Powered by
Oxford Corpus

Tracking the language

Every day we collect thousands of examples of words in order to monitor English as it is being used by everyone, everywhere, every day.

This body of language forms the Oxford English Corpus, a unique electronic database that makes it possible for us to see exactly how English is developing and to discover exciting facts about our language:

- How many words are there in English?
- What is the most common word?
- What new words are entering the language?
- Where do new words come from?

Now containing more than two billion words, the Oxford English Corpus gives us the most up-to-date information available about how words and meanings are changing—and means that Oxford dictionaries offer the fullest, most accurate picture of the English language today.

For more information on the Oxford English Corpus visit:

www.oxforddictionaries.com

New Oxford American Dictionary

New Oxford American Dictionary

THIRD EDITION

Edited by

Angus Stevenson

Christine A. Lindberg

FIRST EDITION

Elizabeth J. Jewell

Frank Abate

OXFORD
UNIVERSITY PRESS

Oxford University Press, Inc., publishes works that further
Oxford University's objective of excellence
in research, scholarship, and education.

Oxford New York

Auckland Cape Town Dar es Salaam Hong Kong Karachi
Kuala Lumpur Madrid Melbourne Mexico City Nairobi
New Delhi Shanghai Taipei Toronto

With offices in

Argentina Austria Brazil Chile Czech Republic France Greece
Guatemala Hungary Italy Japan Poland Portugal Singapore
South Korea Switzerland Thailand Turkey Ukraine Vietnam

First edition 2001
Second edition 2005
Third edition 2010

Published by Oxford University Press, Inc.
198 Madison Avenue, New York, NY 10016
www.oup.com

The Library of Congress Cataloging-in-Publication Data
Data available

ISBN 978-0-19-539288-3

11 13 15 17 19 18 16 14 12

Printed in the United States of America
on acid-free paper

Contents

Editorial staff

Project manager
Angus Stevenson

Principal editor
Christine A. Lindberg

Lexicographers
Carol Braham
Orin Hargraves

Illustrations
Debra Argosy
Lizann Michaud

Pronunciations
Catherine Sangster
Katherine Sietsema

Research and editorial assistance
Debra Argosy
Wade Guyitt
Grace Labatt

Design
Michael Johnson

Production coordinator
Karen Bunn

Publishing manager
Judy Pearsall

For the first edition

Principal Editors
Elizabeth J. Jewell
Frank R. Abate

Senior Project Editor
Christine A. Lindberg

Senior Staff Editors
Suzanne Stone Burke
Erin McKean
Joseph Patwell

Staff Editors
Martin Coleman
Andrea Nagy
Laurie Ongley

Consulting Editors
Donna Farina
Mark LaFlaur
Maurice Lee
Julie Marsh
Lois Principe
Susan Sigalis
Dawn Thornton
Wendy Vidou

Contributors, New Entries
Jeri Famighetti
Archie Hobson
Christine Grove
Orin Hargraves
Nancy LaRoche
Sidney Landau
Paul Lagassé
Eric Sinkins
Sue Ellen Thompson

Pronunciations Editor
Linda Costa

Consulting Pronunciations Editors
John Bollard
Sharon Goldstein
Anne Marie Hamilton
Katherine Isaacs
Ellen Johnson
William Kretzschmar
Rima McKinzey
Lisa Cohen Minnick
Katherine Sietsema
Susan Tamasi
Matthew Zimmerman

Editorial Assistants
Karen Fisher
Kimberly Roberts

Etymologies Editor
Martha Mayou

Illustrations Editor
Debra Argosy

Assistant Illustrations Editors
Katherine Adzima
Lisa Barnett
Benjamin Keene
James Marra
David Roberts

Illustrators
Debra Argosy
Marta Cone
Elizabeth Gaus
Matthew Hansen
Mike Malkovas
Susan Van Winkle

Advisory board for the first edition

Ronald Butters, Professor of English and Cultural Anthropology; Chair, Linguistics Program, Duke University

William J. Frawley, Professor of Linguistics, University of Delaware

Joan Houston Hall, Chief Editor, Dictionary of American Regional English

Willam A. Kretzschmar, Jr., Professor of English and Linguistics, University of Georgia

Mark Liberman, Director, Linguistic Data Consortium, University of Pennsylvania

Specialist subject consultants

AGRICULTURE

Farming	**Robert C. Hughes**, farmer

ARTS

Architecture	**Benjamin E. Northrup**, Lecturer, Yale University
Art	**Michael Harvey**
Ballet/Dance	**Dominique Bourassa**
Bell-Ringing	**Richard Parsons**, Tower Captain, St. James Church, Hendersonville, NC
Film	**Peter DeCherney**, Postdoctoral Fellow, Center for Research on Culture and Literature, Johns Hopkins University
Handwriting	**David R. Evans**, Professor of English and Chair, Department of English, Speech, and Journalism, Georgia College and State University
Musical Direction	**Marguerite L. Brooks**, Associate Professor, Choral Director, Yale University
Musical Instruments	**Nicholas Renouf**, Associate Curator, Yale University Collection of Musical Instruments
Music, Classical and General	**James Haar**, Professor, Department of Music, College of Arts & Sciences, The University of North Carolina–Chapel Hill
Music, General	**Frederick T. Gerhardt**, musician and educator
Music, Popular	**Elysia M. Stobbe**, Director, Market Development, Marketing One, Baltimore, MD
Photography	**Peter Craig**, photographer and instructor
Theater	**Joseph V. Melillo**, Executive Producer, Brooklyn Academy of Music, Brooklyn, NY

ASTRONOMY

Astronomy/Space	**Jennifer Wiseman**, Hubble Fellow, Department of Physics and Astronomy, Johns Hopkins University

BIOLOGY

Biology	**Pamela Mulligan**, Ph.D. in Biology
Birds	**Jacqueline Weicker**, Scientific Assistant, Department of Ornithology, American Museum of Natural History
Breeds	**Carole A. Zerbe**, Assistant Professor of Internal Medicine, School of Veterinary Medicine, University of Pennsylvania
Ecology	**Daniel B. Botkin**, Research Professor, University of California–Santa Barbara
Falconry	**Frederick W. Holderman**, Master Falconer
Insects	**Phillip J. Pellitteri**, Department of Entomology, University of Wisconsin–Madison
Invertebrates	**Alan J. Kohn**, Professor Emeritus, Zoology, University of Wisconsin
Lower Plants	**Carol Brittnacher**, undergraduate researcher, University of Washington–St. Louis
Mammals	**Link Olsen**, Professor, Department of Cell and Molecular Biology, Northwestern University Medical School
Paleontology	**Carl Mendelson**, Professor, Department of Geology, Benoit College
Reptiles	**Robert B. Stuebing**, Associate Professor of Biology, National University of Malaysia and Research Associate, Field Museum of Natural History, Chicago

CHEMISTRY

Biochemistry — **Pamela Mulligan**, Ph.D. in Biology

Chemistry, Inorganic — **Thomas Schweiger**, Research Associate, E.I. du Pont de Nemours & Co., Inc.

Chemistry, Organic — **Robert C. Everich**, Senior Scientist, Makhteshim-Agan of North America, Inc.

COMMERCE

Commerce — **Ellen M. Whitener**, Professor of Commerce, McIntire School of Commerce, University of Virginia

Currency/Finance — **Mark A. White**, Associate Professor of Commerce, McIntire School of Commerce, University of Virginia

Economics — **Donna M. Bombino**, credit analyst

Stock Market — **Richard F. DeMong**, Chaired Professor, Investments and Corporate Finance, McIntire School of Commerce, University of Virginia

COMPUTING

Computing — **Gareth Branwyn**, Editor of "Jargon Watch," *Wired*

Jeff Prucher, author of *Brave New Words*

CRAFTS

Carpentry — **Kevin Ireton**, Chief Editor, *Fine Homebuilding*

Printing/Bookbinding — **David R. Evans**, Professor of English and Chair, Department of English, Speech, and Journalism, Georgia College and State University

EARTH SCIENCES

Epochs — **Dale A. Springer**, Professor, Geosciences, Department of Geography and Geosciences, Bloomsburg University

Geology/Rocks — **Michael J. Soreghan**, Lecturer/Researcher, School of Geology and Geophysics, University of Oklahoma

Minerals — **Lois K. Ongley**, Professor, Geology Department, Bates College

Mining — **Helen Mango**, Professor, Department of Natural Science, Castleton State College

EDUCATION

Education — **Ronald D. Anderson**, Professor of Education, University of Colorado

FASHION

Clothing/Dyeing/Needlework/Textiles/Hairdressing — **Ursula McCarty**

Jewelry — **Gary A. Melillo**, jewelry designer and sculptor

Knitting — **Suzanne Stone Burke**, Editor, Oxford University Press

FISHING

Fishing/Commercial Fishing — **Edward J. Everich**, independent marine consultant

FOOD

Food and Beverages — **Mary Deirdre Donovan**, Senior Editor, The Culinary Institute of America

FORESTRY

Forestry — **Daniel B. Botkin**, Research Professor, University of California–Santa Barbara

Timber — **R. Bruce Hoadley**, Professor, Wood Science and Technology, University of Massachusetts–Amherst

HERALDRY

Heraldry — **David Robert Wooten**, Fellow, Board of Governors; Secretary-Treasurer, Editor, *The Armiger's News*, American College of Heraldry

HISTORY

Archaeology/Greek Antiquities — **Joseph Patwell**, Editor, Oxford University Press

HORTICULTURE

Flowers, Trees, and Shrubs — **Christine A. Lindberg**, Senior Project Editor, Oxford University Press

HUMAN BODY

Anatomy — **William E. Burkel**, Director of Medical Anatomy, University of Michigan Medical School

Physiology — **Tomuo Hoshiko**, Professor Emeritus of Physiology and Biophysics, Case Western Reserve University School of Medicine

HUNTING

Hunting — **Ronald D. Anderson**, Professor of Education, University of Colorado

Stephen E. Lindberg, hunter

LANGUAGE

Black Slang/Black English — **Elysia M. Stobbe**, Director, Market Development, Marketing One, Baltimore, MD

Grammar/Greek Letters — **Joseph Patwell**, Editor, Oxford University Press

Linguistics — **William J. Frawley**, Professor of Linguistics, University of Delaware

Phonetics — **John Bollard**, lexicographer and phonetician

Vulgar Slang/Homosexual Terms — **Ronald R. Butters**, Professor of English and Cultural Anthropology; Chair, Linguistics Program, Duke University

LAW

Law — **Bryan A. Garner**, attorney and lexicographer; President, LawProse, Inc

Archie Hobson, lexicographer

LITERATURE

Literature — **David R. Evans**, Professor of English; Chair, Department of English, Speech, and Journalism, Georgia College and State University

Prosody — **Sue Ellen Thompson**, lexicographer and poet

Rhetoric — **Joseph Patwell**, Editor, Oxford University Press

MATHEMATICS

Mathematics/Geometry	**Michelle LeMasurier**, Assistant Professor, Mathematics, Franklin and Marshall College
Statistics	**Ingram Olkin**, Professor, Statistics and Education, Stanford University

MECHANICAL ENGINEERING

Aeronautics/Engineering	**Ralph Costa**, mechanical engineer
Building	**Faith Gavin Kuhn**, Connecticut Builders & Industry Association (CBIA)
Mechanical Engineering	**Benson H. Tongue**, Professor of Mechanical Engineering, University of California–Berkeley
Railroads	National Railway Historical Society

MEDICINE

Medicine	**John M. Last**, Professor Emeritus, Epidemiology, University of Ottawa
Microbiology	**Robert C. Everich**, Senior Scientist, Makhteshim-Agan of North America, Inc.
Surgery	**William Silen**, Johnson & Johnson Distinguished Professor of Surgery; Dean, Faculty Development and Diversity, Harvard Medical School

MILITARY

Weapons/Medals/Rank	**William L. Faistenhammer**, Colonel, US Army
Military History	**Mary R. Habeck**, Assistant Professor, Department of History, Yale University

MYTHOLOGY

Mythology	**Joseph Patwell**, Editor, Oxford University Press

NAUTICAL TERMS

Nautical/Knots	**Alan H. Hartley**, lexicographer

NUMISMATICS

Numismatics	**Robert W. Hoge**, Curator, Museum of the American Numismatic Association

PHARMACOLOGY

Drugs	**Gail Winger**, Senior Research Scientist, Department of Pharmacology, University of Michigan–Ann Arbor

PHILATELY

Philately	**American Philatelic Society**, State College, PA

PHILOSOPHY

Philosophy/Logic	**Barry Stroud**, Mills Professor of Metaphysics and Epistemology, University of California–Berkeley

PHYSICS

Elements	**Robert C. Everich**, Senior Scientist, Makhteshim-Agan of North America, Inc.
Optics	**Steve E. Watkins**, Associate Professor of Electrical and Computer Engineering, University of Missouri–Rolla
Physics	**Harry Lustig**, Professor of Physics Emeritus, City College, City University of New York; Treasurer Emeritus, American Physical Society

PSYCHIATRY

Psychiatry	**Samuel B. Guze**, Spencer T. Olin Professor of Psychiatry, Department of Psychiatry, Washington University School of Medicine

PSYCHOLOGY

Psychology	**Alan E. Kazdin**, Professor and Chair, Department of Psychology, Yale University

RELIGION

Bible	**Timothy E. Haut**, minister, Congregational Church, Deep River, CT
Buddhism/Hinduism	**Leonard Zwilling**, University of Wisconsin; Dictionary of American Regional English, Madison, WI
Christianity/Ecclesiology	**Peter Rodgers**, Rector, St. John's Episcopal Church, New Haven, CT
Islam	**Abdulaziz A. Sachedina**, Professor, Islamic Studies, Department of Religious Studies, University of Virginia
Roman Catholic Church	**Joseph Patwell**, Editor, Oxford University Press
Theology	**Maurice Lee**, Researcher, Systematic Theology, Yale University

SOCIOLOGY

American Indians	**Richard B. Buckley**
Ethnic Groups	**Alan Hartley**, lexicographer
Sociology	**Ned Polsky**, Professor of Sociology, State University of New York

SPORTS and GAMES

Billiards	**Ned Polsky**, Professor of Sociology, SUNY; international billiard tournament referee
Bridge/Cards	**Carrie Estill**, former editor, *Dictionary of American Regional English*
Chess	**Peter J. Kurzdorfer**, US Chess Federation titles
Golf	**Anthony F. Salvati**
Horse Racing	**The Jockey Club**
Lawn Bowling	**Jack Phillips**, President, American Lawn Bowls Association
Riding	**Jennifer Bryant**, Editor-at-Large, *USDF Connection* (US Dressage Federation magazine)
Sports	**Frank R. Abate**, lexicogapher **Archie Hobson**, lexicographer

TELEVISION

Video	**Michael Harvey**

Preface

The first edition of the groundbreaking *New Oxford American Dictionary* was published in 2001. For this third edition, more than 2,000 new words, senses, and phrases have been added, and key areas of vocabulary have been reanalyzed, reviewed, and revised. Fast-moving areas such as computing, mobile technology, the media, finance, and the environment have provided many of the new terms, and there is also a great deal of new informal and slang material.

New entries tend to be the focus of attention when a dictionary is published, but in the case of this edition, the revisions to existing entries are at least as significant. In countries such as the US, the UK, and Australia more than 70 percent of households now have Internet access. People not only work and access information and entertainment online, but also conduct their social lives via the Internet. These changes in society are reflected in the language, and in the dictionary: items of core vocabulary such as *bookmark*, *browse*, *favorite*, *feed*, and *friend* have new meanings, and other computing-related definitions have been revised to take account of the fact that computers are now part of everyday life.

Oxford Dictionaries is responsible for the largest language research program in the world, constantly monitoring language use of all types in all parts of the English-speaking world. Our primary source for new and revised material is the Oxford English Corpus, a dynamic database of more than two billion words which provides a detailed picture of 21st-century English as an international language. In compiling this new edition, we have also drawn on other sources within Oxford's language research program, including the database of the Oxford Reading Programme, which now consists of around 100 million words.

Entries for proper names have been revised, with death dates and other changes noted as necessary. For example, the Indian cities formerly known as Bombay, Calcutta, and Madras are now referred to as Mumbai, Kolkata, and Chennai. All population figures have been researched, and where possible, recent census figures are given.

The Oxford Dictionaries team work alongside the staff of the full historical *Oxford English Dictionary*, and are very fortunate in being able to call on their resources and expertise. Apart from the contributors listed on the separate credits page, we would like to thank Graeme Diamond and his group for help with drafting new words, Philip Durkin and Katrin Thier for work on etymologies, and Bill Trumble, Alan Hughes, and Jeremy Marshall for advice on scientific entries.

The third edition of the *New Oxford American Dictionary* is available online as well as in print, via Oxford Dictionaries Online. The site, which is updated regularly, allows much fuller exploration of the dictionary text, and beyond: the user can follow links from dictionary to thesaurus and dictionary to dictionary, consult extra information on usage, grammar, and writing, and view more than 1.9 million illustrative examples of real English. However, although the online dictionary brings undoubted advantages in access and searching, consulting a book can still be the quickest and most convenient way of finding a definition, as well as being an enjoyable method of browsing in its own right.

Preface to the first edition

The *New Oxford American Dictionary* is a completely new American dictionary, written on new principles. It builds on the excellence of the lexicographical traditions of scholarship and analysis of evidence as set down by the *Oxford English Dictionary* over a century ago, but it is also a new departure. The *New Oxford American Dictionary* is a dictionary of current American English, based on currently available evidence and current thinking about language and cognition. It is an inventory of the words and meanings of present-day English, both those in actual use and those found in the literature of the past. The compilers have gone to the heart of the traditional practices of dictionary making and reappraised the principles on which lexicography is based. In particular, the focus has been on a different approach to an understanding of "meaning" and how this relates to the structure, organization, and selection of material for the dictionary.

Linguists, cognitive scientists, and others have been developing new techniques for analyzing usage and meaning, and the *New Oxford American Dictionary* has taken full advantage of these developments. Foremost among them is an emphasis on identifying what is "central and typical," as distinct from the time-honored search for "necessary conditions" of meaning (that is, a statement of the conditions that would enable someone to pick out all and only the cases of the term being defined). Past attempts to cover the meaning of all possible uses of a word have tended to lead to a blurred, unfocused result, in which the core of the meaning is obscured by many minor uses. In the *New Oxford American Dictionary*, meanings are linked to central norms of usage as observed in the language. The result is fewer meanings, with sharper, crisper definitions.

The style of definition adopted for the *New Oxford American Dictionary* aims in part to account for the dynamism, imaginativeness, and flexibility of ordinary American usage. The *New Oxford American Dictionary* records and explains all normal meanings and uses of well-attested words, but also illustrates transferred, figurative, and derivative meanings, insofar as these are conventional within the language.

The layout and organization of each entry in the dictionary reflect this new approach to meaning. Each entry has at least one core meaning, to which a number of subsenses, logically connected to it, may be attached. The text design is open and accessible, making it easy to find the core meanings and so to navigate the entry as a whole.

At the heart of this dictionary lies the evidence. This evidence forms the basis for everything that we, as lexicographers, are able to say about the language and the words within it. In particular, the large databank of searchable electronic texts collected by Oxford gives, with its 100 million words, a selection of real, modern, and everyday language, equivalent to an ordinary person's reading over ten years or more. Using computational tools to analyze this databank and other corpora, the editors have been able to look at the behavior of each word in detail in its natural contexts, and so to build up a picture for every word in the dictionary.

Databank analysis has been complemented by analysis of other types of evidence: the *New Oxford American Dictionary* makes extensive use of the citation database of the Oxford North American Reading Program, a collection of citations (currently standing at over 64 million words and growing at a rate of about 4.5 million words a year) taken from a variety of sources from all the English-speaking countries of the world. In addition, a specially commissioned reading program has targeted previously neglected specialist fields as diverse as computing, alternative medicine, antique collecting, and sports.

The general approach to defining in the *New Oxford American Dictionary* has particular application for specialist vocabulary. Here, in the context of dealing with highly technical information that may be unfamiliar to the nonspecialist reader, the focus on clarity of expression is of great importance. Avoidance of overtechnical terminology and an emphasis on explaining and describing as well as defining are balanced by the need to maintain a high level of technical information and accuracy. In many cases, additional technical information is presented separately in an easily recognizable alternative format.

The *New Oxford American Dictionary* views the language from the perspective that English, although a world language, is now centered in the United States, and that American vocabulary and usage deserve special attention. Although the focus is on American English, a network of consultants throughout the English-speaking world has enabled us to ensure excellent coverage of world English, from the United Kingdom and Canada to the Caribbean, India, South Africa, Australia, and New Zealand. We have been indebted to the opportunities provided for communication by the Internet; lively discussions by e-mail across the oceans have formed an everyday part of the dictionary-making process.

Many people have been involved in the preparation of this dictionary, and thanks are due to them all. The US Dictionaries Program would like to give special thanks to Judy Pearsall, Patrick Hanks, and the lexicographers of the Current English Dictionaries department in the United Kingdom for creating the foundation on which we have built. We would also like to express our gratitude to Stephen Perkins of dataformat.com, without whose patience and intelligence this dictionary would not have been possible.

Introduction

The *New Oxford American Dictionary* has been compiled according to principles that are quite different from those of traditional American dictionaries. New types of evidence are now available in sufficient quantity to allow lexicographers to construct a picture of the language that is more accurate than has been possible before. The approach to structure and organization within individual entries has been rethought, as has the approach to the selection and presentation of information in every aspect of the dictionary: definitions, choice of examples, grammar, word histories, and every other category. New approaches have been adopted in response to a reappraisal of the workings of language in general and its relationship to the presentation of information in a dictionary in particular. The aim of this introduction is to give the reader background information for using this dictionary and to explain some of the thinking behind these new approaches.

The making of the New Oxford American Dictionary

The information presented in the *New Oxford American Dictionary* is based on close analysis of how words behave in real, natural language. Behind every dictionary entry are examples of the word in use—often hundreds and thousands of them— which have been analyzed to give information about typical usage, about distribution (whether typically British or typically Canadian, for example), about register (whether informal or derogatory, for example), about currency (whether archaic or dated, for example), and about subject (whether used chiefly in Medicine, Finance, Chemistry, or Sport, for example).

The Oxford English Corpus

A corpus is a collection of texts of written (or spoken) language presented in electronic form. It provides the evidence of how language is used in real situations, from which lexicographers can write accurate and meaningful dictionary entries. Whereas compilers of previous dictionaries were able to base their work on only a limited selection of citations, lexicographers on the *New Oxford American Dictionary* could analyze hundreds or thousands of examples of each word to see how real language behaves today.

The corpus used on the first edition was the British National Corpus, a database of 100 million words. Revisions made to to this third edition, and new material added to it, have been derived largely from analysis of the new Oxford English Corpus, which contains more than two billion words. All content dates from 2000 at the earliest, and the corpus is regularly updated with the latest material, allowing a true picture of language change to build up.

The Oxford English Corpus represents all types of English, from fiction and specialist journals to everyday newspapers and magazines, and from official reports to the language of Internet message boards, chat rooms, and Twitter. And, as English is a global language, used by an estimated one third of the world's population, the Oxford English Corpus contains language from all parts of the world—not only from the US and the UK but also from Canada, Australia, the Caribbean, India, Singapore, and South Africa. It is the largest English corpus of its type: the most representative slice of the English language available.

Meanings of words and phrases change and so do spellings, despite the existence of "standard" or "correct" spelling. A strength of the corpus is that it contains not only published works in which the text has been edited but also unpublished and unedited writing like emails and blogs. Some of the most inventive uses and deliberate exploitations of language (as well as simple mistakes) start out in this kind of informal and unselfconscious language, so tracking them is an essential part of tracking the language as a whole.

Analyzing the corpus lets us identify items that occur there but are not covered in the dictionary, and so helps us to draw up a shortlist of potential new entries. It tells us which words are more common than they were ten years ago, and which are rarer; and which words are increasingly being used in a different way, or in a different sense. It also lets us define familiar, established words more accurately, by telling us more about them.

Concordances show at a glance that some combinations of words (called "collocations") occur together much more often than others. For example, in the concordance on page xv, "end in," "end the," and "end up" all occur quite often. But are any of these combinations important enough to be given special treatment in the dictionary?

Recent research has focused on identifying combinations that are not merely frequent but also statistically significant. In the Oxford English Corpus, the two words "end the" occur very frequently together, but they do not form a statistically significant unit, since the word "the" is the most common in the language. The combinations **end up** and **end in**, on the other hand, are shown to be more significant and tell us something about the way the verb **end** behaves in normal use. Of course, a dictionary for general use cannot go into detailed statistical analysis of word combinations, but it can present examples that are typical of normal usage. In the *New Oxford American Dictionary,* particularly significant or important patterns are highlighted, in bold or in bold italics, e.g.,

> **end**
>
> [no obj.] (**end in**) have as its final part or result: *one in three marriages is now likely to end in divorce.*
>
> [no obj.] (**end up**) eventually reach or come to a specified place, state, or course of action: ***I ended up in** Connecticut* | *you could **end up with** a higher income.*

For further details, see the section on *Grammar*.

The corpus also shows that the verb **cause** is typically used to describe negative events, with typical objects being *death, damage, chaos, disturbance,* and *problems*. Most dictionaries define the word neutrally, for example as "make (something) happen," but armed with the corpus information we have redefined it as "make (something, especially something bad)

sport	football . Ethics , shmethics.) </p><p> " Sometime this will	**end**	, " DuBose said after Saturday 's loss to Louisiana State ,
arts	humanity . This painting shows that the life of a people does not	**end**	, despite the atrocities of a genocide . " The Red Lake , "
news	that we were going to have to end , or do the best we could to	**end**	, global terrorism . </p><p> And if you think about the role
arts	, but otherwise there is no forward motion from beginning to	**end**	. But the section titles in Lip Service are orderly and archaic
sport	2.10 ERA , and has left us no reason to think that trend will	**end**	. His splitter is as good as any pitch in the Majors , maybe
sport	scowling all the way to June 20 - the latest date the playoffs can	**end**	. Something to watch in the Finals : Whichever team wins the
sport	. More goals , no . More odd-man rushes , yes . When does it	**end**	? </p><p> Ty : It is early , and this team hasn't found its identity
society	huge government spending packages under Obuchi have failed to	**end**	a decade of economic stagnation in Japan and left the country
sport	the only , blindingly obvious conclusion that the game must	**end**	after eleven . </p><p> And as if that wasn't enough , instead
business	. Are they saying this rebate is going to be the be all and	**end**	all ? Because President Bush the other day said , because of
business	nothing " aspect of our tax system . In other words , we must	**end**	all deductions , special breaks , loopholes , and rate progressivity
news	report also calls for a number of legal measures that would	**end**	arbitrary detentions and torture during questioning . It called
arts	of terrain . They aren't made for getting from beginning to	**end**	as quickly as possible . Prewitt is making a case for traveling
sport	against the Phillies and Marlins , the two teams most likely to	**end**	Atlanta 's run of consecutive division titles . </p><p> CHICAGO
arts	comments on the film were : " You 're absorbed from beginning to	**end**	because the characters are enormously interesting and likable
sport	six games . He had good throws and bad throws . I think tight	**end**	Clark Harris is overrated Â… South Florida RB Andre Hall runs
business	Treasury note . </p><p> Mutual fund fees used to be a sure way to	**end**	conversation at a party . But congressional hearings , regulatory
society	their own feelings and fears with children . It is important to	**end**	group discussions on a positive note , promoting a sense of
society	the 1973 Supreme Court decision affirming a woman 's right to	**end**	her pregnancy . </p><p> I am writing this in response to the
life_and_leisure	third entry in this ongoing serial , but the challenge doesn't	**end**	here . </p><p> Art is an intelligible image of a real or imaginary
society	over the seven-year fund-raising campaign , which was slated to	**end**	in 2003 , making its mark in the record books for fund-raising
science	cosmic order , which nature has failed to provide us , seems to	**end**	in a kind of cyber-chaos , a new war of all against all . </p>
life_and_leisure	it Up ! Brewery and Grill . I 'm not big on restaurants that	**end**	in an exclamation point , not after my misadventures with Artichokes
science	between a female and all of her potential mates that did not	**end**	in copulation (mean = 4.48 0.4 courtships per female , 108
news	of our past military dictators , such a conference will only	**end**	in deadlock and even lead to the violent break-up of the country
arts	sustainable logic and any attempt at analyzing reason can only	**end**	In despair . Such a situation may of course pass as highly
news	new round of multilateral trade negotiations , scheduled to	**end**	in January 2005 , could see Jamaica taking on new obligations
life_and_leisure	now customary were then nearly nonexistent . Fights that now	**end**	in semi-automatic-weapon fire were settled with knives then
society	Evangelista centers his analysis . Chechnya was not fated to	**end**	in violence . War came about because elites in Moscow thought
life_and_leisure	know about my four-year relationship . He hasn't asked me to	**end**	it , but he 's indicated that when " things fall apart " with
humanities	sealed these identities . The Left opposed the war and tried to	**end**	it ; the Right denounced such efforts as disloyal and appropriated
sport	Jackie Shipp . </p><p> Then there are tackle Tommie Harris and	**end**	Jimmy Wilkerson , the stars on what for now is perceived as
arts	not reviewing Lethal Weapon 5 , 6 , and 7 as the series can	**end**	now at 4 without my feeling a loss . Warner has done another
society	federally-backed loans . </p><p> University of California workers	**end**	strike without contract </p><p> University of California clerical
news	violence was erupting again in Ivory Coast . France 's efforts to	**end**	the civil war in its former colony looked shaky . There is
humanities	slight visitation in summer 1942 . It was the perfect time to	**end**	the feeding shows for good . </p><p> The park 's announcement
society	business community watches meekly as the government 's attempts to	**end**	the financial crisis fail to revive the nation 's banks or
humanities	succeeded in reintegrating the Biafrans into Nigeria , it did not	**end**	the problems of ethnicity in the country . In the years that
life_and_leisure	She is so uncomfortable that she tries to persuade her son to	**end**	the relationship every opportunity she has alone with him .
life_and_leisure	relationship ? Should I just get a tourniquet for my heart and	**end**	the whole thing ? HELP ! - In Love , </p><p> Get the tourniquet
arts	Romeo , who is filled with love for his new cousin , tries to	**end**	their boldness . Before escaping , Tybalt plunges his sword
arts	these rock legends , it would definitely be a fantastic way to	**end**	their great career , because : </p><p> 1 . This band blew the
science	legality of its sovereignty claim to the High Arctic did not	**end**	there . However , the immediate challenge had been dealt with
life_and_leisure	in Toronto in the bill it will almost certainly introduce to	**end**	this strike . </p><p> That 's the scenario Lastman 's shenanigans
sport	Germany , that 's where he first learned to ride . How did he	**end**	up a medalist for the U.S. ? While vacationing in California
business	Dole-style " stop lying about my record " bitterness , he will	**end**	up a net loser . The right course is to offer concrete ideas
arts	The Punisher is patently absurd Â… and if they would , it would	**end**	up at big Paramount . Classics has never released a thriller
news	with our principal allies , the Europeans , so that we do not	**end**	up being isolated internationally and perhaps with a regional
science	. However , it is not foolproof - a deeply flawed paper can	**end**	up being published under a number of different potential circumstances
news	people 's opinions on this issue . I find that they inevitably	**end**	up being split along childhood lines . </p><p> If they paddled
business	answer . " </p><p> Atos Origin 's team in Barcelona , Spain , will	**end**	up closest to the action - at the Olympics themselves . They
news	family did not pay a certain amount of money , Changoor would	**end**	up dead . </p><p> Changoor 's kidnapping came the day after the
news	Have fun . Head over to The Jacksonville Landing . Just don't	**end**	up drinking on the wrong corner with the wrong people . Or
business	cancer patients are operated on , 50 % are cured , and 50 % will	**end**	up dying in 6 to 8 years , but we don't know who is in which
society	initiative stipulating that people convicted of three felonies could	**end**	up facing life in prison . The judicial system in Eva 's Man
arts	impatient than Bill , he is very close to Bill . The two brothers	**end**	up fighting for opposing sides during the war . </p><p> Nancy
arts	goes smooth until Ricky starts to open his mouth which could	**end**	up getting he and Bobby into big trouble - and maybe even killed
news	8 , they will also be ruling on those 18,000 couples who did	**end**	up getting married . We are hopeful that even if the Supreme
sport	respect is that the 20 % of the license fee would basically just	**end**	up going to pay - you can't do the things such as the permitting
business	the company 's cafeteria kitchens , for example , does in fact	**end**	up in local landfills . </p><p> Which makes us feel somewhat
news	going to work in the hotel industry and in fact you 're going to	**end**	up in the illicit sex trade , " he said . </p><p> " You 're being
science	peacefully for the benefit of humankind ? Or will those technologies	**end**	up in the hands of a society that is not mature enough to wield
society	consequence of this is that most refugees (or displaced persons)	**end**	up in the major cities which can best absorb a stream of individuals
news	out . And you know , where do they go . We don't want them to	**end**	up in the streets . We want these kids to be able to learn
sport	<p> Keyshawn . He claims he was singled out , but really he 'll	**end**	up just like every other Buc : a non-factor in the NFL playoffs
life_and_leisure	about the main bad-guys of the movie being troubled teens who	**end**	up making terrible choices . If we feel sorry for the villains
society	province of the most well-off kids , " Haycock says . " You	**end**	up maybe advantaging a few more kids , but creating huge and
life_and_leisure	get out of college , work more in film and maybe eventually	**end**	up on Broadway - if I can learn how to dance and sing . </p>
sport	call in his last appearance there . The Yankees always seem to	**end**	up on top in this clash , and it is boring rooting for the
news	bondholders are crammed down and they take equity , they essentially	**end**	up owning the economy . And so if you think about management
society	when the duties became operative . (74) This resolution did	**end**	up passing . (75) But by and large the references to Chase
business	information . I think that one way or the other the taxpayer will	**end**	up paying a lot . I don't see how we can keep AIG in its current
business	entire debt ! </p><p> Don't worry , it get worse . You would also	**end**	up paying almost $ 14,000 on your $ 7,000 loan . </p><p> So getting
sport	person 's last name , followed by the pound sign . " I usually	**end**	up pressing any button , hoping to get a real person who can
life_and_leisure	little offended that I thought he might be offended ! : -) I	**end**	up promising to withhold final judgment until I meet her (

Figure 1 Extract from a short concordance from the Oxford English Corpus, showing the word "end."

happen." Similarly, **decline** is often defined simply as "become smaller, fewer, or less," but a look at the corpus shows us that the typical subject is something regarded as good, such as standards, output, or income—when something such as crime decreases it doesn't decline, it falls. This level of precision and accuracy across a huge range of meaning and usage is part of what makes the Oxford English Corpus unique.

The Oxford Reading Programme

The citation database created by the Oxford Reading Programme is an ongoing research project in which readers around the world select short extracts from a huge variety of specialist and non-specialist sources in all varieties of English. It is a direct development of the program first created when the original *Oxford English Dictionary* was being compiled in the 19th century. This database currently stands at around 100 million words, and tens of thousands of new citations are added every year.

Illustrative examples

The *New Oxford American Dictionary* contains many more examples of words in use than any other comparable dictionary. Generally, the examples are there to show typical uses of the word or sense. All examples are authentic, in that they represent actual usage. In the past dictionaries used invented examples, partly because not enough authentic text was available and partly through an assumption that invented examples were better because they could be tailored to the precise needs of the dictionary entry. Such a view finds little favor today, and it is now generally recognized that the "naturalness" provided by authentic examples is of the utmost importance in providing an accurate picture of language in use.

Word trends

Through our analysis of the Oxford English Corpus for the third edition, we have been able to identify some high-profile words whose use has changed significantly since the beginning of the century. Thus, for example, *terror* is now commonly used as shorthand for *terrorism*, and *web* primarily relates to the Internet rather than to spiders. Some of these findings have been presented in a new feature called Word Trends, which give an informal account of the word's development.

Structure: Core Sense and Subsense

Within an entry the first part of speech is the primary one for that word: thus, for **bag** and **balloon** the senses of the noun are given before those for the verb, while for **babble** and **bake** the senses of the verb are given before those of the noun.

Within each part of speech, the first definition given is the **core sense**. The general principle on which the senses in the *New Oxford American Dictionary* are organized is that each word has at least one core meaning, to which a number of subsenses may be attached. If there is more than one core sense, this is introduced by a bold sense number. Core meanings represent typical, central uses of the word in question in modern standard English, as established by research on and analysis of American and World English through corpora (language databanks) and citation databases.

The core meaning is the one that represents the most literal sense that the word has in ordinary modern American usage. This is not necessarily the same as the oldest meaning, because word meanings change over time. Nor is it necessarily the most frequent meaning, because figurative senses are sometimes the most frequent. It is the meaning accepted by native speakers as the one that is most established as literal and central.

The core sense also acts as a gateway to other, related subsenses. These subsenses are grouped under the core sense, each one being introduced by a solid square symbol.

> **co·coon** /kəˈko͞on/ ▶ **n.** a silky case spun by the larvae of many insects for protection in the pupal stage. ■ a covering that prevents the corrosion of metal equipment. ■ something that envelops or surrounds, esp. in a protective or comforting way: ***the cocoon of her kimono*** | figurative ***a warm cocoon of love.***

There is a logical relationship between each subsense and the core sense under which it appears. The organization of senses according to this logical relationship is designed to help the user, not only in being able to navigate the entry more easily and find relevant senses more readily, but also in building up an understanding of how senses in the language relate to one another and how the language is constructed on this model. The main types of relationship of core sense to subsense are as follows:

(a) figurative extension of the core sense, e.g.,

barbed

CORE SENSE having a barb or barbs: *barbed arrows.*

SUBSENSE ■ (of a remark or joke) deliberately hurtful: *a fair degree of barbed wit.*

boiling point

CORE SENSE the temperature at which a liquid boils and turns to vapor.

SUBSENSE ■ the point at which anger or excitement breaks out into violent expression: *emotions had reached boiling point and could spill over into violence.*

(b) specialized case of the core sense, e.g.,

zone

CORE SENSE [usu. with modifier] an area or stretch of land having a particular characteristic, purpose, or use, or subject to particular restrictions: *a pedestrian zone.*

SUBSENSE ■ Geography a well-defined region extending around the earth between definite limits, esp. between two parallels of latitude: *a zone of easterly winds.*

SUBSENSE ■ Sports in basketball, football, and hockey, a specific area of the court, field, or rink, esp. one to be defended by a particular player.

demand

CORE SENSE an insistent and peremptory request, made as if by right: *a series of **demands for** far-reaching reforms.*

SUBSENSE ■ Economics the desire of purchasers, consumers, clients, employers, etc., for a particular commodity, service, or other item: *a recent slump in demand* | *a demand for specialists.*

(c) other extension or shift in meaning, retaining one or more elements of the core sense, e.g.,

bamboo

CORE SENSE a giant woody grass that grows chiefly in the tropics, where it is widely cultivated.

SUBSENSE ■ the hollow jointed stem of this plant, used as a cane or to make furniture and implements: [as modifier] *a bamboo serving tray.*

management

CORE SENSE the process of dealing with or controlling things or people: *the management of elk herds.*

SUBSENSE ■ Medicine & Psychiatry the treatment or control of diseases, injuries, or disorders, or the care of patients who suffer from them: *the use of combination chemotherapy in the management of breast cancer.*

mandarin

CORE SENSE an official in any of the nine top grades of the former imperial Chinese civil service.

SUBSENSE ■ a powerful official or senior bureaucrat, esp. one perceived as reactionary and secretive: *a civil service mandarin.*

Many entries have just one core sense. However, some entries are more complex and have different strands of meaning, each constituting a core sense. In this case, each core sense is introduced by a bold sense number, and each potentially has its own block of subsenses relating to it.

belt /belt/ ▶ **n. 1** a strip of leather or other material worn around the waist or across the chest, esp. in order to support clothes or carry weapons: *a sword belt* | [as modifier] *a belt buckle.* ■ short for SEAT BELT. ■ a belt worn as a sign of rank or achievement: *he was awarded the victor's belt.* ■ a belt of a specified color, marking the attainment of a particular level in judo, karate, or similar sports: [as modifier] *brown-belt level.* ■ a person who has reached such a level: *I am a karate black belt.* ■ (**the belt**) the punishment of being struck with a belt.
2 a strip of material used in various technical applications, in particular: ■ a continuous band of material used in machinery for transferring motion from one wheel to another. ■ a conveyor belt. ■ a flexible strip carrying machine-gun cartridges.

Specialist Vocabulary

One of the most important uses of a dictionary is to provide explanations of terms in specialized fields that are unfamiliar to a general reader. Yet in many traditional dictionaries, the definitions have been written by specialists as if for other specialists, and as a result the definitions are often opaque and difficult to understand.

One of the primary aims of the *New Oxford American Dictionary* has been to break down the barriers to understanding specialist vocabulary. The challenge has been, on the one hand, to give information that is comprehensible, relevant, and readable, while on the other hand maintaining the high level of technical information and accuracy suitable for the more specialist reader.

This has been achieved in some cases, notably entries for plants and animals and chemical substances, by separating technical information from the rest of the definition:

A·mer·i·can croc·o·dile ▶ **n.** a crocodile with a long tapering head, occurring from southernmost Florida to Ecuador. ● *Crocodylus acutus*, family Crocodylidae.

ben·zo·py·rene /ˌbenzōˈpīrēn/ ▶ **n.** Chemistry a compound that is the major carcinogen present in cigarette smoke. It also occurs in coal tar. ● A polycyclic aromatic hydrocarbon; chem. formula: $C_{20}H_{12}$.

In other cases, it is achieved by giving additional explanatory information within the definition itself:

curl·ing /ˈkərliNG/ ▶ **n.** a game played on ice, esp. in Scotland and Canada, in which large, round, flat stones are slid across the surface toward a mark. Members of a team use brooms to sweep the surface of the ice in the path of the stone to control its speed and direction.

al·che·my /ˈalkəmē/ ▶ **n.** the medieval forerunner of chemistry, based on the supposed transformation of matter. It was concerned particularly with attempts to convert base metals into gold or to find a universal elixir. ■ a seemingly magical process of transformation, creation, or combination: *finding the person who's right for you requires a very subtle alchemy.*

As elsewhere, the purpose is to give information that is relevant and interesting, aiming not just to define the word but also to describe and explain its context in the real world. Additional information of this type, where it is substantial, is given in the form of separate boxed features:

earth /ərTH/ ▶ **n. 1** (also **Earth**) the planet on which we live; the world: *the diversity of life on earth.* ■ the surface of the world as distinct from the sky or the sea: *it plummeted back to earth at 60 mph.* ■ the present abode of humankind, as distinct from heaven or hell.

> The earth is the third planet from the sun in the solar system, orbiting between Venus and Mars at an average distance of 90 million miles (149.6 million km) from the sun, and has one natural satellite, the moon. It has an equatorial diameter of 7,654 miles (12,756 km), an average density 5.5 times that of water, and is believed to have formed about 4,600 million years ago. The earth, which is three-quarters covered by oceans and has a dense atmosphere of nitrogen and oxygen, is the only planet known to support life.

E·o·cene /ˈēəˌsēn/ ▶ **adj.** Geology of, relating to, or denoting the second epoch of the Tertiary period, between the Paleocene and Oligocene epochs. ■ (as noun **the Eocene**) the Eocene epoch or the system of rocks deposited during it.

> The Eocene epoch lasted from 56.5 million to 35.4 million years ago. It was a time of rising temperatures, and there was an abundance of mammals, including the first horses, bats, and whales.

An especially important feature of the *New Oxford American Dictionary* is the coverage of American animals and plants. In-depth research and a thorough review have been carried out for animals and plants in the Americas and throughout the world and, as a result, a large number of entries have been included that have never before been included in general American dictionaries. The style and presentation of these entries follow the general principles for specialist vocabulary in the *New Oxford American Dictionary*: the entries not only give the technical information, but also describe, in everyday English, the appearance and other characteristics (of behavior, medicinal or culinary use, mythological significance, reason for the name, etc.), and the typical habitat and distribution:

mes·o·saur /ˈmezəˌsôr, ˈmē-/ (also **mesosaurus** /ˌmezəˈsôrəs/) ▶ **n.** an extinct small aquatic reptile of the early Permian period, with an elongated body, flattened tail, and a long narrow snout with numerous needlelike teeth. ● Genus *Mesosaurus*, order Mesosauria, subclass Anapsida.

black·tail deer /ˈblak,tāl/ (also **black-tailed deer**) ▶ **n.** a type of mule deer with black markings on the upper side of its tail, found west of the crest of the Cascade Mountains. ● *Odocoileus hemionus* subsp. *columbianus*, family Cervidae.

chi·a /ˈCHēə/ ▶ **n.** a plant of the mint family with clusters of small two-lipped purple flowers. Chia is common throughout California and the Great Basin. ● *Salvia columbariae*, family Labiatae.

Encyclopedic Material

Some dictionaries do not include entries for the names of people and places and other proper names, or include them only in separate sections. The argument for this is based on a distinction between "words" and "facts," by which dictionaries are about "words" while encyclopedias and other reference works are about "facts." The distinction is an interesting theoretical one, but in practice there is a considerable overlap: names such as Shakespeare and Mississippi are as much part of the language as words such as drama or river, and they belong in a large dictionary.

The *New Oxford American Dictionary* includes all those terms forming part of the enduring common knowledge of English speakers, regardless of whether they are classified as "words" or "names." The information given is the kind of information that people are likely to need from a dictionary, however that information may traditionally be classified. Both the style of definitions in the *New Oxford American Dictionary* and the inclusion of additional material in separate blocks reflect this approach.

The *New Oxford American Dictionary* includes more than 5,000 place-name entries, 4,000 biographical entries, and just under 3,000 other proper names. The biographical entries are designed to provide not just the basic facts (such as birth and death dates, full name, and nationality), but also a brief context giving information about, for example, a person's life and why he or she is important. For a few particularly important encyclopedic entries—for example, countries—a fuller treatment is given and additional information appears in a separate boxed note.

Grammar

In recent years, grammar has begun to enjoy greater prominence than in the past few decades. It is once again being taught explicitly in schools throughout the United States. In addition, there is a recognition that different meanings of a word are closely associated with different lexical and syntactic patterns. The *New Oxford American Dictionary* records and exemplifies the most important of these patterns at the relevant senses of each word, thus giving guidance on language use as well as word meaning.

For example, with the word **bomb**, it is possible to distinguish the main senses of the verb simply on the basis of the grammar: whether the verb is transitive (takes a direct object) or intransitive (no direct object):

CORE SENSE	attack *(a place or vehicle)* with a bomb or bombs: *London* was bombed, night after night.
grammar	[with obj.]

(the asterisks shown here match the direct object in the example with the parenthetical item in the definition)

CORE SENSE	informal (of a movie, play, or other event) fail miserably: *a big-budget movie that bombed at the box office.*
grammar	[no obj.]

This has particular relevance for a dictionary such as the *New Oxford American Dictionary*, where the aim is to present information in such a way that it helps to explain the structure of the language itself, not just the meanings of individual senses. For this reason, special attention has been paid to the grammar of each word, and grammatical structures are given explicitly.

Where possible, the syntactic behavior of a word is presented directly: for example, if a verb is normally found in a particular sense followed by a certain preposition, this is indicated before the definition, in bold:

build

(**build on**) use as a basis for further progress or development: *the nation should build on the talents of its workforce.*

In other cases, collocations that are typical of the term in use, although not obligatory, are shown highlighted within the example sentence:

ball game

a particular situation, esp. one that is completely different from the previous situation: *making the film was* ***a whole new ball game*** *for her.*

bet

a candidate or course of action to choose; an option: ***your best bet*** *is to call a professional exterminator.*

Great efforts have been made to use a minimum of specialist terminology. Nevertheless, a small number of terms are essential in explaining the grammar of a word. The less familiar terms are explained below. All terms are, of course, defined and explained under their own entries in the dictionary.

Terms relating to nouns

[as modifier]: used to mark a noun that can be placed before another noun in order to modify its meaning, e.g.,

boom

[often as modifier] a movable arm over a television or movie set, carrying a microphone or camera: *a boom mike.*

bedside

the space beside a bed, typically that of someone who is ill: *he was summoned to the bedside of a dying man* | [as modifier] *a bedside lamp.*

[treated as sing.]: used to mark a noun that is plural in form but is used with a singular verb, e.g., **mumps** in *mumps is one of the major childhood diseases* or **genetics** in *genetics has played a major role in this work.*

[treated as sing. or pl.]: used to mark a noun that can be used with either a singular or a plural verb without any change in meaning or in the form of the headword (often called *collective nouns*, because they typically denote groups of people considered collectively), e.g., *the staff are committed to this policy* or *the staff is trying to gag its critics.*

[in sing.]: used to mark a noun that is used as a count noun but is never or rarely found in the plural, e.g., **ear** in *an ear for rhythm.*

Terms relating to verbs

[with obj.]: used to mark a verb that is transitive, i.e., takes a direct object (the type of direct object often being shown in parentheses in the definition), e.g.,

> **escort**
>
> [with obj.] accompany (someone or something) somewhere, esp. for protection or security, or as a mark of rank: *Shiona escorted Janice to the door | the shipment was escorted by armed patrol boats.*

[no obj.]: used to mark a verb that is intransitive, i.e., takes no direct object, e.g.,

> **quibble**
>
> [no obj.] argue or raise objections about a trivial matter: *they are always quibbling about the amount they are prepared to pay.*

[with adverbial]: used to mark a verb that takes an obligatory adverbial, typically a prepositional phrase, without which the sentence in which the verb occurs would sound unnatural or weird, e.g.,

> **glare**
>
> **[with adverbial]** (of the sun or an electric light) shine with a strong or dazzling light: *the sun glared out of a clear blue sky.*

Terms relating to adjectives

[attrib.]: used to mark an adjective that is normally used attributively, i.e., comes before the noun that it modifies, e.g., **certain** in *a certain man* (not *the man is certain*, which has a very different meaning). Note that attributive use is standard for many adjectives, especially in specialist fields: the [attrib.] label is used only to mark those cases in which predicative use would be less usual.

[predic.]: used to mark an adjective that is normally used predicatively, i.e., comes after the verb, e.g., **alike** in *the brothers were alike* (not *the alike brothers*).

[postpositive]: used to mark an adjective that is used postpositively, i.e., typically comes immediately after the noun that it modifies (such uses are unusual in English and generally arise because the adjective has been adopted from a language where postpositive use is standard), e.g., **galore** in *there were prizes galore*.

Terms relating to adverbs

[sentence adverb]: used to mark an adverb that stands outside a sentence or clause, providing commentary on it as a whole or showing the speaker's or writer's attitude to what is being said, rather than the manner in which something was done. Sentence adverbs most frequently express the speaker's or writer's point of view, although they may also be used to set a context by stating a field of reference, e.g.,

> **certainly**
>
> [sentence adverb] undoubtedly; definitely; surely: *the prestigious address certainly adds to the firm's appeal | it certainly isn't worth risking your life.*

[as submodifier]: used to mark an adverb that is used to modify an adjective or another adverb, e.g.,

> **comparatively**
>
> [as submodifier] to a moderate degree as compared to something else; relatively: *inflation was comparatively low.*

Word Histories

The etymologies in standard dictionaries explain the language from which a word was brought into English, the period at which it is first recorded in English, and the development of modern word forms. While the *New Oxford American Dictionary* does this, it also goes further. It explains sense development as well as morphological (or form) development. Information is presented clearly and with a minimum of technical terminology, and the perspective taken is that of the general reader who would like to know about word origins but who is not a philological specialist. In this context, the history of how and why a particular meaning developed from an apparently quite different older meaning is likely to be at least as interesting as, for example, what the original form was in Latin or Greek.

For example, the word history for the word **oaf** shows how the present meaning developed from the meaning 'elf,' while the entry for **compass** shows how the sense 'magnetic compass' may have been influenced by Italian:

> **oaf** /ōf/ ▶ **n.** a stupid, uncultured, or clumsy person.
> – ORIGIN early 17th cent.: variant of obsolete *auf*, from Old Norse *álfr* 'elf.' The original meaning was 'elf's child, changeling,' later 'idiot child' and 'halfwit,' generalized in the current sense.

> **com·pass** /ˈkəmpəs/ ▶ **n. 1** (also **magnetic compass**) an instrument containing a magnetized pointer that shows the direction of magnetic north and bearings from it.
> – ORIGIN Middle English: from Old French *compas* (noun), *compasser* (verb), based on Latin *com-* 'together' + *passus* 'a step or pace.' Several senses ('measure,' 'artifice,' 'circumscribed area,' and 'pair of compasses') that appeared in Middle English are also found in Old French, but their development and origin are uncertain. The transference of sense to the magnetic compass is held to have occurred in the related Italian word *compasso*, from the circular shape of the compass box.

Additional special features of the *New Oxford American Dictionary* include "internal etymologies" and "folk etymologies." Internal etymologies are given within entries to explain the origin of particular senses, phrases, or idioms. For example, how did the figurative use of **red herring** come about? Why do we call something a **flash in the pan**?

> **red her·ring** ▶ **n. 1** a dried smoked herring, which is turned red by the smoke.
> **2** something, esp. a clue, that is or is intended to be misleading or distracting: *the book is fast-paced, exciting, and full of red herrings.* [so named from the practice of using the scent of red herring in training hounds.]

> – PHRASES **flash in the pan** a thing or person whose sudden but brief success is not repeated or repeatable: *our start to the season was just a flash in the pan.* [with allusion to the priming of a firearm, the flash arising from an explosion of gunpowder from the pan within the lock.]

The *New Oxford American Dictionary* presents the information in a straightforward, user-friendly fashion immediately following the relevant definition. In a similar vein, folk etymologies—those explanations that are unfounded but nevertheless well known to many people—have traditionally simply been ignored in dictionaries. The *New Oxford American Dictionary* gives an account of widely held but often erroneous folk etymologies for the benefit of the general reader, explaining competing theories and assessing their relative merits where applicable.

posh /päSH/ informal ▶ **adj.** elegant or stylishly luxurious: *a posh Munich hotel.* ■ chiefly Brit. typical of or belonging to the upper class of society: *she had a posh accent.*
– ORIGIN early 20th cent.: perhaps from slang *posh*, denoting a dandy. There is no evidence to support the folk etymology that *posh* is formed from the initials of *port out starboard home* (referring to the practice of using the more comfortable accommodations, out of the heat of the sun, on ships between England and India).

snob /snäb/ ▶ **n.** a person with an exaggerated respect for high social position or wealth who seeks to associate with social superiors and dislikes people or activities regarded as lower-class. ■ [with adj. or noun modifier] a person who believes that their tastes in a particular area are superior to those of other people: *a musical snob.*
– DERIVATIVES **snob·bism** /-ˌbizəm/ **n.**, **snob·by adj.** (**snobbier, snobbiest**).
– ORIGIN late 18th cent. (originally dialect in the sense 'cobbler'): of unknown origin; early senses conveyed a notion of 'lower status or rank,' later denoting a person seeking to imitate those of superior social standing or wealth. Folk etymology connects the word with Latin *sine nobilitate* 'without nobility' but the earliest recorded sense has no connection with this.

Researching word histories is similar in some respects to archaeology: the evidence is often partial or not there at all, and etymologists must make informed decisions using the evidence available, however inadequate it may be. From time to time, new evidence becomes available, and the known history of a word may need to be reconsidered. In this, the *New Oxford American Dictionary* has been able to draw on the extensive expertise and ongoing research of the *Oxford English Dictionary*.

Usage Notes

Interest in questions of good usage is widespread among English speakers everywhere, and many issues are hotly debated. In the *New Oxford American Dictionary*, traditional issues have been reappraised, and guidance is given on various points, old and new. The aim is to help people to use the language more accurately, more clearly, and more elegantly, and to give information and offer reassurance in the face of some of the more baffling assertions about "correctness" that are sometimes made.

This reappraisal has involved looking carefully at evidence of actual usage (in the Oxford English Corpus, the citations collected by the Oxford Reading Programme, and other sources) in order to find out where mistakes are actually being made, and where confusion and ambiguity actually arise. The issues on which journalists and others tend to comment have been reassessed and a judgment made about whether their comments are justified.

From the 15th century onward, traditionalists have been objecting to particular senses of certain English words and phrases, for example, "due to" and "hopefully." Certain grammatical structures, too, have been singled out for adverse comment, notably the split infinitive and the use of a preposition at the end of a clause. Some of these objections are founded on very dubious arguments, for example, the notion that English grammatical structures should precisely parallel those of Latin or that meaning change of any kind is inherently suspect.

USAGE There is a traditional view, as set forth by the 17th-century poet and dramatist John Dryden, that it is incorrect to put a preposition at the end of a sentence, as in *where do you come from?* or *she's not a writer I've ever come across.* The rule was formulated on the basis that, since in Latin a preposition cannot come after the word it governs or is linked with, the same should be true of English. What this rule fails to take into account is that English is not like Latin in this respect, and in many cases (particularly in questions and with phrasal verbs) the attempt to move the preposition produces awkward, unnatural-sounding results. Winston Churchill famously objected to the rule, saying *"This is the sort of English up with which I will not put."* In standard English the placing of a preposition at the end of a sentence is widely accepted, provided the use sounds natural and the meaning is clear.

USAGE The use of **due to** as a prepositional phrase meaning 'because of,' as in *he had to retire **due to** an injury* first appeared in print in 1897, and traditional grammarians have opposed this prepositional usage for more than a century on the grounds that it is a misuse of the adjectival phrase **due to** in the sense of 'attributable to, likely or expected to' (*the train is due to arrive at 11:15*), or 'payable or owed to' (*render unto Caesar what is due to Caesar*). Nevertheless, this prepositional usage is now widespread and common in all types of literature and must be regarded as standard English.The phrase **due to the fact that** is very common in speech, but it is wordy, and, especially in writing, one should use the simple word 'because.'

USAGE The traditional sense of **hopefully**, 'in a hopeful manner' (*he stared hopefully at the trophy*), has been used since 1593. The first recorded use of **hopefully** as a sentence adverb, meaning 'it is to be hoped that' (*hopefully, we'll see you tomorrow*), appears in 1702 in the *Magnalia Christi Americana*, written by Massachusetts theologian and writer Cotton Mather. This use of **hopefully** is now the most common one. Sentence adverbs in general (*frankly, honestly, regrettably, seriously*) are found in English since at least the 1600s, and their use has become common in recent decades. However, most traditionalists take the view that all sentence adverbs are inherently suspect. Although they concede that the battle over **hopefully** is lost on the popular front, they continue to withhold approval of its use as a sentence adverb. Attentive ears are particularly bothered when the sentence that follows does not match the promise of the introductory adverb, as when *frankly* is followed not by an expression of honesty but by a self-serving proclamation (*frankly, I don't care if you go or not*). See also usage at SENTENCE ADVERB and THANKFULLY.

The usage notes in the *New Oxford American Dictionary* take the view that English is English, not Latin, and that English is, like all living languages, subject to change. Good usage is usage that gets the speaker's or writer's message across, not usage that conforms to some arbitrary rules that fly in the face of historical fact or current evidence. The editors of the *New Oxford American Dictionary* are well aware that the prescriptions of pundits in the past have had remarkably little practical effect on the way the language is actually used. A good dictionary reports the language as it is, not as the editors (or anyone else) would wish it to be, and the usage notes must give guidance that accords with observed facts about present-day usage.

This is not to imply that the issues are straightforward or that there are simple solutions, however. Much of the debate about use of language is highly political, and controversy is, occasionally, inevitable. Changing social attitudes have stigmatized long-established uses, such as the word "man" to denote the human race in general, and have highlighted the absence of a gender-neutral singular pronoun meaning both "he" and "she" (for which purpose "they" is now often used). Similarly, words such as "race" and "native" are now associated with particular problems of sensitivity in use. The usage notes in the *New Oxford American Dictionary* offer information and practical advice on such issues.

> **USAGE** Traditionally, the word **man** has been used to refer not only to adult males but also to human beings in general, regardless of sex. There is a historical explanation for this: in Old English, the principal sense of **man** was 'a human being,' and the words **wer** and **wif** were used to refer specifically to 'a male person' and 'a female person,' respectively. Subsequently, **man** replaced **wer** as the normal term for 'a male person,' but at the same time the older sense 'a human being' remained in use. In the second half of the 20th century, the generic use of **man** to refer to 'human beings in general' (as in *reptiles were here long before man appeared on the earth*) became problematic; the use is now often regarded as sexist or old-fashioned. In some contexts, terms such as **the human race** or **humankind** may be used instead of **man** or **mankind**. Certain fixed phrases and sayings, such as *time and tide wait for no man* can be easily rephrased (e.g., *time and tide wait for no one*). Alternatives for other related terms exist as well: the noun **manpower**, for example, can usually be replaced with **staff** or **crew**, and in most cases, the verbal form **to man** can be expressed as **to staff** or **to operate**.

> **USAGE** In contexts such as *a **native** of Boston* or *New York in the summer was too hot even for the **natives***, the noun **native** is quite acceptable. But when it is used to mean 'a nonwhite original inhabitant of a country,' as in *this dance is a favorite with the **natives***, it is more problematic. This meaning has an old-fashioned feel and, because of its associations with a colonial European outlook, it may cause offense.

Standard English

Unless otherwise stated, the words and senses recorded in this dictionary are all part of standard English; that is, they are in normal use in both speech and writing everywhere in the world, at many different levels of formality, ranging from official documents to casual conversation. Some words, however, are appropriate only in particular contexts, and these are labeled accordingly. The technical term for a particular level of use in language is **register**.

The *New Oxford American Dictionary* uses the following register labels:

formal: normally used only in writing, in contexts such as official documents.

informal: normally used only in contexts such as conversations or letters between friends.

dated: no longer used by the majority of English speakers, but still encountered occasionally, especially among the older generation.

archaic: very old-fashioned language, not in ordinary use at all today, but sometimes used to give a deliberately old-fashioned effect, or found in works of the past that are still widely read.

historical: still used today, but only to refer to some practice or artifact that is no longer part of the modern world.

literary: found only or mainly in literature written in an "elevated" style.

technical: normally used only in technical and specialist language, though not necessarily restricted to any specific subject field.

rare: not in normal use.

humorous: used with the intention of sounding funny or playful.

dialect: not used in standard American English, but still widely used in certain local regions of the United States.

offensive: language that is likely to cause offense, particularly ethnic or racial offense, whether the speaker intends it or not.

derogatory: language intended to convey a low opinion or cause personal offense.

vulgar slang: informal language that may cause offense, often because it refers to the bodily functions of sexual activity or excretion, which are still widely regarded as taboo.

World English

English is spoken as a first language by more than 300 million people throughout the world, and used as a second language by many millions more. It is the language of international communication in business, diplomacy, sports, science, technology, and countless other fields.

The main regional standards are American, British, Canadian, Australian and New Zealand, South African, Indian, and West Indian. Within each of these regional varieties, a number of highly differentiated local dialects may be found. For example, within American English, Southern and Appalachian English have a long history and a number of distinctive features, which have in turn influenced other varieties.

The scope of a dictionary such as the *New Oxford American Dictionary*, given the breadth of material it aims to cover, must be limited for the most part to the vocabulary of the standard language of the United States rather than world English variation. Nevertheless, the *New Oxford American Dictionary* includes thousands of regionalisms encountered in standard contexts in the different English-speaking areas of the world, e.g.,

bun·yip /ˈbənyip/ ▶ **n.** Austral. **1** a mythical amphibious monster inhabiting inland waterways. **2** [often as modifier] an impostor or pretender: *Australia's bunyip aristocracy.*
– ORIGIN from Wemba-Wemba *banib*.

ka·ross /kəˈräs/ ▶ **n.** S. African a rug or blanket of sewn animal skins, formerly used as a garment by African people, now used as a bed or floor covering.
– ORIGIN South African Dutch, from Khoikhoi *karos*.

par·kade /pärˈkād/ ▶ **n.** Canadian a multistory parking garage.
– ORIGIN 1950s: from PARK, on the pattern of *arcade*.

ser·vi·ette /ˌsərvēˈet/ ▶ **n.** Brit. & Canadian a table napkin.
– ORIGIN late 15th cent.: from Old French, from *servir* 'to serve.'

snog /snäg/ Brit. informal ▶ **v.** (**snogs, snogging, snogged**) [with obj.] kiss and caress amorously.
▶ **n.** an act or spell of amorous kissing and caressing.
– DERIVATIVES **snog·ger n.**
– ORIGIN 1940s: of unknown origin.

tuque /t(y)o͞ok/ ▶ **n.** Canadian a close-fitting knitted stocking cap.
– ORIGIN Canadian French form of TOQUE.

tyke /tīk/ (also **tike**) ▶ **n. 1** [usu. with adj.] informal a small child: ***is the little tyke up to his tricks again?***
■ [usu. as modifier] Canadian an initiation level of sports competition for young children: *tyke hockey*.
2 dated, chiefly Brit. an unpleasant or coarse man.
3 a dog, esp. a mongrel.
– ORIGIN late Middle English (sense 2 and sense 3): from Old Norse *tík* 'bitch.'

The underlying approach has been to get away from the traditional, parochial notion that "correct" English belongs to a chosen few in any one geographical area or social class. A network of consultants in all parts of the English-speaking world has assisted in this by giving information and answering queries—by e-mail, on a regular, often daily basis—on all aspects of the language in a particular region. Often, the aim has been to find out whether a particular word, sense, or expression, well known and standard in American English, is used anywhere else. The picture that emerges is one of complex interactions among an overlapping set of regional standards.

The vast majority of words and senses in the *New Oxford American Dictionary* are common to all the major regional standard varieties of English, but where important local differences exist, the *New Oxford American Dictionary* records them. There are over 6,000 geographical labels on words and senses in this dictionary, but this contrasts with more than ten times that number that are not labeled at all.

The complexity of the overall picture has necessarily been simplified, principally for reasons of space and clarity of presentation. For example, a label such as "chiefly Brit." implies, but does not state, that a term is not standard in American English, though it may nevertheless be found in some local varieties in the United States. The label "Brit.," on the other hand, implies that the use is found typically in standard British English but is not found in standard American English, though it may be found elsewhere.

Spelling

It is often said that English spelling is both irregular and illogical, and it is certainly true that it is only indirectly related to contemporary pronunciation. English spelling reflects not modern pronunciation but the pronunciation of the 16th and 17th centuries, in particular through the influence of the works of Shakespeare and the Authorized Version of the Bible. However, in the two centuries between Chaucer and Shakespeare, English pronunciation had undergone huge changes, but spelling had failed to follow.

In the 18th century, standard spelling became almost completely fixed. The dictionaries written in this period, particularly Samuel Johnson's *Dictionary of the English Language* (1755), helped establish this standard, which, with only minor change and variation, is the standard accepted in British English today. Just over fifty years after the American colonies became independent, in 1828, Noah Webster published a dictionary with many of the spellings that we recognize today as being distinctly American rather than British. The complex history of the English language, together with the absence of any ruling body imposing "spelling reform," has ensured that many idiosyncrasies and anomalies in standard spelling have not only arisen but have also been preserved.

The *New Oxford American Dictionary* gives advice and information on spelling, particularly those cases that are irregular or that otherwise cause difficulty for native speakers. The main categories are summarized below.

Variant spellings

The main form of each word given in the *New Oxford American Dictionary* is always the standard American spelling. If there is a standard variant, e.g., a standard British spelling variant, this is indicated at the top of the entry and is cross-referred if its alphabetical position is more than five entries distant from the main entry.

esophagus (Brit. **oesophagus**)

oesophagus British spelling of ESOPHAGUS.

phyllo (also **filo**)

filo variant spelling of PHYLLO.

Other variants, such as archaic, old-fashioned, or informal spellings, are cross-referred to the main entry, but are not themselves listed at the parent entry.

cyder archaic spelling of CIDER.

Hyphenation

Although standard spelling in English is fixed, the use of hyphenation is not. In standard American English, a few general rules are followed, and these are outlined below.

Hyphenation of noun compounds: There is no hard-and-fast rule to determine whether, for example, **airstream**, **air stream**, or **air-stream** is correct. All forms are found in use: all are recorded in the Oxford English Corpus and other standard texts. However, there is a broad tendency to avoid hyphenation for noun compounds in modern English (except when used to show grammatical function: see below). Thus there is, for example, a preference for **airstream** rather than **air-stream**, and for **air raid** rather than **air-raid**. Although this is a tendency in both American and British English, there is an additional preference in American English for the form to be one word and in British English for the form to be two words—e.g., **airfare** tends to be the most common form in American English, while **air fare** tends to be the most common form in British English. To save space and avoid confusion, only one of the three potential forms of each noun compound (the standard American one) is generally used as the headword form in the *New Oxford American Dictionary*. This does not, however, imply that other forms are incorrect or not used.

Grammatical function: Hyphens are also used to perform certain grammatical functions. When a noun compound made up of two separate words (e.g., **credit card**) is placed before another noun and used to modify it, the general rule is that the noun compound becomes hyphenated, e.g., *I have overused my credit card and am now in credit-card debt*. This sort of regular alternation is seen in example sentences in the *New Oxford American Dictionary* but is not otherwise explicitly mentioned in the dictionary entries.

A similar alternation is found in compound adjectives such as **well intentioned**. When used predicatively (i.e., after the verb), such adjectives are unhyphenated, but when used attributively (i.e., before the noun), they are hyphenated: *his remarks were well intentioned*; *a well-intentioned remark*.

A general rule governing verb compounds means that, where a noun compound is two words (e.g., **beta test**), any verb derived from it is normally hyphenated (**to beta-test**: *the system was beta-tested*). Similarly, verbal nouns and adjectives are more often hyphenated than ordinary noun or adjective compounds (e.g., **epoch-making**, **nation-building**).

Inflection

Compared with other languages, English has comparatively few inflections, and those that exist are remarkably regular. We add an *-s* to most nouns to make a plural; we add *-ed* to most verbs to make a past tense or a past participle, and *-ing* to make a present participle.

Occasionally, a difficulty arises: for example, a single consonant after a short stressed vowel is doubled before adding *-ed* or *-ing* (**hum**, **hums**, **humming**, **hummed**). In addition, words borrowed from other languages generally bring their foreign inflections with them, causing problems for English speakers who are not proficient in those languages.

In all such cases, guidance is given in the *New Oxford American Dictionary*. The main areas covered are outlined below.

Verbs

The following forms are regarded as regular and are therefore not shown in the dictionary:

- third person singular present forms adding *-s* to the stem (or *-es* to stems ending in *-s*, *-x*, *-z*, *-sh*, or soft *-ch*), e.g., **find ➤ finds; crush ➤ crushes**
- past tenses and past participles dropping a final silent *e* and adding *-ed* to the stem, e.g., **change ➤ changed; dance ➤ danced**
- present participles dropping a final silent *e* and adding *-ing* to the stem, e.g., **change ➤ changing; dance ➤ dancing**

Other forms are given in the dictionary, notably for:

- verbs that inflect by doubling a consonant, e.g., **bat ➤ bats, batting, batted**
- verbs ending in *-y* that inflect by changing *-y* to *-i*, e.g., **try ➤ tries, trying, tried**
- verbs in which past tense and past participle do not follow the regular *-ed* pattern, e.g., **feel ➤** past **felt; awake ➤** past **awoke; ➤** past part. **awoken**
- present participles that add *-ing* but retain a final *e* (in order to make clear that the pronunciation of *g* remains soft), e.g., **singe ➤ singeing**

Nouns

Plurals formed by adding *-s* (or *-es* when they end in *-s*, *-x*, *-z*, *-sh*, or soft *-ch*) are regarded as regular and are not shown, e.g., **dog ➤ dogs; lunch ➤ lunches**

Other plural forms are given in the dictionary, notably for:

- nouns ending in *-i* or *-o*, e.g., **agouti ➤ agoutis; albino ➤ albinos**
- nouns ending in *-a*, *-um*, or *-us* that are or appear to be Latinate forms, e.g., **alumna ➤ alumnae; spectrum ➤ spectra; alveolus ➤ alveoli**
- nouns ending in *-y*, e.g., **fly ➤ flies; party ➤ parties**
- nouns with more than one plural form, e.g., **crux ➤ cruxes** or **cruces; money ➤ moneys** or **monies**
- nouns with plurals showing a change in the stem, e.g., **foot ➤ feet; louse ➤ lice**
- nouns with plurals unchanged from the singular form, e.g., **sheep ➤** (pl. same); **bonsai ➤** (pl. same)

Adjectives

The following forms for comparative and superlative are regarded as regular and are not shown in the dictionary:

- words of one syllable adding *-er* and *-est*, e.g., **great ➤ greater, greatest**
- words of one syllable ending in silent *e*, which drop the *-e* and add *-er* and *-est*, e.g., **brave ➤ braver, bravest**
- words that form the comparative and superlative by adding "more" and "most"; e.g., **beautiful ➤ more beautiful, most beautiful**

Other forms are given in the dictionary, notably for:

- adjectives that form the comparative and superlative by doubling a final consonant, e.g., **hot ➤ hotter, hottest**
- two-syllable adjectives that form the comparative and superlative with *-er* and *-est* (typically adjectives ending in *-y* and their negative forms), e.g., **happy ➤ happier, happiest; unhappy ➤ unhappier, unhappiest.**

How to use this dictionary

New part of speech (indicated by ▶) | Part of speech

Core sense

Subsenses (introduced by ■)

ear[1] /i(ə)r/ ▶ **n.** the organ of hearing and balance in humans and other vertebrates, esp. the external part of this. ■ an organ sensitive to sound in other animals. ■ [in sing.] an ability to recognize, appreciate, and reproduce sounds, esp. music or language: ***an ear for melody.*** ■ used to refer to a person's willingness to listen and pay attention to something: ***she offers a sympathetic ear to worried pet owners.*** ■ an ear-shaped thing, esp. the handle of a jug.

Encyclopedic information (in separate block)

> The ear of a mammal is composed of three parts. The outer or external ear consists of a fleshy external flap and a tube leading to the eardrum or tympanum. The middle ear is an air-filled cavity connected to the throat, containing three small linked bones that transmit vibrations from the eardrum to the inner ear. The inner ear is a complex fluid-filled labyrinth including the spiral cochlea (where vibrations are converted to nerve impulses) and the three semicircular canals (forming the organ of balance). The ears of other vertebrates are broadly similar.

Label (showing level of formality)

Phrases

Example (showing typical use)

– PHRASES **be all ears** informal be listening eagerly and attentively. **bring something (down) about one's ears** bring something, esp. misfortune, on oneself: *she brought her world crashing about her ears.* **one's ears are burning** one is subconsciously aware of being talked about or criticized. **grin** (or **smile**) **from ear to ear** smile broadly. **have something coming out of one's ears** informal have a substantial or excessive amount of something: *that man's got money coming out of his ears.* **have someone's ear** have access to and influence with someone: *he claimed to have the prime minister's ear.* **have** (or **keep**) **an ear to the ground** be well informed about events and trends. **in one ear and out the other** heard but disregarded or quickly forgotten: *whatever he tells me seems to go in one ear and out the other.* **listen with half an ear** not give one's full attention. **be out on one's ear** informal be dismissed or ejected ignominiously. **up to one's ears in** informal very busy with or deeply involved in: *I'm up to my ears in work here.*

Derivatives (in alphabetical order)

– DERIVATIVES **eared adj.** [in combination] *long-eared,* **ear·less adj.**

– ORIGIN Old English *ēare,* of Germanic origin; related to Dutch *oor* and German *Ohr,* from an Indo-European root shared by Latin *auris* and Greek *ous.*

Homonym number (indicates different word with the same spelling)

ear[2] ▶ **n.** the seed-bearing head or spike of a cereal plant. ■ a head of corn.

– ORIGIN Old English *ēar,* of Germanic origin; related to Dutch *aar* and German *Ähre.*

Grammatical information (in square brackets)

Common collocation (highlighted within example)

earn /ərn/ ▶ **v.** [with obj.] (of a person) obtain (money) in return for labor or services: ***they earn $35 per hour | he now earns his living as a truck driver.*** ■ [with two objs.] (of an activity or action) cause (someone) to obtain (money): ***this latest win earned them $50,000 in prize money.*** ■ (of capital invested) gain (money) as interest or profit. ■ gain or incur deservedly in return for one's behavior or achievements: ***through the years she has earned affection and esteem.***

– PHRASES **earn one's keep** work in return for food and accommodations. ■ be worth the time, money, or effort spent on one.

Phrasal verbs

– PHRASAL VERBS **earn out** (or **earn something out**) (of an author, book, recording artist, etc.) generate sufficient income through sales to equal the amount paid in an advance or royalty: *my experience is that most authors don't earn out | don't confuse earning out the advance with being profitable.*

– ORIGIN Old English *earnian,* from a base shared by Old English *esne* 'laborer.'

Label (showing regional distribution)

Technical information

Label (showing currency)

Word history

ear·wig /ˈi(ə)rˌwig/ ▶ **n.** a small elongated insect with a pair of terminal appendages that resemble pincers. The females typically care for their eggs and young until they are grown. ● Order Dermaptera: several families.
▶ **v.** (**earwigs, earwigging, earwigged**) [no obj.] informal, chiefly Brit. eavesdrop on a conversation: *he looked behind him to see if anyone was earwigging.* ■ [with obj.] archaic influence (someone) by secret means.
– ORIGIN Old English *ēarwicga*, from *ēare* 'ear' + *wicga* 'earwig' (probably related to *wiggle*). The insect is so named because it was once thought to crawl into the human ear.

Encyclopedic entry (biography)

Earp /ərp/, Wyatt (Berry Stapp) (1848–1929), US marshal and frontiersman. He is best known for the gunfight at the OK Corral (1881), in which he, his brothers, and his friend Doc Holliday fought the Clanton brothers at Tombstone, Arizona.

Pronunciation (respelling)

Subject label

ec·dy·sis /ˈekdəsis/ ▶ **n.** Zoology the process of shedding the old skin (in reptiles) or casting off the outer cuticle (in insects and other arthropods).
– DERIVATIVES **ec·dys·i·al** /ekˈdizēəl/ **adj.**
– ORIGIN mid 19th cent.: from Greek *ekdusis*, from *ekduein* 'put off,' from *ek-* 'out, off' + *duein* 'put.'

Encyclopedic entry (place name)

Additional information (in separate block)

Ec·ua·dor /ˈekwəˌdôr/ a republic in northwestern South America, on the Pacific coast; pop. 14,573,100 (est. 2009); capital, Quito; languages, Spanish (official), Quechua.

Formerly part of the Inca empire, Ecuador was conquered by the Spanish in 1534. It remained part of Spain's American empire until 1822, when independence was gained.

– DERIVATIVES **Ec·ua·dor·i·an** /ˌekwəˈdôrēən/ (also **Ecuadorean**) **adj. & n.**

Verb inflections

Typical form (in bold)

Typical pattern (in bold)

ed·it /ˈedit/ ▶ **v.** (**edits, editing, edited**) [with obj.]
1 prepare (written material) for publication by correcting, condensing, or otherwise modifying it: *Volume I was edited by J. Johnson.* ■ choose material for (a movie or a radio or television program) and arrange it to form a coherent whole: *the footage wasn't good enough to be edited into broadcast form* | (as adj. **edited**) *an edited version drawn from several prerecorded performances.* ■ change (text) on a computer. ■ (**edit something out**) remove unnecessary or inappropriate words, sounds, or scenes from a text, movie, or radio or television program.
2 be editor of (a newspaper or magazine).
▶ **n.** a change or correction made as a result of editing.
– ORIGIN late 18th cent. (as a verb): partly a back-formation from EDITOR, reinforced by French *éditer* 'to edit' (from *édition* 'edition').

Cross-reference entry

Plural form

e·o·hip·pus /ˌēōˈhipəs/ ▶ **n.** (pl. **eohippuses**) another term for HYRACOTHERIUM.
– ORIGIN late 19th cent.: from Greek *ēōs* 'dawn' + *hippos* 'horse.'

Variant spelling

ep·i·cen·ter /ˈepiˌsentər/ (Brit. **epicentre**) ▶ **n.** the point on the earth's surface vertically above the focus of an earthquake. ■ the central point of something, typically a difficult or unpleasant situation: *the patient was at the epicenter of concern.*
– DERIVATIVES **ep·i·cen·tral** /ˌepiˈsentrəl/ **adj.**
– ORIGIN late 19th cent.: from Greek *epikentros* 'situated on a center,' from *epi* 'upon' + *kentron* 'center.'

Key to pronunciations

This dictionary uses a simple respelling system to show how entries are pronounced, using the symbols listed below. Generally, only the first of two or more identical headwords will have a pronunciation respelling. Where a derivative simply adds a common suffix such as **-less**, **-ness**, or **-ly** to the headword, the derivative may not have a pronunciation respelling unless some other element of the pronunciation also changes.

a	*as in* **hat** /hat/, **fashion** /ˈfasHən/, **carry** /ˈkarē/
ā	*as in* **day** /dā/, **rate** /rāt/, **maid** /mād/, **prey** /prā/
ä	*as in* **lot** /lät/, **father** /ˈfäT͟Hər/, **barnyard** /ˈbärnˌyärd/
b	*as in* **big** /big/
CH	*as in* **church** /CHərCH/, **picture** /ˈpikCHər/
d	*as in* **dog** /dôg/, **bed** /bed/
e	*as in* **men** /men/, **bet** /bet/, **ferry** /ˈferē/
ē	*as in* **feet** /fēt/, **receive** /riˈsēv/
e(ə)r	*as in* **air** /e(ə)r/, **care** /ke(ə)r/
ə	*as in* **about** /əˈbout/, **soda** /ˈsōdə/, **mother** /ˈməT͟Hər/, **person** /ˈpərsən/
f	*as in* **free** /frē/, **graph** /graf/, **tough** /təf/
g	*as in* **get** /get/, **exist** /igˈzist/, **egg** /eg/
h	*as in* **her** /hər/, **behave** /biˈhāv/
i	*as in* **fit** /fit/, **guild** /gild/, **women** /ˈwimin/
ī	*as in* **time** /tīm/, **guide** /gīd/, **hire** /hī(ə)r/, **sky** /skī/
i(ə)r	*as in* **ear** /i(ə)r/, **beer** /bi(ə)r/, **pierce** /pi(ə)rs/
j	*as in* **judge** /jəj/, **carriage** /ˈkarij/
k	*as in* **kettle** /ˈketl/, **cut** /kət/, **quick** /kwik/
l	*as in* **lap** /lap/, **cellar** /ˈselər/, **cradle** /ˈkrādl/
m	*as in* **main** /mān/, **dam** /dam/
n	*as in* **need** /nēd/, **honor** /ˈänər/, **maiden** /ˈmādn/
NG	*as in* **sing** /siNG/, **anger** /ˈaNGgər/
ō	*as in* **go** /gō/, **promote** /prəˈmōt/
ô	*as in* **law** /lô/, **thought** /thôt/, **lore** /lôr/
oi	*as in* **boy** /boi/, **noisy** /ˈnoizē/
o͝o	*as in* **wood** /wo͝od/, **football** /ˈfo͝otˌbôl/, **sure** /SHo͝or/
o͞o	*as in* **food** /fo͞od/, **music** /ˈmyo͞ozik/
ou	*as in* **mouse** /mous/, **coward** /ˈkou(ə)rd/
p	*as in* **put** /po͝ot/, **cap** /kap/
r	*as in* **run** /rən/, **fur** /fər/, **spirit** /ˈspirit/
s	*as in* **sit** /sit/, **lesson** /ˈlesən/, **face** /fās/
SH	*as in* **shut** /SHət/, **social** /ˈsōSHəl/, **action** /ˈakSHən/
t	*as in* **top** /täp/, **seat** /sēt/, **forty** /ˈfôrtē/
TH	*as in* **thin** /THin/, **truth** /tro͞oTH/
T͟H	*as in* **then** /T͟Hen/, **father** /ˈfäT͟Hər/
v	*as in* **never** /ˈnevər/, **very** /ˈverē/
w	*as in* **wait** /wāt/, **quit** /kwit/
(h)w	*as in* **when** /(h)wen/, **which** /(h)wiCH/
y	*as in* **yet** /yet/, **accuse** /əˈkyo͞oz/
z	*as in* **zipper** /ˈzipər/, **musician** /myo͞oˈziSHən/
ZH	*as in* **measure** /ˈmeZHər/, **vision** /ˈviZHən/

Foreign Sounds

KH *as in* **Bach** /bäKH/
A fricative consonant pronounced with the tongue in the same position as for /k/, as in German *Buch* and *ich*, or Scottish *loch*.

N *as in* **en route** /äN ˈro͞ot/, **Rodin** /rōdaN/
The /N/ does not represent a separate sound; it indicates that the preceding vowel is nasalized, as in French *bon* (bon voyage) and *en* (en route).

œ *as in* **hors d'oeuvre** /ôr ˈdœvrə/, **Goethe** /ˈgœtə/
A vowel made by rounding the lips as with /ô/ while saying /e/ or /ā/, as in French *boeuf* and *feu*, or German *Hölle* and *Höhle*.

Y *as in* **Lully** /lYˈlē/, **Utrecht** /ˈYˌtreKHt/
A vowel made by rounding the lips as with /o͝o/ or /o͞o/ while saying /i/ or /ē/, as in French *rue* or German *fühlen*.

Stress Marks

Stress (or accent) is represented by marks placed before the affected syllable. The primary stress mark is a short, raised vertical line /ˈ/ which signifies that the heaviest emphasis should be placed on the syllable that follows. The secondary stress mark is a short, lowered vertical line /ˌ/ which signifies a somewhat weaker emphasis than on the syllable with primary stress.

Variant Pronunciations

There are several ways in which variant pronunciations are indicated in the respellings.

Some respellings show a pronunciation symbol within parentheses to indicate a possible variation in pronunciation; for example, in **sandwich** /ˈsan(d)wiCH/ sometimes the /d/ is pronounced, while at other times it is not.

Variant pronunciations may be respelled in full, separated by semicolons. The more common pronunciation is listed first, if this can be determined, but many variants are so common and widespread as to be of equal status.

Variant pronunciations may be indicated by respelling only the part of the word that changes. A hyphen will replace the part of the pronunciation that has remained the same. These 'cutback' respellings will occur primarily in three areas:

a) where the headword has a variant pronunciation:
quasiparticle /ˌkwāzīˈpärtikəl; ˌkwäzē-/

b) in derivative forms:
dangle /ˈdaNGgəl/ **dangler** /-glər/ **dangly** /-glē/

Note: Cutbacks in derivatives always refer back to the headword respelling, not the preceding derivative.

c) at irregular plurals:
parenthesis /pəˈrenTHəsis/ **parentheses** /-ˌsēz/

Note: A hyphen sometimes serves to separate syllables where the respelling might otherwise look confusing, as at reinforce /ˌrē-inˈfôrs/.

Key to abbreviations

abbr.	abbreviation
adj.	adjective
adv.	adverb
attrib.	attributive
Austral.	Australian
Brit.	British
C	Celsius
c.	circa ('about, around')
cent.	century
chem.	chemical
cm	centimeter, centimeters
comb.	combining
conj.	conjunction
cu.	cubic
e.g.	exempli gratia ('for example')
esp.	especially
etc.	et cetera ('and other things')
exclam.	exclamation
F	Fahrenheit
fem.	feminine
fl.	flourished
fl. oz.	fluid ounce, fluid ounces
ft.	foot, feet
i.e.	id est ('that is')
in.	inch, inches
intrans.	intransitive
kg	kilogram, kilograms
km	kilometer, kilometers
l	liter, liters
lb.	pound, pounds
m	meter, meters
masc.	masculine
mi.	mile, miles
ml	milliliter, milliliters
mm	millimeter, millimeters
mph	miles per hour
n.	noun
N. Amer.	North American
N. English	Northern English
N. Irish	Northern Irish
NZ	New Zealand
obj.	object
oz.	ounce, ounces
part.	participle
pl.	plural
pop.	population
predic.	predicative
prep.	preposition
pron.	pronoun
rpm	revolutions per minute
S. African	South African
sc.	scilicet ('that is to say')
sing.	singular
sq.	square
trans.	transitive
UK	United Kingdom
US	United States
usu.	usually
v.	verb
var.	variety
vs.	versus
W. Indian	West Indian
yd.	yard, yards

New Oxford American Dictionary

Ready Reference

British and American Terminology

American readers of British writing are well aware of the spelling differences that exist between American and British English. The *u* in *colour,* the *re* in *centre,* the *s* in *analyse,* the *que* in *cheque,* the *ae* in *anaemia,* the *c* in *defence,* the *ugh* in *draught,* the single *l* in *enrolment,* the double *l* in *dishevelled,* the *c* in *mollusc,* the *s* in *practise,* the *me* in *programme,* the *y* in *tyre* — just to name a few — are familiar indicators of British, rather than American, English. However, in addition to spelling differences there are a number of terminology distinctions — that is, one term in British English and a different term in American English, both with the same meaning. Some British words and expressions are listed here, with their American equivalents.

British English	American English
accommodation	accommodations
action replay	instant replay
advert	ad; advertisement
aeroplane	airplane
afters	dessert
agony aunt	advice columnist
air bridge	jetway
airscrew	aircraft propeller
Alice band	headband
Allen key	Allen wrench
Alsatian	German shepherd
aluminium	aluminum
American football	football
amusement arcade	video arcade
angel cake	angel food cake
aniseed	anise
anticlockwise	counterclockwise
arse	ass
articulated lorry	tractor-trailer
asymmetric bars	uneven bars
athletics	track and field
aubergine	eggplant
bags of	lots of
bain-marie	double boiler
baking tray	cookie sheet
banger	sausage
bank holiday	legal holiday
bedhead	headboard
beetle crushers	heavy boots
beetroot	beet(s)
big wheel	Ferris wheel
bill	check
bin bag	trash bag
biscuit	cookie; cracker
black economy	underground economy
blanket bath	sponge bath
blind	(window) shade
block of flats	condominium
bloke	guy
blowlamp	blowtorch
board and lodging	room and board
bobble	pompom
boiler suit	coveralls
bonnet	hood (*of a car*)
boob tube	tube top
boot	trunk (*of a car*)
bottom drawer	hope chest
bowls	lawn bowling
box spanner	lug wrench
braces	suspenders
breakdown van	tow truck
breeze block	cinder block
brent goose	brant
bridging loan	bridge loan
bumbag	fanny pack
candyfloss	cotton candy
capstan lathe	turret lathe
car park	parking lot
caravan	camper; RV
carer	caregiver
casualty	emergency room
catapult	slingshot
central reservation	median strip
chat show	talk show
cheeky	sassy; impudent
chips	French fries
chuffed	pleased
cinema	movie theater; the movies
cinemagoer	moviegoer
cling film	plastic wrap
close season	closed season
codswallop	nonsense
cold store	freezer
collywobbles	queasiness
common seal	harbor seal
conker	horse chestnut
consumer durables	durable goods
cooker	stove; range
cookery book	cookbook
cookery	cooking
corn	wheat; grain; cereal crop
cornet	cone (*for ice cream*)
cornflour	cornstarch
cos (lettuce)	Romaine
cot	crib
cotton bud	cotton swab
cotton wool	absorbent cotton
council estate	(housing) project
courgette	zucchini
court card	face card
covering letter	cover letter
cow gum	rubber cement
crash barrier	guardrail
crisps	chips; potato chips
crockery	dishes
crocodile clip	alligator clip
cross wires	crosshairs
crotchet	quarter note
crumbed	breaded

British English	American English
cuckoo pint	jack-in-the-pulpit
current account	checking account
curtain rail	curtain rod
cutthroat razor	straight razor
damp	dampness
danger money	hazard pay
deadlock	deadbolt
deaf aid	hearing aid
demister	defroster (*in a car*)
dialling tone	dial tone
diamante	rhinestone
dicky	shaky; unsound
dotty	loony; crazy
double cream	heavy cream
double-declutch	double-clutch
draughts	checkers (*game*)
drawing pin	thumbtack
dressing gown	robe; bathrobe
drink-driving	drunk driving
drinks cupboard	liquor cabinet
drinks party	cocktail party
drive	driveway
driving licence	driver's license
drophead	convertible (*car*)
dual carriageway	divided highway
dummy	pacifier
dust sheet	drop cloth
dustbin	garbage can
earth closet	outhouse
earth	ground (*electrical*)
egg flip	eggnog
engaged	busy (*of a telephone*)
estate agent	real estate agent; realtor
estate car	station wagon
ex-directory	unlisted
extension lead	extension cord
eyebath	eyecup
fag	cigarette
fairy cake	cupcake
fairy story	fairy tale
faith school	parochial school
Father Christmas	Santa Claus
fibre tip	felt-tip pen
filler cap	gas cap
filmsetting	photocomposition
financial year	fiscal year
fire brigade/service	fire company/ department
fire raiser	arsonist
first floor	second floor
first-name terms	first-name basis
fish finger	fish stick
fish slice	spatula
fitted carpet	wall-to-wall carpeting
fizzy	carbonated
flagstaff	flagpole
flannel	washcloth
flat battery	dead battery
flat	apartment
flex	electric cord
flexitime	flextime
flick knife	switchblade
flyover	overpass
football	soccer

British English	American English
footway	sidewalk
forage cap	service cap
forklift truck	forklift
fringe	bangs (*hair*)
full board	American plan (*in hotels*)
full stop	period (*punctuation*)
funnel	smokestack
in future	in the future
garden	yard; lawn
gearing	leverage (*finance*)
gear lever	gearshift
goods train	freight train
gramophone	phonograph
greaseproof paper	wax paper/waxed paper
green fingers	green thumb
grill (*noun*)	broiler
grill (*verb*)	broil
ground floor	first floor
groundsman	groundskeeper
hairslide	barrette
hatstand	hatrack
hen night	bachelorette party
hire car	rental car
hire purchase	installment plan
hoarding	billboard
hob	stovetop
holdall	carryall
holiday	vacation
holidaymaker	vacationer
homely	homey
Hoover	vacuum cleaner
hosepipe	(garden) hose
in hospital	in the hospital
hot flush	hot flash
house agent	real estate agent; realtor
housing estate	housing development
hundreds and thousands	sprinkles; jimmies
ice lolly	popsicle
icing sugar	confectioners' sugar
immersion heater	electric water heater
indicator	turn signal (*on a car*)
industrial action	strike
industrial estate	industrial park
infant school	kindergarten
insanitary	unsanitary
inside leg	inseam
inspection pit	grease pit
insurance cover	insurance coverage
interval	intermission
inverted commas	quotation marks
jacket potato	baked potato
jelly babies	jelly beans
jemmy	jimmy
jim-jams	jammies
on the jobs front	on the job front
Joe Bloggs	Joe Blow
Joe Public	John Q. Public
joint	roast; cut (*of meat*)
jotter	small notebook; notepad
judder	shudder; wobble

British English	American English
jumble sale	rummage sale
jump lead	jumper cable
jumper	sweater
junior school	elementary school
kennel	doghouse
key money	rent deposit
kit	outfit (*of clothing*)
kitchen paper	paper towel(s)
knackered	exhausted
knave	jack (*card*)
knickers	underpants; panties
knob	small lump (*of butter, coal, etc.*)
knock up	rouse; waken
lace-up	walking shoe; Oxford
lacquer	hair spray
ladder	run (*in hosiery*)
ladies' fingers	okra
ladybird	ladybug
larder	pantry
lashings of	lots of
last but one	next to last
law court	court of law
lead piping	lead pipe
leat	flume
lettings	rental units
a lettuce	a head of lettuce
level crossing	grade crossing
library ticket	library card
on licence	on parole
licensed house	bar; tavern
lie doggo	lie in wait
life assurance	life insurance
lift	elevator
line of country	field of expertise
liquid paraffin	mineral oil
litter lout	litterbug
liver sausage	liverwurst
lodging house	rooming house
lolly	Popsicle
lollipop lady (*or* man)	crossing guard
longsighted	farsighted
loo	john (*toilet*)
loose chippings	gravel
loose cover	slipcover
lorry	truck
loudhailer	bullhorn
lounge	living room
lounge suit	business suit
low loader	flatbed truck
lucerne	alfalfa
lucky dip	grab bag
luggage van	baggage car
made road	paved road
maize	corn
maize cob	corn on the cob
mangetout pea	snow pea
market garden	truck farm
marshalling yard	railroad yard
mash	mashed potatoes
matchboard	tongue-and-groove lumber
maths	math
mean	stingy
metalled road	paved road

British English	American English
metals	rails (*of a railroad*)
milometer	odometer
mincer	food grinder
minim	half note
mobile phone	cell phone
monkey nut	peanut
monkey tricks	monkeyshines
mortgage repayment	mortgage payment
motor mechanic	auto mechanic
motorcar	car; automobile
motorway	expressway; highway
mouse mat	mouse pad
mug	fool (*noun*)
mug/mug up	study hard; cram
mum/mummy	mom/mommy
musical box	music box
muzzy	confused; blurred
nail varnish	nail polish
nappy	diaper
nark	stool pigeon
needlecord	pinwale
newsreader	newscaster
nit	nitwit
noughts and crosses	tic-tac-toe
number plate	license plate
nutter	nutcase
occupier	occupant
off colour	ill
off-licence	liquor store; package store
off pat	down pat
oik	lout; jerk
Old Bill	policeman; the police
old sweat	veteran (*soldier*)
opencast mining	open-pit mining; strip-mining
operating theatre	operating room
ordinary share	common stock
oven glove	oven mitt
oxyacetylene torch	acetylene torch
pack of cards	deck of cards
paddling pool	wading pool
paddy	tantrum
pair of steps	stepladder
panda car	patrol car
paper handkerchief	tissue
paperknife	letter opener
paracetamol	acetaminophen
paraffin	kerosene
parky	chilly
parting	part (*in hair*)
passage	hall or hallway; corridor
patience	solitaire
pavement	sidewalk
pay packet	pay envelope
pea-souper	heavy fog
pedestrian crossing	crosswalk
peg	clothespin
off the peg	off the rack; ready-made
pelmet	valance
penfriend	pen pal
pepper-and-salt	salt-and-pepper
perished	worn out; rotted; decayed
perishing	(*of weather*) extremely cold
pernickety	persnickety
petrol	gas; gasoline
physiotherapy	physical therapy
pie dish	pie plate
pinafore dress	jumper
pink	ping (*engine knock*)
pinny	apron
pitch	field; playing field
plain chocolate	dark chocolate
plain flour	all-purpose flour
plaster; sticking plaster	Band-Aid
plughole	drain (*of a sink, bathtub, etc.*)
plum	very good; highly desirable
pocketbook	notebook *or* wallet
point duty	traffic control
polling day	election day
polo neck	turtleneck
pop shop	pawn shop
positive discrimination	reverse discrimination
post	mail
postal vote	absentee ballot
postbox	mailbox
postcode	zip code
pot plant	houseplant
potato crisp	potato chip
potter	putter; dawdle
power point	electrical outlet
pram	baby carriage; stroller
prawn	shrimp
preference share	preferred stock
presenter	host; commentator
press stud	snap (*fastener*)
press-up	pushup
prise	pry; use a lever
private soldier	private; GI
professor	conductor (*of an orchestra*)
propeller shaft	drive shaft
proprietary name	trademark
pub; public house	bar; tavern
public school	private school
public transport	public transportation
punchbag	punching bag
puncture	flat tire
punt	bet; gamble
punter	gambler or customer
purchase tax	sales tax
pushchair	stroller
pylon	utility pole
quantity surveyor	estimator
quaver	eighth note
queue	line
quieten	quiet (*verb*)
racecourse	racetrack
racing car	race car
rail	rack (*of clothing*)
railway	railroad
at a rate of knots	very fast
ratepayer	taxpayer
rating	sailor; seaman (*in the navy*)
ratty	irritable
razor shell	razor clam
reach-me-downs	hand-me-downs
reader's ticket	library card
readies	cash (*noun*)
recorded delivery	certified mail
redundant	laid-off
registration plate	license plate
remould	retread (*tire*)
residential school	boarding school
return ticket	round-trip ticket
reverse the charges	call collect
reversing lights	backup lights
right-angled triangle	right triangle
ring road	beltway
ring up	call (*on the telephone*)
ring-a-ring-o'-roses	ring-around-the-rosy
room only	European plan
ropey	inferior
roundabout	merry-go-round; carousel
roundabout	traffic circle
rowing boat	rowboat
rowlock	oarlock
rubber	eraser
rubbish tip	dump (*noun*)
rubbish	nonsense
rum	odd; strange
running flush	straight flush
running knot	slip knot
sailing boat	sailboat
saloon	sedan (car)
salt pot	salt shaker
sandpit	sandbox
sandwich cake	layer cake
sanitary towel	sanitary napkin
scarper	run away
scatty	harebrained
scraperboard	scratchboard
screenwasher	windshield washer
scurf	dandruff
seal	sear (*a roast, etc.*)
secateurs	garden shears
secondary smoke	secondhand smoke
self-raising flour	self-rising flour
semibreve	whole note
semitone	half step
service lift	dumbwaiter
serviette	napkin
sewage farm	sewage treatment plant
share option	stock option
shift	move (*an object*)
ship's biscuit	hardtack
shoot	hunting trip
shopper	shopping bag
shopping trolley	shopping cart
shop-soiled	shopworn
shortcrust	pie crust
shortsighted	nearsighted
shovelboard	shuffleboard
show house/home	model home

British English	American English
side plate	bread plate
side	arrogance
sideboards	sideburns
silencer	muffler (*on a car*)
silverside	rump roast
singlet	wife-beater (*undershirt*)
single ticket	one-way ticket
skeleton in the cupboard	skeleton in the closet
skimmed milk	skim milk
skint	broke; penniless
skipping rope	jump rope
skirting board	baseboard
skive	shirk
slap bang	slam bang
slating	scolding; reprimand
sledge	sled
sleep rough	sleep outdoors
sleeper	railroad tie
sleeping partner	silent partner
sleeping policeman	speed bump
slowcoach	slowpoke
smartish	quickly
snakes and ladders	chutes and ladders
snout	informer
solicitor	lawyer
soya/soya bean	soy/soybean
spanner	wrench
sparking plug	spark plug
sparkling	carbonated
spatula	tongue depressor
spiky	irritable
spirits	liquor
splashback	backsplash
split pulse	split peas
sponge bag	shaving kit; cosmetics bag
sports player	athlete
spot on	dead on; exactly right
spring onion	green onion
spyhole	peephole
squashbox	squeezebox; accordion
squib	firecracker
squiffy	drunk
stag night	bachelor party
standard lamp	floor lamp
Stanley knife	utility knife
starkers	naked
starter	appetizer
state school	public school
stewing steak	stew meat
sticking plaster	adhesive tape
stone	14 pounds (*weight*)
stony broke	stone broke
storm in a teacup	tempest in a teapot
street lamp	streetlight
strip cartoon	comic strip
stump up	pay up
subway	underpass
sugar basin	sugar bowl
sun cream	sunblock
superannuation	retirement age
surgical spirit	rubbing alcohol
surtitle	supertitle
swallow dive	swan dive
swede	rutabaga
sweet(s)	candy
sweet plate	dessert plate
sweet trolley	pastry (*or* dessert) cart
swimming bath	swimming pool
switchback	roller coaster
swizz	swindle (*noun*)
tailboard	tailgate
tailplane	horizontal stabilizer
takeaway	takeout (*food*)
to take away	to go (*food*)
taxi rank	taxi stand
teaching block	school building
tea towel	dish towel
tearaway	hoodlum; juvenile delinquent
telly	television
terrace house	row house
theme tune	theme song
thingummy	thingamajig
tick	check mark
ticket tout	scalper
tiddly	tipsy
tights	pantyhose
timber	lumber
tin/tinned	can/canned
tipper	dump truck
tip-up seat	folding seat (*in a theater, etc.*)
titbit	tidbit
titchy	tiny
toffee apple	candy apple
top of the table	head of the table
top up	top off
torch	flashlight
tosh	nonsense
touch wood	knock on wood
trade union	labor union
trading estate	industrial park
trainers	sneakers
tram	streetcar; cable car
transport cafe	truck stop
trapezium	trapezoid
trapezoid	trapezium
traybake	sheet cake
treacle	molasses
tripper	tourist
trolley	shopping cart *or* gurney
trotters	pig's feet
truckle bed	trundle bed
tumble drier	(clothes) dryer
tunny	tuna fish
tup	ram (*male sheep*)
turf out	throw out; dismiss; expel
turkeycock	tom turkey
turps	turpentine
twelve-bore	twelve-gauge
twig	catch on; understand
tyke	mongrel
tyre lever	tire iron
unalike	unlike
underground	subway
unit trust	mutual fund
at university	at college
unmade track	dirt road
up one's street	up one's alley
vacuum flask	thermos bottle
valency	valence
verge	shoulder (*of a road*)
vest	undershirt
veterinary surgeon	veterinarian
viewpoint	scenic lookout
vulgar fraction	common fraction
wagon	car (*on a train*)
waistcoat	vest
walking frame	walker
warder	guard; prison guard
washeteria	laundromat
washing line	clothesline
waste ground	vacant lot
water biscuit	water cracker
water ice	Italian ice
weatherboard	clapboard
whinge	whine; complain
white coffee	coffee with cream
white spirit	mineral spirits
wholemeal bread	wholewheat bread
windcheater	windbreaker
windmill	pinwheel (*toy*)
windscreen	windshield
wing	fender (*of a car*)
wire screen	screen door
wire wool	steel wool
witter	chatter
wodge	chunk; lump
wonky	shaky; unreliable
wood	woods; forest
Worcester sauce	Worcestershire sauce
works outing	company picnic
worktop	countertop
Yale lock	cylinder lock
zebra crossing	crosswalk
zed	zee (*letter Z*)
zip	zipper

Alphabets

Arabic

Alone	Final	Medial	Initial		
ا	ـا			'alif	'
ب	ـب	ـبـ	بـ	bā'	b
ت	ـت	ـتـ	تـ	tā'	t
ث	ـث	ـثـ	ثـ	thā'	th
ج	ـج	ـجـ	جـ	jīm	j
ح	ـح	ـحـ	حـ	ḥā'	ḥ
خ	ـخ	ـخـ	خـ	khā'	kh
د	ـد			dāl	d
ذ	ـذ			dhāl	dh
ر	ـر			rā'	r
ز	ـز			zāy	z
س	ـس	ـسـ	سـ	sīn	s
ش	ـش	ـشـ	شـ	shīn	sh
ص	ـص	ـصـ	صـ	ṣād	ṣ
ض	ـض	ـضـ	ضـ	ḍād	ḍ
ط	ـط	ـطـ	طـ	ṭā'	ṭ
ظ	ـظ	ـظـ	ظـ	ẓā'	ẓ
ع	ـع	ـعـ	عـ	'ayn	'
غ	ـغ	ـغـ	غـ	ghayn	gh
ف	ـف	ـفـ	فـ	fā'	f
ق	ـق	ـقـ	قـ	qāf	q
ك	ـك	ـكـ	كـ	kāf	k
ل	ـل	ـلـ	لـ	lām	l
م	ـم	ـمـ	مـ	mīm	m
ن	ـن	ـنـ	نـ	nūn	n
ه	ـه	ـهـ	هـ	hā'	h
و	ـو			wāw	w
ي	ـي	ـيـ	يـ	yā'	y

Hebrew

א	aleph	'
ב	beth	b, bh
ג	gimel	g, gh
ד	daleth	d, dh
ה	he	h
ו	waw	w
ז	zayin	z
ח	ḥeth	ḥ
ט	ṭeth	ṭ
י	yodh	y
ך כ	kaph	k, kh
ל	lamedh	l
ם מ	mem	m
ן נ	nun	n
ס	samekh	s
ע	'ayin	'
ף פ	pe	p, ph
ץ צ	ṣadhe	ṣ
ק	qoph	q
ר	resh	r
שׂ	śin	ś
שׁ	shin	sh
ת	taw	t, th

Greek

Α α	alpha	a
Β β	beta	b
Γ γ	gamma	g
Δ δ	delta	d
Ε ε	epsilon	e
Ζ ζ	zeta	z
Η η	eta	ē
Θ θ	theta	th
Ι ι	iota	i
Κ κ	kappa	k
Λ λ	lambda	l
Μ μ	mu	m
Ν ν	nu	n
Ξ ξ	xi	x
Ο ο	omicron	o
Π π	pi	p
Ρ ρ	rho	r, rh
Σ σ ς	sigma	s
Τ τ	tau	t
Υ υ	upsilon	u
Φ φ	phi	ph
Χ χ	chi	kh
Ψ ψ	psi	ps
Ω ω	omega	ō

Russian

А а	a
Б б	b
В в	v
Г г	g
Д д	d
Е е	e, ye
Ё ё	yo
Ж ж	zh
З з	z
И и	i
Й й	ĭ
К к	k
Л л	l
М м	m
Н н	n
О о	o
П п	p
Р р	r
С с	s
Т т	t
У у	u
Ф ф	f
Х х	kh
Ц ц	ts
Ч ч	ch
Ш ш	sh
Щ щ	shch
Ъ ъ	" ('hard sign')
Ы ы	y
Ь ь	' ('soft sign')
Э э	e
Ю ю	yu
Я я	ya

Chemical Elements

Element	Symbol	Atomic no.	Element	Symbol	Atomic no.	Element	Symbol	Atomic no.
actinium	Ac	89	gold	Au	79	praseodymium	Pr	59
aluminum	Al	13	hafnium	Hf	72	promethium	Pm	61
americium	Am	95	hassium	Hs	108	protactinium	Pa	91
antimony	Sb	51	helium	He	2	radium	Ra	88
argon	Ar	18	holmium	Ho	67	radon	Rn	86
arsenic	As	33	hydrogen	H	1	rhenium	Re	75
astatine	At	85	indium	In	49	rhodium	Rh	45
barium	Ba	56	iodine	I	53	roentgenium	Rg	111
berkelium	Bk	97	iridium	Ir	77	rubidium	Rb	37
beryllium	Be	4	iron	Fe	26	ruthenium	Ru	44
bismuth	Bi	83	krypton	Kr	36	rutherfordium	Rf	104
bohrium	Bh	107	lanthanum	La	57	samarium	Sm	62
boron	B	5	lawrencium	Lr	103	scandium	Sc	21
bromine	Br	35	lead	Pb	82	seaborgium	Sg	106
cadmium	Cd	48	lithium	Li	3	selenium	Se	34
calcium	Ca	20	lutetium	Lu	71	silicon	Si	14
californium	Cf	98	magnesium	Mg	12	silver	Ag	47
carbon	C	6	manganese	Mn	25	sodium	Na	11
cerium	Ce	58	meitnerium	Mt	109	strontium	Sr	38
cesium	Cs	55	mendelevium	Md	101	sulfur	S	16
chlorine	Cl	17	mercury	Hg	80	tantalum	Ta	73
chromium	Cr	24	molybdenum	Mo	42	technetium	Tc	43
cobalt	Co	27	neodymium	Nd	60	tellurium	Te	52
copper	Cu	29	neon	Ne	10	terbium	Tb	65
curium	Cm	96	neptunium	Np	93	thallium	Tl	81
darmstadtium	Ds	110	nickel	Ni	28	thorium	Th	90
dubnium	Db	105	niobium	Nb	41	thulium	Tm	69
dysprosium	Dy	66	nitrogen	N	7	tin	Sn	50
einsteinium	Es	99	nobelium	No	102	titanium	Ti	22
erbium	Er	68	osmium	Os	76	tungsten	W	74
europium	Eu	63	oxygen	O	8	uranium	U	92
fermium	Fm	100	palladium	Pd	46	vanadium	V	23
fluorine	F	9	phosphorus	P	15	xenon	Xe	54
francium	Fr	87	platinum	Pt	78	ytterbium	Yb	70
gadolinium	Gd	64	plutonium	Pu	94	yttrium	Y	39
gallium	Ga	31	polonium	Po	84	zinc	Zn	30
germanium	Ge	32	potassium	K	19	zirconium	Zr	40

Pending agreement on their permanent names, newly discovered elements are given provisional names (IUPAC) based on the atomic number and formed systematically from the numerical roots *nil* (= 0), *un* (= 1), *bi* (= 2), etc. (*ununbium* = 112, *ununquadium* = 114, *ununhexium* = 116, *ununoctium* = 118).

Standard Weights and Measures with Metric Equivalents and Conversions

Equivalents

Linear Measure

1 inch	= 2.54 centimeters
1 foot = 12 inches	= 0.3048 meter
1 yard = 3 feet = 36 inches	= 0.9144 meter
1 (statute) mile = 1,760 yards = 5,280 feet	= 1.609 kilometers

Square Measure

1 square inch	= 6.45 square centimeters
1 square foot = 144 square inches	= 9.29 square decimeters
1 square yard = 9 square feet	= 0.836 square meter
1 acre = 4,840 square yards	= 0.405 hectare
1 square mile = 640 acres	= 259 hectares

Cubic Measure

1 cubic inch	= 16.4 cubic centimeters
1 cubic foot = 1,728 cubic inches	= 0.0283 cubic meter
1 cubic yard = 27 cubic feet	= 0.765 cubic meter

Capacity Measure

DRY MEASURE

1 pint = 33.60 cubic inches	= 0.550 liter
1 quart = 2 pints	= 1.101 liters
1 peck = 8 quarts	= 8.81 liters
1 bushel = 4 pecks	= 35.3 liters

LIQUID MEASURE

1 fluid ounce	= 29.573 milliliters
1 gill = 4 fluid ounces	= 118.294 milliliters
1 pint = 16 fluid ounces = 28.88 cubic inches	= 0.473 liter
1 quart = 2 pints	= 0.946 liter
1 gallon = 4 quarts	= 3.785 liters

Avoirdupois Weight

1 grain	= 0.065 gram
1 dram	= 1.772 grams
1 ounce = 16 drams	= 28.35 grams
1 pound = 16 ounces = 7,000 grains	= 0.4536 kilograms
1 stone (British) = 14 pounds	= 6.35 kilograms
1 short ton = 2,000 pounds	= 907.19 kilograms
1 long ton = 2,240 pounds	= 1016.05 kilograms
1 hundredweight (US) = 100 pounds	
20 hundredweight (US) = 2,000 pounds	

Conversions

Standard	Multiply By	To Get Metric
Length		
inches	2.5	centimeters
feet	30	centimeters
yards	0.9	meters
miles	1.6	kilometers
Area		
square inches	6.5	square centimeters
square feet	0.09	square meters
square yards	0.8	square meters
square miles	2.6	square kilometers
acres	0.4	hectares
Weight		
ounces	28	grams
pounds	0.45	kilograms
short tons	0.91	metric tons
long tons	1.02	metric tons
Volume		
teaspoons	5	milliliters
tablespoons	15	milliliters
cubic inches	16	milliliters
fluid ounces	30	milliliters
cups	0.24	liters
pints	0.47	liters
quarts	0.95	liters
gallons	3.8	liters
cubic feet	0.03	cubic meters
cubic yards	0.76	cubic meters
Temperature		
degrees Fahrenheit	subtract 32, then multiply by 5/9	degrees Celsius

Metric Weights and Measures with Standard Equivalents and Conversions

Equivalents

Linear Measure

1 millimeter	= 0.039 inch
1 centimeter = 10 millimeters	= 0.394 inch
1 decimeter = 10 centimeters	= 3.94 inches
1 meter = 10 decimeters	= 1.094 yards
1 decameter = 10 meters	= 10.94 yards
1 hectometer = 100 meters	= 109.4 yards
1 kilometer = 1,000 meters	= 0.6214 mile

Square Measure

1 square centimeter	= 0.155 square inch
1 square meter = 10,000 square centimeters	= 1.196 square yards
1 are = 100 square meters	= 119.6 square yards
1 hectare = 100 ares	= 2.471 acres
1 square kilometer = 100 hectares	= 0.386 square mile

Cubic Measure

1 cubic centimeter	= 0.061 cubic inch
1 cubic meter = 1,000,000 cubic centimeters	= 1.308 cubic yards

Capacity Measure

DRY MEASURE

1 liter	= 1.82 pints
1 liter	= 0.91 quart
1 liter	= 0.03 bushel
1 hectoliter = 100 liters	= 2.84 bushels

LIQUID MEASURE

1 milliliter	= 0.034 fluid ounce
1 centiliter = 10 milliliters	= 0.34 fluid ounce
1 deciliter = 10 centiliters	= 3.38 fluid ounces
1 liter = 10 deciliters	= 2.11 pints
1 liter	= 1.06 quarts
1 decaliter = 10 liters	= 2.64 gallons

Weight

1 milligram	= 0.015 grain
1 centigram = 10 milligrams	= 0.154 grain
1 decigram = 10 centigrams	= 1.543 grains
1 gram = 10 decigrams	= 15.43 grains
1 decagram = 10 grams	= 5.64 drams
1 hectogram = 100 grams	= 3.527 ounces
1 kilogram = 1,000 grams	= 2.205 pounds
1 metric ton = 1,000 kilograms	= 1.1 short tons
1 metric ton = 1,000 kilograms	= 0.984 long ton

Conversions

Metric	Multiply By	To Get Standard
Length		
millimeters	0.04	inches
centimeters	0.39	inches
centimeters	0.03	feet
meters	3.3	feet
meters	1.1	yards
kilometers	0.6	miles
Area		
square centimeters	0.16	square inches
square meters	10.76	square feet
square meters	1.2	square yards
square kilometers	0.4	square miles
hectares	2.5	acres
Weight		
grams	0.035	ounces
kilograms	2.2	pounds
metric tons	1.1	short tons
metric tons	0.984	long tons
Volume		
milliliters	0.2	teaspoons
milliliters	0.07	tablespoons
milliliters	0.06	cubic inches
milliliters	0.034	fluid ounces
liters	4.23	cups
liters	2.1	pints
liters	1.06	quarts
liters	0.26	gallons
cubic meters	35	cubic feet
cubic meters	1.3	cubic yards
Temperature		
degrees Celsius	multiply by 9/5, then add 32	degrees Fahrenheit

The Mayflower Compact

Before the passengers of the Mayflower *went ashore at Cape Cod (Massachusetts) in November 1620, a group of them (the English Separatists we know as "the Pilgrims") feared disruption by those not affiliated with them or their cause. The group's original objective had been to settle in the northern Virginia Territory, under the auspices of the British Crown and Virginia law, but the* Mayflower *had veered off on a more northerly course, leaving them outside the domain of a governing structure. To establish clear intent for the common good, an agreement, then and there, was drawn up. Conceived and signed as a voluntary commitment to support a self-administered communal government, the Mayflower Compact was America's first written constitution.*

The original document does not exist. Its first printing was in a 1622 book recounting the settlement of Plymouth Colony, and the oldest known handwritten copy was penned by William Bradford sometime between 1630 and 1654. (The earliest extant list of signers is from 1669.) Appearing as the "Mayflower Compact" in 1793, it was previously referred to as "an association and agreement," a "solemn contract," and "the covenant." The version seen here is a modernized transcription:

In the Name of God, Amen. We whose names are underwritten, the loyal subjects of our dread sovereign Lord, King James, by the grace of God, of Great Britain, France and Ireland King, Defender of the Faith, etc. Having undertaken, for the glory of God, and advancement of the Christian faith and honor of our King and Country, a voyage to plant the first colony in the northern parts of Virginia, do by these presents solemnly and mutually in the presence of God, and one of another, covenant and combine ourselves together into a civil body politic, for our better ordering and preservation and furtherance of the ends aforesaid; and by virtue hereof to enact, constitute and frame such just and equal laws, ordinances, acts, constitutions and offices, from time to time as shall be thought most meet and convenient for the general good of the Colony: unto which we promise all due submission and obedience. In witness whereof we have hereunder subscribed our names at Cape Cod the 11 of November, in the year of the reign of our sovereign Lord, King James of England, France and Ireland the eighteenth, and of Scotland the fifty-fourth Ano. Dom. 1620.

John Carver
William Bradford
Edward Winslow
William Brewster
Isaac Allerton
Miles Standish
John Alden
Samuel Fuller
Christopher Martin
William Mullins
William White
Richard Warren
John Howland
Stephen Hopkins
Edward Tilley
John Tilley
Francis Cooke
Thomas Rogers
Thomas Tinker
John Ridgdale
Edward Fuller
John Turner
Francis Eaton
James Chilton
John Crackstone
John Billington
Moses Fletcher
John Goodman
Digery Priest
Thomas Williams
Gilbert Winslow
Edmund Margeson
Peter Browne
Richard Britteridge
George Soule
Richard Clarke
Richard Gardiner
John Allerton
Thomas English
Edward Doty
Edward Leister

Signed November 11, 1620
(under the current Gregorian calendar, this date would have been November 21, 1620)

Voices of the American Revolution

The most effective asset in the American struggle for independence from Great Britain may have been the voices behind the Revolution. Directing this movement were a number of respected politicians and other members of educated American society noted for their eloquence and leadership. Much of what they had to say in the 1770s continues to be quoted today and is widely regarded as enduring in relevance. Here are some selected quotations from the early days of the American Revolution.

August 1774
Thomas Jefferson (*A Summary View of the Rights of British America*)

"The God who gave us life, gave us liberty at the same time; the hand of force may destroy, but cannot disjoin them."

March 23, 1775
Patrick Henry (speech to the Virginia House of Burgesses)

"Why stand we here idle? What is it that gentlemen wish? What would they have? Is life so dear, or peace so sweet, as to be purchased at the price of chains and slavery? Forbid it, Almighty God! I know not what course others may take; but as for me, give me liberty or give me death!"

April 16, 1775
Samuel Adams (letter to James Warren)

"Our unalterable resolution would be to be free. They have attempted to subdue us by force, but God be praised! in vain. Their arts may be more dangerous then their arms. Let us then renounce all treaty with them upon any score but that of total separation, and under God trust our cause to our swords."

April 26, 1775
Joseph Warren (American account of the Battle of Lexington)

"To the persecution and tyranny of his cruel ministry we will not tamely submit—appealing to Heaven for the justice of our cause, we determine to die or be free."

July 3, 1776
John Adams (letter to his wife, Abigail Adams)

"Yesterday the greatest question was decided, which was ever debated in America; and a greater perhaps never was, nor will be, decided among men. A resolution was passed without one dissenting colony, that these United Colonies are, and of right ought to be, free and independent states."

July 4, 1776
John Hancock (reported, but unsubstantiated, remark upon penning the first, and largest, signature to the Declaration of Independence)

"There, I guess King George will be able to read that."

July 4, 1776
Benjamin Franklin (reported, but unsubstantiated, remark at the signing of the Declaration of Independence)

"We must indeed all hang together, or, most assuredly, we shall all hang separately."

August 23, 1776
George Washington (General Orders)

"The hour is fast approaching, on which the Honor and Success of this army, and the safety of our bleeding Country depend. Remember officers and Soldiers, that you are Freemen, fighting for the blessings of Liberty—that slavery will be your portion, and that of your posterity, if you do not acquit yourselves like men."

September 22, 1776
Nathan Hale (last words before being hanged as a spy by the British)

"I only regret that I have but one life to lose for my country."

December 1776
Thomas Paine (*The Crisis*)

"These are the times that try men's souls. The summer soldier and the sunshine patriot will, in this crisis, shrink from the service of their country; but he that stands it now, deserves the love and thanks of man and woman."

The Declaration of Independence

Action of Second Continental Congress, July 4, 1776

The unanimous Declaration of the thirteen United States of America

WHEN in the Course of human Events, it becomes necessary for one People to dissolve the Political Bands which have connected them with another, and to assume among the Powers of the Earth, the separate and equal Station to which the Laws of Nature and of Nature's God entitle them, a decent Respect to the Opinions of Mankind requires that they should declare the causes which impel them to the Separation.

WE hold these Truths to be self-evident, that all Men are created equal, that they are endowed by their Creator with certain unalienable Rights, that among these are Life, Liberty and the Pursuit of Happiness — That to secure these Rights, Governments are instituted among Men, deriving their just Powers from the Consent of the Governed, that whenever any Form of Government becomes destructive of these Ends, it is the Right of the People to alter or to abolish it, and to institute new Government, laying its Foundation on such Principles, and organizing its Powers in such Form, as to them shall seem most likely to effect their Safety and Happiness. Prudence, indeed, will dictate that Governments long established should not be changed for light and transient Causes; and accordingly all Experience hath shewn, that Mankind are more disposed to suffer, while Evils are sufferable, than to right themselves by abolishing the Forms to which they are accustomed. But when a long Train of Abuses and Usurpations, pursuing invariably the same Object, evinces a Design to reduce them under absolute Despotism, it is their Right, it is their Duty, to throw off such Government, and to provide new Guards for their future Security. Such has been the patient Sufferance of these Colonies; and such is now the Necessity which constrains them to alter their former Systems of Government. The History of the present King of Great-Britain is a History of repeated Injuries and Usurpations, all having in direct Object the Establishment of an absolute Tyranny over these States. To prove this, let Facts be submitted to a candid World.

HE has refused his Assent to Laws, the most wholesome and necessary for the public Good.

HE has forbidden his Governors to pass Laws of immediate and pressing Importance, unless suspended in their Operation till his Assent should be obtained; and when so suspended, he has utterly neglected to attend to them.

HE has refused to pass other Laws for the Accommodation of large Districts of People, unless those People would relinquish the Right of Representation in the Legislature, a Right inestimable to them, and formidable to Tyrants only.

HE has called together Legislative Bodies at Places unusual, uncomfortable, and distant from the Depository of their public Records, for the sole Purpose of fatiguing them into Compliance with his Measures.

HE has dissolved Representative Houses repeatedly, for opposing with manly Firmness his Invasions on the Rights of the People.

HE has refused for a long Time, after such Dissolutions, to cause others to be elected; whereby the Legislative Powers, incapable of the Annihilation, have returned to the People at large for their exercise; the State remaining in the mean time exposed to all the Dangers of Invasion from without, and Convulsions within.

HE has endeavoured to prevent the Population of these States; for that Purpose obstructing the Laws for Naturalization of Foreigners; refusing to pass others to encourage their Migrations hither, and raising the Conditions of new Appropriations of Lands.

HE has obstructed the Administration of Justice, by refusing his Assent to Laws for establishing Judiciary Powers.

HE has made Judges dependent on his Will alone, for the Tenure of their Offices, and the Amount and Payment of their Salaries.

HE has erected a Multitude of new Offices, and sent hither Swarms of Officers to harrass our People, and eat out their Substance.

HE has kept among us, in Times of Peace, Standing Armies, without the consent of our Legislatures.

HE has affected to render the Military independent of and superior to the Civil Power.

HE has combined with others to subject us to a Jurisdiction foreign to our Constitution, and unacknowledged by our Laws; giving his Assent to their Acts of pretended Legislation:

FOR quartering large Bodies of Armed Troops among us:

FOR protecting them, by a mock Trial, from Punishment for any Murders which they should commit on the Inhabitants of these States:

FOR cutting off our Trade with all Parts of the World:

FOR imposing Taxes on us without our Consent:

FOR depriving us, in many Cases, of the Benefits of Trial by Jury:

FOR transporting us beyond Seas to be tried for pretended Offences:

FOR abolishing the free System of English Laws in a neighbouring Province, establishing therein an arbitrary Government, and enlarging its Boundaries, so as to render it at once an Example and fit Instrument for introducing the same absolute Rules into these Colonies:

FOR taking away our Charters, abolishing our most valuable Laws, and altering fundamentally the Forms of our Governments:

FOR suspending our own Legislatures, and declaring themselves invested with Power to legislate for us in all Cases whatsoever.

HE has abdicated Government here, by declaring us out of his Protection and waging War against us.

HE has plundered our Seas, ravaged our Coasts, burnt our Towns, and destroyed the Lives of our People.

HE is, at this Time, transporting large Armies of foreign Mercenaries to compleat the Works of Death, Desolation, and Tyranny, already begun with circumstances of Cruelty and Perfidy, scarcely paralleled in the most barbarous Ages, and totally unworthy the Head of a civilized Nation.

HE has constrained our fellow Citizens taken Captive on the high Seas to bear Arms against their Country, to become the Executioners of their Friends and Brethren, or to fall themselves by their Hands.

HE has excited domestic Insurrections amongst us, and has endeavoured to bring on the Inhabitants of our Frontiers, the merciless Indian Savages, whose known Rule of Warfare, is an undistinguished Destruction, of all Ages, Sexes and Conditions.

IN every stage of these Oppressions we have Petitioned for Redress in the most humble Terms: Our repeated Petitions have been answered only by repeated Injury. A Prince, whose Character is thus marked by every act which may define a Tyrant, is unfit to be the Ruler of a free People.

NOR have we been wanting in Attentions to our British Brethren. We have warned them from Time to Time of Attempts by their Legislature to extend an unwarrantable Jurisdiction over us. We have reminded them of the Circumstances of our Emigration and Settlement here. We have appealed to their native Justice and Magnanimity, and we have conjured them by the Ties of our common Kindred to disavow these Usurpations, which, would inevitably interrupt our Connections and Correspondence. They too have been deaf to the Voice of Justice and of Consanguinity. We must, therefore, acquiesce in the Necessity, which denounces our Separation, and hold them, as we hold the rest of Mankind, Enemies in War, in Peace, Friends.

WE, therefore, the Representatives of the UNITED STATES OF AMERICA, in GENERAL CONGRESS, Assembled, appealing to the Supreme Judge of the World for the Rectitude of our Intentions, do, in the Name, and by Authority of the good People of these Colonies, solemnly Publish and Declare, That these United Colonies are, and of Right ought to be, FREE AND INDEPENDENT STATES; that they are absolved from all Allegiance to the British Crown, and that all political Connection between them and the State of Great-Britain, is and ought to be totally dissolved; and that as FREE AND INDEPENDENT STATES, they have full Power to levy War, conclude Peace, contract Alliances, establish Commerce, and to do all other Acts and Things which INDEPENDENT STATES may of right do. And for the support of this Declaration, with a firm Reliance on the Protection of divine Providence, we mutually pledge to each other our Lives, our Fortunes, and our sacred Honor.

Signed by ORDER AND IN BEHALF of the CONGRESS,

JOHN HANCOCK, President.

Attest:

CHARLES THOMSON, Secretary.

SIGNERS:

Connecticut:
Roger Sherman
Saml. Huntington
Wm. Williams
Oliver Wolcott

Delaware:
Caesar Rodney
Geo. Read
Tho. McKean

Georgia:
Button Gwinnett
Lyman Hall
Geo. Walton

Maryland:
Samuel Chase
Wm. Paca
Thos. Stone
Charles Carroll, of Carrollton

Massachusetts-Bay:
John Hancock
Saml. Adams
John Adams
Robt. Treat Paine
Elbridge Gerry

New-Hampshire:
Josiah Bartlett
Wm. Whipple
Matthew Thornton

New-Jersey:
Richd. Stockton
Jno. Witherspoon
Fras. Hopkinson
John Hart
Abra. Clark

New-York:
Wm. Floyd
Phil. Livingston
Frans. Lewis
Lewis Morris

North-Carolina:
Wm. Hooper
Joseph Hewes
John Penn

Pennsylvania:
Robt. Morris
Benjamin Rush
Benja. Franklin
John Morton
Geo. Clymer
Jas. Smith
Geo. Taylor
James Wilson
Geo. Ross

Rhode-Island and Providence, &c.:
Step. Hopkins
William Ellery

South-Carolina:
Edward Rutledge
Thos. Heyward, Jr.
Thomas Lynch, Jr.
Arthur Middleton

Virginia:
George Wythe
Richard Henry Lee
Ths. Jefferson
Benja. Harrison
Thos. Nelson, Jr.
Francis Lightfoot Lee
Carter Braxton

The Constitution of the United States

PREAMBLE.

We the People of the United States, in Order to form a more perfect Union, establish Justice, insure domestic Tranquility, provide for the common defense, promote the general Welfare, and secure the Blessings of Liberty to ourselves and our Posterity, do ordain and establish this Constitution for the United States of America.

Article I.

Section 1.

All legislative Powers herein granted shall be vested in a Congress of the United States, which shall consist of a Senate and House of Representatives.

Section 2.

Clause 1:
The House of Representatives shall be composed of Members chosen every second Year by the People of the several States, and the Electors in each State shall have the Qualifications requisite for Electors of the most numerous Branch of the State Legislature.

Clause 2:
No Person shall be a Representative who shall not have attained to the Age of twenty five Years, and been seven Years a Citizen of the United States, and who shall not, when elected, be an Inhabitant of that State in which he shall be chosen.

Clause 3:
[*Representatives and direct Taxes shall be apportioned among the several States which may be included within this Union, according to their respective Numbers, which shall be determined by adding to the whole Number of free Persons, including those bound to Service for a Term of Years, and excluding Indians not taxed, three fifths of all other Persons.*][1] The actual Enumeration shall be made within three Years after the first Meeting of the Congress of the United States, and within every subsequent Term of ten Years, in such Manner as they shall by Law direct. The Number of Representatives shall not exceed one for every thirty Thousand, but each State shall have at Least one Representative; and until such enumeration shall be made, the State of New Hampshire shall be entitled to chuse three, Massachusetts eight, Rhode-Island and Providence Plantations one, Connecticut five, New-York six, New Jersey four, Pennsylvania eight, Delaware one, Maryland six, Virginia ten, North Carolina five, South Carolina five, and Georgia three.

Clause 4:
When vacancies happen in the Representation from any State, the Executive Authority thereof shall issue Writs of Election to fill such Vacancies.

Clause 5:
The House of Representatives shall chuse their Speaker and other Officers; and shall have the sole Power of Impeachment.

Section 3.

Clause 1:
The Senate of the United States shall be composed of two Senators from each State, [*chosen by the Legislature thereof,*][2] for six Years; and each Senator shall have one Vote.

Clause 2:
Immediately after they shall be assembled in Consequence of the first Election, they shall be divided as equally as may be into three Classes. The Seats of the Senators of the first Class shall be vacated at the Expiration of the second Year, of the second Class at the Expiration of the fourth Year, and of the third Class at the Expiration of the sixth Year, so that one third may be chosen every second Year; [*and if Vacancies happen by Resignation, or otherwise, during the Recess of the Legislature of any State, the Executive thereof may make temporary Appointments until the next Meeting of the Legislature, which shall then fill such Vacancies.*][3]

Clause 3:
No Person shall be a Senator who shall not have attained to the Age of thirty Years, and been nine Years a Citizen of the United States, and who shall not, when elected, be an Inhabitant of that State for which he shall be chosen.

Clause 4:
The Vice President of the United States shall be President of the Senate, but shall have no Vote, unless they be equally divided.

Clause 5:
The Senate shall chuse their other Officers, and also a President pro tempore, in the Absence of the Vice President, or when he shall exercise the Office of President of the United States.

Clause 6:
The Senate shall have the sole Power to try all Impeachments. When sitting for that Purpose, they shall be on Oath or Affirmation. When the President of the United States is tried, the Chief Justice shall preside: And no Person shall be convicted without the Concurrence of two thirds of the Members present.

1 Modified by Amendment XIV, Section 2.

2 Modified by Amendment XVII, Section 1.

3 Modified by Amendment XVII, Section 2.

Clause 7:
Judgment in Cases of Impeachment shall not extend further than to removal from Office, and disqualification to hold and enjoy any Office of honor, Trust or Profit under the United States: but the Party convicted shall nevertheless be liable and subject to Indictment, Trial, Judgment and Punishment, according to Law.

Section 4.

Clause 1:
The Times, Places and Manner of holding Elections for Senators and Representatives, shall be prescribed in each State by the Legislature thereof; but the Congress may at any time by Law make or alter such Regulations, except as to the Places of chusing Senators.

Clause 2:
The Congress shall assemble at least once in every Year, and such Meeting [*shall be on the first Monday in December*][4], unless they shall by Law appoint a different Day.

Section 5.

Clause 1:
Each House shall be the Judge of the Elections, Returns and Qualifications of its own Members, and a Majority of each shall constitute a Quorum to do Business; but a smaller Number may adjourn from day to day, and may be authorized to compel the Attendance of absent Members, in such Manner, and under such Penalties as each House may provide.

Clause 2:
Each House may determine the Rules of its Proceedings, punish its Members for disorderly Behaviour, and, with the Concurrence of two thirds, expel a Member.

Clause 3:
Each House shall keep a Journal of its Proceedings, and from time to time publish the same, excepting such Parts as may in their Judgment require Secrecy; and the Yeas and Nays of the Members of either House on any question shall, at the Desire of one fifth of those Present, be entered on the Journal.

Clause 4:
Neither House, during the Session of Congress, shall, without the Consent of the other, adjourn for more than three days, nor to any other Place than that in which the two Houses shall be sitting.

Section 6.

Clause 1:
The Senators and Representatives shall receive a Compensation for their Services, to be ascertained by Law, and paid out of the Treasury of the United States. They shall in all Cases, except Treason, Felony and Breach of the Peace, be privileged from Arrest during their Attendance at the Session of their respective Houses, and in going to and returning from the same; and for any Speech or Debate in either House, they shall not be questioned in any other Place.

Clause 2:
No Senator or Representative shall, during the Time for which he was elected, be appointed to any civil Office under the Authority of the United States, which shall have been created, or the Emoluments whereof shall have been increased during such time; and no Person holding any Office under the United States, shall be a Member of either House during his Continuance in Office.

Section 7.

Clause 1:
All Bills for raising Revenue shall originate in the House of Representatives; but the Senate may propose or concur with Amendments as on other Bills.

Clause 2:
Every Bill which shall have passed the House of Representatives and the Senate, shall, before it become a Law, be presented to the President of the United States; If he approve he shall sign it, but if not he shall return it, with his Objections to that House in which it shall have originated, who shall enter the Objections at large on their Journal, and proceed to reconsider it. If after such Reconsideration two thirds of that House shall agree to pass the Bill, it shall be sent, together with the Objections, to the other House, by which it shall likewise be reconsidered, and if approved by two thirds of that House, it shall become a Law. But in all such Cases the Votes of both Houses shall be determined by Yeas and Nays, and the Names of the Persons voting for and against the Bill shall be entered on the Journal of each House respectively. If any Bill shall not be returned by the President within ten Days (Sundays excepted) after it shall have been presented to him, the Same shall be a Law, in like Manner as if he had signed it, unless the Congress by their Adjournment prevent its Return, in which Case it shall not be a Law.

Clause 3:
Every Order, Resolution, or Vote to which the Concurrence of the Senate and House of Representatives may be necessary (except on a question of Adjournment) shall be presented to the President of the United States; and before the Same shall take Effect, shall be approved by him, or being disapproved by him, shall be repassed by two thirds of the Senate and House of Representatives, according to the Rules and Limitations prescribed in the Case of a Bill.

Section 8.

Clause 1:
The Congress shall have Power To lay and collect Taxes, Duties, Imposts and Excises, to pay the Debts and provide for the common Defence and general Welfare of the United States; but all Duties, Imposts and Excises shall be uniform throughout the United States;

Clause 2:
To borrow Money on the credit of the United States;

Clause 3:
To regulate Commerce with foreign Nations, and among the several States, and with the Indian Tribes;

Clause 4:
To establish a uniform Rule of Naturalization, and uniform Laws on the subject of Bankruptcies throughout the United States;

Clause 5:
To coin Money, regulate the Value thereof, and of foreign Coin, and fix the Standard of Weights and Measures;

Clause 6:
To provide for the Punishment of counterfeiting the Securities and current Coin of the United States;

Clause 7:
To establish Post Offices and post Roads;

4 Modified by Amendment XX, Section 2.

Clause 8:
To promote the Progress of Science and useful Arts, by securing for limited Times to Authors and Inventors the exclusive Right to their respective Writings and Discoveries;

Clause 9:
To constitute Tribunals inferior to the supreme Court;

Clause 10:
To define and punish Piracies and Felonies committed on the high Seas, and Offences against the Law of Nations;

Clause 11:
To declare War, grant Letters of Marque and Reprisal, and make Rules concerning Captures on Land and Water;

Clause 12:
To raise and support Armies, but no Appropriation of Money to that Use shall be for a longer Term than two Years;

Clause 13:
To provide and maintain a Navy;

Clause 14:
To make Rules for the Government and Regulation of the land and naval Forces;

Clause 15:
To provide for calling forth the Militia to execute the Laws of the Union, suppress Insurrections and repel Invasions;

Clause 16:
To provide for organizing, arming, and disciplining, the Militia, and for governing such Part of them as may be employed in the Service of the United States, reserving to the States respectively, the Appointment of the Officers, and the Authority of training the Militia according to the discipline prescribed by Congress;

Clause 17:
To exercise exclusive Legislation in all Cases whatsoever, over such District (not exceeding ten Miles square) as may, by Cession of particular States, and the Acceptance of Congress, become the Seat of the Government of the United States, and to exercise like Authority over all Places purchased by the Consent of the Legislature of the State in which the Same shall be, for the Erection of Forts, Magazines, Arsenals, dock-Yards, and other needful Buildings;—And

Clause 18:
To make all Laws which shall be necessary and proper for carrying into Execution the foregoing Powers, and all other Powers vested by this Constitution in the Government of the United States, or in any Department or Officer thereof.

Section 9.

Clause 1:
The Migration or Importation of such Persons as any of the States now existing shall think proper to admit, shall not be prohibited by the Congress prior to the Year one thousand eight hundred and eight, but a Tax or duty may be imposed on such Importation, not exceeding ten dollars for each Person.

Clause 2:
The Privilege of the Writ of Habeas Corpus shall not be suspended, unless when in Cases of Rebellion or Invasion the public Safety may require it.

Clause 3:
No Bill of Attainder or ex post facto Law shall be passed.

Clause 4:
No Capitation, or other direct, Tax shall be laid, [*unless in Proportion to the Census or Enumeration herein before directed to be taken.*][5]

Clause 5:
No Tax or Duty shall be laid on Articles exported from any State.

Clause 6:
No Preference shall be given by any Regulation of Commerce or Revenue to the Ports of one State over those of another: nor shall Vessels bound to, or from, one State, be obliged to enter, clear, or pay Duties in another.

Clause 7:
No Money shall be drawn from the Treasury, but in Consequence of Appropriations made by Law; and a regular Statement and Account of the Receipts and Expenditures of all public Money shall be published from time to time.

Clause 8:
No Title of Nobility shall be granted by the United States: And no Person holding any Office of Profit or Trust under them, shall, without the Consent of the Congress, accept of any present, Emolument, Office, or Title, of any kind whatever, from any King, Prince, or foreign State.

Section 10.

Clause 1:
No State shall enter into any Treaty, Alliance, or Confederation; grant Letters of Marque and Reprisal; coin Money; emit Bills of Credit; make any Thing but gold and silver Coin a Tender in Payment of Debts; pass any Bill of Attainder, ex post facto Law, or Law impairing the Obligation of Contracts, or grant any Title of Nobility.

Clause 2:
No State shall, without the Consent of the Congress, lay any Imposts or Duties on Imports or Exports, except what may be absolutely necessary for executing its inspection Laws: and the net Produce of all Duties and Imposts, laid by any State on Imports or Exports, shall be for the Use of the Treasury of the United States; and all such Laws shall be subject to the Revision and Controul of the Congress.

Clause 3:
No State shall, without the Consent of Congress, lay any Duty of Tonnage, keep Troops, or Ships of War in time of Peace, enter into any Agreement or Compact with another State, or with a foreign Power, or engage in War, unless actually invaded, or in such imminent Danger as will not admit of delay.

Article II.

Section 1.

Clause 1:
The executive Power shall be vested in a President of the United States of America. He shall hold his Office during the Term of four Years, and, together with the Vice President, chosen for the same Term, be elected, as follows:

Clause 2:
Each State shall appoint, in such Manner as the Legislature thereof may direct, a Number of Electors, equal to the whole Number of Senators and Representatives to which

5 Modified by Amendment XVI.

the State may be entitled in the Congress: but no Senator or Representative, or Person holding an Office of Trust or Profit under the United States, shall be appointed an Elector.

Clause 3:
[The Electors shall meet in their respective States, and vote by Ballot for two Persons, of whom one at least shall not be an Inhabitant of the same State with themselves. And they shall make a List of all the Persons voted for, and of the Number of Votes for each; which List they shall sign and certify, and transmit sealed to the Seat of the Government of the United States, directed to the President of the Senate. The President of the Senate shall, in the Presence of the Senate and House of Representatives, open all the Certificates, and the Votes shall then be counted. The Person having the greatest Number of Votes shall be the President, if such Number be a Majority of the whole Number of Electors appointed; and if there be more than one who have such Majority, and have an equal Number of Votes, then the House of Representatives shall immediately chuse by Ballot one of them for President; and if no Person have a Majority, then from the five highest on the List the said House shall in like Manner chuse the President. But in chusing the President, the Votes shall be taken by States, the Representation from each State having one Vote; A quorum for this Purpose shall consist of a Member or Members from two thirds of the States, and a Majority of all the States shall be necessary to a Choice. In every Case, after the Choice of the President, the Person having the greatest Number of Votes of the Electors shall be the Vice President. But if there should remain two or more who have equal Votes, the Senate shall chuse from them by Ballot the Vice President.][6]

Clause 4:
The Congress may determine the Time of choosing the Electors, and the Day on which they shall give their Votes; which Day shall be the same throughout the United States.

Clause 5:
No Person except a natural born Citizen, or a Citizen of the United States, at the time of the Adoption of this Constitution, shall be eligible to the Office of President; neither shall any Person be eligible to that Office who shall not have attained to the Age of thirty five Years, and been fourteen Years a Resident within the United States.

Clause 6:
[In Case of the Removal of the President from Office, or of his Death, Resignation, or Inability to discharge the Powers and Duties of the said Office, the Same shall devolve on the Vice President, and the Congress may by Law provide for the Case of Removal, Death, Resignation or Inability, both of the President and Vice President, declaring what Officer shall then act as President, and such Officer shall act accordingly, until the Disability be removed, or a President shall be elected.][7]

Clause 7:
The President shall, at stated Times, receive for his Services, a Compensation, which shall neither be encreased nor diminished during the Period for which he shall have been elected, and he shall not receive within that Period any other Emolument from the United States, or any of them.

Clause 8:
Before he enter on the Execution of his Office, he shall take the following Oath or Affirmation:—"I do solemnly swear (or affirm) that I will faithfully execute the Office of President of the United States, and will to the best of my Ability, preserve, protect and defend the Constitution of the United States."

6 Modified by Amendment XII.

7 Modified by Amendment XXV.

Section 2.

Clause 1:
The President shall be Commander in Chief of the Army and Navy of the United States, and of the Militia of the several States, when called into the actual Service of the United States; he may require the Opinion, in writing, of the principal Officer in each of the executive Departments, upon any Subject relating to the Duties of their respective Offices, and he shall have Power to grant Reprieves and Pardons for Offences against the United States, except in Cases of Impeachment.

Clause 2:
He shall have Power, by and with the Advice and Consent of the Senate, to make Treaties, provided two thirds of the Senators present concur; and he shall nominate, and by and with the Advice and Consent of the Senate, shall appoint Ambassadors, other public Ministers and Consuls, Judges of the supreme Court, and all other Officers of the United States, whose Appointments are not herein otherwise provided for, and which shall be established by Law: but the Congress may by Law vest the Appointment of such inferior Officers, as they think proper, in the President alone, in the Courts of Law, or in the Heads of Departments.

Clause 3:
The President shall have Power to fill up all Vacancies that may happen during the Recess of the Senate, by granting Commissions which shall expire at the End of their next Session.

Section 3.
He shall from time to time give to the Congress Information of the State of the Union, and recommend to their Consideration such Measures as he shall judge necessary and expedient; he may, on extraordinary Occasions, convene both Houses, or either of them, and in Case of Disagreement between them, with Respect to the Time of Adjournment, he may adjourn them to such Time as he shall think proper; he shall receive Ambassadors and other public Ministers; he shall take Care that the Laws be faithfully executed, and shall Commission all the Officers of the United States.

Section 4.
The President, Vice President and all civil Officers of the United States, shall be removed from Office on Impeachment for, and Conviction of, Treason, Bribery, or other high Crimes and Misdemeanors.

Article III.

Section 1.
The judicial Power of the United States shall be vested in one supreme Court, and in such inferior Courts as the Congress may from time to time ordain and establish. The Judges, both of the supreme and inferior Courts, shall hold their Offices during good Behaviour, and shall, at stated Times, receive for their Services, a Compensation, which shall not be diminished during their Continuance in Office.

Section 2.

Clause 1:
The judicial Power shall extend to all Cases, in Law and Equity, arising under this Constitution, the Laws of the United States, and Treaties made, or which shall be made, under their Authority;—to all Cases affecting Ambassadors, other public Ministers and Consuls;—to all Cases of admiralty and maritime Jurisdiction;—to Controversies to which the United States shall be a Party;—to Controversies between

two or more States;—[*between a State and Citizens of another State;—*][8] between Citizens of different States,—between Citizens of the same State claiming Lands under Grants of different States, [*and between a State, or the Citizens thereof, and foreign States, Citizens or Subjects.*][9]

Clause 2:
In all Cases affecting Ambassadors, other public Ministers and Consuls, and those in which a State shall be Party, the supreme Court shall have original Jurisdiction. In all the other Cases before mentioned, the supreme Court shall have appellate Jurisdiction, both as to Law and Fact, with such Exceptions, and under such Regulations as the Congress shall make.

Clause 3:
The Trial of all Crimes, except in Cases of Impeachment, shall be by Jury; and such Trial shall be held in the State where the said Crimes shall have been committed; but when not committed within any State, the Trial shall be at such Place or Places as the Congress may by Law have directed.

Section 3.

Clause 1:
Treason against the United States, shall consist only in levying War against them, or in adhering to their Enemies, giving them Aid and Comfort. No Person shall be convicted of Treason unless on the Testimony of two Witnesses to the same overt Act, or on confession in open Court.

Clause 2:
The Congress shall have Power to declare the Punishment of Treason, but no Attainder of Treason shall work Corruption of Blood, or Forfeiture except during the Life of the Person attainted.

Article IV.

Section 1.

Full Faith and Credit shall be given in each State to the public Acts, Records, and judicial Proceedings of every other State. And the Congress may by general Laws prescribe the Manner in which such Acts, Records and Proceedings shall be proved, and the Effect thereof.

Section 2.

Clause 1:
The Citizens of each State shall be entitled to all Privileges and Immunities of Citizens in the several States.

Clause 2:
A Person charged in any State with Treason, Felony, or other Crime, who shall flee from Justice, and be found in another State, shall on Demand of the executive Authority of the State from which he fled, be delivered up, to be removed to the State having Jurisdiction of the Crime.

Clause 3:
[*No Person held to Service or Labour in one State, under the Laws thereof, escaping into another, shall, in Consequence of any Law or Regulation therein, be discharged from such Service or Labour, but shall be delivered up on Claim of the Party to whom such Service or Labour may be due.*][10]

8 Modified by Amendment XI.

9 Modified by Amendment XI.

10 Modified by Amendment XIII.

Section 3.

Clause 1:
New States may be admitted by the Congress into this Union; but no new State shall be formed or erected within the Jurisdiction of any other State; nor any State be formed by the Junction of two or more States, or Parts of States, without the Consent of the Legislatures of the States concerned as well as of the Congress.

Clause 2:
The Congress shall have Power to dispose of and make all needful Rules and Regulations respecting the Territory or other Property belonging to the United States; and nothing in this Constitution shall be so construed as to Prejudice any Claims of the United States, or of any particular State.

Section 4.

The United States shall guarantee to every State in this Union a Republican Form of Government, and shall protect each of them against Invasion; and on Application of the Legislature, or of the Executive (when the Legislature cannot be convened) against domestic Violence.

Article V.

The Congress, whenever two thirds of both Houses shall deem it necessary, shall propose Amendments to this Constitution, or, on the Application of the Legislatures of two thirds of the several States, shall call a Convention for proposing Amendments, which, in either Case, shall be valid to all Intents and Purposes, as Part of this Constitution, when ratified by the Legislatures of three fourths of the several States, or by Conventions in three fourths thereof, as the one or the other Mode of Ratification may be proposed by the Congress; Provided that no Amendment which may be made prior to the Year One thousand eight hundred and eight shall in any Manner affect the first and fourth Clauses in the Ninth Section of the first Article; and that no State, without its Consent, shall be deprived of its equal Suffrage in the Senate.

Article VI.

Clause 1:
All Debts contracted and Engagements entered into, before the Adoption of this Constitution, shall be as valid against the United States under this Constitution, as under the Confederation.

Clause 2:
This Constitution, and the Laws of the United States which shall be made in Pursuance thereof; and all Treaties made, or which shall be made, under the Authority of the United States, shall be the supreme Law of the Land; and the Judges in every State shall be bound thereby, any Thing in the Constitution or Laws of any State to the Contrary notwithstanding.

Clause 3:
The Senators and Representatives before mentioned, and the Members of the several State Legislatures, and all executive and judicial Officers, both of the United States and of the several States, shall be bound by Oath or Affirmation, to support this Constitution; but no religious Test shall ever be required as a Qualification to any Office or public Trust under the United States.

Article VII.

The Ratification of the Conventions of nine States, shall be sufficient for the Establishment of this Constitution between the States so ratifying the Same.

Done in Convention by the Unanimous Consent of the States present the Seventeenth Day of September in the Year of our Lord one thousand seven hundred and Eighty seven and of the Independence of the United States of America the Twelfth In witness whereof We have hereunto subscribed our Names,

GEORGE WASHINGTON—
Presidt. and deputy from Virginia

New Hampshire
John Langdon
Nicholas Gilman

Delaware
Geo: Read
Gunning Bedford jun
John Dickinson
Richard Bassett
Jaco: Broom

Massachusetts
Nathaniel Gorham
Rufus King

Maryland
James McHenry
Dan: of St. Thos. Jenifer
Danl Carroll

Connecticut
Wm. Saml. Johnson
Roger Sherman

Virginia
John Blair
James Madison, Jr.

New York
Alexander Hamilton

New Jersey
Wil: Livingston
David Brearley
Wm. Paterson
Jona: Dayton

North Carolina
Wm. Blount
Richd. Dobbs Spaight
Hu Williamson

Pennsylvania
B Franklin
Thomas Mifflin
Robt Morris
Geo. Clymer
Thos. FitzSimons
Jared Ingersoll
James Wilson
Gouv Morris

South Carolina
J. Rutledge
Charles Cotesworth Pinckney
Charles Pinckney
Pierce Butler

Georgia
William Few
Abr Baldwin

Attest:
William Jackson,
Secretary

Amendments to the Constitution of the United States

ARTICLES in addition to, and Amendment of, the Constitution of the United States of America, proposed by Congress, and ratified by the Legislatures of the several States, pursuant to the fifth Article of the original Constitution.[1]

Amendment I.

Congress shall make no law respecting an establishment of religion, or prohibiting the free exercise thereof; or abridging the freedom of speech, or of the press; or the right of the people peaceably to assemble, and to petition the Government for a redress of grievances.

Amendment II.

A well regulated Militia, being necessary to the security of a free State, the right of the people to keep and bear Arms, shall not be infringed.

Amendment III.

No Soldier shall, in time of peace be quartered in any house, without the consent of the Owner, nor in time of war, but in a manner to be prescribed by law.

Amendment IV.

The right of the people to be secure in their persons, houses, papers, and effects, against unreasonable searches and seizures, shall not be violated, and no Warrants shall issue, but upon probable cause, supported by Oath or affirmation, and particularly describing the place to be searched, and the persons or things to be seized.

Amendment V.

No person shall be held to answer for a capital, or otherwise infamous crime, unless on a presentment or indictment of a Grand Jury, except in cases arising in the land or naval forces, or in the Militia, when in actual service in time of War or public danger; nor shall any person be subject for the same offence to be twice put in jeopardy of life or limb; nor shall be compelled in any criminal case to be a witness against himself, nor be deprived of life, liberty, or property, without due process of law; nor shall private property be taken for public use, without just compensation.

Amendment VI.

In all criminal prosecutions, the accused shall enjoy the right to a speedy and public trial, by an impartial jury of the State and district wherein the crime shall have been committed, which district shall have been previously ascertained by law, and to be informed of the nature and cause of the accusation; to be confronted with the witnesses against him; to have compulsory process for obtaining witnesses in his favor, and to have the Assistance of Counsel for his defence.

Amendment VII.

In Suits at common law, where the value in controversy shall exceed twenty dollars, the right of trial by jury shall be preserved, and no fact tried by a jury, shall be otherwise re-examined in any Court of the United States, than according to the rules of the common law.

Amendment VIII.

Excessive bail shall not be required, nor excessive fines imposed, nor cruel and unusual punishments inflicted.

Amendment IX.

The enumeration in the Constitution, of certain rights, shall not be construed to deny or disparage others retained by the people.

Amendment X.

The powers not delegated to the United States by the Constitution, nor prohibited by it to the States, are reserved to the States respectively, or to the people.

Amendment XI.

The Judicial power of the United States shall not be construed to extend to any suit in law or equity, commenced or prosecuted against one of the United States by Citizens of another State, or by Citizens or Subjects of any Foreign State.

Ratification was completed on February 7, 1795.

Amendment XII.

The Electors shall meet in their respective states, and vote by ballot for President and Vice-President, one of whom, at least, shall not be an inhabitant of the same state with themselves; they shall name in their ballots the person voted for as President, and in distinct ballots the person voted for as Vice-President, and they shall make distinct lists of all persons voted for as President, and of all persons voted for as Vice-President, and of the number of votes for each, which lists they shall sign and certify, and transmit sealed to the seat of the government of the United States, directed to the President of the Senate;—The President of the Senate shall, in the presence of the Senate and House of Representatives, open all the certificates and the votes shall then be counted;—The person having the greatest number of votes for President, shall be the President, if such number be a majority of the whole number of Electors appointed; and if no person have such majority, then from the persons having the highest numbers not exceeding three on the list of those voted for as President, the House of Representatives shall choose immediately, by ballot, the President. But in choosing the President, the votes shall be taken by states, the representation from each state having one vote; a quorum for this purpose shall consist of a member or members from two-thirds of the states,

1 On September 25, 1789, Congress transmitted to the states twelve proposed amendments. Two of these, which involved congressional representation and pay, were not adopted. The remaining ten amendments (that is, Amendments I–X) were ratified on December 15, 1791, and are known as the Bill of Rights.

and a majority of all the states shall be necessary to a choice. [*And if the House of Representatives shall not choose a President whenever the right of choice shall devolve upon them, before the fourth day of March next following, then the Vice-President shall act as President, as in the case of the death or other constitutional disability of the President.*—][2] The person having the greatest number of votes as Vice-President, shall be the Vice-President, if such number be a majority of the whole number of Electors appointed, and if no person have a majority, then from the two highest numbers on the list, the Senate shall choose the Vice-President; a quorum for the purpose shall consist of two-thirds of the whole number of Senators, and a majority of the whole number shall be necessary to a choice. But no person constitutionally ineligible to the office of President shall be eligible to that of Vice-President of the United States.

Ratification was completed on June 15, 1804.

Amendment XIII.

Section 1.

Neither slavery nor involuntary servitude, except as a punishment for crime whereof the party shall have been duly convicted, shall exist within the United States, or any place subject to their jurisdiction.

Section 2.

Congress shall have power to enforce this article by appropriate legislation.

Ratification was completed on December 6, 1865.

Amendment XIV.

Section 1.

All persons born or naturalized in the United States, and subject to the jurisdiction thereof, are citizens of the United States and of the State wherein they reside. No State shall make or enforce any law which shall abridge the privileges or immunities of citizens of the United States; nor shall any State deprive any person of life, liberty, or property, without due process of law; nor deny to any person within its jurisdiction the equal protection of the laws.

Section 2.

Representatives shall be apportioned among the several States according to their respective numbers, counting the whole number of persons in each State, excluding Indians not taxed. But when the right to vote at any election for the choice of electors for President and Vice President of the United States, Representatives in Congress, the Executive and Judicial officers of a State, or the members of the Legislature thereof, is denied to any of the male inhabitants of such State, being twenty-one years of age, and citizens of the United States, or in any way abridged, except for participation in rebellion, or other crime, the basis of representation therein shall be reduced in the proportion which the number of such male citizens shall bear to the whole number of male citizens twenty-one years of age in such State.

Section 3.

No person shall be a Senator or Representative in Congress, or elector of President and Vice President, or hold any office, civil or military, under the United States, or under any State, who, having previously taken an oath, as a member of Congress, or as an officer of the United States, or as a member of any State legislature, or as an executive or judicial officer of any State, to support the Constitution of the United States, shall have engaged in insurrection or rebellion against the same, or given aid or comfort to the enemies thereof. But Congress may by a vote of two-thirds of each House, remove such disability.

Section 4.

The validity of the public debt of the United States, authorized by law, including debts incurred for payment of pensions and bounties for services in suppressing insurrection or rebellion, shall not be questioned. But neither the United States nor any State shall assume or pay any debt or obligation incurred in aid of insurrection or rebellion against the United States, or any claim for the loss or emancipation of any slave; but all such debts, obligations and claims shall be held illegal and void.

Section 5.

The Congress shall have power to enforce, by appropriate legislation, the provisions of this article.

Ratification was completed on July 9, 1868.

Amendment XV.

Section 1.

The right of citizens of the United States to vote shall not be denied or abridged by the United States or by any State on account of race, color, or previous condition of servitude.

Section 2.

The Congress shall have power to enforce this article by appropriate legislation.

Ratification was completed on February 3, 1870 (unless the withdrawal of ratification by New York on January 5, 1870, was effective; in which event, ratification was completed on February 17, 1870, when Nebraska ratified).

Amendment XVI.

The Congress shall have power to lay and collect taxes on incomes, from whatever source derived, without apportionment among the several States, and without regard to any census or enumeration.

Ratification was completed on February 3, 1913.

Amendment XVII.

The Senate of the United States shall be composed of two Senators from each State, elected by the people thereof, for six years; and each Senator shall have one vote. The electors in each State shall have the qualifications requisite for electors of the most numerous branch of the State legislatures. When vacancies happen in the representation of any State in the Senate, the executive authority of such State shall issue writs of election to fill such vacancies: *Provided,* That the legislature of any State may empower the executive thereof to make temporary appointments until the people fill the vacancies by election as the legislature may direct. This amendment shall not be so construed as to affect the election or term of any Senator chosen before it becomes valid as part of the Constitution.

Ratification was completed on April 8, 1913.

Amendment XVIII.

Section 1.

After one year from the ratification of this article the manufacture, sale, or transportation of intoxicating liquors within, the importation thereof into, or the exportation thereof from the United States and all territory subject to the jurisdiction thereof for beverage purposes is hereby prohibited.

Section 2.

The Congress and the several States shall have concurrent power to enforce this article by appropriate legislation.

2 Modified by Amendment XX, Section 3.

Section 3.

This article shall be inoperative unless it shall have been ratified as an amendment to the Constitution by the legislatures of the several States, as provided in the Constitution, within seven years from the date of the submission hereof to the States by the Congress.

Ratification was completed on January 16, 1919.

Amendment XIX.

The right of citizens of the United States to vote shall not be denied or abridged by the United States or by any State on account of sex. Congress shall have power to enforce this article by appropriate legislation.

Ratification was completed on August 18, 1920.

Amendment XX.

Section 1.

The terms of the President and Vice President shall end at noon on the 20th day of January, and the terms of Senators and Representatives at noon on the 3d day of January, of the years in which such terms would have ended if this article had not been ratified; and the terms of their successors shall then begin.

Section 2.

The Congress shall assemble at least once in every year, and such meeting shall begin at noon on the 3d day of January, unless they shall by law appoint a different day.

Section 3.

If, at the time fixed for the beginning of the term of the President, the President elect shall have died, the Vice President elect shall become President. If a President shall not have been chosen before the time fixed for the beginning of his term, or if the President elect shall have failed to qualify, then the Vice President elect shall act as President until a President shall have qualified; and the Congress may by law provide for the case wherein neither a President elect nor a Vice President elect shall have qualified, declaring who shall then act as President, or the manner in which one who is to act shall be selected, and such person shall act accordingly until a President or Vice President shall have qualified.

Section 4.

The Congress may by law provide for the case of the death of any of the persons from whom the House of Representatives may choose a President whenever the right of choice shall have devolved upon them, and for the case of the death of any of the persons from whom the Senate may choose a Vice President whenever the right of choice shall have devolved upon them.

Section 5.

Sections 1 and 2 shall take effect on the 15th day of October following the ratification of this article.

Section 6.

This article shall be inoperative unless it shall have been ratified as an amendment to the Constitution by the legislatures of three-fourths of the several States within seven years from the date of its submission.

Ratification was completed on January 23, 1933.

Amendment XXI.

Section 1.

The eighteenth article of amendment to the Constitution of the United States is hereby repealed.

Section 2.

The transportation or importation into any State, Territory, or possession of the United States for delivery or use therein of intoxicating liquors, in violation of the laws thereof, is hereby prohibited.

Section 3.

This article shall be inoperative unless it shall have been ratified as an amendment to the Constitution by conventions in the several States, as provided in the Constitution, within seven years from the date of the submission hereof to the States by the Congress.

Ratification was completed on December 5, 1933.

Amendment XXII.

Section 1.

No person shall be elected to the office of the President more than twice, and no person who has held the office of President, or acted as President, for more than two years of a term to which some other person was elected President shall be elected to the office of the President more than once. But this Article shall not apply to any person holding the office of President when this Article was proposed by the Congress, and shall not prevent any person who may be holding the office of President, or acting as President, during the term within which this Article becomes operative from holding the office of President or acting as President during the remainder of such term.

Section 2.

This article shall be inoperative unless it shall have been ratified as an amendment to the Constitution by the legislatures of three-fourths of the several States within seven years from the date of its submission to the States by the Congress.

Ratification was completed on February 27, 1951.

Amendment XXIII.

Section 1.

The District constituting the seat of Government of the United States shall appoint in such manner as the Congress may direct:

> A number of electors of President and Vice President equal to the whole number of Senators and Representatives in Congress to which the District would be entitled if it were a State, but in no event more than the least populous State; they shall be in addition to those appointed by the States, but they shall be considered, for the purposes of the election of President and Vice President, to be electors appointed by a State; and they shall meet in the District and perform such duties as provided by the twelfth article of amendment.

Section 2.

The Congress shall have power to enforce this article by appropriate legislation.

Ratification was completed on March 29, 1961.

Amendment XXIV.

Section 1.

The right of citizens of the United States to vote in any primary or other election for President or Vice President, for electors for President or Vice President, or for Senator or Representative in Congress, shall not be denied or abridged by the United States or any State by reason of failure to pay any poll tax or other tax.

Section 2.

The Congress shall have power to enforce this article by appropriate legislation.

Ratification was completed on January 23, 1964.

Amendment XXV.

Section 1.

In case of the removal of the President from office or of his death or resignation, the Vice President shall become President.

Section 2.

Whenever there is a vacancy in the office of the Vice President, the President shall nominate a Vice President who shall take office upon confirmation by a majority vote of both Houses of Congress.

Section 3.

Whenever the President transmits to the President pro tempore of the Senate and the Speaker of the House of Representatives his written declaration that he is unable to discharge the powers and duties of his office, and until he transmits to them a written declaration to the contrary, such powers and duties shall be discharged by the Vice President as Acting President.

Section 4.

Whenever the Vice President and a majority of either the principal officers of the executive departments or of such other body as Congress may by law provide, transmit to the President pro tempore of the Senate and the Speaker of the House of Representatives their written declaration that the President is unable to discharge the powers and duties of his office, the Vice President shall immediately assume the powers and duties of the office as Acting President.

Thereafter, when the President transmits to the President pro tempore of the Senate and the Speaker of the House of Representatives his written declaration that no inability exists, he shall resume the powers and duties of his office unless the Vice President and a majority of either the principal officers of the executive department or of such other body as Congress may by law provide, transmit within four days to the President pro tempore of the Senate and the Speaker of the House of Representatives their written declaration that the President is unable to discharge the powers and duties of his office. Thereupon Congress shall decide the issue, assembling within forty-eight hours for that purpose if not in session. If the Congress, within twenty-one days after receipt of the latter written declaration, or, if Congress is not in session, within twenty-one days after Congress is required to assemble, determines by two-thirds vote of both Houses that the President is unable to discharge the powers and duties of his office, the Vice President shall continue to discharge the same as Acting President; otherwise, the President shall resume the powers and duties of his office.

Ratification was completed on February 10, 1967.

Amendment XXVI.

Section 1.

The right of citizens of the United States, who are eighteen years of age or older, to vote shall not be denied or abridged by the United States or by any State on account of age.

Section 2.

The Congress shall have power to enforce this article by appropriate legislation.

Ratification was completed on July 1, 1971.

Amendment XXVII.

No law, varying the compensation for the services of the Senators and Representatives, shall take effect, until an election of Representatives shall have intervened.

Ratification was completed on May 7, 1992.[3]

3 This amendment, being the second of twelve articles proposed by the First Congress on September 25, 1789, was declared by the Archivist of the United States on May 18, 1992, to have been ratified by the legislatures of 40 of the 50 states.

The Gettysburg Address / The New Colossus

The Gettysburg Address

The dedication of the Soldiers' National Cemetery at Gettysburg in Pennsylvania took place on November 19, 1863, at the site of the Battle of Gettysburg (July 1–3, 1863), the costliest battle of the American Civil War. At the dedication, the opening speech was dellvered by renowned orator Edward Everett, who spoke for two hours. Following Everett was President Abraham Lincoln, who spoke for just two minutes. Lincoln's brief address, which includes the remark, "The world will little note, nor long remember what we say here," has been remembered ever since, and is regarded among the most important speeches in American history.

Fourscore and seven years ago our fathers brought forth on this continent a new nation, conceived in liberty and dedicated to the proposition that all men are created equal. Now we are engaged in a great civil war, testing whether that nation, or any nation so conceived and so dedicated, can long endure. We are met on a great battlefield of that war. We have come to dedicate a portion of that field as a final resting-place for those who here gave their lives that that nation might live. It is altogether fitting and proper that we should do this. But, in a larger sense, we cannot dedicate — we cannot consecrate — we cannot hallow — this ground. The brave men, living and dead, who struggled here have consecrated it, far above our poor power to add or detract. The world will little note, nor long remember what we say here, but it can never forget what they did here. It is for us the living, rather, to be dedicated here to the unfinished work which they who fought here have thus far so nobly advanced. It is rather for us to be here dedicated to the great task remaining before us — that from these honored dead we take increased devotion to that cause for which they gave the last full measure of devotion — that we here highly resolve that these dead shall not have died in vain — that this nation shall have a new birth of freedom and that government of the people, by the people, for the people, shall not perish from the earth.

President Abraham Lincoln
November 19, 1863

The New Colossus

"Give me your tired, your poor, Your huddled masses . . ."

Mounted on the inside of the Statue of Liberty, on the second floor of the pedestal, is a bronze plaque engraved with the words of an 1883 sonnet by American poet Emma Lazarus (1849–87). Written as a donation to an auction raising funds for the pedestal's construction, the poem was largely forgotten by the time of the statue's official dedication on October 28, 1886. In 1903, Lazarus and her words were finally memorialized with the creation and installation of the plaque.

The New Colossus

Not like the brazen giant of Greek fame,
With conquering limbs astride from land to land;
Here at our sea-washed, sunset gates shall stand
A mighty woman with a torch, whose flame
Is the imprisoned lightning, and her name
Mother of Exiles. From her beacon-hand
Glows world-wide welcome; her mild eyes command
The air-bridged harbor that twin cities frame.
"Keep, ancient lands, your storied pomp!" cries she
With silent lips. "Give me your tired, your poor,
Your huddled masses yearning to breathe free,
The wretched refuse of your teeming shore.
Send these, the homeless, tempest-tossed to me,
I lift my lamp beside the golden door!"

Emma Lazarus

The Pledge of Allegiance

A timeline of the US Pledge of Allegiance

1892
In August 1892, Francis Bellamy (1855–1931), an American socialist and Baptist minister, wrote a pledge of allegiance, which was published in the September 8, 1892, issue of the *Youth's Companion*, a national magazine for young readers. The original pledge read as follows:

> "I pledge allegiance to my Flag and the Republic for which it stands, one nation, indivisible, with liberty and justice for all."

October 1892 marked the 400th anniversary of Christopher Columbus's arrival in the Americas. Featured in school observances nationwide was the ceremonial raising of the US flag, along with a recitation of Bellamy's pledge, which by then had been amended with the addition of the word 'to':

> "I pledge allegiance to my Flag and to the Republic for which it stands, one nation, indivisible, with liberty and justice for all."

1923
When the National Flag Conference suggested in 1923 that immigrants might interpret "my Flag" as reference to their native land, the wording was replaced with "the Flag of the United States":

> "I pledge allegiance to the Flag of the United States and to the Republic for which it stands, one nation, indivisible, with liberty and justice for all."

1924
The pledge's now-familiar "of America" was added in 1924:

> "I pledge allegiance to the Flag of the United States of America and to the Republic for which it stands, one nation, indivisible, with liberty and justice for all."

1942
The pledge was officially recognized by the US Congress in 1942 and was formally incorporated into the US Flag Code.

1945
It was not until 1945 that the "Pledge of Allegiance" was adopted as the official name.

1954
The most recent revision to the pledge was made on Flag Day (June 14) in 1954. By an act of Congress, with the support of President Dwight D. Eisenhower (who considered it an affirmation of anti-Communism), the words "under God" were added. Since then, the official national pledge, as it appears in the US Flag Code, is this:

> "I pledge allegiance to the Flag of the United States of America and to the Republic for which it stands, one Nation under God, indivisible, with liberty and justice for all."

Manner of delivery

According to the US Flag Code, the Pledge of Allegiance "should be rendered by standing at attention facing the flag with the right hand over the heart. When not in uniform, men should remove their headdress with their right hand and hold it at the left shoulder, the hand being over the heart. Persons in uniform should remain silent, face the flag, and render the military salute."

This delivery was not the original custom. Up until World War II, America's Pledge of Allegiance was recited by schoolchildren giving the so-called Bellamy salute, which Francis Bellamy had instructively described in 1892 as "right hand lifted, palm downward, to a line with the forehead." By 1942, this gesture of respect had become uncomfortably suggestive of Hitler's Nazi salute, so President Franklin D. Roosevelt called for an official modification (as now appears in the US Flag Code).

US Presidents

	Name	Nickname	Life dates	Birthplace	Party	Years in office	Vice president(s)
1	George Washington	Father of His Country	1732–1799	Virginia	—	1789–1797	John Adams
2	John Adams	Atlas of Independence	1735–1826	Massachusetts	Federalist	1797–1801	Thomas Jefferson
3	Thomas Jefferson	Pen of the Revolution	1743–1826	Virginia	Democratic-Republican	1801–1809	Aaron Burr George Clinton
4	James Madison	Father of the Constitution	1751–1836	Virginia	Democratic-Republican	1809–1817	George Clinton* Elbridge Gerry*
5	James Monroe	Last of the Cocked Hats	1758–1831	Virginia	Democratic-Republican	1817–1825	Daniel D. Tompkins
6	John Quincy Adams	Old Man Eloquent	1767–1848	Massachusetts	Federalist	1825–1829	John C. Calhoun
7	Andrew Jackson	Old Hickory	1767–1845	the Carolinas	Democratic	1829–1837	John C. Calhoun† Martin Van Buren
8	Martin Van Buren	Old Kinderhook	1782–1862	New York	Democratic	1837–1841	Richard M. Johnson
9	William Henry Harrison*	Old Tippecanoe	1773–1841	Virginia	Whig	1841	John Tyler
10	John Tyler	His Accidency	1790–1862	Virginia	Whig/Democratic	1841–1845	
11	James Knox Polk	Young Hickory	1795–1849	North Carolina	Democratic	1845–1849	George M. Dallas
12	Zachary Taylor*	Old Rough and Ready	1784–1850	Virginia	Whig	1849–1850	Millard Fillmore
13	Millard Fillmore	Last of the Whigs	1800–1874	New York	Whig	1850–1853	—
14	Franklin Pierce	Handsome Frank	1804–1869	Hew Hampshire	Democratic	1853–1857	William R. King*
15	James Buchanan	Old Buck	1791–1868	Pennsylvania	Democratic	1857–1861	John C. Breckinridge
16	Abraham Lincoln*	Honest Abe	1809–1865	Kentucky	Republican	1861–1865	Hannibal Hamlin Andrew Johnson
17	Andrew Johnson	Tennessee Tailor	1808–1875	North Carolina	Democratic	1865–1869	—
18	Ulysses Simpson Grant	Hero of Appomattox	1822–1885	Ohio	Republican	1869–1877	Schuyler Colfax Henry Wilson*
19	Rutherford Birchard Hayes	Dark-Horse President	1822–1893	Ohio	Republican	1877–1881	William A. Wheeler
20	James Abram Garfield*	Boatman Jim	1831–1881	Ohio	Republican	1881	Chester A. Arthur
21	Chester Alan Arthur	Elegant Arthur	1829–1886	Vermont	Republican	1881–1885	—
22	Grover Cleveland	Veto President	1837–1908	New Jersey	Democratic	1885–1889	Thomas A. Hendricks*
23	Benjamin Harrison	Little Ben	1833–1901	Ohio	Republican	1889–1893	Levi P. Morton
24	Grover Cleveland	Veto President	1837–1908	New Jersey	Democratic	1893–1897	Adlai E. Stevenson
25	William McKinley*	Idol of Ohio	1843–1901	Ohio	Republican	1897–1901	Garret A. Hobart* Theodore Roosevelt
26	Theodore "Teddy" Roosevelt	TR	1858–1919	New York	Republican	1901–1909	Charles W. Fairbanks
27	William Howard Taft	Big Bill/Old Bill	1857–1930	Ohio	Republican	1909–1913	James S. Sherman*
28	Woodrow Wilson	Schoolmaster	1856–1924	Virginia	Democratic	1913–1921	Thomas R. Marshall
29	Warren Gamaliel Harding*	Normalcy President	1865–1923	Ohio	Republican	1921–1923	Calvin Coolidge
30	Calvin Coolidge	Silent Cal	1872–1933	Vermont	Republican	1923–1929	Charles G. Dawes
31	Herbert Clark Hoover	Chief	1874–1964	Iowa	Republican	1929–1933	Charles Curtis
32	Franklin Delano Roosevelt*	FDR	1882–1945	New York	Democratic	1933–1945	John Nance Garner Henry A. Wallace Harry S. Truman
33	Harry S. Truman	Man from Independence	1884–1972	Missouri	Democratic	1945–1953	Alben W. Barkley
34	Dwight David Eisenhower	Ike	1890–1969	Texas	Republican	1953–1961	Richard M. Nixon
35	John Fitzgerald Kennedy*	JFK	1917–1963	Massachusetts	Democratic	1961–1963	Lyndon B. Johnson
36	Lyndon Baines Jonhson	LBJ	1908–1973	Texas	Democratic	1963–1969	Hubert H. Humphrey
37	Richard "Dick" Milhous Nixon†	—	1913–1994	California	Republican	1969–1974	Spiro T. Agnew† Gerald R. Ford
38	Gerald "Jerry" Rudolph Ford	Mr. Nice Guy	1913–2006	Nebraska	Republican	1974–1977	Nelson A. Rockefeller
39	James "Jimmy" Earl Carter, Jr.	Peacemaker	1924–	Georgia	Democratic	1977–1981	Walter F. Mondale
40	Ronald Wilson Reagan	Great Communicator	1911–2004	Illinois	Republican	1981–1989	George H. W. Bush
41	George Herbert Walker Bush	Bush the Elder	1924–	Massachusetts	Republican	1989–1993	J. Danforth Quayle
42	William "Bill" Jefferson Clinton	—	1946–	Arkansas	Democratic	1993–2001	Albert A. Gore, Jr.
43	George Walker Bush	George Dubya (W)	1946–	Connecticut	Republican	2001–2009	Richard B. Cheney
44	Barack Hussein Obama	—	1961–	Hawaii	Democratic	2009–	Joseph R. Biden

* *died in office*

† *resigned*

US Chief Justices / Landmark US Supreme Court Cases

US Chief Justices

	Chief Justice	Life dates	Birthplace	Years presiding	Nominated by
1	John Jay	1745–1829	New York	1789–1795	George Washington
2	John Rutledge	1739–1800	South Carolina	1795	George Washington
3	Oliver Ellsworth	1745–1807	Connecticut	1796–1800	George Washington
4	John Marshall*	1755–1835	Virginia	1801–1835	John Adams
5	Roger Brooke Taney*	1777–1864	Maryland	1836–1864	Andrew Jackson
6	Salmon Portland Chase*	1808–1873	New Hampshire	1864–1873	Abraham Lincoln
7	Morrison Remick Waite*	1816–1888	Connecticut	1874–1888	Ulysses S. Grant
8	Melville Weston Fuller*	1833–1910	Maine	1888–1910	Grover Cleveland
9	Edward Douglass White*	1845–1921	Louisiana	1910–1921	William Howard Taft
10	William Howard Taft	1857–1930	Ohio	1921–1930	Warren G. Harding
11	Charles Evans Hughes	1862–1948	New York	1930–1941	Herbert Hoover
12	Harlan Fiske Stone*	1872–1946	New Hampshire	1941–1946	Franklin D. Roosevelt
13	Frederick Moore Vinson*	1890–1953	Kentucky	1946–1953	Harry S. Truman
14	Earl Warren	1891–1974	California	1953–1969	Dwight D. Eisenhower
15	Warren Earl Burger	1907–1995	Minnesota	1969–1986	Richard M. Nixon
16	William Hubbs Rehnquist*	1924–2005	Wisconsin	1986–2005	Ronald Reagan
17	John Glover Roberts, Jr.	1955–	New York	2005–	George W. Bush

* *died in office*

Landmark US Supreme Court Cases

Twenty selected landmark cases since 1800

Date	Case	Decision/effect
1803	*Marbury v. Madison*	secured the Court's power of judicial review
1819	*McCulloch v. Maryland*	affirmed the constitutional doctrine of Congress's implied powers
1824	*Gibbons v. Ogden*	preserved the exclusive power of Congress to regulate interstate commerce
1857	*Dred Scott v. Sandford*	ruled that no person of African descent (slave or free descendant) was entitled to the constitutional rights of citizenship
1896	*Plessy v. Ferguson*	established the legality of racial segregation by upholding the doctrine of "separate but equal"
1925	*Gitlow v. New York*	applied to states the Fourteenth Amendment's protection of speech through the due process clause
1940	*Cantwell v. Connecticut*	recognized absolute freedom of belief by applying First Amendment's free exercise of religion clause to states
1942	*Chaplinsky v. New Hampshire*	ruled that "fighting words" which cause harm or breach the peace do not have First Amendment protection
1944	*Korematsu v. United States*	agreed with the constitutionality of the executive order to hold Japanese Americans in internment camps
1954	*Brown v. Board of Education*	overturned *Plessy v. Ferguson* by asserting that "separate educational facilities are inherently unequal"
1957	*Roth v. United States*	ruled that obscenity and the publication of obscene material are not protected by First Amendment
1961	*Mapp v. Ohio*	prohibited the use of unconstitutionally obtained evidence in criminal cases
1963	*Gideon v. Wainwright*	bound state courts to comply with the constitutional assurance of free counsel for defendants unable to pay
1964	*New York Times v. Sullivan*	found that First Amendment allows any statement about public officials unless statement is an intentional defaming lie
1965	*Griswold v. Connecticut*	determined that a married couple's use of birth control cannot be subject to government regulation
1966	*Miranda v. Arizona*	established code of conduct in which police must inform suspect of constitutional right to remain silent
1969	*Tinker v. Des Moines*	ruled that "symbolic speech" of students' wearing antiwar black armbands is protected by First Amendment
1973	*Roe v. Wade*	decided that the right of personal privacy includes the decision of abortion
1974	*United States v. Nixon*	found there is no absolute presidential executive privilege from judicial process, unless to safeguard national security
1989	*Texas v. Johnson*	ruled that flag burning as a political protest is "symbol speech" protected by First Amendment

US States

State	Postal abbr.	Capital	Motto(s)	Nickname(s)	Date of statehood	Order of statehood	Resident
Alabama	AL	Montgomery	*Audemus jura nostra defendere* (We dare to defend our rights)	Heart of Dixie Yellowhammer State	Dec. 14, 1819	22	Alabaman
Alaska	AK	Juneau	North to the future	The Last Frontier	Jan. 3, 1959	49	Alaskan
Arizona	AZ	Phoenix	*Ditat Deus* (God enriches)	Grand Canyon State Copper State	Feb. 14, 1912	48	Arizonan
Arkansas	AR	Little Rock	*Regnat populus* (The people rule)	Natural State	June 15, 1836	25	Arkansan
California	CA	Sacramento	*Eureka* (I have found it)	Golden State	Sept. 9, 1850	31	Californian
Colorado	CO	Denver	*Nil sine numine* (Nothing without providence)	Centennial State	Aug. 1, 1876	38	Coloradan
Connecticut	CT	Hartford	*Qui transtulit sustinet* (He who transplanted sustains)	Constitution State Nutmeg State	Jan. 9, 1788	5	Connecticuter Nutmegger
Delaware	DE	Dover	Liberty and independence	First State Diamond State	Dec. 7, 1787	1	Delawarean
Florida	FL	Tallahassee	In God we trust	Sunshine State	Mar. 3, 1845	27	Floridian
Georgia	GA	Atlanta	Wisdom, justice, and moderation Agriculture and commerce	Peach State Empire State of the South	Jan. 2, 1788	4	Georgian
Hawaii	HI	Honolulu	*Ua Mau ke Ea o ka Āina i ka Pono* (The life of the land is perpetuated in righteousness)	Aloha State	Aug. 21, 1959	50	Hawaiian
Idaho	ID	Boise	*Esto perpetua* (Let it be perpetual)	Gem State	July 3, 1890	43	Idahoan
Illinois	IL	Springfield	State sovereignty, national union	Prairie State Land of Lincoln	Dec. 3, 1818	21	Illinoisan
Indiana	IN	Indianapolis	The crossroads of America	Hoosier State	Dec. 11, 1816	19	Indianan/ Indianian Hoosier
Iowa	IA	Des Moines	Our liberties we prize and our rights we will maintain	Hawkeye State Tall Corn State	Dec. 28, 1846	29	Iowan
Kansas	KS	Topeka	*Ad astra per aspera* (To the stars through difficulties)	Sunflower State Wheat State	Jan. 29, 1861	34	Kansan
Kentucky	KY	Frankfort	United we stand, divided we fall *Deo gratiam habeamus* (Let us be grateful to God)	Bluegrass State	June 1, 1792	15	Kentuckian
Louisiana	LA	Baton Rouge	Union, justice, and confidence	Pelican State Bayou State	April 30, 1812	18	Louisianan Louisianian
Maine	ME	Augusta	*Dirigo* (I direct)	Pine Tree State	March 15, 1820	23	Mainer Down Easter
Maryland	MD	Annapolis	*Fatti maschii, parole femine* (Manly deeds, womanly words)	Old Line State Free State	April 28, 1788	7	Marylander
Massachusetts	MA	Boston	*Ense petit placidam sub libertate quietem* (By the sword we seek peace, but peace only under liberty)	Bay State	Feb. 6, 1788	6	Bay Stater
Michigan	MI	Lansing	*Si quaeris peninsulam amoenam, circumspice* (If you seek a pleasant peninsula, look about you)	Great Lakes State Wolverine State	Jan. 26, 1837	26	Michiganite Michigander
Minnesota	MN	St. Paul	*L'Etoile du nord* (The star of the north)	North Star State Land of 10,000 Lakes	May 11, 1858	32	Minnesotan
Mississippi	MS	Jackson	*Virtute et armis* (By valor and arms)	Magnolia State Hospitality State	Dec. 10, 1817	20	Mississippian

State	Postal abbr.	Capital	Motto(s)	Nickname(s)	Date of statehood	Order of statehood	Resident
Missouri	MO	Jefferson City	*Salus populi suprema lex esto* (The welfare of the people shall be the supreme law)	Show Me State	Aug. 10, 1821	24	Missourian
Montana	MT	Helena	*Oro y plata* (Gold and silver)	Big Sky Country Treasure State	Nov. 8, 1889	41	Montanan
Nebraska	NE	Lincoln	Equality before the law	Cornhusker State	March 1, 1867	37	Nebraskan
Nevada	NV	Carson City	All for our country	Silver State Sagebrush State	Oct. 31, 1864	36	Nevadan
New Hampshire	NH	Concord	Live free or die	Granite State	June 21, 1788	9	New Hampshirite
New Jersey	NJ	Trenton	Liberty and prosperity	Garden State	Dec. 18, 1787	3	New Jerseyite
New Mexico	NM	Santa Fe	*Crescit eundo* (It grows as it goes)	Land of Enchantment	Jan. 6, 1912	47	New Mexican
New York	NY	Albany	*Excelsior* (Ever upward)	Empire State	July 26, 1788	11	New Yorker
North Carolina	NC	Raleigh	*Esse quam videri* (To be, rather than to seem)	Old North State Tar Heel State	Nov. 21, 1789	12	North Carolinian
North Dakota	ND	Bismarck	Liberty and union now and forever, one and inseparable	Peace Garden State Roughrider State	Nov. 2, 1889	39	North Dakotan
Ohio	OH	Columbus	With God, all things are possible	Buckeye State	March 1, 1803	17	Ohioan
Oklahoma	OK	Oklahoma City	*Labor omnia vincit* (Labor conquers all things)	Sooner State	Nov. 16, 1907	46	Oklahoman
Oregon	OR	Salem	*Alis volat propiis* (She flies with her own wings)	Beaver State	Feb. 14, 1859	33	Oregonian
Pennsylvania	PA	Harrisburg	Virtue, Liberty, and Independence	Keystone State Quaker State	Dec. 12, 1787	2	Pennsylvanian
Rhode Island	RI	Providence	Hope	Ocean State Little Rhody	May 29, 1790	13	Rhode Islander
South Carolina	SC	Columbia	*Animis opibusque parati* (Prepared in mind and resources) *Dum spiro spero* (While I breathe, I hope)	Palmetto State	May 23, 1788	8	South Carolinian
South Dakota	SD	Pierre	Under God the people rule	Mount Rushmore State	Nov. 2, 1889	40	South Dakotan
Tennessee	TN	Nashville	Agriculture and commerce	Big Bend State Volunteer State	June 1, 1796	16	Tennessean
Texas	TX	Austin	Friendship	Lone Star State	Dec. 29, 1845	28	Texan
Utah	UT	Salt Lake City	Industry	Beehive State	Jan. 4, 1896	45	Utahan Utahn
Vermont	VT	Montpelier	Freedom and Unity	Green Mountain State	March 4, 1791	14	Vermonter
Virginia	VA	Richmond	*Sic semper tyrannis* (Thus always to tyrants)	Old Dominion State Mother of Presidents	June 25, 1788	10	Virginian
Washington	WA	Olympia	*Al-ki* (By and by)	Evergreen State	Nov. 11, 1889	42	Washingtonian
West Virginia	WV	Charleston	*Montani simper liberi* (Mountaineers are always free)	Mountain State	June 20, 1863	35	West Virginian
Wisconsin	WI	Madison	Forward	America's Dairyland Badger State	May 29, 1848	30	Wisconsite
Wyoming	WY	Cheyenne	Equal rights	Cowboy State Equality State	July 10, 1890	44	Wyomingite

Countries of the World

Country	Capital	Continent/Area	Nationality	Population (2009 estimate)
Afghanistan	Kabul	Asia	Afghan	28,395,700
Albania	Tirana	Europe	Albanian	3,639,500
Algeria	Algiers	Africa	Algerian	34,178,200
Andorra	Andorra la Vella	Europe	Andorran	83,900
Angola	Luanda	Africa	Angolan	12,799,300
Antigua and Barbuda	St. John's	North America	Antiguan, Barbudan	85,600
Argentina	Buenos Aires	South America	Argentinian, Argentine	40,913,600
Armenia	Yerevan	Asia	Armenian	2,967,000
Australia	Canberra	Australia	Australian	21,262,600
Austria	Vienna	Europe	Austrian	8,210,300
Azerbaijan	Baku	Asia	Azerbaijani	8,238,700
Bahamas	Nassau	North America	Bahamian	307,600
Bahrain	Manama	Asia	Bahraini	728,700
Bangladesh	Dhaka	Asia	Bangladeshi	156,050,900
Barbados	Bridgetown	North America	Barbadian	284,600
Belarus	Minsk	Europe	Belarusian	9,648,500
Belgium	Brussels	Europe	Belgian	10,414,300
Belize	Belmopan	North America	Belizean	307,900
Benin	Porto Novo	Africa	Beninese	8,791,800
Bhutan	Thimphu	Asia	Bhutanese	691,100
Bolivia	La Paz; Sucre	South America	Bolivian	9,775,200
Bosnia and Herzegovina	Sarajevo	Europe	Bosnian, Herzegovinian	4,613,400
Botswana	Gaborone	Africa	Motswana, *sing.*, Batswana, *pl.*	1,990,900
Brazil	Brasilia	South America	Brazilian	198,739,300
Brunei	Bandar Seri Begawan	Asia	Bruneian	388,200
Bulgaria	Sofia	Europe	Bulgarian	7,204,700
Burkina Faso	Ouagadougou	Africa	Burkinese	15,746,200
Burma	Naypyidaw	Asia	Burmese	48,137,700
Burundi	Bujumbura	Africa	Burundian, *n.*; Burundi, *adj.*	9,511,300
Cambodia	Phnom Penh	Asia	Cambodian	14,494,300
Cameroon	Yaoundé	Africa	Cameroonian	18,879,300
Canada	Ottawa	North America	Canadian	33,487,200
Cape Verde	Praia	Africa	Cape Verdean	429,500
Central African Republic	Bangui	Africa	Central African	4,511,500
Chad	N'Djamena	Africa	Chadian	10,329,200
Chile	Santiago	South America	Chilean	16,601,700
China	Beijing	Asia	Chinese	1,338,613,000
Colombia	Bogotá	South America	Colombian	43,677,400
Comoros	Moroni	Africa	Comoran	752,400
Congo, Democratic Republic of the (*formerly* Zaire)	Kinshasa	Africa	Congolese	68,692,500
Congo, Republic of the	Brazzaville	Africa	Congolese	4,012,800
Costa Rica	San José	North America	Costa Rican	4,253,900
Côte d'Ivoire	Yamoussoukro	Africa	Ivorian	20,617,100
Croatia	Zagreb	Europe	Croat, *n.*; Croatian, *adj.*	4,489,400
Cuba	Havana	North America	Cuban	11,451,700
Cyprus	Nicosia	Europe	Cypriot	1,084,700

Country	Capital	Continent/Area	Nationality	Population (2009 estimate)
Czech Republic	Prague	Europe	Czech	10,211,900
Denmark	Copenhagen	Europe	Dane, *n.*; Danish, *adj.*	5,500,500
Djibouti	Djibouti	Africa	Djiboutian	724,600
Dominica	Roseau	North America	Dominican	72,700
Dominican Republic	Santo Domingo	North America	Dominican	9,650,100
East Timor	Dili	Asia	East Timorese	1,131,600
Ecuador	Quito	South America	Ecuadorian	14,573,100
Egypt	Cairo	Africa	Egyptian	78,866,600
El Salvador	San Salvador	North America	Salvadorean	7,185,200
Equatorial Guinea	Malabo	Africa	Equatorial Guinean *or* Equatoguinean	633,400
Eritrea	Asmara	Africa	Eritrean	5,647,200
Estonia	Tallinn	Europe	Estonian	1,299,400
Ethiopia	Addis Ababa	Africa	Ethiopian	85,237,300
Fiji	Suva	Oceania	Fijian	944,700
Finland	Helsinki	Europe	Finn, *n.*; Finnish, *adj.*	5,250,300
France	Paris	Europe	French	64,420,100
Gabon	Libreville	Africa	Gabonese	1,515,000
Gambia	Banjul	Africa	Gambian	1,778,100
Georgia	Tbilisi	Asia	Georgian	4,615,800
Germany	Berlin	Europe	German	82,329,800
Ghana	Accra	Africa	Ghanaian	23,887,800
Greece	Athens	Europe	Greek	10,737,400
Grenada	St. George's	North America	Grenadian	90,700
Guatemala	Guatemala City	North America	Guatemalan	13,276,500
Guinea	Conakry	Africa	Guinean	10,058,000
Guinea-Bissau	Bissau	Africa	Guinea-Bissauan	1,534,000
Guyana	Georgetown	South America	Guyanese	752,900
Haiti	Port-au-Prince	North America	Haitian	9,035,500
Honduras	Tegucigalpa	North America	Honduran	7,833,700
Hungary	Budapest	Europe	Hungarian	9,905,600
Iceland	Reykjavik	Europe	Icelander, *n.*; Icelandic, *adj.*	306,700
India	New Delhi	Asia	Indian	1,156,897,800
Indonesia	Jakarta	Asia	Indonesian	240,271,500
Iran	Tehran	Asia	Iranian	66,429,300
Iraq	Baghdad	Asia	Iraqi	28,945,600
Ireland, Republic of	Dublin	Europe	Irish	4,203,200
Israel	Jerusalem	Asia	Israeli	7,233,700
Italy	Rome	Europe	Italian	58,126,200
Ivory Coast *see* Côte d'Ivoire				
Jamaica	Kingston	North America	Jamaican	2,825,900
Japan	Tokyo	Asia	Japanese	127,078,700
Jordan	Amman	Asia	Jordanian	6,269,300
Kazakhstan	Astana	Asia	Kazakhstani	15,399,400
Kenya	Nairobi	Africa	Kenyan	39,002,800
Kiribati	Bairiki (on Tarawa)	Oceania	I-Kiribati	112,900
Korea, North *see* North Korea				
Korea, South *see* South Korea				
Kuwait	Kuwait City	Asia	Kuwaiti	2,692,500
Kyrgyzstan	Bishkek	Asia	Kyrgyz	5,431,700
Laos	Vientiane	Asia	Lao *or* Laotian	6,834,300
Latvia	Riga	Europe	Latvian	2,231,500
Lebanon	Beirut	Asia	Lebanese	4,017,100
Lesotho	Maseru	Africa	Mosotho, *sing.*; Basotho, *pl.*; Basotho, *adj.*	2,130,800
Liberia	Monrovia	Africa	Liberian	3,441,800
Libya	Tripoli	Africa	Libyan	6,324,400
Liechtenstein	Vaduz	Europe	Liechtensteiner, *n.*; Liechtenstein, *adj.*	34,800
Lithuania	Vilnius	Europe	Lithuanian	3,555,200
Luxembourg	Luxembourg	Europe	Luxembourger, *n.*; Luxembourg, *adj.*	491,800
Macedonia	Skopje	Europe	Macedonian	2,066,700

Country	Capital	Continent/Area	Nationality	Population (2009 estimate)
Madagascar	Antananarivo	Africa	Malagasy	20,653,600
Malawi	Lilongwe	Africa	Malawian	15,028,800
Malaysia	Kuala Lumpur	Asia	Malaysian	25,715,800
Maldives	Male	Asia	Maldivian	396,300
Mali	Bamako	Africa	Malian	13,443,200
Malta	Valletta	Europe	Maltese	405,200
Marshall Islands	Majuro	Oceania	Marshallese	64,500
Mauritania	Nouakchott	Africa	Mauritanian	3,129,500
Mauritius	Port Louis	Africa	Mauritian	1,284,300
Mexico	Mexico City	North America	Mexican	111,211,800
Micronesia	Palikir	Oceania	Micronesian	107,400
Moldova	Chişinău	Europe	Moldovan	4,320,700
Monaco	Monaco	Europe	Monacan *or* Monegasque	33,000
Mongolia	Ulaanbaatar	Asia	Mongolian	3,041,100
Montenegro	Podgorica	Europe	Montenegrin	672,200
Morocco	Rabat	Africa	Moroccan	31,285,200
Mozambique	Maputo	Africa	Mozambican	21,669,300
Myanmar *see* Burma				
Namibia	Windhoek	Africa	Namibian	2,108,700
Nauru	Yaren District	Oceania	Nauruan	14,000
Nepal	Kathmandu	Asia	Nepalese	28,563,400
Netherlands	Amsterdam; The Hague	Europe	Dutchman *or* Dutchwoman, *n.*; Dutch, *adj.*	16,716,000
New Zealand	Wellington	Oceania	New Zealander, *n.*; New Zealand, *adj.*	4,213,400
Nicaragua	Managua	North America	Nicaraguan	5,891,200
Niger	Niamey	Africa	Nigerien	15,306,300
Nigeria	Abuja	Africa	Nigerian	149,229,100
North Korea	Pyongyang	Asia	North Korean	22,665,300
Norway	Oslo	Europe	Norwegian	4,660,500
Oman	Muscat	Asia	Omani	3,418,100
Pakistan	Islamabad	Asia	Pakistani	174,578,600
Palau	Melekeok	Oceania	Palauan	20,800
Panama	Panama City	North America	Panamanian	3,360,500
Papua New Guinea	Port Moresby	Oceania	Papua New Guinean	5,940,800
Paraguay	Asunción	South America	Paraguayan	6,995,700
Peru	Lima	South America	Peruvian	29,547,000
Philippines	Manila	Asia	Filipino, *n.*; Philippine, *adj.*	97,976,600
Poland	Warsaw	Europe	Pole, *n.*; Polish, *adj.*	38,482,900
Portugal	Lisbon	Europe	Portuguese	10,707,900
Qatar	Doha	Asia	Quatari	833,300
Romania	Bucharest	Europe	Romanian	22,215,400
Russia	Moscow	Europe & Asia	Russian	140,041,200
Rwanda	Kigali	Africa	Rwandan, Rwandese	10,746,300
St. Kitts and Nevis	Basseterre	North America	Kittsian; Nevisian	40,100
St. Lucia	Castries	North America	St. Lucian	160,300
St. Vincent and the Grenadines	Kingstown	North America	St. Vincentian *or* Vincentian	104,600
Samoa	Apia	Oceania	Samoan	220,000
San Marino	San Marino	Europe	Sammarinese	30,200
São Tomé and Príncipe	São Tomé	Africa	Sao Tomean	212,700
Saudi Arabia	Riyadh	Asia	Saudi *or* Saudi Arabian	28,686,600
Senegal	Dakar	Africa	Senegalese	13,711,600
Serbia	Belgrade	Europe	Serbian	7,379,300
Seychelles	Victoria	Indian Ocean	Seychellois, *n.*; Seychelles, *adj.*	87,500
Sierra Leone	Freetown	Africa	Sierra Leonean	5,132,100
Singapore	Singapore	Asia	Singaporean, *n.*; Singapore, *adj.*	4,657,500
Slovakia	Bratislava	Europe	Slovak	5,463,000
Slovenia	Ljubljana	Europe	Slovene, *n.*; Slovenian, *adj.*	2,005,700
Solomon Islands	Honiara	Oceania	Solomon Islander	595,600
Somalia	Mogadishu	Africa	Somali	9,832,000

Country	Capital	Continent/Area	Nationality	Population (2009 estimate)
South Africa	Pretoria; Cape Town; Bloemfontein	Africa	South African	49,052,500
South Korea	Seoul	Asia	South Korean	48,509,000
Spain	Madrid	Europe	Spanish	40,525,000
Sri Lanka	Colombo	Asia	Sri Lankan	21,324,800
Sudan	Khartoum	Africa	Sudanese	41,087,800
Suriname	Paramaribo	South America	Surinamer, *n.*; Surinamese, *adj.*	481,300
Swaziland	Mbabane	Africa	Swazi	1,337,200
Sweden	Stockholm	Europe	Swede, *n.*; Swedish, *adj.*	9,059,700
Switzerland	Berne	Europe	Swiss	7,604,500
Syria	Damascus	Asia	Syrian	21,763,000
Taiwan	Taipei	Asia	Taiwanese	22,974,300
Tajikistan	Dushanbe	Asia	Tajik	7,349,100
Tanzania	Dar es Salaam	Africa	Tanzanian	41,048,500
Thailand	Bangkok	Asia	Thai	65,998,400
Togo	Lomé	Africa	Togolese	6,031,800
Tonga	Nuku'alofa	Oceania	Tongan	120,900
Trinidad and Tobago	Port-of-Spain	South America	Trinidadian; Tobagonian	1,230,000
Tunisia	Tunis	Africa	Tunisian	10,486,300
Turkey	Ankara	Asia & Europe	Turk, *n.*; Turkish, *adj.*	76,805,500
Turkmenistan	Ashgabat	Asia	Turkmen	4,884,900
Tuvalu	Funafuti	Oceania	Tuvaluan	12,400
Uganda	Kampala	Africa	Ugandan	32,369,600
Ukraine	Kiev	Europe	Ukrainian	45,700,400
United Arab Emirates	Abu Dhabi	Africa	Emirian	4,798,500
United Kingdom	London	Europe	Briton, *n.*; British, *adj.*	61,113,200
United States of America	Washington, DC	North America	American	304,059,724
Uruguay	Montevideo	South America	Uruguayan	3,494,400
Uzbekistan	Tashkent	Asia	Uzbek	27,606,000
Vanuatu	Vila	Oceania	Ni-Vanuatu	218,500
Vatican City	Vatican City	Europe		800
Venezuela	Caracas	South America	Venezuelan	26,814,800
Vietnam	Hanoi	Asia	Vietnamese	88,576,800
Yemen	Sana'a	Asia	Yemeni	22,858,200
Zaire *see* Congo, Democratic Republic of the				
Zambia	Lusaka	Africa	Zambian	11,862,700
Zimbabwe	Harare	Africa	Zimbabwean	11,392,600

World Maps

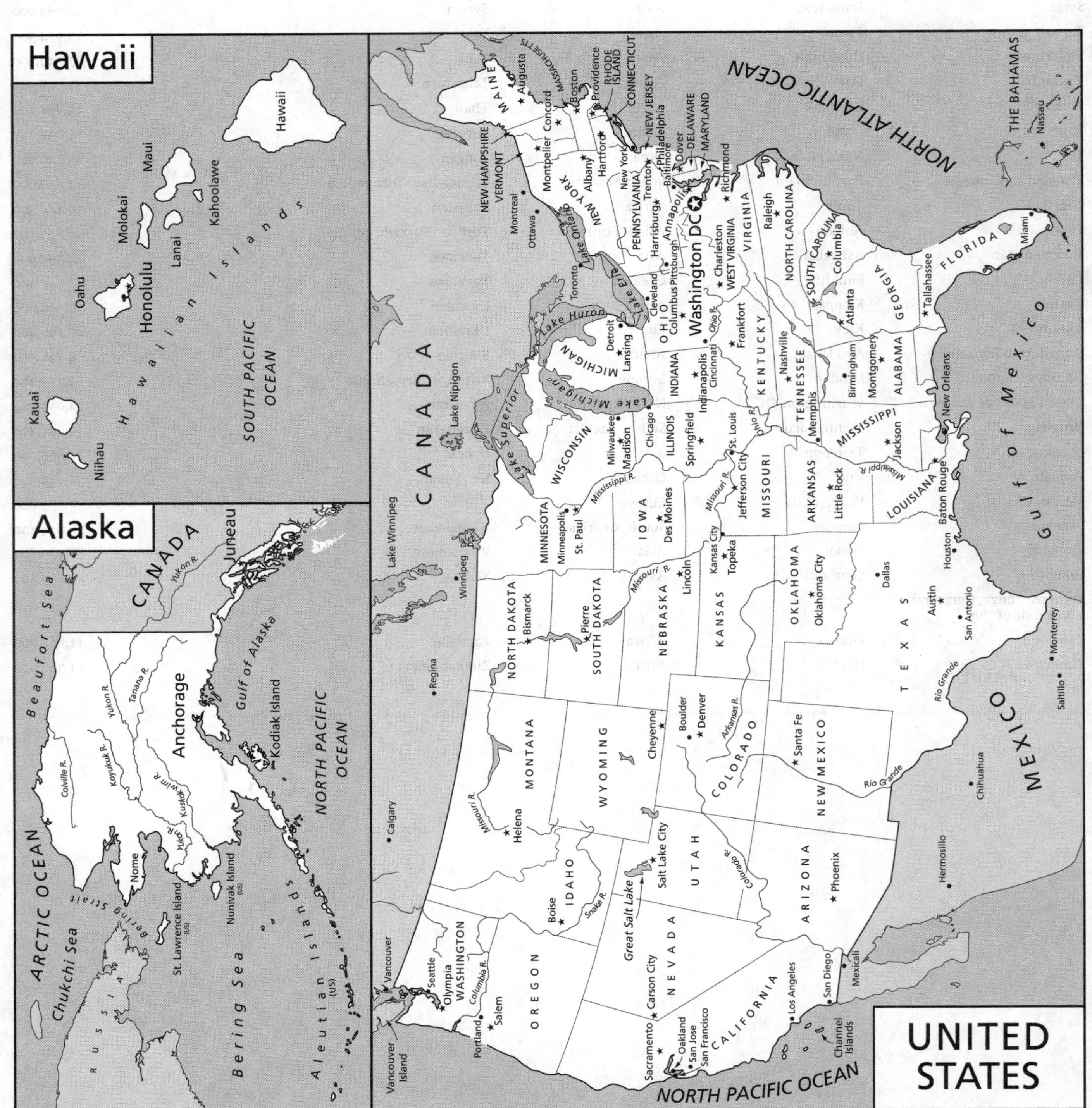
Hawaii
Niihau
Kauai
Oahu
Honolulu
Molokai
Lanai
Maui
Kahoolawe
Hawaii
Hawaiian Islands
SOUTH PACIFIC OCEAN
Alaska
CANADA
Beaufort Sea
ARCTIC OCEAN
Chukchi Sea
RUSSIA
Bering Strait
Bering Sea
Nome
St. Lawrence Island (US)
Nunivak Island (US)
Aleutian Islands (US)
Anchorage
Gulf of Alaska
Kodiak Island
Juneau
NORTH PACIFIC OCEAN
Yukon R.
Tanana R.
Koyukuk R.
Colville R.
Kuskokwim R.
UNITED STATES
CANADA
NORTH ATLANTIC OCEAN
NORTH PACIFIC OCEAN
Gulf of Mexico
MEXICO
THE BAHAMAS
Nassau
WASHINGTON
Olympia
Seattle
OREGON
Salem
Portland
CALIFORNIA
Sacramento
Oakland
San Jose
San Francisco
Los Angeles
San Diego
Channel Islands
NEVADA
Carson City
IDAHO
Boise
MONTANA
Helena
WYOMING
Cheyenne
UTAH
Salt Lake City
Great Salt Lake
ARIZONA
Phoenix
COLORADO
Denver
Boulder
NEW MEXICO
Santa Fe
NORTH DAKOTA
Bismarck
SOUTH DAKOTA
Pierre
NEBRASKA
Lincoln
KANSAS
Topeka
Kansas City
OKLAHOMA
Oklahoma City
TEXAS
Austin
Dallas
Houston
San Antonio
MINNESOTA
St. Paul
Minneapolis
IOWA
Des Moines
MISSOURI
Jefferson City
St. Louis
ARKANSAS
Little Rock
LOUISIANA
Baton Rouge
New Orleans
WISCONSIN
Madison
Milwaukee
ILLINOIS
Springfield
Chicago
MICHIGAN
Lansing
Detroit
INDIANA
Indianapolis
OHIO
Columbus
Cleveland
Cincinnati
KENTUCKY
Frankfort
TENNESSEE
Nashville
Memphis
MISSISSIPPI
Jackson
ALABAMA
Montgomery
Birmingham
GEORGIA
Atlanta
FLORIDA
Tallahassee
Miami
SOUTH CAROLINA
Columbia
NORTH CAROLINA
Raleigh
VIRGINIA
Richmond
WEST VIRGINIA
Charleston
Washington DC
MARYLAND
Annapolis
Baltimore
DELAWARE
Dover
PENNSYLVANIA
Harrisburg
Pittsburgh
Philadelphia
NEW JERSEY
Trenton
NEW YORK
Albany
New York
CONNECTICUT
Hartford
RHODE ISLAND
Providence
MASSACHUSETTS
Boston
VERMONT
Montpelier
NEW HAMPSHIRE
Concord
MAINE
Augusta
Lake Superior
Lake Michigan
Lake Huron
Lake Erie
Lake Ontario
Lake Winnipeg
Lake Nipigon
Mississippi R.
Missouri R.
Ohio R.
Arkansas R.
Rio Grande
Colorado R.
Snake R.
Columbia R.
Vancouver
Vancouver Island
Calgary
Regina
Winnipeg
Toronto
Ottawa
Montreal
Chihuahua
Hermosillo
Monterrey
Saltillo
Mexicali

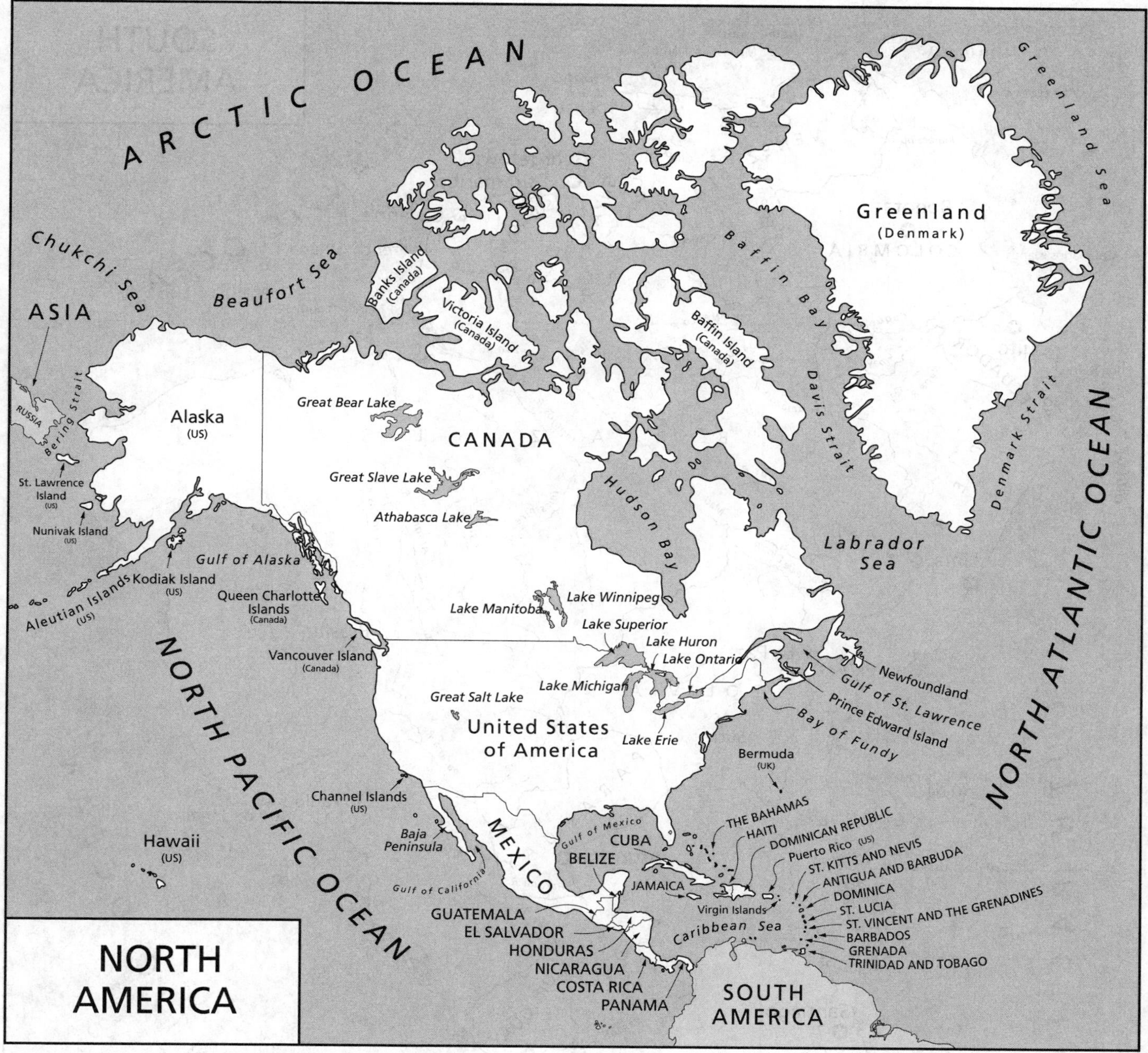
ARCTIC OCEAN
Greenland Sea
Greenland
(Denmark)
Baffin Bay
Chukchi Sea
Beaufort Sea
Banks Island
(Canada)
Victoria Island
(Canada)
Baffin Island
(Canada)
ASIA
RUSSIA
Bering Strait
Davis Strait
Denmark Strait
Alaska
(US)
Great Bear Lake
CANADA
Great Slave Lake
Athabasca Lake
Hudson Bay
St. Lawrence
Island
(US)
Nunivak Island
(US)
Labrador
Sea
NORTH ATLANTIC OCEAN
Gulf of Alaska
Kodiak Island
(US)
Aleutian Islands
(US)
Queen Charlotte
Islands
(Canada)
Lake Winnipeg
Lake Manitoba
Lake Superior
Lake Huron
Lake Ontario
Vancouver Island
(Canada)
Newfoundland
Gulf of St. Lawrence
Prince Edward Island
Bay of Fundy
Lake Michigan
Great Salt Lake
United States
of America
Lake Erie
Bermuda
(UK)
NORTH PACIFIC OCEAN
Channel Islands
(US)
Hawaii
(US)
Baja
Peninsula
Gulf of California
MEXICO
Gulf of Mexico
CUBA
BELIZE
JAMAICA
THE BAHAMAS
HAITI
DOMINICAN REPUBLIC
Puerto Rico (US)
ST. KITTS AND NEVIS
ANTIGUA AND BARBUDA
DOMINICA
ST. LUCIA
ST. VINCENT AND THE GRENADINES
BARBADOS
GRENADA
TRINIDAD AND TOBAGO
Virgin Islands
Caribbean Sea
GUATEMALA
EL SALVADOR
HONDURAS
NICARAGUA
COSTA RICA
PANAMA
SOUTH
AMERICA
NORTH
AMERICA

SOUTH AMERICA
Caribbean Sea
Aruba (Netherlands)
Netherland Antilles (Netherlands)
Margarita Island (Venezuela)
TRINIDAD AND TOBAGO
PANAMA
Lake Maracaibo
Caracas
VENEZUELA
Orinoco R.
Georgetown
Paramaribo
GUYANA
SURINAME
Cayenne
French Guiana
ATLANTIC OCEAN
Bogota
COLOMBIA
Galapagos Islands (Ecuador)
Marajó Island
Quito
ECUADOR
Puna Island
Gulf of Guayaquil
Caquetá R.
Putumayo R.
Napa R.
Negro R.
Japurá R.
Amazon R.
BRAZIL
PERU
Juruá R.
Purus R.
Madeira R.
Tapajós R.
Teles Pires R.
Xingú R.
Araguaia R.
Tocantins R.
São Francisco R.
Ucayali R.
Madre de Dios R.
Lima
Brasilia
La Paz
Lake Titicaca
BOLIVIA
Sucre
Paraná R.
PARAGUAY
São Paulo
Rio de Janeiro
San Felix Island (Chile)
San Ambrosia Island (Chile)
CHILE
Asunción
Iguaçu Falls
SOUTH PACIFIC OCEAN
Uruguay R.
URUGUAY
Santiago
ARGENTINA
Buenos Aires
Montevideo
SOUTH ATLANTIC OCEAN
Gulf of San Matias
Gulf of San Jorge
Patagonia
Strait of Magellan
Falkland Islands (UK)
Stanley
Tierra del Fuego
South Georgia Island (UK)
Drake Passage
Scotia Sea

CANADA

Chukchi Sea
ARCTIC OCEAN
Greenland Sea
GREENLAND
ALASKA (US)
ICELAND
Baffin Bay
Great Bear Lake
YUKON TERRITORY
PACIFIC OCEAN
Great Slave Lake
NUNAVUT
NORTHWEST TERRITORIES
Labrador Sea
ATLANTIC OCEAN
BRITISH COLUMBIA
ALBERTA
Edmonton
SASKATCHEWAN
Hudson Bay
NEWFOUNDLAND AND LABRADOR
MANITOBA
Vancouver
Saskatchewan R.
ONTARIO
QUEBEC
PRINCE EDWARD ISLAND
Quebec
Ottawa
UNITED STATES
L. Superior
L. Huron
Montreal
NOVA SCOTIA
Toronto
NEW BRUNSWICK
L. Michigan
L. Ontario
L. Erie

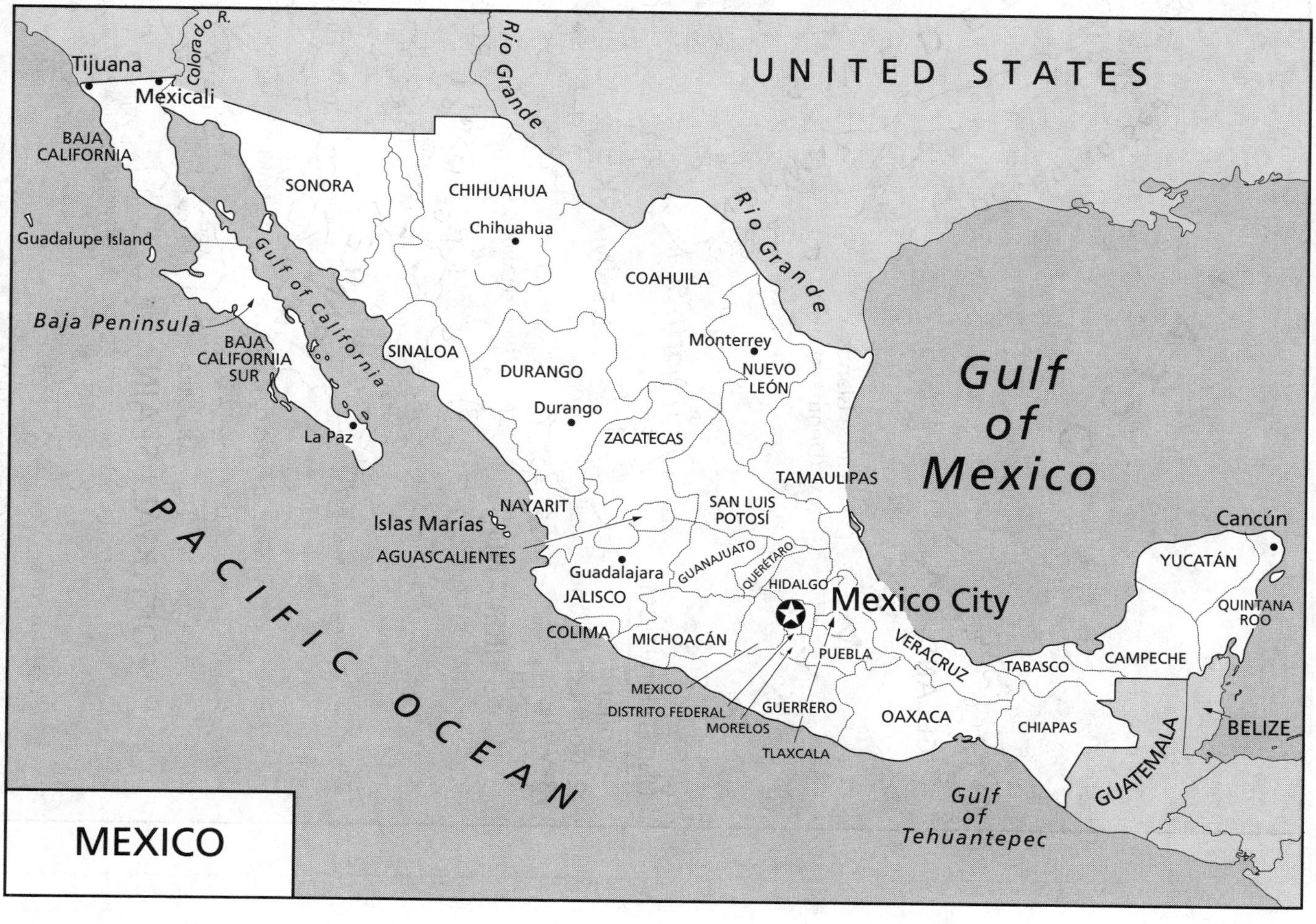

MEXICO

Colorado R.
Rio Grande
Tijuana
Mexicali
UNITED STATES
BAJA CALIFORNIA
SONORA
CHIHUAHUA
Chihuahua
Rio Grande
Guadalupe Island
Gulf of California
COAHUILA
Baja Peninsula
BAJA CALIFORNIA SUR
SINALOA
DURANGO
Monterrey
NUEVO LEÓN
Gulf of Mexico
Durango
La Paz
ZACATECAS
TAMAULIPAS
PACIFIC OCEAN
NAYARIT
SAN LUIS POTOSÍ
Islas Marías
AGUASCALIENTES
Cancún
Guadalajara
GUANAJUATO
QUERÉTARO
YUCATÁN
HIDALGO
Mexico City
JALISCO
QUINTANA ROO
COLIMA
MICHOACÁN
VERACRUZ
PUEBLA
TABASCO
CAMPECHE
MEXICO
DISTRITO FEDERAL
GUERRERO
OAXACA
CHIAPAS
BELIZE
MORELOS
TLAXCALA
GUATEMALA
Gulf of Tehuantepec

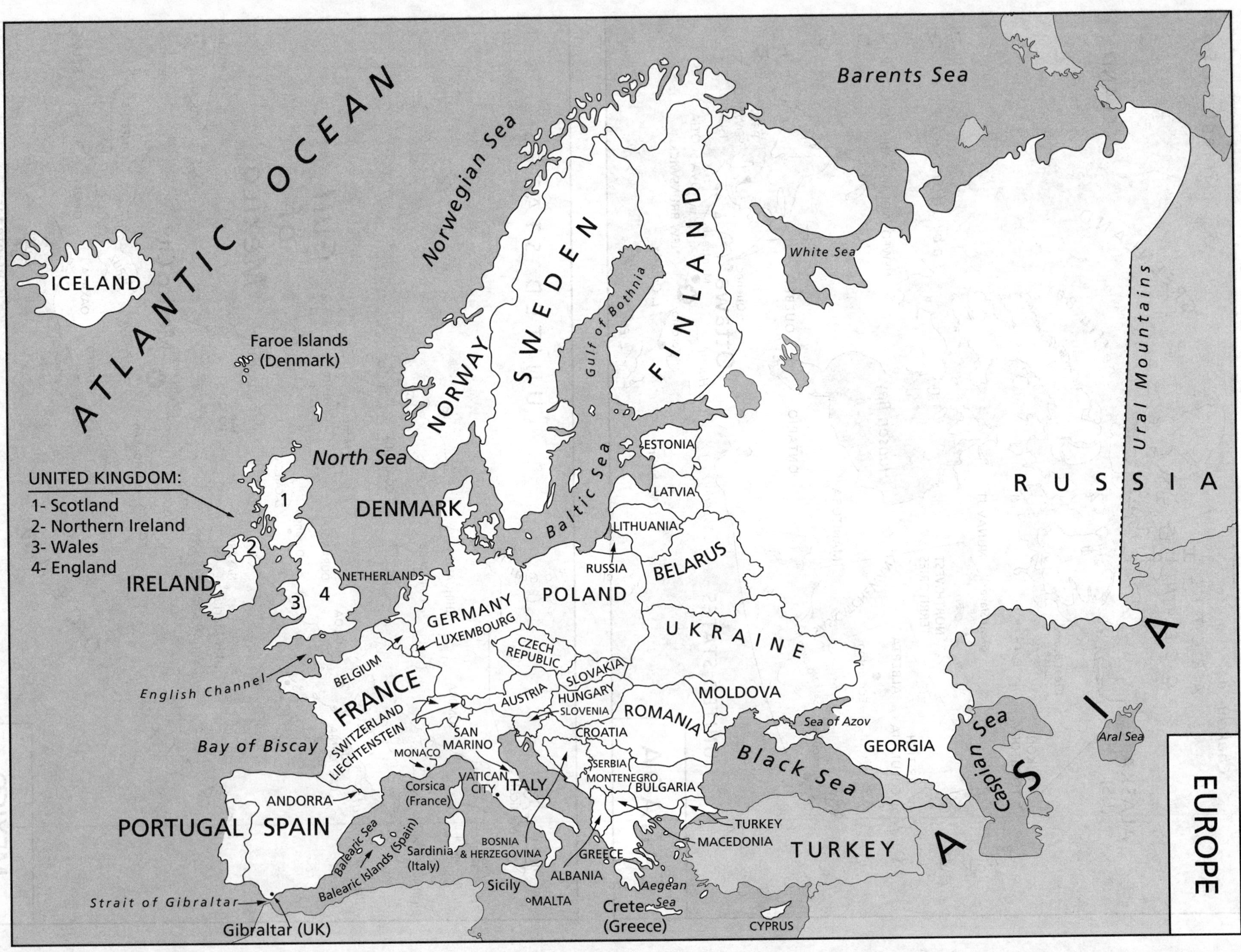
EUROPE
ATLANTIC OCEAN
Norwegian Sea
Barents Sea
White Sea
Ural Mountains
RUSSIA
ASIA
Aral Sea
Caspian Sea
ICELAND
Faroe Islands (Denmark)
NORWAY
SWEDEN
FINLAND
Gulf of Bothnia
Baltic Sea
North Sea
UNITED KINGDOM:
1- Scotland
2- Northern Ireland
3- Wales
4- England
IRELAND
DENMARK
ESTONIA
LATVIA
LITHUANIA
RUSSIA
BELARUS
POLAND
NETHERLANDS
GERMANY
LUXEMBOURG
CZECH REPUBLIC
UKRAINE
SLOVAKIA
HUNGARY
AUSTRIA
SLOVENIA
MOLDOVA
ROMANIA
Sea of Azov
GEORGIA
English Channel
BELGIUM
FRANCE
SWITZERLAND
LIECHTENSTEIN
SAN MARINO
MONACO
CROATIA
Black Sea
Bay of Biscay
SERBIA
MONTENEGRO
BULGARIA
VATICAN CITY
ITALY
Corsica (France)
ANDORRA
PORTUGAL
SPAIN
Balearic Sea
Balearic Islands (Spain)
Sardinia (Italy)
BOSNIA & HERZEGOVINA
GREECE
TURKEY
MACEDONIA
TURKEY
ALBANIA
Sicily
Aegean Sea
MALTA
Crete (Greece)
CYPRUS
Strait of Gibraltar
Gibraltar (UK)

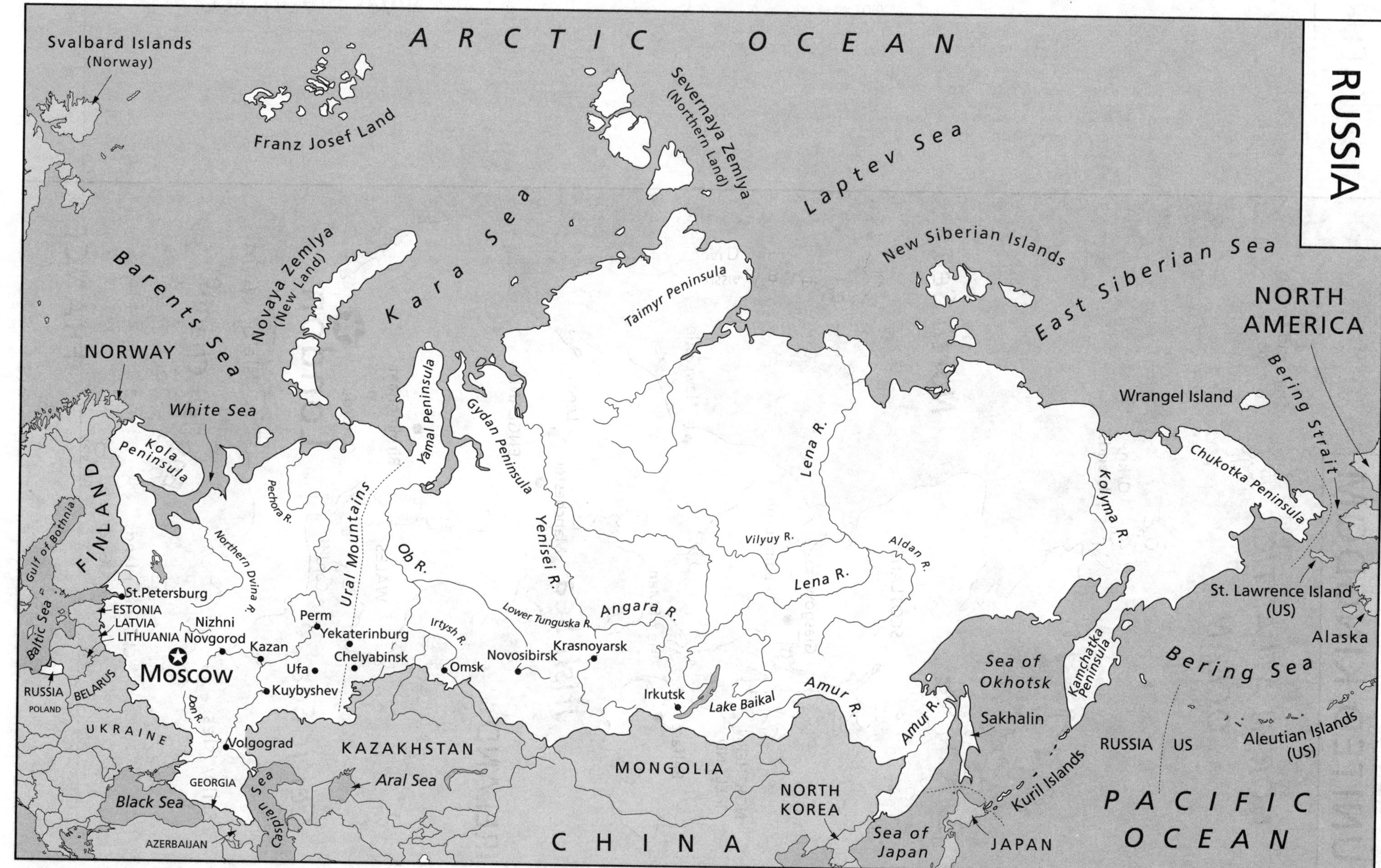
RUSSIA
ARCTIC OCEAN
Svalbard Islands (Norway)
Franz Josef Land
Severnaya Zemlya (Northern Land)
Laptev Sea
New Siberian Islands
East Siberian Sea
NORTH AMERICA
Bering Strait
Wrangel Island
Barents Sea
Novaya Zemlya (New Land)
Kara Sea
Taimyr Peninsula
NORWAY
White Sea
Kola Peninsula
Yamal Peninsula
Gydan Peninsula
Lena R.
Chukotka Peninsula
Kolyma R.
FINLAND
Gulf of Bothnia
Pechora R.
Ural Mountains
Yenisei R.
Northern Dvina R.
Ob R.
Vilyuy R.
Aldan R.
Lena R.
St. Lawrence Island (US)
Baltic Sea
St.Petersburg
ESTONIA
LATVIA
LITHUANIA
Nizhni Novgorod
Perm
Yekaterinburg
Irtysh R.
Lower Tunguska R.
Angara R.
Alaska
Kazan
Chelyabinsk
Novosibirsk
Krasnoyarsk
Moscow
Ufa
Omsk
Sea of Okhotsk
Kamchatka Peninsula
Bering Sea
RUSSIA
BELARUS
POLAND
Kuybyshev
Irkutsk
Lake Baikal
Amur R.
Don R.
Amur R.
Sakhalin
UKRAINE
Volgograd
KAZAKHSTAN
RUSSIA
US
Aleutian Islands (US)
MONGOLIA
Kuril Islands
GEORGIA
Caspian Sea
Aral Sea
NORTH KOREA
PACIFIC OCEAN
Black Sea
AZERBAIJAN
CHINA
Sea of Japan
JAPAN

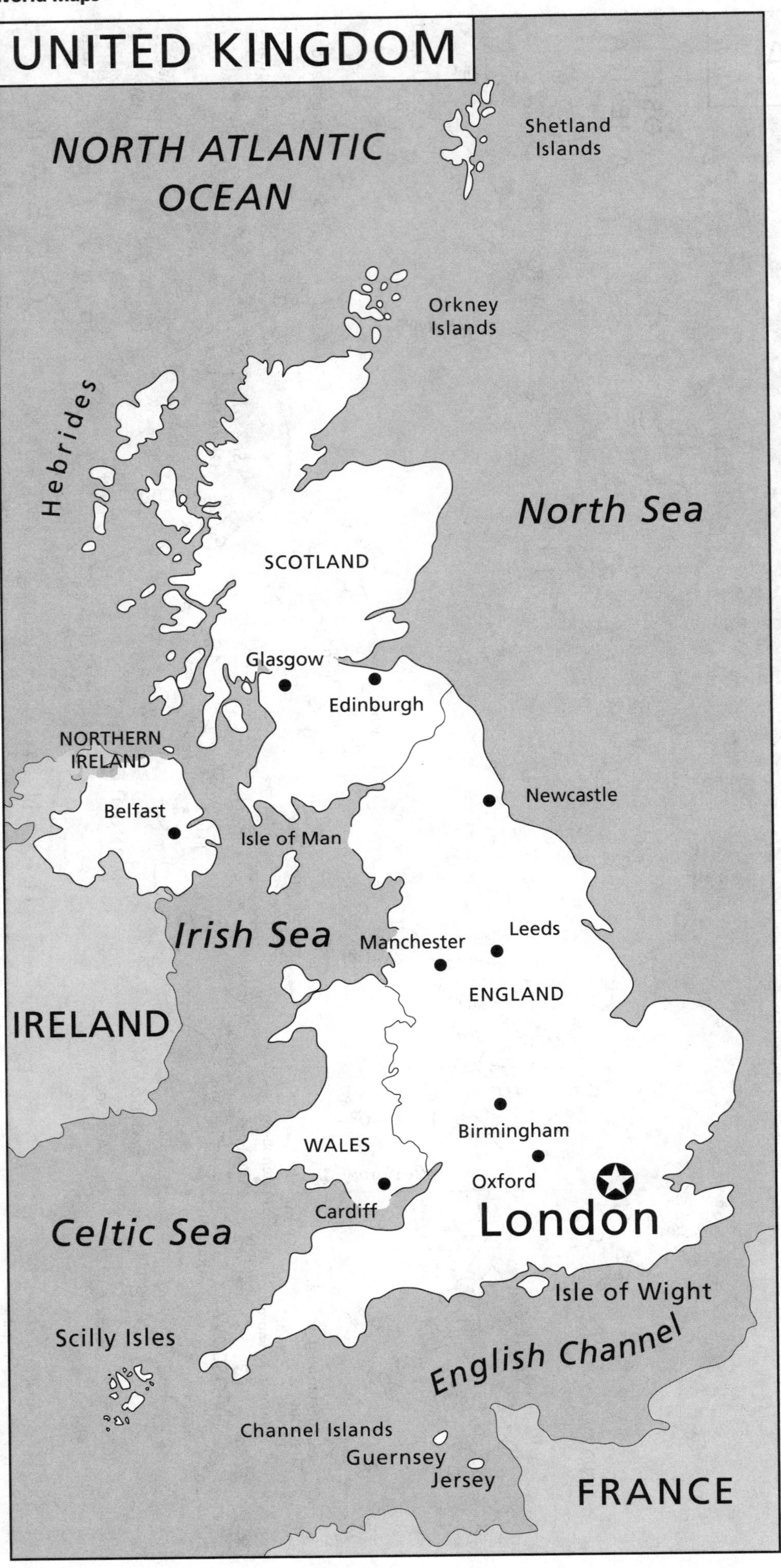
UNITED KINGDOM
NORTH ATLANTIC OCEAN
Shetland Islands
Orkney Islands
Hebrides
North Sea
SCOTLAND
Glasgow
Edinburgh
NORTHERN IRELAND
Belfast
Isle of Man
Newcastle
Irish Sea
Manchester
Leeds
ENGLAND
IRELAND
Birmingham
WALES
Oxford
Cardiff
London
Celtic Sea
Isle of Wight
Scilly Isles
English Channel
Channel Islands
Guernsey
Jersey
FRANCE

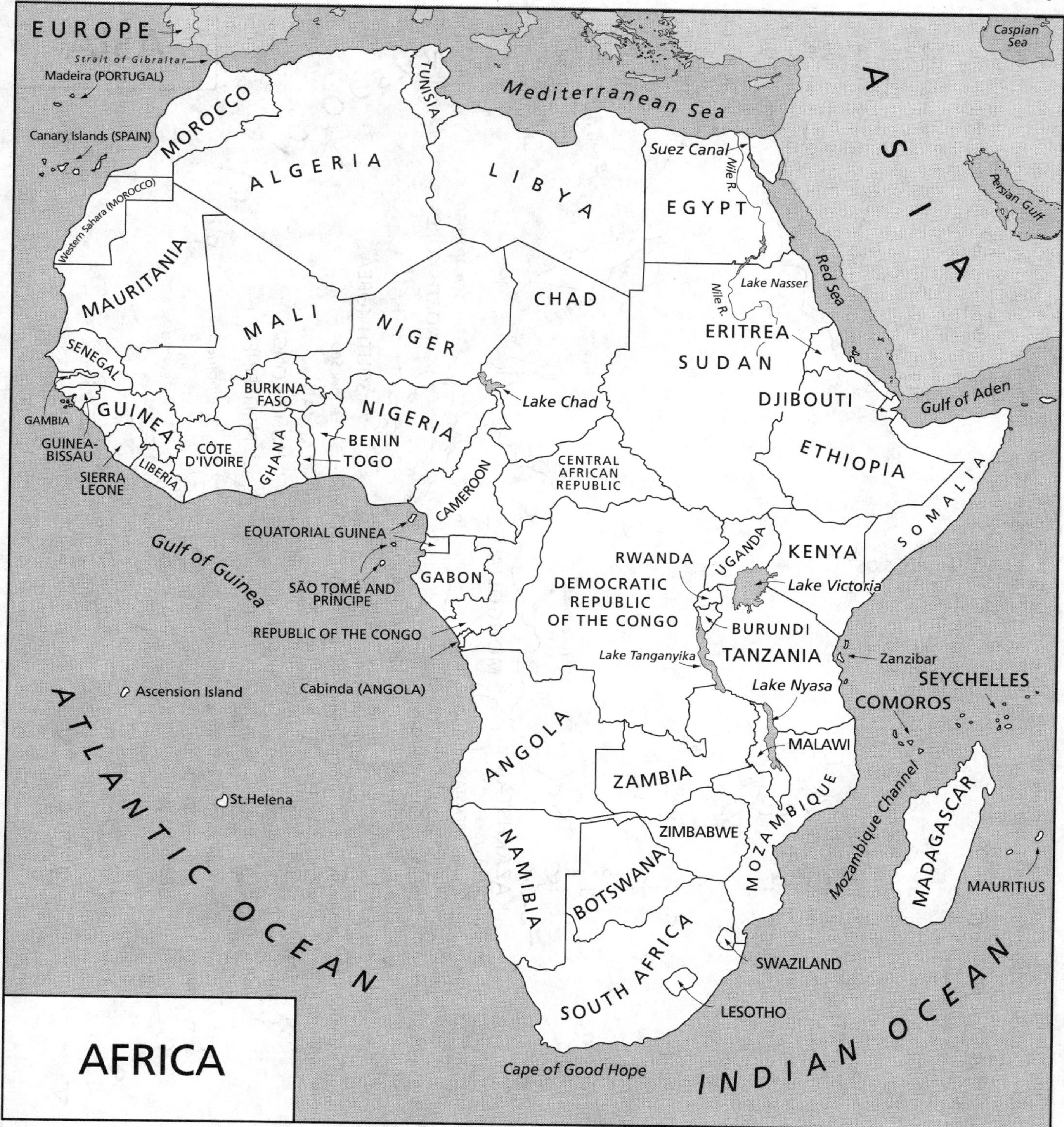
EUROPE
Strait of Gibraltar
Madeira (PORTUGAL)
Canary Islands (SPAIN)
MOROCCO
Western Sahara (MOROCCO)
ALGERIA
TUNISIA
Mediterranean Sea
LIBYA
EGYPT
Suez Canal
Nile R.
Caspian Sea
ASIA
Persian Gulf
Red Sea
Lake Nasser
MAURITANIA
MALI
NIGER
CHAD
SUDAN
ERITREA
DJIBOUTI
Gulf of Aden
SENEGAL
GAMBIA
GUINEA-BISSAU
GUINEA
SIERRA LEONE
LIBERIA
BURKINA FASO
CÔTE D'IVOIRE
GHANA
TOGO
BENIN
NIGERIA
Lake Chad
CAMEROON
CENTRAL AFRICAN REPUBLIC
ETHIOPIA
SOMALIA
EQUATORIAL GUINEA
Gulf of Guinea
SÃO TOMÉ AND PRÍNCIPE
GABON
REPUBLIC OF THE CONGO
Cabinda (ANGOLA)
DEMOCRATIC REPUBLIC OF THE CONGO
RWANDA
UGANDA
KENYA
Lake Victoria
BURUNDI
Lake Tanganyika
TANZANIA
Zanzibar
Lake Nyasa
SEYCHELLES
COMOROS
Ascension Island
ATLANTIC OCEAN
ANGOLA
ZAMBIA
MALAWI
MOZAMBIQUE
Mozambique Channel
MADAGASCAR
MAURITIUS
St.Helena
NAMIBIA
ZIMBABWE
BOTSWANA
SOUTH AFRICA
SWAZILAND
LESOTHO
Cape of Good Hope
INDIAN OCEAN

AFRICA

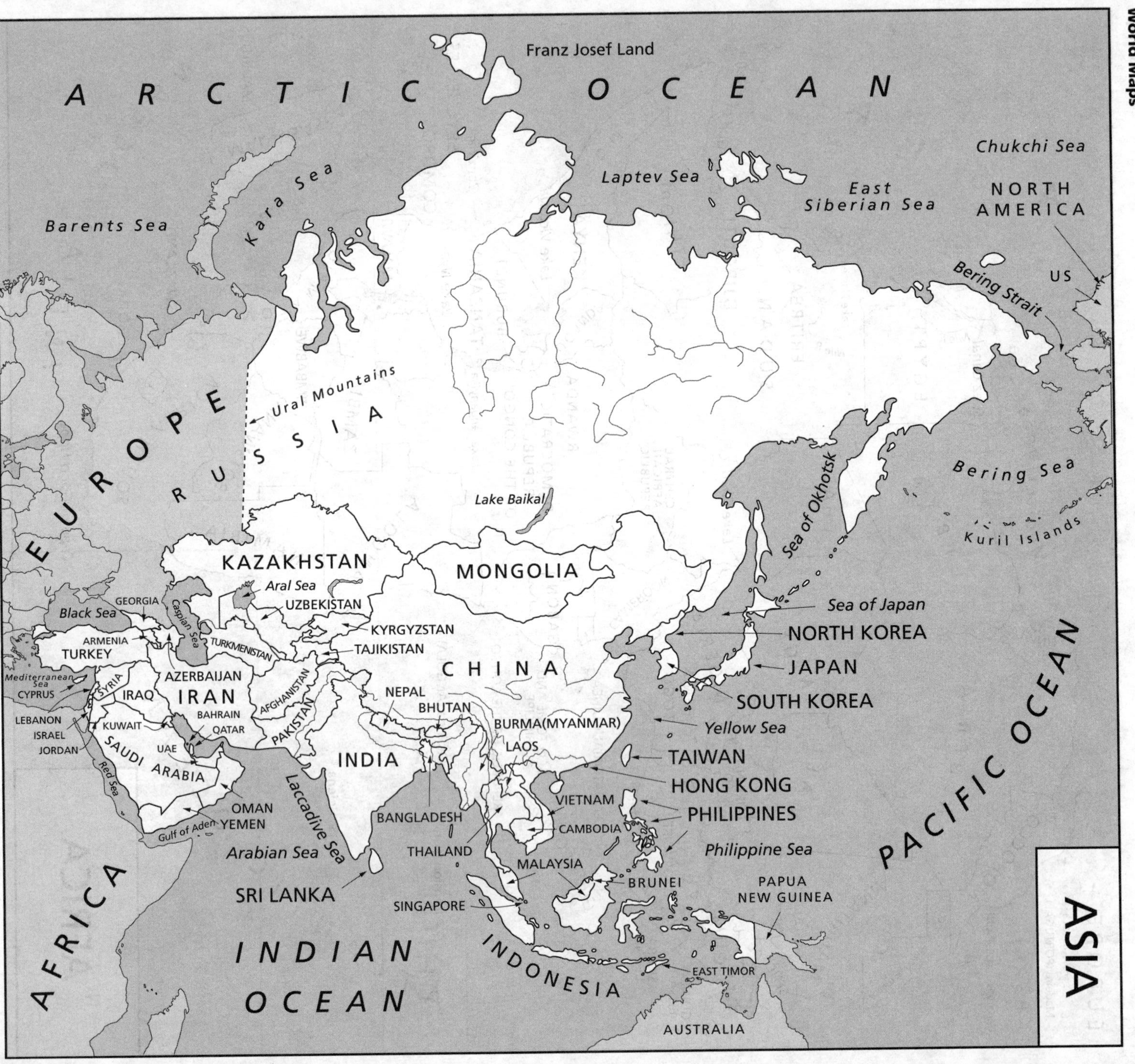
ASIA
Franz Josef Land
ARCTIC OCEAN
Barents Sea
Kara Sea
Laptev Sea
East Siberian Sea
Chukchi Sea
NORTH AMERICA
US
Bering Strait
Bering Sea
Kuril Islands
Sea of Okhotsk
EUROPE
RUSSIA
Ural Mountains
Lake Baikal
KAZAKHSTAN
Aral Sea
UZBEKISTAN
MONGOLIA
KYRGYZSTAN
TAJIKISTAN
TURKMENISTAN
GEORGIA
Black Sea
Caspian Sea
ARMENIA
TURKEY
AZERBAIJAN
Mediterranean Sea
CYPRUS
SYRIA
IRAQ
IRAN
LEBANON
ISRAEL
JORDAN
KUWAIT
BAHRAIN
QATAR
UAE
SAUDI ARABIA
Red Sea
OMAN
YEMEN
Gulf of Aden
AFGHANISTAN
PAKISTAN
CHINA
NEPAL
BHUTAN
INDIA
BURMA(MYANMAR)
LAOS
BANGLADESH
THAILAND
VIETNAM
CAMBODIA
MALAYSIA
SINGAPORE
BRUNEI
Laccadive Sea
Arabian Sea
SRI LANKA
Sea of Japan
NORTH KOREA
JAPAN
SOUTH KOREA
Yellow Sea
TAIWAN
HONG KONG
PHILIPPINES
Philippine Sea
PACIFIC OCEAN
PAPUA NEW GUINEA
INDONESIA
EAST TIMOR
AUSTRALIA
AFRICA
INDIAN OCEAN

CHINA

RUSSIA
KAZAKHSTAN
MONGOLIA
RUSSIA
HEILONGJIANG
JILIN
XINJIANG
KYRGYZSTAN
TAJIKISTAN
AFGHANISTAN
PAKISTAN
INNER MONGOLIA
LIAONING
Sea of Japan
GANSU
BEIJING
Beijing
NORTH KOREA
HEBEI
TIANJIN
QINGHAI
NINGXIA
Huang Ha R.
SHANXI
SHANDONG
SOUTH KOREA
Yellow Sea
SHAANXI
HENAN
JIANGSU
JAPAN
XIZANG (TIBET)
SICHUAN
HUBEI
Yangtze R.
ANHUI
Shanghai
SHANGHAI
NEPAL
East China Sea
BHUTAN
HUNAN
ZHEJIANG
GUIZHOU
JIANGXI
INDIA
FUJIAN
BANGLADESH
YUNNAN
GUANGXI
PACIFIC OCEAN
GUANGDONG
TAIWAN
Hong Kong
BURMA (MYANMAR)
VIETNAM
LAOS
Bay of Bengal
HAINAN
South China Sea
THAILAND
PHILIPPINES

AFGHANISTAN
PAKISTAN
CHINA
JAMMU & KASHMIR
HIMACHAL PRADESH
PUNJAB
UTTARAKHAND
HARYANA
New Delhi
UTTAR PRADESH
NEPAL
SIKKIM
BHUTAN
ARUNACHAL PRADESH
RAJASTHAN
Ganges R.
BIHAR
ASSAM
NAGALAND
MEGHALAYA
MANIPUR
TRIPURA
MIZORAM
JHARKHAND
WEST BENGAL
Kolkata
GUJARAT
Narmada R.
MADHYA PRADESH
CHHATTISGARH
ORISSA
BANGLADESH
BURMA (MYANMAR)
MAHARASHTRA
Mumbai
Godavari R.
ANDHRA PRADESH
Krishna R.
GOA
KARNATAKA
Arabian Sea
Bay of Bengal
TAMIL NADU
KERALA
SRI LANKA
ANDAMAN & NICOBAR ISLANDS
Andaman Sea
INDIAN OCEAN
INDIA

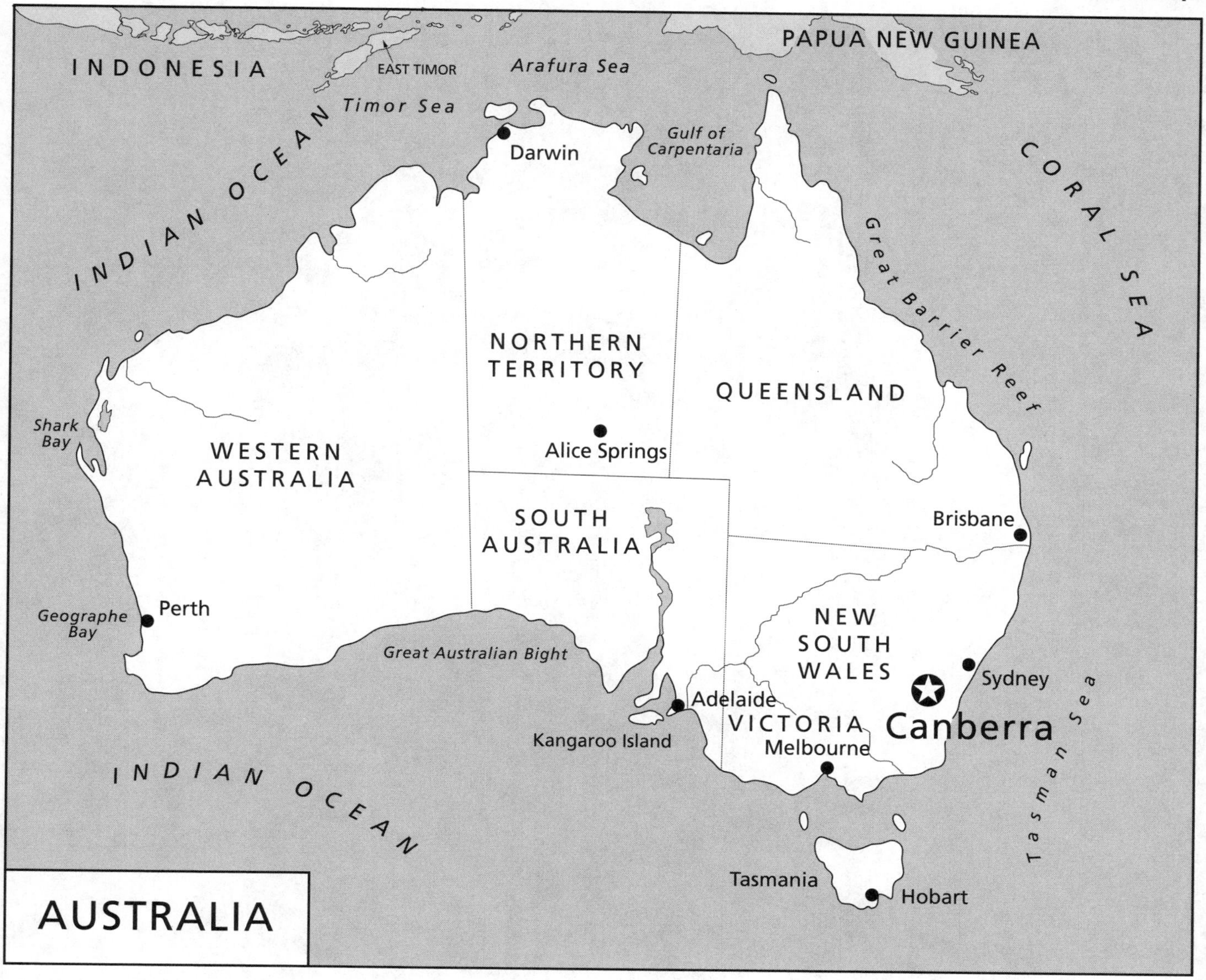

AUSTRALIA
INDONESIA
EAST TIMOR
Arafura Sea
PAPUA NEW GUINEA
Timor Sea
INDIAN OCEAN
Darwin
Gulf of Carpentaria
CORAL SEA
Great Barrier Reef
NORTHERN TERRITORY
QUEENSLAND
Shark Bay
WESTERN AUSTRALIA
Alice Springs
SOUTH AUSTRALIA
Brisbane
NEW SOUTH WALES
Geographe Bay
Perth
Great Australian Bight
Sydney
Adelaide
Canberra
VICTORIA
Kangaroo Island
Melbourne
Tasman Sea
INDIAN OCEAN
Tasmania
Hobart

NEW ZEALAND
PACIFIC OCEAN
Auckland
North Island
Cook Strait
Wellington
Tasman Sea
Christchurch
South Island
PACIFIC OCEAN
Stewart Island

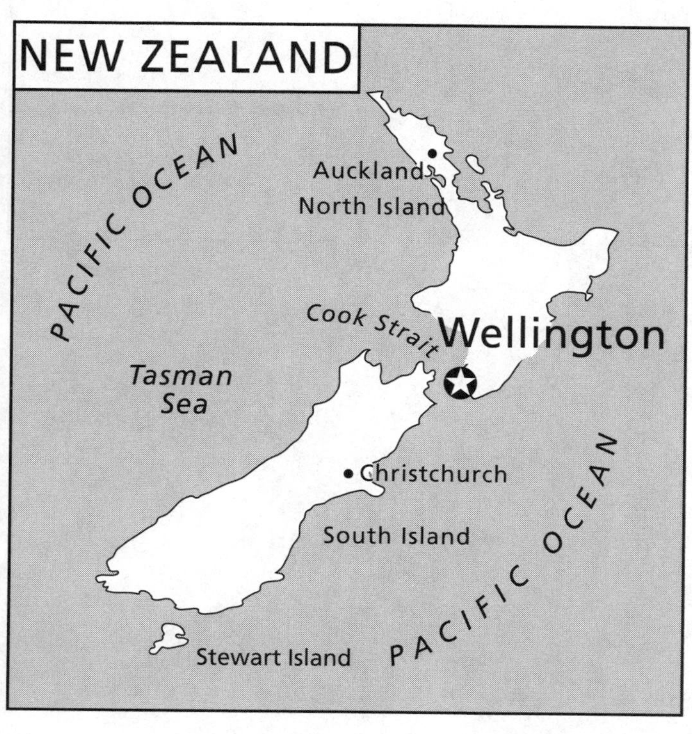

Aa

A[1] /ā/ (also **a**) ▸ **n.** (pl. **As** or **A's**) **1** the first letter of the alphabet. ■ denoting the first in a set of items, categories, sizes, etc. ■ denoting the first of two or more hypothetical people or things: *suppose A had killed B.* ■ the highest class of academic mark. ■ **(a)** Chess denoting the first file from the left, as viewed from white's side of the board. ■ (usu. *a*) the first fixed quantity in an algebraic expression. ■ **(A)** the human blood type (in the ABO system) containing the A agglutinogen and lacking the B.
2 a shape like that of a capital A: [in combination] *an A-shape.* See also **A-FRAME**, **A-LINE**.
3 Music the sixth note of the diatonic scale of C major. ■ a key based on a scale with A as its keynote.
– PHRASES **from A to B** from one's starting point to one's destination: *most road atlases will get you from A to B.* **from A to Z** over the entire range; completely: *make sure you understand the subject from A to Z.*

A[2] ▸ **abbr.** ■ ace (used in describing play in bridge and other card games): *you cash AK of hearts.* ■ ampere(s). ■ **(Å)** ångstrom(s). ■ answer: *Q: What's the senator's zodiac sign? A: He's a Leo.* ■ (in personal ads) Asian. ■ a dry cell battery size. ■ Brit. informal A level.

a /ā, ə/ (**an** before a vowel sound) [called the indefinite article] ▸ **determiner 1** used when referring to someone or something for the first time in a text or conversation: *a man came out of the room | it has been an honor to have you | we need people with a knowledge of languages.* Compare with **THE**. ■ used with units of measurement to mean one such unit: *a hundred | a quarter of an hour.* ■ [with negative] one single; any: *I simply haven't a thing to wear.* ■ used when mentioning the name of someone not known to the speaker: *a Mr. Smith telephoned.* ■ someone like (the name specified): *you're no better than a Hitler.*
2 used to indicate membership of a class of people or things: *he is a lawyer | this car is a BMW.*
3 used when expressing rates or ratios; in, to, or for each; per: *typing 60 words a minute | cost as much as eight dollars a dozen.*
– ORIGIN Middle English: weak form of Old English *ān* 'one.'

> **USAGE 1** The article a can be pronounced either /ā/, when stressed ("He gave you a flower?"—that is, only one flower), or /ə/, when unstressed ("He gave you a *flower*?"—that is, the emphasis is on *flower*, not on the number of flowers). The form **an** is used before words beginning with a vowel sound. **2** On the question of using a or an before words beginning with **h**, see also usage at **AN**.

a-[1] ▸ **prefix** not; without: *atheistic | atypical.*
– ORIGIN from Greek.

a-[2] ▸ **prefix** to; toward: *aside | ashore.* ■ in a specified state or manner: *asleep | aloud.* ■ in the process of (an activity): *a-hunting.* ■ on: *afoot.* ■ in: *nowadays.*
– ORIGIN Old English, unstressed form of **ON**.

a-[3] ▸ **prefix** variant spelling of **AD-** assimilated before *sc, sp,* and *st* (as in *ascend, aspire,* and *astringent*).

a-[4] ▸ **prefix 1** of: *anew.* [unstressed form of **OF**.]
2 utterly: *abash.* [from Anglo-Norman French (corresponding to Old French *e-, es-*), from Latin *ex.*]

-a[1] ▸ **suffix** forming: **1** ancient or Latinized modern names of animals and plants: *primula.*
2 names of oxides: *baryta.*
3 geographical names: *Africa.*
4 ancient or Latinized modern feminine forenames: *Lydia.*
5 nouns from Italian, Portuguese, and Spanish: *duenna | stanza.*
– ORIGIN representing a Greek, Latin, or Romance feminine singular.

-a[2] ▸ **suffix** forming plural nouns: **1** from Greek or Latin neuter plurals corresponding to a singular in *-um* or *-on* (such as *addenda, phenomena*).
2 in names (often from modern Latin) of zoological groups: *Protista | Insectivora.*

-a[3] ▸ **suffix** informal **1** of: *coupla.*
2 have: *mighta.*
3 to: *oughta.*
– ORIGIN representing a casual pronunciation.

A1 ▸ **adj.** informal very good or well; excellent: *guitar in A1 condition.* ■ Nautical (of a vessel) equipped to the highest standard, esp. as certified by a classification society; first-class.

A3 ▸ **n.** a standard European size of paper, 420 × 297 mm: [as modifier] *A3 posters.* ■ paper of this size: *a prospectus printed on A3.*

A4 ▸ **n.** a standard European size of paper, 210 × 297 mm: [as modifier] *an A4 page.* ■ paper of this size: *several sheets of A4.*

A5 ▸ **n.** a standard European size of paper, 210 × 148 mm: [as modifier] *a little A5 booklet.* ■ paper of this size: *printed on A5.*

AA ▸ **abbr.** ■ Alcoholics Anonymous. ■ antiaircraft. ■ administrative assistant. ■ Associate of Arts. ■ (pronounced as **double A**) a dry cell battery size.

aa /ˈä,ä/ ▸ **n.** Geology basaltic lava forming very rough jagged masses with a light frothy texture. Often contrasted with **PAHOEHOE**.
– ORIGIN mid 19th cent.: from Hawaiian *'a-'a.*

AAA /ˌtripəl ˈā/ ▸ **abbr.** ■ American Automobile Association. ■ Baseball see **TRIPLE A**. ■ a 1.5 volt dry cell battery size.

AAAS ▸ **abbr.** American Association for the Advancement of Science.

Aa·chen /ˈäKHən/ an industrial city and spa in western Germany, in North Rhine–Westphalia; pop. 258,800 (est. 2006). French name **AIX-LA-CHAPELLE**.

AAD ▸ **abbr.** analog analog digital, indicating that a musical recording was made and mastered in analog form before being stored digitally.

Aal·borg /ˈôl,bôr(g)/ (also **Ålborg**) an industrial city and port in northern Jutland, Denmark; pop. 101,497 (2009).

Aal·to /ˈältō/, Alvar (1898–1976), Finnish architect and designer; full name *Hugo Alvar Henrik Aalto.* He is known as the inventor of bent plywood furniture.

AAM ▸ **abbr.** air-to-air missile.

A & M ▸ **abbr.** Agricultural and Mechanical (college): *Texas A&M.*

A & R ▸ **abbr.** artist(s) and repertory, used to denote employees of a record company who select and sign new artists.

aard·vark /ˈärd,värk/ ▸ **n.** a nocturnal burrowing mammal with long ears, a tubular snout, and a long extensible tongue, feeding on ants and termites. Aardvarks are native to Africa and have no close relatives. Also called **ANT BEAR**. ● *Orycteropus afer,* the only living member of the family Orycteropidae and order Tubulidentata.
– ORIGIN late 18th cent.: from South African Dutch, from *aarde* 'earth' + *vark* 'pig.'

aard·wolf /ˈärd,wo͝olf/ ▸ **n.** (pl. **aardwolves**) a nocturnal black-striped African mammal of the hyena family, feeding mainly on termites. ● *Proteles cristatus,* family Hyaenidae.
– ORIGIN mid 19th cent.: from South African Dutch, from *aarde* 'earth' + *wolf* 'wolf.'

aargh /är, ärg/ ▸ **exclam.** used as an expression of anguish, horror, rage, or other strong emotion, often with humorous intent.
– ORIGIN late 18th cent.: imitative, lengthened form of **AH**, to express a prolonged cry.

Aar·hus /ˈôr,ho͞os/ (also **Århus**) a city on the coast of eastern Jutland, Denmark; pop. 239,865 (2009).

Aar·on[1] /ˈe(ə)rən, ˈar-/ (in the Bible) brother of Moses and traditional founder of the Jewish priesthood.

Aar·on[2] /ˈe(ə)rən, ˈar-/, Hank (1934–), US baseball player; full name *Henry Louis Aaron.* His career record for home runs (755) was unbroken until 2007. Baseball Hall of Fame (1982).

Aar·on's beard ▸ **n.** a name given to various plants, esp. the **ROSE OF SHARON** (sense 2).
– ORIGIN early 19th cent.: alluding to **AARON[1]**, whose beard "went down to the skirts of his garments" (Psalms 133:2), because of the prominent hairy stamens or the long runners that some of these plants put out.

Aar·on's rod ▸ **n.** another term for the great or common mullein.
– ORIGIN mid 18th cent.: alluding to **AARON[1]**, whose staff was said to have flowered (Numbers 17:8).

AARP /ärp, ˈā ˈā ˈär ˈpē/ ▸ **abbr.** American Association of Retired Persons.

AAU ▸ **abbr.** Amateur Athletic Union.

AAUP ▸ **abbr.** ■ American Association of University Presses. ■ American Association of University Professors.

AAVE ▸ **abbr.** Linguistics African-American Vernacular English.

AB[1] ▸ **n.** a human blood type (in the ABO system) containing both the A and B agglutinogens. In blood transfusion, a person with blood of this group is a potential universal recipient.

AB[2] ▸ **abbr.** ■ able seaman; able-bodied seaman. [from *able-bodied.*] ■ Bachelor of Arts. [from Latin *Artium Baccalaureus.*] ■ airman basic. ■ Baseball at bat. ■ Alberta (in official postal use).

Ab[1] /äb, äv/ (also **Av**) ▸ **n.** (in the Jewish calendar) the eleventh month of the civil year and the fifth month of the religious year, usually coinciding with parts of July and August.
– ORIGIN from Hebrew *'āb.*

Ab[2] ▸ **abbr.** Biology antibody.

ab- (also **abs-**) ▸ **prefix** away; from: *abaxial | abominate.*
– ORIGIN from Latin.

ABA ▸ **abbr.** ■ American Bar Association. ■ American Basketball Association. ■ American Bankers Association. ■ American Booksellers Association.

a·ba·ca /ˌabəˈkä/ ▸ **n.** a large herbaceous Philippine plant of the banana family that yields Manila hemp. ● *Musa textilis,* family Musaceae. ■ Manila hemp.
– ORIGIN mid 18th cent.: via Spanish from Tagalog *abaká.*

a·back /əˈbak/ ▸ **adv. 1** archaic toward or situated to the rear: *the little strip of pasture aback of the house.*
2 Sailing with the sail pressed backward against the mast by a headwind.
– PHRASES **take someone aback** shock or surprise someone: *he was taken aback by the sharpness in her voice.*

PRONUNCIATION KEY ə *ago, up;* ər *over, fur;* a *hat;* ā *ate;* ä *car;* e *let;* ē *see;* i *fit;* ī *by;* NG *sing;* ō *go;* ô *law, for;* oi *toy;* o͝o *good;* o͞o *goo;* ou *out;* TH *thin;* T͟H *then;* ZH *vision*

a

–ORIGIN Old English *on bæc*. Long written as two words, the term came to be treated as a single word in nautical use.

ab·a·cus /'abəkəs/ ▶ **n.** (pl. **abacuses**) **1** an oblong frame with rows of wires or grooves along which beads are slid, used for calculating. **2** Architecture the flat slab on top of a capital, supporting the architrave.
–ORIGIN late Middle English (denoting a board strewn with sand on which to draw figures): from Latin, from Greek *abax, abak-* 'slab, drawing board,' of Semitic origin; probably related to Hebrew *'ābāq* 'dust.'

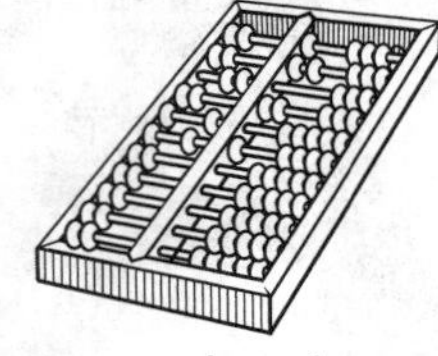
abacus 1

A·ba·dan /,äbə'dän, ,abə'dan/ a major port and oil-refining center on an island of the same name on the Shatt al-Arab waterway in western Iran; pop. 219,772 (2006).

A·bad·don /ə'badn/ (in the Bible) a name for the Devil or for hell.
–ORIGIN late Middle English: via Greek from Hebrew *'ăbaddōn* 'destruction.' Its use for 'hell' arose in the late 17th cent.

a·baft /ə'baft/ Nautical ▶ **adv.** in or behind the stern of a ship.
▶ **prep.** nearer the stern than; behind: *the yacht has a shower just abaft the galley.*
–ORIGIN Middle English (in the sense 'backward'): from **A-**[2] (expressing motion) + archaic *baft* 'in the rear.'

A·ba·kan /,äbə'kän, əbə-/ an industrial city in south central Russia, capital of the republic of Khakassia; pop. 163,200 (est. 2008). Former name (until 1931) **Ust-Abakanskoe.**

ab·a·lo·ne /,abə'lōnē, 'abə,lōnē/ ▶ **n.** an edible mollusk of warm seas that has a shallow ear-shaped shell lined with mother-of-pearl and pierced with respiratory holes. Also called **ear shell.** ● Genus *Haliotis*, family Haliotidae, class Gastropoda.
–ORIGIN mid 19th cent.: via Latin American Spanish from *aulun*, from an American Indian language of Monterey Bay, California.

a·ban·don /ə'bandən/ ▶ **v.** [with obj.] **1** give up completely (a course of action, a practice, or a way of thinking): *he had clearly abandoned all pretense of trying to succeed.* ■ discontinue (a scheduled event) before completion: *against the background of perceived threats, the tour was abandoned.*
2 cease to support or look after (someone); desert: *her natural mother had abandoned her at an early age.* ■ leave (a place or vehicle) empty or uninhabited, without intending to return: *derelict houses were abandoned.* ■ (**abandon someone/something to**) condemn someone or something to (a specified fate) by ceasing to take an interest in or look after them: *it was an attempt to persuade businesses not to abandon the area to inner-city deprivation.*
3 (**abandon oneself to**) allow oneself to indulge in (a desire or impulse): *abandoning herself to moony fantasies.*
▶ **n.** complete lack of inhibition or restraint: *she sings and sways with total abandon.*
–PHRASES **abandon ship** leave a ship because it is sinking. ■ hurriedly leave an organization or enterprise: *he would rather abandon ship now than resign in shame in two years.*
–ORIGIN late Middle English: from Old French *abandoner*, from *a-* (from Latin *ad* 'to, at') + *bandon* 'control,' based on late Latin *bannus, bannum* (see **ban**[1]). The original sense was 'bring under control,' later 'give in to the control of, surrender to' (sense 3).

a·ban·doned /ə'bandənd/ ▶ **adj. 1** having been deserted or cast off: *an abandoned car | abandoned pets.*
2 unrestrained; uninhibited: *a wild, abandoned dance.*

a·ban·don·ment /ə'bandənmənt/ ▶ **n.** the action or fact of abandoning or being abandoned: *she had a feeling of utter abandonment and loneliness.*

a·base /ə'bās/ ▶ **v.** [with obj.] behave in a way so as to belittle or degrade (someone): *I watched my colleagues abasing themselves before the board of trustees.*
–ORIGIN late Middle English: from Old French *abaissier*, from *a-* (from Latin *ad* 'to, at') + *baissier* 'to lower,' based on late Latin *bassus* 'short of stature.' The spelling has been influenced by **base**[2].

a·base·ment /ə'bāsmənt/ ▶ **n.** the action or fact of abasing or being abased; humiliation or degradation.

a·bash /ə'basн/ ▶ **v.** [with obj.] (usu. as adj. **abashed**) cause to feel embarrassed, disconcerted, or ashamed: *she was not abashed at being caught.*
–DERIVATIVES **a·bash·ment n.**
–ORIGIN Middle English: from Anglo-Norman French *abaïss-*; compare with Old French *esbaïss-*, lengthened stem of *esbaïr*, from *es-* 'utterly' + *baïr* 'astound.'

a·bate /ə'bāt/ ▶ **v.** [no obj.] (of something perceived as hostile, threatening, or negative) become less intense or widespread: *the storm suddenly abated.* ■ [with obj.] cause to become smaller or less intense: *nothing abated his crusading zeal.* ■ [with obj.] Law lessen, reduce, or remove (esp. a nuisance): *this action would not have been sufficient to abate the odor nuisance.*
–ORIGIN Middle English (in the legal sense 'put a stop to (a nuisance)'): from Old French *abatre* 'to fell,' from *a-* (from Latin *ad* 'to, at') + *batre* 'to beat' (from Latin *battere, battuere* 'to beat').

a·bate·ment /ə'bātmənt/ ▶ **n.** (often in legal use) the ending, reduction, or lessening of something: *noise abatement | an abatement in the purchase price.*
–ORIGIN Middle English: from Anglo-Norman French, from Old French *abatre* 'fell, put an end to' (see **abate**).

ab·at·toir /'abə,twär/ ▶ **n.** a slaughterhouse.
–ORIGIN early 19th cent.: from French, from *abattre* 'to fell.'

a bat·tu·ta /,ä bä'to͞otä/ ▶ **adv.** Music (typically as a direction) returning to strict tempo.
–ORIGIN Italian, literally 'to the beating.'

ab·ax·i·al /ab'aksēəl/ ▶ **adj.** Botany facing away from the stem of a plant (esp. denoting the lower surface of a leaf). The opposite of **adaxial.**

abaya /ə'bīə/ ▶ **n.** a full-length, sleeveless outer garment worn by some Arab women.
–ORIGIN mid 19th cent.: from Arabic *'abāya*.

Ab·ba /'äbä, 'abä/ ▶ **n.** (in the New Testament) an intimate term for God as father. ■ (in the Syrian Orthodox and Coptic churches) a title given to bishops and patriarchs.
–ORIGIN via Greek from Aramaic *'abbā* 'daddy.'

ab·ba·cy /'abəsē/ ▶ **n.** (pl. **abbacies**) the office or period of office of an abbot or abbess.
–ORIGIN late Middle English: from ecclesiastical Latin *abbacia*, from *abbas, abbat-* (see **abbot**).

Ab·bas[1] /ä'bäs/, Ferhat (1899–1989), Algerian nationalist leader. He was president of the Algerian provisional government from 1958 and then president of the constituent assembly of independent Algeria 1962–63.

Ab·bas[2] /ä'bäs/, Mahmoud (1935–), Palestinian statesman, president of the Palestinian National Authority since 2005, and chairman of the PLO since 2004; also known as **Abu Mazen.**

Ab·bas·id /'abəsid, ə'basid/ ▶ **adj.** of or relating to a dynasty of caliphs who ruled in Baghdad from 750 to 1258.
▶ **n.** a member of this dynasty.

ab·ba·tial /ə'bāsнəl/ ▶ **adj.** of or relating to an abbey, abbot, or abbess.
–ORIGIN late 17th cent.: from medieval Latin *abbatialis*, from *abbas, abbat-* (see **abbot**).

ab·bé /a'bā/ ▶ **n.** (in France) an abbot or other cleric: *the abbé was his confessor* | [as title] *Abbé Pierre.*
–ORIGIN mid 16th cent.: French, from ecclesiastical Latin *abbas, abbat-* (see **abbot**).

ab·bess /'abis/ ▶ **n.** a woman who is the head of an abbey of nuns.
–ORIGIN Middle English: from Old French *abbesse* 'female abbot,' from ecclesiastical Latin *abbatissa*, from *abbas, abbat-* (see **abbot**).

Abbe·vill·i·an /ab'vilēən, ,abə-/ (also **Abbevillean**) ▶ **adj.** Archaeology, dated of, relating to, or denoting the first Paleolithic culture in Europe. It is now usually referred to as the Lower Acheulean. ■ (as noun **the Abbevillian**) the Abbevillian culture or period.
–ORIGIN 1930s: from French *Abbevillien* 'from *Abbeville*,' a town in northern France where tools from this culture were discovered.

ab·bey /'abē/ ▶ **n.** (pl. **abbeys**) the building or buildings occupied by a community of monks or nuns. ■ a church or house that was formerly an abbey.
–ORIGIN Middle English: from Old French *abbeïe*, from medieval Latin *abbatia* 'abbacy,' from *abbas, abbat-* (see **abbot**).

ab·bot /'abət/ ▶ **n.** a man who is the head of an abbey of monks.
–ORIGIN Old English *abbod*, from ecclesiastical Latin *abbas, abbat-*, from Greek *abbas* 'father,' from Aramaic *'abbā* (see **Abba**).

Ab·bott[1] /'abət/ Berenice, (1898–1991), US photographer and teacher of photography. She is noted for her documentation of New York City in the 1930s, published in *Changing New York* (1939). She edited *The World of Atget* (1964).

Ab·bott[2], Sir John Joseph Caldwell (1821–93), Canadian Conservative statesman; prime minister 1891–92.

abbr. ▶ **abbr.** abbreviation.

ab·bre·vi·ate /ə'brēvē,āt/ ▶ **v.** [with obj.] (usu. **be abbreviated**) shorten (a word, phrase, or text): *the business of artists and repertory, commonly abbreviated to A&R.*
–ORIGIN late Middle English: from late Latin *abbreviat-* 'shortened,' from the verb *abbreviare*, from Latin *brevis* 'short.'

ab·bre·vi·at·ed /ə'brēvē,ātid/ ▶ **adj.** shortened; cut short: *an abbreviated version of the earlier work | we intended to run an abbreviated event.*

ab·bre·vi·a·tion /ə,brēvē'āsнən/ (abbr.: **abbr.**) ▶ **n.** a shortened form of a word or phrase. ■ the process or result of abbreviating.

ABC[1] ▶ **n.** the alphabet. ■ (also **ABCs**) the rudiments of a subject: *the ABCs of emergency heart-lung resuscitation.* ■ an alphabetical guide: *an ABC of Civil War battlefields.*
–PHRASES **easy** (or **simple**) **as ABC** extremely easy or straightforward.

ABC[2] ▶ **abbr.** American Broadcasting Company.

ABC Is·lands an acronym for the Caribbean islands of Aruba, Bonaire, and Curaçao.

ABD ▶ **abbr.** all but dissertation, used to denote a student who has completed all other parts of a doctorate: *ABDs will be considered, but receipt of the doctorate will be a condition of tenure.*

ab·di·cate /'abdi,kāt/ ▶ **v.** [no obj.] (of a monarch) renounce one's throne: *in 1918 Kaiser Wilhelm abdicated as German emperor* | [with obj.] *Ferdinand abdicated the throne in favor of the emperor's brother.* ■ [with obj.] fail to fulfill or undertake (a responsibility or duty): *the government was accused of abdicating its responsibility* | [no obj.] *the secretary of state should not* ***abdicate from*** *leadership on educational issues.*
–ORIGIN mid 16th cent.: from Latin *abdicat-* 'renounced,' from the verb *abdicare*, from *ab-* 'away, from' + *dicare* 'declare.'

ab·di·ca·tion /,abdi'kāsнən/ ▶ **n. 1** an act of abdicating or renouncing the throne: *Edward VIII did not marry until after his abdication.*
2 failure to fulfill a responsibility or duty: *we are witnessing an abdication of responsibility on the part of state governments.*

ab·do·men /'abdəmən, ab'dōmən/ ▶ **n.** the part of the body of a vertebrate containing the digestive organs; the belly. In humans and other mammals, it is bounded by the diaphragm and the pelvis. ■ Zoology the posterior part of the body of an arthropod, esp. the segments of an insect's body behind the thorax.
–ORIGIN mid 16th cent.: from Latin.

ab·dom·i·nal /ab'dämənl/ ▶ **adj.** relating to the abdomen: *abdominal pain.*
▶ **n.** (usu. **abdominals**) an abdominal muscle.
–DERIVATIVES **ab·dom·i·nal·ly adv.**

ab·do·min·o·plas·ty /ab'dämənə,plastē/ ▶ **n.** (pl. **abdominoplasties**) Medicine a surgical operation involving the removal of excess flesh from the abdomen.

ab·du·cens nerve /ab'd(y)o͞osənz/ ▶ **n.** Anatomy each of the sixth pair of cranial nerves, supplying the muscles concerned with the lateral movement of the eyeballs.
–ORIGIN early 19th cent.: *abducens* (modern Latin, 'leading away'), from the Latin verb *abducere*.

ab·duct /ab'dəkt/ ▶ **v.** [with obj.] **1** take (someone) away illegally by force or deception; kidnap: *the millionaire who disappeared may have been abducted.*
2 Physiology (of a muscle) move (a limb or part) away from the midline of the body or from another part. The opposite of **adduct**[1].
–ORIGIN early 17th cent.: from Latin *abduct-* 'led away,' from *abducere*, from *ab-* 'away, from' + *ducere* 'to lead.'

ab·duct·ee /,abdək'tē/ ▶ **n.** a person who has been abducted.

ab·duc·tion /ab'dəksнən/ ▶ **n. 1** the action or an instance of forcibly taking someone away against their will: *they organized the abduction of Mr. Cordes on his way to the airport | abductions by armed men in plain clothes.* ■ (in legal use) the illegal removal of a child from parents or guardians.
2 Physiology the movement of a limb or other part away from the midline of the body, or from another part. The opposite of **adduction** (see **adduct**[1]).

ab·duc·tor /ab'dəktər/ ▶ **n. 1** a person who abducts another person.

2 (also **abductor muscle**) Anatomy a muscle whose contraction moves a limb or part away from the midline of the body, or from another part. Compare with **ADDUCTOR**. ■ any of a number of specific muscles in the hand, forearm, or foot: [followed by Latin genitive] *abductor pollicis*.
– ORIGIN early 17th cent. (as a term in anatomy): modern Latin (see **ABDUCT**).

Ab·dul Ha·mid II /ˌäbdo͝ol häˈmēd/ (1842–1918), the last sultan of Turkey 1876–1909. An autocratic ruler, he was deposed after the revolt of the Young Turks.

Ab·dul-Jab·bar /abˈdo͝ol jəˈbär/, Kareem, (1947–), US basketball player; former name *Lewis Ferdinand Alcindor*. He played professionally for the Milwaukee Bucks 1969–75 and the Los Angeles Lakers 1975–89 and holds several records.

Ab·dul·lah ibn Hus·sein /ˌäbdo͝olˈä ˌibən ho͞oˈsān/ (1882–1951), king of Jordan 1946–51. After serving as emir of Transjordan from 1921, he became king of Jordan at the time of independence. He was assassinated in 1951.

Ab·dul·lah II /ˌäbdo͝olˈä/ (1962–), king of Jordan since 1999; full name *Abdullah ibn al-Hussein*. The son of King Hussein, he maintained a moderate political stance and initiated economic reforms.

Abdullah II

Ab·dul Rah·man /äbˈdo͝ol ˈrämən, ˈräkhmän, räkhˈmän/, Tunku (1903–90), Malayan statesman; prime minister of Malaya 1957–63 and of Malaysia 1963–70.

a·beam /əˈbēm/ ▶ **adv.** on a line at right angles to a ship's or an aircraft's length. ■ (**abeam of**) opposite the middle of (a ship or aircraft): *she was lying almost abeam of us* | [as prep.] *before I knew it, I was abeam the ship*.
– ORIGIN mid 19th cent.: from **A-**[2] (expressing general direction) + **BEAM**.

a·be·ce·dar·i·an /ˌābēsēˈde(ə)rēən/ ▶ **adj.**
1 arranged alphabetically: *in abecedarian sequence*.
2 rudimentary; elementary: *abecedarian technology*.
▶ **n.** a person who is just learning; a novice.
– ORIGIN mid 17th cent.: from late Latin *abecedarius* 'alphabetical' (from the names of the letters *a*, *b*, *c*, *d*) + **-AN**.

a·bed /əˈbed/ ▶ **adv.** archaic in bed.
– ORIGIN Middle English: from **A-**[2] 'in, on' + **BED**.

A·bel[1] /ˈābəl/ (in the Bible) the second son of Adam and Eve, murdered by his brother Cain.

A·bel[2] /ˈäbəl/, Niels Henrik (1802–29), Norwegian mathematician. He developed the concept of elliptic functions, independently of Jacobi, and did work on integral equations and power series.

Ab·e·lard /ˈabəˌlärd/, Peter (1079–1142), French scholar, theologian, and philosopher. He is famous for his tragic love affair with his student Héloïse. See also **HÉLOÏSE**.

a·bele /əˈbēl/ ▶ **n.** the white poplar.
– ORIGIN Middle English: via Old French from medieval Latin *albellus*, diminutive of *albus* 'white.' The term was reintroduced in the late 16th cent. from Dutch *abeel* (from Old French *abel*), when specimens were imported into England from the Netherlands.

a·be·li·an /əˈbēlēən, -yən/ ▶ **adj.** Mathematics (of a group) having members related by a commutative operation (e.g., $a \times b = b \times a$).
– ORIGIN mid 19th cent.: named after N. H. *Abel* (see **ABEL**[2]).

A·be·na·ki /ˌabəˈnakē, ˌäbəˈnä-/ ▶ **n.** variant spelling of **ABNAKI**.

A·be·o·ku·ta /äˈbā-ōko͞oˌtä/ a city in southwestern Nigeria, capital of the state of Ogun; pop. 487,600 (est. 2005).

Ab·er·deen /ˌabərˈdēn, ˈabərˌdēn/ **1** a city and seaport in northeastern Scotland, a center of the offshore North Sea oil industry; pop. 166,900 (est. 2009).
2 a town in northeastern Maryland, on Chesapeake Bay; pop. 13,993 (est. 2008). A major military test range is nearby.
3 a city in northeastern South Dakota, a dairy center; pop. 24,460 (est. 2008).

Ab·er·deen An·gus ▶ **n.** an animal of a Scottish breed of hornless black beef cattle. Also called **BLACK ANGUS**.
– ORIGIN mid 19th cent.

Ab·er·nath·y /ˈabərˌnaTHē/, Ralph David (1926–90), US minister and civil rights activist. He served as president of the Southern Christian Leadership Conference (SCLC) from 1968 until 1977. His autobiography, *And the Walls Came Tumbling Down*, was published in 1989.

ab·er·rant /ˈabərənt, əˈber-/ ▶ **adj.** departing from an accepted standard. ■ chiefly Biology diverging from the normal type: *aberrant chromosomes*.
– DERIVATIVES **ab·er·rance** n., **ab·er·ran·cy** n., **ab·er·rant·ly** adv.
– ORIGIN mid 16th cent.: from Latin *aberrant-* 'wandering away,' from the verb *aberrare*, from *ab-* 'away, from' + *errare* 'to stray.'

ab·er·ra·tion /ˌabəˈrāSHən/ ▶ **n.** a departure from what is normal, usual, or expected, typically one that is unwelcome: *they described the outbreak of violence in the area as an aberration*. ■ Biology a characteristic that deviates from the normal type: *color aberrations*. ■ Optics the failure of rays to converge at one focus because of limitations or defects in a lens or mirror. ■ Astronomy the apparent displacement of a celestial object from its true position, caused by the relative motion of the observer and the object.
– DERIVATIVES **ab·er·ra·tion·al** /-SHənl/ adj.
– ORIGIN late 16th cent.: from Latin *aberratio(n-)*, from *aberrare* 'to stray' (see **ABERRANT**).

Ab·er·ta·we /ˌabərˈtou-ē/ see **SWANSEA**.

a·bet /əˈbet/ ▶ **v.** (**abets, abetting, abetted**) [with obj.] encourage or assist (someone) to do something wrong, in particular, to commit a crime or other offense: *he was not guilty of murder but was guilty of aiding and abetting others*. ■ encourage or assist someone to commit (a crime): *we are aiding and abetting this illegal traffic*.
– DERIVATIVES **a·bet·ment** n., **a·bet·tor** (also **abetter**) n.
– ORIGIN late Middle English (in the sense 'urge to do something good or bad'): from Old French *abeter*, from *a-* (from Latin *ad* 'to, at') + *beter* 'hound, urge on.'

a·bey·ance /əˈbāəns/ ▶ **n.** a state of temporary disuse or suspension: *matters were held in abeyance pending further inquiries*. ■ Law the position of being without, or waiting for, an owner or claimant.
– DERIVATIVES **a·bey·ant** /əˈbāənt/ adj.
– ORIGIN late 16th cent. (in the legal sense): from Old French *abeance* 'aspiration to a title,' from *abeer* 'aspire after,' from *a-* 'toward' + *beer* 'to gape.'

ab·hor /abˈhôr/ ▶ **v.** (**abhors, abhorring, abhorred**) [with obj.] formal regard with disgust and hatred: *professional tax preparers abhor a flat tax because it would dry up their business*.
– DERIVATIVES **ab·hor·rer** n.
– ORIGIN late Middle English: from Latin *abhorrere*, from *ab-* 'away from' + *horrere* 'to shudder.'

ab·hor·rence /abˈhôrəns, -ˈhär-/ ▶ **n.** a feeling of repulsion; disgusted loathing: *the thought of marrying him filled her with abhorrence* | *society's abhorrence of crime*.

ab·hor·rent /abˈhôrənt, -ˈhär-/ ▶ **adj.** inspiring disgust and loathing; repugnant: *racial discrimination was abhorrent to us all*.
– ORIGIN late 16th cent.: from Latin *abhorrent-* 'shuddering away from in horror,' from the verb *abhorrere* (see **ABHOR**).

a·bide /əˈbīd/ ▶ **v.** **1** [no obj.] (**abide by**) accept or act in accordance with (a rule, decision, or recommendation): *I said I would abide by their decision*.
2 [with obj.] (**can/could not abide**) informal be unable to tolerate (someone or something): *if there is one thing I cannot abide it is a lack of discipline*.
3 [no obj.] (of a feeling or a memory) continue without fading or being lost. ■ archaic live; dwell.
– ORIGIN Old English *ābīdan* 'wait,' from *ā-* 'onward' + *bīdan* (see **BIDE**).

a·bid·ing /əˈbīdiNG/ ▶ **adj.** [attrib.] (of a feeling or a memory) lasting a long time; enduring: *he had an abiding respect for her*.
– DERIVATIVES **a·bid·ing·ly** adv. [as submodifier] *an abidingly mysterious quality*.

Ab·i·djan /ˌabiˈjän/ the chief port of Côte d'Ivoire (Ivory Coast), the capital 1935–83; pop. 4,000,000 (est. 2009).

Abi·lene /ˈabəˌlēn/ **1** a city in east central Kansas; pop. 6,400 (est. 2008). It was the first terminus of the Chisholm Trail.
2 a city in north central Texas, an agricultural and oil industry center; pop. 116,484 (est. 2008).

a·bil·i·ty /əˈbilitē/ ▶ **n.** (pl. **abilities**) **1** [in sing., with infinitive] possession of the means or skill to do something: *the manager had lost his ability to motivate the players* | *they'll examine your ability to pay*.
2 talent, skill, or proficiency in a particular area: *a man of exceptional ability* | *students of all abilities*.
– ORIGIN late Middle English: from Old French *ablete*, from Latin *habilitas*, from *habilis* 'able.'

-ability ▶ **suffix** forming nouns of quality corresponding to adjectives ending in *-able* (such as *suitability* corresponding to *suitable*).
– ORIGIN from French *-abilité* or Latin *-abilitas*, noun endings.

Ab·ing·ton /ˈabiNGtən/ a township in southeastern Pennsylvania, north of Philadelphia; pop. 53,980 (est. 2008).

ab in·i·ti·o /ˌab əˈniSHē,ō/ ▶ **adv.** from the beginning (used chiefly in formal or legal contexts): *the agreement should be declared void ab initio*.
▶ **adj.** [attrib.] starting from the beginning: *he was instructing ab initio pilots*.
– ORIGIN early 17th cent.: Latin.

a·bi·o·gen·e·sis /ˌābī-ōˈjenəsis/ ▶ **n.** technical term for **SPONTANEOUS GENERATION**.
– ORIGIN late 19th cent.: from **A-**[1] 'not' + Greek *bios* 'life' + **GENESIS**.

a·bi·ot·ic /ˌābīˈätik/ ▶ **adj.** physical rather than biological; not derived from living organisms. ■ devoid of life; sterile.

Ab·i·qui·u /ˌabəˈkē-o͞o/ a ranching community in northern New Mexico, the longtime home of artist Georgia O'Keeffe.

ab·ject /ˈabˌjekt, abˈjekt/ ▶ **adj.** **1** [attrib.] (of a situation or condition) extremely bad, unpleasant, and degrading: *abject poverty*. ■ (of an unhappy state of mind) experienced to the maximum degree: *his letter plunged her into abject misery*.
2 (of a person or their behavior) completely without pride or dignity; self-abasing: *an abject apology*.
– DERIVATIVES **ab·jec·tion** /abˈjekSHən/ n., **ab·ject·ly** adv., **ab·ject·ness** n.
– ORIGIN late Middle English (in the sense 'rejected'): from Latin *abjectus*, past participle of *abjicere* 'reject,' from *ab-* 'away' + *jacere* 'to throw.'

ab·jure /abˈjo͝or/ ▶ **v.** [with obj.] formal solemnly renounce (a belief, cause, or claim): *his refusal to abjure the Catholic faith*.
– PHRASES **abjure the realm** historical swear an oath to leave a country or realm forever.
– DERIVATIVES **ab·ju·ra·tion** /ˌabjəˈrāSHən/ n.
– ORIGIN late Middle English: from Latin *abjurare*, from *ab-* 'away' + *jurare* 'swear.'

Ab·khaz /äbˈkäz, abˈkaz, əbˈKHäz/ (also **Abkhazian** /abˈkazHən, -zēən, äbˈkä-/) ▶ **adj.** of or relating to Abkhazia, its people, or their language.
▶ **n.** **1** a member of a Caucasian people living in Abkhazia.
2 a Northwest Caucasian language.

Ab·kha·zi·a /äbˈkäzēə, abˈkāZH(ē)ə/ an autonomous territory in northwestern Georgia, south of the Caucasus mountains on the Black Sea; pop. 215,972 (2003); capital, Sokhumi. In 1992, Abkhazia unilaterally declared itself independent, sparking ongoing armed conflict with Georgia.

ab·la·tion /əˈblāSHən/ ▶ **n.** **1** the surgical removal of body tissue.
2 the removal of snow and ice by melting or evaporation, typically from a glacier or iceberg. ■ the erosion of rock, typically by wind action. ■ the loss of surface material from a spacecraft or meteorite through evaporation or melting caused by friction with the atmosphere.
– DERIVATIVES **ab·late** /əˈblāt/ v.
– ORIGIN late Middle English (in the general sense 'taking away, removal'): from late Latin *ablatio(n-)*, from Latin *ablat-* 'taken away,' from *ab-* 'away' + *lat-* 'carried' (from the verb *ferre*).

ab·la·tive /ˈablətiv/ ▶ **adj.** [attrib.] **1** Grammar relating to or denoting a case (esp. in Latin) of nouns and pronouns (and words in grammatical agreement with them) indicating separation or an agent, instrument, or location.
2 (of surgical treatment) involving ablation.
3 of, relating to, or subject to ablation through melting or evaporation: *the spacecraft's ablative heat shield*.
▶ **n.** Grammar a word in the ablative case. ■ (**the ablative**) the ablative case.
– ORIGIN late Middle English: from Old French *ablative* (feminine of *ablatif*), Latin *ablativus*, from *ablat-* 'taken away' (see **ABLATION**).

PRONUNCIATION KEY ə *ago, up*; ər *over, fur*; a *hat*; ā *ate*; ä *car*; e *let*; ē *see*; i *fit*; ī *by*; NG *sing*; ō *go*; ô *law, for*; oi *toy*; o͝o *good*; o͞o *goo*; ou *out*; TH *thin*; T͟H *then*; ZH *vision*

ab·la·tive ab·so·lute ▶ n. a construction in Latin that consists of a noun and participle or adjective in the ablative case and that is syntactically independent of the rest of the sentence.

ab·laut /ˈabˌlout/ ▶ n. a change of vowel in related words or forms, e.g., in Germanic strong verbs (e.g., in *sing, sang, sung*).
– ORIGIN mid 19th cent.: from German, from *ab* 'off' + *Laut* 'sound.'

a·blaze /əˈblāz/ ▶ adj. [predic.] burning fiercely: *his clothes were ablaze* | [as complement] *farm buildings were set ablaze*. ■ very brightly colored or lighted: *New England is **ablaze with** color in autumn* | figurative *his eyes were **ablaze with** anger*. ■ filled with anger or another strong emotion: *in 1848 the whole of Europe was **ablaze with** revolution*.

a·ble /ˈābəl/ ▶ adj. (**abler**, **ablest**) **1** [with infinitive] having the power, skill, means, or opportunity to do something: *he was able to read Greek at the age of eight* | *he would never be able to afford such a big house*.
2 having considerable skill, proficiency, or intelligence: *the dancers were technically very able*.
– ORIGIN late Middle English (also in the sense 'easy to use, suitable'): from Old French *hable*, from Latin *habilis* 'handy,' from *habere* 'to hold.'

-able /əbəl/ ▶ suffix forming adjectives meaning:
1 able to be: *calculable*.
2 due to be: *payable*.
3 subject to: *taxable*.
4 relevant to or in accordance with: *fashionable*.
5 having the quality to: *suitable* | *comfortable*.
– ORIGIN from French *-able* or Latin *-abilis*, adjectival endings; originally found in words only from these forms but later used to form adjectives directly from English verbs ending in *-ate*, e.g., *educable* from *educate*. The unrelated ABLE has probably influenced terms such as *bearable*, *salable*.

a·ble-bod·ied ▶ adj. fit, strong, and healthy; not physically disabled: *he was the only able-bodied man on the farm*.

a·ble-bod·ied sea·man ▶ n. (also **able seaman**) a merchant seaman qualified to perform all routine duties.

a·bled /ˈābəld/ ▶ adj. having a full range of physical or mental abilities; not disabled. See also DIFFERENTLY ABLED.
– ORIGIN 1980s: back-formation from DISABLED.

a·ble·ism /ˈābəˌlizəm/ (also **ablism**) ▶ n. discrimination in favor of able-bodied people.
– DERIVATIVES **a·ble·ist** n. & adj.

a·ble sea·man ▶ n. an able-bodied seaman.

a·bloom /əˈblo͞om/ ▶ adj. [predic.] covered in flowers.

ab·lu·tion /əˈblo͞oshən/ ▶ n. (usu. **ablutions**) the act of washing oneself (often used for humorously formal effect): *the women performed their ablutions*. ■ a ceremonial act of washing parts of the body or sacred containers.
– DERIVATIVES **ab·lu·tion·ar·y** adj.
– ORIGIN late Middle English: from Latin *ablutio(n-)*, from *abluere*, from *ab-* 'away' + *luere* 'wash.' The original use was as a term in chemistry and alchemy meaning 'purification by using liquids,' hence 'purification of the body by washing' (mid 16th cent).

a·bly /ˈāblē/ ▶ adv. skillfully; competently: *Steven has summed up our concerns very ably*.

-ably ▶ suffix forming adverbs corresponding to adjectives ending in *-able* (such as *suitably* corresponding to *suitable*).

ABM ▶ abbr. antiballistic missile.

Ab·na·ki /abˈnakē, äbˈnä-/ (also **Abenaki** /ˌabəˈnakē, ˌäbəˈnä-/) ▶ n. (pl. **same** or **Abnakis**) **1** a member of a North American Indian people of Maine on the Atlantic coast to southern Quebec.
2 either or both of two Algonquian languages, **Eastern Abnaki** and **Western Abnaki**, now nearly extinct.
▶ adj. of or relating to this people or their language.
– ORIGIN from French *Abénaqui*, from Eastern Abnaki.

ab·ne·gate /ˈabniˌgāt/ ▶ v. [with obj.] renounce or reject (something desired or valuable): *he attempts to abnegate personal responsibility*.
– DERIVATIVES **ab·ne·ga·tor** /-ˌgātər/ n.
– ORIGIN early 17th cent.: from Latin *abnegat-* 'renounced,' from the verb *abnegare*, from *ab-* 'away, off' + *negare* 'deny.'

ab·ne·ga·tion /ˌabniˈgāshən/ ▶ n. the act of renouncing or rejecting something: *abnegation of political lawmaking power*. ■ self-denial.
– ORIGIN Middle English: from Latin *abnegatio(n-)*, from the verb *abnegare* (see ABNEGATE).

ab·nor·mal /abˈnôrməl/ ▶ adj. deviating from what is normal or usual, typically in a way that is undesirable or worrying: *the illness is recognizable from the patient's abnormal behavior*.
– DERIVATIVES **ab·nor·mal·ly** adv.
– ORIGIN mid 19th cent.: alteration (by association with Latin *abnormis* 'monstrosity') of 16th-cent. *anormal*, from French, variant of *anomal*, via Latin from Greek *anōmalos* (see ANOMALOUS).

ab·nor·mal·i·ty /ˌabnôrˈmalitē/ ▶ n. (pl. **abnormalities**) an abnormal feature, characteristic, or occurrence, typically in a medical context: *a chromosome abnormality*. ■ the quality or state of being abnormal.

A·bo /ˈabō/ (also **abo**) Austral. informal, offensive ▶ n. (pl. **Abos**) an Aborigine.
▶ adj. Aboriginal.
– ORIGIN early 20th cent.: abbreviation.

Å·bo /ˈôbo͞o/ Swedish name for TURKU.

a·board /əˈbôrd/ ▶ adv. & prep. on or into (a ship, aircraft, train, or other vehicle): [as adv.] *the plane crashed, killing all 158 people aboard* | figurative *he came aboard as IBM's new chairman* | [as prep.] *climbing aboard the yacht*. ■ on or onto (a horse): [as adv.] *with Migliore aboard, he won the cup at a gallop*. ■ Baseball on base as a runner: *putting their first batter aboard*.
– PHRASES **all aboard!** a call warning passengers to get on a ship, train, or bus that is about to depart.
– ORIGIN late Middle English: from A-[2] (expressing motion) + BOARD, reinforced by Old French *à bord*.

a·bode[1] /əˈbōd/ ▶ n. formal or literary a place of residence; a house or home: *her current abode* | humorous *my humble abode*. ■ residence: *a place of abode*. ■ archaic a stay; a sojourn.
– ORIGIN Middle English (in the sense 'act of waiting'): verbal noun from ABIDE.

a·bode[2] ▶ v. archaic past of ABIDE.

a·bol·ish /əˈbälish/ ▶ v. [with obj.] formally put an end to (a system, practice, or institution): *the tax was abolished in 1977*.
– DERIVATIVES **a·bol·ish·er** n., **a·bol·ish·ment** n.
– ORIGIN late Middle English: from Old French *aboliss-*, lengthened stem of *abolir*, from Latin *abolere* 'destroy.'

ab·o·li·tion /ˌabəˈlishən/ ▶ n. the action or an act of abolishing a system, practice, or institution: *the abolition of child labor*.
– ORIGIN early 16th cent.: from Latin *abolitio(n-)*, from *abolere* 'destroy.'

ab·o·li·tion·ist /ˌabəˈlishənist/ ▶ n. a person who favors the abolition of a practice or institution, esp. capital punishment or (formerly) slavery.
– DERIVATIVES **ab·o·li·tion·ism** n.

ab·o·ma·sum /ˌabəˈmāsəm/ ▶ n. (pl. **abomasa** /-sə/) Zoology the fourth stomach of a ruminant, which receives food from the omasum and passes it to the small intestine.
– ORIGIN late 17th cent.: modern Latin, from *ab-* 'away, from' + *omasum* (see OMASUM).

A-bomb ▶ n. short for ATOM BOMB.

Ab·o·mey /ˌabəˈmā, əˈbōmē/ a town in southern Benin, capital of the former kingdom of Dahomey; pop. 87,941 (2006).

a·bom·i·na·ble /əˈbäm(ə)nəbəl/ ▶ adj. causing moral revulsion: *the uprising was suppressed with abominable cruelty*. ■ very bad or unpleasant: *a cup of abominable tea*.
– DERIVATIVES **a·bom·i·na·bly** /-blē/ adv.
– ORIGIN Middle English: via Old French from Latin *abominabilis*, from *abominari* (see ABOMINATE). The term was once widely believed to be from AB- 'away from' + Latin *homine* (from *homo* 'human being'), thus 'inhuman, beastly,' and frequently spelled *abhominable* until the 17th cent.

A·bom·i·na·ble Snow·man ▶ n. (pl. **Abominable Snowmen**) another term for YETI.

a·bom·i·nate /əˈbäməˌnāt/ ▶ v. [with obj.] formal detest; loathe: *they abominated the very idea of monarchy*.
– DERIVATIVES **a·bom·i·na·tor** /-ˌnātər/ n.
– ORIGIN mid 17th cent.: from Latin *abominat-* 'deprecated,' from the verb *abominari*, from *ab-* 'away, from' + *omen, omin-* 'omen.'

a·bom·i·na·tion /əˌbäməˈnāshən/ ▶ n. a thing that causes disgust or hatred: *this bill is an abomination to all mankind* | informal *concrete abominations masquerading as hotels*. ■ a feeling of hatred: *their abomination of indulgence*.
– ORIGIN Middle English: from Latin *abominatio(n-)*, from the verb *abominari* (see ABOMINATE).

ab·o·ral /abˈôrəl/ ▶ adj. Zoology relating to or denoting the side or end that is furthest from the mouth, esp. in animals that lack clear upper and lower sides, such as echinoderms. ■ moving or leading away from the mouth: *propagated in an aboral direction*.
– DERIVATIVES **ab·o·ral·ly** adv.

ab·o·rig·i·nal /ˌabəˈrijənl/ ▶ adj. (of human races, animals, and plants) inhabiting or existing in a land from the earliest times or from before the arrival of colonists; indigenous. ■ (**Aboriginal**) of or relating to the Australian Aborigines or their languages.
▶ n. an aboriginal inhabitant of a place. ■ (**Aboriginal**) a person belonging to one of the indigenous peoples of Australia.
– ORIGIN mid 17th cent.: from Latin *aborigines* 'original inhabitants' (see ABORIGINE) + -AL.

Ab·o·rig·i·nal·i·ty /ˌabəˌrijəˈnalitē/ ▶ n. the distinctive culture of aboriginal peoples, esp. those in Australia: *their music reflects their Aboriginality*.

ab·o·rig·i·ne /ˌabəˈrijənē/ ▶ n. a person, animal, or plant that has been in a country or region from earliest times. ■ (**Aborigine**) an aboriginal inhabitant of Australia.
– ORIGIN mid 19th cent.: back-formation from the 16th-cent. plural *aborigines* 'original inhabitants' (in classical times referring to those of Italy and Greece), from the Latin phrase *ab origine* 'from the beginning.'

> **USAGE** Both **Aboriginal** and **Aborigine** may be used as nouns referring to a member of an Australian Aboriginal people, but the term **Aborigine** is more common and is often preferred, especially in the plural.

a·born·ing /əˈbôrning/ ▶ adv. while being born or produced: *the idea died aborning*.
▶ adj. [predic.] being born or produced: *in the early 1960s, hippiedom was aborning*.
– ORIGIN 1930s: from *a-* 'in the process of' + *borning*, verbal noun from *born* (North American dialect usage) 'to be born.'

a·bort /əˈbôrt/ ▶ v. [with obj.] **1** carry out or undergo the abortion of (a fetus). ■ [no obj.] (of a pregnant woman or female animal) have a miscarriage, with loss of the fetus. ■ [no obj.] Biology (of an embryonic organ or organism) remain undeveloped; fail to mature.
2 bring to a premature end because of a problem or fault: *the pilot aborted his landing*.
▶ n. informal or technical an act of aborting a flight, space mission, or other enterprise: *there was an abort because of bad weather*.
– ORIGIN mid 16th cent.: from Latin *aboriri* 'miscarry,' from *ab-* 'away, from' + *oriri* 'be born.'

a·bor·ti·fa·cient /əˌbôrtəˈfāshənt/ Medicine ▶ adj. (chiefly of a drug) causing abortion.
▶ n. an abortifacient drug.

a·bor·tion /əˈbôrshən/ ▶ n. **1** the deliberate termination of a human pregnancy, most often performed during the first 28 weeks of pregnancy. ■ the expulsion of a fetus from the uterus by natural causes before it is able to survive independently. ■ Biology the arrest of the development of an organ, typically a seed or fruit.
2 an object or undertaking regarded by the speaker as unpleasant or badly made or carried out.
– ORIGIN mid 16th cent.: from Latin *abortio(n-)*, from *aboriri* 'miscarry' (see ABORT).

a·bor·tion·ist /əˈbôrshənist/ ▶ n. a person who carries out abortions (typically applied to someone not working in a hospital, or used to convey disapproval of abortion).

a·bor·tion pill ▶ n. informal a drug that can induce abortion, esp. mifepristone.

a·bor·tive /əˈbôrtiv/ ▶ adj. **1** failing to produce the intended result: *an abortive attempt to overthrow the government*.
2 Biology, dated (of an organ or organism) rudimentary; arrested in development: *abortive medusae*. ■ Medicine (of a virus infection) failing to produce symptoms.
3 rare causing or resulting in abortion: *abortive techniques*.
– DERIVATIVES **a·bor·tive·ly** adv.
– ORIGIN Middle English (as a noun denoting a stillborn child or animal): via Old French from Latin *abortivus*, from *aboriri* 'miscarry' (see ABORT).

a·bor·tus fe·ver /əˈbôrtəs/ ▶ n. the most common form of undulant fever in humans. ● This disease is caused by the bacterium *Brucella abortus*, which is also the chief cause of brucellosis in cattle.
– ORIGIN 1920s: from Latin *abortus* 'miscarriage.'

ABO system ▶ n. a system of four basic types (A, AB, B, and O) into which human blood may be classified, based on the presence or absence of certain inherited antigens.

a·bou·li·a /əˈbo͞olēə/ ▶ n. variant spelling of ABULIA.

a·bound /əˈbound/ ▶ v. [no obj.] exist in large numbers or amounts: *rumors of a further scandal abound*. ■ (**abound in/with**) have in large numbers or amounts: *this land abounds with wildlife*.
– ORIGIN Middle English (in the sense 'overflow, be abundant'): from Old French *abunder*, from Latin *abundare* 'overflow,' from *ab-* 'from' + *undare* 'surge' (from *unda* 'a wave').

a·bound·ing /əˈbounding/ ▶ adj. very plentiful; abundant: *his abounding creative talent*.

a·bout /əˈbout/ ▶ **prep. 1** on the subject of; concerning: *I was thinking about you | an article about yellow fever | it's* ***all about*** *having fun.* ■ so as to affect: *there's nothing we can do about it.*
2 used to indicate movement within a particular area: *she looked about the room.*
3 used to express location in a particular place: *rugs strewn about the hall | he produced a knife from somewhere about his person.* ■ used to describe a quality apparent in a person: *there was a look about her that said everything.*
▶ **adv. 1** used to indicate movement in an area: *men were floundering about | finding my way about.*
2 used to express location in a particular place: *there was a lot of flu about | a thief about in the hotel.*
3 (used with a number or quantity) approximately: *reduced by about 5 percent | he's about 35.*
– PHRASES **about to do something** intending to do something or close to doing something very soon: *the ceremony was about to begin.* **be not about to do something** be unwilling to do something: *he is not about to step down after so long.* **how about** see HOW[1]. **just about** see JUST. **know what one is about** informal be aware of the implications of one's actions or of a situation, and of how best to deal with them. **up and about** see UP. **what about** see WHAT.
– ORIGIN Old English *onbūtan*, from *on* + *būtan* 'outside of.'

a·bout-face ▶ **n.** (chiefly in military contexts) a turn made so as to face the opposite direction: *he did an about-face and marched out of the tent.* ■ a complete change of opinion or policy: *he threatened to stop helping us, but did a complete about-face.*
▶ **v.** [no obj.] turn so as to face the opposite direction.
▶ **exclam.** (**about face!**) (in military contexts) a command to make an about-face.
– ORIGIN mid 19th cent.: shortening of *right-about face.*

a·bove /əˈbəv/ ▶ **prep. 1** in extended space over and not touching: *a display of fireworks above the town |* [with verb] *a cable runs above the duct.* ■ extending upward over: *her arms above her head.* ■ higher than and to one side of; overlooking: *in the hills above the capital | on the wall above the altar.*
2 at a higher level or layer than: *bruises above both eyes | small windows above the aisles.* ■ higher in grade or rank than: *at a level above the common people.* ■ considered of higher status or worth than; too good for: *she* ***married above her*** *| above reproach.* ■ in preference to: *they cynically chose profit above car safety.* ■ at a higher volume or pitch than: *above a whisper | it went unheard above the din.*
3 higher than (a specified amount, rate, or norm): *above average | above freezing | above sea level | the unemployment rate will* ***soar above*** *its present level.*
▶ **adv.** at a higher level or layer: *place a quantity of mud in a jar with water above.* ■ higher in grade or rank: *an officer of the rank of superintendent or above.* ■ higher than a specified amount, rate, or norm: *boats of 31 ft. or above.* ■ (in printed text) mentioned earlier or further up on the same page: *the two cases described above | see above left |* [as adj.] *at the above address |* [as noun] *since writing* ***the above****, I have reconsidered.*
– PHRASES **above all (else)** more so than anything else: *he was concerned above all to speak the truth.* **above oneself** conceited; arrogant. **from above** from overhead: *branches rained from above.* ■ from a position of higher rank or authority: *mass culture is imposed from above.* **not be above** be capable of stooping to (an unworthy act): *he was not above practical jokes.* **over and above** see OVER.
– ORIGIN Old English *abufan* (as an adverb), from *a-* 'on' + *bufan* (from *bi* 'by' + *ufan* 'above').

a·bove·board /əˈbəvˌbôrd/ (also **above board**) ▶ **adj. & adv.** legitimate, honest, and open: [as adj.] *certain transactions were not totally aboveboard |* [as adv.] *the accountants acted completely above board.*

ab o·vo /ab ˈōˌvō, äb/ ▶ **adv.** from the very beginning.
– ORIGIN early 18th cent.: Latin, literally 'from the egg.'

Abp. ▶ **abbr.** Archbishop.

ab·ra·ca·dab·ra /ˌabrəkəˈdabrə/ ▶ **exclam.** a word said by magicians when performing a magic trick.
▶ **n.** informal the implausibly easy achievement of difficult feats: *where a computer and a little abracadabra turn a freeze-dried steak into a romantic dinner.* ■ language, typically in the form of gibberish, used to give the impression of arcane knowledge or power: *I get so fed up with all the mumbo jumbo and abracadabra.*
– ORIGIN late 17th cent. (as a mystical word engraved and used as a charm to ward off illness): from Latin, first recorded in a 2nd-cent. poem by Q. Serenus Sammonicus, from a Greek base.

a·brade /əˈbrād/ ▶ **v.** [with obj.] scrape or wear away by friction or erosion: *a landscape slowly abraded by a fine, stinging dust.*
– DERIVATIVES **a·brad·er n.**
– ORIGIN late 17th cent.: from Latin *abradere*, from *ab-* 'away, from' + *radere* 'to scrape.'

A·bra·ham /ˈābrəˌham/ (in the Bible) the Hebrew patriarch from whom all Jews trace their descent.

A·bra·ham, Plains of see PLAINS OF ABRAHAM.

A·bra·ham·ic /ˌābrəˈhamik/ ▶ **adj. 1** denoting any or all of the religions (Judaism, Christianity, and Islam) that revere Abraham, the Biblical patriarch: *the monotheistic faiths that grew out of the Abrahamic heritage.*
2 relating specifically to the Biblical patriarch Abraham.

A·bra·hams /ˈābrəˌhamz/, Harold (Maurice) (1899–1978), English athlete. In 1924 he became the first Englishman to win the 100 meters in the Olympic Games. His story was retold in the movie *Chariots of Fire* (1981).

a·bra·sion /əˈbrāZHən/ ▶ **n.** the process of scraping or wearing away: *the metal is resistant to abrasion.* ■ an area damaged by scraping or wearing away: *there were cuts and abrasions to the lips and jaw.*
– ORIGIN mid 17th cent.: from Latin *abrasio(n-)*, from the verb *abradere* (see ABRADE).

a·bra·sive /əˈbrāsiv, -ziv/ ▶ **adj. 1** (of a substance or material) capable of polishing or cleaning a hard surface by rubbing or grinding. ■ tending to rub or graze the skin: *the trees were abrasive to the touch.*
2 (of a person or manner) showing little concern for the feelings of others; harsh: *her abrasive and arrogant personal style won her few friends.*
▶ **n.** a substance used for grinding, polishing, or cleaning a hard surface.
– DERIVATIVES **a·bra·sive·ly adv.**, **a·bra·sive·ness n.**
– ORIGIN mid 19th cent. (as a noun): from Latin *abras-* 'abraded,' from the verb *abradere* (see ABRADE), + -IVE.

a·bra·zo /əˈbräsō/ ▶ **n.** (pl. **abrazos**) an embrace.
– ORIGIN Spanish.

ab·re·act /ˌabrēˈakt/ ▶ **v.** [with obj.] Psychology release (an emotion) by abreaction. ■ cause (someone) to undergo abreaction.
– ORIGIN early 20th cent.: back-formation from ABREACTION.

ab·re·ac·tion /ˌabrēˈakSHən/ ▶ **n.** Psychology the expression and consequent release of a previously repressed emotion, achieved through reliving the experience that caused it (typically through hypnosis or suggestion).
– DERIVATIVES **ab·re·ac·tive** /-tiv/ **adj.**
– ORIGIN early 20th cent.: from AB- 'away from' + REACTION, translating German *Abreagierung.*

a·breast /əˈbrest/ ▶ **adv. 1** side by side and facing the same way: *the path was wide enough for two people to walk abreast | they were riding three abreast.*
2 alongside or even with something: *the cart came abreast of the Americans in their rickshaw.* ■ up to date with the latest news, ideas, or information: ***keeping abreast of*** *developments.*
– ORIGIN late Middle English: from A-[2] 'in' + BREAST.

a·bridge /əˈbrij/ ▶ **v.** [with obj.] **1** shorten (a book, movie, speech, or other text) without losing the sense: *the cassettes have been abridged from the original stories |* (as adj. **abridged**) *an abridged text of his speech.*
2 Law curtail (rights or privileges): *even the right to free speech can be abridged.*
– DERIVATIVES **a·bridg·er n.**
– ORIGIN Middle English (in the sense 'deprive of'): from Old French *abregier*, from late Latin *abbreviare* 'cut short' (see ABBREVIATE).

a·bridg·ment /əˈbrijmənt/ (also **abridgement**) ▶ **n. 1** a shortened version of a larger work: *an abridgment of Shakespeare's Henry VI.*
2 Law a curtailment of rights: *the abridgment of the rights of ownership.*
– ORIGIN late Middle English: from Old French *abregement*, from the verb *abreg(i)er* (see ABRIDGE).

a·broad /əˈbrôd/ ▶ **adv. 1** in or to a foreign country or countries: *we usually* ***go abroad*** *for a week in May | competition from companies* ***at home and abroad.*** ■ dated or humorous out of doors: *few people ventured abroad from their warm houses.*
2 in different directions; over a wide area: *millions of seeds are annually scattered abroad.* ■ (of a feeling or rumor) widely current: *there is a new buccaneering spirit abroad.* ■ freely moving about: *con artists abroad on the streets of the town.*
3 archaic wide of the mark; in error.
▶ **n.** foreign countries considered collectively: *servicemen returning* ***from abroad.***
– ORIGIN Middle English: from A-[2] 'on' + BROAD.

ab·ro·gate /ˈabrəˌgāt/ ▶ **v.** [with obj.] formal repeal or do away with (a law, right, or formal agreement): *a proposal to abrogate temporarily the right to strike.*
– DERIVATIVES **ab·ro·ga·tion** /ˌabrəˈgāSHən/ **n.**
– ORIGIN early 16th cent.: from Latin *abrogat-* 'repealed,' from the verb *abrogare*, from *ab-* 'away, from' + *rogare* 'propose a law.'

ab·rupt /əˈbrəpt/ ▶ **adj. 1** sudden and unexpected: *I was surprised by the abrupt change of subject | our round of golf came to an abrupt end on the 13th hole.*
2 brief to the point of rudeness; curt: *you were rather abrupt with that young man.* ■ (of a style of speech or writing) not flowing smoothly; disjointed.
3 steep; precipitous: *the abrupt double peak of the mountain.*
– DERIVATIVES **ab·rupt·ly adv.**, **ab·rupt·ness n.**
– ORIGIN late 16th cent.: from Latin *abruptus* 'broken off, steep,' past participle of *abrumpere*, from *ab-* 'away, from' + *rumpere* 'break.'

ab·rup·tion /əˈbrəpSHən/ ▶ **n.** technical the sudden breaking away of a portion from a mass. ■ (also **placental abruption**) Medicine separation of the placenta from the wall of the uterus, esp. when it occurs prematurely during pregnancy.
– ORIGIN early 17th cent.: from Latin *abruptio(n)-*, from *abrumpere* 'break off' (see ABRUPT).

ABS ▶ **abbr.** ■ acrylonitrile-butadiene-styrene, a composite plastic used to make car bodies and cases for computers and other appliances. ■ antilock braking system (for motor vehicles).

abs /abz/ informal ▶ **n.** the abdominal muscles.

abs- ▶ **prefix** variant spelling of AB- before *c*, *q*, and *t* (as in *abscond, abstain*).

Ab·sa·ro·ka Range /abˈsärəkə/ a range of the Rocky Mountains in Montana and Wyoming.

ab·scess /ˈabˌses/ ▶ **n.** a swollen area within body tissue, containing an accumulation of pus.
– ORIGIN mid 16th cent.: from Latin *abscessus* 'a going away,' from the verb *abscedere*, from *ab-* 'away from' + *cedere* 'go,' referring to the elimination of infected matter via the pus.

ab·scise /abˈsīz/ ▶ **v.** [with obj.] cut off or away. ■ [no obj.] Botany separate by abscission; fall off.

ab·scis·ic ac·id /abˈsisik/ ▶ **n.** Biochemistry a plant hormone that promotes leaf detachment, induces seed and bud dormancy, and inhibits germination.
– ORIGIN 1960s: *abscisic* from the earlier name for the hormone *abscisin*, from ABSCISSION.

ab·scis·sa /abˈsisə/ ▶ **n.** (pl. **abscissae** /-ˈsisē/ or **abscissas**) Mathematics (in a system of coordinates) the *x*-coordinate, the distance from a point to the vertical or *y*-axis measured parallel to the horizontal or *x*-axis. Compare with ORDINATE.
– ORIGIN early 17th cent. (denoting the part of a line between a point on it and the point of intersection with an ordinate): from modern Latin *abscissa (linea)* 'cutoff (line),' feminine past participle of *abscindere* (see ABSCISSION).

y-axis
abscissa
ordinate
x-axis

abscissa and ordinate

ab·scis·sion /abˈsiZHən/ ▶ **n.** Botany the natural detachment of parts of a plant, typically dead leaves and ripe fruit.
– ORIGIN early 17th cent.: from Latin *abscissio(n-)*, from *abscindere*, from *ab-* 'off, away' + *scindere* 'to cut.'

ab·scond /abˈskänd/ ▶ **v.** [no obj.] leave hurriedly and secretly, typically to avoid detection of or arrest for an unlawful action such as theft: *she absconded with the remaining thousand dollars.* ■ (of someone on bail) fail to surrender oneself for custody at the appointed time. ■ (of a person kept in detention or under supervision) escape: *176 detainees absconded.* ■ (of a colony of honeybees, esp. Africanized ones) entirely abandon a hive or nest.
– DERIVATIVES **ab·scond·er n.**
– ORIGIN mid 16th cent. (in the sense 'hide, conceal (oneself)'): from Latin *abscondere* 'hide,' from *ab-* 'away, from' + *condere* 'stow.'

ab·seil /ˈäpˌzīl, ˈabˌsāl/ ▶ **n. & v.** another term for RAPPEL.
– DERIVATIVES **ab·seil·er n.**
– ORIGIN 1930s: from German *abseilen*, from *ab* 'down' + *Seil* 'rope.'

a

ab·sence /ˈabsəns/ ▶ **n.** the state of being away from a place or person: *the letter had arrived during his absence* | *I supervised the rehearsal* ***in the absence*** *of the director.* ■ an occasion or period of being away from a place or person: *repeated absences from school.* ■ (**absence of**) the nonexistence or lack of: *she found his total absence of facial expression disconcerting.*
– PHRASES **absence makes the heart grow fonder** proverb you feel more affection for those you love when parted from them. **absence of mind** failure to concentrate on or remember what one is doing.
– ORIGIN late Middle English: from Old French, from Latin *absentia*, from *absens, absent-* (see **ABSENT**).

ab·sent ▶ **adj.** /ˈabsənt/ **1** not present in a place, at an occasion, or as part of something: *most students were* ***absent from*** *school at least once* | *absent colleagues* | *wings are absent in several species of crane flies.* **2** (of an expression or manner) showing that someone is not paying attention to what is being said or done: *she looked up with an absent smile.*
▶ **v.** /abˈsent/ [with obj.] (**absent oneself**) stay or go away: *various people absented themselves because of his presence* | *halfway through the meal, he* ***absented himself from*** *the table.*
▶ **prep.** /abˈsent/ formal without: *employees could not be fired absent other evidence.*
– DERIVATIVES **ab·sent·ly adv.** (sense 2 of the adjective).
– ORIGIN Middle English: via Old French from Latin *absens, absent-* 'being absent,' present participle of *abesse*, from *ab-* 'from, away' + *esse* 'to be.'

ab·sen·tee /ˌabsənˈtē/ ▶ **n.** a person who is expected or required to be present at a place or event but is not.

ab·sen·tee bal·lot ▶ **n.** a ballot completed and typically mailed in advance of an election by a voter who is unable to be present at the polls.

ab·sen·tee·ism /ˌabsənˈtēˌizəm/ ▶ **n.** the practice of regularly staying away from work or school without good reason.

ab·sen·tee land·lord ▶ **n.** a landlord who does not live at and rarely visits the property rented out.

ab·sent-mind·ed /ˈabsəntˌmīndid/ ▶ **adj.** (of a person or a person's behavior or manner) having or showing a habitually forgetful or inattentive disposition: *an absentminded smile.*
– DERIVATIVES **ab·sent·mind·ed·ly adv.**, **ab·sent·mind·ed·ness n.**

ab·sinthe /ˈabˌsinTH/ (also **absinth**) ▶ **n. 1** the shrub wormwood. ■ an essence made from this. **2** a potent green aniseed-flavored liqueur that turns milky when water is added. Prepared from wormwood, it is now largely banned because of its toxicity.
– ORIGIN late Middle English: from French *absinthe*, from Latin *absinthium*, from Greek *apsinthion* 'wormwood.'

ab·sit o·men /ˈabsit/ ▶ **exclam.** used to express the hope that a reference to something undesirable should not foreshadow its arrival or occurrence.
– ORIGIN late 16th cent.: Latin, literally 'may this (evil) omen be absent.'

ab·so·lute /ˈabsəˌlo͞ot, ˌabsəˈlo͞ot/ ▶ **adj. 1** not qualified or diminished in any way; total: *absolute secrecy* | *absolute silence* | *the attention he gave you was absolute.* ■ used for general emphasis when expressing an opinion: *the policy is absolute folly.* ■ (of powers or rights) not subject to any limitation; unconditional: *no one dared challenge her absolute authority* | *human right to life is absolute.* ■ (of a ruler) having unrestricted power: *he proclaimed himself absolute monarch.* ■ Law (of a decree) final: *the decree of nullity was made absolute.* ■ Law see **ABSOLUTE TITLE**. **2** viewed or existing independently and not in relation to other things; not relative or comparative: *absolute moral standards.* ■ Grammar (of a construction) syntactically independent of the rest of the sentence, as in: *dinner being over, we left the table.* ■ Grammar (of a transitive verb) used without an expressed object (e.g., *guns kill*). ■ Grammar (of an adjective) used without an expressed noun (e.g., *the brave*).
▶ **n.** Philosophy a value or principle that is regarded as universally valid or that may be viewed without relation to other things: *good and evil are presented as absolutes.* ■ (**the absolute**) Philosophy that which exists without being dependent on anything else. ■ (**the absolute**) Theology ultimate reality; God.
– DERIVATIVES **ab·so·lute·ness n.**
– ORIGIN late Middle English: from Latin *absolutus* 'freed, unrestricted,' past participle of *absolvere* (see **ABSOLVE**).

ab·so·lute ad·van·tage ▶ **n.** Economics the ability of an individual or group to carry out a particular economic activity more efficiently than another individual or group.

ab·so·lute al·co·hol ▶ **n.** ethanol containing less than one percent of water by weight.

ab·so·lute·ly /ˌabsəˈlo͞otlē/ ▶ **adv. 1** with no qualification, restriction, or limitation; totally: *she trusted him absolutely* | [as submodifier] *you're absolutely right.* ■ used to emphasize a strong or exaggerated statement: *he absolutely adores that car* | *it's absolutely pouring out there* | [as submodifier] *Dad was absolutely furious.* ■ [with negative] none whatsoever: *she had absolutely no idea what he was talking about.* ■ [as exclamation] informal used to express and emphasize one's assent or agreement: *"Did they give you a free hand when you joined the band?" "Absolutely!"* **2** independently; not viewed in relation to other things or factors: *white-collar crime increased both absolutely and in comparison with other categories.* ■ Grammar (of a verb) without a stated object.

ab·so·lute mag·ni·tude ▶ **n.** Astronomy the magnitude (brightness) of a celestial object as it would be seen at a standard distance of 10 parsecs. Compare with **APPARENT MAGNITUDE**.

ab·so·lute ma·jor·i·ty ▶ **n.** a majority over all rivals combined; more than half.

ab·so·lute mu·sic ▶ **n.** instrumental music composed purely as music, and not intended to represent or illustrate something else. Compare with **PROGRAM MUSIC**.

ab·so·lute pitch ▶ **n.** Music the ability to recognize the pitch of a note or produce any given note; perfect pitch. ■ pitch according to a fixed standard defined by the frequency of the sound vibration.

ab·so·lute tem·per·a·ture ▶ **n.** a temperature measured from absolute zero in kelvins. (Symbol: **T**)

ab·so·lute ti·tle ▶ **n.** Law guaranteed title to the ownership of a property or lease.

ab·so·lute u·nit ▶ **n.** a unit of measurement that is defined in terms of the fundamental units of a system (mass, length, and time) and is not based on arbitrary definitions.

ab·so·lute val·ue ▶ **n. 1** Mathematics the magnitude of a real number without regard to its sign. Also called **MODULUS**. ● The absolute value of a complex number $a + ib$ is the positive square root of $a^2 + b^2$. **2** technical the actual magnitude of a numerical value or measurement, irrespective of its relation to other values.

ab·so·lute ze·ro ▶ **n.** the lowest temperature that is theoretically possible, at which the motion of particles that constitutes heat would be minimal. It is zero on the Kelvin scale, equivalent to −273.15°C or −459.67°F.

ab·so·lu·tion /ˌabsəˈlo͞oSHən/ ▶ **n.** formal release from guilt, obligation, or punishment. ■ an ecclesiastical declaration of forgiveness of sins: *the priest administered absolution.*
– ORIGIN Middle English: via Old French from Latin *absolutio(n-)*, from the verb *absolvere* (see **ABSOLVE**).

ab·so·lut·ism /ˈabsəlo͞oˌtizəm/ ▶ **n.** the acceptance of or belief in absolute principles in political, philosophical, ethical, or theological matters.
– DERIVATIVES **ab·so·lut·ist n. & adj.**

ab·so·lut·ize /ˈabsəlo͞oˌtīz/ ▶ **v.** [with obj.] chiefly Philosophy & Theology make (or treat as) absolute.
– DERIVATIVES **ab·so·lut·i·za·tion** /ˌabsəˌlo͞otiˈzāSHən/ **n.**

ab·solve /əbˈzälv, -ˈsälv/ ▶ **v.** [with obj.] set or declare (someone) free from blame, guilt, or responsibility: *the pardon* ***absolved*** *them* ***of*** *any crimes.* ■ Christian Theology give absolution for (a sin).
– ORIGIN late Middle English: from Latin *absolvere* 'set free, acquit,' from *ab-* 'from' + *solvere* 'loosen.'

ab·so·nant /ˈabsənənt/ ▶ **adj.** archaic discordant or unreasonable.
– ORIGIN mid 16th cent.: from Latin *ab-* 'away, from' + *sonant-* 'sounding,' from *sonare*, on the pattern of words such as *dissonant*.

ab·sorb /əbˈzôrb, -ˈsôrb/ ▶ **v.** [with obj.] **1** take in or soak up (energy, or a liquid or other substance) by chemical or physical action, typically gradually: *buildings can be designed to absorb and retain heat* | *steroids are* ***absorbed into*** *the bloodstream.* ■ take in and assimilate (information, ideas, or experience): *she absorbed the information in silence.* ■ take control of (a smaller or less powerful entity), making it a part of oneself by assimilation: *the family firm was* ***absorbed into*** *a larger group.* ■ use or take up (time or resources): *arms spending absorbs roughly 2 percent of the national income.* ■ take up and reduce the effect or intensity of (sound or an impact): *deep-pile carpets absorbed all sound of the outside world.* **2** engross the attention of (someone): *the work absorbed him and continued to make him happy.*
– DERIVATIVES **ab·sorb·er n.**
– ORIGIN late Middle English: from Latin *absorbere*, from *ab-* 'from' + *sorbere* 'suck in.'

ab·sorb·a·ble /əbˈzôrbəbəl, -ˈsôr-/ ▶ **adj.** able to be absorbed, esp. into the body.
– DERIVATIVES **ab·sorb·a·bil·i·ty** /əbˌzôrbəˈbilitē, -ˌsôr-/ **n.**

ab·sorb·ance /əbˈzôrbəns, -ˈsôr-/ ▶ **n.** Physics a measure of the capacity of a substance to absorb light of a specified wavelength. It is equal to the logarithm of the reciprocal of the transmittance.

ab·sorbed /əbˈzôrbd, -ˈsôrbd/ ▶ **adj.** [predic.] intensely engaged; engrossed: *she sat in an armchair,* ***absorbed in*** *a book.*
– DERIVATIVES **ab·sorb·ed·ly** /-bidlē/ **adv.**

ab·sorbed dose ▶ **n.** Physics the energy of ionizing radiation absorbed per unit mass by a body, often measured in rads.

ab·sorb·ent /əbˈzôrbənt, -ˈsôr-/ ▶ **adj.** (of a material) able to soak up liquid easily: *drain on absorbent paper towels.*
▶ **n.** a substance or item that soaks up liquid easily.
– DERIVATIVES **ab·sorb·en·cy n.**
– ORIGIN early 18th cent.: from Latin *absorbent-* 'swallowing up,' from the verb *absorbere* (see **ABSORB**).

ab·sorb·ent cot·ton ▶ **n.** fluffy wadding of a kind originally made from raw cotton, used for cleansing wounds, removing cosmetics, and padding delicate objects.

ab·sorb·ing /əbˈzôrbiNG, -ˈsôr-/ ▶ **adj.** intensely interesting; engrossing: *an absorbing account of their marriage.*
– DERIVATIVES **ab·sorb·ing·ly adv.**

ab·sorp·tion /əbˈzôrpSHən, -ˈsôrp-/ ▶ **n. 1** the process or action by which one thing absorbs or is absorbed by another: *East Germany's* ***absorption into*** *West Germany* | *shock absorption.* **2** the fact or state of being engrossed in something: *her* ***absorption in*** *the problems of the Third World.*
– DERIVATIVES **ab·sorp·tive** /-tiv/ **adj.**
– ORIGIN late 16th cent. (in the sense 'the swallowing up of something'): from Latin *absorptio(n-)*, from *absorbere* 'swallow up' (see **ABSORB**).

ab·sorp·tion neb·u·la ▶ **n.** Astronomy another term for **DARK NEBULA**.

ab·sorp·tion spec·trum ▶ **n.** Physics a spectrum of electromagnetic radiation transmitted through a substance, showing dark lines or bands due to absorption of specific wavelengths. Compare with **EMISSION SPECTRUM**.

ab·squat·u·late /abˈskwäCHəˌlāt/ ▶ **v.** [no obj.] humorous leave abruptly: *some overthrown dictator who had absquatulated to the U.S.A.*
– DERIVATIVES **ab·squat·u·la·tion** /abˌskwäCHəˈlāSHən/ **n.**
– ORIGIN mid 19th cent.: blend, simulating a Latin form, of *abscond, squattle* 'depart,' and *perambulate*.

ab·stain /abˈstān/ ▶ **v.** [no obj.] **1** restrain oneself from doing or enjoying something: ***abstaining from*** *chocolate.* ■ refrain from drinking alcohol: *most pregnant women abstain or drink very little.* **2** formally decline to vote either for or against a proposal or motion: *forty-one voted with the opposition, and some sixty more abstained.*
– DERIVATIVES **ab·stain·er n.**
– ORIGIN late Middle English: from Old French *abstenir*, from Latin *abstinere*, from *ab-* 'from' + *tenere* 'hold.'

ab·ste·mi·ous /abˈstēmēəs/ ▶ **adj.** not self-indulgent, esp. when eating and drinking: *"We only had a bottle." "Very abstemious of you."*
– DERIVATIVES **ab·ste·mi·ous·ly adv.**, **ab·ste·mi·ous·ness n.**
– ORIGIN early 17th cent.: from Latin *abstemius* (from *ab-* 'from' + a word related to *temetum* 'strong drink') + **-OUS**.

ab·sten·tion /abˈstenCHən/ ▶ **n. 1** an instance of declining to vote for or against a proposal or motion: *a resolution passed by 126 votes to none, with six abstentions.* **2** the fact or practice of restraining oneself from indulging in something; abstinence: *alcohol consumption versus abstention.*
– DERIVATIVES **ab·sten·tion·ism** /-ˌnizəm/ **n.**
– ORIGIN early 16th cent. (denoting the act of keeping back or restraining): from late Latin *abstentio(n-)*, from the verb *abstinere* (see **ABSTAIN**).

ab·sti·nence /ˈabstənəns/ ▶ **n.** the fact or practice of restraining oneself from indulging in something, typically alcohol: *I started drinking again after six years of abstinence.*
– DERIVATIVES **ab·sti·nent adj.**, **ab·sti·nent·ly adv.**
– ORIGIN Middle English: from Old French, from Latin *abstinentia*, from the verb *abstinere* (see **ABSTAIN**).

ab·stract ▶ **adj.** /abˈstrakt, ˈabˌstrakt/ existing in thought or as an idea but not having a physical or concrete existence: *abstract concepts such as love or beauty.* ■ dealing with ideas rather than events: *the*

novel was too abstract and esoteric to sustain much attention. ■ not based on a particular instance; theoretical: *we have been discussing the problem in a very abstract manner.* ■ (of a word, esp. a noun) denoting an idea, quality, or state rather than a concrete object: *abstract words like truth or equality.* ■ of or relating to abstract art: *abstract pictures that look like commercial color charts.*
▶ **v.** /ab'strakt/ [with obj.] **1** consider (something) theoretically or separately from something else: *to **abstract** science and religion **from** their historical context can lead to anachronism* | [no obj.] *he cannot form a general notion by **abstracting from** particulars.*
2 extract or remove (something): *applications to **abstract** more water **from** streams.* ■ used euphemistically to say that someone has stolen something: *his pockets contained all he had been able to **abstract from** the apartment.* ■ (**abstract oneself**) withdraw: *as our relationship deepened you seemed to abstract yourself.*
3 make a written summary of (an article or book): *staff who index and abstract material for an online database.*
▶ **n.** /'ab,strakt/ **1** a summary of the contents of a book, article, or formal speech: *an abstract of his inaugural address.*
2 an abstract work of art: *a big unframed abstract.*
3 (**the abstract**) that which is abstract; the theoretical consideration of something: *the abstract must be made concrete by examples.*
– PHRASES **in the abstract** in a general way; without reference to specific instances: *there's a fine line between promoting US business interests in the abstract and promoting specific companies.*
– DERIVATIVES **ab·stract·ly adv.**, **ab·strac·tor** /-tər/ **n.** (sense 3 of the verb).
– ORIGIN Middle English: from Latin *abstractus*, literally 'drawn away,' past participle of *abstrahere*, from *ab-* 'from' + *trahere* 'draw off.'

ab·stract art ▶ **n.** art that does not attempt to represent external, recognizable reality but seeks to achieve its effect using shapes, forms, colors, and textures.

ab·stract·ed /ab'straktid/ ▶ **adj.** showing a lack of concentration on what is happening around one: *she seemed abstracted and unaware of her surroundings* | *an abstracted smile.*
– DERIVATIVES **ab·stract·ed·ly adv.**

ab·stract ex·pres·sion·ism ▶ **n.** a development of abstract art that originated in New York in the 1940s and 1950s and aimed at subjective emotional expression with particular emphasis on the creative spontaneous act (e.g., action painting). Leading figures were Jackson Pollock and Willem de Kooning.
– DERIVATIVES **ab·stract ex·pres·sion·ist n.**

ab·strac·tion /ab'strakSHən/ ▶ **n. 1** the quality of dealing with ideas rather than events: *topics will vary in degrees of abstraction.* ■ something that exists only as an idea: *the question can no longer be treated as an academic abstraction.*
2 freedom from representational qualities in art: *geometric abstraction has been a mainstay in her work.* ■ an abstract work of art.
3 a state of preoccupation: *she sensed his momentary abstraction.*
4 the process of considering something independently of its associations, attributes, or concrete accompaniments: *duty is no longer determined **in abstraction from** the consequences.*
5 the process of removing something, esp. water from a river or other source: *the abstraction of water from springs and wells.*
– ORIGIN late Middle English: from Latin *abstractio(n-)*, from the verb *abstrahere* 'draw away' (see **ABSTRACT**).

ab·strac·tion·ism /ab'strakSHə,nizəm/ ▶ **n.** the principles and practice of abstract art. ■ the presentation of ideas in abstract terms.
– DERIVATIVES **ab·strac·tion·ist n.**

ab·stract of ti·tle /'ab,strakt/ ▶ **n.** Law a summary giving details of the title deeds and documents that prove an owner's right to dispose of land, together with any encumbrances that relate to the property.

ab·struse /ab'stro͞os/ ▶ **adj.** difficult to understand; obscure: *an abstruse philosophical inquiry.*
– DERIVATIVES **ab·struse·ly adv.**, **ab·struse·ness n.**
– ORIGIN late 16th cent.: from Latin *abstrusus* 'put away, hidden,' from *abstrudere* 'conceal,' from *ab-* 'from' + *trudere* 'to push.'

ab·surd /əb'sərd, -'zərd/ ▶ **adj.** (of an idea or suggestion) wildly unreasonable, illogical, or inappropriate: *the allegations are patently absurd* | *so you think I'm a spy? How absurd!* | (as noun **the absurd**) *he had a keen eye for the incongruous and the absurd.* ■ (of a person or a person's behavior or actions) foolish; unreasonable: *she was being absurd—and imagining things.* ■ (of an object or situation) arousing amusement or derision; ridiculous: *gym shorts and knee socks looked absurd on such a tall girl.*
– DERIVATIVES **ab·surd·ly adv.**
– ORIGIN mid 16th cent.: from Latin *absurdus* 'out of tune,' hence 'irrational'; related to *surdus* 'deaf, dull.'

ab·surd·ism /əb'sərd,izəm, -'zərd-/ ▶ **n.** the belief that human beings exist in a purposeless, chaotic universe.
– DERIVATIVES **ab·surd·ist adj. & n.**

ab·surd·i·ty /əb'sərditē, -'zərd-/ ▶ **n.** (pl. **absurdities**) the quality or state of being ridiculous or wildly unreasonable: *Duncan laughed at the absurdity of the situation* | *the absurdities of haute cuisine.*
– ORIGIN late Middle English (in the sense 'dissonance'): from Latin *absurditas*, from *absurdus* (see **ABSURD**).

a·bub·ble /ə'bəbəl/ ▶ **adj.** [predic.] full of excitement and enthusiasm: *he was **abubble with** the news.*
– ORIGIN 1930s: from **A-**[2] 'in the process of' + **BUBBLE**.

A·bu Dha·bi /,äbo͞o 'T͟Häbē, 'däbē/ the largest of the seven member states of the United Arab Emirates, lying between Oman and the Gulf coast; pop. 2,061,100 (est. 2009). The former sheikhdom joined the federation of the United Arab Emirates in 1971. ■ the capital of this state; pop. 896,800 (est. 2009). It is also the federal capital of the United Arab Emirates.

A·bu·ja /ä'bo͞oyä/ a newly built city in central Nigeria, designated in 1982 to replace Lagos as the national capital; pop. 776,300 (est. 2006).

a·bu·li·a /ə'bo͞olēə/ (also **aboulia**) ▶ **n.** an absence of willpower or an inability to act decisively, as a symptom of mental illness.
– ORIGIN mid 19th cent.: coined from **A-**[1] 'without' + Greek *boulē* 'the will.'

Abu Mu·sa /,äbo͞o 'mo͞osə/ a small island in the Persian Gulf. Formerly held by the emirate of Sharjah, it was occupied by Iran by agreement from 1971 until it was taken over by them in 1992.

A·bu·na /ə'bo͞onə/ ▶ **n.** a title given to the Patriarch of the Ethiopian Orthodox Church.
– ORIGIN Amharic, from Arabic *'abūnā* 'our father.'

a·bun·dance /ə'bəndəns/ ▶ **n.** a very large quantity of something: *the tropical island boasts an **abundance of** wildlife.* ■ the quantity or amount of something, e.g., a chemical element or an animal or plant species, present in a particular area, volume, sample, etc.: *estimates of abundance of harp seals* | *the **relative abundances** of carbon and nitrogen.* ■ (in solo whist) a bid by which a player undertakes to make nine or more tricks. ■ the state or condition of having a copious quantity of something; plentifulness: *vines and figs grew **in abundance**.* ■ plentifulness of the good things of life; prosperity: *the growth of industry promised wealth and abundance.*
– ORIGIN Middle English: from Latin *abundantia*, from *abundant-* 'overflowing,' from the verb *abundare* (see **ABOUND**).

a·bun·dant /ə'bəndənt/ ▶ **adj.** existing or available in large quantities; plentiful: *there was abundant evidence to support the theory.* ■ [predic.] (**abundant in**) having plenty of something: *the riverbanks were abundant in wild plants.*
– ORIGIN late Middle English: from Latin *abundant-* 'abounding,' from the verb *abundare* (see **ABOUND**).

a·bun·dant·ly /ə'bəndəntlē/ ▶ **adv.** in large quantities; plentifully: *the plant grows abundantly in the wild.* ■ [as submodifier] extremely: *my boss **made it abundantly clear** that if I didn't like it, I should look for another job.*

a·buse ▶ **v.** /ə'byo͞oz/ [with obj.] **1** use (something) to bad effect or for a bad purpose; misuse: *the judge abused his power by imposing the fines.* ■ make excessive and habitual use of (alcohol or drugs, esp. illegal ones).
2 treat (a person or an animal) with cruelty or violence, esp. regularly or repeatedly: *riders who abuse their horses should be prosecuted.* ■ assault (someone, esp. a woman or child) sexually: *he was a depraved man who had abused his two young daughters* | (as adj. **abused**) *abused children.* ■ (**abuse oneself**) euphemistic masturbate. ■ use or treat in such a way as to cause damage or harm: *he had been abusing his body for years.*
3 speak in an insulting and offensive way to or about (someone): *the referee was abused by players from both teams.*
▶ **n.** /ə'byo͞os/ **1** the improper use of something: *alcohol abuse* | *an **abuse of** public funds.* ■ unjust or corrupt practice: *protection against fraud and abuse* | *human rights abuses.*
2 cruel and violent treatment of a person or animal: *a black eye and other signs of physical abuse.* ■ violent treatment involving sexual assault, esp. on a repeated basis: *young people who have suffered sexual abuse.*
3 insulting and offensive language: *waving his fists and **hurling abuse at** the driver.*
– ORIGIN late Middle English: via Old French from Latin *abus-* 'misused,' from the verb *abuti*, from *ab-* 'away' (i.e., 'wrongly') + *uti* 'to use.'

a·bus·er /ə'byo͞ozər/ ▶ **n.** [usu. with modifier] someone who regularly or habitually abuses someone or something, in particular: ■ someone who makes excessive use of alcohol or illegal drugs: *intravenous drug abusers.* ■ someone who sexually assaults another person, esp. a woman or child: *an alleged child abuser.*

A·bu Sim·bel /,äbo͞o 'simbəl/ the site of two huge rock-cut temples in southern Egypt, built during the reign of Ramses II in the 13th century BC, and commemorating him and his first wife **Nefertari**. Following the building of the High Dam at Aswan, the monument was rebuilt higher on the hillside.

a·bu·sive /ə'byo͞osiv, -ziv/ ▶ **adj. 1** extremely offensive and insulting: *abusive language* | *he became quite abusive and swore at her.*
2 engaging in or characterized by habitual violence and cruelty: *abusive parents* | *an abusive relationship.*
3 involving injustice or illegality: *the abusive and predatory practices of businesses.*
– DERIVATIVES **a·bu·sive·ly adv.**, **a·bu·sive·ness n.**

a·bus·tle /ə'bəsəl/ ▶ **adj.** [predic.] bustling; busy: *the main drag is always **abustle with** inventive sidewalk artists.*
– ORIGIN 1930s: from **A-**[2] 'in the process of' + **BUSTLE**[1].

a·but /ə'bət/ ▶ **v.** (**abuts, abutting, abutted**) [with obj.] (of an area of land or a building) be next to or have a common boundary with: *gardens abutting Prescott Street* | [no obj.] *a park **abutting on** an area of wasteland.* ■ touch or lean upon: *masonry may crumble where a roof abuts it.*
– ORIGIN late Middle English: the sense 'have a common boundary' from Anglo-Latin *abuttare*, from *a-* (from Latin *ad* 'to, at') + Old French *but* 'end'; the sense 'lean upon' (late 16th cent.) from Old French *abouter*, from *a-* (from Latin *ad* 'to, at') + *bouter* 'strike, butt,' of Germanic origin.

a·bu·ti·lon /ə'byo͞otl,än/ ▶ **n.** a herbaceous plant or shrub of the mallow family, native to warm climates and typically bearing showy yellow, red, or mauve flowers. ● Genus *Abutilon*, family Malvaceae.
– ORIGIN modern Latin, from Arabic *ūbūtīlūn* 'Indian mallow.'

a·but·ment /ə'bətmənt/ ▶ **n.** a structure built to support the lateral pressure of an arch or span, e.g., at the ends of a bridge. ■ the process of supporting something with such a structure. ■ a point at which something abuts against something else.

a·but·ter /ə'bətər/ ▶ **n.** the owner of property that abuts (touches on) another.

a·buzz /ə'bəz/ ▶ **adj.** [predic.] filled with a continuous humming sound: *the room was **abuzz with** mosquitoes* | figurative *the city was **abuzz with** rumors.*

ABV ▶ **abbr.** alcohol by volume.

a·bysm /ə'bizəm/ ▶ **n.** a literary or poetic term for **ABYSS**: *the abysm from which nightmares crawl.*
– ORIGIN Middle English: from Old French *abisme*, medieval Latin *abysmus*, alteration of late Latin *abyssus* 'bottomless pit,' the ending being assimilated to the Greek ending *-ismos*.

a·bys·mal /ə'bizməl/ ▶ **adj. 1** informal extremely bad; appalling: *the quality of her work is abysmal.*
2 literary very deep.
– DERIVATIVES **a·bys·mal·ly adv.**
– ORIGIN mid 17th cent. (sense 2): from **ABYSM**. Sense 1 dates from the early 19th cent.

a·byss /ə'bis/ ▶ **n.** a deep or seemingly bottomless chasm: *a rope led down into the dark abyss.* ■ a wide or profound difference between people; a gulf: *the **abyss between** the two nations.* ■ the regions of hell conceived of as a bottomless pit: *Satan's dark abyss.* ■ (**the abyss**) a catastrophic situation seen as likely to occur: *teetering **on the edge of the abyss** of a total political wipeout.*
– ORIGIN late Middle English (in the sense 'infernal pit'): via late Latin from Greek *abussos* 'bottomless,' from *a-* 'without' + *bussos* 'depth.'

a·byss·al /ə'bisəl/ ▶ **adj.** chiefly technical relating to or denoting the depths or bed of the ocean, esp. between about 10,000 and 20,000 feet (3,000 and 6,000 m) down: *the genera found in the abyssal North Atlantic.* ■ Geology another term for **PLUTONIC** (sense 1).
– ORIGIN mid 17th cent.: from late Latin *abyssalis* 'belonging to an abyss' (see **ABYSS**).

Ab·ys·sin·i·a /,abə'sinēə/ former name for **ETHIOPIA**.

Ab·ys·sin·i·an /ˌabəˈsinēən/ ▶ **adj.** historical of or relating to Abyssinia or its people.
▶ **n. 1** historical a native of Abyssinia.
2 (also **Abyssinian cat**) a domestic cat of a breed having long ears and short brown hair flecked with gray.

Ab·zug /ˈabˌzo͝og/, Bella (Savitsky) (1920–98), US politician, lawyer, and women's rights activist. She helped to found Women Strike for Peace in 1961. Serving in Congress as a Democrat from New York, she fought for the rights of women and of the poor.

AC ▶ **abbr.** ■ (also **ac**) alternating current. ■ (also **ac**) air conditioning: *a sedan with power steering and AC.* ■ before Christ. [from Latin *ante Christum.*] ■ appellation contrôlée: *AC Sauvignon and Chardonnay.* ■ athletic club. ■ (**ac.**) acre: *a 22-ac. site.*

Ac ▶ **symbol** the chemical element actinium.

a/c ▶ **abbr.** ■ account. [from the obsolete phrase *account current* denoting a continuous account detailing sums paid and received.] ■ (also **A/C**) air conditioning.

ac- ▶ **prefix** variant spelling of **AD-** assimilated before *c* and *q* (as in *accept, acquit,* and *acquiesce*).

-ac ▶ **suffix** forming adjectives that are also often (or only) used as nouns, such as *maniac*. Compare with **-ACAL**.
– ORIGIN from Greek *-akos* via Latin *-acus* or French *-aque*.

a·ca·cia /əˈkāsHə/ (also **acacia tree**) ▶ **n.** a tree or shrub of warm climates that bears spikes or clusters of yellow or white flowers and is frequently thorny. ● Genus *Acacia*, family Leguminosae: numerous species, including *A. senegal*, which yields gum arabic. ■ see **FALSE ACACIA**.
– ORIGIN late Middle English: via Latin from Greek *akakia*.

ac·a·deme /ˌakəˈdēm, ˈakəˌdēm/ ▶ **n.** the academic environment or community; academia: ***bridging the gap between industry and academe** | **the groves of academe.***
– ORIGIN late 16th cent. (in the sense 'academy'): from Latin *academia*, reinforced by Greek *Akadēmos* (see **ACADEMY**).

ac·a·de·mi·a /ˌakəˈdēmēə/ ▶ **n.** the environment or community concerned with the pursuit of research, education, and scholarship: *he spent his working life in academia.*
– ORIGIN 1950s: from Latin (see **ACADEMY**).

ac·a·dem·ic /ˌakəˈdemik/ ▶ **adj. 1** of or relating to education and scholarship: *academic achievement | he had no academic qualifications.* ■ of or relating to an educational or scholarly institution or environment: *students resplendent in academic dress.* ■ (of an institution or a course of study) placing a greater emphasis on reading and study than on technical or practical work: *an academic high school that prepares students for the best colleges and universities.* ■ (of a person) interested in or excelling at scholarly pursuits and activities: *Ben is not an academic child but he tries hard.* ■ (of an art form) conventional, esp. in an idealized or excessively formal way: *academic painting.*
2 not of practical relevance; of only theoretical interest: *the debate has been largely academic.*
▶ **n.** a teacher or scholar in a college or institute of higher education.
– DERIVATIVES **ac·a·dem·i·cal·ly adv.**
– ORIGIN mid 16th cent.: from French *académique* or medieval Latin *academicus*, from *academia* (see **ACADEMY**).

ac·a·de·mi·cian /ˌakədəˈmisHən, əˌkadə-/ ▶ **n. 1** an academic; an intellectual.
2 a member of an academy, esp. of the Royal Academy of Arts, the Académie Française, or the Russian Academy of Sciences.
– ORIGIN mid 18th cent.: from French *académicien*, from medieval Latin *academicus* (see **ACADEMIC**).

ac·a·dem·i·cism /ˌakəˈdeməˌsizəm/ (also **academism** /əˈkadəˌmizəm/) ▶ **n.** adherence to formal or conventional rules and traditions in art or literature: *the opposition between academicism and creative authenticity.*

ac·a·dem·ic year ▶ **n.** the period of the year during which students attend an educational institution, usually from September to June. Also called **SCHOOL YEAR**.

a·cad·e·my /əˈkadəmē/ ▶ **n.** (pl. **academies**) **1** a place of study or training in a special field: *a police academy.* ■ historical a place of study. ■ a secondary school, typically a private one: *he had passed all his finals at Ephebus Academy.* ■ (**the Academy**) the teaching school founded by Plato.
2 a society or institution of distinguished scholars, artists, or scientists, that aims to promote and maintain standards in its particular field: *the National Academy of Sciences.* ■ the community of scholars; academe: *a writing and publishing world outside the academy.*
– ORIGIN late Middle English (denoting the garden where Plato taught): from French *académie* or Latin *academia*, from Greek *akadēmeia*, from *Akadēmos*, the hero after whom Plato's garden was named.

A·cad·e·my A·ward ▶ **n.** trademark any of a series of awards of the Academy of Motion Picture Arts and Sciences in Hollywood given annually since 1928 for achievement in the movie industry in various categories; an Oscar.

A·ca·di·a /əˈkādēə/ a former French colony established in 1604 in the territory that now includes Nova Scotia, New Brunswick, and Prince Edward Island in Canada. Contested by France and Britain, it was ceded to Britain in 1763, and many French Acadians were deported to other parts of North America, esp. Louisiana.
– ORIGIN from *Acadie*, the French name for what became (chiefly) Nova Scotia.

A·ca·di·an /əˈkādēən/ chiefly historical ▶ **adj.** of or relating to Acadia or its people.
▶ **n.** a native or inhabitant of Acadia. ■ chiefly Canadian a French-speaking descendant of the early French settlers in Acadia. ■ a descendant of the Acadians deported to Louisiana in the 18th century; a Cajun.

aç·a·í /ˈasīē/ ▶ **n.** (pl. **same**) a South American palm tree producing small edible blackish-purple berries. ● Genus *Euterpe*, esp. *E. oleracea*.
– ORIGIN mid 19th cent.: from Portuguese *açaí*, from Tupi-Guarani *asaí*.

ac·a·jou /ˈakəˌZHo͞o, -ˌjo͞o/ ▶ **n. 1** the wood of certain tropical timber-yielding trees, esp. mahogany.
2 another term for **CASHEW**.
– ORIGIN late 16th cent.: from French, via Portuguese from Tupi *acajú*.

-acal ▶ **suffix** forming adjectives from nouns and adjectives usually ending in *-ac*, such as *maniacal*, often making a distinction from nouns ending in *-ac* (as in *maniacal* compared with *maniac*).

a·cal·cu·li·a /ˌākalˈkyo͞olēə/ ▶ **n.** Medicine loss of the ability to perform simple arithmetic calculations, typically resulting from disease or injury of the parietal lobe of the brain.
– ORIGIN early 20th cent.: from **A-**[1] 'not' + Latin *calculare* 'calculate' + **-IA**[1].

acantho- (also **acanth-** before a vowel) ▶ **comb. form** having thornlike characteristics.
– ORIGIN from Greek *akantha* 'thorn.'

A·can·tho·ceph·a·la /əˌkanTHōˈsefələ/ Zoology a small phylum of parasitic invertebrates that comprises the thorny-headed worms.
– DERIVATIVES **a·can·tho·ceph·a·lan adj. & n.**, **a·can·tho·ceph·a·lid** /-lid/ **adj. & n.**
– ORIGIN modern Latin, from **ACANTHO-** 'thorn' + Greek *kephalē* 'head.'

ac·an·tho·di·an /ˌakənˈTHōdēən/ ▶ **n.** a small spiny-finned, jawed fossil fish of a group found chiefly in the Devonian period. ● Class (or subclass) Acanthodii.
– ORIGIN mid 19th cent.: from modern Latin *Acanthodii* (from **ACANTHO-**) + **-AN**.

a·can·thus /əˈkanTHəs/ ▶ **n. 1** a herbaceous plant or shrub with bold flower spikes and spiny decorative leaves, native to Mediterranean regions. [via Latin from Greek *akanthos*, from *akantha* 'thorn,' from *akē* 'sharp point.'] ● Genus *Acanthus*, family Acanthaceae: many species.
2 Architecture a conventionalized representation of an acanthus leaf, used esp. as a decoration for Corinthian column capitals.

acanthus 2

a cap·pel·la /ˌä kəˈpelə/ ▶ **adj. & adv.** (with reference to choral music) without instrumental accompaniment: [as adj.] *an a cappella Mass* | [as adv.] *the trio usually performs a cappella.*
– ORIGIN Italian, literally 'in chapel style.'

A·ca·pul·co /ˌäkəˈpo͞olkō, ˌak-, -ˈpo͞olkō/ a port and resort in southern Mexico, on the Pacific coast; pop. 616,384 (2005). Full name **Acapulco de Juárez**.

Ac·a·ri /ˈakəˌrī/ (also **Acarina** /akəˈrīnə/) Zoology a large order (or subclass) of small arachnids that comprises the mites and ticks. They are distinguished by an apparent lack of body divisions.
– DERIVATIVES **ac·a·rid** /-rid/ **n. & adj.**
– ORIGIN modern Latin (plural), from *acarus*, from Greek *akari* 'mite.'

a·car·i·cide /əˈkarəˌsīd, ˈakərə-/ ▶ **n.** a substance poisonous to mites or ticks.
– ORIGIN late 19th cent.: from Greek *akari* 'mite, tick' + **-CIDE**.

ac·a·rine /ˈakəˌrīn, -ˌrēn/ Zoology ▶ **n.** a small arachnid of the order Acari; a mite or tick. ▶ **adj.** relating to or denoting acarines.

ac·a·rol·o·gy /ˌakəˈräləjē/ ▶ **n.** the study of mites and ticks.
– DERIVATIVES **ac·a·rol·o·gist** /-jist/ **n.**
– ORIGIN early 20th cent.: from Greek *akari* 'mite, tick' + **-LOGY**.

a·cat·a·lec·tic /āˌkatlˈektik/ Prosody ▶ **adj.** (of a line of verse) having the full number of syllables.
▶ **n.** a line of verse of such a type.

Ac·ca·di·an /əˈkādēən/ ▶ **n.** variant spelling of **AKKADIAN**.

ac·cede /akˈsēd/ ▶ **v.** [no obj.] formal **1** assent or agree to a demand, request, or treaty: ***the authorities did not accede to the strikers' demands.***
2 assume an office or position: ***he acceded to the post of director in September.*** ■ become a member of a community or organization: ***Albania acceded to the IMF in 1990.***
– ORIGIN late Middle English (in the general sense 'come forward, approach'): from Latin *accedere*, from *ad-* 'to' + *cedere* 'give way, yield.'

ac·cel·er·an·do /äkˌseləˈrändō, ak-, äˌCHelə-/ Music ▶ **adj. & adv.** with a gradual increase of speed (used chiefly as a direction).
▶ **n.** (pl. **accelerandos** or **accelerandi** /-dē/) a passage to be performed with such an acceleration.
– ORIGIN Italian.

ac·cel·er·ant /akˈselərənt/ ▶ **n.** a substance used to aid the spread of fire: ***stolen accelerants could be used as firebombs.***
▶ **adj.** accelerating or causing acceleration: *accelerant factors for carcinoma.*

ac·cel·er·ate /akˈseləˌrāt/ ▶ **v.** [no obj.] (of a vehicle or other physical object) begin to move more quickly: *the car accelerated toward her.* ■ increase in amount or extent: *inflation started to accelerate* | [with obj.] *the key question is whether stress accelerates aging* | (as adj. **accelerating**) *accelerating industrial activity.* ■ Physics undergo a change in velocity.
– DERIVATIVES **ac·cel·er·a·tive** /-ərətiv, -ˌrātiv/ **adj.**
– ORIGIN early 16th cent. (in the sense 'hasten the occurrence of'): from Latin *accelerat-* 'hastened,' from the verb *accelerare*, from *ad-* 'toward' + *celer* 'swift.'

ac·cel·er·at·ed learn·ing ▶ **n. 1** an intensive method of study employing techniques that enable material to be learned in a relatively short time.
2 a program of learning that allows certain students, esp. those more academically able, to progress through school more rapidly than others.

ac·cel·er·a·tion /akˌseləˈrāsHən/ ▶ **n.** increase in the rate or speed of something: *the acceleration of the industrialization process | an acceleration in the divorce rate.* ■ Physics the rate of change of velocity per unit of time. ■ a vehicle's capacity to gain speed within a short time: *a Formula One car is superior to an Indy car in its acceleration.*

ac·cel·er·a·tor /akˈseləˌrātər/ ▶ **n.** something that brings about acceleration, in particular: ■ the device, typically a pedal, that controls the speed of a vehicle's engine. ■ Physics an apparatus for accelerating charged particles to high velocities.

ac·cel·er·om·e·ter /akˌseləˈrämitər/ ▶ **n.** an instrument for measuring acceleration, typically that of an automobile, ship, aircraft, or spacecraft, or that involved in the vibration of a machine, building, or other structure.
– ORIGIN early 20th cent.: from **ACCELERATE** + **-METER**.

ac·cent ▶ **n.** /ˈakˌsent/ **1** a distinctive mode of pronunciation of a language, esp. one associated with a particular nation, locality, or social class: *a strong German accent.*
2 a distinct emphasis given to a syllable or word in speech by stress or pitch. ■ a mark on a letter, typically a vowel, to indicate pitch, stress, or vowel quality. ■ Music an emphasis on a particular note or chord.
3 [in sing.] a special or particular emphasis: ***the accent is on participation.*** ■ a feature that gives a distinctive visual emphasis to something: ***blue woodwork and accents of red.***
▶ **v.** /ˈakˌsent, akˈsent/ [with obj.] emphasize (a particular feature): ***fabrics that accent the background colors in the room.*** ■ Music play (a note, a beat of the bar, etc.) with an accent.
– DERIVATIVES **ac·cen·tu·al** /akˈsenCHo͞oəl/ **adj.**
– ORIGIN late Middle English (in the sense 'intonation'): from Latin *accentus* 'tone, signal, or intensity' (from *ad-* 'to' + *cantus* 'song'), translating Greek *prosōidia* 'a song sung to music, intonation.'

ac·cent·ed /ˈakˌsentid, akˈsen-/ ▶ **adj. 1** spoken with or characterized by a particular accent: ***he spoke in slightly accented English.***
2 (of a word or syllable) marked with a stress or other accent.

ac·cen·tor /'aksentər/ ▶ **n.** a small Eurasian songbird with generally drab-colored plumage. ● Family Prunellidae and genus *Prunella*: several species.
– ORIGIN early 19th cent.: from late Latin, from *ad-* 'to' + *cantor* 'singer.'

ac·cen·tu·ate /ak'senCHōō,āt/ ▶ **v.** [with obj.] make more noticeable or prominent: *his jacket unfortunately accentuated his paunch.*
– ORIGIN mid 18th cent.: from medieval Latin *accentuat-* 'accented,' from the verb *accentuare*, from *accentus* 'tone' (see ACCENT).

ac·cen·tu·a·tion /ak,senCHōō'āSHən/ ▶ **n.** the action of emphasizing something: *the accentuation of the Treasury's currency policy.* ■ the prominence of a thing relative to the normal: *a condition where there is an accentuation of female characteristics.* ■ the manner in which accents are apparent in pronunciation, or indicated in writing.

ac·cept /ak'sept/ ▶ **v.** [with obj.] **1** consent to receive (a thing offered): *he accepted a pen as a present.* ■ give an affirmative answer to (an offer or proposal); say yes to: *he would accept their offer and see what happened* | [no obj.] *Tim offered Brian a lift home and he accepted.* ■ dated say yes to a proposal of marriage from (a man): *Ronald is a good match and she ought to accept him.* ■ receive as adequate, valid, or suitable: *the college accepted her as a student* | *credit cards are widely accepted.* ■ regard favorably or with approval; welcome: *the Harvard literati never accepted him as one of them.* ■ (of a thing) be designed to allow (something) to be inserted or applied: *vending machines that accepted 100-yen coins for cans of beer.*
2 believe or come to recognize (an opinion, explanation, etc.) as valid or correct: *this tentative explanation came to be accepted by the group* | [with clause] *it is accepted that aging is a continuous process.* ■ take upon oneself (a responsibility or liability); acknowledge: *Jenkins is willing to accept his responsibility* | [with clause] *he accepts that he made a mistake.* ■ tolerate or submit to (something unpleasant or undesired): *they accepted the need to cut expenses.*
– DERIVATIVES **ac·cept·er** n.
– ORIGIN late Middle English: from Latin *acceptare*, frequentative of *accipere* 'take something to oneself,' from *ad-* 'to' + *capere* 'take.'

> **USAGE** Accept, which means 'take (that which is offered),' may be confused with the verb **except**, which means 'exclude.' Thus: *I* **accept** *the terms of your offer, but I wish to* **except** *the clause calling for repayment of the deposit.*

ac·cept·a·ble /ak'septəbəl/ ▶ **adj. 1** able to be agreed on; suitable: *has tried to find a solution* ***acceptable to*** *everyone.* ■ adequate; satisfactory: *an acceptable substitute for champagne.* ■ pleasing; welcome: *some coffee would be most acceptable.*
2 able to be tolerated or allowed: *pollution in the city had reached four times the acceptable level.*
– PHRASES **the acceptable face of** the tolerable or attractive manifestation or aspect of: *he presents himself as the acceptable face of gambling.*
– DERIVATIVES **ac·cept·a·bil·i·ty** /-,septə'bilitē/ n., **ac·cept·a·ble·ness** n., **ac·cept·a·bly** /-blē/ adv.
– ORIGIN late Middle English: from Old French, from late Latin *acceptabilis*, from *acceptare* (see ACCEPT).

ac·cept·ance /ak'septəns/ ▶ **n. 1** the action of consenting to receive or undertake something offered: *charges involving the acceptance of bribes* | [as modifier] *an acceptance speech* | *he had an acceptance from the magazine.* ■ a draft or bill that is accepted by being signed.
2 the action or process of being received as adequate or suitable, typically to be admitted into a group: *you must wait for acceptance into the club.*
3 agreement with or belief in an idea, opinion, or explanation: *acceptance of the teaching of the church.* ■ willingness to tolerate a difficult or unpleasant situation: *a mood of resigned acceptance.*
– ORIGIN mid 16th cent.: from Old French, from *accepter* (see ACCEPT).

ac·cept·ant /ak'septənt/ ▶ **adj.** (**acceptant of**) rare willingly accepting.
– ORIGIN late 16th cent.: from French, 'accepting,' present participle of *accepter* 'to accept.'

ac·cep·ta·tion /,aksep'tāSHən/ ▶ **n.** a particular sense or the generally recognized meaning (**common acceptation**) of a word or phrase.
– ORIGIN late Middle English (originally in the sense 'favorable reception, approval'): from late Latin *acceptatio(n-)*, from the verb *acceptare* (see ACCEPT). The current sense dates from the early 17th cent.

ac·cept·ed /ak'septid/ ▶ **adj.** generally believed or recognized to be valid or correct: *he wasn't handsome in the accepted sense.*

ac·cep·tor /ak'septər/ ▶ **n.** a person or thing that accepts something, in particular: ■ Chemistry an atom or molecule that is able to bind to or accept an electron or other species. ■ Physics such an atom forming a positive hole in a semiconductor.

ac·cess /'ak,ses/ ▶ **n. 1** a means of approaching or entering a place: *the staircase gives access to the top floor* | *wheelchair access* | *the building has a side access.* ■ the right or opportunity to use or benefit from something: *do you have access to a computer?* | *awards to help people gain access to training.* ■ the right or opportunity to approach or see someone: *we were* ***denied access to*** *our grandson.* ■ the action or process of obtaining or retrieving information stored in a computer's memory: *this prevents unauthorized access or inadvertent deletion of the file.* ■ [as modifier] denoting noncommercial broadcasting produced by local independent groups, rather than by professionals: ***public-access television.***
2 [in sing.] an attack or outburst of an emotion: *I was suddenly overcome with* ***an access of*** *rage.*
▶ **v.** [with obj.] **1** approach or enter (a place): *single rooms have private baths accessed via the balcony.*
2 Computing obtain, examine, or retrieve (data or a file).
– ORIGIN Middle English (in the sense 'sudden attack of illness'): from Latin *accessus*, from the verb *accedere* 'to approach' (see ACCEDE). Sense 1 is first recorded in the early 17th cent.

> **USAGE** The verb **access** is standard and common in computing and related terminology (*employees can* **access** *the office network*). But its use outside computing contexts, although well established in the language, is sometimes criticized as being 'jargon' (*we lacked adequate supply to* **access** *the markets we needed to reach*). Other words or phrases such as 'enter' or 'gain access to' are suggested as ready substitutes. For another example of a controversial formation of a verb from a noun, see usage at IMPACT.

ac·cess charge (also **access fee**) ▶ **n.** a charge made for the use of computer or local telephone-network facilities.

ac·cess course ▶ **n.** an educational course enabling those without traditional qualifications to become eligible for higher education.

ac·ces·si·ble /ak'sesəbəl/ ▶ **adj. 1** (of a place) able to be reached or entered: *the town is* ***accessible by*** *bus* | *this room is not* ***accessible to*** *elderly people.* ■ (of an object, service, or facility) able to be easily obtained or used: *making learning opportunities more* ***accessible to*** *adults.* ■ easily understood: *his Latin grammar is lucid and accessible.* ■ able to be reached or entered by people who have a disability: *features such as nonslip floors and accessible entrances.*
2 (of a person, typically one in a position of authority or importance) friendly and easy to talk to; approachable: *he is more accessible than most tycoons.*
– DERIVATIVES **ac·ces·si·bil·i·ty** /-,sesə'bilitē/ n., **ac·ces·si·bly** /-blē/ adv.
– ORIGIN late Middle English: from late Latin *accessibilis*, from Latin *access-* 'approached,' from the verb *accedere* (see ACCEDE).

> **WORD TRENDS** Although the frequency of use of **accessible** has remained fairly static in the last few decades, the way it is being used has changed significantly. A new sense referring specifically to the way in which something can be used or accessed by people with a disability emerged in 1970. Used most literally, **accessibility** refers to the ease with which disabled people can physically enter a place, or use a service: *they're actively trying to expand the accessible bus network* | *facilities include a fully accessible sauna.* **Accessible** is also used to refer to computing tools and websites that can easily be used by people with disabilities.

ac·ces·sion /ak'seSHən/ ▶ **n. 1** the attainment or acquisition of a position of rank or power, typically that of monarch or president: *the queen's* ***accession to the throne*** | *lost the vote on the Fortas accession to the chief justiceship.* ■ the action or process of formally joining or being accepted by an association, institution, or group: *the accession of Spain and Portugal into the European Community.*
2 a new item added to an existing collection of books, paintings, or artifacts. ■ an amount added to an existing quantity of something: *did not anticipate any further accession of wealth from the man's estate.*
3 the formal acceptance of a treaty or agreement: *accession to the Treaty of Paris.*
▶ **v.** [with obj.] (usu. **be accessioned**) record the addition of (a new item) to a library, museum, or other collection.
– ORIGIN late 16th cent. (in the general sense 'something added'): from Latin *accession-*, from the verb *accedere* 'approach, come to' (see ACCEDE).

ac·ces·so·rize /ak'sesə,rīz/ ▶ **v.** [with obj.] provide or complement (a garment) with a fashion accessory: *the leisure suits were accessorized with white vinyl loafers and matching belts.*

ac·ces·so·ry /ak'ses(ə)rē/ (also **accessary**) ▶ **n.** (pl. **accessories**) **1** a thing that can be added to something else in order to make it more useful, versatile, or attractive: *a range of bathroom accessories.* ■ a small article or item of clothing carried or worn to complement a garment or outfit: *among the hottest items are hair accessories such as rhinestone-studded barrettes.*
2 Law someone who gives assistance to the perpetrator of a crime, without directly committing it, sometimes without being present: *she was charged as an* ***accessory to*** *murder.*
▶ **adj.** [attrib.] chiefly technical contributing to or aiding an activity or process in a minor way; subsidiary or supplementary: *functionally the maxillae are a pair of accessory jaws.*
– PHRASES **accessory before** (or **after**) **the fact** Law, dated a person who incites or assists someone to commit a crime (or knowingly aids someone who has committed a crime).
– ORIGIN late Middle English: from medieval Latin *accessorius* 'additional thing,' from Latin *access-* 'increased,' from the verb *accedere* (see ACCEDE).

ac·ces·so·ry cell ▶ **n.** Physiology any of various cells of the immune system that interact with T cells in the initiation of the immune response.

ac·ces·so·ry min·er·al ▶ **n.** Geology a constituent mineral present in small quantity and not taken into account in identifying a rock.

ac·ces·so·ry nerve ▶ **n.** Anatomy each of the eleventh pair of cranial nerves, supplying certain muscles in the neck and shoulder.

ac·cess pro·vid·er ▶ **n.** another term for SERVICE PROVIDER.

ac·cess road ▶ **n.** a road giving access to a place or to another road.

ac·cess time ▶ **n.** Computing the time taken to retrieve data from storage.

ac·ciac·ca·tu·ra /ä,CHäkə'tōōrə/ ▶ **n.** (pl. **acciaccaturas** or **acciaccature** /-'tōōrä, -'tōōrē/) Music a grace note performed as quickly as possible before an essential note of a melody, and falling before the beat.
– ORIGIN Italian, from *acciaccare* 'to crush.'

ac·ci·dence /'aksidəns/ ▶ **n.** the part of grammar that deals with the inflections of words.
– ORIGIN early 16th cent.: from late Latin *accidentia* (translation of Greek *parepomena* 'things happening alongside'), neuter plural of the present participle of *accidere* 'happen' (see ACCIDENT).

ac·ci·dent /'aksidənt/ ▶ **n. 1** an unfortunate incident that happens unexpectedly and unintentionally, typically resulting in damage or injury: *he had an accident at the factory* | *if you are unable to work owing to accident or sickness* | [as modifier] *an accident investigator.* ■ a crash involving road or other vehicles, typically one that causes serious damage or injury: *four people were killed in a car accident.* ■ informal used euphemistically to refer to an incidence of incontinence, typically by a child or an animal.
2 an event that happens by chance or that is without apparent or deliberate cause: *the pregnancy was an accident* | ***it is no accident that*** *my tale features a tragic romance.* ■ the working of fortune; chance: *my faith is an* ***accident of birth****, not a matter of principled commitment* | *he came to Harvard largely through accident.*
3 Philosophy (in Aristotelian thought) a property of a thing that is not essential to its nature.
– PHRASES **an accident waiting to happen 1** a potentially disastrous situation, typically caused by negligent or faulty procedures. **2** a person certain to cause trouble. **accidents will happen** however careful you try to be, it is inevitable that some unfortunate or unforeseen events will occur: *problems like these should not occur, but accidents will happen.* **by accident** unintentionally; by chance: *she didn't get where is today by accident.*
– ORIGIN late Middle English (in the general sense 'an event'): via Old French from Latin *accident-* 'happening,' from the verb *accidere*, from *ad-* 'toward, to' + *cadere* 'to fall.'

ac·ci·den·tal /,aksi'dentl/ ▶ **adj. 1** happening by chance, unintentionally, or unexpectedly: *a verdict of accidental death* | *the damage might have been accidental.*
2 incidental; subsidiary: *the location is accidental and contributes nothing to the tension between the characters in the poem.*

3 Philosophy (in Aristotelian thought) relating to or denoting properties that are not essential to a thing's nature.
▶ **n. 1** Music a sign indicating a momentary departure from the key signature by raising or lowering a note.
2 Ornithology another term for VAGRANT.
– DERIVATIVES **ac·ci·den·tal·ly adv.**
– ORIGIN late Middle English (in sense 2 of the adjective and sense 3 of the adjective): from late Latin *accidentalis*, from Latin *accident-* 'happening' (see ACCIDENT).

ac·ci·dent-prone ▶ **adj.** tending to be involved in a greater than average number of accidents.

ac·ci·die /ˈaksidē/ ▶ **n.** acedia.
– ORIGIN Middle English: via Old French from medieval Latin *accidia*, alteration of ACEDIA. Obsolete after the 16th cent., the term was revived in the late 19th cent.

ac·cip·i·ter /akˈsipitər/ ▶ **n.** Ornithology a hawk of a group distinguished by short, broad wings and relatively long legs, adapted for fast flight in wooded country. ● *Accipiter* and related genera, family Accipitridae: numerous species, including the goshawk.
– ORIGIN late 19th cent.: Latin, literally 'hawk, bird of prey.'

ac·cip·i·trine /akˈsipitrin, -ˌtrīn/ ▶ **adj.** [attrib.] Ornithology of or relating to birds of a family that includes most diurnal birds of prey other than falcons, New World vultures, and the osprey.
● Family Accipitridae; treated as a subfamily (Accipitrinae) in this sense when the osprey is included in this family.
– ORIGIN mid 19th cent.: from French, from Latin *accipiter* 'bird of prey.'

ac·claim /əˈklām/ ▶ **v.** [with obj.] praise enthusiastically and publicly: *the conference was* ***acclaimed as*** *a considerable success* | [with obj. and complement] *he was acclaimed a great painter.*
▶ **n.** enthusiastic and public praise: *she has won acclaim for her commitment to democracy.*
– ORIGIN early 17th cent. (in the sense 'express approval'): from Latin *acclamare*, from *ad-* 'to' + *clamare* 'to shout.' The spelling has been influenced by association with CLAIM. Current senses date from the 17th cent.

ac·cla·ma·tion /ˌakləˈmāsHən/ ▶ **n.** loud and enthusiastic approval, typically to welcome or honor someone or something: *the tackle brought the fans to their feet in acclamation* | *the president was again greeted by the acclamations of all present.*
– PHRASES **by acclamation 1** (of election, agreement, etc.) by overwhelming vocal approval and without ballot. **2** Canadian (of election) by virtue of being the sole candidate.
– ORIGIN mid 16th cent.: from Latin *acclamatio(n-)*, from *acclamare* 'shout at,' later 'shout in approval' (see ACCLAIM).

ac·cli·mate /ˈakləˌmāt, əˈklīmit/ ▶ **v.** [no obj.] (usu. **be acclimated**) become accustomed to a new climate or to new conditions: *it will take a few days to get* ***acclimated to*** *the altitude.* ■ Biology respond physiologically or behaviorally to a change in a single environmental factor: *trees may acclimate to high* CO_2 *levels by reducing the number of stomata.* Compare with ACCLIMATIZE. ■ [with obj.] Botany & Horticulture harden off (a plant).
– DERIVATIVES **ac·cli·ma·tion** /ˌakləˈmāsHən/ **n.**
– ORIGIN late 18th cent.: from French *acclimater*, from *a-* (from Latin *ad* 'to, at') + *climat* 'climate.'

ac·cli·ma·tize /əˈklīməˌtīz/ ▶ **v.** [no obj.] acclimate: *they acclimatized themselves before ascending Everest.* ■ Biology respond physiologically or behaviorally to changes in a complex of environmental factors. Compare with ACCLIMATE. ■ [with obj.] Botany & Horticulture harden off (a plant).
– DERIVATIVES **ac·cli·ma·ti·za·tion** /əˌklīmətəˈzāsHən/ **n.**
– ORIGIN mid 19th cent.: from French *acclimater* 'acclimatize' + -IZE.

ac·cliv·i·ty /əˈklivitē/ ▶ **n.** (pl. **acclivities**) an upward slope.
– DERIVATIVES **ac·cliv·i·tous** /-itəs/ **adj.**
– ORIGIN early 17th cent.: from Latin *acclivitas*, from *acclivis*, from *ad-* 'toward' + *clivus* 'a slope.'

ac·co·lade /ˈakəˌlād, -ˌläd/ ▶ **n. 1** an award or privilege granted as a special honor or as an acknowledgment of merit: *the ultimate official accolade of a visit by the president.* ■ an expression of praise or admiration.
2 a touch on a person's shoulders with a sword at the bestowing of a knighthood.
– ORIGIN early 17th cent.: from French, from Provençal *acolada*, literally 'embrace around the neck (when bestowing knighthood),' from Latin *ad-* 'at, to' + *collum* 'neck.'

ac·com·mo·date /əˈkäməˌdāt/ ▶ **v.** [with obj.] **1** (of physical space, esp. a building) provide lodging or sufficient space for: *the cabins accommodate up to 6 people.*
2 fit in with the wishes or needs of: *any language must accommodate new concepts.* ■ [no obj.] (**accommodate to**) adapt to: *making consumers accommodate to the realities of today's marketplace.*
– DERIVATIVES **ac·com·mo·da·tive** /-ˌdātiv/ **adj.**
– ORIGIN mid 16th cent.: from Latin *accommodat-* 'made fitting,' from the verb *accommodare*, from *ad-* 'to' + *commodus* 'fitting.'

ac·com·mo·dat·ing /əˈkäməˌdātiNG/ ▶ **adj.** fitting in with someone's wishes or demands in a helpful way.
– DERIVATIVES **ac·com·mo·dat·ing·ly adv.**

ac·com·mo·da·tion /əˌkäməˈdāsHən/ ▶ **n. 1** (usu. **accommodations**) a room, group of rooms, or building in which someone may live or stay: *the cost includes airfare and hotel accommodations.* ■ (**accommodations**) lodging; room and board: *the company offers a number of guesthouse accommodations in Cape Cod.* ■ the available space for occupants in a building, vehicle, or vessel: *there was lifeboat accommodation for 1,178 people.* ■ the provision of a room or lodging: *the building is used exclusively for the accommodation of guests.*
2 a convenient arrangement; a settlement or compromise: *management was seeking an accommodation with labor.*
3 the process of adapting or adjusting to someone or something: *accommodation to a separate political entity was not possible.* ■ the automatic adjustment of the focus of the eye by flattening or thickening of the lens.
– ORIGIN early 17th cent.: from Latin *accommodatio(n-)*, from *accommodare* 'fit one thing to another' (see ACCOMMODATE).

ac·com·mo·da·tion·ist /əˌkäməˈdāsHənist/ ▶ **n.** a person who seeks compromise with an opposing point of view, typically a political one.

ac·com·mo·da·tion lad·der ▶ **n.** a ladder or stairway up the side of a ship allowing access, esp. to and from a small boat, or from a dock.

ac·com·pa·ni·ment /əˈkəmp(ə)nimənt/ ▶ **n.**
1 a musical part that supports or partners a solo instrument, voice, or group: *she sang to a guitar accompaniment* | *sonatas for piano with violin accompaniment.* ■ a piece of music played to complement or as background to an activity: *lush string accompaniments to romantic scenes in movies.*
2 something that is supplementary to or complements something else, typically food: *sugar snap peas make a delicious accompaniment for salmon.*
– PHRASES **to the accompaniment of 1** with accompanying or background music or sound from: *we filed out to the accompaniment of the organ.* **2** with another event happening at the same time as: *the dam was completed to the accompaniment of numerous scandals.*
– ORIGIN early 18th cent.: from French *accompagnement*, from *accompagner* 'accompany.'

ac·com·pa·nist /əˈkəmpənist/ ▶ **n.** a person who provides a musical accompaniment to another musician or to a singer.

ac·com·pa·ny /əˈkəmp(ə)nē/ ▶ **v.** (**accompanies, accompanying, accompanied**) [with obj.] **1** go somewhere with (someone) as a companion or escort: *the two sisters were to accompany us to New York* | *he was at the banquet accompanied by his daughter.*
2 be present or occur at the same time as (something else): *the illness is often accompanied by nausea* | (as adj. **accompanying**) *the accompanying documentation.* ■ provide (something) as a complement or addition to something else: *home-cooked ham accompanied by brown bread.*
3 play a musical accompaniment for.
– ORIGIN late Middle English: from Old French *accompagner*, from *a-* (from Latin *ad* 'to, at') + *compagne*, from Old French *compaignon* 'companion.' The spelling change was due to association with COMPANY.

ac·com·plice /əˈkämplis/ ▶ **n.** a person who helps another commit a crime.
– ORIGIN mid 16th cent.: alteration (probably by association with ACCOMPANY) of Middle English *complice* 'an associate,' via Old French from late Latin *complex, complic-* 'allied,' from *com-* 'together' + the root of *plicare* 'to fold.'

ac·com·plish /əˈkämplisH/ ▶ **v.** [with obj.] achieve or complete successfully: *the planes accomplished their mission.*
– ORIGIN late Middle English: from Old French *acompliss-*, lengthened stem of *acomplir*, based on Latin *ad-* 'to' + *complere* 'to complete.'

ac·com·plished /əˈkämplisHt/ ▶ **adj.** highly trained or skilled: *an accomplished pianist.* ■ dated having a higher level of education than average and good social skills.

ac·com·plish·ment /əˈkämplisHmənt/ ▶ **n.** something that has been achieved successfully: *the reduction of inflation was a remarkable accomplishment.* ■ the successful achievement of a task: *the accomplishment of planned objectives.* ■ an activity that a person can do well, typically as a result of study or practice: *long-distance running was another of her accomplishments.* ■ skill or ability in an activity: *a poet of considerable accomplishment.*

ac·cord /əˈkôrd/ ▶ **v. 1** [with obj.] give or grant someone (power, status, or recognition): *the powers* ***accorded to*** *the head of state* | [with two objs.] *the young man had accorded her little notice.*
2 [no obj.] (**accord with**) (of a concept or fact) be harmonious or consistent with.
▶ **n.** an official agreement or treaty. ■ agreement or harmony: *the government and the rebels are in accord on one point* | *function and form in harmonious accord.*
– PHRASES **in accord with** according to. **of one's own accord** voluntarily or without outside intervention: *he would not seek treatment of his own accord* | *the rash may go away of its own accord.* **with one accord** in a united way.
– ORIGIN Old English, from Old French *acorder* 'reconcile, be of one mind,' from Latin *ad-* 'to' + *cor, cord-* 'heart'; influenced by CONCORD.

ac·cord·ance /əˈkôrdns/ ▶ **n.** (in phrase **in accordance with**) in a manner conforming with: *the product is disposed of in accordance with federal regulations.*
– ORIGIN Middle English: from Old French *acordance*, from *acorder* 'bring to an agreement' (see ACCORD).

ac·cord·ant /əˈkôrdnt/ ▶ **adj.** [predic.] archaic agreeing or compatible: *I found the music* ***accordant with*** *the words of the service.*
– ORIGIN Middle English: from Old French *acordant*, from *acorder* 'bring to an agreement' (see ACCORD).

ac·cord·ing /əˈkôrdiNG/ ▶ **adv. 1** (usu. **according to**) as stated by or in: *the outlook for investors is not bright, according to financial experts* | *he may have only weeks to live, according to a source close to the family.* ■ in a manner corresponding or conforming to: *cook the rice according to the instructions.* ■ in proportion or relation to: *salary will be fixed according to experience.*
2 (**according as**) depending on whether.

ac·cord·ing·ly /əˈkôrdiNGlē/ ▶ **adv. 1** in a way that is appropriate to the particular circumstances: *we have to discover what his plans are and act accordingly.*
2 [sentence adverb] consequently; therefore: *There was no breach of the rules. Accordingly, there will be no disciplinary inquiry.*

ac·cor·di·on /əˈkôrdēən/ ▶ **n.** a portable musical instrument with metal reeds blown by bellows, played by means of keys and buttons: [as modifier] *an accordion player.* ■ [as modifier] folding like the bellows of an accordion: *an accordion pleat.*
– DERIVATIVES **ac·cor·di·on·ist** /-nist/ **n.**
– ORIGIN mid 19th cent.: from German *Akkordion*, from Italian *accordare* 'to tune.'

accordion

ac·cost /əˈkôst, əˈkäst/ ▶ **v.** [with obj.] approach and address (someone) boldly or aggressively: *reporters accosted him in the street* | *a man tried to accost the girl on her way to school.*
– ORIGIN late 16th cent. (originally in the sense 'lie or go alongside'): from French *accoster*, from Italian *accostare*, from Latin *ad-* 'to' + *costa* 'rib, side.'

ac·couche·ment /ˌäko͞osHˈmän, əˈko͞osHmənt/ ▶ **n.** archaic the process of giving birth to a baby.
– ORIGIN late 18th cent.: French, from *accoucher* 'act as midwife,' from *a-* (from Latin *ad* 'to, at') + *coucher* 'put to bed' (see COUCH).

ac·cou·cheur /ˌäko͞oˈsHər/ ▶ **n.** a male midwife.
– ORIGIN mid 18th cent.: French, from *accoucher* (see ACCOUCHEMENT).

ac·count /əˈkount/ ▶ **n. 1** a report or description of an event or experience: *a detailed account of what has been achieved.* ■ an interpretation or rendering of a piece of music: *a lively account of Offenbach's score.*
2 (abbr.: **acct.**) a record or statement of financial expenditure or receipts relating to a particular period or purpose: *the ledger contains all the income and expense accounts* | *he submitted a quarterly account.* ■ the department of a company that deals with such records.
3 (abbr.: **acct.**) an arrangement by which a body holds funds on behalf of a client or supplies goods or services to the client on credit: *a bank account* |

charge it to my account | *I began buying things* ***on account.*** ■ a client having such an arrangement with a supplier: *selling bibles to established accounts in the North.* ■ a contract to do work periodically for a client: *another agency was awarded the account.* **4** importance: *money was* ***of no account*** *to her.*
▶ **v.** [with obj. and complement] consider or regard in a specified way: *her visit could not be accounted a success* | *he* ***accounted himself*** *the unluckiest man alive.*
– PHRASES **by** (or **from**) **all accounts** according to what one has heard or read: *by all accounts he is a pretty nice guy.* **call** (or **bring**) **someone to account** require someone to explain a mistake or poor performance. **give a good** (or **bad**) **account of oneself** make a favorable (or unfavorable) impression through one's performance. **keep an account of** keep a record of. **leave something out of account** fail or decline to consider a factor. **on someone's account** for a specified person's benefit: *don't bother on my account.* **on account of** because of. **on no account** under no circumstances: *on no account let anyone know we're interested.* **on one's own account** with one's own money or assets, rather than for an employer or client: *he began trading on his own account.* **settle** (or **square**) **accounts with** pay money owed to (someone). ■ have revenge on: *the potential danger of using the bill for settling accounts with political opponents.* **take something into account** (or **take account of**) consider a specified thing along with other factors before reaching a decision or taking action. **there's no accounting for tastes** (or **taste**) proverb it is impossible to explain why different people like different things, esp. those things that the speaker considers unappealing. **turn something to** (**good**) **account** turn something to one's advantage.
– PHRASAL VERBS **account for 1** give a satisfactory record of (something, typically money, that one is responsible for). ■ provide or serve as a satisfactory explanation or reason for: *he was brought before the Board to account for his behavior.* ■ know the fate or whereabouts of (someone or something), esp. after an accident: *everyone was accounted for after the floods.* ■ succeed in killing, destroying, or defeating: *the fifth inning accounted for Lyons, who gave up three back-to-back home runs.* **2** supply or make up a specified amount or proportion of: *social security accounts for about a third of total public spending.*
– ORIGIN Middle English (in the sense 'counting,' 'to count'): from Old French *acont* (noun), *aconter* (verb), based on *conter* 'to count.'

ac·count·a·bil·i·ty /əˌkountəˈbilitē/ ▶ **n.** the fact or condition of being accountable; responsibility: *their lack of accountability has corroded public respect.*

ac·count·a·ble /əˈkountəbəl/ ▶ **adj. 1** (of a person, organization, or institution) required or expected to justify actions or decisions; responsible: *government must be* ***accountable to*** *its citizens* | *parents could be* ***held accountable for*** *their children's actions.* **2** explicable; understandable: *the delayed introduction of characters' names is accountable, if we consider that names have a low priority.*

ac·count·an·cy /əˈkount(ə)nsē/ ▶ **n.** the profession or duties of an accountant.

ac·count·ant /əˈkount(ə)nt/ (abbr.: **acct.**) ▶ **n.** a person whose job is to keep or inspect financial accounts.
– ORIGIN Middle English: from legal French, present participle of Old French *aconter* (see ACCOUNT). The original use was as an adjective meaning 'liable to give an account,' hence denoting a person who must do so.

ac·count ex·ec·u·tive ▶ **n.** a business executive who manages the interests of a particular client, typically in advertising.

ac·count·ing /əˈkountiNG/ ▶ **n.** the action or process of keeping financial accounts.

ac·counts pay·a·ble ▶ **plural n.** money owed by a company to its creditors.

ac·counts re·ceiv·a·ble ▶ **plural n.** money owed to a company by its debtors.

ac·cou·tre /əˈko͞otər/ (also **accouter**) ▶ **v.** (**accoutres, accoutring, accoutred** or **accouters, accoutering, accoutered**) [with obj.] (usu. **be accoutred**) clothe or equip, typically in something noticeable or impressive.
– ORIGIN mid 16th cent.: from French *accoutrer*, from Old French *acoustrer*, from *a-* (from Latin *ad* 'to, at') + *cousture* 'sewing' (see COUTURE).

ac·cou·tre·ment /əˈko͞otərmənt, -trə-/ (also **accouterment**) ▶ **n.** (usu. **accoutrements**) additional items of dress or equipment, or other items carried or worn by a person or used for a particular activity: *the accoutrements of religious ritual.* ■ a soldier's outfit other than weapons and garments.
– ORIGIN mid 16th cent.: from French, from *accoutrer* 'clothe, equip' (see ACCOUTRE).

Ac·cra /ˈäkrə, ˈakrə, əˈkrä/ the capital of Ghana, a port on the Gulf of Guinea; pop. 1,970,400 (est. 2005).

ac·cred·it /əˈkredit/ ▶ **v.** (**accredits, accrediting, accredited**) [with obj.] (usu. **be accredited**) **1** give credit to (someone) for: *he was accredited with being one of the world's fastest sprinters.* ■ attribute (an action, saying, or quality) to: *the discovery of distillation is usually accredited to the Arabs.* **2** (of an official body) give authority or sanction to (someone or something) when recognized standards have been met: *institutions that do not meet the standards will not be accredited for teacher training.* **3** give official authorization for (someone, typically a diplomat or journalist) to be in a particular place or to hold a particular post: *an ambassador accredited to a northern European country.*
– DERIVATIVES **ac·cred·i·ta·tion** /əˌkrediˈtāSHən/ **n.**, **accreditor n.**
– ORIGIN early 17th cent. (sense 2): from French *accréditer*, from *a-* (from Latin *ad* 'to, at') + *crédit* 'credit.'

ac·cred·it·ed /əˈkreditid/ ▶ **adj.** (of a person, organization, or course of study) officially recognized or authorized: *an accredited chiropractic school.*

ac·crete /əˈkrēt/ ▶ **v.** [no obj.] grow by accumulation or coalescence: *ice that had accreted grotesquely into stalactites.* ■ [with obj.] form (a composite whole or a collection of things) by gradual accumulation: *the collection of art he had accreted was to be sold.* ■ Astronomy (with reference to matter or a body) come or bring together under the influence of gravitation: *the gas will cool and then accrete to the galaxy's core.*
– ORIGIN late 18th cent.: from Latin *accret-* 'grown,' from the verb *accrescere*, from *ad-* 'to' + *crescere* 'grow.'

ac·cre·tion /əˈkrēSHən/ ▶ **n.** the process of growth or increase, typically by the gradual accumulation of additional layers or matter: *the accretion of sediments in coastal mangroves* | figurative *the growing accretion of central government authority.* ■ a thing formed or added by such growth or increase: *about one-third of California was built up by accretions* | *the city has a historic core surrounded by recent accretions.* ■ Astronomy the coming together and cohesion of matter under the influence of gravitation to form larger bodies.
– DERIVATIVES **ac·cre·tive** /əˈkrētiv/ **adj.**
– ORIGIN early 17th cent.: from Latin *accretion-*, from *accrescere* 'become larger' (see ACCRETE).

ac·cre·tion·ar·y prism /əˈkrēSHəˌnerē/ (also **accretionary wedge**) ▶ **n.** Geology a mass of sedimentary material scraped off a region of oceanic crust during subduction and piled up at the edge of the overriding plate.

ac·cre·tion disk ▶ **n.** Astronomy a rotating disk of matter formed by accretion around a massive body (such as a black hole) under the influence of gravitation.

ac·crue /əˈkro͞o/ ▶ **v.** (**accrues, accruing, accrued**) [no obj.] (of sums of money or benefits) be received by someone in regular or increasing amounts over time: *financial benefits will accrue from restructuring* | (as adj. **accrued**) *the accrued interest.* ■ [with obj.] accumulate or receive (such payments or benefits). ■ [with obj.] make provision for (a charge) at the end of a financial period for work that has been done but not yet invoiced.
– DERIVATIVES **ac·cru·al** /əˈkro͞oəl/ **n.**
– ORIGIN late Middle English: from Old French *acreue*, past participle of *acreistre* 'increase,' from Latin *accrescere* 'become larger' (see ACCRETE).

acct. ▶ **abbr.** ■ account. ■ accountant.

ac·cul·tur·ate /əˈkəlCHəˌrāt/ ▶ **v.** assimilate or cause to assimilate a different culture, typically the dominant one: [no obj.] *those who have acculturated to the US* | [with obj.] *the next weeks were spent acculturating the field staff* | (as adj. **acculturated**) *an acculturated Cherokee.*
– DERIVATIVES **ac·cul·tur·a·tion** /əˌkəlCHəˈrāSHən/ **n.**, **ac·cul·tur·a·tive** /-ərətiv, -əˌrātiv/ **adj.**
– ORIGIN mid 20th cent.: from AC- + CULTURE + -ATE[1]. The noun *acculturation* dates from the late 19th cent.

ac·cum·bent ▶ **adj.** Botany (of a cotyledon) lying edgewise against the folded radicle in the seed.
– ORIGIN early 19th cent.: from Latin *accumbent-* 'reclining,' from *accumbere*, from *ad-* 'to' + a verb related to *cubare* 'to lie.'

ac·cu·mu·late /əˈkyo͞omyəˌlāt/ ▶ **v.** [with obj.] gather together or acquire an increasing number or quantity of: *investigators have yet to accumulate enough evidence.* ■ gradually gather or acquire (a resulting whole): *her goal was to accumulate a huge fortune.* ■ [no obj.] gather or build up: *the toxin accumulated in their bodies.*
– ORIGIN late 15th cent.: from Latin *accumulat-* 'heaped up,' from the verb *accumulare*, from *ad-* 'to' + *cumulus* 'a heap.'

ac·cu·mu·la·tion /əˌkyo͞omyəˈlāSHən/ ▶ **n.** the acquisition or gradual gathering of something: *the accumulation of wealth.* ■ a mass or quantity of something that has gradually gathered or been acquired: *the accumulation of paperwork on her desk.* ■ the growth of a sum of money by the regular addition of interest.

ac·cu·mu·la·tive /əˈkyo͞omyələtiv, -ˌlātiv/ ▶ **adj.** [attrib.] gathering or growing by gradual increases: *the accumulative effects of pollution.*

ac·cu·mu·la·tor /əˈkyo͞omyəˌlātər/ ▶ **n.** a person or thing that accumulates things: ***accumulator of capital.*** ■ Computing a register used to contain the results of an arithmetical or logical operation.

ac·cu·ra·cy /ˈakyərəsē/ ▶ **n.** (pl. **accuracies**) the quality or state of being correct or precise: *we have confidence in the accuracy of the statistics* | *she hit the ball with great accuracy.* ■ technical the degree to which the result of a measurement, calculation, or specification conforms to the correct value or a standard: *the accuracy of radiocarbon dating* | *accuracies of 50–70%.* Compare with PRECISION.

ac·cu·rate /ˈakyərit/ ▶ **adj. 1** (of information, measurements, statistics, etc.) correct in all details; exact: *accurate information about the illness is essential.* ■ (of an instrument or method) capable of giving such information: *an accurate thermometer.* ■ (of a piece of work) meticulously careful and free from errors. ■ faithfully or fairly representing the truth about someone or something: *the portrait is an accurate likeness of Mozart* | *we were fairly accurate in our predictions.* **2** (with reference to a weapon, missile, or shot) capable of or successful in reaching the intended target: *reliable, accurate rifles* | *a player who can deliver long accurate passes.*
– DERIVATIVES **ac·cu·rate·ly adv.**
– ORIGIN late 16th cent.: from Latin *accuratus* 'done with care,' past participle of *accurare*, from *ad-* 'toward' + *cura* 'care.'

ac·curs·ed /əˈkərst, əˈkərsid/ ▶ **adj. 1** literary under a curse: *the Angel of Death walks this accursed house.* **2** [attrib.] informal, dated used to express strong dislike of or anger toward someone or something: *those accursed books!*
– ORIGIN Middle English: past participle of obsolete *accurse*, from *a-* (expressing intensity) + CURSE.

ac·cu·sal /əˈkyo͞ozəl/ ▶ **n.** another term for ACCUSATION.

ac·cu·sa·tion /ˌakyəˈzāSHən, ˌakyo͞o-/ ▶ **n.** a charge or claim that someone has done something illegal or wrong: *accusations of bribery.* ■ the action or process of making such a charge or claim: *there was accusation in Brian's voice.*
– ORIGIN late Middle English: from Old French, from Latin *accusatio(n-)*, from *accusare* 'call to account' (see ACCUSE).

ac·cu·sa·tive /əˈkyo͞ozətiv/ Grammar ▶ **adj.** relating to or denoting a case of nouns, pronouns, and adjectives that expresses the object of an action or the goal of motion.
▶ **n.** a word in the accusative case. ■ (**the accusative**) the accusative case.
– ORIGIN late Middle English: from Latin *casus) accusativus*, literally 'relating to an accusation or (legal) case,' translating Greek *((ptōsis) aitiatikē* '(the case) showing cause.'

ac·cu·sa·to·ri·al /əˌkyo͞ozəˈtôrēəl/ ▶ **adj.** [attrib.] Law (esp. of a trial or legal procedure) involving accusation by a prosecutor and a verdict reached by an impartial judge or jury. Often contrasted with INQUISITORIAL.

ac·cu·sa·to·ry /əˈkyo͞ozəˌtôrē/ ▶ **adj.** indicating or suggesting that one believes a person has done something wrong: *he pointed an accusatory finger in her direction.*

ac·cuse /əˈkyo͞oz/ ▶ **v.** [with obj.] charge (someone) with an offense or crime: *he was* ***accused of*** *murdering his wife's lover.* ■ claim that (someone) has done something wrong: *he was accused of favoritism.*
– DERIVATIVES **ac·cus·er n.**
– ORIGIN Middle English: from Old French *acuser*, from Latin *accusare* 'call to account,' from *ad-* 'toward' + *causa* 'reason, motive, lawsuit.'

ac·cused /əˈkyo͞ozd/ ▶ **n.** [treated as sing.] (or pl. **the accused**) a person or group of people who are charged with or on trial for a crime: *the accused was ordered to stand trial on a number of charges.*

a

ac·cus·ing /əˈkyo͞oziNG/ ▶ **adj.** (of an expression, gesture, or tone of voice) indicating a belief in someone's guilt or culpability: *she stared at him with accusing eyes.*
– DERIVATIVES **ac·cus·ing·ly adv.**

ac·cus·tom /əˈkəstəm/ ▶ **v.** [with obj.] make (someone or something) accept something as normal or usual: *I accustomed my eyes to the lenses* | *they tried to accustom him to their lighthearted ways.* ■ (**be accustomed to**) be used to: *my eyes gradually became accustomed to the darkness.*
– ORIGIN late Middle English: from Old French *acostumer*, from *a-* (from Latin *ad* 'to, at') + *costume* 'custom.'

ac·cus·tomed /əˈkəstəmd/ ▶ **adj.** [attrib.] customary or usual: *his accustomed route.*

AC/DC ▶ **adj.** alternating current/direct current. ■ informal bisexual.

ACE ▶ **abbr.** Army Corps of Engineers.

ace /ās/ ▶ **n. 1** a playing card with a single spot on it, ranked as the highest card in its suit in most card games: *the ace of diamonds* | figurative *life had started dealing him aces again.* ■ Golf, informal a hole in one.
2 [often with modifier] informal a person who excels at a particular sport or other activity: *a motorcycle ace.* ■ a pilot who has shot down many enemy aircraft, esp. in World War I or World War II.
3 (in tennis and similar games) a service that an opponent is unable to touch and thus wins a point.
▶ **adj.** informal very good: *an ace swimmer.*
▶ **v.** [with obj.] informal (in tennis and similar games) serve an ace against (an opponent). ■ Golf score an ace on (a hole) or with (a shot). ■ get an A or its equivalent in (a test or exam): *I aced my grammar test.* ■ (**ace someone out**) outdo someone in a competitive situation: *the magazine won an award, acing out its rivals* | *it wasn't our intention to ace Phil out of a job.*
– PHRASES **an ace up one's sleeve** (or **in the hole**) a plan or piece of information kept secret until it becomes necessary to use it. **hold all the aces** have all the advantages. **play one's ace** use one's best resource: *deciding to play her ace, Emily showed the letter to Vic.* **within an ace of** very close to: *they came within an ace of death.*
– ORIGIN Middle English (denoting the "one" on dice): via Old French from Latin *as* 'unity, a unit.'

-acea ▶ **suffix** Zoology forming the names of zoological groups: *Crustacea.* Compare with **-ACEAN**.
– ORIGIN from Latin, 'of the nature of,' neuter plural adjectival ending.

-aceae ▶ **suffix** Botany forming the names of families of plants: *Liliaceae.*
– ORIGIN from Latin, 'of the nature of,' feminine plural adjectival ending.

-acean ▶ **suffix** Zoology forming adjectives and nouns from taxonomic names ending in *-acea* (such as *crustacean* from *Crustacea*).
– ORIGIN from Latin *-aceus*, adjectival ending meaning 'of the nature of.'

Ace band·age ▶ **n.** trademark an elastic bandage, used to wrap sprained or strained ankles, wrists, or other joints.

a·ce·di·a /əˈsēdēə/ ▶ **n.** spiritual or mental sloth; apathy.
– ORIGIN early 17th cent.: late Latin, from Greek *akēdia* 'listlessness,' from *a-* 'without' + *kēdos* 'care.'

a·cel·lu·lar /āˈselyələr/ ▶ **adj.** Biology not consisting of, divided into, or containing cells. ■ (esp. of protozoa) consisting of one cell only.

-aceous ▶ **suffix 1** Botany forming adjectives from nouns ending in *-aceae* (such as *ericaceous* from: *Ericaceae*).
2 chiefly Biology & Geology forming adjectives describing similarity, esp. in shape, texture, or color: *arenaceous* | *foliaceous* | *olivaceous.*
– ORIGIN from Latin *-aceus*, adjectival ending meaning 'of the nature of.'

a·ceph·a·lous /āˈsefələs/ ▶ **adj. 1** no longer having a head: *an acephalous skeleton.* ■ Zoology not having a head. ■ having no leader or chief: *an acephalous society.*
2 Prosody lacking a syllable or syllables in the first foot.
– ORIGIN mid 18th cent.: via medieval Latin from Greek *akephalos* 'headless' (from *a-* 'without' + *kephalē* 'head') + **-OUS**.

a·cerb /əˈsərb/ ▶ **adj.** another term for **ACERBIC**.
– ORIGIN early 17th cent.: from Latin *acerbus* 'sour-tasting.'

a·cer·bic /əˈsərbik/ ▶ **adj. 1** (esp. of a comment or style of speaking) sharp and forthright: *his acerbic wit.*
2 archaic or technical tasting sour or bitter.
– DERIVATIVES **a·cer·bi·cal·ly adv.**, **a·cer·bi·ty** /-bitē/ **n.**
– ORIGIN mid 19th cent.: from Latin *acerbus* 'sour-tasting' + **-IC**.

acet- ▶ **prefix** variant spelling of **ACETO-** shortened before a vowel (as in *acetaldehyde*).

ac·e·tab·u·lum /ˌasiˈtabyələm/ ▶ **n.** (pl. **acetabula** /-lə/) Anatomy the socket of the hipbone, into which the head of the femur fits. ■ Zoology any cup-shaped structure, esp. a sucker.
– DERIVATIVES **ac·e·tab·u·lar adj.**
– ORIGIN late Middle English (denoting a vinegar cup, hence a cup-shaped cavity): from Latin, from *acetum* 'vinegar' + *-abulum*, denoting a container.

ac·e·tal /ˈasiˌtal/ ▶ **n.** Chemistry an organic compound formed by the condensation of two alcohol molecules with an aldehyde molecule. ● Acetals have the general formula $R^1CH(OR^2)_2$, where R^1 and R^2 are alkyl groups.
– ORIGIN mid 19th cent.: from **ACETIC** + *-al* from *alcohol, aldehyde.*

ac·et·al·de·hyde /ˌasiˈtaldəˌhīd/ ▶ **n.** Chemistry a colorless volatile liquid aldehyde obtained by oxidizing ethanol. ● Alternative name: **ethanal**; chem. formula: CH_3CHO.

a·cet·am·ide /əˈsetəˌmīd/ ▶ **n.** Chemistry the crystalline amide of acetic acid. ● Chem. formula: CH_3CONH_2.
– ORIGIN mid 19th cent.: from **ACETYL** + **AMIDE**.

a·ce·ta·min·o·phen /əˌsētəˈminəfən/ ▶ **n.** an analgesic drug used to treat headaches, arthritis, etc., and also to reduce fever, often as an alternative to aspirin. Proprietary names include *Tylenol.* ● Chem. formula: $C_8H_9NO_2$. ■ a tablet of this drug.

ac·et·an·i·lide /ˌasiˈtanəˌlīd/ ▶ **n.** Chemistry a crystalline solid prepared by acetylation of aniline, used in dye manufacture. ● Chem. formula: $C_6H_5NHCOCH_3$.
– ORIGIN mid 19th cent.: from *acet(yl)* + *anil(ine)* + **-IDE**.

ac·e·tate /ˈasiˌtāt/ ▶ **n. 1** Chemistry a salt or ester of acetic acid, containing the anion CH_3COO^- or the group $-OOCCH_3$.
2 cellulose acetate, esp. as used to make textile fibers or plastic: [as modifier] *acetate silk.* ■ a transparency made of cellulose acetate film. ■ a recording disk coated with cellulose acetate.
– ORIGIN late 18th cent.: from **ACETIC** + **-ATE**[1].

a·ce·tic /əˈsētik/ ▶ **adj.** of or like vinegar or acetic acid.
– ORIGIN late 18th cent.: from French *acétique*, from Latin *acetum* 'vinegar.'

a·ce·tic ac·id /əˈsētik/ ▶ **n.** Chemistry the acid that gives vinegar its characteristic taste. The pure acid is a colorless viscous liquid or glassy solid. ● Chem. formula: CH_3COOH.
– ORIGIN late 18th cent.: *acetic* from French *acétique*, from Latin *acetum* 'vinegar.'

a·ce·tic an·hy·dride ▶ **n.** Chemistry the anhydride of acetic acid. It is a colorless pungent liquid, used in making synthetic fibers. ● Chem. formula: $(CH_3CO)_2O$.

aceto- (also **acet-** before a vowel) ▶ **comb. form** Chemistry representing **ACETIC** or **ACETYL**.

a·ce·to·bac·ter /əˌsētəˈbaktər, ˌasitə-/ ▶ **n.** bacteria that oxidize organic compounds to acetic acid, as in vinegar formation. ● Genus *Acetobacter*; Gram-negative oval or rod-shaped bacteria.
– ORIGIN modern Latin (genus name), from **ACETO-** + **BACTERIUM**.

a·ce·to·gen·ic /əˌsētəˈjenik, ˌasitə-/ ▶ **adj.** (of bacteria) forming acetate or acetic acid as a product of metabolism.

ac·e·tone /ˈasiˌtōn/ ▶ **n.** Chemistry a colorless volatile liquid ketone made by oxidizing isopropanol, used as an organic solvent and synthetic reagent. ● Chem. formula: CH_3COCH_3.
– ORIGIN mid 19th cent.: from **ACETIC** + **-ONE**.

a·ce·to·ne·mi·a /əˌsētəˈnēmēə, ˌasitə-/ ▶ **n.** another term for **KETONEMIA**.

ac·e·to·ni·trile /ˌasitōˈnītril, -trēl, əˌsētō-/ ▶ **n.** Chemistry a toxic odoriferous liquid, used as a solvent in high-performance liquid chromatography. ● Alternative name: **methyl cyanide**; chem. formula: $CH_3C{\equiv}N$.

ac·e·tous /əˈsētəs, ˈasitəs/ ▶ **adj.** producing or resembling vinegar: *acetous fermentation.*
– ORIGIN late Middle English (rare before the late 18th cent.): from late Latin *acetosus* 'sour,' from Latin *acetum* 'vinegar.'

a·ce·tyl /əˈsētl, ˈasitl/ ▶ **n.** [as modifier] Chemistry the acyl radical $-C(O)CH_3$, derived from acetic acid: *acetyl chloride* | *an acetyl group.*
– ORIGIN mid 19th cent.: from **ACETIC** + **-YL**.

a·cet·y·late /əˈsetlˌāt/ ▶ **v.** [with obj.] Chemistry introduce an acetyl group into (a molecule or compound): (as adj. **acetylated**) *the acetylated forms of chloramphenicol.*
– DERIVATIVES **a·cet·y·la·tion** /əˌsetlˈāSHən/ **n.**

a·ce·tyl·cho·line /əˌsētlˈkōˌlēn, ˌasitl-/ ▶ **n.** Biochemistry a compound that occurs throughout the nervous system, in which it functions as a neurotransmitter.

a·ce·tyl·cho·lin·es·ter·ase /əˈsētlˌkōləˈnestəˌrās, -ˌrāz, ˈasitl-/ ▶ **n.** Biochemistry an enzyme that causes rapid hydrolysis of acetylcholine. Its action serves to stop excitation of a nerve after transmission of an impulse.

a·ce·tyl·co·en·zyme A ▶ **n.** Biochemistry the acetyl ester of coenzyme A, involved as an acetylating agent in many biochemical processes.

a·cet·y·lene /əˈsetlən, -ˌēn/ ▶ **n.** Chemistry a colorless pungent-smelling hydrocarbon gas, which burns with a bright flame, used in welding and formerly in lighting. ● Alternative name: **ethyne**; chem. formula: C_2H_2.
– ORIGIN mid 19th cent.: from **ACETIC** + **-YL** + **-ENE**.

a·cet·y·lide /əˈsetlˌīd/ ▶ **n.** Chemistry a saltlike compound formed from acetylene and a metal, containing the anion $(C{\equiv}C)^{2-}$ or $HC{\equiv}C^-$. Acetylides are typically unstable or explosive.

a·ce·tyl·sal·i·cyl·ic ac·id /əˌsētlˌsaliˈsilik/ ▶ **n.** systematic chemical name for **ASPIRIN**.

ACH ▶ **abbr.** Automated Clearinghouse.

A·chae·a /əˈkēə, əˈkāə/ a region of ancient Greece on the north coast of the Peloponnesus.

A·chae·an /əˈkēən/ ▶ **adj.** of or relating to Achaea in ancient Greece. ■ literary (esp. in Homeric contexts) Greek.
▶ **n.** an inhabitant of Achaea. ■ literary (esp. in Homeric contexts) a Greek.

> The Achaeans were among the earliest Greek-speaking inhabitants of Greece, being established there well before the 12th century BC. Some scholars identify them with the Mycenaeans of the 14th–13th centuries BC. The Greek protagonists in the Trojan War are regularly called Achaeans in the *Iliad*, though this may have referred only to the leaders.

A·chae·me·nid /əˈkēmənid/ (also **Achaemenian** /ˌakəˈmēnēən/) ▶ **adj.** of or relating to the dynasty ruling in Persia from Cyrus I to Darius III (553–330 BC).
▶ **n.** a member of this dynasty.
– ORIGIN from Greek *Akhaimenēs* 'Achaemenes' (the reputed ancestor of the dynasty) + **-ID**[1].

ach·a·la·sia /ˌakəˈlāZH(ē)ə/ ▶ **n.** Medicine a condition in which the muscles of the lower part of the esophagus fail to relax, preventing food from passing into the stomach.
– ORIGIN early 20th cent.: from **A-**[1] 'without, not' + Greek *khalasis* 'loosening' (from *khalan* 'relax') + **-IA**[1].

a·cha·ry·a /əˈCHə-rēə/ ▶ **n.** (in India) a Hindu or Buddhist spiritual teacher or leader. ■ an influential mentor.
– ORIGIN early 19th cent.: from Sanskrit *ācārya* 'master, teacher.'

A·cha·tes /əˈkātēz/ Greek & Roman Mythology a companion of Aeneas. His loyalty to his friend was so exemplary as to become proverbial, hence the term *fidus Achates* ('faithful Achates').

ache /āk/ ▶ **n. 1** a continuous or prolonged dull pain in a part of one's body: *the ache in her head worsened.*
2 [in sing.] an emotion experienced with painful or bittersweet intensity: *an ache in her heart.*
▶ **v.** [no obj.] **1** (of a person) suffer from a continuous dull pain: *I'm aching all over.* ■ (of a part of one's body) be the source of such a pain: *my legs ached from the previous day's exercise.*
2 feel intense sadness or compassion: *she sat still and silent, her heart aching* | *she looked so tired that my heart ached for her.*
3 feel an intense desire for: *she ached for his touch* | [with infinitive] *he was aching to get his hands on the ball.*
– PHRASES **aches and pains** minor pains and discomforts, typically in the muscles.
– ORIGIN Old English *æce* (noun), *acan* (verb). In Middle and early modern English the noun was spelled *atche* and pronounced so as to rhyme with 'batch,' the verb was spelled and pronounced as it is today. The noun began to be pronounced like the verb around 1700. The modern spelling is largely due to Dr. Johnson, who mistakenly assumed its derivation to be from Greek *akhos* 'pain.'

A·che·be /äˈCHābā/, Chinua (1930–), Nigerian novelist, poet, short-story writer, and essayist; born *Albert Chinualumgu.* Notable works: *Things Fall Apart* (1958), *A Man of the People* (1966), and *Anthills of the Savannah* (1988). Nobel Prize for Literature (1989).

a·chene /ā'kēn/ ▶ **n.** Botany a small, dry, one-seeded fruit that does not open to release the seed.
– ORIGIN mid 19th cent.: from modern Latin *achaenium*, derived irregularly from *a-* 'not' + Greek *khainein* 'to gape.'

A·cher·nar /'akər,när, 'āk-/ Astronomy the ninth brightest star in the sky, and the brightest in the constellation Eridanus. It marks the southern limit of Eridanus, and is only visible to observers in the southern hemisphere.
– ORIGIN from Arabic, 'end of the river (i.e., Eridanus).'

Ach·er·on /'akə,rän, -rən/ Greek Mythology one of the rivers of Hades. ■ literary hell.
– ORIGIN early 16th cent.: Latin from Greek *Akherōn*.

Ach·e·son /'acHəsən/, Dean Gooderham (1893–1971), US statesman; secretary of state 1949–53. He urged international control of nuclear power, was instrumental in the formation of NATO, and implemented the Marshall Plan and the Truman Doctrine.

A·cheu·le·an /ə'sHōōlēən/ (also **Acheulian**) ▶ **adj.** Archaeology of, relating to, or denoting the main Lower Paleolithic culture in Europe, represented by hand-ax industries, and dated to about 1,500,000–150,000 years ago. See also **ABBEVILLIAN**. ■ (as noun **the Acheulean**) the Acheulean culture or period.
– ORIGIN early 20th cent.: from French *Acheuléen*, from *St-Acheul* near Amiens in northern France, where objects from this culture were found.

a·chieve /ə'CHēv/ ▶ **v.** [with obj.] reach or attain (a desired objective, level, or result) by effort, skill, or courage: *he achieved his ambition to become a journalist* | [no obj.] *people striving to achieve*. ■ accomplish or bring about: *the entire sequence is achieved in a single shot*.
– DERIVATIVES **a·chiev·a·ble** adj., **a·chiev·er** n.
– ORIGIN Middle English (in the sense 'complete successfully'): from Old French *achever* 'come or bring to a head,' from *a chief* 'to a head.'

a·chieve·ment /ə'CHēvmənt/ ▶ **n. 1** a thing done successfully, typically by effort, courage, or skill: *to reach this stage is a great achievement*.
2 the process or fact of achieving something: *the achievement of professional recognition* | *sense of achievement*. ■ a child's or student's progress in a course of learning, typically as measured by standardized tests or objectives: *assessing ability in terms of academic achievement* | [as modifier] *an achievement test*.
3 Heraldry a representation of a coat of arms with all the adjuncts to which a bearer of arms is entitled.

ach·il·le·a /,akə'lēə/ ▶ **n.** a plant of the daisy family, which typically has heads of small white or yellow flowers and fernlike leaves. ● Genus *Achillea*, family Compositae: numerous species, including the common yarrow.
– ORIGIN via Latin from Greek *Akhilleios*, denoting a plant supposed to have been used medicinally by Achilles.

A·chil·les /ə'kilēz/ Greek Mythology a hero of the Trojan War, son of Peleus and Thetis. During his infancy his mother plunged him in the Styx, thus making his body invulnerable except for the heel by which she held him. During the Trojan War, Achilles killed Hector but was later wounded in the heel by an arrow shot by Paris and died.

A·chil·les heel ▶ **n.** a weakness or vulnerable point.
– ORIGIN early 19th cent.: alluding to the vulnerability of **ACHILLES**.

A·chil·les ten·don ▶ **n.** the tendon connecting calf muscles to the heel.

a·chim·e·nes /ə'kimə,nēz/ ▶ **n.** (pl. **same**) a tropical American plant with tubular or trumpet-shaped flowers. ● Genus *Achimenes*, family Gesneriaceae.
– ORIGIN modern Latin, either from Greek *akhaimenis*, denoting a different plant (euphorbia), or from *a-* 'not' + *kheimanein* 'expose to the cold.'

ach·ing /'ākiNG/ ▶ **adj. 1** sore; throbbing with pain: *the cool air was a relief to my aching head*.
2 feeling intense or wistful sadness; sorrowful: *an aching feeling of nostalgia*.
– DERIVATIVES **ach·ing·ly** adv. [as submodifier] *a sound which was achingly familiar to me*.

a·chi·o·te /,äCHē'ōtē, ,äkē-/ ▶ **n.** annatto.
– ORIGIN mid 17th cent.: from Spanish, from Nahuatl *achiotl*.

a·chlor·hy·dri·a /,āklôr'hīdrēə/ ▶ **n.** Medicine absence of hydrochloric acid in the gastric secretions.

A·cho·li /ə'kōlē, ə'CHō-/ ▶ **n. 1** (pl. **same**) a member of a farming and pastoral people of northern Uganda and southern Sudan.
2 the Nilotic language of this people.
▶ **adj.** of or relating to this people or their language.
– ORIGIN the name in Acholi.

a·chon·dro·pla·sia /ā,kändrə'plāZH(ē)ə/ ▶ **n.** a hereditary condition in which the growth of long bones by ossification of cartilage is retarded, resulting in very short limbs and sometimes a face that is small in relation to the (normal-sized) skull.
– DERIVATIVES **a·chon·dro·plas·tic** /-'plastik/ adj.
– ORIGIN late 19th cent.: from **A-**[1] 'without' + Greek *khondros* 'cartilage' + *plasis* 'molding' + **-IA**[1].

ach·ro·mat /'akrə,mat/ ▶ **n.** another term for **ACHROMATIC LENS**.

ach·ro·mat·ic /,akrə'matik, ,ākrə-/ ▶ **adj.** [attrib.] **1** relating to, employing, or denoting lenses that transmit light without separating it into constituent colors.
2 literary without color: *achromatic gloom*.
– ORIGIN late 18th cent.: via French from Greek *a-* 'without' + *khrōmatikos* (from *khrōma* 'color').

ach·ro·mat·ic lens ▶ **n.** a lens that transmits light without separating it into constituent colors.

ach·y /'ākē/ ▶ **adj.** [predic.] suffering from continuous dull pain: *she felt tired and achy*.

a·cic·u·lar /ə'sikyələr/ ▶ **adj.** technical (chiefly of crystals) needle-shaped.
– ORIGIN early 18th cent.: from late Latin *acicula* 'small needle,' diminutive of *acus*.

ac·id /'asid/ ▶ **n. 1** a chemical substance that neutralizes alkalis, dissolves some metals, and turns litmus red; typically, a corrosive or sour-tasting liquid of this kind: *rainwater is a very weak acid* | *traces of acid*. Often contrasted with **ALKALI** or **BASE**[1]. ■ bitter or cutting remarks or tone of voice: *she was unable to quell the acid in her voice*.
2 Chemistry a molecule or other entity that can donate a proton or accept an electron pair in reactions.
3 informal the drug LSD.

> Acids are compounds that release hydrogen ions (H^+) when dissolved in water. Any solution with a pH of less than 7 is acidic, strong acids such as sulfuric or hydrochloric acid having a pH as low as 1 or 2. Most organic acids (**carboxylic** or **fatty acids**) contain the carboxyl group –COOH.

▶ **adj. 1** containing acid or having the properties of an acid; in particular, having a pH of less than 7: *poor, acid soils*. Often contrasted with **ALKALINE** or **BASIC**. ■ Geology (of rock, esp. lava) containing a relatively high proportion of silica. ■ Metallurgy relating to or denoting steelmaking processes involving silica-rich refractories and slags.
2 sharp-tasting or sour: *acid fruit*. ■ (of a person's remarks or tone) bitter or cutting. ■ (of a color) intense or bright: *an acid green*.
– DERIVATIVES **ac·id·y** adj.
– ORIGIN early 17th cent. (in the sense 'sour-tasting'): from Latin *acidus*, from *acere* 'be sour.'

ac·id·head /'asid,hed/ ▶ **n.** informal a habitual user of the drug LSD.

ac·id house ▶ **n.** a kind of popular synthesized dance music with a fast repetitive beat, popular in the 1980s and associated with the taking of drugs such as Ecstasy.

a·cid·ic /ə'sidik/ ▶ **adj. 1** having the properties of an acid, or containing acid; having a pH below 7. Often contrasted with **ALKALINE** or **BASIC**. ■ Geology (of rock, esp. lava) relatively rich in silica. ■ Metallurgy relating to or denoting steelmaking processes involving silica-rich refractories and slags.
2 sharp-tasting or sour: *acidic wine*. ■ (of a person's remarks or tone) bitter or cutting: *the occasional acidic comment*. ■ (of a color) intense or bright: *an acidic yellow*.
3 of or relating to acid rock or acid house music.

a·cid·i·fy /ə'sidə,fī/ ▶ **v.** (**acidifies**, **acidifying**, **acidified**) make or become acid: [with obj.] *pollutants can acidify surface water* | [no obj.] *the paper was acidifying*.
– DERIVATIVES **a·cid·i·fi·ca·tion** /ə,sidəfi'kāsHən/ n.

ac·i·dim·e·try /,asi'dimitrē/ ▶ **n.** measurement of the strengths of acids.

a·cid·i·ty /ə'siditē/ ▶ **n. 1** the level of acid in substances such as water, soil, or wine. ■ such a level in the gastric juices, typically when excessive and causing discomfort.
2 the bitterness or sharpness of a person's remarks or tone: *the cutting acidity in his voice*.

ac·id jazz ▶ **n.** a kind of popular dance music incorporating elements of jazz, funk, soul, and hip-hop.
– ORIGIN apparently coined from **ACID HOUSE** and popularized by the *Acid Jazz* record label founded in 1988.

ac·id·ly /'asidlē/ ▶ **adv.** with bitterness or sarcasm: *"Is it up to you to make that decision?" she asked acidly*.

a·cid·o·phil /ə'sidə,fil, 'asidə-/ ▶ **n.** Biology an acidophilic white blood cell.

a·cid·o·phil·ic /ə,sidə'filik, ,asidə-/ ▶ **adj.** Biology **1** (of a cell or its contents) readily stained with acid dyes.
2 (of a microorganism or plant) growing best in acidic conditions.
– ORIGIN early 20th cent.: from **ACID** + *-philic* (see **-PHILIA**).

ac·i·doph·i·lus /,asi'däfələs/ ▶ **n.** a bacterium that is used to make yogurt and to supplement the intestinal flora. ● *Lactobacillus acidophilus*, a Gram-positive rod-shaped bacterium.
– ORIGIN 1920s: modern Latin, literally 'acid-loving.'

ac·i·do·sis /,asi'dōsis/ ▶ **n.** Medicine an excessively acid condition of the body fluids or tissues.
– DERIVATIVES **ac·i·dot·ic** /-'dätik/ adj.

ac·id rad·i·cal ▶ **n.** Chemistry a radical formed by the removal of hydrogen ions from an acid.

ac·id rain ▶ **n.** rainfall made sufficiently acidic by atmospheric pollution that it causes environmental harm, typically to forests and lakes. The main cause is the industrial burning of coal and other fossil fuels, the waste gases from which contain sulfur and nitrogen oxides, which combine with atmospheric water to form acids.

ac·id re·flux ▶ **n.** a condition in which gastric acid is regurgitated.

ac·id rock ▶ **n.** a type of rock music, mainly of the late 1960s, associated with or inspired by the use of hallucinogenic drugs.

ac·id salt ▶ **n.** Chemistry a salt formed by incomplete replacement of the hydrogen of an acid, e.g., potassium hydrogen sulfate ($KHSO_4$).

ac·id test ▶ **n.** [in sing.] a conclusive test of the success or value of something: *the pact with the rebels is an acid test of the government's sincerity*.
– ORIGIN figuratively, from the original use denoting a test for gold using nitric acid.

a·cid·u·late /ə'sijə,lāt/ ▶ **v.** [with obj.] (usu. as adj. **acidulated**) make slightly acidic: *acidulated water*.
– DERIVATIVES **a·cid·u·la·tion** /ə,sijə'lāsHən/ n.
– ORIGIN mid 18th cent.: from Latin *acidulus* (from *acidus* 'sour') + **-ATE**[3].

a·cid·u·lous /ə'sijələs/ ▶ **adj.** sharp-tasting or sour. ■ (of a person's remarks or tone) bitter or cutting.
– ORIGIN mid 18th cent.: from Latin *acidulus* (from *acidus* 'sour') + **-OUS**.

ac·i·nus /'asənəs/ ▶ **n.** (pl. **acini** /-,nī/) Anatomy **1** a small saclike cavity in a gland, surrounded by secretory cells.
2 a region of the lung supplied with air from one of the terminal bronchioles.
– DERIVATIVES **ac·i·nar** adj.
– ORIGIN mid 18th cent.: Latin, literally 'a kernel.'

-acious ▶ **suffix** (forming adjectives) inclined to; having as a capacity: *audacious* | *capacious*.
– ORIGIN from the Latin ending *-ax*, *-acis* (esp. forming adjectives from verbal stems) + **-OUS**.

-acity ▶ **suffix** forming nouns of quality or state corresponding to adjectives ending in *-acious* (such as *audacity* corresponding to *audacious*).
– ORIGIN from French *-acité* or Latin *-acitas*, noun endings.

ack-ack /'ak ,ak/ Military, informal ▶ **n.** antiaircraft gunfire: [as modifier] *a quick burst of ack-ack fire*.
– ORIGIN World War II: signalers' name for the letters *AA*.

ac·kee ▶ **n.** variant spelling of **AKEE**.

ac·knowl·edge /ak'nälij/ ▶ **v. 1** [reporting verb] accept or admit the existence or truth of: [with obj.] *the plight of the refugees was acknowledged by the authorities* | [with clause] *the government acknowledged that the tax was unfair* | [with direct speech] *"That's true," she acknowledged*.
2 [with obj.] (of a body of opinion) recognize the fact or importance or quality of: *the art world has begun to acknowledge his genius* | *he's generally acknowledged to be the game's finest coach*. ■ express or display gratitude for or appreciation of: *he received a letter acknowledging his services*. ■ accept the validity or legitimacy of: *Henry acknowledged Richard as his heir*.
3 [with obj.] show that one has noticed or recognized (someone) by making a gesture or greeting: *she refused to acknowledge my presence*. ■ confirm (receipt of something).
– ORIGIN late 15th cent.: from the obsolete Middle English verb *knowledge*, influenced by obsolete *acknow* 'acknowledge, confess.'

ac·knowl·edged /ak'nälijd/ ▶ **adj.** recognized as being good or important: *he's an acknowledged expert in the field*. ■ accepted as valid or legitimate: *an acknowledged brand leader*.

ac·knowl·edg·ment /ak'nälijmənt/ (also **acknowledgement**) ▶ **n. 1** acceptance of the

truth or existence of something: *there was no acknowledgment of the family's trauma.*
2 the action of expressing or displaying gratitude or appreciation for something: *he received an* ***award in acknowledgment of*** *his work.* ■ the action of showing that one has noticed someone or something: *he touched his hat* ***in acknowledgment of*** *the salute.* ■ a letter confirming receipt of something: *I received an acknowledgment of my application.*
3 (usu. **acknowledgments**) an author's or publisher's statement of indebtedness to others, typically one printed at the beginning of a book.

ACL ▶ **abbr.** anterior cruciate ligament.

a·clin·ic line /āˈklinik/ ▶ **n.** another term for MAGNETIC EQUATOR.
– ORIGIN mid 19th cent.: *aclinic* from Greek *aklinēs*, from *a-* 'not' + *klinein* 'to bend.'

ACLU ▶ **abbr.** American Civil Liberties Union.

ac·me /ˈakmē/ ▶ **n.** [in sing.] the point at which someone or something is best, perfect, or most successful: *physics is the acme of scientific knowledge.*
– ORIGIN late 16th cent.: from Greek *akmē* 'highest point.' Until the 18th cent. it was often consciously used as a Greek word and often written in Greek letters.

Ac·me·ist /ˈakmē-ist/ ▶ **adj.** denoting or relating to an early 20th century movement in Russian poetry that rejected the values of symbolism in favor of formal technique and clarity of exposition. Notable members were Anna Akhmatova and Osip Mandelstam.
▶ **n.** a member of this movement.
– DERIVATIVES **Ac·me·ism** /-ˌizəm/ **n.**

ac·ne /ˈaknē/ ▶ **n.** the occurrence of inflamed or infected sebaceous glands in the skin; in particular, a condition characterized by red pimples on the face, prevalent chiefly among teenagers.
– DERIVATIVES **ac·ned adj.**
– ORIGIN mid 19th cent.: via modern Latin from Greek *aknas*, a misreading of *akmas*, accusative plural of *akmē* 'highest point, peak, or facial eruption'; compare with ACME.

ac·o·lyte /ˈakəˌlīt/ ▶ **n.** a person assisting the celebrant in a religious service or procession. ■ an assistant or follower.
– ORIGIN Middle English: from Old French *acolyt* or ecclesiastical Latin *acolytus*, from Greek *akolouthos* 'follower.'

A·con·ca·gua /ˌakənˈkägwə, ˌäk-/ an extinct volcano in the Andes, on the border between Chile and Argentina, rising to 22,834 feet (6,960 m). It is the highest mountain in the western hemisphere.

ac·o·nite /ˈakəˌnīt/ ▶ **n.** a poisonous plant of the buttercup family, which bears hooded pink or purple flowers. It is native to temperate regions of the northern hemisphere. ● Genus *Aconitum*, family Ranunculaceae: many species, including monkshood and wolfsbane. ■ an extract of such a plant, used as a poison or in medicinal preparations.
– ORIGIN mid 16th cent.: via French and Latin from Greek *akoniton*.

a·con·i·tine /əˈkäniˌtēn/ ▶ **n.** Chemistry a poisonous alkaloid obtained from monkshood and related plants.

a·corn /ˈāˌkôrn/ ▶ **n.** the fruit of the oak, a smooth oval nut in a rough cuplike base.
– ORIGIN Old English *æcern*, of Germanic origin; related to Dutch *aker*, also to ACRE, later associated with OAK and CORN[1].

a·corn bar·na·cle ▶ **n.** a stalkless barnacle that attaches itself to a variety of surfaces including rocks, ships, and marine animals. Large numbers of individuals may form a heavy encrustation that can affect the progress of a ship. ● Genus *Balanus*, family Balanidae.

a·corn squash ▶ **n.** a winter squash, typically of a dark green variety, with a longitudinally ridged rind.

a·corn worm ▶ **n.** a burrowing wormlike marine animal of shallow waters. Its body consists of a proboscis, a collar, and a long trunk with gill slits, and contains a notochordlike structure. ● Class Enteropneusta, phylum Hemichordata.

a·cot·y·le·don /āˌkätlˈēdn/ ▶ **n.** a plant with no distinct seed leaves, esp. a fern or moss.
– DERIVATIVES **a·cot·y·le·don·ous adj.**
– ORIGIN mid 18th cent.: from modern Latin plural *acotyledones* (see A-[1], COTYLEDON).

a·cous·tic /əˈko͞ostik/ ▶ **adj.** [attrib.] **1** relating to sound or the sense of hearing: *dogs have a much greater acoustic range than humans.* ■ (of building materials) used for soundproofing or modifying sound: *acoustic tiles.* ■ (of an explosive mine or other weapon) able to be set off by sound waves.
2 (of music or musical instruments) not having electrical amplification: *acoustic guitar.* ■ (of a person or group) playing such instruments.
▶ **n. 1** (usu. **acoustics**) the properties or qualities of a room or building that determine how sound is transmitted in it: *Symphony Hall has perfect acoustics.*
2 (**acoustics**) [treated as sing.] the branch of physics concerned with the properties of sound.
3 a musical instrument without electrical amplification, typically a guitar.
– DERIVATIVES **a·cous·ti·cal adj.**, **a·cous·ti·cal·ly** /-ik(ə)lē/ **adv.**
– ORIGIN mid 17th cent.: from Greek *akoustikos*, from *akouein* 'hear.'

a·cous·tic cou·pler ▶ **n.** Electronics see COUPLER.

ac·ous·ti·cian /ˌako͞oˈstisHən/ ▶ **n.** an expert in the branch of physics concerned with the properties of sound.

a·cous·tic im·ped·ance ▶ **n.** Physics the ratio of the pressure over an imaginary surface in a sound wave to the rate of particle flow across the surface.

a·cous·tic shock ▶ **n.** damaged hearing suffered by the user of a listening device as a result of sudden excessive noise.

ac·quaint /əˈkwānt/ ▶ **v.** [with obj.] (**acquaint someone with**) make someone aware of or familiar with: *new staff should be acquainted with fire exit routes | you need to* ***acquaint yourself with*** *the house style.* ■ (**be acquainted**) be an acquaintance: *I am not* ***acquainted with*** *any young lady of that name | I'll leave you two to* ***get acquainted****.*
– ORIGIN Middle English: from Old French *acointier* 'make known,' from late Latin *accognitare*, from Latin *accognoscere*, from *ad-* 'to' + *cognoscere* 'come to know.'

ac·quaint·ance /əˈkwāntns/ ▶ **n. 1** a person's knowledge or experience of something: *the students had little* ***acquaintance with*** *the language.* ■ one's slight knowledge of or friendship with someone: *I renewed my* ***acquaintance with*** *Herbert | most men of her acquaintance were in uniform now.*
2 a person one knows slightly, but who is not a close friend: *a wide circle of friends and acquaintances.* ■ such people considered collectively: *his extensive acquaintance included Oscar Wilde and Yeats.*
– PHRASES **make the acquaintance of** (or **make someone's acquaintance**) meet someone for the first time and become only slightly familiar: *they are anxious to make your acquaintance.*
– DERIVATIVES **ac·quaint·ance·ship** /-ˌsHip/ **n.**
– ORIGIN Middle English (in the sense 'mutual knowledge, being acquainted'): from Old French *acointance*, from *acointier* 'make known' (see ACQUAINT).

ac·quaint·ance rape ▶ **n.** rape by a person who is known to the victim.

ac·qui·esce /ˌakwēˈes/ ▶ **v.** [no obj.] accept something reluctantly but without protest: *Sara* ***acquiesced in*** *his decision.*
– ORIGIN early 17th cent.: from Latin *acquiescere*, from *ad-* 'to, at' + *quiescere* 'to rest.'

ac·qui·es·cence /ˌakwēˈesəns/ ▶ **n.** the reluctant acceptance of something without protest: *in silent acquiescence, she rose to her feet.*

ac·qui·es·cent /ˌakwēˈesənt/ ▶ **adj.** ready to accept something without protest, or to do what someone else wants: *the unions were acquiescent and there was no overt conflict.*
– ORIGIN early 17th cent.: from Latin *acquiescent-* 'remaining at rest,' from the verb *acquiescere* (see ACQUIESCE).

ac·quire /əˈkwī(ə)r/ ▶ **v.** [with obj.] buy or obtain (an object or asset) for oneself. ■ learn or develop (a skill, habit, or quality): *you must acquire the rudiments of Greek | I've never acquired a taste for whiskey.* ■ achieve (a particular reputation) as a result of one's behavior or activities.
– PHRASES **acquired taste 1** a thing that one has come to like only through experience: *pumpkin pie is an acquired taste.* **2** a liking of this kind: *an acquired taste for tobacco.*
– DERIVATIVES **ac·quir·a·ble adj.**, **ac·quir·er n.**
– ORIGIN late Middle English *acquere*, from Old French *aquerre*, based on Latin *acquirere* 'get in addition,' from *ad-* 'to' + *quaerere* 'seek.' The English spelling was modified (*c.*1600) by association with the Latin word.

ac·quired char·ac·ter·is·tic (also **acquired character**) ▶ **n.** Biology a modification or change in an organ or tissue during the lifetime of an organism due to use, disuse, or environmental effects, and not inherited.

ac·quired im·mune de·fi·cien·cy syn·drome see **AIDS**.

ac·quire·ment /əˈkwī(ə)rmənt/ ▶ **n.** the action of acquiring: *the acquirement of self control.* ■ something acquired, typically a skill.

ac·qui·si·tion /ˌakwəˈzisHən/ ▶ **n. 1** an asset or object bought or obtained, typically by a library or museum. ■ an act of purchase of one company by another: *there were many acquisitions among travel agents | expanding by growth or acquisition.* ■ buying or obtaining an asset or object: *Western culture places a high value on material acquisition.*
2 the learning or developing of a skill, habit, or quality: *the acquisition of management skills.*
– ORIGIN late Middle English (in the sense 'act of acquiring something'): from Latin *acquisitio(n-)*, from the verb *acquirere* (see ACQUIRE).

ac·quis·i·tive /əˈkwizitiv/ ▶ **adj.** excessively interested in acquiring money or material things.
– DERIVATIVES **ac·quis·i·tive·ly adv.**
– ORIGIN mid 19th cent.: from French *acquisitif, -tive*, from late Latin *acquisitivus*. from Latin *acquisit-* 'acquired,' from the verb *acquirere* (see ACQUIRE).

ac·quis·i·tive·ness /əˈkwizitivnis/ ▶ **n.** excessive interest in acquiring money or material things: *a culture of acquisitiveness permeated his administration.*

ac·quit /əˈkwit/ ▶ **v.** (**acquits, acquitting, acquitted**) **1** [with obj.] (usu. **be acquitted**) free (someone) from a criminal charge by a verdict of not guilty: *she was acquitted on all counts | the jury* ***acquitted*** *him* ***of*** *murder.*
2 (**acquit oneself**) conduct oneself or perform in a specified way: *all the young women in the contest acquitted themselves well.* ■ (**acquit oneself of**) archaic discharge (a duty or responsibility): *they acquitted themselves of their charge with vigilance.*
– ORIGIN Middle English (originally in the sense 'pay a debt, discharge a liability'): from Old French *acquiter*, from medieval Latin *acquitare* 'pay a debt,' from *ad-* 'to' + *quitare* 'set free.'

ac·quit·tal /əˈkwitl/ ▶ **n.** a judgment that a person is not guilty of the crime with which the person has been charged: *the trial resulted in an acquittal | the women felt their chances of acquittal were poor.*

ac·quit·tance /əˈkwitns/ ▶ **n.** Law, dated a written receipt attesting the settlement of a fine or debt.
– ORIGIN Middle English: from Old French, from *aquiter* 'discharge (a debt)' (see ACQUIT).

a·cra·sia /əˈkrāzH(ē)ə/ ▶ **n.** variant spelling of AKRASIA.

A·cre 1 /ˈäkər, ˈākər/ an industrial seaport of Israel; pop. 46,300 (est. 2008). Also called **Akko**.
2 /ˈäkrə, ˈäkrā/ a state in western Brazil, on the border with Peru; capital, Rio Branco.

a·cre /ˈākər/ ▶ **n.** a unit of land area equal to 4,840 square yards (0.405 hectare): [as modifier] *a 15-acre estate.* ■ (**acres of**) informal a large extent or amount of something: *acres of space.*
– DERIVATIVES **a·cred** /ˈākərd/ **adj.** [in combination:] *a many-acred park.*
– ORIGIN Old English *æcer* (denoting the amount of land a yoke of oxen could plow in a day), of Germanic origin; related to Dutch *akker* and German *Acker* 'field,' from an Indo-European root shared by Sanskrit *ajra* 'field,' Latin *ager*, and Greek *agros*.

a·cre·age /ˈāk(ə)rij/ ▶ **n.** an area of land, typically when used for agricultural purposes, but not necessarily measured in acres: *a 35% increase in net acreage.*

a·cre-foot ▶ **n.** (pl. **acre-feet**) a unit of volume equal to the volume of a sheet of water one acre (0.405 hectare) in area and one foot (30.48 cm) in depth; 43,560 cubic feet (1233.5 cu m).

ac·rid /ˈakrid/ ▶ **adj.** having an irritatingly strong and unpleasant taste or smell: *acrid fumes.* ■ angry and bitter: *an acrid farewell.*
– DERIVATIVES **a·crid·i·ty** /əˈkriditē/ **n.**, **ac·rid·ly adv.**
– ORIGIN early 18th cent.: formed irregularly from Latin *acer, acri-* 'sharp, pungent' + -ID[1], probably influenced by *acid*.

ac·ri·dine /ˈakriˌdēn/ ▶ **n.** Chemistry a colorless solid compound obtained from coal tar, used in the manufacture of dyes and drugs. ● Chem. formula: $C_{13}H_9N$.
– ORIGIN late 19th cent.: coined in German from ACRID + -INE[4].

ac·ri·fla·vine /ˌakrəˈflāvēn/ ▶ **n.** a bright orange-red dye derived from acridine, used as an antiseptic.
– ORIGIN early 20th cent.: formed irregularly from ACRIDINE and FLAVINE.

Ac·ri·lan /ˈakrəˌlan/ ▶ **n.** trademark a synthetic acrylic textile fiber.
– ORIGIN 1950s: from ACRYLIC + Latin *lana* 'wool.'

ac·ri·mo·ni·ous /ˌakrəˈmōnēəs/ ▶ **adj.** (typically of speech or a debate) angry and bitter: *an acrimonious dispute about wages.*
– DERIVATIVES **ac·ri·mo·ni·ous·ly adv.**
– ORIGIN early 17th cent. (in the sense 'bitter, pungent'): from ACRIMONY + -OUS.

ac·ri·mo·ny /ˈakrəˌmōnē/ ▶ **n.** bitterness or ill feeling: *a quagmire of lawsuits, acrimony, and finger-pointing.*
– ORIGIN mid 16th cent. (in the sense 'bitter taste or smell'): from French *acrimonie* or Latin *acrimonia*, from *acer, acri-* 'pungent, acrid.'

ac·ro·bat /ˈakrəˌbat/ ▶ **n. 1** an entertainer who performs gymnastic feats.
2 a person noted for constant change of mind, allegiance, etc.
– ORIGIN early 19th cent.: from French *acrobate*, from Greek *akrobatēs*, from *akrobatos* 'walking on tiptoe,' from *akron* 'tip' + *bainein* 'to walk.'

ac·ro·bat·ic /ˌakrəˈbatik/ ▶ **adj.** performing, involving, or adept at spectacular gymnastic feats: *an acrobatic dive.*
– DERIVATIVES **ac·ro·bat·i·cal·ly** /-ik(ə)lē/ **adv.**

ac·ro·bat·ics /ˌakrəˈbatiks/ ▶ **plural n.** [usu. treated as sing.] gymnastic feats: figurative *goes through all sorts of financial acrobatics to make the monthly payments.*

ac·ro·cy·a·no·sis /ˌakrōˌsīəˈnōsis/ ▶ **n.** Medicine bluish or purple coloring of the hands and feet caused by slow circulation.
– ORIGIN late 19th cent.: from Greek *akron* 'tip' + CYANOSIS.

ac·ro·lect /ˈakrəˌlekt/ ▶ **n.** Linguistics the most prestigious dialect or variety of a particular language (used esp. in the study of Creoles). Compare with BASILECT, MESOLECT.
– DERIVATIVES **ac·ro·lec·tal** /akrəˈlektl/ **adj.**
– ORIGIN 1960s: from Greek *akron* 'summit' + *-lect* as in *dialect*.

ac·ro·meg·a·ly /ˌakrōˈmegəlē/ ▶ **n.** Medicine abnormal growth of the hands, feet, and face, caused by overproduction of growth hormone by the pituitary gland.
– DERIVATIVES **ac·ro·me·gal·ic** /-məˈgalik/ **adj.**
– ORIGIN late 19th cent.: coined in French from Greek *akron* 'tip, extremity' + *megas, megal-* 'great.'

ac·ro·nym /ˈakrəˌnim/ ▶ **n.** an abbreviation formed from the initial letters of other words and pronounced as a word (e.g., *ASCII, NASA*).
– ORIGIN 1940s: from Greek *akron* 'end, tip' + *onuma* 'name,' on the pattern of *homonym*.

a·crop·e·tal /əˈkräpitl/ ▶ **adj.** Botany (of growth or development) upward from the base or point of attachment. The opposite of BASIPETAL. ■ (of the movement of dissolved substances) outward toward the shoot and root apexes.
– DERIVATIVES **a·crop·e·tal·ly adv.**
– ORIGIN late 19th cent.: from Greek *akron* 'tip' + Latin *petere* 'seek.'

ac·ro·pho·bi·a /ˌakrəˈfōbēə/ ▶ **n.** extreme or irrational fear of heights.
– DERIVATIVES **ac·ro·pho·bic** /-ˈfōbik/ **adj. & n.**
– ORIGIN late 19th cent.: from Greek *akron* 'summit' + -PHOBIA.

a·crop·o·lis /əˈkräpəlis/ ▶ **n.** a citadel or fortified part of an ancient Greek city, typically built on a hill. ■ (**the Acropolis**) the ancient citadel at Athens, containing the Parthenon and other notable buildings, mostly dating from the 5th century BC.
– ORIGIN Greek, from *akron* 'summit' + *polis* 'city.'

a·cross /əˈkrôs, əˈkräs/ ▶ **prep. & adv.** from one side to the other of (something). ■ expressing movement over a place or region: *I ran across the street* | *traveling across Europe* | [as adv.] *he had swum across.* ■ expressing position or orientation: *they lived across the street from one another* | *the bridge across the river* | [as adv.] *he looked across at me* | *halfway across, Jenny jumped.* ■ [as adv.] used with an expression of measurement: *can grow to 4 feet across.* ■ [as adv.] with reference to a crossword puzzle answer that reads horizontally: *19 across.*
– PHRASES **across from** opposite: *she sat across from me.* **across the board** applying to all: *the cutbacks might be across the board.* ■ (in horse racing) denoting a bet in which equal amounts are staked on the same horse to win, place, or show in a race.
– ORIGIN Middle English (as an adverb meaning 'in the form of a cross'): from Old French *a croix, en croix* 'in or on a cross,' later regarded as being from A-² + CROSS.

a·cros·tic /əˈkrôstik, əˈkräs-/ ▶ **n.** a poem, word puzzle, or other composition in which certain letters in each line form a word or words.
– ORIGIN late 16th cent.: from French *acrostiche*, from Greek *akrostikhis*, from *akron* 'end' + *stikhos* 'row, line of verse.' The spelling change was due to association with -IC.

A·crux /ˈāˌkrəks/ the star Alpha Crucis, the brightest star in the Southern Cross (Crux). It is the twelfth brightest star in the sky.
– ORIGIN from *A* for 'alpha' + CRUX.

a·cryl·a·mide /əˈkriləˌmīd, ˌakrəˈlamīd/ ▶ **n.** Chemistry a colorless crystalline solid that readily forms water-soluble polymers. ● The amide of acrylic acid; chem. formula: $CH_2{=}CHCONH_2$.
– ORIGIN late 19th cent.: from ACRYLIC + AMIDE.

a·cryl·ic /əˈkrilik/ ▶ **adj.** (of synthetic resins and textile fibers) made from polymers of acrylic acid or acrylates: *a red acrylic sweater.* ■ of, relating to, or denoting paints based on acrylic resin as a medium: *acrylic colors* | *an acrylic painting.*
▶ **n. 1** an acrylic textile fiber: *a sweater in four-ply acrylic.*
2 (often **acrylics**) an acrylic paint: *washes of white acrylic.*
– ORIGIN mid 19th cent.: from the liquid aldehyde *acrolein* (from Latin *acer, acri-* 'pungent' + *ol(eum)* 'oil' + -IN¹) + -YL + -IC.

a·cryl·ic ac·id ▶ **n.** Chemistry a pungent liquid organic acid that can be polymerized to make synthetic resins. ● Chem. formula: $CH_2CH{=}COOH$.
– DERIVATIVES **ac·ry·late** /ˈakrəˌlāt/ **n.**

ac·ry·lo·ni·trile /ˌakrəlōˈnītril, -trēl, -trīl/ ▶ **n.** Chemistry a pungent, toxic liquid, used in making artificial fibers and other polymers. ● The nitrile of acrylic acid: chem. formula: $CH_2{=}CHCN$.

ACT ▶ **abbr.** ■ American College Test. ■ Australian Capital Territory.

act /akt/ ▶ **v.** [no obj.] **1** take action; do something: *they urged Washington to act* | [with infinitive] *governments must act to reduce pollution.* ■ (**act on**) take action according to or in the light of: *I shall certainly act on his suggestion.* ■ (**act for**) take action in order to bring about: *one's ability to act for community change.* ■ (**act for/on behalf of**) represent (someone) on a contractual, legal, or paid basis: *he chose an attorney to act for him.* ■ (**act from/out of**) be motivated by: *you acted from greed.*
2 [with adverbial] behave in the way specified: *they followed the man who was seen acting suspiciously* | *he acts as if he owned the place.* ■ (**act as/like**) behave in the manner of: *try to act like civilized adults.*
3 (**act as**) fulfill the function or serve the purpose of: *they need volunteers to act as foster parents.* ■ have the effect of: *a five-year sentence will act as a deterrent.*
4 take effect; have a particular effect: *bacteria* ***act on*** *proteins and sugar.*
5 perform a fictional role in a play, movie, or television production: *she acted in her first professional role at the age of six.* ■ [with obj.] perform (a part or role): *he acted the role of the dragon* | *he got the chance to* ***act out*** *other people's jobs.* ■ [with complement] behave so as to appear to be; pretend to be: *I acted dumb at first.* ■ [with obj.] (**act something out**) perform a narrative as if it were a play: *encouraging students to act out the stories.* ■ [with obj.] (**act something out**) Psychoanalysis express repressed or unconscious feelings in overt behavior: *the impulses of hatred and killing which some human beings act out.*
▶ **n. 1** a thing done; a deed: *a criminal act* | *the act of writing down one's thoughts* | *an act of heroism.*
2 [in sing.] a pretense: *she was* ***putting on an act*** *and laughing a lot.* ■ [with adj. or noun modifier] a particular type of behavior or routine: *he did his Sir Galahad act.*
3 Law a written ordinance of Congress, or another legislative body; a statute: *the act to abolish slavery.* ■ a document attesting a legal transaction. ■ (often **acts**) dated the recorded decisions or proceedings of a committee or an academic body.
4 a main division of a play, ballet, or opera. ■ a set performance: *her one-woman poetry act.* ■ a performing group: *an act called the Apple Blossom Sisters.*
– PHRASES **act of God** an instance of uncontrollable natural forces in operation (often used in insurance claims). **act of grace** a privilege or concession that cannot be claimed as a right. **catch someone in the act** (usu. **be caught in the act**) surprise someone in the process of doing something wrong: *the thieves were caught in the act.* **clean up one's act** behave in a more acceptable manner. **get one's act together** informal organize oneself in the manner required in order to achieve something. **get** (or **be**) **in on the act** informal become or be involved in a particular activity, in order to gain profit or advantage. **in the act of** in the process of: *they photographed him in the act of reading other people's mail.* **read someone the Riot Act** see RIOT ACT. **a tough** (or **hard**) **act to follow** an achievement or performance that sets a standard regarded as being difficult for others to measure up to.
– PHRASAL VERBS **act out** misbehave, esp. when unhappy or stressed: *many children who act out while awaiting placement in a health care facility end up in juvenile detention.* **act up** (of a thing) fail to function properly: *the plane's engine was acting up.* ■ (of a person) misbehave.
– DERIVATIVES **act·a·bil·i·ty** /ˌaktəˈbilitē/ **n.** (sense 5 of the verb), **act·a·ble adj.** (sense 5 of the verb).
– ORIGIN late Middle English: from Latin *actus* 'event, thing done,' *act-* 'done,' from the verb *agere*, reinforced by the French noun *acte*.

Ac·tae·on /akˈtēən/ Greek Mythology a hunter who, because he accidentally saw Artemis bathing, was changed into a stag and killed by his own hounds.

ac·tant /ˈaktənt/ ▶ **n.** (in literary theory) a person, creature, or object playing any of a set of active roles in a narrative: *the room has become an actant, a surrogate for the heroine herself.*

ACTH ▶ **abbr.** Biochemistry adrenocorticotropic (or adrenocorticotrophic) hormone.

ac·tin /ˈaktən/ ▶ **n.** Biochemistry a protein that forms (together with myosin) the contractile filaments of muscle cells, and is also involved in motion in other types of cells.
– ORIGIN 1940: from Greek *aktis, aktin-* 'ray' + -IN¹.

act·ing /ˈaktiNG/ ▶ **n.** the art or occupation of performing in plays, movies, or television productions: *she studied acting in New York.*
▶ **adj.** [attrib.] temporarily doing the duties of another person: *acting director.*

ac·tin·i·an /akˈtinēən/ ▶ **n.** Zoology a sea anemone.
– ORIGIN mid 18th cent.: from the modern Latin genus name *Actinia* (from Greek *aktis, aktin-* 'ray') + -AN.

ac·tin·ic /akˈtinik/ ▶ **adj.** [attrib.] (of light or lighting) able to cause photochemical reactions, as in photography, through having a significant short wavelength or ultraviolet component. ■ relating to or caused by such light: *actinic degradation.*
– DERIVATIVES **ac·tin·ism** /ˈaktəˌnizəm/ **n.**
– ORIGIN mid 19th cent.: from Greek *aktis, aktin-* 'ray' + -IC.

ac·ti·nide /ˈaktəˌnīd/ ▶ **n.** Chemistry any of the series of fifteen metallic elements from actinium (atomic number 89) to lawrencium (atomic number 103) in the periodic table. They are all radioactive, the heavier members being extremely unstable and not of natural occurrence.
– ORIGIN 1940s: from ACTINIUM + -IDE, on the pattern of *lanthanide*.

ac·tin·i·um /akˈtinēəm/ ▶ **n.** the chemical element of atomic number 89, a radioactive metallic element of the actinide series. It is rare in nature, occurring as an impurity in uranium ores. (Symbol: **Ac**)
– ORIGIN early 20th cent.: from Greek *aktis, aktin-* 'ray' + -IUM.

ac·ti·nom·e·ter /ˌaktəˈnämitər/ ▶ **n.** Physics an instrument for measuring the intensity of radiation, typically ultraviolet radiation.
– ORIGIN mid 19th cent.: from Greek *aktis, aktin-* 'ray' + -METER.

ac·tin·o·mor·phic /ˌaktənōˈmôrfik/ ▶ **adj.** Biology characterized by radial symmetry, such as a starfish or the flower of a daisy. Compare with ZYGOMORPHIC.
– DERIVATIVES **ac·tin·o·mor·phy** /akˈtinəˌmôrfē/ **n.**
– ORIGIN late 19th cent.: from Greek *aktis, aktin-* 'ray' + *morphē* 'form' + -IC.

ac·tin·o·my·cete /ˌaktənōˈmīˌsēt, -mīˈsēt/ ▶ **n.** a bacterium of an order of typically nonmotile filamentous form. They include the economically important streptomycetes, and were formerly regarded as fungi. ● Order Actinomycetales; Gram-positive.
– ORIGIN 1920s (originally only in the plural): modern Latin, from Greek *aktis, aktin-* 'ray' + *mukētes*, plural of *mukēs* 'fungus.'

ac·tion /ˈakSHən/ ▶ **n. 1** the fact or process of doing something, typically to achieve an aim: *he vowed to take tougher action against persistent offenders* | *if there is a breach of regulations, we will* ***take action.*** ■ the way in which something such as a chemical has an effect or influence: *the seeds require the catalytic action of water to release hotness.* ■ armed conflict: *servicemen listed as* ***missing in action*** *during the war.* ■ a military engagement: *a rearguard action.* ■ the events represented in a story or play: *the action is set in the country.* ■ informal exciting or notable activity: *the nonstop action of mountain biking* | *people in the media want to be* ***where the action is.*** ■ informal betting. ■ [as exclamation] used by a movie director as a command to begin: *lights, camera, action!*
2 a thing done; an act: *she frequently questioned his actions* | *I would not be responsible for my actions if I saw him.* ■ a legal process; a lawsuit: *an action for damages.* ■ a gesture or movement: *his actions emphasized his words.*
3 a manner or style of doing something, typically the way in which a mechanism works or a person moves: *the weapon has speed and smooth action.*

PRONUNCIATION KEY ə *ago, up;* ər *over, fur;* a *hat;* ā *ate;* ä *car;* e *let;* ē *see;* i *fit;* ī *by;* NG *sing;* ō *go;* ô *law, for;* oi *toy;* o͝o *good;* o͞o *goo;* ou *out;* TH *thin;* T͟H *then;* ZH *vision*

a

■ the mechanism that makes a machine or instrument work: *a piano with an escapement action.*
– PHRASES **go into action** start work or activity. **in action** engaged in a certain activity; in operation. **out of action** temporarily unable to engage in a certain activity; not working: *a heart attack put him out of action | the ship was out of action for 16 days.* **put into action** put into effect; carry out.
– ORIGIN late Middle English: via Old French from Latin *actio(n-)*, from *agere* 'do, act.'

ac·tion·a·ble /'akSHənəbəl/ ▶ **adj.** Law **1** giving sufficient reason to take legal action: *slanderous remarks are actionable.*
2 able to be done or acted on; having practical value: *insightful and actionable information on the effect advertising is having on your brand.*

ac·tion com·mit·tee (also **action group**) ▶ **n.** a body formed to campaign politically, typically on a particular issue.

ac·tion fig·ure ▶ **n.** a doll representing a person or fictional character known for vigorous action, such as a soldier or superhero. The figure typically is posable, with jointed limbs.

ac·tion paint·ing ▶ **n.** a technique and style of abstract painting in which paint is randomly splashed, thrown, or poured on the canvas. It was made famous by Jackson Pollock, and formed part of the more general movement of abstract expressionism.

ac·tion point ▶ **n.** a specific proposal for action to be taken, typically one arising from a discussion or meeting.

ac·tion po·ten·tial ▶ **n.** Physiology the change in electrical potential associated with the passage of an impulse along the membrane of a muscle cell or nerve cell.

Ac·ti·um, Bat·tle of /'aktēəm, 'akSHēəm/ a naval battle which took place in 31 BC off the promontory of Actium in western Greece, in the course of which Octavian defeated Mark Antony.

ac·ti·vate /'aktə,vāt/ ▶ **v.** [with obj.] make (something) active or operative: *fumes from cooking are enough to activate the alarm.* ■ convert (a substance, molecule, etc.) into a reactive form: (as adj. **activated**) *activated chlorine.*
– DERIVATIVES **ac·ti·va·tion** /,aktə'vāSHən/ **n.**, **ac·ti·va·tor** /-,vātər/ **n.**

ac·ti·vat·ed car·bon (also **activated charcoal**) ▶ **n.** charcoal that has been heated or otherwise treated to increase its adsorptive power.

ac·ti·vat·ed sludge ▶ **n.** aerated sewage containing aerobic microorganisms that help to break it down.

ac·ti·va·tion a·nal·y·sis /,aktə'vāSHən/ ▶ **n.** Chemistry a technique of analysis in which atoms of a particular element in a sample are made radioactive, typically by irradiation with neutrons, and their concentration is then determined radiologically.

ac·ti·va·tion en·er·gy ▶ **n.** Chemistry the minimum quantity of energy that the reacting species must possess in order to undergo a specified reaction.

ac·tive /'aktiv/ ▶ **adj. 1** (of a person) engaging or ready to engage in physically energetic pursuits: *I needed to change my lifestyle and become more active.* ■ moving or tending to move about vigorously or frequently: *active fish need a larger tank.* ■ characterized by energetic activity: *they enjoyed an active social life.* ■ (of a person's mind or imagination) alert and lively.
2 doing things for an organization, cause, or campaign, rather than simply giving it one's support: *she was an active member of the church | he had never been very active in the affairs of the institute | he enjoyed the active support of the government.* ■ (of a person) participating or engaged in a particular sphere or activity: *a politically active student body.* ■ [predic.] (of a person or animal) pursuing their usual occupation or activity, typically at a particular place or time: *tigers are active mainly at night.*
3 working; operative: *the old mill was active until 1960.* ■ (of a bank account) in continuous use. ■ (of an electrical circuit) capable of modifying its state or characteristics automatically in response to input or feedback. ■ (of a volcano) currently erupting, or that has erupted within historical times. Often contrasted with DORMANT or EXTINCT. ■ (of a disease) in which the symptoms are manifest; not in remission or latent: *active colitis.* ■ having a chemical or biological effect on something: *350 active ingredients have been banned from pesticides.*
4 Grammar relating to or denoting the voice that attributes the action of a verb to the person or thing from which it logically proceeds (e.g., of the verbs in *guns kill* and *we saw him*). The opposite of PASSIVE.
▶ **n.** Grammar an active form of a verb. ■ (**the active**) the active voice.
– DERIVATIVES **ac·tive·ly adv.**, **ac·tive·ness n.**
– ORIGIN Middle English (in the sense 'preferring action to contemplation'): from Latin *activus*, from *act-* 'done,' from the verb *agere*.

ac·tive bar·ri·er ▶ **n.** a barrier that allows passage of defined agents while preventing or impeding others, in particular: ■ a security barrier that responds to attempted entries with sensors or personnel. ■ a physical or chemical barrier that intercepts contaminants, debris, or other unwanted substances.

ac·tive du·ty ▶ **n.** full-time service in the police or armed forces. ■ the playing of a direct role in the operational work of the police or armed forces as opposed to doing administrative work.

ac·tive im·mu·ni·ty ▶ **n.** Physiology the immunity that results from the production of antibodies by the immune system in response to the presence of an antigen. Compare with PASSIVE IMMUNITY.

ac·tive lay·er ▶ **n.** Geography the seasonally thawed surface layer above permafrost.

ac·tive list ▶ **n.** a list of the officers in an armed service who are liable to be called on for duty.

ac·tive ma·trix ▶ **n.** Electronics a display system in which each pixel is individually controlled.

ac·tive serv·ice ▶ **n.** direct participation in warfare as a member of the armed forces.

ac·tive site ▶ **n.** Biochemistry a region on an enzyme that binds to a protein or other substance during a reaction.

ac·tive trans·port ▶ **n.** Biology the movement of ions or molecules across a cell membrane into a region of higher concentration, assisted by enzymes and requiring energy.

ac·tive·wear /'aktiv,we(ə)r/ ▶ **n.** clothing designed to be worn for sports, exercise, and outdoor activities.

ac·tiv·ism /'aktə,vizəm/ ▶ **n.** the policy or action of using vigorous campaigning to bring about political or social change.
– DERIVATIVES **ac·tiv·ist n. & adj.**

ac·tiv·i·ty /ak'tivitē/ ▶ **n.** (pl. **activities**) **1** the condition in which things are happening or being done: *there has been a sustained level of activity in the economy | 16, they say, is too young for sexual activity.* ■ busy or vigorous action or movement: *the room was a hive of activity.*
2 (usu. **activities**) a thing that a person or group does or has done: *the firm's marketing activities.* ■ a recreational pursuit or pastime: *a range of sports activities.* ■ (**activities**) actions taken by a group in order to achieve their aims: *the police were investigating anarchist activities.*
3 the degree to which something displays its characteristic property or behavior: *abnormal liver enzyme activities.* ■ Chemistry a thermodynamic quantity representing the effective concentration of a particular component in a solution or other system, equal to its concentration multiplied by an **activity coefficient**.
– ORIGIN late Middle English: from French *activité* or late Latin *activitas*, from Latin *act-* 'done,' from the verb *agere*.

act of con·tri·tion ▶ **n.** (in the Roman Catholic Church) a penitential prayer. ■ something done to make amends for an offense.

ac·to·my·o·sin /,aktə'mīəsin/ ▶ **n.** Biochemistry a complex of actin and myosin of which the contractile protein filaments of muscle tissue are composed.
– ORIGIN 1940s: from ACTIN + MYOSIN.

ac·tor /'aktər/ ▶ **n.** a person whose profession is acting on the stage, in movies, or on television. ■ a person who behaves in a way that is not genuine: *in war one must be a good actor.* ■ a participant in an action or process: *employers are key actors within industrial relations.*
– ORIGIN late Middle English (originally denoting an agent or administrator): from Latin, 'doer, actor,' from *agere* 'do, act.' The theater sense dates from the 16th cent.

ac·tor·ly /'aktərlē/ ▶ **adj.** characteristic of an actor or actress: *he seems to lack the actorly range that the role requires.* ■ affected or excessively dramatic: *she eschews the actorly flourishes of her co-star.*

Ac·tors' Stu·di·o an acting workshop in New York City, founded in 1947 by Elia Kazan and others, and a leading center of method acting.

ac·tress /'aktris/ ▶ **n.** a female actor.

ac·tress·y /'aktrisē/ ▶ **adj.** characteristic of an actress; stereotypically being self-consciously theatrical or emotionally volatile: *her actressy manner was an irritant to the others.*

Acts /akts/ (also **Acts of the Apostles**) a New Testament book immediately following the Gospels and relating the history of the early Church.

ac·tu·al /'akCHo͞oəl/ ▶ **adj. 1** existing in fact; typically as contrasted with what was intended, expected, or believed: *the estimate was much less than the actual cost | those were his actual words.* ■ used to emphasize the important aspect of something: *the book could be condensed into half the space, but what of the actual content?*
2 existing now; current: *using actual income to measure expected income.*
– PHRASES **in actual fact** used to emphasize a comment, typically one that modifies or contradicts a previous statement: *people talk as if he were a monster—in actual fact he was a very kind guy.*
– ORIGIN Middle English: from Old French *actuel* 'active, practical,' from late Latin *actualis*, from *actus* (see ACT).

ac·tu·al·i·ty /,akCHo͞o'alitē/ ▶ **n.** (pl. **actualities**) actual existence, typically as contrasted with what was intended, expected, or believed: *the building looked as impressive in actuality as it did in magazines | a mission was sent to investigate the actuality of the situation.* ■ (**actualities**) existing conditions or facts: *the grim actualities of prison life.*
– ORIGIN late Middle English (in the sense 'activeness'): from Old French *actualite* or medieval Latin *actualitas*, from *actualis* 'active, practical,' from *actus* (see ACT).

ac·tu·al·ize /'akCHo͞oə,līz/ ▶ **v.** [with obj.] make a reality of: *he had actualized his dream and achieved the world record.*
– DERIVATIVES **ac·tu·al·i·za·tion** /,akCHo͞oələ'zāSHən/ **n.**

ac·tu·al·ly /'akCHo͞oəlē/ ▶ **adv. 1** as the truth or facts of a situation; really: *we must pay attention to what young people are actually doing | the time actually worked on a job.*
2 [as sentence adverb] used to emphasize that something someone has said or done is surprising: *he actually expected me to be pleased about it!* ■ used when expressing an opinion, typically one that is not expected: *"Actually," she said icily, "I don't care who you go out with."* ■ used when expressing a contradictory opinion or correcting someone: *"Tom seems to be happy." "He isn't, actually, not any more."* ■ used to introduce a new topic or to add information to a previous statement: *he had a thick Brooklyn accent—he sounded like my grandfather actually.*

ac·tu·ar·y /'akCHo͞o,erē/ ▶ **n.** (pl. **actuaries**) a person who compiles and analyzes statistics and uses them to calculate insurance risks and premiums.
– DERIVATIVES **ac·tu·ar·i·al** /,akCHo͞o'e(ə)rēəl/ **adj.**, **ac·tu·ar·i·al·ly adv.**
– ORIGIN mid 16th cent. (originally denoting a clerk or registrar of a court): from Latin *actuarius* 'bookkeeper,' from *actus* (see ACT). The current sense dates from the mid 19th cent.

ac·tu·ate /'akCHo͞o,āt/ ▶ **v. 1** [with obj.] cause (a machine or device) to operate: *the pendulum actuates an electrical switch.*
2 (usu. **be actuated**) cause (someone) to act in a particular way; motivate: *the defendants were actuated by malice.*
– DERIVATIVES **ac·tu·a·tion** /,akCHo͞o'āSHən/ **n.**, **ac·tu·a·tor** /-'ātər/ **n.**
– ORIGIN late 16th cent.: from medieval Latin *actuat-* 'carried out, caused to operate,' from the verb *actuare*, from Latin *actus* (see ACT). The original sense was 'carry out in practice,' later 'stir into activity, enliven'; sense 1 dates from the mid 17th cent.

ac·tus re·us /,aktəs 'rēəs, 'rāəs/ ▶ **n.** Law action or conduct that is a constituent element of a crime, as opposed to the mental state of the accused. Compare with MENS REA.
– ORIGIN early 20th cent.: Latin, literally 'guilty act.'

a·cu·i·ty /ə'kyo͞oitē/ ▶ **n.** sharpness or keenness of thought, vision, or hearing: *intellectual acuity | visual acuity.*
– ORIGIN late Middle English: from Old French *acuite* or medieval Latin *acuitas*, from Latin *acuere* 'sharpen' (see ACUTE).

a·cu·le·ate /ə'kyo͞olēət, -,āt/ ▶ **adj. 1** Entomology (of an insect) having a sting.
2 Botany sharply pointed; prickly.
▶ **n.** Entomology a stinging insect of a group that includes the bees, wasps, and ants. ● Section Aculeata, suborder Apocrita, order Hymenoptera.
– ORIGIN mid 17th cent.: from Latin *aculeatus*, from *aculeus* 'a sting,' diminutive of *acus* 'needle.'

a·cu·men /ə'kyo͞omən, 'akyə-/ ▶ **n.** the ability to make good judgments and quick decisions, typically in a particular domain: *business acumen.*
– ORIGIN late 16th cent.: from Latin, 'sharpness, point,' from *acuere* 'sharpen' (see ACUTE).

a·cu·mi·nate /ə'kyo͞omənit, -,nāt/ ▶ **adj.** Biology (of a plant or animal structure, e.g., a leaf) tapering to a point.
– ORIGIN late 16th cent.: from late Latin *acuminatus* 'pointed,' from *acuminare* 'sharpen to a point,' from *acuere* 'sharpen' (see ACUTE).

ac·u·pres·sure /ˈakyəˌpresHər/ ▶ **n.** another term for **SHIATSU.**
– ORIGIN 1950s: blend of **ACUPUNCTURE** and **PRESSURE.**

ac·u·punc·ture /ˈakyəˌpəNGkCHər/ ▶ **n.** a system of complementary medicine that involves pricking the skin or tissues with needles, used to alleviate pain and to treat various physical, mental, and emotional conditions. Originating in ancient China, acupuncture is now widely practiced in the West.
– DERIVATIVES **ac·u·punc·tur·ist** /-ist/ **n.**
– ORIGIN late 17th cent.: from Latin *acu* 'with a needle' + **PUNCTURE.**

a·cut·ance /əˈkyo͞otns/ ▶ **n.** the sharpness of a photographic or printed image. ■ a measure of this.
– ORIGIN 1950s: from **ACUTE** + **-ANCE.**

a·cute /əˈkyo͞ot/ ▶ **adj.** **1** (of a bad, difficult, or unwelcome situation or phenomenon) present or experienced to a severe or intense degree: *an acute housing shortage* | *the problem is acute and getting worse.* ■ (of a disease or its symptoms) of short duration but typically severe: *acute appendicitis.* Often contrasted with **CHRONIC.** ■ denoting or designed for patients with such conditions: *acute hospital services* | *acute patients.*
2 having or showing a perceptive understanding or insight: shrewd: *an acute awareness of changing fashions.* ■ (of a physical sense or faculty) highly developed; keen: *an acute sense of smell.*
3 (of an angle) less than 90°. ■ having a sharp end; pointed. ■ (of a sound) high; shrill.
▶ **n.** short for **ACUTE ACCENT.**
– DERIVATIVES **a·cute·ness n.**
– ORIGIN late Middle English (sense 2 of the adjective): from Latin *acutus*, past participle of *acuere* 'sharpen,' from *acus* 'needle.'

a·cute ac·cent ▶ **n.** a mark (´) placed over certain letters in some languages to indicate an alteration of a sound, as of quality, quantity, or pitch, e.g., in *risqué.*

a·cute·ly /əˈkyo͞otlē/ ▶ **adv.** [as submodifier] **1** (with reference to something unpleasant or unwelcome) intensely: *the whole situation was acutely embarrassing.*
2 in a way that shows a perceptive understanding or insight: *we are all* **acutely aware** *of the fragility of our world.*

-acy ▶ **suffix** forming nouns of state or quality: *celibacy* | *lunacy.*
– ORIGIN a branch of the suffix **-CY**, from Latin *-atia* (medieval Latin *-acia*), or from Greek *-ateia*, noun suffixes.

a·cy·clic /āˈsīklik, āˈsik-/ ▶ **adj.** not displaying or forming part of a cycle. ■ (of a woman) not having a menstrual cycle. ■ Chemistry (of a compound or molecule) containing no rings of atoms.

a·cy·clo·vir /āˈsīkləˌvi(ə)r/ ▶ **n.** Medicine an antiviral drug used esp. in the treatment of herpes and AIDS. Also called **ZOVIRAX** (trademark).

ac·yl /ˈasəl/ ▶ **n.** [as modifier] Chemistry a radical of general formula –C(O)R, where R is an alkyl group, derived from a carboxylic acid: *acyl groups.*
– ORIGIN late 19th cent.: formed in German, from Latin *acidus* (see **ACID**) + **-YL.**

ac·yl·ate /ˈasəˌlāt/ ▶ **v.** [with obj.] Chemistry introduce an acyl group into (a molecule or compound): (as adj. **acylated**) *an acylated glycine derivative.*
– DERIVATIVES **ac·yl·a·tion** /ˌasəˈlāsHən/ **n.**

AD ▶ **abbr.** ■ Military active duty. ■ armored division. ■ (usu. AD) Anno Domini (used to indicate that a date comes the specified number of years after the accepted date of Christ's birth). ■ athletic director.

> **USAGE** The abbreviation for Anno Domini, AD, typically is written in small capitals and should be placed before the numerals, as in *AD 375* (not *375 AD*). However, when the date is spelled out, it is normal to write, for example, *the third century AD* (not *AD the third century*). The abbreviation BC (before Christ) appears after the date: *Plato was born in 427 BC*—that is to say, in the fifth century BC. In recent years, some writers have begun using the abbreviations CE (of the Common Era) in place of AD, and BCE (before the Common Era) in place of BC, in consideration of a more secular and international readership.

ad[1] /ad/ ▶ **n.** informal an advertisement.
– ORIGIN mid 19th cent.: abbreviation.

ad[2] ▶ **n.** Tennis, informal short for **ADVANTAGE.**

ad- ▶ **prefix** denoting motion or direction to: *advance* | *adduce.* ■ reduction or change into: *adapt* | *adulterate.* ■ addition, increase, or intensification: *adjunct* | *adhere* | *admixture.*
– ORIGIN from Latin *ad* 'to'; in the 16th cent. the use of *ad-* and its variants was extended to replace *a-* from a different origin such as Latin *ab-* (e.g., *advance*, from French *avancer*, based on late Latin *abante* 'in front').

A/D ▶ **abbr.** Electronics analog to digital.

-ad[1] ▶ **suffix** forming nouns: **1** in collective numerals: *pentad* | *triad.* ■ in groups, periods, or aggregates: *Olympiad.*
2 in names of females in classical mythology, such as *Dryad* and *Naiad.* ■ in names of districts such as *Troad.*
3 in names of poems and similar compositions: *Iliad* | *jeremiad.*
4 forming names of members of some taxonomic groupings: *bromeliad.*
– ORIGIN from Greek *-ad-* (from nouns ending in *-as*).

-ad[2] ▶ **suffix** forming nouns such as *ballad, salad.* Compare with **-ADE**[1].
– ORIGIN representing the French noun ending *-ade.*

A·da /ˈādə/ ▶ **n.** a high-level computer programming language used esp. in real-time computerized control systems, e.g., for aircraft navigation.
– ORIGIN 1980s: from the name of *Ada* Lovelace (see **LOVELACE**[1]).

ad·age /ˈadij/ ▶ **n.** a proverb or short statement expressing a general truth: *the old adage "out of sight out of mind."*
– ORIGIN mid 16th cent.: from French, from Latin *adagium* 'saying,' based on an early form of *aio* 'I say.'

a·da·gio /əˈdäjō, əˈdäzHēˌō/ Music ▶ **adj. & adv.** (esp. as a direction) in slow tempo.
▶ **n.** (also **Adagio**) (pl. **adagios**) a movement or composition marked to be played adagio.
– ORIGIN Italian, from *ad agio* 'at ease.'

Ad·am[1] /ˈadəm/ (in the biblical and Koranic traditions) the first man. According to the Book of Genesis, Adam was created by God as the progenitor of the human race and lived with Eve in the Garden of Eden.
– PHRASES **not know someone from Adam** not know or be completely unable to recognize the person in question.
– ORIGIN from Hebrew *'āḏām* 'man,' later taken to be a name.

Ad·am[2], Robert (1728–92), Scottish architect and furniture designer. With his brother **James** (1730–94), he was influential in the change from the prevailing Palladian fashion to a neoclassical style.

ad·a·mant /ˈadəmənt/ ▶ **adj.** refusing to be persuaded or to change one's mind: *he is* **adamant** *that he is not going to resign.*
▶ **n.** archaic a legendary rock or mineral to which many, often contradictory, properties were attributed, formerly associated with diamond or lodestone.
– DERIVATIVES **ad·a·mance n.**, **ad·a·man·cy** /-mənsē/ **n.**, **ad·a·mant·ly adv.**
– ORIGIN Old English (as a noun), from Old French *adamaunt-*, via Latin from Greek *adamas, adamant*, 'untamable, invincible' (later used to denote the hardest metal or stone, hence diamond), from *a-* 'not' + *daman* 'to tame.' The phrase *to be adamant* dates from the 1930s, although adjectival use had been implied in such collocations as "an adamant heart" since the 16th cent.

ad·a·man·tine /ˌadəˈmanˌtīn, -tin-, -ˌtēn/ ▶ **adj.** literary unbreakable: *adamantine chains* | figurative *her adamantine will.*

Ad·ams[1] /ˈadəmz/, Abigail (Smith) (1744–1818), US first lady 1797–1801, the wife of President John Adams and mother of President John Quincy Adams. She is noted for her letters that gave an insider's view of the times.

Abigail Adams

Ad·ams[2], Alice (1926–99), US writer and editor. She wrote about women's lives in her novels *Families and Survivors* (1975), *Superior Women* (1984), and *A Southern Exposure* (1995), among others, and in short stories that are collected in such works as *To See You Again* (1982).

Ad·ams[3], Ansel (Easton) (1902–84), US photographer, noted for his black-and-white photographs of American landscapes. Many of his collections, such as *My Camera in the National Parks* (1950) and *This Is the American Earth* (1960), reflect his interest in conservation.

Ad·ams[4], John (1735–1826), 2nd president of the US 1797–1801. A Massachusetts Federalist, he was a delegate to the Continental Congress 1774–78 and helped draft the Declaration of Independence in 1776. With John Jay and Benjamin Franklin, he negotiated the Treaty of Paris, which ended the American Revolution in 1783. Adams was minister to Great Britain 1785–88 before becoming the first vice president of the US 1789–97.

John Adams

Ad·ams[5], John Couch (1819–92), English astronomer. He postulated the existence of an eighth planet in 1843, three years before Le Verrier discovered Neptune.

Ad·ams[6], John Quincy (1767–1848), 6th president of the US 1825–29; a Massachusetts Democratic-Republican; eldest son of President John Adams. His ministerial positions from 1794 to 1801 included appointments to the Netherlands, Portugal, and Prussia. After serving in the US Senate 1803–08, he was minister to Russia, then to England. He helped negotiate the Treaty of Ghent 1814, which ended the War of 1812. As President Monroe's secretary of state 1817–25, he was the chief architect of the Monroe Doctrine. Two of his impassioned causes were the abolition of slavery and the safeguarding of freedom of speech, which defined his post-presidency as a member of the US House of Representatives 1831–48.

John Quincy Adams

Ad·ams[7], Samuel (1722–1803), US patriot. One of the leaders of the Boston Tea Party in 1773, he was active in the pre-Revolution anti-British activities that took place in that city. He served in the First and Second Continental Congresses 1774–75 and was a signer of the Declaration of Independence 1776.

Ad·am's ale ▶ **n.** dated, humorous water.

Ad·am's ap·ple ▶ **n.** the projection at the front of the neck formed by the thyroid cartilage of the larynx, often prominent in men.

Ad·am's Bridge a line of shoals lying between northwestern Sri Lanka and the southeastern coast of Tamil Nadu in India. It separates the Palk Strait from the Gulf of Mannar.

Ad·am's nee·dle (also **Adam's needle-and-thread**) ▶ **n.** a frost-hardy yucca native

Adam's needle

PRONUNCIATION KEY ə *ago, up*; ər *over, fur*; a *hat*; ā *ate*; ä *car*; e *let*; ē *see*; i *fit*; ī *by*; NG *sing*; ō *go*; ô *law, for*; oi *toy*; o͝o *good*; o͞o *goo*; ou *out*; TH *thin*; T͟H *then*; ZH *vision*

to the eastern US, with long leaves that are edged with white threads. ● *Yucca filamentosa*, family Agavaceae.

Ad·am's Peak a mountain in south central Sri Lanka, rising to 7,360 feet (2,243 m). It is regarded as sacred by Buddhists, Hindus, and Muslims.

A·da·na /ˌädəˈnä/ a town in southern Turkey, capital of a province of the same name; pop. 1,366,000 (est. 2007).

a·dapt /əˈdapt/ ▶ **v.** [with obj.] make (something) suitable for a new use or purpose; modify: *hospitals have had to be* ***adapted for*** *modern medical practice* | *the policies can be adapted to suit individual needs and requirements* | (as adj. **adapted**) *mink are well adapted to hunting prey.* ■ [no obj.] become adjusted to new conditions: *a large organization can be slow to adapt to change.* ■ alter (a text) to make it suitable for filming, broadcasting, or the stage: *the miniseries was* ***adapted from*** *Wouk's novel.*
– ORIGIN late Middle English: from French *adapter*, from Latin *adaptare*, from *ad-* 'to' + *aptare* (from *aptus* 'fit').

> **USAGE** Avoid confusing **adapt** with **adopt**. Trouble sometimes arises because in *adapting* to new conditions, an animal or plant can be said to *adopt* something, such as a new color or behavior pattern.

a·dapt·a·ble /əˈdaptəbəl/ ▶ **adj.** able to adjust to new conditions: *rats are highly* ***adaptable to*** *change.* ■ able to be modified for a new use or purpose: *a workforce with adaptable skills.*
– DERIVATIVES **a·dapt·a·bil·i·ty** /əˌdaptəˈbilitē/ **n.**, **a·dapt·a·bly** /-blē/ **adv.**

ad·ap·ta·tion /ˌadapˈtāsHən, ˌadəp-/ ▶ **n.** the action or process of adapting or being adapted: *the adaptation of teaching strategy to meet students' needs* | *adaptations to the school curriculum.* ■ a movie, television drama, or stage play that has been adapted from a written work, typically a novel: *filming her adaptation of a beloved children's book.* ■ Biology a change by which an organism or species becomes better suited to its environment: *living in groups is an adaptation that increases the efficiency of hunting.* ■ the process of making such changes: *biochemical adaptation in parasites.*
– ORIGIN early 17th cent.: from French, from late Latin *adaptatio(n-)*, from Latin *adaptare* (see **ADAPT**).

ad·ap·ta·tion·ism /ˌadapˈtāsHəˌnizəm, ˌadəp-/ ▶ **n.** Biology the belief or assumption, now generally held, that each feature of an organism is the result of evolutionary adaptation for a particular function.
– DERIVATIVES **ad·ap·ta·tion·ist n. & adj.**

a·dapt·er /əˈdaptər/ (also **adaptor**) ▶ **n. 1** a device for connecting pieces of equipment that cannot be connected directly.
2 a person who adapts a text to make it suitable for filming, broadcasting, or the stage.

a·dap·tion /əˈdapsHən/ ▶ **n.** another term for **ADAPTATION**.

a·dapt·ive /əˈdaptiv/ ▶ **adj.** chiefly technical characterized by or given to adaptation: *mutation is ultimately essential for adaptive evolution in all populations.*
– DERIVATIVES **a·dapt·ive·ly adv.**, **a·dapt·iv·i·ty** ▶ **n.**

a·dap·tive ex·pec·ta·tions hy·poth·e·sis ▶ **n.** Economics a hypothesis that supposes that expectations of future values of a variable can be based primarily on its values in the recent past. Compare with **RATIONAL EXPECTATIONS HYPOTHESIS**.

a·dap·tive ra·di·a·tion ▶ **n.** Biology the diversification of a group of organisms into forms filling different ecological niches.

a·dapt·o·gen /əˈdaptəjən/ ▶ **n.** (in herbal medicine) a natural substance considered to help the body adapt to stress and to exert a normalizing effect upon bodily processes. A well-known example is ginseng.
– DERIVATIVES **a·dapt·o·gen·ic** /əˌdaptəˈjenik/ **adj.**
– ORIGIN 1960s: a term used by N. V. Lazarev, Russian scientist, from **ADAPT** + **-GEN**.

A·dar /ˈädär, ˈäˌdär/ ▶ **n.** (in the Jewish calendar) the sixth month of the civil and twelfth of the religious year, usually coinciding with parts of February and March. It is known in leap years as **SECOND ADAR**. ■ an intercalary month preceding this in leap years. Also called **FIRST ADAR**.
– ORIGIN from Hebrew *'ădār*.

ad·ax·i·al /adˈaksēəl/ ▶ **adj.** Botany facing toward the stem of a plant (esp. denoting the upper surface of a leaf). The opposite of **ABAXIAL**.

ADC ▶ **abbr.** ■ aide-de-camp. ■ Aid to Dependent Children. ■ Air Defense Command. ■ analog-to-digital converter.

ADD ▶ **abbr.** ■ analog digital digital, indicating that a music recording was made in analog format before being mastered and stored digitally. ■ attention deficit disorder.

add /ad/ ▶ **v.** [with obj.] **1** join (something) to something else so as to increase the size, number, or amount: *a new wing was* ***added to*** *the building* | *some box offices now* ***add on*** *a handling charge* | (as adj. **added**) *one vitamin tablet daily will give added protection* | [no obj.] *this development* ***added to*** *the problems facing the staff.* ■ [no obj.] (**add up**) increase in amount, number, or degree: *watch those air miles add up!* ■ put or mix (an ingredient) together with another as one of the stages in the preparation of a dish: *add the flour to the eggs, stirring continuously.* ■ put (something) in or on something else so as to improve or alter its quality or nature: *chlorine is added to the water to kill bacteria* | (as adj. **added**) *the fruit juice contains no added sugar.* ■ contribute (an enhancing quality) to something: *the canopy will add a touch of class to your bedroom.*
2 put together (two or more numbers or amounts) to calculate their total value: *they* ***added*** *all the figures* ***up*** | ***add*** *the two numbers* ***together*** | [no obj.] *children learned to add and subtract quickly and accurately.* ■ [no obj.] (**add up to**) amount to: *this adds up to a total of 400 calories* | figurative *these isolated incidents don't add up to a true picture of the situation.* ■ [no obj., usu. with negative] (**add up**) informal seem reasonable or consistent; make sense: *many things in her story didn't add up.*
3 [reporting verb] say as a further remark: [with direct speech] *"I hope we haven't been too much trouble," she added politely* | [with obj.] *we would like to add our congratulations* | [with clause] *he* ***added that*** *few of America's allies would support military action.*
– ORIGIN late Middle English: from Latin *addere*, from *ad-* 'to' + the base of *dare* 'put.'

Ad·dams[1] /ˈadəmz/, Charles (Samuel) (1912–88), US cartoonist, noted for his macabre characters, which were brought to life in the television series *The Addams Family* (1964–66), which was the basis for two movies in the 1990s. His cartoons appeared in *The New Yorker* magazine from 1935.

Ad·dams[2], Jane (1860–1935), US social reformer, feminist, and pacifist. In 1889 she founded Hull House, a center for the care and education of Chicago's poor and a national model for combating urban poverty and treating youthful offenders. She was a leader of the suffrage movement and an active pacifist. Nobel Peace Prize (1931).

Jane Addams

ad·dax /ˈadˌaks/ ▶ **n.** a large antelope with a mainly grayish and white coat, native to the deserts of North Africa. ● *Addax nasomaculatus*, family Bovidae.
– ORIGIN late 17th cent.: from Latin, from an African word recorded by Pliny.

ad·den·dum /əˈdendəm/ ▶ **n.** (pl. **addenda** /-də/, **addendums**) **1** an item of additional material, typically omissions, added at the end of a book or other publication.
2 Engineering the radial distance from the pitch circle of a cogwheel, worm wheel, etc., to the crests of the teeth or ridges. Compare with **DEDENDUM**.
– ORIGIN late 17th cent.: Latin, 'that which is to be added,' gerundive of *addere* (see **ADD**).

ad·der /ˈadər/ ▶ **n.** a small venomous Eurasian snake that has a dark zigzag pattern on its back and bears live young. Also called **VIPER**. ● *Vipera berus*, family Viperidae. ■ used in names of similar or related snakes, e.g., **death adder**, **puff adder**.
– ORIGIN Old English *nædre* 'serpent, adder,' of Germanic origin; related to Dutch *adder* and German *Natter*. The initial *n* was lost in Middle English by wrong division of *a naddre*; compare with **APRON**, **AUGER**, and **UMPIRE**.

ad·der's tongue ▶ **n. 1** a widely distributed atypical fern that has a single pointed oval leaf and a straight unbranched spore-bearing stem. ● Genus *Ophioglossum*, family Ophioglossaceae, in particular *O. vulgatum*.
2 another term for **DOGTOOTH VIOLET**, esp. a trout lily.

ad·dict /ˈadikt/ ▶ **n.** a person who is addicted to a particular substance, typically an illegal drug: *a former heroin addict.* ■ [with modifier] informal an enthusiastic devotee of a specified thing or activity: *a must-buy book for the crossword-puzzle addict* | *a self-confessed chocolate addict.*
– ORIGIN early 20th cent.: from the obsolete verb *addict*, which was a back-formation from **ADDICTED**.

ad·dict·ed /əˈdiktid/ ▶ **adj.** physically and mentally dependent on a particular substance, and unable to stop taking it without incurring adverse effects: *she became* ***addicted to*** *alcohol and diet pills.* ■ enthusiastically devoted to a particular thing or activity: *he's* ***addicted to*** *computers.*
– ORIGIN mid 16th cent.: from the obsolete adjective *addict* 'bound or devoted (to someone),' from Latin *addict-* 'assigned,' from the verb *addicere*, from *ad-* 'to' + *dicere* 'say.'

ad·dic·tion /əˈdiksHən/ ▶ **n.** the fact or condition of being addicted to a particular substance, thing, or activity: *he committed the theft to finance his drug addiction* | *an addiction to gambling.*
– ORIGIN late 16th cent. (denoting a person's inclination or proclivity): from Latin *addictio(n-)*, from *addicere* 'assign' (see **ADDICT**).

ad·dic·tive /əˈdiktiv/ (also informal **addicting**) ▶ **adj.** (of a substance, thing, or activity) causing or likely to cause someone to become addicted to it: *a highly addictive drug* | *gambling can become addictive.* ■ of, relating to, or susceptible to being or becoming addicted to something: *addictive behavior* | *I have a very addictive personality.*

add-in ▶ **n.** a device or piece of software that can be added to a computer to give extra features or functions.

Ad·dis A·ba·ba /ˌadəs ˈabəbə, ˌädəs ˈäbəbə/ (also **Adis Abeba**) the capital of Ethiopia, in the central part of the country, at an altitude of about 8,000 feet (2,440 m); pop. 3,101,000 (est. 2007).

Ad·di·so·ni·an /ˌadəˈsōnēən/ ▶ **adj. 1** of, relating to, or characteristic of the works or style of Joseph Addison.
2 Medicine of, relating to, or characterized by Addison's disease.

Ad·di·son's dis·ease ▶ **n.** a disease characterized by progressive anemia, low blood pressure, great weakness, and bronze discoloration of the skin. It is caused by inadequate secretion of hormones by the adrenal cortex.
– ORIGIN mid 19th cent.: named after Thomas *Addison* (1793–1860), the English physician who described the disease.

ad·di·tion /əˈdisHən/ (abbr.: **addn.**) ▶ **n. 1** the action or process of adding something to something else: *the hotel has been extended* ***with the addition of*** *more rooms.* ■ a person or thing added or joined, typically in order to improve something: *you will find the coat a useful* ***addition to*** *your wardrobe.*
2 (abbr.: **addn.**) the process or skill of calculating the total of two or more numbers or amounts: *she began with simple arithmetic, addition and then subtraction.* ■ Mathematics the process of combining matrices, vectors, or other quantities under specific rules to obtain their sum.
– PHRASES **in addition** as an extra person, thing, or circumstance: *members of the board were paid a small allowance* ***in addition to*** *their normal salary.*
– ORIGIN late Middle English: from Latin *additio(n-)*, from the verb *addere* (see **ADD**).

ad·di·tion·al /əˈdisHənl/ ▶ **adj.** added, extra, or supplementary to what is already present or available: *we require additional information.*

ad·di·tion·al·ly /əˈdisHənl-ē/ ▶ **adv.** as an extra factor or circumstance: *brokers finance themselves additionally by short-term borrowing.* ■ [as sentence adverb] used to introduce a new fact or argument: *Additionally, the regulations require escape hatches.*

ad·di·tion re·ac·tion ▶ **n.** Chemistry a reaction in which one molecule combines with another to form a larger molecule with no other products.

ad·di·tive /ˈaditiv/ ▶ **n.** a substance added to something in small quantities, typically to improve or preserve it: *many foods contain chemical additives.*
▶ **adj.** characterized by, relating to, or produced by addition: *an additive process* | *the combination of these factors has an additive effect.* ■ technical of or relating to the reproduction of colors by the superimposition of primary colors: *the video monitor uses the additive colors red, green, and blue.*
– ORIGIN late 17th cent. (as an adjective): from late Latin *additivus*, from Latin *addit-* 'added,' from the verb *addere* (see **ADD**). The noun dates from the 1940s.

ad·dle /'adl/ ▶ **v.** [with obj.] chiefly humorous make unable to think clearly; confuse: *being in love must have addled your brain.*
▶ **adj.** archaic (of an egg) rotten.
– ORIGIN Middle English: from Old English *adela* 'liquid filth,' of Germanic origin; related to Dutch *aal* and German *Adel* 'mire, puddle.'

ad·dle·brained /'adl,brānd/ (also **addleheaded** /-,hedid/, **addlepated** /-,pātid/) ▶ **adj.** lacking in common sense; having a muddled mind: *made the addlebrained decision to install an uncertain rookie at point guard.*

ad·dled /'adld/ ▶ **adj. 1** unable to think clearly; confused: *this might just be my addled brain playing tricks* | [in combination] *his persona as a drug-addled hell-raiser.*
2 (of an egg) rotten.

addn. ▶ **abbr.** addition.

add-on ▶ **n.** something that has been or can be added to an existing object or arrangement: *we offer skiing lessons as add-ons to our chalet vacations* | [as modifier] *cars with add-on extras.* ■ an accessory device or piece of software designed to increase the capability of a computer or hi-fi system. ■ a unit of construction added to an existing construction: *the new kitchen replaces an add-on that was torn down in 1980.*

ad·dress /ə'dres, 'a,dres/ ▶ **n. 1** the particulars of the place where someone lives or an organization is situated: *they exchanged addresses and agreed to keep in touch.* ■ the place itself: *our officers went to the address.* ■ Computing a string of characters that identifies a destination for e-mail messages or the location of a website. ■ Computing a binary number that identifies a particular location in a data storage system or computer memory.
2 a formal speech delivered to an audience: *delivered an address to the National Council of Teachers.* ■ archaic a person's manner of speaking to someone else: *his address was abrupt and unceremonious.* ■ (**addresses**) archaic courteous or amorous approaches to someone: *he persecuted her with his addresses.*
3 dated skill, dexterity, or readiness: *he rescued me with the most consummate address.*
▶ **v.** [with obj.] **1** write the name and address of the intended recipient on (an envelope, letter, or package): *I* ***addressed*** *my letter* ***to*** *him personally* | (as adj. **addressed**) *an addressed envelope.*
2 speak to (a person or an assembly), typically in a formal way: *she addressed an audience of the most important Shawnee chiefs* | *they* ***addressed themselves to*** *my father.* ■ (**address someone as**) name someone in a specified way when talking or writing: *she addressed my father as "Mr. Stevens."* ■ (**address something to**) say or write remarks or a protest to (someone): *address your complaints to the Board of Review.*
3 think about and begin to deal with (an issue or problem): *a fundamental problem has still to be addressed.*
4 Golf take up one's stance and prepare to hit (the ball).
– PHRASES **form of address** a name or title used in speaking or writing to a person of a specified rank or function: *"Venerable" was the usual form of address for a priest at that time.*
– DERIVATIVES **ad·dress·er n.**
– ORIGIN Middle English (as a verb in the senses 'set upright' and 'guide, direct,' hence 'write directions for delivery on' and 'direct spoken words to'): from Old French, based on Latin *ad-* 'toward' + *directus* (see **DIRECT**). The noun is of mid 16th-cent. origin in the sense 'act of approaching or speaking to someone.'

ad·dress·a·ble /ə'dresəbəl/ ▶ **adj.** Computing relating to or denoting a memory unit in which all locations can be separately accessed by a particular program.

ad·dress·ee /,adre'sē, ə,dre'sē/ ▶ **n.** the person to whom something, typically a letter, is addressed.

Ad·dres·so·graph /ə'dresə,graf/ ▶ **n.** trademark a machine for printing addresses on envelopes.

ad·duce /ə'd(y)o͞os/ ▶ **v.** [with obj.] cite as evidence: *a number of factors are adduced to explain the situation.*
– DERIVATIVES **ad·duc·i·ble adj.**
– ORIGIN late Middle English: from Latin *adducere*, from *ad-* 'toward' + *ducere* 'to lead.'

ad·duct[1] /ə'dəkt/ ▶ **v.** [with obj.] (of a muscle) move (a limb or other part of the body) toward the midline of the body or toward another part. The opposite of **ABDUCT**.
– DERIVATIVES **ad·duc·tion** /ə'dəkSHən/ **n.**
– ORIGIN mid 19th cent.: back-formation from late Middle English *adduction*, from late Latin *adductio(n-)* 'bringing forward,' from the verb *adducere* 'bring in' (see **ADDUCE**).

ad·duct[2] ▶ **n.** Chemistry the product of an addition reaction between two compounds.
– ORIGIN 1940s: from German *Addukt* (blend of *Addition* and *Produkt*).

ad·duc·tor /ə'dəktər/ (also **adductor muscle**) ▶ **n.** Anatomy a muscle whose contraction moves a limb or other part of the body toward the midline of the body or toward another part. Compare with **ABDUCTOR**. ■ any of a number of specific muscles in the hand, foot, or thigh: [followed by Latin genitive] *adductor hallucis.*
– ORIGIN early 17th cent.: modern Latin, from Latin *adduct-* 'brought in,' from the verb *adducere* (see **ADDUCE**).

ad·dy /'adē/ ▶ **n.** (pl. **addies**) informal an address, esp. an e-mail address: *I just sent you a note from my other addy.*
– ORIGIN by shortening and alteration.

-ade[1] ▶ **suffix** forming nouns: **1** denoting an action that is completed: *barricade* | *blockade.*
2 denoting the body concerned in an action or process: *brigade* | *cavalcade.*
3 denoting the product or result of an action or process: *arcade* | *lemonade* | *marmalade.*
– ORIGIN from French via Portuguese, Provençal, and Spanish *-ada* or via Italian *-ata*, from Latin *-atus* (past participial suffix of verbs ending in *-are*).

-ade[2] ▶ **suffix** forming nouns such as *decade.* Compare with **-AD**[1].
– ORIGIN representing the French noun ending *-ade*, from Greek.

-ade[3] ▶ **suffix** forming nouns: **1** equivalent to **-ADE**[1]: *brocade.*
2 denoting a person: *renegade.*
– ORIGIN from Spanish or Portuguese *-ado*, masculine form of *-ada* (see **-ADE**[1]).

Ad·e·laide /'adl,ād/ a city in southern Australia, the capital and chief port of the state of South Australia; pop. 1,172,105 (2008).

a·del·gid /ə'deljid/ ▶ **n.** an insect of the family Adelgidae, which comprises sap-feeding hemipteran insects resembling aphids.
– ORIGIN 1920s: from family name *Adelgidae*, perhaps from Greek *adelos* 'unseen' + *gē* 'earth.'

A·dé·lie Land /ə'dālē, 'adl-ē/ (also **Adélie Coast**) a section of the Antarctic continent situated east of Wilkes Land.

A·dé·lie pen·guin /ə'dālē/ ▶ **n.** a gregarious and territorial penguin of Antarctica, perhaps the most familiar of all the penguins. The adults have a distinctive white ring around the eye. ● *Pygoscelis adeliae*, family Spheniscidae.

Adélie penguin

A·den /'ādn, 'ädn/ a port in Yemen at the mouth of the Red Sea; pop. 588,900 (est. 2004). Formerly under British rule, first as part of British India from 1839 and then from 1935 as a Crown Colony, it was capital of former South Yemen 1967–90.

A·den, Gulf of a part of the eastern Arabian Sea that lies between the southern coast of Yemen and the Horn of Africa.

A·de·nau·er /'adn,ou(ə)r/, Konrad (1876–1967), German statesman, first chancellor of the Federal Republic of Germany 1949–63.

ad·e·nine /'adn,ēn, -,īn/ ▶ **n.** Biochemistry a compound that is one of the four constituent bases of nucleic acids. A purine derivative, it is paired with thymine in double-stranded DNA. ● Alternative name: **6-aminopurine**; chem. formula: $C_5H_5N_5$.
– ORIGIN late 19th cent.: coined in German from Greek *adēn* 'gland' + **-INE**[4].

adeno- ▶ **comb. form** relating to a gland or glands: *adenocarcinoma.*
– ORIGIN from Greek *adēn* 'gland.'

ad·e·no·car·ci·no·ma /,adn-ō,kärsə'nōmə/ ▶ **n.** (pl. **adenocarcinomas** or **adenocarcinomata** /-'nōmətə/) Medicine a malignant tumor formed from glandular structures in epithelial tissue.

ad·e·noids /'adn,oidz/ ▶ **plural n.** a mass of enlarged lymphatic tissue between the back of the nose and the throat, often hindering speaking and breathing in young children.
– DERIVATIVES **ad·e·noi·dal** /,adn'oidl/ **adj.**
– ORIGIN late 19th cent.: from Greek *adēn* 'gland' + **-OID**.

ad·e·no·ma /,adn'ōmə/ ▶ **n.** (pl. **adenomas** or **adenomata** /-mətə/) Medicine a benign tumor formed from glandular structures in epithelial tissue.
– ORIGIN late 19th cent.: from Latin, from Greek *adēn* 'gland' + **-OMA**.

a·den·o·sine /ə'denə,sēn, -sin/ ▶ **n.** Biochemistry a compound consisting of adenine combined with ribose, one of four nucleoside units in RNA.
– ORIGIN early 20th cent.: blend of **ADENINE** and **RIBOSE**.

a·den·o·sine de·am·i·nase /dē'amə,nās, -,nāz/ ▶ **n.** Biochemistry an enzyme that catalyzes the deamination of adenosine to inosine.

a·den·o·sine mon·o·phos·phate /,mänō'fäs,fāt/ (abbr.: **AMP**) ▶ **n.** Biochemistry a compound consisting of an adenosine molecule bonded to one acidic phosphate group, present in most DNA and RNA. It often exists in a cyclic form with the phosphate bonded to the nucleoside at two points.

a·den·o·sine tri·phos·phate /trī'fäs,fāt/ (abbr.: **ATP**) ▶ **n.** Biochemistry a compound consisting of an adenosine molecule bonded to three phosphate groups, present in all living tissue. The breakage of one phosphate linkage (to form **adenosine diphosphate, ADP**) provides energy for physiological processes such as muscular contraction.

ad·e·no·vi·rus /,adn-ō'vīrəs/ ▶ **n.** Medicine any of a group of DNA viruses first discovered in adenoid tissue, most of which cause respiratory diseases.

a·den·yl·ate cy·clase /ə'denl,āt 'sī,klās, -,klāz, ə'denl-it/ (also **adenyl cyclase** /'adn-il/) ▶ **n.** Biochemistry an enzyme that catalyzes the formation of cyclic adenylic acid from adenosine triphosphate.

ad·e·nyl·ic ac·id /,adn'ilik/ ▶ **n.** another term for **ADENOSINE MONOPHOSPHATE**.
– ORIGIN late 19th cent.: *adenylic* from **ADENINE** + **-YL** + **-IC**.

a·dept ▶ **adj.** /ə'dept/ very skilled or proficient at something: *he is* ***adept at*** *cutting through red tape* | *an adept negotiator.*
▶ **n.** /'adept, ə'dept/ a person who is skilled or proficient at something: *they are adepts at kung fu and karate.*
– DERIVATIVES **a·dept·ly adv.**, **a·dept·ness n.**
– ORIGIN mid 17th cent.: from Latin *adeptus* 'achieved,' past participle of *adipisci* 'obtain, attain.'

ad·e·qua·cy /'adikwəsē/ ▶ **n.** the state or quality of being adequate: *the adequacy of testing procedures.*

ad·e·quate /'adikwit/ ▶ **adj.** satisfactory or acceptable in quality or quantity: *this office is perfectly* ***adequate for*** *my needs* | *the law is* ***adequate to*** *deal with the problem* | *adequate resources and funding.*
– DERIVATIVES **ad·e·quate·ly adv.**
– ORIGIN early 17th cent.: from Latin *adaequatus* 'made equal to,' past participle of the verb *adaequare*, from *ad-* 'to' + *aequus* 'equal.'

à deux /ä 'dœ/ ▶ **adv.** for or involving two people: *dinner à deux.*
– ORIGIN late 19th cent.: French.

ADF ▶ **abbr.** automatic direction finder, a device used by pilots to aid navigation.

ad fin. ▶ **adv.** at or near the end of a piece of writing.
– ORIGIN mid 17th cent.: from Latin *ad finem* 'at the end.'

ADH ▶ **abbr.** Biochemistry antidiuretic hormone.

ad·han /əd'hän/ ▶ **n.** variant spelling of **AZAN**.

ADHD ▶ **abbr.** attention deficit hyperactivity disorder.

ad·here /ad'hi(ə)r/ ▶ **v.** [no obj.] (**adhere to**) stick fast to (a surface or substance): *paint won't adhere well to a greasy surface.* ■ believe in and follow the practices of: *the people adhere to the Muslim religion.* ■ represent truthfully and in detail: *the account adhered firmly to fact.*
– ORIGIN late 15th cent.: from Latin *adhaerere*, from *ad-* 'to' + *haerere* 'to stick.'

ad·her·ent /ad'hi(ə)rənt, -'her-/ ▶ **n.** someone who supports a particular party, person, or set of ideas: *he was a strong* ***adherent of*** *monetarism.*
▶ **adj.** sticking fast to an object or surface: *the eggs have thick sticky shells to which debris is often adherent.*
– DERIVATIVES **ad·her·ence n.**
– ORIGIN late Middle English: from Old French *adherent*, from Latin *adhaerent-* 'sticking to,' from the verb *adhaerere* (see **ADHERE**).

ad·he·sion /ad'hēZHən/ ▶ **n. 1** the action or process of adhering to a surface or object: *the adhesion of the Scotch tape to the paper.* ■ the frictional grip of wheels, shoes, etc., on a road, track, or other surface: *the front tires were struggling for adhesion.* ■ Physics the sticking together of particles of

PRONUNCIATION KEY ə *ago, up*; ər *over, fur*; a *hat*; ā *ate*; ä *car*; e *let*; ē *see*; i *fit*; ī *by*; NG *sing*; ō *go*; ô *law, for*; oi *toy*; o͝o *good*; o͞o *goo*; ou *out*; TH *thin*; T͟H *then*; ZH *vision*

a

different substances. ■ allegiance or faithfulness to a particular person, party, or set of ideas: *he was harshly criticized for his adhesion to the old bureaucracy.*
2 Medicine an abnormal union of membranous surfaces due to inflammation or injury: *endoscopic surgery for pelvic adhesions.*
– ORIGIN late 15th cent.: from French *adhésion*, from Latin *adhaesio(n-)*, from the verb *adhaerere* (see ADHERE).

ad·he·sive /ad'hēsiv, -ziv/ ▶ **adj.** able to stick fast to a surface or object; sticky: *an adhesive label.*
▶ **n.** a substance used for sticking objects or materials together; glue.
– DERIVATIVES **ad·he·sive·ly adv.**, **ad·he·sive·ness n.**
– ORIGIN late 17th cent. (in the sense 'tending to adhere or cling to'): from French *adhésif, -ive*, from the verb *adhérer*, from Latin *adhaerere* 'stick to' (see ADHERE).

ad·he·sive cap·sul·i·tis /ˌkapsə'lītis/ ▶ **n.** extreme stiffness or immobility in the shoulder joint, usu. following injury and caused by the adhesions in the joint and inflammation of the capsule of the humerus. Also called FROZEN SHOULDER.

ad·hib·it /ad'hibit/ ▶ **v.** (**adhibits, adhibiting, adhibited**) [with obj.] formal apply or affix (something) to something else: *signed by a partner who would either adhibit the firm's signature or his own.*
– DERIVATIVES **ad·hi·bi·tion** /ˌad(h)ə'bisHən/ **n.**
– ORIGIN early 16th cent. (in the sense 'take in, include'): from Latin *adhibit-* 'brought in,' from the verb *adhibere*, from *ad-* 'to' + *habere* 'hold, have.'

ad hoc /'ad 'häk, 'hōk/ ▶ **adj. & adv.** formed, arranged, or done for a particular purpose only: [as adj.] *an ad hoc committee* | *the discussions were on an ad hoc basis* | [as adv.] *the group was constituted ad hoc.*
– ORIGIN mid 16th cent.: Latin, literally 'for this.'

ad·hoc·ra·cy /ad'häkrəsē/ ▶ **n.** a flexible, adaptable, and informal organizational structure without bureaucratic policies or procedures.
– ORIGIN 1970s: blend of AD HOC and -CRACY.

ad ho·mi·nem /'ad 'hämənəm/ ▶ **adv. & adj. 1** (of an argument or reaction) arising from or appealing to the emotions and not reason or logic. ■ attacking an opponent's motives or character rather than the policy or position they maintain: *vicious ad hominem attacks.*
2 relating to or associated with a particular person: [as adv.] *the office was created ad hominem for Fenton* | [as adj.] *an ad hominem response.*
– ORIGIN late 16th cent.: Latin, literally 'to the person.'

ad·i·a·bat·ic /ˌādīə'batik, ˌadēə-/ Physics ▶ **adj.** relating to or denoting a process or condition in which heat does not enter or leave the system concerned. ■ impassable to heat.
▶ **n.** a curve or formula representing adiabatic phenomena.
– DERIVATIVES **ad·i·a·bat·i·cal·ly** /-ik(ə)lē/ **adv.**
– ORIGIN late 19th cent.: from Greek *adiabatos* 'impassable,' from *a-* 'not' + *dia* 'through' + *batos* 'passable' (from *bainein* 'go'), + -IC.

ad·i·a·bat·ic lapse rate ▶ **n.** Meteorology the rate at which atmospheric temperature decreases with increasing altitude in conditions of thermal equilibrium.

ad·i·an·tum /ˌadē'antəm/ ▶ **n.** technical term for MAIDENHAIR.

a·dieu /ə'd(y)o͞o, ä'dyœ/ chiefly literary ▶ **exclam.** another term for GOODBYE.
▶ **n.** (pl. **adieus** or **adieux**) a goodbye: *he whispered a fond adieu* | *they bade us all adieu.*
– ORIGIN late Middle English: from Old French, from *à* 'to' + *Dieu* 'God'; compare with ADIOS.

A·di Granth /ˌädē 'grənt/ another term for GURU GRANTH SAHIB.
– ORIGIN from Sanskrit *ādigrantha*, literally 'first book,' based on *grantha* 'literary composition,' from *granth* 'to tie.'

ad in·fi·ni·tum /ˌad infə'nītəm/ ▶ **adv.** again and again in the same way; forever: *registration is for seven years and may be renewed ad infinitum.*
– ORIGIN early 17th cent.: Latin, literally 'to infinity.'

ad·i·os /ˌädē'ōs, ˌadē-/ ▶ **exclam. & n.** Spanish term for GOODBYE.
– ORIGIN Spanish *adiós*, from *a* 'to' + *Dios* 'God'; compare with ADIEU.

a·dip·ic ac·id /ə'dipik/ ▶ **n.** Chemistry a crystalline fatty acid obtained from natural fats and used esp. in the manufacture of nylon. ● Alternative name: **hexanedioic acid**; chem. formula: $HOOC(CH_2)_4COOH$.
– DERIVATIVES **ad·i·pate** /'adəˌpāt/ **n.**
– ORIGIN mid 19th cent.: from Latin *adeps, adip-* 'fat' (because the acid was first prepared by oxidizing fats) + -IC.

ad·i·po·cere /'adəpōˌsi(ə)r/ ▶ **n.** a grayish waxy substance formed by the decomposition of soft tissue in dead bodies subjected to moisture.
– ORIGIN early 19th cent.: from French *adipocire*, from Latin *adeps, adip-* 'fat' + French *cire* 'wax' (from Latin *cera*).

ad·i·po·cyte /'adəpəˌsīt/ ▶ **n.** Biology a cell specialized for the storage of fat, found in connective tissue.
– ORIGIN 1930s: from ADIPOSE + -CYTE.

ad·i·pose /'adəˌpōs/ ▶ **adj.** technical (esp. of body tissue) used for the storage of fat.
– DERIVATIVES **ad·i·pos·i·ty** /ˌadə'päsitē/ **n.**
– ORIGIN mid 18th cent.: from modern Latin *adiposus*, from *adeps, adip-* 'fat.'

ad·i·pose fin ▶ **n.** Zoology a small, rayless, fleshy dorsal fin present in certain fishes, notably in the salmon family.

Ad·i·ron·dack chair /ˌadə'ränˌdak/ ▶ **n.** an outdoor wooden armchair constructed of wide slats. The seat typically slants downward toward the sloping back.

Adirondack chair

Ad·i·ron·dack Moun·tains (also **the Adirondacks**) a range of mountains in New York, source of the Hudson and Mohawk rivers.

Adi·ron·dack Park a state preserve in north central New York, the largest park in the contiguous US.

A·dis A·be·ba variant spelling of ADDIS ABABA.

ad·it /'adit/ ▶ **n.** a horizontal passage leading into a mine for the purposes of access or drainage.
– ORIGIN early 17th cent.: from Latin *aditus* 'approach, entrance,' from *adit-* 'approached,' from the verb *adire*, from *ad-* 'toward' + *ire* 'go.'

adj. ▶ **abbr.** ■ adjective. ■ adjustment. ■ adjunct. ■ (**Adj.**) adjutant.

ad·ja·cent /ə'jāsənt/ ▶ **adj. 1** next to or adjoining something else: *adjacent rooms* | *the area **adjacent to** the fire station.*
2 Geometry (of angles) having a common vertex and a common side.
– DERIVATIVES **ad·ja·cen·cy n.**
– ORIGIN late Middle English: from Latin *adjacent-* 'lying near to,' from *adjacere*, from *ad-* 'to' + *jacere* 'lie down.'

ad·jec·tive /'ajiktiv/ ▶ **n.** Grammar a word or phrase naming an attribute, added to or grammatically related to a noun to modify or describe it.
– DERIVATIVES **ad·jec·ti·val** /ˌajik'tīvəl/ **adj.**, **ad·jec·ti·val·ly** /ˌajik'tīvəlē/ **adv.**
– ORIGIN late Middle English: from Old French *adjectif, -ive*, from Latin *adject-* 'added,' from the verb *adjicere*, from *ad-* 'toward' + *jacere* 'throw.' The term was originally used in the phrase *noun adjective*, translating Latin *nomen adjectivum*, the latter being a translation of Greek *onoma epitheton* 'attributive name.'

ad·join /ə'join/ ▶ **v.** [with obj.] be next to and joined with (a building, room, or piece of land): *the dining room adjoins a small library.*
– ORIGIN Middle English: from Old French *ajoindre*, from Latin *adjungere*, from *ad-* 'to' + *jungere* 'to join.'

ad·join·ing /ə'joiniNG/ ▶ **adj.** (of a building, room, or piece of land) next to or joined with: *I was in an adjoining room and could hear voices* | *they ended up buying the adjoining land.*

ad·joint /'ajoint/ Mathematics ▶ **adj.** relating to or denoting a function or quantity related to a given function or quantity by a particular process of transposition. ■ denoting a matrix that is the transpose of the cofactors of a given square matrix.
▶ **n.** an adjoint matrix, function, or quantity.
– ORIGIN late 19th cent.: from French, literally 'joined to,' from *adjoindre* (see ADJOIN).

ad·journ /ə'jərn/ ▶ **v.** [with obj.] break off (a meeting, legal case, or game) with the intention of resuming it later: *the meeting was adjourned until December 4* | [no obj.] *let's adjourn and reconvene at 2 o'clock.* ■ [no obj.] (of people who are together) go somewhere else, typically for refreshment: *they **adjourned to** a local bar.* ■ put off or postpone (a resolution or sentence): *the sentence was adjourned.*
– ORIGIN Middle English (in the sense 'summon someone to appear on a particular day'): from Old French *ajorner*, from the phrase *a jorn (nome)* 'to an (appointed) day.'

ad·journ·ment /ə'jərnmənt/ ▶ **n.** an act or period of adjourning or being adjourned: *she sought an adjournment of the trial* | *I suggest we have a short adjournment.*

ad·judge /ə'jəj/ ▶ **v.** [with obj.] consider or declare to be true or the case: *she was adjudged guilty* | *he was adjudged to be offensive.* ■ (**adjudge something to**) (in legal use) award something judicially to (someone): *the court adjudged damages to her.* ■ (in legal use) condemn (someone) to pay a penalty: *the defaulter was adjudged to pay the whole amount.*
– DERIVATIVES **ad·judg·ment** (also **adjudgement**) **n.**
– ORIGIN late Middle English: from Old French *ajuger*, from Latin *adjudicare*, from *ad-* 'to' + *judicare*, from *judex, judic-* 'a judge.'

ad·ju·di·cate /ə'jo͞odiˌkāt/ ▶ **v.** [no obj.] make a formal judgment or decision about a problem or disputed matter: *the committee **adjudicates on** all betting disputes* | [with obj.] *the case was adjudicated in the Supreme Court.* ■ act as a judge in a competition: *we asked him to adjudicate at the local flower show.* ■ [with obj. and complement] pronounce or declare judicially: *he was adjudicated bankrupt.*
– DERIVATIVES **ad·ju·di·ca·tive** /-ˌkātiv/ **adj.**
– ORIGIN early 18th cent. (in the sense 'award judicially'): from Latin *adjudicat-* 'awarded judicially,' from the verb *adjudicare* (see ADJUDGE). The noun *adjudication* dates from the early 17th cent.

ad·ju·di·ca·tion /əˌjo͞odi'kāsHən/ ▶ **n.** the action or process of adjudicating: *the matter may have to go to court for adjudication.* ■ a formal judgment on a disputed matter: *an adjudication had found a degree of unwarranted infringement of privacy.*

ad·ju·di·ca·tor /ə'jo͞odiˌkātər/ ▶ **n.** a person who adjudicates: *the proposal to close the school will have to go before an adjudicator.*

ad·junct /'ajəNGkt/ ▶ **n. 1** a thing added to something else as a supplementary rather than an essential part: *computer technology is **an adjunct to** learning.* ■ a person who is another's assistant or subordinate.
2 Grammar a word or phrase used to amplify or modify the meaning of another word or words in a sentence.
▶ **adj.** [attrib.] connected or added to something, typically in an auxiliary way: *other alternative or adjunct therapies include immunotherapy.* ■ (of an academic post) attached to the staff of a college in a temporary or assistant capacity: *an adjunct professor of entomology* | [as noun] *both adjuncts and tenured professors tend to inflate grades.*
– DERIVATIVES **ad·junc·tive** /ə'jəNG(k)tiv/ **adj.**
– ORIGIN early 16th cent. (as an adjective meaning 'joined on, subordinate'): from Latin *adjunctus*, past participle of *adjungere* (see ADJOIN).

ad·junc·tion /ə'jəNG(k)sHən/ ▶ **n. 1** Mathematics the joining of two sets that without overlapping jointly constitute a larger set, or the relation between two such sets.
2 Logic the asserting in a single formula of two previously asserted formulae.
– ORIGIN late 16th cent.: from Latin *adjunctio(n-)*, from the verb *adjungere* (see ADJOIN).

ad·jure /ə'jo͝or/ ▶ **v.** [with obj.] formal urge or request (someone) solemnly or earnestly to do something: *I adjure you to tell me the truth.*
– DERIVATIVES **ad·ju·ra·tion** /ˌajə'rāsHən/ **n.**, **ad·jur·a·to·ry** /-əˌtôrē/ **adj.**
– ORIGIN late Middle English (in the sense 'put a person on oath'): from Latin *adjurare*, from *ad-* 'to' + *jurare* 'swear' (from *jus, jur-* 'oath').

ad·just /ə'jəst/ ▶ **v. 1** [with obj.] alter or move (something) slightly in order to achieve the desired fit, appearance, or result: *he smoothed his hair and adjusted his tie* | *the interest rate should be **adjusted for** inflation.* ■ [no obj.] permit small alterations or movements so as to allow a desired fit, appearance, or result to be achieved: *a harness that **adjusts to** the correct fit.* ■ [no obj.] adapt or become used to a new situation: *she must be allowed to grieve and to adjust in her own way* | *his eyes had **adjusted to** semidarkness.*
2 [with obj.] assess (loss or damages) when settling an insurance claim.
– DERIVATIVES **ad·just·er n.**
– ORIGIN early 17th cent. (in the senses 'harmonize discrepancies' and 'assess (loss or damages)'): from obsolete French *adjuster*, from Old French *ajoster* 'to approximate,' based on Latin *ad-* 'to' + *juxta* 'near.'

ad·just·a·ble /ə'jəstəbəl/ ▶ **adj.** able to be adjusted: *the car has fully adjustable seats and steering wheel.*
– DERIVATIVES **ad·just·a·bil·i·ty** /əˌjəstə'bilitē/ **n.**

adjustable-rate mortgage (abbr.: **ARM**) ▶ **n.** a mortgage whose rate of interest is adjusted periodically to reflect market conditions. Also called VARIABLE-RATE MORTGAGE.

ad·just·ment /ə'jəstmənt/ ▶ **n.** a small alteration or movement made to achieve a desired fit, appearance, or result: *I've made a few adjustments to my diet* | *only slight adjustments to the boat are necessary.* ■ the process of adapting or becoming used to a new situation: *for many couples there may need to be a period of adjustment.*

ad·ju·tant /'ajətənt/ ▶ **n.** **1** a military officer who acts as an administrative assistant to a senior officer. ■ a person's assistant or deputy.
2 (also **adjutant stork** or **adjutant bird**) a large black-and-white stork with a massive bill and a bare head and neck, found in India and Southeast Asia. ● Genus *Leptoptilos*, family Ciconiidae: two species.
– DERIVATIVES **ad·ju·tan·cy** n.
– ORIGIN early 17th cent. (in the sense 'assistant, helper'): from Latin *adjutant-* 'being of service to,' from *adjutare*, frequentative of *adjuvare* 'assist' (see ADJUVANT).

ad·ju·tant gen·er·al ▶ **n.** (pl. **adjutants general**) the adjutant of a unit having a general staff. ■ (**the Adjutant General**) (in the US Army) the chief administrative officer. ■ the senior officer in the National Guard of a US state.

ad·ju·vant /'ajəvənt/ ▶ **adj.** Medicine (of therapy) applied after initial treatment for cancer, esp. to suppress secondary tumor formation.
▶ **n.** Medicine a substance that enhances the body's immune response to an antigen.
– ORIGIN late 16th cent.: from Latin *adjuvant-* 'helping toward,' from the verb *adjuvare*, from *ad-* 'toward' + *juvare* 'to help.'

Ad·ler /'adlər, 'äd-/, Alfred (1870–1937), Austrian psychologist and psychiatrist. Adler disagreed with Freud's idea that mental illness was caused by sexual conflicts in infancy, arguing that society and culture were significant factors. He introduced the concept of the inferiority complex.
– DERIVATIVES **Ad·le·ri·an** /ad'li(ə)rēən, äd-, -'ler-/ adj. & n.

ad lib /'ad 'lib/ ▶ **v.** (**ad libs, ad libbing, ad libbed**) [no obj.] speak or perform in public without previously preparing one's words: *Charles had to ad lib because he'd forgotten his script* | [with obj.] *she ad libbed half the speech.*
▶ **n.** something spoken or performed in such a way: *he came up with an apt ad lib.*
▶ **adv. & adj.** **1** spoken or performed without previous preparation: *an ad lib commentary* | [as adv.] *speaking ad lib.*
2 as much and as often as desired: [as adv.] *the price includes meals and drinks ad lib* | [as adj.] *the pigs are fed on an ad lib system.*
3 Music (in directions) in an improvised manner with freedom to vary tempo and instrumentation.
– ORIGIN early 19th cent. (as an adverb): abbreviation of AD LIBITUM.

ad lib·i·tum /ad 'libitəm/ ▶ **adv. & adj.** more formal term for AD LIB (sense 2 of the adverb).
– ORIGIN early 17th cent.: Latin, literally 'according to pleasure.'

ad li·tem /ad 'lītəm/ ▶ **adj.** Law (esp. of a guardian) appointed to act in a lawsuit on behalf of a child or other person who is not considered capable of representing themselves.
– ORIGIN mid 18th cent.: Latin, literally 'for the lawsuit.'

ad loc. ▶ **abbr.** to or at that place.

Adm. ▶ **abbr.** Admiral.

ad·man /'ad,man/ ▶ **n.** (pl. **admen**) informal a person who works in advertising.

ad·min /'ad,min/ ▶ **n.** informal the administration of a business, organization, etc.: [as modifier] *admin staff.*
– ORIGIN 1940s: abbreviation.

ad·min·is·ter /əd'minəstər/ ▶ **v.** [with obj.] **1** manage and be responsible for the running of (a business, organization, etc.): *each school was administered separately.* ■ be responsible for the implementation or use of (law or resources): *a federal agency would administer new regulations.*
2 dispense or apply (a remedy or drug): *paramedic crews are capable of administering drugs.* ■ deal out or inflict (punishment): *retribution was administered to those found guilty.* ■ (of a priest) perform the rites of (a sacrament, typically the Eucharist). ■ archaic or Law direct the taking of (an oath): *the chief justice will administer the oath of office.*
3 [no obj.] give help or service: *we must selflessly* ***administer to*** *his needs.*
– DERIVATIVES **ad·min·is·tra·ble** /-strəbəl/ adj.
– ORIGIN late Middle English: via Old French from Latin *administrare*, from *ad-* 'to' + *ministrare* (see MINISTER).

ad·min·is·trate /əd'minə,strāt/ ▶ **v.** [with obj.] less common term for ADMINISTER (sense 1).
– ORIGIN mid 16th cent.: from Latin *administrat-* 'managed,' from the verb *administrare* (see ADMINISTER).

ad·min·is·tra·tion /əd,minə'strāsʜən/ (abbr.: **admin.**) ▶ **n.** **1** the process or activity of running a business, organization, etc.: *the day-to-day administration of the company* | *a career in arts administration* | [as modifier] *administration costs.* ■ (**the administration**) the people responsible for this, regarded collectively: *the university administration took their demands seriously.* ■ the management of public affairs; government: *the inhabitants of the island voted to remain under French administration.* ■ Law the management and disposal of the property of an intestate, deceased person, debtor, or other individual, or of an insolvent company, by a legally appointed administrator: *the company* ***went into administration*** | [as modifier] *an administration order.*
2 the officials in the executive branch of government under a particular chief executive: *the Kennedy administration sought to use the conference to repair US prestige.* ■ the term of office of a political leader or government: *the early years of the Reagan Administration.* ■ a government agency: *the US Food and Drug Administration.*
3 the action of dispensing, giving, or applying something: *the oral administration of the antibiotic* | *the administration of justice.*
– ORIGIN Middle English: from Latin *administratio(n-)*, from the verb *administrare* (see ADMINISTER).

ad·min·is·tra·tive /əd'mini,strātiv, -strətiv/ ▶ **adj.** of or relating to the running of a business, organization, etc.: *administrative problems* | *administrative staff.*
– DERIVATIVES **ad·min·is·tra·tive·ly** adv.
– ORIGIN mid 18th cent.: from Latin *administrativus*, from *administrat-* 'managed,' from the verb *administrare* (see ADMINISTRATE).

ad·min·is·tra·tive law ▶ **n.** the body of law that regulates the operation and procedures of government agencies.

ad·min·is·tra·tor /əd'minə,strātər/ ▶ **n.** a person responsible for running a business, organization, etc. ■ Law a person legally appointed to manage and dispose of the estate of an intestate, deceased person, debtor, or other individual, or of an insolvent company. ■ a person who performs official duties in some sphere, esp. dealing out punishment or giving a religious sacrament: *administrators of justice.*

ad·min·is·tra·trix /əd,minə'strātriks/ ▶ **n.** Law a female administrator of an estate.

ad·mi·ra·ble /'admərəbəl/ ▶ **adj.** arousing or deserving respect and approval: *he has one admirable quality—he is totally honest* | *what is admirable in one sex is disdained in the other.*
– DERIVATIVES **ad·mi·ra·bly** /-blē/ adv.
– ORIGIN late Middle English: via Old French from Latin *admirabilis* 'to be wondered at,' from *admirari* (see ADMIRE).

ad·mi·ral /'admərəl/ ▶ **n.** **1** a commander of a fleet or naval squadron, or a naval officer of very high rank. ■ a commissioned officer of very high rank in the US Navy or Coast Guard, ranking above a vice admiral. ■ short for VICE ADMIRAL or REAR ADMIRAL.
2 [with modifier] a butterfly that has dark wings with bold colorful markings. ● Several species in the subfamilies Limenitidinae and Nymphalinae, family Nymphalidae. See RED ADMIRAL, WHITE ADMIRAL.
– DERIVATIVES **ad·mi·ral·ship** /-,sʜip/ n.
– ORIGIN Middle English (denoting an emir or Saracen commander): from Old French *amiral*, *admirail*, via medieval Latin from Arabic *'amīr* 'commander' (from *'amara* 'to command'). The ending *-al* was from Arabic *-al-* in the sense 'of the' used in forming titles (e.g., *'amīr-al-'umarā* 'ruler of rulers'), later assimilated to the familiar Latinate suffix -AL.

Ad·mi·ral of the Fleet ▶ **n.** the highest rank of admiral in the Royal Navy. Compare with FLEET ADMIRAL.

ad·mi·ral·ty /'admərəltē/ ▶ **n.** (pl. **admiralties**) **1** the rank or office of an admiral.
2 Law the jurisdiction of courts of law over cases concerning ships or the sea and other navigable waters (maritime law).
3 (**Admiralty**) the department of the British government that once administered the Royal Navy.
– ORIGIN late Middle English: from Old French *admiralte*, from *admirail* 'emir, leader' (see ADMIRAL).

Ad·mi·ral·ty Is·lands /'admərəltē/ a group of about 40 islands in the western Pacific, part of Papua New Guinea. In 1884 the islands became a German protectorate, but after 1920 they were administered as an Australian mandate.

ad·mi·ra·tion /,admə'rāsʜən/ ▶ **n.** respect and warm approval: *their admiration for each other was genuine.* ■ (**the admiration of**) the object of such feelings: *her house was the admiration of everyone.* ■ pleasurable contemplation: *they were lost in admiration of the scenery.*
– ORIGIN late Middle English (in the sense 'marveling, wonder'): from Latin *admiratio(n-)*, from the verb *admirari* (see ADMIRE).

ad·mire /əd'mī(ə)r/ ▶ **v.** [with obj.] regard (an object, quality, or person) with respect or warm approval: *I admire your courage* | (as adj. **admiring**) *she couldn't help but notice his admiring glance.* ■ look at with pleasure: *we were just admiring your garden.*
– DERIVATIVES **ad·mir·ing·ly** adv.
– ORIGIN late 16th cent.: from Latin *admirari*, from *ad-* 'at' + *mirari* 'wonder.'

ad·mir·er /əd'mī(ə)rər/ ▶ **n.** someone who has a particular regard for someone or something: *he was a great admirer of Mark Twain.* ■ a man who is attracted to a particular woman or a woman who is attracted to a particular man: *she's got a secret admirer.*

ad·mis·si·ble /əd'misəbəl/ ▶ **adj.** **1** acceptable or valid, esp. as evidence in a court of law: *the Court unanimously held that the hearsay was admissible* | *legally admissible evidence.*
2 having the right to be admitted to a place: *foreigners were admissible only as temporary workers.*
– DERIVATIVES **ad·mis·si·bil·i·ty** /-,misə'bilitē/ n.
– ORIGIN early 17th cent.: from medieval Latin *admissibilis*, from Latin *admittere* (see ADMIT).

ad·mis·sion /əd'misʜən/ ▶ **n.** **1** a statement acknowledging the truth of something: *an admission of guilt* | *a tacit* ***admission that*** *things had gone wrong* | *a man who,* ***by his own admission,*** *fell in love easily.*
2 the process or fact of entering or being allowed to enter a place, organization, or institution: *I had some difficulty securing admission to the embassy* | *the country's admission to the UN* | *her condition required frequent hospital admissions* | (as modifier **admissions**) *the university admissions office.* ■ the money charged for allowing someone to enter a public place: *admission is $1 for adults and 50 cents for children.* ■ (**admissions**) the number of people entering a place: *hospital admissions decreased nearly 65 percent.*
– ORIGIN late Middle English: from Latin *admission-*, from the verb *admittere* (see ADMIT).

> **USAGE** Admission traditionally referred to the price paid for entry or the right to enter: *admission was $5.* **Admittance** more often referred to physical entry: *we were denied* ***admittance*** *by a large man with a forbidding scowl.* In the sense of 'permission or right to enter,' these words have become almost interchangeable, although *admittance* is more formal and technical.

ad·mit /əd'mit/ ▶ **v.** (**admits, admitting, admitted**) **1** [reporting verb] confess to be true or to be the case, typically with reluctance: [with clause] *the office finally* ***admitted that*** *several prisoners had been injured* | ***I have to admit*** *I was relieved when he left* | [with direct speech] *"I am feeling pretty tired," Jan admitted* | [with obj.] *she admitted her terror of physical contact.* ■ [with obj.] confess to (a crime or fault, or one's responsibility for it): *he was sentenced to prison after admitting 47 charges of burglary* | [no obj.] *he had* ***admitted to*** *a long history of sexual misconduct.* ■ acknowledge (a failure or fault): *after searching for an hour, she finally had to* ***admit defeat*** | [no obj.] *he* ***admits to*** *having lied.*
2 [with obj.] allow (someone) to enter a place: *senior citizens are* ***admitted*** *free* ***to*** *the museum.* ■ (of a ticket) give (someone) the right to enter a place: *the voucher* ***admits*** *up to four people* ***to*** *the theme park.* ■ carry out the procedures necessary for (someone) to be received into a hospital for treatment: *she was* ***admitted to*** *the hospital suffering from a chest infection.* ■ allow (a person, country, or organization) to join an organization or group: *Canada was* ***admitted to*** *the League of Nations.* ■ allow (someone) to share in a privilege: *the doctrine held that only a chosen few were* ***admitted to*** *the covenant.* ■ [with obj.] accept as valid: *the courts can refuse to admit police evidence that has been illegally obtained.*
3 [no obj.] (**admit of**) allow the possibility of: *the need to inform him was too urgent to admit of further delay.*
– ORIGIN late Middle English: from Latin *admittere*, from *ad-* 'to' + *mittere* 'send.'

ad·mit·tance /əd'mitns/ ▶ **n.** **1** the process or fact of entering or being allowed to enter a place or institution: *people were unable to* ***gain admittance*** *to the hall.*
2 Physics a measure of electrical conduction, numerically equal to the reciprocal of the impedance.

> **USAGE** See usage at ADMISSION.

PRONUNCIATION KEY ə *ago, up*; ər *over, fur*; a *hat*; ā *ate*; ä *car*; e *let*; ē *see*; i *fit*; ī *by*; NG *sing*; ō *go*; ô *law, for*; oi *toy*; o͝o *good*; o͞o *goo*; ou *out*; TH *thin*; T͟H *then*; ZH *vision*

a

ad·mit·ted·ly /əd'mitidlē/ ▶ **adv.** [sentence adverb] used to introduce a concession or recognition that something is true or is the case: *admittedly, the salary was not wonderful, but the duties were light* | *this is admittedly an extreme case.*

ad·mix /ad'miks/ ▶ **v.** [with obj.] chiefly technical mix (something) with something else.
– ORIGIN late Middle English: back-formation from the obsolete adjective *admixt*, from Latin *admixtus* 'mixed together,' past participle of *admiscere*, from *ad-* 'to' + *miscere* 'to mix.'

ad·mix·ture /ad'miksCHər/ ▶ **n.** a mixture: *he felt that his work was an admixture of aggression and creativity.* ■ something mixed with something else, typically as a minor ingredient: *green with an admixture of black.* ■ the action of adding such an ingredient.
– ORIGIN early 17th cent. (in the sense 'act of admixing'): from **AD-** (expressing addition) + **MIXTURE**.

ad·mon·ish /əd'mäniSH/ ▶ **v.** [with obj.] warn or reprimand someone firmly: *she admonished me for appearing at breakfast unshaven* | *"You mustn't say that, Shiona," Ruth admonished her.* ■ [with obj. and infinitive] advise or urge (someone) earnestly: *she admonished him to drink no more than one glass of wine.* ■ archaic warn (someone) of something to be avoided: *he* ***admonished*** *the people* ***against*** *the evil of such practices.*
– DERIVATIVES **ad·mon·ish·ment** n.
– ORIGIN Middle English *amonest* 'urge, exhort,' from Old French *amonester*, based on Latin *admonere* 'urge by warning.' In late Middle English, the final *t* of *amonest* was taken to indicate the past tense, and its present tense *admonesse* changed on the pattern of verbs such as *abolish*; the prefix *a-* became *ad-* in the 16th cent. by association with the Latin form.

ad·mo·ni·tion /,admə'niSHən/ ▶ **n.** an act or action of admonishing; authoritative counsel or warning: *the old judge's admonition to the jury on this point was particularly weighty.*
– ORIGIN late Middle English: from Old French *amonition*, from Latin *admonitio(n-)* '(cautionary) reminder' (see **ADMONISH**).

ad·mon·i·to·ry /əd'mänə,tôrē/ ▶ **adj.** giving or conveying a warning or reprimand: *the sergeant lifted an admonitory finger.*
– ORIGIN late 16th cent.: from medieval Latin *admonitorius*, from *admonit-* 'urged,' from Latin *admonere* (see **ADMONISH**).

ad·nate /'ad,nāt/ ▶ **adj.** Botany joined by having grown together.
– ORIGIN mid 17th cent.: from Latin *adnatus*, variant of *agnatus* (see **AGNATE**), by association with **AD-**.

ad nau·se·am /ad 'nôzēəm/ ▶ **adv.** referring to something that has been done or repeated so often that it has become annoying or tiresome: *the inherent risks of nuclear power have been debated ad nauseam.*
– ORIGIN mid 18th cent.: Latin, literally 'to sickness.'

ad·nex·a /ad'neksə/ ▶ **plural n.** Anatomy the parts adjoining an organ.
– DERIVATIVES **ad·nex·al** adj.
– ORIGIN late 19th cent.: Latin, neuter plural of *adnexus* 'joined,' from *adnectere* 'fasten to.'

ad·nom·i·nal /ad'nämənl/ ▶ **adj.** Grammar attached to or modifying a noun.
– ORIGIN mid 19th cent.: from Latin *adnomen* 'added name' + **-AL**.

a·do /ə'do͞o/ ▶ **n.** trouble or difficulty: *she had much ado to keep up with him.* ■ fuss, esp. about something that is unimportant: *on the face of it, this is much ado about almost nothing.*
– PHRASES **without further** (or **more**) **ado** without any fuss or delay; immediately.
– ORIGIN late Middle English (originally in the sense 'action, business'): from northern Middle English *at do* 'to do,' from Old Norse *at* (used to mark an infinitive) and **DO**[1].

-ado ▶ **suffix** forming nouns such as *bravado, desperado*. Compare with **-ADE**[3].
– ORIGIN representing Spanish and Portuguese noun ending *-ado* or refashioning of Italian *-ata*, Spanish *-ada*, based on Latin *-atus* (past participial suffix of verbs ending in *-are*).

a·do·be /ə'dōbē/ ▶ **n.** a kind of clay used as a building material, typically in the form of sun-dried bricks: [as modifier] *adobe houses.* ■ a brick of such a type. ■ a building constructed from such material.
– ORIGIN mid 18th cent.: from Spanish, from *adobar* 'to plaster,' from Arabic *aṭ-ṭūb*, from *al* 'the' + *ṭūb* 'bricks.'

a·do·bo /ə'dōbō/ ▶ **n.** (pl. **adobos**) a spicy dish or sauce, in particular: ■ a Filipino dish of chicken or pork stewed in vinegar, garlic, soy sauce, bay leaves, and peppercorns. ■ a paste or marinade made from chili peppers, vinegar, herbs, and spices, used in Mexican cooking.
– ORIGIN Spanish, literally 'marinade.'

ad·o·les·cence /,adl'esəns/ ▶ **n.** the period following the onset of puberty during which a young person develops from a child into an adult.
– ORIGIN late Middle English: from French, from Latin *adolescentia*, from *adolescere* 'grow to maturity' (see **ADOLESCENT**).

ad·o·les·cent /,adl'esənt/ ▶ **adj.** (of a young person) in the process of developing from a child into an adult. ■ relating to or characteristic of this process: *his adolescent years* | *adolescent problems.*
▶ **n.** an adolescent boy or girl.
– ORIGIN late Middle English (as a noun): via French from Latin *adolescent-* 'coming to maturity,' from *adolescere*, from *ad-* 'to' + *alescere* 'grow, grow up,' from *alere* 'nourish.' The adjective dates from the late 18th cent.

A·do·nai /,ädō'nī, -'noi/ ▶ **n.** a Hebrew name for God.
– ORIGIN from Hebrew *'ăḏōnāy*; see also **JEHOVAH**.

A·don·is /ə'dōnis, ə'dänis/ Greek Mythology a beautiful youth loved by both Aphrodite and Persephone. He was killed by a boar, but Zeus decreed that he should spend the winter of each year in the underworld with Persephone and the summer months with Aphrodite. ■ (as noun **an Adonis**) an extremely handsome young man.

A·don·is blue ▶ **n.** a small Eurasian butterfly, the male of which has vivid sky-blue wings. ● *Lysandra bellargus*, family Lycaenidae.

a·dopt /ə'däpt/ ▶ **v.** [with obj.] legally take another's child and bring it up as one's own: *there are many people eager to adopt a baby.* ■ take up or start to use or follow (an idea, method, or course of action): *this approach has been adopted by many big banks.* ■ take on or assume (an attitude or position): *he adopted a patronizing tone* | *adopt a slightly knees-bent position.* ■ (**adopt someone as**) choose someone to receive special recognition: *at least 23 people adopted as "prisoners of conscience" remain in jail.* ■ formally approve or accept (a report or suggestion): *the committee voted 5–1 to adopt the proposal.* ■ choose (a textbook) as standard or required for a course of study. ■ choose (an animal) to become a house pet: *the best way to know a dog's traits is to adopt a mature dog.* ■ (of a local authority) accept responsibility for the maintenance of (a road).
– DERIVATIVES **a·dopt·a·ble** adj., **a·dopt·ee** /-'tē/ n., **a·dopt·er** n.
– ORIGIN late 15th cent.: via French from Latin *adoptare*, from *ad-* 'to' + *optare* 'choose.'

USAGE See usage at **ADAPT**.

a·dop·tion /ə'däpSHən/ ▶ **n.** the action or fact of adopting or being adopted: *she gave up her children for adoption* | *the widespread adoption of agricultural technology* | [as modifier] *an adoption agency.*
– ORIGIN Middle English: from Latin *adoptio(n-)*, from *ad-* 'to' + *optio(n-)* 'choosing' (see **OPTION**).

A·dop·tion·ist /ə'däpSHənist/ ▶ **n.** Christian Theology, chiefly historical a person holding the view that Jesus is the Son of God by adoption only.
– DERIVATIVES **A·dop·tion·ism** /-,nizəm/ n.

a·dop·tive /ə'däptiv/ ▶ **adj.** [attrib.] as a result of the adoption of another's child: *adoptive parents.* ■ denoting a country or city to which a person has moved and in which they have chosen to make their permanent place of residence.
– DERIVATIVES **a·dop·tive·ly** adv.
– ORIGIN late Middle English: via Old French from Latin *adoptivus*, from *adoptare* 'select for oneself' (see **ADOPT**).

a·dor·a·ble /ə'dôrəbəl/ ▶ **adj.** inspiring great affection; delightful; charming: *she looked just adorable* | *I have four adorable Siamese cats.*
– DERIVATIVES **a·dor·a·bil·i·ty** /ə,dôrə'bilitē/ n., **a·dor·a·ble·ness** n., **a·dor·a·bly** /-blē/ adv.
– ORIGIN early 17th cent. (in the sense 'worthy of divine worship'): from French, from Latin *adorabilis*, from the verb *adorare* (see **ADORE**).

ad·o·ral /ad'dôrəl/ ▶ **adj.** Zoology relating to or denoting the side or end where the mouth is situated, esp. in animals, such as echinoderms, that lack clear upper and lower sides.
– DERIVATIVES **ad·o·ral·ly** adv.
– ORIGIN late 19th cent.: from **AD-** 'at' + **ORAL**.

ad·o·ra·tion /,adə'rāSHən/ ▶ **n. 1** deep love and respect: *he gave her a look of adoration.*
2 worship; veneration: *the Adoration of the Magi.*

a·dore /ə'dôr/ ▶ **v.** [with obj.] love and respect (someone) deeply: *he adored his mother.* ■ worship; venerate: *he adored the Sacred Host.* ■ informal like (something or someone) very much: *she adores Mexican cuisine* | (as adj. **adoring**) *blowing a farewell kiss to an adoring crowd.*
– DERIVATIVES **a·dor·er** n., **a·dor·ing·ly** adv.
– ORIGIN late Middle English: via Old French from Latin *adorare* 'to worship,' from *ad-* 'to' + *orare* 'speak, pray.'

a·dorn /ə'dôrn/ ▶ **v.** [with obj.] make more beautiful or attractive: *pictures and prints adorned his walls.*
– DERIVATIVES **a·dorn·er** n.
– ORIGIN late Middle English: via Old French from Latin *adornare*, from *ad-* 'to' + *ornare* 'deck, add luster.'

a·dorn·ment /ə'dôrnmənt/ ▶ **n.** a thing that adorns or decorates; an ornament: *the necktie is no longer a necessary male adornment.* ■ the action of adorning something: *precious stones have been used for the purposes of adornment for over 7,000 years.*

A·dor·no /ä'dôrnō/, Theodor Wiesengrund (1903–69), German philosopher, sociologist, and musicologist; born *Theodor Wiesengrund.*

ADP ▶ **abbr.** ■ Biochemistry adenosine diphosphate. ■ automatic data processing.

ad·pressed /ad'prest/ ▶ **adj.** Botany lying closely against the adjacent part, or against the ground.
– ORIGIN early 19th cent.: from Latin *adpress-* 'pressed near,' from *adprimere*, from *ad* 'to, at' + *premere* 'to press,' + **-ED**[2].

ADR ▶ **abbr.** ■ alternative dispute resolution. ■ American depositary receipt.

Adrar des Ifo·ras /ä'drär dāz ,ēfôr'ä/ a massif region in the central Sahara, on the border between Mali and Algeria.

ad rem /'ad 'rem/ ▶ **adv. & adj.** formal relevant to what is being done or discussed at the time.
– ORIGIN late 16th cent.: Latin, literally 'to the matter.'

ad·re·nal /ə'drēnl/ ▶ **adj.** of, relating to, or denoting a pair of ductless glands situated above the kidneys. Each consists of a core region (**adrenal medulla**) secreting epinephrine and norepinephrine, and an outer region (**adrenal cortex**) secreting corticosteroids.
▶ **n.** (usu. **adrenals**) an adrenal gland.
– ORIGIN late 19th cent.: from **AD-** + **RENAL**.

a·dren·al·ine /ə'drenl-in/ (also **adrenalin**) ▶ **n.** another term for **EPINEPHRINE**: *performing live really gets your adrenaline going.* ■ (**Adrenalin**) trademark the hormone epinephrine extracted from animals or prepared synthetically for medicinal purposes.
– ORIGIN early 20th cent.: from **ADRENAL** + **-IN**[1].

a·dre·nal·ized /ə'drēnl,īzd/ ▶ **adj.** affected with adrenaline. ■ informal excited, charged, or tense: *they possess an adrenalized vigor that distinguishes them from other bands.*

ad·ren·er·gic /,adrə'nərjik/ ▶ **adj.** Physiology relating to or denoting nerve cells in which epinephrine (adrenaline), norepinephrine (noradrenaline), or a similar substance acts as a neurotransmitter. Contrasted with **CHOLINERGIC**.
– ORIGIN 1930s: from **ADRENALINE** + Greek *ergon* 'work' + **-IC**.

a·dre·no·cor·ti·co·trop·ic hor·mone /ə'drēnō,kôrtikō'träpik, -'trōpik/ (also **adrenocorticotrophic hormone** /-'träfik, -'trōfik/) (abbr.: **ACTH**) ▶ **n.** Biochemistry a hormone secreted by the pituitary gland and stimulating the adrenal cortex.
– ORIGIN 1930s: from *adreno-* and *cortico-* (combining forms of **ADRENAL** and **CORTEX**) + **-TROPHIC** or **-TROPIC**.

a·dre·no·cor·ti·co·tro·pin /ə'drēnō,kôrtikō'trōpin/ (also **adrenocorticotrophin** /-'trōfin/) ▶ **n.** another term for **ADRENOCORTICOTROPIC HORMONE**.

A·dri·an IV /'ādrēən/ (*c.*1100–59), pope 1154–59; born *Nicholas Breakspear*. He is the only person from England to have held the office of pope.

A·dri·at·ic /,ādrē'atik/ ▶ **adj.** of or relating to the region comprising the Adriatic Sea and its coasts and islands.
▶ **n.** (**the Adriatic**) the Adriatic Sea or its coasts and islands.

A·dri·at·ic Sea an arm of the Mediterranean Sea between the Balkans and the Italian peninsula.

a·drift /ə'drift/ ▶ **adj. & adv.** (of a boat or its passengers) floating without being either moored or steered: [as adv.] *a cargo ship went adrift* | [as adj.] *the seamen are adrift in lifeboats.* ■ (of a person) without purpose or guidance; lost and confused: [as predic. adj.] *he was adrift in a strange country* | [as adv.] *they were cast adrift in a sea of events.*
– ORIGIN late 16th cent.: from **A-**[2] 'on, in' + **DRIFT**.

a·droit /ə'droit/ ▶ **adj.** clever or skillful in using the hands or mind: *he was adroit at tax avoidance.*
– DERIVATIVES **a·droit·ly** adv.
– ORIGIN mid 17th cent.: from French, from *à droit* 'according to right, properly.'

a·droit·ness /ə'droitnis/ ▶ **n.** cleverness or skill: *he lacks political adroitness.*

ad·sci·ti·tious /,adsi'tiSHəs/ ▶ **adj.** rare forming an addition or supplement; not integral or intrinsic.
– ORIGIN early 17th cent.: from Latin *adscit-* 'admitted, adopted,' from *adsciscere*, + **-ITIOUS**[1], on the pattern of *adventitious*.

ADSL ▶ **abbr.** asymmetric (or asynchronous) digital subscriber line, a method of routing digital data on copper telephone wires, allowing high-speed Internet access and simultaneous use of the line for voice transmission.

ad·sorb /adˈzôrb, -ˈsôrb/ ▶ **v.** [with obj.] (of a solid) hold (molecules of a gas or liquid or solute) as a thin film on the outside surface or on internal surfaces within the material: *charcoal will not adsorb nitrates* | *the dye is **adsorbed onto** the fiber.*
– DERIVATIVES **ad·sorb·a·ble adj.**, **ad·sorp·tion n.**, **ad·sorp·tive adj.**
– ORIGIN late 19th cent.: blend of AD- (expressing adherence) + ABSORB.

ad·sorb·ate /adˈzôrbit, -ˈsôr-, -ˌbāt/ ▶ **n.** a substance adsorbed.

ad·sorb·ent /adˈzôrbənt, -ˈsôr-/ ▶ **n.** a substance that adsorbs another.
▶ **adj.** able to adsorb substances.

ad·stra·tum /adˈstrātəm, -ˈstratəm/ ▶ **n.** (pl. **adstrata** /-ˈstrātə, -ˈstratə/) Linguistics a language or group of elements within it that is responsible for changes in a neighboring language.
– DERIVATIVES **ad·strate** /ˈadˌstrāt/ **adj.**
– ORIGIN 1930s: modern Latin, from Latin *ad* 'to' + *stratum* 'something laid down.'

ad·su·ki /adˈso͞okē, -ˈzo͞o-/ ▶ **n.** variant spelling of ADZUKI.

ADT ▶ **abbr.** Atlantic Daylight Time (see ATLANTIC TIME).

ad·u·late /ˈajəˌlāt/ ▶ **v.** [with obj.] praise (someone) excessively or obsequiously.
– DERIVATIVES **ad·u·la·tor** /-ˌlātər/ **n.**
– ORIGIN mid 18th cent.: from Latin *adulat-* 'fawned on,' from the verb *adulari.*

ad·u·la·tion /ˌajəˈlāsʜən/ ▶ **n.** obsequious flattery; excessive admiration or praise: *he found it difficult to cope with the adulation of the fans.*
– ORIGIN late Middle English: from Latin *adulatio(n-)*, from *adulari* 'fawn on.'

ad·u·la·to·ry /ˌajəˈlātôrē/ ▶ **adj.** excessively praising or admiring: *an adulatory review* | *the tone here is adulatory and uncritical.*

a·dult /əˈdəlt, ˈadˌəlt/ ▶ **n.** a person who is fully grown or developed: *children should be accompanied by an adult.* ■ a fully developed animal. ■ Law a person who has reached the age of majority. See MAJORITY (sense 2).
▶ **adj.** (of a person or animal) fully grown or developed: *the adult inhabitants of the U.S.* ■ of or for adult people: *adult education* | *the responsibilities of adult life.* ■ emotionally and mentally mature: *an effort to be adult and civilized.* ■ sexually explicit or pornographic (used euphemistically to refer to a movie, book, or magazine).
– DERIVATIVES **a·dult·hood** /-ˌho͝od/ **n.**
– ORIGIN mid 16th cent.: from Latin *adultus*, past participle of *adolescere* 'grow to maturity' (see ADOLESCENT).

a·dult chil·dren ▶ **n.** [pl.] adults considered in relation to childhood trauma associated with parents: *adult children of divorce.*

a·dult ed·u·ca·tion ▶ **n.** educational programs or courses for adults who are out of school or college.

a·dul·ter·ant /əˈdəltərənt/ ▶ **n.** a substance used to adulterate another.
▶ **adj.** used in adulterating something.
– ORIGIN mid 18th cent.: from Latin *adulterant-* 'corrupting,' from the verb *adulterare* (see ADULTERATE).

a·dul·ter·ate /əˈdəltəˌrāt/ ▶ **v.** [with obj.] render (something) poorer in quality by adding another substance, typically an inferior one: *the meat was ground fine and adulterated with potato flour.*
– DERIVATIVES **a·dul·ter·a·tion** /əˌdəltəˈrāsʜən/ **n.**, **a·dul·ter·a·tor** /-ˌrātər/ **n.**
– ORIGIN early 16th cent. (as an adjective meaning 'spurious'): from Latin *adulterat-* 'corrupted,' from the verb *adulterare.*

a·dul·ter·er /əˈdəltərər/ ▶ **n.** a person who commits adultery.
– ORIGIN early 16th cent.: from the obsolete verb *adulter* 'commit adultery,' from Latin *adulterare* 'debauch, corrupt,' replacing an earlier Middle English noun *avouterer*, from Old French *avoutrer* 'commit adultery,' likewise from Latin *adulterare.*

a·dul·ter·ess /əˈdəlt(ə)ris/ ▶ **n.** a female adulterer.

a·dul·ter·ine /əˈdəltəˌrēn, -ˌrīn/ ▶ **adj.** (of a child) born as the result of an adulterous relationship. ■ archaic & historical illegal, unlicensed, or spurious: *an adulterine castle.*
– ORIGIN mid 18th cent. (in the sense 'due to adulteration'): from Latin *adulterinus*, from *adulterare* 'debauch, corrupt.'

a·dul·ter·ous /əˈdəlt(ə)rəs/ ▶ **adj.** of or involving adultery: *an adulterous affair.*
– DERIVATIVES **a·dul·ter·ous·ly adv.**
– ORIGIN mid 16th cent.: from the obsolete noun *adulter* 'adulterer' (see ADULTERY) + -OUS.

a·dul·ter·y /əˈdəlt(ə)rē/ ▶ **n.** voluntary sexual intercourse between a married person and a person who is not his or her spouse: *she was **committing adultery** with a much younger man.*
– ORIGIN late 15th cent.: from the obsolete noun *adulter*, from Latin *adulter* 'adulterer,' replacing an earlier form *avoutrie*, from Old French *avouterie*, likewise based on Latin *adulter.*

ad·ult·es·cent /ˌadlˈtesənt, əˌdəl-/ ▶ **n.** informal a middle-aged person whose clothes, interests, and activities are typically associated with youth culture.
– ORIGIN 1990s: blend of *adult* and *adolescent.*

ad·um·brate /ˈadəmˌbrāt, əˈdəm-/ ▶ **v.** [with obj.] formal report or represent in outline: *James Madison adumbrated the necessity that the Senate be somewhat insulated from public passions.* ■ indicate faintly: *the walls were not more than adumbrated by the meager light.* ■ foreshadow or symbolize: *what qualities in Christ are adumbrated by the vine?* ■ overshadow: *her happy reminiscences were adumbrated by consciousness of something else.*
– DERIVATIVES **ad·um·bra·tion** /ˌadəmˈbrāsʜən/ **n.**, **ad·um·bra·tive** /əˈdəmbrətiv, ˈadəmˌbrā-/ **adj.**
– ORIGIN late 16th cent.: from Latin *adumbrat-* 'shaded,' from the verb *adumbrare*, from *ad-* 'to' (as an intensifier) + *umbrare* 'cast a shadow' (from *umbra* 'shade').

Ad·vai·ta /ədˈvītə/ ▶ **n.** Hinduism a Vedantic doctrine that identifies the individual self (atman) with the ground of reality (brahman). It is associated esp. with the Indian philosopher Shankara (c 788–820).
– ORIGIN Sanskrit, literally 'nonduality.'

ad va·lo·rem /ˌad vəˈlôrəm/ ▶ **adv. & adj.** (of the levying of tax or customs duties) in proportion to the estimated value of the goods or transaction concerned.
– ORIGIN late 17th cent.: Latin, literally 'according to the value.'

ad·vance /ədˈvans/ ▶ **v. 1** [no obj.] move forward, typically in a purposeful way: *the troops **advanced on** the capital* | *she stood up and advanced toward him.* ■ make progress: *our knowledge is advancing all the time.* ■ [with obj.] cause (an event) to occur at an earlier date than planned: *I advanced the date of the meeting by several weeks.* ■ [with obj.] promote or help the progress of (a person, cause, or plan): *it was a chance to advance his own interests.* ■ [with obj.] put forward (a theory or suggestion): *the hypothesis I wish to advance in this article.* ■ (esp. of shares of stock) increase in price: *two stocks advanced for every one that fell.*
2 [with two objs.] lend (money) to (someone): *the bank advanced them a loan.* ■ pay (money) to (someone) before it is due: *he advanced me a month's salary.*
▶ **n. 1** a forward movement: *the rebels' advance on Madrid was well under way* | figurative *the advance of civilization.* ■ a development or improvement: *genuine advances in engineering techniques* | *decades of great scientific advance.* ■ an increase or rise in amount, value, or price: *bond prices posted vigorous advances.*
2 an amount of money paid before it is due or for work only partly completed: *the author was paid a $250,000 advance* | *I asked for an advance on next month's salary.* ■ a loan: *an advance from the bank.*
3 (usu. **advances**) an approach made to someone, typically with the aim of initiating a sexual encounter: *women accused him of **making** improper **advances.***
▶ **adj.** done, sent, or supplied beforehand: *advance notice* | *advance payment.*
– PHRASES **in advance** ahead in time: *you need to book weeks in advance.* **in advance of** ahead of in time or space; before: *we went on ahead in advance of the main group.*
– DERIVATIVES **ad·vanc·er n.**
– ORIGIN Middle English: from Old French *avance* (noun), *avancer* (verb), from late Latin *abante* 'in front,' from *ab* 'from' + *ante* 'before.' The initial *a-* was erroneously assimilated to AD- in the 16th cent.

ad·vanced /ədˈvanst/ ▶ **adj.** far on or ahead in development or progress: *negotiations are at an advanced stage* | *the cancer is hopelessly advanced* | *people of advanced years.* ■ new and not yet generally accepted: *his advanced views made him unpopular.*

ad·vanced de·gree ▶ **n.** a postgraduate degree, esp. a master's degree or a doctorate.

ad·vanced gas-cooled re·ac·tor (abbr.: **AGR**) ▶ **n.** a nuclear reactor in which the coolant is carbon dioxide, with uranium oxide fuel clad in steel and using graphite as a moderator.

ad·vance di·rec·tive ▶ **n.** a written statement of a person's wishes regarding medical treatment, often including a living will, made to ensure those wishes are carried out should the person be unable to communicate them to a doctor.

ad·vanced place·ment (abbr.: **AP**) ▶ **n.** the placement of a student in a high school course that offers college credit if successfully completed: [as modifier] *advanced placement English and chemistry courses.*

ad·vance guard ▶ **n.** a body of soldiers preceding and making preparations for the main body of an army.

ad·vance man ▶ **n.** a person who visits a location before the arrival of an important visitor to make the appropriate arrangements.

ad·vance·ment /ədˈvansmənt/ ▶ **n.** the process of promoting a cause or plan: *their lives were devoted to the advancement of science.* ■ the promotion of a person in rank or status: *opportunities for career advancement.* ■ development or improvement: *technological advancements.*
– ORIGIN Middle English: from Old French *avancement*, from *avancer* 'to advance.'

ad·van·tage /ədˈvantij/ ▶ **n.** a condition or circumstance that puts one in a favorable or superior position: *companies with a computerized database are **at an advantage*** | *she had an advantage **over** her mother's generation.* ■ the opportunity to gain something; benefit or profit: *you could learn something **to your advantage*** | *he saw some advantage in the proposal.* ■ a favorable or desirable circumstance or feature; a benefit: *the village's proximity to the town is an advantage.* ■ Tennis a player's score in a game when they have won the first point after deuce (and will win the game if they win the next point).
▶ **v.** [with obj.] put in a favorable or more favorable position.
– PHRASES **have the advantage of** dated be in a stronger position than. **take advantage of 1** make unfair demands on (someone) who cannot or will not resist; exploit or make unfair use of for one's own benefit: *people tend to take advantage of a placid nature.* ■ dated (used euphemistically) seduce. **2** make good use of the opportunities offered by (something): *take full advantage of the facilities available.* **to advantage** in a way that displays or makes good use of the best aspects of something: *her shoes showed off her legs to advantage* | *plan your space to its best advantage.* **turn something to advantage** (or **to one's advantage**) handle or respond to something in such a way as to benefit from it.
– ORIGIN Middle English: from Old French *avantage*, from *avant* 'in front,' from late Latin *abante* (see ADVANCE).

ad·van·taged /ədˈvantijd/ ▶ **adj.** having a comparatively favorable position, typically in terms of economic or social circumstances: *children from less advantaged homes.*

ad·van·ta·geous /ˌadvənˈtājəs/ ▶ **adj.** involving or creating favorable circumstances that increase the chances of success or effectiveness; beneficial: *the scheme is **advantageous to** your company* | *we are in an advantageous position.*
– DERIVATIVES **ad·van·ta·geous·ly adv.**

ad·vec·tion /adˈveksʜən/ ▶ **n.** the transfer of heat or matter by the flow of a fluid, esp. horizontally in the atmosphere or the sea.
– DERIVATIVES **ad·vect** /-ˈvekt/ **v.**, **ad·vec·tive** /-tiv/ **adj.**
– ORIGIN early 20th cent.: from Latin *advectio(n-)*, from *advehere* 'bring,' from *ad-* 'to' + *vehere* 'carry.'

ad·vent /ˈadˌvent/ ▶ **n.** [in sing.] the arrival of a notable person, thing, or event: *the advent of television.* ■ (**Advent**) the first season of the Christian church year, leading up to Christmas and including the four preceding Sundays. ■ (**Advent**) Christian Theology the coming or second coming of Christ.
– ORIGIN Old English, from Latin *adventus* 'arrival,' from *advenire*, from *ad-* 'to' + *venire* 'come.'

Ad·vent cal·en·dar ▶ **n.** a calendar containing small numbered flaps, one of which is opened on each day of Advent, typically to reveal a picture appropriate to the season.

Ad·vent·ist /ˈadˌventist/ ▶ **n.** a member of any of various Christian sects emphasizing belief in the imminent second coming of Christ. See also SEVENTH-DAY ADVENTIST.
– DERIVATIVES **Ad·vent·ism** /-ˌtizəm/ **n.**

ad·ven·ti·tia /ˌadvenˈtisʜ(ē)ə/ ▶ **n.** the outermost layer of the wall of a blood vessel.
– DERIVATIVES **ad·ven·ti·tial adj.**
– ORIGIN late 19th cent.: from modern Latin (*tunica*) *adventitia* 'additional (sheath).'

a

ad·ven·ti·tious /ˌadvenˈtisHəs/ ▶ **adj.** happening or carried on according to chance rather than design or inherent nature: *my adventures were always adventitious, always thrust on me.* ■ coming from outside; not native: *the adventitious population.* ■ Biology formed accidentally or in an unusual anatomical position: *propagation of sour cherries by adventitious shoots.* ■ Botany (of a root) growing directly from the stem or other upper part of a plant.
– DERIVATIVES **ad·ven·ti·tious·ly adv.**
– ORIGIN early 17th cent.: from Latin *adventicius* 'coming to us from abroad' (from *advenire* 'arrive') + **-OUS** (see also **-ITIOUS**[2]).

Ad·vent Sun·day ▶ **n.** the first Sunday in Advent, falling on or near November 30.

ad·ven·ture /ədˈvenCHər, əd-/ ▶ **n.** an unusual and exciting, typically hazardous, experience or activity: *her recent adventures in Italy.* ■ daring and exciting activity calling for enterprise and enthusiasm: *she traveled the world in search of adventure | a sense of adventure.* ■ archaic a commercial speculation.
▶ **v.** [no obj.] dated engage in hazardous and exciting activity, esp. the exploration of unknown territory: *they had* ***adventured into*** *the forest.* ■ [with obj.] dated put (something, esp. money or one's life) at risk: *he adventured $3,000 in the purchase of land.*
– ORIGIN Middle English: from Old French *aventure* (noun), *aventurer* (verb), based on Latin *adventurus* 'about to happen,' from *advenire* 'arrive.'

ad·ven·ture game ▶ **n.** a type of computer game in which the participant plays a fantasy role in an episodic adventure story.

ad·ven·tur·er /ədˈvenCHərər, əd-/ ▶ **n.** a person who enjoys or seeks adventure. ■ a person willing to take risks or use dishonest methods for personal gain: *a political adventurer.* ■ archaic a financial speculator. ■ archaic a mercenary soldier.
– ORIGIN late 15th cent. (denoting a gambler): from French *aventurier*, from *aventurer* 'venture upon' (see **ADVENTURE**).

ad·ven·ture·some /ədˈvenCHərsəm, əd-/ ▶ **adj.** given to adventures or to running risks; adventurous: *three adventuresome, energetic boys.*
– DERIVATIVES **ad·ven·ture·some·ness n.**

ad·ven·tur·ess /ədˈvenCHəris, əd-/ ▶ **n.** a woman who enjoys or seeks adventure. ■ a woman who seeks social or financial advancement by dishonest or unscrupulous methods: *a sexual adventuress scheming to make a profitable marriage.*

ad·ven·tur·ism /ədˈvenCHəˌrizəm, əd-/ ▶ **n.** the willingness to take risks in business or politics (esp. in the context of foreign policy); actions, tactics, or attitudes regarded as daring or reckless.
– DERIVATIVES **ad·ven·tur·ist n. & adj.**

ad·ven·tur·ous /ədˈvenCHərəs, əd-/ ▶ **adj.** willing to take risks or to try out new methods, ideas, or experiences: *let's be adventurous | an adventurous traveler.* ■ involving new ideas or methods: *they wanted more adventurous meals.* ■ full of excitement: *my life couldn't be more adventurous.*
– DERIVATIVES **ad·ven·tur·ous·ly adv.**, **ad·ven·tur·ous·ness n.**
– ORIGIN Middle English: from Old French *aventureus*, from *aventure* (see **ADVENTURE**).

Ad·vent wreath ▶ **n.** a wreath of evergreen foliage in which four candles are set, one to be lit on each Sunday of Advent.

ad·verb /ˈadˌvərb/ ▶ **n.** Grammar a word or phrase that modifies or qualifies an adjective, verb, or other adverb or a word-group, expressing a relation of place, time, circumstance, manner, cause, degree, etc. (e.g., *gently, quite, then, there*).
– ORIGIN late Middle English: from Latin *adverbium*, from *ad-* 'to' (expressing addition) + *verbum* 'word, verb.'

ad·ver·bi·al /adˈvərbēəl/ Grammar ▶ **adj.** like or relating to an adverb.
▶ **n.** a word or phrase functioning like an adverb.
– DERIVATIVES **ad·ver·bi·al·ly adv.**

ad·ver·game /ˈadvərˌgām/ ▶ **n.** a downloadable or Internet-based computer game that advertises a brand-name product by featuring it as part of the game.
– DERIVATIVES **ad·ver·gam·ing n.**
– ORIGIN blend of *advertisement* and *game*.

ad·ver·sar·i·al /ˌadvərˈse(ə)rēəl/ ▶ **adj.** involving or characterized by conflict or opposition: *industry and government had an adversarial relationship.* ■ opposed; hostile: *the reviewer's presumed adversarial relationship to his subject.* ■ Law (of a trial or legal procedure) in which the parties in a dispute have the responsibility for finding and presenting evidence: *equality between prosecution and defense is essential in an adversarial system of justice.* Compare with **INQUISITORIAL**.
– DERIVATIVES **ad·ver·sar·i·al·ly adv.**

ad·ver·sar·y /ˈadvərˌserē/ ▶ **n.** (pl. **adversaries**) one's opponent in a contest, conflict, or dispute: *Davis beat his old adversary in the quarterfinals.* ■ (**the Adversary**) the Devil.
▶ **adj.** another term for **ADVERSARIAL**: *the confrontations of adversary politics.*
– ORIGIN Middle English: from Old French *adversarie*, from Latin *adversarius* 'opposed, opponent,' from *adversus* (see **ADVERSE**).

ad·ver·sa·tive /ədˈvərsətiv/ ▶ **adj.** Grammar (of a word or phrase) expressing opposition or antithesis.
– ORIGIN late Middle English: from French *adversatif, -ive* or late Latin *adversativus*, from Latin *adversari* 'oppose,' from *adversus* (see **ADVERSE**).

ad·verse /adˈvərs, ˈadvərs/ ▶ **adj.** preventing success or development; harmful; unfavorable: *taxes are having an* ***adverse effect*** *on production | adverse weather conditions.*
– DERIVATIVES **ad·verse·ly adv.**
– ORIGIN late Middle English: from Old French *advers*, from Latin *adversus* 'against, opposite,' past participle of *advertere*, from *ad-* 'to' + *vertere* 'to turn.' Compare with **AVERSE**.

> **USAGE** **Adverse** means 'hostile, unfavorable, opposed,' and is usually applied to situations, conditions, or events—not to people: *the dry weather has had an* ***adverse*** *effect on the garden.* **Averse** is related in origin and also has the sense of 'opposed,' but is usually employed to describe a person's attitude: *I would not be* ***averse*** *to making the repairs myself.* See also usage at **AVERSE**.

ad·verse pos·ses·sion ▶ **n.** Law the occupation of land to which another person has title with the intention of possessing it as one's own.

ad·ver·si·ty /adˈvərsitē/ ▶ **n.** (pl. **adversities**) difficulties; misfortune: *resilience in the face of adversity | she overcame many adversities.*
– ORIGIN Middle English: from Old French *adversite*, from Latin *adversitas*, from *advertere* 'turn toward.'

ad·vert[1] /ˈadˌvərt/ ▶ **n.** Brit. informal an advertisement.
– ORIGIN mid 19th cent.: abbreviation.

ad·vert[2] /adˈvərt, ədˈvərt/ ▶ **v.** [no obj.] (**advert to**) formal refer to in speaking or writing: *he had failed to advert to the consequences that his conduct was having.*
– ORIGIN late Middle English: from Old French *avertire*, from Latin *advertere* 'turn toward' (see **ADVERSE**). The original sense was 'turn one's attention to,' later 'bring to someone's attention.'

ad·ver·tise /ˈadvərˌtīz/ ▶ **v.** [with obj.] describe or draw attention to (a product, service, or event) in a public medium in order to promote sales or attendance: *a billboard advertising beer | many rugs are* ***advertised as*** *machine washable* | [no obj.] *we had a chance to advertise on television.* ■ seek to fill (a vacancy) by putting a notice in a newspaper or other medium: *for every job we advertise we get a hundred applicants* | [no obj.] *he* ***advertised for*** *dancers in the trade papers.* ■ make (a quality or fact) known: *Meryl coughed briefly to advertise her presence.* ■ archaic notify (someone) of something: *some prisoners* ***advertised*** *the French* ***of*** *this terrible danger.*
– DERIVATIVES **ad·ver·tis·er n.**
– ORIGIN late Middle English: from Old French *advertiss-*, lengthened stem of *advertir*, from Latin *advertere* 'turn toward' (see **ADVERT**[2]).

ad·ver·tise·ment /ˈadvərˌtīzmənt, ədˈvərtiz-/ ▶ **n.** a notice or announcement in a public medium promoting a product, service, or event or publicizing a job vacancy: ***advertisements for*** *alcoholic drinks | we received only two replies to our advertisement.* ■ (**advertisement for**) informal a person or thing regarded as a means of recommending something: *unhappy clients are not a good advertisement for the company.* ■ archaic a notice to readers in a book.
– ORIGIN late Middle English (denoting a statement calling attention to something): from Old French *advertissement*, from the verb *advertir* (see **ADVERTISE**).

ad·ver·tis·ing /ˈadvərˌtīziNG/ ▶ **n.** the activity or profession of producing advertisements for commercial products or services: *movie audiences are receptive to advertising* | [as modifier] *an advertising agency.*

ad·ver·to·ri·al /ˌadvərˈtôrēəl/ ▶ **n.** a newspaper or magazine advertisement giving information about a product in the style of an editorial or objective journalistic article.
– ORIGIN 1960s: blend of **ADVERTISEMENT** and **EDITORIAL**.

ad·vice /ədˈvīs/ ▶ **n.** guidance or recommendations concerning prudent future action, typically given by someone regarded as knowledgeable or authoritative: *she visited the island* ***on*** *her doctor's* ***advice*** *| even successful businessmen asked his advice.* ■ a formal notice of a financial transaction: *remittance advices.* ■ archaic information; news: *fresh advices from Europe.*
– PHRASES **take advice** obtain information and guidance, typically from an expert: *he should take advice from his accountant.* ■ (usu. **take someone's advice**) act according to recommendations given: *he took my advice and put his house up for sale.*
– ORIGIN Middle English: from Old French *avis*, based on Latin *ad* 'to' + *visum*, past participle of *videre* 'to see.' The original sense was 'way of looking at something, judgment,' hence later 'an opinion given.'

ad·vis·a·bil·i·ty /ədˌvīzəˈbilətē/ ▶ **n.** the quality of being advisable or sensible; wisdom: *many questioned the advisability of this policy.*

ad·vis·a·ble /ədˈvīzəbəl/ ▶ **adj.** [often with infinitive] (of a course of action) to be recommended; sensible: *it is advisable to carry one of the major credit cards | early booking is advisable.*
– DERIVATIVES **ad·vis·a·bly** /-blē/ **adv.**

ad·vise /ədˈvīz/ ▶ **v.** [reporting verb] offer suggestions about the best course of action to someone: [with obj. and infinitive] *I advised him to go home* | [with obj.] *he advised caution* | [no obj.] *we* ***advise against*** *sending cash by mail* | [with direct speech] *"Go to Paris," he advised.* ■ [with obj.] recommend (something): *sleeping pills are not advised.* ■ [with obj.] inform (someone) about a fact or situation, typically in a formal or official way: *you will be* ***advised of*** *the requirements* | [with obj. and clause] *the lawyer advised the court that his client wished to give evidence.*
– ORIGIN Middle English: from Old French *aviser*, based on Latin *ad-* 'to' + *visere*, frequentative of *videre* 'to see.' The original senses included 'look at' and 'consider,' hence 'consider jointly, consult with others.'

ad·vised /ədˈvīzd/ ▶ **adj.** behaving as someone, esp. the speaker, would recommend; sensible; wise: *the department* ***would be advised to*** *do some research.*

ad·vis·ed·ly /ədˈvīzidlē/ ▶ **adv.** deliberately and after consideration (used esp. of what might appear a mistake or oversight): *I've used the term "old" advisedly.*

ad·vi·see /adˌvīˈzē, ˌadvī-/ ▶ **n.** a person who meets with an adviser.

ad·vise·ment /ədˈvīzmənt/ ▶ **n.** careful consideration. ■ advice or counsel.
– PHRASES **take something under advisement** reserve judgment while considering something.
– ORIGIN Middle English: from Old French *avisement*, from *aviser* 'look at' (see **ADVISE**).

ad·vis·er /ədˈvīzər/ (also **advisor**) ▶ **n.** a person who gives advice, typically someone who is expert in a particular field: *the military* ***adviser to*** *the president.* ■ in a school, college, or university, a teacher or staff counselor who helps a student plan a course of study: *my adviser might switch me back into Wasserman's class.*

> **USAGE** The spellings **adviser** and **advisor** are both correct. **Adviser** is more common, but **advisor** is also widely used, especially in North America. **Adviser** may be seen as less formal, while **advisor** often suggests an official position.

ad·vi·so·ry /ədˈvīzərē/ ▶ **adj.** having or consisting in the power to make recommendations but not to take action enforcing them: *an independent advisory committee | the Commission acts in an advisory capacity to the government.* ■ recommended but not compulsory: *universities may treat the recommendations as advisory.*
▶ **n.** (pl. **advisories**) an official announcement, typically a warning about bad weather conditions: *a frost advisory.*

ad·vo·ca·cy /ˈadvəkəsē/ ▶ **n.** public support for or recommendation of a particular cause or policy: ***their advocacy of*** *traditional family values.* ■ the profession or work of a legal advocate.
– ORIGIN late Middle English: via Old French from medieval Latin *advocatia*, from *advocare* 'summon, call to one's aid' (see **ADVOCATE**).

ad·vo·cate ▶ **n.** /ˈadvəkit/ a person who publicly supports or recommends a particular cause or policy: *he was an untiring* ***advocate of*** *economic reform.* ■ a person who pleads on someone else's behalf: *care managers can become advocates for their clients.* ■ a pleader in a court of law; a lawyer: *Marshall was a skilled advocate but a mediocre judge.*
▶ **v.** /-ˌkāt/ [with obj.] publicly recommend or support: *they advocated an ethical foreign policy.*
– DERIVATIVES **ad·vo·ca·tion** /ˌadvəˈkāsHən/ **n.**, **ad·vo·ca·tor** /-ˌkātər/ **n.**
– ORIGIN Middle English: from Old French *avocat*, from Latin *advocatus*, past participle (used as a noun) of *advocare* 'call (to one's aid),' from *ad-* 'to' + *vocare* 'to call.'

ad·vow·son /adˈvouzən/ ▶ **n.** (in English ecclesiastical law) the right to recommend a

member of the Anglican clergy for a vacant benefice, or to make such an appointment.
– ORIGIN Middle English (in the sense 'guardianship or patronage of a religious house or benefice,' with the obligation to defend it and speak for it): from Old French *avoeson*, from Latin *advocatio(n-)*, from *advocare* 'summon' (see ADVOCATE).

advt. ▶ **abbr.** advertisement.

ad·ware /ˈadˌwe(ə)r/ ▶ **n.** Computing software that automatically displays or downloads advertising material (often unwanted) when a user is online.

A·dy·gea /ˌädəˈgāə/ an autonomous republic in the northwestern Caucasus in southwestern Russia; pop. 440,500 (est. 2009); capital, Maikop. Its population is largely Muslim. Full name **Adygei Autonomous Republic**.

ad·y·tum /ˈaditəm/ ▶ **n.** (pl. **adyta** /-tə/) the innermost sanctuary of an ancient Greek temple.
– ORIGIN Latin, from Greek *aduton*, neuter singular of *adutos* 'impenetrable,' from *a-* 'not' + *duein* 'enter.'

adze /adz/ (**adz**) ▶ **n.** a tool similar to an ax with an arched blade at right angles to the handle, used for cutting or shaping large pieces of wood.
– ORIGIN Old English *adesa*, of unknown origin.

ad·zu·ki /adˈzo͞okē/ (also **adzuki bean**) ▶ **n. 1** a small, round, dark-red edible bean.
2 the bushy leguminous Asian plant that produces this bean. ● *Vigna angularis*, family Leguminosae.
– ORIGIN early 18th cent.: from Japanese *azuki*.

AE ▶ **abbr.** autoexposure.

Æ (also **æ**) ▶ **n.** a ligatured letter used in Old English to represent either a long sound like that in modern American English *hair* or the short vowel of *hat*; currently used in some phonetic alphabets to represent the vowel of *hat*, which is symbolized in this dictionary by /a/ (see ASH[2]).

-ae ▶ **suffix** forming plural nouns: **1** used in names of animal and plant families and other groups: *Felidae* | *Gymnospermae*.
2 used instead of *-as* in the plural of many nonnaturalized or unfamiliar nouns ending in *-a* derived from Latin or Greek: *alumnae* | *larvae*.
– ORIGIN representing Latin plural, or the Greek plural ending *-ai* of some nouns.

AEC ▶ **abbr.** historical Atomic Energy Commission.

ae·dile /ˈēˌdīl/ ▶ **n.** Roman History either of two (later four) Roman magistrates responsible for public buildings and originally also for the public games and the supply of grain to the city.
– DERIVATIVES **ae·dile·ship** /-ˌSHip/ **n.**
– ORIGIN mid 16th cent.: from Latin *aedilis* 'concerned with buildings,' from *aedes* 'building.'

AEF ▶ **abbr.** American Expeditionary Force.

Ae·ge·an /iˈjēən/ ▶ **adj.** of or relating to the region comprising the Aegean Sea and its coasts and islands.
▶ **n.** (**the Aegean**) the Aegean Sea or its region.
– ORIGIN early 17th cent.: via Latin from Greek *Aigaios* + -EAN.

Ae·ge·an Is·lands a group of islands in the Aegean Sea that form a region of Greece. The principal islands in the group are Chios, Samos, Lesbos, the Cyclades, and the Dodecanese.

Ae·ge·an Sea a part of the Mediterranean Sea that lies between Greece and Turkey, bounded on the south by Crete and Rhodes and linked to the Black Sea by the Dardanelles, the Sea of Marmara, and the Bosporus.

ae·gis /ˈējis/ ▶ **n.** [in sing.] the protection, backing, or support of a particular person or organization: *negotiations were conducted* ***under the aegis of*** *the UN*. ■ (in classical art and mythology) an attribute of Zeus and Athena (or their Roman counterparts Jupiter and Minerva) usually represented as a goatskin shield.
– ORIGIN early 17th cent. (denoting armor or a shield, esp. that of a god): via Latin from Greek *aigis* 'shield of Zeus.'

Ae·gis·thus /ēˈjisTHəs/ Greek Mythology the son of Thyestes and lover of Agamemnon's wife Clytemnestra.

Ael·fric /ˈalfrik/ (*c.*955–*c.*1020) Anglo-Saxon monk, writer, and grammarian; called **Grammaticus**. He wrote *Lives of the Saints* (993–996).

-aemia ▶ **comb. form** British spelling of -EMIA.

Ae·ne·as /iˈnēəs/ Greek & Roman Mythology a Trojan leader, son of Anchises and Aphrodite, and legendary ancestor of the Romans. When Troy fell to the Greeks he escaped and after wandering for many years eventually reached Italy. The story of his voyage is recounted in Virgil's *Aeneid*.

Ae·ne·id /iˈnēid/ a Latin epic poem in twelve books by Virgil, which relates the travels and experiences of Aeneas after the fall of Troy.

ae·o·li·an /ēˈōlēən, āˈō-/ (also **eolian**) ▶ **adj.** **1** Greek Mythology of or relating to Aeolus. ■ literary characterized by a sighing or moaning sound as if produced by the wind: *there is a pure aeolian quality, a music as of storms telling their secret*.
2 chiefly Geology see EOLIAN.
– ORIGIN early 17th cent.: from the name AEOLUS + -IAN.

ae·o·li·an harp ▶ **n.** a stringed instrument that produces musical sounds when a current of air passes through it.

Ae·o·li·an Is·lands /ēˈōlēən, āˈōlēən/ ancient name for LIPARI ISLANDS.

Ae·o·li·an mode ▶ **n.** Music the mode represented by the natural diatonic scale A–A (containing a minor 3rd, 6th, and 7th).
– ORIGIN late 18th cent.: from Latin *Aeolius* 'from *Aeolis*' (an ancient coastal district of Asia Minor) + -AN.

Ae·o·lus /ˈēələs/ Greek Mythology the god of the winds.
– ORIGIN from Greek *Aiolos*, from *aiolos* 'swift, changeable.'

ae·on ▶ **n.** Brit. variant spelling of EON.

ae·py·or·nis /ˌēpēˈôrnis/ ▶ **n.** another term for ELEPHANT BIRD.
– ORIGIN mid 19th cent.: modern Latin, from Greek *aipus* 'high' + *ornis* 'bird.'

aer·ate /ˈe(ə)rāt/ ▶ **v.** [with obj.] introduce air into (a material): *she would aerate the lawn with high heels*.
– DERIVATIVES **aer·a·tion** /e(ə)rˈāSHən/ **n.**, **aer·a·tor** /-ātər/ **n.**
– ORIGIN late 18th cent.: from Latin *aer* 'air' + -ATE[3], influenced by French *aérer*.

aer·en·chy·ma /e(ə)ˈreNGkəmə/ ▶ **n.** Botany a soft plant tissue containing air spaces, found esp. in many aquatic plants.
– DERIVATIVES **aer·en·chy·ma·tous** /-mətəs/ **adj.**
– ORIGIN late 19th cent.: from Greek *aēr* 'air' + *enkhuma* 'infusion.'

aer·i·al /ˈe(ə)rēəl/ ▶ **adj.** [attrib.] existing, happening, or operating in the air: *an aerial battle* | *an intrepid aerial adventurer*. ■ coming or carried out from the air, esp. using aircraft: *aerial bombardment of civilian targets* | *aerial photography*. ■ (of part of a plant) growing above ground: *knobby sections of aerial roots*. ■ (of a bird) spending much of its time in flight. ■ of or in the atmosphere; atmospheric. ■ insubstantial and hard to grasp or define: *the church may draw fine and aerial distinctions*.
▶ **n. 1** another term for ANTENNA (sense 2): *jiggle the aerial on the radio*.
2 (**aerials**) a type of maneuver in gymnastics, skiing, or surfing involving freestyle jumps or somersaults.
– DERIVATIVES **aer·i·al·ly adv.**
– ORIGIN late 16th cent. (in the sense 'thin as air, imaginary'): via Latin *aerius* from Greek *aerios* (from *aēr* 'air') + -AL.

aer·i·al·ist /ˈe(ə)rēəlist/ ▶ **n.** a person who performs acrobatics high above the ground on a tightrope or trapezes.

aer·i·al lad·der ▶ **n.** a long extension ladder, esp. on a fire engine, used to reach high places.

aer·i·al per·spec·tive ▶ **n.** Art the technique of representing more distant objects as fainter and more blue.

aer·ie /ˈe(ə)rē, ˈi(ə)rē/ (also **eyrie**) ▶ **n.** a large nest of a bird of prey, esp. an eagle, typically built high in a tree or on a cliff.
– ORIGIN late 15th cent.: from medieval Latin *aeria, aerea, eyria*, probably from Old French *aire*, from Latin *area* 'level piece of ground,' in late Latin 'nest of a bird of prey.'

aer·o /ˈe(ə)rō/ ▶ **adj. 1** short for AERODYNAMIC: *the cars have a lower, more aero front end*.
2 archaic short for AERONAUTICAL (see AERONAUTICS): *an aero club* | *an aero engine*.

aero- ▶ **comb. form 1** of or relating to air: *aerobe* | *aerobics*.
2 of or relating to aviation: *aerodynamics* | *aeronautics*.
– ORIGIN from Greek *aēr* 'air.'

aer·o·bat·ics /ˌe(ə)rəˈbatiks/ ▶ **plural n.** [usu. treated as sing.] feats of spectacular flying performed in one or more aircraft to entertain an audience on the ground.
– DERIVATIVES **aer·o·bat·ic adj.**
– ORIGIN World War I: from AERO- + a shortened form of ACROBATICS.

aer·obe /ˈe(ə)rˌōb/ ▶ **n.** a microorganism that grows in the presence of air or requires oxygen for growth.
– ORIGIN late 19th cent.: coined in French from Greek *aēr* 'air' + *bios* 'life.'

aer·o·bic /əˈrōbik, e(ə)ˈrō-/ ▶ **adj.** Biology relating to, involving, or requiring free oxygen: *simple aerobic bacteria*. ■ relating to or denoting exercise that improves or is intended to improve the efficiency of the body's cardiovascular system in absorbing and transporting oxygen.
– DERIVATIVES **aer·o·bi·cal·ly adv.**
– ORIGIN late 19th cent.: from AERO- + Greek *bios* 'life' + -IC.

aer·o·bics /əˈrōbiks, e(ə)ˈrō-/ ▶ **plural n.** [often treated as sing.] vigorous exercises, such as swimming or walking, designed to strengthen the heart and lungs.

aer·o·bi·ol·o·gy /ˌe(ə)rōbīˈäləjē/ ▶ **n.** the study of airborne microorganisms, pollen, spores, and seeds, esp. as agents of infection.

aer·o·brake /ˈe(ə)rōˌbrāk/ ▶ **v.** [no obj.] technical cause a spacecraft to slow down by flying through a planet's rarefied atmosphere to produce aerodynamic drag.
▶ **n.** a mechanism for aerobraking.

aer·o·drome /ˈe(ə)rəˌdrōm/ ▶ **n.** British term for AIRDROME.

aer·o·dy·nam·ic /ˌe(ə)rōdīˈnamik/ ▶ **adj.** of or relating to aerodynamics: *aerodynamic forces*. ■ of or having a shape that reduces the drag from air moving past: *the plane has a more aerodynamic shape*.
– DERIVATIVES **aer·o·dy·nam·i·cal·ly adv.**

aer·o·dy·nam·ics /ˌe(ə)rōdīˈnamiks/ ▶ **plural n.** [treated as sing.] the study of the properties of moving air, and esp. of the interaction between the air and solid bodies moving through it. ■ the properties of a solid object regarding the manner in which air flows around it. ■ [treated as pl.] these properties insofar as they result in maximum efficiency of motion.
– DERIVATIVES **aer·o·dy·nam·i·cist** /-ˈnaməsist/ **n.**

aer·o·dyne /ˈe(ə)rəˌdīn/ ▶ **n.** any heavier-than-air aircraft that derives its lift principally from aerodynamic forces.

aer·o·e·las·tic·i·ty /ˌe(ə)rō-iˌlaˈstisitē, -ˌēla-/ ▶ **n.** the science of the interaction between aerodynamic forces and nonrigid structures.
– DERIVATIVES **aer·o·e·las·tic** /-iˈlastik/ **adj.**

aer·o·foil /ˈe(ə)rəˌfoil/ ▶ **n.** British term for AIRFOIL.

aer·o·gel /ˈe(ə)rəˌjel/ ▶ **n.** a solid material of extremely low density, produced by removing the liquid component from a conventional gel. Also called FROZEN SMOKE.

aer·o·lite /ˈe(ə)rəˌlīt/ ▶ **n.** a stony meteorite, composed mainly of silicates.

aer·ol·o·gy /e(ə)ˈräləjē/ ▶ **n.** dated the study of the atmosphere, esp. away from ground level.
– DERIVATIVES **aer·o·log·i·cal** /ˌe(ə)rəˈläjikəl/ **adj.**

aer·o·mag·net·ic /ˌe(ə)rōmagˈnetik/ ▶ **adj.** relating to or denoting the measurement of the earth's magnetic field using airborne instruments.

aer·o·med·i·cal /ˌe(ə)rōˈmedikəl/ ▶ **adj. 1** of or relating to the use of aircraft for medical purposes such as transporting patients to a hospital.
2 relating to medical issues associated with air travel.

aer·o·med·i·cine /ˌe(ə)rōˈmedəsən/ ▶ **n.** a branch of medicine relating to conditions specific to flight.

aer·o·naut /ˈe(ə)rəˌnôt/ ▶ **n.** chiefly historical a traveler in a hot-air balloon, airship, or other flying craft.
– ORIGIN late 18th cent.: from French *aéronaute*, from Greek *aēr* 'air' + *nautēs* 'sailor.'

aer·o·nau·tics /ˌe(ə)rəˈnôtiks/ ▶ **plural n.** [treated as sing.] the science or practice of travel through the air.
– DERIVATIVES **aer·o·nau·tic adj.** (rare), **aer·o·nau·ti·cal adj.**
– ORIGIN early 19th cent.: from modern Latin *aeronautica* 'matters relating to aeronautics' (see AERONAUT).

ae·ron·o·my /eˈränəmē/ ▶ **n.** the science of the upper atmosphere, esp. those regions where there is significant ionization of gases.

aer·o·pha·gia /ˌe(ə)rəˈfājə, -jēə/ ▶ **n.** Medicine the swallowing of air, whether deliberately to stimulate belching, accidentally, or as an involuntary habit.

aer·o·phone /ˈe(ə)rəˌfōn/ ▶ **n.** Music a wind instrument.

aer·o·plane /ˈe(ə)rəˌplān/ ▶ **n.** British term for AIRPLANE.
– ORIGIN late 19th cent.: from French *aéroplane*, from *aéro-* 'air' + Greek *-planos* 'wandering.'

aer·o·pon·ics /ˌe(ə)rōˈpäniks/ ▶ **plural n.** [treated as sing.] a plant-cultivation technique in which the roots hang suspended in the air while nutrient solution is delivered to them in the form of a fine mist.
– DERIVATIVES **aer·o·pon·ic adj.**
– ORIGIN 1950s: blend of AERO- and HYDROPONICS.

PRONUNCIATION KEY ə *ago, up*; ər *over, fur*; a *hat*; ā *ate*; ä *car*; e *let*; ē *see*; i *fit*; ī *by*; NG *sing*; ō *go*; ô *law, for*; oi *toy*; o͝o *good*; o͞o *goo*; ou *out*; TH *thin*; T͟H *then*; ZH *vision*

a

aer·o·shell /ˈe(ə)rō,SHel/ ▸ **n.** a casing that protects a spacecraft during re-entry.

aer·o·sol /ˈerə,sôl, -,säl/ ▸ **n.** a substance enclosed under pressure and able to be released as a fine spray, typically by means of a propellant gas. ■ a container holding such a substance. ■ Chemistry a colloidal suspension of particles dispersed in air or gas.
– ORIGIN 1920s: from AERO- + SOL².

aer·o·sol·ize /ˈe(ə)rəsô,līz, -sä-/ ▸ **v.** [with obj.] technical convert into a fine spray or colloidal suspension in air: (as adj. **aerosolized**) *the drug is being tested in an aerosolized form.*

aer·o·space /ˈe(ə)rō,spās/ ▸ **n.** the branch of technology and industry concerned with both aviation and space flight.

aer·o·stat /ˈe(ə)rə,stat/ ▸ **n.** an airship or hot-air balloon, esp. one that is tethered.
– ORIGIN late 18th cent.: from French *aérostat*, from Greek *aēr* 'air' + *statos* 'standing.'

Aes·chi·nes /ˈeskə,nēz/ (*c.*390–*c.*314 BC), Athenian orator and statesman. He opposed Demosthenes' efforts to unite the Greek city states against Macedon.

Aes·chy·lus /ˈeskələs/ (*c.*525–*c.*456 BC), Greek dramatist. He is best known for his trilogy, the *Oresteia* (458 BC), consisting of the tragedies *Agamemnon*, *Choephoroe*, and *Eumenides*.

Aes·cu·la·pi·an /,esk(y)əˈlāpēən/ ▸ **adj.** archaic of or relating to medicine or physicians.
– ORIGIN late 16th cent.: from *Aesculapius*, the name of the Roman god of medicine, + -IAN.

Aes·cu·la·pi·an snake ▸ **n.** a long, slender olive-brown to grayish snake found in Europe and southwestern Asia. In ancient times it was protected because of its mythical link with the god of healing, Aesculapius. ● *Elaphe longissima*, family Colubridae.

Ae·sir /ˈāzir, ˈāsir/ Scandinavian Mythology the Norse gods and goddesses collectively, including Odin, Thor, and Balder.

Ae·sop /ˈē,säp, ˈēsəp/ (6th century BC), Greek storyteller. The moral animal fables associated with Aesop were probably collected from many sources and initially communicated orally.

aes·thete /ˈes,THēt/ (also **esthete**) ▸ **n.** a person who has or affects to have a special appreciation of art and beauty.
– ORIGIN late 19th cent.: from Greek *aisthētēs* 'a person who perceives,' or from AESTHETIC, on the pattern of the pair *athlete, athletic*.

aes·thet·ic /esˈTHetik/ (also **esthetic**) ▸ **adj.** concerned with beauty or the appreciation of beauty: *the pictures give great aesthetic pleasure.* ■ giving or designed to give pleasure through beauty; of pleasing appearance.
▸ **n.** [in sing.] a set of principles underlying and guiding the work of a particular artist or artistic movement: *the Cubist aesthetic.*
– DERIVATIVES **aes·thet·i·cal·ly** /-ik(ə)lē/ **adv.** [as submodifier] *an aesthetically pleasing color combination.*
– ORIGIN late 18th cent. (in the sense 'relating to perception by the senses'): from Greek *aisthētikos*, from *aisthēta* 'perceptible things,' from *aisthesthai* 'perceive.' The sense 'concerned with beauty' was coined in German in the mid 18th cent. and adopted into English in the early 19th cent., but its use was controversial until late in the century.

aes·the·ti·cian /,esTHəˈtiSHən/ (also **esthetician**) ▸ **n. 1** a person who is knowledgeable about the nature and appreciation of beauty, esp. in art.
2 a beautician.

aes·thet·i·cism /esˈTHetə,sizəm/ ▸ **n.** the approach to art exemplified by (but not restricted to) the Aesthetic Movement.

aes·thet·i·cize /esˈTHetə,sīz/ ▸ **v.** [with obj.] represent (something) as being beautiful or artistically pleasing.

Aes·thet·ic Move·ment a literary and artistic movement that flourished in England in the 1880s, devoted to "art for art's sake" and rejecting the notion that art should have a social or moral purpose. Its chief exponents included Oscar Wilde, Max Beerbohm, and Aubrey Beardsley.

aes·thet·ics /esˈTHetiks/ (also **esthetics**) ▸ **plural n.** [usu. treated as sing.] a set of principles concerned with the nature and appreciation of beauty, esp. in art. ■ the branch of philosophy that deals with the principles of beauty and artistic taste.

aes·ti·val ▸ **adj.** variant spelling of ESTIVAL.

aes·ti·vate ▸ **v.** variant spelling of ESTIVATE.

aes·ti·va·tion ▸ **n.** variant spelling of ESTIVATION.

aet. (also **aetat.**) ▸ **abbr.** aetatis.

ae·ta·tis /īˈtātis, ēˈtātis/ ▸ **adj.** of or at the age of: *his son, aetatis 13, learned in nothing.*
– ORIGIN early 19th cent.: Latin.

ae·ther ▸ **n.** variant spelling of ETHER (sense 2, sense 3).

AF ▸ **abbr.** ■ air force. ■ audio frequency. ■ autofocus.

af- ▸ **prefix 1** variant spelling of AD-.
2 assimilated before *f* (as in *affiliate, affirm*).

AFAIK ▸ **abbr.** informal as far as I know: *none of his stories have been filmed, AFAIK.*

A·far /ˈä,fär/ ▸ **n. 1** (pl. **same** or **Afars**) a member of a people living in Djibouti, Eritrea, and Ethiopia.
2 the Cushitic language of this people.
▸ **adj.** of or relating to this people or their language.
– ORIGIN from Afar *qafar*.

a·far /əˈfär/ ▸ **adv.** chiefly literary at or to a distance: *our hero traveled afar | for months he had loved her from afar.*
– ORIGIN Middle English *of feor* 'from far.'

A·fars and Is·sas, French Territory of the /ˈä,färz ənd ēˈsäz/ former name (1946–77) of DJIBOUTI.

AFB ▸ **abbr.** Air Force Base.

AFC ▸ **abbr.** ■ American Football Conference. ■ automatic frequency control, a system in radios and television that keeps them tuned to an incoming signal.

AFDC ▸ **abbr.** Aid to Families with Dependent Children, a federal assistance program replaced by TANF in 1997.

a·feard /əˈfi(ə)rd/ (also **afeared**) ▸ **adj.** archaic or dialect afraid.
– ORIGIN Old English, from *āfǣran* 'frighten,' from *ā-* (expressing intensity) + *fǣran* (see FEAR); used commonly by Shakespeare, but rarely after 1700 in written form.

a·fe·brile /āˈfebrəl, -ˈfē-/ ▸ **adj.** Medicine not feverish.
– ORIGIN late 19th cent.: from A-¹ 'not' + FEBRILE.

af·fa·bil·i·ty /,afəˈbilitē/ ▸ **n.** the quality of being affable; geniality: *an air of benign affability.*

af·fa·ble /ˈafəbəl/ ▸ **adj.** friendly, good-natured, or easy to talk to: *an affable and agreeable companion.*
– DERIVATIVES **af·fa·bly** /-blē/ **adv.**
– ORIGIN late Middle English: via Old French from Latin *affabilis*, from the verb *affari*, from *ad-* 'to' + *fari* 'speak.'

af·fair /əˈfe(ə)r/ ▸ **n. 1** an event or sequence of events of a specified kind or that has previously been referred to: *the board admitted responsibility for the affair | I wanted the funeral to be a family affair.* ■ a matter that is a particular person's concern or responsibility: *what you do in your spare time is your affair.* ■ (**affairs**) matters of public interest and importance: *commissions were created to advise on foreign affairs.* ■ (**affairs**) business and financial dealings: *his time was spent in winding up his affairs.* ■ [with adj.] informal an object of a particular type: *her dress was a black low-cut affair.*
2 a love affair: *his wife is having an affair.*
– ORIGIN Middle English: from Old French *afaire*, from *à faire* 'to do'; compare with ADO.

af·faire /əˈfe(ə)r, äˈfer/ (also **affaire de** or **du cœur** /də ˈkœr/) ▸ **n.** a love affair.
– ORIGIN early 19th cent.: French, literally 'affair (of the heart).'

af·fect¹ /əˈfekt/ ▸ **v.** [with obj.] have an effect on; make a difference to: *the dampness began to affect my health* | [with clause] *your attitude will affect how successful you are.* ■ touch the feelings of (someone); move emotionally: *the atrocities he witnessed have affected him most deeply.*
– ORIGIN late Middle English (in the sense 'attack as a disease'): from French *affecter* or Latin *affect-* 'influenced, affected,' from the verb *afficere* (see AFFECT²).

> **USAGE** **Affect** and **effect** are both verbs and nouns, but only **effect** is common as a noun, usually meaning 'a result, consequence, impression, etc.': *my father's warnings had no **effect** on my adventurousness.* The noun **affect** is restricted almost entirely to psychology (see AFFECT³). As verbs, they are used differently. **Affect** most commonly means 'produce an effect on, influence': *smoking during pregnancy can **affect** the baby's development.* **Affect** also means 'pretend to have or feel (something)' (see AFFECT²): *she affected a concern for those who had lost their jobs.* **Effect** means 'bring about': *the negotiators **effected** an agreement despite many difficulties.*

af·fect² /əˈfekt/ ▸ **v.** [with obj.] pretend to have or feel (something): *as usual I affected a supreme unconcern* | [with infinitive] *a book that affects to loathe the modern world.* ■ use, wear, or assume (something) pretentiously or so as to make an impression on others: *an American who had affected a British accent.*
– ORIGIN late Middle English: from French *affecter* or Latin *affectare* 'aim at,' frequentative of *afficere* 'work on, influence,' from *ad-* 'at, to' + *facere* 'do.' The original sense was 'like, love,' hence '(like to) use, assume, etc.'

> **USAGE** See usage at AFFECT¹.

af·fect³ /ˈafekt, əˈfekt/ ▸ **n.** Psychology emotion or desire, esp. as influencing behavior or action.
– DERIVATIVES **af·fect·less adj.**, **af·fect·less·ness n.**
– ORIGIN late 19th cent.: coined in German from Latin *affectus* 'disposition,' from *afficere* 'to influence' (see AFFECT²).

> **USAGE** See usage at AFFECT¹.

af·fec·ta·tion /,afekˈtāSHən/ ▸ **n.** behavior, speech, or writing that is artificial and designed to impress: *the affectations of a man who measures every word for effect | she called the room her boudoir, which he thought an affectation.* ■ a studied display of real or pretended feeling: *an affectation of calm.*
– ORIGIN mid 16th cent.: from Latin *affectatio(n-)*, from the verb *affectare* (see AFFECT²).

af·fect·ed /əˈfektid/ ▸ **adj. 1** influenced or touched by an external factor: *apply moist heat to the affected area.*
2 artificial, pretentious, and designed to impress: *the gesture appeared both affected and stagy.*
3 [predic.] archaic disposed or inclined in a specified way: *you might become differently affected toward him.*
– DERIVATIVES **af·fect·ed·ly adv.** (sense 2).

af·fect·ed class ▸ **n.** a group adversely affected from a common cause, as defined by legislation, litigation, or prevailing practice: *any employee in an affected class may volunteer to be laid off.*

af·fect·ing /əˈfektiNG/ ▸ **adj.** touching the emotions; moving: *a highly affecting account of her experiences in prison.*
– DERIVATIVES **af·fect·ing·ly adv.**

af·fec·tion /əˈfekSHən/ ▸ **n. 1** a gentle feeling of fondness or liking: *she felt **affection for** the wise old lady | he won a place in her affections.* ■ physical expressions of these feelings: *the prisoners crave affection and hence participate in sexual relationships.*
2 archaic the act or process of affecting or being affected. ■ a condition of disease: *an affection of the skin.* ■ a mental state; an emotion.
– DERIVATIVES **af·fec·tion·al** /-SHənl/ **adj.**
– ORIGIN Middle English: via Old French from Latin *affectio(n-)*, from *afficere* 'to influence' (see AFFECT²).

af·fec·tion·ate /əˈfekSHənit/ ▸ **adj.** readily feeling or showing fondness or tenderness: *a happy and affectionate family.* ■ expressing fondness: *an affectionate kiss.*
– DERIVATIVES **af·fec·tion·ate·ly adv.**
– ORIGIN late 15th cent. (in the sense 'disposed, inclined toward'): from French *affectionné* 'beloved' or medieval Latin *affectionatus* 'devoted,' from *affectio(n-)*, from *afficere* 'to influence' (see AFFECT²).

af·fec·tive /əˈfektiv/ ▸ **adj.** chiefly Psychology relating to moods, feelings, and attitudes: *affective disorders.*
– DERIVATIVES **af·fec·tive·ly adv.**, **af·fec·tiv·i·ty** /,afekˈtivitē/ **n.**
– ORIGIN late Middle English: via French from late Latin *affectivus*, from *afficere* (see AFFECT²).

Af·fen·pin·scher /ˈäfən,pinCHər/ ▸ **n.** a dog of a small breed resembling a griffin.
– ORIGIN early 20th cent.: from German, from *Affe* 'monkey' + *Pinscher* 'terrier.'

af·fer·ent /ˈaf(ə)rənt/ ▸ **adj.** Physiology conducting or conducted inward or toward something (for nerves, the central nervous system; for blood vessels, the organ supplied). The opposite of EFFERENT.
▸ **n.** an afferent nerve fiber or vessel.
– ORIGIN mid 19th cent.: from Latin *afferent-* 'bringing toward,' from the verb *afferre*, from *ad-* 'to' + *ferre* 'bring.'

af·fi·ance /əˈfīəns/ ▸ **v.** (**be affianced**) literary be engaged to marry: *Ann Elliott was affianced to Col. Lewis Morris.*
– ORIGIN late 15th cent.: from Old French *afiancer*, from *afier* 'promise, entrust,' from medieval Latin *affidare* 'declare on oath,' from *ad-* 'toward' + *fides* 'trust.'

af·fi·ant /əˈfīənt/ ▸ **n.** Law a person who swears to an affidavit.
– ORIGIN early 19th cent.: from French, present participle of *afier*, from medieval Latin *affidare* 'declare on oath' (see AFFIANCE).

af·fi·da·vit /,afiˈdāvit/ ▸ **n.** Law a written statement confirmed by oath or affirmation, for use as evidence in court.
– ORIGIN mid 16th cent.: from medieval Latin, literally 'he has stated on oath,' from *affidare*.

af·fil·i·ate ▶ **v.** /ə'filē,āt/ [with obj.] (usu. **be affiliated with**) officially attach or connect (a subsidiary group or a person) to an organization: *the college is affiliated with the University of Wisconsin.* ■ [no obj.] officially join or become attached to an organization: *the membership of the National Writers Union voted to affiliate with the United Auto Workers.*
▶ **n.** /-it/ a person or organization officially attached to a larger body: *the company established links with British affiliates.*
– DERIVATIVES **af·fil·i·a·tive** /-ətiv, -,ātiv/ **adj.**
– ORIGIN mid 18th cent.: from medieval Latin *affiliat-* 'adopted as a son,' from the verb *affiliare*, from *ad-* 'toward' + *filius* 'son.'

af·fil·i·at·ed /ə'filē,ātid/ ▶ **adj.** (of a subsidiary group or a person) officially attached or connected to an organization: *affiliated union members | Microsoft and its affiliated companies.*

af·fil·i·a·tion /ə,filē'āsнən/ ▶ **n.** the state or process of affiliating or being affiliated: *he had no particular affiliation, no close associates | his political affiliations.*
– ORIGIN late 18th cent.: from French, from medieval Latin *affiliatio(n-)*, from the verb *affiliare* (see **AFFILIATE**).

af·fine /ə'fīn, 'afīn/ ▶ **adj.** Mathematics allowing for or preserving parallel relationships.
▶ **n.** Anthropology a relative by marriage.
– ORIGIN early 16th cent. (as a noun): from Old French *afin* or Latin *affinis* 'related' (see **AFFINITY**). The mathematical sense dates from the early 20th cent.

af·fined /ə'fīnd/ ▶ **adj.** archaic related or connected.
– ORIGIN late 16th cent.: from Latin *affinis* 'related' (see **AFFINITY**) + **-ED**[1].

af·fin·i·ty /ə'finitē/ ▶ **n.** (pl. **affinities**) (often **affinity between/for/with**) a spontaneous or natural liking or sympathy for someone or something: *he has an affinity for the music of Berlioz.* ■ a similarity of characteristics suggesting a relationship, esp. a resemblance in structure between animals, plants, or languages: *a building with no affinity to contemporary architectural styles.* ■ relationship, esp. by marriage as opposed to blood ties. ■ chiefly Biochemistry the degree to which a substance tends to combine with another: *the affinity of hemoglobin for oxygen.*
– ORIGIN Middle English (in the sense 'relationship by marriage'): via Old French from Latin *affinitas*, from *affinis* 'related' (literally 'bordering on'), from *ad-* 'to' + *finis* 'border.'

af·fin·i·ty card ▶ **n.** a credit card carrying the name of an organization to which a portion of the money spent using the card is paid.

af·fin·i·ty group ▶ **n.** a group of people linked by a common interest or purpose.

af·firm /ə'fərm/ ▶ **v. 1** [reporting verb] state as a fact; assert strongly and publicly: [with obj.] *he affirmed the country's commitment to peace* | [with clause] *he affirmed that she was, indeed, a good editor* | [with direct speech] *"Pessimism," she affirmed, "is the most rational view."* ■ [with obj.] declare one's support for; uphold or defend: *the referendum affirmed the republic's right to secede.* ■ Law [with obj.] accept or confirm the validity of (a judgment or agreement); ratify. ■ [no obj.] Law make a formal declaration rather than taking an oath (e.g., to testify truthfully). ■ Law [with obj.] (of a court) uphold (a decision) on appeal.
2 [with obj.] offer (someone) emotional support or encouragement: *there are five common ways parents fail to affirm their children | good teachers know that students need to be both affirmed and challenged.*
– DERIVATIVES **af·firm·er n.**
– ORIGIN Middle English (in the sense 'make firm'): via Old French from Latin *affirmare*, from *ad-* 'to' + *firmus* 'strong.'

af·firm·a·tion /,afər'māsнən/ ▶ **n. 1** the action or process of affirming something or being affirmed: *he nodded in affirmation | an affirmation of basic human values.* ■ Law a formal declaration by a person who declines to take an oath for reasons of conscience.
2 emotional support or encouragement: *the lack of one or both parents' affirmation leaves some children emotionally crippled.*
– ORIGIN late Middle English: from Latin *affirmation-*, from the verb *affirmare* (see **AFFIRM**).

af·firm·a·tive /ə'fərmətiv/ ▶ **adj.** agreeing with a statement or to a request: *an affirmative answer.* ■ (of a vote) expressing approval or agreement. ■ supportive, hopeful, or encouraging: *the music's natural buoyancy and affirmative character.* ■ active or obligatory: *they have an affirmative duty to stop crime in their buildings | using affirmative measures to influence human rights policies.* ■ Grammar & Logic stating that a fact is so; making an assertion. Contrasted with **INTERROGATIVE** and **NEGATIVE**.
▶ **n.** a statement of agreement with an assertion or request: *he accepted her reply as an affirmative.* ■ (**the affirmative**) a position of agreement or confirmation: *his answer veered toward the affirmative.* ■ Grammar a word or particle used in making assertions. ■ Logic a statement asserting that something is true of the subject of a proposition.
▶ **exclam.** expressing agreement with a statement or request; yes.
– PHRASES **in the affirmative** so as to accept or agree to a statement or request: *he answered the question in the affirmative.*
– DERIVATIVES **af·firm·a·tive·ly adv.**
– ORIGIN late Middle English (in the sense 'assertive, positive'): via Old French from late Latin *affirmativus*, from *affirmare* 'assert' (see **AFFIRM**).

af·firm·a·tive ac·tion ▶ **n.** an action or policy favoring those who tend to suffer from discrimination, esp. in relation to employment or education; positive discrimination.

af·fix ▶ **v.** /ə'fiks/ [with obj.] stick, attach, or fasten (something) to something else: *he licked the stamp and affixed it to the envelope.*
▶ **n.** /'a,fiks/ Grammar an additional element placed at the beginning or end of a root, stem, or word, or in the body of a word, to modify its meaning. See also **INFIX, PREFIX, SUFFIX**.
– DERIVATIVES **af·fix·a·tion** /,afik'sāsнən/ **n.**
– ORIGIN late Middle English: from Old French *affixer* or medieval Latin *affixare*, frequentative of Latin *affigere*, from *ad-* 'to' + *figere* 'to fix.'

af·fla·tus /ə'flātəs/ ▶ **n.** formal a divine creative impulse or inspiration.
– ORIGIN mid 17th cent.: from Latin, from the verb *afflare*, from *ad-* 'to' + *flare* 'to blow.'

af·flict /ə'flikt/ ▶ **v.** [with obj.] (of a problem or illness) cause pain or suffering to; affect or trouble: *serious ills afflict the industry | his younger child was afflicted with a skin disease* | (as plural noun **the afflicted**) *he comforted the afflicted.* ■ Astrology (of a celestial body) be in a stressful aspect with (another celestial body or a point on the ecliptic): *Jupiter is afflicted by Mars in opposition.*
– DERIVATIVES **af·flic·tive** /-tiv/ **adj.** (archaic).
– ORIGIN late Middle English (in the sense 'deject, humiliate'): from Latin *afflictare* 'injure, harass,' or from *afflict-* 'knocked down, weakened': both from the verb *affligere*, from *ad-* 'to' + *fligere* 'to strike, dash.'

af·flic·tion /ə'fliksнən/ ▶ **n.** something that causes pain or suffering: *a crippling affliction of the nervous system.* ■ pain or suffering: *poor people in great affliction.* ■ Astrology an instance of one celestial body afflicting another.
– ORIGIN Middle English (originally in the sense 'infliction of pain or humiliation,' specifically 'religious self-mortification'): via Old French from Latin *afflictio(n-)*, from the verb *affligere* (see **AFFLICT**).

af·flu·ence /'aflōōəns/ ▶ **n.** the state of having a great deal of money; wealth: *a sign of our growing affluence.*

af·flu·ent /'aflōōənt, ə'flōō-/ ▶ **adj. 1** (esp. of a group or area) having a great deal of money; wealthy: *the affluent societies of the western world* | (as plural noun **the affluent**) *only the affluent could afford to travel abroad.*
2 archaic (of water) flowing freely or in great quantity.
▶ **n.** archaic a tributary stream.
– DERIVATIVES **af·flu·ent·ly adv.**
– ORIGIN late Middle English (sense 2 of the adjective): via Old French from Latin *affluent-* 'flowing toward, flowing freely,' from the verb *affluere*, from *ad-* 'to' + *fluere* 'to flow.'

af·flu·en·tial /,aflōō'encнəl/ informal ▶ **adj.** rich and socially influential: *the daughter of an affluential businessman.*
▶ **n.** a rich and socially influential person: *the local affluentials have driven up property values.*
– ORIGIN 1970s: blend of *affluent* and *influential*.

af·flu·en·za /,aflōō'enzə/ ▶ **n.** a psychological malaise supposedly affecting wealthy young people, symptoms of which include a lack of motivation, feelings of guilt, and a sense of isolation.
– ORIGIN 1970s: blend of *affluent* and *influenza*.

af·flux /'a,fləks/ ▶ **n.** archaic a flow of something, esp. water or air.
– ORIGIN early 17th cent.: from medieval Latin *affluxus*, from *affluere* 'flow freely' (see **AFFLUENT**).

af·ford /ə'fôrd/ ▶ **v.** [with obj.] **1** (**can/could afford**) have enough money to pay for: *the best that I could afford was a first-floor room* | [with infinitive] *we could never have afforded to heat the place.* ■ have (a certain amount of something, esp. money or time) available or to spare: *it was taking up more time than he could afford.* ■ [with infinitive] be able to do something without risk of adverse consequences: *kings could afford to be wrathful.*
2 provide or supply (an opportunity or facility): *the rooftop terrace affords beautiful views* | [with two objs.] *they were afforded the luxury of bed and breakfast.*
– ORIGIN late Old English *geforthian*, from *ge-* + *forthian* 'to further,' from **FORTH**. The original sense was 'promote, perform, accomplish,' later 'manage, be in a position to do.'

af·ford·a·ble /ə'fôrdəbəl/ ▶ **adj.** inexpensive; reasonably priced: *affordable housing.*
– DERIVATIVES **af·ford·a·bil·i·ty** /ə,fôrdə'bilitē/ **n.**

af·for·est /ə'fôrist, ə'fär-/ ▶ **v.** [with obj.] convert (land) into forest, esp. for commercial use.
– DERIVATIVES **af·for·est·a·tion** /ə,fôrə'stāshən, ə,fär-/ **n.**
– ORIGIN early 16th cent.: from medieval Latin *afforestare*, from *ad-* 'to' (expressing change) + *foresta* 'forest.'

af·fran·chise /ə'fran,cнīz/ ▶ **v.** [with obj.] archaic release from servitude.
– ORIGIN late 15th cent.: from Old French *afranchiss-*, lengthened stem of *afranchir*, from *a-* (from Latin *ad* 'to, at') + *franc* 'free.'

af·fray /ə'frā/ ▶ **n.** Law, dated an instance of fighting in a public place that disturbs the peace: *Lowe was charged with causing an affray | a person guilty of affray.*
– ORIGIN Middle English (in the general sense 'disturbance, fray'): from Anglo-Norman French *afrayer* 'disturb, startle,' based on an element of Germanic origin related to Old English *frithu* 'peace, safety' (compare with German *Friede* 'peace').

af·fri·cate /'afrikit/ ▶ **n.** Phonetics a phoneme that combines a plosive with an immediately following fricative or spirant sharing the same place of articulation, e.g., *ch* as in *chair* and *j* as in *jar*.
– ORIGIN late 19th cent.: from Latin *affricatus*, past participle of *affricare*, from *ad-* 'to' + *fricare* 'to rub.'

af·fright /ə'frīt/ archaic ▶ **v.** [with obj.] frighten (someone): *ghosts could never affright her.*
▶ **n.** fright: *the deer gazed at us in affright.*
– ORIGIN late Middle English: in early use from *āfyrhted* 'frightened' in Old English; later by vague form association with **FRIGHT**.

Af·fri·la·chi·an /,afri'lātcн(ē)ən/ ▶ **n.** an African American who is native to or resides in Appalachia: [as modifier] *Affrilachian poets.*
– ORIGIN blend of *African* (*American*) and *Appalachian*.

af·front /ə'frənt/ ▶ **n.** an action or remark that causes outrage or offense: *he took his son's desertion as a personal affront | privilege publicly worn is an affront to democracy.*
▶ **v.** [with obj.] (usu. **be affronted**) offend the modesty or values of: *she was affronted by his familiarity.*
– ORIGIN Middle English (as a verb): from Old French *afronter* 'to slap in the face, insult,' based on Latin *ad frontem* 'to the face.'

af·fron·té /,afrən'tā, ə'frəntē/ (also **affronty** /ə'frəntē/) ▶ **adj.** [predic. or postpositive] Heraldry (esp. of an animal's head) facing the observer.
– ORIGIN mid 16th cent. (as *affronty*): French, past participle of *affronter* 'to face.'

Af·ghan /'af,gan/ ▶ **n. 1** a native or inhabitant of Afghanistan, or a person of Afghan descent.
2 another term for **PASHTO**.
3 (**afghan**) a woolen blanket or shawl, typically one knitted or crocheted in strips or squares.
4 short for **AFGHAN HOUND**.
▶ **adj.** of or relating to Afghanistan, its people, or their language.
– ORIGIN from Pashto *afghānī*.

Af·ghan hound ▶ **n.** a tall hunting dog of a breed with long silky hair.

Afghan hound

af·ghan·i /af'ganē, -'gä-/ ▶ **n.** (pl. **afghanis**) the basic monetary unit of Afghanistan, equal to 100 puls.
– ORIGIN from Pashto *afghānī*.

a

Af·ghan·i·stan /af'ganə,stan/ a mountainous landlocked republic in central Asia; pop. 28,395,700 (est. 2009); capital, Kabul; official languages, Pashto and Dari (the local form of Persian).

> Part of the Indian Mogul empire, Afghanistan became independent in the mid 18th century. It was occupied by Soviet forces 1979–89; after they withdrew, the country was thrown into turmoil with various Islamic groups struggling for power. The Taliban seized power in 1996; following the attacks of September 11, 2001, US-led forces invaded Afghanistan and toppled the Taliban. A new government was formed, and a constitution was signed January 16, 2004, but instability continued in many areas of the country.

a·fi·ci·o·na·do /ə,fisн(ē)ə'nädō, ə,fisyə-/ ▶ **n.** (pl. **aficionados**) a person who is very knowledgeable and enthusiastic about an activity, subject, or pastime: *aficionados of the finest wines.*
– ORIGIN mid 19th cent. (denoting a devotee of bullfighting): from Spanish, 'amateur,' past participle of *aficioner* 'become fond of' used as a noun, based on Latin *affectio(n-)* '(favorable) disposition toward' (see AFFECTION).

a·field /ə'fēld/ ▶ **adv.** **1** to or at a distance: *competitors from **as far afield** as Hong Kong.*
2 in the field (usually in reference to hunting): *the satisfaction of a day afield.*
– ORIGIN Middle English (sense 2): from A-² 'on, in' + FIELD.

a·fire /ə'fī(ə)r/ ▶ **adv. & adj.** chiefly literary on fire; burning: [as predic. adj.] *the whole mill was afire.*

a·flame /ə'flām/ ▶ **adv. & adj.** in flames; burning: [as adv.] *pour brandy over the steaks and then set aflame.*

af·la·tox·in /,aflə'täksən/ ▶ **n.** Chemistry any of a class of toxic compounds that are produced by certain molds found in food, and can cause liver damage and cancer. ● These are produced by fungi of the *Aspergillus flavus* group, subdivision Deuteromycotina.
– ORIGIN 1960s: from elements of the modern Latin taxonomic name (see above) + TOXIN.

AFL-CIO ▶ **abbr.** American Federation of Labor and Congress of Industrial Organizations.

a·float /ə'flōt/ ▶ **adj. & adv.** **1** floating in water; not sinking: [as adv.] *they trod water to keep afloat* | [as predic. adj.] *the canoes were still afloat.* ■ on board a ship or boat: [as adv.] *flotilla sailing is a sociable way to explore while living afloat.* ■ in general circulation; current: [as predic. adj.] *the rumor has been afloat that I am far advanced in years.*
2 out of debt or difficulty: [as adv.] *I contrived to stay afloat in honest self-employment.*
– ORIGIN Old English *on flote* (see A-², FLOAT), influenced in Middle English by Old Norse *á flot(i)* and Old French *en flot*.

a·foot /ə'fo͝ot/ ▶ **adv. & adj.** **1** in preparation or progress; happening or beginning to happen: [as predic. adj.] *plans are afoot for a festival.*
2 on foot: [as adv.] *they were forced to go afoot.*

a·fore /ə'fôr/ ▶ **prep.** archaic or dialect before.
– ORIGIN Old English *onforan* (see A-², FORE).

afore- ▶ **prefix** before; previously.

a·fore·men·tioned /ə'fôr,mensнənd/ ▶ **adj.** denoting a thing or person previously mentioned: *songs from the aforementioned album.*

a·fore·said /ə'fôr,sed/ ▶ **adj.** another term for AFOREMENTIONED.

a·fore·thought /ə'fôr,тнôt/ ▶ **adj.** see MALICE AFORETHOUGHT.

a for·ti·o·ri /'ä ,fôrtē'ôrē, 'ā ,fôrtē'ôrī, -sнē'ôrē, -sнē'ôrī/ ▶ **adv. & adj.** used to express a conclusion for which there is stronger evidence than for a previously accepted one: [as adv.] *they reject all absolute ideas of justice, and a fortiori the natural-law position.*
– ORIGIN early 17th cent.: Latin, from *a fortiori argumento* 'from stronger argument.'

a·foul /ə'foul/ ▶ **adv.** into conflict or difficulty with.
– PHRASES **fall afoul of** see FALL. **run afoul of** see RUN.

a·fraid /ə'frād/ ▶ **adj.** [predic.] feeling fear or anxiety; frightened: *I'm afraid of dogs* | *she tried to think about the future without feeling afraid.* ■ worried that something undesirable will occur or be done: *he was afraid that the farmer would send the dog after them* | *she was **afraid of** antagonizing him.* ■ [with infinitive] unwilling or reluctant to do something for fear of the consequences: *I'm often afraid to go out on the streets.* ■ (**afraid for**) anxious about the well-being or safety of someone or something: *William was suddenly afraid for her.*
– PHRASES **I'm afraid** [with clause] used to express polite or formal apology or regret: *I'm afraid I don't understand.*

– ORIGIN Middle English: past participle of the obsolete verb *affray*, from Anglo-Norman French *afrayer* (see AFFRAY).

A-frame ▶ **n.** a frame shaped like a capital letter A. ■ a house built around such a timber frame.

A-frame

af·reet /'afrēt, ə'frēt/ (also **afrit**) ▶ **n.** (in Arabian and Muslim mythology) a powerful jinn or demon.
– ORIGIN late 18th cent.: from Arabic *'ifrīt*.

a·fresh /ə'fresн/ ▶ **adv.** in a new or different way: *she left the job to start afresh.*

Af·ri·ca /'afrikə/ the second largest continent (11.62 million square miles; 30.1 million sq km), a southward projection of the Old World landmass divided roughly in half by the equator and surrounded by sea except where the Isthmus of Suez joins it to Asia.

Af·ri·can /'afrikən/ ▶ **n.** a person from Africa, esp. a black person. ■ a person of black African descent.
▶ **adj.** of or relating to Africa or people of African descent.
– ORIGIN from Latin *Africanus*, from *Africa (terra)* '(land) of the *Afri*,' an ancient people of North Africa.

Af·ri·ca·na /,afri'kanə, -'känə/ ▶ **plural n.** books, artifacts, and other collectors' items connected with Africa, in particular southern Africa.

Af·ri·can A·mer·i·can ▶ **n.** a black American.
▶ **adj.** of or relating to black Americans.

> **USAGE** See usage at BLACK.

Af·ri·can buf·fa·lo ▶ **n.** a buffalo with large horns, native to Africa south of the Sahara. ● *Syncerus caffer*, family Bovidae; sometimes considered to be two species, the **Cape buffalo** and the **forest** (or **dwarf**) **buffalo**.

Af·ri·can dai·sy ▶ **n.** a plant of the daisy family, sometimes cultivated for its bright flowers. ● Family Compositae: several genera, in particular *Dimorphotheca*, *Arctotis*, and *Gerbera*.

Af·ri·can·der ▶ **n.** variant spelling of AFRIKANDER.

Af·ri·can el·e·phant ▶ **n.** the elephant native to Africa, which is larger than the Indian elephant and has larger ears and a two-lipped trunk. ● *Loxodonta africana*, family Elephantidae.

Af·ri·can Eve hy·poth·e·sis ▶ **n.** another term for EVE HYPOTHESIS.

Af·ri·can horse sick·ness ▶ **n.** a notifiable viral disease of horses, which is usually fatal. It is transmitted by biting insects and occurs chiefly in Africa, the Middle East, and the Mediterranean.

Af·ri·can·ism /'afrikə,nizəm/ ▶ **n.** **1** a feature of language or culture regarded as characteristically African.
2 the belief that black Africans and their culture should predominate in Africa.
– DERIVATIVES **Af·ri·can·ist** **n. & adj.**

Af·ri·can·ize /'afrikə,nīz/ ▶ **v.** [with obj.] **1** make African in character: (as adj. **Africanized**) *an Africanized form of Cajun music.* ■ (in Africa) restructure (an organization) by replacing white employees with black Africans.
2 (usu. as adj. **Africanized**) hybridize (honeybees of European stock) with bees of African stock, producing an aggressive strain. In recent years hybrids have spread from Brazil to the US, where they have become known colloquially as "killer bees."
– DERIVATIVES **Af·ri·can·i·za·tion** /,afrikənə'zāsнən/ **n.**

Af·ri·can lynx ▶ **n.** another term for CARACAL.

Af·ri·can Na·tion·al Con·gress (abbr.: **ANC**) a South African political party and black nationalist organization. Having been banned by the South African government 1960–90, the ANC was victorious in the country's first democratic elections in 1994 and its leader, Nelson Mandela, became the country's president.

Af·ri·can vi·o·let ▶ **n.** a small East African plant with heart-shaped velvety leaves and violet, pink, or white flowers. ● Genus *Saintpaulia*, family Gesneriaceae: several species, in particular *S. ionantha*, a popular houseplant.

Af·ri·kaans /,afri'känz/ ▶ **n.** a language of southern Africa, derived from the form of Dutch brought to the Cape by Protestant settlers in the 17th century, and an official language of South Africa.
▶ **adj.** relating to the Afrikaner people, their way of life, or their language.
– ORIGIN the name in Afrikaans, from Dutch, literally 'African.'

Af·ri·ka Korps /'afrikə ,kôr, 'äfrēkä/ a German army force sent to North Africa in 1941 under General Rommel.

Af·ri·kan·der /,afri'kandər/ ▶ **n.** an animal of a South African breed of sheep or longhorn cattle.
– ORIGIN early 19th cent. (an early form of AFRIKANER, having the same senses): via Afrikaans from South African Dutch.

Af·ri·ka·ner /,afri'känər/ ▶ **n.** an Afrikaans-speaking person in South Africa, esp. one descended from the Dutch and Huguenot settlers of the 17th century.
– DERIVATIVES **Af·ri·ka·ner·dom** /-dəm/ **n.**
– ORIGIN Afrikaans, from South African Dutch *Africander*, from Dutch *Afrikaan* 'an African' + the personal suffix *-der*, on the pattern of *Hollander* 'Dutchman.'

af·rit ▶ **n.** variant spelling of AFREET.

Af·ro /'afrō/ ▶ **n.** (pl. **Afros**) a thick hairstyle with very tight curls that sticks out all around the head, like the natural hair of some black people.
– ORIGIN 1930s: independent usage of AFRO-, or an abbreviation of AFRICAN.

Afro- ▶ **comb. form** African; African and ...: *Afro-Asiatic* | *Afro-Belizean.* ■ relating to Africa: *Afrocentric.*
– ORIGIN from Latin *Afer, Afr-* 'African.'

Af·ro-A·mer·i·can ▶ **adj. & n.** another term for AFRICAN AMERICAN.

> **USAGE** See usage at BLACK.

Af·ro-A·si·at·ic ▶ **adj.** relating to or denoting a family of languages spoken in the Middle East and North Africa. The family is commonly divided into five groups: Semitic, Omotic, Berber, Cushitic, and Chadic. Ancient Egyptian was also a member of this family. Also called HAMITO-SEMITIC.

Af·ro·beat /'afrō,bēt/ ▶ **n.** a style of popular music incorporating elements of African music and jazz, soul, and funk.

Af·ro-Car·ib·be·an ▶ **n.** a person of African descent living in or coming from the Caribbean.
▶ **adj.** of or relating to Afro-Caribbeans.

Af·ro·cen·tric /,afrō'sentrik/ ▶ **adj.** regarding African or black culture as preeminent.
– DERIVATIVES **Af·ro·cen·trism** /-trizəm/ **n.**, **Af·ro·cen·trist** /-trist/ **n.**

Af·ro·trop·i·cal another term for ETHIOPIAN (sense 2 of the adjective).

aft /aft/ ▶ **adv. & adj.** at, near, or toward the stern of a ship or tail of an aircraft: [as adv.] *Travis made his way aft* | [as adj.] *the aft cargo compartment.*
– ORIGIN early 17th cent.: probably from obsolete *baft* (see ABAFT), influenced by Low German and Dutch *achter* 'abaft, after.'

af·ter /'aftər/ ▶ **prep.** **1** during the period of time following (an event): *shortly after Christmas* | *there's only one thing to do after an experience like that* | [as conjunction] *bathtime ended in a flood after the faucets were left running* | [as adv.] *Duke Frederick died soon after.* ■ with a period of time rather than an event: *after a while he returned.* ■ in phrases indicating something happening continuously or repeatedly: ***day after day** we kept studying.* ■ (used in specifying a time) past: *I strolled in about ten minutes after two.* ■ during the time following the departure of (someone): *she cooks for him and cleans up after him.*
2 behind: *she went out, shutting the door after her.* ■ (with reference to looking or speaking) in the direction of someone who is moving further away: *she stared after him.*
3 in pursuit or quest of: *chasing after something you can't have* | *most of them are after money* | *Jenny still yearned after him.*
4 next to and following in order or importance: *in their order of priorities health **comes after** housing* | *x comes after y in the series.*
5 in allusion to (someone or something with the same or a related name): *they named her Pauline, after Barbara's mother.* ■ in imitation of: *a drawing after Millet's The Reapers.*
6 concerning or about: *she has asked after Iris's mother.*
▶ **adj.** [attrib.] **1** archaic later: *he was sorry in after years.*
2 Nautical nearer the stern: *the after cabin.*
– PHRASES **after all** in spite of any indications or expectations to the contrary: *I called and told her I couldn't come after all* | *you are my counselor, after all.* **after hours** after normal working or opening hours, typically those of bars and nightclubs: [as adv.]

she was going in to work after hours | [as adj.] *an after-hours jazz club.* **after you** a polite formula used to suggest that someone goes in front of or takes a turn before oneself: *after you, Mr. Pritchard.*
– ORIGIN Old English *æfter*, of Germanic origin; related to Dutch *achter*.

af·ter·birth /'aftər,bərTH/ ▶ **n.** the placenta and fetal membranes discharged from the uterus after the birth of offspring.

af·ter·burn·er /'aftər,bərnər/ ▶ **n.** an auxiliary burner fitted to the exhaust system of a turbojet engine to increase thrust.

af·ter·care /'aftər,ke(ə)r/ ▶ **n. 1** subsequent care or maintenance, in particular: ■ care of a patient after a stay in the hospital or of a person on release from prison.
2 childcare for the period between the end of the school day and the end of a parent's working day: [as modifier] *an aftercare facility at the local YMCA.*

af·ter·damp /'aftər,damp/ ▶ **n.** choking gas, rich in carbon monoxide, left after an explosion of firedamp in a mine.

af·ter·deck /'aftər,dek/ ▶ **n.** an open deck toward the stern of a ship.

af·ter·ef·fect /'aftəri,fekt/ ▶ **n.** an effect that follows after the primary action of something: *he was suffering the aftereffects of the drug.*

af·ter·glow /'aftər,glō/ ▶ **n.** [in sing.] light or radiance remaining in the sky after the sun has set. ■ good feelings remaining after a pleasurable or successful experience: *basking in the afterglow of victory.*

af·ter·im·age /'aftər,imij/ ▶ **n.** an impression of a vivid sensation (esp. a visual image) retained after the stimulus has ceased.

af·ter·life /'aftər,līf/ ▶ **n.** [usu. in sing.] **1** (in some religions) life after death: *most Christians believe in an afterlife.*
2 later life: *they spent much of their afterlife trying to forget the fire.*

af·ter·mar·ket /'aftər,märkit/ ▶ **n.** the market for spare parts, accessories, and components, esp. for motor vehicles. ■ Stock Market the market for shares and bonds after their original issue.

af·ter·math /'aftər,maTH/ ▶ **n. 1** the consequences or aftereffects of a significant unpleasant event: *food prices soared* ***in the aftermath of*** *the drought.*
2 Farming new grass growing after mowing or harvest.
– ORIGIN late 15th cent. (sense 2): from AFTER (as an adjective) + dialect *math* 'mowing,' of Germanic origin; related to German *Mahd*.

af·ter·most /'aftər,mōst/ ▶ **adj.** [attrib.] nearest the stern of a ship or tail of an aircraft.
– ORIGIN late 18th cent.: from AFTER (as an adjective) + -MOST.

af·ter·noon /,aftər'nōōn/ ▶ **n.** the time from noon or lunchtime to evening: *I telephoned this* ***afternoon*** | *I'll be back at three in the afternoon* | *she worked on Tuesday afternoons* | [as modifier] *the afternoon sunshine.* ■ this time on a particular day, characterized by a specified type of activity or particular weather conditions: *it was an afternoon of drama and tension.*
▶ **adv.** (**afternoons**) informal in the afternoon; every afternoon.
▶ **exclam.** informal short for GOOD AFTERNOON.

af·ter·pains /'aftər,pānz/ ▶ **plural n.** pains after childbirth caused by contraction of the uterus.

af·ter-par·ty ▶ **n.** a party held after an event, esp. a concert or another party.

af·ters /'aftərz/ ▶ **plural n.** Brit. informal dessert: *there was apple pie for afters.*

af·ter·shave /'aftər,SHāv/ ▶ **n.** an astringent, typically scented lotion for applying to the skin after shaving.

af·ter·shock /'aftər,SHäk/ ▶ **n.** a smaller earthquake following the main shock of a large earthquake.

af·ter·sun /'aftər,sən/ ▶ **adj.** denoting a product intended for application to the skin after exposure to the sun: *aftersun lotion.*

af·ter·taste /'aftər,tāst/ ▶ **n.** a taste, typically an unpleasant one, remaining in the mouth after eating or drinking something.

af·ter-tax ▶ **adj.** relating to income that remains after the deduction of taxes due.

af·ter·thought /'aftər,THôt/ ▶ **n.** an item or thing that is thought of or added later: *as an afterthought she said "Thank you."*

af·ter·touch /'aftər,təCH/ ▶ **n.** a facility on an electronic music keyboard by which an effect is produced by the player depressing a key after striking it.

af·ter·ward /'aftərwərd/ (also **afterwards** /-wərdz/) ▶ **adv.** at a later or future time; subsequently: *the offender was arrested shortly afterward.*
– ORIGIN Old English *æftewearde*, from *æftan* (see AFT) + -WARD, influenced by AFTER. *Afterwards* from *afterward* + adverbial genitive *-es, -s*.

af·ter·word /'aftər,wərd/ ▶ **n.** a concluding section in a book, typically by a person other than the author.

af·ter·world /'aftər,wərld/ ▶ **n.** a world entered after death.

AG ▶ **abbr.** ■ adjutant general. ■ Aktiengesellschaft, used in the names of German joint-stock companies. ■ attorney general.

Ag[1] ▶ **symbol** the chemical element silver.
– ORIGIN from Latin *argentum*.

Ag[2] ▶ **abbr.** Biochemistry antigen.

ag informal ▶ **adj.** short for AGRICULTURAL.
▶ **n.** short for AGRICULTURE.

ag- ▶ **prefix** variant spelling of AD- assimilated before *g* (as in *aggravate*, *aggress*).

a·ga /'ägə/ ▶ **n.** chiefly historical (in Muslim countries, esp. under the Ottoman Empire) a military commander or official.
– ORIGIN mid 16th cent.: from Turkish *ağa* 'master, lord,' from Mongolian *aqa*.

A·ga·dir /,ägə'di(ə)r/ a seaport and resort on the Atlantic coast of Morocco; pop. 487,954 (2004).

a·gain /ə'gen, ə'gān/ ▶ **adv.** another time; once more: *it was great to meet old friends again* | *they were disappointed* ***yet again***. ■ returning to a previous position or condition: *he rose, tidied the bed, and sat down again.* ■ in addition to what has already been mentioned: *the wages were low, but they made half as much again in tips.* ■ [sentence adverb] used to introduce a further point for consideration, supporting or contrasting with what has just been said: *I never saw any signs, but* ***then again***, *maybe I wasn't looking.* ■ used to ask someone to repeat something: *what was your name again?*
– PHRASES **again and again** repeatedly: *I read this author again and again.*
– ORIGIN Old English *ongēan, ongægn*, etc., of Germanic origin; related to German *entgegen* 'opposite.'

a·gainst /ə'genst, ə'gānst/ ▶ **prep. 1** in opposition to: *the fight against crime* | *he decided against immediate publication* | *swimming against the tide.* ■ in opposition to, with reference to legal action: *allegations against police officers* | *the first victim gave evidence against him.* ■ in opposition to, with reference to an athletic contest: *the championship game against Virginia.* ■ (in betting) in anticipation of the failure of: *the odds were 5–1 against Pittsburgh.*
2 in anticipation of and preparation for (a problem or difficulty): *insurance against sickness and unemployment.* ■ in resistance to; as protection from: *he turned up his collar against the wind.* ■ in relation to (an amount of money owed or due) so as to reduce or cancel it: *money was advanced against the value of the property.*
3 in conceptual contrast to: *the benefits must be weighed against the costs* | *the instilling of habits* ***as against*** *the development of understanding.* ■ in visual contrast to: *he was silhouetted against the light of the window.*
4 in or into physical contact with (something), typically so as to be supported by or collide with it: *she stood with her back against the door* | *his lips brushed against her hair.*
– PHRASES **have something against someone** dislike or bear a grudge against someone: *I have nothing against you personally.*
– ORIGIN Middle English: from AGAIN + *-s* (adverbial genitive) + *-t* probably by association with superlatives (as in *amongst*).

A·ga Khan /,ägə 'kän/ ▶ **n.** the title of the spiritual leader of the Nizari sect of Ismaili Muslims. The first Aga Khan was given his title in 1818 by the shah of Persia. The present (fourth) Aga Khan (**Karim al-Hussain Shah**, b.1937) inherited the title in 1957.

a·gal /ä'gäl/ ▶ **n.** a headband worn by Bedouin Arab men to keep the keffiyeh in place.
– ORIGIN mid 19th cent.: representing a Bedouin pronunciation of Arabic *'iḳāl* 'bond, hobble.'

ag·a·ma /ə'gämə, 'agəmə/ ▶ **n.** an Old World lizard with a large head and a long tail, typically showing a marked difference in color and form between the sexes. ● Genus *Agama*, family Agamidae: many species.
– ORIGIN late 18th cent.: perhaps from Carib.

A game ▶ **n.** informal used in reference to performing to the very best of one's ability: *she'll bring her A game tonight—she understands how important it is.*

Ag·a·mem·non /,agə'mem,nän/ Greek Mythology king of Mycenae and brother of Menelaus, commander in chief of the Greek expedition against Troy. On his return home from Troy, he was murdered by his wife Clytemnestra and her lover Aegisthus; his murder was avenged by his son Orestes and daughter Electra.

a·gam·ic /ā'gamik, ə'gam-/ ▶ **adj.** Biology asexual; reproducing asexually: *winged agamic females.*
– ORIGIN mid 19th cent.: from Greek *agamos* 'unmarried' + -IC.

ag·a·mid /'agə,mid/ ▶ **n.** Zoology a lizard of the agama family (Agamidae).
– ORIGIN late 19th cent.: from modern Latin *Agamidae*, from AGAMA.

a·gam·ma·glob·u·li·ne·mi·a /,āgamə,gläbyələ'nēmēə/ ▶ **n.** Medicine lack of gamma globulin in the blood plasma, causing immune deficiency.

ag·a·mo·sper·my /ā'gamə,spərmē, 'agəmō-/ ▶ **n.** Botany asexual reproduction in which seeds are produced from unfertilized ovules.
– DERIVATIVES **ag·a·mo·sper·mous** /ā,gamə'spərməs, ,agəmō-/ **adj.**
– ORIGIN 1930s: from Greek *agamos* 'unmarried' + *sperma* 'seed.'

ag·a·pan·thus /,agə'panTHəs/ ▶ **n.** a South African plant of the lily family, with funnel-shaped bluish flowers that grow in rounded clusters. Also called LILY-OF-THE-NILE. ● Genus *Agapanthus*, family Liliaceae (or Alliaceae).
– ORIGIN modern Latin, from Greek *agapē* 'love' + *anthos* 'flower.'

a·gape[1] /ə'gāp/ ▶ **adj.** [predic.] (of the mouth) wide open, esp. with surprise or wonder: *Downes listened, mouth agape with incredulity.*
– ORIGIN mid 17th cent.: from A-[2] 'on' + GAPE.

a·ga·pe[2] /ä'gä,pā, 'agəpī/ ▶ **n.** Christian Theology Christian love, esp. as distinct from erotic love or emotional affection. ■ a communal meal in token of Christian fellowship, as held by early Christians in commemoration of the Last Supper.
– ORIGIN early 17th cent.: from Greek *agapē* 'selfless love.'

a·gar /'ä,gär, 'ā,gär/ (also **agar-agar** /'ägär 'ä,gär, 'āgär 'ā,gär/) ▶ **n.** a gelatinous substance obtained from various kinds of red seaweed and used in biological culture media and as a thickener in foods.
– ORIGIN early 19th cent.: from Malay.

ag·a·ric /'agərik, ə'gar-/ ▶ **n.** a fungus with a fruiting body that resembles the ordinary mushroom, having a convex or flattened cap with gills on the underside. ● Order Agaricales, class Basidiomycetes, in particular the mushroom family Agaricaceae.
– ORIGIN late Middle English (originally denoting various bracket fungi with medicinal or other uses): from Latin *agaricum*, from Greek *agarikon* 'tree fungus.'

a·gar·ose /'agə,rōs, -,rōz/ ▶ **n.** Biochemistry a substance that is the main constituent of agar and is used esp. in gels for electrophoresis. It is a polysaccharide mainly containing galactose residues.

A·gar·ta·la /,əgərtə'lä/ a city in northeastern India, capital of the state of Tripura, situated near the border with Bangladesh; pop. 218,000 (est. 2009).

Ag·as·si /'agəsē/, André (1970–), US tennis player. During 1992–2003, he won the men's singles title at one Wimbledon, two US Open, one French Open, and four Australian Open tournaments.

Ag·as·siz /'agəsē/, Jean Louis Rodolphe (1807–73), US zoologist, geologist, and paleontologist; born in Switzerland. In 1837, he was the first to propose that much of Europe had once been in the grip of an ice age.

Ag·as·siz, Lake /'agə,sē/ a prehistoric glacial lake of the Pleistocene epoch that covered parts of present-day Minnesota and North Dakota in the US and Manitoba and Ontario in Canada.

ag·ate /'agit/ ▶ **n.** an ornamental stone consisting of a hard variety of chalcedony, typically banded in appearance. ■ a colored toy marble resembling a banded gemstone.
– ORIGIN late 15th cent.: from French, via Latin from Greek *akhatēs*.

a·ga·ve /ə'gävē/ ▶ **n.** a succulent plant with rosettes of narrow spiny leaves and tall flower spikes, native to the southern US and tropical America. ● Genus *Agave*, family Agavaceae: numerous species, including the century plant.
– ORIGIN Latin, from Greek *Agauē*, the name of one of the daughters of Cadmus in Greek mythology, from *agauos* 'illustrious.'

AGC ▶ **abbr.** Electronics automatic gain control.

age /āj/ ▶ **n. 1** the length of time that a person has lived or a thing has existed: *he died from a heart attack at the age of 51* | *his wife is the same age as Carla* | *he must be nearly 40 years* **of age** | *young people between the ages of 11 and 18.* ■ a particular stage in someone's life: *children of primary school age.* ■ the latter part of life or existence; old age: *with age this gland can become sluggish.*
2 a distinct period of history: *an age of technological growth* | *a child of the television age.* ■ Geology a division of time that is a subdivision of an epoch, corresponding to a stage in chronostratigraphy. ■ archaic a lifetime taken as a measure of time; a generation: *Nestor is said to have lived three ages when he was ninety years old.* ■ **(ages/an age)** informal a very long time: *I haven't seen her for ages* | *it would take an age to tell her everything.*
▶ **v.** (**ages, ageing** or **aging, aged**) [no obj.] grow old or older, esp. visibly and obviously so: *you haven't aged a lot* | *the tiredness we feel as we age.* ■ [with obj.] cause to grow, feel, or appear older: *he even tried aging the painting with a spoonful of coffee.* ■ (esp. with reference to an alcoholic drink) mature or allow to mature: [no obj.] *the wine ages in open vats or casks.* ■ [with obj.] determine how old (something) is: *we didn't have a clue how to age these animals.*
– PHRASES **act** (or **be**) **one's age** [usu. in imperative] behave in a manner appropriate to someone of one's age and not to someone much younger: *"Act your age" is not advice to behave like an adolescent.* **come of age** (of a person) reach adult status. ■ (of a movement or activity) become fully established: *space travel will then finally come of age.* **of an age 1** old enough to be able or expected to do something: *the sons are of an age to marry.* **2** (of two or more people or things) of a similar age: *the children all seemed of an age.* **through the ages** throughout history.
– ORIGIN Middle English: from Old French, based on Latin *aetas, aetat-*, from *aevum* 'age, era.'

-age ▶ **suffix** forming nouns: **1** denoting an action: *leverage* | *voyage.* ■ the product of an action: *spillage* | *wreckage.* ■ a function; a sphere of action: *homage* | *peerage.*
2 denoting an aggregate or number of: *mileage* | *percentage* | *signage.* ■ fees payable for; the cost of using: *postage* | *tonnage.* ■ informal denoting a large number of something (typically forming nouns whose plurals are correctly formed with -s): *decibelage* | *kissage.*
3 denoting a place or abode: *vicarage* | *village.*
– ORIGIN from Old French, based on Latin *-aticum*, neuter form of the adjectival ending *-aticus.*

aged ▶ **adj. 1** /ājd/ [predic. or postpositive] having lived for a specified length of time; of a specified age: *young people aged 14 to 18* | *he died aged 60.* ■ (of a horse or farm animal) over a certain defined age of maturity, typically 6 to 12 years for horses, 3 or 4 years for cattle.
2 /'ājid/ having lived or existed for a long time; old: *aged men with white hair* | (as plural noun **the aged**) *Methodist homes for the aged.*
3 /ājd/ that has been subjected to aging: *jeans in hardrock wash give a unique aged appearance.*

A·gee /'ājē/, James (Rufus) (1909–55), US writer. He wrote *Let Us Now Praise Famous Men* (1941) after touring the South with photographer Walker Evans and *A Death in the Family* (1957), for which he was posthumously awarded a Pulitzer Prize. He also wrote the screenplays for *The African Queen* (1951) and *The Night of the Hunter* (1955).

age gap ▶ **n.** a difference in age between people, esp. as a potential source of misunderstanding.

age group ▶ **n.** a number of people or things classed together as being of similar age.

age hard·en·ing ▶ **n.** spontaneous hardening of a metal that occurs if it is quenched and then stored at ambient temperature or treated with mild heat.
– DERIVATIVES **age-hard·ened adj.**

age·ing /'ājiNG/ ▶ **adj. & n.** variant spelling of **AGING**.

age·ism /'āj,izəm/ ▶ **n.** prejudice or discrimination on the basis of a person's age.
– DERIVATIVES **age·ist adj. & n.**

age·less /'ājlis/ ▶ **adj.** never growing or appearing to grow old: *the town retains an ageless charm.*
– DERIVATIVES **age·less·ness n.**

age-long ▶ **adj.** [attrib.] having existed for a very long time: *the will to change age-long habits.*

age-mate ▶ **n.** a person or animal that is the same age as another.

a·gen·cy /'ājənsē/ ▶ **n. 1** [often with adj. or noun modifier] a business or organization established to provide a particular service, typically one that involves organizing transactions between two other parties: *an advertising agency* | *aid agencies.* ■ a department or body providing a specific service for a government or similar organization: *the Environmental Protection Agency.*
2 Law the office or function of an agent: *a contract of agency.*
3 action or intervention, esp. such as to produce a particular effect: *canals carved* **by the agency of** *running water* | *a belief in various forms of supernatural agency.* ■ a thing or person that acts to produce a particular result: *the movies could be an agency molding the values of the public.*
– ORIGIN mid 17th cent.: from medieval Latin *agentia*, from *agent-* 'doing' (see **AGENT**).

a·gen·da /ə'jendə/ ▶ **n. 1** a list of items to be discussed at a formal meeting: *the question of nuclear weapons had been removed from the agenda.* ■ a plan of things to be done or problems to be addressed: *he vowed to put jobs at the top of his agenda* | *the government had its own agenda.* ■ the underlying intentions or motives of a particular person or group: *Miller has his own agenda and it has nothing to do with football.*
2 an appointment diary.
– PHRASES **on the agenda** scheduled for discussion at a meeting: *the rights of minorities would be high on the agenda at the conference.* ■ likely or needing to be dealt with or done: *his release was not on the agenda* | *national problems loomed large on the domestic agenda.* **set the agenda** draw up a list of items to be discussed at a meeting. ■ influence or determine a program of action: *the activists set the agenda, and timorous administrators usually go along.*
– ORIGIN early 17th cent. (in the sense 'things to be done'): from Latin, neuter plural of *agendum*, gerund of *agere* 'do.'

> **USAGE** Although **agenda** ('things to be done') is the plural of *agendum* in Latin, in standard modern English it is a normal singular noun with a normal plural form (**agendas**). See also usage at **DATA** and **MEDIA**¹.

a·gent /'ājənt/ ▶ **n. 1** a person who acts on behalf of another, in particular: ■ a person who manages business, financial, or contractual matters for an actor, performer, or writer. ■ a person or company that provides a particular service, typically one that involves organizing transactions between two other parties: *a travel agent* | *shipping agents* | *a real-estate agent.* ■ a person who obtains information for a government or other official body, typically in secret: *a trained intelligence agent* | *KGB agents* | *an FBI agent.*
2 a person or thing that takes an active role or produces a specified effect: *agents of change* | *bleaching agents.* ■ Grammar the doer of an action, typically expressed as the subject of an active verb or in a *by* phrase with a passive verb.
– ORIGIN late Middle English (in the sense 'someone or something that produces an effect'): from Latin *agent-* 'doing,' from *agere.*

a·gent-gen·er·al ▶ **n.** (pl. **agents-general**) the representative of an Australian state or Canadian province in a major foreign city.

a·gent noun ▶ **n.** a noun denoting someone or something that performs the action of a verb, typically ending in *-er* or *-or*, e.g., *worker, accelerator.*

A·gent Or·ange ▶ **n.** a defoliant chemical used by the US in the Vietnam War.

a·gent pro·vo·ca·teur /ä,ZHän(t) prə,väkə'tər/ ▶ **n.** (pl. **agents provocateurs** pronunc. **same** or /-'tərz/) a person who induces others to break the law so that they can be convicted.
– ORIGIN late 19th cent.: French, literally 'provocative agent.'

age of con·sent ▶ **n.** the age at which a person's, typically a girl's, consent to sexual intercourse is valid in law.

age of dis·cre·tion ▶ **n.** the age at which someone is considered able to manage their own affairs or take responsibility for their actions.

age-old ▶ **adj.** having existed for a very long time: *the haunting, age-old love call of the prairie chicken.*

ag·glom·er·ate ▶ **v.** /ə'glämə,rāt/ collect or form into a mass or group: [with obj.] *companies agglomerate multiple sites such as chains of stores* | [no obj.] *these small particles soon agglomerate together.*
▶ **n.** /-rit/ a mass or collection of things: *a multimedia agglomerate.* ■ Geology a volcanic rock consisting of large fragments bonded together.
▶ **adj.** /-rit/ collected or formed into a mass.
– DERIVATIVES **ag·glom·er·a·tive** /-,rātiv, -rətiv/ **adj.**
– ORIGIN late 17th cent.: from Latin *agglomerat-* 'added to,' from the verb *agglomerare*, from *ad-* 'to' + *glomerare* (from *glomus* 'ball').

ag·glom·er·a·tion /ə,glämə'rāSHən/ ▶ **n.** a mass or collection of things; an assemblage: *the arts center is an agglomeration of theaters, galleries, shops, restaurants, and bars.*

ag·glu·ti·nate /ə'glo͞otn,āt/ ▶ **v.** firmly stick or be stuck together to form a mass: (as adj. **agglutinated**) *rhinoceros horns are agglutinated masses of hair.* ■ Biology (with reference to bacteria or red blood cells) clump together: [with obj.] *these strains agglutinate human red cells* | [no obj.] *cell fragments agglutinate and form intricate meshes.* ■ [with obj.] Linguistics combine (simple words or parts of words) without change of form to express compound ideas.
– DERIVATIVES **ag·glu·ti·na·tion** /ə,glo͞otn'āSHən/ **n.**
– ORIGIN mid 16th cent.: from Latin *agglutinat-* 'caused to adhere,' from the verb *agglutinare*, from *ad-* 'to' + *glutinare* (from *gluten* 'glue').

ag·glu·ti·na·tive /ə'glo͞otn-ətiv/ ▶ **adj.** Linguistics (of a language) forming words predominantly by agglutination, rather than by inflection or by using isolated elements. Examples include Hungarian, Turkish, Korean, and Swahili.

ag·glu·ti·nin /ə'glo͞otn-in/ ▶ **n.** Biology an antibody, lectin, or other substance that causes agglutination.
– ORIGIN late 19th cent.: from **AGGLUTINATE** + **-IN**¹.

ag·glu·tin·o·gen /ə'glo͞otn-əjən/ ▶ **n.** Biology an antigen that stimulates the production of an agglutinin.

ag·gra·da·tion /,agrə'dāSHən/ ▶ **n.** the deposition of material by a river, stream, or current.
– ORIGIN late 19th cent.: from **AG-** (expressing increase) + *(de)gradation.*

ag·gran·dize /ə'gran,dīz/ ▶ **v.** [with obj.] increase the power, status, or wealth of: *an action intended to aggrandize the Frankish dynasty.* ■ enhance the reputation of (someone) beyond what is justified by the facts: *he hoped to aggrandize himself by dying a hero's death.*
– DERIVATIVES **ag·gran·dize·ment** /-,dīzmənt, -diz-/ **n.**, **ag·gran·diz·er n.**
– ORIGIN mid 17th cent. (in the general sense 'increase, magnify'): from French *agrandiss-*, lengthened stem of *agrandir*, probably from Italian *aggrandire*, from Latin *grandis* 'large.' The ending was changed by association with verbs ending in **-IZE**.

ag·gra·vate /'agrə,vāt/ ▶ **v.** [with obj.] **1** make (a problem, injury, or offense) worse or more serious: *military action would only aggravate the situation.*
2 informal annoy or exasperate (someone), esp. persistently: *the gesture aggravated me even more* | (as adj. **aggravating**) *she found him thoroughly aggravating and unprofessional.*
– DERIVATIVES **ag·gra·vat·ing·ly adv.**
– ORIGIN mid 16th cent.: from Latin *aggravat-* 'made heavy,' from the verb *aggravare*, from *ad-* (expressing increase) + *gravis* 'heavy.'

> **USAGE Aggravate** in the sense 'annoy or exasperate' dates back to the 17th century and has been so used by respected writers ever since. This use is still regarded as incorrect by some traditionalists on the grounds that it is too radical a departure from the etymological meaning of 'make heavy.' It is, however, comparable to meaning changes in hundreds of other words that have long been accepted without comment.

ag·gra·vat·ed /'agrə,vātid/ ▶ **adj.** [attrib.] (of an offense) made more serious by attendant circumstances (such as frame of mind): *aggravated burglary.* ■ (of a penalty) made more severe in recognition of the seriousness of an offense: *aggravated damages.*

ag·gra·va·tion /,agrə'vāSHən/ ▶ **n. 1** an intensification of a negative quality or aspect: *Negotiators were optimistic despite the aggravation of the standoff caused by the press release.* ■ (in homeopathy) the temporary appearance or worsening of symptoms that a remedy is intended to eliminate, taken to be caused by too strong a dose.
2 the state of being aggravated: *Internet users' aggravation with the deluge of pop-up ads.*
3 a cause of annoyance or irritation: *the aggravations of living with a self-confessed sports junkie.*

ag·gre·gate ▶ **n.** /'agrigit/ **1** a whole formed by combining several (typically disparate) elements: *the council was an aggregate of three regional assemblies.* ■ the total number of points scored by a player or team in a series of sporting contests: *the result put the sides even* **on aggregate**.
2 a material or structure formed from a loosely compacted mass of fragments or particles. ■ pieces of broken or crushed stone or gravel used to make concrete, or more generally in building and construction work.
▶ **adj.** [attrib.] formed or calculated by the combination of many separate units or items; total: *the aggregate amount of grants made.* ■ Botany (of a group of species) comprising several very similar species formerly regarded as a single species. ■ Economics denoting the total supply or demand for goods and services in an economy at a particular time: *aggregate demand* | *aggregate supply.*
▶ **v.** /-,gāt/ form or group into a class or cluster: [no obj.] *the butterflies aggregate in dense groups.*

– PHRASES **in (the) aggregate** in total; as a whole.
– DERIVATIVES **ag·gre·ga·tion** /ˌagriˈgāSHən/ **n.**, **ag·gre·ga·tive** /-ˌgātiv/ **adj.**
– ORIGIN late Middle English: from Latin *aggregat-* 'herded together,' from the verb *aggregare*, from *ad-* 'toward' + *grex*, *greg-* 'a flock.'

ag·gre·gate fruit ▶ **n.** Botany a fruit formed from several carpels derived from the same flower, e.g., a raspberry.

ag·gre·ga·tor /ˈagriˌgātər/ ▶ **n. 1** Computing a website or program that collects related items of content and displays them or links to them.
2 a wholesale buyer or broker of a utility service, such as electricity or long-distance telephone service, who packages it and sells it to consumers.

ag·gres·sion /əˈgreSHən/ ▶ **n.** hostile or violent behavior or attitudes toward another; readiness to attack or confront: *his chin was jutting with aggression* | *territorial aggression between individuals of the same species.* ■ the action of attacking without provocation, esp. in beginning a quarrel or war: *the dictator resorted to armed aggression* | *he called for an end to foreign aggression against his country.* ■ forceful and sometimes overly assertive pursuit of one's aims and interests.
– ORIGIN early 17th cent. (in the sense 'an attack'): from Latin *aggressio(n-)*, from *aggredi* 'to attack,' from *ad-* 'toward' + *gradi* 'proceed, walk.'

ag·gres·sive /əˈgresiv/ ▶ **adj.** ready or likely to attack or confront; characterized by or resulting from aggression: *he's very uncooperative and aggressive* | *aggressive behavior.* ■ pursuing one's aims and interests forcefully, sometimes unduly so: *an aggressive businessman.*
– DERIVATIVES **ag·gres·sive·ly** **adv.**, **ag·gres·sive·ness** **n.**
– ORIGIN early 19th cent.: from Latin *aggress-* 'attacked' (from the verb *aggredi*) + **-IVE**; compare with French *agressif*, *-ive*.

ag·gres·sor /əˈgresər/ ▶ **n.** a person or country that attacks another first.
– ORIGIN mid 17th cent.: from late Latin, from *aggredi* 'to attack' (see **AGGRESSION**).

ag·grieved /əˈgrēvd/ ▶ **adj.** feeling resentment at having been unfairly treated: *they were aggrieved at the outcome* | *she did not see herself as the aggrieved party.*
– DERIVATIVES **ag·griev·ed·ly** /-vidlē/ **adv.**
– ORIGIN Middle English (in the sense 'distressed'): past participle of *aggrieve*, from Old French *agrever* 'make heavier,' based on Latin *aggravare* (see **AGGRAVATE**).

ag·gro /ˈagrō/ ▶ **n.** Brit. informal aggressive, violent behavior. ■ problems and difficulties.
– ORIGIN 1960s: abbreviation of *aggravation* (see **AGGRAVATE**), or of **AGGRESSION**.

a·ghast /əˈgast/ ▶ **adj.** [predic.] filled with horror or shock: *when the news came out they were aghast.*
– ORIGIN late Middle English: past participle of the obsolete verb *agast*, *gast* 'frighten,' from Old English *gǣsten*. The spelling with *gh* (originally Scots) became general by about 1700, probably influenced by **GHOST**; compare with **GHASTLY**.

ag·ile /ˈajəl/ ▶ **adj.** able to move quickly and easily: *Ruth was as agile as a monkey.* ■ able to think and understand quickly: *his vague manner concealed an agile mind.*
– DERIVATIVES **ag·ile·ly** /ˈajə(l)lē/ **adv.**, **a·gil·i·ty** /əˈjilitē/ **n.**
– ORIGIN late Middle English: via French from Latin *agilis*, from *agere* 'do.'

ag·ile gib·bon ▶ **n.** a gibbon with color varying from light buff to black, found in Southeast Asia. ● *Hylobates agilis*, family Hylobatidae.

a·gin /əˈgin/ ▶ **prep.** dialect form of **AGAINST**.
– ORIGIN early 19th cent.: variant of the obsolete preposition *again*, with the same meaning.

Ag·in·court, Bat·tle of /ˈajinˌkôrt, äZHanˈko͝or/ a battle in northern France in 1415 during the Hundred Years War, in which the English under Henry V defeated a large French army. The victory, achieved largely by use of the longbow, allowed Henry to occupy Normandy.

ag·ing /ˈājiNG/ (also **ageing**) ▶ **n.** the process of growing old: *the external signs of aging* | [as modifier] *the aging process.* ■ the process of change in the properties of a material occurring over a period, either spontaneously or through deliberate action.
▶ **adj.** (of a person) growing old; elderly: *looking after aging relatives* | *an aging population.* ■ (of a thing) reaching the end of useful life; obsolescent: *the world's aging fleet of oil tankers.*

ag·ism ▶ **n.** variant spelling of **AGEISM**.
– DERIVATIVES **ag·ist** **adj. & n.**

ag·i·tate /ˈajiˌtāt/ ▶ **v.** [with obj.] make (someone) troubled or nervous: *the thought of questioning Toby agitated him extremely.* ■ [no obj.] campaign to arouse public concern about an issue in the hope of prompting action: *they agitated for a reversal of the decision.* ■ stir or disturb (something, esp. a liquid) briskly: *agitate the water to disperse the oil.*
– ORIGIN late Middle English (in the sense 'drive away'): from Latin *agitat-* 'agitated, driven,' from *agitare*, frequentative of *agere* 'do, drive.'

ag·i·tat·ed /ˈajiˌtātid/ ▶ **adj.** feeling or appearing troubled or nervous: *there's no point getting agitated.*
– DERIVATIVES **ag·i·tat·ed·ly** **adv.**

ag·i·ta·tion /ˌajiˈtāSHən/ ▶ **n. 1** a state of anxiety or nervous excitement: *she was wringing her hands in agitation.* ■ the action of arousing public concern about an issue and pressing for action on it: *widespread agitation for social reform.*
2 the action of briskly stirring or disturbing something, esp. a liquid.
– ORIGIN mid 16th cent. (in the sense 'action, being active'): from Latin *agitatio(n-)*, from the verb *agitare* (see **AGITATE**).

a·gi·ta·to /ˌajiˈtätō/ ▶ **adv. & adj.** Music (esp. as a direction after a tempo marking) in an agitated manner: *allegro agitato.*
– ORIGIN Italian, literally 'agitated.'

ag·i·ta·tor /ˈajiˌtātər/ ▶ **n. 1** a person who urges others to protest or rebel: *an activist and agitator who fought for striking miners.*
2 an apparatus for stirring liquid, as in a washing machine or a photographic developing tank.
– ORIGIN mid 17th cent. (denoting a delegate of private soldiers in the Parliamentary Army during the English Civil War (1642–49)) from Latin, from *agitare* (see **AGITATE**). Sense 1 dates from the mid 18th cent.

ag·it·prop /ˈajitˌpräp/ ▶ **n.** political (originally communist) propaganda, esp. in art or literature: [as modifier] *agitprop painters.*
– ORIGIN 1930s: Russian, blend of *agitatsiya* 'agitation' and *propaganda* 'propaganda.'

a·gleam /əˈglēm/ ▶ **adj.** [predic.] gleaming: *yellow fur agleam in the sun.*

ag·let /ˈaglit/ ▶ **n.** a metal or plastic tube fixed tightly around each end of a shoelace.
– ORIGIN late Middle English: from French *aiguillette* 'small needle,' diminutive of *aiguille* (see **AIGUILLE**).

a·gley /əˈglā, əˈglē/ ▶ **adv.** Scottish askew; awry.
– ORIGIN late 18th cent.: from **A-²** 'on' + Scots *gley* 'squint,' of unknown origin.

a·glow /əˈglō/ ▶ **adj.** [predic.] glowing: *his bald head aglow under the lights.*

ag·ma /ˈagmə/ ▶ **n.** the speech sound represented by *ng* as in *thing*, a velar nasal consonant represented by ŋ in the International Phonetic Alphabet.
– ORIGIN 1950s: from late Greek, from Greek, literally 'fragment.'

ag·nail /ˈagˌnāl/ ▶ **n.** another term for **HANGNAIL**.

ag·nate /ˈagˌnāt/ chiefly Law ▶ **n.** a person descended from the same male ancestor as another specified or implied person, esp. through the male line.
▶ **adj.** descended from the same male ancestor as a specified or implied subject, esp. through the male line. Compare with **COGNATE** (sense 2 of the adjective). ■ of the same clan or nation.
– DERIVATIVES **ag·nat·ic** /agˈnatik/ **adj.**, **ag·na·tion** /agˈnāSHən/ **n.**
– ORIGIN late 15th cent. (as a noun): from Latin *agnatus*, from *ad-* 'to' + *gnatus*, *natus* 'born.'

Ag·na·tha /ˈagnəTHə/ Zoology a group of primitive jawless vertebrates that includes the lampreys, hagfishes, and many fossil fishlike forms. Compare with **CYCLOSTOME**. ● Superclass Agnatha: the living forms are in the classes Myxini (hagfishes) and Cephalaspidomorphi (lampreys).
– DERIVATIVES **ag·na·than** **n. & adj.**
– ORIGIN from modern Latin *Agnatha* (superclass name), from **A-¹** 'without' + Greek *gnathos* 'jaw.'

Ag·nes, St.¹ /ˈagnəs/ (died *c.*304), Roman martyr. The patron saint of virgins, her emblem is a lamb (Latin *agnus*). Feast day, January 21.

Ag·nes, St.² (c.1211–82), patron saint of Bohemia. She was canonized in 1989. Feast day, March 2.

Agne·si /änˈyāzē/, Maria Gaetana (1718–99), Italian mathematician and philosopher. She wrote a mathematics textbook and was the first woman appointed to a university chair in mathematics.

Ag·new /ˈagn(y)o͞o/, Spiro Theodore (1918–96), US politician. He served as Richard Nixon's vice president 1969–73 but was forced to resign because of corruption charges against him that stemmed from his time as governor of Maryland 1967–69.

Ag·ni /ˈagnē, ˈəg-/ the Vedic god of fire, the priest of the gods and the god of the priests.

a·gno·lot·ti /ˌanyəˈlätē/ ▶ **n.** pasta squares stuffed with a variety of fillings, like small ravioli.
– ORIGIN Italian.

ag·no·sia /agˈnōZH(ē)ə/ ▶ **n.** Medicine inability to interpret sensations and hence to recognize things, typically as a result of brain damage.
– ORIGIN early 20th cent.: coined in German from Greek *agnōsia* 'ignorance.'

ag·nos·tic /agˈnästik/ ▶ **n.** a person who believes that nothing is known or can be known of the existence or nature of God or of anything beyond material phenomena; a person who claims neither faith nor disbelief in God.
▶ **adj.** of or relating to agnostics or agnosticism. ■ (in a nonreligious context) having a doubtful or noncommittal attitude toward something: *until now I've been fairly agnostic about electoral reform.*
– DERIVATIVES **ag·nos·ti·cism** /-təˌsizəm/ **n.**
– ORIGIN mid 19th cent.: from **A-¹** 'not' + **GNOSTIC**.

Ag·nus De·i /ˈagnəs ˈdāˌē, ˈdēˌī, ˈänyo͞os/ ▶ **n. 1** a figure of a lamb bearing a cross or flag, as an emblem of Christ.
2 Christian Church an invocation beginning with the words "Lamb of God" forming a set part of the liturgy. ■ a musical setting of this.
– ORIGIN late Middle English: from Latin, literally 'Lamb of God.'

a·go /əˈgō/ ▶ **adv.** (used after a measurement of time) before the present; earlier: *he went five minutes ago* | *as long ago as 1942* | *not long ago he came across a rattlesnake outside his house.*
– ORIGIN Middle English *ago*, *agone*, past participle of the obsolete verb *ago* 'pass,' used to express passage of time.

> **USAGE** When **ago** is followed by a clause, the clause is normally introduced by *that* rather than *since*: *it was sixty years ago* **that** *I left this place* (not *it was sixty years ago* **since** *I left this place*). The use of *since* is redundant and is not correct in standard English.

a·gog /əˈgäg/ ▶ **adj.** [predic.] very eager or curious to hear or see something: *I'm all agog to see London* | *New York is agog at the gossip.*
– ORIGIN mid 16th cent.: from Old French *en gogues*, from *en* 'in' + the plural of *gogue* 'fun.'

a·gog·ic /əˈgäjik, əˈgō-/ Music ▶ **adj.** relating to or denoting an accent produced by lengthening the time value of a note.
▶ **plural n.** (**agogics**) [usu. treated as sing.] the use of agogic accents.
– ORIGIN late 19th cent.: coined in German from Greek *agōgos* 'leading,' from *agein* 'to lead,' + **-IC**.

a·go·go /əˈgōgō/ ▶ **n.** a small bell made of two metal cones, used as a percussion instrument in African and Latin music.
– ORIGIN from Yoruba.

a go·go /ə ˈgōˌgō/ ▶ **adj.** [postpositive] informal in abundance; galore: *Gershwin à gogo—all the hits.*
– ORIGIN 1960s: from French *à gogo*, from Old French *gogue* 'fun.'

a·gon·ic line /āˈgänik/ ▶ **n.** an imaginary line around the earth passing through both the north pole and the north magnetic pole, at any point on which a compass needle points to true north.
– ORIGIN mid 19th cent.: from Greek *agōnios*, *agōnos* (from *a-* 'without' + *gonia* 'angle') + **-IC**.

ag·o·nist /ˈagənist/ ▶ **n. 1** Biochemistry a substance that initiates a physiological response when combined with a receptor. Compare with **ANTAGONIST**.
2 Anatomy a muscle whose contraction moves a part of the body directly. Often contrasted with **ANTAGONIST**.
3 another term for **PROTAGONIST**.
– DERIVATIVES **ag·o·nism** /-ˌnizəm/ **n.**
– ORIGIN early 20th cent.: from Greek *agōnistēs* 'contestant' (a sense reflected in English in the early 17th cent.), from *agōn* 'contest.'

ag·o·nis·tic /ˌagəˈnistik/ ▶ **adj.** combative; polemical. ■ Zoology (of animal behavior) associated with conflict. ■ Biochemistry of, relating to, or acting as an agonist.
– DERIVATIVES **ag·o·nis·ti·cal·ly** /-ik(ə)lē/ **adv.**
– ORIGIN mid 17th cent.: via late Latin from Greek *agōnistikos*, from *agōnistēs* 'contestant,' from *agōn* 'contest.'

ag·o·nize /ˈagəˌnīz/ ▶ **v.** [no obj.] undergo great mental anguish through worrying about something: *I didn't agonize over the problem.* ■ [with obj.] cause mental anguish to (someone).
– ORIGIN late 16th cent.: from French *agoniser* or late Latin *agonizare*, from Greek *agōnizesthai* 'contend,' from *agōn* 'contest.'

ag·o·nized /ˈagəˌnīzd/ ▶ **adj.** manifesting, suffering, or characterized by great physical or mental pain: *she gave an agonized cry* | *months of agonized discussion.*

ag·o·niz·ing /ˈagəˌnīziNG/ (also **agonising**) ▶ **adj.** causing great physical or mental pain: *there is an agonizing choice to make | an agonizing death.*
– DERIVATIVES **ag·o·niz·ing·ly adv.** [as submodifier] *agonizingly slow steps.*

ag·o·ny /ˈagənē/ ▶ **n.** (pl. **agonies**) extreme physical or mental suffering: *he crashed to the ground in agony.* ■ the final stages of a difficult or painful death: *his last agony | the death agony.*
– ORIGIN late Middle English (originally denoting mental anguish alone): via Old French and late Latin from Greek *agōnia,* from *agōn* 'contest.' The sense of physical suffering dates from the early 17th cent.

ag·o·ny col·umn ▶ **n.** Brit. informal a column in a newspaper or magazine offering advice on personal problems to readers who write in. ■ dated a personal column.

ag·o·ra[1] /ˈagərə/ ▶ **n.** (pl. **agorae** /-rē/ or **agoras**) (in ancient Greece) a public open space used for assemblies and markets.
– ORIGIN from Greek.

a·go·ra[2] /əˈgôrə, ˌägôˈrä/ ▶ **n.** (pl. **agorot** /əˈgôrōt, ˌägôˈrōt/ or **agoroth** /əˈgôrōt, ˌägôˈrōt/) a monetary unit of Israel, equal to one hundredth of a shekel.
– ORIGIN from Hebrew *'ăgōrāh* 'small coin.'

ag·o·ra·pho·bi·a /ˌagərəˈfōbēə/ ▶ **n.** extreme or irrational fear of crowded spaces or enclosed public places.
– DERIVATIVES **ag·o·ra·pho·bic** /-ˈfōbik/ **adj. & n.**, **ag·o·ra·phobe** /ˈagərəˌfōb/ **n.**
– ORIGIN late 19th cent.: from Greek *agora* 'place of assembly, marketplace' + **-PHOBIA**.

a·gou·ti /əˈgo͞otē/ ▶ **n.** (pl. **same** or **agoutis**) a large, long-legged burrowing rodent related to the guinea pig, native to Central and South America. ● Genera *Cuniculus* and *Dasyprocta,* family Dasyproctidae: several species. ■ fur in which each hair has alternate dark and light bands, producing a grizzled appearance. ■ a rodent, esp. a mouse, having fur of this type.
– ORIGIN mid 16th cent.: via French or from Spanish *aguti,* from Tupi *akutí.*

A·gra /ˈägrə/ a city on the Jumna River in Uttar Pradesh state, northern India; pop. 1,638,200 (est. 2009). The capital of the Mogul empire 1566–1658, it is the site of the Taj Mahal.

a·gran·u·lo·cy·to·sis /āˌgranyəlōsīˈtōsis/ ▶ **n.** Medicine a deficiency of granulocytes in the blood, causing increased vulnerability to infection.

a·grar·i·an /əˈgre(ə)rēən/ ▶ **adj.** of or relating to cultivated land or the cultivation of land. ■ relating to landed property. ■ relating to a social system upon which agriculture is the sustaining foundation.
▶ **n.** a person who advocates a redistribution of landed property, esp. as part of a social movement.
– DERIVATIVES **a·grar·i·an·ism n.**
– ORIGIN early 17th cent. (originally designating a Roman law for the division of conquered lands): from Latin *agrarius,* from *ager, agr-* 'field.'

a·gree /əˈgrē/ ▶ **v.** (**agrees, agreeing, agreed**) [no obj.] **1** have the same opinion about something; concur: *I completely **agree with** your recent editorial | we both agreed on issues such as tougher penalties for criminals* | [with clause] *I agree that consumers are always right* | [with direct speech] *"Yes, it's dreadful, isn't it," she agreed.* ■ (**agree with**) approve of (something) with regard to its moral correctness: *I'm not sure I agree with abortion.*
2 (**agree to** or **to do something**) consent to do something that has been suggested by another person: *she had agreed to go and see a movie with him.* ■ [no obj.] reach agreement about (something), typically after a period of negotiation: *the commission **agreed on** a proposal to limit imports* | [with obj.] chiefly Brit. *if they had agreed a price, the deal would have gone through.*
3 (**agree with**) be consistent with: *your body language does not agree with what you are saying.* ■ Grammar have the same number, gender, case, or person as: *the writer made the verb agree with the subject.* ■ [usu. with negative] be healthy or appropriate for someone: *she's eaten something that did not agree with her.*
– PHRASES **agree to differ** see **DIFFER**.
– ORIGIN late Middle English: from Old French *agreer,* based on Latin *ad-* 'to' + *gratus* 'pleasing.'

> **USAGE** Note the distinction between **agreeing to** something like a plan, scheme, or project and **agreeing with** somebody: *I **agree to** the repayment schedule suggested; Danielle **agrees with** Eric that we should all go hiking on Saturday; humid weather does not **agree with** me.* The construction **agree with** is also used regarding two things that go together: *that story does not **agree with** the facts; the verb must **agree with** the noun in person and number.*

a·gree·a·ble /əˈgrēəbəl/ ▶ **adj. 1** enjoyable and pleasurable; pleasant: *a cheerful and agreeable companion.*
2 [predic.] willing to agree to something: *they were agreeable to its publication.* ■ (of a course of action) acceptable: *a compromise that might be agreeable to both management and unions.*
– DERIVATIVES **a·gree·a·ble·ness n.**, **a·gree·a·bly** /-blē/ **adv.** [as submodifier] *an agreeably warm day.*
– ORIGIN late Middle English: from Old French *agreable,* from *agreer* 'make agreeable to' (see **AGREE**).

a·greed /əˈgrēd/ ▶ **adj.** [attrib.] discussed or negotiated and then accepted by all parties: *the agreed time | the **agreed upon** percentage.* ■ [predic.] (of two or more parties) holding the same view or opinion on something: *all the republics are agreed on the necessity of a common defense policy* | [with clause] *we are **agreed that** what is needed is a catchy title.*

a·gree·ment /əˈgrēmənt/ ▶ **n.** harmony or accordance in opinion or feeling; a position or result of agreeing: *the governments **failed to reach agreement** | the two officers **nodded in agreement** | there is wide **agreement that** investment is necessary.* ■ a negotiated and typically legally binding arrangement between parties as to a course of action: *a trade agreement | a verbal agreement to sell.* ■ the absence of incompatibility between two things; consistency: *agreement between experimental observations and theory.* ■ Grammar the condition of having the same number, gender, case, or person.
– ORIGIN late Middle English: from Old French, from *agreer* 'make agreeable to' (see **AGREE**).

a·gres·tal /əˈgrestl/ ▶ **adj.** Botany growing wild in cultivated fields.
– ORIGIN mid 19th cent.: from Latin *agrestis* 'relating to the country' (see **AGRESTIC**) + **-AL**.

a·gres·tic /əˈgrestik/ ▶ **adj.** chiefly literary of or relating to the country; rural; rustic.
– ORIGIN early 17th cent.: from Latin *agrestis,* from *ager, agr-* 'field' + **-IC**.

agri- ▶ **comb. form** variant spelling of **AGRO-**: *agriculture | agribusiness.*

ag·ri·busi·ness /ˈagrəˌbiznis/ ▶ **n. 1** agriculture conducted on commercial principles, esp. using advanced technology. ■ an organization engaged in this.
2 the group of industries dealing with agricultural produce and services required in farming.
– DERIVATIVES **ag·ri·busi·ness·man n.** (pl. **agribusinessmen**).
– ORIGIN 1950s (originally US): blend of **AGRICULTURE** and **BUSINESS**.

ag·ri·chem·i·cal ▶ **n. & adj.** variant form of **AGROCHEMICAL**.

A·gric·o·la /əˈgrikələ/, Gnaeus Julius (AD 40–93), Roman general and governor of Britain 78–84. As governor he completed the subjugation of Wales and defeated the Scottish Highland tribes.

ag·ri·cul·tur·al /ˌagriˈkəlCHərəl/ ▶ **adj.** of or relating to agriculture: *agricultural land | an agricultural worker.*
– DERIVATIVES **ag·ri·cul·tur·al·ist** /-ist/ **n.**, **ag·ri·cul·tur·al·ly adv.** *agriculturally fertile plains.*

ag·ri·cul·tur·al fair ▶ **n.** see **FAIR[2]**.

ag·ri·cul·ture /ˈagriˌkəlCHər/ ▶ **n.** the science or practice of farming, including cultivation of the soil for the growing of crops and the rearing of animals to provide food, wool, and other products.
– DERIVATIVES **ag·ri·cul·tur·ist** /-rist/ **n.**
– ORIGIN late Middle English: from Latin *agricultura,* from *ager, agr-* 'field' + *cultura* 'growing, cultivation.'

ag·ri·mo·ny /ˈagrəˌmōnē/ ▶ **n.** (pl. **agrimonies**) a plant of the rose family bearing slender flower spikes and spiny fruits. Native to north temperate regions, it has been used traditionally in herbal medicine and dyeing. ● Genus *Agrimonia,* family Rosaceae: several species, in particular *A. eupatoria,* which has small yellow flowers.
– ORIGIN late Middle English: directly or (in early use) via Old French from Latin *agrimonia,* alteration of *argemonia,* from Greek *argemōnē* 'poppy.'

A·grip·pa /əˈgripə/, Marcus Vipsanius (63–12 BC), Roman general. Augustus's adviser and son-in-law, he played an important part in the naval victories over Mark Antony.

ag·ri·sci·ence /ˈagriˌsīəns/ ▶ **n.** the application of science to agriculture.
– DERIVATIVES **ag·ri·sci·en·tist** /-tist/ **n.**

agro- (also **agri-**) ▶ **comb. form** agricultural: *agro-industry | agrobiology | agribusiness.* ■ agriculture and ...: *agroforestry.*
– ORIGIN from Greek *agros* 'field.'

ag·ro·bi·ol·o·gy /ˌagrōbīˈäləjē/ ▶ **n.** the branch of biology that deals with soil science and plant nutrition and its application to crop production.
– DERIVATIVES **ag·ro·bi·o·log·i·cal** /-bīəˈläjikəl/ **adj.**, **ag·ro·bi·ol·o·gist** /-jist/ **n.**

ag·ro·chem·i·cal /ˌagrōˈkemikəl/ (also **agrichemical**) ▶ **n.** a chemical used in agriculture, such as a pesticide or a fertilizer.

ag·ro·for·est·ry /ˌagrōˈfôrəstrē, -ˈfär-/ ▶ **n.** agriculture incorporating the cultivation and conservation of trees.

ag·ro-in·dus·try ▶ **n.** industry connected with agriculture. ■ agriculture developed along industrial lines.
– DERIVATIVES **ag·ro-in·dus·tri·al adj.**

a·grol·o·gy /əˈgräləjē/ ▶ **n.** Canadian the application of science to agriculture.
– DERIVATIVES **a·grol·o·gist** /-jist/ **n.**

a·gron·o·my /əˈgränəmē/ ▶ **n.** the science of soil management and crop production.
– DERIVATIVES **ag·ro·nom·ic** /ˌagrəˈnämik/ **adj.**, **ag·ro·nom·i·cal** /ˌagrəˈnämikəl/ **adj.**, **ag·ro·nom·i·cal·ly** /ˌagrəˈnämik(ə)lē/ **adv.**, **a·gron·o·mist** /-mist/ **n.**
– ORIGIN early 19th cent.: from French *agronomie,* from *agronome* 'agriculturist,' from Greek *agros* 'field' + *-nomos* 'arranging' (from *nemein* 'arrange').

Agro Pontino Italian name for **PONTINE MARSHES**.

ag·ros·tol·o·gy /ˌagrəˈstäləjē/ ▶ **n.** the branch of botany concerned with grasses.
– ORIGIN mid 19th cent.: from Greek *agrōstis* (denoting a kind of grass) + **-LOGY**.

ag·ro·ter·ror·ism /ˌagrəˈterəˌrizəm/ ▶ **n.** terrorist acts intended to disrupt or damage a country's agriculture, esp. the use of a biological agent against crops or livestock.
– DERIVATIVES **ag·ro·ter·ror·ist n.**

a·ground /əˈground/ ▶ **adj. & adv.** (with reference to a ship) on or onto the bottom in shallow water: [as adv.] *the ships must slow to avoid **running aground*** | [as predic. adj.] *a cargo ship aground in the Mediterranean.*
– ORIGIN Middle English (in the sense 'on the ground'): from **A-[2]** 'on' + **GROUND[1]**.

Ag·ua Pri·e·ta /ˈägwə prēˈātə/ a city in Sonora, in northwestern Mexico, near the Arizona border; pop. 66,856 (2005).

a·guar·dien·te /ˌägwärˈdyentā/ ▶ **n.** (in Spanish-speaking regions) a distilled liquor resembling brandy, esp. as made in South America from sugar cane.
– ORIGIN from Spanish, from *agua* 'water' + *ardiente* 'fiery.'

A·guas·ca·lien·tes /ˌägwäˌskälˈyenˌtās, ˌäwä-/ a state in central Mexico. ■ its capital, a health resort noted for its hot springs; pop. 663,671 (2005).
– ORIGIN Spanish, literally 'hot waters.'

a·gue /ˈāˌgyo͞o/ ▶ **n.** archaic malaria or some other illness involving fever and shivering. ■ a fever or shivering fit.
– DERIVATIVES **a·gued adj.**, **a·gu·ish adj.**
– ORIGIN Middle English: via Old French from medieval Latin *acuta (febris)* 'acute (fever).'

A·gul·has, Cape /əˈgələs/ the most southern point of the continent of Africa, in Western Cape province, South Africa.

A·gul·has Cur·rent an ocean current in the Indian Ocean that flows southward along the east coast of Africa.

AH ▶ **abbr.** in the year of the Hegira (used in the Muslim calendar for reckoning years from Muhammad's departure from Mecca in AD 622); of the Muslim era: *a Koran dated 556 AH.*
– ORIGIN from Latin *anno Hegirae.*

ah /ä/ ▶ **exclam.** used to express a range of emotions including surprise, pleasure, sympathy, and realization: *ah, there you are! | ah, this is the life.*
– ORIGIN Middle English: from Old French.

AHA ▶ **abbr.** ■ alpha-hydroxy acid. ■ American Heart Association.

a·ha /äˈhä/ ▶ **exclam.** used to express satisfaction, triumph, or surprise: *aha! So that's your secret plan!*
– ORIGIN Middle English: from **AH** + **HA[1]**.

A·hag·gar Moun·tains /əˈhägər, ˌähəˈgär/ another name for **HOGGAR MOUNTAINS**.

a·head /əˈhed/ ▶ **adv.** further forward in space; in the line of one's forward motion: *he had to give his attention to the road ahead | he was striding ahead toward the stream.* ■ further forward in time; in advance; in the near future: *he contemplated the day ahead | we have to plan ahead.* ■ onward so as to make progress. ■ in the lead: *the Bucks were ahead by four | he was slightly ahead on points.* ■ higher in number, amount, or value than previously: *profits were slightly ahead.*

–PHRASES **ahead of** in front of or before: *she walked ahead of him along the corridor.* ■ in store for; awaiting: *we have a long drive ahead of us.* ■ earlier than planned or expected: *elimination of trade barriers came five years ahead of schedule.* **ahead of one's** (or **its**) **time** innovative and radical by the standards of the time; more characteristic of a later age.
–ORIGIN mid 16th cent. (originally in nautical use): from **A-**[2] 'in, at' + **HEAD**.

a·hem /ə'hem, ə'hm/ ▶ **exclam.** used to represent the noise made when clearing the throat, typically to attract attention or express disapproval or embarrassment.
–ORIGIN mid 18th cent.: lengthened form of **HEM**[2].

a·hi /'ähē/ ▶ **n.** a large tuna, esp. as an item of food.
–ORIGIN Hawaiian *'ahi.*

a·him·sa /ə'him,sä/ ▶ **n.** (in the Hindu, Buddhist, and Jain tradition) the principle of nonviolence toward all living things.
–ORIGIN Sanskrit, from *a* 'non-, without' + *hiṃsā* 'violence.'

a·his·tor·i·cal /,āhi'stôrikəl, -'stär-/ ▶ **adj.** lacking historical perspective or context: *ahistorical nostalgia that misunderstands cultural history.*

Ah·mad·a·bad /'ämədə,bäd/ (also **Ahmedabad**) an industrial city in the state of Gujarat in western India; pop. 3,913,800 (est. 2009).

a·ho·le·ho·le /ə'hōlē'hōlē/ ▶ **n.** a small silvery fish occurring only in the shallow waters around the Hawaiian islands, where it is a food fish. ● *Kuhlia sandvicensis*, family Kuhliidae.
–ORIGIN from Hawaiian.

-aholic (also **-oholic**) ▶ **suffix** denoting a person addicted to something: *shopaholic | workaholic.*
–ORIGIN on the pattern of (*alc*)*oholic.*

a·hoy /ə'hoi/ ▶ **exclam.** Nautical a call used in hailing: *ahoy there! | ship ahoy!*
–PHRASES **land ahoy!** an exclamation announcing the sighting of land from a ship.
–ORIGIN mid 18th cent.: from **AH** + **HOY**[1].

Ah·ri·man /'ärimən/ the evil spirit in the doctrine of Zoroastrianism, the opponent of Ahura Mazda.

A·hu·ra Maz·da /ə,hŏŏrə 'mäzdə/ the creator god of Zoroastrianism, the force for good and the opponent of Ahriman. Also called **Ormazd**.
–ORIGIN Avestan, literally 'wise deity.'

Ah·vaz /ä'väz/ (also **Ahwaz** /ä'wäz/) a town in western Iran; pop. 985,614 (2006).

Ah·ve·nan·maa /'ävə,nän,mä/ Finnish name for **Åland Islands**.

AI ▶ **abbr.** ■ Amnesty International. ■ artificial insemination. ■ artificial intelligence.

AID ▶ **abbr.** ■ Agency for International Development. ■ artificial insemination by donor.

aid /ād/ ▶ **n.** help, typically of a practical nature: *he saw the pilot slumped in his cockpit and went to his* ***aid*** *| within six weeks he was walking* ***with the aid of*** *a walker.* ■ financial or material help given to a country or area in need: *700,000 tons of food aid* | [as modifier] *aid convoys.* ■ a person or thing that is a source of help or assistance: *exercise is an important* ***aid to*** *recovery after heart attacks | a teaching aid.* ■ historical a grant of subsidy or tax to a king.
▶ **v.** [with obj.] help, assist, or support (someone or something) in the achievement of something: *women were aided in childbirth by midwives* | [no obj.] *the heel was slanted to aid in climbing hilly terrain.* ■ promote or encourage (something): *diet and exercise aid healthy skin.*
–PHRASES **aid and abet** see **ABET**. **in aid of** chiefly Brit. in support of; for the purpose of raising money for: *a concert in aid of Armenia.*
–ORIGIN late Middle English: from Old French *aïde* (noun), *aïdier* (verb), based on Latin *adjuvare*, from *ad-* 'toward' + *juvare* 'to help.'

Ai·dan, St. /'ādn/ (d. AD 651), Irish missionary. While a monk in the monastery at Iona he set out to Christianize Northumbria, founding a church and monastery on the island of Lindisfarne in 635 and becoming its first bishop.

aid climb·ing ▶ **n.** rock climbing using the assistance of objects such as pitons placed in the rock. Compare with **FREE CLIMBING**.
–DERIVATIVES **aid climb n.**, **aid-climb v.**

aide /ād/ ▶ **n.** an assistant to an important person, esp. to a political leader: *a presidential aide.* ■ short for **AIDE-DE-CAMP**.

aide-de-camp /,ād də 'kamp/ ▶ **n.** (pl. **aides-de-camp** pronunc. **same** or /'ādz/) a military officer acting as a confidential assistant to a senior officer.
–ORIGIN late 17th cent.: from French, 'camp adjutant.'

aide-me·moire /,ād mem'wär/ ▶ **n.** (pl. **aides-memoires** or **aides-memoire** pronunc. **same**) an aid to the memory, esp. a book or document. ■ an informal diplomatic message.
–ORIGIN mid 19th cent.: from French *aide-mémoire*, from *aider* 'to help' and *mémoire* 'memory.'

AIDS /ādz/ ▶ **n.** a disease in which there is a severe loss of the body's cellular immunity, greatly lowering the resistance to infection and malignancy.

> AIDS was first identified in the early 1980s and now affects millions of people. The cause is a virus (called the human immunodeficiency virus or HIV) transmitted in blood and in sexual fluids, and although the incubation period may be long and treatment can slow the course of the disease there is currently no cure or vaccine. In the developed world the disease first spread among homosexuals, intravenous drug users, and recipients of infected blood transfusions, before reaching the wider population. This has tended to overshadow a greater epidemic in parts of Africa, where transmission is mainly through heterosexual contact.

–ORIGIN 1980s: acronym for *acquired immune deficiency syndrome.*

AIDS-re·lat·ed com·plex ▶ **n.** the symptoms of a person who is infected with HIV but does not necessarily develop the disease.

ai·grette /ā'gret/ ▶ **n.** a headdress consisting of a white egret's feather or other decoration such as a spray of gems.
–ORIGIN mid 18th cent.: French, literally 'egret.'

ai·guille /ā'gwēl/ ▶ **n.** a sharp pinnacle of rock in a mountain range.
–ORIGIN mid 18th cent.: French, literally 'needle.'

ai·guil·lette /,āgwə'let/ ▶ **n.** an ornament on some military and naval uniforms, consisting of braided loops hanging from the shoulder and on dress uniforms ending in points.
–ORIGIN mid 16th cent.: from French, literally 'small needle,' diminutive of *aiguille.*

aiguillette

ai·ki·do /,īkē'dō, ī'kēdō/ ▶ **n.** a Japanese form of self-defense and martial art that uses locks, holds, throws, and the opponent's own movements.
–ORIGIN 1950s: from Japanese *aikidō*, literally 'way of adapting the spirit,' from *ai* 'together, unify' + *ki* 'spirit' + *dō* 'way.'

ail /āl/ ▶ **v.** [with obj.] trouble or afflict (someone) in mind or body: *exercise is good for whatever ails you.*
–ORIGIN Old English *eglian, eglan*, from *egle* 'troublesome,' of Germanic origin; related to Gothic *agls* 'disgraceful.'

ai·lan·thus /ā'lanTHəs/ ▶ **n.** a tall large-leaved deciduous tree that is widely grown as an ornamental or shade tree. Native to Asia and Australasia, it has been naturalized in North America and central and southern Europe. ● Genus *Ailanthus*, family Simaroubaceae: several species, in particular the tree of heaven.
–ORIGIN modern Latin, from French *ailante*, from Amboinese *ailanto*, literally 'tree of heaven' (the ending being influenced by names ending with *-anthus*, from Greek *anthos* 'flower').

ai·ler·on /'ālə,rän/ ▶ **n.** a hinged surface in the trailing edge of an airplane wing, used to control lateral balance.
–ORIGIN early 20th cent.: French, literally 'small wing.'

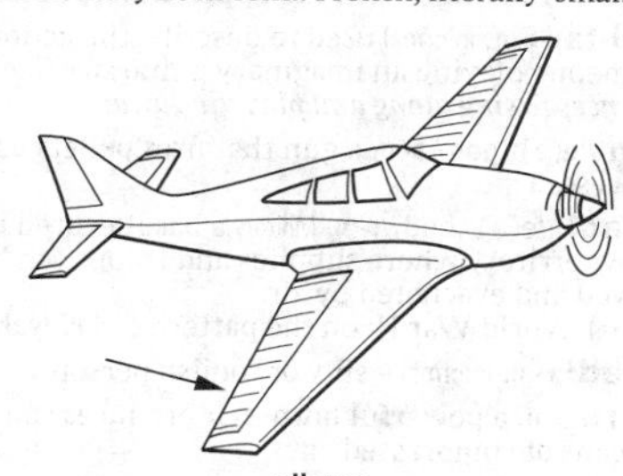

aileron

Ai·ley /'ālē/, Alvin (1931–89), US dancer and choreographer. He founded the Alvin Ailey American Dance Theater in 1958 and helped to establish modern dance as an American art form; he incorporated ballet, jazz, and Afro-Caribbean idioms in his choreography.

ail·ing /'āliNG/ ▶ **adj.** in poor health: *I went to see my ailing mother* | figurative *the ailing economy.*

ail·ment /'ālmənt/ ▶ **n.** an illness, typically a minor one.

ai·lur·o·phile /ī'lŏŏrə,fīl, ā'lŏŏr-/ ▶ **n.** a cat lover.
–ORIGIN 1930s: from Greek *ailuros* 'cat' + **-PHILE**.

ai·lu·ro·pho·bi·a /ī,lŏŏrə'fōbēə, ā,lŏŏr-/ ▶ **n.** extreme or irrational fear of cats.
–DERIVATIVES **ai·lu·ro·phobe** /ī'lŏŏrə,fōb, ā'lŏŏr-/ **n.**

AIM /ām/ ▶ **abbr.** American Indian Movement.

aim /ām/ ▶ **v. 1** [with obj.] point or direct (a weapon or camera) at a target: ***aim*** *the camcorder* ***at*** *some suitable object* | [no obj.] ***aim for*** *the middle of the target.* ■ direct (an object or blow) at someone or something: *she had* ***aimed*** *the bottle* ***at*** *his head.* ■ (**aim something at**) direct information or an action toward (a particular group): *the TV campaign is aimed at the 16-24 age group.*
2 [no obj.] have the intention of achieving: *new French cooking* ***aims at*** *producing clear, fresh flavors and light textures* | [with infinitive] *we aim to give you the best possible service.*
▶ **n. 1** a purpose or intention; a desired outcome: *our primary aim is to achieve financial discipline.*
2 [in sing.] the directing of a weapon or object at a target: *his aim was perfect, and the guard's body collapsed backward.*
–PHRASES **aim high** be ambitious. **take aim** point a weapon or camera at a target.
–ORIGIN Middle English: from Old French *amer*, variant of *esmer* (from Latin *aestimare* 'assess, estimate'), reinforced by *aemer, aesmer* (from late Latin *adaestimare*, intensified form of *aestimare*).

aim·less /'āmlis/ ▶ **adj.** without purpose or direction: *an aimless, ungratifying life.*
–DERIVATIVES **aim·less·ly adv.**, **aim·less·ness n.**

ai·nhum /'īnəm/ ▶ **n.** Medicine a condition in which a band of fibrous tissue grows around the base of a toe, esp. the fifth, eventually resulting in loss of the digit. It occurs mainly in the tropics and is associated with going barefoot, though its cause is unknown.
–ORIGIN late 19th cent.: from Portuguese, based on Yoruba *eyun* 'saw.'

ain't /ānt/ informal ▶ **contraction** am not; are not; is not: *if it ain't broke, don't fix it.* [originally representing London dialect.] ■ has not; have not: *they ain't got nothing to say.* [from dialect *hain't*.]

> **USAGE** The use of **ain't** was widespread in the 18th century and is still perfectly normal in many dialects and informal contexts in both North America and Britain. Today, however, it does not form part of standard English and should not be used in formal contexts.

Ain·tab /īn'täb/ former name (until 1921) of **Gaziantep**.

Ai·nu /'ī,nŏŏ/ ▶ **n. 1** (pl. **same** or **Ainus**) a member of an aboriginal people of Japan, physically distinct (with light skin color and round eyes) from the majority population.
2 the language of this people, of unknown affinity.
▶ **adj.** of or relating to this people or their language.
–ORIGIN early 19th cent.: the name in Ainu, literally 'man, person.'

ai·o·li /ī'ōlē, ā'ō-/ (also **aïoli**) ▶ **n.** mayonnaise seasoned with garlic.
–ORIGIN French, from Provençal *ai* 'garlic' + *oli* 'oil.'

air /e(ə)r/ ▶ **n. 1** the invisible gaseous substance surrounding the earth, a mixture mainly of oxygen and nitrogen. ■ this substance regarded as necessary for breathing: *the air was stale | the doctor told me to get some fresh air.* ■ the free or unconfined space above the surface of the earth: *he celebrated by tossing his hat high in the air.* ■ [as modifier] used to indicate that something involves the use of aircraft: *air travel.* ■ the earth's atmosphere as a medium for transmitting radio waves: *radio stations have successfully sold products over the air.* ■ air considered as one of the four elements in ancient philosophy and in astrology (associated with the signs of Gemini, Aquarius, and Libra). ■ a breeze or light wind. See also **LIGHT AIR**. ■ air conditioning. ■ a jump off the ground on a snowboard. [Middle English: from Old French *air*, from Latin *aer*, from Greek *aēr*, denoting the gas.]
2 an impression of a quality or manner given by someone or something: *she answered with a faint air of boredom | he leaned over with a confidential air.* ■ (**airs**) an annoyingly affected and condescending manner: *he began to* ***put on airs*** *and think he could boss us around.* [late 16th cent.: from French *air*,

PRONUNCIATION KEY ə *ago, up*; ər *over, fur*; a *hat*; ā *ate*; ä *car*; e *let*; ē *see*; i *fit*; ī *by*; NG *sing*; ō *go*; ô *law, for*; oi *toy*; ŏŏ *good*; ōō *goo*; ou *out*; TH *thin*; TH *then*; ZH *vision*

probably from Old French *aire* 'site, disposition,' from Latin *ager, agr-* 'field' (influenced by sense 1).] **3** Music a tune or short melodious composition, typically a song. [late 16th cent.: from Italian *aria* (see **ARIA**).]
▶ **v. 1** [with obj.] express (an opinion or grievance) publicly: *a meeting in which long-standing grievances were aired.* ■ broadcast (a program) on radio or television: *the programs were aired on India's state TV network.* ■ archaic parade or show (something) ostentatiously: *airing a snowy hand and signet ring.* **2** [with obj.] expose (a room) to the open air in order to ventilate it: *the window sashes were lifted regularly to air the room.* ■ (**air oneself**) archaic go out in the fresh air.
– PHRASES **airs and graces** derogatory an affectation of superiority. **by air** in an aircraft: *all goods must come in by air.* **in the air** noticeable all around; becoming prevalent: *I smell violence in the air.* **on** (or **off**) **the air** being (or not being) broadcast on radio or television. **take the air** go out of doors. **up in the air** (of a plan or issue) still to be settled; unresolved: *the fate of the power station is up in the air.* **walk on air** feel elated.

airbag /'e(ə)r,bag/ ▶ **n.** a safety device fitted inside a road vehicle, consisting of a cushion designed to inflate rapidly in the event of a collision and positioned so as to protect passengers from being flung against the vehicle's structure.

air ball ▶ **n.** Basketball, informal a shot that misses the backboard, rim, and net entirely.

air·base /'e(ə)r,bās/ ▶ **n.** a base for the operation of military aircraft.

air bear·ing ▶ **n.** a bearing in which moving surfaces are kept apart by a layer of air provided by jets.

air bed ▶ **n.** an inflatable mattress.

air blad·der ▶ **n.** an air-filled bladder or sac found in certain animals and plants. ■ another term for **SWIM BLADDER**.

air·boat /'e(ə)r,bōt/ ▶ **n.** a shallow-draft boat powered by an aircraft engine, for use in swamps.

air·borne /'e(ə)r,bôrn/ ▶ **adj.** transported by air: *airborne pollutants.* ■ (of an aircraft) in the air after taking off.

air brake ▶ **n.** a brake worked by air pressure. ■ a movable flap or other device on an aircraft to reduce its speed.

air bridge ▶ **n.** British term for **JETWAY**.

air·brush /'e(ə)r,brəsh/ ▶ **n.** an artist's device for spraying paint by means of compressed air.
▶ **v.** [with obj.] paint with an airbrush: *a cab airbrushed with a mural of a sunset.* ■ alter or conceal (a photograph or a detail in one) using an airbrush: *a picture of a man with wings airbrushed onto his shoulders.* ■ (usu. as adj. **airbrushed**) represent or describe (someone or something) as better or more beautiful than they in fact are: *an airbrushed vision of the decade.*

airbrush

air·burst /'e(ə)r,bərst/ ▶ **n.** an explosion in the air, typically of a nuclear bomb or large meteor.
▶ **v.** [no obj.] explode in the air.

air·bus /'e(ə)r,bəs/ ▶ **n.** trademark an aircraft designed to carry a large number of passengers economically, esp. over relatively short routes.

air clean·er another term for **AIR FILTER**.

air com·mand ▶ **n.** a high-level organizational unit in the US Air Force.

air con·di·tion·ing ▶ **n.** a system for controlling the humidity, ventilation, and temperature in a building or vehicle, typically to maintain a cool atmosphere in warm conditions.
– DERIVATIVES **air con·di·tioned adj.**, **air con·di·tion·er n.**

air-cooled ▶ **adj.** cooled by means of a flow of air.

air cor·ri·dor ▶ **n.** a route to which aircraft are restricted, esp. over a foreign country.

air cov·er ▶ **n.** protection from aircraft for land-based or naval operations in war situations.

air·craft /'e(ə)r,kraft/ ▶ **n.** (pl. **same**) an airplane, helicopter, or other machine capable of flight.

air·craft car·ri·er ▶ **n.** a large warship equipped to serve as a base for aircraft that can take off from and land on its deck.

air·crew /'e(ə)r,kroō/ ▶ **n.** (pl. **aircrews**) [treated as sing. or pl.] the crew staffing an aircraft. ■ (pl. **same**) a member of such a crew: *each aircraft carried three aircrew.*

air cush·ion ▶ **n. 1** an inflatable cushion. **2** the layer of air supporting a hovercraft or similar vehicle.

air dam ▶ **n.** a streamlining device below the front bumper of a vehicle; a front spoiler.

air date ▶ **n.** the date on which a recorded program is to be broadcast.

air·drome /'e(ə)r,drōm/ ▶ **n.** an airport. ■ a military air base.

air·drop /'e(ə)r,dräp/ ▶ **n.** an act of dropping supplies, troops, or equipment by parachute from an aircraft.
▶ **v.** (**airdrops, airdropping, airdropped**) [with obj.] drop (such things) by parachute.

air-dry ▶ **v.** make or become dry through contact with unheated air.
▶ **adj.** not giving off any moisture on exposure to air.

Aire·dale /'e(ə)r,dāl/ ▶ **n.** a large terrier of a rough-coated black and tan breed.
– ORIGIN late 19th cent.: from *Airedale*, a district in Yorkshire, England, where the dog was bred.

Airedale

air·fare /'e(ə)r,fe(ə)r/ ▶ **n.** the price of a passenger ticket for travel by aircraft: *save a bundle in airfare by flying standby.*

air·field /'e(ə)r,fēld/ ▶ **n.** an area of land set aside for the takeoff, landing, and maintenance of aircraft.

air fil·ter ▶ **n.** a device for filtering particles of dust, soot, etc., from the air passing through it, esp. one protecting the air inlet of an internal combustion engine.

air·flow /'e(ə)r,flō/ ▶ **n.** the flow of air, esp. that encountered by a moving aircraft or vehicle.

air·foil /'e(ə)r,foil/ ▶ **n.** a structure with curved surfaces designed to give the most favorable ratio of lift to drag in flight, used as the basic form of the wings, fins, and horizontal stabilizer of most aircraft.

air force ▶ **n.** (often **the air force** or **the Air Force**) the branch of a nation's armed services that conducts military operations in the air.

Air Force One the designation (when the president of the US is aboard) of any of several specially equipped jetliners maintained by the US Air Force.

air·frame /'e(ə)r,frām/ ▶ **n.** the body of an aircraft as distinct from its engine.

air·freight /'e(ə)r,frāt/ ▶ **n.** the transportation of goods by aircraft. ■ goods in transit, or to be carried, by aircraft.
▶ **v.** [with obj.] carry or send (goods) by aircraft.
▶ **adv.** by airfreight: *the exhibit was flown airfreight.*

air fresh·en·er ▶ **n.** a substance or device for making the air in a room smell fresh or clean.

air·glow /'e(ə)r,glō/ ▶ **n.** a glow in the night sky caused by radiation from the upper atmosphere.

air gui·tar ▶ **n.** informal used to describe the actions of someone playing an imaginary guitar: *we like our audiences to sing along and play air guitar.*

airgun /'e(ə)r,gən/ ▶ **n.** a gun that fires pellets using compressed air.

air·head[1] /'e(ə)r,hed/ ▶ **n.** Military a base secured in enemy territory where supplies and troops can be received and evacuated by air.
– ORIGIN World War II: on the pattern of *bridgehead*.

air·head[2] ▶ **n.** informal a silly or foolish person.

air horn ▶ **n.** a powerful horn that produces sound by means of compressed air.

air·i·ly /'e(ə)rəlē/ ▶ **adv.** in a way that shows that one is not treating something as serious; casually: *he was airily dismissive of the question.*

air·ing /'e(ə)riNG/ ▶ **n.** [in sing.] **1** an exposure to warm or fresh air, for the purpose of ventilating or removing dampness from something: *somebody had given the place a thorough airing.* ■ a walk or outing to take air or exercise: *taking the baby out for an airing.* **2** a public expression of an opinion or subject: *these are ideas I feel might be worth an airing.* ■ a transmission of a television or radio program.

air-kiss ▶ **v.** [with obj.] purse the lips as if kissing (someone), without making contact: *the media crowd who lunch, gossip, and air-kiss one another.*
▶ **n.** (**air kiss**) a simulated kiss, without physical contact.

air lane ▶ **n.** a path or course regularly used by aircraft.

air lay·er·ing ▶ **n.** Horticulture a form of layering in which the branch is potted or wrapped in a moist growing medium to promote root growth.

air·less /'e(ə)rlis/ ▶ **adj.** stuffy; not ventilated: *a dusty, airless basement.* ■ without wind or breeze; still: *a hot, airless night.*
– DERIVATIVES **air·less·ness n.**

air let·ter ▶ **n.** another term for **AEROGRAMME**.

air·lift /'e(ə)r,lift/ ▶ **n.** an act of transporting supplies by aircraft, typically in a blockade or other emergency: *a massive airlift of food, blankets, and medical supplies.*
▶ **v.** [with obj.] transport (troops or supplies) by aircraft, typically when transportation by land is difficult: *helicopters were employed to airlift the troops out of danger.*

air·line /'e(ə)r,līn/ ▶ **n. 1** an organization providing a regular public service of air transportation on one or more routes. ■ (usu. **air line**) a route that forms part of a system regularly used by aircraft. **2** (usu. **air line**) a pipe supplying air: *use an air line to inflate those tires.*

air·lin·er /'e(ə)r,līnər/ ▶ **n.** a large passenger aircraft.

air·lock /'e(ə)r,läk/ (also **air lock**) ▶ **n. 1** a blockage of the flow in a pump or pipe, caused by an air bubble. **2** a compartment with controlled pressure and parallel sets of doors, to permit movement between areas at different pressures.

air·mail /'e(ə)r,māl/ ▶ **n.** a system of transporting mail by aircraft, typically overseas. ■ a letter carried by aircraft.
▶ **v.** [with obj.] send (mail) by aircraft: *a recent letter that I airmailed to Miss Sifton.*

air·man /'e(ə)rmən/ ▶ **n.** (pl. **airmen**) a pilot or member of the crew of an aircraft, esp. in an air force. ■ a member of the US Air Force of the lowest rank, below sergeant. ■ a member of the US Navy whose general duties are concerned with aircraft.

air·man·ship /'e(ə)rmən,SHip/ ▶ **n.** skill in flying an aircraft.

air mass ▶ **n.** Meteorology a body of air with horizontally uniform temperature, humidity, and pressure.

air mat·tress ▶ **n.** an inflatable mattress.

air mile ▶ **n.** a nautical mile used as a measure of distance flown by aircraft. ■ (**Air Miles**) trademark points (equivalent to miles of free air travel) accumulated by buyers of airline tickets and other products and redeemable against the cost of air travel with a particular airline.

air·mo·bile /'e(ə)r,mōbəl/ ▶ **adj.** (of troops) moved about by helicopters.

air pis·tol ▶ **n.** a pistol that fires pellets using compressed air.

air·plane /'e(ə)r,plān/ ▶ **n.** a powered flying vehicle with fixed wings and a weight greater than that of the air it displaces.

air plant ▶ **n.** a typically epiphytic, sometimes rootless, tropical American plant with grasslike or fingerlike leaves through which water and airborne or waterborne nutrients are absorbed. ● Genus *Tillandsia*, family Bromeliaceae: several species, including Spanish moss.

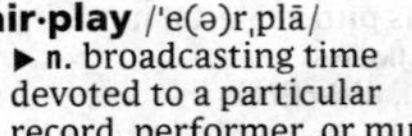
air plant

air·play /'e(ə)r,plā/ ▶ **n.** broadcasting time devoted to a particular record, performer, or musical genre.

air pock·et ▶ **n.** a cavity containing air. ■ a region of low pressure causing an aircraft to lose altitude suddenly.

air·port /'e(ə)r,pôrt/ ▶ **n.** a complex of runways and buildings for the takeoff, landing, and maintenance of civil aircraft, with facilities for passengers. ■ [as modifier] relating to or denoting light popular fiction such as is offered for sale to travelers in airports: *another airport thriller.*

air·pot /ˈe(ə)rˌpät/ ▶ **n.** a container for storing and dispensing coffee or other beverages that maintains a constant temperature by use of glass insulation.

air pow·er ▶ **n.** airborne military forces.

air pump ▶ **n.** a device for pumping air into or out of an enclosed space.

air qual·i·ty ▶ **n.** the degree to which the ambient air is pollution-free, assessed by measuring a number of indicators of pollution.

air quotes ▶ **plural n.** informal a pair of quotation marks gestured by a speaker's fingers in the air, to indicate that what is being said is ironic or mocking, or is not a turn of phrase the speaker would typically employ.

air rage ▶ **n.** violent anger directed mainly at inflight airline personnel and arising from the frustrations and stresses of air travel.

air raid ▶ **n.** an attack in which bombs are dropped from aircraft onto a ground target.

air-raid shel·ter ▶ **n.** a building or structure designed to protect people from bombs dropped during air raids.

air ri·fle ▶ **n.** a rifle that fires pellets using compressed air.

air sac ▶ **n.** a lung compartment containing air; an alveolus. ■ an extension of a bird's lung cavity into a bone or other part of the body.

air·screw /ˈe(ə)rˌskro͞o/ ▶ **n.** Brit. an aircraft propeller.

air-sea res·cue ▶ **n.** a rescue from the sea using aircraft.

air shaft ▶ **n.** a straight, typically vertical passage admitting air into a mine, tunnel, or building.

air·ship /ˈe(ə)rˌSHip/ ▶ **n.** a power-driven aircraft that is kept buoyant by a body of gas (typically helium, formerly hydrogen) that is lighter than air.

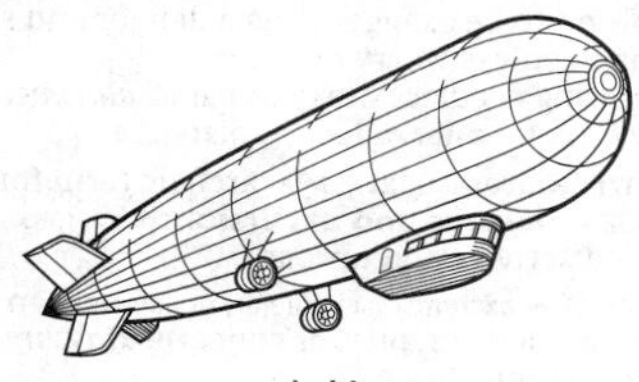

airship

air show ▶ **n.** a show at which aircraft perform aerial displays.

air·sick /ˈe(ə)rˌsik/ ▶ **adj.** affected with nausea due to travel in an aircraft.
– DERIVATIVES **air·sick·ness** **n.**

air·sick·ness bag ▶ **n.** a paper bag provided in an aircraft or ship as a receptacle for vomit.

air·side /ˈe(ə)rˌsīd/ ▶ **n.** the side of an airport terminal from which aircraft can be observed; the area beyond security checks and passport and customs control.
▶ **adv.** on or to this side of an airport terminal: *a new executive lounge has opened airside.*

air·space /ˈe(ə)rˌspās/ ▶ **n.** space available in the atmosphere immediately above the earth: *temples and mosques fight for airspace with skyscrapers.* ■ the air available to aircraft to fly in, esp. the part subject to the jurisdiction of a particular country: *the airliner was refused permission to enter Maltese airspace.* ■ Law the right of a private landowner to the space above his land and any structures on it, which he can use for ordinary purposes such as the erection of signposts or fences. ■ space left to be occupied by air for purposes of insulation.

air·speed /ˈe(ə)rˌspēd/ ▶ **n.** the speed of an aircraft relative to the air through which it is moving. Compare with GROUNDSPEED.

air sta·tion ▶ **n.** an airfield operated by a navy or marine corps.

air·stream /ˈe(ə)rˌstrēm/ ▶ **n.** a current of air.

air strike ▶ **n.** an attack made by aircraft.

air·strip /ˈe(ə)rˌstrip/ ▶ **n.** a strip of ground set aside for the takeoff and landing of aircraft.

air sup·port ▶ **n.** assistance given to ground or naval forces in an operation by their own or allied aircraft.

air·tight /ˈe(ə)rˌtīt/ ▶ **adj.** not allowing air to escape or pass through. ■ having no weaknesses; unassailable: *Scamp had an airtight alibi.*

air·time /ˈe(ə)rˌtīm/ ▶ **n.** time during which a broadcast is being transmitted. ■ time during which a cellular phone is in use, including calls made and received.

air-to-air ▶ **adj.** [attrib.] directed or operating from one aircraft to another in flight.

air-to-ground ▶ **adj.** directed or operating from an aircraft in flight to the land surface.

air-to-sur·face ▶ **adj.** directed or operating from an aircraft in flight to the surface of the sea or other body of water.

air traf·fic con·trol ▶ **n.** the ground-based personnel and equipment concerned with monitoring and controlling air traffic within a particular area.
– DERIVATIVES **air traf·fic con·troll·er** **n.**

air·waves /ˈe(ə)rˌwāvz/ ▶ **plural n.** the radio frequencies used for broadcasting: *football pervades the airwaves.*

air·way /ˈeərˌwā/ ▶ **n. 1** the passage by which air reaches a person's lungs. ■ a tube for supplying air to a person's lungs in an emergency. ■ a ventilating passage in a mine.
2 a recognized route followed by aircraft. ■ (**Airways**) in names of airlines: *British Airways.*

air·wor·thy /ˈe(ə)rˌwərT͟Hē/ ▶ **adj.** (of an aircraft) safe to fly.
– DERIVATIVES **air·wor·thi·ness** **n.**

air·y /ˈe(ə)rē/ ▶ **adj.** (**airier**, **airiest**) **1** (of a room or building) spacious, well lit, and well ventilated. ■ delicate, as though filled with or made of air: *airy clouds.* ■ giving an impression of light gracefulness and elegance: *her airy presence filled the house.*
2 giving an impression of being unconcerned or not serious, typically about something taken seriously by others: *her airy unconcern for economy.*
– DERIVATIVES **air·i·ness** **n.**

air·y-fair·y ▶ **adj.** informal, derogatory, chiefly Brit. impractical and foolishly idealistic: *love might seem an airy-fairy, romantic concept.*

aisle /īl/ ▶ **n.** a passage between rows of seats in a building such as a church or theater, an airplane, or a train: *the musical had the audience dancing in the aisles.* ■ a passage between shelves of goods in a supermarket or other building. ■ Architecture (in a church) a lower part parallel to and at the side of a nave, choir, or transept, from which it is divided by pillars.
– PHRASES **lead someone up the aisle** get married to someone.
– DERIVATIVES **aisled** /īld/ **adj.**
– ORIGIN late Middle English *ele, ile*, from Old French *ele*, from Latin *ala* 'wing.' The spelling change in the 17th cent. was due to confusion with *isle* and influenced by French *aile* 'wing.'

aitch /āCH/ ▶ **n.** the name of the letter H.
– PHRASES **drop one's aitches** fail to pronounce the letter *h* at the beginning of words, a common feature of dialect speech.
– ORIGIN mid 16th cent.: from Old French *ache*.

aitch·bone /ˈāCHˌbōn/ ▶ **n.** the buttock or rump bone of cattle. ■ a cut of beef lying over this.
– ORIGIN late 15th cent.: from dialect *nache* 'rump,' from Old French, based on Latin *natis* 'buttock(s),' + BONE. The initial *n* in *a nache-bone* was lost by wrong division; compare with ADDER.

Aix-en-Pro·vence /ˌeks än prōˈväNs, ˌāks/ a city in Provence in southern France; pop. 145,721 (2006).

Aix-la-Cha·pelle /ˌeks lä SHäˈpel, ˌāks/ French name for AACHEN.

Ai·zawl /īˈzoul/ a city in northeastern India, capital of the state of Mizoram; pop. 295,900 (est. 2009).

A·jac·cio /ˌäˌZHäkˈsyō/ a port on the west coast of Corsica; pop. 59,320.

A·jan·ta Caves /əˈjəntə/ a series of caves in the state of Maharashtra, south central India, that contain Buddhist frescos and sculptures dating from the 1st century BC to the 7th century AD.

a·jar[1] /əˈjär/ ▶ **adv. & adj.** (of a door or other opening) slightly open: [as adv.] *she had left the window ajar that morning* | [as predic. adj.] *the door to the sitting room was ajar.*
– ORIGIN late 17th cent.: from A-[2] 'on' + obsolete *char* (Old English *cerr*) 'a turn, return.'

a·jar[2] ▶ **adv.** archaic out of harmony.
– ORIGIN mid 19th cent.: from A-[2] 'in, at' + JAR[2].

A·jax /ˈāˌjaks/ Greek Mythology **1** a Greek hero of the Trojan War, son of Telamon, king of Salamis. He was proverbial for his size and strength.
2 a Greek hero, son of Oileus, king of Locris.

a·ji·no·mo·to /ˌäjēnōˈmōtō/ ▶ **n.** the Japanese name for MONOSODIUM GLUTAMATE.

Aj·man /ajˈmän, -ˈman/ one of the seven member states of the United Arab Emirates; pop. 387,300 (est. 2009). ■ its capital city.

Aj·mer /ˌəjˈmi(ə)r/ a city in northwestern India, in the state of Rajasthan; pop. 549,600 (est. 2009).

aj·o·wan /ˈajəˌwan/ ▶ **n.** an annual plant (*Trachyspermum ammi*) of the parsley family, with feathery leaves and white flowers, native to India. ■ the aromatic seeds of the ajowan plant, used as a culinary spice. ■ the essential oil of the ajowan plant.

– ORIGIN from Hindi *ajvāyn*.

a·ju·ga /ˈajəgə/ ▶ **n.** a plant of a genus that includes bugle. ● Genus *Ajuga*, family Labiatae: numerous species.
– ORIGIN modern Latin, from medieval Latin *ajuga*.

AK ▶ **abbr.** Alaska (in official postal use).

AK-47 ▶ **n.** a type of assault rifle, originally manufactured in the former Soviet Union.
– ORIGIN acronym for Russian *Avtomat Kalashnikova 1947*, the designation of the original model, designed in 1947 by Mikhail T. Kalashnikov (b. 1919).

aka ▶ **abbr.** also known as: *John Merrick, aka the Elephant Man.*

A·kan /ˈäˌkän/ ▶ **n. 1** (pl. **same**) a member of a people inhabiting southern Ghana and adjacent parts of Côte d'Ivoire (Ivory Coast).
2 the Kwa language spoken by this people. There are two main dialects, Ashanti and Fante. Also called TWI.
▶ **adj.** of or relating to this people or their language.
– ORIGIN the name in Akan.

a·ka·sha /äˈkäSHä/ ▶ **n.** chiefly Hinduism a supposed universal etheric field in which a record of past events is imprinted.
– DERIVATIVES **a·ka·shic** /-SHik/ **adj.**
– ORIGIN from Sanskrit *ākāśa*.

A·ka·shi /äˈkäSHē/ an industrial port city in west central Japan, on southwestern Honshu Island; pop. 292,966 (2008). Standard time for Japan is set here.

ak·a·this·ia /ˌakəˈTHiZHə, -ˈTHizēə/ ▶ **n.** a state of agitation, distress, and restlessness that is an occasional side-effect of antipsychotic and antidepressant drugs.

Ak·bar /ˈäkˌbär, ˈakbər/, Jalaludin Muhammad (1542–1605), Mogul emperor of India 1556–1605; known as **Akbar the Great**. Akbar expanded the Mogul empire to incorporate northern India.

AKC ▶ **abbr.** American Kennel Club.

a·ke·bi·a /əˈkēbēə/ ▶ **n.** a climbing shrub with purplish flowers, deeply divided leaves, and purple berries. Native to eastern Asia, it is grown as an ornamental in North America. ● *Akebia quinata*, family Lardizabalaceae.
– ORIGIN 1837: modern Latin, coined by J. Decaisne, French botanist, from Japanese *akebi*.

a·kee /aˈkē, ˈakē/ (also **ackee**) ▶ **n.** a tropical tree that is cultivated for its fruit. Native to West Africa, it has been introduced into the West Indies and elsewhere. ● *Blighia sapida*, family Sapindaceae. ■ the fruit of this tree, widely eaten as a vegetable, but which can be poisonous unless cooked.
– ORIGIN late 18th cent.: from Kru *ākee*.

A·khe·na·ten /ˌäk(ə)ˈnätn/ (also **Akhenaton** or **Ikhnaton** /ikˈnätn/) (14th century BC), Egyptian pharaoh of the 18th dynasty; reigned 1379–1362 BC; came to the throne as *Amenhotep IV*. He renounced polytheism, introducing a monotheistic cult based on worship of the sun disk, Aten, in whose honor he changed his name. The husband of Nefertiti, he moved the capital from Thebes to the newly built city of Akhetaten. The empire began to disintegrate during his reign.

Akh·ma·to·va /äKHˈmätəvə/, Anna (1889–1966), Russian poet; pseudonym of *Anna Andreevna Gorenko*. Akhmatova was a member of the Acmeist group of poets.

A·ki·hi·to /ˌäkēˈhētō/, (1933–), emperor of Japan 1989–; full name *Tsugu Akihito*. He is the son of Emperor Hirohito.

a·kim·bo /əˈkimbō/ ▶ **adv.** with hands on the hips and elbows turned outward: *she stood with arms akimbo, frowning at the small boy.* ■ (of other limbs) flung out widely or haphazardly.
– ORIGIN late Middle English: from *in kenebowe* in Middle English, probably from Old Norse.

a·kin /əˈkin/ ▶ **adj.** of similar character: *something akin to gratitude overwhelmed her* | *genius and madness are akin.* ■ related by blood.
– ORIGIN mid 16th cent.: contracted form of *of kin*.

a·ki·ne·sia /ˌākiˈnēZHə, ˌaki-/ ▶ **n.** Medicine loss or impairment of the power of voluntary movement.
– DERIVATIVES **a·ki·net·ic** /-ˈnetik/ **adj.**
– ORIGIN mid 19th cent.: from Greek *akinēsia* 'quiescence,' from *a-* 'without' + *kinēsis* 'motion.'

A·ki·ta[1] /äˈkētə/ an industrial port city in northeastern Japan, on northern Honshu Island; pop. 326,309 (2008).

PRONUNCIATION KEY ə **a**go, **u**p; ər **over**, **fur**; a **hat**; ā **ate**; ä **car**; e **let**; ē **see**; i **fit**; ī **by**; NG **sing**; ō **go**; ô **law**, **for**; oi **toy**; o͝o **good**; o͞o **goo**; ou **out**; TH **thin**; T͟H **then**; ZH **vision**

a

A·ki·ta² ▸ **n.** a spitz (dog) of a Japanese breed.
– ORIGIN early 20th cent.: from *Akita*, the name of a district in northern Japan.

Akita²

Ak·kad /ˈak,ad, ˈäk,äd/ the capital city that gave its name to an ancient kingdom, traditionally founded by Sargon in north central Mesopotamia. Its location is unknown.

Ak·ka·di·an /əˈkādēən, əˈkäd-/ ▸ **adj.** of or relating to Akkad in ancient Babylonia or its people or their language.
▸ **n. 1** an inhabitant of Akkad.
2 the Semitic language of Akkad.

Akkadian, known from cuneiform inscriptions, is the oldest Semitic language for which records exist. It was used in Mesopotamia from about 3500 BC; two dialects, Assyrian and Babylonian, were widely spoken in the Middle East for the next 2,000 years, and the Babylonian form functioned as a lingua franca until replaced by Aramaic around the 6th century BC.

Ak·ko /ˈäkō/ another name for **ACRE** (sense 1).

Ak-Me·chet /ˌäk miˈCHet/ former name for **SIMFEROPOL**.

a·kra·sia /əˈkrāZH(ē)ə/ (also **acrasia**) ▸ **n.** chiefly Philosophy the state of mind in which someone acts against their better judgment through weakness of will.
– DERIVATIVES **a·krat·ic** /əˈkratik/ (also **acratic**) **adj.**
– ORIGIN early 19th cent.: from Greek, from *a-* 'without' + *kratos* 'power, strength.' The term is used esp. with reference to Aristotle's *Nicomachean Ethics*.

Ak·ron /ˈakrən/ a city in northeastern Ohio; pop. 207,510 (est. 2008). Noted as a center for the rubber industry; the first rubber factory was established in 1870 by B. F. Goodrich.

Ak·sai Chin /ˈak,sī ˈCHin/ a region of the Himalayas occupied by China since 1950, but claimed by India as part of Kashmir.

Ak·sum /ˈäk,so͞om/ (also **Axum**) a town in the province of Tigray in northern Ethiopia. A religious center, it was the capital of the powerful Axumite kingdom between the 1st and 6th centuries AD.
– DERIVATIVES **Ak·sum·ite** /ˈäkso͞o,mīt/ **adj. & n.**

ak·va·vit /ˈäkvə,vēt/ ▸ **n.** variant spelling of **AQUAVIT**.

AL ▸ **abbr.** ■ Alabama (in official postal use). ■ Baseball American League. ■ American Legion.

Al ▸ **symbol** the chemical element aluminum.

al- ▸ **prefix** variant spelling of **AD-** assimilated before *-l* (as in *alleviate*, *allocate*).

-al ▸ **suffix 1** (forming adjectives) relating to; of the kind of. ■ from Latin words: *annual* | *infernal*. ■ from Greek words: *historical* | *comical*. ■ from English nouns: *tidal*.
2 forming nouns chiefly denoting verbal action: *arrival* | *transmittal*.
– ORIGIN sense 1 from French *-el* or Latin *-alis*; sense 2 from French *-aille* or from Latin *-alis* functioning as a noun ending.

Ala. ▸ **abbr.** Alabama.

à la /ˈä ,lä, ˈä lə/ ▸ **prep.** (of a dish) cooked or prepared in a specified style or manner: *fish cooked à la meunière*. ■ informal in the style or manner of: *afternoon talk shows à la Oprah*.
– ORIGIN French, from **À LA MODE**.

Al·a·bam·a /ˌaləˈbamə/ a state in the southeastern US, on the Gulf of Mexico; pop. 4,661,900 (est. 2008); capital, Montgomery; statehood, Dec. 14, 1819 (22). Visited by Spanish explorers in the mid 16th century and later settled by the French, it passed to Britain in 1763 and to the US in 1783.
– DERIVATIVES **Al·a·bam·an adj. & n.**

Al·a·bam·a Riv·er a river in southern Alabama that flows for 315 miles (507 km) to meet the Mobile River.

al·a·bas·ter /ˈalə,bastər/ ▸ **n.** a fine-grained, translucent form of gypsum, typically white, often carved into ornaments.
▸ **adj.** made of alabaster. ■ literary like alabaster in whiteness and smoothness: *her alabaster cheeks flushed with warmth*.
– ORIGIN late Middle English: via Old French from Latin *alabaster*, *alabastrum*, from Greek *alabastos*, *alabastros*.

à la carte /ˌä lä ˈkärt, lə/ ▸ **adj.** (of a menu or restaurant) listing or serving food that can be ordered as separate items, rather than part of a set meal. ■ (of food) available on such a menu.
▸ **adv.** as separately priced items from a menu, not as part of a set meal: *wine and good food served à la carte*.
– ORIGIN early 19th cent.: French, literally 'according to the (menu) card.'

a·lack /əˈlak/ (also **alack-a-day**) ▸ **exclam.** archaic an expression of regret or dismay.
– ORIGIN late Middle English: probably from **AH** + **LACK**.

a·lac·ri·ty /əˈlakritē/ ▸ **n.** brisk and cheerful readiness: *she accepted the invitation with alacrity*.
– ORIGIN late Middle English: from Latin *alacritas*, from *alacer* 'brisk.'

A·lad·din /əˈladn/ the hero of a story in the *Arabian Nights*, who finds an old lamp that, when rubbed, summons a genie who obeys the will of the owner.
– ORIGIN from Arabic *ʻAlā' al-dīn*.

A·lad·din's lamp ▸ **n.** a talisman enabling its holder to gratify any wish.
– ORIGIN from **ALADDIN**.

Alain-Four·nier /ä,laN ˈfo͝orn,yā/ (1886–1914), French novelist; pseudonym of *Henri-Alban Fournier*.

à la king /ˌä l(ə) ˈkiNG, ˌal (ə)/ ▸ **adj.** (of a dish) with diced meat in a cream sauce, usually with green peppers and pimientos.

Al·a·me·da /ˌaləˈmēdə, -ˈmādə/ a port city in north central California, on San Francisco Bay, just southwest of Oakland; pop. 70,580 (est. 2008).

al·a·me·da /ˌaləˈmādə/ ▸ **n.** (in Spain and Spanish-speaking regions) a public walkway or promenade shaded with trees.
– ORIGIN late 18th cent.: Spanish, from *álamo* 'cottonwood' + *-eda* 'grove' from Latin *-etum* (see **-ETUM**).

A·la·mein /ˌaləˈmān/ see **EL ALAMEIN, BATTLE OF**.

Al·a·mo /ˈalə,mō/ (**the Alamo**) a mission in San Antonio, Texas, site of a siege in 1836 by Mexican forces, in which all 180 defenders were killed.

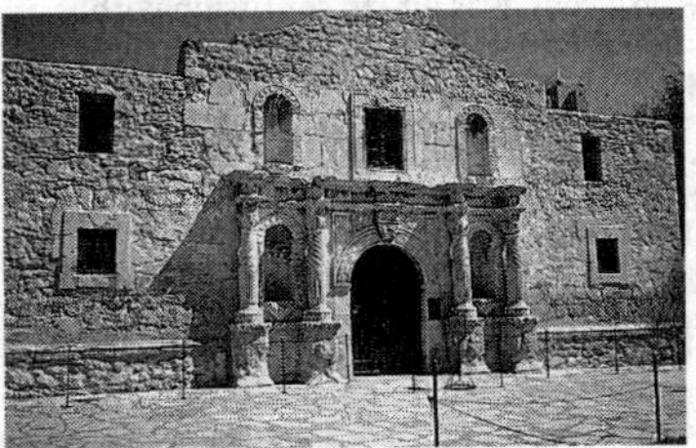

the Alamo

à la mode /ˌä lä ˈmōd/ ▸ **adv. & adj. 1** in fashion; up to date.
2 served with ice cream.
3 (of beef) braised in wine, typically with vegetables.
– ORIGIN late 16th cent.: French, literally 'in the fashion.'

Al·a·mo·gor·do /ˌaləməˈgôrdō/ a city in southern New Mexico; pop. 35,757 (est. 2008). White Sands and other military and aerospace facilities are nearby.

Å·land Is·lands /ˈōlənd/ a group of islands in the Gulf of Bothnia that forms an autonomous region in Finland; capital, Mariehamn (known in Finnish as Maarianhamina). Finnish name **AHVENANMAA**.

al·a·nine /ˈalə,nēn/ ▸ **n.** Biochemistry an amino acid that is a constituent of most proteins. ● Alternative name: 2-aminopropanoic acid; chem. formula: $CH_3CH(NH_2)COOH$. β-**alanine**, an isomer of this, is 3-aminopropanoic acid, $(NH_2)CH_2CH_2COOH$.
– ORIGIN mid 19th cent.: coined in German as *Alanin*, from **ALDEHYDE** + *-an* (for ease of pronunciation) + **-INE**⁴.

Al-A·non /ˈal ə,nän/ a mutual support organization for the families and friends of alcoholics, esp. those of members of Alcoholics Anonymous.

a·lap /ˈäl,äp/ ▸ **n.** (in Indian music) the improvised section of a raga, forming a prologue to the formal expression.
– ORIGIN from Hindi *alāp*.

a la plan·cha /ˌä lə ˈplänCHə/ ▸ **adj. & adv.** (of meat or fish) pan-fried or cooked on a griddle.
– ORIGIN Spanish.

A·lar /ˈā,lär/ ▸ **n.** trademark for **DAMINOZIDE**.

a·lar /ˈālər/ ▸ **adj.** chiefly Zoology of or relating to a wing or wings. ■ Anatomy winglike or wing-shaped. ■ Botany another term for **AXILLARY**.
– ORIGIN mid 19th cent.: from Latin *alaris*, from *ala* 'wing.'

A·lar·cón /ˌälärˈkôn/, Pedro Antonio de (1833–91), Spanish novelist and short-story writer. His notable works include *The Three-Cornered Hat* (1874).

A·lar·cón y Men·do·za see **RUIZ DE ALARCÓN Y MENDOZA**.

Al·a·ric /ˈalərik/ (*c.*370–410), king of the Visigoths 395–410. He captured Rome in 410.

a·larm /əˈlärm/ ▸ **n.** an anxious awareness of danger: *the boat tilted and the boatmen cried out in **alarm** | he views the right-wing upsurge in Europe **with alarm***. ■ [in sing.] a warning of danger: *I hammered on several doors to **raise the alarm** | Oliver smelled smoke and **gave the alarm***. ■ a warning sound or device: *a burglar alarm*. ■ an alarm clock.
▸ **v. 1** [with obj.] cause (someone) to feel frightened, disturbed, or in danger: *the government was alarmed by an outbreak of unrest*.
2 (**be alarmed**) be fitted or protected with an alarm: *this door is locked and alarmed between 11 p.m. and 6 a.m.*
– ORIGIN late Middle English (as an exclamation meaning 'to arms!'): from Old French *alarme*, from Italian *allarme*, from *all' arme!* 'to arms!'

a·larm bell ▸ **n.** a bell rung as a warning of danger: *the alarm bell rang out* | figurative *the proposal has set **alarm bells ringing***.

a·larm call ▸ **n.** a warning cry made by a bird or other animal when startled.

a·larm clock ▸ **n.** a clock with a device that can be made to sound at the time set in advance, used to wake someone up.

a·larm·ing /əˈlärmiNG/ ▸ **adj.** worrying or disturbing: *our countryside is disappearing at an alarming rate*.
– DERIVATIVES **a·larm·ing·ly adv.** *the water swirls alarmingly* | [as submodifier] *an alarmingly high rate*.

a·larm·ist /əˈlärmist/ ▸ **n.** someone who is considered to be exaggerating a danger and so causing needless worry or panic.
▸ **adj.** creating needless worry or panic: *alarmist rumors*.
– DERIVATIVES **a·larm·ism** /-,mizəm/ **n.**

a·lar·um /əˈlärəm, əˈlar-/ ▸ **n.** archaic term for **ALARM**.
– PHRASES **alarums and excursions** humorous confused activity and uproar.

a·las /əˈlas/ ▸ **exclam.** chiefly literary or humorous an expression of grief, pity, or concern: *alas, my funds have some limitations*.
– ORIGIN Middle English: from Old French *a las, a lasse*, from *a* 'ah' + *las(se)* (from Latin *lassus* 'weary').

Alas. ▸ **abbr.** Alaska.

A·las·ka /əˈlaskə/ the largest state in the US, in northwestern North America, with coasts on the Arctic and North Pacific oceans and on the Bering Sea, separated from the contiguous 48 US states by Canada; pop. 686,293 (est. 2008); capital, Juneau; statehood: Jan. 3, 1959 (49). The territory was purchased from Russia in 1867. After oil was discovered in 1968, a pipeline was completed in 1977 to carry the oil from the North Slope to Valdez.
– DERIVATIVES **A·las·kan adj. & n.**

A·las·ka, Gulf of a part of the northeastern Pacific Ocean between the Alaska Peninsula and the Alexander Archipelago.

A·las·ka ce·dar ▸ **n.** another term for **NOOTKA CYPRESS**.

A·las·ka High·way see **ALCAN HIGHWAY**.

A·las·kan mal·a·mute /əˈlaskən/ (also **Alaskan malemute**) ▸ **n.** a powerful dog of a breed with a thick, gray coat, bred by the Inuit and typically used to pull sleds.
– ORIGIN late 19th cent.: from Inuit *malimiut*, the name of a people of Kotzebue Sound, Alaska, who developed the breed.

A·las·ka Pen·in·su·la a peninsula on the south coast of Alaska. It extends southwestward into the northeastern Pacific Ocean and is continued in the Aleutian Islands.

A·las·ka Range a mountain chain that lies across southern Alaska. Mt. McKinley, rising to 20,320 feet (6,194 m), is its high point.

a·late /ˈā,lāt/ ▸ **adj.** Botany & Entomology (chiefly of insects or seeds) having wings or winglike appendages.
– ORIGIN mid 17th cent.: from Latin *alatus*, from *ala* 'wing.'

alb /alb/ ▸ **n.** a white vestment worn by clergy and servers in some Christian Churches.

alb

–ORIGIN Old English *albe*, from ecclesiastical Latin *tunica* (or *vestis*) *alba* 'white garment,' from Latin *albus* 'white.'

al·ba /'albə/ ▶ **n.** a shrub rose of a variety with gray-green leaves and pinkish-white, sweet-scented flowers.
–ORIGIN mid 19th cent.: from Latin *alba*, feminine of *albus* 'white,' from the name *rosa alba*, an old white garden rose.

Al·ba·ce·te /ˌälvä'sātā/ a city in Albacete Province in southeastern Spain; pop. 166,909 (2008).

al·ba·core /'albəˌkôr/ (also **albacore tuna**) ▶ **n.** a tuna that travels in large schools and is of commercial importance as a food fish. ● Two species in the family Scombridae: *Thunnus alalunga* and the **false albacore** (*Euthynus alletteratus*).
–ORIGIN late 16th cent.: from Portuguese *albacora*, from Arabic *al-bakūra*, perhaps from *al* 'the' + *bakūr* 'premature, precocious.'

albacore

Al·ba Iu·lia /ˌälbə 'yo͞olyə/ a city in west central Romania, north of the Transylvanian Alps; pop. 66,747 (2006). Founded by the Romans in the 2nd century AD, it was the capital of Transylvania.

Al·ban, St. /'ôlbən, 'al-/ (3rd century), the first English Christian martyr, a native of Verulamium (now St. Albans). He was put to death for sheltering a fugitive priest. Feast day, June 22.

Al·ba·ni·a /al'bānēə, ôl-/ a republic in southeastern Europe that borders on the Adriatic Sea; pop. 3,639,500 (est. 2009); capital, Tirana; official language, Albanian.

> Previously part of the Byzantine and later the Ottoman empires, Albania gained independence in 1912. It became a Stalinist regime under Enver Hoxha after World War II and remained extremely isolationist in policy and outlook until the Communists lost power in 1992.

Al·ba·ni·an /al'bānēən, ôl-/ ▶ **adj.** of or relating to Albania or its people or their language.
▶ **n. 1** a native or inhabitant of Albania, or a person of Albanian descent.
2 the language of Albania.

> Albanian constitutes a separate branch of the Indo-European language group, spoken in Albania, Serbia (Kosovo), and elsewhere.

Al·ba·ny /'ôlbənē/ **1** a city in southwestern Georgia; pop. 75,831 (est. 2008).
2 the capital of New York, in the eastern part of the state, on the western bank of the Hudson River; pop. 93,539 (est. 2008).
3 a city in northwestern Oregon; pop. 48,081 (est. 2008).

al·ba·tross /'albəˌtrôs, -ˌträs/ ▶ **n.** (pl. **albatrosses**) **1** a very large oceanic bird related to the shearwaters, with long narrow wings. Albatrosses, some species of which have wingspans greater than 10 feet (3.3 m), are found mainly in the southern oceans, with three kinds in the North Pacific. ● Genera *Diomedea* and *Phoebetria*, family Diomedeidae: several species, including the **sooty albatross** (*P. fusca*), **Laysan albatross** (*D. immutablis*), and **wandering albatross** (*D. exulans*). ■ a source of frustration or guilt; an encumbrance (in allusion to Coleridge's *The Rime of the Ancient Mariner*): *an albatross of a marriage*.
2 Golf another term for **DOUBLE EAGLE**.
–ORIGIN late 17th cent.: alteration (influenced by Latin *albus* 'white') of 16th-cent. *alcatras*, applied to various seabirds including the frigate bird and pelican, from Spanish and Portuguese *alcatraz*, from Arabic *al-ġaṭṭās* 'the diver.'

Laysan albatross

al·be·do /al'bēdō/ ▶ **n.** (pl. **albedos**) chiefly Astronomy the proportion of the incident light or radiation that is reflected by a surface, typically that of a planet or moon.
–ORIGIN mid 19th cent.: ecclesiastical Latin, 'whiteness,' from Latin *albus* 'white.'

Al·bee /'ôlbē, 'albē/, Edward Franklin, III (1928–), US playwright. Notable works: *Who's Afraid of Virginia Woolf?* (1962), *A Delicate Balance* (1966), *Seascape* (1975), and *The Goat, or Who Is Sylvia?* (2001).

al·be·it /ôl'bē-it, al-/ ▶ **conj.** although: *he was making progress, albeit rather slowly*.
–ORIGIN late Middle English: from the phrase *all be it* 'although it be (that).'

Al·be·marle Sound /'albəˌmärl/ an inlet of the Atlantic Ocean in northeastern North Carolina, inside the Outer Banks.

Al·bers /'albərz, 'ôl-/, Josef (1888–1976), US artist, designer, and teacher; born in Germany. He is associated with the Bauhaus and constructivism and is best known for his series of abstract canvases *Homage to the Square*, which he began in 1950.

al·bert /'albərt/ (also **albert chain**) ▶ **n.** Brit. a watch chain with a bar at one end for attaching to a buttonhole.
–ORIGIN mid 19th cent.: named after *Prince Albert* (see **ALBERT, PRINCE**).

Al·bert, Lake /'albərt/ a lake in the Rift Valley of eastern central Africa, on the border between the Democratic Republic of the Congo (formerly Zaire) and Uganda. It is linked to Lake Edward by the Semliki River and to the White Nile by the Albert Nile. Also called **MOBUTU SESE SEKO, LAKE**.

Al·bert, Prince /'albərt/ (1819–61), consort to Queen Victoria and prince of Saxe-Coburg-Gotha; full name *Albert Francis Charles Augustus Emmanuel*.

Al·ber·ta /al'bərtə/ a prairie province in western Canada, bounded on the south by the US and on the west by the Rocky Mountains; capital, Edmonton; pop. 3,290,350 (2006).

Al·ber·ta Clip·per ▶ **n.** Meteorology a fast-moving winter weather system originating in the lee of the Canadian Rockies that typically brings snow, high winds, and cold temperatures across the northern US.

Al·ber·ti /äl'bertē/, Leon Battista (1404–72), Italian architect, humanist, painter, and art critic. He wrote *On Painting* (1435), which was the first account of the theory of perspective in the Renaissance.

Al·bert Nile the upper part of the Nile River that flows through northwestern Uganda between Lake Albert and the Ugandan–Sudanese border.

Al·ber·tus Mag·nus, St. /al'bərtəs 'magnəs/ (*c.*1200–80), Dominican theologian, philosopher, and scientist; known as **Doctor Universalis**. A teacher of St. Thomas Aquinas, he was a pioneer in the study of Aristotle. Feast day, November 15.

al·bes·cent /al'besənt/ ▶ **adj.** chiefly literary growing or shading into white: *the albescent waves on the horizon*.
–ORIGIN early 18th cent.: from Latin *albescere* 'become white,' from *albus* 'white.'

Al·bi·gen·ses /ˌalbi'jensēz/ ▶ **plural n.** the members of a heretical sect in southern France in the 12th–13th centuries, identified with the Cathars. Their teaching was a form of Manichaean dualism, with an extremely strict moral and social code.
–DERIVATIVES **Al·bi·gen·si·an** /-'jentsēən, -SHən/ **adj.**
–ORIGIN medieval Latin, from *Albiga*, the Latin name of *Albi* in southern France.

al·bi·no /al'bīnō/ ▶ **n.** (pl. **albinos**) a person or animal having a congenital absence of pigment in the skin and hair (which are white) and the eyes (which are typically pink). ■ informal an abnormally white animal or plant: [as modifier] *an albino tiger*.
–DERIVATIVES **al·bi·nism** /'albəˌnizəm/ **n.**
–ORIGIN early 18th cent.: from Portuguese (originally denoting albinos among African blacks) and Spanish, from *albo* (from Latin *albus* 'white') + the suffix *-ino* (see **-INE**[1]).

Al·bi·nus /'albīnəs/ see **ALCUIN**.

Al·bi·on /'albēən/ ▶ **n.** a poetic or literary term for Britain or England (often used in referring to ancient or historical times).
–ORIGIN Old English, from Latin, probably of Celtic origin and related to Latin *albus* 'white' (in allusion to the white cliffs of Dover). The phrase *perfidious Albion* (mid 19th cent.) translates the French *la perfide Albion*, alluding to alleged treachery to other nations.

al·bite /'alˌbīt/ ▶ **n.** a sodium-rich mineral of the plagioclase feldspar group, typically white, occurring widely in igneous rocks.
–ORIGIN early 19th cent.: from Latin *albus* 'white' + **-ITE**[1].

al·biz·zi·a /al'bizēə, -'bitsēə/ (also **albizia**) ▶ **n.** a leguminous tree or shrub with feathery leaves and densely clustered plumelike flowers. Native to warm climates, it is sometimes grown as a shade tree or ornamental. ● Genus *Albizia*, family Leguminosae: several species.
–ORIGIN modern Latin, named after Filippo degli *Albizzi*, a Tuscan nobleman who introduced the silk tree *A. julibrizzen* into Italy in the mid 18th cent.

al·bon·di·gas /älbôn'dēgäs/ ▶ **plural n.** small meatballs, prepared in the Mexican, Spanish, or South American way.
–ORIGIN Spanish, from Arabic *al-bunduq* 'hazel nut.'

Ål·borg /'ôlˌbôrg/ variant spelling of **AALBORG**.

Al·bright /'ôlˌbrīt/, Madeleine Korbel (1937–), US secretary of state 1997–2001; born in Czechoslovakia. After serving as US ambassador to the United Nations 1993–1997, she became the first woman to head the US Department of State. She emigrated to the US with her family in 1948 during the Communist takeover in Czechoslovakia.

Madeleine Albright

al·bum /'albəm/ ▶ **n. 1** a blank book for the insertion of photographs, stamps, or pictures: *the wedding pictures had pride of place in the family album*.
2 a collection of recordings, on CD, record, or cassette, that are issued as a single item.
–ORIGIN early 17th cent.: from Latin, neuter of *albus* 'white' used as a noun meaning 'a blank tablet.' Taken into English from the German use of the Latin phrase *album amicorum* 'album of friends,' it was originally used consciously as a Latin word with Latin inflections.

al·bu·men /al'byo͞omən/ ▶ **n.** egg white, or the protein contained in it.
–ORIGIN late 16th cent.: from Latin, 'egg white,' from *albus* 'white.'

al·bu·min /al'byo͞omən/ ▶ **n.** Biochemistry a simple form of protein that is soluble in water and coagulable by heat, such as that found in egg white, milk, and (in particular) blood serum.
–ORIGIN mid 19th cent.: from French *albumine*, based on Latin *albumen*, *albumin-* (see **ALBUMEN**).

al·bu·mi·noid /al'byo͞oməˌnoid/ ▶ **n.** another term for **SCLEROPROTEIN**.

al·bu·mi·nous /al'byo͞omənəs/ ▶ **adj.** consisting of, resembling, or containing albumen.

al·bu·mi·nu·ri·a /alˌbyo͞omə'n(y)o͝orēə/ ▶ **n.** Medicine the presence of albumin in the urine, typically as a symptom of kidney disease.

Al·bu·quer·que[1] /'alb(y)əˌkərkē/ city in central New Mexico, on the Rio Grande; pop. 521,999 (est. 2008). It is the largest city in the state.

Al·bu·quer·que[2], Alfonso de (1453–1515), Portuguese colonial statesman. He conquered Goa (1510) and made it the capital of the Portuguese empire in the east.

Al·cae·us /al'sēəs/ (*c.*620–*c.*580 BC), Greek lyric poet. He invented a new form of lyric meter called the alcaic. His works were a model for the Roman poet Horace and the verse of the Renaissance.

al·ca·hest /'alkəˌhest/ ▶ **n.** variant spelling of **ALKAHEST**.

al·ca·ic /al'kā-ik/ Prosody ▶ **adj.** a four-line verse stanza in the meter invented by the Greek poet Alcaeus, and later used in a slightly altered form by the Roman poet Horace.
▶ **n.** (usu. **alcaics**) alcaic verse.
–ORIGIN mid 17th cent.: via late Latin from Greek *alkaikos*, from *Alkaios* (see **ALCAEUS**).

Al·ca·lá de He·na·res /ˌälkə'lä dā ä'näräs/ a city in central Spain, on the Henares River, 15 miles (25 km) northeast of Madrid; pop. 203,645 (2008).

al·cal·de /äl'käldē, al-/ ▶ **n.** a magistrate or mayor in a Spanish, Portuguese, or Latin American town.
–ORIGIN mid 16th cent.: Spanish, from Arabic *al-ḳāḍī* 'the judge' (see **CADI**).

Al·can High·way /'alˌkan/ (also **Alaska Highway**) a military road, built during World War II to link Dawson Creek in the Yukon Territory with

a

Fairbanks in Alaska, as part of a supply route to the former Soviet Union and the Pacific Ocean.

Al·ca·traz /ˈalkəˌtraz/ a rocky island in San Francisco Bay, California. It was the site of a top-security federal prison between 1934 and 1963 and since 1972 has been administered by the National Park Service.

al·ca·zar /ˌalkəˈzär, alˈkazər/ (often **Alcazar**) ▶ **n.** a Spanish palace or fortress of Moorish origin.
– ORIGIN early 17th cent.: from Spanish *alcázar*, from Arabic *al-ḳaṣr* 'the castle.'

Al·ces·tis /alˈsestis/ Greek Mythology wife of Admetus, king of Pherae in Thessaly, whose life she saved by consenting to die on his behalf.

al·che·my /ˈalkəmē/ ▶ **n.** the medieval forerunner of chemistry, based on the supposed transformation of matter. It was concerned particularly with attempts to convert base metals into gold or to find a universal elixir. ■ a seemingly magical process of transformation, creation, or combination: *finding the person who's right for you requires a very subtle alchemy.*
– DERIVATIVES **al·chem·ic** /alˈkemik/ **adj.**, **al·chem·i·cal** /alˈkemikəl/ **adj.**, **al·che·mist** /-mist/ **n.**, **al·che·mize** /-ˌmīz/ **v.**
– ORIGIN late Middle English: via Old French and medieval Latin from Arabic *alkīmiyā'*, from *al* 'the' + *kīmiyā'* (from Greek *khēmia, khēmeia* 'art of transmuting metals').

Al·ci·an blue /ˈalsēən/ ▶ **n.** trademark a water-soluble copper-containing blue dye used as a histological stain for glycosaminoglycans.
– ORIGIN 1940s: *Alcian* perhaps from *(phth)al(o) cyan(ine)* with a phonetic respelling.

Al·ci·bi·a·des /ˌalsəˈbīəˌdēz/ (*c.*450–404 BC), Athenian general and statesman who held commands during the Peloponnesian Wars against Sparta (431–404).

al·cid /ˈalsid/ ▶ **n.** Ornithology a bird of the auk family (Alcidae); an auk or puffin.
– ORIGIN late 19th cent.: modern Latin *Alcidae*, from *Alca* (genus name), based on Old Norse *álka* 'razorbill'; compare with **AUK**.

Al·clad /ˈalˌklad/ ▶ **n.** trademark a composite material consisting of sheets of aluminum alloy coated with pure aluminum or a different alloy to increase corrosion resistance.
– ORIGIN 1920s: from *al(uminum)* + **CLAD**[1].

Al·cock /ˈôlˌkäk/, Sir John William (1892–1919), English aviator. With Sir Arthur Whitten Brown, he made the first nonstop transatlantic flight in June 1919.

al·co·hol /ˈalkəˌhôl, -ˌhäl/ ▶ **n.** a colorless volatile flammable liquid that is the intoxicating constituent of wine, beer, spirits, and other drinks, and is also used as an industrial solvent and as fuel. ● Alternative names: ethanol, ethyl alcohol; chem. formula: C_2H_5OH. ■ drink containing this: *he has not taken alcohol in twenty-five years.* ■ Chemistry any organic compound whose molecule contains one or more hydroxyl groups attached to a carbon atom.
– ORIGIN mid 16th cent.: French (earlier form of *alcool*), or from medieval Latin, from Arabic *al-kuḥl* 'the kohl.' In early use the term denoted powders, specifically kohl, and esp. those obtained by sublimation; later 'a distilled or rectified spirit' (mid 17th cent).

al·co·hol-free ▶ **adj. 1** (of a drink) not containing alcohol (denoting varieties of normally alcoholic drinks from which the alcohol has been removed): *alcohol-free wines.*
2 where, or during which, alcoholic drinks are not consumed: *the hotel has an alcohol-free bar.*

al·co·hol·ic /ˌalkəˈhôlik, -ˈhäl-/ ▶ **adj.** containing or relating to alcoholic liquor: *beer is the favorite alcoholic drink.* ■ caused by the excessive consumption of alcohol: *alcoholic liver disease.* ■ suffering from alcoholism: *his alcoholic daughter was the cause of his anxiety.*
▶ **n.** a person suffering from alcoholism.

Al·co·hol·ics A·non·y·mous (abbr.: **AA**) a self-help organization for people fighting alcoholism, founded in the US in 1935 and now having branches worldwide.

al·co·hol·ism /ˈalkəhôˌlizəm, -hä-/ ▶ **n.** an addiction to the consumption of alcoholic liquor or the mental illness and compulsive behavior resulting from alcohol dependency: *he had a long history of depression, drug abuse and alcoholism.*

al·co·hol·om·e·ter /ˌalkəhôˈlämitər, -hä-/ ▶ **n.** an instrument for measuring the concentration of alcohol in a liquid.
– DERIVATIVES **al·co·hol·om·e·try** /-trē/ **n.**

Al·cott[1] /ˈôlkət, ˈal-, -ˌkät/, (Amos) Bronson (1799–1888), US educator; father of Louisa May Alcott. He advocated radical reforms in education, including racial integration in the classroom. Appointed superintendent of schools in Concord, Massachusetts, in 1859, he created the first parent–teacher association.

Al·cott[2], Louisa May (1832–88), US novelist. Her novel *Little Women* (1868–69) was based on her New England childhood and was written for adolescent girls. She wrote a number of sequels to this, as well as novels for adults. Alcott was involved in the women's suffrage movement and served as a nurse during the Civil War.

al·cove /ˈalˌkōv/ ▶ **n.** a recess, typically in the wall of a room or of a garden.
– ORIGIN late 16th cent.: from French *alcôve*, from Spanish *alcoba*, from Arabic *al-ḳubba* 'the vault.'

Al·cuin /ˈalkwən/ (*c.*735–804) English scholar, theologian, and adviser to Charlemagne; also known as **Albinus**. He is credited with the transformation of Charlemagne's court into a cultural center during the Carolingian Renaissance.

Al·dab·ra /alˈdabrə/ a coral island group in the Indian Ocean, northwest of Madagascar. Formerly part of the British Indian Ocean Territory, it became an outlying dependency of the Seychelles in 1976.

Al·dan Riv·er /ˌəlˈdän/ a river in the eastern Siberian area of Russia that rises in the Stanovoy Khrebet Mountains and flows for 1,400 miles (2,240 km) into the Lena River east of Yakutsk.

Al·deb·a·ran /alˈdebərən/ the brightest star in the constellation Taurus. It is a binary system of which the main star is a red giant.
– ORIGIN Arabic, 'the follower (of the Pleiades).'

al·de·hyde /ˈaldəˌhīd/ ▶ **n.** Chemistry an organic compound containing the group –CHO, formed by the oxidation of alcohols. Typical aldehydes include methanal (formaldehyde) and ethanal (acetaldehyde).
– DERIVATIVES **al·de·hy·dic** /ˌaldəˈhidik/ **adj.**
– ORIGIN mid 19th cent.: shortened from Latin *alcohol dehydrogenatum* 'alcohol deprived of hydrogen.'

al den·te /äl ˈdentā, al/ ▶ **adj. & adv.** (of food, typically pasta) cooked so as to be still firm when bitten.
– ORIGIN Italian, literally 'to the tooth.'

al·der /ˈôldər/ (also **alder tree**) ▶ **n.** a widely distributed tree of the birch family that has toothed leaves and bears male catkins and woody female cones. ● Genus *Alnus*, family Betulaceae: many species, including the **European** (or **black**) **alder** (*A. glutinosa*), common in damp ground and on riverbanks.
– ORIGIN Old English *alor, aler*, of Germanic origin; related to German *Erle*; forms spelled with *d* are recorded from the 14th cent.

al·der·fly /ˈôldərˌflī/ (also **alder fly**) ▶ **n.** (pl. **alderflies**) a brownish flylike insect that lives near water and has predatory aquatic larvae. ● Family Sialidae, order Neuroptera: several genera.

al·der·man /ˈôldərmən/ ▶ **n.** (pl. **aldermen**) an elected member of a municipal council. ■ (in England before 1974) a member of a county or borough council, next in status to the Mayor. ■ (in Anglo-Saxon England) a noble serving the king as a chief officer in a district or shire.
– DERIVATIVES **al·der·man·ic** /ˌôldərˈmanik/ **adj.**, **al·der·man·ship** /-ˌSHip/ **n.**
– ORIGIN Old English *aldormann* (originally in the general sense 'a man of high rank'), from *aldor, ealdor* 'chief, patriarch,' from *ald* 'old' + **MAN**. Later the sense 'warden of a guild' arose; then, as the guilds became identified with the ruling municipal body, 'local magistrate, municipal officer,' the status and method of appointment varying in different times and places.

Al·der·ney /ˈôldərnē/ an island in the English Channel, to the northeast of Guernsey; pop. 2,000 (est. 2009). It is the third largest of the Channel Islands.

al·der·per·son /ˈôldərˌpərsən/ ▶ **n.** an alderman or alderwoman (used as a neutral alternative).

al·der·wom·an /ˈôldərˌwo͝omən/ ▶ **n.** (pl. **alderwomen**) an elected female member of a municipal council.

al·di·carb /ˈaldiˌkärb/ ▶ **n.** a systemic agricultural pesticide used particularly against some mites, insects, and nematode worms.
– ORIGIN 1970s: blend of **ALDEHYDE** and *carbamide* (from **CARBO-** + **AMIDE**).

Al·dine /ˈôlˌdīn, -ˌdēn/ ▶ **adj.** of or relating to the Venetian printer Aldus Manutius, or to the books printed by him, or to certain styles of display types.
– ORIGIN early 19th cent.: from Latin *Aldinus*, from *Aldus*, the printer's given name.

Al·dis lamp /ˈôldis/ ▶ **n.** trademark a handheld lamp for signaling in Morse code.
– ORIGIN World War I: named after A. C. W. *Aldis* (1878–1953), its British inventor.

Al·diss /ˈôldəs/, Brian (Wilson) (1925–), English novelist and critic, best known for his science fiction. He wrote *Frankenstein Unbound* (1973).

al·dol /ˈalˌdôl, -ˌdäl/ ▶ **n.** Chemistry a viscous liquid obtained when acetaldehyde dimerizes in dilute alkali or acid. ● Alternative name: **3-hydroxybutanal**; chem. formula: $CH_3CH(OH)CH_2CHO$.
– ORIGIN late 19th cent.: from *ald(ehyde)* + **-OL**.

al·dos·te·rone /alˈdästəˌrōn/ ▶ **n.** Biochemistry a corticosteroid hormone that stimulates absorption of sodium by the kidneys and so regulates water and salt balance.
– ORIGIN 1950s: blend of **ALDEHYDE** and **STEROID**, + **-ONE**.

al·do·ster·on·ism /ˌaldōˈsterəˌnizəm, alˈdästərə-/ ▶ **n.** Medicine a condition in which there is excessive secretion of aldosterone. This disturbs the balance of sodium, potassium, and water in the blood and so leads to high blood pressure.

Al·drin /ˈôldrin/, Buzz (1930–), US astronaut; full name *Edwin Eugene Aldrin*. He became an astronaut in 1963, and walked in space for 5 hours and 37 minutes during the 1966 Gemini 12 mission. In 1969 he took part in the first moon landing, the Apollo 11 mission, becoming the second person, after Neil Armstrong, to set foot on the moon.

al·drin /ˈôldrin/ ▶ **n.** a toxic synthetic insecticide, now generally banned. ● A chlorinated polycyclic hydrocarbon; chem. formula: $C_{12}H_8Cl_6$.
– ORIGIN 1940s: from the name of K. *Alder* (see **DIELS–ALDER REACTION**) + **-IN**[1].

Al·dus Ma·nu·ti·us /ˈôldəs məˈn(y)o͞osH(ē)əs/ (1450–1515), Italian scholar, printer, and publisher; Latinized name of *Teobaldo Manucci*; also known as **Aldo Manuzio**.

ale /āl/ ▶ **n.** a type of beer with a bitter flavor and higher alcoholic content: *amber-colored beers, ales, and stouts.* ■ chiefly Brit. beer.
– ORIGIN Old English *alu, ealu*, of Germanic origin; related to Old Norse *ǫl*. Formerly the word referred esp. to unhopped or paler-colored varieties of beer.

a·le·a·tor·ic /ˌālēəˈtôrik, ˌal-/ ▶ **adj.** another term for **ALEATORY**.
– ORIGIN 1960s: from Latin *aleatorius*, from *aleator* 'dice player,' from *alea* 'die,' + **-IC**.

a·le·a·to·ry /ˈālēəˌtôrē, ˈal-/ ▶ **adj.** depending on the throw of a die or on chance; random. ■ relating to or denoting music or other forms of art involving elements of random choice (sometimes using statistical or computer techniques) during their composition, production, or performance.
– ORIGIN late 17th cent.: from Latin *aleatorius* (see **ALEATORIC**).

al·ec /ˈalik/ (also **aleck** or **alick**) ▶ **n.** Austral. informal a stupid person: *what sort of alec do you take me for?*
– ORIGIN late 20th cent.: shortening of **SMART ALECK**.

ale·cost /ˈālˌkôst, -ˌkäst/ ▶ **n. 1** a wild plant with small daisylike flowers that has culinary and folk-medicinal uses. ● *Chrysanthemum balsamita*, family Compositae.
2 another name for **COSTMARY**.

A·lec·to /əˈlektō/ (also **Allecto**) Greek Mythology one of the Furies.

a·lee /əˈlē/ ▶ **adv. & adj.** [predic.] on the side of a ship that is sheltered from the wind. ■ (of the helm) moved around to leeward in order to tack a vessel or to bring its bows up into the wind.
– ORIGIN late Middle English: from **A-**[2] 'on' + **LEE**.

ale·house /ˈālˌhous/ ▶ **n.** dated a tavern.

A·lei·chem /əˈlākHəm, -kəm/ see **SHOLOM ALEICHEM**.

Ale·khine /ˌəlˈyôKH(y)in/, Alexander (1892–1946), French chess player; born in Russia; world champion 1927–35 and 1937–46.

A·lek·san·dro·pol /ˌalikˈsändrəˌpōl, ˌəlyiksənˈdrôpəl/ (also **Alexandropol**) former name (1840–1924) for **GYUMRI**.

A·lek·san·drovsk /ˌəlyikˈsändrəfsk/ former name (until 1921) of **ZAPORIZHZHYA**.

a·lem·bic /əˈlembik/ ▶ **n.** a distilling apparatus, now obsolete, consisting of a rounded, necked flask and a cap with a long beak for condensing and conveying the products to a receiver.
– ORIGIN Middle English: via Old French from medieval Latin *alembicus*, from Arabic *al-'anbīḳ*, from *al-* 'the' + *'anbīḳ* 'still' (from Greek *ambix, ambik-* 'cup, cap of a still').

alembic

a·leph /ˈälif, ˈälef/ ▶ **n.** the first letter of the Hebrew alphabet.

– ORIGIN Middle English: from Hebrew *'ālep*, literally 'ox' (the character in Phoenician and ancient Hebrew possibly being derived from a hieroglyph of an ox's head).

A·lep·po /ə'lepō/ a city in northern Syria; pop. 1,693,800 (est. 2009).

A·lep·po gall ▶ **n.** a hard nutlike gall that forms on the Valonia oak (formerly known as the Aleppo oak) in response to the developing larva of a gall wasp. It is used as a source of gallic acid and tannin. ● The wasp is *Cynips tinctoria*, family Cynipidae.

a·ler·ce /ə'lərsə/ ▶ **n.** a cypress tree that is valued for its timber. ● Several species in the family Cupressaceae, in particular the **sandarac tree** (*Tetraclinis articulata*) of southern Spain and northwestern Africa, from which the resin sandarac is obtained. ■ the wood of such a tree, esp. the sandarac tree.
– ORIGIN mid 19th cent.: from Spanish, 'larch.'

a·lert /ə'lərt/ ▶ **adj.** quick to notice any unusual and potentially dangerous or difficult circumstances; vigilant: *an alert police officer discovered a truck full of explosives | schools need to be constantly alert to this problem.* ■ able to think clearly; intellectually active: *she remained active and alert until well into her eighties.*
▶ **n.** the state of being watchful for possible danger: *security forces were placed* ***on alert***. ■ an announcement or signal warning of danger: *a bomb alert | an alert sounded and all the fighters took off.* ■ a period of vigilance in response to such a warning: *traffic was halted during the alert.*
▶ **v.** [with obj.] warn (someone) of a danger, threat, or problem, typically with the intention of having it avoided or dealt with: ***he alerted people to the*** *dangers of smoking | police were alerted after three men drove away without paying.*
– PHRASES **on the alert** vigilant and prepared: *the security forces must be on the alert for an upsurge in violence.*
– DERIVATIVES **a·lert·ly adv.**
– ORIGIN late 16th cent. (originally in military use): from French *alerte*, from Italian *all' erta* 'to the watchtower.'

a·lert·ness /ə'lərtnis/ ▶ **n.** the quality of being alert: *a lack of mental alertness.*

-ales ▶ **suffix** Botany forming the names of orders of plants: *Rosales.*
– ORIGIN from the plural of the Latin adjectival suffix *-alis* (see **-AL**).

a·leth·ic /ə'lēTHik, ə'lē-/ ▶ **adj.** Philosophy denoting modalities of truth, such as necessity, contingency, or impossibility.
– ORIGIN 1950s: from Greek *alētheia* 'truth' + **-IC**.

A·letsch·horn /'äliCH,hôrn/ a mountain in Switzerland, in the Bernese Alps, that rises to 13,763 feet (4,195 m). Its glaciers are among the largest in Europe.

al·eu·rone /'alyə,rōn, ə'lŏŏrōn/ ▶ **n.** Botany protein stored as granules in the cells of plant seeds.
– ORIGIN mid 19th cent.: from Greek *aleuron* 'flour.'

Al·eut /ə'lŏŏt, 'alē,ŏŏt/ ▶ **n. 1** a member of a people inhabiting the Aleutian Islands, other islands in the Bering Sea, and parts of western Alaska.
2 the language of this people, related to Eskimo.
▶ **adj.** of or relating to this people or their language.
– ORIGIN from Russian, from an unknown source.

A·leu·tian Is·lands /ə'lŏŏSHən/ (also **the Aleutians**) a chain of US volcanic islands that extend southwest from the Alaska Peninsula.

A·leu·tian Range /ə'lŏŏSHən/ an extension of the Coast Ranges in southwestern Alaska. It contains many volcanoes.

A lev·el ▶ **n.** (in the UK except Scotland) the higher of the two main levels of standardized examinations in secondary schools. Compare with **O LEVEL**.
– ORIGIN short for *advanced level.*

al·e·vin /'alәvәn/ ▶ **n.** a newly spawned salmon or trout still carrying the yolk.
– ORIGIN mid 19th cent.: from Old French, based on Latin *allevare* 'raise up.'

ale·wife /'āl,wīf/ ▶ **n.** (pl. **alewives** /-,wīvz/) a northwestern Atlantic fish of the herring family that swims up rivers to spawn and is found also in the Great Lakes. ● *Alosa pseudoharengus*, family Clupeidae. ■ another term for MENHADEN.
– ORIGIN mid 17th cent.: possibly from earlier *alewife* 'woman who keeps an alehouse,' with reference to the fish's large belly.

Al·ex·an·der[1] /,alig'zandər/ (356–323 BC), king of Macedon 336–323; son of Philip II; known as **Alexander the Great**. He conquered Persia, Egypt, Syria, Mesopotamia, Bactria, and the Punjab; he founded the city of Alexandria in Egypt.

Al·ex·an·der[2] three kings of Scotland. ■ **Alexander I** (c.1077–1124), son of Malcolm III; reigned 1107–24. ■ **Alexander II** (1198–1249), son of William I of Scotland; reigned 1214–49. ■ **Alexander III** (1241–86), son of Alexander II; reigned 1249–86. He annexed the Hebrides and the Isle of Man in 1266.

Al·ex·an·der[3] three tsars of Russia. ■ **Alexander I** (1777–1825), reigned 1801–25. During his reign, Napoleon unsuccessfully invaded Russia 1812. ■ **Alexander II** (1818–81), son of Nicholas I; reigned 1855–81; known as **Alexander the Liberator**. His reforms included limited emancipation of the serfs. ■ **Alexander III** (1845–94), son of Alexander II; reigned 1881–94.

Al·ex·an·der[4], Grover Cleveland (1887–1950), US baseball player; known as **Pete**. A 20-season pitcher for the Philadelphia Phillies 1911–17, the Chicago Cubs 1917–26, and the St. Louis Cardinals 1926–30, he retired with 373 career wins and 90 shutouts. Baseball Hall of Fame (1938).

Al·ex·an·der[5], Harold (Rupert Leofric George), 1st Earl Alexander of Tunis (1891–1969), British field marshal and statesman.

Al·ex·an·der Ar·chi·pel·a·go a group of more than 1,000 US islands off the coast of southeastern Alaska.

Al·ex·an·der Nev·sky, St. /'nefskē/ (also **Nevski**) (c.1220–63), prince of Novgorod 1236-63; born *Aleksandr Yaroslavich*. He defeated the Swedes on the banks of the Neva River in 1240. Feast day, August 30 or November 23.

Al·ex·an·der tech·nique a system of body awareness designed to promote well-being by ensuring minimum effort in maintaining postures and carrying out movements.
– ORIGIN 1930s: named after Frederick Matthias *Alexander* (1869–1955), Australian-born actor and physical therapist who developed it.

Al·ex·an·dret·ta /,aligzan'dretə/ former name for **ISKENDERUN**.

Al·ex·an·dri·a /,alig'zandrēə/ **1** the chief port of Egypt; pop. 4,084,700 (est. 2006). Founded in 332 BC by Alexander the Great, it was a major center of Hellenistic culture, renowned for its library and for the Pharos lighthouse.
2 an industrial city in central Louisiana, on the Red River; pop. 48,639 (est. 2008).
3 a city in northern Virginia, on the Potomac River, across from Washington, DC; pop. 143,885 (est. 2008).

Al·ex·an·dri·an /,alig'zandrēən/ ▶ **adj.** of or relating to Alexandria in Egypt. ■ belonging to or akin to the schools of literature and philosophy of ancient Alexandria. ■ (of a writer) derivative or imitative rather than creative; fond of recondite learning.

al·ex·an·drine /,alig'zandrin, -,drēn/ Prosody ▶ **adj.** (of a line of verse) having six iambic feet.
▶ **n.** (usu. **alexandrines**) an alexandrine line.
– ORIGIN late 16th cent.: from French *alexandrin*, from *Alexandre* (see **ALEXANDER[1]**), the subject of an Old French poem in this meter.

al·ex·an·drite /,alig'zan,drīt/ ▶ **n.** a gem variety of chrysoberyl that appears green in daylight and red in artificial light.
– ORIGIN mid 19th cent.: from the name of Tsar *Alexander* II of Russia (see **ALEXANDER[3]**) + **-ITE[1]**.

Al·ex·an·dro·pol variant spelling of **ALEKSANDROPOL**.

a·lex·i·a /ə'leksēə/ ▶ **n.** the inability to see words or to read, caused by a defect of the brain. Also called **WORD BLINDNESS**. Compare with **DYSLEXIA**.
– ORIGIN late 19th cent.: from **A-[1]** 'without' + Greek *lexis* 'speech,' from *legein* 'speak,' which was confused with Latin *legere* 'read.'

al·fal·fa /al'falfə/ ▶ **n.** a leguminous plant with cloverlike leaves and bluish flowers. Native to southwestern Asia, it is widely grown for fodder. Also called **LUCERNE**. ● *Medicago sativa*, family Leguminosae.
– ORIGIN mid 19th cent.: from Spanish, from Arabic *al-faṣfaṣa*, a green fodder.

al-Fa·tah see **FATAH**.

al·fi·sol /'alfi,sôl, -,säl/ ▶ **n.** Soil Science a soil of an order comprising leached basic or slightly acid soils with a clay-enriched B horizon (subsoil).
– ORIGIN 1960s: from the arbitrary element *Alfi-* + **-SOL**.

Al·fon·so XIII /al'fänsō, äl'fônsō/ (1886–1941), king of Spain 1886–1931. He was forced into exile after elections indicating a preference for a republic.

Al·fred /'alfrəd/ (849–99), king of Wessex 871–899; known as **Alfred the Great**. His military resistance saved southwestern England from Viking occupation.

Al·fre·do /al'frādō/ ▶ **n.** a sauce for pasta incorporating butter, cream, garlic, and Parmesan cheese.
– ORIGIN named after *Alfredo* di Lelio, the Italian chef and restaurateur who invented the sauce.

al fres·co /al 'freskō, äl-/ ▶ **adv. & adj.** in the open air: [as adj.] *an al fresco luncheon.*
– ORIGIN mid 18th cent.: Italian, 'in the fresh (air).'

al-Fu·jay·rah /,äl fə'jīrə, ,al/ another name for **FUJAIRAH**.

Alf·vén /äl'vān/, Hannes Olof Gösta (1908–95), Swedish theoretical physicist. His work was important for controlled thermonuclear fusion. He shared the 1970 Nobel Prize for Physics with Louis Néel (1904–2000).

Alf·vén wave ▶ **n.** Physics a hydromagnetic shear wave in a plasma that moves along magnetic field lines. The velocity of such waves (the **Alfvén velocity** or **speed**) is characteristic for a plasma of given properties.

al·ga /'algə/ ▶ **n.** (usu. in pl. **algae** /-jē/) a simple nonflowering plant of a large group that includes the seaweeds and many single-celled forms. Algae contain chlorophyll but lack true stems, roots, leaves, and vascular tissue. ● Divisions Chlorophyta (**green algae**), Heterokontophyta (**brown algae**), and Rhodophyta (**red algae**); some (or all) are frequently placed in the kingdom Protista. See also **BLUE-GREEN ALGAE**.
– DERIVATIVES **al·gal** /-gəl/ **adj.**
– ORIGIN mid 16th cent.: from Latin, 'seaweed.'

al·ge·bra /'aljəbrə/ ▶ **n.** the part of mathematics in which letters and other general symbols are used to represent numbers and quantities in formulae and equations. ■ a system of this based on given axioms.
– DERIVATIVES **al·ge·bra·ist** /-,brā-ist/ **n.**
– ORIGIN late Middle English: from Italian, Spanish, and medieval Latin, from Arabic *al-jabr* 'the reunion of broken parts,' 'bone setting,' from *jabara* 'reunite, restore.' The original sense, 'the surgical treatment of fractures,' probably came via Spanish, in which it survives; the mathematical sense comes from the title of a book, *'ilm al-jabr wa'l-mukābala* 'the science of restoring what is missing and equating like with like,' by the mathematician al-Ḵwārizmī (see **ALGORITHM**).

al·ge·bra·ic /,aljə'brā-ik/ ▶ **adj.** relating to or involving algebra. ■ (of a mathematical expression or equation) in which a finite number of symbols is combined using only the operations of addition, subtraction, multiplication, division, and exponentiation with constant rational exponents. Compare with **TRANSCENDENTAL**.
– DERIVATIVES **al·ge·bra·i·cal adv.**, **al·ge·bra·i·cal·ly adv.**

Al·ge·ci·ras /,älKHā'THē,räs, -'sē,räs/ a ferry port and resort in southern Spain, on the Strait of Gibraltar; pop. 115,333 (2008).

Al·ger /'aljər/, Horatio, Jr. (1832–99), US author. His novels, most notably *Ragged Dick* (1867), were infused with the message that honest hard work can overcome poverty.

Al·ge·ri·a /al'ji(ə)rēə/ a republic in northwestern Africa, on the Mediterranean coast; pop. 34,178,200 (est. 2009); capital, Algiers; official language, Arabic.

> Algeria was colonized by France in the mid 19th century and was for a time closely integrated with metropolitan France. Following civil war in the 1950s, it achieved independence in 1962. A brief period of multiparty democracy was ended by a military takeover in 1992 after the fundamentalist Islamic Salvation Front had won the first round of the national elections. This prompted a low-level civil war until 2000 when the Islamic Salvation Army, the armed segment of the Islamic Salvation Front, was dissolved.

– DERIVATIVES **Al·ge·ri·an adj. & n.**

-algia ▶ **comb. form** denoting pain in a specified part of the body: *neuralgia | myalgia.*
– ORIGIN from Greek *algos* 'pain.'

-algic ▶ **comb. form** in adjectives corresponding to nouns ending in *-algia* (such as *neuralgic* corresponding to *neuralgia*).

al·gi·cide /'aljə,sīd/ ▶ **n.** a substance that is poisonous to algae.

Al·giers /al'ji(ə)rz/ the capital of Algeria and one of the leading Mediterranean ports of North Africa; pop. 2,203,700 (est. 2009).

al·gin·ic ac·id /al'jinik/ ▶ **n.** Chemistry an insoluble gelatinous carbohydrate found (chiefly as salts) in many brown seaweeds. The sodium salt is used as a thickener in foods and many other materials.
– DERIVATIVES **al·gi·nate** /'aljə,nāt/ **n.**
– ORIGIN late 19th cent.: *alginic* from **ALGA** + **-IN[1]** + **-IC**.

algo- ▶ **comb. form** pain: *algolagnia.*

a

AL·GOL /ˈalˌgôl, -ˌgäl/ ▶ **n.** one of the early high-level computer programming languages that was devised to carry out scientific calculations.
– ORIGIN 1950s: from *algo(rithmic)* + the initial letter of LANGUAGE.

Al·gol /ˈalˌgôl, -ˌgäl/ Astronomy a variable star or star system in the constellation Perseus, regarded as the prototype of eclipsing binary stars.
– ORIGIN from Arabic *al ġūl* 'the ghoul.'

al·go·lag·ni·a /ˌalgōˈlagnēə/ ▶ **n.** Psychiatry desire for sexual gratification through inflicting pain on oneself or others; sadomasochism.
– ORIGIN early 20th cent.: coined in German from Greek *algos* 'pain' + *lagneia* 'lust.'

al·gol·o·gy /alˈgäləjē/ ▶ **n.** the study of algae.
– DERIVATIVES **al·go·log·i·cal** /ˌalgəˈläjikəl/ **adj.**, **al·gol·o·gist** /-jist/ **n.**

Al·gon·qui·an /alˈgäNGk(w)ēən/ (also **Algonkian** /-kēən/) ▶ **adj.** denoting, belonging to, or relating to a family of North American Indian languages formerly spoken across a vast area from the Atlantic seaboard to the Great Lakes and the Great Plains.
▶ **n. 1** this family of languages.
2 a speaker of any of these languages.

> Algonquian is one of the largest groups of American Indian languages, including Abnaki, Mohegan, Pequot, Ojibwa, Cree, Blackfoot, Cheyenne, Fox, Menomini, and Delaware. Although the Algonquian languages are today spoken from the east coast of North America to the Rockies, the speakers are few and several of the languages are endangered. Many English words have been adopted from these languages, e.g., *moccasin, moose,* and *toboggan.*

– ORIGIN from ALGONQUIN + -IAN.

Al·gon·quin /alˈgäNGk(w)in/ (also **Algonkin** /-kin/) ▶ **n. 1** a member of a North American Indian people living in Canada along the Ottawa River and its tributaries and westward to the north of Lake Superior.
2 the dialect of Ojibwa spoken by this people.
▶ **adj.** of or relating to this people or their language.
– ORIGIN French, contraction of obsolete *Algoumequin*, probably from Malecite *elægómogwik* meaning 'they are our relatives or allies.'

> **USAGE** The use of **Algonquin** to refer generically to the Algonquian peoples or their languages is incorrect.

al·go·rithm /ˈalgəˌriTHəm/ ▶ **n.** a process or set of rules to be followed in calculations or other problem-solving operations, esp. by a computer: *a basic* ***algorithm for*** *division.*
– DERIVATIVES **al·go·rith·mic** /ˌalgəˈriTHmik/ **adj.**, **al·go·rith·mi·cal·ly** /ˌalgəˈriTHmik(ə)lē/ **adv.**
– ORIGIN late 17th cent.: variant (influenced by Greek *arithmos* 'number') of Middle English *algorism*, via Old French from medieval Latin *algorismus*. The Arabic source, *al-Ḵwārizmī* 'the man of Ḵwārizm' (now Khiva), was a name given to the 9th-cent. mathematician Abū Ja'far Muhammad ibn Mūsa.

Al·gren /ˈôlgrən/, Nelson (Abraham) (1909–81), US novelist. He drew on his childhood experiences in the slums of Chicago for his vivid, realistic novels of social protest, such as *Somebody in Boots* (1935).

al·ha·ji /älˈhäjē, alˈhajē/ ▶ **n.** (pl. **alhajis**; fem. **alhaja**) (in West Africa) a Muslim who has been to Mecca as a pilgrim (often used as a title).
– ORIGIN Hausa, from Turkish, from *al* 'the' + *hājī* 'pilgrim.'

Al·ham·bra[1] /alˈhambrə/ a city in southwestern California, northeast of Los Angeles; pop. 85,953 (est. 2008).

Al·ham·bra[2] (**the Alhambra**) a fortified Moorish palace, the last stronghold of the Muslim kings of Granada, built between 1248 and 1354 near Granada in Spain.

the Alhambra

al-Hu·day·da /ˌal (h)o͝oˈdīdə/ Arabic name for HODEIDA.

A·li[1] /äˈlē/, Muhammad, see MUHAMMAD ALI[1].

A·li[2] /äˈlē, ˈälē/, Muhammad (1942–), US boxer; born *Cassius Marcellus Clay*. He won the world heavyweight title in 1964, 1974, and 1978, becoming the only boxer to be world heavyweight champion three times. After converting to Islam and changing his name, he was stripped of his title for refusing army service on conscientious objector grounds. This decision was overturned by the US Supreme Court in 1976, and his title was reinstated.

a·li·as /ˈālēəs/ ▶ **adv.** used to indicate that a named person is also known or more familiar under another specified name: *Eric Blair, alias George Orwell.* ■ informal indicating another term or synonym: *the catfish—alias bullhead—is a mighty tasty fry-up.*
▶ **n.** a false or assumed identity: *a spy operating* ***under the alias*** *Barsad.* ■ Computing an alternative name or label that refers to a file, command, address, or other item, and can be used to locate or access it. ■ Telecommunications each of a set of signal frequencies that, when sampled at a given uniform rate, would give the same set of sampled values, and thus might be incorrectly substituted for one another when reconstructing the original signal.
▶ **v.** [with obj.] (usu. **be aliased**) Physics & Telecommunications misidentify (a signal frequency), introducing distortion or error.
– ORIGIN late Middle English: from Latin, 'at another time, otherwise.'

a·li·as·ing /ˈālēəsiNG/ ▶ **n. 1** Physics & Telecommunications the misidentification of a signal frequency, introducing distortion or error.
2 Computing in computer graphics, the jagged, or saw-toothed appearance of curved or diagonal lines on a low-resolution monitor.

A·li Ba·ba /ˌälē ˈbäbə/ the hero of a story supposed to be from the *Arabian Nights*, who discovered the magic formula ("Open Sesame!") that opened a cave where forty robbers kept their treasure.

al·i·bi /ˈaləˌbī/ ▶ **n.** (pl. **alibis**) a claim or piece of evidence that one was elsewhere when an act, typically a criminal one, is alleged to have taken place: *she* ***has an alibi*** *for the whole of yesterday evening | a defense of alibi.* ■ informal an excuse or pretext: *a catch-all* ***alibi for*** *failure and inadequacy.*
▶ **v.** (**alibis, alibied, alibiing**) [with obj.] informal offer an excuse or defense for (someone), esp. by providing an account of their whereabouts at the time of an alleged act: *her friend agreed to alibi her.* ■ [no obj.] make excuses: *not once do I recall him whining or alibiing.*
– ORIGIN late 17th cent. (as an adverb in the sense 'elsewhere'): from Latin, 'in another place; elsewhere.' The noun use dates from the late 18th cent.

> **USAGE** The weakened nonlegal use of **alibi** to mean simply 'an excuse' is a fairly common and natural extension of the core meaning. It is acceptable in standard English, although regarded as incorrect by some traditionalists.

Al·i·can·te /ˌaliˈkantē, ˌäləˈkäntā/ a seaport on the Mediterranean coast of southeastern Spain, the capital of Alicante Province; pop. 331,750 (2008).

Al·ice-in-Won·der·land /ˌalis in ˈwəndərˌland/ ▶ **adj.** [attrib.] not logically explicable or predictable: *this Alice-in-Wonderland economic system.*

Al·ice Springs /ˈalis/ a railroad terminus and supply center serving the outback of Northern Territory, Australia; pop. 27,481 (2008).

al·i·cy·clic /ˌaləˈsīklik, -ˈsik-/ Chemistry ▶ **adj.** relating to or denoting organic compounds that combine cyclic structure with aliphatic properties, e.g., cyclohexane and other saturated cyclic hydrocarbons. Compare with AROMATIC.
▶ **n.** (usu. **alicyclics**) an alicyclic compound.
– ORIGIN late 19th cent.: blend of ALIPHATIC and CYCLIC.

al·i·dade /ˈaliˌdād/ ▶ **n.** a sighting device or pointer for determining directions or measuring angles, used in surveying and (formerly) astronomy.
– ORIGIN late Middle English: directly or (in modern use) via French and Spanish from Arabic *al-ʿiḍāda* 'the revolving radius,' probably based on *ʿaḍud* 'upper arm.'

a·li·en /ˈālyən, ˈālēən/ ▶ **adj.** belonging to a foreign country or nation. ■ unfamiliar and disturbing or distasteful: *bossing anyone around was* ***alien to*** *him | they found the world of adult education a little alien.* ■ [attrib.] relating to or denoting beings supposedly from other worlds; extraterrestrial: *an alien spacecraft.* ■ (of a plant or animal species) introduced from another country and later naturalized.
▶ **n.** a foreigner, esp. one who is not a naturalized citizen of the country where they are living: *an illegal alien.* ■ a hypothetical or fictional being from another world. ■ a plant or animal species originally introduced from another country and later naturalized.
– DERIVATIVES **al·ien·ness n.**
– ORIGIN Middle English: via Old French from Latin *alienus* 'belonging to another,' from *alius* 'other.'

al·ien·a·ble /ˈālēənəbəl, ˈālyənə-/ ▶ **adj.** Law able to be transferred to new ownership.
– DERIVATIVES **a·lien·a·bil·i·ty** /ˌālēənəˈbilitē, ˌālyən-/ **n.**

al·ien·age /ˈālēənij, ˈālyə-/ ▶ **n.** the state or condition of being an alien.

al·ien·ate /ˈālēəˌnāt, ˈālyə-/ ▶ **v.** [with obj.] **1** cause (someone) to feel isolated or estranged: *an urban environment that would alienate its inhabitants* | (as adj. **alienated**) *an alienated angst-ridden 22-year-old.* ■ cause (someone) to become unsympathetic or hostile: *the association does not wish to alienate its members.*
2 Law transfer ownership of (property rights) to another person or group.
– PHRASES **alienate someone's affections** Law induce someone to transfer their affection from a person (such as a spouse) with legal rights or claims on them.
– ORIGIN early 16th cent.: from Latin *alienat-* 'estranged,' from the verb *alienare*, from *alienus* 'of another' (see ALIEN).

al·ien·a·tion /ˌālēəˈnāSHən, ˌālyə-/ ▶ **n.** the state or experience of being isolated from a group or an activity to which one should belong or in which one should be involved: *unemployment may generate a sense of political alienation.* ■ loss or lack of sympathy; estrangement: *public* ***alienation from*** *bureaucracy.* ■ (in Marxist theory) a condition of workers in a capitalist economy, resulting from a lack of identity with the products of their labor and a sense of being controlled or exploited. ■ Psychiatry a state of depersonalization or loss of identity in which the self seems unreal, thought to be caused by difficulties in relating to society and the resulting prolonged inhibition of emotion. ■ a type of faulty recognition in which familiar situations or people appear unfamiliar. Compare with DÉJÀ VU. ■ (also **alienation effect**) Theater an effect, sought by some dramatists, whereby the audience remains objective and does not identify with the actors. ■ Law the transfer of the ownership of property rights.
– ORIGIN late Middle English: from Latin *alienatio(n-)*, from the verb *alienare* 'estrange,' from *alienus* (see ALIEN). The term *alienation effect* (1940s) is a translation of German *Verfremdungseffekt*.

al·ien·ee /ˌālēəˈnē, ˌālyə-/ ▶ **n.** Law dated term for GRANTEE.

al·ien·ist /ˈālēənist, ˈālyə-/ ▶ **n.** former term for PSYCHIATRIST. ■ a psychiatrist who assesses the competence of a defendant in a court of law.
– ORIGIN mid 19th cent.: from French *aliéniste*, based on Latin *alienus* 'of another' (see ALIEN).

al·ien·or /ˈālēənər, ˈālyə-/ ▶ **n.** Law dated term for GRANTOR.

a-life /ˈā ˌlīf/ ▶ **n.** short for ARTIFICIAL LIFE.

al·i·form /ˈaləˌfôrm, ˈālə-/ ▶ **adj.** wing-shaped.
– ORIGIN early 18th cent.: from modern Latin *aliformis*, from Latin *ala* 'wing' + *-formis* (see -FORM).

A·li·ghie·ri /ˌaləgˈyerē/, Dante, see DANTE.

a·light[1] /əˈlīt/ ▶ **v.** [no obj.] (of a bird) descend from the air and settle: *a lovely blue swallow* ***alighted on*** *a branch.* ■ descend from a train, bus, or other form of transportation: *the conductor alights to push the cable car completely around.*
– PHRASAL VERBS **alight on** find by chance; notice: *her eyes alighted on the item in question.*
– ORIGIN Old English *ālīhtan*, from *ā-* (as an intensifier) + *līhtan* 'descend' (see LIGHT[3]).

a·light[2] ▶ **adv. & adj.** on fire; burning: [as adj.] *the house was well alight when the firemen arrived* | [as adv.] *flammable liquid was* ***set alight.*** ■ shining brightly: [as adj.] *a single lamp was alight* | figurative *the boy's face was* ***alight with*** *excitement.*
– ORIGIN late Middle English: probably from the phrase *on a light* (= lighted) *fire*.

a·lign /əˈlīn/ ▶ **v. 1** [with obj.] place or arrange (things) in a straight line: *gently brush the surface to align the fibers.* ■ put (things) into correct or appropriate relative positions: *the fan blades are carefully aligned* | figurative *aligning domestic prices with prices in world markets.* ■ [no obj.] lie in a straight line, or in correct relative positions: *the pattern of the border at the seam should align perfectly.*
2 (**align oneself with**) give support to (a person, organization, or cause): *newspapers usually align themselves with certain political parties.* ■ [no obj.]

come together in agreement or alliance: *all of them must now align against the foe* | (as adj. **aligned**) *forces aligned with Russia.*
– ORIGIN late 17th cent.: from French *aligner*, from *à ligne* 'into line.'

a·lign·ment /əˈlīnmənt/ ▶ n. **1** arrangement in a straight line, or in correct or appropriate relative positions: *the tiles had slipped out of alignment.* ■ the act of aligning parts of a machine: *oil changes, lube jobs, and wheel alignments.* ■ the route or course of a road or railroad: *four railroads, all on different alignments.*
2 a position of agreement or alliance: *a firm famous for its liberal alignment.*
– ORIGIN late 18th cent.: from French *alignement*, from *aligner* (see ALIGN).

a·like /əˈlīk/ ▶ adj. [predic.] (of two or more subjects) similar to each other: *the brothers were very much alike* | *the houses all looked alike.*
▶ adv. in the same or a similar way: *the girls dressed alike in black pants and jackets.* ■ used to show that something applies equally to a number of specified subjects: *he talked in a friendly manner to staff and patients alike.*
– ORIGIN Old English *gelīc*, of Germanic origin; related to Dutch *gelijk* and German *gleich*, reinforced in Middle English by Old Norse *álíkr* (adjective) and *álíka* (adverb).

al·i·ment /ˈaləmənt/ ▶ n. archaic food; nourishment. ■ support; sustenance.
▶ v. provide with nourishment or sustenance.
– ORIGIN late 15th cent.: from Latin *alimentum*, from *alere* 'nourish.'

al·i·men·ta·ry /ˌaləˈment(ə)rē/ ▶ adj. of or relating to nourishment or sustenance.
– ORIGIN late 16th cent.: from Latin *alimentarius*, from *alimentum* 'nourishment' (see ALIMENT).

al·i·men·ta·ry ca·nal ▶ n. the whole passage along which food passes through the body from mouth to anus. It includes the esophagus, stomach, and intestines.

al·i·men·ta·tion /ˌaləmenˈtāSHən/ ▶ n. formal the provision of nourishment or other necessities of life.
– ORIGIN late 16th cent. (in the sense 'maintenance, support'): from medieval Latin *alimentatio(n-)*, from late Latin *alimentare* 'to feed,' from *alimentum* 'nourishment' (see ALIMENT).

al·i·mo·ny /ˈaləˌmōnē/ ▶ n. a husband's or wife's court-ordered provision for a spouse after separation or divorce.
– ORIGIN early 17th cent. (in the sense 'nourishment, means of subsistence'): from Latin *alimonia* 'nutriment,' from *alere* 'nourish.'

A-line /ˈā ˌlīn/ ▶ adj. (of a garment) slightly flared from a narrow waist or shoulders: *A-line skirts.*

al·i·phat·ic /ˌaləˈfatik/ Chemistry ▶ adj. relating to or denoting organic compounds in which carbon atoms form open chains (as in the alkanes), not aromatic rings. Compare with ALICYCLIC.
▶ n. (usu. **aliphatics**) an aliphatic compound.
– ORIGIN late 19th cent. (originally used of the fatty acids): from Greek *aleiphar, aleiphat-* 'fat' + -IC.

al·i·quot /ˈalikwət/ ▶ n. a portion of a larger whole, esp. a sample taken for chemical analysis or other treatment. ■ (also **aliquot part** or **portion**) Mathematics a quantity that can be divided into another an integral number of times.
▶ v. [with obj.] (usu. **be aliquoted**) divide (a whole) into aliquots; take aliquots from (a whole).
– ORIGIN late 16th cent.: from French *aliquote*, from Latin *aliquot* 'some, so many,' from *alius* 'one of two' + *quot* 'how many.'

al·i·sphe·noid /ˌaləˈsfēˌnoid/ ▶ n. (also **alisphenoid bone**) Anatomy & Zoology a winglike cartilaginous bone within the mammalian skull, forming part of the socket of the eye.
– ORIGIN mid 19th cent.: from Latin *ala* 'wing' + SPHENOID.

A-list /ˈā ˌlist/ (or **B-list** /ˈbē ˌlist/) ▶ n. a real or imaginary list of the most (or, for B-list, second-most) celebrated or sought-after individuals, esp. in show business: [as modifier] *an A-list celebrity.*

a·lit·er·ate /āˈlitərit/ ▶ adj. unwilling to read, although able to do so.
▶ n. an aliterate person.
– DERIVATIVES **a·lit·er·a·cy** /-əsē/ n.

a·live /əˈlīv/ ▶ adj. [predic.] **1** (of a person, animal, or plant) living, not dead: *hopes of finding anyone still alive were fading* | *he was kept alive by a feeding-tube.* ■ (of a feeling or quality) continuing in existence: *keeping hope alive.* ■ continuing to be supported or in use: *militarism was kept alive by pure superstition.*
2 (of a person or animal) alert and active; animated: *Ken comes alive when he hears his music played.* ■ having interest and meaning: *we hope we will make history come alive for the children.*
3 (**alive to**) aware of and interested in; responsive to: *always alive to new ideas.*
4 (**alive with**) swarming or teeming with: *in spring those cliffs are alive with auks and gulls.*
– PHRASES **alive and kicking** informal prevalent and very active: *bigotry is still alive and kicking.* **alive and well** still existing or active (often used to deny rumors or beliefs that something has disappeared or declined): *Jefferson's ideas are alive and well today in Washington.* **look alive** another term for LOOK LIVELY (see LIVELY).
– DERIVATIVES **a·live·ness** n.
– ORIGIN Old English *on līfe*, literally 'in life.'

a·li·yah /ˌäləˈä/ ▶ n. (pl. **aliyoth** /ˌäləˈōt/) Judaism **1** immigration to Israel: *students making aliyah.* **2** the honor of being called upon to read from the Torah: *I was called up for an aliyah.*
– ORIGIN from Hebrew *'ălīyāh* 'ascent.'

a·liz·a·rin /əˈlizərin/ ▶ n. Chemistry a red pigment present in madder root, used in dyeing.
● Alternative name: **1,2-dihydroxyanthraquinone**; chem. formula: $C_{14}H_8O_4$. ■ [as modifier] denoting dyes derived from or similar to this pigment: *alizarin crimson.*
– ORIGIN mid 19th cent.: from French *alizarine*, from *alizari* 'madder,' from Arabic *al-'iṣāra* 'pressed juice,' from *'aṣara* 'to press fruit.'

al-Ji·zah /ˌal ˈjēzə/ Arabic name for GIZA.

al·ka·hest /ˈalkəˌhest/ (also **alcahest**) ▶ n. historical the hypothetical universal solvent sought by alchemists.
– ORIGIN mid 17th cent.: sham Arabic, probably invented by Paracelsus.

al·ka·li /ˈalkəˌlī/ ▶ n. (pl. **alkalis**) a chemical compound that neutralizes or effervesces with acids and turns litmus blue; typically, a caustic or corrosive substance of this kind such as lime or soda. Often contrasted with ACID; compare with BASE¹.

> Alkalis release hydroxide ions (OH^-) when dissolved in water. An alkaline solution has a pH greater than 7.

– ORIGIN late Middle English (denoting a saline substance derived from the ashes of various plants, including glasswort): from medieval Latin, from Arabic *al-ḳalī* 'calcined ashes (of the glasswort, etc.),' from *ḳalā* 'fry, roast.'

al·kal·ic ▶ adj. Geology (of a rock or mineral) richer in sodium and/or potassium than is usual for its type.

al·ka·li feld·spar ▶ n. Geology any of the group of feldspars rich in sodium and/or potassium.

al·ka·li met·al ▶ n. Chemistry any of the elements lithium, sodium, potassium, rubidium, cesium, and francium, occupying Group IA (1) of the periodic table. They are very reactive, electropositive, monovalent metals forming strongly alkaline hydroxides.

al·ka·line /ˈalkəlin, -ˌlīn/ ▶ adj. having the properties of an alkali, or containing alkali; having a pH greater than 7. Often contrasted with ACID or ACIDIC; compare with BASIC.
– DERIVATIVES **al·ka·lin·i·ty** /ˌalkəˈlinitē/ n.

al·ka·line bat·ter·y ▶ n. a long-lived dry cell with an alkaline electrolyte of potassium hydroxide, which deters corrosion.

al·ka·line earth (also **alkaline earth metal**) ▶ n. any of the elements beryllium, magnesium, calcium, strontium, barium, and radium, occupying Group IIA (2) of the periodic table. They are reactive, electropositive, divalent metals, and form basic oxides that react with water to form comparatively insoluble hydroxides.

al·ka·lize /ˈalkəˌlīz/ (also **alkalinize** /ˈalkəliˌnīz/) ▶ v. [with obj.] (usu. as adj. **alkalized** or **alkalizing**) treat with alkali.
– DERIVATIVES **al·ka·li·za·tion** /ˌalkəliˈzāSHən/ n., **al·ka·liz·er** n.

al·ka·loid /ˈalkəˌloid/ ▶ n. Chemistry any of a class of nitrogenous organic compounds of plant origin that have pronounced physiological actions on humans. They include many drugs (morphine, quinine) and poisons (atropine, strychnine).
– ORIGIN early 19th cent.: coined in German from ALKALI.

al·ka·lo·sis /ˌalkəˈlōsis/ ▶ n. Medicine an excessively alkaline condition of the body fluids or tissues that may cause weakness or cramps.

al·kane /ˈalˌkān/ ▶ n. Chemistry any of the series of saturated hydrocarbons including methane, ethane, propane, and higher members. ● Alkanes have the general formula: C_nH_{2n+2}.
– ORIGIN late 19th cent.: from ALKYL + -ANE².

al·kene /ˈalˌkēn/ ▶ n. Chemistry any of the series of unsaturated hydrocarbons containing a double bond, including ethylene and propylene. ● Alkenes have the general formula: C_nH_{2n}.
– ORIGIN late 19th cent.: from ALKYL + -ENE.

al·ky /ˈalkē/ (also **alkie**) ▶ n. (pl. **alkies**) informal an alcoholic.

al·kyd /ˈalkid/ ▶ n. Chemistry any of a group of synthetic polyester resins derived from various alcohols and acids, used in varnishes, paints, and adhesives.
– ORIGIN 1920s: blend of ALKYL and ACID.

al·kyl /ˈalkəl/ ▶ n. [as modifier] Chemistry of or denoting a hydrocarbon radical derived from an alkane by removal of a hydrogen atom.
– ORIGIN late 19th cent.: German, from *Alkohol* 'alcohol' + -YL.

al·kyl·ate /ˈalkəˌlāt/ ▶ v. [with obj.] (usu. as adj. **alkylating** or **alkylated**) Chemistry introduce an alkyl radical into (a compound): *alkylating agents.*
– DERIVATIVES **al·kyl·a·tion** /ˌalkəˈlāSHən/ n.

al·kyne /ˈalˌkīn/ ▶ n. Chemistry any of the series of unsaturated hydrocarbons containing a triple bond, including acetylene. ● Alkynes have the general formula: C_nH_{2n-2}.
– ORIGIN early 20th cent.: from ALKYL + -YNE.

all /ôl/ ▶ **predeterminer, determiner, & pron.** used to refer to the whole quantity or extent of a particular group or thing: [as predeterminer] *all the people I met* | *she left all her money to him* | [as determiner] *10% of all cars sold* | *he slept all day* | [as pronoun] *four bedrooms, all with balconies* | *carry **all of** the blame* | *the men are all bearded.* ■ [determiner] any whatever: *assured beyond all doubt* | *he denied all knowledge.* ■ [determiner] used to emphasize the greatest possible amount of a quality: *they were in all probability completely unaware* | ***with all due respect.*** ■ informal dominated by a particular feature or characteristic: *an eleven-year-old string bean, all elbows and knees.* ■ [pronoun with clause] the only thing (used for emphasis): *all I want is to be left alone.* ■ [pronoun] (used to refer to surroundings or a situation in general) everything: *all was well* | *it was all very strange.* ■ informal used to indicate more than one person or thing: *a team of specialists who all know the patient.* ■ dialect consumed; finished; gone: *the cake is all.*
▶ adv. **1** used for emphasis. ■ completely: *dressed all in black* | *she's been all around the world* | *all by himself.* ■ consisting entirely of: *all leather varsity jacket.*
2 (in games) used after a number to indicate an equal score: *after extra time it was still two all.*
▶ n. the whole of one's possessions, energy, or interest: ***giving their all** for what they believed.*
– PHRASES **all along** all the time; from the beginning: *she'd known all along.* **all and sundry** everyone: *insolent drivers crying to all and sundry to get out of the way.* **all around** (also Brit. **all round**) **1** in all respects: *it was a bad day all around.* **2** for or by each person: *drinks all around* | *good acting all around.* **all but 1** very nearly: *the subject was all but forgotten.* **2** all except: *we have support from all but one of the networks.* **all comers** chiefly informal anyone who chooses to take part in an activity, typically a competition: *the champion took on all comers.* **all for** informal strongly in favor of: *I was all for tolerance.* **all in** informal exhausted: *he was all in by halftime.* **all in all** everything considered; on the whole: *all in all it's been a good year.* **all kinds** (or **sorts**) **of** many different kinds of: *how to install paneling on all kinds of walls.* **all manner of** see MANNER. **all of** as much as (typically used ironically of a quantity considered small by the speaker): *the show lasted all of six weeks.* **all of a sudden** see SUDDEN. **all out** using all one's strength or resources: *going all out to win* | [as adj.] *an all-out effort.* **all over 1** completely finished: *it's all over between us.* **2** informal everywhere: *there were bodies all over.* ■ with reference to all parts of the body: *I was shaking all over.* **3** informal typical of the person mentioned: *that's our management all over!* **4** informal effusively attentive to (someone): *James was all over her.* **all over the place** (or **map**) informal everywhere: *we've been all over the place looking for you.* ■ in a state of disorder: *my hair was all over the place.* **all sorts of** see ALL KINDS OF above. **all's well that ends well** proverb if the outcome of a situation is happy, this compensates for any previous difficulty or unpleasantness. **all that ——** see THAT. **all the same** see SAME. **all the ——** see THE (sense 6). **all there** [usu. with negative] informal in full possession of one's mental faculties: *he's not quite all there.* **all the time** see TIME. **all together** all in one place or in a group; all at once: *5,000 people all together* | *they arrived all together.* Compare with ALTOGETHER. **all told** in total: *they tried a dozen times all told.* **all the way**

informal without limit or reservation: *I'm with you all the way.* See also **GO ALL THE WAY** at **WAY**. **—— and all** used to emphasize something additional that is being referred to: *she threw her coffee over him, mug and all.* ■ informal as well: *it must hit him hard, being so young and all.* **at all** [with negative or in questions] (used for emphasis) in any way; to any extent: *I don't like him at all | did he suffer at all?* **be all one to someone** make no difference to someone: *simple cases or hard cases, it's all one to me.* **be all that** informal be very attractive or good: *he thinks he's all that—yeah, God's gift.* **be all up with** see **UP**. **be all very well** informal used to express criticism or rejection of a favorable or consoling remark: *your proposal is all very well in theory, but in practice it will not pay.* **for all ——** in spite of ——: *for all its clarity and style, the book is not easy reading.* **in all** in total number; altogether: *there were about 5,000 people in all.* **of all** see **OF**. **on all fours** see **FOUR**. **one and all** see **ONE**.
– ORIGIN Old English *all, eall,* of Germanic origin; related to Dutch *al* and German *all.*

al·la bre·ve /ˌälə 'brev(ā)/ ▶ **n.** Music a time signature indicating 2 or 4 half-note beats in a bar.
– ORIGIN Italian, literally 'according to the breve.'

Al·la·gash Riv·er /'aləˌgasн/ a river in northern Maine, noted as a canoeing route.

Al·lah /'älə, 'alə/ the name of God among Muslims (and Arab Christians).
– ORIGIN from Arabic *'allāh,* contraction of *al-'ilāh* 'the god.'

Al·lah·a·bad /'äləhəˌbäd, 'aləhəˌbad/ a city in Uttar Pradesh state, in north central India; pop. 1,125,000 (est. 2009). Situated at the confluence of the sacred Jumna and Ganges rivers, it is a place of Hindu pilgrimage.

al·la·man·da /ˌalə'mandə/ ▶ **n.** any of a number of tropical shrubs or climbers that bear showy flowers, typically of yellow or purple. ● Species in several families, in particular members of the genus *Allamanda,* family Apocynaceae, including the South American **yellow allamanda** (*A. cathartica*), which is cultivated as an ornamental.
– ORIGIN modern Latin, from the name of Jean-Nicholas-Sébastien *Allamand* (1713–87), Swiss naturalist.

all-A·mer·i·can ▶ **adj. 1** possessing qualities characteristic of American ideals, such as honesty, industriousness, and health: *his all-American wholesomeness.*
2 having members or contents drawn only from America or the US: *an all-American anthology.* ■ involving or representing the whole of America or the US: *an all-American final.* ■ (also **all-America**) (of a sports player) honored as one of the best amateur competitors in the US: *an all-American wrestler.*
▶ **n.** (also **all-America**) a sports player honored as one of the best amateurs in the US.

al·lan·to·in /ə'lantō-in/ ▶ **n.** Biochemistry a crystalline compound formed in the nitrogen metabolism of many mammals (excluding primates). ● A cyclic compound related to hydantoin; chem. formula: $C_4H_6N_4O_3$.
– ORIGIN mid 19th cent.: from **ALLANTOIS** (because it was discovered in the allantoic fluid of cows) + **-IN**[1].

al·lan·to·is /ə'lantō-is/ ▶ **n.** (pl. **allantoides** /ˌalən'tō-idēz/) the fetal membrane lying below the chorion in many vertebrates, formed as an outgrowth of the embryo's gut. In birds and reptiles it grows to surround the embryo; in eutherian mammals it forms part of the placenta.
– DERIVATIVES **al·lan·to·ic** /ˌalən'tō-ik/ **adj.**, **al·lan·toid** /-toid/ **adj.**
– ORIGIN mid 17th cent.: modern Latin, based on Greek *allantoeidēs* 'sausage-shaped.'

al·lar·gan·do /ˌälär'gändō/ ▶ **adv. & adj.** Music (esp. as a direction) getting slower and slower, and often also fuller in tone.
– ORIGIN Italian, 'broadening.'

all-a·round (Brit. **all-round**) ▶ **adj.** having many uses or abilities; versatile: *an all-around artist.* ■ in many or all respects: *his all-around excellence.* ■ comprehensive; extensive: *the need of college students for an all-around education.*
▶ **n.** Gymnastics an event in which the scores of each individual exercise are totaled to determine the winner.

al·lay /ə'lā/ ▶ **v.** [with obj.] diminish or put at rest (fear, suspicion, or worry): *the report attempted to educate the public and allay fears.* ■ relieve or alleviate (pain or hunger): *some stale figs partly allayed our hunger.*
– ORIGIN Old English *ālecgan* 'lay down or aside.'

all-clear ▶ **n.** a signal that danger or difficulty is over: *she was given* **the all-clear** *to travel home.*

all-day ▶ **adj.** lasting or available throughout the day: *an all-day barn-raising event.*

al·lée /ä'lā/ ▶ **n.** an alley in a formal garden or park, bordered by trees or bushes.
– ORIGIN mid 18th cent.: French.

al·le·ga·tion /ˌali'gāsнən/ ▶ **n.** a claim or assertion that someone has done something illegal or wrong, typically one made without proof: *he made allegations of corruption against the administration |* **allegations that** *the army was operating a shoot-to-kill policy.*
– ORIGIN late Middle English: from Latin *allegatio(n-),* from *allegare* 'allege.'

al·lege /ə'lej/ ▶ **v.** [reporting verb] claim or assert that someone has done something illegal or wrong, typically without proof that this is the case: [with clause] *he* **alleged that** *he had been assaulted |* [with obj. and infinitive] *the offenses are alleged to have been committed outside the woman's home | he is* **alleged to have** *assaulted five men.* ■ (usu. **be alleged**) suppose or affirm to be the case: *the first artifact ever alleged to be from Earhart's aircraft.*
– ORIGIN Middle English (in the sense 'declare on oath'): from Old French *esligier,* based on Latin *lis, lit-* 'lawsuit'; confused in sense with Latin *allegare* 'allege.'

al·leged /ə'lejd/ ▶ **adj.** [attrib.] (of an incident or a person) said, without proof, to have taken place or to have a specified illegal or undesirable quality: *the alleged conspirators.*

al·leg·ed·ly /ə'lejidlē/ ▶ **adv.** [sentence adverb] used to convey that something is claimed to be the case or have taken place, although there is no proof: *he was allegedly a leading participant in the coup attempt |* [as submodifier] *allegedly obscene material.*

Al·le·ghe·ny Moun·tains /ˌalə'gānē, -'genē/ (also **the Alleghenies**) a mountain range, part of the Appalachian system in the eastern US, which extends from West Virginia through Pennsylvania.

Al·le·ghe·ny Riv·er a river that flows for 325 miles (523 km) through New York and Pennsylvania to Pittsburgh where it joins the Monongahela River to form the Ohio River.

al·le·giance /ə'lējəns/ ▶ **n.** loyalty or commitment of a subordinate to a superior or of an individual to a group or cause: *those wishing to receive citizenship must* **swear allegiance to** *the republic | a complex pattern of cross-party allegiances.*
– ORIGIN late Middle English: from Anglo-Norman French, variant of Old French *ligeance,* from *lige, liege* (see **LIEGE**), perhaps by association with Anglo-Latin *alligantia* 'alliance.'

al·le·gor·i·cal /ˌali'gôrikəl, -'gär-/ ▶ **adj.** constituting or containing allegory: *an allegorical painting.*
– DERIVATIVES **al·le·gor·ic adj.**, **al·le·gor·i·cal·ly adv.**

al·le·go·rize /'aligəˌrīz/ ▶ **v.** [with obj.] interpret or represent symbolically: *the picture is interpreted as allegorizing an alienated society.*
– DERIVATIVES **al·le·go·ri·za·tion** /ˌaliˌgôri'zāsнən/ **n.**

al·le·go·ry /'aləˌgôrē/ ▶ **n.** (pl. **allegories**) a story, poem, or picture that can be interpreted to reveal a hidden meaning, typically a moral or political one: *Pilgrim's Progress is an allegory of the spiritual journey.* ■ the genre to which such works belong. ■ a symbol.
– DERIVATIVES **al·le·go·rist** /-ist/ **n.**
– ORIGIN late Middle English: from Old French *allegorie,* via Latin from Greek *allēgoria,* from *allos* 'other' + *-agoria* 'speaking.'

al·le·gret·to /ˌali'gretō/ Music ▶ **adj. & adv.** (esp. as a direction) at a fairly brisk tempo.
▶ **n.** (pl. **allegrettos**) a movement or piece to be played fairly briskly.
– ORIGIN Italian, diminutive of **ALLEGRO**.

al·le·gro /ə'legrō/ Music ▶ **adj. & adv.** (esp. as a direction) at a brisk tempo.
▶ **n.** (pl. **allegros**) a passage or movement in an allegro tempo.
– ORIGIN Italian, literally 'lively, gay.'

al·lele /ə'lēl/ ▶ **n.** Genetics one of two or more alternative forms of a gene that arise by mutation and are found at the same place on a chromosome. Also called **ALLELOMORPH**.
– DERIVATIVES **al·lel·ic** /ə'lēlik, ə'lel-/ **adj.**
– ORIGIN 1930s: from German *Allel,* abbreviation of **ALLELOMORPH**.

al·le·lo·chem·i·cal /əˌlēlō'kemikəl, ə'lel-/ ▶ **n.** a chemical produced by a living organism, exerting a detrimental physiological effect on the individuals of another species when released into the environment.
– ORIGIN 1970s: from Greek *allēl-* 'one another' + **CHEMICAL**.

al·le·lo·morph /əˌlēlə'môrf, əˌlel-/ ▶ **n.** another term for **ALLELE**.
– DERIVATIVES **al·le·lo·mor·phic** /-'môrfik/ **adj.**
– ORIGIN early 20th cent.: from Greek *allēl-* 'one another' + *morphē* 'form.'

al·le·lop·a·thy /əlē'läpəтнē, ˌalə-/ ▶ **n.** the chemical inhibition of one plant (or other organism) by another, due to the release into the environment of substances acting as germination or growth inhibitors.
– ORIGIN 1950s: from Greek *allēl-* 'one another' + **-PATHY**.

al·le·lu·ia /ˌalə'lōōyə/ ▶ **exclam.** variant spelling of **HALLELUJAH**.
– ORIGIN Old English, via ecclesiastical Latin from Greek *allēlouia* (in the Septuagint), from Hebrew *hallĕlūyāh* 'praise ye the Lord.'

al·le·mande /'aləˌmand, -ˌmänd/ ▶ **n.** any of a number of German dances. ■ the music for any of these, esp. as a movement of a suite. ■ a figure in country dancing in which adjacent dancers link arms or join or touch hands and make a full or partial turn.
– ORIGIN late 16th cent.: from French, 'German (dance).'

all-em·brac·ing ▶ **adj.** including or covering everything or everyone; comprehensive: *the goal is not one all-embracing religion.*

Al·len[1] /'alən/, Ethan (1738–89), American soldier. He fought the British in the American Revolution and led the Green Mountain Boys in their campaign to gain independence for the state of Vermont. He died two years before Vermont achieved statehood.

Al·len[2], Steve (1921–2000), US television pioneer, humorist, and songwriter; full name *Stephen Valentine Patrick William Allen.* He was host and creator of "The Tonight Show" (1954–57) and host of "The Steve Allen Show" (1956–64). He also played the title role in the movie *The Benny Goodman Story* (1963).

Al·len[3], Woody (1935–), US movie director, writer, and actor; born *Allen Stewart Konigsberg.* He has starred in most of his movies, many of which humorously explore themes of neuroses and sexual inadequacy. Notable movies: *Bananas* (1971), *Play It Again, Sam* (1972), *Sleeper* (1973), *Annie Hall* (1977), *Hannah and Her Sisters* (1986), *Crimes and Misdemeanors* (1989), and *Small Time Crooks* (2000).

Al·len·by /'alənbē/, Edmund Henry Hynman, 1st Viscount (1861–1936), British soldier. Commander of the Egyptian Expeditionary Force against the Turks, he captured Jerusalem in 1917 and defeated the Turkish forces at Megiddo in 1918.

Al·len·de /ä'yenˌdā/, Salvador (1908–73), Chilean statesman; president 1970–73. The first avowed Marxist to win a presidency in a free election, he was overthrown and killed in a military coup.

Al·len·stein /'älənˌsнtīn/ German name for **OLSZTYN**.

Al·len·town /'alənˌtoun/ a commercial and industrial city in eastern Pennsylvania, on the Lehigh River; pop. 107,250 (est. 2008).

Al·len wrench (also **allen wrench**) ▶ **n.** an L-shaped metal bar with a hexagonal head at each end, used to turn bolts and screws having hexagonal sockets.
– ORIGIN 1960s: from the name of the manufacturer, the *Allen* Manufacturing Company, of Hartford, Connecticut.

al·ler·gen /'alərjən/ ▶ **n.** a substance that causes an allergic reaction.
– DERIVATIVES **al·ler·gen·ic** /ˌalər'jenik/ **adj.**, **al·ler·ge·nic·i·ty** /ˌalərjə'nisitē/ **n.**
– ORIGIN early 20th cent.: blend of **ALLERGY** and **-GEN**.

al·ler·gic /ə'lərjik/ ▶ **adj.** caused by or relating to an allergy: *an allergic reaction to penicillin.* ■ having an allergy to (a substance): *Heather was allergic to the sting of bees.* ■ (**allergic to**) informal having a strong dislike for: *it's just that I'm allergic to the hype.*

al·ler·gist /'alərjist/ ▶ **n.** a medical practitioner specializing in the diagnosis and treatment of allergies.

al·ler·gy /'alərjē/ ▶ **n.** (pl. **allergies**) a damaging immune response by the body to a substance, esp. pollen, fur, a particular food, or dust, to which it has become hypersensitive. ■ informal an antipathy: *their allergy to free enterprise.*
– ORIGIN early 20th cent.: from German *Allergie,* from Greek *allos* 'other,' on the pattern of *Energie* 'energy.'

Al·le·rød /'aləˌrōōd, -ˌrœd/ ▶ **n.** (**the Allerød**) Geology the second climatic stage of the late-glacial period in northern Europe, between the two Dryas stages (about 12,000 to 10,800 years ago). It was an interlude of warmer weather marked by the spread of birch, pine, and willow.
– ORIGIN 1920s: place name near Copenhagen in Denmark.

al·le·vi·ate /ə'lēvēˌāt/ ▶ **v.** [with obj.] make (suffering, deficiency, or a problem) less severe: *he couldn't prevent her pain, only alleviate it | measures to alleviate unemployment.*

–DERIVATIVES **al·le·vi·a·tion** /əˌlēvēˈāsHən/ **n.**, **al·le·vi·a·tor** /-ˌātər/ **n.**
–ORIGIN late Middle English: from late Latin *alleviat-* 'lightened,' from the verb *alleviare*, from Latin *allevare*, from *ad-* 'to' + *levare* 'raise,' influenced by *levis* 'light.'

al·ley[1] /ˈalē/ ▶ **n.** (pl. **alleys**) a narrow passageway between or behind buildings. ■ a path lined with trees, bushes, or stones. Compare with **ALLÉE**. ■ [with modifier] a long, narrow area in which games such as bowling are played. ■ Tennis either of the two areas of the court between the doubles sideline and the singles or service sideline. ■ Baseball the area between the outfielders in left center or right center field.
–PHRASES **(right) up one's alley** informal well suited to one's tastes, interests, or abilities: *this job would be right up your alley*.
–ORIGIN late Middle English: from Old French *alee* 'walking or passage,' from *aler* 'go,' from Latin *ambulare* 'to walk.'

al·ley[2] (also **ally**) ▶ **n.** (pl. **alleys**) a toy marble made of marble, alabaster, or glass.
–ORIGIN early 18th cent.: perhaps a diminutive of **ALABASTER**.

al·ley cat ▶ **n.** a cat that lives wild in a town.

al·ley-oop /ˌalē ˈo͞op/ ▶ **exclam.** used to encourage or draw attention to the performance of some physical, esp. acrobatic, feat.
▶ **n.** (also **alley-oop pass**) Basketball a high pass caught by a leaping teammate who tries to dunk the ball before landing.
–ORIGIN early 20th cent.: perhaps from French *allez!* 'go on!' (expressing encouragement) + a supposedly French pronunciation of **UP**.

al·ley·way /ˈalēˌwā/ ▶ **n.** another term for **ALLEY[1]**.

all-fired informal ▶ **adv.** informal extremely: *if I was so all-fired bright . . . why did I have to keep learning this same thing over and over?*
▶ **adj.** extreme.

All Fools' Day ▶ **n.** another term for **APRIL FOOL'S DAY**.

all fours ▶ **n.** a card game, now rarely played, in which points are scored for being dealt the highest or lowest trump, capturing the jack of trump, and taking the highest value of cards in tricks.
–PHRASES **on all fours** on hands and knees or (of an animal) on all four legs rather than just the hind ones: *Frankie scuttled away on all fours*.

all hail ▶ **exclam.** archaic or humorous a cry of greeting: *all hail the new kids on the block*.

All Hal·lows ▶ **n.** another term for **ALL SAINTS' DAY**.

all·heal /ˈôlˌhēl/ ▶ **n.** any of a number of plants, in particular valerian, used in herbal medicine and traditionally considered to be effective in treating a variety of conditions.

al·li·a·ceous /ˌalēˈāsHəs/ ▶ **adj.** Botany of, relating to, or denoting plants of a group that comprises the onions and other alliums.
–ORIGIN late 18th cent.: from Latin *allium* 'garlic' + **-ACEOUS**; compare with the modern Latin taxonomic family name *Alliaceae*.

al·li·ance /əˈlīəns/ ▶ **n.** a union or association formed for mutual benefit, esp. between countries or organizations: *a defensive alliance between Australia and New Zealand | divisions within the alliance*. ■ a relationship based on an affinity in interests, nature, or qualities: *an alliance between medicine and morality*. ■ a state of being joined or associated: *his party is in alliance with the Greens*.
–ORIGIN Middle English: from Old French *aliance*, from *aliere* 'to ally' (see **ALLY[1]**).

al·li·cin /ˈalisin/ ▶ **n.** Chemistry a pungent oily liquid with antibacterial properties, present in garlic. ● Chem. formula: $(C_3H_5S)_2O$.
–ORIGIN from Latin *allium* 'garlic' + **-IN[1]**.

al·lied /əˈlīd, ˈalˌīd/ ▶ **adj.** joined by or relating to members of an alliance: *allied territories | the allied fleet*. ■ (usu. **Allied**) of or relating to the US and its allies in World War I and World War II and after: *the liberation of Paris by Allied troops*. ■ **(allied to/with)** in combination or working together with: *skilled craftsmanship allied to advanced technology*. ■ connected or related: *members of the medical and allied professions*.

Al·lier /älˈyā/ a river in central France that rises in the Cévennes Mountains and flows northwest for 258 miles (410 km) to meet the Loire River.

al·li·ga·tor /ˈaliˌgātər/ ▶ **n.** a large semiaquatic reptile similar to a crocodile but with a broader and shorter head, native to the Americas and China. ● Genus *Alligator*, family Alligatoridae, order Crocodylia: the **American alligator** (*A. mississippiensis*) and the **Chinese alligator** (*A. sinensis*). ■ the skin of the alligator or material resembling it.
–ORIGIN late 16th cent.: from Spanish *el lagarto* 'the lizard,' probably based on Latin *lacerta*.

American alligator

al·li·ga·tor clip ▶ **n.** a sprung metal clip with long, serrated jaws, used attached to an electric cable for making a temporary connection to a battery or other component.

alligator clip

al·li·ga·tor fish ▶ **n.** a slender bottom-dwelling fish of the northwestern Atlantic, with an armor of bony plates and two curved spines on the snout. ● *Aspidophoroides monopterygius*, family Agonidae.

al·li·ga·tor liz·ard ▶ **n.** a short-limbed, long-tailed, slim lizard native to the North American west coast. ● Genus *Gerrhonotus*, family Anguidae: several species, including the **northern alligator lizard** (*G. coerulus*) and the **panamint alligator lizard** (*G. panamintinus*).

al·li·ga·tor pear ▶ **n.** another term for **AVOCADO**.

al·li·ga·tor snap·ping tur·tle (also **alligator snapper**) ▶ **n.** a large-headed, long-tailed snapping turtle of the southeastern US, found esp. in the Gulf States. Weighing up to 150 pounds (67.5 kg), it is the largest freshwater turtle in North America. ● *Macroclemys temminckii*, family Chelydridae.

all-im·por·tant ▶ **adj.** vitally important; crucial: *the town's all-important tourist industry*.

all-in·clu·sive ▶ **adj.** including everything or everyone: *the tab for the all-inclusive dinner is $38*.

all-in-one ▶ **adj.** [attrib.] combining two or more items or functions in a single unit: *an all-in-one shampoo/conditioner*.

al·lit·er·ate /əˈlitəˌrāt/ ▶ **v.** [no obj.] (of a phrase or line of verse) contain words that begin with the same sound or letter: *his first and last names alliterated*. ■ use words that begin with the same sound or letter.
–ORIGIN late 18th cent.: back-formation from **ALLITERATION**.

al·lit·er·a·tion /əˌlitəˈrāsHən/ ▶ **n.** the occurrence of the same letter or sound at the beginning of adjacent or closely connected words.
–ORIGIN early 17th cent.: from medieval Latin *alliteratio(n-)*, from Latin *ad-* (expressing addition) + *littera* 'letter.'

al·lit·er·a·tive /əˈlitərətiv, -ˌrātiv/ ▶ **adj.** relating to or marked by alliteration.
–DERIVATIVES **al·lit·er·a·tive·ly** **adv.**

al·li·um /ˈalēəm/ ▶ **n.** (pl. **alliums**) a bulbous plant of a genus that includes the onion and its relatives (e.g., garlic, leek, and chives). ● Genus *Allium*, family Liliaceae (or Alliaceae).
–ORIGIN early 19th cent.: Latin, literally 'garlic.'

all-night ▶ **adj.** [attrib.] lasting, open, or operating throughout the night: *an all-night party*.

all-night·er /ˌôl ˈnītər/ ▶ **n.** informal an event or task that continues throughout the night, esp. a study session before an examination: *he would do an all-nighter, the way he used to in school*.

allo- ▶ **comb. form** other; different: *allopatric | allotrope*.
–ORIGIN from Greek *allos* 'other.'

al·lo·cate /ˈaləˌkāt/ ▶ **v.** [with obj.] distribute (resources or duties) for a particular purpose: *the authorities allocated 50,000 places to refugees* | [with two objs.] *he has been allocated a generous slice of the annual budget*.
–DERIVATIVES **al·lo·ca·ble** /-kəbəl/ **adj.**, **al·lo·ca·tor** /-ˌkātər/ **n.**
–ORIGIN mid 17th cent.: from medieval Latin *allocat-* 'allotted,' from the verb *allocare*, from *ad-* 'to' + *locare* (see **LOCATE**).

al·lo·ca·tion /ˌaləˈkāsHən/ ▶ **n.** the action or process of allocating or distributing something: *more efficient allocation of resources | ticket allocation*. ■ an amount or portion of a resource assigned to a particular recipient.
–DERIVATIVES **al·lo·ca·tive** /ˈaləˌkātiv/ **adj.** (chiefly Economics).
–ORIGIN late Middle English: from medieval Latin *allocatio(n-)*, from the verb *allocare* (see **ALLOCATE**).

al·loch·tho·nous /əˈläkTHənəs/ ▶ **adj.** Geology denoting sediment or rock that originated at a distance from its present position. Often contrasted with **AUTOCHTHONOUS**.
–ORIGIN early 20th cent.: from **ALLO-** 'other' + Greek *khthōn* 'earth' + **-OUS**.

al·lo·cu·tion /ˌaləˈkyo͞osHən/ ▶ **n.** a formal speech giving advice or a warning.
–ORIGIN early 17th cent.: from Latin *allocutio(n-)*, from *alloqui* 'speak to,' from *ad-* 'to' + *loqui* 'speak.'

al·log·a·my /əˈlägəmē/ ▶ **n.** Botany the fertilization of a flower by pollen from another flower, esp. one on a different plant. Compare with **AUTOGAMY**.
–DERIVATIVES **al·log·a·mous** /-məs/ **adj.**
–ORIGIN late 19th cent.: from **ALLO-** 'other, different' + Greek *-gamia* (from *gamos* 'marriage').

al·lo·ge·ne·ic /ˌaləjəˈnē-ik/ ▶ **adj.** Immunology denoting, relating to, or involving tissues or cells that are genetically dissimilar and hence immunologically incompatible, although from individuals of the same species. Compare with **XENOGENEIC**.
–ORIGIN 1960s: from **ALLO-** 'different' + Greek *genea* 'race, stock' + **-IC**.

al·lo·gen·ic /ˌaləˈjenik/ ▶ **adj. 1** Geology (of a mineral or sediment) transported to its present position from elsewhere. Often contrasted with **AUTHIGENIC**. **2** Ecology (of a successional change) caused by nonliving factors in the environment.

al·lo·graft /ˈaləˌgraft/ ▶ **n.** a tissue graft from a donor of the same species as the recipient but not genetically identical. Compare with **HOMOGRAFT**.

al·lo·graph /ˈaləˌgraf/ ▶ **n.** Linguistics each of two or more alternative forms of a letter of an alphabet or other grapheme. The capital, lowercase, italic, and various handwritten forms of the letter A are allographs. ■ Phonetics each of two or more letters or letter-combinations representing a single phoneme in different words. Allographs of the phoneme include the (f) of "fake" and the (ph) of "phase."
–ORIGIN 1950s: from **ALLO-** 'other, different' + **GRAPHEME**.

al·lom·e·try /əˈlämitrē/ ▶ **n.** Biology the growth of body parts at different rates, resulting in a change of body proportions. ■ the study of such growth.
–DERIVATIVES **al·lo·met·ric** /ˌaləˈmetrik/ **adj.**

al·lo·morph /ˈaləˌmôrf/ ▶ **n.** Linguistics any of the versions of a morpheme, such as the plural endings /s/ (as in *bats*), /z/ (as in *bugs*), and /iz/ (as in *buses*) for the plural morpheme.
–DERIVATIVES **al·lo·mor·phic** /ˌaləˈmôrfik/ **adj.**
–ORIGIN 1940s: from **ALLO-** 'other, different' + **MORPHEME**.

al·lo·path /ˈaləˌpaTH/ ▶ **n.** a person who practices allopathy.

al·lop·a·thy /əˈläpəTHē/ ▶ **n.** the treatment of disease by conventional means, i.e., with drugs having opposite effects to the symptoms. Often contrasted with **HOMEOPATHY**.
–DERIVATIVES **al·lo·path·ic** /ˌaləˈpaTHik/ **adj.**, **al·lop·a·thist** /-THist/ **n.**

al·lo·pat·ric /ˌaləˈpatrik/ ▶ **adj.** Biology (of animals or plants, esp. of related species or populations) occurring in separate non-overlapping geographical areas. Compare with **SYMPATRIC**. ■ (of speciation) taking place as a result of such separation.
–DERIVATIVES **al·lop·a·try** /ˈaləˌpatrē/ **n.**
–ORIGIN 1940s: from **ALLO-** 'other' + Greek *patra* 'fatherland' + **-IC**.

al·lo·phone[1] /ˈaləˌfōn/ ▶ **n.** Linguistics any of the speech sounds that represent a single phoneme, such as the aspirated *k* in *kit* and the unaspirated *k* in *skit*, which are allophones of the phoneme *k*.
–DERIVATIVES **al·lo·phon·ic** /ˌaləˈfänik/ **adj.**
–ORIGIN 1930s: from **ALLO-** 'other, different' + **PHONEME**.

al·lo·phone[2] /ˈaləˌfōn/ ▶ **n.** Canadian (esp. in Quebec) an immigrant whose first language is neither French nor English.

al·lo·pu·ri·nol /aləˈpyo͝oriˌnôl, -ˌnäl/ ▶ **n.** Medicine a synthetic drug that inhibits uric acid formation in the body and is used to treat gout and related conditions.
–ORIGIN 1960s: from **ALLO-** 'other' + **PURINE** + **-OL**.

all-or-none ▶ **adj.** another way of saying **ALL-OR-NOTHING**. ■ Physiology (of a response) having a strength independent of the strength of the stimulus that caused it.

all-or-noth·ing ▶ **adj.** having no middle position or compromise available: *an all-or-nothing decision*.

al·lo·saur /ˈaləˌsôr/ (also **allosaurus** /ˌaləˈsôrəs/) ▶ **n.** a large bipedal carnivorous dinosaur of the

PRONUNCIATION KEY ə *ago, up*; ər *over, fur*; a *hat*; ā *ate*; ä *car*; e *let*; ē *see*; i *fit*; ī *by*; NG *sing*; ō *go*; ô *law, for*; oi *toy*; o͝o *good*; o͞o *goo*; ou *out*; TH *thin*; T͟H *then*; ZH *vision*

late Jurassic period. ● Genus *Allosaurus*, suborder Theropoda, order Saurischia.
– DERIVATIVES **al·lo·sau·ri·an** adj.
– ORIGIN modern Latin, from Greek *allos* 'other' + *sauros* 'lizard.'

al·lo·sta·sis /ˌaləˈstāsis/ ▸ **n.** the process by which the body responds to stressors in order to regain homeostasis.
– DERIVATIVES **al·lo·sta·tic** /-ˈstatik/ **adj.**

al·lo·ster·ic /ˌaləˈsterik, -ˈsti(ə)r-/ ▸ **adj.** Biochemistry relating to or denoting the alteration of the activity of a protein through the binding of an effector molecule at a specific site.
– DERIVATIVES **al·lo·ster·i·cal·ly** adv.

al·lot /əˈlät/ ▸ **v.** (**allots, allotting, allotted**) [with obj.] give or apportion (something) to someone as a share or task: *equal time was allotted to each* | [with two objs.] *I was allotted a little room in the servants' block.*
– ORIGIN late 15th cent.: from Old French *aloter*, from *a-* (from Latin *ad* 'to') + *loter* 'divide into lots.'

al·lot·ment /əˈlätmənt/ ▸ **n.** the amount of something allocated to a particular person: *the gadget shuts off the television set when a kid has used up his allotment.* ■ chiefly historical a piece of land deeded by the government to a Native American, as part of the division of tribally held land. ■ the action of allotting: *the allotment of equity securities.*

al·lo·trope /ˈaləˌtrōp/ ▸ **n.** Chemistry each of two or more different physical forms in which an element can exist. Graphite, charcoal, and diamond are all allotropes of carbon.
– ORIGIN late 19th cent.: back-formation from ALLOTROPY.

al·lot·ro·py /əˈlätrəpē/ ▸ **n.** Chemistry the existence of two or more different physical forms of a chemical element.
– DERIVATIVES **al·lo·trop·ic** /ˌaləˈträpik, -ˈtrō-/ **adj.**
– ORIGIN mid 19th cent.: from Greek *allotropos* 'of another form,' from *allo-* 'other' + *tropos* 'manner' (from *trepein* 'to turn').

al·lot·tee /ˌaləˈtē, əˌläˈtē/ ▸ **n.** a person to whom something is allotted, esp. land or shares.

all-ov·er ▸ **adj.** [attrib.] covering the whole of something: *a carpet with an all-over pattern.*

al·low /əˈlou/ ▸ **v.** [with obj.] **1** admit (an event or activity) as legal or acceptable: *a plan to allow Sunday shopping* | *a reservoir with no hunting or overnight camping allowed.* ■ [with obj. and infinitive] give (someone) permission to do something: *the dissident was allowed to leave the country.* ■ [with two objs.] permit (someone) to have (something): *he was allowed his first sip of Scotch and soda.* ■ permit (someone) to enter a place or go in a particular direction: *the river was patrolled and few people were allowed across.* ■ [with obj. and infinitive] fail to prevent (something) from happening: *I could not believe that we would allow the opportunity to slip away.*
2 give the necessary time or opportunity for: *they agreed to a ceasefire to allow talks with the government* | [with obj. and infinitive] *he stopped for a moment to allow his eyes to adjust* | [no obj.] dated *my household duties were too many to* **allow of** *a visit to the hospital.* ■ [no obj.] (**allow for**) make provision or provide scope for (something): *the house was demolished to allow for road widening.* ■ [no obj.] (**allow for**) take (something) into consideration when making plans or calculations: *income rose by 11 percent allowing for inflation.* ■ provide or set aside (a specified amount of something) for a specific purpose: *allow an hour or so for driving.*
3 [reporting verb] admit the truth of; concede: [with clause] *he* **allowed that** *the penalty appeared too harsh for the crime* | [with direct speech] *"Could happen," she allowed indifferently.* ■ [with clause] informal or dialect assert; be of the opinion: *Lincoln* **allowed that** *he himself could never support the man.*
– ORIGIN Middle English (originally in the senses 'commend, sanction' and 'assign as a right'): from Old French *alouer*, from Latin *allaudare* 'to praise,' reinforced by medieval Latin *allocare* 'to place' (see ALLOCATE).

al·low·a·ble /əˈlouəbəl/ ▸ **adj.** **1** allowed, esp. within a set of regulations; permissible: *the loan deal has been extended to the maximum allowable three months.*
2 (of an amount of money) not considered as income for tax purposes: *tax is payable after deduction of allowable expenses.*
– DERIVATIVES **al·low·a·bly** /-əblē/ **adv.**

al·low·ance /əˈlou-əns/ ▸ **n.** the amount of something that is permitted, esp. within a set of regulations or for a specified purpose: *a seventy-five-pound baggage allowance.* ■ a sum of money paid regularly to a person, typically to meet specified needs or expenses. ■ a small amount of money that a parent regularly gives a child. ■ an amount of money that can be earned or received free of tax: *a personal allowance.* ■ a reduction in price, typically for the exchange of used goods: *he made the down payment with the trade-in allowance.* ■ Horse Racing a deduction in the weight that a horse is required to carry in a race. ■ archaic tolerance; sufferance: *the allowance of slavery in the South.*
▸ **v.** [with obj.] archaic give (someone) a sum of money regularly as an allowance.
– PHRASES **make allowance(s) for 1** take into consideration when planning or making calculations: *a special circuit makes allowances for changes in the ambient temperature.* **2** regard or treat leniently on account of mitigating circumstances: *she liked them and made allowances for their faults.*
– ORIGIN late Middle English: from Old French *alouance*, from *alouer* (see ALLOW).

al·low·ed·ly /əˈlou-idlē/ ▸ **adv.** [sentence adverb] as is generally admitted to be true.

al·lox·an /əˈläksən/ ▸ **n.** Chemistry an acidic compound obtained by the oxidation of uric acid and isolated as an efflorescent crystalline hydrate. ● Chem. formula: $C_4H_2N_2O_4$.
– ORIGIN mid 19th cent.: from *all(antoin)* + *ox(alic)* + -AN.

al·loy ▸ **n.** /ˈaˌloi/ a metal made by combining two or more metallic elements, esp. to give greater strength or resistance to corrosion: *an alloy of nickel, bronze, and zinc* | *flat pieces of alloy* | [as modifier] *alloy wheels.* ■ an inferior metal mixed with a precious one.
▸ **v.** /ˈaˌloi, əˈloi/ [with obj.] mix (metals) to make an alloy: *alloying tin with copper to make bronze.* ■ debase (something) by adding something inferior.
– ORIGIN late 16th cent.: from Old French *aloi* (noun) and French *aloyer* (verb), both from Old French *aloier, aleier* 'combine,' from Latin *alligare* 'bind.'

all-par·ty ▸ **adj.** [attrib.] involving all political parties: *the measure received all-party support.*

all-per·vad·ing (also **all-pervasive**) ▸ **adj.** having an effect on everything or throughout something: *the all-pervading excitement.*

all-points bul·le·tin (abbr.: **APB**) ▸ **n.** a radio message sent to every officer in a police force giving details of a suspected criminal or stolen vehicle.

all-pow·er·ful ▸ **adj.** having complete power; almighty: *an all-powerful dictator.*

all-pur·pose ▸ **adj.** having many uses, esp. all that might be expected from something of its type: *an all-purpose kitchen knife.*

all right ▸ **adj.** satisfactory but not especially good; acceptable: *the tea was all right.* ■ (of a person) in a satisfactory mental or physical state: *"Are you all right? You were screaming."* ■ permissible; allowable: *it's all right for you to go now.*
▸ **adv. 1** in a satisfactory manner or to a satisfactory extent; fairly well: *everything will turn out all right.* **2** used to emphasize how certain one is about something: *"Are you sure it's him?" "It's him all right."*
▸ **exclam.** expressing or asking for assent, agreement, or acceptance: *all right, I'll tell you.*

USAGE See usage at ALRIGHT.

all-round ▸ **adj.** British term for ALL-AROUND.

All Saints' Day ▸ **n.** a Christian festival in honor of all the saints, held (in the Western Church) on November 1.

all·seed /ˈôlˌsēd/ ▸ **n.** any of a number of plants producing a great deal of seed for their size, such as knotgrass and goosefoot.

All Souls' Day ▸ **n.** a festival in some Christian churches with prayers for the souls of the dead, held on November 2.

all·spice /ˈôlˌspīs/ ▸ **n. 1** the dried aromatic fruit of a West Indian tree, used whole or ground as a culinary spice.
2 a tree of the myrtle family from which this spice is obtained. Also called PIMENTO. ● *Pimenta dioica*, family Myrtaceae.
3 an aromatic North American tree or shrub. ● Genus *Calycanthus*, family Calycanthaceae: several species, in particular **Carolina allspice** (*C. floridus*) and **smooth allspice** (*C. fertilis*).

all-star ▸ **adj.** [attrib.] composed wholly of outstanding performers or players: *an all-star cast.*
▸ **n.** a member of such a group or team.

All·ston /ˈôlstən/, Washington (1779–1843), US landscape painter, the first major artist of the American romantic movement. His paintings exhibit a taste for the monumental, apocalyptic, and melodramatic. Notable works: *The Deluge* (1804), *Belshazzar's Feast* (1817–43), and *Moonlit Landscape* (1819).

all-ter·rain ve·hi·cle (abbr.: **ATV**) ▸ **n.** a small open motor vehicle with one or two seats and three or more wheels fitted with large tires, designed for use on rough ground.

all-time ▸ **adj.** [attrib.] unsurpassed: *all-time favorite* | *interest rates hit an all-time high.*

al·lude /əˈlo͞od/ ▸ **v.** [no obj.] (**allude to**) suggest or call attention to indirectly; hint at: *she had a way of alluding to Jean but never saying her name.* ■ mention without discussing at length: *we will allude briefly to the main points.* ■ (of an artist or a work of art) recall (an earlier work or style) in such a way as to suggest a relationship with it: *the photographs allude to Italian Baroque painting.*
– ORIGIN late 15th cent. (in the sense 'hint at, suggest'): from Latin *alludere*, from *ad-* 'toward' + *ludere* 'to play.'

al·lure /əˈlo͝or/ ▸ **n.** the quality of being powerfully and mysteriously attractive or fascinating: *people for whom gold holds no allure.*
▸ **v.** [with obj.] powerfully attract or charm; tempt.
– DERIVATIVES **al·lure·ment** n.
– ORIGIN late Middle English (in the sense 'tempt, entice'): from Old French *aleurier* 'attract,' from *a-* (from Latin *ad* 'to') + *luere* 'a lure' (originally a falconry term).

al·lur·ing /əˈlo͝oriNG/ ▸ **adj.** powerfully and mysteriously attractive or fascinating; seductive: *the town offers alluring shops and restaurants.*
– DERIVATIVES **al·lur·ing·ly** adv.

al·lu·sion /əˈlo͞oZHən/ ▸ **n.** an expression designed to call something to mind without mentioning it explicitly; an indirect or passing reference: ***an allusion to** Shakespeare* | *a classical allusion.* ■ the practice of making such references, esp. as an artistic device.
– ORIGIN mid 16th cent. (denoting a pun, metaphor, or parable): from French, or from late Latin *allusio(n-)*, from the verb *alludere* (see ALLUDE).

al·lu·sive /əˈlo͞osiv/ ▸ **adj.** (of a remark or reference) working by suggestion rather than explicit mention: *allusive references to the body.*
– DERIVATIVES **al·lu·sive·ly** adv., **al·lu·sive·ness** n.

al·lu·vi·al /əˈlo͞ovēəl/ ▸ **adj.** of, relating to or derived from alluvium: *rich alluvial soils.*

al·lu·vi·al fan ▸ **n.** a fan-shaped mass of alluvium deposited as the flow of a river decreases in velocity.

al·lu·vi·on /əˈlo͞ovēən/ ▸ **n.** Law the action of the sea or a river in forming new land by deposition. Compare with AVULSION.
– ORIGIN mid 16th cent. (originally denoting a flood, esp. one in which the water carries suspended material that is then deposited): from French, from Latin *alluvion-*, from *ad-* 'toward' + *luere* 'to wash.'

al·lu·vi·um /əˈlo͞ovēəm/ ▸ **n.** a deposit of clay, silt, sand, and gravel left by flowing streams in a river valley or delta, typically producing fertile soil.
– ORIGIN mid 17th cent.: Latin, neuter of *alluvius* 'washed against,' from *ad-* 'toward' + *luere* 'to wash.'

all-weath·er ▸ **adj.** including or suitable for all types of weather: *all-weather tennis courts.*

all-wheel drive ▸ **n.** a transmission system that always operates in four-wheel drive and does not alternate with two-wheel drive.

al·ly[1] ▸ **n.** /ˈalī/ (pl. **allies**) a state formally cooperating with another for a military or other purpose, typically by treaty. ■ a person or organization that cooperates with or helps another in a particular activity: *he was forced to dismiss his closest political ally.* ■ (**the Allies**) a group of nations taking military action together, in particular the countries that fought with the US in World War I and World War II.
▸ **v.** /əˈlī/ (**allies, allying, allied**) [with obj.] (**ally something to/with**) combine or unite a resource or commodity with (another) for mutual benefit: *he allied his racing experience with his father's business acumen.* ■ (**ally oneself with**) side with or support (someone or something): *he allied himself with the forces of change.*
– ORIGIN Middle English (as a verb): from Old French *alier*, from Latin *alligare* 'bind together,' from *ad-* 'to' + *ligare* 'to bind'; the noun is partly via Old French *alie* 'allied.' Compare with ALLOY.

al·ly[2] ▸ **n.** (pl. **allies**) variant spelling of ALLEY[2].

-ally ▸ **suffix** forming adverbs from adjectives ending in *-al* (such as *radically* from *radical*). Compare with -AL, -LY[2], -ICALLY.

al·lyl /ˈalil/ ▸ **n.** [as modifier] Chemistry the unsaturated hydrocarbon radical $-CH{=}CH_2$: *allyl alcohol.*
– DERIVATIVES **al·lyl·ic** /əˈlilik/ **adj.**
– ORIGIN mid 19th cent.: from Latin *allium* 'garlic' + -YL.

Al·ma-A·ta variant spelling of ALMATY.

al-Ma·di·nah /ˌal mäˈdēnə/ Arabic name for MEDINA.

Al·ma·gest /ˈalməˌjest/ ▸ **n.** (**the Almagest**) an Arabic version of Ptolemy's astronomical treatise. ■ (also **almagest**) (in the Middle Ages) any celebrated textbook on astrology and alchemy.

–ORIGIN late Middle English: from Old French *almageste*, based on Arabic, from *al* 'the' + Greek *megistē* 'greatest (composition).'

al·ma ma·ter /'älmə 'mätər, 'almə/ ▶ **n.** (**one's Alma Mater**) the school, college, or university that one once attended. ■ the anthem of a school, college, or university.
–ORIGIN mid 17th cent. (in the general sense 'someone or something providing nourishment'): Latin, literally 'bounteous mother.'

al·ma·nac /'ôlmə,nak, 'al-/ (also, esp. in titles, **almanack**) ▶ **n.** an annual calendar containing important dates and statistical information such as astronomical data and tide tables. ■ a handbook, typically published annually, containing information of general interest or on a sport or pastime.
–ORIGIN late Middle English: via medieval Latin from Greek *almenikhiaka*, of unknown origin.

al·man·dine /'almən,dēn/ ▶ **n.** a kind of garnet with a violet tint.
–ORIGIN late Middle English: from obsolete French, alteration of *alabandine*, from medieval Latin *alabandina (gemma)* 'jewel from *Alabanda*,' an ancient city in Asia Minor where these stones were cut.

Al·ma·ty /,älmə'tē/ (also **Alma-Ata** /,älmə ə'tä/) the largest city and former capital of Kazakhstan, in the southeastern part of the republic; pop. 1,247,900 (est. 2006). Former name (until 1921) **VERNY**.

Al·me·ría /,älmä'rēə/ a town in Almeria Province in southern Spain; pop. 187,521 (2008).

al·might·y /ôl'mītē/ ▶ **adj.** having complete power; omnipotent: *God almighty.* ■ (**the Almighty**) a name or title for God: *I wanted to beg the Almighty for mercy.* ■ informal very great; enormous: *the silence was broken by an almighty roar.*
–ORIGIN Old English *ælmihtig* (see **ALL**, **MIGHTY**).

Al·mo·had /'almə,had/ (also **Almohade** /-,hād, -,had/) ▶ **n.** (pl. **Almohads**) a member of a Berber Muslim movement and dynasty that conquered the Spanish and North African empire of the Almoravids in the 12th century.

al·mond /'ä(l)mənd, 'a(l)-/ ▶ **n. 1** the oval nutlike seed (kernel) of the almond tree, used as food.
2 (also **almond tree**) the tree that produces this nut, belonging to the rose family and related to the peach and plum. Native to western Asia, it is widely cultivated in warm climates. ● Genus *Prunus*, family Rosaceae: one species, *P. dulcis* (**sweet almond**), and a variety, *P. dulcis amara* (**bitter almond**).
▶ **adj.** made of or flavored with almonds: *almond cookies.* ■ of an oval shape, pointed at one or both ends: *her almond eyes.* ■ a pale tan color, as of an almond shell: *the kitchen was done in almond.*
–ORIGIN Middle English: from Old French *alemande*, from medieval Latin *amandula*, from Greek *amugdalē*.

al·mond oil ▶ **n.** oil expressed from bitter almonds, used for cosmetic preparations, flavoring, and medicinal purposes.

al·mond paste ▶ **n.** another term for **MARZIPAN**.

al·mon·er /'almənər, 'äm-/ ▶ **n.** historical an official distributor of alms.
–ORIGIN Middle English: from Old French *aumonier*, based on medieval Latin *eleemosynarius*, from *eleemosyna* 'alms' (see **ALMS**).

al·mon·ry /'almənrē, 'äm-/ ▶ **n.** (pl. **almonries**) a building or place where alms were formerly distributed.
–ORIGIN late Middle English: from Old French *au(l)mosnerie*, from medieval Latin *eleemosynarius* (see **ALMONER**).

Al·mo·ra·vid /,almə'rävid, äl'môrə-/ (also **Almoravide** /-vīd/) ▶ **n.** (pl. **Almoravids**) a member of a federation of Muslim Berber peoples that established an empire in Morocco, Algeria, and Spain in the 11th century. They were in turn driven out by the Almohads.

al·most /ôl'mōst, 'ôl,mōst/ ▶ **adv.** not quite; very nearly: *he almost knocked Georgina over | Rachel laughed, almost apologetically | the place was almost empty | it will eat almost anything | the storm was almost upon them.*
–ORIGIN Old English *æl mæst* 'for the most part' (see **ALL**, **MOST**).

alms /ä(l)mz/ ▶ **plural n.** (in historical contexts) money or food given to poor people.
–ORIGIN Old English *ælmysse, ælmesse*, from Christian Latin *eleemosyna*, from Greek *eleēmosunē* 'compassion,' from *eleēmōn* 'compassionate,' from *eleos* 'mercy.'

alms·house /'ä(l)mz,hous/ ▶ **n.** a house built originally by a charitable person or organization for poor people to live in.

al-Nak·ba /al 'nakbä/ ▶ **n.** the Arabic term for the events of 1948, when many Palestinians were displaced from their homeland by the creation of the new state of Israel.
–ORIGIN from Arabic, literally 'the disaster.'

al·oe /'alō/ ▶ **n. 1** a succulent plant, typically having a rosette of toothed fleshy leaves and bell-shaped or tubular flowers on long stems. Native to the Old World tropics, several species are cultivated commercially or as ornamentals. ● Genus *Aloe*, family Liliaceae (or Aloaceae). ■ (**aloes** or **bitter aloes**) a strong laxative obtained from the bitter juice of various kinds of aloe. ■ (also **American aloe**) another term for **CENTURY PLANT**.
2 (**aloes**) (also **aloeswood**) the fragrant heartwood of a tropical Asian tree. ● The wood is obtained from two trees of the genus *Aquilaria*, family Thymelaeaceae, esp. *A. agallocha*. ■ the resin obtained from this wood, used in perfume, incense, and medicine.
–ORIGIN Old English *alewe, alwe* (denoting the fragrant resin or heartwood of certain Oriental trees), via Latin from Greek *aloē*; reinforced in late Middle English by Old French *aloes* 'aloe,' hence frequently used in the plural.

al·oe ver·a /'alō 'verə, 'vi(ə)rə/ ▶ **n. 1** a gelatinous substance obtained from a kind of aloe, used esp. in cosmetics as an emollient and for the treatment of burns.
2 the plant that yields this substance, grown chiefly in the Caribbean area and the southern US. ● *Aloe vera*, family Liliaceae (or Aloaceae).
–ORIGIN early 20th cent.: modern Latin, literally 'true aloe,' probably in contrast to the American agave, which closely resembles aloe vera: both plants were formerly classified together in the lily family.

a·loft /ə'lôft/ ▶ **adj. & adv.** up in or into the air; overhead: *the congregation sways, hands aloft* | [as adv.] *she held her glass aloft.* ■ up the mast or into the rigging of a sailing vessel.
–ORIGIN Middle English: from Old Norse *á lopt, á lopti*, from *á* 'in, on, to' + *lopt* 'air.'

a·log·i·cal /ā'läjikəl/ ▶ **adj.** opposed to or lacking in logic.

A·lo·ha /ə'lō,hä/ a community in northwestern Oregon, west of Portland; pop. 41,741 (2000).

a·lo·ha /ə'lō,hä/ ▶ **exclam. & n.** Hawaiian word used when greeting or parting from someone.

a·lo·ha shirt ▶ **n.** a loose, brightly patterned Hawaiian shirt.

A·lo·ha State a nickname for the state of **HAWAII**.

a·lone /ə'lōn/ ▶ **adj. & adv. 1** having no one else present; on one's own: [as predic. adj.] *she was alone that evening* | [as adv.] *he lives alone.* ■ without others' help or participation; single-handed: *team members are more effective than individuals working alone.* ■ [as adj.] isolated and lonely: *she was terribly alone and exposed.* ■ having no companions in a particular position or course of action: *they were not alone in dissenting from the advice.*
2 [as adv.] indicating that something is confined to the specified subject or recipient: *we agreed to set up such a test for him alone | it is Congress alone that can declare war.* ■ used to emphasize that only one factor out of several is being considered and that the whole is greater or more extreme: *there were fifteen churches in the town center alone.*
–PHRASES **go it alone** informal act by oneself without assistance. **leave** (or **let**) **someone/something alone 1** abandon or desert someone or something. **2** stop disturbing or interfering with someone or something. **let alone** **LET**[1].
–DERIVATIVES **a·lone·ness** /ə'lōn(n)əs/ **n.**
–ORIGIN Middle English: from **ALL** + **ONE**.

a·long /ə'lôNG, ə'läNG/ ▶ **prep. 1** moving in a constant direction on (a path or any more or less horizontal surface): *soon we were driving along a narrow road | he saw Gary run along the top of the wall* | [as adv.] *she sailed along | we continued to plod along.* ■ used metaphorically to refer to the passage of time or the making of progress: *they can be helped along the road to modernity | we passed along snatches of information | you'll pick up some valuable tips along the way* | [as adv.] *they asked how the construction was coming along.*
2 extending in a more or less horizontal line on: *cars were parked along the grass border | the path along the cliff | hotels are springing up all along the coast.*
▶ **adv.** in or into company with others: *he had brought along a friend of his | I went along to see Ray.* ■ at hand; with one: *take along a camcorder when you visit.*
–PHRASES **along about** informal or dialect around about (a specified time or date): *he generally leaves there along about daylight.* **along of** archaic or dialect **1** on account of: *the trouble I've had along of that lady's crankiness.* **2** with: *you'll have to make a break for it along of me.* **along the lines (of)** in conformity with: *a highway patrol organized along the lines of the New Jersey State Police.* **along with** in company with or at the same time as: *I was chosen, along with twelve other artists.* **be** (or **come**) **along** arrive: *she'll be along soon | a chance like this doesn't come along every day.*
–ORIGIN Old English *andlang*; related to **LONG**[1].

a·long·shore /ə'lôNG'SHôr, ə'läNG-/ ▶ **adv.** along or by the shore: *currents flowing alongshore.*

a·long·side /ə'lôNG'sīd, ə'läNG-/ ▶ **prep.** (also **alongside of**) close to the side of; next to: *she was sitting alongside him | the road passes alongside the viaduct* | [as adv.] *the boat came alongside.* ■ together and in cooperation with: *a care assistant was working alongside him.* ■ at the same time as or in coexistence with: *alongside the development of full-time courses there had to be provision for the part-time student.*

a·loof /ə'lo͞of/ ▶ **adj.** not friendly or forthcoming; cool and distant: *they were courteous but faintly aloof | an aloof and somewhat austere figure.* ■ conspicuously uninvolved and uninterested, typically through distaste: *he stayed* ***aloof from*** *the bickering.*
–DERIVATIVES **a·loof·ly adv.**, **a·loof·ness n.**
–ORIGIN mid 16th cent.: from **A-**[2] (expressing direction) + **LUFF**. The term was originally an adverb in nautical use, meaning 'away and to windward!,' i.e., with the ship's head kept close to the wind away from a lee shore, etc., toward which it might otherwise drift. From this arose the sense 'at a distance' literally or figuratively.

al·o·pe·ci·a /,alə'pēSH(ē)ə/ ▶ **n.** Medicine the partial or complete absence of hair from areas of the body where it normally grows; baldness.
–ORIGIN late Middle English: via Latin from Greek *alōpekia*, literally 'fox mange,' from *alōpēx* 'fox.'

A·lor Se·tar /,al,ôr sē'tär, ,äl,ôr/ a city near the west coast of the central Malay Peninsula in Malaysia; pop. 223,200 (est. 2009).

a·loud /ə'loud/ ▶ **adv. 1** audibly; not silently or in a whisper: *he read the letter aloud.*
2 archaic loudly: *he wept aloud.*
–ORIGIN Middle English: from **A-**[2] (expressing manner) + **LOUD**.

a·low /ə'lō/ ▶ **adv.** archaic or dialect below; downward. ■ Nautical in or into the lower part of a ship, e.g., down from the rigging, or below deck.
–ORIGIN late Middle English (in nautical use since the early 16th cent.): from **A-**[2] 'on' + **LOW**[1].

alp /alp/ ▶ **n.** a high mountain, esp. a snowcapped one. ■ (in Switzerland) an area of green pasture on a mountainside.
–ORIGIN late Middle English: singular of **ALPS**.

al·pac·a /al'pakə/ ▶ **n.** (pl. **same** or **alpacas**) a long-haired domesticated South American mammal related to the llama, valued for its wool. ● *Lama pacos*, family Camelidae, probably descended from the wild guanaco. ■ the wool of the alpaca. ■ fabric made from this wool, with or without other fibers: [as modifier] *an alpaca jersey.*
–ORIGIN late 18th cent.: from Spanish, from Aymara *allpaca*.

alpaca

al·par·ga·ta /,alpər'gätə/ ▶ **n.** a light canvas shoe with a plaited fiber sole; an espadrille.
–ORIGIN early 19th cent.: from Spanish.

al·pen·glow /'alpən,glō/ ▶ **n.** the rosy light of the setting or rising sun seen on high mountains.
–ORIGIN late 19th cent.: a partial translation of German *Alpenglühen*, literally 'Alp glow.'

al·pen·horn /'alpən,hôrn/ (also **alphorn** /'alp,hôrn/) ▶ **n.** a valveless wooden horn up to 12 feet (4 m) long, used for signaling in the Alps.
–ORIGIN late 19th cent.: from German, literally 'Alp horn.'

al·pen·stock /'alpən,stäk/ ▶ **n.** a long iron-tipped staff used by hikers and mountain climbers.
–ORIGIN early 19th cent.: from German, literally 'Alp stick.'

al·pha /'alfə/ ▶ **n. 1** the first letter of the Greek alphabet (Α, α), transliterated as 'a.' ■ [as modifier] denoting the first of a series of items or categories, e.g., forms of a chemical compound: *alpha interferon | the α and β chains of hemoglobin.*

a

■ denoting the dominant animal or person in a particular group: *Turner soon proved to be the alpha male.* ■ short for ALPHA TEST. ■ **(Alpha)** [followed by Latin genitive] the first (typically the brightest) star in a constellation: *Alpha Centauri.* ■ [as modifier] relating to alpha decay or alpha particles: *an alpha emitter.*
2 a code word representing the letter A, used in radio communication. ▶ **symbol** ■ (α) a plane angle. ■ (α) angular acceleration. ■ (α) Astronomy right ascension.
– PHRASES **alpha and omega** ■ the beginning and the end (esp. used by Christians as a title for Jesus). ■ the essence or most important features: *collective bargaining is seen as the alpha and omega of trade unionism.*
– ORIGIN from Semitic; cf. Phoenician *'alp*, lit. 'ox,' and Hebrew *'aleph* 'aleph.'

al·pha·bet /'alfə,bet, -bit/ ▶ **n.** a set of letters or symbols in a fixed order, used to represent the basic sounds of a language; in particular, the set of letters from A to Z. ■ the basic elements in a system that combine to form complex entities: *DNA's 4-letter alphabet.*

> The alphabet has its roots in Phoenician writing of the 2nd millennium BC, from which the modern Hebrew and Arabic systems are ultimately derived. The Greek alphabet, which emerged in 1000–900 BC, developed two branches, Cyrillic (which became the script of Russian) and Etruscan (from which derives the Roman alphabet used in the West).

– ORIGIN early 16th cent.: from late Latin *alphabetum*, from Greek *alpha, bēta*, the first two letters of the Greek alphabet.

al·pha·bet·i·cal /,alfə'betikəl/ ▶ **adj.** of or relating to an alphabet: *alphabetical characters.* ■ in the order of the letters of the alphabet: *an alphabetical index* | *in alphabetical order.*
– DERIVATIVES **al·pha·bet·ic adj.**, **al·pha·bet·i·cal·ly** /-ik(ə)lē/ **adv.**

al·pha·bet·ize /'alfəbi,tīz/ ▶ **v.** [with obj.] arrange (words or phrases) in alphabetical order: *the listings are arranged by state and alphabetized by city.*
– DERIVATIVES **al·pha·bet·i·za·tion** /,alfə,betə'zāsHən/ **n.**

al·pha·bet soup ▶ **n.** informal incomprehensible or confusing language, typically containing many abbreviations or symbols.
– ORIGIN early 20th cent.: alluding to a kind of clear soup containing pasta in the shapes of letters.

al·pha block·er ▶ **n.** Medicine any of a class of drugs that prevent the stimulation of the adrenergic receptors responsible for increased blood pressure.

Al·pha Cen·tau·ri /sen'tôrē/ Astronomy the third brightest star in the sky, in the constellation Centaurus, visible only to observers in the southern hemisphere. It is the nearest bright star to the solar system (distance 4.34 light years), and is a visual binary. Also called RIGIL KENTAURUS.

al·pha-fe·to·pro·tein /,fētō'prōtē(ə)n/ ▶ **n.** Medicine a protein produced by a fetus that is present in amniotic fluid and the bloodstream of the mother. Levels of the protein can be measured to detect certain congenital defects such as spina bifida and Down syndrome.

alpha globulin ▶ **n.** see GLOBULIN.

al·pha-hy·drox·y ac·id /hī'dräksē/ ▶ **n.** Chemistry an organic acid containing a hydroxyl group bonded to the carbon atom adjacent to the carboxylic acid group. A number of such compounds are used in skin-care preparations for their exfoliating properties. Also called FRUIT ACID.

al·pha·nu·mer·ic /,alfən(y)o͞o'merik/ ▶ **adj.** consisting of or using both letters and numerals: *alphanumeric data* | *an alphanumeric keyboard.*
▶ **n.** a character that is either a letter or a number.
– DERIVATIVES **al·pha·nu·mer·i·cal adj.**
– ORIGIN 1950s: blend of ALPHABETICAL and NUMERICAL.

al·pha par·ti·cle ▶ **n.** Physics a helium nucleus emitted by some radioactive substances, originally regarded as a ray.

al·pha ra·di·a·tion ▶ **n.** ionizing radiation consisting of alpha particles, emitted by some substances undergoing radioactive decay.

Al·pha·ret·ta /,alfə'retə/ a city in northwestern Georgia, a suburb of Atlanta; pop. 49,903 (est. 2008).

al·pha rhythm ▶ **n.** Physiology the normal electrical activity of the brain when conscious and relaxed, consisting of oscillations (**alpha waves**) with a frequency of 8 to 13 hertz.

al·pha test ▶ **n.** a trial of machinery, software, or other products carried out by a developer before a product is made available for beta testing.
▶ **v.** **(alpha-test)** [with obj.] subject (a product) to a test of this kind.

alp·horn /'alp,hôrn/ ▶ **n.** another term for ALPENHORN.

al·pine /'al,pīn/ ▶ **adj.** [usu. attrib.] of or relating to high mountains: *alpine and subalpine habitats.* ■ (in the names of plants and animals) growing or found on high mountains: *the alpine forget-me-not.* ■ **(Alpine)** of or relating to the Alps: *the major Alpine ski venues.* ■ (also **Alpine**) (of skiing) involving downhill racing: *an alpine ski team.*
▶ **n. 1** a plant native to mountain districts, often suitable for growing in rock gardens.
2 a North American butterfly that typically has brownish-black wings with orange-red markings. ● Genus *Erebia*, subfamily Satyrinae, family Nymphalidae: several species.
– ORIGIN late Middle English: from Latin *Alpinus*, from *Alpes* 'Alps' (see ALPS).

al·pine house ▶ **n.** an unheated greenhouse used to grow alpine plants.

al·pin·ist /'alpənist/ ▶ **n.** a climber of high mountains, esp. in the Alps.
– ORIGIN late 19th cent.: from French *alpiniste*, from *alpin* (see ALPINE).

al·pra·zo·lam /al'prazə,lam/ ▶ **n.** Medicine a drug of the benzodiazepine group, used in the treatment of anxiety.
– ORIGIN 1970s: from *al-* of unknown origin + *p(henyl)* + *(t)r(i)azol(e)* + *(-azep)am.*

Alps /alps/ a mountain system in Europe that extends in a curve from the coast of southeastern France through northwestern Italy, Switzerland, Liechtenstein, southern Germany, and Austria, into Slovenia. The highest peak, Mont Blanc, rises to a height of 15,771 feet (4,807 m).
– ORIGIN late Middle English: via French from Latin *Alpes*, from Greek *Alpeis*, of unknown origin.

al-Qae·da /al 'kīdə, 'kādə, kä'ēdə/ (also **al-Qaida**) a militant Islamic fundamentalist group.
– ORIGIN Arabic *al-qā'ida*, literally 'the base.'

al-Qa·hi·ra /,al kä'hērə/ Arabic name for CAIRO.

al-Qods /al 'kôdz/ the Arabic name for JERUSALEM.

al·read·y /ôl'redē/ ▶ **adv. 1** before or by now or the time in question: *Anna has suffered a great deal already.* ■ as surprisingly soon or early as this: *at 31, he already suffers from arthritis* | *already it was past four o' clock.*
2 informal used as an intensive after a word or phrase to express impatience: *enough already with these crazy kids and their wacky dances!*
– ORIGIN Middle English: from ALL (as an adverb) + READY; sense 2 is influenced by Yiddish use.

al·right /ôl'rīt/ variant spelling of ALL RIGHT.

> **USAGE** The merging of *all* and *right* to form the one-word spelling **alright** is first recorded toward the end of the 19th century (unlike other similar merged spellings such as **altogether** and **already**, which date from much earlier). There is no logical reason for insisting that **all right** be two words when other single-word forms such as **altogether** have long been accepted. Nevertheless, although found widely, **alright** remains nonstandard.

ALS ▶ **abbr.** amyotrophic lateral sclerosis.

Al·sace /al'sas, -'sās/ a region of northeastern France, on the borders with Germany and Switzerland. It was annexed by Prussia, along with part of Lorraine, to form **Alsace-Lorraine** after the Franco-Prussian War of 1870–71. It was restored to France after World War I.

Al·sa·tian /al'sāsHən/ ▶ **n. 1** chiefly Brit. another term for GERMAN SHEPHERD.
2 a native or inhabitant of Alsace.
▶ **adj.** of or relating to Alsace or its inhabitants.
– ORIGIN from medieval Latin *Alsatia* 'Alsace' + -AN.

al·sike /'al,sik, -,sīk/ (also **alsike clover**) ▶ **n.** a tall clover that is widely grown for fodder. Native to Europe, it has become naturalized in North America. ● *Trifolium hybridum*, family Leguminosae.
– ORIGIN mid 19th cent.: named after *Alsike* in Sweden; Linnaeus mentions the plant growing there.

al·so /'ôlsō/ ▶ **adv.** in addition; too: *a brilliant linguist, he was also interested in botany* | *dyslexia, also known as word-blindness* | [sentence adverb] *also, a car is very expensive to run.*
– ORIGIN Old English *alswā* 'quite so, in that manner, similarly' (see ALL, SO[1]).

al·so-ran ▶ **n.** (pl. **also-rans**) a loser in a race or contest, esp. by a large margin. ■ an undistinguished or unsuccessful person or thing.
– ORIGIN late 19th cent.: originally applied to racehorses that did not finish in the first three.

al·stroe·mer·i·a /,alstrə'mi(ə)rēə/ ▶ **n.** a South American plant with showy lilylike flowers, often cultivated as an ornamental. ● Genus *Alstroemeria*, family Liliaceae: several species, in particular the Peruvian lily.
– ORIGIN late 18th cent.: modern Latin, named after Klas von *Alstroemer* (1736–96), Swedish naturalist.

Alt /ôlt/ ▶ **n.** short for ALT KEY.

alt.[1] ▶ **abbr.** ■ alternate. ■ altimeter. ■ altitude.

alt.[2] (also **alt-**) ▶ **comb. form** denoting a version of something that is intended as a challenge to the traditional version: *an alt.classical quartet.*
– ORIGIN 1990s: abbr. of *alternative*, influenced by the *alt.* prefix of some Usenet newsgroups.

Alta. ▶ **abbr.** Alberta.

Al·ta·de·na /,altə'dēnə/ a residential suburb in southwestern California, just north of Pasadena; pop. 42,610 (2000).

Al·tai /'al,tī, 'äl-/ (also **Altay**) a krai (administrative territory) of Russia in southwestern Siberia, on the border with Kazakhstan; capital, Barnaul.

Al·ta·ic /al'tāik/ ▶ **adj. 1** of or relating to the Altai Mountains.
2 denoting or belonging to a phylum of languages that includes the Turkic, Mongolian, Tungusic, and Manchu languages. They are characterized by agglutination and vowel harmony.
▶ **n.** the Altaic family of languages.

Al·tai Moun·tains a mountain system in central Asia that extends east for about 1,000 miles (1,600 km) from Kazakhstan into western Mongolia and northern China.

Al·tair /'al,te(ə)r, -,tī(ə)r, al'tī(ə)r, -'te(ə)r/ Astronomy the brightest star in the constellation Aquila.
– ORIGIN Arabic, literally 'flying eagle.'

Al·ta·mi·ra /,altə'mi(ə)rə/ the site of a cave with Paleolithic rock paintings, south of Santander in northern Spain, discovered in 1879.

al·tar /'ôltər/ ▶ **n.** the table in a Christian church at which the bread and wine are consecrated in communion services. ■ a table or flat-topped block used as the focus for a religious ritual, esp. for making sacrifices or offerings to a deity.
– PHRASES **lead someone to the altar** marry. **sacrifice someone/something on/at the altar of someone/something** cause someone or something to suffer in the interests of someone or something else: *no businessman is going to sacrifice his company on the altar of such altruism.*
– ORIGIN Old English *altar, alter*, based on late Latin *altar, altarium*, from Latin *altus* 'high.'

al·tar boy ▶ **n.** a boy who acts as a priest's assistant, esp. in the Roman Catholic Church.

al·tar call ▶ **n.** a summons to the altar at a Christian worship service to those wishing to show their commitment: *I never responded to an altar call, or if my pastor gave an altar call, I didn't think it applied to me.*

al·tar girl ▶ **n.** a girl who acts as a priest's assistant during a service, esp. in the Roman Catholic Church.

al·tar·piece /'ôltər,pēs/ ▶ **n.** a work of art, esp. a painting on wood, set above and behind an altar.

al·tar rail ▶ **n.** a railing in front of the altar, separating the chancel from the nave.

Al·tay variant spelling of ALTAI.

alt·az·i·muth /al'tazəməTH/ ▶ **n. 1** (also **altazimuth mount** or **mounting**) Astronomy a telescope mounting that moves in azimuth (about a vertical axis) and in altitude (about a horizontal axis). Compare with EQUATORIAL MOUNT. ■ (also **altazimuth telescope**) a telescope on such a mounting.
2 a surveying instrument for measuring vertical and horizontal angles, resembling a theodolite but larger and more precise.
– ORIGIN mid 19th cent.: blend of ALTITUDE and AZIMUTH.

alt.coun·try /'ôlt 'kəntrē/ (also **alt-country**) ▶ **n.** a style of country music that is influenced by alternative rock.

Alt·dor·fer /'ält,dôrfər/, Albrecht (*c.*1485–1538), German painter and engraver. He was the principal artist of the Danube School.

al·ter /'ôltər/ ▶ **v.** change or cause to change in character or composition, typically in a comparatively small but significant way: [with obj.] *Eliot was persuaded to alter the passage* | *nothing alters the fact that children are our responsibility* | [no obj.] *our outward appearance alters as we get older* | (as adj. **altered**) *an altered state.* ■ [with obj.] make structural changes to (a building): *plans to alter the dining hall.* ■ [with obj.] tailor (clothing) for a better fit or to conform to fashion: *skirts with the hemlines altered a dozen different times.* ■ [with obj.] castrate or spay (a domestic animal).
– DERIVATIVES **al·ter·a·ble adj.**
– ORIGIN late Middle English: from Old French *alterer*, from late Latin *alterare*, from Latin *alter* 'other.'

al·ter·a·tion /,ôltə'rāsHən/ ▶ **n.** the action or process of altering or being altered: *timetables are subject to alteration without notice* | *alterations had to be made.*

–ORIGIN late Middle English: from Old French, or from late Latin *alteratio(n-)*, from the verb *alterare* (see ALTER).

al·ter·cate /ˈôltər,kāt/ ▶ v. [no obj.] archaic dispute or argue noisily and publicly.
–ORIGIN mid 16th cent.: from Latin *altercat-* 'wrangled,' from *altercari*.

al·ter·ca·tion /,ôltərˈkāSHən/ ▶ n. a noisy argument or disagreement, esp. in public: *I had an altercation with the conductor*.
–ORIGIN late Middle English: from Latin *altercatio(n-)*, from the verb *altercari* (see ALTERCATE).

al·tered state ▶ n. a state of mind that differs from the normal state of consciousness, typically one induced by drugs, hypnosis, or mental disorder.

al·ter e·go ▶ n. (pl. **alter egos**) a person's secondary or alternative personality. ■ an intimate and trusted friend.
–ORIGIN mid 16th cent.: Latin, 'other self.'

al·ter·i·ty /ôlˈteritē/ ▶ n. formal the state of being other or different; otherness.
–ORIGIN mid 17th cent.: from late Latin *alteritas*, from *alter* 'other.'

al·ter·nant /ˈôltərnənt/ ▶ n. an alternative form of a word or other linguistic unit; a variant.
▶ adj. alternating; changing from one to the other.
–ORIGIN mid 17th cent.: from Latin *alternant-* 'doing things by turns,' from the verb *alternare* (see ALTERNATE).

al·ter·nate ▶ v. /ˈôltər,nāt/ [no obj.] occur in turn repeatedly: *the governorship **alternated between** the Republican and Democratic parties | bouts of depression **alternate with** periods of elation* | (as adj. **alternating**) *a season of alternating hot days and cool nights*. ■ [with obj.] do or perform in turn repeatedly: *some adults who wish to **alternate** work **with** education*.
▶ adj. /ˈôltərnit/ (abbr.: **alt.**) [attrib.] **1** every other; every second: *she was asked to attend on alternate days*. ■ (of two things) each following and succeeded by the other in a regular pattern: *alternate bouts of intense labor and of idleness*. ■ (of a sequence) consisting of alternate items. ■ Botany (of leaves or shoots) placed alternately on the two sides of the stem.
2 taking the place of; alternative: *the rerouted traffic takes a variety of alternate routes*.
▶ n. /-nit/ (abbr.: **alt.**) a person who acts as a deputy or substitute.
–DERIVATIVES **al·ter·nate·ly** /-nitlē/ adv., **al·ter·na·tion** /,ôltərˈnāSHən/ n.
–ORIGIN early 16th cent. (earlier (late Middle English) as *alternation*): from Latin *alternat-* 'done by turns,' from *alternare*, from *alternus* 'every other,' from *alter* 'other, the other.'

USAGE See usage at ALTERNATIVE.

al·ter·nate an·gles ▶ plural n. two angles, not adjoining one another, that are formed on opposite sides of a line that intersects two other lines. If the original two lines are parallel, the alternate angles are equal.

al·ter·nat·ing cur·rent (abbr.: **AC** or **ac**) ▶ n. an electric current that reverses its direction many times a second at regular intervals, typically used in power supplies. Compare with DIRECT CURRENT.

al·ter·na·tion of gen·er·a·tions ▶ n. Biology a pattern of reproduction occurring in the life cycles of many lower plants and some invertebrates, involving a regular alternation between two distinct forms. The generations are alternately sexual and asexual (as in ferns) or dioecious and parthenogenetic (as in some jellyfish).

al·ter·na·tive /ôlˈtərnətiv/ ▶ adj. [attrib.] (of one or more things) available as another possibility: *the various alternative methods for resolving disputes | the alternative definition of democracy as popular power*. ■ (of two things) mutually exclusive: *the facts fit two alternative scenarios*. ■ of or relating to behavior that is considered unconventional and is often seen as a challenge to traditional norms: *an alternative lifestyle | they have one foot in alternative music and the other in rock*.
▶ n. one of two or more available possibilities: *audiocassettes are an interesting **alternative to** reading | she had no alternative but to break the law*.
–ORIGIN mid 16th cent. (in the sense 'alternating, alternate'): from French *alternatif, -ive* or medieval Latin *alternativus*, from Latin *alternare* 'interchange' (see ALTERNATE).

USAGE **1** **Alternate** can be a verb, noun, or adjective, while **alternative** can be a noun or adjective. In both American and British English, the adjective **alternate** means 'every other' (*there will be a dance on **alternate** Saturdays*) and the adjective **alternative** means 'available as another choice' (*an **alternative** route; **alternative** medicine; **alternative** energy sources*). In American usage, however, **alternate** can also be used to mean 'available as another choice': *an **alternate** plan called for construction to begin immediately rather than waiting for spring*. Likewise, a book club may offer an 'alternate selection' as an alternative to the main selection. **2** Some traditionalists maintain, from an etymological standpoint, that you can have only two alternatives (from the Latin *alter* 'other (of two); the other') and that uses of more than two alternatives are erroneous. Such uses are, however, normal in modern standard English.

al·ter·na·tive dis·pute res·o·lu·tion (abbr.: **ADR**) ▶ n. the use of methods such as mediation and arbitration to resolve a dispute instead of litigation.

al·ter·na·tive en·er·gy ▶ n. energy generated in ways that do not deplete natural resources or harm the environment, esp. by avoiding the use of fossil fuels and nuclear power.

al·ter·na·tive fu·el ▶ n. a fuel other than gasoline for powering motor vehicles, such as natural gas, methanol, or electricity.

al·ter·na·tive·ly /ôlˈtərnətivlē/ ▶ adv. [sentence adverb] as another option or possibility: *alternatively, you may telephone us direct*.

al·ter·na·tive med·i·cine ▶ n. any of a range of medical therapies that are not regarded as orthodox by the medical profession, such as herbalism, homeopathy, and acupuncture. See also COMPLEMENTARY MEDICINE.

al·ter·na·tor /ˈôltər,nātər/ ▶ n. a generator that produces an alternating current.

Al·thing /ˈôl,THiNG, ˈäl-/ the bicameral legislative assembly of Iceland.
–ORIGIN Icelandic, from Old Norse.

alt·horn /ˈalt,hôrn/ ▶ n. a musical instrument of the saxhorn family, esp. the alto or tenor saxhorn in E flat.
–ORIGIN mid 19th cent.: from German, from *alt* 'high' (from Latin *altus*) + *Horn* 'horn.'

al·though /ôlˈT͟Hō/ ▶ conj. in spite of the fact that; even though: *although the sun was shining it wasn't that warm | although small, the room has a spacious feel*. ■ however; but: *he says he has the team jersey, although I've never seen him wear it*.
–ORIGIN Middle English: from ALL (as an adverb) + THOUGH.

USAGE **Although** and **though** are interchangeable in the senses listed above, the only difference being that use of **though** tends to be less formal than that of **although**. In formal writing, **although** tends to sound better than **though** as the opening word of a sentence. Some uses of **though**, however, are not interchangeable with **although**—e.g., adverbial uses (*it was nice of him to phone, though*) and uses in conjunction with 'as' or 'even' (*she doesn't look as though she's listening*).

Alt·hus·ser /ˈält,ho͞osər, ält(h)o͞oˈsā/, Louis (1918–90), French philosopher. He reinterpreted traditional Marxism in the light of structuralist theories. Notable works: *For Marx* (1965) and *Reading Capital* (1970).

al·tim·e·ter /alˈtimitər/ (abbr.: **alt.**) ▶ n. an instrument for determining altitude attained, esp. a barometric or radar device used in an aircraft.
–ORIGIN early 20th cent.: from Latin *altus* 'high' + -METER.

al·tim·e·try /alˈtimitrē/ ▶ n. the measurement of height or altitude.
–DERIVATIVES **al·ti·met·ric** /,altəˈmetrik/ adj., **al·ti·met·ri·cal·ly** /,altəˈmetrik(ə)lē/ adv.
–ORIGIN late Middle English: from medieval Latin *altimetria*.

al·ti·pla·no /altiˈplänō/ ▶ n. (pl. **altiplanos**) the high tableland of central South America.
–ORIGIN early 20th cent.: from Spanish.

al·tis·si·mo /alˈtisə,mō, äl-/ ▶ adj. Music very high in pitch: *the extreme altissimo range of his horn*.
–ORIGIN Italian, superlative of *alto* 'high.'

al·ti·tude /ˈalti,t(y)o͞od/ (abbr.: **alt.**) ▶ n. the height of an object or point in relation to sea level or ground level: *flight data including airspeed and altitude | flying at altitudes over 15,000 feet*. ■ great height: *the mechanism can freeze at altitude*. ■ Astronomy the apparent height of a celestial object above the horizon, measured as an angle. ■ Geometry the length of the perpendicular line from a vertex to the opposite side of a figure.
–DERIVATIVES **al·ti·tu·di·nal** /,altiˈt(y)o͞odn-əl/ adj.
–ORIGIN late Middle English: from Latin *altitudo*, from *altus* 'high.'

al·ti·tude sick·ness ▶ n. illness caused by ascent to a high altitude and the resulting shortage of oxygen, characterized chiefly by hyperventilation, nausea, exhaustion, and cerebral edema.

Alt key /ôlt/ ▶ n. Computing a key on a keyboard that when pressed at the same time as another key gives the second key an alternative function.
–ORIGIN late 20th cent.: abbreviation of *alt(ernative) key*.

Alt·man /ˈôltmən/, Robert (1925–2006), US movie director. He made his name with *M*A*S*H* (1970), a black comedy about an army surgical hospital at the front in the Korean War. Other notable movies: *Nashville* (1975), *The Player* (1992), and *Gosford Park* (2001).

al·to /ˈaltō/ ▶ n. (pl. **altos**) Music a voice, instrument, or part below the highest range and above tenor, in particular: ■ the highest adult male singing voice; countertenor. ■ the lowest female singing voice; contralto. ■ [as modifier] denoting the member of a family of instruments pitched second or third highest: *alto flute*. ■ an alto instrument, esp. an alto saxophone.
–ORIGIN late 16th cent.: from Italian *alto (canto)* 'high (song).'

al·to clef ▶ n. a clef placing middle C on the middle line of the staff, now used chiefly for viola music.

al·to·cu·mu·lus /,altōˈkyo͞omyələs/ ▶ n. (pl. **altocumuli** /-,lī/) cloud forming a layer of rounded masses with a level base, occurring at medium altitude, usually 6,500–23,000 feet (2–7 km).
–ORIGIN late 19th cent.: from modern Latin *alto-* (from Latin *altus* 'high') + CUMULUS.

al·to·geth·er /,ôltəˈgeT͟Hər/ ▶ adv. completely; totally: *I stopped seeing her altogether* | [as submodifier] *I'm not altogether sure that I'd trust him*. ■ including everything or everyone; in total: *he had married several times and had forty-six children altogether*. ■ [sentence adverb] taking everything into consideration; on the whole: *altogether it was a great evening*.
–PHRASES **in the altogether** informal without any clothes on; naked: *she's agreed to pose in the altogether*.
–ORIGIN Old English (see ALL, TOGETHER).

USAGE Note that **altogether** and **all together** do not mean the same thing. **Altogether** means 'in total, totally' as in *there are six bedrooms altogether, or that is a different matter altogether*, whereas **all together** means 'all in one place' or 'all at once,' as in *it was good to have a group of friends all together, or they came in all together*.

al·to·ist /ˈaltōist/ ▶ n. a person who plays an alto instrument, in particular a saxophone.

Al·too·na /alˈto͞onə/ a city in south central Pennsylvania, in the Allegheny Mountains; pop. 46,144 (est. 2008). A noted railroad center, it is near Horseshoe Curve, where rails first crossed the Alleghenies.

al·to-re·lie·vo /ˈaltō rəˈlēvō/ ▶ n. (pl. **alto-relievos**) Sculpture another term for HIGH RELIEF at RELIEF (sense 4). ■ a sculpture or carving in high relief.
–ORIGIN mid 17th cent.: from Italian *alto-rilievo*.

al·to·stra·tus /,altōˈstrātəs, -ˈstratəs/ ▶ n. cloud forming a continuous uniform layer that resembles stratus but occurs at medium altitude, usually 6,500–23,000 feet (2–7 km).
–ORIGIN late 19th cent.: from modern Latin *alto-* (from Latin *altus* 'high') + STRATUS.

al·tri·cial /alˈtriSHəl/ Zoology ▶ adj. (of a young bird or other animal) hatched or born in an undeveloped state and requiring care and feeding by the parents. Also called NIDICOLOUS. Often contrasted with PRECOCIAL. ■ (of a particular species) having such young.
▶ n. an altricial bird.
–ORIGIN late 19th cent.: from Latin *altrix, altric-*, feminine of *altor* 'nourisher,' from *alere* 'nourish.'

al·tru·ism /ˈaltro͞o,izəm/ ▶ n. the belief in or practice of disinterested and selfless concern for the well-being of others: *some may choose to work with vulnerable elderly people out of altruism*. ■ Zoology behavior of an animal that benefits another at its own expense.
–DERIVATIVES **al·tru·ist** n.
–ORIGIN mid 19th cent.: from French *altruisme*, from Italian *altrui* 'somebody else,' from Latin *alteri huic* 'to this other.'

al·tru·is·tic /ˌaltro͞o'istik/ ▶ **adj.** showing a disinterested and selfless concern for the well-being of others; unselfish: *it was an entirely altruistic act.*
– DERIVATIVES **al·tru·is·ti·cal·ly adv.**

ALU ▶ **abbr.** Computing arithmetic logic unit.

al·u·del /'alyəˌdel/ ▶ **n.** a pear-shaped earthenware or glass pot, open at both ends to enable a series to be fitted one above another, formerly used in sublimation and other chemical processes.
– ORIGIN late Middle English: from Old French *alutel*, via Spanish from Arabic *al-'uṯāl* 'the sublimation vessel.'

al·u·la /'alyələ/ ▶ **n.** (pl. **alulae** /-yəˌlē/) technical term for **BASTARD WING**.
– ORIGIN late 18th cent.: modern Latin, literally 'small wing,' diminutive of *ala*.

a·lum[1] /'aləm/ ▶ **n.** Chemistry a colorless astringent compound that is a hydrated double sulfate of aluminum and potassium, used in solution medicinally and in dyeing and tanning. Also called **POTASH ALUM**. ● Chem. formula: $AlK(SO_4)_2.12H_2O$. ■ any of a number of analogous crystalline double sulfates of a monovalent metal (or group) and a trivalent metal.
– ORIGIN late Middle English: via Old French from Latin *alumen, alumin-*; related to *aluta* 'tawed leather.'

a·lum[2] /ə'ləm/ ▶ **n.** informal an alumnus or alumna: *a fellow Wellesley alum.*
– ORIGIN early 20th cent.: abbreviation.

a·lu·mi·na /ə'lo͞omənə/ ▶ **n.** a white solid, aluminum oxide, that occurs in bauxite and is found in crystalline form as the main constituent of corundum, sapphire, and other minerals. ● Aluminum oxide; chem. formula: Al_2O_3.
– ORIGIN late 18th cent.: from Latin *alumen* (see **ALUM**[1]), on the pattern of words such as *magnesia*.

a·lu·mi·nize /ə'lo͞oməˌnīz/ ▶ **v.** [with obj.] (usu. as adj. **aluminized**) coat with aluminum: *an aluminized reflector.*

a·lu·mi·no·sil·i·cate /əˌlo͞omənə'silikit/ ▶ **n.** Chemistry a silicate in which aluminum replaces some of the silicon, esp. a rock-forming mineral such as a feldspar or a clay mineral.
– ORIGIN early 20th cent.: from *alumino-* (combining form of **ALUMINUM**) + **SILICATE**.

a·lu·mi·nous /ə'lo͞omənəs/ ▶ **adj.** (chiefly of minerals and rocks) containing alumina or aluminum.
– ORIGIN late Middle English: from Latin *aluminosus*, from *alumen, alumin-* (see **ALUM**[1]).

a·lu·mi·num /ə'lo͞omənəm/ (Brit. **aluminium** /ˌalyə'minēəm/) ▶ **n.** the chemical element of atomic number 13, a light silvery-gray metal. (Symbol: **Al**)

> Aluminum is the most abundant metal in the earth's crust and is obtained mainly from bauxite. Its lightness, resistance to corrosion, and strength (esp. in alloys) have led to widespread use in domestic utensils, engineering parts, and aircraft construction.

– ORIGIN early 19th cent.: from *alumin(a)* + *(i)um*.

a·lu·mi·num bronze ▶ **n.** an alloy of copper and aluminum.

a·lum·na /ə'ləmnə/ ▶ **n.** (pl. **alumnae** /-nē, -nī/) a female graduate or former student of a particular school, college, or university.
– ORIGIN late 19th cent.: from Latin, feminine of *alumnus* (see **ALUMNUS**).

> **USAGE** See usage at **ALUMNUS**.

a·lum·nus /ə'ləmnəs/ ▶ **n.** (pl. **alumni** /-nī, -nē/) a graduate or former student, esp. male, of a particular school, college, or university: *a Harvard alumnus.*
– ORIGIN mid 17th cent.: from Latin, 'nursling, pupil,' from *alere* 'nourish.'

> **USAGE** In the singular, **alumnus** nearly always means a male, but the plural **alumni** usually refers to graduates or former students of either sex. See also **ALUMNA**.

al·um·root /'aləmˌro͞ot, -ˌro͝ot/ (also **alum root**) ▶ **n.** a heuchera, esp. the green-flowered *H. americana* and the white-flowered *H. parvifolia*.

al-Uq·sur /ˌal 'o͝okˌso͝or/ Arabic name for **LUXOR**.

Al·va·rez /'alvəˌrez/, Luis Walter (1911–88), US physicist. In particle physics, he made the first measurement of the neutron's magnetic moment. He also developed the bubble chamber. In 1980 Alvarez and his son identified iridium in sediment from the Cretaceous–Tertiary boundary and proposed that this resulted from a catastrophic meteorite impact. Nobel Prize for Physics (1968).

al·ve·o·lar /al'vēələr/ ▶ **adj.** of or relating to an alveolus, in particular: ■ Anatomy relating to or denoting the bony ridge that contains the sockets of the upper teeth. ■ Phonetics (of a consonant) pronounced with the tip of the tongue on or near this ridge (e.g., *n, s, t*). ■ Anatomy of or relating to an alveolus or the alveoli of the lung.
▶ **n.** Phonetics an alveolar consonant.

al·ve·o·lus /al'vēələs/ ▶ **n.** (pl. **alveoli** /-ˌlī/) chiefly Anatomy a small cavity, pit, or hollow, in particular: ■ any of the many tiny air sacs in the lungs where the exchange of oxygen and carbon dioxide takes place. ■ the bony socket for the root of a tooth. ■ an acinus in a gland.
– DERIVATIVES **al·ve·o·late** /-lit, -ˌlāt/ **adj.**
– ORIGIN late 17th cent.: from Latin, 'small cavity,' diminutive of *alveus*.

al·ways /'ôlˌwāz, -wēz/ (archaic **alway**) ▶ **adv. 1** at all times; on all occasions: *the sun always rises in the east.* ■ throughout a long period of the past: *she had always been an obstinate sort.* ■ for all future time; forever: *she will always be missed.* ■ repeatedly and annoyingly: *she is always making derogatory remarks.*
2 as a last resort; failing all else: *if the marriage doesn't work out, we can always get divorced.*
– ORIGIN Middle English: genitive case of *all way*, the inflection probably giving the sense 'at every time' as opposed to 'at one uninterrupted time'; the difference between the two is no longer distinct.

a·lys·sum /ə'lisəm/ ▶ **n.** (pl. **alyssums**) a herbaceous Eurasian plant that bears small flowers in a range of colors, typically white or yellow. Several kinds are widely cultivated in gardens. ● Genera *Alyssum* and *Lobularia*, family Brassicaceae: many species, including **sweet alyssum** (*L. maritima*), with fragrant white flowers.
– ORIGIN mid 16th cent. (used loosely to denote various medicinal herbs): modern Latin, from Latin *alysson*, from Greek *alusson*, from *a-* 'without' + *lussa* 'rabies' (referring to early herbalist use).

Alz·hei·mer's dis·ease /'älts,hīmərz, 'ôlts-, 'älz-, 'ôlz-/ ▶ **n.** progressive mental deterioration that can occur in middle or old age, due to generalized degeneration of the brain. It is the most common cause of premature senility.
– ORIGIN early 20th cent.: named after Alois *Alzheimer* (1864–1915), German neurologist who first identified it.

AM ▶ **abbr.** ■ amplitude modulation. ■ Master of Arts. [Latin *artium magister*.]

Am ▶ **symbol** the chemical element americium.

am /am/ 1st person singular present of **BE**.

a.m. ▶ **abbr.** before noon, used with times of day between midnight and noon: *we can deliver your most time-sensitive shipments by 10:30 a.m.*
– ORIGIN from Latin *ante meridiem*.

AMA ▶ **abbr.** ■ American Management Association. ■ American Medical Association. ■ American Motorcycle Association.

a·mah /'ämə/ ▶ **n.** a nursemaid or maid in East Asia or India.
– ORIGIN from Portuguese *ama* 'nurse.'

A·mal /ä'mäl/ a Lebanese Shiite Muslim organization founded in 1975 and having political and paramilitary wings.
– ORIGIN from Arabic *'amal* 'hope.'

a·mal·gam /ə'malgəm/ ▶ **n.** a mixture or blend: *a curious amalgam of the traditional and the modern.* ■ Chemistry an alloy of mercury with another metal, esp. one used for dental fillings.
– ORIGIN late 15th cent.: from French *amalgame* or medieval Latin *amalgama*, from Greek *malagma* 'an emollient.'

a·mal·ga·mate /ə'malgəˌmāt/ ▶ **v.** combine or unite to form one organization or structure: [with obj.] *he amalgamated his company with another* | [no obj.] *numerous small railroad companies amalgamated* | (as adj. **amalgamated**) *his true genius lies in synthesis, in an amalgamated vision.* ■ [with obj.] Chemistry alloy (a metal) with mercury: (as adj. **amalgamated**) *amalgamated zinc.*
– ORIGIN early 17th cent.: from medieval Latin *amalgamat-* 'formed into a soft mass,' from the verb *amalgamare*, from *amalgama* (see **AMALGAM**).

a·mal·ga·ma·tion /əˌmalgə'māSHən/ ▶ **n.** the action, process, or result of combining or uniting: *the threat of amalgamation with a competitor* | *an amalgamation of two separate companies.* ■ Chemistry the action or process of alloying a metal with mercury.
– ORIGIN early 17th cent.: from medieval Latin *amalgamare* (see **AMALGAMATE**).

Am·al·the·a /ˌaməl'THēə, əmal-/ Astronomy satellite V of Jupiter, the third closest to the planet. It is reddish in color and heavily cratered, with a diameter of 106 miles (170 km).
– ORIGIN from the name of a goat in Greek mythology, which suckled the infant Zeus.

A·man·a Col·o·nies /ə'manə/ a group of seven villages in east central Iowa. Settled by a German religious group, they are famous for manufacturing appliances.

a·man·dine /ˌämən'dēn, ˌamən-/ ▶ **adj.** (of a dish) prepared or garnished with sliced almonds.

a·man·u·en·sis /əˌmanyo͞o'ensis/ ▶ **n.** (pl. **amanuenses** /-ˌsēz/) a literary or artistic assistant, in particular one who takes dictation or copies manuscripts.
– ORIGIN early 17th cent.: Latin, from (*servus*) *a manu* '(slave) at hand(writing), secretary' + *-ensis* 'belonging to.'

am·a·ranth /'aməˌranTH/ ▶ **n. 1** any plant of the genus *Amaranthus*, typically having small green, red, or purple tinted flowers. Certain varieties are grown for food. ● Family Amaranthaceae: several genera, esp. *Amaranthus*.
2 an imaginary flower that never fades.
3 a purple color.
– DERIVATIVES **am·a·ran·thine** /ˌamə'ranTHin, -ˌTHīn/ **adj.**
– ORIGIN mid 16th cent.: from French *amarante* or modern Latin *amaranthus*, alteration (on the pattern of plant names ending in *-anthus*, from Greek *anthos* 'flower') of Latin *amarantus*, from Greek *amarantos* 'everlasting,' from *a-* 'not' + *marainein* 'wither.'

am·a·ret·ti /ˌamə'retē/ ▶ **plural n.** Italian almond-flavored cookies.
– ORIGIN Italian, based on *amaro* 'bitter'; compare with **AMARETTO**.

am·a·ret·to /ˌamə'retō, ˌäm-/ ▶ **n.** (pl. **amarettos**) a sweet, almond-flavored liqueur.
– ORIGIN Italian, diminutive of *amaro* 'bitter' (with reference to bitter almonds).

Ama·ril·lo /ˌamə'rilō/ an industrial and commercial city in northwestern Texas, in the Panhandle; pop. 187,236 (est. 2008).

am·a·ryl·lis /ˌamə'rilis/ ▶ **n.** a bulbous plant with white, pink, or red flowers and straplike leaves, of the type genus of the amaryllis family, Amaryllidaceae. ● A South African plant (*Amaryllis belladonna*, also called **BELLADONNA LILY**), and (popularly) a tropical South American plant that is frequently grown as a houseplant (hybrids of the genus *Hippeastrum*, formerly *Amaryllis*).
– ORIGIN modern Latin, from Latin *Amaryllis* (from Greek *Amarullis*), a name for a country girl in pastoral poetry.

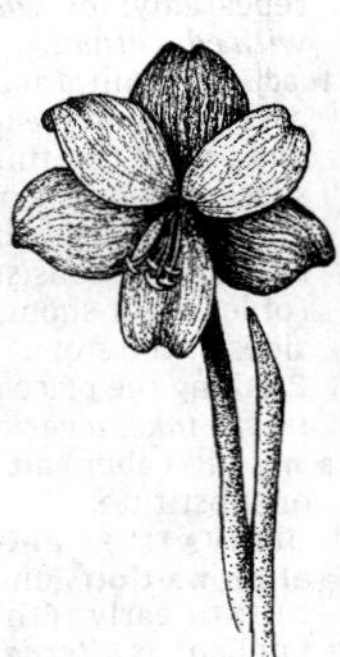
amaryllis

a·mass /ə'mas/ ▶ **v.** [with obj.] gather together or accumulate (a large amount or number of valuable material or things) over a period of time: *starting from nothing he had amassed a huge fortune.* ■ [no obj.] archaic (of people) gather together in a crowd or group: *the soldiers were amassing from all parts of Spain.*
– DERIVATIVES **a·mass·er n.**
– ORIGIN late 15th cent.: from French *amasser* or medieval Latin *amassare*, based on Latin *massa* 'lump' (see **MASS**).

A·ma·te·ra·su /ˌämäte'räso͞o/ the principal deity of the Japanese Shinto religion, the sun goddess and ancestor of Jimmu, founder of the imperial dynasty.

am·a·teur /'amətər, -ˌtər, -ˌCHo͝or, -CHər/ ▶ **n.** a person who engages in a pursuit, esp. a sport, on an unpaid basis. ■ a person considered contemptibly inept at a particular activity: *that bunch of stumbling amateurs.*
▶ **adj.** engaging or engaged in without payment; nonprofessional: *an amateur archaeologist* | *amateur athletics.* ■ inept or unskillful: *it's all so amateur!*
– DERIVATIVES **am·a·teur·ism** /-ˌrizəm/ **n.**
– ORIGIN late 18th cent.: from French, from Italian *amatore*, from Latin *amator* 'lover,' from *amare* 'to love.'

am·a·teur·ish /ˌamə'tərisH, -'t(y)o͝or-, -'CHo͝or-/ ▶ **adj.** unskillful; inept: *the editing is choppy and amateurish* | *amateurish actors.*
– DERIVATIVES **am·a·teur·ish·ly adv.**, **am·a·teur·ish·ness n.**

A·ma·ti /ä'mätē/ the name of a family of Italian violin-makers from Cremona. In the 16th and 17th centuries, three generations, including **Andrea** (*c.*1520–80), his sons **Antonio** (1550–1638) and **Girolamo** (1551–1635), and the latter's son **Nicolò** (1596–1684), developed the basic proportions of the violin, viola, and cello.

am·a·tol /'aməˌtôl, -ˌtäl/ ▶ **n.** a high explosive consisting of a mixture of TNT and ammonium nitrate.

–ORIGIN early 20th cent.: formed irregularly from *am(monium)* + *tol(uene)*.

am·a·to·ry /'amə,tôrē/ ▶ **adj.** [attrib.] relating to or induced by sexual love or desire: *his amatory exploits.*
–ORIGIN late 16th cent.: from Latin *amatorius*, from *amator* (see AMATEUR).

am·au·ro·sis /,amô'rōsis/ ▶ **n.** Medicine partial or total blindness without visible change in the eye, typically due to disease of the optic nerve, spinal cord, or brain.
–DERIVATIVES **am·au·rot·ic** /-'rätik/ **adj.**
–ORIGIN mid 17th cent.: from Greek *amaurōsis*, from *amauroun* 'darken,' from *amauros* 'dim.'

a·maze /ə'māz/ ▶ **v.** [with obj.] surprise (someone) greatly; fill with astonishment: *he was amazed at how modern everything was* | [with obj. and clause] *she was amazed that Paul should notice her* | (as adj. **amazed**) *she shook her head in amazed disbelief.*
–ORIGIN Old English *āmasian*, of unknown origin.

a·maze·ment /ə'māzmənt/ ▶ **n.** a feeling of great surprise or wonder: *she shook her head* ***in amazement*** | *he found* ***to his amazement*** *that it was a passageway.*

a·maz·ing /ə'māziNG/ ▶ **adj.** causing great surprise or wonder; astonishing: *an amazing number of people registered* | *it is amazing how short your memory is.* ■ informal startlingly impressive: *she makes the most amazing cakes.*
–DERIVATIVES **a·maz·ing·ly adv.** [sentence adverb] *amazingly, Alan escaped with a few cuts and bruises* | [as submodifier] *an amazingly good idea.*

Am·a·zon[1] /'amə,zän, -zən/ a river in South America that flows more than 4,150 miles (6,683 km) through Peru, Colombia, and Brazil into the Atlantic Ocean. It drains two-fifths of the continent and, in terms of water-flow, is the largest river in the world.
–DERIVATIVES **Am·a·zo·ni·an** /,amə'zōnēən/ **adj.**
–ORIGIN the river bore various names after its discovery in 1500 and was finally called *Amazon* after a legendary tribe of female warriors believed to live on its banks.

Am·a·zon[2] ▶ **n.** **1** a member of a legendary race of female warriors believed by the ancient Greeks to exist in Scythia (near the Black Sea in modern Russia) or elsewhere on the edge of the known world. ■ (also **amazon**) a tall and strong or athletic woman.
2 (**amazon**) a parrot, typically green and with a broad rounded tail, found in Central and South America. ● Genus *Amazona*, family Psittacidae: numerous species.
–DERIVATIVES **Am·a·zo·ni·an adj.**
–ORIGIN late Middle English: via Latin from Greek *Amazōn*, explained by the Greeks as 'without a breast' (as if from *a-* 'without' + *mazos* 'breast'), referring to the fable that the Amazons cut off the right breast so as not to interfere with the use of a bow, but probably a popular etymology of an unknown foreign word.

am·a·zon ant ▶ **n.** a small reddish ant that captures the pupae of other ant colonies to raise as slaves. ● Genus *Polyergus*, family Formicidae.

Am·a·zo·ni·a /,amə'zōnēə/ the area around the Amazon River in South America, principally in Brazil, but also extending into Peru, Colombia, and Bolivia. This region comprises approximately one-third of the world's remaining tropical rain forest.

am·bas·sa·dor /am'basədər, -,dôr/ ▶ **n.** an accredited diplomat sent by a country as its official representative to a foreign country: *the French* ***ambassador to*** *Portugal.* ■ a person who acts as a representative or promoter of a specified activity: *he is a good ambassador for the industry.*
–DERIVATIVES **am·bas·sa·do·ri·al** /am,basə'dôrēəl/ **adj.**, **am·bas·sa·dor·ship** /-,SHip/ **n.**
–ORIGIN late Middle English: from French *ambassadeur*, from Italian *ambasciator*, based on Latin *ambactus* 'servant.'

am·bas·sa·dor-at-large ▶ **n.** an ambassador with special duties, not appointed to a particular country.

am·bas·sa·dress /am'basədris/ ▶ **n.** a female ambassador. ■ archaic an ambassador's wife.

Am·ba·to /äm'bätō/ a market town in the Andes of central Ecuador; pop. 209,000 (est. 2008).

am·ber /'ambər/ ▶ **n.** hard translucent fossilized resin produced by extinct coniferous trees of the Tertiary period, typically yellowish in color.

> Amber has been used in jewelry since antiquity. It is found chiefly along the southern shores of the Baltic Sea; pieces often contain the bodies of trapped insects. When rubbed, amber becomes charged with static electricity: the word *electric* is derived from the Greek word for amber.

■ a honey-yellow color typical of this substance. ■ a yellow light used as a cautionary signal between green for "go" and red for "stop": *the lights were at amber.*
▶ **adj.** made of amber: *amber beads.* ■ having the yellow color of amber: *her amber eyes.*
–ORIGIN late Middle English (also in the sense 'ambergris'): from Old French *ambre*, from Arabic *'anbar* 'ambergris,' later 'amber.'

AMBER A·lert /'ambər ə,lərt/ (also **Amber Alert**) ▶ **n.** an emergency response system that disseminates information about a missing person (usually a child), by media broadcasting or electronic roadway signs: *our state's AMBER Alert became operational last September.* ■ a public announcement or alert that uses this system: *the AMBER alert gave a description of the suspected abductor.*
–ORIGIN acronym from America's Missing: Broadcast Emergency Response, named after Amber Hagerman, a child kidnapped in Texas in 1996.

am·ber·gris /'ambər,gris, -,grē(s)/ ▶ **n.** a waxlike substance that originates as a secretion in the intestines of the sperm whale, found floating in tropical seas and used in perfume manufacture.
–ORIGIN late Middle English: from Old French *ambre gris* 'gray amber,' as distinct from *amber jaune* 'yellow amber' (the resin).

am·ber·jack /'ambər,jak/ ▶ **n.** a large marine game fish found in inshore tropical and subtropical waters of the Atlantic and South Pacific. ● Genus *Seriola*, family Carangidae: several species.
–ORIGIN late 19th cent.: from AMBER (because of its yellowish tail) + JACK[1].

am·bi·ance ▶ **n.** variant spelling of AMBIENCE.

am·bi·dex·trous /,ambi'dekst(ə)rəs/ ▶ **adj.** (of a person) able to use the right and left hands equally well: *few of us are naturally ambidextrous.* ■ (of an implement) designed to be used by left-handed and right-handed people with equal ease.
–DERIVATIVES **am·bi·dex·ter·i·ty** /-dek'steritē/ **n.**, **am·bi·dex·trous·ly adv.**
–ORIGIN mid 17th cent.: from late Latin *ambidexter* (from Latin *ambi-* 'on both sides' + *dexter* 'right-handed') + -OUS.

am·bi·ence /'ambēəns/ (also **ambiance**) ▶ **n.** [usu. in sing.] the character and atmosphere of a place: *the relaxed ambience of the cocktail lounge is popular with guests.* ■ background noise added to a musical recording to give the impression that it was recorded live.
–ORIGIN late 19th cent.: from AMBIENT + -ENCE, or from French *ambiance*, from *ambiant* 'surrounding.'

am·bi·ent /'ambēənt/ ▶ **adj.** [attrib.] of or relating to the immediate surroundings of something: *the liquid is stored at below ambient temperature.*
▶ **n.** (also **ambient music**) a style of instrumental music with electronic textures and no persistent beat, used to create or enhance a mood or atmosphere.
–ORIGIN late 16th cent.: from French *ambiant* or Latin *ambient-* 'going around,' from *ambire*.

am·bi·gu·i·ty /,ambi'gyo͞oitē/ ▶ **n.** (pl. **ambiguities**) uncertainty or inexactness of meaning in language: *we can detect no ambiguity in this section of the Act* | *ambiguities in such questions are potentially very dangerous.* ■ a lack of decisiveness or commitment resulting from a failure to make a choice between alternatives: *the film is fraught with moral ambiguity.*
–ORIGIN late Middle English: from Old French *ambiguite* or Latin *ambiguitas*, from *ambiguus* 'doubtful' (see AMBIGUOUS).

am·big·u·ous /am'bigyo͞oəs/ ▶ **adj.** (of language) open to more than one interpretation; having a double meaning: *the question is rather ambiguous* | *ambiguous phrases.* ■ unclear or inexact because a choice between alternatives has not been made: *this whole society is morally ambiguous* | *the election result was ambiguous.*
–DERIVATIVES **am·big·u·ous·ly adv.**, **am·big·u·ous·ness n.**
–ORIGIN early 16th cent. (in the sense 'indistinct, obscure'): from Latin *ambiguus* 'doubtful' (from *ambigere* 'waver, go around,' from *ambi-* 'both ways' + *agere* 'to drive') + -OUS.

am·bi·sex·u·al /,ambi'sekSHo͞oəl/ ▶ **adj.** bisexual or androgynous.
▶ **n.** an ambisexual person.
–DERIVATIVES **am·bi·sex·u·al·ly adv.**
–ORIGIN 1930s: from Latin *ambi-* 'on both sides' + SEXUAL.

am·bi·son·ic /,ambi'sänik/ ▶ **adj.** denoting or relating to a high-fidelity audio system that reproduces the directional and acoustic properties of recorded sound using two or more channels.
▶ **n.** (**ambisonics**) [treated as sing.] ambisonic reproduction or systems.
–ORIGIN 1970s: from Latin *ambi-* 'on both sides' + SONIC.

am·bit /'ambit/ ▶ **n.** [in sing.] the scope, extent, or bounds of something: *within the ambit of federal law.*
–ORIGIN late Middle English (in the sense 'precincts, environs'): from Latin *ambitus* 'circuit,' from *ambire* 'go around.'

am·bi·tion /am'bisHən/ ▶ **n.** a strong desire to do or to achieve something, typically requiring determination and hard work: *her ambition was to become a model* | *he achieved his ambition of making a fortune.* ■ desire and determination to achieve success: *life offered few opportunities for young people with ambition.*
–ORIGIN Middle English: via Old French from Latin *ambitio(n-)*, from *ambire* 'go around (canvassing for votes).'

am·bi·tious /am'bisHəs/ ▶ **adj.** having or showing a strong desire and determination to succeed: *his mother was hard-working and ambitious for her four children.* ■ (of a plan or piece of work) intended to satisfy high aspirations and therefore difficult to achieve: *the scope of the book is very ambitious* | *an ambitious enterprise.*
–DERIVATIVES **am·bi·tious·ly adv.**, **am·bi·tious·ness n.**
–ORIGIN late Middle English: from Old French *ambitieux* or Latin *ambitiosus*, from *ambitio* (see AMBITION).

am·biv·a·lence /am'bivələns/ ▶ **n.** the state of having mixed feelings or contradictory ideas about something or someone: *government ambivalence toward the arts.*

am·biv·a·lent /am'bivələnt/ ▶ **adj.** having mixed feelings or contradictory ideas about something or someone: *some loved her, some hated her, few were ambivalent about her* | *an ambivalent attitude to technology.*
–DERIVATIVES **am·biv·a·lent·ly adv.**
–ORIGIN early 20th cent.: from *ambivalence* (from German *Ambivalenz*), on the pattern of *equivalent*.

am·bi·vert /'ambə,vərt/ ▶ **n.** Psychology a person whose personality has a balance of extrovert and introvert features.
–DERIVATIVES **am·bi·ver·sion** /,ambi'vərZHən/ **n.**
–ORIGIN 1920s: from Latin *ambi-* 'on both sides,' on the pattern of *extrovert* and *introvert*.

am·ble /'ambəl/ ▶ **v.** [no obj.] walk or move at a slow, relaxed pace: *they ambled along the riverbank* | *he ambled into the foyer.*
▶ **n.** a walk at a slow, relaxed pace, esp. for pleasure: *a peaceful riverside amble.*
–DERIVATIVES **am·bler** /-blər/ **n.**
–ORIGIN Middle English (originally denoting a horse's gait): from Old French *ambler*, from Latin *ambulare* 'to walk.'

am·bly·o·pi·a /,amblē'ōpēə/ ▶ **n.** Medicine impaired or dim vision without obvious defect or change in the eye.
–DERIVATIVES **am·bly·op·ic** /-'äpik/ **adj.**
–ORIGIN early 18th cent.: from Greek *ambluōpia* 'dim-sightedness,' from *ambluōpos* (adjective), from *amblus* 'dull' + *ōps*, *ōp-* 'eye.'

am·bo /'am,bō/ ▶ **n.** (pl. **ambos** or **ambones** /am'bōnēz/) (in an early Christian church) an oblong pulpit with steps at each end.
–ORIGIN mid 17th cent.: via medieval Latin from Greek *ambōn* 'rim' (in medieval Greek 'pulpit').

Am·boi·na wood /am'boinə/ (also **Amboyna wood**) ▶ **n.** the decorative wood of a rapidly growing Southeast Asian tree, often used for furniture making. ● The tree is *Pterocarpus indicus*, family Leguminosae.
–ORIGIN mid 19th cent.: named after *Amboina* Island (see AMBON).

Am·boi·nese /,amboi'nēz, -'nēs, ,äm-/ ▶ **adj.** of or relating to the island of Ambon, its people, or their language.
▶ **n.** **1** a native or inhabitant of Ambon.
2 the Indonesian language of this people.
–ORIGIN from *Amboina* (see AMBON) + -ESE.

Am·bon /äm'bôn, 'am,bän/ (also **Amboina** /am'boinə/) a mountainous island in eastern Indonesia, one of the Molucca Islands. ■ a port on this island, the capital of the Molucca Islands; pop. 204,200 (est. 2005).

Am·brose, St. /'am,brōz, -,brōs/ (*c.*339–397), doctor of the Church. As bishop of Milan from 374, he introduced much Eastern theology and liturgical practice into the West. Feast day, December 7.

am·bro·sia /am'brōZH(ē)ə/ ▶ **n.** Greek & Roman Mythology the food of the gods. ■ something very pleasing to taste or smell: *the tea was ambrosia after the slop I'd been drinking.* ■ a fungal product used as food by ambrosia beetles. ■ another term for BEE

PRONUNCIATION KEY ə *ago, up*; ər *over, fur*; a *hat*; ā *ate*; ä *car*; e *let*; ē *see*; i *fit*; ī *by*; NG *sing*; ō *go*; ô *law, for*; oi *toy*; o͝o *good*; o͞o *goo*; ou *out*; TH *thin*; T͟H *then*; ZH *vision*

BREAD. ■ a dessert made with oranges and shredded coconut.
– DERIVATIVES **am·bro·sial** adj.
– ORIGIN mid 16th cent.: via Latin from Greek, 'elixir of life,' from *ambrotos* 'immortal.'

am·bro·sia bee·tle ▶ n. a small dark wood-boring beetle, the adults and larvae of which feed on a fungus that they cultivate, called ambrosia. ● Genus *Platypus* (family Platypodidae), and *Xyleborus* and other genera (family Scolytidae).

am·bry /'ômbrē/ (also **aumbry**) ▶ n. (pl. **ambries**) a small recess or cupboard in the wall of a church.
– ORIGIN Middle English: from Old French *armarie*, from Latin *armarium* 'closet, chest,' from *arma* 'utensils.'

am·bu·lac·rum /,ambyə'lakrəm, -'lākrəm/ ▶ n. (pl. **ambulacra** /-'lakrə, -'lākrə/) Zoology (in a starfish or other echinoderm) each of the radially arranged bands, together with their underlying structures, through which the double rows of tube feet protrude.
– DERIVATIVES **am·bu·lac·ral** /-rəl/ adj.
– ORIGIN early 19th cent.: Latin, 'avenue,' from *ambulare* 'to walk.'

am·bu·lance /'ambyələns/ ▶ n. a vehicle specially equipped for taking sick or injured people to and from the hospital, esp. in emergencies.
– ORIGIN early 19th cent.: French, from *hôpital ambulant* 'mobile (horse-drawn) field hospital,' from Latin *ambulant-* 'walking' (see AMBULANT).

am·bu·lance chas·er ▶ n. derogatory a lawyer who specializes in bringing cases seeking damages for personal injury.
– ORIGIN late 19th cent.: from the reputation gained by certain lawyers for attending accidents and encouraging victims to sue.

am·bu·lant /'ambyələnt/ ▶ adj. Medicine (of a patient) able to walk around; not confined to bed. ■ (of treatment) not confining a patient to bed.
– ORIGIN early 17th cent.: from Latin *ambulant-* 'walking,' from *ambulare*.

am·bu·late /'ambyə,lāt/ ▶ v. [no obj.] formal or technical walk; move about: *making use of crutches to ambulate* | *tortoises are diurnally active, ambulating mainly over the course of the day.*
– DERIVATIVES **am·bu·la·tion** /,ambyə'lāsHən/ n.
– ORIGIN early 17th cent.: from Latin *ambulat-* 'walked,' from the verb *ambulare*.

am·bu·la·to·ry /'ambyələ,tôrē/ ▶ adj. relating to or adapted for walking. ■ Medicine able to walk; not bedridden: *ambulatory patients.* ■ Medicine relating to patients who are able to walk: *an ambulatory care facility.* ■ movable; mobile: *an ambulatory ophthalmic service.*
▶ n. (pl. **ambulatories**) a place for walking, esp. an aisle around the apse or a cloister in a church or monastery.
– ORIGIN mid 16th cent. (as a noun): from Latin *ambulatorius*, from *ambulare* 'to walk.'

am·bu·lo·ce·tus /,ambyələ'sētəs/ ▶ n. a large carnivorous amphibian (*Ambulocetus natans*, order Cetacea) of the Eocene epoch, an early ancestor of today's whales.
– ORIGIN 1990s: modern Latin, from Latin *ambulare* 'to walk' + *cetus* 'whale.'

am·bus·cade /'ambə,skād, ,ambə'skād/ ▶ n. dated an ambush.
▶ v. [with obj.] archaic attack from an ambush. ■ [no obj.] archaic lie in ambush: (as adj. **ambuscaded**) *ambuscaded thousands might swarm up over the embankment.*
– ORIGIN late 16th cent.: from French *embuscade*, from Italian *imboscata*, Spanish *emboscada*, or Portuguese *embuscada*, based on a late Latin word meaning 'to place in a wood'; related to BUSH.

am·bush /'am,bŏŏsH/ ▶ n. a surprise attack by people lying in wait in a concealed position: *seven members of a patrol were killed in an ambush* | *kidnappers waiting in ambush.*
▶ v. [with obj.] make a surprise attack on (someone) from a concealed position: *they were ambushed and taken prisoner by the enemy.* ■ confront (someone) suddenly and unexpectedly with unwelcome questions: *representatives were ambushed by camera crews.*
– ORIGIN Middle English (in the sense 'place troops in hiding in order to surprise an enemy'): from Old French *embusche* (noun), *embuschier* (verb), based on a late Latin word meaning 'to place in a wood'; related to BUSH. The noun use dates from the late 15th cent.

am·bush mar·ket·ing ▶ n. the practice by which a rival company attempts to associate its products with an event that already has official sponsors.

am-dram /'am ,dram/ ▶ n. informal, chiefly Brit. [treated as sing. or pl.] amateur dramatics: *a performance poised somewhere between slapstick and below-average am-dram.*
– ORIGIN blend.

AME ▶ abbr. African Methodist Episcopal.

a·me·ba /ə'mēbə/ (also **amoeba**) ▶ n. (pl. **amebas** or **amebae** /-bē/) a single-celled animal that catches food and moves about by extending fingerlike projections of protoplasm. Amebas are either free-living in damp environments or parasitic. ● Many families and genera in the phylum Rhizopoda, kingdom Protista, including the aquatic *Amoeba proteus*.
– DERIVATIVES **a·me·bic** /-bik/ adj., **a·me·boid** /-boid/ adj.
– ORIGIN mid 19th cent.: modern Latin, from Greek *amoibē* 'change, alternation.'

am·e·bi·a·sis /,amə'bīəsis/ (also **amoebiasis**) ▶ n. Medicine infection with amebas, esp. as causing dysentery.
– ORIGIN early 20th cent.: from AMEBA + -ASIS.

a·me·bic dys·en·ter·y /ə'mēbik/ ▶ n. dysentery caused by infection of the intestines by the protozoan *Entamoeba histolytica*, mostly in warm climates, and spread by contaminated food and water.

am·e·lan·chi·er /,amə'laNGkēər/ ▶ n. a tree or shrub of a genus that includes the juneberries. ● Genus *Amelanchier*, family Rosaceae.
– ORIGIN from French dialect *amelancier* 'medlar.'

a·me·lio·rate /ə'mēlyə,rāt, ə'mēlēə-/ ▶ v. [with obj.] make (something bad or unsatisfactory) better: *the reform did much to ameliorate living standards.*
– DERIVATIVES **a·me·lio·ra·tive** /-rətiv, -,rātiv/ adj., **a·me·lio·ra·tor** /-,rātər/ n.
– ORIGIN mid 18th cent.: alteration of MELIORATE, influenced by French *améliorer*, from *meilleur* 'better.'

a·me·lio·ra·tion /ə,mēlyə'rāsHən/ ▶ n. formal the act of making something better; improvement: *progress brings with it the amelioration of the human condition.*

a·men /'ä'men, ā'men/ ▶ exclam. uttered at the end of a prayer or hymn, meaning 'so be it.' ■ used to express agreement or assent: *amen to that!*
▶ n. an utterance of "amen."
– ORIGIN Old English, from ecclesiastical Latin, from Greek *amēn*, from Hebrew *'āmēn* 'truth, certainty,' used adverbially as expression of agreement or consent, and adopted in the Septuagint as a solemn expression of belief or affirmation.

a·me·na·ble /ə'mēnəbəl, ə'men-/ ▶ adj. (of a person) open and responsive to suggestion; easily persuaded or controlled: *parents who have had easy babies and amenable children.* ■ [predic.] (**amenable to**) (of a thing) capable of being acted upon in a particular way; susceptible to: *the patients had cardiac failure not amenable to medical treatment.*
– DERIVATIVES **a·me·na·bil·i·ty** /ə,mēnə'bilitē, ə,men-/ n., **a·me·na·bly** /-blē/ adv.
– ORIGIN late 16th cent. (in the sense 'liable to answer (to a law or tribunal)'): an Anglo-Norman French legal term, from Old French *amener* 'bring to,' from *a-* (from Latin *ad*) 'to' + *mener* 'bring' (from late Latin *minare* 'drive (animals),' from Latin *minari* 'threaten').

a·men cor·ner ▶ n. (in some Protestant churches) seats, usually near the preacher, occupied by those who lead responses from the congregation. ■ informal a group of people that give unwavering support.
– ORIGIN mid. 19th cent.

a·mend /ə'mend/ ▶ v. [with obj.] make minor changes in (a text) in order to make it fairer, more accurate, or more up-to-date: *the rule was amended to apply only to nonmembers.* ■ modify formally, as a legal document or legislative bill: *did she amend her original will later on?* | *pressuring Panama to amend its banking laws.* ■ make better; improve: *if you can amend or alter people's mindset.* ■ archaic put right: *a few things had gone wrong, but these had been amended.*
– DERIVATIVES **a·mend·a·ble** adj., **a·mend·er** n.
– ORIGIN Middle English: from Old French *amender*, based on Latin *emendare* (see EMEND).

a·mend·ment /ə'men(d)mənt/ ▶ n. a minor change in a document. ■ a change or addition to a legal or statutory document: *an amendment to existing bail laws.* ■ (**Amendment**) an article added to the US Constitution: *the First Amendment.* ■ something that is added to soil in order to improve its texture or fertility.
– ORIGIN Middle English (in the sense 'improvement, correction'): from Old French *amendement*, from *amender* (see AMEND).

a·mends /ə'mendz/ ▶ plural n. [treated as sing.] reparation or compensation.
– PHRASES **make amends** do something in order to make up for a wrong inflicted on someone: *try to make amends for the rude way you spoke to Lucy.* **an offer of amends** Law an offer to publish a correction and an apology for an act of libel.
– ORIGIN Middle English: from Old French *amendes* 'penalties, fine,' plural of *amende* 'reparation,' from *amender* (see AMEND).

a·men·i·ty /ə'menitē, ə'mē-/ ▶ n. (pl. **amenities**) (usu. **amenities**) a desirable or useful feature or facility of a building or place: *heating is regarded as a basic amenity.* ■ the pleasantness of a place or a person: *the exertion of amenity toward the boss.*
– ORIGIN late Middle English: from Old French *amenite* or Latin *amoenitas*, from *amoenus* 'pleasant.'

a·men·or·rhe·a /ā,menə'rēə/ (Brit. **amenorrhoea**) ▶ n. an abnormal absence of menstruation.
– ORIGIN early 19th cent.: from A-[1] 'without' + MENO- + -RRHEA.

am·ent /'āment, 'am-/ ▶ n. Botany a catkin.
– ORIGIN mid 18th cent.: from Latin *amentum* 'thong.'

a·men·tia /ā'mencHēə/ ▶ n. severe congenital mental handicap.
– ORIGIN late Middle English: from Latin, literally 'madness,' from *amens, ament-* 'mad,' from *a-* 'without' + *mens* 'the mind.'

Am·er·a·sian /,amər'āZHən/ ▶ adj. having one American and one Asian parent.
▶ n. a person with one American and one Asian parent.
– ORIGIN 1960s: blend of AMERICAN and ASIAN.

a·merce·ment /ə'mərsmənt/ ▶ n. English Law, historical a fine.
– DERIVATIVES **a·merce** v.
– ORIGIN late Middle English: from Anglo-Norman French *amerciment*, based on *estre amercie* 'be at the mercy of another' (with respect to the amount of a fine), from *a merci* 'at (the) mercy.'

A·mer·i·ca /ə'merikə/ (also **the Americas**) a landmass in the western hemisphere that consists of the continents of North and South America joined by the Isthmus of Panama. The continent was originally inhabited by American Indians and Inuits. The northeast coastline of North America was visited by Norse seamen in the 8th or 9th century, but for the modern world the continent was first reached by Christopher Columbus in 1492. ■ used as a name for the United States.
– ORIGIN the name *America* dates from the early 16th cent. and is believed to derive from the Latin form (*Americus*) of the name of Amerigo Vespucci, who sailed along the west coast of South America in 1501.

A·mer·i·can /ə'merikən/ ▶ adj. of, relating to, or characteristic of the United States or its inhabitants: *the election of a new American president.* ■ relating to or denoting the continents of America: *the American continent south of the tropic of Cancer.*
▶ n. **1** a native or citizen of the United States. ■ [usu. with adj.] a native or inhabitant of any of the countries of North, South, or Central America.
2 the English language as it is used in the United States; American English.
– DERIVATIVES **A·mer·i·can·ness** n.
– ORIGIN from modern Latin *Americanus*, from AMERICA.

A·mer·i·ca·na /ə,meri'känə, -'kanə/ ▶ plural n. things associated with the culture and history of America, esp. the United States.

A·mer·i·can al·oe another term for CENTURY PLANT.

A·mer·i·can bald ea·gle ▶ n. another term for BALD EAGLE.

A·mer·i·can cheese ▶ n. a type of mild-flavored semisoft processed cheese.

A·mer·i·can Civ·il War the war between the northern US states (usually known as the Union) and the Confederate states of the South, 1861–65.

> The war was fought over the issues of slavery and states' rights. The pro-slavery southern states seceded from the Federal Union following the election of Abraham Lincoln on an anti-slavery platform, but were defeated by the North.

A·mer·i·can croc·o·dile ▶ n. a crocodile with a long tapering head, occurring from southernmost Florida to Ecuador. ● *Crocodylus acutus*, family Crocodylidae.

American crocodile

A·mer·i·can de·pos·i·tar·y re·ceipt (abbr.: ADR) (also **American depositary share**) ▶ n. (in the

US) a negotiable certificate of title to a number of shares in a non-US company that are deposited in an overseas bank.

A·mer·i·can dream ▶ **n.** the traditional social ideals of the US, such as equality, democracy, and material prosperity.

A·mer·i·can ea·gle ▶ **n.** another term for BALD EAGLE.

A·mer·i·can e·gret ▶ **n.** another term for GREAT EGRET.

A·mer·i·can Eng·lish ▶ **n.** the English language as spoken and written in the US.

A·mer·i·can Falls see NIAGARA FALLS.

A·mer·i·can Fed·er·a·tion of La·bor a federation of North American labor unions, merged in 1955 with the Congress of Industrial Organizations to form the American Federation of Labor and Congress of Industrial Organizations (AFL–CIO).

A·mer·i·can foot·ball ▶ **n.** British term for FOOTBALL.

A·mer·i·can Goth·ic ▶ **n.** a noted 1930 painting by Grant Wood (1891–1942), depicting a dour-faced farmer and his daughter in front of their house, with a Gothic-style window in the background. It is representative of traditional American rural values, and is widely copied and parodied. ■ [as modifier] conservative in moral and social views.

A·mer·i·can In·de·pend·ence, War of British term for AMERICAN REVOLUTION.

A·mer·i·can In·di·an ▶ **n.** a member of any of the indigenous peoples of North, Central, and South America, esp. those of North America.
▶ **adj.** of or relating to any of these groups.

> **USAGE** The term **American Indian** has been steadily replaced, especially in official contexts, by the more recent term **Native American** (first recorded in the 1950s and becoming prominent in the 1970s). The latter is preferred by some as being a more accurate description (the word *Indian* recalling Columbus's assumption that, on reaching America, he had reached the east coast of India). **American Indian** is still widespread in general use, however, partly because it is not normally regarded as offensive by American Indians themselves. See also NATIVE AMERICAN, AMERINDIAN, and INDIAN.

A·mer·i·can·ism /əˈmerikəˌnizəm/ ▶ **n.** a word or phrase peculiar to or originating in the US. ■ the qualities regarded as definitive of America or Americans: *the same Americanism that Whitman sees in the farmer.*

A·mer·i·can·ize /əˈmerikəˌnīz/ ▶ **v.** [with obj.] make American in character or nationality: *trying to Americanize the immigrant children* | (as adj. **Americanized**) *an Americanized accent.*
– DERIVATIVES **A·mer·i·can·i·za·tion** /əˌmerikəniˈzāsʜən/ **n.**

A·mer·i·can League ▶ **n.** one of the two major leagues in American professional baseball.

A·mer·i·can Le·gion an association of former US servicemen formed in 1919.

A·mer·i·can lin·den another name for BASSWOOD.

A·mer·i·can lo·tus ▶ **n.** see LOTUS.

A·mer·i·ca·no /əˌmeriˈkänō/ (also **café Americano**) ▶ **n.** (pl. **Americanos**) a drink of espresso diluted with hot water.
– ORIGIN American Spanish, literally 'American (coffee).'

A·mer·i·can or·gan ▶ **n.** a type of reed organ resembling the harmonium but in which air is sucked (not blown) through reeds.

A·mer·i·can plan ▶ **n.** (in hotels) a system of paying a single daily rate that covers the room and all meals. Often contrasted with EUROPEAN PLAN.

A·mer·i·can Rev·o·lu·tion the war of 1775–83 in which the American colonists won independence from British rule. Called in Britain the WAR OF AMERICAN INDEPENDENCE.

> The war was triggered by resentment at the economic policies of Britain, particularly the right of Parliament to tax the colonies, and by the exclusion of the colonists from participation in political decisions affecting their interests. Following disturbances such as the Boston Tea Party of 1773, fighting broke out in 1775; a year later the Declaration of Independence was signed. The Americans gained the support of France and Spain, and French sea power eventually played a crucial role in the decisive surrender of a British army at Yorktown in 1781.

Amer·i·can Riv·er a river in north central California that joins the Sacramento River at Sacramento. Gold was discovered here in 1848, setting off the California gold rush.

A·mer·i·can Sad·dle Horse ▶ **n.** a light, strong horse of a breed developed in Kentucky to be comfortable to ride over long distances.

A·mer·i·can Sa·mo·a /səˈmōə/ an unincorporated overseas territory of the US that is composed of a group of islands in the southern Pacific Ocean, east of Western Samoa and south of Kiribati; pop. 65,600 (est. 2009); capital, Fagatogo. The US acquired rights to the islands by agreement with Germany and Britain in 1899, and the two main islands were ceded to the US by their chiefs in April 1900.

A·mer·i·can Sign Lan·guage (abbr.: **ASL**) ▶ **n.** a form of sign language developed in the US for the use of people who are deaf, consisting of over 4,000 signs.

A·mer·i·can Stand·ard Ver·sion (abbr.: **ASV**) ▶ **n.** an English translation of the Bible published in the US in 1901, based on the Revised Version of 1881–95 with the incorporation of material produced by American scholars.

A·mer·i·cas /əˈmerikəz/ (**the Americas**) another name for AMERICA.

A·mer·i·ca's Cup an international yachting race held every three to four years.

A·mer·i·ca's Dair·y·land a nickname for the state of WISCONSIN[1].

am·er·i·ci·um /aməˈrisʜēəm/ ▶ **n.** the chemical element of atomic number 95, a radioactive metal of the actinide series. (Symbol: **Am**)

> Americium does not occur naturally and was first made by bombarding plutonium with neutrons. It has been used in industrial measuring equipment as a source of gamma rays.

– ORIGIN 1940s: from AMERICA (where it was first made) + -IUM.

Am·er·in·di·an /ˌaməˈrindēən/ (also **Amerind** /ˈamərind/) ▶ **adj. & n.** another term for AMERICAN INDIAN, used chiefly in anthropological and linguistic contexts.
– ORIGIN late 19th cent.: blend of AMERICAN and INDIAN.

> **USAGE** See usage at INDIAN.

Ames /āmz/ a city in central Iowa, home to Iowa State University; pop. 56,510 (est. 2008).

Am·e·slan /ˈam(i)ˌslan/ another term for AMERICAN SIGN LANGUAGE.
– ORIGIN 1970s: acronym.

Ames test /āmz/ ▶ **n.** Medicine a test to determine the mutagenic activity of chemicals by observing whether they cause mutations in sample bacteria.
– ORIGIN 1970s: named after Bruce N. *Ames* (born 1928), the American biochemist who devised it.

am·e·thyst /ˈaməTHəst/ ▶ **n.** a precious stone consisting of a violet or purple variety of quartz. ■ a violet or purple color.
– DERIVATIVES **am·e·thys·tine** /ˌaməˈTHistin, -ˌtīn/ **adj.**
– ORIGIN Middle English: via Old French from Latin *amethystus*, from Greek *amethustos* 'not drunken' (because the stone was believed to prevent intoxication).

Amex /ˈameks/ ▶ **abbr.** ■ trademark American Express. ■ American Stock Exchange.

Am·ha·ra /ämˈhärə/ ▶ **n.** (pl. **same** or **Amharas**) a member of an Amharic-speaking Semitic people of central Ethiopia.

Am·har·ic /amˈharik/ ▶ **n.** the Semitic language descended from Ge'ez that is the official language of Ethiopia.
▶ **adj.** of or relating to this language.
– ORIGIN mid 18th cent.: from AMHARA + -IC.

Am·herst[1] /ˈam(h)ərst/ **1** a town in west central Massachusetts, home to several colleges and universities; pop. 35,565 (est. 2008).
2 a town in western New York, northeast of Buffalo; pop. 115,563 (est. 2008).

Am·herst[2] /ˈaməst/, Lord Jeffrey (1717–97), English soldier and military commander in North America. He was appointed governor general of British North America 1760–63 and served as commander in chief of the British army 1772–95.

a·mi·a·bil·i·ty /ˌāmēəˈbilitē/ ▶ **n.** the quality of having a friendly and pleasant manner; geniality: *his good-natured amiability.*

a·mi·a·ble /ˈāmēəbəl/ ▶ **adj.** having or displaying a friendly and pleasant manner: *an amiable, unassuming fellow.*
– DERIVATIVES **a·mi·a·bly** /-blē/ **adv.**, **a·mi·a·ble·ness n.**
– ORIGIN late Middle English (originally in the senses 'kind' and 'lovely, lovable'): via Old French from late Latin *amicabilis* 'amicable.' The current sense, influenced by modern French *aimable* 'trying to please,' dates from the mid 18th cent.

am·i·ca·ble /ˈamikəbəl/ ▶ **adj.** (of relations between people) having a spirit of friendliness; without serious disagreement or rancor: *there will be an amicable settlement of the dispute.*
– DERIVATIVES **am·i·ca·bil·i·ty** /ˌamikəˈbilitē/ **n.**, **am·i·ca·bly** /-blē/ **adv.**
– ORIGIN late Middle English (in the sense 'pleasant, benign,' applied to things): from late Latin *amicabilis*, from Latin *amicus* 'friend.'

am·ice[1] /ˈamis/ ▶ **n.** a white linen cloth worn on the neck and shoulders, under the alb, by a priest celebrating the Eucharist.
– ORIGIN late Middle English: from medieval Latin *amicia, amisia*, of unknown origin.

am·ice[2] ▶ **n.** a cap, hood, or cape worn by members of certain religious orders.
– ORIGIN late Middle English: from Old French *aumusse*, from medieval Latin *almucia*, of unknown origin.

a·mi·cus /əˈmēkəs, əˈmī-/ (in full **amicus curiae** /ˈkyŏŏrēˌī, -ēˌē/) ▶ **n.** (pl. **amici** /əˈmēkē, əˈmīkī/, **amici curiae**) an impartial adviser, often voluntary, to a court of law in a particular case: [as modifier] *he was planning to advance this position in an amicus brief.*
– ORIGIN early 17th cent.: from modern Latin *amicus curiae*, literally 'friend of the court.'

a·mid /əˈmid/ ▶ **prep.** surrounded by; in the middle of: *our dream home, set amid magnificent rolling countryside.* ■ in an atmosphere or against a background of: *talks broke down amid accusations of a hostile takeover bid.*
– ORIGIN Middle English *amidde(s)*.

A·mi·dah /əˈmēdä/ ▶ **n.** Judaism a prayer, part of the Jewish liturgy, consisting of a varying number of blessings recited while the worshipers stand.
– ORIGIN late 19th cent.: Hebrew, literally 'standing.'

am·ide /ˈamīd, -id/ ▶ **n.** Chemistry an organic compound containing the group $-C(O)NH_2$, related to ammonia by replacing a hydrogen atom by an acyl group. ■ a compound derived from ammonia by replacement of a hydrogen atom by a metal, containing the anion NH_2^-.
– ORIGIN mid 19th cent.: from AMMONIA + -IDE.

a·mid·ships /əˈmidˌsʜips/ (also **amidship**) ▶ **adv. & adj.** in the middle of a ship: [as adv.] *the destroyer rammed her amidships* | [as adj.] *an amidships engine.*
– ORIGIN late 17th cent.: from A-[2] (expressing position or direction) + MIDSHIPS (as a noun meaning 'midship'), influenced by AMID.

a·midst /əˈmidst/ ▶ **prep.** variant of AMID.

Am·i·ens /ˈamēənz, ämˈyeɴ/ a town in northern France; pop. 139,271 (2006).

a·mi·go /əˈmēgō/ ▶ **n.** (pl. **amigos**) informal used to address or refer to a friend, chiefly in Spanish-speaking areas: *I will think about it, amigo.*
– ORIGIN mid 19th cent.: Spanish.

A·min /äˈmēn/, Idi (1925–2003), Ugandan soldier and head of state 1971–79; full name *Idi Amin Dada*. He was deposed after a rule that was characterized by the murder of political opponents.

A·min·di·vi Is·lands /ˌəmənˈdēvē/ the northernmost group of islands in Lakshadweep, India's Union Territory in the Indian Ocean.

a·mine /əˈmēn, ˈamēn/ ▶ **n.** Chemistry an organic compound derived from ammonia by replacement of one or more hydrogen atoms by organic radicals.
– ORIGIN mid 19th cent.: from AMMONIA + -INE[4].

a·mi·no /əˈmēnō/ ▶ **n.** [as modifier] Chemistry the group $-NH_2$, present in amino acids, amides, and many amines.
– ORIGIN late 19th cent.: from AMINE.

amino- ▶ **comb. form** designating or containing the group $-NH_2$: *aminobutyric.*

a·mi·no ac·id ▶ **n.** Biochemistry a simple organic compound containing both a carboxyl ($-COOH$) and an amino ($-NH_2$) group.

> Amino acids occur naturally in plant and animal tissues and are the basic constituents of proteins.

a·mir /əˈmi(ə)r/ ▶ **n.** an Arab ruler.
– ORIGIN late 16th cent.: from Persian and Urdu, from Arabic *'amīr* 'commander,' from *'amara* 'to command'; compare with ADMIRAL, EMIR.

Am·i·rante Is·lands /ˈaməˌrant/ a group of coral islands in the Indian Ocean that form part of the Seychelles.

A·mis[1] /ˈāməs/, Sir Kingsley (1922–95), English novelist and poet, who achieved popular success with his first novel, *Lucky Jim* (1954). Other notable works: *The Old Devils* (1986), *The Folks that Live on the Hill* (1990), and *You Can't Do Both* (1994).

A·mis[2], Martin (Louis) (1949–), English novelist, son of Kingsley Amis. Notable works: *The Rachel Papers* (1973), *Money* (1984), and *Night Train* (1997).

A·mish /ˈämisʜ/ ▶ **plural n.** the members of a strict Mennonite sect that established major settlements in Pennsylvania, Ohio, and elsewhere in North America from 1720 onward.
▶ **adj.** of or relating to this sect.
– ORIGIN mid 19th cent.: apparently from German *amisch*.

Am·ish Coun·try name for areas, chiefly in southeastern Pennsylvania and northeastern Ohio, that are inhabited by the Amish.

a·miss /əˈmis/ ▶ **adj.** [predic.] not quite right; inappropriate or out of place: *there was something amiss about his calculations.*
▶ **adv.** wrongly or inappropriately: *how terrible was the danger of her loving amiss.*
– PHRASES **take something amiss** be offended by something that is said, typically through misinterpreting the intentions behind it: *don't take this amiss, it's all good-humored teasing.*
– ORIGIN Middle English: probably from Old Norse *á mis* 'so as to miss,' from *á* 'on' + *mis* (related to MISS[1]).

am·i·tot·ic /ˌāmīˈtätik, ˌamī-/ ▶ **adj.** Biology relating to or denoting the division of a cell nucleus into two parts by constriction without the involvement of a mitotic apparatus.
– DERIVATIVES **am·i·to·sis** /-ˈtōsis/ **n.**, **am·i·tot·i·cal·ly** /-ik(ə)lē/ **adv.**

am·i·trip·ty·line /ˌamiˈtriptəˌlēn, -lin/ ▶ **n.** Medicine an antidepressant drug of the tricyclic group, with a mild tranquilizing action.
– ORIGIN 1960s: from *ami(ne)* + TRI- + *(he)ptyl* + -INE[4].

am·i·ty /ˈamitē/ ▶ **n.** a friendly relationship: *international amity and goodwill.*
– ORIGIN late Middle English: from Old French *amitie*, based on Latin *amicus* 'friend.'

Am·man /äˈmän, əˈmän, əˈman/ the capital of Jordan, located in the northwestern part of the country; pop. 1,307,017 (2004).

am·me·ter /ˈa(m)ˌmētər/ ▶ **n.** an instrument for measuring electric current in amperes.
– ORIGIN late 19th cent.: from AMPERE + -METER.

am·mo /ˈamō/ ▶ **n.** informal term for AMMUNITION.

Am·mon /ˈamən/ Greek and Roman form of AMUN.

am·mo·nia /əˈmōnyə, -nēə/ ▶ **n.** a colorless gas with a characteristic pungent smell. It dissolves in water to give a strongly alkaline solution. ● Chem. formula: NH_3. ■ a solution of this gas, used as a cleaning fluid.
– ORIGIN late 18th cent.: modern Latin, from *sal ammoniacus* (see SAL AMMONIAC).

am·mo·ni·a·cal /ˌaməˈnīikəl/ ▶ **adj.** of or containing ammonia.
– ORIGIN mid 18th cent.: from Middle English *ammoniac*, via Old French from Latin *ammoniacus*. This represented the Greek word *ammōniakos* 'of Ammon,' used as a name for the salt and gum obtained near the temple of *Jupiter Ammon* (the Greek name for the Egyptian deity *Amen*) at Siwa in Egypt. Compare with SAL AMMONIAC.

am·mo·ni·at·ed /əˈmōnēˌātid/ ▶ **adj.** combined or treated with ammonia.
– DERIVATIVES **am·mo·ni·a·tion** /əˌmōnēˈāsʜən/ **n.**

am·mo·nite /ˈaməˌnīt/ ▶ **n.** an ammonoid that belongs to the order *Ammonitida*, typically having elaborately frilled suture lines. ● Typified by ammonoids of the order Ammonitida.
– ORIGIN mid 18th cent.: from modern Latin *ammonites*, from medieval Latin *cornu Ammonis* 'horn of Ammon,' from the fossil's resemblance to the ram's horn associated with Jupiter Ammon (see AMMONIACAL).

ammonite

am·mo·ni·um /əˈmōnēəm/ ▶ **n.** [as modifier] Chemistry the cation NH_4^+, present in solutions of ammonia and in salts derived from ammonia.
– ORIGIN early 19th cent.: from AMMONIA + -IUM.

am·mo·ni·um car·bon·ate ▶ **n.** Chemistry a white crystalline solid that slowly decomposes giving off ammonia and is an ingredient of sal volatile. ● Chem. formula: $(NH_4)_2CO_3$. Commercial forms often contain other, related, salts.

am·mo·ni·um chlo·ride ▶ **n.** Chemistry a white crystalline salt used chiefly in dry cells, as a mordant, and as soldering flux. Also called SAL AMMONIAC. ● Chem. formula: NH_4Cl.

am·mo·ni·um ni·trate ▶ **n.** Chemistry a white crystalline solid used as a fertilizer and as a component of some explosives. ● Chem. formula: NH_4NO_3.

am·mo·noid /ˈaməˌnoid/ Paleontology ▶ **n.** an extinct cephalopod mollusk with a flat-coiled spiral shell, found commonly as a fossil in marine deposits from the Devonian to the Cretaceous periods. ● Subclass Ammonoidea, class Cephalopoda: numerous families. See AMMONITE, CERATITE, and GONIATITE.
▶ **adj.** of or relating to the ammonoids.
– ORIGIN mid 19th cent.: from modern Latin *Ammonoidea*, based on AMMON (see AMMONITE).

am·mu·ni·tion /ˌamyəˈnisʜən/ ▶ **n. 1** a supply or quantity of bullets and shells.
2 considerations that can be used to support one's case in debate: *these figures provide ammunition to the argument for more resources.*
– ORIGIN late 16th cent.: from obsolete French *amunition*, alteration (by wrong division) of *la munition* 'the munition' (see MUNITION).

am·ne·sia /amˈnēzʜə/ ▶ **n.** a partial or total loss of memory.
– DERIVATIVES **am·ne·si·ac** /amˈnēzēˌak, -zʜēˌak/ **n. & adj.**, **am·ne·sic** /-zik, -sik/ **adj. & n.**, **am·nes·tic** /amˈnestik/ **adj.**
– ORIGIN late 18th cent.: from Greek *amnēsia* 'forgetfulness.'

am·nes·ty /ˈamnistē/ ▶ **n.** (pl. **amnesties**) an official pardon for people who have been convicted of political offenses: *an amnesty for political prisoners* | *the new law granted amnesty to those who illegally left the country.* ■ an undertaking by the authorities to take no action against specified offenses or offenders during a fixed period: *a month-long weapons amnesty.*
▶ **v.** (**amnesties, amnestying, amnestied**) [with obj.] grant an official pardon to: *the guerrillas would be amnestied and allowed to return to civilian life.*
– ORIGIN late 16th cent.: via Latin from Greek *amnēstia* 'forgetfulness.'

Am·nes·ty In·ter·na·tion·al an independent international organization in support of human rights, esp. for prisoners of conscience. It was awarded the Nobel Peace Prize in 1977.

am·ni·o /ˈamnēˌō/ ▶ **n.** (pl. **amnios**) informal term for AMNIOCENTESIS.

am·ni·o·cen·te·sis /ˌamnēōsenˈtēsis/ ▶ **n.** (pl. **amniocenteses** /-sēz/) Medicine the sampling of amniotic fluid using a hollow needle inserted into the uterus, to screen for developmental abnormalities in a fetus.
– ORIGIN 1950s: from AMNION + Greek *kentēsis* 'pricking' (from *kentein* 'to prick').

am·ni·on /ˈamnēˌän, -ən/ ▶ **n.** (pl. - or **amnionia** /-nēə/) the innermost membrane that encloses the embryo of a mammal, bird, or reptile.
– DERIVATIVES **am·ni·ot·ic** /ˌamnēˈätik/ **adj.**
– ORIGIN mid 17th cent.: from Greek, 'caul,' diminutive of *amnos* 'lamb.'

am·ni·ote /ˈamnēˌōt/ ▶ **n.** Zoology an animal whose embryo develops in an amnion and chorion and has an allantois; a mammal, bird, or reptile.
– ORIGIN late 19th cent.: from modern Latin *Amniota*, back-formation from *amniotic* (see AMNION).

am·ni·ot·ic flu·id /ˌamnēˈätik/ ▶ **n.** the fluid surrounding a fetus within the amnion.

amn't /ant, ˈamənt/ chiefly Scottish & Irish ▶ **contraction** am not.

USAGE see usage at AREN'T.

a·moe·ba ▶ **n.** (pl. **amoebas** or **amoebae** /-bē/) variant spelling of AMEBA.
– DERIVATIVES **a·moe·bic adj.**, **a·moe·boid adj.**

a·mok /əˈmək, əˈmäk/ (also **amuck**) ▶ **adv.** (in phrase **run amok**) behave uncontrollably and disruptively: *stone-throwing anarchists running amok* | figurative *her feelings seemed to be running amok.*
– ORIGIN mid 17th cent.: via Portuguese *amouco*, from Malay *amok* 'rushing in a frenzy.' Early use was as a noun denoting a Malay in a homicidal frenzy; the adverb use dates from the late 17th cent.

a·mo·le /əˈmōlā, -lē/ ▶ **n.** a plant of a group native to Mexico and the southern US whose roots are used as detergent, esp. the soap plant or the lechuguilla.
– ORIGIN mid 19th cent.: Mexican Spanish.

A·mon variant spelling of AMUN.

a·mong /əˈməɴɢ/ (chiefly Brit. also **amongst** /əˈməɴɢst/) ▶ **prep. 1** surrounded by; in the company of: *wild strawberries hidden among the roots of the trees* | *you're among friends.*
2 being a member or members of (a larger set): *he was among the first 29 students enrolled* | *snakes are among the animals most feared by humans.*
3 occurring in or practiced by (some members of a community): *a drop in tooth decay among children* | *this pronunciation is not popular among the general public* | *rooting out abuses among the clergy.* ■ involving most or all members of a group reciprocally: *members of the government bickered among themselves.*
4 indicating a division, choice, or differentiation involving three or more participants: *the king called the three princesses to divide his kingdom among them* | *choosing a privatization scheme from among five models.*
– ORIGIN Old English *ongemang* (from *on* 'in' + *gemang* 'assemblage, mingling'). The *-st* of *amongst* represents *-s* (adverbial genitive) + *-t* probably by association with superlatives (as in *against*).

USAGE See usage at BETWEEN.

a·mon·til·la·do /əˌmäntlˈädō, -təˈyädō/ ▶ **n.** (pl. **amontillados**) a medium dry sherry.
– ORIGIN Spanish, from *Montilla*, the name of a town in southern Spain where the original wine was produced.

a·mor·al /āˈmôrəl/ ▶ **adj.** lacking a moral sense; unconcerned with the rightness or wrongness of something: *an amoral attitude to sex.*
– DERIVATIVES **a·mo·ral·i·ty** /ˌāməˈralitē/ **n.**, **a·mor·al·ism** /-ˌlizəm/ **n.**, **a·mor·al·ist** /-list/ **n.**

USAGE See usage at IMMORAL.

am·o·ret·to /ˌaməˈretō/ ▶ **n.** (pl. **amoretti** /-ˈretē/) a representation of Cupid in a work of art.
– ORIGIN late 17th cent. (denoting a lover or a love song): Italian, diminutive of *amore* 'love,' from Latin *amor*.

am·o·rist /ˈamərist/ ▶ **n.** a person who is in love or who writes about love.
– ORIGIN late 16th cent.: from Latin *amor* or French *amour* 'love' + -IST.

Am·o·rite /ˈaməˌrīt/ ▶ **n.** a member of seminomadic people living in Mesopotamia, Palestine, and Syria in the 3rd millennium BC, founders of Mari on the Euphrates and the first dynasty of Babylon.
▶ **adj.** of or relating to this people.
– ORIGIN from Hebrew *'ĕmōrī*, from Akkadian *'amurrū* + -ITE[1].

a·mo·ro·so[1] /ˌäməˈrōsō/ ▶ **adv. & adj.** Music (esp. as a direction) in a loving or tender manner.
– ORIGIN Italian, from medieval Latin *amorosus* (see AMOROUS).

a·mo·ro·so[2] ▶ **n.** a sweetened oloroso sherry.
– ORIGIN late 19th cent.: Spanish, literally 'amorous,' from medieval Latin *amorosus* (see AMOROUS).

am·o·rous /ˈamərəs/ ▶ **adj.** showing, feeling, or relating to sexual desire: *she rejected his amorous advances.*
– DERIVATIVES **am·o·rous·ly adv.**, **am·o·rous·ness n.**
– ORIGIN Middle English: via Old French from medieval Latin *amorosus*, from Latin *amor* 'love.'

a·mor·phous /əˈmôrfəs/ ▶ **adj.** without a clearly defined shape or form: *amorphous blue forms and straight black lines.* ■ vague; ill-organized; unclassifiable: *make explicit the amorphous statements.* ■ (of a group of people or an organization) lacking a clear structure or focus: *an amorphous and leaderless legislature.* ■ Mineralogy & Chemistry (of a solid) noncrystalline; having neither definite form nor apparent structure.
– DERIVATIVES **a·mor·phous·ly adv.**, **a·mor·phous·ness n.**
– ORIGIN mid 18th cent.: from modern Latin *amorphus*, from Greek *amorphos* 'shapeless' (from *a-* 'without' + *morphē* 'form') + -OUS.

am·or·tize /ˈamərˌtīz/ ▶ **v.** [with obj.] reduce or extinguish (a debt) by money regularly put aside: *loan fees can be amortized over the life of the mortgage.* ■ gradually write off the initial cost of (an asset): *they want to amortize the tooling costs quickly.*
– DERIVATIVES **am·or·ti·za·tion** /ˌamərtiˈzāsʜən, əˌmôrti-/ **n.**
– ORIGIN late Middle English (in the senses 'deaden' and 'transfer (land) to a corporation in mortmain'): from Old French *amortiss-*, lengthened stem of *amortir*, based on Latin *ad* 'to, at' + *mors, mort-* 'death.'

A·mos /ˈāməs/ a Hebrew minor prophet (*c.*760 BC), a shepherd of Tekoa, near Jerusalem. ■ a book of the Bible containing his prophecies.

am·o·site /ˈaməˌsīt/ ▶ **n.** an iron-rich amphibole asbestos, mined in South Africa.
– ORIGIN early 20th cent.: from the initial letters of *Asbestos Mines of South Africa* + -ITE[1].

a·mount /əˈmount/ ▶ **n.** a quantity of something, typically the total of a thing or things in number,

size, value, or extent: *the sport gives an enormous* ***amount of*** *pleasure to many people | the substance is harmless if taken in small amounts.* ■ a sum of money: *they have spent a colossal amount rebuilding the stadium.*
▶ **v.** [no obj.] **(amount to)** come to be (the total) when added together: *losses amounted to over 10 million dollars.* ■ be the equivalent of: *their actions amounted to a conspiracy | what this guy was doing clearly did amount to persecution.* ■ develop into; become: *you'll never amount to anything.*
– PHRASES **any amount of** a great deal or number of: *a good marriage can withstand any amount of external pressure.* **no amount of** not even the greatest possible amount of: *no amount of talk is going to change anything.*
– ORIGIN Middle English (as a verb): from Old French *amunter*, from *amont* 'upward,' literally 'uphill,' from Latin *ad montem*. The noun use dates from the early 18th cent.

a·mour /ə'mo͝or, ä'mo͝or/ ▶ **n.** a secret or illicit love affair or lover.
– ORIGIN Middle English (originally in the sense 'love, affection'): via Old French from Latin *amor* 'love.' The current sense dates from the late 16th cent.

a·mour fou /ä'mo͝or 'fo͞o/ ▶ **n.** uncontrollable or obsessive passion.
– ORIGIN 1970s: French, literally 'insane love.'

a·mour pro·pre /ä,mo͝or 'prôpr(ə)/ ▶ **n.** a sense of one's own worth; self-respect: *few indications in him of ordinary amour propre or common vanity.*
– ORIGIN late 18th cent.: French, literally 'self-esteem, vanity.'

a·mox·i·cil·lin /ə,mäksə'silin/ (also **amoxycillin**) ▶ **n.** a broad-spectrum semisynthetic penicillin, closely related to ampicillin but better absorbed when taken orally, used esp. for ear and upper respiratory infections.
– ORIGIN late 20th cent.: blend of AMINO + contractions of HYDROXY- + PENICILLIN.

A·moy /ä'moi/ another name for **XIAMEN**.

AMP ▶ **abbr.** Biochemistry adenosine monophosphate.

amp[1] /amp/ ▶ **n.** short for AMPERE.

amp[2] ▶ **n.** informal short for AMPLIFIER.
▶ **v.** [with obj.] **1** (often **amp something up**) play (music) through electric amplification: *their willingness to amp up traditional songs virtually began the folk-rock genre.*
2 (as adj. **amped** or **amped up**) informal full of nervous energy: *third-ranked Ohio State visits an amped-up Madison.*

Am·pa·kine /'ampə,kīn/ ▶ **n.** trademark any of a class of synthetic compounds that facilitate transmission of nerve impulses in the brain and appear to improve memory and learning capacity.
– ORIGIN 1990s: from *AMPA* (an acronym denoting certain receptors in the brain) + Greek *kinein* 'to move.'

am·pe·log·ra·pher /,ampə'lägrəfər/ ▶ **n.** an expert in the study and classification of cultivated varieties of grape.
– DERIVATIVES **am·pe·log·ra·phy** **n.**
– ORIGIN late 19th cent.: via French from Greek *ampelos* 'vine' + -GRAPHER.

am·pe·lop·sis /,ampə'läpsis/ ▶ **n.** (pl. **same**) any of several woody vines of the grape family. ● Genus *Ampelopsis*, family Vitaceae: several species, including **American ampelopsis** (*A. cordata*), the PEPPER VINE (*ampelopsis arborea*) and the PORCELAINBERRY (*A. brevipedunculata*).
– ORIGIN modern Latin, from Greek *ampelos* 'vine' + *opsis* 'appearance.'

am·per·age /'amp(ə)rij/ ▶ **n.** the strength of an electric current in amperes.

am·pere /'am,pi(ə)r/ (abbr.: **A**) ▶ **n.** a unit of electric current equal to a flow of one coulomb per second. ● The SI base unit of electric current, 1 ampere is precisely defined as that constant current which, if maintained in two straight parallel conductors of infinite length, of negligible circular cross-section, and placed 1 meter apart in a vacuum, would produce between these conductors a force of 2×10^{-7} newton per meter.
– ORIGIN late 19th cent.: named after A. M. AMPÈRE.

Am·père /äN'per/, André-Marie (1775–1836), French physicist, mathematician, and philosopher, who analyzed the relationship between magnetic force and electric current.

am·per·sand /'ampər,sand/ ▶ **n.** the sign & (standing for *and*, as in *Smith & Co.*, or the Latin *et*, as in *&c.*
– ORIGIN mid 19th cent.: alteration of *and per se and* '& by itself is *and*,' chanted as an aid to learning the sign.

am·phet·a·mine /am'fetə,mēn, -min/ ▶ **n.** a synthetic, addictive, mood-altering drug, used illegally as a stimulant and legally as a prescription drug to treat children with ADD and adults with narcolepsy. ● Alternative name: **1-phenyl-2-aminopropane** (or one of its salts, esp. **amphetamine sulfate**); chem. formula: $C_6H_5CH_2CH(CH_3)NH_2$.
– ORIGIN 1930s: abbreviation of its chemical name, *a(lpha-)m(ethyl) phe(ne)t(hyl)amine.*

amphi- ▶ **comb. form 1** both: *amphibian.* ■ of both kinds: *amphipod.* ■ on both sides: *amphiprostyle.*
2 around: *amphitheater.*
– ORIGIN from Greek.

am·phib·i·an /am'fibēən/ ▶ **n.** Zoology a cold-blooded vertebrate animal of a class that comprises the frogs, toads, newts, and salamanders. They are distinguished by having an aquatic gill-breathing larval stage followed (typically) by a terrestrial lung-breathing adult stage. ● Class Amphibia: orders Urodela (newts and salamanders), Anura (frogs and toads), and Gymnophiona (caecilians). ■ a seaplane, tank, or other vehicle that can operate on land and on water.
▶ **adj.** Zoology of or relating to this class of animals: *reptile and amphibian biology.*
– ORIGIN mid 17th cent. (in the sense 'having two modes of existence or of doubtful nature'): from modern Latin *amphibium* 'an amphibian,' from Greek *amphibion* (noun use of *amphibios* 'living both in water and on land,' from *amphi* 'both' + *bios* 'life').

am·phib·i·ous /am'fibēəs/ ▶ **adj.** relating to, living in, or suited for both land and water: *amphibious habitats | an amphibious vehicle.* ■ (of a military operation) involving forces landed from the sea: *an amphibious assault.* ■ (of forces) trained for such operations.
– ORIGIN mid 17th cent.: from modern Latin *amphibium*, from Greek *amphibion* (see AMPHIBIAN) + -OUS.

am·phi·bole /'amfə,bōl/ ▶ **n.** any of a class of rock-forming silicate or aluminosilicate minerals typically occurring as fibrous or columnar crystals.
– ORIGIN early 19th cent.: from French, from Latin *amphibolus* 'ambiguous' (so called because of the varied structure of these minerals), from Greek *amphibolos*, from *amphi-* 'both, on both sides' + *ballein* 'to throw.'

am·phib·o·lite /am'fibə,līt/ ▶ **n.** Geology a granular metamorphic rock consisting mainly of hornblende and plagioclase.
– ORIGIN early 19th cent.: from AMPHIBOLE + -ITE[1].

am·phi·bol·o·gy /,amfə'bäləjē/ ▶ **n.** (pl. **amphibologies**) a phrase or sentence that is grammatically ambiguous, such as *she sees more of her children than her husband.*
– DERIVATIVES **am·phib·o·lous** /am'fibələs/ **adj.**
– ORIGIN late Middle English: from Old French *amphibologie*, from late Latin *amphibologia*, from Latin *amphibolia*, from Greek *amphibolos* 'ambiguous' (see AMPHIBOLE).

am·phib·o·ly /am'fibəlē/ ▶ **n.** (pl. **amphibolies**) another term for AMPHIBOLOGY.

am·phi·brach /'amfə,brak/ ▶ **n.** Prosody a metrical foot consisting of a stressed syllable between two unstressed syllables or (in Greek and Latin) a long syllable between two short syllables.
– ORIGIN late 16th cent. (originally in the Latin forms *amphibrachus*, *amphibrachys*): via Latin from Greek *amphibrakhus* 'short at both ends.'

am·phi·mix·is /,amfə'miksis/ ▶ **n.** Botany sexual reproduction involving the fusion of two different gametes to form a zygote. Often contrasted with APOMIXIS.
– DERIVATIVES **am·phi·mic·tic** /-'miktik/ **adj.**
– ORIGIN late 19th cent.: from AMPHI- + Greek *mixis* 'mingling.'

am·phi·ox·us /,amfē'äksəs/ ▶ **n.** a lancelet that is caught for food in parts of Asia. ● Genus *Branchiostoma* (formerly *Amphioxus*), family Branchiostomidae.
– ORIGIN mid 19th cent.: modern Latin, from AMPHI- + Greek *oxus* 'sharp.'

am·phi·path·ic /,amfə'paTHik/ ▶ **adj.** Biochemistry (of a molecule, esp. a protein) having both hydrophilic and hydrophobic parts.
– ORIGIN 1930s: from AMPHI- + Greek *pathikos* (from *pathos* 'experience').

am·phi·phil·ic /,amfə'filik/ ▶ **adj.** Biochemistry another term for AMPHIPATHIC.

am·phi·pod /'amfə,päd/ ▶ **n.** Zoology a crustacean of the chiefly marine order Amphipoda.

Am·phip·o·da /am'fipədə/ Zoology an order of crustaceans with a laterally compressed body and a large number of leglike appendages.
– ORIGIN modern Latin (plural), from AMPHI- 'of both kinds' (because some legs are specialized for swimming and some for feeding) + Greek *pous*, *pod-* 'foot.'

am·phip·ro·style /am'fiprə,stīl, ,amfə'prō-/ ▶ **adj.** (of a classical building) having a portico at each end and no columns along the sides.
– ORIGIN early 18th cent.: via Latin from Greek *amphiprostulos*, from *amphi-* 'both, on both sides' + *prostulos* 'having pillars in front' (see PROSTYLE).

am·phis·bae·na /,amfəs'bēnə/ ▶ **n.** a legendary serpent with a head at each end.
– ORIGIN late Middle English: via Latin from Greek *amphisbaina*, from *amphis* 'both ways' + *bainein* 'go.'

Am·phis·bae·ni·a /,amfis'bēnēə/ Zoology a group of reptiles that comprises the worm lizards. ● Suborder Amphisbaenia, order Squamata.
– DERIVATIVES **am·phis·bae·ni·an** **n. & adj.**
– ORIGIN modern Latin, from Greek *amphisbaina*, from *amphis* 'both' + *bainein* 'go, walk.'

am·phi·the·a·ter /'amfə,THēətər/ ▶ **n.** (esp. in Greek and Roman architecture) a round or oval building, typically unroofed, with a central space for the presentation of dramatic or sporting events. Tiers of seats for spectators surround the central space. ■ a sloping, semicircular seating gallery: *I was permitted to attend a lecture in the amphitheater of the hospital.* ■ a large circular hollow in rocks or hills: *that vast amphitheater chiseled out of the mountain.*
– ORIGIN late Middle English: via Latin from Greek *amphitheatron*, from *amphi* 'on both sides' + *theatron* (see THEATER).

amphitheater

Am·phi·tri·te /,amfi'trītē/ Greek Mythology a sea goddess, wife of Poseidon and mother of Triton.

am·phi·u·ma /,amfē'yo͞omə/ ▶ **n.** a fully aquatic eellike amphibian with very small limbs, found in stagnant water and swamps in the southeastern US. ● Family Amphiumidae and genus *Amphiuma*: three species (identified by the number of toes on each limb), the one-toed *A. pholeter*, the two-toed *A. means*, and the three-toed *A. tridactylum.*

am·pho·ra /'amfərə/ ▶ **n.** (pl. **amphorae** /-,rē/ or **amphoras**) a tall ancient Greek or Roman jar with two handles and a narrow neck.
– ORIGIN Latin, from Greek *amphoreus*, or from French *amphore.*

am·pho·ter·ic /,amfə'terik/ ▶ **adj.** Chemistry (of a compound, esp. a metal oxide or hydroxide) able to react both as a base and as an acid.
– ORIGIN mid 19th cent.: from Greek *amphoteros*, comparative of *amphō* 'both,' + -IC.

am·pi·cil·lin /,ampi'silin/ ▶ **n.** Medicine a semisynthetic form of penicillin used chiefly to treat infections of the urinary and respiratory tracts.
– ORIGIN 1960s: blend of AMINO and a contraction of PENICILLIN.

am·ple /'ampəl/ ▶ **adj.** (**ampler**, **amplest**) enough or more than enough; plentiful: *there is ample time for discussion | an ample supply of consumer goods.* ■ large and accommodating: *he leaned back in his ample chair.* ■ used euphemistically to convey that someone is fat: *she stood with her hands on her ample hips.*
– DERIVATIVES **am·ple·ness** **n.**, **am·ply** /-p(ə)lē/ **adv.**
– ORIGIN late Middle English: via French from Latin *amplus* 'large, capacious, abundant.'

am·plex·i·caul /am'pleksi,kôl/ ▶ **adj.** Botany (of a leaf) embracing and surrounding the stem.

am·plex·us /am'pleksəs/ ▶ **n.** Zoology the mating position of frogs and toads, in which the male clasps the female about the back.
– ORIGIN 1930s: from Latin, literally 'an embrace.'

am·pli·fi·er /'amplə,fīər/ ▶ **n.** an electronic device for increasing the amplitude of electrical signals, used chiefly in sound reproduction. ■ a device of this kind combined with a loudspeaker, used to amplify electric guitars and other musical instruments.

am·pli·fy /'amplə,fī/ ▶ **v.** (**amplifies**, **amplifying**, **amplified**) [with obj.] increase the volume of (sound),

a

esp. using an amplifier: *the accompanying chords have been amplified in our arrangement.* ■ increase the amplitude of (an electrical signal or other oscillation). ■ cause to become more marked or intense: *urban policy initiatives amplified social polarization.* ■ Genetics make multiple copies of (a gene or DNA sequence). ■ enlarge upon or add detail to (a story or statement): *the notes amplify information contained in the statement.*
– DERIVATIVES **am·pli·fi·ca·tion** /ˌampləfiˈkāSHən/ **n.**
– ORIGIN late Middle English (in the general sense 'increase, augment'): from Old French *amplifier*, from Latin *amplificare*, from *amplus* 'large, abundant.'

am·pli·tude /ˈampliˌt(y)o͞od/ ▶ **n. 1** Physics the maximum extent of a vibration or oscillation, measured from the position of equilibrium. ■ the maximum difference of an alternating electrical current or potential from the average value.
2 Astronomy the angular distance of a celestial object from the true east or west point of the horizon at rising or setting.
3 breadth, range, or magnitude: *the amplitude of the crime of manslaughter lies beneath murder.*
4 Mathematics the angle between the real axis of an Argand diagram and a vector representing a complex number.
– ORIGIN mid 16th cent. (in the senses 'physical extent' and 'grandeur'): from Latin *amplitudo*, from *amplus* 'large, abundant.'

am·pli·tude mod·u·la·tion (abbr.: **AM**) ▶ **n.** the modulation of a wave by varying its amplitude, used chiefly as a means of radio broadcasting, in which an audio signal is combined with a carrier wave. Often contrasted with FREQUENCY MODULATION.

am·poule /ˈamˌp(y)o͞ol/ (also **ampul** or **ampule**) ▶ **n.** a sealed glass capsule containing a liquid, esp. a measured quantity ready for injecting: *an ampoule of epinephrine.*
– ORIGIN early 20th cent.: from French, from Latin *ampulla* (see AMPULLA).

am·pul·la /amˈpo͝olə, -ˈpələ/ ▶ **n.** (pl. **ampullae** /-lē/) a roughly spherical flask with two handles, used in ancient Rome. ■ a flask for sacred uses such as holding holy oil. ■ Anatomy & Zoology a cavity, or the dilated end of a duct, shaped like a Roman ampulla.
– ORIGIN late Middle English: from Latin, diminutive of *ampora*, variant of *amphora* (see AMPHORA).

am·pu·tate /ˈampyəˌtāt/ ▶ **v.** [with obj.] cut off (a limb), typically by surgical operation: *surgeons had to amputate her left hand | the wounded had to have legs or arms **amputated**.*
– DERIVATIVES **am·pu·ta·tion** /ˌampyəˈtāSHən/ **n.**
– ORIGIN mid 16th cent.: from Latin *amputat-* 'lopped off,' from *amputare*, from *am-* (for *amb-* 'around') + *putare* 'to prune.'

am·pu·tee /ˌampyəˈtē/ ▶ **n.** a person who has had a limb amputated.

AMRAAM /ˈamˌram/ ▶ **abbr.** advanced medium range air-to-air missile.

am·rit /ˈəmrit/ (also **amrita** /əmˈrētə/) ▶ **n.** a syrup considered divine by Sikhs and taken by them in religious observances.
– ORIGIN from Sanskrit *amṛta* 'immortal.'

Am·rit·sar /ˌəmˈritsər, äm-/ a city in the state of Punjab in northwestern India; pop. 1,194,700 (est. 2009). The center of the Sikh faith, it is the site of its Golden Temple.

am·scray /ˈamˌskrā/ ▶ **v.** [no obj.] informal, dated leave quickly: *just amscray and be done with it.*
– ORIGIN 1930s: pig Latin from *scram.*

Am·ster·dam /ˈamstərˌdam/ the capital and largest city of the Netherlands; pop. 747,093 (2008) . It is an important port and financial center, esp. known for its diamond industry.

AMT ▶ **abbr.** alternative minimum tax, introduced to prevent companies and individuals using deductions and credits to pay no tax.

am·trac /ˈamˌtrak/ (also **amtrack, amtrak**) ▶ **n.** an amphibious tracked vehicle used for landing assault troops on a shore.
– ORIGIN World War II: blend of AMPHIBIOUS and TRACTOR.

Am·trak /ˈamˌtrak/ trademark a federal passenger railroad service in the US, operated by the National Railroad Passenger Corporation.

amu ▶ **abbr.** atomic mass unit.

a·muck /əˈmək/ ▶ **adv.** variant spelling of AMOK.

A·mu Dar·ya /ˌämo͞o ˈdäryə/ a river in central Asia that rises in the Pamirs and flows 1,500 miles (2,400 km) into the Aral Sea. In classical times, it was known as the Oxus.

am·u·let /ˈamyəlit/ ▶ **n.** an ornament or small piece of jewelry thought to give protection against evil, danger, or disease.
– ORIGIN late 16th cent.: from Latin *amuletum*, of unknown origin.

A·mun /ˈämən/ (also **Amon**) Egyptian Mythology a supreme god of the ancient Egyptians, identified with the sun god Ra and in Greek and Roman times with Zeus and Jupiter (under the name **Ammon**).

A·mund·sen /ˈämənsən/, Roald (1872–1928), Norwegian explorer. Amundsen was the first to navigate the Northwest Passage (1903–06), during which expedition he located the site of the magnetic North Pole. In 1911, he became the first person to reach the South Pole.

A·mur /äˈmo͝or/ a river of northeastern Asia that forms, for much of its length, the boundary between Russia and China. Its length is about 2,737 miles (4,350 km). Chinese name HEILONG.

a·muse /əˈmyo͞oz/ ▶ **v.** [with obj.] **1** cause (someone) to find something funny; entertain: *he made faces to amuse her* | (as adj. **amused**) *people looked on with amused curiosity.*
2 provide interesting and enjoyable occupation for (someone): *the hotel has planned many activities to amuse its guests | they **amused themselves** digging through an old encyclopedia* | (as adj. **amused**) *elegant shops that will keep any browser amused for hours.*
– DERIVATIVES **a·mus·ed·ly** /-zidlē/ **adv.** (sense 1).
– ORIGIN late 15th cent. (in the sense 'delude, deceive'): from Old French *amuser* 'entertain, deceive,' from *a-* (expressing causal effect) + *muser* 'stare stupidly.' The current senses date from the mid 17th cent.

a·muse-gueule /ˌämo͞oz ˈgəl/ ▶ **n.** (pl. **amuse-gueules** pronunc. **same**) a small, savory item of food served as an appetizer before a meal.
– ORIGIN late 20th cent.: French, literally 'amuse mouth.'

a·muse·ment /əˈmyo͞ozmənt/ ▶ **n.** the state or experience of finding something funny: *we looked with amusement at our horoscopes.* ■ the provision or enjoyment of entertainment: *an evening's amusement.* ■ something that causes laughter or provides entertainment: *his daughter was an amusement to him.*
– ORIGIN early 17th cent. (in the sense 'musing, diversion of the attention'): from French, from the verb *amuser* (see AMUSE).

a·muse·ment park ▶ **n.** a large outdoor area with fairground rides, shows, refreshments, games of chance or skill, and other entertainments.

a·mus·ing /əˈmyo͞oziNG/ ▶ **adj.** causing laughter or providing entertainment: *such a likable, amusing man!*
– DERIVATIVES **a·mus·ing·ly adv.**

a·myg·da·la /əˈmigdələ/ ▶ **n.** (pl. **amygdalae** /-lē/) Anatomy a roughly almond-shaped mass of gray matter inside each cerebral hemisphere, involved with the experiencing of emotions.
– ORIGIN late Middle English: via Latin from Greek *amugdalē* 'almond.'

a·myg·da·lin /əˈmigdəlin/ ▶ **n.** Chemistry a bitter crystalline compound, found in bitter almonds and the stones of peaches, apricots, and other fruit.
– ORIGIN mid 19th cent.: from Latin *amygdala* 'almond' + -IN[1].

a·myg·da·loid /əˈmigdəˌloid/ ▶ **adj.** technical shaped like an almond.
▶ **n. 1** (also **amygdaloid nucleus**) Anatomy another term for AMYGDALA.
2 Geology volcanic rock with amygdules.
– ORIGIN mid 18th cent.: from Latin *amygdala* 'almond' + -OID.

a·myg·da·loi·dal /əˌmigdəˈloidl/ ▶ **adj.** Geology relating to or containing amygdules.

a·myg·dule /əˈmigˌd(y)o͞ol/ (also **amygdale** /-ˌdāl/) ▶ **n.** Geology a vesicle in an igneous rock, containing secondary minerals.
– ORIGIN late 19th cent.: from French, from Latin *amygdala* (see AMYGDALA).

am·yl /ˈaməl/ ▶ **n.** [as modifier] Chemistry the straight-chain pentyl radical $-C_5H_{11}$. ■ informal short for AMYL NITRITE.
– ORIGIN mid 19th cent.: from Latin *amylum* 'starch' + -YL.

am·yl·ase /ˈaməˌlās, -ˌlāz/ ▶ **n.** Biochemistry an enzyme, found chiefly in saliva and pancreatic fluid, that converts starch and glycogen into simple sugars.

am·yl ni·trate ▶ **n.** Chemistry a colorless synthetic liquid used as an additive in diesel fuel to improve its ignition properties. ● Chem. formula: $C_5H_{11}NO_3$.

> **USAGE** **Amyl nitrate** and **amyl nitrite** are quite distinct substances, but **amyl nitrate** is often mistakenly used to refer to the street drug (inhaled and used as a stimulant and vasodilator), which is correctly called **amyl nitrite.**

am·yl ni·trite ▶ **n.** a yellowish volatile synthetic liquid used medicinally as a vasodilator. It is rapidly absorbed by the body on inhalation, and is sometimes used for its stimulatory effects. ● Chem. formula: $C_5H_{11}NO_2$.

> **USAGE** See usage at AMYL NITRATE.

am·y·loid /ˈaməˌloid/ Medicine ▶ **n.** a starchlike protein that is deposited in the liver, kidneys, spleen, or other tissues in certain diseases. ■ another term for AMYLOIDOSIS.

am·y·loi·do·sis /ˌaməloiˈdōsis/ ▶ **n.** Medicine a disorder marked by deposition of amyloid in the body.

am·y·lo·pec·tin /ˌaməlōˈpektin/ ▶ **n.** Biochemistry the noncrystallizable form of starch, consisting of branched polysaccharide chains.

am·yl·ose /ˈaməˌlōs, -ˌlōz/ ▶ **n.** Biochemistry the crystallizable form of starch, consisting of long unbranched polysaccharide chains.

a·my·o·troph·ic lat·er·al scle·ro·sis /ˌāmīəˈträfik/ (abbr.: **ALS**) ▶ **n.** a progressive degeneration of the motor neurons of the central nervous system, leading to wasting of the muscles and paralysis. Also called LOU GEHRIG'S DISEASE.

a·my·ot·ro·phy /ˌāmīˈätrəfē/ ▶ **n.** Medicine muscular atrophy.
– DERIVATIVES **a·my·o·troph·ic** /ˌāmīəˈträfik, -əˈtrō-/ **adj.**
– ORIGIN late 19th cent.: from A-[1] 'not' + Greek *mus, muo-* 'muscle' + -TROPHY (see -TROPHIC).

Am·y·tal /ˈaməˌtôl, -ˌtal/ ▶ **n.** trademark a barbiturate drug used as a sedative and a hypnotic.
● Alternative name: 5-ethyl-5-isopropylbarbituric acid, or its sodium salt (**sodium amytal**); chem. formula: $C_{11}H_{18}N_2O_3$.
– ORIGIN 1920s: from AMYL + *-t-* (for ease of pronunciation) + -AL.

an /an/ ▶ **adj.** the form of the indefinite article (see A) used before words beginning with a vowel sound.

> **USAGE** Is it 'a historical document' or 'an historical document'? '**A** hotel' or '**an** hotel'? There is still some divergence of opinion over which form of the indefinite article should be used before words that begin with **h-** and have an unstressed first syllable. In the 18th and 19th centuries, people often did not pronounce the initial **h** for these words, and so **an** was commonly used. Today the **h** is pronounced, and so it is logical to use **a** rather than **an**. However, the indefinite article **an** is still encountered before the **h** in both British and American English, particularly with **historical**: in the Oxford English Corpus around a quarter of examples of **historical** are preceded with **an** rather than **a**.

an-[1] ▶ **prefix** variant spelling of A-[1] before a vowel (as in *anemia, anechoic*).
– ORIGIN from Greek.

an-[2] ▶ **prefix** variant spelling of AD- assimilated before *n* (as in *annihilate, annotate*).

an-[3] ▶ **prefix** variant spelling of ANA- shortened before a vowel (as in *aneurysm*).

-an (also **-ean** or **-ian**) ▶ **suffix 1** forming adjectives and nouns, esp. from: ■ names of places: *Ohioan | Russian.* ■ names of systems: *Anglican | Presbyterian.* ■ names of zoological classes or orders: *crustacean.* ■ names of founders or leaders when referring to them as sources: *Chomskyan | Lutheran.*
2 Chemistry forming names of organic compounds, chiefly polysaccharides: *dextran.*
– ORIGIN based on Latin *-(i)anus, -aeus*, adjectival endings.

ana- (usu. **an-** before a vowel) ▶ **prefix 1** up: *anabasis.*
2 back: *anamnesis.*
3 again: *anabiosis.*
– ORIGIN from Greek *ana* 'up.'

-ana ▶ **suffix** (forming plural nouns) denoting things associated with a person, place, or field of interest: *Americana | Victoriana.*
– ORIGIN from the neuter plural of the Latin adjectival ending *-anus.*

An·a·bap·tism /ˌanəˈbapˌtizəm/ ▶ **n.** the doctrine that baptism should only be administered to believing adults, held by a radical Protestant sect that emerged during the 1520s and 1530s.
– DERIVATIVES **An·a·bap·tist n. & adj.**
– ORIGIN mid 16th cent.: via ecclesiastical Latin from Greek *anabaptismos*, from *ana-* 'over again' + *baptismos* 'baptism.'

an·a·bas /ˈanəˌbas/ ▶ **n.** any of the freshwater fish of the climbing perch family native to Asia and Africa, esp. the genus *Anabas*, able to breathe air and move on land.

a·nab·a·sis /əˈnabəsis/ ▶ **n.** (pl. **anabases** /-ˌsēz/) rare a march from a coast into the interior, as that of the younger Cyrus into Asia in 401 BC, as narrated by Xenophon in his work *Anabasis.* ■ a military advance.
– ORIGIN early 18th cent.: Greek, literally 'ascent.'

a

an·a·bat·ic /ˌanəˈbatik/ ▶ **adj.** Meteorology (of a wind) caused by local upward motion of warm air. Compare with KATABATIC.
– ORIGIN early 20th cent.: from Greek *anabatikos*, from *anabatēs* 'a person who ascends,' from *anabainein* 'walk up.'

an·a·bi·o·sis /ˌanəbīˈōsis/ ▶ **n.** Zoology a temporary state of suspended animation or greatly reduced metabolism.
– DERIVATIVES **an·a·bi·ot·ic** /-ˈätik/ **adj.**
– ORIGIN late 19th cent.: from Greek *anabiōsis*, from *anabioein* 'return to life.'

an·a·bol·ic /ˌanəˈbälik/ ▶ **adj.** Biochemistry relating to or promoting anabolism.

an·a·bol·ic ste·roid ▶ **n.** a synthetic steroid hormone that resembles testosterone in promoting the growth of muscle. Such hormones are used medicinally to treat some forms of weight loss and (illegally) by some athletes and others to enhance physical performance.

a·nab·o·lism /əˈnabəˌlizəm/ ▶ **n.** Biochemistry the synthesis of complex molecules in living organisms from simpler ones together with the storage of energy; constructive metabolism.
– ORIGIN late 19th cent.: from Greek *anabolē* 'ascent,' from *ana-* 'up' + *ballein* 'to throw.'

a·nach·ro·nism /əˈnakrəˌnizəm/ ▶ **n.** a thing belonging or appropriate to a period other than that in which it exists, esp. a thing that is conspicuously old-fashioned: *everything was as it would have appeared in centuries past apart from one anachronism, a bright yellow construction crane.* ■ an act of attributing a custom, event, or object to a period to which it does not belong.
– DERIVATIVES **a·nach·ro·nis·tic** /əˌnakrəˈnistik/ **adj.**, **a·nach·ro·nis·ti·cal·ly** /-ˈnistik(ə)lē/ **adv.**
– ORIGIN mid 17th cent.: from Greek *anakhronismos*, from *ana-* 'backward' + *khronos* 'time.'

an·a·clit·ic /ˌanəˈklitik/ ▶ **adj.** Psychoanalysis relating to or characterized by a strong emotional dependence on another or others: *anaclitic depression.*
– ORIGIN 1920s: from Greek *anaklitos* 'for reclining,' from *anaklinein* 'recline.'

an·a·co·lu·thon /ˌanəkəˈlo͞oTHän/ ▶ **n.** (pl. **anacolutha** /-THə/) a sentence or construction that lacks grammatical sequence, such as *while in the garden, the door banged shut.*
– DERIVATIVES **an·a·co·lu·thic** /-THik/ **adj.**
– ORIGIN early 18th cent.: via late Latin from Greek *anakolouthon*, from *an-* 'not' + *akolouthos* 'following.'

an·a·con·da /ˌanəˈkändə/ ▶ **n.** a semiaquatic snake of the boa family that may grow to a great size, native to tropical South America. ● Genus *Eunectes*, family Boidae: several species, in particular the **green anaconda** (*E. murinus*).
– ORIGIN mid 18th cent. (originally denoting a kind of Sri Lankan snake): unexplained alteration of Latin *anacandaia* 'python,' from Sinhalese *henakaňdayā* 'whipsnake,' from *hena* 'lightning' + *kaňda* 'stem.'

A·nac·re·on /əˈnakrēən, -ˌän/ (*c.*570–*c.*487 BC), Greek lyric poet, best known for his celebrations of love and wine.

a·nac·re·on·tic /əˌnakrēˈäntik/ (also **Anacreontic**) Prosody ▶ **adj.** (of a poem) composed in the manner of the Greek poet Anacreon, known for his lyrics praising wine, women, and song.
▶ **n.** (usu. **anacreontics**) an anacreontic poem.
– ORIGIN early 17th cent. (as an adjective): from late Latin *anacreonticus*, from Greek *Anakreōn* (see ANACREON).

an·a·cru·sis /ˌanəˈkro͞osis/ ▶ **n.** (pl. **anacruses** /-sēz/)
1 Prosody one or more unstressed syllables at the beginning of a verse.
2 Music one or more unstressed notes before the first bar line of a piece or passage.
– ORIGIN mid 19th cent.: modern Latin, from Greek *anakrousis* 'prelude,' from *ana-* 'up' + *krousis*, from *krouein* 'to strike.'

an·a·dam·a bread /ˌanəˈdamə ˌbred/ ▶ **n.** a type of yeast bread typically made with cornmeal and dark molasses.

a·nad·ro·mous /əˈnadrəməs/ ▶ **adj.** Zoology (of a fish, such as the salmon) migrating up rivers from the sea to spawn. The opposite of CATADROMOUS.
– ORIGIN mid 18th cent.: from Greek *anadromos* (from *ana-* 'up' + *dromos* 'running') + **-ous**.

a·nae·mi·a ▶ **n.** British spelling of ANEMIA.

a·nae·mic ▶ **adj.** British spelling of ANEMIC.

an·aer·obe /ˈanəˌrōb/ ▶ **n.** Biology an organism that grows without air, or requires oxygen-free conditions to live.
– ORIGIN late 19th cent.: from AN-[1] + AEROBE.

an·aer·o·bic /ˌane(ə)ˈrōbik, ˌanə-/ ▶ **adj.** Biology relating to, involving, or requiring an absence of free oxygen: *anerobic bacteria.* ■ relating to or denoting exercise that does not improve or is not intended to improve the efficiency of the body's cardiovascular system in absorbing and transporting oxygen.
– DERIVATIVES **an·aer·o·bi·cal·ly** /-bik(ə)lē/ **adv.**

an·aes·the·sia, etc. ▶ **n.** British spelling of ANESTHESIA, etc.

an·a·gen·e·sis /ˌanəˈjenəsis/ ▶ **n.** Biology species formation without branching of the evolutionary line of descent. Compare with CLADOGENESIS.
– DERIVATIVES **an·a·ge·net·ic** /-jəˈnetik/ **adj.**

an·a·glyph /ˈanəˌglif/ ▶ **n. 1** Photography a stereoscopic photograph with the two images superimposed and printed in different colors, producing a stereo effect when the photograph is viewed through correspondingly colored filters.
2 an object, such as a cameo, embossed or carved in low relief.
– DERIVATIVES **an·a·glyph·ic** /ˌanəˈglifik/ **adj.**
– ORIGIN late 16th cent. (sense 2): from Greek *anagluphē*, from *ana-* 'up' + *gluphē* (from *gluphein* 'carve'). Sense 1 dates from the late 19th cent.

an·a·gram /ˈanəˌgram/ ▶ **n.** a word, phrase, or name formed by rearranging the letters of another, such as *cinema*, formed from *iceman*.
▶ **v.** (**anagrams, anagramming, anagrammed**) another term for ANAGRAMMATIZE.
– DERIVATIVES **an·a·gram·mat·ic** /ˌanəgrəˈmatik/ **adj.**, **an·a·gram·mat·i·cal** /ˌanəgrəˈmatikəl/ **adj.**
– ORIGIN late 16th cent.: from French *anagramme* or modern Latin *anagramma*, from Greek *ana-* 'back, anew' + *gramma* 'letter.'

an·a·gram·ma·tize /ˌanəˈgraməˌtīz/ ▶ **v.** [with obj.] make an anagram of (a word, phrase, or name).
– DERIVATIVES **an·a·gram·ma·ti·za·tion** /-ˌgramətəˈzāSHən/ **n.**

An·a·heim /ˈanəˌhīm/ a city in California, southeast of Los Angeles; pop. 335,288 (est. 2008). It is home to Disneyland.

a·nal /ˈānl/ ▶ **adj.** involving, relating to, or situated near the anus. ■ (in Freudian psychoanalysis) relating to or denoting a stage of infantile psychosexual development supposedly preoccupied with the anus and defecation. ■ informal anal-retentive: *he's anal about things like that.*
– DERIVATIVES **a·nal·ly** **adv.**
– ORIGIN mid 18th cent.: from modern Latin *analis*, from Latin *anus* (see ANUS).

an·a·lects /ˈanlˌek(t)s/ (also **analecta** /ˌanlˈektə/) ▶ **plural n.** a collection of short literary or philosophical extracts.
– ORIGIN late Middle English: via Latin from Greek *analekta* 'things gathered up,' from *analegein* 'pick up,' from *ana-* 'up' + *legein* 'gather.'

an·a·lep·tic /ˌanəˈleptik/ Medicine ▶ **adj.** (chiefly of a drug) tending to restore a person's health or strength; restorative.
▶ **n.** a restorative drug. ■ a drug that stimulates the central nervous system.
– ORIGIN late 16th cent.: via late Latin from Greek *analēptikos* 'restorative.'

a·nal fin ▶ **n.** Zoology an unpaired fin located on the underside of a fish posterior to the anus.

an·al·ge·si·a /ˌanlˈjēzēə, -ZHə/ ▶ **n.** Medicine the inability to feel pain.
– ORIGIN early 18th cent.: from Greek *analgēsia* 'painlessness,' from *an-* 'not' + *algein* 'feel pain.'

an·al·ge·sic /ˌanlˈjēzik, -sik/ Medicine ▶ **adj.** (chiefly of a drug) acting to relieve pain.
▶ **n.** an analgesic drug.

an·a·log /ˈanlˌôg, -ˌäg/ (also **analogue**) ▶ **n.** a person or thing seen as comparable to another: *the idea that the fertilized egg contains a miniature analog of every adult structure.* ■ Chemistry a compound with a molecular structure closely similar to that of another.
▶ **adj.** relating to or using signals or information represented by a continuously variable physical quantity such as spatial position or voltage. Often contrasted with DIGITAL (sense 1). ■ (of a clock or watch) showing the time by means of hands rather than displayed digits.
– ORIGIN early 19th cent.: from French, from Greek *analogon*, neuter of *analogos* 'proportionate.'

a·nal·o·gize /əˈnaləˌjīz/ ▶ **v.** [with obj.] make a comparison of (something) with something else to assist understanding: *he could analogize birth to the coming into being of a poem.*

a·nal·o·gous /əˈnaləgəs/ ▶ **adj.** (often **analogous to**) comparable in certain respects, typically in a way that makes clearer the nature of the things compared: *they saw the relationship between a ruler and his subjects as analogous to that of father and children.* ■ Biology (of structures) performing a similar function but having a different evolutionary origin, such as the wings of insects and birds. Often contrasted with HOMOLOGOUS.
– DERIVATIVES **a·nal·o·gous·ly** **adv.**
– ORIGIN mid 17th cent.: via Latin from Greek *analogos* 'proportionate' + **-ous**.

an·a·log-to-dig·it·al con·vert·er (abbr.: **ADC**) ▶ **n.** a device for converting analog signals to digital form.

an·a·logue ▶ **n. & adj.** variant spelling of ANALOG.

a·nal·o·gy /əˈnaləjē/ ▶ **n.** (pl. **analogies**) a comparison between two things, typically on the basis of their structure and for the purpose of explanation or clarification: *an analogy between the workings of nature and those of human societies | he interprets logical functions by analogy with machines.* ■ a correspondence or partial similarity: *the syndrome is called deep dysgraphia because of its analogy to deep dyslexia.* ■ a thing that is comparable to something else in significant respects: *works of art were seen as an analogy for works of nature.* ■ Logic a process of arguing from similarity in known respects to similarity in other respects. ■ Linguistics a process by which new words and inflections are created on the basis of regularities in the form of existing ones. ■ Biology the resemblance of function between organs that have a different evolutionary origin.
– DERIVATIVES **an·a·log·i·cal** /ˌanəˈläjikəl/ **adj.**, **an·a·log·i·cal·ly** **adv.**
– ORIGIN late Middle English (in the sense 'appropriateness, correspondence'): from French *analogie*, Latin *analogia* 'proportion,' from Greek, from *analogos* 'proportionate.'

an·al·pha·bet·ic /ˌanalfəˈbetik/ ▶ **adj.**
1 representing sounds by composite signs rather than by single letters or symbols: *Chinese has an analphabetic writing system.*
2 completely illiterate.

a·nal-re·ten·tive Psychoanalysis ▶ **adj.** (of a person) excessively orderly and fussy (supposedly owing to conflict over toilet-training in infancy).
▶ **n.** (also **anal retentive**) a person who is excessively orderly and fussy.
– DERIVATIVES **a·nal re·ten·tion** **n.**, **a·nal re·ten·tive·ness** **n.**

a·nal·y·sand /əˈnaləˌsand, -ˌzand/ ▶ **n.** a person undergoing psychoanalysis.

an·a·lyse ▶ **v.** British spelling of ANALYZE.

a·nal·y·sis /əˈnaləsis/ ▶ **n.** (pl. **analyses** /-ˌsēz/) detailed examination of the elements or structure of something, typically as a basis for discussion or interpretation: *statistical analysis | an analysis of popular culture.* ■ the process of separating something into its constituent elements. Often contrasted with SYNTHESIS. ■ the identification and measurement of the chemical constituents of a substance or specimen. ■ short for PSYCHOANALYSIS. ■ Linguistics the use of separate, short words and word order rather than inflection or agglutination to express grammatical structure. ■ Mathematics the part of mathematics concerned with the theory of functions and the use of limits, continuity, and the operations of calculus.
– PHRASES **in the final** (or **last**) **analysis** when everything has been considered (used to suggest that a statement expresses the basic truth about a complex situation): *in the final analysis it is a question of political history.*
– ORIGIN late 16th cent.: via medieval Latin from Greek *analusis*, from *analuein* 'unloose,' from *ana-* 'up' + *luein* 'loosen.'

an·a·lyst /ˈanl-ist/ ▶ **n.** a person who conducts analysis, in particular: ■ an investment expert, typically in a specified field: *rising consumer confidence and falling oil prices are the keys to any upturn, many analysts believe.* ■ short for PSYCHOANALYST. ■ a chemist who analyzes substances. ■ short for SYSTEMS ANALYST.
– ORIGIN mid 17th cent.: from French *analyste*, from the verb *analyser* (see ANALYZE).

an·a·lyte /ˈanəˌlīt/ ▶ **n.** Chemistry a substance whose chemical constituents are being identified and measured.

an·a·lyt·ic /ˌanlˈitik/ ▶ **adj.** another term for ANALYTICAL. ■ Logic true by virtue of the meaning of the words or concepts used to express it, so that its denial would be a self-contradiction. Compare with SYNTHETIC. ■ Linguistics (of a language) tending not to alter the form of its words and to use word order rather than inflection or agglutination to express grammatical structure. Often contrasted with SYNTHETIC.

PRONUNCIATION KEY ə *ago, up*; ər *over, fur*; a *hat*; ā *ate*; ä *car*; e *let*; ē *see*; i *fit*; ī *by*; NG *sing*; ō *go*; ô *law, for*; oi *toy*; o͝o *good*; o͞o *goo*; ou *out*; TH *thin*; T͟H *then*; ZH *vision*

– ORIGIN early 17th cent.: via Latin from Greek *analutikos*, from *analuein* 'unloose.' The term was adopted in the late 16th cent. as a noun denoting the branch of logic dealing with analysis, with specific reference to Aristotle's treatises on logic, the Analytics (Greek *analutika*).

an·a·lyt·i·cal /ˌanlˈitikəl/ ▶ **adj.** relating to or using analysis or logical reasoning: *analytical methods* | *a suave, analytical type who missed his calling as a lawyer.*
– DERIVATIVES **an·a·lyt·i·cal·ly** /-ik(ə)lē/ **adv.**

an·a·lyt·i·cal ge·om·e·try ▶ **n.** geometry using coordinates.

an·a·lyt·i·cal phi·los·o·phy (also **analytic philosophy**) ▶ **n.** a method of approaching philosophical problems through analysis of the terms in which they are expressed, associated with Anglo-American philosophy of the early 20th century.

an·a·lyt·i·cal psy·chol·o·gy ▶ **n.** the psychoanalytic system of psychology developed and practiced by Carl Jung.

an·a·lyze /ˈanlˌīz/ (Brit. **analyse**) ▶ **v.** [with obj.] examine methodically and in detail the constitution or structure of (something, esp. information), typically for purposes of explanation and interpretation: *we need to analyze our results more clearly.* ■ discover or reveal (something) through such examination: *I intend to analyze the sexism in such texts* | [with clause] *he tried to analyze exactly what was going on.* ■ psychoanalyze (someone). ■ identify and measure the chemical constituents of (a substance or specimen). ■ Grammar resolve (a sentence) into its grammatical elements; parse.
– DERIVATIVES **an·a·lyz·a·ble** /ˌanəˈlīzəbəl/ **adj.**, **an·a·lyz·er n.**
– ORIGIN late 16th cent.: influenced by French *analyser*, from medieval Latin *analysis* (see ANALYSIS).

an·am·ne·sis /ˌanəmˈnēsis/ ▶ **n.** (pl. **anamneses** /-sēz/) recollection, in particular: ■ the remembering of things from a supposed previous existence (often used with reference to Platonic philosophy). ■ Medicine a patient's account of a medical history. ■ Christian Church the part of the Eucharist in which the Passion, Resurrection, and Ascension of Christ are recalled.
– ORIGIN late 16th cent.: from Greek *anamnēsis* 'remembrance.'

an·am·nes·tic /ˌanamˈnestik/ ▶ **adj.** Medicine denoting an enhanced reaction of the body's immune system to an antigen that is related to an antigen previously encountered.

an·a·mor·pho·sis /ˌanəˈmôrfəsis/ ▶ **n.** (pl. **anamorphoses** /-fəˌsēz/) **1** a distorted projection or drawing that appears normal when viewed from a particular point or with a suitable mirror or lens. ■ the process by which such images are produced.
2 Biology a gradual, ascending progression or change of form to a higher type. ■ development of the adult form through a series of small changes, esp. in some arthropods, the acquisition of additional body segments after hatching.
– DERIVATIVES **an·a·mor·phic** /-fik/ **adj.**
– ORIGIN early 18th cent.: from Greek *anamorphōsis* 'transformation,' from *ana-* 'back, again' + *morphosis* 'a shaping' (from *morphoun* 'to shape,' from *morphē* 'shape, form').

a·nan·da /ˈänəndə/ ▶ **n.** (in Hinduism, Buddhism, and Jainism) extreme happiness, one of the highest states of being.
– ORIGIN from Sanskrit *ānanda* 'blessedness, bliss.'

an·an·da·mide /əˈnandəˌmīd/ ▶ **n.** a naturally occurring arachidonic acid derivative, present in some foods and in mammalian brains, where it acts as a messenger molecule and plays a role in pain, depression, appetite, memory, and fertility.

An·a·ni·as /ˌanəˈnīəs/ two figures in the New Testament. ■ the husband of Sapphira, struck dead because he lied. ■ the Jewish high priest before whom St. Paul was brought.

an·a·pest /ˈanəˌpest/ (Brit. **anapaest**) ▶ **n.** Prosody a metrical foot consisting of two short or unstressed syllables followed by one long or stressed syllable.
– DERIVATIVES **an·a·pes·tic** /ˌanəˈpestik/ **adj.**
– ORIGIN late 16th cent.: via Latin from Greek *anapaistos* 'reversed,' from *ana-* 'back' + *paiein* 'strike' (so called because it is the reverse of a dactyl).

an·a·phase /ˈanəˌfāz/ ▶ **n.** Genetics the stage of meiotic or mitotic cell division in which the chromosomes move away from one another to opposite poles of the spindle.

an·a·phor /ˈanəˌfôr/ ▶ **n.** a word or phrase that refers to an earlier word or phrase (e.g., in *my cousin said she was coming*, *she* is used as an anaphor for *my cousin*).
– ORIGIN 1970s: back-formation from ANAPHORA.

a·naph·o·ra /əˈnafərə/ ▶ **n. 1** Grammar the use of a word referring to or replacing a word used earlier in a sentence, to avoid repetition, such as *do* in *I like it and so do they.*
2 Rhetoric the repetition of a word or phrase at the beginning of successive clauses.
– DERIVATIVES **an·a·phor·ic** /ˌanəˈfôrik/ **adj.**
– ORIGIN late 16th cent.: senses 1 and 2 via Latin from Greek, 'repetition,' from *ana-* 'back' + *pherein* 'to bear.'

an·aph·ro·dis·i·ac /anˌafrəˈdizēˌak, -ˈdēzē-, -ˈdēzhē-/ Medicine ▶ **adj.** (chiefly of a drug) tending to reduce sexual desire.
▶ **n.** an anaphrodisiac drug.

an·a·phy·lac·tic /ˌanəfəˈlaktik/ ▶ **adj.** Medicine relating to or caused by anaphylaxis.

an·a·phy·lact·ic shock ▶ **n.** Medicine an extreme, often life-threatening allergic reaction to an antigen to which the body has become hypersensitive.

an·a·phy·lax·is /ˌanəfəˈlaksis/ ▶ **n.** Medicine an acute allergic reaction to an antigen (e.g., a bee sting) to which the body has become hypersensitive.
– ORIGIN early 20th cent.: modern Latin, from Greek *ana-* 'again' + *phulaxis* 'guarding.'

a·nap·sid /əˈnapsid/ ▶ **n.** Zoology a reptile of a group characterized by the lack of temporal openings in the skull, including the turtles and their relatives. ● Sometimes placed in a subclass Anapsida, though this taxon is now often not recognized.
– ORIGIN 1930s: from modern Latin *Anapsida*, from Greek *an-* 'without' + *apsis, apsid-* 'arch.'

an·ap·tyx·is /ˌanapˈtiksis/ ▶ **n.** Phonetics the insertion of a vowel between two consonants in pronunciation, as in *filim* for *film*.
– DERIVATIVES **anaptyctic** /-ˈtiktik/ **adj.**
– ORIGIN late 19th cent.: modern Latin, from Greek *anaptuxis* 'unfolding,' from *ana-* 'back, again' + *ptuxis* 'folding.'

an·arch /ˈanˌärk/ ▶ **n.** literary an anarchist.
▶ **adj.** anarchic.
– ORIGIN mid 17th cent.: from Greek *anarkhos* 'without a chief' (see ANARCHY).

an·ar·chic /aˈnärkik/ ▶ **adj.** with no controlling rules or principles to give order: *an anarchic and bitter civil war.* ■ (of comedy or a person's sense of humor) uncontrolled by convention: *his anarchic wit.*
– DERIVATIVES **an·ar·chi·cal** /-kikəl/ **adj.**, **an·ar·chi·cal·ly adv.**

an·ar·chism /ˈanərˌkizəm/ ▶ **n.** belief in the abolition of all government and the organization of society on a voluntary, cooperative basis without recourse to force or compulsion. ■ anarchists as a political force or movement: *ruling-class fears of international anarchism during the 1890s.*
– ORIGIN mid 17th cent.: from Greek *anarkhos* 'without a chief' (see ANARCHY) + -ISM; later influenced by French *anarchisme*.

an·ar·chist /ˈanərkist/ ▶ **n.** a person who believes in or tries to bring about anarchy.
▶ **adj.** relating to or supporting anarchy or anarchists: *an anarchist newspaper.*
– DERIVATIVES **an·ar·chis·tic** /ˌanərˈkistik/ **adj.**
– ORIGIN mid 17th cent.: from Greek *anarkhos* 'without a chief' (see ANARCHY) + -IST; later influenced by French *anarchiste*.

an·ar·chy /ˈanərkē/ ▶ **n.** a state of disorder due to absence or nonrecognition of authority: *he must ensure public order in a country threatened with anarchy.* ■ absence of government and absolute freedom of the individual, regarded as a political ideal.
– ORIGIN mid 16th cent.: via medieval Latin from Greek *anarkhia*, from *anarkhos*, from *an-* 'without' + *arkhos* 'chief, ruler.'

A·na·sa·zi /ˌanəˈsäzē/ ▶ **n.** (pl. **same** or **Anasazis**) a member of an ancient American Indian people of the southwestern US, who flourished between *c.*200 BC and AD 1500. The earliest phase of their culture, typified by pit dwellings, is known as the Basket Maker period; the present day Pueblo culture developed from a later stage.
– ORIGIN 1930s: from Navajo, literally 'ancestors of our enemies (the Pueblo peoples).'

an·as·tig·mat /ˌanəˈstigˌmat/ ▶ **n.** an anastigmatic lens system.

an·as·tig·mat·ic /ˌanəstigˈmatik/ ▶ **adj.** (of a lens system) constructed so that the astigmatism of each element is canceled out.
– ORIGIN late 19th cent.: from AN-[1] 'not' + *astigmatic* (see ASTIGMATISM).

a·nas·to·mose /əˈnastəˌmōz, -ˌmōs/ ▶ **v.** [no obj.] Medicine be linked by anastomosis: *adjacent veins may anastomose.* ■ [with obj.] (usu. **be anastomosed**) link by anastomosis: *the graft is anastomosed to the vein of the recipient.*
– ORIGIN late 17th cent.: coined in French from Greek *anastomōsis* (see ANASTOMOSIS).

a·nas·to·mo·sis /əˌnastəˈmōsis/ ▶ **n.** (pl. **anastomoses** /-sēz/) technical a cross-connection between adjacent channels, tubes, fibers, or other parts of a network. ■ Medicine a connection made surgically between adjacent blood vessels, parts of the intestine, or other channels of the body, or the operation in which this is constructed.
– DERIVATIVES **a·nas·to·mot·ic** /-ˈmätik/ **adj. & n.**
– ORIGIN late 16th cent.: modern Latin, from Greek *anastomōsis*, from *anastomoun* 'provide with a mouth.'

a·nas·tro·phe /əˈnastrəfē/ ▶ **n.** Rhetoric the inversion of the usual order of words or clauses.
– ORIGIN mid 16th cent.: from Greek *anastrophē* 'turning back,' from *ana-* 'back' + *strephein* 'to turn.'

an·as·tro·zole /anˈastrəˌzōl/ ▶ **n.** a nonsteroidal aromatase inhibitor used in the treatment and prevention of breast cancer. It has been observed to have fewer adverse side effects than tamoxifen.

anat. ▶ **abbr.** ■ anatomical. ■ anatomy.

an·a·tase /ˈanəˌtās, -ˌtāz/ ▶ **n.** one of the tetragonal forms of titanium dioxide, usually found as brown crystals, used as a pigment in paints and inks.
– ORIGIN early 19th cent.: from French, from Greek *anatasis* 'extension,' with allusion to the length of the crystals.

a·nath·e·ma /əˈnaTHəmə/ ▶ **n. 1** something or someone that one vehemently dislikes: *racial hatred was **anathema to** her.*
2 a formal curse by a pope or a council of the Church, excommunicating a person or denouncing a doctrine. ■ literary a strong curse: *the sergeant clutched the ruined communicator, muttering anathemas.*
– ORIGIN early 16th cent.: from ecclesiastical Latin, 'excommunicated person, excommunication,' from Greek *anathema* 'thing dedicated,' (later) 'thing devoted to evil, accursed thing,' from *anatithenai* 'to set up.'

a·nath·e·ma·tize /əˈnaTHəməˌtīz/ ▶ **v.** [with obj.] curse; condemn: *she anathematized Tom as the despoiler of a helpless widow.*
– ORIGIN mid 16th cent.: from French *anathématiser*, from Latin *anathematizare*, from Greek *anathematizein*, from *anathema* (see ANATHEMA).

An·a·to·li·a /ˌanəˈtōlēə/ the western peninsula of Asia, bounded by the Black, Aegean, and Mediterranean seas, that forms the greater part of Turkey.

An·a·to·li·an /ˌanəˈtōlēən/ ▶ **adj.** of or relating to Anatolia, its inhabitants, or their ancient languages.
▶ **n. 1** a native or inhabitant of Anatolia.
2 an extinct group of ancient languages constituting a branch of the Indo-European language family and including Hittite, Luwian, Lydian, and Lycian.

an·a·tom·i·cal /ˌanəˈtämikəl/ (abbr.: **anat.**) ▶ **adj.** of or relating to bodily structure: *anatomical abnormalities.* ■ of or relating to anatomy: *anatomical lectures.*
– DERIVATIVES **an·a·tom·i·cal·ly** /-ik(ə)lē/ **adv.**
– ORIGIN late 16th cent.: from late Latin *anatomicus*, from *anatomia* (see ANATOMY), + -AL.

a·nat·o·mist /əˈnatəmist/ ▶ **n.** an expert in anatomy; a dissector.
– ORIGIN mid 16th cent.: from French *anatomiste*, from a medieval Latin derivative of *anatomizare* (see ANATOMIZE).

a·nat·o·mize /əˈnatəˌmīz/ ▶ **v.** [with obj.] dissect (a body). ■ examine and analyze in detail: *successful comedy is notoriously difficult to anatomize.*
– ORIGIN late Middle English: from medieval Latin *anatomizare*, from *anatomia* (see ANATOMY).

a·nat·o·my /əˈnatəmē/ (abbr.: **anat.**) ▶ **n.** (pl. **anatomies**) **1** the branch of science concerned with the bodily structure of humans, animals, and other living organisms, esp. as revealed by dissection and the separation of parts. ■ the bodily structure of an organism: *descriptions of the cat's anatomy and behavior.* ■ informal, humorous a person's body: *he left dusty handprints on his lady customers' anatomies.*
2 a study of the structure or internal workings of something: *Machiavelli's anatomy of the art of war.*
– ORIGIN late Middle English: from Old French *anatomie* or late Latin *anatomia*, from Greek, from *ana-* 'up' + *tomia* 'cutting' (from *temnein* 'to cut').

a·nat·to /əˈnätō/ ▶ **n.** variant spelling of ANNATTO.

An·ax·ag·o·ras /ˌanəkˈsagərəs, ˌanak-/ (*c.*500–*c.*428 BC), Greek philosopher. He believed that all matter was infinitely divisible and motionless until animated by mind (*nous*).

A·nax·i·man·der /əˌnaksəˈmandər, əˈnaksəˌmandər/ (*c.*610–*c.*545 BC), Greek scientist from Miletus. He believed the earth to be cylindrical and poised in space and is reputed to have taught that life began in water and that humans originated from fish.

An·ax·im·e·nes /ˌanakˈsiməˌnēz/ (*c.*546 BC), Greek philosopher and scientist from Miletus. He believed the earth to be flat and shallow, a view of astronomy that was a retrograde step from that of Anaximander.

ANC ▶ **abbr.** African National Congress.

-ance /əns, ns/ ▶ **suffix** forming nouns: **1** denoting a quality or state or an instance of one: *allegiance* | *extravagance* | *perseverance*.
2 denoting an action: *appearance* | *utterance*.
– ORIGIN representing French suffix *-ance*, from Latin nouns ending in *-antia, -entia* (from present participial stems *-ant-, -ent-*).

an·ces·tor /ˈanˌsestər/ ▶ **n.** a person, typically one more remote than a grandparent, from whom one is descended: *my ancestor Admiral Anson circumnavigated the globe 250 years ago*. ■ an early type of animal or plant from which others have evolved. ■ an early version of a machine, system, etc.: *this instrument is an ancestor of the lute*.
– ORIGIN Middle English: from Old French *ancestre*, from Latin *antecessor*, from *antecedere*, from *ante* 'before' + *cedere* 'go.'

an·ces·tral /anˈsestrəl/ ▶ **adj.** [attrib.] of, belonging to, inherited from, or denoting an ancestor or ancestors: *the family's ancestral home* | *the only records of the ancestral forms are their fossils*.
– ORIGIN late Middle English: from Old French *ancestrel*, from *ancestre* (see **ANCESTOR**).

an·ces·tress /ˈanˌsestris/ ▶ **n.** a female ancestor.

an·ces·try /ˈanˌsestrē/ ▶ **n.** (pl. **ancestries**) [usu. in sing.] **1** one's family or ethnic descent: *his Viking ancestry*. ■ the evolutionary or genetic line of descent of an animal or plant: *the ancestry of the rose is extremely complicated*.
2 the origin or background of something: *the book traces the ancestry of women's poetry*.
– ORIGIN Middle English: alteration of Old French *ancesserie*, from *ancestre* (see **ANCESTOR**).

An·chi·ses /anGˈkīsēz/ Greek & Roman Mythology the father of the Trojan hero Aeneas.

an·cho /ˈanCHō, ˈän-/ (also **ancho chili**) ▶ **n.** (pl. **anchos**) a large aromatic variety of chili, used (usually dried) in dishes of Mexican origin or style.
– ORIGIN from Mexican Spanish (*chile*) *ancho* 'wide (chili).'

an·choï·ade (also **anchoiade** /ˌanSHwīˈäd, -CHoiˈäd/) ▶ **n.** a purée of anchovies, crushed garlic, and olive oil that is served with vegetables as a dip or spread on bread.
– ORIGIN Provençal, from French *anchois* 'anchovy.'

an·chor /ˈaNGkər/ ▶ **n.** **1** a heavy object attached to a rope or chain and used to moor a vessel to the sea bottom, typically one having a metal shank with a ring at one end for the rope and a pair of curved and/or barbed flukes at the other. ■ a person or thing that provides stability or confidence in an otherwise uncertain situation: *the European Community is the economic anchor of the New Europe*. ■ (in full **anchor store**) a store, e.g., a department store, that is the principal tenant of a mall or a shopping center.
2 an anchorman or anchorwoman, esp. in broadcasting or athletics: *he signed off after nineteen years as CBS news anchor*.
▶ **v.** [with obj.] **1** moor (a ship) to the sea bottom with an anchor: *the ship was anchored in the lee of the island* | [no obj.] *we anchored in the harbor*. ■ secure firmly in position: *with cords and pitons they **anchored** him **to** the rock* | *the tail is used as a hook with which the fish **anchors** itself **to** coral* | figurative *the first baseman is anchored to the bag*. ■ provide with a firm basis or foundation: *it is important that policy be anchored to some acceptable theoretical basis*.
2 act as an anchor for (a television program or sporting event): *she anchored a television documentary series in the early 1980s*.
– PHRASES **at anchor** (of a ship) moored by means of an anchor. **drop anchor** (of a ship) let down the anchor and moor. **weigh** (or **raise** or **heave**) **anchor** (of a ship) take up the anchor when ready to depart.
– ORIGIN Old English *ancor, ancra*, via Latin from Greek *ankura*; reinforced in Middle English by Old French *ancre*. The current form is from *anchora*, an erroneous Latin spelling. The verb (from Old French *ancrer*) dates from Middle English.

anchor with arm and flukes mushroom anchor
types of anchor

An·chor·age /ˈaNGk(ə)rij/ a seaport in southern Alaska, on an inlet of the Pacific Ocean, the state's largest city; pop. 279,243 (est. 2008).

an·chor·age /ˈaNGk(ə)rij/ ▶ **n.** **1** an area that is suitable for a ship to anchor in. ■ the action of securing something to a base or the state of being secured: *the plant needs firm anchorage* | figurative *the mother provides emotional anchorage*.
2 historical an anchorite's dwelling place.

an·cho·ress /ˈaNGkəris/ ▶ **n.** historical a female anchorite.

an·cho·rite /ˈaNGkəˌrīt/ ▶ **n.** historical a religious recluse.
– DERIVATIVES **an·cho·rit·ic** /ˌaNGkəˈritik/ **adj.**
– ORIGIN late Middle English: from medieval Latin *anchorita* (ecclesiastical Latin *anchoreta*), from ecclesiastical Greek *anakhōrētēs*, from *anakhōrein* 'retire,' from *ana-* 'back' + *khōra, khōr-* 'a place.'

an·chor·man /ˈaNGkərˌman/ ▶ **n.** (pl. **anchormen**) a man who presents and coordinates a live television or radio program involving other contributors. ■ a man who plays the most crucial part or is the most dependable contributor. ■ the member of a relay team who runs the last leg.

an·chor·per·son /ˈaNGkərˌpərsən/ ▶ **n.** (pl. **anchorpersons** or **anchorpeople**) an anchorman or anchorwoman (used as a neutral alternative).

an·chor text ▶ **n.** the text that appears highlighted in a hypertext link and that can be clicked to open the target web page.

an·chor·wom·an /ˈaNGkərˌwo͝omən/ ▶ **n.** (pl. **anchorwomen**) a woman who presents and coordinates a live television or radio program involving other contributors.

an·cho·vy /ˈanˌCHōvē, anˈCHōvē/ ▶ **n.** (pl. **anchovy**) a small shoaling fish of commercial importance as a food fish and as bait. It is strongly flavored and is usually preserved in salt and oil. ● Genus *Engraulis*, family Engraulidae: several species, including *E. encrasicolus* of European waters.
– ORIGIN late 16th cent.: from Spanish and Portuguese *anchova*, of unknown origin.

an·chu·sa /anGˈkyo͞osə/ ▶ **n.** an Old World plant of the borage family, often cultivated for its bright, typically blue, flowers. ● Genus *Anchusa*, family Boraginaceae.
– ORIGIN via Latin from Greek *ankhousa*.

an·cien ré·gime /änˈsyan räˈZHēm/ ▶ **n.** (pl. **anciens régimes** pronunc. **same**) a political or social system that has been displaced, typically by one more modern. ■ (**Ancien Régime**) the political and social system in France before the Revolution of 1789.
– ORIGIN late 18th cent.: French, literally 'old rule.'

an·cient¹ /ˈānCHənt/ ▶ **adj.** belonging to the very distant past and no longer in existence: *the ancient civilizations of the Mediterranean*. ■ having been in existence for a very long time: *an ancient gateway* | *ancient forests*. ■ chiefly humorous showing or feeling signs of age or wear: *an ancient pair of jeans* | *you make me feel ancient*.
▶ **n.** archaic or humorous an old person: *a solitary ancient in a tweed jacket*.
– PHRASES **the Ancient of Days** a biblical title for God. **the ancients** the people of ancient times, esp. the Greeks and Romans of classical antiquity. ■ the classical Greek and Roman authors: *a thorough knowledge of the ancients is a prerequisite of criticism*.
– DERIVATIVES **an·cient·ness** **n.**
– ORIGIN late Middle English: from Old French *ancien*, based on Latin *ante* 'before.'

an·cient² ▶ **n.** archaic a standard, flag, or ensign.
– ORIGIN mid 16th cent.: alteration of **ENSIGN** by association with *ancien*, an early form of **ANCIENT¹**.

an·cient his·to·ry ▶ **n.** the history of the ancient civilizations of the Mediterranean area and the Near East up to the fall of the Western Roman Empire in AD 476. ■ informal something that is already long familiar and no longer new, interesting, or relevant: *the New Wave is ancient history now*.
– DERIVATIVES **an·cient his·to·ri·an** **n.**

an·cient·ly /ˈānCHəntlē/ ▶ **adv.** long ago: *the area was anciently called Dalriada*.

an·cient world ▶ **n.** the region around the Mediterranean and the Near East before the fall of the Western Roman Empire in AD 476.

an·cil·lar·y /ˈansəˌlerē/ ▶ **adj.** providing necessary support to the primary activities or operation of an organization, institution, industry, or system: *the development of ancillary services to support its products*. ■ additional; subsidiary: ***paragraph 19 was merely ancillary to paragraph 16***.
▶ **n.** (pl. **ancillaries**) a person whose work provides necessary support to the primary activities of an organization, institution, or industry: *the employment of specialist teachers and ancillaries*. ■ something that functions in a supplementary or supporting role: *undergraduate courses of three main subjects with related ancillaries*.
– ORIGIN mid 17th cent.: from Latin *ancillaris*, from *ancilla* 'maidservant.'

an·con /ˈanGˌkän/ ▶ **n.** (pl. **ancones** /ˌanGˈkōnēz/) Architecture **1** a console or bracket, typically with two volutes, that supports or appears to support a cornice.
2 each of a pair of projections on either side of a block of stone or other material, used for lifting it.
– ORIGIN early 18th cent. (denoting the corner or quoin of a wall or rafter): via Latin from Greek *ankōn* 'bend, elbow.'

ancon 1

An·co·na¹ /anGˈkōnə, anˈkōnə/ a port on the Adriatic coast of central Italy, capital of Marche region; pop. 102,047 (2008).

An·co·na² ▶ **n.** a chicken of a breed with mottled black and white plumage.
– ORIGIN mid 19th cent.: from the place name *Ancona* (see **ANCONA¹**).

-ancy ▶ **suffix** (forming nouns) denoting a quality or state: *buoyancy* | *expectancy*. Compare with **-ANCE**.
– ORIGIN representing Latin suffix *-antia* (see also **-ENCY**).

an·cy·lo·sto·mi·a·sis /ˌaNGkəlōstəˈmīəsis, ˌansə-/ (also **ankylostomiasis**) ▶ **n.** Medicine hookworm infection of the small intestine, often leading to anemia. ● The infecting organism is typically *Ancylostoma duodenale*, class Phasmida (or Secernentea).
– ORIGIN late 19th cent.: from modern Latin *Ancylostoma* (from Greek *ankulos* 'crooked' + *stoma* 'mouth') + **-IASIS**.

An·cy·ra /anˈsīrə/ ancient Roman name for **ANKARA**.

and /and/ ▶ **conj.** **1** used to connect words of the same part of speech, clauses, or sentences that are to be taken jointly: *bread and butter* | *red and black tiles* | *they can read and write* | *a hundred and fifty*. ■ used to connect two clauses when the second happens after the first: *he turned around and walked out* | *she washed and dried her hair*. ■ used to connect two clauses, the second of which results from the first: *do that once more, and I'll skin you alive*. ■ connecting two identical comparatives, to emphasize a progressive change: *getting better and better* | *he felt more and more like an outsider*. ■ connecting two identical words, implying great duration or great extent: *I cried and cried* | *it takes hours and hours*. ■ used to connect two identical words to indicate that things of the same name or class have different qualities: *all human conduct is determined or caused—but there are causes and causes*. ■ used to connect two numbers to indicate that they are being added together: *six and four make ten*. ■ archaic used to connect two numbers, implying succession: *a line of men marching two and two*.
2 used to introduce an additional comment or interjection: *if it came to a choice—and this was the worst thing—she would turn her back on her parents* | *they believe they are descended from him, and quite right, too*. ■ used to introduce a question in connection with what someone else has just said: *"I found the letter in her bag." "And did you steam it open?"* ■ (esp. in broadcasting) used to introduce a statement about a new topic: *and now to the dessert*.
3 informal used after some verbs and before another verb to indicate intention, instead of "to": *I would **try and** do what he said* | ***come and** see me*.
▶ **n.** (usu. **AND**) Logic & Electronics a Boolean operator that gives the value one if and only if all the operands are one, and otherwise has a value of zero. ■ (also **AND gate**) a circuit that produces an output signal only when signals are received simultaneously through all input connections.
– PHRASES **and/or** either or both of two stated possibilities: *audio and/or video components*.
– ORIGIN Old English *and, ond*, of Germanic origin; related to Dutch *en* and German *und*.

USAGE **1** It is still widely taught and believed that conjunctions such as **and** (and also **but** and **because**) should not be used to start a sentence, the argument being that a sentence starting with **and** expresses an incomplete thought and is therefore incorrect. Writers down the

a

centuries have readily ignored this advice, however, using **and** to start a sentence, typically for rhetorical effect: *What are the government's chances of winning in court? And what are the consequences?* **2** A small number of verbs—notably **try**, **come**, and **go**—can be followed by 'and' with another verb, as in sentences like *we're going to **try and** explain it to them or why don't you **come and** see the film?* Such structures in these verbs correspond to the use of the infinitive 'to,' as in *we're going to **try to** explain it to them or why don't you **come to** see the film?* Since these structures are grammatically odd and, though extremely common, are mainly restricted to informal English, they are regarded as wrong by some and should be avoided in formal standard English. **3** On whether it is more correct to say *both **the boys** and **the girls*** or *both **the boys** and **girls***, see usage at **BOTH**. **4** Where a number of items are separated by **and**, the following verb needs to be in the plural: see usage at **OR**[1].

-and ▶ **suffix** (forming nouns) denoting a person or thing to be treated in a specified way: *analysand*.
– ORIGIN from Latin gerundive ending *-andus*.

An·da·lu·sia /ˌandəˈlo͞ozн(ē)ə/ the southernmost region of Spain, bordering on the Atlantic Ocean and the Mediterranean Sea; capital, Seville. The region was under Moorish rule from 711 to 1492.

An·da·lu·sian /ˌandəˈlo͞ozн(ē)ən, -sн(ē)ən/ ▶ **adj.** of or relating to Andalusia or its people or their dialect.
▶ **n. 1** a native or inhabitant of Andalusia.
2 the dialect of Spanish spoken in Andalusia.
3 a light horse of a strong breed from Andalusia.

an·da·lu·site /ˌandlˈo͞oˌsīt/ ▶ **n.** a gray, green, brown, or pink aluminosilicate mineral occurring mainly in metamorphic rocks as elongated rhombic prisms, sometimes of gem quality.
– ORIGIN early 19th cent.: from the name of the Spanish region of **ANDALUSIA** + **-ITE**[1].

An·da·man and Nic·o·bar Is·lands /ˈandəmən and ˈnikəˌbär, ˈandəˌman/ two groups of islands in the Bay of Bengal that constitute a Union Territory in India; pop. 423,700 (est. 2009); capital, Port Blair.

an·dan·te /änˈdänˌtā/ Music ▶ **adj. & adv.** (esp. as a direction) in a moderately slow tempo.
▶ **n.** a movement or composition marked to be played andante.
– ORIGIN Italian, literally 'going,' present participle of *andare*.

an·dan·ti·no /ˌändänˈtēnō/ Music ▶ **adj. & adv.** (esp. as a direction) more lighthearted than andante, and in most cases quicker.
▶ **n.** (pl. **andantinos**) a movement or composition marked to be played andantino.
– ORIGIN Italian, diminutive of **ANDANTE**.

An·de·an /ˈandēən, anˈdē-/ ▶ **adj.** of or relating to the Andes.
▶ **n.** a native or inhabitant of the Andes.

An·de·an con·dor see **CONDOR**.

An·der·sen /ˈandərsən, ˈänərsən/, Hans Christian (1805–75), Danish author. He is noted for his fairy tales, published from 1835, such as "The Snow Queen," "The Ugly Duckling," and "The Little Match Girl."

An·der·son[1] /ˈandərsən/ an industrial city in east central Indiana; pop. 57,282 (est. 2008).

An·der·son[2], Carl David (1905–91), US physicist. In 1932, he discovered the positron—the first antiparticle known. Nobel Prize for Physics (1936), shared with Victor F. Hess.

An·der·son[3], Elizabeth Garrett (1836–1917), English physician. In 1866 she established a dispensary for women and children in London.

An·der·son[4], Marian (1902–93), US opera singer. Initially barred from giving concerts in the US because of racial discrimination, she gained international success during several European tours 1925–35. Her US career flourished from 1936; in 1955, she became the first black singer to perform at the Metropolitan Opera House in New York.

An·der·son[5], Maxwell (1888–1959), US playwright. His plays, many of which are written in verse, deal with social and moral problems. He also wrote many historical dramas. Notable works: *Elizabeth the Queen* (1930), *Key Largo* (1939), *Anne of the Thousand Days* (1948), and *The Bad Seed* (1954).

An·der·son[6], Philip Warren (1923–), American physicist. He made significant contributions to the study of solid-state physics, investigating magnetism and superconductivity. Nobel Prize for Physics (1977).

An·der·son[7], Sherwood (1876–1941), US author. He is noted for *Winesburg, Ohio* (1919), a collection of interrelated short stories that explore the loneliness and frustration of small-town life.

An·der·son·ville /ˈandərsənˌvil/ a village in southwestern Georgia, near Americus, that was the site of a large and infamous Confederate prison camp during the Civil War.

An·des /ˈandēz/ a major mountain system that runs the length of the Pacific coast of South America. It extends more than 5,000 miles (8,000 km), with a continuous height of more than 10,000 feet (3,000 m). Its highest peak is Aconcagua.

an·des·ite /ˈandiˌzīt/ ▶ **n.** Geology a dark, fine-grained, brown or grayish volcanic rock that is intermediate in composition between rhyolite and basalt.
– DERIVATIVES **an·de·sit·ic** /ˌandiˈzitik/ **adj.**
– ORIGIN mid 19th cent.: named after the **ANDES** mountains, where it is found + **-ITE**[1].

An·dhra Pra·desh /ˌəndrə prəˈdāsн, ˈändrə, prəˈdesн/ a state in southeastern India, on the Bay of Bengal; capital, Hyderabad.

and·i·ron /ˈanˌdīərn/ ▶ **n.** a metal support, typically one of a pair, that holds wood burning in a fireplace.
– ORIGIN Middle English: from Old French *andier*, of unknown origin. The ending was altered by association with **IRON**.

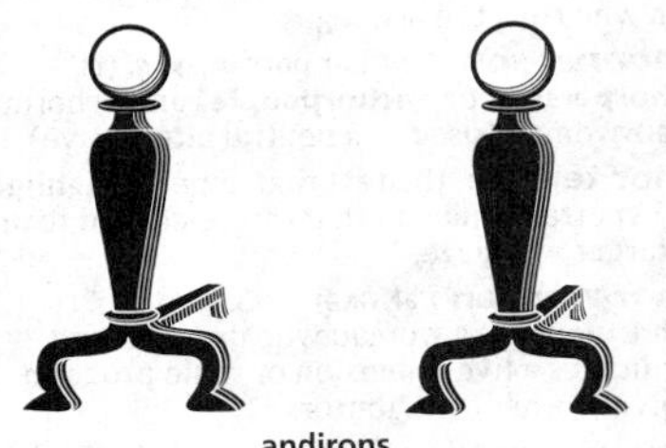

andirons

An·dor·ra /anˈdôrə/ a small autonomous principality in southwestern Europe, in the southern Pyrenees, between France and Spain; pop. 83,900 (est. 2009); capital, Andorra la Vella; languages, Catalan (official) and French.

Andorra's independence dates from the late 8th century, when Charlemagne is said to have granted the Andorrans self-government for their help in defeating the Moors. Since World War II, tourism has driven the economy.

– DERIVATIVES **An·dor·ran adj. & n.**

an·dou·ille /anˈdo͞o-ē/ ▶ **n.** a spicy pork sausage seasoned with garlic, used esp. in Cajun cooking.
– ORIGIN early 17th cent.: French.

an·douil·lette /ˌandwēˈyet/ ▶ **n.** a very small French sausage similar to andouille.
– ORIGIN French.

An·do·ver /ˈanˌdōvər, ˈandəvər/ a town in northeastern Massachusetts, home to Phillips Academy, a noted prep school; pop. 33,418 (est. 2008).

andr- ▶ **comb. form** **ANDRO-** shortened before a vowel (as in *androecium*).

an·dra·dite /ˈandrəˌdīt/ ▶ **n.** a mineral of the garnet group, containing calcium and iron. It occurs as yellow, green, brown, or black crystals, sometimes of gem quality.
– ORIGIN mid 19th cent.: named after J. B. de *Andrada e Silva* (c.1763–1838), Brazilian geologist, + **-ITE**[1].

An·dre /ˈänˌdrā/, Carl (1935–), US sculptor. Many of his works are ready-made units, such as bricks, stacked according to a mathematical system and without adhesives or joints.

An·dré /ˈandrē/, John (1750–80), British soldier. He successfully negotiated with Benedict Arnold for the betrayal of West Point to the British 1779–80. Captured while returning from West Point, he was tried and hanged as a spy.

An·dre·an·of Is·lands /ˌandrēˈanôf, -əf, ˌändrēˈänəf/ an island group in southwestern Alaska, part of the Aleutian Islands.

An·dret·ti /anˈdretē/, Mario (Gabriele) (1940–), US race car driver, born in Italy. He won the Daytona 500 in 1967, the Indianapolis 500 in 1969, and the Grand Prix world driving championship in 1978.

An·drew, Prince /ˈandro͞o/, (1960–), British prince; second son of Elizabeth II; full name *Andrew Albert Christian Edward, Duke of York*. He married **Sarah Ferguson** in 1986, but the couple divorced in 1996; they have two children, **Princess Beatrice** (1988–) and **Princess Eugenie** (1990–).

An·drew, St., an Apostle; the brother of St. Peter. The X-shaped cross is associated with him because he is said to have been crucified on such a cross. He is the patron saint of Scotland and Russia. Feast day, November 30.

An·drews[1] /ˈanˌdro͞oz/, Julie (1935–), English actress and singer; born *Julia Elizabeth Wells*. Best known for her lead roles in *Mary Poppins* (1964) and *The Sound of Music* (1965), she also starred in a number of other movies, including *Darling Lili* (1970), *Victor/Victoria* (1982), and *The Princess Diaries* (2001).

An·drews[2], Thomas (1813–85), Irish physical chemist. He discovered the critical temperature of carbon dioxide and showed that ozone is an allotrope of oxygen.

an·dro /ˈandrō/ another term for **ANDROSTENEDIONE**.

andro- (usu. **andr-** before a vowel) ▶ **comb. form** man (as opposed to woman): *androcentric* | *androgenize*.

an·dro·cen·tric /ˌandrōˈsentrik/ ▶ **adj.** focused or centered on men: *in the radical feminist view science is sexist and androcentric*.
– DERIVATIVES **an·dro·cen·trism n.**
– ORIGIN early 20th cent.: from Greek *anēr, andr-* 'man' + **-CENTRIC**.

An·dro·cles /ˈandrəˌklēz/ a runaway slave in a story by **Aulus Gellius** (2nd century AD) who extracted a thorn from the paw of a lion, which later recognized him and refrained from attacking him when he faced it in the arena.

an·droc·ra·cy /anˈdräkrəsē/ ▶ **n.** (pl. **androcracies**) a social system ruled or dominated by men.
– DERIVATIVES **an·dro·crat·ic** /ˌandrəˈkratik/ **adj.**

an·droe·ci·um /anˈdrēsн(ē)əm/ ▶ **n.** (pl. **androecia** /-sн(ē)ə/) Botany the stamens of a flower collectively.
– ORIGIN mid 19th cent.: modern Latin, from Greek *anēr, andr-* 'man' + *oikion* 'house.'

an·dro·gen /ˈandrəjən/ ▶ **n.** Biochemistry a male sex hormone, such as testosterone.
– DERIVATIVES **an·dro·gen·ic** /ˌandrəˈjenik/ **adj.**
– ORIGIN 1930s: from Greek *anēr, andr-* 'man' + **-GEN**.

an·dro·gen·ize /anˈdräjəˌnīz/ ▶ **v.** [with obj.] (usu. as adj. **androgenized**) treat with or expose to male hormones, typically resulting in the production of male sexual characteristics.
– DERIVATIVES **an·drog·e·ni·za·tion** /anˌdräjənəˈzāsнən/ **n.**

an·dro·gyne /ˈandrəˌjīn/ ▶ **n.** an androgynous individual. ■ a hermaphrodite.
– ORIGIN mid 16th cent. (as a noun): via Latin from Greek *androgunos*, from *anēr, andr-* 'man' + *gunē* 'woman.'

an·drog·y·nous /anˈdräjənəs/ ▶ **adj.** partly male and partly female in appearance; of indeterminate sex. ■ having the physical characteristics of both sexes; hermaphrodite.
– DERIVATIVES **an·drog·y·ny** /-nē/ **n.**
– ORIGIN early 17th cent.: from Latin *androgynus* (see **ANDROGYNE**) + **-OUS**.

an·droid /ˈanˌdroid/ ▶ **n.** (in science fiction) a robot with a human appearance.
– ORIGIN early 18th cent. (in the modern Latin form): from modern Latin *androides*, from Greek *anēr, andr-* 'man' + **-OID**.

an·drol·o·gy /anˈdräləjē/ ▶ **n.** the branch of physiology and medicine that deals with diseases and conditions specific to men.
– DERIVATIVES **an·drol·o·gist n.**

An·drom·a·che /anˈdräməkē/ Greek Mythology the wife of Hector. She became the slave of Neoptolemus (son of Achilles) after the fall of Troy.

An·drom·e·da /anˈdrämidə/ **1** Greek Mythology an Ethiopian princess whose mother Cassiopeia boasted that she herself (or, in some stories, her daughter) was more beautiful than the Nereids. In revenge, Poseidon sent a sea monster to ravage the country; to placate him, Andromeda was fastened to a rock and exposed to the monster, from which she was rescued by Perseus.
2 Astronomy a large northern constellation between Perseus and Pegasus, with few bright stars. It is chiefly notable for the **Andromeda Galaxy** (or **Great Nebula of Andromeda**), a conspicuous spiral galaxy probably twice as massive as our own and located 2 million light years away. ■ (as genitive **Andromedae** /anˈdrämiˌdē/) used with a preceding letter or numeral to designate stars in this constellation: *the star Gamma Andromedae*.

an·drom·e·da /anˈdrämidə/ ▶ **n.** an evergreen shrub of the heath family, typically with clusters of small bell-like flowers. ● Two genera in the family Ericaceae: several species, including the **bog rosemary** (*Andromeda glaucophylla* and *A. polifolia*) of north temperate regions, and the widely cultivated **Japanese andromeda** (*Pieris japonica*).

an·dro·pause /ˈandrəˌpôz/ ▶ **n.** a collection of symptoms, including fatigue and a decrease in libido, experienced by some middle-aged men and attributed to a gradual decline in testosterone levels.
– DERIVATIVES **an·dro·pau·sal adj.**
– ORIGIN 1960s: from **ANDRO-**, on the pattern of *menopause*.

An·dro·pov[1] /anˈdräpôf, änˈdrôpəf/ former name (1984–89) for **RYBINSK**.

An·dro·pov[2] /än'drôpəf/, Yuri (Vladimirovich) (1914–84), Soviet statesman; general secretary of the Communist Party of the former Soviet Union 1982–84 and president 1983–84. As president, he initiated the reform process that was carried out by Mikhail Gorbachev, his successor.

An·dro·scog·gin Riv·er /,andrə'skägən/ a river that flows for 175 miles (280 km) from northern New Hampshire through southwestern Maine to the Atlantic Ocean.

an·dro·stene·di·one /,andrə,stēn'dīōn/ ▶ **n.** a naturally occurring steroid hormone, also available as a dietary supplement, believed to increase levels of serum testosterone. Also called ANDRO.

an·dros·ter·one /an'drästə,rōn/ ▶ **n.** Biochemistry a relatively inactive male sex hormone produced by metabolism of testosterone.
– ORIGIN 1930s: from Greek *anēr, andr-* 'man' + STEROL + -ONE.

-androus ▶ **comb. form** Botany & Zoology having male organs or stamens of a specified number: *monandrous* | *protandrous.*
– ORIGIN based on modern Latin *-andrus*, from Greek *-andros*, from *andros*, genitive of *anēr* 'man.'

-ane[1] ▶ **suffix** variant spelling of -AN, usually with a distinction of sense (such as *humane* compared with *human*) but sometimes with no corresponding form in *-an* (such as *mundane*).

-ane[2] ▶ **suffix** Chemistry forming names of saturated hydrocarbons: *methane* | *propane.*
– ORIGIN on the pattern of words such as *-ene, -ine.*

an·ec·dot·age /'anik,dōtij/ ▶ **n. 1** anecdotes collectively: *a number of reports cannot be dismissed as anecdotage.* [early 19th cent.: from ANECDOTE + -AGE.]
2 humorous old age, esp. in someone who is inclined to be garrulous. [late 18th cent.: from a blend of ANECDOTE and DOTAGE.]

an·ec·do·tal /,anik'dōtl/ ▶ **adj.** (of an account) not necessarily true or reliable, because based on personal accounts rather than facts or research: *while there was much anecdotal evidence there was little hard fact* | *these claims were purely anecdotal.* ■ characterized by or fond of telling anecdotes: *her book is anecdotal and chatty.* ■ [attrib.] (of a painting) depicting small narrative incidents: *nineteenth-century French anecdotal paintings.*
– DERIVATIVES **an·ec·do·tal·ist** /-tl-ist/ **n.**, **an·ec·do·tal·ly adv.**

an·ec·dote /'anik,dōt/ ▶ **n.** a short and amusing or interesting story about a real incident or person: *told anecdotes about his job* | *he had a rich store of anecdotes.* ■ an account regarded as unreliable or hearsay: *his wife's death has long been the subject of rumor and anecdote.* ■ the depiction of a minor narrative incident in a painting.
– ORIGIN late 17th cent.: from French, or via modern Latin from Greek *anekdota* 'things unpublished,' from *an-* 'not' + *ekdotos*, from *ekdidōnai* 'publish.'

an·e·cho·ic /ane'kō-ik/ ▶ **adj.** technical free from echo: *an anechoic chamber.* ■ (of a coating or material) tending to deaden sound.

a·nele /ə'nēl/ ▶ **v.** [with obj.] archaic anoint (someone), esp. as part of the Christian rite of giving extreme unction to the dying.
– ORIGIN Middle English: from *an-* 'on' + archaic *elien* 'to oil' (from Old English *ele*, from Latin *oleum* 'oil').

a·ne·mi·a /ə'nēmēə/ (Brit. **anaemia**) ▶ **n.** a condition marked by a deficiency of red blood cells or of hemoglobin in the blood, resulting in pallor and weariness.
– ORIGIN early 19th cent.: via modern Latin from Greek *anaimia*, from *an-* 'without' + *haima* 'blood.'

a·ne·mic /ə'nēmik/ (Brit. **anaemic**) ▶ **adj.** suffering from anemia. ■ lacking in color, spirit, or vitality.

anemo- ▶ **comb. form** wind: *anemometer.*

a·nem·o·graph /ə'nemə,graf/ ▶ **n.** an anemometer that records on paper the speed, duration, and sometimes also the direction of the wind.
– ORIGIN mid 19th cent.: from Greek *anemos* 'wind' + -GRAPH.

an·e·mom·e·ter /,anə'mämitər/ ▶ **n.** an instrument for measuring the speed of the wind, or of any current of gas.
– DERIVATIVES **an·e·mom·e·try** /-trē/ **n.**, **an·e·mo·met·ric** /-mə'metrik/ **adj.**
– ORIGIN early 18th cent.: from Greek *anemos* 'wind' + -METER.

anemometer

a·nem·o·ne /ə'nemənē/ ▶ **n.**
1 a plant of the buttercup family, typically bearing brightly colored flowers. Anemones are widely distributed in the wild, and several kinds are popular garden plants. ● Genus *Anemone*, family Ranunculaceae: numerous species, including the North American **wood anemone** (*A. quinquefolia*).
2 short for SEA ANEMONE.
– ORIGIN mid 16th cent.: from Latin, said to be from Greek *anemōnē* 'windflower,' literally 'daughter of the wind,' from *anemos* 'wind,' thought to be so named because the flowers open only when the wind blows.

a·nem·o·ne fish ▶ **n.** another term for CLOWNFISH.

an·e·moph·i·lous /,anə'mäfələs/ ▶ **adj.** Botany (of a plant) wind-pollinated.
– DERIVATIVES **an·e·moph·i·ly** /-lē/ **n.**
– ORIGIN late 19th cent.: from Greek *anemos* 'wind' + *-philous* (see -PHILIA).

an·en·ce·phal·ic /,anensə'falik/ Medicine ▶ **adj.** having part or all of the cerebral hemispheres and the rear of the skull congenitally absent.
▶ **n.** an anencephalic fetus or infant.
– DERIVATIVES **an·en·ceph·a·ly** /-'sefəlē/ **n.**
– ORIGIN mid 19th cent.: from Greek *anenkephalos* 'without brain' + -IC.

a·nent /ə'nent/ ▶ **prep.** chiefly archaic concerning; about: *I'll say a few words anent the letter.*
– ORIGIN Old English *on efen* 'in line with, in company with.'

-aneous ▶ **suffix** forming adjectives from Latin words: *cutaneous* | *spontaneous.*
– ORIGIN from the Latin suffix *-aneus* + -OUS.

an·er·gi·a /a'nərj(ē)ə/ ▶ **n.** Psychiatry abnormal lack of energy.
– ORIGIN late 19th cent.: modern Latin, from Greek *an-* 'without' + *ergon* 'work.'

an·er·gy /'anərjē/ ▶ **n. 1** Medicine absence of the normal immune response to a particular antigen or allergen.
2 another term for ANERGIA.
– DERIVATIVES **anergic** /ə'nərjik/ **adj.**
– ORIGIN early 20th cent.: from German *Anergie*, from Greek *an-* 'not,' on the pattern of *Allergie* 'allergy.'

an·er·oid /'anə,roid/ ▶ **adj.** relating to or denoting a barometer that measures air pressure by the action of the air in deforming the elastic lid of an evacuated box or chamber.
▶ **n.** a barometer of this type.
– ORIGIN mid 19th cent.: coined in French from Greek *a-* 'without' + *nēros* 'water.'

an·es·the·sia /,anəs'THēZHə/ (Brit. **anaesthesia**) ▶ **n.** insensitivity to pain, esp. as artificially induced by the administration of gases or the injection of drugs before surgical operations. ■ the induction of this state, or the branch of medicine concerned with it.
– ORIGIN early 18th cent.: from modern Latin *anaesthesia*, from Greek *anaisthēsia*, from *an-* 'without' + *aisthēsis* 'sensation.'

an·es·the·si·ol·o·gy /,anəs,THēzē'äləjē/ (Brit. **anaesthesiology**) ▶ **n.** the branch of medicine concerned with anesthesia and anesthetics.
– DERIVATIVES **an·es·the·si·ol·o·gist** /-jist/ **n.**

an·es·thet·ic /,anəs'THetik/ (Brit. **anaesthetic**) ▶ **n.**
1 a substance that induces insensitivity to pain.
2 (**anesthetics**) [treated as sing.] the study or practice of anesthesia.
▶ **adj.** inducing or relating to insensitivity to pain.
– ORIGIN mid 19th cent.: from Greek *anaisthētos* 'insensible,' related to *anaisthēsia* (see ANESTHESIA), + -IC.

an·es·the·tist /ə'nesTHitist/ (Brit. **anaesthetist**) ▶ **n.** a medical specialist who administers anesthetics.

an·es·the·tize /ə'nesTHi,tīz/ (Brit. **anaesthetize**) ▶ **v.** [with obj.] administer an anesthetic to (a person or animal), esp. so as to induce a loss of consciousness. ■ deprive of feeling or awareness: *tragedy of a magnitude that anesthetizes the mind.*
– DERIVATIVES **an·es·the·ti·za·tion** /-THitə'zāSHən/ **n.**

an·eu·ploid /'anyoo͞,ploid/ ▶ **adj.** Genetics having particular genes or chromosomal regions present in extra or fewer copies than in the normal type.
– DERIVATIVES **an·eu·ploi·dy n.**

an·eu·rysm /'anyə,rizəm/ (also **aneurism**) ▶ **n.** Medicine an excessive localized enlargement of an artery caused by a weakening of the artery wall.
– DERIVATIVES **an·eu·rys·mal** /-,rizməl/ **adj.**
– ORIGIN late Middle English: from Greek *aneurusma* 'dilatation,' from *aneurunein* 'widen out.'

a·new /ə'n(y)oo͞/ ▶ **adv.** chiefly literary in a new or different, typically more positive, way: *her career had begun anew, with a lucrative Japanese modeling contract.* ■ once more; again: *tears filled her eyes anew.*

an·frac·tu·ous /an'frakCHoo͞əs/ ▶ **adj.** rare sinuous or circuitous.
– DERIVATIVES **an·frac·tu·os·i·ty** /-,frakCHoo͞'äsitē/ **n.**
– ORIGIN late 16th cent.: from late Latin *anfractuosus*, from Latin *anfractus* 'a bending.'

An·ga·ra Riv·er /,änGgə'rä, ,əNG-/ a river in the southeastern part of Siberia in Russia that flows northwest and west for 1,039 miles (1,779 km) from Lake Baikal to meet the Yenisei River south of Yeniseysk.

an·gel /'ānjəl/ ▶ **n. 1** a spiritual being believed to act as an attendant, agent, or messenger of God, conventionally represented in human form with wings and a long robe: *God sent an angel to talk to Gideon* | *the Angel of Death* | figurative *Ella, ever the angel of mercy, organized the girls into baking cookies.* ■ an attendant spirit, esp. a benevolent one: *there was an angel watching over me.* See also GUARDIAN ANGEL. ■ informal a financial backer of an enterprise, typically in the theater. ■ in traditional Christian angelology, a being of the lowest order of the celestial hierarchy.
2 a person of exemplary conduct or virtue: *women were then seen as angels or whores* | *I know I'm no angel.* ■ used in similes or comparisons to refer to a person's outstanding beauty, qualities, or abilities: *you sang like an angel.* ■ used in approval when a person has been or is expected to be kind or willing to oblige: *be an angel and let us come in.* ■ used as a term of endearment: *I miss you too, angel.*
3 historical an English coin minted between 1470 and 1634 and bearing the figure of the archangel Michael killing a dragon.
4 (**angels**) Aviation, informal an aircraft's altitude (often used with a numeral indicating thousands of feet): *we rendezvous at angels nine.*
5 Aviation, informal an unexplained radar echo.
– PHRASES **the angel in the house** chiefly ironic a woman who is completely devoted to her husband and family. [phrase from a poem by Coventry Patmore.] **on the side of the angels** on the side of what is right and just.
– ORIGIN Old English *engel*, ultimately via ecclesiastical Latin from Greek *angelos* 'messenger'; superseded in Middle English by forms from Old French *angele.*

an·gel dust ▶ **n.** informal **1** the hallucinogenic drug phencyclidine hydrochloride.
2 another term for CLENBUTEROL.

An·ge·le·no /,anjə'lēnō/ (also **Los Angeleno, Angelino**) ▶ **n.** (pl. **Angelenos**) a native or inhabitant of Los Angeles: [as modifier] *Angeleno sports fans.*
– ORIGIN late 19th cent.: from American Spanish.

An·gel Falls /'ānjəl/ a waterfall in the Guiana Highlands of southeastern Venezuela. The highest waterfall in the world, it has an uninterrupted descent of 3,210 feet (978 m). The falls were discovered in 1935 by US aviator and prospector **James Angel** (*c.*1899–1956).

an·gel·fish /'ānjəl,fiSH/ ▶ **n.** (pl. **same** or **angelfishes**) any of a number of laterally compressed deep-bodied fish with extended dorsal and anal fins, typically brightly colored or boldly striped, including. ● a freshwater fish native to the Amazon basin (genus *Pterophyllum*, family Cichlidae), in particular *P. scalare*, popular in tropical aquariums. ● a coastal marine fish (several genera in the family Pomacanthidae), including the blue and yellow **queen angelfish** (*Holacanthus ciliaris*) and the more drably colored **gray angelfish** (*Pomacanthus arcuatus*). ● another term for BATFISH (sense 2).

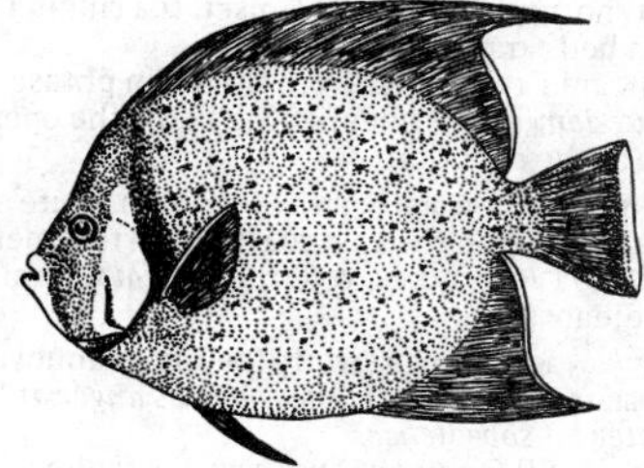

gray angelfish

an·gel food cake (Brit. **angel cake**) ▶ **n.** a light, pale sponge cake made of flour, egg whites, and no fat, typically baked in a ring shape and covered with soft icing.

an·gel hair (also **angel's hair**) ▶ **n.** a type of pasta consisting of very fine long strands.

an·gel·ic /an'jelik/ ▶ **adj.** of or relating to angels: *the angelic hosts.* ■ (of a person) exceptionally

a

beautiful, innocent, or kind: *she looks remarkably young and angelic.*
– DERIVATIVES **an·gel·i·cal** adj., **an·gel·i·cal·ly** /-ik(ə)lē/ adv.
– ORIGIN late Middle English: from French *angélique*, via late Latin from Greek *angelikos*, from *angelos* (see ANGEL).

an·gel·i·ca /an'jelikə/ ▶ n. a tall aromatic plant of the parsley family, with large leaves and yellowish-green flowers. Native to both Eurasia and North America, it is used in cooking and herbal medicine. ● Genus *Angelica*, family Umbelliferae: many species, esp. the cultivated *A. archangelica*. ■ the candied stalk of this plant.
– ORIGIN early 16th cent.: from medieval Latin (*herba*) *angelica* 'angelic (herb),' so named because it was believed to be efficacious against poisoning and disease.

an·gel·i·ca tree ▶ n. another term for DEVIL'S WALKING STICK (see HERCULES-CLUB).

An·gel·ic Doc·tor the nickname of St. Thomas Aquinas.

An·ge·li·co /än'jelikō/, Fra (*c.*1400–55), Italian painter and Dominican friar; born *Guido di Pietro*; monastic name *Fra Giovanni da Fiesole*. Notable works: the frescos in the convent of San Marco, Florence (*c.*1438–47).

An·ge·li·no ▶ n. variant spelling of ANGELENO.

An·gel Is·land an island in San Francisco Bay, in north central California, that was the chief immigration station on the US western coast. It is now a state park.

An·gel·man syn·drome /'aNG(g)əlmən/ (also **Angelman's syndrome**) ▶ n. a rare congenital disorder characterized by mental disability and a tendency toward jerky movement, caused by the absence of certain genes normally present on the copy of chromosome 15 inherited from the mother.
– ORIGIN 1970s: named after Harold *Angelman*, British doctor who described the condition.

an·gel·ol·o·gy /ˌānjə'läləjē/ ▶ n. theological dogma or speculation concerning angels: *Gnostic angelology influenced Pseudo-Dionysius.*
– DERIVATIVES **an·gel·ol·o·gist** /-jist/ n.
– ORIGIN mid 19th cent.

An·ge·lou /'anjəˌlō, -ˌlo͞o/, Maya (1928–), US novelist and poet; born *Marguerite Ann Johnson*. The first volume of her autobiography, *I Know Why the Caged Bird Sings* (1970), which recounts her harrowing experiences as a black child in the US South, was followed by five more: *Gather Together in My Name* (1974), *Singin' and Swingin' and Gettin' Merry Like Christmas* (1976), *The Heart of a Woman* (1981), *All God's Children Need Traveling Shoes* (1986), and *A Song Flung Up to Heaven* (2002).

an·gel shark ▶ n. an active bottom-dwelling cartilaginous fish with broad winglike pectoral fins. ● Family Squatinidae and genus *Squatina*: several species, in particular the **Atlantic angel shark** (*S. dumerili*).

an·gel's trum·pet ▶ n. a South American shrub or small tree of the nightshade family, with distinctive trumpet-shaped flowers, cultivated as an ornamental and in some regions consumed for its narcotic properties. ● Genus *Brugmansia*, family Solanaceae.

An·ge·lus /'anjələs/ (also **angelus**) ▶ n. [in sing.] a Roman Catholic devotion commemorating the Incarnation of Jesus and including the Hail Mary, said at morning, noon, and sunset. ■ a ringing of church bells announcing this.
– ORIGIN mid 17th cent.: from the Latin phrase *Angelus domini* 'the angel of the Lord,' the opening words of the devotion.

an·gel wings ▶ plural n. [treated as sing.] a white edible piddock found on the east coast of North America and in the West Indies. ● *Barnea costata*, family Pholadidae.

an·ger /'aNGgər/ ▶ n. a strong feeling of annoyance, displeasure, or hostility: *the colonel's anger at his daughter's disobedience.*
▶ v. [with obj.] fill (someone) with such a feeling; provoke anger in: *she was angered by his terse answer* | [with obj. and infinitive] *I was angered to receive a further letter from them* | [with obj. and clause] *he was angered that he had not been told.*
– ORIGIN Middle English: from Old Norse *angr* 'grief,' *angra* 'vex.' The original use was in the Old Norse senses; current senses date from late Middle English.

An·gers /'anjərz, äN'ZHā/ a town in western France, capital of the former province of Anjou; pop. 156,965 (2006).

An·ge·vin /'anjəvən/ ▶ n. a native, inhabitant, or ruler of Anjou. ■ any of the Plantagenet kings of England, esp. those who were also counts of Anjou (Henry II, Richard I, and John).
▶ adj. of or relating to Anjou. ■ of, relating to, or denoting the Plantagenets.
– ORIGIN from French, from medieval Latin *Andegavinus*, from *Andegavum* 'Angers' (see ANGERS).

an·gi·na /an'jīnə/ ▶ n. **1** (also **angina pectoris** /'pektəris/) a condition marked by severe pain in the chest, often also spreading to the shoulders, arms, and neck, caused by an inadequate blood supply to the heart.
2 [with modifier] any of a number of disorders in which there is an intense localized pain: *Ludwig's angina.*
– ORIGIN mid 16th cent. (in the Latin sense): from Latin, 'quinsy,' from Greek *ankhonē* 'strangling'; *pectoris* (sense 1): Latin, 'of the chest.'

angio- ▶ comb. form relating to blood vessels: *angiography.* ■ relating to seed vessels: *angiosperm.*
– ORIGIN from Greek *angeion* 'vessel.'

an·gi·o·gen·e·sis /ˌanjē-ō'jenəsis/ ▶ n. Medicine the development of new blood vessels.
– DERIVATIVES **an·gi·o·gen·ic** /-'jenik/ adj.

an·gi·o·gram /'anj(ē)əˌgram/ ▶ n. an X-ray photograph of blood or lymph vessels, made by angiography.

an·gi·og·ra·phy /ˌanjē'ägrəfē/ ▶ n. examination by X-ray of blood or lymph vessels, carried out after introduction of a radiopaque substance.
– DERIVATIVES **an·gi·o·graph·ic** /-ə'grafik/ adj., **an·gi·o·graph·i·cal·ly** /-ə'grafik(ə)lē/ adv.

an·gi·o·ma /ˌanjē'ōmə/ ▶ n. (pl. **angiomas** or **angiomata** /-mətə/) Medicine an abnormal growth produced by the dilatation or new formation of blood vessels.
– ORIGIN late 19th cent.: from Greek *angeion* 'vessel' + -OMA.

an·gi·o·plas·ty /'anjēəˌplastē/ ▶ n. (pl. **angioplasties**) surgical repair or unblocking of a blood vessel, esp. a coronary artery. See also BALLOON ANGIOPLASTY.

an·gi·o·sperm /'anjēəˌspərm/ ▶ n. Botany a plant that has flowers and produces seeds enclosed within a carpel. The angiosperms are a large group and include herbaceous plants, shrubs, grasses, and most trees. Compare with GYMNOSPERM. ● Subdivision Angiospermae, division Spermatophyta.

an·gi·o·sta·tin /ˌanjēō'statn/ ▶ n. Medicine a drug used to inhibit the growth of new blood vessels in malignant tumors.

an·gi·o·ten·sin /ˌanjē-ō'tensin/ ▶ n. Biochemistry a protein whose presence in the blood promotes aldosterone secretion and tends to raise blood pressure.
– ORIGIN 1950s: from ANGIO- + (*hyper*)*tens*(*ion*) + -IN[1].

Ang·kor /'aNGkər, 'aNGˌkôr/ the capital of the ancient kingdom of Khmer in northwestern Cambodia; noted for its temples, esp. **Angkor Wat** (mid 12th century), the site was rediscovered in 1860.

Angkor Wat

An·gle /'aNGgəl/ ▶ n. a member of a Germanic people, originally inhabitants of what is now Schleswig-Holstein, who migrated to England in the 5th century AD. The Angles founded kingdoms in Mercia, Northumbria, and East Anglia and gave their name to England and the English.
– ORIGIN from Latin *Anglus*, (plural) *Angli* 'the people of *Angul*,' a district of Schleswig (now in northern Germany), so called because of its shape; of Germanic origin, related to Old English *angul* (see ANGLE[2]). Compare with ENGLISH.

an·gle[1] /'aNGgəl/ ▶ n. **1** the space (usually measured in degrees) between two intersecting lines or surfaces at or close to the point where they meet. ■ a corner, esp. an external projection or an internal recess of a part of a building or other structure: *a skylight in the angle of the roof.* ■ slope; a measure of the inclination of two lines or surfaces with respect to each other, equal to the amount that one would have to be turned in order to point in the same direction as the other: *sloping at an angle of 33° to the horizontal* | *he trudged back, the angle of his shoulders spelling dejection.* ■ a position from which something is viewed or along which it travels or acts, often as measured by its inclination from an implicit horizontal or vertical baseline: *from this angle, Maggie could not see Naomi's face* | *camera angles.*
2 a particular way of approaching or considering an issue or problem: *discussing the problems from every conceivable angle* | *he always had a fresh angle on life.* ■ one part of a larger subject, event, or problem: *a black prosecutor who downplayed the racial angle* | *his chosen angle was the language of the Old Testament.* ■ a bias or point of view: *Zimmer saw the world from an angle that few could understand.*

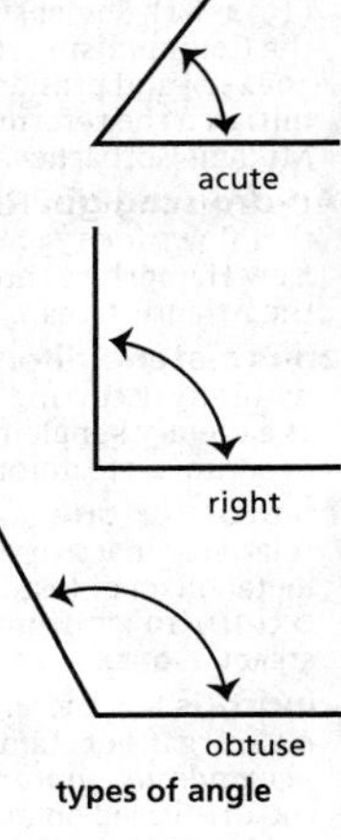

types of angle

3 [often with modifier] Astrology each of the four mundane houses (the first, fourth, seventh, and tenth of the twelve divisions of the heavens) that extend counterclockwise from the cardinal points of the compass.
4 angle iron or a similar construction material made of another metal.
▶ v. [with obj.] direct or incline at an angle: *Anna angled her camera toward the tree* | *he angled his chair so that he could watch her.* ■ [no obj.] move or be inclined at an angle: *the cab angled across two lanes and skidded to a stop* | *the sun angled into the dining room.* ■ present (information) to reflect a particular view or have a particular focus.
– PHRASES **at an angle** in a direction or at an inclination markedly different from parallel, vertical, or horizontal with respect to an implicit baseline: *she wore her beret at an angle* | *an armchair was drawn up at an angle to his desk.* **from all angles** from every direction or point of view: *they come shooting at us from all angles* | *looking at the problem from all angles.*
– ORIGIN late Middle English: from Old French, from Latin *angulus* 'corner.'

an·gle[2] ▶ v. [no obj.] fish with rod and line: *there are no big fish left to angle for.* ■ seek something desired by indirectly prompting someone to offer it: *Ralph had begun to angle for an invitation* | [with infinitive] *her husband was angling to get into the Cabinet.*
▶ n. archaic a fishhook.
– ORIGIN Old English *angul* (noun); the verb dates from late Middle English.

an·gle brack·et ▶ n. **1** either of a pair of marks in the form < >, used to enclose words or figures so as to separate them from their context.
2 another term for BRACKET (sense 3 of the noun).

an·gled /'aNGgəld/ ▶ adj. **1** placed or inclined at an angle to something else: *he sent an angled shot into the net* | *a sharply angled flight of stairs.*
2 [in combination] (of an object or shape) having an angle or angles of a specified type or number: *a right-angled bend* | *an obtuse-angled triangle.* ■ (of information) presented so as to reflect a particular view or to have a particular focus.

an·gle i·ron ▶ n. a construction material consisting of pieces of steel with an L-shaped cross-section, able to be bolted together. ■ a piece of metal of this kind.

an·gle of at·tack ▶ n. the angle between the chord of an airfoil and the direction of the surrounding undisturbed flow of gas or liquid.

an·gle of in·ci·dence ▶ n. Physics the angle that an incident line or ray makes with a perpendicular to the surface at the point of incidence.

an·gle of re·flec·tion ▶ n. Physics the angle made by a reflected ray with a perpendicular to the reflecting surface.

an·gle of re·frac·tion ▶ n. Physics the angle made by a refracted ray with a perpendicular to the refracting surface.

an·gle of re·pose ▶ n. the steepest angle at which a sloping surface formed of a particular loose material is stable.

an·gler /'aNGglər/ ▶ n. a person who fishes with a rod and line. ■ short for ANGLERFISH.

an·gler·fish /'aNGglərˌfiSH/ ▶ n. (pl. **same** or **anglerfishes**) a fish that lures prey with a fleshy lobe attached to a filament that arises from the snout and hangs in front of the mouth. Most anglerfishes have a very large head and wide mouth, with a small body and tail. ● Order Lophiiformes: several families. Some rest motionless on the seabed, in particular those of the family Lophiidae; many others are deep-sea fish.

An·gle·sey /ˈaNGgəlsē/ an island in northwestern Wales, separated from the mainland by the Menai Strait; pop. 70,000 (est. 2009).

an·gle shades ▶ **plural n.** [treated as sing.] a European moth with wings patterned in muted green, red, and pink. ● *Phlogophora meticulosa*, family Noctuidae and other species.

An·gli·an /ˈaNGglēən/ ▶ **adj.** of or relating to the ancient Angles.
– ORIGIN 1960s: from Latin *Angli* (see **ANGLE**) + **-IAN**.

An·gli·can /ˈaNGglikən/ ▶ **adj.** of, relating to, or denoting the Church of England or any Church in communion with it.
▶ **n.** a member of any of these Churches.
– DERIVATIVES **An·gli·can·ism** /-ˌnizəm/ **n.**
– ORIGIN early 17th cent.: from medieval Latin *Anglicanus* (its adoption suggested by *Anglicana ecclesia* 'the English church' in the Magna Carta), from *Anglicus*, from *Angli* (see **ANGLE**).

An·gli·can chant ▶ **n.** a method of singing unmetrical psalms and canticles to short harmonized melodies, the first note being extended to accommodate as many syllables as necessary.

An·gli·can Com·mun·ion the group of Christian Churches derived from or related to the Church of England, including the Episcopal Church in the US and other national, provincial, and independent churches. The body's primate is the Archbishop of Canterbury.

An·gli·cism /ˈaNGgləˌsizəm/ ▶ **n.** **1** a word or phrase that is peculiar to British English: *this new autobiography is studded with Anglicisms like lorries, plimsolls, and doing a bunk.* ■ the quality of being typically English or of favoring English things. **2** a word or phrase borrowed from English into a foreign language: *"purists" condemn the use of "fin de semaine" because it is an anglicism.*
– ORIGIN mid 17th cent.: from Latin *Anglicus*, from *Angli* (see **ANGLE**) + **-ISM**.

an·gli·cize /ˈaNGgləˌsīz/ ▶ **v.** [with obj.] make English in form or character: *he anglicized his name to Goodman* | (as adj. **anglicized**) *an anglicized form of a Navajo word.*
– DERIVATIVES **an·gli·ci·za·tion** /ˌaNGgləsəˈzāSHən/ **n.**

an·gling /ˈaNGg(ə)liNG/ ▶ **n.** the sport or pastime of fishing with a rod and line: [as modifier] *an angling club* | *an angling license.*

An·glo /ˈaNGglō/ ▶ **n.** (pl. **Anglos**) a white, English-speaking American as distinct from a Hispanic American: [as modifier] *Anglo neighborhoods.*
– ORIGIN early 19th cent.: independent usage of **ANGLO-**.

Anglo- ▶ **comb. form** English: *anglophone.* ■ of English origin: *Anglo-Saxon.* ■ English and ...: *Anglo-Latin.* ■ British and ...: *Anglo-Indian.*
– ORIGIN modern Latin, from Latin *Anglus* 'English.'

An·glo-A·mer·i·can ▶ **adj.** of or relating to both Britain and the US: *the older Anglo-American conception of the American as an offshoot of the Anglo-Saxons.* ■ of English descent, but born or living in the US.
▶ **n.** an American born in England or of English ancestry. ■ an American whose native tongue is English.

An·glo-Cath·o·lic ▶ **adj.** of or relating to Anglo-Catholicism.
▶ **n.** a member of an Anglo-Catholic Church.

An·glo-Ca·thol·i·cism ▶ **n.** a tradition within the Anglican Church that is close to Catholicism in its doctrine and worship and is broadly identified with High Church Anglicanism. Anglo-Catholicism grew out of the Oxford Movement of the 1830s and 1840s.

An·glo-Celt ▶ **n.** a person of British or Irish descent (typically used outside Britain and Ireland).
– DERIVATIVES **An·glo-Celt·ic adj.**

An·glo·cen·tric /ˌaNGglōˈsentrik/ ▶ **adj.** centered on or considered in terms of England or Britain: *an Anglocentric, white view of Australian history.*

An·glo-In·di·an ▶ **adj.** of, relating to, or involving both Britain and India: *Anglo-Indian business cooperation.* ■ (esp. of a person living in South Asia) of mixed British and Indian parentage. ■ chiefly historical of British descent or birth but living or having lived long in India. ■ (of a word) adopted into English from an Indian language.
▶ **n.** an Anglo-Indian person.

An·glo-I·rish ▶ **adj.** of or relating to both Britain and Ireland (or specifically the Republic of Ireland). ■ of English descent but born or resident in Ireland. ■ (as plural noun **the Anglo-Irish**) people of English descent but born or resident in Ireland. ■ of mixed English and Irish parentage.
▶ **n.** the English language as used in Ireland.

An·glo-I·rish Trea·ty an agreement signed in 1921 by representatives of the British government and the provisional Irish Republican government, whereby the Irish Free State was established.

An·glo-Lat·in ▶ **adj.** of, in, or relating to Latin as used in medieval England.
▶ **n.** this form of Latin.

An·glo·ma·ni·a /ˌaNGglōˈmānēə/ ▶ **n.** excessive admiration of English customs.

An·glo-Nor·man French (also **Anglo-Norman**) ▶ **n.** the variety of Norman French used in England after the Norman Conquest. It remained the language of the English nobility for several centuries and has had a strong influence on legal phraseology in English.
▶ **adj.** of or relating to this language.

An·glo·phile /ˈaNGgləˌfīl/ ▶ **n.** a person who is fond of or greatly admires England or Britain.
▶ **adj.** fond of or admiring of England or Britain.
– DERIVATIVES **An·glo·phil·ia** /ˌaNGgləˈfilēə/ **n.**

An·glo·phobe /ˈaNGgləˌfōb/ ▶ **n.** a person who greatly hates or fears England or Britain.
▶ **adj.** greatly hating or fearing England or Britain.
– DERIVATIVES **An·glo·pho·bi·a** /ˌaNGgləˈfōbēə/ **n.**

an·glo·phone /ˈaNGgləˌfōn/ ▶ **adj.** English-speaking: *anglophone students* | *the population is largely anglophone.*
▶ **n.** an English-speaking person.
– ORIGIN early 20th cent. (as a noun; rare before the 1960s): from **ANGLO-** + **-PHONE**, on the pattern of *francophone.*

An·glo-Sax·on ▶ **adj.** relating to or denoting the Germanic inhabitants of England from their arrival in the 5th century up to the Norman Conquest. ■ of English descent. ■ of, in, or relating to the Old English language. ■ informal (of an English word or expression) plain, in particular vulgar: *using a lot of good old Anglo-Saxon expletives.*
▶ **n.** **1** a Germanic inhabitant of England between the 5th century and the Norman Conquest. ■ a person of English descent. ■ any white, English-speaking person. **2** another term for **OLD ENGLISH**. ■ informal plain English, in particular vulgar slang.
– ORIGIN from modern Latin *Anglo-Saxones* (plural), medieval Latin *Angli Saxones.*

An·glo·sphere /ˈaNGgləˌsfi(ə)r/ ▶ **n.** (**the Anglosphere**) the countries where English is the main native language, considered collectively.

An·go·la /aNGˈgōlə, anˈgōlə/ a republic on the western coast of southern Africa; pop. 12,799,300 (est. 2009); capital, Luanda; languages, Portuguese (official), Bantu languages.

> Angola was a Portuguese possession from the end of the 16th century until it achieved independence in 1975. Independence was followed by years of civil war, chiefly between the ruling Marxist MPLA and the UNITA movement.

– DERIVATIVES **An·go·lan adj. & n.**

An·go·ra /aNGˈgôrə/ former name (until 1930) of **ANKARA**.

an·go·ra /aNGˈgôrə/ ▶ **n.** [often as modifier] a cat, goat, or rabbit of a long-haired breed: *angora rabbits.* ■ a fabric made from the hair of the angora goat or rabbit: *an angora cardigan.*
– ORIGIN early 19th cent. (denoting a long-haired breed): from the place name **ANGORA**.

an·go·ra wool ▶ **n.** a mixture of sheep's wool and angora rabbit hair.

An·gos·tu·ra /ˌaNGgəˈst(y)o͝orə/ former name (until 1846) for **CIUDAD BOLÍVAR**.

an·gos·tu·ra /ˌaNGgəˈst(y)o͝orə/ (also **angostura bark**) ▶ **n.** an aromatic bitter bark from some South American trees, used as a flavoring, and formerly as a tonic and to reduce fever. ● This bark is taken from the trees *Angostura febrifuga* and *Galipea officinalis*, family Rutaceae. ■ short for **ANGOSTURA BITTERS**.
– ORIGIN late 18th cent.: from the place name **ANGOSTURA**.

An·gos·tu·ra bit·ters ▶ **n.** trademark a kind of tonic first made in Angostura.

an·gry /ˈaNGgrē/ ▶ **adj.** (**angrier, angriest**) having a strong feeling of or showing annoyance, displeasure, or hostility; full of anger: *why are you angry with me?* | *an angry customer* | *Christine had made him angry* | *I'm angry that she didn't call me.* ■ (of the sea or sky) stormy, turbulent, or threatening: *the wild, angry sea.* ■ (of a wound or sore) red and inflamed: *her skin was splotched with angry red burns.*
– DERIVATIVES **an·gri·ly** /-grəlē/ **adv.**

an·gry white male ▶ **n.** derogatory a politically conservative or antiliberal white man.

an·gry young man ▶ **n.** a young man dissatisfied with and outspoken against existing social and political structures. ■ (**Angry Young Men**) a number of British playwrights and novelists of the early 1950s whose work was marked by irreverence toward the Establishment and disgust at the survival of class distinctions and privilege. Notable members of the group were John Osborne and Kingsley Amis.

angst /aNG(k)st, äNG(k)st/ ▶ **n.** a feeling of deep anxiety or dread, typically an unfocused one about the human condition or the state of the world in general: *adolescent angst.* ■ informal a feeling of persistent worry about something trivial: *my hair causes me angst.*
– ORIGIN 1920s: from German, 'fear, anxiety.'

Ång·ström /ˈôNGstrəm, ˈaNG-/, Anders Jonas (1814–1874), Swedish physicist. He proposed a relationship between the emission and absorption spectra of chemical elements and measured optical wavelengths in the unit later named in his honor.

ang·strom /ˈaNGstrəm/ (also **ångström, angstrom unit**) (abbr.: **Å**) ▶ **n.** a unit of length equal to one hundred-millionth of a centimeter, 10^{-10} meter, used mainly to express wavelengths and interatomic distances.
– ORIGIN late 19th cent.: named after A. J. **ÅNGSTRÖM**.

An·guil·la /aNGˈgwilə, an-/ the northernmost island of the Leeward Islands in the West Indies; pop. 14,400 (est. 2009); capital, The Valley. Formerly a British colony and briefly united with St. Kitts and Nevis in 1967, it is now a self-governing British overseas territory.
– DERIVATIVES **An·guil·lan adj. & n.**

an·guish /ˈaNGgwiSH/ ▶ **n.** severe mental or physical pain or suffering: *she shut her eyes in anguish* | *Philip gave a cry of anguish.*
▶ **v.** [no obj.] be extremely distressed about something: *he anguished over how to reply.*
– ORIGIN Middle English: via Old French from Latin *angustia* 'tightness,' (plural) 'straits, distress,' from *angustus* 'narrow.'

an·guished /ˈaNGgwiSHt/ ▶ **adj.** experiencing or expressing severe mental or physical pain or suffering: *he gave an anguished cry* | *when she turned, her face was anguished.*
– ORIGIN early 17th cent.: past participle of **ANGUISH** (verb) in the rare sense 'distress with severe mental or physical pain,' from Old French *anguissier*, from ecclesiastical Latin *angustiare* 'to distress,' from Latin *angustia* (see **ANGUISH**).

an·gu·lar /ˈaNGgyələr/ ▶ **adj.** **1** (of an object, outline, or shape) having angles or sharp corners: *angular chairs* | *Adam's angular black handwriting.* ■ (of a person or part of their body) lean and having a prominent bone structure: *her angular face.* ■ (of a person's way of moving) not flowing smoothly; awkward or jerky: *his movements were stiff and angular* | figurative *the music is angular and sardonic.* ■ placed or directed at an angle: *the large angular writing was typical of the officers and the noncoms.* **2** chiefly Physics denoting physical properties or quantities measured with reference to or by means of an angle, esp. those associated with rotation: *angular acceleration.* **3** Astrology located in or relating to one of the houses that begin at the four cardinal points.
– DERIVATIVES **an·gu·lar·i·ty** /ˌaNGgyəˈlaritē/ **n.**, **an·gu·lar·ly adv.**
– ORIGIN late Middle English (as an astrological term): from Latin *angularis*, from *angulus* (see **ANGLE**[1]).

an·gu·lar di·am·e·ter ▶ **n.** Astronomy the apparent diameter of a planet or other celestial object measured by the angle that it subtends at the point of observation.

an·gu·lar mo·men·tum ▶ **n.** Physics the quantity of rotation of a body, which is the product of its moment of inertia and its angular velocity.

an·gu·lar ve·loc·i·ty ▶ **n.** Physics the rate of change of angular position of a rotating body.

an·gu·late /ˈaNGgyəˌlāt/ ▶ **v.** [with obj.] technical hold, bend, or distort (a part of the body, esp. of an animal) so as to form an angle or angles: (as adj. **angulated**) *the hindquarters are more strongly angulated than the forequarters.* ■ Skiing incline (the upper body) sideways and outward during a turn: [no obj.] *angulate slightly with the knees.*
– DERIVATIVES **an·gu·la·tion** /ˌaNGgyəˈlāSHən/ **n.**
– ORIGIN late 15th cent. (as *angulated*, used chiefly as a botanical or zoological term): from Latin *angulatus*, past participle of *angulare*, from *angulus* 'angle.'

a

ang·wan·ti·bo /ANG'(g)wäntə,bō/ ▶ **n.** (pl. **angwantibos**) a small rare nocturnal primate of west central Africa, related to the potto. ● *Arctocebus calabarensis*, family Lorisidae.
– ORIGIN mid 19th cent.: from Efik.

an·har·mon·ic /,anhär'mänik/ ▶ **adj.** Physics relating to or denoting motion that is not simple harmonic.
– DERIVATIVES **an·har·mo·nic·i·ty** /an,härmə'nisitē/ **n.**

an·he·do·ni·a /,anhē'dōnēə, -hi-/ ▶ **n.** Psychiatry inability to feel pleasure.
– DERIVATIVES **an·he·don·ic** /-'dänik/ **adj.**
– ORIGIN late 19th cent.: from French *anhédonie*, from Greek *an-* 'without' + *hēdonē* 'pleasure.'

an·he·dral /an'hēdrəl/ ▶ **adj.** Crystallography (of a crystal) having no plane faces.
▶ **n.** Aeronautics downward inclination of an aircraft's wing, or the angle of this. Compare with DIHEDRAL.
– ORIGIN late 19th cent. (as an adjective): from AN-[1] 'not' + *-hedral* (see -HEDRON).

an·hin·ga /an'hiNGgə/ ▶ **n.** a long-necked fish-eating bird related to the cormorants, typically found in fresh water. Anhingas spear fish with their long pointed bills and frequently swim submerged to the neck. Also called DARTER, SNAKEBIRD. ● Family Anhingidae and genus *Anhinga*: four species.
– ORIGIN mid 18th cent.: from Portuguese, from Tupi *áyinga*.

An·hui /'än'hwā/ (also **Anhwei**) a province in eastern China; capital, Hefei.

an·hy·dride /an'hī,drīd/ ▶ **n.** Chemistry the compound obtained by removing the elements of water from a particular acid. ■ [usu. with modifier] an organic compound containing the group –C(O)OC(O)–, derived from a carboxylic acid.
– ORIGIN mid 19th cent.: from Greek *anudros* (see ANHYDROUS) + -IDE.

an·hy·drite /an'hī,drīt/ ▶ **n.** a white mineral consisting of anhydrous calcium sulfate. It typically occurs in evaporite deposits.
– ORIGIN early 19th cent.: from Greek *anudros* (see ANHYDROUS) + -ITE[1].

an·hy·drous /an'hīdrəs/ ▶ **adj.** Chemistry (of a substance, esp. a crystalline compound) containing no water.
– ORIGIN early 19th cent.: from Greek *anudros* (from *an-* 'without' + *hudōr* 'water') + -OUS.

a·ni /ä'nē/ ▶ **n.** (pl. **anis**) a glossy black long-tailed bird of the cuckoo family, with a large deep bill, found in Central and South America. ● Genus *Crotophaga*, family Cuculidae: three species.
– ORIGIN early 19th cent.: from Spanish *ani*, Portuguese *anum*, from Tupi *anu-*.

an·i·line /'anl-in/ ▶ **n.** Chemistry a colorless oily liquid present in coal tar. It is used in the manufacture of dyes, drugs, and plastics, and was the basis of the earliest synthetic dyes. ● Chem. formula: $C_6H_5NH_2$.
– ORIGIN mid 19th cent.: from *anil* 'indigo' (from which it was originally obtained), via French and Portuguese from Arabic *an-nīl* (from Sanskrit *nīlī*, from *nīla* 'dark blue').

an·i·line dye ▶ **n.** chiefly historical a synthetic dye, esp. one made from aniline.

a·ni·lin·gus /,ānə'liNGgəs/ ▶ **n.** sexual stimulation of the anus by the tongue or mouth.
– ORIGIN 1960s: from Latin *anus* 'anus' on the pattern of *cunnilingus*.

an·i·ma /'anəmə/ ▶ **n.** Psychology Jung's term for the feminine part of a man's personality. Often contrasted with ANIMUS (sense 3). ■ the part of the psyche that is directed inward, and is in touch with the subconscious. Often contrasted with PERSONA.
– ORIGIN 1920s: from Latin, literally 'mind, soul.'

an·i·mad·ver·sion /,anəmad'vərZHən/ ▶ **n.** formal criticism or censure: *her animadversion against science*. ■ a comment or remark, esp. a critical one: *animadversions that the poet receives quite humbly*.
– ORIGIN mid 16th cent.: from French, or from Latin *animadversio(n-)*, from the verb *animadvertere* (see ANIMADVERT).

an·i·mad·vert /,anəmad'vərt/ ▶ **v.** [no obj.] **(animadvert on/upon/against)** formal pass criticism or censure on; speak out against: *we shall be obliged to animadvert most severely upon you in our report* | *many travelers animadvert against their own towns and cities*.
– ORIGIN late Middle English (in the sense 'pay attention to'): from Latin *animadvertere*, from *animus* 'mind' + *advertere* (from *ad-* 'toward' + *vertere* 'to turn').

an·i·mal /'anəməl/ ▶ **n.** a living organism that feeds on organic matter, typically having specialized sense organs and nervous system and able to respond rapidly to stimuli: *animals such as spiders* | *wild animals adapt badly to a caged life* | *humans are the only animals who weep*. ■ any such living organism other than a human being: *are humans superior to animals, or just different?* ■ a mammal, as opposed to a bird, reptile, fish, or insect: *the snowfall seemed to have chased all birds, animals, and men indoors*. ■ a person whose behavior is regarded as devoid of human attributes or civilizing influences, esp. someone who is very cruel, violent, or repulsive: *those men have to be animals—what they did to that boy was savage*. ■ [with adj. or noun modifier] a particular type of person or thing: *a regular party animal* | *the government that followed the election was a very different animal*.

> Animals are generally distinguished from plants by being unable to synthesize organic molecules from inorganic ones, so that they have to feed on plants or on other animals. They are typically able to move about, although this ability is sometimes restricted to a particular stage in the life cycle. The great majority of animals are invertebrates, of which there are some thirty phyla; the vertebrates constitute but a single subphylum. See also HIGHER ANIMALS, LOWER ANIMALS.

▶ **adj.** [attrib.] of, relating to, or characteristic of animals: *the evolution of animal life* | *animal welfare*. ■ of animals as distinct from plants: *tissues of animal and vegetable protein*. ■ characteristic of the physical and instinctive needs of animals; of the flesh rather than the spirit or intellect: *a crude surrender to animal lust*.
– ORIGIN Middle English: as a noun from Latin *animal*, based on Latin *animalis* 'having breath,' from *anima* 'breath'; as an adjective via Old French, from Latin *animalis*.

an·i·mal crack·er ▶ **n.** a type of sweet cracker made in various animal shapes.

an·i·mal·cule /,anə'mal,kyōōl/ ▶ **n.** archaic a microscopic animal.
– ORIGIN late 16th cent.: from modern Latin *animalculum*, from *animal* 'an animal' + -CULE.

an·i·mal hus·band·ry ▶ **n.** the science of breeding and caring for farm animals.

an·i·mal·ism /'anəmə,lizəm/ ▶ **n.** behavior that is characteristic of or appropriate to animals, particularly in being physical and instinctive. ■ religious worship of or concerning animals.
– DERIVATIVES **an·i·mal·is·tic** /,anəmə'listik/ **adj.**

an·i·mal·i·ty /,anə'malitē/ ▶ **n.** animal nature or character: *a prehuman condition of animality*. ■ physical, instinctive behavior or qualities: *what attracted me to her was her animality*.
– ORIGIN early 17th cent.: from French *animalité*, from *animal* (adjective), from Latin *animalis* 'animate, living' (see ANIMAL).

an·i·mal·ize /'anəmə,līz/ ▶ **v.** [with obj.] make into or like an animal.
– DERIVATIVES **an·i·mal·i·za·tion** /,anəməli'zāSHən/ **n.**

an·i·mal mag·net·ism ▶ **n. 1** a quality of sexual attractiveness: *he had an animal magnetism that women found irresistible*.
2 historical a supposed emanation to which the action of hypnotism was ascribed.

an·i·mal pole ▶ **n.** Biology the portion of an egg that contains the nucleus and less yolk, opposite the vegetal pole.

an·i·mal rights ▶ **plural n.** rights believed to belong to animals to live free from use in medical research, hunting, and other services to humans.

an·i·mal spir·its ▶ **plural n.** natural exuberance.

an·i·mate ▶ **v.** /'anə,māt/ [with obj.] **1** bring to life: *the desert is like a line drawing waiting to be animated with color*. ■ give inspiration, encouragement, or renewed vigor to: *she has animated the nation with a sense of political direction*.
2 (usu. **be animated**) give (a movie or character) the appearance of movement using animation techniques.
▶ **adj.** /-mit/ alive or having life (often as a contrast with INANIMATE): *all of creation, animate and inanimate*. ■ lively and active: *party photos of animate socialites*.
– ORIGIN late Middle English: from Latin *animat-* 'instilled with life,' from the verb *animare*, from *anima* 'life, soul.'

an·i·mat·ed /'anə,mātid/ ▶ **adj. 1** full of life or excitement; lively: *an animated conversation*.
2 (of a movie) made using animation techniques: *an animated version of the classic fairy tale*. ■ moving or appearing to move as if alive: *animated life-size figures*.
– DERIVATIVES **an·i·mat·ed·ly adv.**

an·i·mat·ic /,anə'matik/ ▶ **n.** a preliminary version of a movie, produced by shooting successive sections of a storyboard and adding a soundtrack.
– ORIGIN 1970s: from *animat(ed)* + -IC, or a blend of ANIMATED and SCHEMATIC.

an·i·ma·tion /,anə'māSHən/ ▶ **n. 1** the state of being full of life or vigor; liveliness: *they started talking with animation*. ■ chiefly archaic the state of being alive.
2 the technique of photographing successive drawings or positions of puppets or models to create an illusion of movement when the movie is shown as a sequence: [as modifier] *animation techniques* | *animations as backdrops for live action*. ■ (also **computer animation**) the manipulation of electronic images by means of a computer in order to create moving images.
– ORIGIN mid 16th cent. (in the sense 'encouragement'): from Latin *animatio(n-)*, from *animare* 'instill with life' (see ANIMATE). Sense 1 dates from the early 19th cent.

a·ni·ma·to /,anə'mätō/ Music ▶ **adj. & adv.** (esp. as a direction) in an animated manner.
▶ **n.** (pl. **animatos** or **animati** /-'mätē/) a passage marked animato.
– ORIGIN Italian.

an·i·ma·tor /'anə,mātər/ ▶ **n.** a person who animates something, esp. a person who prepares animated movies.

an·i·ma·tron·ics /,anəmə'träniks/ ▶ **plural n.** [treated as sing.] the technique of making and operating lifelike robots, typically for use in film or other entertainment.
– DERIVATIVES **an·i·ma·tron·ic adj.**
– ORIGIN 1970s: blend of ANIMATED and ELECTRONICS.

an·i·me /'anə,mā/ ▶ **n.** Japanese movie and television animation, often having a science fiction theme and sometimes including violent or explicitly sexual material. Compare with MANGA.
– ORIGIN 1980s: Japanese.

an·i·mism /'anə,mizəm/ ▶ **n. 1** the attribution of a soul to plants, inanimate objects, and natural phenomena.
2 the belief in a supernatural power that organizes and animates the material universe.
– DERIVATIVES **an·i·mist n.**, **an·i·mis·tic** /,anə'mistik/ **adj.**
– ORIGIN mid 19th cent.: from Latin *anima* 'life, soul' + -ISM.

an·i·mos·i·ty /,anə'mäsitē/ ▶ **n.** (pl. **animosities**) strong hostility: *he no longer felt any* **animosity** *toward her* | *the* **animosity** *between the king and his brother* | *the five decided to put aside their* **animosities**.
– ORIGIN late Middle English (originally in the sense 'spirit, courage'): from Old French *animosité* or late Latin *animositas*, from *animosus* 'spirited,' from Latin *animus* 'spirit, mind.' The current sense dates from the early 17th cent.

an·i·mus /'anəməs/ ▶ **n. 1** hostility or ill feeling: *the author's animus toward her*.
2 motivation to do something: *the reformist animus came from within the Party*.
3 Psychology Jung's term for the masculine part of a woman's personality. Often contrasted with ANIMA.
– ORIGIN early 19th cent.: from Latin, 'spirit, mind.'

an·i·on /'an,īən/ ▶ **n.** Chemistry a negatively charged ion, i.e., one that would be attracted to the anode in electrolysis. The opposite of CATION.
– DERIVATIVES **an·i·on·ic** /,anī'änik/ **adj.**
– ORIGIN mid 19th cent.: from ANODE or ANA- + ION.

an·ise /'anis/ ▶ **n. 1** a Mediterranean plant of the parsley family, cultivated for its aromatic seeds, which are used in cooking and herbal medicine. ● *Pimpinella anisum*, family Umbelliferae. See also ANISEED.
2 an Asian or American tree or shrub that bears fruit with an aniseedlike odor. ● Genus *Illicium*, family Illiciaceae: many species, esp. **star anise** (*I. verum*), used in Chinese cooking.
– ORIGIN Middle English: via Old French from Latin *anisum*, from Greek *anison* 'anise, dill.'

an·i·seed /'anə(s),sēd/ ▶ **n.** the seed of the anise, used in cooking and herbal medicine.
– ORIGIN late Middle English: from ANISE + SEED.

an·i·sette /,ani'set, -'zet/ ▶ **n.** a liqueur flavored with aniseed.
– ORIGIN mid 19th cent.: from French, diminutive of *anis* (see ANISE).

an·i·sog·a·my /,anī'sägəmē/ ▶ **n.** Biology sexual reproduction by the fusion of dissimilar gametes. Often contrasted with ISOGAMY.
– DERIVATIVES **an·i·sog·a·mous** /-məs/ **adj.**
– ORIGIN late 19th cent.: from Greek *anisos* 'unequal' + *-gamy* (from *gamos* 'marriage').

an·i·so·trop·ic /an,īsə'trōpik, -'träpik/ ▶ **adj.** Physics (of an object or substance) having a physical property that has a different value when measured in different directions. A simple example is wood, which is stronger along the grain than across it. ■ (of a property or phenomenon) varying in magnitude according to the direction of measurement.
– DERIVATIVES **an·i·sot·ro·py** /,anī'sätrəpē/ **n.**

–ORIGIN late 19th cent.: from Greek *anisos* 'unequal' + *tropos* 'turn' + **-IC**.

An·jou¹ /ˈanjo͞o, äNˈZHo͞o/ a former province of western France, on the Loire River. It was an English possession 1154–1204.

An·jou² (also **Anjou pear**) ▶ **n.** an egg-shaped variety of pear. The most popular type has bright green skin.

An·ka·ra /ˈäNGkərə, ˈaNG-/ the capital of Turkey since 1923; pop. 3,763,600 (est. 2007). Prominent in Roman times as Ancyra, it later declined in importance until chosen by Kemal Atatürk in 1923 as his seat of government. Former name (until 1930) **ANGORA**.

ankh /äNGk/ ▶ **n.** an object or design resembling a cross but having a loop instead of the top arm, used in ancient Egypt as a symbol of life.
–ORIGIN late 19th cent.: from Egyptian, literally 'life, soul.'

ankh

an·kle /ˈaNGkəl/ ▶ **n.** the joint connecting the foot with the leg: [as modifier] *an ankle injury*. ■ the narrow part of the leg between the foot and the calf: *her slim ankles* | *I stood up to my ankles in snow* | *the men are ankle-deep in mud* | [as modifier] *ankle socks*.
▶ **v. 1** [with obj.] informal leave: *he ankled the series to do a movie*. ■ [no obj.] walk.
2 [no obj.] (usu. as noun **ankling**) flex the ankles while cycling in order to increase pedaling efficiency.
–ORIGIN Old English *ancleow*, of Germanic origin; superseded in Middle English by forms from Old Norse; related to Dutch *enkel* and German *Enkel*, from an Indo-European root shared by **ANGLE¹**.

an·kle-bit·er ▶ **n.** humorous a child: *traveling overseas with an ankle-biter has its advantages*.

an·kle bone ▶ **n.** the chief bone of the ankle joint; the talus.

an·klet /ˈaNGklit/ ▶ **n. 1** a sock that reaches just above the ankle.
2 an ornament worn around an ankle.
–ORIGIN early 19th cent.: from **ANKLE** + **-LET**, on the pattern of *bracelet*.

an·ky·lo·saur /ˈaNGkiləˌsôr/ (also **ankylosaurus** /ˌaNGkiləˈsôrəs/) ▶ **n.** a heavily built quadrupedal herbivorous dinosaur primarily of the Cretaceous period, armored with bony plates. ● Infraorder Ankylosauria, order Ornithischia: several genera, in particular *Ankylosaurus*.
–DERIVATIVES **an·ky·lo·sau·ri·an adj.**
–ORIGIN early 20th cent.: from modern Latin *Ankylosaurus*, from Greek *ankulos* (see **ANKYLOSIS**) + *sauros* 'lizard.'

an·ky·lose /ˈaNGkəˌlōs, -ˌlōz/ ▶ **v.** Medicine (**be/become ankylosed**) (of bones or a joint) be or become stiffened or united by ankylosis.
–ORIGIN late 18th cent.: back-formation from **ANKYLOSIS**, on the pattern of words such as *anastomose*.

an·ky·los·ing spon·dy·li·tis /ˈaNGkəˌlōsiNG ˌspəndlˈītis, -ˌlōziNG/ ▶ **n.** Medicine a form of spinal arthritis, chiefly affecting young males, that eventually causes ankylosis of vertebral and sacroiliac joints.

an·ky·lo·sis /ˌaNGkəˈlōsis/ ▶ **n.** Medicine abnormal stiffening and immobility of a joint due to fusion of the bones.
–DERIVATIVES **an·ky·lot·ic** /-ˈlätik/ **adj.**
–ORIGIN early 18th cent.: from Greek *ankulōsis*, from *ankuloun* 'to crook,' from *ankulos* 'crooked.'

an·la·ge /ˈänˌlägə/ ▶ **n.** (pl. **anlagen** /-ˌlägən/) Biology the rudimentary basis of a particular organ or other part, esp. in an embryo.
–ORIGIN late 19th cent.: from German, 'foundation, basis.'

Ann, Cape /an/ a peninsula in northeastern Massachusetts, noted for its resorts and scenery.

An·na·ba /anˈäbə/ a port of northeastern Algeria; pop. 205,600 (est. 2009). The modern town is adjacent to the site of Hippo Regius, a prominent city in Roman Africa and the home and bishopric of St. Augustine of Hippo from 396 to 430. Former name **BÔNE**.

an-Na·jaf /ˌan ˈnajaf/ another name for **NAJAF**.

an·nal·ist /ˈanl-ist/ ▶ **n.** a person who writes annals.
–DERIVATIVES **an·nal·is·tic** /ˌanlˈistik/ **adj.**

an·nals /ˈanlz/ ▶ **plural n.** a record of events year by year: *eighth-century Northumberland annals*. ■ historical records: *the annals of the famous European discoverers* | figurative *the deed will live forever in the annals of infamy*. ■ (**Annals**) used in the titles of learned journals: *Annals of Internal Medicine*.
–ORIGIN mid 16th cent.: from Latin *annales* (*libri*) 'yearly (books),' from *annus* 'year.'

An·nan /əˈnän/, Kofi (Atta) (1938–), Ghanaian diplomat; secretary general of the United Nations 1997–2007.

Kofi Annan

An·nan·dale /ˈanənˌdāl/ a residential suburb in northern Virginia, southwest of Washington, DC; pop. 54,994 (2000).

An·nap·o·lis /əˈnap(ə)ləs/ the state capital of Maryland, on the western coast of Chesapeake Bay; pop. 36,524 (est. 2008). It is the home of the US Naval Academy.

An·na·pur·na /ˌanəˈpərnə/ a ridge of the Himalayas, in north central Nepal. Its highest peak rises to 26,503 ft. (8,078 m.).

Ann Ar·bor /ˌan ˈärbər/ a city in southeastern Michigan, home to the University of Michigan; pop. 114,386 (est. 2008).

An·na's hum·ming·bird /ˈanəz/ ▶ **n.** a North American hummingbird that lives chiefly in California. The male has an iridescent rose-red head and throat. ● *Calypte anna*, family Trochilidae.
–ORIGIN mid 19th cent.: named after *Anna*, the wife of Prince François Massena (*c.*1795–1863), Duc de Ravoli, who obtained the original specimen.

an·nat·to /əˈnätō/ (also **anatto**) ▶ **n.** (pl. **annattos**)
1 an orange-red dye obtained from the pulp of a tropical fruit, used for coloring foods and fabric.
2 the tropical American tree from which this fruit is obtained. ● *Bixa orellana*, family Bixaceae.
–ORIGIN early 17th cent.: from Carib.

Anne /an/ (1665–1714), queen of England and Scotland (known as Great Britain from 1707) and Ireland 1702–14. The last of the Stuart monarchs and daughter of the Catholic James II (but herself a Protestant), she succeeded her brother-in-law William III to the throne.

Anne, Princess, (1950–), daughter of Queen Elizabeth II; full name *Anne Elizabeth Alice Louise, the Princess Royal*. Her two children are Peter (1977–) and Zara (1981–), by her former husband, Mark Philips (1948–).

Anne, St., traditionally the mother of the Virgin Mary; first mentioned by name in the apocryphal gospel of James (2nd century). Feast day, July 26.

an·neal /əˈnēl/ ▶ **v.** [with obj.] heat (metal or glass) and allow it to cool slowly, in order to remove internal stresses and toughen it. ■ Biochemistry recombine (DNA) in the double-stranded form following separation by heat. ■ [no obj.] Biochemistry (of DNA) undergo this process.
–DERIVATIVES **an·neal·er n.**
–ORIGIN Old English *onǣlan*, from *on* + *ǣlan* 'burn, bake,' from *āl* 'fire, burning.' The original sense was 'set on fire,' hence (in late Middle English) 'subject to fire, alter by heating'; sense 1 dates from the mid 17th cent.

Anne Bol·eyn see **BOLEYN**.

an·ne·lid /ˈanlid/ Zoology ▶ **n.** a segmented worm of the phylum Annelida, such as an earthworm or leech.
▶ **adj.** relating to or denoting annelids.
–DERIVATIVES **an·nel·i·dan** /əˈnelidn/ **n. & adj.**

An·nel·i·da /əˈnelidə/ Zoology a large phylum that comprises the segmented worms, which include earthworms, lugworms, and leeches.
–ORIGIN modern Latin (plural), from French (*animaux*) *annelés* 'ringed (animals),' from Old French *anel* 'a ring,' from Latin *anellus*, diminutive of *anulus* 'a ring.'

Anne of Cleves /klēvz/ (1515–57), fourth wife of Henry VIII. The politically arranged marriage was dissolved after only six months.

an·nex ▶ **v.** /əˈneks, ˈaneks/ [with obj.] append or add as an extra or subordinate part, esp. to a document: *the first ten amendments were annexed to the Constitution in 1791* | (as adj. **annexed**) *the annexed diagram*. ■ add (territory) to one's own territory by appropriation: *the left bank of the Rhine was annexed by France in 1797*. ■ informal take for oneself; appropriate: *it was bad enough that Richard should have annexed his girlfriend*. ■ archaic add or attach as a condition or consequence.
▶ **n.** /ˈaneks, -iks/ (chiefly Brit. also **annexe**) (pl. **annexes**) **1** a building joined to or associated with a main building, providing additional space or accommodations.
2 an addition to a document: *an annex to the report*.
–ORIGIN late Middle English: from Old French *annexer*, from Latin *annectere* 'connect,' from *ad-* 'to' + *nectere* 'tie, fasten.'

an·nex·a·tion /ˌanekˈsāSHən, ˌanik-/ ▶ **n.** the action of annexing something, esp. territory: *the annexation of Austria*.
–DERIVATIVES **an·nex·a·tion·ist n. & adj.**

An·ni·go·ni /ˌänəˈgōnē/, Pietro (1910–88), Italian painter. One of the few 20th-century artists to practice the techniques of the Old Masters, he is noted for his portraits of Queen Elizabeth II (1955, 1970) and of President John F. Kennedy (1961).

an·ni·hi·late /əˈnīəˌlāt/ ▶ **v.** [with obj.] destroy utterly; obliterate: *a simple bomb of this type could annihilate them all* | *a crusade to annihilate evil*. ■ defeat utterly: *the stronger force annihilated its opponent virtually without loss*. ■ Physics convert (a subatomic particle) into radiant energy.
–DERIVATIVES **an·ni·hi·la·tor** /-ˌlātər/ **n.**, **an·ni·hi·la·tion** /əˌnīəˈlāSHən/ **n.**
–ORIGIN late Middle English (originally as an adjective meaning 'destroyed, annulled'): from late Latin *annihilatus* 'reduced to nothing,' from the verb *annihilare*, from *ad-* 'to' + *nihil* 'nothing.' The verb sense 'destroy utterly' dates from the mid 16th cent.

an·ni·ver·sa·ry /ˌanəˈvərsərē/ ▶ **n.** (pl. **anniversaries**) the date on which an event took place in a previous year: *the 50th anniversary of the start of World War II* | [as modifier] *anniversary celebrations*. ■ the date on which a country or other institution was founded in a previous year: *Canada's 125th anniversary*. ■ the date on which a couple was married in a previous year: *he even forgot our tenth anniversary!* ■ informal the date on which a romance began in a previous month or week.
–ORIGIN Middle English: from Latin *anniversarius* 'returning yearly,' from *annus* 'year' + *versus* 'turning.'

An·no Dom·i·ni /ˈanō ˈdämənē, -nī, ˈänō/ ▶ **adv.** full form of **AD**.
–ORIGIN mid 16th cent.: Latin, literally 'in the year of the Lord.'

an·no·tate /ˈanəˌtāt/ ▶ **v.** [with obj.] add notes to (a text or diagram) giving explanation or comment: *documentation should be annotated with explanatory notes* | (as adj. **annotated**) *an annotated bibliography*.
–DERIVATIVES **an·no·tat·a·ble adj.**, **an·no·ta·tor** /-ˌtātər/ **n.**
–ORIGIN late 16th cent.: from Latin *annotat-* 'marked,' from the verb *annotare*, from *ad-* 'to' + *nota* 'a mark.'

an·no·ta·tion /ˌanəˈtāSHən/ ▶ **n.** a note of explanation or comment added to a text or diagram: *marginal annotations*. ■ the action of annotating a text or diagram: *annotation of prescribed texts*.
–ORIGIN late Middle English: from French, or from Latin *annotatio(n-)*, from the verb *annotare* (see **ANNOTATE**).

an·nounce /əˈnouns/ ▶ **v.** [reporting verb] make a public and typically formal declaration about a fact, occurrence, or intention: [with clause] *the president's office announced that the state of siege would be lifted* | [with obj.] *he announced his retirement from football* | [with direct speech] *"I have a confession to make," she announced*. ■ [with obj.] make known: *we announce our failures by warring against ourselves and others* | *these glossy and expensive volumes announce anxiety*. ■ [with obj.] give information about (transportation) in a station or airport via a public address system: *they were announcing her train*. ■ [with obj.] (of a notice, letter, sound, etc.) give information to (someone) via the senses of sight or hearing: *storms came announced by long wisps that lashed out from a snow cloud's body* | *she heard the traditional strains of music announcing her arrival in the church*. ■ [with obj.] make known the arrival or imminence of (a guest or a meal) at a formal social occasion: *dinner was announced*.
–ORIGIN late 15th cent.: from French *annoncer*, from Latin *annuntiare*, from *ad-* 'to' + *nuntiare* 'declare, announce' (from *nuntius* 'messenger').

an·nounce·ment /əˈnounsmənt/ ▶ **n.** a public and typically formal statement about a fact, occurrence, or intention: *the spokesperson was about to **make an announcement** | a policy announcement | he was shaken by her announcement.* ■ the action of making such a statement: *the announcement of the decision of the president.* ■ a notice appearing in a newspaper or public place and announcing something such as a birth, death, or marriage: *an announcement is appearing in the Morning Post tomorrow.* ■ a statement of information given over a public address system: *a loudspeaker announcement echoed across the field.*

an·nounc·er /əˈnounsər/ ▶ **n.** a person who announces something, in particular someone who introduces or gives information about programs on radio or television.

an·noy /əˈnoi/ ▶ **v.** [with obj.] irritate (someone); make (someone) a little angry: *your damned cheerfulness has always annoyed me* | [no obj.] *rock music loud enough to annoy.* ■ archaic harm or attack repeatedly: *a gallant Saxon, who annoyed this Coast.*
– ORIGIN Middle English (in the sense 'be hateful to'): from Old French *anoier* (verb), *anoi* (noun), based on Latin *in odio* in the phrase *mihi in odio est* 'it is hateful to me.'

an·noy·ance /əˈnoi-əns/ ▶ **n.** the feeling or state of being annoyed; irritation: *a look of annoyance on his face | **annoyance at** government interference | he turned his charm on Tara, **much to** Herbert's **annoyance**.* ■ a thing that annoys someone; a nuisance: *the Council found him an annoyance.*
– ORIGIN late Middle English: from Old French *anoiance*, from *anoier* (see **ANNOY**).

an·noyed ▶ **adj.** slightly angry; irritated: *Kelly was **annoyed with** him | he was **annoyed at** being woken up so early.*
– DERIVATIVES **an·noy·ed·ly** adv.

an·noy·ing /əˈnoi-iNG/ ▶ **adj.** causing irritation or annoyance: *annoying habits | unsolicited calls are annoying.*
– DERIVATIVES **an·noy·ing·ly** adv.

an·nu·al /ˈanyo͞oəl/ ▶ **adj.** occurring once every year: *the union's annual conference | the sponsored walk became an annual event | an annual report.* ■ calculated over or covering a period of a year: *annual accounts | an annual rate of increase | his basic annual income.* ■ (of a plant) living for a year or less, perpetuating itself by seed: *annual flowers.* ▶ **n.** a book or magazine that is published once a year under the same title but with different contents: *a Christmas annual | trade journals, annuals, and directories.* ■ an annual plant: *sow annuals in spring.*
– ORIGIN late Middle English: from Old French *annuel*, from late Latin *annualis*, based on Latin *annus* 'year.'

an·nu·al·ized /ˈanyo͞oəˌlīzd/ ▶ **adj.** (of a rate of interest, inflation, or return on an investment) recalculated as an annual rate: *an annualized yield of about 11.5%.*

an·nu·al·ly /ˈanyo͞oəlē/ ▶ **adv.** once a year; every year: *the prize is awarded annually | sales are increasing by about 17% annually.*

an·nual ring ▶ **n.** another term for **TREE RING**.

an·nu·i·tant /əˈn(y)o͞oitənt/ ▶ **n.** formal a person who receives an annuity.
– ORIGIN early 18th cent.: from **ANNUITY**, on the pattern of *accountant*.

an·nu·i·ty /əˈn(y)o͞oitē/ ▶ **n.** (pl. **annuities**) a fixed sum of money paid to someone each year, typically for the rest of their life: *he left her an annuity of $1,000 in his will.* ■ a form of insurance or investment entitling the investor to a series of annual sums: [as modifier] *an annuity plan.*
– ORIGIN late Middle English: from French *annuité*, from medieval Latin *annuitas*, from Latin *annuus* 'yearly,' from *annus* 'year.'

an·nul /əˈnəl/ ▶ **v.** (**annuls, annulling, annulled**) [with obj.] declare invalid (an official agreement, decision, or result): *the elections were annulled by the general amid renewed protests.* ■ declare (a marriage) to have had no legal existence: *her first marriage was finally annulled by His Holiness.*
– ORIGIN late Middle English: from Old French *anuller*, from late Latin *annullare*, from *ad-* 'to' + *nullum* 'nothing.'

an·nu·lar /ˈanyələr/ ▶ **adj.** technical ring-shaped.
– DERIVATIVES **an·nu·lar·ly** adv.
– ORIGIN late 16th cent.: from French *annulaire* or Latin *annularis*, from *anulus, annulus* 'a ring.'

an·nu·lar e·clipse ▶ **n.** an eclipse of the sun in which the edge of the sun remains visible as a bright ring around the moon.

an·nu·late /ˈanyəlit, -ˌlāt/ ▶ **adj.** chiefly Zoology having rings; marked with or formed of rings: *an annulate worm.*
– DERIVATIVES **an·nu·lat·ed** adj., **an·nu·la·tion** /ˌanyəˈlāSHən/ n.
– ORIGIN early 19th cent.: from Latin *annulatus*, from *anulus, annulus* 'a ring.'

an·nu·let /ˈanyəlit/ ▶ **n. 1** Architecture a small fillet or band encircling a column.
2 Heraldry a charge in the form of a small ring.
– ORIGIN late Middle English (sense 2): from Old French *anelet*, from Latin *anulus, annulus* 'ring' + **-ET**[1]. The spelling change in the 16th cent. was due to association with the Latin.

an·nul·ment /əˈnəlmənt/ ▶ **n.** the act of annulling something: *the applicant sought the annulment of the decision | grounds for an annulment.*

an·nu·lus /ˈanyələs/ ▶ **n.** (pl. **annuli** /-ˌlī/) technical a ring-shaped object, structure, or region.
– ORIGIN mid 16th cent.: from Latin *anulus, annulus*.

an·nun·ci·ate /əˈnənsēˌāt/ ▶ **v.** [with obj.] archaic announce (something).
– ORIGIN late Middle English (originally as a past participle): from medieval Latin *annunciat-*, variant spelling of Latin *annuntiat-* 'announced,' from the verb *annuntiare*.

an·nun·ci·a·tion /əˌnənsēˈāSHən/ ▶ **n.** (usu. **the Annunciation**) the announcement of the Incarnation by the angel Gabriel to Mary (Luke 1:26–38). ■ the church festival commemorating this, held on March 25 (Lady Day). ■ a painting or sculpture depicting this. ■ formal or archaic the announcement of something: *the annunciation of a set of rules applying to the relationships between states.*
– ORIGIN Middle English: from Old French *annonciation*, from late Latin *annuntiatio(n-)*, from the verb *annuntiare* (see **ANNUNCIATE**).

an·nun·ci·a·tor /əˈnənsēˌātər/ ▶ **n.** a bell, light, or other device that provides information on the state or condition of something by indicating which of several electrical circuits has been activated: [as modifier] *the annunciator panel and warning lights.*

an·nus hor·ri·bi·lis /ˈanəs həˈribəlis/ ▶ **n.** a year of disaster or misfortune.
– ORIGIN late 20th cent.: modern Latin on the pattern of **ANNUS MIRABILIS**.

an·nus mi·ra·bi·lis /ˈanəs məˈräbəlis/ ▶ **n.** a remarkable or auspicious year.
– ORIGIN mid 17th cent.: modern Latin, literally 'wonderful year.'

a·no·a /əˈnōə/ ▶ **n.** (pl. **same** or **anoas**) a small deerlike water buffalo, native to Sulawesi. ● Genus *Bubalus*, family Bovidae: two species.
– ORIGIN mid 19th cent.: a local name.

an·ode /ˈanōd/ ▶ **n.** the positively charged electrode by which the electrons leave a device. The opposite of **CATHODE**. ■ the negatively charged electrode of a device supplying current such as a primary cell.
– DERIVATIVES **an·od·al** /anˈōdl, āˈnōdl/ adj., **an·od·ic** /anˈädik/ adj.
– ORIGIN mid 19th cent.: from Greek *anodos* 'way up,' from *ana* 'up' + *hodos* 'way.'

an·o·dize /ˈanəˌdīz/ ▶ **v.** [with obj.] (usu. as adj. **anodized**) coat (a metal, esp. aluminum) with a protective oxide layer by an electrolytic process in which the metal forms the anode.
– DERIVATIVES **an·o·diz·er** n.

an·o·dyne /ˈanəˌdīn/ ▶ **adj.** not likely to provoke dissent or offense; inoffensive, often deliberately so: *anodyne New Age music | I attempted to keep the conversation as anodyne as possible.*
▶ **n.** a painkilling drug or medicine.
– ORIGIN mid 16th cent.: via Latin from Greek *anōdunos* 'painless,' from *an-* 'without' + *odunē* 'pain.'

a·no·gen·i·tal /ˌānōˈjenitl/ ▶ **adj.** Medicine & Anatomy of or relating to the anus and genitals.
– ORIGIN early 20th cent.: from Latin *ano-* (combining form of **ANUS**) + **GENITAL**.

a·noint /əˈnoint/ ▶ **v.** [with obj.] smear or rub with oil, typically as part of a religious ceremony: *high priests were **anointed with** oil | bodies were anointed after death for burial.* ■ (**anoint something with**) smear or rub something with (any other substance): *Cuna Indians anoint the tips of their arrows with poison.* ■ ceremonially confer divine or holy office upon (a priest or monarch) by smearing or rubbing with oil: *the Lord has anointed me to preach to the poor* | [with obj. and complement] *Samuel anointed him king.* ■ nominate or choose (someone) as successor to or leading candidate for a position: *he was anointed as the organizational candidate of the party* | (as adj. **anointed**) *his officially anointed heir.*
– PHRASES **Anointing of the Sick** (in the Roman Catholic Church) the sacramental anointing of the ill or infirm with blessed oil; unction. **God's** (or **the Lord's**) **anointed** a monarch ruling by divine right.
– DERIVATIVES **a·noint·er** n., **a·noint·ment** n.
– ORIGIN Middle English: from Old French *enoint* 'anointed,' past participle of *enoindre*, from Latin *inungere*, from *in-* 'upon' + *ungere* 'anoint, smear with oil.'

a·no·le /əˈnōlē/ ▶ **n.** a small, mainly arboreal American lizard with a throat fan that (in the male) is typically brightly colored. Anoles have some ability to change color. Also called **CHAMELEON**. ● Genus *Anolis*, family Iguanidae: numerous species, in particular the **green anole** (*A. carolinensis*), which is popular as a pet.
– ORIGIN early 18th cent.: from Carib.

a·nom·a·lis·tic month /əˌnäməˈlistik/ ▶ **n.** a month measured between successive perigees of the moon (approximately 27 1/2 days).

a·nom·a·lis·tic year ▶ **n.** a year measured between successive perihelia of the earth (approximately 365 1/4 days).

a·nom·a·lous /əˈnäməlәs/ ▶ **adj.** deviating from what is standard, normal, or expected: *an anomalous situation | sentences that are grammatically anomalous.*
– DERIVATIVES **a·nom·a·lous·ly** adv., **a·nom·a·lous·ness** n.
– ORIGIN mid 17th cent.: via late Latin from Greek *anōmalos* (from *an-* 'not' + *homalos* 'even') + **-OUS**.

a·nom·a·ly /əˈnäməlē/ ▶ **n.** (pl. **anomalies**)
1 something that deviates from what is standard, normal, or expected: *there are a number of anomalies in the present system | a legal anomaly* | [with clause] *the apparent **anomaly that** those who produced the wealth were the poorest | the position abounds in anomaly.*
2 Astronomy the angular distance of a planet or satellite from its last perihelion or perigee.
– ORIGIN late 16th cent.: via Latin from Greek *anōmalia*, from *anōmalos* (see **ANOMALOUS**).

a·no·mi·a /əˈnōmēə/ ▶ **n.** Medicine a form of aphasia in which the patient is unable to recall the names of everyday objects.
– DERIVATIVES **a·nom·ic** /əˈnämik, əˈnō-/ adj.
– ORIGIN early 20th cent.: formed irregularly from **A-**[1] 'without, not' + Latin *nomen* 'name' + **-IA**[1].

an·o·mie /ˈanəˌmē/ (also **anomy**) ▶ **n.** lack of the usual social or ethical standards in an individual or group: *the theory that high-rise architecture leads to anomie in the residents.*
– DERIVATIVES **a·nom·ic** /əˈnämik, əˈnō-/ adj.
– ORIGIN 1930s: from French, from Greek *anomia*, from *anomos* 'lawless.'

a·non /əˈnän/ ▶ **adv.** archaic soon; shortly: *I'll see you anon.*
– ORIGIN Old English *on ān* 'into one,' *on āne* 'in one.' The original sense was 'in or into one state, course, etc.,' which developed into the temporal sense 'at once.'

anon. ▶ **abbr.** anonymous.

an·o·nym·i·ty /ˌanəˈnimitē/ ▶ **n.** the condition of being anonymous: *most people who agreed to talk requested anonymity.* ■ lack of outstanding, individual, or unusual features; impersonality: *the anonymity of big city life definitely has its advantages.*

a·non·y·mize /əˈnänəˌmīz/ ▶ **v.** [with obj.] make anonymous: *manuscripts will be anonymized by the editorial assistant.* ■ (usu. as adj. **anonymized**) Medicine remove identifying particulars from (test results) for statistical or other purposes: *anonymized testing of routine blood samples.*
– ORIGIN 1970s: from **ANONYMOUS** + **-IZE**.

a·non·y·mous /əˈnänəməs/ ▶ **adj.** (of a person) not identified by name; of unknown name: *the anonymous author of Beowulf | the donor's wish to remain anonymous | an anonymous phone call.* ■ having no outstanding, individual, or unusual features; unremarkable or impersonal: *the anonymous black car waiting to take him to the airport | a faceless, anonymous group.* ■ [postpositive] used in names of support groups for addicts of a substance or behavior to indicate the confidentiality maintained among members of the group: *Alcoholics Anonymous | Debtors Anonymous.*
– DERIVATIVES **a·non·y·mous·ly** adv.
– ORIGIN late 16th cent.: via late Latin from Greek *anōnumos* 'nameless' (from *an-* 'without' + *onoma* 'name') + **-OUS**.

a·non·y·mous FTP ▶ **n.** Computing part of the File Transfer Protocol (FTP) on the Internet that lets anyone log on to an FTP server, using a general username and without a password.

a·noph·e·les /əˈnäfəˌlēz/ (also **anopheles mosquito**) ▶ **n.** a mosquito of a genus that is particularly common in warmer countries and includes the mosquitoes that transmit the malarial parasite to humans. Compare with **CULEX**. ● Genus *Anopheles*, subfamily Anophelinae, family Culicidae.
– DERIVATIVES **a·noph·e·line** /-ˌlīn, -lin/ adj. & n.

– ORIGIN late 19th cent.: modern Latin, from Greek *anōphelēs* 'unprofitable, useless.'

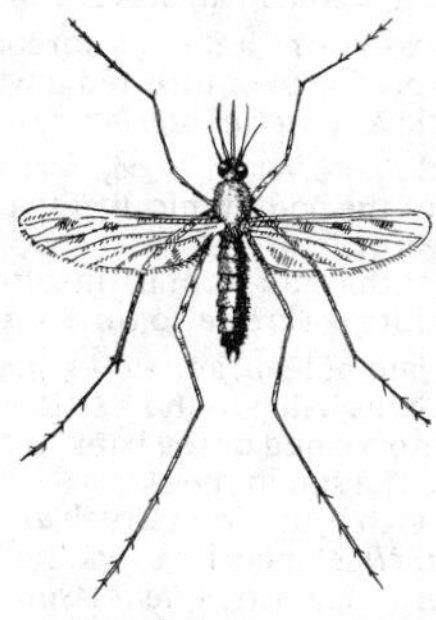

anopheles mosquito

An·o·plu·ra /ˌanəˈplo͝orə/ Entomology an order of insects that comprises the sucking lice. Also called **Siphunculata**. See also **Phthiraptera**.
– DERIVATIVES **an·o·plu·ran** n. & adj.
– ORIGIN modern Latin (plural), from *anoplos* 'unarmed' + *oura* 'tail.'

an·o·rak /ˈanəˌrak/ ▶ n. a waterproof jacket, typically with a hood, of a kind originally used in polar regions.
– ORIGIN 1920s: from Greenland Eskimo *anoraq*.

an·o·rec·tal /ˈanəˈrektəl/ ▶ adj. Medicine & Anatomy of or relating to the anus and rectum.
– ORIGIN late 19th cent.: from French *ano-rectal*, from Latin *ano-* (combining form of **anus**) + *rectal* (see **rectal**).

an·o·rex·i·a /ˌanəˈreksēə/ ▶ n. a lack or loss of appetite for food (as a medical condition). ■ (also **anorexia nervosa** /nərˈvōsə/) an emotional disorder characterized by an obsessive desire to lose weight by refusing to eat. Compare with **bulimia**.
– ORIGIN late 16th cent.: via late Latin from Greek, from *an-* 'without' + *orexis* 'appetite.'

an·o·rex·ic /ˌanəˈreksik/ (also **anorectic** /ˌanəˈrektik/) ▶ adj. relating to, characterized by, or suffering from anorexia. ■ informal extremely thin.
▶ n. **1** a person suffering from anorexia.
2 (**anorectic**) a medicine that produces a loss of appetite.

an·or·gas·mi·a /ˌanôrˈgazmēə/ ▶ n. Medicine persistent inability to achieve orgasm despite responding to sexual stimulation.
– DERIVATIVES **an·or·gas·mic** /-mik/ adj.
– ORIGIN 1970s: from **an-**[1] + **orgasm** + **-ia**[1].

an·or·thite /anˈôrˌTHīt/ ▶ n. a calcium-rich mineral of the plagioclase feldspar group, typically white, occurring esp. in limestones metamorphosed by contact with an igneous intrusion.
– ORIGIN mid 19th cent.: from **an-**[1] + Greek *orthos* 'straight' + **-ite**[1].

an·or·tho·site /əˈnôrTHəˌsīt/ ▶ n. Geology a plutonic rock composed largely of calcic plagioclase.
– ORIGIN mid 19th cent.: from French *anorthose* 'plagioclase' + **-ite**[1].

an·os·mi·a /aˈnäzmēə, aˈnäs-/ ▶ n. Medicine the loss of the sense of smell, either total or partial. It may be caused by head injury, infection, or blockage of the nose.
– DERIVATIVES **an·os·mic** /-mik/ adj.
– ORIGIN early 19th cent.: from **an-**[2] + Greek *osmē* 'smell.'

an·oth·er /əˈnəT͟Hər/ ▶ determiner & pron. **1** used to refer to an additional person or thing of the same type as one already mentioned or known about; one more; a further: [as determiner] *have another drink* | *I didn't say another word* | [as pronoun] *they have two practices, one in the morning and another in the afternoon* | *she was to become* ***another*** *of his stars*. ■ [usu. as determiner] used with a proper name to indicate someone or something's similarity to the person or event specified: *they said she was another Jennifer Aniston* | *this will not be another Vietnam*.
2 used to refer to a different person or thing from one already mentioned or known about: [as determiner] *come back another day* | *his wife left him for another man* | [as pronoun] *moving from one place to another* | ***it is one thing*** *to formulate policies and* ***quite another*** *to implement them*. ■ [determiner] used to refer to someone sharing an attribute in common with the person already mentioned: *his kiss with another man caused a tabloid rumpus*.
– ORIGIN Middle English: as *an other* until the 16th cent.

A·nouilh /ˈänōōē, änˈwē/, Jean (1910–87), French playwright. Notable works: *Ring Around the Moon* (1947), *Thieves' Carnival* (1932), and *Antigone* (1944).

ANOVA /ˈanōvə/ ▶ n. analysis of variance, a statistical method in which the variation in a set of observations is divided into distinct components.
– ORIGIN 1960s: acronym.

an·ov·u·lant /anˈävyələnt/ Medicine ▶ adj. (chiefly of a drug) preventing ovulation.
▶ n. an anovulant drug.
– ORIGIN 1960s: from **an-**[1] + *ovul(ation)* + **-ant**.

an·ov·u·la·to·ry /anˈävyələˌtôrē/ ▶ adj. Medicine (of a menstrual cycle) in which ovulation does not occur.

an·ox·i·a /aˈnäksēə/ ▶ n. technical an absence of oxygen. ■ Medicine an absence or deficiency of oxygen reaching the tissues; severe hypoxia.
– DERIVATIVES **an·ox·ic** /-sik/ adj.
– ORIGIN 1930s: from **an-**[1] + *ox(ygen)* + **-ia**[1].

ANS ▶ abbr. autonomic nervous system.

An·schluss /ˈänˌSHlo͞os/ the annexation of Austria by Germany in 1938. Hitler had forced the resignation of the Austrian chancellor by demanding that he admit Nazis into his Cabinet. The new chancellor, a pro-Nazi, invited German troops to enter the country on the pretext of restoring law and order.
– ORIGIN German, from *anschliessen* 'to join.'

An·selm, St. /ˈanˌselm/ (*c.*1033–1109), English philosopher and theologian; born in Italy; archbishop of Canterbury 1093–1109. Feast day, April 21.

An·shan /anˈSHan/ a city in Liaoning, China; pop. 1,293,000 (est. 2006). It is situated close to major iron-ore deposits, and China's largest iron and steel complex is nearby.

ANSI /ˈansē/ ▶ abbr. American National Standards Institute.

an·swer /ˈansər/ ▶ n. a thing said, written, or done to deal with or as a reaction to a question, statement, or situation: *he knocked and entered without waiting for an answer*. ■ a thing written or said in reaction to a question in a test or quiz: *write your answers on a postcard*. ■ the correct solution to such a question: *the answer is 280°*. ■ a solution to a problem or dilemma: ***the answer to*** *poverty and unemployment is a properly funded range of services*. ■ [in sing.] (**answer to**) a thing or person that imitates or fulfills the same role as something or someone else: *the press called her Britain's answer to Marilyn Monroe*. ■ Law the defendant's reply to the plaintiff's charges.
▶ v. **1** [reporting verb] say or write something to deal with or as a reaction to someone or something: [with direct speech] *"Of course I can," she answered* | [with clause] *she answered that she would take nothing but the ring* | [with obj.] *she tried to answer his questions truthfully* | *I didn't answer him* | [no obj.] *Steve was about to answer, but Hazel spoke first*. ■ [with obj.] provide the required responses to (a test or quiz): *answer the questions below for a chance to win a vacation*. ■ [no obj.] (**answer back**) respond impudently or disrespectfully to someone, esp. when being criticized or told to do something: *one couldn't argue with a parent; one couldn't answer back* | [with obj.] *Mary resisted the temptation to answer her mother back*.
2 [with obj.] act in reaction to (a sound such as a telephone ringing or a knock or ring on a door): *David answered the door* | [no obj.] *she called Edward's house, hoping he would answer*.
3 [no obj.] (**answer to**) be responsible or report to (someone): *I answer to the assistant commissioner*.
4 [with obj.] defend oneself against (a charge, accusation, or criticism): *he said he would return to Spain to answer all charges*. ■ [no obj.] (**answer to**) be required to explain or justify oneself to (someone): *you will have the police to answer to*. ■ [no obj.] (**answer for**) be responsible or to blame for: *the dust mite* ***has a lot to answer for****, especially if you are asthmatic*.
5 [with obj.] be suitable for fulfilling (a need); satisfy: *entrepreneurship is necessary to answer the needs of national and international markets* | [no obj.] *nothing short of that would answer*.
– PHRASES **answer the description of** correspond to a description, esp. one of a suspect issued by the police: *he answers the description of being slightly taller than his two supposed companions*. **answer to (the name of)** often humorous be called: *an attractive woman answering to the name of Suzanne*. **have** (or **know**) **all the answers** informal be confident in one's knowledge of something, typically unjustifiably so: *it was his air of knowing all the answers that riled Mrs. Farrar*. **in answer to** as a response to or as a result of: *in answer to the stresses on modern woman, we have developed a range of beauty treatments*.
– DERIVATIVES **an·swer·er** n., **an·swer·less** adj.
– ORIGIN Old English *andswaru* (noun), *andswarian* (verb), of Germanic origin; from a base shared by **swear**.

an·swer·a·ble /ˈansərəbəl/ ▶ adj. **1** [predic.] (**answerable to**) required to explain or justify one's actions to; responsible or having to report to: *I'm not answerable to you for my every movement*. ■ (**answerable for**) responsible for: *an employer is answerable for the negligence of his employees*.
2 (of a question) able to be answered: *straightforward and answerable questions*.

an·swer·ing ma·chine ▶ n. a tape recorder or digital device that supplies a recorded answer to a telephone call and can record a message from the caller.

an·swer·ing serv·ice ▶ n. a business that receives and answers telephone calls for its clients.

ant /ant/ ▶ n. a small insect, often with a sting, that usually lives in a complex social colony with one or more breeding queens. It is wingless except for fertile adults, which often form large mating swarms, and is proverbial for industriousness.
● Family Formicidae, order Hymenoptera: several subfamilies.
– PHRASES **have ants in one's pants** informal be fidgety or restless.
– ORIGIN Old English *ǣmete*; related to German *Ameise*. Compare with **emmet**.

ant- ▶ prefix variant spelling of **anti-** before a vowel or *h* (as in *Antarctic*).

-ant ▶ suffix **1** (forming adjectives) denoting attribution of an action or state: *arrogant* | *expectant*.
2 (forming nouns) denoting an agent: *deodorant* | *propellant*.
– ORIGIN from Latin or French present participial verb stems (see also **-ent**).

Ant·a·buse /ˈantəˌbyo͞os/ ▶ n. trademark for **disulfiram**.
– ORIGIN 1940s: from **anti-** + **abuse**.

ant·ac·id /antˈasid/ ▶ adj. (chiefly of a medicine) preventing or correcting acidity, esp. in the stomach.
▶ n. an antacid medicine.

An·tae·us /anˈtēəs, -ˈtā-/ Greek Mythology a giant, the son of Poseidon and Earth, who compelled all comers to wrestle with him, overcoming and killing them all them until he was defeated by Hercules.

an·tag·o·nism /anˈtagəˌnizəm/ ▶ n. active hostility or opposition: ***the antagonism between them*** | ***his antagonism toward the local people*** | *petty antagonisms and jealousies*. ■ Biochemistry inhibition of or interference with the action of one substance or organism by another.
– ORIGIN early 19th cent.: from French *antagonisme*, from Greek *antagōnizesthai* 'struggle against' (see **antagonist**).

an·tag·o·nist /anˈtagənist/ ▶ n. a person who actively opposes or is hostile to someone or something; an adversary: *he turned to confront his antagonist*. ■ Biochemistry a substance that interferes with or inhibits the physiological action of another. Compare with **agonist**. ■ Anatomy a muscle whose action counteracts that of another specified muscle. Compare with **agonist**.
– ORIGIN late 16th cent.: from French *antagoniste* or late Latin *antagonista*, from Greek *antagōnistēs*, from *antagōnizesthai* 'struggle against' (see **antagonize**).

an·tag·o·nis·tic /anˌtagəˈnistik/ ▶ adj. showing or feeling active opposition or hostility toward someone or something: *he was* ***antagonistic to*** *the government's reforms* | *an antagonistic group of bystanders*. ■ Biochemistry & Physiology of or relating to an antagonist or its action.
– DERIVATIVES **an·tag·o·nis·ti·cal·ly** /-ik(ə)lē/ adv.

an·tag·o·nize /anˈtagəˌnīz/ ▶ v. [with obj.] cause (someone) to become hostile: *he antagonized many colleagues during the budget wars*. ■ Biochemistry (of a substance) act as an antagonist of (a substance or its action): *two other drugs antagonized the antidepressantlike effect*.
– ORIGIN mid 18th cent. (in the sense 'struggle against'): from Greek *antagōnizesthai*, from *ant-* 'against' + *agōnizesthai* 'struggle' (from *agōn* 'contest').

An·ta·kya /ˌäntäkˈyä/ Turkish name for **Antioch**.

An·tal·ya /ˌänˌtälˈyä, ˌäntlˈyä/ a port in southern Turkey; pop. 775,200 (est. 2007).

An·ta·na·na·ri·vo /ˌäntəˌnänəˈrēvō, ˌantəˌnanə-/ the capital of Madagascar, located in the central plateau; pop. 1,697,000 (est. 2007). Former name (until 1975) **Tananarive**.

Ant·arc·tic /antˈär(k)tik/ ▶ adj. of or relating to the south polar region or Antarctica. ■ Botany of, relating to, or denoting a phytogeographical kingdom comprising New Zealand, southern parts of Chile and Argentina, and islands in the South Atlantic and southern Indian Ocean.
▶ n. (**the Antarctic**) the Antarctic region.
– ORIGIN late Middle English: from Old French *antartique* or Latin *antarcticus*, from Greek

PRONUNCIATION KEY ə *ago, up*; ər *over, fur*; a *hat*; ā *ate*; ä *car*; e *let*; ē *see*; i *fit*; ī *by*; NG *sing*; ō *go*; ô *law, for*; oi *toy*; o͝o *good*; o͞o *goo*; ou *out*; TH *thin*; T͟H *then*; ZH *vision*

antarktikos 'opposite to the north,' from *ant-* 'against' + *arktikos* (see ARCTIC).

Ant·arc·ti·ca /ant'ärktikə, -'ärtikə/ a continent around the South Pole, situated mainly within the Antarctic Circle and almost entirely covered by ice sheets. Its exploitation is governed by an international treaty of 1959, which was renewed in 1991.

Ant·arc·tic Cir·cle the parallel of latitude 66° 33' south of the equator. It marks the southernmost point at which the sun is visible on the southern winter solstice and the northernmost point at which the midnight sun can be seen on the southern summer solstice.

Ant·arc·tic Con·ver·gence the zone of the Antarctic Ocean where the cold, nutrient-laden Antarctic surface water sinks beneath the warmer waters to the north.

Ant·arc·tic O·cean another name (esp. formerly) for SOUTHERN OCEAN.

Ant·arc·tic Pen·in·su·la a mountainous peninsula of Antarctica between the Bellingshausen and Weddell seas that extends northward toward Cape Horn and the Falkland Islands.

An·tar·es /an'te(ə)rēz, -'tar-/ the brightest star in the constellation Scorpius. It is a binary star of which the main component is a red supergiant.
– ORIGIN Greek, literally 'simulating Mars (in color).'

ant bear ▶ **n.** **1** another term for AARDVARK.
2 another term for GIANT ANTEATER (see ANTEATER).

ant·bird /'ant,bərd/ ▶ **n.** an insectivorous, long-legged, short-tailed bird that typically has dark gray plumage in the male and brown in the female. Antbirds, found mainly in the tropical forests of South America, often feed on insects that have been disturbed by swarms of army ants. ● Family Formicariidae: several genera, in particular *Myrmeciza*, *Cercomacra*, and *Drymophila*.

an·te /'antē/ ▶ **n.** a stake put up by a player in poker and similar games before receiving cards.
▶ **v.** (**antes, anteing, anted**) [with obj.] (**ante something up**) put up an amount as an ante in poker and similar games. ■ informal pay an amount of money in advance: *he anted up $925,000 of his own money.* ■ [no obj.] (**ante up**) informal put up one's money; pay up: *the owners have to ante up if they want to attract the best talent.*
– PHRASES **up** (or **raise**) **the ante** increase what is at stake or under discussion, esp. in a conflict or dispute: *he decided to up the ante in the trade war.*
– ORIGIN early 19th cent.: from Latin, literally 'before.'

ante- ▶ **prefix** before; preceding: *antechapel* | *antecedent.*
– ORIGIN from Latin *ante* 'before.'

ant·eat·er /'ant,ētər/ ▶ **n.** a mammal that feeds on ants and termites. It has a long snout and sticky tongue. ● Most anteaters are edentates of the Central and South American family Myrmecophagidae, which includes the **giant anteater** and the tamanduas. The echidna, numbat, and pangolin are also known as **spiny anteater**, **banded anteater**, and **scaly anteater**, respectively.

an·te·bel·lum /,antē'beləm/ ▶ **adj.** [attrib.] occurring or existing before a particular war, esp. the American Civil War: *the conventions of the antebellum South.*
– ORIGIN mid 19th cent.: from Latin, from *ante* 'before' and *bellum* 'war.'

an·te·ced·ent /,antə'sēdnt/ ▶ **n.** a thing or event that existed before or logically precedes another: *some antecedents to the African novel might exist in Africa's oral traditions.* ■ (**antecedents**) a person's ancestors or family and social background: *her early life and antecedents have been traced.* ■ Grammar a word, phrase, clause, or sentence to which another word (esp. a following relative pronoun) refers. ■ Logic the statement contained in the "if" clause of a conditional proposition. ■ Mathematics the first term in a ratio.
▶ **adj.** preceding in time or order; previous or preexisting: *the antecedent events that prompt you to break a diet.* ■ denoting a grammatical antecedent.
– DERIVATIVES **an·te·ced·ence** **n.**
– ORIGIN late Middle English: from Old French or from Latin *antecedent-* 'going before,' from *antecedere*, from *ante* 'before' + *cedere* 'go.'

an·te·cham·ber /'antē,CHāmbər/ ▶ **n.** a small room leading to a main one.
– ORIGIN mid 17th cent. (as *antichamber*): from French *antichambre*, from Italian *anticamera*, from *anti-* 'preceding' + *camera* (see CHAMBER).

an·te·chap·el /'antē,CHapəl/ ▶ **n.** a vestibule for a college chapel, lying beyond the west end of the nave.

an·te·chi·nus /,antē'kīnəs/ ▶ **n.** a marsupial mouse of shrewlike habits and appearance, found in Australia, New Guinea, and Tasmania. ● Genera *Antechinus* and *Parantechinus*, family Dasyuridae: several species.
– ORIGIN modern Latin, from Greek *anti-* 'simulating' + *ekhinos* 'sea urchin, hedgehog' (from its bristly fur).

an·te·date /'anti,dāt/ ▶ **v.** [with obj.] precede in time; come before (something) in date: *a civilization that antedated the Roman Empire.* ■ indicate or discover that (a document, event, or word) should be assigned to an earlier date: *there are no references to him that would antedate his birth.*

an·te·dat·ing /'anti,dātiNG/ ▶ **n.** an example or instance of a word, phrase, etc., at a date earlier than previously known or recorded: *antedatings of some prize-fighting terms.*

an·te·di·lu·vi·an /,antēdə'lo͞ovēən/ ▶ **adj.** [attrib.] of or belonging to the time before the biblical Flood: *gigantic bones of antediluvian animals.* ■ chiefly humorous ridiculously old-fashioned: *they maintain antediluvian sex-role stereotypes.*
– ORIGIN mid 17th cent.: from ANTE- + Latin *diluvium* 'deluge' + -AN.

an·te·lope /'antl,ōp/ ▶ **n.** (pl. **same** or **antelopes**) a swift-running deerlike ruminant with smooth hair and upward-pointing horns, native to Africa and Asia. ● Many genera and species, in the family Bovidae. ■ another term for PRONGHORN.
– ORIGIN late Middle English (originally the name of a fierce mythical creature with long serrated horns, said to live on the banks of the Euphrates): via Old French and medieval Latin from late Greek *antholops*, of unknown origin and meaning.

an·te·mor·tem /,antē'môrtəm/ ▶ **adj. & adv.** before death: [as adj.] *the antemortem instructions of the dead leader* | [as adv.] *abnormalities of the sinus are difficult to demonstrate antemortem.*
– ORIGIN late 19th cent.: Latin, literally 'before death.'

an·te·na·tal /,antē'nātl/ ▶ **adj.** [attrib.] before birth; during or relating to pregnancy; prenatal: *antenatal care.*
▶ **n.** informal a medical examination during pregnancy.
– DERIVATIVES **an·te·na·tal·ly** **adv.**

an·ten·na /an'tenə/ ▶ **n.** **1** Zoology (pl. **antennae** /-'tenē/) either of a pair of long, thin sensory appendages on the heads of insects, crustaceans, and some other arthropods. ■ (**antennae**) the faculty of instinctively detecting and interpreting subtle signs: *he has the political antennae of a party whip.*
2 (pl. **antennas**) a rod, wire, or other device used to transmit or receive radio or television signals.
– DERIVATIVES **an·ten·nal** /-'tenl/ **adj.** (sense 1), **an·ten·na·ry** /-'tenərē/ **adj.** (sense 1).
– ORIGIN mid 17th cent.: from Latin, alteration of *antemna* 'yard' (of a ship), used in the plural to translate Greek *keraioi* 'horns (of insects),' used by Aristotle.

an·ten·nule /an'ten,yo͞ol/ ▶ **n.** Zoology a small antenna, esp. either of the first pair of antennae in a crustacean.
– ORIGIN mid 19th cent.: diminutive of ANTENNA.

an·te·par·tum /,antē'pärtəm/ ▶ **adj.** [attrib.] Medicine occurring not long before childbirth.
– ORIGIN late 19th cent.: from Latin, 'before birth.'

an·te·pe·nul·ti·mate /,antēpə'nəltəmit/ ▶ **adj.** [attrib.] last but two in a series; third last: *the antepenultimate item on the agenda* | *the antepenultimate syllable.*

an·te·ri·or /an'ti(ə)rēər/ ▶ **adj.** **1** technical, chiefly Anatomy & Biology nearer the front, esp. situated in the front of the body or nearer to the head: *the veins anterior to the heart.* The opposite of POSTERIOR. ■ Botany (of a part of a flower or leaf) situated further away from the main stem.
2 formal coming before in time; earlier: *there are few examples of gold and silver work anterior to the dynasty of the Romanoffs.*
– DERIVATIVES **an·te·ri·or·i·ty** /an,ti(ə)rē'ôritē, -'är-/ **n.**, **an·te·ri·or·ly** **adv.**
– ORIGIN mid 16th cent.: from French *antérieur* or Latin *anterior*, comparative of *ante* 'before.'

antero- ▶ **comb. form** chiefly Anatomy representing ANTERIOR: *anteroposterior.*

an·ter·o·grade /'antərō,grād/ ▶ **adj.** directed forward in time. The opposite of RETROGRADE. ■ of or denoting a type of amnesia involving inability to remember any new information.
– ORIGIN late 19th cent.: from ANTERIOR, on the pattern of *retrograde.*

an·ter·o·lat·er·al /,antərō'latərəl/ ▶ **adj.** chiefly Anatomy both anterior and lateral.

an·te·room /'antē,ro͞om, -,ro͝om/ ▶ **n.** an antechamber, typically serving as a waiting room. ■ Military a sitting room in an officers' mess.

an·ter·o·pos·te·ri·or /,antərōpä'stirēər, -pō-/ ▶ **adj.** chiefly Anatomy relating to or directed toward both front and back: *an anteroposterior axis.*

an·te·vert·ed /'antē,vərtid/ ▶ **adj.** Anatomy & Medicine (of an organ of the body, typically the uterus) inclined forward.
– ORIGIN mid 19th cent.: from Latin *antevertere*, from *ante* 'before' + *vertere* 'to turn' + -ED².

ant·he·li·on /ant'hēlēən, an'THē-/ ▶ **n.** (pl. **anthelia** /-lēə/) a luminous halo around a shadow projected by the sun onto a cloud or fog bank. ■ a parhelion seen opposite the sun in the sky.
– ORIGIN late 17th cent.: from Greek *anthēlion*, neuter of *anthēlios* 'opposite to the sun,' from *anth-* (variant of *anti-* 'against') + *hēlios* 'sun.'

ant·hel·min·tic /,ant-hel'mintik, ,anTHel-/ Medicine ▶ **adj.** [attrib.] (chiefly of medicines) used to destroy parasitic worms.
▶ **n.** an anthelmintic medicine.
– ORIGIN late 17th cent. (as an adjective): from *anth-* (variant of *anti* 'against') + Greek *helmins*, *helminth-* 'worm' + -IC.

an·them /'anTHəm/ ▶ **n.** **1** a rousing or uplifting song identified with a particular group, body, or cause: *the song became the anthem for hippie activists.* ■ (also **national anthem**) a solemn patriotic song officially adopted by a country as an expression of national identity.
2 a choral composition based on a biblical passage, for singing by a choir in a church service.
– ORIGIN Old English *antefn*, *antifne* (denoting a composition sung antiphonally), from late Latin *antiphona* (see ANTIPHON). The spelling with *th*, which began in the 16th cent., was on the pattern of similar words, such as *Antony*, *Anthony* or *amarant*, *amaranth*.

an·the·mic /an'THēmik, -'THemik/ ▶ **adj.** (of a song) like an anthem in being rousing or uplifting.

an·the·mi·on /an'THēmēən/ ▶ **n.** (pl. **anthemia** /-mēə/) a flowerlike ornament used in the decorative arts.
– ORIGIN mid 19th cent.: from Greek, literally 'flower.'

an·ther /'anTHər/ ▶ **n.** Botany the part of a stamen that contains the pollen.
– ORIGIN early 18th cent.: from French *anthère* or modern Latin *anthera*, from Greek *anthēra* 'flowery,' from *anthos* 'flower.'

an·ther·id·i·um /,anTHə'ridēəm/ ▶ **n.** (pl. **antheridia** /-THə'ridēə/) Botany the male sex organ of algae, mosses, ferns, fungi, and other nonflowering plants.
– DERIVATIVES **an·ther·id·i·al** /-THə'ridēəl/ **adj.**
– ORIGIN mid 19th cent.: modern Latin, from *anthera* (see ANTHER) + *-idium* (from the Greek diminutive suffix *-idion*).

an·ther·o·zo·id /,anTHərə'zō-id, 'anTHərə,zoid/ ▶ **n.** Botany another term for SPERMATOZOID.
– ORIGIN mid 19th cent.: from ANTHER + ZOOID.

an·the·sis /an'THēsis/ ▶ **n.** Botany the flowering period of a plant, from the opening of the flower bud.
– ORIGIN mid 19th cent.: from Greek *anthēsis* 'flowering,' from *anthein* 'to blossom.'

ant·hill /'ant,hil/ ▶ **n.** a moundlike nest built by ants or termites.

antho- ▶ **comb. form** of or relating to flowers: *anthophilous.*
– ORIGIN from Greek *anthos* 'flower.'

an·tho·cy·a·nin /,anTHə'sīənin/ ▶ **n.** Chemistry a blue, violet, or red flavonoid pigment found in plants.
– ORIGIN mid 19th cent.: from German *Anthocyan*, from Greek *anthos* 'flower' + *kuanos* 'blue' + -IN¹.

an·thol·o·gize /an'THälə,jīz/ ▶ **v.** [with obj.] (usu. as adj. **anthologized**) include (an author or work) in an anthology: *the most anthologized of today's poets.*

an·thol·o·gy /an'THäləjē/ ▶ **n.** (pl. **anthologies**) a published collection of poems or other pieces of writing: *an anthology of European poetry.* ■ a similar collection of songs or musical compositions issued in one album.
– DERIVATIVES **an·thol·o·gist** /-jist/ **n.**
– ORIGIN mid 17th cent.: via French or medieval Latin from Greek *anthologia*, from *anthos* 'flower' + *-logia* 'collection' (from *legein* 'gather'). In Greek, the word originally denoted a collection of the "flowers" of verse, i.e., small choice poems or epigrams, by various authors.

An·tho·ny /'anTHənē/, Susan B. (1820–1906), US social reformer and leader of the woman suffrage movement.; full name *Susan Brownell Anthony*. She traveled, lectured, and campaigned throughout her life for women's rights. With Elizabeth Cady Stanton, she organized the National Woman Suffrage Association in 1869. With Stanton and

Matilda Joslyn Gage, she compiled the *History of Woman Suffrage* (1881–1902).

Susan B. Anthony

An·tho·ny, St. /'anTHənē/ (also **Antony** /'antənē/) (*c.*251–356), Egyptian hermit; the founder of monasticism. Feast day, January 17.

An·tho·ny of Pad·u·a, St. (also **Antony** /'antənē/) (1195–1231), Portuguese Franciscan friar. His devotion to the poor is commemorated by alms known as St. Anthony's bread; he is invoked to find lost articles. Feast day, June 13.

an·thoph·i·lous /an'THäfələs/ ▶ **adj.** Zoology (of insects or other animals) frequenting flowers.

An·tho·zo·a /,anTHə'zōə/ Zoology a large class of sedentary marine coelenterates that includes the sea anemones and corals. They are either solitary or colonial, and have a central mouth surrounded by tentacles.
– ORIGIN modern Latin (plural), from Greek *anthos* 'flower' + *zōia* 'animals.'

an·tho·zo·an /,anTHə'zōən/ Zoology ▶ **n.** a member of a large class of marine coelenterates (the Anthozoa), such as a sea anemone or coral.
▶ **adj.** relating to or denoting anthozoans.

an·thra·cene /'anTHrə,sēn/ ▶ **n.** Chemistry a colorless crystalline aromatic hydrocarbon obtained by the distillation of crude oils and used in chemical manufacture. ● A tricyclic compound; chem. formula: $C_{14}H_{10}$.
– ORIGIN mid 19th cent.: from Greek *anthrax*, *anthrak-* 'coal' + **-ENE**.

an·thra·cite /'anTHrə,sīt/ ▶ **n.** coal of a hard variety that contains relatively pure carbon and burns with little flame and smoke. Also called **HARD COAL**.
– DERIVATIVES **an·thra·cit·ic** /,anTHrə'sitik/ **adj.**
– ORIGIN late 16th cent. (denoting a gem described by Pliny and said to resemble coals, supposedly hydrophane): from Greek *anthrakitēs*, from *anthrax*, *anthrak-* 'coal.'

an·thrac·nose /an'THrak,nōs/ ▶ **n.** a mainly fungal disease of plants, causing dark lesions. ● This is usually caused by fungi of the subdivision Deuteromycotina.
– ORIGIN late 19th cent.: coined in French from Greek *anthrax*, *anthrak-* 'coal' + *nosos* 'disease.'

an·thra·qui·none /,anTHrəkwi'nōn, -'kwēnōn/ ▶ **n.** Chemistry a yellow crystalline compound obtained by oxidation of anthracene. It is the basis of many natural and synthetic dyes. ● Chem. formula: $C_{14}H_8O_2$.
– ORIGIN late 19th cent.: from *anthra(cene)* + **QUINONE**.

an·thrax /'an,THraks/ ▶ **n.** a notifiable bacterial disease of sheep and cattle, typically affecting the skin and lungs. It can be transmitted to humans, causing severe skin ulceration or a form of pneumonia (also called **WOOL-SORTER'S DISEASE**).
– ORIGIN late Middle English: Latin, 'carbuncle' (the earliest sense in English), from Greek *anthrax*, *anthrak-* 'coal, carbuncle,' with reference to the skin ulceration in humans.

an·throp·ic prin·ci·ple /an'THräpik/ ▶ **n.** the cosmological principle that theories of the universe are constrained by the necessity to allow human existence.

> In its 'weak' form the principle affirms that a universe in which living observers cannot exist is inherently unobservable. 'Strong' forms take this line of reasoning further, seeking to explain features of the universe as being so because they are necessary for human existence.

– ORIGIN 1970s: *anthropic* from Greek *anthrōpikos*, from *anthrōpos* 'human being.'

anthropo- ▶ **comb. form** human; of a human being: *anthropometry*. ■ relating to humankind: *anthropology*.
– ORIGIN from Greek *anthrōpos* 'human being.'

An·thro·po·cene /'anTHrəpə,sēn/ ▶ **n.** the current geological age, viewed as having begun about 200 years ago with the significant impact of human activity on the ecosphere.
– ORIGIN 2000: based on Greek *anthrōpos* 'human being' + *kainos* 'recent'; reportedly coined by chemist Paul Crutzen (1933–).

an·thro·po·cen·tric /,anTHrəpō'sentrik/ ▶ **adj.** regarding humankind as the central or most important element of existence, esp. as opposed to God or animals.
– DERIVATIVES **an·thro·po·cen·tri·cal·ly** /-trik(ə)lē/ **adv.**, **an·thro·po·cen·trism** /-,trizəm/ **n.**

an·thro·po·gen·ic /,anTHrəpō'jenik/ ▶ **adj.** (chiefly of environmental pollution and pollutants) originating in human activity: *anthropogenic emissions of sulfur dioxide*.
– DERIVATIVES **an·thro·po·gen·i·cal·ly** /-ik(ə)lē/ **adv.**

an·thro·pog·e·ny /,anTHrə'päjənē/ ▶ **n.** the study of the origin of humankind.

an·thro·poid /'anTHrə,poid/ ▶ **adj.** resembling a human being in form: *cartoons of anthropoid frogs*. ■ Zoology of or relating to the group of higher primates, which includes monkeys, apes, and humans. ■ Zoology (of an ape) belonging to one of the families of great apes. ■ informal, derogatory (of a person) apelike in appearance or behavior: *his crewcut sloped down from the back of his head to a low-cut, anthropoid forehead*.
▶ **n.** Zoology a higher primate, esp. an ape or apeman. ● Suborder Anthropoidea, order Primates. ■ informal, derogatory a person that resembles an ape in appearance or behavior: *anthropoids ruled the streets*.
– ORIGIN mid 19th cent.: from Greek *anthrōpoeidēs*, from *anthrōpos* 'human being' + **-OID**.

an·thro·pol·o·gy /,anTHrə'päləjē/ ▶ **n.** the study of humankind, in particular: ■ (also **cultural** or **social anthropology**) the comparative study of human societies and cultures and their development. ■ (also **physical anthropology**) the science of human zoology, evolution, and ecology.
– DERIVATIVES **an·thro·po·log·i·cal** /-pə'läjikəl/ **adj.**, **an·thro·po·log·i·cal·ly** **adv.**, **an·thro·pol·o·gist** /-jist/ **n.**

an·thro·pom·e·try /,anTHrə'pämitrē/ ▶ **n.** the scientific study of the measurements and proportions of the human body.
– DERIVATIVES **an·thro·po·met·ric** /-pō'metrik/ **adj.**

an·thro·po·mor·phic /,anTHrəpə'môrfik/ ▶ **adj.** relating to or characterized by anthropomorphism. ■ having human characteristics: *anthropomorphic bears and monkeys*.
– DERIVATIVES **an·thro·po·mor·phi·cal·ly** /-ik(ə)lē/ **adv.**
– ORIGIN early 19th cent.: from Greek *anthrōpomorphos* (see **ANTHROPOMORPHOUS**) + **-IC**.

an·thro·po·mor·phism /,anTHrəpə'môr,fizəm/ ▶ **n.** the attribution of human characteristics or behavior to a god, animal, or object.
– DERIVATIVES **an·thro·po·mor·phize** /-,fīz/ **v.**

an·thro·po·mor·phous /,anTHrəpə'môrfəs/ ▶ **adj.** (of a god, animal, or object) human in form or nature.
– ORIGIN mid 18th cent.: from Greek *anthrōpomorphos* (from *anthrōpos* 'human being' + *morphē* 'form') + **-OUS**.

an·thro·poph·a·gus /,anTHrə'päfəjəs, -gəs/ ▶ **n.** a cannibal, esp. in legends or fables.
– ORIGIN mid 16th cent.: from Latin, from Greek *anthrōpophagos* 'man-eating,' from *anthrōpos* 'human being' + *-phagos* (see **-PHAGOUS**).

an·thro·poph·a·gy /,anTHrə'päfəjē/ ▶ **n.** the eating of human flesh by human beings.
– DERIVATIVES **an·thro·poph·a·gous** /-gəs/ **adj.**
– ORIGIN mid 17th cent.: from Greek *anthrōpophagia*, from *anthrōpophagos* (see **ANTHROPOPHAGUS**).

an·thro·pos·o·phy /,anTHrə'päsəfē/ ▶ **n.** a formal educational, therapeutic, and creative system established by Rudolf Steiner, seeking to use mainly natural means to optimize physical and mental health and well-being.
– DERIVATIVES **an·thro·po·soph·i·cal** /-pə'säfikəl/ **adj.**
– ORIGIN early 20th cent.: from **ANTHROPO-** + Greek *sophia* 'wisdom.'

an·thu·ri·um /an'THo͝orēəm/ ▶ **n.** (pl. **anthuriums**) a tropical American plant often grown elsewhere for its ornamental foliage or brightly colored flowering spathes. ● Genus *Anthurium*, family Araceae.
– ORIGIN modern Latin, from Greek *anthos* 'flower' + *oura* 'tail.'

an·ti /'an,tī, 'antē/ ▶ **prep.** opposed to; against: *I'm anti the abuse of drink and the hassle that it causes*.
▶ **adj.** [predic.] informal opposed: *neither side in the debate, whether anti or pro, has offered a particularly convincing case*.
▶ **n.** (pl. **antis**) informal a person opposed to a particular policy, activity, or idea: *a shadow army of antis who endanger your sport*.
– ORIGIN late 18th cent. (as a noun): independent usage of **ANTI-**.

anti- (also **ant-**) ▶ **prefix** opposed to; against: *antiaircraft*. ■ preventing or suppressing: *antibacterial*. ■ reversing or undoing: *anticoagulant* | *antigravity* | *antipruritic*. ■ the opposite of: *anticlimax*. ■ Physics the opposite state of matter or of a specified particle: *antimatter* | *antiproton*. ■ acting as a rival: *antipope*. ■ unlike the conventional form: *antihero*.
– ORIGIN representing Greek *anti* 'against.'

an·ti·a·bor·tion /,antēə'bôrSHən, ,antī-/ ▶ **adj.** [attrib.] opposing or legislating against medically induced abortion.
– DERIVATIVES **an·ti·a·bor·tion·ist** **n.**

an·ti·air·craft /,antē'er,kraft, ,antī-/ (abbr.: **AA**) ▶ **adj.** [attrib.] (esp. of a gun or missile) used to attack enemy aircraft.

an·ti·a·li·as·ing /,antē'ālēəsiNG, ,antī-/ ▶ **n.** (in computer graphics) a technique used to add greater realism to a digital image by smoothing jagged edges on curved lines and diagonals.

an·ti-A·mer·i·can /,antēə'merikən, ,antī-/ ▶ **adj.** hostile to the interests of the United States; opposed to Americans.
– DERIVATIVES **an·ti-A·mer·i·can·ism** **n.**

an·ti·bac·te·ri·al /,antēbak'ti(ə)rēəl, ,antī-/ ▶ **adj.** [attrib.] active against bacteria.

an·ti·bal·lis·tic mis·sile /,antēbə'listik, ,antī-/ (abbr.: **ABM**) ▶ **n.** a missile designed for intercepting and destroying a ballistic missile while in flight.

An·tibes /äN'tēb/ a fishing port and resort in southeastern France; pop. 76,925 (2006).

an·ti·bi·o·sis /,antēbī'ōsis, ,antī-/ ▶ **n.** Biology an antagonistic association between two organisms (esp. microorganisms), in which one is adversely affected. See also **SYMBIOSIS**.
– ORIGIN late 19th cent.: from **ANTI-** + a shortened form of **SYMBIOSIS**.

an·ti·bi·ot·ic /,antēbī'ätik, ,antī-/ ▶ **n.** a medicine (such as penicillin or its derivatives) that inhibits the growth of or destroys microorganisms.
▶ **adj.** relating to, involving, or denoting antibiotics.
– ORIGIN mid 19th cent. (in the sense 'doubting the possibility of life in a particular environment'): from **ANTI-** + Greek *biōtikos* 'fit for life' (from *bios* 'life').

an·ti·bod·y /'anti,bädē/ ▶ **n.** (pl. **antibodies**) a blood protein produced in response to and counteracting a specific antigen. Antibodies combine chemically with substances that the body recognizes as alien, such as bacteria, viruses, and foreign substances in the blood.
– ORIGIN early 20th cent.: from **ANTI-** + **BODY**, translating German *Antikörper*, from *anti-* 'against' + *Körper* 'body.'

an·ti·bub·ble /'antē,bəbəl, 'antī-/ ▶ **n.** a membrane of air, submerged in liquid and surrounding a sphere of liquid.

an·tic /'antik/ ▶ **adj.** literary grotesque or bizarre.
– ORIGIN early 16th cent.: from Italian *antico* 'antique,' used to mean 'grotesque.'

an·ti·cap·i·tal·ist /,anti'kapitl-ist, ,antī-/ ▶ **adj.** opposed to capitalism.
▶ **n.** a person who is opposed to capitalism.

an·ti·cath·ode /,antē'ka,THōd, ,antī-/ ▶ **n.** Physics the target (or anode) of an X-ray tube that is struck by electrons from the cathode and from which X-rays are emitted.

an·ti·choice /,antē'CHois, ,antī-/ ▶ **adj.** opposed to a pregnant woman's choice of a medically induced abortion. Compare with **PRO-LIFE**.

an·ti·cho·lin·er·gic /,antē,kōlə'nərjik, ,antī-/ ▶ **adj.** Medicine (chiefly of a drug) inhibiting the physiological action of acetylcholine, esp. as a neurotransmitter.
▶ **n.** an anticholinergic drug.

An·ti·christ /'antē,krīst, 'antī-/ ▶ **n.** (**the Antichrist**) a great personal opponent of Christ who will spread evil throughout the world before being conquered at Christ's Second Coming. ■ a person or force seen as opposing Christ or the Christian Church.
– ORIGIN Old English, via Old French or ecclesiastical Latin from Greek *antikhristos*, from *anti* 'against' + *Khristos* (see **CHRIST**).

an·ti-Chris·tian /,antē'krisCHən, ,antī-/ ▶ **adj.** opposed to Christianity or Christian values. ■ of or relating to the Antichrist.
▶ **n.** a person who opposes Christianity.

PRONUNCIATION KEY ə *ago, up*; ər *over, fur*; a *hat*; ā *ate*; ä *car*; e *let*; ē *see*; i *fit*; ī *by*; NG *sing*; ō *go*; ô *law, for*; oi *toy*; o͝o *good*; o͞o *goo*; ou *out*; TH *thin*; TH *then*; ZH *vision*

an·tic·i·pate /an'tisə,pāt/ ▶ **v.** [with obj.] **1** regard as probable; expect or predict: *she anticipated scorn on her return to the theater* | [with clause] *it was anticipated that the rains would slow the military campaign.* ■ guess or be aware of (what will happen) and take action in order to be prepared: *they failed to anticipate a full scale invasion.* ■ look forward to: *Stephen was eagerly anticipating the break from the routine of business.*
2 act as a forerunner or precursor of: *he anticipated Bates's theories on mimicry and protective coloration.* ■ come or take place before (an event or process expected or scheduled for a later time). ■ react or respond to (someone) too quickly, without giving them a chance to do or say something. ■ pay (a debt) before it is due.
– DERIVATIVES **an·tic·i·pa·tor** /-,pātər/ **n.**
– ORIGIN mid 16th cent. (in the senses 'to take something into consideration,' 'mention something before the proper time'): from Latin *anticipat-* 'acted in advance,' from *anticipare*, based on *ante-* 'before' + *capere* 'take.'

an·tic·i·pa·tion /an,tisə'pāsʜən/ ▶ **n.** the action of anticipating something; expectation or prediction: *her eyes sparkled with anticipation.* ■ Music the introduction in a composition of part of a chord that is about to follow in full.
– PHRASES **in anticipation** with the probability or expectation of something happening: *they manned the telephones **in anticipation of** a flood of calls.*
– ORIGIN late Middle English: from Latin *anticipatio(n-)*, from the verb *anticipare* (see **ANTICIPATE**).

an·tic·i·pa·to·ry /an'tisəpə,tôrē/ ▶ **adj.** happening, performed, or felt in anticipation of something: *an anticipatory flash of excitement.* ■ Law (of a breach of contract) taking the form of an announcement or indication that a contract will not be honored.

an·ti·cler·i·cal /,antē'klərikəl, ,antī-/ chiefly historical ▶ **adj.** opposed to the power or influence of the clergy, esp. in politics.
▶ **n.** a person holding such views.
– DERIVATIVES **an·ti·cler·i·cal·ism** /-,lizəm/ **n.**

an·ti·cli·max /,antē'klī,maks, ,antī-/ ▶ **n.** a disappointing end to an exciting or impressive series of events: *the rest of the journey was an anticlimax by comparison* | *a sense of anticlimax and incipient boredom.*
– DERIVATIVES **an·ti·cli·mac·tic** /-klī'maktik/ **adj.**, **an·ti·cli·mac·ti·cal·ly** /-klī'maktik(ə)lē/ **adv.**

an·ti·cline /'antē,klīn, 'antī-/ ▶ **n.** Geology a ridge-shaped fold of stratified rock in which the strata slope downward from the crest. Compare with **SYNCLINE**.
– DERIVATIVES **an·ti·cli·nal** /,antē'klīnl, ,antī-/ **adj.**
– ORIGIN mid 19th cent.: from **ANTI-** + Greek *klinein* 'lean,' on the pattern of *incline.*

an·ti·clock·wise /,antē'kläk,wīz, ,antī-/ ▶ **adv. & adj.** British term for **COUNTERCLOCKWISE**.

an·ti·co·ag·u·lant /,antēkō'agyələnt, ,antī-/ ▶ **adj.** having the effect of retarding or inhibiting the coagulation of the blood.
▶ **n.** an anticoagulant substance.

an·ti·co·don /,antē'kōdn, ,antī-/ ▶ **n.** Biochemistry a sequence of three nucleotides forming a unit of genetic code in a transfer RNA molecule, corresponding to a complementary codon in messenger RNA.

an·ti·com·pet·i·tive /,antēkəm'petitiv, ,antī-/ ▶ **adj.** tending to stifle or suppress competition, esp. when this violates antitrust laws: *an anticompetitive advantage in the software industry.*
– DERIVATIVES **an·ti·com·pet·i·tive·ly** **adv.**, **an·ti·com·pet·i·tive·ness** **n.**

an·ti·con·vul·sant /,antēkən'vəlsənt, ,antī-/ ▶ **adj.** (chiefly of a drug) used to prevent or reduce the severity of epileptic fits or other convulsions.
▶ **n.** an anticonvulsant drug.

an·tics /'antiks/ ▶ **plural n.** foolish, outrageous, or amusing behavior: *the antics of our political parties.*
– ORIGIN early 16th cent.: from **ANTIC**.

an·ti·cy·clone /,antē'sīklōn, ,antī-/ ▶ **n.** a weather system with high atmospheric pressure at its center, around which air slowly circulates in a clockwise (northern hemisphere) or counterclockwise (southern hemisphere) direction. Anticyclones are associated with calm, fine weather.
– DERIVATIVES **an·ti·cy·clon·ic** /-sī'klänik/ **adj.**

an·ti·dem·o·crat·ic /,antē,demə'kratik, ,antī-/ ▶ **adj.** in conflict with the principles of democracy: *these antidemocratic measures have severely curtailed political freedom.*

an·ti·de·pres·sant /,antēdə'presnt, ,antī-/ ▶ **adj.** (chiefly of a drug) used to alleviate depression.
▶ **n.** an antidepressant drug.

an·ti·di·ar·rhe·al /,antē,dīə'rēəl, ,antī-/ ▶ **adj.** (of a drug) used to alleviate diarrhea.
▶ **n.** an antidiarrheal drug.

an·ti·di·u·ret·ic hor·mone /,antē,dīə'retik, ,antī-/ (abbr.: **ADH**) ▶ **n.** another term for **VASOPRESSIN**.

an·ti·dote /'anti,dōt/ ▶ **n.** a medicine taken or given to counteract a particular poison. ■ something that counteracts or neutralizes an unpleasant feeling or situation: *laughter is a good antidote to stress.* ■ (in homeopathy) a substance that cancels or opposes the effect of a remedy.
▶ **v.** [with obj.] (**antidotes, antidoting, antidoted**) counteract or cancel with an antidote: *What remedy will antidote henbane?*
– DERIVATIVES **an·ti·dot·al** /,anti'dōtl/ **adj.**
– ORIGIN late Middle English: via Latin, from Greek *antidoton*, neuter of *antidotos* 'given against,' from *anti-* 'against' + *didonai* 'give.'

an·ti·drom·ic /,anti'drämik/ ▶ **adj.** Physiology (of an impulse) traveling in the opposite direction to that normal in a nerve fiber. The opposite of **ORTHODROMIC**.
– ORIGIN early 20th cent.: from **ANTI-** + Greek *dromos* 'running' + **-IC**.

an·ti·e·met·ic /,antēə'metik, ,antī-/ ▶ **adj.** (chiefly of a drug) preventing vomiting.
▶ **n.** an antiemetic drug.

an·ti·es·tab·lish·ment /,antē-i'stablisʜmənt, ,antī-/ ▶ **adj.** against the establishment or established authority.

An·tie·tam /an'tētəm/ historic site in northwestern Maryland, on Antietam Creek, southeast of Sharpsburg, scene of a major Civil War battle in September 1862.

an·ti·feed·ant /,antē'fēdnt, ,antī-/ ▶ **n.** a naturally occurring substance in certain plants that adversely affects insects or other animals that eat them.
– ORIGIN 1960s: from **ANTI-** + **FEED** + **-ANT**.

an·ti·fer·ro·mag·net·ic /,antē,ferōməg'netik, ,antī-/ ▶ **adj.** Physics designating or exhibiting a form of magnetism characterized by an antiparallel alignment of adjacent electron spins in a crystal lattice. Compare with **FERRIMAGNETIC**.

an·ti·foul·ing /,antē'fouliɴɢ, ,antī-/ ▶ **n.** treatment of a boat's hull with a paint or similar substance designed to prevent fouling. ■ an antifouling substance.

an·ti·fraud /,antē'frôd, ,antī-/ ▶ **adj.** designed to prevent fraudulent practices: *new antifraud measures will save the taxpayer millions in lost revenue.*

an·ti·freeze /'anti,frēz/ ▶ **n.** a liquid, typically one based on ethylene glycol, which can be added to water to lower the freezing point, chiefly used in the radiator of a motor vehicle.

an·ti-g /,antē'jē, ,antī-/ ▶ **adj.** short for **ANTIGRAVITY**.
– ORIGIN 1940s: from **ANTI-** + *g*, the symbol for acceleration due to gravity.

an·ti·gen /'antijən/ ▶ **n.** a toxin or other foreign substance that induces an immune response in the body, esp. the production of antibodies.
– DERIVATIVES **an·ti·gen·ic** /,anti'jenik/ **adj.**
– ORIGIN early 20th cent.: via German from French *antigène* (see **ANTI-**, **-GEN**).

an·ti·gen·ic de·ter·mi·nant ▶ **n.** Biochemistry another term for **EPITOPE**.

an·ti·glob·al·i·za·tion /,antē,glōbələ'zāsʜən, ,antī-/ ▶ **n.** opposition to the increase in the global power and influence of businesses, esp. multinational corporations: [as modifier] *antiglobalization protesters.*

An·tig·o·ne /an'tigənē/ Greek Mythology daughter of Oedipus and Jocasta, the subject of a tragedy by Sophocles. She was sentenced to death for defying her uncle Creon, king of Thebes, but she took her own life before the sentence could be carried out, and Creon's son Haemon, who was engaged to her, killed himself over her body.

an·tig·o·rite /an'tigə,rīt/ ▶ **n.** a mineral of the serpentine group, occurring typically as thin green plates.

an·ti·gov·ern·ment /,antē'gəvər(n)mənt, ,antī-/ ▶ **adj.** against a government or the administration in office.

an·ti·grav·i·ty /,antē'gravitē, ,antī-/ ▶ **n.** Physics a hypothetical force opposing gravity.
▶ **adj.** [attrib.] (chiefly of clothing for a pilot or astronaut) designed to counteract the effects of high acceleration.

An·ti·gua /an'tēgwə, -'tigwə/ (also **Antigua Guatemala** /,gwätə'mälə/) a town in the central highlands of Guatemala; pop. 54,100 (est. 2009).

An·ti·gua and Bar·bu·da /bär'bo͞odə/ a country in the western West Indies, in the Leeward Islands, that consists of two main islands (Antigua and Barbuda) and Redonda, a smaller island to the southwest of Antigua; pop. 85,600 (est. 2009); capital, St. John's (on Antigua); languages, English (official), Creole.

> Discovered in 1493 by Columbus and settled by the English in 1632, Antigua became a British colony with Barbuda as its dependency; the islands gained independence within the Commonwealth of Nations in 1981.

– DERIVATIVES **An·ti·guan** **adj. & n.**

an·ti·he·ro /'antē,hi(ə)rō, 'antī-/ ▶ **n.** (pl. **antiheroes**) a central character in a story, movie, or drama who lacks conventional heroic attributes.

an·ti·her·o·ine /'antē,herōin, 'antī-/ ▶ **n.** a female antihero.

an·ti·his·ta·mine /,antē'histəmin, -mēn/ ▶ **n.** a drug or other compound that inhibits the physiological effects of histamine, used esp. in the treatment of allergies.

an·ti·in·fec·tive /,antēin'fektiv, ,antī-/ ▶ **adj.** (of a drug) used to prevent infection.
▶ **n.** an anti-infective drug.

an·ti·in·flam·ma·to·ry /,antēin'flamə,tôrē, ,antī-/ ▶ **adj.** (chiefly of a drug) used to reduce inflammation.
▶ **n.** (pl. **anti-inflammatories**) an anti-inflammatory drug.

an·ti·in·tel·lec·tu·al /,antē,intl'ekcʜo͞oəl, ,antī-/ ▶ **n.** a person who scorns intellectuals and their views and methods.
▶ **adj.** characteristic of an anti-intellectual person.
– DERIVATIVES **an·ti-in·tel·lec·tu·al·ism** **n.**

an·ti·knock /,antē'näk, ,antī-/ ▶ **n.** a substance (such as tetraethyl lead) added to gasoline to inhibit preignition.

An·ti-Leb·a·non Moun·tains /,antē 'lebənən, -ə,nän/ a range of mountains that run north to south along the border between Lebanon and Syria, east of the Lebanon range.

an·ti·life /,antē'līf, ,antī-/ ▶ **adj.** opposed to or restricting the full development of life: *the new industrial age was antilife.* ■ opposing the development of life by advocating abortion.

An·til·les /an'tilēz/ a group of islands that form the greater part of the West Indies. The **Greater Antilles** extend roughly east to west and comprise Cuba, Jamaica, Hispaniola (Haiti and the Dominican Republic), and Puerto Rico; the **Lesser Antilles**, to the southeast, include the Virgin, Leeward, and Windward islands, as well as various small islands to the north of Venezuela. See also **NETHERLANDS ANTILLES**.

an·ti·lock /,antē'läk, ,antī-/ ▶ **adj.** [attrib.] (of brakes) designed so as to prevent the wheels from locking and the vehicle from skidding if applied suddenly.

an·ti·log /'antē,lôg, 'antī-, -,läg/ ▶ **n.** short for **ANTILOGARITHM**.

an·ti·log·a·rithm /,antē'lôgə,riᴛʜəm, -'läg-, ,antī-/ ▶ **n.** the number to which a logarithm belongs.

an·ti·ma·cas·sar /,antēmə'kasər/ ▶ **n.** chiefly historical a piece of cloth put over the back of a chair to protect it from grease and dirt or as an ornament.
– ORIGIN mid 19th cent.: from **ANTI-** + **MACASSAR**.

an·ti·mag·net·ic /,antēmag'netik, ,antī-/ ▶ **adj.** (esp. of watches) resistant to magnetization.

an·ti·mat·ter /'antē,matər, 'antī-/ ▶ **n.** Physics molecules formed by atoms consisting of antiprotons, antineutrons, and positrons. Stable antimatter does not appear to exist in our universe.

an·ti·me·tab·o·lite /,antēmi'tabə,līt, ,antī-/ ▶ **n.** Physiology a substance that interferes with the normal metabolic processes within cells, typically by combining with enzymes.

an·ti·mon·ar·chist /,antē'mänərkist, ,antī-/ ▶ **n.** an opponent of monarchy.

an·ti·mo·ny /'antə,mōnē/ ▶ **n.** the chemical element of atomic number 51, a brittle silvery-white metalloid. (Symbol: **Sb**)

> Antimony was known from ancient times; the naturally occurring black sulfide was used as the cosmetic kohl. The element is used in alloys, usually with lead, such as pewter, type-metal, and Britannia metal.

– DERIVATIVES **an·ti·mo·ni·al** /,antə'mōnēəl/ **adj.**, **an·ti·mo·nic** /,antə'mänik/ **adj.**, **an·ti·mo·ni·ous** /,antə'mōnēəs/ **adj.**
– ORIGIN late Middle English (denoting stibnite, the most common ore of the metal): from medieval Latin *antimonium*, of unknown origin. The current sense dates from the early 19th cent.

an·ti·na·tion·al /,antē'nasʜənl, ,antī-/ ▶ **adj.** opposed to national interests or nationalism: *an antinational party.*

an·ti·neu·tron /,antē'n(y)o͞oträn, ,antī-/ ▶ **n.** Physics the antiparticle of a neutron.

an·ti·node /'anti,nōd/ ▶ **n.** Physics the position of maximum displacement in a standing wave system.

an·ti·noise /ˌantēˈnoiz, ˌantī-/ ▶ **adj.** [attrib.] promoting the suppression or reduction of noise: *stringent antinoise regulations.*
▶ **n.** sound generated for the purpose of reducing noise by interference.

an·ti·no·mi·an /ˌantiˈnōmēən/ ▶ **adj.** of or relating to the view that Christians are released by grace from the obligation of observing the moral law.
▶ **n.** a person holding this view.
– DERIVATIVES **an·ti·no·mi·an·ism** /-ˌnizəm/ **n.**
– ORIGIN mid 17th cent.: from medieval Latin *Antinomi*, the name of a 16th-cent. sect in Germany alleged to hold this view, from Greek *anti-* 'opposite, against' + *nomos* 'law.'

an·tin·o·my /anˈtinəmē/ ▶ **n.** (pl. **antinomies**) a contradiction between two beliefs or conclusions that are in themselves reasonable; a paradox.
– ORIGIN late 16th cent. (in the sense 'a conflict between two laws'): from Latin *antinomia*, from Greek, from *anti* 'against' + *nomos* 'law.'

an·ti·nu·cle·ar ▶ **adj.** [attrib.] opposed to the development of nuclear weapons or nuclear power.

An·ti·och /ˈäntēˌäk/ **1** a city in southern Turkey, near the Syrian border; pop. 186,200 (est. 2007). Antioch was the ancient capital of Syria under the Seleucid kings, who founded it *c.*300 BC. Turkish name **Antakya.**
2 a city in ancient Phrygia.
3 a city in north central California; pop. 100,219 (est. 2008).

An·ti·o·chus /anˈtīəkəs/ the name of eight Seleucid kings, notably. ■ **Antiochus III** (*c.*242–187 BC), reigned 223–187 BC; known as **Antiochus the Great.** He restored and expanded the Seleucid empire.
■ **Antiochus IV** (*c.*215–163 BC), son of Antiochus III; reigned 175–163 BC; known as **Antiochus Epiphanes.** His attempt to Hellenize the Jews resulted in the revival of Jewish nationalism and the Maccabean revolt.

an·ti·ox·i·dant /ˌantēˈäksidənt, ˌantī-/ ▶ **n.** a substance that inhibits oxidation, esp. one used to counteract the deterioration of stored food products. ■ a substance such as vitamin C or E that removes potentially damaging oxidizing agents in a living organism.

an·ti·par·al·lel /ˌantēˈparəˌlel, ˌantī-/ ▶ **adj.** Physics parallel but moving or oriented in opposite directions.

an·ti·par·ti·cle /ˈantēˌpärtikəl, ˈantī-/ ▶ **n.** Physics a subatomic particle having the same mass as a given particle but opposite electric or magnetic properties. Every kind of subatomic particle has a corresponding antiparticle, e.g., the positron has the same mass as the electron but an equal and opposite charge.

an·ti·pas·to /ˌantēˈpastō, ˌäntēˈpästō/ ▶ **n.** (pl. **antipasti** /-ˈpästē/) (in Italian cooking) an appetizer typically consisting of olives, anchovies, cheeses, and meats.
– ORIGIN Italian, from *anti-* 'before' + *pasto* (from Latin *pastus* 'food').

an·ti·pa·thet·ic /anˌtipəˈTHetik/ ▶ **adj.** showing or feeling a strong aversion: *it is human nature to be **antipathetic to** change.*
– ORIGIN mid 19th cent.: from **antipathy**, on the pattern of *pathetic.*

an·tip·a·thy /anˈtipəTHē/ ▶ **n.** (pl. **antipathies**) a deep-seated feeling of dislike; aversion: *his fundamental **antipathy to** capitalism | a thinly disguised mutual antipathy.*
– ORIGIN late 16th cent. (in the sense 'opposition of feeling, nature, or disposition'): from French *antipathie* or Latin *antipathia*, from Greek *antipatheia*, from *antipathēs* 'opposed in feeling,' from *anti* 'against' + *pathos* 'feeling.'

an·ti·per·son·nel /ˌantēˌpərsəˈnel, ˌantī-/ ▶ **adj.** [attrib.] (of weapons, esp. bombs) designed to kill or injure people rather than to damage buildings or equipment.

an·ti·per·spi·rant /ˌantiˈpərspərənt/ ▶ **n.** a substance that is applied to the skin, esp. under the arms, to prevent or reduce perspiration.

an·ti·phon /ˈantəˌfän/ ▶ **n.** (in traditional Western Christian liturgy) a short sentence sung or recited before or after a psalm or canticle. ■ a musical setting of such a sentence or sentences.
– ORIGIN late Middle English: via ecclesiastical Latin from Greek *antiphōna* 'harmonies,' neuter plural of *antiphōnos* 'responsive,' from *anti* 'in return' + *phōnē* 'sound.'

an·tiph·o·nal /anˈtifənl/ ▶ **adj.** (in traditional Western Christian liturgy) (of a short sentence or its musical setting) sung, recited, or played alternately by two groups.
▶ **n.** another term for **antiphonary.**
– DERIVATIVES **an·tiph·o·nal·ly** **adv.**

an·tiph·o·nar·y /anˈtifəˌnerē/ ▶ **n.** (pl. **antiphonaries**) a collection of antiphons.
– ORIGIN early 17th cent.: from ecclesiastical Latin *antiphonarium*, from *antiphona* (see **antiphon**).

an·tiph·o·ny /anˈtifənē/ ▶ **n.** antiphonal singing, playing, or chanting.

an·ti·pi·ra·cy /ˌantēˈpīrəsē, ˌantī-/ ▶ **adj.** **1** designed to prevent the unauthorized use or reproduction of copyright material: *the music industry's antipiracy campaign.*
2 denoting activities or measures designed to prevent or thwart piracy on the seas: *the law will allow direct involvement by Japanese vessels in antipiracy patrols.*

an·tip·o·dal /anˈtipədl/ ▶ **adj.** relating to or situated on the opposite side of the earth. ■ (**antipodal to**) diametrically opposed to something. ■ Botany relating to or denoting cells formed at the chalazal end of the embryo sac.

an·ti·pode /ˈantiˌpōd/ ▶ **n.** the direct opposite of something else: *the pole and its antipode.*
– ORIGIN early 17th cent. (denoting an inhabitant of the opposite side of the earth): back-formation from **antipodes.**

an·tip·o·des /anˈtipədēz/ ▶ **plural n.** (**the Antipodes**) Australia and New Zealand (used by inhabitants of the northern hemisphere). ■ the direct opposite of something: *we are the very **antipodes of** labor unions.*
– DERIVATIVES **an·tip·o·de·an** /anˌtipəˈdēən/ **adj. & n.**
– ORIGIN late Middle English: via French or late Latin from Greek *antipodes* 'having the feet opposite,' from *anti* 'against, opposite' + *pous, pod-* 'foot.' The term originally denoted the inhabitants of opposite sides of the earth, or of the side opposite to oneself, and was later transferred to the places where they live (mid 16th cent).

an·ti·pope /ˈantiˌpōp/ ▶ **n.** a person established as pope in opposition to one held by others to be canonically chosen.
– ORIGIN late Middle English *antipape*, via French from medieval Latin *antipapa* (on the pattern of *Antichrist*). The spelling change in the 17th cent. was due to association with **pope**[1].

an·ti·pro·ton /ˈantēˌprōtän, ˈantī-/ ▶ **n.** Physics the negatively charged antiparticle of a proton.

an·ti·pru·rit·ic /ˌantēprəˈritik, ˌantī-/ ▶ **adj.** [attrib.] (chiefly of a drug) used to relieve itching.
▶ **n.** an antipruritic drug.
– ORIGIN late 19th cent.: from **anti-** + *pruritic* (see **pruritus**).

an·ti·psy·chot·ic /ˌantēsīˈkätik, ˌantī-/ ▶ **adj.** [attrib.] (chiefly of a drug) used to treat psychotic disorders.
▶ **n.** an antipsychotic drug.

an·ti·py·ret·ic /ˌantēˌpīˈretik, ˌantī-/ ▶ **adj.** (chiefly of a drug) used to prevent or reduce fever.
▶ **n.** an antipyretic drug.

an·ti·quar·i·an /ˌantiˈkwe(ə)rēən/ ▶ **adj.** relating to or dealing in antiques or rare books. ■ valuable because rare or old: *out-of-print and antiquarian books.*
▶ **n.** a person who studies or collects antiques or antiquities.
– DERIVATIVES **an·ti·quar·i·an·ism** /-ˌnizəm/ **n.**
– ORIGIN early 17th cent.: from Latin *antiquarius* (see **antiquary**).

an·ti·quark /ˈantēˌkwôrk, ˈantī-/ ▶ **n.** Physics the antiparticle of a quark.

an·ti·quar·y /ˈantiˌkwerē/ ▶ **n.** (pl. **antiquaries**) another term for **antiquarian.**
– ORIGIN mid 16th cent.: from Latin *antiquarius*, from *antiquus* (see **antique**).

an·ti·quat·ed /ˈantiˌkwātid/ ▶ **adj.** old-fashioned or outdated: *this antiquated central heating system.*
– ORIGIN late 16th cent. (in the sense 'old, of long standing'): from ecclesiastical Latin *antiquare* 'make old,' from *antiquus* (see **antique**).

an·tique /anˈtēk/ ▶ **n.** a collectible object such as a piece of furniture or work of art that has a high value because of its considerable age: *Pauline loves collecting antiques* | [as modifier] *an antique dealer.*
▶ **adj.** **1** (of a collectible object) having a high value because of considerable age: *an antique clock.* ■ (of a method of finishing a wooden surface) intended to resemble the appearance of antique furniture: *bookshelves with an antique finish.*
2 belonging to ancient times: *statues of antique gods.* ■ old-fashioned or outdated: *trade unions defending antique work practices.* ■ often humorous showing signs of great age or wear: *an antique divorcee in reduced circumstances.*
▶ **v.** **1** (**antiques, antiquing, antiqued**) [with obj.] (usu. as adj. **antiqued**) make (something) resemble an antique by artificial means: *an antiqued door.*
2 (**go antiquing**) shop in stores where antiques are sold: *we would often go antiquing in search of furnishings.*
– ORIGIN late 15th cent. (as an adjective): from Latin *antiquus, anticus* 'former, ancient,' from *ante* 'before.'

an·tiq·ui·ty /anˈtikwitē/ ▶ **n.** (pl. **antiquities**) **1** the ancient past, esp. the period before the Middle Ages: *the great civilizations of antiquity.* ■ [with adj.] a specified historical period during the ancient past: *cameos dating from classical antiquity.* ■ (usu. **antiquities**) an object, building, or work of art from the ancient past: *an extensive collection of Greek antiquities.*
2 great age: *a church of great antiquity.*
– ORIGIN Middle English: from Old French *antiquite*, from Latin *antiquitas*, from *antiquus* 'old, former' (see **antique**).

an·ti·rac·ism ▶ **n.** the policy or practice of opposing racism and promoting racial tolerance.
– DERIVATIVES **an·ti·rac·ist** **n. & adj.**

an·ti·re·tro·vi·ral /ˌantēˌretrōˈvīrəl, ˌantī-/ ▶ **adj.** working against or targeted against retroviruses, esp. HIV: *antiretroviral therapy.*
▶ **n.** an antiretroviral drug.

an·ti·roll bar ▶ **n.** a rubber-mounted bar fitted in the suspension of a vehicle to increase its stability, esp. when cornering.

an·tir·rhi·num /ˌantiˈrīnəm/ ▶ **n.** (pl. **antirrhinums**) a plant of the figwort family, with showy two-lipped flowers. ● Genus *Antirrhinum*, family Scrophulariaceae: several species, in particular the snapdragon.
– ORIGIN from Latin, from Greek *antirrhinon*, from *anti-* 'counterfeiting' + *rhis, rhin-* 'nose,' from the resemblance of the flower to an animal's snout.

an·ti·scor·bu·tic /ˌantēskôrˈbyo͞otik, ˌantī-/ Medicine ▶ **adj.** (chiefly of a drug) having the effect of preventing or curing scurvy.
▶ **n.** an antiscorbutic food or drug.

an·ti-Sem·i·tism ▶ **n.** hostility to or prejudice against Jews.
– DERIVATIVES **an·ti-Sem·ite** **n.**, **an·ti-Se·mit·ic** **adj.**

an·ti·sense /ˈantēˌsens, ˈantī-/ ▶ **adj.** Genetics having a sequence of nucleotides complementary to (and hence capable of binding to) a coding sequence, which may be either that of the strand of a DNA double helix that undergoes transcription, or that of a messenger RNA molecule.

an·ti·sep·sis /ˈantiˌsepsis/ ▶ **n.** the practice of using antiseptics to eliminate the microorganisms that cause disease. Compare with **asepsis.**

an·ti·sep·tic /ˌantiˈseptik/ ▶ **adj.** **1** of, relating to, or denoting substances that prevent the growth of disease-causing microorganisms. ■ (of medical techniques) based on the use of such substances.
2 scrupulously clean or pure, esp. so as to be bland or characterless: *the antiseptic modernity of a conference center.*
▶ **n.** an antiseptic compound or preparation.
– DERIVATIVES **an·ti·sep·ti·cal·ly** /-ik(ə)lē/ **adv.**

an·ti·se·rum /ˈantiˌsi(ə)rəm/ ▶ **n.** (pl. **antisera** /-ˌsi(ə)rə/) a blood serum containing antibodies against specific antigens, injected to treat or protect against specific diseases.

an·ti·sla·ver·y /ˌantēˈslāvərē, ˌantī-/ ▶ **adj.** opposed to the practice or system of slavery.

an·ti·so·cial /ˌantēˈsōSHəl, ˌantī-/ ▶ **adj.** **1** contrary to the laws and customs of society; devoid of or antagonistic to sociable instincts or practices: *a dangerous, unprincipled, antisocial type of man.*
2 not sociable; not wanting the company of others.

USAGE See usage at **unsociable.**

an·ti·spas·mod·ic /ˌantēspazˈmätik, ˌantī-/ ▶ **adj.** (chiefly of a drug) used to relieve spasm of involuntary muscle.
▶ **n.** an antispasmodic drug.

an·ti·stat·ic ▶ **adj.** [attrib.] preventing the buildup of static electricity or reducing its effects.

an·tis·tro·phe /anˈtistrəfē/ ▶ **n.** the second section of an ancient Greek choral ode or of one division of it. Compare with **strophe** and **epode** (sense 2).
– ORIGIN mid 16th cent. (as a term in rhetoric denoting the repetition of words in reverse order): via late Latin from Greek *antistrophē*, from *antistrephein* 'turn against,' from *anti* 'against' + *strephein* 'to turn.'

an·ti·sym·met·ric /ˌantēsəˈmetrik, ˌantī-/ ▶ **adj.** Mathematics & Physics unaltered in magnitude but changed in sign by exchange of two variables or by a particular symmetry operation.

an·ti·tank ▶ **adj.** [attrib.] for use against enemy tanks: *new antitank missiles.*

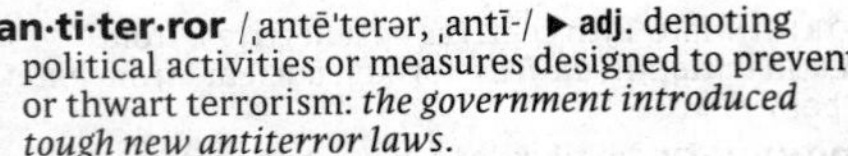

an·ti·ter·ror /ˌantēˈterər, ˌantī-/ ▶ **adj.** denoting political activities or measures designed to prevent or thwart terrorism: *the government introduced tough new antiterror laws.*

an·ti·ter·ror·ism /ˌantēˈterəˌrizəm, ˌantī-/ ▶ **n.** the prevention or abatement of terrorism: *a meeting of experts on antiterrorism* | [as modifier] *antiterrorism measures.*
– DERIVATIVES **an·ti·ter·ror·ist** **n. & adj.**

an·ti·tet·a·nus ▶ **adj.** Medicine preventing or effective against tetanus: *an antitetanus injection.*

an·tith·e·sis /anˈtiTHəsis/ ▶ **n.** (pl. **antitheses** /-ˌsēz/) a person or thing that is the direct opposite of someone or something else: *love is the antithesis of selfishness.* ■ a contrast or opposition between two things: *the antithesis between occult and rational mentalities.* ■ a figure of speech in which an opposition or contrast of ideas is expressed by parallelism of words that are the opposites of, or strongly contrasted with, each other, such as "hatred stirs up strife, but love covers all sins": *his sermons were full of startling antitheses.* ■ (in Hegelian philosophy) the negation of the thesis as the second stage in the process of dialectical reasoning. Compare with **SYNTHESIS**.
– ORIGIN late Middle English (originally denoting the substitution of one grammatical case for another): from late Latin, from Greek *antitithenai* 'set against,' from *anti* 'against' + *tithenai* 'to place.' The earliest current sense, denoting a rhetorical or literary device, dates from the early 16th cent.

an·ti·thet·i·cal /ˌantəˈTHetikəl/ ▶ **adj.** **1** directly opposed or contrasted; mutually incompatible: *people whose religious beliefs are antithetical to mine* | *two antithetical emotions pulled at her.*
2 [attrib.] connected with, containing, or using the rhetorical device of antithesis.
– DERIVATIVES **an·ti·thet·ic** **adj.**, **an·ti·thet·i·cal·ly** **adv.**
– ORIGIN late 16th cent. (sense 2): from Greek *antithetikos*, from *antithetos* 'placed in opposition,' from *antitithenai* 'set against.'

an·ti·tox·in /ˌantēˈtäksin/ ▶ **n.** Physiology an antibody that counteracts a toxin.
– DERIVATIVES **an·ti·tox·ic** /-sik/ **adj.**

an·ti·trades /ˈantiˌtrādz/ ▶ **plural n.** (also **antitrade winds**) steady winds that blow in the opposite direction to and overlie the trade winds.

an·ti·trust /ˌantēˈtrəst, ˌantī-/ ▶ **adj.** [attrib.] of or relating to legislation preventing or controlling trusts or other monopolies, with the intention of promoting competition in business.

an·ti·tus·sive /ˌantēˈtəsiv/ ▶ **adj.** (esp. of a drug) used to prevent or relieve a cough.
▶ **n.** an antitussive drug.

an·ti·type /ˈantiˌtīp/ ▶ **n.** **1** a person or thing that represents the opposite of someone or something else.
2 something that is represented by a symbol: *the ship in danger is easily understood to be its old antitype, the Commonwealth.*
– DERIVATIVES **an·ti·typ·i·cal** /ˌantiˈtipikəl/ **adj.**
– ORIGIN early 17th cent.: from late Latin *antitypus*, from Greek *antitupos* 'corresponding as an impression to the die,' from *anti* 'against, opposite' + *tupos* 'type, a stamp.'

an·ti·ven·in /ˌantēˈvenin, ˌantī-/ ▶ **n.** an antiserum containing antibodies against specific poisons, esp. those in the venom of snakes, spiders, and scorpions. Also called **ANTIVENOM**.
– ORIGIN late 19th cent.: from **ANTI-** + *ven(om)* + **-IN**[1].

an·ti·ven·om /ˌantēˈvenəm, ˌantī-/ another term for **ANTIVENIN**.

an·ti·vi·ral /ˌantēˈvīrəl, ˌantī-/ ▶ **adj.** **1** Medicine (chiefly of a drug or treatment) effective against viruses.
2 Computing (of software) designed to detect, remove, or offer protection against computer viruses.
▶ **n.** Medicine an antiviral drug or medicine.

an·ti·vi·rus /ˌantēˈvīrəs, ˌantī-/ ▶ **adj.** [attrib.] Computing (of software) designed to detect and destroy computer viruses.

an·ti·viv·i·sec·tion /ˌantēˌviviˈsekSHən, ˌantī-/ ▶ **adj.** [attrib.] opposed to operations on live animals for scientific research.
– DERIVATIVES **an·ti·viv·i·sec·tion·ism** /-ˌnizəm/ **n.**, **an·ti·viv·i·sec·tion·ist** /-nist/ **n. & adj.**

an·ti·war /ˌantēˈwôr, ˌantī-/ ▶ **adj.** opposed to war in general or to the conduct of a specific war: *his speech was interrupted by antiwar protesters.*

an·ti-Wes·tern ▶ **adj.** hostile to the interests of Europe and North America, esp. the United States: *another wave of anti-Western sentiment could emerge as a result of such an attack.*

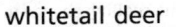

ant·ler /ˈantlər/ ▶ **n.** one of the branched horns on the head of an adult (usually male) deer, which are made of bone and are grown and cast off annually. ■ one of the branches on such a horn.
– DERIVATIVES **ant·lered** **adj.**
– ORIGIN late Middle English (originally denoting the lowest (forward-directed) branch of the antler): from Anglo-Norman French, variant of Old French *antoillier*, of unknown origin. The current sense dates from the early 19th cent.

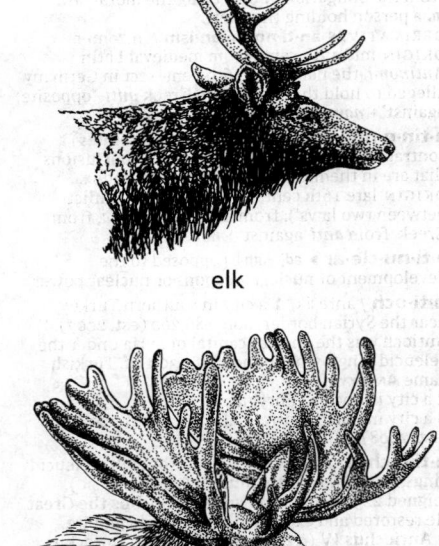

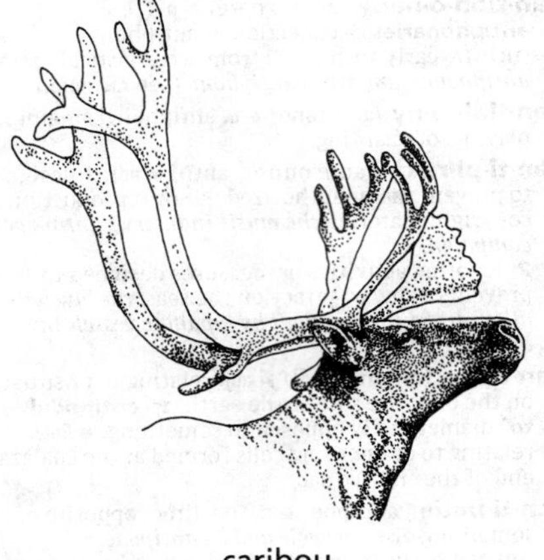

caribou

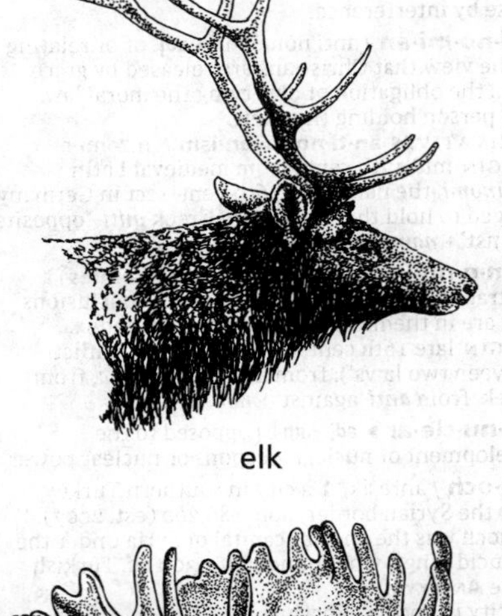

elk

whitetail deer

moose

antlers

Ant·li·a /ˈantlēə/ Astronomy a small and faint southern constellation (the Air Pump), between Hydra and Vela. ■ (as genitive **Antliae** /ˈantlēˌē/) used with a preceding letter or numeral to designate stars in the constellation: *the star Alpha Antliae.*
– ORIGIN Latin, from Greek.

ant li·on ▶ **n.** an insect that resembles a dragonfly, with predatory larvae that construct conical pits into which insect prey, esp. ants, fall. ● Family Myrmeleontidae, order Neuroptera.

An·to·fa·gas·ta /ˌäntōfəˈgästə/ a port in northern Chile, capital of Antofagasta region; pop. 341,900 (est. 2006).

An·to·nine /ˈantəˌnīn/ ▶ **adj.** [attrib.] of or relating to the Roman emperors Antoninus Pius and Marcus Aurelius or their rules (AD 137–80).
▶ **plural n.** (**the Antonines**) the Antonine emperors.

An·to·ni·nus Pi·us /ˌantəˈnīnəs ˈpīəs/ (86–161), Roman emperor 138–161, the adopted son and successor of Hadrian. His reign was generally peaceful.

An·to·nio·ni /ˌantōnēˈōnē, -təˈnyō-/, Michelangelo (1912–2007), Italian movie director. Notable movies: *L'avventura* (1960), *Blow-Up* (1966), *Zabriskie Point* (1970), and *Beyond the Clouds* (1995).

an·to·no·ma·sia /anˌtänəˈmāZH(ē)ə/ ▶ **n.** Rhetoric the substitution of an epithet or title for a proper name (e.g., *the Bard* for Shakespeare). ■ the use of a proper name to express a general idea (e.g., *a Scrooge* for a miser).
– ORIGIN mid 16th cent.: via Latin from Greek, from *antonomazein* 'name instead,' from *anti-* 'against, instead' + *onoma* 'a name.'

An·to·ny /ˈantənē, ˈanTHənē/, Mark (*c.*83–30 BC), Roman general and triumvir; Latin name *Marcus Antonius*. Following Julius Caesar's assassination in 44 BC, he took charge of the Eastern Empire, where he established his association with Cleopatra. Quarrels with Octavian led finally to his defeat at the battle of Actium and to his suicide.

An·to·ny, St. see **ANTHONY, ST.**

an·to·nym /ˈantəˌnim/ ▶ **n.** Linguistics a word opposite in meaning to another (e.g., *bad* and *good*).
– DERIVATIVES **an·ton·y·mous** /anˈtänəməs/ **adj.**
– ORIGIN mid 19th cent.: from French *antonyme*, from *ant-* (from Greek *anti-* 'against') + Greek *onuma* 'name.'

An·to·ny of Pad·u·a, St. see **ANTHONY OF PADUA, ST.**

an·trec·to·my /anˈtrektəmē/ ▶ **n.** surgical removal of an antrum, esp. the antrum of the stomach.

An·trim /ˈantrəm/ one of the six counties of Northern Ireland, formerly an administrative area. ■ a town in this county, on the northeastern shore of Lough Neagh; pop. 22,000 (est. 2009).

An·tron /ˈanˈträn/ ▶ **n.** trademark a type of strong, light nylon fiber used chiefly in making carpets and upholstery.
– ORIGIN 1960s: invented name.

an·trum /ˈantrəm/ ▶ **n.** (pl. **antra** /-trə/) Anatomy a natural chamber or cavity in a bone or other anatomical structure. ■ the part of the stomach just inside the pylorus.
– DERIVATIVES **an·tral** /-trəl/ **adj.**
– ORIGIN early 19th cent.: from Latin, from Greek *antron* 'cave.'

ant·sy /ˈantsē/ ▶ **adj.** agitated, impatient, or restless: *he was too antsy to stay in one place for long.*
– ORIGIN mid 19th cent.: probably from the phrase *have ants in one's pants* (see **ANT**).

ant-thrush ▶ **n.** any of a number of thrush-sized ant-eating birds. ● a large antbird (three genera in the family Formicariidae). ● an African thrush (genus *Neocossyphus*, subfamily Turdinae, family Muscicapidae: four species). ● another term for **PITTA**[2].

An·tung /ˈänˈdŏŏNG/ former name for **DANDONG**.

Ant·werp /ˈanˌtwərp/ a port in northern Belgium, on the Scheldt River; pop. 472,071 (2008). By the 16th century, it was a leading European commercial and financial center. Flemish name **Antwerpen**. French name **ANVERS**. ■ a province of Belgium of which Antwerp is the capital.

A·nu·bis /əˈnōōbis/ Egyptian Mythology the god of mummification, protector

Anubis

of tombs, typically represented as having the head of a jackal.

An·u·ra /əˈn(y)o͝orə/ Zoology an order of tailless amphibians that comprises the frogs and toads. Also called **Salientia** or **Batrachia**. ■ (as plural noun **anura**) amphibians of this order; frogs and toads.
– ORIGIN modern Latin, from **an-**[1] + Greek *oura* 'tail.'

A·nu·ra·dha·pu·ra /ˌənəˌrädəˈpo͝orə/ a city in north central Sri Lanka; pop. 81,500 (est. 2007). The ancient capital of Sri Lanka, it is a center of Buddhist pilgrimage.

an·u·ran /əˈn(y)o͝orən/ Zoology ▶ **n.** a tailless amphibian of the order Anura; a frog or toad.
▶ **adj.** relating to or denoting anurans.

an·u·ri·a /əˈn(y)o͝orēə/ ▶ **n.** Medicine failure of the kidneys to produce urine.
– DERIVATIVES **an·u·ric** /-ik/ **adj.**
– ORIGIN mid 19th cent.: from **an-**[1] + **-uria**.

a·nus /ˈānəs/ ▶ **n.** Anatomy & Zoology the opening at the end of the alimentary canal through which solid waste matter leaves the body.
– ORIGIN late Middle English: from Latin, originally 'a ring.'

An·vers /änˈver(s)/ French name of **Antwerp**.

an·vil /ˈanvil/ ▶ **n.** a heavy steel or iron block with a flat top, concave sides, and typically a pointed end, on which metal can be hammered and shaped. ■ the horizontally extended upper part of a cumulonimbus cloud: [as modifier] *anvil clouds*.
■ Anatomy another term for **incus**.
– ORIGIN Old English *anfilte*, from the Germanic base of **on** + a verbal stem meaning 'beat.'

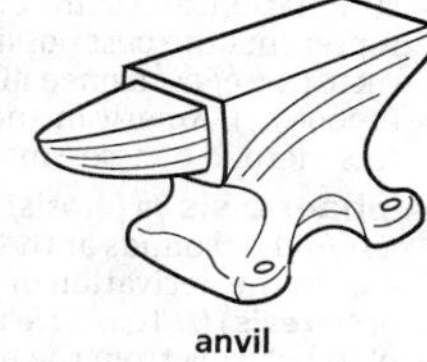
anvil

ANWR ▶ **n.** the Arctic National Wildlife Refuge, a wilderness area in Alaska. ■ a Congressional bill that would open up this area to oil exploration and drilling: [as modifier] *to date, ANWR language has not gained enough bipartisan backing*.

anx·i·e·ty /aNGˈzī-itē/ ▶ **n.** (pl. **anxieties**) a feeling of worry, nervousness, or unease, typically about an imminent event or something with an uncertain outcome: *he felt a surge of anxiety* | *anxieties about the moral decline of today's youth*. ■ [with infinitive] desire to do something, typically accompanied by unease: *the housekeeper's eager anxiety to please*.
■ Psychiatry a nervous disorder characterized by a state of excessive uneasiness and apprehension, typically with compulsive behavior or panic attacks.
– ORIGIN early 16th cent.: from French *anxiété* or Latin *anxietas*, from *anxius* (see **anxious**).

anx·i·o·lyt·ic /ˌaNGzēəˈlitik/ Medicine ▶ **adj.** (chiefly of a drug) used to reduce anxiety.
▶ **n.** an anxiolytic drug.
– ORIGIN 1960s: from **anxiety** + **-lytic**.

anx·ious /ˈaNG(k)SHəs/ ▶ **adj. 1** experiencing worry, unease, or nervousness, typically about an imminent event or something with an uncertain outcome: *she was extremely anxious about her exams*. ■ [attrib.] (of a period of time or situation) causing or characterized by worry or nervousness: *there were some anxious moments*.
2 [usu with infinitive] wanting something very much, typically with a feeling of unease: *the company was anxious to avoid any trouble* | [with clause] *my parents were anxious that I get an education*.
– DERIVATIVES **anx·ious·ly adv.**, **anx·ious·ness n.**
– ORIGIN early 17th cent.: from Latin *anxius* (from *angere* 'to choke') + **-ous**.

> **USAGE** **Anxious** and **eager** both mean 'looking forward to something,' but they have different connotations. **Eager** suggests enthusiasm about something, a positive outlook: *I'm eager to get started on my vacation*. **Anxious** implies worry about something: *I'm anxious to get started before it rains*.

an·y /ˈenē/ ▶ **determiner & pron. 1** [usu. with negative or in questions] used to refer to one or some of a thing or number of things, no matter how much or many: [as determiner] *I don't have any choice* | *do you have any tips to pass on?* | [as pronoun] *someone asked him for a match, but Joe didn't have any* | *you don't know* ***any*** *of my friends* | *if there is any left, throw it away*. ■ [as pronoun] anyone: *they are unlikely to be known by name to any but specialists*.
2 whichever of a specified class might be chosen: [as determiner] *these constellations are visible at any hour of the night* | *any fool knows that* | [as pronoun] *the illness may be due to* ***any of*** *several causes*.
▶ **adv.** [usu. with negative or in questions, as submodifier] (used for emphasis) at all; in some degree: *he wasn't any good at basketball* | *why look any further?* | *no one would be* ***any the wiser***. ■ informal used alone, not qualifying another word: *I didn't hurt you any*.
– PHRASES **any amount of** see **amount**. **any old** see **old**. **any time** (also **anytime**) **1** at whatever time: *she can come any time*. **2** without exception or doubt: *I can handle a shrimp like him anytime*. **any time** (or **day** or **minute**, etc.) **now** informal very soon: *we'll get them back any day now*. **be not having any (of it)** informal be unwilling to cooperate: *I tried to make polite conversation, but he wasn't having any*. **hardly any** see **hardly**. **not just any** — a particular or special thing of its type rather than an ordinary one of that type: *he had an acting job at last, and not just any part, but the lead in a new film*.
– ORIGIN Old English *ǣnig* (see **one**, **-y**[1]), of Germanic origin; related to Dutch *eenig* and German *einig*.

> **USAGE** When used as a pronoun, **any** can be used with either a singular or a plural verb, depending on the context: *we needed more sugar but there wasn't any left* (singular verb) or *are any of the new videos available?* (plural verb).

an·y·bod·y /ˈenēˌbädē, -ˌbədē/ ▶ **pron. 1** anyone: *there wasn't anybody around*.
2 a person of any importance: *everybody who was anybody in state government turned out to be involved*.
– PHRASES **anybody's guess** see **guess**.

an·y·how /ˈenēˌhou/ ▶ **adv. 1** another term for **anyway**.
2 in a careless or haphazard way: *two suitcases flung anyhow*.

an·y·more /ˌenēˈmôr/ (also **any more**) ▶ **adv.** [usu. with negative or in questions] to any further extent; any longer: *she refused to listen anymore* | *you don't get men like him anymore*.

an·y·one /ˈenēˌwən/ ▶ **pron. 1** [usu. with negative or in questions] any person or people: *there wasn't anyone there* | *does anyone remember him?* | *I was afraid to tell anyone*. ■ [without negative] used for emphasis: *anyone could do it*.
2 a person of importance or authority: *they are read by* ***anyone who's anyone***.
– PHRASES **be anyone's** informal (of a person) be open to sexual advances from anyone: *three drinks and he's anyone's*. **anyone's game** an evenly balanced contest: *it was still anyone's game at halftime*. **anyone's guess** see **guess**.

> **USAGE** **Any one** is not the same as **anyone**, and the two forms should not be used interchangeably. **Any one**, meaning 'any single (person or thing),' is written as two words to emphasize singularity: *any one of us could do the job; not more than ten new members are chosen in any one year*. Otherwise it is written as one word: *anyone who wants to come is welcome*. Note that this distinction is structurally similar to, although not identical with, the difference between *every day* and *everyday*: see usage at **everyday**.

an·y·place /ˈenēˌplās/ ▶ **adv.** informal term for **anywhere**: *Miami is hotter than anyplace else*.

an·y·thing /ˈenēˌTHiNG/ ▶ **pron.** [usu. with negative or in questions] used to refer to a thing, no matter what: *nobody was saying anything* | *have you found anything?* | *he inquired whether there was anything he could do*. ■ [without negative] used for emphasis: *I was ready for anything*. ■ used to indicate a range: *he trains anything from seven to eight hours a day*.
– PHRASES **anything but** not at all (used for emphasis): *he is anything but racist*. **anything like** — [with negative] at all like— (used for emphasis): *it doesn't taste anything like wine*. **(as) — as anything** informal extremely—: *she said it out loud, clear as anything*. **if anything** see **if**. **like anything** see **like**[1]. **or anything** [usu. with negative or in questions] informal added as a general reference to other things similar to the thing mentioned: *no strings attached, you don't have to join up or anything*.

an·y·time /ˈenēˌtīm/ ▶ **adv.** variant of **any time** at **any**.

An·y·town /ˈenēˌtoun/ (also **Anytown USA**) ▶ **n.** any real or fictional place regarded as being typical of American small-town appearance or values: *the party was looking for that elusive candidate from Anytown*.

an·y·way /ˈenēˌwā/ ▶ **adv. 1** used to confirm or support a point or idea just mentioned: *I told you, it's all right, and anyway, it was my fault* | *it's too late now anyway*. ■ used in questions to emphasize the speaker's wish to obtain the truth: *What are you doing here, anyway?*
2 used in conversations: ■ to change the subject or to resume a subject after interruption: *How she lives with him is beyond me. Anyway, I really like her*. ■ to indicate that the speaker wants to end the conversation: *Anyway, Dot, I must go*. ■ to indicate that the speaker is passing over less significant aspects of an account in order to focus on the most important points: *Poor John always enjoyed a drink. Anyway, he died last year*.
3 used to indicate that something happened or will happen in spite of something else: *nobody invited Miss Honey to sit down so she sat down anyway*.

an·y·ways /ˈenēˌwāz/ ▶ **adv.** informal or dialect form of **anyway**: *you wouldn't understand all them long words anyways*.

an·y·where /ˈenēˌ(h)we(ə)r/ ▶ **adv.** [usu. with negative or in questions] in or to any place: *he couldn't be found anywhere*. ■ [without negative] used for emphasis: *I could go anywhere in the world*. ■ used to indicate a range: *this iron garden seat dates anywhere from 1890 to 1920* | *she could have been* ***anywhere between*** *twenty-five and forty*.
▶ **pron.** any place: *he doesn't have anywhere to live*.
– PHRASES **anywhere near** [with negative or in questions] (used for emphasis) at all near: *I wouldn't dream of letting a surgeon anywhere near my eyes*. ■ remotely close to in extent, level, or scope: *imitations rarely look anywhere near as good as the real thing*.

an·y·wheres /ˈenēˌ(h)we(ə)rz/ ▶ **adv. & pron.** informal or dialect form of **anywhere**: [as adv.] *I'll see if I can find your clothes anywheres*.

an·y·wise /ˈenēˌwīz/ ▶ **adv.** archaic in any manner or way.
– ORIGIN Old English *on ǣnige wisan* 'in any wise.'

An·zac /ˈanˌzak/ ▶ **n.** a soldier in the Australian and New Zealand Army Corps (1914–18). ■ dated a person, esp. a member of the armed services, from Australia or New Zealand.
– ORIGIN acronym.

An·zio /ˈäntsēˌō, ˈanzēō/ a seaport in western Italy, south of Rome; pop. 52,192 (2008). It was a popular resort for citizens of ancient Rome. Allied troops landed here in January 1944, amid fierce fighting, to begin their drive to capture Rome.

AOC ▶ **abbr.** *appellation d'origine contrôlée* (see **appellation contrôlée**).

ao dai /ˈou ˌdī, ˈō/ ▶ **n.** (pl. **ao dais**) a Vietnamese woman's long-sleeved tunic with ankle-length panels at front and back, worn over trousers.
– ORIGIN 1960s: Vietnamese.

A-OK (also **A-okay**) informal ▶ **adj.** in good order or condition; all right: *everything will be A-OK* | *the pictures look A-OK to me*.
▶ **adv.** in a good manner or way; all right: *we hit it off A-OK*.
– ORIGIN 1960s (originally an astronauts' term): from *all systems OK*.

AOR ▶ **n.** [usu. as modifier] a type of popular music in which a hard rock background is combined with softer or more melodic elements.
– ORIGIN 1970s: from *album-oriented rock* or *adult-oriented rock*.

Ao·ra·ki/Mount Cook /ouˈrakē ˌmount ˈko͝ok/ official name (since 1999) for Mount Cook, the highest peak in New Zealand: 12,349 feet (3,764 m).

a·o·rist /ˈāərist/ Grammar ▶ **n.** (esp. in Greek) an unqualified past tense of a verb without reference to duration or completion of the action.
▶ **adj.** relating to or denoting this tense.
– DERIVATIVES **a·o·ris·tic** /ˌāəˈristik/ **adj.**
– ORIGIN late 16th cent.: from Greek *aoristos* 'indefinite,' from *a-* 'not' + *horizein* 'define, limit.'

a·or·ta /āˈôrtə/ ▶ **n.** the main artery of the body, supplying oxygenated blood to the circulatory system. In humans it passes over the heart from the left ventricle and runs down in front of the backbone.
– DERIVATIVES **a·or·tic** /-tik/ **adj.**
– ORIGIN mid 16th cent.: from Greek *aortē* (used in the plural by Hippocrates for the branches of the windpipe, and by Aristotle for the great artery), from *aeirein* 'raise.'

Ao·te·a·ro·a /ouˌtäəˈrōə/ the Maori name for **New Zealand**.
– ORIGIN Maori, literally 'land of the long white cloud.'

a·ou·dad /ˈä-o͞oˌdad/ ▶ **n.** another term for **Barbary sheep**.
– ORIGIN early 19th cent.: from French, from Berber *udād*.

à ou·trance /ˌä o͞oˈträns/ ▶ **adv.** literary to the death or the very end: *a duel à outrance*.
– ORIGIN early 17th cent.: French, literally 'to the utmost.'

Aou·zou Strip /ouˈzo͞o/ a narrow corridor of disputed desert land in northern Chad. It forms the border between Chad and Libya. In 1994, Libya agreed to withdraw its troops from the area.

AP ▶ **abbr.** ■ advanced placement. ■ American plan. ■ Associated Press.

ap-[1] ▶ **prefix** variant spelling of AD- assimilated before *p* (as in *apposite, apprehend*).

ap-[2] ▶ **prefix** variant spelling of APO- before *h* (as in *aphelion*).

a·pace /əˈpās/ ▶ **adv.** literary swiftly; quickly: *work continues apace.*
– ORIGIN late Middle English: from Old French *a pas* 'at (a considerable) pace.'

A·pach·e ▶ **n.** /əˈpaCHē/ **1** (pl. **same** or **Apaches**) a member of a North American Indian people living chiefly in New Mexico and Arizona. The Apache put up fierce resistance to the European settlers and were, under the leadership of Geronimo, the last American Indian people to be conquered. **2** the Athabaskan language of this people.
▶ **adj.** of or relating to the Apache or their language.
– ORIGIN from Mexican Spanish, probably from Zuni *Apachu*, literally 'enemy.'

a·pache /əˈpasн, äˈpäsн/ ▶ **n.** (pl. **apaches** pronunc. **same**) a violent street ruffian, originally in Paris.
– ORIGIN early 20th cent.: French, from APACHE, by association with the reputed ferocity of the American Indian people.

Apa·la·chi·co·la Riv·er /ˌapəlaCHiˈkōlə/ see CHATTAHOOCHEE RIVER.

a·part /əˈpärt/ ▶ **adv.** **1** (of two or more people or things) separated by a distance; at a specified distance from each other in time or space: *his parents are now living apart* | *two stone gateposts some thirty feet apart* | *countries* ***as far apart as*** *New Zealand and the US* | figurative *the two sides remained far apart on the issue.* **2** to or on one side; at a distance from the main body: *Isabel stepped away from Joanna and stood apart* | figurative *their religious commitment sets them apart.* ■ used after a noun to indicate that someone or something has distinctive qualities that mark them out from other people or things: *wrestlers were a breed apart.* ■ used after a noun to indicate that someone or something has been dealt with sufficiently or is being excluded from what follows: *Alaska apart, much of America's energy business concentrates on producing gas.* **3** so as to be shattered; into pieces: *he leapt out of the car just before it was blown apart.*
– PHRASES **apart from 1** except for: *the whole world seemed to be sleeping, apart from Barbara.* **2** in addition to; as well as: *quite apart from all the work, he had such financial problems.* **tell apart** distinguish or separate one from another: *the twins were so identical that it was impossible to tell them apart.*
– DERIVATIVES **a·part·ness n.**
– ORIGIN late Middle English: from Old French, from Latin *a parte* 'at the side.'

a·part·heid /əˈpärt,(h)āt, -,(h)īt/ ▶ **n.** historical (in South Africa) a policy or system of segregation or discrimination on grounds of race. ■ segregation in other contexts: *sexual apartheid.*

> Adopted by the successful Afrikaner National Party as a slogan in the 1948 election, apartheid extended and institutionalized existing racial segregation. Despite rioting and terrorism at home and isolation abroad from the 1960s onward, the white regime maintained the apartheid system with only minor relaxation until February 1991.

– ORIGIN 1940s: Afrikaans, literally 'separateness,' from Dutch *apart* 'separate' + *-heid* (equivalent of -HOOD).

a·part·ment /əˈpärtmənt/ (abbr.: **apt.**) ▶ **n.** a suite of rooms forming one residence, typically in a building containing a number of these. ■ a large building containing such suites; an apartment building. ■ (**apartments**) a suite of rooms in a very large or grand house set aside for the private use of a monarch or noble: *the Imperial apartments.*
– ORIGIN mid 17th cent. (denoting a suite of rooms for the use of a particular person or group): from French *appartement*, from Italian *appartamento*, from *appartare* 'to separate,' from *a parte* 'apart.'

a·part·ment build·ing (also **apartment block** or **apartment house**) ▶ **n.** a large building divided into separate apartments.

ap·a·thet·ic /ˌapəˈTHetik/ ▶ **adj.** showing or feeling no interest, enthusiasm, or concern: *apathetic slackers who don't vote.*
– DERIVATIVES **ap·a·thet·i·cal·ly** /-ik(ə)lē/ **adv.**
– ORIGIN mid 18th cent.: from APATHY, on the pattern of *pathetic.*

ap·a·thy /ˈapəTHē/ ▶ **n.** lack of interest, enthusiasm, or concern: *widespread apathy among students.*
– ORIGIN early 17th cent.: from French *apathie*, via Latin from Greek *apatheia*, from *apathēs* 'without feeling,' from *a-* 'without' + *pathos* 'suffering.'

ap·a·tite /ˈapə,tīt/ ▶ **n.** a widely occurring pale green to purple mineral, consisting of calcium phosphate with some fluorine, chlorine, and other elements. It is used in the manufacture of fertilizers.
– ORIGIN early 19th cent.: coined in German from Greek *apatē* 'deceit' (from the mineral's diverse forms and colors).

a·pa·to·saur /əˈpatō,sôr/ (also **apatosaurus** /ə,patōˈsôrəs/) ▶ **n.** a huge herbivorous dinosaur of the late Jurassic period, with a long neck and tail. Also called BRONTOSAUR. ● Genus *Apatosaurus* (popularly *Brontosaurus*), infraorder Sauropoda, order Saurischia.
– DERIVATIVES **a·pa·to·sau·ri·an adj.**
– ORIGIN modern Latin, from Greek *apatē* 'deceit' + *sauros* 'lizard.'

APB ▶ **abbr.** all-points bulletin.

APC ▶ **abbr.** ■ armored personnel carrier. ■ aspirin, phenacetin, and caffeine, a compound used in some analgesics.

ape /āp/ ▶ **n.** a large primate that lacks a tail, including the gorilla, chimpanzees, orangutan, and gibbons. See also GREAT APE, GIBBON. ● Families Pongidae and Hylobatidae. ■ used in names of macaque monkeys with short tails, e.g., **Barbary ape.** ■ (in general use) any monkey. ■ an unintelligent or clumsy person. ■ archaic an inferior imitator or mimic: *cunning is but the ape of wisdom.*
▶ **v.** [with obj.] imitate the behavior or manner of (someone or something), esp. in an absurd or unthinking way: *new architecture can respect the old without aping its style.*
– PHRASES **go ape** informal express wild excitement or anger: *your kids will go ape over these Popsicles!* | *a washerwoman gone ape with a butcher knife.*
– DERIVATIVES **ape·like adj.**
– ORIGIN Old English *apa*, of Germanic origin; related to Dutch *aap* and German *Affe.*

APEC /ˈā,pek/ ▶ **abbr.** Asia Pacific Economic Cooperation, a regional economic forum established in 1989, including the US, Japan, China, Australia, Indonesia, Hong Kong, and Thailand.

A·pel·doorn /ˈapəl,dôrn/ a town in the east central Netherlands; pop. 155,108 (2008). It is the site of the summer residence of the Dutch royal family.

ape·man /ˈāp,man/ ▶ **n.** (pl. **apemen**) an extinct apelike primate believed to be related or ancestral to present-day humans.

Ap·en·nines /ˈapə,nīnz/ a mountain range in Italy that extends for 880 miles (1,400 km) from the northwest to the southern tip of the country.

a·per·çu /äperˈso͞o/ ▶ **n.** (pl. **aperçus** pronunc. **same**) a comment or brief reference that makes an illuminating or entertaining point.
– ORIGIN early 19th cent.: from French, past participle of *apercevoir* 'perceive.'

a·per·i·ent /əˈpi(ə)rēənt/ Medicine ▶ **adj.** (chiefly of a drug) used to relieve constipation.
▶ **n.** an aperient drug.
– ORIGIN early 17th cent.: from Latin *aperient-* 'opening,' from *aperire.*

a·pe·ri·od·ic /ˌāpi(ə)rēˈädik/ ▶ **adj.** technical not periodic; irregular: *aperiodic fluctuations.* ■ Physics denoting a potentially oscillating or vibrating system (such as an instrument with a pointer) that is damped to prevent oscillation or vibration.
– DERIVATIVES **a·pe·ri·o·dic·i·ty** /ā,pi(ə)rēəˈdisitē/ **n.**

a·pe·ri·tif /ä,periˈtēf, -ə,per-/ ▶ **n.** an alcoholic drink taken before a meal to stimulate the appetite.
– ORIGIN late 19th cent.: from French *apéritif*, from medieval Latin *aperitivus*, based on Latin *aperire* 'to open.'

ap·er·ture /ˈapər,CHər/ ▶ **n.** chiefly technical an opening, hole, or gap: *the bell ropes passed through apertures in the ceiling.* ■ a space through which light passes in an optical or photographic instrument, esp. the variable opening by which light enters a camera.
– DERIVATIVES **ap·er·tur·al adj.**
– ORIGIN late Middle English: from Latin *apertura*, from *apert-* 'opened,' from *aperire* 'to open.'

ap·er·ture pri·or·i·ty ▶ **n.** Photography an exposure system used in some automatic cameras in which the aperture is selected by the user and the appropriate shutter speed is controlled automatically. Compare with SHUTTER PRIORITY.

ap·er·y /ˈāpərē/ ▶ **n.** archaic the act of imitating the behavior or manner of someone, esp. in an absurd or unthinking way.

ape·shit /ˈāp,SHit/ ▶ **n.**
– PHRASES **go apeshit** vulgar slang another way of saying GO APE (see APE).

a·pet·al·ous /āˈpetl-əs/ ▶ **adj.** Botany (of a flower) having no petals.
– ORIGIN early 18th cent.: from modern Latin *apetalus*, from Greek *apetalos* 'leafless' (from *a-* 'without' + *petalon* 'leaf') + -OUS.

A·pex /ˈāpeks/ ▶ **n.** [usu. as modifier] a system of reduced fares for scheduled airline flights and railroad journeys that must be booked and paid for before a certain period in advance of departure: *Apex fares.*
– ORIGIN 1970s: from Advance Purchase Excursion.

a·pex /ˈāpeks/ ▶ **n.** (pl. **apexes** or **apices** /ˈāpə,sēz, ˈapə-/) the top or highest part of something, esp. one forming a point: *the living room extends right up into the apex of the roof* | figurative *the apex of his career was when he hoisted aloft the World Cup.* ■ Geometry the highest point in a plane or solid figure, relative to a base line or plane. ■ Botany the growing point of a shoot. ■ the highest level of a hierarchy, organization, or other power structure regarded as a triangle or pyramid: *the central bank is at the apex of the financial system.*
▶ **v.** [no obj.] reach a high point or climax: *melodic lines build up to the chorus and it apexes at the solo.*
– ORIGIN early 17th cent.: from Latin, 'peak, tip.'

Ap·gar score /ˈap,gär/ ▶ **n.** Medicine a measure of the physical condition of a newborn infant. It is obtained by adding points (2, 1, or 0) for heart rate, respiratory effort, muscle tone, response to stimulation, and skin coloration; a score of ten represents the best possible condition.
– ORIGIN 1960s: named after Virginia *Apgar* (1909–74), American anesthesiologist who devised this method of assessment in 1953.

a·phaer·e·sis /əˈferəsis/ ▶ **n.** Linguistics the loss of a sound or sounds at the beginning of a word, e.g., in the derivation of *adder* from *nadder.* (usu. **apheresis**) Medicine /ˌafəˈrēsis/ the removal of blood plasma from the body by the withdrawal of blood, its separation into plasma and cells, and the reintroduction of the cells, used esp. to remove antibodies in treating autoimmune diseases.
– ORIGIN mid 16th cent.: via late Latin from Greek *aphairesis*, from *aphairein* 'take away,' from *apo* 'from' + *hairein* 'take.'

a·pha·sia /əˈfāZHə, əˈfāziə/ ▶ **n.** Medicine loss of ability to understand or express speech, caused by brain damage. Compare with APHONIA.
– DERIVATIVES **a·pha·sic** /-zik/ **adj. & n.**
– ORIGIN mid 19th cent.: from Greek, from *aphatos* 'speechless,' from *a-* 'not' + *phanai* 'speak.'

a·phe·li·on /əˈfēlyən, əˈfēlēən/ ▶ **n.** (pl. **aphelia** /əˈfēlyə, əˈfēlēə/ or **aphelions**) Astronomy the point in the orbit of a planet, asteroid, or comet at which it is furthest from the sun: *Mars is* ***at aphelion.*** The opposite of PERIHELION.
– ORIGIN mid 17th cent.: alteration of modern Latin *aphelium* (by substitution of the Greek inflection *-on*), from Greek *aph' hēlion* 'from the sun.'

aph·e·sis /ˈafisis/ ▶ **n.** Linguistics the loss of an unstressed vowel at the beginning of a word (e.g., of *a* from *around* to form *round*).
– DERIVATIVES **a·phet·ic** /əˈfetik/ **adj.**, **a·phet·i·cal·ly** /əˈfetik(ə)lē/ **adv.**
– ORIGIN late 19th cent.: from Greek, literally 'letting go,' from *apo* 'from' + *hienai* 'let go, send.'

a·phi·cide /ˈāfi,sīd, ˈaf-/ ▶ **n.** an insecticide used against aphids.

a·phid /ˈāfid, ˈaf-/ ▶ **n.** a minute bug that feeds by sucking sap from plants. It reproduces rapidly, often producing live young without mating, and may live in large colonies that cause extensive damage to crops. ● Superfamily Aphidoidea, suborder Homoptera.

aphid

– ORIGIN late 19th cent.: back-formation from *aphides*, plural of APHIS.

a·phis /ˈāfis, ˈaf-/ ▶ **n.** (pl. **aphides** /ˈāfi,dēz, ˈafi-/) an aphid, esp. one of the genus *Aphis.*
– ORIGIN late 18th cent.: modern Latin, from Greek, perhaps a misreading of *koris* 'bug' (misinterpreting the Greek characters κορ 'kor' as αφ 'aph').

a·pho·ni·a /āˈfōnēə/ (also **aphony** /ˈafənē/) ▶ **n.** Medicine loss of ability to speak through disease of or damage to the larynx or mouth. Compare with APHASIA.
– ORIGIN late 17th cent.: modern Latin, from Greek *aphōnia*, from *aphōnos* 'voiceless,' from *a-* 'without' + *phōnē* 'voice.'

aph·o·rism /ˈafə,rizəm/ ▶ **n.** a pithy observation that contains a general truth, such as, "if it ain't broke, don't fix it." ■ a concise statement of a scientific principle, typically by an ancient classical author.
– DERIVATIVES **aph·o·rist n.**, **aph·o·ris·tic** /ˌafəˈristik/ **adj.**, **aph·o·ris·ti·cal·ly** /ˌafəˈristik(ə)lē/ **adv.**, **aph·o·rize** /-,rīz/ **v.**

– ORIGIN early 16th cent.: from French *aphorisme* or late Latin *aphorismus*, from Greek *aphorismos* 'definition,' from *aphorizein* 'define.'

aph·ro·dis·i·ac /ˌafrəˈdizēˌak, -ˈdēzē-, -ˈdēzHē-/ ▶ **n.** a food, drink, or drug that stimulates sexual desire: *the Romans worshiped the apple as an aphrodisiac* | [as adj.] *aphrodisiac powers.* ■ a thing that causes excitement: *for a few seconds she'd fallen for the powerful aphrodisiac of music | power is an aphrodisiac.*
– ORIGIN early 18th cent.: from Greek *aphrodisiakos*, from *aphrodisios*, from *Aphroditē* (see **APHRODITE**).

Aph·ro·di·te /ˌafrəˈdītē/ Greek Mythology the goddess of beauty, fertility, and sexual love. She is variously described as the daughter of Zeus and Dione, or as being born from the sea. Roman equivalent **VENUS**.
– ORIGIN Greek, literally 'foam-born,' from *aphros* 'foam.'

aph·tha /ˈafTHə/ ▶ **n.** (pl. **aphthae** /-THē/) Medicine a small ulcer occurring in groups in the mouth or on the tongue. ■ a condition in which such ulcers occur.
– DERIVATIVES **aph·thous** /-THəs/ **adj.**
– ORIGIN mid 17th cent.: via Latin from Greek, connected with *haptein* 'set on fire.'

API ▶ **abbr.** ■ American Petroleum Institute. ■ Computing application programming interface.

A·pi·a /əˈpēə, äˈpēə/ the capital of Samoa; pop. 43,000 (est. 2007).

a·pi·an /ˈāpēən/ ▶ **adj.** [attrib.] of or relating to bees.
– ORIGIN early 19th cent.: from Latin *apianus*, from *apis* 'bee.'

a·pi·ar·y /ˈāpēˌerē/ ▶ **n.** (pl. **apiaries**) a place where bees are kept; a collection of beehives.
– DERIVATIVES **a·pi·ar·i·an** /ˌāpēˈe(ə)rēən/ **adj.**, **a·pi·a·rist** /-əˌrist/ **n.**
– ORIGIN mid 17th cent.: from Latin *apiarium*, from *apis* 'bee.'

a·pi·cal /ˈāpikəl, ˈap-/ ▶ **adj.** technical of, relating to, or denoting an apex. ■ Phonetics (of a consonant) formed with the tip of the tongue.
– ORIGIN early 19th cent.: from Latin *apex, apic-* (see **APEX**) + **-AL**.

a·pi·ces /ˈāpəˌsēz, ˈapə-/ plural form of **APEX**.

A·pi·com·plex·a /ˌāpikəmˈpleksə/ another term for **SPOROZOA**.

a·pi·cul·ture /ˈāpiˌkəlCHər/ ▶ **n.** technical term for **BEEKEEPING**.
– DERIVATIVES **a·pi·cul·tur·al** /ˌāpiˈkəlCHərəl/ **adj.**, **a·pi·cul·tur·ist** /ˌāpiˈkəlCHərist/ **n.**
– ORIGIN mid 19th cent.: from Latin *apis* 'bee' + **CULTURE**, on the pattern of words such as *agriculture*.

a·piece /əˈpēs/ ▶ **adv.** (used after a noun or an amount) to, for, or by each one of a group: *we sold 385 prints at $10 apiece.*
– ORIGIN late Middle English: from **A** + **PIECE**.

A·pis /ˈāpis/ Egyptian Mythology a god depicted as a bull, symbolizing fertility and strength in war.

ap·ish /ˈāpisH/ ▶ **adj.** of or resembling an ape in appearance: *Australopithecus had an apish cranium and a humanlike jaw.* ■ resembling or likened to an ape in being foolish or silly.
– DERIVATIVES **ap·ish·ly adv.**, **ap·ish·ness n.**

a·pi·ther·a·py /ˌāpiˈTHerəpē/ ▶ **n.** the use of products derived from bees as medicine, including venom, honey, pollen, and royal jelly.

ap·la·nat /ˈapləˌnat/ ▶ **n.** Physics a reflecting or refracting surface that is free from spherical aberration.
– DERIVATIVES **ap·la·nat·ic** /ˌapləˈnatik/ **adj.**
– ORIGIN late 19th cent.: coined in German from Greek *aplanētos* 'free from error,' from *a-* 'not' + *planan* 'wander.'

a·pla·sia /əˈplāzHə/ ▶ **n.** Medicine the failure of an organ or tissue to develop or to function normally.
– DERIVATIVES **a·plas·tic** /āˈplastik/ **adj.**
– ORIGIN late 19th cent.: from **A-**[1] 'without' + Greek *plasis* 'formation.'

a·plas·tic a·ne·mi·a /āˈplastik əˈnēmēə/ ▶ **n.** Medicine deficiency of all types of blood cells caused by failure of bone marrow development.

a·plen·ty /əˈplentē/ ▶ **adj.** [postpositive] in abundance: *there are going to be disasters aplenty in the garden.*

a·plomb /əˈpläm, əˈpləm/ ▶ **n.** self-confidence or assurance, esp. when in a demanding situation: *Diana passed the test with aplomb.*
– ORIGIN late 18th cent. (in the sense 'perpendicularity, steadiness'): from French, from *à plomb* 'according to a plummet.'

ap·ne·a /ˈapnēə, apˈnēə/ (Brit. **apnoea**) ▶ **n.** Medicine temporary cessation of breathing, esp. during sleep: *thousands suffer from sleep apnea.*
– DERIVATIVES **ap·ne·ic adj.**
– ORIGIN early 18th cent.: modern Latin, from Greek *apnoia*, from *apnous* 'breathless.'

APO ▶ **abbr.** ■ (US) Air Force Post Office. ■ (US) Army Post Office.

apo- ▶ **prefix 1** away from: *apocrypha* | *apostrophe.* ■ separate: *apocarpous.*
2 Astronomy denoting the furthest point in the orbit of a body in relation to the primary: *apolune.* Compare with **PERI-**.
– ORIGIN from Greek *apo* 'from, away, quite, un-.'

Apoc. ▶ **abbr.** ■ Apocalypse. ■ Apocrypha. ■ Apocryphal.

a·poc·a·lypse /əˈpäkəˌlips/ ▶ **n. 1** (often **the Apocalypse**) the complete final destruction of the world, esp. as described in the biblical book of Revelation. See also **FOUR HORSEMEN OF THE APOCALYPSE**. ■ (**the Apocalypse**) (esp. in the Vulgate Bible) the book of Revelation.
2 an event involving destruction or damage on an awesome or catastrophic scale: *a stock market apocalypse | an era of ecological apocalypse.*
– ORIGIN Old English, via Old French and ecclesiastical Latin from Greek *apokalupsis*, from *apokaluptein* 'uncover, reveal,' from *apo-* 'un-' + *kaluptein* 'to cover.'

a·poc·a·lyp·tic /əˌpäkəˈliptik/ ▶ **adj.** describing or prophesying the complete destruction of the world: *the apocalyptic visions of ecologists.* ■ resembling the end of the world; momentous or catastrophic: *the struggle between the two countries is assuming apocalyptic proportions.* ■ of or resembling the biblical Apocalypse: *apocalyptic imagery.*
– DERIVATIVES **a·poc·a·lyp·ti·cal·ly** /-ik(ə)lē/ **adv.**
– ORIGIN early 17th cent. (as a noun denoting the writer of the Apocalypse, St. John): from Greek *apokaluptikos*, from *apokaluptein* 'uncover' (see **APOCALYPSE**).

ap·o·car·pous /ˌapəˈkärpəs/ ▶ **adj.** Botany (of a flower, fruit, or ovary) having distinct carpels that are not joined together. The opposite of **SYNCARPOUS**.
– ORIGIN mid 19th cent.: from **APO-** + Greek *karpos* 'fruit' + **-OUS**.

ap·o·chro·mat /ˌapəˈkrōmat/ ▶ **n.** Physics a lens or lens system that reduces spherical and chromatic aberration.
– DERIVATIVES **ap·o·chro·mat·ic** /-krōˈmatik/ **adj.**
– ORIGIN early 20th cent.: from **APO-** + **CHROMATIC**.

a·poc·o·pe /əˈpäkəpē/ ▶ **n.** Linguistics the loss of a sound or sounds at the end of a word, e.g., in the derivation of *curio* from *curiosity*.
– ORIGIN mid 16th cent.: from late Latin, from Greek *apokoptein* 'cut off,' from *apo-* 'from' + *koptein* 'to cut.'

Apocr. ▶ **abbr.** Apocrypha.

ap·o·crine /ˈapəkrin, -ˌkrīn, -ˌkrēn/ ▶ **adj.** Physiology relating to or denoting multicellular glands that release some of their cytoplasm in their secretions, esp. the sweat glands associated with hair follicles in the armpits and pubic regions. Compare with **ECCRINE**.
– ORIGIN early 20th cent.: from **APO-** + Greek *krinein* 'to separate.'

A·poc·ry·pha /əˈpäkrəfə/ ▶ **plural n.** [treated as sing. or pl.] biblical or related writings not forming part of the accepted canon of Scripture. ■ (**apocrypha**) writings or reports not considered genuine.
– ORIGIN late Middle English: from ecclesiastical Latin *apocrypha (scripta)* 'hidden (writings),' from Greek *apokruphos*, from *apokruptein* 'hide away.'

a·poc·ry·phal /əˈpäkrəfəl/ ▶ **adj.** (of a story or statement) of doubtful authenticity, although widely circulated as being true: *an apocryphal story about a former president.* ■ (also **Apocryphal**) of or belonging to the Apocrypha: *the Apocryphal Gospel of Thomas.*

ap·o·dal /ˈāpōdl/ ▶ **adj.** Zoology without feet or having undeveloped feet. ■ (of fish) without ventral fins.
– ORIGIN early 19th cent.: from Greek *apous, apod-* 'footless' (from *a-* 'without' + *pous, pod-* 'foot') + **-OUS**.

ap·o·dic·tic /ˌapəˈdiktik/ (also **apodeictic** /-ˈdiktik/) ▶ **adj.** formal clearly established or beyond dispute.
– ORIGIN mid 17th cent.: via Latin from Greek *apodeiktikos*, from *apodeiknunai* 'show off, demonstrate.'

a·pod·o·sis /əˈpädəsis/ ▶ **n.** (pl. **apodoses** /-ˌsēz/) Grammar the main (consequent) clause of a conditional sentence (e.g., *I would agree* in *if you asked me I would agree*). Often contrasted with **PROTASIS**.
– ORIGIN early 17th cent.: via late Latin from Greek, from *apodidonai* 'give back.'

ap·o·dous /ˈapədəs/ ▶ **adj.** Zoology without feet or having only rudimentary feet.

ap·o·gee /ˈapəjē/ ▶ **n. 1** the highest point in the development of something; the climax or culmination: *the White House is considered the apogee of American achievement.*
2 Astronomy the point in the orbit of the moon or a satellite at which it is furthest from the earth. The opposite of **PERIGEE**.
– ORIGIN late 16th cent.: from French *apogée* or modern Latin *apogaeum*, from Greek *apogaion (diastēma)* '(distance) away from earth,' from *apo* 'from' + *gaia, gē* 'earth.'

a·po·lar /āˈpōlər/ ▶ **adj.** chiefly Biochemistry having no electrical polarity.

a·po·lit·i·cal /ˌāpəˈlitikəl/ ▶ **adj.** not interested or involved in politics: *a former apolitical housewife.*

A·pol·li·naire /əˌpäləˈne(ə)r/, Guillaume (1880–1918), French poet; pseudonym of *Wilhelm Apollinaris de Kostrowitzki*. He coined the term *surrealist* and was acknowledged by the surrealist poets as their precursor. Notable works: *Les Alcools* (1913) and *Calligrammes* (1918).

A·pol·li·nar·is /əˌpäləˈne(ə)ris/ (c.310–c.390), bishop of Laodicea in Asia Minor. He upheld the heretical doctrine that Jesus Christ had a human body and soul but no human spirit, this being replaced by the divine Logos.
– DERIVATIVES **A·pol·li·nar·i·an adj. & .n.**

A·pol·lo /əˈpälō/ **1** Greek Mythology a god, son of Zeus and Leto and brother of Artemis. He is associated with music, poetic inspiration, archery, prophecy, medicine, pastoral life, and in later poetry with the sun; the sanctuary at Delphi was dedicated to him.
2 the American space program for landing astronauts on the moon. *Apollo 8* was the first mission to orbit the moon (1968), *Apollo 11* was the first to land astronauts (July 20, 1969), and five further landings took place up to 1972.

Ap·ol·lo·ni·an /ˌapəˈlōnēən/ ▶ **adj. 1** Greek Mythology of or relating to the god Apollo.
2 of or relating to the rational, ordered, and self-disciplined aspects of human nature: *the struggle between cold Apollonian categorization and Dionysiac lust and chaos.* Compare with **DIONYSIAN**.

Ap·ol·lo·ni·us[1] /ˌapəˈlōnēəs/ (c.260–190 BC), Greek mathematician; known as **Apollonius of Perga**. He examined and redefined the various conic sections and was the first to use the terms *ellipse, parabola,* and *hyperbola* for these classes of curve.

Ap·ol·lo·ni·us[2] (3rd century BC), Greek poet and grammarian; known as **Apollonius of Rhodes**. He wrote *Argonautica*, an epic poem in Homeric style.

A·pol·lyon /əˈpälyən/ a name for the Devil (Rev. 9:11).
– ORIGIN from late Latin (Vulgate), from Greek *Apolluōn* 'destroyer' (translating **ABADDON**), from *apollunai*, from *apo-* 'quite' + *ollunai* 'destroy.'

a·pol·o·get·ic /əˌpäləˈjetik/ ▶ **adj.** regretfully acknowledging or excusing an offense or failure: *she was very apologetic about the whole incident.* ■ of the nature of a formal defense or justification of something such as a theory or religious doctrine: *the apologetic proposition that production for profit is the same thing as production for need.*
▶ **n.** a reasoned argument or writing in justification of something, typically a theory or religious doctrine: *free market apologetics.*
– DERIVATIVES **a·pol·o·get·i·cal·ly** /-ik(ə)lē/ **adv.**
– ORIGIN late Middle English (as a noun denoting a formal defense or justification): from French *apologétique* or late Latin *apologeticus*, from Greek *apologētikos*, from *apologeisthei* 'speak in one's own defense,' from *apologia* (see **APOLOGY**). The current sense dates from the mid 19th cent.

a·pol·o·get·ics /əˌpäləˈjetiks/ ▶ **plural n.** [treated as sing. or pl.] reasoned arguments or writings in justification of something, typically a theory or religious doctrine.
– ORIGIN mid 18th cent.: from **APOLOGETIC**.

ap·o·lo·gi·a /ˌapəˈlōj(ē)ə/ ▶ **n.** a formal written defense of one's opinions or conduct: *an apologia for book banning.*
– ORIGIN late 18th cent.: from Latin (see **APOLOGY**).

a·pol·o·gist /əˈpäləjist/ ▶ **n.** a person who offers an argument in defense of something controversial: *an enthusiastic* ***apologist for*** *fascism in the 1920s.*
– ORIGIN mid 17th cent.: from French *apologiste*, from Greek *apologizesthai* 'give an account' (see **APOLOGIZE**).

a·pol·o·gize /əˈpäləˌjīz/ ▶ **v.** [no obj.] express regret for something that one has done wrong: *I must* ***apologize for*** *disturbing you like this* | *we* ***apologize to*** *him for our error.*
– ORIGIN late 16th cent. (in the sense 'make a defensive argument, offer a justification'): from Greek *apologizesthai* 'give an account,' from *apologos*

a

(see **APOLOGUE**). In English the verb has always been used as if it were a direct derivative of *apology*.

ap·o·logue /ˈapəˌlôg, -ˌläg/ ▶ **n.** a moral fable, esp. one with animals as characters.
– ORIGIN mid 16th cent.: from French, via Latin from Greek *apologos* 'story.'

a·pol·o·gy /əˈpäləjē/ ▶ **n.** (pl. **apologies**) **1** a regretful acknowledgment of an offense or failure: *we owe you an apology | my apologies for the delay | I make no apologies for supporting that policy.* ■ a formal, public statement of regret, such as one issued by a newspaper, government, or other organization: *the Prime Minister demanded an apology from the ambassador.* ■ (**apologies**) used to express formally one's regret at being unable to attend a meeting or social function: ***apologies for absence*** *were received from Miss Brown.*
2 (**an apology for**) a very poor or inadequate example of: *we were shown into an apology for a bedroom.*
3 a reasoned argument or writing in justification of something, typically a theory or religious doctrine: *a specious apology for capitalism.*
– PHRASES **with apologies to** used before the name of an author or artist to indicate that something is a parody or adaptation of their work: *here, with apologies to Rudyard Kipling, is a more apt version of "If."*
– ORIGIN mid 16th cent. (denoting a formal defense against an accusation): from French *apologie*, or via late Latin from Greek *apologia* 'a speech in one's own defense,' from *apo* 'away' + *-logia* (see **-LOGY**).

ap·o·lune /ˈapəˌlo͞on/ ▶ **n.** the point at which a spacecraft in lunar orbit is furthest from the moon. The opposite of **PERILUNE**.
– ORIGIN 1960s: from **APO-** + Latin *luna* 'moon,' on the pattern of *apogee*.

ap·o·mict /ˈapəˌmikt/ ▶ **n.** Botany a plant that reproduces by apomixis.

ap·o·mix·is /ˌapəˈmiksis/ ▶ **n.** Botany asexual reproduction in plants, in particular agamospermy. Often contrasted with **AMPHIMIXIS**.
– DERIVATIVES **ap·o·mic·tic** /-ˈmiktik/ **adj.**
– ORIGIN early 20th cent.: from **APO-** + Greek *mixis* 'mingling.'

ap·o·mor·phine /ˌapəˈmôrfēn, -fin/ ▶ **n.** Medicine a white crystalline compound used as an emetic and in the treatment of Parkinson's disease. ● A morphine derivative; chem. formula: $C_{17}H_{17}NO_2$.

ap·o·neu·ro·sis /ˌapən(y)o͝oˈrōsis/ ▶ **n.** (pl. **aponeuroses** /-ˌsēz/) Anatomy a sheet of pearly-white fibrous tissue that takes the place of a tendon in sheetlike muscles having a wide area of attachment.
– DERIVATIVES **ap·o·neu·rot·ic** /-ˈrätik/ **adj.**
– ORIGIN late 17th cent.: modern Latin, from Greek *aponeurōsis*, from *apo* 'off, away' + *neuron* 'sinew' + **-OSIS**.

ap·o·pha·tic /ˌapəˈfatik/ ▶ **adj.** Theology (of knowledge of God) obtained through negation. The opposite of **CATAPHATIC**.
– DERIVATIVES **ap·o·pha·ti·cal·ly** /-ik(ə)lē/ **adv.**, **ap·o·pha·ti·cism** /-ˌsizəm/ **n.**
– ORIGIN mid 19th cent.: from Greek *apophatikos* 'negative,' from *apophasis* 'denial,' from *apo-* 'other than' + *phanai* 'speak.'

ap·o·phthegm ▶ **n.** British spelling of **APOTHEGM**.

a·poph·yl·lite /əˈpäfəˌlīt, ˌapəˈfilīt/ ▶ **n.** a mineral occurring typically as white glassy prisms, usually as a secondary mineral in volcanic rocks. It is a hydrated silicate and fluoride of calcium and potassium.
– ORIGIN early 19th cent.: from **APO-** + Greek *phullon* 'leaf' + **-ITE**[1].

a·poph·y·sis /əˈpäfəsis/ ▶ **n.** (pl. **apophyses** /-ˌsēz/) Zoology & Anatomy a natural protuberance from a bone, or inside the shell or exoskeleton of a sea urchin or insect, for the attachment of muscles. ■ Botany a swelling at the base of the sporangium in some mosses. ■ Geology a small offshoot extending from an igneous intrusion into the surrounding rock.
– DERIVATIVES **ap·o·phys·e·al** /əˌpäfəˈsēəl/ **adj.**
– ORIGIN late 16th cent.: modern Latin, from Greek *apophusis* 'offshoot,' from *apo-* 'from, away' + *phusis* 'growth.'

ap·o·plec·tic /ˌapəˈplektik/ ▶ **adj.** informal overcome with anger; extremely indignant: *Mark was* ***apoplectic with rage*** *at the decision.* ■ dated relating to or denoting apoplexy (stroke): *an apoplectic attack.*
– DERIVATIVES **ap·o·plec·ti·cal·ly** /-ik(ə)lē/ **adv.**
– ORIGIN early 17th cent.: from French *apoplectique* or late Latin *apoplecticus*, from Greek *apoplēktikos*, from *apoplēssein* 'disable by a stroke' (see **APOPLEXY**).

ap·o·plex·y /ˈapəˌpleksē/ ▶ **n.** (pl. **apoplexies**) dated unconsciousness or incapacity resulting from a cerebral hemorrhage or stroke. ■ informal incapacity or speechlessness caused by extreme anger: *this drives the social engineers of government into apoplexy.*
– ORIGIN late Middle English: from Old French *apoplexie*, from late Latin *apoplexia*, from Greek *apoplēxia*, from *apoplēssein* 'disable by a stroke.'

ap·o·pro·tein /ˌapəˈprōˌtēn, -ˈprōtēən/ ▶ **n.** Biochemistry a protein that together with a prosthetic group forms a particular biochemical molecule such as a hormone or enzyme.

ap·op·to·sis /ˌapə(p)ˈtōsis/ ▶ **n.** Physiology the death of cells that occurs as a normal and controlled part of an organism's growth or development. Also called **PROGRAMMED CELL DEATH**.
– DERIVATIVES **ap·op·tot·ic** /-ˈtätik/ **adj.**
– ORIGIN 1970s: from Greek *apoptōsis* 'falling off,' from *apo* 'from' + *ptōsis* 'falling, a fall.'

a·po·ri·a /əˈpôrēə/ ▶ **n.** an irresolvable internal contradiction or logical disjunction in a text, argument, or theory: *the celebrated aporia whereby a Cretan declares all Cretans to be liars.* ■ Rhetoric the expression of doubt.
– ORIGIN mid 16th cent.: via late Latin from Greek, from *aporos* 'impassable,' from *a-* 'without' + *poros* 'passage.'

ap·o·se·mat·ic /ˌapəsiˈmatik/ ▶ **adj.** Zoology (of coloration or markings) serving to warn or repel predators. ■ (of an animal) having such coloration or markings.
– DERIVATIVES **ap·o·se·ma·tism** /ˌapəˈsēməˌtizəm/ **n.**

ap·o·si·o·pe·sis /ˌapəˌsīəˈpēsis/ ▶ **n.** (pl. **aposiopeses** /-sēz/) Rhetoric the device of suddenly breaking off in speech.
– DERIVATIVES **ap·o·si·o·pet·ic** /-ˈpetik/ **adj.**
– ORIGIN late 16th cent.: via Latin from Greek *aposiōpēsis*, from *aposiōpan* 'be silent.'

a·pos·ta·sy /əˈpästəsē/ ▶ **n.** the abandonment or renunciation of a religious or political belief.
– ORIGIN Middle English: from ecclesiastical Latin *apostasia*, from a late Greek alteration of Greek *apostasis* 'defection.'

a·pos·tate /əˈpäsˌtāt, -tit/ ▶ **n.** a person who renounces a religious or political belief or principle. ▶ **adj.** abandoning a religious or political belief or principle.
– DERIVATIVES **ap·o·stat·i·cal** /ˌapəˈstatikəl/ **adj.**
– ORIGIN Middle English: from ecclesiastical Latin *apostata*, from Greek *apostatēs* 'apostate, runaway slave.'

a·pos·ta·tize /əˈpästəˌtīz/ ▶ **v.** [no obj.] renounce a religious or political belief or principle.
– ORIGIN mid 16th cent.: from medieval Latin *apostatizare*, from *apostata* (see **APOSTATE**).

a pos·te·ri·o·ri /ˈā päˌsti(ə)rēˈôrē, -ˈôrˌī/ ▶ **adj.** relating to or denoting reasoning or knowledge that proceeds from observations or experiences to the deduction of probable causes. Compare with **A PRIORI**. ■ (loosely) of the nature of an afterthought or subsequent rationalization.
▶ **adv.** in a way based on reasoning from known facts or past events rather than by making assumptions or predictions. ■ [sentence adverb] (loosely) with hindsight; as an afterthought.
– ORIGIN early 17th cent.: Latin, 'from what comes after.'

a·pos·tle /əˈpäsəl/ ▶ **n.** (often **Apostle**) each of the twelve chief disciples of Jesus Christ. ■ any important early Christian teacher, esp. St. Paul. ■ (**Apostle of**) the first successful Christian missionary in a country or to a people: *Kiril and Metodije, the Apostles of the Slavs.* ■ a vigorous and pioneering advocate or supporter of a particular policy, idea, or cause: *Leo Buscaglia, leading apostle of love and okayness.* ■ a messenger or representative: *apostles of doom and defeat.* ■ one of the twelve administrative officers of the Mormon church.

> The twelve Apostles were Peter, Andrew, James, John, Philip, Bartholomew, Thomas, Matthew, James (the Less), Judas (or Thaddaeus), Simon, and Judas Iscariot. After the suicide of Judas Iscariot his place was taken by Matthias.

– DERIVATIVES **a·pos·tle·ship** /-ˌSHip/ **n.**
– ORIGIN Old English *apostol*, via ecclesiastical Latin from Greek *apostolos* 'messenger,' from *apostellein* 'send forth.'

A·pos·tle Is·lands an island group in northern Wisconsin, in Lake Superior.

A·pos·tles' Creed a statement of Christian belief used in the Western Church, dating from the 4th century and traditionally ascribed to the twelve Apostles.

A·pos·tle spoon (also **Apostle teaspoon**) ▶ **n.** a teaspoon with the figure of an Apostle or saint on the handle.

a·pos·to·late /əˈpästəˌlāt, -lit/ ▶ **n.** (chiefly in Roman Catholic contexts) the position or authority of an Apostle or a religious leader. ■ a group of Apostles or religious leaders. ■ religious or evangelistic activity or works: *our apostolate of hospitality to the elderly.*
– ORIGIN late Middle English: from ecclesiastical Latin *apostolatus*, from *apostulus* (see **APOSTLE**).

ap·os·tol·ic /ˌapəˈstälik/ ▶ **adj.** Christian Church of or relating to the Apostles: *apostolic writings | a simple apostolic life.* ■ of or relating to the pope, esp. when he is regarded as the successor to St. Peter: *an apostolic nuncio.*
– ORIGIN Middle English: from French *apostolique* or ecclesiastical Latin *apostolicus*, from Greek *apostolikos*, from *apostolos* (see **APOSTLE**).

Ap·os·tol·ic Fa·thers ▶ **plural n.** the Christian leaders immediately succeeding the Apostles.

ap·os·tol·ic suc·ces·sion ▶ **n.** (in Christian thought) the uninterrupted transmission of spiritual authority from the Apostles through successive popes and bishops, taught by the Roman Catholic Church but denied by most Protestants.

a·pos·tro·phe[1] /əˈpästrəfē/ ▶ **n.** a punctuation mark (') used to indicate either possession (e.g., *Harry's book; boys' coats*) or the omission of letters or numbers (e.g., *can't; he's; class of '99*).
– ORIGIN mid 16th cent. (denoting the omission of one or more letters): via late Latin, from Greek *apostrophos* 'accent of elision,' from *apostrephein* 'turn away,' from *apo* 'from' + *strephein* 'to turn.'

> **USAGE** The apostrophe is used to indicate missing letters or numbers (*bo'sun; the summer of '63*), to form some possessives (see usage at **POSSESSIVE**), and to form some plurals (see usage at **PLURAL**).

a·pos·tro·phe[2] ▶ **n.** Rhetoric an exclamatory passage in a speech or poem addressed to a person (typically one who is dead or absent) or thing (typically one that is personified).
– ORIGIN mid 16th cent.: via Latin from Greek *apostrophē* 'turning away,' from *apostrephein* 'turn away' (see **APOSTROPHE**[1]).

a·pos·tro·phize /əˈpästrəˌfīz/ ▶ **v.** [with obj.] **1** Rhetoric address an exclamatory passage in a speech or poem to (someone or something).
2 punctuate (a word) with an apostrophe.

a·poth·e·car·ies' meas·ure /əˈpäTHiˌkerēz/ (also **apothecaries' weight**) ▶ **n.** historical systems of units formerly used in pharmacy for liquid volume (or weight). They were based respectively on the fluid ounce (= 8 drachms or 480 minims) and the ounce troy (= 8 drams or 24 scruples or 480 grains).

a·poth·e·car·y /əˈpäTHiˌkerē/ ▶ **n.** (pl. **apothecaries**) archaic a person who prepared and sold medicines and drugs.
– ORIGIN late Middle English: via Old French from late Latin *apothecarius*, from Latin *apotheca*, from Greek *apothēkē* 'storehouse.'

ap·o·thegm /ˈapəˌTHem/ (Brit. **apophthegm** /ˈapəˌTHem/) ▶ **n.** a concise saying or maxim; an aphorism.
– DERIVATIVES **ap·o·theg·mat·ic** /ˌapəTHegˈmatik/ **adj.**
– ORIGIN mid 16th cent.: from French *apophthegme* or modern Latin *apothegma*, from Greek, from *apophthengesthai* 'speak out.'

ap·o·them /ˈapəˌTHem/ ▶ **n.** Geometry a line from the center of a regular polygon at right angles to any of its sides.
– ORIGIN late 19th cent.: from Greek *apotithenai* 'put aside, deposit,' from *apo* 'away' + *tithenai* 'to place.'

a·poth·e·o·sis /əˌpäTHēˈōsis, ˌapəˈTHēəsis/ ▶ **n.** (pl. **apotheoses** /-ˌsēz/) [usu. in sing.] the highest point in the development of something; culmination or climax: *his appearance as Hamlet was the apotheosis of his career.* ■ the elevation of someone to divine status; deification.
– ORIGIN late 16th cent.: via ecclesiastical Latin from Greek *apotheōsis*, from *apotheoun* 'make a god of,' from *apo* 'from' + *theos* 'god.'

a·poth·e·o·size /əˈpäTHēəˌsīz, ˌapəˈTHēə-/ ▶ **v.** [with obj.] elevate to, or as if to, the rank of a god; idolize.

ap·o·tro·pa·ic /ˌapətrəˈpā-ik/ ▶ **adj.** supposedly having the power to avert evil influences or bad luck: *apotropaic statues.*
– DERIVATIVES **ap·o·tro·pa·i·cal·ly** /-ik(ə)lē/ **adv.**
– ORIGIN late 19th cent.: from Greek *apotropaios* 'averting evil,' from *apotrepein* 'turn away or from' + **-IC**.

app /ap/ ▶ **n.** Computing short for **APPLICATION** (sense 5).

Ap·pa·la·chi·a /ˌapəˈlāCH(ē)ə, -ˈlaCH-, -ˈlāSH-/ a term for areas in the Appalachian Mountains of the eastern US that exhibit long-term poverty and distinctive folkways.
– DERIVATIVES **Ap·pa·la·chi·an adj.**

Ap·pa·la·chi·an dul·ci·mer ▶ **n.** see **DULCIMER**.

Ap·pa·la·chi·an Moun·tains /ˌapəˈlāCH(ē)ən, -ˈlaCH-, -ˈlāSH-/ (also **the Appalachians**) a mountain system in eastern North America that stretches from Quebec and Maine in the north to Georgia and Alabama in the south. Its highest peak, Mount Mitchell in North Carolina, rises to 6,684 feet (2,037 m).

Ap·pa·la·chi·an Trail an approximately 2,000-mi. (3,200-km.) footpath through the Appalachian Mountains from Mount Katahdin in Maine to Springer Mountain in Georgia.

ap·pall /ə'pôl/ ▶ v. (**appalls, appalling, appalled**) [with obj.] greatly dismay or horrify: *bankers are appalled at the economic incompetence of some officials* | (as adj. **appalled**) *Alison looked at me, appalled.*
– ORIGIN Middle English: from Old French *apalir* 'grow pale,' from *a-* (from Latin *ad* 'to, at') + *palir* 'to pale.' The original sense was 'grow pale,' later 'make pale,' hence 'dismay, horrify' (late Middle English).

ap·pall·ing /ə'pôliNG/ ▶ adj. informal awful; terrible: *his conduct was appalling.*
– DERIVATIVES **ap·pall·ing·ly** adv.

Ap·pa·loo·sa /ˌapə'lo͞osə/ ▶ n. a horse of a North American breed having dark spots on a light background.
– ORIGIN 1920s: from *Opelousas* in Louisiana, or *Palouse*, a river in Idaho.

ap·pa·nage /'apənij/ (also **apanage**) ▶ n. archaic a gift of land, an official position, or money given to the younger children of kings and princes to provide for their maintenance. ■ a necessary accompaniment: *there is a tendency to make microbiology an appanage of organic chemistry.*
– ORIGIN early 17th cent.: from French, based on medieval Latin *appanare* 'provide with the means of subsistence,' from *ad-* 'to' + *panis* 'bread.'

ap·pa·rat /'äpəˌrät, ˌäpə-/ ▶ n. chiefly historical the administrative system of a communist party, typically in a communist country.
– ORIGIN 1940s: Russian, from German, literally 'apparatus.'

ap·pa·rat·chik /ˌäpə'räCHik/ ▶ n. (pl. **apparatchiks** or **apparatchiki** /-CHiˌkē/) derogatory or humorous an official in a large organization, typically a political one: *Tory apparatchiks.* ■ chiefly historical a member of a communist party apparat.
– ORIGIN 1940s: from Russian, from *apparat* (see APPARAT).

ap·pa·rat·us /ˌapə'ratəs, -'rātəs/ ▶ n. (pl. **apparatuses**) **1** the technical equipment or machinery needed for a particular activity or purpose: *laboratory apparatus.* ■ the organs used to perform a particular bodily function: *the specialized male and female sexual apparatus.*
2 a complex structure within an organization or system: *the apparatus of government.*
3 (also **critical apparatus** or **apparatus criticus**) a collection of notes, variant readings, and other matter accompanying a printed text.
– ORIGIN early 17th cent.: from Latin, from *apparare* 'make ready for,' from *ad-* 'toward' + *parare* 'make ready.'

ap·par·el /ə'parəl/ ▶ n. formal clothing. ■ (**apparels**) embroidered ornamentation on ecclesiastical vestments.
▶ v. (**apparels, appareling, appareled**; Brit. **apparels, apparelling, apparelled**) [with obj.] archaic clothe (someone): *all the vestments in which they used to apparel their Deities.*
– ORIGIN Middle English (as a verb in the sense 'make ready or fit'; as a noun 'furnishings, equipment'): from Old French *apareillier*, based on Latin *ad-* 'to' (expressing change) + *par* 'equal.'

ap·par·ent /ə'parənt, ə'pe(ə)r-/ ▶ adj. clearly visible or understood; obvious: [with clause] *it became apparent that he was talented* | *for no apparent reason she laughed.* ■ seeming real or true, but not necessarily so: *his apparent lack of concern.*
– ORIGIN late Middle English: from Old French *aparant*, from Latin *apparent-* 'appearing,' from the verb *apparere* (see APPEAR).

ap·par·ent ho·ri·zon ▶ n. see HORIZON (sense 1).

ap·par·ent·ly /ə'parəntlē, ə'pe(ə)r-/ ▶ adv. [sentence adverb] as far as one knows or can see: *the child nodded, apparently content with the promise.* ■ used by speakers or writers to avoid committing themselves to the truth of what they are saying: *foreign ministers met but apparently failed to make progress.*

ap·par·ent mag·ni·tude ▶ n. Astronomy the magnitude of a celestial object as it is actually measured from the earth. Compare with ABSOLUTE MAGNITUDE.

ap·par·ent so·lar time ▶ n. Astronomy time as calculated by the motion of the apparent (true) sun. The time indicated by a sundial corresponds to apparent solar time. Compare with MEAN SOLAR TIME.

ap·par·ent time ▶ n. another term for MEAN SOLAR TIME.

ap·pa·ri·tion /ˌapə'riSHən/ ▶ n. a ghost or ghostlike image of a person. ■ the appearance of something remarkable or unexpected, typically an image of this type: *twentieth-century apparitions of the Virgin.*
– DERIVATIVES **ap·pa·ri·tion·al** /-SHənl/ adj.
– ORIGIN late Middle English (in the sense 'the action of appearing'): from Latin *apparitio(n-)* 'attendance,' from the verb *apparere* (see APPEAR).

ap·peal /ə'pēl/ ▶ v. [no obj.] **1** make a serious or urgent request, typically to the public: *police are appealing for information about the incident* | *she appealed to Germany for political asylum.*
2 Law apply to a higher court for a reversal of the decision of a lower court: *he said he would appeal against the conviction* | [with obj.] *they have 48 hours to appeal the decision.* ■ Baseball (of the team in the field) call on the umpire to rule a strike or out on a completed play. ■ (**appeal to**) address oneself to (a principle or quality in someone) in anticipation of a favorable response: *I appealed to his sense of justice.*
3 be attractive or interesting: *the range of topics will appeal to youngsters.*
▶ n. **1** a serious or urgent request, typically one made to the public: *his mother made an appeal for the return of the ring.* ■ an attempt to obtain financial support: *a public appeal to raise $120,000.* ■ entreaty: *a look of appeal on his face.*
2 Law an application to a higher court for a decision to be reversed: *he has 28 days in which to lodge an appeal* | *the right of appeal.* ■ an address to a principle or quality in anticipation of a favorable response: *an appeal to black pride.*
3 the quality of being attractive or interesting: *the popular appeal of football.*
– DERIVATIVES **ap·peal·er** n.
– ORIGIN Middle English (in legal contexts): from Old French *apel* (noun), *apeler* (verb), from Latin *appellare* 'to address,' based on *ad-* 'to' + *pellere* 'to drive.'

ap·peal·ing /ə'pēliNG/ ▶ adj. **1** attractive or interesting: *the rural life is somehow more appealing* | *an appealing young woman.*
2 (of an expression or tone of voice) showing that one wants help or sympathy: *an appealing look.*
– DERIVATIVES **ap·peal·ing·ly** adv.

ap·peals court ▶ n. a court that hears appeals from a lower court.

ap·pear /ə'pi(ə)r/ ▶ v. [no obj.] **1** come into sight; become visible or noticeable, typically without visible agent or apparent cause: *smoke appeared on the horizon.* ■ come into existence or use: *the major life forms appeared on earth.* ■ (of a book) be published: *the paperback edition didn't appear for another two years.* ■ feature or be shown: *the symbol appears in many paintings of the period.* ■ perform publicly in a movie, play, etc.: *he appeared on Broadway.* ■ (of an accused person, witness, or lawyer) make an official appearance in a court of law: *he appeared on six charges of theft.* ■ informal arrive at a place: *by ten o'clock Bill still hadn't appeared.*
2 seem; give the impression of being: [with infinitive] *she appeared not to know what was happening* | [with clause] *it appears unlikely that interest rates will fall* | [with complement] *he appeared unaware of the rebuke.*
– ORIGIN Middle English: from Old French *apareir*, from Latin *apparere*, from *ad-* 'toward' + *parere* 'come into view.'

ap·pear·ance /ə'pi(ə)rəns/ ▶ n. **1** the way that someone or something looks: *I like the appearance of stripped antique pine* | *they are similar in appearance.* ■ an impression given by someone or something, although this may be misleading: *she read it with every appearance of interest.*
2 an act of performing or participating in a public event: *he is well-known for his television appearances.*
3 [usu. in sing.] an act of becoming visible or noticeable; an arrival: *the sudden appearance of her daughter startled her.* ■ a process of coming into existence or use: *the appearance of the railroad.*
– PHRASES **keep up appearances** maintain an impression of wealth or well-being, typically to hide the true situation. **make** (or **put in**) **an appearance** attend an event briefly, typically out of courtesy. **to** (or **by**) **all appearances** as far as can be seen: *to all appearances, it had been a normal day.*
– ORIGIN late Middle English: from Old French *aparance, aparence*, from late Latin *apparentia*, from Latin *apparere* (see APPEAR).

ap·pear·ance mon·ey ▶ n. money paid to secure the appearance of a celebrity, typically a sports figure, at a particular event.

ap·pease /ə'pēz/ ▶ v. [with obj.] **1** pacify or placate (someone) by acceding to their demands: *amendments have been added to appease local pressure groups.*
2 relieve or satisfy (a demand or a feeling): *we give to charity because it appeases our guilt.*
– DERIVATIVES **ap·peas·er** n.
– ORIGIN Middle English: from Old French *apaisier*, from *a-* (from Latin *ad* 'to, at') + *pais* 'peace.'

ap·pease·ment /ə'pēzmənt/ ▶ n. the action or process of appeasing: *a policy of appeasement.*

Ap·pel /'äpəl/, Karel (1921–2006), Dutch painter, sculptor, and graphic artist.

ap·pel·lant /ə'pelənt/ ▶ n. Law a person who applies to a higher court for a reversal of the decision of a lower court.
– ORIGIN late Middle English: from French *apelant*, literally 'appealing,' from the verb *apeler* (see APPEAL).

ap·pel·late /ə'pelit/ ▶ adj. [attrib.] Law (typically of a court) concerned with or dealing with applications for decisions to be reversed.
– ORIGIN late Middle English (originally in the sense 'appealed against, accused'): from Latin *appellatus* 'appealed against,' from the verb *appellare* (see APPEAL). The current sense dates from the mid 18th cent.

ap·pel·la·tion[1] /ˌapə'lāSHən/ ▶ n. formal a name or title: *the city fully justifies its appellation "the Pearl of the Orient."* ■ the action of giving a name to a person or thing.
– ORIGIN late Middle English: via Old French from Latin *appellatio(n-)*, from the verb *appellare* (see APPEAL).

ap·pel·la·tion[2] /äpelä'syôN/ ▶ n. an appellation contrôlée. ■ a wine bearing such a guarantee. ■ the district in which such wine is produced.
– ORIGIN late 20th cent.: abbreviation of *appellation (d'origine) contrôlée.*

ap·pel·la·tion con·trô·lée /äpelä'syôN ˌkôNtrô'lā/ (also **appellation d'origine contrôlée** /dôrē'ZHēN/) ▶ n. a description awarded to French wine guaranteeing that it was produced in the region specified, using vines and production methods that satisfy the regulating body.
– ORIGIN mid 20th cent.: French, literally 'controlled appellation.'

ap·pel·la·tive /ə'pelətiv/ ▶ adj. formal relating to or denoting the giving of a name.
▶ n. Grammar a common noun, such as "doctor," "mother," or "sir," used as a vocative.
– ORIGIN late Middle English: from late Latin *appellativus*, from *appellat-* 'addressed,' from the verb *appellare* (see APPEAL).

ap·pel·lee /ˌapə'lē/ ▶ n. Law the respondent in a case appealed to a higher court.
– ORIGIN mid 16th cent.: from French *appelé*, past participle of *appeler* 'call,' from Latin *appellare* 'to address' (see APPEAL).

ap·pend /ə'pend/ ▶ v. [with obj.] add (something) as an attachment or supplement: *the results of the survey are appended to this chapter.*
– ORIGIN late Middle English: from Latin *appendere* 'hang on,' from *ad-* 'to' + *pendere* 'hang.'

ap·pend·age /ə'pendij/ ▶ n. (often with negative or pejorative connotations) a thing that is added or attached to something larger or more important: *they treat Scotland as a mere appendage of England.* ■ Biology a projecting part of an invertebrate or other living organism, with a distinct appearance or function: *many species have specialized clutching appendages.*

ap·pend·ant /ə'pendənt/ formal ▶ adj. attached or added, typically in a subordinate capacity.
▶ n. a subordinate person or thing.
– ORIGIN late Middle English (in legal contexts): from Old French *apendant*, from *apendre* 'depend on, belong to,' from Latin *appendere* (see APPEND).

ap·pen·dec·to·my /ˌapən'dektəmē/ (Brit. also **appendicectomy** /əˌpendə'sektəmē/) ▶ n. (pl. **appendectomies**) a surgical operation to remove the appendix.

ap·pen·di·ci·tis /əˌpendə'sītis/ ▶ n. a serious medical condition in which the appendix becomes inflamed and painful.

ap·pen·dic·u·lar /apən'dikyələr/ ▶ adj. technical relating to or denoting an appendage or appendages. ■ Anatomy of or relating to a limb or limbs: *the appendicular skeleton.*
– ORIGIN mid 17th cent.: from Latin *appendicula* 'small appendage,' diminutive of *appendix*, + -AR[1].

ap·pen·dix /ə'pendiks/ ▶ n. (pl. **appendices** /-diˌsēz/; **appendixes**) **1** Anatomy a tube-shaped sac attached to and opening into the lower end of the large intestine in humans and some other mammals. Also called VERMIFORM APPENDIX.

In humans the appendix is small and has no known function, but in rabbits, hares, and some other herbivores it is involved in the digestion of cellulose.

2 a section or table of additional matter at the end of a book or document.
– ORIGIN mid 16th cent. (sense 2): from Latin, from *appendere* 'hang upon' (see APPEND). Sense 1 dates from the early 17th cent.

USAGE **Appendix** typically has the plural **appendixes** in the anatomical sense, and **appendices** when referring to a part of a book or document.

ap·per·cep·tion /ˌapərˈsepSHən/ ▶ **n.** Psychology, dated the mental process by which a person makes sense of an idea by assimilating it to the body of ideas he or she already possesses. ■ fully conscious perception: *an immediate apperception of a unity lying beyond.*
– DERIVATIVES **ap·per·cep·tive** /-tiv/ **adj.**
– ORIGIN mid 18th cent.: from French *aperception* or modern Latin *aperceptio(n-)*, from Latin *ad-* 'to' + *percipere* 'perceive.'

ap·per·tain /ˌapərˈtān/ ▶ **v.** [no obj.] **1** (**appertain to**) relate to; concern: *the answers generally appertain to improvements in standards of service.*
2 be appropriate or applicable: *the institutional arrangements that appertain under the system.*
– ORIGIN late Middle English: from Old French *apertenir*, from late Latin *appertinere*, from *ad-* 'to' + Latin *pertinere* 'to pertain.'

ap·pe·stat /ˈapəˌstat/ ▶ **n.** Physiology the region of the hypothalamus of the brain that is believed to control a person's appetite for food.
– ORIGIN 1950s: from APPETITE, probably on the pattern of *thermostat*.

ap·pe·ten·cy /ˈapitənsē/ ▶ **n.** (pl. **appetencies**) archaic a longing or desire. ■ a natural tendency or affinity.
– ORIGIN early 17th cent.: from Latin *appetentia*, from *appetere* 'seek after' (see APPETITE).

ap·pe·tite /ˈapiˌtīt/ ▶ **n.** [usu. in sing.] a natural desire to satisfy a bodily need, esp. for food: *he has a healthy appetite | they suffered from loss of appetite.* ■ a strong desire or liking for something: *an unquenchable appetite for life.*
– ORIGIN Middle English: from Old French *apetit* (modern *appétit*), from Latin *appetitus* 'desire for,' from *appetere* 'seek after,' from *ad-* 'to' + *petere* 'seek.'

ap·pe·ti·tive /ˈapiˌtitiv/ ▶ **adj.** characterized by a natural desire to satisfy bodily needs: *the appetitive behavior of animals.*
– DERIVATIVES **ap·pe·ti·tive·ness n.**, **ap·pe·ti·tive·ly adv.**
– ORIGIN mid 16th cent.: from French *appétitif* or medieval Latin *appetitivus*, from *appetire* 'seek after' (see APPETITE).

ap·pe·tiz·er /ˈapiˌtīzər/ ▶ **n.** a small dish of food or a drink taken before a meal or the main course of a meal to stimulate one's appetite.

ap·pe·tiz·ing /ˈapiˌtīziNG/ (also **appetising**) ▶ **adj.** stimulating one's appetite: *the appetizing aroma of sizzling bacon.*
– DERIVATIVES **ap·pe·tiz·ing·ly adv.**
– ORIGIN mid 17th cent.: from French *appétissant*, irregular formation from *appétit* (see APPETITE).

Ap·pi·an Way /ˈapēən/ in classical times, the principal road south from Rome, named after the censor **Appius Claudius Caecus**, who built the section to Capua in 312 BC; it was later extended to Brindisi. Latin name **Via Appia**.

ap·plaud /əˈplôd/ ▶ **v.** [no obj.] show approval or praise by clapping: *the crowd whistled and applauded | [with obj.] his speech was loudly applauded.* ■ [with obj.] show strong approval of (a person or action); praise: *Jill applauded the decision.*
– ORIGIN late 15th cent.: from Latin *applaudere*, from *ad-* 'to' + *plaudere* 'to clap,' reinforced by French *applaudir*.

ap·plause /əˈplôz/ ▶ **n.** approval or praise expressed by clapping: *they gave him a round of applause.*
– ORIGIN late Middle English: from medieval Latin *applausus*, from the verb *applaudere* (see APPLAUD).

ap·ple /ˈapəl/ ▶ **n.** **1** the round fruit of a tree of the rose family, which typically has thin red or green skin and crisp flesh. Many varieties have been developed as dessert or cooking fruit or for making cider. ■ [with modifier] an unrelated fruit that resembles this in some way. See also CUSTARD APPLE, THORN APPLE.
2 (also **apple tree**) the tree bearing such fruit.
● Genus *Malus*, family Rosaceae: numerous hybrids and cultivars.
3 (**the Apple**) short for **Big Apple**.
– PHRASES **the apple never falls far from the tree** proverb family characteristics are usually inherited. **the apple of one's eye** a person of whom one is extremely fond and proud. [originally denoting the pupil of the eye, considered to be a globular solid body, extended as a symbol of something cherished.] **apples and oranges** (of two people or things) irreconcilably or fundamentally different. **a rotten** (or **bad**) **apple** informal a bad or corrupt person in a group, typically one whose behavior is likely to have a detrimental influence on his or her associates. [with reference to the effect that a rotten apple has on fruit with which it is in contact.] **upset the applecart** spoil a plan or disturb the status quo.
– ORIGIN Old English *æppel*, of Germanic origin; related to Dutch *appel* and German *Apfel*.

ap·ple but·ter ▶ **n.** a paste of spiced stewed apple used as a spread or condiment, typically made with cider.

ap·ple-cheeked ▶ **adj.** (of a person) having round rosy cheeks.

ap·ple green ▶ **n.** a bright yellowish green.

Ap·ple Isle (also **Apple Island**) Austral. a nickname for Tasmania.

ap·ple·jack /ˈapəlˌjak/ ▶ **n.** an alcoholic drink distilled from fermented cider.
– ORIGIN early 19th cent.: from APPLE + JACK[1].

ap·ple pie ▶ **n.** [in sing.] used to represent a cherished ideal of comfort and familiarity: *to say I'm fed up with the Olympics is like being against* **motherhood and apple pie**.
– PHRASES **as American as apple pie** typically American in character.

ap·ple-pie or·der ▶ **n.** perfect order or neatness: *everything was* **in apple-pie order**.

ap·ple pol·ish·er ▶ **n.** informal a person who behaves obsequiously to someone important.
– DERIVATIVES **ap·ple-pol·ish·ing n.**

ap·ple·sauce /ˈapəlˌsôs/ ▶ **n.** **1** a purée of stewed apples, typically sweetened.
2 informal nonsense: *Equal Opportunity for All—Elmer says that's all applesauce.*

Ap·ple·seed /ˈapəlˌsēd/, Johnny (1774–1845), US folk hero; born *John Chapman*. A missionary, he traveled throughout Ohio and Indiana planting and caring for apple orchards.

ap·plet /ˈaplit/ ▶ **n.** Computing a very small application, esp. a utility program performing one or a few simple functions.
– ORIGIN 1990s: blend of APPLICATION and -LET.

Ap·ple·ton[1] /ˈapəltən/ an industrial and academic city in east central Wisconsin; pop. 70,305 (est. 2008).

Ap·ple·ton[2], Sir Edward Victor (1892–1965), English physicist. He discovered a region of ionized gases (the Appleton layer) in the atmosphere above the Heaviside or E layer. Nobel Prize for Physics (1947).

Ap·ple Val·ley 1 a town in southwestern California, northeast of Los Angeles; pop. 70,200 (est. 2008).
2 a city in southeastern Minnesota, south of Minneapolis; pop. 50,004 (est. 2008).

ap·ple·wood /ˈapəlˌwo͝od/ ▶ **n.** the timber of the apple tree, used in carpentry and to smoke food.

ap·pli·ance /əˈplīəns/ ▶ **n.** **1** a device or piece of equipment designed to perform a specific task, typically a domestic one. ■ an apparatus fitted by a surgeon or a dentist for corrective or therapeutic purpose: *electrical and gas appliances.*
2 Brit. the action or process of bringing something into operation: *the appliance of science could increase crop yields.*

ap·pli·anced /əˈplīənst/ ▶ **adj.** (of a kitchen) having or fitted with appliances.

ap·pli·ca·ble /ˈaplikəbəl, əˈplik-/ ▶ **adj.** relevant or appropriate: *the same considerations are equally applicable to accident claims.*
– DERIVATIVES **ap·pli·ca·bil·i·ty** /ˌaplikəˈbilitē/ **n.**, **ap·pli·ca·bly** /-blē/ **adv.**
– ORIGIN mid 16th cent. (in the sense 'compliant'): from Old French, or from medieval Latin *applicabilis*, from the verb *applicare* (see APPLY).

ap·pli·cant /ˈaplikənt/ ▶ **n.** a person who makes a formal application for something, typically a job.
– ORIGIN early 19th cent.: from APPLICATION + -ANT.

ap·pli·ca·tion /ˌapliˈkāSHən/ ▶ **n.** **1** a formal request to an authority for something: *an application for leave | [with infinitive] an application to join the forum | [as modifier] application form.* ■ the action or process of making such a request: *licenses are available on application.*
2 the action of putting something into operation: *the application of general rules to particular cases | massage has far-reaching medical applications.* ■ [often with negative] practical use or relevance: *this principle has no application to the present case.*
3 the action of putting something on a surface: *a fresh application of makeup | paints suitable for application on fabric.* ■ a medicinal substance put on the skin.
4 sustained effort; hard work: *the job takes a great deal of patience and application.*
5 Computing a program or piece of software designed and written to fulfill a particular purpose of the user: *a database application.*
– DERIVATIVES **ap·pli·ca·tion·al** /-SHənl/ **adj.**
– ORIGIN Middle English: via Old French from Latin *applicatio(n-)*, from the verb *applicare* (see APPLY).

ap·pli·ca·tion pro·gram ▶ **n.** another term for APPLICATION (sense 5).

ap·pli·ca·tion pro·gram·ming in·ter·face (abbr.: **API**) ▶ **n.** Computing a system of tools and resources in an operating system, enabling developers to create software applications.

ap·pli·ca·tive /ˈapliˌkātiv, əˈplikə-/ ▶ **adj.** relating to or involving the application of a subject or idea; practical or applied: *applicative algebra.*
– ORIGIN mid 17th cent.: from Latin *applicat-* 'set close or in contact, fastened to,' from the verb *applicare* (see APPLY).

ap·pli·ca·tor /ˈapliˌkātər/ ▶ **n.** a device used for inserting something or for applying a substance to a surface. ■ a person who applies a substance or installs something, such as house siding.
– ORIGIN mid 17th cent.: from Latin *applicat-* 'fastened to' (from the verb *applicare*) + -OR[1].

ap·plied /əˈplīd/ ▶ **adj.** [attrib.] (of a subject or type of study) put to practical use as opposed to being theoretical: *applied chemistry.* Compare with PURE.

ap·plied math·e·mat·ics see MATHEMATICS.

ap·pli·qué /ˌapliˈkā/ ▶ **n.** ornamental needlework in which pieces of fabric are sewn or stuck onto a large piece of fabric to form pictures or patterns.
▶ **v.** (**appliqués**, **appliquéing**, **appliquéd**) [with obj.] (usu. **be appliquéd**) decorate (a piece of fabric) in such a way: *the coat is* **appliquéd with** *exotic-looking cloth | (as adj.* **appliquéd***) 19th-century appliquéd silks.* ■ sew or stick (pieces of fabric) onto a large piece of fabric to form pictures or patterns: *the floral motifs are* **appliquéd to** *christening robes.*
– ORIGIN mid 18th cent.: from French, past participle of *appliquer* 'apply,' from Latin *applicare* (see APPLY).

ap·ply /əˈplī/ ▶ **v.** (**applies**, **applying**, **applied**) **1** [no obj.] make a formal application or request: *you need to* **apply to** *the local authorities* **for** *a grant | [with infinitive] a number of people have applied to vote by proxy.* ■ put oneself forward formally as a candidate for a job: *she had* **applied for** *a number of positions.*
2 [no obj.] be applicable or relevant: *the offer does not apply to unionized workers | normal rules apply.*
3 [with obj.] put or spread (something) on a surface: *the sealer can be* **applied to** *new wood.* ■ administer: *smooth over with a cloth, applying even pressure.*
4 (**apply oneself**) give one's full attention to a task; work hard.
5 [with obj.] bring or put into operation or practical use: *the oil industry has failed to apply appropriate standards of care.*
– ORIGIN late Middle English: from Old French *aplier*, from Latin *applicare* 'fold, fasten to,' from *ad-* 'to' + *plicare* 'to fold.'

ap·pog·gia·tu·ra /əˌpäjəˈto͝orə/ ▶ **n.** (pl. **appoggiaturas** or **appoggiature** /-ˈto͝orā/) Music a grace note performed before a note of the melody and falling on the beat.
– ORIGIN Italian, from *appoggiare* 'lean upon, rest.'

ap·point /əˈpoint/ ▶ **v.** [with obj.] **1** assign a job or role to (someone): *she has been* **appointed to** *the board | [with obj. and infinitive] a delegated engineer will be appointed to oversee each graduate | they* **appointed** *her* **as** *personnel manager.*
2 determine or decide on (a time or a place): *they appointed a day in May for the meeting.* ■ archaic decree: *such laws are appointed by God.*
3 Law decide the disposal of (property of which one is not the owner) under powers granted by the owner: *trustees appoint the capital to the beneficiaries.*
– DERIVATIVES **ap·point·ee** /əˌpoinˈtē/ **n.**, **ap·point·er n.**
– ORIGIN late Middle English: from Old French *apointer*, from *a point* 'to a point.'

ap·point·ed /əˈpointid/ ▶ **adj.** **1** (of a time or place) decided on beforehand; designated: *she arrived at the appointed time.*
2 (of a building or room) equipped or furnished in a specified way or to a specified standard: *a luxuriously appointed lobby.*

ap·poin·tive /əˈpointiv/ ▶ **adj.** (of a job) relating to or filled by appointment rather than election.

ap·point·ment /əˈpointmənt/ ▶ **n.** **1** an arrangement to meet someone at a particular time and place: *she* **made an appointment with** *my receptionist.*
2 an act of appointing; assigning a job or position to someone: *his appointment as president.* ■ a job

or position: *she took up an appointment as head of communications.* ■ a person appointed to a job or position.
3 (**appointments**) furniture or fittings: *the room was spartan in its appointments.*
– PHRASES **by appointment** having previously made an arrangement to do something: *visits are by appointment only.* **power of appointment** **1** power to select the holder of a particular job or position. **2** Law power to decide the disposal of property, in exercise of a right conferred by the owner.
– ORIGIN Middle English: from Old French *apointement*, from *apointer* (see APPOINT).

Ap·po·mat·tox /ˌapəˈmatəks/ a historic site in central Virginia, at the head of the Appomattox River, where Robert E. Lee's surrender of his Confederate forces in April 1865 ended the Civil War.

ap·por·tion /əˈpôrSHən/ ▶ **v.** [with obj.] divide and allocate: *voting power will be apportioned according to contribution.* ■ assign: *they did not apportion blame or liability to any one individual.*
– ORIGIN late 16th cent.: from Old French *apportionner* or medieval Latin *apportionare*, from *ad-* 'to' + *portionare* 'divide into portions.'

ap·por·tion·ment /əˈpôrSHənmənt/ ▶ **n.** the action or result of apportioning something: *an exercise in apportionment of blame.* ■ the determination of the proportional number of members each US state sends to the House of Representatives, based on population figures.

ap·pose /əˈpōz/ ▶ **v.** [with obj.] technical place (something) in proximity to or juxtaposition with something else: *the specimen was apposed to X-ray film.*
– ORIGIN late 16th cent.: from Latin *apponere*, on the pattern of words such as *compose*, *expose*.

ap·po·site /ˈapəzit/ ▶ **adj.** apt in the circumstances or in relation to something: *an apposite quotation* | *the observations are* **apposite to** *the discussion.*
– DERIVATIVES **ap·po·site·ly** **adv.**, **ap·po·site·ness** **n.**
– ORIGIN late 16th cent.: from Latin *appositus*, past participle of *apponere* 'apply,' from *ad-* 'toward' + *ponere* 'put.'

ap·po·si·tion /ˌapəˈziSHən/ ▶ **n.** **1** chiefly technical the positioning of things or the condition of being side by side or close together.
2 Grammar a relationship between two or more words or phrases in which the two units are grammatically parallel and have the same referent (e.g., *my friend Sue*; *the first US president, George Washington*.
– ORIGIN late Middle English: from late Latin *appositio(n-)*, from *apponere* 'to apply' (see APPOSITE).

ap·po·si·tion·al /ˌapəˈziSHənl/ Grammar ▶ **adj.** of or relating to apposition.
▶ **n.** a term standing in apposition.

ap·pos·i·tive /əˈpäzitiv/ ▶ **adj. & n.** Grammar another term for APPOSITIONAL.
– ORIGIN late 17th cent.: from late Latin *appositivus* 'subsidiary.'

ap·prais·al /əˈprāzəl/ ▶ **n.** an act of assessing something or someone: *treatment begins with a thorough appraisal of the patient's condition* | *the report has been subject to appraisal.* ■ an expert estimate of the value of something: *the final figure is just a little more than triple the appraisal.*

ap·prais·al drill·ing ▶ **n.** drilling undertaken to establish the quality, quantity, and other characteristics of oil or gas in a newly discovered field.

ap·praise /əˈprāz/ ▶ **v.** [with obj.] assess the value or quality of: *she stealthily appraised him in a pocket mirror* | [no obj.] *the interviewer's job is to appraise and evaluate.* ■ (of an official or expert) set a price on; value: *they appraised the painting at $200,000.*
– DERIVATIVES **ap·prais·er** **n.**, **ap·prais·ing·ly** **adv.**
– ORIGIN late Middle English (in the sense 'set a price on'): alteration of APPRIZE, by association with PRAISE. The current sense dates from the mid 19th cent.

> **USAGE** Appraise, meaning 'evaluate,' should not be confused with **apprise**, which means 'inform': *the painting was appraised at $3,000,000; they gasped when apprised of this valuation.*

ap·pre·ci·a·ble /əˈprēSH(ē)əbəl/ ▶ **adj.** large or important enough to be noticed: *tea and coffee both contain appreciable amounts of caffeine.*
– ORIGIN early 19th cent.: from French *appréciable*, from *apprécier* (see APPRECIATE).

ap·pre·ci·a·bly /əˈprēSH(ē)əblē/ ▶ **adv.** to an appreciable extent; considerably: *profits have grown appreciably over the last four years* | [as submodifier] *an appreciably higher risk.*

ap·pre·ci·ate /əˈprēSHēˌāt/ ▶ **v.** [with obj.] **1** recognize the full worth of: *she feels that he does not appreciate her.* ■ be grateful for (something): *I'd appreciate any information you could give me.*
2 understand (a situation) fully; recognize the full implications of: *they failed to appreciate the pressure he was under* | [with clause] *I appreciate that you cannot be held totally responsible.*
3 [no obj.] rise in value or price: *they expected the house to* **appreciate in value.**
– DERIVATIVES **ap·pre·ci·a·tor** /-ˌātər/ **n.**
– ORIGIN mid 16th cent.: from late Latin *appretiat-* 'set at a price, appraised,' from the verb *appretiare*, from *ad-* 'to' + *pretium* 'price.'

ap·pre·ci·a·tion /əˌprēSHēˈāSHən/ ▶ **n.** **1** the recognition and enjoyment of the good qualities of someone or something: *I smiled in appreciation* | *she shows a fine appreciation of obscure thinkers.* ■ gratitude for something: *they would be the first to* **show their appreciation.** ■ a piece of writing in which the qualities of a person or the person's work are discussed and assessed. ■ sensitive understanding of the aesthetic value of something: *courses in music appreciation.*
2 a full understanding of a situation: *they have an appreciation of the needs of users* | *the bank's lack of appreciation of their problems.*
3 increase in monetary value: *the appreciation of the franc against the dollar.*
– ORIGIN early 17th cent.: from French *appréciation*, from late Latin *appretiatio(n-)*, from the verb *appretiare* 'set at a price, appraise' (see APPRECIATE).

ap·pre·cia·tive /əˈprēSH(ē)ətiv/ ▶ **adj.** feeling or showing gratitude or pleasure: *the team is very* **appreciative of** *your support* | *an appreciative audience.*
– DERIVATIVES **ap·pre·cia·tive·ly** **adv.**, **ap·pre·ci·a·tive·ness** **n.**

ap·pre·hend /ˌapriˈhend/ ▶ **v.** [with obj.] **1** arrest (someone) for a crime: *a warrant was issued but he has not been apprehended.*
2 understand or perceive: *great art invites us to apprehend beauty.* ■ archaic anticipate (something) with uneasiness or fear.
– ORIGIN late Middle English (originally in the sense 'grasp, get hold of (physically or mentally)'): from French *appréhender* or Latin *apprehendere*, from *ad-* 'toward' + *prehendere* 'lay hold of.'

ap·pre·hen·si·ble /ˌapriˈhensəbəl/ ▶ **adj.** archaic or literary capable of being understood or perceived: *a bat whirred, apprehensible only from the displacement of air.*
– ORIGIN early 17th cent.: from late Latin *apprehensibilis*, from Latin *apprehendere* (see APPREHEND).

ap·pre·hen·sion /ˌapriˈhenSHən/ ▶ **n.** **1** anxiety or fear that something bad or unpleasant will happen: *he felt sick with apprehension* | *she had some apprehensions about the filming.*
2 understanding; grasp: *the pure apprehension of the work of art.*
3 the action of arresting someone: *they acted with intent to prevent lawful apprehension.*
– ORIGIN late Middle English (in the sense 'learning, acquisition of knowledge'): from late Latin *apprehensio(n-)*, from *apprehendere* 'seize, grasp' (see APPREHEND).

ap·pre·hen·sive /ˌapriˈhensiv/ ▶ **adj.** **1** anxious or fearful that something bad or unpleasant will happen: *he felt apprehensive about going home* | [with clause] *they were apprehensive that something might go wrong.*
2 archaic or literary of or relating to perception or understanding.
– DERIVATIVES **ap·pre·hen·sive·ly** **adv.**, **ap·pre·hen·sive·ness** **n.**
– ORIGIN late Middle English (sense 2): from French *appréhensif* or medieval Latin *apprehensivus*, from Latin *apprehendere* 'seize, grasp' (see APPREHENSION).

ap·pren·tice /əˈprentis/ ▶ **n.** a person who is learning a trade from a skilled employer, having agreed to work for a fixed period at low wages: [as modifier] *an apprentice electrician.* ■ [usu. as modifier] a beginner at something: *an apprentice confidence trickster.*
▶ **v.** [with obj.] employ (someone) as an apprentice: *Edward was* **apprenticed to** *a printer.* ■ [no obj.] serve as an apprentice: *she apprenticed with midwives in San Francisco.*
– ORIGIN Middle English: from Old French *aprentis* (from *apprendre* 'learn,' from Latin *apprehendere* 'apprehend'), on the pattern of words ending in *-tis*, *-tif*, from Latin *-tivus* (see -IVE).

ap·pren·tice·ship /əˈprentisˌSHip/ ▶ **n.** the position of an apprentice: *six young chefs have completed their apprenticeships.*

ap·press /əˈpres/ ▶ **v.** [with obj.] (usu. **be appressed**) technical press (something) close to something else: *the two cords can be closely* **appressed to** *one another.*
– ORIGIN early 17th cent.: from Latin *appress-* 'pressed close,' from the verb *apprimere*, from *ad-* 'to' + *premere* 'to press.'

ap·prise /əˈprīz/ ▶ **v.** [with obj.] inform or tell (someone): *I thought it right to* **apprise** *Chris* **of** *what had happened.*
– ORIGIN late 17th cent.: from French *appris*, *apprise*, past participle of *apprendre* 'learn, teach,' from Latin *apprehendere* (see APPREHEND).

> **USAGE** See usage at APPRAISE.

ap·prize /əˈprīz/ ▶ **v.** [with obj.] archaic put a price upon; appraise: *the sheriff was to apprize the value of the lands.* ■ value highly; esteem: *how highly your Highness apprizeth peace.*
– ORIGIN late Middle English: from Old French *aprisier*, from *a-* (from Latin *ad* 'to, at') + *prisier* 'to price, prize,' from *pris* (see PRICE). The spelling change in the 17th cent. was due to association with PRIZE[1].

ap·proach /əˈprōCH/ ▶ **v.** [with obj.] **1** come near or nearer to (someone or something) in distance: *the train approached the main line* | [no obj.] *she hadn't heard him approach* | (as adj. **approaching**) *an approaching car.* ■ come near or nearer to (a future time or event): *he was approaching retirement.* ■ [no obj.] (of a future time) come near: *the time is approaching when you will be destroyed.* ■ come close to (a number, level, or standard) in quality or quantity: *the population will approach 12 million by the end of the decade.* ■ (of an aircraft) descend toward and prepare to land on (an airfield, runway, etc.): *the single-seater plane hit a post as it was approaching the runway.* ■ archaic bring nearer: *all those changes shall serve to approach him the faster to the blest mansion.*
2 speak to (someone) for the first time about something, typically with a proposal or request: *the department had been approached about funding.*
3 start to deal with (something) in a certain way: *one must approach the matter with caution.*
▶ **n.** **1** a way of dealing with something: *we need a whole new* **approach to** *the job.*
2 an act of speaking to someone for the first time about something, typically a proposal or request: *the landowner made an approach to the developer.* ■ (**approaches**) dated behavior intended to propose personal or sexual relations with someone: *feminine resistance to his approaches.*
3 [in sing.] the action of coming near or nearer to someone or something in distance or time: *the approach of winter.* ■ (**approach to**) an approximation to something: *the past is impossible to recall with any approach to accuracy.* ■ the part of an aircraft's flight in which it descends gradually toward an airfield or runway for landing.
4 (usu. **approaches**) a road, sea passage, or other way leading to a place: *the eastern* **approach to** *the town.*
– ORIGIN Middle English: from Old French *aprochier*, *aprocher*, from ecclesiastical Latin *appropiare* 'draw near,' from *ad-* 'to' + *propius* (comparative of *prope* 'near').

ap·proach·a·ble /əˈprōCHəbəl/ ▶ **adj.** **1** friendly and easy to talk to: *managers should be approachable.*
2 (of a place) able to be reached from a particular direction or by a particular means: *at night parrotfish are approachable as they sleep in nooks and crannies on the reef.*
– DERIVATIVES **ap·proach·a·bil·i·ty** /əˌprōCHəˈbilitē/ **n.**

ap·proach shot ▶ **n.** Golf a stroke that sends the ball from the fairway onto or nearer to the green.

ap·pro·bate /ˈaprəˌbāt/ ▶ **v.** [with obj.] rare approve formally; sanction: *a letter approbating the affair.*
– ORIGIN late Middle English: from Latin *approbat-* 'approved,' from the verb *approbare*, from *ad-* 'to' + *probare* 'try, test' (from *probus* 'good').

ap·pro·ba·tion /ˌaprəˈbāSHən/ ▶ **n.** formal approval or praise: *the opera met with high approbation.*
– DERIVATIVES **ap·pro·ba·tive** /ˈaprəˌbātiv, əˈprōbətiv/ **adj.**, **ap·pro·ba·to·ry** /əˈprōbəˌtôrē/ **adj.**
– ORIGIN late Middle English: via Old French from Latin *approbatio(n-)*, from the verb *approbare* (see APPROBATE).

ap·pro·pri·ate ▶ **adj.** /əˈprōprē-it/ suitable or proper in the circumstances: *a measure appropriate to a wartime economy.*
▶ **v.** /-ˌāt/ [with obj.] **1** take (something) for one's own use, typically without the owner's permission: *his images have been appropriated by advertisers.*
2 devote (money or assets) to a special purpose: *there can be problems in* **appropriating funds for** *legal expenses.*

a

– DERIVATIVES **ap·pro·pri·ate·ly** /-itlē/ **adv.** [sentence adverb] *appropriately, the first recital will be given at the festival*, **ap·pro·pri·ate·ness** /-itnis/ **n.**, **ap·pro·pri·a·tor** /-ˌātər/ **n.**
– ORIGIN late Middle English: from late Latin *appropriatus*, past participle of *appropriare* 'make one's own,' from *ad-* 'to' + *proprius* 'own, proper.'

ap·pro·pri·a·tion /əˌprōprēˈāsHən/ ▶ **n.** **1** the action of taking something for one's own use, typically without the owner's permission: *the appropriation of parish funds*. ■ often derogatory the artistic practice or technique of reworking images from well-known paintings, photographs, etc., in one's own work. **2** a sum of money or total of assets devoted to a special purpose.
– ORIGIN late Middle English: from late Latin *appropriatio(n-)*, from *appropriare* 'make one's own' (see APPROPRIATE).

ap·pro·pri·a·tion·ist /əˌprōprēˈāsHənist/ ▶ **n.** often derogatory an artist whose work contains reworkings of well-known images by other artists: [as modifier] *appropriationist art*.

ap·prov·al /əˈpro͞ovəl/ ▶ **n.** **1** the action of officially agreeing to something or accepting something as satisfactory: *the road plans have been given approval | they have delayed the launch to await project approvals*. ■ the belief that someone or something is good or acceptable: *step-parents need to win a child's approval*. **2** (usu. **approvals**) Philately stamps sent by request to a collector or potential customer.
– PHRASES **on approval** (of goods) supplied on condition that they may be returned if not satisfactory. **seal** (or **stamp**) **of approval** an official statement or indication that something is accepted or regarded favorably.

ap·prove /əˈpro͞ov/ ▶ **v.** [with obj.] **1** officially agree to or accept as satisfactory: *the budget was approved by Congress* | (as adj. **approved**) *an approved profit-sharing plan*. ■ [no obj.] believe that someone or something is good or acceptable: *I don't approve of the way she pampers my father and brothers*. **2** archaic prove; show: *he approved himself ripe for military command*.
– ORIGIN Middle English: from Old French *aprover*, from Latin *approbare* (see APPROBATE). The original sense was 'prove, demonstrate,' later 'corroborate, confirm,' hence 'pronounce to be satisfactory' (late Middle English).

ap·prov·ing /əˈpro͞oviNG/ ▶ **adj.** showing or feeling approval of someone or something: *the wine drew approving comments from across the table*.
– DERIVATIVES **ap·prov·ing·ly adv.**

approx. ▶ **abbr.** approximate(ly).

ap·prox·i·mate ▶ **adj.** /əˈpräksəmit/ close to the actual, but not completely accurate or exact: *the calculations are very approximate*.
▶ **v.** /-ˌmāt/ [no obj.] come close or be similar to something in quality, nature, or quantity: *a leasing agreement approximating to ownership* | [with obj.] *reality can be approximated by computational techniques*. ■ [with obj.] estimate or calculate (a quantity) fairly accurately: *I had to approximate the weight of my horse*.
– ORIGIN late Middle English (in the adjectival sense 'close, similar'): from late Latin *approximatus*, past participle of *approximare*, from *ad-* 'to' + *proximus* 'very near.' The verb (originally meaning 'bring close') arose in the mid 17th cent.; the current adjectival sense dates from the early 19th cent.

ap·prox·i·mate·ly /əˈpräksəmətlē/ ▶ **adv.** used to show that something is almost, but not completely, accurate or exact; roughly: *a journey of approximately two hours*.

ap·prox·i·ma·tion /əˌpräksəˈmāsHən/ ▶ **n.** a value or quantity that is nearly but not exactly correct: *these figures are only approximations*. ■ a thing that is similar to something else, but is not exactly the same: *the band smashed up their equipment in an approximation of rock star behavior*.

ap·prox·i·ma·tive /əˈpräksəˌmātiv/ ▶ **adj.** (of a method, description, etc.) giving only an approximation to something: *a crudely approximative outline*.

ap·pur·te·nance /əˈpərtn-əns/ ▶ **n.** (usu. **appurtenances**) an accessory or other item associated with a particular activity or style of living: *all the appurtenances of luxurious travel*.
– ORIGIN Middle English: from Old French *apertenance*, based on late Latin *appertinere* 'belong to' (see APPERTAIN).

ap·pur·te·nant /əˈpərtn-ənt/ ▶ **adj.** belonging; pertinent: *secondary buildings that are appurtenant to the main building*.
– ORIGIN late Middle English: from Old French *apartenant* 'appertaining,' from the verb *apartenir* (see APPERTAIN).

APR ▶ **abbr.** annual or annualized percentage rate, typically of interest on loans or credit.

Apr. ▶ **abbr.** April.

a·prax·i·a /āˈpraksēə/ ▶ **n.** Medicine inability to perform particular purposive actions, as a result of brain damage.
– DERIVATIVES **a·prax·ic** /-sik/ **adj.**
– ORIGIN late 19th cent.: from German *Apraxie*, from Greek *apraxia* 'inaction.'

après- ▶ **prefix** informal, humorous coming after in time, typically specifying a period following an activity: *a low-fat, après-workout snack*.
– ORIGIN mid 20th cent.: French, literally 'after,' used in combinations on the pattern of *après-ski*.

a·près-ski /ˌäprā ˈskē/ ▶ **n.** the social activities and entertainment following a day's skiing: [as modifier] *the après-ski disco*.
– DERIVATIVES **a·près-ski·ing n.**
– ORIGIN 1950s: French, literally 'after skiing.'

ap·ri·cot /ˈapriˌkät, ˈāpri-/ ▶ **n.** **1** a juicy, soft fruit, resembling a small peach, of an orange-yellow color. ■ an orange-yellow color like the skin of a ripe apricot. **2** (also **apricot tree**) the tree bearing this fruit. ● *Prunus armeniaca*, family Rosaceae.
– ORIGIN mid 16th cent.: from Portuguese *albricoque* or Spanish *albaricoque*, from Spanish Arabic *al* 'the' + *barḳūḳ* (from late Greek *praikokion*, from Latin *praecoquum*, variant of *praecox* 'early ripe'); influenced by Latin *apricus* 'ripe' and by French *abricot*.

A·pril /ˈāprəl/ ▶ **n.** the fourth month of the year, in the northern hemisphere usually considered the second month of spring: *the prison was to close in April* | [as modifier] *April showers*.
– ORIGIN Old English, from Latin *Aprilis*.

A·pril Fool ▶ **n.** a person who is the victim of a trick or hoax on April 1: [as exclamation] *Lucy was waiting right outside. "April Fool!" she said*. ■ a trick or hoax on April 1: [as modifier] *an April Fool joke*.

A·pril Fool's Day (also **April Fools' Day**) ▶ **n.** April 1, in many Western countries traditionally an occasion for playing tricks. This custom has been observed for hundreds of years, but its origin is unknown. Also called ALL FOOLS' DAY.

a pri·o·ri /ˈä prēˈôrē, prīˈôrī, ˈā/ ▶ **adj.** relating to or denoting reasoning or knowledge that proceeds from theoretical deduction rather than from observation or experience: *a priori assumptions about human nature*.
▶ **adv.** in a way based on theoretical deduction rather than empirical observation: *sexuality may be a factor, but it cannot be assumed a priori* | [sentence adverb] *a priori, it would seem that his government was an extension of that power*.
– DERIVATIVES **a·pri·o·rism** /ˌāprīˈôrizəm, -prē-, ˌäprē-/ **n.**
– ORIGIN late 16th cent.: Latin, 'from what is before.'

a·pron /ˈāprən/ ▶ **n.** **1** a protective or decorative garment worn over the front of one's clothes and tied at the back. ■ a similar garment worn as part of official dress, as by an Anglican bishop or a Freemason. ■ a sheet of lead worn to shield the body during an X-ray examination. **2** a small area adjacent to another larger area or structure: *a tiny apron of garden*. ■ a hard-surfaced area on an airfield used for maneuvering or parking aircraft. ■ (also **apron stage**) a projecting strip of stage for playing scenes in front of the curtain. ■ a broadened area of pavement at the end of a driveway. ■ the narrow strip of the floor of a boxing ring lying outside the ropes. ■ the outer edge or border of a golf green. ■ Geology an extensive outspread deposit of sediment, typically at the foot of a glacier or mountain. **3** an object resembling an apron in shape or function, in particular: ■ a covering protecting an area or structure, for example, from water erosion. ■ [often as modifier] an endless conveyor made of overlapping plates: *apron feeders bring coarse ore to a grinding mill*. ■ Medicine a pendulous fold of abdominal fat that obscures the genital region.
– PHRASES **(tied to) someone's apron strings** (too much under) the influence and control of someone: *we have all met sturdy adults who are tied to mother's apron strings*.
– ORIGIN Middle English *naperon*, from Old French, diminutive of *nape, nappe* 'tablecloth,' from Latin *mappa* 'napkin.' The *n* was lost by wrong division of *a napron*; compare with ADDER.

ap·ro·pos /ˌaprəˈpō/ ▶ **prep.** with reference to; concerning: *she remarked apropos of the initiative, "It's not going to stop the abuse."*
▶ **adv.** [sentence adverb] (**apropos of nothing**) used to state a speaker's belief that someone's comments or acts are unrelated to any previous discussion or situation: *Isabel kept smiling apropos of nothing*.
▶ **adj.** [predic.] very appropriate to a particular situation: *the composer's reference to child's play is apropos*.
– ORIGIN mid 17th cent.: from French *à propos* '(with regard) to (this) purpose.'

ap·sa·ra /ˈəpsərə/ (also **apsaras** /-sərəs/) ▶ **n.** (pl. **apsaras** or **apsarases** /-rəsiz/) Hindu Mythology a celestial nymph, typically the consort of a gandharva or heavenly musician.
– ORIGIN from Hindi *apsarā*, from Sanskrit *apsarās*.

apse /aps/ ▶ **n.** **1** a large semicircular or polygonal recess in a church, arched or with a domed roof, typically at the eastern end, and usually containing the altar. **2** another term for APSIS.
– DERIVATIVES **ap·si·dal** /ˈapsidl/ **adj.**
– ORIGIN early 19th cent. (sense 2): from Latin *apsis* (see APSIS).

ap·sis /ˈapsis/ ▶ **n.** (pl. **apsides** /-siˌdēz/) either of two points on the orbit of a planet or satellite that are nearest to or furthest from the body around which it moves.
– DERIVATIVES **ap·si·dal** /ˈapsidl/ **adj.**
– ORIGIN early 17th cent. (denoting the orbit of a planet): via Latin from Greek *apsis, hapsis* 'arch, vault,' perhaps from *haptein* 'fasten, join.'

apt /apt/ ▶ **adj.** **1** appropriate or suitable in the circumstances: *an apt description of her nature*. **2** [predic.] (**apt to do something**) having a tendency to do something: *she was apt to confuse the past with the present*. **3** quick to learn: *he proved an apt scholar*.
– DERIVATIVES **apt·ly adv.**
– ORIGIN late Middle English (in the sense 'suited, appropriate'): from Latin *aptus* 'fitted,' past participle of *apere* 'fasten.'

apt. ▶ **abbr.** ■ apartment. ■ aptitude.

ap·ter·ous /ˈaptərəs/ ▶ **adj.** Entomology (of an insects) having no wings.
– ORIGIN late 18th cent.: from Greek *apteros* (from *a-* 'without' + *pteron* 'wing') + -OUS.

Ap·ter·y·go·ta /apˌteriˈgōtə/ Entomology a group of insects that includes the bristletails and springtails. They have a primitive body form that lacks wings and typically have no distinct larval stage. Compare with PTERYGOTA. ● Subclass Apterygota, class Insecta (or Hexapoda): several orders, some of which are sometimes not included with the Insecta.
– ORIGIN modern Latin *Apterygota*, from Greek *a-* 'not' + *pterugōtos* 'winged.'

ap·ter·y·gote /apˈteriˌgōt/ ▶ **n.** Entomology a primitive wingless insect of the group Apterygota, which includes the bristletails and springtails.

ap·ti·tude /ˈaptiˌt(y)o͞od/ ▶ **n.** **1** (often **aptitude for**) a natural ability to do something: *he had a remarkable aptitude for learning words*. ■ a natural tendency: *his natural aptitude for failure*. **2** archaic suitability or fitness: *aptitude of expression*.
– ORIGIN late Middle English: via Old French from late Latin *aptitudo*, from *aptus* (see APT).

ap·ti·tude test ▶ **n.** a test designed to determine a person's ability in a particular skill or field of knowledge.

apt·ness /ˈaptnis/ ▶ **n.** the quality of being appropriate or suitable: *the aptness of the punishment*.

APU ▶ **abbr.** auxiliary power unit, a device used on aircraft to provide power while on the ground and to start the main engines.

Ap·u·le·ius /ˌapyəˈlēəs/ (born *c.* AD 123), Roman writer; born in Africa. He wrote *Metamorphoses* (*The Golden Ass*).

A·pus /ˈāpəs/ Astronomy a faint southern constellation, the Bird of Paradise, close to the south celestial pole. ■ (as genitive **Apodis** /ˈapədis/) used with a preceding letter or numeral to designate stars: *the star Beta Apodis*.
– ORIGIN Latin, denoting a kind of bird, from Greek *apous*.

A·qa·ba /ˈäkəbə, ˈak-/ Jordan's only port, at the head of the Gulf of Aqaba; pop. 79,839 (2004).

A·qa·ba, Gulf of part of the Red Sea that extends northward between the Sinai and Arabian peninsulas.

aq·ua /ˈäkwə, ˈak-/ ▶ **n.** a light bluish-green color; aquamarine: *houses of yellow and aqua* | [as modifier] *aqua blue*.
– ORIGIN 1930s: abbreviation of AQUAMARINE.

aqua- ▶ **comb. form** relating to water: *aquaculture*. ■ relating to water sports or aquatic entertainment: *aquacade*.
– ORIGIN from Latin *aqua* 'water.'

aq·ua·cade /ˈäkwəˌkād, ˈak-/ ▶ **n.** a spectacle involving swimming and diving, usually with musical accompaniment.

aq·ua·cul·ture /ˈäkwəˌkəlCHər, ˈak-/ ▶ **n.** Botany the rearing of aquatic animals or the cultivation of aquatic plants for food.
– ORIGIN mid 19th cent.: from Latin *aqua* 'water' + **CULTURE**, on the pattern of words such as *agriculture*.

aq·ua for·tis /ˈäkwə ˈfôrtis, ˈak-/ ▶ **n.** archaic term for **NITRIC ACID**.
– ORIGIN late 15th cent.: from Latin, literally 'strong water.'

aq·ua·lung /ˈäkwəˌləNG, ˈak-/ (also trademark **Aqua-Lung**) ▶ **n.** a portable breathing apparatus for divers, consisting of cylinders of compressed air strapped on the diver's back, feeding air automatically through a mask or mouthpiece.
▶ **v.** [no obj.] dated swim underwater using such an apparatus.
– ORIGIN 1950s (originally a proprietary name in the US): from Latin *aqua* 'water' + **LUNG**.

aq·ua·ma·rine /ˌäkwəməˈrēn, ˌak-/ ▶ **n.** a precious stone consisting of a light bluish-green variety of beryl. ■ a light bluish-green color: *the aquamarine of the Atlantic Ocean* | [as modifier] *the aquamarine water*.
– ORIGIN early 18th cent.: from Latin *aqua marina* 'seawater.'

aq·ua·naut /ˈäkwəˌnôt, ˈak-/ ▶ **n.** a person who swims underwater using an aqualung.
– ORIGIN late 19th cent.: from Latin *aqua* 'water' + Greek *nautēs* 'sailor.'

aq·ua·plane /ˈäkwəˌplān, ˈak-/ ▶ **n.** a board for riding on water, pulled by a speedboat.
▶ **v.** [no obj.] (often as noun **aquaplaning**) ride standing on an aquaplane. ■ (of a vehicle) slide uncontrollably on a wet surface: *the plane is believed to have aquaplaned on the runway*.
– ORIGIN early 20th cent.: from Latin *aqua* 'water' + **PLANE**[1].

aq·ua re·gi·a /ˈäkwə ˈrejēə, ˈak-/ ▶ **n.** Chemistry a mixture of concentrated nitric and hydrochloric acids. It is a highly corrosive liquid that will dissolve gold and other resistant substances.
– ORIGIN early 17th cent.: Latin, literally 'royal water.'

aq·ua·relle /ˌäkwəˈrel, ˌak-/ ▶ **n.** a style of painting using thin, typically transparent, watercolors. ■ a painting in such a style.
– ORIGIN mid 19th cent.: from French, from Italian *acquarella* 'watercolor,' diminutive of *acqua*, from Latin *aqua* 'water.'

A·quar·i·an /əˈkwe(ə)rēən/ Astrology ▶ **n.** a person born under the sign of Aquarius.
▶ **adj.** of or relating to people born under the sign of Aquarius. ■ of or relating to the Age of Aquarius or the New Age.

a·quar·ist /əˈkwe(ə)rist/ ▶ **n.** a person who keeps an aquarium.

a·quar·i·um /əˈkwe(ə)rēəm/ ▶ **n.** (pl. **aquariums** or **aquaria** /-ēə/) a transparent tank of water in which fish and other water creatures and plants are kept. ■ a building containing such tanks, esp. one that is open to the public.
– ORIGIN mid 19th cent.: from Latin, neuter of *aquarius* 'of water,' on the pattern of *vivarium*.

A·quar·i·us /əˈkwe(ə)rēəs/ **1** Astronomy a large constellation, the Water-carrier or Water-bearer, said to represent a man pouring water from a jar. It contains no bright stars but has several planetary nebulae. ■ (as genitive **Aquarii** /əˈkwe(ə)rēˌī/) used with a preceding letter or numeral to designate stars: *the star Alpha Aquarii*.
2 Astrology the eleventh sign of the zodiac, which the sun enters about January 21. ■ (**an Aquarius**) a person born when the sun is in this sign.
– PHRASES **Age of Aquarius** an age that the world has just entered or is about to enter, believed by some to signal a period of peace and harmony.
– ORIGIN Latin *aquarius* 'of water,' used as a noun to mean 'water carrier.'

a·quat·ic /əˈkwätik, əˈkwat-/ ▶ **adj.** of or relating to water. ■ (of a plant or animal) growing or living in or near water: *the bay could support aquatic life*. ■ (of a sport) played in or on water. ■ (of a shop or dealer) specializing in products for ponds or aquariums.
▶ **n. 1** an aquatic plant or animal, typically one suitable for a pond or aquarium.
2 (**aquatics**) sports played in or on water.
– ORIGIN late 15th cent. (in the sense 'watery, rainy'): from Old French *aquatique* or Latin *aquaticus*, from *aqua* 'water.'

aq·ua·tint /ˈäkwəˌtint, ˈak-/ ▶ **n.** a print resembling a watercolor, produced from a copper plate etched with nitric acid. ■ the technique or process of making pictures in such a way.
▶ **v.** [with obj.] create (a scene or picture) in such a way.
– ORIGIN late 18th cent.: from French *aquatinte*, from Italian *acqua tinta* 'colored water.'

aq·ua·vit /ˈäkwəˌvēt, ˈak-/ (also **akvavit** /ˈäkväˌvēt/) ▶ **n.** an alcoholic spirit made from potatoes or other starchy plants.
– ORIGIN late 19th cent.: from Norwegian, Swedish, and Danish *akvavit* (see **AQUA VITAE**).

aq·ua vi·tae /ˈäkwə ˈvītē, ˈvēˌtī, ˈakwə/ ▶ **n.** strong alcoholic spirit, esp. brandy.
– ORIGIN late Middle English: from Latin, literally 'water of life'; compare with **AQUAVIT**, **EAU-DE-VIE**, **USQUEBAUGH**, and **WHISKEY**.

aq·ue·duct /ˈäkwəˌdəkt, ˈak-/ ▶ **n.** an artificial channel for conveying water, typically in the form of a bridge supported by tall columns across a valley. ■ Anatomy a small canal containing fluid.
– ORIGIN mid 16th cent.: from obsolete French (now *aqueduc*), from Latin *aquae ductus* 'conduit,' from *aqua* 'water' + *ducere* 'to lead.'

Roman aqueduct

a·que·ous /ˈākwēəs, ˈak-/ ▶ **adj.** of or containing water, typically as a solvent or medium: *an aqueous solution of potassium permanganate*. ■ like water; watery: *a great hall of aqueous marble*.
– ORIGIN mid 17th cent.: from medieval Latin *aqueus*, from Latin *aqua* 'water.'

a·que·ous hu·mor ▶ **n.** the clear fluid filling the space in the front of the eyeball between the lens and the cornea. Compare with **VITREOUS HUMOR**.

A·quid·neck /əˈkwidˌnek/ the former name of Rhode Island, the largest island in Narragansett Bay, part of the state of Rhode Island.

aq·ui·fer /ˈäkwəfər, ˈak-/ ▶ **n.** a body of permeable rock that can contain or transmit groundwater.
– ORIGIN early 20th cent.: from Latin *aqui-* (from *aqua* 'water') + *-fer* 'bearing' (from *ferre* 'to bear').

A·quil·a /əˈkwilə, ˈakwilə/ Astronomy a small northern constellation, the Eagle, said to represent the eagle that carried Ganymede to Olympus. It contains the bright star Altair, and some rich star fields of the Milky Way. ■ (as genitive **Aquilae** /əˈkwilē, ˈakwilē/) used with a preceding letter or numeral to designate stars: *the star Beta Aquilae*.
– ORIGIN Latin.

aq·ui·le·gi·a /ˌakwəˈlēj(ē)ə/ ▶ **n.** a plant of the buttercup family, bearing showy flowers with backward-pointing spurs. Native to temperate regions of the northern hemisphere, it is widely grown in gardens. ● Genus *Aquilegia*, family Ranunculaceae. See also **COLUMBINE**.
– ORIGIN from medieval Latin, probably from Latin *aquilegus* 'water collecting.'

aq·ui·line /ˈakwəˌlīn, -lin/ ▶ **adj.** like an eagle. ■ (of a person's nose) hooked or curved like an eagle's beak.
– ORIGIN mid 17th cent.: from Latin *aquilinus*, from *aquila* 'eagle.'

A·qui·nas, St. Thom·as /əˈkwīnəs/ (1225–74), Italian philosopher, theologian, and Dominican friar; known as *the Angelic Doctor*. He is regarded as the greatest figure of scholasticism. One of his most important achievements was the introduction of the work of Aristotle to Christian western Europe. His works include commentaries on Aristotle as well as the *Summa Contra Gentiles* and *Summa Theologiae*. Feast day, January 28.

A·qui·no /äˈkēnō, əˈkē-/, Corazón (1933–2009), Filipino stateswoman; full name *Maria Corazón Sumulong Cojuangco Aquino*. She was president of the Philippines 1986–92.

Aq·ui·taine[1] /ˈakwəˌtān/ a region and former province in southwestern France, on the Bay of Biscay. It became an English possession as a result of the marriage of Eleanor of Aquitaine to Henry II in 1152 and remained so until 1453.

Aq·ui·taine[2], Eleanor of, see **ELEANOR OF AQUITAINE**.

a·quiv·er /əˈkwivər/ ▶ **adj.** [predic.] quivering; trembling: *her face aquiver with pleasure*.

AR ▶ **abbr.** ■ (also **A/R**) accounts receivable. ■ Arkansas (in official postal use). ■ Army Regulation. ■ Autonomous Republic.

Ar ▶ **symbol** the chemical element argon.

ar- ▶ **prefix** variant spelling of **AD-** assimilated before *r* (as in *arrive*, *arrogate*).

-ar[1] ▶ **suffix 1** (forming adjectives) of the kind specified; relating to: *lunar* | *molecular*.
2 forming nouns such as *scholar*.
– ORIGIN from Old French *-aire*, *-ier*, or from Latin *-aris*.

-ar[2] ▶ **suffix** forming nouns such as *pillar*.
– ORIGIN from French *-er* or representing Latin *-ar*, *-are* (neuter of *-aris*).

-ar[3] ▶ **suffix** forming nouns such as *bursar*, *vicar*.
– ORIGIN from Old French *-aire*, *-ier*, or from Latin *-arius*, *-arium*.

-ar[4] ▶ **suffix** alteration of **-ER**[1], **-OR**[1] (as in *beggar*, *liar*).

A·ra /ˈārə, ˈe(ə)rə/ Astronomy a small and faint southern constellation, the Altar, in the Milky Way near Scorpius. ■ (as genitive **Arae** /ˈārē, ˈe(ə)rē/) used with a preceding letter or numeral to designate stars: *the star Delta Arae*.
– ORIGIN Latin.

Ar·ab /ˈarəb/ ▶ **n. 1** a member of a Semitic people, originally from the Arabian peninsula and neighboring territories, inhabiting much of the Middle East and North Africa.
2 an Arabian horse.
▶ **adj.** of or relating to Arabia and the people of Arabia: *Arab countries*.
– ORIGIN from French *Arabe*, via Latin and Greek from Arabic *ʻarab*.

> **USAGE** See usage at **ARABIAN**.

ar·a·besque /ˌarəˈbesk/ ▶ **n. 1** an ornamental design consisting of intertwined flowing lines, originally found in Arabic or Moorish decoration: [as modifier] *arabesque scrolls*. ■ Music a passage or composition with fanciful ornamentation of the melody.
2 Ballet a posture in which the body is supported on one leg, with the other leg extended horizontally backward.
– ORIGIN mid 17th cent.: from French, from Italian *arabesco* 'in the Arabic style,' from *arabo* 'Arab.'

arabesque 1

A·ra·bi·a /əˈrābēə/ (also **Arabian peninsula**) a peninsula in southwestern Asia, largely desert, that lies between the Red Sea and the Persian Gulf and is bounded on the north by Jordan and Iraq. The original homeland of the Arabs and the historic center of Islam, it comprises the states of Saudi Arabia, Yemen, Oman, Bahrain, Kuwait, Qatar, and the United Arab Emirates.

A·ra·bi·an /əˈrābēən/ ▶ **adj.** historical of or relating to Arabia or Arabs.
▶ **n.** historical **1** a native or inhabitant of Arabia.
2 (also **Arabian horse**) a horse of a breed originating in Arabia, with a distinctive dished face and high-set tail.

> **USAGE** Arab is now generally used in reference to people; the use of **Arabian** in this sense is historical.

A·ra·bi·an cam·el ▶ **n.** the domesticated one-humped camel, probably native to the deserts of North Africa and southwestern Asia. See also **DROMEDARY**. ● *Camelus dromedarius*, family Camelidae.

A·ra·bi·an Des·ert /əˈrābēən/ a desert in eastern Egypt, between the Nile River and the Red Sea. Also called **EASTERN DESERT**.

A·ra·bi·an Gulf another name for **PERSIAN GULF**.

A·ra·bi·an Nights a collection of stories and romances written in Arabic, called in full *The Arabian Nights' Entertainment*. The stories include the tales of Aladdin and Sinbad the Sailor. Also called the **THOUSAND AND ONE NIGHTS**.

A·ra·bi·an pen·in·su·la another name for **ARABIA**.

A·ra·bi·an Sea the northwestern part of the Indian Ocean, between Arabia and India.

Ar·a·bic /ˈarəbik/ ▶ **n.** the Semitic language of the Arabs, spoken by some 150 million people throughout the Middle East and North Africa.
▶ **adj.** of or relating to the literature or language of Arab people.

> Arabic is written from right to left in a characteristic cursive script of twenty-eight consonants, the vowels being indicated by additional signs. The script has been adapted for various languages, including Persian, Urdu, Malay, and (formerly) Turkish.

a

– ORIGIN Middle English: via Latin from Greek *arabikos*, from *Araps, Arab-* 'Arab.'

a·rab·i·ca /əˈrabikə/ ▶ n. **1** coffee from the most widely grown kind of coffee plant.
2 the bush of the bedstraw family that produces these beans, native to the Old World tropics. ● *Coffea arabica*, family Rubiaceae.
– ORIGIN 1920s: from Latin, feminine of *arabicus* (see ARABIC).

Ar·a·bic nu·mer·al ▶ n. any of the numerals 0, 1, 2, 3, 4, 5, 6, 7, 8, and 9. Arabic numerals reached western Europe through Arabia, replacing Roman numerals, by about AD 1200, but probably originated in India.

a·rab·i·nose /əˈrabəˌnōs, ˈarəbə-/ ▶ n. Chemistry a sugar of the pentose class that is a constituent of many plant gums.
– ORIGIN late 19th cent.: from *arabin*, a carbohydrate derived from gum arabic, (based on GUM ARABIC + -IN[1]) + -OSE[2].

ar·a·bis /ˈarəbəs/ ▶ n. a low-growing herbaceous plant that typically bears white or pink flowers and is frequently grown in rock gardens. Also called ROCK CRESS. ● Genus *Arabis*, family Brassicaceae.
– ORIGIN via medieval Latin from Greek, feminine of *Araps, Arab-* (see ARAB).

Ar·ab·ism /ˈarəˌbizəm/ ▶ n. **1** Arab culture or identity. ■ support for Arab nationalism or political interests.
2 an Arabic linguistic usage, word, or phrase.

Ar·ab·ist /ˈarəbist/ ▶ n. a person who studies Arabic civilization or language. ■ a person who supports Arab nationalism or political interests.

Ar·ab·ize /ˈarəˌbīz/ ▶ v. [with obj.] (usu. as adj. **Arabized**) give (someone or something) an Arab or Arabic character: *an Arabized script.*
– DERIVATIVES **Ar·ab·i·za·tion** /ˌarəbəˈzāshən/ n.

ar·a·ble /ˈarəbəl/ ▶ adj. (of land) used or suitable for growing crops. ■ (of crops) able to be grown on such land. ■ concerned with growing such crops: *arable farming.*
▶ n. land or crops of this type.
– ORIGIN late Middle English: from Old French, or from Latin *arabilis*, from *arare* 'to plow.'

A·ra·ca·jú /ˌäräkəˈzhoo/ a port in eastern Brazil, on the Atlantic coast; pop. 520,303 (2007).

a·ra·ca·ri /ˌäräˈsärē/ ▶ n. (pl. **aracaris**) a small toucan with a serrated bill, and typically with a green back and wings, yellow underside, and red rump. ● Genus *Pteroglossus*, family Ramphastidae: several species.
– ORIGIN early 19th cent.: via Portuguese from Tupi *arasa'ri.*

ar·a·chi·don·ic ac·id /ˌarəkiˈdänik/ ▶ n. Biochemistry a polyunsaturated fatty acid present in animal fats. It is important in metabolism, esp. in the synthesis of prostaglandins and leukotrienes, and is an essential constituent of the diet. ● Alternative name: **eicosa-5,8,11,14-enoic acid**; chem. formula: $C_{19}H_{31}COOH$.
– ORIGIN early 20th cent.: *arachidonic* formed irregularly from *arachidic* (a saturated fatty acid) + -ONE + -IC.

A·rach·ne /əˈraknē/ Greek Mythology a woman of Colophon in Lydia, a skillful weaver who challenged Athena to a contest. Athena destroyed Arachne's work and Arachne tried to hang herself, but Athena changed her into a spider.
– ORIGIN from Greek *arakhnē* 'spider.'

a·rach·nid /əˈraknid/ Zoology ▶ n. an arthropod of the class Arachnida, such as a spider or scorpion.
▶ adj. relating to or denoting arachnids.

A·rach·ni·da /əˈraknidə/ Zoology a class of chelicerate arthropods that includes spiders, scorpions, mites, and ticks. They have become adapted for a terrestrial life and possess book lungs and tracheae, and many have silk or poison glands.
– ORIGIN modern Latin (plural), from Greek *arakhnē* 'spider.'

a·rach·noid /əˈrakˌnoid/ ▶ adj. like a spider or arachnid.
▶ n. (also **arachnoid membrane** or **arachnoid mater**) Anatomy a fine, delicate membrane, the middle one of the three membranes or meninges that surround the brain and spinal cord, situated between the dura mater and the pia mater.
– ORIGIN mid 18th cent.: from modern Latin *arachnoides*, from Greek *arakhnoeidēs* 'like a cobweb,' from *arakhnē* 'spider.'

a·rach·no·pho·bi·a /əˌraknəˈfōbēə/ ▶ n. extreme or irrational fear of spiders.
– DERIVATIVES **a·rach·no·phobe** /əˈraknəˌfōb/ n., **a·rach·no·pho·bic** /-bik/ adj.
– ORIGIN 1920s: modern Latin, from Greek *arakhnē* 'spider' + -PHOBIA.

Ar·a·fat /ˈarəˌfat/, Yasser (1929–2004), Palestinian statesman, chairman of the Palestine Liberation Organization 1968–2004 and Palestinian president 1996–2004. He became leader of the new Palestine National Authority in 1994, following the signing of a PLO–Israeli peace accord for which he shared the 1994 Nobel Peace Prize with Yitzhak Rabin and Shimon Peres.

A·ra·fu·ra Sea /ˌarəˈfoorə/ a sea that lies between northern Australia and eastern Indonesia and New Guinea.

A·ra·gon[1] /ˈarəˌgän, -gən/ an autonomous region in northeastern Spain, bounded on the north by the Pyrenees and on the east by Catalonia and Valencia; capital, Saragossa. Formerly an independent kingdom, it was united with Catalonia in 1137 and with Castile in 1479. Spanish name **Aragón**.

A·ra·gon[2], Catherine of, see CATHERINE OF ARAGON.

a·rag·o·nite /əˈragəˌnīt, ˈarəgə-/ ▶ n. a mineral consisting of calcium carbonate, typically occurring in white seashells and as colorless prisms in deposits in hot springs.
– ORIGIN early 19th cent.: from the place name ARAGON[1] + -ITE[1].

ar·ak ▶ n. variant spelling of ARRACK.

a·ra·li·a /əˈrālēə, -yə/ ▶ n. a plant of a diverse group of trees and shrubs of the ginseng family, native to America and Asia. Several kinds are cultivated for their foliage and profusion of tiny flowers, and some are used in herbal medicine. ● Genus *Aralia*, family Araliaceae: several species, including the **bristly sarsaparilla** (*A. hispida*).
– ORIGIN modern Latin, of unknown origin.

Ar·al Sea /ˈarəl/ an inland sea in central Asia, on the border between Kazakhstan and Uzbekistan. Its area was reduced by one-third and serious environmental consequences resulted between 1960 and 1990 after water was diverted for irrigation.

Ar·a·mae·an /ˌarəˈmāən, -ˈmēən/ ▶ n. a member of an ancient Aramaic-speaking people inhabiting Aram (modern Syria) and part of Babylonia in the 11th–8th centuries BC.
▶ adj. of or relating to Aram or the Aramaeans.
– ORIGIN from Latin *Aramaeus* (from Greek *Aramaios*: see ARAMAIC) + -AN.

Ar·a·ma·ic /ˌarəˈmāik/ ▶ n. a Semitic language, a Syrian dialect of which was used as a lingua franca in the Near East from the 6th century BC. It gradually replaced Hebrew as the language of the Jews in those areas and was itself supplanted by Arabic in the 7th century AD.
▶ adj. of or in this language.
– ORIGIN mid 19th cent.: from Greek *Aramaios* 'of *Aram*' (the biblical name of Syria) + -IC.

ar·a·me /ˈarəˌmā, əˈrä-/ ▶ n. an edible Pacific seaweed with broad brown leaves, used in Japanese cooking. ● *Ecklonia bicyclis*, class Phaeophyceae.

ar·a·mid /ˈarəmid/ ▶ n. any of a class of synthetic polymers, related to nylon, that yield fibers of exceptional strength and thermal stability.
– ORIGIN 1970s: from *ar(omatic)* + *(poly)amid(e)*.

Ar·an /ˈarən/ ▶ adj. denoting a type of knitwear with traditional patterns, typically involving a raised cable stitch and large diamond designs.
– ORIGIN 1960s: from the ARAN ISLANDS.

a·ra·ne·id /əˈrānēid/ ▶ n. Zoology an invertebrate of an order that comprises the spiders. ● Order Araneae, in particular the family Araneidae.
– ORIGIN late 19th cent.: from modern Latin *Araneida* (former order name), from *aranea* 'spider.'

Ar·an Is·lands three islands, Inishmore, Inishmaan, and Inisheer, located off the west coast of the Republic of Ireland.

A·ran·ya·ka /äˈrənyəkə/ ▶ n. each of a set of Hindu sacred treatises based on the Brahmanas, composed in Sanskrit *c.*700 BC. Intended only for initiates, the Aranyakas contain mystical and philosophical material and explications of esoteric rites.

A·rap·a·ho /əˈrapəˌhō/ ▶ n. **1** (pl. **same** or **Arapahos**) a member of a North American Indian people living chiefly on the Great Plains, esp. in Wyoming.
2 the Algonquian language of this people.
▶ adj. of or relating to this people or their language.
– ORIGIN from Crow *aaraxpéahu*, probably literally 'those having many tattoo marks.'

ar·a·pai·ma /ˌarəˈpīmə/ ▶ n. a large, long edible freshwater fish native to tropical South America. ● *Arapaima gigas*, family Osteoglossidae.
– ORIGIN mid 19th cent.: from Tupi.

Ar·a·rat, Mount /ˈarəˌrat/ two volcanic peaks in eastern Turkey, near the borders with Armenia and Iran. The higher peak, which rises to 16,946 feet (5,165 m), is the traditional site of the resting place of Noah's ark after the Flood (Gen. 8:4).

a·ra·tion·al /āˈrashənl/ ▶ adj. not based on or governed by reason.

Ar·au·ca·ni·an /ˌarôˈkānēən/ ▶ n. **1** a member of a group of South American Indian peoples of Chile and adjacent parts of Argentina, of which the only people that has a surviving cultural identity is the Mapuche.
2 the family of languages spoken by this people.
▶ adj. relating to or denoting this people or their language. See also MAPUCHE.
– ORIGIN from Spanish *Araucania*, a region in Chile, + -AN.

ar·au·car·i·a /ˌarôˈke(ə)rēə/ ▶ n. an evergreen conifer of a genus that includes the monkey puzzle and the Norfolk Island pine, having stiff sharp leaves. ● Genus *Araucaria*, family Araucariaceae.
– ORIGIN modern Latin, from Spanish *Arauco*, the name of a province of Araucania, Chile.

Ar·a·wak /ˈarəˌwäk/ ▶ n. (pl. **same** or **Arawaks**)
1 a member of a people originally of the Greater Antilles and adjacent South America, now living mainly in Guiana. They were forced out of the Antilles by the more warlike Caribs shortly before Spanish expansion in the Caribbean.
2 any of the Arawakan languages of these peoples.
▶ adj. designating or relating to this people or their languages.

Ar·a·wak·an /ˌarəˈwäkən/ ▶ adj. **1** of or relating to the Arawak people.
2 denoting or belonging to a widely scattered family of South American Indian languages, most of which are now extinct or nearly so.
▶ n. this family of languages.

arb /ärb/ ▶ n. informal short for ARBITRAGEUR.

ar·ba·lest /ˈärbəlist/ ▶ n. historical a crossbow with a special mechanism for drawing back and releasing the string.
– ORIGIN Old English *arblast*, from Old French *arbaleste*, from late Latin *arcubalista*, from Latin *arcus* 'bow' + *ballista* (see BALLISTA).

ar·bi·ter /ˈärbitər/ ▶ n. a person who settles a dispute or has ultimate authority in a matter: *the military acted as arbiter of conflicts between political groups.* ■ a person whose views or actions have great influence over trends in social behavior: *an arbiter of taste.*
– ORIGIN late Middle English: from Latin, 'judge, supreme ruler.'

ar·bi·ter e·le·gan·ti·a·rum /ˌeliˌganshēˈärəm/ (also **arbiter elegantiae** /ˌeliˈganshēˌē, -ī/) ▶ n. a judge of artistic taste and etiquette.
– ORIGIN early 19th cent.: Latin, 'judge of elegance,' used by Tacitus to describe PETRONIUS, arbiter of taste at Nero's court.

ar·bi·trage /ˈärbiˌträzh/ ▶ n. the simultaneous buying and selling of securities, currency, or commodities in different markets or in derivative forms in order to take advantage of differing prices for the same asset.
▶ v. [no obj.] buy and sell assets in such a way.
– ORIGIN late Middle English (originally denoting the exercise of individual judgment): from French, from *arbitrer* 'give judgment,' from Latin *arbitrari* (see ARBITRATE). The current sense dates from the late 19th cent.

ar·bi·tra·geur /ˌärbiträˈzhər, ˈärbiˌträzhər/ (also **arbitrager** /ˈärbiˌträzhər/) ▶ n. a person who engages in arbitrage.
– ORIGIN late 19th cent.: from French, from *arbitrer* 'give judgment,' from Latin *arbitrari* (see ARBITRATE).

ar·bi·tral /ˈärbitrəl/ ▶ adj. [attrib.] relating to or resulting from the use of an arbitrator to settle a dispute.
– ORIGIN late 15th cent.: from late Latin *arbitralis*, from *arbiter* 'judge, supreme ruler.'

ar·bit·ra·ment /ärˈbitrəmənt/ ▶ n. the settling of a dispute by an arbitrator. ■ an authoritative decision made by an arbitrator.
– ORIGIN late Middle English: from Old French *arbitrement*, from medieval Latin *arbitramentum*, from *arbitrari* (see ARBITRATE).

ar·bi·trar·y /ˈärbiˌtrerē/ ▶ adj. based on random choice or personal whim, rather than any reason or system: *his mealtimes were entirely arbitrary.* ■ (of power or a ruling body) unrestrained and autocratic in the use of authority: *arbitrary rule by King and bishops has been made impossible.* ■ Mathematics (of a constant or other quantity) of unspecified value.
– DERIVATIVES **ar·bi·trar·i·ly** /ˌärbiˈtre(ə)rəlē/ adv., **ar·bi·trar·i·ness** n.
– ORIGIN late Middle English (in the sense 'dependent on one's will or pleasure, discretionary'): from Latin *arbitrarius*, from *arbiter* 'judge, supreme ruler,' perhaps influenced by French *arbitraire*.

ar·bi·trate /ˈärbiˌtrāt/ ▶ v. [no obj.] (of an independent person or body) reach an authoritative judgment or settlement: *the board has the power to arbitrate in disputes* | [with obj.] *it set up a commission to arbitrate border tensions.*
– ORIGIN mid 16th cent.: from Latin *arbitrat-* 'judged,' from *arbitrari*, from *arbiter* 'judge, supreme ruler.'

ar·bi·tra·tion /ˌärbiˈtrāSHən/ ▶ **n.** the use of an arbitrator to settle a dispute.
– PHRASES **go to arbitration** submit a dispute to an arbitrator.

ar·bi·tra·tor /ˈärbiˌtrātər/ ▶ **n.** an independent person or body officially appointed to settle a dispute.

ar·bor[1] /ˈärbər/ ▶ **n.** an axle or spindle on which something revolves. ■ a device holding a tool in a lathe.
– ORIGIN mid 17th cent.: from French *arbre* 'tree, axis.' The spelling change was due to association with Latin *arbor* 'tree.'

ar·bor[2] (Brit. **arbour**) ▶ **n.** a shady garden alcove with sides and a roof formed by trees or climbing plants trained over a wooden framework.
– ORIGIN Middle English (also denoting a lawn or flower bed): from Old French *erbier*, from *erbe* 'grass, herb,' from Latin *herba*. The phonetic change to *ar-* (common in words having *er-* before a consonant) was assisted by association with Latin *arbor* 'tree.'

Ar·bor Day ▶ **n.** a day dedicated annually to public tree-planting in the US, Australia, and other countries. It is usually observed in late April or early May.
– ORIGIN from Latin *arbor* 'tree.'

ar·bo·re·al /ärˈbôrēəl/ ▶ **adj.** (chiefly of animals) living in trees: *arboreal rodents*. ■ of or relating to trees.
– DERIVATIVES **ar·bo·re·al·i·ty** /ärˌbôrēˈalitē/ **n.**
– ORIGIN mid 17th cent.: from Latin *arboreus*, from *arbor* 'tree,' + -AL.

ar·bo·res·cent /ˌärbəˈresənt/ ▶ **adj.** chiefly Botany treelike in growth or appearance: *arborescent ferns*.
– DERIVATIVES **ar·bo·res·cence n.**
– ORIGIN late 17th cent.: from Latin *arborescent-* 'growing into a tree,' from *arborescere*, from *arbor* 'tree.'

ar·bo·re·tum /ˌärbəˈrētəm/ ▶ **n.** (pl. **arboretums** or **arboreta** /-ˈrētə/) a botanical garden devoted to trees.
– ORIGIN early 19th cent.: from Latin, 'a place with trees,' from *arbor* 'tree' + -ETUM.

ar·bor·i·cul·ture /ˈärbəriˌkəlCHər, ärˈbôri-/ ▶ **n.** the cultivation of trees and shrubs.
– DERIVATIVES **ar·bor·i·cul·tur·al** /ˌärbəriˈkəlCHərəl, ärˈbôriˌkəl-/ **adj.**, **ar·bor·i·cul·tur·ist** /ˌärbəriˈkəlCHərist, ärˈbôrəˌkəl-/ **n.**
– ORIGIN early 19th cent.: from Latin *arbor* 'tree' + CULTURE, on the pattern of words such as *agriculture*.

Ar·bo·ri·o /ärˈbôrē-ō/ ▶ **n.** a variety of round-grained rice produced in Italy and used in making risotto.
– ORIGIN Italian.

ar·bor·ist /ˈärbərist/ ▶ **n.** a tree surgeon.

ar·bor·i·za·tion /ˌärbərəˈzāSHən/ ▶ **n.** Anatomy a fine branching structure at the end of a nerve fiber.

ar·bor vi·tae /ˈärbər ˈvītē/ (also **arborvitae**) ▶ **n.**
1 a North American and eastern Asian evergreen coniferous tree of the cypress family. ● Genus *Thuja*, family Cupressaceae: several species, in particular the northern white cedar (see WHITE CEDAR).
2 the arborescent appearance of the white matter in a vertical section of the cerebellum.
– ORIGIN mid 16th cent.: from Latin, literally 'tree of life,' probably with reference to its medicinal use.

ar·bour ▶ **n.** British spelling of ARBOR[2].

ar·bo·vi·rus /ˈärbəˌvīrəs/ ▶ **n.** Medicine any of a group of viruses that are transmitted by mosquitoes, ticks, or other arthropods. They include encephalitis, dengue, and yellow fever.
– ORIGIN 1950s: from *ar(thropod)-bo(rne)* + VIRUS.

Ar·bus /ˈärbəs/, Diane (1923–71), US photographer. She is best known for her disturbing images of people, esp. the poor or unusual, on city streets.

Ar·buth·not /ärˈbəTHnət, ˈärbəTHˌnät/, John (1667–1735), Scottish physician and writer. His satirical *History of John Bull* (1712) was the origin of John Bull as the personification of the typical Englishman.

ar·bu·tus /ärˈbyo͞otəs/ ▶ **n.** either of two evergreen plants of the family Ericaceae (heath family). ● a tree or shrub of the genus *Arbutus*, which includes the strawberry tree. ● (in full **trailing arbutus**) a North American trailing plant that bears pink or white flowers (*Epigaea repens*). Also called MAYFLOWER.
– ORIGIN from Latin.

ARC /ärk/ ▶ **abbr.** ■ Medicine AIDS-related complex. ■ American Red Cross.

arc /ärk/ ▶ **n. 1** a part of the circumference of a circle or other curve. ■ a curved shape, or something shaped like a curve: *the huge arc of the sky*. ■ a curving trajectory: *he swung his flashlight in a wide arc*. ■ [as modifier] Mathematics indicating the inverse of a trigonometrical function. [from the former method of defining trigonometrical functions by arcs.]
2 (also **electric arc**) a luminous electrical discharge between two electrodes or other points.
3 (in a novel, play, or movie) the development or resolution of the narrative or principal theme: *his transformation provides the emotional arc of the story*.
▶ **v.** (**arcs, arcing, arced**) [no obj.] **1** [with adverbial of direction] move with a curving trajectory: *the ball arced across the room*.
2 (usu. as noun **arcing**) form an electric arc: *check that switches operate properly with no sign of arcing*.
– PHRASES **minute of arc** see MINUTE[1] (sense 2). **second of arc** see SECOND[2] (sense 2).
– ORIGIN late Middle English (denoting the path of a celestial object, esp. the sun, from horizon to horizon): via Old French from Latin *arcus* 'bow, curve.'

Tudor

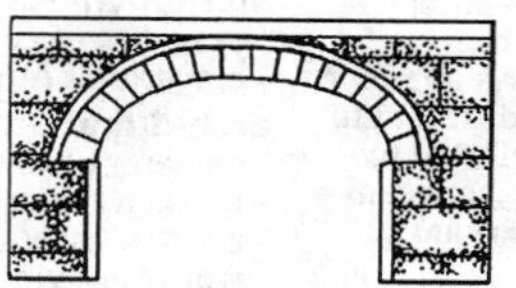
basket handle

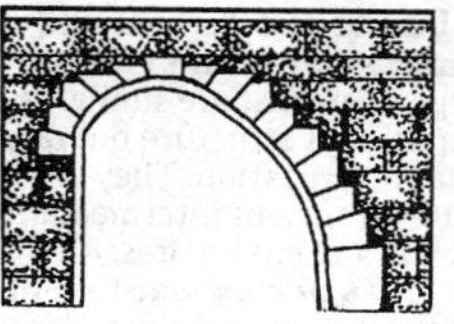
rampant

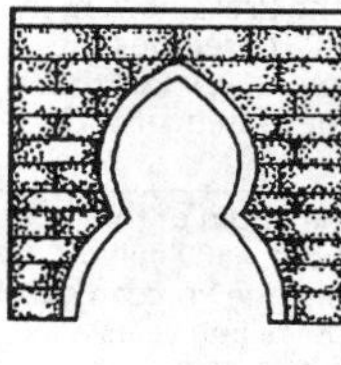
trefoil

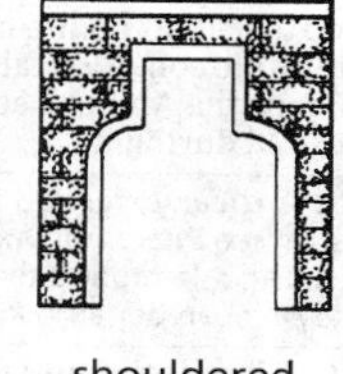
shouldered

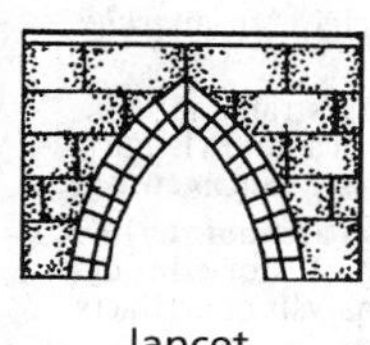
lancet

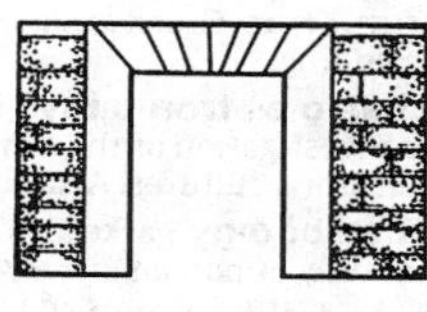
flat

horseshoe

equilateral

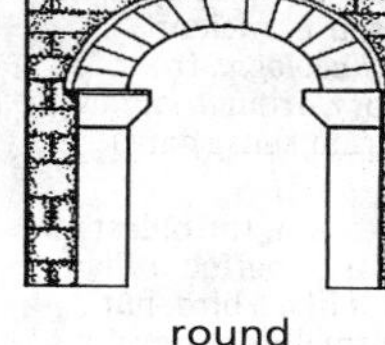
round

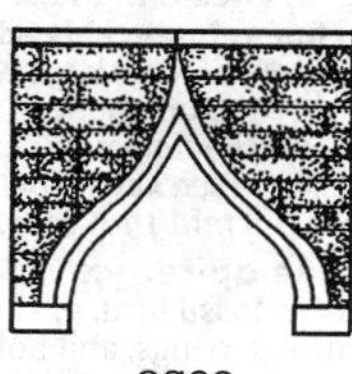
ogee

types of arch

ar·cade /ärˈkād/ ▶ **n. 1** a covered passageway with arches along one or both sides. ■ a covered walk with stores along one or both sides. ■ Architecture a series of arches supporting a wall, or set along it.
2 short for VIDEO ARCADE.
– DERIVATIVES **ar·cad·ed adj.**, **ar·cad·ing n.**
– ORIGIN late 17th cent.: from French, from Provençal *arcada* or Italian *arcata*, based on Latin *arcus* 'bow' (see ARC).

Ar·ca·di·a /ärˈkādēə/ **1** a mountainous district in the Peloponnese of southern Greece. In poetic fantasy it represents a pastoral paradise, and in Greek mythology it is the home of Pan.
2 a city in southwestern California, northeast of Los Angeles; pop. 56,248 (est. 2008). The Santa Anita racetrack is here.

Ar·ca·di·an /ärˈkādēən/ ▶ **n.** a native of Arcadia. ■ literary an idealized country dweller.
▶ **adj.** of or relating to Arcadia. ■ literary of or relating to an ideal rustic paradise.
– ORIGIN late 16th cent.: from Latin *Arcadius*, from Greek *Arkadia* (see ARCADIA).

Ar·ca·dy /ˈärkədē/ ▶ **n.** literary an ideal rustic paradise.
– ORIGIN late 16th cent.: from Greek *Arkadia* (see ARCADIA).

ar·ca·na /ärˈkānə/ ▶ **plural n.** [treated as sing. or pl.] (sing. **arcanum** /-nəm/) secrets or mysteries: *his knowledge of federal budget arcana is legendary*. ■ [treated as sing.] either of the two groups of cards in a tarot pack: the twenty-two trump cards (the **major arcana**) and the fifty-six suit cards (the **minor arcana**).
– ORIGIN mid 16th cent.: from Latin, neuter plural of *arcanus* (see ARCANE).

ar·cane /ärˈkān/ ▶ **adj.** understood by few; mysterious or secret: *modern math and its arcane notation*.
– DERIVATIVES **ar·cane·ly adv.**
– ORIGIN mid 16th cent.: from Latin *arcanus*, from *arcere* 'to shut up,' from *arca* 'chest.'

Ar·ca·ro /ärˈkarō, -ˈke(ə)rō/, Eddie (1916–97), US jockey; full name *George Edward Arcaro*. He was the first two-time Triple Crown winner, riding Whirlaway in 1941 and Citation in 1948.

Arc de Tri·omphe /ˈärk də trēˈôNf/ a ceremonial arch standing at the top of the Champs-Élysées in Paris, commissioned by Napoleon to commemorate his victories in 1805–06. Inspired by the Arch of Constantine in Rome, it was completed in 1836.

Arc de Triomphe

arc fur·nace ▶ **n.** a furnace that uses an electric arc as a heat source, esp. for steelmaking.

arch[1] /ärCH/ ▶ **n.** a curved symmetrical structure spanning an opening and typically supporting the weight of a bridge, roof, or wall above it. ■ a structure of this type forming a passageway or a ceremonial monument: *a triumphal arch*. ■ a shape resembling such a structure or a thing with such a shape: *the delicate arch of his eyebrows*. ■ the inner side of the foot.
▶ **v. 1** [no obj.] have the curved shape of an arch: *a beautiful bridge that arched over a canal*. ■ form or cause to form the curved shape of an arch: *her eyebrows arched in surprise* | [with obj.] *she arched her back*.
2 [with obj.] (usu. as adj. **arched**) provide (a bridge, building, or part of a building) with an arch: *high arched windows*. ■ archaic or literary span (something) by or as if by an arch: *the vine arched his evening seat*.
– ORIGIN Middle English: from Old French *arche*, based on Latin *arcus* 'bow' (see ARC).

arch[2] ▶ **adj.** deliberately or affectedly playful and teasing: *arch observations about even the most mundane matters*.
– DERIVATIVES **arch·ly adv.**, **arch·ness n.**
– ORIGIN mid 16th cent. (in the sense 'chief, principal'): from ARCH-, because of its association with words such as *rogue*.

arch- ▶ **comb. form** chief; principal: *archbishop*. ■ preeminent of its kind: *archenemy*. ■ (in unfavorable senses) out-and-out: *arch-scoundrel*.
– ORIGIN via Latin from Greek *arkhi-*, from *arkhos* 'chief.'

ar·chae·a /ärˈkēə/ ▶ **plural n.** another term for ARCHAEBACTERIA.
– DERIVATIVES **ar·chae·an** (also **archaeal**) **adj.** & **n.**

Ar·chae·an ▶ **adj.** British spelling of ARCHEAN.

PRONUNCIATION KEY ə *ago, up*; ər *over, fur*; a *hat*; ā *ate*; ä *car*; e *let*; ē *see*; i *fit*; ī *by*; NG *sing*; ō *go*; ô *law, for*; oi *toy*; o͝o *good*; o͞o *goo*; ou *out*; TH *thin*; TH *then*; ZH *vision*

a

ar·chae·bac·te·ri·a /ˌärkēˌbakˈti(ə)rēə/ ▶ **plural n.** (sing. **archaebacterium** /-ˈti(ə)rēəm/) Biology microorganisms that are similar to bacteria in size and simplicity of structure but radically different in molecular organization. They are now believed to constitute an ancient intermediate group between the bacteria and eukaryotes. Also called ARCHAEA.
– DERIVATIVES **ar·chae·bac·te·ri·al** adj.
– ORIGIN modern Latin (plural), from Greek *arkhaios* 'primitive.'

archaeo- (also **archeo-**) ▶ **comb. form** relating to archaeology or prehistoric times: *archaeoastronomy* | *archaeomagnetism*.
– ORIGIN from Greek *arkhaios* 'ancient,' from *arkhē* 'beginning.'

ar·chae·o·as·tron·o·my /ˌärkēō-əˈstränəmē/ ▶ **n.** the investigation of the astronomical knowledge of prehistoric cultures. Also called ASTROARCHAEOLOGY.

ar·chae·ol·o·gy /ˌärkēˈäləjē/ (also **archeology**) ▶ **n.** the study of human history and prehistory through the excavation of sites and the analysis of artifacts and other physical remains.
– DERIVATIVES **ar·chae·o·log·ic** /-əˈläjik/ adj., **ar·chae·o·log·i·cal** /-əˈläjikəl/ adj., **ar·chae·o·log·i·cal·ly** adv., **ar·chae·ol·o·gist** /-jist/ n.
– ORIGIN early 17th cent. (in the sense 'ancient history'): from modern Latin *archaeologia*, from Greek *arkhaiologia* 'ancient history,' from *arkhaios* 'ancient' (see ARCHAEO-). The current sense dates from the mid 19th cent.

ar·chae·op·ter·yx /ˌärkēˈäptəriks/ ▶ **n.** the oldest known fossil bird, of the late Jurassic period. It had feathers, wings, and hollow bones like a bird, but teeth, a bony tail, and legs like a small coelurosaur dinosaur. ● *Archaeopteryx lithographica*, subclass Archaeornithes.
– ORIGIN from Greek *arkhaios* 'ancient' (see ARCHAEO-) + *pterux* 'wing.'

ar·cha·ic /ärˈkāik/ ▶ **adj.** very old or old-fashioned: *prisons are run on archaic methods*. ■ (of a word or a style of language) no longer in everyday use but sometimes used to impart an old-fashioned flavor. ■ of an early period of art or culture, esp. the 7th–6th centuries BC in Greece: *the archaic temple at Corinth*.
– DERIVATIVES **ar·cha·i·cal·ly** adv.
– ORIGIN mid 19th cent.: from French *archaïque*, from Greek *arkhaikos*, from *arkhaios*, from *arkhē* 'beginning.'

ar·cha·ism /ˈärkēˌizəm, ˈärkā-/ ▶ **n.** a thing that is very old or old-fashioned. ■ an archaic word or style of language or art. ■ the use or conscious imitation of very old or old-fashioned styles or features in language or art.
– DERIVATIVES **ar·cha·is·tic** /ˌärkēˈistik, ˌärkā-/ adj.
– ORIGIN mid 17th cent.: from modern Latin *archaismus*, from Greek *arkhaismos*, from *arkhaizein* 'imitate archaic styles,' from *arkhaios* 'ancient,' from *arkhē* 'beginning.'

ar·cha·iz·ing /ˈärkēˌīziNG, ˈärkā-/ ▶ **adj.** consciously imitating a word or a style of language or art that is very old or old-fashioned: *some archaizing poetry*.

Arch·an·gel /ˈärkˌānjəl/ a port in northwestern Russia, on the White Sea; pop. 348,700 (est. 2008). It is named after the monastery of the Archangel Michael that is situated here. Russian name ARKHANGELSK.

arch·an·gel /ˈärkˌānjəl/ ▶ **n.** an angel of high rank. ■ in traditional Christian angelology, a being of the eighth order of the ninefold celestial hierarchy.
– DERIVATIVES **arch·an·gel·ic** /ˌärkanˈjelik/ adj.
– ORIGIN Middle English, from Anglo-Norman French *archangele*, via ecclesiastical Latin from ecclesiastical Greek *arkhangelos*, from *arkhi-* 'chief' + *angelos* 'messenger, angel.'

arch·bish·op /ˈärCHˈbiSHəp/ ▶ **n.** the chief bishop responsible for an archdiocese.
– ORIGIN Old English, from ARCH- 'chief' + *biscop* (see BISHOP), replacing earlier *heah-biscop* 'high bishop.'

arch·bish·op·ric /ˌärCHˈbiSHəprik/ ▶ **n.** the office of an archbishop. ■ an archdiocese.
– ORIGIN Old English *arcebiscoprice* (see ARCH-, BISHOPRIC).

arch·dea·con /ˈärCHˈdēkən/ ▶ **n.** a senior Christian cleric (in the early Church a deacon, in the modern Anglican church a priest) to whom a bishop delegates certain responsibilities.
– ORIGIN Old English *arce-*, *ercediacon*, from ecclesiastical Latin *archidiaconus*, from ecclesiastical Greek *arkhidiakonos*, from *arkhi-* 'chief' + *diakonos* (see DEACON).

arch·dea·con·ry /ˌärCHˈdēkənrē/ ▶ **n.** (pl. **archdeaconries**) the office of an archdeacon. ■ the district for which an archdeacon is responsible. ■ the residence of an archdeacon.

arch·di·o·cese /ˌärCHˈdīəsis, -ˌsēz/ ▶ **n.** the district for which an archbishop is responsible.
– DERIVATIVES **arch·di·oc·e·san** /ˌärCHdīˈäsəsən/ adj.

arch·duch·ess /ˈärCHˈdəCHis/ ▶ **n.** historical the wife or widow of an archduke. ■ a daughter of the emperor of Austria.

arch·duke /ˈärCHˈd(y)o͞ok/ ▶ **n.** historical a son of the emperor of Austria.
– DERIVATIVES **arch·du·cal** /ˌärCHˈd(y)o͞okəl/ adj.
– ORIGIN early 16th cent.: from Old French *archeduc*, from Merovingian Latin *archidux*, *archiduc-*, from *archi-* 'chief' + *dux*, *duc-* (see DUKE).

Ar·che·an /ärˈkēən/ (Brit. **Archaean**) ▶ **adj.** Geology of, relating to, or denoting the eon that constitutes the earlier (or middle) part of the Precambrian, in which there was no life on earth. It precedes the Proterozoic eon. Also called AZOIC. ■ (as noun **the Archean**) the Archean eon or the system of rocks deposited during it.

> The Archean extended from the origin of the earth (see PRECAMBRIAN) to about 2,500 million years ago. In models that include the Priscoan eon, the Archean began about 4,000 million years ago.

– ORIGIN late 19th cent.: from Greek *arkhaios* 'ancient' + -AN.

ar·che·go·ni·um /ˌärkiˈgōnēəm/ ▶ **n.** (pl. **archegonia** /-nēə/) Botany the female sex organ in mosses, liverworts, ferns, and most conifers.
– ORIGIN mid 19th cent.: modern Latin, from Greek *arkhegonos*, from *arkhe-* 'first' + *gonos* 'race.'

arch·en·e·my /ˈärCHˈenəmē/ ▶ **n.** a person who is extremely hostile or opposed to someone or something: *the twins were archenemies*. ■ (**the Archenemy**) the Devil.

arch·en·ter·on /ärkˈentəˌrän/ ▶ **n.** Embryology the rudimentary alimentary cavity of an embryo at the gastrula stage.
– ORIGIN late 19th cent.: from Greek *arkhē* 'beginning' + *enteron* 'intestine.'

archeo- ▶ **comb. form** ARCHAEO-.

ar·che·ol·o·gy ▶ **n.** variant of ARCHAEOLOGY.

arch·er /ˈärCHər/ ▶ **n.** a person who shoots with a bow and arrows, esp. at a target for sport. ■ (**the Archer**) the zodiacal sign or constellation Sagittarius.
– ORIGIN Middle English: from Old French *archier*, based on Latin *arcus* 'bow.'

ar·cher·fish /ˈärCHərˌfiSH/ ▶ **n.** (pl. **same** or **archerfishes**) a freshwater fish that knocks insect prey off overhanging vegetation by spitting water at it. It is native to Asia, Australia, and the Philippines. ● Genus *Toxotes*, family Toxotidae: several species, in particular *T. jaculator*.

ar·cher·y /ˈärCHərē/ ▶ **n.** the sport or skill of shooting with a bow and arrows, esp. at a target.
– ORIGIN late Middle English: from Old French *archerie*, from *archier* (see ARCHER).

arch·es /ˈärCHiz/ ▶ **plural n.** [treated as sing.] used in names of moths with curving archlike patterns on the wings, such as **dark arches**. ● Several genera in the families Noctuidae and Notodontidae.

ar·che·typ·al /ˌärk(i)ˈtīpəl/ ▶ **adj.** very typical of a certain kind of person or thing: *the archetypal country doctor*. ■ recurrent as a symbol or motif in literature, art, or mythology: *an archetypal journey representing the quest for identity*. ■ of, relating to, or denoting an original that has been imitated: *the archetypal believer, Abraham*. ■ relating to or denoting Jungian archetypes.

ar·che·type /ˈärk(i)ˌtīp/ ▶ **n.** a very typical example of a certain person or thing: *the book is a perfect archetype of the genre*. ■ an original that has been imitated: *the archetype of faith is Abraham*. ■ a recurrent symbol or motif in literature, art, or mythology: *mythological archetypes of good and evil*. ■ Psychoanalysis (in Jungian psychology) a primitive mental image inherited from the earliest human ancestors, and supposed to be present in the collective unconscious.
– DERIVATIVES **ar·che·typ·i·cal** /ˌärk(i)ˈtipikəl/ adj.
– ORIGIN mid 16th cent.: via Latin from Greek *arkhetupon* 'something molded first as a model,' from *arkhe-* 'primitive' + *tupos* 'a model.'

arch·fiend /ˈärCHˈfēnd/ ▶ **n.** literary a chief fiend, esp. the Devil.

ar·chi·di·ac·o·nal /ˌärkidīˈakənl/ ▶ **adj.** of or relating to an archdeacon.
– DERIVATIVES **ar·chi·di·ac·o·nate** /-nit/ n.
– ORIGIN late Middle English: from medieval Latin *archidiaconalis*, from *archi-* 'chief' + *diaconalis* (see DIACONAL).

ar·chi·e·pis·co·pal /ˌärkēəˈpiskəpəl/ ▶ **adj.** of or relating to an archbishop.
– DERIVATIVES **ar·chi·e·pis·co·pa·cy** /-əˈpiskəpəsē/ n. (pl. **archiepiscopacies**), **ar·chi·e·pis·co·pate** /-pit, -ˌpāt/ n.
– ORIGIN early 17th cent.: via ecclesiastical Latin from Greek *arkhiepiskopos* 'archbishop' (from *arkhi-* 'chief' + *episkopos* 'bishop') + -AL.

ar·chil /ˈärkəl, -CHəl/ ▶ **n.** archaic spelling of ORCHIL.

Ar·chil·o·chus /ärˈkiləkəs/ (8th or 7th century BC), Greek poet. He is credited with the invention of iambic meter.

ar·chi·man·drite /ˌärkəˈmanˌdrīt/ ▶ **n.** the head of a large monastery or group of monasteries in the Orthodox Church. ■ an honorary title given to a monastic priest.
– ORIGIN mid 17th cent.: via ecclesiastical Latin, from ecclesiastical Greek *arkhimandritēs*, from *arkhi-* 'chief' + *mandra* 'monastery.'

Ar·chi·me·de·an screw /ˌärkəˈmēdēən/ ▶ **n.** a device invented by Archimedes for raising water by means of a spiral within a tube.

Ar·chi·me·des /ˌärkəˈmēdēz/ (*c*.287–212 BC), Greek mathematician and inventor from Syracuse. He is noted for his discovery of Archimedes' principle (legend has it that he made this discovery while taking a bath and ran through the streets shouting "Eureka!"). Among his mathematical discoveries are the ratio of the radius of a circle to its circumference and formulas for the surface area and volume of a sphere and of a cylinder.
– DERIVATIVES **Ar·chi·me·de·an** /-ˈmēdēən/ adj.

Ar·chi·me·des' prin·ci·ple Physics a result stating that a body totally or partially immersed in a fluid is subject to an upward force equal in magnitude to the weight of fluid it displaces.

ar·chi·pel·a·go /ˌärkəˈpeləˌgō/ ▶ **n.** (pl. **archipelagos** or **archipelagoes**) a group of islands. ■ a sea or stretch of water containing many islands.
– ORIGIN early 16th cent.: from Italian *arcipelago*, from Greek *arkhi-* 'chief' + *pelagos* 'sea.' The word was originally used as a proper name (*the Archipelago* 'the Aegean Sea'): the generalization of meaning occurred because the Aegean Sea is remarkable for its large numbers of islands.

Ar·chi·pen·ko /ˌärkəˈp(y)eNGkō/, Aleksandr (Porfirevich) (1887–1964), US sculptor; born in Russia. He adapted cubist techniques to sculpture.

Ar·chi·pié·la·go de Co·lón /ˌärCHēˈpyāləˌgō dā kōˈlōn/ official Spanish name for GALAPAGOS ISLANDS.

ar·chi·tect /ˈärkiˌtekt/ ▶ **n.** a person who designs buildings and in many cases also supervises their construction. ■ a person who is responsible for inventing or realizing a particular idea or project: *a chief architect of the plan to slash income taxes*.
▶ **v.** [with obj.] (usu. **be architected**) Computing design and make: *few software packages were architected with Ethernet access in mind*.
– ORIGIN mid 16th cent.: from French *architecte*, from Italian *architetto*, via Latin from Greek *arkhitektōn*, from *arkhi-* 'chief' + *tektōn* 'builder.'

ar·chi·tec·ton·ic /ˌärkitekˈtänik/ ▶ **adj.** of or relating to architecture or architects. ■ (of an artistic composition or physical appearance) having a clearly defined structure, esp. one that is artistically pleasing: *the painting's architectonic harmony*.
▶ **n.** (**architectonics**) [usu. treated as sing.] the scientific study of architecture. ■ musical, literary, or artistic structure: *the architectonics of Latin prose*.
– DERIVATIVES **ar·chi·tec·ton·i·cal·ly** /-ik(ə)lē/ adv.
– ORIGIN mid 17th cent.: via Latin from Greek *arkhitektonikos*, from *arkhitektōn* (see ARCHITECT).

ar·chi·tec·ture /ˈärkiˌtekCHər/ ▶ **n. 1** the art or practice of designing and constructing buildings. ■ the style in which a building is designed or constructed, esp. with regard to a specific period, place, or culture: *Victorian architecture*. **2** the complex or carefully designed structure of something: *the chemical architecture of the human brain*. ■ the conceptual structure and logical organization of a computer or computer-based system: *a client/server architecture*.
– DERIVATIVES **ar·chi·tec·tur·al** /ˌärkiˈtekCHərəl/ adj., **ar·chi·tec·tur·al·ly** /ˌärkiˈtekCHərəlē/ adv.
– ORIGIN mid 16th cent.: from Latin *architectura*, from *architectus* (see ARCHITECT).

ar·chi·trave /ˈärkiˌtrāv/ ▶ **n. 1** (in classical architecture) a main beam resting across the tops of columns, specifically the lower third entablature. **2** the molded frame around a doorway or window. ■ a molding around the exterior of an arch.
– ORIGIN mid 16th cent.: from French, from Italian, from *archi-* 'chief' + *-trave* from Latin *trabs*, *trab-* 'a beam.'

ar·chive /ˈärˌkīv/ (usu. **archives**) ▶ **n.** a collection of historical documents or records providing information about a place, institution, or group of people: *source materials in local archives* | [as modifier] *a section of archive film*. ■ the place where such documents or records are kept: *to get into the archives I had to fill in a request form*.
▶ **v.** [with obj.] place or store (something) in such a collection or place. ■ Computing transfer (data) to a less frequently used storage medium such as

magnetic tape, typically external to the computer system and having a greater storage capacity.
– DERIVATIVES **ar·chi·val** /är'kīvəl/ **adj.**
– ORIGIN early 17th cent. (in the sense 'place where records are kept'): from French *archives* (plural), from Latin *archiva, archia*, from Greek *arkheia* 'public records,' from *arkhē* 'government.' The verb dates from the late 19th cent.

ar·chi·vist /'ärkəvist, -ˌkī-/ ▶ **n.** a person who maintains and is in charge of archives.

ar·chi·volt /'ärkəˌvōlt/ ▶ **n.** a band of molding, resembling an architrave, around the lower curve of an arch. ■ the lower curve itself from impost to impost of the columns.
– ORIGIN mid 17th cent.: from French *archivolte* or Italian *archivolto*, based on Latin *arcus* 'bow, arch' + *volvere* 'to roll.'

arch·lute /'ärCHˌlo͞ot/ ▶ **n.** a bass lute with an extended neck and unstopped bass strings.
– ORIGIN mid 17th cent.: from French *archiluth*, from *archi-* 'chief' + *luth* (see LUTE[1]).

ar·chon /'ärˌkän/ ▶ **n.** each of the nine chief magistrates in ancient Athens. ■ any ruler: *rock's archons are disc jockeys and concert promoters.*
– DERIVATIVES **ar·chon·ship** /-ˌSHip/ **n.**
– ORIGIN late 16th cent.: from Greek *arkhōn* 'ruler,' noun use of the present participle of *arkhein* 'to rule.'

ar·cho·saur /'ärkəˌsôr/ (also **archosaurus** /ˌärkə'sôrəs/) ▶ **n.** Zoology & Paleontology a reptile of a large group that includes the dinosaurs and pterosaurs, represented today only by the crocodilians. ● Subdivision Archosauria, subclass Diapsida.
– DERIVATIVES **ar·cho·sau·ri·an** /ˌärkə'sôrēən/ **adj.**
– ORIGIN 1930s: from modern Latin *Archosauria*, from Greek *arkhos* 'chief' or *arkhōn* 'ruler' + -SAUR.

arch·priest /'ärCH'prēst/ ▶ **n.** a chief priest.

arch·way /'ärCHˌwā/ ▶ **n.** a curved structure forming a passage or entrance.

arc light (also **arc lamp**) ▶ **n.** a light source using an electric arc.

arc min·ute /'minit/ ▶ **n.** see MINUTE[1] (sense 2).

arc sec·ond (also **second of arc**) ▶ **n.** see SECOND[2] (sense 2).

arc sine (abbr.: **arcsin**) ▶ **n.** a mathematical function that is the inverse of the sine function.

arc tan·gent (abbr.: **arctan**) ▶ **n.** a mathematical function that is the inverse of the tangent function.

Arc·tic /'ärktik, 'ärtik/ ▶ **adj. 1** of or relating to the regions around the North Pole: *an Arctic explorer.* ■ (of animals or plants) living or growing in such regions. ■ designed for use in such regions: *Arctic clothing.*
2 (**arctic**) informal (of weather conditions) very cold.
▶ **n. 1** (**the Arctic**) the regions around the North Pole.
2 (**arctics** /'ärtiks/) thick waterproof overshoes extending to the ankle or above.
3 (**arctic**) a drab-colored hairy butterfly of the arctic and subarctic regions of the New World. ● Genus *Oenis*, subfamily Satyrinae, family Nymphalidae.
– ORIGIN late Middle English: via Old French from Latin *arcticus, articus*, from Greek *arktikos*, from *arktos* 'bear, Ursa Major, North Star.'

Arc·tic Ar·chi·pel·a·go the name for all of the islands that lie north of mainland Canada and the Arctic Circle. Sparsely populated, they have varied mineral resources and wildlife. Baffin Island is the largest of the group.

Arc·tic char ▶ **n.** see CHAR[4].

Arc·tic Cir·cle the parallel of latitude 66° 33′ north of the equator. It marks the northernmost point at which the sun is visible on the northern winter solstice and the southernmost point at which the midnight sun can be seen on the northern summer solstice.

Arc·tic fox ▶ **n.** a fox with a thick coat that turns white in winter, found on the tundra of North America and Eurasia. ● *Alopex lagopus*, family Canidae.

Arc·tic hare ▶ **n.** a hare whose coat turns white in winter, found in the arctic areas of North America. ● *Lepus arcticus*, family Leporidae.

Arc·tic O·cean a sea that surrounds the North Pole and lies within the Arctic Circle. Much of the sea is covered with pack ice throughout the year.

Arc·tic tern ▶ **n.** a red-billed tern that breeds in the Arctic and adjacent areas, migrating to Antarctic regions for the winter. ● *Sterna paradisaea*, family Sternidae.

Arc·tic wil·low (also **arctic willow**) ▶ **n.** a shrub, *Salix arctica*, found in the Canadian tundra.

Arc·to·gae·a /ˌärktə'jēə/ (also **Arctogea**) Zoology a major zoogeographical area comprising the Palaearctic, Nearctic, Ethiopian, and Oriental regions.
– DERIVATIVES **Arc·to·gae·an adj.**
– ORIGIN modern Latin, from Greek *arktos* 'northern' + *gaia* 'earth.'

arc·to·phile /'ärktəˌfīl/ ▶ **n.** a person who collects or is very fond of teddy bears.
– DERIVATIVES **arc·to·phil·i·a** /ˌärktə'filēə/ **n.**, **arc·toph·il·ist** /ärk'täfilist/ **n.**, **arc·toph·il·y** /-'täfilē/ **n.**
– ORIGIN 1970s: from Greek *arktos* 'bear' + *philos* 'loving.'

Arc·tu·rus /ärk't(y)o͞orəs/ Astronomy the fourth brightest star in the sky, and the brightest in the constellation Boötes. It is an orange giant.
– ORIGIN from Greek *arktos* 'bear' + *ouros* 'guardian' (because of its position in line with the tail of Ursa Major).

ar·cu·ate /'ärkyo͞oit, -ˌāt/ ▶ **adj.** technical shaped like a bow; curved: *the arcuate sweep of the chain of islands.*
– ORIGIN late Middle English: from Latin *arcuatus*, past participle of *arcuare* 'to curve,' from *arcus* 'bow, curve.'

ar·cus se·ni·lis /'ärkəs sə'nīlis/ ▶ **n.** Medicine a narrow opaque band encircling the cornea, common in old age.
– ORIGIN late 18th cent.: Latin, literally 'senile bow.'

arc weld·ing ▶ **n.** a technique in which metals are welded using heat generated by an electric arc.

-ard ▶ **suffix** forming nouns such as *bollard, wizard.* ■ forming nouns having a depreciatory sense: *drunkard | dullard.*
– ORIGIN Middle English and Old French, from German *-hard* 'hard, hardy.'

Ar·den /'ärdn/, Elizabeth (*c.*1880–1966), US executive in the cosmetics industry; born in Canada; born *Florence Nightingale Graham.*

Ar·dennes /är'den/ a forested upland region extending over parts of southeastern Belgium, northeastern France, and Luxembourg. It was the scene of fierce fighting in both world wars.

ar·dent /'ärdnt/ ▶ **adj.** enthusiastic or passionate: *an ardent baseball fan | an ardent suitor.* ■ archaic or literary burning; glowing: *the ardent flames.*
– DERIVATIVES **ar·dent·ly adv.**
– ORIGIN Middle English: from Old French *ardant*, from Latin *ardens, ardent-*, from *ardere* 'to burn.'

Ar·di /'ärdē/ the nickname of a partial female skeleton of a fossil hominid found in Ethiopia in 1994, about 4.4 million years old and 4 feet (1.2 m) in height. ● *Ardipithecus ramidus*, family Hominidae. The species is believed to have been bipedal on the ground and quadrupedal when in trees.

ar·dor /'ärdər/ (Brit. **ardour**) ▶ **n.** enthusiasm or passion: *they felt the stirrings of revolutionary ardor.*
– ORIGIN late Middle English: via Old French from Latin *ardor*, from *ardere* 'to burn.'

ar·du·ous /'ärjo͞oəs/ ▶ **adj.** involving or requiring strenuous effort; difficult and tiring: *an arduous journey.*
– DERIVATIVES **ar·du·ous·ly adv.**, **ar·du·ous·ness n.**
– ORIGIN mid 16th cent.: from Latin *arduus* 'steep, difficult' + -OUS.

are[1] /är/ 2nd person singular present and 1st, 2nd, 3rd person plural present of BE.

are[2] /är, er(ə)r/ ▶ **n.** historical a metric unit of measure, equal to 100 square meters (about 119.6 square yards).
– ORIGIN late 18th cent.: from French, from Latin *area* (see AREA).

ar·e·a /'e(ə)rēə/ ▶ **n. 1** a region or part of a town, a country, or the world: *rural areas of New Jersey | people living in the area are at risk.* ■ [with modifier] a space allocated for a specific purpose: *the dining area.* ■ a part of an object or surface: *areas of the body.* ■ a subject or range of activity or interest: *the key areas of science.* ■ [usu. as modifier] Brit. a sunken enclosure giving access to the basement of a building: *a bicycle padlocked to the area railing.*
2 the extent or measurement of a surface or piece of land: *the area of a triangle | the room is twelve square feet in area.*
– DERIVATIVES **ar·e·al adj.**
– ORIGIN mid 16th cent. (in the sense 'space allocated for a specific purpose'): from Latin, literally 'vacant piece of level ground.'

ar·e·a code ▶ **n.** a three-digit number that identifies one of the telephone service regions into which the US, Canada, and certain other countries are divided and that is dialed when calling from one area to another.

ar·e·a rug ▶ **n.** a rug that covers only a part of a floor in a room.

ar·e·a·way /'e(ə)rēəˌwā/ ▶ **n.** a sunken enclosure giving access to the basement of a building. ■ a passageway between buildings.

a·re·ca /ə'rēkə, 'arikə, 'e(ə)r-/ (also **areca palm**) ▶ **n.** a tropical Asian palm. ● Genus *Areca*, family Palmae: several species, in particular *A. catechu*.
– ORIGIN via Portuguese from Malayalam *ḍekka*.

a·re·ca nut ▶ **n.** the astringent seed of an areca palm (*Areca catechu*), which is often chewed with betel leaves. Also called BETEL NUT.

A·re·ci·bo /ˌärə'sēbō/ a community in northwestern Puerto Rico, west of San Juan; pop. 47,300 (est. 2009). It is an academic center noted for its huge radio telescope facility.

a·re·li·gious /ˌāri'lijəs/ ▶ **adj.** not influenced by or practicing religion: *the sexual mores of today's secular and areligious culture.*

a·re·na /ə'rēnə/ ▶ **n.** a level area surrounded by seats for spectators, in which sports, entertainments, and other public events are held. ■ a place or scene of activity, debate, or conflict: *he has re-entered the political arena.*
– ORIGIN early 17th cent.: from Latin *harena, arena* 'sand, sand-strewn place of combat.'

ar·e·na·ceous /ˌarə'nāSHəs/ ▶ **adj.** Geology consisting of sand or sandlike particles. ■ Biology (of animals or plants) living or growing in sand.
– ORIGIN mid 17th cent.: from Latin *arenaceus*, from *arena, harena* 'sand.'

Ar·endt /'ärənt/, Hannah (1906–75), US philosopher and political theorist; born in Germany. A student of Martin Heidegger, she established her reputation as a political thinker with one of the first works to propose that Nazism and Stalinism had common roots. Notable works: *The Origins of Totalitarianism* (1951), *Eichmann in Jerusalem* (1963), and *On Violence* (1970).

a·re·no·sol /ə'rēnəˌsôl, -ˌsäl/ ▶ **n.** a soil type consisting mainly of sand with very little organic matter and supporting limited amounts of specialized vegetation.

aren't /är(ə)nt/ ▶ **contraction** are not: *they aren't here.* ■ am not (only used in questions): *I'm right, aren't I? | why aren't I being given a pay raise?*

> **USAGE** The contraction **aren't** is used in standard English to mean 'am not' in questions, as in *I'm right, aren't I?* Outside of questions, it is incorrect to use **aren't** to mean 'am not' (for example, *I aren't going* is clearly wrong). The nonstandard (although logical) form **amn't** is restricted to Scottish, Irish, and dialect use.

a·re·o·la /ə'rēələ/ ▶ **n.** (pl. **areolae** /-ˌlē/) Anatomy a small circular area, in particular the ring of pigmented skin surrounding a nipple. ■ Biology any of the small spaces between the veins on a leaf or the nervures on an insect's wing. ■ Medicine a reddened patch around a spot or papule.
– DERIVATIVES **a·re·o·lar adj.**, **a·re·o·late** /-lit, -ˌlāt/ **adj.**
– ORIGIN mid 17th cent. (in the sense 'small space or interstice'): from Latin, literally 'small open space,' diminutive of *area* (see AREA).

ar·e·ole /'e(ə)rēˌōl/ ▶ **n.** Biology an areola, esp. a small area bearing spines or hairs on a cactus.
– ORIGIN mid 19th cent.: from French *aréole*, from Latin (see AREOLA).

ar·e·ol·o·gy /ˌe(ə)rē'äləjē/ ▶ **n.** the study of the planet Mars.
– DERIVATIVES **ar·e·o·log·i·cal** /ˌe(ə)rēə'läjikəl/ **adj.**, **ar·e·ol·o·gist n. & adj.**
– ORIGIN late 19th cent.: from *Ares* (Greek equivalent of the Roman war god Mars) + *-ology*.

Ar·e·op·a·gus /ˌarē'äpəgəs/ (in ancient Athens) a hill on which met the highest governmental council and later a judicial court.
– ORIGIN from Greek *Areios pagos* 'hill of *Ares*'; the name for the site came to denote the court itself.

a·re·pa /ə'rāpə/ ▶ **n.** a corn pancake, sweetened or unsweetened, eaten in Venezuela and Colombia.
– ORIGIN Cariban.

A·re·qui·pa /ˌärə'kēpə/ a city in southern Peru, in the Andes; pop. 784,700 (est. 2007).

Ar·es /'e(ə)rēz/ Greek Mythology the Greek war god, son of Zeus and Hera. Roman equivalent MARS.

a·rête /ə'rāt/ ▶ **n.** a sharp mountain ridge.
– ORIGIN early 19th cent.: from French, from Latin *arista* 'ear of wheat, fish bone, spine.'

ar·e·thu·sa /ˌarə'THo͞ozə/ ▶ **n.** a pinkish-red North American wild orchid that grows in boggy ground.

PRONUNCIATION KEY ə *ago, up*; ər *over, fur*; a *hat*; ā *ate*; ä *car*; e *let*; ē *see*; i *fit*; ī *by*; NG *sing*; ō *go*; ô *law, for*; oi *toy*; o͝o *good*; o͞o *goo*; ou *out*; TH *thin*; T͟H *then*; ZH *vision*

a

Also called **DRAGON'S MOUTH.** ● *Arethusa bulbosa*, family Orchidaceae.

arf /ärf/ ▶ **exclam.** (usu. **arf arf**) used to imitate or represent a dog's bark.

ar·ga·li /'ärgəlē/ ▶ **n.** (pl. **same**) the largest wild sheep, which has massive horns and is found in mountainous areas of Asia. ● *Ovis ammon*, family Bovidae.
– ORIGIN late 18th cent.: from Mongolian.

Ar·gand di·a·gram /'ärgənd, -gand/ ▶ **n.** Mathematics a diagram on which complex numbers are represented geometrically using Cartesian axes, the horizontal coordinate representing the real part of the number and the vertical coordinate the complex part.
– ORIGIN early 20th cent.: named after J. R. *Argand* (1768–1822), French mathematician.

Ar·gand lamp ▶ **n.** historical an oil or gas lamp equipped with a tubular wick that allowed air to pass both inner and outer surfaces of the flame, securing more perfect combustion and brighter light.
– ORIGIN late 18th cent.: named after A. *Argand* (1755–1803), French physicist.

ar·gan oil /'ärgən/ ▶ **n.** an aromatic culinary oil expressed from the seeds of the argan tree, native to an area of southwestern Morocco. ● *Argania spinosa*, family Sapotaceae.

ar·gent /'ärjənt/ ▶ **adj.** literary & Heraldry silver; silvery white: *the argent moon.*
▶ **n.** Heraldry silver as a heraldic tincture.
– ORIGIN late Middle English (denoting silver coins): via Old French from Latin *argentum* 'silver.'

ar·gen·tif·er·ous /,ärjən'tifərəs/ ▶ **adj.** (of rocks or minerals) containing silver.
– ORIGIN late 18th cent.: from Latin *argentum* 'silver' + **-FEROUS.**

Ar·gen·ti·na /,ärjən'tēnə/ a republic that occupies much of the southern part of South America; pop. 40,913,600 (est. 2009); capital, Buenos Aires; official language, Spanish.

> Colonized by the Spanish in the 16th century, Argentina declared its independence in 1816. It emerged as a democratic republic in the mid 19th century, but has periodically fallen under military rule. In 1982, Argentina's claim to the Falkland Islands led to an unsuccessful war with Britain.

– DERIVATIVES **Ar·gen·tine** /'ärjən,tēn, -,tīn/ **adj. & n., Ar·gen·tin·i·an** /-'tinēən/ **adj. & n.**

ar·gen·tine /'ärjən,tīn, -,tēn/ ▶ **adj.** archaic of or resembling silver.
▶ **n.** a small marine fish with a silvery sheen. ● Family Argentinidae: two genera and several species, in particular *Argentina silus* of the North Atlantic.
– ORIGIN late Middle English: from Old French *argentin, argentine*, from *argent* 'silver,' from Latin *argentum.*

Ar·gen·tine ant ▶ **n.** a small South American ant that has become established in parts of the US. ● *Iridomyrmex humilis*, family Formicidae.

ar·gil·la·ceous /,ärjə'lāsʜəs/ ▶ **adj.** Geology (of rocks or sediment) consisting of or containing clay.
– ORIGIN late 17th cent.: from Latin *argillaceus* (from *argilla* 'clay') + **-OUS.**

ar·gil·lite /'ärjə,līt/ ▶ **n.** Geology a sedimentary rock that does not split easily, formed from consolidated clay.
– ORIGIN late 18th cent.: from Latin *argilla* 'clay' + **-ITE**[1].

ar·gi·nine /'ärjə,nēn, -,nīn/ ▶ **n.** Biochemistry a basic amino acid that is a constituent of most proteins. It is an essential nutrient in the diet of vertebrates. ● Chem. formula: $HN{=}C(NH_2)NH(CH_2)_3CH(NH_2)COOH$.
– ORIGIN late 19th cent.: from German *Arginin*, perhaps from Greek *arginoeis* 'bright-shining, white.'

Ar·give /'är,jīv, -,gīv/ ▶ **adj.** of or relating to the ancient city of Argos. ■ (esp. in Homer) Greek.
▶ **n.** a citizen of Argos. ■ (esp. in Homer) a Greek person.
– ORIGIN from Latin *Argivus*, from Greek *Argeios* 'relating to Argos.'

ar·gle-bar·gle /,ärgəl 'bärgəl/ ▶ **n.** informal, chiefly Brit.
1 copious but meaningless talk or writing; nonsense: *bureaucratic argle-bargle.*
2 another term for **ARGY-BARGY.**
– ORIGIN early 19th cent.: reduplication of dialect *argle*, a late 16th-cent. alteration of **ARGUE.**

Ar·go /'ärgō/ (in full **Argo Navis**) Astronomy, historical a large southern constellation (the ship *Argo*), which is now divided into the constellations Carina, Puppis, and Vela.
– ORIGIN Latin.

ar·gol /'ärgəl/ ▶ **n.** tartar obtained from wine fermentation.
– ORIGIN Middle English: from Anglo-Norman French *argoile*, of unknown origin.

ar·gon /'är,gän/ ▶ **n.** the chemical element of atomic number 18, an inert gaseous element of the noble gas group. Argon is the most common noble gas, making up nearly one percent of the earth's atmosphere. (Symbol: **Ar**)
– ORIGIN late 19th cent.: from Greek, neuter of *argos* 'idle,' from *a-* 'without' + *ergon* 'work.'

ar·go·naut /'ärgə,nôt/ ▶ **n.** a small floating octopus, the female of which has webbed arms like sails and secretes a thin, coiled, papery shell in which the eggs are laid. Also called **PAPER NAUTILUS.** ● Genus *Argonauta*, order Octopoda.

Ar·go·nauts /'ärgə,nôts/ Greek Mythology a group of heroes who accompanied Jason on board the ship *Argo* in the quest for the Golden Fleece.
– ORIGIN *argonaut* from Greek *argonautēs* 'sailor in the ship *Argo*.'

Ar·gonne /är'gän, 'är,gän/ a wooded plateau in northeastern France, near the Belgian border. The region is thinly populated. A major Allied offensive was staged here during World War I; during World War II the region was occupied by Germany from 1940 until 1944.

Ar·gos /'ärgəs, -gôs/ a city in southern Greece, in the northeastern Peloponnese; pop. 23,600 (est. 2009). One of the oldest cities of ancient Greece, it dominated the Peloponnese and the western Aegean in the 7th century BC.

ar·go·sy /'ärgəsē/ ▶ **n.** (pl. **argosies**) literary a large merchant ship, originally one from Ragusa (now Dubrovnik) or Venice.
– ORIGIN late 16th cent.: apparently from Italian *Ragusea* (*nave*) '(vessel) of *Ragusa*' (see **RAGUSA**).

ar·got /'ärgō, -gət/ ▶ **n.** the jargon or slang of a particular group or class: *teenage argot.*
– ORIGIN mid 19th cent. (originally denoting the jargon or slang of criminals): from French, of unknown origin.

ar·gu·a·ble /'ärgyōōəbəl/ ▶ **adj.** able to be argued or asserted: *an arguable case for judicial review* | [with clause] *it is **arguable that** egg donation raises a series of moral and practical problems.* ■ open to disagreement; not obviously correct: *a highly arguable assumption.*

ar·gu·a·bly /'ärgyōōəblē/ ▶ **adv.** [sentence adverb] it may be argued (used to qualify the statement of an opinion or belief): *she is arguably the greatest woman tennis player of all time.*

ar·gue /'ärgyōō/ ▶ **v.** (**argues, arguing, argued**)
1 [reporting verb] give reasons or cite evidence in support of an idea, action, or theory, typically with the aim of persuading others to share one's view: [with clause] *defense attorneys **argue that** the police lacked "probable cause" to arrest the driver* | [with direct speech] *"It stands to reason," she argued.* ■ [with obj.] (**argue someone into/out of**) persuade someone to do or not to do (something) by giving reasons: *I tried to argue him out of it.*
2 [no obj.] exchange or express diverging or opposite views, typically in a heated or angry way: *don't **argue with** me* | figurative *I wasn't going to **argue with** a gun* | [with obj.] *she was too tired to **argue the point**.*
– DERIVATIVES **ar·gu·er** n.
– ORIGIN Middle English: from Old French *arguer*, from Latin *argutari* 'prattle,' frequentative of *arguere* 'make clear, prove, accuse.'

ar·gu·fy /'ärgyə,fī/ ▶ **v.** (**argufies, argufying, argufied**) [no obj.] humorous or dialect argue or quarrel, typically about something trivial: *it won't do to argufy, I tell you.*
– ORIGIN late 17th cent.: fanciful formation from **ARGUE**; compare with *speechify.*

ar·gu·ment /'ärgyəmənt/ ▶ **n. 1** an exchange of diverging or opposite views, typically a heated or angry one: *I've had **an argument with** my father* | *heated arguments over public spending* | *there was some argument about the decision.*
2 a reason or set of reasons given with the aim of persuading others that an action or idea is right or wrong: *there is a strong argument for submitting a formal appeal* | [with clause] *he rejected **the argument that** keeping the facility would be costly.*
3 Mathematics an independent variable associated with a function and determining the value of the function. For example, in the expression $y = F(x_1, x_2)$, the arguments of the function F are x_1 and x_2, and the value is y. ■ another term for **AMPLITUDE** (sense 4). ■ Computing a value or address passed to a procedure or function at the time of call. ■ Linguistics any of the noun phrases in a clause that are related directly to the verb, typically the subject, direct object, and indirect object. ■ Logic the middle term in a syllogism.
4 archaic a summary of the subject matter of a book.
– PHRASES **for the sake of argument** as a basis for discussion or reasoning.
– ORIGIN Middle English (in the sense 'process of reasoning'): via Old French from Latin *argumentum*, from *arguere* 'make clear, prove, accuse.'

ar·gu·men·ta·tion /,ärgyəmən'tāsʜən/ ▶ **n.** the action or process of reasoning systematically in support of an idea, action, or theory: *lines of argumentation used to support his thesis.*
– ORIGIN late Middle English: via Old French from Latin *argumentatio(n-)*, from *argumentat-* 'conducted as an argument,' from *argumentari.*

ar·gu·men·ta·tive /,ärgyə'mentətiv/ ▶ **adj. 1** given to expressing divergent or opposite views: *an argumentative child.*
2 using or characterized by systematic reasoning: *the highest standards of argumentative rigor.*
– DERIVATIVES **ar·gu·men·ta·tive·ly adv., ar·gu·men·ta·tive·ness n.**
– ORIGIN late Middle English: from Old French *argumentatif, -ive* or late Latin *argumentativus*, from *argumentari* 'conduct an argument.'

ar·gu·ment from de·sign ▶ **n.** Christian Theology the argument that God's existence is demonstrable from the evidence of design in the universe.

ar·gus /'ärgəs/ ▶ **n. 1** (**Argus**) Greek Mythology a monster with a hundred eyes, used by Hera to watch over Io. He was killed by Hermes, and Hera then used his eyes to deck the peacock's tail. ■ an alert, watchful guardian.
2 (also **argus pheasant**) a long-tailed pheasant with generally brown plumage, found in Southeast Asia and Indonesia. ● Two species in the family Phasianidae: the male **great argus** (*Argusianus argus*) has lengthened secondary wing feathers bearing eyespots, spread during display; the **crested argus** (*Rheinartia ocellata*) has the longest tail feathers of any bird.
3 a small brown or bluish Eurasian butterfly that typically has eyelike markings near the wing margins. ● *Aricia* and other genera, family Lycaenidae.
4 (also **argus fish**) a silvery deep-bodied fish with round spots, widely distributed throughout the tropical Indo-Pacific region in both fresh and salt water. ● *Scatophagus argus*, family Scatophagidae.
– ORIGIN late Middle English: from Latin, from Greek *Argos*, the name of the mythical watchman with a hundred eyes.

Ar·gus-eyed /'ärgəs/ ▶ **adj.** literary vigilant.

ar·gy-bar·gy /,ärjē 'bärjē/ ▶ **n.** (pl. **argy-bargies**) informal, chiefly Brit. noisy quarreling or wrangling.
– ORIGIN late 19th cent. (originally Scots): rhyming jingle based on **ARGUE.**

ar·gyle /'är,gīl/ ▶ **n.** [usu. as modifier] a pattern composed of diamonds of various colors on a plain background, used in knitted garments such as sweaters and socks. ■ a sock with such a pattern.
– ORIGIN 1940s: from *Argyll*, a family name and a former county of Scotland. The pattern is based on the tartan of the *Argyll* branch of the Campbell clan.

argyle

ar·hat /'ärhət/ ▶ **n.** (in Buddhism and Jainism) someone who has attained the goal of the religious life.
– ORIGIN late 19th cent.: from Sanskrit, literally 'meritorious.'

År·hus variant spelling of **AARHUS.**

a·rhyth·mic ▶ **adj.** variant spelling of **ARRHYTHMIC.**

a·ri·a /'ärēə/ ▶ **n.** Music a long, accompanied song for a solo voice, typically one in an opera or oratorio.
– ORIGIN early 18th cent.: from Italian, from Latin *aer* 'air.'

Ar·i·ad·ne /,arē'adnē/ Greek Mythology the daughter of King Minos of Crete and Pasiphaë. She helped Theseus to escape from the Minotaur's labyrinth by giving him a ball of thread, which he unraveled as he went in and used to trace his way out again after killing the Minotaur.

Ar·i·an /'e(ə)rēən/ ▶ **n. 1** an adherent of the doctrine of Arianism.
2 a person born under the sign of Aries.
▶ **adj. 1** of or concerning Arianism.
2 of or relating to a person born under the sign of Aries.

-arian ▶ **suffix** (forming adjectives and corresponding nouns) having a concern or belief in a specified thing: *antiquarian* | *humanitarian* | *vegetarian.*
– ORIGIN from the Latin suffix *-arius.*

Ar·i·an·ism /'e(ə)rēə,nizəm/ ▶ **n.** Christian Theology an influential heresy denying the divinity of Christ, originating with the Alexandrian priest

Arius (c.250–c.336). Arianism maintained that the Son of God was created by the Father and was therefore neither coeternal with the Father, nor consubstantial.

A·ri·as San·chez /ˈärē-äs ˈsäncHes/, Oscar (1941–), Costa Rican president 1986–90 and 2006–10. He worked to achieve peace in Central America, particularly in Nicaragua. Nobel Peace Prize (1987).

ar·id /ˈarid/ ▶ **adj. 1** (of land or a climate) having little or no rain; too dry or barren to support vegetation: *hot and arid conditions.*
2 lacking in interest, excitement, or meaning: *his arid years in suburbia.*
– DERIVATIVES **a·rid·i·ty** /əˈriditē/ **n.**, **ar·id·ly adv.**, **ar·id·ness n.**
– ORIGIN mid 17th cent.: from French *aride* or Latin *aridus*, from *arere* 'be dry or parched.'

a·rid·i·sol /əˈridi,sôl, -,säl/ ▶ **n.** Soil Science a soil of an order comprising typically saline or alkaline soils with very little organic matter, characteristic of arid regions.

Ar·i·el /ˈe(ə)rēəl/ **1** Astronomy a satellite of Uranus discovered in 1851, the twelfth closest to the planet and the fourth largest, with a diameter of 721 miles (1,160 km).
2 a series of six American and British satellites devoted to studies of the ionosphere and X-ray astronomy (1962–79).
– ORIGIN named after a fairy or spirit in Shakespeare's *The Tempest.*

ar·i·el /ˈe(ə)rēəl/ ▶ **n.** a gazelle found in the Middle East and North Africa. ● Genus *Gazella*, family Bovidae: the mountain gazelle (*G. gazella*) or the dorcas gazelle (*G. dorcas*).
– ORIGIN mid 19th cent.: from Arabic *ʼaryal.*

Ar·ies /ˈe(ə)rēz, ˈe(ə)rē-ēz/ **1** Astronomy a small constellation (the Ram), said to represent the ram whose Golden Fleece was sought by Jason and the Argonauts. ■ (as genitive **Arietis** /əˈrī-itis/) used with a preceding letter or numeral to designate stars: *the star Beta Arietis.*
2 Astrology the first sign of the zodiac, which the sun enters at the vernal equinox (about March 20). ■ (**an Aries**) (pl. **same**) a person born when the sun is in this sign.
– PHRASES **First Point of Aries** Astronomy the point on the celestial sphere where the path of the sun crosses the celestial equator from south to north in March, marking the zero point of right ascension. Owing to precession of the equinoxes, it has moved from Aries into Pisces, and is now approaching Aquarius. Also called VERNAL EQUINOX.
– ORIGIN Latin.

a·right /əˈrīt/ ▶ **adv.** dialect correctly; properly: *I wondered if I'd heard aright.*
– ORIGIN Old English *on riht, ariht* (see A-[2] 'in,' RIGHT).

ar·il /ˈarəl/ ▶ **n.** Botany an extra seed-covering, typically colored and hairy or fleshy, e.g., the red fleshy cup around a yew seed.
– DERIVATIVES **ar·il·late** /-lit, -,lāt/ **adj.**
– ORIGIN mid 18th cent.: from modern Latin *arillus*, of unknown origin; perhaps related to medieval Latin *arilli* 'dried grape stones.'

a·rio·so /,ärēˈōsō, -zō/ Music ▶ **adj. & adv.** in a melodious, expressive, songlike style.
▶ **n.** (pl. **ariosos**) a piece of music to be performed in this way.
– ORIGIN Italian, from ARIA.

A·ri·os·to /,ärēˈästō, -ˈōstō/, Ludovico (1474–1533), Italian poet; noted for his romantic epic *Orlando Furioso* (final version 1532).

-arious ▶ **suffix** forming adjectives such as *gregarious, vicarious.*
– ORIGIN from the Latin suffix *-arius* + -OUS.

a·rise /əˈrīz/ ▶ **v.** (past **arose** /əˈrōz/; past participle **arisen** /əˈrizən/) [no obj.] **1** (of a problem, opportunity, or situation) emerge; become apparent: *new difficulties had arisen.* ■ come into being; originate: *the practice arose in the nineteenth century.* ■ (**arise from/out of**) occur as a result of: *most conflicts arise from ignorance or uncertainty.*
2 formal or literary get or stand up: *he arose at 9:30 and went out for a walk.*
– ORIGIN Old English *ārīsan*, from *ā-* 'away' (as an intensifier) + the verb RISE.

Ar·is·tar·chus[1] /,arəˈstärkəs/ (3rd century BC), Greek astronomer; known as **Aristarchus of Samos.** Founder of an important school of Hellenic astronomy, he was aware of the rotation of the earth around the sun and so was able to account for the seasons.

Ar·is·tar·chus[2] (c.217–145 BC), Greek scholar; known as **Aristarchus of Samothrace.** He is noted for his editions of the writings of Homer and other Greek authors.

A·ri·stide /ärēˈstēd/, Jean-Bertrand (1953–), Haitian president 1991, 1994–96, and 2001–04. He led a movement against the dictatorship of Duvalier in the 1980s and was elected president of Haiti in 1990, but was forced into exile 1991–94 by a military coup. US troops facilitated his return, and he served as president 1994–96 and 2001–04, when he was again forced into exile.

Ar·is·ti·des /,arəˈstī,dēz/ (5th century BC), Athenian statesman and general; known as **Aristides the Just.** He commanded the Athenian army at the battle of Plataea (479 BC).

Ar·is·tip·pus /,arəˈstipəs/ (late 5th century BC), Greek philosopher; known as **Aristippus the Elder (of Cyrene).** He is considered the founder of the Cyrenaic school.

a·ris·to /əˈristō/ ▶ **n.** (pl. **aristos**) informal term for ARISTOCRAT.

ar·is·toc·ra·cy /,ariˈstäkrəsē/ ▶ **n.** (pl. **aristocracies**) [treated as sing.] (or pl., usu. **the aristocracy**) the highest class in certain societies, esp. those holding hereditary titles or offices: *the ancient Polish aristocracy had hereditary right to elect the king.* ■ a form of government in which power is held by the nobility. ■ a state governed in this way. ■ a group regarded as privileged or superior in a particular sphere: *high-level technocrats make up a large part of this "technical aristocracy."*
– ORIGIN late 15th cent.: from Old French *aristocratie*, from Greek *aristokratia*, from *aristos* 'best' + *-kratia* 'power.' The term originally denoted the government of a state by its best citizens, later by the rich and well-born, hence the sense 'nobility,' regardless of the form of government (mid 17th cent).

> **USAGE** Aristocracy, oligarchy, and plutocracy are sometimes confused. All mean some form of rule by a small elite. **Aristocracy** is rule by a traditional elite, held to be made up of 'the best' people, and is usually hereditary. **Oligarchy** is literally rule by a few. **Plutocracy** is rule by the (necessarily few) very rich.

a·ris·to·crat /əˈristə,krat/ ▶ **n.** a member of the aristocracy: *an aristocrat by birth.* ■ something believed to be the best of its kind: *the trout is the aristocrat of freshwater fish.*
– ORIGIN late 18th cent.: from French *aristocrate* (a word of the French Revolution), from *aristocratie* (see ARISTOCRACY).

a·ris·to·crat·ic /ə,ristəˈkratik/ ▶ **adj.** of or relating to the aristocracy: *an aristocratic family.* ■ distinguished in manners or bearing: *a stately, aristocratic manner.* ■ grand; stylish: *aristocratic-sounding names | a snob with aristocratic aspirations.*
– DERIVATIVES **a·ris·to·crat·i·cal·ly** /-ik(ə)lē/ **adv.**
– ORIGIN early 17th cent.: from French *aristocratique*, from Greek *aristokratikos*, from *aristokratia* (see ARISTOCRACY).

Ar·is·toph·a·nes /,arəˈstäfə,nēz/ (c.450–c.385 BC), Greek comic playwright. Notable works: *Lysistrata, The Birds*, and *The Frogs.*

Ar·is·to·te·lian /ə,ristəˈtēlyən, ,aristə-, -lēən/ ▶ **adj.** of or relating to Aristotle or his philosophy.
▶ **n.** a student of Aristotle or an adherent of his philosophy.

Ar·is·to·te·lian log·ic ▶ **n.** the traditional system of logic expounded by Aristotle and developed in the Middle Ages, concerned chiefly with deductive reasoning as expressed in syllogisms. Compare with SYMBOLIC LOGIC.

Ar·is·tot·le /ˈarə,stätl, ,arəˈstätl/ (384–322 BC), Greek philosopher and scientist. A student of Plato and tutor to Alexander the Great, he founded a school (the Lyceum) outside Athens. He is one of the most influential thinkers in the history of Western thought. His surviving works cover a vast range of subjects, including logic, ethics, metaphysics, politics, natural science, and physics.

Ar·is·tot·le's lan·tern ▶ **n.** Zoology a conical structure of calcareous plates and muscles supporting the rasping teeth of a sea urchin.

A·ri·ta /əˈrētə/ ▶ **n.** a type of Japanese porcelain characterized by asymmetric decoration.
– ORIGIN late 19th cent.: named after *Arita*, a town in Japan, where it is made.

a·rith·me·tic ▶ **n.** /əˈriTHmə,tik/ the branch of mathematics dealing with the properties and manipulation of numbers: *the laws of arithmetic.* ■ the use of numbers in counting and calculation: *he could do arithmetic in his head.*
▶ **adj.** (**arithmetic** /,ariTHˈmetik/) (also **arithmetical**) of or relating to arithmetic: *perform arithmetic functions.*
– DERIVATIVES **a·rith·me·tic·al·ly adv.**, **a·rith·me·ti·cian** /ə,riTHməˈtisHən/ **n.**
– ORIGIN Middle English: from Old French *arismetique*, based on Latin *arithmetica*, from Greek *arithmētikē (tekhnē)* '(art) of counting,' from *arithmos* 'number.'

ar·ith·met·ic log·ic u·nit /,ariTHˈmetik/ ▶ **n.** a unit in a computer that carries out arithmetic and logical operations.

ar·ith·met·ic mean /,ariTHˈmetik/ ▶ **n.** the average of a set of numerical values, calculated by adding them together and dividing by the number of terms in the set.

ar·ith·met·ic pro·gres·sion /,ariTHˈmetik/ (also **arithmetic series**) ▶ **n.** a sequence of numbers in which each differs from the preceding by a constant quantity (e.g., 3, 6, 9, 12, etc.; 9, 7, 5, 3, etc.). ■ the relationship between numbers in such a sequence: *the numbers are in arithmetic progression.*

ar·ith·met·ic u·nit ▶ **n.** another term for ARITHMETIC LOGIC UNIT.

a·rith·me·tize /əˈriTHmə,tīz/ ▶ **v.** [with obj.] express arithmetically; reduce to arithmetic form.

-arium ▶ **suffix** forming nouns usually denoting a place: *planetarium | vivarium.*
– ORIGIN from Latin, neuter ending of adjectives in *-arius.*

Ariz. ▶ **abbr.** Arizona.

Ar·i·zo·na /,arəˈzōnə/ a state in the southwestern US, on the border with Mexico; pop. 6,500,180 (est. 2008); capital, Phoenix; statehood, Feb. 14, 1912 (48). Part of New Spain until 1821, it was organized as a US territory in 1863 from lands ceded by the Treaty of Guadalupe Hidalgo in 1848 and the Gadsden Purchase in 1853.
– DERIVATIVES **Ar·i·zo·nan n. & adj.**

Ar·ju·na /ˈärjənə, ˈər-/ Hinduism a hero prince in the Mahabharata, one of the two main characters in the Bhagavadgita.

Ark. ▶ **abbr.** Arkansas.

ark /ärk/ ▶ **n. 1** (**the ark**) (in the Bible) the ship built by Noah to save his family and two of every kind of animal from the Flood; Noah's ark. ■ a vessel or sanctuary that serves as protection against extinction: *a starship ark built by their android protectors.* ■ archaic a chest or box: *the ark was of Italian walnut.* ■ a large, flat-bottomed boat.
2 short for ARK OF THE COVENANT. ■ (also **Holy Ark**) a chest or cupboard housing the Torah scrolls in a synagogue.
3 (also **ark shell**) a widely distributed bivalve mollusk that typically attaches itself to rocks with byssus threads. ● Order Arcoidea: *Arca* and other genera.
– ORIGIN Old English *ærc*, from Latin *arca* 'chest.'

Ar·kan·sas /ˈärkən,sô/ a state in the southern central US, on the western banks of the Mississippi River; pop. 2,855,390 (est. 2008); capital, Little Rock; statehood, June 15, 1836 (25). Arkansas seceded from the Union in 1861 to fight for the Confederacy during the Civil War and rejoined the Union in 1868. In 1957, federal troops were needed to enforce school desegregation in Little Rock.

Ar·kan·sas Riv·er /ˈärkən,sô, ärˈkanzəs/ a river in the southwestern US, which flows for 1,450 miles (2,320 km) from the Rockies in Colorado to join the Mississippi River in Arkansas. It has been made navigable for oceangoing vessels as far west as Tulsa, Oklahoma.

Ar·khan·gelsk /ärˈKHängilsk, ärˈkaNG,gelsk/ Russian name for ARCHANGEL.

Ark of the Cov·e·nant (also **Ark of the Testimony**) the wooden chest that contained the tablets of the laws of the ancient Israelites. Carried by the Israelites on their wanderings in the wilderness, it was later placed by Solomon in the Temple at Jerusalem.

ar·kose /ˈär,kōs/ ▶ **n.** Geology a coarse-grained sandstone that is at least 25 percent feldspar.
– DERIVATIVES **ar·ko·sic** /ärˈkōsik/ **adj.**
– ORIGIN mid 19th cent.: from French, probably from Greek *arkhaios* 'ancient.'

Ark·wright /ˈärk,rīt/, Sir Richard (1732–92), English inventor and industrialist. In 1767 he patented a water-powered spinning machine known as the spinning jenny.

Arles /ärl/ a city in southeastern France; pop. 53,058 (2006). It was the capital of the medieval kingdom of Arles, formed in the 10th century by the union of the kingdoms of Provence and Burgundy.

Ar·ling·ton /ˈärliNGtən/ **1** a county in northern Virginia, forming a suburb of Washington. It is the site of the Pentagon and Arlington National Cemetery.

2 a town in eastern Massachusetts, northwest of Boston; pop. 40,993 (est. 2008).
3 an industrial city in northern Texas, between Dallas and Fort Worth; pop. 374,417 (est. 2008).

Arlington National Cemetery

Ar·ling·ton Heights a village in northeastern Illinois, northwest of Chicago; pop. 73,399 (est. 2008).

ARM ▶ **abbr.** ADJUSTABLE-RATE MORTGAGE.

arm[1] /ärm/ ▶ **n. 1** each of the two upper limbs of the human body from the shoulder to the hand: *she held the baby in her arms.* ■ (in technical use) each of these upper limbs from the shoulder to the elbow. ■ each of the forelimbs of an animal. ■ a flexible limb of an invertebrate animal, e.g., an octopus. ■ a sleeve of a garment. ■ an ability to throw a ball skillfully: *he has a good arm.* ■ an athlete with such an ability: *he wasn't the best arm in the outfield, but his performance at the plate more than compensated.* ■ used to refer to the holding of a person's arm in support or companionship: *as they walked he offered her his arm | he arrived with a pretty girl on his arm.* ■ used to refer to something perceived as powerful or protective: *the comforting arms of the church.*
2 a thing resembling an arm in form or function, in particular: ■ a side part of a chair or other seat on which a sitter's arm can rest. ■ a narrow strip of water or land projecting from a larger body. ■ a large branch of a tree. ■ a long, narrow shape or object: *a long arm of sunshine.*
3 a branch or division of a company or organization: *the political arm of the separatist group.* ■ one of the types of troops of which an army is composed, such as infantry or artillery. [also understood as a figurative use of ARM[2].]
4 Mathematics each of the lines enclosing an angle.
– PHRASES **arm in arm** (of two or more people) with arms linked. **the long arm of the law** used to refer to the criminal justice system as far-reaching: *act now before the long arm of the law catches up with you.* **as long as one's** (or **someone's**) **arm** informal very long: *I have a list of vices as long as your arm.* **at arm's length** away from the body, with the arm fully extended: *I held the telephone at arm's length.* **cost an arm and a leg** informal be extremely expensive. **get one's arms around** informal fully understand an issue or situation: *doctors are having difficulty getting their arms around these new findings.* **give one's right arm** informal used to convey a strong desire to have or do something: *I'd give my right arm to go with them.* **in arms** (of a baby) too young to walk: *a babe in arms.* **into the arms of** into the possession or control of: *the violin passed into the arms of a wealthy dilettante.* **keep someone/something at arm's length** avoid intimacy or close contact with someone or something. **put the arm on** informal attempt to force or coerce (someone) to do something: *she started putting the arm on them for donations.* **under one's arm** between one's arm and one's body: *Barbara tucked the papers under her arm.* **with open arms** with great affection or enthusiasm: *schools have welcomed such arrangements with open arms.* **within arm's reach** near enough to reach by extending one's arm.
– DERIVATIVES **arm·ful** /-ˌfo͝ol/ **n.** (pl. **armfuls**). **arm·less adj.**
– ORIGIN Old English *arm, earm,* of Germanic origin; related to Dutch *arm* and German *Arm.*

arm[2] ▶ **v.** [with obj.] supply or provide with weapons: *both sides* **armed themselves with** *grenades and machine guns.* ■ supply or provide with equipment, tools, or other items in preparation or readiness for something: *she* **armed** *them* **with** *brushes and mops.* ■ activate the fuse of (a bomb or other device) so that it is ready to explode.
▶ **n.** see ARMS.
– ORIGIN Middle English: from Old French *armer* (verb), from Latin *armare,* from *arma* 'armor, arms.'

ar·ma·da /ärˈmädə/ ▶ **n.** a fleet of warships: *an armada of destroyers, minesweepers, and gunboats.* ■ (**the Spanish Armada**) a Spanish naval invasion force sent against England by Philip II of Spain in 1588. It was defeated by the English fleet and almost completely destroyed by storms off the Hebrides.
– ORIGIN mid 16th cent.: from Spanish, from *armata,* feminine past participle of Latin *armare* 'to arm.' Compare with ARMY.

ar·ma·dil·lo /ˌärməˈdilō/ ▶ **n.** (pl. **armadillos**) a nocturnal omnivorous mammal that has large claws for digging and a body covered in bony plates. Armadillos are native to the south central US and Central and South America. ● Family Dasypodidae, order Xenarthra (or Edentata): several genera and species, including the **nine-banded armadillo** (*Dasypus novemcinctus*), which has spread into the southern US.
– ORIGIN late 16th cent.: from Spanish, diminutive of *armado* 'armed man,' from Latin *armatus,* past participle of *armare* 'to arm.'

nine-banded armadillo

Ar·ma·ged·don /ˌärməˈgedn/ ▶ **n.** (in the New Testament) the last battle between good and evil before the Day of Judgment. ■ a biblical hill of Megiddo, an archaeological site on the plain of Esdraelon, south of present-day Haifa in Israel. See also MEGIDDO. ■ the place where the last battle between good and evil will be fought. ■ a dramatic and catastrophic conflict, typically seen as likely to destroy the world or the human race: *nuclear Armageddon.*
– ORIGIN Greek, from Hebrew *har mĕgiddôn* 'hill of Megiddo' (Rev. 16:16.).

Ar·magh /ärˈmä, ˈärˌmä/ one of the six counties of Northern Ireland, formerly an administrative area. ■ the chief town of this county; pop. 15,100 (est. 2009).

Ar·mag·nac /ˌärmənˈyak, -ˈyäk/ ▶ **n.** a type of brandy, traditionally made in Aquitaine in southwestern France.

Ar·ma·lite /ˈärməˌlīt/ ▶ **n.** trademark a type of light automatic rifle.

ar·ma·ment /ˈärməmənt/ ▶ **n.** (also **armaments**) military weapons and equipment: *chemical weapons and other unconventional armaments.* ■ the process of equipping military forces for war. ■ archaic a military force equipped for war.
– ORIGIN late 17th cent. (in the sense 'force equipped for war'): from Latin *armamentum,* from *armare* 'to arm' (see ARM[2]).

ar·ma·men·tar·i·um /ˌärməmənˈte(ə)rēəm/ ▶ **n.** (pl. **armamentaria** /-ˈte(ə)rēə/) the medicines, equipment, and techniques available to a medical practitioner. ■ a collection of resources available for a certain purpose: *the entire armamentarium of electronic surveillance.*
– ORIGIN late 19th cent.: from Latin, 'arsenal, armory.'

Ar·ma·ni /ärˈmänē/, Giorgio (1934–), Italian fashion designer.

ar·ma·ture /ˈärməCHər, -ˌCHo͝or/ ▶ **n. 1** the rotating coil or coils of a dynamo or electric motor. ■ any moving part of an electrical machine in which a voltage is induced by a magnetic field. ■ a piece of iron or other object acting as a keeper for a magnet.
2 a metal framework on which a sculpture is molded with clay or similar material. ■ a framework or formal structure, esp. of a literary work: *Shakespeare's plots have served as the armature for many novels.*
3 Biology the protective covering of an animal or plant. ■ archaic armor.
– ORIGIN late Middle English: from French, from Latin *armatura* 'armor,' from *armare* 'to arm' (see ARM[2]). The original sense was 'armor,' hence 'protective covering' (sense 3, early 18th cent.), later 'keeper of a magnet,' source of sense 1 (mid 19th cent.).

arm·band /ˈärmˌband/ ▶ **n.** a band worn around a person's upper arm to hold up a shirtsleeve or as a symbol.

arm can·dy ▶ **n.** informal a sexually attractive companion accompanying a person, esp. a celebrity, at social events: *the athletes and their arm candy clustered around the bar.*

arm·chair /ˈärmˌCHe(ə)r/ ▶ **n.** a comfortable chair, typically upholstered, with side supports for a person's arms.
▶ **adj.** [attrib.] lacking or not involving practical or direct experience of a particular subject or activity: *armchair adventurers.*

Arm·co /ˈärmkō/ ▶ **n.** trademark a very pure soft iron, used in particular for roadside guardrails.
– ORIGIN early 20th cent.: acronym from *American Rolling Mill Company.*

armed /ärmd/ ▶ **adj. 1** equipped with or carrying a weapon or weapons: *the security forces are* **armed with** *automatic rifles | heavily armed troops.* ■ involving the use of firearms: *armed robbery.* ■ (of a bomb, alarm, or other device) prepared to activate or explode. ■ supplied with equipment, tools, or other items in preparation or readiness for something: *he is* **armed with** *a list of questions.*
2 Heraldry having claws, a beak, etc., of a specified tincture.
– PHRASES **armed to the teeth** see TEETH.

armed camp ▶ **n.** a town, territory, or group of people fully armed for war.

armed forc·es (also **armed services**) ▶ **plural n.** a country's military forces, esp. its army, navy, and air force.

Ar·me·ni·a /ärˈmēnēə/ a landlocked country in southwestern Asia, in the Caucasus; pop. 2,967,000 (est. 2009); capital, Yerevan; official languages, Armenian and Russian.

> The Armenian homeland fell under Turkish rule from the 16th century and with the decline of the Ottomans was divided among Turkey, Iran, and Russia. In 1915 the Turks forcibly deported 1,750,000 Armenians to the deserts of Syria and Mesopotamia; more than 600,000 were killed or died on forced marches. Russian Armenia was absorbed into the former Soviet Union in 1922 and gained independence as a member of the Commonwealth of Independent States in 1991. Since 1988 there has been conflict with neighboring Azerbaijan over the ethnically Armenian enclave of Nagorno-Karabakh and the predominantly Azerbaijani territory of Naxçivan.

Ar·me·ni·an /ärˈmēnēən, -yən/ ▶ **adj.** of or relating to Armenia, its language, or the Christian Church established there.
▶ **n. 1** a native of Armenia or a person of Armenian descent.
2 the Indo-European language of Armenia, spoken by around 4 million people and written in a distinctive alphabet of thirty-eight letters.

Ar·me·ni·an Church (also **Armenian Apostolic Orthodox Church**) an independent Christian Church established in Armenia since *c.*300 and influenced by Roman and Byzantine as well as Syrian traditions. A small Armenian Catholic Church also exists (see UNIATE).

arm·guard /ˈärmˌgärd/ ▶ **n.** another term for BRACER[2].

arm·hole /ˈärmˌhōl/ ▶ **n.** each of two openings in a garment through which the wearer puts their arms.

ar·mi·ger /ˈärmijər/ ▶ **n.** a person entitled to heraldic arms.
– DERIVATIVES **ar·mig·er·ous** /ärˈmijərəs/ **adj.**
– ORIGIN mid 16th cent.: Latin, literally 'bearing arms,' from *arma* 'arms' + *gerere* 'to bear.'

ar·mil·lar·y sphere /ˈärməˌlerē/ ▶ **n.** a model of the celestial globe constructed from rings and hoops representing the equator, the tropics, and other celestial circles, and able to revolve on its axis.
– ORIGIN mid 17th cent.: from modern Latin *armillaris* 'relating to an *armilla,*' an astronomical instrument consisting of a hoop fixed in the plane of the equator (sometimes crossed by one in the plane of the meridian), used by the ancient astronomers to show the recurrence of equinoxes and solstices; from Latin *armilla* 'bracelet.'

Ar·min·i·an /ärˈminēən/ ▶ **adj.** relating to the doctrines of **Jacobus Arminius** (Latinized name of Jakob Hermandszoon, 1560–1609), a Dutch Protestant theologian, who rejected the Calvinist doctrine of predestination. His teachings had a considerable influence on Methodism.
▶ **n.** an adherent of these doctrines.
– DERIVATIVES **Ar·min·i·an·ism** /-ˌnizəm/ **n.**

ar·mi·stice /ˈärməstis/ ▶ **n.** an agreement made by opposing sides in a war to stop fighting for a certain time; a truce.
– ORIGIN early 18th cent.: from French, or from modern Latin *armistitium,* from *arma* 'arms' (see ARM[2]) + *-stitium* 'stoppage.'

Ar·mi·stice Day ▶ **n.** the anniversary of the armistice of November 11, 1918, observed since 1954 as Veterans Day in the US.

arm·let /ˈärmlit/ ▶ **n. 1** a band or bracelet worn around the upper part of a person's arm.
2 a small inlet of a sea or branch of a river.

arm·load /ˈärmˌlōd/ ▶ **n.** the amount that can be carried with one arm or in both arms.

arm·lock /ˈärmˌläk/ ▶ **n.** a method of restraining someone by holding an arm tightly behind their back.

ar·moire /ärmˈwär, ˈärmˌwär/ ▶ **n.** a wardrobe or movable cabinet, typically one that is ornate or antique.
– ORIGIN late 16th cent.: from French, from Old French *armarie* (see AMBRY).

armoire

ar·mor /ˈärmər/ (Brit. **armour**) ▶ **n.** the metal coverings formerly worn by soldiers or warriors to protect the body in battle: *knights in armor | a suit of armor.* ■ (also **armor plate**) the tough metal layer covering a military vehicle or ship to defend it from attack. ■ military vehicles collectively: *the contingent includes infantry, armor, and logistic units.* ■ the protective layer or shell of some animals and plants. ■ a person's emotional, social, or other defenses: *his armor of self-confidence.*
▶ **v.** [with obj.] provide (someone) with emotional, social, or other defenses: *the knowledge armored him against her.*
– DERIVATIVES **ar·mor-plat·ed adj.**
– ORIGIN Middle English: from Old French *armure*, from Latin *armatura*, from *armare* 'to arm' (see ARM²).

ar·mored /ˈärmərd/ (Brit. **armoured**) ▶ **adj.** (of a military vehicle or ship) covered with a tough metal layer as a defense against attack: *armored vehicles.* ■ (of troops) equipped with such vehicles: *the 2nd Armored Division.* ■ (of some animals and plants) having a protective layer or shell: *armored fish.* ■ historical (of a soldier) wearing armor: *armored and mounted knights.*

ar·mored per·son·nel car·ri·er ▶ **n.** an armored military vehicle used to transport troops.

ar·mor·er /ˈärmərər/ (Brit. **armourer**) ▶ **n. 1** a maker, supplier, or repairer of weapons or armor.
2 an official in charge of the arms of a military unit.
– ORIGIN Middle English: from Old French *armurier*, from *armure* (see ARMOR).

ar·mo·ri·al /ärˈmôrēəl/ ▶ **adj.** of or relating to heraldry or heraldic devices: *armorial shields.*
▶ **n.** a book of heraldic devices.
– ORIGIN late Middle English: from Old French *armoierie* (see ARMORY¹).

ar·mor·y¹ /ˈärmərē/ (Brit. **armoury**) ▶ **n.** (pl. **armories**) **1** a place where arms are kept. ■ a supply of arms: *the most powerful weapon in our armory.* ■ a place where arms are manufactured.
2 an array of resources available for a particular purpose: *his armory of comic routines.*
3 a place where military reservists are trained or headquartered.
– ORIGIN Middle English (in the sense 'armor'): from Old French *armoirie, armoierie*, from *armoier* 'to blazon,' from *arme* 'weapon' (see ARMS). The spelling change in the 17th cent. was due to association with ARMOR.

ar·mor·y² ▶ **n.** heraldry.
– ORIGIN late Middle English: from Old French *armoierie* (see ARMORY¹).

Ar·mour /ˈärmər/, Philip Danforth (1832–1901), US industrialist. He reorganized his brother Herman's grain commission house into the Armour & Co. meatpacking plant in 1870.

ar·mour /ˈärmər/ ▶ **n.** British spelling of ARMOR.

ar·mour·er ▶ **n.** British spelling of ARMORER.

ar·mour·y ▶ **n.** British spelling of ARMORY¹.

arm·pit /ˈärmˌpit/ ▶ **n.** a hollow under the arm at the shoulder. Also called AXILLA. ■ informal a place regarded as extremely unpleasant: *they call the region the armpit of America.*
– PHRASES **up to one's armpits** deeply involved in a particular unpleasant situation or enterprise: *the country is up to its armpits in drug trafficking.*

arm·rest /ˈärmˌrest/ ▶ **n.** a padded or upholstered arm of a chair or other seat on which a sitter's arm can comfortably rest.

arms /ärmz/ ▶ **plural n. 1** weapons and ammunition; armaments: *they were subjugated by force of arms |* [as modifier] *arms exports.*
2 distinctive emblems or devices, originally borne on shields in battle and now forming the heraldic insignia of families, corporations, or countries. See also COAT OF ARMS.
– PHRASES **a call to arms** a call to prepare for confrontation: *a call to arms to defend against a takeover.* **take up arms** begin fighting. **under arms** equipped and ready for war or battle: *the Empire now had half a million men under arms.* **up in arms (about/over)** protesting vigorously about something: *teachers are up in arms about new school tests.*
– ORIGIN Middle English: from Old French *armes*, from Latin *arma.*

arms con·trol ▶ **n.** international disarmament or arms limitation, esp. by mutual consent.

arm's-length ▶ **adj.** [attrib.] avoiding intimacy or close contact: *an arm's-length relationship.*

arms race ▶ **n.** a competition between nations for superiority in the development and accumulation of weapons, esp. between the US and the former Soviet Union during the Cold War.

Arm·strong¹ /ˈärmˌstrôNG/, Edwin Howard (1890–1954), US electrical engineer, inventor of the superheterodyne radio receiver and the frequency modulation (FM) system.

Arm·strong², Lance (1971–) US cyclist. He won the Tour de France in 1999 after successfully battling advanced testicular cancer. He repeated the win in 2000, 2001, 2002, 2003, 2004, and 2005.

Arm·strong³, Louis (1901–71), US jazz musician; nicknamed **Satchmo**; full name *Daniel Louis Armstrong.* A major influence on Dixieland jazz, he was a trumpet and cornet player, as well as a bandleader and a distinctive singer. He also appeared in many movies, including *The Birth of the Blues* (1941).

Arm·strong⁴, Neil (Alden) (1930–), US astronaut. He commanded the Apollo 11 mission, during which he became the first man to set foot on the Moon (July 20, 1969).

Neil Armstrong

arm-twist·ing ▶ **n.** informal persuasion by the use of physical force or moral pressure: *eight years of arguing and diplomatic arm-twisting.*
– DERIVATIVES **arm-twist v.**

arm-wres·tling ▶ **n.** a trial of strength in which two people sit opposite each other with one elbow resting on a table, clasp each other's hands, and try to force each other's arm down onto the table.
– DERIVATIVES **arm-wres·tle v.**

ar·my /ˈärmē/ ▶ **n.** (pl. **armies**) an organized military force equipped for fighting on land: *the two armies were in position.* ■ (**the army** or **the Army**) the branch of a nation's armed services that conducts military operations on land: *an enlisted man in the army |* [as modifier] *army officers.* ■ (**an army of** or **armies of**) a large number of people or things, typically formed or organized for a particular purpose: *an army of photographers | armies of cockroaches.*
– PHRASES **an army marches on its stomach** see STOMACH. **you and whose army?** informal used as an expression of disbelief in someone's ability to carry out a threat: *"One word to him and I'll nail you." "You and whose army?"*
– ORIGIN late Middle English: from Old French *armee*, from *armata*, feminine past participle of Latin *armare* 'to arm.'

ar·my ant ▶ **n.** a blind nomadic tropical ant that forages in large columns, preying chiefly on insects and spiders. Also called DRIVER ANT. ● Subfamily Dorylinae, family Formicidae.

ar·my brat ▶ **n.** informal a child of a career soldier, esp. one who has lived in various places as a result of military transfers.

ar·my is·sue ▶ **n.** [usu. as modifier] equipment or clothing supplied by the army.

ar·my-na·vy ▶ **adj.** denoting the type of store that specializes in military surplus equipment, or the goods sold there.

ar·my sur·plus ▶ **n.** goods and equipment that are in excess of the army's requirements: [as modifier] *an army surplus store.*

ar·my worm ▶ **n.** any of a number of insect larvae that occur in large numbers, in particular: ● the caterpillars of some moths, which feed on cereals and other crops, moving *en masse* when the food is exhausted (*Spodoptera* and other genera, family Noctuidae). ● the small maggots of certain fungus gnats, which move in very large numbers within secreted slime (genus *Sciara*, family Mycetophilidae).

Arne /ärn/, Thomas (1710–78), English composer of the music for "Rule, Britannia."

Ar·nel /ärˈnel/ ▶ **n.** trademark a synthetic fiber made from cellulose triacetate. ■ fabric made from fibers of this type.

Arn·hem /ˈärnəm, ˈärnˌhem/ a town in the eastern Netherlands, situated on the Rhine River; pop. 143,582 (2008).

Arn·hem Land a peninsula in Northern Territory, Australia.

ar·ni·ca /ˈärnikə/ ▶ **n.** a plant of the daisy family that bears yellow daisylike flowers. Native to cooler regions of the northern hemisphere, it is sometimes cultivated as an ornamental. ● Genus *Arnica*, family Compositae: many species, esp. mountain tobacco (*A. montana*) of central Europe. ■ a preparation of this plant used medicinally, esp. for the treatment of bruises.
– ORIGIN mid 18th cent.: modern Latin, of unknown origin.

Ar·no /ˈärnō/ a river that rises in the Apennines in northern Italy and flows west for 150 miles (240 km) through Florence and Pisa to the Ligurian Sea.

Ar·nold¹ /ˈärnld/, Benedict (1741–1801), American general and traitor. During the American Revolution, with Ethan Allan, he was instrumental in the capture of Fort Ticonderoga but later planned to betray West Point to the British. He fled behind British lines and lived the rest of his life in Britain. His name became synonymous with 'traitor.'

Ar·nold², Matthew (1822–88), English poet, essayist, and social critic. He is known for such poems as "The Scholar-Gipsy" and "Dover Beach" and was professor of poetry at Oxford 1857–67.

ar·oid /ˈaroid/ (also **aroid lily**) ▶ **n.** Botany a plant of the arum family (Araceae).
– ORIGIN late 19th cent.: from ARUM + -OID.

a·rol·la /əˈrälə, əˈrō-/ (also **arolla pine**) ▶ **n.** a tall pine tree native to the Alps and Carpathian mountains, often planted in dense clumps as an avalanche break. ● *Pinus cembra*, family Pinaceae.
– ORIGIN late 19th cent.: from Swiss French *arol(l)e.*

a·ro·ma /əˈrōmə/ ▶ **n.** a distinctive, typically pleasant smell: *the tantalizing aroma of fresh coffee.* ■ a subtle, pervasive quality or atmosphere of a particular type: *the aroma of officialdom.*
– ORIGIN Middle English (usually in the plural denoting fragrant plants or spices): via Latin from Greek *arōma* 'spice.'

a·ro·ma·tase /əˈrōməˌtās/ ▶ **n.** an adrenal enzyme that converts androstenedione and estrone to estrogen. Inhibiting its action is one approach to breast cancer prevention and treatment.

a·ro·ma·ther·a·py /əˌrōməˈTHerəpē/ ▶ **n.** the use of aromatic plant extracts and essential oils in massage or baths.
– DERIVATIVES **a·ro·ma·ther·a·peu·tic** /-ˌTHerəˈpyōōtik/ **adj.**, **a·ro·ma·ther·a·pist** /-pist/ **n.**

ar·o·mat·ic /ˌarəˈmatik/ ▶ **adj. 1** having a pleasant and distinctive smell: *a massage with aromatic oils.*
2 Chemistry (of an organic compound) containing a planar unsaturated ring of atoms that is stabilized by an interaction of the bonds forming the ring. Such compounds are typified by benzene and its derivatives. Compare with ALICYCLIC.
▶ **n. 1** a substance or plant emitting a pleasant and distinctive smell.
2 (usu. **aromatics**) Chemistry an aromatic compound.
– DERIVATIVES **ar·o·mat·i·cal·ly adv.**, **ar·o·ma·tic·i·ty** /-məˈtisitē/ **n.** (Chemistry).
– ORIGIN late Middle English: via Old French from late Latin *aromaticus*, from Greek *arōmatikos*, from *arōma* (see AROMA).

a·ro·ma·tize /əˈrōməˌtīz/ ▶ **v.** [with obj.] **1** Chemistry convert (a compound) into an aromatic structure.
2 cause to have a pleasant and distinctive smell: *vinegar aromatized with plant juices and honey.*
– DERIVATIVES **a·ro·ma·ti·za·tion** /əˌrōmətiˈzāSHən/ **n.**
– ORIGIN late Middle English: from Old French *aromatiser*, from late Latin *aromatizare*, from Greek *arōmatizein* 'to spice.'

a·ro·nia /əˈrōnyə, -nēə/ ▶ **n.** a plant of the genus *Aronia* in the rose family, esp. (in gardening) a chokeberry.
– ORIGIN modern Latin, from Greek *arōnia* 'medlar.'

a

a·rose /əˈrōz/ past of **ARISE**.

a·round /əˈround/ ▶ **adv.** **1** (Brit. also **round**) located or situated on every side: *the mountains towering all around* | *a building visible for miles around.* ■ so as to surround someone or something: *everyone crowded around* | *a pool with banks all the way around.* ■ so as to give support and companionship: *if one girl is distraught, the others will rally around.* ■ with circular motion: *the boats were spun around by waterspouts.* ■ so as to cover or take in the whole area surrounding a particular center: *she paused to glance around admiringly at the decor.* ■ so as to reach everyone in a particular group or area: *he passed a newspaper clipping around.*
2 (Brit. also **round**) so as to rotate and face in the opposite direction: *Jack seized her by the shoulders and turned her around* | figurative *having him in my corner has turned my career around.* ■ so as to lead in another direction: *it was the last house before the road curved around.* ■ used in describing the position of something, typically with regard to the direction in which it is facing or its relation to other items: *the picture shows the pieces the wrong way around.* ■ used to describe a situation in terms of the relation between people, actions, or events: *it was he who was attacking her, not the other way around.*
3 (Brit. also **round**) so as to reach a new place or position, typically by moving from one side of something to the other: *he made his way around to the back of the building* | *they went **the long way around** by the main road.* ■ in or to many places throughout a locality: *his only ambition is to drive around in a sports car* | *word got around that he was on the verge of retirement.* ■ used to convey an ability to navigate or orient oneself: *I like pupils to **find their own way around**.* ■ informal used to convey the idea of visiting someone else: *why don't you come around to my office?* ■ randomly or unsystematically; here and there: *John tried to focus on her but she kept moving around* | *one of them was glancing nervously around.*
4 (Brit. also **round**) in existence, in the vicinity, or in active use: *there was no one around* | *by being around I threaten her happiness* | *barley has been around for a long time.* ■ near at hand: *he would want to have her around as much as possible.*
5 approximately; about: *software costs would be around $1,500* | [as prep.] *I returned to my hotel around 3 a.m.*
▶ **prep.** (Brit. also **round**) **1** on every side of: *the palazzo is built around a courtyard* | *the hills around the city.* ■ (of something abstract) having (the thing mentioned) as a focal point: *our entire culture is built around those loyalties* | *you can organize your essay around an existing critical controversy.*
2 in or to many places throughout (a community or locality): *cycling around the village* | *a number of large depots around the country.* ■ on the other side of (a corner or obstacle): *Steven parked the car around the corner.* ■ so as to hit (something) in passing: *if he didn't shut up, he might get a slap around the ear.*
3 so as to encircle or embrace (someone or something): *he put his arm around her* | *warming her hands around a cup of coffee* | *the polar vortex around Antarctica.* ■ (of a person's arm or arms) partially encircling (another person) as part of a gesture of affection: *Mike put an arm around Mary and kissed her.* ■ following an approximately circular route: *he walked around the airfield* | *it can drill around corners* | *the contour followed around a curve to the north.* ■ so as to cover or take in the whole area of (a place): *she went around the house and saw that all the windows were barred.*
– PHRASES **around the bend** see **BEND**[1]. **have been around** informal have a lot of varied experience and understanding of the world.
– ORIGIN Middle English: from **A-**[2] 'in, on' + **ROUND**.

> **USAGE** Are around and round (as preposition and adverbial particle) interchangeable? In US English, the normal form in most contexts is **around**; **round** is generally regarded as informal or nonstandard and is standard only in certain fixed expressions, as in *the park is open **year round*** and *they went **round and round** in circles.*

a·rous·al /əˈrouzəl/ ▶ **n.** the action or fact of arousing or being aroused: *sexual arousal in dreams is common.*

a·rouse /əˈrouz/ ▶ **v.** [with obj.] **1** evoke or awaken (a feeling, emotion, or response): *something about the man aroused the guard's suspicions* | *the letter **aroused in** him a sense of urgency.* ■ excite or provoke (someone) to anger or strong emotions: *an ability to influence the audience and to arouse the masses.* ■ excite (someone) sexually.
2 awaken (someone) from sleep: *she had been aroused by the telephone.*
– ORIGIN late 16th cent.: from **ROUSE**, on the pattern of the pair of *rise, arise.*

ARP ▶ **abbr.** adjustable-rate preferred.

Arp /ärp/, Jean (1887–1966), French painter, sculptor, and poet; also known as **Hans Arp**. He was a cofounder of the Dada movement.

ar·peg·gi·ate /ärˈpejēˌāt/ ▶ **v.** [with obj.] Music play (a chord) as a series of ascending or descending notes.
– DERIVATIVES **ar·peg·gi·a·tion** /ärˌpejēˈāsHən/ **n.**, **ar·peg·gi·a·tor** /-ˌātər/ **n.**

ar·peg·gi·o /ärˈpejēˌō/ ▶ **n.** (pl. **arpeggios**) Music the notes of a chord played in succession, either ascending or descending.
– ORIGIN Italian, from *arpeggiare* 'play the harp,' from *arpa* 'harp.'

ar·peg·gio·ne /ärˌpejēˈōnē, ˌärpeˈjyōnē/ ▶ **n.** an early 19th-century stringed instrument resembling a guitar in shape and having six strings and frets, but played with a bow like a cello.
– ORIGIN late 19th cent.: from German, from **ARPEGGIO**.

ar·pent /ˈärpənt, ˈärpäN/ ▶ **n.** Canadian **1** an old French unit of land area equivalent to 3,420 square meters (about 1 acre), the standard measure of land in those areas settled during the French regime and in use until the 1970s.
2 a unit of linear measure equivalent to about 190 feet (58 m), used in New France.
– ORIGIN French.

ar·que·bus /ˈärk(w)əbəs/ (also **harquebus**) ▶ **n.** historical an early type of portable gun supported on a tripod or a forked rest.
– ORIGIN mid 16th cent.: from French *harquebuse*, based on Middle Low German *hakebusse*, from *hake* 'hook' + *busse* 'gun.'

arr. ▶ **abbr.** ■ (of a piece of music) arranged by: *Variations on a theme of Corelli (arr. Wild).* ■ (with reference to the arrival time of a bus, train, or airplane) arrives.

ar·rab·bi·a·ta /ˌärəˈbēätə/ ▶ **adj.** denoting a spicy pasta sauce made with tomatoes and hot peppers.
– ORIGIN Italian, literally 'angry,' feminine past participle of *arrabbiare* 'make angry.'

ar·rack /ˈarək, əˈrak/ (also **arak**) ▶ **n.** an alcoholic liquor typically distilled from the sap of the coconut palm or from rice.
– ORIGIN early 17th cent.: from Arabic *ʿarak* 'sweat,' from the phrase *ʿarak al-tamr*, denoting an alcoholic spirit made from dates.

ar·raign /əˈrān/ ▶ **v.** [with obj.] call or bring (someone) before a court to answer a criminal charge: *her sister was **arraigned on** attempted murder charges.* ■ find fault with (someone or something); censure: *the soldiers bitterly arraigned the government for failing to keep its word.*
– ORIGIN late Middle English: from Old French *araisnier*, based on Latin *ad-* 'to' + *ration-* 'reason, account.'

ar·raign·ment /əˈrānmənt/ ▶ **n.** the action of arraigning someone in court: *he's scheduled for arraignment in New York on Thursday* | *she pleaded not guilty at her arraignment.*

Ar·ran /ˈarən/ an island in the Firth of Clyde, in the west of Scotland.

ar·range /əˈrānj/ ▶ **v.** [with obj.] **1** put (things) in a neat, attractive, or required order: *she had just finished arranging the flowers* | *the columns are **arranged in** 12 rows.*
2 organize or make plans for (a future event): *they hoped to arrange a meeting* | *we've arranged the funeral **for** Saturday* | [no obj.] *my aunt **arranged for** the furniture to be stored.* ■ [no obj.] reach agreement about an action or event in advance: *I **arranged with** my boss to have the time off* | [with infinitive] *they **arranged to** meet at eleven o'clock.* ■ ensure that (something) is done or provided by organizing it in advance: *accommodations can be arranged if required.*
3 Music adapt (a composition) for performance with instruments or voices other than those originally specified: *songs **arranged for** viola and piano.*
4 archaic settle (a dispute or claim): *the quarrel, partly by the interference of the crown prince, was arranged.*
– DERIVATIVES **ar·range·a·ble adj.**, **ar·rang·er n.**
– ORIGIN late Middle English: from Old French *arangier*, from *a-* (from Latin *ad* 'to, at') + *rangier* 'to range' (see **RANGE**).

ar·ranged mar·riage ▶ **n.** a marriage planned and agreed to by the families or guardians of the bride and groom, who have little or no say in the matter themselves.

ar·range·ment /əˈrānjmənt/ ▶ **n.** **1** the action, process, or result of arranging or being arranged: *the arrangement of the furniture in the room.* ■ a thing that has been arranged in a neat or attractive way: *flower arrangements* | *an intricate arrangement of gravel paths.*
2 (usu. **arrangements**) plans or preparations for a future event: *all the **arrangements for** the wedding were made.* ■ an agreement with someone: *the travel agents have an **arrangement with** the hotel* | ***by special arrangement**, students can take a course in other degree programs.*
3 Music a composition adapted for performance with different instruments or voices than those originally specified: *Mozart's symphonies in **arrangements for** cello and piano.*
4 archaic a settlement of a dispute or claim.

ar·rant /ˈarənt/ ▶ **adj.** [attrib.] dated complete, utter: *what arrant nonsense!*
– ORIGIN Middle English: variant of **ERRANT**, originally in phrases such as *arrant thief* 'outlawed, roving thief.'

Ar·ras /äˈräs, ˈarəs/ a town in northeastern France; pop. 43,663 (2006). In medieval times, it was a center for the manufacture of tapestries.

ar·ras /ˈarəs/ ▶ **n.** a rich tapestry, typically hung on the walls of a room or used to conceal an alcove.
– ORIGIN late Middle English (originally denoting the fabric itself): named after the French town of **ARRAS**.

ar·ray /əˈrā/ ▶ **n.** **1** an impressive display or range of a particular type of thing: *there is a vast array of literature on the topic* | *a bewildering array of choices.*
2 an ordered arrangement, in particular: ■ an arrangement of troops. ■ Mathematics an arrangement of quantities or symbols in rows and columns; a matrix. ■ Computing an indexed set of related elements. ■ Law a list of jurors empaneled.
3 literary elaborate or beautiful clothing: *he was clothed in fine array.*
▶ **v.** [with obj.] **1** display or arrange (things) in a particular way: *arrayed across the table was a buffet* | *the forces arrayed against him.*
2 (usu. **be arrayed in**) dress someone in (the clothes specified): *they were arrayed in Hungarian national dress.*
3 Law empanel (a jury).
– ORIGIN Middle English (in the senses 'preparedness' and 'place in readiness'): from Old French *arei* (noun), *areer* (verb), based on Latin *ad-* 'toward' + a Germanic base meaning 'prepare.'

ar·rears /əˈri(ə)rz/ ▶ **plural n.** money that is owed and should have been paid earlier: *he was suing the lessee for the arrears of rent.*
– PHRASES **in arrears** (also chiefly Law **in arrear**) behind in paying money that is owed: *two out of three tenants are in arrears.* ■ (of payments made or due for wages, rent, etc.) at the end of each period of work or occupancy: *you will be paid monthly in arrears.*
– DERIVATIVES **ar·rear·age** /əˈri(ə)rij/ **n.**
– ORIGIN Middle English (first used in the phrase *in arrear*): from *arrear* (adverb) 'behind, overdue,' from Old French *arere*, from medieval Latin *adretro*, from *ad-* 'toward' + *retro* 'backward.'

ar·rest /əˈrest/ ▶ **v.** [with obj.] **1** seize (someone) by legal authority and take into custody: *the police **arrested** him **for** possession of marijuana* | *two youths aged 16 were arrested.*
2 stop or check (progress or a process): *the spread of the disease can be arrested* | (as adj. **arrested**) *arrested development may occur.* ■ [no obj.] suffer a heart attack: *they were trying to resuscitate a patient who had arrested.*
3 attract the attention of (someone): *his attention was arrested by a strange sound.*
▶ **n.** **1** the action of seizing someone to take into custody: *I have a warrant for your arrest* | *they placed her **under arrest*** | *at least 69 arrests were made.*
2 a stoppage or sudden cessation of motion: *a respiratory arrest.*
– ORIGIN late Middle English: from Old French *arester*, based on Latin *ad-* 'at, to' + *restare* 'remain, stop.'

ar·rest·ee /əˌresˈtē/ ▶ **n.** a person who has been arrested.

ar·rest·er /əˈrestər/ (also **arrestor**) ▶ **n.** [usu. with modifier] a device that prevents or stops a specified thing: *a spark arrester* | *a lightning arrester.* ■ a device on an aircraft carrier that slows aircraft after landing by means of a hook and cable.

ar·rest·ing /əˈrestiNG/ ▶ **adj.** **1** striking; eye-catching: *at 6 feet 6 inches he was an arresting figure.*
2 a person or agency that seizes and detains (someone or something) by legal authority: *the arresting officer.*
– DERIVATIVES **ar·rest·ing·ly adv.**

ar·rest of judg·ment ▶ **n.** Law a postponement or stay of a court decision because of a legal challenge or problem.

Ar·re·tine /ˈariˌtīn, -ˌtēn/ ▶ **adj.** denoting fine red pottery made at Arretium, an ancient city in central Italy, and elsewhere from *c.*100 BC until the late 1st century AD.
– ORIGIN late 18th cent.: from the name of the city *Arretium* (modern Arezzo) + **-INE**[1].

Ar·rhe·ni·us /ə'rēnēəs, -'rā-/, Svante August (1859–1927), Swedish chemist, noted for his work on electrolytes. Nobel Prize for Chemistry (1903).

ar·rhyth·mi·a /ā'riT͟Hmēə, ə'riT͟H-/ ▶ **n.** Medicine a condition in which the heart beats with an irregular or abnormal rhythm.
– ORIGIN late 19th cent.: from Greek *arruthmia* 'lack of rhythm,' from *a-* 'without' + *rhuthmos* (see RHYTHM).

ar·rhyth·mic /ə'riT͟Hmik/ (also **arhythmic**) ▶ **adj.** not rhythmic; without rhythm or regularity: *the arrhythmic clip-clop of pony steps.* ■ Medicine of, relating to, or suffering from cardiac arrhythmia.
– DERIVATIVES **ar·rhyth·mi·cal** adj., **ar·rhyth·mi·cal·ly** /-mik(ə)lē/ adv.

ar·rière-pen·sée /ä,ryer pän'sā/ ▶ **n.** a concealed thought or intention; an ulterior motive.
– ORIGIN early 19th cent.: French, literally 'behind thought.'

ar·ris /'aris/ ▶ **n.** Architecture a sharp edge formed by the meeting of two flat or curved surfaces.
– ORIGIN late 17th cent.: alteration of early modern French *areste* 'sharp ridge,' earlier form of ARÊTE.

ar·ri·val /ə'rīvəl/ ▶ **n.** the action or process of arriving: *Ruth's arrival in New York* | *he was dead on arrival at the hospital.* ■ a person who has arrived somewhere: *hotel staff greeted the late arrivals.* ■ the emergence or appearance of a new development, phenomenon, or product: *the arrival of democracy.* ■ such a new development, phenomenon, or product: *sociology is a relatively new arrival on the academic scene.*
– ORIGIN late Middle English: from Anglo-Norman French *arrivaille*, from Old French *arriver* (see ARRIVE).

ar·rive /ə'rīv/ ▶ **v.** [no obj.] reach a place at the end of a journey or a stage in a journey: *we arrived at his house and knocked at the door* | *the team arrived in New Delhi on July 30* | *they had recently arrived from Turkey.* ■ (of a thing) be brought or delivered: *the invitation arrived a few days later.* ■ (**arrive at**) reach (a conclusion or decision): *they arrived at the same conclusion.* ■ (of an event or a particular moment) happen or come: *we will be in touch with them when the time arrives.* ■ (of a new development or product) come into existence or use: *microcomputers arrived at the start of the 1970s.* ■ (of a baby) be born: *he will feel jealous when a new baby arrives.* ■ informal achieve success or recognition.
– ORIGIN Middle English (in the sense 'reach the shore after a voyage'): from Old French *ariver*, based on Latin *ad-* 'to' + *ripa* 'shore.'

ar·ri·viste /,ärē'vēst/ ▶ **n.** an ambitious or ruthlessly self-seeking person, esp. one who has recently acquired wealth or social status.
– ORIGIN early 20th cent.: from French, from *arriver* (see ARRIVE).

ar·ro·gance /'arəgəns/ ▶ **n.** the quality of being arrogant: *the arrogance of this man is astounding.*

ar·ro·gant /'arəgənt/ ▶ **adj.** having or revealing an exaggerated sense of one's own importance or abilities: *he's arrogant and opinionated* | *a typically arrogant assumption.*
– DERIVATIVES **ar·ro·gant·ly** adv.
– ORIGIN late Middle English: via Old French from Latin *arrogant-* 'claiming for oneself,' from the verb *arrogare* (see ARROGATE).

ar·ro·gate /'arə,gāt/ ▶ **v.** [with obj.] take or claim (something) for oneself without justification: *they arrogate to themselves the ability to divine the nation's true interests.*
– DERIVATIVES **ar·ro·ga·tion** /,arə'gāSHən/ n.
– ORIGIN mid 16th cent.: from Latin *arrogat-* 'claimed for oneself,' from the verb *arrogare*, from *ad-* 'to' + *rogare* 'ask.'

ar·ron·disse·ment /ə'rändismənt, ä'rändēs,män/ ▶ **n.** a subdivision of a department in France, for purposes of local government administration. ■ an administrative district of certain large French cities, in particular Paris.
– ORIGIN French, from *arrondir* 'make round.'

Ar·row /'arō/, Kenneth Joseph (1921–), US economist, noted chiefly for his work on general economic equilibrium and social choice. His *Social Choices and Individual Values* (1951) argued the impossibility of aggregating the preferences of individuals into a single combined order of priorities for society as a whole. Nobel Prize for Economics (1972), shared with John R. Hicks.

ar·row /'arō/ ▶ **n.** a shaft sharpened at the front and with feathers or vanes at the back, shot from a bow as a weapon or for sport: *his ability to launch an arrow accurately.* ■ a mark or sign resembling an arrow, used to show direction or position; a pointer: *we drove in the main gate and followed a series of arrows* | [as modifier] *you can use the up and down arrow keys.*
– PHRASES **arrow of time** (or **time's arrow**) the direction of travel from past to future in time considered as a physical dimension. **straight as an arrow** perfectly straight, with no deviation.
– DERIVATIVES **ar·row·y** adj.
– ORIGIN Old English *arewe*, *arwe*, from Old Norse.

ar·row·head /'arō,hed/ ▶ **n.** **1** the pointed end of an arrow, typically wedge-shaped. ■ a decorative device resembling an arrowhead. **2** an aquatic or semiaquatic plant with arrow-shaped leaves and three-petaled white flowers. ● Genus *Sagittaria*, family Alismataceae: several species, in particular the common **broad-leaved arrowhead** *S. latifolia*.

broad-leaved arrowhead

ar·row·root /'arō,rōōt, -,rŏŏt/ ▶ **n.** a West Indian herbaceous plant from which a starch is prepared. ● *Maranta arundinacea*, family Marantaceae. ■ the fine-grained starch obtained from this plant, used in cooking and medicine.
– ORIGIN late 17th cent.: alteration of Arawak *aru-aru* (literally 'meal of meals') by association with ARROW and ROOT[1], the tubers being used to absorb poison from arrow wounds.

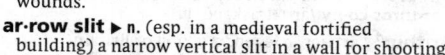

ar·row slit ▶ **n.** (esp. in a medieval fortified building) a narrow vertical slit in a wall for shooting or looking through, or to admit light and air.

ar·row-straight ▶ **adj. & adv.** completely straight: [as adj.] *the roads are empty and arrow-straight* | [as adv.] *an index leads the reader arrow-straight to documents of interest.*

ar·row worm ▶ **n.** a slender transparent wormlike animal with fins, having spines on the head for grasping prey. It is common in marine plankton. Also called CHAETOGNATH (see CHAETOGNATHA). ● Phylum Chaetognatha.

Ar·roy·o /ə'roi,ō/, Grace (1947–), president of the Philippines since 2001; full name *Maria Gloria Macapagal-Arroyo*.

ar·roy·o /ə'roi,ō/ ▶ **n.** (pl. **arroyos**) a steep-sided gully cut by running water in an arid or semiarid region.
– ORIGIN mid 19th cent.: from Spanish.

ar·roz /ä'rōs/ ▶ **n.** Spanish word for RICE, used in the names of various dishes.

arse /ärs/ British spelling of ASS[2].
– ORIGIN Old English *ærs*, of Germanic origin; related to Dutch *aars* and German *Arsch*.

ar·se·nal /'ärs(ə)-nl/ ▶ **n.** a collection of weapons and military equipment stored by a country, person, or group: *Britain's nuclear arsenal.* ■ a place where weapons and military equipment are stored or made. ■ an array of resources available for a certain purpose: *an arsenal of computers at our disposal.*
– ORIGIN early 16th cent. (denoting a dock for the construction and repair of ships): from French, or from obsolete Italian *arzanale*, based on Arabic *dār-aṣ-ṣinā'a*, from *dār* 'house' + *al-* '(of) the' + *ṣinā'a* 'art, industry' (from *ṣana'a* 'make, fabricate').

ar·se·nate /'ärs(ə)nit, -,nāt/ ▶ **n.** Chemistry a salt or ester of arsenic acid.

ar·se·nic ▶ **n.** /'ärs(ə)nik/ the chemical element of atomic number 33, a brittle steel-gray metalloid. (Symbol: **As**)

> Arsenic compounds (and their poisonous properties) have been known since ancient times, and the metallic form was isolated in the Middle Ages. Arsenic occurs naturally in orpiment, realgar, and other minerals, and rarely as the free element. Arsenic is used in semiconductors and some specialized alloys; its toxic compounds are widely used in wood preservation.

▶ **adj.** (**arsenic** /är'senik/) of or relating to arsenic. ■ Chemistry of arsenic with a valence of five; of arsenic (V).
– ORIGIN late Middle English (denoting yellow orpiment, arsenic sulfide): via Old French from Latin *arsenicum*, from Greek *arsenikon* 'yellow orpiment,' identified with *arsenikos* 'male,' but in fact from Arabic *al-zarnīk* 'the orpiment,' based on Persian *zar* 'gold.'

ar·sen·ic ac·id /är'senik/ ▶ **n.** Chemistry a weakly acidic crystalline solid with oxidizing properties, formed when arsenic reacts with nitric acid. ● Chem. formula: H_3AsO_4.

ar·sen·i·cal /är'senikəl/ ▶ **adj.** of or containing arsenic.
▶ **n.** (usu. **arsenicals**) an arsenical drug or other compound.

ar·se·nide /'ärs(ə),nīd/ ▶ **n.** Chemistry a binary compound of arsenic with a metallic element.

ar·se·no·py·rite /,ärsənō'pī,rīt, är,senō-/ ▶ **n.** a silvery-gray mineral consisting of an arsenide and sulfide of iron. ● Chem. formula FeAsS.

ar·sine /'ärsēn, är'sēn/ ▶ **n.** Chemistry a poisonous gas smelling slightly of garlic, made by the reaction of some arsenides with acids. ● Arsenic trihydride; chem. formula: AsH_3.
– ORIGIN late 19th cent.: from ARSENIC, on the pattern of *amine*.

ar·sis /'ärsis/ ▶ **n.** (pl. **arses** /-,sēz/) Prosody the unstressed syllable of a metrical foot. The opposite of THESIS (sense 3). To the Greeks, the two terms designated the raising and lowering of the foot in walking, but their meanings became reversed in the Latin tradition, where grammarians identified them with the lowering and raising of the voice.
– ORIGIN late Middle English: via late Latin from Greek, literally 'lifting,' from *airein* 'raise.'

ar·son /'ärsən/ ▶ **n.** the criminal act of deliberately setting fire to property: *police are treating the fire as arson* | [as modifier] *an arson attack.*
– ORIGIN late 17th cent.: an Anglo-Norman French legal term, from medieval Latin *arsio(n-)*, from Latin *ardere* 'to burn.'

ar·son·ist /'ärsənist/ ▶ **n.** a person who commits arson: *police believe arsonists were responsible for both fires.*

ars·phen·a·mine /ärs'fenəmən, -,mēn/ ▶ **n.** Medicine a synthetic organic arsenic compound formerly used to treat syphilis and other diseases.
– ORIGIN early 20th cent.: blend of ARSENIC, PHENYL, and AMINE.

ar·sy-ver·sy /,ärsē 'vərsē/ informal, chiefly Brit. ▶ **adj.** in a confused, disordered, or perversely contrary state or condition: *the whole place was arsy-versy* | *they got things all arsy-versy.*
– ORIGIN mid 16th cent.: from ARSE + Latin *versus* 'turned,' the addition of -Y[1] to both elements forming a jingle.

art[1] /ärt/ ▶ **n.** **1** the expression or application of human creative skill and imagination, typically in a visual form such as painting or sculpture, producing works to be appreciated primarily for their beauty or emotional power: *the art of the Renaissance* | *great art is concerned with moral imperfections* | *she studied art in Paris.* ■ works produced by such skill and imagination: *his collection of modern art* | *an exhibition of Mexican art* | [as modifier] *an art critic.* ■ creative activity resulting in the production of paintings, drawings, or sculpture: *she's good at art.*
2 (**the arts**) the various branches of creative activity, such as painting, music, literature, and dance: *the visual arts* | [in sing.] *the art of photography.*
3 (**arts**) subjects of study primarily concerned with the processes and products of human creativity and social life, such as languages, literature, and history (as contrasted with scientific or technical subjects): *the belief that the arts and sciences were incompatible* | *the Faculty of Arts.*
4 a skill at doing a specified thing, typically one acquired through practice: *the art of conversation.*
– PHRASES **art for art's sake** used to convey the idea that the chief or only aim of a work of art is the self-expression of the individual artist who creates it. **art is long, life is short** proverb there is so much knowledge (or skill) to acquire that a lifetime is not sufficient. **art of war** the strategy, tactics, and techniques of combat.
– ORIGIN Middle English: via Old French from Latin *ars*, *art-*.

art[2] archaic or dialect 2nd person singular present of BE.

art. ▶ **abbr.** ■ article. ■ artificial. ■ artillery.

Ar·taud /är'tō/, Antonin (1896–1948), French actor, director, and poet. He developed the concept of the nonverbal Theater of Cruelty.

art dec·o ▶ **n.** the predominant decorative art style of the 1920s and 1930s, characterized by precise and boldly delineated geometric shapes and strong colors, and used most notably in household objects and in architecture.
– ORIGIN 1960s: shortened from French *art décoratif* 'decorative art,' from the 1925 *Exposition des Arts décoratifs* in Paris.

ar·te·fact ▶ **n.** British spelling of ARTIFACT.

ar·tel /är'tel/ ▶ **n.** historical (in prerevolutionary Russia) a cooperative association of craftsmen living and working together.
– ORIGIN from Russian *artel'*.

Ar·te·mis /'ärtəməs/ Greek Mythology a goddess, daughter of Zeus and sister of Apollo. She was a huntress and is typically depicted with a bow and arrows. Roman equivalent DIANA.

ar·te·mis·i·a /ˌärtə'mēZH(ē)ə/ ▶ **n.** an aromatic or bitter-tasting plant of a genus that includes wormwood, mugwort, and sagebrush. Several kinds of artemisia are used in herbal medicine and many are cultivated for their feathery gray foliage. ● Genus *Artemisia*, family Compositae.
– ORIGIN Middle English: via Latin from Greek, 'wormwood,' named after the goddess ARTEMIS, to whom it was sacred.

ar·te·mis·in·in /ˌärtə'mēsənin, -'mis-/ ▶ **n.** another term for QINGHAOSU.
– ORIGIN 1970s: blend of ARTEMISIA and QUININE.

Ar·te Po·ver·a /'ärtā 'pōvərə, 'pô-/ ▶ **n.** a style and movement in art originating in Italy in the 1960s combining aspects of conceptual, minimalist, and performance art, and making use of worthless or common materials such as stones or newspapers, in the hope of subverting the commercialization of art.
– ORIGIN 1960s: Italian, literally 'impoverished art,' from *arte* 'art' + *povera* (feminine of *povero* 'needy').

ar·te·ri·al /är'ti(ə)rēəl/ ▶ **n.** a through road: *sabotaged arterials needed for evacuation of civilians.*
▶ **adj.** [attrib.] of or relating to an artery or arteries. ■ denoting an important route in a system of roads, railroad lines, or rivers: *one of the main arterial routes from New York.*
– ORIGIN late Middle English: from medieval Latin *arterialis*, from Latin *arteria* (see ARTERY).

ar·te·ri·al·ize /är'ti(ə)rēəˌlīz/ ▶ **v.** [with obj.] (usu. as adj. **arterialized**) convert venous into arterial (blood) by reoxygenation, esp. in the lungs.
– DERIVATIVES **ar·te·ri·al·i·za·tion** /ärˌti(ə)rēələ'zāSHən/ **n.**

arterio- ▶ **comb. form** of or relating to the arteries: *arteriosclerosis.*
– ORIGIN from Greek *artēria* (see ARTERY).

ar·te·ri·og·ra·phy /ärˌti(ə)rē'ägrəfē/ ▶ **n.** Medicine radiography of an artery, carried out after injection of a radio-opaque substance.

ar·te·ri·ole /är'ti(ə)rēˌōl/ ▶ **n.** Anatomy a small branch of an artery leading into capillaries.
– DERIVATIVES **ar·te·ri·o·lar** /ärˌti(ə)rē'ōlər/ **adj.**
– ORIGIN mid 19th cent.: from French *artériole*, diminutive of *artère* (see ARTERY).

ar·te·ri·o·scle·ro·sis /ärˌti(ə)rēōsklə'rōsis/ ▶ **n.** Medicine the thickening and hardening of the walls of the arteries, occurring typically in old age.
– DERIVATIVES **ar·te·ri·o·scle·rot·ic** /-'rätik/ **adj.**

ar·te·ri·o·ve·nous /ärˌti(ə)rēō'vēnəs/ ▶ **adj.** Anatomy of, relating to, or affecting an artery and a vein.

ar·te·ri·tis /ˌärtə'rītis/ ▶ **n.** Medicine inflammation of the walls of an artery.

ar·ter·y /'ärtərē/ ▶ **n.** (pl. **arteries**) any of the muscular-walled tubes forming part of the circulation system by which blood (mainly that which has been oxygenated) is conveyed from the heart to all parts of the body. Compare with VEIN (sense 1). ■ an important route in a system of roads, rivers, or railroad lines: *the east-west artery between San Francisco and Sacramento.*
– ORIGIN late Middle English: from Latin *arteria*, from Greek *artēria*, probably from *airein* 'raise.'

ar·te·sian /är'tēZHən/ ▶ **adj.** relating to or denoting a well bored perpendicularly into water-bearing strata lying at an angle, so that natural pressure produces a constant supply of water with little or no pumping: *the water from artesian wells makes agriculture possible.*
– ORIGIN mid 19th cent.: from French *artésien* 'from *Artois*' (see ARTOIS), where such wells were first made.

art form ▶ **n.** a conventionally established form of artistic composition, such as the novel, sonata, or sonnet. ■ any activity regarded as a medium of imaginative or creative self-expression: *he elevates stage managing to an art form.*

art·ful /'ärtfəl/ ▶ **adj. 1** (of a person or action) clever or skillful, typically in a crafty or cunning way: *her artful wiles.*
2 showing creative skill or taste: *an artful photograph of a striking woman.*
– DERIVATIVES **art·ful·ly adv.**, **art·ful·ness n.**

art his·to·ry ▶ **n.** the academic study of the history and development of painting, sculpture, and the other visual arts.
– DERIVATIVES **art his·to·ri·an n.**, **art his·tor·i·cal adj.**

art house ▶ **n.** a movie theater that specializes in films that are artistic or experimental rather than merely entertaining.

ar·thral·gia /är'THralj(ē)ə/ ▶ **n.** Medicine pain in a joint.
– ORIGIN mid 19th cent.: from Greek *arthron* 'joint' + -ALGIA.

ar·thri·tis /är'THrītis/ ▶ **n.** painful inflammation and stiffness of the joints.
– DERIVATIVES **ar·thrit·ic** /-'THritik/ **adj. & n.**
– ORIGIN mid 16th cent.: via Latin from Greek, from *arthron* 'joint.' *Arthritic* was already used in late Middle English.

arthro- ▶ **comb. form** of a joint; relating to joints: *arthroscope.*
– ORIGIN from Greek *arthron* 'joint.'

ar·throd·e·sis /är'THrädəsis/ ▶ **n.** surgical immobilization of a joint by fusion of the adjacent bones.
– ORIGIN early 20th cent.: from ARTHRO- + Greek *desis* 'binding together.'

ar·thro·pod /'ärTHrəˌpäd/ ▶ **n.** Zoology an invertebrate animal of the large phylum Arthropoda, such as an insect, spider, or crustacean.

Ar·throp·o·da /är'THräpədə/ Zoology a large phylum of invertebrate animals that includes insects, spiders, crustaceans, and their relatives. They have a segmented body, an external skeleton, and jointed limbs, and are sometimes divided among several phyla.
– ORIGIN late 19th cent.: modern Latin (plural), from Greek *arthron* 'joint' + *pous*, *pod-* 'foot.'

ar·thro·scope /'ärTHrəˌskōp/ ▶ **n.** Medicine an instrument through which the interior of a joint may be inspected or operated on.
– DERIVATIVES **ar·thro·scop·ic** /ˌärTHrə'skäpik/ **adj.**, **ar·thros·co·py** /är'THräskəpē/ **n.**

Ar·thur[1] /'ärTHər/ a legendary king of Britain, historically perhaps a 5th- or 6th-century Romano-British chieftain or general. Stories of his life, the exploits of his knights, and the Round Table of the court at Camelot were developed by Malory, Chrétien de Troyes, and other medieval writers and became the subject of many legends.
– DERIVATIVES **Ar·thu·ri·an** /är'THo͝orēən/ **adj.**

Ar·thur[2], Chester Alan (1829–86), 21st president of the US 1881–85. A New York Republican, he became James Garfield's vice president in March 1881, succeeding to the presidency upon the assassination of Garfield six months later. During his term of office, he was responsible for the enactment of Civil Service reforms and for improving the strength of the US Navy.

Chester Alan Arthur

ar·ti·choke /'ärtiˌCHōk/ ▶ **n. 1** (also **globe artichoke**) a European plant cultivated for its large thistlelike flower heads. ● *Cynara scolymus*, family Compositae. ■ the unopened flower head of this, of which the heart and the fleshy bases of the bracts are edible.
2 see JERUSALEM ARTICHOKE.
– ORIGIN mid 16th cent.: from northern Italian *articiocco*, from Spanish *alcarchofa*, from Arabic *al-ḵaršūfa*.

artichoke 1

ar·ti·choke gall ▶ **n.** a hard egg-shaped gall that forms inside an artichoke bud in response to the developing larva of a gall wasp. ● The wasp is *Andricus fecundator*, family Cynipidae.

ar·ti·cle /'ärtikəl/ ▶ **n. 1** a particular item or object, typically one of a specified type: *small household articles | articles of clothing.*
2 a piece of writing included with others in a newspaper, magazine, or other publication: *an article about middle-aged executives.*
3 a separate clause or paragraph of a legal document or agreement, typically one outlining a single rule or regulation: [as modifier] *it is an offense under Article 7 of the treaty.*
4 Grammar see DEFINITE ARTICLE, INDEFINITE ARTICLE.
▶ **v.** [with obj.] (usu. **be articled**) bind by the terms of a contract, as one of apprenticeship.
– PHRASES **an article of faith** a firmly held belief: *it was an article of faith with this circle that women must free themselves.* **the genuine article** a person or thing considered to be an authentic and excellent example of their kind.
– ORIGIN Middle English (denoting a separate clause of the Apostles' Creed): from Old French, from Latin *articulus* 'small connecting part,' diminutive of *artus* 'joint.'

Ar·ti·cle 15 ▶ **n.** a section of the Uniform Code of Military Justice allowing commanders to carry out discretionary punishments without judicial proceedings. ■ a judgment or punishment issued under this provision: *if I agree to accept the Article 15, am I admitting guilt?*

Ar·ti·cles of Con·fed·er·a·tion ▶ **n.** the original constitution of the US, ratified in 1781, which was replaced by the US Constitution in 1789.

ar·tic·u·lar /är'tikyələr/ ▶ **adj.** [attrib.] of or relating to a joint or the joints: *articular cartilage.*
– ORIGIN late Middle English: from Latin *articularis*, from *articulus* 'small connecting part' (see ARTICLE).

ar·tic·u·late ▶ **adj.** /är'tikyəlit/ **1** (of a person or a person's words) having or showing the ability to speak fluently and coherently: *an articulate account of their experiences.*
2 having joints or jointed segments. ■ Zoology denoting a brachiopod that has projections and sockets that form a hinge joining the two halves of the shell.
▶ **v.** /-ˌlāt/ **1** [with obj.] express (an idea or feeling) fluently and coherently: *they were unable to articulate their emotions.* ■ pronounce (something) clearly and distinctly: *he articulated each word with precision* | [no obj.] *people who do not articulate well are more difficult to lip-read.*
2 [no obj.] form a joint: *the mandible is a solid piece articulating with the head.* ■ (**be articulated**) be connected by joints: *the wing is articulated to the thorax.*
– DERIVATIVES **ar·tic·u·la·ble adj.**, **ar·tic·u·la·cy** /-ləsē/ **n.**, **ar·tic·u·late·ly adv.**, **ar·tic·u·late·ness n.**, **ar·tic·u·la·tor** /-ˌlātər/ **n.**
– ORIGIN mid 16th cent.: from Latin *articulatus*, past participle of *articulare* 'divide into joints, utter distinctly,' from *articulus* 'small connecting part' (see ARTICLE).

ar·tic·u·lat·ed /är'tikyəˌlātid/ ▶ **adj. 1** having two or more sections connected by a flexible joint: *eight articulated trailer coaches | the trilobite's thorax has a variable number of articulated segments.*
2 (of an idea or feeling) expressed; put into words: *the lack of a clearly articulated policy.*

ar·tic·u·la·tion /ärˌtikyə'lāSHən/ ▶ **n. 1** the action of putting into words an idea or feeling of a specified type: *it would involve the articulation of a theory of the just war.* ■ the formation of clear and distinct sounds in speech: *the articulation of vowels and consonants.* ■ Music clarity in the production of successive notes: *beautifully polished articulation from the violins.* ■ Phonetics the act or manner of uttering a speech sound, esp. a consonant.
2 the state of being jointed: *the area of articulation of the lower jaw.* ■ [with modifier] a specified joint: *the leg articulation.*
– ORIGIN late Middle English (in the senses 'joint,' 'joining'): from Latin *articulatio(n-)*, from the verb *articulare* (see ARTICULATE).

ar·tic·u·la·to·ry /är'tikyələˌtôrē/ ▶ **adj.** [attrib.] of or relating to the formation of speech sounds.

ar·ti·fact /'ärtəfakt/ (Brit. **artefact**) ▶ **n. 1** an object made by a human being, typically an item of cultural or historical interest: *gold and silver artifacts.* ■ Archaeology such an object as distinguished from a similar object naturally produced.
2 something observed in a scientific investigation or experiment that is not naturally present but occurs as a result of the preparative or investigative procedure: *widespread tissue infection may be a technical artifact.*
– DERIVATIVES **ar·ti·fac·tu·al** /ˌärtə'fakCHo͞oəl/ **adj.**
– ORIGIN early 19th cent.: from Latin *arte* 'by or using art' + *factum* 'something made' (neuter past participle of *facere* 'make').

ar·ti·fice /'ärtəfis/ ▶ **n.** clever or cunning devices or expedients, esp. as used to trick or deceive others: *artifice and outright fakery | the style is not free from the artifices of the period.*

– ORIGIN late Middle English (in the sense 'workmanship'): from Old French, from Latin *artificium*, based on *ars, art-* 'art' + *facere* 'make.'

ar·tif·i·cer /är'tifəsər/ ▶ **n.** archaic a skilled craftsman or inventor. ■ Brit. Military a skilled mechanic in the armed forces.
– ORIGIN late Middle English: from Anglo-Norman French, probably an alteration of Old French *artificien*, from *artifice* (see **ARTIFICE**).

ar·ti·fi·cial /,ärtə'fisHəl/ ▶ **adj. 1** made or produced by human beings rather than occurring naturally, typically as a copy of something natural: *her skin glowed in the artificial light | an artificial limb | artificial flowers.* ■ (of a situation or concept) not existing naturally; contrived or false: *the artificial division of people into age groups.* ■ Bridge (of a bid) conventional as opposed to natural.
2 (of a person or a person's behavior) insincere or affected: *an artificial smile.*
– DERIVATIVES **ar·ti·fi·ci·al·i·ty** /-,fisHē'alitē/ **n.**, **ar·ti·fi·cial·ly adv.**
– ORIGIN late Middle English: from Old French *artificiel* or Latin *artificialis*, from *artificium* 'handicraft' (see **ARTIFICE**).

ar·ti·fi·cial climb·ing ▶ **n.** the sport of climbing on an indoor or outdoor wall whose surface simulates a mountain.

ar·ti·fi·cial ho·ri·zon ▶ **n.** a gyroscopic instrument or a fluid surface, typically one of mercury, used to provide a horizontal reference plane for navigational measurement.

ar·ti·fi·cial in·sem·i·na·tion (abbr.: **AI**) ▶ **n.** the injection of semen into the vagina or uterus other than by sexual intercourse.

ar·ti·fi·cial in·tel·li·gence (abbr.: **AI**) ▶ **n.** the theory and development of computer systems able to perform tasks that normally require human intelligence, such as visual perception, speech recognition, decision-making, and translation between languages.

ar·ti·fi·cial life ▶ **n.** the production or action of computer programs or computerized systems that simulate the behavior, population dynamics, or other characteristics of living organisms.

ar·ti·fi·cial res·pi·ra·tion ▶ **n.** the restoration or substitution of someone's breathing by manual, mechanical, or mouth-to-mouth methods.

ar·ti·fi·cial sat·el·lite ▶ **n.** another term for **SATELLITE** (sense 1).

ar·ti·fi·cial sur·face ▶ **n.** Sports (also **artificial turf**) a carpetlike playing surface used in stadiums instead of natural grass.

ar·til·ler·y /är'tilərē/ ▶ **n.** (pl. **artilleries**) large-caliber guns used in warfare on land: *tanks and heavy artillery.* ■ a military detachment or branch of the armed forces that uses such guns.
– DERIVATIVES **ar·til·ler·ist** /-rist/ **n.**, **ar·til·ler·y·man** /-mən/ **n.**
– ORIGIN late Middle English: from Old French *artillerie*, from *artiller*, alteration of *atillier* 'equip, arm,' probably a variant of *atirier*, from *a-* (from Latin *ad* 'to, at') + *tire* 'rank, order.'

ar·ti·o·dac·tyl /,ärtē-ō'daktl/ Zoology ▶ **n.** a mammal of the order Artiodactyla, such as a cow, sheep, camel, or pig.
▶ **adj.** relating to or denoting artiodactyls.

Ar·ti·o·dac·ty·la /,ärtē-ō'daktl-ə/ Zoology an order of mammals that comprises the even-toed ungulates. Compare with **PERISSODACTYLA**.
– ORIGIN modern Latin (plural), from Greek *artios* 'even' + *daktulos* 'finger, toe.'

ar·ti·san /'ärtizən/ ▶ **n.** a worker in a skilled trade, esp. one that involves making things by hand.
– DERIVATIVES **ar·ti·san·al** /-zənl/ **adj.**
– ORIGIN mid 16th cent.: from French, from Italian *artigiano*, based on Latin *artitus*, past participle of *artire* 'instruct in the arts,' from *ars, art-* 'art.'

art·ist /'ärtist/ ▶ **n.** a person who produces paintings or drawings as a profession or hobby. ■ a person who practices any of the various creative arts, such as a sculptor, novelist, poet, or filmmaker. ■ a person skilled at a particular task or occupation: *a surgeon who is an artist with the scalpel.* ■ a performer, such as a singer, actor, or dancer. ■ [with modifier] informal a habitual practitioner of a specified reprehensible activity: *a con artist | rip-off artists.*
– ORIGIN early 16th cent. (denoting a master of the liberal arts): from French *artiste*, from Italian *artista*, from *arte* art, from Latin *ars, art-*.

ar·tiste /är'tēst/ ▶ **n.** a professional entertainer, esp. a singer or dancer: *cabaret artistes.*
– ORIGIN early 19th cent.: from French (see **ARTIST**).

ar·tis·tic /är'tistik/ ▶ **adj.** having or revealing natural creative skill: *my lack of artistic ability.* ■ of, relating to, or characteristic of art or artistry: *a denial of artistic freedom | her artistic temperament.* ■ aesthetically pleasing: *computer programs that produce artistic designs.*
– DERIVATIVES **ar·tis·ti·cal·ly** /-ik(ə)lē/ **adv.**

ar·tis·tic di·rec·tor ▶ **n.** the person with overall responsibility for the selection and interpretation of the works performed by a theater, ballet, or opera company.

art·ist·ry /'ärtistrē/ ▶ **n.** creative skill or ability: *the artistry of the pianist.*

art·ist's fun·gus ▶ **n.** a bracket fungus with a reddish-brown upper surface and a pale lower surface on which scratches remain visible as dark marks, found in both Eurasia and North America. ● *Ganoderma applanatum*, family Ganodermataceae, class Hymenomycetes.

art·ist's im·pres·sion ▶ **n.** a sketch or drawing of someone or something, produced when no photograph is available.

art·less /'ärtlis/ ▶ **adj.** without guile or deception: *an artless, naive girl | artless sincerity.* ■ without effort or pretentiousness; natural and simple: *an artless literary masterpiece.* ■ without skill or finesse: *her awkward, artless prose.*
– DERIVATIVES **art·less·ly adv.**

art nou·veau /är(t) no͞o'vō/ ▶ **n.** a style of decorative art, architecture, and design prominent in western Europe and the US from about 1890 until World War I and characterized by intricate linear designs and flowing curves based on natural forms.
– ORIGIN early 20th cent.: from French, literally 'new art.'

Ar·tois /är'twä/ a region and former province of northwestern France.

art pa·per ▶ **n.** high-quality paper coated with china clay or a similar substance to give it a smooth surface.

arts and crafts ▶ **plural n.** decorative design and handicraft.

Arts and Crafts Move·ment an English decorative arts movement of the second half of the 19th century that sought to revive the ideal of craftsmanship in an age of increasing mechanization and mass production. William Morris was its most prominent member.

art song ▶ **n.** Music a song written to be sung in recital, typically with piano accompaniment and often set to a poem.

art·sy /'ärtsē/ (also **arty** /'ärtē/) ▶ **adj.** (**artsier, artsiest**) informal making a strong, affected, or pretentious display of being artistic or interested in the arts: *the artsy town of Taos | artsy French flicks.*
– DERIVATIVES **art·si·ness n.**

art·sy-craft·sy /,ärtsē 'kraftsē/ informal ▶ **adj.** interested or involved in making decorative, artistic objects, typically ones perceived as quaint or homespun: *artsy-craftsy gift shops.*

art·sy-fart·sy /,ärtsē 'färtsē/ ▶ **adj.** informal, derogatory associated with or showing a pretentious interest in the arts: *you can wear a turtleneck to join your artsy-fartsy friends.*

art ther·a·py ▶ **n.** a form of psychotherapy involving the encouragement of free self-expression through painting, drawing, or modeling, used as a remedial activity or an aid to diagnosis.

art·work /'ärt,wərk/ ▶ **n.** illustrations, photographs, or other nontextual material prepared for inclusion in a publication. ■ paintings, drawings, or other artistic works: *a collection of artwork from tribal cultures | each artwork is reproduced in color on a full page.*

A·ru·ba /ə'ro͞obə/ an island in the Caribbean Sea, close to the Venezuelan coast; pop. 103,100 (est. 2009); capital, Oranjestad. Formerly part of the Netherlands Antilles, it separated in 1986 to become a self-governing territory of the Netherlands.

a·ru·gu·la /ə'ro͞ogələ/ (also **rucola, rugola**) ▶ **n.** the rocket plant, used in cooking.
– ORIGIN 1970s: from Italian dialect, ultimately a diminutive of Latin *eruca*, 'downy-stemmed plant.'

ar·um /'arəm/ ▶ **n.** a North American and European plant that has arrow-shaped leaves and a broad leafy spathe enclosing a club-shaped spadix, and that bears bright red berries in late summer. ● *Arum, Arisaema*, and other genera, family Araceae (the **arum family**): several species, including jack-in-the-pulpit, cuckoopint, and skunk cabbage. The arum family also contains a number of popular houseplants, such as philodendrons and calla lilies.
– ORIGIN late Middle English: from Latin, from Greek *aron*.

ar·um lil·y ▶ **n.** chiefly British term for **CALLA LILY** (see **CALLA**).

Ar·u·na·chal Pra·desh /,ärə'näcHəl prə'desH/ a mountainous state in far northeastern India that lies on the border of Tibet to the north and Burma (Myanmar) to the east; capital, Itanagar. It became a state of India in 1986.

Ar·va·da /är'vadə, -'vädə/ a city in north central Colorado, northwest of Denver; pop. 107,361 (est. 2008).

-ary[1] ▶ **suffix 1** forming adjectives such as *budgetary, primary.*
2 forming nouns such as *dictionary, granary.*
– ORIGIN from French *-aire* or Latin *-arius* 'connected with.'

-ary[2] ▶ **suffix** forming adjectives such as *capillary, military.*
– ORIGIN from French *-aire* or Latin *-aris* 'belonging to.'

Ar·ya·bha·ta I /,äryə'bətə/, (476–c.550), Indian astronomer and mathematician. His surviving work, *Aryabhatiya* (499), deals with mathematics, the measurement of time, planetary models, the sphere, and eclipses.

Ar·yan /'e(ə)rēən, 'ar-, -yən/ ▶ **n.** a member of a people speaking an Indo-European language who invaded northern India in the 2nd millennium BC, displacing the Dravidian and other aboriginal peoples. ■ dated term for **PROTO-INDO-EUROPEAN** or for **INDO-IRANIAN**. ■ (in Nazi ideology) a person of Caucasian race not of Jewish descent.

> The idea that there was an "Aryan" race corresponding to the parent Indo-European language was proposed by certain 19th century writers and was taken up by Hitler and other proponents of racist ideology, but it has been generally rejected by scholars.

▶ **adj.** of or relating to this people or their language.
– ORIGIN from Sanskrit *ārya* 'noble' + **-AN**.

ar·yl /'arəl/ ▶ **n.** [as modifier] Chemistry of or denoting a radical derived from an aromatic hydrocarbon by removal of a hydrogen atom: *aryl groups.*
– ORIGIN early 20th cent.: from **AROMATIC** + **-YL**.

ar·y·te·noid /ə'ritn,oid, ,arə'tē,noid, ,er-/ Anatomy ▶ **adj.** [attrib.] of, relating to, or denoting a pair of cartilages at the back of the larynx.
▶ **n.** either of these cartilages.
– ORIGIN early 18th cent.: from modern Latin *arytaenoides*, from Greek *arutainoeidēs*, from *arutaina* 'funnel.'

AS ▶ **abbr.** American Samoa. ■ Anglo-Saxon. ■ Asperger's syndrome. ■ Associate in Science.

As ▶ **symbol** the chemical element arsenic.

as[1] /az/ ▶ **adv.** (usu. **as —— as**) used in comparisons to refer to the extent or degree of something: *hailstones as big as tennis balls | go as fast as you can | it tasted like grape juice but not as sweet.* ■ used to emphasize an amount: ***as many as** twenty-two rare species may be at risk.*
▶ **conj. 1** used to indicate that something happens during the time when something is taking place: *Frank watched him as he ambled through the crowd | as she grew older, she kept more to herself.*
2 used to indicate by comparison the way that something happens or is done: *dress as you would if you were having guests | they can do as they wish |* [as adv.] *she kissed him goodbye, **as usual** | as in the past, a collection is to be taken.* ■ used to add or interject a comment relating to the statement of a fact: *as you can see, I didn't go after all | he has, as you know, called for a referendum.*
3 because; since: *I must stop now as I have to go out.*
4 even though: *sweet as he is, he doesn't pay his bills | try as he might, he failed to pull it off.*
▶ **prep. 1** used to refer to the function or character that someone or something has: *he got a job as a cook | they were treated as foreigners | it came as a shock | as a dairy producer, you should evaluate and analyze your farm from many viewpoints.*
2 during the time of being (the thing specified): *he had often been sick as a child | as a student, my nickname was Space.*
– PHRASES **as and when** at the time when (used to refer to an uncertain future event): *they deal with an issue as and when it rears its head.* **as for** with regard to: *as for you, you'd better be quick.* **as if** (or **as though**) as would be the case if: *she behaved as if he weren't there.* **as if!** informal I very much doubt it: *You know how lottery winners always say it won't change their lives? Yeah, as if!* **as (it) is** in the existing circumstances: *I've got enough on my plate as it is.* **as it were** in a way (used to be less precise): *areas that have been, as it were, pushed aside.* **as long as** see **LONG[1]**. **as much** see **MUCH**. **as of** used to indicate the time or date from which something starts: *as of January 1, a free market will be created | I'm on unemployment as of today.* **as per** see **PER**. **as**

a

such see **SUCH**. **as though** see **AS IF** above. **as to** with respect to; concerning: *decisions as to which patients receive treatment*. **as well** see **WELL**[1]. **as yet** [usu. with negative] until now or a particular time in the past: *the damage is as yet undetermined*.
– ORIGIN Middle English: reduced form of Old English *alswā* 'similarly' (see **ALSO**).

USAGE 1 A small, seemingly innocent word, **as** is so frequently misused (or not used where needed) that interested writers are advised to consult a full-length usage guide for counsel on its proper use. **As** is often used in causal senses in place of *because* or *since* (*As Julie wasn't hungry, she ordered only a cup of coffee*); in such constructions, where **as** may cause confusion, it is generally advisable to use the unambiguous *because*, or *since*. 2 On whether it is more correct to say *he's not as shy* **as I** rather than *he's not as shy as me*, or *I live in the same street* **as she** rather than *I live in the same street* **as her**, see usage at **PERSONAL PRONOUN**. 3 For a discussion of when to use **as** rather than **like**, see usage at **LIKE**[1].

as[2] /as/ ▶ **n.** (pl. **asses**) an ancient Roman copper coin.
– ORIGIN early 17th cent.: Latin, literally 'a unit.'

as- ▶ **prefix** variant spelling of **AD-** assimilated before *s* (as in *assemble*, *assess*).

ASA ▶ **abbr.** American Standards Association (esp. in film-speed specification): *color film from 50 to 400 ASA*.

a·sa·fet·i·da /ˌasəˈfetidə/ (Brit. **asafoetida**) ▶ **n.** 1 a fetid resinous gum obtained from the roots of a herbaceous plant, used in herbal medicine and Indian cooking.
2 a Eurasian plant of the parsley family, from which this gum is obtained. ● *Ferula*, family Apiaceae.
– ORIGIN late Middle English: from medieval Latin *asafoetida*, from *asa* (from Persian *azā* 'mastic') + *foetida* (see **FETID**).

a·sa·na /ˈäsənə/ ▶ **n.** a posture adopted in performing hatha yoga.
– ORIGIN from Sanskrit *āsana*.

A·san·sol /ˌəsənˈsōl/ an industrial city in northeastern India, in West Bengal, northwest of Kolkata (Calcutta); pop. 499,300 (est. 2009).

A·san·te /əˈsänˌtē/ variant spelling of **ASHANTI**[1].

ASAP (also **asap**) ▶ **abbr.** as soon as possible.

as·bes·tos /asˈbestəs, az-/ ▶ **n.** a heat-resistant fibrous silicate mineral that can be woven into fabrics, and is used in fire-resistant and insulating materials such as brake linings: *asbestos was used for pipe insulation* | [as modifier] *asbestos shingles*. ■ fabric containing such a mineral.

The asbestos minerals include chrysotile (**white asbestos**) and several kinds of amphibole, notably amosite (**brown asbestos**) and crocidolite (**blue asbestos**). The danger to health caused by breathing in highly carcinogenic asbestos particles has led to stringent control of its use.

– ORIGIN early 17th cent.: via Latin from Greek *asbestos* 'unquenchable' (applied by Dioscurides to quicklime), from *a-* 'not' + *sbestos* (from *sbennumi* 'quench').

as·bes·to·sis /ˌasbesˈtōsis, ˌaz-/ ▶ **n.** a lung disease resulting from the inhalation of asbestos particles, marked by severe fibrosis and a high risk of mesothelioma (cancer of the pleura).

As·bury Park /ˈazˌberē, -b(ə)rē/ a city in east central New Jersey, on the Atlantic Ocean, long a noted resort; pop. 16,546 (est. 2008).

ASCAP ▶ **abbr.** American Society of Composers, Authors, and Publishers.

as·ca·ri·a·sis /ˌaskəˈrīəsis/ ▶ **n.** Medicine infection of the intestine with ascarids.

as·ca·rid /ˈaskərid/ (also **ascaris** /-ris/) ▶ **n.** Zoology a parasitic nematode worm of a family (Ascaridae) whose members typically live in the intestines of vertebrates.
– ORIGIN late 17th cent.: back-formation from Greek *askarides*, plural of *askaris* 'intestinal worm.'

as·cend /əˈsend/ ▶ **v.** 1 [with obj.] go up or climb: *she ascended the stairs* | [no obj.] *new magmas were created and ascended to the surface*. ■ climb to the summit of (a mountain or hill): *the first traveler to ascend the mountain*. ■ (of a fish or boat) move upstream along (a river).
2 [no obj.] rise through the air: *we had ascended 3,000 ft*. ■ (of a road or flight of steps) slope or lead up: *the road* **ascends to** *the lake*. ■ move up the social or professional scale: *he took exams to* **ascend through the ranks**. ■ (**ascend to**) rise to (an important position or a higher level): *some executives ascend to top-level positions*. ■ (of a spiritual being or soul) rise into heaven: *the Prophet* **ascended to heaven** | (as adj. **ascended**) *the risen and ascended Christ*. ■ (of a voice or sound) rise in pitch: *Carolyn's voice had ascended into high-pitched giggles*.
– PHRASES **ascend the throne** become king or queen.
– ORIGIN late Middle English: from Latin *ascendere*, from *ad-* 'to' + *scandere* 'to climb.'

as·cend·an·cy /əˈsendənsē/ (also **ascendency**) ▶ **n.** occupation of a position of dominant power or influence: *the ascendancy of good over evil* | *they have a moral ascendancy over the rich*.

as·cend·ant /əˈsendənt/ (also **ascendent**) ▶ **adj.** 1 rising in power or influence: *ascendant moderate factions in the party*.
2 Astrology (of a planet, zodiacal degree, or sign) just above the eastern horizon.
▶ **n.** Astrology the point on the ecliptic at which it intersects the eastern horizon at a particular time, typically that of a person's birth. ■ the point on an astrological chart representing this.
– PHRASES **in the ascendant** rising in power or influence: *the reformers are in the ascendant*.
– ORIGIN late Middle English: via Old French from Latin *ascendent-* 'climbing up,' from the verb *ascendere* (see **ASCEND**).

as·cend·er /əˈsendər/ ▶ **n.** a person or thing that ascends, in particular: ■ a part of a letter that extends above the main part (as in *b* and *h*). ■ a letter having such a part. ■ a device used in climbing that can be clipped to a rope to act as a foothold or handhold, or to keep something in position.

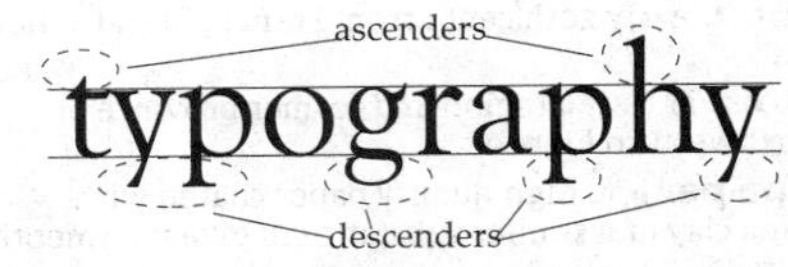

ascenders and descenders

as·cend·ing /əˈsendiNG/ ▶ **adj.** [attrib.] 1 increasing in size or importance: *incomes ranked* **in ascending order** *of size*.
2 sloping or leading upward: *a gently ascending forest path* | *blood pressure in the ascending aorta*.

as·cend·ing co·lon ▶ **n.** Anatomy the first main part of the large intestine, which passes upward from the cecum on the right side of the abdomen.

as·cen·sion /əˈsenSHən/ ▶ **n.** [in sing.] the act of rising to an important position or a higher level: *his* **ascension to** *the ranks of pop star*. ■ (**Ascension**) the ascent of Christ into heaven on the fortieth day after the Resurrection.
– ORIGIN Middle English (referring to the ascent of Christ): via Old French from Latin *ascensio(n-)*, from the verb *ascendere* (see **ASCEND**).

As·cen·sion Day the fortieth day after Easter, on which Christ's Ascension is celebrated in the Christian Church. Also called **HOLY THURSDAY**.

As·cen·sion Is·land /əˈsenSHən/ a small island in the South Atlantic Ocean; with St. Helena it is a dependency of the UK; pop. 1,100 (est. 2009).

as·cent /əˈsent/ ▶ **n.** 1 a climb or walk to the summit of a mountain or hill: *the first ascent of the Matterhorn* | *the routes of ascent can be retraced*. ■ an upward slope or path: *the ascent grew steeper*.
2 [in sing.] an instance of rising through the air: *the first balloon ascent was in 1783*. ■ [in sing.] a rise to an important position or a higher level: *his ascent to power*.
– ORIGIN late 16th cent.: from **ASCEND**, on the pattern of the pair of *descend*, *descent*.

as·cer·tain /ˌasərˈtān/ ▶ **v.** [with obj.] find (something) out for certain; make sure of: *an attempt to ascertain the cause of the accident* | [with clause] *management should ascertain whether adequate funding can be provided*.
– DERIVATIVES **as·cer·tain·a·ble** **adj.**, **as·cer·tain·ment** **n.**
– ORIGIN late Middle English (in the sense 'assure, convince'): from Old French *acertener*, based on Latin *certus* 'settled, sure.'

as·cet·ic /əˈsetik/ ▶ **adj.** characterized by or suggesting the practice of severe self-discipline and abstention from all forms of indulgence, typically for religious reasons: *an ascetic life of prayer, fasting, and manual labor* | *a narrow, humorless, ascetic face*.
▶ **n.** a person who practices such self-discipline and abstention.
– DERIVATIVES **as·cet·i·cal·ly** /-ik(ə)lē/ **adv.**
– ORIGIN mid 17th cent.: from medieval Latin *asceticus* or Greek *askētikos*, from *askētēs* 'monk,' from *askein* 'to exercise.'

as·cet·i·cism /əˈsetiˌsizəm/ ▶ **n.** severe self-discipline and avoidance of all forms of indulgence, typically for religious reasons: *acts of physical asceticism*.

As·cham /ˈaskəm/, Roger (*c.*1515–68), English humanist scholar and writer. He was noted for his treatise on archery, *Toxophilus* (1545), and for *The Scholemaster* (1570), a practical and influential tract on education.

asc·hel·minth /ˈaskhelˌminTH, ˈaSHhel-/ ▶ **n.** (pl. **aschelminths** or **aschelminthes** /ˌaskhelˈminTHēz, ˌaSHhel-/) Zoology an invertebrate animal belonging to a group of phyla that are distinguished by the lack of a well-developed coelom and blood vessels. Most aschelminths are minute wormlike animals, including the nematode worms, rotifers, and water bears. ● Phylum Nematoda and about seven minor phyla, formerly placed in a phylum Aschelminthes.
– ORIGIN from modern Latin *Aschelminthes* (former phylum name), from Greek *askos* 'sac' + *helminth* 'worm' (from the former belief that animals of this group had a fluid-filled internal sac).

as·ci /ˈasī, -kī, -kē/ plural form of **ASCUS**.

as·cid·i·an /əˈsidēən/ ▶ **n.** Zoology a sea squirt. ● Phylum Chordata, Subphylum Urochordata, class Ascidiacea.
– ORIGIN mid 19th cent.: from modern Latin plural *Ascidia* (genus name), from Greek *askidion*, diminutive of *askos* 'wineskin.'

ASCII /ˈaskē/ ▶ **abbr.** Computing American Standard Code for Information Interchange, a set of digital codes representing letters, numerals, and other symbols, widely used as a standard format in the transfer of text between computers.

as·ci·tes /əˈsītēz/ ▶ **n.** Medicine the accumulation of fluid in the peritoneal cavity, causing abdominal swelling.
– DERIVATIVES **as·cit·ic** /əˈsitik/ **adj.**
– ORIGIN late Middle English: via late Latin from Greek *askitēs*, from *askos* 'wineskin.'

As·cle·pi·us /əˈsklēpēəs/ Greek Mythology a hero and god of healing, son of Apollo.

as·co·my·cete /ˌaskəˈmīsēt, -mīˈsēt/ ▶ **n.** Botany a fungus whose spores develop within asci. The ascomycetes include most molds, mildews, and yeasts, the fungal component of most lichens, and a few large forms such as morels and truffles. Compare with **BASIDIOMYCETE**. ● Phylum Ascomycota (formerly subdivision Ascomycotina), class Ascomycetes.
– ORIGIN mid 19th cent.: from modern Latin *Ascomycetes* (former class name), from Greek *askos* 'sac' + *muskētes* 'fungi.'

as·con /ˈaskän/ ▶ **n.** Zoology a sponge of the simplest structure, with a tubelike or baglike form lined with choanocytes. Compare with **LEUCON** and **SYCON**. ● Phylum Porifera.
– DERIVATIVES **as·co·noid** /-kəˌnoid/ **adj.**
– ORIGIN late 19th cent.: modern Latin (genus name), from Greek *askos* 'bag.'

a·scor·bic ac·id /əˈskôrbik/ ▶ **n.** a vitamin found particularly in citrus fruits and green vegetables. It is essential in maintaining healthy connective tissue, and is also thought to act as an antioxidant. Severe deficiency causes scurvy. Also called **VITAMIN C**. ● A lactone; chem. formula: $C_6H_8O_6$.
– DERIVATIVES **a·scor·bate** /-bāt, -bit/ **n.**
– ORIGIN 1930s: from **A-**[1] 'without' + medieval Latin *scorbutus* 'scurvy' + **-IC**.

As·cot /ˈasˌkät, -kət/ a town in southern England, southwest of London. It is the site of an annual horse race.

as·cot /ˈasˌkät, -kət/ ▶ **n.** (also **ascot tie**) a man's broad silk necktie.
– ORIGIN early 20th cent.: from the place name **ASCOT**, by association with formal dress at race meetings held there.

ascot

as·cribe /əˈskrīb/ ▶ **v.** [with obj.] (**ascribe something to**) attribute something to (a cause): *he ascribed Jane's short temper to her upset stomach*. ■ (usu. **be ascribed to**) attribute (a text, quotation, or work of art) to a particular person or period: *a quotation ascribed to Thomas Cooper*. ■ (usu. **be ascribed to**) regard (a quality) as belonging to: *tough-mindedness is a quality commonly ascribed to top bosses*.
– DERIVATIVES **a·scrib·a·ble** **adj.**
– ORIGIN Middle English: from Latin *ascribere*, from *ad-* 'to' + *scribere* 'write.'

as·crip·tion /əˈskripSHən/ ▶ **n.** the attribution of something to a cause: *an* **ascription of** *effect* **to** *cause*. ■ the attribution of a text, quotation, or work of art to a particular person or period: *her ascription of the text to Boccaccio* | *questions of authorial ascription*. ■ the action of regarding a quality as belonging to someone or something: *the author's* **ascription of** *human attributes* **to** *his hero or villain*. ■ a preacher's words ascribing praise to God at the end of a sermon.

–ORIGIN late 16th cent.: from Latin *ascriptio(n-)*, from the verb *ascribere* (see ASCRIBE).

as·cus /ˈaskəs/ ▶ n. (pl. **asci** /ˈasī, ˈaskī, -kē/) Botany a sac, typically cylindrical in shape, in which the spores of ascomycete fungi develop.
–ORIGIN mid 19th cent.: modern Latin, from Greek *askos* 'bag.'

ASDIC /ˈazˌdik/ ▶ n. chiefly Brit. an early form of sonar used to detect submarines.
–ORIGIN World War II: acronym from *Allied Submarine Detection Investigation Committee*.

-ase ▶ suffix Biochemistry forming names of enzymes: *amylase*.
–ORIGIN from *(diast)ase*.

ASEAN /ˈäsēˌän, ˈas-/ ▶ abbr. Association of Southeast Asian Nations.

a·seis·mic /āˈsīzmik/ ▶ adj. Geology not characterized by earthquake activity.

a·sep·sis /āˈsepsis/ ▶ n. the absence of bacteria, viruses, and other microorganisms. ■ the exclusion of bacteria and other microorganisms, typically during surgery. Compare with ANTISEPSIS.

a·sep·tic /āˈseptik/ ▶ adj. free from contamination caused by harmful bacteria, viruses, or other microorganisms. ■ [attrib.] (of surgical practice) aiming at the complete exclusion of harmful microorganisms. ■ [attrib.] (of a wound, instrument, or dressing) surgically sterile or sterilized.

a·sex·u·al /āˈsekSHo͞oəl/ ▶ adj. without sex or sexuality, in particular: ■ Biology (of reproduction) not involving the fusion of gametes. ■ Biology without sex or sexual organs: *asexual parasites*. ■ without sexual feelings or associations: *she rested her hand on the back of his head, in a maternal, wholly asexual, gesture*.
▶ n. a person who has no sexual feelings or desires.
–DERIVATIVES **a·sex·u·al·i·ty** /ˌāsekSHo͞oˈalitē/ n., **a·sex·u·al·ly** adv.

As·gard /ˈasˌgärd, ˈaz-/ Scandinavian Mythology a region in the center of the universe, inhabited by the gods.

ash¹ /asH/ ▶ n. the powdery residue left after the burning of a substance: *cigarette ash* | *a day's worth of paper burned to ashes*. ■ (**ashes**) the remains of something destroyed; ruins: *the people are really living in the ashes of those traditions and institutions*. ■ (**ashes**) the remains of the human body after cremation or burning: *his ashes were scattered on a Welsh mountainside*. ■ powdery material thrown out by a volcano: *the plains have been showered by volcanic ash*. ■ the mineral component of an organic substance, as assessed from the residue left after burning: *coal contains higher levels of ash than premium fuels*.
–PHRASES (**turn to**) **ashes in one's mouth** (become) something that is bitterly disappointing or worthless: *they found words such as "heroic" turn to ashes in their mouths during the scandal*. **rise** (or **emerge**) **from the ashes** be renewed after destruction: *Atlanta has risen from the ashes*. [compare with *rise like a phoenix from the ashes* (see PHOENIX).]
–ORIGIN Old English *æsce*, *axe*, of Germanic origin; related to Dutch *as* and German *Asche*.

ash² ▶ n. **1** (also **ash tree**) a tree with silver-gray bark and compound leaves. The ash is widely distributed throughout north temperate regions where it can form forests. ● Genus *Fraxinus*, family Oleaceae: many species, including the North American **white ash** (*F. americana*) and the **European ash** (*F. excelsior*). ■ the hard pale wood of this tree. ■ [with modifier] any of a number of unrelated trees with similar leaves. See also MOUNTAIN ASH.
2 an Old English runic letter (so named from the word of which it was the first letter). ■ the symbol æ or Æ, used in the Roman alphabet in place of the runic letter, and as a phonetic symbol. See also Æ.
–ORIGIN Old English *æsc*, of Germanic origin; related to Dutch *es* and German *Esche*.

a·shamed /əˈSHāmd/ ▶ adj. [predic.] embarrassed or feeling guilt because of something one has done or a characteristic one has: *you should be ashamed of yourself* | [with clause] *she felt ashamed that she had hit him*. ■ (**ashamed to do something**) reluctant to do something through fear of embarrassment or humiliation: *I'm ashamed to say I followed him home* | *I am not ashamed to be seen with them*. ■ embarrassed or humiliated to be associated with a person: *his clothes and manners made me ashamed of him*.
–DERIVATIVES **a·sham·ed·ly** /əˈSHāmidlē/ adv.
–ORIGIN Old English *āscamod*, past participle of *āscamian* 'feel shame,' from *ā-* (as an intensifier) + the verb SHAME.

A·shan·ti¹ /əˈSHäntē, əˈSHantē/ (also **Asante** /əˈsäntē, əˈsantē/) a region of central Ghana. Annexed by Britain in 1902, it became part of the former British colony of the Gold Coast.

A·shan·ti² (also **Asante**) ▶ n. (pl. **same**) **1** a member of a people of south central Ghana.
2 the dialect of Akan spoken by this people.
▶ adj. relating to or denoting this people or their language.
–ORIGIN the name in Akan.

ash blond (also **ash blonde**) ▶ adj. (of a person or their hair) very pale blond.
▶ n. a very pale blond color. ■ a person with hair of such a color.

ash·can /ˈasHˌkan/ ▶ n. a metal receptacle for trash or ashes. ■ military slang a depth charge.

Ash·can School /ˈasHˌkan/ a group of American realist painters active from *c.*1908 until World War I, who painted scenes from the slums of New York. The school grew out of the group called "the Eight."

Ash·croft /ˈasHˌkrôft/, John (1942–), US attorney general 2001–05. Under him, the Justice Department was reorganized to focus on antiterrorism, a national concern that had heightened following the terrorist attacks of September 11, 2001.

Ashe /asH/, Arthur (Robert) (1943–93), US tennis player. He won the men's singles title at the US Open 1968 and Wimbledon 1975, becoming the first black male player to achieve world rankings.

ash·en¹ /ˈasHən/ ▶ adj. of the pale gray color of ash: *the ashen morning sky*. ■ (of a person's face) very pale with shock, fear, or illness. ■ of or resembling ashes: *the volcano's ashen breath*.

ash·en² ▶ adj. archaic or literary made of timber from the ash tree.

Ash·er /ˈasHər/ (in the Bible) a Hebrew patriarch, son of Jacob and Zilpah. ■ the tribe of Israel traditionally descended from him.

Ashe·ville /ˈasHvəl, -ˌvil/ a city in western North Carolina, a resort in the Blue Ridge Mountains; pop. 74,543 (est. 2008). The Biltmore estate is here.

Ash·ga·bat /ˈäsHgəˌbät, ˈasHgəˌbat/ (also **Ashkhabad** /ˈäsHkəˌbäd, ˈasHkəˌbad/) the capital of the central Asian republic of Turkmenistan; pop. 744,000 (est. 2007). Former name (1919–27) POLTORATSK.

a·shine /əˈSHīn/ ▶ adj. [predic.] literary shining: *eyes ashine in the darkness*.

A-shirt ▶ n. a sleeveless undershirt, with straps over the shoulders.

Ash·ke·naz·i /ˌasHkəˈnazē, ˌäsHkəˈnäzē/ ▶ n. (pl. **Ashkenazim** /-ˈnazim, -ˈnäzim/) a Jew of central or eastern European descent. More than 80 percent of Jews today are Ashkenazim; they preserve Palestinian rather than Babylonian Jewish traditions, and some still use Yiddish. Compare with SEPHARDI.
–DERIVATIVES **Ash·ke·naz·ic** /-ˈnazik, -ˈnä-/ adj.
–ORIGIN from modern Hebrew, from *Ashkenaz*, son of Japheth, one of the sons of Noah (Gen. 10:3).

Ash·ke·na·zy /ˌasHkəˈnäzē, ˌäsH-/, Vladimir (Davidovich) (1937–), Russian pianist. A child prodigy, he left the former Soviet Union in 1963, finally settling in Iceland in 1973.

Ash·kha·bad /ˈäsHkəˌbäd/ variant spelling of ASHGABAT.

Ash·land /ˈasHlənd/ a city in northeastern Kentucky, on the Ohio River; pop. 21,346 (est. 2008). It is a center of the area's coal industry.

ash·lar /ˈasHlər/ ▶ n. masonry made of large square-cut stones, typically used as a facing on walls of brick or stone. ■ a stone used in such masonry.
–ORIGIN Middle English: from Old French *aisselier*, from Latin *axilla*, diminutive of *axis* 'plank.'

ash·lar·ing /ˈasHləriNG/ ▶ n. **1** ashlar masonry.
2 upright boarding fixed from the joists to the rafters of an attic to cut off the acute angle between the roof and the floor.

Ash·ley /ˈasHlē/, Laura (1925–85), Welsh fashion and textile designer; known for her use of floral patterns and romantic Victorian and Edwardian styles.

Ash·mo·le·an Mu·se·um /asHˈmōlēən/ a museum of art and antiquities in Oxford, England. It opened in 1683 and was the first public institution of its kind in England.

Ash·more and Car·ti·er Is·lands /ˈasHˌmôr, ˈkärtēˌā, ˌkärtēˈā/ uninhabited islands in the Indian Ocean, an external territory of Australia.

A·sho·ka variant spelling of ASOKA.

a·shore /əˈSHôr/ ▶ adv. to or on the shore from the direction of the sea: *the seals come ashore to breed*. ■ on land as opposed to at sea: *we spent the day ashore*.

ash pan ▶ n. a tray fixed beneath a grate in which ashes can be collected and removed.

ash·ram /ˈäsHrəm/ ▶ n. (in South Asia) a hermitage, monastic community, or other place of religious retreat for Hindus. ■ a place of religious retreat or community life modeled on the Indian ashram.
–ORIGIN from Sanskrit *āśrama* 'hermitage.'

Ash Sha·ri·qah /ˌäsH ˈSHärēkə/ variant form of SHARJAH.

Ash·ta·bu·la /ˌasHtəˈbyo͞olə/ a port city in northeastern Ohio, on Lake Erie; pop. 19,689 (est. 2008).

ash·tang·a /asHˈtäNGə/ (also **asthtanga**; **astanga** /as-/) ▶ n. a type of yoga based on eight principles and consisting of a series of poses executed in swift succession, combined with deep, controlled breathing.
–ORIGIN from Hindi *aṣṭaṅ* or its source, Sanskrit *aṣṭaṅga* 'having eight parts,' from *aṣṭán* 'eight.'

ash·tray /ˈasHˌtrā/ ▶ n. a receptacle for tobacco ash and cigarette butts.

A·shur·ba·ni·pal /ˌäsHo͝orˈbäniˌpäl/, king of Assyria *c.*668–627 BC; grandson of Sennacherib. A patron of the arts, he established a library of more than 20,000 clay tablets at Nineveh.

Ash Wednes·day ▶ n. the first day of Lent in the Western Christian Church, marked by services of penitence.
–ORIGIN from the custom of marking the foreheads of penitents with ashes on that day.

ash·y /ˈasHē/ ▶ adj. **1** of a pale grayish color; ashen: *the ashy shadows of the mountains*.
2 covered with, consisting of, or resembling ashes: *an ashy sediment*.

ASI ▶ abbr. airspeed indicator.

A·sia /ˈāZHə/ the largest of the world's continents, constituting nearly one-third of the landmass, lying entirely north of the equator except for some Southeast Asian islands. It is connected to Africa by the Isthmus of Suez and borders Europe (part of the same landmass) along the Ural Mountains and across the Caspian Sea.

as·i·a·go /ˌäsēˈägō, äˈsyä-/ ▶ n. a strong-flavored cow's milk cheese originally made in northern Italy.
–ORIGIN named after *Asiago*, the plateau and town in northern Italy where the cheese was first made.

A·sia Mi·nor /ˈmīnər/ a western peninsula of Asia that now constitutes most of modern Turkey.

A·sian /ˈāZHən/ ▶ adj. of or relating to Asia or its people, customs, or languages.
▶ n. a native of Asia or a person of Asian descent.
–ORIGIN late Middle English: from Latin *Asianus*, from Greek *Asianos*, from *Asia* (see ASIA).

> **USAGE** In North America, **Asian** refers to people from China, Japan, and other countries of East Asia, while in Britain it is used to refer to people who come from (or whose parents came from) India, Pakistan, or elsewhere in South Asia. See also usage at ORIENTAL.

A·sian A·mer·i·can ▶ n. an American who is of Asian (chiefly East Asian) descent.
▶ adj. of or relating to such people.

A·sian co·bra ▶ n. another term for SPECTACLED COBRA.

A·sian De·vel·op·ment Bank a bank with forty-seven member countries (thirty-two are from the Asia-Pacific region) located in Manila. Its aim is to promote the economic and social progress of its developing member countries.

A·sian el·e·phant ▶ n. another term for INDIAN ELEPHANT.

A·sian long-horned bee·tle ▶ n. a large black beetle with white spots whose larvae feed on hardwoods. Infestations in the US have led to large-scale destruction of trees in order to eradicate the pest. ● *Anoplophora glabripennis*, family Cerambycidae.

A·sian pear ▶ n. the crisp apple-shaped fruit of a tree that is native to Japan and China and cultivated in Australia and New Zealand. Also called NASHI. ● This fruit is obtained from varieties of *Pyrus pyrifolia*, family Rosaceae.

A·sian swamp eel ▶ n. a freshwater eel that can breathe air and traverse land. Its introduction in the southeastern US threatens some native aquatic fauna. ● *Monopterus albus*, family Synbranchidae.

A·sia-Pa·cif·ic ▶ n. (also **Asia-Pacific region**) a business region consisting of the whole of Asia as well as the countries of the Pacific Rim.

A·si·at·ic /ˌāZHēˈatik, ˌāzē-/ ▶ adj. relating to or deriving from Asia: *Asiatic cholera* | *Asiatic coastal regions*.
▶ n. often offensive an Asian person.

– ORIGIN via Latin *Asiaticus* from Greek *Asiatikos*, from *Asia* (see **Asia**).

> **USAGE** The standard and accepted term when referring to individual people is **Asian** rather than **Asiatic**, which can be offensive. However, **Asiatic** is standard in scientific and technical use, for example in biological and anthropological classifications. See also usage at **ORIENTAL**.

ASIC /ˈāsik/ ▶ **abbr.** Electronics application specific integrated circuit.

a·side /əˈsīd/ ▶ **adv.** to one side; out of the way: *he pushed his plate aside | they stood aside to let a car pass | she must put aside all her antagonistic feelings.* ■ in reserve; for future use: *she set aside some money for rent.* ■ used to indicate that one is dismissing something from consideration, or that one is shifting from one topic or tone of discussion to another: ***joking aside**, I've certainly had my fill.*
▶ **n. 1** a remark or passage by a character in a play that is intended to be heard by the audience but unheard by the other characters in the play. ■ a remark not intended to be heard by everyone present: *"Does that make him a murderer?" whispered Alice in an aside to Fred.*
2 a remark that is not directly related to the main topic of discussion: *the recipe book has little asides about the importance of home and family.*
– PHRASES **aside from** apart from. **set something aside 1** remove land from agricultural production for fallow or other use: *with 15% of land set aside, cereal production will fall* | [as adj.] *using his set-aside acreage to work clover into his rotation.* **2** annul a legal decision or process. **3** put in reserve: *he was setting aside a few dollars a week.* **take** (or **draw**) **someone aside** move someone away from a group of people in order to talk privately.
– ORIGIN Middle English (originally *on side*): see **A-**[2], **SIDE**.

A-side ▶ **n.** the side of a pop single record regarded as the main release.

As·i·mov /ˈazə,môv, -,môf/, Isaac (1920–92), US writer and scientist; born in Russia; particularly known for his works of science fiction, his books on science for nonscientists, and his essays on a wide variety of subjects. Building on Karel Čapek's concept of the robot, in 1941, Asimov coined the term *robotics*. Notable science-fiction works: *I, Robot* (1950) and *Foundation* (trilogy, 1951–53).

as·i·nine /ˈasə,nīn/ ▶ **adj.** extremely stupid or foolish: *Lydia ignored his asinine remark.*
– DERIVATIVES **as·i·nin·i·ty** /,asəˈninitē/ **n.**
– ORIGIN late 15th cent.: from Latin *asininus*, from *asinus* 'ass.'

A·sir Moun·tains /äˈsi(ə)r/ a range of mountains in southwestern Saudi Arabia that run parallel to the Red Sea.

-asis (often **-iasis**) ▶ **suffix** forming the names of diseases: *onchocerciasis | psoriasis.*
– ORIGIN via Latin from Greek in nouns denoting a state or condition.

as·i·ty /ˈasitē/ ▶ **n.** (pl. **asities**) a stocky perching bird related to the pittas, found only in Madagascar. ● Family Philepittidae: two genera, in particular *Philepitta* (two species). See also **FALSE SUNBIRD**.
– ORIGIN probably a local name.

ask /ask/ ▶ **v. 1** [reporting verb] say something in order to obtain an answer or some information: [with clause] *he **asked if** she wanted coffee | he **asked whether** his electric wheelchair would fit through their doors* | [with obj.] *people are always asking questions* | [with direct speech] *"How much further?" I asked* | [no obj.] *the old man **asked about** her job.* ■ [no obj.] (**ask around**) talk to various people in order to find something out: *there are fine meals to be had if you ask around.* ■ [no obj.] (**ask after**) inquire about the health or well-being of: *Mrs. Savage asked after Iris's mother.*
2 [with obj.] request (someone) to do or give something: *Mary **asked** her father **for** money* | [with obj. and infinitive] *I asked him to call the manager* | [no obj.] *don't be afraid to **ask for** advice.* ■ [with clause] request permission to do something: *she **asked if** she could move in* | [with infinitive] *he asked to see the officer involved.* ■ [no obj.] (**ask for**) request to speak to: *when I arrived, I asked for Catherine.* ■ request (a specified amount) as a price for selling something: *he was **asking** $250 **for** the guitar.* ■ expect or demand (something) of someone: *it's asking a lot, but could you look through Billy's things?*
3 [with obj.] invite (someone) to one's home or a function: *it's about time we **asked** Pam **to** dinner.* ■ (**ask someone along**) invite someone to join one on an outing: *do you want to ask him along?* ■ (**ask someone out**) invite someone out socially, typically on a date.
▶ **n.** [in sing.] **1** a request, esp. for a donation: *it was an awkward ask for more funding.*
2 the price at which an item, esp. a financial security, is offered for sale: [as modifier] *ask prices for bonds.*
– PHRASES **be asking for it** (or **trouble**) informal behave in a way that is likely to result in difficulty for oneself: *they accused me of asking for it | you're asking for trouble.* **don't ask me!** informal used to indicate that one does not know the answer to a question and that one is surprised or irritated to be questioned: *"Is he her boyfriend then?" "Don't ask me!"* **for the asking** used to indicate that something can be easily obtained: *the job was his for the asking.* **I ask you!** informal an exclamation of shock or disapproval intended to elicit agreement from one's listener: *A toaster for a birthday present? I ask you!* **if you ask me** informal used to emphasize that a statement is one's personal opinion: *if you ask me, it's just an excuse for laziness.*
– DERIVATIVES **ask·er n.**
– ORIGIN Old English *āscian, āhsian, āxian.*

a·skance /əˈskans/ (also **askant** /əˈskant/) ▶ **adv.** with an attitude or look of suspicion or disapproval: *the reformers **looked askance at** the mystical tradition | a waiter **looked askance at** Charlie's jeans.*
– ORIGIN late 15th cent.: of unknown origin.

as·ka·ri /ˈaskərē/ ▶ **n.** (pl. **same** or **askaris**) (in East Africa) a soldier or police officer.
– ORIGIN late 19th cent.: from Arabic *'askarī* 'soldier.'

as·ke·sis /əˈskēsis/ (also **ascesis** /əˈsēsis/) ▶ **n.** the practice of severe self-discipline, typically for religious reasons.
– ORIGIN late 19th cent.: from Greek *askēsis* 'training,' from *askein* 'to exercise.'

a·skew /əˈskyo͞o/ ▶ **adv. & adj.** not in a straight or level position: [as adv.] *the door was hanging askew on one twisted hinge* | [as predic. adj.] *her hat was slightly askew.* ■ wrong; awry: [as adv.] *the plan went sadly askew* | [as adj.] *outrageous humor with a decidedly askew point of view.*
– ORIGIN mid 16th cent.: from **A-**[2] 'on' + **SKEW**.

ask·ing price ▶ **n.** the price at which something is offered for sale.

ASL ▶ **abbr.** American Sign Language.

a·slant /əˈslant/ ▶ **adv.** at an angle or in a sloping direction: *some of the paintings hung aslant.*
▶ **prep.** across at an angle or in a sloping direction: *rays of light fell aslant a door.*

a·sleep /əˈslēp/ ▶ **adj. & adv.** in or into a state of sleep: [as adj.] *she had been asleep for over three hours* | [as adv.] *Bob regularly **fell asleep** in his recliner.* ■ not attentive or alert; inactive: [as adj.] *the competition was not asleep.* ■ (of a limb) having no feeling; numb: [as adj.] *his legs were asleep.* ■ literary used euphemistically to say that someone is dead.
– PHRASES **asleep at the switch** (or **wheel**) informal not attentive or alert; inactive: *someone must have been asleep at the switch to allow this.*

a·slope /əˈslōp/ ▶ **adv. & adj.** archaic or literary in a sloping position: [as adj.] *the steps are aslope and broken* | [as adv.] *against the mast he leans aslope.*
– ORIGIN late Middle English: origin uncertain; this form appears earlier than **SLOPE**.

ASM ▶ **abbr.** ■ air-to-surface missile. ■ assistant stage manager.

As·ma·ra /äzˈmärə/ (also **Asmera** /azˈmerə/) the capital of Eritrea; pop. 601,000 (est. 2007).

a·so·cial /āˈsōshəl/ ▶ **adj.** avoiding social interaction; inconsiderate of or hostile to others: *the cat's independence has encouraged a view that it is asocial.*

A·so·ka /əˈsōkə/ (also **Ashoka** /əˈshōkə/) (died *c.*232 BC), emperor of India *c.*269–232 BC. He converted to Buddhism and established it as the state religion.

A·so·ka pil·lar (also **Ashoka pillar**) the pillar of the Emperor Asoka with four lions on the capital, built at Sarnath in Uttar Pradesh to mark the spot where the Buddha publicly preached his doctrine, and adopted as a symbol by the government of India.
– ORIGIN *Asoka* from Sanskrit *aśoka*.

ASP ▶ **abbr.** application service provider, a company providing Internet access to software applications that would otherwise have to be installed on individual computers.

asp /asp/ ▶ **n.** (also **asp viper**) a small southern European viper with an upturned snout. ● *Vipera aspis*, family Viperidae. ■ another term for **EGYPTIAN COBRA**.
– ORIGIN Middle English: from Latin *aspis*, from Greek.

as·par·a·gine /əˈsparə,jēn, -jin/ ▶ **n.** Biochemistry a hydrophilic amino acid that is a constituent of most proteins. ● An amide of aspartic acid; chem. formula: $CONH_2CH_2CH(NH_2)COOH$.
– ORIGIN early 19th cent.: from **ASPARAGUS** (which contains it) + **-INE**[4].

as·par·a·gus /əˈsparəgəs/ ▶ **n.** a tall plant of the lily family with fine feathery foliage, cultivated for its edible shoots. ● *Asparagus officinalis*, family Liliaceae. ■ the tender young shoots of this plant, eaten as a vegetable and considered a delicacy.
– ORIGIN mid 16th cent.: via Latin from Greek *asparagos*.

as·par·a·gus bee·tle ▶ **n.** a small, boldly marked leaf beetle whose adults and larvae feed on the leaves of asparagus. ● *Crioceris asparagi*, family Chrysomelidae.

as·par·a·gus fern ▶ **n.** a decorative indoor or greenhouse plant with feathery foliage, related to the edible asparagus. ● Genus *Asparagus*, family Liliaceae: several species, in particular *A. plumosus*.

as·par·tame /ˈaspär,tām/ ▶ **n.** a very sweet substance used as an artificial sweetener, chiefly in low-calorie products. It is a derivative of aspartic acid and phenylalanine.

as·par·tic ac·id /əˈspärtik/ ▶ **n.** Biochemistry an acidic amino acid that is a constituent of most proteins and also occurs in sugar cane. It is important in the metabolism of nitrogen in animals and also acts as a neurotransmitter. ● Chem. formula: $COOHCH_2CH(NH_2)COOH$.
– DERIVATIVES **as·par·tate** /-tāt/ **n.**
– ORIGIN mid 19th cent.: *aspartic* from French *aspartique*, formed arbitrarily from Latin *asparagus* (see **ASPARAGUS**).

ASPCA ▶ **abbr.** American Society for the Prevention of Cruelty to Animals.

as·pect /ˈaspekt/ ▶ **n. 1** a particular part or feature of something: *the financial aspect can be overstressed.* ■ a specific way in which something can be considered: *from every aspect, theirs was a changing world.* ■ [in sing.] a particular appearance or quality: *the air of desertion lent the place a sinister aspect | a man of decidedly foreign aspect.*
2 [usu. in sing.] the positioning of a building or thing in a specified direction: *a greenhouse with a southern aspect.* ■ the side of a building facing a particular direction: *the front aspect of the hotel was unremarkable.* ■ Astrology a particular position of a planet or other celestial body relative to another, as measured by angular distance: *the sun in Aries formed an adverse aspect with Uranus in Capricorn.*
3 Grammar a grammatical category or form that expresses the way in which time is denoted by the verb: *the semantics of tense and aspect | four verbal aspects.*

> There are two aspects in English, the progressive or continuing aspect (expressing duration, typically using the auxiliary verb *be* with a form in *-ing*, as in *I was reading a book*) and the perfect or perfective (expressing completed action, typically using the auxiliary verb *have* with a past participle, as in *I have read the book*).

▶ **v.** [with obj.] Astrology (of a planet) form an aspect with (another celestial body): *the sun is superbly aspected by your ruler Mars on the 19th.*
– DERIVATIVES **as·pec·tu·al** /aˈspekcho͞oəl/ **adj.**
– ORIGIN late Middle English (denoting the action or a way of looking at something): from Latin *aspectus*, from *aspicere* 'look at,' from *ad-* 'to, at' + *specere* 'to look.'

as·pect ra·tio ▶ **n.** the ratio of two dimensions of something as considered from a specific direction, in particular: ■ the ratio of the width to the height of the image on a television screen. ■ Aeronautics the ratio of the span to the mean chord of an airfoil.

As·pen /ˈaspən/ a resort in south central Colorado; pop. 5,902 (est. 2008) A thriving recreational center, it is noted particularly for its skiing facilities.

as·pen /ˈaspən/ ▶ **n.** a poplar tree with rounded, long-stalked, and typically coarsely toothed leaves that tremble in even a slight breeze. ● Genus *Populus*, family Salicaceae: several species, in particular the North American **quaking aspen** (*P. tremuloides*) and **bigtooth aspen** (*P. grandidentata*) and the European *P. tremula*.
– ORIGIN late Middle English: from dialect *asp* (in the same sense) + **-EN**[2], forming an adjective later used as a noun (late 16th cent).

As·per·ger's syn·drome /ˈaspərgərz/ ▶ **n.** a developmental disorder related to autism and characterized by higher than average intellectual ability coupled with impaired social skills and restrictive, repetitive patterns of interest and activities.

as·per·ges /əˈsparjəz/ ▶ **n.** Christian Church the rite of sprinkling holy water at the beginning of the Mass, still used occasionally in Catholic churches. ■ another term for **ASPERGILLUM**.
– ORIGIN late 16th cent.: the first word of the Latin (Vulgate) text of Psalms 51:9 (literally 'thou shalt purge'), recited before Mass during the sprinkling of holy water.

as·per·gil·lo·sis /ˌaspərjəˈlōsis/ ▶ **n.** a condition in which certain fungi infect the tissues. It most commonly affects the lungs, owing to inhalation of spores from moldy hay, and is then informally called **farmer's lung**. ● The fungi that cause this condition are blackish molds of the genus *Aspergillus*, phylum Ascomycota.
– ORIGIN late 19th cent.: from modern Latin *Aspergillus*, from ASPERGILLUM, + -OSIS.

as·per·gil·lum /ˌaspərˈjiləm/ ▶ **n.** (pl. **aspergilla** /-ˈjilə/ or **aspergillums**) an implement for sprinkling holy water.
– ORIGIN mid 17th cent.: from Latin.

as·per·i·ty /əˈsperitē/ ▶ **n.** (pl. **asperities**) harshness of tone or manner: *he pointed this out with some asperity.* ■ (**asperities**) harsh qualities or conditions: *the asperities of a harsh and divided society.* ■ (usu. **asperities**) a rough edge on a surface: *the asperities of the metal surfaces.*
– ORIGIN Middle English (in the sense 'hardship, rigor'): from Old French *asperite*, or Latin *asperitas*, from *asper* 'rough.'

a·sper·mi·a /āˈspərmēə/ ▶ **n.** Medicine failure to produce semen, or absence of sperm in the semen.

as·perse /əˈspərs/ ▶ **v.** [with obj.] rare attack or criticize the reputation or integrity of: *he aspersed the place and its inhabitants.*
– ORIGIN late 15th cent. (in the sense 'sprinkle or spatter with liquid'): from Latin *aspers-* 'sprinkled,' from the verb *aspergere*, from *ad-* 'to' + *spargere* 'sprinkle.'

aspergillum

as·per·sion /əˈspərZHən/ ▶ **n.** (usu. **aspersions**) an attack on the reputation or integrity of someone or something: *I don't think anyone is casting **aspersions on** you.*
– ORIGIN late Middle English (denoting the sprinkling of water, esp. at baptism): from Latin *aspersio(n-)*, from *aspergere* (see ASPERSE).

as·phalt /ˈasfôlt/ ▶ **n.** a mixture of dark bituminous pitch with sand or gravel, used for surfacing roads, flooring, roofing, etc. ■ the pitch used in this mixture, sometimes found in natural deposits but usually made by the distillation of crude oil.
▶ **v.** [with obj.] cover with asphalt.
– DERIVATIVES **as·phal·tic** /asˈfôltik/ **adj.**
– ORIGIN late Middle English: from French *asphalte*, based on late Latin *asphalton*, *asphaltum*, from Greek *asphalton*.

as·phalt jun·gle ▶ **n.** the modern city, esp. when considered as a place of poverty and crime.

a·spher·i·cal /āˈsferikəl/ ▶ **adj.** (esp. of the surface of an optical lens) not spherical.
– DERIVATIVES **a·spher·ic adj.**

as·pho·del /ˈasfəˌdel/ ▶ **n.** **1** a Eurasian plant of the lily family, typically having long slender leaves and flowers borne on a spike. ● Genera *Asphodelus* and *Asphodeline*, family Liliaceae. See also BOG ASPHODEL.
2 literary an immortal flower said to grow in the Elysian fields.
– ORIGIN late Middle English: via Latin from Greek *asphodelos*; compare with DAFFODIL.

as·phyx·i·a /asˈfiksēə/ ▶ **n.** a condition arising when the body is deprived of oxygen, causing unconsciousness or death; suffocation.
– DERIVATIVES **as·phyx·i·al adj.**, **as·phyx·i·ant** /-sēənt/ **adj. & n.**
– ORIGIN early 18th cent. (in the sense 'stopping of the pulse'): modern Latin, from Greek *asphuxia*, from *a-* 'without' + *sphuxis* 'pulse.'

as·phyx·i·ate /asˈfiksēˌāt/ ▶ **v.** [with obj.] (usu. **be asphyxiated**) kill (someone) by depriving them of air: *they were asphyxiated by the carbon monoxide fumes* | (as adj. **asphyxiating**) figurative *avoiding asphyxiating government control.* ■ [no obj.] die in this way: *they slowly asphyxiated.*
– DERIVATIVES **as·phyx·i·a·tion** /asˌfiksēˈāSHən/ **n.**

as·pic /ˈaspik/ ▶ **n.** a savory jelly made with meat stock, set in a mold and used to contain pieces of meat, seafood, or eggs: *chicken in aspic* | figurative *a world preserved in aspic, far removed from mass unemployment.*
– ORIGIN late 18th cent.: from French, literally 'asp,' from the colors of the jelly as compared with those of the snake.

as·pi·dis·tra /ˌaspiˈdistrə/ ▶ **n.** a bulbous plant with broad tapering leaves, native to eastern Asia and often grown as a houseplant. ● Genus *Aspidistra*, family Liliaceae.
– ORIGIN early 19th cent.: modern Latin, from Greek *aspis, aspid-* 'shield' (because of the shape of the stigma), on the pattern of *Tupistra*, a related genus.

As·pie /ˈaspē/ (also **aspie**) ▶ **n.** informal a person with Asperger's syndrome.

as·pir·ant /ˈaspərənt, əˈspī-/ ▶ **adj.** [attrib.] (of a person) having ambitions to achieve something, typically to follow a particular career: *an aspirant politician.*
▶ **n.** a person who has ambitions to achieve something: *an **aspirant to** the throne.*
– ORIGIN mid 18th cent. (as a noun): from Latin *aspirant-* 'aspiring,' from the verb *aspirare* (see ASPIRE).

as·pi·rate ▶ **v.** /ˈaspəˌrāt/ [with obj.] **1** (often as adj. **aspirated**) Phonetics pronounce (a sound) with an exhalation of breath: *the aspirated allophone of p occurs in "pie."* ■ [no obj.] pronounce the sound *h* at the beginning of a word.
2 Medicine draw (fluid) by suction from a vessel or cavity. ■ draw fluid in such a way from (a vessel or cavity). ■ breathe (something) in; inhale: *some drowning victims don't aspirate any water.*
3 (usu. as adj. **aspirated**) provide (an internal combustion engine) with air: *the superchargers produce twice the power of standard aspirated engines.* See also NORMALLY ASPIRATED.
▶ **n.** /ˈasp(ə)rit/ **1** Phonetics an aspirated consonant. ■ the sound *h* or a character used to represent this sound.
2 Medicine matter that has been drawn from the body by aspiration: *gastric aspirate* | *esophageal aspirates.*
▶ **adj.** /ˈasp(ə)rit/ Phonetics, rare (of a sound) pronounced with an exhalation of breath; aspirated.
– ORIGIN mid 16th cent. (as an adjective): from Latin *aspiratus* 'breathed,' past participle of *aspirare* (see ASPIRE).

as·pi·ra·tion /ˌaspəˈrāSHən/ ▶ **n.** **1** (usu. **aspirations**) a hope or ambition of achieving something: *he had nothing tangible to back up his literary aspirations* | *the yawning gulf between aspiration and reality.* ■ the object of such an ambition; a goal: *fabrics and oriental rugs were my aspirations.*
2 Medicine the action or process of drawing breath. ■ the action of drawing fluid by suction from a vessel or cavity.
3 Phonetics the action of pronouncing a sound with an exhalation of breath.
– DERIVATIVES **as·pi·ra·tion·al** /-SHənl/ **adj.** (sense 1).
– ORIGIN late Middle English (sense 3): from Latin *aspiratio(n-)*, from the verb *aspirare* (see ASPIRE).

as·pi·ra·tor /ˈaspəˌrātər/ ▶ **n.** Medicine an instrument or apparatus for aspirating fluid from a vessel or cavity.

as·pire /əˈspī(ə)r/ ▶ **v.** [no obj.] direct one's hopes or ambitions toward achieving something: *we never thought that we might **aspire to** those heights* | [with infinitive] *other people will aspire to be like you.* ■ literary rise high; tower: *above the domes of loftiest mosques, these pinnacles of death aspire.*
– ORIGIN late Middle English: from French *aspirer* or Latin *aspirare*, from *ad-* 'to' + *spirare* 'breathe.'

as·pi·rin /ˈasp(ə)rin/ ▶ **n.** a synthetic compound used medicinally to relieve mild or chronic pain and to reduce fever and inflammation. ● Alternative name: **acetylsalicylic acid**; chem. formula: $C_6H_4(OCOCH_3)COOH$. ■ (pl. **same** or **aspirins**) a tablet containing this.
– ORIGIN late 19th cent.: from German, from *acetylierte Spirsäure* 'acetylated salicylic acid' (the element *Spir-* being from the plant genus name *Spiraea*).

as·pir·ing /əˈspī(ə)riNG/ ▶ **adj.** [attrib.] directing one's hopes or ambitions toward becoming a specified type of person: *an aspiring artist.*

as·por·ta·tion /ˌaspərˈtāSHən/ ▶ **n.** Law, rare the detachment, movement, or carrying away of property, considered an essential component of the crime of larceny.
– ORIGIN late 15th cent.: from Latin *asportation-*, from *asportare* 'carry away.'

a·sprawl /əˈsprôl/ ▶ **adv. & adj.** sprawling: [as adv.] *he slipped on the greasy tiles and fell asprawl* | [as predic. adj.] *she lay, legs and arms asprawl.*

a·squint /əˈskwint/ ▶ **adv. & adj.** with a glance to one side or from the corner of the eyes: [as adv.] *a woman looked asquint at me.*
– ORIGIN Middle English: perhaps from A-[2] 'on' + a Low German or Dutch word related to modern Dutch *schuinte* 'slant.'

As·quith /ˈaskwəTH/, Herbert Henry, 1st Earl of Oxford and Asquith (1852–1928), British statesman; prime minister 1908–16.

ass[1] /as/ ▶ **n.** **1** a hoofed mammal of the horse family with a braying call, typically smaller than a horse and with longer ears. ● Genus *Equus*, family Equidae: *E. africanus* of Africa, which is the ancestor of the domestic ass or donkey, and *E. hemionus* of Asia. ■ (in general use) a donkey.
2 informal a foolish or stupid person: *that ass of a young man.*
– PHRASES **make an ass of oneself** informal behave in a way that makes one look foolish or stupid: *he is stewed and about to make an ass of himself.*
– ORIGIN Old English *assa*, from a Celtic word related to Welsh *asyn*, Breton *azen*, based on Latin *asinus*.

ass[2] (Brit. **arse**) ▶ **n.** vulgar slang a person's buttocks or anus. ■ a stupid, irritating, or contemptible person. ■ women regarded as a source of sexual gratification. ■ oneself (used in phrases for emphasis): *get your ass in here fast* | *the bureaucrat who wants everything in writing so as to cover his ass.*
– PHRASES **bust one's ass** try very hard to do something. **bust** (or **whip**) **someone's ass** beat someone in a fight or contest. **chew** (**someone's**) **ass** reprimand severely. **get your ass in** (or **into**) **gear** [in imperative] hurry: *if you get your ass in gear, you can make it out of here tonight.* **get off one's ass** stop being lazy. **haul** (or **drag** or **tear**) **ass** hurry or move fast: *I just turn around and haul ass right out of there.* **kick** (**some**) **ass** (or **kick someone's ass**) see KICK[1]. **kiss ass** see KISS. **my ass** used to convey that one does not believe something that has just been said: *sold out, my ass!* **not give a rat's ass** not care at all about something. **not know one's ass from a hole in the ground** (or **from one's elbow**) be totally ignorant or incompetent. **a pain in the ass** see PAIN. **a piece of ass** see PIECE. **put** (or **have**) **someone's ass in a sling** get someone in trouble: *you managed to put his ass in a sling along with your own.* **up your ass** used to express contempt for someone or something. **you bet your ass** you can be very sure: [with clause] *you can bet your ass I'll go for it every time.*
– DERIVATIVES **assed** /ast/ **adj.** [in combination] *fat-assed guys.*

-ass ▶ **comb. form** used in slang terms as an intensifier, often with depreciatory reference: *smart-ass* | *lame-ass.*
– ORIGIN see ASS[2].

As·sad /äˈsäd, ˈäˌsäd/, Hafiz al- (1928–2000), Syrian statesman; president 1971–2000. While in office, he ensured the strengthening of Syria's oil-based economy and suppressed political opposition such as the uprising of Muslim extremists (1979–82). He supported the coalition forces during the 1991 Gulf War. His son **Bashar al-Assad** (1965–) succeeded him in 2000.

as·sa·gai ▶ **n. & v.** variant spelling of ASSEGAI.

as·sa·i /äˈsī/ ▶ **adv.** Music (esp. as a direction after a tempo marking) very: *allegro assai.*
– ORIGIN Italian, 'very much.'

as·sail /əˈsāl/ ▶ **v.** [with obj.] make a concerted or violent attack on: *the Scots army assailed Edward's army from the rear.* ■ (usu. **be assailed**) (of an unpleasant feeling or physical sensation) come upon (someone) suddenly and strongly: *she was assailed by doubts and regrets.* ■ criticize (someone) strongly.
– DERIVATIVES **as·sail·a·ble adj.**
– ORIGIN Middle English: from Old French *asaill-*, stressed stem of *asalir*, from medieval Latin *assalire*, from Latin *assilire*, from *ad-* 'to' + *salire* 'to leap'; compare with ASSAULT.

as·sail·ant /əˈsālənt/ ▶ **n.** a person who physically attacks another.

As·sam /äˈsäm, əˈsam, ˈasˌam/ a state in northeastern India, much of which lies in the valley of the Brahmaputra River, noted for its production of tea; capital, Dispur.

As·sa·mese /ˌäsəˈmēz/ ▶ **n.** (pl. **same**) **1** a native or inhabitant of Assam.
2 the Indic language, related to Bengali, that is the official language of Assam.
▶ **adj.** of or relating to Assam, its people, or its language.

as·sas·sin /əˈsasin/ ▶ **n.** a murderer of an important person in a surprise attack for political or religious reasons. ■ (**Assassin**) historical a member of the Nizari branch of Ismaili Muslims at the time of the Crusades, when the newly established sect ruled part of northern Persia (1094–1256). They were renowned as militant fanatics, and were popularly reputed to use hashish before going on murder missions.
– ORIGIN mid 16th cent.: from French, or from medieval Latin *assassinus*, from Arabic *ḥašīšī* 'hashish eater.'

as·sas·si·nate /əˈsasəˌnāt/ ▶ **v.** murder (an important person) in a surprise attack for political or religious reasons.

PRONUNCIATION KEY ə *ago, up*; ər *over, fur*; a *hat*; ā *ate*; ä *car*; e *let*; ē *see*; i *fit*; ī *by*; NG *sing*; ō *go*; ô *law, for*; oi *toy*; o͝o *good*; o͞o *goo*; ou *out*; TH *thin*; T͟H *then*; ZH *vision*

–ORIGIN early 17th cent.: from medieval Latin *assassinat-* 'killed,' from the verb *assassinare*, from *assassinus* (see ASSASSIN).

as·sas·si·na·tion /ə,sasəˈnāSHən/ ▶ **n.** the action of assassinating someone: *the assassination of President Kennedy* | [as modifier] *a failed assassination attempt.*

as·sas·sin bug ▶ **n.** a long-legged predatory or bloodsucking bug that occurs chiefly in the tropics and feeds mainly on other arthropods. Some of those that bite humans can transmit microorganisms such as the one causing Chagas' disease. ● Family Reduviidae, suborder Heteroptera: numerous species.

As·sa·teague Is·land /ˈasə,tēg/ a barrier island in southeastern Maryland and northeastern Virginia, on the Atlantic Ocean, noted for its wild ponies.

as·sault /əˈsôlt/ ▶ **v.** [with obj.] make a physical attack on: *he pleaded guilty to assaulting a police officer* | *she was sexually assaulted as a child.* ■ attack or bombard (someone or the senses) with something undesirable or unpleasant: *her right ear was assaulted with a tide of music.* ■ carry out a military attack or raid on (an enemy position): *they left their strong position to assault the hill.* ■ rape.
▶ **n. 1** a physical attack: *his imprisonment for an* ***assault on*** *the film director* | *sexual assaults.* ■ Law an act, criminal or tortious, that threatens physical harm to a person, whether or not actual harm is done: *he appeared in court charged with assault.* ■ a military attack or raid on an enemy position: *troops began an* ***assault on*** *the city* | [as modifier] *an assault boat.* ■ a strong verbal attack: *the* ***assault on*** *the party's tax policies.*
2 a concerted attempt to do something demanding: *a winter* ***assault on*** *Mt. Everest.*
–DERIVATIVES **as·sault·er n.**
–ORIGIN Middle English: from Old French *asaut* (noun), *assauter* (verb), based on Latin *ad-* 'to' + *saltare*, frequentative of *salire* 'to leap.' Compare with ASSAIL.

as·sault and bat·ter·y ▶ **n.** Law the crime of threatening a person together with the act of making physical contact with them.

as·saul·tive /əˈsôltiv/ ▶ **adj.** tending or likely to commit an assault: *they found that assaultive men had abusive parents.* ■ extremely aggressive or forcefully assertive: *his loud, assaultive playing style can leave you cowering.*

as·sault ri·fle ▶ **n.** a rapid-fire, magazine-fed automatic rifle designed for infantry use.

as·say /ˈa,sā, aˈsā/ ▶ **n.** the testing of a metal or ore to determine its ingredients and quality: *submission of plate for assay.* ■ a procedure for measuring the biochemical or immunological activity of a sample: *each assay was performed in duplicate* | *the results of sequential assays of serum were analyzed* | *immunofluorescence assay.*
▶ **v.** [with obj.] **1** determine the content or quality of (a metal or ore). ■ determine the biochemical or immunological activity of (a sample): *cell contents were* ***assayed for*** *enzyme activity.* ■ examine (something) in order to assess its nature: *stepping inside, I quickly assayed the clientele.*
2 archaic attempt: *I assayed a little joke of mine on him.*
–DERIVATIVES **as·say·er n.**
–ORIGIN Middle English (in the general sense 'testing, or a test of, the merit of someone or something'): from Old French *assai* (noun), *assaier* (verb), variant of *essai* 'trial,' *essayer* 'to try' (see ESSAY).

ass-back·wards ▶ **adv. & adj.** informal, derogatory backwards or in a contrary way.

ass ban·dit ▶ **n.** vulgar slang (also **ass burglar**) **1** a male homosexual sodomite or pederast.
2 an eager seducer of young women.

as·se·gai /ˈasə,gī/ (also **assagai**) ▶ **n.** (pl. **assegais**)
1 a slender, iron-tipped, hardwood spear used chiefly by southern African peoples.
2 (also **assegai wood**) a South African tree of the dogwood family that yields hard timber. ● *Curtisia dentata*, family Cornaceae.
▶ **v.** (**assegais, assegaing, assegaied**) [with obj.] wound or kill with an assegai.
–ORIGIN early 17th cent.: from obsolete French *azagaie* or Portuguese *azagaia*, from Arabic *az-zaḡāyah*, from *az, al* 'the' + Berber *zaḡāyah* 'spear.'

as·sem·blage /əˈsemblij/ ▶ **n.** a collection or gathering of things or people: *a wondrous assemblage of noble knights, cruel temptresses, and impossible loves.* ■ a machine or object made of pieces fitted together: *some vast assemblage of gears and cogs.* ■ a work of art made by grouping found or unrelated objects. ■ the action of gathering or fitting things together.

as·sem·ble /əˈsembəl/ ▶ **v. 1** [no obj.] (of people) gather together in one place for a common purpose: *a crowd had assembled outside the gates.* ■ [with obj.] bring (people or things) together for a common purpose: *he assembled the surviving members of the group for a tour.* ■ (usu. as noun **assembling**) Entomology (of male moths) gather for mating in response to a pheromone released by a female.
2 [with obj.] fit together the separate component parts of (a machine or other object): *a factory that assembled parts for trucks.* ■ Computing translate (a program) from assembly language into machine code.
–ORIGIN Middle English: from Old French *asembler*, based on Latin *ad-* 'to' + *simul* 'together.'

as·sem·bler /əˈsemblər/ ▶ **n. 1** a person who assembles a machine or its parts.
2 Computing a program for converting instructions written in low-level symbolic code into machine code. ■ another term for ASSEMBLY LANGUAGE.

as·sem·bly /əˈsemblē/ ▶ **n.** (pl. **assemblies**) **1** a group of people gathered together in one place for a common purpose: *an assembly of scholars and poets.* ■ a group of people elected to make laws or decisions for a particular country or region, esp. the lower legislative house in some US states: *the Connecticut General Assembly.*
2 the action of gathering together as a group for a common purpose: *a decree guaranteeing freedom of assembly.* ■ a regular gathering of the teachers and students of a school: *catcalling occurred during the assembly.* ■ (usu. **the assembly**) chiefly historical a signal for troops to assemble, given by drum or bugle.
3 [often as modifier] the action of fitting together the component parts of a machine or other object: *a car assembly plant.* ■ a unit consisting of components that have been fitted together: *the tail assembly of the aircraft.* ■ [usu. as modifier] Computing the conversion of instructions in low-level code to machine code by an assembler.
–ORIGIN Middle English: from Old French *asemblé*, feminine past participle of *asembler* (see ASSEMBLE).

as·sem·bly lan·guage ▶ **n.** Computing a low-level symbolic code converted by an assembler.

as·sem·bly line ▶ **n.** a series of workers and machines in a factory by which a succession of identical items is progressively assembled: *their latest economy car rolled off the assembly line last August* | figurative *new teenage idols were pouring off the assembly line.* Compare with PRODUCTION LINE.

as·sem·bly·man /əˈsemblēmən/ ▶ **n.** (pl. **assemblymen**) a person who is a member of a legislative assembly.

as·sem·bly·wo·man /əˈsemblē,wo͝omən/ ▶ **n.** (pl. **assemblywomen**) a woman who is a member of a legislative assembly.

as·sent /əˈsent/ ▶ **n.** the expression of approval or agreement: *a loud murmur of assent* | *he nodded assent.* ■ official agreement or sanction: *the governor has power to withhold his assent from a bill.*
▶ **v.** [no obj.] express approval or agreement, typically officially: *Roosevelt assented to the agreement* | [with direct speech] *"Guest house, then," Frank assented cheerfully.*
–DERIVATIVES **as·sent·er n.**
–ORIGIN Middle English: from Old French *as(s)enter* (verb), *as(s)ente* (noun), based on Latin *assentiri*, from *ad-* 'toward' + *sentire* 'feel, think.'

as·sert /əˈsərt/ ▶ **v.** [reporting verb] state a fact or belief confidently and forcefully: [with clause] *the company asserts that the cuts will not affect development* | [with obj.] *he asserted his innocence* | [with direct speech] *"I don't know why she came," he asserted.* ■ [with obj.] cause others to recognize (one's authority or a right) by confident and forceful behavior: *the good librarian is able to assert authority when required.* ■ (**assert oneself**) behave or speak in a confident and forceful manner: *it was time to assert himself.*
–DERIVATIVES **as·sert·er n.**
–ORIGIN early 17th cent.: from Latin *asserere* 'claim, affirm,' from *ad-* 'to' + *serere* 'to join.'

as·ser·tion /əˈsərSHən/ ▶ **n.** a confident and forceful statement of fact or belief: [with clause] *his assertion that his father had deserted the family.* ■ the action of stating something or exercising authority confidently and forcefully: *the assertion of his legal rights.*

as·ser·tive /əˈsərtiv/ ▶ **adj.** having or showing a confident and forceful personality: *patients should be more assertive with their doctors.*
–DERIVATIVES **as·ser·tive·ly adv., as·ser·tive·ness n.**

as·ses /ˈasiz/ plural form of AS², ASS¹, ASS².

as·sess /əˈses/ ▶ **v.** [with obj.] evaluate or estimate the nature, ability, or quality of: *the committee must assess the relative importance of the issues* | [with clause] *it is difficult to assess whether this is a new trend.* ■ (usu. **be assessed**) calculate or estimate the price or value of: *the damage was assessed at $5 billion.* ■ set the value of a tax, fine, etc., for (a person or property) at a specified level: *all empty properties will be* ***assessed at*** *50 percent.*
–DERIVATIVES **as·sess·a·ble adj.**
–ORIGIN late Middle English: from Old French *assesser*, based on Latin *assidere* 'sit by' (in medieval Latin 'levy tax'), from *ad-* 'to, at' + *sedere* 'sit.' Compare with ASSIZE.

as·sess·ment /əˈsesmənt/ ▶ **n.** the evaluation or estimation of the nature, quality, or ability of someone or something: *the assessment of educational needs* | *he made a rapid assessment of the situation* | *assessments of market value.*

as·ses·sor /əˈsesər/ ▶ **n.** a person who assesses someone or something, in particular: ■ a person who calculates or estimates the value of something or an amount to be paid, chiefly for tax or insurance purposes. ■ a person who is knowledgeable in a particular field and is called upon for advice, typically by a judge or committee of inquiry.
–ORIGIN late Middle English: from Old French *assessour*, from Latin *assessor* 'assistant judge' (in medieval Latin 'assessor of taxes'), from Latin *assidere* (see ASSESS).

as·set /ˈaset/ ▶ **n.** a useful or valuable thing, person, or quality: *quick reflexes were his chief asset* | *the school is an asset to the community.* ■ (usu. **assets**) property owned by a person or company, regarded as having value and available to meet debts, commitments, or legacies: *growth in net assets* | [as modifier] *debiting the asset account.* ■ (**assets**) military equipment, such as planes, ships, communications and radar installations, employed or targeted in military operations.
–ORIGIN mid 16th cent. (in the plural in the sense 'sufficient estate to allow discharge of a will'): from an Anglo-Norman French legal term, from Old French *asez* 'enough,' based on Latin *ad* 'to' + *satis* 'enough.'

as·set-backed ▶ **adj.** [attrib.] denoting securities having as collateral the return on a series of mortgages, credit agreements, or other forms of lending.

as·set-strip·ping ▶ **n.** the practice of taking over a company in financial difficulties and selling each of its assets separately at a profit without regard for the company's future.
–DERIVATIVES **as·set-strip·per n.**

as·sev·er·a·tion /ə,sevəˈrāSHən/ ▶ **n.** the solemn or emphatic declaration or statement of something: *I fear that you offer only unsupported asseveration* | *the dogmatic outlook marks many of his asseverations.*
–DERIVATIVES **as·sev·er·ate** /əˈsevə,rāt/ **v.**
–ORIGIN mid 16th cent.: from Latin *asseveratio(n-)*, from the verb *asseverare*, from *ad-* 'to' + *severus* 'serious.'

ass·hat /ˈashat/ ▶ **n.** vulgar slang a stupid person.

ass·hole /ˈas,hōl/ ▶ **n.** vulgar slang the anus. ■ an irritating or contemptible person.

as·sib·i·late /əˈsibə,lāt/ ▶ **v.** [with obj.] Phonetics pronounce (a sound) as a sibilant or affricate ending in a sibilant (e.g., sound *t* as *ts*).
–DERIVATIVES **as·sib·i·la·tion** /ə,sibəˈlāSHən/ **n.**
–ORIGIN mid 19th cent.: from Latin *assibilat-* 'hissed at,' from the verb *assibilare*, from *ad-* 'to' + *sibilare* 'to hiss.'

as·si·du·i·ty /,asiˈd(y)o͞oitē/ ▶ **n.** (pl. **assiduities**) constant or close attention to what one is doing: *the assiduity with which he could wear down his opponents.* ■ (**assiduities**) archaic or literary constant attentions to someone.
–ORIGIN late Middle English: from Latin *assiduitas*, from *assiduus* 'occupied with' (see ASSIDUOUS).

as·sid·u·ous /əˈsijəwəs/ ▶ **adj.** showing great care and perseverance: *she was* ***assiduous in*** *pointing out every feature.*
–DERIVATIVES **as·sid·u·ous·ly adv., as·sid·u·ous·ness n.**
–ORIGIN mid 16th cent.: from Latin *assiduus*, from *assidere* 'be engaged in doing' (see ASSESS), + -OUS.

as·sign /əˈsīn/ ▶ **v.** [with obj.] **1** allocate (a job or duty): *Congress* ***assigned*** *the task* ***to*** *the agency* | [with two objs.] *his leader assigned him this mission.* ■ appoint (someone) to a particular job, task, or organization: *she has been* ***assigned to*** *a new job* | [with obj. and infinitive] *he was assigned to prosecute the case.*
2 designate or set (something) aside for a specific purpose: *managers happily assign large sums of money to travel budgets.* ■ (**assign something to**) attribute something as belonging to: *it is difficult to decide whether to assign the victory to Goodwin.*
3 transfer (legal rights or liabilities): *they will ask you to assign your rights against the airline.*
▶ **n.** Law another term for ASSIGNEE (sense 1).
–DERIVATIVES **as·sign·a·ble adj.** (sense 3 of the verb), **as·sign·er n., as·sign·or** /əˈsīnər/ **n.** (sense 3 of the verb).
–ORIGIN Middle English: from Old French *asigner*, *assiner*, from Latin *assignare*, from *ad-* 'to' + *signare* 'to sign.'

a

as·sig·na·tion /ˌasigˈnāSHən/ ▶ **n.** **1** an appointment to meet someone in secret, typically one made by lovers: *his **assignation with** an older woman.*
2 the allocation or attribution of someone or something as belonging to something.
– ORIGIN late Middle English (in the senses 'command, appointment to office, or allotment of revenue'): via Old French from Latin *assignatio(n-)*, from the verb *assignare* (see ASSIGN).

as·sign·ee /əˌsīˈnē/ ▶ **n.** chiefly Law **1** a person to whom a right or liability is legally transferred.
2 a person appointed to act for another.
– ORIGIN Middle English: from Old French *assigne*, past participle of *assigner* 'allot' (see ASSIGN).

as·sign·ment /əˈsīnmənt/ ▶ **n.** **1** a task or piece of work assigned to someone as part of a job or course of study: *a homework assignment.* ■ the allocation of a job or task to someone: *the effective assignment of tasks.* ■ the task or post to which one has been appointed: *his assignment was to the County Court | I was **on assignment** for a German magazine.*
2 the attribution of someone or something as belonging: *the **assignment** of individuals **to** particular social positions.*
3 an act of making a legal transfer of a right, property, or liability: *an assignment of leasehold property.* ■ a document effecting such a transfer.
– ORIGIN late Middle English: from Old French *assignement*, from medieval Latin *assignamentum*, from Latin *assignare* 'allot' (see ASSIGN).

as·sim·i·late /əˈsiməˌlāt/ ▶ **v.** [with obj.] **1** take in (information, ideas, or culture) and understand fully: *Marie tried to assimilate the week's events.* ■ (usu. **be assimilated**) absorb and integrate (people, ideas, or culture) into a wider society or culture: *pop trends are **assimilated into** the mainstream with alarming speed | [no obj.] the converts were assimilated into the society of their conquerors.* ■ absorb or integrate and use for one's own benefit: *the music business assimilated whatever aspects of punk it could turn into profit.* ■ (usu. **be assimilated**) (of the body or any biological system) absorb and digest (food or nutrients): *the sugars in the fruit are readily assimilated by the body.*
2 cause (something) to resemble; liken: *philosophers had **assimilated** thought **to** perception.* ■ [no obj.] come to resemble: *the churches **assimilated to** a certain cultural norm.* ■ Phonetics make (a sound) more like another in the same or next word.
– DERIVATIVES **as·sim·i·la·ble** /-ləbəl/ **adj.**, **as·sim·i·la·tion** /əˌsiməˈlāSHən/ **n.**, **as·sim·i·la·tive** /-ˌlātiv, -lətiv/ **adj.**, **as·sim·i·la·tor** /-ˌlātər/ **n.**, **as·sim·i·la·to·ry** /-ləˌtôrē/ **adj.**
– ORIGIN late Middle English: from Latin *assimilat-* 'absorbed, incorporated,' from the verb *assimilare*, from *ad-* 'to' + *similis* 'like.'

as·sim·i·la·tion·ist /əˌsiməˈlāSHəˌnist/ ▶ **n.** a person who advocates or participates in racial or cultural integration: [as modifier] *the assimilationist policies of the right.*

As·sin·i·boin /əˈsinəˌboin/ (also **Assiniboine**) ▶ **n.** (pl. **same** or **Assiniboins**) **1** a member of an American Indian people formerly living in southern Manitoba, but now living in Montana, Alberta, and Saskatchewan.
2 the Siouan language of this people.
▶ **adj.** of or relating to the Assiniboin or their language.
– ORIGIN late 17th cent.: from Canadian French, from Ojibwa *assini:pwa:n* 'stone Sioux,' from *assin* 'stone' + *pwa:n* 'Sioux.'

As·si·ni·boine Riv·er /əˈsinəˌboin/ a river in south central Canada that flows for 590 miles (950 km) from eastern Saskatchewan into Manitoba to join the Red River at Winnipeg.

As·si·si[1] /əˈsēsē, -zē/ a town in the province of Umbria in central Italy; pop. 27,507 (2008). It is the birthplace of St. Francis, whose tomb is located there.

As·si·si[2] see CLARE OF ASSISI, ST.

As·si·si[3] see FRANCIS OF ASSISI, ST.

as·sist /əˈsist/ ▶ **v.** [with obj.] help (someone), typically by doing a share of the work: *a senior academic would assist him in his work | [with obj.] he assisted her to find employment | [no obj.] their presence would **assist in** keeping the peace.* ■ help by providing money or information: *they were assisting police with their inquiries | [no obj.] funds to **assist with** capital investment.* ■ [no obj.] be present as a helper or spectator: *two midwives who **assisted at** a water birth.*
▶ **n.** an act of help, typically by providing money: *the budget must have an assist from tax policies.* ■ (chiefly in ice hockey, basketball, or baseball) the act of touching the puck or ball in a play in which a teammate scores or an opposing batter is put out: *he led the league with 14 outfield assists.* ■ [in combination] a mechanical device that provides help: *the implant is a ventricular-assist device.*
– DERIVATIVES **as·sist·er** **n.**, **as·sist·ive** **adj.**
– ORIGIN late Middle English: from Old French *assister*, from Latin *assistere* 'take one's stand by,' from *ad-* 'to, at' + *sistere* 'take one's stand.'

as·sis·tance /əˈsistəns/ ▶ **n.** the provision of money, resources, or information to help someone: *plans offering financial **assistance to** employers | she will be glad to give advice and assistance.* ■ the action of helping someone with a job or task: *the work was completed **with the assistance of** carpenters.*
– PHRASES **be of assistance** be of practical use or help: *the guide will **be of assistance to** development groups.* **come to someone's assistance** act to help someone.
– ORIGIN late Middle English: from Old French, or from medieval Latin *assistentia*, from Latin *assistere* (see ASSIST).

as·sis·tant /əˈsistənt/ ▶ **n.** a person who ranks below a senior person: *the managing director and his assistant | [as modifier] an assistant manager.* ■ [with adj. or noun modifier] a person who helps in particular work: *a laboratory assistant.*
– ORIGIN late Middle English: from Old French, or from medieval Latin *assistent-* 'taking one's stand beside,' from the verb *assistere* (see ASSIST).

as·sis·tant pro·fes·sor ▶ **n.** a college teacher ranking immediately below an associate professor.

as·sis·tant·ship /əˈsistəntˌSHip/ ▶ **n.** a paid academic appointment made to a graduate student that involves part-time teaching or research.

as·sist·ed liv·ing ▶ **n.** housing for elderly or disabled people that provides nursing care, housekeeping, and prepared meals as needed.

as·sist·ed su·i·cide ▶ **n.** the suicide of a patient suffering from an incurable disease, effected by the taking of lethal drugs provided by a doctor for this purpose.

as·size /əˈsīz/ ▶ **n.** (usu. **assizes**) historical a court that formerly sat at intervals in each county of England and Wales to administer the civil and criminal law. In 1972 the civil jurisdiction of assizes was transferred to the High Court, and the criminal jurisdiction to the Crown Court.
– ORIGIN Middle English: from Old French *assise*, feminine past participle of *asseeir* 'sit, settle, assess,' from Latin *assidere* (see ASSESS).

ass-kick·ing ▶ **adj.** vulgar slang forceful or aggressive.

ass-kiss·ing ▶ **n.** vulgar slang the use of compliments, flattery, or other obsequious behavior in order to gain favor.
– DERIVATIVES **ass-kiss·er** **n.**

ass-lick·ing vulgar slang another term for ASS-KISSING.

ass·load /ˈaslōd/ ▶ **n.** vulgar slang a large number or amount of something.

assn. ▶ **abbr.** association.

Assoc. ▶ **abbr.** ■ Associate. ■ (as part of a title) Association.

as·so·ci·ate ▶ **v.** /əˈsōsēˌāt, -SHē-/ [with obj.] connect (someone or something) with something else in one's mind: *I **associated** wealth **with** freedom.* ■ (usu. **be associated**) connect (something) with something else because they occur together or one produces another: *the environmental problems **associated with** nuclear waste.* ■ (**associate oneself with**) allow oneself to be connected with or seen to be supportive of: *I cannot associate myself with some of the language used.* ■ (**be associated with**) be involved with: *she has been associated with the project from the first.* ■ [no obj.] meet or have dealings with someone commonly regarded with disapproval: *they are at risk of **associating with** criminals.*
▶ **n.** /-it/ **1** a partner or colleague in business or at work: *he arranged for a close associate to take control of the institute.* ■ a companion or friend: *his old friend and hearty associate.*
2 a person with limited or subordinate membership in an organization. ■ a person who holds an academic degree conferred by a junior college (only in titles or set expressions): *an associate's degree in science | an Associate of Arts.*
3 chiefly Psychology a concept connected with another.
▶ **adj.** /-it/ [attrib.] joined or connected with an organization or business: *an associate company.* ■ denoting shared function or membership but with a lesser status: *the associate director of the academy.*
– DERIVATIVES **as·so·ci·a·bil·i·ty** /əˌsōSH(ē)əˈbilitē, -SHē-/ **n.**, **as·so·ci·a·ble** /əˈsōSH(ē)əbəl, -SHē-/ **adj.**, **as·so·ci·ate·ship** /-ˌSHip/ **n.**
– ORIGIN late Middle English (as a verb in the sense 'join with in a common purpose'; as an adjective in the sense 'allied'): from Latin *associat-* 'joined,' from the verb *associare*, from *ad-* 'to' + *socius* 'sharing, allied.'

as·so·ci·at·ed /əˈsōsēˌātid, -SHē-/ ▶ **adj.** (of a person or thing) connected with something else: *two associated events.* ■ (of a company) connected or amalgamated with another company or companies. ■ Chemistry (of liquids) in which the molecules are held together by hydrogen bonding or other weak interaction.

As·so·ci·at·ed Press (abbr.: **AP**) an international news agency based in New York City.

As·so·ci·ate of Arts (abbr.: **AA**) (also **Associate's degree**) ▶ **n.** a degree granted after a two-year course of study, esp. by a community or junior college.

as·so·ci·ate pro·fes·sor ▶ **n.** an academic ranking immediately below full professor.

as·so·ci·a·tion /əˌsōsēˈāSHən, -SHē-/ ▶ **n.** **1** (abbr.: **assn.**) (often in names) a group of people organized for a joint purpose: *the National Association of Broadcasters.* ■ Ecology a plant community defined by a characteristic group of dominant plant species.
2 a connection or cooperative link between people or organizations: *he developed a close **association** with the university | the program was promoted **in association with** the Department of Music.* ■ the action or state of becoming a member of an organization with subordinate status: [as modifier] *Slovenia signed association agreements with the European Union.* ■ Chemistry the linking of molecules through hydrogen bonding or other interaction short of full bond formation.
3 (usu. **associations**) a mental connection between ideas or things: *the word bureaucracy has unpleasant associations.* ■ the action of making such a connection: *the association of alchemy with "hieroglyphics" and "cabala."* ■ the fact of occurring with something else; co-occurrence: *cases of cancer found **in association with** colitis.*
– DERIVATIVES **as·so·ci·a·tion·al** /-SHənl/ **adj.**
– ORIGIN mid 16th cent. (in the sense 'uniting in a common purpose'): from medieval Latin *associatio(n-)*, from Latin *associare* 'to unite, ally' (see ASSOCIATE).

as·so·ci·a·tion ar·e·a ▶ **n.** Anatomy a region of the cortex of the brain that connects sensory and motor areas, and that is thought to be concerned with higher mental activities.

As·so·ci·a·tion foot·ball ▶ **n.** more formal term for SOCCER.
– ORIGIN so called because it is played according the rules of the Football *Association*.

as·so·ci·a·tion·ism /əˌsōsēˈāSHəˌnizəm, -ˌsōSHē-/ ▶ **n.** a theory in philosophy or psychology that regards the simple association or co-occurrence of ideas or sensations as the primary basis of meaning, thought, or learning.
– DERIVATIVES **as·so·ci·a·tion·ist** **n.** & **adj.**

As·so·ci·a·tion of South·east A·sian Na·tions (abbr.: **ASEAN**) a regional organization intended to promote economic cooperation and now comprising the countries of Indonesia, Malaysia, the Philippines, Singapore, Thailand, Brunei, Vietnam, Laos, Burma (Myanmar), and Cambodia.

as·so·ci·a·tive /əˈsōsēˌātiv, -SHē-, -sēətiv, -SHətiv/ ▶ **adj.** **1** of or involving the action of associating ideas or things: *an associative, nonlinear mode of thought.* ■ [attrib.] Computing of or denoting computer storage in which items are identified by content rather than by address.
2 Mathematics involving the condition that a group of quantities connected by operators gives the same result whatever their grouping, as long as their order remains the same, e.g., $(a \times b) \times c = a \times (b \times c)$.

as·so·ci·a·tive mem·o·ry ▶ **n.** Computing a memory capable of determining whether a given datum (the search word) is contained in one of its addresses or locations.

as·so·nance /ˈasənəns/ ▶ **n.** in poetry, the repetition of the sound of a vowel or diphthong in nonrhyming stressed syllables near enough to each other for the echo to be discernible (e.g., *penitence, reticence*). Compare with ALLITERATION.
– DERIVATIVES **as·so·nant** **adj.**, **as·so·nate** /-ˌnāt/ **v.**
– ORIGIN early 18th cent.: from French, from Latin *assonare* 'respond to,' from *ad-* 'to' + *sonare* (from *sonus* 'sound').

as·sort /əˈsôrt/ ▶ **v.** **1** [no obj.] Genetics (of genes or characters) become distributed among cells or progeny.
2 [with obj.] archaic place in a group; classify: *he would assort it with the fabulous dogs as a monstrous invention.*
– ORIGIN late 15th cent.: from Old French *assorter*, from *a-* (from Latin *ad* 'to, at') + *sorte* 'sort, kind.'

as·sort·a·tive /əˈsôrtətiv/ ▶ **adj.** [attrib.] denoting or involving the preferential mating of animals or marrying of people with similar characteristics.

a

as·sort·ed /əˈsôrtid/ ▶ **adj.** [attrib.] of various sorts put together; miscellaneous: *bowls in assorted colors.*

as·sort·ment /əˈsôrtmənt/ ▶ **n.** a miscellaneous collection of things or people: *the room was filled with an assortment of clothes.*

ASSR ▶ **abbr.** historical Autonomous Soviet Socialist Republic.

Asst. ▶ **abbr.** Assistant.

as·suage /əˈswāj/ ▶ **v.** [with obj.] make (an unpleasant feeling) less intense: *the letter assuaged the fears of most members.* ■ satisfy (an appetite or desire): *an opportunity occurred to assuage her desire for knowledge.*
– DERIVATIVES **as·suage·ment** **n.**
– ORIGIN Middle English: from Old French *assouagier, asouagier,* based on Latin *ad-* 'to' (expressing change) + *suavis* 'sweet.'

As Su·lay·ma·ni·yah /äs ˌsoolīˌmäˈnē(y)ə/ variant form of **Sulaymaniyah.**

as·sume /əˈsoom/ ▶ **v.** [with obj.] **1** suppose to be the case, without proof: *you're afraid of what people are going to assume about me* | [with clause] *it is reasonable to assume that such changes have significant social effects* | [with obj. and infinitive] *they were assumed to be foreign.*
2 take or begin to have (power or responsibility): *he assumed full responsibility for all organizational work.* ■ seize (power or control): *the rebels assumed control of the capital.*
3 take on (a specified quality, appearance, or extent): *militant activity had assumed epidemic proportions.* ■ take on or adopt (a manner or identity), sometimes falsely: *Oliver assumed an expression of penitence* | (as adj. **assumed**) *a man living under an assumed name.*
– DERIVATIVES **as·sum·ed·ly** /-midlē/ **adv.**
– ORIGIN late Middle English: from Latin *assumere,* from *ad-* 'toward' + *sumere* 'take.'

as·sum·ing /əˈsoomiNG/ ▶ **conj.** used for the purpose of argument to indicate a premise on which a statement can be based: ***assuming that the treaty is*** *ratified, what is its relevance?*
▶ **adj.** archaic arrogant or presumptuous.

as·sump·tion /əˈsəm(p)SHən/ ▶ **n. 1** a thing that is accepted as true or as certain to happen, without proof: *they made certain assumptions about the market* | [with clause] *we're working on the assumption that the time of death was after midnight.*
2 the action of taking or beginning to take power or responsibility: *the assumption of an active role in regional settlements.*
3 (**Assumption**) the reception of the Virgin Mary bodily into heaven. This was formally declared a doctrine of the Roman Catholic Church in 1950. See also **Dormition.** ■ the feast in honor of this, celebrated on August 15.
4 archaic arrogance or presumption.
– ORIGIN Middle English (sense 3): from Old French *asompsion* or Latin *assumptio(n-),* from the verb *assumere* (see **assume**).

as·sump·tive /əˈsəm(p)tiv/ ▶ **adj. 1** rare of the nature of an assumption.
2 archaic apt to seize something for oneself.
– ORIGIN mid 16th cent. (in the sense 'taken, adopted'): from Latin *assumptivus,* from the verb *assumere* (see **assume**).

as·sur·ance /əˈSHoorəns/ ▶ **n. 1** a positive declaration intended to give confidence; a promise: [with clause] *he gave an assurance that work would not recommence until Wednesday.*
2 confidence or certainty in one's own abilities: *she drove with assurance.* ■ certainty about something: *the crowd's assurance of Joe's guilt.*
3 chiefly Brit. insurance, specifically life insurance.
– ORIGIN late Middle English (sense 2): from Old French, from *assurer* 'assure.'

as·sure /əˈSHoor/ ▶ **v. 1** [reporting verb] tell someone something positively or confidently to dispel any doubts they may have: [with obj. and clause] *Tony assured me that there was a supermarket in the village* | [with obj. and direct speech] *"I quite understand," Mrs. Lewis assured her* | [with obj.] *they assured him of their full confidence.* ■ make (someone) sure of something: *you would be assured of a fine welcome* | *she assured herself that he was asleep.*
2 [with obj.] make (something) certain to happen: *victory was now assured* | [with clause] *their influence assured that the report would be tough.* ■ chiefly Brit. cover (a person) with life insurance. ■ secure the future payment of (an amount) with insurance.
– DERIVATIVES **as·sur·er** **n.**
– ORIGIN late Middle English: from Old French *assurer,* based on Latin *ad-* 'to' (expressing change) + *securus* (see **secure**).

as·sured /əˈSHoord/ ▶ **adj. 1** confident: *"Certainly not," was her assured reply.*
2 [attrib.] protected against discontinuance or change: *an assured tenancy.*
– DERIVATIVES **as·sur·ed·ly** /əˈSHooridlē/ **adv.** [sentence adverb] *if they lose their hold, they will assuredly drown.*

As·syr·i·a /əˈsi(ə)rēə/ an ancient country in what is now northern Iraq. From the early part of the 2nd millennium BC, Assyria was the center of a succession of empires.

As·syr·i·an /əˈsi(ə)rēən/ ▶ **n. 1** an inhabitant of ancient Assyria.
2 the language of ancient Assyria, a dialect of Akkadian.
3 a dialect of Aramaic still spoken by a group of people of mainly Christian faith living in the mountains of Syria, northern Iraq, and surrounding regions.
▶ **adj. 1** of or relating to ancient Assyria or its language.
2 relating to or denoting modern Assyrian or its speakers.

As·syr·i·ol·o·gy /əˌsi(ə)rēˈäləjē/ ▶ **n.** the study of the language, history, and antiquities of ancient Assyria.
– DERIVATIVES **As·syr·i·o·log·i·cal** /əˌsi(ə)rēəˈläjikəl/ **adj., As·syr·i·ol·o·gist** /-jist/ **n.**

AST ▶ **abbr.** Atlantic Standard Time (see **Atlantic time**).

a·sta·ble /āˈstābəl/ ▶ **adj.** chiefly Electronics of or relating to a system or electric circuit that oscillates spontaneously between unstable states.

A·staire /əˈste(ə)r/, Fred (1899–1987), US dancer, singer, and actor; born *Frederick Austerlitz.* He starred in a number of movie musicals, including *Top Hat* (1935) and *Shall We Dance?* (1937) with Ginger Rogers and *Easter Parade* (1948) with Judy Garland.

As·ta·na /asˈtänə/ the capital of Kazakhstan (since 1998); pop. 550,400 (est. 2006). Formerly called ***Aqmola*** and, earlier, ***Tselinograd.***

as·tang·a /asˈtäNGə/ ▶ **n.** variant spelling of **ashtanga.**

As·tar·te /əˈstärtē/ Mythology a Phoenician goddess of fertility and sexual love who corresponds to the Babylonian and Assyrian goddess Ishtar and who became identified with the Egyptian Isis, the Greek Aphrodite, and others.

a·stat·ic /āˈstatik/ ▶ **adj.** not keeping a steady position or direction, in particular: ■ Physics (of a system or instrument) consisting of or employing a combination of magnets suspended in a uniform magnetic field on a single wire or thread in such a way that no torque is present (e.g., to minimize the effect of the earth's magnetic field).
– ORIGIN early 19th cent.: from Greek *astatos* 'unstable' + **-ic.**

as·ta·tine /ˈastəˌtēn, -tin/ ▶ **n.** the chemical element of atomic number 85, a radioactive member of the halogen group. Astatine was first produced by bombarding bismuth with alpha particles, and it occurs in traces in nature as a decay product. (Symbol: **At**)
– ORIGIN 1940s: from Greek *astatos* 'unstable' + **-ine**[4].

as·ter /ˈastər/ ▶ **n. 1** a plant of the daisy family that has bright rayed flowers, typically of purple or pink. ● Genus *Aster,* family Compositae: numerous species, many of which bloom in autumn, including the wild purple **New England aster** (*A. novae-angliae*). See also **China aster.**
2 Biology a star-shaped structure formed during division of the nucleus of an animal cell.
– ORIGIN early 17th cent. (in the Greek sense): via Latin from Greek *astēr* 'star.'

New England aster

-aster ▶ **suffix** forming nouns:
1 denoting poor quality: *criticaster* | *poetaster.*
2 Botany denoting incomplete resemblance: *oleaster.*
– ORIGIN from Latin.

as·ter·isk /ˈastəˌrisk/ ▶ **n.** a symbol (*) used to mark printed or written text, typically as a reference to an annotation or to stand for omitted matter. ■ a thing resembling a star in shape: *soft asterisks of pollen.*
▶ **v.** [with obj.] (usu. as adj. **asterisked**) mark (printed or written text) with an asterisk: *asterisked entries.*
– ORIGIN late Middle English: via late Latin from Greek *asteriskos* 'small star,' diminutive of *astēr.*

> **USAGE** Even though **asterisk** does not look like a tricky word to pronounce, it can be problematic. In both its singular and plural forms, it is often mispronounced as if it ends with **-rix.** Pronounced correctly, it ends with a *-risk* sound when singular and *-risks* when plural.

as·ter·ism /ˈastəˌrizəm/ ▶ **n. 1** Astronomy a prominent pattern or group of stars, typically having a popular name but smaller than a constellation.
2 a group of three asterisks (***) drawing attention to following text.
– ORIGIN late 16th cent.: from Greek *asterismos,* from *astēr* 'star.'

a·stern /əˈstərn/ ▶ **adv. 1** behind or toward the rear of a ship or aircraft: *the engine rooms lay astern.*
2 (of a ship) backward: *the lifeboat was carried astern by the tide.*
– ORIGIN late Middle English: from **a-**[2] (expressing position or direction) + **stern**[2].

as·ter·oid /ˈastəˌroid/ ▶ **n. 1** a small rocky body orbiting the sun. Large numbers of these, ranging in size from nearly 600 miles (1,000 km) across (Ceres) to dust particles, are found (as the **asteroid belt**) esp. between the orbits of Mars and Jupiter, though some have more eccentric orbits, and a few pass close to the earth or enter the atmosphere as meteors.
2 Zoology an echinoderm of the class Asteroidea; a starfish.
▶ **adj.** Zoology relating to echinoderms of the class Asteroidea.
– DERIVATIVES **as·ter·oi·dal** /ˌastəˈroidl/ **adj.**
– ORIGIN early 19th cent.: from Greek *asteroeidēs* 'starlike,' from *astēr* 'star.'

As·ter·oi·de·a /ˌastəˈroidēə/ Zoology a class of echinoderms that comprises the starfishes.
– ORIGIN modern Latin (plural), from Greek *asteroeidēs* 'starlike,' from *astēr* 'star.'

as·the·ni·a /asˈTHēnēə/ ▶ **n.** Medicine abnormal physical weakness or lack of energy.
– ORIGIN late 18th cent.: modern Latin, from Greek *astheneia,* from *asthenēs* 'weak.'

as·then·ic /asˈTHenik/ ▶ **adj.** Medicine relating to, involving, or suffering from asthenia.
– ORIGIN late 18th cent.: from Greek *asthenikos,* from *asthenēs* 'weak.'

as·then·o·sphere /asˈTHenəˌsfi(ə)r/ ▶ **n.** Geology the upper layer of the earth's mantle, below the lithosphere, in which there is relatively low resistance to plastic flow and convection is thought to occur.
– DERIVATIVES **as·then·o·spher·ic** /asˌTHenəˈsfi(ə)rik, -ˈsferik/ **adj.**
– ORIGIN early 20th cent.: from Greek *asthenēs* 'weak' + **sphere.**

asth·ma /ˈazmə/ ▶ **n.** a respiratory condition marked by spasms in the bronchi of the lungs, causing difficulty in breathing. It usually results from an allergic reaction or other forms of hypersensitivity.
– ORIGIN late Middle English: from medieval Latin *asma,* from Greek *asthma,* from *azein* 'breathe hard.'

asth·mat·ic /azˈmatik/ ▶ **adj.** relating to or suffering from asthma.
▶ **n.** a person who suffers from asthma.
– DERIVATIVES **asth·mat·i·cal·ly** /-ik(ə)lē/ **adv.**
– ORIGIN early 16th cent.: via Latin from Greek *asthmatikos,* from *asthma* (see **asthma**).

asth·tang·a /asˈtäNGə/ ▶ **n.** variant spelling of **ashtanga.**

As·ti /ˈästē/ ▶ **n. 1** a white wine from the Italian province of Asti and neighboring parts of Piedmont.
2 a light sparkling wine from this region.

a·stig·ma·tism /əˈstigməˌtizəm/ ▶ **n.** a defect in the eye or in a lens caused by a deviation from spherical curvature, which results in distorted images, as light rays are prevented from meeting at a common focus.
– DERIVATIVES **as·tig·mat·ic** /ˌastigˈmatik/ **adj.**
– ORIGIN mid 19th cent.: from **a-**[1] 'without' + Greek *stigma* 'point' + **-ism.**

a·stil·be /əˈstilbē/ ▶ **n.** an Old World plant of the saxifrage family, with plumes of tiny white, pink, or red flowers. ● Genus *Astilbe,* family Saxifragaceae.
– ORIGIN modern Latin, from Greek *a-* 'not' + *stilbē,* feminine of *stilbos* 'glittering' (because the individual flowers are small and inconspicuous).

a·stir /əˈstər/ ▶ **adj.** [predic.] in a state of excited movement: *the streets are all astir.* ■ awake and out of bed: *he woke before anyone else was astir.*
– ORIGIN late 18th cent.: from **a-**[2] 'on' + the noun **stir**[1].

As·ti Spu·man·te /ˈästē sp(y)ooˈmäntē/ former term for **Asti** (sense 2).

As·ton /ˈastən/, Francis William (1877–1945), English physicist. He invented the mass spectrograph (with J. J. Thomson) and eventually discovered many of the 287 naturally occurring isotopes of nonradioactive elements. Nobel Prize for Chemistry (1922).

as·ton·ish /əˈstäniSH/ ▶ **v.** [with obj.] surprise or impress (someone) greatly: *you never fail to astonish me* | [with obj. and clause] *it astonished her that Mrs. Browing could seem so anxious.*
– ORIGIN early 16th cent. (as *astonished,* in the sense 'stunned, bewildered, dismayed'): from obsolete

astone 'stun, stupefy,' from Old French *estoner*, based on Latin *ex-* 'out' + *tonare* 'to thunder.'

as·ton·ished /ə'stänisHt/ ▶ **adj.** greatly surprised or impressed; amazed: *he was* **astonished at** *the change in him | an astonished expression on her face.*

as·ton·ish·ing /ə'stänisHiNG/ ▶ **adj.** extremely surprising or impressive; amazing: *an astonishing achievement | I find it astonishing that they ever thought it could work.*
– DERIVATIVES **as·ton·ish·ing·ly adv.** [as submodifier] *an astonishingly successful program.*

as·ton·ish·ment /ə'stänisHmənt/ ▶ **n.** great surprise: *she looked at him* **in astonishment**.

As·tor[1] /'astər/, John Jacob (1763–1848), US merchant; born in Germany. He emigrated to the US in 1784 and made a fortune in the fur trade.

As·tor[2], Nancy Witcher Langhorne, Viscountess (1879–1964), British politician; born in the US. She became the first woman to sit in the House of Commons when she succeeded her husband as a member of Parliament.

As·to·ri·a /ə'stôrēə/ **1** a city in northwestern Oregon, near the mouth of the Columbia River on the Pacific coast; pop. 9,851 (est. 2008). In the 19th century it was a noted fur-trading center.
2 a section of northwestern Queens in New York City, noted for its large Greek-American population.

as·tound /ə'stound/ ▶ **v.** [with obj.] shock or greatly surprise: *her bluntness astounded him.*
– ORIGIN Middle English (as an adjective in the sense 'stunned'): from *astoned*, past participle of obsolete *astone* (see **ASTONISH**).

as·tound·ing /ə'stoundiNG/ ▶ **adj.** surprisingly impressive or notable: *the summit offers astounding views.*
– DERIVATIVES **as·tound·ing·ly adv.** [as submodifier] *an astoundingly good performance.*

a·strad·dle /ə'stradl/ ▶ **prep.** with the legs stretched widely on each side of: *policemen sitting astraddle motorcycles.*
▶ **adj. & adv.** with the legs stretched widely on each side.

As·trae·a /a'strēə/ Astronomy asteroid 5, discovered in 1845 (diameter 125 km).
– ORIGIN from the name of a Roman goddess associated with justice.

as·tra·gal /'astrəgəl/ ▶ **n.** a convex molding or wooden strip across a surface or separating panels, typically semicircular in cross-section. ■ Architecture a small semicircular molding around the top or bottom of a column. ■ a wooden molding that covers the gap between a pair of doors or casement windows. ■ a glazing bar, typically one used in cabinetmaking.
– ORIGIN mid 17th cent.: from **ASTRAGALUS**, partly via French *astragale.*

as·trag·a·lus /ə'stragələs/ ▶ **n.** (pl. **astragali** /-,lī/) chiefly Zoology another term for **TALUS**[1].
– ORIGIN mid 16th cent.: via Latin from Greek *astragalos* 'ankle bone, molding,' also the name of a vetch.

As·tra·khan /'astrə,kan, -kən/ a city in southern Russia, on the delta of the Volga River; pop. 503,100 (est. 2008).

as·tra·khan /'astrəkən, -,kan/ ▶ **n.** the dark curly fleece of young karakul lambs from central Asia: [as modifier] *an astrakhan collar.* ■ a cloth imitating this.
– ORIGIN mid 18th cent.: named after the city of **ASTRAKHAN** in Russia, from which the fleeces were exported.

as·tral /'astrəl/ ▶ **adj.** [attrib.] of, connected with, or resembling the stars: *astral navigation.* ■ of or relating to a supposed nonphysical realm of existence to which various psychic and paranormal phenomena are ascribed, and in which the physical human body is said to have a counterpart.
– ORIGIN early 17th cent.: from late Latin *astralis*, from *astrum* 'star.'

a·stray /ə'strā/ ▶ **adv. 1** away from the correct path or direction: *we went astray but a man redirected us.*
2 into error or morally questionable behavior: *he was led astray by boozy colleagues.*
– PHRASES **go astray** (of an object) become lost or mislaid: *the money had gone astray.*
– ORIGIN Middle English (in the sense 'distant from the correct path'): from an Anglo-Norman French variant of Old French *estraie*, past participle of *estraier*, based on Latin *extra* 'out of bounds' + *vagari* 'wander.'

a·stride /ə'strīd/ ▶ **prep.** with a leg on each side of: *he was* **sitting astride** *the bike | a figure astride a horse |* [as adv.] *he sat on the chair astride.* ■ extending across: *the port* **stands astride** *an international route | why do people build their dream homes astride some seismic fault?* ■ [as adv.] with legs apart: *he stood, legs astride.*

as·trin·gent /ə'strinjənt/ ▶ **adj. 1** causing the contraction of body tissues, typically of the skin: *an astringent skin lotion.*
2 sharp or severe in manner or style: *her astringent words had their effect.* ■ (of taste or smell) sharp or bitter: *an astringent smell of rotting apples.*
▶ **n.** a substance that causes the contraction of body tissues, typically used to protect the skin and to reduce bleeding from minor abrasions.
– DERIVATIVES **as·trin·gen·cy n.**, **as·trin·gent·ly adv.** (sense 2 of the adjective).
– ORIGIN mid 16th cent.: from French, from Latin *astringent-* 'pulling tight,' from the verb *astringere*, from *ad-* 'toward' + *stringere* 'bind, pull tight.'

astro- ▶ **comb. form** relating to the stars, celestial objects, or outer space: *astrocompass | astrophysics | astrochemistry | astrophotography.*
– ORIGIN from Greek *astron* 'star.'

as·tro·ar·chae·ol·o·gy /'astrō,ärkē'äləjē/ ▶ **n.** another term for **ARCHAEOASTRONOMY**.

as·tro·bi·o·lo·gy /,astrōbī'äləjē/ ▶ **n.** the branch of biology concerned with the study of life on earth and in space.

as·tro·bleme /'astrə,blēm/ ▶ **n.** Geology an eroded remnant of a large crater made by the impact of a meteorite or comet.
– ORIGIN mid 20th cent.: from Greek *astron* 'star' + *blēma* 'wound.'

as·tro·chem·is·try /,astrō'keməstrē/ ▶ **n.** the study of the chemical substances and species occurring in stars and interstellar space.
– DERIVATIVES **as·tro·chem·i·cal** /-kəl/ **adj.**, **as·tro·chem·ist** /'astrō,kemist/ **n.**

as·tro·com·pass /'astrō,kəmpəs, -,käm-/ ▶ **n.** an instrument designed to indicate direction with respect to the stars.

as·tro·cyte /'astrə,sīt/ ▶ **n.** Anatomy a star-shaped glial cell of the central nervous system.
– DERIVATIVES **as·tro·cyt·ic** /,astrə'sitik/ **adj.**

as·tro·dome /'astrə,dōm/ ▶ **n. 1** a domed window in an aircraft for astronomical observations.
2 (**the Astrodome**) an enclosed stadium in Houston with a domed roof.

as·tro·ga·tion /,astrə'gāsHən/ ▶ **n.** (in science fiction) navigation in outer space.
– DERIVATIVES **as·tro·ga·tor** /'astrə,gātər/ **n.**
– ORIGIN 1930s: blend of **ASTRO-** and **NAVIGATION**.

as·troid /'astroid/ ▶ **n.** Mathematics a hypocycloid with four cusps (like a square with concave sides).

as·tro·labe /'astrə,lāb/ ▶ **n.** chiefly historical an instrument formerly used to make astronomical measurements, typically of the altitudes of celestial bodies, and in navigation for calculating latitude, before the development of the sextant. In its basic form (known from classical times), it consists of a disk with the edge marked in degrees and a pivoted pointer.
– ORIGIN late Middle English: from Old French *astrelabe*, from medieval Latin *astrolabium*, from Greek *astrolabon*, neuter of *astrolabos* 'star-taking.'

as·trol·o·gy /ə'sträləjē/ ▶ **n.** the study of the movements and relative positions of celestial bodies interpreted as having an influence on human affairs and the natural world.

> Ancient observers of the heavens developed elaborate systems of explanation based on the movements of the sun, moon, and planets through the constellations of the zodiac, for predicting events and for casting horoscopes. By 1700 astrology had lost intellectual credibility in the West, but continued to have popular appeal. Modern astrology is based on that of the Greeks, but other systems are extant, notably those of China and India.

– DERIVATIVES **as·trol·o·ger** /-jər/ **n.**, **as·tro·log·i·cal** /,astrə'läjikəl/ **adj.**, **as·trol·o·gist** /-jist/ **n.**
– ORIGIN late Middle English: from Old French *astrologie*, from Latin *astrologia*, from Greek, from *astron* 'star.' The term (in full *natural astrology*) originally denoted the practical uses of astronomy, applied in the measurement of time and the prediction of natural phenomena. The current sense (in full *judicial astrology*, relating to human affairs) dates from the mid 16th cent.

as·tro·met·ric bi·na·ry /,astrō'metrik 'bīnərē/ ▶ **n.** Astronomy a binary star system in which one companion is invisible, but is known to be present from its effect on measurements relating to the other.

as·trom·e·try /ə'strämitrē/ ▶ **n.** the measurement of the positions, motions, and magnitudes of stars.
– DERIVATIVES **as·tro·met·ric** /,astrō'metrik/ **adj.**

as·tro·naut /'astrə,nôt/ ▶ **n.** a person who is trained to travel in a spacecraft.
– DERIVATIVES **as·tro·nau·ti·cal** /,astrə'nôtikəl/ **adj.**
– ORIGIN 1920s: from **ASTRO-**, on the pattern of *aeronaut* and *aquanaut.*

as·tro·nau·tics /,astrə'nôtiks/ ▶ **n.** the science and technology of human space travel and exploration.

as·tro·nav·i·ga·tion /,astrō,navi'gāsHən/ ▶ **n.** determination of the position and course of an aircraft or a spacecraft by means of observation of the stars.
– DERIVATIVES **as·tro·nav·i·ga·tor** /-'navi,gātər/ **n.**
– ORIGIN mid 20th cent.: from **ASTRO-** + **NAVIGATION**.

as·tron·o·mer /ə'stränəmər/ ▶ **n.** an expert in or student of astronomy.

as·tro·nom·i·cal /,astrə'nämikəl/ ▶ **adj. 1** of or relating to astronomy.
2 informal (of an amount) extremely large: *he wanted an astronomical fee.*
– DERIVATIVES **as·tro·nom·ic adj.** (sense 2), **as·tro·nom·i·cal·ly** /-ik(ə)lē/ **adv.**
– ORIGIN mid 16th cent.: via Latin from Greek *astronomikos*, from *astronomia* (see **ASTRONOMY**).

as·tro·nom·i·cal u·nit (abbr.: **AU**) ▶ **n.** Astronomy a unit of measurement equal to 149.6 million kilometers, the mean distance from the center of the earth to the center of the sun.

as·tro·nom·i·cal year See **YEAR** (sense 1).

as·tron·o·my /ə'stränəmē/ ▶ **n.** the branch of science that deals with celestial objects, space, and the physical universe as a whole.

> In ancient times, observation of the sun, moon, stars, and planets formed the basis of timekeeping and navigation. Astronomy was greatly furthered by the invention of the optical telescope, but modern observations are made in all parts of the spectrum, including X-ray and radio frequencies, using terrestrial and orbiting instruments and space probes.

– ORIGIN Middle English (also denoting astrology): from Old French *astronomie*, from Latin *astronomia*, from Greek, from *astronomos* (adjective) 'star-arranging.'

as·tro·pho·tog·ra·phy /,astrōfə'tägrəfē/ ▶ **n.** the use of photography in astronomy; the photographing of celestial objects and phenomena.
– DERIVATIVES **as·tro·pho·tog·ra·pher** /-fər/ **n.**, **as·tro·pho·to·graph·ic** /-,fōtə'grafik/ **adj.**

as·tro·phys·ics /,astrō'fiziks/ ▶ **n.** the branch of astronomy concerned with the physical nature of stars and other celestial bodies, and the application of the laws and theories of physics to the interpretation of astronomical observations.
– DERIVATIVES **as·tro·phys·i·cal** /-ikəl/ **adj.**, **as·tro·phys·i·cist** /-isist/ **n.**

As·tro·Turf /'astrō,tərf/ ▶ **n.** trademark an artificial grass surface, used for athletic fields.
– DERIVATIVES **As·tro·Turfed adj.**
– ORIGIN 1960s: from **ASTRODOME** (sense 1), where it was first used, + **TURF**.

As·tu·ri·as[1] /ə'st(y)o͝orēəs/ an autonomous region and former principality in northwestern Spain; capital, Oviedo.

As·tu·ri·as[2], Miguel Ángel (1899–1974), Guatemalan novelist and poet, best known for his experimental novel *The President* (1946). Nobel Prize for Literature (1967).

as·tute /ə'st(y)o͞ot/ ▶ **adj.** having or showing an ability to accurately assess situations or people and turn this to one's advantage: *an astute businessman.*
– DERIVATIVES **as·tute·ly adv.**, **as·tute·ness n.**
– ORIGIN early 17th cent.: from obsolete French *astut* or Latin *astutus*, from *astus* 'craft.'

a·sty·lar /ā'stīlər/ ▶ **adj.** Architecture (of a classical building) lacking columns or pilasters.
– ORIGIN mid 19th cent.: from **A-**[1] 'without' + Greek *stulos* 'column' + **-AR**[1].

A·sun·ción /ä,so͞onsē'ōn, -'syōn/ the capital and chief port of Paraguay, on the Paraguay River; pop. 519,100 (est. 2007).

a·sun·der /ə'səndər/ ▶ **adv.** archaic or literary apart; divided: *those whom God hath joined together let no man put asunder.* ■ into pieces: *the desk burst asunder.*
– ORIGIN Old English *on sundran* 'in or into a separate place'; compare with **SUNDER**.

a·su·ra /'äsərə/ ▶ **n.** a member of a class of divine beings in the Vedic period, which in Indian mythology tend to be evil and in Zoroastrianism are benevolent. Compare with **DEVA**, **AHURA MAZDA**.

As·wan /as'wän, äs-/ a city on the Nile River in southern Egypt, 10 miles (16 km), north of Lake Nasser; pop. 266,000 (est. 2006). Two dams across the Nile have been built nearby. The controlled release of water from Lake Nasser behind the High Dam produces the greater part of Egypt's electricity.

a·swarm /ə'swôrm/ ▶ **adj.** [predic.] crowded; full of moving beings or objects: *the streets were aswarm with vendors.*

a·swim /ə'swim/ ▶ **adj.** [predic.] swimming: *sardines aswim in oil.*

a·swirl /ə'swərl/ ▶ **adj. & adv.** swirling; covered or surrounded with something swirling: [predic. adj.] *flowers aswirl with bees* | [adv.] *she shook her head, sending the streamers aswirl.*

a·sy·lee /əsī'lē/ ▶ **n.** a person who is seeking or has been granted political asylum.

a·sy·lum /ə'sīləm/ ▶ **n. 1** (also **political asylum**) the protection granted by a nation to someone who has left their native country as a political refugee: *granting asylum to foreigners persecuted for political reasons.* ■ shelter or protection from danger: *asylum for those too ill to care for themselves.*
2 dated an institution offering shelter and support to people who are mentally ill: *he'd been committed to an asylum.*
– ORIGIN late Middle English (in the sense 'place of refuge,' esp. for criminals): via Latin from Greek *asulon* 'refuge,' from *asulos* 'inviolable,' from *a-* 'without' + *sulon* 'right of seizure.' The current senses date from the 18th cent.

a·sym·met·ri·cal /ˌāsə'metrikəl/ ▶ **adj.** having parts that fail to correspond to one another in shape, size, or arrangement; lacking symmetry: *the church has an asymmetrical plan with an aisle only on one side.* ■ having parts or aspects that are not equal or equivalent; unequal in some respect: *the asymmetrical relationship between a landlord and a tenant.*
– DERIVATIVES **a·sym·met·ric adj.**, **a·sym·met·ri·cal·ly** /-ik(ə)lē/ **adv.**

a·sym·met·ri·cal war·fare ▶ **n.** warfare involving surprise attacks by small, simply armed groups on a nation armed with modern high-tech weaponry.

a·sym·met·ric bars /ˌāsə'metrik/ ▶ **plural n.** British term for **UNEVEN BARS.**

a·sym·me·try /ā'simitrē/ ▶ **n.** (pl. **asymmetries**) lack of equality or equivalence between parts or aspects of something; lack of symmetry.
– ORIGIN mid 17th cent.: from Greek *asummetria*, from *a-* 'without' + *summetria* (see **SYMMETRY**).

a·symp·to·mat·ic /ˌāsim(p)tə'matik/ ▶ **adj.** Medicine (of a condition or a person) producing or showing no symptoms.

as·ymp·tote /'asəm(p)ˌtōt/ ▶ **n.** a line that continually approaches a given curve but does not meet it at any finite distance.
– DERIVATIVES **as·ymp·tot·ic** /ˌasəm(p)'tätik/ **adj.**, **as·ymp·tot·i·cal·ly** /-ik(ə)lē/ **adv.**
– ORIGIN mid 17th cent.: from modern Latin *asymptota (linea)* '(line) not meeting,' from Greek *asumptōtos* 'not falling together,' from *a-* 'not' + *sun* 'together' + *ptōtos* 'apt to fall' (from *piptein* 'to fall').

a·syn·chro·nous /ā'siNGkrənəs/ ▶ **adj. 1** Computing & Telecommunications of or requiring a form of computer control timing protocol in which a specific operation begins upon receipt of an indication (signal) that the preceding operation has been completed.
2 not going at the same rate and exactly together with something else, in particular: ■ (of a machine or motor) not working in time with the alternations of current. ■ Astronomy (of a satellite) revolving around the parent planet at a different rate from that at which the planet rotates. ■ Astronomy (of an orbit) such that a satellite in it is asynchronous.
3 (of two or more objects or events) not existing or happening at the same time.
– DERIVATIVES **a·syn·chro·nous·ly adv.**

a·syn·de·ton /ə'sindəˌtän/ ▶ **n.** (pl. **asyndeta** /-dətə/) the omission or absence of a conjunction between parts of a sentence.
– DERIVATIVES **as·yn·det·ic** /ˌasən'detik/ **adj.**
– ORIGIN mid 16th cent.: modern Latin, from Greek *asundeton*, neuter of *asundetos* 'unconnected,' from *a-* 'not' + *sundetos* 'bound together.'

At ▶ **symbol** the chemical element astatine.

at¹ /at/ ▶ **prep. 1** expressing location or arrival in a particular place or position: *they live at Conway House* | *she was constantly at the telex machine* | *they stopped at a small trattoria.* ■ used in speech to indicate the sign @ in e-mail addresses, separating the address holder's name from their location.
2 expressing the time when an event takes place: *the children go to bed at nine o'clock* | *his death came at a time when the movement was split.* ■ [without adj.] denoting a particular period of time: *the sea is cooler at night.* ■ [without adj.] denoting the time spent by someone attending an educational institution, a workplace, or their home: *we all need to get involved in fighting crime whether it's at work, at home, or at school.*
3 denoting a particular point or segment on a scale: *prices start at $18,500* | *driving at 50 mph.* ■ referring to someone's age: *at fourteen he began to work as a mailman.*
4 expressing a particular state or condition: *placed them at a serious disadvantage* | *the coroner accepted that the machines were at fault.* ■ expressing a relationship between an individual and a skill: *boxing was the only sport I was any good at* | *he is poor at giving instructions.*
5 expressing the object of a look, gesture, thought, action, or plan: *I looked at my watch* | *Leslie pointed at him.* ■ expressing the target of a shot from a weapon: *they tore down the main street, firing at anyone in sight.* ■ emphasizing the directing of an action toward a specified object: *she clutched at the thin gown* | *he hit at her face with the gun.*
6 expressing the means by which something is done: *holding a corrections officer at knifepoint* | figurative *her pride had taken a beating at his hands.*
– PHRASES **at all** see **ALL**. **at first** see **FIRST**. **at it** engaged in some activity, typically a reprehensible one: *oh dear, they are at it again.* **at last** see **LAST¹**. **at least** see **LEAST**. **at most** see **MOST**. **at once** see **ONCE**. **at that** in addition; furthermore: *it was not fog but smoke, and very thick at that.* **not at all** see **NOT**. **where it's at** informal the fashionable place, possession, or activity: *New York is where it's at, stylewise.* **where someone is at** informal someone's true or fundamental nature or character: *I think we've got enough information to have an idea of where he's at.*
– ORIGIN Old English *æt*, of Germanic origin; related to Old Frisian *et* and Old Norse *at*, from an Indo-European root shared by Latin *ad* 'to.'

at² /ät/ ▶ **n.** a monetary unit of Laos, equal to one hundredth of a kip.

at- ▶ **prefix** variant spelling of **AD-** assimilated before *t* (as in *attend, attenuate*).

At·a·brine /'atəbrin, -ˌbrēn/ trade name for **QUINACRINE.**

A·ta·ca·ma Des·ert /ˌätə'kämə, ˌatə-/ an arid region in western Chile that extends roughly 600 miles (965 km) south from the Peruvian border.

a·tac·tic /ā'taktik/ ▶ **adj.** Chemistry (of a polymer or polymer structure) in which the repeating units have no regular stereochemical configuration.
– ORIGIN mid 19th cent.: from Greek *ataktos*, from *a-* 'not' + *taktos* 'arranged' + **-IC.**

At·a·lan·ta /ˌätə'läntə/ Greek Mythology a huntress who would marry only someone who could beat her in a foot race. She was beaten when a suitor threw down three golden apples which she stopped to pick up.

at·a·man /'atəmən/ ▶ **n.** (pl. **atamans**) a Cossack leader. See also **HETMAN.**
– ORIGIN mid 19th cent.: from Russian.

at·a·rax·y /'atəˌraksē/ (also **ataraxia** /ˌatə'raksēə/) ▶ **n.** a state of serene calmness.
– DERIVATIVES **at·a·rac·tic** /ˌatə'raktik/ **adj.**, **at·a·rax·ic** /ˌatə'raksik/ **adj.**
– ORIGIN early 17th cent.: from French *ataraxie*, from Greek *ataraxia* 'impassiveness,' from *a-* 'not' + *tarassein* 'disturb.'

A·ta·türk /ˌatə'tərk/, Kemal (1881–1938), Turkish general and statesman; president 1923–38; born *Mustafa Kemal*; also called **Kemal Pasha**. As the first president of the Turkish republic, he abolished the caliphate and introduced other policies designed to make Turkey a modern secular state.

at·a·vis·tic /ˌatə'vistik/ ▶ **adj.** relating to or characterized by reversion to something ancient or ancestral: *atavistic fears and instincts.*
– DERIVATIVES **at·a·vism** /'atəˌvizəm/ **n.**, **at·a·vis·ti·cal·ly** /-tik(ə)lē/ **adv.**
– ORIGIN late 19th cent.: based on Latin *atavus* 'forefather,' via French *atavisme*, + **-IC.**

a·tax·i·a /ə'taksēə/ (also **ataxy** /ə'taksē/) ▶ **n.** Medicine the loss of full control of bodily movements.
– DERIVATIVES **a·tax·ic** /-sik/ **adj.**
– ORIGIN late 19th cent.: modern Latin, from Greek, from *a-* 'without' + *taxis* 'order.' The original sense was 'irregularity, disorder,' later (in medical use) denoting irregularity of function or symptoms.

ATB ▶ **abbr.** all-terrain bike.

at-bat Baseball ▶ **n.** a player's turn at batting, as officially recorded: *O'Neill had three singles in four at-bats.* Compare with **PLATE APPEARANCE.**
▶ **adv.** batting.

ATC ▶ **abbr.** ■ air traffic control. ■ air traffic controller.

A·tchaf·a·lay·a Riv·er /(ə)ˌCHafə'līə/ a river in south central Louisiana that flows south for 170 miles (275 km) to the Gulf of Mexico. It is used to control flooding on the Red and Mississippi rivers.

ATE ▶ **abbr.** automated test equipment.

ate /āt/ past of **EAT.**

-ate¹ ▶ **suffix** forming nouns: **1** denoting status or office: *doctorate* | *episcopate.* ■ a state or function: *curate* | *mandate.*
2 denoting a group: *electorate.*
3 Chemistry denoting a salt or ester, esp. of an acid with a corresponding name ending in *-ic*: *chlorate* | *nitrate.*
4 denoting a product (of a chemical process): *condensate* | *filtrate.*
– ORIGIN representing Old French *-at* or *-é(e)*, or from Latin *-atus* (as a noun or past participial form).

-ate² ▶ **suffix 1** forming adjectives and nouns such as *associate, duplicate, separate.*
2 forming adjectives from Latin: *caudate.*
– ORIGIN representing French *-é* or its Latin source *-atus* (past participial suffix).

-ate³ ▶ **suffix** forming verbs such as *fascinate, hyphenate.*
– ORIGIN representing French *-er* or its Latin source *-are.* Originally forms were based on existing past participial adjectives ending in *-atus*, later extended to any verb ending in *-are.*

A-team ▶ **n.** a group of elite soldiers or the top advisers or workers in an organization.
– ORIGIN 1970s: from sports terminology in which an organization's A-team is its best team.

at·e·lec·ta·sis /ˌatl'ektəsis/ ▶ **n.** Medicine partial or complete collapse of the lung.
– ORIGIN mid 19th cent.: from Greek *atelēs* 'imperfect' + *ektasis* 'extension.'

at·el·ier /ˌatl'yā/ ▶ **n.** a workshop or studio, esp. one used by an artist or designer.
– ORIGIN late 17th cent.: from French, from Old French *astelle* 'splinter of wood,' from Latin *astula.*

a tem·po /ä 'tempō/ ▶ **adv.** Music (esp. as a direction) in the previous or original tempo.
– ORIGIN Italian, literally 'in time.'

a·tem·po·ral /ā'temp(ə)rəl/ ▶ **adj.** existing or considered without relation to time.
– DERIVATIVES **a·tem·po·ral·i·ty** /ˌātempə'ralitē/ **n.**

A·ten /'ätn/ (also **Aton**) Egyptian Mythology the sun or solar disk, the deity of a strong monotheistic cult, particularly during the reign of Akhenaten.

a·ten·o·lol /ə'tenəˌlôl, -ˌläl/ ▶ **n.** Medicine a beta blocker used mainly to treat angina and high blood pressure.
– ORIGIN 1970s: perhaps from *a(ngina)* + *ten(sion)* + *(propran)olol*, a related compound.

ATF ▶ **abbr.** (Federal Bureau of) Alcohol, Tobacco, and Firearms.

Ath·a·bas·ca Riv·er /ˌaTHə'baskə/ a river in Canada that flows northeast for 765 miles (1,230 km) from the Rocky Mountains across Alberta to Lake Athabasca, Canada's fourth-largest lake. The river valley has large oil tar deposits.

Ath·a·bas·kan /ˌaTHə'baskən/ (also **Athapaskan** /-'pas-/) ▶ **adj.** denoting, belonging to, or relating to a family of North American Indian languages including esp. Navajo and various Apache languages of the southwest US, several languages of coastal California and Oregon, and many languages of Alaska and northwestern Canada, including Chipewyan.
▶ **n. 1** this family of languages.
2 a speaker of any of these languages.
– ORIGIN from *Athabasca*, the name of a lake in western Canada, from Cree *athapaskaw* 'grass and reeds here and there,' + **-AN.**

Ath·a·na·sian Creed /ˌaTHə'nāZHən/ a summary of Christian doctrine formerly attributed to St. Athanasius, but probably dating from the 5th century.

Ath·a·na·sius, St. /ˌaTHə'nāSHəs/ (c.296–373), Greek theologian and upholder of Christian orthodoxy against the Arian heresy. Feast day, May 2.

ath·a·nor /'aTHəˌnôr/ ▶ **n.** a type of furnace used by alchemists, able to maintain a steady heat for long periods.
– ORIGIN late 15th cent.: from Arabic *at-tannūr*, from *al-* 'the' + *tannūr* 'baker's oven.' Compare with **TANDOOR.**

A·thar·va Ve·da /ə'tärvə 'vādə, 'vēdə/ Hinduism a collection of hymns and ritual utterances, written in early Sanskrit and added at a later stage to the existing Vedic material.
– ORIGIN from Sanskrit *Atharvan* (the name of Brahma's eldest son, said to be the author of the collection) + *vēda* '(sacred) knowledge.'

a·the·ism /'āTHēˌizəm/ ▶ **n.** disbelief in the existence of God or gods.
– ORIGIN late 16th cent.: from French *athéisme*, from Greek *atheos*, from *a-* 'without' + *theos* 'god.'

a·the·ist /'āTHēˌist/ ▶ **n.** a person who does not believe in the existence of God or gods: *he is a committed atheist.*

– DERIVATIVES **a·the·is·tic** /ˌāTHēˈistik/ **adj.**, **a·the·is·ti·cal** /-ˈistikəl/ **adj.**

ath·el·ing /ˈaTHəliNG, ˈaT͟H-/ ▶ **n.** historical a prince or lord in Anglo-Saxon England.
– ORIGIN Old English *ætheling*, from a base meaning 'race, family.'

Ath·el·stan /ˈaTHəlˌstan/ (*c.*893/4–939), king of England 925–939.

a·the·mat·ic /ˌāTHiˈmatik/ ▶ **adj. 1** Music (of a composition) not based on the use of themes.
2 Grammar (of a verb form) having a suffix attached to the stem without a connecting (thematic) vowel.

A·the·na /əˈTHēnə/ (also **Athene** /-nē/) Greek Mythology the patron goddess of Athens, worshiped as the goddess of wisdom, handicrafts, and warfare. She is often allegorized into a personification of wisdom. Also called **Pallas**. Identified with the Roman goddess **Minerva**.

Ath·e·nae·um /ˌaTHəˈnēəm/ (also **Atheneum**) ▶ **n.** used in the names of libraries or institutions for literary or scientific study: *the Boston Athenaeum*. ■ used in the titles of periodicals concerned with literature, science, and art.
– ORIGIN mid 18th cent.: via Latin from Greek *Athēnaion*, denoting the temple of Athena.

A·the·ni·an em·pire /əˈTHēnēən/ see **Delian League**.

Ath·ens /ˈaTHənz/ **1** the capital of Greece, in the southern part of the country; pop. 745,500 (est. 2009). A flourishing city state in ancient Greece, it was an important cultural center in the 5th century BC. It came under Roman rule in 146 BC and fell to the Goths in AD 267. After its capture by the Turks in 1456, Athens declined to the status of a village until chosen as the capital of a newly independent Greece in 1834. Greek name **Athínai**.
2 a city in northeastern Georgia, the seat of the University of Georgia; since a 1991 merger, is part of Athens–Clarke County; consolidated pop. 113,398 (est. 2008).
3 a city in southeastern Ohio, the seat of Ohio University; pop. 22,088 (est. 2008).
– DERIVATIVES **A·the·ni·an** /əˈTHēnēən/ **adj. & n.**

ath·er·o·gen·ic /ˌaTH(ə)rōˈjenik/ ▶ **adj.** Physiology tending to promote the formation of fatty plaques in the arteries.
– DERIVATIVES **ath·er·o·gen·e·sis** /-əsis/ **n.**
– ORIGIN 1950s: from **atheroma** + **-genic**.

ath·er·o·ma /ˌaTHəˈrōmə/ ▶ **n.** Medicine degeneration of the walls of the arteries caused by accumulated fatty deposits and scar tissue, and leading to restriction of the circulation and a risk of thrombosis. See also **atherosclerosis**. ■ the fatty material that forms plaques in the arteries.
– DERIVATIVES **ath·er·om·a·tous** /-ˈrämətəs, -ˈrō-/ **adj.**
– ORIGIN late 16th cent.: via Latin from Greek *athērōma*, from *athērē*, *atharē* 'groats.'

ath·er·o·scle·ro·sis /ˌaTHərōskləˈrōsis/ ▶ **n.** Medicine a disease of the arteries characterized by the deposition of plaques of fatty material on their inner walls. See also **atheroma** and **arteriosclerosis**.
– DERIVATIVES **ath·er·o·scle·rot·ic** /-ˈrätik/ **adj.**
– ORIGIN early 20th cent.: coined in German from Greek *athērē* 'groats' + *sklērōsis* 'hardening' (see **sclerosis**).

ath·e·tize /ˈaTHiˌtīz/ ▶ **v.** [with obj.] rare reject (a passage in a text) as spurious.
– DERIVATIVES **ath·e·te·sis** /ˌaTHiˈtēsis/ **n.**
– ORIGIN late 19th cent.: from Greek *athetos* 'without position' + **-ize**, rendering the Greek verb *athetein*.

ath·e·to·sis /ˌaTHiˈtōsis/ ▶ **n.** Medicine a condition in which abnormal muscle contractions cause involuntary writhing movements. It affects some people with cerebral palsy, impairing speech and use of the hands.
– DERIVATIVES **ath·e·toid** /ˈaTHiˌtoid/ **adj.**, **ath·e·tot·ic** /-ˈtätik/ **adj.**
– ORIGIN late 19th cent.: from Greek *athetos* 'without position' + **-osis**.

A·thí·nai /äˈTHēne/ variant spelling of **Athens**.

a·thirst /əˈTHərst/ ▶ **adj.** [predic.] archaic thirsty. ■ very eager to get something: *she was athirst for news.*
– ORIGIN Old English *ofthyrst*, shortened from *ofthyrsted*, past participle of *ofthyrstan* 'be thirsty.'

ath·lete /ˈaTHˌlēt/ ▶ **n.** a person who is proficient in sports and other forms of physical exercise. ■ chiefly Brit. a person who is skilled in competitive track and field events (athletics).
– ORIGIN late Middle English: from Latin *athleta*, from Greek *athlētēs*, from *athlein* 'compete for a prize,' from *athlon* 'prize.'

ath·lete's foot ▶ **n.** a fungal infection affecting the skin between the toes. It is a form of ringworm.

ath·let·ic /aTHˈletik/ ▶ **adj. 1** [attrib.] of or relating to athletes or athletics: *athletic events | an athletic club.*
2 physically strong, fit, and active: *big, muscular, athletic boys.*
– DERIVATIVES **ath·let·i·cal·ly** /-ik(ə)lē/ **adv.**, **ath·let·i·cism** /-ˌsizəm/ **n.**
– ORIGIN mid 17th cent.: from French *athlétique* or Latin *athleticus*, from Greek *athlētikos*, from *athlētēs* (see **athlete**).

ath·let·ics /aTHˈletiks/ ▶ **plural n.** [usu. treated as sing.] physical sports and games of any kind. ■ chiefly Brit. the sport of competing in track and field events, including running races and various competitions in jumping and throwing: [as modifier] *athletics championships*.

ath·let·ic sup·port·er ▶ **n.** another term for **jockstrap**.

at-home ▶ **n.** an informal party in a person's home. ■ dated a period when a person has announced that they will receive visitors in their home.
▶ **adj.** occurring in or suited to one's home: *at-home athletic equipment.*

Ath·os, Mount /ˈaTHˌäs, ˈāˌTHäs/ a narrow, mountainous peninsula in northeastern Greece that projects into the Aegean Sea. It is inhabited by Greek Orthodox monks, who forbid women and even female animals to set foot on the peninsula.
– DERIVATIVES **Ath·o·nite** /ˈaTHəˌnīt/ **adj. & n.**

a·thwart /əˈTHwôrt/ ▶ **prep. 1** from side to side of; across: *a long counter thrown athwart the entranceway.*
2 in opposition to; counter to: *these statistics run sharply* **athwart** *conventional presumptions.*
▶ **adv. 1** across from side to side; transversely: *one table running athwart was all the room would hold.*
2 so as to be perverse or contradictory: *our words ran athwart and we ended up at cross purposes.*
– ORIGIN late Middle English: from **a-**[2] 'on' + **thwart**.

-atic ▶ **suffix** forming adjectives and nouns such as *aquatic*, *idiomatic*.
– ORIGIN from French *-atique* or Latin *-aticus*, often based on Greek *-atikos*.

-ation ▶ **suffix** (forming nouns) denoting an action or an instance of it: *exploration | hesitation.* ■ denoting a result or product of action: *plantation.*
– ORIGIN representing French *-ation* or Latin *-ation-*.

At·i·van /ˈatiˌvan/ ▶ **n.** trademark for **lorazepam**.

-ative ▶ **suffix** (forming adjectives) denoting a characteristic or propensity: *pejorative | talkative.*
– ORIGIN representing French *-atif*, *-ative*, or from Latin *-ativus*.

At·kins di·et /ˈatkinz/ ▶ **n.** trademark a diet high in protein and fat and low in carbohydrates, prescribed for weight loss.
– ORIGIN 1972: after its originator, cardiologist Dr. Robert C. *Atkins* (1930–2003) and his book *Dr. Atkins' Diet Revolution* (1972).

At·lan·ta /ətˈlantə, at-/ the capital of the state of Georgia in the US, in northwest central Georgia; pop. 537,958 (est. 2008). It was burned by Union forces under Gen. William T. Sherman in 1864 during the Civil War.

at·lan·tes /atˈlantēz/ plural form of **atlas** (sense 3).

At·lan·tic /ətˈlantik, at-/ ▶ **adj.** [attrib.] of or adjoining the Atlantic Ocean: *an Atlantic storm | the Atlantic coast of Europe.*
▶ **n.** short for **Atlantic Ocean**.
– ORIGIN late Middle English: via Latin from Greek *Atlantikos*, from *Atlas*, *Atlant-* (see **atlas**). The term originally referred to the Atlas Mountains in Libya, hence to the sea near the west African coast, later being extended to the whole ocean.

At·lan·tic, Battle of the a succession of sea operations during World War II in which Axis naval and air forces attempted to destroy shipping carrying supplies from North America to the UK.

At·lan·tic Char·ter a declaration of eight common principles in international relations drawn up by Winston Churchill and Franklin Roosevelt in August 1941, which provided the ideological basis for the United Nations organization.

At·lan·tic Cit·y a resort city in southeastern New Jersey, on the Atlantic Ocean; pop. 39,408 (est. 2008). It is noted for its gambling casinos and its boardwalk.

At·lan·tic In·tra·coast·al Wa·ter·way a water route in the US that allows sheltered boat passage for 1,900 miles (3,100 km) along the Atlantic coast between Boston and Key West.

At·lan·ti·cism /ətˈlantiˌsizəm/ ▶ **n.** belief in or support for a close relationship between western Europe and the US, or particularly for NATO.
– DERIVATIVES **At·lan·ti·cist n. & adj.**

At·lan·tic O·cean the ocean that lies between Europe and Africa on the east and North and South America on the west. It is divided by the equator into the North Atlantic and the South Atlantic oceans.

At·lan·tic Prov·in·ces another name for **Maritime Provinces**.

At·lan·tic seal ▶ **n.** another term for **gray seal**.

At·lan·tic time the standard time in a zone including the easternmost parts of mainland Canada, Puerto Rico, and the Virgin Islands, specifically. ● (**Atlantic Standard Time**, abbrev.: **AST**) standard time based on the mean solar time at the longitude 60° W, four hours behind GMT. ● (**Atlantic Daylight Time**, abbrev.: **ADT**) Atlantic time during daylight savings, three hours behind GMT.

At·lan·tis /ətˈlantis, at-/ a legendary island, beautiful and prosperous, which sank into the sea.
– DERIVATIVES **At·lan·te·an** /ˌatlanˈtēən, atˈlantēən/ **adj.**

At·las /ˈatləs/ Greek Mythology one of the Titans, who was punished for his part in their revolt against Zeus by being made to support the heavens. He became identified with the Atlas Mountains.
– DERIVATIVES **At·lan·te·an** /ˌatlanˈtēən, atˈlantēən/ **adj.**

at·las /ˈatləs/ ▶ **n. 1** (pl. **atlases**) a book of maps or charts: *I looked in the atlas to find a map of Italy | a road atlas.* ■ a book of illustrations or diagrams on any subject: *Atlas of Surgical Operations.*
2 (pl. **atlases**) (also **atlas vertebra**) Anatomy the topmost vertebra of the backbone, articulating with the occipital bone of the skull.
3 (pl. **atlantes** /atˈlantēz/) Architecture a stone carving of a male figure, used as a column to support the entablature of a Greek or Greek-style building.
– ORIGIN late 16th cent. (originally denoting a person who supported a great burden): via Latin from Greek **Atlas**, the god who held up the pillars of the universe and whose picture appeared at the front of early atlases.

at·las moth ▶ **n.** a very large, boldly marked silkworm moth that occurs in both the Old and New World tropics. ● Genus *Attacus*, family Saturniidae: several species, in particular *A. atlas* of Asia, which is the largest moth in the world.

At·las Moun·tains a range of mountains in North Africa that extends from Morocco to Tunisia in a series of chains, including the Anti-Atlas, High Atlas, Middle Atlas, Rif Mountains, Tell Atlas, and Sahara Atlas.

at·latl /ˌätˈlätl/ ▶ **n.** a stick used by Eskimos and early American Indians to propel a spear or dart. ■ a similar device used in modern sport.
– ORIGIN Nahuatl *atlatl* 'spear-thrower.'

ATM ▶ **abbr.** ■ Telecommunications asynchronous transfer mode. ■ automated (or automatic) teller machine.

atm ▶ **abbr.** Physics atmosphere(s), as a unit of pressure.

at·man /ˈätmən/ (also **Atman**) ▶ **n.** Hinduism the spiritual life principle of the universe, esp. when regarded as inherent in the real self of the individual. ■ a person's soul.
– ORIGIN from Sanskrit *ātman*, literally 'essence, breath.'

at·mos·phere /ˈatməsˌfi(ə)r/ ▶ **n.** [usu. in sing.] **1** the envelope of gases surrounding the earth or another planet: *part of the sun's energy is absorbed by the earth's atmosphere.* ■ the air in any particular place: *we couldn't breathe in the dusty atmosphere of his apartment.* ■ (abbr.: **atm**) Physics a unit of pressure equal to mean atmospheric pressure at sea level, 101,325 pascals.
2 the pervading tone or mood of a place, situation, or work of art: *the hotel is famous for its friendly, welcoming atmosphere | this crisis further compounded the prevailing atmosphere of gloom.* ■ a pleasurable and interesting or exciting mood: *a superb restaurant, full of atmosphere.*
– ORIGIN mid 17th cent.: from modern Latin *atmosphaera*, from Greek *atmos* 'vapor' + *sphaira* 'ball, globe.'

at·mos·pher·ic /ˌatməsˈfi(ə)rik, -ˈferik/ ▶ **adj.**
1 of or relating to the atmosphere of the earth or (occasionally) another planet: *atmospheric conditions such as fog, snow, rain.*
2 creating a distinctive mood, typically of romance, mystery, or nostalgia: *atmospheric lighting.*
– DERIVATIVES **at·mos·pher·i·cal adj.** (archaic), **at·mos·pher·i·cal·ly adv.**

at·mos·pher·ic pres·sure ▶ **n.** the pressure exerted by the weight of the atmosphere, which at sea level has a mean value of 101,325 pascals (roughly 14.6959 pounds per square inch). Also called **barometric pressure**.

at·mos·pher·ics /ˌatməsˈfi(ə)riks, -ˈferiks/ ▶ **plural n. 1** electrical disturbances in the atmosphere due to lightning and other phenomena, esp. as they interfere with telecommunications.

a

2 effects intended to create a particular atmosphere or mood, esp. in music: *a jazz sound with spooky atmospherics.*

at·oll /'at,ôl, 'at,äl, 'ā,tôl, 'ā,täl/ ▶ **n.** a ring-shaped reef, island, or chain of islands formed of coral.
– ORIGIN early 17th cent.: from Maldivian *atolu.*

at·om /'atəm/ ▶ **n.** the basic unit of a chemical element. ■ such particles as a source of nuclear energy: *the power of the atom.* ■ [usu. with negative] an extremely small amount of a thing or quality: *I shall not have one atom of strength left.*

> An atom, roughly 10^{-8} cm in diameter, consists of a tiny, dense, positively charged nucleus made of neutrons and protons, surrounded by a cloud of negatively charged electrons. Each chemical element consists of atoms that possess a characteristic number of protons. Atoms are held together in molecules by sharing electrons.

– ORIGIN late 15th cent.: from Old French *atome,* via Latin from Greek *atomos* 'indivisible,' based on *a-* 'not' + *temnein* 'to cut.'

at·om bomb (also **atomic bomb**) ▶ **n.** a bomb that derives its destructive power from the rapid release of nuclear energy by fission of heavy atomic nuclei, causing damage through heat, blast, and radioactivity. Compare with HYDROGEN BOMB.

> In such a bomb two pieces of a fissile material are brought together by a conventional explosion to form a super critical mass. Neutrons then cause an uncontrolled fission chain reaction that quickly releases large amounts of energy.

a·tom·ic /ə'tämik/ ▶ **adj.** of or relating to an atom or atoms: *the atomic nucleus.* ■ Chemistry (of a substance) consisting of uncombined atoms rather than molecules: *atomic hydrogen.* ■ of or forming a single irreducible unit or component in a larger system: *a society made up of atomic individuals pursuing private interests.* ■ relating to, denoting, or using the energy released in nuclear fission or fusion: *the atomic age required a new way of political thinking | atomic weapons.*
– DERIVATIVES **a·tom·i·cal·ly** /-ik(ə)lē/ **adv.**
– ORIGIN late 17th cent.: from modern Latin *atomicus,* from *atomus* 'indivisible' (see ATOM).

a·tom·ic age ▶ **n.** another term for NUCLEAR AGE.

a·tom·ic clock ▶ **n.** an extremely accurate type of clock that is regulated by the vibrations of an atomic or molecular system such as cesium or ammonia.

a·tom·ic en·er·gy ▶ **n.** another term for NUCLEAR ENERGY.

at·o·mic·i·ty /,atə'misitē/ ▶ **n.** 1 Chemistry the number of atoms in the molecules of an element.
2 the state or fact of being composed of indivisible units.

a·tom·ic mass ▶ **n.** the mass of an atom of a chemical element expressed in atomic mass units. It is approximately equivalent to the number of protons and neutrons in the atom (the mass number) or to the average number allowing for the relative abundances of different isotopes.

a·tom·ic mass u·nit (abbr.: **amu**) ▶ **n.** a unit of mass used to express atomic and molecular weights, equal to one-twelfth of the mass of an atom of carbon-12. It is equal to approximately 1.66×10^{-27} kg.

a·tom·ic num·ber ▶ **n.** Chemistry & Physics the number of protons in the nucleus of an atom, which determines the chemical properties of an element and its place in the periodic table. (Symbol: **Z**)

a·tom·ic phys·ics ▶ **plural n.** [treated as sing.] the branch of physics concerned with the structure of the atom, its energy states, and its interactions with particles and fields.

a·tom·ic pile ▶ **n.** dated term for NUCLEAR REACTOR.

a·tom·ic pow·er ▶ **n.** another term for NUCLEAR POWER.

a·tom·ic spec·trum ▶ **n.** the spectrum of frequencies of electromagnetic radiation emitted or absorbed during transitions of electrons between energy levels within an atom. Each element has a characteristic spectrum by which it can be recognized.

a·tom·ic the·o·ry ▶ **n.** the theory that all matter is made up of tiny indivisible particles (atoms). According to the modern version, the atoms of each element are effectively identical, but differ from those of other elements, and unite to form compounds in fixed proportions. ■ in any field, a theory that proposes the existence of distinct, separable, independent components: *an atomic theory of heredity.*

a·tom·ic vol·ume ▶ **n.** Chemistry the volume occupied by one gram-atom of an element under standard conditions.

a·tom·ic weight ▶ **n.** Chemistry another term for ATOMIC MASS.

at·om·ism /'atə,mizəm/ ▶ **n.** chiefly Philosophy a theoretical approach that regards something as interpretable through analysis into distinct, separable, and independent elementary components. The opposite of HOLISM.
– DERIVATIVES **at·om·ist n., at·om·is·tic** /,atə'mistik/ **adj.**

at·om·ize /'atə,mīz/ ▶ **v.** [with obj.] convert (a substance) into very fine particles or droplets: *the CO_2 depressurized, atomizing the paint into a mist of even-size particles.* ■ reduce (something) to atoms or other small distinct units: *by disrupting our ties with our neighbors, crime atomizes society.*
– DERIVATIVES **at·om·i·za·tion** /,atəmə'zāSHən/ **n.**

at·om·iz·er /'atə,mīzər/ (Brit. also **atomiser**) ▶ **n.** a device for emitting water, perfume, or other liquids as a fine spray.

atomizer

at·om smash·er ▶ **n.** informal term for PARTICLE ACCELERATOR.

at·o·my /'atəmē/ ▶ **n.** (pl. **atomies**) archaic a skeleton or emaciated body.
– ORIGIN late 16th cent.: from ANATOMY, taken as *an atomy.*

A·ton variant spelling of ATEN.

a·ton·al /ā'tōnl/ ▶ **adj.** Music not written in any key or mode.
– DERIVATIVES **a·ton·al·ism** /-,izəm/ **n., a·ton·al·ist** /-ist/ **n., a·to·nal·i·ty** /,ātō'nalitē/ **n.**

a·tone /ə'tōn/ ▶ **v.** [no obj.] make amends or reparation: *he was being helpful, to atone for his past mistakes.*
– ORIGIN Middle English (originally in the sense 'make or become united or reconciled,' rare before the 16th cent.): from *at one* in early use; later by back-formation from ATONEMENT.

a·tone·ment /ə'tōnmənt/ ▶ **n.** reparation for a wrong or injury: *she wanted to make atonement for her husband's behavior.* ■ (in religious contexts) reparation or expiation for sin: *an annual ceremony of confession and atonement for sin.* ■ (**the Atonement**) Christian Theology the reconciliation of God and humankind through Jesus Christ.
– ORIGIN early 16th cent. (denoting unity or reconciliation, esp. between God and man): from *at one* + -MENT, influenced by medieval Latin *adunamentum* 'unity,' and earlier *onement* from an obsolete verb *one* 'to unite.'

a·ton·ic /ā'tänik/ ▶ **adj.** 1 Linguistics (of a syllable) without accent or stress.
2 Physiology lacking muscular tone.
– DERIVATIVES **at·o·ny** /'atnē/ **n.**

a·top /ə'täp/ ▶ **prep.** on the top of: *the weathervane is perched atop the barn.*
▶ **adv.** on the top: *the air raid siren atop of the courthouse.*

a·top·ic /ā'täpik/ ▶ **n.** denoting a form of allergy in which a hypersensitivity reaction such as dermatitis or asthma may occur in a part of the body not in contact with the allergen.
– DERIVATIVES **at·o·py** /'atəpē/ **adj.**
– ORIGIN early 20th cent.: from Greek *atopia* 'a being out of place,' from *atopos* 'out of place,' from *a-* 'without' + *topos* 'place.'

-ator ▶ **suffix** forming agent nouns such as *agitator.* ■ used in names of implements, machines, etc.: *escalator.*
– ORIGIN from Latin, or sometimes representing French *-ateur.*

-atory ▶ **suffix** (forming adjectives) relating to or involving an action: *explanatory | predatory.*
– ORIGIN from Latin *-atorius.*

ATP ▶ **abbr.** Biochemistry adenosine triphosphate.

at·ra·bil·ious /,atrə'bilēəs, -'bilyəs/ ▶ **adj.** literary melancholy or ill-tempered.
– DERIVATIVES **at·ra·bil·ious·ness n.**
– ORIGIN mid 17th cent. (in the sense 'affected by black bile,' one of the four supposed cardinal humors of the body, believed to cause melancholy): from Latin *atra bilis* 'black bile,' translation of Greek *melankholia* 'melancholy,' + -IOUS.

a·trau·mat·ic /,ātrə'matik, ,ātrou-, ,ātrô-/ ▶ **adj.** (of a medical or surgical procedure) causing minimal tissue injury.

at·ra·zine /'atrə,zēn/ ▶ **n.** a synthetic compound used as an agricultural herbicide. ● A triazine derivative; chem. formula: $C_8H_{14}N_5Cl$.
– ORIGIN 1960s: blend of AMINO and TRIAZINE.

a·trem·ble /ə'trembəl/ ▶ **adj.** [predic.] literary trembling: *the breeze failed to set a single leaf atremble.*

a·tre·sia /ə'trēZH(ē)ə/ ▶ **n.** 1 Medicine absence or abnormal narrowing of an opening or passage in the body.
2 Physiology the degeneration of those ovarian follicles that do not ovulate during the menstrual cycle.
– ORIGIN early 19th cent.: from A-[1] 'without' + Greek *trēsis* 'perforation' + -IA[1].

A·tre·us /'ātrēəs, 'ātrōōs/ Greek Mythology the son of Pelops and father of Agamemnon and Menelaus. He quarreled with his brother Thyestes and invited him to a banquet at which he served up the flesh of Thyestes' own children.

a·tri·o·ven·tric·u·lar /,ātrē-ōven'trikyələr/ ▶ **adj.** Anatomy & Physiology relating to the atrial and ventricular chambers of the heart, or the connection or coordination between them.

at-risk ▶ **adj.** vulnerable, esp. to abuse or deliquency: *a church-run school for the most at-risk children.*

a·tri·um /'ātrēəm/ ▶ **n.** (pl. **atria** /'ātrēə/ or **atriums**) 1 Architecture an open-roofed entrance hall or central court in an ancient Roman house. ■ a central hall or court in a modern building, with rooms or galleries opening off it, often glass-covered.
2 Anatomy each of the two upper cavities of the heart from which blood is passed to the ventricles. The right atrium receives deoxygenated blood from the veins of the body; the left atrium receives oxygenated blood from the pulmonary vein. Also called AURICLE.
– DERIVATIVES **a·tri·al** /'ātrēəl/ **adj.**
– ORIGIN late 16th cent.: from Latin.

a·tro·cious /ə'trōSHəs/ ▶ **adj.** horrifyingly wicked: *atrocious cruelties.* ■ of a very poor quality; extremely bad or unpleasant: *he attempted an atrocious imitation of my English accent | atrocious weather.*
– DERIVATIVES **a·tro·cious·ly adv., a·tro·cious·ness n.**
– ORIGIN mid 17th cent.: from Latin *atrox, atroc-* 'cruel' + -IOUS.

a·troc·i·ty /ə'träsitē/ ▶ **n.** (pl. **atrocities**) an extremely wicked or cruel act, typically one involving physical violence or injury: *war atrocities | scenes of hardship and atrocity.* ■ humorous a highly unpleasant or distasteful object: *the house was a split-level atrocity.*
– ORIGIN mid 16th cent. (in the sense 'cruelty'): from French *atrocité* or Latin *atrocitas,* from *atrox, atroc-* 'cruel.'

at·ro·phy /'atrəfē/ ▶ **v.** (**atrophies, atrophying, atrophied**) [no obj.] 1 (of body tissue or an organ) waste away, typically due to the degeneration of cells, or become vestigial during evolution: *without exercise, the muscles will atrophy* | (as adj. **atrophied**) *in some beetles, the hind wings are atrophied.*
2 gradually decline in effectiveness or vigor due to underuse or neglect: *her artistic skills atrophied from lack of use.*
▶ **n.** the process of atrophying or state of having atrophied: *gastric atrophy | extensive TV viewing may lead to atrophy of children's imaginations.*
– DERIVATIVES **a·troph·ic** /ā'trōfik, ā'träfik/ **adj.**
– ORIGIN late 16th cent.: from French *atrophier* (verb), *atrophie* (noun), from late Latin *atrophia,* from Greek, 'lack of food,' from *a-* 'without' + *trophē* 'food.'

at·ro·pine /'atrə,pēn/ ▶ **n.** Chemistry a poisonous compound found in deadly nightshade and related plants. It is used in medicine as a muscle relaxant, e.g., in dilating the pupil of the eye. ● An alkaloid; chem. formula: $C_{17}N_{23}NO_3$.
– ORIGIN mid 19th cent.: modern Latin *Atropa belladonna* 'deadly nightshade,' from ATROPOS + -INE[4].

At·ro·pos /'atrə,päs/ Greek Mythology one of the three Fates.
– ORIGIN Greek, literally 'inflexible.'

at sign ▶ **n.** the symbol @.

At·si·na /at'sēnə/ ▶ **n.** (pl. **same** or **Atsinas**) a member of a North American Indian people living chiefly in the north central plains region. They speak an Algonquian language. Also called GROS VENTRE.
▶ **adj.** of or relating to the Atsina.

at·ta·boy /'atə,boi/ ▶ **exclam.** an informal expression of encouragement or admiration, typically to a man or boy.
▶ **n.** a piece of encouragement or congratulations, esp. a letter: *our boss will write you guys an attaboy.*
– ORIGIN early 20th cent.: probably representing a casual pronunciation of *that's the boy.*

at·tach /ə'taCH/ ▶ **v.** [with obj.] 1 fasten; join: *he made certain that the trailer was securely attached to the van.* ■ fasten (a related document) to another, or to an e-mail: *I attach a copy of the memo for your information.* ■ include (a condition) as part of an agreement: *the Commission can attach appropriate conditions to the operation of the agreement.* ■ (**attach oneself to**) join (someone or something)

without being invited: *they were all too ready to attach themselves to you for the whole day.* ■ (usu. **be attached**) appoint (someone) for special or temporary duties: *I was attached to another department.*
2 (**attach something to**) attribute importance or value to: *he doesn't attach too much importance to radical ideas.* ■ [no obj.] (**attach to**) (of importance or value) be attributed to: *great importance is attached to the family role.*
3 Law seize (a person's property) by legal authority: *the court attached his wages for child support.*
– DERIVATIVES **at·tach·a·ble** adj.
– ORIGIN Middle English (in the sense 'seize by legal authority'): from Old French *atachier* or *estachier* 'fasten, fix,' based on an element of Germanic origin related to STAKE[1]; compare with ATTACK.

at·ta·ché /ˌatəˈSHā ˌata-/ ▶ n. **1** a person on the staff of an ambassador, typically with a specialized area of responsibility: *military attachés.*
2 short for ATTACHÉ CASE.
– ORIGIN early 19th cent.: from French, literally 'attached,' past participle of *attacher.*

at·ta·ché case ▶ n. a small, flat, rectangular case used for carrying documents.

at·tached /əˈtaCHt/ ▶ adj. **1** joined or fastened to something: *please complete the attached form.* ■ (of a building or room) adjacent to and typically connected with another building or room: *a ground-floor bedroom with a bathroom attached.*
2 full of affection or fondness: *during his visit, Mark became increasingly attached to Tara.*
3 (**attached to**) (of a person) appointed to an organization or group for special or temporary duties: *he was attached to military intelligence.* ■ (of an organization or body) affiliated to another larger organization or body: *a public relations agency attached to the university.*

at·tach·ment /əˈtaCHmənt/ ▶ n. **1** an extra part or extension that is or can be attached to something to perform a particular function: *the food processor comes with a blender attachment.* ■ a computer file appended to an e-mail.
2 the condition of being attached to something or someone, in particular: ■ affection, fondness, or sympathy for someone or something: *she felt a sentimental attachment to the place.* ■ an affectionate relationship between two people: *he formed an attachment with a young widow.*
3 the action of attaching something: *the case has a loop for attachment to your belt.* ■ legal seizure of property.
– ORIGIN late Middle English (in the sense 'arrest for contempt of court'): from Old French *attachement,* from *atachier* 'fasten, fix' (see ATTACH).

at·tack /əˈtak/ ▶ v. [with obj.] take aggressive action against (a place or enemy forces) with weapons or armed force, typically in a battle or war: *in December, the Japanese attacked Pearl Harbor* | [no obj.] *Italian forces attacked in October.* ■ (of a person or animal) act against (someone or something) aggressively in an attempt to injure or kill: *a doctor was attacked by two youths.* ■ (of a disease, chemical substance, or insect) act harmfully on: *HIV is thought to attack certain cells in the brain.* ■ criticize or oppose fiercely and publicly: *he attacked the government's defense policy.* ■ begin to deal with (a problem or task) in a determined and vigorous way: *a plan of action to attack unemployment.* ■ [no obj.] make an aggressive or forceful attempt to score a goal or point, or gain or exploit an advantage in a game against an opposing team or player: (as adj. **attacking**) *the home team showed some good attacking play.* ■ Chess move into or be in a position to capture (an opponent's piece).
▶ n. an aggressive and violent action against a person or place: *he was killed in an **attack on** a checkpoint* | *three classrooms were gutted in the arson attack.* ■ destructive action by a disease, chemical, or insect: *the tissue is open to attack by fungus.* ■ a sudden short bout of an illness or stress: *an attack of nausea* | *an asthma attack.* ■ an instance of fierce public criticism or opposition: *he launched a stinging **attack on** the White House.* ■ a determined attempt to tackle a problem or task: *an **attack on** inflation.* ■ Music the manner of beginning to play or sing a passage. ■ forceful and decisive style in performing music or another art: *the sheer attack of Hendrix's playing.* ■ an aggressive attempt to score a goal, win points, or gain or exploit an advantage in a game. ■ Chess a threat to capture an opponent's piece.
– PHRASES **under attack** subject to aggressive, violent, or harmful action: *his paintings have come under attack for their satanic content.*
– ORIGIN early 17th cent.: from French *attaque* (noun), *attaquer* (verb), from Italian *attacco* 'an attack,' *attaccare* 'join battle,' based on an element of Germanic origin (see ATTACH).

at·tack dog ▶ n. a dog trained to attack on command and kept for this purpose. ■ a person who is very aggressive in defense or support of someone or something: *he was accused of being an all-purpose attack dog for the party.*

at·tack·er /əˈtakər/ ▶ n. a person or animal that attacks someone or something. ■ (in soccer and other games) a player that makes an assertive or aggressive attempt to score; a forward.

at·ta·girl /ˈatəˌgərl/ ▶ exclam. an informal expression of encouragement or admiration to a woman or girl.
– ORIGIN 1920s: on the pattern of *attaboy.*

at·tain /əˈtān/ ▶ v. [with obj.] succeed in achieving (something that one desires and has worked for): *clarify your objectives and ways of attaining them* | *he attained the rank of admiral* | *human beings can attain happiness.* ■ reach (a specified age, size, or amount): *dolphins can attain remarkable speeds in water.*
– ORIGIN Middle English (in the senses 'bring to justice' and 'reach (a state)'): from Old French *ateindre,* from Latin *attingere,* from *ad-* 'at, to' + *tangere* 'to touch.'

at·tain·a·ble /əˈtānəbəl/ ▶ adj. able to be attained; achievable: *yields in excess of 6% are easily attainable* | *an attainable target.*
– DERIVATIVES **at·tain·a·bil·i·ty** /əˌtānəˈbilitē/ n.

at·tain·der /əˈtāndər/ ▶ n. historical the forfeiture of land and civil rights suffered as a consequence of a sentence of death for treason or felony.
– PHRASES **bill of attainder** an item of legislation (prohibited by the US Constitution) that inflicts attainder without judicial process.
– ORIGIN late Middle English: from Anglo-Norman French, variant (used as a noun) of Old French *ateindre* in the sense 'convict, bring to justice' (see ATTAIN).

at·tain·ment /əˈtānmənt/ ▶ n. the action or fact of achieving a goal toward which one has worked: *the attainment of a complete collection is the measure of a collector's success.* ■ (often **attainments**) a thing achieved, esp. a skill or educational achievement: *scholarly attainments.*

at·taint /əˈtānt/ ▶ v. [with obj.] **1** (usu. **be attainted**) historical subject to attainder.
2 archaic affect or infect with disease or corruption.
– ORIGIN Middle English (in the sense 'touch, reach, attain'): from obsolete *attaint* (adjective), from Old French *ataint, ateint,* past participle of *ateindre* 'bring to justice' (see ATTAIN); influenced in meaning by TAINT.

At·ta·lid /ˈatlˌid/ ▶ n. a member of a Hellenistic dynasty centered on the city of Pergamum in Asia Minor and named after **Attalus I** (reigned 241–197 BC), which flourished in the 3rd and 2nd centuries BC.
▶ adj. of or relating to this dynasty.

at·tar /ˈatər/ (also **otto** /ˈätō/) ▶ n. a fragrant essential oil, typically made from rose petals.
– ORIGIN late 17th cent.: via Persian from Arabic *'iṭr* 'fragrant.'

at·tempt /əˈtem(p)t/ ▶ v. [with obj.] make an effort to achieve or complete (something, typically a difficult task or action): *she attempted a comeback in 1989* | [with infinitive] *those who attempted to flee were captured at the border.* ■ try to climb to the top of (a mountain): *the group's next plan was to attempt Everest.* ■ archaic try to take (a life): *he would not have attempted the life of a friend.*
▶ n. an act of trying to achieve something, typically one that is unsuccessful or not certain to succeed: [with infinitive] *an attempt to halt the bombings* | *any **attempt at** talking politics ended in a fit of laughter* | *an abortive coup attempt.* ■ an effort to surpass a record or conquer a mountain: *we made an **attempt on** the southwest buttress.* ■ a bid to kill someone: *Karakozov made an **attempt on** the tsar's life.* ■ a thing produced as a result of trying to make or achieve something: *her first **attempt at** a letter ended up in the wastebasket.*
– ORIGIN late Middle English: from Old French *attempter,* from Latin *attemptare,* from *ad-* 'to' + *temptare* 'to tempt.'

At·ten·bor·ough /ˈatnb(ə)rə/, Sir Richard (Samuel), Baron Attenborough of Richmond-upon-Thames (1923–), English movie actor, producer, and director. He directed *Oh! What a Lovely War* (1969), *A Bridge Too Far* (1977), *Gandhi* (1982), and *Shadowlands* (1993).

at·tend /əˈtend/ ▶ v. **1** [with obj.] be present at (an event, meeting, or function): *the entire sales force attended the conference* | *she was unable to attend the wedding.* ■ go regularly to (an educational, religious, social, or clinical institution): *all children are required to attend school.*
2 [no obj.] (**attend to**) deal with: *he muttered that he had business to attend to.* ■ give practical help and care to; look after: *the severely wounded had two medics to attend to their wounds* | [with obj.] *each of the beds in the intensive care unit is attended by a nurse.* ■ pay attention to: *Alice hadn't attended to a word of his sermon.*
3 [with obj.] (usu. **be attended**) occur with or as a result of: *people feared that the switch to a peacetime economy would be attended by a severe slump.* ■ escort or accompany (a member of royalty or other important personage) so as to assist them; wait on: *Her Royal Highness was attended by two capable women.*
– DERIVATIVES **at·tend·er** /əˈtendər/ n.
– ORIGIN Middle English (in the sense 'apply one's mind, one's energies to'): from Old French *atendre,* from Latin *attendere,* from *ad-* 'to' + *tendere* 'stretch.'

at·tend·ance /əˈtendəns/ ▶ n. the action or state of going regularly to or being present at a place or event: *my **attendance at** church was very irregular.* ■ the number of people present at a particular event, function, or meeting: *reports placed the attendance at 500,000.*
– PHRASES **in attendance** present at a function or a place. ■ accompanying a member of royalty or the aristocracy in the capacity of an assistant or servant.
– ORIGIN late Middle English: from Old French, from *atendre* 'give one's attention to' (see ATTEND).

at·tend·ant /əˈtendənt/ ▶ n. **1** a person employed to provide a service to the public in a particular place: *a flight attendant* | *a gas station attendant.* ■ an assistant to an important person; a servant or courtier.
2 a person who is present at an event, meeting, or function: *he had become a regular attendant at chapel.*
▶ adj. occurring with or as a result of; accompanying: *the sea and its attendant attractions* | *he warns against the dangers **attendant on** solitary life.* ■ (of a person or animal) accompanying another as a companion or assistant: *a pair of blind tourists with their attendant dogs.*
– ORIGIN late Middle English (as an adjective): from Old French, from *atendre* 'give one's attention to' (see ATTEND).

at·tend·ee /əˌtenˈdē, ˌaten-/ ▶ n. a person who attends a conference or other gathering.

at·ten·tion /əˈtenCHən/ ▶ n. **1** notice taken of someone or something; the regarding of someone or something as interesting or important: *he **drew attention to** three spelling mistakes* | *you've never **paid** that much **attention to** her opinions.* ■ the mental faculty of considering or taking notice of someone or something: *he **turned his attention to** the educational system.*
2 the action of dealing with or taking special care of someone or something: *the business needed her attention* | *he failed to give the patient adequate medical attention.* ■ (**attentions**) a person's interest in someone, esp. when unwelcome or regarded as excessive: *his primary aim was to avoid the attentions of the newspapers.* ■ (**attentions**) a person's actions intended to express interest of a sexual or romantic nature in someone, sometimes when unwelcome: *she felt flattered by his attentions.*
3 Military a position assumed by a soldier, standing very straight with the heels together and the arms straight down the sides of the body: *the squadron **stood to attention** when we arrived* | *midshipmen **standing at attention.*** ■ [as exclamation] an order to assume such a position.
– DERIVATIVES **at·ten·tion·al** /-CHənl/ adj.
– ORIGIN late Middle English: from Latin *attentio(n-),* from the verb *attendere* (see ATTEND).

at·ten·tion def·i·cit dis·or·der (also **attention deficit hyperactivity disorder**) (abbr.: **ADD** or **ADHD**) ▶ n. any of a range of behavioral disorders occurring primarily in children, including such symptoms as poor concentration, hyperactivity, and impulsivity.

at·ten·tion span ▶ n. the length of time for which a person is able to concentrate mentally on a particular activity.

at·ten·tive /əˈtentiv/ ▶ adj. paying close attention to something: *never before had she had such an attentive audience* | *Congress should be more **attentive to** the interests of taxpayers.* ■ assiduously attending to the comfort or wishes of others; very polite or courteous: *the hotel has a pleasant atmosphere and attentive service.*
– DERIVATIVES **at·ten·tive·ly** adv., **at·ten·tive·ness** n.
– ORIGIN late Middle English: from Old French *attentif, -ive,* from *atendre* 'give one's attention to' (see ATTEND).

at·ten·u·ate ▶ v. /əˈtenyo͞oˌāt/ [with obj.] reduce the force, effect, or value of: *her intolerance was attenuated by a rather unexpected liberalism.* ■ reduce the amplitude of (a signal, electric

a

current, or other oscillation). ■ [no obj.] (of a signal, electric current, or other oscillation) be reduced in amplitude. ■ (usu. as adj. **attenuated**) reduce the virulence of (a pathogenic organism or vaccine): *attenuated strains of rabies virus*. ■ reduce in thickness; make thin: *the trees are attenuated from being grown too close together*.
▶ **adj.** /-wit, -ˌwāt/ rare reduced in force, effect, or physical thickness.
– DERIVATIVES **at·ten·u·a·tion** /əˌtenyoo͞ˈāsHən/ **n.**
– ORIGIN mid 16th cent.: from Latin *attenuat-* 'made slender,' from the verb *attenuare*, from *ad-* 'to' + *tenuare* 'make thin' (from *tenuis* 'thin').

at·ten·u·at·ed /əˈtenyo͞oˌātid/ ▶ **adj.** unnaturally thin: *she was a drooping, attenuated figure*. ■ weakened in force or effect: *Roman influence became attenuated*.

at·ten·u·a·tor /əˈtenyo͞oˌātər/ ▶ **n.** a device consisting of an arrangement of resistors that reduces the strength of a radio or audio signal.

at·test /əˈtest/ ▶ **v.** [with obj.] provide or serve as clear evidence of: *his status is attested by his recent promotion* | [no obj.] *his numerous drawings of ships **attest to** his fascination with them*. ■ [no obj.] declare that something exists or is the case: *I can **attest to** his tremendous energy* | [with clause] *the deceased's attorney attested that he had been about to institute divorce proceedings*. ■ be a witness to; certify formally: *the witnesses must attest and sign the will in the testator's presence*.
– DERIVATIVES **at·tes·ta·tion** /ˌateˈstāsHən/ **n.**
– ORIGIN early 16th cent.: from French *attester*, from Latin *attestari*, from *ad-* 'to' + *testari* 'to witness' (from *testis* 'a witness').

At·tic /ˈatik/ ▶ **adj.** of or relating to Athens or Attica, or the dialect of Greek spoken there in ancient times.
▶ **n.** the dialect of Greek used by the ancient Athenians, the chief literary form of classical Greek.
– ORIGIN late 16th cent.: via Latin from Greek *Attikos*.

at·tic /ˈatik/ ▶ **n.** a space or room just below the roof of a building.
– ORIGIN late 17th cent. (as an architectural term designating a small order (column and entablature) above a taller one): from French *attique*, from Latin *Atticus* 'relating to Athens or Attica.'

At·ti·ca /ˈatikə/ **1** a triangular promontory in eastern Greece. With the islands in the Saronic Gulf, it forms a department of Greece, of which Athens is the capital.
2 a town in western New York, the scene of a bloody 1971 prison uprising; pop. 7,533 (est. 2008).

At·ti·cism /ˈatəˌsizəm/ (often **atticism**) ▶ **n.** a word or form characteristic of Attic Greek.
– ORIGIN late 16th cent.: from Greek *Attikismos*, from *Attikos* (see ATTIC). From the original sense of 'the Greek language as used by the Athenians,' arose the meaning 'refined, elegant Greek,' later extended to language in general.

At·ti·la /əˈtilə, ˈatl-ə/ (406–453), king of the Huns 434–453. He ravaged vast areas between the Rhine and the Caspian Sea before being defeated by the joint forces of the Roman army and the Visigoths at Châlons in 451.

at·tire /əˈtī(ə)r/ ▶ **n.** clothes, esp. fine or formal ones: *holiday attire*.
▶ **v.** (**be attired**) be dressed in clothes of a specified kind: *Donna **was attired in** an elaborate evening gown* | [as adj., with submodifier] (**attired**) *the outrageously attired rock star*.
– ORIGIN Middle English: from Old French *atirier*, *atirer* 'equip,' from *a tire* 'in order,' of unknown origin.

At·tis /ˈatis/ Anatolian Mythology the youthful consort of Cybele. His death and resurrection were associated with the spring festival.

at·ti·tude /ˈatiˌt(y)o͞od/ ▶ **n.** a settled way of thinking or feeling about someone or something, typically one that is reflected in a person's behavior: *she took a tough attitude toward other people's indulgences* | *being competitive is **an attitude of mind*** | *differences in attitude were apparent between groups*. ■ a position of the body proper to or implying an action or mental state: *the boy was standing in an **attitude of** despair, his chin sunk on his chest*. ■ informal truculent or uncooperative behavior; a resentful or antagonistic manner: *I asked the waiter for a clean fork, and all I got was attitude*. ■ informal individuality and self-confidence as manifested by behavior or appearance; style: *she snapped her fingers **with attitude***. ■ the orientation of an aircraft or spacecraft, relative to the direction of travel. ■ Ballet a position in which one leg is lifted behind with the knee bent at right angles and turned out, and the corresponding arm is raised above the head, the other extended to the side.
– DERIVATIVES **at·ti·tu·di·nal** /ˌatiˈt(y)o͞odn-əl/ **adj.**
– ORIGIN late 17th cent. (denoting the placing or posture of a figure in art): from French, from Italian *attitudine* 'fitness, posture,' from late Latin *aptitudo*, from *aptus* 'fit.'

at·ti·tu·di·nize /ˌatiˈt(y)o͞odnˌīz/ ▶ **v.** [no obj.] adopt or express a particular attitude or attitudes, typically just for effect.
– DERIVATIVES **at·ti·tu·di·niz·er** **n.**
– ORIGIN late 16th cent.: from Italian *attitudine* (see ATTITUDE) + -IZE.

Att·lee /ˈatlē/, Clement Richard, 1st Earl Attlee (1883–1967), British Labour statesman; Labour prime minister 1945–51. His term saw the creation of the modern welfare state and the nationalization of major industries.

attn. ▶ **abbr.** (on an envelope, packet, package, or cover letter) attention (i.e., for the attention of): *attn.: Harold Carter*.

atto- ▶ **comb. form** Mathematics (used in units of measurement) denoting a factor of 10^{-18}: *attowatt*.
– ORIGIN from Danish or Norwegian *atten* 'eighteen.'

at·torn /əˈtərn/ ▶ **v.** [no obj.] Law formally make or acknowledge a transfer of something. ■ [with obj.] archaic transfer (something) to someone else.
– PHRASES **attorn tenant** Law formally make or acknowledge a transfer of tenancy.
– ORIGIN Middle English (in the senses 'turn, change, transform'): from Old French *atorner* 'appoint, assign,' from *a-* (from Latin *ad* 'to, at') + *torner* 'to turn.'

at·tor·ney /əˈtərnē/ ▶ **n.** (pl. **attorneys**) **1** a person appointed to act for another in business or legal matters.
2 a lawyer.
– DERIVATIVES **at·tor·ney·ship** /-ˌsHip/ **n.**
– ORIGIN Middle English: from Old French *atorne*, past participle of *atorner* 'assign,' from *a* 'toward' + *torner* 'turn.'

at·tor·ney-at-law ▶ **n.** a lawyer who is qualified to represent a client in court.

at·tor·ney gen·er·al (abbr.: **AG** or **Atty. Gen.**) ▶ **n.** (pl. **attorneys general**) the principal legal officer who represents a country or a state in legal proceedings and gives legal advice to the government. ■ the head of the US Department of Justice.

at·tract /əˈtrakt/ ▶ **v.** [with obj.] cause to come to a place or participate in a venture by offering something of interest, favorable conditions, or opportunities: *a campaign to attract more visitors to West Virginia* | *he hoped this strategy would attract foreign investment by multinationals*. ■ evoke (a specified reaction): *I did not want to attract attention* | *his criticism of the government attracted widespread support*. ■ cause (someone) to have a liking for or interest in something: *I **was attracted to** the idea of working for a ballet company*. ■ cause (someone) to have a sexual or romantic interest in someone: *it was her beauty that attracted him*. ■ exert a force on (an object) that is directed toward the source of the force: *the negatively charged ions attract particles of dust*.
– DERIVATIVES **at·trac·tor** /-tər/ **n.**
– ORIGIN late Middle English: from Latin *attract-* 'drawn near,' from the verb *attrahere*, from *ad-* 'to' + *trahere* 'draw.'

at·tract·ant /əˈtraktənt/ ▶ **n.** a substance that attracts something (esp. animals): *a sex attractant given off by female moths to attract a mate*.
▶ **adj.** attracting.

at·trac·tion /əˈtraksHən/ ▶ **n.** the action or power of evoking interest, pleasure, or liking for someone or something: *she has romantic ideas about sexual attraction* | *the timeless attraction of a good tune*. ■ a quality or feature of something or someone that evokes interest, liking, or desire: *this reform has many **attractions for** those on the left* | *the main attraction of Peking duck is the crackling texture of its skin*. ■ a thing or place that draws visitors by providing something of interest or pleasure: *the church is the town's main tourist attraction*. ■ Physics a force under the influence of which objects tend to move toward each other: *gravitational attraction*. ■ Grammar the influence exerted by one word on another that causes it to change to an incorrect form, e.g., *the wages of sin is* (for *are*) *death*.
– ORIGIN late Middle English (denoting the action of a poultice in drawing matter from the tissues): from Latin *attractio(n-)*, from the verb *attrahere* (see ATTRACT).

at·trac·tive /əˈtraktiv/ ▶ **adj.** (of a thing) pleasing or appealing to the senses: *an attractive home* | *foliage can be as attractive as flowers*. ■ (of a person) appealing to look at; sexually alluring: *an attractive, charismatic man*. ■ (of a thing) having beneficial qualities or features that induce someone to accept what is being offered: *the site is close to the high-rent district, which should make it **attractive** to developers*. ■ of or relating to attraction between physical objects.
– DERIVATIVES **at·trac·tive·ly** **adv.**, **at·trac·tive·ness** **n.**
– ORIGIN late Middle English (in the sense 'absorbent'): from French *attractif*, *-ive*, from late Latin *attractivus*, from the verb *attrahere* (see ATTRACT).

at·trib·ute ▶ **v.** /əˈtriˌbyo͞ot/ [with obj.] (**attribute something to**) regard something as being caused by (someone or something): *he attributed the firm's success to the efforts of the managing director* | *the bombing was attributed to the IRA*. ■ ascribe a work or remark to (a particular author, artist, or speaker): *the building was attributed to Frank Lloyd Wright*. ■ regard a quality or feature as characteristic of or possessed by (someone or something): *ancient peoples attributed magic properties to certain stones*.
▶ **n.** /ˈatrəˌbyo͞ot/ **1** a quality or feature regarded as a characteristic or inherent part of someone or something: *flexibility and mobility are the key attributes of our army*. ■ a material object recognized as symbolic of a person, esp. a conventional object used in art to identify a saint or mythical figure.
2 Computing a piece of information that determines the properties of a field or tag in a database or a string of characters in a display.
3 Grammar an attributive adjective or noun.
4 Statistics a real property that a statistical analysis is attempting to describe.
– DERIVATIVES **at·trib·ut·a·ble** /əˈtribyətəbəl/ **adj.**, **at·tri·bu·tion** /ˌatrəˈbyo͞osHən/ **n.**, **at·tri·bu·tion·al** **adj.**
– ORIGIN late 15th cent.: as a noun from Old French *attribut*, and as a verb from Latin *attribut-* 'allotted,' both from the verb *attribuere*, from *ad-* 'to' + *tribuere* 'assign.'

at·tri·bu·tion the·o·ry /ˌatrəˈbyo͞osHən/ ▶ **n.** Psychology a theory that supposes that one attempts to understand the behavior of others by attributing feelings, beliefs, and intentions to them.

at·trib·u·tive /əˈtribyətiv/ ▶ **adj.** Grammar (of an adjective or noun) preceding the word it qualifies or modifies and expressing an attribute, as *old* in *the old dog* (but not in *the dog is old*) and *expiration* in *expiration date* (but not in *date of expiration*). Often contrasted with PREDICATIVE.
– DERIVATIVES **at·trib·u·tive·ly** **adv.**
– ORIGIN mid 18th cent. (as a noun in the sense 'a word expressing an attribute'): from French *attributif*, *-ive*, from *attribut* 'an attribute,' from Latin *attribuere* 'add to' (see ATTRIBUTE).

at·trit /əˈtrit/ ▶ **v.** (**attrits, attriting, attritted**) [with obj.] informal wear down (an opponent or enemy) by sustained action: *his defense was designed to attrit us*.
– ORIGIN 1950s: back-formation from ATTRITION.

at·tri·tion /əˈtrisHən/ ▶ **n.** **1** the action or process of gradually reducing the strength or effectiveness of someone or something through sustained attack or pressure: *the council is trying to wear down the opposition by attrition* | *the squadron suffered severe attrition of its bombers*. ■ the gradual reduction of a workforce by employees' leaving and not being replaced rather than by their being laid off: *with so few retirements since March, the year's attrition was insignificant*. ■ wearing away by friction; abrasion: *the skull shows attrition of the edges of the teeth*.
2 (in scholastic theology) sorrow, but not contrition, for sin.
– DERIVATIVES **at·tri·tion·al** /-sHənl/ **adj.**
– ORIGIN late Middle English (sense 2): from late Latin *attritio(n-)*, from *atterere* 'to rub.'

At·tu /ˈaˌto͞o/ an island in southwestern Alaska, the westernmost of the Aleutian Islands. During World War II, it was occupied by Japanese forces.

At·tucks /ˈatəks/, Crispus (c.1723–70), American revolutionary. Believed to have been either an escaped or freed slave, he was one of five colonists killed by British soldiers in the Boston Massacre on March 5, 1770.

at·tune /əˈt(y)o͞on/ ▶ **v.** [with obj.] (usu. **be attuned**) make receptive or aware: *a society more **attuned to** consumerism than ideology* | (as adj. **attuned**) *the department is very attuned politically*. ■ accustom or acclimatize: *students are not **attuned to** making decisions*. ■ [no obj.] become receptive to or aware of: *a conscious attempt **to attune to** the wider audience*. ■ make harmonious: *the interests of East and West are now closely attuned*.
– ORIGIN late 16th cent.: from AT- + TUNE.

Atty. ▶ **abbr.** Attorney.

Atty. Gen. ▶ **abbr.** Attorney General.

ATV ▶ **abbr.** all-terrain vehicle.

At·wood /ˈatˌwo͝od/, Margaret (Eleanor) (1939–), Canadian novelist, poet, critic, and short-story writer. Notable works: *The Edible Woman* (1969), *The Handmaid's Tale* (1985), *Cat's Eye* (1989), and *Alias Grace* (1996).

a·typ·i·cal /āˈtipikəl/ ▶ **adj.** not representative of a type, group, or class: *a sample of people who are rather atypical of the target audience | there were somewhat atypical results in May and November.*
– DERIVATIVES **a·typ·i·cal·ly adv.**

AU ▶ **abbr.** ångström unit(s). ■ (also **a.u.**) astronomical unit(s).

Au ▶ **symbol** the chemical element gold.
– ORIGIN from Latin *aurum.*

au·bade /ōˈbäd/ ▶ **n.** a poem or piece of music appropriate to the dawn or early morning.
– ORIGIN late 17th cent.: from French, from Spanish *albada*, from *alba* 'dawn.'

au·berge /ōˈberzh/ ▶ **n.** an inn in France or another French-speaking country.
– ORIGIN French, from Provençal *alberga* 'lodging.'

au·ber·gine /ˈōbərˌzhēn/ ▶ **n.** chiefly Brit. another term for EGGPLANT. ■ a dark purple color like that of eggplant.

Au·brey /ˈôbrē/, John (1626–97), English antiquarian and author. He is noted for *Brief Lives*, a collection of biographies of eminent people.

au·brie·tia /ôˈbrēsh(ē)ə/ (also **aubretia**) ▶ **n.** a dwarf evergreen Eurasian trailing plant with dense masses of foliage and purple, pink, or white flowers. It is widely cultivated in rock gardens and on banks. ● *Aubrieta deltoidea*, family Brassicaceae.
– ORIGIN early 19th cent.: modern Latin, named after Claude *Aubriet* (1668–1743), French botanist.

> **USAGE** Aubretia is named after French botanist Claude *Aubriet*, and the original spelling was **aubrieta**, which is the plant's genus name. In nontechnical use, however, the forms **aubrietia** and **aubretia** are now more usual.

Au·burn /ˈôbərn/ **1** an academic city in eastern Alabama, home to Auburn University; pop. 56,088 (est. 2008).
2 an industrial city in southwestern Maine, on the Androscoggin River, across from Lewiston; pop. 23,177 (est. 2008).
3 an industrial city in west central Washington; pop. 55,426 (est. 2008).

au·burn /ˈôbərn/ ▶ **adj.** (chiefly of a person's hair) of a reddish-brown color.
▶ **n.** a reddish-brown color.
– ORIGIN late Middle English: from Old French *auborne, alborne*, from Latin *alburnus* 'whitish,' from *albus* 'white.' The original sense was 'yellowish white,' but the word became associated with *brown* because in the 16th and 17th centuries it was often written *abrune* or *abroun.*

Au·bus·son /ˈōbəˌsôn/ ▶ **n.** a kind of French tapestry or carpet, principally from the 18th century.
– ORIGIN from *Aubusson*, the name of a town in central France where the tapestries were made.

AUC ▶ **abbr.** used to indicate a date reckoned from 753 BC, the year of the foundation of Rome: *765 auc.*
– ORIGIN from Latin *ab urbe condita* 'from the foundation of the city,' also *anno urbis conditae* 'in the year of the founding of the city.'

Au·chin·closs /ˈôkənˌkläs/, Louis Stanton (1917–2010), US lawyer and author; early pseudonym *Andrew Lee*. His novels often depict life among the elite of New York City.

Auck·land /ˈôklənd/ the largest city and chief seaport of New Zealand, on North Island; pop. 404,658 (2006). It was the capital of New Zealand until 1865.

au con·traire /ō ˌkänˈtre(ə)r/ ▶ **exclam.** often humorous on the contrary.
– ORIGIN French.

au cou·rant /ˌō ko͝oˈrän/ ▶ **adj.** aware of what is going on; well informed: *they were **au courant** with the literary scene.* ■ fashionable: *light, low-fat, au courant recipes.*
– ORIGIN mid 18th cent.: from French, literally 'in the (regular) course.'

auc·tion /ˈôkshən/ ▶ **n.** a public sale in which goods or property are sold to the highest bidder: *the books are expected to fetch a six-figure sum at tomorrow's auction* | [as modifier] *an auction sale.* ■ the action or process of selling something in this way: *the Ferrari sold **at auction** for $10 million.* ■ Bridge the part of the play in which players bid to decide the contract in which the hand shall be played.
▶ **v.** [with obj.] sell or offer for sale at an auction: *his collection of vintage cars is to be **auctioned off** tomorrow.*
– PHRASES **on the auction block** see ON THE BLOCK at BLOCK.
– ORIGIN late 16th cent.: from Latin *auctio(n)-* 'increase, auction,' from the verb *augere* 'to increase.'

auc·tion bridge ▶ **n.** an obsolete form of the card game bridge, in which all tricks won count toward the game whether bid or not.

auc·tion·eer /ˌôkshəˈni(ə)r/ ▶ **n.** a person who conducts auctions by accepting bids and declaring goods sold.
– DERIVATIVES **auc·tion·eer·ing n.**

auc·tion house ▶ **n.** a company that runs auctions.

au·da·cious /ôˈdāshəs/ ▶ **adj. 1** showing a willingness to take surprisingly bold risks: *a series of audacious takeovers.*
2 showing an impudent lack of respect: *an audacious remark.*
– DERIVATIVES **au·da·cious·ly adv., au·da·cious·ness n.**
– ORIGIN mid 16th cent.: from Latin *audax, audac-* 'bold' (from *audere* 'dare') + -IOUS.

au·dac·i·ty /ôˈdasitē/ ▶ **n. 1** the willingness to take bold risks: *her audacity came in handy during our most recent emergency.*
2 rude or disrespectful behavior; impudence: *she **had the audacity to** pick up the receiver and ask me to hang up.*
– ORIGIN late Middle English: from medieval Latin *audacitas*, from *audax, audac-* 'bold' (see AUDACIOUS).

Au·den /ˈôdn/, W. H. (1907–73), British poet; full name *Wystan Hugh Auden*. He was a leading left-wing poet and was awarded the Pulitzer Prize for *The Age of Anxiety* (1947).

Audh variant spelling of OUDH.

au·di·al /ˈôdēəl/ ▶ **adj.** relating to or perceived through the sense of hearing.
– ORIGIN late 20th cent.: formed irregularly from Latin *audire* 'hear' (compare with AUDILE), on the pattern of *visual.*

au·di·ble /ˈôdəbəl/ ▶ **adj.** able to be heard: *ultrasound is audible to dogs.*
▶ **n.** Football a change in the offensive play called by the quarterback at the line of scrimmage.
– DERIVATIVES **au·di·bil·i·ty** /ˌôdəˈbilitē/ **n., au·di·bly** /-blē/ **adv.**
– ORIGIN late 15th cent.: from late Latin *audibilis*, from *audire* 'hear.'

au·di·ence /ˈôdēəns/ ▶ **n. 1** the assembled spectators or listeners at a public event, such as a play, movie, concert, or meeting: *the orchestra was given an enthusiastic ovation from the audience.* ■ the people who watch or listen to a television or radio program: *the program attracted an audience of almost twenty million.* ■ the readership of a book, magazine, or newspaper: *the newspaper has a sophisticated audience.* ■ the people giving or likely to give attention to something: *there will always be an audience for romantic literature.*
2 a formal interview with a person in authority: *he demanded an audience with the pope.*
3 archaic formal hearing.
– ORIGIN late Middle English: from Old French, from Latin *audientia*, from *audire* 'hear.'

au·dile /ˈôˌdīl/ ▶ **adj.** another term for AUDITORY.
– ORIGIN late 19th cent.: formed from Latin *audire* 'hear,' on the pattern of *tactile.*

au·di·o /ˈôdēˌō/ ▶ **n.** [usu. as modifier] sound, esp. when recorded, transmitted, or reproduced: *audio equipment | the machine can retrieve and play audio from a CD-ROM.*
– ORIGIN 1930s: independent usage of AUDIO-.

audio- ▶ **comb. form** relating to hearing or sound: *audiometer | audiovisual.*
– ORIGIN from Latin *audire* 'hear.'

Au·di·o-An·i·ma·tron·ics /ˌanəməˈträniks/ ▶ **plural n.** trademark for ANIMATRONICS.
– DERIVATIVES **Au·di·o-An·i·ma·tron·ic adj.**

au·di·o·book /ˈôdē-ōˌbo͝ok/ (also **audio book**) ▶ **n.** an audiocassette or CD recording of a reading of a book, typically a novel.

au·di·o·cas·sette /ˌôdē-ōkəˈset/ ▶ **n.** a cassette of audiotape.

au·di·o fre·quen·cy ▶ **n.** a frequency of oscillation capable of being perceived by the human ear, generally between 20 and 20,000 Hz.

au·di·o·gram /ˈôdēəˌgram/ ▶ **n.** a graphic record produced by audiometry.

au·di·o guide ▶ **n.** a handheld device that provides recorded information for visitors touring a museum, gallery, or other place of interest.

au·di·ol·o·gy /ˌôdēˈäləjē/ ▶ **n.** the branch of science and medicine concerned with the sense of hearing.
– DERIVATIVES **au·di·o·log·i·cal** /-əˈläjikəl/ **adj., au·di·ol·o·gist** /-jist/ **n.**

au·di·om·e·try /ˌôdēˈämitrē/ ▶ **n.** measurement of the range and sensitivity of a person's sense of hearing.
– DERIVATIVES **au·di·om·e·ter** /-itər/ **n., au·di·o·met·ric** /-əˈmetrik/ **adj.**

au·di·o·phile /ˈôdē-ōˌfīl/ ▶ **n.** a hi-fi enthusiast.

au·di·o·tape /ˈôdē-ōˌtāp/ ▶ **n.** magnetic tape on which sound can be recorded. ■ a length of this, typically in the form of a cassette.
▶ **v.** [with obj.] record (sound) on tape: *each interview was audiotaped and transcribed.*

au·di·o·vis·u·al /ˌôdē-ōˈvizho͞oəl/ ▶ **adj.** using both sight and sound, typically in the form of slides or video and recorded speech or music: *audiovisual presentations.*

au·dit /ˈôdit/ ▶ **n.** an official inspection of an individual's or organization's accounts, typically by an independent body. ■ a systematic review or assessment of something: *a complete audit of flora and fauna at the site.*
▶ **v.** (**audits, auditing, audited**) [with obj.] **1** conduct an official financial examination of (an individual's or organization's accounts): *companies must have their accounts audited.* ■ conduct a systematic review of: *auditing obstetrical and neonatal care.*
2 attend (a class) informally, not for academic credit.
– ORIGIN late Middle English: from Latin *auditus* 'hearing,' from *audire* 'hear,' in medieval Latin *auditus (compoti)* 'audit (of an account),' an audit originally being presented orally.

au·di·tion /ôˈdishən/ ▶ **n.** an interview for a particular role or job as a singer, actor, dancer, or musician, consisting of a practical demonstration of the candidate's suitability and skill.
▶ **v.** [no obj.] perform an audition: *he was **auditioning for** the lead role in the play.* ■ [with obj.] assess the suitability of (someone) for a role by means of an audition: *she was **auditioning** people **for** her new series.*
– ORIGIN late 16th cent. (in the sense 'power of hearing or listening'): from Latin *auditio(n)-*, from *audire* 'hear.' The current sense of the noun dates from the late 19th cent.

au·di·tive /ˈôditiv/ ▶ **adj.** another term for AUDITORY.

au·di·tor /ˈôditər/ ▶ **n. 1** a person who conducts an audit.
2 a listener: *so low was Jim's voice that his auditors had to give it close attention.* ■ a person who attends a class informally without working for academic credit.
– DERIVATIVES **au·di·to·ri·al** /ˌôdəˈtôrēəl/ **adj.**
– ORIGIN Middle English: from Old French *auditeur*, from Latin *auditor*, from *audire* 'to hear.'

au·di·to·ri·um /ˌôdiˈtôrēəm/ ▶ **n.** (pl. **auditoriums** or **auditoria** /-ˈtôrēə/) **1** the part of a theater, concert hall, or other public building in which the audience sits.
2 a large building or hall used for public gatherings, typically concerts or sports events. ■ a large room for such gatherings, esp. in a school.
– ORIGIN early 17th cent. (originally in the general sense 'a place for hearing'): from Latin, neuter of *auditorius* 'relating to hearing' (see AUDITORY).

au·di·to·ry /ˈôdiˌtôrē/ ▶ **adj.** of or relating to the sense of hearing: *the auditory nerves | teaching methods use both visual and auditory stimulation.*
– ORIGIN late 16th cent.: from Latin *auditorius*, from *audire* 'hear.'

Au·du·bon /ˈôdəˌbän/, John James (1785–1851), US naturalist and artist. His most notable work is *The Birds of America* (1827–38), in which he portrayed even the largest birds life-size and painted them in action.

Au·er·bach[1] /ˈou-ərˌbäk, -ˌbäkh/, Frank (1931–), British painter, born in Germany.

Au·er·bach[2] /ˈou-ərˌbak, -ˌbäk/, Red (1917–2006), US basketball coach; full name *Arnold Jacob Auerbach*. As coach of the Boston Celtics 1950–66, he led the team to nine National Basketball Association (NBA) championships 1957, 1959–66. Basketball Hall of Fame (1968).

au fait /ˌō ˈfe/ ▶ **adj.** (**au fait with**) having a good or detailed knowledge of something: *you should be reasonably **au fait with** the company and its products.*
– ORIGIN mid 18th cent.: from French, literally 'to the fact, to the point.'

au fond /ˌō ˈfôn/ ▶ **adv.** in essence: *she might be, au fond, quite a pleasant woman.*
– ORIGIN late 18th cent.: French, literally 'at bottom.'

Aug. ▶ **abbr.** August.

Au·ge·an /ôˈjēən/ ▶ **adj.** of or relating to Augeas: *the Augean stables.* ■ (of a task or problem) requiring so much effort to complete or solve as to seem impossible: *Augean amounts of debris to clear.*

a

Au·ge·as /ôˈjēəs/ Greek Mythology a legendary king whose vast stables had never been cleaned. Hercules cleaned them in a day by diverting the Alpheus River to flow through them.

au·ger /ˈôgər/ ▶ **n.** a tool with a helical bit for boring holes in wood. ■ a similar larger tool for boring holes in the ground.
– ORIGIN Old English *nafogār*, from *nafu* (see **NAVE**[2]) + *gār* 'piercer.' The *n* was lost by wrong division of *a nauger*; compare with **ADDER** and **APRON**.

auger

Au·ger ef·fect /ōˈZHā/ ▶ **n.** Physics a process in which an electron in an outer shell of an atom makes a transition to a vacancy in an inner shell. The energy gained is transferred to an electron that escapes from the atom.
– ORIGIN 1930s: named after Pierre V. *Auger* (1899–1944), French physicist.

aught[1] /ôt/ (also **ought**) archaic ▶ **pron.** anything at all: *know you aught of this fellow, young sir?*
– ORIGIN Old English *āwiht* (see **AYE**[2], **WIGHT**).

aught[2] ▶ **n.** the digit 0; zero.

au·gite /ˈôˌjīt/ ▶ **n.** a dark green or black aluminosilicate mineral of the pyroxene group. It occurs in many igneous rocks, including basalt, gabbro, and diabase.
– ORIGIN early 19th cent.: from Latin *augites*, denoting a precious stone (probably turquoise), from Greek *augitēs*, from *augē* 'luster.'

aug·ment ▶ **v.** /ôgˈment/ [with obj.] make (something) greater by adding to it; increase: *he augmented his summer income by painting houses.*
▶ **n.** /ˈôgˌment, -mənt/ Linguistics a vowel prefixed to past tenses of verbs in Greek and other Indo-European languages.
– ORIGIN late Middle English: from Old French *augmenter* (verb), *augment* (noun), or late Latin *augmentare*, from Latin *augere* 'to increase.'

aug·men·ta·tion /ˌôgmenˈtāSHən/ ▶ **n.** the action or process of making or becoming greater in size or amount: *the augmentation of the curriculum with new subjects.* ■ Music the lengthening of the time values of notes in a melodic part. ■ Heraldry an addition to a coat of arms granted as a mark of special honor.
– ORIGIN late Middle English: from late Latin *augmentatio(n-)*, from the verb *augmentare* (see **AUGMENT**).

aug·ment·a·tive /ôgˈmentətiv/ ▶ **adj.** Grammar (of an affix or derived word) reinforcing the idea of the original word, esp. by meaning 'a large —,' as with the Italian suffix *-one* in *borrone* 'ravine,' compared with *borro* 'ditch.'
– ORIGIN late Middle English (in the sense 'having a tendency to increase'): from Old French *augmentatif, -ive* or medieval Latin *augmentativus*, from the verb *augmentare* (see **AUGMENT**).

aug·ment·ed /ôgˈmentid/ ▶ **adj. 1** having been made greater in size or value: *augmented pensions for those retiring at 65.*
2 Music denoting or containing an interval that is one semitone greater than the corresponding major or perfect interval: *augmented fourths.*

aug·men·ted re·al·i·ty ▶ **n.** a technology that superimposes a computer-generated image on a user's view of the real world, thus providing a composite view.

au grat·in /ˌō ˈgrätn, ˈgratn, graˈtaN/ ▶ **adj.** [predic.] sprinkled with breadcrumbs or grated cheese, or both, and browned: *lentils and mushrooms au gratin.*
– ORIGIN early 19th cent.: French, literally 'by grating.'

Augs·burg /ˈôgzˌbərg, ˈouksˌbo͝ork/ a city in southern Germany, in Bavaria; pop. 262,500 (est. 2006).

Augs·burg Con·fes·sion a statement of the Lutheran position, drawn up mainly by Melanchthon and approved by Luther before being presented to the Emperor Charles V at Augsburg on June 25, 1530.

au·gur /ˈôgər/ ▶ **v.** [no obj.] (**augur well/badly/ill**) (of an event or circumstance) portend a good or bad outcome: *the end of the Cold War seemed to augur well | the return to the gold standard augured badly for industry.* ■ [with obj.] portend or bode (a specified outcome): *a new coalition would not augur a new period of social reforms.* ■ [with obj.] (archaic) foresee or predict.
▶ **n.** historical (in ancient Rome) a religious official who observed natural signs, esp. the behavior of birds, interpreting these as an indication of divine approval or disapproval of a proposed action.
– DERIVATIVES **au·gu·ral** /ˈôgyərəl/ **adj.** (archaic).
– ORIGIN late Middle English (as a noun): from Latin, 'diviner.'

au·gu·ry /ˈôgyərē/ ▶ **n.** (pl. **auguries**) a sign of what will happen in the future; an omen: *they heard the sound as an augury of death.* ■ the work of an augur; the interpretation of omens.
– ORIGIN late Middle English (in the sense 'divination'): from Old French *augurie* or Latin *augurium* 'interpretation of omens,' from *augur* (see **AUGUR**).

Au·gust /ˈôgəst/ ▶ **n.** the eighth month of the year, in the northern hemisphere usually considered the last month of summer: *the sultry haze of late August* | [as modifier] *an August cold snap.*
– ORIGIN Old English, from Latin *augustus* 'consecrated, venerable'; named after **AUGUSTUS** Caesar, the first Roman emperor.

au·gust /ôˈgəst/ ▶ **adj.** respected and impressive: *she was in august company.*
– DERIVATIVES **au·gust·ly adv.**
– ORIGIN mid 17th cent.: from French *auguste* or Latin *augustus* 'consecrated, venerable.'

Au·gus·ta /əˈgəstə/ **1** a city in eastern Georgia; since a 1996 merger, is part of Augusta–Richmond County; consolidated pop. 199,486 (est. 2008).
2 the capital of Maine, in the southwestern part of the state, on the Kennebec River; pop. 18,282 (est. 2008).

Au·gus·tan /ôˈgəstən/ ▶ **adj.** connected with or occurring during the reign of the Roman emperor Augustus. ■ relating to or denoting Latin literature of the reign of Augustus, including the works of Virgil, Horace, Ovid, and Livy. ■ relating to or denoting 17th- and 18th-century English literature of a style considered refined and classical, including the works of Pope, Addison, and Swift.
▶ **n.** a writer of the (Latin or English) Augustan age.
– ORIGIN from Latin *Augustanus* 'relating to Augustus' (see **AUGUSTUS**).

Au·gus·tine /ˈôgəˌstēn, ôˈgəstin/ ▶ **n.** an Augustinian friar.
– ORIGIN late Middle English: from Old French *augustin*, from Latin *Augustinus* 'Augustine' (see **AUGUSTINIAN**).

Au·gus·tine, St.[1] /ˈôgəˌstēn, əˈgəstən/ (died *c.*604), Italian churchman; known as **St. Augustine of Canterbury**. Sent from Rome by Pope Gregory the Great, he founded a monastery at Canterbury and became its first archbishop. Feast day, May 26.

Au·gus·tine, St.[2] (354–430), doctor of the Church; known as **St. Augustine of Hippo**. He became bishop of Hippo in North Africa in 396. His writings, such as *Confessions* (400) and *City of God* (412–427), dominated subsequent Western theology. Feast day, August 28.

Au·gus·tin·i·an /ˌôgəˈstinēən/ ▶ **adj. 1** of or relating to St. Augustine of Hippo or his theological doctrines.
2 of or relating to a religious order observing a rule derived from St. Augustine's writings.
▶ **n. 1** a member of an Augustinian order.
2 an adherent of the doctrines of St. Augustine.

Au·gus·tus /əˈgəstəs/ (63 BC–AD 14), the first Roman emperor; born *Gaius Octavianus*; also called **Octavian**. He was adopted in the will of his great-uncle Julius Caesar and gained supreme power by his defeat of Antony in 31 BC. In 27 BC he was given the title Augustus ("venerable") and became in effect emperor.

auk /ôk/ ▶ **n.** a short-winged diving seabird found in northern oceans, typically with a black head and back and white underparts. ● Family Alcidae (the **auk family**), which comprises the guillemots, murres, razorbills, puffins, and their relatives. See also **GREAT AUK, DOVEKIE**.
– ORIGIN late 17th cent.: from Old Norse *álka* 'razorbill.'

auk·let /ˈôklit/ ▶ **n.** a small stubby auk (seabird) found in the North Pacific, typically with gray underparts. ● *Aethia* and three other genera, family Alcidae: several species.

auld /ôld/ ▶ **adj.** Scottish form of **OLD**.
– ORIGIN Old English *ald*, Anglian form of **OLD**.

auld lang syne /ôld laNG ˈzīn, ˈsīn/ ▶ **n.** times long past.
– PHRASES **for auld lang syne** for old times' sake.
– ORIGIN late 18th cent.: Scots (see **AULD, LANG SYNE**). The phrase was popularized as the title and refrain of a song by Robert Burns (1788).

aum·bry /ˈambrē/ ▶ **n.** variant spelling of **AMBRY**.

au na·tu·rel /ˌō ˌnaCHəˈrel/ ▶ **adj. & adv.** with no elaborate treatment, dressing, or preparation: [as adv.] *I wear my hair au naturel these days* | [as adj.] *the cheese is delicious whether au naturel or seasoned.* ■ (humorous) naked.
– ORIGIN early 19th cent.: French, literally 'in the natural (state).'

Aung San /ˈouNG ˈsän/ (1914–47), Burmese nationalist leader. As leader of the Council of Ministers, he negotiated a promise of self-government from the British shortly before his assassination.

Aung San Suu Kyi /ˈouNG ˈsän ˈso͞o ˈCHē/ (1945–), Burmese political leader, daughter of Aung San and leader of the National League for Democracy (NLD) 1988– . She was kept under house arrest 1989–95, and the military government refused to recognize her party's victory in the 1990 elections. Since 2000 she has frequently been detained again. Nobel Peace Prize (1991).

Aung San Suu Kyi

aunt /ant, änt/ ▶ **n.** the sister of one's father or mother or the wife of one's uncle. ■ informal an unrelated older woman friend, esp. of a child.
– ORIGIN Middle English: from Old French *ante*, from Latin *amita*.

aunt·ie /ˈantē, ˈän-/ (also **aunty**) ▶ **n.** (pl. **aunties**) informal term for **AUNT**.

Aunt Sal·ly /ˌant ˈsalē, ˌänt/ ▶ **n.** (pl. **Aunt Sallies**) a game played in some parts of Britain in which players throw sticks or balls at a wooden dummy. ■ a dummy used in this game. ■ a person or thing that is subjected to much criticism, esp. one set up as an easy target for it.

au pair /ˌō ˈpe(ə)r/ ▶ **n.** a young foreign person, typically a woman, who helps with housework or child care in exchange for room and board.
– ORIGIN late 19th cent.: from French, literally 'on equal terms.' The phrase was originally adjectival, describing an arrangement between two parties paid for by the exchange of mutual services; the noun usage dates from the 1960s.

au·ra /ˈôrə/ ▶ **n.** (pl. **auras**) [usu. in sing.] the distinctive atmosphere or quality that seems to surround and be generated by a person, thing, or place: *the ceremony retains an aura of mystery.* ■ a supposed emanation surrounding the body of a living creature, viewed by mystics, spiritualists, and some practitioners of complementary medicine as the essence of the individual, and allegedly discernible by people with special sensibilities. ■ any invisible emanation, esp. a scent or odor: *there was a faint aura of disinfectant.* ■ Medicine (pl. also **aurae** /ˈôrē/) a warning sensation experienced before an attack of epilepsy or migraine.
– ORIGIN late Middle English (originally denoting a gentle breeze): via Latin from Greek, 'breeze, breath.' Current senses date from the 18th cent.

au·ral /ˈôrəl/ ▶ **adj.** of or relating to the ear or the sense of hearing: *aural anatomy | information held in written, aural, or database form.*
– DERIVATIVES **au·ral·ly adv.**
– ORIGIN mid 19th cent.: from Latin *auris* 'ear' + **-AL**.

> **USAGE** The words **aural** and **oral** have the same pronunciation in standard English, which is sometimes a source of confusion. A distinctive pronunciation for **aural** has been proposed, with the first syllable rhyming with *cow*, but it has not become standard.

Au·rang·zeb /ˌôräNGˈzeb/ (1618–1707), Mogul emperor of Hindustan 1658–1707, who increased the Mogul empire to its greatest extent.

au·rar /ˈouˌrär, ˈoi-/ plural form of **EYRIR**.

au·re·ate /ˈôrē-it, -ˌāt/ ▶ **adj.** denoting, made of, or having the color of gold. ■ (of language) highly ornamented or elaborate.
– ORIGIN late Middle English: from late Latin *aureatus*, from Latin *aureus* 'golden,' from *aurum* 'gold.'

Au·re·li·an /ôˈrēlēən/ (*c.*215–275), Roman emperor 270–275; Latin name *Lucius Domitius Aurelianus*.

Au·re·li·us /ôˈrēlēəs/, Marcus (121–80), Roman emperor 161–180; full name *Caesar Marcus*

Aurelius Antoninus Augustus. He was occupied for much of his reign with wars against invading Germanic tribes. His *Meditations* are evidence of his philosophical interest.

au·re·ole /'ôrē,ōl/ (also **aureola** /ô'rēələ/) ▶ **n.** a circle of light or brightness surrounding something, esp. as depicted in art around the head or body of a person represented as holy. ■ another term for CORONA[1] (sense 1). ■ another term for AREOLA. ■ Geology the zone of metamorphosed rock surrounding an igneous intrusion.
– ORIGIN Middle English: from Old French *aureole*, from Latin *aureola (corona)* 'golden (crown),' feminine of *aureolus* (diminutive of *aureus*, from *aurum* 'gold').

au·re·us /'ôrēəs/ ▶ **n.** (pl. **aurei** /'ôrē,ī/) a gold coin of ancient Rome, worth 25 silver denarii.
– ORIGIN Latin, noun use of *aureus* 'golden,' from *aurum* 'gold.'

au re·voir /,ō rəv'wär/ ▶ **exclam.** good-bye until we meet again.
– ORIGIN late 17th cent.: from French, literally 'to the seeing again.'

Au·ric /ô'rēk/, Georges (1899–1983), French composer. He is best known for his scores for movies such as *The Lavender Hill Mob* (1951) and *Moulin Rouge* (1952).

au·ric[1] /'ôrik/ ▶ **adj.** of or relating to the aura supposedly surrounding a living creature.

au·ric[2] ▶ **adj.** Chemistry of gold with a valence of three.
– ORIGIN early 19th cent.: from Latin *aurum* 'gold' + -IC.

au·ri·cle /'ôrikəl/ ▶ **n.** Anatomy & Biology a structure resembling an ear or earlobe. ■ another term for ATRIUM (of the heart). ■ strictly, a small muscular appendage of each atrium. ■ the external part or pinna of the ear.
– ORIGIN late Middle English: from Latin *auricula* 'external part of the ear,' diminutive of *auris* 'ear.'

au·ric·u·lar /ô'rikyələr/ ▶ **adj.** **1** of or relating to the ear or hearing.
2 of, relating to, or shaped like an auricle.
– ORIGIN late Middle English: from late Latin *auricularis*, from *auricula*, diminutive of *auris* 'ear.'

au·ric·u·late /ô'rikyəlit, -,lāt/ ▶ **adj.** Botany & Zoology having one or more structures shaped like an ear or earlobe.
– ORIGIN early 18th cent.: from Latin *auricula* 'external part of the ear' (diminutive of *auris* 'ear') + -ATE[2].

au·ric·u·lo·ther·apy /ô,rikyəlō'THerəpē/ ▶ **n.** a form of acupuncture applied to points on the ear in order to treat other parts of the body.
– ORIGIN 1970s: from Latin *auricula* 'external part of the ear' + *therapy*.

au·rif·er·ous /ô'rifərəs/ ▶ **adj.** (of rocks or minerals) containing gold.
– ORIGIN mid 17th cent.: from Latin *aurifer* 'gold-bearing' (from *aurum* 'gold') + -OUS.

Au·ri·ga /ô'rīgə/ Astronomy a large northern constellation (the Charioteer), said to represent a man holding a whip. ■ (as genitive **Aurigae** /ô'rījē/) used with a preceding letter or numeral to designate stars: *the star Theta Aurigae.*
– ORIGIN Latin.

Au·ri·gna·cian /,ôrig'nāSHən, ,ôrin'yā-/ ▶ **adj.** Archaeology of, relating to, or denoting the early stages of the Upper Paleolithic culture in Europe and the Near East. It is dated in most places to about 34,000–29,000 years ago and is associated with Cro-Magnon Man. ■ (as noun **the Aurignacian**) the Aurignacian culture or period.
– ORIGIN early 20th cent.: from French *Aurignacien*, from *Aurignac* in southwestern France, where remains of this culture were found.

au·ri·scope /'ôri,skōp/ (also **auroscope** /'ôrə-/) ▶ **n.** another term for OTOSCOPE.
– ORIGIN mid 19th cent.: from Latin *auris* 'ear' + -SCOPE.

au·rochs /'ouräks, 'ô,räks/ ▶ **n.** (pl. **same**) a large wild Eurasian ox that was the ancestor of domestic cattle. It was probably exterminated in Britain in the Bronze Age, and the last one was killed in Poland in 1627. Also called URUS. ● *Bos taurus* (formerly *primigenius*), family Bovidae.
– ORIGIN late 18th cent.: from German, early variant of *Auerochs*, from Old High German *ūrohso*, from *ūr* (form also found in Old English, of unknown origin) + *ohso* 'ox.'

Au·ro·ra[1] /ə'rôrə/ **1** a city in north central Colorado, east of Denver; pop. 319,057 (est. 2008).
2 an industrial city in northeastern Illinois; pop. 171,782 (est. 2008).

Au·ro·ra[2] /ə'rôrə, ô'rôrə/ Roman Mythology goddess of the dawn. Greek equivalent **Eos**.

au·ro·ra /ə'rôrə, ô'rôrə/ ▶ **n.** (pl. **auroras** or **aurorae** /ô'rôrē/) **1** a natural electrical phenomenon characterized by the appearance of streamers of reddish or greenish light in the sky, usually near the northern or southern magnetic pole. [*borealis* from Latin, 'northern,' based on Greek *Boreas*, the god of the north wind; *australis* from Latin, 'southern,' from *Auster* 'the south, the south wind.']

> The effect is caused by the interaction of charged particles from the sun with atoms in the upper atmosphere. In northern and southern regions it is respectively called **aurora borealis** or **Northern Lights** and **aurora australis** or **Southern Lights**.

2 [in sing.] literary the dawn.
– DERIVATIVES **au·ro·ral** adj.
– ORIGIN late Middle English (sense 2): from Latin, 'dawn, goddess of the dawn.' Sense 1 dates from the early 18th cent.

AUS (also **A.U.S.**) ▶ **abbr.** Army of the United States.

Ausch·witz /'ousHvits/ a Nazi concentration camp in World War II, near the town of Oświęcim (Auschwitz) in Poland.

aus·cul·ta·tion /,ôskəl'tāSHən/ ▶ **n.** the action of listening to sounds from the heart, lungs, or other organs, typically with a stethoscope, as a part of medical diagnosis.
– DERIVATIVES **aus·cul·tate** /'ôskəl,tāt/ v., **aus·cul·ta·to·ry** /ô'skəltə,tôrē/ adj.
– ORIGIN mid 17th cent.: from Latin *auscultatio(n-)*, from *auscultare* 'listen to.'

Aus·le·se /'ouslāzə/ ▶ **n.** a white wine of German origin or style made from selected bunches of grapes picked later than the general harvest.
– ORIGIN from German, from *aus* 'out' + *Lese* 'picking, vintage.'

aus·pice /'ôspis/ ▶ **n.** archaic a divine or prophetic token.
– PHRASES **under the auspices of** with the help, support, or protection of: *the delegation's visit was arranged under UN auspices.*
– ORIGIN mid 16th cent. (originally denoting the observation of bird flight in divination): from French, or from Latin *auspicium*, from *auspex* 'observer of birds,' from *avis* 'bird' + *specere* 'to look.'

aus·pi·cious /ô'spiSHəs/ ▶ **adj.** conducive to success; favorable: *it was not the most auspicious moment to hold an election.* ■ giving or being a sign of future success: *they said it was an auspicious moon—it was rising.* ■ archaic characterized by success; prosperous: *he was respectful to his auspicious customers.*
– DERIVATIVES **aus·pi·cious·ly** adv., **aus·pi·cious·ness** n.
– ORIGIN late 16th cent.: from AUSPICE + -OUS.

Aus·sie /'ôsē/ ▶ **n.** (pl. **Aussies**) & **adj.** informal term for AUSTRALIA or AUSTRALIAN.

Aus·ten /'ôstən/, Jane (1775–1817), English novelist. Her major novels are *Sense and Sensibility* (1811), *Pride and Prejudice* (1813), *Mansfield Park* (1814), *Emma* (1815), *Northanger Abbey* (1818), and *Persuasion* (1818).

aus·ten·ite /'ôstə,nīt/ ▶ **n.** Metallurgy a solid solution of carbon in a nonmagnetic form of iron, stable at high temperatures. It is a constituent of some forms of steel.
– DERIVATIVES **aus·ten·it·ic** /,ôstə'nitik/ adj.
– ORIGIN early 20th cent.: from the name of Sir William Roberts-*Austen* (1843–1902), English metallurgist, + -ITE[1].

aus·tere /ô'sti(ə)r/ ▶ **adj.** (**austerer, austerest**) severe or strict in manner, attitude, or appearance: *an austere man, with a rigidly puritanical outlook* | *an austere expression.* ■ (of living conditions or a way of life) having no comforts or luxuries; harsh or ascetic: *conditions in the prison could hardly be more austere.* ■ having an extremely plain and simple style or appearance; unadorned: *the cathedral is impressive in its austere simplicity.* ■ (of an economic policy or measure) designed to reduce a budget deficit, esp. by cutting public expenditure.
– DERIVATIVES **aus·tere·ly** adv.
– ORIGIN Middle English: via Old French from Latin *austerus*, from Greek *austēros* 'severe.'

aus·ter·i·ty /ô'steritē/ ▶ **n.** (pl. **austerities**) sternness or severity of manner or attitude: *he was noted for his austerity and his authoritarianism.* ■ extreme plainness and simplicity of style or appearance: *the room was decorated with a restraint bordering on austerity.* ■ (**austerities**) conditions characterized by severity, sternness, or asceticism: *a simple life of prayer and personal austerity.* ■ difficult economic conditions created by government measures to reduce a budget deficit, esp. by reducing public expenditure: *a period of austerity* | [as modifier] *austerity measures.*
– ORIGIN late Middle English: from French *austérité*, from Latin *austeritas*, from *austerus* 'severe' (see AUSTERE).

Aus·ter·litz, Battle of /'ôstər,lits, 'oustər-/ a battle in 1805 near the town of Austerlitz (now in the Czech Republic), in which Napoleon defeated the Austrians and Russians.

Aus·tin[1] /'ôstən/ the capital of Texas; pop. 757,688 (est. 2008). First settled by Anglo-Americans in 1835 (a year before Texas gained independence from Mexico), it was named **Waterloo** until 1839, when it was renamed to honor **Stephen F. Austin**.

Aus·tin[2], J. L. (1911–60), English philosopher; full name *John Langshaw Austin*. Notable works: *Sense and Sensibilia* and *How to Do Things with Words* (both 1962).

Aus·tin[3], John (1790–1859), English jurist. His work is significant for its strict delimitation of the sphere of law and its distinction from that of morality.

Aus·tin[4], Stephen Fuller (1793–1836), colonizer of Texas. He founded the first recognized Anglo-American settlement in Texas 1823 and served briefly as secretary of state of the Republic of Texas 1836. His colonization of Texas was a continuation of the effort begun by his father, **Moses Austin** (1761–1821), who in 1821 became the first man allowed to bring Anglo-American settlers into Spanish Texas.

Aus·tin[5] ▶ **adj.** & **n.** another name for AUGUSTINIAN.

aus·tral /'ôstrəl/ ▶ **adj.** of or relating to the south, in particular: ■ technical of the southern hemisphere: *the austral spring.* ■ (**Austral**) of Australia or Australasia.
– ORIGIN late 15th cent.: from Latin *australis*, from *Auster* 'the south, the south wind.'

Aus·tral·a·sia /,ôstrə'lāZHə/ the region that consists of Australia, New Zealand, New Guinea, and the neighboring islands of the Pacific Ocean.
– DERIVATIVES **Aus·tral·a·sian** adj. & n.

Aus·tral·ia /ô'strālyə, ə'strāl-/ an island country and continent in the southern hemisphere, in the southwestern Pacific Ocean, a member state of the Commonwealth of Nations; pop. 21,262,600 (est. 2009); capital, Canberra; official language, English.

> Inhabited by Aboriginal peoples since prehistoric times, Australia was explored by the Dutch from 1606; British colonization began in 1788, as did the transportation of convicts from Britain, a practice that was discontinued in 1868. Australia was declared a commonwealth in 1901 when the six colonies (New South Wales, Victoria, Queensland, South Australia, Western Australia, and Tasmania) federated as sovereign states. The two mainland federal territories, the Northern Territory and the Australian Capital Territory, became self-governing in 1978 and 1988, respectively. Although an independent nation, Australia is a constitutional monarchy whose formal head of state is Queen Elizabeth II of the United Kingdom.

Aus·tral·ian /ô'strālyən/ ▶ **n.** a native or inhabitant of Australia, or a person of Australian descent.
▶ **adj.** of or relating to Australia. ■ Zoology of, relating to, or denoting a zoogeographical region comprising Australasia together with Indonesia east of Wallace's line, in which monotremes and marsupials dominate the fauna. Compare with NOTOGAEA, ORIENTAL. ■ Botany of, relating to, or denoting a phytogeographical kingdom comprising only Australia and Tasmania.
– DERIVATIVES **Aus·tral·ian·ism** /-,nizəm/ n.
– ORIGIN from French *australien*, from Latin *australis* in the phrase *Terra Australis* 'the southern land,' the name of the supposed southern continent.

Aus·tral·ian Ant·arc·tic Ter·ri·to·ry an area of Antarctica that lies between longitudes 142° east and 136° east. It is administered by Australia.

Aus·tral·ian Cap·i·tal Ter·ri·to·ry a federal territory in New South Wales, Australia, that consists of two enclaves ceded by New South Wales—one in 1911 to contain Canberra, the other in 1915 containing Jervis Bay. The latter became the Jervis Bay Territory in 1988.

Aus·tral·ian crawl ▶ **n.** chiefly Austral. another term for CRAWL (sense 2 of the noun).

Aus·tral·ian La·bor Par·ty (abbr.: **ALP**) Australia's oldest political party, founded in 1891. The party is moderately liberal; it has provided three recent Australian Prime Ministers, Gough Whitlam, Bob Hawke, and Paul Keating.

Aus·tral·ian pine ▶ **n.** another name for the BEEFWOOD.

Aus·tral·ian Rules (also **Australian Rules football**) ▶ **n.** a form of football played on an oval ground with an oval ball by teams of eighteen

a

players. Official name **Australian National football**.

The game dates from 1858. Players may run with the ball if they touch it to the ground every fifteen meters, and may pass it in any direction by punching. There are both inner and outer goalposts: a behind (between the outer posts) scores one point and a goal (between the inner posts) scores six.

Aus·tral·ian salm·on ▸ n. see SALMON (sense 2).

Aus·tral·ian ter·ri·er ▸ n. a wire-haired terrier of a breed originating in Australia.

Aus·tral·ian wil·low ▸ n. another term for WILGA.

Aus·tral Is·lands /ˈôstrəl/ another name for TUBUAI ISLANDS.

aus·tra·lite /ˈôstrəˌlīt/ ▸ n. Geology a tektite from the strewn field in Australia.

Aus·tra·loid /ˈôstrəˌloid/ often offensive ▸ adj. of or belonging to the division of humankind represented by Australian Aboriginal peoples.
▸ n. a person belonging to this division of humankind.

USAGE The term **Australoid**, together with other terms such as **Caucasoid, Negroid**, and **Mongoloid**, belong to the systems of human classification developed by 19th-century anthropologists and physiologists and relate to outdated notions of race that have largely been abandoned. Such terms are potentially offensive today and, when referring to native peoples of a particular region, it is preferable, e.g., to refer to 'Australian Aborigines' or to the names of specific peoples. See also usage at CAUCASIAN and MONGOLOID.

Aus·tra·lo·pith·e·cus /ˌôstrəlōˈpiTHikəs, ôˌstrālō-/ ▸ n. a fossil bipedal primate with both apelike and human characteristics, found in Pliocene and lower Pleistocene deposits (*c.*4 million to 1 million years old) in Africa. ● Genus *Australopithecus*, family Hominidae: several species, including the lightly built *A. africanus*, which is thought to be the immediate ancestor of the human genus *Homo*. The more heavily built forms (often placed in the genus *Paranthropus*), such as *A. robustus* and *A. boisei*, were probably evolutionary dead ends.
– DERIVATIVES **aus·tra·lo·pith·e·cine** /-ˌsēn, -ˌsīn/ n. & adj.
– ORIGIN modern Latin, from Latin *australis* 'southern' (see AUSTRAL) + Greek *pithēkos* 'ape.'

Aus·tral·orp /ˈôstrəˌlôrp/ ▸ n. a black Orpington chicken of an Australian breed.
– ORIGIN early 20th cent.: blend of AUSTRALIAN and ORPINGTON.

Aus·tri·a /ˈôstrēə/ a republic in central Europe; pop. 8,210,300 (est. 2009); capital, Vienna; official language, German.

Austria was dominated from the early Middle Ages by the Habsburg family and became the center of a massive central European empire that lasted until 1918. The country was incorporated within the Nazi Reich in 1938 and after World War II was occupied by the Allies before regaining its sovereignty in 1955. A referendum in 1994 approved Austria's entry into the European Union.

– DERIVATIVES **Aus·tri·an** adj. & n.

Aus·tri·a–Hun·ga·ry (also **Austro-Hungarian Empire** /ˈôstrō/) the dual monarchy established in 1867 by the Austrian emperor Franz Josef, according to which Austria and Hungary became autonomous states under a common sovereign.

Aus·tri·an shade /ˈôstrēən/ ▸ n. a window shade made from fabric shirred in puffy frills or pleats, extending about a third of the way down a window.

Aus·tri·an Suc·ces·sion, War of the a group of several related conflicts (1740–48), involving most of the states of Europe, that were triggered by the death of the Emperor Charles VI and the accession of his daughter Maria Theresa in 1740 to the Austrian throne. See also PRAGMATIC SANCTION.

Austro-[1] ▸ comb. form Austrian; Austrian and ...: *Austro-Hungarian*.

Austro-[2] ▸ comb. form Australian; Australian and ...: *Austro-Malayan*. ■ southern: *Austro-Asiatic*.
– ORIGIN from Latin *australis* 'southern.'

Aus·tro-A·si·at·ic /ˈôstrō ˌāZHēˈatik, -SHē-, -zē-/ ▸ adj. of, relating to, or denoting a phylum of languages spoken in Southeast Asia, consisting of the Mon-Khmer family, the Munda family, and one or two other isolated languages.
▸ n. this phylum of languages.
– ORIGIN early 20th cent.: from AUSTRO-[2] 'southern' + ASIATIC.

Aus·tro·ne·sian /ˌôstrōˈnēZHən/ ▸ adj. of, relating to, or denoting a family of languages spoken in an area extending from Madagascar in the west to the Pacific islands in the east. Also called MALAYO-POLYNESIAN.
▸ n. this family of languages.
– ORIGIN from German *austronesisch*, based on Latin *australis* 'southern' (see AUSTRAL) + Greek *nēsos* 'island.'

aut- ▸ prefix variant spelling of AUTO- shortened before a vowel (as in *autarky*).

au·tarch /ˈôtärk/ ▸ n. a ruler who has absolute power.
– ORIGIN early 19th cent.: from Greek *autarkhos*, from *autos* 'self' + *arkhos* 'leader.'

au·tar·chy /ˈôˌtärkē/ ▸ n. (pl. **autarchies**) **1** another term for AUTOCRACY.
2 variant spelling of AUTARKY.
– DERIVATIVES **au·tar·chic** /ôˈtärkik/ adj.
– ORIGIN mid 17th cent.: from modern Latin *autarchia*, from Greek *autos* 'self' + *-arkhia* (from *arkhein* 'take the lead'), on the pattern of *monarchia* 'monarchy.'

au·tar·ky /ˈôˌtärkē/ ▸ n. economic independence or self-sufficiency. ■ a country, state, or society that is economically independent.
– DERIVATIVES **au·tar·kic** /ôˈtärkik/ adj.
– ORIGIN early 17th cent.: from Greek *autarkeia*, from *autarkēs* 'self-sufficiency,' from *autos* 'self' + *arkein* 'suffice.'

aut·e·col·o·gy /ôtiˈkäləjē/ (also **autoecology**) ▸ n. Biology the ecological study of an individual organism, or sometimes a particular species. Contrasted with SYNECOLOGY.
– DERIVATIVES **aut·ec·o·log·i·cal** /ˌôtekəˈläjikəl, -ēkə-/ adj.

au·teur /ôˈtər/ ▸ n. a filmmaker whose personal influence and artistic control over a movie are so great that the filmmaker is regarded as the author of the movie.
– DERIVATIVES **au·teur·ism** /-ˌizəm/ n., **au·teur·ist** /-ist/ adj.
– ORIGIN 1960s: French, literally 'author.'

auth. ▸ abbr. ■ authentic. ■ author. ■ authority. ■ authorized.

au·then·tic /ôˈTHentik/ (abbr.: **auth.**) ▸ adj. **1** of undisputed origin; genuine: *the letter is now accepted as an authentic document | authentic 14th-century furniture*. ■ made or done in the traditional or original way, or in a way that faithfully resembles an original: *the restaurant serves authentic Italian meals | every detail of the movie was totally authentic*. ■ based on facts; accurate or reliable: *an authentic depiction of the situation*. ■ (in existentialist philosophy) relating to or denoting an emotionally appropriate, significant, purposive, and responsible mode of human life.
2 Music (of a church mode) comprising the notes lying between the principal note or final and the note an octave higher. Compare with PLAGAL.
– DERIVATIVES **au·then·ti·cal·ly** /-ik(ə)lē/ adv. [as submodifier] *the food is authentically Cajun*.
– ORIGIN late Middle English: via Old French from late Latin *authenticus*, from Greek *authentikos* 'principal, genuine.'

au·then·ti·cate /ôˈTHentiˌkāt/ ▸ v. [with obj.] prove or show (something, esp. a claim or an artistic work) to be true or genuine: *they were invited to authenticate artifacts from the Italian Renaissance*. ■ validate: *the nationalist statements authenticated their leadership among the local community*. ■ [no obj.] Computing (of a user or process) have one's identity verified.
– DERIVATIVES **au·then·ti·ca·tion** /ôˌTHentiˈkāSHən/ n., **au·then·ti·ca·tor** /-ˌkātər/ n.
– ORIGIN early 17th cent.: from medieval Latin *authenticat-* 'established as valid,' from the verb *authenticare*, from late Latin *authenticus* 'genuine' (see AUTHENTIC).

au·then·tic·i·ty /ˌôTHenˈtisitē/ ▸ n. the quality of being authentic: *the paper should have established the authenticity of the documents before publishing them*.

au·thi·gen·ic /ˌôTHiˈjenik/ ▸ adj. Geology (of minerals and other materials) formed in their present position. Often contrasted with ALLOGENIC.
– ORIGIN late 19th cent.: from Greek *authigenēs* 'born on the spot' + -IC.

au·thor /ˈôTHər/ (abbr.: **auth.**) ▸ n. a writer of a book, article, or report: *he is the author of several books on the subject*. ■ someone who writes books as a profession: *my favorite authors are Kurt Vonnegut and Aldous Huxley*. ■ the writings of such a person: *I had to read authors I disliked*. ■ an originator or creator of something, esp. a plan or idea: *the authors of the peace plan*.
▸ v. [with obj.] be the author of (a book or piece of writing): *she has authored several articles on wildlife*. ■ be the originator of; create: *the concept has been authored largely by insurance companies*.
– DERIVATIVES **au·tho·ri·al** /ôˈTHôrēəl/ adj.
– ORIGIN Middle English (in the sense 'a person who invents or causes something'): from Old French *autor*, from Latin *auctor*, from *augere* 'increase, originate, promote.' The spelling with *th* arose in the 15th cent., and perhaps became established under the influence of *authentic*.

USAGE In the sense 'be the author of,' the verb **author** is objected to by some traditionalists, who regard it as an awkward or pretentious substitute for *write* or *compose*. It is widespread and well established, though, especially in North America, and has been in use since the end of the 16th century.

au·thor·ess /ˈôTHəris/ ▸ n. a female author.

USAGE See usage at -ESS[1].

au·thor·ing /ˈôTHəriNG/ ▸ n. Computing the creation of programs and databases for computer applications such as computer-assisted learning or multimedia products: [as modifier] *an authoring system*.

au·thor·i·tar·i·an /əˌTHôriˈte(ə)rēən, ôˌTHär-/ ▸ adj. favoring or enforcing strict obedience to authority, esp. that of the government, at the expense of personal freedom: *the transition from an authoritarian to a democratic regime*. ■ showing a lack of concern for the wishes or opinions of others; domineering; dictatorial: *he had an authoritarian and at times belligerent manner*.
▸ n. an authoritarian person.
– DERIVATIVES **au·thor·i·tar·i·an·ism** n.

au·thor·i·ta·tive /əˈTHôriˌtātiv, əˈTHär-/ ▸ adj. **1** able to be trusted as being accurate or true; reliable: *clear, authoritative information and advice | an authoritative source*. ■ (of a text) considered to be the best of its kind and unlikely to be improved upon: *the authoritative study of mollusks*.
2 commanding and self-confident; likely to be respected and obeyed: *she had an authoritative air | his voice was calm and authoritative*. ■ proceeding from an official source and requiring compliance or obedience: *authoritative directives*.
– DERIVATIVES **au·thor·i·ta·tive·ly** adv., **au·thor·i·ta·tive·ness** n.

au·thor·i·ty /əˈTHôritē, ôˈTHär-/ (abbr.: **auth.**) ▸ n. (pl. **authorities**) **1** the power or right to give orders, make decisions, and enforce obedience: *he had absolute* **authority over** *his subordinates | positions of authority | they acted* **under the authority of** *the UN Security Council | a rebellion against those* **in authority**. ■ [often with infinitive] the right to act in a specified way, delegated from one person or organization to another: *military forces have the legal authority to arrest drug traffickers*. ■ official permission; sanction: *the money was spent without congressional authority*.
2 (often **authorities**) a person or organization having power or control in a particular, typically political or administrative, sphere: *the health authorities | the Chicago Transit Authority | the authorities ordered all foreign embassies to close | she wasn't used to dealing with authority*.
3 the power to influence others, esp. because of one's commanding manner or one's recognized knowledge about something: *he has the natural authority of one who is used to being obeyed | he spoke* **with authority** *on the subject*. ■ the confidence resulting from personal expertise: *he hit the ball with authority*. ■ a person with extensive or specialized knowledge about a subject; an expert: *she was an* **authority on** *the stock market*. ■ a book or other source able to supply reliable information or evidence, typically to settle a dispute: *the court cited a series of authorities supporting their decision*.
– PHRASES **have something on good authority** have ascertained something from a reliable source: *I have it on good authority that there is a waiting list of up to five weeks*.
– ORIGIN Middle English: from Old French *autorite*, from Latin *auctoritas*, from *auctor* 'originator, promoter' (see AUTHOR).

au·thor·i·ty fig·ure ▸ n. a person who has or represents authority: *these techniques can help parents re-establish their role as authority figures*.

au·thor·i·za·tion /ˌôTHərəˈzāSHən/ ▸ n. the action or fact of authorizing or being authorized: *the raising of revenue and the authorization of spending | power stations will have to obtain authorizations to continue their operations*. ■ a document giving permission or authority.

au·thor·ize /ˈôTHəˌrīz/ ▸ v. [with obj.] give official permission for or approval to (an undertaking or agent): *the government authorized further aircraft production* | [with obj. and infinitive] *the troops were authorized to use force*.
– ORIGIN late Middle English: from Old French *autoriser*, from medieval Latin *auctorizare*, from *auctor* 'originator, promoter' (see AUTHOR).

a

au·thor·ized /ˈôTHəˌrīzd/ ▶ **adj.** having official permission or approval: *an authorized dealer | authorized access to the computer.*

Au·thor·ized Ver·sion ▶ **n.** chiefly Brit. another name for KING JAMES BIBLE.

au·thor·ship /ˈôTHərˌSHip/ ▶ **n.** the fact or position of someone's having written a book or other written work: *an investigation into the authorship of the Gospels | joint authorship.* ■ the occupation of writing: *he took to authorship.*

au·tism /ˈôˌtizəm/ ▶ **n.** a mental condition, present from early childhood, characterized by difficulty in communicating and forming relationships with other people and in using language and abstract concepts. ■ a mental condition in which fantasy dominates over reality, as a symptom of schizophrenia and other disorders.
– DERIVATIVES **au·tist** **n.**
– ORIGIN early 20th cent.: from Greek *autos* 'self' + -ISM.

au·tis·tic /ôˈtistik/ ▶ **adj.** of, relating to, or affected by autism.
▶ **n.** an autistic person.

au·tis·tic spec·trum dis·or·der ▶ **n.** any condition in which the subject displays autistic characteristics.

au·to /ˈôtō/ ▶ **n.** (pl. **autos**) [usu. as modifier] informal an automobile: *the auto industry.*
– ORIGIN late 19th cent.: abbreviation of AUTOMOBILE.

auto- (usu. **aut-** before a vowel) ▶ **comb. form**
1 self: *autoanalysis.* ■ one's own: *autograph.* ■ by oneself or spontaneous: *autoxidation.* ■ by itself or automatic: *autofocusing.*
2 relating to cars: *autocross.*
– ORIGIN from Greek *autos* 'self.' Sense 2 is a back-formation from *automobile.*

au·to·an·ti·bod·y /ˌôtōˈantiˌbädē/ ▶ **n.** (pl. **autoantibodies**) Physiology an antibody produced by an organism in response to a constituent of its own tissues.

au·to·bahn /ˈôtəˌbän/ ▶ **n.** a German, Austrian, or Swiss expressway.
– ORIGIN 1930s: from German, from *Auto* 'automobile' + *Bahn* 'path, road.'

au·to·bi·o·graph·i·cal /ˌôtəbīəˈgrafikəl/ ▶ **adj.** (of a written work) dealing with the writer's own life: *an autobiographical account | the book is partly autobiographical.*
– DERIVATIVES **au·to·bi·o·graph·ic** /-fik/ **adj.**

au·to·bi·og·ra·phy /ˌôtəbīˈägrəfē/ ▶ **n.** (pl. **autobiographies**) an account of a person's life written by that person: *he gives a vivid description of his childhood in his autobiography.* ■ such writing as a literary genre.
– DERIVATIVES **au·to·bi·og·ra·pher** /-fər/ **n.**

au·to·ca·tal·y·sis /ˌôtōkəˈtaləsis/ ▶ **n.** Chemistry catalysis of a reaction by one of its products.
– DERIVATIVES **au·to·cat·a·lyst** /-ˈkatl-ist/ **n.**, **au·to·cat·a·lyt·ic** /-ˌkatlˈitik/ **adj.**

au·to·ceph·a·lous /ˌôtəˈsefələs/ ▶ **adj.** (of an Eastern Christian Church) appointing its own head, not subject to the authority of an external patriarch or archbishop.
– ORIGIN mid 19th cent.: from Greek *autokephalos* (from *autos* 'self' + *kephalē* 'head') + -OUS.

au·to·chrome /ˈôtəˌkrōm/ ▶ **n.** [usu. as modifier] an early form of color photography using plates coated with dyed starch grains, patented by the Lumière brothers in 1904: *the autochrome process.* ■ a color photograph made by this process.

au·toch·thon /ôˈtäkTHən/ ▶ **n.** (pl. **autochthons** or **autochthones** /-THəˌnēz/) an original or indigenous inhabitant of a place; an aborigine.
– ORIGIN late 16th cent.: from Greek, literally 'sprung from the earth,' from *autos* 'self' + *khthōn* 'earth, soil.'

au·toch·tho·nous /ôˈtäkTHənəs/ ▶ **adj.** (of an inhabitant of a place) indigenous rather than descended from migrants or colonists. ■ Geology (of a deposit or formation) formed in its present position. Often contrasted with ALLOCHTHONOUS.

au·to·clave /ˈôtəˌklāv/ ▶ **n.** a strong, heated container used for chemical reactions and other processes using high pressures and temperatures, e.g., steam sterilization.
▶ **v.** [with obj.] heat (something) in an autoclave.
– ORIGIN late 19th cent.: from French, from *auto-* 'self' + Latin *clavus* 'nail' or *clavis* 'key' (so called because it is self-fastening).

au·to·com·plete /ˌôtōkəmˈplēt/ Computing ▶ **n.** a software function that gives users the option of completing words or forms by a shorthand method on the basis of what has been typed before.
▶ **v.** [with obj.] complete (a word or form) in this way.

au·to·cor·re·la·tion /ˌôtōˌkôrəˈlāSHən/ ▶ **n.** Statistics correlation between the elements of a series and others from the same series separated from them by a given interval. ■ a calculation of such correlation.

au·toc·ra·cy /ôˈtäkrəsē/ ▶ **n.** (pl. **autocracies**) a system of government by one person with absolute power. ■ a regime based on such a principle of government. ■ a country, state, or society governed in such a way. ■ domineering rule or control: *a boss who shifts between autocracy, persuasion, and consultation.*
– ORIGIN mid 17th cent. (in the sense 'autonomy'): from Greek *autokrateia,* from *autokratēs* (see AUTOCRAT).

au·to·crat /ˈôtəˌkrat/ ▶ **n.** a ruler who has absolute power. ■ someone who insists on complete obedience from others; an imperious or domineering person.
– ORIGIN early 19th cent.: from French *autocrate,* from Greek *autokratēs,* from *autos* 'self' + *kratos* 'power.'

au·to·crat·ic /ˌôtəˈkratik/ ▶ **adj.** of or relating to a ruler who has absolute power: *the constitutional reforms threatened his autocratic power.* ■ taking no account of other people's wishes or opinions; domineering: *an autocratic management style.*
– DERIVATIVES **au·to·crat·i·cal·ly** /-ik(ə)lē/ **adv.**

au·to·cross /ˈôtōˌkrôs, -ˌkräs/ ▶ **n.** a form of competition in which cars are driven around an obstacle course, typically marked out by cones.
– ORIGIN 1960s: blend of AUTOMOBILE and CROSS-COUNTRY.

au·to-da-fé /ˌôtō də ˈfā/ ▶ **n.** (pl. **autos-da-fé**) the burning of a heretic by the Spanish Inquisition. ■ a sentence of such a kind.
– ORIGIN early 18th cent.: from Portuguese, literally 'act of the faith.'

au·to·di·al /ˈôtōˌdī(ə)l/ ▶ **n.** a function of telephonic equipment that allows for automatic dialing of preprogrammed or of randomly selected numbers: *have a telephone with autodial by your bed.*
▶ **v.** (**autodials, autodialing, autodialed**; Brit. **autodials, autodialling, autodialled**) automatically dial a telephone number, with or without human prompting: [no obj.] *it had autodialed and been online for over 2hours* | [with obj.] *if the first number is busy the modem autodials the backup number.*

au·to·dial·er /ˈôtōˌdī(ə)lər/ ▶ **n.** an electronic device that dials telephone numbers randomly or from a list and may also leave messages and request information.

au·to·di·dact /ˌôtōˈdīˌdakt/ ▶ **n.** a self-taught person.
– DERIVATIVES **au·to·di·dac·tic** /-ˌdīˈdaktik/ **adj.**
– ORIGIN mid 18th cent.: from Greek *autodidaktos* 'self-taught,' from *autos* 'self' + *didaskein* 'teach.'

au·to·e·col·o·gy /ˌôtō-iˈkäləjē/ ▶ **n.** variant spelling of AUTECOLOGY.

au·to·e·rot·ic /ˌôtō-iˈrätik/ ▶ **adj.** of or relating to sexual excitement generated by stimulating or fantasizing about one's own body.
– DERIVATIVES **au·to·e·rot·i·ci·sm** /-ˌsizəm/ **n.**

au·to·e·rot·ic as·phyx·i·a ▶ **n.** asphyxia that results from intentionally strangling oneself while masturbating, in an attempt to heighten sexual pleasure by limiting the oxygen supply to the brain.

au·to·ex·po·sure /ˈôtō-ikˈspōZHər/ ▶ **n.** a device that sets the exposure automatically on a camera or other piece of equipment. ■ the facility to set exposure automatically.

au·to·fo·cus /ˈôtōˌfōkəs/ ▶ **n.** a device that focuses a camera or other piece of equipment automatically. ■ automatic focusing.
– DERIVATIVES **au·to·fo·cus·ing** /-siNG/ **n.**

au·tog·a·my /ôˈtägəmē/ ▶ **n.** Biology self-fertilization, esp. the self-pollination of a flower.
– DERIVATIVES **au·tog·a·mous** /-məs/ **adj.**
– ORIGIN late 19th cent.: from AUTO- 'self' + Greek *-gamia* (from *gamos* 'marriage').

au·to·ge·net·ic /ˌôtōjəˈnetik/ ▶ **adj.** technical self-generated: *autogenetic succession.*

au·to·gen·ic train·ing /ôtəˈjenik/ ▶ **n.** a form of relaxation therapy involving autosuggestion.

au·tog·e·nous /ôˈtäjənəs/ ▶ **adj.** arising from within or from a thing itself. ■ (of welding) done either without solder or with a filler of the same metal as the pieces being welded.

au·to·gi·ro /ˌôtōˈjīrō/ (also **autogyro**) ▶ **n.** (pl. **autogiros**) a form of aircraft with freely rotating horizontal vanes and a propeller. It differs from a helicopter in that the vanes are not powered but rotate in the slipstream, propulsion being by a conventional mounted engine.
– ORIGIN 1920s: from Spanish, from *auto-* 'self' + *giro* 'gyration.'

au·to·graft /ˈôtəˌgraft/ ▶ **n.** a graft of tissue from one point to another of the same individual's body.

au·to·graph /ˈôtəˌgraf/ ▶ **n.** **1** a signature, esp. that of a celebrity written as a memento for an admirer: *fans surged around the car asking for autographs.*
2 a manuscript or musical score in the author's or musician's own handwriting. ■ a person's handwriting: *a songbook in Purcell's autograph.*
▶ **v.** [with obj.] (of a celebrity) write one's signature on (something); sign: *the whole team autographed a shirt for him* | (as adj. **autographed**) *an autographed photo.*
▶ **adj.** written in the author's own handwriting: *an autograph manuscript.* ■ (of a painting or sculpture) done by the artist, not by a copier.
– ORIGIN early 17th cent.: from French *autographe* or late Latin *autographum,* from Greek *autographon,* neuter of *autographos* 'written with one's own hand,' from *autos* 'self' + *graphos* 'written.'

au·tog·ra·phy /ôˈtägrəfē/ ▶ **n.** (pl. **autographies**) an autobiography: *Arthur Miller's splendid autography, Timebends.*

au·to·harp /ˈôtōˌhärp/ ▶ **n.** trademark a kind of zither with a mechanical device that allows the playing of a chord by damping all the other strings.

au·to·hyp·no·sis /ˌôtōhipˈnōsis/ ▶ **n.** induction of a hypnotic state in oneself; self-hypnosis.
– DERIVATIVES **au·to·hyp·not·ic** /-ˈnätik/ **adj.**

au·to·im·mune /ˌôtōəˈmyōōn/ ▶ **adj.** Medicine of or relating to disease caused by antibodies or lymphocytes produced against substances naturally present in the body: *the infection triggers an autoimmune response.*
– DERIVATIVES **au·to·im·mu·ni·ty** /-nitē/ **n.**

au·to·in·tox·i·ca·tion /ˌôtō-inˌtäksiˈkāSHən/ ▶ **n.** Medicine poisoning by a toxin formed within the body itself.

au·to·load /ˈôtōˌlōd/ ▶ **adj.** self-loading; semiautomatic: *24mm film in autoload cartridges.*
– DERIVATIVES **au·to·load·er** **n.**, **au·to·load·ing** **n.**

au·tol·o·gous /ôˈtäləgəs/ ▶ **adj.** (of cells or tissues) obtained from the same individual: *autologous bone marrow transplants.*

au·tol·y·sis /ôˈtäləsis/ ▶ **n.** Biology the destruction of cells or tissues by their own enzymes, esp. those released by lysosomes.
– DERIVATIVES **au·to·lyt·ic** /ˌôtlˈitik/ **adj.**

au·to·mag·ic·al·ly /ˌôtəˈmajik(ə)lē/ ▶ **adv.** informal (esp. in relation to the operation of a computer process) automatically and in a way that seems ingenious, inexplicable, or magical: *just type in the name of what you want to listen to, and it automagically appears on your computer.*
– ORIGIN 1940s: blend of AUTOMATICALLY and MAGICALLY.

au·to·mat /ˈôtəˌmat/ ▶ **n.** historical a cafeteria in which food and drink were obtained from vending machines.
– ORIGIN late 17th cent. (denoting an automaton): from German, from French *automate,* from Latin *automaton* (see AUTOMATON). The current sense dates from the early 20th cent.

au·to·mate /ˈôtəˌmāt/ ▶ **v.** [with obj.] convert (a process or facility) to largely automatic operation: *industry is investing in automating production* | (as adj. **automated**) *a fully automated process.*
– ORIGIN 1950s: back-formation from AUTOMATION.

Au·to·mat·ed Clear·ing·house /ˈôtəˌmātid ˈkli(ə)riNGˌhous/ ▶ **n.** the clearing and settlement system used by US commercial banks and other institutions.

au·to·mat·ed tell·er ma·chine (also **automatic teller machine**) (abbr.: **ATM**) ▶ **n.** a machine that automatically provides cash and performs other banking services on insertion of a special card by the account holder.

au·to·mat·ic /ˌôtəˈmatik/ ▶ **adj.** **1** (of a device or process) working by itself with little or no direct human control: *an automatic kettle that switches itself off when it boils | calibration is fully automatic.* ■ (of a firearm) self-loading and able to fire continuously until the ammunition is exhausted or the pressure on the trigger is released: *automatic weapons.* ■ (of a motor vehicle or its transmission) using gears that shift by themselves according to speed and acceleration: *a four-speed automatic gearbox.*
2 done or occurring spontaneously, without conscious thought or intention: *automatic physical functions such as breathing | "Nice to meet you," he said, with automatic politeness.* ■ occurring as a matter of course and without debate: *he is the automatic choice for the senior team.* ■ (esp. of a legal sanction) given or imposed as a necessary and

a

inevitable result of a fixed rule or particular set of circumstances: *for missing the team workout, he received an automatic one-game suspension.*
▶ **n. 1** an automatic machine or device, in particular: ■ a gun that continues firing until the ammunition is exhausted or the pressure on the trigger is released. ■ a vehicle with automatic transmission. **2** Football another term for **AUDIBLE**.
– DERIVATIVES **au·to·mat·i·cal·ly** /-ik(ə)lē/ **adv.**, **au·to·ma·tic·i·ty** /-mə'tisitē/ **n.**
– ORIGIN mid 18th cent.: from Greek *automatos* 'acting of itself' (see **AUTOMATON**) + **-IC**.

au·to·mat·ic gain con·trol (abbr.: **AGC**) ▶ **n.** Electronics a feature of certain amplifier circuits that gives a constant output over a wide range of input levels.

au·to·mat·ic pi·lot ▶ **n.** a device for keeping an aircraft on a set course without the intervention of the pilot: figurative *cruising through life **on automatic pilot**.*

au·to·mat·ic writ·ing ▶ **n.** writing said to be produced by a spiritual, occult, or subconscious agency rather than by the conscious intention of the writer.

au·to·ma·tion /ˌôtə'māsʜən/ ▶ **n.** the use of largely automatic equipment in a system of manufacturing or other production process: *unemployment due to the spread of automation* | *the automation of office tasks.*
– ORIGIN 1940s (originally US): irregular formation from **AUTOMATIC** + **-ATION**.

au·tom·a·tism /ô'tämə,tizəm/ ▶ **n.** the performance of actions without conscious thought or intention. ■ Art the avoidance of conscious intention in producing works of art, esp. by using mechanical techniques or subconscious associations. ■ an action performed unconsciously or involuntarily.
– ORIGIN mid 19th cent.: from French *automatisme*, from *automate* 'automaton,' from Greek *automatos* 'acting of itself' (see **AUTOMATON**).

au·tom·a·tize /ô'tämə,tīz/ ▶ **v.** [with obj.] (usu. as adj. **automatized**) make automatic or habitual: *the need to refresh automatized forms of literature.*
– DERIVATIVES **au·tom·a·ti·za·tion** /ô,tämәti'zāsʜən/ **n.**

au·tom·a·ton /ô'tämətən, -,tän/ ▶ **n.** (pl. **automata** /-tə/ or **automatons**) a moving mechanical device made in imitation of a human being. ■ a machine that performs a function according to a predetermined set of coded instructions, esp. one capable of a range of programmed responses to different circumstances. ■ used in similes and comparisons to refer to a person who seems to act in a mechanical or unemotional way: *she went about her preparations like an automaton.*
– ORIGIN early 17th cent.: via Latin from Greek, neuter of *automatos* 'acting of itself,' from *autos* 'self.'

au·to·mim·ic·ry /ˌôtə'mimikrē/ ▶ **n.** the mimicking or accentuation of some characteristic of one's own species as an adaptive response.

au·to·mize /'ôtə,mīz/ ▶ **v. 1** another term for **AUTOMATE**.
2 another term for **AUTOMATIZE**.

au·to·mo·bile /ˌôtəmō'bēl/ ▶ **n.** a road vehicle, typically with four wheels, powered by an internal combustion engine or electric motor and able to carry a small number of people.
– ORIGIN late 19th cent.: from French, from *auto-* 'self' + *mobile* 'mobile.'

au·to·mo·tive /ˌôtə'mōtiv/ ▶ **adj.** [attrib.] of, relating to, or concerned with motor vehicles.

au·to·nom·ic /ˌôtə'nämik/ ▶ **adj.** [attrib.] chiefly Physiology involuntary or unconscious; relating to the autonomic nervous system.
– ORIGIN mid 19th cent. (in the sense 'self-governing'): from **AUTONOMY** + **-IC**.

au·to·nom·ic nerv·ous sys·tem ▶ **n.** the part of the nervous system responsible for control of the bodily functions not consciously directed, such as breathing, the heartbeat, and digestive processes.

au·ton·o·mous /ô'tänəməs/ ▶ **adj.** (of a country or region) having self-government, at least to a significant degree: *the federation included sixteen autonomous republics.* ■ acting independently or having the freedom to do so: *an autonomous committee of the school board* | *autonomous underwater vehicles.* ■ (in Kantian moral philosophy) acting in accordance with one's moral duty rather than one's desires.
– DERIVATIVES **au·ton·o·mous·ly adv.**
– ORIGIN early 19th cent.: from Greek *autonomos* 'having its own laws' + **-OUS**.

au·ton·o·my /ô'tänəmē/ ▶ **n.** (pl. **autonomies**) (of a country or region) the right or condition of self-government, esp. in a particular sphere: *Tatarstan demanded greater autonomy within the Russian Federation.* ■ a self-governing country or region. ■ freedom from external control or influence; independence: *economic autonomy is still a long way off for many women.* ■ (in Kantian moral philosophy) the capacity of an agent to act in accordance with objective morality rather than under the influence of desires.
– DERIVATIVES **au·ton·o·mist** /-mist/ **n. & adj.**
– ORIGIN early 17th cent.: from Greek *autonomia*, from *autonomos* 'having its own laws,' from *autos* 'self' + *nomos* 'law.'

au·to·pa·thog·ra·phy /ˌôtōpə'tʜägrəfē/ ▶ **n.** (pl. **autopathographies**) an autobiography dealing primarily with the influence of a disease, disability, or psychological disorder on the author's life.
– ORIGIN blend of *autobiography* and *pathography*.

au·to·pi·lot /'ôtō,pīlət/ ▶ **n.** short for **AUTOMATIC PILOT**.

au·top·sy /'ô,täpsē/ ▶ **n.** (pl. **autopsies**) a postmortem examination to discover the cause of death or the extent of disease: [as modifier] *an autopsy report.*
▶ **v.** (**autopsies, autopsying, autopsied**) [with obj.] perform a postmortem examination on (a body or organ): (as adj. **autopsied**) *an autopsied brain.*
– ORIGIN mid 17th cent. (in the sense 'personal observation'): from French *autopsie* or modern Latin *autopsia*, from Greek, from *autoptēs* 'eyewitness,' from *autos* 'self' + *optos* 'seen.'

au·to·ra·di·o·gram /ˌôtō'rādēə,gram/ ▶ **n.** another term for **AUTORADIOGRAPH**.

au·to·ra·di·o·graph /ˌôtō'rādēə,graf/ ▶ **n.** a photograph of an object produced by radiation from radioactive material in the object and revealing the distribution or location of labeled material in the object.
▶ **v.** [with obj.] make an autoradiograph of.
– DERIVATIVES **au·to·ra·di·o·graph·ic** /-,rādēə'grafik/ **adj.**, **au·to·ra·di·og·ra·phy** /-,rādē'ägrəfē/ **n.**

au·to·ro·ta·tion /ˌôtōrō'tāsʜən/ ▶ **n.** rotation of an object caused by the flow of moving air or water around the shape of the object (e.g., a winged seed). ■ such rotation in the rotor blades of a helicopter that is descending without engine power.
– DERIVATIVES **au·to·ro·tate** /-'rōtāt/ **v.**

au·to·route /'ôtō,ro͞ot/ ▶ **n.** a highway in a French-speaking country.
– ORIGIN 1960s: from French, from *auto(mobile)* 'car' + *route* 'route.'

au·to·shap·ing /'ôtō,sʜāpiNG/ ▶ **n.** Psychology a method of conditioning in which the conditioned response has not been reinforced by reward or punishment, but is a modified instinctive response to certain stimuli.

au·to·some /'ôtə,sōm/ ▶ **n.** Biology any chromosome that is not a sex chromosome.
– DERIVATIVES **au·to·so·mal** /ˌôtō'sōməl/ **adj.**

au·to·stra·da /'ôtō,strädə/ ▶ **n.** (pl. **autostradas** or **autostrade** /-,strädē/) an Italian highway.
– ORIGIN 1920s: from Italian, from *auto* 'automobile' + *strada* 'road.'

au·to·sug·ges·tion /ˌôtōsə(g)'jesCHən/ ▶ **n.** the hypnotic or subconscious adoption of an idea that one has originated oneself, e.g. through repetition of verbal statements to oneself in order to change behavior.

au·to·tel·ic /ˌôtə'telik/ ▶ **adj.** formal (of an activity or a creative work) having an end or purpose in itself.
– ORIGIN early 20th cent.: from **AUTO-** 'self' + Greek *telos* 'end' + **-IC**.

au·tot·o·my /ô'tätəmē/ ▶ **n.** Zoology the casting off of a part of the body (e.g., the tail of a lizard) by an animal under threat.

au·to·tox·in /'ôtō,täksin/ ▶ **n.** a substance produced by an organism that is toxic to the organism itself.
– DERIVATIVES **au·to·tox·ic** /ˌôtō'täksik/ **adj.**

au·to·trans·form·er /ˌôtōtrans'fôrmər/ ▶ **n.** an electrical transformer that has a single coil winding, part of which is common to both primary and secondary circuits.

au·to·trans·plan·ta·tion /ˌôtō,transplan'tāsʜən/ ▶ **n.** transplantation of tissue from one site to another in the same individual.
– DERIVATIVES **au·to·trans·plant** /-'trans,plant/ **n.**, **au·to·trans·plant·ed** /-trans'plantid/ **adj.**

au·to·troph /'ôtə,träf, -,trōf/ ▶ **n.** Biology an organism that is able to form nutritional organic substances from simple inorganic substances such as carbon dioxide. Compare with **HETEROTROPH**.
– DERIVATIVES **au·to·troph·ic adj.**, **au·tot·ro·phy n.**

au·to·wind·er /'ôtō,wīndər/ ▶ **n.** a device that automatically advances the film in a camera after a picture has been taken.
– DERIVATIVES **au·to·wind n. & v.**

au·to·work·er /'ôtō,wərkər/ ▶ **n.** a worker in the automobile industry.

au·tox·i·da·tion /ô,täksi'dāsʜən/ ▶ **n.** Chemistry spontaneous oxidation of a substance at ambient temperatures in the presence of oxygen.
– DERIVATIVES **au·tox·i·dize** /ô'täksi,dīz/ **v.**

Au·try /'ôtrē/, Gene (1907–98), US singer and actor; full name *Orvon Gene Autry*; known as **the Singing Cowboy**. His credits include the first cowboy song recording (1929) and many musical western movies.

au·tumn /'ôtəm/ ▶ **n.** the third season of the year, when crops and fruits are gathered and leaves fall, in the northern hemisphere from September to November and in the southern hemisphere from March to May: *the countryside is ablaze with color in autumn* | [as modifier] *autumn leaves* | figurative ***he was in the autumn of his life.*** ■ Astronomy the period from the autumnal equinox to the winter solstice.
– ORIGIN late Middle English: from Old French *autompne*, or later directly from Latin *autumnus*.

au·tum·nal /ô'təmnəl/ ▶ **adj.** of, characteristic of, or occurring in autumn: *chilly autumnal weather.*
– ORIGIN late 16th cent.: from Latin *autumnalis*, from *autumnus* 'autumn.'

au·tum·nal e·qui·nox ▶ **n.** the equinox in autumn, on about September 22 in the northern hemisphere and March 20 in the southern hemisphere.

au·tumn cro·cus ▶ **n.** a crocuslike Eurasian plant of the lily family, cultivated for its autumn-blooming flowers. ● Genus *Colchicum*, family Liliaceae: several species, in particular meadow saffron.

au·tun·ite /'ôtənīt, 'ōtn,īt/ ▶ **n.** a yellow or pale green mineral occurring as square crystals that fluoresce in ultraviolet light. It is a hydrated phosphate of calcium and uranium.
– ORIGIN mid 19th cent.: from *Autun*, the name of a town in eastern France, + **-ITE**[1].

Au·vergne /ō'vern(yə), ō'vərn/ a region in south central France that was a province of the Roman Empire. The region is mountainous and contains extinct volcanic cones known as the Puys.
– ORIGIN from Latin *Arverni*, the name of a Celtic tribe that lived there in Roman times.

aux·il·ia·ry /ôg'zilyərē, -'zil(ə)rē/ ▶ **adj.** providing supplementary or additional help and support: *an auxiliary nurse* | *auxiliary airport staff.* ■ (of equipment) held in reserve: *the ship has an auxiliary power source.* ■ (of troops) engaged in the service of a nation at war but not part of the regular army, and often of foreign origin. ■ (of a sailing vessel) equipped with a supplementary engine.
▶ **n.** (pl. **auxiliaries**) a person or thing providing supplementary or additional help and support: *a nursing auxiliary* | *there are two main fuel tanks and two auxiliaries.* ■ a group of volunteers giving supplementary support to an organization or institution: *members of the Volunteer Fire Department's women's auxiliary.* ■ (**auxiliaries**) troops engaged in the service of a nation at war but not part of the regular army, and often of foreign origin. ■ Grammar an auxiliary verb. ■ a naval vessel with a supporting role, not armed for combat.
– ORIGIN late Middle English: from Latin *auxiliarius*, from *auxilium* 'help.'

aux·il·ia·ry verb ▶ **n.** Grammar a verb used in forming the tenses, moods, and voices of other verbs. See also **MODAL VERB**.

> The primary auxiliary verbs in English are *be, do,* and *have*; the modal auxiliaries are *can, could, may, might, must, shall, should, will,* and *would*.

aux·in /'ôksin/ ▶ **n.** a plant hormone that causes the elongation of cells in shoots and is involved in regulating plant growth.
– ORIGIN 1930s: coined in German from Greek *auxein* 'to increase' + **-IN**[1].

aux·o·troph /'ôksə,träf, -,trōf/ ▶ **n.** Biology a mutant organism (typically a bacterium or fungus) that requires a particular additional nutrient that the normal strain does not.
– DERIVATIVES **aux·o·troph·ic** /ˌôksə'träfik, -'trō-/ **adj.**
– ORIGIN 1950s: from Latin *auxilium* 'help' + Greek *trophos* 'feeder.'

AV ▶ **abbr.** ■ audiovisual (teaching aids). ■ Authorized Version.

Av ▶ **n.** variant spelling of **AB**[1].

av·a·da·vat /'avədə,vat/ (also **amadavat** /'am-/) ▶ **n.** a small southern Asian waxbill that is often kept as a caged bird. The male has red or green plumage and a red bill. ● Genus *Amandava*, family Estrildidae: the **red avadavat** (*A. amandava*) and the **green avadavat** (*A. formosa*).
– ORIGIN late 17th cent.: named after the city of **AHMADABAD** in India, where the birds were sold.

a·vail /ə'vāl/ ▶ **v. 1** (**avail oneself of**) use or take advantage of (an opportunity or available resource): *my daughter did not avail herself of my advice.*

2 help or benefit: [with obj.] *no amount of struggle availed Charles* | [no obj.] *the dark and narrow hiding place did not avail to save the fugitives.*
– PHRASES **avail someone nothing** archaic (of an action) be of no help at all to someone: *this protest availed her nothing.* **of little** (or **no**) **avail** not very (or not at all) effective or successful: *Latin was of little avail in the practical affairs of life.* **to little** (or **no**) **avail** with little (or no) success or benefit: *he tried to get his work recognized, but to little avail.*
– ORIGIN Middle English: from obsolete *vail* 'be of use or value' (apparently on the pattern of pairs such as *amount, mount*), from Old French *valoir*, from Latin *valere* 'be strong, be of value.'

a·vail·a·ble /ə'vāləbəl/ ▶ **adj.** able to be used or obtained; at someone's disposal: *refreshments will be available all afternoon* | *a slush fund* ***available to*** *universities.* ■ (of a person) not otherwise occupied; free to do something: *the nurse is only available at certain times* | *the minister was not available for comment.* ■ not currently involved in a sexual or romantic relationship: *there's a dearth of available women here.*
– DERIVATIVES **a·vail·a·bil·i·ty** /ə,vālə'bilitē/ **n.**
– ORIGIN late Middle English (in the senses 'effectual, serviceable' and 'legally valid'): from AVAIL + -ABLE. Sense 1 dates from the early 19th cent.

av·a·lanche /'avə,lanCH/ ▶ **n. 1** a mass of snow, ice, and rocks falling rapidly down a mountainside. ■ a large mass of any material moving rapidly downhill: *an avalanche of mud.*
2 a sudden arrival or occurrence of something in overwhelming quantities: *we have had an avalanche of applications.*
3 Physics a cumulative process in which a fast-moving ion or electron generates further ions and electrons by collision.
▶ **v.** [no obj.] **1** (of a mass of snow, ice, and rocks) descend rapidly down a mountainside. ■ [with obj.] engulf or carry off by such a mass of material: *the climbers were avalanched down the south face of the mountain.*
2 Physics undergo a rapid increase in conductivity due to an avalanche process.
– ORIGIN late 18th cent.: from French, alteration of the Alpine dialect word *lavanche* (of unknown origin), influenced by *avaler* 'descend'; compare with Italian *valanga*.

Av·a·lon /'avə,län/ (in Arthurian legend) the place to which Arthur was conveyed after death.

a·vant- /'ävänt/ ▶ **comb. form** (esp. with reference to popular music) original or innovative; avant-garde: *even in avant-rock, a song's words are usually its focus.*

a·vant-garde /,ävänt 'gärd, ,ävän/ ▶ **n.** (usu. **the avant-garde**) new and unusual or experimental ideas, esp. in the arts, or the people introducing them: *works by artists of the Russian avant-garde.*
▶ **adj.** favoring or introducing such new ideas: *a controversial avant-garde composer.*
– DERIVATIVES **a·vant-gard·ism** /-,dizəm/ **n.**, **a·vant-gard·ist** /-dist/ **n.**
– ORIGIN late Middle English (denoting the vanguard of an army): from French, literally 'vanguard.' Current senses date from the early 20th cent.

av·a·rice /'avəris/ ▶ **n.** extreme greed for wealth or material gain.
– ORIGIN Middle English: from Old French, from Latin *avaritia*, from *avarus* 'greedy.'

av·a·ri·cious /,avə'risHəs/ ▶ **adj.** having or showing an extreme greed for wealth or material gain: *a corrupt and avaricious government.*
– DERIVATIVES **av·a·ri·cious·ly adv.**, **av·a·ri·cious·ness n.**
– ORIGIN late Middle English: from Old French *avaricieux*, based on Latin *avarus* 'greedy' (see AVARICE).

a·vas·cu·lar /ā'vaskyələr, ā'vas-/ ▶ **adj.** Medicine characterized by or associated with a lack of blood vessels.

a·vast /ə'vast/ ▶ **exclam.** Nautical stop; cease: *you, young man, avast there!*
– ORIGIN early 17th cent.: from Dutch *hou'vast, houd vast* 'hold fast!'

av·a·tar /'avə,tär/ ▶ **n. 1** chiefly Hinduism a manifestation of a deity or released soul in bodily form on earth; an incarnate divine teacher. ■ an incarnation, embodiment, or manifestation of a person or idea: *he chose John Stuart Mill as the avatar of the liberal view.*
2 Computing an icon or figure representing a particular person in computer games, Internet forums, etc.
– ORIGIN from Sanskrit *avatāra* 'descent,' from *ava* 'down' + *tar-* 'to cross.'

a·vaunt /ə'vônt/ ▶ **exclam.** archaic go away: *avaunt, you worm-faced fellows of the night!*
– ORIGIN late Middle English: from an Anglo-Norman French variant of Old French *avant*, from Latin *ab* 'from' + *ante* 'before.'

a·ve /'ä,vā/ ▶ **exclam.** literary used to express good wishes on meeting or parting.
▶ **n. 1** (**Ave**) short for AVE MARIA.
2 literary a shout of welcome or farewell.
– ORIGIN Middle English: from Latin, 'fare well!,' singular imperative of *avere*.

Ave. ▶ **abbr.** Avenue.

Ave·bur·y /'āvb(ə)rē, 'āv,berē/ a village in Wiltshire, site of one of Britain's major henge monuments of the late Neolithic period.

A·ve Ma·ri·a /'ävā mə'rēə/ ▶ **n.** a prayer to the Virgin Mary used in Catholic worship. The first line is adapted from Luke 1:28. Also called HAIL MARY.
– ORIGIN Middle English: the opening words in Latin, literally 'Hail, Mary!'

a·venge /ə'venj/ ▶ **v.** [with obj.] inflict harm in return for (an injury or wrong done to oneself or another): *his determination to avenge the murder of his brother* | *they are eager to avenge last year's Super Bowl defeat.* ■ inflict such harm on behalf of (oneself or someone else previously wronged or harmed): *we must avenge our dead* | *she* ***avenged herself*** *after he broke off their engagement* | *the warrior swore he would be* ***avenged on*** *their prince.*
– DERIVATIVES **a·veng·er n.**
– ORIGIN late Middle English: from Old French *avengier*, from *a-* (from Latin *ad* 'to') + *vengier*, from Latin *vindicare* 'vindicate.'

av·ens /'avənz/ ▶ **n.** a plant of the rose family, typically having serrated, divided leaves and seeds bearing small hooks. Several kinds are grown in gardens. ● Genus *Geum*, family Rosaceae: several species, including the widespread **water avens** (*G. rivale*), with drooping pinkish flowers, and the mat-forming **alpine avens** (*G. montanum*).
– ORIGIN Middle English: from Old French *avence* (medieval Latin *avencia*), of unknown origin.

a·ven·tu·rine /ə'vencHə,rēn, -,rīn/ ▶ **n.** brownish glass containing sparkling particles of copper or gold: [as modifier] *aventurine glass.* ■ a translucent mineral containing small reflective particles, typically quartz containing mica or iron compounds, or feldspar containing hematite.
– ORIGIN early 18th cent.: from French, from Italian *avventurino*, from *avventura* 'chance' (because of its accidental discovery).

av·e·nue /'avə,n(y)o͞o/ ▶ **n. 1** a broad road in a town or city, typically having trees at regular intervals along its sides: *tree-lined avenues surround the hotel* | [in proper names] *Euclid Avenue.* ■ [in proper names] a thoroughfare running at right angles to the streets in a city laid out on a grid pattern: *7th Avenue.* ■ a tree-lined road or path, esp. one that leads to a country house or similar building: *an avenue of limes.*
2 a way of approaching a problem or making progress toward something: *three possible avenues of research suggested themselves.*
– ORIGIN early 17th cent. (sense 2): from French, feminine past participle of *avenir* 'arrive, approach,' from Latin *advenire*, from *ad-* 'toward' + *venire* 'come.'

a·ver /ə'vər/ ▶ **v.** (**avers, averring, averred**) [reporting verb] formal state or assert to be the case: [with clause] *he averred that he was innocent of the allegations* | [with direct speech] *"You're the most beautiful girl in the world," he averred.* ■ [with obj.] Law allege as a fact in support of a plea.
– ORIGIN late Middle English (in the sense 'declare or confirm to be true'): from Old French *averer*, based on Latin *ad* 'to' (implying 'cause to be') + *verus* 'true.'

av·er·age /'av(ə)rij/ (abbr.: **avg.**) ▶ **n. 1** the result obtained by adding several quantities together and then dividing this total by the number of quantities; the mean: *the housing prices there are twice the national average.* Compare with MEAN[3] (sense 1 of the noun). ■ an amount, standard, level, or rate regarded as usual or ordinary: *the month's snowfall* ***is below average*** | *they take about thirty minutes* ***on average.***
2 the apportionment of financial liability resulting from loss of or damage to a ship or its cargo. ■ reduction in the amount payable under an insurance policy, e.g., in respect of partial loss.
▶ **adj.** constituting the result obtained by adding together several quantities and then dividing this total by the number of quantities: *the average temperature in May was 64°F.* ■ of the usual or ordinary standard, level, or quantity: *a woman of average height.* ■ having qualities that are seen as typical of a particular person or thing: *the average teenager prefers comfort to high fashion.* ■ mediocre; not very good: *a very average director who made very average movies.*
▶ **v.** [with obj.] achieve or amount to as an average rate or amount over a period of time: *annual inflation averaged 2.4 percent.* ■ calculate or estimate the average of (figures or measurements): *their earnings,* ***averaged out*** *over the month, were only $62 a week.* ■ [no obj.] (**average out**) result in an even distribution; even out: *it is reasonable to hope that the results will average out.* ■ [no obj.] (**average out at/to**) result in an average figure of: *the cost should average out to about $6 per page.*
– DERIVATIVES **av·er·age·ly adv.**
– ORIGIN late 15th cent.: from French *avarie* 'damage to ship or cargo,' earlier 'customs duty,' from Italian *avaria*, from Arabic *'awār* 'damage to goods'; the suffix *-age* is on the pattern of *damage*. Originally denoting a charge or customs duty payable by the owner of goods to be shipped, the term later denoted the financial liability from goods lost or damaged at sea, and specifically the equitable apportionment of this between the owners of the vessel and the cargo (late 16th cent.); this gave rise to the general sense of the equalizing out of gains and losses by calculating the mean (mid 18th cent).

a·ver·ment /ə'vərmənt/ ▶ **n.** formal an affirmation or allegation. ■ Law a formal statement by a party in a case of a fact or circumstance that the party offers to prove or substantiate.
– ORIGIN late Middle English: from Old French *averrement, averement*, from *averer* 'declare true' (see AVER).

A·ver·ro·ës /ə'verō,ēz, ,avə'rō-ēz/ (*c.*1126–98), Islamic philosopher, judge, and physician, born in Spain; Arabic name *ibn-Rushd*. His highly influential commentaries on Aristotle sought to reconcile the Greek philosophical tradition with the Arabic.

a·verse /ə'vərs/ ▶ **adj.** [predic., usu. with negative] (**averse to**) having a strong dislike of or opposition to something: *as a former CIA director, he is not averse to secrecy* | [in combination] *the bank's approach has been risk-averse.*
– ORIGIN late 16th cent.: from Latin *aversus* 'turned away from,' past participle of *avertere* (see AVERT).

> **USAGE** The widespread phrase for expressing dislike, opposition, or hostility (to things, usually not people) is **averse to.** Similarly, one may be said to have an **aversion to** (usually not **aversion from**) certain things or activities (but usually not people): *Katherine was known for her* ***aversion to*** *flying, but she was brave and boarded the plane anyway.* **Averse from** is found more often in British than US English, following the prescription of Samuel Johnson and other traditionalists, who have condemned **averse to** as nonsensical (the Latin origin of **averse** has the meaning 'turn from'). In the US, however, **averse to** is by far the more common occurrence. See also usage at ADVERSE.

a·ver·sion /ə'vərZHən/ ▶ **n.** a strong dislike or disinclination: *he had a deep-seated* ***aversion to*** *most forms of exercise.* ■ someone or something that arouses such feelings.
– DERIVATIVES **a·ver·sive** /-siv, -ziv/ **adj.**
– ORIGIN late 16th cent. (originally denoting the action of turning away or averting one's eyes): from Latin *aversio(n-)*, from *avertere* 'turn away from' (see AVERT).

a·ver·sion ther·a·py ▶ **n.** a type of behavior therapy designed to make a patient give up an undesirable habit by causing them to associate it with an unpleasant effect.

a·vert /ə'vərt/ ▶ **v.** [with obj.] **1** turn away (one's eyes or thoughts): *she averted her eyes during the more violent scenes.*
2 prevent or ward off (an undesirable occurrence): *talks failed to avert a rail strike.*
– ORIGIN late Middle English (in the sense 'divert or deter someone from a place or a course of action'): from Latin *avertere*, from *ab-* 'from' + *vertere* 'to turn'; reinforced by Old French *avertir*.

A·ves /'ävāz/ Zoology a class of vertebrates that comprises the birds.
– ORIGIN Latin, plural of *avis* 'bird.'

A·ves·ta /ə'vestə/ ▶ **n.** the sacred writings of Zoroastrianism, compiled in the 4th century AD.
– ORIGIN Persian.

A·ves·tan /ə'vestən/ ▶ **adj.** of or relating to the Avesta or to the ancient Indo-Iranian language in which it is written, closely related to Vedic Sanskrit.
▶ **n.** the Avestan language.

avg. ▶ **abbr.** average.

av·gas /'av,gas/ ▶ **n.** aircraft fuel.
– ORIGIN mid 20th cent.: from *av(iation)* + GAS.

a·vi·an /'āvēən/ ▶ **adj.** of or relating to birds: *avian tuberculosis.*
▶ **n.** a bird.
– ORIGIN late 19th cent.: from Latin *avis* 'bird' + -AN.

a

a·vi·an in·flu·en·za (also **avian flu**) ▶ **n.** the technical name for **BIRD FLU**.

a·vi·ar·y /ˈāvēˌerē/ ▶ **n.** (pl. **aviaries**) a large cage, building, or enclosure for keeping birds in.
– ORIGIN late 16th cent.: from Latin *aviarium*, from *avis* 'bird.'

a·vi·ate /ˈāvēˌāt/ ▶ **v.** pilot or fly in an airplane: [with obj.] *an aircraft that can be aviated without effort* | [no obj.] *there are fewer opportunities to aviate in winter.*
– ORIGIN late 19th cent.: back-formation from **AVIATION**.

a·vi·a·tion /ˌāvēˈāSHən/ ▶ **n.** the flying or operating of aircraft: [as modifier] *the aviation industry* | *aviation engineering.*
– ORIGIN mid 19th cent.: from French, formed irregularly from Latin *avis* 'bird.'

a·vi·a·tor /ˈāvēˌātər/ ▶ **n.** dated a pilot.

a·vi·a·tor glass·es ▶ **n.** a style of sunglasses with thin wire frames and large lenses.

a·vi·a·trix /ˌāvēˈātriks/ ▶ **n.** (pl. **aviatrices** /-trisēz/) dated a female pilot.

Av·i·cen·na /ˌavəˈsenə/ (980–1037), Islamic philosopher and physician, born in Persia; Arabic name *ibn-Sina*. His philosophical system was the major influence on the development of scholasticism.

a·vic·u·lar·i·um /əˌvikyəˈle(ə)rēəm/ ▶ **n.** (pl. **avicularia** /-ˈle(ə)rēə/) Zoology (in some bryozoans) any of a number of modified zooids that take the form of a pair of snapping jaws resembling a bird's head, serving to prevent other organisms from settling on the colony. Compare with **VIBRACULUM**.
– ORIGIN mid 19th cent.: modern Latin, from *avicula*, diminutive of *avis* 'bird.'

a·vi·cul·ture /ˈāviˌkəlCHər, ˈavi-/ ▶ **n.** the breeding and rearing of birds.
– DERIVATIVES **a·vi·cul·tur·al** /ˌāviˈkəlCHərəl, ˌavi-/ **adj.**, **a·vi·cul·tur·al·ist** /ˌāviˈkəlCHərəlist, ˌavi-/ **n.**, **a·vi·cul·tur·ist** /-rist/ **n.**
– ORIGIN early 20th cent.: from Latin *avis* 'bird' + **CULTURE**.

av·id /ˈavid/ ▶ **adj.** having or showing a keen interest in or enthusiasm for something: *an avid reader of science fiction* | *she took an avid interest in the project.* ■ (**avid for**) having an eager desire for something: *she was avid for information about the murder inquiry.*
– DERIVATIVES **av·id·ly adv.**
– ORIGIN mid 18th cent.: from French *avide* or Latin *avidus*, from *avere* 'crave.'

av·i·din /ˈavidin/ ▶ **n.** Biochemistry a protein found in raw egg white, which combines with biotin and hinders its absorption.
– ORIGIN 1940s: from **AVID** + **-IN**[1].

a·vid·i·ty /əˈviditē/ ▶ **n.** extreme eagerness or enthusiasm: *he read detective stories with avidity.* ■ Biochemistry the overall strength of binding between an antibody and an antigen.
– ORIGIN late Middle English: from French *avidité* or Latin *aviditas*, from *avidus* 'eager, greedy.'

a·vi·fau·na /ˌāvəˈfônə, ˌavə-/ ▶ **n.** the birds of a particular region, habitat, or geological period.
– DERIVATIVES **a·vi·fau·nal adj.**
– ORIGIN late 19th cent.: from Latin *avis* 'bird' + **FAUNA**.

A·vi·gnon /ˌävēnˈyôN/ a city on the Rhône River in southeastern France; pop. 94,787 (2006). From 1309 until 1377, it was the residence of the popes during their exile from Rome, and it was papal property until the French Revolution.

Á·vi·la, Te·re·sa of see **TERESA OF ÁVILA, ST.**

a·vi·on·ics /ˌāvēˈäniks/ ▶ **plural n.** [usu. treated as sing.] electronics as applied to aviation. ■ electronic equipment fitted in an aircraft.
– ORIGIN 1940s: blend of **AVIATION** and **ELECTRONICS**.

a·vir·u·lent /āˈvir(y)ələnt/ ▶ **adj.** (of a microorganism) not virulent.

a·vi·ta·min·o·sis /āˌvītəmiˈnōsis/ ▶ **n.** (pl. **avitaminoses** /-sēz/) Medicine a condition resulting from a deficiency of one or more particular vitamins.

av·o·ca·do /ˌavəˈkädō, ˌävə-/ ▶ **n.** (pl. **avocados**) **1** a pear-shaped fruit with a rough leathery skin, smooth oily edible flesh, and a large stone: *serve with slices of avocado.* Also called **ALLIGATOR PEAR**. ■ a light green color like that of the flesh of avocados. **2** the tropical evergreen tree that bears this fruit. It is native to Central America and widely cultivated elsewhere. ● *Persea americana*, family Lauraceae.
– ORIGIN mid 17th cent.: from Spanish, alteration (influenced by *avocado* 'advocate') of *aguacate*, from Nahuatl *ahuacatl*.

av·o·ca·tion /ˌavəˈkāSHən/ ▶ **n.** a hobby or minor occupation.
– DERIVATIVES **av·o·ca·tion·al** /-SHənl/ **adj.**
– ORIGIN mid 17th cent.: from Latin *avocatio(n-)*, from *avocare* 'call away,' from *ab-* 'from' + *vocare* 'to call.'

av·o·cet /ˈavəˌset/ ▶ **n.** a long-legged wading bird with a slender upturned bill and strikingly patterned plumage. ● Genus *Recurvirostra*, family Recurvirostridae: four species, including the **American avocet** (*R. americana*), which has black and white plumage.
– ORIGIN late 17th cent.: from French *avocette*, from Italian *avosetta*.

A·vo·ga·dro /ˌävəˈgädˌrō, ˌävō-/, Amedeo (1776–1856), Italian chemist and physicist. His law, formulated in 1811, was used to derive both molecular weights and a system of atomic weights.

A·vo·ga·dro's law Chemistry a law stating that equal volumes of gases at the same temperature and pressure contain equal numbers of molecules.

A·vo·ga·dro's num·ber (also **Avogadro's constant**) Chemistry the number of atoms or molecules in one mole of a substance, equal to 6.023×10^{23}.

a·void /əˈvoid/ ▶ **v.** [with obj.] **1** keep away from or stop oneself from doing (something): *avoid excessive exposure to the sun.* ■ contrive not to meet (someone): *boys lined up to meet Gloria, but avoided her bossy sister.* ■ not go to or through (a place): *this route avoids downtown Boston.* ■ prevent from happening: *make the necessary adjustments to avoid an accident.*
2 Law repudiate, nullify, or render void (a decree or contract).
– PHRASES **avoid someone/something like the plague** try hard to avoid someone or something: *a place that Robyn normally avoided like the plague.*
– DERIVATIVES **a·void·ance** /əˈvoidns/ **n.**, **a·void·er n.**
– ORIGIN late Middle English: from Old French *evuider* 'clear out, get rid of,' from *vuide* 'empty' (see **VOID**).

a·void·a·ble /əˈvoidəbəl/ ▶ **adj.** able to be avoided or prevented: *the accident was entirely avoidable* | *avoidable costs.*
– DERIVATIVES **a·void·a·bly adv.**

a·void·ance re·la·tion·ship ▶ **n.** a familial relationship that is forbidden according to rules operating in some traditional societies. In Australian Aboriginal society, for example, mothers-in-law and sons-in-law may not meet face to face or speak directly with one another.

a·void·ant /əˈvoidənt/ ▶ **adj.** Psychology relating to or denoting a type of personality or behavior characterized by the avoidance of intimacy or social interaction.

av·oir·du·pois /ˌävərdəˈpoiz/ ▶ **n.** a system of weights based on a pound of 16 ounces or 7,000 grains, widely used in English-speaking countries: [as modifier] *avoirdupois weights* | [postpositive] *a pound avoirdupois.* Compare with **TROY**. ■ humorous weight; heaviness: *she was putting on the avoirdupois like nobody's business.*
– ORIGIN Middle English (denoting merchandise sold by weight): from Old French *aveir de peis* 'goods of weight,' from *aveir* 'to have' (infinitive used as a noun, from Latin *habere*) + *peis* 'weight' (see **POISE**[1]).

A·von /ˈävən, ˈāˌvän/ **1** a river in central England that rises near the border between the counties of Leicestershire and Northamptonshire and flows 96 miles (154 km) southwest through Stratford to the Severn River.
2 a river in southwestern England that rises near the Gloucestershire–Wiltshire border and flows 75 miles (121 km) through Bath and Bristol to the Severn River.
3 a county in southwestern England; county town, Bristol.

Av·on·dale /ˈavənˌdāl/ a city in south central Arizona, a western suburb of Phoenix; pop. 81,299 (est. 2008).

a·vouch /əˈvouCH/ ▶ **v.** [with obj.] archaic affirm or assert.
– DERIVATIVES **a·vouch·ment n.**
– ORIGIN late 15th cent.: from Old French *avochier*, from Latin *advocare* 'summon in defense,' from *ad-* 'to' + *vocare* 'to call.'

a·vow /əˈvou/ ▶ **v.** [reporting verb] assert or confess openly: [with clause] *he avowed that he had voted Republican in every election* | [with obj.] *he avowed his change of faith.*
– DERIVATIVES **a·vow·al** /əˈvouəl/ **n.**
– ORIGIN Middle English (in the senses 'acknowledge, approve' and 'vouch for'): from Old French *avouer* 'acknowledge,' from Latin *advocare* 'summon in defense' (see **AVOUCH**).

a·vowed /əˈvoud/ ▶ **adj.** [attrib.] that has been asserted, admitted, or stated publicly: *an avowed atheist* | *they came to power with the avowed aim of promoting religious toleration.*
– DERIVATIVES **a·vow·ed·ly** /əˈvou-idlē/ **adv.**

a·vul·sion /əˈvəlSHən/ ▶ **n.** chiefly Medicine the action of pulling or tearing away. ■ Law the sudden separation of land from one property and its attachment to another, esp. by flooding or a change in the course of a river. Compare with **ALLUVION**.
– DERIVATIVES **a·vulse** /əˈvəls/ **v.**
– ORIGIN early 17th cent.: from Latin *avulsion-*, from the verb *avellere*, from *ab-* 'from' + *vallere* 'pluck.'

a·vun·cu·lar /əˈvəNGkyələr/ ▶ **adj. 1** of or relating to an uncle. ■ kind and friendly toward a younger or less experienced person: *an avuncular manner.*
2 Anthropology of or relating to the relationship between men and their siblings' children.
– ORIGIN mid 19th cent.: from Latin *avunculus* 'maternal uncle,' diminutive of *avus* 'grandfather.'

a·vun·cu·late /əˈvəNGkyəlit, -ˌlāt/ ▶ **n.** (**the avunculate**) Anthropology the special relationship in some societies between a man and his sister's son.
– ORIGIN early 20th cent.: from Latin *avunculus* 'maternal uncle' + **-ATE**[2].

aw /ô/ ▶ **exclam.** used to express mild protest, entreaty, commiseration, or disapproval: *aw, Dad, that's not fair.*
– ORIGIN natural exclamation: first recorded in American English in the mid 19th cent.

AWACS /ˈāˌwaks/ ▶ **n.** a long-range airborne radar system for detecting enemy aircraft and missiles and directing attacks on them. ■ an aircraft equipped with this radar system.
– ORIGIN 1960s: acronym from *airborne warning and control system.*

Awadh variant spelling of **OUDH**.

a·wait /əˈwāt/ ▶ **v.** [with obj.] (of a person) wait for (an event): *we await the proposals with impatience* | *prisoners awaiting trial* | [as adj., with submodifier] (**awaited**) *an eagerly awaited debut.* ■ (of an event or circumstance) be in store for (someone): *many dangers await them.*
– ORIGIN Middle English: from Anglo-Norman French *awaitier*, from *a-* (from Latin *ad* 'to, at') + *waitier* 'to wait.'

a·wake /əˈwāk/ ▶ **v.** (past **awoke** /əˈwōk/; past participle **awoken** /əˈwōkən/) [no obj.] stop sleeping; wake from sleep: *she awoke to find the streets covered in snow.* ■ [with obj.] cause (someone) to wake from sleep: *my screams awoke my parents.* ■ regain consciousness: *I awoke six hours after the operation.* ■ (**awake to**) become aware of; come to a realization of: *the authorities finally awoke to the extent of the problem.* ■ make or become active again: *there were echoes and scents that awoke some memory in me.*
▶ **adj.** [predic.] not asleep: *the noise might keep you awake at night.* ■ (**awake to**) aware of: *too few are awake to the dangers.*
– ORIGIN Old English *āwæcnan, āwacian*, both used in the sense 'come out of sleep' (see **A-**[2], **WAKE**[1]).

a·wak·en /əˈwākən/ ▶ **v.** [with obj.] rouse from sleep; cause to stop sleeping: *Anna was awakened by the telephone.* ■ [no obj.] stop sleeping: *he sighed but did not awaken.* ■ rouse (a feeling): *different images can awaken new emotions within us.* ■ (**awaken someone to**) make someone aware of (something) for the first time: *the movie helped to awaken the public to the horrors of apartheid.*
– ORIGIN Old English *onwæcnan*, from *on* 'on' + **WAKEN**.

a·wak·en·ing /əˈwāk(ə)niNG/ ▶ **n.** [in sing.] an act or moment of becoming suddenly aware of something: *the war came as a rude awakening to the hardships of life.* ■ formal an act of waking from sleep. ■ the beginning or rousing of something: *the awakening of democracy in Eastern Europe.*
▶ **adj.** [attrib.] coming into existence or awareness: *his awakening desire* | *an awakening conscience.*

a·ward /əˈwôrd/ ▶ **v.** [with two objs.] give or order the giving of (something) as an official payment, compensation, or prize to (someone): *he was awarded the Purple Heart* | *the 3.5 percent pay raise was awarded to the staff.* ■ grant or assign (a contract or commission) to (a person or organization).
▶ **n.** a prize or other mark of recognition given in honor of an achievement: *the company's annual award for high-quality service* | [as modifier] *an award ceremony.* ■ an amount of money paid to someone as an official payment, compensation, or grant: *a generous award given to promising young dancers.* ■ the action of giving a payment, compensation, or prize: *the award of an honorary doctorate* | *an award of damages.*
– DERIVATIVES **a·ward·ee** /əˌwôrˈdē/ **n.**, **a·ward·er n.**
– ORIGIN late Middle English (in the sense 'issue a judicial decision,' also denoting the decision itself): from Anglo-Norman French *awarder*, variant of Old French *esguarder* 'consider, ordain,' from *es-* (from Latin *ex* 'thoroughly') + *guarder* 'watch (over),' based on a word of Germanic origin related to **WARD**; compare with **GUARD**.

a·ware /ə'we(ə)r/ ▶ **adj.** [predic.] having knowledge or perception of a situation or fact: *most people are **aware of** the dangers of sunbathing* | ***I am well aware of** the problem* | [with clause] *he was aware that a problem existed* | ***as far as I'm aware**, no one has complained.* ■ [with adverbial] concerned and well-informed about a particular situation or development: *unless everyone becomes more **environmentally aware**, catastrophe is inevitable* | *a **politically aware** electorate.*
– ORIGIN Old English *gewær*; related to German *gewahr*, also to **WARE²**.

a·ware·ness /ə'we(ə)rnis/ ▶ **n.** knowledge or perception of a situation or fact: *we need to raise public awareness of the issue.* ■ concern about and well-informed interest in a particular situation or development: *a growing environmental awareness.*

a·wash /ə'wôsʜ, ə'wäsʜ/ ▶ **adj.** [predic.] covered or flooded with water, esp. seawater or rain: *the boat rolled violently, its decks awash.* ■ containing large numbers or amounts of someone or something: *the city was **awash with** journalists.* ■ level with the surface of water, esp. the sea, so that it just washes over: *a rock awash outside the reef entrance.*

a·way /ə'wā/ ▶ **adv. 1** to or at a distance from a particular place, person, or thing: *she landed badly, and crawled away* | *they walked **away from** the church in silence* | *Bernice pushed him away* | *we'll be away for four nights* | *there's a river **not far away**.* ■ at a specified distance: *when he was ten or twelve feet away, he stopped* | *a loud explosion **a short distance away*** | *we have had patients **from as far away as** Toronto.* ■ at a specified future distance in time: *the wedding is only weeks away.* ■ toward a lower level; downward: *in front of them the land fell away to the river.* ■ conceptually to one side, so as no longer to be the focus of attention: *the museum has shifted its emphasis **away from** research toward exhibitions.*
2 into an appropriate place for storage or safekeeping: *he put away the lawn furniture* | *Philip locked away all the cash every night.* ■ toward or into nonexistence: *the sound of hoofbeats died away* | *Marie felt her distress ebbing away.*
3 constantly, persistently, or continuously: *there was little Edgar crooning away* | *have your camera ready and click away when you spot something.*
▶ **adj.** (of a sports competition) played at the opponents' grounds: *tomorrow night's away game at Yankee Stadium.*
– PHRASES **away with** said as an exhortation to overcome or be rid of something; let us be rid of: *away with poverty!*
– ORIGIN Old English *onweg*, *aweg* 'on one's way' (see **A-²**, **WAY**).

a·way mes·sage ▶ **n.** a voice or text message directed to callers of a cellular phone whose owner cannot answer.

awe /ô/ ▶ **n.** a feeling of reverential respect mixed with fear or wonder: *they gazed in awe at the small mountain of diamonds* | *the sight filled me with awe* | *his staff members **are in awe of** him.* ■ archaic capacity to inspire awe: *is it any wonder that Christmas Eve has lost its awe?*
▶ **v.** [with obj.] (usu. **be awed**) inspire with awe: *they were both awed by the vastness of the forest.*
– ORIGIN Old English *ege* 'terror, dread, awe,' replaced in Middle English by forms related to Old Norse *agi*.

awed /ôd/ ▶ **adj.** filled with awe or wonder: *he spoke in a hushed, awed whisper* | *I watched her in awed silence.*

a·weigh /ə'wā/ ▶ **adj.** Nautical (of an anchor) raised just clear of the sea or riverbed.
– ORIGIN early 17th cent.: from **A-²** 'on' + **WEIGH¹**.

awe-in·spir·ing ▶ **adj.** arousing awe through being impressive, formidable, or magnificent: *Michelangelo's awe-inspiring masterpiece.*

awe·some /'ôsəm/ ▶ **adj.** extremely impressive or daunting; inspiring great admiration, apprehension, or fear: *the awesome power of the atomic bomb.* ■ informal extremely good; excellent: *the band is truly awesome!*
– DERIVATIVES **awe·some·ly** adv., **awe·some·ness** n.
– ORIGIN late 16th cent. (in the sense 'filled with awe'): from **AWE** + **-SOME¹**.

awe·struck /'ô,strək/ (also **awestricken** /'ô,strikən/) ▶ **adj.** filled with or revealing awe: *people were awestruck by the pictures sent back to earth.*

aw·ful /'ôfəl/ ▶ **adj. 1** very bad or unpleasant: *the place smelled awful* | *I look awful in a swimsuit* | *an awful speech.* ■ extremely shocking; horrific: *awful, bloody images.* ■ [attrib.] used to emphasize the extent of something, esp. something unpleasant or negative: *I've made an awful fool of myself.* ■ (of a person) very unwell, troubled, or unhappy: *I felt awful for being so angry with him* | *you look awful—you should go and lie down.*
2 archaic inspiring reverential wonder or fear.
▶ **adv.** [as submodifier] informal awfully; very: *we're an awful long way from the main road.*
– PHRASES **an awful lot** a very large amount; a great deal: *we've had an awful lot of letters* | *you've still got an awful lot to learn.*
– DERIVATIVES **aw·ful·ness** n.
– ORIGIN Old English (see **AWE**, **-FUL**).

aw·ful·ize /'ôfə,līz/ ▶ **v.** [with obj.] informal imagine (a situation) to be as bad as it can possibly be: *I awfulized the upcoming confrontation I was planning to have with my boss.*

aw·ful·ly /'ôf(ə)lē/ ▶ **adv. 1** [as submodifier] (used esp. in spoken English) very: *I'm awfully sorry to bother you so late* | *an awfully nice man.*
2 very badly or unpleasantly: *we played awfully.*

a·while /ə'(h)wīl/ ▶ **adv.** for a short time: *stand here awhile.*
– ORIGIN Old English *āne hwīle* '(for) a while.'

> **USAGE** The adverb **awhile**, meaning 'for a short time,' should be written as one word (*we paused awhile*). The noun phrase, meaning 'a period of time,' especially when preceded by a preposition, should be written as two words (*Margaret rested for a while; we'll be there in a while*). See also usage at **WORTHWHILE**.

a·whirl /ə'(h)wərl/ ▶ **adj.** [predic.] in a whirl; whirling: *her mind was **awhirl with** images.*

awk·ward /'ôkwərd/ ▶ **adj. 1** causing difficulty; hard to do or deal with: *one of the most awkward jobs is painting a ceiling* | *some awkward questions* | *the wheelbarrow can be awkward to maneuver.* ■ deliberately unreasonable or uncooperative: *you're being damned awkward!*
2 causing or feeling embarrassment or inconvenience: *he had put her in a very awkward situation.*
3 not smooth or graceful; ungainly: *Luther's awkward movements impeded his progress* | *she was long-legged and rather awkward.* ■ uncomfortable or abnormal: *make sure the baby isn't sleeping in an awkward position.*
– DERIVATIVES **awk·ward·ly** adv.
– ORIGIN late Middle English (in the sense 'the wrong way around, upside down'): from dialect *awk* 'backward, perverse, clumsy' (from Old Norse *afugr* 'turned the wrong way') + **-WARD**.

awk·ward age ▶ **n.** the period of adolescence marked by self-consciousness and moody behavior.

awk·ward·ness /'ôkwərdnis/ ▶ **n.** the quality of being awkward: *there was a moment of awkwardness* | *the awkwardness of youth.*

awl /ôl/ ▶ **n.** a small pointed tool used for piercing holes, esp. in leather.
– ORIGIN Old English *æl*, of Germanic origin; related to German *Ahle*.

awl

awn /ôn/ ▶ **n.** Botany a stiff bristle, esp. one of those growing from the ear or flower of barley, rye, and many grasses.
– DERIVATIVES **awned** adj.
– ORIGIN Old English, from Old Norse *ǫgn*; related to Swedish *agn*, Danish *avn*.

awn·ing /'ôniɴɢ/ ▶ **n.** a sheet of canvas or other material stretched on a frame and used to keep the sun or rain off a storefront, window, doorway, or deck.
– ORIGIN early 17th cent. (originally in nautical use): of unknown origin.

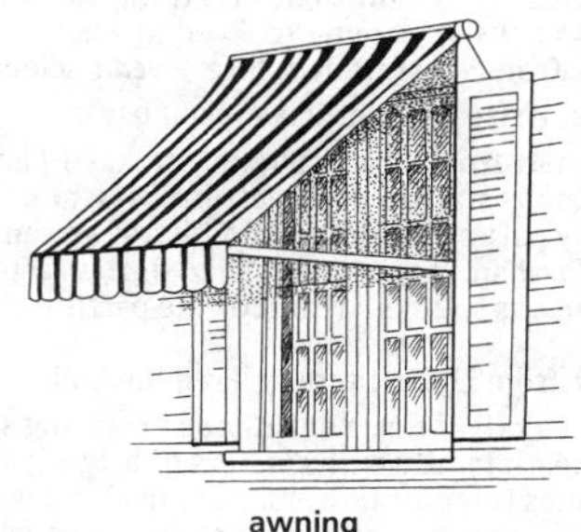

awning

a·woke /ə'wōk/ past of **AWAKE**.

a·wo·ken /ə'wōkən/ past participle of **AWAKE**.

AWOL /'ā,wôl/ ▶ **adj.** [predic.] Military absent from one's post but without intent to desert: *the men have gone AWOL* | humorous *now the parrot has **gone AWOL**.*
– ORIGIN 1920s: acronym from *absent without (official) leave*.

a·wry /ə'rī/ ▶ **adv. & adj.** away from the appropriate, planned, or expected course; amiss: [as adv.] *many youthful romances **go awry*** | [as predic. adj.] *I got the impression that something was awry.* ■ out of the normal or correct position; askew: [as predic. adj.] *he was hatless, his silver hair awry.*
– ORIGIN late Middle English: from **A-²** 'on' + **WRY**.

aw-shucks ▶ **adj.** [attrib.] informal (of a personal quality or manner) self-deprecating and shy: *his aw-shucks niceness disguised his conniving nature.*
– ORIGIN late 20th cent.: from **AW** + *shucks* (see **SHUCK**).

ax /aks/ (also **axe**) ▶ **n. 1** a tool typically used for chopping wood, usually a steel blade attached at a right angle to a wooden handle. ■ a measure intended to reduce costs drastically, esp. one that involves elimination of staff: *thirty workers **are facing the ax** in the assembly department.*
2 informal a musical instrument, esp. one played by a jazz or rock musician.
▶ **v.** [with obj.] **1** end, cancel, or dismiss suddenly and ruthlessly: *the company is axing 125 jobs* | *2,500 staff were axed as part of the realignment.* ■ reduce (costs or services) drastically: *the candidates all promised to ax government spending.*
2 cut or strike with an ax, esp. violently or destructively: *the door had been axed by the firefighters.*
– PHRASES **have an ax to grind** have a self-serving reason for doing or being involved in something: *she joined the board because she had an ax to grind with the school system.*
– ORIGIN Old English *æx*, of Germanic origin; related to Dutch *aaks* and German *Axt*.

ax 1

ax·el /'aksəl/ (also **Axel**) ▶ **n.** Figure Skating a jump with a forward takeoff from the forward outside edge of one skate to the backward outside edge of the other, with one and a half turns in the air.
– ORIGIN 1930s: named after *Axel* R. Paulsen (1885–1938), Norwegian skater.

a·xen·ic /ā'zēnik, ā'zen-/ ▶ **adj.** chiefly Botany of, relating to, or denoting a culture that is free from living organisms other than the species required.
– DERIVATIVES **a·xen·i·cal·ly** /-ik(ə)lē/ adv.
– ORIGIN 1940s: from *a-* 'not' + Greek *xenikos* 'alien, strange' + **-IC**.

ax·es /'ak,sēz/ plural form of **AXIS**.

ax·i·al /'aksēəl/ ▶ **adj.** of, forming, or relating to an axis: *the main axial road.* ■ around an axis: *the axial rotation rate of the earth.*
– DERIVATIVES **ax·i·al·ly** adv.

ax·il /'aksəl/ ▶ **n.** Botany the upper angle between a leaf stalk or branch and the stem or trunk from which it is growing.
– ORIGIN late 18th cent.: from Latin *axilla* 'armpit' (see **AXILLA**).

ax·il·la /ak'silə/ ▶ **n.** (pl. **axillae** /ak'silē/) Anatomy the space below the shoulder through which vessels and nerves enter and leave the upper arm; a person's armpit. ■ Botany an axil.
– ORIGIN early 17th cent.: from Latin, diminutive of *ala* 'wing.'

axil

ax·il·lar·y /'aksə,lerē/ ▶ **adj.** Anatomy of or relating to the armpit: *enlargement of the axillary lymph nodes.* ■ Botany in or growing from an axil: *axillary shoots.* Often contrasted with **TERMINAL**.

ax·il·lar·y bud ▶ **n.** a bud that grows from the axil of a leaf and may develop into a branch or flower cluster. Also called **LATERAL BUD**.

ax·i·om /'aksēəm/ ▶ **n.** a statement or proposition that is regarded as being established, accepted, or self-evidently true: *the axiom that supply equals demand.* ■ chiefly Mathematics a statement or proposition on which an abstractly defined structure is based.
– ORIGIN late 15th cent.: from French *axiome* or Latin *axioma*, from Greek *axiōma* 'what is thought fitting,' from *axios* 'worthy.'

ax·i·o·mat·ic /,aksēə'matik/ ▶ **adj.** self-evident or unquestionable: *it is **axiomatic that** dividends have to be financed.* ■ [attrib.] chiefly Mathematics relating to or containing axioms.
– DERIVATIVES **ax·i·o·mat·i·cal·ly** /-ik(ə)lē/ adv.
– ORIGIN late 18th cent.: from Greek *axiōmatikos*, from *axiōma* 'what is thought fitting' (see **AXIOM**).

a

ax·i·on /ˈaksēˌän/ ▶ **n.** Physics a hypothetical subatomic particle postulated to account for the rarity of processes that break charge-parity symmetry. It is very light, electrically neutral, and pseudoscalar.
– ORIGIN 1970s: from **AXIAL** + **-ON**.

ax·is /ˈaksis/ ▶ **n.** (pl. **axes** /ˈaksēz/) **1** an imaginary line about which a body rotates: *the earth revolves on its axis once every 24 hours.* ■ Geometry an imaginary straight line passing through the center of a symmetrical solid, and about which a plane figure can be conceived as rotating to generate the solid. ■ an imaginary line that divides something into equal or roughly equal halves, esp. in the direction of its greatest length.
2 Mathematics a fixed reference line for the measurement of coordinates: *the variable that is thought of as a cause is placed on the horizontal axis, and the variable that is thought of as an effect on the vertical axis.*
3 a straight central part in a structure to which other parts are connected. ■ Botany the central column of an inflorescence or other growth. ■ Zoology the skull and backbone of a vertebrate animal.
4 Anatomy the second cervical vertebra, below the atlas at the top of the backbone.
5 an agreement or alliance between two or more countries that forms a center for an eventual larger grouping of nations: *the Anglo-American axis.* ■ **(the Axis)** the alliance of Germany and Italy formed before and during World War II, later extended to include Japan and other countries: [as modifier] *the Axis Powers.*
– ORIGIN late Middle English: from Latin, 'axle, pivot.'

ax·is deer (also **axis**) ▶ **n.** a deer that has lyre-shaped antlers and a yellowish-brown coat with white spots, native to India and Sri Lanka. ● *Cervus axis*, family Cervidae.
– ORIGIN early 17th cent.: *axis* from Latin, the name of an Indian animal mentioned by Pliny.

ax·i·sym·met·ric /ˌaksēsəˈmetrik/ ▶ **adj.** Geometry symmetrical about an axis.

ax·le /ˈaksəl/ ▶ **n.** a rod or spindle (either fixed or rotating) passing through the center of a wheel or group of wheels: [as modifier] *axle grease | axle loads.*
– ORIGIN Middle English (originally *axle-tree*): from Old Norse *ǫxultré*.

ax·man /ˈaksˌman/ (also **axeman**) ▶ **n.** (pl. **axmen**)
1 a person who works with an ax: *he was like an axman at work in a tangled thicket.*
2 informal a rock or jazz guitarist.

Ax·min·ster /ˈaksˌminstər/ (also **Axminster carpet**) ▶ **n.** a kind of machine-woven patterned carpet with a cut pile.
– ORIGIN early 19th cent.: named after the town of *Axminster* in southern England, noted since the 18th cent. for the production of carpets.

ax·o·lotl /ˈaksəˌlätl/ ▶ **n.** a Mexican salamander which in natural conditions retains its aquatic newtlike larval form throughout life but is able to breed. ● *Ambystoma mexicanum*, family Ambystomatidae.
– ORIGIN late 18th cent.: from Nahuatl, from *atl* 'water' + *xolotl* 'servant.'

ax·on /ˈakˌsän/ ▶ **n.** the long threadlike part of a nerve cell along which impulses are conducted from the cell body to other cells.
– DERIVATIVES **ax·on·al** /ˈaksənl, akˈsänl/ **adj.**
– ORIGIN mid 19th cent. (denoting the body axis): from Greek *axōn* 'axis.'

ax·o·neme /ˈaksəˌnēm/ ▶ **n.** Biology the central strand of a cilium or flagellum. It is composed of an array of microtubules, typically in nine pairs around two single central ones.
– DERIVATIVES **ax·o·ne·mal** /aksəˈnēməl/ **adj.**
– ORIGIN early 20th cent.: from Greek *axōn* 'axis' + *nēma* 'thread.'

ax·o·no·met·ric /ˌaksənōˈmetrik/ ▶ **adj.** using or designating an orthographic projection of an object, such as a building, on a plane inclined to each of the three principal axes of the object; three-dimensional but without perspective.

ax·o·plasm /ˈaksəˌplazəm/ ▶ **n.** Biology the cytoplasm of a nerve axon.
– DERIVATIVES **ax·o·plas·mic** /ˌaksəˈplazmik/ **adj.**

Ax·um variant spelling of **AKSUM**.

ay /ī, ā/ ▶ **exclam.** & **n.** variant spelling of **AYE**[1].

A·ya·cu·cho /ˌäyəˈko͞ochō/ a city in the Andes in south central Peru; pop. 151,000 (est. 2007).

a·yah /ˈäyə/ ▶ **n.** a native maid or nursemaid employed by Europeans in India.
– ORIGIN Anglo-Indian, from Portuguese *aia* 'nurse,' feminine of *aio* 'tutor.'

a·ya·huas·ca /ˌäyəˈwäskə/ ▶ **n.** a tropical vine native to the Amazon region, noted for its hallucinogenic properties. ● Genus *Banisteriopsis*, family Malpighiaceae: several species, in particular *B. caapi*. ■ a hallucinogenic drink prepared from the bark of this.
– ORIGIN 1940s: from South American Spanish, from Quechua *ayawáskha*, from *aya* 'corpse' + *waskha* 'rope.'

a·ya·tol·lah /ˌäyəˈtōlə/ ▶ **n.** a Shiite religious leader in Iran.
– ORIGIN 1950s: from Persian, from Arabic *āyatu-llāh*, literally 'token of God.'

A·ya·tol·lah Kho·mei·ni see **KHOMEINI**.

Ayck·bourn /ˈākˌbôrn/, Sir Alan (1939–), English playwright. Notable plays: *Relatively Speaking* (1967), *Absurd Person Singular* (1973), and *A Chorus of Disapproval* (1985).

aye[1] /ī/ (also **ay**) ▶ **exclam.** archaic or dialect said to express assent; yes: *aye, you're right about that.* ■ **(aye, aye)** Nautical a response acknowledging an order: *aye, aye, captain.* ■ (in voting) I assent: *all in favor say, "aye."*
▶ **n.** an affirmative answer or assent, esp. in voting: *the House was divided: Ayes 211, Noes 271.*
– PHRASES **the ayes have it** the affirmative votes are in the majority.
– ORIGIN late 16th cent.: probably from *I*, first person personal pronoun, expressing assent.

aye[2] /ā/ ▶ **adv.** archaic or Scottish always or still.
– PHRASES **for aye** forever: *I shall treasure the memory for aye.*
– ORIGIN Middle English: from Old Norse *ei, ey*; related to Latin *aevum* 'age' and Greek *aie(i)* 'ever,' *aiōn*; 'aeon.'

aye-aye /ˈī ī/ ▶ **n.** a rare nocturnal Madagascan primate allied to the lemurs. It has rodentlike incisor teeth and an elongated twiglike finger on each hand with which it pries insects from bark. ● *Daubentonia madagascariensis*, the only member of the family Daubentoniidae.
– ORIGIN late 18th cent.: from French, from Malagasy *aiay*.

Ayer /e(ə)r/, Sir A. J. (1910–89), English philosopher; full name *Alfred Jules Ayer*. He was an important proponent of logical positivism. Notable works: *Language, Truth, and Logic* (1936) and *The Problem of Knowledge* (1956).

Ayers Rock /e(ə)rz/ a red rock mass in Northern Territory, Australia, southwest of Alice Springs. The largest monolith in the world, it is 1,143 feet (348 m) high and about 6 miles (9 km) in circumference. Aboriginal name **ULURU**.

A·ye·sha /äˈ(y)ēshə/ the wife of Muhammad.

Ay·ma·ra /ˌīmäˈrä/ ▶ **n.** (pl. **same** or **Aymaras**)
1 a member of a South American Indian people inhabiting the high plateau region of Bolivia and Peru near Lake Titicaca.
2 the language of this people, related to Quechua.
▶ **adj.** of or relating to this people or their language.
– ORIGIN Spanish.

Ayr·shire /ˈe(ə)rshər, -ˌshi(ə)r/ ▶ **n.** an animal of a mainly white breed of dairy cattle.
– ORIGIN mid 19th cent.: named after *Ayrshire*, a former Scottish county where the cattle were bred.

A·yur·ve·da /ˌäyərˈvādə, -ˈvēdə/ ▶ **n.** the traditional Hindu system of medicine, which is based on the idea of balance in bodily systems and uses diet, herbal treatment, and yogic breathing.
– DERIVATIVES **A·yur·ve·dic** /-ˈvedik/ **adj.**
– ORIGIN from Sanskrit *āyus* 'life' + *veda* 'science.'

AZ ▶ **abbr.** Arizona (in official postal use).

A·zad Kash·mir /ˈäzäd käshˈmi(ə)r, kash-/ an autonomous state in northeastern Pakistan, formerly part of Kashmir; administrative center, Muzzafarabad. It was established in 1949 after Kashmir was split as a result of the partition of India.
– ORIGIN from Urdu, literally 'Free Kashmir.'

a·zal·ea /əˈzālyə/ ▶ **n.** a deciduous flowering shrub of the heath family with clusters of brightly colored, sometimes fragrant flowers. Technically classified as rhododendrons, azaleas are characteristically smaller than most other rhododendrons. ● Genus *Rhododendron*, family Ericaceae: many cultivars.
– ORIGIN mid 18th cent.: modern Latin, from Greek, feminine of *azaleos* 'dry,' because the shrub flourishes in dry soil.

a·zan /äˈzän/ (also **adhan**) ▶ **n.** the Muslim call to ritual prayer, typically made by a muezzin from the minaret of a mosque.
– ORIGIN mid 19th cent.: from Arabic *'aḏān* 'announcement.' Compare with **MUEZZIN**.

a·za·role /ˈazəˌrōl/ ▶ **n.** a small tree related to the hawthorn, cultivated in southern Europe for its small yellow or reddish fruit. ● *Crataegus azarolus*, family Rosaceae.

a·ze·o·trope /āˈzēəˌtrōp/ ▶ **n.** Chemistry a mixture of two liquids that has a constant boiling point and composition throughout distillation.
– DERIVATIVES **a·ze·o·trop·ic** /ˌāzēəˈträpik, -ˈtrōpik/ **adj.**
– ORIGIN early 20th cent.: from **A-**[1] 'without' + Greek *zein* 'to boil' + *tropos* 'turning.'

Az·er·bai·jan /ˌazərˌbīˈjän, ˌäz-, -ˈzhän/ a country in southwestern Asia, in the Caucasus, on the western shore of the Caspian Sea; pop. 8,238,700 (est. 2009); capital, Baku; languages, Azerbaijani (official), Russian.

> Historically, the name Azerbaijan refers to a larger region that formed part of Persia. The northern part of this was ceded to Russia in the early 19th century; the southern part remained a region in northwestern Iran. Russian Azerbaijan was absorbed into the Soviet Union in 1922 and gained independence on the breakup of the Soviet Union in 1991. Azerbaijan contains the predominantly Armenian region of Nagorno-Karabakh, over which open conflict with Armenia broke out in 1988. The Azeri autonomous republic of Naxçivan forms an enclave within the Republic of Armenia and similarly continues to be the subject of armed conflict.

A·zer·bai·ja·ni /ˌazərbīˈjänē, ˌäzər-/ ▶ **adj.** of or relating to Azerbaijan or its people or their language.
▶ **n.** (pl. **Azerbaijanis**) **1** a native or inhabitant of Azerbaijan or a person of Azerbaijani descent.
2 the Turkic language of Azerbaijan.

A·ze·ri /əˈzerē/ ▶ **n.** (pl. **Azeris**) **1** a member of a Turkic people forming the majority population of Azerbaijan, and also living in Armenia and northern Iran.
2 the Azerbaijani language.
▶ **adj.** of, relating to, or denoting this people or their language.
– ORIGIN from Turkish *azerî*.

az·ide /ˈāˌzīd, ˈazˌīd/ ▶ **n.** Chemistry a compound containing the univalent group $-N_3^-$.
– ORIGIN early 20th cent.: from **AZO-** + **-IDE**.

a·zi·do·thy·mi·dine /ˌazidōˈthīməˌdēn, əˌzī-, əˌzē-/ ▶ **n.** former name for the drug **ZIDOVUDINE**.

A·zi·ki·we /ˌäziˈkēwā/, Nnamdi (1904–96), Nigerian statesman; full name *Benjamin Nnamdi Azikiwe* the first governor general of independent Nigeria 1960–63 and its first president 1963–66.

az·i·muth /ˈazəməth/ ▶ **n.** the direction of a celestial object from the observer, expressed as the angular distance from the north or south point of the horizon to the point at which a vertical circle passing through the object intersects the horizon. ■ the horizontal angle or direction of a compass bearing.
– DERIVATIVES **az·i·muth·al** /ˌazəˈməthəl/ **adj.**
– ORIGIN late Middle English (denoting the arc of a celestial circle from the zenith to the horizon): from Old French *azimut*, from Arabic *as-samt*, from *al* 'the' + *samt* 'way, direction.'

az·i·muth·al pro·jec·tion /ˌazəˈməthəl/ ▶ **n.** a map projection in which a region of the earth is projected onto a plane tangential to the surface, typically at a pole or the equator.

az·ine /ˈazˌēn, ˈāˌzēn/ ▶ **n.** Chemistry a cyclic organic compound having a ring including one or (typically) more nitrogen atoms.
– ORIGIN late 19th cent.: from **AZO-** + **-INE**[4].

azo- ▶ **prefix** Chemistry containing two adjacent nitrogen atoms between carbon atoms: *azobenzene*.
– ORIGIN from obsolete *azote* 'nitrogen,' from French, from Greek *azōos* 'without life.'

az·o·ben·zene /ˌazōˈbenzēn, -benˈzēn, ˌāzō-/ ▶ **n.** Chemistry a synthetic crystalline organic compound used chiefly in dye manufacture. ● Chem. formula: $(C_6H_5)N{=}N(C_6H_5)$.

az·o dye /ˈazō, ˈāzō/ ▶ **n.** Chemistry any of a large class of synthetic dyes whose molecules contain two adjacent nitrogen atoms between carbon atoms.

a·zo·ic /āˈzō-ik, əˈzō-/ ▶ **adj.** having no trace of life or organic remains. ■ **(Azoic)** Geology another term for **ARCHEAN**.
– ORIGIN mid 19th cent.: from Greek *azōos* 'without life' + **-IC**.

a·zon·al /āˈzōnl/ ▶ **adj.** (esp. of soils) having no zonal organization or structure.

a·zo·o·sper·mi·a /ˌāzōəˈspərmēə/ ▶ **n.** Medicine absence of motile (and hence viable) sperm in the semen.
– DERIVATIVES **a·zo·o·sper·mic** /-ˈspərmik/ **adj.**

A·zores /əˈzôrz, ˈāˌzôrz/ a group of volcanic islands in the Atlantic Ocean, west of Portugal, a possession of Portugal but partially autonomous; pop. 244,780 (2007); capital, Ponta Delgada.

A·zores High ▶ **n.** Meteorology a semipermanent area of high pressure located over the Azores in winter and early spring. Compare with **Bermuda High**.

az·o·tu·ri·a /ˌazəˈt(y)o͝orēə/ ▶ **n.** Medicine abnormal excess of nitrogen compounds in the urine. ■ Veterinary Medicine a condition of horses that causes stiffness and pain in the muscles of the hindquarters and back, and the production of dark-colored urine containing myoglobin.
– ORIGIN mid 19th cent.: from obsolete *azote* 'nitrogen' + **-uria**.

A·zov, Sea of /ˈazˌôf, ˈāˌzôf/ an inland sea in southern Russia and Ukraine, separated from the Black Sea by the Crimea and linked to it by a narrow strait.

Az·ra·el /ˈazrēˌel, ˌäzrēˈel/ Jewish & Islamic Mythology the angel who severs the soul from the body at death.

AZT ▶ **abbr.** trademark azidothymidine.

Az·tec /ˈazˌtek/ ▶ **n. 1** a member of the American Indian people dominant in Mexico before the Spanish conquest of the 16th century. **2** the extinct language of this people, a Uto-Aztecan language from which modern Nahuatl is descended.
▶ **adj.** of, relating to, or denoting this people or their language.
– ORIGIN from French *Aztèque* or Spanish *Azteca*, from Nahuatl *aztecatl* 'person of Aztlan,' their legendary place of origin.

a·zu·le·jo /ˌazhəˈlāˌhō, ˌazyə-/ ▶ **n.** (pl. **azulejos**) a kind of glazed colored tile traditionally used in Spanish and Portuguese buildings.
– ORIGIN from Spanish, from *azul* 'blue.'

az·ure /ˈazhər/ ▶ **adj.** bright blue in color, like a cloudless sky: *white beaches surrounded by azure seas*. ■ Heraldry blue: [postpositive] *a saltire azure*.
▶ **n. 1** a bright blue color. ■ literary the clear sky. **2** a small butterfly that is typically blue or purplish, with color differences between the sexes. ● *Celastrina* and other genera, family Lycaenidae.
– ORIGIN Middle English (denoting a blue dye): from Old French *asur, azur*, from medieval Latin *azzurum, azolum*, from Arabic *al* 'the' + *lāzaward* (from Persian *lāžward* 'lapis lazuli').

az·ur·ite /ˈazhəˌrīt/ ▶ **n.** a blue mineral consisting of copper hydroxyl carbonate. It occurs as blue prisms or crystal masses, often with malachite.
– ORIGIN early 19th cent.: from **azure** + **-ite**.

Azu·sa /əˈzo͞osə/ a city in southwestern California, northeast of Los Angeles; pop. 46,847 (est. 2008).

az·y·gos vein /ˈazəgəs/ ▶ **n.** Anatomy a large vein on the right side at the back of the thorax, draining into the superior vena cava.
– ORIGIN mid 17th cent.: *azygos* from Greek *azugos*, from *a-* 'without' + *zugon* 'yoke,' the vein not being one of a pair.

az·y·gous /āˈzīgəs, ˈazə-/ ▶ **adj.** Anatomy & Biology (of an organic structure) single; not existing in pairs.
– ORIGIN mid 19th cent.: from Greek *azugos* 'unyoked' (from *a-* 'without' + *zugon* 'yoke') + **-ous**.

az-Zar·qa /az ˈzärˌkä/ variant form of **Zarqa**.

Bb

B¹ /bē/ (also **b**) ▶ **n.** (pl. **Bs** or **B's**) **1** the second letter of the alphabet. ■ the second highest class of academic mark. ■ denoting the second-highest-earning socioeconomic category for marketing purposes, including intermediate management and professional personnel. ■ **(b)** Chess denoting the second file from the left, as viewed from White's side of the board. ■ (usu. **b**) the second constant to appear in an algebraic equation. ■ Geology denoting a soil horizon of intermediate depth, typically the subsoil. ■ the human blood type (in the ABO system) containing the B antigen and lacking the A. **2** (usu. **B**) Music the seventh note of the diatonic scale of C major. ■ a key based on a scale with B as its keynote.
– PHRASES **plan B** an alternative strategy: *it's time I put plan B into action.*

B² ▶ **abbr.** ■ (used in recording moves in chess) bishop: *Be5.* ■ black (used in describing grades of pencil lead): *2HB pencils.* ■ (in personal ads) Black. ■ bomber (in designations of US aircraft types): *a B52.* ■ a dry cell battery size. ▶ **symbol** ■ the chemical element boron. ■ Physics magnetic flux density.

b ▶ **abbr.** ■ Physics barn(s). ■ **(b.)** born (used to indicate a date of birth): *George Lloyd (b. 1913).* ■ billion. ■ bass. ■ basso.

BA ▶ **abbr.** ■ Bachelor of Arts: *David Brown, BA.* ■ Baseball batting average. ■ Buenos Aires.

Ba ▶ **symbol** the chemical element barium.

baa /bä/ ▶ **v.** (**baas, baaing, baaed** /bäd/) [no obj.] (of a sheep or lamb) bleat.
▶ **n.** the cry of a sheep or lamb.
– ORIGIN early 16th cent.: imitative.

Baa·de /'bädə/ (Wilhelm Heinrich) Walter (1893–1960), US astronomer, born in Germany. He proved that the Andromeda galaxy was much farther away than had been thought, which implied that the universe was much older and more extensive than had been supposed. He also contributed to the understanding of the life cycles of stars.

Baa·der–Mein·hof Group /ˌbädər 'mīnhäf/ another name for **Red Army Faction**.

Ba·al /'bā(ə)l/ (also **Bel** /bel/) a fertility god whose cult was widespread in ancient Phoenician and Canaanite lands.
– ORIGIN from Hebrew *ba'al* 'lord.'

Baal·bek /'bälˌbek, 'bāəl-/ a town in eastern Lebanon, site of the ancient city of Heliopolis.

Ba·ath Par·ty /bäTH/ (also **Ba'ath**) a pan-Arab socialist party founded in Syria in 1943. Different factions of the Baath Party hold power in Syria and formerly held power in Iraq.
– DERIVATIVES **Ba·ath·ism** /-izəm/ **n.**, **Ba·ath·ist** /-ist/ **adj. & n.**
– ORIGIN *Baath*, from Arabic *ba'ṯ* 'resurrection, renaissance.'

ba·ba¹ /'bäˌbä/ (also **baba au rhum** /ō 'rəm/) ▶ **n.** a small rich sponge cake, typically soaked in rum-flavored syrup.
– ORIGIN early 19th cent.: via French from Polish, literally 'married peasant woman.'

ba·ba² ▶ **n.** Indian informal **1** father (often as a proper name or as a familiar form of address). ■ a respectful form of address for an older man: *"Sit down, baba, you like tea?"* ■ (often **Baba**) a holy man (often as a proper name or form of address).
2 a child, esp. a male one (often in names or as an affectionate form of address).
– ORIGIN from Hindi *bābā*.

ba·ba gha·nouj /ˌbäbə gə'nOOSH/ (also **baba ganoush** /gə'nOOSH/) ▶ **n.** a thick sauce or spread made from ground eggplant and sesame seeds, olive oil, lemon, and garlic, typical of eastern Mediterranean cuisine.
– ORIGIN from Egyptian Arabic, from Arabic *bābā*, literally 'father' + *gannuug*, perhaps a personal name.

ba·bas·su /ˌbäbə'sOO/ (also **babaçu**) ▶ **n.** a Brazilian palm that yields an edible oil sometimes used in cosmetics. ● Genus *Orbignya*, family Palmae.
– ORIGIN 1920s: from Brazilian Portuguese *babaçu*, from Tupi *ybá* 'fruit' + *guasu* 'large.'

Bab·bage /'babij/, Charles (1791–1871), English mathematician, inventor, and pioneer of machine computing. With Ada Lovelace, he designed a mechanical computer that would perform calculations and print the results, but he was unable to complete it during his lifetime.

Bab·bitt¹, Milton (Byron) (1916–), US composer and mathematician, noted as a pioneer of electronic music. His compositions developed from the twelve-note system of Arnold Schoenberg and Anton von Webern.

Bab·bitt² ▶ **n.** dated a materialistic, complacent, and conformist businessman.
– DERIVATIVES **Bab·bitt·ry** /-trē/ **n.**
– ORIGIN 1922: from the name George *Babbitt*, the protagonist of the novel *Babbitt* by Sinclair Lewis.

bab·ble /'babəl/ ▶ **v.** [no obj.] talk rapidly and continuously in a foolish, excited, or incomprehensible way: *he would **babble on** in his gringo Spanish.* ■ [reporting verb] utter something rapidly and incoherently: [with direct speech] *I gasped and stared and babbled, "Look at this!"* | [with obj.] *he began to babble an apology.* ■ reveal something secret or confidential by talking impulsively or carelessly: *he babbled to another convict while he was in jail* | [with obj.] *my father **babbled out** the truth.* ■ (usu. as adj. **babbling**) (of a stream) make the continuous murmuring sound of water flowing over stones: *a gently babbling brook.*
▶ **n.** [in sing.] the sound of people talking quickly and in a way that is difficult or impossible to understand: *a babble of protest.* ■ foolish, excited, or confused talk: *her soft voice stopped his babble.* ■ the continuous murmuring sound of water flowing over stones in a stream: *the babble of a brook.* ■ background disturbance caused by interference from conversations on other telephone lines.
– ORIGIN Middle English: from Middle Low German *babbelen*, or an independent English formation, as a frequentative based on the repeated syllable *ba*, typical of a child's early speech.

babble ▶ **comb. form** forming nouns denoting confusing or pretentious jargon characteristic of a specified field or group: *psychobabble* | *technobabble*.

bab·bler /'bab(ə)lər/ ▶ **n.** **1** a person who babbles. **2** a thrushlike Old World songbird with a long tail, short rounded wings, and typically a loud discordant or musical voice. ● Family Timaliidae (the **babbler family**): numerous genera.

babe /bāb/ ▶ **n.** **1** chiefly literary a baby: ***a babe in arms**, less than twelve months old.*
2 informal an affectionate form of address, typically for someone with whom one has a sexual or romantic relationship: *I'm the golden boy, babe.*
3 a sexually attractive young woman or girl: *he's been pumping up his pecs to impress the babes.*
– ORIGIN late Middle English: probably imitative of an infant's first attempts at speech. Compare with **baby**.

ba·bel /'babəl, 'bā-/ ▶ **n.** [in sing.] a confused noise, typically that made by a number of voices: *the babel of voices on the road.* ■ a scene of noisy confusion.
– ORIGIN early 16th cent.: from *Babel* (see **Tower of Babel**), where, according to the biblical story in Gen. 11:4–9, God made the builders all speak different languages.

Ba·bel, Tower of see **Tower of Babel**.

ba·be·li·cious /ˌbābə'liSHəs, ˌbab-/ ▶ **adj.** informal (of a woman) sexually very attractive.
– ORIGIN 1992: coined in the film *Wayne's World*.

ba·be·si·o·sis /bəˌbēzē'ōsis/ (also **babesiasis** /ˌbabi'zīəsis, -'sī-/) ▶ **n.** a disease of cattle and other livestock, transmitted by the bite of ticks. It affects the red blood cells and causes the passing of red or blackish urine. Also called **piroplasmosis**. ● This is caused by protozoans of the genus *Babesia*, phylum Sporozoa.
– ORIGIN early 20th cent.: from modern Latin *Babesia*, from the name Victor *Babès* (1854–1926), Romanian bacteriologist.

Ba·bi /'bäbē/ ▶ **n.** an adherent of Babism.

ba·biche /bə'bēSH/ ▶ **n.** rawhide, typically formed into strips, as used by North American Indians for making fastenings, animal snares, snowshoes, etc.
– ORIGIN early 19th cent.: from Canadian French, from Micmac *a:papi:č*.

Ba·bin·ski re·flex /bə'binskē/ ▶ **n.** a reflex action in which the big toe remains extended or extends itself when the sole of the foot is stimulated.
– ORIGIN named for Joseph François Felix Babinski (1857–1932), French neurologist.

bab·i·ru·sa /ˌbäbə'rOOsə, ˌbab-/ ▶ **n.** a forest-dwelling wild pig with several upturned hornlike tusks, native to Malaysia. ● *Babyrousa babyrussa*, family Suidae.
– ORIGIN late 17th cent.: from Malay, from *babi* 'hog' + *rusa* 'deer.'

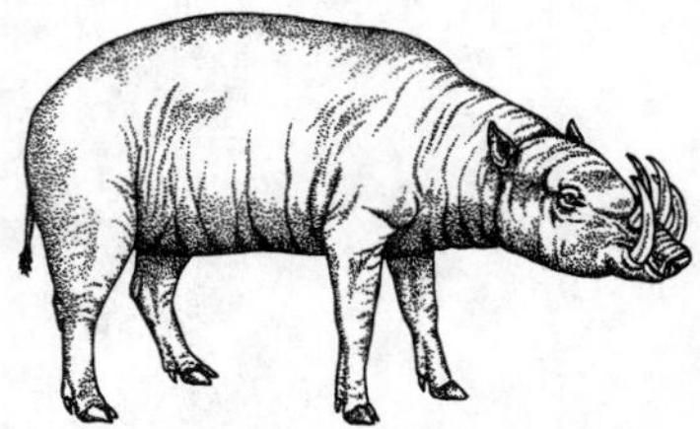

babirusa

Bab·ism /'bäbizəm/ ▶ **n.** a religion founded in 1844 by the Persian **Mirza Ali Muhammad** of Shiraz (1819–50) (popularly known as "the Bab"), who taught that a new prophet would follow Muhammad. See also **Baha'i**.
– ORIGIN mid 19th cent.: via Persian from Arabic *bāb* 'intermediary,' literally 'gate' (taken as a name by the founder) + **-ism**.

bab·ka /'bäbkə/ ▶ **n.** a loaf-shaped coffee cake made with sweet yeast dough to which raisins, chocolate, or nuts may be added.
– ORIGIN Polish, diminutive of *baba* (see **baba¹**).

ba·boon /ba'bOOn/ ▶ **n.** a large Old World ground-dwelling monkey with a long doglike snout, large teeth, and naked callosities on the buttocks. Baboons are social animals and live in troops. ● Genera *Papio* and *Mandrillus*, family Cercopithecidae: several species, including the drill and mandrill. ■ an ugly or uncouth person.
– ORIGIN Middle English (denoting a grotesque figure used in architecture): from Old French *babuin* or medieval Latin *babewynus*, perhaps from Old French *baboue* 'muzzle, grimace.'

Ba·bo·qui·va·ri Moun·tains /ˌbäbōkə'värē/ a range in southern Arizona that rises to 7,734 feet (2,357 m) at Baboquivari Peak.

ba·bouche /bəˈbo͞osн/ ▶ **n.** a heelless slipper, typically in oriental style.
–ORIGIN late 17th cent.: from French, from Arabic *bābūj*, Persian *pāpūš*, literally 'foot covering.'

Ba·bruisk /bäˈbro͞o-isk/ (also **Babruysk**, **Bobruisk**, or **Bobruysk**) a river port in central Belarus, on the Berezina River, southeast of Minsk; pop. 219,000 (est. 2009).

ba·bu /ˈbäbo͞o/ ▶ **n.** (pl. **babus**) Indian a respectful title or form of address for a man, esp. an educated one: *I could see Kana-babu's shop.* ■ an office worker; a clerk.
–ORIGIN from Hindi *bābū*, literally 'father.'

ba·bul /bəˈbo͝ol/ ▶ **n.** (in South Asia) a tropical acacia introduced from Africa, used as a source of fuel, gum arabic, and (formerly) tannin. ● *Acacia nilotica*, family Leguminosae.
–ORIGIN early 19th cent.: from Hindi *babūl*.

Ba·bur /ˈbäbo͝or/ (1483–1530), first Mogul emperor of India *c.*1525–30; descendant of Tamerlane; born *Zahir ad-Din Muhammad*. He invaded India *c.*1525 and conquered the territory that extended from the Oxus to Patna.

ba·bush·ka /bəˈbo͞osнkə/ ▶ **n.** (in Poland and Russia) an old woman or grandmother. ■ a headscarf tied under the chin, typical of those worn by Polish and Russian women.
–ORIGIN mid 20th cent.: Polish, Russian, 'grandmother.'

Ba·bu·yan Is·lands /ˌbäbo͞oˈyän/ a group of 24 volcanic islands lying to the north of the island of Luzon in the northern Philippines.

ba·by /ˈbābē/ ▶ **n.** (pl. **babies**) **1** a very young child, esp. one newly or recently born: *his wife's just had a baby* | [as modifier] *a baby girl.* ■ a young or newly born animal. ■ the youngest member of a family or group: *Clara was the baby of the family.* ■ a timid or childish person: *"Don't be such a baby!" she said witheringly.* ■ (**one's baby**) informal one's particular responsibility, achievement, or concern: *"This is your baby, Gerry," she said, handing him the brief.*
2 informal a young woman or a person with whom one is having a romantic relationship (often as a form of address): *my baby left me for another guy* | *baby, don't cry!* ■ a thing regarded with affection or familiarity: *this baby can reach speeds of 140 mph.*
▶ **adj.** [attrib.] comparatively small or immature of its kind: *a baby grand piano.* ■ (of vegetables) picked before reaching their usual size: *baby carrots.*
▶ **v.** (**babies**, **babying**, **babied**) [with obj.] treat (someone) as a baby; pamper or be overprotective toward: *her aunt babied her and fussed over her clothes.*
–PHRASES **throw the baby out with the bathwater** discard something valuable along with other things that are inessential or undesirable.
–DERIVATIVES **ba·by·hood** /-ˌho͝od/ **n.**
–ORIGIN late Middle English: probably imitative of an infant's first attempts at speech.

Ba·by Bell ▶ **n.** informal a nickname for any of the telephone companies created in 1984 from the breakup of American Telephone and Telegraph Corporation, which was nicknamed "Ma Bell."

ba·by blue ▶ **n.** a pale shade of blue. ■ (**baby blues**) informal blue eyes. ■ (**baby blues**) depression affecting a woman after giving birth; postnatal depression.

ba·by-blue-eyes ▶ **n.** a plant of western North America with blue bowl-shaped flowers. ● Genus *Nemophila*, family Hydrophyllaceae: several species, in particular *N. menziesii* of California and southern Oregon.

ba·by boom ▶ **n.** informal a temporary marked increase in the birth rate, esp. the one following World War II.
–DERIVATIVES **baby boomer n.**

ba·by bug·gy ▶ **n.** a baby carriage.

ba·by bust ▶ **n.** informal a temporary marked decrease in the birth rate.
–DERIVATIVES **ba·by bust·er n.**

ba·by car·riage ▶ **n.** a four-wheeled carriage for a baby, typically with a retractable hood, pushed by a person on foot.

ba·by corn ▶ **n.** individual cobs of corn that have been harvested when very small and immature, eaten as a vegetable.

Baby Doc see **DUVALIER**.

ba·by-doll ▶ **adj.** denoting a style of women's clothing or sleepwear resembling that traditionally worn by a doll or young child, esp. short, high-waisted, short-sleeved dresses.

ba·by face ▶ **n.** a smooth round face like a baby's.

ba·by-faced ▶ **adj.** having a youthful or innocent face: *baby-faced tough guys.*

ba·by fat ▶ **n.** fat on the body of a baby or child that disappears as it grows up. ■ the extra body fat that a woman may develop during pregnancy.

ba·by grand ▶ **n.** the smallest size of grand piano, about 4.5 feet (1.5 m) long.

ba·by·ish /ˈbābē-isн/ ▶ **adj.** derogatory (of appearance or behavior) characteristic of a baby: *he pursed his mouth into a babyish pout.* ■ (of clothes or toys) suitable for a baby: *he declared that dolls were silly, babyish things.*
–DERIVATIVES **ba·by·ish·ly adv.**, **ba·by·ish·ness n.**

Bab·y·lon[1] /ˈbabəˌlän, -ˌlən/ **1** an ancient city in Mesopotamia, the capital of Babylonia in the 2nd millennium BC. The city was on the banks of the Euphrates River and was noted for its luxury, its fortifications, and, particularly, for the Hanging Gardens of Babylon.
2 a town on the southern shore of Long Island in New York that includes the villages of Babylon and Amityville; pop. 219,761 (est. 2008).
–ORIGIN Greek *Babulōn* (from Hebrew *bābel*), also the name of the mystical city of the Apocalypse. Compare with **BABEL**.

Bab·y·lon[2] ▶ **n.** black English (chiefly among Rastafarians) a contemptuous or dismissive term for aspects of a society seen as degenerate or oppressive, esp. the police: *praise them for bringing a new rectitude to Babylon.*
–ORIGIN 1940s: by association with **BABYLON**[1].

Bab·y·lo·ni·a /ˌbabəˈlōnēə/ an ancient region of Mesopotamia, formed when the kingdoms of Akkad in the north and Sumer in the south combined in the first half of the 2nd millennium BC.

Bab·y·lo·ni·an /ˌbabəˈlōnēən/ ▶ **n. 1** an inhabitant of Babylon or Babylonia.
2 the dialect of Akkadian spoken in ancient Babylon.
▶ **adj.** of or relating to Babylon or Babylonia.

Bab·y·lo·ni·an Cap·tiv·i·ty the captivity of the Israelites in Babylon, lasting from their deportation by Nebuchadnezzar in 586 BC until their release by Cyrus the Great in 539 BC.

ba·by·moth·er /ˈbābēˌmə<u>TH</u>ər/ (or **babyfather** /ˈbābēˌfä<u>TH</u>ər/) ▶ **n.** black English the mother (or father) of one or more of one's children: *I knew his babymother, Miss Richards, as we went to school and grew up together.*

ba·by oil ▶ **n.** a mineral oil used to soften the skin.

ba·by's breath ▶ **n.** a herbaceous plant of delicate appearance that bears tiny scented pink or white flowers. ● *Gypsophila paniculata*, family Caryophyllaceae.

ba·by·sit /ˈbābēˌsit/ ▶ **v.** (**babysits**, **babysitting**; past and past participle **babysat**) [no obj.] look after a child or children while the parents are out: *I babysit for my neighbor sometimes* | [with obj.] *she was babysitting Sophie* | (as noun **babysitting**) *part-time jobs such as babysitting.*
–DERIVATIVES **ba·by·sit·ter n.**

ba·by step ▶ **n.** a tentative act or measure that is the first stage in a long or challenging process: *the country is just taking its first baby steps toward the future.*

ba·by talk ▶ **n.** childish talk used by or to young children.

ba·by tooth ▶ **n.** another term for **MILK TOOTH**.

ba·ca·lao /ˌbäkəˈlou/ ▶ **n.** codfish, often dried or salted, as used in Spanish and Latin American cooking.
–ORIGIN Spanish.

Ba·call /bəˈkôl/, Lauren (1924–), US actress; born *Betty Joan Perske*. Her movies with husband Humphrey Bogart include *The Big Sleep* (1946) and *Key Largo* (1948). She received Tonys for her lead roles in the stage musicals *Applause* (1970) and *Woman of the Year* (1981).

Ba·car·di /bəˈkärdē/ ▶ **n.** (pl. **Bacardis**) trademark a West Indian rum produced originally in Cuba.
–ORIGIN named after the Compañía Ron *Bacardi* of Cuba (now *Bacardi* & Co. Ltd., Nassau).

bac·ca·la /ˌbakəˈlä, ˈbakəˌlä/ ▶ **n.** Italian term for **BACALAO**.

bac·ca·lau·re·ate /ˌbakəˈlôrēit/ ▶ **n. 1** a college bachelor's degree.
2 Brit. an examination intended to qualify successful candidates for higher education.
3 Brit. a religious service held at some educational institutions before commencement, containing a farewell sermon to the graduating class.
–ORIGIN mid 17th cent. (sense 1): from French *baccalauréat* or medieval Latin *baccalaureatus*, from *baccalaureus* 'bachelor.' The earlier form *baccalarius* was altered by wordplay to conform with *bacca lauri* 'laurel berry,' because of the laurels awarded to scholars. Sense 2 dates from 1970.

bac·ca·rat /ˈbäkəˌrä, ˌbakəˈrä/ ▶ **n.** a gambling card game in which players hold two- or three-card hands, the winning hand being that giving the highest remainder when its face value is divided by ten.
–ORIGIN mid 19th cent.: from French *baccara*, of unknown origin.

bac·cate /ˈbakˌāt/ ▶ **adj.** bearing berries; berried. ■ of the nature of a berry; berrylike.

Bac·chae /ˈbakē, ˈbäkē/ the priestesses or female devotees of the Greek god Bacchus.

bac·cha·nal /ˌbäkəˈnäl, ˌbak-, ˈbakənl/ chiefly literary ▶ **n. 1** an occasion of wild and drunken revelry. ■ a drunken reveler.
2 a priest, worshiper, or follower of Bacchus.
▶ **adj.** another term for **BACCHANALIAN**.
–ORIGIN mid 16th cent.: from Latin *bacchanalis*, from the name of the god **BACCHUS**.

Bac·cha·na·li·a /ˌbakəˈnālyə, ˌbäk-/ ▶ **plural n.** [also treated as sing.] the Roman festival of Bacchus. ■ (**bacchanalia**) drunken revelry.
–ORIGIN late 16th cent.: from Latin *bacchanalia*, neuter plural of the adjective *bacchanalis* (see **BACCHANAL**).

bac·cha·na·li·an /ˌbäkəˈnālyən, -ˈnālēən, ˌbakə-/ ▶ **adj.** characterized by or given to drunken revelry; riotously drunken: *a bacchanalian orgy.*

bac·chant /bəˈkänt, -ˈkant/ ▶ **n.** (pl. **bacchants** or **bacchantes** /-ˈkäntēz/; fem. **bacchante** /-tē/) a priest, priestess, or follower of Bacchus.
–ORIGIN late 16th cent.: from French *bacchante*, from Latin *bacchari* 'celebrate the feast of Bacchus.'

Bac·chus /ˈbäkəs, ˈbak-/ Greek Mythology another name for **DIONYSUS**.
–DERIVATIVES **Bac·chic** /-kik/ **adj.**
–ORIGIN Latin, from Greek *Bakkhos*.

bac·cy /ˈbakē/ ▶ **n.** chiefly Brit. informal term for **TOBACCO**.

Bach /bäkн, bäk/, Johann Sebastian (1685–1750), German composer. An exceptional and prolific baroque composer, his compositions range from violin concertos, suites, and the six *Brandenburg Concertos* (1720–21) to clavier works and sacred cantatas. Large-scale choral works include *The Passion according to St. John* (1723), *The Passion according to St. Matthew* (1729), and the *Mass in B minor* (1733–38). Three of his sons were also well-known composers: **J. C. Bach** (1735–82), known as **the London Bach**, full name *Johann Christian Bach*; **J. C. F. Bach** (1732–95), known as **the Bückeburg Bach**, full name *Johann Christoph Friedrich Bach*; and **W. F. Bach** (1710–84), known as **the Halle Bach**, full name Wilhelm Friedemann Bach.

Bach·a·rach /ˈbakəˌrak/, Burt (1928–), US writer of popular songs. His songs, many of which were written with lyricist **Hal David** (1921–), include "Walk On By" (1961), "Alfie" (1966), and "Raindrops Keep Falling on My Head" (1969).

ba·cha·ta /bäˈcнätä/ ▶ **n.** a style of romantic music originating in the Dominican Republic. ■ a song in this style.
–ORIGIN Caribbean Spanish, literally 'a party, good time.'

bach·e·lor /ˈbacн(ə)lər/ ▶ **n. 1** a man who is not and has never been married: *Mark is a confirmed bachelor* | *one of the country's most eligible bachelors.* ■ Zoology a male bird or mammal without a mate, esp. one prevented from breeding by a dominant male.
2 a person who holds an undergraduate degree from a university or college (only in titles or set expressions): *he graduated with a bachelor's degree in philosophy* | *a Bachelor of Arts.*
3 historical a young knight serving under another's banner. See also **KNIGHT BACHELOR**. [said to be from French *bas chevalier*, literally 'low knight' (i.e., knight of a low order).]
–DERIVATIVES **bach·e·lor·hood** /-ˌho͝od/ **n.**
–ORIGIN Middle English: from Old French *bacheler*, of uncertain origin.

bach·e·lor a·part·ment ▶ **n.** an apartment occupied by a bachelor. ■ an apartment consisting of a single large room serving as bedroom and living room, with a separate bathroom.

bach·e·lor·ette /ˌbacн(ə)ləˈret/ ▶ **n. 1** a young unmarried woman.
2 a small bachelor apartment: *a bachelorette in a high-rise complex.*

bach·e·lor·ette par·ty ▶ **n.** a party given for a woman who is about to get married, typically one attended by women only.

PRONUNCIATION KEY ə *ago, up*; ər *over, fur*; a *hat*; ā *ate*; ä *car*; e *let*; ē *see*; i *fit*; ī *by*; NG *sing*; ō *go*; ô *law, for*; oi *toy*; o͝o *good*; o͞o *goo*; ou *out*; TH *thin*; <u>TH</u> *then*; ZH *vision*

b

b

bach·e·lor girl ▶ n. an independent, unmarried young woman.

bach·e·lor par·ty (or **bachelorette party**) ▶ n. a party given for a man (or woman) who is about to get married, typically attended by men (or women) only.

bach·e·lor's but·tons ▶ plural n. [treated as sing. or pl.] any of a number of ornamental plants that bear small, buttonlike, double flowers, in particular the vivid blue cornflower *Centaurea cyanus*.

ba·cil·li·form /bəˈsiləˌfôrm/ ▶ adj. chiefly Biology rod-shaped.

ba·cil·lus /bəˈsiləs/ ▶ n. (pl. **bacilli** /-ˈsilī/) a disease-causing bacterium. ■ a rod-shaped bacterium.
– DERIVATIVES **bac·il·lar·y** /ˈbasəˌlerē/ adj.
– ORIGIN late 19th cent.: from late Latin, diminutive of Latin *baculus* 'stick.'

> **USAGE** All bacteria belonging to the genus *Bacillus* are called **bacilli**, but not all bacteria called **bacilli** belong to the genus *Bacillus*.

bac·i·tra·cin /ˌbasiˈtrāsin/ ▶ n. an antibiotic typically used topically for skin and eye infections. ● The drug is obtained from the bacterium *Bacillus subtilis*.

back /bak/ ▶ n. **1** the rear surface of the human body from the shoulders to the hips: *he lay on his back* | *Forbes slapped me on the back* | [as modifier] *back pain*. ■ the corresponding upper surface of an animal's body. ■ the spine of a person or animal. ■ the part of a chair against which the sitter's back rests. ■ the part of a garment that covers a person's back. ■ a person's back regarded as carrying a load or bearing an imposition: *they wanted the government **off their backs**.*
2 the side or part of something that is away from the spectator or from the direction in which it moves or faces; the rear: *at the back of the hotel is a secluded garden* | *an empty spot in the back of the plane*. ■ [in sing.] the position directly behind someone or something: *she unbuttoned her dress from the back*. ■ the side or part of an object opposed to the one that is normally seen or used; the less active, visible, or important part of something: *write on the back of a postcard* | *he wiped his mouth with the back of his hand*.
3 a player in a field game whose initial position is behind the front line: *their backs showed some impressive running and passing*. ■ the position taken by such a player.
▶ adv. **1** toward the rear; in the opposite direction from the one that one is facing or traveling: *she moved back a pace* | *she walked away without looking back*. ■ expressing movement of the body into a reclining position: *he leaned back in his chair* | *sit back and relax*. ■ at a distance away: *I thought you were miles back* | *the officer pushed the crowd back*. ■ (**back of**) behind: *he knew that other people were back of him*.
2 expressing a return to an earlier or normal condition: *she put the book back on the shelf* | *drive to Montreal and back* | *I went back to sleep* | *he was given his job back*. ■ fashionable again: *sideburns are back*.
3 in or into the past: *he made his fortune back in 1955*. ■ at a place previously left or mentioned: *the folks back home are counting on him*.
4 in return: *they wrote back to me*.
▶ v. **1** [with obj.] give financial, material, or moral support to: *he had a newspaper empire backing him* | *go up there and tell them—I'll back you up*. ■ bet money on (a person or animal) winning a race or contest: *he backed the horse at 33–1*. ■ be in favor of: *over 97 percent backed the changes*. ■ supplement in order to reinforce or strengthen: *U.S. troops were **backed up** by forces from European countries*.
2 [with obj.] cover the back of (an object) in order to support, protect, or decorate it: *a mirror backed with tortoiseshell*. ■ (esp. in popular music) provide musical accompaniment to (a singer or musician): *brisk guitar work backed by drums, bass, fiddle, and accordion*. ■ put a song or piece of music on the less important side of (a recording): *the new single is backed with a track from the LP*.
3 [no obj.] walk or drive backward: *she tried to back away* | *backing down the stairs* | figurative *the administration **backed away from** the plan* | [with obj.] *he backed the Mercedes into the yard*. ■ (of the wind) change direction counterclockwise around the points of the compass: *the wind had backed to the northwest*. The opposite of **VEER**[1]. ■ [with obj.] Sailing put (a sail) aback in order to slow the vessel down.
4 [no obj.] (of a property) have its back adjacent to (a piece of land or body of water): *a row of cottages **backed on** the water* | *his garage wall backs onto the neighboring property*. ■ [with obj.] (usu. **be backed**) lie behind or at the back of: *the promenade is backed by lots of cafes*.
▶ adj. [attrib.] **1** of or at the back of something: *the back garden* | *the back pocket of his jeans*. ■ situated in a remote or subsidiary position: *back roads*.
2 (esp. of wages or something published or released) from or relating to the past: *she was owed back pay*.
3 directed toward the rear or in a reversed course: *back currents*.
4 Phonetics (of a sound) articulated at the back of the mouth.
– PHRASES **at someone's back** in pursuit or support of someone. **back and fill** trim the sails of a vessel so that the wind alternately fills and spills out of them, in order to maneuver in a limited space. ■ zigzag or vacillate. **back and forth** to and fro. **someone's back is turned** someone's attention is elsewhere: *he kissed her quickly, when the landlady's back was turned*. **the back of (the) beyond** a remote or inaccessible place. **the back of one's mind** used to express that something is in one's mind but is not consciously thought of or remembered: *she had a little nagging worry at the back of her mind*. **back to front** /ˌbak tə ˈfrənt/ Brit. reversed; backward: *the exhausts had been fitted back to front* | *a back-to-front baseball cap*. **back through the box** see **BOX**[1]. **back water** reverse the action of the oars while rowing, causing a boat to slow down or stop. **back the wrong horse** make a wrong or inappropriate choice. **behind someone's back** without a person's knowledge and in an unfair or dishonorable way: *Carla made fun of him behind his back*. **get** (or **put**) **someone's back up** make someone annoyed or angry. **in back** at the back of something, esp. a building: *my dad demolished an old shed **in back of** his barn*. **know something like the back of one's hand** be entirely familiar with a place or route. **on one's back** in bed recovering from an injury or illness. ■ full-length on the ground: *he slipped off the heap and landed **flat on his back**.* **put one's back into** approach (a task) with vigor. **turn one's back on** ignore (someone) by turning away. ■ reject or abandon: *she turned her back on her career to devote her life to animals*. **with one's back to** (or **up against**) **the wall** in a desperate situation; hard-pressed.
– PHRASAL VERBS **back down** withdraw a claim or assertion in the face of opposition: *the contenders **backed down from** their original pledge*. **back off** draw back from action or confrontation: *they **backed off from** fundamental reform of the system*. ■ another way of saying **BACK DOWN**. **back out** withdraw from a commitment: *if he **backs out of** the deal they'll sue him*. **back up 1** (of vehicles) form a line due to congestion: *the traffic began to back up*. **2** (of running water) accumulate behind an obstruction. **back something up** Computing make a spare copy of data or a disk. ■ (usu. **be backed up**) cause vehicles to form into a queue due to congestion: *the traffic was backed up a couple of miles in each direction*.
– ORIGIN Old English *bæc*, of Germanic origin; related to Middle Dutch and Old Norse *bak*. The adverb use dates from late Middle English and is a shortening of **ABACK**.

back·ache /ˈbakˌāk/ ▶ n. a prolonged pain in one's back.

back al·ley ▶ n. a narrow passage behind or between buildings.
▶ adj. [attrib.] secret or illegal, as might be found in a back alley: *a back-alley drug deal*.

back·bar /ˈbakˌbär/ ▶ n. a structure behind a bar counter, with shelves for holding bottles and other supplies.

Back Bay a historic residential and commercial district in western Boston, Massachusetts, on land along the Charles River that was reclaimed in the 19th century.

back·beat /ˈbakˌbēt/ ▶ n. Music a strong accent on one of the normally unaccented beats of the bar, used esp. in jazz and popular music.

back·bench /ˈbakˈbenCH/ ▶ n. (in the UK) the benches behind the front benches on either side of the House of Commons, occupied by members of parliament who do not hold office in the government or opposition: [as modifier] *backbench MPs*.
– DERIVATIVES **back·bench·er** n.

back·bit·ing /ˈbakˌbītiNG/ ▶ n. malicious talk about someone who is not present.
– DERIVATIVES **back·bite** /-ˌbīt/ v., **back·bit·er** /-tər/ n.

back·board /ˈbakˌbôrd/ ▶ n. a board placed at or forming the back of something, such as a collage or piece of electronic equipment. ■ Basketball an upright board behind the basket, off which the ball may rebound. ■ a board used to support or straighten a person's back, esp. after an accident.

back·bone /ˈbakˌbōn/ ▶ n. **1** the series of vertebrae extending from the skull to the pelvis; the spine. ■ the spine of a book. ■ Biochemistry the main chain of a polymeric molecule.
2 the chief support of a system or organization; the mainstay: *these firms are the backbone of our industrial sector*. ■ strength of character; firmness: *he has the backbone to see us through this difficulty*.
3 Computing & Telecommunications a high-speed, high-capacity digital connection which forms the axis of a local or wide area network.

back·break·ing (also **backbreaking**) ▶ adj. [attrib.] (esp. of manual labor) physically demanding: *a day's back-breaking work*.

back burn·er ▶ n. a state of inaction or suspension; a position of relatively little importance: *priorities that have been **placed on the back burner** year after year*.
▶ v. [with obj.] (usu. **be back-burnered**) postpone consideration of or action on: *a planned test of the new ale has been back-burnered*.

back·cast /ˈbakˌkast/ Fishing ▶ n. a backward swing of a fishing line preparatory to casting.
▶ v. (past and past participle **backcast**) [no obj.] make such a backward swing.

back cat·a·log (also **back catalogue**) ▶ n. all the works previously produced by a recording artist or record company.

back·chan·nel /ˈbakˌCHanl/ (also **back channel**) ▶ n. **1** a secondary or covert route for the passage of information: *the agency offered a reliable backchannel to Washington* | [as modifier] *backchannel briefings*.
2 Psychology a sound or gesture made to give continuity to a conversation by a person who is listening to another.

back·chat /ˈbakˌCHat/ ▶ n. another term for **BACK TALK**.

back·coun·try /ˈbakˌkəntrē/ ▶ n. (**the backcountry**) sparsely inhabited rural areas; wilderness: *exploring the backcountry on horseback* | [as modifier] *backcountry skiing*.

back·court /ˈbakˌkôrt/ ▶ n. (in tennis, basketball, and similar games) the part of each side of the court nearest the back wall or back boundary line. ■ the defensive players in a basketball team.

back·cross /ˈbakˌkrôs/ Genetics ▶ v. [with obj.] cross (a hybrid) with one of its parents or an organism with the same genetic characteristics as one of the parents: (as adj. **backcrossed**) *after five generations the backcrossed dogs were indistinguishable from purebred dalmatians*.
▶ n. an instance or result of backcrossing.

back·date /ˈbakˌdāt/ ▶ v. [with obj.] put an earlier date to (a document or agreement) than the actual one: *they backdated the sale documents to evade a court order*.

back door ▶ n. the door or entrance at the back of a building. ■ a feature or defect of a computer system that allows surreptitious unauthorized access to data.
▶ adj. (also **backdoor**) [attrib.] (of an activity) clandestine; underhanded: *backdoor private deals*.

back·door sell·ing /ˈbakˌdôr/ ▶ n. the selling by wholesalers directly to the public, seen as detrimental to retailers.

back·down /ˈbakˌdoun/ ▶ n. an act of backing down.

back·draft /ˈbakˌdraft/ (Brit. **backdraught**) ▶ n. **1** a current of air or water that flows backward down a chimney, pipe, etc.
2 a phenomenon in which a fire that has consumed all available oxygen suddenly explodes when more oxygen is made available, typically because a door or window has been opened.
– DERIVATIVES **back·draft·ing** n.

back·drop /ˈbakˌdräp/ ▶ n. a painted cloth hung at the back of a theater stage as part of the scenery. ■ the setting or background for a scene, event, or situation: *the conference took place **against a backdrop of** increasing diplomatic activity*.
▶ v. (**backdrops, backdropping, backdropped**) provide a background or setting for: *an ornate fountain, and at its center, backdropped with golden spray, a statue of a young girl*.

back end ▶ n. the end of something that is farthest from the front or the working end: *the back end of the car swung around*. ■ chiefly Brit. the latter part of a period of time or process: *the book takes us up to the back end of last year*.
▶ adj. [attrib.] **1** relating to the end or outcome of a project, process, or investment: *many annuities have back-end surrender charges*.
2 Computing denoting a subordinate processor or program, not directly accessed by the user, which performs a specialized function on behalf of a main processor or software system: *a back-end database server*.

back·er /ˈbakər/ ▶ n. a person, institution, or country that supports something, esp. financially: *$3.3 million was provided by the project's backers*. ■ a person who bets on a horse.

back-fanged ▶ adj. Zoology (of a snake such as a boomslang) having the rear one or two pairs of teeth modified as fangs, with grooves to conduct the venom. Compare with FRONT-FANGED.

back fat ▶ n. fat on the back of a meat-producing animal.

back·field /ˈbak,fēld/ ▶ n. Football the area of play behind either the offensive or defensive line. ■ the players positioned in this area.

back·fill /ˈbak,fil/ ▶ v. [with obj.] refill (an excavated hole) with the material dug out of it: *they backfill the hole to street level.*
▶ n. material used for backfilling.

back·fire /ˈbak,fī(ə)r/ ▶ v. [no obj.] **1** (of an engine) undergo a mistimed explosion in the cylinder or exhaust: *a car backfired in the road.*
2 (of a plan or action) rebound adversely on the originator; have the opposite effect to what was intended: *overzealous publicity backfired on her.*
▶ n. **1** a mistimed explosion in the cylinder or exhaust of a vehicle or engine.
2 a fire set intentionally to arrest the progress of an approaching fire by creating a burned area in its path, thus depriving the fire of fuel.

back·flip /ˈbak,flip/ ▶ n. a backward somersault done in the air with the arms and legs stretched out straight.

back fo·cus ▶ n. Photography the distance between the back of a lens and the image of an object at infinity.

back-for·ma·tion ▶ n. a word that is formed from an already existing word from which it appears to be a derivative, often by removal of a suffix (e.g., *laze* from *lazy* and *edit* from *editor*). ■ the process by which such words are formed.

back·gam·mon /ˈbak,gamən/ ▶ n. a board game in which two players move their pieces around twenty-four triangular points according to the throw of dice, the winner being the first to remove all their pieces from the board. ■ the most complete form of win in this game.
– ORIGIN mid 17th cent.: from BACK + GAMMON[2].

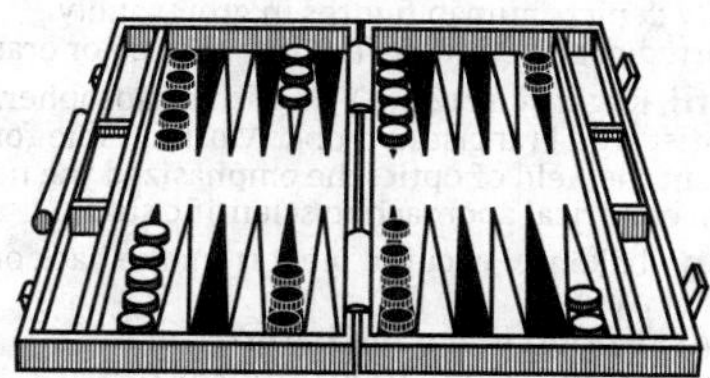
backgammon board and pieces

back·ground /ˈbak,ground/ ▶ n. **1** [in sing.] the area or scenery behind the main object of contemplation, esp. when perceived as a framework for it: *the house stands against a background of sheltering trees.* ■ the part of a picture or design that serves as a setting to the main figures or objects, or that appears furthest from the viewer: *the background shows a landscape of domes and minarets | the word is written in white on a red background.* ■ a position or function that is not prominent or conspicuous: *after that evening, Athens remained* ***in the background.*** ■ Computing used to describe tasks or processes running on a computer that do not need input from the user: *programs can be left running in the background.* ■ Physics low-intensity radiation from radioisotopes present in the natural environment. ■ unwanted signals, such as noise in the reception or recording of sound.
2 the circumstances or situation prevailing at a particular time or underlying a particular event: *the political and economic background* | [as modifier] *background information.* ■ a person's education, experience, and social circumstances: *she has a background in nursing | a mix of students from many different backgrounds.*

back·ground·er /ˈbak,groundər/ ▶ n. an official briefing or handout giving background information: *their departure had to be explained by aides in a backgrounder the next day.*

back·ground mu·sic ▶ n. music intended as an unobtrusive accompaniment to some activity, such as dining in a restaurant, or to provide atmosphere in a movie.

back·ground ra·di·a·tion ▶ n. Astronomy the uniform microwave radiation remaining from the Big Bang.

back·hand /ˈbak,hand/ ▶ n. **1** (in tennis and other racket sports) a stroke played with the back of the hand facing in the direction of the stroke, typically starting with the arm crossing the body: *he drove a backhand into the net* | [as modifier] *a backhand volley.* ■ a blow or stroke of any kind made in this way, or in a direction opposite to the usual: *ground balls hit to my backhand* | [as modifier] *he made a backhand stop of the ball.*
2 handwriting that slopes to the left.
▶ v. [with obj.] strike with a backhanded blow or stroke: *in a flash, he backhanded Ace across the jaw.*

back·hand·ed /bakˈhandid/ ▶ adj. **1** made with the back of the hand facing in the direction of movement: *a backhanded pass.*
2 indirect; ambiguous or insincere: *coming from me, teasing is a* ***backhanded compliment.***
▶ adv. with the back of the hand or with the hand turned backward: *Frank hit him backhanded.*

back·hand·er /ˈbak,handər/ ▶ n. **1** a backhand stroke or shot in a game. ■ a blow made with the back of the hand.
2 Brit. informal a secret payment, typically one made illegally; a bribe.

back·haul /ˈbak,hôl/ ▶ n. **1** cargo carried on a return journey.
2 an unedited video transmission via satellite or other means to a network or station. ■ a frequency on which such transmissions occur.
▶ v. carry (freight) on a return journey.

back·hoe /ˈbak,hō/ (Brit. also **backhoe loader**) ▶ n. a mechanical excavator that draws toward itself a bucket attached to a hinged boom.

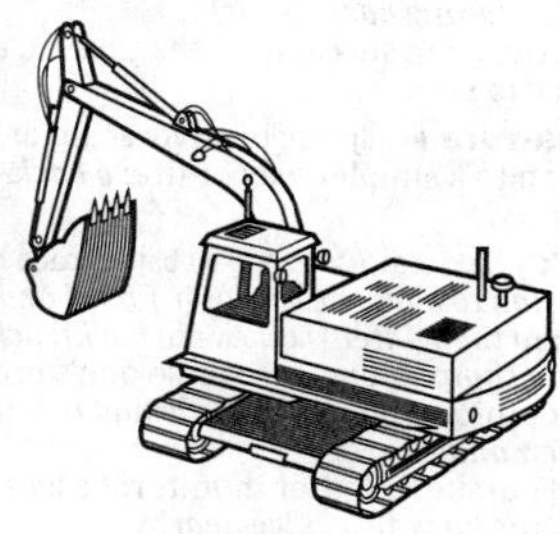
backhoe

back·ing /ˈbakiNG/ ▶ n. **1** support or help: *he accepted the backing of the police group | they had financial backing from local firms.* ■ a layer of material that forms, protects, or strengthens the back of something: *the fabric has a special backing for durability.* ■ (esp. in popular music) the music or singing that accompanies the main singer or soloist: *the trio provided backing to some of the most popular vocalists of the day* | [as modifier] *backing vocals.*
2 Phonetics the movement of the place of formation of a sound toward the back of the mouth.

back·ing track ▶ n. a recorded musical accompaniment, esp. for a soloist to play or sing along with.

back is·sue ▶ n. a past issue of a journal or magazine.

back·land /ˈbak,land/ ▶ n. **1** (also **backlands**) another term for BACKCOUNTRY.
2 land behind or beyond an area that is built on or otherwise developed.

back·lash /ˈbak,lasH/ ▶ n. **1** [in sing.] a strong and adverse reaction by a large number of people, esp. to a social or political development: *a public backlash against racism.*
2 recoil arising between parts of a mechanism. ■ degree of play between parts of a mechanism.

back·less /ˈbaklis/ ▶ adj. (of a woman's garment) cut low at the back: *a backless Lycra dress.*

back·light /ˈbak,līt/ ▶ n. illumination from behind.
▶ v. (past **backlit**; past participle **backlit** or **backlighted**) [with obj.] illuminate from behind: *she was backlit by the morning sun* | (as adj. **backlit**) *a backlit LCD screen.*
– DERIVATIVES **back·light·ing** n.

back·list /ˈbak,list/ ▶ n. a publisher's list of older books still in print.

back·load /ˈbak,lōd/ ▶ v. [with obj.] (usu. **be backloaded**) place more charges at the later stages of (a financial agreement) than at the earlier stages.

back·log /ˈbak,lôg, -,läg/ ▶ n. an accumulation of something, esp. uncompleted work or matters that need to be dealt with: *the company took on extra staff to clear the backlog of work.*

back·lot /ˈbak,lät/ ▶ n. an outdoor area in a movie studio where large exterior sets are made and some outside scenes are filmed.

back num·ber ▶ n. an issue of a periodical earlier than the current one. ■ informal a person or thing seen as old-fashioned.

back of·fice ▶ n. an office or center in which the administrative work of a business is carried out, as opposed to its dealings with customers.

back·or·der /ˈbak,ôrdər/ ▶ n. a retailer's order for a product that is temporarily out of stock with the supplier: *the phone I wanted was* ***on backorder.***
▶ v. [with obj.] place an order for (a product) that is temporarily out of stock.

back·pack /ˈbak,pak/ ▶ n. a bag with shoulder straps that allow it to be carried on one's back. ■ a load or piece of equipment carried on a person's back: *a two-tank scuba backpack.*
▶ v. [no obj.] (usu. as noun **backpacking**) travel or hike carrying one's belongings in a backpack: *a week's backpacking in the Pyrenees | he has backpacked around the world.*
– DERIVATIVES **back·pack·er** n.

back pay ▶ n. payment for work done in the past that was withheld at the time, or for work that could have been done had the worker not been prevented from doing so: *Hickman should be provided back pay plus any expenses.*

back·ped·al /ˈbak,pedl/ ▶ v. (**backpedals, backpedaling, backpedaled**; Brit. **backpedals, backpedalling, backpedalled**) [no obj.] move the pedals of a bicycle backward in order to brake. ■ move hastily backward: *backpedaling furiously, he flipped a perfect pass.* ■ reverse one's previous action or opinion: *you've criticized him for backpedaling on budget reform.*

back·plane /ˈbak,plān/ ▶ n. a board to which the main circuit boards of a computer may be connected and that provides connections between them.

back·plate /ˈbak,plāt/ ▶ n. a plate placed at or forming the back of something.

back-pro·jec·tion ▶ n. another term for REAR PROJECTION.

back·rest /ˈbak,rest/ ▶ n. a support for a person's back when the person is seated.

back·ro·nym /ˈbakrə,nim/ ▶ n. a fanciful expansion of an existing acronym or word, such as "port out, starboard home" for *posh.*
– ORIGIN blend of *back* and *acronym.*

back room ▶ n. a place where secret, administrative, or supporting work is done: *this would lead to weak government and deals in back rooms* | [as modifier] *back-room strategists.*

back·saw /ˈbak,sô/ ▶ n. a type of saw with a reinforced back edge that keeps the thin blade from being distorted.

back·scat·ter /ˈbak,skatər/ ▶ n. Physics deflection of radiation or particles through an angle of 180°. ■ radiation or particles that have been deflected in this way. ■ Photography light from a flashgun or other light source that is deflected directly into a lens: *backscatter causes an underexposed picture with a blizzard effect.*
▶ v. [with obj.] Physics deflect (radiation or particles) through an angle of 180°: (as adj. **backscattered**) *backscattered sound reaches the sonar receiver.*

back·scratch·er /ˈbak,skracHər/ ▶ n. a rod terminating in a clawed hand for scratching one's own back.

back·scratch·ing /ˈbak,skraCHiNG/ ▶ n. the mutual providing of favors or services, esp. when the legitimacy of such dealings is doubtful: *the friendship thrives on little more than mutual backscratching.*

back seat (also **backseat**) ▶ n. a seat at the back of a vehicle.
– PHRASES **take a back seat** take or be given a less important position or role: *printed words will take a back seat to TV and video screens.*

back·seat driv·er /ˈbakˈsēt/ ▶ n. a passenger in a car who gives the driver unwanted advice. ■ a person who is eager to advise without responsibility.
– DERIVATIVES **back·seat driv·ing** n.

back·shift /ˈbak,sHift/ ▶ n. Grammar the changing of a present tense in direct speech to a past tense in reported speech (or a past tense to pluperfect).

back·side /ˈbak,sīd/ ▶ n. informal a person's buttocks or rump. ■ the rear side or view of a thing: *the backside of the hill.*
▶ adj. (of a maneuver in surfing and other board sports) done clockwise for a regular rider and counterclockwise for a goofy rider.

back slang ▶ n. slang in which words are spoken as though they were spelled backward (e.g., *redraw* for *warder*).

back·slap·ping /ˈbak,slapiNG/ ▶ n. the action of effusively congratulating or encouraging someone, typically by slapping a person's back: *effusive displays of backslapping and arm-punching.*
▶ adj. vigorously hearty: *those cheerful, backslapping journalists.*
– DERIVATIVES **back·slap** v. & n., **back·slap·per** n.

b

back·slash /ˈbak,slasʜ/ ▶ **n.** Computing a backward-sloping diagonal line (\), used to separate file and folder names in some path statements.

back·slide /ˈbak,slīd/ ▶ **v.** (past **backslid**; past participle **backslid** or archaic **backslidden** /-,slidn/) [no obj.] relapse into bad ways or error: *converted vegetarians backslide to T-bones* | (as noun **backsliding**) *there would be no backsliding from the administration's sound policies.*
– DERIVATIVES **back·slid·er** n.

back·space /ˈbak,spās/ ▶ **n. 1** a key on a typewriter or computer keyboard that causes the carriage or cursor to move backward.
2 a device on a video recorder or camcorder that produces a slight backward run between shots to eliminate disturbance caused by the interruption of the scanning process.
▶ **v.** [no obj.] move a typewriter carriage or computer cursor back one or more spaces.

back·spin /ˈbak,spin/ ▶ **n.** a backward spin given to a moving ball, causing it to stop more quickly or rebound at a steeper angle on hitting a surface.

back·splash /ˈbak,splasʜ/ ▶ **n.** a panel behind a sink or stove that protects the wall from splashes.

back·stab·bing /ˈbak,stabiɴɢ/ ▶ **n.** the action or practice of criticizing someone in a treacherous manner while feigning friendship.
▶ **adj.** (of a person) behaving in such a way.
– DERIVATIVES **back·stab** v., **back·stab·ber** n.

back·stage /bakˈstāj/ ▶ **n.** the area in a theater out of view of the audience, esp. in the wings or dressing rooms: *backstage was the scene of pleasant pandemonium.*
▶ **adj.** of, relating to, or situated in the area behind the stage in a theater: *a backstage tour of the opera house.* ■ kept from public scrutiny; secret: *backstage deals.*
▶ **adv.** in or to the backstage area in a theater: *I went backstage after the show.* ■ not known to the public; in secret: *we planned our strategies backstage.*

back·stairs /ˈbakˈste(ə)rz/ ▶ **plural n.** stairs at the back or side of a building.
▶ **adj.** [attrib.] underhanded or clandestine: *I won't make backstairs deals with politicians.*

back·stay /ˈbak,stā/ ▶ **n.** a stay on a sailing ship leading downward and aft from the top or upper part of a mast.

back·stitch /ˈbak,sticʜ/ ▶ **n.** sewing with overlapping stitches.
▶ **v.** sew using backstitches: [with obj.] *you can simply backstitch the edges* | [no obj.] *this method avoids having to backstitch through open loops.*

back·stop /ˈbak,stäp/ ▶ **n.** a person or thing placed at the rear of or behind something as a barrier, support, or reinforcement: *bullets volleyed into the backstop of a flood-control canal.* ■ Baseball a high fence or similar structure behind the home plate area. ■ Baseball, informal a catcher: *he tore the chest protector completely off the big Yankee backstop.* ■ an emergency precaution or last resort: *the human operator has to act as the ultimate backstop when things go badly wrong.*
▶ **v.** [with obj.] Baseball act as backstop for. ■ Hockey act as goaltender for. ■ support or reinforce: *the founding banks were backstopping the loans.*

back·sto·ry /ˈbak,stôrē/ ▶ **n.** (pl. **backstories**) a history or background created for a fictional character in a motion picture or television program. ■ similar background information about a real person or thing that promotes fuller understanding of it: *the little-known backstory about the theory of evolution.*

back·street /ˈbak,strēt/ ▶ **n.** a minor street remote from a main road: *the fetid backstreets of the shanty town* | [as modifier] *a backstreet garage.*
▶ **adj.** [attrib.] operating or performed secretly, and typically illegally: *a loophole that allowed backstreet chemists to make methamphetamine.*

back·stretch /ˈbakˈstrecʜ/ ▶ **n.** the part of a racecourse that is farthest from the grandstand and parallel to the homestretch. ■ the area adjacent to a racetrack where the horses are stabled and stable employees have temporary living accommodations.

back·stroke /ˈbak,strōk/ ▶ **n.** [in sing.] a swimming stroke performed on the back with the arms lifted alternately out of the water in a backward circular motion and the legs extended and kicking: *I concentrated on the backstroke most of the time* | [as modifier] *I won the backstroke and breaststroke events* | [as adv.] *they would swim freestyle and then backstroke.* ■ (**the backstroke**) a race, typically of a specified length or kind, in which such a style of swimming is used: *he was fifth in the 200-meter backstroke.*
– DERIVATIVES **back·strok·er** n.

back·swept /ˈbak,swept/ ▶ **adj.** swept, slanted, or sloped backward: *his backswept hair.*

back·swim·mer /ˈbak,swimər/ ▶ **n.** a predatory aquatic bug that swims on its back using its long back legs as oars. It is able to capture large prey such as tadpoles and fish. See also WATER BOATMAN.
● Family Notonectidae, suborder Heteroptera: *Notonecta* and other genera.

backswimmer

back·swing /ˈbak,swiɴɢ/ ▶ **n.** a backward swing, esp. of an arm or of a golf club when about to hit a ball.

back·sword /ˈbak,sôrd/ ▶ **n.** a sword with only one cutting edge.

back talk (also **backtalk**) ▶ **n.** informal rude or impertinent remarks made in reply to someone in authority: *no back talk, I'm warning you.*

back-to-back ▶ **adj.** consecutive: *back-to-back homers in a major league baseball game.*
▶ **adv.** (**back to back**) **1** (of two people) facing in opposite directions with backs touching: *they sat on the ground, leaning back to back.*
2 consecutively; in succession: *the games were played back to back.*

back-to-na·ture ▶ **adj.** [attrib.] advocating or relating to reversion to a simpler way of life: *a back-to-nature lifestyle.*

back·track /ˈbak,trak/ ▶ **v. 1** [no obj.] retrace one's steps: *she had to bypass two closer farms and backtrack to them later* | figurative *to backtrack a little, the case is a complex one.* ■ reverse one's previous action or opinion: *the unions have had to* **backtrack** *on their demands.*
2 [with obj.] pursue, trace, or monitor: *he was able to backtrack the buck to a ridge nearby.*

back·up /ˈbak,əp/ ▶ **n. 1** help or support: *no police backup could be expected.* ■ a person or thing that can be called on if necessary; a reserve: *I've got a security force as backup* | *the filter is an excellent backup to other systems* | [as modifier] *a backup generator.*
2 Computing the procedure for making extra copies of data in case the original is lost or damaged: *automatic online backup* | [as modifier] *a backup system.* ■ a copy of this type.
3 an overflow caused by a stoppage, as in water or automobile traffic: *there are long backups on all routes.*

back·up light ▶ **n.** a light at the rear of a vehicle that comes on when the vehicle is in reverse gear.

back·ward /ˈbakwərd/ ▶ **adj. 1** [attrib.] directed behind or to the rear: *she left the room without a backward glance* | *a gradual backward movement.* ■ looking toward the past, rather than being progressive; retrograde: *he said the decision was a backward step.*
2 (of a person) having learning difficulties: *a lively child but a bit backward.* ■ having made less than normal progress: *economically backward countries.*
▶ **adv.** (also **backwards**) **1** (of a movement) away from one's front; in the direction of one's back: *he took a step backward* | *Harry suddenly fell backward into a somersault.* ■ in reverse of the usual direction or order: *counting backward* | *baseball caps turned backward.*
2 toward or into the past: *a loving look backward at his early life.* ■ toward or into a worse state: *a giant step backward for child-centered education.*
– PHRASES **backward and forward** in both directions alternately; to and fro. **bend** (or **lean**) **over backward to do something** informal make every effort, esp. to be fair or helpful: *Jensen bent over backward to be fair.* **know something backward** (**and forward**) be entirely familiar with something.
– DERIVATIVES **back·ward·ly** adv., **back·ward·ness** n.
– ORIGIN Middle English: from earlier *abackward*, from ABACK.

> **USAGE** In US English, the adverb form is sometimes spelled **backwards** (*the ladder fell backwards*), but the adjective is almost always **backward** (*a backward glance*). Directional words using the suffix *-ward* tend to have no *s* ending in US English, although **backwards** is more common than *afterwards, towards,* or *forwards.* The *s* ending often (but not always) appears in the phrases *backwards and forwards* and *bending over backwards.* In British English, the spelling **backwards** is more common than **backward**.

back·ward-com·pat·i·ble (also **backwards-compatible**) ▶ **adj.** (of computer hardware or software) able to be used with an older piece of hardware or software without special adaptation or modification.
– DERIVATIVES **back·ward com·pat·i·bil·i·ty** n.

back·wash /ˈbak,wôsʜ, -,wäsʜ/ ▶ **n.** the motion of receding waves. ■ a backward current of water or air created by the motion of an object through it: *the backwash of a truck on the highway.* ■ repercussions: *the backwash of the Cuban missile crisis.*
▶ **v.** [with obj.] clean (a filter) by reversing the flow of fluid through it.

back·wa·ter /ˈbak,wôtər, -,wätər/ ▶ **n.** a part of a river not reached by the current, where the water is stagnant: *the eels inhabit backwaters.* ■ an isolated or peaceful place: *a sleepy Midwest backwater.* ■ a place or condition in which no development or progress is taking place: *the country remained an economic backwater.*

back·wind /ˈbak,wind/ Sailing ▶ **v.** [with obj.] (of a sail or vessel) deflect a flow of air into the back of (another sail or vessel).
▶ **n.** a flow of air deflected into the back of a sail.

back·woods /ˈbakˈwo͝odz/ ▶ **plural n.** [often as modifier] remote uncleared forest land: *backwoods homesteads.* ■ a remote or sparsely inhabited region, esp. one considered backward.
– DERIVATIVES **back·woods·man** /-mən/ n.

back·yard /ˈbakˈyärd/ ▶ **n. 1** a yard behind a house or other building, typically surrounded by a fence: *a tree-shaded succession of backyards* | [as modifier] *a casual backyard party.*
2 the area close to where one lives, or the territory close to a particular country, regarded with proprietorial concern: *anything was preferable to a nuclear dump* **in their own backyard.**

Ba·co·lod /bəˈkō,lôd/ a city in the central Philippines, a port on the northwestern coast of the island of Negros; pop. 499,500 (est. 2007).

Ba·con[1] /ˈbākən/, Francis, Baron Verulam and Viscount St. Albans (1561–1626), English statesman and philosopher. As a scientist he advocated the inductive method. Notable works: *The Advancement of Learning* (1605) and *Novum Organum* (1620).

Ba·con[2], Francis (1909–92), Irish painter. His work chiefly depicts human figures in grotesquely distorted postures, their features blurred or erased.

Ba·con[3], Roger (c.1214–94), English philosopher, scientist, and Franciscan monk. Most notable for his work in the field of optics, he emphasized the need for an empirical approach to scientific study.

ba·con /ˈbākən/ ▶ **n.** cured meat from the back or sides of a pig.
– PHRASES **bring home the bacon** informal **1** supply material provision or support; earn a living. **2** achieve success. **save someone's bacon** see SAVE[1].
– ORIGIN Middle English: from Old French, from a Germanic word meaning 'ham, flitch'; related to BACK.

Ba·co·ni·an /bāˈkōnēən/ ▶ **adj.** of or relating to Sir Francis Bacon or his inductive method of reasoning and philosophy. ■ relating to or denoting the theory that Bacon wrote the plays attributed to Shakespeare.
▶ **n.** an adherent of Bacon's philosophical system. ■ a supporter of the theory that Bacon wrote the plays attributed to Shakespeare.

bac·te·re·mi·a /,baktəˈrēmēə/ (Brit. **bacteraemia**) ▶ **n.** Medicine the presence of bacteria in the blood.
– DERIVATIVES **bac·te·re·mic** /-mik/ adj.
– ORIGIN late 19th cent.: from BACTERIUM + -EMIA.

bac·te·ri·a /bakˈti(ə)rēə/ plural form of BACTERIUM.

> **USAGE** **Bacteria** is often mistakenly treated as a singular form, as in this sentence: *the* **bacteria** *causing salmonella* **is** *killed by thorough cooking.* But **bacteria** is the plural form (derived from Latin) of **bacterium**, and like any other plural, it should be used with the plural form of the verb. Hence, the sentence should read: *the* **bacteria** *causing salmonella* **are** *killed by thorough cooking.*

bac·te·ri·cide /bakˈti(ə)rə,sīd/ ▶ **n.** a substance that kills bacteria.
– DERIVATIVES **bac·te·ri·cid·al** /-,ti(ə)rəˈsīdl/ adj.

bacterio- (also **bacteri-**; also **bacter-** before a vowel) ▶ **comb. form** representing BACTERIUM.

bac·te·ri·o·cin /bakˈti(ə)rēəsin/ ▶ **n.** Biology a protein produced by bacteria of one strain and active against those of a closely related strain.
– ORIGIN 1950s: from French *bactériocine*, from Greek *baktērion* 'small cane' + a shortened form of COLICIN.

bac·te·ri·o·log·i·cal /bak,ti(ə)rēəˈläjikəl/ ▶ **adj.** [attrib.] of or relating to bacteriology or bacteria. ■ relating to or denoting germ warfare.
– DERIVATIVES **bac·te·ri·o·log·ic** /-jik/ adj., **bac·te·ri·o·log·i·cal·ly** /-ik(ə)lē/ adv.

bac·te·ri·ol·o·gy /bak,ti(ə)rēˈäləjē/ ▶ **n.** the study of bacteria.
– DERIVATIVES **bac·te·ri·ol·o·gist** /-jist/ n.

b

bac·te·ri·ol·y·sis /bak,ti(ə)rē'äləsis/ ▶ **n.** Biology the rupture of bacterial cells, esp. by an antibody.
– DERIVATIVES **bac·te·ri·o·lyt·ic** /-,ti(ə)rēə'litik/ **adj.**

bac·te·ri·o·phage /bak'ti(ə)rēə,fāj/ ▶ **n.** Biology a virus that parasitizes a bacterium by infecting it and reproducing inside it.
– ORIGIN 1920s: from BACTERIUM + Greek *phagein* 'eat.'

bac·te·ri·o·rho·dop·sin /bak,ti(ə)rēō-rō'däpsin/ ▶ **n.** a protein pigment in the bacterium *Halobacterium halobium* that when illuminated transports protons across the cytoplasmic membrane in large numbers.

bac·te·ri·o·stat /bak'ti(ə)rēə,stat/ ▶ **n.** a substance that prevents the multiplying of bacteria without destroying them.
– DERIVATIVES **bac·te·ri·o·sta·sis** /-,ti(ə)rēə'stāsis/ **n.**, **bac·te·ri·o·stat·ic** /-,ti(ə)rēə'statik/ **adj.**, **bac·te·ri·o·stat·i·cal·ly adv.**
– ORIGIN early 20th cent.: from BACTERIUM + Greek *statos* 'standing.'

bac·te·ri·um /bak'ti(ə)rēəm/ ▶ **n.** (pl. **bacteria** /-'ti(ə)rēə/) a member of a large group of unicellular microorganisms that have cell walls but lack organelles and an organized nucleus, including some that can cause disease.

> Bacteria are widely distributed in soil, water, and air, and on or in the tissues of plants and animals. Formerly included in the plant kingdom, they are now classified separately (as prokaryotes). They play a vital role in global ecology, as the chemical changes they bring about include those of organic decay and nitrogen fixation. Much modern biochemical knowledge has been gained from the study of bacteria because they grow easily and reproduce rapidly in laboratory cultures.

– DERIVATIVES **bac·te·ri·al** /-'ti(ə)rēəl/ **adj.**
– ORIGIN mid 19th cent.: modern Latin, from Greek *baktērion*, diminutive of *baktēria* 'staff, cane' (because the first ones to be discovered were rod-shaped). Compare with BACILLUS.

> **USAGE** See usage at BACTERIA.

bac·te·ri·u·ri·a /bak,ti(ə)rē'yo͝orēə/ ▶ **n.** Medicine the presence of bacteria in the urine.

bac·te·rize /'baktə,rīz/ ▶ **v.** [with obj.] treat with bacteria.
– DERIVATIVES **bac·te·ri·za·tion** /,baktərə'zāsʜən/ **n.**

bac·te·roid /'baktə,roid/ ▶ **adj.** of the nature of or resembling a bacterium.
▶ **n.** a bacteroid organism or structure, esp. a modified cell formed by a symbiotic bacterium in a root nodule of a leguminous plant.

Bac·tri·a /'baktrēə/ an ancient country in central Asia, corresponding to the northern part of modern Afghanistan.
– DERIVATIVES **Bac·tri·an adj. & n.**

Bac·tri·an cam·el /'baktrēən/ ▶ **n.** the two-humped camel, which has been domesticated but is still found wild in central Asia. ● *Camelus bactrianus* (formerly *ferus*), family Camelidae.

bac·u·lo·vi·rus /'bakyəlō,vīrəs/ ▶ **n.** Biology a member of a family of DNA viruses infecting only invertebrate animals. Some have a very specific insect host and may be used in biological pest control.
– ORIGIN 1980s: from Latin *baculum* 'rod, stick' + VIRUS.

bac·u·lum /'bakyo͝oləm/ ▶ **n.** (pl. **bacula** /-lə/) another term for OS PENIS.
– ORIGIN 1930s: modern Latin.

bad /bad/ ▶ **adj.** (**worse** /wərs/; **worst** /wərst/) **1** of poor quality; inferior or defective: *a bad diet* | *bad eyesight.* ■ (of a person) not able to do something well; incompetent: *I'm so* **bad at** *names* | *a bad listener.*
2 not such as to be hoped for or desired; unpleasant or unwelcome: *bad weather* | *we had the worst luck* | (as noun **the bad**) *taking the good with the bad.* ■ (of an unwelcome thing) serious; severe: *bad headaches* | *a bad crash* | *a bad mistake.* ■ unfavorable; adverse: *bad reviews.* ■ harmful: *soap was* **bad for** *his face.* ■ not suitable: *morning was a bad time to ask Andy about anything.*
3 (of food) decayed; putrid: *everything in the fridge would go bad.* ■ (of the atmosphere) polluted; unhealthy: *bad air.*
4 (of parts of the body) injured, diseased, or causing pain: *a bad back.* ■ [as complement] (of a person) unwell: *I feel bad.*
5 [as complement] regretful, guilty, or ashamed about something: *working mothers who feel bad about leaving their children.*
6 morally depraved; wicked: *the bad guys* | *bad language* | *a bad reputation.* ■ naughty; badly behaved: *what a bad girl* | *bad behavior.*
7 worthless; not valid: *he ran up 87 bad checks.*
8 (**badder, baddest**) informal good; excellent: *they want the baddest, best-looking Corvette there is.*
▶ **adv.** informal badly: *he beat her up real bad.*
– PHRASES **come to a bad end** see END. **from bad to worse** into an even worse state: *the country's going from bad to worse.* **in a bad way** ill: *Sammy shivered. He was in a bad way.* ■ in trouble: *the fleet was in a bad way, mainly due to a shortage of spares.* **my bad** informal used to acknowledge responsibility for a mistake: *Sorry about the confusion. It's my bad.* **not** (or **not so**) **bad** informal fairly good: *she discovered he wasn't so bad after all.* **to the bad** to ruin: *I hate to see you going to the bad.* ■ in deficit: *he was $80 to the bad.* **too bad** informal used to indicate that something is regrettable but now beyond retrieval: *too bad, but that's the way it is.*
– DERIVATIVES **bad·dish adj.**, **bad·ness n.**
– ORIGIN Middle English: perhaps representing Old English *bǣddel* 'hermaphrodite, womanish man.'

> **USAGE** Confusion in the use of **bad** versus **badly** usually has to do with verbs called copulas, such as *feel* or *seem*. Thus, standard usage calls for *I feel bad*, not *I feel badly*. As a precise speaker or writer would explain, *I feel badly* means 'I do not have a good sense of touch.' See also usage at GOOD.

> **WORD TRENDS** See SICK[1].

bad·ass /'bad,as/ informal ▶ **n.** a tough, aggressive, or uncooperative person: *one of them is a real badass, the other's pretty friendly.*
▶ **adj. 1** tough or aggressive: *a strange fellow with a badass temper.* ■ particularly bad or severe: *some badass virus I'd caught at sea.*
2 formidable; excellent: *this was one badass camera.*
– ORIGIN 1950s: from the adjective BAD + ASS[2].

bad blood ▶ **n.** ill feeling: *there has always been bad blood between these families.*

bad boy ▶ **n.** informal **1** a man who does not conform to approved standards of behavior, esp. in a particular sphere of activity: *the bad boy of classical music.*
2 a thing that is regarded as extremely impressive or effective: *we went 142 mph in that bad boy.*

bad break ▶ **n.** informal a piece of bad luck: *a weird coincidence and a bad break.*

bad breath ▶ **n.** unpleasant-smelling breath; halitosis.

bad debt ▶ **n.** a debt that cannot be recovered.

bad·de·ley·ite /'bad(ə)lē,īt/ ▶ **n.** a mineral consisting largely of zirconium dioxide, ranging from colorless to yellow, brown, or black.
– ORIGIN late 19th cent.: named after Joseph Baddeley, English traveler, + -ITE[1].

bad·der·locks /'badər,läks/ ▶ **plural n.** chiefly Scottish an edible seaweed with a long greenish frond and prominent midrib, occurring in northern Europe. ● *Alaria esculenta*, class Phaeophyceae.
– ORIGIN late 18th cent.: perhaps from *Balderlocks*, based on the name of the god BALDER.

bad·dy /'badē/ (also **baddie**) informal ▶ **n.** (pl. **baddies**) a villain or criminal in a story, movie, etc.

bade /bad, bād/ past of BID[2].

bad egg ▶ **n.** see EGG[1] (sense 2).

Ba·den /'bädn/ a spa town in eastern Austria, south of Vienna; pop. 25,255 (2006). It is noted for its warm mineral springs.

Ba·den-Ba·den /,bädn 'bädn/ a spa town in the Black Forest in southwestern Germany; pop. 54,900 (est. 2007).

Ba·den-Pow·ell /,bädn 'pōəl, 'pou-əl/, Robert (Stephenson Smyth), 1st Baron Baden-Powell of Gilwell (1857–1941), English soldier and founder of the Boy Scout movement.

Ba·den-Würt·tem·berg /'wərtəm,bərg, 'vʏrtəm,berk/ a state of western Germany; capital, Stuttgart.

bad faith ▶ **n.** intent to deceive: *the owners have bargained* **in bad faith**. ■ (in existentialist philosophy) refusal to confront facts or choices.

bad form ▶ **n.** an offense against current social conventions: *it was considered bad form to talk about money.*

badge /baj/ ▶ **n.** a distinctive emblem worn as a mark of office, membership, achievement, licensed employment, etc.: *name badges* | *a Girl Scout badge.* ■ a distinguishing object or emblem: *a large gold key hung around his neck as his badge of office.* ■ a feature or sign that reveals a particular condition or quality: *my jeans had patches on the knees, like badges of courage marking encounters with barbed wire.*
▶ **v.** [with obj.] mark with a badge or other distinguishing emblem.
– ORIGIN late Middle English: of unknown origin.

badge en·gi·neer·ing ▶ **n.** the practice of marketing a motor vehicle under two or more brand names.

badg·er /'bajər/ ▶ **n. 1** a heavily built omnivorous nocturnal mammal of the weasel family, typically having a gray and black coat. ● Several genera and species in the family Mustelidae, in particular the Eurasian *Meles meles*, which has a white head with two black stripes, and the North American *Taxidea taxus*, with a white stripe on the head.
2 (**Badger**) informal a native of Wisconsin.
▶ **v.** [with obj.] ask (someone) repeatedly and annoyingly for something; pester: *journalists* **badgered** *him* **about** *the deals* | *Tom had finally* **badgered** *her* **into** *going* | [with obj. and infinitive] *his daughter was always badgering him to let her join.*
– ORIGIN early 16th cent.: perhaps from BADGE, with reference to its distinctive head markings. The verb sense (late 18th cent.) originates from the formerly popular sport of badger baiting.

badger 1

Badg·er State a nickname for the state of WISCONSIN[1].

bad hair day ▶ **n.** informal a day on which everything seems to go wrong, characterized as a day on which one's hair is particularly unmanageable.

bad·i·nage /,badn'äzʜ/ ▶ **n.** humorous or witty conversation: *cultured badinage about art and life.*
– ORIGIN mid 17th cent.: from French, from *badiner* 'to joke,' from *badin* 'fool,' based on Provençal *badar* 'gape.'

bad·lands /'bad,landz/ ▶ **plural n.** extensive tracts of heavily eroded, uncultivable land with little vegetation. ■ (**the Badlands**) a barren plateau region of the western US, mainly in southwestern South Dakota and northwestern Nebraska, south of the Black Hills, noted for its harsh terrain.
– ORIGIN mid 19th cent. (originally US): translation of French *mauvaises terres*.

bad·ly /'badlē/ ▶ **adv.** (**worse** /wərs/, **worst** /wərst/) **1** in an unsatisfactory, inadequate, or unsuccessful way: *a badly managed company* | *the war was going badly.* ■ in an unfavorable way: *try not to think badly of me.* ■ in an unacceptable or unpleasant way: *she realized she was behaving rather badly.*
2 to a great or serious degree; severely: *the building was badly damaged by fire* | *I wanted a baby so badly* | *things had begun to go badly wrong.*
▶ **adj.** [as complement] informal guilty or regretful: *I felt badly about my unfriendliness of the previous evening.*
– PHRASES **badly off** in an unfavorable situation; at a disadvantage: *with his pension benefits, he shouldn't be too badly off* | *she was a lot worse off before the divorce.*

> **USAGE** See usage at BAD.

bad man·ners ▶ **plural n.** lack of polite or well-bred social behavior: *it's bad manners to talk with your mouth full.*
– DERIVATIVES **bad-mannered adj.**

bad·min·ton /'badmintn/ ▶ **n.** a game with rackets in which a shuttlecock is played back and forth across a net.
– ORIGIN named after *Badminton*, a country home in southwestern England.

bad-mouth ▶ **v.** [with obj.] informal criticize (someone or something); speak disloyally of: *no one wants to hire an individual who bad-mouths a prior employer.*

bad news ▶ **n.** informal an unpleasant or undesirable person or thing: *dry weather is always bad news for gardeners.*

bad-tem·pered ▶ **adj.** easily annoyed or made angry: *in a heat wave, many people become*

b

increasingly bad-tempered. ■ characterized by anger or ungraciousness: *Mary was feeling very bad-tempered | a bad-tempered exchange.*
–DERIVATIVES **bad-tem·pered·ly** adv.

Bae·de·ker /ˈbādikər, ˈbed-/, Karl (1801–59), German publisher of travel guidebooks. He is remembered chiefly for the series of guidebooks to which he gave his name and which are still published.

Bae·ke·land /ˈbakəˌlänt, ˈbāk(ə)lənd/, Leo Hendrik (1863–1944), US chemist and inventor; born in Belgium. He invented and developed the synthetic resin Bakelite in 1907.

Baer /be(ə)r/, Karl Ernest von (1792–1876), German biologist. He discovered that ova are particles within the ovarian follicles, and he formulated the principle that general characters appear before special ones do in the developing embryo. His studies were used by Darwin in the theory of evolution.

Bae·yer /ˈbāər/, Adolph Johann Friedrich Wilhelm von (1835–1917), German organic chemist. He prepared the first barbiturates, investigated dyes, and synthesized indigo. Nobel Prize for Chemistry (1905).

Ba·ez /ˈbīˌez, bīˈez/, Joan (1941–), US folk singer and civil rights activist. She is best known for her performances at civil rights demonstrations in the early 1960s. Notable albums: *Any Day Now* (1968) and *Diamonds and Rust* (1975).

Baf·fin /ˈbafən/, William (*c.*1584–1622), English navigator and explorer, the pilot of several expeditions in search of the Northwest Passage 1612–16. He discovered the largest island of the Canadian Arctic in 1616; this and the strait between it and Greenland are named after him.

Baf·fin Bay an extension of the North Atlantic Ocean between Baffin Island and Greenland, linked to the Arctic Ocean by three passages. It is largely ice-bound in winter.

Baf·fin Is·land a large island in the Canadian Arctic Ocean, situated at the mouth of Hudson Bay. It is separated from Greenland by Baffin Bay.

baf·fle /ˈbafəl/ ▶ **v.** [with obj.] **1** totally bewilder or perplex: *an unexplained occurrence that baffled everyone.*
2 restrain or regulate (a fluid, sound, etc.): *to baffle the noise further, I pad the gunwales.*
▶ **n.** a device used to restrain the flow of a fluid, gas, or loose material or to prevent the spreading of sound or light in a particular direction.
–DERIVATIVES **baf·fle·ment** n. (sense 1 of the verb).
–ORIGIN late 16th cent. (in the sense 'cheat, deceive'): perhaps related to French *bafouer* 'ridicule' or obsolete French *beffer* 'mock, deceive.'

baf·fle·gab /ˈbafəlˌgab/ ▶ **n.** informal incomprehensible or pretentious language, esp. bureaucratic jargon: *the smooth chairman who had elevated bafflegab to an art form.*

baff·ling /ˈbaf(ə)liNG/ ▶ **adj.** impossible to understand; perplexing: *the crime is a baffling mystery for the police.*
–DERIVATIVES **baf·fling·ly** adv. [as submodifier] *his team selection has been bafflingly erratic.*

bag /bag/ ▶ **n. 1** a container of flexible material with an opening at the top, used for carrying things: *brown paper bags | a shopping bag.* ■ an amount held by such a container: *a bag of apples.* ■ a woman's handbag or purse. ■ a piece of luggage: *she began to unpack her bags.* ■ Baseball a base. ■ (**bags**) informal, chiefly Brit. plenty of something: *I had bags of energy.*
2 the amount of game shot by a hunter.
3 (usu. **bags**) a loose fold of skin under a person's eye: *the bags under his eyes gave him a sad appearance.*
4 informal, derogatory a woman, esp. an older one, perceived as unpleasant, bad-tempered, or unattractive: *an interfering old bag.*
5 (**one's bag**) informal one's particular interest or taste: *if religion and politics are your bag, you'll find something to interest you here.*
▶ **v.** (**bags, bagging, bagged**) [with obj.] **1** put (something) in a bag: *customers bagged their own groceries | we bagged up the apples.*
2 (of a hunter) succeed in killing or catching an animal: *in 1979, handgun hunters bagged 677 deer.* ■ succeed in securing (something): *we've bagged three awards for excellence.*
3 [no obj.] (of clothes, esp. pants) hang loosely or lose shape: *these trousers never bag at the knee.* ■ swell or bulge.
4 quit; give up on: *it was a drag to be in the ninth grade at 17, so he bagged it.*
5 informal fit (a patient) with an oxygen mask or other respiratory aid.
–PHRASES **bag and baggage** with all one's belongings: *he threw her out bag and baggage.* **a bag of bones** an emaciated person or animal: *the pony is just a bag of bones.* **a bag** (or **whole bag**) **of tricks** informal a set of ingenious plans, techniques, or resources: *hoteliers are using a whole new bag of tricks to keep their guests on the premises.* **be left holding the bag** see HOLD¹. **in the bag** informal **1** (of something desirable) as good as secured: *the election is in the bag.* **2** drunk: *I don't think my parents even suspected that I was half in the bag.*
–DERIVATIVES **bag·ful** /-ˌfo͝ol/ n. (pl. **bagfuls**).
–ORIGIN Middle English: perhaps from Old Norse *baggi.*

Ba·gan·da /bəˈgändə/ (also **Ganda**) ▶ **plural n.** (sing. **Muganda** /mo͞oˈgändə/) a Bantu people of the kingdom of Buganda, now forming part of Uganda. Their language is Luganda.
▶ **adj.** of or relating to the Baganda.
–ORIGIN a local name; compare with Kiswahili *Waganda.*

ba·gasse /bəˈgas/ ▶ **n.** the dry pulpy residue left after the extraction of juice from sugar cane, used as fuel for electricity generators, etc.
–ORIGIN early 19th cent.: from French, from Spanish *bagazo* 'pulp.'

bag·a·telle /ˌbagəˈtel/ ▶ **n. 1** a thing of little importance; a very easy task: *dealing with these boats was a mere bagatelle for the world's oldest yacht club.*
2 a game in which small balls are hit and then allowed to roll down a sloping board on which there are holes, each numbered with the score achieved if a ball goes into it, with pins acting as obstructions.
3 a short, light piece of music, esp. one for the piano.
–ORIGIN mid 17th cent. (sense 1): from French, from Italian *bagatella*, perhaps from *baga* 'baggage' or from a diminutive of Latin *baca* 'berry.' Sense 2 dates from the early 19th cent.

ba·gel /ˈbāgəl/ ▶ **n.** a dense bread roll in the shape of a ring, made by boiling dough and then baking it.
–ORIGIN early 20th cent. (as *beigel*): from Yiddish *beygel.*

bag·gage /ˈbagij/ ▶ **n. 1** personal belongings packed in suitcases for traveling; luggage. ■ the portable equipment of an army.
2 past experiences or long-held ideas regarded as burdens and impediments: *the emotional baggage I'm hauling around | the party jettisoned its traditional ideological baggage.*
–ORIGIN late Middle English: from Old French *bagage* (from *baguer* 'tie up'), or *bagues* 'bundles'; perhaps related to BAG.

bag·gage claim ▶ **n.** [in sing.] the area in an airport where arriving passengers collect luggage that has been carried in the hold of the aircraft.

Bag·gie /ˈbagē/ ▶ **n.** (pl. **Baggies**) trademark a plastic bag typically used for storing food. ■ (**baggie**) informal any small plastic bag.

bag·ging /ˈbagiNG/ ▶ **n.** material out of which bags are made.

bag·gy /ˈbagē/ ▶ **adj.** (**baggier, baggiest**) (of clothing) loose and hanging in folds: *baggy pants.* ■ (of eyes) with folds of puffy skin below them: *his eyes were baggy with the fatigue of overwork.*
▶ **n.** (**baggies**) informal loose and wide-legged pants, shorts, or swim trunks.
–DERIVATIVES **bag·gi·ly** /ˈbagəlē/ adv., **bag·gi·ness** n.

Bagh·dad /ˈbagˌdad, bagˈdad/ the capital of Iraq, on the Tigris River; pop. 6,194,800 (est. 2009).

bag la·dy ▶ **n.** informal a homeless woman who carries her possessions in shopping bags.

bag·less /ˈbaglis/ ▶ **adj.** (of a vacuum cleaner) designed to operate without the use of a replaceable bag.

bag lunch ▶ **n.** a cold lunch prepared at home and carried in a bag to work, to school, or on an excursion.

bag·man /ˈbagˌman, -mən/ ▶ **n.** (pl. **bagmen**) **1** informal an agent who collects or distributes the proceeds of illicit activities: *one million dollars cash paid to the general's bagman.*
2 Canadian a political fundraiser: *a Tory bagman.*
3 Brit. informal, dated a traveling salesman.

bagn·io /ˈbanyō, ˈbän-/ ▶ **n.** (pl. **bagnios**) **1** archaic a brothel.
2 historical an oriental prison.
–ORIGIN late 16th cent. (sense 2): from Italian *bagno*, from Latin *balneum* 'bath.'

bag of wa·ters ▶ **n.** the fluid-filled sac that contains and protects the fetus in the womb and that releases its fluids when it breaks during birth.

bag·pipe /ˈbagˌpīp/ ▶ **n.** (usu. **bagpipes**) a musical instrument with reed pipes that are sounded by the pressure of wind emitted from a bag squeezed by the player's arm. Bagpipes are associated esp. with Scotland, but are also used in folk music in Ireland, Northumberland, and France.
–DERIVATIVES **bag·pip·er** /ˈbagˌpīpər/ n.

bagpipes

ba gua /ˌbä ˈgwä/ (also **pa kua**) ▶ **n.** a Chinese religious motif incorporating the eight trigrams of the *I Ching*, typically arranged octagonally around a symbol denoting the balance of yin and yang, or around a mirror. ■ this motif regarded in feng shui as a pattern determining the significance and auspicious qualities of spatial relationships. ■ a Chinese martial art in which movements are focused on a circle and the defense of eight points around it.
–ORIGIN from Chinese *bā* 'eight' + *guà* 'divinatory symbols.'

ba·guette /baˈget/ ▶ **n. 1** a long, narrow loaf of French bread.
2 a gem, esp. a diamond, cut in a long rectangular shape: [often as modifier] *a baguette diamond.*
3 Architecture a small molding, semicircular in section.
4 a slim, rectangular handbag.
–ORIGIN early 18th cent. (sense 3): from French, from Italian *bacchetto*, diminutive of *bacchio*, from Latin *baculum* 'staff.' Sense 1 and sense 2 date from the 20th cent.

bag·worm /ˈbagˌwərm/ ▶ **n.** a drab moth, the caterpillar and flightless female of which live in a portable protective case constructed out of plant debris. ● Family Psychidae: many genera.

bah /bä/ ▶ **exclam.** an expression of contempt or disagreement: *You think it was an accident? Bah!*
–ORIGIN early 19th cent.: probably from French.

Ba·ha·'i /bəˈhī/ (also **Bahai**) ▶ **n.** (pl. **Baha'is**) a monotheistic religion founded in the 19th century as a development of Babism, emphasizing the essential oneness of humankind and of all religions and seeking world peace. The Baha'i faith was founded by the Persian **Baha'ullah** (1817–92) and his son **Abdul Baha** (1844–1921). ■ an adherent of the Baha'i faith.
–DERIVATIVES **Ba·ha·'ism** /-ˌizəm/ n.
–ORIGIN Persian, from Arabic *bahā'* 'splendor.'

Ba·ha·mas /bəˈhäməz/ a country in the northwestern West Indies, an archipelago off the southeastern coast of Florida; pop. 307,600 (est. 2009); capital, Nassau; languages, English (official), Creole.

> It was here that Columbus first landed in the New World (Oct. 12, 1492). The islands were a British colony from the 18th century until they gained independence within the Commonwealth of Nations in 1973.

–DERIVATIVES **Ba·ha·mi·an** /bəˈhāmēən, -ˈhäm-/ adj. & n.

Ba·ha·sa In·do·ne·sia /bəˈhäsə ˌindəˈnēZHə/ ▶ **n.** the official language of Indonesia. See INDONESIAN.
–ORIGIN from Malay *bahasa* 'language.'

Ba·ha·sa Ma·lay·sia /bəˈhäsə məˈlāZHə/ ▶ **n.** the official language of Malaysia. See MALAY.

Ba·ha·wal·pur /bəˈhä-wəlˌpo͝or/ a city in east central Pakistan, in Punjab province; pop. 530,400 (est. 2009).

Ba·hi·a /bäˈēə, bəˈhēə/ **1** a state of eastern Brazil, on the Atlantic coast; capital, Salvador.
2 former name for SALVADOR.

Ba·hí·a Blan·ca /bäˈēə ˈbläNGkə/ a port in Argentina serving the southern part of the country; pop. 315,700 (est. 2008).

Bah·rain /bäˈrān/ a country in western Asia that consists of a group of islands in the Persian Gulf; pop. 728,700 (est. 2009); capital, Manama; official language, Arabic.

> Ruled by the Portuguese in the 16th century and the Persians in the 17th century, Bahrain became a British protectorate in 1861 and gained independence in 1971. Its economy is dependent on the refining and export of oil.

–DERIVATIVES **Bah·rain·i** /-ˈrānē/ adj. & n.

baht /bät/ ▶ **n.** (pl. **same**) the basic monetary unit of Thailand, equal to 100 satangs.
–ORIGIN from Thai *bāt.*

Ba·hu·tu /bäˈho͞oˌto͞o/ plural form of HUTU.

Bai·kal, Lake /bīˈkäl, -ˈkôl, -ˈkal/ (also **Baykal**) a large lake in southern Siberia, in Russia, the largest freshwater lake in Europe and Asia and, with a depth of 5,714 feet (1,743 m), the deepest lake in the world.

bail¹ /bāl/ ▶ **n.** the temporary release of an accused person awaiting trial, sometimes on condition that a sum of money be lodged to guarantee their

appearance in court: *he has been released on bail.* ■ money paid by or for such a person as security.
▶ v. [with obj.] (usu. **be bailed**) release or secure the release of (a prisoner) on payment of bail: *his son called home to get bailed out of jail.* See also **BAIL OUT** at **BAIL³**.
– PHRASES **jump bail** informal fail to appear for trial after being released on bail: *he jumped bail and was on the run until his arrest.* **go bail** (or **stand bail**) act as surety for an accused person. **post bail** pay a sum of money as bail: *I posted bail for him.*
– DERIVATIVES **bail·a·ble** adj.
– ORIGIN Middle English: from Old French, literally 'custody, jurisdiction,' from Old French *bailler* 'take charge of,' from Latin *bajulare* 'bear a burden.'

bail² ▶ n. **1** a bar that holds something in place, in particular: ■ Fishing a bar that guides fishing line on a reel. ■ a bar on a typewriter or computer printer that holds the paper steady. ■ Mountaineering a bar on a crampon that fits into a groove in the sole of a boot. ■ a bar separating horses in an open stable.
2 an arched handle, such as on a bucket or a teapot: [as modifier] *drawers fitted with brass bail handles.*
3 (usu. **bails**) Cricket either of the two crosspieces bridging the stumps, which the bowler and fielders try to dislodge with the ball to get the batsman out.
– ORIGIN Middle English (denoting the outer wall of a castle): from Old French *baile* 'palisade, enclosure,' *baillier* 'enclose,' perhaps from Latin *baculum* 'rod, stick.' Compare with **BAILEY**.

bail³ ▶ v. **1** [with obj.] scoop water out of (a ship or boat): *the first priority is to* **bail out** *the boat with buckets.* ■ scoop (water) out of a ship or boat: *I started to use my hands to* **bail out** *the water.*
2 [no obj.] abandon a commitment, obligation, or responsibility: *after 12 years of this, including Sunday Mass with the family, I bailed.* ■ (**bail on**) let (someone) down by failing to fulfill a commitment, obligation, or responsibility: *he looks a little like the guy who bailed on me.*
– PHRASAL VERBS **bail out** (of a member of an aircrew) make an emergency parachute descent from an aircraft; eject. ■ become free of an obligation or commitment; discontinue an activity: *she felt ready to* **bail out of** *the corporate rat race.* **bail someone/something out** release someone or something from a difficulty; rescue: *the state will not bail out loss-making enterprises.*
– DERIVATIVES **bail·er** n.
– ORIGIN early 17th cent.: from obsolete *bail* 'bucket,' from French *baille*, based on Latin *bajulus* 'carrier.'

bai·le /ˈbīlā/ ▶ n. (in the southwestern US and parts of Central and South America) a gathering for dancing.
– ORIGIN Spanish, 'dance, dancing.'

Bai·le Átha Cli·ath /blä ˈklēə/ Irish name for **DUBLIN**.

bail·ee /bāˈlē/ ▶ n. Law a person or party to whom goods are delivered for a purpose, such as custody or repair, without transfer of ownership.

Bai·ley /ˈbālē/, Frederick Augustus Washington, see **DOUGLASS**.

bai·ley /ˈbālē/ ▶ n. (pl. **baileys**) the outer wall of a castle. ■ a court enclosed by this.
– ORIGIN Middle English: probably from Old French *baile* 'palisade, enclosure' (see **BAIL²**).

bail·ie /ˈbālē/ ▶ n. (pl. **bailies**) chiefly historical a municipal officer and magistrate in Scotland.
– ORIGIN Middle English (originally used interchangeably with **BAILIFF**): from Old French *bailli*.

bail·iff /ˈbālif/ ▶ n. a person who performs certain actions under legal authority, in particular: ■ an official in a court of law who keeps order, looks after prisoners, etc. ■ chiefly Brit. a sheriff's officer who executes writs and processes and carries out distraints and arrests. ■ Brit. the agent or steward of a landlord.
– ORIGIN Middle English: from Old French *baillif*, inflected form of *bailli*, based on Latin *bajulus* 'carrier, manager.'

bail·i·wick /ˈbāləˌwik/ ▶ n. **1** (**one's bailiwick**) one's sphere of operations or particular area of interest: *you never give the presentations—that's my bailiwick.*
2 Law the district or jurisdiction of a bailie or bailiff.
– ORIGIN late Middle English: from **BAILIE** + **WICK²**.

bail·ment /ˈbālmənt/ ▶ n. Law an act of delivering goods to a bailee for a particular purpose, without transfer of ownership.

bail·or /ˈbālər/ ▶ n. Law a person or party that entrusts goods to a bailee.

bail·out /ˈbālˌout/ ▶ n. informal an act of giving financial assistance to a failing business or economy to save it from collapse.

Bain·bridge Island /ˈbānˌbrij/ an island in western Washington, in Puget Sound, west of Seattle.

bain-ma·rie /ˌban məˈrē/ ▶ n. (pl. **bains-marie** pronunc. **same**) a container holding hot water into which a pan is placed for slow cooking. ■ chiefly Brit. a double boiler.
– ORIGIN early 18th cent.: French, translation of medieval Latin *balneum Mariae* 'bath of Maria,' translating Greek *kaminos Marias* 'furnace of Maria,' said to be a Jewish alchemist.

Baird /be(ə)rd/, John Logie (1888–1946), Scottish inventor. He made the first transatlantic transmission and demonstration of color television in 1928 using a mechanical system that was soon superseded by an electronic system.

Bai·ri·ki /ˈbīˌrēkē/ the capital of Kiribati, on South Tarawa Island; pop. 2,766 (2005).

bairn /be(ə)rn/ ▶ n. chiefly Scottish & N. English a child.
– ORIGIN Old English *bearn*, of Germanic origin; related to the verb **BEAR¹**.

Bai·sak·hi /bīˈsäkē/ ▶ n. a Sikh festival held annually to commemorate the founding of the khalsa by Gobind Singh in 1699.
– ORIGIN from Sanskrit *Vaiśākha*, denoting a month of the Hindu lunar year corresponding to April–May, regarded in some areas as the start of the new year.

bait /bāt/ ▶ n. **1** food used to entice fish or other animals as prey: *herrings make excellent bait for pike | fishing with live baits.* ■ an allurement; a thing intended to tempt or entice: *she used the prospect of freedom as bait to trap him into talking | many potential buyers are reluctant to* **take the bait**.
2 variant spelling of **BATE**.
▶ v. [with obj.] **1** deliberately annoy or taunt (someone): *the other boys reveled in* **baiting him about** *his love of literature.* ■ torment (a trapped or restrained animal), esp. by allowing dogs to attack it.
2 prepare (a hook, trap, net, or fishing area) with bait to entice fish or animals as prey: *she baited a trap with carrots and corn.*
– PHRASES **fish or cut bait** informal stop vacillating and act on something or disengage from it: *when it comes to flagging brands, companies are being forced to fish or cut bait.* **rise to the bait** react to a provocation or temptation exactly as intended: *Jenny was being provocatively rude, but he never rose to the bait.* **with baited breath** misspelling of **WITH BATED BREATH** at **BATED**.
– DERIVATIVES **bait·er** n.
– ORIGIN Middle English: from Old Norse *beit* 'pasture, food,' *beita* 'to hunt or chase.'

USAGE See usage at **BATED**.

bait-and-switch ▶ n. the action (generally illegal) of advertising goods that are an apparent bargain, with the intention of substituting inferior or more expensive goods: [as modifier] *a bait-and-switch scheme.*

bait·fish /ˈbātˌfisH/ ▶ n. a fish used as bait to catch a larger fish.

bai·za /ˈbīzə/ ▶ n. (pl. **same** or **baizas**) a monetary unit of Oman, equal to one thousandth of a rial.

baize /bāz/ ▶ n. a coarse, feltlike, woolen material that is typically green, used for covering billiard and card tables and for aprons.
– ORIGIN late 16th cent.: from French *baies*, feminine plural of *bai* 'chestnut-colored' (see **BAY⁴**), treated as a singular noun. The name is presumably from the original color of the cloth, although several colors are recorded.

Ba·ja Ca·li·for·nia /ˈbähä ˌkaləˈfôrnyə/ a mountainous peninsula in northwestern Mexico that extends southward from the border with California and separates the Gulf of California from the Pacific Ocean. It consists of two states of Mexico: **Baja California** (capital, Mexicali) and **Baja California Sur** (capital, La Paz). Also called **LOWER CALIFORNIA**.

ba·ja·da /bəˈhädə/ ▶ n. a broad slope of alluvial material at the foot of an escarpment or mountain.
– ORIGIN mid 19th cent.: from Spanish, 'descent, slope.'

Ba·jan /ˈbājən/ ▶ adj. & n. informal term for **BARBADIAN** (see **BARBADOS**).

Ba·ka /ˈbäkə/ ▶ n. (pl. **same**) **1** a member of a nomadic Pygmy people inhabiting the rain forests of southeastern Cameroon and northern Gabon.
2 the Bantu language of the Baka.
– ORIGIN the name in Baka.

bake /bāk/ ▶ v. [with obj.] **1** cook (food) by dry heat without direct exposure to a flame, typically in an oven or on a hot surface: *they bake their own bread and cakes* | [with two objs.] *I baked him a cake for his birthday* | (as adj. **baked**) *baked apples.* ■ [no obj.] (of food) be cooked in such a way: *the bread was baking on hot stones.*
2 (of the sun or other agency) subject (something) to dry heat, esp. so as to harden it: *the sun has baked the earth a dusty brown.* ■ [no obj.] informal (of a person or place) be or become extremely hot in prolonged sun or hot weather: *the city was baking in a heat wave* | (as adj. **baking**) *the summer's baking heat.*
▶ n. [with modifier] a social gathering at which baked food is eaten: *lobster bakes on deserted islands.*
– ORIGIN Old English *bacan*, of Germanic origin; related to Dutch *bakken* and German *backen*.

baked /bākt/ ▶ adj. **1** (of food) cooked by dry heat in an oven: *baked apples.*
2 informal intoxicated by drink or drugs, esp. marijuana.

baked A·las·ka ▶ n. sponge cake and ice cream in a meringue covering, cooked for a very short time.
– ORIGIN named after the state of **ALASKA**.

baked beans ▶ plural n. short for **BOSTON BAKED BEANS**.

Baked Bean State a nickname for the state of **MASSACHUSETTS**.

bake·house /ˈbākˌhous/ ▶ n. dated a building or area in which bread is made.

Ba·ke·lite /ˈbāk(ə)ˌlīt/ ▶ n. trademark an early form of brittle plastic, typically dark brown, made from formaldehyde and phenol, used chiefly for electrical equipment.
– ORIGIN early 20th cent.: named after Leo H. *Baekeland* (1863–1944), the Belgian-born American chemist who invented it, + **-ITE¹**.

bake-off ▶ n. a contest in which cooks prepare baked goods such as bread and cakes for judging. ■ informal a contest between companies to win a contract.

Bak·er /ˈbākər/, Josephine (1906–75), US dancer. She was a star of the Folies-Bergère in Paris in the 1930s, famed for her exotic dancing and risqué clothing.

bak·er /ˈbākər/ ▶ n. a person who makes bread and cakes, esp. commercially. ■ [often with modifier.] an oven for a particular purpose: *a bread baker.*
– ORIGIN Old English *bæcere*, from *bacan* (see **BAKE**).

Ba·ker Is·land an uninhabited island in the central Pacific Ocean, near the equator, claimed by the US in 1857. Once a guano source, it is now a wildlife refuge.

bak·er's doz·en ▶ n. a group or set of thirteen: *a baker's dozen of love songs.*
– ORIGIN late 16th cent.: from the former bakers' custom of adding an extra loaf to a dozen sold, this constituting the retailer's profit.

Ba·kers·field /ˈbākərzˌfēld/ an industrial city in south central California, an oil industry center in the San Joaquin Valley; pop. 321,078 (est. 2008).

bak·er's yeast ▶ n. a dried preparation of yeast used or suitable for use as leaven.

bak·er·y /ˈbāk(ə)rē/ ▶ n. (pl. **bakeries**) a place where bread and cakes are made or sold: *delicious aromas wafting from the bakery* | [as modifier] *an assortment of bakery goods.* ■ baked goods such as bread and cakes: *a table overflowing with homemade bakery and wine.*

bake sale ▶ n. a sale of home-baked items as a fundraising activity.

bake·shop /ˈbākˌsHäp/ ▶ n. a place where bread and cakes are made or sold.

bake·ware /ˈbākˌwe(ə)r/ ▶ n. tins, trays, and other items placed in the oven during baking.

bak·ing pow·der ▶ n. a mixture of sodium bicarbonate and cream of tartar, used instead of yeast in baking.

bak·ing so·da ▶ n. sodium bicarbonate used in cooking, for cleaning, or in toothpaste.

Bak·ker /ˈbakər/, Robert T. (1945–), US paleontologist. He proposed the controversial idea that dinosaurs were both active and warm-blooded.

ba·kla·va /ˌbäkləˈvä/ ▶ n. a dessert originating in the Middle East made of phyllo pastry filled with chopped nuts and soaked in honey.
– ORIGIN Turkish.

bak·sheesh /ˈbaksHēsH, bakˈsHēsH/ ▶ n. (in parts of Asia) a small sum of money given as alms, a tip, or a bribe.
– ORIGIN based on Persian *bakšiš*, from *bakšīdan* 'give.'

Bakst /bäkst/, Léon (1866–1924), Russian painter and designer; born *Lev Samuilovich Rozenberg*. He was a member of the Ballets Russes, for which he designed exotic, richly colored sets and costumes.

Ba·ku /bäˈko͞o/ the capital of Azerbaijan, on the Caspian Sea; pop. 1,917,000 (est. 2008). It is an industrial port and a center of the oil industry.

Ba·ku·nin /bəˈko͞onyin/, Mikhail (Aleksandrovich) (1814–76), Russian anarchist and writer who participated in the revolutionary movements of 1848–49.

bal·a·cla·va /ˌbaləˈklävə/ (also **balaclava helmet**) ▶ **n.** a close-fitting garment covering the whole head and neck except for parts of the face, typically made of wool.
– ORIGIN late 19th cent. (denoting a garment worn originally by soldiers serving in the Crimean War): named after the village of *Balaclava* in the Crimea (see BALACLAVA, BATTLE OF).

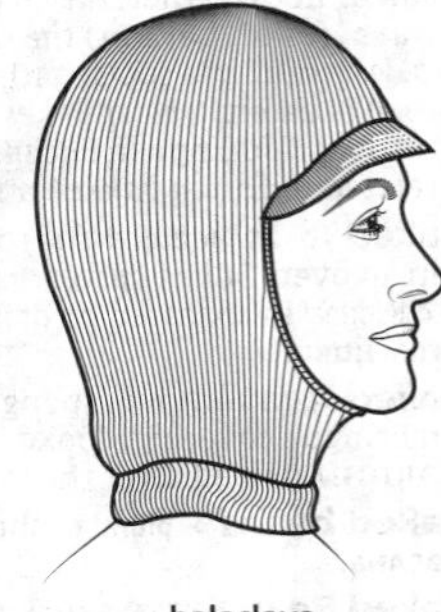
balaclava

Bal·a·cla·va, Battle of /ˌbaləˈklävə/ a battle of the Crimean War, fought between Russia and an alliance of British, French, and Turkish forces in and around the port of Balaclava (now Balaklava) in the southern Crimea in 1854. The battle ended inconclusively; and is chiefly remembered as the scene of the Charge of the Light Brigade.

bal·a·fon /ˈbaləˌfôn/ ▶ **n.** a large xylophone having hollow gourds as resonators, used in West African music.
– ORIGIN late 18th cent.: via French from Manding *bala* 'xylophone' + *fo* 'to play.'

bal·a·lai·ka /ˌbaləˈlīkə/ ▶ **n.** a guitarlike musical instrument with a triangular body and two, three, or four strings, popular in Russia and other Slavic countries.
– ORIGIN late 18th cent.: from Russian, of Tartar origin.

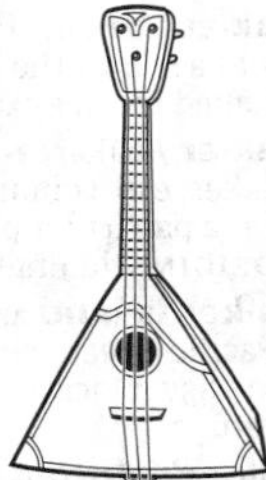
balalaika

bal·ance /ˈbaləns/ ▶ **n. 1** an even distribution of weight enabling someone or something to remain upright and steady: *slipping in the mud but keeping their balance | she lost her balance before falling.* ■ stability of one's mind or feelings: *the way to some kind of peace and personal balance.* ■ Sailing the ability of a boat to stay on course without adjustment of the rudder.
2 a condition in which different elements are equal or in the correct proportions: *overseas investments can add balance to an investment portfolio* | [in sing.] *try to keep a **balance between** work and relaxation.* ■ Art harmony of design and proportion. ■ [in sing.] the relative volume of various sources of sound: *the balance of the voices is good.*
3 an apparatus for weighing, esp. one with a central pivot, beam, and a pair of scales. ■ (**the Balance**) the zodiacal sign or constellation Libra.
4 a counteracting weight or force. ■ (also **balance wheel**) the regulating device in a mechanical clock or watch.
5 a predominating weight or amount; the majority: *the **balance of** opinion was that work was more important than leisure.*
6 a figure representing the difference between credits and debits in an account; the amount of money held in an account: *he accumulated a healthy balance with the savings bank.* ■ the difference between an amount due and an amount paid: *unpaid credit-card balances.* ■ [in sing.] an amount left over.
▶ **v.** [with obj.] **1** keep or put (something) in a steady position so that it does not fall: *a mug that she **balanced on** her knee.* ■ [no obj.] remain in a steady position without falling: *Richard **balanced on** the ball of one foot.*
2 offset or compare the value of (one thing) with another: *the cost of obtaining such information needs to be **balanced against** its benefits.* ■ counteract, equal, or neutralize the weight or importance of: *he **balanced** his radical remarks **with** more familiar declarations.* ■ establish equal or appropriate proportions of elements in: *balancing work and family life.*
3 compare debits and credits in (an account), typically to ensure that they are equal: *the law requires the council to **balance its books** each year.* ■ [no obj.] (of an account) have credits and debits equal.
– PHRASES **balance of payments** the difference in total value between payments into and out of a country over a period. **balance of power 1** a situation in which nations of the world have roughly equal power. **2** the power held by a small group when larger groups are of equal strength. **balance of trade** the difference in value between a country's imports and exports. **in the balance** uncertain; at a critical stage: *his survival hung in the balance for days.* **on balance** with all things considered: *but on balance he was pleased.* **strike a balance** choose a moderate course or compromise: *she's decided to strike a balance between fashionable and accessible.* **throw** (or **catch**) **someone off balance** cause someone to become unsteady and in danger of falling. ■ confuse or bewilder someone.
– DERIVATIVES **bal·anc·er n.**
– ORIGIN Middle English (sense 3 of the noun): from Old French *balance* (noun), *balancer* (verb), based on late Latin *(libra) bilanx* '(balance) having two scalepans,' from *bi-* 'twice, having two' + *lanx* 'scalepan.'

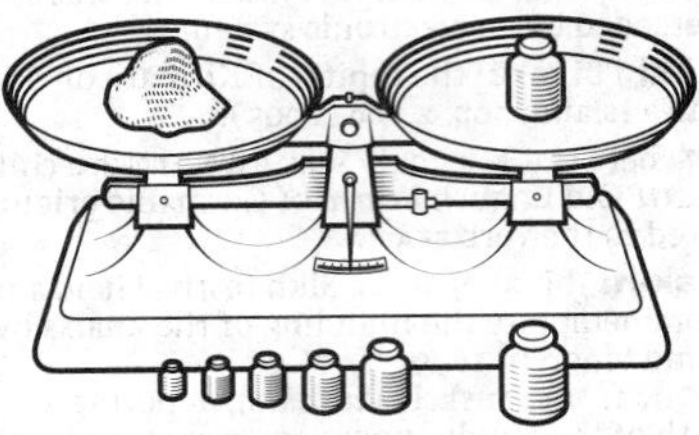
balance 3

bal·ance beam ▶ **n.** a narrow horizontal bar raised off the floor, on which a gymnast balances while performing exercises. ■ [in sing.] the set of exercises performed on such a piece of equipment.

bal·anced /ˈbalənst/ ▶ **adj.** keeping or showing a balance; arranged in good proportions: *she assembled a balanced team.* ■ taking everything into account; fairly judged or presented: *accurate and balanced information.* ■ (esp. of food) having different elements in the correct proportions: *a healthy, balanced diet.* ■ (of a person or state of mind) having no emotion lacking or too strong; stable: *a balanced personality.* ■ (of an electrical circuit or signal) being symmetrical with respect to a reference point, typically ground.

bal·ance sheet ▶ **n.** a statement of the assets, liabilities, and capital of a business or other organization at a particular point in time, detailing the balance of income and expenditure over the preceding period.

bal·ance tab ▶ **n.** a tab on a control surface of an aircraft that reduces the amount of force needed to move the control surface by moving in the opposite direction.

bal·ance wheel ▶ **n.** the regulating device in a watch or clock.

Bal·an·chine /ˌbalənˈCHēn, ˈbalənˌCHēn/, George (1904–83), US ballet dancer and choreographer; born in Russia; born *Georgi Melitonovich Balanchivadze.* He was chief choreographer of Diaghilev's Ballets Russes during the 1920s, and in 1934 he cofounded the company that later became the New York City Ballet. Notable ballets: *The Firebird* (1949) and *A Midsummer Night's Dream* (1962).

bal·anc·ing act ▶ **n.** an action or activity that requires a delicate balance between different situations or requirements: *our balancing act between working more to buy luxuries and having enough leisure to enjoy them.*

bal·as ru·by /ˈbaləs/ ▶ **n.** a spinel of a delicate rose-red variety.
– ORIGIN late Middle English: from Old French *balais,* from Arabic *balakš,* from Persian *Badakšān,* a district of Afghanistan, where it is found.

ba·la·ta /bəˈlätə/ ▶ **n.** a tropical American tree that bears edible fruit and produces latex. ● Several species in the family Sapotaceae, in particular, *Manilkara bidentata.* ■ the dried sap of this tree used as a substitute for rubber.
– ORIGIN early 17th cent.: from Carib *balatá.*

Ba·la·ton, Lake /ˈbôləˌtôn, ˈbäləˌtän/ a large shallow lake in west central Hungary, situated in a wine-producing and resort region south of the Bakony mountains.

Bal·bo·a /balˈbōə/, Vasco Núñez de (1475–1519), Spanish explorer. In 1513 he reached the western coast of the isthmus of Darien (Panama), thereby becoming the first European to see the eastern shores of the Pacific Ocean.

bal·bo·a /balˈbōə/ ▶ **n.** the basic monetary unit of Panama, equal to 100 centésimos.
– ORIGIN named after Vasco Núñez de BALBOA.

bal·brig·gan /balˈbrigən/ ▶ **n.** a fine, unbleached knitted cotton fabric, used for stockings and underwear.
– ORIGIN late 19th cent.: named after the town of *Balbriggan* in Ireland, where it was originally made.

Bal·co·nes Es·carp·ment /balˈkōnəs/ the scarp marking the geologic fault that separates the plains of eastern Texas from highlands to the west. San Antonio, Austin, and Waco lie near or on it.

bal·co·ny /ˈbalkənē/ ▶ **n.** (pl. **balconies**) **1** a platform enclosed by a wall or balustrade on the outside of a building, with access from an upper-floor window or door.
2 (**the balcony**) the upstairs seats in a theater, concert hall, or auditorium.
– DERIVATIVES **bal·co·nied adj.**
– ORIGIN early 17th cent.: from Italian *balcone,* probably ultimately of Germanic origin.

bald /bôld/ ▶ **adj. 1** having a scalp wholly or partly lacking hair: *he had a shiny bald head | he was starting to go bald.* ■ (of an animal) not covered by the usual fur, hair, or feathers: *hedgehogs are born bald.* ■ (of a plant or an area of land) not covered by the usual leaves, bark, or vegetation: *the bald trunks with their empty branches.* ■ (of a tire) having the tread worn away: *my car had two bald tires.*
2 [attrib.] without any extra detail or explanation; plain or blunt: *the bald statement in the preceding paragraph requires amplification.*
– DERIVATIVES **bald·ish adj., bald·ly adv.** (sense 2): *"I want to leave," Stephen said baldly,* **bald·ness n.**
– ORIGIN Middle English: probably from a base meaning 'white patch,' whence the archaic sense 'marked or streaked with white.'

bal·da·chin /ˈbôldəkin/ (also **baldaquin** or **baldacchino** /bôldəˈkinō/) ▶ **n.** a ceremonial canopy of stone, metal, or fabric over an altar, throne, or doorway.
– ORIGIN late 16th cent. (denoting an embroidered material, woven with silk and gold thread): from Italian *baldacchino,* from *Baldacco* 'Baghdad,' place of origin of the original brocade.

bald cy·press ▶ **n.** a deciduous North American conifer with exposed buttress roots and ball-shaped cones, typically growing in swamps and on water margins. ● *Taxodium distichum,* family Taxodiaceae.

bald ea·gle ▶ **n.** a white-headed North American eagle that includes fish among its prey. Now most common in Alaska, it is the national emblem of the US. ● *Haliaetus leucocephalus,* family Accipitridae.

bald eagle

Bal·der /ˈbôldər/ Scandinavian Mythology a son of Odin and god of the summer sun. He was invulnerable to all things except mistletoe, with which the god Loki, by a trick, induced the blind god Hödur to kill him.

bal·der·dash /ˈbôldərˌdaSH/ ▶ **n.** senseless talk or writing; nonsense: *she dismissed talk of plots as "bunkum and balderdash."*
– ORIGIN late 16th cent. (denoting a frothy liquid; later, an unappetizing mixture of drinks): of unknown origin.

bald-faced ▶ **adj.** shameless and undisguised; barefaced: *a bald-faced lie.*

bald·ing /ˈbôldiNG/ ▶ **adj.** going bald: *a man in his late twenties, prematurely balding.*

bald·pate /ˈbôldˌpāt/ ▶ **n.** the American wigeon, in allusion to its white-crowned head.

bal·dric /ˈbôldrik/ ▶ **n.** historical a belt for a sword or other piece of equipment, worn over one shoulder and reaching down to the opposite hip.
– ORIGIN Middle English *baudry,* from Old French *baudre,* of unknown ultimate origin.

Bald·win[1] /ˈbôldwin/, Henry (1780–1844), US Supreme Court associate justice 1830–44. He also served in Congress as a representative from Pennsylvania 1817–22.

Bald·win[2], James (Arthur) (1924–87), US writer and civil rights activist. Notable works: novels *Go Tell It on the Mountain* (1953), *Giovanni's Room* (1956), and *Another Country* (1962); essay collections *Nobody Knows My Name* (1961) and *The Price of a Ticket* (1985).

b

Bald·win[3], Stanley, 1st Earl Baldwin of Bewdley (1867–1947), British statesman; prime minister 1923–24, 1924–29, and 1935–37.

Bald·win Park a city in southwestern California, east of Los Angeles; pop. 77,380 (est. 2008).

bald·y /ˈbôldē/ (also **baldie**) ▶ **n.** (pl. **baldies**) informal, derogatory a baldheaded person.
▶ **adj.** [attrib.] chiefly Scottish & Irish bald: *a baldy head.*

bale[1] /bāl/ ▶ **n.** a bundle of paper, hay, cotton, etc., tightly wrapped and bound with cords or hoops: *the fire destroyed 500 **bales of hay**.* ■ the quantity in a bale as a measure, esp. 500 pounds of cotton.
▶ **v.** [with obj.] make (something) into bales: *they baled a lot of good hay* | (as noun **baling**) *most baling and field work have been finished.*
– ORIGIN Middle English: probably from Middle Dutch, from Old French; ultimately of Germanic origin and related to BALL[1].

bale[2] ▶ **n.** archaic or literary evil considered as a destructive force. ■ evil suffered; physical torment or mental suffering.
– ORIGIN Old English *balu, bealu*, of Germanic origin.

Bâle /bäl/ French name for BASLE.

Bal·e·ar·ic Is·lands /ˌbalēˈarik/ (also **the Balearics**) a group of four large and seven small islands in the Mediterranean off the eastern coast of Spain that form an autonomous region of Spain; capital, Palma (on the island of Majorca).

ba·leen /bəˈlēn/ ▶ **n.** whalebone.
– ORIGIN Middle English (also denoting a whale): from Old French *baleine*, from Latin *balaena* 'whale.'

ba·leen whale ▶ **n.** a whale that has plates of whalebone in the mouth for straining plankton from the water. Baleen whales include the rorquals, humpback, right whales, and gray whale. Also called WHALEBONE WHALE. ● Suborder Mysticeti, order Cetacea: three families and ten species.

bale·fire /ˈbālˌfīr/ ▶ **n.** a large open-air fire; a bonfire.
– ORIGIN Old English (recorded in poetry), from obsolete *bale* 'great fire' + FIRE.

bale·ful /ˈbālfəl/ ▶ **adj.** threatening harm; menacing: *Bill shot a baleful glance in her direction* | *the baleful light cast trembling shadows.* ■ having a harmful or destructive effect: *drug money has had a baleful impact on the country.*
– DERIVATIVES **bale·ful·ly** adv., **bale·ful·ness** n.
– ORIGIN Old English *bealufull* (see BALE[2], -FUL).

Ba·len·ci·a·ga /ˌbälensēˈägə, ˌbälenˈTHyägə/, Cristóbal (1895–1972), Spanish couturier. In the 1950s he contributed to the move away from the tight-waisted New Look originated by Christian Dior to a looser, semifitted style.

bal·er /ˈbālər/ ▶ **n.** a machine for making paper, hay, or cotton into bales.

Bal·four /ˈbalˌfôr/, Arthur James, 1st Earl of Balfour (1848–1930), British statesman; prime minister 1902–05. In 1917, as foreign secretary, he issued the Balfour Declaration that favored a Jewish national home in Palestine.

Ba·li /ˈbälē, ˈbalē/ a mountainous island in Indonesia, east of Java; chief city, Denpasar; pop. 3,470,700 (est. 2009). It is noted for its beauty and the richness of its culture.

Ba·li·nese /ˌbäləˈnēz, ˌbal-, -ˈnēs/ ▶ **adj.** of or relating to Bali or its people or language.
▶ **n.** (pl. **same**) **1** a native of Bali.
2 the Indonesian language of Bali.
– ORIGIN from BALI, on the pattern of Dutch *Balinees*.

balk /bôk/ (Brit. also **baulk**) ▶ **v.** [no obj.] **1** hesitate or be unwilling to accept an idea or undertaking: *any gardener will at first **balk at** enclosing the garden.* ■ [with obj.] thwart or hinder (a plan or person): *the utmost of his influence will be invoked to balk the law.* ■ [with obj.] (**balk someone of**) prevent a person or animal from having (something): *the lions, fearing to be balked of their prey.* ■ (of a horse) refuse to go on. ■ [with obj.] archaic miss or refuse (a chance or invitation).
2 Baseball (of a pitcher) make an illegal motion, penalized by an advance of the base runners: *the rookie balked and permitted Robinson to score.*
▶ **n. 1** Baseball an illegal motion made by a pitcher that may deceive a base runner.
2 a roughly squared timber beam.
3 any area on a pool or billiard table in which play is restricted in some way.
4 a ridge left unplowed between furrows.
– ORIGIN late Old English *balc*, from Old Norse *bálkr* 'partition.' The original use was 'unplowed ridge,' in late Middle English 'land left unplowed by mistake,' hence 'blunder, omission' (giving rise to the verb sense 'miss (a chance)'). A late Middle English sense 'obstacle' gave rise to the verb senses 'hesitate' and 'hinder.'

Bal·kan·ize /ˈbôlkəˌnīz/ ▶ **v.** [with obj.] divide (a region or body) into smaller mutually hostile states or groups.
– DERIVATIVES **Bal·kan·i·za·tion** /ˌbôlkənəˈzāSHən/ **n.**
– ORIGIN 1920s: from *Balkan* Peninsula (where this was done in the late 19th and early 20th cent.) + -IZE.

Bal·kans /ˈbôlkənz/ **1** (also **Balkan Mountains**) a range of mountains stretching east across Bulgaria from the Serbian frontier to the Black Sea. The highest point is Botev Peak (7,793 feet; 2,375 m).
2 the countries occupying the part of southeastern Europe that lies south of the Danube and Sava rivers and forms a peninsula bounded by the Adriatic and Ionian seas in the west, the Aegean and Black seas in the east, and the Mediterranean Sea in the south.
– DERIVATIVES **Bal·kan adj.**

Bal·kan Wars /ˈbôlkən/ two wars of 1912–13 that were fought over the last European territories of the Ottoman Empire.

> In 1912 Bulgaria, Serbia, Greece, and Montenegro forced Turkey to give up Albania and Macedonia, leaving the area around Constantinople (Istanbul) as the only Ottoman territory in Europe. The following year Bulgaria disputed with Serbia, Greece, and Romania for possession of Macedonia, which was partitioned between Greece and Serbia.

balk·line /ˈbôkˌlīn/ (also **balk line**) ▶ **n.** a line on a billiard table marking off an area in which play is restricted.

balk·y /ˈbôkē/ (Brit. also **baulky**) ▶ **adj.** (**balkier, balkiest**) reluctant; uncooperative: *he was trying to get his balky horse to move.*

Ball[1] /bôl/, John (died 1381), English rebel. He was a priest who preached egalitarianism. Following the Peasants' Revolt, he was hanged as a traitor.

Ball[2], Lucille (Désirée) (1911–89), US comedienne known in particular for the popular television series *I Love Lucy* (1951–55). Notable movies: *Stage Door* (1937), *Sorrowful Jones* (1949), and *Yours, Mine, and Ours* (1968).

Lucille Ball

ball[1] /bôl/ ▶ **n. 1** a solid or hollow sphere or ovoid, esp. one that is kicked, thrown, or hit in a game: *a soccer ball.* ■ a ball-shaped object: *a **ball of wool*** | *he crushed the card into a ball.* ■ historical a solid nonexplosive missile for a firearm. ■ a game played with a ball, esp. baseball: *kids have been playing ball in that lot for almost a hundred years.*
2 Baseball a pitch delivered outside the strike zone that the batter does not attempt to hit: *the umpire called it a ball.* ■ Sports a pass of a ball from one player to another: *Whelan sent a long ball to Goddard.*
3 (in full **the ball of the foot**) the rounded protuberant part of the foot at the base of the big toe. ■ (in full **the ball of the thumb**) the rounded protuberant part of the hand at the base of the thumb.
4 (**balls**) vulgar slang testicles. ■ courage or nerve. ■ nonsense; rubbish (often said to express strong disagreement).
▶ **v.** [with obj.] **1** (usu. **ball up**) squeeze or form (something) into a rounded shape: *Robert **balled up** his napkin and threw it onto his plate.* ■ clench or screw up (one's fist) tightly: *she balled her fist so that the nails dug into her palms.* ■ [no obj.] form a round shape: *the fishing nets eventually **ball up** and sink.* ■ wrap the rootball of (a tree or shrub) in burlap to protect it during transportation.
2 vulgar slang have sexual intercourse with.
– PHRASES **balled up** entangled; confused: *I got slightly balled up in my facts.* **the ball is in your court** it is up to you to make the next move. **a ball of fire** a person full of energy and enthusiasm. **keep the ball rolling** maintain the momentum of an activity. **keep one's eye on** (or **take one's eye off**) **the ball** keep (or fail to keep) one's attention focused on the matter in hand. **on the ball** alert to new ideas, methods, and trends: *maintaining contact with customers keeps me on the ball.* ■ indicating competence, alertness, or intelligence: *a woman like that, with so much on the ball.* **play ball** play a ball game such as baseball: *we noticed some youngsters playing ball in a vacant lot.* ■ informal work willingly with others; cooperate: *if his lawyers won't play ball, there's nothing we can do.* ■ Baseball the umpire's command to begin or resume play. **start** (or **get** or **set**) **the ball rolling** set an activity in motion; make a start: *to start the ball rolling, the government was asked to contribute a million dollars to the fund.* **the whole ball of wax** informal everything.
– PHRASAL VERBS **ball** (Brit. **balls**) **something up** bungle something.
– ORIGIN Middle English: from Old Norse *bǫllr*, of Germanic origin.

ball[2] ▶ **n.** a formal social gathering for dancing: *the social season was highlighted by debutante balls* | [as modifier] *a ball gown.*
– PHRASES **have a ball** informal enjoy oneself greatly; have a lot of fun: *I had a ball on my fortieth birthday.*
– ORIGIN early 17th cent.: from French *bal* 'a dance,' from late Latin *ballare* 'to dance'; related to Greek *ballizein* 'to dance' (also *ballein* 'to throw').

bal·lad /ˈbaləd/ ▶ **n.** a poem or song narrating a story in short stanzas. Traditional ballads are typically of unknown authorship, having been passed on orally from one generation to the next as part of the folk culture. ■ a slow sentimental or romantic song.
– ORIGIN late 15th cent. (denoting a light, simple song): from Old French *balade*, from Provençal *balada* 'dance, song to dance to,' from *balar* 'to dance,' from late Latin *ballare* (see BALL[2]). The sense 'narrative poem' dates from the mid 18th cent.

bal·lade /bəˈläd/ ▶ **n. 1** a poem normally composed of three stanzas and an envoi. The last line of the opening stanza is used as a refrain, and the same rhymes, strictly limited in number, recur throughout.
2 a short, lyrical piece of music, esp. one for piano.
– ORIGIN late Middle English: earlier spelling and pronunciation of BALLAD.

bal·lad·eer /ˌbaləˈdi(ə)r/ ▶ **n.** a singer or composer of ballads.

bal·lad op·er·a ▶ **n.** a theatrical entertainment popular in early 18th-century England, taking the form of a satirical play interspersed with traditional or operatic songs. The best-known example is John Gay's *The Beggar's Opera* (1728).

bal·lad·ry /ˈbalədrē/ ▶ **n.** ballads collectively. ■ the art of writing or performing ballads.

bal·lad stan·za ▶ **n.** a four-line stanza in iambic meter in which the first and third unrhymed lines have four metrical feet and the second and fourth rhyming lines have three metrical feet.

ball and chain ▶ **n.** a heavy metal ball secured by a chain to the leg of a prisoner to prevent escape. ■ a crippling encumbrance: *the ball and chain of debt.*

ball-and-sock·et joint ▶ **n.** a natural or manufactured joint or coupling, such as the hip joint, in which a partially spherical end lies in a socket, allowing multidirectional movement and rotation.

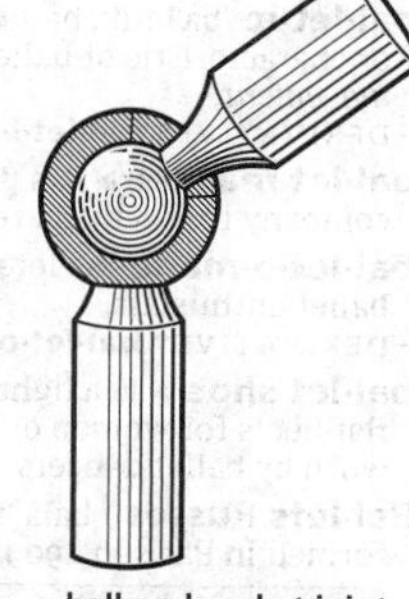
ball-and-socket joint

Bal·lard /ˈbalərd/, J. G. (1930–2009), British novelist and short-story writer; full name *James Graham Ballard*. Notable works: *The Drowned World* (1962), *Crash* (1973), and *Empire of the Sun* (1984).

bal·last /ˈbaləst/ ▶ **n. 1** heavy material, such as gravel, sand, iron, or lead, placed low in a vessel to improve its stability. ■ a substance of this type carried in an airship or on a hot-air balloon to stabilize it, and jettisoned when greater altitude is required. ■ something that gives stability or substance: *the film is an entertaining comedy with some serious ideas thrown in for ballast.*
2 gravel or coarse stone used to form the bed of a railroad track or road. ■ a mixture of coarse and fine aggregate for making concrete.
3 a passive component used in an electric circuit to moderate changes in current.

PRONUNCIATION KEY ə *ago, up*; ər *over, fur*; a *hat*; ā *ate*; ä *car*; e *let*; ē *see*; i *fit*; ī *by*; NG *sing*; ō *go*; ô *law, for*; oi *toy*; o͝o *good*; o͞o *goo*; ou *out*; TH *thin*; T͟H *then*; ZH *vision*

▶ **v.** [with obj.] (usu. **be ballasted**) **1** give stability to (a ship) by putting a heavy substance in its bilge: *the vessel has been ballasted to give the necessary floating stability.*
2 form (the bed of a railroad line or road) with gravel or coarse stone.
– PHRASES **in ballast** (of a ship) laden only with ballast.
– ORIGIN mid 16th cent.: probably of Low German or Scandinavian origin.

ball bear·ing ▶ **n.** a bearing between a wheel and a fixed axle, in which the rotating part and the stationary part are separated by a ring of small solid metal balls that reduce friction. ■ a ball used in such a bearing.

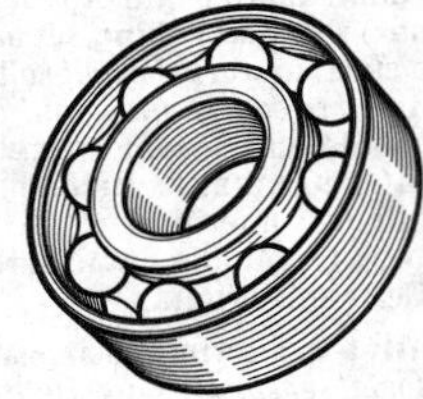
ball bearing

ball boy ▶ **n.** a boy who retrieves balls that go out of play during a game such as tennis or baseball, and who supplies players or umpires with new balls.

ball-break·er (also **ball-buster**) ▶ **n.** informal a sexually demanding woman who destroys men's self-confidence. ■ a tough disciplinarian or taskmaster: *he's an old-school ball-breaker, a real pit bull.*
– DERIVATIVES **ball-break·ing** **adj.**

ball·car·ri·er /'bôl,karēər/ ▶ **n.** Football a player in possession of the ball and attempting to advance it.

ball·cock /'bɔlkɑk/ ▶ **n.** a valve that automatically fills a tank after liquid has been drawn from it. Used, for example, in a flush toilet, a ballcock has a float on the end of a pivoting arm that opens the valve when the arm drops.

bal·le·ri·na /,balə'rēnə/ ▶ **n.** a female ballet dancer.
– ORIGIN late 18th cent.: from Italian, feminine of *ballerino* 'dancing master,' from *ballare* 'to dance,' from late Latin.

Bal·le·ste·ros /,bīyə'stārōs, ,bälə'ste(ə)rōs/, Severiano, known as **Seve** (1957–), Spanish golfer. In 1979, he became the youngest player in the 20th century to win the British Open, and he won it again in 1984 and 1988. In 1980, he was the youngest-ever and the second European to win the US Masters; he won it again in 1983. He holds the record for most European Tour wins (50).

bal·let /'balā, ba'lā/ ▶ **n.** an artistic dance form performed to music using precise and highly formalized set steps and gestures. Classical ballet, which originated in Renaissance Italy and established its present form during the 19th century, is characterized by light, graceful, fluid movements and the use of pointe shoes. ■ a creative work of this form or the music written for it. ■ a group of dancers who regularly perform such works: *the New York City Ballet.*
– ORIGIN mid 17th cent.: from French, from Italian *balletto*, diminutive of *ballo* 'a dance,' from late Latin *ballare* 'to dance' (see BALL[2]).

bal·let·ic /ba'letik, bə-/ ▶ **adj.** of, relating to, or characteristic of ballet: *a graceful, balletic movement.*
– DERIVATIVES **bal·let·i·cal·ly** /-ik(ə)lē/ **adv.**

bal·let mas·ter ▶ **n.** a person employed by a ballet company to teach and rehearse dancers.

bal·let·o·mane /bə'letə,mān, 'baletə,mān/ ▶ **n.** a ballet enthusiast.
– DERIVATIVES **bal·let·o·ma·ni·a** /-,letə'mānēə/ **n.**

bal·let shoe ▶ **n.** a light, round-toed shoe with very flat heels for women or girls, resembling the type worn by ballet dancers.

Bal·lets Russes /,balā 'rōōs/ a ballet company formed in Paris in 1909 by Sergei Diaghilev.

> The company presented a unified whole encompassing music, dance, decor, and costume: music was commissioned from the composers Stravinsky, Satie, and Rimsky-Korsakov, while Picasso and Jean Cocteau designed sets. The company's choreographers and dancers included Michel Fokine, Anna Pavlova, Vaslav Nijinsky, and George Balanchine. It was responsible for reviving ballet as an art form in western Europe.

ball float ▶ **n.** the spherical float attached to the pivoting arm of the ballcock in a toilet tank.

ball game ▶ **n. 1** a game played with a ball. ■ a baseball game: *I took the afternoon off and went to a ball game.*
2 [in sing.] informal a particular situation, esp. one that is completely different from the previous situation: *making the film was **a whole new ball game** for her.*

ball girl ▶ **n.** a girl who retrieves balls that go out of play during a game such as tennis or baseball, and who supplies players or umpires with new balls.

ball·gown /'bôl,goun/ ▶ **n.** a woman's elaborate full-length dress suitable for wearing to balls and similar social gatherings.

ball·hawk /'bôl,hôk/ ▶ **n.** informal a skilled ball player, in particular a football or basketball player adept at stealing or intercepting the ball or an outfielder in baseball skilled at catching fly balls.
– DERIVATIVES **ball·hawk·ing** **n.**

bal·lis·ta /bə'listə/ ▶ **n.** (pl. **ballistae** /-tē/ or **ballistas**) a catapult used in ancient warfare for hurling large stones. ■ a large crossbow for firing a spear.
– ORIGIN early 16th cent.: from Latin, based on Greek *ballein* 'to throw.'

bal·lis·tic /bə'listik/ ▶ **adj.** [attrib.] **1** of or relating to projectiles or their flight.
2 moving under the force of gravity only.
– PHRASES **go ballistic** informal fly into a rage.
– DERIVATIVES **bal·lis·ti·cal·ly** /-ik(ə)lē/ **adv.**
– ORIGIN late 18th cent.: from BALLISTA + -IC.

bal·lis·tic mis·sile ▶ **n.** a missile with a high, arching trajectory, that is initially powered and guided but falls under gravity onto its target. Compare with GUIDED.

bal·lis·tics /bə'listiks/ ▶ **plural n.** [treated as sing.] the science of projectiles and firearms. ■ the study of the effects of being fired on a bullet, cartridge, or gun.

bal·lis·to·car·di·o·gram /bə,listə'kärdēə,gram/ ▶ **n.** a record made by a ballistocardiograph.

bal·lis·to·car·di·o·graph /bə,listə'kärdēə,graf/ ▶ **n.** an instrument for recording the movements of the body caused by ejection of blood from the heart at each beat.

ball light·ning ▶ **n.** a rare and little known kind of lightning having the form of a moving globe of light several centimeters across that persists for periods of up to a minute.

bal·locks ▶ **n.** variant spelling of BOLLOCKS.

bal·lon /bə'lôn/ ▶ **n. 1** (in dancing) the ability to appear effortlessly suspended while performing movements during a jump.
2 variant spelling of BALLOON (sense 4 of the noun).
– ORIGIN French, from Italian *ballone*, from *balla* 'ball.'

bal·lo·net /,balə'nā/ (also **ballonnet**) ▶ **n.** the compartment in a balloon or airship into which air or another gas can be forced in order to maintain the craft's shape as buoyant gas is released.

bal·loon /bə'lōōn/ ▶ **n. 1** a brightly colored rubber sac inflated with air and then sealed at the neck, used as a children's toy or a decoration.
2 (also **hot-air balloon**) a large bag filled with hot air or gas to make it rise in the air, typically carrying a basket for passengers: *he set his sights on crossing the Pacific **by balloon**.*
3 a rounded outline in which the words or thoughts of characters in a comic strip or cartoon are written.
4 (also **balloon glass**) a large rounded drinking glass, used for brandy and other drinks.
▶ **v.** [no obj.] **1** swell out in a spherical shape; billow: *the trousers ballooned out below his waist* | [with obj.] *the wind ballooned her sleeves.* ■ (of an amount of money) increase rapidly: *the company's debt has ballooned in the last five years* | (as adj. **ballooning**) *ballooning government spending.* ■ (of a person) increase rapidly and dramatically in weight: *I had ballooned on the school's starchy diet.*
2 travel by hot-air balloon: *he is famous for ballooning across oceans.*
▶ **adj.** resembling a balloon; puffed: *a flouncy balloon curtain.*
– ORIGIN late 16th cent. (originally denoting a game played with a large inflated leather ball): from French *ballon* or Italian *ballone* 'large ball.'

bal·loon an·gi·o·plas·ty ▶ **n.** Medicine surgical widening of a blocked or narrowed blood vessel, esp. a coronary artery, by means of a balloon catheter.

bal·loon cath·e·ter ▶ **n.** Medicine a type of catheter incorporating a small balloon that may be introduced into a canal, duct, or blood vessel and then inflated in order to clear an obstruction or dilate a narrowed region.

bal·loon·ing /bə'lōōniNG/ ▶ **n.** the sport or pastime of flying in a balloon.
– DERIVATIVES **bal·loon·ist** /-nist/ **n.**

bal·loon mort·gage ▶ **n.** a mortgage in which a large portion of the borrowed principal is repaid in a single payment at the end of the loan period.

bal·loon pay·ment ▶ **n.** a repayment of the outstanding principal sum made at the end of a loan period, interest only having been paid hitherto.

bal·loon tire ▶ **n.** a large tire containing air at low pressure.
– DERIVATIVES **bal·loon-tired** **adj.**

bal·loon vine ▶ **n.** a tropical American vine with inflated balloonlike pods. ● *Cardiospermum halicacabum*, family Sapiondaceae.

bal·lot /'balət/ ▶ **n.** a process of voting, in writing and typically in secret: *next year's primary ballot* | *the commissioners were elected **by ballot**.* ■ (**the ballot**) the total number of votes cast in such a process: *he won 54 percent of the ballot.* ■ the piece of paper used to record someone's vote in such a process.
▶ **v.** (**ballots, balloting, balloted**) [with obj.] (of an organization) elicit a secret vote from (members) on a particular issue: *the union is preparing to ballot its members on the same issue.* ■ [no obj.] cast one's vote on a particular issue: *ambulance crews balloted unanimously to reject the deal.* ■ decide the allocation of (something) to applicants by drawing lots.
– ORIGIN mid 16th cent. (originally denoting a small colored ball placed in a container to register a vote): from Italian *ballotta*, diminutive of *balla* (see BALL[1]).

bal·lot box ▶ **n.** a sealed box into which voters put completed ballots. ■ (**the ballot box**) democratic principles and methods: *the proper remedy was the ballot box and not the court.*

bal·lo·tin /'balətin/ ▶ **n.** a decorative cardboard box, slightly larger at the top and with broad flaps, in which chocolates are sold.
– ORIGIN French, from *ballot* 'a small package of goods.'

bal·lot·tine /'balə,tēn/ ▶ **n.** a dish of meat, poultry, or fish that is stuffed and rolled.
– ORIGIN French.

ball·park /'bôl,pärk/ ▶ **n.** a baseball stadium or field. ■ informal a particular area or range: *we can make a pretty good guess that this figure's in the ballpark.*
▶ **adj.** [attrib.] informal (of prices or costs) approximate; rough: *the **ballpark figure** is $400–500.*

ball-peen ham·mer ▶ **n.** a hammer with a rounded end opposite the face.

ball·point /'bôl,point/ (also **ballpoint pen**) ▶ **n.** a pen with a tiny ball as its writing point. The ball transfers ink from a cartridge to the paper.

ball race ▶ **n.** Mechanics either of the components of a ball bearing that have ring-shaped grooves in which the balls run.

ball·room /'bôl,rōōm, -,rŏŏm/ ▶ **n.** a large room used for dancing.

ball·room danc·ing ▶ **n.** formal social dancing in couples, popular as a recreation and also as a competitive activity. The ballroom dance repertoire includes dances developed from old European folk dances such as the waltz, Latin American dances such as the tango, rumba, and cha-cha, and dances of 20th-century origin such as the foxtrot and quickstep.
– DERIVATIVES **ball·room dance** **n.**

balls-up ▶ **n.** Brit. vulgar slang a bungled or badly carried out task or action; a mess.

balls·y /'bôlzē/ ▶ **adj.** (**ballsier, ballsiest**) informal tough and courageous: *a cool, ballsy woman who could not be intimidated.*
– DERIVATIVES **balls·i·ness** **n.**
– ORIGIN 1950s: from BALL[1] (sense 4 of the noun) + -Y[1].

ball valve ▶ **n. 1** a one-way valve that is opened and closed by pressure on a ball that fits into a cup-shaped opening.
2 Brit. another term for BALLCOCK.

bal·ly·hoo /'balē,hōō/ informal ▶ **n.** extravagant publicity or fuss: *after all the ballyhoo, the film was a flop.*
▶ **v.** (**ballyhoos, ballyhooing, ballyhooed**) [with obj.] praise or publicize extravagantly: (as adj. **ballyhooed**) *a much-ballyhooed musical extravaganza.*
– ORIGIN late 19th cent.: American coinage of unknown origin.

balm /bä(l)m/ ▶ **n. 1** a fragrant ointment or preparation used to heal or soothe the skin. ■ something that has a comforting, soothing, or restorative effect: *the murmur of the water can provide balm for troubled spirits.*
2 a tree that yields a fragrant resinous substance, typically one used in medicine. ● Species in several families, in particular those of the genus *Commiphora* (family Burseraceae). ■ such a substance.
3 (also **lemon balm** or **sweet balm**) a bushy herb of the mint family, with leaves smelling and tasting of lemon. ● *Melissa officinalis*, family Labiatae. ■ used in names of other aromatic herbs of the mint family, e.g., **bee balm**.
– ORIGIN Middle English (in the sense 'preparation for embalming, fragrant resinous substance'): from Old French *basme*, from Latin *balsamum* (see BALSAM).

bal·ma·caan /ˌbalmə'kan, -'kän/ ▶ **n.** a loose overcoat with raglan sleeves.

Bal·mer se·ries /'bämər/ Physics a series of lines in the visible and ultraviolet spectrum of atomic hydrogen, between 656 and 365 nanometers.

balm of Gil·e·ad /'gilēəd/ ▶ **n. 1** a fragrant medicinal resin obtained from certain kinds of tree. **2** a tree that yields such a resin, in particular: ● an Arabian tree traditionally of importance in medicine and perfumery (*Commiphora gileadensis*, family Burseraceae). ● either of two poplars with sticky aromatic buds (*Populus* × *gileadensis* (or *candicans*) and the balsam poplar, family Salicaceae). ● the balsam fir.
– ORIGIN early 16th cent.: *balm* from a translation in Coverdale's Bible (Gen. 37:25), rendered 'resin' in the Vulgate; *Gilead* from the assumption that this resin is the substance mentioned in the Bible as coming from Gilead.

bal·mor·al /bal'môrəl/ (also **Balmoral**) ▶ **n. 1** a type of brimless round cocked hat with a cockade or ribbons attached, worn by certain Scottish regiments. **2** a heavy laced leather walking boot.
– ORIGIN mid 19th cent.: named after **Balmoral Castle** in Scotland.

Bal·mor·al Cas·tle a vacation residence of the British royal family, on the Dee River in Scotland.

balm·y /'bä(l)mē/ ▶ **adj.** (**balmier, balmiest**) **1** (of the weather) pleasantly warm: *the balmy days of late summer*. **2** informal extremely foolish; eccentric: *this is a balmy decision*. ■ mad; crazy: *I think he's gone balmy again*.
– DERIVATIVES **balm·i·ness n.**

bal·ne·ol·o·gy /ˌbalnē'äləjē/ ▶ **n.** the study of therapeutic bathing and medicinal springs. ■ another term for **balneotherapy**.
– DERIVATIVES **bal·ne·o·log·i·cal** /-nēə'läjikəl/ **adj.**, **bal·ne·ol·o·gist** /-jist/ **n.**
– ORIGIN mid 19th cent.: from Latin *balneum* 'bath' + **-logy**.

bal·ne·o·ther·a·py /ˌbalnēə'THerəpē/ ▶ **n.** the treatment of disease by bathing in mineral springs.
– ORIGIN late 19th cent.: from Latin *balneum* 'bath' + **therapy**.

ba·lo·ney /bə'lōnē/ ▶ **n.** informal **1** foolish or deceptive talk; nonsense: *typical salesman's baloney*. [corruption of **bologna**.] **2** variant of **bologna**.

Bal·qash, Lake /bäl'käsH, bal'kasH/ (also **Balkhash**) a shallow salt lake in Kazakhstan.

bal·sa /'bôlsə/ ▶ **n. 1** (also **balsa wood**) a very lightweight wood used in particular for making models and rafts. **2** the fast-growing tropical American tree from which this wood is obtained. ● *Ochroma lagopus* (or *pyramidale*), family Bombacaceae.
– ORIGIN early 17th cent. (denoting a kind of South American raft or fishing boat): from Spanish, 'raft.'

bal·sam /'bôlsəm/ ▶ **n. 1** an aromatic resinous substance, such as balm, exuded by various trees and shrubs and used as a base for certain fragrances and medical and cosmetic preparations. ■ a tree or shrub that yields balsam. **2** a herbaceous plant cultivated for its flowers, which are typically pink or purple and carried high on the stem. ● Genus *Impatiens*, family Balsaminaceae: several species, including **garden balsam** (*I. balsamina*) and **Himalayan balsam** (*I. glandulifera*), which is naturalized in Europe and North America, sometimes to the detriment of the native flora.
– DERIVATIVES **bal·sam·ic** /bôl'samik/ **adj.**
– ORIGIN Old English, via Latin from Greek *balsamon*.

bal·sam ap·ple ▶ **n.** another name for **bitter melon**.

bal·sam fir ▶ **n.** a North American fir tree that yields Canada balsam. ● *Abies balsamea*, family Pinaceae.

bal·sam·ic vin·e·gar ▶ **n.** dark, sweet Italian vinegar that has been matured in wooden barrels.

bal·sam pop·lar ▶ **n.** a North American poplar tree that yields balsam. ● *Populus balsamifera*, family Salicaceae.

Bal·sas, Ri·o /ˌrēō 'bôlsəs/ a river that flows 450 miles (725 km) through central Mexico, through Puebla, Guerrero, and Michoacán states, into the Pacific Ocean.

bal·sa wood ▶ **n.** see **balsa** (sense 1).

Balt /bôlt/ ▶ **n. 1** a speaker of a Baltic language; a Lithuanian or Latvian. **2** a native or inhabitant of one of the Baltic States of Lithuania, Latvia, and Estonia. ■ historical a German-speaking inhabitant of any of these states.
▶ **adj.** of or relating to the Balts.
– ORIGIN late 19th cent.: from late Latin *Balthae* 'dwellers near the Baltic Sea.'

Bal·tha·sar /bôl'THazər, bal-, 'bôlTHəˌzär/ (also **Balthazar**) one of the three Magi.

bal·tha·zar /bôl'THazər, bal-, 'bôlTHəˌzär/ ▶ **n.** a very large wine bottle, with a capacity of 12 liters, equivalent to that of 16 ordinary wine bottles.
– ORIGIN 1930s: from *Balthazar*, the name of the King of Babylon, who "made a great feast...and drank wine before a thousand" (Dan. 5:1).

Bal·tic /'bôltik/ ▶ **adj. 1** of or relating to the Baltic Sea or the region surrounding it. **2** denoting, belonging to, or relating to a branch of the Indo-European family of languages consisting of Lithuanian, Latvian, and Old Prussian.
▶ **n. 1** (**the Baltic**) the Baltic Sea or the Baltic States. **2** the Baltic languages collectively.
– ORIGIN late 16th cent.: from medieval Latin *Balticus*, from late Latin *Balthae* 'dwellers near the Baltic Sea.'

Bal·tic Sea a sea in northern Europe. Almost landlocked, it is linked with the North Sea by Kattegat Strait and the Øresund Channel.

Bal·tic States 1 the independent republics of Estonia, Latvia, and Lithuania. **2** the ten members of the Council of Baltic States established in 1992: Denmark, Estonia, Finland, Germany, Latvia, Lithuania, Norway, Poland, Russia, and Sweden.

Bal·ti·more /'bôltəˌmôr, 'bôlt(ə)mər/ a seaport in northern Maryland, the largest city in Maryland, on Chesapeake Bay; pop. 636,919 (est. 2008).
– ORIGIN named after George Calvert, the first Baron *Baltimore* (c.1580–1632), who in 1632 obtained a grant of land for the colony that later became Maryland.

Bal·ti·more Coun·ty a county in north central Maryland that surrounds but does not include the city of Baltimore; pop. 785,618 (est. 2008). Towson is its seat.

Bal·ti·stan /ˌbôltə'stan, ˌbəl-, -'stän/ a region of the Karakoram range of the Himalayas, to the south of K2 peak. Also called **Little Tibet**.

Bal·to-Slav·ic /ˌbôltō'slävik/ ▶ **n.** a branch of the Indo-European language family that includes the Baltic and Slavic languages.
▶ **adj.** relating to Balto-Slavic.

Ba·lu·chi /bə'lōōCHē/ (also **Baluch** /-'lōōCH/) ▶ **n.** (pl. **same** or **Baluchis**) **1** a native or inhabitant of Baluchistan. **2** the Iranian language of Baluchistan.
▶ **adj.** of or relating to this people or their language.
– ORIGIN from Persian *Balūč* (ī).

Ba·lu·chi·stan /bə'lōōCHiˌstan, -stän/ **1** a mountainous region of western Asia that includes part of southeastern Iran, southwestern Afghanistan, and western Pakistan. **2** a province of western Pakistan; capital, Quetta.

Ba·lun·da /bə'lōōndə, -'lōōn-/ plural form of **Lunda**.

bal·us·ter /'baləstər/ ▶ **n.** a short pillar or column, typically decorative in design, in a series supporting a rail or coping. ■ [as modifier] (of a furniture leg or other decorative item) having the form of a baluster.
– ORIGIN early 17th cent.: from French *balustre*, from Italian *balaustro*, from *balaust(r)a* 'wild pomegranate flower' (via Latin from Greek *balaustion*), so named because part of the pillar resembles the curving calyx tube of the flower.

balustrade

bal·us·trade /balə'strād/ ▶ **n.** a railing supported by balusters, esp. an ornamental parapet on a balcony, bridge, or terrace.
– DERIVATIVES **bal·us·trad·ed adj.**
– ORIGIN mid 17th cent.: from French, from *balustre* (see **baluster**).

Bal·zac /'bôlˌzak, 'bal-/, Honoré de (1799–1850), French novelist; chiefly remembered for his series of ninety-one interconnected novels and stories known collectively as *La Comédie humaine*.
– DERIVATIVES **Bal·zac·i·an** /bôl'zakēən, bal-/ **adj.**

bam /bam/ ▶ **exclam.** used to imitate the sound of a hard blow or to convey the abruptness of an occurrence: *he'll have to make a dash for it, and when he does, bam, he's dead*.
– ORIGIN 1920s: imitative.

Ba·ma·ko /'bäməˌkō, 'bam-/ the capital of Mali, in the south part of the country, on the Niger River; pop. 1,728,400 (est. 2009).

Bam·ba·ra /bäm'bärə/ ▶ **n.** (pl. **same** or **Bambaras**) a member of an indigenous people living chiefly in Mali. ■ the Mande language of this people.
▶ **adj.** of or relating to this people or their language.

bam·bi·no /bam'bēnō/ ▶ **n.** (pl. **bambini** /-nē/) often humorous a baby or young child. ■ an image of the infant Jesus.
– ORIGIN early 18th cent.: Italian, diminutive of *bambo* 'silly.'

bam·boo /ˌbam'bōō/ ▶ **n.** a giant woody grass that grows chiefly in the tropics, where it is widely cultivated. ● *Bambusa* and other genera, family Gramineae. ■ the hollow jointed stem of this plant, used as a cane or to make furniture and implements: [as modifier] *a bamboo serving tray*.
– ORIGIN late 16th cent.: from Dutch *bamboes*, based on Malay *mambu*.

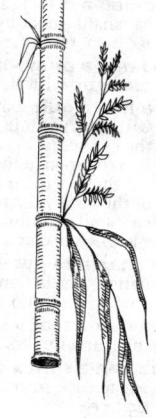

bam·boo cur·tain ▶ **n.** dated (often **the Bamboo Curtain**) a political and economic barrier between China and noncommunist countries.

bam·boo shoot ▶ **n.** a young shoot of bamboo, eaten as a vegetable.

bamboo

bam·boo·zle /bam'bōōzəl/ ▶ **v.** [with obj.] informal fool or cheat (someone): *Tom Sawyer bamboozled the neighborhood boys into doing it for him*. ■ confound or perplex: *bamboozled by the number of savings plans being offered*.
– ORIGIN early 18th cent.: of unknown origin.

bam·my /'bamē/ (also **bammie**) ▶ **n.** (pl. **bammy** or **bammies**) (in the West Indies) a flat roll or pancake made from cassava flour.
– ORIGIN probably from a West African language.

ban[1] /ban/ ▶ **v.** (**bans, banning, banned**) [with obj.] officially or legally prohibit: *he was banned from driving for a year* | *a proposal to ban all trade in ivory*. ■ officially exclude (someone) from a place: *he once was banned from a casino in Reno*.
▶ **n. 1** an official or legal prohibition: *a proposed ban on cigarette advertising* | *a three-year driving ban*. ■ an official exclusion of a person from an organization, country, or activity: *a proposed ban on foreign correspondents was condemned by international leaders*. **2** ■ archaic a curse.
– ORIGIN Old English *bannan* 'summon by a public proclamation,' of Germanic origin, reinforced by Old Norse *banna* 'curse, prohibit'; the noun is partly from Old French *ban* 'proclamation, summons, banishment.'

ban[2] /bän/ ▶ **n.** (pl. **bani** /'bänē/) a monetary unit of Romania, equal to one hundredth of a leu.
– ORIGIN Romanian.

Ba·na·ba /bə'näbə, -'nabə/ an island in the western Pacific, just south of the equator to the west of the Gilbert Islands. Formerly within the Gilbert and Ellice Islands, it has been part of Kiribati since 1979. Also called **Ocean Island**.

ba·nal /'bānl, bə'nal, -'näl/ ▶ **adj.** so lacking in originality as to be obvious and boring: *songs with banal, repeated words*.
– DERIVATIVES **ba·nal·ly adv.**
– ORIGIN mid 18th cent. (originally relating to feudal service in the sense 'compulsory,' hence 'common to all'): from French, from *ban* 'a proclamation or call to arms'; ultimately of Germanic origin and related to **ban**[1].

ba·nal·i·ty /bə'nalitē/ ▶ **n.** (pl. **banalities**) the fact or condition of being banal; unoriginality: *there is an essential banality to the story he tells*. ■ something that is banal: *the banalities of contemporary celebrity culture*.

ba·nan·a /bə'nanə/ ▶ **n. 1** a long curved fruit that grows in clusters and has soft pulpy flesh and yellow skin when ripe. **2** (also **banana plant** or **banana tree**) the tropical and subtropical treelike plant that bears this fruit. It has very large leaves and resembles a palm, but lacks a woody trunk. ● Genus *Musa*, family Musaceae: several species, in particular *M. sapientum*.
▶ **adj.** (**bananas**) informal insane or extremely silly: *he's beginning to think I'm bananas*.
– PHRASES **go bananas** informal go insane: *Roy's customers think the council has gone bananas*. ■ rave; cheer wildly: *I have never had a product that people went so bananas over*. ■ become extremely angry or excited: *she went bananas when I said I was going to leave the job*. **second banana** informal the second most important person in an organization

or activity. **top banana** informal the most important person in an organization or activity.
– ORIGIN late 16th cent.: via Portuguese or Spanish from Mande.

ba·nan·a belt ▶ n. informal a region with a comparatively warm climate.

ba·nan·a oil ▶ n. a colorless liquid with a bananalike odor used in flavorings and as a solvent. ● Chem. formula: $CH_3CO_2C_5H_{11}$.

ba·nan·a plug ▶ n. Electronics, informal a single-pole connector with a curved spring along its tip.

ba·nan·a·quit /bəˈnanəˌkwit/ ▶ n. a small songbird with a curved bill, typically with a white stripe over the eye, a sooty gray back, and yellow underparts. It is common in the West Indies and Central and South America. ● *Coereba flaveola*, the only member of the family Coerebidae (sometimes placed in the subfamily Parulinae, family Emberizidae).
– ORIGIN see QUIT².

ba·nan·a re·pub·lic ▶ n. chiefly derogatory a small nation, esp. in Central America, dependent on one crop or the influx of foreign capital.

ba·nan·a seat ▶ n. a narrow, elongated bicycle seat that curves up toward the rear.

ba·nan·a split ▶ n. a dessert made with a split banana, ice cream, sauce, whipped cream, nuts, and a cherry.

ba·nau·sic /bəˈnôzik, -sik/ ▶ adj. formal not operating on a refined or elevated level; mundane. ■ relating to technical work.
– ORIGIN mid 19th cent.: from Greek *banausikos* 'of or for artisans.'

ban·co /ˈbaNGkō/ ▶ exclam. used in baccarat, chemin de fer, and similar games to express a player's willingness to meet the banker's whole stake single-handed.
– ORIGIN late 18th cent.: via French from Italian.

band¹ /band/ ▶ n. **1** a flat, thin strip or loop of material put around something, typically to hold it together or to decorate it: *wads of banknotes fastened with gummed paper bands.* ■ a plain ring for the finger, esp. a gold wedding ring: *a narrow band of gold was her only jewelry.* ■ Ornithology a ring of metal placed around a bird's leg to identify it. ■ (**bands**) a collar with two hanging strips, worn by certain clerics and academics as part of their formal dress. ■ Mechanics a belt connecting wheels or pulleys.
2 a stripe or elongated area of a different color, texture, or composition than its surroundings: *a long, narrow band of cloud.*
3 a range of frequencies or wavelengths in a spectrum (esp. of radio frequencies): *channels in the UHF band.*
4 archaic a thing that restrains, binds, or unites.
▶ v. [with obj.] **1** surround (an object) with something in the form of a strip or ring, typically for reinforcement or decoration: *doors are banded with iron to make them stronger.* ■ Ornithology put a band on (a bird) for identification.
2 mark (something) with a stripe or stripes of a different color: *the bird's bill is banded across the middle with black* | (as adj. **banded**) *banded agate.*
– ORIGIN late Old English (sense 4 of the noun), from Old Norse, reinforced in late Middle English by Old French *bande*, of Germanic origin; related to BIND.

band² ▶ n. **1** a group of people who have a common interest or purpose: *guerrilla bands* | *a determined band of activists.* ■ Anthropology a subgroup of a tribe.
2 a group of musicians who play together, in particular: ■ a small group of musicians and vocalists who play pop, jazz, or rock music: *the band's last two albums* | *a rock band.* ■ a group of musicians who play brass, wind, or percussion instruments: *a military band.* ■ informal an orchestra.
3 a herd or flock: *moving bands of caribou.*
▶ v. [no obj.] (of people or organizations) form a group for a mutual purpose: *local people banded together to fight the company.*
– ORIGIN late Middle English: from Old French *bande*, of Germanic origin; related to BANNER.

Ban·da /ˈbandə/, Hastings Kamuzu (1906–1997), Malawian statesman; prime minister 1964–94; the first president of the Republic of Malawi 1966–94.

band·age /ˈbandij/ ▶ n. a strip of material used to bind a wound or to protect an injured part of the body: *her leg was swathed in bandages* | *a sterile adhesive bandage with nonstick pad.*
▶ v. [with obj.] bind (a wound or a part of the body) with a protective strip of material: *bandage the foot so that the ankle is supported* | *the doctors bandaged up his wounds.*
– DERIVATIVES **band·ag·ing** n.
– ORIGIN late 16th cent.: from French, from *bande* (see BAND¹).

Band-Aid /ˈband ˌād/ ▶ n. trademark an adhesive bandage with a gauze pad in the center, used to cover minor wounds. ■ (also **band-aid**) a makeshift or temporary solution: [as modifier] *a band-aid solution to a much deeper problem.*

ban·dan·na /banˈdanə/ (also **bandana**) ▶ n. a large handkerchief, typically having a colorful pattern, worn tied around the head or neck.
– ORIGIN mid 18th cent.: probably via Portuguese from Hindi.

Ban·da·ra·nai·ke /ˌbəndərəˈnīkə/, Sirimavo Ratwatte Dias (1916–2000), Sinhalese stateswoman; prime minister of Sri Lanka 1960–65, 1970–77, and 1994–2000. The world's first woman prime minister, she succeeded her husband, **S. W. R. D. Bandaranaike** (1899–1959), after his assassination. Their daughter **Chandrika Bandaranaike Kumaratunga** (1949–) was Sri Lanka's president 1994–2005.

Ban·dar Lam·pung /ˈbəndər ˈlämˌpŏŏNG/ a city at the southern tip of Sumatra, in Indonesia; pop. 916,600 (est. 2009). It was created in the 1980s as a result of the amalgamation of the city of Tanjungkarang and the nearby port of Telukbetung.

Ban·dar Se·ri Be·ga·wan /ˈbänˌdär ˈserē bəˈgäwən/ the capital of Brunei, in the northern part of the country; pop. 32,300 (est. 2008).

Ban·da Sea /ˈbandə, ˈbändə/ a sea in eastern Indonesia, between the central and south Molucca Islands.

B & B ▶ abbr. bed and breakfast.

band·box /ˈbandˌbäks/ ▶ n. a cardboard box, typically circular, for carrying hats.
– ORIGIN mid 17th cent.: from BAND² + BOX¹, the box being used originally for neckbands.

B & E ▶ abbr. breaking and entering.

ban·deau /banˈdō/ ▶ n. (pl. **bandeaux** /-ˈdōz/) a narrow band worn around the head to hold the hair in position: *their dusty blonde hair smoothly combed in bandeaux.* ■ a woman's strapless top formed from a band of fabric fitting around the bust: *white two-piece bathing suit with quilted sateen bandeau top.*
– ORIGIN early 18th cent.: from French, from Old French *bandel*, diminutive of *bande* (see BAND²).

ban·de·ril·la /ˌbandəˈrēə/ ▶ n. a decorated dart thrust into a bull's neck or shoulders during a bullfight.
– ORIGIN Spanish, diminutive of *bandera* 'banner.'

ban·de·ril·le·ro /ˌbandərēˈyerō/ ▶ n. (pl. **banderilleros**) a bullfighter who uses banderillas.
– ORIGIN Spanish.

ban·de·role /ˈbandəˌrōl/ (also **banderol**) ▶ n. a narrow flaglike object, in particular: ■ a long, narrow flag with a cleft end, flown at a masthead. ■ an ornamental streamer on a knight's lance. ■ a ribbonlike stone scroll bearing an inscription.
– ORIGIN mid 16th cent.: from French, from Italian *banderuola*, diminutive of *bandiera* 'banner.'

ban·di·coot /ˈbandiˌko͞ot/ ▶ n. a mainly insectivorous marsupial native to Australia and New Guinea. ● Family Peramelidae: several genera and species, some of which are endangered or extinct, including the **short-nosed** (or **southern brown**) **bandicoot** (*Isodon obesulus*).
– ORIGIN late 18th cent.: from Telugu *pandikokku*, literally 'pig-rat.'

short-nosed bandicoot

ban·di·coot rat ▶ n. an Asian rat that is often a destructive pest. ● Genera *Bandicota* and *Nesokia*, family Muridae: four species, in particular the large *B. indica*.

band·ing /ˈbandiNG/ ▶ n. **1** the presence or formation of visible stripes of contrasting color: *the yellow and black banding of bees and wasps.* ■ Biochemistry the pattern of regions on a chromosome made visible by staining. ■ Biochemistry the separation of molecules into bands of concentration in a gel.
2 the marking of individual birds or other animals with bands or rings: *banding is a useful tool for the study of migration.*

ban·dit /ˈbandit/ ▶ n. (pl. **bandits** or **banditti** /banˈditē/) a robber or outlaw belonging to a gang and typically operating in an isolated or lawless area: *the bandit produced a weapon and demanded money.* ■ military slang an enemy aircraft.
– PHRASES **make out like a bandit** profit greatly from an activity.
– DERIVATIVES **ban·dit·ry** /-trē/ n.
– ORIGIN late 16th cent.: from Italian *bandito*, literally 'banned,' past participle of *bandire*.

band·lead·er /ˈbandˌlēdər/ (also **band leader**) ▶ n. a player or conductor at the head of a musical band.

band·mas·ter /ˈbandˌmastər/ ▶ n. the conductor of a musical band, esp. a brass or military one.

band·mate /ˈbandˌmāt/ ▶ n. a fellow musician or singer in a band.

ban·dog /ˈbanˌdôg/ ▶ n. a dog bred for its strength and ferocity by crossing aggressive breeds.
– ORIGIN Middle English (originally denoting a dog kept on a chain or "band"): from BAND¹ + DOG.

ban·do·lier /ˌbandəˈli(ə)r/ (also **bandoleer**) ▶ n. a shoulder-belt with loops or pockets for cartridges.
– ORIGIN late 16th cent.: from French *bandoulière*; perhaps from Spanish *bandolera* (from *banda* 'sash'), or from Catalan *bandolera* (from *bandoler* 'bandit').

bandolier

ban·do·ne·on /banˈdōnēən/ ▶ n. a type of concertina used esp. in South America.
– ORIGIN via Spanish from German *Bandonion*, named after Heinrich *Band*, the 19th-cent. German musician who invented it, + *-on-* (as in *Harmonika* 'harmonica') + *-ion* (as in *Akkordion* 'accordion').

ban·do·ra /banˈdôrə/ ▶ n. a bass stringed instrument of the cittern family, having a long neck and a scallop-shaped body.
– ORIGIN mid 16th cent.: origin uncertain; compare with Dutch *bandoor*, Spanish *bandurria*, also with BANJO.

band·pass /ˈbandˌpas/ ▶ adj. Electronics (of a filter) transmitting only a set range of frequencies: *a 1–40 Hz bandpass filter.*
▶ n. the range of frequencies transmitted through such a filter.

band·saw /ˈbandˌsô/ (also **band saw**) ▶ n. an endless saw, consisting of a steel band with a serrated edge running over wheels.

band·shell /ˈbandˌSHel/ (also **band shell**) ▶ n. a bandstand in the form of a large concave shell with special acoustic properties.

bands·man /ˈbandzmən/ ▶ n. (pl. **bandsmen**) a player in a musical band, esp. a military or brass one.

band·stand /ˈbandˌstand/ ▶ n. a covered outdoor platform for a band to play on, typically in a park. ■ a raised platform for performing musicians in a restaurant or dance hall.

Ban·dung /ˈbänˌdo͝oNG/ a city in Indonesia; pop. 1,601,800 (est. 2009). Founded by the Dutch in 1810, it was the capital of the former Dutch East Indies.

band·wag·on /ˈbandˌwagən/ ▶ n. **1** a wagon used for carrying a band in a parade or procession.
2 [usu. in sing.] a particular activity or cause that has suddenly become fashionable or popular: *the local deejays are on the home-team bandwagon.*
– PHRASES **jump** (or **climb**) **on the bandwagon** join others in doing or supporting something fashionable or likely to be successful: *scientists and doctors alike have jumped on the bandwagon.*

band·width /ˈbandˌwidTH/ ▶ n. Electronics a range of frequencies within a given band, in particular that used for transmitting a signal. ■ the transmission capacity of a computer network or other telecommunication system.

ban·dy¹ /ˈbandē/ ▶ adj. (**bandier**, **bandiest**) (of a person's legs) curved so as to be wide apart at the knees. ■ (often **bandy-legged**) (of a person) having legs that are curved in such a way; bowlegged.
– ORIGIN late 17th cent.: perhaps from obsolete *bandy* 'curved stick used in hockey.'

ban·dy² ▶ v. (**bandies**, **bandying**, **bandied**) [with obj.] (usu. **be bandied about/around**) pass on or discuss (an idea or rumor) in a casual or uninformed way: *$40,000 is the figure that has been bandied about.*
– PHRASES **bandy words with** argue pointlessly or rudely: *don't bandy words with me, Sir!*
– ORIGIN late 16th cent. (in the sense 'pass (a ball) to and fro'): perhaps from French *bander* 'take sides in a tennis match,' from *bande* 'band, crowd' (see BAND²).

bandy³ ▶ n. a game similar to field hockey. ■ (pl. **bandies**) the stick used to play this game.
– ORIGIN late 17th cent.: perhaps from BANDY².

bane /bān/ ▶ n. [usu. in sing.] a cause of great distress or annoyance: *the bane of the decorator is the long, narrow hall* | *the depressions that were the the bane of her existence.* ■ archaic something, typically poison, that causes death.
– DERIVATIVES **bane·ful** /-fəl/ adj. (archaic).
– ORIGIN Old English *bana* 'thing causing death, poison,' of Germanic origin.

b

bane·ber·ry /ˈbānˌberē/ ▶ **n.** (pl. **baneberries**) a plant of the buttercup family that bears fluffy spikes of creamy-white flowers followed by shiny berries. Native to north temperate regions, it was formerly used in medicine. ● Genus *Actaea*, family Ranunculaceae: many species, including the North American **white baneberry** (*A. pachypoda*), with clusters of black-eyed white berries on red stalks. ■ the bitter, typically poisonous berry of this plant.
–ORIGIN mid 18th cent.: from BANE in the sense 'poison' + BERRY.

bang[1] /baNG/ ▶ **n. 1** a sudden loud noise: *the door slammed with a bang* | *I heard a series of loud bangs.* ■ a sharp blow causing such a loud noise: *I went to answer a bang on the front door.* ■ a sudden painful blow: *a nasty bang on the head.*
2 (**bangs**) a fringe of hair cut straight across the forehead: *she brushed back her wispy bangs.* [from a use of the adverb *bang* to mean 'abruptly.']
3 vulgar slang an act of sexual intercourse.
4 Computing the character "!"
▶ **v.** [with obj.] **1** strike or put down (something) forcefully and noisily, typically in anger or in order to attract attention: *he began to bang the table with his fist* | *Sarah banged the phone down* | [no obj.] *someone was banging on the door.* ■ come into contact with (something) suddenly and sharply, typically by accident: *I banged my head on the low beams* | [no obj.] *she banged into some shelves in the darkness.* ■ [no obj.] make a sudden loud noise, typically repeatedly: *the shutter was banging in the wind.* ■ (with reference to a door) open or close violently and noisily: [with obj. and complement] *he* **banged** *the kitchen door* **shut** *behind him* | [no obj., with complement] *the door* **banged open** *and a man staggered out.* ■ [no obj.] (of a person) move around or do something noisily, esp. as an indication of anger or irritation: *she was banging around the kitchen.* ■ (of a sports player) hit (a ball or a shot) forcefully and successfully: *in his second start he banged out two hits.* ■ vulgar slang (of a man) have sexual intercourse with (a woman).
2 cut (hair) in a fringe.
▶ **adv.** informal, chiefly Brit. exactly: *bang in the middle of town.* ■ completely: *bring your wardrobe bang up to date.*
▶ **exclam. 1** used to express or imitate the sound of a sudden loud noise: *firecrackers went bang* | *Bang, Bang! You're dead.*
2 used to convey the suddenness of an action or process: *the minute something becomes obsolete, bang, it's gone.*
–PHRASES **bang for one's** (or **the**) **buck** informal value for money; performance for cost: *this cross between a sports car and a family sedan gave a lot of bang for the buck.* **bang** (or **knock** or **crack**) **people's heads together** reprimand people severely, esp. in the attempt to make them stop arguing. **get a bang out of** informal derive excitement or pleasure from: *some people get a bang out of reading that stuff.* **with a bang 1** abruptly: *the remark brought me down to earth with a bang.* **2** impressively or spectacularly: *the occasion* **went with a bang** | *the day starts with a bang—the steep climb to the mountain top.*
–PHRASAL VERBS **bang away at** informal do something in a persistent or dogged way: *he was banging away at his novel.* **bang something out** informal **1** play music noisily, enthusiastically, and typically unskillfully: *Dad was annihilating a Beethoven sonata, banging out notes.* **2** produce hurriedly or in great quantities: *they weren't banging out ads in my day the way they are now.* **bang someone/something up** informal damage or injure someone or something: *he banged up his knee.* ■ Brit. informal imprison someone: *they've been banged up for something they didn't do.*
–ORIGIN mid 16th cent.: imitative, perhaps of Scandinavian origin; compare with Old Norse *bang* 'hammering.'

bang[2] ▶ **n.** variant spelling of BHANG.

Ban·ga·lore /ˌbaNGgəˈlôr/ a city in south central India, capital of the state of Karnataka; pop. 5,310,300 (est. 2009).

Ban·ga·lore tor·pe·do (also **bangalore torpedo**) ▶ **n.** a tube containing explosives used by infantry for blowing up barriers.

bang·er /ˈbaNGər/ ▶ **n.** chiefly Brit. **1** informal a sausage: *bangers and beans.*
2 informal a car in poor condition, esp. a noisy one: *they've got an old banger.*
3 a loud explosive firework.

Bang·kok /ˈbaNGˌkäk, baNGˈkäk/ the capital and chief port of Thailand, on the Chao Phraya waterway, 25 miles (40 km) upstream from its outlet into the Gulf of Thailand; pop. 5,705,100 (est. 2007).

Bang·la·desh /ˌbäNGgləˈdesH, ˌbaNGglə-/ a country in southern Asia, in the Ganges River delta, on the Bay of Bengal; pop. 156,050,900 (est. 2009); capital, Dhaka; official language, Bengali.

Formerly part of British India, the region, as East Pakistan, became one of the two geographical units of Pakistan. After civil war, the independent republic of Bangladesh was proclaimed in 1971. Cyclones in the Bay of Bengal cause repeated devastation to the country.

–DERIVATIVES **Bang·la·desh·i** /-ˈdesHē/ **adj. & n.**

ban·gle /ˈbaNGgəl/ ▶ **n.** a rigid bracelet or anklet.
–ORIGIN late 18th cent.: from Hindi *baṅglī* 'glass bracelet.'

Ban·gor /ˈbaNGgər/ an industrial city in east central Maine, on the Penobscot River, formerly a lumbering center; pop. 31,756 (est. 2008).

bang·tail /ˈbaNGˌtāl/ ▶ **n.** a horse's tail that has been cut straight across just below the level of the hocks.

Ban·gui /bäNGˈgē, ˈbäNGˌgē/ the capital of the Central African Republic, in the southwestern part of the country, on the Ugandi River; pop. 672,000 (est. 2007).

bang-up ▶ **adj.** informal excellent: *for a novice, he has done a bang-up job.*

ba·ni /ˈbänē/ plural form of BAN[2].

ban·ian ▶ **n.** variant spelling of BANYAN.

ban·ish /ˈbanisH/ ▶ **v.** [with obj.] send (someone) away from a country or place as an official punishment: *they were* **banished** *to Siberia for political crimes.* ■ forbid, abolish, or get rid of (something unwanted): *it's perfectly feasible to banish the smoke without banning smoking* | *all thoughts of romance were* **banished from** *her head.*
–DERIVATIVES **ban·ish·ment** **n.**
–ORIGIN late Middle English: from Old French *baniss-*, lengthened stem of *banir*; ultimately of Germanic origin and related to BAN[1].

ban·is·ter /ˈbanəstər/ (also **bannister**) ▶ **n.** (also **banisters**) the structure formed by uprights and a handrail at the side of a staircase. ■ a single upright at the side of the staircase: *I stuck my head between the banisters.*
–ORIGIN mid 17th cent.: from earlier *barrister*, alteration of BALUSTER.

Ban·ja Lu·ka /ˌbänyə ˈlo͝okə/ a spa town in northern Bosnia and Herzegovina; pop. 164,200 (est. 2008). It served as a base for Bosnian Serbs during their war against Bosnian Muslims in the 1990s.

Ban·jar·ma·sin /ˌbänjərˈmäsən, ˌban-/ a deep-water port in Indonesia, on the southern part of the island of Borneo; pop. 576,400 (est. 2009).

ban·jo /ˈbanjō/ ▶ **n.** (pl. **banjos** or **banjoes**) a stringed musical instrument with a long neck and a round open-backed body consisting of parchment stretched over a metal hoop like a tambourine, played by plucking or with a plectrum. It is used esp. in American folk music. ■ an object resembling this in shape: [as modifier] *a banjo clock.*
–DERIVATIVES **ban·jo·ist** /-ist/ **n.**
–ORIGIN mid 18th cent.: originally a black American alteration of earlier *bandore*; probably based on Greek *pandoura* 'three-stringed lute.' Compare with BANDORA.

banjo

Ban·jul /ˈbänˌjo͞ol/ the capital of Gambia; pop. 34,828 (2003). Until 1973 it was known as Bathurst.

bank[1] /baNGk/ ▶ **n. 1** the land alongside or sloping down to a river or lake: *willows lined the bank.*
2 a slope, mass, or mound of a particular substance: *a bank of clouds* | *a bank of snow.* ■ an elevation in the seabed or a riverbed; a mudbank or sandbank. ■ a transverse slope given to a road, railroad, or sports track to enable vehicles or runners to maintain speed around a curve. ■ the sideways tilt of an aircraft when turning in flight: *flying with small amounts of bank.*
3 a set or series of similar things, esp. electrical or electronic devices, grouped together in rows: *the DJ had big banks of lights and speakers on either side of his console.* ■ a tier of oars: *the early ships had only twenty-five oars in each bank.*
4 the cushion of a pool table: [as modifier] *a bank shot.*
▶ **v.** [with obj.] **1** heap (a substance) into a mass or mound: *the rain* **banked** *the soil* **up** *behind the gate* | *snow was banked in humps at the roadside.* ■ [no obj.] rise or form into a mass or mound: *purple clouds* **banked up** *over the hills.* ■ heap a mass or mound of a substance against (something): *people were banking their houses with earth.* ■ heap (a fire) with tightly packed fuel so that it burns slowly: *she could have made a fire and banked it with dirt.* ■ edge or surround with a ridge or row of something: *steps banked with pots of chrysanthemums.*
2 (of an aircraft or vehicle) tilt or cause to tilt sideways in making a turn: [no obj.] *the plane banked as if to return to the airport* | [with obj.] *I banked the aircraft steeply and turned.* ■ [no obj.] build (a road, railroad, or sports track) higher at the outer edge of a bend to facilitate fast cornering.
3 (in pool and other games) play (a ball) so that it rebounds off a surface such as a backboard or cushion.
–ORIGIN Middle English: from Old Norse *bakki*, of Germanic origin; related to BENCH. The senses 'set of similar things in sloping rows' and 'tier of oars' are from French *banc*, of the same ultimate origin.

bank[2] ▶ **n.** a financial establishment that invests money deposited by customers, pays it out when required, makes loans at interest, and exchanges currency: *I paid the money straight into my bank.* ■ a stock of something available for use when required: *a blood bank* | *building a bank of test items is the responsibility of teachers.* ■ a site or receptacle where something may be stored: *the computer's memory bank.* ■ (**the bank**) the store of money or tokens held by the banker in some gambling or board games. ■ the person holding this store; the banker. ■ Brit. a site or receptacle where something may be deposited for recycling: *a paper bank.*
▶ **v.** [with obj.] deposit (money or valuables) in a bank: *I banked the check.* ■ [no obj.] have an account at a particular bank: *he did not* **bank with** *the old family banks.* ■ informal (esp. of a competitor in a game or race) win or earn (a sum of money): *he banked $100,000 for a hole-in-one.* ■ store (something, esp. blood, tissue, or sperm) for future use: *the sperm is banked or held in storage for the following spring.*
–PHRASES **break the bank** (in gambling) win more money than is held by the bank. ■ [usu. with negative] informal cost more than one can afford: *Christmas need not break the bank.*
–PHRASAL VERBS **bank on** base one's hopes or confidence on: *they can bank on my winning 25 games next year.*
–ORIGIN late 15th cent. (originally denoting a money dealer's table): from French *banque* or Italian *banca*, from medieval Latin *banca*, *bancus*, of Germanic origin; related to BANK[1] and BENCH.

bank·a·ble /ˈbaNGkəbəl/ ▶ **adj.** (esp. in the entertainment industry) certain to bring profit and success: *he needed some bankable names to star in the film.* ■ reliable: *a bankable assurance.*
–DERIVATIVES **bank·a·bil·i·ty** /ˌbaNGkəˈbilitē/ **n.**

bank ac·count ▶ **n.** an arrangement made with a bank whereby one may deposit and withdraw money and in some cases be paid interest.

bank bal·ance ▶ **n.** the amount of money held in a bank account at a given moment.

bank bill ▶ **n. 1** Brit. a bill of exchange drawn by one bank on another.
2 another term for BANKNOTE.

bank book ▶ **n.** another term for PASSBOOK.

bank card ▶ **n.** a plastic card issued by a bank which enables a customer to withdraw money at an automated teller machine.

bank dis·count ▶ **n.** interest computed on the face value of a loan and deducted in advance from the loan by the lending bank.

bank draft ▶ **n.** a check drawn by a bank on its own funds in another bank.

bank·er /ˈbaNGkər/ ▶ **n.** an officer or owner of a bank or group of banks. ■ the person running the table, controlling play, or acting as dealer in some gambling or board games.
–ORIGIN mid 16th cent.: from French *banquier*, from *banque* (see BANK[2]).

bank·er's hours ▶ **plural n.** short working hours (in reference to the typical opening hours of a bank in former times).

Bank·head /ˈbaNGkˌhed/, Tallulah (1903–68), US actress noted for her uninhibited public persona, rich laugh, and harsh drawl. Her best-known movie appearance was in Alfred Hitchcock's *Lifeboat* (1944).

bank hol·i·day ▶ **n.** Brit. a day on which banks are officially closed, observed as a public holiday.

Ban Ki-moon /ˌban kē ˈmo͞on/ (1944–), South Korean diplomat; secretary general of the United Nations since 2007.

bank·ing /ˈbaNGkiNG/ ▶ **n.** the business conducted or services offered by a bank: *with this account, you are entitled to free banking* | *a 23-year career in banking.*

bank ma·chine ▶ **n.** another term for AUTOMATED TELLER MACHINE.

bank·note /ˈbaNGkˌnōt/ (also **bank note**) ▶ **n.** a piece of paper money, constituting a central bank's promissory note to pay a stated sum to the bearer on demand: *is the $1 bill the only banknote with George Washington's picture on it?*

bank rate ▶ n. the rate of discount set by a central bank.

b

bank·roll /'baNGk,rōl/ ▶ n. a roll of paper money. ■ financial resources: *his bankroll allowed him to run campaigns all over the U.S.*
▶ v. [with obj.] informal support (a person, organization, or project) financially: *the project is bankrolled by wealthy expatriates.*

bank·rupt /'baNGk,rəpt, -rəpt/ ▶ adj. **1** (of a person or organization) declared in law unable to pay outstanding debts: *the company was declared bankrupt* | *his father went* **bankrupt** *and the family had to sell their home.* ■ impoverished or depleted: *a bankrupt country with no natural resources.*
2 completely lacking in a particular quality or value: *their cause is morally bankrupt.*
▶ n. a person judged by a court to be insolvent, whose property is taken and disposed of for the benefit of creditors.
▶ v. [with obj.] reduce (a person or organization) to bankruptcy: *the strike nearly bankrupted the union.*
– ORIGIN mid 16th cent.: from Italian *banca rotta* 'broken bench,' from *banca* (see BANK²) and *rompere* 'to break.' The change in the ending was due to association with Latin *rupt-* 'broken.'

bank·rupt·cy /'baNGk,rəp(t)sē, -rəp(t)sē/ ▶ n. (pl. **bankruptcies**) **1** the state of being bankrupt: *many companies were facing bankruptcy* | *a series of bankruptcies and scandals* | [as modifier] *bankruptcy proceedings.*
2 the state of being completely lacking in a particular quality or value: *the moral bankruptcy of turning away desperate people.*

Banks, Sir Joseph (1743–1820), English botanist. He accompanied Captain James Cook on his first voyage to the Pacific.

bank·si·a /'baNGksēə/ ▶ n. an evergreen Australian shrub that typically has narrow, leathery leaves and spikes of bottlebrushlike flowers. ● Genus *Banksia*, family Proteaceae.
– ORIGIN modern Latin, named after Sir Joseph BANKS.

bank state·ment ▶ n. a printed record of the balance in a bank account and the amounts that have been paid into it and withdrawn from it, issued periodically to the holder of the account.

bank swal·low ▶ n. another term for SAND MARTIN.

bank vole ▶ n. a common reddish-brown Eurasian vole that lives in woodland and scrub. ● *Clethrionomys glareolus*, family Muridae.

Ban·ne·ker /'banikər/, Benjamin (1731–1806), US inventor, astronomer, and mathematician. Born to a slave father and freed slave mother, he published an almanac 1791–1802 that featured his astronomical and tide calculations. On the recommendation of Thomas Jefferson, he was hired to assist in the surveying of the District of Columbia 1790.

ban·ner /'banər/ ▶ n. **1** a long strip of cloth bearing a slogan or design, hung in a public place or carried in a demonstration or procession: *a banner in the front window announced "Grand Reopening"* | *students waved banners and chanted slogans.* ■ a flag on a pole used as the standard of a monarch, army, or knight. ■ an idea or principle used to rally public opinion: *the administration is flying the free trade banner.*
2 a heading or advertisement appearing on a web page in the form of a bar, column, or box: *to get a new banner now, click Step 1* | [as modifier] *a banner ad.*
▶ adj. [attrib.] excellent; outstanding: *I predict that 1998 will be a banner year.*
– PHRASES **under the banner of** claiming to support a particular cause or set of ideas: *campaigns fought under the banner of multiculturalism.* ■ as part of a particular group or organization: *the party is running under the banner of the Left-Wing Alliance.*
– DERIVATIVES **ban·nered** adj.
– ORIGIN Middle English: from Old French *baniere*, ultimately of Germanic origin and related to BAND².

ban·ner·et /'banərit, ,banə'ret/ ▶ n. historical **1** a knight who commanded his own troops in battle under his own banner.
2 a knighthood given on the battlefield for courage.
– ORIGIN Middle English: from Old French *baneret*, literally 'bannered,' from *baniere* 'banner.'

ban·ner head·line ▶ n. a newspaper headline running across a whole page, esp. one on the front page.

Ban·nis·ter /'banəstər/, Sir Roger Gilbert (1929–), British middle-distance runner and neurologist. In 1954, he became the first man to run a mile in under 4 minutes.

ban·nis·ter ▶ n. variant spelling of BANISTER.

ban·nock /'banək/ ▶ n. a round, flat loaf, typically unleavened, associated with Scotland and northern England.
– ORIGIN Old English *bannuc*, of Celtic origin; related to Welsh *ban*, Breton *bannac'h*, *banne*, and Cornish *banna* 'a drop.'

Ban·nock·burn, Battle of /'banək,bərn/ a battle that took place near Stirling in central Scotland in 1314, in which the English army of Edward II, advancing to break the siege of Stirling Castle, was defeated by the Scots under Robert the Bruce.

banns /banz/ ▶ plural n. a notice read out on three successive Sundays in a parish church, announcing an intended marriage and giving the opportunity for objections.
– ORIGIN Middle English: plural of BAN¹.

ban·quet /'baNGkwit/ ▶ n. an elaborate and formal evening meal for many people, often followed by speeches: *the Austrian emperor's lavish banquets* | [as modifier] *a banquet table.* ■ an elaborate and extensive meal; a feast: *a ten-course banquet.*
▶ v. (**banquets, banqueting, banqueted**) [with obj.] entertain with a banquet: *there are halls for banqueting up to 3,000 people* | (as adj. **banqueting**) *a banqueting hall.*
– DERIVATIVES **ban·quet·er** n.
– ORIGIN late 15th cent.: from French, diminutive of *banc* 'bench' (see BANK¹).

ban·quette /baNG'ket/ ▶ n. **1** an upholstered bench along a wall, esp. in a restaurant or bar.
2 a raised step behind a rampart.
– ORIGIN early 17th cent. (sense 2): from French, from Italian *banchetta*, diminutive of *banca* 'bench' (see BANK²). Sense 1 dates from the mid 19th cent.

ban·shee /'banSHē/ ▶ n. (in Irish legend) a female spirit whose wailing warns of an impending death in a house: *the little girl dropped her ice cream and began to howl like a banshee* | [as modifier] *a horrible banshee wail.*
– ORIGIN late 17th cent.: from Irish *bean sídhe*, from Old Irish *ben síde* 'woman of the fairies.'

ban·tam /'bantəm/ ▶ n. **1** a chicken of a small breed, of which the cock is noted for its aggressiveness: figurative *what a wiry bantam he is!*
2 short for BANTAMWEIGHT.
– ORIGIN mid 18th cent.: apparently named after the province of *Bantam* in Java, although the fowl is not native there.

ban·tam·weight /'bantəm,wāt/ ▶ n. a weight in boxing and other sports intermediate between flyweight and featherweight. In boxing it ranges from 112 to 118 pounds (51 to 54 kg). ■ a boxer or other competitor of this weight.

ban·teng /'banteNG/ ▶ n. a Southeast Asian forest ox that resembles the domestic cow. It has been domesticated in Bali. ● *Bos javanicus*, family Bovidae.
– ORIGIN early 19th cent.: from Malay.

ban·ter /'bantər/ ▶ n. the playful and friendly exchange of teasing remarks: *there was much singing and good-natured banter.*
▶ v. [no obj.] talk or exchange remarks in a good-humored teasing way: *the men bantered with the waitresses* | (as adj. **bantering**) *a bantering tone.*
– ORIGIN late 17th cent.: of unknown origin.

Ban·ting /'bantiNG/, Sir Frederick Grant (1891–1941), Canadian physiologist and surgeon. With the assistance of Charles H. Best, Banting discovered insulin 1921–22, using it to treat diabetes. Nobel Prize for Physiology or Medicine (1923), shared with J. J. R. Macleod.

bant·ling /'bantliNG/ ▶ n. archaic a young child.
– ORIGIN late 16th cent.: from BAND¹ + -LING, or a corruption of German *bänkling* 'bastard.'

Ban·tu /'bantō͞o/ ▶ n. (pl. **same** or **Bantus**) **1** a member of an extensive group of indigenous peoples of central and southern Africa.
2 the group of languages spoken by these peoples.

> Bantu languages belong to the Niger-Congo language family, and there are more than 400 of them (with over 100 million speakers), of which Swahili, Xhosa, and Zulu are the most important.

▶ adj. of or relating to these peoples or their languages.
– ORIGIN plural (in certain Bantu languages) of *-ntu* 'person.'

ban·yan /'banyən/ (also **banian**) ▶ n. (also **banyan tree**) an Indian fig tree whose branches produce aerial roots that later become accessory trunks. A mature tree may cover several acres in this manner. ● *Ficus benghalensis*, family Moraceae.
– ORIGIN late 16th cent.: from Portuguese, from Gujarati *vāṇiyo* 'man of the trading caste,' from Sanskrit. Originally denoting a Hindu trader or merchant, the term was applied by Europeans in the mid 17th cent. to a particular tree under which such traders had built a pagoda.

ban·zai /'ban'zī/ ▶ exclam. **1** a Japanese battle cry. [early 20th cent.]
2 a form of greeting used to the Japanese emperor. [late 19th cent.]
▶ adj. (esp. of Japanese troops) attacking fiercely and recklessly: *a banzai charge.*
– ORIGIN Japanese, literally 'ten thousand years (of life to you).'

ba·o·bab /'bāō,bab, 'bä-ō-/ ▶ n. a short tree with an enormously thick trunk and large edible fruit. It can live to a great age. ● Genus *Adansonia*, family Bombacaceae: several species, in particular the African *A. digitata* and the Australian *A. gregorii.*
– ORIGIN mid 17th cent.: probably from an African language; first recorded in Latin (1592), in a treatise on the plants of Egypt by Prosper Alpinus, Italian botanist.

Bao·tou /'bou'tō/ an industrial city in Inner Mongolia, northern China, on the Yellow River; pop. 1,194,600 (est. 2006).

bap·tism /'bap,tizəm/ ▶ n. (in the Christian Church) the religious rite of sprinkling water onto a person's forehead or of immersion in water, symbolizing purification or regeneration and admission to the Christian Church. In many denominations, baptism is performed on young children and is accompanied by name-giving. ■ a ceremony or occasion at which this takes place. ■ a person's initiation into a particular activity or role, typically one perceived as difficult: *this event constituted his baptism as a politician.*
– PHRASES **baptism of fire** a difficult or painful new undertaking or experience. [from the original sense of 'a soldier's first battle.']
– DERIVATIVES **bap·tis·mal** /bap'tizməl/ adj.
– ORIGIN Middle English: from Old French *baptesme*, via ecclesiastical Latin from ecclesiastical Greek *baptismos* 'ceremonial washing,' from *baptizein* 'immerse, baptize.'

bap·tis·mal name ▶ n. a personal name given at baptism.

bap·tist /'baptist/ ▶ n. **1** (**Baptist**) a member of a Protestant Christian denomination advocating baptism only of adult believers by total immersion. Baptists form one of the largest Protestant bodies and are found throughout the world and esp. in the US.
2 a person who baptizes someone.
– ORIGIN Middle English (sense 2): from Old French *baptiste*, via ecclesiastical Latin from ecclesiastical Greek *baptistēs*, from *baptizein* 'immerse, baptize.'

bap·tis·tery /'baptəstrē/ (also **baptistry**) ▶ n. (pl. **baptisteries**) the part of a church used for baptism. ■ historical a building next to a church, used for baptism. ■ (in a Baptist chapel) a sunken receptacle used for baptism by total immersion.
– ORIGIN Middle English: from Old French *baptistere*, via ecclesiastical Latin from ecclesiastical Greek *baptistērion*, from *baptizein* 'immerse, baptize.'

bap·tize /'bap,tīz, bap'tīz/ ▶ v. [with obj. and often with complement] administer baptism to (someone); christen: *he was baptized Joshua.* ■ admit (someone) into a specified church by baptism: *Mark had been baptized a Catholic.* ■ give a name or nickname to: *he baptized the science of narrative "narratology."*
– ORIGIN Middle English: via Old French from ecclesiastical Latin *baptizare*, from Greek *baptizein* 'immerse, baptize.'

bar¹ /bär/ ▶ n. **1** a long rod or rigid piece of wood, metal, or similar material, typically used as an obstruction, fastening, or weapon. ■ an amount of food or another substance formed into a regular narrow block: *a* **bar of** *chocolate* | *gold bars.* ■ a band of color or light, esp. on a flat surface: *bars of sunlight shafting through the broken windows.* ■ see CROSSBAR. ■ a sandbank or shoal at the mouth of a harbor, bay, or estuary. ■ Brit. a rail marking the end of each chamber in the Houses of Parliament. ■ Heraldry a charge in the form of a narrow horizontal stripe across the shield.
2 a counter across which alcoholic drinks or refreshments are served. ■ a room in a restaurant or hotel in which alcohol is served. ■ an establishment where alcohol and sometimes other refreshments are served. ■ [usu. with modifier] a small store or booth serving refreshments or providing a service: *a dairy bar.*
3 a barrier or restriction to an action or advance: *political differences are not necessarily* **a bar to** *a good relationship.*
4 Music a measure of music or the time of a piece of music.
5 (**the bar**) a partition in a courtroom or legislative assembly, now usually notional, beyond which most people may not pass and, in court, at which an accused person stands: *the prisoner at the bar* | *he had to appear at the Bar of the House for a reprimand by the Speaker.* ■ a plea arresting an action or claim in a law case. ■ a particular court of law.

6 (**the Bar**) the legal profession. ■ lawyers collectively. ■ Brit. barristers collectively.
▶ **v.** (**bars, barring, barred**) [with obj.] **1** fasten (something, esp. a door or window) with a bar or bars: *she bolts and bars the door.*
2 prevent or forbid the entrance or movement of: *boulders barred her passage* | *she was* ***barred from*** *a men-only dinner.* ■ prohibit (someone) from doing something: *journalists had been* ***barred from*** *covering the elections.* ■ forbid (an activity) to someone: *the job she loved had been* ***barred to*** *her.* ■ exclude (something) from consideration: *nothing is barred in the crime novel.* ■ Law prevent or delay (an action) by objection.
3 mark (something) with bars or stripes: *his face was barred with light.*
▶ **prep.** chiefly Brit. except for; apart from: *everyone, bar a few ascetics, thinks it desirable.*
– PHRASES **bar none** with no exceptions: *the greatest living American poet bar none.* **behind bars** in prison. **lower** (or **raise** or **lift**) **the bar** lower (or raise) the standards that need to be met in order to qualify for something: *they have drastically lowered the bar for anyone who wants to call themselves a musician.*
– DERIVATIVES **barred** /bärd/ **adj.** *barred windows* | *birds with barred breasts* | [in combination] *a five-barred gate.*
– ORIGIN Middle English: from Old French *barre* (noun), *barrer* (verb), of unknown origin.

bar[2] ▶ **n.** a unit of pressure equivalent to 100,000 newtons per square meter or approximately one atmosphere.
– ORIGIN early 20th cent.: from Greek *baros* 'weight.'

Bar. ▶ **abbr.** Bible Baruch.

Ba·rak /ba'rak/, Ehud (1942–), Israeli Labor statesman; prime minister 1999–2001.

Ba·ra·ta·ria Bay /ˌbärə'tarēə, -'te(ə)rēə/ an inlet of the Gulf of Mexico in southeastern Louisiana, south of New Orleans, associated with Jean Lafitte and other early 19th-century outlaws.

bar·a·the·a /ˌbarə'THēə/ ▶ **n.** a fine woolen cloth, sometimes mixed with silk or cotton, used chiefly for coats and suits.
– ORIGIN mid 19th cent.: of unknown origin.

barb[1] /bärb/ ▶ **n. 1** a sharp projection near the end of an arrow, fishhook, or similar item, angled away from the main point so as to make extraction difficult. ■ a cluster of spikes on barbed wire. ■ a deliberately hurtful remark: *his barb hurt more than she cared to admit.*
2 a beardlike filament at the mouth of some fish, such as barbel and catfish. ■ each of the fine hairlike filaments growing from the shaft of a feather, forming the vane.
3 a freshwater fish that typically has barbels around the mouth, popular in aquariums. ● *Barbus* and other genera, family Cyprinidae: numerous species, including the **tiger barb** (*B. pentazona*) and the **rosy barb** (*B. conchonius*).
– DERIVATIVES **barb·less adj.**
– ORIGIN Middle English: from Old French *barbe*, from Latin *barba* 'beard.'

barb[2] ▶ **n.** a small horse of a hardy breed originally from North Africa.
– ORIGIN mid 17th cent.: from French *barbe*, from Italian *barbero* 'of Barbary.'

Bar·ba·dos /bär'bādəs, -ˌdōs, -ˌdōz/ a country in the eastern West Indies, one of the Windward Islands; pop. 284,600 (est. 2009); capital, Bridgetown; official language, English.

> Barbados was a British colony until it gained independence within the Commonwealth of Nations in 1966. Its economy is based on tourism, sugar, and light manufacturing industries.

– DERIVATIVES **Bar·ba·di·an** /bär'bādēən/ **adj. & n.**

bar·bar·i·an /bär'be(ə)rēən/ ▶ **n.** (in ancient times) a member of a community or tribe not belonging to one of the great civilizations (Greek, Roman, Christian). ■ an uncultured or brutish person.
▶ **adj.** of or relating to ancient barbarians: *barbarian invasions* | *barbarian peoples.* ■ uncultured; brutish.
– ORIGIN Middle English (as an adjective used depreciatively to denote a person with different speech and customs): from Old French *barbarien*, from *barbare*, or from Latin *barbarus* (see BARBAROUS).

bar·bar·ic /bär'barik/ ▶ **adj. 1** savagely cruel; exceedingly brutal: *he had carried out barbaric acts in the name of war.*
2 primitive; unsophisticated: *the barbaric splendor he found in civilizations since destroyed.* ■ uncivilized and uncultured.
– DERIVATIVES **bar·bar·i·cal·ly adv.**
– ORIGIN late Middle English (as a noun in the sense 'a barbarian'): from Old French *barbarique*, or via Latin from Greek *barbarikos*, from *barbaros* 'foreign' (esp. with reference to speech).

bar·ba·rism /'bärbəˌrizəm/ ▶ **n. 1** absence of culture and civilization: *the collapse of civilization and the return to barbarism.* ■ a word or expression that is badly formed according to traditional philological rules, for example a word formed from elements of different languages, such as *breathalyzer* (English and Greek) or *television* (Greek and Latin).
2 extreme cruelty or brutality: *she called the execution an act of barbarism* | *barbarisms from the country's past.*
– ORIGIN late Middle English: from Old French *barbarisme*, via Latin from Greek *barbarismos*, from *barbarizein* 'speak like a foreigner,' from *barbaros* 'foreign.'

bar·bar·i·ty /bär'baritē/ ▶ **n.** (pl. **barbarities**) **1** extreme cruelty or brutality: *the barbarity of the slave trade* | *the barbarities of the last war.*
2 absence of culture and civilization: *beyond the Empire lay barbarity.*

bar·ba·rize /'bärbəˌrīz/ ▶ **v.** [with obj.] (usu. as adj. **barbarizing**) cause to become savage or uncultured: *the barbarizing effect of four decades of rock 'n' roll.*
– DERIVATIVES **bar·ba·ri·za·tion** /ˌbärbərə'zāSHən/ **n.**
– ORIGIN late Middle English (in the sense 'speak using barbarisms'): from late Latin *barbarizare*, from Greek *barbarizein* 'speak like a foreigner.'

Bar·ba·ros·sa[1] /ˌbärbə'räsə, -'rōsə/ see FREDERICK I.

Bar·ba·ros·sa[2], (*c.*1483–1546), Barbary pirate; born *Khair ad-Din.* He was notorious for his successes against Christian vessels in the eastern Mediterranean Sea.

bar·ba·rous /'bärbərəs/ ▶ **adj. 1** savagely cruel; exceedingly brutal: *many early child-rearing practices were barbarous by modern standards.*
2 primitive; uncivilized: *a remote and barbarous country.* ■ (esp. of language) coarse and unrefined.
– DERIVATIVES **bar·ba·rous·ly adv.**
– ORIGIN late Middle English (sense 2): via Latin from Greek *barbaros* 'foreign' + -OUS.

Bar·ba·ry /'bärbərē/ (also **Barbary States**) a former name for the Saracen countries of north and northwestern Africa, together with Moorish Spain. The area was noted between the 16th and 18th centuries as a haunt of pirates. Compare with MAGHRIB.
– ORIGIN based on Arabic *barbar* (see BERBER).

Bar·ba·ry ape ▶ **n.** a tailless macaque monkey that is native to northwestern Africa and also found on the Rock of Gibraltar. ● *Macaca sylvana*, family Cercopithecidae.

Bar·ba·ry Coast a former name for the Mediterranean coast of North Africa from Morocco to Egypt.

Bar·ba·ry sheep ▶ **n.** a short-coated sheep with a long neck ruff, found in the high deserts of northern Africa. Also called AOUDAD. ● *Ammotragus lervia*, family Bovidae.

bar·be·cue /'bärbiˌkyo͞o/ ▶ **n.** a meal or gathering at which meat, fish, or other food is cooked out of doors on a rack over an open fire or on a portable grill. ■ a portable grill used for the preparation of food at a barbecue, or a brick fireplace containing a grill. ■ food cooked in such a way.
▶ **v.** (**barbecues, barbecuing, barbecued**) [with obj.] cook (meat, fish, or other food) on a barbecue: *fish barbecued with herbs* | (as adj. **barbecued**) *barbecued chicken.*
– ORIGIN mid 17th cent.: from Spanish *barbacoa*, perhaps from Arawak *barbacoa* 'wooden frame on posts.' The original sense was 'wooden framework for sleeping on, or for storing meat or fish to be dried.'

> **USAGE** Barbecue is often misspelled as *barbeque*. This form arises understandably from the word's pronunciation and from the informal abbreviations *BBQ* and *Bar-B-Q*. Although almost a quarter of citations in the Oxford English Corpus are for the *-que* spelling, it is not accepted in standard English.

bar·be·cue sauce ▶ **n.** a highly seasoned sauce containing vinegar, spices, and usually chilies.

barbed /bärbd/ ▶ **adj.** having a barb or barbs: *barbed arrows.* ■ (of a remark or joke) deliberately hurtful: *a fair degree of barbed wit.*

barbed wire ▶ **n.** wire with clusters of short, sharp spikes set at intervals along it, used to make fences or in warfare as an obstruction.

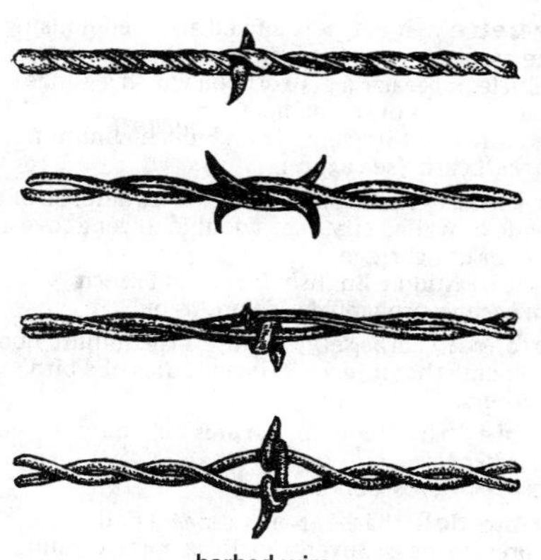

barbed wire

bar·bel /'bärbəl/ ▶ **n. 1** a fleshy filament growing from the mouth or snout of a fish.
2 a large European freshwater fish of the minnow family that has such filaments hanging from its mouth. It lives in running water. ● *Barbus barbus*, family Cyprinidae.
3 [with modifier] a marine or freshwater African fish with barbels around the mouth. ● Species in several families, including *Tachysurus feliceps* (family Aniidae), of southern African coasts and estuaries, whose toxin-coated spines can inflict a dangerous wound.
– ORIGIN late Middle English (sense 2): via Old French from late Latin *barbellus*, diminutive of *barbus* 'barbel,' from *barba* 'beard.'

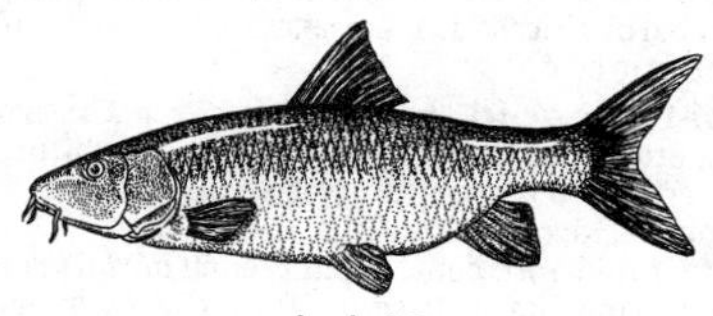

barbel 2

bar·bell /'bärˌbel/ ▶ **n.** a long metal bar to which disks of varying weights are attached at each end, used for weightlifting.
– ORIGIN late 19th cent.: from BAR[1] + BELL[1].

Bar·ber /'bärbər/, Samuel (1910–81), US composer. He developed a style based on romanticism allied to classical forms. Notable works: *Adagio for Strings* (1936) and *Vanessa* (opera, 1958).

bar·ber /'bärbər/ ▶ **n.** a person who cuts hair, esp. men's, and shaves or trims beards as an occupation.
▶ **v.** [with obj.] cut or trim (a man's hair): *his hair was neatly barbered.*
– ORIGIN Middle English: via Anglo-Norman French from Old French *barbe* (see BARB[1]).

bar·ber·ry /'bärˌberē, -bərē/ ▶ **n.** (pl. **barberries**) a thorny shrub that bears yellow flowers and red or blue-black berries. ● Genus *Berberis*, family Berberidaceae: many species, including the **American barberry** (*B. canadensis*), with widely toothed leaves, and the **European barberry** (*B. vulgaris*), with more closely toothed leaves.
– ORIGIN late Middle English: from Old French *berberis*. The change in the ending was due to association with BERRY.

bar·ber·shop /'bärbərˌSHäp/ ▶ **n.** a shop where a barber works. ■ [often as modifier] a popular style of close harmony singing, typically for four male voices: *a barbershop quartet.* [from the custom in the 16th and 17th centuries of passing time in a barbershop by harmonizing to a lute or guitar provided to entertain customers waiting their turn.]

bar·ber's itch ▶ **n.** ringworm of the face or neck communicated by unsterilized shaving apparatus.

bar·ber's pole (also **barber pole**) ▶ **n.** a pole painted with spiraling red and white stripes and hung outside barbershops as a business sign.

bar·bet /'bärbit/ ▶ **n.** a large-headed, brightly colored, fruit-eating bird that has a stout bill with tufts of bristles at the base. Barbets are found on all continents, esp. in the tropics. ● Family Capitonidae: numerous genera and species.
– ORIGIN late 16th cent. (denoting a poodle until the early 19th cent.): from French, from *barbe* 'beard' (see BARB[1]). The current sense dates from the early 19th cent.

b

bar·bette /bär'bet/ ▶ **n.** a fixed armored housing at the base of a gun turret on a warship or armored vehicle. ■ historical a platform on which a gun is placed to fire over a parapet.
– ORIGIN late 18th cent.: from French, diminutive of *barbe* 'beard' (see BARB[1]).

bar·bi·can /'bärbikən/ ▶ **n.** the outer defense of a castle or walled city, esp. a double tower above a gate or drawbridge.
– ORIGIN Middle English: from Old French *barbacane*; probably based on Arabic.

bar·bi·cel /'bärbə,sel/ ▶ **n.** any of the minute hooked filaments that interlock the barbules of a bird's feathers.

bar·bie /'bärbē/ ▶ **n.** (pl. **barbies**) informal, chiefly Austral. a barbecue.
– ORIGIN 1970s: abbreviation.

Bar·bie doll /'bärbē/ ▶ **n.** trademark a doll representing a conventionally attractive young woman. ■ informal a woman who is attractive in a glossily artificial way and is typically considered to be stupid and characterless.
– ORIGIN 1950s: *Barbie*, diminutive of the given name *Barbara*.

bar·bi·tal /'bärbi,täl, -,tôl/ ▶ **n.** a long-acting sedative and sleep-inducing drug of the barbiturate type. ● Alternative name: **diethylbarbituric acid**; chem. formula: $C_6H_{12}O_3N_2$.
– ORIGIN early 20th cent.: from BARBITURIC ACID, on the pattern of *veronal* (an alternative name).

bar·bi·tone /'bärbi,tōn/ ▶ **n.** British term for BARBITAL.
– ORIGIN early 20th cent.: from BARBITURIC ACID + -ONE.

bar·bi·tu·rate /bär'biCHərit, -ə,rāt/ ▶ **n.** any of a class of sedative and sleep-inducing drugs derived from barbituric acid. ■ Chemistry a salt or ester of barbituric acid.

bar·bi·tu·ric ac·id /,bärbi'CHŏŏrik/ ▶ **n.** Chemistry a synthetic organic acid from which the barbiturates are derived. ● A cyclic derivative of urea and malonic acid; chem. formula: $C_4H_4O_3N_2$.
– ORIGIN mid 19th cent.: from French *barbiturique*, from German *Barbitursäure*, from the given name *Barbara* + *Säure* 'acid.'

Bar·bi·zon School /'bärbə,zän/ a mid-19th-century school of French landscape painters who reacted against classical conventions and based their art on direct study of nature. Led by Théodore Rousseau, the group included Charles Daubigny and Jean-François Millet.
– ORIGIN named after *Barbizon*, a small village in the forest of Fontainebleau, near Paris, where Rousseau and others worked.

Bar·bour /'bärbər/, Philip Pendleton (1783–1841), US Supreme Court associate justice 1836–41. He also served in Congress as a representative from Virginia 1814–25; 1827–30.

Bar·bu·da /bär'bŏŏdə/ see **ANTIGUA AND BARBUDA**.
– DERIVATIVES **Bar·bu·dan** /bär'bŏŏdn/ **adj. & n.**

bar·bule /'bär,byŏŏl/ ▶ **n.** a minute filament projecting from the barb of a feather.
– ORIGIN mid 19th cent.: from Latin *barbula*, diminutive of *barba* 'beard.'

barb·wire /'bärb'wīr/ ▶ **n.** barbed wire.

Bar·ca·Loung·er /'bärkə,lounjər/ ▶ **n.** trademark a type of deeply padded reclining chair.
– ORIGIN 1970s: from the name of Edward J. *Barcolo*, who acquired the original license to manufacture the chairs, and *lounger*.

bar·ca·role /'bärkə,rōl/ (also **barcarolle**) ▶ **n.** a song traditionally sung by Venetian gondoliers. ■ a musical composition in the style of such a song.
– ORIGIN late 18th cent.: from French *barcarolle*, from Venetian Italian *barcarola* 'boatman's song,' from *barca* 'boat.'

Bar·ce·lo·na /,bärsə'lōnə/ a city on the coast of northeastern Spain, capital of Catalonia; pop. 1,615,908 (2008).

Bar·ce·lo·na chair ▶ **n.** trademark an armless chair with a curved stainless steel frame and padded leather cushions.

bar·chan /bär'kän/ ▶ **n.** a crescent-shaped shifting sand dune, concave on the leeward side.
– ORIGIN late 19th cent.: from Turkic *barkhan*.

bar chart ▶ **n.** another term for BAR GRAPH.

Bar-Coch·ba /'bär 'kôKHbə/ Jewish rebel leader; known as **Simeon** in Jewish sources. He led the rebellion in AD 132 against the Romans and was accepted by some of his Jewish contemporaries as the Messiah.

bar·code ▶ **n.** a machine-readable code in the form of numbers and a pattern of parallel lines of varying widths, printed on and identifying a product. Also called **UNIVERSAL PRODUCT CODE**.
▶ **v.** [with obj.] mark with a barcode: *all the merchandise is barcoded and scanned.*

bard[1] /bärd/ ▶ **n.** archaic or literary a poet, traditionally one reciting epics and associated with a particular oral tradition. ■ (**the Bard** or **the Bard of Avon**) Shakespeare.
– DERIVATIVES **bard·ic** /-dik/ **adj.**
– ORIGIN Middle English: from Scottish Gaelic *bàrd*, Irish *bard*, Welsh *bardd*, of Celtic origin. In Scotland in the 16th cent. it was a derogatory term for an itinerant musician, but was later romanticized by Sir Walter Scott.

bard[2] ▶ **n.** a slice of bacon placed on meat or game before roasting.
▶ **v.** [with obj.] cover (meat or game) with slices of bacon.
– ORIGIN early 18th cent.: from French *barde*, a transferred sense of *barde* 'armor for the breast and flanks of a warhorse,' based on Arabic *barda'a* 'saddlecloth, padded saddle.'

Bar·deen /bär'dēn/, John (1908–91), US physicist. With William Shockley and Walter Brattain, he developed a point-contact transistor. He also worked on the theory of superconductivity. Nobel Prize for Physics in 1956, shared with Shockley and Brattain, and in 1972, shared with Leon Neil Cooper (1930–) and John Robert Schreiffer (1931–).

bar·do /'bär,dō/ ▶ **n.** (in Tibetan Buddhism) a state of existence between death and rebirth, varying in length according to a person's conduct in life and manner of, or age at, death. ■ an indeterminate, transitional state: *wandering adrift in a bardo of intense negativity, blame, disappointment, criticism, and denial.*
– ORIGIN Tibetan *bár-do*, from *bar* 'interval' + *do* 'two.'

bard·ol·a·try /bär'dälətrē/ ▶ **n.** humorous excessive admiration of Shakespeare.
– DERIVATIVES **bard·ol·a·ter** /-'dälitər/ (or **bardolator**) **n.**

Bar·do·li·no /,bärdl'ēnō/ ▶ **n.** a red wine from the Veneto region of Italy.
– ORIGIN Italian.

Bar·dot /bär'dō/, Brigitte (1934–), French actress; born *Camille Javal*. The movie *And God Created Woman* (1956) established her reputation as an international sex symbol.

bare /be(ə)r/ ▶ **adj. 1** (of a person or part of the body) not clothed or covered: *he was bare from the waist up* | *she padded in bare feet toward the door.* ■ without the appropriate, usual, or natural covering: *a clump of bare aspen trees* | *bare floorboards.* ■ without the appropriate or usual contents: *a bare cell with just a mattress.* ■ unconcealed; without disguise: *an ordeal that would lay bare a troubled family background.*
2 without addition; basic and simple: *he outlined the bare essentials of the story* | *a strange, bare production of Twelfth Night.* ■ [attrib.] only just sufficient: *a bare majority.* ■ [attrib.] surprisingly small in number or amount: *all you need to get started with this program is a bare 10K bytes of memory.*
▶ **v.** [with obj.] uncover (a part of the body or other thing) and expose it to view: *he bared his chest to show his scar.*
– PHRASES **bare all** take off all of one's clothes and display oneself to others: *Lysette bared all for Playboy in 1988.* **the bare bones** the basic facts about something, without any detail: *the bare bones of the plot.* **bare of** without: *the interior, bare of plaster, leaked a smell of old timbers.* **bare one's soul** reveal one's innermost secrets and feelings to someone. **bare one's teeth** show one's teeth, typically when angry. **with one's bare hands** without using tools or weapons.
– DERIVATIVES **bare·ness n.**
– ORIGIN Old English *bær* (noun), *barian* (verb), of Germanic origin; related to Dutch *baar*.

bare·back /'be(ə)r,bak/ ▶ **adj. & adv.** on an unsaddled horse or other animal: [as adj.] *a bareback circus rider* | [as adv.] *riding bareback.*

bare·back·ing /'be(ə)r,bakiNG/ ▶ **n.** vulgar slang anal intercourse without a condom.

bare·boat /'be(ə)r,bōt/ ▶ **adj.** [attrib.] relating to or denoting a boat or ship hired without a crew: *bareboat charters.*
– DERIVATIVES **bare·boat·ing n.**

bare·faced /'be(ə)r,fāst/ ▶ **adj. 1** shameless; undisguised: *a barefaced lie.*
2 having an uncovered face, so as to be exposed or vulnerable to something: *his years of working barefaced, breathing down dust.*

bare·foot /'be(ə)r,fŏŏt/ (also **barefooted** /-,fŏŏtid/) ▶ **adj. & adv.** wearing nothing on the feet: [as adv.] *I won't walk barefoot.*

bare·foot doc·tor ▶ **n.** a paramedical worker with basic medical training working in a rural district in China.

ba·rège /bə'reZH/ (also **barege**) ▶ **n.** a light, silky dress fabric resembling gauze, typically made from wool.
– ORIGIN French, named after the village of *Barèges* in southwestern France, where it was originally made.

bare·hand /'be(ə)r,hand/ ▶ **v.** (in baseball) field with one's bare hand.

bare·hand·ed /'be(ə)r'handid/ ▶ **adj. & adv.** with nothing in or covering one's hands: *his running, barehanded catch in foul territory.* ■ carrying no weapons.

bare·head·ed /'be(ə)r,hedid/ ▶ **adj. & adv.** without a covering for one's head: [as adv.] *he walked bareheaded in the teeming rain.*

Ba·reil·ly /bə'rālē/ an industrial city in northern India, in Uttar Pradesh; pop. 825,100 (est. 2009).

bare-knuck·le (also **bare-knuckled** or **bare-knuckles**) ▶ **adj.** [attrib.] (of a boxer or boxing match) without gloves. ■ informal with no scruples or reservations: *an apostle of bare-knuckled capitalism.*

bare·leg·ged /'be(ə)r,legid/ ▶ **adj. & adv.** without a covering on the legs: *barelegged models strutted down the runway.*

bare·ly /'be(ə)rlē/ ▶ **adv. 1** only just; almost not: *she nodded, barely able to speak* | [as submodifier] *a barely perceptible pause.* ■ only a short time before: *they had barely sat down when forty policemen swarmed in.*
2 in a simple and sparse way: *their barely furnished house.*
3 archaic openly; explicitly.

Bar·en·boim /'barən,boim/, Daniel (1942–), Argentine-born pianist and conductor; husband of Jacqueline du Pré. He was musical director of the Orchestre de Paris 1975–88 and of the Chicago Symphony Orchestra 1991–2006.

Bar·ents /'barənts, 'bär-/, Willem (died 1597), Dutch explorer. The leader of several expeditions in search of the Northeast Passage to Asia, Barents discovered Spitsbergen and reached Novaya Zemlya.

Bar·ents Sea a part of the Arctic Ocean north of Norway and Russia, bounded on the west by Svalbard, on the north by Franz Josef Land, and on the east by Novaya Zemlya.

barf /bärf/ informal ▶ **v.** [no obj.] vomit.
▶ **n.** vomited food.
– ORIGIN 1960s: of unknown origin.

bar·fly /'bär,flī/ ▶ **n.** (pl. **barflies**) informal a person who spends much time drinking in bars.

bar·gain /'bärgən/ ▶ **n. 1** an agreement between two or more parties as to what each party will do for the other: *the extraconstitutional bargain between the northern elite and the southern planters.*
2 a thing bought or offered for sale more cheaply than is usual or expected: *the secondhand table was a real bargain* | [as modifier] *household and electrical goods at bargain prices.*
▶ **v.** [no obj.] negotiate the terms and conditions of a transaction: *he **bargained with** the city council to rent the stadium* | (as noun **bargaining**) *many statutes are passed by political bargaining.* ■ [with obj.] (**bargain something away**) part with something after negotiation but get little or nothing in return: *his determination not to bargain away any of the province's existing economic powers.* ■ (**bargain for/on**) be prepared for; expect: *I got more information than I'd bargained for* | *he didn't bargain on this storm.*
– PHRASES **drive a hard bargain** be uncompromising in making a deal. **into** (or **in**) **the bargain** in addition to what was expected; moreover: *an upstate yokel and a raving paranoiac into the bargain.* **keep one's side of the bargain** carry out the promises one has made as part of an agreement. **strike a bargain** make a bargain; agree to a deal.
– DERIVATIVES **bar·gain·er n.**
– ORIGIN Middle English: from Old French *bargaine* (noun), *bargaignier* (verb); probably of Germanic origin and related to German *borgen* 'borrow.'

bar·gain base·ment ▶ **n.** a part of a store where goods are sold cheaply, typically because they are old or imperfect: [as modifier] *bargain-basement prices* | figurative *a mixture of styles from pop culture's bargain basement.*

bar·gain·ing chip ▶ **n.** a potential concession or other factor that can be used to advantage in negotiations.

barge /bärj/ ▶ **n.** a flat-bottomed boat for carrying freight, typically on canals and rivers, either under its own power or towed by another. ■ a long ornamental boat used for pleasure or ceremony. ■ a boat used by the chief officers of a warship.

▸ **v. 1** [no obj.] move forcefully or roughly: *we can't just **barge into** a private garden.* ■ (**barge in**) intrude or interrupt rudely or awkwardly: *sorry to **barge in** on your cozy evening.* ■ (chiefly in a sporting context) collide with: *displays of dissent, such as deliberately **barging into** the umpire.*
2 [with obj.] convey (freight) by barge.
–ORIGIN Middle English (denoting a small seagoing vessel): from Old French, perhaps ultimately from Greek *baris* 'Egyptian boat.'

barge·board /'bärj,bôrd/ ▸ **n.** a board, typically ornamental, fixed to the gable end of a roof to hide the ends of the roof timbers.
–ORIGIN mid 19th cent.: from mid 16th-cent. *barge-* (used in architectural terms relating to the gable of a building).

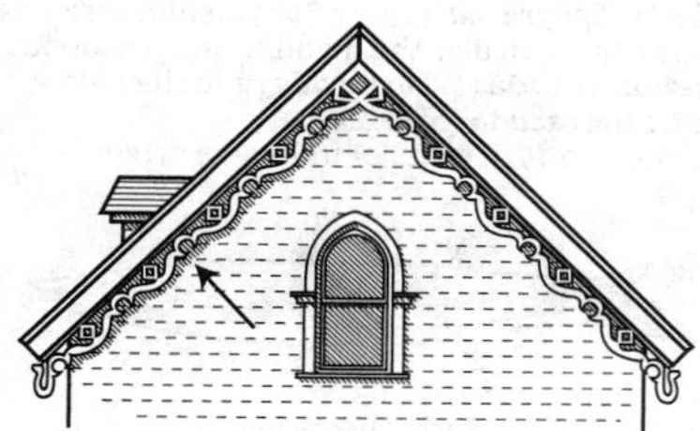
bargeboard

barg·ee /bär'jē/ ▸ **n.** chiefly Brit. a bargeman.

Bar·gel·lo /bär'jelō, -'ZHelō/ (also **bargello**) ▸ **n.** a kind of embroidery, typically worked on upholstery fabrics, in stitch patterns suggestive of flames. Also called FLAME STITCH.
–ORIGIN 1940s: named after *Bargello* Palace, in Florence, Italy, which contains upholstered chairs with such embroidery.

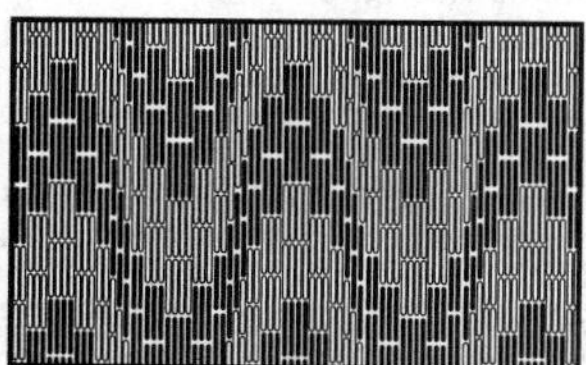
Bargello

barge·man /'bärjmən/ ▸ **n.** (pl. **bargemen**) a person who has charge of, or works on, a barge.

bar graph (also **bar chart**) ▸ **n.** a diagram in which the numerical values of variables are represented by the height or length of lines or rectangles of equal width.

Bar Har·bor /bär/ a resort town in southern central Maine, on Mount Desert Island; pop. 5,129 (est. 2008).

bar·hop /'bär,häp/ ▸ **v.** [no obj.] drink at a number of bars during a single day or evening.

Ba·ri /'bärē/ an industrial seaport on the Adriatic coast of southeastern Italy; pop. 320,677 (2008).

bar·i·at·rics /,barē'atriks/ ▸ **n.** the branch of medicine that deals with the study and treatment of obesity.
–DERIVATIVES **bar·i·at·ric adj.**

bar·i·at·ric sur·ger·y ▸ **n.** surgical removal of parts of the stomach and small intestines to induce weight loss.

ba·ril·la /bə'rilə, -'rēə/ ▸ **n.** an impure alkali formerly made from the ashes of burned plants, esp. saltworts.
–ORIGIN early 17th cent.: from Spanish *barrilla*, diminutive of *barra* 'bar.'

Ba·ri·sal /'barə,sôl/ a river port in southern Bangladesh, on the Ganges delta; pop. 210,374 (2008).

ba·ri·sta /bə'rēstə/ ▸ **n.** a person whose job involves preparing and serving different types of coffee.
–ORIGIN 1980s: Italian, 'barman.'

bar·ite /'be(ə)rīt, 'bar-/ ▸ **n.** a mineral consisting of barium sulfate, typically occurring as colorless prismatic crystals or thin white flakes.

bar·i·tone /'bari,tōn/ ▸ **n. 1** an adult male singing voice between tenor and bass: *he sang in a rich baritone.* ■ a singer with such a voice. ■ a part written for such a voice.
2 (in full **baritone horn**) an instrument that is second lowest in pitch in its family. ■ a large, valved brass instrument in coiled oval form, used esp. in military or street bands.
▸ **adj.** second lowest in musical pitch.
–ORIGIN early 17th cent.: from Italian *baritono*, from Greek *barutonos*, from *barus* 'heavy' + *tonos* (see TONE).

bar·i·ton·ist /'bari,tōnist/ ▸ **n.** a person who plays a baritone instrument, in particular a saxophone or a horn.

bar·i·um /'be(ə)rēəm, 'bar-/ ▸ **n.** the chemical element of atomic number 56, a soft white reactive metal of the alkaline earth group. (Symbol: **Ba**) ■ a mixture of barium sulfate and water, opaque to X-rays, that is swallowed to permit radiological examination of the stomach or intestines: [as modifier] *a barium meal.*

> Barium compounds are used in water purification, the glass industry, and pigments, and as an ingredient of signal flares and fireworks, giving a bright yellowish-green color. Barium oxide is a component of high-temperature superconductors.

–ORIGIN early 19th cent.: from BARYTA + -IUM.

bar·i·um sul·fate ▸ **n.** an odorless, insoluble white powder used in the making of pigments, paper, textiles, and plastics, and ingested as a contrasting agent in X-raying the digestive tract. ● Chem. formula: $BaSO_4$.

bark[1] /bärk/ ▸ **n.** the sharp explosive cry of certain animals, esp. a dog, fox, or seal. ■ a sound resembling this cry, typically one made by someone laughing or coughing: *a short bark of laughter.*
▸ **v. 1** [no obj.] (of a dog or other animal) emit a bark: *a dog **barked at** her.* ■ (of a person) make a sound, such as a cough or a laugh, resembling a bark: *she barked with laughter.*
2 [with obj.] utter (a command or question) abruptly or aggressively: *he began **barking out** his orders* | [with direct speech] *"Nobody is allowed up here," he barked* | [no obj.] *he was **barking at** me to make myself presentable.* ■ [no obj.] call out in order to sell or advertise something: *doormen bark at passersby, promising hot music and cold beer.*
–PHRASES **someone's bark is worse than their bite** someone is not as ferocious as they appear or sound. **be barking up the wrong tree** informal be pursuing a mistaken or misguided line of thought or course of action.
–ORIGIN Old English *beorc* (noun), *beorcan* (verb), of Germanic origin; possibly related to BREAK.

bark[2] ▸ **n.** the tough, protective outer sheath of the trunk, branches, and twigs of a tree or woody shrub. ■ this material used for tanning leather, making dyestuffs, or as a mulch in gardening.
▸ **v.** [with obj.] **1** strip the bark from (a tree or piece of wood). ■ scrape the skin off (one's shin) by accidentally hitting it against something hard.
2 technical tan or dye (leather or other materials) using the tannins found in bark.
–DERIVATIVES **barked adj.** [in combination] *the red-barked dogwood.*
–ORIGIN Middle English: from Old Norse *bǫrkr*; perhaps related to BIRCH.

bark[3] ▸ **n.** (also **barque**) a sailing ship, typically with three masts, in which the foremast and mainmast are square-rigged and the mizzenmast is rigged fore-and-aft. ■ archaic or literary a ship or boat.
–ORIGIN late Middle English: variant of BARQUE.

bark bee·tle ▸ **n.** a small wood-boring beetle that tunnels under the bark of trees, which die if heavily infested. ● Family Scolytidae: many genera and species, including the **smaller European elm bark beetle** (*Scolytus multistriatus*), which is responsible for the spread of the fungus that causes Dutch elm disease.

bark·cloth /'bärk,klôTH/ ▸ **n.** cloth made from the inner bark of the paper mulberry or similar tree.

bar·keep·er /'bär,kēpər/ (also **barkeep**) ▸ **n.** a person who owns or serves drinks in a bar.

bark·en·tine /'bärkən,tēn/ (Brit. **barquentine**) ▸ **n.** a sailing ship similar to a bark but square-rigged only on the foremast.
–ORIGIN late 17th cent.: from BARK[3], on the pattern of *brigantine*.

bark·er /'bärkər/ ▸ **n.** informal a person who stands in front of a theater, sideshow, etc., and calls out to passersby to attract customers.
–ORIGIN late Middle English: from BARK[1] + -ER[1]. The original sense was 'a person or animal that barks; noisy protester,' hence the current sense (late 17th cent).

bark·ing deer ▸ **n.** another term for MUNTJAC.

bar·ley /'bärlē/ ▸ **n.** a hardy cereal that has coarse bristles extending from the ears. It is widely cultivated, chiefly for use in brewing and stockfeed. ● Genus *Hordeum*, family Gramineae. ■ the grain of this plant. See also PEARL BARLEY.
–ORIGIN Old English *bærlic* (adjective), from *bære*, *bere* 'barley' + *-lic* (see -LY[1]).

bar·ley·corn /'bärlē,kôrn/ ▸ **n.** a grain of barley. ■ a former unit of measurement (about a third of an inch) based on the length of a grain of barley.

bar·ley sug·ar ▸ **n.** an amber-colored candy made of boiled sugar, traditionally shaped as a twisted stick.
▸ **adj.** (**barley-sugar**) [attrib.] shaped like twisted barley-sugar sticks.

bar·ley wa·ter ▸ **n.** a drink made from water and a boiled barley mixture, typically flavored with orange or lemon.

bar·ley wine ▸ **n.** a strong English ale.

bar line ▸ **n.** Music a vertical line used in a musical score to mark a division between bars.

Bar·low knife /'bärlō/ ▸ **n.** a large single-bladed pocketknife.
–ORIGIN named for Russell Barlow, 18th-cent. English inventor.

barm /bärm/ ▸ **n.** the froth on fermenting malt liquor. ■ archaic or dialect yeast or leaven.
–ORIGIN Old English *beorma*.

bar·maid /'bär,mād/ ▸ **n. 1** a waitress who serves drinks in a bar.
2 Brit. a woman bartender.

bar·man /'bärmən/ ▸ **n.** (pl. **barmen**) chiefly Brit. a male bartender.

Bar·me·cide /'bärmə,sīd/ (also **Barmecidal** /,bärmə'sīdl/) rare ▸ **adj.** [attrib.] illusory or imaginary and therefore disappointing.
▸ **n.** a person who offers benefits that are illusory or disappointing.
–ORIGIN early 18th cent. (as a noun): from Arabic *Barmaki*, the name of a prince in the *Arabian Nights' Entertainments*, who gave a beggar a feast consisting of ornate but empty dishes.

bar mitz·vah /,bär 'mitsvə/ ▸ **n.** the religious initiation ceremony of a Jewish boy who has reached the age of 13 and is regarded as ready to observe religious precepts and eligible to take part in public worship. ■ the boy undergoing this ceremony.
▸ **v.** [with obj.] (usu. **be bar mitzvahed**) celebrate the bar mitzvah of (a boy).
–ORIGIN mid 19th cent.: from Hebrew *bar miṣwāh*, literally 'son of the commandment.'

barm·y /'bärmē/ ▸ **adj.** (**barmier**, **barmiest**) Brit. another term for BALMY (sense 2).
–DERIVATIVES **barm·i·ly** /-məlē/ **adv.**, **barm·i·ness n.**
–ORIGIN late 15th cent. (in the sense 'frothy'): from BARM + -Y[1].

barn[1] /bärn/ ▸ **n.** a large farm building used for storing grain, hay, or straw or for housing livestock. ■ a large shed used for storing vehicles. ■ a large and unattractive building: *moved into that barn of a house.*
–ORIGIN Old English *bern*, *berern*, from *bere* 'barley' + *ern*, *ærn* 'house.'

barn[2] (abbr.: **b**) ▸ **n.** Physics a unit of area, 10^{-28} square meters, used esp. in particle physics.
–ORIGIN 1940s: apparently from the phrase *as big as a barn door.*

Bar·na·bas, St. /'bärnəbəs/ (died *c.*61), a Cypriot Levite and apostle. The traditional founder of the Cypriot Church, he is said to have been martyred in Cyprus. Feast day, June 11.

bar·na·cle /'bärnəkəl/ ▸ **n.** a marine crustacean with an external shell, which attaches itself permanently to a variety of surfaces. Barnacles feed by filtering particles from the water using their modified feathery legs. ● Class Cirripedia. See ACORN BARNACLE, GOOSE BARNACLE. ■ used figuratively to describe a tenacious person or thing: *buses careered along with men hanging from their doors like barnacles.*
–DERIVATIVES **bar·na·cled adj.**
–ORIGIN late 16th cent.: from medieval Latin *bernaca*, of unknown origin. In Middle English the term denoted the barnacle goose, whose breeding grounds were long unknown and which was believed to hatch from the shell of the crustacean to which it gave its name.

bar·na·cle goose ▸ **n.** a goose with a white face and black neck, breeding in the arctic tundra of Greenland and northern Europe. ● *Branta leucopsis*, family Anatidae.
–ORIGIN mid 18th cent.: see BARNACLE.

Bar·nard /'bärnərd/, Christiaan Neethling (1922–2001), South African surgeon; a pioneer in human heart transplantation. He performed the first heart transplant in December 1967.

Bar·na·ul /,bərnə'o͞ol/ the capital of Altai territory in southern Russia, on the Ob River; pop. 597,200 (est. 2008).

barn burn·er (also **barnburner**) ▸ **n.** informal an event, typically a sports contest, that is very exciting or intense.

b

barn dance ▶ **n.** an informal social gathering for square dancing, originally held in a barn.

barn door ▶ **n.** the large door of a barn. ■ a target too large to be missed: *on the shooting range he could not hit a barn door.* ■ a hinged metal flap fitted to a spotlight to control the direction and intensity of its beam.

Bar·ne·gat Bay /ˈbärni,gat, -gət/ a tidal body in southeastern New Jersey, shielded from the Atlantic Ocean by barrier islands, the site of numerous resorts.

barn owl ▶ **n.** an owl with a heart-shaped face, dark eyes, and relatively long, slender legs. It typically nests in farm buildings or in holes in trees. ● Genus *Tyto*, family Tytonidae: three species, esp. the white-faced *T. alba*, which is found throughout the world.

Barns·ley /ˈbärnzlē/ a town in northern England; pop. 70,100 (est. 2009).

Barn·sta·ble /ˈbärnstəbəl/ a town in southeastern Massachusetts, on the southwestern part of Cape Cod; pop. 46,184 (est. 2008). It is the commercial center for a resort area.

barn·storm /ˈbärn,stôrm/ ▶ **v.** [no obj.] tour rural districts giving theatrical performances, originally often in barns. ■ [with obj.] make a rapid tour of (an area), typically as part of a political campaign. ■ travel around giving exhibitions of flying and performing aeronautical stunts: (as noun **barnstorming**) *barnstorming had become a popular occupation among many trained pilots.*
– DERIVATIVES **barn·storm·er n.**

barn swal·low ▶ **n.** see SWALLOW².

Bar·num /ˈbärnəm/, P. T. (1810–91), US showman; full name *Phineas Taylor Barnum.* He was noted for his extravagant advertising and exhibition of freaks at his museum in New York City. When his circus opened in 1871, he billed it as "The Greatest Show on Earth"; ten years later, he founded the Barnum and Bailey circus with former rival Anthony Bailey (1847–1906).

Bar·num ef·fect ▶ **n.** Psychology the tendency to accept certain information as true, such as character assessments or horoscopes, even when the information is so vague as to be worthless.
– ORIGIN named after P. T. BARNUM; the word *Barnum* was in use from the mid 19th cent. as a noun in the sense 'nonsense, humbug.'

barn·yard /ˈbärn,yärd/ ▶ **n.** the area of open ground around a barn.
▶ **adj.** (esp. of manners or language) characterized by a lack of propriety; coarse, indecent, earthy: *a polite way of avoiding barnyard language.*

baro- ▶ **comb. form** relating to pressure: *barotrauma* | *baroreceptor.*
– ORIGIN from Greek *baros* 'weight.'

bar·o·gram /ˈbarə,gram/ ▶ **n.** a record traced by a barograph.

bar·o·graph /ˈbarə,graf/ ▶ **n.** a barometer that records its readings on a moving chart.
– ORIGIN mid 19th cent.: from Greek *baros* 'weight' + -GRAPH.

Ba·ro·lo /bəˈrōlō/ ▶ **n.** a full-bodied red Italian wine from Barolo, a region of Piedmont.

ba·rom·e·ter /bəˈrämitər/ ▶ **n.** an instrument measuring atmospheric pressure, used esp. in forecasting the weather and determining altitude. ■ something that reflects changes in circumstances or opinions: *furniture is a barometer of changing tastes.*
– DERIVATIVES **bar·o·met·ric** /,barəˈmetrik/ **adj.**, **bar·o·met·ri·cal adj.**, **ba·rom·e·try** /-ˈrämitrē/ **n.**
– ORIGIN mid 17th cent.: from Greek *baros* 'weight' + -METER.

bar·o·met·ric pres·sure ▶ **n.** another term for ATMOSPHERIC PRESSURE.

bar·on /ˈbarən/ ▶ **n.** a member of the lowest order of the British nobility. The term "Baron" is not used as a form of address in Britain, barons usually being referred to as "Lord." ■ a similar member of a foreign nobility. ■ historical a person who held lands or property from the sovereign or a powerful overlord. ■ [with modifier] an important or powerful person in a specified business or industry: *a press baron.*
– ORIGIN Middle English: from Old French, from medieval Latin *baro, baron-* 'man, warrior,' probably of Germanic origin.

bar·on·age /ˈbarənij/ ▶ **n. 1** [treated as sing. or pl.] barons or nobles collectively.
2 an annotated list of barons or peers.
– ORIGIN Middle English: from Old French *barnage* (from *baron*), or from medieval Latin *baronagium*, from *baro* (see BARON).

bar·on·ess /ˈbarənis/ ▶ **n.** the wife or widow of a baron. The term "Baroness" is not used as a form of address in Britain, baronesses usually being referred to as "Lady." ■ a woman holding the rank of baron either as a life peerage or as a hereditary rank.
– ORIGIN late Middle English: from Old French *baronesse*, from *baron* (see BARON).

bar·on·et /ˈbarənit, ,barəˈnet/ ▶ **n.** a member of the lowest hereditary titled British order, with the status of a commoner but able to use the prefix "Sir."
– ORIGIN late Middle English: from Anglo-Latin *baronettus*, from Latin *baro, baron-* 'man, warrior.' The term originally denoted a gentleman, not a nobleman, summoned by the king to attend parliament; the current order was instituted in the early 17th cent.

bar·on·et·age /ˈbarənitij, ,barəˈnetij/ ▶ **n. 1** [treated as sing. or pl.] baronets collectively.
2 an annotated list of baronets.

bar·on·et·cy /ˈbarənitsē/ ▶ **n.** (pl. **baronetcies**) the rank of a baronet.

ba·ro·ni·al /bəˈrōnēəl/ ▶ **adj.** belonging or relating to a baron or barons; suitable for a baron: *a leading baronial family* | *halls of baronial splendor.*

bar·on of beef ▶ **n.** a joint of beef consisting of two sirloins joined at the backbone.

bar·o·ny /ˈbarənē/ ▶ **n.** (pl. **baronies**) **1** the rank and estates of a baron.
2 historical (in Ireland) a division of a county.
3 historical (in Scotland) a large manor or estate.

ba·roque /bəˈrōk/ ▶ **adj.** relating to or denoting a style of European architecture, music, and art of the 17th and 18th centuries that followed mannerism and is characterized by ornate detail. In architecture the period is exemplified by the palace of Versailles and by the work of Bernini in Italy. Major composers include Vivaldi, Bach, and Handel; Caravaggio and Rubens are important baroque artists. ■ highly ornate and extravagant in style: *the candles were positively baroque.*
▶ **n.** the baroque style or period.
– ORIGIN mid 18th cent.: from French (originally designating a pearl of irregular shape), from Portuguese *barroco*, Spanish *barrueco*, or Italian *barocco*; of unknown ultimate origin.

bar·o·re·cep·tor /,barōriˈseptər/ ▶ **n.** Zoology a receptor sensitive to changes in pressure.

bar·o·trau·ma /,barōˈtroumə, -ˈtrô-/ ▶ **n.** Medicine injury caused by a change in air pressure, typically affecting the ear or the lung.

ba·rouche /bəˈro͞osн/ ▶ **n.** historical a four-wheeled horse-drawn carriage with a collapsible hood over the rear half, a seat in front for the driver, and seats facing each other for the passengers, used esp. in the 19th century.
– ORIGIN early 19th cent.: from German dialect *Barutsche*, from Italian *baroccio*, based on Latin *birotus* 'two-wheeled,' from *bi-* 'having two' + *rota* 'wheel.'

barouche

barque /bärk/ ▶ **n.** variant spelling of BARK³.
– ORIGIN Middle English: from Old French, probably from Provençal *barca*, from late Latin *barca* 'ship's boat.'

bar·quen·tine /ˈbärkən,tēn/ ▶ **n.** British spelling of BARKENTINE.

Bar·qui·si·me·to /,bärkēsēˈmātō/ a city in northwestern Venezuela; pop. 1,018,900 (est. 2009).

bar·rack¹ /ˈbarək/ ▶ **v.** [with obj.] provide (soldiers) with accommodations in a building or set of buildings: *the granary in which the platoons were barracked.*
– ORIGIN early 18th cent.: from BARRACKS.

bar·rack² ▶ **v.** [with obj.] Brit. & Austral./NZ jeer loudly at (someone performing or speaking in public) in order to express disapproval or to create a distraction: *opponents barracked him when he addressed the opening parliamentary session* | (as noun **barracking**) *the disgraceful barracking which came from the mob.* ■ [no obj.] (**barrack for**) Austral./NZ give support and encouragement to: *I take it you'll be barracking for Labour tonight?*
– ORIGIN late 19th cent.: probably from Northern Irish dialect.

bar·racks /ˈbarəks/ ▶ **plural n.** [often treated as sing.] a building or group of buildings used to house soldiers: *the troops were ordered back to barracks.* ■ a building or group of buildings used to house large numbers of people.
– ORIGIN late 17th cent.: *barrack* from French *baraque*, from Italian *baracca* or Spanish *barraca* 'soldier's tent,' of unknown origin.

bar·racks bag ▶ **n.** a large cloth bag for carrying clothing, equipment, and personal items; a duffel bag.

bar·ra·coon /,barəˈko͞on/ ▶ **n.** historical an enclosure in which black slaves were confined for a limited period.
– ORIGIN mid 19th cent.: from Spanish *barracón*, from *barraca* 'soldier's tent' (see BARRACKS).

bar·ra·cu·da /,barəˈko͞odə/ ▶ **n.** (pl. **same** or **barracudas**) a large, predatory tropical marine fish with a slender body and large jaws and teeth. ● Genus *Sphyraena*, family Sphyraenidae: several species, in particular the inedible and poisonous **great barracuda** (*S. barracuda*) and the edible **Pacific barracuda** (*S. argentea*).
– ORIGIN late 17th cent.: of unknown origin.

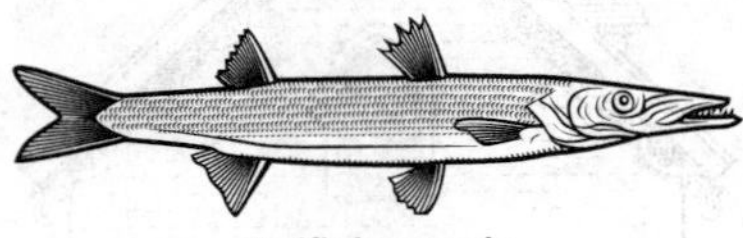
Pacific barracuda

bar·rage /bəˈräzн/ ▶ **n.** a concentrated artillery bombardment over a wide area. ■ a concentrated outpouring, as of questions or blows: *she was not prepared for his barrage of questions* | *a barrage of 60-second television spots.*
▶ **v.** [with obj.] (usu. **be barraged**) bombard (someone) with something: *his doctor was barraged with unsolicited advice.*
– ORIGIN mid 19th cent.: from French, from *barrer* 'to bar,' of unknown origin.

bar·rage bal·loon ▶ **n.** a large balloon anchored to the ground by cables and often with netting suspended from it, serving as an obstacle to low-flying enemy aircraft.

bar·ra·mun·di /,barəˈməndē/ ▶ **n.** (pl. **same** or **barramundis**) any of a number of large, chiefly freshwater, fishes of Australia and Southeast Asia. ● a fish that migrates between the sea and rivers and is valued as a food fish (*Lates calcarifer*, family Centropomidae). ● a mouthbrooder (genus *Scleropages*, family Osteoglossidae), in particular *S. leichardti*, which is popular with fly fishermen.
– ORIGIN late 19th cent.: probably from an Aboriginal language of Queensland, Australia.

bar·ran·ca /bəˈrängkə/ (also **barranco** /-kō/) ▶ **n.** (pl. **barrancas** also **barrancos**) a narrow, winding river gorge.
– ORIGIN late 17th cent.: from Spanish.

Bar·ran·quil·la /,bärənˈkē(y)ə/ the chief port of Colombia; pop. 1,112,889 (2005). Founded in 1629, it lies at the mouth of the Magdalena River, near the Caribbean Sea.

bar·ra·try /ˈbarətrē/ ▶ **n. 1** archaic fraud or gross negligence of a ship's master or crew at the expense of its owners or users.
2 Law vexatious litigation or incitement to it.
3 historical trade in the sale of church or state appointments.
– DERIVATIVES **bar·ra·tor** /ˈbarətər/ **n.** (historical) BARRATRY (sense 2), **bar·ra·trous** /-trəs/ **adj.**
– ORIGIN late Middle English (sense 3): from Old French *baraterie*, from *barater* 'deceive,' based on Greek *prattein* 'do, perform, manage' (sometimes dishonestly); perhaps influenced by Old Norse *barátta* 'contest.'

Barr bod·y /bär/ ▶ **n.** Anatomy & Physiology a small, densely staining structure in the cell nuclei of female mammals, consisting of a condensed, inactive X chromosome. It is regarded as diagnostic of genetic femaleness.

barre /bär/ ▶ **n.** a horizontal bar at waist level on which ballet dancers rest a hand for support during exercises.
– ORIGIN early 20th cent.: French, literally 'bar.'

bar·ré /ˈbä'rā/ ▶ **n.** Music a method of playing a chord on the guitar or similar instrument with a finger laid across the strings at a particular fret, raising their pitch.
– ORIGIN late 19th cent.: French, literally 'barred,' past participle of *barrer*.

barred owl ▶ **n.** large gray-brown North American owl with brown eyes and a barred pattern across the chest. ● *Strix varia*, family Strigidae.

bar·rel /ˈbarəl/ ▶ **n. 1** a cylindrical container bulging out in the middle, traditionally made of wooden staves with metal hoops around them. ■ such a container together with its contents: *a barrel of beer.* ■ a measure of capacity used for oil and beer.

It is usually equal to 36 imperial gallons for beer and 35 imperial gallons or 42 US gallons (roughly 192 liters) for oil.
2 a tube forming part of an object such as a gun or a pen.
3 the belly and loins of a four-legged animal such as a horse.
▶ v. (**barrels, barreling, barreled**; Brit. **barrels, barrelling, barrelled**) **1** [no obj.] informal drive or move fast, often heedless of surroundings or conditions: *we barreled across the Everglades | **barreling along** the Ventura freeway.*
2 [with obj.] put into a barrel or barrels.
– PHRASES **a barrel of laughs** [often with negative] informal a source of fun or amusement: *life is not exactly a barrel of laughs at the moment.* **on the barrel** (of payment) without delay: *I gotta be paid cash on the barrel.* **over a barrel** informal in a helpless position; at someone's mercy. **with both barrels** informal with unrestrained force or emotion.
– ORIGIN Middle English: from Old French *baril,* from medieval Latin *barriclus* 'small cask.'

bar·rel cac·tus ▶ n. a spiny, ribbed cylindrical cactus. ● *Ferocactus, Echinocereus,* and other genera, family Cactaceae: numerous species, including the **Arizona barrel cactus** (*F. wislizenii*), with yellow, orange, or red flower.

bar·rel-chest·ed ▶ adj. having a large rounded chest.

bar·rel dis·tor·tion ▶ n. a type of defect in optical or electronic images in which vertical or horizontal straight lines appear as convex curves.

bar·rel·head /ˈbarəl,hed/ ▶ n. the flat top of a barrel.
– PHRASES **on the barrelhead** another way of saying ON THE BARREL (see BARREL).

bar·rel·house /ˈbarəl,hous/ ▶ n. **1** a cheap or disreputable bar.
2 [usu. as modifier] an unrestrained and unsophisticated style of jazz music.
– ORIGIN late 19th cent.: so named because of the rows of barrels along the walls of such a bar.

bar·rel knot ▶ n. another term for BLOOD KNOT.

bar·rel or·gan ▶ n. a mechanical musical instrument from which predetermined music is produced by turning a handle, played, esp. in former times, by street musicians.

bar·rel roll ▶ n. an aerobatic maneuver in which an aircraft follows a single turn of a spiral while rolling once about its longitudinal axis.

bar·rel vault ▶ n. Architecture a vault forming a half cylinder.
– DERIVATIVES **bar·rel-vault·ed** adj.

bar·ren /ˈbarən/ ▶ adj. **1** (of land) too poor to produce much or any vegetation. ■ (of a tree or plant) not producing fruit or seed. ■ archaic (of a woman) unable to have children. ■ (of a female animal) not pregnant or unable to become so. ■ showing no results or achievements; unproductive: *much of philosophy has been barren.*
2 (of a place or building) bleak and lifeless: *the sports hall turned out to be a rather barren concrete building.* ■ empty of meaning or value: *those young heads were stuffed with barren facts.* ■ (**barren of**) devoid of: *the room was barren of furniture.*
▶ n. (usu. **barrens**) a barren tract or tracts of land: *crossing the barrens was no easy feat.*
– DERIVATIVES **bar·ren·ness** n.
– ORIGIN Middle English: from Old French *barhaine,* of unknown origin.

Bar·rett /ˈbarit/, Elizabeth, see BROWNING[1].

bar·rette /bəˈret/ ▶ n. a typically bar-shaped clip or ornament for the hair.
– ORIGIN early 20th cent.: from French, diminutive of *barre* 'bar.'

bar·ri·cade /ˈbari,kād/ ▶ n. an improvised barrier erected across a street or other thoroughfare to prevent or delay the movement of opposing forces.
▶ v. [with obj.] block or defend with such a barrier: *he barricaded the door with a bureau* | (as adj. **barricaded**) *the heavily barricaded streets.* ■ shut (oneself or someone) into a place by blocking all the entrances: *detainees who **barricaded themselves into** their dormitory.*
– ORIGIN late 16th cent.: from French, from *barrique* 'cask,' from Spanish *barrica;* related to BARREL (barrels being often used to build barricades).

Bar·rie /ˈbarē/, Sir J. M. (1860–1937), Scottish dramatist and novelist; full name *James Matthew Barrie.* He wrote *Peter Pan* (1904), a fantasy for children about a boy who would not grow up. Other notable plays include *The Admirable Crichton* (1902).

bar·ri·er /ˈbarēər/ ▶ n. a fence or other obstacle that prevents movement or access. ■ a circumstance or obstacle that keeps people or things apart or prevents communication or progress: *a language barrier | the cultural barriers to economic growth.* ■ the starting gate of a racecourse. ■ Brit. a gate at a parking lot that controls access by being raised or lowered. ■ (in full **barrier island**) a long narrow island lying parallel and close to the mainland, protecting the mainland from erosion and storms.
– PHRASES **break the barrier** pass or exceed a significant level or amount: *the Tokyo stock exchange reopened to break the 5000-yen barrier.*
– ORIGIN late Middle English (denoting a palisade or fortification defending an entrance): from Old French *barriere,* of unknown origin; related to BARRE.

bar·ri·er meth·od ▶ n. a method of contraception using a device or preparation that prevents live sperm from reaching an ovum.

bar·ri·er reef ▶ n. a coral reef running parallel to the shore but separated from it by a channel of deep water.

bar·ring /ˈbäriNG/ ▶ prep. except for; if not for: *barring a miracle, you'll lose.*
– ORIGIN late 15th cent.: from the verb BAR[1] + -ING[2].

bar·ri·o /ˈbärē,ō/ ▶ n. (pl. **barrios**) a district of a town in Spain and Spanish-speaking countries. ■ (in the US) the Spanish-speaking quarter of a town or city, esp. one with a high poverty level.
– ORIGIN Spanish, perhaps from Arabic.

bar·rique /bəˈrēk/ ▶ n. a wine barrel, esp. a small one made of new oak, in which Bordeaux and other wines are aged.
– ORIGIN late 18th cent.: French.

bar·ris·ter /ˈbarəstər/ (also **barrister-at-law**) ▶ n. chiefly Brit. a lawyer entitled to practice as an advocate, particularly in the higher courts. Compare with ATTORNEY, SOLICITOR.
– ORIGIN late Middle English: from the noun BAR[1], perhaps on the pattern of *minister.*

bar·room /ˈbär,ro͞om, -,ro͝om/ ▶ n. a room where alcoholic drinks are served over a counter.

Bar·row[1] /ˈbarō/ a city in north central Alaska, a commercial center on the Arctic Ocean. It is the northernmost US city; pop. 4,010 (est. 2008). Nearby Point Barrow is the northernmost point in the US.

Bar·row[2], Clyde (1909–34), US bank robber and murderer. He and his partner, Bonnie Parker, shot and killed at least thirteen people during a notorious two-year crime spree across the Southwest. They were finally stopped and shot to death at a Louisiana roadblock.

bar·row[1] /ˈbarō/ ▶ n. a wheelbarrow. ■ a luggage trolley. ■ Brit. a two-wheeled handcart used esp. by street vendors.
– DERIVATIVES **bar·row·load** /-,lōd/ n.
– ORIGIN Old English *bearwe* 'stretcher, bier,' of Germanic origin; related to BEAR[1].

bar·row[2] ▶ n. Archaeology an ancient burial mound.
– ORIGIN Old English *beorg,* of Germanic origin; related to Dutch *berg,* German *Berg* 'hill, mountain.'

bar·row[3] ▶ n. a male pig castrated before maturity.

bar·row boy ▶ n. Brit. a boy or man who sells wares from a barrow in the street.

Bar·ry /ˈbarē/, Sir Charles (1795–1860), English architect, designer of the Houses of Parliament.

bar·ry /ˈbarē/ ▶ adj. Heraldry divided into typically four, six, or eight equal horizontal bars of alternating tinctures.
– ORIGIN late 15th cent.: from French *barré* 'barred, striped,' past participle of *barrer.*

Bar·ry·more /ˈbarə,môr/, a US family of film and stage actors, notably **Lionel** (1878–1954), his sister **Ethel** (1879–1959), their brother **John** (1882–1942), and John's granddaughter **Drew** (1975–).

Bar·sac /ˈbär,sak/ ▶ n. a sweet white wine from the district of Barsac, a department of the Gironde in France.

bar sin·is·ter ▶ n. popular and erroneous term for BEND SINISTER.

bar·stool /ˈbär,sto͞ol/ (also **bar stool**) ▶ n. a tall padded stool for customers at a bar to sit on.

Bar·stow /ˈbär,stō/ a city in south central California, in the Mojave Desert, northeast of Los Angeles; pop. 24,596 (est. 2008).

Bart /bärt/, Lionel (1930–99), English composer and lyricist; born *Lionel Beglieter.* His musicals include *Oliver!* (1960).

Bart. ▶ abbr. Baronet.

bar tack ▶ n. a stitch made to strengthen a potential weak spot in a garment or other sewn item.
– DERIVATIVES **bar-tacked** adj., **bar tack·ing** n.

bar·tend·er /ˈbär,tendər/ ▶ n. a person who mixes and serves drinks at a bar.
– DERIVATIVES **bar·tend** v., **bar·tend·ing** n.

bar·ter /ˈbärtər/ ▶ v. [with obj.] exchange (goods or services) for other goods or services without using money: *he often **bartered** a meal **for** drawings* | [no obj.] *the company is prepared to barter for Russian oil.*
▶ n. the action or system of exchanging goods or services without using money: *it will be paid for by a mixture of barter and cash.* ■ the goods or services used for such an exchange: *I took a supply of coffee and cigarettes to use as barter.*
– DERIVATIVES **bar·ter·er** n.
– ORIGIN late Middle English: probably from Old French *barater* 'deceive' (see BARRATRY).

Barth[1] /bärTH/, John (Simmons) (1930–), US novelist and short-story writer noted for complex experimental novels. Notable works: *The Sot-Weed Factor* (1960), *Giles Goat-Boy* (1966), and *Letters* (1979).

Barth[2] /bärt/, Karl (1886–1968), Swiss theologian. His seminal work *Epistle to the Romans* (1919) established a neo-orthodox or theocentric approach to contemporary religious thought that remains influential in Protestant theology.

Barthes /bärt/, Roland (1915–80), French writer and critic. He was a leading exponent of structuralism and semiology in literary criticism. Notable works: *On Racine* (1963), *Mythologies* (1957), and *Elements of Semiology* (1964).

Bar·thol·di /bärˈtôldē/, (Frédéric) Auguste (1834–1904), French sculptor, known primarily as the designer of the *Statue of Liberty.*

Bar·tho·lin's gland /ˈbärtl-inz/ ▶ n. Anatomy one of a pair of glands lying near the entrance of the vagina, which secrete a fluid that lubricates the vulva.
– ORIGIN early 18th cent.: named by Caspar *Bartholin* (1655–1738), Danish anatomist, as a tribute to his father.

Bar·thol·o·mew, St. /bärˈTHälə,myo͞o/, an Apostle; regarded as the patron saint of tanners. Feast day, August 24.

bar·ti·zan /ˈbärtəzən/ ▶ n. Architecture an overhanging corner turret at the top of a castle or church tower.
– ORIGIN early 19th cent.: from 17th-cent. *bertisene,* Scots variant of *bratticing* 'temporary breastwork or parapet,' from BRATTICE; revived and reinterpreted by Sir Walter Scott.

Bar·tles·ville /ˈbärtlz,vil/ a city in northeastern Oklahoma, noted as an oil industry center; pop. 35,914 (est. 2008).

Bart·lett[1] /ˈbärtlit/ a town in southwestern Tennessee, northeast of Memphis; pop. 47,501 (est. 2008).

Bart·lett[2] (also **Bartlett pear**) ▶ n. a dessert pear of a juicy, early-ripening variety.

Bar·tók /ˈbär,täk, -,tôk/, Béla (1881–1945), Hungarian composer, whose work owes much to Hungarian folk music. Notable works: *Concerto for Orchestra* (1943) and *Duke Bluebeard's Castle* (opera, 1911).

Bar·to·lom·me·o /,bärtōləˈmāō/, Fra (*c.*1472–1517), Italian painter; born *Baccio della Porta.* A Dominican friar, he worked chiefly in Florence. Notable works: *The Vision of St. Bernard* (1507) and *The Mystic Marriage of St. Catherine* (1511).

Bar·ton /ˈbärtn/, Clara (1821–1912), US social activist; full name *Clarissa Harlowe Barton.* She founded the American Red Cross and served as its first president 1882–1904.

Clara Barton

bart·si·a /ˈbärtsēə/ ▶ n. a herbaceous plant of the figwort family. Some kinds obtain additional nourishment by attachment to the roots of other plants, esp. grasses. ● *Bartsia* and related genera, family Scrophulariaceae: several species, in particular the pink-flowered **red bartsia** (*Odontites serotina*).

PRONUNCIATION KEY ə ago, up; ər over, fur; a hat; ā ate; ä car; e let; ē see; i fit; ī by; NG sing; ō go; ô law, for; oi toy; o͝o good; o͞o goo; ou out; TH thin; T͟H then; ZH vision

b

– ORIGIN modern Latin, from the name of Johann *Bartsch* (1709–38), Prussian botanist.

Ba·ruch[1] /bəˈro͞ok/, Bernard Mannes (1870–1965), US financier and economic consultant. As an adviser to Presidents Woodrow Wilson and Franklin D. Roosevelt, he served as chairman of the War Industries Board 1918–19 and US representative on the UN Atomic Energy Commission 1946.

Bar·uch[2] a book of the Apocrypha, attributed in the text to Baruch, the scribe of Jeremiah (Jer. 36).

bar·ware /ˈbär,we(ə)r/ ▶ **n.** glassware of various shapes and sizes used for preparing and serving alcoholic drinks.

bar·y·cen·tric /,barəˈsentrik/ ▶ **adj.** [attrib.] of or relating to the center of gravity.
– DERIVATIVES **bar·y·cen·ter** /ˈbarə,sentər/ **n.**
– ORIGIN late 19th cent.: from Greek *barus* 'heavy' + **-CENTRIC**.

bar·y·on /ˈbarē,än/ ▶ **n.** Physics a subatomic particle, such as a nucleon or hyperon, that has a mass equal to or greater than that of a proton.
– DERIVATIVES **bar·y·on·ic** /,barēˈänik/ **adj.**
– ORIGIN 1950s: from Greek *barus* 'heavy' + **-ON**.

bar·y·on·ic mat·ter ▶ **n.** matter composed of protons and neutrons; ordinary matter, as distinct from exotic forms.

Ba·rysh·ni·kov /bəˈrisʜnə,kôf, -,kôv/, Mikhail (Nikolaevich) (1948–), US ballet dancer, born in Latvia of Russian parents. In 1974 he defected to the West while touring with the Kirov Ballet. He served as the American Ballet Theater's artistic director 1980–89.

Mikhail Baryshnikov

ba·ry·ta /bəˈrītə/ ▶ **n.** Chemistry barium hydroxide. • Chem. formula: $Ba(OH)_2$.
– ORIGIN early 19th cent.: from **BARYTE**, on the pattern of words such as *soda*.

bar·yte /ˈbarīt/ (also **barytes** /bəˈrītēz/) ▶ **n.** Brit. variant spelling of **BARITE**.
– ORIGIN mid 19th cent.: from **BARIUM** + **-ITE**[1].

ba·sal /ˈbāsəl, -zəl/ ▶ **adj.** [attrib.] chiefly technical forming or belonging to a bottom layer or base.

ba·sal bod·y (also **basal granule**) ▶ **n.** an organelle that forms the base of a flagellum or cilium and that is similar to a centriole in structure and function. Also called **KINETOSOME**.

ba·sal cell ▶ **n.** a type of cell in the innermost layer of the epidermis.

ba·sal cell car·ci·no·ma ▶ **n.** technical term for **RODENT ULCER**.

ba·sal gan·gli·a ▶ **plural n.** Anatomy a group of structures linked to the thalamus in the base of the brain and involved in coordination of movement.

ba·sal met·a·bol·ic rate ▶ **n.** the rate at which the body uses energy while at rest to keep vital functions going, such as breathing and keeping warm.
– DERIVATIVES **ba·sal me·tab·o·lism n.**

ba·salt /bəˈsôlt/ ▶ **n.** a dark, fine-grained volcanic rock that sometimes displays a columnar structure. It is typically composed largely of plagioclase with pyroxene and olivine. ■ a kind of black stoneware resembling such rock.
– DERIVATIVES **ba·sal·tic** /-tik/ **adj.**
– ORIGIN early 17th cent. (in the Latin form): from Latin *basaltes* (variant of *basanites*), from Greek *basanitēs*, from *basanos* 'touchstone.'

bas·cule /ˈbaskyo͞ol/ (also **bascule bridge**) ▶ **n.** a type of bridge with a pivoting section that is raised and lowered using counterweights. ■ a moveable section of road forming part of such a bridge.
– ORIGIN late 19th cent.: earlier denoting a lever apparatus of which one end is raised while the other is lowered, from French (earlier *bacule*), 'seesaw,' from *battre* 'to bump' + *cul* 'buttocks.'

base[1] /bās/ ▶ **n. 1** the lowest part or edge of something, esp. the part on which it rests or is supported: *she sat down at the base of a tree.* ■ Architecture the part of a column between the shaft and pedestal or pavement. ■ Botany & Zoology the end at which a part or organ is attached to the trunk or main part: *a shoot is produced at the base of the stem.* ■ Geometry a line or surface on which a figure is regarded as standing: *the base of the triangle.* ■ Surveying a line of known length used in triangulation. ■ Heraldry the lowest part of a shield.
2 a conceptual structure or entity on which something draws or depends: *the town's economic base collapsed.* ■ something used as a foundation or starting point for further work; a basis: *uses existing data as the base for the study.* ■ [with modifier] a group of people regarded as supporting an organization, for example by buying its products: *a client base.*
3 the main place where a person works or stays: *she makes the studio her base.* ■ chiefly Military a place used as a center of operations by the armed forces or others; a headquarters: *the corporal headed back to base | a base for shipping operations.*
4 a main or important element or ingredient to which other things are added: *soaps with a vegetable oil base.* ■ a substance used as a foundation for makeup. ■ a substance such as water or oil into which a pigment is mixed to form paint.
5 Chemistry a substance capable of reacting with an acid to form a salt and water, or (more broadly) of accepting or neutralizing hydrogen ions. Compare with **ALKALI**. ■ Biochemistry a purine or pyrimidine group in a nucleotide or nucleic acid.
6 Electronics the middle part of a bipolar transistor, separating the emitter from the collector.
7 Linguistics the root or stem of a word or a derivative. ■ the uninflected form of a verb.
8 Mathematics a number used as the basis of a numeration scale. ■ a number in terms of which other numbers are expressed as logarithms.
9 Baseball one of the four stations that must be reached in turn to score a run.
▶ **v.** [with obj.] **1** have as the foundation for (something); use as a point from which (something) can develop: *the film is* **based on** *a novel by Pat Conroy | inaccurate conclusions based on incomplete facts.*
2 situate as the center of operations: *a research program* **based at** *the University of Arizona* | [as adj., in combination] **(-based)** *a London-based band.*
– PHRASES **get to first base** [usu. with negative] informal achieve the first step toward one's objective. **first base** (, **second base**, **third base**) informal used to refer to progressive levels of sexual intimacy. **off-base** informal mistaken: *the boy is way off-base.* **touch base(s)** informal briefly make or renew contact with someone.
– ORIGIN Middle English: from Old French, from Latin *basis* 'base, pedestal,' from Greek.

base[2] ▶ **adj.** (of a person or a person's actions or feelings) without moral principles; ignoble: *the electorate's baser instincts of greed and selfishness | we hope his motives are nothing so base as money.* ■ archaic denoting or befitting a person of low social class. ■ (of coins or other articles) not made of precious metal: *the basest coins in the purse were made in the seventh century AD.*
– DERIVATIVES **base·ly adv.**
– ORIGIN late Middle English: from Old French *bas*, from medieval Latin *bassus* 'short' (found in classical Latin as a cognomen). The senses in late Middle English included 'low, short' and 'of inferior quality'; from the latter arose a sense 'low on the social scale, menial,' and hence (mid 16th cent.) 'reprehensibly cowardly, selfish, or mean.'

base·ball /ˈbās,bôl/ ▶ **n.** a ball game played between two teams of nine on a field with a diamond-shaped circuit of four bases. It is played chiefly in the US, Canada, Latin America, and East Asia. ■ the hard ball used in this game.

base·ball cap ▶ **n.** a fabric cap of a kind originally worn by baseball players, with a large brim and an adjustable strap at the back.

base·board /ˈbās,bôrd/ ▶ **n.** a narrow wooden board running along the base of an interior wall.

base·born /ˈbās,bôrn/ ▶ **adj.** [attrib.] archaic of low birth or origin. ■ illegitimate.

base bur·ner ▶ **n.** a coal stove or furnace into which coal is fed automatically from a hopper as the lower layers are burned.

base camp ▶ **n.** a camp from which mountaineering expeditions set out.

base dress·ing ▶ **n.** the application of manure or fertilizer to the earth, which is then plowed or dug in. ■ manure or fertilizer applied in this way.

base ex·change (abbr.: **BX**) ▶ **n.** a nonprofit store for the purchase of personal items, clothing, refreshments, etc., at a naval or air force base.

base·head /ˈbās,hed/ ▶ **n.** informal a habitual abuser of freebase or crack cocaine.
– ORIGIN 1980s: from a shortened form of **FREEBASE** + **-HEAD**[2].

base hit ▶ **n.** Baseball a fair ball hit such that the batter can advance safely to a base without aid of an error committed by the team in the field.

base hos·pi·tal ▶ **n.** a military hospital situated at some distance from the area of active operations during a war.

base jump (also **BASE jump**) ▶ **n.** a parachute jump from a fixed point, typically a high building or promontory, rather than an aircraft.
▶ **v.** [no obj.] (often as noun **base jumping**) perform such a jump.
– DERIVATIVES **base jump·er n.**
– ORIGIN 1980s: *base* from *b*uilding, *a*ntenna tower, *s*pan, *e*arth (denoting the types of structure used).

Ba·sel /ˈbäzəl/ German name for **BASLE**.

base·less /ˈbāslis/ ▶ **adj. 1** without foundation in fact: *baseless allegations.*
2 Architecture (of a column) not having a base between the shaft and pedestal.
– DERIVATIVES **base·less·ly adv.**, **base·less·ness n.**

base·line /ˈbās,līn/ ▶ **n. 1** a minimum or starting point used for comparisons.
2 (in tennis, volleyball, etc.) the line marking each end of the court.
3 Baseball the line between bases, which a runner must stay close to when running.
4 Printing the imaginary straight line on which a line of type rests.

base·man /ˈbāsmən/ ▶ **n.** (pl. **basemen**) Baseball a fielder designated to cover first, second, or third base.

base·ment /ˈbāsmənt/ ▶ **n.** the floor of a building partly or entirely below ground level. ■ Geology the oldest formation of rocks underlying a particular area.
– ORIGIN mid 18th cent.: probably from archaic Dutch *basement* 'foundation,' perhaps from Italian *basamento* 'column base.'

base·ment mem·brane ▶ **n.** Anatomy a thin, delicate membrane of protein fibers and glycosaminoglycans separating an epithelium from underlying tissue.

base met·al ▶ **n.** a common metal not considered precious, such as copper, tin, or zinc.

base·ness /ˈbāsnis/ ▶ **n.** lack of moral principles; bad character: *the baseness of human nature.*

ba·sen·ji /bəˈsenjē/ ▶ **n.** (pl. **basenjis**) a small hunting dog of a central African breed, which growls and yelps but does not bark.
– ORIGIN 1930s: a local word.

base on balls (abbr.: **BB**) ▶ **n.** Baseball another term for **WALK** (sense 3 of the noun).

base pair ▶ **n.** Biochemistry a pair of complementary bases in a double-stranded nucleic acid molecule, consisting of a purine in one strand linked by hydrogen bonds to a pyrimidine in the other. Cytosine always pairs with guanine, and adenine with thymine (in DNA) or uracil (in RNA).
– DERIVATIVES **base pair·ing n.**

base path ▶ **n.** Baseball the straight-line path from one base to the next, defined by the position of the base runner while a play is being made.

base pay ▶ **n.** the base rate of pay for a job or activity, not including any additional payments such as overtime or bonuses.

base·plate /ˈbās,plāt/ ▶ **n.** a sheet of metal forming the bottom of an object.

base run·ner (also **baserunner**) ▶ **n.** Baseball a player on the team at bat who is on a base, or running between bases.
– DERIVATIVES **base-run·ning** (or **baserunning**) **n.**

ba·ses /ˈbāsēz/ plural form of **BASIS**.

base sta·tion ▶ **n. 1** a relay located at the center of any of the cells of a cellular telephone system.
2 a short-range transceiver that connects a cordless phone, computer, or other wireless device to a central hub and allows connection to a network.

base u·nit ▶ **n.** a fundamental unit that is defined arbitrarily and not by combinations of other units. The base units of the SI system are the meter, kilogram, second, ampere, kelvin, mole, and candela.

bash /basʜ/ ▶ **v.** [with obj.] informal strike hard and violently: *bash a mosquito with a newspaper.* ■ **(bash something in)** damage or break something by striking it violently: *the car's rear window had been bashed in.* ■ [no obj.] **(bash into)** collide with: *the other vehicle bashed into the back of them.*

■ criticize severely: *a remark bashing the Belgian brewing industry.*
▶ **n.** informal **1** a heavy blow: *a bash on the head.*
2 [usu. with modifier] informal a party or social event: *a birthday bash.*
– PHRASAL VERBS **bash something out** produce something rapidly without preparation or attention to detail.
– ORIGIN mid 17th cent. (as a verb): imitative, perhaps a blend of BANG¹ and SMASH, DASH, etc. Sense 2 of the noun is a 20th-cent. usage.

ba·shaw /bəˈsHô/ ▶ **n.** another term for PASHA (sense 1).

-bash·er /-ˌbasHər/ ▶ **comb. form** forming nouns denoting a person who harshly criticizes, debunks, or commits violence against the named party: *theory-basher | world-trade basher.*

ba·shert /bäˈsHert/ ▶ **n.** (in Jewish use) a person's soulmate, esp. when considered as an ideal or predestined marriage partner.
– ORIGIN Yiddish 'fate, destiny.'

bash·ful /ˈbasHfəl/ ▶ **adj.** reluctant to draw attention to oneself; shy: *don't be bashful about telling folks how you feel.*
– DERIVATIVES **bash·ful·ly** adv., **bash·ful·ness** n.
– ORIGIN late 15th cent.: from obsolete *bash* 'make or become abashed' (from ABASH) + -FUL.

bash·ing /ˈbasHiNG/ ▶ **n.** [usu. with modifier] informal violent physical assault: *nine incidents of gay bashing were reported to the police.* ■ severe criticism: *press bashing.*

Bash·kir /basHˈki(ə)r/ ▶ **n. 1** a member of a Muslim people living in the southern Urals.
2 the Turkic language of this people.
▶ **adj.** of or relating to this people or their language.
– ORIGIN via Russian from Turkic *Başkurt.*

Bash·kir·i·a /basHˈki(ə)rēə/ an autonomous republic in central Russia, west of the Urals; pop. 4,042,900 (est. 2009); capital, Ufa. Also called **Bashkir Autonomous Republic, Bashkortostan.**

BASIC /ˈbāsik/ ▶ **n.** a simple high-level computer programming language that uses familiar English words, designed for beginners and formerly used widely.
– ORIGIN 1960s: acronym from *Beginners' All-purpose Symbolic Instruction Code.*

ba·sic /ˈbāsik/ ▶ **adj. 1** forming an essential foundation or starting point; fundamental: *certain basic rules must be obeyed | the laying down of arms is basic to the agreement.* ■ offering or consisting in the minimum required without elaboration or luxury; simplest or lowest in level: *basic and unsophisticated resorts | the food was good, if a bit basic.* ■ common to or required by everyone; primary and ineradicable or inalienable: *basic human rights.*
2 Chemistry having the properties of a base, or containing a base; having a pH greater than 7. Often contrasted with ACID or ACIDIC; compare with ALKALINE. ■ Geology (of rock, esp. igneous rock) relatively poor in silica. ■ Metallurgy relating to or denoting steelmaking processes involving lime-rich refractories and slags.
▶ **n.** (**basics**) the essential facts or principles of a subject or skill: *learning the basics of the business | storytelling has re-emerged as people have turned back to basics.* ■ essential food and other supplies: *people are facing a shortage of basics like flour.* ■ Military basic training.
– ORIGIN mid 19th cent.: from BASE¹ + -IC.

ba·si·cal·ly /ˈbāsik(ə)lē/ ▶ **adv.** [often as submodifier] in the most essential respects; fundamentally: *we started from a basically simple idea.* ■ [sentence adverb] used to indicate that a statement summarizes the most important aspects, or gives a roughly accurate account, of a more complex situation: *I basically played the same tunes every night.*

Ba·sic Eng·lish ▶ **n.** a simplified form of English limited to 850 selected words, intended for international communication.

ba·sic·i·ty /bāˈsisitē/ ▶ **n.** Chemistry the number of hydrogen atoms replaceable by a base in a particular acid.

ba·sic train·ing ▶ **n.** Military the initial period of training for new personnel, involving intense physical activity and behavioral discipline.

ba·sid·i·o·my·cete /bəˌsidēōˈmīsēt/ ▶ **n.** Botany a fungus whose spores develop in basidia. Basidiomycetes include the majority of familiar mushrooms and toadstools. Compare with ASCOMYCETE. ● Phylum Basidiomycota: classes Basidiomycetes (mushrooms, toadstools, puffballs, earthstars, stinkhorns, polypores), Teliomycetes (rusts), and Ustomycetes (smuts).
– ORIGIN late 19th cent.: anglicized singular of modern Latin *Basidiomycetes*, from *basidium* (see BASIDIUM) + Greek *mukētes* 'fungi.'

ba·sid·i·o·spore /bəˈsidēōˌspôr/ ▶ **n.** a spore produced by a basidium.

ba·sid·i·um /bəˈsidēəm/ ▶ **n.** (pl. **basidia** /-ˈsidēə/) a microscopic, club-shaped spore-bearing structure produced by certain fungi.
– ORIGIN mid 19th cent.: modern Latin, from Greek *basidion*, diminutive of *basis* (see BASIS).

Ba·sie /ˈbāsē/, Count (1904–84), US jazz pianist, organist, and bandleader; born *William Basie*. In 1935 he formed the Count Basie Orchestra, which became one of the best-known and most successful bands of the swing era.

ba·si·fy /ˈbāsəˌfī/ ▶ **v.** [with obj.] Chemistry change into a base; alkalize.

bas·il /ˈbāzəl, ˈbazəl/ ▶ **n.** an aromatic annual herb of the mint family, native to tropical Asia. ● Genus *Ocimum*, family Labiatae: several species, in particular the common **sweet basil** (*O. basilicum*) and the low-growing, compact **bush basil** *O. minimum*. ■ the leaves of this plant used as a culinary herb, esp. in Mediterranean dishes.
– ORIGIN late Middle English: from Old French *basile*, via medieval Latin from Greek *basilikon*, neuter of *basilikos* 'royal' (see BASILICA).

Bas·il, St. /ˈbazəl, ˈbāzəl/ (*c.*330–379), doctor of the Church; bishop of Caesarea; known as **St. Basil the Great**. Brother of St. Gregory of Nyssa, he staunchly opposed the Arian heresy and established a monastic rule that is still the basis of monasticism in the Eastern Church. Feast day, June 14.

bas·i·lar /ˈbasələr/ ▶ **adj.** [attrib.] of or situated at the base of something, esp. of the skull, or of the organ of Corti in the ear.
– ORIGIN mid 16th cent.: from modern Latin *basilaris*, formed irregularly from Latin *basis* (see BASIS).

bas·i·lar mem·brane ▶ **n.** Anatomy a membrane in the cochlea that bears the organ of Corti.

Ba·sil·don /ˈbazəldən/ a town in southeastern England; pop. 100,600 (est. 2009).

ba·si·lect /ˈbāzəˌlekt, ˈbaz-/ ▶ **n.** Linguistics a less prestigious dialect or variety of a particular language (used esp. in the study of Creoles). Compare with ACROLECT, MESOLECT.
– DERIVATIVES **ba·si·lec·tal** /ˌbāzəˈlektəl, ˌbaz-/ adj.

Ba·sil·i·an /bəˈzilyən, -ˈzilēən/ ▶ **adj.** of or relating to St. Basil the Great, or the order of monks and nuns following his monastic rule.
▶ **n.** a Basilian monk or nun.

ba·sil·i·ca /bəˈsilikə/ ▶ **n.** a large oblong hall or building with double colonnades and a semicircular apse, used in ancient Rome as a court of law or for public assemblies. ■ a similar building used as a Christian church. ■ the name given to certain churches granted special privileges by the pope.
– DERIVATIVES **ba·sil·i·can** adj.
– ORIGIN mid 16th cent.: from Latin, literally 'royal palace,' from Greek *basilikē*, feminine of *basilikos* 'royal,' from *basileus* 'king.'

bas·i·lisk /ˈbasəˌlisk, ˈbaz-/ ▶ **n. 1** a mythical reptile with a lethal gaze or breath, hatched by a serpent from a cock's egg. ■ Heraldry another term for COCKATRICE.
2 a long, slender, and mainly bright green lizard found in Central America, the male of which has a crest running from the head to the tail. It can swim well and is able to run on its hind legs across the surface of water. ● *Basiliscus plumifrons*, family Iguanidae.
– ORIGIN late Middle English: via Latin from Greek *basiliskos* 'little king, serpent,' from *basileus* 'king.'

basilisk 2

bas·i·lo·sau·rus /ˌbasələˈsôrəs/ ▶ **n.** a large marine cetacean of the Eocene epoch, having a long, slender body and vestigial fore and hind limbs. Fossils were discovered in the early 1990s. ● Genus *Basilosaurus*, suborder Archaeoceti, order Cetacea.
– ORIGIN modern Latin, from Greek *basileus* 'king' + *sauros* 'lizard.'

ba·sin /ˈbāsən/ ▶ **n. 1** a bowl for washing, typically attached to a wall and having faucets connected to a water supply; a washbasin.
2 a wide, round open container, esp. one used for holding liquid.
3 a natural depression on the earth's surface, typically containing water: *the Indian Ocean basin.* ■ the tract of country that is drained by a river and its tributaries or drains into a lake or sea: *the Amazon basin | a drainage basin.* ■ an enclosed area of water where vessels can be moored: *a yacht basin.* ■ Geology a circumscribed area within which the rock strata dip toward the center.
– DERIVATIVES **ba·sin·ful** /-ˌfo͝ol/ n.
– ORIGIN Middle English: from Old French *bacin*, from medieval Latin *bacinus*, from *bacca* 'water container,' perhaps of Gaulish origin.

Ba·sin and Range Province a largely arid region of the southwestern US, chiefly in Nevada, Utah, and California. The Great Basin and Death Valley are parts of the region.

bas·i·net /ˌbasəˈnet/ (also **bascinet**) ▶ **n.** a medieval helmet of light steel, fitting close to the wearer's head and typically having a visor.
– ORIGIN Middle English: from Old French *bacinet* 'little basin.'

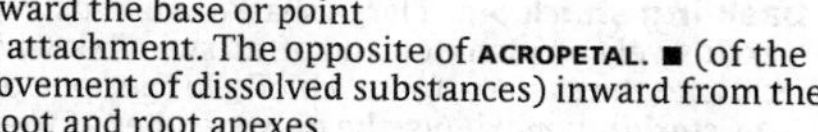

basinet

ba·sip·e·tal /bāˈsipitl/ ▶ **adj.** Botany (of growth or development) downward toward the base or point of attachment. The opposite of ACROPETAL. ■ (of the movement of dissolved substances) inward from the shoot and root apexes.
– DERIVATIVES **ba·sip·e·tal·ly** adv.
– ORIGIN mid 19th cent.: from BASIS + Latin *petere* 'seek' + -AL.

ba·sis /ˈbāsis/ ▶ **n.** (pl. **bases** /-sēz/) the underlying support or foundation for an idea, argument, or process: *trust is the only basis for a good working relationship.* ■ the system or principles according to which an activity or process is carried on: *she needed coaching on a regular basis | flea markets operate on a cash-only basis.* ■ the justification for or reasoning behind something: *on the basis of these statistics, important decisions are made.*
– ORIGIN late 16th cent. (denoting a base or pedestal): via Latin from Greek, 'stepping.' Compare with BASE¹.

ba·sis point ▶ **n.** Finance one hundredth of one percent, used chiefly in expressing differences of interest rates.

bask /bask/ ▶ **v.** [no obj.] lie exposed to warmth and light, typically from the sun, for relaxation and pleasure: *sprawled figures basking in the afternoon sun.* ■ (**bask in**) revel in and make the most of (something pleasing): *he went on basking in the glory of his first book.*
– ORIGIN late Middle English (originally in the sense 'bathe'): perhaps related to Old Norse *batha* 'bathe.'

Bas·ker·ville /ˈbaskərˌvil/ ▶ **n.** a typeface much used in books.
– ORIGIN early 19th cent.: named after John *Baskerville* (1706–75), English printer, designer of the typeface.

bas·ket /ˈbaskit/ ▶ **n. 1** a container used to hold or carry things, typically made from interwoven strips of cane or wire: *a laundry basket.* ■ a structure suspended from a hot-air balloon for carrying the crew, equipment, and ballast. ■ Finance a group or range of currencies or investments: *the European currency unit is made up of a basket of ten currencies.*
2 Basketball a net fixed on a hoop used as the goal. ■ a goal scored.
– ORIGIN Middle English: from Old French *basket*, of unknown ultimate origin.

bas·ket·ball /ˈbaskitˌbôl/ ▶ **n.** a game played between two teams of five players in which goals are scored by throwing a ball through a netted hoop fixed above each end of the court. ■ the inflated ball used in this game.

bas·ket bin·go ▶ **n.** a fundraising event in which players buy tickets to play bingo for prizes of gift baskets that are made up by donors.

bas·ket case ▶ **n.** informal a person or thing regarded as useless or unable to cope.
– ORIGIN early 20th cent.: originally slang denoting a soldier who had lost all four limbs, thus unable to move independently.

bas·ket hilt ▶ **n.** a sword hilt with a guard resembling basketwork.

PRONUNCIATION KEY ə *ago, up*; ər *over, fur*; a *hat*; ā *ate*; ä *car*; e *let*; ē *see*; i *fit*; ī *by*; NG *sing*; ō *go*; ô *law, for*; oi *toy*; o͝o *good*; o͞o *goo*; ou *out*; TH *thin*; T͟H *then*; ZH *vision*

b

– DERIVATIVES **bas·ket-hilt·ed** adj.

bas·ket·mak·er /ˈbaskitˌmākər/ ▶ n. a person who makes baskets.
– DERIVATIVES **bas·ket·mak·ing** n.

Bas·ket Mak·er ▶ n. a member of a culture of the southwestern US, forming the early stages of the Anasazi culture, from the 1st century BC until *c.* AD 700. The name comes from the basketry and other woven fragments found in early cave sites.

bas·ket-of-gold ▶ n. a cultivated evergreen alyssum, with gray-green leaves and numerous small yellow flowers. ● *Alyssum saxatile*, family Brassicaceae.

bas·ket·ry /ˈbaskitrē/ ▶ n. the craft of basket-making. ■ baskets collectively.

bas·ket star ▶ n. a brittlestar having branched arms. ● Genus *Gorgonocephalus*, family Gorgonocephalidae: several species, including the large *G. eucnemis*.

bas·ket weave ▶ n. a style of weave or a pattern resembling basketwork.

bas·ket-weav·ing ▶ n. **1** the art or activity of creating woven baskets.
2 humorous a college course that is thought to be very easy.

bas·ket·work /ˈbaskitˌwərk/ ▶ n. material woven in the style of a basket. ■ the craft of making such material.

bask·ing shark ▶ n. a large shark that feeds exclusively on plankton and often swims slowly close to the surface, found chiefly in the open ocean. ● *Cetorhinus maximus*, the only member of the family Cetorhinidae.

Basle /bäl/ a commercial and industrial city on the Rhine River in northwestern Switzerland; pop. 163,521 (2007). French name **Bâle**, German name **Basel**.

bas·ma·ti /bäsˈmätē/ (also **basmati rice**) ▶ n. a kind of long-grain Indian rice of a high quality.
– ORIGIN from Hindi *bāsmatī*, literally 'fragrant.'

bas mitz·vah /bäs ˈmitsvə/ ▶ n. a variant of **bat mitzvah**.

ba·so·phil /ˈbāsəfil/ ▶ n. Physiology a basophilic white blood cell.

ba·so·phil·i·a /ˌbāsəˈfilēə/ ▶ n. **1** a tendency to stain readily with a basic dye.
2 a condition of the blood marked by the formation and accumulation of an excess of basophil cells.

ba·so·phil·ic /ˌbāsəˈfilik/ ▶ adj. Physiology (of a cell or its contents) readily stained with basic dyes.

Ba·so·tho /bəˈsōˌtō/ ▶ n. (pl. **same** or **Basothos**) a member of the Sotho people of southern Africa, esp. Lesotho.
– ORIGIN from Sesotho, from *ba-* (prefix denoting a plural) + **Sotho**. Compare with **Basutoland**.

Basque /bask/ ▶ n. **1** a member of a people living in the Basque Country of France and Spain. Culturally one of the most distinct groups in Europe, the Basques were largely independent until the 19th century.
2 the language of this people, which has no known relation to any other language.
▶ adj. of or relating to the Basques or their language.
– ORIGIN from French, from Latin *Vasco*; compare with **Gascon**.

basque /bask/ ▶ n. a close-fitting bodice extending from the shoulders to the waist and often with a short continuation below waist level.
– ORIGIN mid 19th cent.: from **Basque**, referring to Basque dress.

Basque Coun·try /bask/ a region of the western Pyrenees in both France and Spain, the homeland of the Basque people. French name **Pays Basque**.

Basque Prov·in·ces an autonomous region consisting of the provinces of Álava, Guipúzcoa, and Vizcaya in northern Spain, on the Bay of Biscay; capital, Vitoria.

Bas·ra /ˈbäsrə, ˈbäz-/ an oil port in Iraq, on the Shatt al-Arab waterway; pop. 870,000 (est. 2007).

bas-re·lief /ˌbä rəˈlēf, bas/ ▶ n. Sculpture see **relief** (sense 4). ■ a sculpture, carving, or molding in bas-relief.
– ORIGIN early 17th cent. (as *basse relieve*): from Italian *basso-rilievo* 'low relief,' later altered to the French form.

bass[1] /bās/ ▶ n. a voice, instrument, or sound of the lowest range, in particular: ■ the lowest adult male singing voice. ■ [as modifier] denoting the member of a family of instruments that is the lowest in pitch: *a bass clarinet* | *a bass drum*. ■ a bass guitar or double bass. ■ the low-frequency output of a radio or audio system, corresponding to the bass in music.
– ORIGIN late Middle English: alteration of **base**[2], influenced by **basso**.

bass[2] /bas/ ▶ n. (pl. **same** or **basses**) **1** the common European freshwater perch.
2 any of a number of fish similar to or related to this, in particular: ● a mainly marine fish found in temperate waters (family Percichthyidae or Moronidae, including *Dicentrarchus labrax* of European waters and genus *Morone* of North America). ● an American freshwater fish of the sunfish family, popular with anglers (genera *Ambloplites* and *Micropterus*, family Centrarchidae). ● a sea bass.
– ORIGIN late Middle English: alteration of dialect *barse*, of Germanic origin; related to Dutch *baars* and German *Barsch*.

bass[3] /bas/ ▶ n. another term for **bast**.
– ORIGIN late 17th cent.: alteration.

bass-ack·wards /ˌbas ˈakwərds/ ▶ adv. & adj. humorous another term for **ass-backwards**.

bass clef /bās klef/ ▶ n. a clef placing F below middle C on the second-highest line of the staff.

bass drum /bās/ ▶ n. a large, two-headed drum that has a low booming sound.

Bas·sein /bəˈsān/ a port on the Irrawaddy delta in southwestern Myanmar (Burma); pop. 215,600 (est. 2004).

Basse-Nor·man·die /ˌbäs ˈnôrmänˈdē/ a region of northwestern France, on the coast of the English Channel, including the Cherbourg peninsula and the city of Caen.

Basse·terre /bäsˈter/ the capital of St. Kitts and Nevis in the Leeward Islands, on the island of St. Kitts; pop. 13,000 (est. 2007).

Basse-Terre /bäs ˈter/ the main island of Guadeloupe in the West Indies.

bas·set horn /ˈbasit/ ▶ n. an alto clarinet in F.
– ORIGIN mid 19th cent.: from German, translation of French *cor de bassette*, from Italian *corno di bassetto*, from *corno* 'horn' + *di* 'of' + *bassetto* (diminutive of *basso* 'low,' from Latin *bassus* 'short').

bas·set hound /ˈbasit hound/ ▶ n. a sturdy hunting dog of a breed with a long body, short legs, and big ears.
– ORIGIN early 17th cent.: from French, diminutive of *bas* 'low,' from medieval Latin *bassus* 'short.'

basset hound

bass fid·dle /bās/ ▶ n. another term for **double bass**.

Bas·si /ˈbäsē/, Laura (1711–78), Bolognese physicist and professor. After receiving her college degree in 1732, she became a professor at the University of Bologna, teaching philosophy, mathematics, and physics. She was the first woman to pursue a scientific career for which she was paid a salary. She also gave private instruction in physics and performed experiments in her home.

bas·si·net /ˌbasəˈnet/ ▶ n. a baby's wicker cradle, usually with a hood.
– ORIGIN mid 19th cent.: from French, diminutive of *bassin* 'basin'; compare with **basinet**.

bas·si pro·fun·di /ˈbasē prəˈfəndē/ plural form of **basso profundo**.

bass·ist /ˈbāsist/ ▶ n. a person who plays a double bass or bass guitar.

bass·let /ˈbaslit/ ▶ n. a small, brightly colored fish related to the sea basses. ● Genera *Gramma* and *Lipogramma*, family Grammidae: several species.

bass·line /ˈbāsˌlīn/ ▶ n. the lowest part or sequence of notes in a piece of music.

bas·so /ˈbasō, bä-/ ▶ n. (pl. **bassos** or **bassi** /ˈbäsē/) a bass voice or vocal part.
– ORIGIN early 18th cent.: Italian, 'low,' from Latin *bassus* 'short, low.'

bas·soon /bəˈso͞on, ba-/ ▶ n. a bass instrument of the oboe family with a double reed.
– DERIVATIVES **bas·soon·ist** /-nist/ n.

bassoon

– ORIGIN early 18th cent.: from French *basson*, from Italian *bassone*, from *basso* 'low,' from Latin *bassus* 'short, low.'

bas·so pro·fun·do /ˈbasō prōˈfəndō, ˈbäsō/ ▶ n. (pl. **basso profundos** or **bassi profundi** /ˈbäsē prōˈfəndē/) a bass singer with an exceptionally low range.
– ORIGIN mid 19th cent.: Italian, from *basso* 'low' + *profondo* 'deep.'

bas·so-re·lie·vo /ˌbasō riˈlēvō/ ▶ n. (pl. **basso-relievos**) Sculpture another term for **bas-relief** (see **relief** (sense 4)).
– ORIGIN mid 17th cent.: from Italian *basso-rilievo*.

Bass Strait /ˈbas/ a channel that separates Tasmania from the mainland of Australia.

bass vi·ol /bās ˈvīəl/ ▶ n. a viola da gamba. ■ a double bass.

bass·wood /ˈbasˌwo͝od/ ▶ n. a North American linden tree, commonly planted along streets. ● Genus *Tilia*, family Tiliaceae: several species, in particular the large-leaved *T. americana* (also called **American linden**) of the northern US and Canada.
– ORIGIN late 17th cent.: from **bass**[3] + **wood**.

bast /bast/ ▶ n. (also **bast fiber**) fibrous material from the phloem of a plant, used as fiber in matting, cord, etc. ■ Botany the phloem or vascular tissue of a plant.
– ORIGIN Old English *bæst*; related to Dutch *bast*, German *Bast*; of unknown origin.

bas·tard /ˈbastərd/ ▶ n. **1** archaic or derogatory a person born of parents not married to each other.
2 informal an unpleasant or despicable person: *he lied to me, the bastard!* ■ [with adj.] a person of a specified kind: *the poor bastard* | *he was a lucky bastard*. ■ a difficult or awkward thing, undertaking, or situation: *it's been an absolute bastard of a week*.
▶ adj. [attrib.] **1** archaic or derogatory born of parents not married to each other; illegitimate: *a bastard child*.
2 (of a thing) no longer in its pure or original form; debased: *a bastard Darwinism*. ■ (of a handwriting script or typeface) showing a mixture of different styles.
– DERIVATIVES **bas·tar·dy** n. (sense 1 of the noun).
– ORIGIN Middle English: via Old French from medieval Latin *bastardus*.

> **USAGE** In the past, the word **bastard** was the standard term in both legal and nonlegal use for 'an illegitimate child.' Today, however, it has little importance as a legal term and is retained today in this older sense only as a term of abuse.

bas·tard·ize /ˈbastərˌdīz/ ▶ v. [with obj.] **1** (often as adj. **bastardized**) corrupt or debase (something such as a language or art form), typically by adding new elements: *a strange, bastardized form of French*.
2 archaic declare (someone) illegitimate: *to annul the marriage and bastardize the child*.
– DERIVATIVES **bas·tard·i·za·tion** /ˌbastərdiˈzāsHən/ n.

bas·tard wing ▶ n. a group of small quill feathers on the first digit of a bird's wing.

baste[1] /bāst/ ▶ v. [with obj.] pour juices or melted fat over (meat) during cooking in order to keep it moist.
– ORIGIN late 15th cent.: of unknown origin.

baste[2] ▶ v. [with obj.] Needlework tack with long, loose stitches in preparation for sewing.
– ORIGIN late Middle English: from Old French *bastir* 'sew lightly,' ultimately of Germanic origin and related to **bast**.

baste[3] ▶ v. [with obj.] informal, dated beat (someone) soundly; thrash: *go baste him one!*
– ORIGIN mid 16th cent.: perhaps a figurative use of **baste**[1].

Bas·tet /ˈbastet/ Egyptian Mythology a goddess usually shown as a woman with the head of a cat, wearing one gold earring. See also **Sekhmet**.

Ba·sti·a /ˈbästēə, bästˈyä/ the chief port of the French island of Corsica, on the northeastern coast; pop. 43,300 (2007).

Bas·tille /baˈstēl/ a fortress in Paris built in the 14th century and used in the 17th–18th centuries as a state prison. Its storming by the mob on July 14, 1789, marked the start of the French Revolution.
– ORIGIN via Old French from Provençal *bastida*, from *bastir* 'build.'

Bas·tille Day ▶ n. July 14, the date of the storming of the Bastille in 1789, celebrated as a national holiday in France.

bas·ti·na·do /ˌbastəˈnādō, -ˈnädō/ chiefly historical ▶ n. a form of punishment or torture that involves caning the soles of someone's feet.
▶ v. (**bastinadoes, bastinadoing, bastinadoed**) [with obj.] (usu. **be bastinadoed**) punish or torture (someone) in such a way.

– ORIGIN late 16th cent. (denoting a blow with a stick): from Spanish *bastonada*, from *bastón* 'stick, cudgel,' from late Latin *bastum* 'stick.'

bas·tion /ˈbasCHən/ ▶ **n. 1** a projecting part of a fortification built at an angle to the line of a wall, so as to allow defensive fire in several directions. ■ a natural rock formation resembling such a fortification.
2 an institution, place, or person strongly defending or upholding particular principles, attitudes, or activities: *the last bastion of male privilege*.
– ORIGIN mid 16th cent.: from French, from Italian *bastione*, from *bastire* 'build.'

bast·naes·ite /ˈbast-nəˌsīt/ ▶ **n.** a yellow to brown mineral consisting of a fluoride and carbonate of cerium and other rare earth metals.
– ORIGIN late 19th cent.: from *Bastnäs*, the name of a district in Västmanland, Sweden, + **-ITE**[1].

Bas·togne /bäˈstōn(yə)/ a town in southeastern Belgium; pop. 14,577 (2008). It was the scene of heavy fighting during the Battle of the Bulge in World War II.

ba·su·co /bəˈso͞okō/ ▶ **n.** impure or low-grade cocaine, esp. when mixed with coca paste and tobacco and marijuana.
– ORIGIN 1980s: from Colombian Spanish; perhaps related to Spanish *bazucar* 'shake violently.'

Ba·su·to·land /bəˈso͞otōˌland/ former name (until 1966) of **LESOTHO**. Compare with **BASOTHO**.

bat[1] /bat/ ▶ **n.** an implement with a handle and a solid surface, usually of wood, used for hitting the ball in games such as baseball, cricket, and table tennis. ■ the person batting, esp. in cricket: *the team's opening bat*. ■ each of a pair of objects resembling table tennis bats, used by a person on the ground to guide a taxiing aircraft.
▶ **v.** (**bats, batting, batted**) **1** [no obj.] (of a team or a player in sports such as baseball) take in turns the role of hitting rather than fielding: *Ruth came to bat in the fifth inning*.
2 [with obj.] hit at (someone or something) with the palm of one's hand: *he batted the flies away*.
– PHRASES **bat a thousand** informal be very successful; achieve perfection: *with the tortellini, I batted a thousand—both kids had seconds*. **go to bat for** informal defend the interests of; support: *his willingness to go to bat for his employees*. **right off the bat** at the very beginning.
– PHRASAL VERBS **bat around** (or **about**) informal travel widely, frequently, or casually: *I'm always batting around between England and America*. **bat something around** (or **about**) informal discuss an idea or proposal casually or idly.
– ORIGIN late Old English *batt* 'club, stick, staff,' perhaps partly from Old French *batte*, from *battre* 'to strike.'

bat[2] ▶ **n. 1** a mainly nocturnal mammal capable of sustained flight, with membranous wings that extend between the fingers and connecting the forelimbs to the body and the hindlimbs to the tail. ● Order Chiroptera: many families and numerous species. The large tropical fruit bats (suborder Megachiroptera) generally have good eyesight and feed mainly on fruit; the numerous smaller bats (suborder Microchiroptera) are mouselike in appearance, mainly insectivorous, and use ultrasonic echolocation.
2 (usu. **old bat**) a woman regarded as unattractive or unpleasant: *some deranged old bat*.
– PHRASES **have bats in the** (or **one's**) **belfry** informal be eccentric or crazy. **like a bat out of hell** informal very fast and wildly.
– ORIGIN late 16th cent.: alteration, perhaps by association with medieval Latin *batta, blacta*, of Middle English *bakke*, of Scandinavian origin.

bat[3] ▶ **v.** (**bats, batting, batted**) [with obj.] flutter one's eyelashes, typically in a flirtatious manner: *she batted her long dark eyelashes at him*.
– PHRASES **not bat** (or **without batting**) **an eyelid** (or **eye** or **eyelash**) informal show (or showing) no reaction: *she paid the bill without batting an eyelid*.
– ORIGIN late 19th cent.: from dialect *bat* 'to wink, blink,' variant of obsolete *bate* 'to flutter.'

Ba·taan /bəˈtan, -ˈtän/ a peninsula and province in the Philippines, on the western part of the island of Luzon, bounded by Manila Bay on the east and the South China Sea on the west; site of World War II battles and the infamous "Death March." Pop. 721,000 (est. 2009).

Ba·tak /bəˈtäk/ ▶ **n. 1** (pl. **same** or **Bataks**) a member of a people of northern Sumatra.
2 the Indonesian language of this people.
▶ **adj.** of or relating to the Batak or their language.
– ORIGIN the name in Batak.

Ba·tan Is·lands /bäˈtän/ the northernmost islands in the Philippines.

ba·ta·ta /bəˈtätə/ ▶ **n.** (in the southern West Indies) sweet potato.
– ORIGIN via Spanish from Taino.

Ba·ta·vi·a /bəˈtāvēə/ former name (until 1949) for **JAKARTA**.

Ba·ta·vi·an /bəˈtāvēən/ historical or archaic ▶ **adj.** of or relating to the ancient Germanic people who inhabited the island of Betuwe between the Rhine and the Waal (now part of the Netherlands). ■ of or relating to the people of the Netherlands. ■ of or relating to Jakarta in Indonesia (formerly the Dutch East Indies).
▶ **n.** a Batavian person.
– ORIGIN from Latin *Batavia* (from *Batavi* 'the people of Betuwe') + **-AN**.

bat·boy /ˈbatˌboi/ ▶ **n.** a boy who is employed to look after and retrieve bats during a baseball game and as a general assistant at other times.

batch /baCH/ ▶ **n.** a quantity or consignment of goods produced at one time: ***a batch of** cookies* | *the company undertakes thirty-six separate quality control checks on every batch*. ■ informal a number of things or people regarded as a group or set: ***a batch of** hostile letters came*. ■ Computing a group of records processed as a single unit, usually without input from a user.
▶ **v.** [with obj.] arrange (things) in sets or groups.
– ORIGIN late 15th cent. (in the senses 'process of baking,' 'quantity produced at one baking'): based on an Old English word related to *bacan* (see **BAKE**). Current senses date from the early 18th cent.

batch file ▶ **n.** a computer file containing a list of instructions to be carried out in turn.

batch proc·ess·ing ▶ **n.** the performing of an industrial process on material in batches of a limited quantity or number. ■ Computing the processing of previously collected jobs in a single batch.

bate /bāt/ ▶ **v.** [no obj.] Falconry (of a hawk) beat the wings in an attempt to escape from the perch: *the hawks bated when the breeze got in their feathers*.
– ORIGIN late Middle English: from Old French *batre* 'to beat' (see also **BATTER**[1]).

ba·teau /baˈtō/ ▶ **n.** (pl. **bateaux** /-ˈtōz/) a light flat-bottomed riverboat used in eastern and central North America.
– ORIGIN early 18th cent.: French, literally 'boat.'

bat·ed /ˈbātid/ ▶ **adj.** (in phrase **with bated breath**) in great suspense; very anxiously or excitedly: *he waited for a reply to his offer with bated breath*.
– ORIGIN late 16th cent.: from the past participle of obsolete *bate* 'restrain,' from **ABATE**.

> **USAGE** The spelling **baited breath** instead of **bated breath** is a common mistake. Almost a third of citations for this idiom in the Oxford English Corpus are for the incorrect spelling.

Bates·i·an mim·ic·ry /ˈbātsēən/ ▶ **n.** Zoology mimicry in which an edible animal is protected by its resemblance to a noxious one that is avoided by predators. Compare with **MÜLLERIAN MIMICRY**.
– ORIGIN late 19th cent.: named after Henry W. *Bates* (1825–92), the English naturalist who first described it.

Bate·son /ˈbātsən/, William (1861–1926), English geneticist. He coined the term *genetics* in its current sense and publicized the work of Gregor Mendel.

bat·fish /ˈbatˌfiSH/ ▶ **n.** (pl. **same** or **batfishes**)
1 a fish of tropical and temperate seas with a flattened body that is round or almost triangular when viewed from above. It typically has a hard or spiny covering. ● Family Ogcocephalidae: several genera and species, including the southern African *Halieuta fitzsimonsi*.
2 a deep-bodied, laterally compressed marine fish of the Indo-Pacific region that resembles an angelfish. ● Genus *Platax*, family Ephippidae: several species, including the large *P. pinnatus* (also called **ANGELFISH**).

bat·fowl /ˈbatˌfoul/ ▶ **v.** [no obj.] catch birds at night by dazing them with a light and knocking them down or netting them.

bat·girl /ˈbatˌgərl/ ▶ **n.** a girl who is employed to look after and retrieve bats during a baseball game and as a general assistant at other times.

Bath /baTH, bäTH/ a spa town in southwestern England; pop. 81,600 (est. 2009).

bath[1] /baTH/ ▶ **n.** (pl. **baths** /baTHs, baT͟Hz/) an act or process of immersing and washing one's body in a large container of water: ***she took a** long, hot **bath***. ■ such a container and its contents; a bathtub: *he lay thinking in the bath*. ■ (usu. **baths**) a public establishment offering bathing facilities. ■ (**baths**) a resort with a mineral spring used for medical treatment. ■ a bathroom. ■ [with modifier] a container holding a liquid or other substance in which something is immersed, typically when undergoing a process such as film developing.
▶ **v.** [with obj.] wash (someone) while immersing him or her in a container of water: *how to bath a baby*.
– PHRASES **take a bath** informal suffer a heavy financial loss.
– ORIGIN Old English *bæth*, of Germanic origin; related to Dutch *bad* and German *Bad*.

bath[2] ▶ **n.** an ancient Hebrew liquid measure equivalent to about 40 liters or 9 gallons.
– ORIGIN from Hebrew *baṯ*.

bath chair ▶ **n.** dated a kind of wheelchair for invalids, typically with a hood.
– ORIGIN early 19th cent.: named after the city of **BATH**, which attracted many invalids because of the supposed curative powers of its hot springs.

bathe /bāT͟H/ ▶ **v.** [no obj.] **1** wash by immersing one's body in water. ■ [with obj.] soak or wipe gently with liquid to clean or soothe: *she bathed and bandaged my knee*. ■ [with obj.] wash (someone) in a bath: *they bathed the baby*.
2 chiefly Brit. spend time in the ocean or a lake, river, or swimming pool for pleasure.
3 [with obj.] (usu. **be bathed**) suffuse or envelop in something: *the park lay bathed in sunshine* | *mussels bathed in garlic butter*.
– DERIVATIVES **bath·er** n.
– ORIGIN Old English *bathian*, of Germanic origin; related to Dutch and German *baden*.

ba·thet·ic /bəˈTHetik/ ▶ **adj.** producing an unintentional effect of anticlimax: *the movie manages to be poignant without becoming bathetic*.

bath·house /ˈbaTHˌhous/ ▶ **n. 1** a building with baths for communal use.
2 a building where swimmers change clothes.

Bath·i·nette /ˌbaTHəˈnet/ ▶ **n.** trademark a portable folding bathtub for infants.
– ORIGIN a play on the word **BASSINET**.

bath·ing beau·ty ▶ **n.** a contestant in a beauty contest in which bathing suits are worn.

bath·ing cap ▶ **n.** a close-fitting elastic cap worn while swimming to keep the hair dry or to reduce friction.

bath·ing ma·chine /ˈbāT͟HiNG/ ▶ **n.** historical a wheeled hut drawn to the edge of the sea, used for changing in and swimming from.

bath·ing suit ▶ **n.** a garment worn for swimming; a swimsuit.

bath mat ▶ **n.** a mat for someone to stand on after getting out of a bathtub. ■ a rubber mat placed in the bottom of a bathtub to prevent someone from slipping while getting in or out.

bath·o·lith /ˈbaTHəˌliTH/ ▶ **n.** Geology a very large igneous intrusion extending deep in the earth's crust.
– ORIGIN early 20th cent.: coined in German from Greek *bathos* 'depth' + **-LITH**.

ba·thos /ˈbāTHäs/ ▶ **n.** (esp. in a work of literature) an effect of anticlimax created by an unintentional lapse in mood from the sublime to the trivial or ridiculous.
– ORIGIN mid 17th cent. (first recorded in the Greek sense): from Greek, literally 'depth.' The current sense was introduced by Alexander Pope in the early 18th cent.

bath·robe /ˈbaTHˌrōb/ ▶ **n.** a robe, typically made of terry cloth, worn esp. before and after taking a bath.

bath·room /ˈbaTHˌro͞om, -ˌro͝om/ ▶ **n.** a room containing a bathtub or a shower and usually also a sink and a toilet. ■ a set of matching units to be fitted in such a room, esp. as sold together. ■ a room containing a toilet: *I have to go to the bathroom*.
– PHRASES **go to** (or **use**) **the bathroom** urinate or defecate.

bath·room break ▶ **n.** informal a break in a meeting or other organized gathering to allow those in attendance to use the bathroom.

bath salts ▶ **plural n.** a crystalline substance that is dissolved in bath water to soften or perfume the water.

Bath·she·ba /ˌbaTHˈSHēbə/ (in the Bible) the mother of Solomon, she was originally the wife of Uriah the Hittite, and later one of the wives of David.

bath sponge ▶ **n.** a marine sponge of warm waters, the fibrous skeleton of which is used as a sponge for washing. ● Genera *Spongia* and *Hippospongia*, family Spongiidae.

bath·tub /ˈbaTHˌtəb/ ▶ **n.** a tub, usually installed in a bathroom, in which to bathe.

Bath·urst /ˈbaTHərst/ former name (until 1973) of **BANJUL**.

b

bathy- ▶ **comb. form** relating to depth: *bathymetry* | *bathysphere.*
– ORIGIN from Greek *bathus* 'deep.'

bath·y·al /ˈbaTHēəl/ ▶ **adj.** of or relating to the zone of the sea between the continental shelf and the abyssal zone.

ba·thym·e·ter /bəˈTHimitər/ ▶ **n.** an instrument used to measure the depth of water in oceans, seas, or lakes.
– ORIGIN late 19th cent.: from Greek *bathos* 'depth' + **-METER.**

ba·thym·e·try /bəˈTHimətrē/ ▶ **n.** the measurement of depth of water in oceans, seas, or lakes.
– DERIVATIVES **bath·y·met·ric** /ˌbaTHəˈmetrik/ **adj.**
– ORIGIN mid 19th cent.: from Greek *bathus* 'deep' + **-METRY.**

bath·y·pe·lag·ic /ˌbaTHəpəˈlajik/ ▶ **adj.** Biology (of fish and other organisms) inhabiting the deep sea where the environment is dark and cold, approximately 3,300–9,800 feet (1,000–3,000 m) below the surface.

bath·y·scaphe /ˈbaTHəˌskaf/ ▶ **n.** chiefly historical a manned submersible vessel of a kind used by the French deep-sea explorer Auguste Piccard (1884–1962).
– ORIGIN 1940s: coined in French by its inventor, Auguste Piccard, from Greek *bathus* 'deep' + *skaphos* 'vessel; hull (of a ship).'

bath·y·sphere /ˈbaTHəˌsfir/ ▶ **n.** a manned spherical chamber for deep-sea observation, lowered by cable from a ship.
– ORIGIN 1930s: from Greek *bathus* 'deep' + **SPHERE.**

ba·tik /bəˈtēk/ ▶ **n.** a method (originally used in Java) of producing colored designs on textiles by dyeing them, having first applied wax to the parts to be left undyed. ■ an item or piece of cloth treated in this way.
– ORIGIN late 19th cent.: from Javanese, literally 'painted.'

Ba·tis·ta /bəˈtēstə/, Fulgencio (1901–73), Cuban soldier and statesman; president 1940–44 and 1952–59; full name *Fulgencio Batista y Zaldívar.* Despite support from the US, his second government was overthrown by Fidel Castro.

ba·tiste /bəˈtēst/ ▶ **n.** a fine, light linen or cotton fabric resembling cambric.
– ORIGIN early 19th cent.: from French (earlier *batiche*); probably related to *battre* 'to beat.'

bat·man /ˈbatmən/ ▶ **n.** (pl. **batmen**) dated (in the British armed forces) an officer's personal servant.
– ORIGIN mid 18th cent. (originally denoting an orderly in charge of the *bat horse* 'packhorse' that carried the officer's baggage): from Old French *bat* (from medieval Latin *bastum* 'packsaddle') + **MAN.**

bat mitz·vah /bät ˈmitsvə/ ▶ **n.** a religious initiation ceremony for a Jewish girl aged twelve years and one day, regarded as the age of religious maturity. ■ the girl undergoing such a ceremony.
– ORIGIN from Hebrew *baṯ miṣwāh* 'daughter of the commandment,' on the pattern of **BAR MITZVAH.**

ba·ton /bəˈtän/ ▶ **n.** a short stick or staff or something resembling one, in particular: ■ a thin stick used by a conductor to direct an orchestra or choir. ■ Track & Field a short stick or tube passed from runner to runner in a relay race. ■ a long stick carried and twirled by a drum major. ■ a police officer's club. ■ a staff symbolizing office or authority, esp. one carried by a field marshal. ■ Heraldry a narrow bend truncated at each end. ■ a short bar replacing some figures on the dial of a clock or watch. ■ (**batons**) one of the suits in some tarot packs, corresponding to wands in others.
– PHRASES **pass (on) the baton** hand over a particular duty or responsibility. **take up** (or **pick up**) **the baton** accept a duty or responsibility. **under the baton of** (of an orchestra or choir) conducted by: *under the baton of Sir Edward Downes.*
– ORIGIN early 16th cent. (denoting a staff or cudgel): from French *bâton,* earlier *baston,* from late Latin *bastum* 'stick.'

Bat·on Rouge /ˌbatn ˈro͞oZH/ the capital of Louisiana, in the southeastern central part of the state, on the Mississippi River; pop. 223,689 (est. 2008).
– ORIGIN French, literally 'red stick,' with reference to a post placed as a boundary marker for the settlement.

Ba·tra·chi·a /bəˈtrākēə/ Zoology another term, esp. formerly, for **ANURA.**
– ORIGIN modern Latin (plural), from Greek *batrakhos* 'frog.'

ba·tra·chi·an /bəˈtrākēən/ ▶ **n. & adj.** Zoology another term for **ANURAN.**

bats /bats/ ▶ **adj.** [predic.] informal, dated (of a person) crazy; insane.
– ORIGIN early 20th cent.: from the phrase *have bats in the belfry* (see **BAT**[2]).

bat·shit /ˈbatˌSHit/ ▶ **adj.** vulgar slang completely mad or crazy.

bats·man /ˈbatsmən/ ▶ **n.** (pl. **batsmen**) a player, esp. in baseball and cricket, who is batting or whose chief skill is in batting.
– DERIVATIVES **bats·man·ship** /-ˌSHip/ **n.**

Bat·swa·na /bätˈswänə/ ▶ **n. & adj.** see **TSWANA.**

batt /bat/ ▶ **n.** a piece of felted material used for lining or insulating items such as quilts and sleeping bags. ■ a piece of fiberglass used to insulate buildings.
– ORIGIN late Middle English (in the general sense 'lump, piece'): of unknown origin.

bat·tal·ion /bəˈtalyən/ ▶ **n.** a large body of troops ready for battle, esp. an infantry unit forming part of a brigade typically commanded by a lieutenant colonel. ■ a large, organized group of people pursuing a common aim or sharing a major undertaking.
– ORIGIN late 16th cent.: from French *bataillon,* from Italian *battaglione,* from *battaglia* 'battle,' from Latin (see **BATTLE**).

Bat·tam·bang /ˈbatəmˌbaNG/ (also **Batdambang**) the capital of a province of the same name in western Cambodia; pop. 182,600 (est. 2009).

batte·ment /ˈbatmənt/ ▶ **n.** [with modifier] Ballet a movement in which one leg is moved outward from the body and in again: *performing battements tendus.*
– ORIGIN mid 19th cent.: French, literally 'beating.'

bat·ten[1] /ˈbatn/ ▶ **n.** a long, flat strip of squared wood or metal used to hold something in place or as a fastening against a wall. ■ a strip of wood or metal for securing the edges of a tarpaulin that covers a ship's hatch. ■ a strip of wood or plastic used to stiffen and extend the leech of a sail.
▶ **v.** [with obj.] strengthen or fasten (something) with battens: *Stephen was* ***battening down*** *the shutters.*
– PHRASES **batten down the hatches** Nautical secure a ship's hatch-tarpaulins, esp. when rough weather is expected. ■ prepare for a difficulty or crisis.
– ORIGIN late 15th cent.: from Old French *batant,* present participle (used as a noun) of *batre* 'to beat,' from Latin *battuere.*

bat·ten[2] ▶ **v.** [no obj.] (**batten on**) thrive or prosper at the expense of (someone): *multinational monopolies batten on the working classes.*
– ORIGIN late 16th cent. (in the sense 'improve in condition, grow fat'): from Old Norse *batna* 'get better,' related to **BETTER**[1].

bat·ten·ing /ˈbatn-iNG/ ▶ **n.** the application or addition of battens. ■ a structure formed with battens.

bat·ter[1] /ˈbatər/ ▶ **v.** [with obj.] strike repeatedly with hard blows; pound heavily and insistently: *a prisoner was* ***battered to death*** *with a table leg* | figurative *their idealism has been battered.* ■ (often as noun **battering**) subject (one's spouse, partner, or child) to repeated violence and assault. ■ (usu. as noun **battering**) censure, criticize, or defeat severely: *the movie* ***took a battering*** *from critics.*
– DERIVATIVES **bat·ter·er** **n.**
– ORIGIN Middle English: from Old French *batre* 'to beat' (from Latin *battuere*) + **-ER**[3].

bat·ter[2] ▶ **n. 1** a semiliquid mixture of flour, egg, and milk or water used in cooking, esp. for making cakes or for coating food before frying.
2 Printing, historical a damaged area of metal type or a printing block.
– ORIGIN late Middle English: from Old French *bateure* 'the action of beating,' from *batre* 'to beat.'

bat·ter[3] ▶ **n.** (in various sports, esp. baseball) a player who is batting.

bat·ter[4] ▶ **n.** a gradual backward slope in a wall or similar structure.
▶ **v.** [no obj.] (of a wall) have a receding slope.
– ORIGIN mid 16th cent. (as a verb): of unknown origin.

bat·tered[1] /ˈbatərd/ ▶ **adj.** injured by repeated blows or punishment: *he finished the day battered and bruised.* ■ having suffered repeated violence from a spouse, partner, or parent: *a battered wife.* ■ (of a thing) damaged by age and repeated use; shabby: *a pair of battered black boots.*

bat·tered[2] ▶ **adj.** (of food) coated in batter and deep-fried until crisp.

bat·tered child syn·drome ▶ **n.** the set of symptoms, injuries, and signs of mistreatment seen on a severely or repeatedly abused child.

bat·tered wom·an syn·drome ▶ **n.** the set of symptoms, injuries, and signs of mistreatment seen in a woman who has been repeatedly abused by a husband or other male figure.

bat·te·rie /ˈbatərē/ ▶ **n.** Ballet the action of beating or crossing the feet or calves together during a leap or jump.
– ORIGIN early 18th cent.: French, literally 'beating.'

bat·te·rie de cui·sine /batˈrē də kwēˈzēn/ ▶ **n.** the apparatus or set of utensils for serving or preparing a meal.
– ORIGIN late 18th cent.: French, literally 'set of equipment for the kitchen.' The sense of 'set' developed from the original meaning of 'collection of artillery equipment (for "beating" the enemy)'; see also **BATTERY.**

bat·ter·ing par·ent syn·drome ▶ **n.** the set of symptoms and signs indicating a psychological disorder in a parent or child-care provider resulting in a tendency toward repeated abuse of a child.

bat·ter·ing ram ▶ **n.** a heavy object swung or rammed against a door to break it down: figurative *a battering ram to crush opposing views.* ■ historical a heavy beam, originally with an end in the form of a carved ram's head, used in breaching fortifications.

Bat·tery /ˈbatərē/ (**the Battery**) a historic area at the southern end of Manhattan Island in New York City.

bat·ter·y /ˈbatərē/ ▶ **n.** (pl. **batteries**) **1** a container consisting of one or more cells, in which chemical energy is converted into electricity and used as a source of power: [as modifier] *battery power.*
2 a fortified emplacement for heavy guns. ■ an artillery subunit of guns, men, and vehicles.
3 a set of similar units of equipment, typically when connected together: *a battery of equipment to monitor blood pressure.* ■ an extensive series, sequence, or range of things: *children given a battery of tests.*
4 Law the crime or tort of unconsented physical contact with another person, even where the contact is not violent but merely menacing or offensive. See also **ASSAULT AND BATTERY.**
5 (**the battery**) Baseball the pitcher and the catcher in a game, considered as a unit.
– ORIGIN Middle English: from French *batterie,* from *battre* 'to strike,' from Latin *battuere.* The original sense was 'metal articles wrought by hammering,' later 'a number of pieces of artillery used together'; on this was based a sense 'a number of Leyden jars connected up so as to discharge simultaneously' (mid 18th cent.), from which sense 1 developed. The general meaning 'a set or series of similar units' (sense 3) dates from the late 19th cent.

bat·ting ▶ **n.** cotton wadding prepared in sheets for use in quilts.

bat·ting av·er·age ▶ **n.** Baseball the average performance of a batter, expressed as a ratio of a batter's safe hits per official times at bat.

bat·ting cage ▶ **n.** Baseball an area for batting practice that is enclosed by fencing or netting.

bat·ting or·der ▶ **n.** Baseball the order in which batters take their turn at bat.

bat·tle /ˈbatl/ ▶ **n.** a sustained fight between large, organized armed forces: [in names] *the Battle of Shiloh* | *he died in battle.* ■ a lengthy and difficult conflict or struggle: *the battle over the future shape of Europe* | *the battle against aging.*
▶ **v.** [no obj.] fight or struggle tenaciously to achieve or resist something: *he has been* ***battling against*** *the illness* | *representatives from eight countries are* ***battling for*** *the title.* ■ [with obj.] engage in a fight or struggle against: *firefighters battled a 9,800-acre brush fire.*
– PHRASES **battle it out** fight or compete to a definite conclusion. **do battle** fight; engage in conflict: *do battle with the forces of evil.* **battle royal** (pl. **battles royal**) a fiercely contested fight or dispute: *there promises to be a battle royal between the two companies.* **battle stations** the positions taken by military personnel in preparation for battle (often used as a command or signal to prepare for battle). **half the battle** an important step toward achieving something: *he never gives in, and that's half the battle.*
– ORIGIN Middle English: from Old French *bataille* (noun), *bataillier* (verb), based on late Latin *battualia* 'military or gladiatorial exercises,' from Latin *battuere* 'to beat.'

bat·tle-ax (also **battle-axe**) ▶ **n. 1** a large broad-bladed ax used in ancient warfare.
2 informal a formidably aggressive older woman.

Bat·tle·born State /ˈbatlˌbôrn/ nickname for **NEVADA.**

Bat·tle Creek a city in southern Michigan, noted as a center of the cereal industry; pop. 52,053 (est. 2008).

bat·tle·cruis·er /ˈbatlˌkro͞ozər/ ▶ **n.** historical a large warship of a type built in the early 20th century, carrying similar armament to a battleship but faster and more lightly armored.

bat·tle cry ▶ n. a word or phrase shouted by soldiers going into battle to express solidarity and intimidate the enemy. ■ a slogan expressing the ideals of people promoting a cause.

bat·tle·dore /ˈbatl,dôr/ ▶ n. historical (also **battledore and shuttlecock**) a game played with a shuttlecock and rackets; a forerunner of badminton. ■ the small racket used in this.
– ORIGIN late Middle English (in the sense 'a paddle-shaped implement used in washing clothes'): perhaps from Provençal *batedor* 'beater, paddle,' from *batre* 'to beat.'

bat·tle fa·tigue ▶ n. another term for SHELL SHOCK.

bat·tle·field /ˈbatl,fēld/ (also **battleground** /-,ground/) ▶ n. the piece of ground on which a battle is or was fought: *death on the battlefield* | [as modifier] *battlefield conditions.* ■ a place or situation of strife or conflict: *an ideological battlefield.*

bat·tle·front /ˈbatl,frənt/ ▶ n. the region or line along which opposing armies engage in combat. ■ the area in which opponents or opposing ideas meet.

bat·tle group ▶ n. a military force created to fight together, typically consisting of several different types of troops.

bat·tle jack·et ▶ n. a style of waist-length jacket worn by army personnel. ■ any jacket of a similar cut.

bat·tle·ment /ˈbatlmənt/ ▶ n. (usu. **battlements**) a parapet at the top of a wall, usually of a fort or castle, that has regularly spaced, squared openings for shooting through. ■ a section of roof enclosed by this.
– DERIVATIVES **bat·tle·ment·ed** adj.
– ORIGIN late Middle English: from Old French *bataillier* 'fortify with movable defense turrets,' possibly related to BATTLE.

battlement

bat·tler /ˈbatlər, ˈbatl-ər/ ▶ n. a person who battles or fights. ■ a person who refuses to admit defeat in the face of difficulty: *a battler taking swings at opponents and rallying friends.*

bat·tle·ship /ˈbatl,sHip/ ▶ n. a heavy warship of a type built chiefly in the late 19th and early 20th centuries, with extensive armor and large-caliber guns.
– ORIGIN late 18th cent.: shortening of *line-of-battle ship*, originally with reference to the largest wooden warships.

bat·tle·ship gray ▶ n. a bluish gray color, typically used for warships to reduce their visibility.

bat·tle star ▶ n. former term for SERVICE STAR.

bat·tle·wag·on /ˈbatl,wagən/ (also **battle wagon**) ▶ n. informal a battleship or an armored vehicle.

bat·tue /baˈto͞o/ ▶ n. the driving of game toward hunters by beaters. ■ a hunting party arranged in such a way.
– ORIGIN early 19th cent.: from French, feminine past participle of *battre* 'to beat,' from Latin *battuere.*

bat·ty /ˈbatē/ ▶ adj. (**battier**, **battiest**) informal crazy; insane: *you'll drive me batty!*
– DERIVATIVES **bat·ti·ly** /ˈbatəlē/ adv., **bat·ti·ness** n.
– ORIGIN early 20th cent.: from BAT[2] + -Y[1]. Compare with BATS.

Ba·twa /baˈtwä/ plural form of TWA.

bat·wing /ˈbat,wiNG/ ▶ adj. [attrib.] (of a sleeve) having a deep armhole and a tight cuff. ■ (of a garment) having such sleeves.

bau·ble /ˈbôbəl/ ▶ n. **1** a small, showy trinket or decoration. ■ something of no importance or worth. **2** historical a baton formerly used as an emblem by jesters.
– ORIGIN Middle English: from Old French *baubel* 'child's toy,' of unknown origin.

Bau·cis /ˈbôsis/ Greek Mythology the wife of Philemon.

baud /bôd/ ▶ n. (pl. **same** or **bauds**) chiefly Computing a unit used to express the speed of transmission of electronic signals, corresponding to one information unit or event per second. ■ a unit of data transmission speed for a modem of one bit per second (in fact there is usually more than one bit per event).
– ORIGIN 1930s: coined in French from the name of J. M. E. *Baudot* (1845–1903), French engineer who invented a telegraph printing system.

Bau·de·laire /,bōdəˈle(ə)r, -dlˈe(ə)r/, Charles (Pierre) (1821–67), French poet and critic. He is noted for *Les Fleurs du mal* (1857), a series of 101 lyrics that explore his isolation and melancholy and the attraction of evil and the macabre.

Bau·dril·lard /,bōdrē'(y)är/, Jean (1929–2007), French sociologist and cultural critic, associated with postmodernism.

Baugh /bô/, Sammy (1914–2008), US football player; full name *Samuel Adrian Baugh*; known as **Slingin' Sammy**. He played for the Washington Redskins 1937–52, where his trademark pinpoint passing revolutionized professional football by making the forward pass a routine play from scrimmage. In 1943, he became the only player to lead the National Football League in passing, punting, and interceptions in the same season. Football Hall of Fame (1963).

Bau·haus /ˈbou,hous/ a school of design established by Walter Gropius in Weimar in 1919, best known for its designs of objects based on functionalism and simplicity.
– ORIGIN German, 'house of architecture,' from *Bau* 'building' + *Haus* 'house.'

baulk ▶ v. & n. Brit. variant spelling of BALK.

baulk·y ▶ adj. British spelling of BALKY.

Baum /bôm, bäm/, L. Frank (1856–1919), US journalist and author; full name *Lyman Frank Baum.* His many children's books include *Father Goose: His Book* (1899), *The Wonderful Wizard of Oz* (1900), and other Oz books.

Bau·mé scale /bōˈmā, ˈbōmā/ ▶ n. a scale with arbitrary markings, used with a hydrometer to measure the relative density of liquids.
– ORIGIN named for Antoine Baumé (1728–1804), French chemist.

Bausch /bousH/, John Jacob (1830–1926), US businessman, born in Germany. He cofounded (with Henry Lomb) the Bausch & Lomb Optical Company in 1853.

baux·ite /ˈbôksīt/ ▶ n. an amorphous clayey rock that is the chief commercial ore of aluminum. It consists largely of hydrated alumina with variable proportions of iron oxides.
– DERIVATIVES **baux·it·ic** /,bôkˈsitik/ adj.
– ORIGIN mid 19th cent.: from French, from *Les Baux* (the name of a village near Arles in southeastern France, near which it was first found) + -ITE[1].

ba·var·dage /,bavərˈdäzH/ ▶ n. idle gossip; chitchat.
– ORIGIN French, from *bavarder* 'to chatter,' from *bavard* 'talkative,' from *bave* 'drivel.'

Ba·var·i·a /bəˈve(ə)rēə/ a state in southern Germany, formerly an independent kingdom; capital, Munich. German name BAYERN.

Ba·var·i·an /bəˈve(ə)rēən/ ▶ adj. of or relating to Bavaria, its people, or their language.
▶ n. **1** a native or inhabitant of Bavaria.
2 the dialect of German used in Bavaria.

ba·va·rois /,bävärˈwä/ (also **bavaroise** /-ˈwäz/) ▶ n. a dessert containing gelatin and whipped cream, served cold.
– ORIGIN mid 19th cent.: French, literally 'Bavarian.'

baw·bee /ˈbôbē/ ▶ n. Scottish & N. Irish a coin of low value. ■ historical a former silver coin worth three (later six) Scottish pennies.
– ORIGIN mid 16th cent.: from the name of the laird of Sille*bawby*, mint master under James V.

bawd /bôd/ ▶ n. archaic a woman in charge of a brothel.
– ORIGIN late Middle English: shortened from obsolete *bawdstrot*, from Old French *baudestroyt* 'procuress,' from *baude* 'shameless.'

bawd·ry /ˈbôdrē/ ▶ n. obscenity in speech or writing.

bawd·y /ˈbôdē/ ▶ adj. (**bawdier**, **bawdiest**) dealing with sexual matters in a comical way; humorously indecent.
▶ n. humorously indecent talk or writing.
– DERIVATIVES **bawd·i·ly** /-dəlē/ adv., **bawd·i·ness** n.

bawd·y house ▶ n. archaic a brothel.

bawl /bôl/ ▶ v. **1** [reporting verb] shout or call out noisily and unrestrainedly: [with direct speech] *"Move!" bawled the drill sergeant* | [with obj.] *lustily bawling out the hymns* | [no obj.] *Joe bawled with laughter.*
2 [no obj.] weep or cry noisily: *she began to bawl like a child* | (as adj. **bawling**) *bawling babies.*
▶ n. a loud, unrestrained shout.
– PHRASAL VERBS **bawl someone out** reprimand someone angrily: *tales of how she bawled out employees.*
– ORIGIN late Middle English (in the sense '(of an animal) howl, bark'): imitative.

Bax·ter State Park /ˈbakstər/ a preserve in northern Maine that incorporates Mount Katahdin and the northern end of the Appalachian Trail.

bay[1] /bā/ ▶ n. a broad inlet of the sea where the land curves inward: [in place names] *San Francisco Bay* | *the Bay of Biscay.* ■ an indentation or recess in a range of hills or mountains.
– ORIGIN late Middle English: from Old French *baie*, from medieval Latin *baia.*

bay[2] ▶ n. **1** (also **bay tree**, **bay laurel**, or **sweet bay**) an evergreen Mediterranean shrub of the laurel family, with deep green leaves and purple berries. Its aromatic leaves are used in cooking and were formerly used to make triumphal crowns for victors. ● *Laurus nobilis*, family Lauraceae.
2 a similarly aromatic tree or shrub of North America, esp. the bayberry used in the preparation of bay rum.
– ORIGIN late Middle English (denoting the laurel berry): from Old French *baie*, from Latin *baca* 'berry.'

bay[3] ▶ n. a recessed or enclosed area, in particular: ■ a space created by a window-line projecting outward from a wall. ■ short for BAY WINDOW. ■ a section of wall between two buttresses or columns, esp. in the nave of a church. ■ [with modifier] a compartment with a particular function in a motor vehicle, aircraft, or ship: *an engine bay* | *a bomb bay.* ■ an area allocated or marked off for a specified purpose: *a loading bay.* ■ Computing a cabinet, or a space in the cabinet, into which an electronic device is installed: *a drive bay.*
– ORIGIN late Middle English: from Old French *baie*, from *baer* 'to gape,' from medieval Latin *batare*, of unknown origin.

bay[4] ▶ adj. (of a horse) brown with black points.
▶ n. a bay horse.
– ORIGIN Middle English: from Old French *bai*, from Latin *badius.*

bay[5] ▶ v. [no obj.] (of a dog, esp. a large one) bark or howl loudly: *the dogs bayed* | *a jackal baying at the moon.* ■ (of a group of people) shout loudly, typically to demand something: *as a mob bayed below, the king was dead.* ■ [with obj.] archaic bay at: *a pack of wolves baying at the moon.*
▶ n. the sound of baying, esp. that of hounds in close pursuit of their quarry.
– PHRASES **at bay** forced to confront one's attackers or pursuers; cornered. **bring someone/something to bay** trap or corner a person or animal being hunted or chased. **hold** (or **keep**) **someone/something at bay** prevent someone or something from approaching or having an effect. **stand at bay** turn to face one's pursuers.
– ORIGIN Middle English (as a noun): from Old French *a)bai* (noun), ((*a*)*baiier* (verb) 'to bark,' of imitative origin.

ba·ya·dère /ˈbīə,de(ə)r/ ▶ n. a Hindu dancing girl, in particular one at a southern Indian temple.
– ORIGIN from French, from Portuguese *bailadeira*, from *bailar* 'to dance' (related to medieval Latin *ballare* 'to dance').

Bay Ar·e·a the region around San Francisco Bay, in north central California. Oakland is the hub of the East Bay, San Jose of the South Bay.

bay·ber·ry /ˈbā,berē/ ▶ n. (pl. **bayberries**) **1** a North American shrub with aromatic leathery leaves and waxy berries. See also WAX MYRTLE. ● Genus *Myrica*, family Myricaceae: several species, in particular **northern bayberry** (*M. pensylvanica*) and **black bayberry** (*M. heterophylla*).
2 a tropical American shrub with aromatic leaves that are used in the preparation of bay rum. Also called BAY RUM TREE. ● *Pimenta racemosa*, family Myrtaceae.
– ORIGIN late 17th cent.: from BAY[2] + BERRY.

Bay Cit·y an industrial city in eastern Michigan, on the Saginaw River, near Lake Huron; pop. 33,874 (est. 2008).

Bay·ern /ˈbīərn/ German name for BAVARIA.

Bayes' the·o·rem /bāz/ Statistics a theorem describing how the conditional probability of each of a set of possible causes for a given observed outcome can be computed from knowledge of the probability of each cause and the conditional probability of the outcome of each cause.
– DERIVATIVES **Bayes·i·an** /ˈbāzēən/ adj.
– ORIGIN mid 19th cent.: named after Thomas *Bayes* (1702–61), English mathematician.

Ba·yeux Tap·es·try /bäˈyo͞o, bāˈyo͞o/ a medieval English embroidery made between 1066 and 1077, telling the story of the Norman Conquest.

Bay·kal, Lake variant spelling of BAIKAL, LAKE.

bay lau·rel ▶ n. another term for BAY[2].

bay leaf ▶ n. the aromatic, usually dried, leaf of the bay tree, used in cooking.

Bay·lor /ˈbālər/, Elgin Gay (1934–), US basketball player. He played for the Lakers (Minneapolis until 1960, then Los Angeles) 1958–72. Basketball Hall of Fame (1976).

b

Bay of Ben·gal, Bay of Fun·dy, etc. see **Bengal, Bay of; Fundy, Bay of,** etc.

bay·o·net /ˈbāənit, ˌbāəˈnet/ ▶ **n. 1** a swordlike stabbing blade that may be fixed to the muzzle of a rifle for use in hand-to-hand fighting.
2 [as modifier] denoting a fitting for a light bulb, camera lens, or other appliance that is engaged by being pushed into a socket and then twisted to lock it in place.

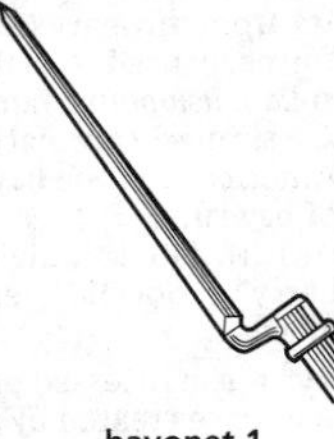
bayonet 1

▶ **v.** (**bayonets, bayoneting, bayoneted**) [with obj.] stab (someone) with a bayonet.
– ORIGIN late 17th cent. (denoting a kind of short dagger): from French *baïonnette*, from *Bayonne*, the name of a town in southwestern France, where they were first made.

Bay·onne /bāˈyōn/ an industrial port city in northeastern New Jersey, on New York Bay; pop. 57,448 (est. 2008).

bay·ou /ˈbīo͞o, ˈbīō/ ▶ **n.** (pl. **bayous**) (in the southern US) a marshy outlet of a lake or river.
– ORIGIN mid 18th cent.: from Louisiana French, from Choctaw *bayuk*.

Bay·ou State a nickname for the state of **Louisiana**.

Bay·ou Teche /ˈbīˌo͞o ˈtesh/ a water route in south central Louisiana, at the heart of Cajun Country. Also called **the Teche**.

Bay·reuth /ˈbīˌroit, bīˈroit/ a town in Bavaria where Wagner is buried and where festivals of his operas are held regularly.

bay rum ▶ **n.** an aromatic liquid, used esp. for the hair or as an aftershave, typically distilled from rum and the leaves of the bayberry.

bay rum tree another name for **bayberry** (sense 2).

bay·side /ˈbāˌsīd/ ▶ **adj.** on or near the shore of a bay.
▶ **n.** the land on the shore of a bay.

Bay State a nickname for the state of **Massachusetts**.

Bay·town /ˈbāˌtoun/ a city in southeastern Texas, east of Houston, a center of the oil industry; pop. 70,330 (est. 2008).

bay tree ▶ **n.** see **bay**[2].

bay win·dow ▶ **n.** a window built to project outward from an outside wall.

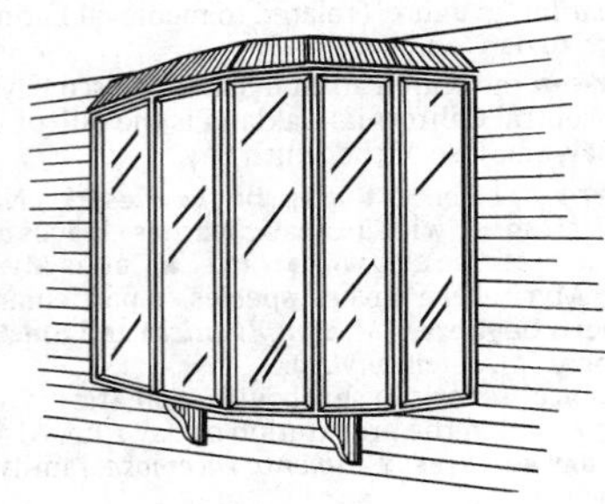
bay window

ba·zaar /bəˈzär/ ▶ **n.** a market in a Middle-Eastern country. ■ a fundraising sale of goods, typically for charity. ■ dated a large shop selling miscellaneous goods.
– ORIGIN late 16th cent.: from Italian *bazarro*, from Turkish, from Persian *bāzār* 'market.'

ba·zil·lion /bəˈzilyən/ ▶ **cardinal number** informal a very large exaggerated number: *you were going a bazillion miles per hour!*
– ORIGIN 1980s: probably a blend of *billion* and *gazillion* (also a large exaggerated number).

ba·zoo /bəˈzo͞o/ ▶ **n.** (pl. **bazoos**) informal **1** a person's mouth.
2 a person's buttocks or anus.
– ORIGIN late 19th cent.: of unknown origin; compare with Dutch *bazuin* 'trombone, trumpet.'

ba·zoo·ka /bəˈzo͞okə/ ▶ **n.**
1 a short-range tubular rocket launcher used against tanks.
2 a trombonelike type of kazoo.
– ORIGIN 1930s sense 2: apparently from slang **bazoo** in the original sense 'kazoo.'

bazooka 1

ba·zoom /bəˈzo͞om/ ▶ **n.** (usu. **bazooms**) informal a woman's breast.
– ORIGIN 1950s: probably an alteration of **bosom**.

BB ▶ **symbol** a standard size of lead pellet used in air rifles.
▶ **abbr.** Baseball base on balls.

b-ball ▶ **n.** informal basketball.

BBC ▶ **abbr.** British Broadcasting Corporation.

BB gun ▶ **n.** an air rifle that fires BBs.

BBIN ▶ **abbr.** Bangladesh, Bhutan, India, and Nepal, considered as a group with regard to development, public health, and economic issues.

bbl. ▶ **abbr.** barrels (esp. of oil).

b-boy ▶ **n.** informal a young man involved with hip-hop culture.
– ORIGIN 1980s: *b*-probably from the noun **beat** or from *breakdancing*.

BBQ ▶ **abbr.** informal barbecue.

BBS ▶ **abbr.** Computing bulletin board system.

BC ▶ **abbr.** ■ before Christ (used to indicate that a date is before the Christian Era). ■ British Columbia (in official postal use). ■ Batallion Commander.

> **USAGE** In recent years, some writers have begun using the abbreviations CE (of the Common Era) in place of AD, and BCE (before the Common Era) in place of BC. See also usage at **AD**.

bcc ▶ **abbr.** blind carbon copy, a copy of an e-mail sent to someone whose name and address isn't visible to other recipients.

BCD ▶ **abbr.** ■ Military bad conduct discharge. ■ binary coded decimal.

BCE ▶ **abbr.** ■ Bachelor of Chemical Engineering. ■ Bachelor of Civil Engineering. ■ before the Common Era (used of dates before the Christian era, esp. by non-Christians).

B cell ▶ **n.** Physiology a lymphocyte not processed by the thymus gland, and responsible for producing antibodies. Also called **B lymphocyte**. Compare with **T cell**.
– ORIGIN *B* for **bursa**, referring to the organ in birds where it was first identified.

BCF ▶ **abbr.** bromochlorodifluoromethane, a substance formerly used in fire extinguishers.

BCG ▶ **abbr.** Bacillus Calmette-Guérin, an antituberculosis vaccine.

B com·plex ▶ **n.** see **vitamin B**.

BD ▶ **abbr.** Bachelor of Divinity.

BDD ▶ **abbr.** body dysmorphic disorder.

Bde ▶ **abbr.** Brigade.

bdel·li·um /ˈdelēəm/ ▶ **n.** a fragrant resin produced by a number of trees related to myrrh, used in perfumes.
– ORIGIN late Middle English: via Latin from Greek *bdellion*, of Semitic origin.

bdrm. ▶ **abbr.** bedroom.

BDU ▶ **abbr.** battle dress uniform.

BE ▶ **abbr.** ■ Bachelor of Education. ■ Bachelor of Engineering. ■ bill of exchange. ■ Black English.

Be ▶ **symbol** the chemical element beryllium.

be /bē/ ▶ **v.** (sing. present **am** /am/; **are** /är/; **is** /iz/; pl. present **are**; 1st and 3rd sing. past **was** /wəz, wäz/; 2nd sing. past and pl. past **were** /wər/; present subjunctive **be**; past subjunctive **were**; present participle **being** /ˈbēiNG/; past participle **been** /bin/) **1** (usu. **there is/are**) exist: *there are no easy answers | there once was a man | there must be something wrong | I think, therefore I am.* ■ be present: *there is a boy sitting on the step | there were no curtains around the showers | Are there any castles in this area?*
2 [with adverbial] occur; take place: *the exhibition will be in November | the opening event is on October 16 | that was before the war.* ■ occupy a position in space: *the Salvation Army store was on his left | she was not at the window.* ■ stay in the same place or condition: *she was here until about ten-thirty | he's a tough customer—let him be.* ■ attend: *the days when she was in school.* ■ come; go; visit: *he's from Missouri | I have just been to Thailand | the doctor's been here twice today.*
3 [as copular verb] having the state, quality, identity, nature, role, etc., specified: *Amy was 91 | the floor was uneven | I want to be a teacher | father was not well | his hair's brown | it will be Christmas soon | "Be careful," Mr. Carter said.* ■ cost: *the tickets were $25.* ■ amount to: *one and one is two | two sixes are twelve.* ■ represent: *let A be a square matrix of order n.* ■ signify: *we were everything to each other.* ■ consist of; constitute: *the monastery was several three-story buildings.*
4 informal say: *when I got there, they were like "What are you doing here?"*
▶ **auxiliary v. 1** used with a present participle to form continuous tenses: *they are coming | he had been reading | she will be waiting.*
2 used with a past participle to form the passive mood: *it was done | it is said | his book will be published.*
3 [with infinitive] used to indicate something due to happen: *construction is to begin next summer | I was to meet him at 6:30.* ■ used to express obligation or necessity: *you are to follow these orders | they said I was to remain on board.* ■ used to express possibility: *these snakes are to be found in North America | she was nowhere to be seen.* ■ used to hypothesize about something that might happen: *if I were to lose | if I was to tell you, you'd think I was crazy | were she to cure me, what could I offer her?*
4 archaic used with the past participle of intransitive verbs to form perfect tenses: *I am returned | all humanity is fallen.*
– PHRASES **as/that was** archaic as someone or something was previously called: *General Dunstaple had married Miss Hughes that was.* **the be-all and end-all** informal a feature of an activity or a way of life that is of greater importance than any other. **be oneself** act naturally, according to one's character and instincts. **be that as it may** see **may**[1]. **be there for someone** be available to support or comfort someone while they are experiencing difficulties or adversities. **been there, done that** see **there**. **not be oneself** not feel well. **-to-be** [in combination] of the future: *my bride-to-be.*
– PHRASAL VERBS **be about** see **about**. **be off** go away; leave: *he was anxious to be off.*
– ORIGIN Old English *bēon*, an irregular and defective verb, whose full conjugation derives from several originally distinct verbs. The forms *am* and *is* are from an Indo-European root shared by Latin *sum* and *est*. The forms *was* and *were* are from an Indo-European root meaning 'remain.' The forms *be* and *been* are from an Indo-European root shared by Latin *fui* 'I was,' *fio* 'I become' and Greek *phuein* 'bring forth, cause to grow.' The origin of *are* is uncertain.

> **USAGE** For a discussion of whether it is correct to say *that must* **be he** *at the door* and *it is* **I** rather than *that must* **be him** *at the door* and *it* **is me**, see usage at **personal pronoun**.

be- ▶ **prefix 1** forming verbs: ■ all over; all around: *bespatter.* ■ thoroughly; excessively: *bewilder.*
2 (added to intransitive verbs) expressing transitive action: *bemoan.*
3 (added to adjectives and nouns) expressing transitive action: *befool | befriend.*
4 (added to nouns) affect with: *befog.* ■ (added to adjectives) cause to be: *befoul.*
5 (forming adjectives ending in *-ed*) having; covered with: *bejeweled.*
– ORIGIN Old English, weak form of *bī* 'by.'

beach /bēch/ ▶ **n.** a pebbly or sandy shore, esp. by the ocean between high- and low-water marks.
▶ **v.** [with obj.] run or haul up (a boat or ship) onto a beach: *at the water's edge a rowboat was beached | [no obj.] crews would not beach for fear of damaging craft.* ■ (often as adj. **beached**) cause (a whale or similar animal) to become stranded out of the water. ■ [no obj.] (of a whale or similar animal) become stranded out of the water. ■ (of an angler) land (a fish) on a beach. ■ cause (someone) to suffer a loss: *competitive procurement seems to have beached several companies.*
– ORIGIN mid 16th cent. (denoting shingle on the seashore): perhaps related to Old English *bæce*, *bece* 'brook' (an element that survives in place names such as Wisbech and Sandbach), assuming an intermediate sense 'pebbly river valley.'

beach ball ▶ **n.** a large inflatable ball used for playing games on the beach.

beach bug·gy ▶ **n.** another term for **dune buggy**.

beach bum ▶ **n.** informal a person who loafs on or around a beach.

beach·comb·er /ˈbēchˌkōmər/ ▶ **n. 1** a vagrant who makes a living by searching beaches for articles of value and selling them.
2 a person who searches beaches for useful or interesting items.
3 a long wave rolling in from the sea; a comber.

beach flea ▶ **n.** a small crustacean of the seashore that typically lives among seaweed and leaps when disturbed. Also called **sand flea, sand hopper**.
● *Orchestia* and other genera, order Amphipoda.

beach·front /ˈbēchˌfrənt/ ▶ **n.** [usu. in sing.] the part of a coastal town next to and directly facing the sea: [as modifier] *beachfront property.*

beach grass ▶ **n.** marram grass, or any related grass of the genus *Ammophila*.

beach·head /ˈbēchˌhed/ ▶ **n.** a defended position on a beach taken from the enemy by landing forces, from which an attack can be launched.

–ORIGIN World War II (originally US): formed on the pattern of *bridgehead*.

Beach-la-mar /ˌbēCH lə ˈmär/ ▶ **n.** another term for **Bislama**.

beach plum ▶ **n.** a maritime shrub related to the plum, native to northeastern North America. ● *Prunus maritima*, family Rosaceae. ■ the edible fruit of this tree.

beach·side /ˈbēCHˌsīd/ ▶ **n.** the area adjacent to a beach.

beach·wear /ˈbēCHˌwe(ə)r/ ▶ **n.** clothing suitable for wearing on the beach, though not necessarily for swimming in.

bea·con /ˈbēkən/ ▶ **n.** a fire or light set up in a high or prominent position as a warning, signal, or celebration: *a chain of beacons carried the news* | figurative *the prospect of a new government was a beacon of hope for millions.* ■ Brit. (often in place names) a hill suitable for such a fire or light: *Ivinghoe Beacon* | *the Brecon Beacons.* ■ a light or other visible object serving as a signal, warning, or guide, esp. at sea or on an airfield. ■ a radio transmitter whose signal helps to fix the position of a ship, aircraft, or spacecraft.
–ORIGIN Old English *bēacn* 'sign, portent, ensign'; related to **beckon**.

Bea·con Hill a historic neighborhood in downtown Boston, Massachusetts, on high ground north of the Boston Common.

bead /bēd/ ▶ **n. 1** a small piece of glass, stone, or similar material, typically rounded and perforated for threading with others as a necklace or rosary or for sewing onto fabric. ■ (**beads**) a necklace made of a string of beads. ■ (**beads**) a rosary.
2 something resembling a bead or a string of beads, in particular: ■ a drop of a liquid on a surface: *beads of sweat.* ■ a long, narrow strip of caulking compound, adhesive or similar material applied to a surface. ■ a small knob forming the front sight of a gun. ■ the reinforced inner edge of a pneumatic tire that grips the rim of the wheel. ■ an ornamental molding resembling a string of beads or of a semicircular cross-section.
▶ **v.** [with obj.] **1** (often as adj. **beaded**) decorate or cover with beads: *a beaded evening bag.* ■ string (beads) together.
2 cover (a surface) with drops of moisture: *his face was beaded with perspiration.*
–PHRASES **draw** (or **get**) **a bead on** take aim at. ■ fully understand or make sense of: *it's hard to draw a bead on the stock market these days.* **tell** (or **say**) **one's beads** use the beads of a rosary in counting prayers.
–ORIGIN Old English *gebed* 'prayer,' of Germanic origin; related to Dutch *bede* and German *Gebet*, also to **bid**[1]. Current senses derive from the use of a rosary, each bead representing a prayer.

bead·ing /ˈbēdiNG/ ▶ **n.** decoration or ornamental molding resembling a string of beads or of a semicircular cross section.

bea·dle /ˈbēdl/ ▶ **n.** Brit. a ceremonial officer of a church, college, or similar institution. ■ Scottish a church officer assisting the minister. ■ historical a minor parish officer dealing with petty offenders.
–ORIGIN Old English *bydel* 'a person who makes a proclamation,' gradually superseded in Middle English by forms from Old French *bedel*, ultimately of Germanic origin; related to German *Büttel*, also to **bid**[1].

bead·work /ˈbēdˌwərk/ ▶ **n.** decorative work made of beads.

bead·y /ˈbēdē/ ▶ **adj.** (of a person's eyes) small, round, and gleaming. ■ (of a look) bright and penetrating: *she fixed him with a beady stare.*
–DERIVATIVES **bead·i·ly** /ˈbēdəlē/ **adv.**

bead·y-eyed ▶ **adj.** having small, glinting eyes. ■ informal keenly observant, typically in a sinister or hostile way.

bea·gle /ˈbēgəl/ ▶ **n.** a small sturdy hound of a breed with a coat of medium length, bred esp. for hunting.
–DERIVATIVES **bea·gler** /-g(ə)lər/ **n.**
–ORIGIN late 15th cent.: perhaps from Old French *beegueule* 'open-mouthed,' from *beer* 'open wide' + *gueule* 'throat.'

beagle

cardinal
heavy, triangular beak for cracking seeds

red-tailed hawk
strong, sharp, hooked beak for tearing flesh

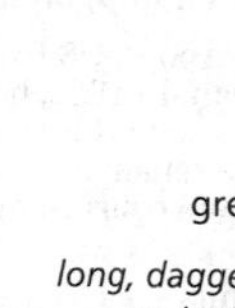

great blue heron
long, daggerlike beak for spearing and seizing fish and frogs

ruby-throated hummingbird
needlelike beak for collecting nectar

mallard
wide bill for scooping and sifting vegetation and insects from water's surface

white pelican
long, flat bill with throat pouch for scooping and swallowing fish

roseate spoonbill
spatulate bill that sweeps through the water to scoop up crustaceans and fish

tree swallow
short, wide-opening beak for catching flying insects

red-bellied woodpecker
tapered beak for boring into wood for insects

beaks and bills

beak /bēk/ ▶ **n.** a bird's horny projecting jaws; a bill. ■ the similar horny projecting jaw of other animals, e.g., a turtle or squid. ■ informal a person's nose, esp. a hooked one: *she can't wait to stick her beak in.* ■ a projection at the prow of an ancient warship, typically shaped to resemble the head of a bird or other animal, used to pierce the hulls of enemy ships.
–DERIVATIVES **beaked adj.** [in combination] *a yellow-beaked alpine chough.*
–ORIGIN Middle English: from Old French *bec*, from Latin *beccus*, of Celtic origin.

beaked whale ▶ **n.** a medium-sized whale with elongated jaws that form a beak, often showing marked differences in size and body form between the sexes. ● Family Ziphiidae: four genera and several species.

beak·er /ˈbēkər/ ▶ **n.** a lipped cylindrical glass container for laboratory use. ■ archaic or literary a large drinking container with a wide mouth. ■ Archaeology a waisted pot characteristic of graves of the Beaker folk.
–ORIGIN Middle English (in the sense 'large drinking container'): from Old Norse *bikarr*, perhaps based on Greek *bikos* 'drinking bowl.'

Beak·er folk /ˈbēkər/ ▶ **plural n.** Archaeology a late Neolithic and early Bronze Age European people (*c.*2700–1700 BC), named after distinctive waisted pots (**Beaker ware**) that were associated with their burials and appear to have been used for alcoholic drinks.

beak·y /ˈbēkē/ ▶ **adj.** informal (of a person's nose) resembling a bird's beak; hooked. ■ (of a person) having such a nose.

Beale /bēl/, Dorothea (1831–1906), English educator. She campaigned for women's suffrage and for higher education.

Beale Street /bēl/ a historic commercial street in downtown Memphis, Tennessee, that is associated with black music and commerce.

beam /bēm/ ▶ **n. 1** a long, sturdy piece of squared timber or metal spanning an opening or part of a building, usually to support the roof or floor above. ■ another term for **balance beam**. ■ a horizontal piece of squared timber or metal supporting the deck and joining the sides of a ship. ■ Nautical the direction of an object visible from the port or starboard side of a ship when it is perpendicular to the center line of the vessel: *there was land in sight on the port beam.* ■ a ship's breadth at its widest point: *a cutter with a beam of 16 feet.* ■ [in sing.] informal the width of a person's hips: *notice how broad in the beam she's getting?* ■ the main stem of a stag's antler. ■ the crossbar of a balance. ■ (esp. in a stationary steam engine) an oscillating shaft through which the vertical piston movement is transmitted to the crank or pump. ■ historical the main timber of a horse-drawn plow.
2 a ray or shaft of light: *a beam of light flashed in front of her* | *the flashlight beam dimmed perceptibly.* ■ a directional flow of particles or radiation: *beams of electrons.* ■ a series of radio or radar signals emitted to serve as a navigational guide for ships or aircraft.
3 [in sing.] a radiant or good-natured look or smile: *a beam of satisfaction.*
▶ **v. 1** [with obj.] transmit (a radio signal or broadcast) in a specified direction: *beaming a distress signal into space* | [no obj.] *the TV station begins beaming into homes in the new year.* ■ (**beam someone up/down**) (in science fiction) transport someone instantaneously to another place, esp. to or from a spaceship: *Scotty, beam me up!* [phrase from the television series *Star Trek*.]
2 [no obj.] (of a light or light source) shine brightly: *the sun's rays beamed down.*
3 [no obj.] smile radiantly: *she beamed with pleasure* | (as adj. **beaming**) *a beaming smile.* ■ [with obj.] express (an emotion) with a radiant smile: *the teacher beamed her approval* | [with direct speech] *"Isn't that wonderful, Beatrice?" beamed the nun.*
4 (**beamed**) construct a ceiling with exposed beams: *vaulted beamed ceilings in the family room.*
–PHRASES **a beam in one's eye** a fault that is greater in oneself than in the person one is finding fault with. [with biblical allusion to Matt. 7:3.] **off** (or **way off**) **beam** informal on the wrong track; mistaken: *you're way off beam on this one.* **on the beam** informal on the right track. **on her** (or **its**) **beam-ends** (of a ship) heeled over on its side; almost capsized.
–ORIGIN Old English *bēam* 'tree, beam'; related to Dutch *boom* and German *Baum*.

beam com·pass (also **beam compasses**) ▶ **n.** a drawing compass consisting of a horizontal rod or beam connected by sliding sockets to two vertical legs, used for drawing large circles.

beam·ish /ˈbēmiSH/ ▶ **adj.** beaming with happiness, optimism, or anticipation.

Bea·mon /ˈbēmən/, Bob (1946–), US long jumper; full name *Robert Beamon*. He set a world record at the 1968 Olympic Games that stood until 1991.

beam sea ▶ **n.** Nautical a sea that is running at approximately right angles to a vessel's heading.

b

beam split·ter ▶ **n.** a device for dividing a beam of light or other electromagnetic radiation into two or more separate beams.

beam·y /ˈbēmē/ ▶ **adj.** (of a ship) broad-beamed.

Bean /bēn/, Roy (*c.*1825–1903), US frontiersman; known as **Judge Roy Bean**. In 1882, he named himself justice of the peace in the Texas settlement of Vinegaroon, which he renamed Langtry for his idol Lillie Langtry. He held court in his saloon, the Jersey Lily.

bean /bēn/ ▶ **n. 1** an edible seed, typically kidney-shaped, growing in long pods on certain leguminous plants. ■ the hard seed of coffee, cocoa, and certain other plants.
2 a leguminous plant that bears such seeds in pods. ● *Phaseolus* and other genera, family Leguminosae: numerous species, including the **scarlet runner** (*P. coccineus*), **kidney bean** (*P. vulgaris*), and **broad bean** (*Vicia faba*).
3 [with negative] (also **beans**) informal a very small amount or nothing at all of something (used emphatically): *there is not a single bean of substance in the report | I didn't know beans about being a step-parent.*
4 informal a person's head, typically when regarded as a source of common sense.
▶ **v.** [with obj.] informal hit (someone) on the head: *Boone was nearly beaned by that wild pitch.*
– PHRASES **full of beans** informal lively; in high spirits. **a hill** (or **row**) **of beans** [with negative] anything of any importance or value: *three little people **don't amount to a hill of beans** in this crazy world.* **old bean** Brit. informal, dated a friendly form of address, usually to a man: *great to see you, old bean!*
– ORIGIN Old English *bēan*, of Germanic origin; related to Dutch *boon* and German *Bohne*.

bean·bag /ˈbēn,bag/ ▶ **n. 1** a small bag filled with dried beans and typically used in children's games. ■ Football a square of colored plastic with a weighted section, used as a penalty flag.
2 a large cushion, typically filled with polystyrene beads, used as a seat.
▶ **v.** [with obj.] (**beanbags, beanbagging, beanbagged**) Football indicate (a penalty) or charge (a player) with a penalty using a beanbag.

bean·ball /ˈbēn,bôl/ ▶ **n.** Baseball, informal a ball pitched, esp. intentionally, at the batter's head.

bean count·er ▶ **n.** informal, derogatory a person, typically an accountant or bureaucrat, perceived as placing excessive emphasis on controlling expenditure and budgets.
– DERIVATIVES **bean count·ing n.**

bean curd ▶ **n.** another term for TOFU.

bean·er /ˈbēnər/ ▶ **n.** informal, offensive a Mexican or a person of Mexican descent.

bean·er·y /ˈbēnərē/ ▶ **n.** (pl. **beaneries**) a cheap restaurant.

bean·ie /ˈbēnē/ ▶ **n.** (pl. **beanies**) a small, close-fitting hat worn on the back of the head.
– ORIGIN 1940s: perhaps from BEAN (in the sense 'head') + -IE.

bean·pole /ˈbēn,pōl/ ▶ **n.** a stick for supporting bean plants. ■ informal a tall, thin person.

bean sprouts ▶ **plural n.** the sprouting seeds of certain beans, esp. mung beans, used in Asian cooking.

bean·stalk /ˈbēn,stôk/ ▶ **n.** the stem of a bean plant, proverbially fast growing and tall.

bear[1] /be(ə)r/ ▶ **v.** (past **bore** /bôr/; past participle **borne** /bôrn/) [with obj.] **1** (of a person) carry: *he was bearing a tray of brimming glasses | the warriors bore lances tipped with iron.* ■ (of a vehicle or boat) convey (passengers or cargo): *steamboats bear the traveler out of Kerrerra Sound.* ■ have or display as a visible mark or feature: *a small boat bearing a white flag | many of the papers bore his flamboyant signature.* ■ be called by (a name or title): *he bore the surname Tiller.* ■ (**bear oneself**) [with adverbial] carry or conduct oneself in a particular manner: *she bore herself with dignity.*
2 support: *walls that cannot bear a stone vault.* ■ take responsibility for: *no one likes to **bear the responsibility** for such decisions | the expert's fee shall be borne by the tenant.* ■ be able to accept or stand up to: *it is doubtful whether either of these distinctions would **bear scrutiny**.*
3 endure (an ordeal or difficulty): *she bore the pain stoically.* ■ [with modal and negative] manage to tolerate (a situation or experience): *she **could hardly bear** his sarcasm | [with infinitive] I cannot bear to see you hurt.* ■ (**cannot bear someone/something**) strongly dislike: *I can't bear caviar.*
4 give birth to (a child): *she bore six daughters | [with two objs.] his wife had borne him a son.* ■ (of a tree or plant) produce (fruit or flowers): *a squash that bears fruit shaped like cucumbers.*
5 [no obj.] turn and proceed in a specified direction: *bear left and follow the old road.*
– PHRASES **be borne in upon** come to be realized by: *the folly of her action was borne in on her with devastating precision.* **bear arms 1** carry firearms. **2** wear or display a coat of arms. **bear the brunt of** see BRUNT. **bear the burden of** suffer the consequences of. **bear fruit** yield positive results: *plans for power-sharing may be about to bear fruit.* **bear someone a grudge** nurture a feeling of resentment against someone. **bear a hand** archaic help in a task or enterprise. **bear someone malice** (or **ill will**) [with negative] wish someone harm. **bear a resemblance** (or **similarity**) **to** resemble. **bear a relation** (or **relationship**) **to** [with negative] be logically consistent with: *the map didn't seem to bear any relation to the roads.* **bear the stamp of** be clearly identifiable with: *every work of mine must inevitably bear the stamp of my own personality.* **bear witness** (or **testimony**) **to** testify to: *little is left to bear witness to the past greatness of the city.* **bring pressure to bear on** attempt to coerce: *they brought pressure to bear on him to resign.* **bring to bear 1** muster and use to effect: *she had reservations about how much influence she could bring to bear.* **2** aim (a weapon): *bringing his rifle to bear on a distant target.* **does not bear thinking about** is too terrible to contemplate. **grin and bear it** see GRIN. **have one's cross to bear** see CROSS.
– PHRASAL VERBS **bear away** another way of saying BEAR OFF. **bear down** (of a woman in labor) exert downward pressure in order to push the baby out. ■ put pressure on someone or something: *he bore down and allowed the Bears only one more run.* **bear down on** move quickly toward someone, in a purposeful or an intimidating manner. ■ take strict measures to deal with: *a commitment to bear down on inflation.* **bear off** Sailing change course away from the wind. ■ Nautical steer away from something, typically the land. **bear on** be relevant to (something): *two kinds of theories that bear on literary studies.* ■ [with adverbial] be a burden on (someone): *a tax that will **bear heavily on** poorer households.* **bear something out** support or confirm something: *this assumption is not borne out by any evidence.* **bear up** remain cheerful in the face of adversity: *she's bearing up remarkably well.* **bear with** be patient or tolerant with.
– ORIGIN Old English *beran*, of Germanic origin; from an Indo-European root shared by Sanskrit *bharati*, Greek *pherein*, and Latin *ferre*.

> **USAGE** In the early 17th century, **borne** and **born** were simply variant forms of the past participle of **bear** used interchangeably with no distinction in meaning. By around 1775, however, the present distinction in use had become established. At that time, **borne** became the standard past participle used in all the senses listed in this dictionary entry, e.g., *she has **borne** you another son, the findings have been **borne** out*, and so on. **Born** became restricted to just one very common use (which remains the case today), in the passive, without **by**, as the standard, neutral way to refer to birth: *she was **born** in 1965, he was **born** lucky*, or *I was **born** and bred in Boston.*

bear[2] ▶ **n. 1** a large, heavy, mammal that walks on the soles of its feet, with thick fur and a very short tail. Bears are related to the dog family, but most species are omnivorous. ● Family Ursidae: several genera and species. ■ a teddy bear. ■ informal a rough, unmannerly, or uncouth person. ■ a large, heavy, cumbersome man: *a lumbering bear of a man.* ■ (**the Bear**) informal a nickname for Russia. ■ (**the Bear**) the constellation Ursa Major or Ursa Minor.
2 Stock Market a person who forecasts that prices of stocks or commodities will fall, esp. a person who sells shares hoping to buy them back later at a lower price: [as modifier] *bear markets.* Often contrasted with BULL[1] (sense 2 of the noun). [said to be from a proverb warning against 'selling the bear's skin before one has caught the bear.']
– PHRASES **loaded for bear** informal fully prepared for any eventuality, typically a confrontation or challenge.
– ORIGIN Old English *bera*; related to Dutch *beer* and German *Bär*.

bear·a·ble /ˈbe(ə)rəbəl/ ▶ **adj.** able to be endured: *a ceiling fan made the heat bearable.*
– DERIVATIVES **bear·a·bly adv.**

bear·bait·ing /ˈbe(ə)r,bātiNG/ ▶ **n.** historical a form of entertainment that involved setting dogs to attack a captive bear.

bear·ber·ry /ˈbe(ə)r,berē/ ▶ **n.** (pl. **bearberries**) a creeping dwarf shrub of the heath family, with pinkish flowers and bright red berries. ● Genus *Arctostaphylos*, family Ericaceae: several species, in particular *A. uva-ursi*, found esp. in circumpolar regions.

bear·cat /ˈbe(ə)r,kat/ ▶ **n. 1** a bearlike climbing mammal, esp. the red panda.
2 a binturong.
3 informal an aggressive or forceful person.

bear claw ▶ **n.** a filled pastry made from a folded circle of dough with slits cut in it.

Beard, James (1903–85), US chef and cookbook author. He hosted the first televised cooking show and founded a cooking school in New York.

beard /bi(ə)rd/ ▶ **n. 1** a growth of hair on the chin and lower cheeks of a man's face: *he had a black beard | three days' growth of beard.* ■ a tuft of hair on the chin of certain mammals, for example a lion or goat. ■ an animal's growth or marking that is likened to a beard, e.g., the gills of an oyster, or the beak bristles of certain birds. ■ a tuft of hairs or bristles on certain plants, esp. the awn of a grass.
2 informal a person who carries out a transaction, typically a bet, for someone else in order to conceal the other's identity. ■ a person who pretends to have a romantic or sexual relationship with someone else in order to conceal the other's true sexual orientation.
▶ **v.** [with obj.] boldly confront or challenge (someone formidable).
– PHRASES **beard the lion in his den** (or **lair**) confront or challenge someone on their own ground.
– DERIVATIVES **beard·ed adj.** [in combination] *a gray-bearded man*, **beard·less adj.**
– ORIGIN Old English; related to Dutch *baard* and German *Bart*.

beard·ed col·lie ▶ **n.** a dog of a shaggy breed of collie with long hair on the face.

beard·ed vul·ture ▶ **n.** another term for LAMMERGEIER.

Beard·more Gla·cier /ˈbi(ə)rd,môr/ a glacier in Antarctica that flows from the Queen Maud Mountains to the Ross Ice Shelf, at the southern edge of the Ross Sea, 260 miles (418 km) long.

Beards·ley /ˈbi(ə)rdzlē/, Aubrey (Vincent) (1872–98), English artist and illustrator, associated with art nouveau and the Aesthetic Movement.

beard·tongue /ˈbi(ə)rd,təNG/ ▶ **n.** a North American plant of the figwort family with showy, five-lobed flowers. Each blossom has a tuft of hair on one of its stamens. ● Genus *Penstemon*, family Scrophulariaceae: several species, including **hairy beardtongue** (*P. hirsutus*) and the widespread **foxglove beardtongue** (*P. digitalis*).

bear·er /ˈbe(ə)rər/ ▶ **n. 1** a person or thing that carries or holds something: *I'm sorry to be the bearer of bad tidings | [in combination] a flag-bearer.* ■ a carrier of equipment on an expedition. ■ a person who carries the coffin at a funeral; pall-bearer.
2 a person who presents a check or other order to pay money: ***promissory notes payable to the bearer.*** ■ [as modifier] payable to the possessor: *bearer bonds.*

bear·grass /ˈbe(ə)r,gras/ (also **bear grass**) ▶ **n.** a North American plant with long, coarse, grasslike leaves, in particular: ● a wild yucca (genus *Yucca*, family Agavaceae). ● a cultivated ornamental plant, the leaves of which were formerly used by American Indians to make watertight baskets (*Xerophyllum tenax*, family Liliaceae). Also called ELK GRASS.

bear hug ▶ **n.** a rough, tight embrace.

bear·ing /ˈbe(ə)riNG/ ▶ **n. 1** [in sing.] a person's way of standing or moving: *a man of precise military bearing.* ■ the way one behaves or conducts oneself: *she has the bearing of a First Lady.*
2 relation or relevance: *the case has no direct bearing on the issues.*
3 the level to which something bad can be tolerated: *school was bad enough, but now it's past bearing.*
4 a part of a machine that bears friction, esp. between a rotating part and its housing. ■ a ball bearing.
5 Architecture a structural part that supports weight, such as a wall that supports a beam. ■ the point at which a structural part rests upon a supporting structure, such as the specific area of a beam that rests upon a wall.
6 the direction or position of something, or the direction of movement, relative to a fixed point. It is typically measured in degrees, usually with magnetic north as zero: *the Point is on a bearing of 015°.* ■ (**one's bearings**) awareness of one's position relative to one's surroundings: *he rose unsteadily to his feet and tried to get his bearings.*
7 Heraldry a device or charge: *armorial bearings.*

bear·ing rein ▶ **n.** a fixed rein that causes the horse to raise its head and arch its neck.

bear·ish /ˈbe(ə)rish/ ▶ **adj. 1** resembling or likened to a bear, typically in being rough, surly, or clumsy: *a bearish figure with muttonchop whiskers.*
2 Stock Market characterized by or associated with falling share prices. ■ (of a dealer) inclined to sell because of an anticipated fall in prices.
– DERIVATIVES **bear·ish·ly** adv., **bear·ish·ness** n.

bear mar·ket ▶ **n.** Stock Market a market in which prices are falling, encouraging selling.

Bé·ar·naise sauce /ˌberˈnāz/ ▶ **n.** a rich sauce thickened with egg yolks and flavored with tarragon.
– ORIGIN *Béarnaise*, feminine of French *Béarnais* 'of *Béarn*,' a region of southwestern France.

bear·skin /ˈbe(ə)rˌskin/ ▶ **n.** the pelt of a bear, esp. when used as a rug or wrap. ■ a tall cap of black fur worn ceremonially by certain military troops.

Be·as /ˈbēˌäs/ a river in northern India that rises in the Himalayas and flows through Himachal Pradesh to join the Sutlej River in Punjab. It is one of the five rivers that gave Punjab ("five waters") its name.

beast /bēst/ ▶ **n.** an animal, esp. a large or dangerous four-footed one: *a wild beast.* ■ (usu. **beasts**) a domestic animal, esp. a bovine farm animal. ■ archaic or humorous an animal as opposed to a human: *the gift of reason differentiates humanity from the beasts.* ■ an inhumanly cruel, violent, or depraved person: *he is a filthy drunken beast.* ■ informal an objectionable or unpleasant person or thing: *a scheming, manipulative little beast.* ■ (**the beast**) a person's brutish or untamed characteristics: ***the beast** in you is rearing its ugly head.* ■ [with adj.] informal a thing or concept possessing a particular quality: *that much-maligned beast, the rave record.*
– ORIGIN Middle English: from Old French *beste*, based on Latin *bestia*.

beast·ie /ˈbēstē/ ▶ **n.** (pl. **beasties**) Scottish or humorous an animal, insect, or germ: *our immune systems are killing millions of wee beasties.* ■ [with adj.] a vehicle or device of a particular kind: *these little beasties only have three wheels.*

beast·ings ▶ **n.** variant spelling of BEESTINGS.

beast·ly /ˈbēstlē/ ▶ **adj.** (**beastlier, beastliest**)
1 informal, chiefly Brit. very unpleasant: *this beastly war.* ■ unkind; malicious: *don't be **beastly to** him.*
2 archaic cruel and unrestrained: *beastly immorality.*
▶ **adv.** [as submodifier] Brit. informal, dated possessing a specified characteristic to an intense and unpleasant degree: *a beastly hot summer.*
– DERIVATIVES **beast·li·ness** n.

beast of bur·den ▶ **n.** an animal such as a mule or donkey that is used for carrying loads.

beast of prey ▶ **n.** an animal, esp. a mammal, that kills and eats other animals.

beat /bēt/ ▶ **v.** (past **beat**; past participle **beaten** /ˈbētn/) [with obj.] **1** strike (a person or an animal) repeatedly and violently so as to hurt or injure them, usually with an implement such as a club or whip: *a woman whose husband would frequently beat her after becoming drunk | the victims were **beaten to death** with baseball bats.* ■ strike (an object) repeatedly so as to make a noise: *he beat the table with his hand.* ■ [no obj.] (of an instrument) make a rhythmical sound by being struck: *drums were beating in the distance.* ■ strike (a carpet, blanket, etc.) repeatedly in order to remove dust. ■ remove (dust) from something by striking it repeatedly. ■ flatten or shape (metal) by striking it repeatedly with a hammer: *pure gold can be **beaten out** to form very thin sheets.* ■ (**beat something against/on**) strike something against (something): *she beat her fists against the wood.* ■ [no obj.] (**beat on/against**) strike repeatedly on: *Sidney beat on the door with the flat of his hand.* ■ [no obj.] (**beat at**) make striking movements toward: *Emmie seized the hearthrug and began to beat at the flames.* ■ move across (an area of land) repeatedly striking at the ground cover in order to raise game birds for shooting.
2 defeat (someone) in a game, competition, election, or commercial venture: *she beat him easily at chess | the Senators **beat out** the Yankees for the 1933 pennant.* ■ informal baffle: ***it beats me how** you manage to work in this heat.* ■ overcome (a problem, or disease): *they are investing their savings in hopes of beating inflation | he beat heroin addiction in 1992.* ■ do or be better than (a record or score): *he beat his own world record.* ■ informal be better than: ***you can't beat** the taste of fresh raspberries.*
3 succeed in getting somewhere ahead of (someone): *I could beat him on my bicycle | the goalie beat him to the ball.* ■ take action to avoid (difficult or inconvenient effects of an event or circumstance): *they set off early to beat the traffic.*
4 [no obj.] (of the heart) pulsate: *her heart beat faster with panic.*
5 (of a bird) move (the wings) up and down. ■ (of a bird or its wings) make rhythmic movements through (the air): *black-tipped wings beat the air.* ■ [no obj.] (of a bird) fly making rhythmic wing movements: *an owl beat low over the salt marsh.*
6 stir (cooking ingredients) vigorously with a fork, whisk, or beater to make a smooth or frothy mixture.
7 (**beat it**) informal leave: [in imperative] *now beat it, will you!*
8 [no obj.] Sailing sail into the wind, following a zigzag course with repeated tacking: *we beat southward all that first day.*
▶ **n. 1** a main accent or rhythmic unit in music or poetry: *the glissando begins on the second beat.* ■ a strong rhythm in popular music: *the music changed to a funky disco beat.* ■ [in sing.] a regular, rhythmic sound or movement: *the beat of the wipers became almost hypnotic.* ■ the sound made when something, typically a musical instrument, is struck: *he heard a regular drumbeat.* ■ a pulsation of the heart. ■ a periodic variation of sound or amplitude due to the combination of two sounds, electrical signals, or other vibrations having similar but not identical frequencies. ■ the movement of a bird's wings.
2 an area allocated to a police officer to patrol: *a patrolman who strived to make his beat a safe one | public clamor for more police officers **on the beat**.* ■ a spell of duty allocated to a police officer: *her beat ended at 6 a.m.* ■ an area regularly frequented by someone, typically a prostitute. ■ a person's area of interest: *his beat is construction, property, and hotels.*
3 a brief pause or moment of hesitation, typically one lasting a specified length: *she waited for a beat of three seconds.* [as a stage direction.]
4 informal short for BEATNIK.
▶ **adj. 1** [predic.] informal completely exhausted: *I'm **dead beat**.*
2 [attrib.] of or relating to the beat generation or its philosophy: *beat poet Allen Ginsberg.*
– PHRASES **beat all** be amazing or impressive: *well, that beats all.* **beat around** (or **beat about**) **the bush** discuss a matter without coming to the point. **beat someone at their own game** see GAME. **beat someone's brains out** see BRAIN. **beat one's breast** see BREAST. **beat the bushes** informal search thoroughly: *I was out **beating the bushes** for investors to split the risk.* **beat the clock** perform a task quickly or within a fixed time limit. **beat a dead horse** waste energy on a lost cause or unalterable situation. **beat the drum for** see DRUM[1]. **beat the hell out of** informal **1** beat (someone) very severely. **2** surpass or defeat easily. ■ totally confuse or puzzle (someone). **beat the living daylights out of** see DAYLIGHT (sense 2). **beat the pants off** informal prove to be vastly superior to. **beat a path to someone's door** (of a large number of people) hasten to make contact with someone regarded as interesting or inspiring, or in association with whom one stands to profit. **beat a** (**hasty**) **retreat** withdraw, typically in order to avoid something unpleasant: *as the bombs started to go off, they beat a hasty retreat across the field.* **beat the shit out of** vulgar slang beat (someone) very severely. **beat the system** succeed in finding a means of getting around rules, regulations, or other means of control. **beat time** indicate or follow a musical tempo with a baton or other means. **beat someone to it** succeed in doing something or getting somewhere before someone else, to their annoyance. **miss a beat** see MISS[1]. **to beat all ——s** that is infinitely better than all the things mentioned: *a PC screen saver to beat all screen savers.* **to beat the band** informal in such a way as to surpass all competition: *they were talking to beat the band.*
– PHRASAL VERBS **beat someone back** (usu. **be beaten back**) force (someone attempting to do something) to retreat: *I tried to get in but was beaten back by the flames.* **beat down** (of the sun) radiate intense heat and brightness. ■ (of rain) fall hard and continuously. **beat something down** quell defense or resistance. **beat someone down** force someone to reduce the price of something. **beat one's meat** vulgar slang (of a man) masturbate. **beat off** vulgar slang (of a man) masturbate. **beat someone/something off** succeed in resisting an attacker or an attack. ■ win against a challenge or rival. **beat something out 1** produce a loud, rhythmic sound by striking something: *he beat out a rhythm on the drums.* **2** extinguish flames by striking at them with a suitable object. **beat someone up 1** assault and severely injure someone by hitting, kicking, or punching them repeatedly. **2** abuse someone verbally. **beat up on** another way of saying BEAT SOMEONE UP.
– DERIVATIVES **beat·a·ble** adj.
– ORIGIN Old English *bēatan*, of Germanic origin.

beat·box /ˈbētˌbäks/ ▶ **n.** informal a drum machine. ■ a radio or radio cassette player used to play loud music, esp. rap. ▶ **v.** [no obj.] imitate the sounds of a drum machine with the voice.
– DERIVATIVES **beat·box·er** n., **beat·box·ing** n.

beat·down /ˈbētˌdoun/ ▶ **n.** informal a physical beating or assault: *a savage beatdown.* ■ a decisive defeat: *the Lakers handed out a beatdown on the Pacers, 99–77.*

beat·en /ˈbētn/ past participle of BEAT.
▶ **adj. 1** having been defeated: *I knew when I was beaten.* ■ exhausted and dejected: *he sat feeling old and beaten.*
2 having been beaten or struck: *he trudged home like a beaten dog.* ■ (of food) whipped to a uniform consistency: *beaten eggs.* ■ (of metal) shaped by hammering, typically so as to give the surface a dimpled texture. ■ (of precious metal) hammered to form thin foil for ornamental use.
3 (of a path) well trodden; much used.
– PHRASES **off the beaten track** (or **path**) in or into an isolated place. ■ unusual: [as adj.] *off-the-beaten-track experiences.*

beat·er /ˈbētər/ ▶ **n. 1** a person who hits someone or something, in particular: ■ a person employed to flush out or drive game animals for shooting by striking at the ground cover. ■ a person who beats metal in manufacturing. ■ [in combination] a person who habitually hits someone: *a wife-beater.*
2 an implement or machine used for beating.
3 [in combination] informal a means of defeating or preventing something: *a recession-beater.*
4 informal a dilapidated but serviceable car: *If you provide the kids with a car, give them an old beater.*

bea·ter bar ▶ **n.** the rotating-brush unit within the powerhead of a vacuum cleaner.

beat fre·quen·cy ▶ **n.** Physics the number of beats per second, equal to the difference in the frequencies of two interacting tones or oscillations.

beat gen·er·a·tion a movement of young people in the 1950s who rejected conventional society and favored Zen Buddhism, modern jazz, free sexuality, and recreational drugs. Among writers associated with the movement were Jack Kerouac and Allen Ginsberg.

be·a·tif·ic /ˌbēəˈtifik/ ▶ **adj.** blissfully happy: *a beatific smile.* ■ Christian Theology imparting holy bliss.
– DERIVATIVES **be·a·tif·i·cal·ly** /-ik(ə)lē/ adv.
– ORIGIN mid 17th cent.: from French *béatifique* or Latin *beatificus*, from *beatus* 'blessed.'

be·at·i·fi·ca·tion /bēˌatəfiˈkāshən/ ▶ **n.** (in the Roman Catholic Church) declaration by the pope that a dead person is in a state of bliss, constituting a step toward canonization and permitting public veneration.
– ORIGIN early 16th cent. (in the sense 'action of making blessed'): from Old French, or from ecclesiastical Latin *beatificatio(n-)*, from *beatificare* 'make blessed,' from Latin *beatus* 'blessed.'

be·at·i·fy /bēˈatəˌfī/ ▶ **v.** (**beatifies, beatifying, beatified**) [with obj.] (in the Roman Catholic Church) announce the beatification of.
– ORIGIN mid 16th cent. (in the sense 'make blessed or supremely happy'): from Old French *beatifier* or ecclesiastical Latin *beatificare*, from Latin *beatus* 'blessed.'

beat·ing /ˈbētiNG/ ▶ **n. 1** a punishment or assault in which the victim is hit repeatedly: *if he got dirt on his clothes, he'd get a beating | torture methods included beating.*
2 pulsation or throbbing, typically of the heart.
3 a defeat in a competitive situation.
– PHRASES **take a beating** informal suffer damage or hurt.

be·at·i·tude /bēˈatiˌt(y)o͞od/ ▶ **n.** supreme blessedness. ■ (**the Beatitudes**) the blessings listed by Jesus in the Sermon on the Mount (Matt. 5:3–11). ■ (**his/your Beatitude**) a title given to patriarchs in the Orthodox Church.
– ORIGIN late Middle English: from Old French *beatitude* or Latin *beatitudo*, from *beatus* 'blessed.'

Beat·les /ˈbētəlz/ (**the Beatles**) a pop and rock group from Liverpool, England, consisting of George Harrison, John Lennon, Paul McCartney, and Ringo Starr. Remembered for the quality and stylistic diversity of their songs (mostly written by Lennon and McCartney), they achieved success with their first single "Love Me Do" (1962) and went on to produce albums such as *Sergeant Pepper's Lonely Hearts Club Band* (1967).

b

b

■ (as modifier **Beatle**) characteristic of the Beatles: *a Beatle jacket.*

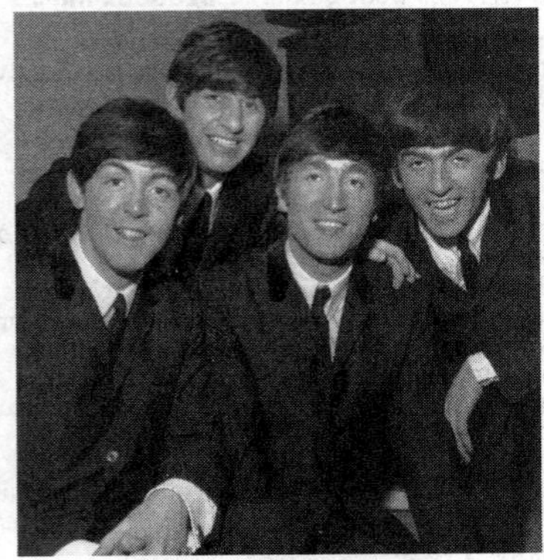
the Beatles

beat·nik /ˈbētnik/ ▶ **n.** a young person in the 1950s and early 1960s belonging to a subculture associated with the beat generation.
– ORIGIN 1950s: from BEAT + *-nik* on the pattern of *sputnik*, perhaps influenced by US use of Yiddish *-nik*, denoting someone or something who acts in a particular way.

Be·a·trix /ˈbāə,triks, ˈbē-/ (1938–), queen of the Netherlands (1980–); full name *Beatrix Wilhelmina Armgard.*

Beat·tie /ˈbētē/, Ann (1947–), US author. Her works include the novels *Chilly Scenes of Winter* (1976), *Picturing Will* (1989), and *Another You* (1995) and the short-story collection *Park City* (1998).

beat-up ▶ **adj.** [attrib.] informal (of a thing) worn out by overuse; in a state of disrepair.

beau /bō/ ▶ **n.** (pl. **beaux** /bōz/ or **beaus**) dated **1** a boyfriend or male admirer.
2 a rich, fashionable young man; a dandy.
– ORIGIN late 17th cent. (sense 2): from French, literally 'handsome,' from Latin *bellus.*

beau·coup /bōˈkoo, ˈbo͞o,ko͞o/ ▶ **adj.** informal many or much: *you can spend beaucoup bucks on software.*
– ORIGIN French.

Beau·fort scale /ˈbōfərt/ a scale of wind speed based on a visual estimation of the wind's effects, ranging from force 0 (less than 1 knot or 1 mph, "calm") to force 12 (64 knots or 74 mph and above, "hurricane").
– ORIGIN mid 19th cent.: named after Sir Francis *Beaufort* (1774–1857), the English admiral and naval hydrographer who devised it.

Beau·fort Sea a part of the Arctic Ocean that lies to the north of Alaska and Canada.
– ORIGIN named after Sir Francis *Beaufort* (see BEAUFORT SCALE).

beau geste /ˌbō ˈzHest/ ▶ **n.** (pl. **beaux gestes** pronunc. **same**) a noble and generous act.
– ORIGIN early 20th cent.: French, literally 'splendid gesture.'

beau i·dé·al /ˌbō ˌēdāˈal, īˈdēl/ ▶ **n.** a person or thing representing the highest possible standard of excellence in a particular respect.
– ORIGIN early 19th cent.: French, literally 'ideal beauty.'

Beau·jo·lais /ˌbōzHəˈlā/ ▶ **n.** a light red or (less commonly) white burgundy wine produced in the Beaujolais district of southeastern France.

Beau·jo·lais Nou·veau /ˌbōzHəˈlā no͞oˈvō/ ▶ **n.** a Beaujolais wine sold in the first year of a vintage.
– ORIGIN from BEAUJOLAIS + French *nouveau* 'new.'

Beau·mar·chais /ˌbōmärˈsHā/, Pierre Augustin Caron de (1732–99), French playwright. He is chiefly remembered for his comedies *The Barber of Seville* (1775) and *The Marriage of Figaro* (1784).

beau monde /ˌbō ˈmônd/ ▶ **n.** (**the beau monde**) fashionable society.
– ORIGIN late 17th cent.: French, literally 'fine world.'

Beau·mont[1] /ˌbō ˈmänt/ an industrial port in southeastern Texas, on the Neches River, a center of the oil industry; pop. 110,553 (est. 2008).

Beau·mont[2], Francis (1584–1616), English playwright. He collaborated with John Fletcher on *Philaster* (1609), *The Maid's Tragedy* (1610–11), and many other plays. *The Knight of the Burning Pestle* (*c.*1607) is attributed to Beaumont alone.

Beaune /bōn/ ▶ **n.** a red burgundy wine from the region around Beaune in eastern France.

Beau·re·gard /ˈbōri,gärd/, Pierre Gustave Toutant (1818–93), Confederate army officer. He served as superintendent of the US Military Academy at West Point; as the Civil War was about to begin in 1861, he resigned to join the Confederate army with the rank of brigadier general.

beaut /byo͞ot/ informal ▶ **n.** a particularly fine example of something: *the idea was a beaut.* ■ a beautiful person.
– ORIGIN mid 19th cent.: abbreviation of BEAUTY or BEAUTIFUL.

beau·te·ous /ˈbyo͞otēəs/ ▶ **adj.** literary beautiful: *his beauteous bride.*
– ORIGIN late Middle English: from BEAUTY, on the pattern of *bounteous* and *plenteous.*

beau·ti·cian /byo͞oˈtisHən/ ▶ **n.** a person whose job is to do hair styling, manicures, and other beauty treatments.

beau·ti·ful /ˈbyo͞otəfəl/ ▶ **adj.** pleasing the senses or mind aesthetically: *beautiful poetry | a beautiful young woman | the mountains were calm and beautiful.* ■ of a very high standard; excellent: *the house had been left in beautiful order | she spoke in beautiful English.*
– PHRASES **the beautiful people 1** fashionable, glamorous, and privileged people. **2** (in the 1960s) hippies. **the body beautiful** an ideal of physical beauty.
– DERIVATIVES **beau·ti·ful·ly** /-f(ə)lē/ **adv.** [as adj.] *the rules are beautifully simple.*

beau·ti·fy /ˈbyo͞otə,fī/ ▶ **v.** (**beautifies, beautifying, beautified**) [with obj.] improve the appearance of.
– DERIVATIVES **beau·ti·fi·ca·tion** /ˌbyo͞otəfiˈkāsHən/ **n.**, **beau·ti·fi·er n.**

beau·ty /ˈbyo͞otē/ ▶ **n.** (pl. **beauties**) **1** a combination of qualities, such as shape, color, or form, that pleases the aesthetic senses, esp. the sight: *I was struck by her beauty | an area of outstanding natural beauty.* ■ a combination of qualities that pleases the intellect or moral sense. ■ [as modifier] denoting something intended to make a woman more attractive: *beauty products | beauty treatment.*
2 a beautiful or pleasing thing or person, in particular: ■ a beautiful woman. ■ an excellent specimen or example of something: *the fish was a beauty, around 14 pounds.* ■ (**the beauties of**) the pleasing or attractive features of something: *the beauties of the Pennsylvania mountains.* ■ [in sing.] the best feature or advantage of something: *the beauty of keeping cats is that they don't tie you down.*
– PHRASES **beauty is in the eye of the beholder** proverb beauty cannot be judged objectively, for what one person finds beautiful or admirable may not appeal to another. **beauty is only skin-deep** proverb a pleasing appearance is not a guide to character.
– ORIGIN Middle English: from Old French *beaute*, based on Latin *bellus* 'beautiful, fine.'

beau·ty bush (also **beautybush**) ▶ **n.** a deciduous Chinese shrub of the honeysuckle family, with clusters of yellow-throated pink tubular flowers, widely cultivated as an ornamental. ● *Kolkwitzia amabilis*, family Caprifoliaceae.

beau·ty con·test ▶ **n.** a competition for a prize given to the woman judged the most beautiful. ■ a contest between rival institutions or political candidates that depends heavily on presentation.

beau·ty mark ▶ **n.** another term for BEAUTY SPOT (sense 2).

beau·ty pag·eant ▶ **n.** see PAGEANT.

beau·ty par·lor (also **beauty salon** or **beauty shop**) ▶ **n.** an establishment in which hairdressing, makeup, and similar cosmetic treatments are carried out professionally.

beau·ty queen ▶ **n.** a woman judged most beautiful in a beauty contest.

beau·ty sleep ▶ **n.** humorous sleep considered to be sufficient to keep one looking young and beautiful.

beau·ty spot ▶ **n. 1** a place known for its beautiful scenery.
2 a small natural or artificial mark such as a mole on a woman's face, considered to enhance another feature.

Beau·voir, Simone de, see DE BEAUVOIR.

beaux /bōz/ plural form of BEAU.

beaux arts /ˌbō ˈzär/ ▶ **plural n. 1** fine arts.
2 (usu. **Beaux Arts**) [as modifier] relating to the classical decorative style maintained by the École des Beaux-Arts in Paris, esp. in the 19th century.
– ORIGIN from French *beaux-arts.*

bea·ver[1] /ˈbēvər/ ▶ **n.** (pl. **same** or **beavers**) a large semiaquatic broad-tailed rodent that is native to North America and northern Eurasia. It is noted for its habit of gnawing through tree trunks to fell the trees in order to feed on the bark and build dams. ● Family Castoridae and genus *Castor*: the North American *C. canadensis* and the Eurasian *C. fiber.* ■ the soft light brown fur of the beaver. ■ (also **beaver hat**) chiefly historical a hat made of felted beaver fur. ■ (also **beaver cloth**) a heavy woolen cloth resembling felted beaver fur. ■ a very hard-working person.
▶ **v.** [no obj.] informal work hard: *Bridget beavered away to keep things running smoothly.*
– ORIGIN Old English *beofor, befor*, of Germanic origin; related to Dutch *bever* and German *Biber*, from an Indo-European root meaning 'brown.'

beaver[1]

bea·ver[2] ▶ **n.** the lower part of the face guard of a helmet in a suit of armor. The term is also used to refer to the upper part or visor, or to a single movable guard.
– ORIGIN late 15th cent.: from Old French *baviere* 'bib,' from *baver* 'to drool.'

bea·ver[3] ▶ **n.** vulgar slang a woman's genitals or pubic area. ■ offensive a woman.
– ORIGIN early 20th cent.: of unknown origin.

bea·ver·board /ˈbēvər,bôrd/ ▶ **n.** a kind of fiberboard used in building.
– ORIGIN early 20th cent.: from BEAVER[1] + BOARD.

Bea·ver State a nickname for the state of OREGON.

Bea·ver·ton /ˈbēvərtən/ a city in northwestern Oregon, west of Portland, noted for its electronics industry; pop. 91,757 (est. 2008).

be·bop /ˈbē,bäp/ ▶ **n.** a type of jazz originating in the 1940s and characterized by complex harmony and rhythms. It is associated particularly with Charlie Parker, Thelonious Monk, and Dizzy Gillespie.
– DERIVATIVES **be·bop·per n.**
– ORIGIN 1940s (originally US): imitative of the typical rhythm of this music.

be·calm /biˈkä(l)m/ ▶ **v.** [with obj.] leave (a sailing vessel) unable to move through lack of wind.

be·came /biˈkām/ past tense of BECOME.

be·cause /biˈkôz, -ˈkəz/ ▶ **conj.** for the reason that; since: *we did it because we felt it our duty | just because I'm inexperienced doesn't mean that I lack perception.*
– PHRASES **because of** on account of; by reason of: *they moved here because of the baby.*
– ORIGIN Middle English: from the phrase *by cause*, influenced by Old French *par cause de* 'by reason of.'

> **USAGE** **1** When **because** follows a negative construction, the meaning can be ambiguous. In the sentence *he did not go* **because** *he was ill*, for example, it is not clear whether it means either 'the reason he did not go was that he was ill' or 'being ill was *not* the reason for his going—there was another reason.' Some usage guides recommend using a comma when the first interpretation is intended (*he did not go, because he was ill*) and no comma where the second interpretation is intended, but in general it is probably safest to try to avoid such constructions altogether. **2** As with other conjunctions such as **but** and **and**, it is still widely believed and taught that it is incorrect to begin a sentence with **because**. It has, however, long been used in this way in both written and spoken English (typically for rhetorical effect), and it is quite correct—however, the sentence-opening **because** should be used sparingly. See also usage at AND. **3** On the construction **the reason…is because**, see usage at REASON. **4** On the use of **since** in the sense of **because**, see usage at SINCE.

bé·cha·mel /ˌbāsHəˈmel/ (also **béchamel sauce**) ▶ **n.** a rich white sauce made with milk infused with herbs and other flavorings.
– ORIGIN named after the Marquis Louis de *Béchamel* (died 1703), steward to Louis XIV of France, who is said to have invented a similar sauce.

be·chance /biˈcHans/ ▶ **v.** archaic happen; befall.

bêche-de-mer /ˌbesH də ˈmer/ ▶ **n.** (pl. **same** or **bêches-de-mer** pronunc. **same**) **1** a large sea cucumber that is eaten as a delicacy in China and Japan. Also called TREPANG.
2 variant spelling of BEACH-LA-MAR.
– ORIGIN late 18th cent.: pseudo-French, alteration of Portuguese *bicho do mar*, literally 'sea worm.'

Bech·stein /ˈbekˌstīn/ ▶ **n.** a piano made by the German piano-builder Friedrich Wilhelm Carl Bechstein (1826–1900) or by the firm that he founded in 1856.

beck[1] /bek/ ▶ **n.** chiefly Brit. a mountain stream.
– ORIGIN Middle English: from Old Norse *bekkr*, of Germanic origin; related to Dutch *beek* and German *Bach*. Used as the common term for a brook in the northern areas of England, *beck* often refers, in literature, to a brook with a stony bed or following a rugged course, typical of such areas.

beck[2] ▶ **n.** literary a gesture requesting attention, such as a nod or wave.
– PHRASES **at someone's beck and call** always having to be ready to obey someone's orders immediately.
– ORIGIN Middle English: from archaic *beck*, abbreviated form of BECKON.

Beck·er /ˈbekər/, Boris (1967–), German tennis player. During 1985–91, he won the men's singles title at one US Open, one Australian Open, and three Wimbledon tournaments.

beck·et /ˈbekit/ ▶ **n.** a loop of rope or similar device for securing loose items on a ship.
– ORIGIN early 18th cent.: of unknown origin.

Beck·et, St. Tho·mas à /ə ˈbekit/ (c.1118–70), English prelate and statesman, archbishop of Canterbury 1162–70. He was assassinated when he opposed Henry II. Feast day, December 29.

Beck·ett /ˈbekit/, Samuel (Barclay) (1906–89), Irish playwright, novelist, and poet. He is well known for *Waiting for Godot* (1952), a seminal work in the Theater of the Absurd. Nobel Prize for Literature (1969).

Beck·mann[1] /ˈbekmən/, Ernst Otto (1853–1923), German chemist. He devised a method for determining a compound's molecular weight by measuring the rise in boiling point of a solvent containing the compound.

Beck·mann[2], Max (1884–1950), German painter and graphic artist. His paintings reflect his first-hand experience of human evil during World War I.

beck·on /ˈbekən/ ▶ **v.** [no obj.] make a gesture with the hand, arm, or head to encourage someone to come nearer or follow: *Miranda* ***beckoned to*** *Adam.* ■ [with obj.] attract the attention of and summon (someone) in this way: *he beckoned Christopher over* | [with obj. and infinitive] *he beckoned Duncan to follow.* ■ seem to be appealing or inviting: *the going is tough, and soft options beckon.*
– ORIGIN Old English *bīecnan*, *bēcnan*; related to BEACON.

be·cloud /biˈkloud/ ▶ **v.** [with obj.] cause to become obscure or muddled: *self-interest beclouds the issue.* ■ (usu. **be beclouded**) cover or surround with clouds.

be·come /biˈkəm/ ▶ **v.** (**becomes**, **becoming**; past **became**; past participle **become**) **1** [no obj., with complement] begin to be: *they became angry* | *it is becoming clear that we are in a totally new situation.* ■ grow to be; turn into: *the child will become an adult.* ■ (of a person) qualify or be accepted as; acquire the status of: *she wanted to become a doctor.* ■ (**become of**) (in questions) happen to: *what would become of her now?*
2 [with obj.] (of clothing) look good on or suit (someone): *the dress becomes her.* ■ be appropriate or suitable to (someone): *minor celebrity status did not become him.*
– ORIGIN Old English *becuman* 'come to a place, come (to be or do something)' (see BE-, COME), of Germanic origin; related to Dutch *bekomen* and German *bekommen* 'get, receive.'

be·com·ing /biˈkəmiNG/ ▶ **adj.** (esp. of clothing) flattering a person's appearance: *what a becoming dress!* | *New beret? It's very becoming.* ■ decorous: *a becoming modesty.*
▶ **n.** Philosophy the process of coming to be something or of passing into a state: *a series of poem sketches in a state of becoming.*
– DERIVATIVES **be·com·ing·ly** adv.

Bec·que·rel /ˌbek(ə)ˈrel/, Antoine-Henri (1852–1908), French physicist. With Marie and Pierre Curie, he discovered the natural radioactivity in uranium salts. Nobel Prize for Physics (1903), shared with the Curies.

bec·que·rel /ˈbekəˌrel/ (abbr.: **Bq**) ▶ **n.** Physics the SI unit of radioactivity, corresponding to one disintegration per second.
– ORIGIN late 19th cent.: named after A. H. BECQUEREL.

BEd ▶ **abbr.** Bachelor of Education.

bed /bed/ ▶ **n. 1** a piece of furniture for sleep or rest, typically a framework with a mattress and coverings: *a large double bed* | *she was* ***in bed*** *by nine* | *getting out of bed is a real struggle.* ■ a place or article used by a person or animal for sleep or rest: *a bed of straw.* ■ the time for sleeping: *a glass of milk before bed.* ■ a bed and associated facilities making up a place for a patient in a hospital or for a guest at a hotel: *a round of hospital staff layoffs and bed closings* | *few can afford a bed in a hotel.* ■ informal used with reference to a bed as the typical place for sexual activity: *some men care very little about pleasing their partners* ***in bed*** | *she'd* ***gone to bed with*** *Tony willingly.*
2 an area of ground, typically in a garden, where flowers and plants are grown: *a bed of tulips* | *vegetable beds.*
3 a flat base or foundation on which something rests or is supported, in particular: ■ the foundation of a road or railroad. ■ the open part of a truck, wagon, or railroad car, where goods are carried. ■ the flat surface beneath the baize of a billiard table.
4 a layer or pile of something, in particular: ■ a layer of food on which other foods are served: *the salad is served on a bed of raw spinach.* ■ a layer of rock or other geological material: *a bed of clay.* ■ any mass or pile resembling a bed: *pots steaming on the fragrant bed of coals* | *a dog knocked the girl into a bed of ants.*
5 the bottom of the sea or a lake or river: *a riverbed.* ■ [with modifier] a place on the seabed where shellfish, esp. oysters or mussels, breed or are bred: *mussel beds.*
▶ **v.** (**beds**, **bedding**, **bedded**) **1** [no obj.] settle down to sleep or rest for the night, typically in an improvised place: *he usually* ***bedded down on*** *newspapers in the church porch.* ■ (**bed someone/something down**) settle a person or animal down to sleep or rest for the night. ■ informal have sexual intercourse with: *he should bed a woman his own age.*
2 transfer (a plant) from a pot or seed tray to a garden plot: *I* ***bedded out*** *these houseplants.*
3 (usu. **be bedded in/on**) fix firmly; embed: *the posts should be firmly bedded in concrete.* ■ lay or arrange (something, esp. stone) in a layer.
– PHRASES **bed of nails** a board with nails pointing out of it, as lain on by fakirs and ascetics. ■ a problematic or uncomfortable situation. **bed of roses** [often with negative] used in reference to a situation or activity that is comfortable or easy: *farming is no bed of roses.* **be brought to bed** archaic (of a woman) give birth to a child: *she was* ***brought to bed of*** *a daughter.* **get up on the wrong side of the bed** start the day in a bad temper. **in bed with** informal having sexual intercourse with: *he found his wife in bed with one of the neighbors.* ■ in undesirably close association with: *these meetings with politicians put the gay movement in bed with the dreaded Establishment.* **make a bed** fit a bed with sheets, blankets, and pillows. **put someone to bed** take or prepare someone, typically a child, for rest in bed: *Clare put her to bed and gave her a mug of cocoa.* **put a newspaper to bed** informal prepare a newspaper for press. **take to one's bed** stay in bed because of illness.
– ORIGIN Old English *bed*, *bedd* (noun), *beddian* (verb), of Germanic origin; related to Dutch *bed* and German *Bett*.

be·dab·ble /biˈdabəl/ ▶ **v.** [with obj.] (usu. **be bedabbled**) archaic stain or splash with dirty liquid or blood: *idols of gold bedabbled all with blood.*

be·dad /biˈdad/ ▶ **exclam.** Irish used to express surprise or for emphasis.
– ORIGIN early 18th cent.: alteration of *by God*; compare with BEGAD and GAD[2].

bed and break·fast (abbr.: **b. & b.**) ▶ **n.** sleeping accommodations for a night and a morning meal, provided in guest houses and small hotels. ■ a guest house or small hotel offering such accommodations.

be·daub /biˈdôb/ ▶ **v.** [with obj.] (usu. **be bedaubed**) literary smear or daub with a sticky substance: *a dozen maidens, all* ***bedaubed with*** *paint.*

be·daz·zle /biˈdazəl/ ▶ **v.** [with obj.] greatly impress (someone) with brilliance or skill: *bedazzled by him, they offered him a job in Paris.* ■ cleverly outwit.
– DERIVATIVES **be·daz·zle·ment** n.

bed·bug /ˈbedˌbəg/ ▶ **n.** a bloodsucking bug that is a parasite of birds and mammals. ● Family Cimicidae, suborder Heteroptera: *Cimex* and other genera, and many species, in particular the chiefly nocturnal *C. lectularius*, which feeds mainly on humans, hiding in crevices or among clothing during the day.

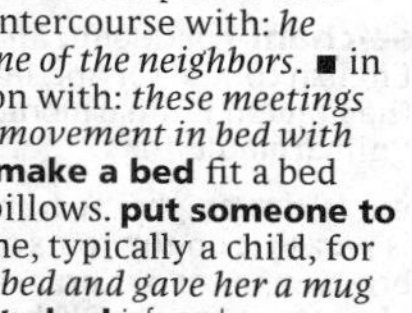

bedbug

bed·cham·ber /ˈbedˌCHāmbər/ ▶ **n.** archaic a bedroom.

bed·clothes /ˈbedˌklō(TH)z/ ▶ **plural n.** coverings for a bed, such as sheets and blankets.

bed·cov·er /ˈbedˌkəvər/ ▶ **n.** a bedspread.

bed·da·ble /ˈbedəbəl/ ▶ **adj.** informal sexually attractive or available.

bed·ded /ˈbedid/ ▶ **adj.** Geology (of rock) deposited in layers or strata, esp. in a way specified: *thinly bedded carbonate mudstones.*

bed·der /ˈbedər/ ▶ **n.** a plant suitable for use as a bedding plant.

bed·ding /ˈbediNG/ ▶ **n. 1** coverings for a bed, such as sheets and blankets. ■ straw or similar material for animals to sleep on.
2 a base or bottom layer: [as modifier] *a bedding course of sand.*
3 a display of bedding plants.
4 Geology the stratification or layering of rocks or other geological materials: [as modifier] *a bedding plane.*

bed·ding plant ▶ **n.** a plant set into a garden bed or container when it is about to bloom, usually an annual used for display and discarded at the end of the season.

bed·dy-bye /ˈbedē ˌbī/ ▶ **n.** informal a baby-talk word for bed or bedtime: *it was time for beddy-bye* | [as modifier] *we got our beddy-bye kisses and trundled up the stairs.*
– PHRASES **go beddy-bye** go to bed: *for the last ten miles, all I could think about was getting home and going beddy-bye.*
– ORIGIN early 20th cent.: from BED + -Y[2] and BYE-BYE.

Bede, St. /bēd/ (c.673–735), English monk, theologian, and historian; known as **the Venerable Bede**. He wrote *The Ecclesiastical History of the English People* (written in Latin and completed in 731), a primary source for early English history. Feast day, May 27.

be·deck /biˈdek/ ▶ **v.** [with obj.] decorate: *he led us into a room* ***bedecked with*** *tinsel.*

bed·e·guar /ˈbediˌgär/ (also **bedeguar gall**) another term for MOSSY ROSE GALL.
– ORIGIN late Middle English: from French *bédégar*, from Persian *bād-āwar*, literally 'wind-brought.'

be·dev·il /biˈdevəl/ ▶ **v.** (**bedevils**, **bedeviling**, **bedeviled**; also chiefly Brit. **bedevils**, **bedevilling**, **bedevilled**) [with obj.] (of something bad) cause great and continual trouble to: *inconsistencies that bedevil modern English spelling.* ■ (of a person) torment or harass: *he bedeviled them with petty practical jokes.*
– DERIVATIVES **be·dev·il·ment** n.

be·dew /biˈd(y)o͞o/ ▶ **v.** [with obj.] literary cover or sprinkle with drops of water or other liquid.

bed·fel·low /ˈbedˌfelō/ ▶ **n.** a person who shares a bed with another. ■ a person or thing allied or closely connected with another: *the treaty will make* ***strange bedfellows*** *of a number of enemies.*

Bed·ford /ˈbedfərd/ a city in northeastern Texas, northeast of Fort Worth; pop. 49,155 (est. 2008).

Bed·ford cord ▶ **n.** a tough woven fabric having prominent ridges, similar to corduroy.
– ORIGIN late 19th cent.: named after the town of Bedford, England.

Bed·ford-Stuy·ve·sant /ˈstīvəsənt/ a residential and commercial section of northern Brooklyn in New York City, home to one of the largest US black communities.

bed head ▶ **n.** informal a casual hairstyle resulting from failure to comb or arrange the hair after sleep.

bed-hop ▶ **v.** [no obj.] informal engage in successive casual sexual affairs: (as noun **bed-hopping**) *a life of bed-hopping.*
– DERIVATIVES **bed-hop·per** n.

be·dight /biˈdīt/ ▶ **adj.** archaic adorned: *a Christmas pudding bedight with holly.*
– ORIGIN late Middle English: past participle of archaic *bedight* 'equip, array' (see BE-, DIGHT).

be·dim /biˈdim/ ▶ **v.** (**bedims**, **bedimming**, **bedimmed**) [with obj.] literary cause to become dim: *a slight cloud would bedim the sky.*

be·di·zened /biˈdīzənd/ ▶ **adj.** literary dressed up or decorated gaudily: *a dress* ***bedizened with*** *resplendent military medals.*
– DERIVATIVES **be·di·zen** v.
– ORIGIN mid 17th cent.: from BE- (as an intensifier) + obsolete *dizen* 'deck out,' probably of Dutch origin.

bed·lam /ˈbedləm/ ▶ **n. 1** a scene of uproar and confusion: *there was bedlam in the courtroom.*
2 ■ archaic an asylum for the insane.
– ORIGIN late Middle English: early form of BETHLEHEM, referring to the hospital of St. Mary of Bethlehem in London, used as an asylum for the insane.

b

bed lin·en ▶ n. sheets, pillowcases, and duvet covers.

Bed·ling·ton ter·ri·er /ˈbedlinɢtən/ ▶ n. a terrier of a breed with a narrow head, long legs, and curly hair.
– ORIGIN mid 19th cent.: named after the village of *Bedlington* in northern England, where the breed originated.

Bedlington terrier

bed·mate /ˈbed,māt/ ▶ n. a person with whom a bed is shared, esp. a sexual partner.

Bed·ou·in /ˈbed(ə)win/ (also **Beduin**) ▶ n. (pl. **same**) a nomadic Arab of the desert.
▶ adj. of or relating to the Bedouin.
– ORIGIN from Old French *beduin*, based on Arabic *badawī*, (plural) *badawīn* 'dwellers in the desert,' from *badw* 'desert.'

bed·pan /ˈbed,pan/ ▶ n. a receptacle used by a bedridden patient as a toilet.

bed·plate /ˈbed,plāt/ ▶ n. a metal plate forming the base of a machine.

bed·post /ˈbed,pōst/ ▶ n. any of the four upright supports of a bedstead.
– PHRASES **between you and me and the bedpost** (or **the gatepost** or **the wall**) informal in strict confidence.

be·drag·gled /biˈdragəld/ ▶ adj. dirty and disheveled: *we got there, tired and bedraggled.*
– DERIVATIVES **be·drag·gle** v.
– ORIGIN early 18th cent.: from BE- 'thoroughly' + DRAGGLE + -ED².

bed rest ▶ n. confinement of an invalid to bed as part of treatment.

bed·rid·den /ˈbed,ridn/ ▶ adj. confined to bed by sickness or old age.
– ORIGIN Middle English: formed irregularly from archaic *bedrid* 'bedridden person,' from the base of the verb RIDE.

bed·rock /ˈbed,räk/ ▶ n. solid rock underlying loose deposits such as soil or alluvium. ■ the fundamental principles on which something is based: *honesty is the bedrock of a good relationship.*

bed·roll /ˈbed,rōl/ ▶ n. a sleeping bag or other bedding rolled into a bundle.

bed·room /ˈbed,ro͞om, -,ro͝om/ (abbr.: **bdrm.**) ▶ n. a room for sleeping in: [in combination] *a three-bedroom house.* ■ [as modifier] relating to sexual relations: *bedroom secrets.* ■ [as modifier] denoting a small town or suburb whose residents travel to work in a nearby city: *a bedroom community.*
– DERIVATIVES **bed·roomed** adj. [in combination] *a three-bedroomed house.*

bed·side /ˈbed,sīd/ ▶ n. the space beside a bed, typically that of someone who is ill: *he was summoned to the bedside of a dying man* | [as modifier] *a bedside lamp.*
– PHRASES **bedside manner** a doctor's approach or attitude toward a patient.

bed·sit /ˈbed,sit/ (also **bedsitter** or **bed-sitting room**) ▶ n. Brit. a one-room apartment typically consisting of a combined bedroom and sitting room with cooking facilities.

bed·skirt /ˈbed,skərt/ ▶ n. a decorative drapery attached to the frame of a bed; a dust ruffle.

bed·sore /ˈbed,sôr/ ▶ n. a sore developed by an invalid because of pressure caused by lying in bed in one position. Also called DECUBITUS ULCER.

bed·spread /ˈbed,spred/ ▶ n. a decorative cloth used to cover a bed.

bed·stead /ˈbed,sted/ ▶ n. the framework of a bed on which the mattress is placed.

bed·straw /ˈbed,strô/ ▶ n. a herbaceous plant with small, lightly perfumed, white or yellow flowers and whorls of slender leaves. It was formerly used for stuffing mattresses. ● Genus *Galium*, family Rubiaceae: several species, including **yellow bedstraw** (*G. verum*).

bed·time /ˈbed,tīm/ ▶ n. [in sing.] the usual time when someone goes to bed: *it was well past her bedtime* | [as modifier] *a bedtime story.*

Bed·u·in ▶ n. & adj. variant spelling of BEDOUIN.

bed warm·er (also **bedwarmer**) ▶ n. historical a device for warming a bed, typically a metal pan filled with warm coals.

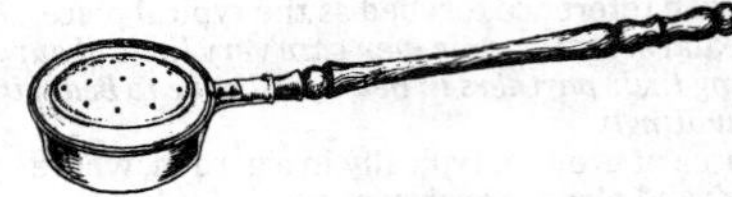
bed warmer

bed-wet·ting ▶ n. involuntary urination during sleep.
– DERIVATIVES **bed-wet·ter** n.

bee /bē/ ▶ n. **1** a honeybee.
2 an insect of a large group to which the honeybee belongs, including many solitary as well as social kinds. ● Superfamily Apoidea, order Hymenoptera: several families, often now placed in the single family Apidae.
3 [with modifier] a meeting for communal work or amusement: *a quilting bee.*
– PHRASES **have a bee in one's bonnet** informal be preoccupied or obsessed about something, esp. a scheme or plan of action. **the bee's knees** informal an outstandingly good person or thing. [first used to denote something small and insignificant, transferred to the opposite sense in US slang.]
– ORIGIN Old English *bēo*, of Germanic origin; related to Dutch *bij* and German dialect *Beie*.

bee balm ▶ n. another term for BERGAMOT (sense 3).

bee bread (also **beebread**) ▶ n. honey or pollen used as food by bees.

beech /bēcн/ ▶ n. (also **beech tree**) a large tree with smooth gray bark, glossy leaves, and hard, pale, fine-grained timber. Its fruit, the beechnut, is an important food for numerous wild birds and mammals. ● Genera *Fagus* (of the north temperate zone) and *Notofagus* (the **southern beeches**, of Australasia and South America), family Fagaceae: many species, esp. the common **American beech** (*F. grandifolia*) and the **European beech** (*F. sylvatica*).
– ORIGIN Old English *bēce*, of Germanic origin; related to BOOK and to Latin *fagus* 'beech,' Greek *phagos* 'edible oak.'

Bee·cham /ˈbēcнəm/, Sir Thomas (1879–1961), English conductor and impresario. He founded the London Philharmonic 1932 and the Royal Philharmonic 1947.

beech·drops /ˈbēcн,dräps/ ▶ n. a broomrape that is parasitic on the roots of beech trees. Unlike most broomrapes, it has branching stems. ● *Epifagus virginiana*, family Orobanchaceae.

Bee·cher¹ /ˈbēcнər/, Catharine Esther (1800–78), US educator. She promoted educational rights for women and founded the American Women's Education Assocation in 1852. She was the sister of Henry Ward Beecher and Harriet Beecher Stowe.

Bee·cher², Henry Ward (1813–87), US clergyman, orator, and writer. Ordained as a Congregationalist in 1837, he became famous as an orator who attacked political corruption and slavery. He was the brother of Catharine Beecher and Harriet Beecher Stowe.

beech fern ▶ n. a fern with triangular, deeply lobed fronds. Native to eastern North America, it favors moist woodland habitats and streamsides. ● Genus *Thelypteris*, family Polypodiaceae: two species, the **broad beech fern** (*T. hexagonptera*) and the **long beech fern** (also **narrow beech fern** or **northern beech fern**) (*T. phegopteris*).

beech mar·ten ▶ n. another term for STONE MARTEN.

beech·mast /ˈbēcн,mast/ ▶ n. (collectively, esp. when on the ground) beechnuts.
– ORIGIN late 16th cent.: from BEECH + MAST².

beech·nut /ˈbēcн,nət/ ▶ n. the small triangular brown fruit of the beech tree, pairs of which are enclosed in a prickly case. See BEECHMAST.

bee dance ▶ n. a series of movements performed in the hive by worker honeybees to inform the colony of the direction and distance to a food source.

bee·di ▶ n. (pl. **beedis**) variant spelling of BIDI.

bee-eat·er ▶ n. a brightly colored insectivorous bird with a large head and a long down-curved bill, and typically with long central tail feathers. ● Family Meropidae: three genera, in particular *Merops*, and including the **European bee-eater** (*M. apiaster*).

beef /bēf/ ▶ n. **1** the flesh of a cow, bull, or ox, used as food. ■ (pl. **beeves** /bēvz/) Farming a cow, bull, or ox fattened for its meat. ■ informal flesh or muscle, typically when well developed: *he needs a little more beef on his bones.* ■ informal strength or power: *he's been brought in to give the team more beef.*
2 (pl. **beefs**) informal a complaint or grievance: *he has a beef with American education: it doesn't teach the basics of investing.*
3 informal a criminal charge: *a drunk-driving beef.*
▶ v. [no obj.] informal complain: *he was beefing about how the recession was killing the business.*
– PHRASAL VERBS **beef something up** informal give more substance or strength to something: *cost-cutting measures are planned to beef up performance.*
– ORIGIN Middle English: from Old French *boef*, from Latin *bos*, *bov-* 'ox.'

beef·a·lo /ˈbēfə,lō/ ▶ n. (pl. **same** or **beefaloes**) a hybrid animal, a cross between cattle and buffalo.
– ORIGIN 1970s: blend of BEEF and BUFFALO.

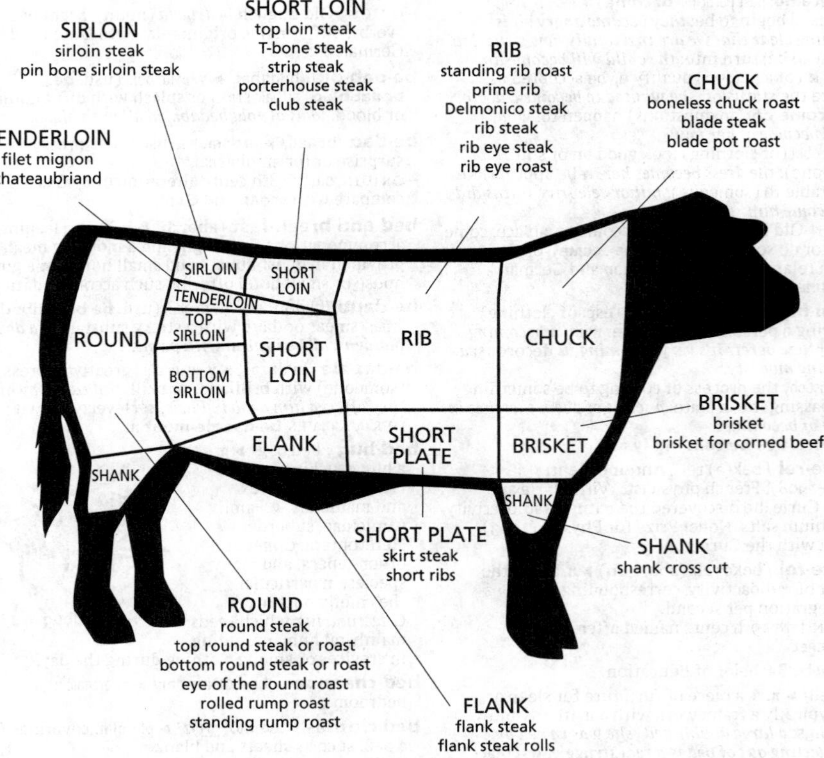

cuts of beef

beef bour·gui·gnon ▶ **n.** variant spelling of **BOEUF BOURGUIGNON**.

beef·cake /ˈbēf,kāk/ ▶ **n.** informal an attractive man with well-developed muscles.

beef·eat·er /ˈbēf,ētər/ ▶ **n.** a Yeoman Warder or Yeoman of the Guard in the Tower of London.
– ORIGIN early 17th cent. (originally a derogatory term for a well-fed servant): the current sense dates from the late 17th cent.

bee fly ▶ **n.** a squat, hairy, beelike fly that hovers to feed from flowers using its long tongue. Its larvae usually parasitize other insects, esp. bees and wasps. ● Family Bombyliidae: many genera.

beef·steak /ˈbēf,stāk/ ▶ **n.** a thick slice of lean beef, typically from the rump and eaten grilled, broiled, or fried.

beef·steak fun·gus (also **beefsteak mushroom**) ▶ **n.** an edible reddish-brown bracket fungus that resembles raw beef. Native to both Eurasia and North America, it usually grows on oak or sweet chestnut trees. ● *Fistulina hepatica*, family Fistulinaceae, class Hymenomycetes.

beef·steak to·ma·to ▶ **n.** a tomato of an exceptionally large and firm variety.

beef tea ▶ **n.** chiefly Brit. a drink made from stewed extract of beef used as nourishment for invalids.

beef Wel·ling·ton ▶ **n.** a dish of beef, typically coated in pâté de foie gras, wrapped in puff pastry, and baked.

beef·wood /ˈbēf,wo͝od/ ▶ **n.** a tropical hardwood tree with close-grained red timber. ● Species in several families, in particular *Casuarina equisetifolia* (family Casuarinaceae), native to Australia and Southeast Asia.

beef·y /ˈbēfē/ ▶ **adj.** (**beefier**, **beefiest**) **1** informal muscular or robust: *he shrugged his beefy shoulders.* ■ [attrib.] large and impressively powerful: *beefy skis.* **2** tasting like beef.
– DERIVATIVES **beef·i·ly** /ˈbēfəlē/ **adv.**, **beef·i·ness** **n.**

bee·hive /ˈbē,hīv/ ▶ **n. 1** a structure in which bees are kept, typically in the form of a dome or box. ■ [usu. as modifier] something having the domed shape of a traditional wicker beehive: *beehive huts | beehive ovens.* ■ a busy, crowded place: *the church became a beehive of activity.* ■ (**the Beehive** or **the Beehive cluster**) another term for **PRAESEPE**.
2 a woman's domed and lacquered hairstyle, esp. popular in the 1960s.
– DERIVATIVES **bee·hived** **adj.** (sense 2).

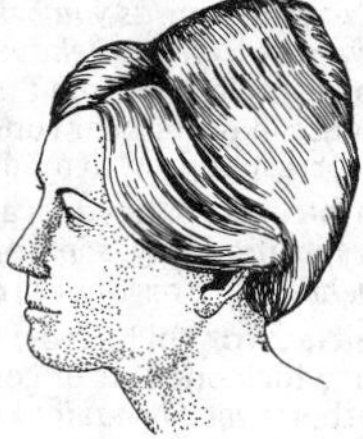
beehive 2

Bee·hive State a nickname for the state of **UTAH**.

bee·keep·ing /ˈbē,kēpiNG/ ▶ **n.** the occupation of owning and breeding bees for their honey.
– DERIVATIVES **bee·keep·er** /-,kēpər/ **n.**

bee·line /ˈbē,līn/ ▶ **n.** a straight line between two places.
– PHRASES **make a beeline for** hurry directly to.
– ORIGIN early 19th cent.: with reference to the straight line supposedly taken instinctively by a bee when returning to the hive.

Be·el·ze·bub /bēˈelzə,bəb/ a name for the Devil.
– ORIGIN from late Latin *Beëlzebub*, translating Hebrew *baʿal zĕbūb* 'lord of flies,' the name of a Philistine god (2 Kings 1:2), and Greek *Beelzeboul* 'the Devil' (Matt. 12:24).

Bee·mer /ˈbēmər/ (also **Beamer**) ▶ **n.** informal a car or motorcycle manufactured by the company BMW.
– ORIGIN 1980s (originally US): representing a pronunciation of the first two letters of *BMW* (Bayerische Motoren Werke AG) + *-er*.

been /bin/ past participle of **BE**.

Beene /bēn/, Geoffrey (1927–2004), US fashion designer.

beep /bēp/ ▶ **n.** a short, high-pitched sound emitted by electronic equipment or a vehicle horn.
▶ **v.** [no obj.] (of a horn or electronic device) produce such a sound: *radio receivers squawked and beeped.* ■ [with obj.] summon (someone) by means of a pager: *they have themselves beeped in restaurants.*
– ORIGIN 1920s: imitative.

beep·er /ˈbēpər/ ▶ **n.** another term for **PAGER**.

beer /bi(ə)r/ ▶ **n.** an alcoholic drink made from yeast-fermented malt flavored with hops: *a pint of beer | I'm dying for a beer.*
– PHRASES **beer and skittles** [often with negative] Brit. amusement or enjoyment: *life isn't all beer and skittles.*
– ORIGIN Old English *bēor*, based on monastic Latin *biber* 'a drink,' from Latin *bibere* 'to drink'; related to Dutch *bier* and German *Bier*.

beer bel·ly (also informal **beer gut**) ▶ **n.** a man's fat stomach, caused by excessive consumption of beer.
– DERIVATIVES **beer-bel·lied** **adj.**

Beer·bohm /ˈbi(ə)r,bōm/, Max (1872–1956), English caricaturist, essayist, and critic; full name *Sir Henry Maximilian Beerbohm*.

Beer·en·aus·le·se /ˌberənˈous,lāzə/ ▶ **n.** a white wine of German origin or style made from selected individual grapes picked later than the general harvest.
– ORIGIN German, from *Beeren* 'berries' + *aus* 'out' + *lese* 'picking.'

beer gar·den ▶ **n.** a garden, typically one attached to a bar or tavern, where beer is served.

beer gog·gles ▶ **plural n.** informal used to refer to the supposed influence of alcohol on one's visual perception, whereby one is sexually attracted to people who would not otherwise be appealing.

beer gut ▶ **n.** another term for **BEER BELLY**.

beer hall ▶ **n.** a large room or building where beer is served.

beer mon·ey ▶ **n.** informal a small amount of money allowed or earned.
– ORIGIN early 19th cent.: so named because the allowance of money was made instead of beer.

beer par·lour ▶ **n.** Canadian a room in a hotel or tavern where beer is served.

Beer·she·ba /bi(ə)rˈSHēbə/ a town in southern Israel on the northern edge of the Negev Desert; pop. 187,200 (est. 2008).

beer-swill·ing ▶ **adj.** drinking a lot of beer. ■ disreputable, rowdy.

beer·y /ˈbi(ə)rē/ ▶ **adj.** informal relating to or characterized by the drinking of beer, typically in large amounts: *many beery pledges were made | stale beery breath.*

beest·ings /ˈbēstiNGz/ (also **beastings**) ▶ **n.** [treated as sing.] the first milk produced by a cow or goat after giving birth.
– ORIGIN Old English *bȳsting*; related to Dutch *biest* and German *Biest(milch)*.

bee-stung ▶ **adj.** [attrib.] informal (of a woman's lips) full, red, and pouting.

bees·wax /ˈbēz,waks/ ▶ **n. 1** the wax secreted by bees to make honeycombs and used to make wood polishes and candles: *turning pollen into beeswax.* **2** informal a person's concern or business: *that's none of your beeswax.*

beet /bēt/ ▶ **n. 1** a herbaceous plant widely cultivated as a source of food for humans and livestock, and for processing into sugar. Some varieties are grown for their leaves and some for their large nutritious root. ● *Beta vulgaris*, family Chenopodiaceae: several subspecies.
2 the edible root of a kind of beet that is typically dark red and spherical and eaten as a vegetable. ■ the variety of beet that produces this root. ● *Beta vulgaris* subsp. *vulgaris*.
– ORIGIN Old English *bēte*, from Latin *beta*, perhaps of Celtic origin; related to Dutch *beet* and German *Bete*.

Bee·tho·ven /ˈbā,tōvən, ˈbāt,ō-/, Ludwig van (1770–1827), German composer. Despite increasing deafness, Beethoven wrote prodigiously: nine symphonies, thirty-two piano sonatas, sixteen string quartets, the opera *Fidelio* (1814), and the Mass in D (the *Missa Solemnis*, 1823).

bee·tle[1] /ˈbētl/ ▶ **n.** an insect of an order distinguished by forewings typically modified into hard wing cases (elytra) that cover and protect the hind wings and abdomen. ● Order Coleoptera: see **COLEOPTERA**.
▶ **v.** [no obj.] informal make one's way hurriedly or with short, quick steps: *the tourist beetled off.*
– ORIGIN Old English *bitula*, *bitela* 'biter,' from the base of *bītan* 'to bite.'

bee·tle[2] ▶ **n.** a tool with a heavy head and a handle, used for tasks such as ramming, crushing, and driving wedges; a maul. ■ a machine used for heightening the luster of cloth by pressure from rollers.
▶ **v.** [with obj.] ram, crush, or drive with a beetle. ■ finish (cloth) with a beetle.
– ORIGIN Old English *bētel*, of Germanic origin; related to **BEAT**.

bee·tle[3] ▶ **v.** [no obj.] (usu. as adj. **beetling**) (of a person's eyebrows) project or overhang threateningly: *piercing eyes glittered beneath a great beetling brow.*
▶ **adj.** [attrib.] (of a person's eyebrows) shaggy and projecting.
– DERIVATIVES **bee·tle-browed** **adj.**
– ORIGIN mid 16th cent. (as an adjective): back-formation from *beetle-browed*. The verb was apparently used as a nonce word by Shakespeare and was later adopted by other writers.

beet leaf·hop·per ▶ **n.** a North American leafhopper found west of the Mississippi River and considered a serious pest to beets and members of the gourd family. It is a principal carrier of the virus that causes curly top. ● *Circulifer tenellus*, family Cicadellidae.

bee tree ▶ **n.** a hollow tree used by bees for a hive: *in the Appalachians, the tupelo is a prime bee tree.*

beet·root /ˈbēt,ro͞ot/ ▶ **n.** chiefly Brit. another term for **BEET** (sense 2).

beet sug·ar ▶ **n.** sugar obtained from sugar beet.

beeves /bēvz/ plural form of **BEEF** (sense 1 of the noun).

BEF ▶ **abbr.** British Expeditionary Force.

be·fall /biˈfôl/ ▶ **v.** (past **befell**; past participle **befallen**) [with obj.] literary (of something bad) happen to someone: *a tragedy befell his daughter* | [no obj.] *she was to blame for anything that befell.*
– ORIGIN Old English *befeallan* 'to fall' (early use being chiefly figurative); related to German *befallen*.

be·fit /biˈfit/ ▶ **v.** (**befits**, **befitting**, **befitted**) [with obj.] be appropriate for; suit: *the ballet ends nobly, as befits a tragedy* | (as adj. **befitting**) *I answered in a befitting manner.*
– DERIVATIVES **be·fit·ting·ly** **adv.**

be·fog /biˈfäg/ ▶ **v.** (**befogs**, **befogging**, **befogged**) [with obj.] cause to become confused: *her brain was befogged with lack of sleep.*

be·fool /biˈfo͞ol/ ▶ **v.** [with obj.] archaic make a fool of: *novels that befool almost every intelligence.*

be·fore /biˈfôr/ ▶ **prep., conj., & adv. 1** during the period of time preceding (a particular event, date, or time): [as prep.] *she had to rest before dinner | the day before yesterday | before the war* | [as conjunction] *they lived rough for four days before they were arrested | it wasn't long before I had my first bite* | [as adv.] *his playing days had ended six years before | it's never happened to me before.*
2 in front of: [as prep.] *Matilda stood before her, panting | the patterns swam before her eyes* | [as adv.] archaic *trotting through the city with guards running before and behind.* ■ [prep.] in front of and required to answer to (a court of law, tribunal, or other authority): *he could be taken before a magistrate for punishment | a fall in the number of cases brought before the courts.*
3 in preference to; with a higher priority than: [as prep.] *a woman who placed duty before all else* | [as conjunction] *they would die before they would cooperate with each other.*
– ORIGIN Old English *beforan* (see **BY**, **FORE**), of Germanic origin; related to German *bevor*.

be·fore·hand /biˈfôr,hand/ ▶ **adv.** before an action or event; in advance: *rooms must be booked beforehand.*
– PHRASES **be beforehand with** archaic anticipate; forestall.
– ORIGIN Middle English (originally as two words): from **BEFORE** + **HAND**; probably influenced by Old French *avant main*.

be·fore·time /biˈfôr,tīm/ ▶ **adv.** archaic previously; formerly.

be·foul /biˈfoul/ ▶ **v.** [with obj.] make dirty; pollute: *they befoul our water with mining.*

be·friend /biˈfrend/ ▶ **v.** [with obj.] act as a friend to (someone) by offering help or support.

be·fud·dle /biˈfədl/ ▶ **v.** [with obj.] (usu. as adj. **befuddled**) make (someone) unable to think clearly: *he has an air of befuddled unworldliness.*
– DERIVATIVES **be·fud·dle·ment** **n.**

beg /beg/ ▶ **v.** (**begs**, **begging**, **begged**) **1** [reporting verb] ask (someone) earnestly or humbly for something: [with obj.] *I begged him for mercy* | [with obj. and infinitive] *she begged me to say nothing to her father* | [no obj.] *I must beg of you not to act impulsively.* ■ ask for (something) earnestly or humbly: *he begged their forgiveness* | [with direct speech] *"Don't leave me," she begged.* ■ ask formally for (permission to do something): *I will now beg leave to make some observations* | [no obj.] *we beg to inform you that we are instructed to wait.*
2 [no obj.] ask for something, typically food or money, as charity or a gift: *they had to beg for food.* ■ [with obj.] acquire (something) from someone in this way: *a piece of bread that I begged from a farmer.* ■ live by acquiring food or money in this way. ■ (of a dog)

PRONUNCIATION KEY ə *ago, up*; ər *over, fur*; a *hat*; ā *ate*; ä *car*; e *let*; ē *see*; i *fit*; ī *by*; NG *sing*; ō *go*; ô *law, for*; oi *toy*; o͝o *good*; o͞o *goo*; ou *out*; TH *thin*; T͟H *then*; ZH *vision*

b

sit up with the front paws raised expectantly in the hope of a reward.
– PHRASES **beg, borrow, or steal** do whatever may be necessary to acquire something greatly desired: *I'm gonna get the money to buy Casey's ring, even if I have to beg, borrow, or steal.* **beg off** request to be excused from a question or obligation: *asked to name her favorites from her films, Hepburn begs off.* **beg one's bread** archaic live by begging. **beg the question 1** (of a fact or action) raise a question or point that has not been dealt with; invite an obvious question. **2** avoid the question; evade the issue. **3** assume the truth of an argument or proposition to be proved, without arguing it. **beg to differ** see DIFFER. **go begging** (of an article) be available for use because unwanted by others: *half the apartments in New York go begging in the summer.* ■ (of an opportunity) not be taken: *we let so many good chances go begging.*
– PHRASAL VERBS **beg off** withdraw from a promise or undertaking.
– ORIGIN Middle English: probably from Old English *bedecian*, of Germanic origin; related to BID[1].

USAGE The original meaning of the phrase **beg the question** belongs to the field of logic and is a translation of the Latin term *petitio principii*, literally meaning 'laying claim to a principle' (that is, assuming something that ought to be proved first), as in the following sentence: *by devoting such a large part of the anti-drug budget to education, we are* ***begging the question*** *of its significance in the battle against drugs.* To some traditionalists, this is still the only correct meaning. However, over the last 100 years or so, another, more general use has arisen: 'invite an obvious question,' as in *some definitions of mental illness* ***beg the question*** *of what constitutes normal behavior.* This is by far the more common use today in modern standard English.

be·gad /bi'gad/ ▶ **exclam.** archaic used to express surprise or for emphasis.
– ORIGIN late 16th cent.: altered form; compare with BEDAD and GAD[2].

be·gan /bi'gan/ past of BEGIN.

be·gat /bi'gat/ archaic past of BEGET.

be·gem /bi'jem/ ▶ **v.** (**begems, begemming, begemmed**) [with obj.] (usu. as adj. **begemmed**) set or stud with gems: *a begemmed cross.*

be·get /bi'get/ ▶ **v.** (**begets, begetting**; past **begot** /-'gat/; past participle **begotten**) [with obj.] literary
1 (typically of a man, sometimes of a man and a woman) bring (a child) into existence by the process of reproduction: *they hoped that the King might beget an heir by his new queen.*
2 give rise to; bring about: *success begets further success.*
– DERIVATIVES **be·get·ter** **n.**
– ORIGIN Old English *begietan* 'get, obtain by effort' (see BE-, GET).

beg·gar /'begər/ ▶ **n. 1** a person, typically a homeless one, who lives by asking for money or food.
2 [with adj.] informal a person of a specified type, often one to be envied or pitied: *poor little beggars.*
▶ **v.** [with obj.] reduce (someone) to poverty: *by being soft to the unfortunate, we beggared ourselves.*
– PHRASES **beggar belief** (or **description**) be too extraordinary to be believed or described. **beggars can't be choosers** proverb people with no other options must be content with what is offered. **set a beggar on horseback and he'll ride to the Devil** proverb someone unaccustomed to power or luxury will abuse or be corrupted by it.
– ORIGIN Middle English: from BEG + -AR[3].

beg·gar·ly /'begərlē/ ▶ **adj.** poverty-stricken. ■ pitifully or deplorably meager or bad: *the stipend was a beggarly $26 | my beggarly physical condition.*
– DERIVATIVES **beg·gar·li·ness** **n.**

beg·gar-my-neigh·bor ▶ **n.** a card game for two players in which the object is to acquire one's opponent's cards. Players alternately turn cards up and if an honor is revealed, the other player must find an honor within a specified number of turns or else forfeit the cards already played.
▶ **adj.** [attrib.] (also **beggar-thy-neighbor**) (esp. of national policy) self-aggrandizing at the expense of competitors: *failure would create a growing risk of trade wars as countries retreated into beggar-thy-neighbor policies.*

beg·gar's purse ▶ **n.** an appetizer consisting of a crêpe stuffed with a savory filling, typically caviar and crème fraiche.

beg·gar·ticks /'begərtiks/ (also **beggar's ticks**) ▶ **plural n.** [often treated as sing.] a plant of the daisy family with inconspicuous yellow flowers and small barbed fruit that cling to passing animals. Several kinds are widespread weeds. Also called BUR MARIGOLD. ● Genus *Bidens*, family Compositae: several species, in particular *B. frondosa*.
– ORIGIN mid 19th cent.: apparently from the resemblance of the seedpods to ticks.

beg·gar·y /'begərē/ ▶ **n.** a state of extreme poverty.

beg·ging bowl ▶ **n.** a bowl held out by a beggar for food or donations: *among them was a wandering mendicant, with wooden staff and begging bowl* | figurative *they went to the government with a begging bowl to seek cash to finance the scheme.*

Be·gin /'bāgin, bə'gēn/, Menachem (1913–92), Israeli statesman, prime minister 1977–84. His hard line on Arab–Israeli relations softened in a series of meetings with President Anwar al-Sadat of Egypt, which led to a peace treaty between the countries. Nobel Peace Prize (1978), shared with Sadat.

be·gin /bi'gin/ ▶ **v.** (**begins, beginning**; past **began** /-'gan/; past participle **begun** /-'gən/) **1** [with obj.] start; perform or undergo the first part of (an action or activity): *theorists have just begun to address these complex questions | she began a double life |* (**begin to do/doing something**) *it was beginning to snow |* [no obj.] *she* ***began by*** *rewriting the syllabus.* ■ [no obj.] come into being or have its starting point at a certain time or place: *the ground campaign had begun | the story* ***begins with*** *the death of her senile father | the tour* ***begins at*** *the active Poas Volcano.* ■ [no obj.] (of a person) hold a specific position or role before holding any other: *he* ***began as*** *a drummer.* ■ [no obj.] (of a thing) originate: *Watts Lake* ***began as*** *a marine inlet.* ■ [no obj.] (**begin with**) have as a first element: *words beginning with a vowel.* ■ [no obj.] (**begin on/upon**) set to work at: *Picasso began on a great canvas.* ■ [with direct speech] start speaking by saying: *"I've got to go to the hotel," she began.* ■ [no obj.] (**begin at**) (of an article) cost at least (a specified amount): *rooms begin at $139.*
2 [no obj. with negative] informal not have any chance or likelihood of doing a specified thing: *circuitry that Karen could not begin to comprehend.*
– PHRASES **to begin with** at first. ■ in the first place: *such a fate is unlikely to befall him: to begin with, his is a genuine talent.*
– ORIGIN Old English *beginnan*, of Germanic origin; related to Dutch and German *beginnen*.

be·gin·ner /bi'ginər/ ▶ **n.** a person just starting to learn a skill or take part in an activity.
– PHRASES **beginner's luck** good luck supposedly experienced by a beginner at a particular activity.

be·gin·ning /bi'giniNG/ ▶ **n.** [usu. in sing.] the point in time or space at which something starts: *he left at the beginning of February | they had reached the beginning of the forest.* ■ the first part or earliest stage of something: *the ending of one relationship and the beginning of another | she had the beginnings of a headache.* ■ (usu. **beginnings**) the background or origins of anything: *the series explores the beginnings of flight | he had risen from humble beginnings to great wealth.*
▶ **adj.** new or inexperienced: *a beginning gardener.* ■ introductory or elementary: *the beginning guitar class.*
– PHRASES **the beginning of the end** the event to which ending or failure can be traced.

be·gird /bi'gərd/ ▶ **v.** [with obj.] chiefly literary gird about or around; encompass. ■ besiege.

Be·glie·ter /bi'glītər/, Lionel, see BART.

be·gone /bi'gôn, -'gän/ ▶ **exclam.** literary go away (as an expression of annoyance): *begone from my sight!*

be·go·nia /bi'gōnyə, -nēə/ ▶ **n.** a herbaceous plant of warm climates, the bright flowers of which have brightly colored sepals but no petals. Numerous cultivated varieties of begonia are grown for their flowers or for their striking foliage. ● Genus *Begonia*, family Begoniaceae.
– ORIGIN modern Latin, named after Michel *Bégon* (1638–1710), French amateur botanist who discovered the plant on the island of Santo Domingo and introduced it to Europe.

be·got /bi'gät/ past of BEGET.

be·got·ten /bi'gätn/ past participle of BEGET.

be·grime /bi'grīm/ ▶ **v.** [with obj.] (often as adj. **begrimed**) blacken with ingrained dirt: *paint flaking from begrimed walls.*

be·grudge /bi'grəj/ ▶ **v. 1** [with two objs.] envy (someone) the possession or enjoyment of (something): *she begrudged Martin his affluence.*
2 [with obj.] give reluctantly or resentfully: *nobody begrudges a single penny spent on health.*
– DERIVATIVES **be·grudg·ing·ly** **adv.**

be·guile /bi'gīl/ ▶ **v.** [with obj.] **1** charm or enchant (someone), sometimes in a deceptive way: *every prominent American artist has been beguiled by Maine |* (as adj. **beguiling**) *a beguiling smile.* ■ trick (someone) into doing something: *they were beguiled into signing a peace treaty.*
2 dated help (time) pass pleasantly: *to beguile some of the time they went to the movie theater.*
– DERIVATIVES **be·guile·ment** **n.**, **be·guil·er** **n.**, **be·guil·ing·ly** **adv.**
– ORIGIN Middle English (in the sense 'deceive, deprive of by fraud'): from BE- 'thoroughly' + obsolete *guile* 'to deceive' (see GUILE).

Beg·uine /'begēn, 'bā,gēn, bə'gēn/ ▶ **n.** (in the Roman Catholic Church) a member of a Dutch lay sisterhood, formed in the 12th century, and not bound by vows.

be·guine /bi'gēn/ ▶ **n.** a popular dance of West Indian origin, similar to the foxtrot.
– ORIGIN 1930s: from West Indian French, from French *béguin* 'infatuation.'

be·gum /'bāgəm, 'bē-/ ▶ **n.** Indian a Muslim lady of high rank. ■ (**Begum**) the title of a married Muslim woman, equivalent to Mrs.
– ORIGIN from Urdu *begam*, from eastern Turkish *bigim* 'princess,' feminine of *big* 'prince.'

be·gun /bi'gən/ past participle of BEGIN.

be·half /bi'haf/ ▶ **n.**
– PHRASES **on** (also **in**) **behalf of** (or **on someone's behalf**) **1** in the interests of a person, group, or principle: *votes cast by labor unions on behalf of their members.* **2** as a representative of: *he had to attend the funeral on Mama's behalf.* **3** on the part of; done by: *this wasn't simply a philanthropic gesture on his behalf.*
– ORIGIN Middle English: from a mixture of the earlier phrases *on his halve* and *bihalve him*, both meaning 'on his side' (see BY, HALF).

be·have /bi'hāv/ ▶ **v.** [no obj.] **1** [with adverbial] act or conduct oneself in a specified way, esp. toward others: *he always behaved like a gentleman | you should* ***behave*** *affectionately* ***toward*** *the patient.* ■ (of a machine or natural phenomenon) work or function in a specified way: *each car behaves differently.*
2 [often in imperative] conduct oneself in accordance with the accepted norms of a society or group: *you can go as long as you behave |* (**behave oneself**) *they were expected to behave themselves.*
– ORIGIN late Middle English: from BE- + HAVE in the sense 'have or bear (oneself) in a particular way' (corresponding to modern German *sich behaben*).

be·haved /bi'hāvd/ ▶ **adj.** conducting oneself in a specified way: *some of the boys had been badly behaved |* [in combination] *a well-behaved child.*

be·hav·ior /bi'hāvyər/ (Brit. **behaviour**) ▶ **n.** the way in which one acts or conducts oneself, esp. toward others: *good behavior | his insulting* ***behavior toward*** *me.* ■ the way in which an animal or person acts in response to a particular situation or stimulus: *the feeding behavior of predators.* ■ the way in which a natural phenomenon or a machine works or functions: *the erratic behavior of the old car.*
– PHRASES **be on one's best behavior** behave well when being observed: *warn them to be on their best behavior.*
– ORIGIN late Middle English: from BEHAVE, on the pattern of *demeanour* (an earlier spelling of DEMEANOR), and influenced by obsolete *haviour* from HAVE.

be·hav·ior·al /bi'hāvyərəl/ ▶ **adj.** involving, relating to, or emphasizing behavior: *closely related species have similar behavioral patterns | a behavioral approach to children's language.*
– DERIVATIVES **be·hav·ior·al·ly** **adv.**

be·hav·ior·al·ism /bi'hāvyərə,lizəm/ ▶ **n.** the methods and principles of the science of animal (and human) behavior. ■ advocacy of or adherence to a behavioral approach to social phenomena.
– DERIVATIVES **be·hav·ior·al·ist** **n. & adj.**

be·hav·ior·al sci·ence ▶ **n.** the scientific study of human and animal behavior.

be·hav·ior·ism /bi'hāvyə,rizəm/ (Brit. **behaviourism**) ▶ **n.** Psychology the theory that human and animal behavior can be explained in terms of conditioning, without appeal to thoughts or feelings, and that psychological disorders are best treated by altering behavior patterns. ■ such study and treatment in practice.
– DERIVATIVES **be·hav·ior·ist** **n. & adj.**, **be·hav·ior·is·tic** /bi,hāvyə'ristik/ **adj.**

be·ha·vior mod·i·fi·ca·tion ▶ **n. 1** the alteration of behavioral patterns through the use of such learning techniques as biofeedback and positive or negative reinforcement.
2 another term for BEHAVIOR THERAPY.

be·hav·ior ther·a·py ▶ **n.** the treatment of neurotic symptoms by training the patient's reactions to stimuli.

be·head /bi'hed/ ▶ **v.** cut off the head of (someone), typically as a form of execution: (as noun **beheading**) *public beheadings.*

– ORIGIN Old English *beheafdian*; from **BE-** 'off' (expressing removal) + *hēafod* (see **HEAD**).

be·held /bi'held/ past and past participle of **BEHOLD**.

be·he·moth /bi'hēməTH, 'bēməTH/ ▶ n. a huge or monstrous creature. ■ something enormous, esp. a big and powerful organization: *shoppers are now more loyal to their local stores than to faceless behemoths* | [as modifier] *behemoth telephone companies*.
– ORIGIN late Middle English: from Hebrew *bĕhēmōt*, intensive plural of *bĕhēmāh* 'beast.'

be·hest /bi'hest/ ▶ n. literary a person's orders or command: *they had assembled* **at his behest** | *the slaughter of the male children* **at the behest of** *Herod*.
– ORIGIN Old English *behǣs* 'a vow,' from a Germanic base meaning 'bid'; related to **HIGHT**.

be·hind /bi'hīnd/ ▶ prep. **1** at or to the far side of (something), typically so as to be hidden by it: *the recording machinery was kept behind screens* | *the sun came out from behind a cloud*. ■ underlying (something) but not apparent to the observer: *the agony behind his decision to retire*. ■ at the back of (someone), after they have passed through a door: *she ran out of the room, slamming the door behind her*.
2 in a line or procession, following or further back than (another member of the line or procession): *stuck behind a slow-moving tractor*.
3 in support of or giving guidance to (someone else): *whatever you decide to do, I'll be behind you* | *the power behind the throne*. ■ guiding, controlling, or responsible for (an event or plan): *the chances were that he was behind the death of the girl* | *the reasoning behind their decisions*.
4 after the departure or death of (the person referred to): *he left behind him a manuscript that was subsequently published*.
5 less advanced than (someone else) in achievement or development: *the government admitted it is ten years behind the West in PC technology*.
6 having a lower score than (another competitor): *Woodnam moved to ten under par, five shots behind Fred Couples*.
▶ adv. **1** at or to the far side or the back side of something: *as I looked behind, my feet crashed into a basket* | *Campbell grabbed him from behind*.
2 in a place or time already past: *the adventure lay behind them*.
3 remaining after someone or something is gone: *blocks of ice left behind by a retreating glacier* | *don't leave me behind*.
4 further back than other members of a group: *Bill led the way, with the others a short distance behind*.
5 (in a game or contest) having a score lower than that of the opposition: *polls showed him as much as 50 points behind*.
6 slow or late in accomplishing a task: *getting* **behind with** *my work* | *things were falling behind*. ■ in arrears: *she was* **behind with** *her rent*.
▶ n. **1** informal the buttocks: *sitting on her behind*.
2 Australian Rules Football a one-point score made by kicking the ball between the outer set of two sets of goalposts (the behind line), or by touching the ball, causing it to pass between the inner posts (goalposts).
– ORIGIN Old English *behindan, bihindan*, from *bi* 'by' + *hindan* 'from behind.'

be·hind·hand /bi'hīnd,hand/ ▶ adj. late or slow in doing something, esp. paying a debt: *the Yoruba have not been* **behindhand in** *economic activity*. ■ archaic unaware of recent events: *you are miserably behindhand—Mr. Cole gave me a hint of it six weeks ago*.
– ORIGIN mid 16th cent.: from **BEHIND** + **HAND**, on the pattern of *beforehand*.

be·hold /bi'hōld/ ▶ v. (past and past participle **beheld** /-'held/) [with obj. often in imperative] archaic or literary see or observe (a thing or person, esp. a remarkable or impressive one): *behold your king!* | *the botanical gardens were a wonder to behold*.
– PHRASES **beauty is in the eye of the beholder** see **BEAUTY**.
– DERIVATIVES **be·hold·er** n.
– ORIGIN Old English *bihaldan*, from *bi-* 'thoroughly' + *haldan* 'to hold.'

be·hold·en /bi'hōldən/ ▶ adj. [predic.] owing thanks or having a duty to someone in return for help or a service: *I don't like to be beholden to anybody*.
– ORIGIN late Middle English: former past participle of **BEHOLD**, in the otherwise unrecorded sense 'bound.'

be·hoof /bi'hoof/ ▶ n. archaic benefit or advantage: *to make laws* **for the behoof of** *the colony*.
– ORIGIN Old English *behōf*; related to Dutch *behoef* and German *Behuf*, also to **HEAVE**.

be·hoove /bi'hoov/ (Brit. **behove** /-'hōv/) ▶ v. [with obj.] (**it behooves someone to do something**) formal it is a duty or responsibility for someone to do something; it is incumbent on: *it behooves any coach to study his predecessors*. ■ [with negative] it is appropriate or suitable; it befits: *it ill behooves the opposition constantly to decry the sale of arms to friendly countries*.
– ORIGIN Old English *behōfian*, from *behōf* (see **BEHOOF**).

Beh·ring /'beriNG/, Emil Adolf von (1854–1917), German bacteriologist; one of the founders of immunology. Nobel Prize for Physiology or Medicine (1901).

Bei·der·becke /'bīdər,bek/, Bix (1903–31), US jazz musician and composer; born *Leon Bismarck Beiderbecke*. A self-taught cornetist and pianist, he profoundly influenced the development of jazz.

beige /bāZH/ ▶ n. a pale sandy yellowish-brown color: *tones of beige and green* | [as modifier] *a beige raincoat*.
– ORIGIN mid 19th cent. (denoting a usually undyed and unbleached woolen fabric of this color): from French, of unknown ultimate origin.

Beige Book ▶ n. a summary and analysis of economic activity and conditions, prepared with the aid of reports from the district Federal Reserve Banks and issued by the central bank of the Federal Reserve for its policy makers before a Federal Open Market Committee meeting: *Wednesday's Beige Book will be scanned for reports of tightness in labor markets*.

bei·gnet /ben'yā/ ▶ n. **1** a fritter: *a cheese beignet*.
2 a square of fried dough eaten hot sprinkled with confectioners' sugar.
– ORIGIN French, from archaic *buyne* 'hump, bump.'

Bei·jing /'bā'jiNG/ the capital of China, in the northeastern part of the country; pop. 8,580,400 (est. 2006). It became the country's capital in 1421, at the start of the Ming period, and survived as the capital of the Republic of China after the revolution of 1912. Also called (esp. formerly) **PEKING**.

be·ing /'bēiNG/ present participle of **BE**.
▶ n. **1** existence: *the railroad* **brought** *many towns* **into being** | *the moment when the universe* **came into being**. ■ living; being alive: *holism promotes a unified way of being*.
2 [in sing.] the nature or essence of a person: *sometimes one aspect of our being has been developed at the expense of the others*.
3 a real or imaginary living creature, esp. an intelligent one: *alien beings* | *a rational being*.

Bei·ra /'bārə/ a port on the coast of Mozambique; pop. 436,240 (2007).

Bei·rut /bā'root/ the capital and chief port of Lebanon; pop. 2,006,500 (est. 2009). It was badly damaged during the Lebanese civil war of 1975–89.

beit din /'bāt 'din/ ▶ n. a rabbinical court that decides questions on the basis of Talmudic law: *would a beit din close Napster down?*
– ORIGIN Hebrew, literally 'house of judgment.'

Be·ja /'bājə/ ▶ n. (pl. **same**) **1** a member of a nomadic people living between the Nile and the Red Sea.
2 the Cushitic language of this people.
▶ adj. of or relating to this people or their language.

be·jab·bers /bi'jabərz/ (also **bejabers** /-'jā-/) ▶ exclam. another way of saying **BEJESUS**.
– ORIGIN early 19th cent.: alteration of *by Jesus*.

Bé·jart /bā'yär/, Maurice (1927–2007), French ballet choreographer; born *Maurice Jean Berger*.

be·je·sus /bi'jēzəs/ (also **bejeezus**) ▶ n. informal an exclamation traditionally attributed to the Irish, used to express surprise or for emphasis: *they were forty minutes late, cocky as bejesus*.
– PHRASES **beat the bejesus out of someone** hit someone very hard or for a long time. **scare the bejesus out of someone** frighten someone very much.

be·jew·eled /bi'jooəld/ (also **bejewelled**) ▶ adj. adorned with jewels: *a wave of his bejeweled hand*.

Bel /bel/ another name for **BAAL**.

bel /bel/ ▶ n. a unit used in the comparison of power levels in electrical communication or of intensities of sound, corresponding to an intensity ratio of 10 to 1. See also **DECIBEL**.
– ORIGIN 1920s: from the name of Alexander Graham *Bell* (see **BELL**[1]).

be·la·bor /bi'lābər/ ▶ v. [with obj.] **1** argue or elaborate (a subject) in excessive detail: *critics thought they belabored the obvious*.
2 attack or assault (someone) physically or verbally: *Tyndale seized every opportunity to belabor the Roman Church*.
– ORIGIN late Middle English: from **BE-** (expressing transitivity) + the verb **LABOR**.

Bel Air /bel 'e(ə)r/ an affluent residential section of Los Angeles, California.

Be·la·rus /,belə'roos, ,bā-/ a country in eastern Europe; pop. 9,648,500 (est. 2009); capital, Minsk; official language, Belorussian. Formerly called **BELORUSSIA, WHITE RUSSIA**.

> Belarus became a republic of the former Soviet Union in 1921. It gained independence as a member of the Commonwealth of Independent States in 1991 but in 1996 signed a treaty with Russia that established a Community of Sovereign Republics. In 1999, Belarus signed another agreement with Russia for closer political and economic integration.

– DERIVATIVES **Be·la·ru·si·an** n. & adj.

be·lat·ed /bi'lātid/ ▶ adj. coming or happening later than should have been the case: *a belated apology*.
– DERIVATIVES **be·lat·ed·ly** adv., **be·lat·ed·ness** n.
– ORIGIN early 17th cent. (in the sense 'overtaken by darkness'): past participle of obsolete *belate* 'delay' (see **BE-**, **LATE**).

be·lay /bi'lā/ ▶ v. [with obj.] **1** fix (a running rope) around a cleat, pin, rock, or other object, to secure it. ■ secure (a mountaineer) in this way: *he belayed his partner across the ice* | [no obj.] *it is possible to belay here*.
2 [usu. in imperative] Nautical slang stop; enough!: *"Belay that, mister. Man your post."*
▶ n. **1** an act of belaying: *the leader may require belays to tackle more difficult sections*.
2 a spike of rock or other hard material used for belaying.
– DERIVATIVES **be·lay·er** n.
– ORIGIN mid 16th cent. (originally in nautical use): from **BE-** + **LAY**[1], on the pattern of Dutch *beleggen*.

Be·la·ya Riv·er /'byeləyə/ a river in the Bashkir Republic, in eastern Russia, that flows northwest for 700 miles (1,210 km) from the Ural Mountains to the Kama River.

be·lay·ing pin ▶ n. a pin or rod, typically of metal or wood, used on board ship and in mountaineering to secure a rope fastened around it.

bel can·to /bel 'käntō, 'kan-/ ▶ n. a lyrical style of operatic singing using a full rich broad tone and smooth phrasing: *a superb piece of bel canto* | [as modifier] *the bel canto arias of Bellini*.
– ORIGIN late 19th cent.: Italian, literally 'fine song.'

belch /belCH/ ▶ v. **1** [no obj.] emit gas noisily from the stomach through the mouth.
2 [with obj.] (often **belch out/forth/into**) (esp. of a chimney) send (smoke or flames) out or up: *a factory chimney belches out smoke*. ■ [no obj.] (often **belch from**) (of smoke or flames) pour out from a chimney or other opening: *flames belch from the wreckage*.
▶ n. an act of belching: *he gave a loud belch*.
– ORIGIN Old English *belcettan*, probably imitative.

bel·dam /'beldəm, -,dam/ (also **beldame**) ▶ n. archaic an old woman. ■ a malicious and ugly woman, esp. an old one; a witch.
– ORIGIN late Middle English (originally in the sense 'grandmother'): from Old French *bel* 'beautiful' + **DAM**[2].

be·lea·guer /bi'lēgər/ ▶ v. [with obj.] (usu. as adj. **beleaguered**) lay siege to: *he is leading a relief force to the aid of the beleaguered city*. ■ beset with difficulties: *the board is supporting the beleaguered director amid calls for his resignation*.
– ORIGIN late 16th cent.: from Dutch *belegeren* 'camp around,' from *be-* '(all) around' + *leger* 'a camp.'

Be·lém /bā'lem, bə-/ a city and port in northern Brazil, at the mouth of the Amazon River; pop. 1,408,847 (2007). It is Brazil's chief commercial center.

bel·em·nite /'beləm,nīt/ ▶ n. an extinct cephalopod mollusk with a bullet-shaped internal shell that is often found as a fossil in marine deposits of the Jurassic and Cretaceous periods. ● Order Belemnoidea, class Cephalopoda: many genera.
– ORIGIN early 17th cent.: from modern Latin *belemnites*, based on Greek *belemnon* 'dart.'

Bel·fast /'bel,fast, bel'fast/ the capital and chief port of Northern Ireland; pop. 260,700 (est. 2009). It suffered damage and population decline from the early 1970s because of sectarian violence by the Irish Republican Army (IRA) and Loyalist paramilitary groups.

Bel·fast sink ▶ n. Brit. a deep rectangular sink with a drain at one end, traditionally made of glazed white porcelain.

bel·fry /'belfrē/ ▶ n. (pl. **belfries**) a bell tower or steeple housing bells, esp. one that is part of a church. ■ a space for hanging bells in a church tower.
– PHRASES **bats in the** (or **one's**) **belfry** see **BAT**[2].

b

–ORIGIN Middle English *berfrey*, from Old French *berfrei*, later *belfrei*. The change in the first syllable was due to association with BELL[1].

Bel·gae /'beljē, 'bel,gī/ ▶ plural n. an ancient Celtic people inhabiting Gaul north of the Seine and Marne rivers.
–ORIGIN from Latin.

Bel·gaum /bel'goum/ an industrial city in western India, in the state of Karnataka; pop. 458,200 (est. 2009).

Bel·gian /'beljən/ ▶ adj. of or relating to Belgium. ▶ n. a native or inhabitant of Belgium or a person of Belgian descent.

Bel·gian en·dive ▶ n. another term for ENDIVE (sense 2).

Bel·gian hare ▶ n. a rabbit of a dark red long-eared domestic breed.

Bel·gian sheep·dog ▶ n. a dog of a medium-sized breed, similar in appearance to a German shepherd.

Bel·gian waf·fle ▶ n. a waffle made with a special tool to have large, deep indentations in it.

Bel·gic /'beljik/ ▶ adj. of or relating to the Belgae.

Bel·gium /'beljəm/ a low-lying country in western Europe, on the southern shore of the North Sea; pop. 10,414,300 (est. 2009); capital, Brussels, official languages, Flemish and French. French name **Belgique**, Flemish name **België**.

> Belgium became independent from the Netherlands after a nationalist revolt in 1830. Occupied and devastated during both world wars, Belgium formed the Benelux Customs Union with the Netherlands and Luxembourg in 1948 and became a founding member of the EEC. Flemish is spoken mainly in the north, and French and Walloon are spoken in the south.

–ORIGIN Latin, from BELGAE.

Bel·go·rod /'byelgərət, 'belgə,räd/ an industrial city in southern Russia, on the Donets River close to the border with Ukraine; pop. 353,000 (est. 2008).

Bel·grade /'bel,grād, -,gräd/ the capital of Serbia, on the Danube River; pop. 1,119,000 (est. 2008).

Be·li·al /'bēlēəl/ a name for the Devil.
–ORIGIN from Hebrew *bĕliyya'al* 'worthlessness.'

be·lie /bi'lī/ ▶ v. (**belies, belying, belied**) [with obj.] **1** (of an appearance) fail to give a true notion or impression of (something); disguise or contradict: *his lively alert manner belied his years.* **2** fail to fulfill or justify (a claim or expectation); betray: *the notebooks belie Darwin's later recollection.*
–ORIGIN Old English *belēogan* 'deceive by lying,' from BE- 'about' + *lēogan* 'to lie' Current senses date from the 17th cent.

be·lief /bi'lēf/ ▶ n. **1** an acceptance that a statement is true or that something exists: *his belief in the value of hard work | a belief that solitude nourishes creativity.* ■ something one accepts as true or real; a firmly held opinion or conviction: *contrary to popular belief, Aramaic is a living language | we're prepared to fight for our beliefs.* ■ a religious conviction: *Christian beliefs | I'm afraid to say belief has gone | local beliefs and customs.* **2** (**belief in**) trust, faith, or confidence in someone or something: *a belief in democratic politics | I've still got belief in myself.*
–PHRASES **be of the belief that** hold the opinion that; think: *I am firmly of the belief that we need to improve our product.* **beyond belief** astonishingly good or bad; incredible: *riches beyond belief | the driving we have witnessed was beyond belief.* **in the belief that** thinking or believing that: *he took the property in the belief that he had consent.* **to the best of my belief** in my genuine opinion; as far as I know: *to the best of my belief, Francis never made a will.*
–ORIGIN Middle English: alteration of Old English *gelēafa*; compare with BELIEVE.

be·liev·a·ble /bi'lēvəbəl/ ▶ adj. (of an account or the person relating it) able to be believed; credible. ■ (of a fictional character or situation) convincing or realistic.
–DERIVATIVES **be·liev·a·bil·i·ty** /bi,lēvə'bilitē/ n., **be·liev·a·bly** adv.

be·lieve /bi'lēv/ ▶ v. [with obj.] **1** accept (something) as true; feel sure of the truth of: *the superintendent believed Lancaster's story* | [with clause] *Christians believe that Jesus rose from the dead.* ■ accept the statement of (someone) as true: *he didn't believe her or didn't want to know.* ■ [no obj.] have faith, esp. religious faith: *there are those on the fringes of the Church who do not really believe.* ■ (**believe something of someone**) feel sure that (someone) is capable of a particular action: *I wouldn't have believed it of Lois—what an extraordinary woman!* **2** [with clause] hold (something) as an opinion; think or suppose: *I believe we've already met | things were not as bad as the experts believed | humuhumu are, I believe, shrimp fritters* | (**believe someone/something to be**) *four men were believed to be trapped.*
–PHRASES **be unable** (or **hardly able**) **to believe something** be amazed by something: *I couldn't believe what was happening | Clarke could hardly believe his luck as he put the ball into the empty net.* **be unable** (or **hardly able**) **to believe one's eyes** (or **ears**) be amazed by what one sees or hears: *I couldn't believe my eyes when I opened the box.* **believe it or not** used to concede that a proposition or statement is surprising: *believe it or not, the speaker was none other than Horace.* **believe me** (or **believe you me**) used to emphasize the truth of a statement or assertion: *believe me, she is a shrewd woman.* **don't you believe it!** used to express disbelief in the truth of a statement: *he says he is left of center, but don't you believe it.* **would you believe it?** used to express surprise at something one is relating: *they're still arguing, would you believe it?*
–PHRASAL VERBS **believe in 1** have faith in the truth or existence of: *I believe in ghosts.* **2** be of the opinion that (something) is right, proper, or desirable: *I don't believe in censorship of the arts | he didn't believe in sex before marriage.* **3** have confidence in (a person or a course of action): *he had finally begun to believe in her.*
–ORIGIN late Old English *belȳfan, belēfan*, alteration of *gelēfan*, of Germanic origin; related to Dutch *geloven* and German *glauben*, also to LIEF.

be·liev·er /bi'lēvər/ ▶ n. **1** a person who believes that a specified thing is effective, proper, or desirable: *a believer in ghosts | a firm believer that party politics has no place in local government.* **2** an adherent of a particular religion; someone with religious faith.

be·like /bi'līk/ ▶ adv. archaic probably; perhaps.

be·lit·tle /bi'litl/ ▶ v. [with obj.] make (someone or something) seem unimportant: *this is not to belittle his role | she felt belittled.*
–DERIVATIVES **be·lit·tle·ment** n., **be·lit·tler** n.
–ORIGIN late 18th cent.: a coinage of Thomas Jefferson originally meaning 'diminish in size, make small'; the current sense dates from the very end of the 18th century.

Be·li·tung /bä'lē,to͝oNG/ an Indonesian island in the Java Sea, between Borneo and Sumatra. Former name BILLITON.

Be·lize /bə'lēz/ a country in northeastern Central America, on the coast of the Caribbean Sea; pop. 307,900 (est. 2009); capital, Belmopan; languages, English (official), Creole, Spanish. Former name (until 1973) **British Honduras**.

> Proclaimed as a British Crown Colony in 1862, Belize became independent within the Commonwealth of Nations in 1981. Guatemala, on the west and south, has always claimed the territory on the basis of old Spanish treaties, although in 1992 it agreed to recognize the existence of Belize.

–DERIVATIVES **Be·li·zi·an** /-zēən/ adj. & n.
–ORIGIN named after a river with a Mayan name meaning 'muddy water.'

Be·lize Cit·y the principal seaport and former capital (until 1970) of Belize; pop. 65,200 (est. 2008).

Bell[1], Alexander Graham (1847–1922), US scientist, born in Scotland. He invented a method for transmitting speech electrically and gave the first public demonstration of the telephone in 1876; he founded the Bell Telephone Company the following year.

Bell[2], Currier, Ellis, and Acton, the pseudonyms used by Charlotte, Emily, and Anne Brontë respectively.

Bell[3], Vanessa (1879–1961), English painter and designer; born *Vanessa Stephen*. Together with her sister, Virginia Woolf, she was a prominent member of the Bloomsbury Group.

bell[1] /bel/ ▶ n. **1** a hollow object, typically made of metal and having the shape of a deep inverted cup widening at the lip, that sounds a clear musical note when struck, typically by means of a clapper inside. ■ a device that includes or sounds like a bell, used to give a signal or warning: *a bicycle bell.* ■ (**the bell**) a bell rung to denote intervals of time, such as (in boxing and other sports) to mark the start or end of a round: *at the bell, we dashed out of Latin class | the fight went to the final bell for a decision.* **2** a bell-shaped object or part of one, such as the end of a trumpet. ■ the corolla of a bell-shaped flower: *a flower with small, pale blue bells.* **3** (**bells**) a musical instrument consisting of a set of cylindrical metal tubes of different lengths, suspended in a frame and played by being struck with a hammer. Also called TUBULAR BELLS. **4** Nautical (preceded by a numeral) the time as indicated every half hour of a watch by the striking of the ship's bell one to eight times: *at five bells in the forenoon of June 11.*
▶ v. **1** [with obj.] provide with a bell or bells; attach a bell or bells to: *the young men were belling and hobbling the horses before releasing them* | (as adj. **belled**) *animals in gaudy belled harnesses.* **2** [no obj.] make a ringing sound likened to that of a bell: *the organ belling away.* **3** [no obj.] spread or flare outward like the lip of a bell: *her shirt belled out behind.*
–PHRASES **be saved by the bell** (in boxing and other sports) avoid being counted out by the ringing of the bell at the end of a round. ■ escape from danger narrowly or by an unexpected intervention. **bell the cat** take the danger of a shared enterprise upon oneself. [an allusion to a fable in which the mice (or rats) suggest hanging a bell around the cat's neck to have warning of its approach.] **bells and whistles** informal attractive additional features or trimmings: *an advocate of more bells and whistles on the income tax code.* [an allusion to the various bells and whistles of old fairground organs.] **(as) clear** (or **sound**) **as a bell** perfectly clear or sound: *Aunt Nora's words came clear as a bell.* **ring a bell** informal revive a distant recollection; sound familiar: *the name Woodall rings a bell.* **with bells on** informal enthusiastically: *everybody's waiting for you with bells on.*
–ORIGIN Old English *belle*, of Germanic origin; related to Dutch *bel*, and perhaps to BELL[2].

bell[2] ▶ n. the cry of a stag or buck at rutting time.
▶ v. [no obj.] (of a stag or buck) make this cry.
–ORIGIN Old English *bellan* 'to bellow,' of Germanic origin; related to German *bellen* 'to bark, bray,' and perhaps also to BELL[1].

bel·la·don·na /,belə'dänə/ ▶ n. deadly nightshade. ■ a drug prepared from the leaves and root of this, containing atropine.
–ORIGIN mid 18th cent.: from modern Latin, from Italian *bella donna* 'fair lady,' perhaps from the use of its juice to add brilliance to the eyes by dilating the pupils.

bel·la·don·na lil·y ▶ n. the South African amaryllis.

bell·bird /'bel,bərd/ ▶ n. **1** a tropical American bird of the cotinga family, with loud explosive calls. There are wattles on the head of the male. ● Genus *Procnias*, family Cotingidae: four species. **2** any of a number of Australasian songbirds with ringing bell-like calls, including. ● (**New Zealand bellbird**) a New Zealand honeyeater (*Anthornis melanura*, family Meliphagidae). ● (**crested bellbird**) an Australian whistler (*Oreoica gutturalis*, family Pachycephalidae). ● the bell miner. See MINER (sense 2).

bell-bot·toms ▶ plural n. trousers with a marked flare below the knee: (as modifier **bell-bottom**) *bell-bottom trousers.*
–DERIVATIVES **bell-bot·tomed** adj.

bell·boy /'bel,boi/ ▶ n. another term for BELLHOP.

bell buoy ▶ n. a buoy equipped with a bell rung by the motion of the sea, warning nearby vessels of shoal waters.

bell cap·tain ▶ n. the supervisor of a group of bellboys.

bell crank (also **bell crank lever**) ▶ n. a lever with two arms that have a common fulcrum at their junction.

bell curve ▶ n. Mathematics a graph of a normal (Gaussian) distribution, with a large rounded peak tapering away at each end.

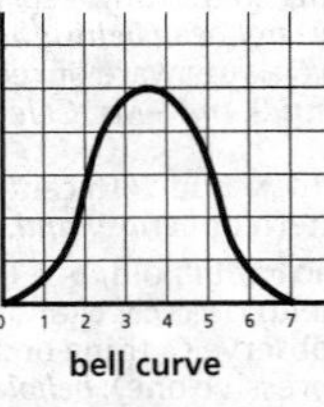

bell curve

belle /bel/ ▶ n. a beautiful girl or woman, esp. the most beautiful at a particular event or in a particular group: *the belle of the season.*
–PHRASES **belle of the ball** the most beautiful and popular girl or woman at a dance.
–ORIGIN early 17th cent.: from French, feminine of *beau*, from Latin *bella*, feminine of *bellus* 'beautiful.'

Bel·leau Wood /be'lō/ (French name *Bois de Belleau*) a forest east of Paris, France, and just east of Château-Thierry, the scene of a June 1918 US victory over the Germans during World War I.

belle é·poque /,bel ā'pôk/ ▶ n. the period of settled and comfortable life preceding World War I: [as modifier] *a romantic, belle-époque replica of a Paris bistro.*
–ORIGIN mid 20th cent.: French, literally 'fine period.'

Bel·ler·o·phon /bə'lerə,fän, -fən/ Greek Mythology a hero who slew the monster Chimera with the help of the winged horse Pegasus.

belles-let·tres /,bel 'letrə/ ▶ plural n. [also treated as sing.] **1** essays, particularly of literary and artistic

criticism, written and read primarily for their aesthetic effect.
2 literature considered as a fine art.
– DERIVATIVES **bel·let·rism** /bel'letrizəm/ **n.**, **bel·let·rist** /bel'letrist/ **n.**, **bel·let·ris·tic** /ˌbelə'tristik/ **adj.**
– ORIGIN mid 17th cent.: from French, literally 'fine letters.'

Belle·ville /'belˌvil/ an industrial city in southwestern Illinois; pop. 41,097 (est. 2008).

Belle·vue /'belˌvyo͞o/ **1** a city in eastern Nebraska; pop. 49,699 (est. 2008).
2 a city in northwestern Washington, across an inlet of Puget Sound to the east of Seattle; pop. 123,771 (est. 2008).

Bell·flow·er /'belˌflou(-ə)r/ a city in southwestern California, southeast of Los Angeles; pop. 73,033 (est. 2008).

bell·flow·er /'belˌflou(-ə)r/ ▶ **n.** a plant with bell-shaped flowers that are usually blue, purple, pink, or white. Many kinds are cultivated as ornamentals. ● Genus *Campanula*, family Campanulaceae: many species, including the Eurasian **clustered bellflower** (*C. glomerata*) and the harebell.

Bell Gardens a city east of Los Angeles, California; pop. 44,692 (est. 2008).

bell·hop /'belˌhäp/ ▶ **n.** an attendant in a hotel who performs services such as carrying guests' luggage.

bel·li·cose /'beliˌkōs/ ▶ **adj.** demonstrating aggression and willingness to fight: *a group of bellicose patriots.*
– DERIVATIVES **bel·li·cos·i·ty** /ˌbelə'käsitē/ **n.**
– ORIGIN late Middle English: from Latin *bellicosus*, from *bellicus* 'warlike,' from *bellum* 'war.'

bel·lig·er·ence /bə'lijərəns/ (also **belligerency** /-ənsē/) ▶ **n.** aggressive or warlike behavior: *the reaction ranged from wild enthusiasm to outright belligerence.*

bel·lig·er·ent /bə'lijərənt/ ▶ **adj.** hostile and aggressive: *a bull-necked, belligerent old man.* ■ engaged in a war or conflict, as recognized by international law.
▶ **n.** a nation or person engaged in war or conflict, as recognized by international law.
– DERIVATIVES **bel·lig·er·ent·ly** **adv.**
– ORIGIN late 16th cent.: from Latin *belligerant-* 'waging war,' from the verb *belligerare*, from *bellum* 'war.'

Bel·ling·ham /'beliNGˌham/ an industrial port city in northwestern Washington, on Bellingham Bay off Puget Sound; pop. 78,905 (est. 2008).

Bel·lings·hau·sen Sea /'beliNGzˌhouzən/ a part of the southeastern Pacific Ocean off the coast of Antarctica, bounded on the east and the south by the Antarctic Peninsula and Ellsworth Land.
– ORIGIN named after the Russian explorer Fabian Gottlieb von *Bellingshausen* (1778–1852), who in 1819–21 became the first to circumnavigate Antarctica.

Bel·li·ni /bə'lēnē/ ▶ **n.** (pl. **Bellinis**) a cocktail consisting of peach juice mixed with champagne.
– ORIGIN from the name of Venetian painter Giovanni *Bellini* (*c.* 1430–1516): the cocktail is said to have been invented in Venice during a major exhibition of the artist's work in 1948.

Bel·li·ni[1] /bə'lēnē/ the name of a family of Italian painters in Venice, including **Jacopo** (*c.*1400–70) and his sons **Gentile** (*c.*1429–1507) and **Giovanni** (*c.*1430–1516).

Bel·li·ni[2], Vincenzo (1801–35), Italian opera composer. Notable works: *La Sonnambula* (1831), *Norma* (1831), and *I Puritani* (1835).

bell jar ▶ **n.** **1** a bell-shaped glass cover used for covering delicate objects or used in a laboratory, typically for enclosing samples.
2 an environment in which someone is protected or cut off from the outside world: *let him stay in his bell jar of perfectionist concentration.*

bell·man /'belmən/ ▶ **n.** (pl. **bellmen**) **1** another term for BELLHOP.
2 historical a town crier.

Bel·loc /bə'lôk/ Hilaire (1870–1953), British writer, historian, and poet; born in France; full name *Joseph Hilaire Pierre René*. He is remembered chiefly for *Cautionary Tales* (1907).

Bel·low /'belō/, Saul (1915–2005), US novelist; born in Canada. Notable works: *The Adventures of Augie March* (1953), *Herzog* (1964), *More Die of Heartbreak* (1987) and *Ravelstein* (2000). Nobel Prize for Literature (1976).

bel·low /'belō/ ▶ **v.** [no obj.] (of a person or animal) emit a deep loud roar, typically in pain or anger: *he bellowed in agony* | (as noun **bellowing**) *the bellowing of a bull.* ■ [reporting verb] shout something with a deep loud roar: [with obj.] *the watchers were bellowing encouragement* | *he* **bellowed out** *the order* | [with direct speech] *"God send the right!" he bellowed* | [with infinitive] *his desperate parents were* **bellowing at** *her to stop.* ■ [with obj.] sing (a song) loudly and tunelessly: *he got thrown out of bars for bellowing Portuguese folk songs.*
▶ **n.** a deep roaring shout or sound: *a bellow of rage* | *he delivers his lines in a bellow.*
– ORIGIN Middle English: perhaps from late Old English *bylgan*.

bel·lows /'belōz/ ▶ **plural n.** [also treated as sing.] **1** (also **a pair of bellows**) a device with an air bag that emits a stream of air when squeezed together with two handles, used for blowing air into a fire. ■ a similar device used in a harmonium or small organ.
2 an object or device with concertinaed sides to allow it to expand and contract, such as a tube joining a lens to a camera body.
– ORIGIN Middle English: probably representing Old English *belga*, plural of *belig* (see BELLY), used as a shortened form of earlier *blǣstbelig* 'blowing bag.'

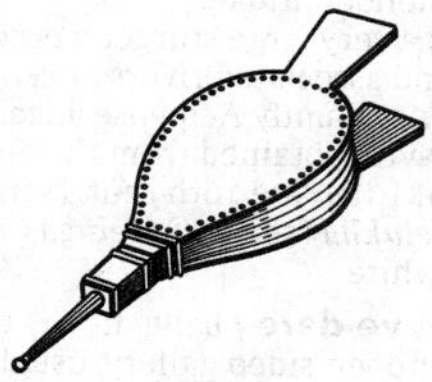

pair of bellows

bell pep·per ▶ **n.** another term for SWEET PEPPER.

bell pull ▶ **n.** a cord or handle that rings a bell when pulled, typically used to summon someone from another room.

bell-ring·ing ▶ **n.** the activity or pastime of ringing church bells or handbells.
– DERIVATIVES **bell-ring·er** **n.**

Bell's pal·sy ▶ **n.** paralysis of the facial nerve, causing muscular weakness in one side of the face.
– ORIGIN mid 19th cent.: named after Sir Charles *Bell* (1774–1842), the Scottish anatomist who first described it.

bell·weth·er /'belˌweT͟Hər/ ▶ **n.** the leading sheep of a flock, with a bell on its neck. ■ an indicator or predictor of something: *college campuses are often the bellwether of change* | [as modifier] *the market's bellwether stock.*

bell·wort /'belˌwərt, -ˌwôrt/ ▶ **n.** a plant of the lily family bearing slender yellow bell-like flowers and found chiefly in eastern North America. ● Genus *Uvularia*, family Liliaceae: several species, including the **large-flowered bellwort** (*U. grandiflora*) and the **perfoliate bellwort** (*U. perfoliata*).

bel·ly /'belē/ ▶ **n.** (pl. **bellies**) the front part of the human trunk below the ribs, containing the stomach and bowels. ■ the stomach, esp. as representing the body's need for food: *they'll fight all the better on empty bellies.* ■ the underside of a bird or other animal. ■ a cut of pork from the underside between the legs. ■ a pig's belly as food, esp. as a traded commodity. ■ the rounded underside of a ship or aircraft. ■ the top surface of an instrument of the violin family, across which the strings are placed.
▶ **v.** (**bellies, bellying, bellied**) **1** swell or cause to swell: [no obj.] *as she leaned forward her sweater* **bellied out** | [with obj.] *the wind bellied the sail out.*
2 [no obj.] (**belly up to**) informal move or sit close to (a bar or table): *regulars who first bellied up to the bar years before.*
– PHRASES **go belly up** informal go bankrupt.
– DERIVATIVES **bel·lied** **adj.** [usu. in combination] *fat-bellied men.*
– ORIGIN Old English *belig* 'bag,' of Germanic origin, from a base meaning 'swell, be inflated.'

bel·ly·ache /'belēˌāk/ informal ▶ **n.** an abdominal pain.
▶ **v.** [no obj.] complain noisily or persistently: *heads of departments* **bellyaching about** *lack of resources* | (as noun **bellyaching**) *there was plenty of bellyaching.*
– DERIVATIVES **bel·ly·ach·er** **n.**

bel·ly·band /'belēˌband/ (also **belly band**) ▶ **n.** **1** a band placed around the belly, in particular: ■ a part of a horse's harness that attaches to the shafts of a cart. ■ a cloth strip used to protect an infant's navel. ■ an absorbent cloth strip used to aid in a male dog's housebreaking. **2** a band wrapped around an item of merchandise, in particular: ■ a band that prevents a product from opening prior to display or purchase. ■ a printed strip wrapped around a book or magazine for promotional purposes.

bel·ly but·ton ▶ **n.** informal a person's navel.

bel·ly dance ▶ **n.** a dance originating in the Middle East, typically performed by a woman and involving undulating movements of the belly and rapid gyration of the hips.
– DERIVATIVES **bel·ly danc·er** **n.**, **bel·ly danc·ing** **n.**

bel·ly·flop /'belēˌfläp/ informal ▶ **n.** **1** a dive into water, landing flat on one's front.
2 a commercial failure: *the film's bellyflop at the box office is unsurprising.*
▶ **v.** (**bellyflops, bellyflopping, bellyflopped**) [no obj.] perform a bellyflop. ■ (of an aircraft) perform a belly landing.

bel·ly·ful /'belēˌfo͝ol/ ▶ **n.** (pl. **bellyfuls**) a quantity of food sufficient to fill one's stomach; a sustaining meal.
– PHRASES **have a** (or **one's**) **bellyful** informal become intolerant of someone or something after lengthy or repeated contact: *he had had his bellyful of hospitals.*

bel·ly land·ing ▶ **n.** a crash-landing of an aircraft on the underside of the fuselage, without lowering the undercarriage.

bel·ly laugh ▶ **n.** a loud, unrestrained laugh.

Bel·mo·pan /'belməˌpan/ the capital of Belize since 1970, in the central part of the country. It is one of the smallest capital cities in the world; pop. 18,100 (est. 2008).

Be·lo Ho·ri·zon·te /ˌbālō ˌhôrə'zôntā/ a city in eastern Brazil, the first planned city in Brazil; pop. 2,412,937 (2007).

Be·loit /bə'loit/ an industrial and academic city in southeastern Wisconsin; pop. 36,160 (est. 2008).

be·long /bi'lôNG/ ▶ **v.** [no obj.] **1** [with adverbial of place] (of a thing) be rightly placed in a specified position: *learning to place the blame where it belongs.* ■ be rightly classified in or assigned to a specified category: *bony fish: the vast majority of living fish belong here.*
2 [usu. with adverbial of place] (of a person) fit in a specified place or environment: *she is a stranger, and doesn't belong here* | *you and me, we belong together* | (as noun **belonging**) *we feel a real sense of belonging.* ■ have the right personal or social qualities to be a member of a particular group: *young people are generally very anxious to belong.* ■ (**belong to**) be a member or part of (a particular group, organization, or class): *they belong to garden and bridge clubs.*
3 (**belong to**) be the property of: *the vehicle did not belong to him.* ■ be the rightful possession of; be due to: *most of the credit belongs to Paul.* ■ (of a contest or period of time) be dominated by: *the race belonged completely to Ferguson.*
– DERIVATIVES **be·long·ing·ness** **n.**
– ORIGIN Middle English (in the sense 'be appropriately assigned to'): from BE- (as an intensifier) + the archaic verb *long* 'belong,' based on Old English *gelang* 'at hand, together with.'

be·long·ings /bi'lôNGiNGz/ ▶ **plural n.** one's movable possessions.

Be·lo·rus·sia /ˌbelō'rəsHə/ (also **Byelorussia**) former name for BELARUS.
– ORIGIN Russian *Belorossiya*, from *belyĭ* 'white' + *Rossiya* 'Russia.'

Be·lo·rus·sian /ˌbelō'rəsHən/ (also **Byelorussian** /ˌbyelō-/) ▶ **adj.** of or relating to Belarus, its people, or its language.
▶ **n.** **1** a native or inhabitant of Belarus. ■ a person of Belorussian descent.
2 the East Slavic language of Belarus.

Be·lo·stok /ˌbyelə'stôk/ Russian name for BIAŁYSTOK.

be·lov·ed /bi'ləv(i)d/ ▶ **adj.** dearly loved. ■ (**beloved by/of**) very popular with or much used by a specified set of people: *being so close, the mountain hut is beloved of families on a day's outing.*
▶ **n.** a much loved person: *he watched his beloved.*
– ORIGIN late Middle English: past participle of obsolete *belove* 'be pleasing,' later 'love.'

be·low /bi'lō/ ▶ **prep.** **1** extending underneath: *the tunnel below the crags* | *cables running below the floorboards* | *hanging space below a top storage shelf.*
2 at a lower level or layer than: *just below the pocket was a stain* | *blistered skin below his collar.* ■ lower in grade or rank than: *they rated its financial soundness below its competitor's.*
3 lower than (a specified amount, rate, or norm): *below average* | *below freezing* | *a dive to below 60 feet.*
▶ **adv.** at a lower level or layer: *he jumped from the window into the moat below.* ■ on earth: *the lot of all that dwells here below.* ■ in hell: *traitors gnash their teeth below.* ■ lower than zero (esp. zero degrees Fahrenheit) in temperature: *there's a north wind blowing, and it's 30 below.* ■ (in printed text) mentioned later or further down on the same page: *our nutritionist is pictured below right* | *the most common methods are shown below.* ■ Nautical below deck: *I'll go below and fix us a drink.*
– PHRASES **below (the) ground** beneath the surface of the ground: *60 feet below ground.*
– ORIGIN late Middle English (as an adverb): from BE- 'by' + the adjective LOW[1]. Not common until the 16th

cent., the word developed a prepositional use and was frequent in Shakespeare.

be·low decks (also **below deck**) ▶ **adj. & adv.** in or into the space below the main deck of a ship: [as adj.] *the sleeping quarters were below decks* | [as adv.] *nuclear weapons stored below decks.*
▶ **plural n.** (**belowdecks**) the space below the main deck of a ship.

Bel Pa·e·se /,bel pä'āzē/ ▶ **n.** trademark a rich, white, mild, creamy cheese of a kind originally made in Italy.
– ORIGIN Italian, literally 'fair country.'

Bel·sen /'belsən/ a Nazi concentration camp in World War II, near the village of Belsen in northwestern Germany.

Bel·shaz·zar /'belsʜə,zär, bel'sʜazər/ (6th century BC), last king of Babylon, son of Nebuchadnezzar. According to the biblical book of Daniel, he was killed in the sacking of the city and his doom was foretold by writing that appeared on the palace walls at a great banquet.

belt /belt/ ▶ **n. 1** a strip of leather or other material worn around the waist or across the chest, esp. in order to support clothes or carry weapons: *a sword belt* | [as modifier] *a belt buckle.* ■ short for SEAT BELT. ■ a belt worn as a sign of rank or achievement: *he was awarded the victor's belt.* ■ a belt of a specified color, marking the attainment of a particular level in judo, karate, or similar sports: [as modifier] *brown-belt level.* ■ a person who has reached such a level: *I am a karate black belt.* ■ (**the belt**) the punishment of being struck with a belt.
2 a strip of material used in various technical applications, in particular: ■ a continuous band of material used in machinery for transferring motion from one wheel to another. ■ a conveyor belt. ■ a flexible strip carrying machine-gun cartridges.
3 a strip or encircling band of something having a specified nature or composition that is different from its surroundings: *the asteroid belt* | *a belt of trees.*
4 a heavy blow: *she ran in to administer a good belt with her stick.*
5 informal a gulp or shot of liquor: *they could probably use a few belts.*
▶ **v.** [with obj.] **1** fasten with a belt: *she paused only to belt a robe about her waist* | *she belted her raincoat firmly.* ■ [no obj.] be fastened with a belt: *the jacket belts at the waist.* ■ attach or secure with a belt: *he was securely belted into the passenger seat.*
2 beat or strike (someone), esp. with a belt, as a punishment. ■ hit (something) hard: *he belted the ball to the left-field fence.*
3 gulp a drink quickly: *belting down shots of a potent drink called arrack.*
4 [no obj.] move quickly in a specified direction: *they belted along the empty road.* ■ (of rain) fall hard: *the rain belted down on the tin roof.*
– PHRASES **below the belt** unfair or unfairly; disregarding the rules: *there has been yet another below-the-belt blow to the workers of Chicago.* [from the notion of an unfair and illegal blow in boxing.] **tighten one's belt** cut one's spending; live more frugally. **under one's belt 1** safely or satisfactorily achieved, experienced, or acquired: *I want to get more experience under my belt* | *he now has almost a year as president under his belt.* **2** (of food or drink) consumed: *Gus already had a large brandy under his belt.*
– PHRASAL VERBS **belt something out** sing or play a song loudly and forcefully.
– DERIVATIVES **belt·ed adj.** (sense 1 of the noun).
– ORIGIN Old English, of Germanic origin, from Latin *balteus* 'girdle.'

Bel·tane /'bel,tān/ ▶ **n.** an ancient Celtic festival celebrated on May Day.
– ORIGIN late Middle English: from Scottish Gaelic *bealltainn.*

belt drive ▶ **n.** a mechanism in which power is transmitted by a continuous flexible belt.

belt·ed gal·lo·way ▶ **n.** an animal belonging to a variety of the galloway breed of cattle (see GALLOWAY).

belt·er /'beltər/ ▶ **n.** informal a loud forceful singer or song.

belt·ing /'beltiɴɢ/ ▶ **n. 1** belts collectively, or material for belts: *a small piece of plastic belting.*
2 a beating, esp. with a belt, as a punishment.

belt sand·er ▶ **n.** a sander that uses a moving abrasive belt to smooth surfaces.

belt-tight·en·ing ▶ **n.** the introduction of rigorous reductions in spending: [as modifier] *belt-tightening measures.*

belt·way /'belt,wā/ ▶ **n.** a highway encircling an urban area. ■ (**Beltway**) [often as modifier] Washington, DC, esp. as representing the perceived insularity of the US government: *conventional beltway wisdom.* [transferred use by association with the beltway encircling Washington.]

Belt·way ban·dit ▶ **n.** informal a company that does a large percentage of its business as a federal government contractor.

be·lu·ga /bə'lo͞ogə/ ▶ **n.** (pl. **same** or **belugas**) **1** a small, white-toothed whale related to the narwhal, living in herds mainly in Arctic coastal waters. Also called WHITE WHALE. ● *Delphinapterus leucas*, family Monodontidae.
2 a very large sturgeon occurring in the inland seas and associated rivers of central Eurasia. ● *Huso huso*, family Acipenseridae. ■ (also **beluga caviar**) caviar obtained from this fish.
– ORIGIN late 16th cent. (sense 2): from Russian *belukha* (sense 1), *beluga* (sense 2), both from *belyĭ* 'white.'

bel·ve·dere /'belvi,di(ə)r/ ▶ **n.** a summerhouse or open-sided gallery, usually at rooftop level, commanding a fine view.
– ORIGIN late 16th cent.: from Italian, literally 'fair view,' from *bel* 'beautiful' + *vedere* 'to view.'

be·ly·ing /bi'lī-iɴɢ/ present participle of BELIE.

BEM ▶ **abbr.** Bachelor of Engineering of Mines.

be·ma /'bēmə/ ▶ **n.** (pl. **bemas** or **bemata** /-mətə/) the altar part or sanctuary in ancient and Orthodox churches. ■ (**bima, bimah**) Judaism the podium or platform in a synagogue from which the Torah and Prophets are read. ■ historical the platform from which orators spoke in ancient Athens.
– ORIGIN late 17th cent.: from Greek *bēma* 'step, raised place.'

Bem·ba /'bembə/ ▶ **n.** (pl. **same**) **1** a member of an indigenous people of Zambia.
2 the Bantu language of this people.
▶ **adj.** of or relating to this people or their language.
– ORIGIN of Bemba origin.

be·mire /bi'mī(ə)r/ ▶ **v.** [with obj.] archaic cover or stain with mud: *his shoes were bemired, as if he had been traveling on foot.* ■ (**be bemired**) be stuck in mud: *men and horses and wagons all bemired.*
– ORIGIN mid 16th cent.: from BE- (expressing transitivity) + MIRE.

be·moan /bi'mōn/ ▶ **v.** [with obj.] often humorous express discontent or sorrow over (something): *single women bemoaning the absence of men.*
– ORIGIN Old English *bemǣnan* 'complain, lament.' The change in the second syllable (16th cent.) was due to association with MOAN, to which it is related.

be·muse /bi'myo͞oz/ ▶ **v.** [with obj.] (usu. as adj. **bemused**) puzzle, confuse, or bewilder (someone): *her bemused expression* | *she was accepted with bemused resignation by her parents as a hippie.*
– DERIVATIVES **be·mus·ed·ly** /-zidlē/ **adv.**, **be·muse·ment n.**
– ORIGIN mid 18th cent.: from BE- (as an intensifier) + MUSE.

ben[1] /ben/ ▶ **n.** Scottish a high mountain or mountain peak (esp. in place names): *Ben Nevis.*
– ORIGIN late 18th cent.: from Scottish Gaelic and Irish *beann.*

ben[2] ▶ **n.** Scottish & N. Irish an inner room in a two-roomed cottage.
– ORIGIN late 18th cent.: dialect variant of Middle English *binne* 'within' (adverb), from Old English *binnan* (related to Dutch and German *binnen*).

Be·na·res /bə'näris, -ēz/ former name for VARANASI.

Ben Bel·la /ben 'belə/, (Muhammad) Ahmed (1918–), Algerian statesman; prime minister 1962–63; president 1963–65. The first president of an independent Algeria, he was overthrown in a military coup.

bench /bencʜ/ ▶ **n. 1** a long seat for several people, typically made of wood or stone.
2 a long, sturdy work table used by a carpenter, mechanic, scientist, or other worker.
3 (**the bench**) the office of judge or magistrate: *his appointment to the civil bench.* ■ a judge's seat in a court. ■ judges or magistrates collectively: *rulings from the bench.*
4 Brit. a seat in Parliament for politicians of a specified party or position: *the Conservative benches* | *the Opposition benches.* ■ the politicians occupying such a seat: *the pledge that was given by the Opposition benches yesterday.*
5 (**the bench**) a seat on which sports coaches and players sit during a game when they are not playing.
6 a flat ledge in masonry or on sloping ground.
▶ **v.** [with obj.] **1** exhibit (a dog) at a show: *Affenpinschers and Afghans were benched side by side.* [from the practice of exhibiting dogs on benches.]
2 withdraw (a sports player) from play; substitute: *the coach benched quarterback Randall Cunningham in favor of Jim McMahon.*
3 short for BENCH PRESS.
– PHRASES **on the bench 1** appointed as or in the capacity of a judge or magistrate: *he retired after twenty-five years on the bench.* **2** acting as one of the possible substitutes in a sports contest.
– ORIGIN Old English *benc*, of Germanic origin; related to Dutch *bank* and German *Bank*, also to BANK[1].

bench·er /'bencʜər/ ▶ **n.** Law (in the UK) a senior member of any of the Inns of Court.

Bench·ley /'bencʜlē/ the name of a family of US writers, including: ■ **Robert Charles** (1889–1945), drama critic, actor, and humorist. He was a theater critic for *Life* magazine (1920–29) and *The New Yorker* (1929–40). ■ **Nathaniel** (1915–81), son of Robert. He was the author of such humorous novels as *Lassiter's Folly* (1971). ■ **Peter** (1940–2006), son of Nathaniel. He wrote *Jaws* (1974), *The Deep* (1976), and *White Shark* (1994).

bench·mark /'bencʜ,märk/ ▶ **n. 1** a standard or point of reference against which things may be compared or assessed: [as modifier] *a benchmark case.* ■ a problem designed to evaluate the performance of a computer system: *Xstones is a graphics benchmark.*
2 a surveyor's mark cut in a wall, pillar, or building and used as a reference point in measuring altitudes.
▶ **v.** [with obj.] evaluate or check (something) by comparison with a standard: *we are* ***benchmarking*** *our performance* ***against*** *external criteria* | [no obj.] *we continue to benchmark against the competition.* ■ [no obj.] show particular results during a benchmark test: *the device should benchmark at between 100 and 150 MHz.*

bench·mark test ▶ **n.** a test using a benchmark to evaluate a computer system's performance.

bench press ▶ **n.** a bodybuilding and weightlifting exercise in which a lifter lies on a bench with feet on the floor and raises a weight with both arms.
▶ **v.** (**bench-press**) [with obj.] raise (a weight) in a bench press: *Josh can bench-press more than 400 pounds* | [no obj.] *my elbow hurts when I bench-press.*

bench run ▶ **n. & v.** another term for BENCH TEST.

bench seat ▶ **n.** a seat across the whole width of a car.

bench test chiefly Computing ▶ **n.** a test carried out on a machine, a component, or software before it is released for use, to ensure that it works properly.
▶ **v.** (**bench-test**) [with obj.] run a bench test on (something): *they are offering you the chance to bench-test their applications.* ■ [no obj.] give particular results during a bench test: *it bench-tests two times faster than the previous version.*

bench·warm·er /'bencʜ,wôrmər/ ▶ **n.** informal a sports player who does not get selected to play; a substitute.

bench war·rant ▶ **n.** a written order issued by a judge authorizing the arrest of a person charged with some contempt, crime, or misdemeanor.

bench·work /'bencʜ,wərk/ ▶ **n.** work carried out at a bench in a laboratory or workshop.

Bend /bend/ a city in central Oregon; pop. 77,181 (est. 2008).

bend[1] /bend/ ▶ **v.** (past and past participle **bent** /bent/)
1 [with obj.] shape or force (something straight) into a curve or angle: *the rising wind bent the long grass.* ■ [no obj.] (of something straight) be shaped or forced into a curve or angle: *the oar bent as Lance heaved angrily at it.* ■ [no obj.] (of a road, river, or path) deviate from a straight line in a specified direction; have a sharply curved course: *the road bent left and then right* | *the river slowly bends around Davenport.*
2 [no obj.] (of a person) incline the body downward from the vertical: *he bent down and picked her up* | *I bent over my plate* | [with infinitive] *he bent to tie his shoelaces.* ■ [with obj.] move (a jointed part of the body) to an angled position: *extend your left leg and bend your right* | *Irene bent her head over her work.*
3 force or be forced to submit: [with obj.] *they want to* ***bend*** *me* ***to their will*** | [no obj.] *a refusal to* ***bend to*** *mob rule.* ■ [with obj.] interpret or modify (a rule) to suit oneself or somebody else: *we cannot bend the rules, even for Darren.*
4 [with obj.] direct or devote (one's attention or energies) to a task: *Eric bent all his efforts to persuading them to donate some blankets* | [no obj.] *she* ***bent*** *once more* ***to*** *the task of diverting the wedding guests.*
5 [with obj.] Nautical attach (a sail or rope) by means of a knot: *sailors were* ***bending*** *sails* ***to*** *the spars.*

▶ **n.** **1** a curve, esp. a sharp one, in a road, river, racecourse, or path.
2 a curved or angled part or form of something: *making a bend in the wire.*
3 a kind of knot used to join two ropes, or to tie a rope to another object, e.g. a carrick bend.
4 (**the bends**) decompression sickness, esp. in divers.
– PHRASES **bend someone's ear** informal talk to someone, esp. with great eagerness or in order to ask a favor: *she regularly bent Michael's ear with her problems.* **bend one's elbow** drink alcohol. **bend one's** (or **the**) **knee** submit: *a country no longer willing to bend its knee to foreign powers.* **bend over backward** see BACKWARD. **on bended knee** (or **knees**) kneeling, esp. when pleading or showing great respect. **around the bend** informal crazy; insane: *I'd tell you if you were going around the bend.*
– DERIVATIVES **bend·a·ble** adj.
– ORIGIN Old English *bendan* 'put in bonds, tension a bow by means of a string,' of Germanic origin; related to BAND[1].

bend[2] ▶ **n.** Heraldry an ordinary in the form of a broad diagonal stripe from top left (dexter chief) to bottom right (sinister base) of a shield or part of one.
– ORIGIN late Middle English: from Anglo-Norman French *bande*, Old French *bende* 'flat strip.'

bend·er /ˈbendər/ informal ▶ **n.** **1** [usu. in combination] an object or person that bends something else: *a fender bender.*
2 a wild drinking spree.
– ORIGIN late 15th cent. (denoting instruments such as pliers, for bending things): from BEND[1] + -ER[1].

bend sin·is·ter ▶ **n.** Heraldry a broad diagonal stripe from top right to bottom left of a shield (a supposed sign of bastardy).

bend sinister

bend·y /ˈbendē/ ▶ **adj.** (**bendier, bendiest**) informal capable of bending; soft and flexible.
– DERIVATIVES **bend·i·ness** n.

be·neath /biˈnēTH/ ▶ **prep.** **1** extending or directly underneath, typically with close contact: *in the labyrinths beneath central Moscow.* ■ underneath so as to be hidden, covered, or protected: *unaltered even after years beneath the sea.*
2 at a lower level or layer than: *beneath this floor there's a cellar* | *her eyes were dull with dark shadows beneath them.* ■ lower in grade or rank than: *relegated to the rank beneath theirs.* ■ considered of lower status or worth than: *taking jobs beneath my abilities.* ■ behind (a physical surface): *they found another layer beneath the stucco.* ■ behind or hidden behind (an appearance): *beneath the gloss of success.*
▶ **adv.** **1** extending or directly underneath something: *a house built on stilts to allow air to circulate beneath.*
2 at a lower level or layer: *the runways had cracked open, exposing the black earth beneath.* ■ behind or hidden behind an appearance: *the smile revealed the evil beneath.*
– ORIGIN Old English *binithan, bineothan*, from *bi* (see BY) + *nithan, neothan* 'below,' of Germanic origin; related to NETHER.

ben·e·dic·i·te /ˌbeniˈdisitē/ ▶ **n.** a blessing, esp. a grace said at table in religious communities. [Middle English.] ■ (**the Benedicite**) the canticle used in the Anglican service of matins beginning "O all ye works of the Lord, bless ye the Lord," the text being taken from the Apocrypha. [mid 17th cent.]
– ORIGIN Latin, 'bless ye!,' plural imperative from *benedicere* 'wish well'; the first word of the canticle in Latin.

Ben·e·dict, St. /ˈbeniˌdikt/ (*c.*480–*c.*550), Italian hermit. He established a monastery at Monte Cassino and his *Regula Monachorum* (known as the Rule of St. Benedict) formed the basis of Western monasticism. Feast day, July 11 (formerly March 21).

Ben·e·dict XVI (1927–), German cleric, pope since 2005; born *Joseph Alois Ratzinger.*

Ben·e·dic·tine /ˌbeniˈdikˌtēn, -tin/ ▶ **n.** **1** a monk or nun of an order following the rule of St. Benedict.
2 trademark a liqueur based on brandy, originally made by Benedictine monks in France.
▶ **adj.** of St. Benedict or the Benedictines.
– ORIGIN from French *bénédictine* or modern Latin *benedictinus*, from the name *Benedictus* (see BENEDICT, ST.).

ben·e·dic·tion /ˌbeniˈdikSHən/ ▶ **n.** the utterance or bestowing of a blessing, esp. at the end of a religious service. ■ (**Benediction**) a service in which the congregation is blessed with the Blessed Sacrament, held mainly in the Roman Catholic Church.
■ devout or formal invocation of blessedness: *her arms outstretched in benediction.* ■ the state of being blessed: *he eventually wins benediction.*
– ORIGIN late Middle English: via Old French from Latin *benedictio(n-)*, from *benedicere* 'wish well, bless,' from *bene* 'well' + *dicere* 'say.'

Ben·e·dict's so·lu·tion /ˈbeniˌdikts/ (also **Benedict's reagent**) ▶ **n.** a chemical solution that changes color in the presence of glucose and other reducing sugars, used in clinical urine tests for diabetes. It is a mixture of sodium or potassium citrate, sodium carbonate, and copper sulfate.
– ORIGIN named after S. R. *Benedict* (1884–1936), American chemist.

Ben·e·dic·tus /ˌbeniˈdiktəs/ ▶ **n.** Christian Church **1** an invocation beginning *Benedictus qui venit in nomine Domini* (Blessed is he who comes in the name of the Lord) forming a set part of the Mass.
2 a canticle beginning *Benedictus Dominus Deus* (Blessed be the Lord God) from Luke 1:68–79.
– ORIGIN mid 16th cent.: Latin, 'blessed,' past participle of *benedicere* 'wish well.'

ben·e·fac·tion /ˌbenəˈfakSHən/ ▶ **n.** a donation or gift.
– ORIGIN mid 17th cent.: from late Latin *benefactio(n-)*, from *bene facere* 'do good (to),' from *bene* 'well' + *facere* 'do.'

ben·e·fac·tive /ˌbenəˈfaktiv/ Grammar ▶ **adj.** denoting a semantic case or construction that expresses the person or thing that benefits from the action of the verb, for example *for you* in *I bought this for you.*
▶ **n.** the benefactive case, or a word or expression in it.
– ORIGIN 1940s: from Latin *benefactus* 'capable of giving' + -IVE.

ben·e·fac·tor /ˈbenəˌfaktər, ˌbenəˈfaktər/ ▶ **n.** a person who gives money or other help to a person or cause.
– ORIGIN late Middle English: from Latin, from *bene facere* 'do good (to)' (see BENEFACTION).

ben·e·fac·tress /ˈbenəˌfaktris, ˌbenəˈfaktris/ ▶ **n.** a female benefactor.

be·nef·ic /bəˈnefik/ ▶ **adj.** rare beneficent or kindly. ■ Astrology relating to or denoting the planets Jupiter and Venus, traditionally considered to have a favorable influence.
– ORIGIN early 17th cent.: from Latin *beneficus*, from *bene facere* 'do good (to).'

ben·e·fice /ˈbenəfis/ ▶ **n.** a permanent Church appointment, typically that of a rector or vicar, for which property and income are provided in respect of pastoral duties.
– DERIVATIVES **ben·e·ficed** adj.
– ORIGIN Middle English: via Old French from Latin *beneficium* 'favor, support,' from *bene* 'well' + *facere* 'do.'

be·nef·i·cent /bəˈnefəsənt/ ▶ **adj.** (of a person) generous or doing good. ■ resulting in good: *a beneficent democracy.*
– DERIVATIVES **be·nef·i·cence** n., **be·nef·i·cent·ly** adv.
– ORIGIN early 17th cent.: from Latin *beneficent-* (stem of *beneficentior*, comparative of *beneficus* 'favorable, generous'), from *bene facere* 'do good (to).'

ben·e·fi·cial /ˌbenəˈfiSHəl/ ▶ **adj.** favorable or advantageous; resulting in good: *the beneficial effect on the economy* | *discoveries beneficial to mankind.* ■ Law of or relating to rights, other than legal title: *the beneficiary will be taxed on the value of his beneficial use of the property.*
– DERIVATIVES **ben·e·fi·cial·ly** adv.
– ORIGIN late Middle English: from late Latin *beneficialis*, from *beneficium* (see BENEFICE).

ben·e·fi·cials /ˌbenəˈfiSHəlz/ ▶ **plural n.** insects that are a boon to gardeners: *daisies that are highly attractive to five key kinds of beneficials (ladybugs, lacewings, hover flies, tachinid flies, and miniwasps).*

ben·e·fi·ci·ar·y /ˌbenəˈfiSHēˌerē/ ▶ **n.** (pl. **beneficiaries**) a person who derives advantage from something, esp. a trust, will, or life insurance policy.
– ORIGIN early 17th cent.: from Latin *beneficiarius*, from *beneficium* (see BENEFICE).

ben·e·fit /ˈbenəfit/ ▶ **n.** **1** an advantage or profit gained from something: *tenants bought their houses with the benefit of a discount* | *enjoy the benefits of being a member* | *uninformed criticism is of benefit to no one.*
2 a payment or gift made by an employer, the state, or an insurance company: *welfare benefits* | *wages and benefits.*
3 a public performance or other entertainment of which the proceeds go to a particular charitable cause.
▶ **v.** (**benefits, benefiting** or **benefitting, benefited** or **benefitted**) [no obj.] receive an advantage; profit; gain: *areas that would benefit from regeneration.* ■ [with obj.] bring advantage to: *the bill will benefit the nation.*
– PHRASES **benefit of clergy** **1** historical exemption of the English clergy and nuns from the jurisdiction of the ordinary civil courts, granted in the Middle Ages but abolished in 1827. **2** ecclesiastical sanction or approval: *they lived together without benefit of clergy.* **the benefit of the doubt** a concession that a person or fact must be regarded as correct or justified, if the contrary has not been proven: *I'll give you the benefit of the doubt as to whether it was deliberate or not.* **for the benefit of** **1** in order to help, guide, or be of service to: *a man who has spent his life fighting evil for the benefit of the community.* **2** in order to interest or impress someone: *it was all an act put on for his benefit.* **give someone the benefit of** often ironic explain or recount to someone at length: *the whole assembly was given the benefit of his opinions.*
– ORIGIN late Middle English (originally denoting a kind deed or something well done): from Old French *bienfet*, from Latin *benefactum* 'good deed,' from *bene facere* 'do good (to).'

Ben·e·lux /ˈbenlˌəks/ a collective name for Belgium, the Netherlands, and Luxembourg, esp. with reference to their economic union.
– ORIGIN 1947: acronym from *Be*lgium, *Ne*therlands, and *Lux*embourg.

be·nev·o·lent /bəˈnevələnt/ ▶ **adj.** well meaning and kindly: *a benevolent smile.* ■ (of an organization) serving a charitable rather than a profit-making purpose: *a benevolent fund.*
– DERIVATIVES **be·nev·o·lence** n., **be·nev·o·lent·ly** adv.
– ORIGIN late Middle English: from Old French *benivolent*, from Latin *bene volent-* 'well wishing,' from *bene* 'well' + *velle* 'to wish.'

Ben·ford's Law /ˈbenfərdz/ ▶ **n.** Mathematics the principle that in any large, randomly produced set of natural numbers, such as tables of logarithms or corporate sales statistics, around 30 percent will begin with the digit 1, 18 percent with 2, and so on, with the smallest percentage beginning with 9. The law is applied in analyzing the validity of statistics and financial records.
– ORIGIN Named for US physicist Frank Benford, whose 1938 paper demonstrated the statistical validity of the phenomenon.

BEng ▶ **abbr.** Bachelor of Engineering.

beng·a /ˈbeNGgə/ ▶ **n.** a style of African popular music originating in Kenya, characterized by a fusion of traditional Kenyan music and a lively arrangement of guitars, bass, and vocals.
– ORIGIN 1980s: from Luo (a Kenyan language).

Ben·gal /benˈgôl, beNG-, -ˈgäl/ a region of South Asia that contains the Ganges and Brahmaputra river deltas. In 1947, the province was divided into West Bengal, which has remained a state of India, and East Bengal, which is now Bangladesh.

Ben·gal, Bay of a part of the Indian Ocean that lies between India on the west and Burma (Myanmar) and Thailand on the east.

Ben·ga·li /ˌbeNGˈgälē/ ▶ **n.** (pl. **Bengalis**) **1** a native of Bengal.
2 the Indic language of Bangladesh and West Bengal.
▶ **adj.** of or relating to Bengal, its people, or their language.
– ORIGIN from Hindi *baṅgālī*.

ben·ga·line /ˈbeNGgəˌlēn/ ▶ **n.** a strong ribbed fabric made of a mixture of silk and either cotton or wool.
– ORIGIN late 19th cent.: from French, so named because of a similarity with archaic *Bengals* denoting fabrics, usually silks, imported from Bengal.

Ben·gal light /ˌbeNGˈgäl/ ▶ **n.** a kind of firework giving off a blue flame and used for lighting or signaling.

Ben·gha·zi /benˈgäzē, beNG-/ a Mediterranean port in northeastern Libya; pop. 670,800 (est. 2006). It was the joint capital (with Tripoli) 1951–72.

Ben·guel·a /benˈgwelə, beNG-/ a port and railroad terminal in Angola, on the Atlantic coast; pop. 115,900 (est. 2004). Copper is brought here from

PRONUNCIATION KEY ə *ago, up*; ər *over, fur*; a *hat*; ā *ate*; ä *car*; e *let*; ē *see*; i *fit*; ī *by*; NG *sing*; ō *go*; ô *law, for*; oi *toy*; o͝o *good*; o͞o *goo*; ou *out*; TH *thin*; T͟H *then*; ZH *vision*

Zambia and the Democratic Republic of the Congo (formerly Zaire).

Ben·guel·a Cur·rent a cold ocean current that flows north from Antarctica along the west coast of southern Africa as far as Angola.

Ben-Gu·rion /ben 'go͝orēən/, David (1886–1973), Israeli statesman; prime minister 1948–53 and 1955–63. He was Israel's first prime minister and minister of defense.

be·night·ed /bi'nītid/ ▶ **adj.** **1** in a state of pitiful or contemptible intellectual or moral ignorance, typically owing to a lack of opportunity: *they saw themselves as bringers of culture to poor benighted peoples.*
2 overtaken by darkness: *a storm developed and we were forced to wait benighted near the summit.*
– DERIVATIVES **be·night·ed·ness** n.
– ORIGIN late 16th cent. (sense 2): past participle of archaic *benight* 'cover in the darkness of night, obscure' (see **BE-**, **NIGHT**).

be·nign /bi'nīn/ ▶ **adj.** **1** gentle; kindly: *her face was calm and benign | his benign but firm manner.* ■ (of a climate or environment) mild and favorable. ■ not harmful to the environment: [in combination] *an ozone-benign refrigerant.*
2 Medicine (of a disease) not harmful in effect: in particular, (of a tumor) not malignant.
– DERIVATIVES **be·nign·ly** adv.
– ORIGIN Middle English: from Old French *benigne*, from Latin *benignus*, probably from *bene* 'well' + *-genus* '-born.' Compare with **GENTLE**.

be·nig·nant /bi'nignənt/ ▶ **adj.** **1** kindly and benevolent: *an old man, with a face noble and benignant.*
2 Medicine less common term for **BENIGN** (sense 2). ■ archaic having a good effect; beneficial: *the benignant touch of love and beauty.*
– DERIVATIVES **be·nig·nan·cy** n., **be·nig·nant·ly** adv.
– ORIGIN late 18th cent.: from **BENIGN**, or Latin *benignus*, on the pattern of *malignant*.

be·nig·ni·ty /bi'nignitē/ ▶ **n.** (pl. **benignities**) kindness or tolerance toward others: *his air of benignity.* ■ archaic an act of kindness.
– ORIGIN late Middle English: from Old French *benignite* or Latin *benignitas*, from *benignus* (see **BENIGN**).

be·nign ne·glect ▶ **n.** a noninterference that is intended to benefit someone or something more than continual attention would.

Be·nin /bə'nēn, -'nin/ a country in West Africa, just west of Nigeria; pop. 8,791,800 (est. 2009); capital, Porto Novo; languages, French (official), West African languages. Former name (until 1975) **DAHOMEY**.

> The country was conquered by the French in 1893 and became part of French West Africa. In 1960, it achieved independence.

– DERIVATIVES **Be·ni·nese** /,benə'nēz, -'nēs/ **adj. & n.**
– ORIGIN name adopted in 1975, formerly used by an African kingdom, powerful in the 14th–17th centuries.

Be·nin, Bight of a wide bay on the coast of Africa north of the Gulf of Guinea, bordered by Togo, Benin, and southwestern Nigeria. Lagos is its chief port.

Be·ni Riv·er /'bānē/ a river that flows for 1,000 miles (1,600 km) from central to northern Bolivia, east of the Andes, into the Madeira River.

ben·i·son /'benəsən, -zən/ ▶ **n.** literary a blessing: *the rewards and benisons of marriage.*
– ORIGIN Middle English: from Old French *beneiçun*, from Latin *benedictio* (see **BENEDICTION**).

Ben·ja·min /'benjəmən/ (in the Bible) a Hebrew patriarch, the youngest son of Jacob and Rachel, and Jacob's favorite (Gen. 35:18, 42, etc.). ■ the smallest tribe of Israel, traditionally descended from him.

ben·ne /'benē/ ▶ **n.** another term for **SESAME**.
– ORIGIN mid 18th cent.: from Malay *bene*.

Ben·nett[1] /'benit/, Richard Bedford (1870–1947), Canadian Conservative statesman; prime minister 1930–35.

Ben·nett[2], Tony (1926–), US singer; born *Anthony Dominick Benedetto*. A popular jazz singer in the early 1950s with such hits as "Because of You" (1951), he made a successful comeback during the 1990s.

Ben Ne·vis /ben 'nevəs/ a mountain in western Scotland. Rising to 4,406 feet (1,343 m), it is the highest mountain in the British Isles.

Ben·ning·ton /'beniNGtən/ a historic town in southwestern Vermont; pop. 15,093 (est. 2008).

Ben·ny /'benē/, Jack (1894–1974), US comedian and actor; born *Benjamin Kubelsky*. His radio series *The Jack Benny Program* ran from 1932 to 1955. Made for television, *The Jack Benny Show* was broadcast 1950–65.

Jack Benny

ben·ny[1] /'benē/ ▶ **n.** (pl. **bennies**) informal a tablet of Benzedrine.

ben·ny[2] ▶ **n.** (pl. **bennies**) informal a benefit attached to employment.

ben·o·myl /'benə,mil/ ▶ **n.** a systemic fungicide used on fruit and vegetable crops, derived from imidazole.
– ORIGIN 1960s: from *ben(z)o-* + *m(eth)yl*.

Be·no·ni /bə'nōnē/ a city in South Africa, east of Johannesburg; pop. 654,500 (est. 2009). It is a gold-mining center.

Ben·sa·lem /ben'sāləm/ a township in southeastern Pennsylvania; pop. 58,304 (est. 2008).

Ben·son·hurst /'bensən,hərst/ a residential section in southwestern Brooklyn in New York City.

bent[1] /bent/ past and past participle of **BEND[1]**.
▶ **adj.** **1** sharply curved or having an angle: *a piece of bent wire | his bent shoulders.*
2 informal, chiefly Brit. dishonest; corrupt: *a bent cop.* ■ stolen. ■ derogatory homosexual.
3 (**bent on**) determined to do or have something: *a missionary bent on saving souls | a mob bent on violence.*
▶ **n.** a natural talent or inclination: *a man of religious bent | she had no natural **bent for** literature.*
– PHRASES **bent out of shape** informal angry or agitated: *it was just a mistake, nothing to get bent out of shape about.*

bent[2] ▶ **n.** **1** (also **bent grass**) a stiff grass that is used for lawns and is a component of pasture and hay grasses. ● *Agrostis* and other genera, family Gramineae: several species, including **common bent** (*A. capillaris* (or *tenuis*)). ■ the stiff flowering stalk of a grass. ■ archaic any stiff-stemmed or rushlike grass or sedge.
2 Brit. archaic or dialect a heath or unenclosed pasture.
– ORIGIN Middle English: representing Old English *beonet* (recorded in place names); related to German *Binse*.

Ben·tham /'benTHəm/, Jeremy (1748–1832), English philosopher and jurist, the first major proponent of utilitarianism. He wrote *Introduction to the Principles of Morals and Legislation* (1789).

ben·thos /'ben,THäs/ ▶ **n.** Ecology the flora and fauna found on the bottom, or in the bottom sediments, of a sea, lake, or other body of water.
– DERIVATIVES **ben·thic** /-THik/ **adj.**
– ORIGIN late 19th cent.: from Greek, 'depth of the sea.'

ben·to /'bentō/ ▶ **n.** (pl. **bentos**) a lacquered or decorated wooden Japanese lunchbox. ■ a Japanese-style packed lunch, consisting of such items as rice, vegetables, and sashimi (raw fish with condiments).
– ORIGIN Japanese.

Ben·ton[1] /'bentn/, Thomas Hart (1782–1858), US politician. A Democratic member of the US Senate from Missouri (1821–51), he supported frontier explorations and opposed extending slavery to the territories.

Ben·ton[2], Thomas Hart (1889–1975), US painter, a grandnephew of Senator Thomas Hart Benton. His paintings, of the American naturalist school, represent life in the Midwest.

ben·ton·ite /'bentn,īt/ ▶ **n.** a kind of absorbent clay formed by the breakdown of volcanic ash, used esp. as a filler.
– ORIGIN late 19th cent.: from the name of Fort *Benton* in Montana, where it is found, + **-ITE[1]**.

Bent's Fort /bents/ a historic site in east central Colorado, northeast of La Junta, on the Arkansas River and the former Santa Fe Trail.

bent·wood /'bent,wo͝od/ ▶ **n.** wood that is artificially shaped for use in making furniture: [as modifier] *bentwood chairs.*

bentwood chair

Be·nue-Con·go /'bān,wā/ ▶ **n.** a major branch of the Niger-Congo family of languages, spoken mainly in Nigeria and including Efik and Fula.
▶ **adj.** of, relating to, or denoting this group of languages.
– ORIGIN from the names of rivers.

Be·nue Riv·er a river that flows for 870 miles (1,400 km) from northern Cameroon into Nigeria, where it joins the Niger River.

be·numb /bi'nəm/
▶ **v.** [with obj.] (often as adj. **benumbed**) deprive of physical or emotional feeling: *a hoarse shout cut through his benumbed senses.*
– ORIGIN late 15th cent.: from obsolete *benome*, past participle of *benim* 'deprive,' from **BE-** (expressing removal) + Old English *niman* 'take.'

Ben·xi /'ben'CHē/ a city in northeastern China, in the province of Liaoning; pop. 846,700 (est. 2006).

Benz /benz, bents/, Karl Friedrich (1844–1929), German engineer and automobile manufacturer. In 1885 he built the first vehicle to be powered by an internal combustion engine.

benz·al·de·hyde /ben'zaldə,hīd/ ▶ **n.** Chemistry a colorless liquid aldehyde with the odor of bitter almonds, used in the manufacture of dyes and perfumes. ● Chem. formula: C_6H_5CHO.

Ben·ze·drine /'benzə,drēn/ ▶ **n.** trademark for **AMPHETAMINE**.
– ORIGIN 1930s: blend of **BENZOIN** and **EPHEDRINE**.

ben·zene /'ben,zēn, ben'zēn/ ▶ **n.** a colorless volatile liquid hydrocarbon present in coal tar and petroleum, used in chemical synthesis. Its use as a solvent has been reduced because of its carcinogenic properties. ● Chem. formula: C_6H_6.
– ORIGIN mid 19th cent.: from **BENZOIN** + **-ENE**.

ben·zene hex·a·chlor·ide /,heksə'klôr,īd/ (abbr.: **BHC**) ▶ **n.** **1** a compound of benzene and chlorine used as an insecticide. ● Chem. formula: $C_6H_6Cl_6$.
2 used as a general term for **LINDANE**.

ben·zene ring ▶ **n.** Chemistry the hexagonal unsaturated ring of six carbon atoms present in benzene and many other aromatic molecules.

ben·ze·noid /'benzə,noid/ ▶ **adj.** Chemistry having the six-membered ring structure or aromatic properties of benzene.

ben·zi·dine /'benzi,dēn/ ▶ **n.** a crystalline base used in making dyes and in detecting blood stains. ● Chem. formula: $NH_2C_6H_4C_6H_4NH_2$.

ben·zine /'ben,zēn, ben'zēn/ (also **benzin** /'benzin/) ▶ **n.** a mixture of liquid hydrocarbons obtained from petroleum.
– ORIGIN mid 19th cent. (denoting benzene): from **BENZOIN** + **-INE[4]**.

ben·zo·caine /'benzə,kān/ ▶ **n.** a white, odorless, crystalline powder used in ointments as a local anesthetic and to protect against sunburn. ● Chem. formula: $NH_2C_6H_4C_6H_4NH_2$.

ben·zo·di·az·e·pine /,benzō,dī'azə,pēn/ ▶ **n.** Medicine any of a class of heterocyclic organic compounds used as tranquilizers, such as Librium and Valium.
– ORIGIN 1930s: from **BENZENE** + **DI-[1]** + **AZO-** + **EPI-** + **-INE[4]**.

ben·zo·ic ac·id /ben'zō-ik/ ▶ **n.** Chemistry a white crystalline substance present in benzoin and other plant resins, and used as a food preservative. ● Chem. formula: C_6H_5COOH.

ben·zo·in /'benzō-in, -,zoin/ ▶ **n.** **1** (also **gum benzoin**) a fragrant gum resin obtained from a tropical tree of eastern Asia, used in medicines, perfumes, and incense. Also called **GUM BENJAMIN**. ● This is obtained from several species of the genus *Styrax*, family Styracaceae, in particular *S. benzoin*.
2 Chemistry a white crystalline aromatic ketone present in this resin. ● Alternative name: **2-hydroxy-1,2-diphenylethanone**; chem. formula: $C_6H_5CHOHCOC_6H_5$.
– ORIGIN mid 16th cent.: from French *benjoin*, based on Arabic *lubānjāwī* 'incense of Java.'

ben·zo·phe·none /,benzōfi'nōn, -'fē,nōn/ ▶ **n.** a white, crystalline ketone that is used in perfume, sunscreen, and as a flavoring agent. ● Chem. formula: $C_6H_5COC_6H_5$.

ben·zo·py·rene /,benzō'pīrēn/ ▶ **n.** Chemistry a compound that is the major carcinogen present in cigarette smoke. It also occurs in coal tar. ● A polycyclic aromatic hydrocarbon; chem. formula: $C_{20}H_{12}$.

ben·zo·qui·none /ˌbenzōkwiˈnōn, -ˈkwinōn/ ▶ **n.** Chemistry a yellow crystalline compound related to benzene but having two hydrogen atoms replaced by oxygen. ● Chem. formula: $C_6H_4O_2$; there are two isomers, with the oxygen atoms on opposite (**1,4-benzoquinone**) or adjacent (**1,2-benzoquinone**) carbon atoms.

ben·zo·yl /ˈbenzō-il/ ▶ **n.** [as modifier] Chemistry the acyl radical $-C(O)C_6H_5$, derived from benzoic acid: *benzoyl peroxide.*

ben·zo·yl per·ox·ide ▶ **n.** an antibacterial ingredient used in acne medications.

ben·zyl /ˈbenzil/ ▶ **n.** [as modifier] Chemistry the radical $-CH_2C_6H_5$, derived from toluene: *benzyl benzoate.*

Be·o·thuk /ˈbāəˌTHo͝ok/ ▶ **n.** (pl. **same** or **Beothuks**) **1** a member of an extinct North American Indian people of Newfoundland.
2 the language of this people, of unknown affinity.
▶ **adj.** of or relating to this people or their language.
– ORIGIN probably the name in Beothuk.

Be·o·wulf /ˈbāəˌwo͝olf/ an Old English epic poem celebrating the legendary Scandinavian hero Beowulf.

Generally dated to the 8th century, it was the first major poem in a European vernacular language and is the only complete Germanic epic that survives. It describes Beowulf's killing of the water monster Grendel and its mother and his death in combat with a dragon, and includes both pagan and Christian elements.

be·queath /biˈkwēTH, -ˈkwē<u>TH</u>/ ▶ **v.** [with obj.] leave (a personal estate or one's body) to a person or other beneficiary by a will: *an identical sum was bequeathed by Margaret | he bequeathed his art collection to the town.* ■ pass (something) on or leave (something) to someone else: *he is ditching the unpopular policies bequeathed to him.*
– DERIVATIVES **be·queath·er n.**
– ORIGIN Old English *becwethan*, from BE- 'about' (expressing transitivity) + *cwethan* 'say' (see QUOTH).

be·quest /biˈkwest/ ▶ **n.** a legacy: *her $135,000 was the largest bequest the library ever has received.* ■ the action of bequeathing something: *a painting acquired by bequest.*
– ORIGIN Middle English: from BE- 'about' + Old English *cwis* 'speech,' influenced by BEQUEATH.

be·rate /biˈrāt/ ▶ **v.** [with obj.] scold or criticize (someone) angrily: *his mother came out and berated me for raising my voice.*
– ORIGIN mid 16th cent.: from BE- 'thoroughly' + RATE².

Ber·ber /ˈbərbər/ ▶ **n. 1** a member of an indigenous people of North Africa. The majority of Berbers are settled farmers or (now) migrant workers.
2 the Afro-Asiatic language of these peoples. There are several different dialects; some of them, e.g., Tamashek, are regarded by some scholars as separate languages.
▶ **adj.** of or relating to these peoples or their language.
– ORIGIN from Arabic *barbar*, from Greek *barbarus* 'foreigner' (see BARBARIAN).

ber·be·rine /ˈbərbəˌrēn/ ▶ **n.** Chemistry a bitter yellow compound of the alkaloid class obtained from barberry and other plants.
– ORIGIN early 19th cent.: from BERBERIS + -INE⁴.

ber·be·ris /ˈbərbəris/ ▶ **n.** a plant of a genus that comprises the barberries. ● Genus *Berberis*, family Berberidaceae.
– ORIGIN modern Latin and Old French, from medieval Latin *barbaris*.

ber·ceuse /berˈso͞oz, -ˈsœz/ ▶ **n.** (pl. **berceuses** pronunc. **same**) a lullaby.
– ORIGIN French, from *bercer* 'to rock.'

Berch·tes·ga·den /ˈberKHtəsˌgädn/ a town in southern Germany, in the Bavarian Alps close to the border with Austria; pop. 8,200 (est. 2006). Adolf Hitler had a fortified retreat there.

be·reave /biˈrēv/ ▶ **v.** (**be bereaved**) be deprived of a loved one through a profound absence, esp. due to the loved one's death: *the year after they had been bereaved* | (as adj. **bereaved**) *bereaved families* | (as plural noun **the bereaved**) *those who counsel the bereaved.*
– DERIVATIVES **be·reave·ment n.**
– ORIGIN Old English *berēafian* (see BE-, REAVE). The original sense was 'deprive of' in general.

be·reft /biˈreft/ archaic past participle of BEREAVE.
▶ **adj.** deprived of or lacking something, esp. a nonmaterial asset: *her room was stark and bereft of color.* ■ (of a person) lonely and abandoned, esp. through someone's death or departure: *his death in 1990 left her bereft.*

Ber·e·ni·ce /ˌberəˈnīsē, -ˈnēs/ (3rd century BC), Egyptian queen; wife of **Ptolemy III**. She offered her hair for the safe return of her husband from an expedition; the hair was stolen and, according to legend, placed in the heavens. The constellation Coma Berenices (*Berenice's hair*) is named after her.

be·ret /bəˈrā/ ▶ **n.** a round flattish cap of felt or cloth.
– ORIGIN early 19th cent.: from French *béret* 'Basque cap,' from Old Provençal *berret*, based on late Latin *birrus* 'hooded cape.' Compare with BIRETTA.

be·ret·ta ▶ **n.** variant spelling of BIRETTA.

Berg /berKH/, Alban (Maria Johannes) (1885–1935), Austrian composer, a leading exponent of twelve-tone composition.

berg /bərg/ ▶ **n.** short for ICEBERG.

ber·ga·mot /ˈbərgəˌmät/ ▶ **n. 1** an oily substance extracted from the rind of the fruit of a dwarf variety of the Seville orange tree. It is used in cosmetics and as flavoring in tea.
2 (also **bergamot orange**) the tree that bears this fruit. ● *Citrus aurantium* subsp. *bergamia*, family Rutaceae.
3 an aromatic North American herb of the mint family, grown for its bright flowers and traditionally used in American Indian medicine. Also called BEE BALM, OSWEGO TEA. ● *Monarda didyma*, family Labiatae.
– ORIGIN late 17th cent. (sense 2): named after the city and province of *Bergamo* in northern Italy.

Ber·gen /ˈbərgən, ˈber-/ a seaport in southwestern Norway; pop. 220,418 (2007). It is a center of the fishing and North Sea oil industries.

Ber·ger¹ /ˈbərgər/, Hans (1873–1941), German psychiatrist. He detected electric currents in the brain's cortex and developed encephalography.

Ber·ger², Thomas (1924–), US writer. His works include *Crazy in Berlin* (1958), *Little Big Man* (1964), *The Feud* (1983), and *Meeting Evil* (1992).

Ber·ge·rac see CYRANO DE BERGERAC.

ber·gère /berˈZHer/ ▶ **n.** a long-seated upholstered armchair fashionable in the 18th century.

Ber·gi·us /ˈbergēo͝os/, Friedrich Karl Rudolf (1884–1949), German industrial chemist. Nobel Prize for Chemistry (1931), shared with Carl Bosch (1874–1940).

Berg·man¹ /ˈbərgmən, ˈber(yə)ˌmän/, (Ernst) Ingmar (1918–2007), Swedish movie and theater director. He used haunting imagery and symbolism. Notable films: *Smiles of a Summer Night* (1955), *The Seventh Seal* (1956), and *Fanny and Alexander* (1982).

Berg·man² /ˈbərgmən/, Ingrid (1915–82), Swedish actress. Notable movies: *Casablanca* (1942), *Gaslight* (1944), *Anastasia* (1956), and *Murder on the Orient Express* (1974).

Berg·son /ˈbergsən, berkˈsôN/, Henri (Louis) (1859–1941), French philosopher. He wrote *Creative Evolution* (1907). Nobel Prize for Literature (1927).

Be·ri·a /ˈbyeryə/, Lavrenti (Pavlovich) (1899–1953), Soviet politician and head of the secret police 1938–53. After Joseph Stalin's death, he was arrested and executed.

be·rib·boned /biˈribənd/ ▶ **adj.** decorated with many ribbons.

ber·i·ber·i /ˈberēˈberē/ ▶ **n.** a disease causing inflammation of the nerves and heart failure, caused by a deficiency of vitamin B_1.
– ORIGIN early 18th cent.: from Sinhalese, from *beri* 'weakness.'

Ber·ing /ˈberiNG/, Vitus (Jonassen) (1681–1741), Danish navigator and explorer. He led several Russian expeditions to determine whether Asia and North America were connected by land. The Bering Sea and Bering Strait are named after him.

Be·rin·gi·a /bəˈrinjēə/ the area comprising the Bering Strait and adjacent parts of Siberia and Alaska, esp. in connection with the migration of animals across the former Bering land bridge. See BERING STRAIT.
– DERIVATIVES **Be·rin·gi·an adj.**

Ber·ing Sea an arm of the North Pacific Ocean that lies between northeastern Siberia in Russia and Alaska, bounded on the south by the Aleutian Islands. It is linked to the Arctic Ocean by the Bering Strait. Both the sea and the strait are named after Vitus Bering.

Ber·ing Strait a narrow sea passage that separates the eastern tip of Siberia in Russia from Alaska and links the Arctic Ocean with the Bering Sea, about 53 miles (85 km) wide at its narrowest point. During the Ice Age, as a result of a drop in sea levels, the **Bering land bridge** formed between the two continents, allowing the migration of animals and dispersal of plants in both directions.

Berke·ley¹ /ˈbərklē/ a city in western California, on San Francisco Bay, site of a campus of the University of California; pop. 101,371 (est. 2008).

Berke·ley² /ˈbərklē/, Busby (1895–1976), US choreographer and movie director; born *William Berkeley Enos*. He is remembered for his spectacular movie sequences in which dancers formed kaleidoscopic patterns on the screen. Notable movies: *Gold Diggers* series (1922–37) and *Babes in Arms* (1939).

Berke·ley³ /ˈbärklē, ˈbər-/, George (1685–1753), Irish philosopher and bishop. He argued that material objects exist only by being perceived.
– DERIVATIVES **Berke·le·ian·ism** /ˈbärklēəˌnizəm, ˈbər-/ **n.**

ber·ke·li·um /bərˈkēlēəm/ ▶ **n.** the chemical element of atomic number 97, a radioactive metal of the actinide series. Berkelium does not occur naturally and was first made by bombarding americium with helium ions. (Symbol: **Bk**)
– ORIGIN 1949: from BERKELEY¹, California (where it was first made) + -IUM.

Berk·shire /ˈbərkSHər, -ˌSHi(ə)r/ (in full **Berkshire Pig**) ▶ **n.** a pig of a black breed, now rarely kept commercially.

Berk·shire Hills /ˈbərkSHər/ an upland in western Massachusetts, noted as a resort area.

Berle /bərl/, Milton (1908–2002), US comedian and actor; born *Milton Berlinger*. He began as a vaudeville entertainer and went on to star on radio, stage, movies and, in particular, on television with the "Texaco Star Theater" from 1948 until 1956 (renamed "The Milton Berle Show" in 1953).

Ber·lin¹ /bərˈlin/ the capital of Germany; pop. 3,404,000 (est. 2006). At the end of World War II, the city was occupied by the Allies and divided into two parts: **West Berlin** and **East Berlin**. Between 1961 and 1989, the Berlin Wall separated the two parts, which were reunited in 1990.

Ber·lin², Irving (1888–1989), US composer of popular music; born in Russia; born *Israel Baline*. His prolific work includes the songs "Alexander's Ragtime Band" (1911) and "God Bless America" (1939), the movie scores for *Top Hat* (1935) and *White Christmas* (1954), and the stage musicals *Annie Get Your Gun* (1946) and *Call Me Madam* (1950).

Ber·li·ner /bərˈlinər/ ▶ **n.** a native or citizen of Berlin.
– ORIGIN mid 19th cent.: German.

Ber·lin Wall a fortified and heavily guarded wall built on the boundary between East and West Berlin in 1961 by the communist authorities, chiefly to curb the flow of East Germans to the West. It was opened in November 1989 after the collapse of the communist regime in East Germany and subsequently was dismantled.

Ber·lin work ▶ **n.** worsted embroidery on canvas.

Ber·li·oz /ˈberlēˌōz, berˈlyōz/, Hector (1803–69), French composer; full name *Louis-Hector Berlioz*. Notable works: *Les Troyens* (opera, 1856–59), *Symphonie fantastique* (1830), and *La Damnation de Faust* (cantata, 1846).

berm /bərm/ ▶ **n.** a flat strip of land, raised bank, or terrace bordering a river or canal. ■ a path or grass strip beside a road. ■ an artificial ridge or embankment, e.g., as a defense against tanks. ■ a narrow space, esp. one between a ditch and the base of a parapet.
– ORIGIN early 18th cent. (denoting a narrow space): from French *berme*, from Dutch *berm*.

Ber·mu·da /bərˈmyo͞odə/ (also **the Bermudas**) a British dependency made up of about 150 small islands about 650 miles (1,046 km) east of the coast of North Carolina; pop. 67,800 (est. 2009); capital, Hamilton. It now has internal self-government.
– DERIVATIVES **Ber·mu·dan** /-ˈmyo͞odn/ **adj. & n.**, **Ber·mu·di·an** /-ˈmyo͞odēən/ **adj. & n.**
– ORIGIN named after a Spanish sailor, Juan *Bermúdez*, who sighted the islands early in the 16th cent.

Ber·mu·da grass ▶ **n.** a creeping grass common in warmer parts of the world, used for lawns and pasture. ● *Cynodon dactylon*, family Gramineae.

Ber·mu·da High ▶ **n.** Meteorology a semipermanent area of high pressure located over Bermuda in summer and fall that steers many storm systems westward across the Atlantic. Compare with AZORES HIGH.

b

Ber·mu·da Hun·dred a locality southeast of Richmond in Virginia, the site of an 1864 Civil War battle.

Ber·mu·da on·ion ▶ **n.** a variety of cultivated onion with a mild flavor and a flattened shape.

Ber·mu·da rig ▶ **n.** a tall yachting rig with a high, tapering fore-and-aft mainsail.

Ber·mu·da shorts (also **Bermudas**) ▶ **plural n.** casual knee-length shorts.

Ber·mu·da Tri·an·gle an area of the western Atlantic Ocean between Florida, Bermuda, and Puerto Rico where a large number of ships and aircraft are said to have disappeared mysteriously.

Ber·na·dette, St. /ˌbərnəˈdet/ (1844–79), French peasant girl; born *Marie Bernarde Soubirous.* Her visions of the Virgin Mary at Lourdes in 1858 led to the town's establishment as a center of pilgrimage. Feast day, February 18.

Ber·na·dotte[1] /ˌbernəˈdät, -ˈdôt/, Count Folke (1895–1948), Swedish statesman. As vice president of the Swedish Red Cross, he arranged the exchange of prisoners of war and in 1945 conveyed a German offer of capitulation to the Allies. Appointed as UN mediator in Palestine in 1948, he was assassinated by the Stern Gang.

Ber·na·dotte[2], Jean Baptiste Jules (1763–1844), French soldier who became king of Sweden as Charles XIV 1818–44. One of Napoleon's marshals, he was adopted by Charles XIII of Sweden in 1810 and later became king, thus founding Sweden's present royal house.

Ber·nard /berˈnär/, Claude (1813–78), French physiologist. He showed the role of the pancreas in digestion, the method of regulation of body temperature, and the function of nerves that supply the internal organs.

Ber·nard, St. /bərˈnärd, berˈnär/ (*c.*996–*c.*1081), French monk. He founded two hospices for travelers in the Alps. The St. Bernard passes, where the hospices were situated, and St. Bernard dogs, once kept by the monks and trained to aid travelers, are named after him. Feast day, May 28.

Ber·nard of Clair·vaux, St. /bərˈnärd əv klerˈvō, berˈnär/ (1090–1153), French theologian and abbot. The first abbot of Clairvaux, his monastery was one of the chief centers of the Cistercian order. Feast day, August 20.

Berne /bern, bərn/ (also **Bern**) the capital of Switzerland, in the west central part of the country; pop. 122,658 (2007). ■ a canton of Switzerland.
– DERIVATIVES **Ber·nese** /berˈnēz, -ˈnēs, bər-/ **adj. & n.**

Ber·nese moun·tain dog /ˈbərnēz, -nēs, bərˈnēz, -ˈnēs/ ▶ **n.** a large muscular dog of a Swiss breed with a silky black coat, having white and russet markings.

Bern·hardt /ˈbərnˌhärt/, Sarah (1844–1923), French actress; born *Henriette Rosine Bernard.* She was noted for her portrayal of Marguerite in *La Dame aux camélias* and of Cordelia in *King Lear.*

Ber·ni·ni /bərˈnēnē/, Gian Lorenzo (1598–1680), Italian sculptor, painter, and architect. His work includes the great canopy over the altar and the colonnade around the piazza at St. Peter's in Rome.

Ber·noul·li /bərˈno͞o(l)ē/ a Swiss family that produced many eminent mathematicians and scientists. ■ **Jakob** (1654–1705), a professor of mathematics; also known as *Jacques* or *James Bernoulli.* He made discoveries in calculus and contributed to geometry and the theory of probabilities. ■ **Johann** (1667–1748), the brother of Jakob; also known as *Jean* or *John Bernoulli.* He contributed to differential and integral calculus. ■ **Daniel** (1700–82), son of Johann. His greatest contributions were to hydrodynamics and mathematical physics.

Ber·noul·li's prin·ci·ple ▶ **n.** the principle in hydrodynamics that an increase in the velocity of a stream of fluid results in a decrease in pressure. Also called **Bernoulli effect** or **Bernoulli theorem**.
– ORIGIN Named for Swiss mathematician Daniel Bernoulli (1700–82).

Bern·stein[1] /ˈbərnˌstēn, -ˌstīn/, Carl (1944–), US journalist. He was the *Washington Post* reporter who, with Bob Woodward, broke the story of the Watergate burglary and traced the financial payoffs to President Nixon. With Woodward, he wrote *All The President's Men* (1974) and *The Final Days* (1976).

Bern·stein[2], Leonard (1918–90), US composer, conductor, and pianist. He was a conductor with the New York Philharmonic Orchestra 1945–48 and 1957–69. Notable works: *The Age of Anxiety* (symphony, 1947–49), *West Side Story* (musical, 1957), and music for the movie *On the Waterfront* (1954).

Leonard Bernstein

Ber·ra /ˈberə/, Yogi (1925–), US baseball player and manager; born *Lawrence Peter Berra.* A New York Yankee (1946–63) for all but one season of his playing career, he set the record for most home runs (313) by a catcher in the American League. Baseball Hall of Fame (1972).

ber·ried /ˈberēd/ ▶ **adj. 1** bearing or covered with berries.
2 like a berry or berries, as in flavor or shape.
3 (of crustaceans or fish) bearing eggs.

Ber·ry /ˈberē/, Chuck (1926–), US rock-and-roll singer, guitarist, and songwriter; born *Charles Edward Berry.* One of the first great rock-and-roll stars, his recording career was interrupted by a period of imprisonment 1962–64. Notable songs: "Maybelline" (1955), "Johnny B Goode" (1958), and "My Ding A Ling" (1972).

ber·ry /ˈberē/ ▶ **n.** (pl. **berries**) a small roundish juicy fruit without a stone: *juniper berries* | [as modifier] *berry clusters.* ■ Botany any fruit that has its seeds enclosed in a fleshy pulp, for example, a banana or tomato. ■ any of various kernels or seeds, such as the coffee bean. ■ a fish egg or the roe of a lobster or similar creature.
– ORIGIN Old English *berie*, of Germanic origin; related to Dutch *bes* and German *Beere*.

ber·ry·ing /ˈberēiNG/ ▶ **n.** the activity of gathering berries: *let's go **berrying**.*

Ber·ry·man /ˈberēmən/, John (1914–72), US poet and educator. His notable works include the Pulitzer Prize-winning *77 Dream Songs* (1964).

ber·seem clo·ver /bərˈsēm/ ▶ **n.** a white-flowered clover. Native to Egypt and Syria, it is an established forage plant in the southern US. Also called **Egyptian clover**. ● *Trifolium alexandrinum*, family Leguminosae.

ber·serk /bərˈzərk, -ˈsərk/ ▶ **adj.** (of a person or animal) out of control with anger or excitement; wild or frenzied: *after she left him, he **went berserk**, throwing things about the apartment.* ■ (of a device, system, or activity) operating in a wild or erratic way; fluctuating wildly: *the climate control went berserk and either roasted or froze us* | *the stock market's gone berserk.*
– ORIGIN early 19th cent. (originally as a noun denoting a wild Norse warrior who fought with frenzy): from Old Norse *berserkr* (noun), probably from *birn-*, *bjǫrn* (see **bear[2]**) + *serkr* 'coat,' but also possibly from *berr* 'bare' (i.e., without armor).

ber·serk·er /bərˈzərkər, -ˈsər-/ ▶ **n.** an ancient Norse warrior who fought in a wild frenzy.

berth /bərTH/ ▶ **n. 1** a ship's allotted place at a wharf or dock.
2 a fixed bed or bunk on a ship, train, or other means of transport.
3 informal (often in a sports context) a situation or position in an organization or event: *today's victory clinched a berth for the Orioles in the playoffs.*
▶ **v.** [with obj.] **1** moor (a ship) in its allotted place: *these modern ships can almost berth themselves.* ■ [no obj.] (of a ship) dock: *the Dutch freighter berthed at the Brooklyn docks.*
2 (of a passenger ship) provide a sleeping place for (someone).
– PHRASES **give a wide berth** steer (a ship) well clear of something while passing it: *ships are advised to give a wide berth to the Outer Banks.* ■ stay away from someone or something: *I'd sworn to give women a wide berth.*
– ORIGIN early 17th cent. (in the sense 'adequate sea room'): probably from a nautical use of **bear[1]** + **-th[2]**.

ber·tha /ˈbərTHə/ ▶ **n.** chiefly historical a deep collar, typically made of lace, attached to the top of a dress that has a low neckline.
– ORIGIN mid 19th cent.: from the given name *Bertha*.

berth·ing /ˈbərTHiNG/ ▶ **n. 1** the action of mooring a ship: *as soon as the berthing was complete, they went ashore.*
2 mooring position; accommodation in berths: *there were more than 12 miles of berthing.*

Ber·til·lon /ˈbərtlˌän, ˌbertēˈyôN/, Alphonse (1853–1914), French criminologist. He devised a system of body measurements (the **Bertillon system**) for the identification of criminals, which was widely used until superseded by the technique of fingerprinting at the beginning of the 20th century.

Ber·to·luc·ci /ˌbertlˈo͞oCHē/, Bernardo (1940–), Italian movie director. Notable works: *The Spider's Stratagem* (1970), *Last Tango in Paris* (1972), *The Last Emperor* (1988), and *The Dreamers* (2003).

Ber·wyn /ˈbərˌwin/ a city in northeastern Illinois, west of Chicago; pop. 49,919 (est. 2008).

ber·yl /ˈberəl/ ▶ **n.** a transparent pale green, blue, or yellow mineral consisting of a silicate of beryllium and aluminum, sometimes used as a gemstone.
– ORIGIN Middle English: from Old French *beril*, via Latin from Greek *bērullos*.

be·ryl·li·o·sis /bəˌrilēˈōsis/ ▶ **n.** Medicine poisoning by beryllium or beryllium compounds, esp. by inhalation causing fibrosis of the lungs.

be·ryl·li·um /bəˈrilēəm/ ▶ **n.** the chemical element of atomic number 4, a hard gray metal. (Symbol: **Be**)

> Beryllium is the lightest of the alkaline earth metals, and its chief source is the mineral beryl. It is used in the manufacture of light corrosion-resistant alloys and in windows in X-ray equipment.

Ber·ze·li·us /bərˈzālēəs, -ˈzē-/, Jöns Jakob (1779–1848), Swedish analytical chemist. He determined the atomic weights of many elements and discovered cerium, selenium, and thorium.

Bes /bes/ Egyptian Mythology a grotesque god depicted as having short legs, an obese body, and an almost bestial face, who dispelled evil spirits.

Be·san·çon /bəzäNˈsôN/ a city in northeastern France; pop. 121,012 (2006).

Besch·loss /ˈbesHlôs/, Michael (1955–), US historian and writer. Among his books on the twentieth-century presidency are *Mayday: Eisenhower, Khrushchev, and the U-2 Affair* (1986), *The Crisis Years: Kennedy and Khrushchev, 1960–1963* (1991), and *The Conquerors: Roosevelt, Truman, and the Destruction of Hitler's Germany, 1941–1945* (2002).

be·seech /biˈsēCH/ ▶ **v.** (past and past participle **besought** /-ˈsôt/ or **beseeched**) [reporting verb] literary ask (someone) urgently and fervently to do something; implore; entreat: [with obj. and infinitive] *they beseeched him to stay* | [with obj.] *they earnestly beseeched his forgiveness* | [with obj. and direct speech] *"You have got to believe me," Gloria beseeched him* | (as adj. **beseeching**) *a beseeching gaze.*
– DERIVATIVES **be·seech·ing·ly adv.**
– ORIGIN Middle English: from **be-** (as an intensifier) + Old English *sēcan* (see **seek**).

be·seem /biˈsēm/ ▶ **v.** [with obj.] archaic seem; befit.

be·set /biˈset/ ▶ **v.** (**besets**, **besetting**; past and past participle **beset**) [with obj.] **1** (of a problem or difficulty) trouble or threaten persistently: *the social problems that beset the inner city* | *she was beset with self-doubt* | [as adj.] *poverty is a besetting problem.* ■ surround and harass; assail on all sides: *I was beset by clouds of flies.* ■ hem in; enclose: *the ship was beset by ice.*
2 (**be beset with**) archaic be covered or studded with: *blades of grass beset with glistening drops of dew.*
– ORIGIN Old English *besettan*, from **be-** 'around' + *settan* (see **set[1]**).

be·shrew /biˈsHro͞o/ ▶ **v.** [with obj.] archaic **1** make wicked; deprave.
2 invoke evil upon; curse; blame for a misfortune.

be·side /biˈsīd/ ▶ **prep. 1** at the side of; next to: *he sat beside me in the front seat* | *on the table beside the bed.* ■ compared with: *beside Beth's idealism, my priorities looked shabby.*
2 in addition to; apart from: *he commissioned work from other artists beside Rivera.*
– PHRASES **beside oneself** overcome with worry or anger; distraught: *she was **beside herself** with anguish.* **beside the point** see **point**.
– ORIGIN Old English *be sīdan* (adverb) 'by the side' (see **by**, **side**).

> **USAGE** It is sometimes said that **beside** should not be used to mean 'apart from' and that **besides** should be used instead (*he commissioned work from other artists **besides** Minton* rather than *he commissioned work from other artists **beside** Minton*). Although there is little logical basis for such a view, and in standard English both **beside**

and **besides** are used for this sense, it is worth being aware of the potential ambiguity in the use of **beside**: *beside the cold meat, there are platters of trout and salmon* means either 'the cold meat is next to the trout and salmon' or 'apart from the cold meat, there are also trout and salmon.' **Beside** is always the word to use in the phrases **beside the point** and **beside oneself**.

be·sides /bi'sīdz/ ▶ **prep.** in addition to; apart from: *I have no other family besides my parents | besides being a player, he was my friend.*
▶ **adv.** in addition; as well: *I'm capable of doing the work, and a lot more besides.* ■ moreover; anyway: *I had no time to warn you. Besides, I wasn't sure.*

USAGE See usage at **BESIDE**.

be·siege /bi'sēj/ ▶ **v.** [with obj.] surround (a place) with armed forces in order to capture it or force its surrender; lay siege to: *the guerrillas continued to besiege other major cities to the north* | (as adj. **besieged**) *the besieged city.* ■ crowd around oppressively; surround and harass: *she spent the whole day besieged by newsmen.* ■ (**be besieged**) be inundated by large numbers of requests or complaints: *the television station was* **besieged with** *calls.*
– DERIVATIVES **be·sieg·er** n.
– ORIGIN Middle English: alteration (by change of prefix) of *assiege*, from Old French *asegier*.

be·smear /bi'smi(ə)r/ ▶ **v.** [with obj.] literary smear or cover with a greasy or sticky substance.
– ORIGIN Old English *bismierwan* (see **BE-**, **SMEAR**).

be·smirch /bi'smərCH/ ▶ **v.** [with obj.] damage the reputation of (someone or something) in the opinion of others: *he had besmirched the good name of his family.* ■ literary make (something) dirty or discolored: *the ground was besmirched with blood.*
– ORIGIN from **BE-** + **SMIRCH**.

be·som /'bēzəm/ ▶ **n.** a broom made of twigs tied around a stick.
– ORIGIN Old English *besema*; related to Dutch *bezem* and German *Besen*.

besom

be·sot·ted /bi'sätid/ ▶ **adj.**
1 strongly infatuated: *he became* **besotted with** *his best friend's sister.*
2 archaic intoxicated; drunk.
– ORIGIN late 16th cent.: past participle of *besot* 'make foolishly affectionate,' from **BE-** 'cause to be' + **SOT**.

be·sought /bi'sôt/ past and past participle of **BESEECH**.

be·spat·ter /bi'spatər/ ▶ **v.** [with obj.] splash small drops of a liquid substance all over (an object or surface): *his shoes were* **bespattered with** *mud.*

be·speak /bi'spēk/ ▶ **v.** (past **bespoke**; past participle **bespoken**) [with obj.] **1** (of an appearance or action) suggest; be evidence of: *the attractive tree-lined road bespoke money.*
2 order or reserve (something) in advance: *obtaining the affidavits that it has been necessary to bespeak.*
3 archaic speak to: *and in disgrace bespoke him thus.*
– ORIGIN Old English *bisprecan* 'speak up, speak out' (see **BE-**, **SPEAK**), later 'discuss, decide on,' hence 'arrange, order' (sense 2, late 16th cent).

be·spec·ta·cled /bi'spektəkəld/ ▶ **adj.** (of a person) wearing eyeglasses: *a bespectacled, studious youth.*

be·spoke /bi'spōk/ past of **BESPEAK**.
▶ **adj.** [attrib.] chiefly Brit. (of goods, esp. clothing) made to order: *a bespoke suit.* ■ (of a trader) making such goods: *bespoke tailors.*

be·spo·ken /bi'spōkən/ past participle of **BESPEAK**.

be·sprent /bi'sprent/ ▶ **adj.** [archaic] sprinkled.

be·sprin·kle /bi'spriNGkəl/ ▶ **v.** [with obj.] literary sprinkle all over with small drops or amounts of a substance: *their lips were* **besprinkled with** *flakes of pastry.*

Bes·sa·ra·bi·a /ˌbesə'rābēə/ a region in eastern Europe between the Dniester and Prut rivers. It was part of Romania 1918–40, but now lies in Moldova and Ukraine.
– DERIVATIVES **Bes·sa·ra·bi·an** adj. & n.

Bes·sel /'besəl/, Friedrich Wilhelm (1784–1846), German astronomer and mathematician. He determined the positions of about 75,000 stars, obtained accurate measurements of stellar distances, and, following a study of the orbit of Uranus, predicted the existence of an eighth planet.

Bes·se·mer[1] /'besəmər/ a city in north central Alabama, a steel and industrial center southwest of Birmingham; pop. 28,542 (est. 2008).

Bes·se·mer[2], Sir Henry (1813–98), English engineer and inventor. By 1860 he had developed the Bessemer process, the first successful method of making steel in quantity at low cost.

Bes·se·mer proc·ess ▶ **n.** a steel-making process, now largely superseded, in which carbon, silicon, and other impurities are removed from molten pig iron by oxidation in a blast of air in a special tilting retort (a **Bessemer converter**).

Best /best/, Charles Herbert (1899–1978), Canadian physiologist; born in the US. He assisted Frederick G. Banting in research leading to the discovery of insulin in 1922.

best /best/ superlative of **GOOD** ▶ **adj.** of the most excellent, effective, or desirable type or quality: *the best pitcher in the league | how to obtain the best results from your machine | her best black suit.* ■ most enjoyable: *some of the best times of my life.* ■ most appropriate, advantageous, or well advised: *do whatever you think best | it's best if we both go.*
▶ **adv.** superlative of **WELL**[1]. ■ to the highest degree; most: *the one we liked best | you knew him best | well-drained soil suits it best.* ■ most excellently or effectively: *the best-dressed man in Hollywood | the things we do best.* ■ most suitably, appropriately, or usefully: *this is best done at home | jokes are best avoided in essays.*
▶ **n.** (usu. **the best**) that which is the most excellent, outstanding, or desirable: *buy the best you can afford | Sarah always had to be* **the best at** *everything | this year's event will cover the best of both domestic and international manufacturing practices.* ■ the most meritorious aspect of a thing or person: *he* **brought out the best** *in people.* ■ (**one's best**) the peak of condition; the highest standard or level that a person or thing can reach: *this is jazz* **at its best** *| try to* **look your best**. ■ (**one's best**) one's finest or most formal clothes: *she dressed in her best.* ■ (in sports) a record of a specified kind, esp. a personal one: *achieving a lifetime best of 12.0 seconds |* **a personal best**.
▶ **v.** [with obj.] informal outwit or get the better of (someone): *she refused to allow herself to be bested.*
– PHRASES **all the best** said or written to wish a person well on ending a letter or parting. **as best one can** (or **may**) as effectively as possible under the circumstances: *I went about my job as best I could.* **at best** taking the most optimistic or favorable view: *signs of recovery are patchy at best.* **at** (or **in**) **the best of times** even in the most favorable circumstances: *his memory is poor at the best of times.* **be best friends** be mutually closest friends: *he's* **best friends with** *Eddie.* **be for** (or **all for**) **the best** be desirable in the end, although not at first seeming so. **one's best friend** one's closest or favorite friend. **best of** (or **in**) **breed** the animal in a show judged to be the best representative of its breed. ■ any item or product considered to be the best of its kind: *their technology is still considered best of breed, and demand for their products is still growing.* **the best of friends** very good friends. **the best of three** (or **five**, etc.) victory achieved by winning the majority of a specified (usually odd) number of games. **the best part of** most of: *it took them the best part of 10 years.* **best wishes** an expression of hope for someone's future happiness or welfare: *we sent our* **best wishes for** *a speedy recovery.* ■ written at the end of a letter: *Best wishes, Celia.* **one's best years** the most vigorous and productive period of one's life; one's prime: *he had spent* **the best years of his life** *working at the stables.* **do** (or **try**) **one's best** do all one can: *Ruth* **did her best** *to reassure her.* **get the best of** overcome (someone): *his drinking got the best of him and he was fired.* **had best do something** find it most sensible or well advised to do the thing mentioned: *I'd best be going.* **make the best of** derive what limited advantage one can from (something unsatisfactory or unwelcome): *you'll just have to make the best of the situation.* ■ use (resources) as well as possible: *he tried to make the best of his talents.* **to the best of one's ability** (or **knowledge**) as far as one can do or know: *the text is free of factual errors, to the best of my knowledge.* **with the best of them** as well or as much as anyone: *he'll be out there dancing with the best of them.*
– ORIGIN Old English *betest* (adjective), *betost, betst* (adverb), of Germanic origin; related to Dutch and German *best*, also to **BETTER**[1].

USAGE On the punctuation of **best** in compound adjectives, see usage at **WELL**[1].

best ball ▶ **n.** Golf the better score at a hole of two or more players competing as a team: [as modifier] *a best-ball match.*

best boy ▶ **n.** the assistant to the chief electrician of a movie crew.

best buy ▶ **n.** an item or product that gives the best value for money out of all its competitors.

bes·tial /'bēsCHəl, 'bes-/ ▶ **adj.** of or like an animal or animals: *Darwin's revelations about our bestial beginnings.* ■ savagely cruel and depraved: *bestial and barbaric acts.*
– DERIVATIVES **bes·tial·ly** adv.
– ORIGIN late Middle English: via Old French from late Latin *bestialis*, from Latin *bestia* 'beast.'

bes·ti·al·i·ty /ˌbēsCHē'alitē, ˌbes-/ ▶ **n. 1** savagely cruel or depraved behavior: *there seems no end to the bestiality of human beings.*
2 sexual intercourse between a person and an animal.
– ORIGIN late Middle English: from Old French *bestialite*, from *bestial* (see **BESTIAL**).

bes·ti·ar·y /'bēsCHēˌerē, 'bes-/ ▶ **n.** (pl. **bestiaries**) a descriptive or anecdotal treatise on various real or mythical kinds of animals, esp. a medieval work with a moralizing tone.
– ORIGIN mid 19th cent.: from medieval Latin *bestiarium*, from Latin *bestia* 'beast.'

be·stir /bi'stər/ ▶ **v.** (**bestirs**, **bestirring**, **bestirred**) (**bestir oneself**) make a physical or mental effort; exert or rouse oneself: *they rarely bestir themselves except in the most pressing of circumstances.*

best man ▶ **n.** [in sing.] a male friend or relative chosen by a bridegroom to assist him at his wedding.

best-of ▶ **n.** a list or collection comprising the best examples of something: *foodies have flocked like sheep to this critic's best-ofs* | [as modifier] *a best-of CD.*

be·stow /bi'stō/ ▶ **v.** [with obj.] confer or present (an honor, right, or gift): *the office was* **bestowed on** *him by the chief of state | thank you for this honor that you have* **bestowed upon** *me* | figurative *she bestowed her nicest smile on Jim.*
– DERIVATIVES **be·stow·al** /-əl/ n.
– ORIGIN Middle English *bistowen* (in the sense 'use for, devote to'): from **BE-** (as an intensifier) + *stowen* 'to place,' from Old English *stōw* 'place.'

best prac·tice ▶ **n.** commercial or professional procedures that are accepted or prescribed as being correct or most effective.

be·strew /bi'strōō/ ▶ **v.** (past participle **bestrewed** or **bestrewn**) [with obj.] literary cover or partly cover (a surface) with scattered objects: *the bride's train was* **bestrewn with** *rose petals.* ■ (of objects) lie scattered over (a surface): *sweeping away the sand and rubbish that bestrewed it.*
– ORIGIN Old English *bestrēowian* (see **BE-**, **STREW**).

be·stride /bi'strīd/ ▶ **v.** (past **bestrode**; past participle **bestridden**) [with obj.] stand astride over; span or straddle: figurative *creatures that bestride the dividing line between amphibians and reptiles.* ■ sit astride on: *he bestrode his horse with the easy grace of a born horseman.*
– ORIGIN Old English *bestrīdan* (see **BE-**, **STRIDE**).

best·sell·er ▶ **n.** a book or other product that sells in very large numbers: *her autobiography is an international bestseller.*

best-sell·ing ▶ **adj.** [attrib.] (of a book or other product) having very large sales; very popular: *a best-selling novel.*

be·suit·ed /bi'sōōtid/ ▶ **adj.** (of a person, esp. a man) wearing a suit: *the personification of Bloated Washington, heaving his besuited bulk from stump to stump.*

bet /bet/ ▶ **v.** (**bets**, **betting**; past and past participle **bet** or **betted**) **1** [no obj.] risk something, usually a sum of money, against someone else's on the basis of the outcome of a future event, such as the result of a race or game: *betting* **on** *horses* | [with clause] *I would be prepared to bet that what he really wanted was to settle down* | [with obj.] *most people would bet their life savings* **on** *this prospect.* ■ [with obj.] risk a sum of money against (someone) on the outcome or happening of a future event: [with two objs.] *I'll bet you $15 you won't find a single scratch.*
2 [with clause] informal feel sure: *I bet this place is really spooky late at night | he'll be surprised to see me, I'll bet.*
▶ **n.** an act of risking a sum of money in this way: *every Saturday she had* **a bet on** *the horses.* ■ a sum of money staked in this way: *the bookies are taking bets on his possible successor.* ■ [with adj.] informal a candidate or course of action to choose; an option: ***your best bet*** *is to call a professional exterminator.* ■ (**one's bet**) informal an opinion, typically one

PRONUNCIATION KEY ə *ago, up*; ər *over, fur*; a *hat*; ā *ate*; ä *car*; e *let*; ē *see*; i *fit*; ī *by*; NG *sing*; ō *go*; ô *law, for*; oi *toy*; ŏŏ *good*; ōō *goo*; ou *out*; TH *thin*; TH *then*; ZH *vision*

formed quickly or spontaneously: *my bet is that the president will veto the bill.*
– PHRASES **all bets are off** informal the outcome of a situation is unpredictable. **bet the farm** informal risk everything that one owns on a bet, investment, or enterprise: *they're betting the farm on this merger bid.* **don't** (or **I wouldn't**) **bet on it** informal used to express doubt about an assertion or situation: *he may be a suitable companion—but don't bet on it.* **want to** (or **wanna**) **bet?** informal used to express vigorous disagreement with a confident assertion: *"You can't be with me every moment." "Want to bet?"* **you bet** informal you may be sure; certainly: *"Would you like this piece of pie?" "You bet!"*
– ORIGIN late 16th cent.: perhaps a shortening of the obsolete noun *abet* 'abetment.'

bet. ▶ abbr. between.

be·ta /ˈbātə/ ▶ n. the second letter of the Greek alphabet (Β, β), transliterated as 'b.' ■ [as modifier] denoting the second of a series of items, categories, forms of a chemical compound, etc.: *beta carotene | beta blocker.* ■ informal short for **BETA TEST**: *their database system is currently **in beta** |* [as modifier] *a beta version.* ■ (**Beta**) [followed by Latin genitive] the second (usually second-brightest) star in a constellation: *Beta Virginis.* ■ [as modifier] relating to beta decay or beta particles: *beta emitters.*

be·ta-ad·ren·er·gic ▶ adj. of, relating to, or affecting beta receptors: *sympathetic nerves that stimulate beta-adrenergic receptors.*

be·ta block·er ▶ n. any of a class of drugs that prevent the stimulation of the adrenergic receptors responsible for increased cardiac action. Beta blockers are used to control heart rhythm, treat angina, and reduce high blood pressure.

Be·ta·cam /ˈbātəˌkam/ ▶ n. trademark a high quality format for video cameras and recorders. ■ a camera using this format.

be·ta-car·o·tene /ˌbātəˈkarəˌtēn/ ▶ n. see **CAROTENE**.

be·ta cell ▶ n. any of the insulin-producing cells in the islets of Langerhans.

be·ta de·cay ▶ n. radioactive decay in which an electron is emitted.

be·ta en·dor·phin ▶ n. an endorphin produced in the pituitary gland that is a powerful pain suppressor.

be·ta glob·u·lin ▶ n. see **GLOBULIN**.

be·ta·ine /ˈbētəˌēn/ ▶ n. Chemistry a crystalline compound with basic properties found in many plant juices. ● Chem. formula: $(CH_3)_3N^+{-}CH_2CO_2^-$. ■ any zwitterionic compound of the same type.
– ORIGIN mid 19th cent.: formed irregularly from Latin *beta* 'beet' (because originally isolated from sugar beet) + **-INE**⁴.

be·take /biˈtāk/ ▶ v. (past **betook**; past participle **betaken**) [with obj.] (**betake oneself to**) literary go to: *I shall betake myself to my room.*

Be·ta·max /ˈbātəˌmaks/ ▶ n. trademark a format for video recorders, now largely obsolete.

be·ta par·ti·cle (also **beta ray**) ▶ n. Physics a fast-moving electron emitted by radioactive decay of substances. (The emission of beta particles was originally regarded as a ray.).

be·ta re·cep·tor ▶ n. an adrenergic receptor in the sympathetic nervous system, stimulation of which results esp. in increased cardiac activity.

be·ta rhythm ▶ n. Physiology the normal electrical activity of the brain when conscious and alert, consisting of oscillations (**beta waves**) with a frequency of 18 to 25 hertz.

be·ta test ▶ n. a trial of machinery, software, or other products, in the final stages of its development, carried out by a party unconnected with its development.
▶ v. (**beta-test**) [with obj.] subject (a product) to such a test.

be·ta·tron /ˈbātəˌträn/ ▶ n. Physics an apparatus for accelerating electrons in a circular path by magnetic induction.
– ORIGIN 1940s: from **BETA** + **-TRON**.

bet·cha /ˈbeCHə/ ▶ v. a nonstandard contraction of "bet you," used in representing informal speech: *betcha can't find a better apartment.*

be·tel /ˈbētl/ ▶ n. **1** the leaf of an Asian evergreen climbing plant that is used in the East as a mild stimulant. Parings of areca nut, lime, and cinnamon are wrapped in the leaf, which is then chewed, causing the saliva to go red and, with prolonged use, the teeth to go black.
2 the plant, related to pepper, from which these leaves are taken. ● *Piper betle*, family Piperaceae.
– ORIGIN mid 16th cent.: via Portuguese from Malayalam *verrila*.

Be·tel·geuse /ˈbētlˌjo͞os, ˈbetl-, -ˌjo͞oz/ (also **Betelgeux**) Astronomy the tenth brightest star in the sky, in the constellation Orion. It is a red supergiant, and variations in its brightness are associated with pulsations in its outer envelope.
– ORIGIN French, alteration of Arabic *yad al-jauzā* 'hand of the giant' (the giant being Orion).

be·tel nut ▶ n. another term for **ARECA NUT**.

be·tel palm ▶ n. another term for **ARECA**.

bête noire /ˌbāt ˈnwär, ˌbet/ ▶ n. (pl. **bêtes noires** pronunc. **same** or /ˈnwärz/) a person or thing that one particularly dislikes: *great-uncle Edward was my father's bête noire.*
– ORIGIN mid 19th cent.: French, literally 'black beast.'

beth /bās, bāt, bet/ ▶ n. the second letter of the Hebrew alphabet.

Beth·el /ˈbeTHəl/ a town in the Catskill Mountains, in southeastern New York; pop. 4,543 (est. 2008). It is the actual site of the 1969 Woodstock music festival.

beth·el /ˈbeTHəl/ ▶ n. **1** a holy place.
2 a chapel for seamen.
3 Brit. a Nonconformist chapel.

Be·thes·da /bəˈTHezdə/ an affluent unincorporated suburb in central Maryland, north of Washington, DC. It is home to the National Institutes of Health; pop. 55,277 (2000).

be·think /biˈTHiNGk/ ▶ v. (past and past participle **bethought**) (**bethink oneself**) formal or archaic think on reflection; come to think: *he **bethought himself** of the verse from the Book of Proverbs |* [with clause] *the council bethought itself that this plan would leave room for future expansion.*
– ORIGIN Old English *bithencan* (see **BE-**, **THINK**).

Beth·le·hem /ˈbeTHliˌhem, -lēəm/ **1** a small town 5 miles (8 km) south of Jerusalem, in the West Bank; pop. 43,100 (est. 2009). It was the native city of King David and is the reputed birthplace of Jesus.
2 an industrial city in eastern Pennsylvania, on the Lehigh River; pop. 72,241 (est. 2008). It is noted for the manufacturing of steel.

Be·thune /bəˈTH(y)o͞on/, Mary McLeod (1875–1955), US educator. In 1904, she founded the Daytona Normal and Industrial Institute for Negro Girls, which, with the Cookman Institute, became Bethune-Cookman College in 1923. Bethune was founder and first president 1935–49 of the National Council of Negro Women.

be·tide /biˈtīd/ ▶ v. [no obj.] literary happen: *I waited with beating heart, as yet not knowing what would betide.* ■ [with obj.] happen to (someone): *she was trembling with fear lest worse might betide her.*
– PHRASES **woe betide** see **WOE**.
– ORIGIN Middle English: from **BE-** (as an intensifier) + obsolete *tide* 'befall,' from Old English *tīdan* 'happen,' from *tīd* (see **TIDE**).

be·times /biˈtīmz/ ▶ adv. literary before the usual or expected time; early: *next morning I was up betimes.*
– ORIGIN Middle English: from obsolete *betime* (see **BY**, **TIME**).

bê·tise /beˈtēz/ ▶ n. a foolish or ill-timed remark or action.
– ORIGIN early 19th cent.: French, literally 'stupidity.'

be·to·ken /biˈtōkən/ ▶ v. [with obj.] literary be a sign of; indicate: *she wondered if his cold, level gaze betokened indifference or anger.* ■ be a warning or indication of (a future event): *the falling comet betokened the true end of Merlin's powers.*
– ORIGIN Old English *betācnian*, from **BE-** (as an intensifier) + *tācnian* 'signify,' of Germanic origin; related to **TOKEN**.

bet·o·ny /ˈbetn-ē/ ▶ n. (pl. **betonies**) a Eurasian plant of the mint family that bears spikes of showy purple flowers. ● *Stachys officinalis*, family Labiatae. ■ used in names of plants that resemble the betony, e.g., **wood betony**.
– ORIGIN Middle English: from Old French *betoine*, based on Latin *betonica*, perhaps from the name of an Iberian tribe.

be·took /biˈto͝ok/ past of **BETAKE**.

be·tray /biˈtrā/ ▶ v. [with obj.] **1** expose (one's country, a group, or a person) to danger by treacherously giving information to an enemy: *a double agent who **betrayed** some 400 British and French agents **to** the Germans.* ■ treacherously reveal (secrets or information): *many of those employed by diplomats betrayed secrets and sold classified documents.* ■ be disloyal to: *his friends were shocked when he betrayed them.*
2 unintentionally reveal; be evidence of: *she drew a deep breath that betrayed her indignation.*
– DERIVATIVES **be·tray·al** /-əl/ n., **be·tray·er** n.
– ORIGIN Middle English: from **BE-** 'thoroughly' + obsolete *tray* 'betray,' from Old French *trair*, based on Latin *tradere* 'hand over.' Compare with **TRAITOR**.

be·troth /bəˈtrō*TH*, -ˈtrôTH/ ▶ v. [with obj.] (usu. **be betrothed**) dated enter into a formal agreement to marry: *soon I shall be betrothed to Isabel.*
– DERIVATIVES **be·troth·al** /-əl/ n.
– ORIGIN Middle English *betreuthe*: from **BE-** (expressing transitivity) + **TRUTH**. The change in the second syllable was due to association with **TROTH**.

be·trothed /bəˈtrō*TH*d, -ˈtrôTHd/ ▶ n. (**one's betrothed**) the person to whom one is engaged: *how long have you known your betrothed?*

Bet·tel·heim /ˈbetlˌhīm/, Bruno (1903–90), US psychologist; born in Austria. His experiences in Nazi Germany helped him to develop revolutionary theories and therapies for autistic children.

bet·ter¹ /ˈbetər/ ▶ adj. **1** comparative of **GOOD** and **WELL**¹. ■ of a more excellent or effective type or quality: *hoping for better weather | the new facilities were far better | I'm **better at** algebra than Alice.* ■ more appropriate, advantageous, or well advised: *there couldn't be a better time to start this job | it might be better to borrow the money.*
2 [predic.] partly or fully recovered from illness, injury, or mental stress; less unwell: *she's much better today | his leg was getting better | we'll feel a lot better after a decent night's sleep.*
▶ adv. comparative of **WELL**¹. ■ more excellently or effectively: *Johnny could do better if he tried | instruments are generally better made these days.* ■ to a greater degree; more: *I liked it better when we lived in the country | you may find alternatives that suit you better.* ■ more suitably, appropriately, or usefully: *the money could be better spent on more urgent cases.*
▶ n. **1** the better one; that which is better: *the Natural History Museum book is by far the better of the two | a change **for the better**.*
2 (**one's betters**) chiefly dated or humorous one's superiors in social class or ability: *amusing themselves by imitating their betters.*
▶ v. [with obj.] improve on or surpass (an existing or previous level or achievement): *bettering his previous time by ten minutes.* ■ make (something) better; improve: *his ideas for bettering the working conditions.* ■ (**better oneself**) achieve a better social position or status: *the residents are mostly welfare mothers who have bettered themselves.* ■ overcome or defeat (someone): *she bettered him at archery.*
– PHRASES **be better off** be in a better position, esp. in financial terms: *the promotion would make her about $750 a year better off |* (as plural noun **the better off**) *a paper read mainly by the better off.* **the —— the better** used to emphasize the importance or desirability of the quality or thing specified: *the sooner we're off, the better | the more people there the better.* **the better part of** almost all of; most of: *it is the better part of a mile.* **better safe than sorry** proverb it's wiser to be cautious than to be hasty or rash and so do something you may later regret. **better than** more than: *he'd lived there for better than twenty years.* **the better to —— so as to —— better**: *he leaned closer the better to hear her.* **for better or (for) worse** whether the outcome is good or bad: *ours, for better or for worse, is the century of youth.* **get the better of** (often of something immaterial) win an advantage over (someone); defeat or outwit: *curiosity got the better of her.* **go one better** narrowly surpass a previous effort or achievement: *I want to go one better this time and score.* ■ narrowly outdo (another person): *he went one better than Jack by reaching the finals.* **had better do something** would find it wiser to do something; ought to do something: *you had better be careful.* **have the better of** be more successful in a contest: *she usually had the better of these debates.* **no** (or **little**) **better than** just (or almost) the same as; merely: *government officials who were often no better than bandits.*
– ORIGIN Old English *betera* (adjective), of Germanic origin; related to Dutch *beter* and German *besser*, also to **BEST**.

> **USAGE 1** In the verb phrase *had better do something*, the word **had** acts like an auxiliary verb; in informal spoken contexts, it is often dropped, as in *you **better** not come tonight.* In writing, the **had** may be contracted to **'d** (*you'd better call*), but it should not be dropped altogether (not *you better call*). **2** On the punctuation of **better** in compound adjectives, see usage at **WELL**¹.

bet·ter² ▶ n. variant spelling of **BETTOR**.

bet·ter half ▶ n. informal a person's wife, husband, or partner.

bet·ter·ment /ˈbetərmənt/ ▶ n. the act or process of improving something: *they believed that what they were doing was vital for the betterment of society |* [as modifier] *working at betterment projects throughout the city.* ■ the enhanced value of real property arising from local improvements: [as modifier] *a betterment charge.*

bet·ting /ˈbetiNG/ ▶ n. the act of gambling money on the outcome of a race, game, or other unpredictable event: *there was a good deal of **betting** on the races going on.*

bet·ting slip ▶ **n.** a slip of paper on which a bet is entered.

bet·tong /bəˈtôNG, -ˈtäNG/ ▶ **n.** a short-nosed rat kangaroo found in Australia. ● Family Potoroidae: two genera, in particular *Bettongia*, and several species.
– ORIGIN early 19th cent.: from Dharuk.

bet·tor /ˈbetər/ (also **better**) ▶ **n.** a person who bets, typically regularly or habitually.

be·tween /biˈtwēn/ (abbr.: **bet.**) ▶ **prep. 1** at, into, or across the space separating (two objects or regions): *the border between Mexico and the United States | the dog crawled between us and lay down at our feet | those who travel by train between London and Paris.* ■ expressing movement from one side or point to the other and back again: *traveling by train between London and Paris.*
2 in the period separating (two points in time): *they snack between meals | the long, cold nights between autumn and spring.*
3 in the interval separating (two points on a scale): *a man aged between 18 and 30 | between 25 and 40 percent off children's clothes | the difference between income and expenditure.*
4 indicating a connection or relationship involving two or more parties: *the relationship between Pauline and Chris | negotiations between the two companies are continuing | links between science and industry.* ■ with reference to a collision or conflict: *a collision in midair between two light aircraft above Geneva | the wars between Carthage and Rome.* ■ with reference to a choice or differentiation involving two or more things being considered together: *if you have to choose between two or three different options.*
5 by combining the resources or actions of (two or more people or other entities): *we have created something between us | oxygen and nitrogen between them account for 99 per cent of air.* ■ shared by (two or more people or things): *they had drunk between them a bottle of Chianti.*
▶ **adv. 1** in or along the space separating two objects or regions: *layers of paper with tar **in between** | from Leipzig to Dresden, with the gentle Elbe flowing between.*
2 in the period separating two points in time: *sets of exercises with no rest **in between**.*
– PHRASES **between ourselves** (or **you and me**) in confidence: *just between you and me, I don't think it is going to happen.* **(in) between times** in the intervals between other actions: *I have seen to the needs of my child, and in between times I have cooked the meals.*
– ORIGIN Old English *betwēonum*, from *be* 'by' + a Germanic word related to TWO.

> **USAGE 1 Between** is used in speaking of two things, people, etc.: *we must choose between two equally unattractive alternatives.* **Among** is used for collective and undefined relations of usually three or more: *agreement on landscaping was reached among all the neighbors.* But where there are more than two parties involved, **between** may be used to express one-to-one relationships of pairs within the group or the sense 'shared by': *there is close friendship between the members of the club; diplomatic relations between the US, Canada, and Mexico.* **2 Between** *you and I, between you and he*, etc., are incorrect; **between** should be followed only by the objective case: *between you and me, between you and him*, etc. See also usage at PERSONAL PRONOUN.

be·twixt /biˈtwikst/ ▶ **prep. & adv.** archaic term for BETWEEN.
– PHRASES **betwixt and between** informal neither one thing nor the other.
– ORIGIN Old English *betwēox*, from *be* 'by' + a Germanic word related to TWO.

beurre blanc /bər ˈbläNGk/ ▶ **n.** a creamy sauce made with butter, onions or shallots, and vinegar or lemon juice, usually served with seafood dishes.
– ORIGIN mid 20th cent.: French, literally 'white butter.'

beurre noir /ˈbər ˈnwär/ ▶ **n.** French term for BLACK BUTTER.

beurre noi·sette /ˈbər nwäˈzet/ ▶ **n.** a sauce of butter cooked until golden or brown, usually flavored with capers, herbs, vinegar, etc.
– ORIGIN French, literally 'hazelnut butter.'

Beu·then /ˈboitn/ German name for **BYTOM**.

BEV ▶ **abbr.** Linguistics Black English Vernacular.

BeV another term for **GEV**.
– ORIGIN 1940s: from *billion* (10^9) *electronvolts*.

bev·a·tron /ˈbevəˌträn/ ▶ **n.** a synchrotron used to accelerate protons to energies in the billion electron-volt range.
– ORIGIN 1940s: from **BEV** + -TRON.

bev·el /ˈbevəl/ ▶ **n.** a slope from the horizontal or vertical in carpentry and stonework; a sloping surface or edge. ■ (in full **bevel square**) a tool for marking angles in carpentry and stonework.
▶ **v.** (**bevels, beveling, beveled** or **bevels, bevelling, bevelled**) [with obj.] (often as adj. **beveled**) reduce (a square edge on an object) to a sloping edge: *a beveled mirror.*
– ORIGIN late 16th cent. (as an adjective in the sense 'oblique'): from an Old French diminutive of *baif* 'open-mouthed,' from *baer* 'to gape' (see BAY[5]).

bev·el gear ▶ **n.** a gear working another gear at an angle to it by means of bevel wheels.

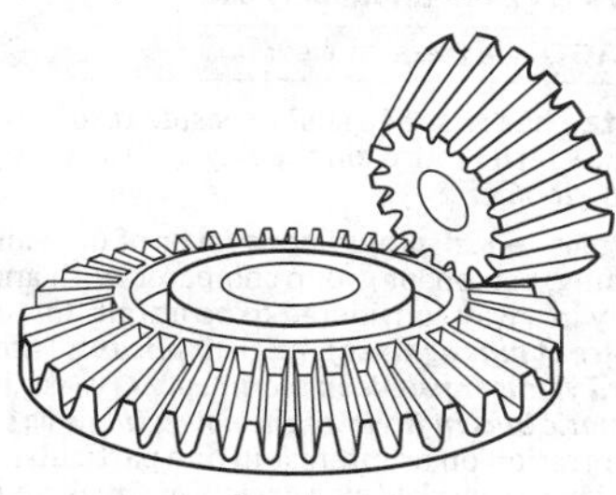
bevel gear

bev·el wheel ▶ **n.** a toothed wheel whose working face is oblique to the axis.

bev·er·age /ˈbev(ə)rij/ ▶ **n.** a drink, esp. one other than water.
– ORIGIN Middle English: from Old French *bevrage*, based on Latin *bibere* 'to drink.'

Bev·er·ly /ˈbevərlē/ an industrial and resort city in northeastern Massachusetts; pop. 39,343 (est. 2008).

Bev·er·ly Hills a largely residential city in California, on the northwestern side of the Los Angeles conurbation; pop. 34,445 (est. 2008). It is known as the home of many movie stars.

Bev·in /ˈbevən/, Ernest (1881–1951), British statesman and trade unionist. As foreign secretary 1945–51, he helped to establish NATO 1949.

bev·y /ˈbevē/ ▶ **n.** (pl. **bevies**) a large group of people or things of a particular kind: *he was surrounded by **a bevy of** beautiful girls.* ■ a group of birds, esp. quail, particularly when closely gathered on the ground.
– ORIGIN late Middle English: of unknown origin.

be·wail /biˈwāl/ ▶ **v.** [with obj.] express great regret, disappointment, or bitterness over (something): *he bewailed the fact that heart trouble had slowed him down.* ■ cry or wail loudly about (something).

be·ware /biˈwe(ə)r/ ▶ **v.** [no obj. in imperative or infinitive] be cautious and alert to the dangers of: *consumers were warned to **beware of** faulty packaging | Beware! Dangerous submerged rocks ahead* | [with obj.] *we should beware the incompetence of legislators.*
– ORIGIN Middle English: from the phrase *be ware* (see BE-, WARE[2]).

be·whisk·ered /biˈ(h)wiskərd/ ▶ **adj.** having hair or whiskers growing on the face.

be·wigged /biˈwigd/ ▶ **adj.** (of a person) wearing a wig.

be·wil·der /biˈwildər/ ▶ **v.** [with obj.] (often as adj. **bewildered**) cause (someone) to become perplexed and confused: *she seemed frightened and bewildered | his reaction had bewildered her* | (as adj. **bewildering**) *there is a bewildering array of desserts to choose from.*
– DERIVATIVES **be·wil·dered·ly adv.**, **be·wil·der·ing·ly adv.**, **be·wil·der·ment n.**
– ORIGIN late 17th cent.: from BE- 'thoroughly' + obsolete *wilder* 'lead or go astray,' of unknown origin.

be·witch /biˈwiCH/ ▶ **v.** [with obj.] cast a spell on and gain control over (someone) by magic: *his relatives were firmly convinced that he was bewitched.* ■ enchant and delight (someone): *they both were bewitched by the country and its culture* | (as adj. **bewitching**) *she was certainly a bewitching woman.*
– DERIVATIVES **be·witch·ing·ly adv.**, **be·witch·ment n.**
– ORIGIN Middle English: from BE- 'thoroughly' + WITCH.

bey /bā/ ▶ **n.** (pl. **beys**) historical the governor of a district or province in the Ottoman Empire. ■ formerly used in Turkey and Egypt as a courtesy title.
– ORIGIN Turkish, modern form of *beg* 'prince, governor.'

be·yond /bēˈänd, biˈyänd/ ▶ **prep. & adv. 1** at or to the further side of: [as prep.] *he pointed to a spot beyond the trees | passengers traveling to destinations beyond Boston* | [as adv.] *there was the terminal and, beyond, an endless line of warehouses.* ■ [prep.] outside the physical limits or range of: *the land sloped away until far beyond sight it reached the Great Plains.* ■ more extensive or extreme than; further-reaching than: [as prep.] *what these children go through is far **beyond** what most adults endure in a lifetime* | [as adv.] *pushing the laws to their limits **and beyond**.*
2 happening or continuing after (a specified time or event): [as prep.] *we can manage another two years, but beyond that the system is not viable* | [as adv.] *music going on into the night **and beyond**.*
3 having progressed or achieved more than (a specified stage or level): [as prep.] *we need to get beyond square one.* ■ above or greater than (a specified amount): [as prep.] *the absenteeism had gone beyond 15%* | [as adv.] *he could count up to a billion now, **and beyond**.*
4 [prep.] to a degree or condition where a specified action is impossible: *the landscape has changed beyond recognition.* ■ too much for (someone) to achieve or understand: *I did something that I thought was beyond me.*
5 [prep. with negative] apart from; except: *beyond telling us that she was well educated, he has nothing to say about her | there was little vegetation beyond scrub and brush.*
▶ **n.** (**the beyond**) the unknown after death: *messages from the beyond.*
– PHRASES **the back of beyond** see BACK.
– ORIGIN Old English *begeondan*, from *be* 'by' + *geondan* of Germanic origin (related to YON and YONDER).

bez·ant /ˈbezənt/ ▶ **n. 1** historical a gold or silver coin originally minted at Byzantium.
2 Heraldry a roundel or (i.e., a solid gold circle).
– ORIGIN Middle English: from Old French *besant*, from Latin *Byzantius* 'Byzantine.' Sense 2 dates from the late 15th cent.

bez·el /ˈbezəl/ ▶ **n.** a grooved ring holding the glass or plastic cover of a watch face or other instrument in position. ■ a groove holding the crystal of a watch or the stone of a gem in its setting.
– ORIGIN late 16th cent.: from Old French, of unknown origin.

be·zique /bəˈzēk/ ▶ **n.** a trick-taking card game for two, played with a double pack of 64 cards, including the seven to ace only in each suit. ■ the holding of the queen of spades and the jack of diamonds in this game.
– ORIGIN mid 19th cent.: from French *bésigue*, perhaps from Persian *bāzīgar* 'juggler' or *bāzī* 'game.'

be·zoar /ˈbēzôr/ ▶ **n.** a small stony concretion that may form in the stomachs of certain animals, esp. ruminants, and which was once used as an antidote for various ailments.
– ORIGIN late 15th cent. (in the general sense 'stone or concretion'): from French *bezoard*, based on Arabic *bāzahr*, *bādizahr*, from Persian *pādzahr* 'antidote.'

BF ▶ **n.** (pl. **BFs**) informal a person's boyfriend: *I've been dating my BF since January.* ■ a person's best friend: *Lottie is my absolute BF.*
– ORIGIN from the syllabic initial letters of *boyfriend*, and the initial letters of *best friend*.

b.f. ▶ **abbr.** ■ Printing boldface. ■ board foot. ■ (also **b/f** or **B/F**) (in bookkeeping) brought forward.

BFF ▶ **n.** (pl. **BFFs**) informal a girl's best friend: *my BFF's boyfriend is cheating on her.*
– ORIGIN 1996: from the initial letters of *best friend forever*.

BG (also **B Gen**) ▶ **abbr.** brigadier general.

BGH ▶ **abbr.** bovine growth hormone.

Bh ▶ **symbol** the chemical element bohrium.

BHA ▶ **abbr.** butylated hydroxyanisole.

Bha·ga·vad·gi·ta /ˌbəgəvədˈgētə, ˌbägəväd-/ (also **Gita**) Hinduism a poem composed between the 2nd century BC and the 2nd century AD and incorporated into the Mahabharata. Presented as a dialogue between the warrior prince Arjuna and his divine charioteer Krishna, it stresses the importance of doing one's duty and of faith in God.

Bhag·wan /ˌbəgˈwän/ ▶ **n.** Indian God. ■ a guru or revered person (often as a proper name or form of address).
– ORIGIN from Hindi *bhagwān*, from Sanskrit *bhagavān*, from the root *bhaj* 'adore.'

PRONUNCIATION KEY ə *ago, up*; ər *over, fur*; a *hat*; ā *ate*; ä *car*; e *let*; ē *see*; i *fit*; ī *by*; NG *sing*; ō *go*; ô *law, for*; oi *toy*; o͝o *good*; o͞o *goo*; ou *out*; TH *thin*; T͟H *then*; ZH *vision*

b

b

bha·jan /'bəjən, 'bä,jän/ ▶ **n.** Hinduism a devotional song.
– ORIGIN from Sanskrit *bhajana.*

bhak·ti /'bəktē, 'bäk-/ ▶ **n.** Hinduism devotional worship directed to one supreme deity, usually Vishnu (esp. in his incarnations as Rama and Krishna) or Shiva, by whose grace salvation may be attained by all regardless of sex, caste, or class. It is practiced by the majority of Hindus today.
– ORIGIN Sanskrit.

bhang /baNG/ (also **bang**) ▶ **n.** the leaves and flower heads of cannabis, used as a narcotic.
– ORIGIN from Hindi *bhāng.*

bhan·gra /'bäNGgrə/ ▶ **n.** a type of popular music combining Punjabi folk traditions with Western pop music.
– ORIGIN 1960s (denoting a traditional folk dance): from Punjabi *bhāngrā.*

Bha·rat /'bə-rət/ Hindi name for **INDIA**.

Bhav·na·gar /bou'nəgər/ an industrial port in northwestern India, in Gujarat, on the Gulf of Cambay; pop. 600,600 (est. 2009).

bhik·khu /'bikoo/ ▶ **n.** a Theravada Buddhist monk.
– ORIGIN Pali.

Bhi·sho /'bēSHō/ a town in southern South Africa, situated near the coast to the northeast of Port Elizabeth; pop. 147,600 (est. 2009). Former name **Bisho**.

Bhn (also **BHN**) ▶ **abbr.** Brinell hardness number.

Bhoj·pu·ri /,bōj'poorē/ ▶ **n.** a Bihari language spoken in western Bihar and eastern Uttar Pradesh.

Bho·pal /bō'päl/ a city in central India, the capital of the state of Madhya Pradesh; pop. 1,752,200 (est. 2009). In December 1984, leakage of poisonous gas from a US-owned pesticide factory in the city caused the death of about 2,500 people.

b.h.p. ▶ **abbr.** brake horsepower.

BHT ▶ **abbr.** butylated hydroxytoluene.

Bhu·ba·nes·war /,boovə'näSHwər/ a city in eastern India, capital of the state of Orissa; pop. 904,200 (est. 2009).

bhu·na /'boonə/ (also **bhoona**) ▶ **n.** a medium-hot, dry curry originating in Bengal, prepared typically by frying meat with spices at a high temperature: *lamb bhuna.*
– ORIGIN 1950s: from Bengali Urdu *bhunnā* 'to be fried,' ultimately from Sanskrit *bhrajj* 'fry, parch, roast.'

Bhu·tan /boo'tän, -'tan/ a small independent kingdom in southern Asia, on the southeastern slopes of the Himalayas, north of India; pop. 691,100 (est. 2009); capital, Thimphu; languages, Dzongkha (official), Nepali.

> A British protectorate from 1910, it became independent in 1949, with continuing help from India regarding its foreign policy and aid.

– DERIVATIVES **Bhu·tan·ese** /,bootn'ēz, -'ēs/ **adj. & n.**

Bhut·to[1] /'bootō/, Benazir (1953–2007), Pakistani stateswoman; prime minister 1988–90 and 1993–96; daughter of Zulfikar Ali Bhutto. She was the first woman prime minister of a Muslim country. She was assassinated in Pakistan while campaigning for re-election as prime minister.

Bhut·to[2], Zulfikar Ali (1928–79), Pakistani statesman; president 1971–73; prime minister 1973–77. He was ousted by a military coup and executed for conspiring to murder a political rival.

BI ▶ **abbr.** Block Island.

Bi ▶ **symbol** the chemical element bismuth.

bi /bī/ ▶ **abbr.** informal bisexual.

bi- (often **bin-** before a vowel) ▶ **comb. form** two; having two: *bicolored | biathlon | binocular.* ■ occurring twice in every one: *biannual | bimonthly.* ■ occurring once in every two: *bicentennial | biennial.* ■ lasting for two: *biennial | biennium.* ■ doubly; in two ways: *biconcave.* ■ Chemistry a substance having a double proportion of the radical, group, etc., indicated by the simple word: *bicarbonate | binoxalate.* ■ Botany & Zoology (of division and subdivision) twice over: *bipinnate.*
– ORIGIN from Latin, earlier *dui-*, related to Greek *di-* 'two' and Sanskrit *dvi-* 'doubly, having two.'

> **USAGE** The meaning of **bimonthly** (and other similar words such as **biweekly** and **biyearly**) is ambiguous. **Bimonthly**, for instance, can mean either 'occurring or produced twice a month' or 'occurring or produced every two months.' So, if an organization holds bimonthly meetings, over the course of a year, will it meet six times or twenty-four times? The only way to avoid this ambiguity is to use alternative expressions like *every two months* and *twice a month.* See also usage at **BIENNIAL**.

Bi·a·fra /bē'afrə, bī-/ a state proclaimed in 1967, when part of eastern Nigeria, inhabited chiefly by the Ibo people, sought independence from the rest of the country. In the ensuing civil war the new state's troops were overwhelmed by numerically superior forces, and by 1970 it had ceased to exist.
– DERIVATIVES **Bi·a·fran adj. & n.**

bi·a·ly /bē'älē/ ▶ **n.** (pl. **bialys**) a flat bread roll topped with chopped onions.
– ORIGIN mid 20th cent.: from *Białystok*, where the bread originated.

Bia·ły·stok /byä'wi,stôk/ an industrial city in northeastern Poland, close to the border with Belarus; pop. 294,817 (2007). Russian name **BELOSTOK**.

bi·an·nu·al /bī'anyooəl/ ▶ **adj.** occurring twice a year: *the biannual meeting of the planning committee.*
– DERIVATIVES **bi·an·nu·al·ly adv.**

> **USAGE** See usage at **BIENNIAL**.

Biar·ritz /,bēə'rits, 'bēə,rits/ a seaside resort in southwestern France, on the Bay of Biscay; pop. 27,398 (2006).

bi·as /'bīəs/ ▶ **n. 1** prejudice in favor of or against one thing, person, or group compared with another, usually in a way considered to be unfair: *there was evidence of **bias against** foreign applicants | the bias toward younger people in recruitment* | [in sing.] *a systematic **bias in favor of** the powerful.* ■ [in sing.] a concentration on or interest in one particular area or subject: *he worked on a variety of Greek topics, with a discernible bias toward philosophy.* ■ Statistics a systematic distortion of a statistical result due to a factor not allowed for in its derivation.
2 in some sports, such as lawn bowling, the irregular shape given to a ball. ■ the oblique course that such a shape causes a ball to run.
3 Electronics a steady voltage, magnetic field, or other factor applied to an electronic system or device to cause it to operate over a predetermined range.
▶ **v.** (**biases, biasing, biased**) [with obj.] **1** (usu. **be biased**) cause to feel or show inclination or prejudice for or against someone or something: *readers said the paper was **biased toward** the conservatives | the tests were **biased against** women and minorities.*
2 give a bias to: *bias the ball.*
– PHRASES **cut on the bias** (of a fabric or garment) cut obliquely or diagonally across the grain.
– ORIGIN mid 16th cent. (in the sense 'oblique line'; also as an adjective meaning 'oblique'): from French *biais*, from Provençal, perhaps based on Greek *epikarsios* 'oblique.'

bi·as-cut ▶ **adj.** (of a garment or fabric) cut obliquely or diagonally across the grain.

bi·ased /'bīəst/ ▶ **adj.** unfairly prejudiced for or against someone or something: *we will not tolerate this biased media coverage.*

bi·as-ply ▶ **adj.** (of a tire) having fabric layers with their threads running diagonally, crosswise to each other. Compare with **RADIAL**.

bi·as tape (also **bias binding**) ▶ **n.** a narrow strip of fabric cut obliquely and used to bind edges or for decoration.

bi·ath·lon /bī'aTHlän/ ▶ **n.** an athletic contest combining two events, esp. cross-country skiing and rifle shooting.
– DERIVATIVES **bi·ath·lete** /-lēt/ **n.**
– ORIGIN 1950s: from **BI-** 'two' + Greek *athlon* 'contest,' on the pattern of *pentathlon.*

bi·ax·i·al /bī'aksēəl/ ▶ **adj.** having or relating to two axes. ■ (of crystals) having two optic axes, as in the orthorhombic, monoclinic, and triclinic systems.

bib[1] /bib/ ▶ **n.** a piece of cloth or plastic fastened around a person's neck to keep their clothes clean while eating. ■ the part above the waist of the front of an apron or pair of overalls. ■ a loose-fitting, sleeveless garment worn for identification, esp. by competitors and officials at sporting events. ■ a patch of color on the throat of a bird or other animal: *a black bird with a white bib.*
– PHRASES **one's best bib and tucker** informal one's finest clothes.
– ORIGIN late 16th cent.: probably from **BIB**[2].

bib[2] ▶ **v.** (**bibs, bibbing, bibbed**) [with obj.] archaic drink (something alcoholic).
– ORIGIN late Middle English: probably from Latin *bibere* 'to drink.'

bib·ber /'bibər/ ▶ **n.** [usu. in combination] a person who regularly drinks a particular drink: *a wine-bibber.*

bibb let·tuce /bib/ (also **Bibb**) ▶ **n.** a variety of butterhead lettuce that has crisp dark-green leaves.
– ORIGIN late 19th cent.: named after Jack Bibb (1789–1884), the American horticulturalist who developed it.

bib·cock /'bib,käk/ ▶ **n.** a faucet with a bent nozzle fixed at the end of a pipe.
– ORIGIN late 18th cent.: perhaps from **BIB**[1] and **COCK**[1].

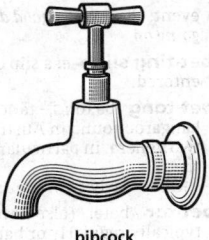

bibcock

bi·be·lot /'bib(ə),lō/ ▶ **n.** a small, decorative ornament or trinket.
– ORIGIN late 19th cent.: from French, fanciful formation based on *bel* 'beautiful.'

bibl. (also **Bibl.**) ▶ **abbr.** biblical.

Bi·ble /'bībəl/ ▶ **n.** (**the Bible**) the Christian scriptures, consisting of the 66 books of the Old and New Testaments. ■ (**the Bible**) the Jewish scriptures, consisting of the Torah or Law, the Prophets, and the Hagiographa or Writings. ■ (also **bible**) a copy of the Christian or Jewish scriptures: *clutching a large black Bible under his arm.* ■ a particular edition or translation of the Bible: *the New English Bible.* ■ (**bible**) informal any authoritative book: *"Larousse Gastronomique," the bible of French cooking.* ■ the scriptures of any religion.
– ORIGIN Middle English: via Old French from ecclesiastical Latin *biblia*, from Greek *biblia* 'books,' from *biblion* 'book,' originally a diminutive of *biblos* 'papyrus, scroll,' of Semitic origin.

Bi·ble Belt ▶ **n.** (**the Bible Belt**) informal those areas of the southern and midwestern US and western Canada where Protestant fundamentalism is widely practiced.

Bi·ble-thump·ing ▶ **adj.** [attrib.] denoting a person who expounds or follows the teachings of the Bible in an aggressively evangelical way: *a Bible-thumping evangelical Protestant.*
– DERIVATIVES **Bi·ble-thump·er n.**

bib·li·cal /'biblikəl/ (also **Biblical**) (abbr.: **bibl.** or **Bibl.**) ▶ **adj.** of, relating to, or contained in the Bible: *the biblical account of creation | biblical times.* ■ resembling the language or style of the Bible: *there is a biblical cadence in the last words he utters.* ■ very great; on a large scale: *we need rainfall of biblical proportions to bring us back to normal.*
– DERIVATIVES **bib·li·cal·ly** /-ik(ə)lē/ **adv.**

bib·li·cist /'bibləsist/ ▶ **n.** one who interprets the Bible literally.
– DERIVATIVES **bib·li·cism** /-,sizəm/ **n.**

biblio- ▶ **comb. form** relating to a book or books: *bibliomania | bibliophile.*
– ORIGIN from Greek *biblion* 'book.'

bibliog. ▶ **abbr.** bibliography.

bib·li·og·ra·phy /,biblē'ägrəfē/ (abbr.: **bibliog.**) ▶ **n.** (pl. **bibliographies**) a list of the books referred to in a scholarly work, usually printed as an appendix. ■ a list of the books of a specific author or publisher, or on a specific subject: *a bibliography of his publications.* ■ the history or systematic description of books, their authorship, printing, publication, editions, etc.: *he regarded bibliography as a science.*
– DERIVATIVES **bib·li·og·ra·pher** /-fər/ **n.**, **bib·li·o·graph·ic** /-lēə'grafik/ **adj.**, **bib·li·o·graph·i·cal** /-'grafikəl/ **adj.**, **bib·li·o·graph·i·cal·ly adv.**
– ORIGIN early 19th cent.: from French *bibliographie* or modern Latin *bibliographia*, from Greek *biblion* 'book' + *-graphia* 'writing.'

bib·li·ol·a·try /,biblē'älətrē/ ▶ **n. 1** an excessive adherence to the literal interpretation of the Bible.
2 an excessive love of books.
– DERIVATIVES **bib·li·ol·a·ter** /-'älətər/ **n.**, **bib·li·ol·a·trous** /-'älətrəs/ **adj.**

bib·li·o·man·cy /'biblēə,mansē/ ▶ **n.** rare foretelling the future by interpreting a randomly chosen passage from a book, esp. the Bible.

bib·li·o·ma·ni·a /,biblēə'mānēə/ ▶ **n.** passionate enthusiasm for collecting and possessing books.
– DERIVATIVES **bibli·o·ma·ni·ac** /-nē,ak/ **n. & adj.**

bib·li·o·phile /'biblēə,fīl/ ▶ **n.** a person who collects or has a great love of books.
– DERIVATIVES **bib·li·o·phil·ic** /,biblēə'filik/ **adj.**, **bib·li·oph·i·ly** /,biblē'äfəlē/ **n.**
– ORIGIN early 19th cent.: from French, from Greek *biblion* 'book' + *philos* 'loving.'

bib·li·o·pole /'biblēə,pōl/ ▶ **n.** archaic a person who buys and sells books, esp. rare ones.
– ORIGIN late 18th cent.: via Latin from Greek *bibliopōlēs*, from *biblion* 'book' + *pōlēs* 'seller.'

bib·li·o·the·ca /,biblēə'THēkə/ ▶ **n.** (pl. **bibliothecae** /-kē/ or **bibliothecas**) a library. ■ a list of books in a catalog, esp. for use by a bookseller.

bib·li·o·ther·a·py /ˌbiblēəˈTHerəpē/ ▶ **n.** the use of books as therapy in the treatment of mental or psychological disorders.

bib·li·ot·ics /ˌbiblēˈätiks/ ▶ **plural n.** [treated as sing.] the study of documents, handwriting, and writing materials to determine authenticity.
– DERIVATIVES **bib·li·ot·ic n.**, **bib·li·o·tist** /ˈbiblēətist/ **n.**

bib o·ver·alls ▶ **n.** see OVERALL (noun).

bib·u·lous /ˈbibyələs/ ▶ **adj.** formal excessively fond of drinking alcohol.
– ORIGIN late 17th cent. (in the sense 'absorbent'): from Latin *bibulus* 'freely or readily drinking' (from *bibere* 'to drink') + -OUS.

bi·cam·er·al /bīˈkamərəl/ ▶ **adj.** (of a legislative body) having two branches or chambers.
– DERIVATIVES **bi·cam·er·al·ism** /-ˌlizəm/ **n.**
– ORIGIN mid 19th cent.: from BI- 'two' + Latin *camera* 'chamber' + -AL.

bi·carb /ˈbīˌkärb/ ▶ **n.** informal sodium bicarbonate.

bi·car·bo·nate /bīˈkärbəˌnāt, -nit/ ▶ **n.** Chemistry a salt containing the anion HCO_3^-. ■ (also **bicarbonate of soda**) sodium bicarbonate.

bice /bīs/ (also **blue bice** or **bice blue**) ▶ **n.** a medium blue pigment made from basic copper carbonate.
– ORIGIN Middle English (originally in the sense 'dark or brownish gray'): from Old French *bis* 'dark gray.'

bi·cen·ten·ar·y /ˌbīsenˈtenərē/ ▶ **n. & adj.** another term for BICENTENNIAL.

bi·cen·ten·ni·al /ˌbīsenˈtenēəl/ ▶ **n.** the two-hundredth anniversary of a significant event: *last year's commemoration of the bicentennial of Mozart's birth.*
▶ **adj.** [attrib.] of or relating to such an anniversary: *the bicentennial celebrations.*

bi·ceph·a·lous /bīˈsefələs/ ▶ **adj.** having two heads.
– ORIGIN early 19th cent.: from BI- 'two' + Greek *kephalē* 'head' + -OUS.

bi·ceps /ˈbīˌseps/ ▶ **n.** (pl. **same** or **bicepses** /-ˌsepsiz, -sɛpsɪz/) a muscle having two points of attachment at one end, in particular: ■ (also **biceps brachii** /ˈbrākēˌī, -kēˌē, ˈbrak-/) the large muscle in the upper arm that turns the hand to face palm uppermost and flexes the arm and forearm: *he clenched his fist and exhibited his bulging biceps.* ■ (also **biceps femoris** /ˈfemərɪs/) Anatomy the muscle in the back of the thigh that helps to flex the leg.
– DERIVATIVES **bi·cep adj.** *bicep curls.*
– ORIGIN mid 17th cent.: from Latin, literally 'two-headed,' from *bi-* 'two' + *-ceps* (from *caput* 'head').

bich·ir /ˈbiCHər/ ▶ **n.** an elongated African freshwater fish with an armor of hard shiny scales and a series of separate fins along its back. ● Genus *Polypterus*, family *Polypteridae*: several species, including *P. senegalus.*
– ORIGIN 1960s: via French from dialect Arabic *abu shīr.*

Bi·chon Fri·sé /ˈbēSHän friˈzā, ˈfrēz, ˈbēSHôN frēˈzā/ (also **Bichon Frise**) ▶ **n.** (pl. **Bichons Frisés** pronunc. **same**) a small sturdy dog of a breed with a curly white coat and a tail that curves over its back.

Bichon Frise

bi·chro·mate /bīˈkrōmāt/ ▶ **adj.** another term for DICHROMATE.

bi·cip·i·tal /bīˈsipitl/ ▶ **adj. 1** two-headed. **2** of or relating to biceps.

bick·er /ˈbikər/ ▶ **v.** [no obj.] **1** argue about petty and trivial matters: *whenever the phone rings, they bicker over who must answer it* | (as noun **bickering**) *the constant bickering between Edgar and his mother.* **2** literary (of water) flow or fall with a gentle repetitive noise; patter: *against the glass the rain did beat and bicker.* ■ (of a flame or light) flash, gleam, or flicker: *the restless wheels whose flashing spokes bicker and burn.*
– ORIGIN Middle English: of unknown origin.

bi·coast·al /bīˈkōstəl/ ▶ **adj.** living on, taking place in, or involving two coasts, esp. the Atlantic and Pacific coasts of the US: *a bicoastal businessman* | *a bicoastal custody settlement.*

ordinary (or penny-farthing) (1880s)

ladies' safety bicycle (1890s)

mountain bike

racing bike

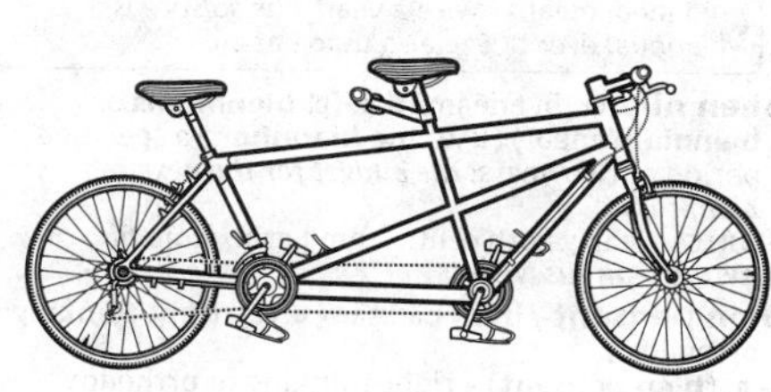
tandem

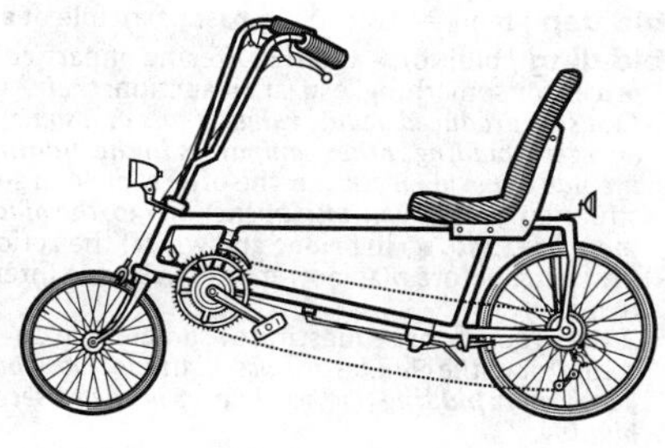
recumbent

bicycles

bi·col·or /ˈbīˌkələr/ ▶ **adj.** having two colors: *a male bicolor damselfish.*
▶ **n.** a bicolor blossom or animal.
– DERIVATIVES **bi·col·ored adj. & n.**

bi·con·cave /bīˈkänˌkāv, ˌbīkänˈkāv/ ▶ **adj.** concave on both sides.

bi·con·vex /bīˈkänˌveks, ˌbīkänˈveks/ ▶ **adj.** convex on both sides.

bi·cul·tur·al /bīˈkəlCHərəl/ ▶ **adj.** having or combining the cultural attitudes and customs of two nations, peoples, or ethnic groups: *there is too little recognition of the children's bilingual and bicultural status.*
– DERIVATIVES **bi·cul·tur·al·ism** /-ˌlizəm/ **n.**

bi·cus·pid /bīˈkəspid/ ▶ **adj.** having two cusps or points.
▶ **n.** a tooth with two cusps, esp. a human premolar tooth.
– ORIGIN mid 19th cent.: from BI- 'two' + Latin *cuspis, cuspid-* 'sharp point.'

bi·cus·pid valve ▶ **n.** Anatomy another term for MITRAL VALVE.

bi·cy·cle /ˈbīsikəl/ ▶ **n.** a vehicle composed of two wheels held in a frame one behind the other, propelled by pedals and steered with handlebars attached to the front wheel.
▶ **v.** [no obj.] ride a bicycle in a particular direction: *they had spent the day bicycling around the island.*
– DERIVATIVES **bi·cy·clist** /-siklist/ **n.**
– ORIGIN mid 19th cent.: from BI- 'two' + Greek *kuklos* 'wheel.'

bi·cy·cle chain ▶ **n.** a chain that transmits the driving power from the pedals of a bicycle to its rear wheel.

bi·cy·cle clip ▶ **n.** either of a pair of metal clips worn by cyclists around their ankles to prevent their pants legs from becoming entangled in the bicycle chain.

bi·cy·cle pump ▶ **n.** a portable pump for inflating bicycle tires.

bi·cy·cle rick·sha ▶ **n.** a three-wheeled bicycle for public hire, with a covered seat for passengers behind the driver.

bi·cy·clic /bīˈsīklik, -ˈsik-/ ▶ **adj.** Chemistry having two rings of atoms in its molecule.

bid[1] /bid/ ▶ **v.** (**bids, bidding**; past and past participle **bid**) [with obj.] offer (a certain price) for something, esp. at an auction: *a consortium of dealers bid a world record price for a snuff box* | *what am I bid?* | [no obj.] *guests will bid for pieces of fine jewelry.* ■ [no obj.] (**bid for**) (of a contractor) offer to do (work) for a stated price; tender for: *nineteen companies have indicated their intention to bid for the contract.* ■ [no

PRONUNCIATION KEY ə *ago, up*; ər *over, fur*; a *hat*; ā *ate*; ä *car*; e *let*; ē *see*; i *fit*; ī *by*; NG *sing*; ō *go*; ô *law, for*; oi *toy*; o͝o *good*; o͞o *goo*; ou *out*; TH *thin*; T͟H *then*; ZH *vision*

b

obj.] (**bid for**) make an effort or attempt to achieve: *the two freshmen are bidding for places in the varsity swim team.* ■ Bridge make a statement during the auction undertaking to make (a certain number of tricks with a stated suit as trumps) if the bid is successful and one becomes the declarer: *North bids four hearts* | [no obj.] *with this hand, South should not bid.*
▶ **n.** an offer of a price, esp. at an auction: *several buyers* ***made bids for*** *the Van Gogh sketches.* ■ an offer to buy the shares of a company in order to gain control of it: *a takeover bid.* ■ an offer to do work or supply goods at a stated price; a tender. ■ an attempt or effort to achieve something: [with infinitive] *an investigation would be carried out* ***in a bid*** *to establish what had happened* | *she did not hesitate to help him* ***make a bid for*** *the presidency.* ■ Bridge an undertaking by a player in the auction to make a stated number of tricks with a stated suit as trumps.
– DERIVATIVES **bid·der** n.
– ORIGIN Old English *bēodan* 'to offer, command,' of Germanic origin; related to Dutch *bieden* and German *bieten.*

bid² ▶ **v.** (**bids, bidding**; past **bid** or **bade** /bad, bād/; past participle **bid**) [with obj.] **1** utter (a greeting or farewell) to: *a chance to bid farewell to their president.*
2 archaic or literary command or order (someone) to do something: *I did as he bade me.* ■ invite (someone) to do something: *he bade his companions enter.*
– PHRASES **bid fair to** archaic or literary seem likely to: *the girl bade fair to be pretty.*
– ORIGIN Old English *biddan* 'ask,' of Germanic origin; related to German *bitten.*

bi·dar·ka /bī'därkə/ ▶ **n.** a canoe covered with animal skins, used by the Inuit of Alaska and adjacent regions.
– ORIGIN early 19th cent.: from Russian *baĭdarka*, diminutive of *baĭdara* 'an umiak.'

bid cal·ler ▶ **n.** one who announces the bids and recognizes bidders at an auction.

bid·da·ble /'bidəbəl/ ▶ **adj. 1** meekly ready to accept and follow instructions; docile and obedient.
2 Bridge strong enough to justify a bid.
– DERIVATIVES **bid·da·bil·i·ty** /ˌbidə'bilitē/ **n.**

Bid·de·ford /'bidəfərd/ an industrial city in southwestern Maine; pop. 21,435 (est. 2008).

bid·den /'bidn/ archaic or literary past participle of **BID²**.

bid·ding /'bidiNG/ ▶ **n. 1** the offering of particular prices for something, esp. at an auction: *their first sale produced a wide range of lots and some energetic bidding* | *other companies* ***in the bidding*** *include General Electric.* ■ the offers made in such a situation: *from a cautious opener of $30, the bidding soared to $450.* ■ (in bridge and whist) the action of stating before play how many tricks one intends to make.
2 the ordering or requesting of someone to do something: *the clandestine associations that would* ***act at their bidding*** | [in sing.] *I never needed a second bidding.*
– PHRASES **do someone's bidding** do what someone orders or requests, typically in a way considered overly slavish.

bid·ding pad·dle ▶ **n.** a paddle-shaped baton, usually marked with an identifying number, used to signal bids at auctions.

bid·ding prayer ▶ **n.** a prayer in the form of an invitation by a minister or leader to the congregation to pray about something.

bid·dy /'bidē/ ▶ **n.** (pl. **biddies**) informal a woman, usually an elderly one regarded as annoying or interfering: *the* ***old biddies*** *were muttering in his direction.*
– ORIGIN early 17th cent. (originally denoting a chicken): of unknown origin; probably influenced by the use of *biddy* denoting an Irish maidservant, from *Biddy*, nickname for the given name *Bridget.*

bide /bīd/ ▶ **v.** [no obj.] archaic or dialect remain or stay somewhere: *how long must I bide here to wait for the answer?*
– PHRASES **bide one's time** wait quietly for a good opportunity to do something: *she bided her time, patiently reading a magazine and planning her escape.*
– ORIGIN Old English *bīdan*, of Germanic origin.

Bi·den /'bīdn/ Joe (1942–) US vice president since 2009; full name *Joseph Robinette Biden, Jr.* A Delaware Democrat, he served in the US Senate 1973–2009.

bi·det /bi'dā/ ▶ **n.** a low oval basin used for washing one's genital and anal area.
– ORIGIN mid 17th cent. (in the sense 'horse'): from French, literally 'pony,' from *bider* 'to trot,' of unknown origin.

bi·di /'bēdē/ (also **beedi** or **biri** /'bērē/) ▶ **n.** (pl. **bidis**) (in South Asia) a type of cheap cigarette made of unprocessed tobacco wrapped in leaves.
– ORIGIN from Hindi *bīṛī* 'betel plug, cigar,' from Sanskrit *vīṭikā.*

bi·di·rec·tion·al /ˌbīdi'rekSHənl/ ▶ **adj.** functioning in two directions.

bi·don·ville /ˌbēdôN'vēl, bi'dôNˌvēl/ ▶ **n.** a shanty town built of oil drums or other metal containers, esp. on the outskirts of a North African city.
– ORIGIN 1950s: from French, from *bidon* 'container for liquids' + *ville* 'town.'

bid price ▶ **n.** the price that a dealer or other prospective buyer is prepared to pay for securities or other assets. Often contrasted with **OFFERING PRICE.**

Bie·der·mei·er /'bēdərˌmīər/ ▶ **adj.** denoting or relating to a style of furniture and interior decoration current in Germany in the period 1815–48, characterized by restraint, conventionality, and utilitarianism.
– ORIGIN from the name of Gottlieb *Biedermeier*, a fictitious German provincial schoolmaster and poet created by German satirist Ludwig Eichrodt (1827–92) in 1854.

Bie·le·feld /'bēləˌfeld/ an industrial city in western Germany, in North Rhine–Westphalia; pop. 325,800 (est. 2006).

Bien Hoa /'byen 'hwä/ an industrial city in southern Vietnam, north of Ho Chi Minh City; pop. 446,400 (est. 2009). A major US airbase was here during the Vietnam War.

biennale /ˌbē-en'älā/ ▶ **n.** a large art exhibition or music festival, usually one held biennially.
– ORIGIN 1930s (used originally as the name of an international art exhibition held in Venice): from Italian, literally 'biennial.'

bi·en·ni·al /bī'enēəl/ ▶ **adj. 1** taking place every other year: *summit meetings are normally biennial.*
2 (esp. of a plant) living or lasting for two years.
▶ **n. 1** a plant that takes two years to grow from seed to fruition and die. Compare with **ANNUAL, PERENNIAL.**
2 an event celebrated or taking place every two years.
– DERIVATIVES **bi·en·ni·al·ly adv.**
– ORIGIN early 17th cent.: from Latin *biennis* (from *bi-* 'twice' + *annus* 'year') + **-AL.**

> **USAGE** **Biennial** and **biannual** are often confused. **Biennial** means 'occurring every two years' (*the biennial Ryder Cup tournament*), while **biannual** means 'twice a year' (*the solstice is a biannual event*). See also usage at **BI-**.

bi·en·ni·um /bī'enēəm/ ▶ **n.** (pl. **bienniums** or **biennia** /-'enēə/) (usu. **the biennium**) a specified period of two years: *the budget for the next biennium.*
– ORIGIN early 20th cent.: from Latin, from *bi-* 'twice' + *annus* 'year.'

bien pensant /ˌbyeN päN'säN/ ▶ **adj.** right-thinking; orthodox.
▶ **n.** (**bien-pensant**) a right-thinking or orthodox person.
– ORIGIN French, from *bien* 'well' + *pensant*, present participle of *penser* 'think.'

bier /bi(ə)r/ ▶ **n.** a movable frame on which a coffin or a corpse is placed before burial or cremation or on which it is carried to the grave.
– ORIGIN Old English *bēr*, of Germanic origin; related to German *Bahre*, also to **BEAR¹**.

Bierce /bi(ə)rs/, Ambrose (Gwinnett) (1842–c.1914), US writer, best known for his sardonic short stories that include "An Occurrence at Owk Creek Bridge" (1891) and his satirical treatment of the English language in *The Devil's Dictionary* (1911). In 1913, he traveled to Mexico and mysteriously disappeared.

bi·face /'bīˌfās/ ▶ **n.** Archaeology a type of prehistoric stone implement flaked on both faces.

bi·fa·cial /bī'fāSHəl/ ▶ **adj.** having two faces, in particular: ■ Botany (of a leaf) having upper and lower surfaces that are structurally different. ■ Archaeology (of a flint or other artifact) worked on both faces.

biff /bif/ informal ▶ **v.** [with obj.] strike (someone) roughly or sharply, usually with the fist: *he biffed me on the nose.*
▶ **n.** a sharp blow with the fist.
– ORIGIN mid 19th cent.: symbolic of a short sharp movement.

bi·fid /'bīfid/ ▶ **adj.** Botany & Zoology (of a part of a plant or animal) divided by a deep cleft or notch into two parts: *a bifid leaf* | *the gut is bifid.*
– ORIGIN mid 17th cent.: from Latin *bifidus*, from *bi-* 'doubly' + *fidus* (from *findere* 'to split').

bi·fi·lar /bī'fīlər/ ▶ **adj.** consisting of or involving two threads or wires.
– ORIGIN mid 19th cent.: from **BI-** 'two' + *filum* 'thread' + **-AR¹**.

bi·fla·gel·late /bī'flajəlit, -ˌlāt/ ▶ **adj.** having two flagella: *various types of biflagellate spermatozoa.*

bi·fo·cal /'bīˌfōkəl/ ▶ **adj.** (usually of a pair of eyeglasses) having lenses each with two parts with different focal lengths, one for distant vision and one for near vision.
▶ **n.** (**bifocals**) a pair of eyeglasses having two such parts.

bi·fold /'bīˌfōld/ ▶ **adj.** double or twofold.

bi·func·tion·al /bī'fəNGkSHənl/ ▶ **adj. 1** having two functions.
2 Chemistry having two highly reactive binding sites in each molecule: *bifunctional enzymes retain stable levels of activity.*

bi·fur·cate ▶ **v.** /'bīfərˌkāt/ divide into two branches or forks: [no obj.] *just below Cairo the river bifurcates* | [with obj.] *the trail was bifurcated by a mountain stream.*
▶ **adj.** /bī'fərkāt, 'bīfərkit/ forked; branched: *a bifurcate tree.*
– ORIGIN early 17th cent.: from medieval Latin *bifurcat-* 'divided into two forks,' from the verb *bifurcare*, from Latin *bifurcus* 'two-forked,' from *bi-* 'having two' + *furca* 'a fork.'

bi·fur·ca·tion /ˌbīfər'kāSHən/ ▶ **n.** the division of something into two branches or parts: *the bifurcation of the profession into social do-gooders and self-serving iconoclasts.* ■ a thing divided in this way or either of the branches: *the bifurcation of the aorta is a site commonly affected first.*

big /big/ ▶ **adj.** (**bigger, biggest**) **1** of considerable size, extent, or intensity: *big hazel eyes* | *big buildings* | *big cuts in staff.* ■ [attrib.] of a large or the largest size: *my big toe.* ■ grown up: *I'm a big girl now.* ■ elder: *my big sister.* ■ [attrib.] informal doing a specified action very often or on a very large scale: *a big eater* | *a big gambler.* ■ informal on an ambitiously large scale: *a small company with big plans.* ■ informal popular or exciting interest among the public: *Latino bands that are big in Los Angeles.* ■ showing great enthusiasm: *a big tennis fan* | *he tells me the Inuits of the Arctic are very* ***big on*** *Jim Reeves.* ■ (**big with**) archaic advanced in pregnancy: *my wife was big with child* | figurative *a word big with fate.*
2 of considerable importance or seriousness: *it's a big decision* | *Mark's biggest problem is money* | *he made a big mistake.* ■ informal holding an important position or playing an influential role: *as a senior in college, he was a big man on campus.*
3 [predic.] informal, often ironic generous: *"I'm inclined to take pity on you." "That's big of you!"*
▶ **n.** (**the bigs**) informal the major league in a professional sport: *the day he made it to the bigs, he forgot every minor league ballpark he ever played in.*
– PHRASES **big bucks** informal large amounts of money, esp. as pay or profit: *Emily earns big bucks on Wall Street.* **the big idea** chiefly ironic a clever or important intention or scheme: *okay, what's the big idea?* **the big lie** a gross distortion or misrepresentation of the facts, esp. when used as a propaganda device by a politician or official body. **the big screen** informal the movies: *the play was adapted for the big screen.* **big shot** (also **big noise**) informal an important or influential person. **big stick** informal the use or threat of force or power: *the authorities used quiet persuasion instead of a big stick.* **the Big Three,** (**Four,** etc.) informal the dominant group of three, four, etc.: *increased competition between the Big Three networks.* **go over big** informal have a great effect; be a success: *the story went over big with the children.* **in a big way** informal on a large scale; with great enthusiasm: *he contributed to the project in a big way* | *they went for it in a big way.* **make it big** informal become very successful or famous: *Simon had made it big in the financial world.* **talk big** informal talk confidently or boastfully: *he talked big, blinding her with legal jargon.* **think big** informal be ambitious: *to trade in a heavyweight world market we must think big.* **too big for one's britches** (or **breeches**) informal conceited.
– DERIVATIVES **big·gish adj., big·ness n.**
– ORIGIN Middle English (in the sense 'strong, mighty'): of unknown origin.

big air ▶ **n.** informal a high jump in sports such as skateboarding, snowboarding, and BMX.

big·a·my /'bigəmē/ ▶ **n.** the act of going through a marriage ceremony while already married to another person.
– DERIVATIVES **big·a·mist** /-mist/ **n., big·a·mous** /-məs/ **adj.**
– ORIGIN Middle English: from Old French *bigamie*, from *bigame* 'bigamous,' from late Latin *bigamus*, from *bi-* 'twice' + Greek *-gamos* 'married.'

Big Ap·ple a nickname for New York City.

big band ▶ **n.** a large group of musicians playing jazz or dance music: [as modifier] *the big band sound.*

Big Bang ▶ **n.** Astronomy the explosion of dense matter that, according to current cosmological theories, marked the origin of the universe.

> In the beginning, a fireball of radiation at extremely high temperature and density, but occupying a tiny volume, is believed to have formed. This expanded and cooled, extremely fast at first, but more slowly as subatomic particles condensed into matter that later accumulated to form galaxies and stars. The galaxies are currently still retreating from one another. What was left of the original radiation continued to cool and has been detected as a uniform background of weak microwave radiation.

Big Bear Lake a reservoir and recreational center in southern California, in the San Bernardino Mountains, east northeast of Los Angeles.

big beat ▶ **n.** popular music with a steady, prominent beat: [as modifier] *had my big beat box and I was jammin'.*

Big Ben the great clock tower of the Houses of Parliament in London and its bell.

Big Bend Na·tion·al Park a US national park in a bend of the Rio Grande, in the desert lands of southern Texas on the border with Mexico. In 1975, fossil remains of the pterosaur were discovered here.

Big Bend State a nickname for the state of **Tennessee**.

Big Black Riv·er a river in Mississippi that flows 330 miles (530 km) into the Mississippi River near Vicksburg.

Big Board informal the New York Stock Exchange.

big box ▶ **n.** [usu. as modifier] informal a very large store that sells goods at discount prices, esp. one specializing in a particular type of merchandise: *a big box store in the 'burbs.*

Big Broth·er ▶ **n.** informal a person or organization exercising total control over people's lives.
– DERIVATIVES **Big Broth·er·ism** /ˈbrəT͟Hər,izəm/ **n.**
– ORIGIN 1950s: from the name of the head of state in George Orwell's *Nineteen Eighty-Four* (1949).

big busi·ness ▶ **n.** large-scale or important financial or commercial activity: *the children's toy market is big business now.*

big cat ▶ **n.** any of the large members of the cat family, including the lion, tiger, leopard, jaguar, snow leopard, clouded leopard, cheetah, and cougar. ● *Panthera* and other genera, family Felidae.

big crunch ▶ **n.** Astronomy a contraction of the universe to a state of extremely high density and temperature, hypothesized as a possible scenario for its demise.

Big Dad·dy (also **Big Chief**) ▶ **n.** informal a person in authority; the head of an organization or enterprise.

Big Dip·per ▶ **n. 1** a prominent group of seven stars in the constellation Ursa Major (the Great Bear), containing the Pointers that indicate the direction to Polaris.
2 Brit. (also **big dipper**) a roller coaster.

Big Eas·y a nickname for New Orleans.

bi·gem·i·ny /bīˈjemənē/ ▶ **n.** a cardiac rhythm in which each normal beat is followed by an abnormal one.
– DERIVATIVES **bi·gem·i·nal** /-ˈjemənl/ **adj.**

big end ▶ **n.** (in an engine) the end of the connecting rod that encircles the crankpin.

bi·ge·ner·ic /ˌbījəˈnerik/ ▶ **adj.** Botany relating to or denoting a hybrid between two genera.

big·eye /ˈbigˌī/ ▶ **n. 1** (also **bigeye tuna**) a large migratory tuna that is very important to the commercial fishing industry. ● *Thunnus obesus*, family Scombridae.
2 a reddish, large-eyed fish that lives in moderately deep waters of the tropical Atlantic and the western Indian Ocean. Also called **catalufa**. ● *Priacanthus arenatus*, family Priacanthidae.

Big·foot /ˈbigˌfo͝ot/ ▶ **n.** (pl. **Bigfeet**) a large, hairy, apelike creature resembling a yeti, supposedly found in northwestern America. Also called **Sasquatch**.
– ORIGIN so named because of the size of its footprints.

big game ▶ **n.** large animals hunted for sport: [as modifier] *a big-game hunter.*

big·gie /ˈbigē/ ▶ **n.** (pl. **biggies**) informal a big, important, or successful person or thing: *composers including most of the biggies like Brahms, Wagner, Mendelssohn.*

big·git·y /ˈbigitē/ (also **biggety**) informal ▶ **adj.** conceited, self-important, or boastful: *we had no truck with biggity Yankees.*
▶ **adv.** rudely; impudently: *so that's why you talked to him so biggity.*

big gov·ern·ment ▶ **n.** government perceived as excessively interventionist and intruding into all aspects of the lives of its citizens.

big hair ▶ **n.** informal a bouffant hairstyle, typically one that has been teased, permed, or sprayed to create volume.

big·head /ˈbigˌhed/ ▶ **n.** informal a conceited or arrogant person.

big-head·ed /ˈbig ˌhedid/ ▶ **adj.** informal conceited or arrogant: *I'm trying not to get too big-headed.*
– DERIVATIVES **big-head·ed·ness** **n.**

big-heart·ed /ˈbig ˌhärtid/ ▶ **adj.** (of a person or action) kind and generous.

big hit·ter another term for **heavy hitter**.

big·horn /ˈbigˌhôrn/ (in full **American bighorn sheep**) ▶ **n.** a stocky brown North American wild sheep, found esp. in the Rocky Mountains. Also called **mountain sheep**. ● *Ovis canadensis*, family Bovidae.

bighorn (male)

Big·horn Moun·tains /ˈbigˌhôrn/ a range of the Rocky Mountains in Montana and Wyoming. The Bighorn River flows along its west side.

big house ▶ **n.** informal a prison: *he's doing a stint in the big house.*

bight /bīt/ ▶ **n.** a curve or recess in a coastline, river, or other geographical feature. ■ a loop of rope, as distinct from the rope's ends.
– ORIGIN Old English *byht* 'a bend or angle,' of Germanic origin; related to **bow**[2].

Big Is·land a popular name for the island of **Hawaii**.

big league ▶ **n.** a group of teams in a professional sport, esp. baseball, competing for a championship at the highest level: [as modifier] *big league teams.*
■ (**the big league**) informal a very successful or important group: *the film brought him into the movie world's big league.*
– DERIVATIVES **big lea·guer** **n.**

big me·di·a ▶ **n.** [treated as sing. or pl.] the main means of mass communication (i.e., television, radio, and the press), as opposed to blogs or other personal websites.

big·mouth /ˈbigˌmouTH/ ▶ **n. 1** informal an indiscreet or boastful person.
2 Another term for largemouth bass; see **black bass**.
– DERIVATIVES **big·mouthed** **adj.**

Big Mud·dy a popular name for the Missouri River, whose waters are muddier than those of the Mississippi River.

big name ▶ **n.** informal a person who is famous in a certain sphere: *he's a big name in gymnastics.*

big·o·rex·i·a /ˌbigəˈreksēə/ ▶ **n.** informal term for **muscle dysmorphia**.
– DERIVATIVES **big·o·rex·ic** **adj.** & **n.**
– ORIGIN *big*+Greek *orexis* 'appetite,' on the pattern of *anorexia*.

big·ot /ˈbigət/ ▶ **n.** a person who is bigoted: *religious bigots.*
– ORIGIN late 16th cent. (denoting a superstitious religious hypocrite): from French, of unknown origin.

big·ot·ed /ˈbigətid/ ▶ **adj.** having or revealing an obstinate belief in the superiority of one's own opinions and a prejudiced intolerance of the opinions of others: *a bigoted group of reactionaries* | *a thoughtless and bigoted article.*

big·ot·ry /ˈbigətrē/ ▶ **n.** bigoted attitudes; intolerance toward those who hold different opinions from oneself: *the report reveals racism and right-wing bigotry.*
– ORIGIN late 17th cent.: from **bigot**, reinforced by French *bigoterie*.

big rig ▶ **n.** informal another term for **tractor-trailer**.

Big Rip ▶ **n.** a theory about the end of the universe holding that the accelerating forces driving its expansion will eventually rend all currently organized matter.
– ORIGIN early 21st cent.: on the pattern of *Big Bang*.

big sci·ence ▶ **n.** informal scientific research that is expensive and involves large teams of scientists.

Big Sioux Riv·er a river in South Dakota and Iowa that flows for 420 miles (680 km) to the Missouri River.

Big Sky Coun·try a nickname for the state of **Montana**[1].

Big Sur /ˈsər/ a scenic locality in west central California, south of Monterey on the Pacific coast.

big tent ▶ **n.** used in reference to a political party's policy of permitting or encouraging a broad spectrum of views among its members: *the struggle to change Wyoming takes place inside the Republican Party and its "big tent."*

Big Thick·et a forested area in eastern Texas, north of Beaumont, noted for its biological diversity.

big-tick·et ▶ **adj.** [attrib.] informal constituting a major expense: *big-ticket items such as cars, houses, and expensive vacations.*

big time informal ▶ **n.** (**the big time**) the highest or most successful level in a career, esp. in entertainment: *a bit-part actor who finally made the big time in Hollywood.*
▶ **adv.** on a large scale; to a great extent: *this time they've messed up big time.*
– DERIVATIVES **big-tim·er** **n.**

big top ▶ **n.** the main tent in a circus.

big tree ▶ **n.** another term for giant redwood (see **redwood**).

big·wig /ˈbigˌwig/ ▶ **n.** informal an important person, usually in a particular sphere. Also called **big wheel**.

Bi·har /biˈhär/ a state in northeastern India; capital, Patna.

Bi·ha·ri /biˈhärē/ ▶ **n. 1** a native or inhabitant of Bihar.
2 a group of three closely related Indic languages, Bhojpuri, Maithili, and Magahi, spoken principally in Bihar.
▶ **adj.** of or relating to this people, their languages, or Bihar.
– ORIGIN from Hindi *Bihārī*.

bi·jou /ˈbēZHo͞o/ ▶ **adj.** (esp. of a residence or business establishment) small and elegant: *the greasy spoons have given way to bijou restaurants.*
▶ **n.** (pl. **bijoux** /-ZHo͞o(z)/) archaic a jewel or trinket.
– ORIGIN French, from Breton *bizou* 'finger ring,' from *biz* 'finger.'

bi·jou·te·rie /bēˈZHo͞otərē/ ▶ **n.** jewelry or trinkets: *strewn about were bric-a-brac and bijouterie.*
– ORIGIN French, from **bijou**.

bike /bīk/ informal ▶ **n.** a bicycle or motorcycle: *I'm going by bike* | [as modifier] *a bike ride.*
▶ **v.** [no obj.] ride a bicycle or motorcycle: *we hope to encourage as many people as possible to bike to work* | (as noun **biking**) *the terrain is perfect for biking.*
– ORIGIN late 19th cent.: abbreviation.

bike lane ▶ **n.** a division of a road marked off with painted lines, for use by cyclists.

bike path ▶ **n.** a path or road for bicycles and not motor vehicles.

bik·er /ˈbīkər/ ▶ **n.** informal a motorcyclist, esp. one who is a member of a motorcycle gang or club: [as modifier] *her biker boyfriend.* ■ a cyclist: *a mountain biker.*

bike·way /ˈbīkˌwā/ ▶ **n.** a path or lane for the use of bicycles.

Bi·ki·ni /biˈkēnē/ an atoll in the Marshall Islands, in the western Pacific Ocean, used by the US 1946–58 as a site for testing nuclear weapons.

bi·ki·ni /biˈkēnē/ ▶ **n.** (pl. **bikinis**) a very brief two-piece swimsuit for women. ■ (also **bikinis**) scanty underpants.
– ORIGIN 1940s: named after **Bikini**, where an atomic bomb was exploded in 1946 (because of the supposed 'explosive' effect created by the garment).

bi·ki·ni line ▶ **n.** the area of skin around the edge of the bottom half of a bikini, used esp. with reference to the cosmetic removal of the pubic hair in this area.

bi·ki·ni wax ▶ **n.** a cosmetic treatment in which unwanted pubic hair is removed from the bikini line by applying hot wax and then peeling off the wax and hair together.

Bi·ko /ˈbēkō/, Steve (1946–77), South African radical leader; full name *Stephen Biko.* He was banned from political activity in 1973. After his death in police custody, he became a symbol of heroic resistance to apartheid.

Bi·kol /bi'kōl/ (also **Bicol**) ▶ n. (pl. **same** or **Bikols**) a member of an indigenous people of southeastern Luzon in the Philippines. ■ the Austronesian language of this people.
▶ adj. of or relating to this people or their language.

Bik·ram yo·ga /'bikram/ ▶ n. trademark a type of hatha yoga characterized by a set series of postures and breathing exercises, performed in a room heated to a very high temperature.
– ORIGIN named after the Indian yoga teacher *Bikram* Choudhury (1946–), who developed it.

bi·la·bi·al /bī'lābēəl/ ▶ adj. Phonetics (of a speech sound) formed by closure or near closure of the lips, as in *p, b, m, w*.
▶ n. a consonant sound made in such a way.

bi·lat·er·al /bī'latərəl/ ▶ adj. having or relating to two sides; affecting both sides: *bilateral hearing is essential for sound location.* ■ involving two parties, usually countries: *the recently concluded bilateral agreements with Japan.*
– DERIVATIVES **bi·lat·er·al·ly** adv.

bi·lat·er·al sym·me·try ▶ n. the property of being divisible into symmetrical halves on either side of a unique plane.

bi·lay·er /'bī,lāər/ ▶ n. Biochemistry a film two molecules thick (formed, e.g., by lipids), in which each molecule is arranged with its hydrophobic end directed inward toward the opposite side of the film and its hydrophilic end directed outward.

Bil·ba·o /bil'bou/ a seaport and industrial city in northern Spain; pop. 353,340 (2008).

bil·ber·ry /'bil,berē/ ▶ n. (pl. **bilberries**) a hardy dwarf shrub closely related to the blueberry, with red drooping flowers and dark blue edible berries. ● Genus *Vaccinium*, family Ericaceae: several species, including the **tundra bilberry** (*V. uliginosum*). ■ the small blue edible berry of this plant.
– ORIGIN late 16th cent.: probably of Scandinavian origin; compare with Danish *bøllebær*.

bil·bo /'bilbō/ ▶ n. (pl. **bilbos** or **bilboes**) a sword used in former times, noted for the temper and elasticity of its blade.
– ORIGIN mid 16th cent.: from *Bilboa*, an earlier English form of the name BILBAO, noted for the manufacture of fine blades.

bil·boes /'bilbōz/ ▶ plural n. an iron bar with sliding shackles formerly used for confining a prisoner's ankles.
– ORIGIN mid 16th cent.: of unknown origin.

Bil·dungs·ro·man /'bildŏŏNGzrō,män, 'bēldŏŏNGks-/ ▶ n. a novel dealing with one person's formative years or spiritual education.
– ORIGIN German, from *Bildung* 'education' + *Roman* 'a novel.'

bile /bīl/ ▶ n. **1** a bitter greenish-brown alkaline fluid that aids digestion and is secreted by the liver and stored in the gallbladder.
2 anger; irritability: *that topic is sure to stir up plenty of bile.*
– ORIGIN mid 16th cent.: from French, from Latin *bilis*.

bile duct ▶ n. the duct that conveys bile from the liver and the gallbladder to the duodenum.

bi-lev·el ▶ adj. [attrib.] having or functioning on two levels; arranged on two planes: *the unit's bi-level design keeps water in the sink.* ■ denoting a style of two-story house in which the lower story is partially sunk below ground level, and the main entrance is between the two stories; split-level. ■ denoting a railroad passenger coach or a bus with seats on two levels.
▶ n. a bi-level house: *a three-bedroom bi-level.*

bilge /bilj/ ▶ n. **1** the area on the outer surface of a ship's hull where the bottom curves to meet the vertical sides. ■ (**bilges**) the lowest internal portion of the hull. ■ (also **bilgewater**) dirty water that collects inside the bilges.
2 informal nonsense; rubbish: *romantic bilge dreamed up by journalists.*
▶ v. [with obj.] archaic break a hole in the bilge of (a ship): *she was hopelessly bilged, her back broken.*
– ORIGIN late 15th cent.: probably a variant of BULGE.

bilge keel ▶ n. each of a pair of plates or timbers fastened under the sides of the hull of a ship to provide lateral resistance to the water, prevent rolling, and support its weight in dry dock.

bil·har·zi·a /bil'härzēə/ ▶ n. a chronic disease, endemic in parts of Africa and South America, caused by infestation with blood flukes (schistosomes). Also called BILHARZIASIS or SCHISTOSOMIASIS. ■ the fluke (schistosome) itself.
– ORIGIN mid 19th cent.: modern Latin, former name of the genus *Schistosoma*, named after T. Bilharz (1825–62), the German physician who discovered the parasite.

bil·har·zi·a·sis /,bilhär'zīəsis/ ▶ n. Medicine another term for BILHARZIA (the disease).

bil·i·ar·y /'bilē,erē, 'bilyərē/ ▶ adj. Medicine of or relating to bile or the bile duct.
– ORIGIN mid 18th cent.: from French *biliaire*, from *bile* 'bile.'

bi·lin·e·ar /bī'linēər/ ▶ adj. Mathematics **1** rare of, relating to, or contained by two straight lines.
2 of, relating to, or denoting a function of two variables that is linear and homogeneous in both independently.

bi·lin·gual /bī'liNGgwəl/ ▶ adj. (of a person) speaking two languages fluently: *a bilingual secretary.* ■ (of a text or an activity) written or conducted in two languages: *bilingual dictionaries | bilingual education.* ■ (of a country, city, or other community) using two languages, esp. officially: *the town is virtually bilingual in Dutch and German.*
▶ n. a person fluent in two languages.
– DERIVATIVES **bi·lin·gual·ism** /-,lizəm/ n.
– ORIGIN mid 19th cent.: from Latin *bilinguis*, from *bi-* 'having two' + *lingua* 'tongue' + -AL.

bil·ious /'bilyəs/ ▶ adj. **1** affected by or associated with nausea or vomiting: *I had eaten something that didn't agree with me and I was a little bilious.* ■ (of a color) lurid or sickly: *a bilious olive hue.*
2 spiteful; bad-tempered: *outbursts of bilious misogyny.*
3 Physiology of or relating to bile.
– DERIVATIVES **bil·ious·ly** adv., **bil·ious·ness** n.
– ORIGIN mid 16th cent. (in the sense 'biliary'): from Latin *biliosus*, from *bilis* 'bile.'

bil·i·ru·bin /,bili'ro͞obin/ ▶ n. Biochemistry an orange-yellow pigment formed in the liver by the breakdown of hemoglobin and excreted in bile.
– ORIGIN late 19th cent.: coined in German from Latin *bilis* 'bile' + *ruber* 'red' + -IN[1].

bil·i·ver·din /,bilə'vərdn, 'bili,vərdn/ ▶ n. Biochemistry a green pigment excreted in bile. It is an oxidized derivative of bilirubin.

bilk /bilk/ informal ▶ v. [with obj.] **1** obtain or withhold money from (someone) by deceit or without justification; cheat or defraud: *government waste has bilked the taxpayer of billions of dollars.* ■ obtain (money) fraudulently: *some businesses bilk thousands of dollars from unsuspecting elderly consumers.*
2 archaic evade; elude: *I ducked into the pantry, bilking Edward for the third time this week.*
– DERIVATIVES **bilk·er** n.
– ORIGIN mid 17th cent. (originally used in cribbage meaning 'spoil one's opponent's score'): perhaps a variant of BALK.

bill[1] /bil/ ▶ n. **1** an amount of money owed for goods supplied or services rendered, set out in a printed or written statement of charges: *he was running up a bill of hundreds of dollars | the bill for their meal came to $17.*
2 a draft of a proposed law presented to parliament for discussion: *a debate over the civil rights bill.*
3 a program of entertainment, esp. at a theater: *she was top of the bill at America's leading vaudeville house.*
4 a banknote; a piece of paper money: *a ten-dollar bill.*
5 a poster or handbill: *the circus promoters were posting bills all over town.*
▶ v. [with obj.] **1** (usu. **be billed**) list (a person or event) in a program: *they were billed to appear but didn't show up.* ■ (**bill someone/something as**) describe someone or something in a particular, usually promotional, way, esp. as a means of advertisement: *he was billed as "the new Sean Connery."*
2 send a note of charges to (someone): *we shall be billing them for the damage caused* | [with two objs.] *he had been billed $3,000 for his license.* ■ charge (a sum of money): *we billed her $400,000.*
– PHRASES **fit** (or **fill**) **the bill** be suitable for a particular purpose: *a partner is an ally or a companion, and you don't seem to fit the bill.* **foot** (or **pick up**) **the bill** see FOOT (sense 1 of the verb).
– DERIVATIVES **bill·a·ble** adj.
– ORIGIN Middle English (denoting a written list or catalog): from Anglo-Norman French *bille*, probably based on medieval Latin *bulla* 'seal, sealed document' (see also BULL[2]).

bill[2] ▶ n. the beak of a bird, esp. when it is slender, flattened, or weak, or belongs to a web-footed bird or a bird of the pigeon family. ■ the muzzle of a platypus. ■ the point of an anchor fluke. ■ a stiff brim at the front of a cap.
▶ v. [no obj.] (of birds, esp. doves) stroke bill with bill during courtship.
– PHRASES **bill and coo** informal exchange caresses or affectionate words; behave or talk in a very loving or sentimental way.
– DERIVATIVES **billed** adj. [usu. in combination] *the red-billed weaverbird.*
– ORIGIN Old English *bile*, of unknown origin.

bill[3] ▶ n. a medieval weapon like a halberd with a hook instead of a blade.
– ORIGIN Old English *bil*; related to German *Bille* 'ax.'

bil·la·bong /'bilə,bôNG/ ▶ n. Austral. a branch of a river forming a backwater or stagnant pool, made by water flowing from the main stream during a flood.
– ORIGIN mid 19th cent.: from Wiradhuri *bilabang* (originally as the name of the Bell River, New South Wales), from *billa* 'water' + *bang* 'channel that is dry except after rain.'

bill·board /'bil,bôrd/ ▶ n. a large outdoor board for displaying advertisements.

bill·bug /'bil,bəg/ ▶ n. a typically large weevil that feeds on various grasses and grains. ● Genus *Sphenophorus*, subfamily Rhynchophorinae, family Curculionidae: numerous species, including the **maize billbug** (*S. maidis*), which can cause serious damage to corn plants and can harm or kill poultry by clamping onto the bird's throat or tongue.

Bille·rica /bil'rikə, ,belə-/ a town in northeastern Massachusetts, south of Lowell; pop. 41,844 (est. 2008).

bil·let[1] /'bilit/ ▶ n. a place, usually a civilian's house or other nonmilitary facility, where soldiers are lodged temporarily.
▶ v. (**billets, billeting, billeted**) [with obj.] lodge (soldiers) in a particular place, esp. a civilian's house or other nonmilitary facility: *he didn't belong to the regiment billeted at the hotel.*
– ORIGIN late Middle English (originally denoting a short written document): from Anglo-Norman French *billette*, diminutive of *bille* (see BILL[1]). The verb is recorded in the late 16th cent., and the noun sense 'a written order requiring a householder to lodge the bearer, usually a soldier,' from the mid 17th cent.; hence the current meaning.

bil·let[2] ▶ n. a thick piece of wood. ■ a small bar of metal for further processing. ■ Architecture each of a series of short cylindrical pieces inserted at intervals in decorative hollow moldings. ■ Heraldry a rectangle placed vertically as a charge.
– ORIGIN late Middle English: from Old French *billette* and *billot*, diminutives of *bille* 'tree trunk,' from medieval Latin *billa, billus* 'branch, trunk,' probably of Celtic origin.

bil·let-doux /,bilā 'do͞o, ,bēyā-/ ▶ n. (pl. **billets-doux** pronunc. **same** or /-'do͞oz/) dated or humorous a love letter.
– ORIGIN late 17th cent.: French, literally 'sweet note.'

bill·fish /'bil,fisH/ ▶ n. (pl. **same** or **billfishes**) a large, fast-swimming fish of open seas, with a streamlined body and a long, pointed, spearlike snout. It occurs on the surface in warmer waters and is a popular sporting fish. ● Family Istiophoridae: three genera and several species, including the marlins, sailfish, and spearfishes.

bill·fold /'bil,fōld/ ▶ n. a wallet, typically made of leather, esp. a thin one with few compartments.

bill·hook /'bil,ho͝ok/ ▶ n. a tool with a sickle-shaped blade with a sharp inner edge, used for pruning or lopping branches or other vegetation.

bil·liard /'bilyərd/ ▶ n. **1** (**billiards**) [usu. treated as sing.] a game usually for two people, played on a billiard table, in which three balls are struck with cues into pockets around the edge of the table: *play billiards at home* | [as modifier] (**billiard**) *billiard ball | billiard room.* ■ (in full **English billiards**) a game played on a billiard table with pockets, in which points are made by caroms, pocketing an object ball, or caroming the cue ball into a pocket.
2 a stroke in which the cue ball strikes two balls successively.
– ORIGIN late 16th cent.: from French *billard*, denoting both the game and the cue, diminutive of *bille* (see BILLET[2]).

bil·liard ta·ble ▶ n. a smooth rectangular cloth-covered table used for billiards and some forms of pool, with six pockets at the corners and sides into which the balls can be struck. ■ a similar table but without pockets used for playing carom billiards.

bill·ing /'biliNG/ ▶ n. **1** the action or fact of publicizing or being publicized in a particular way: *they can justify their billing as the American League favorites.* ■ prominence in publicity, esp. as an indication of importance: *he shared top billing with his wife.*
2 the process of making out or sending invoices: *faster, more accurate order fulfillment and billing.* ■ the total amount of business conducted in a given time, esp. that of an advertising agency: *the account was worth about $2 million a year in billings.*

Bil·lings /'biliNGz/ a commercial city in south central Montana, the state's largest city; pop. 103,994 (est. 2008).

Bil·lings meth·od ▶ n. a system for finding the time of ovulation by examining cervical mucus. It can be used as a form of birth control by avoiding sexual intercourse at that time.

b

–ORIGIN 1960s: named after Drs. John and Evelyn *Billings*, who devised the method.

bil·lion /'bilyən/ ▶ **cardinal number** (pl. **billions** or (with numeral or quantifying word) **same**) the number equivalent to the product of a thousand and a million; 1,000,000,000 or 10^9: *a world population of over 6 billion | half a billion dollars*. ■ (**billions**) informal a very large number or amount of something: *our immune systems are killing billions of germs right now*. ■ a billion dollars (or pounds, etc.): *the problem persists despite the billions spent on it*. ■ dated, chiefly Brit. a million million (1,000,000,000,000 or 10^{12}).
–DERIVATIVES **bil·lionth** /-yənTH/ **ordinal number**.
–ORIGIN late 17th cent.: from French, from *million*, by substitution of the prefix *bi-* 'two' for the initial letters.

bil·lion·aire /'bilyə,ne(ə)r/ ▶ **n.** a person possessing assets worth at least a billion dollars (or pounds, etc.).
–ORIGIN mid 19th cent.: from **BILLION**, on the pattern of *millionaire*.

Bil·li·ton /bi'lē,tōn/ former name of **BELITUNG**.

bill of at·tain·der ▶ **n.** see **ATTAINDER**.

bill of ex·change ▶ **n.** a written order to a person requiring the person to make a specified payment to the signatory or to a named payee; a promissory note.

bill of fare ▶ **n.** dated a menu. ■ informal the selection of food available to or consumed by (a person or animal): *our bill of fare in Alaska included clams, mussels, and herring*. ■ a program for a theatrical event.

bill of goods ▶ **n.** a consignment of merchandise.
–PHRASES **sell someone a bill of goods** deceive someone, usually by persuading them to accept something untrue or undesirable: *she was sold a bill of goods about that dog's pedigree*.

bill of health ▶ **n.** a certificate relating to the incidence of infectious disease on a ship or in the port from which it has sailed.
–PHRASES **a clean bill of health** a declaration or confirmation that someone is healthy or that something is in good condition: *a survey gave the property a clean bill of health*.

bill of in·dict·ment ▶ **n.** a written accusation as presented to a grand jury.

bill of lad·ing ▶ **n.** a detailed list of a shipment of goods in the form of a receipt given by the carrier to the person consigning the goods.

Bill of Rights ▶ **n.** Law a statement of the rights of a class of people, in particular: ■ the first ten amendments to the US Constitution, ratified in 1791 and guaranteeing such rights as the freedoms of speech, assembly, and worship. ■ the English constitutional settlement of 1689, confirming the deposition of James II and the accession of William and Mary, guaranteeing the Protestant succession, and laying down the principles of parliamentary supremacy.

bill of sale ▶ **n.** a certificate of transfer of personal property.

bil·lon /'bilən/ ▶ **n.** an alloy formerly used for coinage, containing gold or silver with a predominating amount of copper or other base metal.
–ORIGIN early 18th cent.: from French, literally 'bronze or copper money,' in Old French 'ingot,' from *bille* (see **BILLET**[2]).

bil·low /'bilō/ ▶ **n.** a large undulating mass of something, typically cloud, smoke, or steam. ■ archaic a large sea wave.
▶ **v.** [no obj.] (of fabric) fill with air and swell outward: *her dress billowed out around her*. ■ (of smoke, cloud, or steam) move or flow outward with an undulating motion: *smoke was billowing from the chimney*.
–DERIVATIVES **bil·low·ing adj.**, **bil·low·y** /'bilō-ē/ **adj.**
–ORIGIN mid 16th cent.: from Old Norse *bylgja*.

bill·post·er /'bil,pōstər/ ▶ **n.** a person who posts advertisements, notices, or posters.
–DERIVATIVES **bill·post·ing** /-,pōstiNG/ **n.**

bil·ly /'bilē/ ▶ **n.** (pl. **billies**) **1** short for **BILLY GOAT**.
2 (also **billy club**) a truncheon; a cudgel.
–ORIGIN mid 19th cent.: from *Billy*, nickname for the given name *William*.

bil·ly goat ▶ **n.** a male goat.

Bil·ly the Kid see **BONNEY**.

bi·lobed /bī'lōbd/ (also **bilobate** /-'lōbāt/) ▶ **adj.** having or consisting of two lobes.

bi·lo·ca·tion /,bīlō'kāSHən/ ▶ **n.** the supposed phenomenon of being in two places simultaneously.

Bi·loxi /bi'ləksē, -'läksē/ a city in southeastern Mississippi, on the Gulf of Mexico; pop. 45,670 (est. 2008). It is a noted fishing and tourist center.

bil·tong /'bil,tôNG/ ▶ **n.** chiefly S. African lean meat that is salted and dried in strips.
–ORIGIN Afrikaans, from Dutch *bil* 'buttock' + *tong* 'tongue.'

bi·man·u·al /bī'manyo͞oəl/ ▶ **adj.** performed with both hands.
–DERIVATIVES **bi·man·u·al·ly adv.**

bim·bo /'bimbō/ (also **bimbette** /bim'bet/) ▶ **n.** (pl. **bimbos**) informal an attractive but empty-headed young woman, esp. one perceived as a willing sex object.
–ORIGIN early 20th cent. (originally in the sense 'fellow, man'): from Italian, literally 'little child.'

bi·me·tal·lic /,bīmə'talik/ ▶ **adj.** made or consisting of two metals. ■ historical of or relating to bimetallism.
–ORIGIN late 19th cent.: from French *bimétallique*, from *bi-* 'two' + *métallique* 'metallic.'

bi·me·tal·lic strip ▶ **n.** a temperature-sensitive electrical contact used in some thermostats, consisting of two bands of different metals joined face to face along their lengths. When heated, the metals expand at different rates, causing the strip to bend.

bi·met·al·lism /bī'metl,izəm/ ▶ **n.** historical a system allowing the unrestricted currency of two metals (e.g., gold and silver) as legal tender at a fixed ratio to each other.
–DERIVATIVES **bi·met·al·list n.**

bi·mil·le·nar·y /bī'milə,nerē/; ▶ **adj.** [attrib.] of or relating to a period of two thousand years or a two-thousandth anniversary.
▶ **n.** (pl. **bimillenaries**) a period of two thousand years or a two-thousandth anniversary.

Bim·i·ni /'bimənē/ (also **Biminis**) resort islands in the northwestern Bahamas. The legendary Fountain of Youth sought by Ponce de León was thought to be here.

bi·mod·al /bī'mōdl/ ▶ **adj.** having or involving two modes, in particular (of a statistical distribution) having two maxima.

bi·mo·lec·u·lar /,bīmə'lekyələr/ ▶ **adj.** Chemistry consisting of or involving two molecules.

bi·month·ly /bī'mənTHlē/ ▶ **adj.** occurring or produced twice a month or every two months: *a bimonthly newsletter*.
▶ **adv.** twice a month or every two months: *the magazine appears bimonthly*.
▶ **n.** (pl. **bimonthlies**) a periodical produced twice a month or every two months.

> **USAGE** On the ambiguity of words like bimonthly, biweekly, etc., see usage at **BI-**.

bin /bin/ ▶ **n.** [with modifier] a receptacle for storing a specified substance: *a vegetable bin*. ■ a receptacle in which to deposit trash or recyclables: *we tossed the soda cans in the bin marked "aluminum only."* ■ Statistics each of a series of ranges of numerical value into which data are sorted in statistical analysis. ■ short for **LOONY BIN**: *back in the bin, she suffers from dreadful nightmares*.
▶ **v.** (**bins, binning, binned**) [with obj.] place (something) in a bin. ■ Statistics group together (data) in bins.
–ORIGIN Old English *bin(n)*, *binne*, of Celtic origin; related to Welsh *ben* 'cart.' The original meaning was 'receptacle' in a general sense; also specifically 'a receptacle for provender in a stable' and 'a receptacle for storing grain, bread, or other foodstuffs.' The sense 'receptacle for trash' dates from the mid 19th cent.

bin- ▶ **prefix** variant spelling of **BI-** before a vowel (as in *binaural*).

bi·na·ry /'bī,nerē, -nərē/ ▶ **adj. 1** relating to, using, or expressed in a system of numerical notation that has 2 rather than 10 as a base.
2 relating to, composed of, or involving two things: *testing the so-called binary, or dual-chemical, weapons*.
▶ **n.** (pl. **binaries**) **1** the binary system: binary notation: *the device is counting in binary*.
2 something having two parts. ■ a binary star.
–ORIGIN late Middle English (in the sense 'duality, a pair'): from late Latin *binarius*, from *bini* 'two together.'

bi·na·ry code ▶ **n.** Electronics a coding system using the binary digits 0 and 1 to represent a letter, digit, or other character in a computer or other electronic device.

bi·na·ry cod·ed dec·i·mal (abbr.: **BCD**) ▶ **n.** Electronics a system for coding a number in which each digit of a decimal number is represented individually by its binary equivalent. ■ a number represented in this way.

bi·na·ry dig·it ▶ **n.** one of two digits (0 or 1) in a binary system of notation.

bi·na·ry op·er·a·tion ▶ **n.** a mathematical operation, such as addition or multiplication, performed on two elements of a set to derive a third element.

bi·na·ry star ▶ **n.** a system of two stars in which one star revolves around the other or both revolve around a common center.

bi·na·ry sys·tem ▶ **n. 1** a system in which information can be expressed by combinations of the digits 0 and 1.
2 a system consisting of two parts: *the binary system of state and public schools*. ■ Astronomy a star system containing two stars orbiting around each other.

bi·na·ry tree ▶ **n.** Computing a data structure in which a record is linked to two successor records, usually referred to as the left branch when greater and the right when less than the previous record.

bi·nate /'bīnāt/ ▶ **adj.** Botany growing in pairs. ■ composed of two equal parts.
–ORIGIN early 19th cent.: from modern Latin *binatus*, from Latin *bini* 'two together.'

bi·na·tion·al /bī'naSHənl/ ▶ **adj.** concerning or consisting of two nations.

bin·au·ral /bī'nôrəl, bin-/ ▶ **adj.** of, relating to, or used with both ears: *human hearing is binaural*. ■ of or relating to sound recorded using two microphones and usually transmitted separately to the two ears of the listener.

bind /bīnd/ ▶ **v.** (past and past participle **bound** /bound/) [with obj.] **1** tie or fasten (something) tightly: *floating bundles of logs **bound together** with ropes | the magician bound her wrists with a silk scarf*. ■ restrain (someone) by the tying up of hands and feet: *the raider then bound and gagged Mr. Glenn*. ■ wrap (something) tightly: *her hair was **bound up** in a towel*. ■ bandage (a wound): *he cleaned the wound and **bound** it **up** with a clean dressing | she had bound his wounds with a poultice of herbs*. ■ (**be bound with**) (of an object) be encircled by something, typically metal bands, in order to strengthen it: *an ancient oak chest, bound with brass braces*. ■ Linguistics (of a rule or set of grammatical conditions) determine the relationship between (coreferential noun phrases).
2 ■ cohere or cause to cohere in a single mass: [with obj.] *mix the flour with the coconut and enough egg white to bind them* | [no obj.] *clay is made up chiefly of tiny soil particles that **bind together** tightly*. ■ cause (painting pigments) to form a smooth medium by mixing them with oil: *use a white that is bound in linseed oil*. ■ hold by chemical bonding: *a protein in a form that can bind DNA*. ■ [no obj.] (**bind to**) combine with (a substance) through chemical bonding: *these proteins have been reported to **bind to** calmodulin*.
3 cause (people) to feel united: *the comradeship that had **bound** such a disparate bunch of young men **together***. ■ (**bind someone to**) cause someone to feel strongly attached to (a person or place): *loosened the ties that had bound him to the university*.
4 formal impose a legal or contractual obligation on: *a party who signs a document will normally be bound by its terms*. ■ indenture (someone) as an apprentice: *he was **bound apprentice** at the age of sixteen*. ■ (**bind oneself**) formal make a contractual or enforceable undertaking: *the government cannot bind itself as to the form of subsequent legislation*. ■ secure (a contract), typically with a sum of money. ■ (**be bound by**) be hampered or constrained by: *Sarah did not want to be bound by a rigid timetable*.
5 fix together and enclose (the pages of a book) in a cover: *a small, fat volume, bound in red morocco*.
6 trim (the edge of a piece of material) with a decorative strip: *a ruffle with the edges **bound** in a contrasting color*.
7 Logic (of a quantifier) be applied to (a given variable) so that the variable falls within its scope. ● For example, in an expression of the form 'For every *x*, if *x* is a dog, *x* is an animal,' the universal quantifier is binding the variable *x*.
▶ **n. 1** a problematical situation: *he is in a political bind over the welfare issue*.
2 formal a statutory constraint: *the moral bind of the law*.
3 Brit. Music another term for **TIE**.
4 another term for **BINE**.
–PHRASES **bind someone hand and foot** see **HAND**.
–PHRASAL VERBS **bind off** cast off in knitting. **bind someone over** (usu. **be bound over**) (of a court of law) require someone to fulfill an obligation, typically by paying a sum of money as surety: *he was bound over for trial on a felony charge*.

– ORIGIN Old English *bindan*, of Germanic origin; related to Dutch and German *binden*, from an Indo-European root shared by Sanskrit *bandh*.

bind·er /ˈbīndər/ ▶ **n.** a thing or person that binds something, in particular: ■ a cover for holding loose sheets of paper, magazines, etc., together. ■ a substance that acts cohesively. ■ a reaping machine that binds grain into sheaves. ■ a bookbinder.

bind·er twine ▶ **n.** (in farming) strong cord made from plastic or natural fiber, used in a baling machine or binder to tie hay and straw bales.

bind·er·y /ˈbīndərē/ ▶ **n.** (pl. **binderies**) a workshop or factory in which books are bound.

bin·di /ˈbindē/ ▶ **n.** a decorative mark worn in the middle of the forehead by Indian women.
– ORIGIN from Hindi *bindī*.

bin·di-eye ▶ **n.** a small perennial Australian plant of the daisy family that has a burlike fruit. ● *Calotis cuneifolia*, family Compositae.
– ORIGIN early 20th cent.: perhaps from an Aboriginal language.

bind·ing /ˈbīndiNG/ ▶ **n. 1** a strong covering holding the pages of a book together. ■ fabric such as braid used for binding the edges of a piece of material.
2 (also **ski binding**) a mechanical device fixed to a ski to grip a ski boot, esp. either of a pair used for downhill skiing that hold the toe and heel of the boot and release it automatically in a fall.
3 the action of fastening, holding together, or being linked by chemical bonds: *the binding of antibodies to cell surfaces*. ■ (in Chomskyan linguistics) the relationship between a referentially dependent form (such as a reflexive) and the independent noun phrase that determines its reference.
▶ **adj.** (of an agreement or promise) involving an obligation that cannot be broken: *business agreements are intended to be legally binding*.

bind·ing en·er·gy ▶ **n.** Physics the energy that holds a nucleus together, equal to the mass defect of the nucleus.

bind·ing post ▶ **n.** Electronics a connector consisting of a threaded screw to which bare wires are attached and held in place by a nut.

bin·dle·stiff /ˈbindlˌstif/ ▶ **n.** informal a tramp or a hobo, esp. one carrying a bundle containing a bedroll and other gear.
– ORIGIN early 20th cent.: probably from an alteration of **BUNDLE** + **STIFF** (in the sense 'useless person').

bind·weed /ˈbīndˌwēd/ ▶ **n.** a twining plant with trumpet-shaped flowers. Several kinds are invasive weeds. ● Genera *Convolvulus* and *Calystegia*, family Convolvulaceae: several species, including the widespread **hedge bindweed** (or **wild morning glory**) (*Calystegia* (or *Convolvulus*) *sepium*). ■ used in names of similar twining plants, e.g., **black bindweed**.

bine /bīn/ ▶ **n.** a long flexible stem of a climbing plant, esp. the hop.
– ORIGIN early 19th cent.: originally a dialect form of **BIND**.

Bi·net /bəˈnā/, Alfred (1857–1911), French psychologist. He devised a mental age scale that described performance in relation to the average performance of students of the same physical age. With psychiatrist **Théodore Simon** (1873–1961), he was responsible for a pioneering system of intelligence tests.

Bi·net–Si·mon scale /biˈnā ˈsīmən/ ▶ **n.** the measurement of intelligence by the application of a test (see **BINET–SIMON TEST**) consisting of tasks and problems graded in terms of mental age.

Bi·net–Si·mon test /biˈnā ˈsīmən/ (also **Binet test**) ▶ **adj.** Psychology a test used to measure intelligence, esp. that of children.

Bing /biNG/, Sir Rudolf (1902–97), British opera conductor and manager; born in Austria. He was conductor and director of the Metropolitan Opera in New York City 1950–72. In 1955, he hired Marian Anderson, ending the Met's unwritten ban against African Americans. He was knighted in 1971.

bing /biNG/ ▶ **exclam.** indicating a sudden action or event: *Bing! They've hit you with something.*
– ORIGIN late 19th cent. (originally dialect in the sense 'sudden bang'): imitative.

Bing cher·ry /biNG/ ▶ **n.** a large heart-shaped cherry, juicy, sweet and dark blackish-red.

binge /binj/ informal ▶ **n.** a short period devoted to indulging in an activity to excess, esp. drinking alcohol or eating: *he* **went on a binge** *and was in no shape to drive* | *a spending binge* | [as modifier] *binge eating*.
▶ **v.** (**binges**, **binging** or **bingeing**, **binged**) [no obj.] indulge in an activity, esp. eating, to excess: *some dieters say they cannot help* **binging on** *chocolate* | (as noun **binging**) *her secret binging and vomiting*.
– DERIVATIVES **bing·er n.**
– ORIGIN early 19th cent.: of unknown origin.

binge drink·ing ▶ **n.** the consumption of an excessive amount of alcohol in a short period of time: *teenagers as young as 16 admit to binge drinking*.
– DERIVATIVES **binge-drink v.**, **binge drink·er n.**

binge-eat·ing syn·drome ▶ **n.** see **BULIMIA**.

binge-purge syn·drome ▶ **n.** see **BULIMIA**.

Bing·ham /ˈbiNGəm/, George Caleb (1811–79), US artist. His paintings of the US frontier include *The Fur Traders Descending the Missouri* (1845), *The Trappers Return* (1851), and *The Country Election* (1851–52).

Bing·ham·ton /ˈbiNGəmtən/ an industrial city in south central New York, on the Susquehanna River, near the Pennsylvania border; pop. 44,729 (est. 2008).

bin·go /ˈbiNGgō/ ▶ **n.** a game in which players mark off numbers on cards as the numbers are drawn randomly by a caller, the winner being the first person to mark off five numbers in a row or another required pattern.
▶ **exclam.** used to express satisfaction or surprise at a sudden positive event or outcome: *bingo, she leapfrogged into a sales trainee position*. ■ a call by someone who wins a game of bingo.
– ORIGIN 1920s (as an interjection): of unknown origin.

bin·na·cle /ˈbinəkəl/ ▶ **n.** a built-in housing for a ship's compass.
– ORIGIN late 15th cent. (as *bittacle*): from Spanish *bitácula*, *bitácora* or Portuguese *bitacola*, from Latin *habitaculum* 'dwelling place,' from *habitare* 'inhabit.' The change to *binnacle* occurred in the mid 18th cent.

binnacle

bin·ocs /biˈnäks/ ▶ **plural n.** informal short for **BINOCULARS**.

bin·oc·u·lar /biˈnäkyələr/ ▶ **adj.** adapted for or using both eyes: *a binocular microscope*.
– ORIGIN early 18th cent. (in the sense 'having two eyes'): from Latin *bini* 'two together' + *oculus* 'eye,' on the pattern of *ocular*.

bin·oc·u·lars /biˈnäkyələrz/ ▶ **plural n.** an optical instrument with a lens for each eye, used for viewing distant objects.
– ORIGIN late 19th cent.: plural of **BINOCULAR**.

bin·oc·u·lar vi·sion ▶ **n.** vision using two eyes with overlapping fields of view, allowing good perception of depth.

bi·no·mi·al /bīˈnōmēəl/ ▶ **n. 1** Mathematics an algebraic expression of the sum or the difference of two terms.
2 a two-part name, esp. the Latin name of a species of living organism (consisting of the genus followed by the specific epithet).
3 Grammar a noun phrase with two heads joined by a conjunction, in which the order is relatively fixed (as in *knife and fork*).
▶ **adj. 1** Mathematics consisting of two terms. ■ of or relating to a binomial or to the binomial theorem.
2 having or using two names, used esp. of the Latin name of a species of living organism.
– ORIGIN mid 16th cent.: from French *binôme* or modern Latin *binomium* (from *bi-* 'having two' + Greek *nomos* 'part, portion') + **-AL**.

bi·no·mi·al dis·tri·bu·tion ▶ **n.** Statistics a frequency distribution of the possible number of successful outcomes in a given number of trials in each of which there is the same probability of success.

bi·no·mi·al no·men·cla·ture ▶ **n.** Biology the system of nomenclature in which two terms are used to denote a species of living organism, the first one indicating the genus and the second the specific epithet. Compare with **SYSTEMATIC NAME**.

bi·no·mi·al the·o·rem ▶ **n.** a formula for finding any power of a binomial without multiplying at length.

bin·tu·rong /binˈto͝orôNG/ ▶ **n.** a tree-dwelling Asian civet with a coarse blackish coat and a muscular prehensile tail. ● *Arctictis binturong*, family Viverridae.
– ORIGIN early 19th cent.: from Malay.

bi·nu·cle·ate /bīˈn(y)o͞oklēit, -ˌāt/ ▶ **adj.** having two nuclei.

bi·o /ˈbīō/ informal ▶ **n.** (pl. **bios**) **1** biology: [as modifier] *he dated a bio major in college*.
2 a biography: *the latest in a series of unauthorized bios*.
▶ **adj. 1** biological: *studying the effects of bio treatment*.
2 biographical: *it was excluded from her official bio material*.
– ORIGIN mid 20th cent.: abbreviation.

bio- ▶ **comb. form 1** of or relating to life: *biosynthesis*. ■ biological; relating to biology: *biohazard*. ■ of living beings: *biogenesis*.
2 relating to or involving the use of toxic biological or biochemical substances as weapons of war: *bioterrorism*.
– ORIGIN from Greek *bios* '(course of) human life.' The sense is extended in modern scientific usage to mean 'organic life.'

bi·o·ac·cu·mu·late /ˌbīōəˈkyo͞omyəˌlāt/ ▶ **v.** [no obj.] (of a substance) become concentrated inside the bodies of living things.
– DERIVATIVES **bi·o·ac·cu·mu·la·tion** /-ˌkyo͞omyəˈlāSHən/ **n.**

bi·o·a·cous·tics /ˌbīōəˈko͞ostiks/ ▶ **plural n.** [treated as sing.] the branch of acoustics concerned with sounds produced by or affecting living organisms, esp. as relating to communication.

bi·o·ac·tive /ˌbīōˈaktiv/ ▶ **adj.** (of a substance) having a biological effect.
– DERIVATIVES **bi·o·ac·tiv·i·ty** /-akˈtivitē/ **n.**

bi·o·as·say /ˌbīōəˈsā, -ˈasā/ ▶ **n.** measurement of the concentration or potency of a substance by its effect on living cells or tissues.
– ORIGIN early 20th cent.: from **BIO-** 'life' + **ASSAY**.

bi·o·a·vail·a·bil·i·ty /ˌbīōˌəvāləˈbilitē/ ▶ **n.** Physiology the proportion of a drug or other substance that enters the circulation when introduced into the body and so is able to have an active effect.
– DERIVATIVES **bi·o·a·vail·a·ble** /-əˈvāləbəl/ **adj.**

bi·o·cat·a·lyst /ˌbīōˈkatl-ist/ ▶ **n.** a substance, such as an enzyme or hormone, that initiates or increases the rate of a chemical reaction.
– DERIVATIVES **bi·o·cat·a·lyt·ic** /ˌbīōˌkatlˈitik/ **adj.**

bi·o·ce·no·sis /ˌbīōsiˈnōsis/ (also **biocoenosis**) ▶ **n.** (pl. **biocenoses** /-ˈnōsēz/) Ecology an association of different organisms forming a closely integrated community.
– ORIGIN late 19th cent.: modern Latin, from **BIO-** 'life' + Greek *koinōsis* 'sharing' (from *koinos* 'common').

bi·o·cen·trism /ˌbīōˈsentrizəm/ ▶ **n.** the view or belief that the rights and needs of humans are not more important than those of other living things.
– DERIVATIVES **bi·o·cen·tric** /-trik/ **adj.**, **bi·o·cen·trist n.**

bi·o·chem·i·cal ox·y·gen de·mand /ˌbīōˈkemikəl/ (abbr.: **BOD**) ▶ **n.** the amount of dissolved oxygen that must be present in water in order for microorganisms to decompose the organic matter in the water, used as a measure of the degree of pollution. Also called **BIOLOGICAL OXYGEN DEMAND**.

bi·o·chem·is·try /ˌbīōˈkeməstrē/ ▶ **n.** the branch of science concerned with the chemical and physicochemical processes that occur within living organisms. ■ processes of this kind: *abnormal brain biochemistry*.
– DERIVATIVES **bi·o·chem·i·cal** /-ˈkemikəl/ **adj.**, **bi·o·chem·i·cal·ly adv.**, **bi·o·chem·ist** /-ˈkemist/ **n.**

bi·o·chip /ˈbīōˌCHip/ ▶ **n.** a microchip intended to function in a biological environment, esp. inside a living organism. ■ a logical device analogous to the silicon chip, whose components are formed from biological molecules or structures.

bi·o·cide /ˈbīəˌsīd/ ▶ **n. 1** a poisonous substance, esp. a pesticide.
2 the destruction of life: *our whims have brought us to the brink of biocide*.
– DERIVATIVES **bi·o·cid·al** /ˌbīəˈsīdl/ **adj.**
– ORIGIN 1940s: from **BIO-** 'life' + **-CIDE**.

bi·o·cir·cuit /ˈbīōˌsərkit/ ▶ **n.** an integrated circuit incorporating biological molecules or structures.
– DERIVATIVES **bi·o·cir·cuit·ry** /ˌbīōˈsərkitrē/ **n.**

bi·o·cli·mat·ic /ˌbīōklīˈmatik/ ▶ **adj.** Ecology of or relating to the interrelation of climate and the activities and distribution of living organisms.

bi·o·com·pat·i·ble /ˌbīōkəmˈpatəbəl/ ▶ **adj.** (esp. of materials used in surgical implants) not harmful to living tissue.
– DERIVATIVES **bi·o·com·pat·i·bil·i·ty** /-ˌpatəˈbilitē/ **n.**

bi·o·com·pu·ter /ˈbīōkəmˌpyo͞otər/ ▶ **n.** a hypothetical computer based on circuits and components formed from biological molecules or structures that would be smaller and faster than an equivalent computer built from semiconductor components. ■ a human being, or the human mind, regarded as a computer.

bi·o·com·put·ing /ˌbīōkəmˈpyo͞otiNG/ ▶ **n.** the design and construction of computers using biochemical components. ■ an approach to programming that seeks to emulate or model biological processes. ■ computing in a biological context or environment.

bi·o·con·trol /ˌbīōkənˈtrōl/ ▶ **n.** short for **BIOLOGICAL CONTROL**.

bi·o·con·ver·sion /ˌbīōkənˈvərZHən/ ▶ n. the conversion of organic matter, such as animal or plant waste, into a source of energy through the action of microorganisms.

bi·o·de·grad·a·ble /ˌbīōdiˈgrādəbəl/ ▶ adj. (of a substance or object) capable of being decomposed by bacteria or other living organisms.
– DERIVATIVES **bi·o·de·grad·a·bil·i·ty** /-ˌgrādəˈbilitē/ n.

bi·o·de·grade /ˌbīōdiˈgrād/ ▶ v. [no obj.] (of a substance or object) be decomposed by bacteria or other living organisms: *most plastics will not biodegrade at all.*
– DERIVATIVES **bi·o·deg·ra·da·tion** /-ˌdegrəˈdāSHən/ n.

bi·o·die·sel /ˈbīō,dēzəl, -səl/ ▶ n. a biofuel intended as a substitute for diesel.

bi·o·di·verse /ˌbīōdiˈvərs, ˌbīōdī-/ ▶ adj. (of a habitat or region) having a high level of biodiversity: *Australia is one of the most biodiverse regions on earth.*

bi·o·di·ver·si·ty /ˌbīōdiˈvərsitē/ ▶ n. the variety of life in the world or in a particular habitat or ecosystem.

bi·o·dy·nam·ics /ˌbīōdīˈnamiks/ ▶ plural n. [treated as sing.] **1** the study of physical motion or dynamics in living systems.
2 a method of organic farming involving such factors as the observation of lunar phases and planetary cycles and the use of incantations and ritual substances.
– DERIVATIVES **bi·o·dy·nam·ic** adj.

bi·o·e·lec·tric /ˌbīōiˈlektrik/ ▶ adj. of or relating to electricity or electrical phenomena produced within living organisms.
– DERIVATIVES **bi·o·e·lec·tri·cal** adj.

bi·o·e·lec·tron·ics /ˌbīōilekˈträniks, -ˌēlek-/ ▶ plural n. [usu. treated as sing.] **1** the study and application of electronics in medicine and biological processes.
2 the integration of biological principles in electronic technology: *the impact of bioelectronics on computer hardware.*
– DERIVATIVES **bi·o·e·lec·tron·ic** adj., **bi·o·e·lec·tron·i·cal·ly** /-ik(ə)lē/ adv.

bi·o·en·er·get·ics /ˌbīō,enərˈjetiks/ ▶ plural n. [treated as sing.] **1** the study of the transformation of energy in living organisms.
2 a system of alternative psychotherapy based on the belief that emotional healing can be aided through resolution of bodily tension.
– DERIVATIVES **bi·o·en·er·get·ic** adj.

bi·o·en·er·gy /ˌbīōˈenərjē/ ▶ n. renewable energy produced by living organisms.

bi·o·en·gi·neer·ing /ˌbīō,enjəˈni(ə)riNG/ ▶ n.
1 another term for **GENETIC ENGINEERING**.
2 the use of artificial tissues, organs, or organ components to replace damaged or absent parts of the body, such as artificial limbs and heart pacemakers.
3 the use in engineering or industry of biological organisms or processes.
– DERIVATIVES **bi·o·en·gi·neer** n. & v.

bi·o·eth·a·nol /ˌbīōˈeTHə,nôl/ ▶ n. ethanol produced from plants such as sugar cane or corn, used as an alternative to gasoline.

bi·o·eth·ics /ˌbīōˈeTHiks/ ▶ plural n. [treated as sing.] the ethics of medical and biological research.
– DERIVATIVES **bi·o·eth·i·cal** /-ˈeTHikəl/ adj., **bi·o·eth·i·cist** /-ˈeTHəsist/ n.

bi·o·feed·back /ˌbīōˈfēd,bak/ ▶ n. the use of electronic monitoring of a normally automatic bodily function in order to train someone to acquire voluntary control of that function.

bi·o·film /ˈbīō,film/ ▶ n. a thin, slimy film of bacteria that adheres to a surface.

bi·o·fla·vo·noid /ˌbīōˈflāvə,noid/ ▶ n. any of a group of compounds occurring mainly in citrus fruits and black currants, formerly regarded as vitamins. Also called **CITRIN**. See also **VITAMIN P**.

bi·o·foul·ing /ˈbīō,fouliNG/ ▶ n. the fouling of pipes and underwater surfaces by organisms such as barnacles and algae.

bi·o·fu·el /ˈbīō,fyo͞oəl/ ▶ n. a fuel derived directly from living matter.

bi·o·gas /ˈbīō,gas/ ▶ n. gaseous fuel, esp. methane, produced by the fermentation of organic matter.

bi·o·gen·e·sis /ˌbīōˈjenəsis/ ▶ n. the synthesis of substances by living organisms. ■ historical the hypothesis that living matter arises only from other living matter.
– DERIVATIVES **bi·o·ge·net·ic** /-jəˈnetik/ adj.

bi·o·ge·net·ic law /ˌbīōjəˈnetik/ ▶ n. the theory that evolutionary stages are repeated in the growth of a young animal. Also called **RECAPITULATION THEORY**.

bi·o·gen·ic /ˌbīōˈjenik/ ▶ adj. [attrib.] produced or brought about by living organisms: *biogenic sediments.*

bi·o·ge·o·chem·i·cal /ˌbīō,jēōˈkemikəl/ ▶ adj. relating to or denoting the cycle in which chemical elements and simple substances are transferred between living systems and the environment.
– DERIVATIVES **bi·o·ge·o·chem·ist** /-ˈkemist/ n., **bi·o·ge·o·chem·is·try** /-ˈkeməstrē/ n.

bi·o·ge·og·ra·phy /ˌbīōjēˈägrəfē/ ▶ n. the branch of biology that deals with the geographical distribution of plants and animals.
– DERIVATIVES **bi·o·ge·og·ra·pher** /-fər/ n., **bi·o·ge·o·graph·ic** /-ˌjēəˈgrafik/ adj., **bi·o·ge·o·graph·i·cal** /-ˌjēəˈgrafikəl/ adj., **bi·o·ge·o·graph·i·cal·ly** adv.

bi·og·ra·phee /bīˌägrəˈfē/ ▶ n. one who is the subject of a biography.

bi·og·ra·phy /bīˈägrəfē/ ▶ n. (pl. **biographies**) an account of someone's life written by someone else. ■ writing of such a type as a branch of literature. ■ a human life in its course: *although their individual biographies are different, both are motivated by a similar ambition.*
– DERIVATIVES **bi·og·ra·pher** /-fər/ n., **bi·o·graph·ic** /ˌbīəˈgrafik/ adj., **bi·o·graph·i·cal** /ˌbīəˈgrafikəl/ adj.
– ORIGIN late 17th cent.: from French *biographie* or modern Latin *biographia*, from medieval Greek, from *bios* 'life' + *-graphia* 'writing.'

bi·o·haz·ard /ˈbīō,hazərd/ ▶ n. a risk to human health or the environment arising from biological work, esp. with microorganisms.

bi·o·in·di·ca·tor /ˌbīōˈindi,kātər/ ▶ n. an organism whose status in an ecosystem is analyzed as an indication of the ecosystem's heath.
– DERIVATIVES **bi·o·in·di·ca·tion** /-ˌindiˈkāSHən/ n.

bi·o·in·for·mat·ics /ˌbīō,infərˈmatiks/ ▶ plural n. [treated as sing.] the science of collecting and analyzing complex biological data such as genetic codes.
– DERIVATIVES **bi·o·in·for·mat·ic** adj.

Bi·o·ko /bēˈōkō/ an island in Equatorial Guinea, in the eastern part of the Gulf of Guinea. Its chief town is Malabo, which is also the capital of Equatorial Guinea. Known as Fernando Póo until 1973, it was called Macias Nguema 1973–79.

biol. ▶ abbr. ■ biological. ■ biologist. ■ biology.

bi·o·log·i·cal /ˌbīəˈläjikəl/ (abbr.: **biol.**) ▶ adj. of or relating to biology or living organisms. ■ genetically related; related by blood: *the alleged rights of the biological father.* ■ (of a detergent or other cleaning product) containing enzymes to assist the process of cleaning.
▶ n. a therapeutic substance, such as a vaccine or drug, derived from biological sources: [usu. pl.] *an international biotechnology company with interests in biologicals, agriculture, and pharmaceutical products.*
– DERIVATIVES **bi·o·log·i·cal·ly** /-ik(ə)lē/ adv.

bi·o·log·i·cal clock ▶ n. an innate mechanism that controls the physiological activities of an organism that change on a daily, seasonal, yearly, or other regular cycle.

bi·o·log·i·cal con·trol ▶ n. the control of a pest by the introduction of a natural enemy or predator.

bi·o·log·i·cal ox·y·gen de·mand (abbr.: **BOD**) ▶ n. another term for **BIOCHEMICAL OXYGEN DEMAND**.

bi·o·log·i·cal war·fare ▶ n. the use of toxins of biological origin or microorganisms as weapons of war: *opposed to chemical and biological warfare.*

bi·ol·o·gism /bīˈälə,jizəm/ ▶ n. the interpretation of human life from a strictly biological point of view.
– DERIVATIVES **bi·ol·o·gis·tic** /-ˌäləˈjistik/ adj.

bi·ol·o·gy /bīˈäləjē/ (abbr.: **biol.**) ▶ n. the study of living organisms, divided into many specialized fields that cover their morphology, physiology, anatomy, behavior, origin, and distribution. ■ the plants and animals of a particular area: *the biology of Chesapeake Bay.* ■ the physiology, behavior, and other qualities of a particular organism or class of organisms: *human biology.*
– DERIVATIVES **bi·ol·o·gist** /-jist/ n.
– ORIGIN early 19th cent.: coined in German, via French from Greek *bios* 'life' + **-LOGY**.

bi·o·lu·mi·nes·cence /ˌbīō,lo͞oməˈnesəns/ ▶ n. the biochemical emission of light by living organisms such as fireflies and deep-sea fishes. ■ the light emitted in such a way.
– DERIVATIVES **bi·o·lu·mi·nes·cent** /-ˈnesənt/ adj.

bi·o·mag·net·ism /ˌbīōˈmagni,tizəm/ ▶ n. the interaction of living organisms with magnetic fields.

bi·o·mag·ni·fi·ca·tion /ˌbīō,magnifiˈkāSHən/ ▶ n. the concentration of toxins in an organism as a result of its ingesting other plants or animals in which the toxins are more widely disbursed.
– DERIVATIVES **bi·o·mag·ni·fy** v.

bi·o·mark·er /ˈbīō,märkər/ ▶ n. a measurable substance in an organism whose presence is indicative of some phenomenon such as disease, infection, or environmental exposure: *a biomarker that may predict aggressive disease recurrence in liver transplant recipients.*

bi·o·mass /ˈbīō,mas/ ▶ n. the total mass of organisms in a given area or volume. ■ organic matter used as a fuel, esp. in a power station for the generation of electricity.

bi·o·ma·ter·i·al /ˌbīōməˈti(ə)rēəl/ ▶ n. synthetic or natural material suitable for use in constructing artificial organs and prostheses or to replace bone or tissue.

bi·o·math·e·mat·ics /ˌbīō,maTHəˈmatiks/ ▶ plural n. [treated as sing.] the science of the application of mathematics to biology.

bi·ome /ˈbī,ōm/ ▶ n. Ecology a large naturally occurring community of flora and fauna occupying a major habitat, e.g., forest or tundra.
– ORIGIN early 20th cent.: from **BIO-** 'life' + **-OME**.

bi·o·me·chan·ics /ˌbīōməˈkaniks/ ▶ plural n. [treated as sing.] the study of the mechanical laws relating to the movement or structure of living organisms.

bi·o·med·i·cal /ˌbīōˈmedikəl/ ▶ adj. of or relating to both biology and medicine.
– DERIVATIVES **bi·o·med·i·cine** /-ˈmedəsən/ n.

bi·o·me·te·or·ol·o·gy /ˌbīō,mētēəˈräləjē/ ▶ n. the study of the relationship between living organisms and weather.
– DERIVATIVES **bi·o·me·te·or·o·log·i·cal** /-ərəˈläjikəl/ adj.

bi·o·met·ric read·er /ˌbīōˈmetrik/ ▶ n. an electronic device that determines identity by detecting and matching physical characteristics.

bi·o·met·rics /ˌbīōˈmetriks/ ▶ n. **1** another term for **BIOMETRY**.
2 another term for **BIOSTATISTICS**.

bi·o·met·ric sig·na·ture ▶ n. the unique pattern of a bodily feature such as the retina, iris, or voice, encoded on an identity card and used for recognition and identification purposes.

bi·om·e·try /bīˈämitrē/ ▶ n. the application of statistical analysis to biological data. Also called **BIOMETRICS**.
– DERIVATIVES **bi·o·met·ric** /ˌbīōˈmetrik/ adj., **bi·o·met·ri·cal** /ˌbīōˈmetrikəl/ adj., **bi·o·me·tri·cian** /ˌbīōməˈtriSHən/ n.

bi·o·mi·met·ic /ˌbīōmiˈmetik/ ▶ adj. Biochemistry relating to or denoting synthetic methods that mimic biochemical processes.
– DERIVATIVES **bi·o·mi·met·ics** n.

bi·o·mim·ic·ry /ˌbīōˈmiməkrē/ ▶ n. the design and production of materials, structures, and systems that are modeled on biological entities and processes.

bi·o·morph /ˈbīō,môrf/ ▶ n. a decorative form or object based on or resembling a living organism. ■ a graphical representation of an organism generated on a computer, used to model evolution.
– DERIVATIVES **bi·o·mor·phic** /ˌbīōˈmôrfik/ adj.

bi·on·ic /bīˈänik/ ▶ adj. having artificial body parts, esp. electromechanical ones. ■ informal having ordinary human powers increased by or as if by the aid of such devices (real or fictional): *working out in gymnasiums to become bionic men.* ■ of or relating to bionics.
– DERIVATIVES **bi·on·i·cal·ly** /-ik(ə)lē/ adv.
– ORIGIN 1960s: from **BIO-** 'human,' on the pattern of *electronic.*

bi·on·ics /bīˈäniks/ ▶ plural n. [treated as sing.] the study of mechanical systems that function like living organisms or parts of living organisms.

bi·o·nom·ics /bīəˈnämiks/ ▶ plural n. [treated as sing.] the study of the mode of life of organisms in their natural habitat and their adaptations to their surroundings; ecology.
– DERIVATIVES **bi·o·nom·ic** adj.
– ORIGIN late 19th cent.: from **BIO-** 'life,' on the pattern of *economics.*

bi·o·phar·ma·ceu·ti·cal /ˌbīō,färməˈso͞otikəl/ ▶ n. a biological macromolecule or cellular component, such as a blood product, used as a pharmaceutical.

bi·o·phar·ma·ceu·tics /ˌbīō,färməˈso͞otiks/ ▶ plural n. [treated as sing.] the study of the chemical and physical properties of drugs and the biological effects they produce.

bi·o·phys·ics /ˌbīōˈfiziks/ ▶ plural n. [treated as sing.] the science of the application of the laws of physics to biological phenomena.

PRONUNCIATION KEY ə *ago, up*; ər *over, fur*; a *hat*; ā *ate*; ä *car*; e *let*; ē *see*; i *fit*; ī *by*; NG *sing*; ō *go*; ô *law, for*; oi *toy*; o͝o *good*; o͞o *goo*; ou *out*; TH *thin*; T͟H *then*; ZH *vision*

b

– DERIVATIVES **bi·o·phys·i·cal** /-ˈfizikəl/ **adj.**, **bi·o·phys·i·cist** /-ˈfizəsist/ **n.**

bi·o·pic /ˈbīōˌpik/ ▶ **n.** informal a biographical movie.
– ORIGIN 1950s: blend of *biographical* (see **BIOGRAPHY**) and **PIC**.

bi·o·pi·ra·cy /ˌbīōˈpīrəsē/ ▶ **n.** bioprospecting that exploits plant and animal species by claiming patents to restrict their general use.

bi·o·plas·tic /ˌbīōˈplastik/ ▶ **n.** a type of biodegradable plastic derived from biological substances rather than from petroleum.

bi·o·pol·y·mer /ˌbīōˈpäləmər/ ▶ **n.** a polymeric substance occurring in living organisms, e.g., a protein, cellulose, or DNA.

bi·o·pros·pect·ing /ˌbīōˈpräspektiNG/ ▶ **n.** the search for plant and animal species from which medicinal drugs and other commercially valuable compounds can be obtained.
– DERIVATIVES **bi·o·pros·pec·tor** /-ˈpräspektər/ **n.**
– ORIGIN 1990s: from *bio(diversity) prospecting*.

bi·op·sy /ˈbīˌäpsē/ ▶ **n.** (pl. **biopsies**) an examination of tissue removed from a living body to discover the presence, cause, or extent of a disease.
– ORIGIN late 19th cent.: coined in French from Greek *bios* 'life' + *opsis* 'sight,' on the pattern of *necropsy*.

bi·o·psy·chol·o·gy /ˌbīōsīˈkäləjē/ ▶ **n.** the branch of psychology concerned with its biological and physiological aspects.

bi·o·re·ac·tor /ˌbīōrēˈaktər/ ▶ **n.** an apparatus in which a biological reaction or process is carried out, esp. on an industrial scale.

bi·o·re·gion /ˈbīōˌrējən/ ▶ **n.** a region defined by characteristics of the natural environment rather than by man-made divisions.
– DERIVATIVES **bi·o·re·gion·al** /ˌbīōˈrējənl/ **adj.**

bi·o·re·gion·al·ism /ˌbīōˈrējənlˌizəm/ ▶ **n.** advocacy of the belief that human activity should be largely restricted to distinct ecological and geographical regions.
– DERIVATIVES **bi·o·re·gion·al·ist n.**

bi·o·re·me·di·a·tion /ˌbīōriˌmēdēˈāsHən/ ▶ **n.** the use of either naturally occurring or deliberately introduced microorganisms or other forms of life to consume and break down environmental pollutants, in order to clean up a polluted site.

bi·o·rhythm /ˈbīōˌriT͟Həm/ ▶ **n.** a recurring cycle in the physiology or functioning of an organism, such as the daily cycle of sleeping and waking. ■ a cyclic pattern of physical, emotional, or mental activity said to occur in the life of a person.
– DERIVATIVES **bi·o·rhyth·mic** /ˌbīōˈriT͟Hmik/ **adj.**

BIOS /ˈbīōs/ ▶ **n.** Computing a set of computer instructions in firmware that control input and output operations.
– ORIGIN acronym from *Basic Input-Output System*.

bi·o·safe·ty /ˌbīōˈsāftē/ ▶ **n.** another term for **BIOSECURITY**.

bi·o·sat·el·lite /ˌbīōˈsatlˌīt/ ▶ **n.** an artificial satellite that serves as an automated laboratory, conducting biological experiments on living organisms.

bi·o·sci·ence /ˈbīōˌsīəns/ ▶ **n.** any of the life sciences.
– DERIVATIVES **bi·o·sci·en·tist** /ˌbīōˈsīəntist/ **n.**

bi·o·se·cur·i·ty /ˌbīōsiˈkyo͝oritē/ ▶ **n.** [often as modifier] procedures intended to protect humans or animals against disease or harmful biological agents: *biosecurity risks*.

bi·o·sen·sor /ˈbīōˌsensər/ ▶ **n.** a device that uses a living organism or biological molecules, esp. enzymes or antibodies, to detect the presence of chemicals.

bi·o·so·cial /ˌbīōˈsōsHəl/ ▶ **adj.** of or relating to the interaction of biological and social factors.

bi·o·sol·ids /ˈbīōˌsälidz/ ▶ **plural n.** organic matter recycled from sewage, esp. for use in agriculture.

bi·o·sphere /ˈbīəˌsfi(ə)r/ ▶ **n.** the regions of the surface, atmosphere, and hydrosphere of the earth (or analogous parts of other planets) occupied by living organisms.
– DERIVATIVES **bi·o·spher·ic** /ˌbīəˈsfi(ə)rik, -ˈsfer-/ **adj.**
– ORIGIN late 19th cent.: coined in German from Greek *bios* 'life' + *sphaira* (see **SPHERE**).

bi·o·sta·tis·tics /ˌbīōstəˈtistiks/ ▶ **plural n.** [treated as sing.] the branch of statistics that deals with data relating to living organisms. Also called **BIOMETRICS**.
– DERIVATIVES **bi·o·sta·tis·ti·cal** /-tikəl/ **adj.**, **bi·o·stat·is·ti·cian** /-ˌstatəˈstisHən/ **n.**

bi·o·stra·tig·ra·phy /ˌbīōstrəˈtigrəfē/ ▶ **n.** the branch of stratigraphy concerned with fossils and their use in dating rock formations.
– DERIVATIVES **bi·o·stra·tig·ra·pher** /-fər/ **n.**, **bi·o·strat·i·graph·ic** /-ˌstratiˈgrafik/ **adj.**, **bi·o·strat·i·graph·i·cal** /-ˌstratiˈgrafikəl/ **adj.**, **bi·o·strat·i·graph·i·cal·ly adv.**

bi·o·sur·ge·ry /ˌbīōˈsərjərē/ ▶ **n.** the medical use of maggots to clean infected wounds, esp. in cases where a patient is resistant to conventional antibiotic treatment.

bi·o·syn·the·sis /ˌbīōˈsinTHəsis/ ▶ **n.** the production of complex molecules within living organisms or cells.
– DERIVATIVES **bi·o·syn·thet·ic** /-ˌsinˈTHetik/ **adj.**

bi·o·sys·tem·at·ics /ˌbīōˌsistəˈmatiks/ ▶ **plural n.** [treated as sing.] taxonomy based on the study of the genetic evolution of plant and animal populations.
– DERIVATIVES **bi·o·sys·tem·a·tist** /-ˈsistəməˌtist/ **n.**

bi·o·ta /bīˈōtə/ ▶ **n.** Ecology the animal and plant life of a particular region, habitat, or geological period: *the biota of the river*.
– ORIGIN early 20th cent.: modern Latin, from Greek *biotē* 'life.'

bi·o·tech /ˌbīōˈtek, ˈbīōˌtek/ ▶ **n.** informal short for **BIOTECHNOLOGY**.
▶ **adj.** informal genetically modified: *biotech corn*.

bi·o·tech·nol·o·gy /ˌbīōtekˈnäləjē/ ▶ **n.** the exploitation of biological processes for industrial and other purposes, esp. the genetic manipulation of microorganisms for the production of antibiotics, hormones, etc.

bi·o·te·lem·e·try /ˌbīōtəˈlemitrē/ ▶ **n.** the detection or measurement of human or animal physiological functions from a distance using a telemeter: *a review of underwater biotelemetry, with emphasis on ultrasonic techniques*.
– DERIVATIVES **bi·o·tel·e·me·tric** /-ˌteləˈmetrik/ **adj.**

bi·o·ter·ror·ism /ˌbīōˈterəˌrizəm/ ▶ **n.** terrorism involving the release of toxic biological agents.

bi·o·ther·a·py /ˌbīōˈTHerəpē/ ▶ **n.** (pl. **biotherapies**) the treatment of disease using substances obtained or derived from living organisms.

bi·ot·ic /bīˈätik/ ▶ **adj.** of, relating to, or resulting from living things, esp. in their ecological relations: *the preservation of biotic diversity*.
– ORIGIN mid 19th cent.: from French *biotique*, or via late Latin from Greek *biōtikos*, from *bios* 'life.'

bi·o·tin /ˈbīətin/ ▶ **n.** Biochemistry a vitamin of the B complex, found in egg yolk, liver, and yeast. It is involved in the synthesis of fatty acids and glucose. Also called **VITAMIN H**.
– ORIGIN 1930s: coined in German from Greek *bios* 'life' + **-IN**[1].

bi·o·tite /ˈbīəˌtīt/ ▶ **n.** a black, dark brown, or greenish black variety of mica, occurring in many igneous and metamorphic rocks.
– ORIGIN mid 19th cent.: named after Jean-Baptiste *Biot* (1774–1862), French mineralogist.

bi·o·tope /ˈbīəˌtōp/ ▶ **n.** Ecology the region of a habitat associated with a particular ecological community.
– ORIGIN 1920s: from German *Biotop*, based on Greek *topos* 'place.'

bi·o·trans·for·ma·tion /ˌbīōˌtransfərˈmāsHən/ ▶ **n.** the alteration of a substance, such as a drug, within the body.

bi·o·tur·ba·tion /ˌbīōtərˈbāsHən/ ▶ **n.** Geology the disturbance of sedimentary deposits by living organisms.
– DERIVATIVES **bi·o·tur·ba·ted** /-ˈtərbātid/ **adj.**

bi·o·type /ˈbīəˌtīp/ ▶ **n.** a group of organisms having an identical genetic constitution.

bi·o·war·fare /ˌbīōˈwôrˌfe(ə)r/ ▶ **n.** biological warfare, including the use of toxins of biological origin or microorganisms as weapons of war.

bi·o·weap·on /ˈbīōˌwepən/ ▶ **n.** a biological weapon: *fears mount about smallpox as a bioweapon*.

bi·par·ti·san /bīˈpärtəzən/ ▶ **adj.** of or involving the agreement or cooperation of two political parties that usually oppose each other's policies: *educational reform received considerable bipartisan approval*.
– DERIVATIVES **bi·par·ti·san·ship** /-ˌsHip/ **n.**

USAGE See usage at **CROSS-PARTY**.

bi·par·tite /bīˈpärˌtīt/ ▶ **adj.** involving or made by two separate parties: *the bipartite system of elementary and secondary schools*. ■ technical consisting of two parts: *a bipartite uterus*.
– ORIGIN late Middle English (in the sense 'divided into two parts'): from Latin *bipartitus*, past participle of *bipartire*, from *bi-* 'two' + *partire* 'to part.'

bi·ped /ˈbīped/ ▶ **n.** an animal that uses two legs for walking.
▶ **adj.** using two legs for walking.
– ORIGIN mid 17th cent. (earlier (early 17th cent.) as *bipedal*): from Latin *bipes*, *biped-* (from *bi-*'having two' + *pes*, *ped-*'foot').

bi·ped·al /bīˈpedl/ ▶ **adj.** Zoology (of an animal) using only two legs for walking.
– DERIVATIVES **bi·ped·al·ism** /bīˈpedlˌizəm/ **n.**, **bi·pe·dal·i·ty** /ˌbīpiˈdalitē/ **n.**
– ORIGIN early 17th cent.: from Latin *bipes*, *biped-* (from *bi-* 'having two' + *pes*, *ped-* 'foot') + **-AL**.

bi·pha·sic /bīˈfāzik/ ▶ **adj.** technical having two phases: *the patient's biphasic recovery curve*.

bi·phen·yl /bīˈfenl/ ▶ **n.** Chemistry an organic compound containing two phenyl groups bonded together, e.g., the PCBs.

bi·pin·nate /bīˈpinˌāt/ ▶ **adj.** Botany (of a pinnate leaf) having leaflets that are further subdivided in a pinnate arrangement.

bi·plane /ˈbīˌplān/ ▶ **n.** an early type of aircraft with two pairs of wings, one above the other.

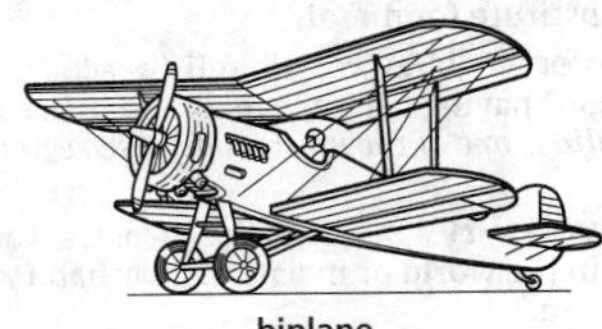

biplane

bi·pod /ˈbīˌpäd/ ▶ **n.** a two-legged stand or support.

bi·po·lar /bīˈpōlər/ ▶ **adj. 1** having or relating to two poles or extremities: *a sharply bipolar division of affluent and underclass*. ■ relating to or occurring in both North and South polar regions: *bipolar species*.
2 (of psychiatric illness) characterized by both manic and depressive episodes, or manic ones only. ■ (of a person) suffering from bipolar disorder.
3 (of a nerve cell) having two axons, one either side of the cell body.
4 Electronics (of a transistor or other device) using both positive and negative charge carriers.
– DERIVATIVES **bi·po·lar·i·ty** /ˌbīpōˈlaritē, -pə-/ **n.**

bi·po·lar dis·or·der ▶ **n.** a mental disorder marked by alternating periods of elation and depression. Also called (esp. formerly) **MANIC DEPRESSION**. Compare with **UNIPOLAR**.

USAGE See usage at **MANIC DEPRESSION**.

bi·ra·cial /bīˈrāsHəl/ ▶ **adj.** concerning or containing members of two racial groups.

bi·ra·mous /bīˈrāməs/ ▶ **adj.** Zoology (esp. of crustacean limbs and antennae) dividing to form two branches.
– ORIGIN late 19th cent.: from **BI-** 'two' + **RAMUS** + **-OUS**.

birch /bərCH/ ▶ **n. 1** (also **birch tree**) a slender, fast-growing tree that has thin bark (often peeling) and bears catkins. Birch trees grow chiefly in north temperate regions, some reaching the northern limit of tree growth. ● Genus *Betula*, family Betulaceae: many species, including the **yellow birch** (*B. alleghaniensis*) of North America. ■ (also **birchwood**) the hard fine-grained pale wood of any of these trees.
2 (**the birch**) chiefly historical a formal punishment in which a person is flogged with a bundle of birch twigs.
▶ **v.** [with obj.] chiefly historical beat (someone) with a bundle of birch twigs as a formal punishment.
– DERIVATIVES **birch·en** /-CHən/ **adj.** (archaic).
– ORIGIN Old English *bierce*, *birce*, of Germanic origin; related to German *Birke*.

birch·bark /ˈbərCHˌbärk/ (also **birch bark**) ▶ **n.** the impervious bark of the North American paper birch, *Betula papyrifera*, used, esp. formerly by American Indians, to make canoes and containers: *stretch the birchbark over a cedar frame* | [as modifier] *birchbark baskets*. ■ a canoe of this material.

Birch·er /ˈbərCHər/ ▶ **n.** a member or supporter of the John Birch Society, a conservative anticommunist American organization founded in 1958.
– ORIGIN from the name of John *Birch*, a Baptist missionary and US Army Air Force officer and called the "first casualty of the Cold War," killed by Chinese communists in 1945.

bird /bərd/ ▶ **n. 1** a warm-blooded egg-laying vertebrate distinguished by the possession of feathers, wings, and a beak and (typically) by being able to fly. ● Class Aves; birds probably evolved in the Jurassic period from small dinosaurs that may already have been warm-blooded. ■ an animal of this type that is hunted for sport or used for food: *carve the bird at the dinner table*. ■ informal an aircraft, spacecraft, satellite, or guided missile: *the crews worked frantically to ready their birds for flight*.
2 [usu. with adj.] informal a person of a specified kind or character: *I'm a pretty tough old bird*. ■ Brit. informal a young woman; a girlfriend.
– PHRASES **a bird in the hand is worth two in the bush** proverb it's better to be content with what you have than to risk losing everything by seeking more. **the birds and the bees** basic facts about sex and

reproduction, as told to a child. **birds of a feather flock together** proverb people of the same sort or with the same tastes and interests will be found together: *these health professionals were birds of a feather*. **eat like a bird** see EAT. **flip someone the bird** informal stick one's middle finger up at someone as a sign of contempt or anger, meaning 'fuck you'. Compare with *give someone the finger* in FINGER. **(strictly) for the birds** informal not worth consideration; unimportant: *this piece of legislation is for the birds*. **give someone the bird** another way of saying FLIP SOMEONE THE BIRD. **have a bird** informal be very shocked or agitated: *the press corps would have a bird if the president-to-be appointed his wife to a real job*. **kill two birds with one stone** see KILL[1]. **a little bird told me** humorous used to say that the speaker knows something but prefers to keep the identity of the informant a secret: *a little bird told me it was your birthday*.
– ORIGIN Old English *brid* 'chick, fledgling,' of unknown origin.

bird band·ing ▶ **n.** the practice of catching birds, marking them with an identifying band around the leg, and then releasing them.
– DERIVATIVES **bird band·er n.**

bird·bath /ˈbərd,baTH/ ▶ **n.** a small basin filled with water for birds to bathe in, typically found in a garden.

bird·brain /ˈbərd,brān/ ▶ **n.** informal an annoyingly stupid and shallow person.
– DERIVATIVES **bird·brained adj.**

bird·cage /ˈbərd,kāj/ ▶ **n.** a cage for pet birds, typically made of wire or cane.

bird call ▶ **n.** a note uttered by a bird for the purpose of contact, alarm, or marking its territory. ■ an instrument imitating such a sound, used esp. by hunters.

bird cher·ry ▶ **n.** a small wild cherry tree or shrub, with bitter black fruit that is eaten by birds.
● Genus *Prunus*, family Rosaceae: many species, including the **pin cherry** (*P. pensylvanica*) of North America.

bird colo·nel ▶ **n.** informal a full colonel.
– ORIGIN mid 20th cent.; from the silver eagle indicating the rank of full colonel.

bird dog ▶ **n.** a gun dog trained to retrieve birds.
■ informal a person whose job involves searching, esp. a talent scout for a sports team.
▶ **v.** (**bird-dog**) [with obj.] search out or pursue with dogged determination: *he ordered the vice president to bird-dog Congress for funds*.

bird·er /ˈbərdər/ ▶ **n.** informal a bird-watcher.

bird flu ▶ **n.** a severe, often fatal flu virus of birds, esp. poultry, that is transmissible from them to humans.

bird·house /ˈbərd,hous/ ▶ **n.** a box, typically made to resemble a house, provided for a bird to make its nest in.

bird·ie /ˈbərdē/ ▶ **n.** (pl. **birdies**) **1** informal a child's term for a bird.
2 Golf a score of one stroke under par at a hole.
▶ **v.** (**birdieing**) [with obj.] Golf play (a hole) with a score of one stroke under par: *she wound up birdieing the hole from 20 feet*.
– ORIGIN late 18th cent.: diminutive of BIRD; the golf term from slang *bird*, denoting any first-rate thing.

bird·ing /ˈbərdiNG/ ▶ **n.** the observation of birds in their natural habitats as a hobby.

bird·lime /ˈbərd,līm/ ▶ **n.** a sticky substance spread on twigs to trap small birds.
▶ **v.** spread with birdlime: *he birdlimed the branch*.
■ catch or trap with birdlime.

bird of par·a·dise ▶ **n.** **1** (pl. **birds of paradise**) a tropical Australasian bird, the male of which is noted for the beauty and brilliance of its plumage and its spectacular courtship display. Most kinds are found in New Guinea, where their feathers are used in ornamental dress. [early 17th cent.: *paradise* suggested by the modern Latin family name *Paradisaeidae* (plural).] ● Family Paradisaeidae: numerous genera.
2 (also **bird of paradise flower**) a southern African plant related to the banana. It bears a showy irregular flower with a long projecting tongue. [late 19th cent.: named from the protrusion of flowers from a green spathe, resembling a bird of paradise in flight.] ● Genus *Strelitzia*, family Strelitziaceae: several species, in particular *S. regina*, whose orange and dark blue flowers are pollinated by a sunbird.

bird of pas·sage ▶ **n.** dated a migratory bird. ■ a person who passes through or visits a place without staying for long.

bird of prey ▶ **n.** a predatory bird, distinguished by a hooked bill and sharp talons; a raptor. ● Orders Falconiformes (the diurnal birds of prey) and Strigiformes (the owls).

bird pep·per ▶ **n.** a tropical American pepper thought to be the ancestor of both sweet and chili peppers. ● *Capsicum annuum* var. glabriusculum (or *C. frutescens* var. *typicum*), family Solanaceae. ■ the small, red, very hot fruit of this plant. ■ a variety of small hot pepper grown in Asia or Africa.

bird·seed /ˈbərd,sēd/ ▶ **n.** any seed or blend of seed for feeding birds.

Birds·eye /ˈbərd,zī/, Clarence (1886–1956), US businessman and inventor. A former fur trader, he had observed food preservation techniques practiced by the people of Labrador. He developed a process of rapidly freezing foods in small packages that were suitable for retail sale and created a revolution in eating habits.

bird's-eye ▶ **n.** **1** [usu. as modifier] any of a number of plants with small flowers that have contrasting petals and centers, in particular: ● (also **bird's-eye primrose**) a primrose with yellow-centered purple flowers (*Primula farinosa*, family Primulaceae).
● (also **bird's-eye speedwell**) a speedwell with bright blue flowers,also known as GERMANDER SPEEDWELL.
2 (also **bird's-eye chili** or **bird's-eye pepper**) a small, very hot chili pepper.
3 a small geometric pattern woven with a dot in the center, typically used in suiting and lining fabrics.

bird's-eye ma·ple ▶ **n.** the lumber from an American maple, typically the sugar maple, that contains eyelike markings, used in decorative woodwork.

bird's-eye view ▶ **n.** a general view from above, or as if from above.

bird's-foot tre·foil (also **birdsfoot trefoil**) ▶ **n.** a small plant of the pea family with leaves that consist of three leaflets, yellow flowers streaked with red, and triple pods that resemble the feet of a bird.
● *Lotus corniculatus*, family Leguminosae.

bird·shot /ˈbərd,SHät/ ▶ **n.** the smallest size of shot for shotguns.

bird's-nest ▶ **n.** **1** a North American brownish or yellowish flowering plant of the wintergreen family, with scalelike leaves. The bird's-nest is a saprophyte that lacks chlorophyll. Also called **giant bird's-nest**.
● *Pterospora andromeda*, family Monotropaceae.
2 (also **bird's-nest fungus**) a fungus of worldwide distribution that grows on dead wood and other plant debris. It produces a small bowl-shaped fruiting body that opens to reveal egg-shaped organs containing the spores. ● Family Nidulariaceae, class Basidiomycetes: several genera and species, including the common *Crucibulum levis*.

bird's-nest or·chid ▶ **n.** a European woodland orchid that lacks chlorophyll, the whole plant being yellowish-brown. It obtains nourishment by linking its nestlike mass of thick roots to a soil-dwelling fungus from which it absorbs nutrients. ● *Neottia nidus-avis*, family Orchidaceae.

bird's nest soup ▶ **n.** a Chinese soup made from the dried gelatinous coating of the nests of swifts and other birds.

bird·song /ˈbərd,sôNG/ ▶ **n.** the musical vocalizations of a bird or birds, typically uttered by a male songbird in characteristic bursts or phrases for territorial purposes.

bird strike ▶ **n.** a collision between a bird or flock of birds and an aircraft.

bird-watch·er (also **birdwatcher**) ▶ **n.** a person who observes birds in their natural surroundings as a hobby.
– DERIVATIVES **bird-watch·ing n.**

bi·re·frin·gent /,bīriˈfrinjənt/ ▶ **adj.** Physics having two different refractive indices.
– DERIVATIVES **bi·re·frin·gence n.**

bi·reme /ˈbī,rēm/ ▶ **n.** an ancient warship with two files of oarsmen on each side.
– ORIGIN late 16th cent.: from Latin *biremis*, from *bi-* 'having two' + *remus* 'oar.'

bi·ret·ta /bəˈretə/ (also **beretta**) ▶ **n.** a square cap with three flat projections on top, worn by Roman Catholic clergymen.
– ORIGIN late 16th cent.: from Italian *berretta* or Spanish *birreta*, based on late Latin *birrus* 'hooded cape.' Compare with BERET.

Bir·git·ta, St. /birˈgitə/ see BRIDGET, ST.[2]

bi·ri /ˈbi(ə)rē/ ▶ **n.** (pl. **biris**) variant spelling of BIDI.

bi·ri·a·ni /,birēˈänē/ ▶ **n.** variant spelling of BIRYANI.

Bir·ken·head /ˈbərkən,hed/ a town in northwestern England on the Wirral Peninsula on the Mersey River, opposite Liverpool; pop. 79,700 (est. 2009).

Bir·ken·stock /ˈbərkən,stäk/ ▶ **n.** trademark a type of shoe or sandal with a contoured cork-filled sole and a thick leather upper. ■ [as modifier] denoting people concerned with political correctness or conservationist issues: *home builders are no longer content to leave environmentalism to the Birkenstock crowd*.
– ORIGIN 1970s: from the name of the manufacturer.

Bir·man /ˈbərmən/ ▶ **n.** a cat of a long-haired breed, typically with a cream body, a dark head, tail, and legs, and white paws.

b

Bir·ming·ham 1 /ˈbərmiNG,ham/ an industrial city in north central Alabama; pop. 228,798 (est. 2008).
2 /ˈbərmiNGəm/ an industrial city in west central England; pop. 945,700 (est. 2009).

birr /bər/ ▶ **n.** the basic monetary unit of Ethiopia, equal to 100 cents.
– ORIGIN from Amharic.

birth /bərTH/ ▶ **n.** the emergence of a baby or other young from the body of its mother; the start of life as a physically separate being: *he was blind from birth* | *despite a difficult birth he's fit and healthy*. ■ the beginning or coming into existence of something: *the birth of democracy*. ■ a person's origin, descent, or ancestry: *the mother is American by birth* | *he is not of noble birth*.
▶ **v.** [with obj.] informal give birth to (a baby or other young): *she had carried him and birthed him* | [no obj.] *in spring the cows birthed*.
– PHRASES **give birth** bear a child or young: *she's due to give birth in March* | *she gave* **birth to** *a son*.
– ORIGIN Middle English: from Old Norse *byrth*; related to BEAR[1].

birth ca·nal ▶ **n.** the passageway from the womb through the cervix, the vagina, and the vulva through which a fetus passes during birth.

birth cer·tif·i·cate ▶ **n.** an official document issued to record a person's birth, including such identifying data as name, gender, date of birth, place of birth, and parentage.

birth con·trol ▶ **n.** the practice of preventing unwanted pregnancies, typically by use of contraception.

birth con·trol pill ▶ **n.** a contraceptive pill.

birth·date /ˈbərTH,dāt/ ▶ **n.** the date on which a person was born: *her baptismal record puts her birthdate as April 26, 1741*.

birth·day /ˈbərTH,dā/ ▶ **n.** the annual anniversary of the day on which a person was born, typically treated as an occasion for celebration and present-giving: *I'm getting a dollhouse for my birthday* | [as modifier] *a birthday cake* | *the birthday boy*. ■ the day of one's birth: *she shares a birthday with Paul McCartney*. ■ the anniversary of something starting or being founded: *the staff celebrated the twenty-fifth birthday of the paper*.
– PHRASES **in one's birthday suit** humorous naked.

birth de·fect ▶ **n.** a physical or biochemical abnormality that is present at birth and that may be inherited or the result of environmental influence.

birth fam·i·ly ▶ **n.** one's biological parents and siblings, as opposed to adoptive relatives.

birth·ing /ˈbərTHiNG/ ▶ **n.** the action or process of giving birth: [as modifier] *a birthing pool*.

birth·ing cen·ter ▶ **n.** a medical facility, specializing in childbirth, that is less restrictive and more homelike than a hospital.

birth·ing room ▶ **n.** a room in a hospital or other medical facility that is equipped for labor and childbirth and is designed to be comfortable and homelike.

birth·mark /ˈbərTH,märk/ ▶ **n.** an unusual and typically permanent brown or red mark on someone's body from birth.

birth moth·er ▶ **n.** a woman who has given birth to a child, as opposed to an adoptive mother; a biological mother.

birth pang ▶ **n.** [usu. in pl.] another term for LABOR PAIN.

birth par·ent ▶ **n.** a biological as opposed to an adoptive parent.

birth·place /ˈbərTH,plās/ ▶ **n.** the place where a person was born. ■ the place where something started or originated: *Florence was the birthplace of the Renaissance*.

birth rate ▶ **n.** the number of live births per thousand of population per year.

birth·right /ˈbərTH,rīt/ ▶ **n.** a particular right of possession or privilege one has from birth, esp. as an eldest child. ■ a natural or moral right, possessed by everyone: *she saw a liberal education as the birthright of every child*.

birth·stone /ˈbərTH,stōn/ ▶ **n.** a gemstone popularly associated with the month or astrological sign of one's birth.

b

birth·weight /ˈbərTH,wāt/ ▶ n. the weight of a baby at birth.

birth·wort /ˈbərTH,wərt, -,wôrt/ ▶ n. a climbing or herbaceous plant that typically has heart-shaped leaves and deep-throated, often pipe-shaped, flowers. It was formerly used as an aid to childbirth and to induce abortion. ● Genus *Aristolochia*, family Aristolochiaceae.

bi·ry·a·ni /,birēˈänē/ (also **biriani**) ▶ n. an Indian dish made with highly seasoned rice and meat, fish, or vegetables.
– ORIGIN Urdu, from Persian *biryānī*, from *biriyān* 'fried, grilled.'

bis /bis/ ▶ adv. again, as a direction in a musical score indicating that a passage is to be repeated.
– ORIGIN via French and Italian from Latin, literally 'twice.'

bis- ▶ comb. form Chemistry used to form the names of compounds containing two groups identically substituted or coordinated: *bis(2-aminoethyl) ether*.

Bis·bee /ˈbizbē/ a town in southeastern Arizona, near the Mexican border; pop. 5,991 (est. 2008). An artists' colony, it was a copper mining center in the early 1900s and is noted as the source of ***Bisbee turquoise***, an incidental byproduct of the copper mining.

Bis·cay, Bay of /ˈbis,kā/ a part of the North Atlantic Ocean between the northern coast of Spain and the western coast of France, noted for its strong currents and storms.

Bis·cayne Bay /bisˈkān/ an inlet of the Atlantic Ocean in southeastern Florida, south of Miami, noted for its islands and resorts.

bis·cot·ti /biˈskätē/ ▶ plural n. small, crisp rectangular twice-baked cookies typically containing nuts, made originally in Italy.
– ORIGIN Italian.

bis·cuit /ˈbiskit/ ▶ n. **1** a small, typically round cake of bread leavened with baking powder, baking soda, or sometimes yeast. ■ Brit. a cookie or cracker.
2 another term for BISQUE[3]: [as modifier] *biscuit ware*.
3 a light brown color.
4 a small flat piece of wood used to join two mortised planks together.
▶ adj. light brown in color.
– DERIVATIVES **bis·cuit·y** adj.
– ORIGIN Middle English: from Old French *bescuit*, based on Latin *bis* 'twice' + *coctus*, past participle of *coquere* 'to cook' (so named because originally biscuits were cooked in a twofold process: first baked and then dried out in a slow oven so that they would keep).

bi·sect /bīˈsekt, ˈbī,sekt/ ▶ v. [with obj.] divide into two parts: *a landscape of farmland bisected by long straight roads*. ■ Geometry divide (a line, angle, shape, etc.) into two equal parts.
– DERIVATIVES **bi·sec·tion** /bīˈsekSHən/ n., **bi·sec·tor** /bīˈsektər, ˈbī,sek-/ n.
– ORIGIN mid 17th cent.: from BI- 'two' + Latin *sect-* (from *secare* 'to cut').

bi·se·ri·al /bīˈsi(ə)rēəl/ ▶ adj. Statistics referring to the correlation between two sets measurements, one of which is dichotomous. ■ Botany & Zoology arranged in or consisting of two series or rows.

bi·sex·u·al /bīˈsekSHo͞oəl/ ▶ adj. sexually attracted to both men and women. ■ Biology having characteristics of both sexes.
▶ n. a person who is sexually attracted to both men and women.
– DERIVATIVES **bi·sex·u·al·i·ty** /,bīsekSHo͞oˈalitē/ n.

Bish·kek /biSHˈkek/ the capital of Kyrgyzstan; pop. 837,000 (est. 2007). From 1926 to 1991, the city was named Frunze. Former name (until 1926) PISHPEK.

Bish·op /ˈbiSHəp/, Elizabeth (1911–79), US poet. Her poetry contrasts her experiences in South America 1952–67 with her New England origins. She was awarded the Pulitzer Prize for her first two collections, *North and South* (1946) and *A Cold Spring* (1955). Other notable works include *Geography III* (1976).

bish·op /ˈbiSHəp/ ▶ n. **1** a senior member of the Christian clergy, typically in charge of a diocese and empowered to confer holy orders.
2 (also **bishop bird**) an African weaverbird, the male of which has red, orange, yellow, or black plumage. ● Genus *Euplectes*, family Ploceidae: several species, including the **red bishop** (*E. orix*), which has scarlet plumage with a black face and underparts.
3 a chess piece, typically with its top shaped like a miter, that can move in any direction along a diagonal on which it stands. Each player starts the game with two bishops, one moving on white squares and the other on black.
4 mulled and spiced wine.
– ORIGIN Old English *biscop, bisceop*, based on Greek *episkopos* 'overseer,' from *epi* 'above' + *-skopos* '-looking.'

bish·op·ric /ˈbiSHəprik/ ▶ n. the office or rank of a bishop. ■ a district under a bishop's control; a diocese.
– ORIGIN Old English *bisceoprīce*, from *bisceop* (see BISHOP) + *rīce* 'realm.'

Bis·la·ma /bisˈlämə/ ▶ n. an English-based pidgin language used as a lingua franca in Fiji and the Solomon Islands and as an official language in Vanuatu. Also called BEACH-LA-MAR.
– ORIGIN alteration of Portuguese *bicho do mar* 'sea cucumber' (traded as a commodity, the word later being applied to the language of trade). Compare with BÊCHE-DE-MER.

Bis·marck[1] /ˈbiz,märk/ the capital of North Dakota, in the south central part of the state, on the Missouri River; pop. 60,389 (est. 2008). It took the name of German Chancellor Bismarck in order to attract German capital for railroad building.

Bis·marck[2], Otto Eduard Leopold von, Prince of Bismarck, Duke of Lauenburg (1815–98), Prussian minister and German statesman; chancellor of the German Empire 1871–90; also known as the **Iron Chancellor**. He was the driving force behind the unification of Germany and orchestrated wars with Denmark 1864, Austria 1866, and France 1870–71 in order to achieve this end.

Bis·marck Ar·chi·pel·a·go an island group in the western Pacific Ocean, part of Papua New Guinea. Held by Germany from 1884 to World War I, it includes New Britain, New Ireland, and several hundred other islands.

Bis·marck Sea an arm of the Pacific Ocean, northeast of New Guinea and north of New Britain. In March 1943, the US destroyed a large Japanese naval force in these waters.

bis·mil·lah /bisˈmilə/ ▶ exclam. in the name of Allah (an invocation used by Muslims at the beginning of any undertaking).
– ORIGIN from Arabic *bi-smi-llāh(i)*, the first phrase of the Koran.

bis·muth /ˈbizməTH/ ▶ n. the chemical element of atomic number 83, a brittle reddish-gray metal. (Symbol: **Bi**) ■ a compound of this element used medicinally.
– ORIGIN mid 17th cent.: from modern Latin *bisemutum*, Latinization of German *Wismut*, of unknown origin.

bi·son /ˈbīsən, -zən/ ▶ n. (pl. **same**) a humpbacked shaggy-haired wild ox native to North America and Europe. ● Genus *Bison*, family Bovidae: *B. bison* of North American prairies (also called BUFFALO), and *B. bonasus* of European forests (also called WISENT), now found only in Poland. These are sometimes regarded as a single species.
– ORIGIN late Middle English: from Latin, ultimately of Germanic origin and related to WISENT.

bis·phe·nol A /bisˈfēnôl/ ▶ n. Chemistry a synthetic organic compound used in the manufacture of epoxy resins and other polymers. ● A bicyclic phenol; chem. formula: $C(CH_3)_2(C_6H_4OH)_2$.

bisque[1] /bisk/ ▶ n. a rich, creamy soup typically made with shellfish, esp. lobster.
– ORIGIN mid 17th cent.: French, literally 'crayfish soup.'

bisque[2] ▶ n. an extra turn, point, or stroke allowed to a weaker player in croquet or court tennis.
– ORIGIN mid 17th cent. (originally a term in court tennis): from French, of unknown ultimate origin.

bisque[3] ▶ n. **1** fired unglazed pottery: *using bisque for doll heads* | [as modifier] *bisque figurines*.
2 a light brown color: *shades of bisque, taupe, and chocolate brown*.
▶ adj. light brown in color.

Bis·sau /biˈsou/ the capital of Guinea-Bissau, in the western part of the country; pop. 330,000 (est. 2007).

bi·sta·ble /bīˈstābəl/ ▶ n. an electronic circuit that has two stable states.
▶ adj. (of a system) having two stable states.

bis·ter /ˈbistər/ (also **bistre**) ▶ n. a brownish-yellowish pigment made from the soot of burned wood. ■ the color of this pigment.
– ORIGIN early 18th cent.: from French *bistre*, of unknown origin.

bis·tort /ˈbistôrt/ ▶ n. a Eurasian herbaceous plant with a spike of flesh-colored flowers and twisted root that is sometimes used medicinally. ● Genus *Polygonum*, family Polygonaceae: several species, in particular *P. bistorta*.
– ORIGIN early 16th cent.: from French *bistorte* or medieval Latin *bistorta*, from *bis* 'twice' + *torta* (feminine past participle of *torquere* 'to twist').

bis·tou·ry /ˈbistərē/ ▶ n. (pl. **bistouries**) a surgical knife with a long, narrow, straight or curved blade.
– ORIGIN mid 18th cent.: from French *bistouri*, originally *bistorie* 'dagger,' of unknown origin.

bis·tro /ˈbistrō, ˈbē-/ ▶ n. (pl. **bistros**) a small restaurant.
– ORIGIN 1920s: French; perhaps related to *bistouille*, a colloquial term meaning 'bad alcohol,' perhaps from Russian *bystro* 'rapidly.'

bi·sul·fate /bīˈsəl,fāt/ (chiefly Brit. also **bisulphate**) ▶ n. Chemistry a salt of the anion HSO_4^-.

bi·sul·fide /bīˈsəl,fīd/ (chiefly Brit. **bisulphide**) ▶ n. another term for DISULFIDE.

bi·sul·fite /bīˈsəl,fīt/ (chiefly Brit. also **bisulphite**) ▶ n. an acid sulfite containing the radical HSO_3.

bit[1] /bit/ ▶ n. **1** a small piece, part, or quantity of something: *give the duck **a bit of** bread* | *he read bits of his work to me*. ■ **(a bit)** a fair amount: *there's a bit to talk about there*. ■ **(a bit)** a short time or distance: *I fell asleep for a bit*. ■ [with adj.] informal a set of actions or ideas associated with a specific group or activity: *she's gone off to do her theatrical bit*.
2 informal, dated a unit of 12½ cents (used only in even multiples): *the sideshow admission was twenty-five cents, two bits, the fourth of a dollar*.
– PHRASES **a bit** somewhat; to some extent: *he came back looking a bit annoyed*. **bit by bit** gradually: *the school was built bit by bit over the years*. **a bit of a —** used to suggest that something is not severe or extreme, or is true only to a limited extent: *he's a bit of a womanizer*. ■ only a little —; a mere —: *we went on a bit of a walk*. **bits and pieces** an assortment of small items: *weird bits and pieces of paraphernalia*. **do one's bit** informal make a useful contribution to an effort or cause: *she was keen to do her bit to help others*. **every bit as** see EVERY. **not a bit** not at all: *I'm not a bit tired*. **to bits 1** into pieces: *he smashed it to bits with a hammer*. **2** informal very much; to a great degree: *we've got two great kids whom I love to bits*.
– ORIGIN Old English *bita* 'bite, mouthful,' of Germanic origin; related to German *Bissen*, also to BITE.

bit[2] past of BITE.

bit[3] ▶ n. **1** a mouthpiece, typically made of metal, that is attached to a bridle and used to control a horse.
2 a tool or piece for boring or drilling, typically of metal: *a drill bit*. ■ the cutting or gripping part of a plane, pliers, or other tool. ■ the part of a key that engages with the lock lever. ■ the copper head of a soldering iron.
▶ v. [with obj.] put a bit into the mouth of (a horse). ■ restrain: *my own hysteria was bitted by upbringing and respect*.
– PHRASES **above the bit** (of a horse) carrying its head too high so that it evades correct contact with the bit. **behind the bit** (of a horse) carrying its head with the chin tucked in so that it evades contact with the bit. **off the bit** (or **bridle**) (of a horse) ridden on a loose rein to allow it to gallop freely, esp. at the end of a race. **on the bit** (or **bridle**) (of a horse) ridden with a light but firm contact on the mouth, and accepting the bit in a calm and relaxed manner. **take** (or **get** or **have**) **the bit in** (or **between**) **one's teeth** begin to tackle a problem or task in a determined or independent way.
– DERIVATIVES **bit·ted** adj. [in combination] *a double-bitted ax*.
– ORIGIN Old English *bite* 'biting, a bite,' of Germanic origin; related to Dutch *beet* and German *Biss*, also to BITE.

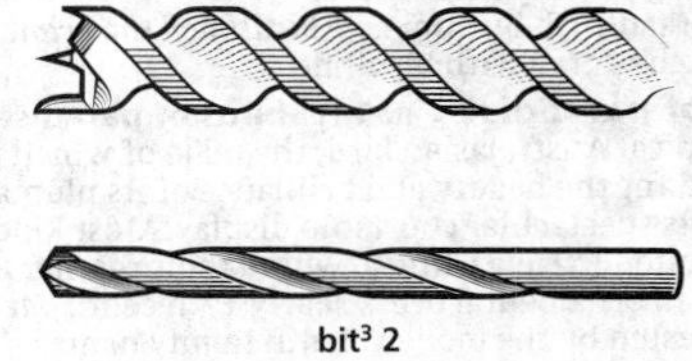

bit[3] 2

bit[4] ▶ n. Computing a unit of information expressed as either a 0 or 1 in binary notation.
– ORIGIN 1940s: blend of BINARY and DIGIT.

bi·tar·trate /bīˈtär,trāt/ ▶ n. an acid tartrate containing the radical $C_4H_5O_6$.

bitch /biCH/ ▶ n. **1** a female dog, wolf, fox, or otter.
2 informal, derogatory a spiteful or unpleasant woman. ■ black slang a woman. ■ a person who is completely subservient to another: *he will always be her bitch*.
3 (a bitch) informal a difficult or unpleasant situation or thing: *the stove is a bitch to fix*.
4 informal a complaint: *my big bitch is that there's nothing new here*.
▶ v. [no obj.] informal express displeasure; grumble: *they bitch about everything* | (as noun **bitching**) *we're tired of your bitching*.
– ORIGIN Old English *bicce*, of Germanic origin.

bitch·er·y /ˈbiCHərē/ ▶ **n.** bitchy behavior.

bitch·ing /ˈbiCHiNG/ (also **bitchen** or **bitchin'** /ˈbiCHən/) ▶ **adj.** informal excellent: *a bitching new album.*
▶ **adv.** [as submodifier] extremely: *it's bitchin' hot, ain't it?*

bitch-slap ▶ **v.** (**bitch-slaps, bitch-slapping, bitch-slapped**) informal [with obj.] deliver a stinging blow to (someone), typically in order to humiliate them: *I'd bitch-slap her too if she mouthed off to me like that.*
–ORIGIN 1990s: originally black English, referring to a woman hitting or haranguing her male partner.

bitch·y /ˈbiCHē/ informal ▶ **adj.** (**bitchier, bitchiest**) (of a person's comments or behavior) malicious or unpleasant: *bitchy remarks.*
–DERIVATIVES **bitch·i·ly** /ˈbiCHəlē/ **adv.**, **bitch·i·ness n.**

bite /bīt/ ▶ **v.** (past **bit** /bit/; past participle **bitten** /ˈbitn/) [no obj.] **1** (of a person or animal) use the teeth to cut into something in order to eat it: *Rosa bit into a cupcake* | [with obj.] *he bit a mouthful from the sandwich.* ■ [with obj.] (of an animal or a person) use the teeth in order to inflict injury on: *she had bitten, scratched, and kicked her assailant.* ■ [with obj.] (of a snake, insect, or spider) wound with fangs, pincers, or a sting: *she was bitten by an adder.* ■ (**bite at**) (of an animal) snap at; attempt to bite: *it is not unusual for this dog to bite at its owner's hand.* ■ (of an acid) corrode a surface: *chemicals have bitten deep into the stone.* ■ (of a fish) take the bait or lure on the end of a fishing line into the mouth. ■ (of a person) be persuaded to accept a deal or offer: *a hundred or so retailers should bite.*
2 (of a tool, tire, boot, etc.) grip a surface: *once on the wet grass, my boots failed to bite.* ■ (of an object) press into a part of the body, causing pain: *the handcuffs bit into his wrists.* ■ cause emotional pain: *Cheryl's betrayal had bitten deep.* ■ (of a policy or situation) take effect, with unpleasant consequences: *when the cuts in art education start to bite.* ■ informal be very bad, unpleasant, or unfortunate: *it bites that your mom won't let you go.*
▶ **n. 1** an act of biting into something in order to eat it: *Stephen ate a hot dog in three big bites.* ■ a piece cut off by biting: *Robyn took a large bite out of her sandwich.* ■ informal a quick snack: *I plan to stop off in the village and have a bite to eat.* ■ a small morsel of prepared food, intended to constitute one mouthful: *minced bacon bites with cheese.* ■ a short piece of information: *snack-sized bites of information.* See also SOUND BITE. ■ a wound inflicted by an animal's or a person's teeth: *Perry's dog had given her a nasty bite.* ■ a wound inflicted by a snake, insect, or spider: *his face was covered in mosquito bites.* ■ an act of bait being taken by a fish: *by four o'clock he still hadn't had a single bite.* ■ Dentistry the bringing together of the teeth in occlusion. ■ Dentistry the imprint of this in a plastic material.
2 a sharp or pungent flavor: *a fresh, lemony bite.* ■ incisiveness or cogency of style: *his colorful characterizations brought added bite to the story.* ■ a feeling of cold in the air or wind: *by early October there's a bite in the air.*
–PHRASES **one's bark is worse than one's bite** proverb said of someone whose fierce and intimidating manner is not felt by the speaker to reflect the person's nature. **be bitten by the —— bug** develop a passionate interest in a specified activity: *Joe was bitten by the showbiz bug at the age of four.* **bite the big one** informal die. **bite the bullet** decide to do something difficult or unpleasant that one has been putting off or hesitating over. [from the old custom of giving wounded soldiers a bullet to bite on when undergoing surgery without anesthetic.] **bite the dust** informal be killed: *and the bad guys bite the dust with lead in their bellies.* ■ fail; come to an end: *she hoped the new program would not bite the dust for lack of funding.* **bite the hand that feeds one** deliberately hurt or offend a benefactor. **bite someone's head off** see HEAD. **bite one's lip** dig one's front teeth into one's lip in embarrassment, grief, or annoyance, to prevent oneself from saying something, or to control oneself when experiencing physical pain: *he could have mocked Carol's obnoxious behavior, but he bit his lip.* **bite off more than one can chew** take on a commitment one cannot fulfill. **bite one's tongue** make a desperate effort to avoid saying something: *I had to bite my tongue and accept his explanation.* **one could have bitten one's tongue off** used to show that someone profoundly and immediately regrets having said something. **once bitten, twice shy** proverb an unpleasant experience induces caution. **put the bite on** informal borrow or extort money from. [1930s: *bite* in the slang sense 'cadging.'] **take a bite out of** informal reduce by a significant amount: *insurance costs that can take a bite out of your retirement funds.*
–PHRASAL VERBS **bite something back** refrain with difficulty from saying something, making a sound, or expressing an emotion: *Melissa bit back a scathing comment.*
–DERIVATIVES **bit·er n.**
–ORIGIN Old English *bītan*, of Germanic origin; related to Dutch *bijten* and German *beissen*.

bite-sized (also **bite-size**) ▶ **adj.** (of a piece of food) small enough to be eaten in one mouthful: *cut the potatoes into bite-sized pieces.* ■ informal very small or short: *a series of bite-sized essays.*

bite·wing /ˈbīt,wiNG/ ▶ **n.** a dental film for X-raying the crowns of upper and lower teeth simultaneously and that is held in place by a tab between the teeth.

bit·ing /ˈbītiNG/ ▶ **adj.** (of insects and certain other animals) able to wound the skin with a sting or fangs: *ridding the premises of biting red ants.* ■ (of wind or cold) so cold as to be painful: *he leaned forward to protect himself against the biting wind.* ■ (of wit or criticism) harsh or cruel: *his biting satire on corruption and power.*
–DERIVATIVES **bit·ing·ly adv.**

bit·ing midge ▶ **n.** a very small fly that typically occurs in large swarms. The female has piercing mouthparts and feeds on the blood of a variety of animals including humans. ● Family Ceratopogonidae: numerous genera and species, including the punkie (*Culicoides* and related genera).

bit·map /ˈbit,map/ Computing ▶ **n.** a representation in which each item corresponds to one or more bits of information, esp. the information used to control the display of a computer screen.
▶ **v.** (**bitmaps, bitmapping, bitmapped**) [with obj.] represent (an item) as a bitmap.

BITNET /ˈbit,net/ (also **Bitnet**) trademark a data transmission network founded in 1981 to link North American academic institutions and to interconnect with other information networks.

bi·ton·al /bīˈtōnl/ ▶ **adj.** (of music) having parts in two different keys sounding together.
–DERIVATIVES **bi·ton·al·i·ty n.**

bit part ▶ **n.** a small acting role in a play or a movie.

bit rate ▶ **n.** Electronics the number of bits per second that can be transmitted along a digital network.

bit·stream /ˈbit,strēm/ ▶ **n.** Electronics a stream of data in binary form. ■ (**Bitstream**) trademark a system of digital-to-analog signal conversion used in some audio CD players, in which the signal from the CD is digitally processed to give a signal at a higher frequency before being converted to an analog signal.

bitt /bit/ ▶ **n.** [usu. in pl.] any of the posts fixed in pairs on the deck of a ship, for fastening cables, belaying ropes, etc.
▶ **v.** [with obj.] coil or fasten around the bitts.

bit·ten /ˈbitn/ past participle of BITE.

bit·ter /ˈbitər/ ▶ **adj. 1** having a sharp, pungent taste or smell; not sweet: *the raw berries have an intensely bitter flavor.* ■ (of chocolate) dark and unsweetened.
2 (of people or their feelings or behavior) angry, hurt, or resentful because of one's bad experiences or a sense of unjust treatment: *I don't feel jealous or bitter.* ■ (of a conflict, argument, or opponent) full of anger and acrimony: *a bitter, five-year legal battle.*
3 (often used for emphasis) painful or unpleasant to accept or contemplate: *today's decision has come as a bitter blow.*
4 (of wind, cold, or weather) intensely cold: *a bitter wind blowing from the east.*
▶ **n. 1** Brit. beer that is strongly flavored with hops and has a bitter taste.
2 (**bitters**) [treated as sing.] liquor that is flavored with the sharp pungent taste of plant extracts and is used as an additive in cocktails or as a medicinal substance to promote appetite or digestion.
–PHRASES **to the bitter end** used to say that one will continue doing something until it is finished, no matter what: *the workers would fight to the bitter end for safer conditions.* [perhaps associated with a nautical word *bitter* denoting the last part of a cable inboard of the BITTS, perhaps influenced by the biblical phrase 'her end is bitter as wormwood' (Prov. 5:4).]
–DERIVATIVES **bit·ter·ly adv.**
–ORIGIN Old English *biter*, of Germanic origin; related to Dutch and German *bitter*, and probably to BITE.

bit·ter al·mond ▶ **n.** see ALMOND (sense 2 of the noun).

bit·ter al·oes ▶ **n.** see ALOE.

bit·ter ap·ple ▶ **n.** another term for COLOCYNTH.

bit·ter·cress /ˈbitər,kres/ ▶ **n.** a plant with small white flowers that grows widely as a weed of temperate areas, esp. in damp soils. ● Genus *Cardamine*, family Brassicaceae: several species, in particular the **Pennsylvania bittercress** (*C. pensylvanica*) of North America.

bit·ter·end·er ▶ **n.** a person who holds out until the end no matter what.

bit·ter gourd ▶ **n.** another term for BITTER MELON.

bit·ter greens ▶ **plural n.** mixed green leaves of a variety of salad vegetables with a bitter taste, such as kale, mustard, collard, endive, chicory, or spinach.

b

bit·ter mel·on ▶ **n.** a warty, green-colored, unripe fruit of an annual tropical vine, used in Asian cooking and for its medicinal properties. Also called BITTER GOURD. ■ the widespread plant of the gourd family that produces this fruit. ● *Momordica charantia*, family Cucurbitaceae.

bit·tern[1] /ˈbitərn/ ▶ **n.** a large marsh bird of the heron family, typically smaller than a heron, with brown streaked plumage. The larger kinds are noted for the deep booming call of the male in the breeding season. ● Genera *Botaurus* and *Ixobrychus*, family Ardeidae: several species, esp. the **American bittern** (*B. lentiginosus*) and the **least bittern** (*I. exilis*).
–ORIGIN late Middle English *bitore*, from Old French *butor*, based on Latin *butio* 'bittern' + *taurus* 'bull' (because of its call). The *-n* was added in the 16th cent., perhaps by association with *hern*, obsolete variant of HERON.

bit·tern[2] (also **bitterns**) ▶ **n.** a concentrated solution of various salts remaining after the crystallization of salt from seawater.
–ORIGIN late 17th cent.: probably from the adjective BITTER.

bit·ter·ness /ˈbitərnis/ ▶ **n. 1** sharpness of taste; lack of sweetness: *the lime juice imparts a slight bitterness.*
2 anger and disappointment at being treated unfairly; resentment: *he expressed bitterness over his dismissal without notice.*

bit·ter or·ange ▶ **n.** another term for SEVILLE ORANGE.

bit·ter·root /ˈbitər,ro͞ot, -,ro͝ot/ ▶ **n.** a plant of the purslane family with showy pinkish-white flowers on short stems. Found throughout the rocky areas of western North America, it is particularly abundant in Montana, of which it is the state flower. ● *Lewisia rediviva*, family Portulacaceae.

Bit·ter·root Range part of the Rocky Mountains in western Montana and eastern Idaho.

bit·ter rot ▶ **n.** a disease of apples, characterized by sunken brown spots, caused by the fungus *Glomerella cingulata*.

bit·ter·sweet /ˈbitər,swēt/ ▶ **adj.** (of food, drink, or flavor) sweet with a bitter aftertaste. ■ arousing pleasure tinged with sadness or pain: *the room, with all its bittersweet memories.*
▶ **n. 1** another term for woody nightshade (see NIGHTSHADE).
2 (also **climbing bittersweet**) a vinelike climbing plant that bears clusters of bright orange pods. ● Genus *Celastrus*, family Celastraceae: several species, in particular *C. scandens*.

Bit·Tor·rent /ˈbit,tôrənt/ ▶ **n.** Computing, trademark a peer-to-peer file transfer protocol for sharing large amounts of data over the Internet, in which each part of a file downloaded by a user is transferred to other users.
–ORIGIN early 21st cent.: blend of BIT[4] and TORRENT.

bitts /bits/ ▶ **plural n.** a pair of posts on the deck of a ship for fastening mooring lines or cables.
–ORIGIN Middle English: probably of Low German origin.

bit·ty /ˈbitē/ informal ▶ **adj.** (**bittier, bittiest**) tiny: *a little bitty house.*
–DERIVATIVES **bit·ti·ly** /ˈbitəlē/ **adv.**, **bit·ti·ness n.**

bi·tu·men /biˈt(y)o͞omən, bī-/ ▶ **n.** a black viscous mixture of hydrocarbons obtained naturally or as a residue from petroleum distillation. It is used for road surfacing and roofing.
–ORIGIN late Middle English (denoting naturally occurring asphalt used as mortar): from Latin.

bi·tu·mi·nize /biˈt(y)o͞omə,nīz, bī-/ ▶ **v.** [with obj.] convert into, impregnate with, or cover with bitumen.
–DERIVATIVES **bi·tu·mi·ni·za·tion** /-,t(y)o͞oməniˈzāSHən/ **n.**

bi·tu·mi·nous /biˈt(y)o͞omənəs, bī-/ ▶ **adj.** [attrib.] of, containing, or of the nature of bitumen.
–ORIGIN mid 16th cent.: from French *bitumineux*, from Latin *bituminosus*.

bi·tu·mi·nous coal ▶ **n.** black coal having a relatively high volatile content. It burns with a characteristically bright smoky flame.

b

bit·wise /ˈbit,wīz/ ▶ **adj.** Computing designating an operator in a programming language that manipulates the individual bits in a byte or word.

bi·va·lence /bīˈvāləns/ ▶ **n.** Logic the existence of only two states or truth values (e.g., true and false).

bi·va·lent /bīˈvālənt/ ▶ **adj.** **1** Biology (of homologous chromosomes) associated in pairs.
2 Chemistry another term for **DIVALENT**.
▶ **n.** Biology a pair of homologous chromosomes.
– ORIGIN mid 19th cent.: from **BI-** 'two' + Latin *valent-* 'being strong' (from the verb *valere*).

bi·valve /ˈbī,valv/ ▶ **n.** an aquatic mollusk that has a compressed body enclosed within a hinged shell, such as oysters, clams, mussels, and scallops. Also called **PELECYPOD** or **LAMELLIBRANCH**. ● Class Bivalvia (formerly Pelecypoda or Lamellibranchia).
▶ **adj.** (also **bivalved**) Zoology (of a mollusk or other aquatic invertebrate) with a hinged shell. ■ Botany having two valves.

bi·var·i·ate /bīˈve(ə)rēit, -ˈve(ə)rē,āt/ ▶ **adj.** Statistics involving or depending on two variables.

biv·ou·ac /ˈbivōō,ak, ˈbivwak/ ▶ **n.** a temporary camp without tents or cover, used esp. by soldiers or mountaineers.
▶ **v.** [no obj.] (**bivouacked**, **bivouacking**) stay in such a camp: *he'd bivouacked on the north side of the town* | *the battalion was now bivouacked in a field.*
– ORIGIN early 18th cent. (denoting a night watch by the whole army): from French, probably from Swiss German *Bîwacht* 'additional guard at night,' apparently denoting a citizens' patrol supporting the ordinary town watch.

bi·week·ly /bīˈwēklē/ ▶ **adj. & adv.** appearing or taking place every two weeks or twice a week: [as adj.] *a biweekly bulletin* | [as adv.] *she followed her doctor's instructions to undergo health checks biweekly.*
▶ **n.** (pl. **biweeklies**) a periodical that appears every two weeks or twice a week.

> **USAGE** On the ambiguity of words like **biweekly**, **bimonthly**, etc., see usage at **BI-**.

bi·year·ly /bīˈyi(ə)rlē/ ▶ **adj. & adv.** appearing or taking place every two years or twice a year.

> **USAGE** On the ambiguity of words like **biyearly**, **bimonthly**, etc., see usage at **BI-**.

biz /biz/ ▶ **n.** [usu. in sing., usu. with modifier] informal a business, typically one connected with entertainment: *the music biz.*
– ORIGIN mid 19th cent. (originally US): abbreviation.

bi·zarre /biˈzär/ ▶ **adj.** very strange or unusual, esp. so as to cause interest or amusement: *her bizarre dresses and outrageous hairdos.*
– DERIVATIVES **bi·zarre·ness n.**
– ORIGIN mid 17th cent.: from French, from Italian *bizzarro* 'angry.'

bi·zarre·ly ▶ **adv.** in a very strange or unusual manner: *bizarrely attired musicians.* ■ [sentence adverb] used to express the opinion that something is very strange or unusual: ***bizarrely enough**, he began to trust his abductors.*

bi·zar·re·rie /biˈzärərē/ ▶ **n.** (pl. **bizarreries**) a thing considered extremely strange and unusual, typically in an amusing way: *the bizarreries of small talk.*
– ORIGIN mid 18th cent.: from French, from **BIZARRE**.

bi·zar·ro /biˈzärō/ ▶ **adj.** informal bizarre: *a whacked-out frontman for a bizarro fringe rock n' roll band.*
– ORIGIN perhaps from *Bizarro*, the name of a character in DC Comics' *Superman* comic books, or from *Bizarro*, the name of a comic strip.

Bi·zet /biˈzā/, Georges (1838–75), French composer; born *Alexandre César Léopold Bizet*. He is best known for the opera *Carmen* (1875).

BJ ▶ **abbr. BLOW JOB.**

Bjerk·nes /ˈbyerknəs/, Vilhelm Frimann Koren (1862–1951), Norwegian geophysicist and meteorologist. He developed a theory of physical hydrodynamics for atmosphere and oceanic circulation and mathematical models for weather prediction.

Bk ▶ **symbol** the chemical element berkelium.

bk ▶ **abbr.** ■ bank. ■ book. ■ brick.

BL ▶ **abbr.** ■ Bachelor of Law. ■ Bachelor of Letters. ■ bill of lading.

bl ▶ **abbr.** ■ bale. ■ barrel. ■ black. ■ blue.

blab /blab/ informal ▶ **v.** (**blabs**, **blabbing**, **blabbed**) [no obj.] reveal secrets by indiscreet talk: *she blabbed to the press* | [with obj.] *there's no need to blab the whole story.*
▶ **n.** a person who blabs.
– ORIGIN Middle English (as a noun): probably of Germanic origin; ultimately imitative.

blab·ber /ˈblabər/ informal ▶ **v.** [no obj.] talk foolishly, mindlessly, or excessively: *she **blabbered on and on**.*
▶ **n.** a person who talks foolishly or indiscreetly. ■ foolish or mindless talk: *annoyed by their endless blabber.*

blab·ber·mouth /ˈblabər,mouTH/ ▶ **n.** informal a person who talks excessively or indiscreetly.

Black[1] /blak/, Hugo Lafayette (1886–1971), US Supreme Court associate justice 1937–71, noted as an advocate of First Amendment rights. He was also a US senator from Alabama 1927–37.

Black[2], Joseph (1728–99), Scottish chemist. He developed accurate techniques for following chemical reactions by weighing reactants and products.

black /blak/ ▶ **adj.** **1** of the very darkest color; the opposite of white; colored like coal, due to the absence of or complete absorption of light: *black smoke* | *her hair was black.* ■ (of the sky or night) completely dark due to nonvisibility of the sun, moon, or stars, normally because of dense cloud cover: *the sky was moonless and black.* ■ deeply stained with dirt: *his clothes were absolutely black.* ■ (of a plant or animal) dark in color as distinguished from a lighter variety: *Japanese black pine.* ■ (of coffee or tea) served without milk or cream. ■ of or denoting the suits spades and clubs in a deck of cards. ■ (of a ski run) of the highest level of difficulty, as indicated by black markers positioned along it.
2 (also **Black**) of any human group having dark-colored skin, esp. of African or Australian Aboriginal ancestry: *black adolescents of Jamaican descent.* ■ of or relating to black people: *black culture.*
3 (of a period of time or situation) characterized by tragic or disastrous events; causing despair or pessimism: *five thousand men were killed on the blackest day of the war* | *the future looks black for those of us interested in freedom.* ■ (of a person's state of mind) full of gloom or misery; very depressed: *Jean had disappeared and Mary was in a black mood.* ■ (of humor) presenting tragic or harrowing situations in comic terms: *"Good place to bury the bodies," she joked with black humor.* ■ full of anger or hatred: *Roger shot her a black look.* ■ archaic very evil or wicked: *my soul is steeped in the blackest sin.*
▶ **n.** **1** black color or pigment: *a tray decorated in black and green* | *a series of paintings done only in grays and blacks.* ■ black clothes or material, often worn as a sign of mourning: *dressed in the black of widowhood.* ■ darkness, esp. of night or an overcast sky: *the only thing visible in the black was the light of the lantern.*
2 (also **Black**) a member of a dark-skinned people, esp. one of African or Australian Aboriginal ancestry: *a coalition of blacks and whites against violence.*
3 (in a game or sport) a black piece or ball, in particular: ■ (often **Black**) the player of the black pieces in chess or checkers. ■ the black pieces in chess.
▶ **v.** [with obj.] make black, esp. by the application of black polish: *blacking the prize bull's hooves.* ■ make (one's face, hands, and other visible parts of one's body) black with polish or makeup, so as not to be seen at night or, esp. formerly, to play the role of a black person in a musical show, play, or movie: *white extras **blacking up** their faces to play Ethiopians.*
– PHRASES **black someone's eye** hit someone in the eye so as to cause bruising. **in the black** (of a person or organization) not owing any money; solvent. **look on the black side** informal view a situation pessimistically. **men in black** informal anonymous dark-clothed men who supposedly visit people who have reported an encounter with a UFO or an alien in order to prevent their publicizing it. **the new black** a color that is currently so popular that it rivals the traditional status of black as the most reliably fashionable color: *brown is the new black this season.* ■ something that is suddenly extremely popular or fashionable: *retro sci-fi is the new black.* **not as black as one is painted** informal not as bad as one is said to be.
– PHRASAL VERBS **black out** (of a person) undergo a sudden and temporary loss of consciousness: *they knocked me around and I blacked out.* **black something out** **1** (usu. **be blacked out**) extinguish all lights or completely cover windows, esp. for protection against an air attack or in order to provide darkness in which to show a movie: *the bombers began to come nightly and the city was blacked out.* ■ subject a place to an electricity failure: *Chicago was blacked out yesterday after a freak flood.* **2** obscure something completely so that it cannot be read or seen: *the license plate had been blacked out with masking tape.* ■ (of a television company) suppress the broadcast of a program: *they blacked out the women's finals on local television.*
– DERIVATIVES **black·ish adj.**, **black·ly adv.**, **black·ness n.**
– ORIGIN Old English *blæc*, of Germanic origin.

> **USAGE** **Black**, designating Americans of African heritage, became the most widely used and accepted term in the 1960s and 1970s, replacing **Negro**. It is not usually capitalized: *black Americans*. Through the 1980s, the more formal **African American** replaced **black** in much usage, but both are now generally acceptable. **Afro-American**, first recorded in the 19th century and popular in the 1960s and 1970s, is now heard mostly in anthropological and cultural contexts. **Colored people**, common in the early part of the 20th century, is now usually regarded as offensive, although the phrase survives in the full name of the NAACP, the National Association for the Advancement of Colored People. An inversion, **people of color**, has gained some favor, but is also used in reference to other nonwhite ethnic groups: *a gathering spot for African Americans and other people of color interested in reading about their cultures.* See also usage at **COLORED** and **PERSON OF COLOR**.

black Af·ri·ca the area of Africa, generally south of the Sahara, where black people predominate.

black·a·moor /ˈblakə,mŏŏr/ ▶ **n.** dated, offensive a black African; a very dark-skinned person.
– ORIGIN early 16th cent.: from **BLACK** + **MOOR**.

black and blue ▶ **adj.** discolored by bruising: *a black-and-blue mark on his arm.* ■ (of a person) covered in bruises: *they were both black and blue the day after the accident.*

black and tan ▶ **n.** **1** a terrier of a breed with a black back and tan markings on face, flanks, and legs.
2 a drink composed of stout (or porter) and ale.
3 informal an event or establishment that is attended or frequented by both blacks and whites: *takes this guy out to the black and tan every night* | [as modifier] *a black and tan nightclub.*

Black and Tans an armed force recruited by the British government to fight Sinn Fein in Ireland in 1920–21. Their harsh methods caused an outcry in Britain and the US.
– ORIGIN so named because of the mixture of military khaki and black constabulary colors of their uniform.

black and white ▶ **adj.** **1** (of a photograph, movie, television program, or illustration) in black, white, shades of gray, and no other color: *old black-and-white movies.* ■ (of a television) displaying images only in black, white, and shades of gray.
2 (of a situation or debate) involving clearly defined opposing principles or issues: *there is nothing black and white about these matters.*
▶ **n.** informal a police car.
– PHRASES **in black and white** **1** in writing or in print, and regarded as more reliable, credible, or formal than by word of mouth: *getting her contract down in black and white.* **2** in terms of clearly defined opposing principles or issues: *children think in black and white, good and bad.*

Black An·gus ▶ **n.** another term for **ABERDEEN ANGUS**.

black ant ▶ **n.** an ant that is black and is often found in and around houses. ● Several species in the family Formicidae.

black art ▶ **n.** (usu. **the black art**) another term for **BLACK MAGIC**. ■ often humorous a technique or practice considered mysterious and sinister: *the black art of political news management.*

black·ball /ˈblak,bôl/ ▶ **v.** [with obj.] reject (someone, usually a candidate applying to become a member of a private club), typically by means of a secret ballot: *her husband was blackballed when he tried to join the country club.*
– ORIGIN late 18th cent.: from the practice of registering an adverse vote by placing a black ball in a ballot box.

black bass /bas/ ▶ **n.** a North American freshwater fish of the sunfish family. It is a popular sporting and food fish. ● Genus *Micropterus*, family Centrarchidae: several species, in particular the **largemouth bass** (*M. salmoides*) and the **smallmouth bass** (*M. dolomieui*).

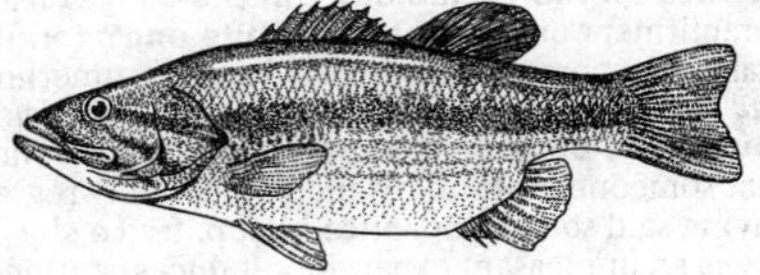

black bass

black bean ▶ **n.** **1** either of two cultivated varieties of bean plant having small black seeds. ● a variety of soybean, used fermented in Asian cooking. ● a Mexican variety of string bean. ■ the dried seed of such a plant used as a vegetable.

2 either of two Australian plants of the pea family. ● a large tree with red or yellow flowers, dark beanlike seeds, and a hard and decorative wood (*Castanospermum australe*, family Leguminosae). ● a liana with blackish flowers (*Kennedia nigricans*, family Leguminosae).

black bear ▶ n. a medium-sized forest-dwelling bear with blackish fur and a paler face, found in North America and eastern Asia. ● Two species, family Ursidae: the **American black bear** (*Ursus americanus*), with a wide range of coat color, and the smaller **Asian black bear** (*Selenarctos thibetanus*).

American black bear

Black·beard /ˈblakˌbi(ə)rd/ (died 1718), English pirate; real name *Edward Teach.* Originally a privateer during the War of the Spanish Succession 1701–14, he turned to piracy and concentrated on the West Indies and the Virginia–North Carolina coast of America.

Black Belt an agricultural district in central Alabama and Mississippi, named for its rich soils.

black belt ▶ n. a black belt worn by an expert in judo, karate, and other martial arts. ■ a person qualified to wear this.

Black·Ber·ry /ˈblakˌberē/ ▶ n. trademark a handheld wireless electronic device that provides Internet access along with e-mail, telephone, and text messaging services.

black·ber·ry /ˈblakˌberē/ ▶ n. (pl. **blackberries**)
1 an edible soft fruit, consisting of a cluster of soft purple-black drupelets.
2 the prickly climbing shrub of the rose family that bears this fruit and that grows extensively in the wild. ● *Rubus fruticosus*, family Rosaceae (sometimes treated as an aggregate of many species).
▶ v. (**blackberries, blackberrying, blackberried**) [no obj.] (usu. as noun **blackberrying**) gather blackberries in the wild.

black bile ▶ n. (in medieval science and medicine) one of the four bodily humors, believed to be associated with a melancholy temperament. Also called MELANCHOLY.
– ORIGIN late 18th cent.: translation of Greek *melankholia* (see MELANCHOLY). Compare with ATRABILIOUS.

black bind·weed ▶ n. a twining weed of the dock family, with arrowhead-shaped leaves and small greenish flowers. ● *Polygonum convolvulus*, family Polygonaceae.

black birch ▶ n. another term for SWEET BIRCH.

black·bird /ˈblakˌbərd/ ▶ n. 1 a European thrush with mainly black plumage. ● Genus *Turdus*, subfamily Turdinae, family Muscicapidae: four species, in particular *T. merula*, the male of which has all-black plumage and a yellow bill.
2 an American bird with a strong pointed bill. The male has black plumage that is iridescent or has patches of red or yellow. ● Family Icteridae: several genera and species, including the abundant **red-winged blackbird** (*Agelaius phoeniceus*).

black·board /ˈblakˌbôrd/ ▶ n. a large board with a smooth, typically dark, surface attached to a wall or supported on an easel and used for writing on with chalk, esp. by teachers in schools.

black book ▶ n. a book containing a list of secret contacts, or of the names of people liable to be punished: *he lists his sexual conquests in his little black book.*

black bot·tom ▶ n. a popular US dance of the 1920s.

black bot·tom pie ▶ n. pie with a bottom layer of chocolate cream or custard and a contrasting top layer, usually of whipped cream.

black box ▶ n. a flight recorder in an aircraft. ■ any complex piece of equipment, typically a unit in an electronic system, with contents that are mysterious to the user.

black bread ▶ n. a coarse, dark-colored type of rye bread.

black bry·o·ny ▶ n. see BRYONY (sense 2).

black·buck /ˈblakˌbək/ ▶ n. a small Indian gazelle, the horned male of which has a black back and white underbelly, the female being hornless. ● *Antilope cervicapra*, family Bovidae.

Black·burn /ˈblakbərn/ an industrial town in northwestern England; pop. 104,100 (est. 2009).

black but·ter ▶ n. a sauce made by heating butter until it is dark brown. It is often flavored with vinegar and herbs.

black·cap /ˈblakˌkap/ ▶ n. 1 a mainly European warbler with a black cap in the male and a reddish-brown one in the female. ● *Sylvia atricapilla*, family Sylviidae.
2 the black-capped chickadee. See CHICKADEE.

black cau·cus ▶ n. a political caucus composed of black people interested in advancing the concerns of blacks. ■ (**Black Caucus**) a caucus of this kind composed of black members of the US Congress.

black cher·ry ▶ n. a large North American cherry tree that yields valuable close-grained hard wood. ● *Prunus serotina*, family Rosaceae. ■ the bitter blackish fruit of this tree, sometimes used for jellies and regularly eaten by wild birds and animals.

black·cock /ˈblakˌkäk/ ▶ n. (pl. **same**) the male of the black grouse.

black co·hosh /ˈkōhäsн/ ▶ n. see COHOSH.

black con·scious·ness ▶ n. awareness of one's identity as a black person. ■ a political movement or ideology (particularly in the US and South Africa) seeking to unite black people in affirming their common identity.

black cur·rant ▶ n. (Brit. **blackcurrant**) 1 a small round edible black berry that grows in loose hanging clusters.
2 the shrub that produces this fruit. ● Genus *Ribes*, family Grossulariaceae: several species, in particular the widely cultivated *Ribes nigrum*.

black·damp /ˈblakˌdamp/ ▶ n. choking or suffocating gas, typically carbon dioxide, that is found in mines and other underground spaces.

Black Death the great epidemic of bubonic plague that killed a large part of the population of Europe in the mid 14th century. It originated in central Asia and China and spread rapidly through Europe, carried by the fleas of black rats, reaching England in 1348 and killing between one third and one half of the population in a matter of months.
– ORIGIN a modern term (compare with earlier *the (great) pestilence, great death, the plague*), said to have been introduced into English history by Mrs. Markham (pseudonym of Mrs. Penrose) in 1823, and into medical literature by a translation of German *der Schwarze Tod* (1833). The epithet *Black* is of uncertain origin; its equivalent was first found in Swedish and Danish chroniclers.

black dia·mond ▶ n. 1 informal a lump of coal.
2 [usu. as modifier] a difficult ski slope: *a steep, black diamond run.*
3 another term for CARBONADO.

black dog ▶ n. informal used as a metaphor for melancholy or depression: *I'm very happy, but the black dog is there, lurking around the corner.*
– ORIGIN late 18th cent.: figuratively from a cant name used during Queen Anne's reign (1702–14) for a base silver coin (usually a bad shilling).

black duck ▶ n. a duck with black plumage, esp. the **American black duck** (*Anas rubripes*) of northeastern North America.

black·en /ˈblakən/ ▶ v. become or make black or dark, esp. as a result of burning, decay, or bruising: [no obj.] *he set fire to the paper, watching the end blacken as it burned* | [with obj.] *she blackened George's eye before he knew what had happened* | (as adj. **blackened**) *her smile revealed blackened teeth.* ■ [with obj.] dye or color (the face or hair) black for camouflage or cosmetic effect: *in full combat gear with blackened faces.* ■ [with obj.] damage or destroy (someone's good reputation); defame: *she won't thank you for blackening her husband's name.*

black Eng·lish ▶ n. any of various nonstandard forms of English spoken by black people, esp. as an urban dialect in the US.

Black·ett /ˈblakit/, Patrick Maynard Stuart, Baron (1897–1974), English physicist. He was a member of the Maud Committee, which dealt with the development of the atom bomb. He also modified the cloud chamber for the study of cosmic rays. Nobel Prize for Physics (1948).

black eye ▶ n. 1 a bruised and discolored area around the eye resulting from a blow: *it's gonna be a doozy of a black eye.*
2 a mark or source of dishonor or shame: *legislators have caused the state to suffer yet another black eye.*

black-eyed pea ▶ n. another term for COWPEA.

black-eyed Su·san ▶ n. any of a number of flowers that have yellowish petals and a dark center, in particular: ● a daisylike North American flower with bristly leaves and stems (*Rudbeckia hirta* and its hybrids, family Compositae). ● a slender tropical climber, grown as a popular indoor or greenhouse plant (*Thunbergia alata*, family Acanthaceae).

black·face /ˈblakˌfās/ ▶ n. the makeup used by a nonblack performer playing a black role. The role played is typically comedic or musical and usually is considered offensive: *he appeared in blackface* | [as modifier] *the blackface components of the minstrel era.* ■ used to imply patronization of blacks by whites or by institutions perceived to be insincerely or ineffectively nonracist.

black·fish /ˈblakˌfisн/ ▶ n. (pl. **same** or **blackfishes**)
1 any of a number of dark-colored fish, in particular: ● an open-ocean fish related to the perches (genera *Centrolophus* and *Schedophilus*, family Centrolophidae), in particular the large and widespread *C. niger*. ● (**Alaska blackfish**) a small fish occurring along the Arctic coasts of Alaska and Siberia, noted for its ability to withstand freezing (*Dallia pectoralis*, family Umbridae). ● (**river blackfish**) a large fish of Australian rivers (*Gadopsis marmoratus*, family Gadopsidae). ● a salmon just after spawning.
2 another term for PILOT WHALE.

black flag ▶ n. 1 historical a pirate's ensign, typically thought to feature a white skull and crossbones on a black background; Jolly Roger.
2 Auto Racing a black flag used to signal a driver to make an immediate pit stop as punishment for violating a rule or driving dangerously, or to force inspection of a hazardous condition such as an oil leak.

black fly ▶ n. (pl. **black flies**) 1 a small black fly, the female of which sucks blood and can transmit a number of serious human and animal diseases. Large swarms sometimes cause distress to livestock and humans. ● Family Simuliidae: *Simulium* and other genera.
2 a black or dark green aphid that is a common pest of crops and gardens. ● Several species in the family Aphididae, in particular *Aphis fabae*.

Black·foot /ˈblakˌfo͝ot/ ▶ n. (pl. **same** or **Blackfeet**)
1 a member of a confederacy of North American Indian peoples of the northwestern plains. The Blackfoot confederacy comprised three closely related tribes: the Blackfeet proper, the Bloods, and the Piegan.
2 the Algonquian language of this people.
3 a subdivision of the Teton Sioux.
▶ adj. of or relating to these peoples or the language of the Blackfeet proper.

Black For·est a hilly wooded region of southwestern Germany that lies to the east of the Rhine River valley. German name SCHWARZWALD.

Black For·est cake ▶ n. a chocolate sponge cake with layers of morello cherries or cherry jam and whipped cream and topped with chocolate icing.
– ORIGIN *Black Forest*, a translation of German *Schwarzwald*, the name of a forested area in southwestern Germany.

Black Fri·ar ▶ n. a Dominican friar.
– ORIGIN early 16th cent.: so named because of the color of the order's habit.

Black Fri·day ▶ n. 1 (in the US) the day after Thanksgiving, noted as the first day of traditional Christmas shopping, during which crowds of consumers are drawn to special offers by retailers.
2 September 24, 1869. On this date, an attempt by a few speculators to corner the US gold market was thwarted when President Ulysses S. Grant released government gold for sale, making gold prices plummet and creating a panic in the stock market.

black frost ▶ n. a dry, nonvisible killing frost that turns vegetation black.

black gold ▶ n. informal petroleum.

black grouse ▶ n. (pl. **same**) a large Eurasian grouse, the male of which has glossy blue-black plumage and a lyre-shaped tail. The males display in communal leks. ● *Tetrao tetrix*, family Tetraonidae (or Phasianidae); the male is called a **blackcock** and the female a **greyhen**.

black·guard /ˈblagərd, ˈblakˌgärd/ ▶ n. dated a person, particularly a man, who behaves in a dishonorable or contemptible way.
▶ v. [with obj.] dated abuse or disparage (someone) scurrilously.
– DERIVATIVES **black·guard·ly** adj.
– ORIGIN early 16th cent. (originally as two words): from BLACK + GUARD. The term originally denoted a body of attendants or servants, esp. the menials who had charge of kitchen utensils, but the exact significance of the epithet 'black' is uncertain. The

PRONUNCIATION KEY ə *ago, up*; ər *over, fur*; a *hat*; ā *ate*; ä *car*; e *let*; ē *see*; i *fit*; ī *by*; NG *sing*; ō *go*; ô *law, for*; oi *toy*; o͝o *good*; o͞o *goo*; ou *out*; TH *thin*; T̲H̲ *then*; ZH *vision*

b

b

sense 'scoundrel, villain' dates from the mid 18th cent., and was formerly considered highly offensive.

black guil·le·mot ▶ n. a seabird of the auk family with black summer plumage and large white wing patches, breeding on the coasts of the Arctic and North Atlantic. ● *Cepphus grylle*, family Alcidae.

black gum ▶ n. another term for SOURGUM.

Black Hand ▶ n. a secret criminal and terrorist society in New York during the early 20th century. ■ any similar society.

Black Hawk (1767–1838), American Indian leader, chief of the Sauk and Fox Indians; native name *Makataimeshekiakiak*. He fought to repossess Indian lands in the Black Hawk War 1832.

black·head /ˈblakˌhed/ ▶ n. **1** a plug of sebum in a hair follicle, darkened by oxidation.
2 an infectious disease of turkeys producing discoloration of the head, caused by a protozoan.

Black Hills a mountain range in eastern Wyoming and western South Dakota. The highest point is Harney Peak (7,242 feet; 2,207 m); Mount Rushmore is also part of this range.

black hole ▶ n. Astronomy a region of space having a gravitational field so intense that no matter or radiation can escape. ■ informal a place where people or things, esp. money, disappear without trace: *the moribund economy has been a black hole for federal funds | juveniles lost for good in the black hole of the criminal justice system.*

Black holes are probably formed when a massive star exhausts its nuclear fuel and collapses under its own gravity. If the star is massive enough, no known force can counteract the increasing gravity, and it will collapse to a point of infinite density. Before this stage is reached, within a certain radius (the event horizon), light itself becomes trapped and the object becomes invisible.

Black Hole of Cal·cut·ta a dungeon 20 feet (6 m) square in Fort William, Calcutta (now Kolkata), where perhaps as many as 146 English prisoners were confined overnight following the capture of Calcutta by the nawab of Bengal, in 1756. Only twenty-three of them were still alive the next morning.

black ice ▶ n. a transparent coating of ice, found esp. on a road or other paved surface.

black·jack /ˈblakˌjak/ ▶ n. **1** a gambling card game in which players try to acquire cards with a face value as close as possible to 21 without going over. Also called TWENTY-ONE, VINGT-ET-UN.
2 a short, leather-covered, typically lead-filled club with a flexible handle, used as a weapon.
3 historical a pirate's black ensign.
4 historical a tarred-leather container used for alcoholic drinks.

Black Jew ▶ n. another term for FALASHA.

black·lead /ˈblakˌled/ ▶ n. another term for GRAPHITE.

black·leg /ˈblakˌleg/ ▶ n. **1** any of a number of plant diseases in which part of the stem blackens and decays, in particular: ● a fungal disease of cabbages and related plants (caused by *Leptosphaeria*, *Pleospora*, and other genera). ● a bacterial disease of potatoes (caused by *Erwinia carotovora* subsp. *atroseptica*).
2 an acute infectious bacterial disease of cattle and sheep, causing necrosis in one or more legs. ● This disease is caused by *Clostridium chauvoei*.
3 Brit. derogatory a strikebreaker. [the reason for the name remains unknown.]

black let·ter ▶ n. an early, ornate, bold style of type, typically resembling Gothic.

black light ▶ n. ultraviolet or infrared radiation, invisible to the eye.

black·list /ˈblakˌlist/ ▶ n. a list of people or products viewed with suspicion or disapproval.
▶ v. [with obj.] put (a person or product) on such a list: *workers were blacklisted after being quoted in the newspaper.*

black lo·cust ▶ n. a North American tree with compound leaves and dense, hanging clusters of fragrant white flowers, widely grown as an ornamental. ● *Robinia pseudoacacia*, family Leguminosae.

black lung ▶ n. pneumoconiosis caused by inhalation of coal dust.

black mag·ic ▶ n. magic involving the supposed invocation of evil spirits for evil purposes.

black·mail /ˈblakˌmāl/ ▶ n. the action, treated as a criminal offense, of demanding money from a person in return for not revealing compromising or injurious information about that person: *they were acquitted of charges of blackmail.* ■ money demanded in this way: *we do not pay blackmail.* ■ the use of threats or the manipulation of someone's feelings to force them to do something: *out of fear, she submitted to Jim's **emotional blackmail** | they are trying to blackmail us with hunger.*
▶ v. [with obj.] demand money from (a person) in return for not revealing compromising or injurious information about that person: *trying to blackmail him for $400,000.* ■ force (someone) to do something by using threats or manipulating their feelings: *he had **blackmailed** her **into** sailing with him.*
– DERIVATIVES **black·mail·er** n.
– ORIGIN mid 16th cent. (denoting protection money levied by Scottish chiefs): from BLACK + obsolete *mail* 'tribute, rent,' from Old Norse *mál* 'speech, agreement.'

black mam·ba ▶ n. a highly venomous, slender, olive-brown to dark gray snake that moves with great speed and agility. Native to eastern and southern Africa, it is the largest poisonous snake on the continent. ● *Dendroaspis polylepis*, family Elapidae.

Black Ma·ri·a /ˌblak məˈrīə/ ▶ n. informal a police vehicle for transporting prisoners.
– ORIGIN mid 19th cent.: said to be named after a black woman, *Maria* Lee, who kept a boarding house in Boston and helped police in escorting drunk and disorderly customers to jail.

black mark ▶ n. informal used to indicate that someone is remembered and regarded with disfavor: *an arrest will be a black mark on your record | **a black mark** went down **against** him for turning down the job.*

black mar·ket ▶ n. (**the black market**) an illegal traffic or trade in officially controlled or scarce commodities: *they planned to sell the meat **on the black market** |* [as modifier] *black market currency trading.*
– DERIVATIVES **black mar·ke·teer** (also **black-marketeer**) n., **black-mar·ke·teer** v., **black mar·ket·er** n.

black mass (often **Black Mass**) ▶ n. a travesty of the Roman Catholic Mass in worship of Satan.

Black Me·sa an upland in northeastern Arizona, home to many of the Navajo. The Hopi live on extensions to the south.

black met·al ▶ n. a type of heavy metal music having lyrics that deal with Satan and the supernatural.

Black Mon·day ▶ n. Monday, October 19, 1987. On this date, the collapse of stock prices on Wall Street triggered similar declines in markets around the world.

black mon·ey ▶ n. income illegally obtained or not declared for tax purposes.

Black Monk ▶ n. a Benedictine monk.
– ORIGIN Middle English: so named because of the color of the order's habit.

Black·more /ˈblakˌmôr/, R. D. (1825–1900), English novelist and poet; full name *Richard Doddridge Blackmore*. He is noted for his romantic novel *Lorna Doone* (1869).

Black Moun·tains a range of the Appalachian Mountains in western North Carolina. Mount Mitchell at 6,684 feet (2,039 m) is the high point.

Black·mun /ˈblakmən/, Harry Andrew (1908–99), US Supreme Court associate justice 1970–94. He is noted as the author of *Roe v. Wade*, which ruled on the right to legal abortion in 1973.

Black Mus·lim ▶ n. a member of the NATION OF ISLAM.

black na·tion·al·ism ▶ n. the advocacy of separate national status for black people, esp. in the US.
– DERIVATIVES **black na·tion·al·ist** n.

black-on-black ▶ adj. designating harmful actions in which both the perpetrator and the victim are black: *black-on-black violence.*

black op·er·a·tions (also **black ops**) ▶ plural n. covert military or political operations that may employ measures not generally authorized.

black·out /ˈblakˌout/ ▶ n. **1** [often with modifier] a failure of electrical power supply: *due to a power blackout, their hotel was in total darkness.* ■ a period when all lights must be turned out or covered to prevent them being seen by the enemy during an air raid: *people found it difficult to travel in the blackout |* [as modifier] *she peered out through the blackout curtains.* ■ (usu. **blackouts**) dark curtains put up in windows to cover lights during an air raid. ■ a moment in the theater when the lights on stage are suddenly turned off.
2 a suppression of information, esp. one imposed on the media by government: *there is a total information **blackout on** minority interests.* ■ a period during which a particular activity is prohibited: *there are no blackout days during the travel period.*
3 a temporary loss of consciousness: *she was suffering from blackouts.*

black oys·ter plant ▶ n. another term for SCORZONERA.

Black Pan·ther ▶ n. a member of a militant political organization set up in the US in 1966 to fight for black rights.

black pan·ther ▶ n. a leopard that has black fur rather than the typical spotted coat.

black pep·per ▶ n. the dried black berries of the pepper (see PEPPER (sense 2 of the noun)), which are harvested while still green and unripe. Black pepper is widely used as a spice and a condiment and may be used whole (peppercorns) or ground.

black·poll /ˈblakˌpōl/ (also **blackpoll warbler**) ▶ n. a North American warbler, the male of which has a black cap, white cheeks, and white underparts streaked with black. ● *Dendroica striata*, subfamily Parulinae, family Emberizidae.

Black·pool /ˈblakˌpo͞ol/ a seaside resort in northwestern England; pop. 142,600 (est. 2009).

black pop·lar ▶ n. a Eurasian poplar with a blackish-brown trunk and arching lower branches. ● *Populus nigra*, family Salicaceae.

black pow·der ▶ n. the original gunpowder, composed of charcoal, saltpeter, and sulfur, now used chiefly in antique firearms and in fireworks.

Black Pow·er ▶ n. a movement in support of rights and political power for black people, esp. prominent in the US in the 1960s and 1970s.

Black Prince (1330–76), eldest son of Edward III of England; name given to *Edward, Prince of Wales and Duke of Cornwall*, most likely because of the black armor he wore when fighting. He was responsible for the British victory at Poitiers in 1356. He predeceased his father, and his son became King Richard II.

black pud·ding ▶ n. blood sausage.

black rasp·ber·ry ▶ n. **1** an edible soft fruit related to the blackberry, consisting of a cluster of black drupelets.
2 the prickly arching shrub of the rose family that bears this fruit. ● *Rubus occidentalis*, family Rosaceae.

black rat ▶ n. a rat with dark fur, large ears, and a long tail. It is found throughout the world, being particularly common in the tropics, and is the chief host of the plague-transmitting flea. Also called ROOF RAT. ● *Rattus rattus*, family Muridae.

black rhi·noc·er·os ▶ n. a two-horned rhinoceros with a prehensile upper lip, found in Africa south of the Sahara. ● *Diceros bicornis*, family Rhinocerotidae.

Black Riv·er a river that flows southeast for 300 miles (480 km) through Missouri and Arkansas, along the eastern edge of the Ozark Plateau.

Black Rod (in full **Gentleman Usher of the Black Rod**) ▶ n. (in the UK) the chief usher of the Lord Chamberlain's department of the royal household, who is also usher to the House of Lords.
– ORIGIN mid 17th cent.: so named because of the black wand carried as a symbol of office.

black rot ▶ n. a disease of fruits and vegetables caused by bacteria or fungi, producing blackening, rotting, and shriveling.

black sal·si·fy ▶ n. another term for SCORZONERA.

Blacks·burg /ˈblaksˌbərg/ a town in southwestern Virginia, in the Appalachian Mountains, home to Virginia Polytechnic Institute; pop. 41,796 (est. 2008).

Black Sea a tideless almost landlocked sea bounded by Ukraine, Russia, Georgia, Turkey, Bulgaria, and Romania. It is connected to the Mediterranean Sea through the Bosporus and the Sea of Marmara.

black sheep ▶ n. informal a member of a family or group who is regarded as a disgrace to them: *the **black sheep of the family**.*
– ORIGIN late 18th cent.: from the proverb *there is a black sheep in every flock.*

black·shirt /ˈblakˌsHərt/ ▶ n. a member of a fascist organization, in particular: ■ (in Italy) a member of a paramilitary group founded by Mussolini. ■ (in Nazi Germany) a member of the SS.
– ORIGIN 1920s: so named because of the color of the Italian Fascist uniform.

black·smith /ˈblakˌsmiTH/ ▶ n. a person who makes and repairs things in iron by hand. ■ a farrier.

black smok·er ▶ n. Geology a geothermal vent on the seabed that ejects superheated water containing much suspended matter, typically black sulfide minerals.

black·snake /ˈblakˌsnāk/ ▶ n. a long black American racer, esp. the common **Northern blacksnake** (*Coluber constrictor constrictor*), the adult of which is a patternless black, above and below.

b

black spot ▶ **n.** a disease of plants, esp. of roses, producing black blotches on leaves.

Black·stone Riv·er /ˈblakˌstōn/ a river that flows south for 50 miles (80 km) through Worcester, Massachusetts, to Pawtucket, Rhode Island, below which it is called the Seekonk River. The Blackstone Valley was a site of early US industrial development.

black·strap /ˈblakˌstrap/ ▶ **n.** a dark, viscous molasses, the byproduct of the final extraction phase of sugar refining, used chiefly in cattle feed and in the industrial production of citric acid and vinegar.

black swan ▶ **n.** a mainly black swan with white flight feathers, which is common in Australia and Tasmania and has been introduced widely elsewhere. ● *Cygnus atratus*, family Anatidae.

black·tail deer /ˈblakˌtāl/ (also **black-tailed deer**) ▶ **n.** a type of mule deer with black markings on the upper side of its tail, found west of the crest of the Cascade Mountains. ● *Odocoileus hemionus* subsp. *columbianus*, family Cervidae.

black tea ▶ **n. 1** tea of the most usual type, that is fully fermented before drying. Compare with GREEN TEA.
2 tea served without milk or cream.

black·thorn /ˈblakˌTHôrn/ ▶ **n.** a thorny Eurasian shrub that bears white flowers before the leaves appear and astringent blue-black fruits. Also called SLOE. ● *Prunus spinosa*, family Rosaceae. ■ a walking stick or cudgel made from the wood of this shrub.

Black Thurs·day ▶ **n.** October 24, 1929. On this date, a then-record number of shares were traded on the New York Stock Exchange by panicked investors, marking the onset of the stock market crash that precipitated the Great Depression.

black tie ▶ **n.** a black bow tie worn with a dinner jacket. ■ formal evening dress: *the audience wears black tie* | [as modifier] *evening meals were black-tie affairs.*

black·top /ˈblakˌtäp/ ▶ **n.** asphalt, or other black material used for surfacing roads: [as modifier] *blacktop roads.* ■ a road or area surfaced with such material: *playing hopscotch on the blacktop behind the school.*
▶ **v.** (**blacktops, blacktopping, blacktopped**) [with obj.] surface (a road or area) with such material: *41 miles had been blacktopped to date.*

Black Tues·day ▶ **n.** October 29, 1929. On this date, share prices on the New York Stock Exchange completely collapsed, becoming a pivotal factor in the emergence of the Great Depression.

black tu·pe·lo ▶ **n.** another term for SOURGUM.

black vel·vet ▶ **n.** a drink consisting of a mixture of stout and champagne.

black vul·ture ▶ **n. 1** a large, aggressive American vulture with black plumage and a short square tail. Also called CARRION CROW. ● *Coragyps atratus*, family Cathartidae.
2 a very large Old World vulture with blackish-brown plumage, now rare in Europe. Also called CINEREOUS VULTURE. ● *Aygypius monachus*, family Accipitridae.

black wal·nut ▶ **n.** see WALNUT.

Black War·ri·or Riv·er a river that flows 178 miles (287 km) across northern Alabama to join the Tombigbee River. Tuscaloosa and the Birmingham area lie along its course.

black wa·ter ▶ **n.** technical waste water from toilets. Compare with GRAY WATER.

black·wa·ter fe·ver /ˈblakˌwôtər, -ˌwätər/ ▶ **n.** a severe form of malaria in which blood cells are rapidly destroyed, resulting in dark urine.

Black·well /ˈblakwəl, -ˌwel/, Elizabeth (1821–1910), US physician, born in England. She was the first woman to receive a medical degree in the US (1849) and the first woman listed in the Medical Register of the United Kingdom (1859).

black wid·ow ▶ **n.** a highly venomous American spider that has a black body with red markings. ● *Latrodectus mactans*, family Theridiidae; races also occur on other continents.

black widow

black·work /ˈblakˌwərk/ ▶ **n.** a type of embroidery done in black thread on white cloth, esp. popular in England during the Tudor period.

blad /blad/ ▶ **n.** a promotional flyer or mockup for a product, esp. for a book.

blad·der /ˈbladər/ ▶ **n. 1** a membranous sac in humans and other animals, in which urine is collected for excretion.
2 anything inflated and hollow: *an air bladder in the arch and collar of the shoe.* ■ Botany an inflated fruit or vesicle in various plants: *a dried bladder of seaweed.*
– ORIGIN Old English *blǣdre*, of Germanic origin; related to Dutch *blaar* and German *Blatter*, also to BLOW[1].

blad·dered /ˈbladərd/ ▶ **adj.** Brit. informal extremely drunk.

blad·der fern ▶ **n.** a small delicate fern with rounded spore cases, growing on rocks and walls. Bladder ferns are native to both Eurasia and North America. Also called BRITTLE FERN. ● Genus *Cystopteris*, family Dryopteridaceae: several species.

blad·der·nut /ˈbladərˌnət/ ▶ **n.** (also **bladder nut**) a shrub or small tree of north temperate regions that bears white flowers and inflated seed capsules. ● Genus *Staphylea*, family Staphyleaceae: several species, in particular the **American bladdernut** (*S. trifolia*) of the eastern US. ■ the fruit of this shrub or tree.

blad·der sen·na ▶ **n.** a Mediterranean shrub of the pea family that bears yellow flowers followed by inflated reddish pods. ● *Colutea arborescens*, family Leguminosae.

blad·der worm ▶ **n.** an immature form of a tapeworm, which lives in the flesh of the secondary host. Further development is suspended until it is eaten by the primary host.

blad·der·wort /ˈbladərˌwərt, -ˌwôrt/ ▶ **n.** an aquatic plant of north temperate regions with small air-filled bladders that keep the plant afloat and trap tiny animals that provide additional nutrients. ● Genus *Utricularia*, family Lentibulariaceae.

blad·der·wrack /ˈbladərˌrak/ (also **bladder wrack**) ▶ **n.** a common brown shoreline seaweed that has tough straplike fronds containing air bladders that give buoyancy. ● *Fucus vesiculosus*, class Phaeophyceae.

blade /blād/ ▶ **n. 1** the flat cutting edge of a knife, saw, or other tool or weapon. ■ short for RAZOR BLADE. ■ literary a sword. ■ Archaeology a long, narrow flake.
2 the flat, wide section of an implement or device such as an oar or a propeller. ■ a thin, flat metal runner on an ice skate. ■ a shoulder bone in a cut of meat, or the cut of meat itself. ■ the flat part of the tongue behind the tip.
3 a long, narrow leaf of grass or another similar plant: ***a blade of grass.*** ■ Botany the broad thin part of a leaf apart from the stalk.
4 informal, dated a dashing or energetic young man.
▶ **v.** [no obj.] informal skate using in-line skates: *we bladed into the parking lot behind Mensky's.*
– DERIVATIVES **blad·ed adj.** [in combination] *double-bladed paddles.*
– ORIGIN Old English *blæd* 'leaf of a plant' (also sense 2 of the noun), of Germanic origin; related to Dutch *blad* and German *Blatt*.

blague /bläg/ ▶ **n.** a joke or piece of nonsense.
– ORIGIN mid 19th cent.: French, literally 'claptrap, nonsense.'

bla·gueur /bläˈgər/ ▶ **n.** a person who talks nonsense.
– ORIGIN French, from BLAGUE.

blah /blä/ informal used to substitute for actual words in contexts where they are felt to be too tedious or lengthy to give in full: *the typical kid, going out every night, blah, blah, blah.*
▶ **n. 1** (also **blah-blah**) used to refer to something that is boring or without meaningful content: *talking all kinds of blah to him* | [as modifier] *his blah feeling.*
2 (**the blahs**) depression: *he battled a case of the blahs* | *the winter blahs.*
– ORIGIN early 20th cent. (originally US): imitative.

blain /blān/ ▶ **n.** rare an inflamed swelling or sore on the skin. See CHILBLAIN.
– ORIGIN Old English *blegen*; related to Dutch *blein*.

Blaine /blān/ a city in southeastern Minnesota, north of Minneapolis; pop. 55,042 (est. 2008).

Blair[1] /ble(ə)r/, Bonnie (1964–), US speed skater. She is the only US woman to win five Olympic gold medals—in the 500-meter race in 1988, 1992, and 1994 and in the 1,000-meter race in 1992 and 1994.

Blair[2], John (1732–1800), US Supreme Court associate justice 1789–96. He was a member of the Constitutional Convention 1787 and signed the US Constitution. He favored a strong federal government.

Blair[3], Tony (1953–), British statesman; prime minister 1997–2007; full name *Anthony Charles Lynton Blair*. He was elected leader of the Labour Party in 1994. His landslide victory in the election of 1997 gave his party its biggest-ever majority and made him the youngest prime minister since Lord Liverpool in 1812.

Blake[1] /blāk/, Eubie (1883–1983), US jazz pianist and composer. One of the foremost ragtime pianists, he wrote over 300 songs, many in collaboration with lyricist Noble Sissle (1889–1975).

Blake[2], Peter (1932–), English painter. He was prominent in the pop art movement in the late 1950s and early 1960s.

Blake[3], William (1757–1827), English artist and poet. His poems mark the beginning of romanticism and a rejection of the Age of Enlightenment. His watercolors and engravings, like his writings, were not fully appreciated until after his death. Notable collections of poems: *Songs of Innocence* (1789) and *Songs of Experience* (1794).

Bla·key /ˈblākē/, Art (1919–90), US jazz drummer; full name *Arthur Blakey*. A pioneer of the bebop movement, he was known for his group, the Jazz Messengers.

blame /blām/ ▶ **v.** [with obj.] assign responsibility for a fault or wrong: *the inquiry blamed the engineer for the accident.* ■ (**blame something on**) assign the responsibility for something bad to (someone or something): *they blame youth crime on unemployment.*
▶ **n.** responsibility for a fault or wrong: *his players had to take the blame* | *they are trying to put the blame on us.*
– PHRASES **be to blame** be responsible for a fault or wrong: *he was to blame for their deaths.* **I don't** (or **can't**) **blame you** (or **her**, etc.) used to indicate that one agrees that the action or attitude taken was reasonable: *he was becoming impatient, and I couldn't blame him.* **have only oneself to blame** be solely responsible for something bad that has happened.
– DERIVATIVES **blam·a·ble** (also **blameable**) **adj.**, **blame·ful** /-fəl/ **adj.**
– ORIGIN Middle English: from Old French *blamer*, *blasmer* (verb), from a popular Latin variant of ecclesiastical Latin *blasphemare* 'reproach, revile, blaspheme,' from Greek *blasphēmein* (see BLASPHEME).

blamed /blāmd/ ▶ **adj. & adv.** informal used for emphasis, esp. to express disapprobation or annoyance: *a blamed old sodden-headed conservative.*

blame game ▶ **n.** informal a situation in which one party blames others for something bad or unfortunate rather than attempting to seek a solution.
– DERIVATIVES **blame-gam·ing n.**

blame·less /ˈblāmlis/ ▶ **adj.** innocent of wrongdoing: *he led a blameless life.*
– DERIVATIVES **blame·less·ly adv.**, **blame·less·ness n.**

blame·storm·ing /ˈblāmˌstôrmiNG/ ▶ **n.** group discussion regarding the assigning of responsibility for a failure or mistake.
– ORIGIN 1990s: on the pattern of *brainstorming*.

blame·wor·thy /ˈblāmˌwərT͟Hē/ ▶ **adj.** responsible for wrongdoing and deserving of censure or blame.
– DERIVATIVES **blame·wor·thi·ness n.**

blanc fixe /ˈblaNGk ˈfiks, blän ˈfēks/ ▶ **n.** barium sulfate in the form of a white powder used in making pigments and paper.

blanch /blanCH/ ▶ **v. 1** [with obj.] make white or pale by extracting color; bleach: *the cold light blanched her face.* ■ [with obj.] whiten (a plant) by depriving it of light: *blanch endive by covering plants with large flowerpots.*
2 [no obj.] (of a person) grow pale from shock, fear, or a similar emotion: ***many people blanch at the suggestion*** | *their faces blanched with fear.*
3 [with obj.] prepare (vegetables) for freezing or further cooking by immersing briefly in boiling water. ■ peel (almonds) by scalding them: (as adj. **blanched**) *blanched almonds.*
– ORIGIN Middle English: from Old French *blanchir*, from *blanc* 'white,' ultimately of Germanic origin.

Blan·chard /ˈblanCHärd, blänˈSHär/, Jean Pierre François (1753–1809), French balloonist. Together with an American, **John Jeffries** (1744–1819), he made the first air crossing of the English Channel, in a balloon, on January 7, 1785.

blanc·mange /bləˈmänj, -ˈmänZH/ ▶ **n.** a sweet opaque gelatinous dessert made with cornstarch and milk.
– ORIGIN late Middle English *blancmanger*, from Old French *blanc mangier*, from *blanc* 'white' + *mangier* 'eat' (used as a noun to mean 'food'). The shortened form without *-er* arose in the 18th cent.

b

bland /bland/ ▶ **adj.** lacking strong features or characteristics and therefore uninteresting: *rebelling against the bland uniformity.* ■ (of food or drink) mild or insipid: *bland and unadventurous vegetarian dish | bland beers of mediocre quality.* ■ (of a person or behavior) showing no strong emotion; dull and unremarkable: *offering bland reassurance | his expression was bland and unreadable.*
– DERIVATIVES **bland·ly** adv., **bland·ness** n.
– ORIGIN late Middle English (in the sense 'gentle in manner'): from Latin *blandus* 'soft, smooth.'

Blan·da /'blandə/, George Frederick (1927–), US football player. The all-time leading scorer (2,002 points) in professional football, he played the most games (340) for the most seasons (26). Football Hall of Fame (1981).

bland·ish /'blandisн/ ▶ **v.** [with obj.] archaic coax (someone) with kind words or flattery: *I was blandishing her with imprudences to get her off the subject.*
– ORIGIN Middle English: from Old French *blandiss-*, lengthened stem of *blandir*, from Latin *blandiri*, from *blandus* 'soft, smooth.'

bland·ish·ment /'blandisнmənt/ ▶ **n.** (usu. **blandishments**) a flattering or pleasing statement or action used to persuade someone gently to do something: *the blandishments of the travel brochure.*

blank /blaNGk/ ▶ **adj. 1** (of a surface or background) unrelieved by decorative or other features; bare, empty, or plain: *the blank skyline | a blank wall.* ■ not written or printed on: *a blank sheet of paper.* ■ (of a document) with spaces left for a signature or details: *blank tax-return forms.* ■ (of a tape) with nothing recorded on it: *blank cassettes.*
2 showing incomprehension or no reaction: *we were met by blank looks.* ■ having temporarily no knowledge or understanding: *her mind went blank.* ■ lacking incident or result: *those blank moments aboard airplanes.*
3 [attrib.] complete; absolute (used emphatically with negative force): *he was met with a blank refusal to discuss the issue.*
▶ **n. 1** a space left to be filled in a document: *leave blanks to type in the appropriate names | this measure required subjects to* ***fill in the blanks*** *in a story.* ■ a document with blank spaces to be filled.
2 (also **blank cartridge**) a cartridge containing gunpowder but no bullet, used for training or as a signal.
3 an empty space or period of time, esp. in terms of a lack of knowledge or understanding: *my mind was a total blank.*
4 an object that has no mark or design on it, in particular: ■ a roughly cut metal or wooden block intended for further shaping or finishing. ■ a domino with one or both halves blank. ■ a plain metal disk from which a coin is made by stamping a design on it.
5 a dash written instead of a word or letter, esp. instead of an obscenity or profanity. ■ used euphemistically in place of a noun regarded as obscene, profane, or abusive.
▶ **v.** [with obj.] **1** cover up, obscure, or cause to appear blank or empty: *electronic countermeasures* ***blanked out*** *the radar signals.* ■ [no obj.] become blank or empty: *the picture* ***blanked out.*** ■ cut (a metal blank): *the complete core disk can be* ***blanked out*** *in one piece.*
2 informal defeat (a sports opponent) without allowing the opposition to score: *Baltimore blanked Toronto in a 7–0 victory.*
– PHRASES **draw a blank** elicit no successful response; fail: *the search drew a blank.* **firing blanks** informal (of a man) infertile.
– DERIVATIVES **blank·ly** adv., **blank·ness** n.
– ORIGIN Middle English (in the sense 'white, colorless'): from Old French *blanc* 'white,' ultimately of Germanic origin.

blank check ▶ **n.** a bank check with the amount left for the payee to fill in. ■ [in sing.] an unlimited freedom of action: *he was effectively granted a blank check to conduct a war without congressional authorization.*

blan·ket /'blaNGkit/ ▶ **n. 1** a large piece of woolen or similar material used as a bed covering or other covering for warmth. ■ a thick mass or layer of a specified material that covers something completely: *a dense gray blanket of cloud.*
2 Printing a rubber surface used for transferring the image in ink from the plate to the paper in offset printing.
▶ **adj.** covering all cases or instances; total and inclusive: *a blanket ban on tobacco advertising.*
▶ **v.** (**blankets, blanketing, blanketed**) [with obj.] cover completely with a thick layer of something: *the countryside* ***was blanketed in*** *snow.* ■ stifle or keep quiet (sound): *the double glazing blankets the noise a bit.* ■ Sailing take wind from the sails of (another craft) by passing to windward.
– PHRASES **born on the wrong side of the blanket** dated born of parents not lawfully married to each other.
– ORIGIN Middle English (denoting undyed woolen cloth): via Old Northern French from Old French *blanc* 'white,' ultimately of Germanic origin.

blan·ket·flow·er /'blaNGkit,flou(ə)r/ ▶ **n.** another term for GAILLARDIA.

blan·ket·ing /'blaNGkitiNG/ ▶ **n.** material used for making blankets.

blan·ket roll ▶ **n.** a blanket or sleeping bag made into a cylindrical roll for ease of carrying, often with utensils and other personal supplies inside; a bedroll.

blan·ket stitch ▶ **n.** a buttonhole stitch used on the edges of a blanket or other material too thick to be hemmed.

blan·ket·weed /'blaNGkit,wēd/ ▶ **n.** a common green freshwater alga that forms long unbranched filaments. It can be a problem in overenriched water and garden ponds. ● Genus *Spirogyra*, phylum Chlorophyta, kingdom Plantae (or Protista).

blank·e·ty /'blaNGkitē/ (also **blankety-blank**) ▶ **adj. & n.** informal used euphemistically to replace a word considered coarse or vulgar: *it's time to ditch the blankety-blank tax code.*

blank verse ▶ **n.** verse without rhyme, esp. that which uses iambic pentameter.

blan·quette /bläNG'ket/ ▶ **n.** a dish consisting of white meat in a white sauce.
– ORIGIN French, based on *blanc* 'white.'

Blan·tyre /'blan,tī(ə)r/ the chief commercial and industrial city in Malawi; pop. 661,444 (2008). It is named after explorer David Livingstone's birthplace in Scotland.

blare /ble(ə)r/ ▶ **v.** make or cause to make a loud, harsh sound: [no obj.] *the ambulance arrived outside, siren blaring* | [with obj.] *the radio was* ***blaring out*** *organ music.*
▶ **n.** a loud harsh sound: *a blare of trumpets.*
– DERIVATIVES **blar·ing** adj.
– ORIGIN late Middle English (in the sense 'roar, bellow'): from Middle Dutch *blaren*, *bleren*, or Low German *blaren*, of imitative origin. Current senses date from the late 18th cent.

blar·ney /'blärnē/ ▶ **n.** talk that aims to charm, pleasantly flatter, or persuade: *he had the "street charm" of an Irish politician, but this blarney concealed his inner self.* ■ amusing and harmless nonsense: *this story is perhaps just a bit of blarney.*
▶ **v.** (**blarneys, blarneying, blarneyed**) [with obj.] influence or persuade (someone) using charm and pleasant flattery.
– ORIGIN late 18th cent.: named after *Blarney*, a castle near Cork in Ireland, where there is a stone said to give the gift of persuasive speech to anyone who kisses it.

bla·sé /blä'zā/ ▶ **adj.** unimpressed or indifferent to something because one has experienced or seen it so often before: *she was becoming quite blasé about the dangers.*
– ORIGIN early 19th cent.: French, past participle of *blaser* 'cloy,' probably ultimately of Germanic origin.

blas·pheme /blas'fēm, 'blas,fēm/ ▶ **v.** [no obj.] speak irreverently about God or sacred things: *he has* ***blasphemed against*** *God.*
– DERIVATIVES **blas·phem·er** /blas'fēmər, 'blasfəmər/ n.
– ORIGIN Middle English: via Old French from ecclesiastical Latin *blasphemare* 'reproach, revile, blaspheme,' from Greek *blasphēmein*, from *blasphēmos* 'evil-speaking.' Compare with BLAME.

blas·phe·mous /'blasfəməs/ ▶ **adj.** sacrilegious against God or sacred things; profane: *blasphemous and heretical talk.*
– DERIVATIVES **blas·phe·mous·ly** adv.
– ORIGIN late Middle English: via ecclesiastical Latin from Greek *blasphēmos* 'evil-speaking' + -OUS.

blas·phe·my /'blasfəmē/ ▶ **n.** (pl. **blasphemies**) the act or offense of speaking sacrilegiously about God or sacred things; profane talk: *he was detained on charges of blasphemy | screaming incomprehensible blasphemies.*
– ORIGIN Middle English: from Old French, via ecclesiastical Latin from Greek *blasphēmia* 'slander, blasphemy.'

blast /blast/ ▶ **n. 1** a destructive wave of highly compressed air spreading outward from an explosion: *they were thrown backward by the blast.* ■ an explosion or explosive firing, esp. of a bomb: *a bomb blast | a shotgun blast.* ■ a forceful attack or assault: *he defeated his weakest opponent in such a blast that the fans left unimpressed.*
2 a strong gust of wind or air: *the icy blast hit them.* ■ a strong current of air used in smelting.
3 a single loud note of a horn, whistle, or other noisemaking device: *a blast of the ship's siren.*
4 informal a severe reprimand: *I braced myself for the inevitable blast.*
5 informal an enjoyable experience or lively party: *it could turn out to be a real blast.*
▶ **v.** [with obj.] **1** blow up or break apart (something solid) with explosives: *quantities of solid rock had to be* ***blasted away*** *| the explosion* ***blasted out*** *hundreds of windows.* ■ produce (damage or a hole) by means of an explosion: *the force of the collision* ***blasted out*** *a tremendous crater.* ■ [with obj.] force or throw (something) in a specified direction by impact or explosion: *the car was blasted thirty feet into the sky.* ■ shoot with a gun: *Fowler was blasted with an air rifle.* ■ [no obj.] move very quickly and loudly in a specified direction: *driving rain blasted through the smashed window.* ■ informal criticize fiercely: *the school was blasted by government inspectors.*
2 make or cause to make a loud continuous musical or other noise: [no obj.] *music blasted out at full volume* | [with obj.] *an impatient motorist blasted his horn.*
3 kick, strike, or throw (a ball) hard: *Ripken blasted the ball into the gap in right field.*
4 literary (of a wind or other natural force) wither, shrivel, or blight (a plant): *crops blasted on the eve of harvest.* ■ strike with divine anger: *damn and blast this awful place!* ■ destroy or ruin: *a candidate whose only strategy is to blast the opposition.*
▶ **exclam.** chiefly Brit. informal expressing annoyance: *"Blast! The car won't start!"*
– PHRASES **a blast from the past** informal something forcefully nostalgic: *a request for a real old blast from the past.* **(at) full blast** at maximum power or intensity: *the heat is on full blast.*
– PHRASAL VERBS **blast off** (of a rocket or spacecraft) take off from a launching site.
– ORIGIN Old English *blǣst*, of Germanic origin; related to BLAZE[3].

-blast ▶ **comb. form** Biology denoting an embryonic cell: *erythroblast.* Compare with -CYTE. ■ denoting a germ layer of an embryo: *epiblast.*
– ORIGIN from Greek *blastos* 'sprout.'

blast cell ▶ **n.** a primitive, undifferentiated blood cell, often found in the blood of those with acute leukemia.

blast·ed /'blastid/ ▶ **adj. 1** [attrib.] informal used to express annoyance: *make your own blasted coffee!*
2 [attrib.] literary withered or blighted; laid waste: *an area of blasted trees.*
3 [predic.] informal drunk: *the waiter kept bringing us free cocktails; so I got really blasted.*

blas·te·ma /bla'stēmə/ ▶ **n.** (pl. **blastemas** or **blastemata** /-mətə/) the primary formative material of plants and animals, from which cells are developed.
– DERIVATIVES **blas·te·mal** adj., **blas·te·mat·ic** /,blastə'matik/ adj.

blast·er /'blastər/ ▶ **n.** a person or thing that blasts: *Jake was an explosives specialist, a blaster.* ■ (in science fiction) a weapon that emits a destructive blast. ■ a computer game in which the objective is to shoot as many enemies as possible: *the game is a blaster requiring a gun-happy trigger finger.* ■ short for GHETTO BLASTER.

blast fur·nace ▶ **n.** a smelting furnace in the form of a tower into which a blast of hot compressed air can be introduced from below. Such furnaces are used chiefly to make iron from a mixture of iron ore, coke, and limestone.

blast·ing gel·a·tin ▶ **n.** another term for GELATIN.

blasto- ▶ **comb. form** relating to germination: *blastoderm.*
– ORIGIN from Greek *blastos* 'germ, sprout.'

blas·to·coel /'blastə,sēl/ (also **blastocoele**) ▶ **n.** the fluid-filled cavity of a blastula. Also called SEGMENTATION CAVITY.
– DERIVATIVES **blas·to·coel·ic** /,blastə'sēlik/ adj.

blas·to·cyst /'blastə,sist/ ▶ **n.** Embryology a mammalian blastula in which some differentiation of cells has occurred. Also called BLASTODERMIC VESICLE.

blas·to·derm /'blastə,dərm/ ▶ **n.** Embryology the layer of embryonic tissue that forms prior to the development of the embryonic axis. ■ the outer layer of cells that forms the wall of a blastula.
– DERIVATIVES **blas·to·der·mic** /,blastə'dərmik/ adj.

blas·to·der·mic ves·i·cle another term for BLASTOCYST.

blas·to·disk /'blastə,disk/ (also **blastodisc**) ▶ **n.** Embryology a blastula having the form of a disk of cells on top of the yolk in the eggs of reptiles and birds.

blast-off /'blast,ôf, -,äf/ ▶ **n.** the launching of a rocket or spacecraft.

blas·to·gen·e·sis /,blastə'jenəsis/ ▶ **n. 1** the theory of the transmission of inherited characteristics by germ plasm.
2 asexual reproduction of an organism by budding.

3 the development of lymphocytes into larger undifferentiated cells that can undergo mitosis.
– DERIVATIVES **blas·to·gen·ic** /-'jenik/ **adj.**

blas·to·ma /bla'stōmə/ ▶ **n.** (pl. **blastomas** or **blastomata** /-mətə/) a neoplasm consisting of immature undifferentiated cells.

blas·to·mere /'blastə,mi(ə)r/ ▶ **n.** Embryology a cell formed by cleavage of a fertilized ovum.

blas·to·my·co·sis /,blastəmī'kōsis/ ▶ **n.** Medicine a disease caused by infection with parasitic fungi affecting the skin or the internal organs. ● The fungi (**blastomycetes**) belong to the genus *Blastomyces*, subdivision Deuteromycotina.

blas·to·pore /'blastə,pôr/ ▶ **n.** the opening of the central cavity of an embryo in the early stage of development.

blas·to·sphere /'blastə,sfi(ə)r/ another term for BLASTULA.

blas·tu·la /'blascHələ/ ▶ **n.** (pl. **blastulas** or **blastulae** /-,lē/) Embryology an animal embryo at the early stage of development when it is a hollow ball of cells. Also called BLASTOSPHERE.
– ORIGIN late 19th cent.: modern Latin, from Greek *blastos* 'sprout.'

blat /blat/ ▶ **v.** (**blats, blatting, blatted**) [no obj.] make a bleating sound.
▶ **n.** a bleat or similar noise: *the blat of Jack's horn.*
– ORIGIN mid 19th cent.: imitative.

bla·tant /'blātnt/ ▶ **adj.** (of bad behavior) done openly and unashamedly: *blatant lies.* ■ completely lacking in subtlety; very obvious: *forcing herself to resist his blatant charm.*
– DERIVATIVES **bla·tan·cy** /'blātnsē/ **n.**
– ORIGIN late 16th cent.: perhaps an alteration of Scots *blatand* 'bleating' It was first used by Spenser as an epithet for a thousand-tongued monster produced by Cerberus and Chimera, a symbol of calumny, which he called the *blatant beast*. It was subsequently used to mean 'clamorous, offensive to the ear,' first of people (mid 17th cent.), later of things (late 18th cent.); the sense 'obtrusive to the eye, unashamedly conspicuous' arose in the late 19th cent.

bla·tant·ly /'blātntlē/ ▶ **adv.** in an unsubtle and unashamed manner: *the general staff blatantly manipulated press coverage of the war.* ■ [usu. as submodifier] used to emphasize the speaker's opinion that something disapproved of is clearly the case: *he found her remarks blatantly racist.*

Blatch·ford /blacHfərd/, Samuel (1820–93), US Supreme Court associate justice 1882–93. He was a circuit judge before being appointed to the Court by President Arthur. His specialty was patent law.

blath·er /'blaTHər/ (also **blether** /'bleTHər/ or **blither** /'bliTHər/) ▶ **v.** [no obj.] talk long-windedly without making very much sense: *she began blathering on about spirituality and life after death* | (as noun **blathering**) *now stop your blathering and get back to work.*
▶ **n.** long-winded talk with no real substance.
– ORIGIN late Middle English (as a verb; originally Scots and northern English dialect): from Old Norse *blathra* 'talk nonsense,' from *blathr* 'nonsense.'

blath·er·skite /'blaTHər,skīt/ ▶ **n.** a person who talks at great length without making much sense. ■ foolish talk; nonsense: *politicians get away all the time with their blatherskite.*
– ORIGIN mid 17th cent.: from BLATHER + *skite*, a Scottish derogatory term adopted into American colloquial speech during the American Revolution, from the Scottish song *Maggie Lauder*, by F. Semphill, which was popular with American troops.

Blau·e Rei·ter /'blouə 'rītər/ a group of German expressionist painters formed in 1911, based in Munich. The group included Wassily Kandinsky, Jean Arp, and Paul Klee.
– ORIGIN German, literally 'blue rider,' the title of a painting by Kandinsky.

Bla·vat·sky /blə'vatskē, -'vätskē/, Helena (Petrovna) (1831–91), Russian spiritualist; born in Ukraine; born *Helena Petrovna Hahn*; known as **Madame Blavatsky**. In 1875, she cofounded the Theosophical Society in New York.

blax·ploi·ta·tion /,blaksploi'tāsHən/ ▶ **n.** the exploitation of black people, esp. with regard to stereotyped roles in movies.
– ORIGIN 1970s: blend of *blacks* (plural of noun BLACK) and *exploitation* (see EXPLOIT).

blaze¹ /blāz/ ▶ **n. 1** a very large or fiercely burning fire: *twenty fireman fought the blaze.* ■ [in sing.] a very bright display of light or color: *the gardens in summer are a blaze of color.* ■ [in sing.] a conspicuous display or outburst of something: *their relationship broke up in a blaze of publicity.*
2 (**blazes**) informal used in various expressions of anger, bewilderment, or surprise as a euphemism for "hell": *"Go to blazes!" he shouted* | *what in blue blazes are you all talking about?* [with reference to the flames associated with hell.]
▶ **v.** [no obj.] **1** burn fiercely or brightly: *the fire blazed merrily.* ■ shine brightly or powerfully: *the sun blazed down* | figurative *Barbara's eyes were blazing with anger.*
2 (of a gun or a person firing a gun) fire repeatedly or indiscriminately: *we go in with guns blazing.*
3 informal achieve something in an impressive manner: *she blazed to a gold medal in the 200-meter sprint.* ■ [with obj.] hit (a ball) with impressive strength: *he blazed a drive into the rough.*
– PHRASES **like blazes** informal very fast or forcefully: *I ran like blazes toward home.* [see sense 2 of the noun.] **with all guns blazing** informal with great determination and energy, typically without thought for the consequences.
– PHRASAL VERBS **blaze up** burst into flame: *he attacked the fire with poker and tongs until it blazed up.* ■ suddenly become angry: *he blazed up without warning.*
– ORIGIN Old English *blæse* 'torch, bright fire,' of Germanic origin; related ultimately to BLAZE².

blaze² ▶ **n. 1** a white spot or stripe on the face of a mammal or bird. ■ a broad white stripe running the length of a horse's face.
2 a mark made on a tree by cutting the bark so as to mark a route.
▶ **v.** (**blaze a trail**) **1** set an example by being the first to do something; pioneer: *small firms would set the pace, blazing a trail for others to follow.*
2 mark out a path or route.
– ORIGIN mid 17th cent.(sense 1 of the noun): ultimately of Germanic origin; related to German *Blässe* 'blaze' and *blass* 'pale,' also to BLAZE¹, and probably to BLEMISH.

blaze³ ▶ **v.** [with obj.] (of a newspaper) present or proclaim (news) in a prominent, typically sensational, manner.
– ORIGIN late Middle English (in the sense 'blow out on a trumpet'): from Middle Low German or Middle Dutch *blāzen* 'to blow'; related to BLOW¹.

blaz·er /'blāzər/ ▶ **n.** a lightweight jacket, typically solid-colored, often worn as part of a uniform by members of a club, sports team, or school. ■ a plain jacket, typically dark blue, not forming part of a suit but considered appropriate for formal or semiformal wear.
– ORIGIN late 19th cent.: from BLAZE¹ + -ER¹. The original general sense was 'a thing that blazes or shines' (mid 17th cent.), giving rise to the term for a brightly colored sport coat.

blaz·ing star ▶ **n.** any of a number of North American plants, some of which are cultivated for their flowers, in particular: ● a plant of the daisy family with tall spikes of purple or white flowers (genus *Liatris*, family Compositae. ● a plant of the western US with toothed leaves and yellow flowers (genus *Mentzelia*, family Loasaceae), esp. the gray-leaved, large-flowered **giant blazing star** (*M. laevicaulis*. ● devil's bit.

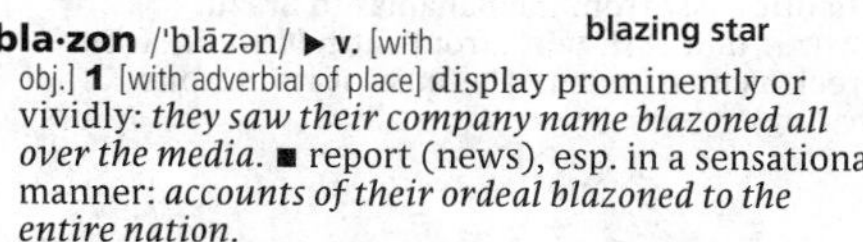
blazing star

bla·zon /'blāzən/ ▶ **v.** [with obj.] **1** [with adverbial of place] display prominently or vividly: *they saw their company name blazoned all over the media.* ■ report (news), esp. in a sensational manner: *accounts of their ordeal blazoned to the entire nation.*
2 Heraldry describe or depict (armorial bearings) in a correct heraldic manner. ■ inscribe or paint (an object) with arms or a name.
▶ **n.** Heraldry a correct description of armorial bearings. ■ archaic a coat of arms.
– ORIGIN Middle English (denoting a shield, later one bearing a heraldic device): from Old French *blason* 'shield,' of unknown origin. The sense of the verb has been influenced by BLAZE³.

bla·zon·ry /'blāzənrē/ ▶ **n.** Heraldry the art of describing or painting heraldic devices or armorial bearings. ■ [plural noun] devices or bearings of this type.

bldg. ▶ **abbr.** building.

bleach /blēcH/ ▶ **v.** [with obj.] **1** whiten by exposure to sunlight or by a chemical process: *paper products are bleached with chlorine* | (as adj. **bleached**) *permed and bleached hair.* ■ deprive of vitality or substance: *his contributions to the album are bleached of personality.*
2 clean and sterilize: *a new formula to bleach and brighten clothing.*
▶ **n.** a chemical (typically a solution of sodium hypochlorite or hydrogen peroxide) used to whiten or sterilize materials.
– ORIGIN Old English *blǣcan* (verb), *blǣce* (noun), from *blǣc* 'pale,' of Germanic origin; related to BLEAK¹.

bleach·er /'blēcHər/ ▶ **n. 1** a person or thing that bleaches.
2 (usu. **bleachers**) a cheap bench seat at a sports arena, typically in an outdoor uncovered stand. ■ (also **bleacherite** /'blēcHə,rīt/) a person occupying such a seat: *the bleachers cheered.*

bleach·ing pow·der ▶ **n.** a powder containing calcium hypochlorite, used chiefly to remove color from materials.

bleak¹ /blēk/ ▶ **adj.** (of an area of land) lacking vegetation and exposed to the elements: *a bleak and barren moor.* ■ (of a building or room) charmless and inhospitable; dreary: *he looked around the bleak little room in despair.* ■ (of the weather) cold and miserable: *a bleak midwinter's day.* ■ (of a situation or future prospect) not hopeful or encouraging; unlikely to have a favorable outcome: *he paints a bleak picture of a company that has lost its way.* ■ (of a person or a person's expression) cold and forbidding: *his bleak, near vacant eyes grew remote.*
– DERIVATIVES **bleak·ly adv.**, **bleak·ness n.**
– ORIGIN Old English *blāc* 'shining, white,' or in later use from synonymous Old Norse *bleikr*; ultimately of Germanic origin and related to BLEACH.

bleak² ▶ **n.** a small silvery shoaling fish of the minnow family, found in Eurasian rivers. ● Genera *Alburnus* and *Chalcalburnus*, family Cyprinidae: several species, in particular *A. alburnus*.
– ORIGIN late 15th cent.: from Old Norse *bleikja*.

blear /bli(ə)r/ archaic ▶ **v.** [with obj.] make dim; blur: *you would blear your eyes with books.*
▶ **adj.** dim, dull, or filmy: *a medicine to lay to sore and blear eyes.*
▶ **n.** a film over the eyes; a blur: *he forced his eyes open and shut to rid them of blear.*
– ORIGIN Middle English (as a verb): probably related to Middle High German *blerre* 'blurred vision' and Low German *blarroged* 'bleary-eyed.'

blear·y /'bli(ə)rē/ ▶ **adj.** (**blearier, bleariest**) (of the eyes) unfocused or filmy from sleep or tiredness: *you hate to face the world with bleary, tear-soaked, itching eyes.*
– DERIVATIVES **blear·i·ly** /'bli(ə)rəlē/ **adv.**, **blear·i·ness n.**

blear·y-eyed (also **blear-eyed**) ▶ **adj.** (of a person) having bleary eyes.

bleat /blēt/ ▶ **v.** [no obj.] (of a sheep, goat, or calf) make a characteristic wavering cry: *the lamb was bleating weakly* | figurative *handing the mike to some woman who starts bleating out rap rhymes* | (as noun **bleating**) *the silence was broken by the plaintive bleating of sheep.* ■ [reporting verb] speak or complain in a weak, querulous, or foolish way: *he bleated incoherently about the report.*
▶ **n.** [in sing.] the wavering cry made by a sheep, goat, or calf: *the distant bleat of sheep in the field.* ■ a person's plaintive cry: *his despairing bleat touched her heart.* ■ informal a complaint: *they're hoping that I'll bow to their idiotic arrangements without a bleat.*
– ORIGIN Old English *blǣtan*, of imitative origin.

bleb /bleb/ ▶ **n.** a small blister on the skin. ■ a small bubble in glass or in a fluid. ■ Biology a rounded outgrowth on the surface of a cell.
– ORIGIN early 17th cent.: variant of BLOB.

bleed /blēd/ ▶ **v.** (past and past participle **bled** /bled/)
1 [no obj.] lose blood from the body as a result of injury or illness: *the cut was bleeding steadily* | *some casualties were left to* **bleed to death** | (as noun **bleeding**) *the bleeding has stopped now.* ■ (of a dye or color) seep into an adjacent color or area: *I worked loosely with the oils, allowing colors to bleed into one another.* ■ Printing (with reference to an illustration or design) print or be printed so that it runs off the page after trimming: *the picture bleeds on three sides* | [with obj.] *Faye showed us how to bleed the images for our brochure layout.*
2 [with obj.] draw blood from (someone), esp. as a once-common method of treatment in medicine. ■ remove blood from (an animal carcass): *the first steer rolled out on the floor to be bled, skinned, and dressed.* ■ [with obj.] informal drain (someone) of money or resources: *his policy of attempting to bleed unions of funds.* ■ [with obj.] allow (fluid or gas) to escape from a closed system through a valve: *open the valves and bleed air from the pump chamber.*

PRONUNCIATION KEY ə ago, up; ər over, fur; a hat; ā ate; ä car; e let; ē see; i fit; ī by; NG sing; ō go; ô law, for; oi toy; o͝o good; o͞o goo; ou out; TH thin; TH then; ZH vision

■ [with obj.] treat (a system) in this way: *bleeding the radiator at the air vent.*
▶ **n.** an instance of bleeding: *a lot of blood was lost from the placental bleed.* ■ Printing an instance of printing an illustration, design, or text to the edge of the page: *it allows printing of a tabloid page with full bleed.* ■ the escape of fluid or gas from a closed system through a valve: *the amount of air bleed from the compressor.* ■ the action or process of a dye, ink, or color seeping into an adjacent color or area: *color bleed is apparent on brighter hues.*
– PHRASES **bleed someone dry** (or **white**) drain someone of all money or resources: *the railroads claimed that personnel costs were bleeding them dry.* **my heart bleeds** (**for you**) used ironically to express the speaker's belief that the person spoken about does not deserve the sympathetic response sought: *"I flew out here feeling tired and overworked." "My heart bleeds for you!" she replied.*
– ORIGIN Old English *blēdan*, of Germanic origin; related to **BLOOD**.

bleed·er /ˈblēdər/ ▶ **n. 1** informal a person who bleeds easily, esp. a hemophiliac. ■ a blood vessel that bleeds freely during surgery.
2 Baseball a ground ball that barely passes between two infielders.

bleed·ing /ˈblēdiNG/ ▶ **adj.** [attrib.] Brit. informal used for emphasis or to express annoyance.

bleed·ing edge ▶ **n.** the very forefront of technological development: [as modifier] *an architecture that many people believe is still too bleeding edge for large mission-critical systems.*
– ORIGIN 1980s: on the pattern of *leading edge, cutting edge.*

bleed·ing heart ▶ **n. 1** informal, derogatory a person considered to be dangerously softhearted, typically someone considered too liberal in political beliefs: [as modifier] *a tirade against bleeding-heart environmentalists.*
2 any of a number of plants that have heart-shaped flowers, typically pink or red, in particular: ● a popular herbaceous garden plant (genus *Dicentra*, family Fumariaceae, in particular *D. spectabilus*). ● a tropical twining shrub with cream and red flowers, often cultivated under glass (*Clerodendrum thomsoniae*, family Verbenaceae).

bleeding heart 2

bleep /blēp/ ▶ **n.** a short high-pitched sound made by an electronic device as a signal or to attract attention: *the autopilot sent back an acknowledgment bleep.* ■ a sound of this type used in broadcasting as a substitute for a censored word or phrase.
▶ **v.** [no obj.] (of an electronic device) make a short high-pitched sound or repeated sequence of sounds: *the screen flickered for a few moments and bleeped.* ■ [with obj.] substitute a bleep or bleeps for (a censored word or phrase): *cable operators have* ***bleeped out*** *the accuser's name.* ■ used in place of an expletive: *"what the bleep are we going to do?" he asked.*
– ORIGIN 1950s: imitative.

bleep·er /ˈblēpər/ ▶ **n.** British term for **PAGER**.

bleep·ing /ˈblēpiNG/ ▶ **adj.** (of an electronic device) making a short high-pitched sound or sounds: *a bleeping red display on the exercise machine.* ■ informal, often humorous used to express exasperation or annoyance, in place of an expletive: *we didn't do a bleeping thing, and we're still getting hung.*
– ORIGIN 1950s: euphemistically for **BLEEDING**, by association with the "bleeps" used to dub expletives in broadcast texts.

blem·ish /ˈblemiSH/ ▶ **n.** a small mark or flaw that spoils the appearance of something: *the merest blemish on a Rolls Royce might render it unsalable.* ■ a moral defect or fault: *the offenses were an uncharacteristic blemish on an otherwise clean record* | *local government is not without blemish.*
▶ **v.** [with obj.] (often as adj. **blemished**) spoil the appearance of (something) that is otherwise aesthetically perfect: *thousands of Web pages are blemished with embarrassing typos* | figurative *his reign as world champion has been blemished by controversy.*
– ORIGIN late Middle English (as a verb): from Old French *ble(s)miss-*, lengthened stem of *ble(s)mir* 'make pale, injure'; probably of Germanic origin.

blench[1] /blenCH/ ▶ **v.** [no obj.] make a sudden flinching movement out of fear or pain: *he blenched and struggled to regain his composure.*
– ORIGIN Old English *blencan* 'deceive,' of Germanic origin; later influenced by **BLINK**.

blench[2] ▶ **v.** chiefly dialect variant spelling of **BLANCH**.

blend /blend/ ▶ **v.** [with obj.] mix (a substance) with another substance so that they combine together as a mass: *blend the cornstarch with a tablespoon of water* | [no obj.] *add the grated cheese and blend well.* ■ (often as adj. **blended**) mix (different types of the same substance, such as tea, coffee, liquor, etc.) together so as to make a product of the desired quality: *a blended whiskey.* ■ put or combine (abstract things) together: *blend basic information for the novice with some scientific gardening for the more experienced* | (as noun **blending**) *a blending of romanticism with a more detached modernism.* ■ merge (a color) with another so that one is not clearly distinguishable from the other. ■ [no obj.] form a harmonious combination: *costumes, music, and lighting all blend together beautifully.* ■ (**blend in/into**) be unobtrusive or harmonious by being similar in appearance or behavior: *she would have to employ a permanent bodyguard in the house, someone who would blend in.*
▶ **n.** a mixture of different things or qualities: *knitting yarns in mohair blends* | *Ontario offers a cultural blend you'll find nowhere else on earth.* ■ a mixture of different types or grades of a substance, such as tea, coffee, whiskey, etc. ■ a word made up of the parts of others and combining their meanings, for example *motel* from *motor* and *hotel*.
– ORIGIN Middle English: probably of Scandinavian origin and related to Old Norse *blanda* 'to mix.'

blende /blend/ ▶ **n.** another term for **SPHALERITE**.
– ORIGIN late 17th cent.: from German, from *blenden* 'deceive' (so named because it often resembles galena, but is deceptive in that it yields no lead).

blend·ed fam·i·ly ▶ **n.** a family consisting of a couple and their children from this and all previous relationships.

blend·er /ˈblendər/ ▶ **n.** a person or thing that mixes things together, in particular an electric mixing machine used in food preparation for liquefying, chopping, or puréeing.

Blen·heim[1] /ˈblenəm/ a battle in 1704 in Bavaria, near the village of Blindheim, in which the English, under the Duke of Marlborough, defeated the French and the Bavarians. See **MARLBOROUGH**[2].

Blen·heim[2] ▶ **n.** a dog of a small red and white breed of spaniel.
– ORIGIN mid 19th cent.: from the name of *Blenheim* palace, the Duke of Marlborough's seat in central England, given to the Duke in honor of his victory at Blenheim.

blen·ny /ˈblenē/ ▶ **n.** (pl. **blennies**) a small, spiny-finned marine fish with scaleless skin and a blunt head, typically living in shallow inshore or intertidal waters. ● Family Blenniidae: several genera, in particular *Blennius*. ■ any of a number of other small fishes that resemble or are related to the true blennies, including the **hairy blenny** (*Labrisomus nuchipinnis*, family Clinidae), found esp. along the Atlantic coast from the Bahamas to Brazil.
– ORIGIN mid 18th cent.: from Latin *blennius*, from Greek *blennos* 'mucus' (because of its mucous coating).

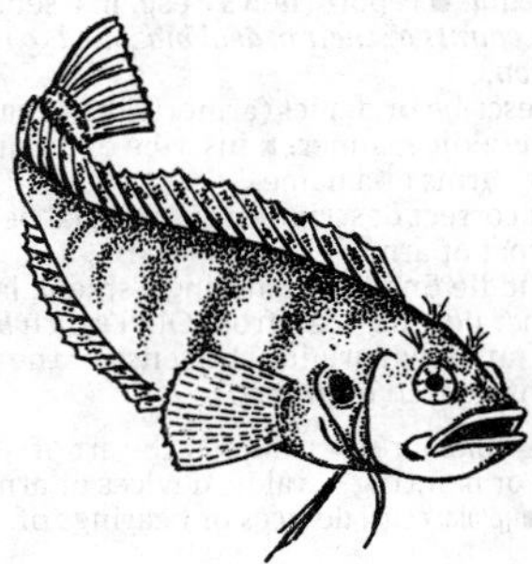

hairy blenny

blent /blent/ literary past and past participle of **BLEND**.

ble·o·my·cin /ˌblēəˈmīsin/ ▶ **n.** Medicine an antibiotic used to treat Hodgkin's disease and other cancers. ● The drug is obtained from the bacterium *Streptomyces verticillus*.
– ORIGIN 1960s: an arbitrary alteration of earlier *phleomycin*, the name of a related antibiotic.

bleph·a·ri·tis /ˌblefəˈrītis/ ▶ **n.** Medicine inflammation of the eyelid.
– ORIGIN mid 19th cent.: from Greek *blepharon* 'eyelid' + **-ITIS**.

bleph·a·ro·plas·ty /ˈblefərəˌplastē/ ▶ **n.** Medicine surgical repair or reconstruction of an eyelid.
– ORIGIN mid 19th cent.: from Greek *blepharon* 'eyelid' + **-PLASTY**.

bleph·a·ro·spasm /ˈblefərəˌspazəm/ ▶ **n.** involuntary tight closure of the eyelids.
– ORIGIN late 19th cent.: from Greek *blepharon* 'eyelid' + **SPASM**.

Blé·riot /ˈblārēˌō, ble(ə)rˈyō/, Louis (1872–1936), French aviation pioneer. On July 25, 1909, he became the first person to cross the English Channel (Calais to Dover) in a monoplane.

bles·bok /ˈblesˌbäk/ ▶ **n.** an antelope with a mainly reddish-brown coat and white face, found in southwestern South Africa. It belongs to the same species as the bontebok. ● *Damaliscus dorcas phillipsi*, family Bovidae.
– ORIGIN early 19th cent.: from Afrikaans, from Dutch *bles* 'blaze' (because of the white mark on its forehead) + *bok* 'buck.'

bless /bles/ ▶ **v.** [with obj.] (of a priest) pronounce words in a religious rite, to confer or invoke divine favor upon; ask God to look favorably on: *he blessed the dying man and anointed him.* ■ consecrate (something) by a religious rite, action, or spoken formula. ■ (esp. in Christian Church services) call (God) holy; praise (God). ■ (**bless someone with**) (of God or some notional higher power) endow (someone) with a particular cherished thing or attribute: *God has blessed us with free will.* ■ express or feel gratitude to; thank: *she silently blessed the premonition which had made her pack her best dress.* ■ (**bless oneself**) make the Christian gesture of the sign of the cross: *the poor parson, blessing himself, brought up the rear.* ■ used in expressions of surprise, endearment, gratitude, etc.: *bless my soul, Alan, what are you doing?* | *Lenore,* ***bless her heart,*** *had done just that.*
– PHRASES **bless you!** said to a person who has just sneezed. [from the phrase *(may) God bless you.*]
– ORIGIN Old English *blēdsian, blētsian*, based on *blōd* 'blood' (i.e., originally perhaps 'mark or consecrate with blood'). The meaning was influenced by its being used to translate Latin *benedicere* 'to praise, worship,' and later by association with **BLISS**.

bless·ed /blest, ˈblesid/ ▶ **adj. 1** made holy; consecrated. ■ a title preceding the name of a dead person considered to have led a holy life, esp. a person formally beatified by the Roman Catholic Church: *the Convent of the Blessed Agnes.* ■ used respectfully in reference to a dead person: *a gracious lady of blessed memory.* ■ endowed with divine favor and protection: *blessed are the meek.* ■ bringing pleasure or relief as a welcome contrast to what one has previously experienced: *he half stumbled out of the room up to his bed and blessed, blessed sleep.* ■ (**blessed with**) endowed with (a particular quality or attribute): *a beautiful city, steeped in history and blessed with huge sandy beaches.*
2 informal used in mild expressions of annoyance or exasperation: *there wasn't a blessed thing anybody could have done.*
▶ **plural n.** (**the Blessed** /ˈblesid/) those who live with God in heaven.
– DERIVATIVES **bless·ed·ly** /ˈblesidlē/ **adv.**

bless·ed·ness /ˈblesidnis/ ▶ **n.** the state of being blessed with divine favor.

Bless·ed Vir·gin Mar·y /ˈblesid/ (also **Blessed Virgin**) (abbr.: **BVM**) a title given to Mary, the mother of Jesus. See **MARY**[1].

bless·ing /ˈblesiNG/ ▶ **n.** [in sing.] God's favor and protection: *may God continue to give us his blessing.* ■ a prayer asking for such favor and protection: *a priest gave a blessing as the ship was launched.* ■ grace said before or after a meal. ■ a beneficial thing for which one is grateful; something that brings well-being: *great intelligence can be a curse as well as a blessing* | *it's a blessing we're alive.* ■ a person's sanction or support: *he gave the plan his blessing even before it was announced.*
– PHRASES **a blessing in disguise** an apparent misfortune that eventually has good results. **count one's blessings** see **COUNT**[1].

blest /blest/ ▶ **adj.** archaic or literary term for **BLESSED**.

bleth·er /ˈbleTHər/ ▶ **n.** another term for **BLATHER**.

bleu cheese /bloo͞/ ▶ **n.** variant spelling of **BLUE CHEESE**.

blew /bloo͞/ past of **BLOW**[1] and **BLOW**[3].

blew·it /ˈbloo͞it/ (also **blewits**) ▶ **n.** an edible wild mushroom of Europe and North America, with a pale buff or lilac cap and a lilac stem. ● Genus *Lepista*, family Tricholomataceae, class

Basidiomycetes: several species, including **common blewit** (*L. saeva*) and **wood blewit** (*L. nuda*).
– ORIGIN early 19th cent.: probably from **BLUE**.

Bligh /blī/, William (1754–1817), British naval officer; captain of HMS *Bounty*. In 1789, part of his crew, led by the first mate Fletcher Christian, mutinied and set Bligh adrift in an open boat. Bligh landed safely at Timor, nearly 4,000 miles (6,400 km) away, a few weeks later.

blight /blīt/ ▶ **n.** a plant disease, esp. one caused by fungi such as mildews, rusts, and smuts: *the vines suffered blight and disease* | *potato blight.* ■ [in sing.] a thing that spoils or damages something: *her remorse could be a blight on that happiness.* ■ an ugly, neglected, or rundown condition of an urban area: *the depressing urban blight that lies to the south of the city.*
▶ **v.** [with obj.] infect (plants or a planted area) with blight: *a peach tree blighted by leaf curl.* ■ spoil, harm, or destroy: *the scandal blighted the careers of several leading politicians* | (as adj. **blighted**) *his father's blighted ambitions.* ■ (usu. as adj. **blighted**) subject (an urban area) to neglect: *plans to establish enterprise zones in blighted areas.*
– ORIGIN mid 16th cent. (denoting inflammation of the skin): of unknown origin.

blight·er /ˈblītər/ ▶ **n.** [with adj.] Brit. informal a person who is regarded with contempt, irritation, or pity: *you little blighter!*
– ORIGIN early 19th cent.: from **BLIGHT** + **-ER**[1].

Blight·y /ˈblītē/ ▶ **n.** Brit. an informal and typically affectionate term for Britain or England, chiefly as used by soldiers of World War I and World War II. ■ military slang a wound suffered by a soldier in World War I that was sufficiently serious to merit being shipped home to Britain: *he had copped a Blighty and was on his way home.*
– ORIGIN first used by soldiers in the Indian army; Anglo-Indian alteration of Urdu *bilāyatī, wilāyatī* 'foreign, European,' from Arabic *wilāyat, wilāya* 'dominion, district.'

bli·mey /ˈblīmē/ ▶ **exclam.** Brit. informal used to express one's surprise, excitement, or alarm.
– ORIGIN late 19th cent.: altered form of (*God*) *blind* (or *blame*) *me!*

blimp /blimp/ ▶ **n. 1** informal a small nonrigid airship. ■ an obese person: *I could work out four hours a day and still end up a blimp.*
2 (also **Colonel Blimp**) Brit. a pompous, reactionary type of person: *no Colonel Blimp could have been more nationalistic.*
3 a soundproof cover for a movie camera.
– DERIVATIVES **blimp·ish** adj.
– ORIGIN World War I (sense 1): of uncertain origin. Sense 2 derives from the character invented by cartoonist David Low (1891–1963), used in anti-German or antigovernment drawings before and during World War II.

blin /blin/ singular form of **BLINI**.

blind /blīnd/ ▶ **adj. 1** unable to see; sightless: *she suffered from glaucoma, which has left her completely blind* | *he was blind in one eye.* ■ [attrib.] (of an action, esp. a test or experiment) done without being able to see or without being in possession of certain information: *a blind tasting of eight wines.* ■ Aeronautics (of flying) using instruments only: *blind landings during foggy conditions.*
2 [predic.] lacking perception, awareness, or discernment: *he's absolutely blind where you're concerned, isn't he?* | *she was blind to the realities of her position.* ■ [attrib.] (of an action or state of mind) not controlled by reason or judgment: *they left in blind panic.* ■ [attrib.] not governed by purpose: *moving purposelessly in a world of blind chance.*
3 [attrib.] concealed or closed, in particular: ■ (of a corner or bend in a road) impossible to see around: *two trucks collided on a blind curve in the road.* ■ (of a door or window) walled up. ■ closed at one end: *a blind pipe.* ■ (of a plant) without buds, eyes, or terminal flowers: *planting too shallowly is the most common cause of bulbs coming up blind.*
4 [attrib. with negative] Brit. informal (used in emphatic expressions) not the slightest: *you don't know a blind thing!*
5 informal drunk.
▶ **v.** [with obj.] **1** cause (someone) to be unable to see, permanently or temporarily: *the injury temporarily blinded him* | *eyes blinded with tears.*
2 (**be blinded**) deprive (someone) of understanding, judgment, or perception: *a clever tactician blinded by passion* | *somehow Clare and I were blinded to the truth.* ■ (**blind someone with**) confuse or overawe someone with something difficult to understand: *they try to blind you with science.*
▶ **n. 1** (as plural noun **the blind**) people who are unable to see: *guide dogs for the blind.*
2 an obstruction to sight or light, in particular: ■ a screen for a window, esp. one on a roller or made of slats: *she pulled down the blinds.* ■ Brit. an awning over a shop window.
3 [in sing.] something designed to conceal one's real intentions: *he phoned again from his own home: that was just a blind for his wife.* ■ a hiding place: *you can sometimes use your car as a blind.* ■ a camouflaged shelter used by hunters to get close to wildlife: *a duck blind.*
4 Brit. informal, dated a heavy drinking bout: *he's off on a blind again.*
5 Brit. a legitimate business concealing a criminal enterprise.
▶ **adv.** without being able to see clearly: *he was the first pilot in history to fly blind.* ■ without having all the relevant information; unprepared: *he was going into the interview blind.* ■ (of a stake in poker and other games) put up by a player before the cards dealt are seen.
– PHRASES (**as**) **blind as a bat** informal having very bad eyesight. **blind drunk** informal extremely drunk. **effing and blinding** Brit. see **EFF**. **rob** (or **steal**) **someone blind** informal rob or cheat someone in a comprehensive or merciless way. **turn a blind eye** pretend not to notice. [said to be in allusion to Nelson, who lifted a telescope to his blind eye at the Battle of Copenhagen (1801), in order to avoid seeing the signal to 'discontinue the action.']
– DERIVATIVES **blind·ness** n.
– ORIGIN Old English, of Germanic origin; related to Dutch and German *blind*.

blind al·ley ▶ **n.** an alley or road that is closed at one end. ■ a course of action leading nowhere: *many technologies that show early promise lead up blind alleys.*

blind date ▶ **n.** a social engagement or date with a person one has not previously met: *a blind date arranged by well-meaning friends.* ■ either person of the couple on a blind date: *where do you take a blind date, anyway?*

blind·ers /ˈblīndərz/ ▶ **plural n.** a pair of small leather screens attached to a horse's bridle to prevent it seeing sideways and behind. Also called **BLINKERS** (see **BLINKER**). ■ something that prevents someone from gaining a full understanding of a situation: *they will wear their cultural blinders to the grave.*

blind·fish /ˈblīnd,fisн/ ▶ **n.** another term for **CAVEFISH**.

blind·fold /ˈblīnd,fōld/ ▶ **v.** [with obj.] deprive (someone) of sight by tying a piece of cloth around the head so as to cover the eyes.
▶ **n.** a piece of cloth tied around the head to cover someone's eyes.
▶ **adj.** literary wearing a blindfold. ■ (of a game of chess) conducted without sight of board and pieces.
▶ **adv.** with a blindfold covering the eyes: *the reporter was driven blindfold to meet the gangster.* ■ done with great ease and confidence, as if it could have been done wearing a blindfold: *missing putts that he would normally hole blindfold.*
– ORIGIN mid 16th cent.: alteration, by association with **FOLD**[1], of *blindfeld*, past participle of obsolete *blindfell* 'strike blind, blindfold,' from Old English *geblindfellan* (see **BLIND**, **FELL**[2]).

blind gut ▶ **n.** the cecum.

blind·ing /ˈblīndiNG/ ▶ **n.** Brit. the process of covering a newly made road with grit to fill cracks. ■ the grit used in such a process.
▶ **adj.** [attrib.] (of light) very bright and likely to dazzle or temporarily blind someone: *a massive explosion with a blinding flash of light.* ■ (of a thing) temporarily obstructing a person's vision: *he saw the school bus approaching through almost blinding rain.* ■ (of pain or an emotion) so intense as to block out everything else: *I've got a blinding headache.* ■ (of a process or action) remarkably fast or skillful; dazzling: *a blinding fastball.*
– DERIVATIVES **blind·ing·ly** adv. [as submodifier] *the reason was blindingly obvious.*

blind·ly /ˈblīndlē/ ▶ **adv.** as if blind; without seeing or noticing: *I continued to stare blindly into my coffee.* ■ without reasoning or questioning: *solutions must be assessed, not blindly accepted.*

blind·man's bluff /ˈblīndmənz/ (also **blindman's buff**) ▶ **n.** a children's game in which a blindfolded player tries to catch others.
– ORIGIN early 17th cent.: *bluff*, alteration of *buff* 'a blow,' from Old French *bufe* (see **BUFFET**[2]).

blind pig ▶ **n.** another term for **BLIND TIGER**.
– ORIGIN late 19th cent.: see **BLIND TIGER**.

blind pool ▶ **n.** a company that sells stock without specifying how invested money will be spent.

blind side ▶ **n.** [in sing.] a direction in which a person has a poor view, typically of approaching danger: *a minivan nearly clipped him on his blind side.* ■ the side opposite the one toward which a person is looking: *they came at me from my blind side* | [as modifier] *the crushing blind-side sack of the quarterback.*
▶ **v.** (**blindside**) [with obj.] hit or attack (someone) on the blind side: *Jenkins blindsided Adams, knocking him to the sidewalk.* ■ catch (someone) unprepared; attack from an unexpected position: *protection against being technologically blindsided.*

blind·sight /ˈblīnd,sīt/ ▶ **n.** Medicine the ability to respond to visual stimuli without consciously perceiving them. This condition can occur after certain types of brain damage.

blind snake ▶ **n.** a small burrowing insectivorous snake that lacks a distinct head and has very small inefficient eyes. Also called **WORM SNAKE**.
● Infraorder Scolecophidia: three families, in particular Typhlopidae, and several genera.

blind spot ▶ **n. 1** Anatomy the point of entry of the optic nerve on the retina, insensitive to light.
2 an area where a person's view is obstructed: *the angle rearview mirror eliminates blind spots on both sides of the car.* ■ an area in which a person lacks understanding or impartiality: *Ed had a blind spot where these ethical issues were concerned.*
3 Telecommunications a point within the normal range of a transmitter where there is unusually weak reception.

blind stamp·ing (also **blind tooling**) ▶ **n.** the impressing of text or a design on a book cover without the use of color or gold leaf.

blind stitch ▶ **n.** a sewing stitch producing stitches visible on one side only.
▶ **v.** (**blind-stitch**) [with obj.] sew (something) using such a stitch.

blind ti·ger ▶ **n.** informal an illegal bar.
– ORIGIN mid 19th cent.: probably so named because in order to evade prohibition laws, the bars were disguised as exhibition halls for natural curiosities.

blind trust ▶ **n.** a financial arrangement in which a person in public office gives the administration of private business interests to an independent trust in order to prevent conflict of interest. Under the trust, the owner does not know how the assets are managed.

blind·worm /ˈblīnd,wərm/ ▶ **n.** another term for **SLOW-WORM**.

bling /bliNG/ ▶ **n.** informal expensive, ostentatious clothing and jewelry, or the wearing of them: *behind the bling: are diamonds worth it?*
– ORIGIN 1990s: perhaps imitative of light reflecting off jewelry, or of jewelry clashing together.

blin·i /ˈblinē, ˈblē-/ (also **bliny** or **blinis**) ▶ **plural n.** (sing. **blin** /blin/) pancakes made from buckwheat flour and served with sour cream.
– ORIGIN Russian (plural); compare with **BLINTZ**.

blink /bliNGk/ ▶ **v.** [no obj.] **1** shut and open the eyes quickly: *she blinked, momentarily blinded* | [with obj.] *he blinked his eyes nervously.* ■ [with obj.] (**blink back**) try to control or prevent (tears) by such an action: *Elizabeth blinked back tears.* ■ (**blink at**) [usu. with negative] react to (something) with surprise or disapproval: *he doesn't blink at the unsavory aspects of his subject.* ■ back down from a confrontation: *the government blinked in the face of a coordinated public sector strike.*
2 (of a light or light source) shine intermittently or unsteadily: *the icon for his e-mail was blinking.*
▶ **n.** [in sing.] **1** an act of shutting and opening the eyes quickly: *he was observing her every blink.* ■ a moment's hesitation: *Thompson would have given her all this without a blink.*
2 a momentary gleam of light.
– PHRASES **not blink an eye** show no reaction. **in the blink of an eye** (or **in a blink**) informal very quickly. **on the blink** informal (of a machine) not working properly; out of order: *the computer's on the blink.*
– ORIGIN Middle English: from *blenk*, Scots variant of **BLENCH**[1], reinforced by Middle Dutch *blinken* 'to shine.' Early senses included 'deceive,' 'flinch' (compare with **BLENCH**[1]), also 'open the eyes after sleep': hence sense 1 (mid 16th cent).

blink·er /ˈbliNGkər/ ▶ **n. 1** a device that blinks, esp. a vehicle's turn signal.
2 (**blinkers**) another term for **BLINDERS**.
▶ **v.** [with obj.] put blinders on (a horse). ■ cause (someone) to have a narrow or limited outlook on a situation: *college education blinkers researchers so that they see poverty in terms of their own specialization.*

blink·ered /ˈbliNGkərd/ ▶ **adj.** (of a horse) wearing blinders. ■ having or showing a limited outlook: *a small-minded, blinkered approach.*

blink·ing /ˈbliNGkiNG/ ▶ **adj.** [attrib.] Brit. informal used to express annoyance: *computers can be a blinking nuisance to operators.*

blintz /blints/ (also **blintze** /ˈblintsə/) ▶ **n.** a thin rolled pancake filled with cheese or fruit and then fried or baked.
– ORIGIN from Yiddish *blintse*, from Russian *blinets* 'little pancakes'; compare with **BLINI**.

blin·y ▶ **plural n.** variant spelling of **BLINI**.

blip /blip/ ▶ **n. 1** a short high-pitched sound made by an electronic device.
2 a flashing point of light on a radar screen representing an object, typically accompanied by a high-pitched sound.
3 an unexpected, minor, and typically temporary deviation from a general trend: *an upward blip in house prices.*
▶ **v.** (**blips, blipping, blipped**) **1** [no obj.] (of an electronic device) make a short high-pitched sound or succession of sounds.
2 [with obj.] open (the throttle of a motor vehicle) momentarily.
– ORIGIN late 19th cent. (denoting a sudden rap or tap): imitative; the noun sense 'unexpected deviation' dates from the 1970s.

Bliss /blis/, Sir Arthur (Edward Drummond) (1891–1975), English composer.

bliss /blis/ ▶ **n.** perfect happiness; great joy: *she gave a sigh of bliss.* ■ a state of spiritual blessedness, typically that reached after death.
– PHRASAL VERBS **bliss out** (often as adj. **blissed out**) informal reach a state of perfect happiness, typically so as to be oblivious of everything else: *blissed-out hippies.*
– ORIGIN Old English *bliths, bliss*, of Germanic origin; related to **BLITHE**.

bliss·ful /ˈblisfəl/ ▶ **adj.** extremely happy; full of joy: *a blissful couple holding a baby.* ■ providing perfect happiness or great joy: *the blissful caress of cool cotton sheets.*
– PHRASES **blissful ignorance** fortunate unawareness of something unpleasant.
– DERIVATIVES **bliss·ful·ly adv.**, **bliss·ful·ness n.**

B-list /ˈbē ˌlist/ ▶ **n.** see **A-LIST**.

blis·ter /ˈblistər/ ▶ **n. 1** a small bubble on the skin filled with serum and caused by friction, burning, or other damage. ■ a similar swelling, filled with air or fluid, on the surface of a plant, heated metal, painted wood, or other object. ■ Medicine, chiefly historical a preparation applied to the skin to cause a blister.
2 Brit. informal, dated an annoying person: *the child is a disgusting little blister.*
▶ **v.** [no obj.] form swellings filled with air or fluid on the surface of something: *the surface of the door began to blister* | (as adj. **blistered**) *he had blistered feet.* ■ [with obj.] cause blisters to form on the surface of: *a caustic liquid that blisters the skin.*
– ORIGIN Middle English: perhaps from Old French *blestre* 'swelling, pimple.'

blis·ter a·gent ▶ **n.** a chemical weapon that burns and blisters the skin or other tissues.

blis·ter bee·tle ▶ **n.** a beetle that, when alarmed or crushed, gives off a substance that causes blisters. The larvae are typically parasites of other insects. ● *Lytta* and other genera, family Meloidae: several species. See also **SPANISH FLY**.

blis·ter cop·per ▶ **n.** partly purified copper with a blistered surface formed during smelting.

blis·ter·ing /ˈblistəriNG/ ▶ **adj.** (of heat) intense: *the blistering heat of the desert.* ■ (of criticism) expressed with great vehemence: *blistering diatribes.* ■ extremely fast, forceful, or impressive: *Burke set a blistering pace.*

blis·ter pack ▶ **n.** a type of packaging in which a product is sealed in plastic, often with a cardboard backing.

blis·ter rust ▶ **n.** any of several destructive diseases of pine trees caused by fungi of the genus *Conartium*, resulting in orange blisters on the bark and tips of branches.

blithe /blīT͟H, blīTH/ ▶ **adj.** showing a casual and cheerful indifference considered to be callous or improper: *a blithe disregard for the rules of the road.* ■ happy or joyous: *a blithe seaside comedy.*
– DERIVATIVES **blithe·ly adv.**, **blithe·ness n.**, **blithe·some** /-səm/ **adj.** (literary).
– ORIGIN Old English *blīthe*, of Germanic origin; related to Dutch *blijde*, also to **BLISS**.

blith·er /ˈbliT͟Hər/ ▶ **v. & n.** another term for **BLATHER**.

blith·er·ing /ˈbliT͟HəriNG/ ▶ **adj.** [attrib.] informal senselessly talkative, babbling; used chiefly as an intensive to express annoyance or contempt: *a blithering idiot.*
– ORIGIN late 19th cent.: from **BLITHER** + **-ING**[2].

BLitt (also **BLit**) ▶ **abbr.** ■ Bachelor of Letters. ■ Bachelor of Literature.
– ORIGIN from Latin *Baccalaureus Litterarum*.

blitz /blits/ ▶ **n. 1** an intensive or sudden military attack. ■ (**the Blitz**) the German air raids on Britain in 1940–41.
2 informal a sudden, energetic, and concerted effort, typically on a specific task: *a major press blitz.* ■ Football a charge of the passer by the defensive linebackers just after the ball is snapped.
3 a form of chess in which moves must be made at very short intervals.
▶ **v.** [with obj.] **1** attack or damage (a place or building) in a blitz: *news came that Rotterdam had been blitzed* | figurative *organizations blitzed Capitol Hill with mailgrams and postcards.*
2 Football attack (the passer) in a blitz.
– PHRASES **Blitz spirit** (also **the spirit of the Blitz**) Brit. stoicism and determination in a difficult or dangerous situation, esp. as displayed by a group of people: *he urged the British public to show their Blitz spirit in the face of the recession.*
– DERIVATIVES **blitz·er n.**
– ORIGIN World War II: abbreviation of **BLITZKRIEG**.

blitzed /blitst/ ▶ **adj.** informal intoxicated by drink or drugs.

blitz·krieg /ˈblitsˌkrēg/ ▶ **n.** an intense military campaign intended to bring about a swift victory.
– ORIGIN World War II: from German, literally 'lightning war.'

Blix·en /ˈbliksən/, Karen (Christentze), Baroness Blixen-Finecke (1885–1962), Danish novelist and short-story writer; born *Karen Dinesen*; also known by the pseudonym of **Isak Dinesen**. She is best known for *Seven Gothic Tales* (1934) and her autobiography *Out of Africa* (1937), which was made into a movie in 1985.

bliz·zard /ˈblizərd/ ▶ **n.** a severe snowstorm with high winds and low visibility. ■ an overabundance; a deluge: *a blizzard of legal forms.*
– ORIGIN early 19th cent. (originally US, denoting a violent blow): of unknown origin.

bloat[1] /blōt/ ▶ **v.** make or become swollen with fluid or gas: [with obj.] *the fungus has bloated their abdomens* | (as noun **bloating**) *she suffered from abdominal bloating.*
▶ **n.** a disease of livestock characterized by an accumulation of gas in the stomach.
– ORIGIN late 17th cent. (in the sense 'cause to swell'): from obsolete *bloat* 'swollen, soft,' perhaps from Old Norse *blautr* 'soft, flabby.' The noun sense dates from the late 19th cent.

bloat[2] ▶ **v.** [with obj.] cure (a herring) by salting and smoking it lightly.
– ORIGIN late 16th cent.: related to the adjective *bloat* used in the compound *bloat herring* 'bloater' from the late 16th to mid 17th cent.; of obscure origin.

bloat·ed /ˈblōtid/ ▶ **adj.** (of part of the body) swollen with fluid or gas: *he had a bloated, unshaven face.* ■ excessive in size or amount: *the company trimmed its bloated labor force.* ■ (of a person) excessively wealthy and pampered: *the bloated captains of industry.*

bloat·er[1] /ˈblōtər/ ▶ **n.** a herring cured by salting and light smoking.

bloat·er[2] ▶ **n.** another term for **CISCO**.

bloat·ware /ˈblōtˌwe(ə)r/ ▶ **n.** Computing, informal software whose usefulness is reduced because of the excessive disk space and memory it requires.

BLOB /bläb/ ▶ **n.** Computing binary large objects.

blob /bläb/ ▶ **n.** a drop of a thick liquid or other viscous substance: *blobs of paint.* ■ a spot of color: *a badly printed blob on shopping bags.* ■ an indeterminate mass or shape: *a leathery blob commonly known as a sea squirt.*
▶ **v.** (**blobs, blobbing, blobbed**) [with obj.] put small drops of thick liquid or spots of color on: *her nose was blobbed with paint.*
– DERIVATIVES **blob·by adj.**
– ORIGIN late Middle English (denoting a bubble): perhaps symbolic of a drop of liquid; compare with **BLOTCH**, **BLUBBER**[1], and **PLOP**.

bloc /bläk/ ▶ **n.** a combination of countries, parties, or groups sharing a common purpose: *a center-left voting bloc.*
– ORIGIN early 20th cent.: from French, literally 'block.'

Bloch /bläk/, Ernest (1880–1959), US composer; born in Switzerland. His work reflects the influence of the late 19th-century romanticism of Franz Liszt and Richard Strauss and of Jewish musical forms. Notable works: *Israel Symphony* (1912–16) and *Solomon* (1916).

block /bläk/ ▶ **n. 1** a large solid piece of hard material, esp. rock, stone, or wood, typically with flat surfaces on each side: *a block of marble.* ■ a sturdy, flat-topped block used as a work surface, typically for chopping food. ■ (usu. **blocks**) any of a set of solid cubes used as a child's toy. ■ (usu. **blocks**) a starting block: *the thrust a sprinter gets when coming out of the blocks.* ■ Printing a piece of wood or metal engraved for printing on paper or fabric. ■ (also **cylinder block** or **engine block**) the main body of an internal combustion engine, containing the pistons. ■ a head-shaped mold used for shaping hats or wigs.
2 the area bounded by four streets in a town or suburb: *she went for a run around the block* | *ours was the ugliest house on the block.* ■ the length of one side of such an area, typically as a measure of distance: *he lives a few blocks away from the museum.*
3 [with modifier] a building, esp. part of a complex, used for a particular purpose: *a cell block.* ■ chiefly Brit. a large single building subdivided into separate rooms, apartments, or offices: *an apartment block.*
4 a large quantity or allocation of things regarded as a unit: *a block of shares* | [as modifier] *block grants.* ■ Computing a large piece of text processed as a unit. ■ chiefly Brit. a set of sheets of paper glued along one edge, used for drawing or writing on: *a sketching block.* ■ an unseparated unit of at least four postage stamps in at least two rows, generally a group of four.
5 an obstacle to the normal progress or functioning of something: *substantial demands for time off may constitute **a block to** career advancement* | *an emotional block.* ■ Sports a hindering or stopping of an opponent's movement or action. ■ Tennis a shot in which the racket is held stationary rather than being swung back, esp. a stop volley. ■ short for **MENTAL BLOCK**. ■ short for **NERVE BLOCK**. ■ a chock for stopping the motion of a wheel.
6 a flat area of something, typically a solid area of color: *cover the eyelid with a neutral block of color.*
7 a pulley or system of pulleys mounted in a case.
8 informal a person's head: *"I'll knock your block off," he said.*
▶ **v.** [with obj.] **1** make the movement or flow in (a passage, pipe, road, etc.) difficult or impossible: ***block up** the holes with sticky tape* | *a police cordon **blocked off** roads* | (as adj. **blocked**) *a blocked nose.* ■ put an obstacle in the way of (something proposed or attempted): *he stood up, blocking her escape* | *the administration tried to block an agreement on farm subsidies.* ■ restrict the use or conversion of (currency or any other asset). ■ Sports hinder or stop the movement or action of (an opponent, a ball, etc.). ■ Medicine produce insensibility in (a part of the body) by injecting an anesthetic close to the nerves that supply it. ■ Bridge play in such a way that an opponent cannot establish (a long suit).
2 impress text or a design on (a book cover).
3 Theater design or plan the movements of actors on a stage or movie set.
4 shape or reshape (a hat) using a wooden mold.
– PHRASES **have been around the block** (**a few times**) informal (of a person) have a lot of experience. **the new kid on the block** informal a newcomer to a particular place or sphere of activity, typically someone who has yet to prove themselves. **on the** (**auction**) **block** for sale at auction: *the original first manuscript for Ravel's Bolero goes on the block today* | figurative *the company put its subsidiary on the block because it did not fit its core business interests.* **put** (or **lay**) **one's head** (or **neck**) **on the block** informal put one's standing or reputation at risk by proceeding with a particular course of action. [with reference to the executioner's block.]
– PHRASAL VERBS **block something in 1** mark something out roughly. ■ add something in a unit: *it's a good idea to block in regular periods of exercise.* ■ paint something with solid areas of color. **2** park one's car in such a way as to prevent another car from moving away: *he blocked in Vera's minivan.* **block something out 1** stop something, typically light or noise, from reaching somewhere: *you're blocking out my sun.* ■ exclude something unpleasant from one's thoughts or memory. **2** mark or sketch something out roughly.
– ORIGIN Middle English (denoting a log or tree stump): from Old French *bloc* (noun), *bloquer* (verb), from Middle Dutch *blok*, of unknown ultimate origin.

block·ade /bläˈkād/ ▶ **n.** an act or means of sealing off a place to prevent goods or people from entering or leaving: *there was a blockade of humanitarian aid* | *the police pulled down blockades on the highway.* ■ an obstruction of a physiological or mental function, esp. of a biochemical receptor.
▶ **v.** [with obj.] seal off (a place) to prevent goods or people from entering or leaving.
– PHRASES **run a blockade** (of a ship) manage to enter or leave a blockaded port.
– DERIVATIVES **block·ad·er n.**
– ORIGIN late 17th cent.: from **BLOCK** + **-ADE**[1], probably influenced by *ambuscade*.

block·ade run·ner ▶ n. **1** a vessel that runs or attempts to run into or out of a blockaded port. **2** the owner, master, or one of the crew of such a vessel.

block·age /ˈbläkij/ ▶ n. an obstruction that makes movement or flow difficult or impossible: *a blockage in the pipes | the pumps are prone to blockage.*

block and tack·le ▶ n. a mechanism consisting of ropes and one or more pulley-blocks, used for lifting or pulling heavy objects.

block and tackle

block·bust·er /ˈbläk,bəstər/ ▶ n. informal a thing of great power or size, in particular a movie, book, or other product that is a great commercial success: [as modifier] *a blockbuster pay-per-view special event.*
– ORIGIN 1940s (denoting a huge aerial bomb capable of destroying a whole block of streets): from BLOCK + BUSTER.

block·bust·ing /ˈbläk,bəstiNG/ ▶ adj. [attrib.] very successful commercially: *his blockbusting novel.*
▶ n. the practice of persuading owners to sell property cheaply because of the fear of people of another race or class moving into the neighborhood, and thus profiting by reselling at a higher price.

block cap·i·tals ▶ plural n. another term for BLOCK LETTERS.

block di·a·gram ▶ n. a diagram showing in schematic form the general arrangement of parts or components of a complex system or process, such as an industrial apparatus or an electronic circuit.

block·er /ˈbläkər/ ▶ n. a person or thing that blocks, in particular: ■ Football a player whose task it is to block for the ballcarrier or kicker. ■ a substance that prevents or inhibits a given physiological function.

block grant ▶ n. a grant from a central government that a local authority can allocate to a wide range of services.

block·head /ˈbläk,hed/ ▶ n. informal a stupid person.
– DERIVATIVES **block·head·ed** adj.

block heat·er ▶ n. a device for heating the engine block of a vehicle.

block·house /ˈbläk,hous/ ▶ n. a reinforced concrete shelter used as an observation point. ■ historical a one-storied timber building with loopholes, used as a fort. ■ a house made of squared logs.

block·ing /ˈbläkiNG/ ▶ n. **1** the action or process of obstructing movement, progress, or activity, in particular: ■ obstructing or impeding the actions of an opponent in a game, esp. (in ball sports) one who does not have control of the ball. ■ Psychiatry the sudden halting of the flow of thought or speech, as a symptom of schizophrenia or other mental disorder. ■ failure to recall or consider an unpleasant memory or train of thought.
2 the grouping or treatment of things (e.g., items of data or shades of color) in blocks. ■ the physical arrangement of actors on a stage or movie set.

block·ish /ˈbläkiSH/ ▶ adj. **1** big, bulky, or crude in form or appearance: *his blockish architecture is ugly if functional.*
2 unintelligent and stupid.

Block Is·land (abbr.: **BI**) a resort island in southern Rhode Island, in the Atlantic Ocean at the eastern end of Long Island Sound.

block let·ters ▶ plural n. plain capital letters.

block moun·tain ▶ n. Geology a mountain consisting of a block or blocks bounded by normal faults in the earth's crust. See NORMAL.

block par·ty ▶ n. a party for all the residents of a block or neighborhood, typically held on a closed-off city street.

block plane ▶ n. a carpenter's plane with a blade set at an acute angle, used esp. for planing across the end grain of wood.

block sys·tem ▶ n. a system of railroad signaling that divides the track into sections and allows no train to enter a section that is not completely clear.

block vote ▶ n. a vote proportional in power to the number of people a delegate represents.

block·y /ˈbläkē/ ▶ adj. of the nature of or resembling a block or blocks: *blocky granite.*

Bloem·fon·tein /ˈblo͞omfän,tān/ a city in central South Africa, judicial capital of the country, capital of Orange Free State; pop. 583,300 (est. 2009).

blog /bläg/ ▶ n. a personal website or web page on which an individual records opinions, links to other sites, etc. on a regular basis.
▶ v. (**blogs, blogging, blogged**) [no obj.] add new material to or regularly update a blog: *it's about a week since I last blogged.*
– DERIVATIVES **blog·ger** n.
– ORIGIN 1990s: shortening of WEBLOG.

blog·o·sphere /ˈblägə,sfi(ə)r/ ▶ n. informal personal websites and blogs collectively.

blog·roll /ˈbläg,rōl/ ▶ n. informal (on a blog) a list of hyperlinks to other blogs or websites.

bloke /blōk/ ▶ n. Brit. informal a man; a fellow.
– ORIGIN mid 19th cent.: from Shelta.

blond /bländ/ ▶ adj. (of hair) fair or pale yellow: *short-cropped blond hair | her hair was dyed blond.* ■ (of a person) having hair of a fair or pale yellow color: *a slim blond woman.* ■ (of a person) having fair hair and a light complexion, typically regarded as a racial characteristic. ■ (of wood and other substances) light in color or tone: *a New York office full of blond wood.*
▶ n. a person with fair hair and skin.
– DERIVATIVES **blond·ish** adj., **blond·ness** n.

> **USAGE** The spellings **blonde** and **blond** correspond to the feminine and masculine forms in French. Although the distinction is often retained in Britain, American usage since the 1970s has generally preferred the gender-neutral **blond**. The adjective **blonde** may still refer to a woman's (but not a man's) hair color, although use of the noun risks offense (*see that blonde over there?*): the offense arises from the fact that the color of hair is not the person. The adjective applied to inanimate objects (such as *wood* or *beer*) is typically spelled **blond**.

blonde /bländ/ ▶ adj. (of a woman or a woman's hair) blond.
▶ n. a blond-haired woman.
– ORIGIN late 17th cent. (earlier as *blond*): from French, feminine of *blond*.

blonde mo·ment ▶ n. humorous an instance of being silly or scatterbrained.
– ORIGIN late 20th cent.: from the stereotypical perception of blonde-haired women as unintelligent.

Blood /bləd/ ▶ n. (pl. **same** or **Bloods**) a member of a North American Indian people belonging to the Blackfoot Confederacy.

blood /bləd/ ▶ n. **1** the red liquid that circulates in the arteries and veins of humans and other vertebrate animals, carrying oxygen to and carbon dioxide from the tissues of the body: *drops of blood.* ■ an internal bodily fluid, not necessarily red, that performs a similar function in invertebrates.

> Blood consists of a mildly alkaline aqueous fluid (plasma) containing red cells (erythrocytes), white cells (leukocytes), and platelets; it is red when oxygenated and purple when deoxygenated. Red blood cells carry the protein hemoglobin, which gives blood its color and can combine with oxygen, thus enabling the blood to carry oxygen from the lungs to the tissues. White blood cells protect the body against the invasion of foreign agents (e.g., bacteria). Platelets and other factors present in plasma are concerned in the clotting of blood, preventing hemorrhage. In medieval science and medicine, blood was regarded as one of the four bodily humors, believed to be associated with a confident and optimistic temperament.

2 violence involving bloodshed: *a commando operation full of blood and danger.*
3 temperament or disposition, esp. when passionate: *a ritual that fires up his blood.*
4 [with adj.] family background; descent or lineage: *she must have Irish blood in her.* ■ [in combination] a person of specified descent: *a mixed-blood.* ■ informal a fellow black person.
5 (usu. **Blood**) a member of a Los Angeles street gang.
6 dated, chiefly Brit. a fashionable and dashing young man: *a group of young bloods.*
▶ v. [with obj.] initiate (someone) in a particular activity: *clubs are too slow in blooding young players.* ■ (in hunting) smear the face of (a novice) with the blood of the kill. ■ (in hunting) give (a hound) a first taste of blood.
– PHRASES **be like getting blood out of** (or **from**) **a stone** (or **turnip**) be extremely difficult (said in reference to obtaining something from someone): *getting a story out of her is like getting blood out of a stone!* **blood and guts** informal violence and bloodshed, typically in fiction. **blood and thunder** informal, chiefly Brit. unrestrained and violent action or behavior, typically in sports or fiction. **blood is thicker than water** proverb relationships and loyalties within a family are the strongest and most important ones. **blood, sweat, and tears** extremely hard work; unstinting effort. **blood will tell** proverb family characteristics cannot be concealed. **first blood 1** the first shedding of blood, esp. in a boxing match or formerly in dueling with swords. **2** the first point or advantage gained in a contest: *King drew first blood when he took the opening set.* **give blood** allow blood to be removed medically from one's body in order to be stored for use in transfusions. **have blood on one's hands** be responsible for someone's death. **have** (or **get**) **one's blood up** be in a fighting mood. **in one's blood** ingrained in or fundamental to one's character: *racing is in his blood.* **in cold blood** ruthlessly; without feeling: *proving that he can kill in cold blood.* **make someone's blood boil** informal infuriate someone. **make someone's blood run cold** horrify someone. **new** (or **fresh**) **blood** new members admitted to a group, typically as an invigorating force. **out for** (**someone's**) **blood** set on getting revenge. **taste blood** achieve an early success that stimulates further efforts: *the speculators have tasted blood and could force a devaluation of the franc.* **young blood** a younger member or members of a group, typically as an invigorating force.
– ORIGIN Old English *blōd*, of Germanic origin; related to German *Blut* and Dutch *bloed*.

blood bank ▶ n. a place where supplies of blood or plasma for transfusion are stored.

blood·bath /ˈbləd,baTH/ ▶ n. an event or situation in which many people are killed in a violent manner: *he allowed the protest to go ahead despite warnings that it would spark a bloodbath |* figurative *the bad publicity would be a media bloodbath.*

blood boost·ing ▶ n. another term for BLOOD DOPING.

blood-borne ▶ adj. (typically of a disease or pathogen) carried by the blood.

blood–brain bar·ri·er ▶ n. Physiology a filtering mechanism of the capillaries that carry blood to the brain and spinal cord tissue, blocking the passage of certain substances.

blood broth·er ▶ n. a brother by birth. ■ a man who has sworn to treat another man as a brother, sometimes with a ceremonial mingling of blood.

blood cell ▶ n. any of the kinds of cells normally found circulating in the blood.

blood clot ▶ n. a gelatinous or semisolid mass of coagulated blood.

blood count ▶ n. a determination of the number of corpuscles in a specific volume of blood. ■ the number found in such a procedure: *a low blood count.*

blood-cur·dling /ˈbləd ,kərd(ə)liNG/ ▶ adj. causing terror or horror: *the warrior's blood-curdling cry.*

blood cur·rant ▶ n. another term for RED-FLOWERING CURRANT (see FLOWERING CURRANT).

blood do·nor ▶ n. a person who gives blood for transfusion.

blood dop·ing (also **blood boosting**) ▶ n. the injection of oxygenated blood into an athlete before an event in an attempt to enhance athletic performance.

blood·ed /ˈblədid/ ▶ adj. [usu. in combination] having blood or a temperament of a specified kind: *warm-blooded animals.* ■ (of horses or cattle) of good pedigree: *a blooded stallion.*

blood feud ▶ n. a lengthy conflict between families involving a cycle of retaliatory killings or injury.

blood film ▶ n. a specimen of blood on a glass slide, used for microscopic investigation of possible abnormalities or pathogens.

blood·fin /ˈbləd,fin/ ▶ n. a small South American freshwater fish that is silvery-yellow with bright red fins. It is popular in aquariums. ● *Aphyocharax rubripinnis*, family Characidae.

blood fluke ▶ n. another term for SCHISTOSOME.

blood group ▶ n. any of the various types of human blood whose antigen characteristics determine compatibility in transfusion. The best known blood groups are those of the ABO system.

blood·guilt /ˈbləd,gilt/ ▶ n. guilt resulting from murder or bloodshed.
– DERIVATIVES **blood·guilt·i·ness** n., **blood·guilt·y** adj.

blood·hound /ˈbləd,hound/ ▶ n. a large hound of a breed with a very keen sense of smell, used in tracking.

bloodhound

blood knot ▶ n. a type of knot used by anglers to join two fishing lines. Also called BARREL KNOT.

blood·less /ˈblədlis/ ▶ adj. **1** (of a revolution or conflict) without violence or killing: *a bloodless coup.*
2 (of the skin or a part of the body) drained of color: *his bloodless lips.* ■ (of a person) cold or unemotional: *a shrewd and bloodless Hollywood mogul.* ■ lacking in vitality; feeble: *their occasionally bloodless chamber jazz.*
– DERIVATIVES **blood·less·ly** adv., **blood·less·ness** n.

blood·let·ting /ˈbləd,letiNG/ ▶ n. chiefly historical the surgical removal of some of a patient's blood for therapeutic purposes. ■ the violent killing and wounding of people during a war or conflict: *gang members have halted their internecine bloodletting.* ■ bitter division and quarreling within an organization.

blood·line /ˈbləd,līn/ ▶ n. an animal's set of ancestors or pedigree, typically considered with regard to the desirable characteristics bred into it. ■ a set of ancestors or line of descent of a person.

blood·lust /ˈbləd,ləst/ ▶ n. uncontrollable desire to kill or maim others.

blood meal ▶ n. dried blood used for feeding animals and as a fertilizer.

blood·mo·bile /ˈblədmə,bēl/ ▶ n. a motor vehicle equipped for collecting blood from volunteer donors.

blood mon·ey ▶ n. money paid in compensation to the family of someone who has been killed. ■ money paid to a hired killer. ■ money paid by the police or the media for information about a killer or killing.

blood or·ange ▶ n. an orange of a variety with red or red-streaked flesh.

blood plate·let ▶ n. see PLATELET.

blood poi·soning ▶ n. the presence of microorganisms or their toxins in the blood, causing disease; septicemia.

blood pres·sure ▶ n. the pressure of the blood in the circulatory system, often measured for diagnosis since it is closely related to the force and rate of the heartbeat and the diameter and elasticity of the arterial walls.

blood pud·ding ▶ n. another term for BLOOD SAUSAGE.

blood red ▶ n. a deep red: [as modifier] *a blood-red lipstick.*

blood re·la·tion (also **blood relative**) ▶ n. a person related to another by birth rather than by marriage.

blood·root /ˈbləd,ro͞ot, -,ro͝ot/ ▶ n. **1** a North American plant of the poppy family that has white flowers and fleshy underground rhizomes that exude red sap when cut. ● *Sanguinaria canadensis*, family Papaveraceae.
2 a lilylike Australian plant with a red rhizome that is roasted and eaten by some Aborigines. ● *Haemodorum coccineum*, family Haemodoraceae.

bloodroot 1

blood sau·sage (also **blood pudding**) ▶ n. a dark sausage containing pork, dried pig's blood, and suet.

blood·shed /ˈbləd,SHed/ ▶ n. the killing or wounding of people, typically on a large scale during a conflict.

blood·shot /ˈbləd,SHät/ ▶ adj. (of the eyes) inflamed or tinged with blood, typically as a result of tiredness.

blood sport ▶ n. (usu. **blood sports**) a sport involving the shedding of blood, esp. the hunting or killing of animals: *cockfighting, bullfighting, fox hunting, and other blood sports* | figurative *politics is a blood sport.*

blood·stain /ˈbləd,stān/ ▶ n. a stain or a spot caused by blood.
– DERIVATIVES **blood·stained** adj.

blood·stock /ˈbləd,stäk/ ▶ n. [treated as sing. or pl.] thoroughbred horses considered collectively.

blood·stone /ˈbləd,stōn/ ▶ n. a type of green chalcedony spotted or streaked with red, used as a gemstone.

blood·stream /ˈbləd,strēm/ ▶ n. [in sing.] the blood circulating through the body of a person or animal.

blood·suck·er /ˈbləd,səkər/ ▶ n. **1** an animal or insect that sucks blood, esp. a leech or a mosquito.
2 a long-tailed arboreal Asian lizard that carries its head in a raised position. Its ability to change color is most marked in the male, whose head and shoulders become bright red when excited. ● *Calotes versicolor*, family Agamidae.
3 a person who extorts money. ■ a person who lives off others; a parasite.
– DERIVATIVES **blood·suck·ing** /-,səkiNG/ adj.

blood sug·ar ▶ n. the concentration of glucose in the blood.

blood test ▶ n. a scientific examination of a sample of blood, typically for the diagnosis of illness or for the detection and measurement of drugs or other substances.

blood·thirst·y /ˈbləd,THərstē/ ▶ adj. (**bloodthirstier**, **bloodthirstiest**) eager to shed blood: *a bloodthirsty dictator.* ■ (of a story or movie) containing or depicting much violence: *a bloodthirsty novel.*
– DERIVATIVES **blood·thirst·i·ly** /-stəlē/ adv., **blood·thirst·i·ness** n.

blood trans·fu·sion ▶ n. Medicine the process of transferring the blood of a person into the veins of another.

blood type ▶ n. another term for BLOOD GROUP.

blood typ·ing ▶ n. the testing of a sample of blood to determine an individual's blood group.

blood ves·sel ▶ n. a tubular structure carrying blood through the tissues and organs; a vein, artery, or capillary.

blood·wood /ˈbləd,wo͝od/ ▶ n. any of a number of hardwood trees with deep red timber, in particular: ● an Australian gum tree (genus *Eucalyptus*, family Myrtaceae, in particular *E. gummifera*). ● a tree of the Old World tropics (genus *Pterocarpus*, family Leguminosae).

blood·worm /ˈblədwərm/ ▶ n. **1** the bright red aquatic larva of a nonbiting midge, the blood of which contains hemoglobin that allows it to live in poorly oxygenated water. ● Genus *Chironomus*, family Chironomidae.
2 another term for TUBIFEX.

blood·wort /ˈbləd,wərt, -,wôrt/ ▶ n. any of various plants having red roots or leaves, esp. the red-veined dock.

blood·y[1] /ˈblədē/ ▶ adj. (**bloodier**, **bloodiest**)
1 covered, smeared, or running with blood: *a bloody body.* ■ composed of or resembling blood: *a bloody discharge.*
2 involving or characterized by bloodshed or cruelty: *a bloody coup* | *the bloody tyrannies of Europe.*
▶ v. (**bloodies**, **bloodying**, **bloodied**) [with obj.] cover or stain with blood: *he ended the fight with his face bloodied and battered* | figurative *she has been bloodied in her three years on the commission.*
– PHRASES **bloody** (or **bloodied**) **but unbowed** proud of what one has achieved despite having suffered great difficulties or losses.
– DERIVATIVES **blood·i·ly** /ˈblədəlē/ adv., **blood·i·ness** n.
– ORIGIN Old English *blōdig* (see BLOOD, -Y[1]).

blood·y[2] ▶ adj. **1** [attrib.] informal, chiefly Brit. used to express anger, annoyance, or shock, or simply for emphasis: *took your bloody time* | [as exclamation] *bloody Hell!—what was that?* | [as submodifier] *it's bloody cold outside.*
2 Brit. dated unpleasant or perverse: *don't be too bloody to poor Jack.*
– ORIGIN mid 17th cent.: from BLOODY[1]. The use of *bloody* to add emphasis to an expression is of uncertain origin, but is thought to have a connection with the "bloods" (aristocratic rowdies) of the late 17th and early 18th centuries; hence the phrase *bloody drunk* (= as drunk as a blood) meant 'very drunk indeed' After the mid 18th cent. until quite recently, *bloody* used as a swearword was regarded as unprintable, probably from the mistaken belief that it implied a blasphemous reference to the blood of Christ, or that the word was an alteration of "by Our Lady"; hence a widespread caution in using the term even in phrases such as *bloody battle* merely referring to bloodshed.

Blood·y Mar·y[1] the nickname of Mary I of England (see MARY[2]).

Blood·y Mar·y[2] ▶ n. a drink consisting of vodka and seasoned tomato juice.

blood·y-mind·ed ▶ adj. Brit. informal deliberately uncooperative.
– DERIVATIVES **blood·y-mind·ed·ly** adv., **blood·y-mind·ed·ness** n.

bloo·ey /ˈblo͞oē/ (also **blooie**) informal ▶ adv. & adj. awry; amiss: [as adv.] *the ignition switch went blooey* | *my head for figures has gone blooey.*
▶ exclam. used to convey that something has happened in an abrupt way: *and, blooey! He shot himself dead.*
– ORIGIN 1920s: of unknown origin.

bloom[1] /blo͞om/ ▶ n. **1** a flower, esp. one cultivated for its beauty: *an exotic bloom* | *the hydrangea has a wealth of bloom.* ■ the state or period of flowering: *the apple trees were* ***in bloom.*** ■ the state or period of greatest beauty, freshness, or vigor: *a young girl, still* ***in the bloom of youth.***
2 [in sing.] a youthful or healthy glow in a person's complexion: *her face had lost its usual bloom.*
3 a delicate powdery surface deposit on certain fresh fruits, leaves, or stems. ■ (also **algal bloom**) a rapid growth of microscopic algae or cyanobacteria in water, often resulting in a colored scum on the surface. ■ a grayish-white appearance on chocolate caused by cocoa butter rising to the surface.
4 a full bright sound, esp. in a musical recording: *the remastering has lost some of the bloom of the strings.*
▶ v. [no obj.] produce flowers; be in flower: *a rose tree bloomed on a ruined wall.* ■ come into or be in full beauty or health; flourish: *she bloomed as an actress under his tutelage.* ■ (of fire, color, or light) become radiant and glowing: *color bloomed in her cheeks.*
– PHRASES **the bloom is off the rose** something is no longer new, fresh, or exciting.
– ORIGIN Middle English: from Old Norse *blóm* 'flower, blossom,' *blómi* 'prosperity,' *blómar* 'flowers.'

bloom[2] ▶ n. a mass of iron, steel, or other metal hammered or rolled into a thick bar for further working. ■ historical an unworked mass of puddled iron.
▶ v. [with obj.] (usu. as noun **blooming**) make (metal) into such a mass.
– ORIGIN Old English *blōma*, of unknown origin.

Bloom·er /ˈblo͞omər/, Amelia Jenks (1818–94), US suffragette and social reformer. She founded and edited 1849–55 the feminist paper *Lily*, and she wore full pants that came to be known as "bloomers."

bloom·er[1] /ˈblo͞omər/ ▶ n. [usu. in combination] a plant that produces flowers at a specified time: *fragrant night-bloomers such as nicotiana.* ■ [with adj.] a person who matures or flourishes at a specified time: *he was a late bloomer.*

bloom·er[2] ▶ n. Brit. informal, dated a serious or stupid mistake.
– ORIGIN late 19th cent.: equivalent to *blooming error.*

bloo·mers /ˈblo͞omərz/ ▶ plural n. women's loose-fitting knee-length underpants, considered old-fashioned. ■ historical women's and girls' loose-fitting trousers, gathered at the knee or, originally, the ankle.
– ORIGIN mid 19th cent.: named after Mrs. Amelia J. *Bloomer* (1818–94), an American social reformer who advocated a similar garment.

Bloom·field[1] /ˈblo͞om,fēld/ a township in northeastern New Jersey, north of Newark; pop. 43,885 (est. 2008).

Bloom·field[2], Leonard (1887–1949), US linguist. One of the founders of American structural linguistics, his primary aim was to establish linguistics as an autonomous and scientific discipline. He wrote *Language* (1933).

bloom·ing /ˈblo͞omiNG/ ▶ adj. & adv. Brit. informal used for emphasis or to express annoyance: [as adj.] *I didn't learn a blooming thing* | [as submodifier] *a blooming good read.*

Bloom·ing·ton /ˈblo͞omiNGtən/ **1** a commercial city in central Illinois; pop. 73,026 (est. 2008).
2 a city in south central Indiana, noted for its limestone industry and home to Indiana University; pop. 71,819 (est. 2008).
3 a city in southeastern Minnesota, south of Minneapolis. It is home to the huge Mall of America; pop. 81,280 (est. 2008).

Blooms·bur·y /ˈblo͞omzbərē, -,berē/ an area of central London noted for its large squares and gardens and for its associations with the Bloomsbury Group. The British Museum is located here. ■ [as adj.] associated with or similar to the Bloomsbury Group.

Blooms·bur·y Group a group of writers, artists, and philosophers living in or associated with Bloomsbury in the early 20th century. Members of the group, which included Virginia Woolf, Lytton Strachey, Vanessa Bell, Duncan Grant, and Roger Fry, were known for their unconventional lifestyles and attitudes and were a powerful force in the growth of modernism.

bloop /blo͞op/ ▶ **v. 1** [no obj.] informal make a mistake: *the company admitted it had blooped.* ■ [with obj.] Baseball hit a ball weakly or make (a hit) from a poorly hit fly ball landing just beyond the reach of the infielders.
2 [no obj.] chiefly Brit. (of an electronic device) emit a short low-pitched noise.
▶ **n. 1** informal a mistake: *a typical beginner's bloop.* ■ Baseball another term for **BLOOPER** (sense 2): [as modifier] *a bloop single.*
2 chiefly Brit. a short low-pitched noise emitted by an electronic device.
– DERIVATIVES **bloop·y adj.**
– ORIGIN 1920s: imitative.

bloop·er /'blo͞opər/ ▶ **n.** informal **1** an embarrassing error: *he poked fun at his own tendency to utter bloopers.* ■ a brief television or radio segment containing a humorous error, often collected with others for broadcast as a group: *a selection of bloopers and outtakes from the evening.*
2 Baseball a weakly hit fly ball landing just beyond the reach of the infielders: *a blooper over the shortstop's head.*
– ORIGIN 1926 (originally denoting a radio that caused others to *bloop*, i.e., emit a loud howling noise): from imitative **BLOOP** + **-ER**[1].

blos·som /'bläsəm/ ▶ **n.** a flower or a mass of flowers on a tree or bush: *tiny white blossoms | the slopes were ablaze with almond blossom.* ■ the state or period of flowering: *fruit trees* ***in blossom.***
▶ **v.** [no obj.] (of a tree or bush) produce flowers or masses of flowers: *the mango trees have shed their fruit and blossomed again.* ■ mature or develop in a promising or healthy way: *their friendship* ***blossomed into*** *romance* | (as noun **blossoming**) *the blossoming of experimental theater.*
– DERIVATIVES **blos·som·y adj.**
– ORIGIN Old English *blōstm, blōstma* (noun), *blōstmian* (verb), of Germanic origin; related to Dutch *bloesem*, also to **BLOOM**[1].

blot /blät/ ▶ **n.** a dark mark or stain, typically one made by ink, paint, or dirt: *an ink blot.* ■ a shameful act or quality that tarnishes an otherwise good character or reputation: *the only blot on an otherwise clean campaign.* ■ Biochemistry a procedure in which proteins or nucleic acids separated on a gel are transferred directly to an immobilizing medium for identification.
▶ **v. (blots, blotting, blotted)** [with obj.] **1** dry (a wet surface or substance) using an absorbent material: *Guy blotted his face with a dust rag.* ■ Biochemistry transfer by means of a blot.
2 mark or stain (something): (as adj. **blotted**) *the writing was messy and blotted.* ■ tarnish the good character or reputation of: *the turmoil blotted his memory of the school.*
3 (**blot something out**) cover writing or pictures with ink or paint so that they cannot be seen. ■ obscure a view: *a dust shield blotting out the sun.* ■ obliterate or disregard something painful in one's memory or existence: *the concentration necessary to her job blotted out all the feelings.*
– ORIGIN late Middle English: probably of Scandinavian origin and related to Old Norse *blettr.*

blotch /bläCH/ ▶ **n.** an irregular patch or unsightly mark on a surface, typically the skin: *red blotches on her face.*
▶ **v.** cover with blotches: *her face was blotched and swollen with crying.*
– ORIGIN early 17th cent. (as a verb): partly an alteration of obsolete *plotch* in the same sense (of unknown origin), influenced by **BLOT**; partly a blend of **BLOT** and **BOTCH**.

blotch·y /'bläCHē/ ▶ **adj. (blotchier, blotchiest)** covered with blotches; patchy: *discoloration or blotchy skin on the legs.*

blot·ter /'blätər/ ▶ **n. 1** a sheet or pad of blotting paper inserted into a frame and kept on a desk.
2 a temporary recording book, esp. a police charge sheet: *the boys ended up on police blotters for property crimes.*

blot·ting pa·per ▶ **n.** absorbent paper used for soaking up excess ink when writing.

blot·to /'blätō/ ▶ **adj.** informal extremely drunk: *we got blotto.*
– ORIGIN early 20th cent.: from **BLOT** + **-O**.

blouse /blous, blouz/ ▶ **n.** a woman's loose upper garment resembling a shirt, typically with a collar, buttons, and sleeves. ■ a loose linen or cotton garment of a type worn by peasants and manual workers, typically belted at the waist. ■ a type of jacket worn as part of military uniform.
▶ **v.** [with obj.] make (a garment) hang in loose folds: *I bloused my trousers over my boots* | [no obj.] *my dress bloused out above my waist.*
– ORIGIN early 19th cent. (denoting a belted loose garment worn by peasants): from French, of unknown origin.

blous·on /'blou,sän, -,zän/ ▶ **n.** a short loose-fitting jacket, typically bloused and finishing at the waist.
– ORIGIN early 20th cent.: from French, diminutive of **BLOUSE**.

blo·vi·ate /'blōvē,āt/ ▶ **v.** [no obj.] informal talk at length, esp. in an inflated or empty way.
– DERIVATIVES **blo·vi·ation n., blo·vi·ator n.**
– ORIGIN mid 19th cent.: perhaps from **BLOW**[1].

blow[1] /blō/ ▶ **v.** (past **blew** /blo͞o/; past participle **blown** /blōn/) **1** [no obj.] (of wind) move creating an air current: *a cold wind began to blow.* ■ [with obj.] (of wind) cause to move; propel: *a gust of wind blew a cloud of smoke into his face | the spire was blown down during a gale.* ■ be carried, driven, or moved by the wind or an air current: *it was so windy that the tent nearly blew away | cotton curtains blowing in the breeze.* ■ [with obj.] informal leave (a place): *I'm ready to blow town* | [no obj.] *I'd better blow.*
2 [no obj.] (of a person) expel air through pursed lips: *Willie took a deep breath, and blew | he* ***blew on*** *his coffee to cool it.* ■ [with obj.] use one's breath to propel: *he blew cigar smoke in her face.* ■ breathe hard; pant: *Uncle Albert was soon puffing and blowing.* ■ [with obj.] cause to breathe hard; exhaust of breath: (as adj. **blown**) *an exhausted, blown horse.* ■ [with obj.] (of a person) force air through the mouth into (an instrument) in order to make a sound: *the umpire blew his whistle.* ■ (of such an instrument) make a noise through being blown into in such a way: *police whistles blew.* ■ [with obj.] sound (the horn of a vehicle). ■ informal play jazz or rock music in an unrestrained style: *it took him maybe five choruses to warm up, but then he could really blow.* ■ [with obj.] force air through a tube into (molten glass) in order to create an artifact. ■ [with obj.] remove the contents of (an egg) by forcing air through it. ■ [with adverbial of place] (of flies) lay eggs in or on something: *to repel the hordes of flies that would otherwise blow on the buffalo hide.* ■ (of a whale) eject air and vapor through the blowhole.
3 [with obj.] (of an explosion or explosive device) displace violently or send flying: *the blast had blown the windows out of the van | the back of his head had been blown away.* ■ [no obj.] (of a vehicle tire) burst suddenly while the vehicle is in motion. ■ burst or cause to burst due to pressure or overheating: [no obj.] *the engines sounded as if their exhausts had blown* | [with obj.] *frost will have blown a compression joint.* ■ (of an electrical circuit) burn out or cause to burn out through overloading: [no obj.] *the fuse in the plug had blown* | [with obj.] *the floodlights blew a fuse.*
4 [with obj.] informal spend recklessly: *they blew $100,000 in just eighteen months.*
5 [with obj.] informal completely lose or miss (an opportunity): *the wider issues were to show that politicians had blown it.* ■ expose (a stratagem): *a man whose cover was blown.*
6 (past participle **blowed**) [with obj., usu. as imperative] Brit. informal damn: *"Well, blow me," he said, "I never knew that"* | [with clause] ***I'm blowed if*** *I want to see him again.*
7 [with obj.] vulgar slang perform fellatio.
▶ **n. 1** [in sing.] a strong wind: *we're in for a blow.*
2 an act of blowing on an instrument: *a number of blows on the whistle.* ■ [in sing.] an act of blowing one's nose: *give your nose a good blow.* ■ [in sing.] informal a spell of playing jazz or rock music. ■ (in steelmaking) an act of sending an air or oxygen blast through molten metal in a converter.
3 informal cocaine.
– PHRASES **be blown off course** (of a project) be disrupted by some circumstance. **be blown out of the water** (of a person, idea, or project) be shown to lack all credibility. **blow away the cobwebs** refresh oneself when feeling weary, typically by having some fresh air. **blow someone's brains out** informal kill someone with a shot in the head with a firearm. **blow chunks** informal vomit. **blow the doors off** informal be considerably better or more successful than: *a package that blows the doors off anything on the market.* **blow a fuse** see **FUSE**[1]. **blow a gasket** informal lose one's temper. **blow one's own horn** see **HORN**. **blow hot and cold** vacillate. **blow someone a kiss** kiss the tips of one's fingers then blow across them toward someone as a gesture of affection. **blow one's lid** (or **top** or **stack** or **cool**) informal lose one's temper. **blow the lid off** see **LID**. **blow me down** Brit. an exclamation of surprise. **blow someone's mind** informal affect someone very strongly. **blow one's nose** clear one's nose of mucus by blowing through it into a handkerchief. **blow off steam** see **LET OFF STEAM** at **STEAM**. **blow a raspberry** see **RASPBERRY**. **blow someone's socks off** see **SOCK**. **blow something to bits** (or **pieces** or **smithereens**) use bombs or other explosives to destroy something, typically a building, completely. **blow something out of proportion** exaggerate the importance of something. **blow up in one's face** (of an action, project, or situation) go drastically wrong with damaging effects to oneself. **blow the whistle on** see **WHISTLE**. **blow with the wind** be incapable of maintaining a consistent course of action.
– PHRASAL VERBS **blow someone away** informal **1** kill someone using a firearm. **2** (**be blown away**) be extremely impressed: *I'm blown away by his new poem.* **blow in** informal (of a person) arrive casually and unannounced. **blow off** lose one's temper and shout. **blow someone off** informal fail to keep an appointment with someone. ■ end a romantic or sexual relationship with someone. **blow something off** informal ignore or make light of something. ■ fail to attend something: *Ivy blew off class.* **blow out 1** be extinguished by an air current: *the candles blew out.* **2** (of a tire) puncture while the vehicle is in motion. **3** (of an oil or gas well) emit gas suddenly and forcefully. **4** (**blow itself out**) (of a storm) finally lose its force: figurative *the recession may finally have blown itself out.* **blow someone out** informal defeat someone convincingly. **blow something out 1** use one's breath to extinguish a flame: *he blew out the candle.* **2** informal render a part of the body useless: *he blew out his arm trying to snap a curveball.* **blow over** (of trouble) fade away without serious consequences. **blow up 1** explode. ■ (of a person) lose one's temper: *Meg* ***blows up at*** *Patrick for always throwing his tea bags in the sink.* **2** (of a wind or storm) begin to develop. ■ (of a scandal or dispute) emerge or become public. **3** inflate: *my stomach had started to blow up.* **blow something up 1** cause something to explode. **2** inflate something: *a small pump for blowing up balloons.* ■ enlarge a photograph or text.
– ORIGIN Old English *blāwan*, of Germanic origin; related to German *blähen* 'blow up, swell,' from an Indo-European root shared by Latin *flare* 'blow.'

blow[2] ▶ **n.** a powerful stroke with a hand, weapon, or hard object: *he received a blow to the skull.* ■ a sudden shock or disappointment: *the news came as a crushing blow.*
– PHRASES **at one blow** by a single stroke; in one operation: *the letter had destroyed his certainty at one blow.* **come to blows** start fighting after a disagreement. **soften** (or **cushion**) **the blow** make it easier to cope with a difficult change or upsetting news: *monetary compensation was offered to soften the blow.* **strike a blow for** (or **against**) act in support of (or opposition to): *a chance to strike a blow for freedom.*
– ORIGIN late Middle English: of unknown origin.

blow[3] archaic or literary ▶ **v.** (past **blew** /blo͞o/; past participle **blown** /blōn/) [no obj.] produce flowers or be in flower: *I know a bank where the wild thyme blows.*
▶ **n.** the state or period of flowering: *stocks in fragrant blow.*
– ORIGIN Old English *blōwan*, of Germanic origin; related to Dutch *bloeien* and German *blühen*, also to **BLOOM**[1] and **BLOSSOM**.

blow·back /'blō,bak/ ▶ **n. 1** a process in which gases expand or travel in a direction opposite to the usual one, esp. through escape of pressure or delayed combustion.
2 the unintended adverse results of a political action or situation: *this is the blowback from all those aggressive public health campaigns.*

blow-by-blow ▶ **adj.** [attrib.] (of a description of an event) giving all the details in the order in which they occurred: *he gave them a* ***blow-by-blow account*** *of your rescue.*

blow·dart /'blō,därt/ ▶ **n.** a dart shot from a blowpipe.

blow·down /'blō,doun/ ▶ **n. 1** a tree or trees that have been blown down by the wind: *crews will be removing blowdown for a number of days.* ■ the blowing down of a tree or trees: *the measures did not prevent mass blowdown.*
2 the removal of solids or liquids from a container or pipe using pressure.

blow-dry ▶ **v.** [with obj.] arrange (the hair) into a particular style while drying it with a handheld dryer. ■ (as adj. **blow-dried**) (of a person) well groomed, polished, and assured.
▶ **n.** [in sing.] an act of arranging the hair in such a way.
– DERIVATIVES **blow-dry·er** (also **blowdrier**) **n.**

blow·er /'blōər/ ▶ **n. 1** a person or thing that blows, typically a mechanical device for creating a current of air used to dry or heat something.
2 informal, chiefly Brit. a telephone.

b

blow·fish /ˈblōˌfisн/ ▶ **n.** (pl. **same** or **blowfishes**) any of a number of fishes that are able to inflate their bodies when alarmed, such as a globefish.

blow·fly /ˈblōˌflī/ ▶ **n.** (pl. **blowflies**) a large and typically metallic-colored fly that lays its eggs on meat and carcasses. ● Family Calliphoridae: numerous species, including the bluebottle.

blow·gun /ˈblōˌgən/ ▶ **n.** a primitive weapon consisting of a long tube through which an arrow or dart is propelled by force of the breath.

blow·hard /ˈblōˌhärd/ informal ▶ **n.** a person who blusters and boasts in an unpleasant way: *a bunch of pompous blowhards trying to get on the news* | [as modifier] *local blowhard politicians*.

blow·hole /ˈblōˌhōl/ ▶ **n.** a hole for blowing or breathing through, in particular: ■ the nostril of a whale on the top of its head. ■ a hole in ice to which seals, whales, and other aquatic animals come to breathe. ■ a vent for air or smoke in a tunnel or other structure. ■ a cavity in a metal casting, produced by the escape of air through the liquid metal.

blow job (**BJ**) ▶ **n.** vulgar slang an act of fellatio.

blown /blōn/ past participle of **BLOW**[1].
▶ **adj.** destroyed; spoiled: *a blown fuse* | *your cover is blown*. ■ informal (of a vehicle or its engine) provided with a turbocharger.
– PHRASES **blown away** extremely surprised; flabbergasted: *Sharon was blown away by the place*. **blown to bits** (or **smithereens**) completely destroyed.

blow·off /ˈblōˌôf/ ▶ **n.** the action of emitting a gas, typically to reduce pressure to a safe level.

blow·out /ˈblōˌout/ ▶ **n.** **1** a sudden rupture or malfunction of a part or an apparatus due to pressure, in particular the bursting of an automobile tire. ■ an outburst of anger; an argument: *that exchange led to a big blowout five years ago*. ■ an uprush of oil or gas from a well. ■ informal a melting of an electric fuse.
2 informal an easy victory in a sporting contest or an election: *they had lost seven games—four by blowouts and three by slim margins*.
3 informal a large or lavish meal or social gathering.
4 a hollow eroded by the wind.

blow·pipe /ˈblōˌpīp/ ▶ **n.** **1** another term for **BLOWGUN**.
2 a long tube by means of which molten glass is blown into the required shape. ■ a tube used to intensify the heat of a flame by blowing air or other gas through it at high pressure.

blows·y /ˈblouzē/ (also **blowzy**) ▶ **adj.** (of a woman) coarse, untidy, and red-faced: *a blowsy woman wearing Bermuda shorts and a Bally's sweatshirt* | figurative *blowsy, old-fashioned roses*.
– DERIVATIVES **blows·i·ly** /-zəlē/ **adv.**, **blows·i·ness n.**
– ORIGIN early 17th cent.: from obsolete *blowze* 'beggar's female companion,' of unknown origin.

blow·torch /ˈblōˌtôrcн/ ▶ **n.** a portable device producing a hot flame that is directed onto a surface, typically to solder metal.

blow·up /ˈblōˌəp/ ▶ **n.** **1** an enlargement of a photograph.
2 informal an outburst of anger.
▶ **adj.** [attrib.] inflatable: *a blowup neck pillow*.

blow·y /ˈblō-ē/ ▶ **adj.** (**blowier**, **blowiest**) having or affected by strong winds; windy or windswept: *a blowy day*.

BLT ▶ **n.** informal a sandwich filled with bacon, lettuce, and tomato.

blub·ber[1] /ˈbləbər/ ▶ **n.** the fat of sea mammals, esp. whales and seals. ■ informal, derogatory excessive human fat.
▶ **adj.** [attrib.] archaic (of a person's lips) swollen or protruding. [alteration of obsolete *blabber* 'swollen.']
– DERIVATIVES **blub·ber·y adj.**
– ORIGIN late Middle English (denoting the foaming of the sea, also a bubble on water): perhaps symbolic; compare with **BLOB** and **BLOTCH**.

blub·ber[2] ▶ **v.** [no obj.] informal sob noisily and uncontrollably: *he was blubbering like a child* | [with direct speech] *"I don't like him," blubbered Jonathan*.
– ORIGIN late Middle English: probably symbolic; compare with **BLOB** and **BLUBBER**[1].

blu·chers /ˈblo͞okərz, -cнərz/ ▶ **plural n.** historical strong leather half-boots or high shoes.
– ORIGIN mid 19th cent.: named after G. L. von *Blücher* (1742–1819), Prussian general.

bludg·eon /ˈbləjən/ ▶ **n.** a thick stick with a heavy end, used as a weapon: figurative *a rhetorical bludgeon in the war against liberalism*.
▶ **v.** [with obj.] beat (someone) repeatedly with a bludgeon or other heavy object. ■ force or bully (someone) to do something: *she was determined not to be bludgeoned into submission*. ■ (**bludgeon one's way**) make one's way by brute force.

– ORIGIN mid 18th cent.: of unknown origin.

blue /blo͞o/ ▶ **adj.** (**bluer**, **bluest**) **1** of a color intermediate between green and violet, as of the sky or sea on a sunny day: *the clear blue sky* | *blue jeans* | *deep blue eyes*. ■ (of a person's skin) having or turning such a color, esp. with cold or breathing difficulties: *Annie went blue, and I panicked*. ■ (of a bird or other animal) having blue markings: *a blue jay*. ■ (of cats, foxes, or rabbits) having fur of a smoky gray color: *the blue fox*. ■ (of a ski run) of the second lowest level of difficulty, as indicated by colored markers positioned along it. ■ Physics denoting one of three colors of quark.
2 informal (of a person or mood) melancholy, sad, or depressed: *he's feeling blue*.
3 informal (of a movie, joke, or story) with sexual or pornographic content: *the blue movies are hugely profitable*. ■ (of language) marked by cursing, swearing, and blasphemy.
4 informal, dated rigidly religious or moralistic; puritanical.
▶ **n.** **1** blue color or pigment: *she was dressed in blue* | *the dark blue of his eyes* | *armchairs in pastel blues and greens*. ■ blue clothes or material: *Susan wore blue*. ■ (usu. **Blue**) the Union army in the Civil War, or a member of that army. [because Union soldiers wore blue uniforms.]
2 a blue thing, in particular: ■ a blue ball, piece, etc., in a game or sport. ■ (**the blue**) literary the sky or sea; the unknown: *a lark went trilling up, up into the blue*.
3 [usu. with modifier] a small butterfly, the male of which is predominantly blue while the female is typically brown. ● Numerous genera in the family Lycaenidae.
4 another term for **BLUING**.
▶ **v.** (**blues**, **bluing** or **blueing**, **blued**) **1** make or become blue: [with obj.] *the light dims, bluing the retina* | (as adj. **blued**) *blued paper* | [no obj.] *the day would haze, the air bluing with afternoon*. ■ [with obj.] heat (metal) so as to give it a grayish-blue finish: (as adj. **blued**) *nickel-plated or blued hooks*.
2 [with obj.] wash (white clothes) with bluing.
– PHRASES **do something until** (or **till**) **one is blue in the face** informal put all one's efforts into doing something to no avail: *she could talk to him until she was blue in the face, but he was just not hearing*. **men in blue** informal police officers. **once in a blue moon** informal very rarely. [because a "blue moon" is a phenomenon that occurs very rarely.] **out of the blue** (or **out of a clear blue sky**) informal without warning; unexpectedly: *she phoned me out of the blue*. [with reference to a "blue" (i.e., clear) sky, from which nothing unusual is expected.] **talk a blue streak** informal speak continuously and at great length.
– DERIVATIVES **blue·ness n.**
– ORIGIN Middle English: from Old French *bleu*, ultimately of Germanic origin and related to Old English *blǣwen* 'blue' and Old Norse *blár* 'dark blue.'

blue ba·by ▶ **n.** a baby with a blue complexion from lack of oxygen in the blood due to a congenital defect of the heart or major blood vessels.

blue·back /ˈblo͞oˌbak/ ▶ **n.** a bird or fish, esp. a trout or a sockeye salmon, having a bluish back.

Blue·beard /ˈblo͞oˌbi(ə)rd/ a character in a tale by Charles Perrault, who killed several wives in turn for disobeying his order to avoid a locked room, which contained the bodies of his previous wives. Local tradition in Brittany identifies him with **Gilles de Rais** (*c.*1400–40), a perpetrator of atrocities, although he had only one wife (who left him). ■ (as noun **a Bluebeard**) a man who murders his wives.

blue beat ▶ **n.** another term for **SKA**.

blue·bell /ˈblo͞oˌbel/ ▶ **n.** **1** (also **English bluebell**) a widely cultivated European woodland plant of the lily family that produces clusters of bell-shaped blue flowers in spring. ● *Hyacinthoides* (or *Endymion*) *nonscripta*, family Liliaceae.
2 any of a number of other plants with blue bell-shaped flowers, in particular: ● another term for **BELLFLOWER** ● chiefly Scottish term for **HAREBELL** ● another term for **SQUILL** and other scillas ● short for **VIRGINIA BLUEBELL** ● a plant of the bellflower family (genus *Wahlenbergia*, family Campanulaceae), distributed mostly in the southern hemisphere, e.g., the **Australian bluebell** (*W. gloriosa*).

blue·ber·ry /ˈblo͞oˌberē/ ▶ **n.** (pl. **blueberries**) **1** a hardy dwarf shrub of the heath family, with small, whitish drooping flowers and dark blue edible berries. ● Genus *Vaccinium*, family Ericaceae: several North American species, including the **common highbush blueberry** (*V. corymbosum*), from which many cultivated varieties originate.
2 the small, sweet edible berry of this plant.

blue bice ▶ **n.** see **BICE**.

blue·bill /ˈblo͞oˌbil/ ▶ **n.** any of a number of ducks with blue bills, esp. the scaup.

blue·bird /ˈblo͞oˌbərd/ ▶ **n.** an American songbird of the thrush subfamily, the male of which has a blue head, back, and wings. See also **FAIRY BLUEBIRD**. ● Genus *Sialia*, subfamily Turdinae, family Muscicapidae: three species, including the **eastern bluebird** (*S. sialis*).

blue-black ▶ **adj.** black with a tinge of blue.

blue blood ▶ **n.** noble birth: *blue blood is no guarantee of any particular merit, competence, or expertise*. ■ (also **blueblood**) a person of noble birth: *a comforting figure among that crowd of blue bloods*.
– DERIVATIVES **blue-blood·ed adj.**

blue·bon·net /ˈblo͞oˌbänit/ ▶ **n.** a blue-flowered lupine, esp. common in Texas. ● Genus *Lupinus*, family Leguminosae: several species, in particular the **Texas bluebonnet** (*L. texensis*) and the **shy bluebonnet** (*L. subcarnosus*).

Blue Book ▶ **n.** **1** an official book listing government officials. ■ Brit. a report bound in a blue cover and issued by Parliament or the Privy Council. ■ (in full **Kelley Blue Book**) trademark a reference book listing the prices of used cars. ■ (usu. **blue book**) an authoritative handbook, e.g., a listing of socially prominent people.
2 (**blue book**) a blank book used for written examinations in high school and college.

blue·bot·tle /ˈblo͞oˌbätl/ ▶ **n.** **1** a common blowfly with a metallic-blue body, the female of which often comes into houses searching for a suitable food source on which to lay her eggs. ● *Calliphora vomitoria*, family Calliphoridae.
2 the wild cornflower.

blue box ▶ **n.** an electronic device used to access long-distance telephone lines illegally.

blue cheese ▶ **n.** cheese containing veins of blue mold, such as Gorgonzola and Danish Blue.

blue-chip ▶ **adj.** [attrib.] denoting companies or their shares considered to be a reliable investment, though less secure than gilt-edged stock. ■ of the highest quality: *blue-chip art*.
– ORIGIN early 20th cent. (originally US): from the *blue chip* used in gambling games, which usually has a high value.

blue chip·per ▶ **n.** a highly valued person, esp. an athlete.

blue coat ▶ **n.** a person who wears a blue uniform, in particular: ■ a soldier, esp. a Union soldier during the Civil War. ■ a police officer.

blue co·hosh ▶ **n.** see **COHOSH**.

blue-col·lar ▶ **adj.** of or relating to manual work or workers, particularly in industry: *their speech and attitudes mark them as blue-collar guys*. Compare with **WHITE-COLLAR**.

blue corn ▶ **n.** a variety of corn with bluish grains.

blue crab ▶ **n.** a large edible swimming crab of the Atlantic coast of North America. ● *Callinectes sapidus*, family Portunidae.

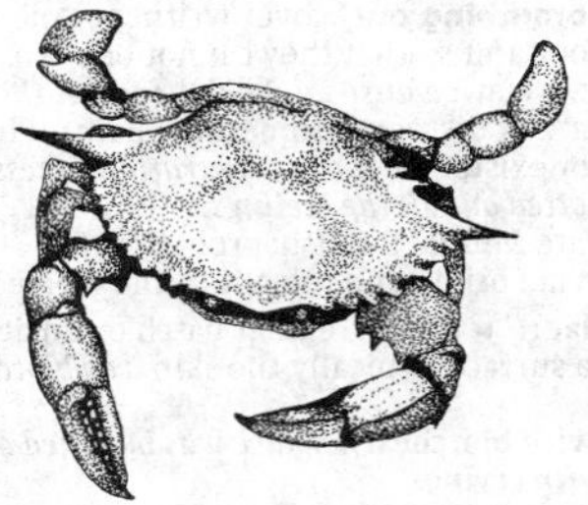

blue crab

blue crane ▶ **n.** a large South African crane with blue-gray plumage. Also called **STANLEY CRANE**. ● *Anthropoides paradisea*, family Gruidae. ■ this bird as the national bird of South Africa.

blue·curls /ˈblo͞oˌkərlz/ ▶ **n.** a North American plant of the mint family, with small blue flowers and blue-stalked, deeply curled stamens. ● Genus *Trichtostema*, family Labiatae: several species, in particular *T. dichotomum*, found esp. in the northeastern US, and the typically more southern *T. setaceum*.

blue dev·il ▶ **n.** informal **1** a blue capsule containing a barbiturate.
2 (**blue devils**) a feeling of despondency or low spirits.
3 (**blue devils**) another term for **DELIRIUM TREMENS**.

blue dog Dem·o·crat (also **Blue Dog Democrat**) ▶ **n.** informal in the US, a Democrat from a southern state who has a conservative voting record.

– ORIGIN From the name of a coalition of Southern Democrats in the US Congress formed in 1995. Their name alludes to an older term, "yellow dog Democrat," for a party loyalist who allegedly "would vote for a yellow dog if it were on the ballot as a Democrat." The blue dog Democrats claim that their conservative views have been choked off by their own party to the point that these yellow dogs have turned blue.

blue-eyed boy ▶ n. informal a person highly regarded by someone and treated with special favor.

blue-eyed grass ▶ n. a North American plant of the iris family, cultivated for its blue flowers. ● Genus *Sisyrinchium*, family Iridaceae: several species, including the flat-stemmed *S. montanum*.

blue-eyed Mar·y ▶ n. a low-growing plant of the borage family that bears bright blue flowers and spreads by means of runners. ● *Omphalodes verna*, family Boraginaceae.

blue·fin /ˈblo͞oˌfin/ (also **bluefin tuna**) ▶ n. the most common large tuna, which occurs worldwide in warm seas. It is probably the largest bony fish, and is very important as a food and game fish. ● *Thunnus thynnus*, family Scombridae.

blue·fish /ˈblo͞oˌfisн/ ▶ n. (pl. **same** or **bluefishes**) a predatory blue-colored marine fish that inhabits tropical and temperate waters and is popular as a game fish. ● *Pomatomus saltatrix*, the only member of the family Pomatomidae.

blue flag ▶ n. **1** a violet-flowered iris that grows in marshy places and wet meadows. ● Genus *Iris*, family Iridaceae: several species, in particular the **larger blue flag** (*I. versicolor*) and the **slender blue flag** (*I. prismatica*).
2 a European award for beaches based on cleanliness and safety.

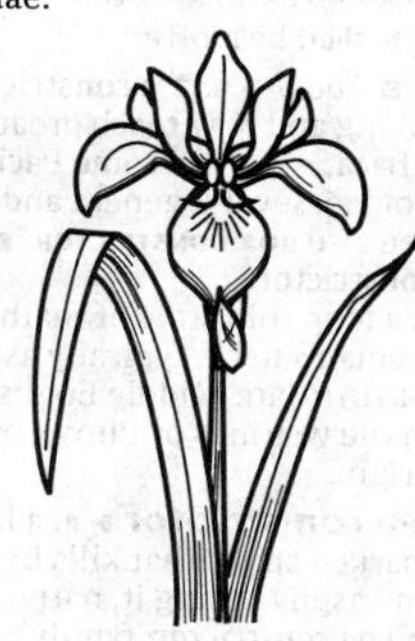
larger blue flag

blue flu ▶ n. a strike action, esp. among police officers, in which workers are absent on the pretext of sickness.

blue·gill /ˈblo͞oˌgil/ ▶ n. an edible North American freshwater fish of the sunfish family, with a deep body and bluish cheeks and gill covers. It is popular with anglers. ● *Lepomis macrochirus*, family Centrarchidae.

blue·grass /ˈblo͞oˌgras/ ▶ n. **1** (also **Kentucky bluegrass**) a bluish-green grass that was introduced into North America from northern Europe. It is widely grown for fodder, esp. in Kentucky and Virginia. See also MEADOW GRASS.
2 a kind of country music influenced by jazz and blues and characterized by virtuosic playing of banjos and guitars and high-pitched, close-harmony vocals.

Blue·grass State a nickname for the state of KENTUCKY.

blue-green al·gae ▶ plural n. another term for CYANOBACTERIA.

blue ground ▶ n. another term for KIMBERLITE.

blue gum ▶ n. a eucalyptus tree with blue-green aromatic leaves and smooth bark. ● Genus *Eucalyptus*, family Myrtaceae: several species, in particular *E. regnans*.

blue·head /ˈblo͞oˌhed/ ▶ n. a small wrasse (fish) of the tropical eastern Atlantic that is sometimes kept in aquariums. Large males have a blue head and green body with vertical stripes in between, and females and smaller males are predominantly yellowish. ● *Thalassoma bifasciatum*, family Labridae.

blue hel·met ▶ n. a member of a UN peacekeeping force.

Blue Hen State a nickname for the state of DELAWARE[1].

blue ice ▶ n. clean, dense ice of a vivid blue color, formed in glaciers by the recrystallization of snow.

blue·ing /ˈblo͞oiNG/ ▶ n. variant spelling of BLUING.

blue·ish /ˈblo͞oisн/ ▶ adj. variant spelling of BLUISH.

blue·jack·et /ˈblo͞oˌjakit/ ▶ n. informal a sailor in the navy.

blue jay ▶ n. a common North American jay with a blue crest, back, wings, and tail. ● *Cyanocitta cristata*, family Corvidae.

blue jeans ▶ n. jeans made of blue denim.

blue law ▶ n. a law prohibiting certain activities, such as shopping, on a Sunday. ■ (in colonial New England) a strict religious law, particularly one preventing entertainment or leisure activities on a Sunday.

Blue Law State a nickname for the state of CONNECTICUT.

blue line ▶ n. Ice Hockey either of the two lines midway between the center of the rink and each goal.

blue mold ▶ n. a bluish fungus that grows on food. Blue molds are deliberately introduced into some cheeses, and some kinds are used to produce antibiotics such as penicillin. ● *Penicillium* and other genera, phylum Ascomycota.

Blue Nile one of the two principal headwaters of the Nile River. It rises from Lake Tana in northwestern Ethiopia and flows about 1,000 miles (1,600 km) south and then northwest into Sudan, where it meets the White Nile at Khartoum.

blue·nose /ˈblo͞oˌnōz/ ▶ n. informal **1** a priggish or puritanical person: [as modifier] *the most restrictive, bluenose standards*.
2 (**Bluenose**) a person from Nova Scotia.
– DERIVATIVES **bluenosed** adj. (sense 1).

blue note ▶ n. Music a minor interval where a major would be expected, used esp. in jazz.

blue-pen·cil ▶ v. [with obj.] edit or make cuts in (a manuscript, movie, or other work).

Blue Pe·ter ▶ n. a blue flag with a white square in the center, raised by a ship about to leave port.

blue plate ▶ adj. [attrib.] (of a restaurant meal) consisting of a full main course ordered as a single menu item: *the blue plate special*.
– ORIGIN mid 20th cent.: with reference to the original blue plates divided into compartments, on which fixed-price restaurant meals were served.

blue·point /ˈblo͞oˌpoint/ ▶ n. a small oyster, in particular one harvested from the oyster beds in Great South Bay, at Blue Point, Long Island. Bluepoints are typically served raw, on the half shell.

blue·print /ˈblo͞oˌprint/ ▶ n. a design plan or other technical drawing. ■ something that acts as a plan, model, or template: *a vague* ***blueprint for*** *fundamental land redistribution*.
▶ v. [with obj.] draw up (a plan or model): (as adj. **blueprinted**) *a neatly blueprinted scheme*.
– ORIGIN late 19th cent.: from the original process in which prints were composed of white lines on a blue ground or of blue lines on a white ground.

blue ra·cer ▶ n. a grayish-blue variety of blacksnake (*Coluber constrictor foxii*), found in the central US.

blue rib·bon ▶ n. (Brit. also **blue riband**) a badge made of blue ribbon and given as first prize to the winner of a competition. ■ (in the UK) a badge worn by members of the Order of the Garter.

blue-rib·bon ▶ adj. [attrib.] of the highest quality; first-class: *blue-ribbon service*. ■ (of a jury or committee) carefully or specially selected: *the SEC's blue-ribbon committee on auditor independence*.

Blue Ridge Moun·tains a range in the Appalachian Mountains in the eastern US that stretches from southern Pennsylvania to northern Georgia. Mount Mitchell is the highest peak, rising to a height of 6,684 feet (2,037 m).

blue rinse ▶ n. a preparation used as a rinse on gray or white hair intended to make it look more silver.
▶ adj. (**blue-rinse** or **blue-rinsed**) [attrib.] informal, derogatory of or relating to elderly and conservative women: *the blue-rinse brigade*.

blue roan ▶ adj. denoting an animal's coat consisting of black-and-white hairs evenly mixed, giving it a blue-gray hue.
▶ n. an animal with such a coat.

blues /blo͞oz/ ▶ plural n. **1** [treated as sing.] (or pl. often **the blues**) melancholic music of black American folk origin, typically in a twelve-bar sequence. It developed in the rural southern US toward the end of the 19th century, finding a wider audience in the 1940s as blacks migrated to the cities. This urban blues gave rise to rhythm and blues and rock and roll. ■ [treated as sing.] a piece of such music: *we'll do a blues in C*.
2 (**the blues**) informal feelings of melancholy, sadness, or depression: *she's got the blues*.
– DERIVATIVES **blues·man** n. (pl. **bluesmen**) (sense 1), **blues·y** adj. (sense 1).
– ORIGIN mid 18th cent. (in sense 2): elliptically from *blue devils* 'depression or delirium tremens.'

blue screen ▶ n. [often as modifier] (in film and video techniques such as chromakey) a blue (or green) background in front of which moving subjects are filmed and which allows a separately filmed background to be added to the final image: *a blue-screen effect*. Also called GREEN SCREEN.

blue shark ▶ n. a long slender shark with an indigo-blue back and white underparts, typically occurring in the open sea. ● *Prionace glauca*, family Carcharhinidae.

blue·shift /ˈblo͞oˌsнift/ (also **blue shift**) ▶ n. Astronomy the displacement of the spectrum to shorter wavelengths in the light coming from distant celestial objects moving toward the observer. Compare with REDSHIFT.

blue-sky (also **blue-skies**) informal ▶ adj. [attrib.] not yet practical or profitable: *blue-sky research*.
▶ v. [no obj.] make impractical or as yet unachievable plans.

blue-sky law ▶ n. a law regulating the sale of securities, intended to protect the public from fraud.

Blue Springs a city in west central Missouri, east of Kansas City; pop. 55,698 (est. 2008).

blue spruce ▶ n. a North American spruce with sharp, stiff blue-green needles, growing wild in the central Rocky Mountains. Its many cultivated varieties tend to be bluer in color than the wild ones. Also called COLORADO BLUE SPRUCE, COLORADO SPRUCE. ● *Picea pungens*, family Pinaceae.

blue state ▶ n. a US state that predominantly votes for or supports the Democratic Party. Compare with RED STATE.
– ORIGIN from the typical color used to represent the Democratic Party on maps during elections.

blue·stem /ˈblo͞oˌstem/ ▶ n. a coarse North American prairie grass with bluish leaf sheaths, often cultivated as forage. ● Genus *Andropogon*, family Gramineae.

blue·stock·ing /ˈblo͞oˌstäkiNG/ ▶ n. often derogatory an intellectual or literary woman.
– ORIGIN late 17th cent.: originally used to describe a man wearing blue worsted (instead of formal black silk) stockings; extended to mean 'in informal dress.' Later the term denoted a person who attended the literary assemblies held (*c*.1750) by three London society ladies, where some of the men favored less formal dress. The women who attended became known as *blue-stocking ladies* or *blue-stockingers*.

blue·stone /ˈblo͞oˌstōn/ ▶ n. any of various bluish or gray building stones. ■ any of the smaller stones made of dolerite found in the inner part of Stonehenge.

blu·et /ˈblo͞oit/ ▶ n. a low-growing North American plant of the bedstraw family, with small four-petaled flowers and paired leaves. Bluets often grow in large groups. ● Genus *Houstonia* (or *Hedyotis*), family Rubiaceae: several species, esp. *H. caerulea*, with milky-blue or white flowers, and **long-leaved bluets** (*H. longifolia*), with white or lavender flowers.
– ORIGIN early 18th cent.: from French, diminutive of *bleu* 'blue.'

blue·throat /ˈblo͞oˌтнrōt/ ▶ n. a small, lively thrush found in northern Eurasia and Alaska. The male has a blue throat with a reddish spot in the center. ● *Luscinia svecica*, subfamily Turdinae, family Muscicapidae.

blue tit ▶ n. a small titmouse with a blue cap, greenish-blue back, and yellow underparts, widespread in Eurasia and northwestern Africa. ● *Parus caeruleus*, family Paridae.

blue-tongued skink (also **blue-tongued lizard**) ▶ n. a heavily built Australian skink with a large head, short limbs, and a blue tongue, which is displayed in defense. ● Genus *Tiliqua*, family Scincidae: several species, in particular *T. scincoides*, which is commonly kept as a pet.

Blue·tooth /ˈblo͞oˌto͞oтн/ ▶ n. trademark a standard for the short-range wireless interconnection of cellular phones, computers, and other electronic devices.
– ORIGIN 1990s: said to be named after King Harald *Bluetooth* (910–985), credited with uniting Denmark and Norway, as Bluetooth technology unifies the telecommunications and computing industries.

blue vit·ri·ol ▶ n. archaic crystalline copper sulfate.

blue-wa·ter ▶ adj. relating to or associated with the open sea; oceangoing: *a blue-water navy*.

blue·weed /ˈblo͞oˌwēd/ ▶ n. another term for VIPER'S BUGLOSS.

blue whale ▶ n. a migratory, mottled bluish-gray rorqual, found in all oceans of the world. Known to grow as long as 110 feet (33 m) and weigh as much as 150 tons (136,000 kg), it is the largest animal ever to inhabit the earth. ● *Balaenoptera musculus*, family Balaenopteridae.

bluff[1] /bləf/ ▶ n. an attempt to deceive someone into believing that one can or will do something: *the offer was denounced as a bluff | his game of bluff*.

▸ **v.** [no obj.] try to deceive someone as to one's abilities or intentions: *he's been bluffing all along* | *he bluffed his way onto an Antarctic supply vessel* | [with obj.] *the object is to* ***bluff*** *your opponent* ***into*** *submission.* ■ (in a card game) bet heavily on a weak hand in order to deceive opponents.
– PHRASES **call someone's bluff** challenge someone thought to be bluffing: *she was tempted to call his bluff, hardly believing he'd carry out his threat.*
– DERIVATIVES **bluff·er** n.
– ORIGIN late 17th cent. (originally in the sense 'blindfold, hoodwink'): from Dutch *bluffen* 'brag,' or *bluf* 'bragging.' The current sense (originally US, mid 19th cent.) originally referred to bluffing in the game of poker.

bluff² ▸ **adj.** direct in speech or behavior but in a good-natured way: *a big, bluff, hearty man.*
– DERIVATIVES **bluff·ly** adv., **bluff·ness** n.
– ORIGIN early 18th cent. (in the sense 'surly, abrupt in manner'): figurative use of BLUFF³. The current positive connotation dates from the early 19th cent.

bluff³ ▸ **n. 1** a steep cliff, bank, or promontory.
2 Canadian a grove or clump of trees.
▸ **adj.** (of a cliff or a ship's bow) having a vertical or steep broad front.
– ORIGIN early 17th cent. (as an adjective, originally in nautical use): of unknown origin. The Canadian sense dates from the mid 18th cent.

blu·ing /ˈblo͞oiNG/ (also **blueing**) ▸ **n. 1** chiefly historical blue powder used to preserve the whiteness of laundry.
2 a grayish-blue finish on metal produced by heating.

blu·ish /ˈblo͞oiSH/ (also **blueish**) ▸ **adj.** having a blue tinge; somewhat blue.

Blum /ˈblo͞om/, Léon (1872–1950), French statesman; prime minister 1936–37, 1938, and 1946–47. As France's first socialist and Jewish prime minister, Blum introduced significant labor reforms.

Blume /blo͞om/, Judy Sussman (1938–), US author, mostly of fiction for young adults. Her works include *Are You There, God? It's Me, Margaret* (1970), *Tales of a Fourth Grade Nothing* (1972), *Forever...* (1975), and, for adults, *Wifey* (1977) and *Summer Sisters* (1998).

Blu·men·bach /ˈblo͞omənˌbäKH/, Johann Friedrich (1752–1840), German physiologist and anatomist. He is regarded as the founder of physical anthropology, although his approach has since been much modified. He classified modern human beings into five broad categories (Caucasian, Mongoloid, Malayan, Ethiopian, and American), based mainly on cranial measurements.

blun·der /ˈbləndər/ ▸ **n.** a stupid or careless mistake.
▸ **v.** [no obj.] make such a mistake; act or speak clumsily: *the mayor and the City Council have blundered in an ill-advised campaign* | ***I blundered on*** *in my explanation* | (as adj. **blundering**) *blundering actors.* ■ move clumsily or as if unable to see: *we were blundering around in the darkness.*
– DERIVATIVES **blun·der·er** n., **blun·der·ing·ly** adv.
– ORIGIN Middle English: probably of Scandinavian origin and related to BLIND.

blun·der·buss /ˈbləndərˌbəs/ ▸ **n. 1** historical a short-barreled large-bored gun with a flared muzzle, used at short range.
2 an action or way of doing something regarded as lacking in subtlety and precision: *economists resort too quickly to the blunderbuss of regulation.*
– ORIGIN mid 17th cent.: alteration (by association with BLUNDER) of Dutch *donderbus*, literally 'thunder gun.'

blunderbuss

blunge /blənj/ ▸ **v.** [with obj.] mix (clay or other materials) with water in a revolving apparatus for use in ceramics.
– DERIVATIVES **blung·er** n.
– ORIGIN early 19th cent.: blend of BLEND and PLUNGE.

blunt /blənt/ ▸ **adj. 1** (of a knife, pencil, etc.) having a worn-down edge or point; not sharp: *a blunt knife.* ■ having a flat or rounded end: *the blunt tip of the leaf.*
2 (of a person or remark) uncompromisingly forthright: *he is as blunt as a kick in the shins* | *a blunt statement of fact.*
▸ **n.** informal a hollowed-out cigar filled with marijuana.
▸ **v.** make or become less sharp: [with obj.] *wood can blunt your ax* | [no obj.] *the edge may blunt very rapidly.* ■ [with obj.] weaken or reduce (something): *their determination had been blunted.*
– DERIVATIVES **blunt·ly** adv., **blunt·ness** n.
– ORIGIN Middle English (in the sense 'dull, insensitive'): perhaps of Scandinavian origin and related to Old Norse *blunda* 'shut the eyes.'

blunt in·stru·ment ▸ **n.** a heavy object without a sharp edge or point, used as a weapon. ■ an imprecise or heavy-handed way of doing something: *as a promotional method, direct mail has been a blunt instrument.*

blur /blər/ ▸ **v.** (**blurs**, **blurring**, **blurred**) make or become unclear or less distinct: [with obj.] *tears blurred her vision* | *his novels blur the boundaries between criticism and fiction* | [no obj.] *as daylight waned, the pages blurred.*
▸ **n.** a thing that cannot be seen or heard clearly: *the pale blur of her face* | *the words were a blur.* ■ an indistinct memory or impression of events, typically because they happened very fast: *the day before was a blur.*
– DERIVATIVES **blur·ry** adj. (**blurrier**, **blurriest**).
– ORIGIN mid 16th cent. (in the sense 'smear that partially obscures something'): perhaps related to BLEAR.

Blu-ray /ˈblo͞oˌrā/ ▸ **n.** a format of DVD designed for the storage of high-definition video and data.
– ORIGIN early 21st cent.: from *blu*, a respelling of BLUE (from the color of the laser used to read and write this type of DVD), + RAY¹.

blurb /blərb/ ▸ **n.** a short description of a book, movie, or other product written for promotional purposes and appearing on the cover of a book or in an advertisement.
▸ **v.** [with obj.] informal write or contribute such a passage for (a book, movie, or other product).
– ORIGIN early 20th cent.: coined by Gelett Burgess (died 1951), American humorist.

blurred /blərd/ ▸ **adj.** unable to see or be seen clearly: *blurred vision* | *the camera caught only two blurred images.* ■ not clear or distinct; hazy: *the blurred distinctions between childhood and adulthood.*

blurt /blərt/ ▸ **v.** [with obj.] say (something) suddenly and without careful consideration: *she wouldn't* ***blurt out*** *words she did not mean* | [with direct speech] *"It wasn't my idea," Gordon blurted.*
– ORIGIN late 16th cent.: probably imitative.

blush /bləSH/ ▸ **v.** [no obj.] develop a pink tinge in the face from embarrassment or shame: *she blushed at the unexpected compliment* | [with complement] *Kate felt herself blushing scarlet.* ■ feel embarrassed or ashamed: [with infinitive] *he blushed to think of how he'd paraded himself.* ■ (often as adj. **blushing**) (of a flower or other thing) be or become pink or pale red: *the trees are loaded with blushing blossoms.*
▸ **n. 1** a reddening of the face as a sign of embarrassment or shame: *he had brought a faint blush to her cheeks.* ■ a pink or pale red tinge: *the roses were white with a lovely pink blush.* ■ another term for BLUSHER (sense 1).
2 (also **blush wine**) a wine with a slight pink tint made in the manner of white wine but from red grape varieties.
– PHRASES **at first blush** at the first glimpse or impression.
– ORIGIN Old English *blyscan*; related to modern Dutch *blozen.*

blush·er /ˈbləSHər/ ▸ **n. 1** a cosmetic of a powder or cream consistency used to give a warm color to the cheeks. Also called BLUSH.
2 (**the blusher**) a woodland toadstool that has a buff cap bearing fluffy white spots and white flesh that turns pink when bruised or cut. It is native to both Eurasia and North America. ● *Amanita rubescens*, family Amanitaceae, class Basidiomycetes.

blus·ter /ˈbləstər/ ▸ **v.** [no obj.] talk in a loud, aggressive, or indignant way with little effect: *you threaten and bluster, but won't carry it through* | [with direct speech] *"I don't care what he says," I blustered* | (as adj. **blustering**) *a blustering bully.* ■ (of a storm, wind, or rain) blow or beat fiercely and noisily: *a winter gale blustered against the sides of the house* | (as adj. **blustering**) *the blustering wind.*
▸ **n.** loud, aggressive, or indignant talk with little effect: *their threats contained a measure of bluster.*
– DERIVATIVES **blus·ter·er** n.
– ORIGIN late Middle English: ultimately imitative.

blus·ter·y /ˈbləstərē/ ▸ **adj.** (of weather or a period of time) characterized by strong winds: *a gusty, blustery day.* ■ (of a wind) blowing in strong gusts.

blvd. ▸ **abbr.** boulevard.

Bly /blī/, Nellie (1867–1922), US journalist and social reformer; pseudonym of *Elizabeth Jane Cochrane.* As a reporter for the *Pittsburgh Dispatch*, she wrote about child labor and unsafe working conditions in factories .

B lym·pho·cyte ▸ **n.** Physiology another term for B CELL.

BM ▸ **abbr.** ■ Bachelor of Medicine. ■ Bachelor of Music. ■ bowel movement. ■ basal metabolism. ■ board measure. ■ black male. ■ British Museum.

BMI ▸ **abbr.** body mass index.

BMOC ▸ **abbr.** big man on campus.

B-mov·ie ▸ **n.** a low-budget movie, esp. (formerly) one made for use as a companion to the main attraction in a double feature: [as modifier] *a B-movie actress.*

BMR ▸ **abbr.** basal metabolic rate.

BMus ▸ **abbr.** Bachelor of Music.

BMX ▸ **n.** organized bicycle racing on a dirt track, esp. for youngsters: [as modifier] *a BMX track.* ■ a kind of bicycle designed to be used for such racing.
– ORIGIN 1970s: from the initial letters of *bicycle motocross*, with *X* standing for *cross.*

bn ▸ **abbr.** billion.

Bn. ▸ **abbr.** ■ Baron. ■ Battalion.

B'nai B'rith /bəˈnā ˈbriTH/ a Jewish organization founded in New York in 1843. It pursues educational, humanitarian, and cultural activities and attempts to safeguard the rights and interests of Jews around the world.
– ORIGIN Hebrew, literally 'sons of the covenant.'

BO ▸ **abbr.** ■ informal body odor. ■ best offer. ■ box office. ■ back order. ■ (also **B/O** or **b/o**) (in bookkeeping) brought over.

bo ▸ **abbr.** best offer.

bo·a /ˈbōə/ ▸ **n. 1** a constrictor snake that bears live young and may reach great size, native to America, Africa, Asia, and some Pacific islands. ● Family Boidae, several genera and numerous species. See also BOA CONSTRICTOR. ■ any snake that is a constrictor.
2 a long thin stole of feathers or fur worn around a woman's neck, typically as part of evening dress.
– ORIGIN late Middle English: from Latin (mentioned in the writings of Pliny), of unknown ultimate origin.

bo·a con·stric·tor ▸ **n.** a large and typically boldly marked snake that kills by coiling around its prey and asphyxiating it, native to tropical America. ● *Boa constrictor*, family Boidae.

boar /bôr/ ▸ **n.** (pl. **same** or **boars**) **1** (also **wild boar**) a tusked Eurasian wild pig from which domestic pigs are descended. ● *Sus scrofa*, family Suidae. ■ the flesh of the wild boar as food.
2 an uncastrated domestic male pig. ■ the full-grown male of certain other animals, esp. a badger, guinea pig, or hedgehog.
– ORIGIN Old English *bār*; related to Dutch *beer* and German *Bär.*

board /bôrd/ ▸ **n. 1** a long, thin, flat piece of wood or other hard material, used for floors or other building purposes: *loose boards creaked as I walked on them* | *sections of board.* ■ (**the boards**) informal the stage of a theater.
2 a thin, flat, rectangular piece of wood or other stiff material used for various purposes, in particular: ■ a vertical surface on which to write or pin notices. ■ a horizontal surface on which to cut things, play games, or perform other activities. ■ a flat insulating sheet used as a mounting for an electronic circuit: *a graphics board.* ■ the piece of equipment on which a person stands in surfing, skateboarding, snowboarding, and certain other sports. ■ (**boards**) the wooden structure surrounding an ice-hockey rink. ■ (usu. **boards**) Basketball informal term for BACKBOARD, referring specifically to rebounding: *the absence of center David Robinson to dominate* ***on the boards.*** ■ (**boards**) pieces of thick stiff cardboard or, originally, wood used for book covers.
3 [treated as sing. or pl.] a group of people constituted as the decision-making body of an organization: *he sits on the board of directors* | [in names] *the Federal Reserve Board* | [as modifier] *a board meeting.*
4 the provision of regular meals when one stays somewhere, in return for payment or services: *your* ***room and board*** *will be free.* ■ archaic a table set for a meal.
5 Sailing a distance covered by a vessel in a single tack.
▸ **v. 1** [with obj.] get on or into (a ship, aircraft, or other vehicle): *we boarded the plane for Oslo* | [no obj.] *they would not be able to board without a ticket.* ■ (**be boarding**) (of an aircraft) be ready for passengers to embark: *flight 172 to Istanbul is now boarding at gate 37.*
2 [no obj.] live and receive regular meals in a house in return for payment or services: *the cousins boarded for a while with Ruby.* ■ (of a student) live at school during the semester in return for payment. ■ [with obj.] provide (a person or animal) with regular meals and somewhere to live in return for payment: *dogs may have to be* ***boarded*** *at kennels.*

3 [with obj.] (**board something up**) cover or seal a window, storefront, or other structure with pieces of wood: *the shop was still boarded up*.
4 [no obj.] ride on a snowboard.
–PHRASES **go by the board** (of something planned or previously upheld) be abandoned, rejected, or ignored: *my education just went by the board*. [earlier in nautical use meaning 'fall overboard,' used of a mast falling past the *board*, i.e., the side of the ship.] **on board** on or in a ship, aircraft, or other vehicle. ■ informal onto a team or group as a member: *the need to bring on board a young manager*. ■ informal (of a jockey) riding. ■ Baseball on base. **take something on board** informal fully consider or assimilate a new idea or situation: *we've got to take accusations of sexism on board*. **tread the boards** informal appear on stage as an actor.
–ORIGIN Old English *bord*, of Germanic origin; related to Dutch *boord* and German *Bort*; reinforced in Middle English by Old French *bort* 'edge, ship's side' and Old Norse *borth* 'board, table.'

board cer·ti·fi·ca·tion ▶ **n.** the process of examining and certifying the qualifications of a physician or other professional by a board of specialists in the field.

board-cer·ti·fied ▶ **adj.** having satisfied the requirements for board certification.

board·ed /ˈbôrdid/ ▶ **adj.** (of a floor, roof, or other structure) built with pieces of wood. ■ (of a window, storefront, or other structure) covered or sealed with pieces of wood.

board·er /ˈbôrdər/ ▶ **n. 1** a person who receives regular meals when staying somewhere, in return for payment or services. ■ a student who lives at school during the semester in return for payment.
2 a person who boards a ship during or after an attack.
3 a person who takes part in a sport using a board, such as surfing or snowboarding.

board foot ▶ **n.** (pl. **board feet**) a unit of volume for timber equal to 144 cubic inches, notionally twelve inches by twelve inches by one inch.

board game ▶ **n.** any game played on a board, esp. one that involves the movement of pieces on the board, such as chess or checkers.

board·ing /ˈbôrdiNG/ ▶ **n. 1** long, flat, thin pieces of wood used to build or cover something.
2 the procedure according to which students live at school during the semester in return for payment.
3 the action of getting on or into a ship, aircraft, or other vehicle.

board·ing house ▶ **n.** a house providing food and lodging for paying guests.

board·ing ken·nel ▶ **n.** a place in which dogs are kept and fed, typically while their owners are on vacation.

board·ing pass (also **boarding card**) ▶ **n.** a pass for boarding an aircraft, given to a passenger when the ticket is issued or upon check-in at the airport.

board·ing school ▶ **n.** a school where students reside during the semester.

board of ed·u·ca·tion ▶ **n.** a body of officials elected or appointed to oversee a local or statewide school system or systems. Compare with SCHOOL BOARD.

Board of Trade ▶ **n. 1** another term for CHAMBER OF COMMERCE. ■ (also **Chicago Board of Trade**) the Chicago futures exchange.
2 (**Board of Trade**) a now nominal British government department within the Department of Trade and Industry concerned with commerce and industry.

board·room /ˈbôrd,ro͞om/ ▶ **n.** a room in which the members of a board meet regularly. ■ the directors of a company or organization considered collectively.

board·sail·ing /ˈbôrd,sāliNG/ ▶ **n.** another term for WINDSURFING.
–DERIVATIVES **board·sail·or** /-,sālər/ **n.**

board·slide /ˈbôrd,slīd/ ▶ **n.** (in skateboarding and snowboarding) a maneuver in which the board slides along a rail, ledge, edge of a ramp, etc., on the flat part of its underside between the trucks.

board·walk /ˈbôrd,wôk/ ▶ **n.** a wooden walkway across sand or marshy ground. ■ a promenade along a beach or waterfront, typically made of wood.

Bo·as /ˈbō,az/, Franz (1858–1942), US anthropologist; born in Germany. A pioneer of modern anthropology, he developed the linguistic and cultural components of ethnology. His most notable work was *Race, Language, and Culture* (1940).

boast[1] /bōst/ ▶ **v. 1** [reporting verb] talk with excessive pride and self-satisfaction about one's achievements, possessions, or abilities: [with direct speech] *Ted used to boast, "I manage ten people"* | [with clause] *he boasted that he had taken part in the crime* | [no obj.] *she* **boasted about** *her many conquests*.
2 [with obj.] (of a person, place, or thing) possess (a feature that is a source of pride): *the hotel boasts high standards of comfort*.
▶ **n.** an act of talking with excessive pride and self-satisfaction: *I said I would score, and it wasn't an idle boast*.
–DERIVATIVES **boast·er n.**, **boast·ing·ly adv.**
–ORIGIN Middle English (as a noun): of unknown origin.

boast[2] ▶ **n.** (in squash) a stroke in which the ball is made to hit one of the sidewalls before hitting the front wall.
–ORIGIN late 19th cent.: perhaps from French *bosse* denoting a rounded projection in the wall of a court for court tennis.

boast·ful /ˈbōstfəl/ ▶ **adj.** showing excessive pride and self-satisfaction in one's achievements, possessions, or abilities.
–DERIVATIVES **boast·ful·ly adv.**, **boast·ful·ness n.**

boat /bōt/ ▶ **n. 1** a small vessel propelled on water by oars, sails, or an engine: *a fishing boat* | [as modifier] *a boat trip*. ■ (in general use) a ship of any size.
2 a serving dish in the shape of a boat: *a gravy boat*.
▶ **v.** [no obj.] travel or go in a boat for pleasure: *they boated through fjords* | (as noun **boating**) *she likes to go boating*. ■ [with obj.] transport (someone or something) in a boat in a specified direction: *they boated the timber down the lake*. ■ [with obj.] (of an angler) bring a caught fish into a boat.
–PHRASES **be in the same boat** informal be in the same unfortunate circumstances as others. **miss the boat** see MISS[1]. **off the boat** informal, often offensive recently arrived from a foreign country, and by implication naive or an outsider: *what are you, fresh off the boat?* **rock the boat** informal say or do something to disturb an existing situation.
–DERIVATIVES **boat·ful** /-,fo͝ol/ **n.** (pl. **boatfuls**).
–ORIGIN Old English *bāt*, of Germanic origin.

boat·bill /ˈbōt,bil/ ▶ **n.** (also **boat-billed heron**) a small Central and South American heron with a broad, flattened bill and a prominent black crest. ● *Cochlearius cochlearius*, family Ardeidae.

boat·build·ing /ˈbōt,bildiNG/ ▶ **n.** the occupation or industry of building boats.
–DERIVATIVES **boat·build·er** /-,bildər/ **n.**

boat deck ▶ **n.** the deck from which a ship's lifeboats are launched.

boat·el /,bōˈtel/ ▶ **n. 1** a waterside hotel with facilities for mooring boats.
2 a ship moored at a wharf and used as a hotel.
–ORIGIN 1950s: blend of BOAT and HOTEL.

boat·er /ˈbōtər/ ▶ **n. 1** a flat-topped hardened straw hat with a brim. [so named because originally worn while boating.]
2 a person who uses or travels in a boat for pleasure.

boat·hook /ˈbōt,ho͝ok/ ▶ **n.** a long pole with a hook and a spike at one end, used for fending off or pulling a boat.

boat·house /ˈbōt,hous/ ▶ **n.** a shed at the edge of a river or lake used for housing boats.

boat·ing /ˈbōtiNG/ ▶ **n.** rowing or sailing in boats as a sport or form of recreation.

boat·load /ˈbōt,lōd/ ▶ **n.** a number of passengers or amount of cargo that will fill a ship or boat: *a boatload of coal*. ■ informal a large amount: *a boatload of new regulations* | *the festival brought together a boatload of guitarists from all corners of the world*.

boat·man /ˈbōtmən/ ▶ **n.** (pl. **boatmen**) a person who rents out or works on boats.

boat neck (also **boatneck**) ▶ **n.** a type of wide neckline on a garment that passes just below the collarbone.
–ORIGIN from its shape.

boat peo·ple ▶ **plural n.** refugees who have left a country by sea, in particular the Vietnamese who fled in small boats to Hong Kong, Australia, and elsewhere after the conquest of South Vietnam by North Vietnam in 1975.

boat shoe ▶ **n.** a flat canvas or leather shoe with rubber soles to provide good traction on boat decks. Also called DECK SHOE.

boat·swain /ˈbōsən/ (also **bo'sun** or **bosun**) ▶ **n.** a ship's officer in charge of equipment and the crew.
–ORIGIN late Old English *bātswegen* (see BOAT, SWAIN).

boat·swain's chair ▶ **n.** a seat suspended from ropes, used in rescues and for work on the body or masts of a ship or the face of a building.

boat train ▶ **n.** a train scheduled to connect with the arrival or departure of a boat.

boat·yard /ˈbōt,yärd/ ▶ **n.** a place where boats are built, repaired, or stored.

Bo·a Vis·ta /ˈbōə ˈvistə/ a town in northern Brazil; pop. 249,853 (2007).

bob[1] /bäb/ ▶ **v.** (**bobs, bobbing, bobbed**) [no obj.] (of a thing) make a quick short movement up and down: *I could see his red head bobbing around* | *the boat bobbed up and down*. ■ [with obj.] cause (something) to make such a movement: *she bobbed her head*. ■ make a sudden move in a particular direction so as to appear or disappear: *a lady* **bobbed up** *from beneath the counter*. ■ move up and down briefly in a curtsy.
▶ **n.** a movement up and down: *she could only manage a slight bob of her head*. ■ another term for BOBBER. ■ a curtsy.
–PHRASES **bob and weave** make rapid bodily movements up and down and from side to side, for example as an evasive tactic by a boxer. **bob for apples** try to catch floating or hanging apples with one's mouth alone, as a game.
–ORIGIN late Middle English: of unknown origin.

bob[2] ▶ **n. 1** a style in which the hair is cut short and evenly all around so that it hangs above the shoulders.
2 a weight on a pendulum, plumb line, or kite-tail.
3 a bobsled.
4 a short line at or near the end of a stanza.
5 a horse's tail docked short.
▶ **v.** (**bobs, bobbing, bobbed**) **1** [with obj.] (usu. as adj. **bobbed**) cut (someone's hair) in a bob: *she tied a headscarf over her bobbed brown hair*.
2 [no obj.] ride on a bobsled.
–ORIGIN late Middle English (denoting a bunch or cluster): of unknown origin.

bob[3] Brit. informal ▶ **n.** (pl. **same**) a shilling. ■ used with reference to a moderately large but unspecified amount of money: *those vases are worth a few bob*.
–ORIGIN late 18th cent.: of unknown origin.

bob[4] ▶ **n.** a change of order in bell-ringing. ■ used in names of change-ringing methods: *plain bob* | *bob minor*.
–ORIGIN late 17th cent.: perhaps connected with BOB[1] in the noun sense 'sudden movement up and down.'

bo·ba tea ▶ **n.** another term for BUBBLE TEA.

bob·ber /ˈbäbər/ ▶ **n.** a small float placed on a fishing line to hold the hook at the desired depth.

bob·bin /ˈbäbin/ ▶ **n.** a cylinder or cone holding thread, yarn, or wire, used esp. in weaving, machine sewing, and lacemaking. ■ a spool or reel.
–ORIGIN mid 16th cent.: from French *bobine*, of unknown origin.

bob·bi·net /,bäbəˈnet/ ▶ **n.** machine-made cotton net (imitating lace made with bobbins on a pillow).
–ORIGIN mid 19th cent.: from BOBBIN + NET[1].

bob·bin lace ▶ **n.** lace made by hand with thread wound on bobbins.

bob·ble[1] /ˈbäbəl/ ▶ **n.** a small ball made of strands of wool used as a decoration on a hat or on furnishings.
–DERIVATIVES **bob·bly** /ˈbäb(ə)lē/ **adj.**
–ORIGIN 1920s: diminutive of BOB[2].

bob·ble[2] informal ▶ **v. 1** [with obj.] mishandle (a ball): *Andy bobbled the ball, so his throw home was too late*.
2 [no obj.] move with an irregular bouncing motion: *the glare of the snow made the landscape bobble*.
▶ **n. 1** a mishandling of a ball: *a once-a-season bobble by Jordan en route to a breakaway jam*.
2 an irregular bouncing motion.
–ORIGIN early 19th cent.: frequentative of BOB[1].

Bobb·sey twins /ˈbäbzē/ ▶ **n.** humorous a name for two people who are often seen together or who look and act alike.
–ORIGIN From the characters in a long-running series of children's books (1904–1992), written under the pen name Laura Lee Hope.

bob·by /ˈbäbē/ ▶ **n.** (pl. **bobbies**) Brit. informal a police officer.
–ORIGIN mid 19th cent.: nickname for *Robert*, given name of Sir Robert PEEL.

bob·by pin ▶ **n.** a kind of sprung hairpin or small clip.
▶ **v.** (**bobby-pin**) [with obj.] fix (hair) in place with such a pin or clip.
–ORIGIN 1930s: from BOB[2] (because bobby pins were originally used with bobbed hair) + -Y[2].

bob·by socks (also **bobby sox**) ▶ **plural n.** dated short socks reaching just above the ankle (used chiefly in the 1940s and 1950s to refer to the socks worn by teenage girls).
–ORIGIN 1940s: compare with BOB[2] in the sense 'cut short.'

bob·by-sox·er /ˈbäbē ,säksər/ ▶ **n.** informal, dated an adolescent girl.

bob·cat /ˈbäb,kat/ ▶ **n.** a small North American cat species with a barred and spotted coat and a short

PRONUNCIATION KEY ə *ago, up*; ər *over, fur*; a *hat*; ā *ate*; ä *car*; e *let*; ē *see*; i *fit*; ī *by*; NG *sing*; ō *go*; ô *law, for*; oi *toy*; o͝o *good*; o͞o *goo*; ou *out*; TH *thin*; T͟H *then*; ZH *vision*

b

tail. ● *Lynx rufus*, family Felidae. Compare with **LYNX**.
– ORIGIN late 19th cent.: from **BOB²** (with reference to its short tail) + **CAT¹**.

b

bob·o·link /ˈbäbəˌlingk/ ▶ **n.** a North American songbird of the American blackbird family, with a finchlike bill. The male has black, buff, and white plumage. ● *Dolichonyx oryzivorus*, family Icteridae.
– ORIGIN late 18th cent. (originally *Bob o'Lincoln*, *Bob Lincoln*): imitative of its call.

bobolink

bob·sled /ˈbäbˌsled/ ▶ **n.** a mechanically steered and braked sled, typically manned by crews of two or four, used for racing down a steep ice-covered run with banked curves.
▶ **v.** ride on a bobsled.
– ORIGIN mid 19th cent. (originally denoting a sled made of two short sleds coupled together and used for hauling logs): from **BOB²** in the sense 'short' + **SLED**.

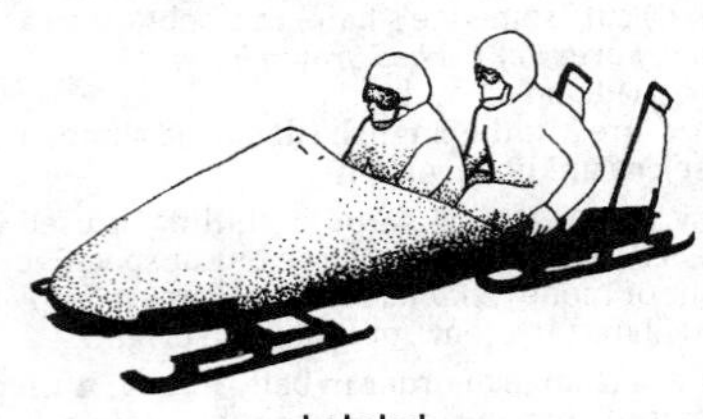
bobsled

bob·sled·ding /ˈbäbˌsleding/ ▶ **n.** riding in a bobsled, esp. as a winter sport.

bob·sleigh /ˈbäbˌslā/ ▶ **n.** another term for **BOBSLED**.

bob·stay /ˈbäbˌstā/ ▶ **n.** a rope used to hold down the bowsprit of a ship against the upward pull of the forestay.
– ORIGIN mid 18th cent.: probably from **BOB¹** + **STAY²**.

bob·tail /ˈbäbˌtāl/ ▶ **n.** a docked tail of a horse or dog.
▶ **adj.** (also **bobtailed**) cut short; abbreviated: *the bobtailed 1995 baseball season*.
– ORIGIN mid 16th cent.: probably from **BOB²** + **TAIL¹**. It was originally recorded as a humorous term for a kind of broad-headed arrow, probably because it looked as though it had been cut short.

bob weight ▶ **n.** a component used as a counterweight to a moving part in a machine.

bob·white /ˈbäbˈ(h)wīt/ (also **bobwhite quail**) ▶ **n.** a New World quail with mottled reddish-brown plumage, and typically a pale throat and eyestripe. ● Genus *Colinus*, family Phasianidae: two species, in particular the **northern** (or **common**) **bobwhite** (*C. virginianus*).
– ORIGIN early 19th cent.: imitative of its call.

northern bobwhite

bo·cac·cio /bəˈkächō, -chē-ō, bō-/ ▶ **n.** (pl. **bocaccios**) an edible rockfish, of particular commercial importance in California. ● *Sebastes paucispinis*, family Scorpaenidae.
– ORIGIN ultimately from American Spanish *bocacho* 'big-mouth(ed).'

bo·cage /bōˈkäzh/ ▶ **n.** (in France) pastureland divided into small hedged fields interspersed with groves of trees.
– ORIGIN late 16th cent.: from French, from Old French *boscage* (see **BOSCAGE**).

Bo·ca Ra·ton /ˌbōkə rəˈtōn/ a city and resort in southeastern Florida, on the Atlantic Ocean, north of Fort Lauderdale; pop. 85,670 (est. 2008).

Boc·cac·ci·o /bəˈkächēˌō/, Giovanni (1313–75), Italian writer, poet, and humanist. He is most noted for the *Decameron* (1348–58), a collection of 100 tales told by ten young people living in the country in order to escape the Black Death.

boc·ce /ˈbächē/ (also **boccie** or **bocci**) ▶ **n.** an Italian game similar to lawn bowling but played on a shorter, narrower green.
– ORIGIN Italian, 'bowls,' plural of *boccia* 'ball.'

Boc·che·ri·ni /ˌbäkəˈrēnē, ˌbōkə-/, Luigi (1743–1805), Italian composer and cellist.

boc·con·ci·ni /ˌbäkənˈchēnē/ ▶ **plural n.** small balls of mozzarella cheese.
– ORIGIN Italian.

Boche /bôsh, bäsh/ dated, offensive ▶ **n.** a German, esp. a soldier. ■ (**the Boche**) Germans, esp. German soldiers, considered collectively.
▶ **adj.** German.
– ORIGIN late 19th cent.: French soldiers' slang, originally in the sense 'rascal,' later used in World War I meaning 'German.'

Bo·chum /ˈbōkhŏŏm, ˈbōkəm/ an industrial city in the Ruhr valley, in North Rhine–Westphalia, Germany; pop. 383,700 (est. 2006).

bock /bäk/ (also **bock beer**) ▶ **n.** a strong dark beer brewed in the fall and drunk in the spring.
– ORIGIN mid 19th cent.: via French from an abbreviation of German *Eimbockbier* 'beer from *Einbeck*,' a town in Hanover.

BOD ▶ **abbr.** biochemical oxygen demand.

bod /bäd/ ▶ **n.** informal a body or physique: *shake your bod* | *Roger was proud of his bod*. ■ chiefly Brit. a person: *some clever bod wrote a song about them*.
– ORIGIN late 18th cent. (originally Scots): abbreviation of **BODY**.

bo·da·cious /bōˈdāshəs/ ▶ **adj.** informal excellent, admirable, or attractive: *the restaurant serves bodacious grilled lobster*. ■ audacious in a way considered admirable: *those bodacious dudes have an excellent time playing games with death*.
– ORIGIN mid 19th cent.: perhaps a variant of southwestern English dialect *boldacious*, blend of **BOLD** and **AUDACIOUS**.

bode /bōd/ ▶ **v.** [no obj.] (**bode well/ill**) be an omen of a particular outcome: *their argument did not bode well for the future* | [with obj.] *the 12 percent interest rate bodes dark days ahead for retailers*.
– ORIGIN Old English *bodian* 'proclaim, foretell,' from *boda* 'messenger,' of Germanic origin; related to German *Bote*, also to **BID¹**.

bo·de·ga /bōˈdāgə/ ▶ **n.** a small grocery store in a Spanish-speaking neighborhood. ■ a wine shop or wine cellar.
– ORIGIN mid 19th cent.: from Spanish, via Latin from Greek *apothēkē* 'storehouse.' Compare with **APOTHECARY**, **BOUTIQUE**.

Bo·den·see /ˈbōdnˌzā/ German name for Lake Constance (see **CONSTANCE, LAKE**).

Bodh·ga·ya /ˌbōdˈgīə/ (also **Bodh Gaya**, **Buddh Gaya** /ˈbŏŏdˈgīə/) a village in the state of Bihar in northeastern India, where Buddha attained enlightenment.

bo·dhi·satt·va /ˌbōdiˈsätvə, -ˈsət-/ (also **Bodhisattva**) ▶ **n.** (in Mahayana Buddhism) a person who is able to reach nirvana but delays doing so out of compassion in order to save suffering beings.
– ORIGIN early 19th cent.: Sanskrit, 'a person whose essence is perfect knowledge,' from *bodhi-* 'perfect knowledge' (from *budh-* 'awaken' [see **BUDDHA**]) + *sattva* 'being, essence.'

bo·dhi tree /ˈbōdē/ ▶ **n.** another term for **BO TREE**.

bod·hrán /ˈbôˌrän, -rən/ ▶ **n.** a shallow one-sided Irish drum typically played with a short two-headed drumstick.
– ORIGIN Irish.

bod·ice /ˈbädis/ ▶ **n.** the part of a woman's dress (excluding sleeves) that is above the waist. ■ a woman's vest, esp. a laced vest worn as an outer garment. ■ a woman's vestlike undergarment.
– ORIGIN mid 16th cent. (originally *bodies*): plural of **BODY**, retaining the original pronunciation. The term probably first denoted an undergarment, then known as a *pair of bodice*, although this sense is not recorded until the early 17th cent.

bodice

bod·ice-rip·per ▶ **n.** informal, derogatory or humorous a sexually explicit romantic novel or movie with a historical setting.
– DERIVATIVES **bod·ice-rip·ping adj.**

bod·i·less /ˈbädēlis/ ▶ **adj.** lacking a body: *a bodiless head*. ■ having no material existence; insubstantial: *a sinister, bodiless voice*.

bod·i·ly /ˈbädl-ē/ ▶ **adj.** [attrib.] of or concerning the body: *children learn to control their bodily functions*. ■ material or actual as opposed to spiritual or incorporeal: *the idea of angels taking human bodily form when they come to earth*.
▶ **adv.** by taking hold of a person's body, esp. with force: *he hauled her bodily from the van*. ■ with one's whole body and with great force: *he launched himself bodily at the door*.

bod·kin /ˈbädkin/ ▶ **n.** a blunt, thick needle with a large eye used esp. for drawing tape or cord through a hem. ■ a small pointed instrument used to pierce cloth or leather. ■ historical a long pin used for fastening hair. ■ Printing, historical a pointed tool used for removing pieces of metal type for correction.
– ORIGIN Middle English: perhaps of Celtic origin and related to Irish *bod*, Welsh *bidog*, Scottish Gaelic *biodag* 'dagger.'

Bod·lei·an Li·brar·y /ˈbädlēən/ the main research library of Oxford University, and one of six copyright libraries in the UK.

Bo·do·ni /bōˈdōnē/, Giambattista (1740–1813), Italian printer. He designed a typeface that is named after him.

bod·y /ˈbädē/ ▶ **n.** (pl. **bodies**) **1** the physical structure of a person or an animal, including the bones, flesh, and organs: *it's important to keep your body in good condition* | [as modifier] *body temperature*. ■ a corpse: *they found his body washed up on the beach*. ■ the physical and mortal aspect of a person as opposed to the soul or spirit: *a duality of body and soul*. ■ informal a person's body regarded as an object of sexual desire: *he was just after her body*. ■ informal, dated a person, often one of a specified type or character: *a motherly body*.
2 the trunk apart from the head and the limbs: *the blow almost severed his head from his body*. ■ [in sing.] (**the body of**) the main or central part of something, esp. a building or text: *information that changes regularly is kept apart from the main body of the text*. ■ the main section of a car or aircraft: *the body of the aircraft was filled with smoke*. ■ a large or substantial amount of something; a mass or collection of something: *a rich* **body of** *Canadian folklore* | *large* **bodies of** *seawater*. ■ (in pottery) a clay used for making the main part of ceramic ware, as distinct from a glaze.
3 a group of people with a common purpose or function acting as an organized unit: *a regulatory body* | *international bodies of experts*.
4 [often with adj.] technical a distinct material object: *the path taken by the falling body*.
5 a full or substantial quality of flavor in wine. ■ fullness or thickness of a person's hair: *designed to add body to limp and straight hair*.
▶ **v.** (**bodies**, **bodying**, **bodied**) [with obj.] **1** (**body something forth**) give material form to something abstract: *he bodied forth the traditional Prussian remedy for all ills*.
2 build the bodywork of (a motor vehicle): *an era when automobiles were bodied over wooden frames*.
– PHRASES **body and soul** involving every aspect of a person; completely: *the company owned them body and soul*. **in a body** all together; as a group: *they departed in a body*. **keep body and soul** (or **soul and body**) **together** stay alive, esp. in difficult circumstances: *do you think a man can keep body and soul together by selling coconuts?* **over my dead body** informal used to emphasize that one opposes something and would do anything to prevent it from happening: *she moves into our home over my dead body*.
– DERIVATIVES **bod·ied adj.** [in combination] *a wide-bodied jet*.
– ORIGIN Old English *bodig*, of unknown origin.

bod·y ar·mor ▶ **n.** clothing worn by military and police personnel to protect against gunfire.

bod·y art ▶ **n.** **1** items of jewelry or clothing worn on the body and regarded as art. ■ the practice of decorating the body by means of tattooing, piercing, plastic surgery, etc.
2 an artistic movement originating in the 1970s in which the physical presence of the artist (or of a model) is regarded as an integral part of the work.

bod·y bag ▶ **n.** a bag used for carrying a corpse from a battlefield or the scene of an accident or crime.

bod·y blow ▶ **n.** a heavy punch to the body. ■ a severe disappointment or crushing setback: *a tax on books would be a body blow for education*.

bod·y·board /ˈbädēˌbôrd/ ▶ **n.** a short light type of surfboard ridden in a prone position.
– DERIVATIVES **bod·y·board·er n.**, **bod·y·board·ing n.**

bod·y·build·ing /ˈbädēˌbilding/ ▶ **n.** the practice of strengthening and enlarging the muscles of the body through exercise.
– DERIVATIVES **bod·y·build·er** /-ˌbildər/ **n.**

bod·y-cen·tered ▶ **adj.** denoting a crystal structure in which there is an atom at each vertex and at the center of the unit cell. Compare with **FACE-CENTERED**.

bod·y check ▶ **n.** a deliberate obstruction of a player (esp. in ice hockey) by placing one's body in the way.

▶ v. (**body-check**) [with obj.] obstruct (a player) in such a way.

bod·y clock ▶ n. a person's or animal's biological clock.

bod·y col·or ▶ n. an opaque pigment.

bod·y cor·po·rate ▶ n. formal term for CORPORATION.

bod·y count ▶ n. a list or total of casualties.

bod·y dou·ble ▶ n. a stand-in for a movie actor used during stunt or nude scenes.

bod·y dys·mor·phic dis·or·der (abbr.: **BDD**) ▶ n. a psychological disorder in which a person becomes obsessed with imaginary defects in their appearance.

bod·y Eng·lish ▶ n. a bodily action after throwing, hitting, or kicking a ball, intended as an attempt to influence the ball's trajectory: *see him waving and using body English to try to keep the ball from going foul.*

bod·y·guard /ˈbädēˌgärd/ ▶ n. a person or group of people hired to escort and protect another person, esp. a dignitary.

bod·y im·age ▶ n. the subjective picture or mental image of one's own body.

bod·y·kit /ˈbädēˌkit/ (also **body kit**) ▶ n. a packaged set of decorations and fittings for customizing a car or motorcycle body.

bod·y lan·guage ▶ n. the process of communicating nonverbally through conscious or unconscious gestures and movements: *his intent was clearly expressed in his body language.*

bod·y louse ▶ n. a louse of a variety that infests the human body and is particularly prevalent where hygiene is poor. It can transmit several diseases through its bite, including typhus. ● *Pediculus humanus humanus*, family Pediculidae, order Anoplura. See also HEAD LOUSE.

body louse

bod·y mass in·dex (abbr.: **BMI**) ▶ n. (pl. **body mass indices** /-dəsēz/ or **body mass indexes**) a weight-to-height ratio, calculated by dividing one's weight in kilograms by the square of one's height in meters and used as an indicator of obesity and underweight.

bod·y me·chan·ics ▶ plural n. [treated as sing. or pl.] exercises designed to improve posture, coordination, and stamina.

bod·y o·dor ▶ n. the smell of the human body, esp. when unpleasant.

bod·y pierc·ing ▶ n. the piercing of holes in parts of the body other than the earlobes in order to insert rings or other decorative objects.

bod·y pol·i·tic ▶ n. (usu. **the body politic**) the people of a nation, state, or society considered collectively as an organized group of citizens.

bod·y press ▶ n. Wrestling a move in which a wrestler uses their body weight to pin an opponent to the floor.

bod·y scrub ▶ n. an exfoliating cosmetic preparation, applied to the body to cleanse the skin. ■ a type of beauty treatment in which the skin is cleaned and exfoliated.

bod·y search ▶ n. a search, typically conducted by customs officials or the police, of a person's body and clothing for illicit weapons, drugs, or other articles.

bod·y shirt ▶ n. a close-fitting woman's garment for the upper body that is closed at the crotch. ■ a close-fitting blouse or shirt.

bod·y shop ▶ n. a garage where repairs to the bodies of vehicles are carried out.

bod·y·side /ˈbädeˌsīd/ ▶ n. the side of the body of a vehicle: [as modifier] *bodyside panels.*

bod·y slam ▶ n. Wrestling a move (illegal in some codes) in which the opponent's body is lifted and then thrown hard onto the floor.

bod·y·snatch·er /ˈbädēˌsnachər/ ▶ n. historical a person who stole corpses from a graveyard for dissection, for which there was no legal provision until 1832.
–DERIVATIVES **bod·y·snatch·ing** /-ˌsnachiNG/ n.

bod·y stock·ing ▶ n. a woman's one-piece undergarment that covers the torso and legs.

bod·y·suit /ˈbädēˌso͞ot/ ▶ n. a close-fitting one-piece stretch garment for women, typically worn for sports.

bod·y·surf /ˈbädēˌsərf/ ▶ v. [no obj.] (often as noun **bodysurfing**) float on the crest of incoming waves without using a board.

bod·y text ▶ n. (usu. **the body text**) the main part of a printed text, excluding items such as headings and footnotes.

bod·y wall ▶ n. the external surface of an animal body that encloses the body cavity and consists of ectoderm and mesoderm.

bod·y wave ▶ n. a soft, light permanent wave designed to give hair fullness.

bod·y·work /ˈbädēˌwərk/ ▶ n. **1** the metal outer shell of a vehicle.
2 therapies and techniques in complementary medicine that involve touching or manipulating the body.
–DERIVATIVES **bod·y·work·er** n. (sense 2).

bod·y wrap ▶ n. a type of beauty treatment involving the application of skin-cleansing ingredients to the body, which is then wrapped in hot towels.

boehm·ite /ˈbāmīt, ˈbō-/ ▶ n. a crystalline mineral compound composed of aluminum oxide and hydroxide and found in bauxite. ● Chem. formula: AlO(OH).

Boe·ing /ˈbō-iNG/, William Edward (1881–1956), US industrialist. In 1927, he founded United Aircraft and Transport, which, in 1934, was divided into Boeing Aircraft, United Aircraft, and United Airlines.

Boe·o·tia /bēˈōsHə/ a department in central Greece, north of the Gulf of Corinth, and a region of ancient Greece of which the chief city was Thebes.
–DERIVATIVES **Boe·o·tian** adj. & n.

Boer /bôr, bo͝or/ chiefly historical ▶ n. a member of the Dutch and Huguenot population that settled in southern Africa in the late 17th century.

> The Boers were Calvinist in religion and fiercely self-sufficient. Conflict with the British administration of Cape Colony after 1806 led to the Great Trek of 1835–37 and the Boer Wars, after which the Boer republics of Transvaal and Orange Free State became part of the Republic of South Africa. The Boers' present-day descendants are the Afrikaners.

▶ adj. of or relating to the Boers.
–ORIGIN from Dutch *boer* 'farmer.' Compare with BOOR.

boer·bull /ˈbôrˌbo͝ol, ˈbo͝or-/ (also **boerbul**) ▶ n. S. African a large dog crossbred from the mastiff and indigenous African dogs.
–ORIGIN 1960s: from Afrikaans *boerboel*, from *boer* (commonly applied to indigenous plants and animals) + *boel*, from Dutch *bul* (as in *bulhond* 'mastiff').

boer goat /bôr, bo͝or/ ▶ n. a goat of a hardy breed, originally from South Africa.
–ORIGIN from Afrikaans *boer* 'farmer' + GOAT.

Boer Wars two wars fought by Great Britain in southern Africa.

> The first war (1880–81) began with the revolt of the Boer settlers in Transvaal against British rule and ended with the establishment of an independent Boer Republic under British suzerainty. The second (1899–1902) was caused by the Boer refusal to grant equal rights to recent British immigrants and by the imperialist ambitions of Cecil Rhodes. The British eventually won through superior numbers and the employment of concentration camps to control the countryside.

boeuf /bœf/ ▶ n. Cooking French word for BEEF, used in the names of various beef dishes.

boeuf bour·gui·gnon /ˈbœf ˌbo͝orgēˈnyôN/ ▶ n. a dish consisting of beef stewed in red wine.
–ORIGIN early 20th cent.: French, literally 'Burgundy beef.'

boff /bäf/ informal ▶ v. [with obj.] have sexual intercourse with (someone).
▶ n. an act of sexual intercourse.
–ORIGIN 1920s (in the sense 'blow, punch'): imitative. The current sense dates from the 1950s.

bof·fin /ˈbäfin/ ▶ n. informal, chiefly Brit. a person engaged in scientific or technical research: *a computer boffin.* ■ a person with knowledge or a skill considered to be complex, arcane, and difficult: *he had a reputation as a tax boffin, a learned lawyer.*
–DERIVATIVES **bof·fin·y** adj.
–ORIGIN World War II: of unknown origin.

bof·fo /ˈbäfō/ informal ▶ adj. **1** (of a theatrical production or movie, or a review of one) very successful or wholeheartedly commendatory: *a boffo box-office certainty.*
2 (of a laugh) deep and unrestrained.
■ boisterously funny.
▶ n. (pl. **boffos**) a success: *the finale is a genuine boffo.*
–ORIGIN 1940s: from *boff* 'roaring success' + -O.

bof·fo·la /bäˈfōlə/ informal ▶ n. a joke or a line in a script meant to get a laugh.
▶ adj. (of a laugh) hearty and unrestrained.
–ORIGIN 1940s: extension of BOFF.

Bo·fors gun /ˈbōfôrz/ ▶ n. a type of light antiaircraft gun.
–ORIGIN 1930s: named after *Bofors* in Sweden, where it was first manufactured.

bog /bäg, bôg/ ▶ n. **1** wet muddy ground too soft to support a heavy body: *the island is a wilderness of bog* | *a peat bog* | figurative *a bog of legal complications.* ■ Ecology wetland with acid, peaty soil, typically dominated by peat moss. Compare with FEN[1].
2 (usu. **the bog**) Brit. informal a bathroom.
▶ v. (**bogs, bogging, bogged**) [with obj.] (usu. **be bogged down**) cause (a vehicle, person, or animal) to become stuck in mud or wet ground: *the car became bogged down on the beach road.* ■ (**be bogged down**) (of a person or process) be unable to make progress: *you must not get bogged down in detail.*
–ORIGIN Middle English: from Irish or Scottish Gaelic *bogach*, from *bog* 'soft.'

Bo·gart /ˈbōˌgärt/, Humphrey (DeForest) (1899–1957), US actor. His role on stage as a ruthless gangster in *The Petrified Forest* was repeated in the movie of 1936. His other movies include *Casablanca* (1942), *The Big Sleep* (1946), and *The African Queen* (1951).

bo·gart /ˈbōgärt/ ▶ v. [with obj.] informal selfishly appropriate or keep (something, esp. a lit marijuana cigarette).
–ORIGIN 1960s: from US actor Humphrey *Bogart* (1899–1957), who often smoked in films.

bog as·pho·del ▶ n. a yellow-flowered marsh plant of the lily family. ● Genus *Narthecium*, family Liliaceae: several species, including *N. ossifragum* of Europe and *N. americanum* of the eastern US, esp. New Jersey.

bog·bean /ˈbägˌbēn/ ▶ n. another term for BUCKBEAN.

bo·gey[1] /ˈbōgē/ Golf ▶ n. (pl. **bogeys**) a score of one stroke over par at a hole. ■ archaic term for PAR[1] (sense 1 of the noun).
▶ v. (**bogeys, bogeying, bogeyed**) [with obj.] play (a hole) in one stroke over par.
–ORIGIN late 19th cent.: perhaps from *Bogey*, denoting the Devil (see BOGEY[2]), regarded as an imaginary player.

bo·gey[2] /ˈbo͝ogē/ (also **bogy**) ▶ n. (pl. **bogeys**) a person or thing that causes fear or alarm: *the bogey of recession.* ■ an evil or mischievous spirit. ■ military slang an enemy aircraft.
–ORIGIN mid 19th cent. (as a proper name applied to the Devil): of unknown origin; probably related to BOGLE.

bo·gey·man /ˈbo͝ogēˌman, ˈbō-/ (also **boogeyman, bogyman**) ▶ n. (pl. **bogeymen**) (usu. **the bogeyman**) an imaginary evil spirit, referred to typically to frighten children: *with the blankets pulled over our heads to keep out the bogeyman.* ■ a person or thing that is widely regarded as an object of fear: *nuclear power is the environmentalists' bogeyman.*

bog·gle /ˈbägəl/ ▶ v. [no obj.] informal (of a person or a person's mind) be astonished or overwhelmed when trying to imagine something: *the mind boggles at the spectacle.* ■ [with obj.] cause (a person or a person's mind) to be astonished in such a way: *the inflated salary of a CEO boggles the mind* | (as adj. **boggling**) *the total was a boggling 1.5 trillion miles.* ■ (**boggle at**) (of a person) hesitate or be anxious at: *you never boggle at plain speaking.*
–ORIGIN late 16th cent.: probably of dialect origin and related to BOGLE and BOGEY[2].

bog·gy /ˈbôgē/ ▶ adj. (**boggier, boggiest**) too wet and muddy to be easily walked on; marshy: *the shrub grows naturally in boggy ground.*
–DERIVATIVES **bog·gi·ness** n.

bo·gie /ˈbōgē/ ▶ n. (pl. **bogies**) chiefly Brit. an undercarriage with four or six wheels pivoted beneath the end of a railroad car.
–ORIGIN early 19th cent. (originally in northern English dialect use): of unknown origin.

bog i·ron ▶ n. soft, spongy goethite deposited in bogs.

bog·land /ˈbägˌland/ ▶ n. chiefly Brit. marshy land.

bo·gle /ˈbōgəl/ ▶ n. a phantom or goblin. ■ Scottish & N. English a scarecrow.
–ORIGIN early 16th cent.: of unknown origin; probably related to BOGEY[2].

bog moss ▶ n. another term for PEAT MOSS (sense 1).

b

bog myr·tle ▶ **n.** another term for SWEET GALE.

bog oak ▶ **n.** an ancient oak tree that has been preserved in a black state in peat.

BOGOF /ˈbägôf/ ▶ **abbr.** buy one, get one free.

Bog·o·mil /ˈbägəmil/ ▶ **n.** historical a member of a heretical medieval Balkan sect professing a modified form of Manichaeism.
– DERIVATIVES **Bog·o·mil·ism** /-ˌlizəm/ **n.**
– ORIGIN mid 19th cent.: from medieval Greek *Bogomilos*, from *Bogomil*, literally 'beloved of God,' the name of the person who first disseminated the heresy, from Old Church Slavic.

bo·gong /ˈbōgông, -gäng/ (also **bogong moth**) ▶ **n.** Austral. a large brown moth native to southern Australia, formerly used as food by Aborigines. ● *Agrotis infusa*, family Noctuidae.
– ORIGIN mid 19th cent.: from Ngayawuh.

Bo·go·tá /ˌbōgəˌtä, ˌbōgəˈtô/ the capital of Colombia, in the eastern Andes at about 8,560 feet (2,610 m); pop. 6,778,691 (2005). It was founded by the Spanish in 1538 on the site of a pre-Columbian center of the Chibcha culture. Official name SANTA FÉ DE BOGOTÁ.

bog rose·mar·y ▶ **n.** See ANDROMEDA.

bog spav·in ▶ **n.** a soft swelling of the joint capsule of the hock of horses that most commonly occurs in young, fast-growing horses.

bog·trot·ter /ˈbägˌträtər/ ▶ **n.** a person who lives or works among bogs. ■ informal, offensive an Irish person.

bo·gus /ˈbōgəs/ ▶ **adj.** not genuine or true; fake: *a bogus insurance claim.*
– DERIVATIVES **bo·gus·ly adv.**, **bo·gus·ness n.**
– ORIGIN late 18th cent. (originally US, denoting a machine for making counterfeit money): of unknown origin.

bo·gy /ˈbōgē, ˈbo͝ogē/ ▶ **n.** (pl. **bogies**) variant spelling of BOGEY[2].

bo·gy·man ▶ **n.** variant spelling of BOGEYMAN.

Bo Hai /ˈbō ˈhī/ (also **Po Hai**) a large inlet of the Yellow Sea, on the coast of eastern China. Also called CHIHLI, GULF OF.

bo·hea /bōˈhē/ ▶ **n.** a black China tea that comes from the last crop of the season and is typically regarded as of low quality.
– ORIGIN early 18th cent.: named after the *Bu-yi* (*Wuyi*) hills in China, from where black tea first came to Britain.

Bo·he·mi·a /bōˈhēmēə/ a region that forms the western part of the Czech Republic. Formerly a Slavic kingdom, it became a province in the newly formed Czechoslovakia by the Treaty of Versailles in 1919.

Bo·he·mi·an /bōˈhēmēən/ ▶ **n. 1** a native or inhabitant of Bohemia.
2 (also **bohemian**) a person who has informal and unconventional social habits, esp. an artist or writer: *the young bohemians with their art galleries and sushi bars.* [mid 19th cent.: from French *bohémien* 'Gypsy' (because Gypsies were thought to come from Bohemia, or because they perhaps entered the West through Bohemia).]
▶ **adj. 1** of or relating to Bohemia or its people.
2 (also **bohemian**) having informal and unconventional social habits: *the bohemian writer's drafty-garret existence.*
– DERIVATIVES **Bo·he·mi·an·ism** /-ˌnizəm/ **n.** (sense 2 of the adjective).

bo·ho /ˈbōˌhō/ ▶ **n.** (pl. **bohos**) informal term for BOHEMIAN (sense 2 of the noun).
▶ **adj.** informal term for BOHEMIAN (sense 2 of the adjective).

Bo·hol /bōˈhôl/ an island in the central Philippines, north of Mindanao; pop. 1,384,800 (est. 2009); chief town, Tagbilaran.

Bohr /bôr/, Niels Henrik David (1885–1962), Danish physicist and pioneer in quantum physics. His theory of the structure of the atom incorporated quantum theory for the first time and is the basis for present-day quantum-mechanical models. Bohr helped to develop the atom bomb in Britain and then in the US. Nobel Prize for Physics (1922).

Bohr ef·fect ▶ **n.** a decrease in the amount of oxygen associated with hemoglobin and other respiratory compounds in response to a lowered blood pH resulting from an increased concentration of carbon dioxide in the blood.
– ORIGIN named for Danish physiologist Christian Bohr (1855–1911).

bohr·i·um /ˈbôrēəm/ ▶ **n.** the chemical element of atomic number 107, a very unstable element made by high-energy atomic collisions. (Symbol: **Bh**)

Bohr the·o·ry ▶ **n.** Physics a theory of the structure of atoms stating that electrons revolve in discrete orbits around a positively charged nucleus and that radiation is given off or absorbed only when an electron moves from one orbit to another.
– ORIGIN named for Danish physicist N. BOHR.

bo·hunk /ˈbōˌhəNGk/ ▶ **n.** informal, offensive an immigrant from central or southeastern Europe, esp. a laborer. ■ informal a rough or uncivilized person.
– ORIGIN early 20th cent.: apparently from BOHEMIAN + *-hunk*, alteration of HUNGARIAN.

boil[1] /boil/ ▶ **v. 1** (with reference to a liquid) reach or cause to reach the temperature at which it bubbles and turns to vapor: [with obj.] *we tried to get people to boil their drinking water* | *I'll boil up the stock* | [no obj.] *he waited for the water to boil.* ■ (with reference to a kettle, pan, or other container) heat or be heated until the liquid inside reaches such a temperature: [with obj.] *she boiled the kettle and took down a couple of mugs* | [no obj.] *the kettle boiled and he filled the teapot.*
2 [with obj.] subject (something) to the heat of boiling liquid, in particular: ■ (with reference to food) cook or be cooked by immersing in boiling water or stock: [with obj.] *boil the potatoes until well done* | (as adj. **boiled**) *two boiled eggs* | [no obj.] *make the sauce while the lobsters are boiling.* ■ [no obj.] (of food) be cooked in boiling water: *make the sauce while the lobsters are boiling.* ■ wash or sterilize (clothes) in very hot water. ■ historical execute (someone) by subjecting them to the heat of boiling liquid.
3 [no obj.] (of the sea or clouds) be turbulent and stormy: *a huge cliff with the black sea boiling below.* ■ (of a person or strong emotion) be stirred up or inflamed: *he was* **boiling with** *rage.*
▶ **n. 1** [in sing.] the temperature at which a liquid bubbles and turns to vapor: *stir in cream and bring* **to a boil**. ■ an act or process of heating a liquid to such a temperature. ■ a state of vigorous activity or excitement. ■ an area of churning water: *massive current differentials, boils, and braided channels.* ■ Fishing a sudden rise of a fish at a fly.
2 an outdoor meal at which seafood is boiled: *everything for a traditional Louisiana seafood boil can be carried down to the beach.* ■ a blend of seasonings added to water to enhance the flavor of boiled seafood.
– PHRASES **keep the pot boiling** maintain the momentum or interest value of something. **make one's blood boil** see BLOOD.
– PHRASAL VERBS **boil down to** be in essence a matter of: *everything boiled down to cash in the end.* **boil something down** reduce the volume of a liquid by boiling: *they boil down the syrup until it is very thick.* **boil over** (of a liquid) flow over the sides of the container in boiling. ■ (of a situation or strong emotion) become so excited or tense as to get out of control: *one woman's anger boiled over.*
– ORIGIN Middle English: from Old French *boillir*, from Latin *bullire* 'to bubble,' from *bulla* 'bubble.'

boil[2] ▶ **n.** an inflamed pus-filled swelling on the skin, typically caused by the infection of a hair follicle.
– ORIGIN Old English *bȳle, bȳl*; related to Dutch *buil* and German *Beule*.

Boi·leau /bwäˈlō/, Nicholas (1636–1711), French critic and poet; full name *Nicholas Boileau-Despréaux*. One of the founders of French literary criticism, his didactic poem *Art poétique* (1674) defined principles of composition and criticism.

boiled shirt ▶ **n.** dated a dress shirt with a starched front.

boil·er /ˈboilər/ ▶ **n.** a fuel-burning apparatus or container for heating water, in particular: ■ a household device providing a hot-water supply or serving a central heating system. ■ a tank for generating steam under pressure in a steam engine. See also STEAM BOILER. ■ dated a metal tub for washing or sterilizing clothes at a very high temperature.

boil·er·mak·er /ˈboilərˌmākər/ ▶ **n. 1** a person who makes boilers. ■ a metalworker in heavy industry.
2 a shot of whiskey followed by a glass of beer as a chaser.

boil·er·plate /ˈboilərˌplāt/ ▶ **n. 1** rolled steel for making boilers.
2 (**boilerplates**) Mountaineering smooth, overlapping, and undercut slabs of rock: *the ice-worn boilerplates.*
3 writing that is clichéd or expresses a generally accepted opinion or belief: *the same dreary boilerplate he's been dishing up for years.*
■ standardized pieces of text for use as clauses in contracts or as part of a computer program: *some sections have been written as boilerplate for use in all proposals.*

boil·er room ▶ **n.** a room in a building (typically in the basement) or a compartment in a ship containing a boiler and related heating or steam-generating equipment. ■ a room used for intensive telephone selling: [as modifier] *boiler-room stock salesmen.*

boil·er suit ▶ **n.** British term for COVERALLS (see COVERALL).

boil·ing /ˈboiliNG/ ▶ **adj.** (for fresh water at sea level) at 212°F (100°C). ■ (also **boiling hot**) informal (used hyperbolically) extremely hot: *Saturday is forecast to be boiling and sunny.*
▶ **n.** the action of bringing a liquid to the temperature at which it bubbles and turns to vapor. ■ the temperature at which such an event occurs: *reheat gently to just below boiling.*

boil·ing point ▶ **n.** the temperature at which a liquid boils and turns to vapor. ■ the point at which anger or excitement breaks out into violent expression: *emotions had reached boiling point and could spill over into violence.*

boil·ing-wa·ter re·ac·tor (abbr.: **BWR**) ▶ **n.** a nuclear reactor in which the fuel is uranium oxide clad in zircaloy and the coolant and moderator is water, which is boiled to produce steam for driving turbines.

boing /boiNG/ ▶ **exclam.** representing the noise of a compressed spring suddenly released.
▶ **n.** such a noise.
▶ **v.** [no obj.] make such a noise.
– ORIGIN 1950s: imitative.

Boi·se /ˈboisē, -zē/ a city in southwestern Idaho, the capital of the state; pop. 205,314 (est. 2008).

boi·se·rie /bwäzəˈrē/ ▶ **n.** wooden paneling.
– ORIGIN mid 19th cent.: French.

bois·ter·ous /ˈboist(ə)rəs/ ▶ **adj.** (of a person, event, or behavior) noisy, energetic, and cheerful; rowdy: *the boisterous conviviality associated with taverns of that period.* ■ (of wind, weather, or water) wild or stormy: *the boisterous wind was lulled.*
– DERIVATIVES **bois·ter·ous·ly adv.**, **bois·ter·ous·ness n.**
– ORIGIN late Middle English (in the sense 'rough, stiff'): variant of earlier *boistuous* 'rustic, coarse, boisterous,' of unknown origin.

boîte /bwät/ ▶ **n.** (pl. **same** or **boîtes**) a small restaurant or nightclub.
– ORIGIN French, literally 'box.'

Bo·kas·sa /bəˈkäsə/, Jean Bédel (1921–96), Central African Republic statesman and military leader; president 1972–76; self-styled emperor 1976–79.

bok choy /ˈbäk ˈCHoi/ ▶ **n.** Chinese cabbage of a variety with smooth-edged tapering leaves. Also called PAK CHOI.

bok choy

bok·ken /ˈbäkən/ ▶ **n.** a wooden sword used as a practice weapon in kendo.

Bok·mål /ˈbo͝okˌmôl/ ▶ **n.** one of two standard forms of the Norwegian language, a modified form of Danish. See NORWEGIAN.
– ORIGIN from Norwegian *bok* 'book' + *mål* 'language.'

bo·la /ˈbōlə/ (also **bolas**) ▶ **n.** (esp. in South America) a weapon consisting of a number of balls connected by strong cord, which when thrown entangles the limbs of the quarry.
– ORIGIN early 19th cent.: from Spanish and Portuguese *bolas*, plural of *bola* 'ball.'

bo·la tie /ˈbōlə/ ▶ **n.** variant spelling of BOLO TIE.

bold /bōld/ ▶ **adj. 1** (of a person, action, or idea) showing an ability to take risks; confident and courageous: *a bold attempt to solve the crisis* | *he was the only one bold enough to air his dislike.* ■ dated (of a person or manner) so confident as to suggest a lack of shame or modesty: *she tossed him a bold look.*
2 (of a color or design) having a strong or vivid appearance: *a coat with bold polka dots.* ■ of a kind of typeface having dark, heavy strokes, used esp. for emphasis.
▶ **n.** a bold typeface or letter: *difficult words and phrases are highlighted in bold.*
– PHRASES **be** (or **make**) **so bold** (**as to do something**) formal dare to do something (often used when politely asking a question or making a suggestion): *what would he be calling for, if I might make so bold as to ask?* (**as**) **bold as brass** confident to the point of impudence: *she marched into the library as bold as brass.* **a bold stroke** a daring action or initiative. **put a bold face on something** see FACE.
– DERIVATIVES **bold·ly adv.**, **bold·ness n.**
– ORIGIN Old English *bald*, of Germanic origin; related to Dutch *boud* and to German *bald* 'soon.'

bold·face /ˈbōld,fās/ ▶ **n.** a typeface with thick strokes.
▶ **adj.** printed or displayed in such a typeface.
– DERIVATIVES **bold·faced** adj.

bole¹ /bōl/ ▶ **n.** the trunk of a tree.
– ORIGIN Middle English: from Old Norse *bolr*; perhaps related to BALK.

bole² ▶ **n.** fine, compact, earthy clay, typically of a reddish color, used as a pigment.
– ORIGIN Middle English: from late Latin *bolus* 'rounded mass' (see BOLUS).

bo·lec·tion /bōˈleksʜən/ ▶ **n.** [usu. as modifier] Architecture a decorative molding that separates two planes (or surfaces), esp. around a wooden panel, usually convex.
– ORIGIN mid 17th cent.: of unknown origin.

bo·le·ro /bəˈle(ə)rō/ ▶ **n.** (pl. **boleros**) **1** a Spanish dance in simple triple time. ■ a piece of music for this dance.
2 (also **bolero jacket**) a woman's short open jacket.
– ORIGIN late 18th cent.: from Spanish.

bolero 2

bo·lete /bōˈlēt/ (also **boletus** /bōˈlētəs/) ▶ **n.** (pl. **boletes** or **boletuses** /-ˈlētəsəz/) a mushroom or toadstool with pores rather than gills on the underside of the cap. Boletes often have a thick stem, and several kinds are edible. See also CEP. ● Genus *Boletus*, family Boletaceae, class Basidiomycetes.
– ORIGIN from Latin, from Greek *bōlitēs*, perhaps from *bōlos* 'lump.'

Bol·eyn /bŏŏˈlin, ˈbŏŏlən/, Anne (1507–36), second wife of Henry VIII; mother of Elizabeth I. Henry divorced Catherine of Aragon in order to marry Anne in 1533, but she fell from favor when she failed to provide him with a male heir. She was eventually executed because of alleged infidelities.

bo·lide /ˈbōlīd, ˈbōlid/ ▶ **n.** a large meteor that explodes in the atmosphere.
– ORIGIN early 19th cent.: from French, from Latin *bolis, bolid-*, from Greek *bolis* 'missile.'

Bol·ing·broke /ˈbōliɴɢ,brŏŏk, ˈbäl-, -,brōk/, the surname of Henry IV of England (see HENRY¹).

Bo·ling·brook /ˈbōliɴɢ,brŏŏk/ a village in northeastern Illinois, southwest of Chicago; pop. 70,823 (est. 2008).

bol·i·var /bəˈlē,vär, ˈbälәvәr/ ▶ **n.** the basic monetary unit of Venezuela, equal to 100 centimos.
– ORIGIN named after S. BOLÍVAR.

Bol·í·var /bəˈlē,vär, ˈbäləvər/, Simón (1783–1830), Venezuelan patriot and statesman; known as **the Liberator**. He succeeded in driving the Spanish from Venezuela, Colombia, Peru, and Ecuador. Upper Peru was named Bolivia in his honor.

Bo·liv·i·a /bəˈlivēə/ a landlocked country in western South America; pop. 9,775,200 (est. 2009); capital, La Paz; legal capital and seat of the judiciary, Sucre; languages, Spanish (official), Aymara, and Quechua.

> After the defeat of the Incas, Bolivia became part of Spain's empire in the Americas. Freed from Spanish rule in 1825, it has suffered continually from political instability.

– DERIVATIVES **Bo·liv·i·an** adj. & n.
– ORIGIN named after Simón *Bolívar*, who liberated the country from Spanish rule.

bo·liv·i·a·no /bə,livēˈänō/ ▶ **n.** (pl. **bolivianos**) the basic monetary unit of Bolivia (1863–1962 and since 1987), equal to 100 centavos or cents.
– ORIGIN late 19th cent.: Spanish, literally 'Bolivian,' from BOLIVIA.

boll /bōl/ ▶ **n.** the rounded seed capsule of plants such as cotton or flax.
– ORIGIN Middle English (originally denoting a bubble): from Middle Dutch *bolle* 'rounded object'; related to BOWL¹.

Böll /bœl/, Heinrich (Theodor) (1917–85), German novelist and short-story writer. Notable works: *Billiards at Half Past Nine* (1959) and *The Lost Honor of Katharina Blum* (1974). Nobel Prize for Literature (1972).

bol·lard /ˈbälərd/ ▶ **n.** **1** a short, thick post on the deck of a ship or on a wharf, to which a ship's rope may be secured.
2 Brit. a short post used to divert traffic from an area or road.
– ORIGIN Middle English (sense 1): perhaps from Old Norse *bolr* (see BOLE¹) + -ARD.

bol·li·to mis·to /bōˈlētō ˈmistō/ ▶ **n.** (pl. **bolliti misti** /bōˈlētē ˈmistē/) a dish of mixed kinds of meat, such as chicken, veal, and sausage, boiled with vegetables in broth.
– ORIGIN Italian, 'boiled mixed meat,' from *bollito* past participle of *bollire* 'to boil' and *misto* 'mixed.'

bol·lix /ˈbäliks/ vulgar slang ▶ **v.** [with obj.] (usu. **bollix something up**) bungle (a task).
▶ **plural n.** variant spelling of BOLLOCKS.

bol·locks /ˈbäləks/ (also **ballocks** or **bollix**) vulgar slang, chiefly Brit. ▶ **n.** **1** [in pl.] the testicles.
2 used to express contempt, annoyance, or defiance.
– ORIGIN mid 18th cent.: plural of *bollock*, variant of earlier *ballock*, of Germanic origin; related to BALL¹.

boll wee·vil ▶ **n.** a small weevil that feeds on the fibers of the cotton boll. It is a major pest of the American cotton crop. ● *Anthonomus grandis*, family Curculionidae.
■ informal in the US, a conservative Southern Democrat, esp. a member of Congress.

boll weevil

boll·worm /ˈbōl,wərm/ ▶ **n.** a moth caterpillar that attacks the cotton boll, in particular: ● (**pink bollworm**) a small moth that is a serious pest of the North American cotton crop (*Pectinophora gossypiella*, family Gelechiidae). ● (also **cotton bollworm**) another term for CORN EARWORM.

Bol·ly·wood /ˈbälē,wŏŏd/ ▶ **n.** the Indian movie industry, based in Mumbai (Bombay).
– ORIGIN 1970s: blend of BOMBAY and HOLLYWOOD.

bo·lo /ˈbōlō/ ▶ **n.** **1** (pl. **bolos**) a large single-edged knife used in the Philippines.
2 variant of BOLA.
3 short for BOLO TIE.
– ORIGIN Spanish.

Bo·lo·gna /bəˈlōnyə/ a city in northern Italy, northeast of Florence; pop. 374,944 (2008). Its university, which dates from the 11th century, is the oldest in Europe.

bo·lo·gna /bəˈlōnē/ (also **bologna sausage**) ▶ **n.** a large smoked, seasoned sausage made of various meats, esp. beef and pork.
– ORIGIN from BOLOGNA.

bo·lom·e·ter /bōˈlämitər/ ▶ **n.** a sensitive electrical instrument for measuring radiant energy.
– DERIVATIVES **bo·lo·met·ric** /,bōləˈmetrik/ adj.
– ORIGIN late 19th cent.: from Greek *bolē* 'ray of light' + -METER.

bo·lo·ney ▶ **n.** old-fashioned spelling of BALONEY.

bo·lo tie (also **bola tie** /ˈbōlə/) ▶ **n.** a type of tie consisting of a cord worn around the neck with a large, sliding, ornamental fastening at the throat.

Bol·she·vik /ˈbōlsʜə,vik/ ▶ **n.** historical a member of the majority faction of the Russian Social Democratic Party, which was renamed the Communist Party after seizing power in the October Revolution of 1917. ■ chiefly derogatory (in general use) a person with politically subversive or radical views; a revolutionary.
▶ **adj.** of, relating to, or characteristic of Bolsheviks or their views or policies.
– DERIVATIVES **Bol·she·vism** /-,vizəm/ n., **Bol·she·vist** /-vist/ n.
– ORIGIN Russian, from *bol'she* 'greater' (with reference to the greater faction).

bolo tie

Bol·shie /ˈbōlsʜē/ (also **Bolshy**) ▶ **n.** (pl. **Bolshies**) Brit. informal a Bolshevik or socialist.
▶ **adj.** (**bolshie**) Brit. informal or dated (of a person or attitude) deliberately combative or uncooperative: *policemen with bolshie attitudes*.
– DERIVATIVES **bol·shi·ness** n.
– ORIGIN early 20th cent.: abbreviation of BOLSHEVIK.

bol·ster /ˈbōlstər/ ▶ **n.** (also **bolster pillow**) a long, thick pillow that is placed under other pillows for support. ■ a part of a vehicle or tool providing structural support. ■ Building a short timber cap over a post designed to increase the bearing of the beams it supports.
▶ **v.** [with obj.] support or strengthen; prop up: *the fall in interest rates is starting to bolster confidence* | *he wished to bolster up his theories with hard data*.
■ provide (a seat) with padded support: (as adj. **bolstered**) *I snuggled down into the heavily bolstered seat*.
– ORIGIN Old English (in the sense 'long, thick pillow'), of Germanic origin; related to Dutch *bolster* and German *Polster*.

Bolt¹ /bōlt/, Robert (Oxton) (1924–95), English writer. His play *A Man for All Seasons* (1960) was made into a movie in 1967. He also wrote the screenplays for *Lawrence of Arabia* (1962), *Dr. Zhivago* (1965), and *The Mission* (1986).

Bolt², Usain (St. Leo) (1986–), Jamaican athlete. At the 2008 Olympic Games in Beijing, he won gold medals in the 100 meter and 200 meter races, setting a new world record time for each. He also won a gold medal, and set a new world record, as part of the Jamaican 4×100 meter relay team.

bolt¹ /bōlt/ ▶ **n.** **1** a metal pin or bar, in particular: ■ a bar that slides into a socket to fasten a door or window. ■ a threaded pin that screws into a nut and is used to fasten things together. ■ the sliding piece of the breech mechanism of a rifle. ■ (in rock climbing) a long pin that is driven into a rock face so that a rope can be attached to it.
2 a short heavy arrow shot from a crossbow.
3 a flash of lightning leaving a jagged line across the sky.
▶ **v.** [with obj.] fasten (something) with a metal pin or bar, in particular: ■ fasten (a door or window) with a bar that slides into a socket: *all the doors were locked and bolted*. ■ fasten (an object) to something else with a bolt: *the lid was put into position and bolted down* | *a camera was bolted to the aircraft*.
– PHRASES **a bolt from** (or **out of**) **the blue** a sudden and unexpected event or piece of news: *the job came like a bolt from the blue*. **bolt upright** upright, with the back rigid and straight: *she sat bolt upright in bed*. **have shot one's bolt** informal have done all that one is able.
– ORIGIN Old English, 'arrow,' of unknown origin; related to Dutch *bout* and German *Bolzen* 'arrow, bolt for a door.'

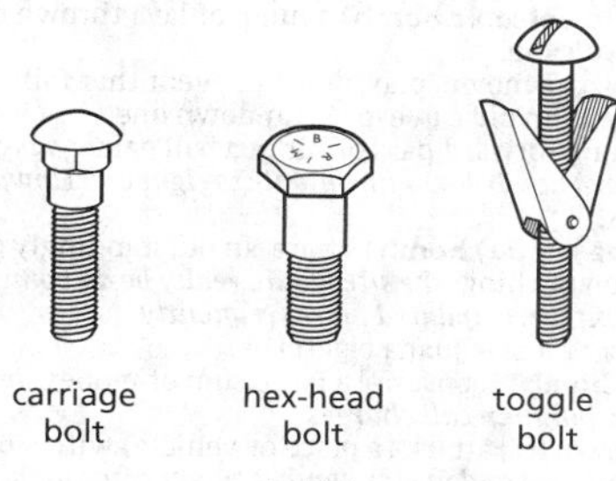

bolt¹ 1

bolt² ▶ **v.** **1** [no obj.] (of a horse or other animal) run away suddenly out of control: *the horses shied and bolted*. ■ (of a person) move or run away suddenly: *they bolted down the stairs*. ■ [with obj.] (in hunting) cause (a rabbit or fox) to run out of its burrow or hole. ■ (of a plant) grow tall quickly and stop flowering as seeds develop: *the lettuces have bolted*.
2 [with obj.] (often **bolt something down**) eat or swallow (food) quickly: *it is normal for puppies to bolt down their food*.
– PHRASES **make a bolt for** try to escape by moving suddenly toward (something): *Ellie made a bolt for the door*. **shut the stable door after the horse has bolted** try to avert something bad or unwelcome when it is already too late to do so.
– ORIGIN Middle English: from BOLT¹, expressing the sense 'fly like an arrow.'

bolt³ ▶ **n.** a roll of fabric, originally as a measure: *the room is stacked with bolts of cloth*.
– ORIGIN Middle English: transferred use of BOLT¹.

bolt⁴ (also **boult**) ▶ **v.** [with obj.] archaic pass (flour, powder, or other material) through a sieve.
– ORIGIN Middle English: from Old French *bulter*, of unknown ultimate origin. The change in the first syllable was due to association with BOLT¹.

bolt-ac·tion ▶ **adj.** (of a gun) having a breech that is opened by turning a bolt and sliding it back.

bolt-hole ▶ **n.** a place where a person can escape and hide: *he thought of Antwerp as a possible bolt-hole*. ■ chiefly Brit. a hole or burrow by which a rabbit or other wild animal can escape.

bolt·ing /ˈbōltiɴɢ/ ▶ **n.** (in rock climbing) the action of driving metal pins into rock faces so that ropes can be attached to them.

Bol·ton /ˈbōltn/ a town in northwestern England, northwest of Manchester; pop. 135,200 (est. 2009).

bolt-on ▶ **adj.** [attrib.] (of an extra part of a machine) able to be fastened on with a bolt or catch.
▶ **n.** an extra part that can be fastened onto a machine with a bolt or catch.

bolt rope ▶ **n.** a rope sewn around the edge of a vessel's sail to prevent tearing.

b

Boltz·mann /ˈbôltsmən/, Ludwig (1844–1906), Austrian physicist. He made contributions to the kinetic theory of gases, statistical mechanics, and thermodynamics. He also derived the Maxwell–Boltzmann equation for the distribution of energy among colliding atoms.

Boltz·mann dis·tri·bu·tion another term for MAXWELL–BOLTZMANN DISTRIBUTION.

Boltz·mann's con·stant Chemistry the ratio of the gas constant to Avogadro's number, equal to 1.381×10^{-23} joule per kelvin. (Symbol: **k**)

bo·lus /ˈbōləs/ ▶ n. (pl. **boluses**) a small rounded mass of a substance, esp. of chewed food at the moment of swallowing. ■ a type of large pill used in veterinary medicine. ■ Medicine a single dose of a drug or other medicinal preparation given all at once.
– ORIGIN mid 16th cent. denoting a large pill of medicine: via late Latin from Greek *bōlos* 'clod.'

Bol·za·no /bōltˈsänō, bōldˈzänō/ a city in northeastern Italy; pop. 102,000 (2009).

bomb /bäm/ ▶ n. **1** a container filled with explosive, incendiary material, smoke, gas, or other destructive substance, designed to explode on impact or when detonated by a time mechanism, remote-control device, or lit fuse. ■ [with modifier] an explosive device fitted into a specified object: *a package bomb.* See also CAR BOMB, LETTER BOMB. ■ (**the bomb**) nuclear weapons considered collectively as agents of mass destruction: *she joined the fight against the bomb.* ■ a small pressurized container that sprays liquid, foam, or gas: *the bug bombs we tried did not kill the cockroaches.*
2 (also **volcanic bomb**) a lump of lava thrown out by a volcano.
3 informal a movie, play, or other event that fails badly. ■ an old car, esp. a run-down one.
4 a long forward pass or hit in a ball game: *a big 40-yard bomb down the middle to tight end Howard Cross.*
5 (**the** (or **da**) **bomb**) informal an outstandingly good person or thing: *the site would really be da bomb if its content were updated more frequently.*
6 informal a marijuana cigarette.
7 (**a bomb**) Brit. informal a large sum of money: *it will cost a bomb in call charges.*
▶ v. **1** [with obj.] attack (a place or vehicle) with a bomb or bombs: *London was bombed, night after night* | (as noun **bombing**) *a series of bombings.*
2 [no obj.] informal (of a movie, play, or other event) fail miserably: *a big-budget movie that bombed at the box office* | *he **bombed out** at several tournaments.*
3 [no obj., with adverbial of direction] Brit. informal move very quickly: *the bus came bombing along.*
– PHRASES **go down a bomb** Brit. informal be very well received: *those gigs we did went down a bomb.* **it looks like a bomb's hit it** informal used to describe a place that is extremely messy or untidy in appearance.
– ORIGIN late 17th cent.: from French *bombe,* from Italian *bomba,* probably from Latin *bombus* 'booming, humming,' from Greek *bombos,* of imitative origin.

bom·bard ▶ v. /bämˈbärd/ [with obj.] attack (a place or person) continuously with bombs, shells, or other missiles: *the city was bombarded by federal forces* | *supporters **bombarded** police **with** bottles.* ■ assail (someone) persistently, as with questions, criticisms, or information: *they will be **bombarded with** complaints.* ■ Physics direct a high-speed stream of particles at (a substance).
▶ n. /ˈbäm,bärd/ historical a cannon of the earliest type, which originally fired a stone ball.
– ORIGIN late Middle English (as a noun denoting an early form of cannon, also a shawm): from Old French *bombarde,* probably based on Latin *bombus* 'booming, humming' (see BOMB). The verb (late 16th cent.) is from French *bombarder.*

bom·barde /ˈbäm,bärd/ ▶ n. Music a medieval alto-pitched shawm.
– ORIGIN late Middle English: from Old French, denoting a shawm (see BOMBARD).

bom·bar·dier /,bämbə(r)ˈdi(ə)r/ ▶ n. **1** a member of a bomber crew in the US Air Force responsible for sighting and releasing bombs.
2 a rank of noncommissioned officer in certain Canadian and British artillery regiments, equivalent to corporal.
– ORIGIN mid 16th cent. (denoting a soldier in charge of a *bombard,* an early form of cannon): from French, from Old French *bombarde* 'cannon' (see BOMBARD).

bom·bar·dier bee·tle ▶ n. a ground beetle that when alarmed discharges a puff of hot irritant vapor from its anus with an audible pop. ● Genus *Brachinus,* family Carabidae: several species.

bom·bard·ment /bämˈbärdmənt/ ▶ n. a continuous attack with bombs, shells, or other missiles: *an aerial bombardment will precede the attack.* ■ a continuous flow of questions, criticisms, or information: *a steady bombardment of e-mails and phone calls.*

bom·bar·don /ˈbämbərdən, bämˈbärdn/ ▶ n. Music a type of valved bass tuba. ■ an organ stop imitating this.
– ORIGIN mid 19th cent.: from Italian *bombardone,* from *bombardo* 'cannon.' Compare with BOMBARDE.

bom·bast /ˈbämbast/ ▶ n. high-sounding language with little meaning, used to impress people.
– ORIGIN mid 16th cent. (denoting raw cotton or absorbent cotton used as padding, later used figuratively): from Old French *bombace,* from medieval Latin *bombax, bombac-,* alteration of *bombyx* 'silkworm' (see BOMBAZINE).

bom·bas·tic /bämˈbastik/ ▶ adj. high-sounding but with little meaning; inflated: *bombastic rhetoric* | *bombastic music that drowned out anyone was saying.*
– DERIVATIVES **bom·bas·ti·cal·ly** /bämˈbastik(ə)lē/ adv.

Bom·bay /bämˈbā/ former name (until 1995) for MUMBAI.

Bom·bay duck ▶ n. the bummalo (fish), esp. when dried and eaten as an accompaniment with curry.
– ORIGIN mid 19th cent.: alteration of BUMMALO by association with BOMBAY in India (now Mumbai), from which bummalo were exported.

bom·ba·zine /,bämbəˈzēn, ˈbämbə,zēn/ ▶ n. a twilled dress fabric of worsted and silk or cotton.
– ORIGIN mid 16th cent. (denoting raw cotton): from French *bombasin,* from medieval Latin *bombacinum,* from *bombycinum,* neuter of *bombycinus* 'silken,' based on Greek *bombux* 'silkworm.'

bomb bay ▶ n. a compartment in the fuselage of an aircraft in which bombs are held and from which they may be dropped.

bomb dis·pos·al ▶ n. the defusing or removal and detonation of unexploded and delayed-action bombs.

bombe /bäm(b)/ ▶ n. a frozen dome-shaped dessert. ■ a dome-shaped mold in which this dessert is made.
– ORIGIN late 19th cent.: French, literally 'bomb.'

bom·bé /bämˈbā/ ▶ adj. (of furniture) rounded.
– ORIGIN early 20th cent.: French, literally 'swollen out.'

bombed /bämd/ ▶ adj. **1** (of an area or building) subjected to bombing: *the rubble of a bombed house.*
2 informal intoxicated by drink or drugs: *"we might as well get **bombed out of our minds**," he said, downing another bottle.*

bombed-out ▶ adj. **1** [attrib.] (of a building or city) destroyed by bombing.
2 informal another term for BOMBED (sense 2).

bomb·er /ˈbämər/ ▶ n. **1** an aircraft designed to carry and drop bombs.
2 a person who plants, detonates, or throws bombs in a public place, esp. as a terrorist.
3 informal a cigarette containing marijuana.
4 short for BOMBER JACKET.

bomb·er jack·et ▶ n. a short jacket, usually leather, tightly gathered at the waist and cuffs by elasticized bands and typically having a zipper front.

bom·bi·nate /ˈbämbə,nāt/ ▶ v. [no obj.] literary buzz; hum: (as adj. **bombinating**) *her head had become a bombinating vacuum.*
– ORIGIN late 19th cent.: from medieval Latin *bombinat-* 'buzzed,' from the verb *bombinare,* from Latin *bombus* 'humming' (see BOMBARD).

bomb·ing run ▶ n. the part of the flight path of a bomber that brings it into position to release its weapons.

bomb·let /ˈbämlit/ ▶ n. a small bomb.

bom·bor·a /bämˈbôrə/ ▶ n. Austral. a wave that forms over a submerged offshore reef or rock, sometimes breaking heavily and producing a dangerous stretch of broken water.
– ORIGIN 1930s: from an Aboriginal word, perhaps Dharuk *bumbora.*

bomb·proof /ˈbäm,pro͞of/ ▶ adj. strong enough to resist the effects of blast from a bomb.

bomb·shell /ˈbäm,SHel/ ▶ n. **1** an overwhelming surprise or disappointment: *the news came as a bombshell.*
2 informal a very attractive woman: *a twenty-year-old blonde bombshell.*
3 dated an artillery shell.

bomb·sight /ˈbäm,sīt/ ▶ n. a mechanical or electronic device used in an aircraft for aiming bombs.

bomb squad ▶ n. a division of a police force assigned to defuse explosive devices.

Bon /bôn/ (also **O-Bon** /ō ˈbôn/) ▶ n. a Japanese Buddhist festival held annually in August to honor the dead. Also called FESTIVAL OF THE DEAD or LANTERN FESTIVAL.

Bon, Cape /bôN/ a peninsula in northeastern Tunisia.

bo·na fide /ˈbōnə ,fīd, ˈbänə/ ▶ adj. genuine; real: *only bona fide members of the company are allowed to use the logo.*
▶ adv. chiefly Law sincerely; without intention to deceive: *the court will assume that they have acted bona fide.*
– ORIGIN mid 16th cent.: Latin, literally 'with good faith,' ablative singular of BONA FIDES.

bo·na fi·des /ˈbōnə ,fīdz, ˈfīdēz, ˈbänə/ ▶ n. a person's honesty and sincerity of intention: *he went to great lengths to establish his liberal bona fides.* ■ [treated as pl.] informal documentary evidence showing a person's legitimacy; credentials: *are you satisfied with my bona fides?*
– ORIGIN late 18th cent.: Latin, literally 'good faith.'

Bon·aire /bəˈne(ə)r/ one of the two principal islands of the Netherlands Antilles (the other is Curaçao); chief town, Kralendijk; pop.12,877 (2009).

bo·nan·za /bəˈnanzə/ ▶ n. a situation or event that creates a sudden increase in wealth, good fortune, or profits: *a bonanza in military sales* | [as modifier] *a bonanza year for the computer industry.* ■ a large amount of something desirable: *the festive feature film bonanza.*
– ORIGIN early 19th cent. (originally US, esp. with reference to success when mining): from Spanish, literally 'fair weather, prosperity,' from Latin *bonus* 'good.'

Bo·na·parte /ˈbōnə,pärt/ (Italian **Buonaparte** /,bwōnäˈpärtā/) a Corsican family, including the three French rulers named Napoleon.

bon ap·pé·tit /ˈbōn ,apəˈtē/ ▶ exclam. used as a salutation to a person about to eat.
– ORIGIN mid 19th cent.: French, literally 'good appetite.'

Bon·a·ven·tu·ra, St. /,bōnə,venˈto͝orə/ (1221–74), Franciscan theologian; born *Giovanni di Fidanza;* known as **the Seraphic Doctor**. He wrote the official biography of St. Francis. Feast day, July 15 (formerly 14).

bon·bon /ˈbän,bän/ ▶ n. a piece of candy, esp. one covered with chocolate.
– ORIGIN late 18th cent.: from French, reduplication of *bon* 'good,' from Latin *bonus.*

bond /bänd/ ▶ n. **1** (**bonds**) physical restraints used to hold someone or something prisoner, esp. ropes or chains. ■ a thing used to tie something or to fasten things together: *she brushed back a curl that had strayed from its bonds* | figurative *chaos could result if the bonds of obedience and loyalty were broken.* ■ adhesiveness; ability of two objects to stick to each other: *a total lack of effective bond between the concrete and the steel.* ■ a force or feeling that unites people; a common emotion or interest: *there was a bond of understanding between them.*
2 an agreement with legal force, in particular: ■ Law a deed by which a person is committed to make payment to another. ■ a certificate issued by a government or a public company promising to repay borrowed money at a fixed rate of interest at a specified time. ■ an insurance policy held by a company, which protects against losses resulting from circumstances such as bankruptcy or misconduct by employees. ■ a sum of money paid as bail.
3 (also **chemical bond**) a strong force of attraction holding atoms together in a molecule or crystal, resulting from the sharing or transfer of electrons.
4 [with modifier] Building any of the various patterns in which bricks are conventionally laid in order to ensure the strength of the resulting structure. See ENGLISH BOND, FLEMISH BOND.
5 short for BOND PAPER.
▶ v. **1** join or be joined securely to something else, typically by means of an adhesive substance, heat, or pressure: [with obj.] *press the material to bond the layers together* | [no obj.] *this material will bond well to stainless steel rods* | (as adj. **bonding**) *a bonding agent.* ■ [no obj.] establish a relationship with someone based on shared feelings, interests, or experiences: *the failure to properly **bond with** their children* | *the team has **bonded together** well* | (as noun **bonding**) *the film has some great male bonding scenes.*
2 join or be joined by a chemical bond.
3 [with obj.] (usu. as adj. **bonding**) lay (bricks) in an overlapping pattern so as to form a strong structure: *a bonding course.*
4 (usu. as noun **bonding**) place (dutiable goods) in bond.
– ORIGIN Middle English: variant of BAND[1].

bond·age /ˈbändij/ ▶ n. **1** the state of being a slave: *the deliverance of the Israelites from Egypt's bondage* | figurative *the bondage of drug addiction.*
2 sexual practice that involves the tying up or restraining of one partner.

–ORIGIN Middle English: from Anglo-Latin *bondagium*, from Middle English *bond* 'serf' (earlier 'peasant, householder'), from Old Norse *bóndi* 'tiller of the soil,' based on *búa* 'dwell'; influenced in sense by BOND.

bond·ed /ˈbändid/ ▶ **adj.** [attrib.] **1** (of a thing) joined securely to another thing, esp. by an adhesive, a heat process, or pressure: *bonded metal plates.* ■ emotionally or psychologically linked: *a strongly bonded group of females.* ■ held by a chemical bond: *bonded atoms.*
2 (of a person or company) bound by a legal agreement, in particular: ■ (of a debt) secured by bonds. ■ (of a worker or workforce) obliged to work for a particular employer, often in a condition close to slavery.
3 (of dutiable goods) placed in bond.

bond·ed ware·house ▶ **n.** a customs-controlled warehouse for the retention of imported goods until the duty owed is paid.

bond·hold·er /ˈbänd,hōldər/ ▶ **n.** a person owning a bond or bonds issued by a government or a public company.

bond·maid /ˈbänd,mād/ ▶ **n.** archaic a slave girl.

bond·man /ˈbänd,mən/ ▶ **n.** archaic a serf; a slave.

bond pa·per ▶ **n.** high-quality writing paper.

bond·serv·ant /ˈbänd,sərvənt/ ▶ **n.** a person bound in service without wages. ■ a slave or serf.

bonds·man /ˈbändzmən/ ▶ **n.** (pl. **bondsmen**)
1 a person who stands surety for a bond. [early 18th cent.: from BOND + MAN.]
2 archaic a slave. [mid 18th cent.: variant of Middle English *bondman*, from obsolete *bond* 'serf' (see also BONDAGE).]

bond·wom·an /ˈbänd,wo͝omən/ ▶ **n.** (pl. **bondwomen**) a female bondservant or slave.

Bône /bōn/ former name for ANNABA.

bone /bōn/ ▶ **n.** **1** any of the pieces of hard, whitish tissue making up the skeleton in humans and other vertebrates: *his injuries included many broken bones | a shoulder bone.*

> The substance of bones is formed by specialized cells (osteoblasts) that secrete around themselves a material containing calcium salts (which provide hardness and strength in compression) and collagen fibers (which provide tensile strength). Many bones have a central cavity containing marrow.

■ (**bones**) a person's body: *he hauled his tired bones upright.*
■ (**bones**) a corpse or skeleton: *the diggers turned up the bones of a fifteen-year-old girl | bones of prehistoric mammals.*
■ a bone of an animal with meat on it, used as food for people or dogs: *stewed in stock made with a ham bone | dogs yelping over a bone.*
2 the calcified material of which bones consist: *an earring of bone.* ■ a substance similar to this such as ivory, dentin, or whalebone. ■ (often **bones**) a thing made of, or once made of, such a substance, for example a pair of dice. ■ the whitish color of bone: *the sandals she had dyed bone to match the small purse.*
3 (**bones**) the basic or essential framework of something: *you need to put some flesh on the bones of your idea.*
4 vulgar slang a penis.
▶ **v.** **1** [with obj.] remove the bones from (meat or fish): *while the gumbo is simmering, bone the cooked chicken.*
2 [no obj.] (**bone up on**) informal study (a subject) intensively, often in preparation for something: *she boned up on languages she had learned long ago and went back to New Guinea.*
3 [with obj.] vulgar slang (of a man) have sexual intercourse with (someone).
–PHRASES **a bag of bones** see BAG. **the bare bones** see BARE. **be skin and bones** see SKIN. **a bone of contention** a subject or issue over which there is continuing disagreement: *the examination system has long been a serious bone of contention.* **close to** (or **near**) **the bone** **1** (of a remark) penetrating and accurate to the point of causing hurt or discomfort. **2** destitute; hard up. **cut** (or **pare**) **something to the bone** reduce something to the bare minimum: *costs will have to be cut to the bone.* (**as**) **dry as a bone** see DRY. **have a bone to pick with someone** informal have reason to disagree or be annoyed with someone. **have not a —— bone in one's body** (of a person) have not the slightest trace of the specified quality: *there's not a conservative bone in his body.* **in one's bones** felt, believed, or known deeply or instinctively: *he has rhythm in his bones | something good was bound to happen; he could feel it in his bones.* **make no bones about something** have no hesitation in stating or dealing with something, however awkward or distasteful it is: *the film is an op-ed piece, and the director makes no bones about its biases.* **to the bone** **1** (of a wound) so deep as to expose a person's bone: *his thigh had been axed open to the bone* | figurative *his contempt cut her to the bone.* ■ (esp. of cold) affecting a person in a penetrating way: *chilled to the bone.* **2** (or **to one's bones**) used to emphasize that a person has a specified quality in an overwhelming or fundamental way: *she's a New Englander to her bones | he's a cop to the bone.* **throw a bone to** give someone only a token concession: *was the true purpose of the minimum wage hike to throw a bone to the unions?* **what's bred in the bone will come out in the flesh** (or **blood**) proverb a person's behavior or characteristics are determined by heredity. **work one's fingers to the bone** work very hard: *Tracy can work her fingers to the bone, but it's Ms. Green who gets the thanks.*
–ORIGIN Old English *bān*, of Germanic origin; related to Dutch *been* and German *Bein.*

bone ash ▶ **n.** the mineral residue of calcined bones, used chiefly in the production of bone china and fertilizers.

bone black ▶ **n.** fine charcoal made by burning animal bones in a closed container, used as a pigment and in the refining of sugar.

bone chi·na ▶ **n.** fine china made of clay mixed with bone ash.

boned /bōnd/ ▶ **adj.** [attrib.] **1** (of meat or fish) having had the bones removed before cooking or serving: *boned turkey with cranberry stuffing.*
2 [in combination] (of a person) having bones of the specified type: *she was fine-boned and boyishly slim.*
3 (of a garment) stiffened with strips of plastic or whalebone to give shape to the figure or the garment.

bone-dry ▶ **adj.** extremely or completely dry.

bone·fish /ˈbōn,fisн/ ▶ **n.** (pl. **same** or **bonefishes**) a silvery game fish of warm coastal waters. Also called LADYFISH. ● Family Albulidae and genus *Albula*: several species, in particular *A. vulpes.*

bone·head /ˈbōn,hed/ ▶ **n.** informal a stupid person.
–DERIVATIVES **bone·head·ed** **adj.**

bone·less /ˈbōnlis/ ▶ **adj.** (of a piece of meat or fish) having had the bones removed. ■ lacking physical or mental strength: *the slack and boneless character of his writing.*
–DERIVATIVES **bone·less·ly** **adv.** *he collapsed bonelessly into an easy chair.*

bone mar·row ▶ **n.** see MARROW (sense 1).

bone·meal /ˈbōn,mēl/ ▶ **n.** crushed or ground bones used as a fertilizer.

bon·er /ˈbōnər/ ▶ **n.** **1** informal a stupid mistake.
2 vulgar slang an erection of the penis.
–ORIGIN early 20th cent. (originally US): from BONE + -ER[1].

bone·set /ˈbōn,set/ ▶ **n.** a North American plant of the daisy family that bears clusters of small flowers and is used in herbal medicine. ● Genus *Eupatorium*, family Compositae, several species, in particular the white-flowered *E. perfoliatum* and its purple-flowered form, **purple boneset.** ■ another term for COMFREY. [its ground-up root was formerly used as a 'plaster' to set broken bones.]

bone·set·ter /ˈbōn,setər/ ▶ **n.** historical a person, typically not formally qualified, who sets broken or dislocated bones.

bone spav·in ▶ **n.** osteoarthritis of the hock in horses, which may cause swelling and lameness.

bone-wea·ry (also **bone-tired**) ▶ **adj.** utterly weary; extremely tired.

bone·yard /ˈbōn,yärd/ ▶ **n.** informal a cemetery.

bon·fire /ˈbän,fīr/ ▶ **n.** a large open-air fire used as part of a celebration, for burning trash, or as a signal.
–ORIGIN late Middle English: from BONE + FIRE. The term originally denoted a large open-air fire on which bones were burned (sometimes as part of a celebration), also one for burning heretics or proscribed literature. Dr. Johnson accepted the mistaken idea that the word came from French *bon* 'good.'

bong[1] /bäng/ ▶ **n.** a low-pitched sound as of a bell: *the clock had struck the hour, and it was only three bongs.*
▶ **v.** [no obj.] emit such a sound.
–ORIGIN 1920s (originally US): imitative.

bong[2] ▶ **n.** a water pipe used for smoking marijuana or other drugs.
–ORIGIN 1970s: from Thai *baung*, literally 'wooden tube.'

bong[3] ▶ **n.** Mountaineering a large piton.
–ORIGIN 1960s: probably imitative of the sound of its being hammered into rock.

bon·go[1] /ˈbäNGgō, ˈbôNG-/ (also **bongo drum**) ▶ **n.** (pl. **bongos**) either of a pair of small, long-bodied drums typically held between the knees and played with the fingers.
–ORIGIN 1920s: from Latin American Spanish *bongó.*

bongo[1]

bon·go[2] ▶ **n.** (pl. **same** or **bongos**) a forest antelope that has a chestnut coat with narrow white vertical stripes, native to central Africa. ● *Tragelaphus euryceros*, family Bovidae.
–ORIGIN mid 19th cent.: from Kikongo.

Bon·hoef·fer /ˈbän,hôfər/, Dietrich (1906–45), German Lutheran theologian and pastor. He was an active opponent of Nazism and was involved in the German resistance movement. Arrested in 1943, he was sent to Buchenwald concentration camp and later executed.

bon·ho·mie /ˈbänə,mē, ,bänəˈmē/ ▶ **n.** cheerful friendliness; geniality: *he exuded good humor and bonhomie.*
–ORIGIN late 18th cent.: from French, from *bonhomme* 'good fellow.'

bon·ho·mous /ˈbänəməs/ ▶ **adj.** full of cheerful friendliness: *her relaxed, bonhomous nature.*
–ORIGIN early 20th cent.: from BONHOMIE + -OUS.

bo·ni·a·to /,bānēˈätō/ ▶ **n.** (pl. **boniatos**) a variety of sweet potato with white flesh.
–ORIGIN American Spanish.

Bon·i·face, St. /ˈbänəfəs/ (680–754), Anglo-Saxon missionary; born *Wynfrith*; known as **the Apostle of Germany.** He was sent to Frisia and Germany to spread the Christian faith and was appointed primate of Germany in 732. He was martyred in Frisia. Feast day, June 5.

bo·ni·to /bəˈnētō/ ▶ **n.** (pl. **bonitos**) a smaller relative of the tunas, with dark oblique stripes on the back and important as a food and game fish. ● *Sarda* and related genera, family Scombridae: several species. ■ (also **ocean bonito**) another term for SKIPJACK (sense 1).
–ORIGIN late 16th cent.: from Spanish.

bonk /bäNGk/ informal ▶ **v.** **1** [with obj.] knock or hit (something) so as to cause a reverberating sound: *he bonked his head on the plane's low bulkhead.*
2 [with obj.] have sexual intercourse with (someone).
3 [no obj.] (of a cyclist or runner) reach a point of exhaustion that makes one unable to go further: *I bonked and couldn't pedal another stroke.*
▶ **n.** **1** an act of knocking or hitting something that causes a reverberating sound: *give it a bonk with a hammer.*
2 an act of sexual intercourse.
3 (**the bonk**) a level of exhaustion that makes a cyclist or runner unable to go further: *we had the bonk when we were saddle sore.*
–ORIGIN 1930s: imitative.

bon·kers /ˈbäNGkərz/ ▶ **adj.** [predic.] informal mad; crazy: *and the fans* **go bonkers** *| he's driving me bonkers.*
–ORIGIN 1940s: of unknown origin.

bon mot /ˈbän ˈmō, ,bôN ˈmō/ ▶ **n.** (pl. **bons mots** pronunc. **same** or /ˈmōz/) a witty remark.
–ORIGIN mid 18th cent.: French, literally 'good word.'

Bonn /bän/ a city in the state of North Rhine–Westphalia in Germany; pop. 314,300 (est. 2006). From 1949 until the reunification of Germany in 1990, it was the capital of the Federal Republic of Germany (West Germany).

Bon·nard /bôˈnär/, Pierre (1867–1947), French painter and graphic artist; member of the Nabi Group.

bonne femme /,bän ˈfam/ ▶ **adj.** [postpositive] (of fish dishes, stews, and soups) cooked in a simple way.
–ORIGIN French, from the phrase *à la bonne femme* 'in the manner of a good housewife.'

bon·net /ˈbänit/ ▶ **n.** **1** a woman's or child's hat tied under the chin, typically with a brim framing the face. ■ (also **war bonnet**) the ceremonial feathered headdress of an American Indian. ■ a soft round brimless hat like a beret, esp. as worn by men and

boys in Scotland. ■ Heraldry the velvet cap within a coronet.
2 a protective cover or cap over a machine or object, in particular: ■ a cowl on a chimney. ■ Brit. the hood of an automobile.
3 Sailing, historical an additional canvas laced to the foot of a sail to catch more wind.
– DERIVATIVES **bon·net·ed adj.** (sense 1).
– ORIGIN late Middle English (denoting a soft brimless hat for men): from Old French *bonet,* from medieval Latin *abonnis* 'headgear.' Sense 1 dates from the late 15th cent.

Bon·ne·ville Dam /'bänə,vil/ hydroelectric dam built in the 1930s on the Columbia River, east of Portland in Oregon.

Bon·ne·ville Salt Flats a desert in northwestern Utah, west of the Great Salt Lake, noted as the site of automotive speed trials.

Bon·ney /'bänē/, William H. (1859–81), US outlaw; born *Henry McCarty*; known as **Billy the Kid**. A notorious robber and murderer, he was captured by Sheriff Pat Garrett in 1880 and was shot by Garrett after he had escaped from jail.

Bon·nie Prince Char·lie /'bänē ,prins 'CHärlē/ see **STUART**[1].

bon·ny /'bänē/ (also **bonnie**) chiefly Scottish & N. English ▶ **adj.** (**bonnier, bonniest**) attractive; beautiful: *a bonny lass.* ■ (of a baby) plump and healthy-looking. ■ sizable; considerable (usually expressing approval): *it's worth a thousand pounds, a bonny sum.*
▶ **n.** (**my bonny**) literary used as a form of address for one's beloved or baby.
– DERIVATIVES **bon·ni·ly** /'bänəlē/ **adv.**, **bon·ni·ness n.**
– ORIGIN late 15th cent.: perhaps related to Old French *bon* 'good.'

bon·ny clab·ber ▶ **n.** another term for **CLABBER**.
– ORIGIN early 17th cent.: from Irish *bainne clabair,* denoting thick milk for churning.

bo·no·bo /bə'nōbō/ ▶ **n.** (pl. **bonobos**) a chimpanzee with a black face and black hair, found in the rain forests of the Democratic Republic of the Congo (formerly Zaire). Also called **PYGMY CHIMPANZEE**. ● *Pan paniscus,* family Pongidae.
– ORIGIN 1950s: a local word.

bon·sai /bän'sī, 'bänsī/ ▶ **n.** (pl. **same**) (also **bonsai tree**) an ornamental tree or shrub grown in a pot and artificially prevented from reaching its normal size. ■ the art of growing trees or shrubs in such a way.
– ORIGIN 1950s: from Japanese, from *bon* 'tray' + *sai* 'planting.'

bons mots /'mō/ plural form of **BON MOT**.

bon·spiel /'bän,spēl/ ▶ **n.** chiefly Scottish & Canadian a curling tournament.
– ORIGIN mid 16th cent.: probably of Low German origin.

bon·te·bok /'bäntē,bäk/ ▶ **n.** (pl. **same** or **bonteboks**) an antelope with a mainly reddish-brown coat and white face, found in eastern South Africa. It belongs to the same species as the blesbok. ● *Damaliscus dorcas dorcas,* family Bovidae.
– ORIGIN late 18th cent.: from Afrikaans, from Dutch *bont* 'pied' + *bok* 'buck.'

bon ton /bän 'tän, bôN 'tôN/ ▶ **n.** the fashionable world.
– ORIGIN French, literally 'good taste.'

bo·nus /'bōnəs/ ▶ **n.** an amount of money added to wages on a seasonal basis, esp. as a reward for good performance: *big Christmas bonuses.* ■ something welcome and often unexpected that accompanies and enhances something that is itself good: *good weather is* ***an added bonus*** *but the real appeal is the landscape.* ■ Basketball an extra free throw awarded to a fouled player when the opposing team has exceeded the number of team fouls allowed during a period. ■ Brit. an extra dividend or issue paid to the shareholders of a company. ■ Brit. a distribution of profits to holders of an insurance policy.
– ORIGIN late 18th cent. (probably originally London stock-exchange slang): from Latin *bonus* (masculine) 'good,' used in place of *bonum* (neuter) 'good, good thing.' Compare with **BOON**[2].

bon vi·vant /'bän vē'vänt, ,bôN vē'väN/ ▶ **n.** (pl. **bon vivants** or **bons vivants** pronunc. **same** or /-'vänts/) a person who enjoys a sociable and luxurious lifestyle.
– ORIGIN late 17th cent.: from French, literally 'person living well,' from *bon* 'good' and *vivre* 'to live.'

bon vi·veur /'bän vē'vər, ,bôN vē'vœr/ ▶ **n.** (pl. **bon viveurs** or **bons viveurs** pronunc. **same** or /-'vərz/) another term for **BON VIVANT**.
– ORIGIN mid 19th cent.: pseudo-French, from French *bon* 'good' and *viveur* 'a living person,' on the pattern of *bon vivant.*

bon vo·yage /'bän voi'äZH, 'bôn, bôN/ ▶ **exclam.** used to express good wishes to someone about to go on a journey: *good luck and bon voyage!* | *they had come to wish her bon voyage.*
– ORIGIN late 17th cent.: French, literally 'good journey.'

bon·y /'bōnē/ ▶ **adj.** (**bonier, boniest**) of or like bone: *the bony plates that protect turtles and tortoises.* ■ (of a person or part of the body) so thin that the bones are prominent: *he held up his bony fingers.* ■ (of a fish eaten as food) having many bones.
– DERIVATIVES **bon·i·ness n.**

bon·y fish ▶ **n.** a fish of a large class distinguished by a skeleton of bone, and comprising the majority of modern fishes. Compare with **CARTILAGINOUS FISH**. ● Class Osteichthyes: two or three subclasses.

bon·y lab·y·rinth ▶ **n.** see **LABYRINTH**.

bonze /bänz/ ▶ **n.** a Japanese or Chinese Buddhist monk.
– ORIGIN late 16th cent.: probably from Japanese *bonzō, bonsō* 'priest.'

bon·zer /'bänzər/ ▶ **adj.** Austral./NZ informal excellent, first-rate.
– ORIGIN early 20th cent.: perhaps an alteration of **BONANZA**.

boo[1] /bo͞o/ ▶ **exclam. 1** said suddenly to surprise someone: *"Boo!" she cried, jumping up to frighten him.* [probably an alteration of earlier *bo,* used in the same way since late Middle English.]
2 said to show disapproval or contempt, esp. at a performance or athletic contest.
▶ **n.** an utterance of "boo" to show disapproval or contempt: *the audience greeted this comment with boos and hisses.*
▶ **v.** (**boos, booing, booed**) say "boo" to show disapproval or contempt: [no obj.] *they booed and hissed when he stepped on stage* | [with obj.] *I was practically* ***booed off the stage*** *for talking about cyberpunk.*
– PHRASES **say boo** [with negative] say anything at all; utter a sound: *Walter looked at us, but he didn't say boo.* **wouldn't say boo to a goose** Brit. used to emphasize that someone is very shy or reticent.
– ORIGIN early 19th cent. (sense 2 of the exclamation): imitative of the lowing of oxen. The sound was considered to be derisive; compare with **HISS** and **HOOT**.

boo[2] ▶ **n.** informal a person's boyfriend or girlfriend.
– ORIGIN 1980s: origin uncertain; probably an alteration of French *beau* 'boyfriend, male admirer.'

boob[1] /bo͝ob/ informal ▶ **n. 1** a foolish or stupid person: *why was that boob given a key investigation?*
2 Brit. an embarrassing mistake.
– ORIGIN early 20th cent.: abbreviation of **BOOBY**[1].

boob[2] ▶ **n.** (usu. **boobs**) informal a woman's breast.
– ORIGIN 1950s (originally US): abbreviation of **BOOBY**[2], from dialect *bubby,* of uncertain origin; perhaps related to German dialect *Bübbi* 'teat.'

boob·oi·sie /,bo͞obwä'zē/ ▶ **n.** informal stupid people as a class.
– ORIGIN 1920s: from **BOOB**[1], humorous formation on the pattern of *bourgeoisie.*

boo-boo ▶ **n.** (pl. **boo-boos**) informal a mistake: *you could make a big boo-boo if you leap to any drastic conclusions.* ■ a minor injury, such as a scratch: *there is no one to kiss the boo-boo!*
– ORIGIN 1950s (originally US): reduplication of **BOOB**[1].

boob tube informal ▶ **n.** (usu. **the boob tube**) television or a television set: *librarians are scrambling for ways to compete with the boob tube.*

boo·by[1] /'bo͞obē/ ▶ **n.** (pl. **boobies**) **1** a stupid or childish person.
2 a large tropical seabird of the gannet family, with brown, black, or white plumage and often brightly colored feet. ● Genus *Sula,* family Sulidae: several species, including the common **red-footed booby** (*S. sula*).
– ORIGIN early 17th cent.: probably from Spanish *bobo* (in both senses), from Latin *balbus* 'stammering.'

boo·by[2] ▶ **n.** (pl. **boobies**) (usu. **boobies**) informal a woman's breast.
– ORIGIN 1930s: alteration of dialect *bubby* (see **BOOB**[2]).

boo·by hatch ▶ **n.** informal, offensive a psychiatric hospital.

boo·by prize ▶ **n.** a prize given as a joke to the last-place finisher in a race or competition.

boo·by trap ▶ **n.** a thing designed to catch the unwary, in particular: ■ an apparently harmless object containing a concealed explosive device designed to kill or injure anyone who touches it: *miles of mines, booby traps, and underground fortifications.* ■ a trap intended as a practical joke, such as an object placed on top of a door ajar ready to fall on the next person to pass through.
▶ **v.** (**booby-trap**) [with obj.] place a booby trap in or on (an object or area): (as adj. **booby-trapped**) *the area was heavily mined and booby-trapped.*

boo·dle /'bo͞odl/ ▶ **n. 1** informal money, esp. that gained or spent illegally or improperly: *he spent $30 million of his own boodle trying to buy a Senate seat.*
2 (**boodles**) a great quantity, esp. of money: *Scandinavian Air has boodles of seats for America* | *the men expected to make boodles.*
– ORIGIN early 17th cent. (denoting a pack or crowd): from Dutch *boedel, boel* 'possessions, disorderly mass.' Compare with **CABOODLE**.

boo·ga·loo /'bo͞ogə,lo͞o/ ▶ **n.** (pl. **boogaloos**) a modern dance to rock-and-roll music performed with swiveling and shuffling movements of the body, originally popular in the 1960s.
▶ **v.** (**boogaloos, boogalooing, boogalooed**) [no obj.] perform this dance.
– ORIGIN 1960s: perhaps an alteration of **BOOGIE-WOOGIE** (see **BOOGIE**).

boog·er /'bo͝ogər/ ▶ **n. 1** another term for **BOGEYMAN**.
2 informal a piece of dried nasal mucus.

boog·ey·man ▶ **n.** variant spelling of **BOGEYMAN**.

boog·ie /'bo͝ogē/ ▶ **n.** (also **boogie-woogie** /'wo͝ogē/) (pl. **boogies**) a style of blues played on the piano with a strong, fast beat. ■ informal a dance to fast pop or rock music.
▶ **v.** (**boogies, boogieing, boogied**) [no obj.] informal dance to fast pop or rock music: *ready to boogie down to the music of the house band* | *he can boogie the night away.* ■ move or leave somewhere fast: *I think we'd better boogie on out of here.*
– ORIGIN early 20th cent. (originally US in the sense 'party'): of unknown origin.

boog·ie board ▶ **n.** a short light type of surfboard ridden in a prone position.
– DERIVATIVES **boog·ie board·er n.**

boo·hoo /'bo͞o'ho͞o/ ▶ **exclam.** used to represent the sound of someone crying noisily.
▶ **v.** (**boohoos, boohooing, boohooed**) [no obj.] cry noisily: *she broke down and boohooed.*
– ORIGIN mid 19th cent.: imitative.

boo·jum /'bo͞ojəm/ ▶ **n.** an imaginary dangerous animal.
– ORIGIN late 19th cent.: nonsense word coined by Lewis Carroll.

book /bo͝ok/ ▶ **n. 1** a written or printed work consisting of pages glued or sewn together along one side and bound in covers: *a book of selected poems* | *a book on cats* | [as modifier] *a book report.* ■ a literary composition that is published or intended for publication as such a work: *the book is set in the 1940s* | *I'm writing a book.* ■ (**the books**) used to refer to studying: *he is so deep in his books he would forget to eat.* ■ a main division of a classic literary work, an epic, or the Bible: *the Book of Genesis.* ■ the libretto of an opera or musical, or the script of a play. ■ (**the book**) the local telephone directory: *is your name in the book?* ■ (**the Book**) the Bible. ■ informal a magazine. ■ an imaginary record or list (often used to emphasize the thoroughness or comprehensiveness of someone's actions or experiences): *she felt every emotion in the book of love.*
2 [with modifier] a bound set of blank sheets for writing or keeping records in: *an accounts book.* ■ (**books**) a set of records or accounts: *he can do more than* ***balance the books.*** ■ a bookmaker's record of bets accepted and money paid out.
3 a set of tickets, stamps, matches, checks, samples of cloth, etc., bound together: *a pattern book* | *a book of matches.* ■ (**the book**) the first six tricks taken by the declarer in a hand of bridge.
▶ **v.** [with obj.] **1** reserve (accommodations, a place, etc.); buy (a ticket) in advance: *I have booked a table at the Swan* | [no obj.] *book early to avoid disappointment.* ■ reserve accommodations for (someone): *his secretary had booked him into the Howard Hotel* | [with two objs.] *book me a single room at my usual hotel.* ■ engage (a performer or guest) for an occasion or event. ■ (**be booked** (**up**)) have all appointments or places reserved; be full: *I'm booked till, like, 2014.*
2 make an official record of the name and other personal details of (a criminal suspect or offender): *the cop booked me and took me down to the station.*
– PHRASES **bring someone to book** bring someone to justice; punish. **by the book** strictly according to the rules: *a cop who doesn't exactly* ***play it by the book.*** **close the book on** lay aside; expend no further energy on: *Congress closed the book on wool subsidies.* **in someone's bad** (or **good**) **books** chiefly Brit. in disfavor (or favor) with a person. **in my book** in my opinion: *that counts as a lie in my book.* **make book** take bets on the outcome of an event: figurative *I wouldn't make book on it.* **one for the books** an extraordinary feat or event. **on**

the books contained in a book of laws or records: *discriminatory laws still on the books | the longest pitching career on the books*. **People of the Book** Jews and Christians as regarded by Muslims. **suit one's book** Brit. be convenient to one: *it didn't suit her book at all to be moved*. **take a leaf from** (or **out of**) **someone's book** imitate or emulate someone in a particular way: *Gorbachev must take a leaf from Deng's book and offer tangible benefits*. **throw the book at** informal charge or punish (someone) as severely as possible. **wrote the book** be the leader in the field: *John wrote the book on extreme biking*. **you can't judge a book by its cover** proverb outward appearances are not a reliable indication of true character.
– DERIVATIVES **book·a·ble** adj.
– ORIGIN Old English *bōc* (originally also 'a document or charter'), *bōcian* 'to grant by charter,' of Germanic origin; related to Dutch *boek* and German *Buch*, and probably to **BEECH** (on which runes were carved).

book·bind·er /ˈbo͝okˌbīndər/ ▶ n. a person who binds books as a profession.
– DERIVATIVES **book·bind·ing** /-ˌbīndiNG/ n.

book·case /ˈbo͝okˌkās/ ▶ n. a set of shelves for books set in a surrounding frame or cabinet.

book club ▶ n. an organization that sells selected books to members or subscribers, often from a mail-order catalog.

book·end /ˈbo͝okˌend/ ▶ n. a support for the end of a row of books to keep them upright, often one of a pair.
▶ v. [with obj.] (usu. **be bookended**) informal occur or be positioned at the end or on either side of (something): *the narrative is bookended by a pair of incisive essays*.

book·er /ˈbo͝okər/ ▶ n. short for **BOOKING AGENT**.

Book·er Prize /ˈbo͝okər/ a literary prize awarded annually for a novel published by a British, Irish, or Commonwealth citizen during the previous year, formerly financed by the multinational company Booker McConnell and since 2002 by the investment management firm Man Group plc. Full name **Man Booker Prize**.

book group ▶ n. a group of people who meet regularly to discuss books that all the members have read.

book hand ▶ n. a formal style of handwriting as used by professional copiers of books before the invention of printing.

book·ie /ˈbo͝okē/ ▶ n. (pl. **bookies**) informal term for **BOOKMAKER**.

book·ing /ˈbo͝okiNG/ ▶ n. an act of reserving accommodations, travel, etc., or of buying a ticket in advance: *the hotel does not handle group bookings | early booking is essential*. ■ an engagement for a performance by an entertainer: *TV show bookings were mysteriously canceled*.

book·ing a·gent ▶ n. a person who makes engagements or reservations for others, in particular: ■ a person who arranges concert or club engagements for performers. ■ a person who makes travel arrangements for clients.

book·ing clerk ▶ n. Brit. an official selling tickets, esp. at a railroad station.

book·ing hall (also **booking office**) ▶ n. Brit. a room or area at a railroad station in which tickets are sold.

book·ish /ˈbo͝okiSH/ ▶ adj. (of a person or way of life) devoted to reading and studying rather than worldly interests: *by comparison I was very bookish, intellectual, and wordy in a wrong way*. ■ (of language or writing) literary in style or allusion: *long bookish scholarship | a bookish but eloquent erotic memoir*.
– DERIVATIVES **book·ish·ly** adv., **book·ish·ness** n.

book·keep·ing /ˈbo͝okˌkēpiNG/ ▶ n. the activity or occupation of keeping records of the financial affairs of a business.
– DERIVATIVES **book·keep·er** /-ˌkēpər/ n.

book learn·ing ▶ n. knowledge gained from books or study; mere theory: *knowledge based on experience rather than book learning*.

book·let /ˈbo͝oklit/ ▶ n. a small book consisting of a few sheets, typically with paper covers.

book·louse /ˈbo͝okˌlous/ ▶ n. (pl. **booklice**) a minute insect that typically has reduced or absent wings and often lives in books or papers, where it feeds on mold. ● Liposcelidae and related families in the order Psocoptera: many species.

book lung ▶ n. Zoology (in a spider or other arachnid) each of a pair of respiratory organs composed of many fine leaves. They are situated in the abdomen and have openings on the underside.

book·mak·er /ˈbo͝okˌmākər/ ▶ n. a person who takes bets (esp. on horse races), calculates odds, and pays out winnings.
– DERIVATIVES **book·mak·ing** /-ˌmākiNG/ n.

book·man /ˈbo͝okmən/ ▶ n. (pl. **bookmen**) a literary person, esp. one involved in the business of books.

book·mark /ˈbo͝okˌmärk/ ▶ n. a strip of leather, cardboard, or other material used to mark one's place in a book. ■ a record of the address of a website, file, or other data made to enable quick access in future.
▶ v. [with obj.] record the address of (a website, file, etc.) to enable quick access in future: *if you think politics is the ultimate game, be sure to bookmark eVote*.

book·mo·bile /ˈbo͝okməˌbēl/ ▶ n. a truck, van, or trailer serving as a mobile library.
– ORIGIN 1930s: from **BOOK**, on the pattern of *automobile*.

Book of Chang·es ▶ n. another name for **I CHING**.

Book of Com·mon Prayer ▶ n. the official service book of the Church of England and, with some variation, of other churches of the Anglican Communion. It was compiled by Thomas Cranmer and others and first issued in 1549.

book of hours ▶ n. (in the Christian Church) a book containing the prayers or offices to be said at the canonical hours of the day, particularly popular in the Middle Ages.

book page ▶ n. **1** a page of a book.
2 a page of a newspaper or magazine devoted to book reviews.

book·plate /ˈbo͝okˌplāt/ ▶ n. a decorative label stuck in the front of a book, bearing the name of the book's owner.

book·rack /ˈbo͝okˌrak/ ▶ n. a rack or shelf for books. ■ a stand or rack for holding an open book. Also called **BOOKSTAND**.

book·sell·er /ˈbo͝okˌselər/ ▶ n. a person who sells books, esp. as the owner or manager of a bookstore.
– DERIVATIVES **book·sell·ing** n.

book·shelf /ˈbo͝okˌSHelf/ ▶ n. (pl. **bookshelves**) a shelf on which books can be stored.

book·stall /ˈbo͝okˌstôl/ ▶ n. a stand where books are sold, typically secondhand. ■ chiefly Brit. a newsstand.

book·stand /ˈbo͝okˌstand/ ▶ n. **1** another term for **BOOKSTALL**.
2 another term for **BOOKRACK**.

book·store /ˈbo͝okˌstôr/ (also chiefly Brit. **bookshop** /-ˌSHäp/) ▶ n. a store where books are sold.

book val·ue ▶ n. the value of a security or asset as entered in a company's books. Often contrasted with **MARKET VALUE**.

book·work /ˈbo͝okˌwərk/ ▶ n. **1** the activity of keeping records of accounts: *the bookwork has a tendency to pile up if I don't keep on top of it*.
2 the studying of textbooks, as opposed to practical work: *he concentrates mainly on the flying, but the heavy bookwork is in there too*.

book·worm /ˈbo͝okˌwərm/ ▶ n. **1** informal a person devoted to reading.
2 the larva of a wood-boring beetle that feeds on the paper and glue in books.

Boole /bo͞ol/, George (1815–64), English mathematician; responsible for Boolean algebra. The study of mathematical or symbolic logic developed mainly from his ideas.

Bool·e·an /ˈbo͞olēən/ ▶ adj. denoting a system of algebraic notation used to represent logical propositions, esp. in computing and electronics.
▶ n. Computing a binary variable, having two possible values called "true" and "false."
– ORIGIN mid 19th cent.: from the name of G. **BOOLE** + **-AN**.

boom[1] /bo͞om/ ▶ n. a loud, deep, resonant sound: *the deep boom of the bass drum*. ■ the characteristic resonant call of the bittern.
▶ v. [no obj.] make a loud, deep, resonant sound: *thunder boomed in the sky | her voice **boomed out***. ■ [with direct speech] say in a loud, deep, resonant voice: *the imperative "Silence!" boomed out by Ray himself*. ■ (of a bittern) utter its characteristic resonant call.
– DERIVATIVES **boom·y** adj.
– ORIGIN late Middle English (as a verb): ultimately imitative; perhaps from Dutch *bommen* 'to hum, buzz.'

boom[2] ▶ n. a period of great prosperity or rapid economic growth: *a boom in precious metal mining |* [as modifier] *a boom economy*.
▶ v. [no obj.] enjoy a period of great prosperity or rapid economic growth: *business is booming | the popularity of soy-based foods has boomed in the last two decades*.
– DERIVATIVES **boom·let** /ˈbo͞omlit/ n., **boom·y** adj.
– ORIGIN late 19th cent. (originally US): probably from **BOOM**[1].

boom[3] ▶ n. a long pole or rod, in particular: ■ a spar pivoting on the after side of the mast and to which the foot of a vessel's sail is attached, allowing the angle of the sail to be changed. ■ [often as modifier] a movable arm over a television or movie set, carrying a microphone or camera: *a boom mike*. ■ a long beam extending upward at an angle from the mast of a derrick, for guiding or supporting objects being moved or suspended. ■ a floating beam used to contain oil spills or to form a barrier across the mouth of a harbor or river. ■ a retractable tube for inflight transfer of fuel from a tanker airplane to another airplane.
– ORIGIN mid 16th cent. (in the general sense 'beam, pole'): from Dutch, 'beam, tree, pole'; related to **BEAM**.

boom box ▶ n. informal a portable sound system, typically including radio and cassette or CD player, capable of powerful sound: *teenagers dance to boom boxes on warm April nights*.

boom·er /ˈbo͞omər/ ▶ n. informal **1** short for **BABY BOOMER** (see **BABY BOOM**).
2 something large or notable of its kind, in particular: ■ Austral. a large male kangaroo. ■ a large wave.
3 informal a nuclear submarine with ballistic missiles.
4 a transient construction worker, esp. a bridge builder.
5 another name for **MOUNTAIN BEAVER**.
– ORIGIN early 19th cent.: probably from the verb **BOOM**[1] + **-ER**[1].

boo·mer·ang /ˈbo͞oməˌraNG/ ▶ n. a curved flat piece of wood that can be thrown so as to return to the thrower, traditionally used by Australian Aborigines as a hunting weapon.
▶ v. [no obj.] (of a plan or action) return to the originator, often with negative consequences: *misleading consumers about quality will eventually boomerang on a carmaker*.
– ORIGIN early 19th cent.: from Dharuk.

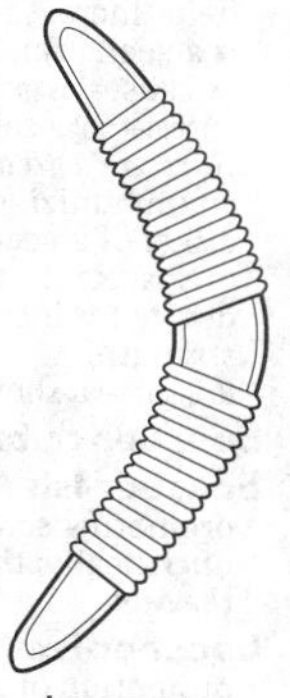
boomerang

Boom·er State a nickname for the state of **OKLAHOMA**.

boom·ing /ˈbo͞omiNG/ ▶ adj. **1** having a period of great prosperity or rapid economic growth: *the booming economy*.
2 (of a sound or voice) loud, deep, and resonant: *his booming voice | a booming laugh*.

boom·slang /ˈbo͞omˌslaNG/ ▶ n. a large, highly venomous southern African tree snake, the male of which is bright green and the female dull olive brown. ● *Dispholidus typus*, family Colubridae.
– ORIGIN late 18th cent.: from Afrikaans, from Dutch *boom* 'tree' + *slang* 'snake.'

boom town (also **boomtown**) ▶ n. a town undergoing rapid growth due to sudden prosperity: *the automobile was in its heady adolescence, and Detroit was America's newest boom town*.

boon[1] /bo͞on/ ▶ n. **1** [usu. in sing.] a thing that is helpful or beneficial: *the navigation system will be a **boon to** both civilian and military users*.
2 archaic a favor or request: *may I have the inestimable boon of a few minutes' conversation?*
– ORIGIN Middle English (originally in the sense 'request for a favor'): from Old Norse *bón*.

boon[2] ▶ adj. (of a companion or friend) close; intimate; favorite: *he debated the question with a few **boon companions** in the barroom*.
– ORIGIN mid 16th cent.: *boon* from Old French *bon*, from Latin *bonus* 'good.' The early literal sense was 'good fellow,' originally denoting a drinking companion.

boon·docks /ˈbo͞onˌdäks/ ▶ plural n. informal rough, remote, or isolated country: *we're out here in the boondocks, miles from a telephone*.
– ORIGIN 1940s: *boondock* from Tagalog *bundok* 'mountain.'

boon·dog·gle /ˈbo͞onˌdägəl, -ˌdôgəl/ informal ▶ n. work or activity that is wasteful or pointless but gives the appearance of having value: *writing off the cold fusion phenomenon as a boondoggle best buried in literature*. ■ a public project of questionable merit that typically involves political patronage and graft: *they each drew $600,000 in the final months of the great boondoggle*.
▶ v. [no obj.] waste money or time on such projects.
– ORIGIN 1930s: of unknown origin.

Boone /bo͞on/, Daniel (*c*.1734–1820), American pioneer. He made trips west from North Carolina into the unexplored area that is now Kentucky, organizing settlements and successfully defending them against hostile Indians. He later moved further west to what is now Missouri, having been granted land there in 1799.

boon·ies /ˈbo͞onēz/ ▶ **plural n.** short for BOONDOCKS.

boor /bo͝or/ ▶ **n.** an unrefined, ill-mannered person: *at last the big obnoxious boor had been dealt a stunning blow for his uncouth and belligerent manner.*
– ORIGIN mid 16th cent. (in the sense 'peasant'): from Low German *būr* or Dutch *boer* 'farmer.' Compare with **BOER**.

boor·ish /ˈbo͝orisH/ ▶ **adj.** rough and bad-mannered; coarse: *boorish behavior.*
– DERIVATIVES **boor·ish·ly adv.**, **boor·ish·ness n.**

boost /bo͞ost/ ▶ **v.** [with obj.] help or encourage (something) to increase or improve: *a range of measures to boost tourism.* ■ push from below; assist: *people they were trying to boost over a wall.* ■ amplify (an electrical signal). ■ informal steal, esp. by shoplifting or pickpocketing.
▶ **n.** a source of help or encouragement leading to increase or improvement: *the cut in interest rates will give a further boost to the economy.* ■ an increase or improvement: *a boost in exports.* ■ a push from below.
– ORIGIN early 19th cent. (originally in the sense 'push from below'): of unknown origin.

boost·er /ˈbo͞ostər/ ▶ **n. 1** a person or thing that helps increase or promote something, in particular: ■ a keen promoter of a person, organization, or cause: [as modifier] *athletic booster clubs.* ■ [in combination] a source of help or encouragement: *job fairs are a great morale booster.* ■ Medicine a dose of an immunizing agent increasing or renewing the effect of an earlier one. ■ the first stage of a rocket or spacecraft, used to give initial acceleration. ■ a device for increasing electrical voltage or signal strength.
2 informal a shoplifter.

boost·er ca·ble ▶ **n.** another term for JUMPER CABLE.

boost·er·ish /ˈbo͞ostərisH/ ▶ **adj.** supporting or promoting something enthusiastically, and often uncritically: *the city's boosterish slogan "La Porte's on the Move."*

boost·er·ism /ˈbo͞ostəˌrizəm/ ▶ **n.** the enthusiastic promotion of a person, organization, or cause: *a barrage of boosterism about the wonderful recreation facilities.*

boost·er seat ▶ **n.** an extra seat or cushion placed on an existing seat for a small child to sit on.

boot[1] /bo͞ot/ ▶ **n. 1** a sturdy item of footwear covering the foot, the ankle, and sometimes the leg below the knee: *walking boots.* ■ a covering or sheath to protect a mechanical connection, as on a gearshift. ■ (also **Denver boot**) a clamp placed by the police on the wheel of an illegally parked vehicle to make it immobile. ■ a covering to protect the lower part of a horse's leg. ■ historical an instrument of torture encasing and crushing the foot.
2 informal a hard kick: *I got a boot in the stomach.*
3 Brit. the trunk of a car.
4 (also **boot up**) [usu. as modifier] the process of starting a computer and putting it into a state of readiness for operation: *a boot disk.*
5 Military informal a navy or marine recruit.
▶ **v.** [with obj.] **1** (usu. as adj. **booted**) place boots on (oneself, another person, or an animal): *thin, booted legs.*
2 kick (something) hard in a specified direction: *he ended up booting the ball into the stands.* ■ (**boot someone off**) force someone to leave a vehicle unceremoniously: *the driver booted two teenagers off the bus.* ■ (**boot someone out**) informal force someone to leave a place, institution, or job unceremoniously: *she had been booted out of school.*
3 start (a computer) and put it into a state of readiness for operation: *the menu will be ready as soon as you boot up your computer* | [no obj.] *the system won't boot from the original drive.* [from BOOTSTRAP.]
4 place a Denver boot on (an illegally parked car).
– PHRASES **die with one's boots on** die in battle or while otherwise actively occupied. **get the boot** informal be dismissed from one's job. **give someone the boot** informal dismiss someone from their job. **one's heart sank** (or **fell**) **into one's boots** used to refer to a sudden onset of depression or dismay: *the way your heart drops to your boots if your foal has terribly crooked legs.* **you** (**can**) **bet your boots** informal used to express certainty about a situation or statement: *you can bet your boots that patrol has raised the alarm.*
– ORIGIN Middle English: from Old Norse *bóti* or its source, Old French *bote*, of unknown ultimate origin.

boot[2] ▶ **n.** (in phrase **to boot**) as well; in addition: *images that are precise, revealing, and often beautiful to boot.*
– ORIGIN originally 'something extra thrown into a bargain,' from Old English *bōt* 'advantage, remedy,' of Germanic origin; related to Dutch *boete* and German *Busse* 'penance, fine,' also to BETTER[1] and BEST.

boot·a·ble /ˈbo͞otəbəl/ ▶ **adj.** (of a disk) containing the software required to boot a computer.

boot·black /ˈbo͞otˌblak/ ▶ **n.** chiefly historical a person employed to polish boots and shoes.

boot camp ▶ **n.** a military training camp for new recruits, with strict discipline. ■ a prison for youthful offenders, run on military lines.

boot-cut (also **bootcut**) ▶ **adj.** (of jeans or other trousers) flared very slightly below the knee, so as to be worn comfortably over boots.

boot·ee /ˈbo͞otē, bo͞oˈtē/ ▶ **n.** (pl. **bootees**) variant spelling of BOOTIE.

Bo·ö·tes /bōˈōtēz/ Astronomy a northern constellation (the Herdsman), said to represent a man holding the leash of two dogs (Canes Venatici) while driving a bear (Ursa Major). It contains the bright star Arcturus. ■ (as genitive **Boötis** /bōˈōtis/) used with a preceding letter or numeral to designate stars: *the star Gamma Boötis.*
– ORIGIN Greek.

Booth[1] /bo͞oTH/, John Wilkes (1838–65), US actor. He is better known as the assassin of President Abraham Lincoln at Ford's Theater in Washington, DC.

Booth[2], William (1829–1912), English religious leader; founder and first general of the Salvation Army.

booth /bo͞oTH/ ▶ **n. 1** a small temporary tent or structure at a market, fair, or exhibition, used for selling goods, providing information, or staging shows. ■ a small room where a vendor sits separated from customers by a window: *a ticket booth.*
2 an enclosure or compartment for various purposes, such as telephoning, broadcasting, or voting: *the phone booth alongside the highway* | *ex-athletes in the broadcast booth.*
3 a set of a table and benches in a restaurant or bar: *I sat in a booth with coffee and a roll.*
– ORIGIN Middle English (in the general sense 'temporary dwelling or shelter'): from Old Norse *buth*, based on *búa* 'dwell.'

Boo·thi·a, Gulf of /ˈbo͞oTHēə/ a gulf in the Canadian Arctic Ocean, in Northwest Territories, between Boothia Peninsula and Baffin Island.
– ORIGIN named in honor of Sir Felix *Booth* (1775–1850), patron of the expedition to the Arctic (1829–33) led by Sir John Ross.

Boo·thi·a Pen·in·su·la a peninsula in northern Canada, in the Northwest Territories, located between Victoria and Baffin islands.

boot·ie /ˈbo͞otē/ (also **bootee**) ▶ **n.** (pl. **booties**) **1** a soft shoe, typically knitted, worn by a baby. ■ any soft, socklike shoe.
2 a protective shoe or lining for a shoe.
3 a woman's short boot.

boot·jack /ˈbo͞otˌjak/ ▶ **n.** a device for holding a boot by the heel to ease withdrawal of one's foot.

boot·lace /ˈbo͞otˌlās/ ▶ **n.** a cord or leather strip for lacing boots.

boot·leg /ˈbo͞otˌleg/ ▶ **adj.** [attrib.] (esp. of liquor, computer software, or recordings) made, distributed, or sold illegally: *bootleg cassettes* | *bootleg whiskey.*
▶ **v.** (**bootlegs, bootlegging, bootlegged**) [with obj.] make, distribute, or sell (illicit goods, esp. liquor, computer software, or recordings) illegally: (as noun **bootlegging**) *domestic bootlegging was almost impossible to control* | (as adj. **bootlegged**) *bootlegged videos.*
▶ **n. 1** an illegal musical recording, esp. one made at a concert.
2 Football a play in which the quarterback fakes a handoff and runs with the ball hidden next to his hip: *he scored on a 29-yard bootleg on fourth down.*
– DERIVATIVES **boot·leg·ger n.**
– ORIGIN late 19th cent.: from the smugglers' practice of concealing bottles in their boots.

boot·less /ˈbo͞otlis/ ▶ **adj.** archaic (of a task or undertaking) ineffectual; useless: *words at this pass were vain and bootless.*
– ORIGIN Old English *bōtlēas* 'not able to be compensated for by payment' (see BOOT[2], -LESS).

boot·lick·er /ˈbo͞otˌlikər/ ▶ **n.** informal an obsequious or overly deferential person; a toady: *bootlickers telling him what a big star he's going to be.*
– DERIVATIVES **boot·lick·ing** /-ˌlikiNG/ **n.**

boots /bo͞ots/ ▶ **n.** Brit. dated a hotel employee who cleans boots and shoes, carries luggage, and performs other menial tasks.
– ORIGIN late 18th cent.: plural of BOOT[1], used as a singular.

boot-scoot·ing ▶ **n.** another term for LINE DANCING.

boot·strap /ˈbo͞otˌstrap/ ▶ **n. 1** a loop at the back of a boot, used to pull it on.
2 Computing a technique of loading a program into a computer by means of a few initial instructions that enable the introduction of the rest of the program from an input device.
3 [usu. as modifier] the technique of starting with existing resources to create something more complex and effective: *we see the creative act as a bootstrap process.*
▶ **v.** (**bootstraps, bootstrapping, bootstrapped**) [with obj.] **1** get (oneself or something) into or out of a situation using existing resources: *the company is bootstrapping itself out of a marred financial past.* ■ start up (an enterprise), esp. one based on the Internet, with minimal resources: *they are bootstrapping their stations themselves, not with lots of dot-com venture capital.*
2 Computing fuller form of BOOT[1] (sense 3 of the verb).
▶ **adj.** (of a person or project) using one's own resources rather than external help: *a bootstrap capitalist's trip up the entrepreneurial ladder.*
– PHRASES **pull oneself up by one's** (**own**) **bootstraps** improve one's position by one's own efforts.

boot top ▶ **n.** the part of a ship's hull just above the waterline, typically marked by a line of contrasting color.

boot-up ▶ **n.** see BOOT[1] (sense 4 of the noun).

boo·ty[1] /ˈbo͞otē/ ▶ **n.** valuable stolen goods, esp. those seized in war: *the militias supply themselves with booty from the raided civilian populations.* ■ informal something gained or won: *now the booty: four winners will receive prizes.*
– ORIGIN late Middle English (denoting plunder acquired in common and destined to be divided among the plunderers): from Middle Low German *būte, buite* 'exchange, distribution,' of uncertain ultimate origin.

boo·ty[2] ▶ **n.** (pl. **booties**) informal a person's buttocks.
– PHRASES **shake one's booty** dance energetically.
– ORIGIN 1920s: probably an alteration of the British word *botty*, a child's term for a person's buttocks.

boo·ty call ▶ **n.** informal a sexual invitation or rendezvous.
– ORIGIN 1990s: from BOOTY[2] and *call.*

boo·ty·li·cious /ˌbo͞otiˈlisHəs/ ▶ **adj.** informal (of a woman) sexually attractive.
– ORIGIN 1990s: from BOOTY[2], on the pattern of *delicious.*

boo word ▶ **n.** informal a word or expression denoting something that is regarded with disapproval or dislike: *positivism has become something of a boo word among many social scientists.*

booze /bo͞oz/ informal ▶ **n.** alcohol, esp. hard liquor: *they turn to booze to beat work pressure.*
▶ **v.** [no obj.] drink alcohol, esp. in large quantities: *you used to booze a lot on expensive hard liquor* | (as noun **boozing**) *Michael is trying to quit boozing.*
– ORIGIN Middle English *bouse*, from Middle Dutch *būsen* 'drink to excess.' The spelling *booze* dates from the 18th cent.

booze cruise ▶ **n.** a cruise with freely available alcohol. ■ Brit. an excursion to Europe by ferry, the aim of which is to bring back cheap or tax-free alcohol.

booze·hound /ˈbo͞ozˌhound/ ▶ **n.** informal a person who drinks alcohol often and heavily.

booz·er /ˈbo͞ozər/ ▶ **n.** informal a person who drinks large quantities of alcohol. ■ Brit. a pub or bar.

booze-up ▶ **n.** informal, chiefly Brit. a drinking spree.

booz·y /ˈbo͞ozē/ ▶ **adj.** (**boozier, booziest**) informal intoxicated; addicted to drink: *the boozy and drugged-out wreckage of his later years.*
– DERIVATIVES **booz·i·ly** /-zəlē/ **adv.**, **booz·i·ness n.**

bop[1] /bäp/ informal ▶ **n.** short for BEBOP.
▶ **v.** (**bops, bopping, bopped**) [no obj.] dance to pop music: *bopping to the radio while they made breakfast.* ■ move or travel energetically: *we had been bopping around the county all morning.*
– DERIVATIVES **bop·per n.**
– ORIGIN 1940s: shortening of BEBOP.

bop[2] informal ▶ **v.** (**bops, bopping, bopped**) [with obj.] hit; punch lightly: *I warned him I'd bop him on the nose if he tried it.*
▶ **n.** a blow or light punch.
– ORIGIN 1930s: imitative.

Bo·phu·that·swa·na /ˌbōpo͞oˌtätˈswänə/ a former homeland established in South Africa for the Tswana people.

bor. ▶ **abbr.** borough.

bo·ra /ˈbôrə/ ▶ **n.** a strong, cold, dry northeast wind blowing in the upper Adriatic.
– ORIGIN mid 19th cent.: dialect variant of Italian *borea*, from Latin *boreas* 'north wind' (see BOREAL).

Bo·ra-Bo·ra /ˌbôrə ˈbôrə/ an island in the Society Islands group in French Polynesia.

bo·rac·ic /bəˈrasik/ ▶ **adj.** another term for BORIC.

– ORIGIN late 18th cent.: from medieval Latin *borax, borac-* (see **BORAX**) + **-IC**.

bor·age /ˈbôrij, ˈbär-/ ▶ **n.** a herbaceous plant with bright blue flowers and hairy leaves, used medicinally and as a salad green. ● *Borago officinalis*, family Boraginaceae (the **borage family**). This family includes many plants that typically have blue or purple flowers, including forget-me-not, comfrey, and bugloss.
– ORIGIN Middle English: from Old French *bourrache*, from medieval Latin *borrago*, probably from Arabic.

bo·rane /ˈbôrān/ ▶ **n.** Chemistry any of a series of unstable binary compounds of boron and hydrogen, analogous to the alkanes. The simplest example is diborane, B_2H_6.
– ORIGIN early 20th cent.: from **BORON** + **-ANE²**.

Bo·rås /bo͞oˈrôs/ an industrial city in southwestern Sweden; pop. 101,487 (2008).

bo·rate /ˈbôrāt/ ▶ **n.** Chemistry a salt in which the anion contains both boron and oxygen, as in borax.

bo·rax /ˈbôraks/ ▶ **n.** a white mineral in some alkaline salt deposits, used in making glass and ceramics, as a metallurgical flux, and as an antiseptic. ● A hydrated sodium borate; chem. formula: $Na_2B_4O_5(OH)_4.8H_2O$.
– ORIGIN late Middle English: from medieval Latin, from Arabic *būraḳ*, from Pahlavi *būrak*.

Bo·ra·zon /ˈbôrəˌzän/ ▶ **n.** trademark an industrial abrasive consisting of boron nitride.
– ORIGIN 1950s: from **BORON**, with the insertion of **AZO-**.

bor·bo·ryg·mus /ˌbôrbəˈrigməs/ ▶ **n.** (pl. **borborygmi** /-mī/) technical a rumbling or gurgling noise made by the movement of fluid and gas in the intestines.
– DERIVATIVES **bor·bo·ryg·mic** /-mik/ **adj.**
– ORIGIN early 18th cent.: modern Latin, from Greek *borborugmos*.

Bor·deaux¹ /bôrˈdō/ a port in southwestern France, on the Garonne River; pop. 235,878 (2006).

Bor·deaux² ▶ **n.** (pl. **same**) a red, white, or rosé wine from the district of Bordeaux.

Bor·deaux mix·ture ▶ **n.** a fungicide for vines, fruit trees, and other plants composed of equal quantities of copper sulfate and calcium oxide in water.
– ORIGIN late 19th cent.: first used in the vineyards of the Bordeaux region.

bor·de·laise /ˌbôrdlˈāz/ ▶ **adj.** served with a sauce of red wine and onions: [postpositive] *lobster bordelaise*.
– ORIGIN French, from *(à la) bordelaise* 'Bordeaux-style.'

bor·del·lo /bôrˈdelō/ ▶ **n.** (pl. **bordellos**) a brothel.
– ORIGIN late 16th cent. (gradually replacing Middle English *bordel*): from Italian, probably from Old French *bordel*, diminutive of *borde* 'small farm, cottage,' ultimately of Germanic origin.

Bor·den¹ /ˈbôrdn/, Lizzie Andrew (1860–1927), US accused murderess. Accused of the murder of her father and stepmother in Fall River, Massachusetts, in 1892, she was acquitted in a trial that became a national sensation.

Bor·den², Robert Laird (1854–1937), Canadian Conservative statesman; prime minister 1911–20.

bor·der /ˈbôrdər/ ▶ **n.** **1** a line separating two political or geographical areas, esp. countries: *the German border with Denmark* | [as modifier] *border patrols*. ■ a district near such a line: *a refugee camp on the border*.
2 the edge or boundary of something, or the part near it: *the northern border of their distribution area* | figurative *the unknown regions at the borders of physics and electronics*.
3 a band or strip, esp. a decorative one, around the edge of something: *put a white border around the picture*. ■ a strip of ground along the edge of a lawn or path for planting flowers or shrubs: *the garden borders are planted with perennials*.
▶ **v.** [with obj.] form an edge along or beside (something): *a pool **bordered by** palm trees*. ■ (of a country or area) be adjacent to (another country or area): *regions bordering Azerbaijan* | [no obj.] *the park is east of San Diego, **bordering on** Mexico*. ■ [no obj.] (**border on**) be close to an extreme condition: *Sam arrived in a state of excitement bordering on hysteria*. ■ (usu. **be bordered with**) provide (something) with a decorative edge: *a curving driveway bordered with chrysanthemums*.
– DERIVATIVES **bor·der·less adj.**
– ORIGIN late Middle English: from Old French *bordeure*; ultimately of Germanic origin and related to **BOARD**.

Bor·der col·lie ▶ **n.** (also **border collie**) a common working sheepdog, typically with a black and white coat, of a medium-sized breed originating near the border between England and Scotland.

bord·er·er /ˈbôrdərər/ ▶ **n.** a person living near a border.

bord·er·land /ˈbôrdərˌland/ ▶ **n.** (usu. **borderlands**) the district near a border. ■ an area of overlap between two things: *the murky borderland between history and myth*.

bord·er·line /ˈbôrdərˌlīn/ ▶ **n.** a line marking a border. ■ a division between two distinct (often extreme) conditions: *the borderline between ritual and custom*.
▶ **adj.** barely acceptable in quality or as belonging to a category; on the borderline: *references may be requested in borderline cases*.

bor·der pa·trol ▶ **n.** **1** a patrol sent to keep watch over an area along a country's border.
2 (**Border Patrol**) an agency within the US Department of Homeland Security responsible for preventing the entry of illegal aliens as well as terrorists and their weapons into the United States.

bor·der state ▶ **n.** any of the slave states that bordered the northern free states during the US Civil War. See also **BORDER STATES**. ■ a US state that borders Canada or Mexico. ■ a small country that borders a larger, more powerful country or that lies between two larger countries.

Bor·der States those US states, including Delaware, Maryland, Kentucky, Virginia, and Missouri, that were slave states but did not secede from the Union during the Civil War.

Bord·er ter·ri·er ▶ **n.** a small terrier of a breed with rough hair, originating in the Cheviot Hills.

Bor·det /bôrˈdā/, Jules (1870–1961), Belgian bacteriologist and immunologist. He discovered the complement system of blood serum, and developed a vaccine for whooping cough.

bor·dure /ˈbôrjər/ ▶ **n.** Heraldry a broad border used as a charge in a coat of arms, often as a mark of difference.
– ORIGIN late Middle English: variant of **BORDER**.

bore¹ /bôr/ ▶ **v.** **1** [with obj.] make (a hole) in something, esp. with a revolving tool: *they bored holes in the sides* | [no obj.] *the drill can bore through rock* | figurative *his eyes bored into hers*. ■ [with obj.] hollow out (a tube or tunnel): *try to bore the tunnel at the correct angle*. ■ hollow out (a gun barrel).
2 [no obj.] make one's way through (a crowd).
▶ **n.** **1** the hollow part inside a gun barrel or other tube. ■ [often in combination] the diameter of this; the caliber: *a small-bore rifle*. ■ [in combination] a gun of a specified bore: *he shot a guard in the leg with a twelve-bore*.
2 short for **BOREHOLE**.
– ORIGIN Old English *borian* (verb), of Germanic origin; related to German *bohren*.

bore² ▶ **n.** a person whose talk or behavior is dull and uninteresting: ***a crashing bore** who tells the same old jokes over and over*. ■ [in sing.] a tedious situation or thing: *it's such a bore cooking when one's alone*.
▶ **v.** [with obj.] make (someone) feel weary and uninterested by tedious talk or dullness: *rather than bore you with all the details, I'll hit some of the bright spots*.
– PHRASES **bore someone to death** (or **to tears**) weary (a person) in the extreme.
– ORIGIN mid 18th cent. (as a verb): of unknown origin.

bore³ ▶ **n.** a steep-fronted wave caused by the meeting of two tides or by the constriction of a tide rushing up a narrow estuary.
– ORIGIN early 17th cent.: perhaps from Old Norse *bára* 'wave'; the term was used in the general sense 'billow, wave' in Middle English.

bore⁴ past of **BEAR¹**.

bo·re·al /ˈbôrēəl/ ▶ **adj.** of the North or northern regions. ■ Ecology relating to or characteristic of the climatic zone south of the Arctic, esp. the cold temperate region dominated by taiga and forests of birch, poplar, and conifers: *northern boreal forest*. ■ (**Boreal**) Botany relating to or denoting a phytogeographical kingdom comprising the arctic and temperate regions of Eurasia and North America.
– ORIGIN late Middle English: from late Latin *borealis*, from Latin *Boreas*, denoting the god of the north wind, from Greek.

bored¹ /bôrd/ ▶ **adj.** feeling weary because one is unoccupied or lacks interest in one's current activity: *she got **bored with** staring out of the window* | *they would hang around all day, **bored stiff**.*
– DERIVATIVES **bored·ly** /ˈbɔːdli/ **adv.**

> **USAGE** The traditional constructions for **bored** are **bored by** or **bored with**. The construction **bored of** emerged more recently, and is extremely common, especially in informal language. Although it is perfectly logical by analogy with constructions such as **tired of**, it is not fully accepted in standard English.

bored² ▶ **adj.** [in combination] (of a gun) having a specified bore: *large-bored guns*.

bore·dom /ˈbôrdəm/ ▶ **n.** the state of feeling bored: *the boredom of afternoon duty could be relieved by friendly conversation*.

bo·reen /bôˈrēn/ ▶ **n.** Irish a narrow country road.
– ORIGIN mid 19th cent.: from Irish *bóithrín*, diminutive of *bóthar* 'road.'

bore·hole /ˈbôrˌhōl/ ▶ **n.** a deep, narrow hole made in the ground, esp. to locate water or oil.

bo·rek /bôˈrek/ ▶ **n.** an envelope of thin pastry filled with cheese, spinach, or ground meat and baked or fried.
– ORIGIN Turkish, 'pie.'

bor·er /ˈbôrər/ ▶ **n.** **1** a worm, mollusk, insect, or insect larva that bores into wood, other plant material, or rock.
2 a tool for boring.

bore·scope /ˈbôrˌskōp/ ▶ **n.** an instrument used to inspect the inside of a structure through a small hole.

Borg /bôrg/, Björn (Rune) (1956–), Swedish tennis player. During 1974–81, he won the men's singles title at six French Open and five consecutive Wimbledon tournaments.

bor·ga·ta /bôrˈgätə/ ▶ **n.** (pl. **borgatas** or **borgate** /-tē/) an organized branch of the Mafia.
– ORIGIN 1960s: Italian, 'district, village.'

Bor·ge /ˈbôrgə/, Victor (1909–2000), US pianist; born in Denmark. He was noted for his clowning while playing classical music. His one-man show, *Comedy in Music*, began an 849-performance run on Broadway in 1953, with a brief revival in 1977.

Bor·ges /ˈbôrˌhās/, Jorge Luis (1899–1986), Argentine poet, short-story writer, and essayist. His volume of short stories *A Universal History of Infamy* (1935, revised 1954) is regarded as one of the first works of magic realism.

Bor·gia¹ /ˈbôrzhə/, Cesare (*c.*1476–1507), Italian statesman, cardinal, and general. He was the illegitimate son of **Cardinal Rodrigo Borgia** (later Pope Alexander VI) and the brother of Lucrezia Borgia.

Bor·gia², Lucrezia (1480–1519), Italian noblewoman; sister of Cesare Borgia. She was the illegitimate daughter of **Cardinal Rodrigo Borgia** (later Pope Alexander VI).

Bor·glum /ˈbôrgləm/, Gutzon (1867–1941) US sculptor; full name *John Gutzon de la Mothe Borglum*. His most famous work is the Mount Rushmore National Memorial in South Dakota, which features the monumental heads of US Presidents Washington, Jefferson, Lincoln, and T. Roosevelt. The work, begun in 1927, was completed in 1941 with the help of his son Lincoln Borglum (1912–86).

bo·ric /ˈbôrik/ ▶ **adj.** Chemistry of boron: *boric oxide*.

bo·ric ac·id ▶ **n.** Chemistry a weakly acid crystalline compound derived from borax, used as a mild antiseptic and in the manufacture of heat-resistant glass and enamels. ● Chem. formula: $B(OH)_3$.

Bo·ri·cua /bôˈrēkwə/ ▶ **n.** informal a Puerto Rican, esp. one living in the United States.

bor·ing /ˈbôriNG/ ▶ **adj.** not interesting; tedious: *I've got a boring job in an office*.
– DERIVATIVES **bor·ing·ly adv.** [as submodifier] *the list is excoriated as boringly predictable*, **bor·ing·ness n.**

Bo·ris Go·du·nov /ˈbôrəs/ see **GODUNOV**.

bork /bôrk/ (also **Bork**) ▶ **v.** [with obj.] informal obstruct (someone, esp. a candidate for public office) through systematic defamation or vilification: (as noun **borking**) *is fear of borking scaring people from public office?*
– ORIGIN 1980s: from the name of Robert *Bork* (born 1927), an American judge whose nomination to the US Supreme Court (1987) was rejected following unfavorable publicity for his allegedly extreme views.

Bor·laug /ˈbôrˌlôg/, Norman Ernest (1914–2009), US agronomist. He worked for many years on the improvement of wheat crops and the adaptation of new strains of wheat to parts of the world where it had not previously been grown. Nobel Peace Prize (1970).

Bor·mann /ˈbôrmən/, Martin (1900–*c.*1945), German Nazi politician. Considered to be Hitler's closest collaborator, he disappeared at the end of World War II; his skeleton, exhumed in Berlin, was identified in 1973.

b

Born /bôrn/, Max (1882–1970), German theoretical physicist, a founder of quantum mechanics. Nobel Prize for Physics (1954), shared with Walther Bothe (1891–1957).

born /bôrn/ past participle of **BEAR**[1] (sense 4).
▶ **adj.** existing as a result of birth: *he was born in Seattle* | *babies **born to** women aged 25–29* | *he was **born into** a family of wine merchants* | *she was born Margaret Roberts* | [in combination] *a German-born philosopher.* ■ [attrib.] having a natural ability to do a particular job or task: *he's a born engineer.* ■ [with infinitive] perfectly suited or trained to do a particular job or task: *they believe that they are born to rule.* ■ (of a thing) brought into existence: *her own business was born.* ■ (**born of**) existing as a result of a particular situation or feeling: *a power born of obsession.*
– PHRASES **born and bred** by birth and upbringing, esp. when considered a typical product of a place: *he was a born and bred product of the Bronx.* **born on the wrong side of the blanket** see **BLANKET**. **born with a silver spoon in one's mouth** see **SILVER**. **I (she, etc.) wasn't born yesterday** used to remind someone that one isn't naive. **in all one's born days** used to express surprise or shock at something one has not encountered before: *in all my born days I've never seen the like of it.* **there's one** (or **a sucker**) **born every minute** there are many gullible people.
– ORIGIN Old English *boren*, past participle of *beran* 'to bear' (see **BEAR**[1]).

USAGE On the difference between **born** and **borne**, see usage at **BEAR**[1].

born-a·gain ▶ **adj.** converted to a personal faith in Christ (with reference to John 3:3): *a born-again Christian.* ■ having the extreme enthusiasm of the newly converted or reconverted: *born-again environmentalists.*
▶ **n.** a born-again Christian.

borne /bôrn/ past participle of **BEAR**[1].
▶ **adj.** [in combination] carried or transported by: *waterborne bacteria* | *insect-borne pollen.*

Bor·ne·o /ˈbôrnēō/ a large island in the Malay Archipelago that is comprised of Kalimantan (a region of Indonesia), Sabah and Sarawak (states of Malaysia), and Brunei.
– DERIVATIVES **Bor·ne·an** /-nēən/ **adj.**

Born·holm /ˈbôrn,hō(l)m/ a Danish island in the Baltic Sea, southeast of Sweden.

Born·holm dis·ease ▶ **n.** a viral infection with fever and pain in the muscles of the ribs.
– ORIGIN 1930s: named after the island of **BORNHOLM**, where it was first described.

born·ite /ˈbôrnīt/ ▶ **n.** a brittle reddish-brown crystalline mineral with an iridescent purple tarnish, consisting of a sulfide of copper and iron.
– ORIGIN early 19th cent.: from the name of Ignatius von *Born* (1742–91), Austrian mineralogist, + **-ITE**[1].

boro- ▶ **comb. form** Chemistry representing **BORON**.

Bo·ro·bu·dur /,bôrəbəˈdo͝or/ a Buddhist monument in central Java, built *c.*800.

Bo·ro·din /,bôrəˈdēn/, Aleksandr (Porfirevich) (1833–87), Russian composer. He is noted for the opera *Prince Igor*, which was completed, after his death, by Nikolai Rimsky-Korsakov and Aleksandr Glazunov (1865–1936).

Bo·ro·di·no, Battle of /,bôrəˈdēnō/ a battle in 1812 at Borodino, a village about 110 km (70 miles) west of Moscow, at which Napoleon's forces defeated the Russian army.

bo·ron /ˈbôrän/ ▶ **n.** the chemical element of atomic number 5, a nonmetallic solid. (Symbol: **B**)

Boron is usually prepared as an amorphous brown powder, but when very pure it forms hard, shiny, black crystals with semiconducting properties. The element has some specialized uses, such as in alloy steels and nuclear control rods.

– DERIVATIVES **bo·ride** /-rīd/ **n.**
– ORIGIN early 19th cent.: from **BORAX**, on the pattern of *carbon* (which it resembles in some respects).

bo·ro·ni·a /bəˈrōnēə/ ▶ **n.** a sweet-scented Australian shrub cultivated for its perfume and for use as a cut flower. ● Genus *Boronia*, family Rutaceae.
– ORIGIN modern Latin, named after Francesco *Borone* (1769–94), Italian botanist.

bo·ro·sil·i·cate /,bôrəˈsilikit, -,kāt/ ▶ **n.** [usu. as modifier] a low-melting-point glass made from a mixture of silica and boric oxide (B_2O_3).

bor·ough /ˈbərō/ (abbr.: **bor.**) ▶ **n.** a town or district that is an administrative unit, in particular: ■ an incorporated municipality in certain US states. ■ each of five divisions of New York City. ■ in Alaska, a district corresponding to a county elsewhere in the US. ■ Brit. a town (as distinct from a city) with a corporation and privileges granted by a royal charter. ■ Brit. historical a town sending representatives to Parliament.
– ORIGIN Old English *burg, burh* 'fortress, citadel,' later 'fortified town,' of Germanic origin; related to Dutch *burg* and German *Burg*. Compare with **BURGH**.

Bor·ro·mi·ni /,bôrəˈmēnē/, Francesco (1599–1667), Italian architect, a leading figure of the Italian baroque style.

bor·row /ˈbärō, ˈbôrō/ ▶ **v.** [with obj.] take and use (something that belongs to someone else) with the intention of returning it: *he had **borrowed** a car **from** one of his colleagues* | (as adj. **borrowed**) *she was wearing a borrowed jacket.* ■ take and use (money) from a person or bank under an agreement to pay it back later: *I borrowed the money for a return plane ticket* | [no obj.] *lower interest rates will make it cheaper for individuals to borrow.* ■ take (a word, idea, or method) from another source and use it in one's own language or work: *the term is **borrowed from** Greek* | [no obj.] *designers consistently **borrow from** the styles of preceding generations.* ■ take and use (a book) from a library for a fixed period of time. ■ in subtraction, take a unit from the next larger denomination. ■ Golf allow (a certain distance) when playing a shot to compensate for sideways motion of the ball due to a slope or other irregularity.
▶ **n.** Golf a slope or other irregularity on a golf course that must be compensated for when playing a shot.
– PHRASES **be (living) on borrowed time** used to say that someone has continued to survive against expectations, with the implication that this will not be for much longer. **borrow trouble** take needless action that may have detrimental effects.
– DERIVATIVES **bor·row·er n.**
– ORIGIN Old English *borgian* 'borrow against security,' of Germanic origin; related to Dutch and German *borgen*.

bor·row·ing /ˈbärō-iNG, ˈbôr-/ ▶ **n.** the action of borrowing something: *the borrowing of clothes.* ■ the action of taking and using money from a bank under an agreement to pay it back later: *a curb on government borrowing* | *the group had total borrowings of $570 million.* ■ a word, idea, or method taken from another source and used in one's own language or work: *a hard-bop musician with some borrowings from free jazz.*

Bor·sa·li·no /,bôrsəˈlēnō/ ▶ **n.** (pl. **Borsalinos**) trademark a man's wide-brimmed felt hat.
– ORIGIN early 20th cent.: from the name of the manufacturer.

borscht /bôrSHt/ (also **borsch**) ▶ **n.** a Russian or Polish soup made with beets and usually served with sour cream.
– ORIGIN Russian *borshch*.

Borscht Belt /bôrSHt/ ▶ **n.** (**the Borscht Belt**) humorous a resort area in the Catskill Mountains frequented chiefly by Jewish guests: [as modifier] *Borscht Belt entertainers.*

bor·stal /ˈbôrstəl/ (also **Borstal**) ▶ **n.** Brit. historical a custodial institution for youthful offenders.
– ORIGIN early 20th cent.: named after the village of *Borstal* in southern England, where the first of these was established.

bort /bôrt/ ▶ **n.** small, granular, opaque diamonds, used as an abrasive in cutting tools. Compare with **CARBONADO**.
– ORIGIN early 17th cent.: from Dutch *boort*.

bor·zoi /ˈbôrzoi/ ▶ **n.** (pl. **borzois**) a large Russian wolfhound of a breed with a narrow head and silky, often white, coat.
– ORIGIN late 19th cent.: from Russian *borzoĭ* (adjective) 'swift.'

borzoi

Bosc /bäsk/ (also **Bosc pear**) ▶ **n.** a medium- to large-sized variety of pear, golden brown in color and often russeted. The Bosc's dense flesh makes it a common choice for baking and cooking.
– ORIGIN named after L. *Bosc* d'Antic (1759–1828), French naturalist.

bos·cage /ˈbäskij/ (also **boskage**) ▶ **n.** massed trees or shrubs: *the lush subtropical boscage.*
– ORIGIN late Middle English: from Old French; ultimately of Germanic origin and related to **BUSH**. Compare with **BOCAGE**.

Bosch /bäSH, bôSH/, Hieronymus (*c.*1450–1516), Dutch painter. His highly detailed works are typically crowded with half-human, half-animal creatures and grotesque demons in settings symbolic of sin and folly.

Bose /bōz/, Satyendra Nath (1894–1974), Indian physicist. With Albert Einstein, he described fundamental particles that later came to be known as *bosons*.

bosh /bäSH/ ▶ **n.** informal something regarded as absurd; nonsense: *I think it's a load of bosh* | [as exclamation] *bosh! You don't want to go with us.*
– ORIGIN mid 19th cent.: from Turkish *boş* 'empty, worthless,' which became widely known in English through James Morier's novel *Ayesha* (1834).

bosk /bäsk/ ▶ **n.** a thicket of bushes; a small wood.

bosk·y /ˈbäskē/ ▶ **adj.** wooded; covered by trees or bushes: *a river meandering between bosky banks.*
– ORIGIN late 16th cent.: from Middle English *bosk*, variant of **BUSH**.

Bos·man rul·ing /ˈbäzmən/ ▶ **n.** a European Court ruling that obliges professional soccer or other sports clubs to allow players over the age of 25 to move freely between clubs once their contracts have expired.
– ORIGIN 1990s: named after Jean-Marc *Bosman* (1964–), a Belgian soccer player who brought a legal case that resulted in the ruling.

bo's'n ▶ **n.** variant spelling of **BOATSWAIN**.

Bos·ni·a /ˈbäznēə/ a region in the Balkans that forms the larger, northern part of Bosnia and Herzegovina.
– DERIVATIVES **Bos·ni·ak** (also **Bosniac**) **adj. & n.**

Bos·ni·a and Her·ze·go·vi·na (also **Bosnia-Herzegovina**) a country in southeastern Europe, in the Balkans, formerly a constituent republic of Yugoslavia; pop. 4,613,400 (est. 2009); capital, Sarajevo; languages, Bosnian, Croatian, Serbian.

Bosnia and Herzegovina were conquered by the Turks in 1463. The province of Bosnia and Herzegovina was annexed by Austria in 1908, an event that contributed to the outbreak of World War I. In 1918, it became part of the Kingdom of Serbs, Croats, and Slovenes, which changed its name to Yugoslavia in 1929. In 1992, Bosnia and Herzegovina followed Slovenia and Croatia in declaring independence, but ethnic conflict among Muslims, Serbs, and Croats quickly reduced the republic to a state of civil war. An accord signed in December 1995 formally brought the conflict to an end.

Bos·ni·an /ˈbäznēən/ ▶ **n. 1** a native or inhabitant of the Balkan country Bosnia and Herzegovina. **2** the Slavic language of the Bosnians.
▶ **adj.** relating to Bosnia and Herzegovina, its people, or their language.

bos·om /ˈbo͝ozəm/ ▶ **n.** a woman's chest: *her ample bosom* | *the dress offered a fair display of bosom.* ■ (usu. **bosoms**) a woman's breast. ■ a part of a woman's dress covering the chest. ■ the space between a person's clothing and chest used for carrying things: *he carried a letter **in his bosom**.* ■ (**the bosom of**) literary the loving care and protection of: *Bruno went home each night **to the bosom of his family*** | *the town has taken the gay community **to its bosom**.* ■ used to refer to the chest as the seat of emotions: *quivering dread was settling in her bosom.*
▶ **adj.** [attrib.] (of a friend) close or intimate: *the two girls had become bosom friends.*
– DERIVATIVES **bos·omed adj.** [in combination] *her small-bosomed physique.*
– ORIGIN Old English *bōsm*; related to Dutch *boezem* and German *Busen*.

bos·om·y /ˈbo͝ozəmē/ ▶ **adj.** (of a woman) having large breasts.

bo·son /ˈbōsän/ ▶ **n.** Physics a subatomic particle, such as a photon, that has zero or integral spin and follows the statistical description given by S. N. Bose and Einstein.
– ORIGIN 1940s: named after S. N. **BOSE** + **-ON**.

Bos·po·rus /ˈbäsp(ə)rəs/ (also **Bosphorus** /ˈbäsf(ə)rəs/) a strait that connects the Black Sea with the Sea of Marmara and separates Europe from the Anatolian peninsula of western Asia. Istanbul is located at its south end.

boss[1] /bôs, bäs/ informal ▶ **n.** a person in charge of a worker or organization: *I asked my boss for a promotion* | *union bosses.* ■ a person in control of a group or situation: *the boss of the largest crime family in the country.*
▶ **v.** [with obj.] give (someone) orders in a domineering manner: *plump old battle-axes **bossing** everyone **around**.*
▶ **adj.** [attrib.] excellent; outstanding: *she's a real boss chick.*

– PHRASES **be one's own boss** be self-employed. **show someone who's boss** make it clear that one is in charge.
– ORIGIN early 19th cent. (originally US): from Dutch *baas* 'master.'

boss² ▶ n. a round knob, stud, or other protuberance, in particular: ■ a stud on the center of a shield. ■ Architecture a piece of ornamental carving covering the point where the ribs in a vault or ceiling cross. ■ Geology a large mass of igneous rock protruding through other strata. ■ Mechanics an enlarged part of a shaft.
– ORIGIN Middle English: from Old French *boce*, of unknown origin.

boss³ ▶ n. informal a cow. Compare with BOSSY².
– ORIGIN early 19th cent.: of unknown origin.

bos·sa no·va /ˈbäsə ˈnōvə, ˈbô-/ ▶ n. a style of Brazilian music derived from samba but placing more emphasis on melody and less on percussion. ■ a dance to this music.
– ORIGIN 1960s: from Portuguese, from *bossa* 'tendency' and *nova* (feminine of *novo*) 'new.'

Bos·sier Cit·y /ˈbōzh, ər/ a city in northwestern Louisiana, on the Red River, just northeast of Shreveport; pop. 62,384 (est. 2008). It is a center for the oil and gas industry.

boss·ism /ˈbôsizəm, ˈbäs-/ ▶ n. a situation in which a political party is controlled by party managers.

boss·y¹ /ˈbôsē, ˈbäs-/ ▶ adj. (**bossier, bossiest**) informal fond of giving people orders; domineering: *she was headlong, bossy, scared of nobody, and full of vinegar.*
– DERIVATIVES **boss·i·ly** /-səlē/ adv., **boss·i·ness** n.

boss·y² ▶ n. (pl. **bossies**) informal a cow or calf. Compare with BOSS³.
– ORIGIN mid 19th cent.: of unknown origin.

Bos·ton¹ /ˈbôstən/ a city in eastern Massachusetts, the capital of the state, on Massachusetts Bay; pop. 609,023 (est. 2008). It was founded *c.*1630 by the Massachusetts Bay Company under its governor, *John Winthrop* (1588–1649). Boston was the scene of many disturbances that led to the American Revolution at the end of the 18th century.
– DERIVATIVES **Bos·to·ni·an** /bôˈstōnēən/ n. & adj.

Bos·ton² ▶ n. **1** a card game resembling solo whist. **2** a variation of the waltz or of the two-step.

Bos·ton baked beans ▶ plural n. a dish of baked beans with salt pork and molasses.

Bos·ton cream pie ▶ n. a round, two-layer cake that is filled with custard or cream and frosted, usually with chocolate.

Bos·ton fern ▶ n. a variety of sword fern, with long, arching bright green fronds, widely cultivated esp. as a hanging houseplant. ● *Nephrolepis exaltata bostoniensis*, family Dryopteridaceae.

Bos·ton i·vy ▶ n. a Virginia creeper with three-lobed leaves, cultivated for its foliage. ● *Parthenocissus tricuspidata*, family Vitaceae.

Bos·ton let·tuce ▶ n. a butterhead lettuce of a variety that has medium or light green leaves.

Bos·ton rock·er ▶ n. a rocking chair with a decorative panel on a high spindled back and with arms and a seat that curves downward at the front.

Bos·ton Tea Par·ty a violent demonstration in 1773 by American colonists before the American Revolution. Colonists boarded vessels in Boston harbor and threw the cargoes of tea into the water in protest at the imposition of a tax on tea by the British Parliament, in which the colonists had no representation.

Bos·ton ter·ri·er ▶ n. a small smooth-coated terrier of a breed originating in Massachusetts from a crossing of the bulldog and terrier.

bo·sun (also **bo'sun**) ▶ n. variant spelling of BOATSWAIN.

Bos·well /ˈbäzwəl, -ˌwel/, James (1740–95), Scottish author, companion and biographer of Samuel Johnson. Notable works: *Journal of a Tour to the Hebrides* (1785) and *The Life of Samuel Johnson* (1791).

Bos·worth Field /ˈbäzwərth/ (also **Battle of Bosworth**) a battle of the Wars of the Roses fought in 1485 near Market Bosworth in Leicestershire. Henry Tudor defeated and killed the Yorkist king Richard III, which enabled him to take the throne as Henry VII.

bot¹ /bät/ ▶ n. the larva of the botfly, which is an internal parasite of animals. It lives typically in the stomach, finally passing through the host's dung and pupating on the ground.
– ORIGIN early 16th cent.: probably of Low German origin.

bot² ▶ n. (chiefly in science fiction) a robot. ■ Computing an autonomous program on a network (esp. the Internet) that can interact with computer systems or users, esp. one designed to respond or behave like a player in an adventure game.
– ORIGIN 1960s: shortening of ROBOT.

bot. ▶ abbr. ■ (with reference to journal titles) botanic; botanical; botany. ■ bottle. ■ bought.

-bot ▶ comb. form used to form nouns denoting a computer program or robot with a very specific function: *fembot* | *adbot*.
– ORIGIN from *robot*.

bo·tan·i·cal /bəˈtanikəl/ ▶ adj. of or relating to plants: *botanical specimens* | *a botanical illustrator*.
▶ n. (usu. **botanicals**) a substance obtained from a plant and used as an additive, esp. in gin or cosmetics.
– DERIVATIVES **bo·tan·i·cal·ly** /-ik(ə)lē/ adv.

bo·tan·i·cal gar·den (also **botanic garden**) ▶ n. an establishment where plants are grown for display to the public and often for scientific study.

bot·a·nize /ˈbätn‚īz/ ▶ v. [no obj.] study plants, esp. in their natural habitat: *I'd always be scheming to go off birdwatching or botanizing.*
– ORIGIN mid 18th cent.: from modern Latin *botanizare*, from Greek *botanizein* 'gather plants,' from *botanē* 'plant.'

Bot·a·ny /ˈbätn-ē/ (also **Botany wool**) ▶ n. merino wool, esp. from Australia.
– ORIGIN late 19th cent.: named after BOTANY BAY, from where the wool originally came.

bot·a·ny /ˈbätn-ē/ ▶ n. the scientific study of plants, including their physiology, structure, genetics, ecology, distribution, classification, and economic importance. ■ the plant life of a particular region, habitat, or geological period: *the botany of North America.*
– DERIVATIVES **bo·tan·ic** /bəˈtanik/ adj., **bot·a·nist** /-ist/ n.
– ORIGIN late 17th cent.: from earlier *botanic* (from French *botanique*, based on Greek *botanikos*, from *botanē* 'plant') + -Y³.

Bot·a·ny Bay an inlet of the Tasman Sea just south of Sydney, Australia. It was the site of Captain James Cook's landing in 1770 and of an early British penal settlement.
– ORIGIN named by Cook after the large variety of plants collected there by his companion, Sir Joseph Banks.

botch /bäch/ ▶ v. [with obj.] informal carry out (a task) badly or carelessly: *the ability to take on any task without botching it* | *he was in a position to hire people, and he* **botched** *that up* | (as adj. **botched**) *a botched attempt to kill them.*
▶ n. (also **botch-up**) informal a bungled or badly carried out task or action: *I've probably* **made a botch of** *things.*
– DERIVATIVES **botch·er** n.
– ORIGIN late Middle English (in the sense 'repair' but originally not implying clumsiness): of unknown origin.

bot·fly /ˈbät‚flī/ ▶ n. (pl. **botflies**) a stout hairy-bodied fly with larvae that are internal parasites of mammals, in particular: ● a fly with larvae (bots) that develop within the guts of horses (*Gasterophilus* and other genera, family Gasterophilidae). ● a fly of the warble fly family (Oestridae).

both /bōth/ ▶ predeterminer, determiner, & pron. used to refer to two people or things, regarded and identified together: [as predeterminer] *both his parents indulged him* | [as determiner] *I urge you to read both these books* | *she held on with both hands* | *he was blind in both eyes* | [as pronoun] *a picture of* **both of** *us together* | *Jackie and I are both self-employed* | *he looked at them both.*
▶ adv. used before the first of two alternatives to emphasize that the statement being made applies to each (the other alternative being introduced by "and"): *they all loved to play, both the boys and the girls* | *it has won favor with both young and old* | *studies of finches, both in the wild and in captivity.*
– PHRASES **have it both ways** benefit from two incompatible ways of thinking or behaving: *countries cannot have it both ways: the cost of a cleaner environment may sometimes be fewer jobs.*
– ORIGIN Middle English: from Old Norse *báthir*.

> **USAGE** When **both** is used in constructions with **and**, the structures following 'both' and 'and' should be symmetrical in well-formed English. Thus, *studies of zebra finches,* **both** *in the wild* **and** *in captivity* is stronger and clearer than *studies of zebra finches,* **both** *in the wild* **and** *captivity*. In the second example, the symmetry or parallelism of 'in the wild' and 'in captivity' has been lost.

Bo·tha¹ /ˈbōtə/, Louis (1862–1919), South African soldier and statesman; first prime minister of the Union of South Africa 1910–19.

Bo·tha², P. W. (1916–2006), South African statesman; full name *Pieter Willem Botha*. As prime minister 1978–84 and state president 1984–89, he was an authoritarian leader who continued to enforce apartheid, but in response to pressure, he introduced limited reforms.

both·er /ˈbäTHər/ ▶ v. **1** [with negative] take the trouble to do something: *nobody bothered locking the doors* | *scientists rarely* **bother with** *such niceties* | [with infinitive] *the driver didn't bother to ask why.* **2** (of a circumstance or event) worry, disturb, or upset (someone): *secrecy is an issue that bothers journalists* | [with obj. and clause] *it* **bothered** *me that I hadn't done anything.* ■ trouble or annoy (someone) by interrupting or causing inconvenience: *she didn't feel she could* **bother** *Mike* **with** *the problem.* ■ [no obj., usu. with negative] feel concern about or interest in: *don't* **bother about** *me—I'll find my own way home* | *he wasn't to* **bother himself with** *day-to-day things* | (as adj. **bothered**) *I'm not particularly* **bothered about** *how I look.*
▶ n. effort, worry, or difficulty: *he* **saved me the bother of** *having to come up with a speech* | *it may seem like too much bother to cook just for yourself.* ■ (**a bother**) a person or thing that causes worry or difficulty: *I hope she hasn't been a bother.* ■ [with negative] a nuisance or inconvenience: ***it's no bother,*** *it's on my way home.*
– PHRASES **can't be bothered** (**to do something**) be unwilling to make the effort to do something: *they couldn't be bothered to look it up.* **hot and bothered** in a state of anxiety or physical discomfort.
– ORIGIN late 17th cent. (as a noun in the dialect sense 'noise, chatter'): of Anglo-Irish origin; probably related to Irish *bodhaire* 'noise,' *bodhraim* 'deafen, annoy.' The verb (originally dialect) meant 'confuse with noise' in the early 18th cent.

both·er·a·tion /‚bäTHəˈrāshən/ informal ▶ n. effort, worry, or difficulty; bother: *he has caused us a deal of unnecessary botheration.*
▶ exclam. dated used to express mild irritation or annoyance.

both·er·some /ˈbäTHərsəm/ ▶ adj. causing bother; troublesome: *most childhood stomachaches, though bothersome, aren't serious.*

Both·ni·a, Gulf of /ˈbäthnēə/ a northern arm of the Baltic Sea, between Sweden and Finland.

both·y /ˈbäthē/ (also **bothie**) ▶ n. (pl. **bothies**) (in Scotland) a small hut or cottage.
– ORIGIN late 18th cent.: obscurely related to Irish and Scottish Gaelic *both, bothan*, and perhaps to BOOTH.

bot·net /ˈbät‚net/ ▶ n. Computing a network of private computers infected with malicious software and controlled as a group without the owners' knowledge, e.g., to send spam messages.
– ORIGIN early 21st cent.: blend of BOT² and NETWORK.

Bo·tox /ˈbō‚täks/ ▶ n. trademark a drug prepared from the bacterial toxin botulin, used medically to treat certain muscular conditions and cosmetically to remove wrinkles by temporarily paralyzing facial muscles.
– DERIVATIVES **Bo·toxed** adj.
– ORIGIN 1990s: from *bo(tulinum) tox(in)*.

bo tree /bō/ (also **bodhi tree** /ˈbōdē/) ▶ n. a fig tree native to India and Southeast Asia, regarded as sacred by Buddhists. Also called PEEPUL, PIPAL. ● *Ficus religiosa*, family Moraceae.
– ORIGIN mid 19th cent.: representing Sinhalese *bōgaha* 'tree of knowledge' (Buddha's enlightenment having occurred beneath such a tree), from *bō* (from Sanskrit *budh* 'understand thoroughly') + *gaha* 'tree.'

bot·ry·oi·dal /‚bätrēˈoidl/ ▶ adj. (chiefly of minerals) having a shape reminiscent of a cluster of grapes.
– ORIGIN late 18th cent.: from Greek *botruoeidēs* (from *botrus* 'bunch of grapes') + -AL.

bo·try·tis /bōˈtrītis/ ▶ n. a fungus that forms a grayish powdery mold on a variety of organic matter. It causes a number of fungal plant diseases, including chocolate spot, and is deliberately cultivated (as noble rot) on the grapes used for certain wines. ● Genus *Botrytis*, phylum Ascomycota: numerous species, in particular the gray mold *B. cinerea*.
– ORIGIN modern Latin, from Greek *botrus* 'cluster of grapes.'

Bot·swa·na /bätˈswänə/ a landlocked country in southern Africa, the western half of which is the Kalahari Desert; pop. 1,990,900 (est. 2009); capital, Gaborone; languages, English (official) and Setswana.

b

Inhabited by Sotho people and, in the Kalahari Desert, San (Bushmen), the area was made the British Protectorate of Bechuanaland in 1885. It became an independent republic within the Commonwealth of Nations in 1966 and adopted the name Botswana.

– DERIVATIVES **Bot·swa·nan** adj. & n.

bot·tar·ga /bō'tärgə/ ▶ n. the dried, pressed roe of the mullet, which is sold in blocks and shaved over Italian dishes.
– ORIGIN Italian, from Arabic *butarkhah*.

Bot·ti·cel·li /ˌbätə'CHelē/, Sandro (1445–1510), Italian painter; born *Alessandro di Mariano Filipepi*. He is noted for his mythological works, such as *Primavera* (c.1478) and *The Birth of Venus* (c.1480).

bot·tle /'bätl/ ▶ n. a container, typically made of glass or plastic and with a narrow neck, used for storing drinks or other liquids: *a bottle of soda pop.* ■ the contents of such a container: *he managed to put away a bottle of wine.* ■ (**the bottle**) informal used in reference to heavy drinking: *more women are taking to the bottle.* ■ a bottle fitted with a nipple for giving milk or other drinks to babies and very young children: *a bottle of formula.* ■ a large metal cylinder holding liquefied gas.
▶ v. [with obj.] place (drinks or other liquid) in bottles or jars: *the wine is then bottled* | (as adj. **bottled**) *bottled beer.* ■ (usu. as adj. **bottled**) store (gas) in a container in liquefied form: *connecting the bottled gas to the stove.*
– PHRASES **hit the bottle** informal begin to drink heavily.
– PHRASAL VERBS **bottle someone up** keep (someone) trapped or contained: *he had to stay bottled up in New York.* **bottle something up** repress or conceal feelings over a period of time: *learning how to express anger instead of bottling it up* | (as adj. **bottled up**) *Lily's bottled-up fury.*
– DERIVATIVES **bot·tler** n.
– ORIGIN late Middle English (denoting a leather bottle): from Old French *boteille*, from medieval Latin *butticula*, diminutive of late Latin *buttis* 'cask, wineskin' (see **BUTT**[4]).

wine bottles

bot·tle age ▶ n. time spent by a wine maturing in its bottle.

bot·tle bill ▶ n. any of several US state laws that require deposits to be paid on beverages sold in recyclable bottles and cans.

bot·tle blond (also **bottle blonde**) derogatory ▶ adj. (of a woman's hair) of a light blond shade, as though artificially lightened or bleached.
▶ n. a woman with such hair.

bot·tle·brush /'bätlˌbrəSH/ ▶ n. an Australian shrub or small tree with spikes of scarlet or yellow flowers that resemble a cylindrical brush in shape. ● Genus *Callistemon*, family Myrtaceae. ■ any of a number of plants bearing similar flowers.

bot·tled gas ▶ n. butane or propane gas stored under pressure in portable tanks.

bot·tle-feed ▶ v. [with obj.] feed (a baby) with milk from a bottle instead of from the mother's breast: (as adj. **bottle-fed**) *a bottle-fed baby.*

bot·tle green ▶ n. a dark shade of green.

bot·tle jack ▶ n. a bottle-shaped hydraulic jack used for lifting heavy objects.

bot·tle·neck /'bätlˌnek/ ▶ n. **1** the neck or mouth of a bottle.
2 a point of congestion or blockage, in particular: ■ a narrow section of road or a junction that impedes traffic flow: *narrow streets and a lack of parking space combine to make the town a bottleneck.* ■ a situation that causes delay in a process or system: *lack of imports is making the bottlenecks in domestic output worse than usual.*
3 a device shaped like the neck of a bottle, worn on a guitarist's finger to produce special sound effects. ■ (also **bottleneck guitar**) the style of guitar playing that uses such a device.

bot·tle·nose dol·phin /'bätlˌnōz/ (also **bottle-nosed dolphin**) ▶ n. a stout-bodied dolphin with a distinct short beak, found in tropical and temperate coastal waters. ● *Tursiops truncatus*, family Delphinidae.

bot·tle tree ▶ n. either of two Australian trees with swollen water-containing trunks. ● the Australian baobab of the Kimberley region (*Adansonia gregorii*, family Bombacaceae). ● a relative of the flame tree occurring in Queensland (*Brachychiton rupestre*, family Sterculiaceae).

bot·tom /'bätəm/ ▶ n. (usu. **the bottom**) **1** the lowest point or part: *the bottom of the page* | *she paused at the bottom of the stairs.* ■ the lowest surface on the inside of a container: *place the fruit on the bottom of the dish.* ■ the part on which a thing rests; the underside: *he sat on the bottom of an upturned bucket.* ■ the ground under a sea, river, or lake: *the liner plunged to the bottom of the sea.* ■ (also **bottoms**) another term for **BOTTOMLAND**. ■ the seat of a chair. ■ the lowest position in a competition or ranking: *he started at the bottom and now has his own business.* ■ the basis or origin: *there's a mad scientist at the bottom of it all.* ■ (also **bottoms**) the lower half of a two-piece garment: *pajama bottoms* | *a skimpy bikini bottom.* ■ the lowest part of the hull of a ship, esp. the relatively flat portion on either side of the keel. ■ archaic a ship, esp. considered as a unit of transport capacity. ■ archaic stamina or strength of character, esp. of a horse.
2 informal the buttocks: *he climbs the side of the gorge, scratching his bottom unselfconsciously.*
3 Baseball the second half of an inning: *the bottom of the ninth.*
4 Physics one of six flavors of quark.
▶ adj. in the lowest position: *the books on the bottom shelf.* ■ in the lowest or last position in a competition or ranking: *households in the bottom income bracket.*
▶ v. [no obj.] (of a performance or situation) reach the lowest point before stabilizing or improving: *interest rates have bottomed out.*
– PHRASES **at bottom** basically; fundamentally: *at bottom, science is exploration.* **bet your bottom dollar** informal stake everything: *you can bet your bottom dollar it'll end in tears.* **the bottom falls** (or **drops**) **out** collapse or failure occurs: *the bottom fell out of the market for classic cars.* **bottoms up!** informal a call to finish one's drink. **from the bottom of one's heart** see **HEART**. **from the bottom up** starting at the lower end or beginning of a hierarchy or process and proceeding to the top or to completion: *we began to study history from the bottom up.* **get to the bottom of** find an explanation for (a mystery): *he hopes to get to the bottom of the scam.*
– DERIVATIVES **bot·tomed** adj. [in combination] *a glass-bottomed boat* | *bare-bottomed toddlers.* **bot·tom·most** /-ˌmōst/ adj.
– ORIGIN Old English *botm*, of Germanic origin; related to Dutch *bodem* 'bottom, ground' and German *Boden* 'ground, earth.'

bot·tom-dwell·ing ▶ adj. (of an aquatic organism) dwelling on or near the bed of the sea, a lake, or other body of water. ■ (of a person or organization) characterized by poor, questionable, or unethical performance.
– DERIVATIVES **bot·tom-dwell·er** n.

bot·tom feed·er ▶ n. **1** an aquatic creature that feeds at the bottom of a body of water.
2 someone who profits from things cast off or left over by others.

bot·tom fer·men·ta·tion ▶ n. a process in the brewing of certain beers in which the yeast falls to the bottom during fermentation.

bot·tom fish ▶ n. a species of fish, such as flounder, that is a bottom feeder.
▶ v. (**bottom-fish**) fish for species that are bottom fish. ■ make profits from investments that are of low value or out of favor.

bot·tom·land /'bätəmˌland/ ▶ n. low-lying land, typically by a river and subject to overflow during floods.

bot·tom·less /'bätəmlis/ ▶ adj. **1** without a bottom: *plant mint in a bottomless bucket sunk into the ground.* ■ very deep: *the cold dark sea in whose bottomless depths monsters swam.* ■ (of a supply of money or other resources) inexhaustible: *I don't have a bottomless pit of money.*
2 naked below the waist.

bot·tom line ▶ n. informal the final total of an account, balance sheet, or other financial document: figurative *the determination of Japanese companies to ignore the bottom line.* ■ the underlying or ultimate outcome or criterion: *the bottom line is I'm still married to Denny* | *the bottom line is, does it work?*

bot·tom round ▶ n. a steak or other cut from the outer part of a round of beef.

bot·tom·ry /'bätəmrē/ ▶ n. dated a system of merchant insurance in which a ship is used as security against a loan to finance a voyage, the lender losing the investment if the ship sinks.
– ORIGIN late 16th cent.: from **BOTTOM** (in the sense 'ship') + **-RY**, influenced by Dutch *bodemerij*.

bot·tom-up ▶ adj. proceeding from the bottom of a hierarchy upward or from the beginning of a process forward.

bot·u·lin /'bäCHəlin/ ▶ n. the bacterial toxin involved in botulism.

bot·u·li·num /ˌbäCHə'līnəm/ ▶ n. a rod-shaped bacterium that produces botulin. ● *Clostridium botulinum*.

bot·u·li·num tox·in /ˌbäCHə'līnəm/ (also **botulinus toxin** /-'līnəs/) ▶ n. another term for **BOTULIN**.

bot·u·lism /'bäCHəˌlizəm/ ▶ n. food poisoning caused by a bacterium (botulinum) growing on improperly sterilized canned meats and other preserved foods.
– ORIGIN late 19th cent.: from German *Botulismus*, originally 'sausage poisoning,' from Latin *botulus* 'sausage.'

bou·bou /'bo͞oˌbo͞o/ ▶ n. **1** (also **boubou shrike**) an African bush shrike with the upper parts mainly blackish in color. It is noted for the duet of bell-like calls produced by the male and female together. ● Genus *Laniarius*, family Laniidae: several species, in particular the **tropical boubou** (*L. aethiopicus*) and the **southern boubou** (*L. ferrugineus*).
2 a long, colorful, loose-fitting garment worn by both sexes in parts of Africa.
– ORIGIN French, from Malinke *bubu*.

bou·chée /bo͞o'SHā/ ▶ n. a small pastry with a sweet or savory filling.

Bou·cher /bo͞o'SHā/, François (1703–70), French painter and decorative artist. One of the foremost artists of the rococo style in France, his works include *The Rising of the Sun* (1753) and *Summer Pastoral* (1749).

bou·clé /ˌbo͞o'klā/ ▶ n. [often as modifier] yarn with a looped or curled ply, or fabric woven from this yarn: *a bouclé sweater.*
– ORIGIN late 19th cent.: French, literally 'buckled, curled.'

Bou·dic·ca /bo͞o'dikə/ (died AD 62), a queen of the Britons; ruler of the Iceni tribe in eastern England; also known as **Boadicea**. She led her forces in revolt against the Romans and sacked Colchester, St. Albans, and London before being defeated by the Roman governor, **Suetonius Paulinus**.

bou·din /bo͞o'dan, -'daN/ ▶ n. (pl. pronunc. **same**) a French type of blood sausage. ■ a spicy sausage used esp. in Louisiana cuisine.
– ORIGIN early 19th cent.: French, literally 'blood sausage.'

bou·doir /'bo͞oˌdwär/ ▶ n. chiefly historical or humorous a woman's bedroom or private room.
– ORIGIN late 18th cent.: French, literally 'sulking place.'

bouf·fant /bo͞o'fänt/ ▶ adj. [attrib.] (of a person's hair) styled so as to puff out in a rounded shape: *a blonde lady with bouffant hair.*
▶ n. a bouffant hairstyle.
– ORIGIN early 19th cent.: from French, literally 'swelling,' present participle of *bouffer*.

Bou·gain·ville[1] /'bo͞ogənˌvil, 'bō-/ a volcanic island in the South Pacific Ocean, the largest of the Solomon Islands.
– ORIGIN named after Louis de *Bougainville* (see **BOUGAINVILLE**[2]), who visited it in 1768.

Bou·gain·ville[2] /ˌbo͞ogaN'vēl/, Louis Antoine de (1729–1811), French explorer. He led the first French circumnavigation of the globe 1766–69, visiting many of the islands of the South Pacific and compiling an invaluable scientific record of his findings.

bou·gain·vil·le·a /ˌbo͞ogən'vilyə, -'vēə, ˌbō-/ (also **bougainvillaea**) ▶ n. an ornamental climbing plant that is widely cultivated in the tropics. The insignificant flowers are surrounded by brightly colored papery bracts that persist on the plant

for a long time. ● Genus *Bougainvillea*, family Nyctaginaceae.
–ORIGIN named after Louis Antoine de *Bougainville* (see **BOUGAINVILLE[2]**).

bough /bou/ ▶ **n.** a main branch of a tree: *apple boughs laden with blossom.*
–ORIGIN Old English *bōg, bōh* 'bough or shoulder,' of Germanic origin; related to Dutch *boeg* 'shoulders or ship's bow,' German *Bug* 'ship's bow' and 'horse's hock or shoulder,' also to **BOW[3]**.

bought /bôt/ past and past participle of **BUY**.

bought·en /'bôtn/ ▶ **adj.** dialect bought rather than homemade: *wooden boxes full of boughten cookies | her first store-boughten doll.*
–ORIGIN late 18th cent.: dialect variant of **BOUGHT**.

bou·gie /'bo͞ojē, -ZHē/ ▶ **n.** (pl. **bougies**) Medicine a thin, flexible surgical instrument for exploring or dilating a passage of the body.
–ORIGIN mid 18th cent.: from French, literally 'wax candle,' from Arabic *Bijāya*, the name of an Algerian town that traded in wax.

bouil·la·baisse /,bo͞o(l)yə'bās, 'bo͞o(l)yə,bās/ ▶ **n.** a rich, spicy stew or soup made with various kinds of fish, originally from Provence.
–ORIGIN French, from modern Provençal *bouiabaisso* 'boil down.'

bouil·lon /'bo͝olyən, -yän/ ▶ **n.** a broth made by stewing meat, fish, or vegetables in water.
–ORIGIN mid 17th cent.: French, literally 'liquid in which something has boiled.'

bouil·lon cube ▶ **n.** a cube of concentrated stock, used for making bouillon.

Boul·der /'bōldər/ a city in north central Colorado, northwest of Denver, home to the University of Colorado; pop. 94,171 (est. 2008).

boul·der /'bōldər/ ▶ **n.** a large rock, typically one that has been worn smooth by erosion.
–DERIVATIVES **boul·der·y adj.**
–ORIGIN late Middle English: shortened from earlier *boulderstone*, of Scandinavian origin.

boul·der clay ▶ **n.** Brit. another term for **TILL[4]**.

boul·der·ing /'bōldəriNG/ ▶ **n.** Mountaineering climbing on large boulders, either for practice or as a sport in its own right.

boule[1] /bo͞ol/ ▶ **n.** (pl. **boules** pronounced same) a metal ball used in the French game of **boules**, a form of lawn bowling played on rough ground.
–ORIGIN 1920s (originally denoting a form of roulette): French, literally 'bowl.'

bou·le[2] /bo͞o'lā, 'bo͞olē/ ▶ **n.** a legislative body of ancient or modern Greece.
–ORIGIN from Greek *boulē* 'senate.'

boul·e·vard /'bo͝olə,värd/ (abbr.: **blvd.**) ▶ **n.** a wide street in a town or city, typically one lined with trees: [in names] *Sunset Boulevard.* ■ another term for **BOULEVARD STRIP**.
–ORIGIN mid 18th cent.: French, literally 'a rampart' (later 'a promenade on the site of one'), from German *Bollwerk* (see **BULWARK**).

bou·le·var·dier /,bo͝oləvär'di(ə)r/ ▶ **n.** a wealthy, fashionable socialite.
–ORIGIN late 19th cent.: from French, originally in the sense 'person who frequents boulevards.'

boul·e·vard strip ▶ **n.** a grassy strip between a road and a sidewalk.

bou·le·ver·se·ment /,bo͞oləversə'mäN/ ▶ **n.** an inversion, esp. a violent one; an upset or upheaval.
–ORIGIN from French *bouleverser* 'overturn.'

Bou·lez /bo͞o'lez/, Pierre (1925–), French composer and conductor. He was principal conductor with the New York Philharmonic Orchestra 1971–78.

boulle /bo͞ol/ ▶ **n.** Brit. variant spelling of **BUHL**.

bounce /bouns/ ▶ **v.** [no obj.] **1** (of an object, esp. a ball) move quickly up, back, or away from a surface after hitting it; rebound (once or repeatedly): *the ball **bounced off** the rim | the ball bounced away, and he chased it* | [with obj.] *he was bouncing the ball against the wall.* ■ (of light, sound, or an electronic signal) come into contact with an object or surface and be reflected: *short sound waves **bounce off** even small objects.* ■ (also **bounce back**) (of an e-mail) be returned to its sender after failing to reach its destination: *I tried to e-mail him, but the message bounced.* ■ (**bounce back**) recover well after a setback: *he was admired for his ability to bounce back from injury.* ■ Baseball hit a ball that bounces before reaching a fielder: *bouncing out with the bases loaded* | [with obj.] *bounced a grounder to third.*
2 (of a person) jump repeatedly up and down, typically on something springy: *bouncing up and down on the mattress.* ■ (of a thing) move up and down while remaining essentially in the same position: *the gangplank bounced under his confident step.* ■ [with obj.] cause (a child) to move lightly up and down on one's knee as a game: *I remember how you used to bounce me on your knee.* ■ [often with adv. or prep. phrase showing direction] move in an energetic or happy manner: *Linda bounced in through the open front door.* ■ [often with adv. or prep. phrase showing direction] (of a vehicle) move jerkily along a bumpy surface: *the car bounced down the narrow track.*
3 informal (of a check) be returned by a bank when there are insufficient funds to meet it: *my rent check bounced.* ■ [with obj.] informal write (a check) on insufficient funds: *I've never bounced a check.*
4 [with obj.] informal eject (a troublemaker) forcibly from a nightclub or similar establishment. ■ dismiss (someone) from a job: *those who put in a dismal performance will be **bounced from** the tour.*
▶ **n. 1** a rebound of a ball or other object: *a bad bounce caused the ball to get away from the second baseman.* ■ the power of rebounding.
2 an act of jumping or an instance of being moved up and down: *every bounce of the truck brought them into fresh contact | a bounce on your knee or a cuddle and pat on the back.* ■ a sudden rise in the level of something: *economists agree that there could be a bounce in prices next year.* ■ exuberant self-confidence: *the bounce was now back in Jenny's step.* ■ health and body in the hair: *use conditioner to help hair regain its bounce.*
–PHRASES **bounce an idea off someone** informal share an idea with another person in order to get feedback on it. **be bouncing off the walls** informal be full of nervous excitement or agitation.
–ORIGIN Middle English *bunsen* 'beat, thump.'

bounce flash ▶ **n.** a device for giving reflected photographic flashlight. ■ flashlight reflected in this way.

bounc·er /'bounsər/ ▶ **n. 1** a person employed by a nightclub or similar establishment to prevent troublemakers from entering or to eject them from the premises.
2 Baseball a batted ball that bounces before being fielded.

bounc·ing /'bounsiNG/ ▶ **adj.** (of a ball) rebounding up and down: *an awkwardly bouncing ball.* ■ (of a baby) vigorous and healthy: *Lisa gave birth to a bouncing baby boy.* ■ lively and confident: *by the next day she was her usual bouncing, energetic self.*

bounc·ing Bet ▶ **n.** another term for **SOAPWORT**.

bounc·y /'bounsē/ ▶ **adj.** (**bouncier, bounciest**) bouncing well: *a bouncy ball.* ■ resilient; springy: *that bouncy artificial grass.* ■ (of a person) confident and lively: *she was still the girl he remembered, bouncy and full of life.* ■ (of music) having a jaunty rhythm: *the bouncy cheerfulness of polka.* ■ (of the hair) in good condition; having bounce: *hair with shiny, bouncy curls.*
–DERIVATIVES **bounc·i·ly** /-səlē/ **adv.**, **bounc·i·ness n.**

bound[1] /bound/ ▶ **v.** [no obj.] walk or run with leaping strides: *Louis came **bounding down** the stairs | the dog **bounded up to** him.* ■ (of an object, typically a round one) rebound from a surface: *bullets **bounded off** the veranda.*
▶ **n.** a leaping movement upward: *I went up the steps in two effortless bounds.*
–ORIGIN early 16th cent. (as a noun): from French *bond* (noun), *bondir* (verb) 'resound,' later 'rebound,' from late Latin *bombitare*, from Latin *bombus* 'humming.'

bound[2] ▶ **n.** (often **bounds**) a territorial limit; a boundary: *the ancient bounds of the forest.* ■ a limitation or restriction on feeling or action: *it is not **beyond the bounds of possibility** that the issue could arise again | enthusiasm to join the union **knew no bounds**.* ■ technical a limiting value.
▶ **v.** [with obj.] (usu. **be bounded**) form the boundary of; enclose: *the ground was bounded by a main road on one side and a meadow on the other.* ■ place within certain limits; restrict: *freedom of action is bounded by law.*
–PHRASES **in bounds** Sports inside the regular playing area. **out of bounds** Sports outside the regular playing area: *he hit his third shot out of bounds at the 17th.* ■ (of a place) outside the limits of where one is permitted to be: *his kitchen was **out of bounds** to me at mealtimes.* ■ beyond what is acceptable: *Paul felt that this conversation was getting out of bounds.*
–ORIGIN Middle English (in the senses 'landmark' and 'borderland'): from Old French *bodne*, from medieval Latin *bodina*, earlier *butina*, of unknown ultimate origin.

bound[3] ▶ **adj.** heading toward somewhere: *trains **bound for** Chicago* | [in combination] *the three moon-bound astronauts.* ■ destined or likely to have a specified experience: *they were **bound for** disaster.*
–ORIGIN Middle English *boun* (in the sense 'ready, dressed'), from Old Norse *búinn*, past participle of *búa* 'get ready'; the final *-d* is euphonic, or influenced by **BOUND[4]**.

bound[4] past and past participle of **BIND**.
▶ **adj. 1** [in combination] restricted or confined to a specified place: *his job kept him city-bound.* ■ prevented from operating normally by the specified conditions: *blizzard-bound Boston.*
2 [with infinitive] certain to do or have something: *there is bound to be a change of plan.* ■ obliged by law, circumstances, or duty to do something: *I'm bound to do what I can to help Sam | I'm **bound to** say that I'm not sure.*
3 [in combination] (of a book) having a specified binding: *fine leather-bound books.*
4 Linguistics (of a morpheme) unable to occur alone, e.g., *dis-* in *dismount*.
5 constipated.
–PHRASES **bound up in** focusing on, to the exclusion of all else: *she was too bound up in her own misery to care that other people were hurt.* **bound up with** (or **in**) closely connected with or related to: *democracy is bound up with a measure of economic and social equality.*

bound·a·ry /'bound(ə)rē/ ▶ **n.** (pl. **boundaries**) a line that marks the limits of an area; a dividing line: *the eastern boundary of the wilderness | the boundary between the US and Canada* | [as modifier] *a boundary wall.* ■ (often **boundaries**) a limit of a subject or sphere of activity: *a community without class or political boundaries.*
–ORIGIN early 17th cent.: variant of dialect *bounder*, from **BOUND[2]** + **-ER[1]**, perhaps on the pattern of *limitary*.

bound·a·ry con·di·tion ▶ **n.** Mathematics a condition that is required to be satisfied at all or part of the boundary of a region in which a set of differential equations is to be solved.

bound·a·ry lay·er ▶ **n.** a layer of more or less stationary fluid (such as water or air) immediately surrounding an immersed object in relative motion with the fluid.

Bound·a·ry Waters a region in northeast Minnesota, along the Ontario border, known as a canoeing wilderness.

bound·en /'boundən/ archaic past participle of **BIND**.
–PHRASES **one's bounden duty** a responsibility regarded as obligatory: *the Pastor believed that it was his bounden duty to keep them on the right path.*

bound·er /'boundər/ ▶ **n.** informal, dated, chiefly Brit. a dishonorable man: *he is nothing but a fortune-seeking bounder.*

bound form ▶ **n.** a morpheme that occurs only as an element of a compound word and cannot stand on its own, such as *-ing* or *-er*.

bound·less /'boundlis/ ▶ **adj.** unlimited; immense: *enthusiasts who devote boundless energy to their hobby.*
–DERIVATIVES **bound·less·ly adv.** [as submodifier] *the land was boundlessly fertile*, **bound·less·ness n.**

boun·te·ous /'bountēəs/ ▶ **adj.** archaic generously given or giving; bountiful: *the earth yields a bounteous harvest.*
–DERIVATIVES **boun·te·ous·ly adv.**, **boun·te·ous·ness n.**
–ORIGIN late Middle English: from Old French *bontif, -ive* 'benevolent' (from *bonte* 'bounty'), on the pattern of *plenteous*.

Boun·ti·ful /'bountəfəl/ a city in northern Utah, north of Salt Lake City; pop. 44,473 (est. 2008).

boun·ti·ful /'bountəfəl/ ▶ **adj.** large in quantity; abundant: *the ocean provided a bountiful supply of fresh food.* ■ giving generously: *he was exceedingly bountiful to persons in distress.*
–DERIVATIVES **boun·ti·ful·ly adv.**
–ORIGIN early 16th cent.: from **BOUNTY** + **-FUL**.

Boun·ty /'bountē/ a ship of the British navy on which in 1789 part of the crew, led by Fletcher Christian, mutinied against their commander, William Bligh, and set him adrift in an open boat with eighteen crewmen.

boun·ty /'bountē/ ▶ **n.** (pl. **bounties**) **1** generosity; liberality: figurative *for millennia the people along the Nile have depended entirely on its bounty.* ■ abundance; plenty: *we ask that growers share their bounty with others.*
2 a monetary gift or reward, typically given by a government, in particular: ■ a sum paid for killing or capturing a person or animal: *there was an increased **bounty on his head**.* ■ historical a sum paid to encourage trade: *bounties were paid to colonial producers of indigo dye.* ■ a sum paid to army or navy recruits upon enlistment. ■ literary something given or occurring in generous amounts: *the bounties of nature.*
–ORIGIN Middle English (denoting goodness or generosity): from Old French *bonte* 'goodness,'

from Latin *bonitas*, from *bonus* 'good.' The sense 'monetary reward' dates from the early 18th cent.

boun·ty hunt·er ▶ n. one who pursues a criminal or seeks an achievement for the sake of the reward.

b

bou·quet /bō'kā, bōō-/ ▶ n. **1** an attractively arranged bunch of flowers, esp. one presented as a gift or carried at a ceremony. ■ an expression of approval; a compliment: *we will happily publish the bouquets*.
2 a characteristic scent, esp. that of a wine or perfume: *the aperitif has a faint bouquet of almonds* | *champagnes have a delicacy of bouquet*.
– ORIGIN early 18th cent.: from French (earlier 'clump of trees'), from a dialect variant of Old French *bos* 'wood.' Sense 2 dates from the mid 19th cent.

bou·quet gar·ni /bō'kā gär'nē, bōō-/ ▶ n. (pl. **bouquets garnis** pronunc. **same**) a bunch of herbs, typically encased in a cheesecloth bag, used for flavoring a stew or soup.
– ORIGIN mid 19th cent.: French, literally 'garnished bouquet.'

Bour·bon[1] /'bŏŏrbən/ the surname of a branch of the royal family of France. The Bourbons ruled France from 1589, when Henry IV succeeded to the throne, until the monarchy was overthrown in 1848, and reached the peak of their power under Louis XIV in the late 17th century. Members of this family have also been kings of Spain (1700–1931 and since 1975).

Bour·bon[2] ▶ n. **1** a reactionary.
2 (also **Bourbon rose**) a rose of a variety that flowers over a long period and has a rich scent. It arose as a natural hybrid on the island of Réunion (formerly Île de Bourbon) and was introduced into Europe in the early 19th century. ● *Rosa* × borboniana, a hybrid of *Rosa chinensis* and *R. damascena*, family Rosaceae.
– ORIGIN mid 19th cent. (sense 1): from the name of the BOURBON[1] family. Sense 2 dates from the 1930s.

bour·bon /'bərbən/ ▶ n. a straight whiskey distilled from a mash having at least 51 percent corn in addition to malt and rye.
– ORIGIN mid 19th cent.: named after *Bourbon* County, Kentucky, where it was first made.

Bour·bon Coun·ty a county in north central Kentucky, in the Bluegrass region, birthplace of the American whiskey type.

Bour·bon·nais /ˌbŏŏrbə'nā/ a former duchy and province in central France; chief town, Moulins.

bour·don /'bŏŏrdn/ ▶ n. **1** Music a low-pitched stop in an organ or harmonium, typically a sixteen-foot stopped diapason.
2 the drone pipe of a bagpipe.
– ORIGIN Middle English (in the sense 'drone of a bagpipe'): from Old French, 'drone,' of imitative origin.

bourg /bŏŏrg/ ▶ n. historical a town or village under the shadow of a castle. ■ a French market town.
– ORIGIN French, from late Latin *burgus* 'castle' (in medieval Latin 'fortified town'), ultimately of Germanic origin and related to BOROUGH.

bour·geois /bŏŏr'ZHwä, 'bŏŏrZHwä/ ▶ adj. of or characteristic of the middle class, typically with reference to its perceived materialistic values or conventional attitudes: *a rich, bored, bourgeois family* | *these views will shock the bourgeois critics*. ■ (in Marxist contexts) upholding the interests of capitalism; not communist: *bourgeois society took for granted the sanctity of property*.
▶ n. (pl. **same**) a bourgeois person: *a self-confessed and proud bourgeois*.
– ORIGIN mid 16th cent.: from French BOURG. Compare with BURGESS.

bour·geoise /bŏŏr'ZHwäz, 'bŏŏrZHwäz/ ▶ adj. of or characteristic of female members of the bourgeoisie.
▶ n. a female member of the bourgeoisie.
– ORIGIN late 18th cent.: French, feminine of *bourgeois* 'citizen' (see BOURGEOIS).

bour·geoi·sie /ˌbŏŏrZHwä'zē/ ▶ n. (usu. **the bourgeoisie**) the middle class, typically with reference to its perceived materialistic values or conventional attitudes. ■ (in Marxist contexts) the capitalist class who own most of society's wealth and means of production.
– ORIGIN early 18th cent.: French, from BOURGEOIS.

Bour·gogne /bŏŏr'gôn(yə)/ French name for BURGUNDY.

Bour·gui·ba /bŏŏr'gēbə/, Habib ibn Ali (1903–2000), Tunisian nationalist and statesman. He was the first president of independent Tunisia 1957–87.

Bourke-White /'bərk ˌ(h)wīt/, Margaret (1906–71), US photojournalist. During World War II, she was the first female photographer with the US armed forces. At the end of the war, she accompanied the Allied forces when they entered the Nazi concentration camps. Later assignments included the Korean War (1950–53) and work in India and South Africa.

bourn[1] /bôrn, bŏŏrn/ (also **bourne**) ▶ n. dialect a small stream, esp. one that flows intermittently or seasonally.
– ORIGIN Middle English: southern English variant of BURN[2].

bourn[2] (also **bourne**) ▶ n. literary **1** a goal; a destination.
2 a limit; a boundary.
– ORIGIN early 16th cent. (denoting a boundary of a field): from French *borne*, from Old French *bodne* (see BOUND[2]).

Bourne·mouth /'bôrnməTH, 'bŏŏrn-/ a resort on the southern coast of England; pop. 159,500 (est. 2009).

bour·rée /bŏŏ'rā/ ▶ n. a lively French dance like a gavotte. ■ Ballet a series of very fast little steps, with the feet close together, typically performed on pointe and giving the impression that the dancer is gliding over the floor.
▶ v. [no obj.] perform a bourrée.
– ORIGIN late 17th cent.: French, literally 'faggot of twigs' (the dance being performed around a fire made with such twigs).

bourse /bŏŏrs/ ▶ n. a stock market in a non-English-speaking country, esp. France. ■ (**Bourse**) the Paris stock exchange.
– ORIGIN mid 16th cent. (as *burse*, the usual form until the mid 19th cent.): from French, literally 'purse,' via medieval Latin from Greek *bursa* 'leather.'

Bour·sin /bŏŏr'saN/ ▶ n. trademark a kind of soft cheese from France.
– ORIGIN French.

bou·stro·phe·don /ˌbōōstrə'fēdn/ ▶ adj. & adv. (of written words) from right to left and from left to right in alternate lines.
– ORIGIN early 17th cent.: from Greek, literally 'as an ox turns in plowing,' from *bous* 'ox' + *-strophos* 'turning.'

bout /bout/ ▶ n. **1** a short period of intense activity of a specified kind: *occasional bouts of strenuous exercise* | *a drinking bout*. ■ an attack of illness or strong emotion of a specified kind: *a severe bout of flu*. ■ a wrestling or boxing match.
2 a curve in the side of a violin, guitar, or other musical instrument.
– ORIGIN mid 16th cent. (denoting a curve or circuit, hence later a "turn" of activity): from dialect *bought* 'bend, loop'; probably of Low German origin.

bou·tade /bōō'täd/ ▶ n. formal a sudden outburst or outbreak.
– ORIGIN early 17th cent.: French, from *bouter* 'to thrust.'

bou·tique /bōō'tēk/ ▶ n. **1** a small store selling fashionable clothes or accessories.
2 a business that serves a sophisticated or specialized clientele: *a small investment boutique* | [as modifier] *a boutique film*.
– DERIVATIVES **bou·tique·y** adj.
– ORIGIN mid 18th cent.: French, literally 'small shop,' via Latin from Greek *apothēkē* 'storehouse.' Compare with BODEGA.

bou·tique brew·er·y ▶ n. another term for MICROBREWERY.

bou·tique ho·tel ▶ n. a small stylish hotel, typically one situated in a fashionable urban location.

bou·ton /bōō'tôn/ ▶ n. Anatomy an enlarged part of a nerve fiber or cell, esp. an axon, where it forms a synapse with another nerve.
– ORIGIN mid 20th cent.: from French, literally 'button.'

bou·ton·nière /ˌbōōtn'i(ə)r/ ▶ n. a spray of flowers worn in a buttonhole.
– ORIGIN late 19th cent.: French, 'buttonhole,' from *bouton* 'button.'

Bou·tros-Gha·li, Boutros (1922–), Egyptian diplomat and politician; secretary general of the United Nations 1992–97.

bou·vier /bōō'vyā/ ▶ n. a large, powerful dog of a rough-coated breed originating in Belgium.
– ORIGIN French 'cowherd.'

bou·zou·ki /bōō'zōōkē/ ▶ n. (pl. **bouzoukis** or **bouzoukia** /-kyä/) a long-necked Greek instrument similar to the mandolin.
– ORIGIN 1950s: from modern Greek *mpouzouki*, possibly related to Turkish *bozuk* 'spoiled' (with reference to roughly made instruments).

bo·vid /'bōvid/ ▶ n. Zoology a mammal of the cattle family (Bovidae).
– ORIGIN late 19th cent.: from modern Latin *Bovidae*, from *bos, bov-* 'ox.'

bo·vine /'bōvīn, -vēn/ ▶ adj. of, relating to, or affecting cattle: *bovine tuberculosis* | *bovine tissue*. ■ (of a person) slow-moving and dull-witted: *amiable bovine faces*.
▶ n. an animal of the cattle group, which also includes buffaloes and bisons.
– DERIVATIVES **bo·vine·ly** adv.
– ORIGIN early 19th cent.: from late Latin *bovinus*, from Latin *bos, bov-* 'ox.'

bo·vine growth hor·mone (abbr.: **BGH**) ▶ n. a natural hormone in cattle that helps regulate growth and milk production and that may be produced artificially and given to dairy cattle to increase the yield of milk. Also called BOVINE SOMATOTROPIN.

bo·vine so·mat·o·tro·pin /sə,matə'trōpin/ (abbr.: **BST**) ▶ n. another term for BOVINE GROWTH HORMONE.

bo·vine spon·gi·form en·ceph·a·lop·a·thy ▶ n. see BSE.

Bow /bō/, Clara (1905–65), US actress. One of the most popular stars and sex symbols of the 1920s, she was known as the "It Girl." Her silent movies include *It* (1927) and *The Wild Party* (1929).

bow[1] /bō/ ▶ n. **1** a knot tied with two loops and two loose ends, used esp. for tying shoelaces and decorative ribbons: *a girl with long hair tied back in a bow*. ■ a decorative ribbon tied in such a knot.
2 a weapon for shooting arrows, typically made of a curved piece of wood whose ends are joined by a taut string. ■ a bowman.
3 a long, partially curved rod with horsehair stretched along its length, used for playing the violin and other stringed instruments. ■ a single passage of such a rod over the strings.
4 a thing that is bent or curved in shape, in particular: ■ a curved stroke forming part of a letter (e.g., *b, p*). ■ a metal ring forming the handle of a key or pair of scissors. ■ a side piece or lens frame of a pair of glasses.
▶ v. [with obj.] **1** play (a stringed instrument or music) using a bow: *the techniques by which the pieces were bowed*.
2 bend into the shape of a bow: *the sides of the image are squeezed in or bowed out*.
– ORIGIN Old English *boga* 'bend, bow, arch,' of Germanic origin; related to Dutch *boog* and German *Bogen*, also to BOW[2].

bow[2] /bou/ ▶ v. [no obj.] **1** bend the head or upper part of the body as a sign of respect, greeting, or shame: *he turned and bowed to his father* | *they refused to **bow down before the king*** | (as adj. **bowed**) *councilors stood **with heads bowed*** | [with obj.] *she knelt and bowed her head*. ■ [with obj.] express (thanks, agreement, or other sentiments) by bending one's head respectfully: *he looked at Hector before bowing grave thanks*. ■ [no obj.] bend the body in order to see or concentrate: [as adj.] *my mother sat bowed over a library book*.
2 bend with age or under pressure: *the grass bowed down before the wind* | [with obj.] *the vines were bowed down with flowers*. ■ submit to pressure or to someone's demands: *the mayor **bowed to public opinion***.
3 (of a movie or product) be premiered or launched: *the trailer bowed in theaters nationwide on December 23*.
▶ n. **1** an act of bending the head or upper body as a sign of respect or greeting: *the man gave a little bow*.
2 the premiere or launch of a movie or product: *the new big screen will make its bow at the game on Saturday* .
– PHRASES **bow and scrape** behave in an obsequious way to someone in authority. **make one's bow** make one's first formal appearance in a particular role: *he made his bow as a science fiction writer*. **take a bow** (of a performer) acknowledge applause after a performance by bowing: figurative *the aides do the grind work while the boss takes the bows*.
– PHRASAL VERBS **bow out** withdraw or retire from an activity, role, or commitment: *many artists are forced to **bow out of the profession** at a relatively early age*.
– ORIGIN Old English *būgan* 'bend, stoop,' of Germanic origin; related to German *biegen*, also to BOW[1].

bow[3] /bou/ (also **bows**) ▶ n. the front end of a ship: *water sprayed high over her bows* | *stand in the bow*.
– PHRASES **on the bow** Nautical within 45° of the point directly ahead. **a (warning) shot across the bows** a statement or gesture intended to frighten someone into changing their course of action: *supporters are firing a warning shot across the President's bows*.
– ORIGIN late Middle English: from Low German *boog*, Dutch *boeg* 'shoulder or ship's bow'; related to BOUGH.

bow com·pass /bō/ (also **bow compasses**) ▶ n. a compass with jointed legs.

bowd·ler·ize /'bōdlə,rīz, 'boud-/ ▶ v. [with obj.] remove material that is considered improper or offensive from (a text or account), esp. with the

result that it becomes weaker or less effective: (as adj. **bowdlerized**) *a bowdlerized version of the story.*
– DERIVATIVES **bowd·ler·ism** /-ˌrizəm/ **n.**, **bowd·ler·i·za·tion** /ˌbōdlərəˈzāSHən, ˌboud-/ **n.**
– ORIGIN mid 19th cent.: from the name of Dr. Thomas *Bowdler* (1754–1825), who published an expurgated edition of Shakespeare in 1818, + **-IZE**.

bow ech·o /bō/ ▶ **n.** Meteorology a bow-shaped radar signature associated with fast-moving storm systems accompanied by damaging winds.

bow·el /ˈbou(ə)l/ (also **bowels**) ▶ **n.** the part of the alimentary canal below the stomach; the intestine. ■ (**the bowels of ——**) the parts deep inside something large: *the train picks up speed for its final plunge into the subterranean bowels of Manhattan.*
– ORIGIN Middle English: from Old French *bouel*, from Latin *botellus*, diminutive of *botulus* 'sausage.'

Bow·ell /ˈbōəl/, Sir Mackenzie (1823–1917), Canadian Conservative statesman; prime minister 1894–96.

bow·el move·ment ▶ **n.** an act of defecation. ■ the feces discharged in an act of defecation.

Bow·en /ˈbōən/, Elizabeth (Dorothea Cole) (1899–1973), British novelist and short-story writer, born in Ireland. Notable works: *The Death of the Heart* (1938) and *The Heat of the Day* (1949).

bow·er[1] /ˈbou(-ə)r/ ▶ **n.** a pleasant shady place under trees or climbing plants in a garden or wood. ■ literary a summerhouse or country cottage. ■ literary a lady's private room or bedroom.
▶ **v.** [with obj.] literary shade or enclose (a place or person): (as adj. **bowered**) *the bowered pathways into the tangle of vines.*
– ORIGIN Old English *būr* 'dwelling, inner room,' of Germanic origin; related to German *Bauer* 'birdcage.'

bow·er[2] (also **bower anchor**) ▶ **n.** each of two anchors carried at a ship's bow.
– ORIGIN late 15th cent.: from **BOW**[3] + **-ER**[1].

bow·er·bird /ˈbou(-ə)rˌbərd/ ▶ **n.** a strong-billed Australasian bird, noted for the male's habit of constructing a bower adorned with feathers, shells, and other objects to attract the female. ● Family Ptilonorhynchidae: several genera and species, esp. the **satin bowerbird** (*Ptilonorhynchus violaceus*), which decorates the bower with blue-colored articles.

Bow·er·y /ˈbou(-ə)rē/ a street and district of lower Manhattan in New York City associated, esp. formerly, with flophouses and rowdies.
– ORIGIN mid 17th cent.: built on the site of governor Peter Stuyvesant's *bowery* 'farm,' from Dutch *bouwerij*.

bow·fin /ˈbōˌfin/ ▶ **n.** a predatory American freshwater fish with a large blunt head and a long dorsal fin. It is able to survive for long periods out of water. ● *Amia calva*, the only living member of the family Amiidae.
– ORIGIN late 19th cent.: from **BOW**[1] + **FIN**.

bow-front·ed /bō/ ▶ **adj.** (of furniture) having a convexly curved front.
– DERIVATIVES **bow front n. & adj.**

bow·head /ˈbōˌhed/ (also **bowhead whale**) ▶ **n.** a black Arctic right whale that feeds by skimming the surface for plankton. Also called **GREENLAND RIGHT WHALE**. ● *Balaena mysticetus*, family Balaenidae.
– ORIGIN late 19th cent.: from **BOW**[1] + **HEAD**.

bow·hunt·ing /ˈbōˌhəntiNG/ ▶ **n.** the practice of hunting animals with a bow rather than a gun.
– DERIVATIVES **bow·hunt·er** /-ˌhəntər/ **n.**

Bow·ie[1] /ˈbōē/ a town in west central Maryland, northeast of Washington, DC; pop. 52,544 (est. 2008).

Bow·ie[2] /ˈbōē, ˈbo͞oē/, Jim (1799–1836), US frontiersman; full name *James Bowie*. The Bowie knife was designed either by him or by his brother Rezin. One of the leaders among the US settlers who opposed Mexican rule in Texas, he shared command of the garrison that resisted the Mexican attack on the Alamo. He died during this battle.

bow·ie knife /ˈbo͞oē, ˈbōē/ ▶ **n.** a long knife with a blade double-edged at the point.
– ORIGIN mid 19th cent.: named after Jim *Bowie* or his brother (see **BOWIE**[2]).

bow·knot /ˈbōˌnät/ ▶ **n.** a double-looped knot in a ribbon, tie, or other fastening.

bowl[1] /bōl/ ▶ **n. 1** a round, deep dish or basin used for food or liquid: *a mixing bowl* | *a sugar bowl.* ■ the contents of such a container: *huge bowls of steaming spaghetti.* ■ [usu. in names] a decorative round dish awarded as a prize in a competition: *the McGeorge Rose Bowl.* ■ a rounded, concave part of an object: *a toilet bowl* | *the bowl of a spoon.* ■ Geography a natural basin.
2 [in names] a stadium for sporting or musical events: *the Hollywood Bowl.* ■ a football game played after the regular season between leading or all-star teams: [as modifier] *their last four bowl games.*
– DERIVATIVES **bowl·ful** /-ˌfo͝ol/ **n.**
– ORIGIN Old English *bolle, bolla*, of Germanic origin; related to Dutch *bol* 'round object,' also to **BOLL**.

bowl[2] ▶ **n.** a ball made slightly asymmetrical so that it runs on a curved course, used in the game of lawn bowling.
▶ **v. 1** [with obj.] roll (a ball or hoop) along the ground: *she snatched her hat off and bowled it ahead of her like a hoop.*
2 [no obj.] play the game of bowling: *I usually bowl Tuesday nights.* ■ achieve (a certain score) in tenpin bowling: *she bowled a 162 high game.*
3 [with obj.] Cricket (of a bowler) propel (the ball) with a straight arm towards the batsman, typically in such a way that the ball bounces once: *Lillee bowled another bouncer* | [no obj.] *Sobers bowled to Willis.* ■ (also **bowl someone out**) dismiss (a batsman) by knocking down the wicket with the ball that one has bowled: *Stewart was bowled for 33 in the one-day international.*
4 [no obj.] move rapidly and smoothly in a specified direction: *they bowled along the country roads.*
– PHRASAL VERBS **bowl someone over** knock someone down. ■ informal completely overwhelm or astonish someone, for example by one's good qualities or looks: *when he met Angela, he was just bowled over by her.*
– ORIGIN late Middle English (in the general sense 'ball'): from Old French *boule*, from Latin *bulla* 'bubble.'

bowl·der ▶ **n.** archaic spelling of **BOULDER**.

bow legs /bō/ ▶ **plural n.** legs that curve outward at the knee; bandy legs.
– DERIVATIVES **bow-leg·ged** /ˈbō ˌlegid/ **adj.**

bowl·er[1] /ˈbōlər/ ▶ **n. 1** a player at tenpin bowling, lawn bowling, or skittles.
2 Cricket a member of the fielding side who bowls or is bowling.

bowl·er[2] (also **bowler hat**) ▶ **n.** a man's hard felt hat with a round dome-shaped crown.
– ORIGIN mid 19th cent.: named after William *Bowler*, the English hatter who designed it in 1850.

Bowles /bōlz/, Paul (Frederick) (1910–99), US writer and composer. In the 1930s, he studied music in Paris and worked as a music critic and composer. His novels, which include *The Sheltering Sky* (1949), *Let It Come Down* (1952), and *The Spider's House* (1966), typically concern Westerners in the Arab world.

bowl hair·cut ▶ **n.** a haircut done by or as if by inverting a bowl on a person's head and cutting off the hair left exposed.

bow·line /ˈbōlīn/ ▶ **n. 1** a rope attached to the weather leech of a square sail and leading forward, thus helping the ship sail nearer the wind.
2 a nonbinding knot for forming a nonslipping nonjamming loop at the end of a rope.
– ORIGIN Middle English: from Middle Low German *bōlīne*, Middle Dutch *boechlijne*, from *boeg* 'ship's bow' + *lijne* 'line.'

bowl·ing /ˈbōliNG/ ▶ **n. 1** the game of tenpin bowling as a sport or recreation. ■ the game of candlepin or duckpin bowling. ■ the game of lawn bowling. ■ the game of skittles.
2 Cricket the delivery of the ball.

bowl·ing al·ley ▶ **n.** a long narrow track along which balls are rolled in the games of bowling (tenpin, candlepin, or duckpin) or skittles. ■ a building containing such tracks.

bowl·ing ball ▶ **n.** a large, heavy ball with holes for the thumb and two fingers, used in tenpin bowling. ■ a smaller, holeless ball used in candlepin and duckpin bowling.

Bowl·ing Green a city in west central Kentucky; pop. 55,097 (est. 2008).

bowl·ing green ▶ **n.** an area of closely mown grass on which the game of lawn bowling is played.

bowls /bōlz/ ▶ **plural n.** [treated as sing.] British term for **LAWN BOWLING**. ■ Brit. tenpin bowling or skittles.

bow·man[1] /ˈbōmən/ ▶ **n.** (pl. **bowmen**) an archer.

bow·man[2] /ˈboumən/ ▶ **n.** (pl. **bowmen**) the rower who sits nearest the bow of a boat, esp. a racing boat.

Bow·man's cap·sule /ˈbōmənz/ ▶ **n.** a capsule-shaped membranous structure surrounding the glomerulus of each nephron in the kidneys of mammals that extracts wastes, excess salts, and water from the blood.

bow saw /bō/ ▶ **n.** a narrow saw stretched like a bowstring on a light frame.

bow·ser /ˈbouzər/ ▶ **n.** trademark a tanker used for fueling aircraft and other vehicles or for supplying water.
– ORIGIN 1920s: from the name of a company of oil storage engineers.

bow·shot /ˈbōˌSHät/ ▶ **n.** [in sing.] the distance to which a bow can send an arrow: *the two armies camped almost within bowshot of each other.*

bow·sprit /ˈbouˌsprit, ˈbō-/ ▶ **n.** a spar extending forward from a ship's bow, to which the forestays are fastened.
– ORIGIN Middle English: from Middle Low German *bōgsprēt*, Middle Dutch *boechspriet*, from *boech* 'bow' + *spriet* 'sprit.'

b

bowsprit

bow·string /ˈbōˌstriNG/ ▶ **n.** the string of an archer's bow, traditionally made of three strands of hemp.
▶ **v.** (past and past participle **bowstrung**) [with obj.] historical strangle with a bowstring (a former Turkish method of execution).

bow·string hemp ▶ **n.** another term for **SANSEVIERIA**.

bow tie /bō/ ▶ **n.** a necktie in the form of a bow or a knot with two loops. ■ a pattern used for patchwork quilts, resembling such a necktie: [as modifier] *a bow-tie quilt.*

bow wave /bou/ ▶ **n.** a wave or system of waves set up at the bows of a moving ship.

bow win·dow /bō/ ▶ **n.** a curved bay window.

bow·wood /ˈbōˌwo͝od/ ▶ **n.** another name for **OSAGE ORANGE**.

bow-wow /ˈbou ˌwou/ ▶ **exclam.** an imitation of a dog's bark.
▶ **n.** informal a child's word for a dog.

bow·yer /ˈbōyər/ ▶ **n.** a person who makes or sells archers' bows.

box[1] /bäks/ ▶ **n. 1** a container with a flat base and sides, typically square or rectangular and having a lid: *a cereal box* | *a hat box.* ■ the contents of such a container: *she ate a whole box of chocolates that night.* ■ informal a casing containing a computer. ■ (**the box**) informal, chiefly Brit. television or a television set: *light entertainment shows on the box.* ■ informal a coffin: *I always thought I'd be in a box when I finally left here.* ■ historical a coachman's seat. ■ vulgar slang a woman's vagina.
2 an area or space enclosed within straight lines, in particular: ■ an area on a printed page that is to be filled in or that is set off by a border: *a picture of Sandy was in the upper right-hand box.* ■ an area on a computer screen for user input or displaying information. ■ (**the box**) (also **the batter's box**) Baseball the rectangular area occupied by the batter. ■ Baseball the rectangular area behind home plate for the catcher (**catcher's box**), or those near first and third bases, in foul territory, for each base coach (**coach's box**). ■ (**the box**) Soccer the penalty area: *he curled in a shot from the edge of the box.*
3 a small structure or building for a specific purpose, in particular: ■ a separate section or enclosed area within a larger building, esp. one reserved for a group of people in a theater or sports ground or for witnesses or the jury in a law court: *a box at the opera* | *the jury was now in the box.* ■ Brit. a small country house for use when hunting or fishing.
4 a protective casing for a piece of a mechanism. ■ informal short for **GEARBOX**.
5 a mailbox at a post office, newspaper office, or other facility where a person may arrange to receive correspondence: *write to me care of PO Box 112.*
▶ **v.** [with obj.] (often as adj. **boxed**) put in or provide with a box: *the books are sold as a boxed set* | *Muriel boxed up all of Christopher's clothes.* ■ enclose (a piece of text) within printed lines: *boxed sections in magazines.* ■ (**box someone in**) restrict the ability of someone to move freely: *a van had double-parked alongside her car and totally boxed her in.*
– PHRASES **back through the box** Baseball (of a batted ball) hit in the direction of the pitcher past second base. **in a box** restricted or limited: *he will find himself in a box on US policy.* **in-a-box** (or **in-the-box**) packaged simply, cheaply, and conveniently:

b

the Butler-in-a-Box is the gadget of your dreams. (**right**) **out of the box** describing a newly purchased product that works immediately, without any special assembly or training: *a completely preconfigured system you can quickly install right out of the box.* **think outside** (**of**) **the box** think in an original or creative way: *you have to give him credit for thinking outside the box.*
– PHRASAL VERBS **box someone out** Basketball block an opponent from an area by the position of one's body: *Miller neglected to box out his man in the final seconds.*
– DERIVATIVES **box·ful** /-ˌfo͝ol/ **n.**, **box·like** /-ˌlīk/ **adj.**
– ORIGIN late Old English, probably from late Latin *buxis*, from Latin *pyxis* 'boxwood box,' from Greek *puxos* (see BOX³).

box² ▶ **v.** [no obj.] fight an opponent using one's fists; compete in the sport of boxing: *he boxed for England* | [with obj.] *he had to box Bennett for the title.*
▶ **n.** [in sing.] a slap with the hand on the side of a person's head given as a punishment or in anger: *she gave him a box on the ear.*
– PHRASES **box someone's ears** slap someone on the side of the head as a punishment or in anger.
– ORIGIN late Middle English (in the general sense 'a blow'): of unknown origin.

box³ ▶ **n. 1** (also **box tree**) a slow-growing European evergreen shrub or small tree with glossy dark green leaves. It is often grown as a hedge and for topiary. ● *Buxus sempervirens*, family Buxaceae. ■ (also **boxwood**) the hard, heavy wood of this tree, formerly widely used for engraving and for musical instruments.
2 any of a number of trees that have similar wood or foliage, in particular: ● several Australian eucalyptus trees (genus *Eucalyptus*, family Myrtaceae). ● the tropical American **Venezuelan** (or **West Indian**) **box** (*Casearia praecox*, family Flacourtiaceae), the wood of which has now largely replaced that of the European box.
– ORIGIN Old English, via Latin from Greek *puxos*.

box⁴ ▶ **v.** (in phrase **box the compass**) chiefly Nautical **1** recite the compass points in correct order.
2 make a complete change of direction: *by now the breeze had boxed the compass.*
– ORIGIN mid 18th cent.: perhaps from Spanish *bojar* 'sail around,' from Middle Low German *bōgen* 'bend,' from the base of BOW¹.

box beam ▶ **n.** another term for BOX GIRDER.

box·board /ˈbäksˌbôrd/ ▶ **n.** a type of stiff cardboard used to make boxes.

box cam·er·a ▶ **n.** a simple box-shaped hand camera, typically lacking an adjustment for shutter speed.

box can·yon ▶ **n.** a narrow canyon with a flat bottom and vertical walls.
– ORIGIN mid 19th cent.: probably a calque from Spanish *cajón* 'large box, canyon.'

box·car /ˈbäksˌkär/ ▶ **n.** an enclosed railroad freight car, typically with sliding doors on the sides.

box-cut·ter ▶ **n.** a thin, inexpensive razor-blade knife designed to open cardboard boxes.

boxed set ▶ **n.** another term for BOX SET.

box el·der ▶ **n.** an American maple of damp soils that has leaves resembling the ash and green or purplish twigs. ● *Acer negundo*, family Aceraceae.

box-end wrench another term for BOX WRENCH.

Box·er /ˈbäksər/ ▶ **n.** a member of a fiercely nationalistic Chinese secret society that flourished in the 19th century. In 1899 the society led a Chinese uprising (**the Boxer Rebellion**) against Western domination that was eventually crushed by a combined European force, aided by Japan and the US.
– ORIGIN from BOXER, translating Chinese *yì hé quán*, literally 'righteous harmony fists.'

box·er /ˈbäksər/ ▶ **n. 1** a person who takes part in boxing, esp. as a sport.
2 a medium-sized dog of a breed with a smooth brown coat and puglike face.

boxer 2

box·er shorts (also **boxers**) ▶ **plural n.** men's loose underpants similar in shape to the shorts worn by boxers.

box·fish /ˈbäksˌfisʜ/ ▶ **n.** (pl. **same** or **boxfishes**) a tropical marine fish that has a shell of bony plates enclosing the body, from which spines project. Also called TRUNKFISH. ● Family Ostraciontidae: numerous genera and species, including the widely distributed *Tetrosomus gibbosus*.

box gird·er ▶ **n.** a hollow girder square in cross section.

box·ing /ˈbäksiNG/ ▶ **n.** the sport or practice of fighting with the fists, esp. with padded gloves in a roped square ring according to prescribed rules.

Box·ing Day ▶ **n.** (in parts of the British Commonwealth) a public holiday celebrated on the first day (strictly, the first weekday) after Christmas Day.
– ORIGIN mid 19th cent.: from the custom of giving tradespeople a Christmas box on this day.

box·ing glove ▶ **n.** a heavily padded mitten worn in boxing.

box jel·ly·fish ▶ **n.** a jellyfish with a box-shaped swimming bell, living in warm seas. See also SEA WASP. ● Class Cubozoa (formerly order Cubomedusae).

box kite ▶ **n.** a tailless kite in the form of a long box open at each end.

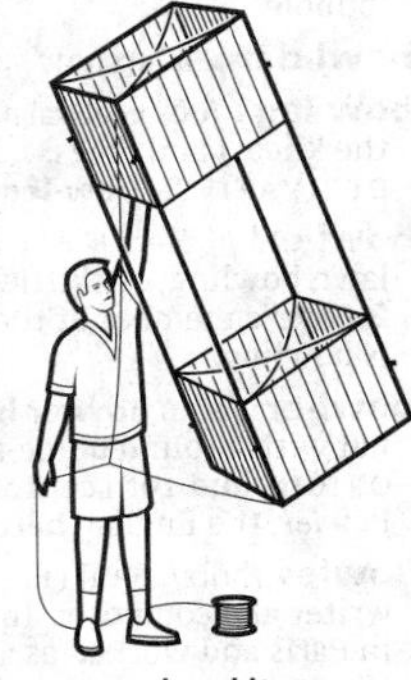
box kite

box lunch ▶ **n.** an individual lunch carried in a box rather than a bag.

box of·fice ▶ **n.** a place at a theater or other arts establishment where tickets are bought or reserved. ■ [in sing.] used to refer to the commercial success of a movie, play, or actor in terms of the audience size or takings they command: [as modifier] *the movie was a huge box-office hit.*

box·out /ˈbäksˌout/ ▶ **n.** a piece of text written to accompany a larger text and printed in a separate area of the page.

box pew ▶ **n.** an old-fashioned church pew enclosed by wooden partitions.

box pleat ▶ **n.** a pleat consisting of two parallel creases facing opposite directions and forming a raised section in between.

box score ▶ **n.** the tabulated results of a baseball game or other sporting event, with statistics given for each player's performance.

box seat ▶ **n. 1** a seat in a box in a theater or sports stadium.
2 historical a coachman's seat.

box set (also **boxed set**) ▶ **n.** a set of related items, typically books or recordings, packaged together in a box and sold as a unit.

box so·cial ▶ **n.** a fundraising event in which box lunches are auctioned off.

box spring ▶ **n.** each of a set of vertical springs housed in a frame in a mattress or upholstered chair base.

box stall ▶ **n.** an enclosed area in a barn in which a single animal can move around freely.

box step ▶ **n.** a dance step in which the feet describe the form of a square or rectangle.

box tur·tle ▶ **n.** a land-living turtle that has a lower shell with hinged lobes that can be drawn up tightly to enclose the animal. It is native to North America and Mexico and is sometimes kept as a pet. ● Genus *Terrapene*, family Emydidae: several species, including the **eastern box turtle** (*T. carolina*) and the **western box turtle** (*T. ornata*).

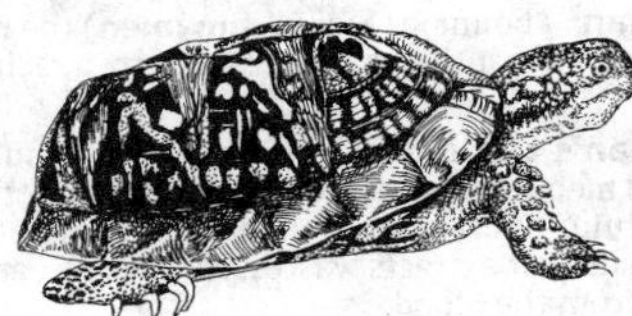
eastern box turtle

box·wood /ˈbäksˌwo͝od/ ▶ **n.** see BOX³ (sense 1).

box wrench ▶ **n.** a cylindrical wrench with a hexagonal end fitting over the head of a nut, used esp. when the nut is difficult to reach. Also called BOX-END WRENCH.

box·y /ˈbäksē/ ▶ **adj.** (**boxier**, **boxiest**) squarish in shape: *a boxy jacket* | *nondescript highrises, boxy and uniform.* ■ (of a room or space) cramped: *the children are too old to share this boxy bedroom.* ■ (of recorded sound) restricted in tone.

boy /boi/ ▶ **n. 1** a male child or young man: *a group of six boys.* ■ a son: *she put her little boy to bed.* ■ [with modifier] a male child or young man who does a specified job: *a delivery boy.*
2 [usu. with adj.] used informally or lightheartedly to refer to a man: *the inspector was a local boy.* ■ dated used as a friendly form of address from one man to another, often from an older man to a young man: *my dear boy, don't say another word!* ■ dated, offensive (often used as a form of address) a black male servant or worker. ■ used as a form of address to a male dog: *down boy, down!*
▶ **exclam.** informal used to express strong feelings, esp. of excitement or admiration: *oh boy, that's wonderful!*
– PHRASES **the big boys** men or organizations considered to be the most powerful and successful. **boys will be boys** used to express the view that mischievous or childish behavior is typical of boys or young men and should not cause surprise when it occurs. **one of the boys** an accepted member of a group, esp. a group of men: *he expected to be treated just like one of the boys* | *Ms. Patton is one of the boys.*
– DERIVATIVES **boy·hood** /-ho͝od/ **n.**
– ORIGIN Middle English (denoting a male servant): of unknown origin.

bo·yar /bōˈyär/ ▶ **n.** historical a member of the old aristocracy in Russia, next in rank to a prince.
– ORIGIN late 16th cent.: from Russian *boyarin* 'grandee.'

boy band (or **girl band**) ▶ **n.** a pop group composed of attractive young men (or young women) whose music and image are designed to appeal primarily to a young teenage audience.

boy·cott /ˈboiˌkät/ ▶ **v.** [with obj.] withdraw from commercial or social relations with (a country, organization, or person) as a punishment or protest. ■ refuse to buy or handle (goods) as a punishment or protest. ■ refuse to cooperate with or participate in (a policy or event).
▶ **n.** a punitive ban that forbids relations with certain groups, cooperation with a policy, or the handling of goods.
– ORIGIN from the name of Captain C. C. *Boycott* (1832–97), an English land agent in Ireland, so treated in 1880, in an attempt instigated by the Irish to get rents reduced.

Boyd /boid/, Nancy, see MILLAY.

boy·friend /ˈboiˌfrend/ ▶ **n. 1** a regular male companion with whom one has a romantic or sexual relationship.
2 [as modifier] denoting an item of clothing for a woman or girl that is designed to be loose-fitting or slightly oversized: *a boyfriend cardigan.*

boy·ish /ˈboi-isʜ/ ▶ **adj.** of, like, or characteristic of a male child or young man: *his boyish charm* | *she looked boyish and defiant.*
– DERIVATIVES **boy·ish·ly adv.**, **boy·ish·ness n.**

Boyle /boil/, Robert (1627–91), Irish scientist. He advanced a corpuscular view of matter and is known for his experiments with the air pump that led to the law named after him.

Boyle's law Chemistry a law stating that the pressure of a given mass of an ideal gas is inversely proportional to its volume at a constant temperature.

Boyne, Battle of the /boin/ a battle fought near the Boyne River in Ireland in 1690, in which the Protestant army of William of Orange, the newly crowned William III, defeated the Catholic army (including troops from both France and Ireland) led by the recently deposed James II. The battle is celebrated annually (on July 12) in Northern Ireland as a victory for the Protestant cause.

Boyn·ton Beach /ˈbointən/ a resort city in southeastern Florida; pop. 68,291 (est. 2008).

boy·o /ˈboiō/ ▶ **n.** (pl. **boyos**) informal, chiefly Welsh & Irish a boy or man (usually used as a form of address).

Boy Scout ▶ **n.** a member of an organization of boys, esp. the **Boy Scouts of America**, that promotes character, outdoor activities, good citizenship, and service to others. ■ an honest, friendly, and typically naive man: [as modifier] *his trademark Boy Scout smile.*

boy·sen·ber·ry /ˈboizənˌberē/ ▶ **n.** (pl. **boysenberries**) **1** a large red edible fruit resembling a blackberry.
2 the shrubby plant that bears this fruit, which is a hybrid of several kinds of bramble. ● *Rubus loganobaccus*, family Rosaceae.

– ORIGIN 1930s: named after Robert *Boysen* (died 1950), the American horticulturalist who developed it.

Boys Town a village in east central Nebraska, just west of Omaha, noted as a home for troubled youth; pop. 977 (est. 2008).

boy toy ▶ **n.** informal, derogatory a young woman who offers herself as a sex object for young men. ■ a young man who offers himself as a sex object.

boy won·der ▶ **n.** an exceptionally talented young man or boy.

Boz /bäz/ the pseudonym used by Charles Dickens in his *Pickwick Papers* and contributions to the *Morning Chronicle.*

Boze·man /ˈbōzmən/ a city in southwestern Montana; pop. 39,442 (est. 2008).

bo·zo /ˈbōzō/ ▶ **n.** (pl. **bozos**) informal a stupid, rude, or insignificant person, esp. a man.
– ORIGIN 1920s: of unknown origin.

BP ▶ **abbr.** ■ before the present (era): *18,000 years BP.* ■ blood pressure. ■ Baseball batting practice. ■ boiling point.

bp ▶ **abbr.** ■ baptized. ■ Biochemistry base pair(s), as a unit of length in nucleic acid chains. ■ Finance basis point(s). ■ (**b.p.**) boiling point.

Bp. ▶ **abbr.** Bishop.

BPH ▶ **abbr.** Medicine benign prostatic hyperplasia (or hypertrophy), an enlargement of the prostate gland common in older men.

BPh ▶ **abbr.** (also **BPhil**) Bachelor of Philosophy.

bpi ▶ **abbr.** Computing bits per inch, used to indicate the density of data that can be stored on magnetic tape or similar media.

B-pic·ture ▶ **n.** another term for **B-MOVIE.**

BPO ▶ **abbr.** business process outsourcing.

BPR ▶ **abbr.** business process re-engineering.

bps ▶ **abbr.** Computing bits per second.

Bq ▶ **abbr.** becquerel.

BR ▶ **abbr.** ■ bedroom(s). ■ bills receivable. ■ (in the UK) British Rail or (formerly) British Railways.

Br ▶ **symbol** the chemical element bromine.

Br. ▶ **abbr.** ■ British. ■ (with reference to religious orders) Brother.

bra /brä/ ▶ **n.** an undergarment worn by women to support the breasts. ■ (also **auto bra** or **car bra**) a carbon-based cover that fits over the front bumper of a car, absorbing the microwaves used in police radar equipment to minimize the risk of detection for the speeding motorist.
– DERIVATIVES **bra·less adj.**
– ORIGIN 1930s: abbreviation of **BRASSIERE.**

Bra·bant /brəˈbant/ a former duchy in western Europe, the capital of which was Brussels. It is now divided into two provinces: North Brabant in the Netherlands, of which the capital is ’s-Hertogenbosch; and Brabant in Belgium, of which the capital remains Brussels.

bra burn·er ▶ **n.** informal a feminist perceived as militant in the struggle for women's rights.
– ORIGIN from the mid 20th-cent. urban legend of women of burning bras to symbolize freedom from societal restraints.

brace /brās/ ▶ **n. 1** a device that clamps things tightly together or that gives support, in particular: ■ a device fitted to a weak or injured neck, leg, or other part of the body for support: *a neck brace.* ■ (also **braces**) a wire device fitted in the mouth to straighten the teeth. ■ a strengthening piece of iron or timber used in building and carpentry. ■ a tool in carpentry having a crank handle and a socket to hold a bit for boring. ■ a rope leading aft from each yardarm, used for trimming the sail. ■ (**braces**) British term for **SUSPENDERS.**
2 (pl. **same**) a pair of something, typically of birds or mammals killed in hunting: *thirty* ***brace of*** *grouse.*
3 either of the two marks { and }, used either to indicate that two or more items on one side have the same relationship as each other to the single item to which the other side points, or in pairs to show that words between them are connected. ■ Music a similar mark connecting staves to be performed at the same time.
▶ **v.** [with obj.] make (a structure) stronger or firmer with wood, iron, or other forms of support: *the posts were braced by lengths of timber.* ■ press (one's body or part of one's body) firmly against something in order to stay balanced: *she* ***braced*** *her feet* ***against*** *a projecting shelf* | (as adj. **braced**) *he stood with legs braced.* ■ prepare (someone or oneself) for something difficult or unpleasant: *both stations are* ***bracing themselves for*** *job losses* | *police are* ***braced for*** *a traffic nightmare.*
– PHRASAL VERBS **brace up** be strong or courageous.
– ORIGIN Middle English (as a verb meaning 'clasp, fasten tightly'): from Old French *bracier* 'embrace,' from *brace* 'two arms,' from Latin *bracchia,* plural of *bracchium* 'arm,' from Greek *brakhiōn.*

brace and bit ▶ **n.** a revolving tool with a D-shaped crank handle for boring.

brace and bit

brace·let /ˈbrāslit/ ▶ **n.** an ornamental band, hoop, or chain worn on the wrist or arm. ■ (**bracelets**) informal handcuffs.
– ORIGIN late Middle English: from Old French, from *bras* 'arm,' from Latin *bracchium.*

brace·let sleeve ▶ **n.** a sleeve on a woman's garment that reaches to just above the wrist.

brac·er[1] /ˈbrāsər/ ▶ **n.** informal an alcoholic drink intended to prepare one for something difficult or unpleasant.

brac·er[2] ▶ **n.** a wristguard used in archery, fencing, and other sports. Also called **ARMGUARD.** ■ historical a portion of a suit of armor covering the arm.
– ORIGIN late Middle English: from Old French *braciere,* from *bras* 'arm' (see **BRACELET**).

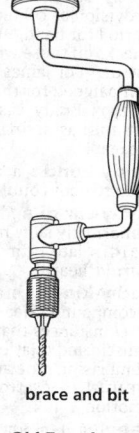

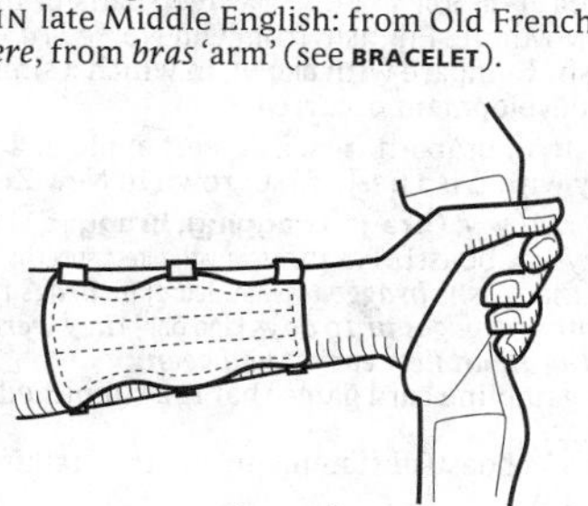
bracer 2

bra·cer·o /brəˈse(ə)rō/ ▶ **n.** (pl. **braceros**) a Mexican laborer allowed into the US for a limited time as a seasonal agricultural worker.
– ORIGIN Spanish 'farm worker,' from *brazo* 'arm.'

bra·chi·al /ˈbrākēəl, ˈbrak-/ ▶ **adj.** Anatomy of or relating to the arm, specifically the upper arm, or an armlike structure: *the brachial artery.* ■ Zoology denoting the upper valve of a brachiopod's shell.
– ORIGIN late Middle English: from Latin *brachialis,* from *brac(c)hium* 'arm.'

bra·chi·ate ▶ **v.** /ˈbrākēˌāt, ˈbrak-/ [no obj.] (of certain apes) move by using the arms to swing from branch to branch: *the gibbons brachiate energetically across their enclosure.*
▶ **adj.** /ˈbrākēˌāt, ˈbrak-, -it/ Biology branched, esp. having widely spread paired branches on alternate sides. ■ having arms.
– DERIVATIVES **bra·chi·a·tion** /ˌbrākēˈāSHən, ˌbrak-/ **n.,** **bra·chi·a·tor** /-ˌātər/ **n.**
– ORIGIN mid 18th cent. (originally in the sense 'having paired branches'): from Latin *brachium* 'arm' + **-ATE**[2].

bra·chi·o·ce·phal·ic /ˈbrākēōsəˈfalik, ˈbrak-/ ▶ **adj.** of or relating to both arm and head.

bra·chi·o·pod /ˈbrākēəˌpäd, ˈbrak-/ ▶ **n.** Zoology a marine invertebrate of the phylum Brachiopoda, which comprises the lamp shells.

Brach·i·op·o·da /ˌbrākēˈäpədə, ˌbrak-/ Zoology a phylum of marine invertebrates that comprises the lamp shells.
– ORIGIN modern Latin (plural), from Greek *brakhiōn* 'arm' + *pous, pod-* 'foot.'

bra·chi·o·saur /ˈbrākēəˌsôr, ˈbrak-/ (also **brachiosaurus** /ˌbrākēəˈsôrəs, ˌbrak-/) ▶ **n.** a huge herbivorous dinosaur of the late Jurassic to mid Cretaceous periods, with forelegs much longer than the hind legs. ● Genus *Brachiosaurus,* infraorder Sauropoda, order Saurischia.
– DERIVATIVES **bra·chi·o·sau·ri·an adj.**
– ORIGIN modern Latin, from Greek *brakhiōn* 'arm' + *sauros* 'lizard.'

bra·chis·to·chrone /brəˈkistəˌkrōn/ ▶ **n.** a curve between two points along which a body can move under gravity in a shorter time than for any other curve.
– ORIGIN late 18th cent.: from Greek *brakhistos* 'shortest' + *khronos* 'time.'

bra·chi·um /ˈbrākēəm, ˈbrak-/ ▶ **n.** the arm, specifically the upper arm from shoulder to elbow.

brachy- ▶ **comb. form** short: *brachycephalic.*
– ORIGIN from Greek *brakhus* 'short.'

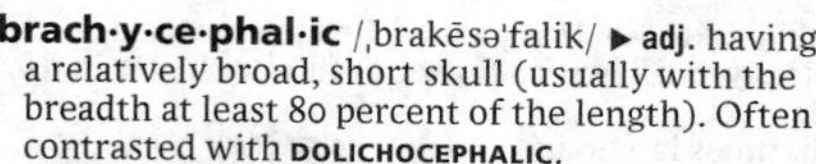

brach·y·ce·phal·ic /ˌbrakēsəˈfalik/ ▶ **adj.** having a relatively broad, short skull (usually with the breadth at least 80 percent of the length). Often contrasted with **DOLICHOCEPHALIC.**
– DERIVATIVES **brach·y·ceph·a·ly** /-ˈsefəlē/ **n.**

brach·y·ther·a·py /ˌbrakēˈTHerəpē/ ▶ **n.** the treatment of cancer, esp. prostate cancer, by the insertion of radioactive implants directly into the tissue.

brach·y·u·ra /ˌbrakēˈyo͝orə/ ▶ **plural n.** a tribe or suborder of crustaceans that have short abdomens folded toward the ventral surface. It includes the true crabs.
– ORIGIN from **BRACHY-** + Greek *oura* 'tail.'

brach·y·u·ran /ˌbrakēˈyo͝orən/ ▶ **n.** a crab belonging to the brachyura suborder of crustaceans.

brac·ing /ˈbrāsiNG/ ▶ **adj. 1** fresh and invigorating: *the bracing sea air.*
2 [attrib.] (of a support) serving to brace a structure: *bracing struts.*
– DERIVATIVES **brac·ing·ly adv.** (sense 1).

bra·ci·o·la /ˌbräCHēˈōlə, bräˈCHō-/ ▶ **n.** a thin slice of beef or other meat wrapped around a filling and cooked in wine.
– ORIGIN Italian.

brack·en /ˈbrakən/ ▶ **n.** a tall fern with coarse lobed fronds that occurs worldwide and can cover large areas. ● *Pteridium aquilinum,* family Dennstaedtiaceae (or Hypolepidaceae). ■ (loosely) any large coarse fern resembling this.
– ORIGIN Middle English: of Scandinavian origin; related to Danish *bregne,* Swedish *bräken.*

brack·et /ˈbrakit/ ▶ **n. 1** each of a pair of marks [ ] used to enclose words or figures so as to separate them from the context: *symbols are* ***given in brackets.***
2 [with adj. or noun modifier] a category of people or things that are similar or fall between specified limits: *those in a high income bracket.*
3 a right-angled support attached to and projecting from a wall for holding a shelf, lamp, or other object. ■ a shelf fixed with such a support to a wall.
4 Military the distance between two artillery shots fired either side of the target to establish range.
▶ **v.** (**brackets, bracketing, bracketed**) [with obj.]
1 enclose (words or figures) in brackets: (as adj. **bracketed**) *the relevant data are included as bracketed points.* ■ Mathematics enclose (a complex expression) in brackets to denote that the whole of the expression rather than just a part of it has a particular relation, such as multiplication or division, to another expression. ■ put (a belief or matter) aside temporarily: *he* ***bracketed off*** *the question of God.*
2 place (one or more people or things) in the same category or group: *he is sometimes* ***bracketed with*** *the "new wave" of film directors.*
3 hold or attach (something) by means of a right-angled support: *pipes should be bracketed.*
4 Military establish the range of (a target) by firing two preliminary shots, one short of the target and the other beyond it. ■ Photography establish (the correct exposure) by taking several pictures with slightly more or less exposure.
– ORIGIN late 16th cent.: from French *braguette* or Spanish *bragueta* 'codpiece, bracket, corbel,' from Provençal *braga,* from Latin *braca,* (plural) *bracae* 'breeches.'

brack·et creep ▶ **n.** movement into a higher tax bracket as taxable income increases.

brack·et fun·gus ▶ **n.** a fungus that grows on living trees or dead wood, forming one or more shelflike projections that are the spore-producing bodies. Hyphae spread through the wood absorbing nutrients and can cause the death of the tree. ● Several families (formerly in the order Aphyllophorales), class Basidiomycetes.

brack·ish /ˈbrakiSH/ ▶ **adj.** (of water) slightly salty, as is the mixture of river water and seawater in estuaries. ■ (of fish or other organisms) living in or requiring such water. ■ unpleasant or distasteful: *the lighting in the movie is brackish.*
– DERIVATIVES **brack·ish·ness n.**
– ORIGIN mid 16th cent.: from obsolete *brack* 'salty,' from Middle Low German, Middle Dutch *brac.*

brac·o·nid /ˈbrakənid/ ▶ **n.** Entomology a small parasitic wasp of a family (Braconidae) that is related to that of the ichneumons. Unlike the latter, braconids lay numerous eggs in a single host.
– ORIGIN late 19th cent.: from modern Latin *Braconidae,* formed irregularly from Greek *brakhus* 'short.'

b

bract /brakt/ ▶ n. Botany a modified leaf or scale, typically small, with a flower or flower cluster in its axil. Bracts are sometimes larger and more brightly colored than the true flower, as in a poinsettia.
– DERIVATIVES **brac·te·ate** /-tēit, -tē,āt/ adj.
– ORIGIN late 18th cent.: from Latin *bractea* 'thin plate of metal.'

bract of a composite flower

brac·te·o·late /ˈbraktēəlit, -ˌlāt/ ▶ adj. having bracteoles.

brac·te·ole /ˈbraktēˌōl/ ▶ n. a small bract, esp. one on a floral stem.

brad /brad/ ▶ n. a small wire nail with a small, often asymmetrical head.
– ORIGIN late Middle English: from Old Norse *broddr* 'spike.'

brad·awl /ˈbradˌôl/ ▶ n. a hand boring tool similar to a small, sharpened screwdriver.
– ORIGIN early 19th cent.: from **BRAD** + **AWL**.

Brad·bur·y /ˈbradˌberē, -bərē/, Ray (1920–), US writer of science fiction; full name *Raymond Douglas Bradbury*. Notable works: *The Martian Chronicles* (1950), *Fahrenheit 451* (1951), and the semiautobiographical Green Town trilogy—*Dandelion Wine* (1957), *Something Wicked This Way Comes* (1962), and *Farewell Summer* (2006).

Brad·dock /ˈbradək/, Edward (1695–1755) British soldier. He was commander in chief of the British forces in America in 1754.

Bra·den·ton /ˈbrādntən/ a city in southwestern Florida, noted as a resort and for citrus processing; pop. 53,513 (est. 2008).

Brad·ford[1] /ˈbradfərd/ an industrial city in northern England; pop. 280,400 (est. 2009).

Brad·ford[2], William (1590–1657), American religious and colonial leader. He was a signer of the Mayflower Compact in 1620 and governor of Plymouth Colony sporadically from 1621 until 1656 (1621–32, 1635, 1637, 1639–43, 1645–56).

Brad·ley[1] /ˈbradlē/, Joseph (1813–92), US Supreme Court associate justice 1870–92. In 1877, he was part of the Electoral College commission that was formed to resolve the indecisiveness of the Hayes-Tilden presidential election and cast the deciding vote in favor of Rutherford B. Hayes.

Brad·ley[2], Milton (1836–1911), US publisher and manufacturer. His board game "The Checkered Game of Life" (1860) led to the formation of Milton Bradley and Company in 1864. Through the company, he also created books and other materials for kindergartens.

Brad·ley[3], Omar Nelson (1893–1981), US army officer. As a general, he commanded the land contingent during the Normandy campaign of 1944–45. After World War II, he served as chief of staff of the US Army 1948–49, chairman of the US Joint Chiefs of Staff 1949–53, and General of the Army 1950.

Omar Bradley

Brad·ley[4] (in full **Bradley Fighting Vehicle**) ▶ n. a medium-sized tank equipped for use in combat.
– ORIGIN named for General Omar *Bradley*.

Brad·street /ˈbradˌstrēt/, Anne Dudley (1612–72), American poet. She came from England with her husband Simon Bradstreet to the Massachusetts Bay Colony in 1630. Her poetry is collected in *The Tenth Muse Lately Sprung Up in America* (1650).

Bra·dy /ˈbrādē/, Mathew W. (c.1823–96) US photographer. His photographs of the Union armies taken during the Civil War became the basis for his National Photographic Collection, and the publication of his *Gallery of Illustrious Americans* (1850) established him as a leading US photographer.

Bra·dy Bill /ˈbrādē/ (also **Brady Law**) ▶ n. a provision of US federal law that requires a waiting period for handgun purchases and background checks on those who wish to purchase handguns.
– ORIGIN For James S. Brady (1940–), who campaigned for the bill, which was signed into law in 1993. Brady was shot and seriously wounded in the 1981 assassination attempt on President Ronald Reagan.

Bra·dy bond ▶ n. a restructured commercial bank loan to poor countries, denominated in US dollars.

brad·y·car·di·a /ˌbradiˈkärdēə/ ▶ n. Medicine abnormally slow heart action.
– ORIGIN late 19th cent.: from Greek *bradus* 'slow' + *kardia* 'heart.'

brad·y·kin·in /ˌbradiˈkinin, -ˈkinin/ ▶ n. Biochemistry a compound released in the blood in some circumstances that causes contraction of smooth muscle and dilation of blood vessels. It is a peptide comprising nine amino-acid residues.
– ORIGIN 1940s: from Greek *bradus* 'slow' + *kinēsis* 'motion' + **-IN**[1].

brae /brā/ ▶ n. Scottish & N. Irish a steep bank or hillside.
– ORIGIN Middle English: from Old Norse *brá* 'eyelash.' Compare with **BROW**[1], in which a similar sense development occurred.

Brae·burn /ˈbrābərn/ ▶ n. a dessert apple of a variety with crisp flesh, first grown in New Zealand.

brag /brag/ ▶ v. (**brags**, **bragging**, **bragged**) [reporting verb] say in a boastful manner: [with direct speech] *"I found them," she bragged* | [with clause] ***he brags that** he wrote 300 pages in 10 days* | [no obj.] ***they were bragging about** how easy it had been.*
▶ n. **1** a gambling card game that is a simplified form of poker.
2 [in sing.] a boastful statement; an act of talking boastfully.
▶ adj. [attrib.] informal excellent; first-rate: *that was my brag heifer.*
– DERIVATIVES **brag·ger** n., **brag·ging·ly** adv.
– ORIGIN Middle English (as an adjective in the sense 'boastful'): of unknown origin (French *braguer* is recorded only later).

Bra·gan·za /brəˈgänzə/ the dynasty that ruled Portugal from 1640 until the end of the monarchy in 1910 and Brazil (on its independence from Portugal) from 1822 until the formation of a republic in 1889.

brag book ▶ n. a scrapbook or photo album intended to show its subject to advantage.

Bragg /brag/, Sir William Henry (1862–1942), English physicist, a founder of solid-state physics. He collaborated with his son, **Sir (William) Lawrence Bragg** (1890–1971), in developing the technique of X-ray diffraction for determining the atomic structure of crystals. Nobel Prize for Physics (1915), shared with his son.

brag·ga·do·ci·o /ˌbragəˈdōsнēˌō/ ▶ n. boastful or arrogant behavior.
– ORIGIN late 16th cent. (denoting a boaster): from *Braggadocchio*, the name of a braggart in Spenser's *The Faerie Queene*, from **BRAG** or **BRAGGART** + the Italian suffix *-occio*, denoting something large of its kind.

brag·gart /ˈbragərt/ ▶ n. a person who boasts about achievements or possessions: [as modifier] *braggart men.*
– ORIGIN late 16th cent.: from French *bragard*, from *braguer* 'to brag.'

brag·ging rights ▶ plural n. a temporary position of ascendancy in a closely contested rivalry: ***he walked off with** a guaranteed $25,000 **and bragging rights** for at least a year.*

Brahe /ˈbräˌhē/, Tycho (1546–1601), Danish astronomer. He built an observatory equipped with precision instruments, but despite demonstrating that comets follow sun-centered paths, he adhered to a geocentric system of planetary motions.

Brah·ma /ˈbrämə/ **1** the creator god in later Hinduism, who forms a triad with Vishnu the preserver and Shiva the destroyer.
2 another term for **BRAHMAN** (sense 2).
– ORIGIN from Sanskrit *brahman*.

brah·ma /ˈbrämə/ ▶ n. short for **BRAHMAPUTRA**.

Brah·ma bull ▶ n. another term for **BRAHMAN** (sense 3).

Brah·man /ˈbrämən/ (also **Brahmin** /-min/) ▶ n. (pl. **Brahmans** also **Brahmins**) **1** a member of the highest Hindu caste, that of the priesthood. [from Sanskrit *brāhmaṇa*.]
2 (in Hinduism) the ultimate reality underlying all phenomena. [from Sanskrit *brahman*.]
3 an ox of a humped breed originally domesticated in India that is tolerant of heat and drought and is now kept widely in tropical and warm-temperate countries. Also called **BRAHMA BULL**; **ZEBU**. ● *Bos indicus*, family Bovidae; now usually included under the name *B. taurus* with other domestic cattle.
– DERIVATIVES **Brah·man·ic** /bräˈmanik/ adj., **Brah·man·i·cal** /bräˈmanikəl/ adj.

Brah·ma·na /ˈbrämənə/ ▶ n. (in Hinduism) any of the lengthy commentaries on the Vedas, composed in Sanskrit c.900–700 BC and containing expository material relating to Vedic sacrificial ritual.

Brah·man·ism /ˈbräməˌnizəm/ (also **Brahminism**) ▶ n. the complex sacrificial religion that emerged in post-Vedic India (c.900 BC) under the influence of the dominant priesthood (Brahmans), an early stage in the development of Hinduism.

Brah·ma·pu·tra /ˌbräməˈpōōtrə/ a river in southern Asia that rises in the Himalayas and flows for 1,800 miles (2,900 km) through Tibet, northeastern India, and Bangladesh to join the Ganges River at its delta on the Bay of Bengal.

Brah·min /ˈbrämin/ ▶ n. **1** variant spelling of **BRAHMAN**.
2 a socially or culturally superior person, esp. a member of the upper classes from New England.
– DERIVATIVES **Brah·min·i·cal** /bräˈminikəl/ adj. (sense 1).

Brahms /brämz/, Johannes (1833–97), German composer and pianist. He eschewed program music and opera and concentrated on traditional forms. He wrote four symphonies, four concertos, chamber and piano music, choral works including the *German Requiem* (1857–68), and nearly 200 songs.

braid /brād/ ▶ n. **1** threads of silk, cotton, or other material woven into a decorative band for edging or trimming garments: *a coat trimmed with gold braid* | *fancy braids.*
2 a length of hair made up of three or more interlaced strands: *women with long black braids.* ■ a length made up of three or more interlaced strands of any flexible material: *a flexible copper braid* | *braids of garlic.*
▶ v. [with obj.] **1** interlace three or more strands of (hair or other flexible material) to form a length: *their long hair was tightly braided* | (as adj. **braided**) *horses with braided manes.*
2 (often as adj. **braided**) edge or trim (a garment) with braid: *braided red trousers.*
3 (usu. as adj. **braided**) (of a river or stream) flow into shallow interwoven channels divided by deposits of sediment.
– ORIGIN Old English *bregdan* 'make a sudden movement,' also 'interweave,' of Germanic origin; related to Dutch *breien* (verb).

braid·ing /ˈbrādiNG/ ▶ n. decorative braid or braided work: *curtains heavy with gold braiding.*

brail /brāl/ Sailing ▶ n. (**brails**) small ropes that are led from the leech of a fore-and-aft sail to pulleys on the mast for temporarily furling it.
▶ v. [with obj.] (**brail a sail up**) furl (a sail) by hauling on such ropes.
– ORIGIN late Middle English: from Old French *braiel*, from medieval Latin *bracale* 'girdle,' from *braca* 'breeches.'

Bră·i·la /brəˈēlä/ an industrial city and port in eastern Romania, on the Danube River; pop. 216,814 (2006).

Braille[1] /brāl/, Louis (1809–52), French educator. Blind from the age of 3, he had developed his own system of raised-point reading and writing by the age of 15. His system was officially adopted two years after his death.

Braille[2] ▶ n. a form of written language for blind people, in which characters are represented by patterns of raised dots that are felt with the fingertips.
▶ v. [with obj.] print or transcribe in Braille.

braille·writ·er /ˈbrālˌrītər/ ▶ n. a machine for writing braille.

brain /brān/ ▶ n. **1** an organ of soft nervous tissue contained in the skull of vertebrates, functioning as the coordinating center of sensation and intellectual and nervous activity. ■ (**brains**) the substance of such an organ, typically that of an animal, used as food. ■ informal an electronic device with functions comparable to those of the human brain.

The human brain consists of three main parts. (i) The forebrain, greatly developed into the cerebrum, consists of two hemispheres joined by a bridge of nerve fibers, and is responsible for thought and control of speech. (ii) The midbrain, the upper part of the tapering brainstem, contains cells involved in eye movements. (iii) The hindbrain, the lower part of the brainstem, contains cells responsible for breathing and for regulating heart action, the flow of digestive juices, and other unconscious actions and processes. The cerebellum, which lies behind the brain stem, plays an important role in the execution of highly skilled movements.

2 intellectual capacity: *I didn't have enough brains for the sciences | success requires brain as well as brawn.* ■ (**the brains**) informal a clever person who supplies the ideas and plans for a group of people: *Tom was the brains of the outfit.* ■ a person's mind: *a tiny alarm bell began to ring in her brain.* ■ an exceptionally intelligent person: *he was known more as a snappy dresser than a brain.*
▶ **v.** [with obj.] informal hit (someone) hard on the head with an object: *she brained me with a rolling pin.*
– PHRASES **beat** (or **blow**) **someone's brains out** informal injure or kill someone with a hard hit on (or gunshot to) the head. **have something on the brain** informal be obsessed with something: *John has cars on the brain.*
– ORIGIN Old English *brægen*; related to Dutch *brein*.

brain cell ▶ **n.** a cell in the tissue of the brain. ■ informal regarded as a unit of intellectual power: *it does help if the student has more than one brain cell.*

brain·child /ˈbrān,CHīld/ ▶ **n.** (pl. **brainchildren**) informal an idea or invention considered to be a particular person's creation: *the statue is the brainchild of a local landscape artist.*

brain cor·al ▶ **n.** a compact coral with a convoluted surface resembling that of the brain. ● *Diploria* and other genera, order Scleractinia.

brain dam·age ▶ **n.** injury to the brain that impairs its functions, esp. permanently.
– DERIVATIVES **brain-dam·aged adj.**

brain-dead ▶ **adj.** having suffered brain death: *brain-dead patients.* ■ informal extremely stupid: *the brain-dead politics of the past.*

brain death ▶ **n.** irreversible brain damage causing the end of independent respiration, regarded as indicative of death.

brain drain ▶ **n.** [in sing.] informal the emigration of highly trained or intelligent people from a particular country.

Braine /brān/, John (Gerard) (1922–86), English novelist, noted for *Room at the Top* (1957), whose opportunistic hero is hailed as a representative example of an "angry young man."

brained /brānd/ ▶ **adj.** [in combination] (of vertebrates) having an organ in the skull of a certain size or kind: *large-brained mammals.* ■ derogatory (of a person) having an intellectual capacity of a certain quality or kind: *pea-brained consumers.*

brain fe·ver ▶ **n.** dated inflammation of the brain.

brain fin·ger·print·ing ▶ **n.** the recording and analysis of an individual's neurological responses to images and words flashed on a screen, esp. to determine if the person is telling the truth.

brain food ▶ **n.** food believed to be beneficial to the brain, esp. in increasing intellectual power.

brain·i·ac /ˈbrānē,ak/ ▶ **n.** informal an exceptionally intelligent person.
– ORIGIN 1950s: from the name of a superintelligent alien character of the Superman comic strip, from a blend of BRAIN and MANIAC.

brain·less /ˈbrānlis/ ▶ **adj.** stupid; foolish: *a brainless bimbo.*
– DERIVATIVES **brain·less·ly adv.**, **brain·less·ness n.**

brain·pan /ˈbrān,pan/ ▶ **n.** informal a person's skull.

brain·pow·er /ˈbrān,pouər/ ▶ **n.** mental ability; intelligence.

brain·sick /ˈbrān,sik/ ▶ **adj.** diseased in the mind; mad or insane.

brain·stem /ˈbrān,stem/ (also **brain stem**) ▶ **n.** Anatomy the central trunk of the mammalian brain, consisting of the medulla oblongata, pons, and midbrain, and continuing downward to form the spinal cord.

brain·storm /ˈbrān,stôrm/ ▶ **n. 1** a spontaneous group discussion to produce ideas and ways of solving problems. ■ informal a sudden clever idea. **2** informal a moment in which one is suddenly unable to think clearly or act sensibly.
▶ **v.** [no obj.] produce an idea or way of solving a problem by holding a spontaneous group discussion: (as noun **brainstorming**) *a brainstorming session.*

brain-teas·er (also **brainteaser**, **brain-twister**) ▶ **n.** informal a problem or puzzle, typically one designed to be solved for amusement.
– DERIVATIVES **brain-teas·ing adj.**

brain trust ▶ **n.** a group of experts appointed to advise a government or politician.

brain·wash /ˈbrān,wôSH, -,wäSH/ ▶ **v.** [with obj.] make (someone) adopt radically different beliefs by using systematic and often forcible pressure: *the organization could brainwash young people | they have been* **brainwashed into** *conformity and subservience.*

brain·wave /ˈbrān,wāv/ ▶ **n.** (usu. **brainwaves**) an electrical impulse in the brain. ■ [usu. in sing.] informal a sudden clever idea.

brain·work /ˈbrān,wərk/ ▶ **n.** mental activity or effort, esp. as opposed to physical labor.

brain·y /ˈbrānē/ ▶ **adj.** (**brainier**, **brainiest**) having or showing intelligence: *a brainy, high-powered lawyer.*
– DERIVATIVES **brain·i·ly** /-nəlē/ **adv.**, **brain·i·ness n.**

braise /brāz/ ▶ **v.** [with obj.] fry (food) lightly and then stew it slowly in a closed container: (as adj. **braised**) *braised veal.*
– ORIGIN mid 18th cent.: from French *braiser*, from *braise* 'live coals' (in which the container was formerly placed).

brake[1] /brāk/ ▶ **n.** a device for slowing or stopping a moving vehicle, typically by applying pressure to the wheels: *he slammed on his brakes* | [as modifier] *a brake pedal.* ■ a thing that slows or hinders a process: *managers have a duty to* **put the brakes on** *growth when it is unsustainable.*
▶ **v.** [no obj.] make a moving vehicle slow down or stop by using a brake: *drivers who brake abruptly* | (as adj. **braking**) *an anti-lock braking system.*
– ORIGIN late 18th cent.: of unknown origin.

brake[2] ▶ **n.** historical an open, horse-drawn, four-wheeled carriage.
– ORIGIN mid 19th cent.

brake[3] ▶ **n.** a toothed instrument used for crushing flax and hemp. ■ (also **brake harrow**) a heavy machine formerly used in agriculture for breaking up large lumps of earth.
– ORIGIN late Middle English: possibly related to Middle Low German *brake* and Dutch *braak*, and perhaps also to BREAK.

brake[4] ▶ **n.** archaic or literary a thicket. See also CANEBRAKE, FERNBRAKE.
– ORIGIN Old English *bracu* (first recorded in the plural in *fearnbraca* 'thickets of fern'), related to Middle Low German *brake* 'branch, stump.'

brake[5] (also **brake fern**) ▶ **n.** a coarse fern of warm and tropical countries, frequently having the fronds divided into long linear segments. ● Genus *Pteris*, family Pteridaceae. ■ archaic term for BRACKEN.
– ORIGIN Middle English: perhaps an abbreviation of BRACKEN (interpreted as plural).

brake[6] archaic past of BREAK.

brake block ▶ **n.** a block of hard material pressed against the rim of a wheel to slow it down by friction, typically one of a pair made of hardened rubber used on a bicycle.

brake disc ▶ **n.** the disc attached to the wheel in a disc brake.

brake drum ▶ **n.** a broad, very short cylinder attached to a wheel, against which the brake shoes press in a drum brake.

brake flu·id ▶ **n.** fluid used in a hydraulic brake system.

brake har·row ▶ **n.** see BRAKE[3].

brake horse·pow·er ▶ **n.** (pl. **same**) the available power of an engine, assessed by measuring the force needed to brake it: *the net brake horsepower is only up by six.*

brake light ▶ **n.** a red light at the back of a vehicle that is automatically illuminated when the brakes are applied.

brake lin·ing ▶ **n.** a layer of asbestos or a similar material attached to a brake shoe to increase friction against the brake drum.

brake·man /ˈbrākmən/ ▶ **n.** (pl. **brakemen**) **1** a railroad worker responsible for a train's brakes and other aspects of its operation. **2** a person in charge of brakes, for instance in a bobsled.

brake pad ▶ **n.** either of the thin blocks that grip the disc in a disc brake.

brake shoe ▶ **n.** either of the long curved blocks that press on the inside of the brake drum.

brak·ing dis·tance ▶ **n.** the approximate distance traveled before coming to a complete stop when the brakes are applied in a vehicle moving at a specified speed.

Bra·man·te /brä'mäntā/, Donato (di Angelo) (1444–1514), Italian architect. He drew up the first plan for St. Peter's Cathedral, which was begun in 1506, and established the concept of a huge central dome.

bram·ble /ˈbrambəl/ ▶ **n.** a prickly scrambling vine or shrub, esp. a blackberry or other wild shrub of the rose family.
– DERIVATIVES **bram·bly** /-b(ə)lē/ **adj.**
– ORIGIN Old English *bræmbel*, *brēmel*, of Germanic origin; related to BROOM.

Bramp·ton /ˈbramtən/ a city in south Ontario, an industrial and residential suburb west of Toronto; pop. 433,806 (2006).

bran /bran/ ▶ **n.** pieces of grain husk separated from flour after milling.
– ORIGIN Middle English: from Old French, of unknown origin.

branch /branCH/ ▶ **n.** a part of a tree that grows out from the trunk or from a bough. ■ a lateral extension or subdivision extending from the main part of something, typically one extending from a river, road, or railway: *a branch of the Susquehanna River.* ■ a division or office of a large business or organization, operating locally or having a particular function: *he went to work at our Boston branch.* ■ a conceptual subdivision of something, esp. a family, group of languages, or a subject: *a branch of mathematics called graph theory.* ■ Computing a control structure in which one of several alternative sets of program statements is selected for execution.
▶ **v.** [no obj.] (of a road or path) divide into one or more subdivisions. ■ (of a tree or plant) bear or send out branches: (as adj. **branched**) *the common sea lavender can be identified by its branched stem.* ■ (**branch off**) diverge from the main route or part: *the road branched off at the town* | figurative *Ellington was constantly branching off with new musical styles.* ■ (**branch out**) extend or expand one's activities or interests in a new direction: *the company is branching out into Europe.*
– DERIVATIVES **branch·let** /-lit/ **n.**, **branch·like** /-,līk/ **adj.**, **branch·y adj.**
– ORIGIN Middle English: from Old French *branche*, from late Latin *branca* 'paw.'

bran·chi·a /ˈbraNGkēə/ ▶ **n.** (pl. **branchiae** /-kē,ē/) the gills of fish and some invertebrate animals.
– DERIVATIVES **bran·chi·al** /-kēəl/ **adj.**
– ORIGIN late 17th cent.: from Latin *branchia*, (plural) *branchiae*, from Greek *brankhia* (plural).

bran·chi·o·pod /ˈbraNGkēə,päd/ ▶ **n.** Zoology a small aquatic crustacean of the class Branchiopoda, such as a water flea or fairy shrimp.

Bran·chi·op·o·da /,braNGkēəˈpōdə/ Zoology a class of small aquatic crustaceans that includes water fleas and fairy shrimps, which are distinguished by having gills on their feet.
– ORIGIN modern Latin (plural), from Greek *brankhia* 'gills' + *pous*, *pod-* 'foot.'

branch line ▶ **n.** a secondary railroad line branching off from a main line.

branch wa·ter (also **branch**) ▶ **n.** ordinary water, esp. when added to alcoholic drinks. ■ water from a stream or brook.

Bran·cu·si /branˈkōōsē, ˈbrän,kōōSH/, Constantin (1876–1957), Romanian sculptor, who spent much of his working life in France. His sculpture represents an attempt to move away from representational art and to capture the essence of forms by reducing them to their ultimate, almost abstract, simplicity.

brand /brand/ ▶ **n. 1** a type of product manufactured by a particular company under a particular name: *a new brand of detergent.* ■ a brand name: *the company will market computer software under its own brand.* ■ a particular identity or image regarded as an asset: *you can still invent your own career, be your own brand | the Michael Jordan brand certainly hasn't hurt them.* ■ a particular type or kind of something: *his incisive brand of intelligence.* **2** an identifying mark burned on livestock or (esp. formerly) criminals or slaves with a branding iron. ■ archaic a branding iron. ■ a habit, trait, or quality that causes someone public shame or disgrace: *the brand of Paula's alcoholism.* **3** a piece of burning or smoldering wood: *he took two burning brands from the fire.* ■ literary a torch. **4** literary a sword.
▶ **v.** [with obj.] **1** mark (an animal, formerly a criminal or slave) with a branding iron. ■ mark indelibly: *an ointment that branded her with unsightly violet-colored splotches.* ■ describe (someone or something) as something bad or shameful: *the do-gooders* **branded us as** *politically incorrect* | [with obj. and complement] *she was branded a liar.* **2** assign a brand name to: (as adj. **branded**) *branded goods at low prices.* ■ (as noun **branding**) the promotion of a particular product or company by means of advertising and distinctive design.
– DERIVATIVES **brand·er n.**
– ORIGIN Old English, of Germanic origin; related to German *Brand*, also to BURN[1]. The word originally meant 'burning' or 'a piece of burning or smoldering wood' (sense 3 of the noun); the verb sense

'mark permanently with a hot iron' dates from late Middle English. The noun sense 'mark of ownership made by branding,' based on the latter, arose in the mid 17th cent., and from it is derived sense 1 (early 19th cent).

WORD TRENDS Once upon a time, people thought about **brands** most often in the grocery store, when selecting a favored make of soap, breakfast cereal, or baked beans. Now a **brand** is primarily something to *build, promote, sell, create*, or *develop*, according to the Oxford English Corpus. Marketing and advertising are so pervasive that organizations, public figures, and even ordinary people may be considered as **brands**: *the first soccer club to promote its brand in Asia | is Beyoncé the brand they're looking for? | by developing a strong personal brand, you'll create a life that's more successful and fulfilling.*

bran·dade /brän'däd/ ▶ **n.** a Provençal dish consisting of salt cod mixed into a purée with olive oil and milk.
– ORIGIN French, from modern Provençal *brandado*, literally 'something that has been shaken.'

brand a·ware·ness ▶ **n.** the extent to which consumers are familiar with the distinctive qualities or image of a particular brand of goods or services.

Bran·deis /'brandīs/, Louis Dembitz (1856–1941), US Supreme Court associate justice 1916–39. He gained an early reputation as the "people's attorney" by defending without a fee Boston residents seeking regulation of local public utilities. His "Brandeis brief" made use of social facts, rather than relying solely on precedent and general arguments.

Bran·den·burg /'brandən,bərg/ a state in northeastern Germany that surrounds but is independent of the city of Berlin; capital, Potsdam.

Bran·den·burg Gate one of the city gates of Berlin. Built 1788–91, it is the only one that survives. After the construction of the Berlin Wall in 1961, it stood in East Berlin, a conspicuous symbol of a divided city. It was reopened in December 1989.

Brandenburg Gate

brand eq·ui·ty ▶ **n.** the commercial value that derives from consumer perception of the brand name of a particular product or service, rather than from the product or service itself.

brand ex·ten·sion ▶ **n.** an instance of using an established brand name or trademark on new products, so as to increase sales.

brand im·age ▶ **n.** the impression of a product held by real or potential consumers.

brand·ing i·ron ▶ **n.** a metal implement that is heated and used to brand livestock or (esp. formerly) criminals or slaves.

bran·dish /'brandisH/ ▶ **v.** [with obj.] wave or flourish (something, esp. a weapon) as a threat or in anger or excitement.
– DERIVATIVES **bran·dish·er n.**
– ORIGIN Middle English: from Old French *brandiss-*, lengthened stem of *brandir*; ultimately of Germanic origin and related to **BRAND**.

brand lead·er ▶ **n.** the best-selling or most highly regarded product or brand of its type.

brand·ling /'brandliNG/ ▶ **n.** a red earthworm that has rings of a brighter color, often found in manure, and used as bait by anglers and in composting kitchen waste. ● *Eisenia fetida*, family Lumbricidae.
– ORIGIN mid 17th cent.: from **BRAND** + **-LING**.

brand loy·al·ty ▶ **n.** the tendency of some consumers to continue buying the same brand of goods rather than competing brands.

brand name ▶ **n.** a name given by the maker to a product or range of products, esp. a trademark. ■ a familiar or widely known name: [as modifier] *younger writers who clamber toward brand-name status.*

brand new ▶ **adj.** completely new.

Bran·do /'brandō/, Marlon (1924–2004), US actor. An exponent of method acting, he first attracted critical acclaim in the stage production of *A Streetcar Named Desire* (1947) and starred in the movie version four years later. Other notable movies: *On the Waterfront* (1954), *The Godfather* (1972), and *Apocalypse Now* (1979).

Brandt /bränt/, Willy (1913–92), German statesman; chancellor of West Germany 1969–74; born *Karl Herbert Frahm*. He achieved international recognition for his policy of détente and the opening of relations with the countries of the Eastern bloc (Ostpolitik). Nobel Peace Prize (1971).

Brand X ▶ **n.** a name used for an unidentified brand contrasted unfavorably with a product of the same type being promoted.

bran·dy /'brandē/ ▶ **n.** (pl. **brandies**) a strong alcoholic spirit distilled from wine or fermented fruit juice.
– ORIGIN mid 17th cent.: from earlier *brandwine, brandewine*, from Dutch *brandewijn*, from *branden* 'burn, distill' + *wijn* 'wine.'

Bran·dy·wine Creek /'brandē,wīn/ a historic stream in southeastern Pennsylvania and northern Delaware, the birthplace of the US gunpowder industry.

brane /brān/ ▶ **n.** Physics an extended object with any given number of dimensions, of which strings in string theory are examples with one dimension. Our universe is a 3-brane.
– ORIGIN 1980s: short for **MEMBRANE**.

branks /braNGks/ ▶ **plural n.** historical an instrument of punishment for a scolding woman, consisting of an iron framework for the head and a sharp metal gag for restraining the tongue.
– ORIGIN mid 16th cent.: origin uncertain; compare with German *Pranger* 'a pillory or bit for a horse' and Dutch *prang* 'a fetter'; also with late Middle English *barnacle(s)*, denoting a powerful bit for restraining a horse.

bran·ni·gan /'branigən/ ▶ **n.** informal a brawl or violent argument.
– ORIGIN late 19th cent.: of unknown origin; perhaps from the surname *Brannigan*.

Bran·son[1] /'bransən/ a city in southwestern Missouri, on the Ozark Plateau, noted as a resort based on country music; pop. 7,651 (est. 2008).

Bran·son[2], Richard (1950–), English businessman and adventurer. He established Virgin Records in 1969 and Virgin Atlantic Airways in 1984. He also made the fastest transatlantic crossing by boat in 1986 and the first by hot-air balloon in 1987.

brant /brant/ ▶ **n.** (pl. **same** or **brants**) a small goose with a mainly black head and neck, breeding in the arctic tundra of Eurasia and Canada. ● *Branta bernicla*, family Anatidae.

Braque /bräk/, Georges (1882–1963), French painter. His collages, which introduced commercial lettering and fragmented objects into pictures to contrast the real with the "illusory" painted image, were the first stage in the development of synthetic cubism.

brash[1] /brasH/ ▶ **adj.** self-assertive in a rude, noisy, or overbearing way: *he could be brash, cocky, and arrogant.* ■ strong, energetic, or irreverent: *I like brash, vibrant flavors.* ■ (of a place or thing) having an ostentatious or tasteless appearance: *the cafe was a brash new building.*
– DERIVATIVES **brash·ly adv., brash·ness n.**
– ORIGIN early 19th cent. (originally dialect); perhaps a form of **RASH**[1].

brash[2] ▶ **n.** a mass of fragments, in particular: ■ loose broken rock or ice.
– ORIGIN late 18th cent.: of unknown origin.

Bra·sil /brə'zil/ Portuguese name for **BRAZIL**[1].

Bra·sil·ia /brə'zilyə/ the capital, since 1960, of Brazil; pop. 2,455,903 (2007). Designed by Lúcio Costa in 1956, the city was built in the center of the country with the intention of drawing people away from the crowded coastal areas.

Bra·şov /brä'SHōv/ a city in Romania; pop. 281,375 (2006). It belonged to Hungary until after World War I and was ceded to Romania in 1920. Hungarian name **BRASSÓ**. German name **KRONSTADT**.

brass /bras/ ▶ **n.** a yellow alloy of copper and zinc: [as modifier] *a brass plate on the door.* ■ a decorative object made of such an alloy: *shining brasses stood on the mantelpiece.* ■ a memorial, typically medieval, consisting of a flat piece of inscribed brass, laid in the floor or set into the wall of a church. ■ a brass block or die used for stamping a design on a book binding. ■ Brit. informal money: *they wanted to spend their newly acquired brass.* ■ Music brass wind instruments (including trumpet, horn, trombone) forming a band or a section of an orchestra: *the brass and percussion were consistently too loud.* ■ (also **top brass**) informal people in authority or of high military rank. ■ informal a person's hardness or effrontery: *he was the only one who **had the brass to** show his face.*
– PHRASES **the brass ring** informal a prize or goal that someone strives for: *Willa went for the brass ring, joining the firm at a whopping salary.* [with reference to the reward of a free ride given on a merry-go-round to the person hooking a brass ring suspended over the horses.]
– ORIGIN Old English *bræs*, of unknown origin.

bras·sard /brə'särd, 'bras,ärd/ ▶ **n.** a band worn on the sleeve, typically having an identifying mark and worn with a uniform. ■ historical a piece of armor for the upper arm.
– ORIGIN late 16th cent. (denoting a piece of armor for the upper arm): from French, from *bras* 'arm.'

brass band ▶ **n.** a group of musicians playing brass instruments and sometimes also percussion.

brass-bound ▶ **adj.** trimmed or banded with brass fittings. ■ (of a person) adhering inflexibly to tradition or belief. ■ (of a person) brazen or impudent.

bras·se·rie /,brasə'rē/ ▶ **n.** (pl. **brasseries**) an informal restaurant, esp. one in France or modeled on a French one and with a large selection of drinks.
– ORIGIN mid 19th cent.: French, originally 'brewery,' from *brasser* 'to brew.'

Bras·sey /'brasē/, Thomas (1805–70), English engineer and railroad contractor. He built more than 6,500 miles (10,000 km) of railroads in Europe, India, South America, and Australia.

brass hat ▶ **n.** informal a high-ranking officer in the armed forces.
– ORIGIN late 19th cent.: so named because of the gilt insignia on the caps of such officers.

bras·si·ca /'brasikə/ ▶ **n.** a plant of a genus that includes cabbage, turnip, Brussels sprout, and mustard. ● Genus *Brassica*, family Brassicaceae.
– ORIGIN early 19th cent.: Latin, literally 'cabbage.'

brass·ie /'brasē/ (also **brassy**) ▶ **n.** (pl. **brassies**) Golf, informal a number two wood.
– ORIGIN late 19th cent.: so named because the wood was originally shod with brass.

bras·siere /brə'zi(ə)r/ ▶ **n.** full form of **BRA**.
– ORIGIN early 20th cent.: from French *brassière*, literally 'bodice, child's vest.'

brass in·stru·ment ▶ **n.** a wind instrument, such as a trumpet or trombone, typically made of brass.

brass knuck·les ▶ **n.** a metal guard worn over the knuckles in fighting, esp. to increase the effect of the blows.

brass knuckles

brass mon·key ▶ **n.** informal used in phrases to refer to extremely cold weather: *it's brass monkey weather tonight.*
– ORIGIN mid 19th cent.: often said to be from a type of brass rack or 'monkey' in which cannonballs were stored and which contracted in very cold weather, ejecting the balls, but this explanation has not been proved.

Bras·só /'bräsH-shō/ Hungarian name for **BRAŞOV**.

brass rub·bing ▶ **n.** the action of rubbing crayon or chalk over paper laid on an engraved brass to reproduce its design. ■ an image created by doing this.

brass·ware /'bras,we(ə)r/ ▶ **n.** utensils or other objects made of brass.

brass·y[1] /'brasē/ ▶ **adj.** (**brassier, brassiest**) resembling brass in colour. ■ sounding like a brass musical instrument; harsh and loud. ■ (of a person, typically a woman) tastelessly showy or loud in appearance or manner: *her brassy, audacious exterior.*
– DERIVATIVES **brass·i·ly** /'brasəlē/ **adv., brass·i·ness n.**

brass·y[2] ▶ **n.** variant spelling of **BRASSIE**.

brat /brat/ ▶ **n.** informal, derogatory or humorous a child, typically a badly behaved one.
– DERIVATIVES **brat·tish adj., brat·tish·ness n., brat·ty adj.**
– ORIGIN mid 16th cent.

Bra·ti·sla·va /,brätə'slävə/ the capital of Slovakia, in the western part of the country, a port on the Danube River; pop. 426,927 (2007). From 1526 to 1784 it was the capital of Hungary. German name **PRESSBURG**; Hungarian name **POZSONY**.

brat pack ▶ **n.** informal a rowdy and ostentatious group of young celebrities, typically movie stars.
– DERIVATIVES **brat pack·er n.**

Brat·tain /'bratn/, Walter Houser (1902–87), US physicist and inventor. He invented the point-contact transistor in 1947 with John Bardeen and William Shockley. Nobel Prize for Physics (1956), shared with Bardeen and Shockley.

brat·tice /'bratis/ ▶ **n.** a partition or shaft lining in a coal mine, typically made of wood or heavy cloth.
– DERIVATIVES **brat·ticed adj.**

–ORIGIN Middle English (denoting a temporary wooden gallery for use in a siege): from Old French *bretesche*, from medieval Latin *britisca*, from Old English *brittisc* 'British.' The current sense dates from the mid 19th cent.

brat·tle /'bratl/ dialect ▶ **n.** a sharp rattling sound: *a distant brattle of thunder.*
▶ **v.** [with obj.] rattle (something). ■ [no obj.] produce a rattling sound.
–ORIGIN early 16th cent.: probably imitative, from a blend of **BREAK** and **RATTLE**.

Brat·tle·bo·ro /'bratl,bərə, -,bərō/ a town in southeastern Vermont, on the Connecticut River; pop. 11,491 (est. 2008).

brat·wurst /'brät,wərst/ ▶ **n.** a type of fine German pork sausage that is typically fried or grilled.
–ORIGIN German, from *Brat* 'a spit' + *Wurst* 'sausage.'

Braun[1] /broun/, Eva (1910–45), German mistress of Adolf Hitler. Braun and Hitler are thought to have married during the fall of Berlin, shortly before committing suicide together in the air-raid shelter of his Berlin headquarters.

Braun[2] /broun/, Karl Ferdinand (1850–1918), German physicist. He invented the coupled system of radio transmission and the Braun tube (forerunner of the cathode ray tube), in which a beam of electrons could be deflected. Nobel Prize for Physics (1909), shared with Guglielmo Marconi.

Braun[3] /brôn, broun/, Wernher Magnus Maximilian von (1912–77), US rocket engineer; born in Germany. He led the development of the V-2 rockets used by Germany during World War II. After the war, he moved to the US, where he worked in the US space program.

Braun·schweig /'broun,SHwīg/ German name for **BRUNSWICK**.

braun·schwei·ger /'broun,SHwīgər/ ▶ **n.** a variety of smoked liver sausage.

bra·va /'brävä, brä'vä/ ▶ **exclam.** feminine of **BRAVO**[1].

bra·va·do /brə'vädō/ ▶ **n.** a bold manner or a show of boldness intended to impress or intimidate.
–ORIGIN late 16th cent.: from Spanish *bravada*, from *bravo* 'bold' (see **BRAVE**, **-ADO**).

brave /brāv/ ▶ **adj.** ready to face and endure danger or pain; showing courage: *a brave soldier* | *he put up a brave fight before losing.* ■ literary fine or splendid in appearance: *his medals made a brave show.*
▶ **n. 1** (as plural noun **the brave**) people who are ready to face and endure danger or pain.
2 dated an American Indian warrior. ■ a young man who shows courage or a fighting spirit.
▶ **v.** [with obj.] endure or face (unpleasant conditions or behavior) without showing fear: *we had to brave the full heat of the sun.*
–PHRASES **brave new world** used to refer, often ironically, to a new and hopeful period in history resulting from major changes in society: *the brave new world of computing.* **put a brave face on something** see **FACE**.
–DERIVATIVES **brave·ly** adv., **brave·ness** n.
–ORIGIN late 15th cent.: from French, from Italian *bravo* 'bold' or Spanish *bravo* 'courageous, untamed, savage,' based on Latin *barbarus* (see **BARBAROUS**).

brav·er·y /'brāv(ə)rē/ ▶ **n.** courageous behavior or character.
–ORIGIN mid 16th cent. (in the sense 'bravado'): from French *braverie* or Italian *braveria*, based on Latin *barbarus* (see **BARBAROUS**).

bra·vis·si·mo /brä'visə,mō, -'vēsē-/ ▶ **exclam.** used to express great approval of a performance or performer.

bra·vo[1] /'brävō/ ▶ **exclam.** used to express approval when a performer or other person has done something well: *people kept on clapping and shouting "bravo!"*
▶ **n.** (pl. **bravos**) **1** a cry of bravo: *bravos rang out.*
2 a code word representing the letter B, used in radio communication.
–ORIGIN mid 18th cent.: from French, from Italian, literally 'bold' (see **BRAVE**).

bra·vo[2] ▶ **n.** (pl. **bravos** or **bravoes**) a thug or hired assassin.
–ORIGIN late 16th cent.: from Italian, from *bravo* 'bold (one)' (see **BRAVE**).

bra·vu·ra /brə'v(y)o͞orə/ ▶ **n.** great technical skill and brilliance shown in a performance or activity: *the recital ended with a blazing display of bravura* | [as modifier] *a bravura performance.* ■ the display of great daring: *the show of bravura hid a guilty timidity.*
–ORIGIN mid 18th cent.: from Italian, from *bravo* 'bold.'

braw /brô/ ▶ **adj.** Scottish fine: *it was a braw day.*
–DERIVATIVES **braw·ly** adv.
–ORIGIN late 16th cent.: variant of **BRAVE**.

brawl /brôl/ ▶ **n.** a rough or noisy fight or quarrel.
▶ **v.** [no obj.] fight or quarrel in a rough or noisy way. ■ literary (of a stream) flow noisily.
–DERIVATIVES **brawl·er** n.
–ORIGIN late Middle English: perhaps ultimately imitative and related to **BRAY**[1].

brawn /brôn/ ▶ **n. 1** physical strength in contrast to intelligence: *commando work required as much brain as brawn.*
2 Brit. meat from a pig's or calf's head that is cooked and pressed in a pot with jelly.
–ORIGIN Middle English: from Old French *braon* 'fleshy part of the leg,' of Germanic origin; related to German *Braten* 'roast meat.'

brawn·y /'brônē/ ▶ **adj.** (**brawnier**, **brawniest**) physically strong; muscular.
–DERIVATIVES **brawn·i·ness** n.

Brax·ton Hicks con·trac·tions /,brakstən 'hiks/ ▶ **plural n.** Medicine intermittent weak contractions of the uterus occurring during pregnancy.
–ORIGIN early 20th cent.: named after John *Braxton Hicks* (1823–97), English gynecologist.

brax·y /'braksē/ ▶ **n.** a fatal bacterial infection of young sheep, caused by ingestion of frozen grass or contaminated feed. ● The bacterium is *Clostridium septicum.*
–ORIGIN late 18th cent.

bray[1] /brā/ ▶ **n.** [usu. in sing.] the loud, harsh cry of a donkey or mule. ■ a sound, voice, or laugh resembling such a cry.
▶ **v.** [no obj.] (of a donkey or mule) utter a bray. ■ (of a person) speak or laugh loudly and harshly: *he brayed with laughter* | [with direct speech] *'Leave!,' brayed a voice behind her.*
–ORIGIN Middle English: from Old French *brait* 'a shriek,' *braire* 'to cry' (the original senses in English), perhaps ultimately of Celtic origin.

bray[2] ▶ **v.** [with obj.] archaic pound or crush (something) to small pieces, typically with a pestle and mortar.
–ORIGIN late Middle English: from Old French *breier*, of Germanic origin; related to **BREAK**, **BRIOCHE**.

braze /brāz/ ▶ **v.** [with obj.] (often as adj. **brazed**) form, fix, or join by soldering with an alloy of copper and zinc at high temperature.
▶ **n.** a brazed joint.
–ORIGIN late 17th cent.: from French *braser* 'solder,' ultimately of Germanic origin.

bra·zen /'brāzən/ ▶ **adj. 1** bold and without shame: *he went about his illegal business with a brazen assurance* | *a brazen hussy!*
2 chiefly literary made of brass. ■ harsh in sound: *the music's brazen chords.*
–PHRASAL VERBS **brazen it** (or **something**) **out** endure an embarrassing or difficult situation by behaving with apparent confidence and lack of shame.
–DERIVATIVES **bra·zen·ly** adv., **bra·zen·ness** n.
–ORIGIN Old English *bræsen* 'made of brass,' from *bræs* 'brass,' of unknown ultimate origin.

bra·zier /'brāZHər/ ▶ **n. 1** a portable heater consisting of a pan or stand for holding lighted coals.
2 a barbecue.
–ORIGIN late 17th cent.: from French *brasier*, from *braise* 'hot coals.'

Bra·zil[1] /brə'zil/ the largest country in South America, in the east-central part of the continent, on the Atlantic Ocean; pop. 198,739,300 (est. 2009); capital, Brasilia; official language, Portuguese. Portuguese name **BRASIL**.

> Brazil is the fifth largest country in the world. Previously inhabited in large part by Tupi and Guarani peoples, Brazil was colonized by the Portuguese, who imported large numbers of slaves from West Africa to work on sugar plantations. The country was proclaimed an independent empire in 1822 and became a republic after the overthrow of the monarchy in 1889.

–DERIVATIVES **Bra·zil·ian** adj. & n.

Bra·zil[2] (also **brazil**) ▶ **n. 1** (also **Brazil nut**) a large three-sided nut with an edible kernel, several of which grow inside a large woody capsule. Brazil nuts grow on a South American forest tree, and most are harvested in the wild. ● *Bertholletia excelsa*, family Lecythidaceae.
2 (also **Brazil wood**) a hard red wood obtained from a tropical tree and from which dyes may be obtained. ● Genus *Caesalpinia*, family Leguminosae: several species.
–ORIGIN Middle English (sense 2): from medieval Latin *brasilium*. The South American country *Brazil* (see **BRAZIL**[1]) takes its name from the wood.

Braz·os Riv·er /'brazəs/ a river that flows southeast for 840 miles (1,350 km) across Texas, from the Panhandle to the Gulf of Mexico. The cities at its mouth are called collectively Brazosport.

Braz·za·ville /'brazə,vil, 'bräzə,vēl/ the capital of Congo, a major port; pop. 1,357,392 (2009). It was founded in 1880 by French explorer **Savorgnan de Brazza** (1852–1905) and was capital of French Equatorial Africa 1910–58.

BRB ▶ **abbr.** informal be right back (used in online conversations): *I'm takin' a juice break, BRB.*

breach /brēCH/ ▶ **n. 1** an act of breaking or failing to observe a law, agreement, or code of conduct: *a breach of confidence* | *I sued for breach of contract.* ■ a break in relations: *a sudden breach between father and son.*
2 a gap in a wall, barrier, or defense, esp. one made by an attacking army.
▶ **v.** [with obj.] **1** make a gap in and break through (a wall, barrier, or defense): *the river breached its bank.* ■ break or fail to observe (a law, agreement, or code of conduct).
2 [no obj.] (of a whale) rise and break through the surface of the water.
–PHRASES **breach of the peace** an act of violent or noisy behavior that causes a public disturbance and is considered a criminal offense. **breach of promise** the action of breaking a sworn assurance to do something, formerly esp. to marry someone. **step into the breach** replace someone who is suddenly unable to do a job or task.
–ORIGIN Middle English: from Old French *breche*, ultimately of Germanic origin; related to **BREAK**.

bread /bred/ ▶ **n. 1** food made of flour, water, and yeast or another leavening agent, mixed together and baked: *a loaf of bread* | [as modifier] *a bread roll* | *Italian breads.* ■ the bread or wafer used in the Eucharist: *altar bread.* ■ the food that one needs in order to live: *his day job puts bread on the table.*
2 informal money: *I hate doing this, but I need the bread.*
–PHRASES **the best** (or **greatest**) **thing since sliced bread** informal used to emphasize one's enthusiasm about a new idea, person, or thing: *they think that she is the greatest thing since sliced bread.* **bread and circuses** a diet of entertainment or political policies on which the masses are fed to keep them happy and docile. [translating Latin *panem et circenses* (Juvenal's *Satires*, x.80).] **bread and water** a frugal diet that is eaten in poverty, chosen in abstinence, or given as a punishment. **bread and wine** the consecrated elements used in the celebration of the Eucharist; the sacrament of the Eucharist. **the bread of life** something regarded as a source of spiritual nourishment: *the Roman Catholic Church and faith were the bread of life to the subordinate classes.* **break bread** celebrate the Eucharist. ■ literary share a meal with someone. **cast one's bread upon the waters** do good without expecting gratitude or reward. [with biblical allusion to Eccles. 11:1.] **daily bread** the money or food that one needs in order to live: *she earned her daily bread by working long hours.* **know which side one's bread is buttered** (**on**) informal know where one's advantage lies. **one cannot live by bread alone** people have spiritual as well as physical needs. [with biblical allusion to Deut. 8:3, Matt. 4:4.] **take the bread out of** (or **from**) **people's mouths** deprive people of their livings by competition or unfair working practices. **want one's bread buttered on both sides** informal want more than is practicable or than is reasonable to expect.
–ORIGIN Old English *brēad*, of Germanic origin; related to Dutch *brood* and German *Brot*.

bread and but·ter ▶ **n.** a person's livelihood or main source of income, typically as earned by routine work: *their bread and butter is reporting local events* | [as modifier] *bread-and-butter occupations.* ■ an everyday or ordinary person or thing: *the bread and butter of non-League soccer* | [as modifier] *a good bread-and-butter player.*

bread-and-but·ter let·ter ▶ **n.** a letter expressing thanks for hospitality.

bread-and-but·ter pick·le ▶ **n.** a variety of sweet pickle made with thin-sliced cucumbers and various seasonings.

Bread and But·ter State a nickname for the state of **MINNESOTA**.

bread·bas·ket /'bred,baskit/ ▶ **n. 1** a part of a region that produces cereals for the rest of it.
2 informal a person's stomach, considered as the target for a blow.

Bread·bas·ket of A·mer·i·ca a nickname for the state of **KANSAS**.

bread·board /'bred,bôrd/ ▶ **n.** a board for making an experimental model of an electric circuit.
▶ **v.** [with obj.] make (an experimental circuit).

PRONUNCIATION KEY ə *ago, up*; ər *over, fur*; a *hat*; ā *ate*; ä *car*; e *let*; ē *see*; i *fit*; ī *by*; NG *sing*; ō *go*; ô *law, for*; oi *toy*; o͝o *good*; o͞o *goo*; ou *out*; TH *thin*; T̲H̲ *then*; ZH *vision*

bread·box /ˈbredˌbäks/ ▶ **n.** a box for storing bread and other baked goods.

bread·crumb /ˈbredˌkrəm/ ▶ **n.** (usu. **breadcrumbs**) a small fragment of bread.
– DERIVATIVES **bread·crumbed adj.**

bread·ed /ˈbredid/ ▶ **adj.** (of food) coated with breadcrumbs and then fried: *lightly breaded chicken strips.*

bread·fruit /ˈbredˌfro͞ot/ ▶ **n. 1** the large, round, starchy fruit of a tropical tree, which is used as a vegetable and sometimes to make a substitute for flour.
2 (also **breadfruit tree**) the large evergreen tree that bears this fruit, which is widely cultivated on the islands of the Pacific and the Caribbean. ● *Artocarpus altilis*, family Moraceae.

bread knife ▶ **n.** a long knife, typically with a serrated edge, for slicing bread.

bread·line /ˈbredˌlīn/ ▶ **n.** a line of people waiting to receive free food.

bread mold ▶ **n.** any of various fungi, esp. of the genus *Rhizopus*, that grow on bread and other foods.

bread pud·ding ▶ **n.** a dessert consisting of slices of bread baked together with dried fruit, sugar, spices, eggs, and milk.

bread·stick /ˈbredˌstik/ ▶ **n.** a long, thin, often crisp piece of bread.

bread·stuff /ˈbredˌstəf/ ▶ **n.** any bread product. ■ grain or flour used in the making of bread.

breadth /bredTH/ ▶ **n.** the distance or measurement from side to side of something; width: *a black sweater outlined the breadth of his shoulders | the boat measured 27 feet **in breadth** | we traveled the length and breadth of India.* ■ wide range or extent: *she has the advantage of breadth of experience | there is a greater breadth of sound in the later recordings.* ■ dated a piece of cloth of standard or full width. ■ overall unity of artistic effect: *these masterpieces showed a new breadth of handling.*
– ORIGIN early 16th cent.: from obsolete *brede* in the same sense (related to BROAD) + -TH[2], on the pattern of *length.*

breadth·wise /ˈbredTHˌwīz/ (also **breadthways** /-ˌwāz/) ▶ **adv.** in a direction parallel with a thing's width.

bread·win·ner /ˈbredˌwinər/ ▶ **n.** a person who earns money to support a family.
– DERIVATIVES **bread·win·ning** /-ˌwiniNG/ **n.**

break /brāk/ ▶ **v.** (past **broke** /brōk/; past participle **broken** /ˈbrōkən/) **1** separate or cause to separate into pieces as a result of a blow, shock, or strain: [no obj.] *the rope broke with a loud snap | the slate fell from my hand and broke in two on the hard floor |* [with obj.] *windows in the street were broken by the blast | break the chocolate into pieces.* ■ sustain an injury involving the fracture of a bone or bones in a part of the body: [with obj.] *she had broken her leg in two places |* [no obj.] *what if his leg had broken?* ■ [with obj.] cause a cut or graze in (the skin): *the bite had scarcely broken the skin.* ■ make or become inoperative: [no obj.] *the machine has broken, and they can't fix it until next week |* [with obj.] *he's broken the video.* ■ (of the amniotic fluid surrounding a fetus) be or cause to be discharged when the sac is ruptured in the first stages of labor: [no obj.] *she realized her water had broken.* ■ [with obj.] open (a safe) forcibly. ■ [with obj.] use (a piece of paper currency) to pay for something and receive change out of the transaction: *she had to break a ten.* ■ [no obj.] (of two boxers or wrestlers) come out of a clinch, typically at the referee's command: *I was acting as referee and telling them to break.* ■ [with obj.] unfurl (a flag or sail). ■ [with obj.] succeed in deciphering (a code). ■ [with obj.] open (a shotgun or rifle) at the breech. ■ [with obj.] disprove (an alibi). ■ [with obj.] invalidate (a will) through legal process.
2 [with obj.] interrupt (a continuity, sequence, or course): *the new government broke the pattern of growth | his concentration was broken by a sound.* ■ put an end to (a silence) by speaking or making contact. ■ make a pause in (a journey): *we will break our journey in Venice.* ■ [no obj.] stop proceedings in order to have a pause or vacation: *at mid-morning they **broke for** coffee.* ■ lessen the impact of (a fall): *she put out an arm to break her fall.* ■ stop oneself from being subject to (a habit). ■ put an end to (a tie in a game) by making a score. ■ [no obj.] (chiefly of an attacking player or team, or of a military force) make a rush or dash in a particular direction: *the flight broke to the right and formed a defensive circle.* ■ surpass (a record): *the movie broke box-office records.* ■ disconnect or interrupt (an electrical circuit). ■ [no obj.] (of a pitched baseball) curve or drop on its way toward the batter. ■ [no obj.] Soccer (of the ball) rebound unpredictably: *the ball broke to Craig but his shot rebounded from the post.* ■ [no obj.] (of a bowled cricket ball) change direction on bouncing, due to spin.
3 [with obj.] fail to observe (a law, regulation, or agreement): *the district attorney says she will prosecute retailers who break the law | a legally binding contract that can only be broken by mutual consent.* ■ fail to continue with (a self-imposed discipline): *diets started without preparation are broken all the time.*
4 [with obj.] crush the emotional strength, spirit, or resistance of: *the idea was to better the prisoners, not to break them.* ■ [no obj.] (of a person's emotional strength) give way: *her self-control finally broke.* ■ destroy the power of (a movement or organization). ■ destroy the effectiveness of (a strike), typically by bringing in other people to replace the striking workers. ■ tame or train (a horse).
5 [no obj.] undergo a change or enter a new state, in particular: ■ (of the weather) change suddenly: *the weather broke, and thunder rumbled through a leaden sky.* ■ (of a storm) begin violently. ■ (of dawn or day) begin with the sun rising: *dawn was just breaking.* ■ (of clouds) move apart and begin to disperse. ■ (of waves) curl over and dissolve into foam: *the Caribbean sea breaking gently on the shore.* ■ (of the voice) falter and change tone, due to emotion: *her voice broke as she relived the experience.* ■ (of a boy's voice) change in tone and register at puberty. ■ Phonetics (of a vowel) develop into a diphthong, under the influence of an adjacent sound. ■ (of prices on the stock exchange) fall sharply. ■ (of news or a scandal) suddenly become public: *since the news broke I've received thousands of wonderful letters.* ■ [with obj.] (**break something to someone**) make bad news known to someone. ■ make the first stroke at the beginning of a game of billiards, pool, or snooker.
▶ **n. 1** an interruption of continuity or uniformity: *the magazine has been published without a break since 1950.* ■ an act of separating oneself from a state of affairs: *a **break with** the past.* ■ a change in the weather. ■ [with modifier] a change of line, paragraph, or page: *dotted lines on the screen show page breaks.* ■ a curve or drop in the path of a pitched baseball. ■ a change of tone in the voice due to emotion: *there was a break in her voice now.* ■ an interruption in an electrical circuit. ■ a rush or dash in a particular direction, esp. by an attacking player or team: *he made a bounce pass for a basket on the break in the second quarter.* ■ a breakout, esp. from prison. ■ a sudden decrease, typically in prices. ■ informal an opportunity or chance, esp. one leading to professional success: *his big break came when a critic gave him a rave review.* ■ (also **break of serve** or **service break**) Tennis the winning of a game against an opponent's serve.
2 a pause in work or during an activity or event: *I need a **break from** mental activity | they take long coffee breaks | those returning to work after a career break.* ■ a short vacation: *the Christmas break.* ■ a short solo or instrumental passage in jazz or popular music.
3 a gap or opening: *the spectacular vistas occasionally offered by a break in the rain forest | he stopped to wait for a break in the traffic.*
4 an instance of breaking; the point where something is broken: *a break in the valve was being repaired.*
5 Billiards & Snooker a player's turn to make the opening shot of a game or a rack. ■ a consecutive series of successful shots, scoring a specified number of points: *a break of 83 put him in front for the first time.*
– PHRASES **break a leg!** theatrical slang good luck! **break bread** see BREAD. **break camp** see CAMP[1]. **break cover** (of game being hunted) emerge into the open. **break someone's heart** see HEART. **break in two** break into two parts. **break of day** dawn. **break ranks** see RANK[1]. **break (someone's) serve** (or **service**) win a game in a tennis match against an opponent's service. **break step** see STEP. **break the back of** do the hardest part of (a task): *we've broken the back of the problem.* ■ overwhelm or defeat: *I thought we really had broken the back of inflation.* **break the bank** see BANK[2]. **break the ice** see ICE. **break the mold** see MOLD[1]. **break wind** release gas from the anus. **give someone a break** [usu. in imperative] informal stop putting pressure on someone about something. ■ (**give me a break**) used to express contemptuous disagreement or disbelief about what has been said: *He's seven times as quick and he's only 20 years old. Give me a break.* **make a break for** make a sudden dash in the direction of, typically in a bid to escape: *he made a break for the door.* **make a clean break** remove oneself completely and finally from a situation or relationship. **those are** (or **them's**) **the breaks** that is the way things turn out.
– PHRASAL VERBS **break away** (of a person) escape from someone's hold. ■ escape from the control of a person, group, or practice: *an attempt to **break away from** the elitism that has dominated the book trade.* ■ (of a competitor in a race) move into the lead. ■ (of a material or object) become detached from its base, typically through decay or under force. **break down 1** (of a machine or motor vehicle) suddenly cease to function: *his van broke down.* ■ (of a person) have the vehicle they are driving cease to function: *she broke down on the highway.* ■ (of a relationship, agreement, or process) cease to continue; collapse: *pay negotiations with management broke down.* ■ lose control of one's emotions when in a state of distress: *if she had tried to utter a word, she would have broken down | the old woman broke down in tears.* ■ (of a person's health or emotional control) fail or collapse: *his health broke down under the strain of overwork.* **2** undergo chemical decomposition: *waste products that **break down into** low-level toxic materials.* **break something down 1** demolish a door or other barrier: *they had to get the police to break the door down |* figurative *race barriers can be broken down by educational reform.* **2** separate something into parts: *each tutorial is broken down into more manageable units.* ■ analyze information: *bar graphs show how the information can be broken down.* ■ convert a substance into simpler compounds by chemical action: *almost every natural substance can be broken down by bacteria.* **break even** reach a point in a business venture when the profits are equal to the costs. **break forth** burst out suddenly; emerge. **break free** another way of saying BREAK AWAY. **break in 1** force entry to a building: *it sounded like someone trying to break in.* **2** [with direct speech] interject: *"I don't want to interfere," Mrs. Hendry broke in.* **break someone in** familiarize someone with a new job or situation: *there was no time to break in a new executive assistant.* ■ (**break a horse**) accustom a horse to a saddle and bridle, and to being ridden. **break something in** wear something, typically a pair of new shoes, until it becomes supple and comfortable. **break in on** interrupt: *the doctor's voice **broke in on** her thoughts.* **break into 1** enter or open a (place, vehicle, or container) forcibly, typically for the purposes of theft: *four men broke into the house | a friend of mine had his car broken into.* ■ succeed in winning a share of (a market or a position in a profession): *Japanese companies failed to break into the US personal-computer market.* ■ interrupt (a conversation). **2** (of a person) suddenly or unexpectedly burst forth into (laughter or song). ■ (of a person's face or mouth) relax into (a smile). **3** change one's pace to (a faster one): *Greg broke into a sprint.* **break off** become severed: *the fuselage had broken off just behind the pilot's seat.* ■ abruptly stop talking: *she broke off, stifling a sob.* **break something off** remove something from a larger unit or whole: *Tucker broke off a piece of bread.* ■ discontinue talks or relations: *the US threatened to break off diplomatic relations.* **break something open** open something forcibly. **break out** (of war, fighting, or similarly undesirable things) start suddenly: *forest fires have broken out across Indonesia.* ■ (of a physical discomfort) suddenly manifest itself: *prickles of sweat had broken out along her backbone.* **break out in** (of a person or a part of their body) be suddenly affected by an unpleasant sensation or condition: *something had caused him to break out in a rash.* **break out of** escape from: figurative *executives looking to break out of the corporate hierarchy.* **break something out** informal open and start using something: *it was time to break out the champagne.* **break through** make or force a way through (a barrier): *demonstrators attempted to break through the police lines | the sun might break through in a few spots.* ■ (of a person) achieve success in a particular area: *so many talented players are struggling to break through.* **break up** disintegrate; disperse: *the bones had broken up into minute fragments | the gray clouds had begun to break up.* ■ (of a gathering) disband; end. ■ Brit. end the school term: *we broke up for the summer.* ■ (of a couple in a relationship) part company. ■ start laughing uncontrollably: *the whole cast broke up.* ■ become emotionally upset. **break someone up** cause someone to become extremely upset. **break something up** cause something to separate into pieces, parts, or sections: *break up the chocolate, and place it in a bowl | he intends to break the company up into strategic business units.* ■ bring a social event or meeting to an end by being the first person to leave: *Richard was sorry to break up the party.* ■ disperse or put an end to a gathering: *police broke up a demonstration in the capital.* **break with** quarrel or cease relations with (someone): *he had broken with his family long before.* ■ act in a way that is not in accordance with (a custom or tradition).
– ORIGIN Old English *brecan* (verb), of Germanic origin; related to Dutch *breken* and German *brechen*, from an Indo-European root shared by Latin *frangere* 'to break.'

break·a·ble /ˈbrākəbəl/ ▶ **adj.** capable of breaking or being broken easily: *breakable ornaments | an encrypted password isn't easily breakable.*
▶ **n.** (**breakables**) things that are fragile and easily broken.

break·age /ˈbrākij/ ▶ **n.** the action of breaking something, or the fact of being broken: *some breakage of bone has occurred | there had been three breakages in the overhead wires.*

break·a·way /ˈbrākəˌwā/ ▶ **n. 1** a divergence or radical change from something established or long standing: *rock was a* ***breakaway from*** *pop* | [as modifier] *the breakaway hit movie.* ■ a secession of a number of people from an organization, typically following conflict or disagreement and resulting in the establishment of a new organization: [as modifier] *the breakaway republic.*
2 Sports a sudden attack or forward movement, esp. in a bicycle race or in hockey or football: *a winning breakaway.*
3 an object, such as a stage prop, designed to break apart easily: [as modifier] *barroom brawls are staged with breakaway furniture.*

break·beat /ˈbrākˌbēt/ ▶ **n.** Music a repeated sample of a drumbeat, usually forming a fast syncopated rhythm, used as a basis for dance music. ■ dance music featuring breakbeats.

break·bone fe·ver /ˈbrākˌbōn/ ▶ **n.** another term for DENGUE.

break-bulk ▶ **adj.** [attrib.] denoting a system of transporting cargo as separate pieces rather than in containers.

break crop ▶ **n.** a crop grown between fields of grain to ensure a varied planting pattern.

break·danc·ing /ˈbrākˌdansiNG/ ▶ **n.** an energetic and acrobatic style of street dancing, developed by American blacks.
– DERIVATIVES **break·dance v. & n., break·danc·er** /-ˌdansər/ **n.**

break·down /ˈbrākˌdoun/ ▶ **n. 1** a mechanical failure.
2 a failure of a relationship or system: *the breakdown of their marriage | a breakdown in military discipline.* ■ a sudden collapse in someone's mental health.
3 the chemical or physical decomposition of something: *the breakdown of ammonia to nitrites.* ■ an explanatory analysis, esp. of statistics: *a detailed cost breakdown.*
4 a lively, energetic American country dance.

break·er /ˈbrākər/ ▶ **n. 1** a heavy sea wave that breaks into white foam on the shore or a shoal.
2 a person or thing that breaks something: [in combination] *a rule-breaker | a code-breaker.* ■ a person who breaks horses. ■ short for CIRCUIT BREAKER.
3 a person who interrupts the conversation of others on a Citizens' Band radio channel, indicating a wish to transmit a message. ■ any CB radio user.
4 a break dancer.

break-e·ven ▶ **n.** the point or state at which a person or company breaks even: [as modifier] *the break-even point.*

break·fall ▶ **n.** (in martial arts) a controlled fall in which most of the impact is absorbed by the arms or legs.

break·fast /ˈbrekfəst/ ▶ **n.** a meal eaten in the morning, the first of the day: *I often have toast for my breakfast | I don't eat breakfast.*
▶ **v.** [no obj.] have this meal: *she* ***breakfasted on*** *French toast and bacon.*
– PHRASES **have** (or **eat**) **someone for breakfast** informal deal with or defeat someone with contemptuous ease.
– DERIVATIVES **break·fast·er n., break·fast·less adj.**
– ORIGIN late Middle English: from the verb BREAK + FAST².

break·front /ˈbrākˌfrənt/ ▶ **n.** a piece of furniture having the line of its front broken by a curve or angle: [as modifier] *a breakfront bookcase.*

break-in ▶ **n.** a forced or unconsented entry into a building, car, computer system, etc., typically to steal something.

break·ing and en·ter·ing ▶ **n.** the crime of entering a building by force so as to commit burglary.

break·ing point ▶ **n.** the moment of greatest strain at which someone or something gives way: *the tense situation* ***reached the breaking point*** *late last week | her nerves were stretched to the breaking point.*

break·neck /ˈbrākˌnek/ ▶ **adj.** [attrib.] dangerously or extremely fast: *he drove at breakneck speed.*

break-off ▶ **n.** an instance of breaking something off or of discontinuing something.

break·out /ˈbrākˌout/ ▶ **n. 1** a forcible escape, typically from prison: *a prison breakout.* ■ [in sing.] (in soccer, hockey, and other sports) a sudden attack by a team that had been defending.
2 [in sing.] an outbreak: *a breakout of hostilities.*
3 a categorized list: *an excellent breakout of websites by topic.*
4 a sudden advance to a new level: *gold was overdue for a breakout.*
5 the deformation or splintering of wood, stone, or other material being drilled or planed.
▶ **adj.** informal **1** suddenly and extremely popular or successful: *a breakout movie.*
2 denoting or relating to groups that break away from a conference or other larger gathering for discussion: *we divided into 15 breakout groups.*

break point ▶ **n. 1** a place or time at which an interruption or change is made. ■ (usu. **breakpoint**) Computing a place in a computer program where the sequence of instructions is interrupted, esp. by another program or by the operator.
2 Tennis the state of a game when the side receiving service needs only one more point to win the game: *he hit a winner to reach break point.*
3 another term for BREAKING POINT.

Break·spear /ˈbrākˌspi(ə)r/, Nicholas, see ADRIAN IV.

break·through /ˈbrākˌTHro͞o/ ▶ **n.** a sudden, dramatic, and important discovery or development: *a major breakthrough in DNA research.*

break·through bleed·ing ▶ **n.** bleeding from the uterus occurring between menstrual periods, a side effect of some oral contraceptives.

break·through pain ▶ **n.** (usually in connection with cancer) severe pain that erupts while a patient is already medicated with a long-acting painkiller.

break·up /ˈbrākˌəp/ ▶ **n.** an end to a relationship, typically a marriage. ■ a division of a country or organization into smaller autonomous units: *the breakup of the two states constituting Czechoslovakia.* ■ a physical disintegration of something: *large quantities of oil are released after the breakup of a tanker | the spring breakup of the ice.*

break·wa·ter /ˈbrākˌwôtər, -ˌwätər/ ▶ **n.** a barrier built out into a body of water to protect a coast or harbor from the force of waves.

bream¹ /brim, brēm/ ▶ **n.** (pl. **same**) a greenish-bronze deep-bodied freshwater fish native to Europe, popular with anglers. ● *Abramis brama*, family Cyprinidae. ■ used in names of other fishes resembling or related to this, e.g., **sea bream**.
– ORIGIN late Middle English: from Old French *bresme*, of Germanic origin; related to German *Brachsen, Brassen.*

bream² /brēm/ ▶ **v.** [with obj.] Nautical, archaic clear (a ship or its bottom) of weeds, shells, or other accumulated matter by burning and scraping it.
– ORIGIN late 15th cent.: probably of Low German origin and related to BROOM.

breast /brest/ ▶ **n.** either of the two soft, protruding organs on the upper front of a woman's body that secrete milk after pregnancy. ■ the corresponding less-developed part of a man's body. ■ a person's chest: *her heart was hammering in her breast.* ■ the corresponding part of a bird or mammal: [as modifier] *the breast feathers of the doves.* ■ a portion of poultry cut from such a part: *a grilled chicken breast.* ■ the part of a garment that covers the chest: [as modifier] *a breast pocket.*
▶ **v.** [with obj.] face and move forward against or through (something): *I watched him breast the wave.* ■ reach the top of (a hill).
– PHRASES **beat one's breast** make an exaggerated show of sorrow, despair, or regret. **make a clean breast of something** see CLEAN.
– DERIVATIVES **breast·ed adj.** [in combination] *a bare-breasted woman | a crimson-breasted bird.*
– ORIGIN Old English *brēost*, of Germanic origin; related to Dutch *borst* and German *Brust.*

breast-beat·ing ▶ **n.** a loud, emotional expression of remorse: *the breast-beating of American media commentators* | [as modifier] *the breast-beating advocates of the people.*

breast·bone /ˈbrestˌbōn/ ▶ **n.** a thin, flat bone running down the center of the chest and connecting the ribs. Also called STERNUM.

breast col·lar ▶ **n.** a thick chest strap that forms part of a horse's harness, often used instead of an ordinary collar on horses pulling lightweight or show vehicles.

breast drill ▶ **n.** a drill on which pressure is brought to bear by the operator's chest.

breastfeed /ˈbrestˌfēd/ ▶ **v.** (past and past participle **breastfed**) [with obj.] (of a woman) feed (a baby) with milk from the breast: *she breastfed her first child* | [no obj.] *sometimes it is not possible to breastfeed.* ■ [no obj.] (of a baby) feed from the breast: *the child began to breastfeed.*

breast·hook /ˈbrestˌho͝ok/ ▶ **n.** a large piece of shaped timber fitted horizontally in the bows of a ship, used to connect the sides to the stem.

breast im·plant ▶ **n.** a prosthesis consisting of a gel-like or fluid material in a flexible sac, implanted behind or in place of a female breast in reconstructive or cosmetic surgery.

breast·plate /ˈbrestˌplāt/ ▶ **n. 1** a piece of armor covering the chest.
2 Judaism in ancient times, a jeweled vestment covering the chest of the Jewish high priest.
3 a set of straps attached to the front of a saddle, which pass across the horse's chest and prevent the saddle from slipping backward. ■ the strap of a harness covering the chest of a horse.

breast pump ▶ **n.** a device for drawing milk from a woman's breasts by suction.

breast·stroke /ˈbrestˌstrōk/ ▶ **n.** [in sing.] a style of swimming on one's front, in which the arms are pushed forward and then swept back in a circular movement, while the legs are tucked in toward the body and then kicked out in a corresponding movement. ■ (**the breaststroke**) a race, typically of a specified length or kind, in which such a style of swimming is used: *she won the 200 m breaststroke.*

breast·work /ˈbrestˌwərk/ ▶ **n.** a low temporary defense or parapet.

breath /breTH/ ▶ **n.** the air taken into or expelled from the lungs: *I was gasping for breath | his breath smelled of garlic.* ■ an inhalation or exhalation of air from the lungs: *she drew in a quick breath | take three deep breaths.* ■ archaic the power of breathing; life. ■ a brief moment; the time required for one act of respiration: *in Las Vegas, they marry you in a breath.* ■ [in sing.] a slight movement of air: *the weather was balmy, not a breath of wind.* ■ [in sing.] a sign, hint, or suggestion: *he avoided the slightest breath of scandal.*
– PHRASES **a breath of fresh air** a small amount of or a brief time in the fresh air. ■ a refreshing change: *the company's no-nonsense attitude is a breath of fresh air.* **the breath of life** a thing that someone needs or depends on: *politics has been the breath of life to her for 50 years.* **catch one's breath 1** cease breathing momentarily in surprise or fear. **2** rest after exercise to restore normal breathing: *she stood for a few moments, catching her breath.* **don't hold your breath** informal used hyperbolically to indicate that something is likely to take a long time: *don't hold your breath waiting for Congress to clean up political action committees.* **draw breath** breathe in. **get one's breath** (**back**) begin to breathe normally again after exercise or exertion. **hold one's breath** cease breathing temporarily. ■ be in a state of suspense or anticipation: *France held its breath while the Senate chose its new president.* **in the same** (or **next**) **breath** at the same time: *he congratulated Simon on his victory but in the same breath dismissed it.* **last breath** the last moment of one's life (often used hyperbolically); death: *she would fight to the last breath to preserve her good name.* **out of breath** gasping for air, typically after exercise: *he arrived on the top floor out of breath.* **save one's breath** stop wasting time in futile talk: *save your breath; I know all about it.* **take someone's breath away** astonish or inspire someone with awed respect or delight. **under** (or **below**) **one's breath** in a very quiet voice; almost inaudibly: *he swore violently under his breath.* Compare with SOTTO VOCE. **waste one's breath** talk or give advice without effect: *I have better things to do than waste my breath arguing.*
– ORIGIN Old English *brǣth* 'smell, scent,' of Germanic origin; related to BROOD.

breath·a·ble /ˈbrēT͟Həbəl/ ▶ **adj.** (of the air) fit or pleasant to breathe. ■ (of clothes or material) admitting air to the skin and allowing sweat to evaporate.

breath·a·lyze /ˈbreTHəˌlīz/ ▶ **v.** [with obj.] (usu. **be breathalyzed**) (of the police) use a breathalyzer.

breath·a·lyz·er /ˈbreTHəˌlīzər/ (also **Breathalyzer**) ▶ **n.** trademark a device used by police for measuring the amount of alcohol in a driver's breath.
– ORIGIN 1960s: blend of BREATH and (*an*)*alyze* + -ER¹.

breath·ar·i·an /breTHˈe(ə)rēən/ ▶ **n.** a person who believes that it is possible, through meditation, to reach a level of consciousness where one can obtain all sustenance from the air or sunlight.

breathe /brēT͟H/ ▶ **v.** [no obj.] take air into the lungs and then expel it, esp. as a regular physiological process: *she was wheezing as she breathed | breathe in through your nose | he breathed out heavily* | [with obj.] *we are polluting the air we breathe.* ■ be or seem to be alive because of this: *at least I'm still breathing.*

PRONUNCIATION KEY ə *ago, up*; ər *over, fur*; a *hat*; ā *ate*; ä *car*; e *let*; ē *see*; i *fit*; ī *by*; NG *sing*; ō *go*; ô *law, for*; oi *toy*; o͝o *good*; o͞o *goo*; ou *out*; TH *thin*; T͟H *then*; ZH *vision*

b

■ literary (of wind) blow softly. ■ [with direct speech] say something with quiet intensity: *"We're together at last," she breathed.* ■ (of an animal or plant) respire or exchange gases: *plants breathe through their roots.* ■ [with obj.] give an impression of (something): *the whole room breathed an air of hygienic efficiency.* ■ (of wine) be exposed to fresh air: *red wine needs untold time to breathe.* ■ (of material or soil) admit or emit air or moisture: *let your lawn breathe by putting air into the soil.* ■ [with obj.] allow (a horse) to rest after exertion. ■ **(breathe upon)** archaic or literary tarnish or taint: *before the queen's fair name was breathed upon.*
– PHRASES **breathe (freely) again** relax after being frightened or tense about something: *she wouldn't breathe freely again until she was airborne.* **breathe down someone's neck** follow closely behind someone. ■ constantly check up on someone. **breathe one's last** die. **breathe (new) life into** fill with enthusiasm and energy; reinvigorate: *spring breathes new life into a wintry woods.* **breathe a sigh of relief** exhale noisily as a sign of relief (often used hyperbolically): *they breathed a great sigh of relief after the election was won.* **live and breathe** see LIVE[1]. **not breathe a word** remain silent about something; keep secret.
– ORIGIN Middle English (in the sense 'exhale, steam'): from BREATH.

breathed /breTHt/ ▶ adj. **1** [usu. in combination] having breath of a specified kind: *a foul-breathed poodle.* **2** (also /brēTHd/) Phonetics unvoiced; voiceless.

breath·er /'brēTHər/ ▶ n. **1** [in sing.] informal a brief pause for rest: *the director is taking a breather from his furious schedule.* **2** a vent or valve to release pressure or to allow air to move freely around something: *a cask breather* | [as modifier] *a breather pipe.* **3** a person or animal that breathes in a particular way, or breathes a particular substance: *a heavy breather* | [in combination] *reptiles are lung-breathers.*

breath·ing /'brēTHiNG/ ▶ n. **1** the process of taking air into and expelling it from the lungs: *his breathing was shallow.* **2** a sign in Greek (ʻ or ʼ) indicating the presence of an aspirate (**rough breathing**) or the absence of an aspirate (**smooth breathing**) at the beginning of a word.

breath·ing room ▶ n. sufficient room to move and breathe comfortably. ■ breathing space.

breath·ing space ▶ n. [in sing.] an opportunity to pause, relax, or decide what to do next.

breath·less /'breTHlis/ ▶ adj. gasping for breath, typically due to exertion: *the climb left me breathless.* ■ short of breath or appearing this way because of excitement or other strong feelings: *her breathless account of what happened in the courtroom.* ■ (of the air or weather) unstirred by a wind or breeze; stiflingly still: *the warm, breathless air.*
– DERIVATIVES **breath·less·ly** adv., **breath·less·ness** n.

breath·tak·ing /'breTH,tākiNG/ ▶ adj. astonishing or awe-inspiring in quality, so as to take one's breath away: *the scene was one of breathtaking beauty.*
– DERIVATIVES **breath·tak·ing·ly** adv.

breath test ▶ n. a test in which a driver is made to blow into a breathalyzer to check the amount of alcohol that has been drunk.
▶ v. **(breath-test)** [with obj.] give (someone) such a test.

breath·y /'breTHē/ ▶ adj. **(breathier, breathiest)** producing or causing an audible sound of breathing, often related to physical exertion or strong feelings: *a breathy laugh.*
– DERIVATIVES **breath·i·ly** /'breTHəlē/ adv., **breath·i·ness** n.

brec·ci·a /'brechēə, 'bresH-/ ▶ n. Geology rock consisting of angular fragments cemented together.
– DERIVATIVES **brec·ci·ate** /-ē,āt/ v., **brec·ci·a·tion** /,brechē'āsHən, ,bresH-/ n.
– ORIGIN late 18th cent.: from Italian, literally 'gravel,' ultimately of Germanic origin and related to BREAK.

Brecht /brekt, brekHt/, (Eugen) Bertolt (Friedrich) (1898–1956), German playwright, producer, and poet. His interest in combining music and drama led to collaboration with Kurt Weill in *The Threepenny Opera* (1928). Brecht's later dramas include *Mother Courage* (1941) and *The Caucasian Chalk Circle* (1948).

bred /bred/ past and participle of BREED.
▶ adj. [usu. in combination] (of a person or animal) reared in a specified environment or way: *a city-bred man.*

Bre·da /brä'dä, 'brädə/ a manufacturing town in the southwestern Netherlands; pop. 170,960 (2008). Historically, it is noted for the Compromise of Breda of 1566; the 1660 manifesto of Charles II; and the Treaty of Breda.

bred-in-the-bone ▶ adj. firmly established; deep-rooted. ■ long established and unlikely to change; inveterate.

breech /brēcH/ ▶ n. **1** the part of a cannon behind the bore. ■ the back part of a rifle or gun barrel. **2** archaic a person's buttocks.
▶ v. [with obj.] archaic put (a boy) into breeches after being in petticoats since birth.
– ORIGIN Old English *brēc* (plural of *brōc*, of Germanic origin; related to Dutch *broek*), interpreted as a singular form. The original sense was 'garment covering the loins and thighs' (compare with BREECHES), hence 'the buttocks' (sense 2 of the noun, mid 16th cent.), later 'the hind part' of anything (late 16th cent).

breech birth (also **breech delivery**) ▶ n. a delivery of a baby so positioned in the uterus that the buttocks or feet are delivered first.

breech·block /'brēcH,bläk/ ▶ n. a metal block that closes the aperture at the back part of a rifle or gun barrel.

breech·clout /'brēcH,klout/ ▶ n. (also **breechcloth**) another term for LOINCLOTH.

breech·es /'bricHiz, 'brē-/ ▶ plural n. short trousers fastened just below the knee, now chiefly worn for riding a horse or as part of ceremonial dress. ■ informal trousers.
– PHRASES **too big for one's breeches** see BIG.
– ORIGIN Middle English: plural of BREECH.

Breech·es Bi·ble ▶ n. the Geneva Bible of 1560, so named because the word *breeches* is used in Gen. 3:7 for the garments made by Adam and Eve.

breech·es bu·oy ▶ n. a lifebuoy with canvas breeches attached that, when suspended from a rope, can be used to transfer a person to safety from a ship.

breech·ing /'brēcHiNG/ ▶ n. **1** a strong leather strap passing around the hindquarters of a horse harnessed to a vehicle. **2** historical a thick rope used to secure the carriage of a cannon on a ship and to absorb the force of the recoil. **3** the hair or wool on the hindquarters of an animal.

breech-load·er ▶ n. a gun designed to have ammunition inserted at the breech rather than through the muzzle.
– DERIVATIVES **breech-load·ing** adj.

breech pre·sen·ta·tion ▶ n. a position of a fetus in which the feet or buttocks appear first during birth.

breed /brēd/ ▶ v. (past and past participle **bred** /bred/) [with obj.] cause (an animal) to produce offspring, typically in a controlled and organized way: *he wants to see the animals his new stock has been bred from.* ■ [no obj.] (of animals) mate and then produce offspring: *toads are said to return to the pond of their birth to breed* | (as adj. **breeding**) *the breeding season.* ■ develop (a kind of animal or plant) for a particular purpose or quality: *these horses are bred for this sport.* ■ rear and train (someone) to behave in a particular way or have certain qualities: *Theresa had been beautifully bred.* ■ cause (something) to happen or occur, typically over a period of time: *success breeds confidence.* ■ Physics create (fissile material) by nuclear reaction.
▶ n. a stock of animals or plants within a species having a distinctive appearance and typically having been developed by deliberate selection. ■ a sort or kind of person or thing: *a new breed of entrepreneurs was brought into being.*
– PHRASES **a breed apart** a sort or kind or person that is very different from the norm: *Japanese capitalism is a breed apart from that found in the US.* **a dying breed** a sort or kind of person that is slowly disappearing: *the country's dying breed of elder statesmen.* **what's bred in the bone will come out in the flesh** (or **blood**) see BONE.
– ORIGIN Old English *brēdan* 'produce (offspring), bear (a child),' of Germanic origin; related to German *brüten*, also to BROOD.

breed·er /'brēdər/ ▶ n. a person who breeds livestock, racehorses, other animals, or plants: *a plant breeder* | *a breeder of fine cattle.* ■ an animal that breeds at a particular time or in a particular way: *emperor penguins are winter breeders.* ■ informal, derogatory (among homosexuals) a heterosexual person.

breed·er doc·u·ment ▶ n. a document, genuine or fraudulent, that can serve as a basis to obtain other identification documents or benefits fraudulently.

breed·er re·ac·tor ▶ n. a nuclear reactor that creates fissile material (typically plutonium-239 by irradiation of uranium-238) at a faster rate than it uses another fissile material (typically uranium-235) as fuel.

breed·ing /'brēdiNG/ ▶ n. the mating and production of offspring by animals: *palolo worms use the moon to time their breeding.* ■ the activity of controlling the mating and production of offspring of animals: *the breeding of rats and mice for experiments.* ■ training and education, esp. in proper social behavior: *a girl of good breeding.* ■ the good manners regarded as characteristic of the aristocracy and conferred by heredity: *a lady of breeding.*

breed·ing ground ▶ n. an area where birds, fish, or other animals habitually breed. ■ [usu. in sing.] a thing that favors the development or occurrence of something: *Austin is a breeding ground for musical talent.*

breeks /brēks/ ▶ plural n. Scottish term for BREECHES.

breeze[1] /brēz/ ▶ n. **1** a gentle wind. ■ [with modifier] a wind of force 2 to 6 on the Beaufort scale (4–27 knots or 4.5-31 mph). **2** informal a thing that is easy to do or accomplish: *traveling through London was a breeze.*
▶ v. [no obj.] informal come or go in a casual or lighthearted manner: *I breezed in as if nothing were wrong.* ■ deal with something with apparently casual ease: *the computer has the power to breeze through huge documents* | *he breezed to victory.*
– PHRASES **shoot the breeze** see SHOOT.
– ORIGIN mid 16th cent.: probably from Old Spanish and Portuguese *briza* 'northeastern wind' (the original sense in English).

breeze[2] ▶ n. small cinders mixed with sand and cement to make cinder blocks.
– ORIGIN late 16th cent.: from French *braise*, (earlier) *brese* 'live coals.'

breeze block ▶ n. British term for CINDER BLOCK.

breeze·way /'brēz,wā/ ▶ n. a roofed outdoor passage, as between a house and a garage.

breez·y /'brēzē/ ▶ adj. **(breezier, breeziest)** **1** pleasantly windy: *it was a bright, breezy day.* **2** appearing relaxed, informal, and cheerily brisk: *the text is written in a breezy, matter-of-fact manner.*
– DERIVATIVES **breez·i·ly** /-zəlē/ adv., **breez·i·ness** n.

Brel /brel/, Jacques (1929–78), Belgian singer and composer.

Brem·en /'brämən, 'bremən/ a state in northeastern Germany. Divided into two parts, which center on the city of Bremen and the port of Bremerhaven, it is surrounded by the state of Lower Saxony. ■ its capital, an industrial city linked by the Weser River to the port of Bremerhaven and the North Sea; pop. 547,900 (est. 2006).

Brem·er·ha·ven /'bremər,hävən/ a seaport in northwestern Germany, on the North Sea coast, north of Bremen; pop. 115,300 (est. 2007). Bremerhaven is one of the largest seaports and fishing centers in Europe. The first regular shipping service between the US and Europe began here. Former name **Wesermünde**.

Brem·er·ton /'bremərtən/ a city in west central Washington, on Puget Sound, home to large naval shipyards; pop. 36,006 (est. 2008).

brems·strah·lung /'brem,sHträləNG/ ▶ n. Physics electromagnetic radiation produced by the acceleration or esp. the deceleration of a charged particle after passing through the electric and magnetic fields of a nucleus.
– ORIGIN 1940s: from German, from *bremsen* 'to brake' + *Strahlung* 'radiation.'

Bren /bren/ (also **Bren gun**) ▶ n. a lightweight quick-firing machine gun used by the Allied Forces in World War II.
– ORIGIN blend of *Brno* (a town in the Czech Republic where it was originally made) and *Enfield* in England (site of the Royal Small Arms Factory where it was later made).

Bren·dan, St. /'brendən/ (c.486–c.575), Irish abbot. Feast day, May 16.

Bren·nan, William Joseph, Jr. (1906–97), US Supreme Court associate justice 1956–90. He was a New Jersey Supreme Court judge 1952–56 before being appointed to the US Supreme Court by President Eisenhower. He was noted for his defense of First Amendment rights.

Bren·ner Pass /'brenər/ an Alpine pass at the border between Austria and Italy, on the route between Innsbruck and Bolzano, at an altitude of 4,450 feet (1,371 m).

brent goose /brent/ ▶ n. British term for BRANT.
– ORIGIN late Middle English: of unknown origin.

Brent·wood /'brent,wo͝od/ **1** a village in central Long Island in New York; pop. 53,917 (2000). **2** a section of West Los Angeles, California, noted for expensive homes and celebrity inhabitants.

bre·sao·la /bre'sōlə, bri'zō-/ ▶ n. an Italian dish of raw beef cured by salting and air-drying, served typically in slices with a dressing of olive oil, lemon juice, and black pepper.
– ORIGIN Italian, from *bresada*, past part. of *brasare* 'braise.'

Bre·scia /'brāsHə, 'bresHə/ an industrial city in northern Italy, in the region of Lombardy; pop. 190,844 (2008).

Bres·lau /'bres,lou/ German name for **Wrocław**.

Bres·lin /'brezlən/, Jimmy (1930–), US journalist and writer. He wrote *The Gang That Couldn't Shoot Straight* (1969), *He Got Hungry and Forgot His Manners* (1988), *Damon Runyon: A Life* (1991), and *I'd Like to Thank My Brain for Remembering Me* (1996). Pulitzer Prize (1986).

Brest /brest/ **1** a port and naval base in northwestern France, on the Atlantic coast of Brittany; pop. 148,316 (2006).
2 a river port and industrial city in Belarus, close to the border with Poland; pop. 318,000 (est. 2009). The peace treaty between Germany and Russia was signed here in March 1918. Former name (until 1921) **Brest-Litovsk**. Polish name **Brzesc nad Bugiem**.

Bre·tagne /brə'tänyə/ French name for **Brittany**.

breth·ren /'breTH(ə)rin/ archaic plural form of **brother**.
▸ **plural n.** fellow Christians or members of a male religious order. See also **brother** (sense 2 of the noun). ▪ used for humorous or rhetorical effect to refer to people belonging to a particular group: *our brethren in the popular press*.

Bret·on[1] /'bretn/ ▸ **n. 1** a native of Brittany.
2 the Celtic language of Brittany, related to Cornish.
▸ **adj.** of or relating to Brittany or its people or language.
– ORIGIN early 19th cent.: from Old French, literally 'Briton.'

Bret·on[2] /bre'tôN/, André (1896–1966), French poet, essayist, and critic. He launched the surrealist movement, outlining the movement's philosophy in his manifesto of 1924.

Bret·ton Woods /'bretn/ a resort in the White Mountains of north central New Hampshire, noted as the site of UN conferences at the end of World War II.

Breu·er /'broiər/, Marcel Lajos (1902–81), US architect; born in Hungary. He designed the UNESCO headquarters in Paris 1953–58 and the Whitney Museum of American Art in New York City 1965–66. He is also known for his chair designs.

Bre·vard Coun·ty /brə'värd/ a county in east central Florida, on the Atlantic Ocean, the site of Cape Canaveral and of large citrus and resort industries; pop. 536,521 (est. 2008).

breve /brēv, brev/ ▸ **n. 1** a musical note having the time value of two semibreves or whole notes.
2 a written or printed mark (˘) indicating a short or unstressed vowel.
3 historical an authoritative letter from a pope or monarch.
– ORIGIN Middle English: variant of **brief**. In the musical sense, the term was originally used in a series where a *long* was of greater time value than a *breve*.

bre·vet /brə'vet, 'brevit/ ▸ **n.** [often as modifier] a former type of military commission conferred esp. for outstanding service by which an officer was promoted to a higher rank without the corresponding pay: *a brevet lieutenant*.
▸ **v.** (**brevets, breveting** or **brevetting, breveted** or **brevetted**) [with obj.] confer a brevet rank on.
– ORIGIN late Middle English (denoting an official letter, esp. a papal indulgence): from Old French *brievet* 'little letter,' diminutive of *bref*.

bre·vi·ar·y /'brēvē,erē, 'brev-/ ▸ **n.** (pl. **breviaries**) a book containing the service for each day, to be recited by those in orders in the Roman Catholic Church.
– ORIGIN late Middle English (also denoting an abridged version of the psalms): from Latin *breviarium* 'summary, abridgment,' from *breviare* 'abridge,' from *brevis* 'short, brief.'

brev·i·ty /'brevitē/ ▸ **n.** concise and exact use of words in writing or speech. ▪ shortness of time: *the brevity of human life*.
– PHRASES **brevity is the soul of wit** proverb the essence of a witty statement lies in its concise wording and delivery. [from Shakespeare's *Hamlet* II. ii. 90.]
– ORIGIN late 15th cent.: from Old French *brievete*, from Latin *brevitas*, from *brevis* 'brief.'

brew /broo/ ▸ **v.** [with obj.] **1** make (beer) by soaking, boiling, and fermentation.
2 make (tea or coffee) by mixing it with hot water: *I've just brewed some coffee* | [no obj.] *he did a crossword while the tea brewed*. ▪ (**brew up**) Brit. informal make tea.
3 [no obj.] (of an unwelcome event or situation) begin to develop: *there was more trouble brewing as the airline pilots went on strike* | *a storm was brewing*.
▸ **n. 1** a kind of beer: *nonalcoholic brews*. ▪ informal a serving of beer.
2 a cup or mug of tea or coffee.
3 a mixture of events, people, or things that interact to form a more potent whole: *a dangerous brew of political turmoil and violent conflict*.
– DERIVATIVES **brew·er n.**
– ORIGIN Old English *brēowan* (verb), of Germanic origin; related to Dutch *brouwen* and German *brauen*.

Brew·er /'brooər/, David Josiah (1837–1910), US Supreme Court associate justice 1889–1910. Appointed to the Court by President Benjamin Harrison, he was considered a moderate conservative and generally opposed a strong central government.

brew·er's yeast ▸ **n.** a yeast that is used in breadmaking, winemaking, and the brewing of top-fermenting beer. It is also consumed as a source of vitamin B and is used in laboratories as an important research organism. ● *Saccharomyces cerevisiae*, phylum Ascomycota.

brew·er·y /'brooərē/ ▸ **n.** (pl. **breweries**) a place where beer is made commercially.
– ORIGIN mid 17th cent.: from **brew**, probably on the pattern of Dutch *brouwerij*.

brew·house /'broo,hous/ ▸ **n.** a brewery.

brew·mas·ter /'broo,mastər/ ▸ **n.** a person who supervises the brewing process in a brewery.

brew·pub /'broo,pəb/ ▸ **n.** an establishment selling beer brewed on the premises and often including a restaurant.

brew·ski /'brooskē/ ▸ **n.** informal a bottle, can, or glass of beer.

Brey·er /'brīər/, Stephen Gerald (1938–), US Supreme Court associate justice 1994–. He is known for his pragmatic judgments.

Brezh·nev /'brezH,nef, 'brezHnyif/, Leonid (Ilich) (1906–82), Soviet statesman; general secretary of the Communist Party of the former Soviet Union 1966–82; president 1977–82. His administration was marked by intensified persecution of dissidents at home and by attempted détente followed by renewed Cold War in 1968; he was largely responsible for the invasion of Czechoslovakia 1968.

bri·ar[1] /'brī(ə)r/ ▸ **n.** variant spelling of **brier**[1].

bri·ar[2] ▸ **n.** variant spelling of **brier**[2].

bri·ar·root ▸ **n.** variant spelling of **brierroot**.

bri·ar·wood ▸ **n.** variant spelling of **brierwood**.

bribe /brīb/ ▸ **v.** [with obj.] persuade (someone) to act in one's favor, typically illegally or dishonestly, by a gift of money or other inducement: *an undercover agent **bribed** the judge **into** giving a lenient sentence* | *you weren't willing to be good to your sister without being bribed with a lollipop* | *he has no money to bribe with*.
▸ **n.** a sum of money or other inducement offered or given in this way.
– DERIVATIVES **brib·a·ble adj.**, **brib·er n.**
– ORIGIN late Middle English: from Old French *briber, brimber* 'beg,' of unknown origin. The original sense was 'rob, extort,' hence (as noun) 'theft, stolen goods,' also 'money extorted or demanded for favors,' later 'offer money as an inducement' (early 16th cent).

brib·er·y /'brīb(ə)rē/ ▸ **n.** the giving or offering of a bribe: *he was convicted of racketeering and bribery* | [as modifier] *a bribery scandal*.

BRIC ▸ **abbr.** Brazil, Russia, India, and China (regarded in terms of their fast-growing economies).

bric-a-brac /'brik ə ,brak/ ▸ **n.** miscellaneous objects and ornaments of little value.
– ORIGIN mid 19th cent.: from French, from obsolete *à bric et à brac* 'at random.'

Brick /brik/ a township in southeastern New Jersey; pop. 78,419 (est. 2008).

brick ▸ **n. 1** a small rectangular block typically made of fired or sun-dried clay, used in building. ▪ bricks collectively as a building material: *this mill was built of brick* | [as modifier] *a large brick building*. ▪ a small, rectangular object: *a brick of ice cream*.
2 Brit. informal, dated a generous, helpful, and reliable person.
▸ **v.** [with obj.] block or enclose with a wall of bricks: *the doors have been bricked up*.
– PHRASES **be built like a brick shithouse** see **shithouse**. **bricks and mortar** buildings: *David knows how inefficient it is to tie up your capital in bricks and mortar*. ▪ [as modifier] used to denote a business that operates conventionally rather than (or as well as) over the Internet: *the bricks-and-mortar banks*. Compare with **clicks and mortar**. **a brick short of a load** see **short**. **hit** (or **run into**) **a brick wall** face an insuperable problem or obstacle while trying to do something. **like a ton of bricks** informal with crushing weight, force, or authority: *all her years of marriage suddenly fell on her like a ton of bricks*. **shit a brick** (or **bricks**) vulgar slang be extremely anxious or nervous. **you can't make bricks without straw** proverb nothing can be made or accomplished without proper or adequate material or information. [with biblical allusion to Exodus 5; "without straw" meant "without having straw provided" (i.e., the Israelites were required to gather the straw for themselves). A misinterpretation has led to the current sense.]
– ORIGIN late Middle English: from Middle Low German, Middle Dutch *bricke, brike*; probably reinforced by Old French *brique*; of unknown ultimate origin.

brick·bat /'brik,bat/ ▸ **n.** a piece of brick, typically when used as a weapon. ▪ a remark or comment which is highly critical and typically insulting: *the plaudits were beginning to outnumber the brickbats*.

brick-built ▸ **adj.** [attrib.] (of a building or structure) made of bricks.

brick·field /'brik,fēld/ ▸ **n.** Brit. an area of ground where bricks are made.

brick·lay·er /'brik,lāər/ ▸ **n.** a person whose job is to build walls, houses, and other structures with bricks.
– DERIVATIVES **brick·lay·ing** /-,lāiNG/ **n.**

brick red ▸ **n.** a deep brownish red: *various shades from blushing pink to angry brick red* | [as modifier] *he had a brick-red face*.

brick ve·neer ▸ **n.** a covering of brick applied to a timber frame. ▪ timber frames covered in brick as a building material.

brick·work /'brik,wərk/ ▸ **n.** the bricks in a wall, house, or other structure, typically in terms of their type or layout: *the patterned brickwork of the gables*. ▪ the craft or occupation of building walls, houses, or other structures with bricks.

brick·yard /'brik,yärd/ ▸ **n.** a place where bricks are made.

bri·co·lage /,brēkō'läzH, ,brikə-/ ▸ **n.** (pl. **same** or **bricolages**) (in art or literature) construction or creation from a diverse range of available things: *the chaotic bricolage of the novel is brought together in a unifying gesture*. ▪ something constructed or created in this way: *bricolages of painted junk*.
– ORIGIN mid 20th cent.: French, from *bricoler* 'do odd jobs, repair.'

bri·co·leur /,brēkō'lər, ,brikə-/ ▸ **n.** a person who engages in bricolage.
– ORIGIN mid 20th cent.: French, literally 'handyman.'

brid·al /'brīdl/ ▸ **adj.** [attrib.] of or concerning a bride or a wedding: *her white bridal gown* | *the **bridal party** came out into the church porch*.
– ORIGIN late Middle English: from Old English *brȳd-ealu* 'wedding feast,' from *brȳd* 'bride' + *ealu* 'ale-drinking' Since the late 16th cent., the word has been associated with adjectives ending in **-al**.

brid·al reg·is·try ▸ **n.** a service offered by a store or other organization in which a bridal couple's gift preferences are recorded so as to be available to family and friends when shopping at the store.

brid·al suite ▸ **n.** a suite of rooms in a hotel for the use of a newly married couple.

brid·al wreath ▸ **n.** a spirea with sprays of white flowers. ● *Spirea prunifolia*, family Rosaceae.

bride /brīd/ ▸ **n.** a woman on her wedding day or just before and after the event.
– ORIGIN Old English *brȳd*, of Germanic origin; related to Dutch *bruid* and German *Braut*.

Bride, St. /brīd, brēd/ see **Bridget, St.**

bride·groom /'brīd,groom/ ▸ **n.** a man on his wedding day or just before and after the event.
– ORIGIN Old English *brȳdguma*, from *brȳd* 'bride' + *guma* 'man' The change in the second syllable was due to association with **groom**.

bride price ▸ **n.** [in sing.] a sum of money or quantity of goods given to a bride's family by that of the groom, esp. in tribal societies: *payments of bride price from the husband's kin*.

brides·maid /'brīdz,mād/ ▸ **n.** a girl or woman who accompanies a bride on her wedding day.
– ORIGIN late 18th cent.: alteration of earlier *bridemaid*.

bride·well /'brīd,wel, -wəl/ ▸ **n.** a prison for petty offenders such as a reform school.
– ORIGIN mid 16th cent.: named after *St. Bride's Well* in the City of London, near which such a building stood.

bridge[1] /brij/ ▸ **n. 1** a structure carrying a road, path, railroad, or canal across a river, ravine, road,

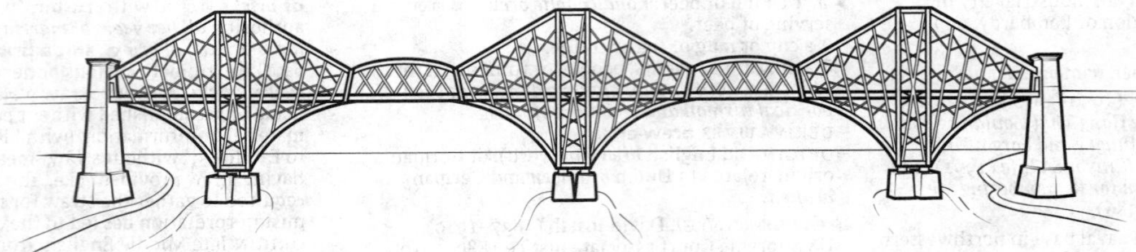

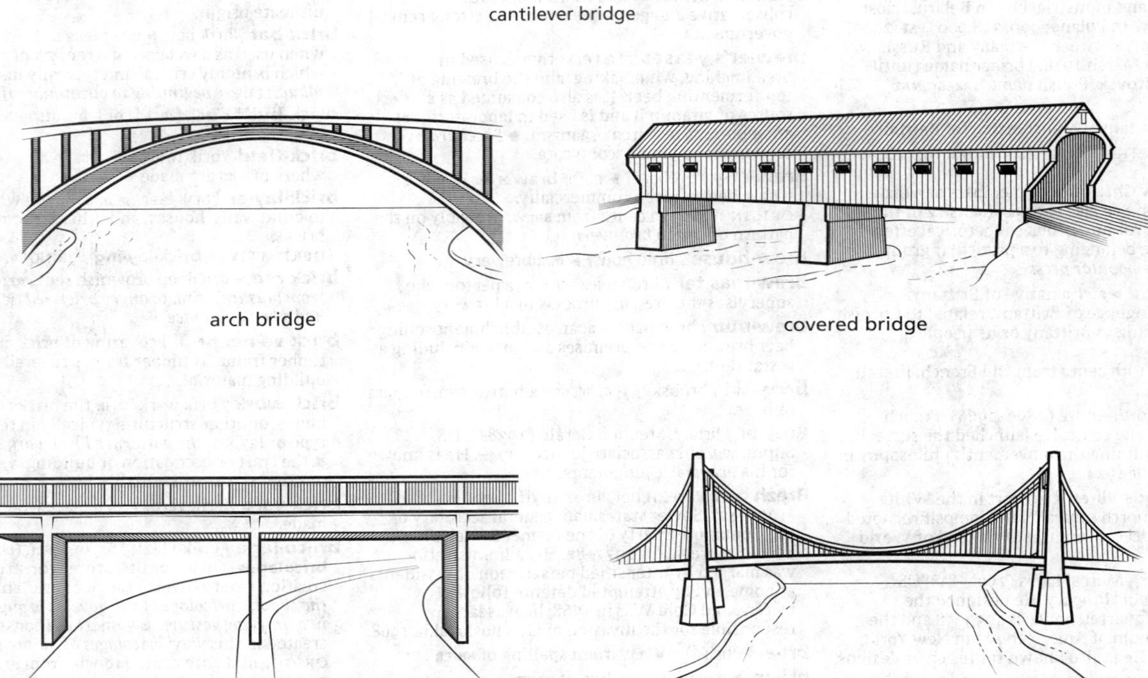

bridge[1]

railroad, or other obstacle: *a bridge across the river | a railroad bridge.* ■ something that is intended to reconcile or form a connection between two things: *a committee that was formed to create a bridge between rival parties.* ■ a partial denture supported by natural teeth on either side. See also BRIDGEWORK. ■ the support formed by the hand for the forward part of a billiard cue. ■ a long stick with a frame at the end that is used to support a cue for a shot that is otherwise hard to reach. ■ Music an upright piece of wood on a string instrument over which the strings are stretched. ■ Music a bridge passage or middle eight. ■ short for LAND BRIDGE.
2 the elevated, enclosed platform on a ship from which the captain and officers direct operations.
3 the upper bony part of a person's nose: *he pushed his spectacles further up the bridge of his nose.* ■ the central part of a pair of glasses, fitting over this: *these sunglasses have a special nose bridge for comfort.*
4 an electric circuit with two branches across which a detector or load is connected. These circuits are used to measure resistance or other property by equalizing the potential across the two ends of a detector, or to rectify an alternating voltage or current.
▶ v. [with obj.] be a bridge over (something): *a covered walkway that bridged the gardens.* ■ build a bridge over (something): *earlier attempts to bridge the channel had failed.* ■ make (a difference between two groups) smaller or less significant: *bridging the gap between avant garde art and popular culture.*
– PHRASES **a bridge too far** a step or act that is regarded as being too drastic to take: *having Botox would be a bridge too far.* ■ something that is very difficult to achieve: *that second goal proved a bridge too far.* **burn one's bridges** see BURN[1]. **cross that bridge when one comes to it** deal with a problem when and if it arises.
– DERIVATIVES **bridge·a·ble** adj.
– ORIGIN Old English *brycg* (noun), of Germanic origin; related to Dutch *brug* and German *Brücke.*

bridge[2] ▶ n. a card game descended from whist, played by two partnerships of two players who at the beginning of each hand bid for the right to name the trump suit, the highest bid also representing a contract to make a specified number of tricks with a specified suit as trumps.
– ORIGIN late 19th cent.: of unknown origin.

bridge-and-tun·nel ▶ adj. informal (of a person) living in the suburbs and perceived as unsophisticated: *clubs catering to the beautiful people and the bridge-and-tunnel crowds.*
– ORIGIN 1980s: with reference to the routes used for commuting into New York.

bridge-build·ing ▶ n. the activity of building bridges. ■ the promotion of friendly relations between groups.
– DERIVATIVES **bridge-build·er** n.

bridge·head /ˈbrij,hed/ ▶ n. a strong position secured by an army inside enemy territory from which to advance or attack: figurative *in the 1970s, academic literary theory established bridgeheads in Britain.*

bridge loan ▶ n. a sum of money lent by a bank to cover an interval between two transactions, typically the buying of one house and the selling of another.

bridge mix ▶ n. a mixture of various bite-size snack foods, such as nuts, raisins, and chocolates, typically served in a bowl at card games, parties, etc.

Bridge of Sighs a 16th-century enclosed bridge in Venice between the Doges' Palace and the state prison, originally crossed by prisoners on their way to torture or execution.

bridge pas·sage ▶ n. a transitional section in a musical composition leading to a new section or theme.

Bridge·port /ˈbrij,pôrt/ an industrial city in southwestern Connecticut, on Long Island Sound; pop. 136,405 (est. 2008).

Bridg·es, Robert (Seymour) (1844–1930), English poet and literary critic; poet laureate 1913–30. His long philosophical poem, *The Testament of Beauty* (1929), was written in the Victorian tradition.

Brig·et, St.[1] /ˈbrijət/ (also **Bride** /brīd, brēd/ or **Brigid** /ˈbrijəd, brēd/) (6th century), Irish abbess; also known as **St. Bridget of Ireland**. She was venerated in Ireland as a virgin saint and noted in miracle stories for her compassion. Feast day, July 23.

Bridg·et, St.[2] (also **Birgitta** /birˈgētə/) (c.1303–73), Swedish nun and visionary; also known as **St. Bridget of Sweden**. She experienced her first vision of the Virgin Mary at the age of seven. Feast day, February 1.

Bridge·town /ˈbrij,toun/ the capital of Barbados, a port on the southern coast; pop. 116,000 (est. 2007).

bridge·work /ˈbrij,wərk/ ▶ n. **1** dental bridges collectively. ■ the construction or insertion of such bridges.
2 Building the component parts of a bridge. ■ the construction of bridges.

bridg·ing /ˈbrijiNG/ ▶ n. the action of putting a bridge over something: *the bridging of a ditch.* ■ Mountaineering a method of climbing a wide chimney by using the left hand and foot on one sidewall and the right hand and foot on the other.

Bridg·man /ˈbrijmən/, Percy Williams (1882–1961), US physicist. He worked with liquids and solids under very high pressures; his techniques were later used in making artificial minerals (including diamonds). Nobel Prize for Physics (1946).

bri·dle /ˈbrīdl/ ▶ n. the headgear used to control a horse, consisting of buckled straps to which a bit and reins are attached. ■ a line, rope, or device that is used to restrain or control the action or movement of something. ■ Nautical a length of rope, chain, or cable fastened at both ends to an object that is to be secured or moved or to a vessel that is to do the towing, a pull being exerted at the center of its length.

horse's bridle

▶ **v. 1** [with obj.] (usu. **be bridled**) put a bridle on (a horse). ■ bring (something) under control; curb: *the fact that he was their servant bridled his tongue.* **2** [no obj.] show one's resentment or anger, esp. by throwing up the head and drawing in the chin: *ranchers have* **bridled** *at excessive federal control.*
– PHRASES **off the bridle** see BIT[3]. **on the bridle** see BIT[3].
– ORIGIN Old English *brīdel* (noun), *brīdlian* (verb), of Germanic origin; related to Dutch *breidel* (noun). Sense 2 of the verb use is from the action of a horse when reined in.

bri·dle path ▶ **n.** a path or track used for horseback riding.

Brie /brē/ ▶ **n.** a kind of soft, mild, creamy cheese with a firm white skin.
– ORIGIN named after *Brie* in northern France, where it was originally made.

brief /brēf/ ▶ **adj.** of short duration: *the president made a brief visit to Moscow.* ■ concise in expression; using few words: *introductions were brief and polite.* ■ (of a piece of clothing) not covering much of the body; scanty: *Alice sported a pair of extremely brief black shorts.*
▶ **n.** a concise statement or summary: *their comments were cribbed right from industry briefs.* ■ a set of instructions given to a person about a job or task: *his brief is to turn around the country's economy.* ■ a written summary of the facts and legal points supporting one side of a case, for presentation to a court. ■ a letter from the pope to a person or community on a matter of discipline.
▶ **v.** [with obj.] instruct or inform (someone) thoroughly, esp. in preparation for a task: *she briefed him on last week's decisions.*
– PHRASES **hold no brief for** not support or argue in favor of: *I hold no brief for the president.* **in brief** in a few words; in short: *he is, in brief, the embodiment of evil* | *the news in brief.*
– DERIVATIVES **brief·ness n.**
– ORIGIN Middle English: from Old French *brief*, from Latin *brevis* 'short.' The noun is via late Latin *breve* 'note, dispatch,' hence 'an official letter.'

brief·case /'brēf,kās/ ▶ **n.** a flat, rectangular container, typically made of leather, for carrying books and papers.

brief·ing /'brēfiNG/ ▶ **n.** a meeting for giving information or instructions: *the daily press briefing.* ■ the action of informing or instructing someone: *today's briefing of NATO allies.*

brief·ly /'brēflē/ ▶ **adv.** for a short time; fleetingly: *he worked briefly as a lawyer.* ■ using few words; concisely: *as I briefly mentioned earlier* | [sentence adverb] *briefly, the plot is as follows.*

briefs /brēfs/ ▶ **plural n.** close-fitting legless underpants that are cut so as to cover the body to the waist, in contrast to a bikini.

bri·er[1] /'brī(ə)r/ (also **briar**) ▶ **n.** any of a number of prickly scrambling shrubs, esp. the sweetbrier and other wild roses.
– DERIVATIVES **bri·er·y adj.**
– ORIGIN Old English *brǣr, brēr*, of unknown origin.

bri·er[2] (also **briar**) ▶ **n. 1** (also **brier pipe**) a tobacco pipe made from nodules borne at ground level by a large woody plant of the heath family. **2** the white-flowered shrub of the heath family that bears these nodules, native chiefly to France and Corsica. ● *Erica arborea*, family Ericaceae.
– ORIGIN mid 19th cent.: from French *bruyère* 'heath, heather,' from medieval Latin *brucus.*

bri·er·root /'brī(ə)r,ro͞ot, -,ro͝ot/ ▶ **n.** wood from the nodules of the brier (*Erica arborea*), used esp. for making tobacco pipes.

bri·er·wood /'brī(ə)r,wo͝od/ ▶ **n.** another term for BRIERROOT.

brig /brig/ ▶ **n.** a two-masted, square-rigged ship with an additional gaff sail on the mainmast. ■ informal a prison, esp. on a warship.
– ORIGIN early 18th cent.: abbreviation of BRIGANTINE (the original sense).

Brig. ▶ **abbr.** ■ brigade. ■ brigadier.

bri·gade /bri'gād/ ▶ **n.** a subdivision of an army, typically consisting of a small number of infantry battalions and/or other units and often forming part of a division: *he commanded a brigade of 3,000 men.* ■ an organization with a specific purpose, typically with a military or quasi-military structure: *the local fire brigade.* ■ [in sing.] informal, often derogatory a group of people with a common characteristic or dedicated to a common cause: *the anti-smoking brigade.*
▶ **v.** [with obj.] rare form into a brigade. ■ associate with (someone or something): *they thought the speech too closely brigaded with illegal action.*
– ORIGIN mid 17th cent.: from French, from Italian *brigata* 'company,' from *brigare* 'contend,' from *briga* 'strife.'

brig·a·dier /,brigə'di(ə)r, 'brigə,di(ə)r/ ▶ **n.** a rank of officer in the British army, above colonel and below major general.
– ORIGIN late 17th cent.: from French (see BRIGADE, -IER).

brig·a·dier gen·er·al ▶ **n.** (pl. **brigadier generals**) an officer in the US Army, Air Force, or Marine Corps ranking above colonel and below major general.

brig·and /'brigənd/ ▶ **n.** literary a member of a gang that ambushes and robs people in forests and mountains.
– DERIVATIVES **brig·and·age** /-dij/ **n.**, **brig·and·ry** /-drē/ **n.**
– ORIGIN late Middle English (also denoting an irregular foot soldier): from Old French, from Italian *brigante*, literally '(person) contending,' from *brigare* 'contend' (see BRIGADE).

brig·an·dine /'brigən,dēn/ ▶ **n.** historical a coat of mail, typically one made of iron rings or plates attached to canvas or other fabric.
– ORIGIN late Middle English: from Old French, from *brigand* (see BRIGAND).

brig·an·tine /'brigən,tēn/ ▶ **n.** a two-masted sailing ship with a square-rigged foremast and a fore-and-aft-rigged mainmast.
– ORIGIN early 16th cent. (denoting a small vessel used by pirates): from Old French, from Italian *brigantino*, from *brigante* (see BRIGAND).

Briggs /brigz/, Henry (1561–1630), English mathematician. Renowned for his work on logarithms, he introduced the decimal base, made the thousands of calculations necessary for the tables, and popularized their use. He also devised the usual method used for long division.

bright /brīt/ ▶ **adj. 1** giving out or reflecting a lot of light; shining: *I have problems seeing when the sun is bright* | *her bright, dark eyes.* ■ full of light: *the rooms are bright and spacious.* ■ (of a period of time) having sunny, cloudless weather: *the long, bright days of June.* ■ having a vivid color: *the bright flowers* | *a bright tie.* ■ (of color) vivid and bold: *the bright green leaves.* **2** (of sound) clear, vibrant, and typically high-pitched: *her voice is fresh and bright.* **3** (of a person, idea, or remark) intelligent and quick-witted: *a bright young journalist* | *a suggestion box for bright ideas.* **4** giving an appearance of cheerful liveliness: *she gave a bright smile.* ■ (of someone's future) likely to be successful and happy: *the bright prospects for her early retirement.*
▶ **adv.** luminously: *a full moon shining bright.*
▶ **n.** (**brights**) **1** bold and vivid colors: *webbed gloves in neon brights.* **2** headlights switched to high beam: *he turned the brights on, and we drove along the dirt road.*
– PHRASES **bright and early** very early in the morning. **the bright lights** the glamor and excitement of the city: *they hankered for the bright lights of the capital.* **look on the bright side** be optimistic or cheerful in spite of difficulties.
– DERIVATIVES **bright·ish adj.**, **bright·ly adv.**, **bright·ness n.**
– ORIGIN Old English *beorht*, of Germanic origin.

bright·en /'brītn/ ▶ **v.** make or become more light: [no obj.] *the day began to brighten in the east* | [with obj.] *the fire began to blaze fiercely, brightening the room.* ■ [with obj.] make (something) more attractively and cheerfully colorful: *this colorful hanging ornament will brighten any room* | *daffodils* **brighten up** *many gardens and parks.* ■ make or become happier and more cheerful: [no obj.] *Sarah brightened up considerably as she thought of Emily's words* | [with obj.] *she seems to brighten his life.*
– ORIGIN Old English *(ge)beorhtnian.*

bright-eyed ▶ **adj. 1** having shining eyes. **2** alert and lively: *bright-eyed young lawyers* | *a bright-eyed optimism.*
– PHRASES **bright-eyed and bushy-tailed** informal alert and lively; eager. [from the conventional description of a squirrel.]

Bright·on /'brītn/ a resort on the southern coast of England; pop. 127,700 (est. 2009).

Brigh·ton Beach /'brītn/ a section of southern Brooklyn in New York City, east of Coney Island, noted for its Jewish community, and now home to a large Russian immigrant population.

Bright's dis·ease ▶ **n.** a disease involving chronic inflammation of the kidneys.
– ORIGIN mid 19th cent.: named after Richard *Bright* (1789–1858), the English physician who established its nature.

bright·work /'brīt,wərk/ ▶ **n.** polished metalwork on ships or vehicles.

Brig·id, St. /'brijəd, brēd/ see BRIDGET, ST.[1]

brill /bril/ ▶ **n.** a European flatfish that resembles a turbot. ● *Scophthalmus rhombus*, family Scophthalmidae (or Bothidae).
– ORIGIN late 15th cent.: of unknown origin.

bril·liance /'brilyəns/ (also **brilliancy** /-sē/) ▶ **n.** intense brightness of light: *the nights were dark, lit only by the brilliance of Aegean stars.* ■ vividness of color. ■ exceptional talent or intelligence: *he's played the stock market with great brilliance.*

bril·liant /'brilyənt/ ▶ **adj. 1** (of light or color) very bright and radiant. **2** exceptionally clever or talented: *a brilliant young mathematician* | *a brilliant idea.* ■ outstanding; impressive: *his brilliant career at Harvard.* ■ Brit. informal very good, excellent, or marvelous: *we had a brilliant time* | [as exclamation] *"Brilliant!" he declared excitedly as she finished telling him what had happened.*
▶ **n.** a diamond of brilliant cut.
– DERIVATIVES **bril·liant·ly adv.**
– ORIGIN late 17th cent.: from French *brillant* 'shining,' present participle of *briller*, from Italian *brillare*, probably from Latin *beryllus* (see BERYL).

bril·liant cut ▶ **n.** a circular cut for diamonds and other gemstones in the form of two many-faceted pyramids joined at their bases, the upper one truncated near its apex.

bril·lian·tine /'brilyən,tēn/ ▶ **n. 1** dated scented oil used on men's hair to make it look glossy. **2** shiny dress fabric made from cotton and mohair or cotton and worsted.
– DERIVATIVES **bril·lian·tined adj.** (sense 1).
– ORIGIN late 19th cent.: from French *brillantine*, from *brillant* 'shining' (see BRILLIANT).

Bril·lo /'brilō/ (also **Brillo pad**) ▶ **adj.** informal denoting hair that is wiry or tightly curled.
– ORIGIN from the trademark *Brillo*, used for soaped, steel-wool scouring pads.

brim /brim/ ▶ **n.** the projecting edge around the bottom of a hat: *a soft hat with a turned-up brim.* ■ the upper edge or lip of a cup, bowl, or other container: *tankards frothing to the brim.*
▶ **v.** (**brims, brimming, brimmed**) (often as adj. **brimming**) fill or be full to the point of overflowing: [no obj.] *a brimming cup* | [with obj.] *seawater brimmed the riverbanks.* ■ fill something so completely as almost to spill out of it: *large tears brimmed in her eyes.* ■ be possessed by or full of feelings or thoughts: *he is brimming with ideas.*
– DERIVATIVES **brimmed adj.** [in combination:] *a wide-brimmed hat*, **brim·less adj.**
– ORIGIN Middle English (denoting the edge of the sea or other body of water): perhaps related to German *Bräme* 'trimming.'

brim·ful /'brim,fo͝ol/ ▶ **adj.** [predic.] filled with something to the point of overflowing: *a jug brimful of custard.*

brim·stone /'brim,stōn/ ▶ **n.** archaic sulfur.
– PHRASES **fire and brimstone** see FIRE.
– ORIGIN late Old English *brynstān*, probably from *bryne* 'burning' + *stān* 'stone.'

brin·dle /'brindl/ ▶ **n.** a brownish or tawny color of animal fur, with streaks of other color. ■ an animal with such a coat.
▶ **adj.** (also **brindled**) (esp. of domestic animals) brownish or tawny with streaks of other color: *a brindle pup.*
– ORIGIN late 17th cent.: back-formation from *brindled*, alteration of Middle English *brinded* in the same sense, probably of Scandinavian origin.

brine /brīn/ ▶ **n.** water saturated or strongly impregnated with salt. ■ seawater: *dolphins and whales can't help taking in the odd gulp of brine as they swallow a fish.* ■ technical a strong solution of a salt or salts: *these brines percolated downward.*
▶ **v.** [with obj.] (often as adj. **brined**) soak in or saturate with salty water: *brined anchovies.*
– ORIGIN Old English *brīne*, of unknown origin.

Bri·nell hard·ness test /bri'nel/ ▶ **n.** a test to determine the hardness of metals and alloys by hydraulically pressing a steel ball into the metal and measuring the resulting indentation.
– ORIGIN named for Johan August *Brinell* (1849–1925), Swedish engineer.

brine shrimp ▶ **n.** a small fairy shrimp that lives in brine pools and salt lakes and is used as food for aquarium fish. ● *Artemia salina*, class Branchiopoda.

bring /briNG/ ▶ **v.** (past **brought** /brôt/) [with obj.] come to a place with (someone or something): *she brought Luke home from the hospital* | [with two objs.] *Liz brought her a glass of water.* ■ cause (someone or something) to come to a place: *what brings you here?* | *a felony case brought before a jury* | figurative *his inner confidence has* ***brought*** *him* ***through*** *his ordeal.* ■ make (someone or something) move in a particular direction or way: *he brought his hands out of his pockets* | *heavy rain* ***brought down*** *part of the ceiling.* ■ cause (something): *the bad weather brought famine* | *her letter* ***brought forth*** *a torrent of criticism.* ■ cause (someone or something) to be in or change to a particular state or condition: *I'll give you some aspirin to* ***bring down*** *his temperature* | *his approach* ***brought*** *him* ***into*** *conflict with government.* ■ (**bring someone in**) involve (someone) in a particular activity: *he has brought in a consultant.* ■ initiate (legal action) against someone: *riot and conspiracy charges should* ***be brought against*** *them.* ■ [usu. with negative] (**bring oneself to do something**) force oneself to do something unpleasant or distressing: *she could not bring herself to mention it.* ■ cause someone to receive (an amount of money) as income or profit: *two important Chippendale lots brought $10,000 each* | [with two objs.] *five more novels brought him $150,000.*

– PHRASES **bring home the bacon** see BACON. **bring something home to someone** see HOME. **bring the house down** make an audience respond with great enthusiasm, typically as shown by their laughter or applause. **bring something into play** cause something to begin operating or to have an effect; activate. **bring it** (**on**) informal used to express confidence in meeting a challenge: *if you want to fight me so bad, bring it on!* **bring something to bear** exert influence or pressure so as to cause a particular result: *he was released after pressure had been brought to bear by the aid agencies.* **bring someone to book** see BOOK. **bring something to light** see LIGHT[1]. **bring someone/something to mind** cause one to remember or think of someone or something: *all that marble brought to mind a mausoleum.* **bring something to pass** chiefly literary cause something to happen.

– PHRASAL VERBS **bring something about** **1** cause something to happen: *she brought about a revolution.* **2** cause a ship to head in a different direction. **bring something back** cause something to return. ■ reintroduce something: *bringing back capital punishment would solve nothing.* **bring someone down** cause someone to fall over, esp. by tackling them during a football game or rugby match. ■ cause someone to lose power: *the vote will not bring down the government.* ■ make someone unhappy. **bring someone/something down** cause an animal or person to fall over by shooting them. ■ cause an aircraft or bird to fall from the sky by shooting it. **bring something forth** archaic or literary give birth to: *why does Elsbeth not bring forth a child?* **bring something forward** **1** move a meeting or event to an earlier date or time. **2** (often as adj. **brought forward**) in bookkeeping, transfer a total sum from the bottom of one page to the top of the next: *a profit and loss balance brought forward of $5,000,000.* **3** propose a plan, subject, or idea for consideration. **bring something in** **1** introduce something, esp. a new law or product: *Congress brought in reforms to prevent abuse of presidential power.* **2** make or earn a particular amount of money: *their fund-raising efforts have brought in more than $1 million.* **3** (of a jury) give a decision in court: *the jury brought in a unanimous verdict.* **bring someone off** **1** be rescued from a ship in difficulties. **2** vulgar slang give someone or oneself an orgasm. **bring something off** achieve something successfully: *a good omelet is very hard to bring off.* **bring someone on** encourage someone who is learning something to develop or improve at a faster rate. **bring something on** cause something, typically something unpleasant, to occur or develop: *ulcers are not brought on by a rich diet.* ■ (**bring something on/upon**) be responsible for something, typically something unpleasant, that happens to oneself or someone else: *the doom that he has* ***brought upon himself.*** **bring someone out** **1** encourage one to feel more confident or sociable: *she needs friends to* ***bring her out of herself.*** **2** introduce (a young woman) formally into society. **3** introduce (a homosexual) into the homosexual subculture. **bring something out** produce and launch a new product or publication: *the band is bringing out a video.* ■ make something more evident; emphasize something: *the shawl brings out the color of your eyes* | *he* ***brought out the best in*** *his team.* **bring someone around** **1** restore someone to consciousness. **2** persuade someone to do something, esp. to adopt one's own point of view: *my wife has brought me around to eating broiled grouper.* **bring someone to** restore someone to consciousness. **bring something to** cause a boat to stop, esp. by turning into the wind. **bring up** (chiefly of a ship) come to a stop. **bring someone up** look after a child until it is an adult. ■ (**be brought up**) be taught as a child to adopt particular behavior or attitudes: *he had been brought up to believe that marriage was forever.* **bring something up** **1** vomit something. **2** raise a matter for discussion or consideration: *she tried repeatedly to bring up the subject of marriage.*

– DERIVATIVES **bring·er** n.

– ORIGIN Old English *bringan*, of Germanic origin; related to Dutch *brengen* and German *bringen*.

bring·down /ˈbriNG,doun/ ▶ n. a disappointment or letdown; comedown.

Brink /briNGk/, André (1935–), South African novelist, short-story writer, and playwright. His anti-apartheid *Looking on Darkness* (1973) became the first novel in Afrikaans to be banned by the South African government. Other notable works: the novel *A Dry White Season* (1979) and the memoir *A Fork in the Road* (2009).

brink /briNGk/ ▶ n. an extreme edge of land before a steep or vertical slope: ***the brink of*** *the cliffs.* ■ a point at which something, typically something unwelcome, is about to happen; the verge: *the country was* ***on the brink of*** *a constitutional crisis.*

– ORIGIN Middle English: of Scandinavian origin.

brink·man·ship /ˈbriNGkmən,SHip/ (also **brinksmanship** /ˈbriNGksmən-/) ▶ n. the art or practice of pursuing a dangerous policy to the limits of safety before stopping, typically in politics.

brin·y /ˈbrīnē/ ▶ adj. of salty water or the sea; salty: *the briny tang of the scallops.*
▶ n. (**the briny**) Brit. informal the sea.

bri·o /ˈbrēō/ ▶ n. vigor or vivacity of style or performance: *she told her story with some brio.* See also CON BRIO.

– ORIGIN mid 18th cent.: from Italian.

bri·oche /brēˈōSH, -ˈôSH/ ▶ n. a light, sweet yeast bread typically in the form of a small, round roll.

– ORIGIN French, from Norman French *brier*, synonym of *broyer*, literally 'split up into very small pieces by pressure;' related to BRAY[2].

bri·quette /briˈket/ (also **briquet**) ▶ n. a block of compressed charcoal or coal dust used as fuel.

– ORIGIN late 19th cent.: from French, diminutive of *brique* 'brick.'

bris /bris/ ▶ n. the Jewish ceremony of circumcision. Also called BRITH.

Bris·bane /ˈbrizbən, -,bān/ the capital of Queensland, Australia; pop. 1,945,639 (2008). It was founded in 1824 as a penal colony.

– ORIGIN named after Sir Thomas *Brisbane* (1773–1860), governor of New South Wales 1821–25.

bri·sé /brēˈzā/ ▶ n. Ballet a jump in which the dancer sweeps one leg into the air to the side while jumping off the other, brings both legs together in the air and beats them before landing.

– ORIGIN late 18th cent.: French, literally 'broken.'

brise-so·leil /,brēzsōˈlā/ ▶ n. a device, such as a perforated screen or louvers, for shutting out direct or excessive sunlight.

– ORIGIN French, literally 'sun-breaker.'

brisk /brisk/ ▶ adj. active, fast, and energetic: *a good brisk walk* | *business appeared to be brisk.* ■ (of the weather or wind) cold but fresh and enlivening. ■ sharp or abrupt: *the brisk, dismissive nod of her head.*

– DERIVATIVES **brisk·ly** adv., **brisk·ness** n.

– ORIGIN late 16th cent.: probably from French *brusque* (see BRUSQUE).

bris·ket /ˈbriskit/ ▶ n. meat cut from the breast of an animal, typically a cow.

– ORIGIN Middle English: perhaps from Old Norse *brjósk* 'cartilage, gristle.'

bris·ling /ˈbrizliNG, ˈbris-/ ▶ n. (pl. **same** or **brislings**) a sprat, typically one seasoned and smoked in Norway and sold in a can.

– ORIGIN early 20th cent.: from Norwegian and Danish.

bris·tle /ˈbrisəl/ ▶ n. (usu. **bristles**) a short stiff hair, typically one of those on an animal's skin, a man's face, or a plant. ■ a stiff animal hair, or a man-made substitute, used to make a brush: *a toothbrush with nylon bristles* | *the heads are made with natural bristle.*
▶ v. [no obj.] **1** (of hair or fur) stand upright away from the skin, esp. in anger or fear: *the hair on the back of his neck bristled.* ■ make one's hair or fur stand on end: *the cat bristled in annoyance.* ■ react angrily or defensively, typically by drawing oneself up: *she* ***bristled at*** *his rudeness.*
2 (**bristle with**) be covered with or abundant in: *the roof bristled with antennas.*

– ORIGIN Middle English: from Old English *byrst* (of Germanic origin, related to German *Borste*) + -LE[1].

bris·tle·cone pine /ˈbrisəl,kōn/ ▶ n. a very long-lived shrubby pine of western North America. It has been used in dendrochronology to correct radiocarbon dating. ● *Pinus longaeva*, family Pinaceae.

bris·tle fern ▶ n. a filmy fern with hairlike bristles protruding from the spore-containing bodies. Most bristle ferns have delicate fronds and live in damp shady places, chiefly in tropical areas. ● Genus *Trichomanes*, family Hymenophyllaceae.

bris·tle·tail /ˈbrisəl,tāl/ ▶ n. a small wingless insect that has bristles at the end of the abdomen. ● Orders Thysanura (the **true bristletails**, with three bristles, including the silverfish) and Diplura (the **two-pronged bristletails**), subclass Apterygota.

bris·tle worm ▶ n. a marine annelid worm that has a segmented body with numerous bristles on the fleshy lobes of each segment. Also called POLYCHAETE. ● Class Polychaeta: numerous species, including ragworms, lugworms, fan worms, and their relatives.

bris·tling /ˈbris(ə)liNG/ ▶ adj. **1** (esp. of hair) close-set, stiff, and spiky: *a bristling beard.*
2 aggressively brisk or tense: *he fills the screen with a restless, bristling energy.*

bris·tly /ˈbrislē/ ▶ adj. (of hair or foliage) having a stiff and prickly texture. ■ covered with short stiff hairs: *he rubbed his bristly chin.*

bris·tly sar·sa·pa·ril·la ▶ n. see ARALIA.

Bris·tol /ˈbristl/ **1** a city in southwestern England; pop. 374,000 (est. 2009). It is located on the Avon River about 6 miles (10 km) from the Bristol Channel.
2 an industrial city and township in west central Connecticut; pop. 60,927 (est. 2008).
3 a township in southeastern Pennsylvania, on the Delaware River; pop. 53,847 (est. 2008).

Bris·tol board ▶ n. fine, smooth pasteboard used for drawing or cutting.

– ORIGIN early 19th cent.: named after the city of BRISTOL in southwestern England.

Bris·tol Chan·nel a wide inlet of the Atlantic Ocean between South Wales and the southwestern peninsula of England that narrows into the estuary of the River Severn.

Brit /brit/ informal ▶ n. a British person.
▶ adj. British.

– ORIGIN early 20th cent.: abbreviation.

Brit·ain /ˈbritn/ an island that consists of England, Wales, and Scotland. The name is broadly synonymous with Great Britain, but the longer form is more usual for the political unit. See also GREAT BRITAIN, UNITED KINGDOM.

– ORIGIN Old English *Breoton*, from Latin *Brittones* 'Britons,' superseded in Middle English by forms from Old French *Bretaigne* (from Latin *Brit(t)annia*).

Bri·tan·ni·a /briˈtanyə, -ˈtanēə/ the personification of Britain, usually depicted as a helmeted woman with shield and trident. The figure had appeared on Roman coins and was revived with the name Britannia on the coinage of Charles II.

– ORIGIN the Latin name for BRITAIN.

Bri·tan·ni·a met·al ▶ n. a silvery alloy consisting of tin with about 5–15 percent antimony and typically some copper, lead, or zinc.

Bri·tan·nic /briˈtanik/ ▶ adj. dated (usually in names or titles) of Britain or the British Empire: *he answered His Britannic Majesty's call to arms.*

– ORIGIN mid 17th cent.: from Latin *Britannicus*, from *Britannia* (see BRITANNIA).

britch·es /ˈbriCHiz/ ▶ plural n. variant spelling of BREECHES.

– PHRASES **too big for one's britches** see BIG.

brith /bris, brit/ ▶ n. another term for BRIS.

– ORIGIN For *brith milah*, from Hebrew *berit mila* 'covenant of circumcision' (Gen 17:9–10).

Brit·i·cism /ˈbriti,sizəm/ (also **Britishism** /ˈbritiSH,izəm/) ▶ n. an idiom used in Britain but not in other English-speaking countries.

– ORIGIN mid 19th cent.: from BRITISH, on the pattern of words such as *Gallicism*.

Brit·ish /ˈbritiSH/ ▶ adj. **1** of or relating to Great Britain or the United Kingdom, or to its people or language.
2 of the British Commonwealth or (formerly) the British Empire.
▶ n. (as plural noun **the British**) the British people.

– DERIVATIVES **Brit·ish·ness** n.

– ORIGIN Old English *Brettisc* 'relating to the ancient Britons,' from *Bret* 'Briton,' from Latin *Britto*, or its Celtic equivalent.

Brit·ish Ant·arc·tic Ter·ri·to·ry that part of Antarctica claimed by Britain. It includes about 150,058 square miles (388,500 sq km) of the continent of Antarctica as well as the South Orkney and South Shetland islands in the South Atlantic Ocean.

Brit·ish Broad·cast·ing Cor·po·ra·tion (abbr.: **BBC**) a public corporation for radio and television broadcasting in Britain.

> The BBC was established in 1927 by royal charter and held a monopoly until the introduction of the first commercial TV station in 1954. It is financed by the sale of television viewing licenses rather than by revenue from advertising and has an obligation to remain impartial in its reporting.

Brit·ish Co·lum·bi·a a province on the western coast of Canada; pop. 4,113,487 (2006); capital, Victoria. Formed in 1866 by the union of Vancouver Island and the mainland area, then called New Caledonia, the province includes the Queen Charlotte Islands.

Brit·ish Com·mon·wealth see **COMMONWEALTH** (sense 2).

Brit·ish Em·pire a former empire consisting of Great Britain and its possessions, dominions, and dependencies.

> Colonization of North America and domination of India began in the 17th century. A series of small colonies, mostly in the West Indies, was gained during the late 17th–early 19th centuries, and Australia, New Zealand, various parts of the Far East, and large areas of Africa were added in the 19th century. Self-government was granted to Canada, Australia, New Zealand, and South Africa in the mid 19th century, and most of the remaining colonies have gained independence since the end of World War II.

Brit·ish Eng·lish ▶ **n.** English as used in Great Britain, as distinct from that used elsewhere.

Brit·ish·er /ˈbritisнər/ ▶ **n.** informal (in North America and old-fashioned British English) a native or inhabitant of Britain.

Brit·ish Ex·pe·di·tion·ar·y Force (abbr.: **BEF**) a British force made available by the army reform of 1908 for service overseas against foreign countries. Such forces were sent to France at the outbreak of both world wars.

Brit·ish In·di·a that part of the Indian subcontinent administered by the British from 1765, when the East India Company acquired control over Bengal, until 1947, when India became independent and Pakistan was created. See also **INDIA**.

Brit·ish In·di·an O·cean Ter·ri·to·ry a British overseas territory in the Indian Ocean that consists of the islands of the Chagos Archipelago and (until 1976) some other groups that now belong to the Seychelles. Ceded to Britain by France in 1814, the islands became a separate dependency in 1965.

Brit·ish Isles a group of islands lying off the coast of northwestern Europe, from which they are separated by the North Sea and the English Channel. They include Britain, Ireland, the Isle of Man, the Isle of Wight, the Hebrides, the Orkney Islands, the Shetland Islands, the Scilly Isles, and the Channel Islands.

Brit·ish·ism /ˈbritəˌsнizəm/ ▶ **n.** variant spelling of **BRITICISM**.

Brit·ish Mu·se·um a national museum of antiquities in Bloomsbury, London. Established with public funds in 1753, it includes among its holdings the Magna Carta, the Elgin Marbles, and the Rosetta Stone.

Brit·ish So·ma·li·land a former British protectorate that was established on the Somali coast of East Africa in 1884. In 1960, it united with a former Italian territory to create the independent republic of Somalia.

Brit·ish ther·mal u·nit (abbr.: **Btu, BTU**) ▶ **n.** the amount of heat needed to raise one pound of water at maximum density through one degree Fahrenheit, equivalent to 1.055×10^3 joules.

Brit·ish Vir·gin Is·lands see **VIRGIN ISLANDS**.

Brit·on /ˈbritn/ ▶ **n.** **1** a citizen or native of Great Britain. ■ a person of British descent.
2 one of the people of southern Britain before and during Roman times.
– ORIGIN from Old French *Breton*, from Latin *Britto*, *Britton-*, or its Celtic equivalent.

Brit·pop /ˈbritˌpäp/ ▶ **n.** pop music by a loose affiliation of British groups of the mid 1990s, typically influenced by the Beatles and other British groups of the 1960s and perceived as a reaction against American grunge music.

Brit·ta·ny /ˈbritn-ē/ a region and former duchy of northwestern France that forms a peninsula between the Bay of Biscay and the English Channel. French name **BRETAGNE**.

Brit·ten /ˈbritn/, Benjamin (1913–76), English composer, pianist, and conductor; full name *Edward Benjamin Britten, Lord Britten of Aldeburgh*. Notable operas: *Peter Grimes* (1945), *A Midsummer Night's Dream* (1960), and *Death in Venice* (1973).

brit·tle /ˈbritl/ ▶ **adj.** hard but liable to break or shatter easily: *her bones became fragile and brittle.* ■ (of a sound, esp. a person's voice) unpleasantly hard and sharp and showing signs of instability or nervousness: *a brittle laugh.* ■ (of a person or behavior) appearing aggressive or hard but unstable or nervous within: *her manner was artificially bright and brittle.*
▶ **n.** a candy made from nuts and set melted sugar: *peanut brittle.*
– DERIVATIVES **brit·tle·ly** (or **brittly**) **adv.**, **brit·tle·ness n.**
– ORIGIN late Middle English, ultimately of Germanic origin and related to Old English *brēotan* 'break up.'

brit·tle bone dis·ease ▶ **n.** Medicine **1** another term for **OSTEOGENESIS IMPERFECTA**.
2 another term for **OSTEOPOROSIS**.

brit·tle fern ▶ **n.** another term for **BLADDER FERN**.

brit·tle frac·ture ▶ **n.** fracture of a metal or other material occurring without appreciable prior plastic deformation.

brit·tle·star /ˈbritlˌstär/ ▶ **n.** an echinoderm related to the starfish, with long, thin, flexible arms radiating from a small central disk. ● Class Ophiuroidea: *Ophiura* and other genera.

Brit·ton·ic /briˈtänik/ ▶ **adj. & n.** variant of **BRYTHONIC**.
– ORIGIN from Latin *Britto*, *Britton-* 'Briton' + **-IC**.

britz·ka /ˈbricнkə, ˈbrits-/ (also **britzska**) ▶ **n.** historical an open carriage with calash top and space for reclining.
– ORIGIN early 19th cent.: from Polish *bryczka*.

Brix scale /briks/ ▶ **n.** a hydrometer scale for measuring the amount of sugar in a solution at a given temperature.
– ORIGIN late 19th cent.: the name of A. F. W. *Brix* (1798–1890), German scientist.

Br·no /ˈbərnō/ an industrial city in the Czech Republic; pop. 366,812 (2007).

bro /brō/ ▶ **n.** informal short for **BROTHER**: *his baby bro.* ■ [in sing.] a friendly greeting or form of address: *"Yo bro!"* ■ (**Bro.**) Brother (used before a first name when referring in writing to a member of a religious order of men): *Bro. Felix.*

broach[1] /brōcн/ ▶ **v.** [with obj.] **1** raise (a sensitive or difficult subject) for discussion: *he broached the subject he had been avoiding all evening.*
2 pierce (a cask) to draw liquor. ■ open and start using the contents of (a bottle or other container).
3 [no obj.] (of a fish or sea mammal) rise through the water and break the surface: *the salmon broach, then fall to slap the water.*
– ORIGIN Middle English: from Old French *brochier*, based on Latin *brocchus*, *broccus* 'projecting.' The earliest recorded sense was 'prick with spurs,' part of the general meaning 'pierce with something sharp,' from which sense 2 arose in late Middle English. Sense 1, a figurative use of this, dates from the late 16th cent.

broach[2] Nautical ▶ **v.** [no obj.] (also **broach to**) (of a ship with the wind on the quarter) veer and pitch forward because of bad steering or a sea hitting the stern, causing it to present a side to the wind and sea, lose steerage, and possibly suffer serious damage: *we had broached badly, side on to the wind and sea | the ship would have broached to if the captain had not sprung to the wheel.*
▶ **n.** a sudden and hazardous veering of a ship having such consequences.
– ORIGIN early 18th cent.: of unknown origin.

broad /brôd/ ▶ **adj.** **1** having an ample distance from side to side; wide: *a broad staircase.* ■ (after a measurement) giving the distance from side to side: *the valley is three miles long and half a mile broad.* ■ large in area; spacious: *a broad expanse of prairie.*
2 covering a large number and wide scope of subjects or areas: *a broad range of experience.* ■ having or incorporating a wide range of meanings, applications, or kinds of things; loosely defined: *three broad categories of mutual funds.* ■ including or coming from many people of many kinds: *broad support for the president's foreign policy.*
3 general; without detail: *a broad outline of NATO's position.* ■ (of a hint) clear and unambiguous; not subtle: *a broad hint.* ■ somewhat coarse and indecent: *what we regard as broad or even bawdy is a fact of nature to him.* ■ (of a phonetic transcription) showing only meaningful distinctions in sound and ignoring minor details.
4 (of a regional accent) very noticeable and strong: *his broad Bronx accent.*
▶ **n.** informal a woman.
– PHRASES **broad in the beam** fat around the hips. **in broad daylight** during the day, when it is light, and surprising or unexpected for this reason: *the kidnapping took place in broad daylight.*
– DERIVATIVES **broad·ness n.**
– ORIGIN Old English *brād*, of Germanic origin; related to Dutch *breed* and German *breit*.

broad ar·row ▶ **n.** a mark resembling a broad arrowhead, formerly used on British prison clothing, Navy timber, and other government property.

broad·ax /ˈbrôdˌaks/ (also **broadaxe**) ▶ **n.** an ax with a wide head and a short handle.

broad·band /ˈbrôdˌband/ ▶ **n.** a high-capacity transmission technique using a wide range of frequencies, which enables a large number of messages to be communicated simultaneously: *our ability to uplink on broadband has been curtailed |* [as modifier] *broadband applications such as video and live audio.*

broad bean ▶ **n.** **1** a large edible flat green bean that is typically eaten without the pod. Also called **FAVA BEAN, HORSEBEAN**.
2 the plant that yields these beans, often cultivated in gardens. ● *Vicia faba*, family Leguminosae.

broad·bill /ˈbrôdˌbil/ ▶ **n.** **1** a small bird of the Old World tropics, with a stocky body, a large head, a flattened bill with a wide gape, and typically very colorful plumage. ● Family Eurylaimidae: several genera.
2 a bird with a broad bill, esp. a duck like the shoveler or the scaup.
3 another term for **SWORDFISH**.

broad-brush ▶ **adj.** lacking in detail and subtlety: *a broad-brush measure of inflation.*
▶ **n.** (**broad brush**) an approach characterized in this way: *the public painted all evangelists with a broad brush.*

broad·cast /ˈbrôdˌkast/ ▶ **v.** (past and past participle **broadcast**) [with obj.] **1** transmit (a program or some information) by radio or television: *the announcement was broadcast live |* (as noun **broadcasting**) *the 1920s saw the dawn of broadcasting.* ■ [no obj.] take part in a radio or television transmission: *the station broadcasts 24 hours a day.* ■ tell (something) to many people; make widely known: *we don't want to broadcast our unhappiness to the world.*
2 scatter (seeds) by hand or machine rather than placing in drills or rows.
▶ **n.** a radio or television program or transmission.
▶ **adj.** of or relating to such programs: *a broadcast journalist.*
▶ **adv.** by scattering: *green manure can be sown broadcast or in rows.*
– DERIVATIVES **broad·cast·er n.**
– ORIGIN mid 18th cent. (in the sense 'sown by scattering'): from **BROAD** + the past participle of **CAST**[1]. Senses relating to radio and television date from the early 20th cent.

Broad Church ▶ **n.** a tradition or group within the Anglican Church favoring a liberal interpretation of doctrine. ■ a group, organization, or doctrine that allows for and caters to a wide range of opinions and people.

broad·cloth /ˈbrôdˌklôтн/ ▶ **n.** clothing fabric of fine twilled wool or worsted, or plain-woven cotton.
– ORIGIN late Middle English: originally denoting cloth made 72 inches wide, as opposed to 'strait' cloth, 36 inches wide. The term now implies quality rather than width.

broad·en /ˈbrôdn/ ▶ **v.** [no obj.] become larger in distance from side to side; widen: *her smile broadened | the river slowed and broadened out slightly.* ■ expand to encompass more people, ideas, or things: *her interests broadened as she grew up |* [with obj.] *efforts to broaden classical music's appeal.*
– PHRASES **broaden one's horizons** expand one's range of interests, activities, and knowledge.

broad gauge ▶ **n.** a railroad gauge that is wider than the standard gauge of 56.5 inches (1.435 m).

broad jump ▶ **n.** another term for **LONG JUMP**.

broad·leaf /ˈbrôdˌlēf/ ▶ **adj.** another term for **BROADLEAVED**.
▶ **n.** (pl. **broadleaves** or **broadleafs**) a tree or plant with wide flat leaves.

broad·leaved ▶ **adj.** [attrib.] (of a tree or plant) having relatively wide, flat leaves rather than needles; nonconiferous. ■ (of a wood or woodland) consisting of trees with such leaves: *ancient broadleaved woodlands.*

broad·loom /ˈbrôdˌlo͞om/ ▶ **n.** carpet woven in wide widths: *wall-to-wall broadloom.*
– DERIVATIVES **broad·loomed adj.**

b

broad·ly /ˈbrôdlē/ ▶ **adv. 1** in general and with the exception of minor details: *the climate is broadly similar in the two regions.*
2 widely and openly: *he was grinning broadly.*

broad-mind·ed ▶ **adj.** tolerant or liberal in one's views and reactions; not easily offended: *a broad-minded approach to religion.*
– DERIVATIVES **broad-mind·ed·ness n., broad-mind·ed·ly adv.**

broad pen·nant (also **broad pendant**) ▶ **n.** a short swallow-tailed pennant distinguishing the commodore's ship in a squadron.

broad reach Sailing ▶ **n.** a point of sailing in which the wind blows over a boat's quarter, between the beam and the stern: *on a broad reach they are magnificent craft.*
▶ **v. (broad-reach)** [no obj.] sail with the wind in this position.

broad·sheet /ˈbrôd,SHēt/ ▶ **n.** a large piece of paper printed on one side only with information; a broadside. ■ (also **broadsheet newspaper**) a newspaper with a large format regarded as more serious and less sensationalist than tabloids.

broad·side /ˈbrôd,sīd/ ▶ **n. 1** a nearly simultaneous firing of all the guns from one side of a warship. ■ a strongly worded critical attack: ***broadsides against** political correctness.* ■ the set of guns that can fire on each side of a warship. ■ the side of a ship above the water between the bow and quarter.
2 a sheet of paper printed on one side only, forming one large page: *a broadside of Lee's farewell address.* Also called BROADSHEET.
▶ **adv.** with the side turned to a particular thing: *the yacht was drifting **broadside to the wind.*** ■ on the side: *her car was hit broadside by another vehicle.*
▶ **v.** [with obj.] collide with the side of (a vehicle): *I had to skid my bike sideways to avoid broadsiding her.*

broad-spec·trum ▶ **adj.** [attrib.] denoting antibiotics, pesticides, etc., effective against a large variety of organisms.

broad·sword /ˈbrôd,sôrd/ ▶ **n.** a sword with a wide blade, used for cutting rather than thrusting.

broad·tail /ˈbrôd,tāl/ ▶ **n.** a karakul sheep. ■ the fleece or wool from a karakul lamb.

Broad·way /ˈbrôdwā/ a street that runs the length of Manhattan in New York City. It is famous for its theaters, and its name has become synonymous with show business. It is also known as the Great White Way, in reference to its brilliant street illuminations.

broad·way /ˈbrôd,wā/ ▶ **n.** (usually in names) a large open or main road.

broast /brōst/ ▶ **v.** prepare food using a cooking process that combines broiling and roasting: [as adj.] *broasted chicken.*

Brob·ding·nag·i·an /,bräbdiNGˈnagēən/ ▶ **adj.** gigantic.
▶ **n.** a giant.
– ORIGIN early 18th cent.: from *Brobdingnag*, the name given by Swift (in *Gulliver's Travels*) to a land where everything is of huge size, + -IAN.

bro·cade /brōˈkād/ ▶ **n.** a rich fabric, usually silk, woven with a raised pattern, typically with gold or silver thread: [as modifier] *a heavy brocade curtain.*
▶ **v.** [with obj.] (usu. as adj. **brocaded**) weave (something) with this design: *a heavily brocaded blanket.*
– ORIGIN late 16th cent.: from Spanish and Portuguese *brocado* (influenced by French *brocart*), from Italian *broccato*, from *brocco* 'twisted thread.'

Bro·ca's ar·e·a /ˈbrōkəz/ ▶ **n.** Anatomy a region of the brain concerned with the production of speech, located in the cortex of the dominant frontal lobe. Damage in this area causes **Broca's aphasia**, characterized by hesitant and fragmented speech with little grammatical structure.
– ORIGIN late 19th cent.: named after P. Paul *Broca* (1824–80), French surgeon.

broc·ci·flow·er /ˈbräkə,flou(ə)r/ (also **broccoflower**) ▶ **n.** a light green vegetable that is a cross between broccoli and cauliflower.
– ORIGIN blend of *broccoli* and *cauliflower*.

broc·co·li /ˈbräk(ə)lē/ ▶ **n.** a cabbage of a variety similar to the cauliflower, bearing heads of green or purplish flower buds. It is widely cultivated as a vegetable. ● There are several kinds of broccoli, in particular those in the "Italica" group.
– ORIGIN mid 17th cent.: from Italian, plural of *broccolo* 'cabbage sprout, head,' diminutive of *brocco* 'shoot,' based on Latin *brocchus, broccus* 'projecting.'

broc·co·li·ni /,bräkəˈlēnē/ ▶ **n.** a vegetable that is a hybrid of broccoli and kale, with small florets on slender stalks. It has a mild, nutty flavor.

broc·co·li rabe /räb/ (also **broccoli raab**) ▶ **n.** a vegetable related to the turnip, grown for its broccoli-like buds and bitter-flavored greens. Also called RAPINI.

bro·chette /brōˈSHet/ ▶ **n.** a skewer or spit on which chunks of meat or fish are barbecued, grilled, or roasted: *beef and lamb en brochette.* ■ a dish of meat or fish chunks cooked in such a way.
– ORIGIN French, diminutive of *broche* (see BROACH[1]).

bro·chure /brōˈSHo͝or/ ▶ **n.** a small book or magazine containing pictures and information about a product or service.
– ORIGIN mid 18th cent.: from French, literally 'something stitched,' from *brocher* 'to stitch' (see BROACH[1]).

bro·chure·ware /brōˈSHo͝or,we(ə)r/ ▶ **n.** websites or web pages produced by converting a company's printed marketing or advertising material into an Internet format.

Brock·en /ˈbräkən/ a mountain in northern central Germany, in the Harz Mountains, that rises to 3,747 feet (1,143 m). It is noted for the optical phenomenon of the Brocken specter, in which a greatly enlarged image appears projected on clouds, and for witches' revels that reputedly took place here on Walpurgis night.

brock·et /ˈbräkit/ (also **brocket deer**) ▶ **n.** a small deer with short, straight antlers, found in Central and South America. ● Genus *Mazama*, family Cervidae: four species.
– ORIGIN late Middle English (denoting any red deer stag in its second year, with straight antlers): from Anglo-Norman French *broquet*, diminutive of *broque*, variant of *broche* (see BROOCH). The current sense dates from the mid 19th cent.

Brock·ton /ˈbräktən/ an industrial city in southeastern Massachusetts, south of Boston, noted esp. for shoe manufacture; pop. 93,007 (est. 2008).

bro·de·rie an·glaise /,brōdəˈrē äNGˈglez, -ˈglāz/ ▶ **n.** open embroidery, typically in white floral patterns, on fine white cotton or linen.
– ORIGIN mid 19th cent.: French, literally 'English embroidery.'

Brod·sky /ˈbrädskē, ˈbrät-/, Joseph (1940–96), US poet; born in Russia; born *Iosif Aleksandrovich Brodsky*; US poet laureate 1991. Writing both in Russian and in English, he was noted for his collection *The End of a Beautiful Era* (1977). Nobel Prize for Literature (1987).

Broe·der·bond /ˈbrōdər,bänd/ a largely secret society in South Africa (founded in 1918) promoting the interests of and restricted in membership to male, Protestant Afrikaners.
– ORIGIN Afrikaans, from *broeder* 'brother' + *bond* 'league.'

bro·gan /ˈbrogən/ ▶ **n.** a coarse, stout leather shoe reaching to the ankle.
– ORIGIN mid 19th cent.: from Irish *brógán*, Scottish Gaelic *brógan*, literally 'small brogue.'

brogue[1] /brōg/ ▶ **n.** a strong outdoor shoe with ornamental perforated patterns in the leather. ■ historical a rough shoe of untanned leather, formerly worn in parts of Ireland and the Scottish Highlands.
– ORIGIN late 16th cent.: from Scottish Gaelic and Irish *bróg*, from Old Norse *brók* (related to BREECH).

brogue[2] ▶ **n.** [usu. in sing.] a marked accent, esp. Irish or Scottish, when speaking English: *a fine Irish brogue | a sweet lilt of brogue in her voice.*
– ORIGIN early 18th cent.: perhaps allusively from BROGUE[1], referring to the rough footwear of Irish peasants.

broi·der /ˈbroidər/ ▶ **v.** [with obj.] archaic ornament with embroidery.

broil[1] /broil/ ▶ **v.** [with obj.] cook (meat or fish) by exposure to direct, intense radiant heat: *he broiled a wedge of sea bass* | (as adj. **broiled**) *a broiled sirloin steak.* ■ [no obj.] become very hot, esp. from the sun: *the countryside lay broiling in the sun.*
– ORIGIN late Middle English (also in the sense 'burn, char'): from Old French *bruler* 'to burn,' of unknown origin.

broil[2] ▶ **n.** archaic a quarrel or a commotion.
– ORIGIN early 16th cent.: from obsolete *broil* 'to muddle' Compare with EMBROIL.

broil·er /ˈbroilər/ ▶ **n. 1** (also **broiler chicken**) a young chicken suitable for roasting, grilling, or barbecuing.
2 a gridiron, grill, or special part of a stove for broiling meat or fish.

broil·ing /broiliNG/ ▶ **adj.** extremely hot; scorching: *the women toil in the broiling sun.*

broke /brōk/ past (and archaic past participle) of BREAK.
▶ **adj.** [predic.] informal having completely run out of money: *many farmers went broke.*
– PHRASES **go for broke** informal risk everything in an all-out effort. **if it ain't broke, don't fix it** informal if something is reasonably successful or effective, there is no need to change or replace it.

bro·ken /ˈbrōkən/ past participle of BREAK ▶ **adj.**
1 having been fractured or damaged and no longer in one piece or in working order: *a broken arm.* ■ (of a relationship) ended, such as through infidelity: *a broken marriage.* ■ disrupted or divided: *broken families.* ■ (of an agreement or promise) not observed by one of the parties involved.
2 (of a person) having given up all hope; despairing: *he went to his grave a broken man.*
3 having breaks or gaps in continuity: *a broken white line across the road.* ■ (of speech or a language) spoken falteringly, as if overcome by emotion, or with many mistakes, as by a foreigner: *a young man talking in broken Italian.*
4 having an uneven and rough surface: *broken ground.*
– PHRASES **broken record** annoying repetition, as likened to a scratched phonograph record that repeats the same brief passage over and over: *the words echoed through his head like a broken record.*
– DERIVATIVES **bro·ken·ly adv., bro·ken·ness n.**

Bro·ken Ar·row a city in northeastern Oklahoma, southeast of Tulsa; pop. 92,931 (est. 2008).

bro·ken chord ▶ **n.** [usu. as modifier] Music a chord in which the notes are played successively: *the second entry is a straight broken-chord figure.*

bro·ken-down ▶ **adj.** [attrib.] worn out and dilapidated by age, use, or ill-treatment: *a broken-down car.* ■ (of a machine or vehicle) not functioning due to a mechanical failure. ■ (of a horse) with serious damage to the legs, in particular the tendons, caused by excessive strain.

bro·ken-field Football ▶ **adj.** relating to or occurring in the area beyond the line of scrimmage where defenders are relatively scattered: *a broken-field run.* ■ informal (of a movement) with starts, stops, and changes of direction, in the manner of a broken-field ballcarrier: *a broken-field chase.*

bro·ken-heart·ed ▶ **adj.** overwhelmed by grief or disappointment.

Bro·ken Hill 1 a town in New South Wales in Australia, a center of lead, silver, and zinc mining; pop. 20,001 (2008).
2 former name (1904–65) for KABWE.

bro·ken home ▶ **n.** a family in which the parents are divorced or separated.

bro·ken wind /wind/ ▶ **n.** another term for **COPD** in horses.
– DERIVATIVES **bro·ken-wind·ed adj.**

bro·ker /ˈbrōkər/ ▶ **n.** a person who buys and sells goods or assets for others.
▶ **v.** [with obj.] arrange or negotiate (a settlement, deal, or plan): *fighting continued despite attempts to broker a ceasefire.*
– ORIGIN Middle English (denoting a retailer or peddler): from Anglo-Norman French *brocour*, of unknown ultimate origin.

bro·ker·age /ˈbrōkərij/ ▶ **n.** the business or service of acting as a broker. ■ a fee or commission charged by a broker: *a revenue of $1,400 less a sales brokerage of $12.50.* ■ a company that buys or sells goods or assets for clients.

bro·ker-deal·er ▶ **n.** a brokerage firm that buys and sells securities on its own account as a principal before selling the securities to customers.

brol·ga /ˈbrälgə/ ▶ **n.** a large gray Australian crane that has an elaborate courtship display that involves much leaping, wing-flapping, and trumpeting. ● *Grus rubicundus*, family Gruidae.
– ORIGIN late 19th cent.: from Kamilaroi *burralga* (also found in other Aboriginal languages).

bro·mance /ˈbrō,mans/ ▶ **n.** informal a close but nonsexual relationship between two men.
– ORIGIN early 21st cent.: blend of BROTHER and ROMANCE.

Brom·berg /ˈbrämbərg/ German name for BYDGOSZCZ.

brome /brōm/ ▶ **n.** an oatlike grass that is sometimes grown for fodder or ornamental purposes. ● Genus *Bromus*, family Gramineae.
– ORIGIN mid 18th cent.: from modern Latin *Bromus*, from Greek *bromos* 'oat.'

bro·me·li·ad /brōˈmēlē,ad/ ▶ **n.** a plant native to tropical and subtropical America, typically having short stems with rosettes of stiff, usually spiny, leaves. Some kinds are epiphytic, and many are cultivated as houseplants. ● Family Bromeliaceae: *Bromelia* and other genera, and numerous species, including the pineapple and Spanish moss.
– ORIGIN mid 19th cent.: from modern Latin *Bromelia* (named by Linnaeus after Olaf *Bromel* (1639–1705), Swedish botanist) + -AD[1].

bro·mic ac·id /ˈbrōmik/ ▶ **n.** Chemistry a strongly oxidizing acid known only in aqueous solutions. ● Chem. formula: $HBrO_3$.
– DERIVATIVES **bro·mate** /ˈbrō,māt/ **n.**

bro·mide /ˈbrōmīd/ ▶ **n. 1** Chemistry a compound of bromine with another element or group, esp. a salt containing the anion Br^- or an organic compound with bromine bonded to an alkyl radical.
2 a trite and unoriginal idea or remark, typically intended to soothe or placate: *feel-good bromides create the illusion of problem solving.* dated a sedative preparation containing potassium bromide.
3 a reproduction or piece of typesetting on bromide paper.
– DERIVATIVES **bro·mid·ic** /brōˈmidik/ **adj.** (sense 2).

bro·mide pa·per ▶ **n.** photographic printing paper coated with silver bromide emulsion.

bro·min·ate /ˈbrōməˌnāt/ ▶ **v.** [with obj.] treat with bromine. ■ (usu. as adj. **brominated**) introduce one or more bromine atoms into a compound or molecule, usually in place of hydrogen: *brominated flame retardants.*
– DERIVATIVES **bro·mi·na·tion** /ˌbrōməˈnāSHən/ **n.**

bro·mine /ˈbrōmēn/ ▶ **n.** the chemical element of atomic number 35, a dark red fuming toxic liquid with a choking, irritating smell. It is a member of the halogen group and occurs chiefly as salts in seawater and brines. (Symbol: **Br**)
– ORIGIN early 19th cent.: from French *brome,* from Greek *brōmos* 'a stink,' + **-INE**[4].

bro·mism /ˈbrōˌmizəm/ ▶ **n.** dated a condition of dullness and weakness due to excessive intake of bromide sedatives.

bromo- (usu. **brom-** before a vowel) ▶ **comb. form** Chemistry representing **BROMINE.**

Bromp·ton cock·tail /ˈbrämptən/ ▶ **n.** a powerful painkiller and sedative consisting of vodka or other liquor laced with morphine and sometimes also cocaine.
– ORIGIN late 20th cent.: said to be from the name of *Brompton* Hospital, London, where the mixture was invented for cancer patients.

bronc /bräNGk/ ▶ **n.** informal short for **BRONCO.**

bron·chi /ˈbräNGkī, -kē/ plural form of **BRONCHUS.**

bron·chi·a /ˈbräNGkēə/ ▶ **n.** rare the ramifications of the two main bronchi in the lungs.

bron·chi·al /ˌbrängkēəl/ ▶ **adj.** of or relating to the bronchi or bronchioles: *bronchial pneumonia.*

bron·chi·al tree ▶ **n.** the branching system of bronchi and bronchioles conducting air from the windpipe into the lungs.

bron·chi·al tube ▶ **n.** a bronchus or a primary branch off of one.

bron·chi·ec·ta·sis /ˌbräNGkēˈektəsis/ ▶ **n.** Medicine abnormal widening of the bronchi or their branches, causing a risk of infection.
– ORIGIN late 19th cent.: from Greek *bronkhia* (denoting the branches of the main bronchi) + *ektasis* 'dilatation.'

bron·chi·ole /ˈbräNGkēˌōl/ ▶ **n.** Anatomy any of the minute branches into which a bronchus divides.
– DERIVATIVES **bron·chi·o·lar** /ˌbräNGkēˈōlər/ **adj.**
– ORIGIN mid 19th cent.: from modern Latin *bronchiolus, bronchiolum,* diminutives of late Latin *bronchia,* denoting the branches of the main bronchi.

bron·chi·o·li·tis /ˌbräNGkēəˈlītis/ ▶ **n.** Medicine inflammation of the bronchioles.

bron·chi·tis /bräNGˈkītis/ ▶ **n.** inflammation of the mucous membrane in the bronchial tubes. It typically causes bronchospasm and coughing.
– DERIVATIVES **bron·chit·ic** /bräNGˈkitik/ **adj. & n.**

bron·chi·um /ˈbräNGkēəm/ ▶ **n.** a bronchial tube smaller than a bronchus and larger than a bronchiole.

broncho- ▶ **comb. form** of or relating to the bronchi: *bronchopneumonia.*
– ORIGIN from Greek *bronkho-,* from *bronkhos* (see **BRONCHUS**).

bron·cho·di·la·tor /ˌbräNGkōdīˈlātər, -di-, -ˈdīlātər/ ▶ **n.** Medicine a drug that causes widening of the bronchi, e.g., any of those taken by inhalation for the alleviation of asthma.

bron·cho·gen·ic /ˌbräNGkōˈjenik/ ▶ **adj.** of bronchial origin.

bron·cho·pneu·mo·nia /ˌbräNGkōn(y)o͞oˈmōnēə, -ˈmōnyə/ ▶ **n.** inflammation of the lungs, arising in the bronchi or bronchioles.

bron·cho·scope /ˈbräNGkəˌskōp/ ▶ **n.** a fiber-optic cable that is passed into the windpipe in order to view the bronchi.
– DERIVATIVES **bron·chos·co·py** /bräNGˈkäskəpē/ **n.**

bron·cho·spasm /ˈbräNGkəˌspazəm/ ▶ **n.** Medicine spasm of bronchial smooth muscle producing narrowing of the bronchi.

bron·chus /ˈbräNGkəs/ ▶ **n.** (pl. **bronchi** /-kī, -kē/) any of the major air passages of the lungs that diverge from the windpipe.
– ORIGIN late 17th cent.: from late Latin, from Greek *bronkhos* 'windpipe.'

bron·co /ˈbräNGkō/ ▶ **n.** (pl. **broncos**) a wild or half-tamed horse, esp. of the western US.
– ORIGIN mid 19th cent.: from Spanish, literally 'rough, rude.'

bron·co·bust·er /ˈbräNGkōˌbəstər/ ▶ **n.** informal a cowboy who breaks in wild or half-tamed horses.

Bron·të /ˈbräntē ˈbräntā/ three English novelists. ■ **Charlotte** (1816–55), author of *Jane Eyre* (1847), *Shirley* (1849), and *Villette* (1853). ■ **Emily** (1818–48), author of *Wuthering Heights* (1847); also a poet. ■ **Anne** (1820–49), author of *Agnes Grey* (1845) and *The Tenant of Wildfell Hall* (1847).

bron·to·saur /ˈbräntəˌsôr/ (also **brontosaurus** /ˌbräntəˈsôrəs/) ▶ **n.** another term for **APATOSAUR.**
– DERIVATIVES **bron·to·sau·ri·an** /ˌbräntəˈsôrēən/ **adj.**
– ORIGIN modern Latin from Greek *brontē* 'thunder' + *sauros* 'lizard.'

bron·to·there /ˈbräntəTHi(ə)r/ ▶ **n.** a large ungulate mammal (*Embolotherium andrewsi*) of the Eocene epoch with a hornlike bony growth on the nose.
– ORIGIN modern Latin, from Greek *brontē* 'thunder' + *thērion* 'wild beast.'

Bronx /bräNGks/ (**the Bronx**) a borough in northeastern New York City.
– ORIGIN named after Jonas *Bronck,* a Dutch settler who purchased land here in 1641.

Bronx cheer ▶ **n.** a sound of derision or contempt made by blowing through closed lips with the tongue between them; a raspberry.
– ORIGIN 1920s: named after the **BRONX** in New York.

bronze /bränz/ ▶ **n.** a yellowish-brown alloy of copper with up to one-third tin. ■ a yellowish-brown color: *rich, gleaming shades of bronze.* ■ a work of sculpture or other object made of bronze. ■ short for **BRONZE MEDAL.**
▶ **v.** [with obj.] (usu. **be bronzed**) make (a person or part of the body) suntanned: *Alison was bronzed by outdoor life.* ■ give a surface of bronze or something resembling bronze to: *the doors were bronzed with sculpted reliefs.*
– DERIVATIVES **bronz·y adj.**
– ORIGIN mid 17th cent. (as a verb): from French *bronze* (noun), *bronzer* (verb), from Italian *bronzo,* probably from Persian *birinj* 'brass.'

Bronze Age a prehistoric period that followed the Stone Age and preceded the Iron Age, when certain weapons and tools came to be made of bronze rather than stone.

> The Bronze Age began in the Near East and southeastern Europe in the late 4th and early 3rd millennium BC. It is associated with the first European civilizations, the beginnings of urban life in China, and the final stages of some Meso-American civilizations, but did not appear in Africa and Australasia at all.

bronzed /bränzd/ ▶ **adj.** attractively and evenly suntanned; tanned: *bronzed and powerful arms.*

bronze med·al ▶ **n.** a medal made of bronze, customarily awarded for third place in a race or competition.

Bronze Star ▶ **n.** a US military decoration awarded for heroic or meritorious achievement not involving participation in aerial flight.

Bron·zi·no /brônˈzēnō/, Agnolo (1503–72), Italian painter; born *Agnolo di Cosimo.*

brooch /brōCH, bro͞oCH/ ▶ **n.** an ornament fastened to clothing with a hinged pin and catch.
– ORIGIN Middle English: variant of *broach,* a noun originally meaning 'skewer, bodkin,' from Old French *broche* 'spit for roasting,' based on Latin *brocchus, broccus* 'projecting.' Compare with **BROACH**[1].

brood /bro͞od/ ▶ **n.** a family of young animals, esp. of a bird, produced at one hatching or birth: *a brood of chicks.* ■ bee or wasp larvae. ■ informal all of the children in a family: *he was the youngest in a brood of six* | figurative *a remarkable brood of writers.*
▶ **v. 1** [no obj.] think deeply about something that makes one unhappy: *he brooded over his need to find a wife.*
2 [with obj.] (of a bird) sit on (eggs) to hatch them. ■ (of a fish, frog, or invertebrate) hold (developing eggs) within the body.
3 [usu. foll. by over] (of silence, a storm, etc.) hang or hover closely: *a winter storm broods over the lake.*
▶ **adj.** [attrib.] (of an animal) kept to be used for breeding: *a brood mare.*
– ORIGIN Old English *brōd,* of Germanic origin; related to Dutch *broed* and German *Brut,* also to **BREED.** Sense 1 of the verb was originally used with an object, i.e., 'to nurse (feelings) in the mind' (late 16th cent.), a figurative use of the notion of a hen nursing chicks under her wings.

brood·er /ˈbro͞odər/ ▶ **n. 1** a heated house for chicks or piglets.
2 a person who broods about something.

brood·ing /ˈbro͞odiNG/ ▶ **adj.** showing deep unhappiness of thought: *he stared with brooding eyes.* ■ appearing darkly menacing: *a dark, brooding landscape.*
– DERIVATIVES **brood·ing·ly adv.**

brood pouch ▶ **n.** a pouch in certain fish, frogs, and invertebrates in which the eggs are protected before hatching.

brood·y /ˈbro͞odē/ ▶ **adj.** (**broodier, broodiest**) **1** (of a hen) wishing or inclined to incubate eggs. ■ informal (of a woman) having a strong desire to have a baby.
2 thoughtful and unhappy: *his broody concern for the future.*
– DERIVATIVES **brood·i·ly** /-dəlē/ **adv., brood·i·ness n.**

brook[1] /bro͝ok/ ▶ **n.** a small stream.
– DERIVATIVES **brook·let** /-lit/ **n.**
– ORIGIN Old English *brōc;* related to Dutch *broek* and German *Bruch* 'marsh.'

brook[2] ▶ **v.** [with obj. with negative] formal tolerate or allow (something, typically dissent or opposition): *Jenny would brook no criticism of Matthew.*
– ORIGIN Old English *brūcan* 'use, possess,' of Germanic origin; related to Dutch *bruiken* and German *brauchen.* The current sense dates from the mid 16th cent., a figurative use of an earlier sense 'digest, stomach.'

Brooke[1] /bro͝ok/, Edward William (1919–), US lawyer and politician. A Republican senator from Massachusetts 1966–79, he was the first African-American senator popularly elected to the US Senate. He was awarded the Spingarn Medal in 1967.

Brooke[2], Rupert (Chawner) (1887–1915), English poet. He is noted for his wartime poetry, *1914 and Other Poems* (1915).

Brook Farm a historic commune that existed in the 1840s in West Roxbury, now a southwestern section of Boston in Massachusetts, associated with Margaret Fuller and other writers.

Brook·field /ˈbro͝okˌfēld/ a city in southeastern Wisconsin, west of Milwaukee; pop. 39,020 (est. 2008).

Brook·ha·ven /ˈbro͝okˌhāvən/ a town in eastern Long Island in New York that includes the villages of Brookhaven and Stony Brook, home to a noted nuclear laboratory; pop. 488,800 (est. 2008).

brook·lime /ˈbro͝okˌlīm/ ▶ **n.** a speedwell with smooth, fleshy leaves and deep blue flowers on long stalks. It grows in wet areas, where the stems take root or float in the water. ● Genus *Veronica,* family Scrophulariaceae: several species, in particular *V. beccabunga* of Eurasia and the **American brooklime** (*V. americana*).
– ORIGIN Middle English *broklemok,* from **BROOK**[1] + *hleomoce,* the name of the plant in Old English.

Brook·line /ˈbro͝okˌlīn/ a town in eastern Massachusetts, on the west side of Boston and almost surrounded by the city; pop. 54,896 (est. 2008).

Brook·lyn /ˈbro͝oklən/ a borough of New York City, at the southwestern corner of Long Island.
– DERIVATIVES **Brook·lyn·ite n.**

Brook·lyn Bridge a suspension bridge between southern Manhattan and northern Brooklyn (on Long Island) in New York City. Constructed 1869-1883, it was one of the period's engineering marvels and is celebrated in art and literature.

Brooklyn Bridge

PRONUNCIATION KEY ə *ago, up;* ər *over, fur;* a *hat;* ā *ate;* ä *car;* e *let;* ē *see;* i *fit;* ī *by;* NG *sing;* ō *go;* ô *law, for;* oi *toy;* o͝o *good;* o͞o *goo;* ou *out;* TH *thin;* T̲H̲ *then;* ZH *vision*

Brook·lyn·ese /ˌbro͝oklə'nēz, -'nēs/ ▸ **n.** a form of New York speech associated esp. with the borough of Brooklyn.

Brook·lyn Park a city in southeastern Minnesota, north of Minneapolis; pop. 71,308 (est. 2008).

Brook·ner /'bro͝oknər/, Anita (1928–), English novelist and art historian. Notable works: *Hotel du Lac* (1984), *Visitors* (1997), *The Bay of Angels* (2001) and *The Rules of Engagement* (2003).

Brooks[1] /bro͝oks/, Cleanth (1906–94), US teacher and critic. A leading proponent of the New Criticism movement, he edited *The Southern Review* 1935–42 and taught at Yale University 1947–75. Notable works: *Modern Poetry and Tradition* (1939) and *The Well-Wrought Urn* (1947).

Brooks[2], Gwendolyn (1917–2000), US poet and writer. She was the first African-American woman named as poetry consultant to the Library of Congress 1985–86 and the first to be awarded a Pulitzer Prize for her poetry collected in *Annie Allen* (1949).

Brooks[3], Mel (1927–), US comedian, screenwriter, director, and actor; born *Melvin Kaminsky*. He was both writer and director for a number of movies, including *The Producers* (1967) and *Young Frankenstein* (1974), both of which he later adapted to the stage as musicals.

Brooks Range /bro͝oks/ a mountain chain that extends across northern Alaska. It is the northwestern end of the Rocky Mountains; the North Slope lies on its north.

brook trout ▸ **n.** see **CHAR**[4].

broom /bro͞om, bro͝om/ ▸ **n. 1** a long-handled brush of bristles or twigs used for sweeping. ■ an implement for sweeping the ice in the game of curling. [formerly made of twigs of broom.] **2** a flowering shrub with long, thin green stems and small or few leaves, that is cultivated for its profusion of flowers. ● Genera *Cytisus* and *Genista*, family Leguminosae: many species and cultivated hybrids. See also **SPANISH BROOM**.
– PHRASES **a new broom sweeps clean** proverb people newly appointed to positions of responsibility tend to be eager to make big or far-reaching changes.
– ORIGIN Old English *brōm* (sense 2), of Germanic origin; related to Dutch *braam*, also to **BRAMBLE**.

broom·corn /'bro͞omˌkôrn, 'bro͝om-/ ▸ **n.** a variety of sorghum whose dried inflorescences are used to make brooms.

broom·rape /'bro͞omˌrāp, 'bro͝om-/ ▸ **n.** a parasitic plant that bears tubular flowers on a leafless brown stem. It is attached by its tubers to the roots of a host plant, which may be any of a number of species. ● Genus *Orobanche*, family Orobanchaceae.
– ORIGIN late 16th cent.: from **BROOM** + Latin *rapum* 'tuber.'

broom·stick /'bro͞omˌstik, 'bro͝om-/ ▸ **n.** the long handle of a broom. ■ a broom (esp. one made of twigs) on which, in children's literature, witches are said to fly.

Bros. ▸ **plural n.** brothers (in names of companies): *Hills Bros. coffee.*

broth /bräTH, brôTH/ ▸ **n. 1** soup consisting of meat or vegetable chunks, and often rice, cooked in stock. ■ meat or fish stock. **2** Microbiology liquid medium containing proteins and other nutrients for the culture of bacteria: [as modifier] *broth cultures of intestinal tissue.* ■ a liquid mixture for the preservation of tissue: *tissue samples were frozen in a cryoprotective broth.*
– PHRASES **a broth of a boy** informal, chiefly Irish used approvingly to refer to a very lively boy.
– ORIGIN Old English, of Germanic origin; related to **BREW**.

broth·el /'bräTHəl, 'brôTHəl/ ▸ **n.** a house where men can visit prostitutes.
– ORIGIN mid 16th cent. (originally *brothel-house*): from late Middle English *brothel* 'worthless man, prostitute,' related to Old English *brēothan* 'degenerate, deteriorate.'

broth·er /'brəT͟Hər/ ▸ **n. 1** a man or boy in relation to other sons and daughters of his parents. ■ a male associate or fellow member of an organization: *fraternity brothers.* ■ (also **brotha** or **brutha**) informal a black man (chiefly used as a term of address among black people). ■ a fellow human being. ■ a thing that resembles or is connected to another thing: *the machine is almost identical to its larger brother.* **2** (pl. also **brethren** /'breT͟Hrin/) Christian Church a (male) fellow Christian. ■ a member of a religious order or congregation of men: *a Benedictine brother.*
▸ **exclam.** used to express annoyance or surprise.
– PHRASES **brothers in arms** soldiers fighting together, esp. in a war.
– ORIGIN Old English *brōthor*, of Germanic origin; related to Dutch *broeder* and German *Bruder*, from an Indo-European root shared by Latin *frater*.

broth·er·hood /'brəT͟Hərˌho͝od/ ▸ **n. 1** the relationship between brothers. ■ the feeling of kinship with and closeness to a group of people or all people: *a gesture of solidarity and brotherhood.* **2** an association, society, or community of people linked by a common interest, religion, or trade: *a religious brotherhood.* ■ a labor union.
– ORIGIN Middle English: probably from obsolete *brotherred* (based on Old English *-rǣden* 'condition, state'; compare with **KINDRED**). The change of suffix was due to association with words ending in **-HOOD** and **-HEAD**[1].

broth·er-in-law ▸ **n.** (pl. **brothers-in-law**) the brother of one's wife or husband. ■ the husband of one's sister or sister-in-law.

broth·er·ly ▸ **adj.** typical of how brothers behave toward each other; fraternal: *he and I had such a brotherly bond.* ■ showing affection and concern; affectionate: *you could feel the warmth and the brotherly kindness.*
– DERIVATIVES **broth·er·li·ness n.**

broth·er·ly love ▸ **n.** feelings of humanity and compassion toward one's fellow humans.

brough·am /'bro͞oəm, 'brōəm/ ▸ **n.** historical a horse-drawn carriage with a roof, four wheels, and an open driver's seat in front. ■ an automobile with an open driver's seat.
– ORIGIN mid 19th cent.: named after Lord *Brougham* (1778–1868), who designed the carriage.

brought /brôt/ past and past participle of **BRING**.

brou·ha·ha /'bro͞ohäˌhä, bro͞o'hähä/ ▸ **n.** a noisy and overexcited reaction or response to something: *24 members resigned over the brouhaha | all that election brouhaha.*
– ORIGIN late 19th cent.: from French, probably imitative.

Brou·wer /'brou-ər/, Adriaen (*c.*1605–38), Flemish painter. Providing an important link between Dutch and Flemish genre painting, his most typical works represent peasant scenes in taverns.

brow[1] /brou/ ▸ **n. 1** a person's forehead: *he wiped his brow.* ■ (usu. **brows**) an eyebrow: *his brows lifted in surprise.* **2** the summit of a hill or pass: *the cottages were built on the brow of a hill.*
– ORIGIN Old English *brū* 'eyelash, eyebrow,' of Germanic origin. The sense 'forehead' dates from Middle English, and 'top of a hill' from late Middle English; compare with **BRAE**.

brow[2] ▸ **n.** a gangway from a ship to the shore. ■ a hinged part of a ferry or landing craft forming a landing platform or ramp.
– ORIGIN mid 19th cent.: probably from Norwegian *bru*, from Old Norse *brú* 'bridge.'

Brow·ard Coun·ty /'brou-ərd/ a county in southeastern Florida, on the Atlantic Ocean, north of Miami; pop. 1,751,234 (est. 2008). Fort Lauderdale is its seat.

brow·beat /'brouˌbēt/ ▸ **v.** (past **browbeat**; past participle **browbeaten**) [with obj.] intimidate (someone), typically into doing something, with stern or abusive words: *a witness is being browbeaten under cross-examination.*

-browed ▸ **comb. form** having a specified kind of brow or brows: [in combination] *furrow-browed | monobrowed.*

Brown[1] /broun/, Sir Arthur Whitten (1886–1948), Scottish aviator. In 1919, he made the first transatlantic flight, with Sir John William Alcock.

Brown[2], Capability (1716–83), English landscape gardener; born *Lancelot Brown.* He evolved an English style of natural-looking landscape parks.

Brown[3], Ford Madox (1821–93), English painter. His early work was inspired by the Pre-Raphaelites, and in 1861 he became a founding member of William Morris's company, designing stained glass and furniture.

Brown[4], Gordon (James) (1951–), British Labour statesman; prime minister 2007–10.

Brown[5], Henry Billings (1836–1913), US Supreme Court associate justice 1890–1906. After serving in several judicial posts in Michigan, he was appointed to the Court by President Benjamin Harrison.

Brown[6], James (1928–2006), US soul and funk singer and songwriter. In the 1960s he played a leading role in the development of funk with songs such as "Papa's Got a Brand New Bag" (1965) and "Sex Machine" (1970).

Brown[7], John (1800–59), US abolitionist. In 1859 he was executed after raiding a government arsenal at Harpers Ferry, Virginia (later part of West Virginia), with the intention of arming slaves and starting a revolt. He became a hero of the abolitionists in the Civil War, and he is commemorated in the song "John Brown's Body."

brown /broun/ ▸ **adj.** of a color produced by mixing red, yellow, and black, as of dark wood or rich soil: *an old brown coat | she had warm brown eyes.* ■ dark-skinned or suntanned: *his face was brown from the sun.* ■ (of bread) made from a dark, unsifted, or unbleached flour.
▸ **n.** brown color or pigment: *the brown of his eyes | a pair of boots in brown | the print is rich with velvety browns.* ■ brown clothes or material: *a woman all in brown.*
▸ **v.** make or become brown, typically by cooking: [with obj.] *a skillet in which food has been browned* | [no obj.] *bake the pizza until the cheese has browned.*
– PHRASES **(as) brown as a berry** (of a person) very suntanned. **do something up brown** do something thoroughly or completely: [as adj.] *a real picnic, done up brown according to all the rules.* **in a brown study** see **STUDY**.
– PHRASAL VERBS **brown someone off** (usu. as adj. **browned off**) make someone feel irritated or depressed: *they are getting browned off with the overtime.*
– DERIVATIVES **brown·ish adj.**, **brown·ness n.**, **brown·y adj.**
– ORIGIN Old English *brūn*, of Germanic origin; related to Dutch *bruin* and German *braun*.

brown al·gae ▸ **plural n.** algae belonging to a large group that includes many seaweeds, typically olive brown or greenish in color. They contain xanthophyll in addition to chlorophyll. ● Class Phaeophyceae, phylum Heterokonta, kingdom Protista; formerly division Phaeophyta.

brown bag ▸ **n.** a bag made of opaque brown paper. ■ a bag of such a kind in which a lunch is packed and carried to work, school, or informal functions: [as modifier] *a brown-bag lunch.*
▸ **v.** [with obj.] **(brown-bag it)** take a packed lunch to work or school: *no school lunch next week, so I'm brown-bagging it.*
– DERIVATIVES **brown-bag·ger n.**

brown bag·ging ▸ **n. 1** the practice of bringing one's own packed lunch to work. **2** the practice of bringing one's own liquor to a restaurant or club that cannot sell alcoholic beverages.

brown bear ▸ **n.** a large bear with a coat color ranging from cream to black, occurring chiefly in forests in Eurasia and North America. See also **GRIZZLY**. ● *Ursus arctos*, family Ursidae.

brown belt ▸ **n.** a brown belt marking a high level of proficiency in judo, karate, or other martial arts, below that of a black belt. ■ a person qualified to wear such a belt.

brown bet·ty ▸ **n.** a baked pudding made with apples or other fruit and breadcrumbs.

brown cloud ▸ **n.** a visible pall of air pollutants that persists over a city or other area: *the Asian brown cloud | throughout the day, air shifts in the valley cause variances in the brown cloud.*

brown coal ▸ **n.** another term for **LIGNITE**.

brown dwarf ▸ **n.** Astronomy a celestial object intermediate in size between a giant planet and a small star, believed to emit mainly infrared radiation.

brown earth ▸ **n.** Soil Science a type of soil having a brown humus-rich surface layer.

brown fat ▸ **n.** a dark-colored adipose tissue with many blood vessels, involved in the rapid production of heat in hibernating animals and human babies.

brown·field /'brounˌfēld/ ▸ **adj.** [attrib.] (of an urban site for potential building development) having had previous development on it. Compare with **GREENFIELD**.
▸ **n.** a former industrial or commercial site where future use is affected by real or perceived environmental contamination.

brown goods ▸ **plural n.** television sets, audio equipment, and similar household appliances: *a supply chain that accommodates highly perishable products, as well as white and brown goods.* Compare with **WHITE GOODS**.

brown hare ▸ **n.** a hare found commonly in much of Eurasia. ● *Lepus europaeus* (or *capensis*), family Leporidae.

brown hol·land ▸ **n.** unbleached holland linen.

Brown·i·an mo·tion /'brounēən/ ▸ **n.** Physics the erratic random movement of microscopic particles in a fluid, as a result of continuous bombardment from molecules of the surrounding medium.
– ORIGIN late 19th cent.: named after Robert *Brown* (1773–1858), the Scottish botanist who first observed the motion.

Brown·ie /'brounē/ ▸ **n.** (pl. **Brownies**) **1** a member of the junior branch of the Girl Scouts, for girls aged

between about 6 and 8. [so named because of the color of the uniform.]
2 (**brownie**) a small square of rich cake, typically chocolate cake with nuts.
3 (**brownie**) a benevolent elf supposed to haunt houses and do housework secretly. [diminutive of BROWN; a "wee brown man" often appears in Scottish ballads and fairy tales; compare with Old Norse *svartálfar*, the dark elves of the Edda.]
– PHRASES **brownie point** informal, humorous an imaginary award given to someone who does good deeds or tries to please: *his policy will win brownie points with voters*.

Brown·ing[1] /ˈbrouniNG/, Elizabeth Barrett (1806–61), English poet; born *Elizabeth Barrett*. She established her reputation with *Poems* (1844). In 1846, she eloped with Robert Browning. Other notable works: *Sonnets from the Portuguese* (1850), *Aurora Leigh* (novel, 1857), and the posthumous *Last Poems* (1862).

Brown·ing[2], Robert (1812–89), English poet. In 1842, he established his name with *Dramatic Lyrics* that contained "The Pied Piper of Hamelin" and "My Last Duchess." A highly creative period followed his elopement with Elizabeth Barrett. Other notable works: *Dramatic Romances and Lyrics* (1845), *Men and Women* (1855), and *The Ring and the Book* (1868–69).

Brown·ing[3] ▶ **n.** (also **Browning machine gun**) a type of water-cooled automatic machine gun. ■ (also **Browning automatic**) a type of automatic pistol. ■ (also **Browning automatic rifle**) a gas-operated automatic rifle, typically fired from a bipod.
– ORIGIN early 20th cent.: named after J. M. *Browning* (1855–1926), American designer of the weapons.

brown-nose (also **brownnose**) informal ▶ **n.** (also **brown-noser**) a person who acts in a grossly obsequious way.
▶ **v.** [with obj.] curry favor with (someone) by acting in such a way: ***academics were brown-nosing the senior faculty*** | [no obj.] *I dedicated a book to him—I was not brown-nosing.*
– ORIGIN the assumed result of ASS-KISSING.

brown·out /ˈbrounˌout/ ▶ **n.** a partial blackout.

brown owl ▶ **n.** another term for TAWNY OWL.

brown rat ▶ **n.** a rat found throughout the world, often living in association with man and regarded as a pest. It is commonly kept as a laboratory animal and as a pet, and is also bred in the albino form. Also called COMMON RAT, NORWAY RAT. ● *Rattus norvegicus*, family Muridae.

brown rec·luse (also **brown recluse spider**) ▶ **n.** a brown venomous North American spider, identifiable by the dark brown violin-shaped marking on the top of its orange-yellow head. Also called FIDDLEBACK, VIOLIN SPIDER. ● *Loxosceles reclusa*, family Loxoscelidae.

brown rice ▶ **n.** unpolished rice with only the husk of the grain removed.

brown rot ▶ **n.** a fungal disease causing the rotting and browning of parts of plants, in particular: ● a disease producing discoloration and shriveling of apples, pears, plums, etc. (caused by fungi of the genus *Monilinia*, phylum Ascomycota). ● a disease resulting in the softening and cracking of timber (caused by bracket fungi of the family Polyporaceae, class Basidiomycetes).

brown sauce ▶ **n.** a savory sauce made with fat and flour cooked to a brown color.

Brown·shirt /ˈbrounˌSHərt/ ▶ **n.** a member of an early Nazi militia founded by Hitler in Munich in 1921, with brown uniforms resembling that of Mussolini's Blackshirts. They aided Hitler's rise to power, but were eclipsed by the SS after the "night of the long knives" in June 1934. Also called STORM TROOPS or STURMABTEILUNG.

brown snake ▶ **n.** **1** a fast-moving, venomous, and aggressive Australian snake, with a variety of color forms. ● *Pseudonaja* and other genera, family Elapidae: several species, in particular *P. textilis*.
2 a small, secretive, harmless North American snake that is typically brownish in color. ● *Storeria dekayi*, family Colubridae.

brown·stone /ˈbrounˌstōn/ ▶ **n.** a kind of reddish-brown sandstone used for building. ■ a building faced with such sandstone.

brown sug·ar ▶ **n.** unrefined or partially refined sugar. ■ a consumer product made by adding molasses to white sugar.

Browns·ville 1 a city in southern Texas, on the Rio Grande and the Mexican border; pop. 175,494 (est. 2008).
2 a section of eastern Brooklyn in New York City, noted in the early 20th century for its Jewish community, today a struggling inner-city neighborhood. Local name ***the 'Ville***.

Brown Swiss ▶ **n.** an animal of a brown breed of dairy cattle, originally bred in Switzerland.

brown-tail (also **brown-tail moth**) ▶ **n.** a white European moth that has a brown tip on the abdomen and is a pest of tree foliage in several areas, including North America. The caterpillars live communally in web tents and bear irritant hairs that can produce an allergic reaction. ● *Euproctis chrysorrhoea*, family Lymantriidae.

brown tree snake ▶ **n.** a nocturnal tree snake of Pacific origin that has escaped captivity as a pet to threaten native fauna in many Pacific Rim locations. ● *Boiga irregularis*, family Colubridae.

brown trout ▶ **n.** (pl. **same**) the common trout of Europe, esp. one of a nonmigratory race with dark spotted skin, that occurs in small rivers and pools. It has been introduced into North America as a game fish. ● *Salmo trutta*, family Salmonidae, in particular *S. trutta fario*. Compare with LAKE TROUT, SEA TROUT.

browse /brouz/ ▶ **v.** [no obj.] **1** survey goods for sale in a leisurely and casual way: ***he stopped to browse around a sporting goods store***. ■ scan through a text, website, or collection of data to gain an impression of the contents: ***she browsed through the newspaper*** | [with obj.] *I decided to spend the night browsing the Internet.*
2 (of an animal) feed on leaves, twigs, or other high-growing vegetation: ***they reach upward to browse on bushes*** | [with obj.] *the animals browse the high foliage of trees.*
▶ **n. 1** [in sing.] an act of casual looking or reading: *the brochure is well worth a browse.*
2 vegetation, such as twigs and young shoots, eaten by animals: *a moose needs to eat forty to fifty pounds of browse a day.*
– DERIVATIVES **brows·a·ble** adj.
– ORIGIN late Middle English (sense 2 of the verb): from Old French *broster*, from *brost* 'young shoot,' probably of Germanic origin.

> **WORD TRENDS** The move of **browse** from the existing sense of 'read or look at something in a leisurely way' into Internet use is a natural one. The metaphor of an animal feeding from vegetation here and there is an apt description of a person moving from link to link rather than searching specifically for a particular term. Almost all of the top collocates of **browse** in the Oxford English Corpus are now Internet-related, with *site*, *Web*, *Internet*, and *website* all appearing as objects far more frequently than *shelf*, *store*, or *book*. **Browse** is typically qualified by adverbs such as *casually* and *idly*, although it can also imply more focused use of the Internet: *after about 45 minutes of intense Web browsing I still couldn't find answers to my questions.*

brows·er /ˈbrouzər/ ▶ **n. 1** a person who looks casually through books or magazines or at things for sale.
2 Computing a program with a graphical user interface for displaying HTML files, used to navigate the World Wide Web: *a Web browser.*
3 an animal that feeds mainly on high-growing vegetation.

brrr /bər/ ▶ **exclam.** used to express someone's reaction to feeling cold: *Brrr! It's a freezing cold day.*

Bru·beck /ˈbro͞oˌbek/, Dave (1920–), US jazz pianist, composer, and bandleader; full name *David Warren Brubeck*. He formed the Dave Brubeck Quartet in 1951 and gained a reputation as an experimental musician. He won international recognition with the album *Time Out* (1959), which included "Take Five."

Bruce[1] /bro͞os/, Lenny (1925–66), US comedian; born *Leonard Alfred Schneider*. He gained notoriety for flouting the bounds of respectability with his humor and was imprisoned for obscenity in 1961. In 1963, he was refused entry to Britain and banned in Australia.

Bruce[2], Robert the, ROBERT I.

bru·cel·lo·sis /ˌbro͞osəˈlōsis/ ▶ **n.** a bacterial disease typically affecting cattle and buffalo and causing undulant fever in humans. ● This disease is caused by Gram-negative bacteria of the genus *Brucella*, in particular *B. abortus*.
– ORIGIN 1930s: from modern Latin *Brucella* + -OSIS: named after Sir David *Bruce* (1855–1931), the Scottish physician who identified the bacterium.

bru·cine /ˈbro͞osēn, -sin/ ▶ **n.** a highly toxic alkaloid present in nux vomica. ● Chem. formula: $C_{23}H_{26}N_2O_4$.

bru·cite /ˈbro͞osīt/ ▶ **n.** a white, gray, or greenish mineral consisting of magnesium hydroxide.
– ORIGIN early 19th cent.: named after Archibald *Bruce* (1777–1818), American mineralogist, + -ITE[1].

Brue·gel /ˈbroigəl/ (also **Breughel** or **Brueghel**) the name of a family of Flemish artists. ■ **Pieter** (*c.*1525–69); known as **Pieter Bruegel the Elder**. He produced landscapes, religious allegories, and satires of peasant life. Notable works: *The Procession to Calvary* (1564). ■ **Pieter Bruegel the Younger** (1564–1638), son of Pieter Bruegel the Elder; known as **Hell Bruegel**. A copyist of his father's work, he is also noted for his paintings of devils. ■ **Jan** (1568–1623), son of Pieter Bruegel the Elder; known as **Velvet**. He was a celebrated painter of flower, landscape, and mythological pictures.

b

Bru·ges /bro͞oZH/ a city in northwestern Belgium; pop. 117,071 (2008). Flemish name BRUGGE.

Brug·ge /ˈbrYgə/ Flemish name for BRUGES.

bru·in /ˈbro͞oin/ ▶ **n.** a bear, esp. in children's fables.
– ORIGIN late 15th cent.: from Dutch *bruin* (see BROWN); used as a name for the bear in the 13th-cent. fable *Reynard the Fox*.

bruise /bro͞oz/ ▶ **n.** an injury appearing as an area of discolored skin on the body, caused by a blow or impact rupturing underlying blood vessels. ■ a similar area of damage on a fruit, vegetable, or plant.
▶ **v.** [with obj.] (often as adj. **bruised**) inflict such an injury on (someone or something): *a bruised knee.* ■ hurt (someone's feelings): *she tried to bolster her bruised pride.* ■ [no obj.] be susceptible to bruising: *potatoes bruise easily, so treat them with care.* ■ crush or pound (something): *bruise the raisins before adding to the mixture.*
– ORIGIN Old English *brȳsan* 'crush, injure or damage with a blow,' reinforced in Middle English by Old French *bruisier* 'break.'

bruis·er /ˈbro͞ozər/ ▶ **n.** informal, chiefly derogatory a person who is tough and aggressive and enjoys a fight or argument. ■ a professional boxer.

bruis·ing /ˈbro͞oziNG/ ▶ **adj.** causing a bruise or bruises: *his legs took the bruising blows.* ■ (of an antagonistic or competitive situation) conducted in an aggressive way and likely to have a stressful effect on those involved: *a bruising congressional battle over public spending.*
▶ **n.** bruises on the skin: *her arm showed signs of bruising.*

bruit /bro͞ot/ ▶ **v.** [with obj.] spread (a report or rumor) widely: ***I didn't want to have our relationship bruited about the office.***
▶ **n. 1** archaic a report or rumor.
2 a sound, typically an abnormal one, heard through a stethoscope; a murmur.
– ORIGIN late Middle English (as a noun): from Old French *bruit* 'noise,' from *bruire* 'to roar.'

Bru·maire /bro͞oˈme(ə)r/ ▶ **n.** the second month of the French Republican calendar (1793–1805), originally running from October 22 to November 20.
– ORIGIN French, from *brume* 'mist.'

bru·mal /ˈbro͞oməl/ ▶ **adj.** literary of or relating to winter; wintry: *'tis a brumal night.*

brume /bro͞om/ ▶ **n.** literary mist or fog: *the birds rise like brume.*
– ORIGIN early 18th cent.: from French, from Latin *bruma* 'winter.'

Brum·ma·gem /ˈbrəməjəm/ (also **brummagem**) ▶ **adj.** [attrib.] cheap, showy, or counterfeit: *a vile Brummagem substitute for the genuine article.*
– ORIGIN mid 17th cent.: dialect form of BIRMINGHAM, England, with reference to counterfeit coins and plated goods once made there.

Brum·mell /ˈbrəməl/, George Bryan (1778–1840), English dandy; known as **Beau Brummell**. He was the arbiter of British fashion for the early 19th century, owing his social position to his friendship with the Prince Regent.

bru·mous /ˈbro͞oməs/ ▶ **adj.** literary foggy; wintry.
– ORIGIN mid 19th cent.: from French *brumeux*, from late Latin *brumosus* (from *bruma* 'winter').

brunch /brənCH/ ▶ **n.** a late morning meal eaten instead of breakfast and lunch.
– ORIGIN late 19th cent.: blend of BREAKFAST and LUNCH.

Brundt·land /ˈbro͞ontˌländ/, Gro Harlem (1939–), Norwegian stateswoman, prime minister 1981, 1986–89, and 1990–96. As Norway's first female prime minister, she chaired the World Commission on Environment and Development (known as the Brundtland Commission), which produced the *Our Common Future* report in 1987.

Bru·nei /bro͞oˈnī, ˈbro͞oˌnī/ a small oil-rich constitutional sultanate on the northwestern coast of Borneo, divided by parts of Malaysia's state of Sarawak; pop. 388,200 (est. 2009); capital,

Bandar Seri Begawan; languages, Malay (official), English (official), Chinese. Official name **Brunei Darussalam**.

In the 16th century Brunei dominated Borneo and parts of the Philippines, but its power declined as that of the Portuguese and Dutch grew. In 1888, it was placed under British protection; it became a fully independent Commonwealth of Nations state in 1984. Brunei has been ruled by the same family for six centuries.

– DERIVATIVES **Bru·nei·an** /-ˈnīən/ **adj. & n.**

Bru·nel /bro͞oˈnel/, Isambard Kingdom (1806–59), English engineer, son of **Sir Marc Isambard Brunel** (1769–1849). He designed the *Great Western* (1838), the first transatlantic steamship, and the *Great Eastern* (1858), the world's largest ship until 1899.

Bru·nel·les·chi /ˌbro͞onlˈeskē/, Filippo (1377–1446), Italian architect; born *Filippo di Ser Brunellesco*. He is noted for the dome of Florence Cathedral (1420–61), which he raised without the use of temporary supports.

bru·nette /bro͞oˈnet/ (also **brunet**) ▶ **adj.** having dark brown hair: *a fresh-faced brunette woman in her thirties.* ■ (of hair) dark brown: *her lustrous brunette tresses.*
– ORIGIN mid 16th cent.: from French, feminine of *brunet*, diminutive of *brun* 'brown.'

brung /brəNG/ dialect past and past participle of **BRING**.

Brun·hild /ˈbro͞onˌhild, -ˌhilt/ Germanic Mythology in the Nibelungenlied, the wife of Gunther, who instigated the murder of Siegfried. In the Norse versions she is a Valkyrie whom Sigurd (the counterpart of Siegfried) wins by penetrating the wall of fire behind which she lies in an enchanted sleep.

Bru·no /ˈbro͞onō/, Giordano (1548–1600), Italian philosopher. A supporter of the heliocentric Copernican view of the solar system, envisaging an infinite universe of numerous worlds moving in space, he was tried by the Inquisition for heresy and burned at the stake.

bru·noise /bro͞onˈwäz/ ▶ **n.** finely diced vegetables that are cooked in butter and used to flavor soups and sauces.

Bru·no, St. /ˈbro͞onō, bryˈnō/ (*c.*1032–1101), French churchman, born in Germany. He founded the Carthusian order at La Grande Chartreuse in 1084. Feast day, October 6.

Bruns·wick /ˈbrənzwik/ **1** a former duchy and state in central Germany, mostly incorporated into Lower Saxony. German name **BRAUNSCHWEIG**. ■ the capital of this former duchy, an industrial city in Lower Saxony, Germany; pop. 245,500 (est. 2006).
2 a town in southwestern Maine, home to Bowdoin College; pop. 21,720 (est. 2008).

Bruns·wick stew ▶ **n.** a stew originally made with squirrel or rabbit, but now consisting of chicken and vegetables including onion and tomatoes.

brunt /brənt/ ▶ **n.** (**the brunt**) the worst part or chief impact of a specified thing: *education will bear* ***the brunt of*** *the cuts.*
– ORIGIN late Middle English (denoting a blow or an attack, also the force or shock of something): of unknown origin.

bru·schet·ta /bro͞oˈsketə/ ▶ **n.** toasted Italian bread drenched in olive oil and served typically with garlic or tomatoes.
– ORIGIN Italian.

brush¹ /brəSH/ ▶ **n.** **1** an implement with a handle, consisting of bristles, hair, or wire set into a block, used for cleaning or scrubbing, applying a liquid or powder to a surface, arranging the hair, or other purposes: *a paint brush.* ■ an act of sweeping, applying, or arranging with such an implement or with one's hand: *he gave the seat a brush.* ■ (usu. **brushes**) a thin stick set with long wire bristles, used to make a soft hissing sound on drums or cymbals. ■ the bushy tail of a fox.
2 a slight and fleeting touch: *the lightest brush of his lips against her cheek.* ■ a brief encounter with someone or something unpleasant or notable: *a* ***brush with death*** | *my first brush with fame.*
3 a piece of carbon or metal serving as an electrical contact with a moving part in a motor or alternator.
▶ **v.** **1** [with obj.] remove (dust or dirt) by sweeping or scrubbing: *we'll be able to* ***brush*** *the mud* ***off*** *easily* | *he* ***brushed*** *himself* ***down.*** ■ use a brush or one's hand to remove dust or dirt from (something): *she* ***brushed down*** *her best coat.* ■ clean (one's teeth) by scrubbing with a brush. ■ arrange (one's hair) by running a brush through it. ■ apply a liquid to (a surface) with a brush: *brush the potatoes with oil.* ■ apply (a liquid or substance) to a surface: ***brush on*** *a floor enamel for a long-lasting base coat.*
2 [no obj.] touch lightly and gently: *stems of grass* ***brush against*** *her legs.* ■ (**brush past**) touch fleetingly and in passing: *she brushed past him to leave the room.* ■ [with obj.] push (something) away with a quick movement of the hand: *she brushed a wisp of hair away from her face.*
– PHRASAL VERBS **brush someone/something aside** dismiss someone or something curtly and confidently: *people brushed aside the possibility of imminent war.* **brush someone back** Baseball, informal (of a pitcher) force a batter to step back to avoid being hit by a ball pitched close to the body. **brush someone/something off** dismiss someone or something in an abrupt way: *the state brushed off the idea as something that would never happen.* **brush up on** improve one's previously good knowledge of or skill at a particular thing: *brush up on your telephone skills.*
– DERIVATIVES **brush·less adj.** (chiefly technical).
– ORIGIN Middle English: noun from Old French *broisse*; verb partly from Old French *brosser* 'to sweep.'

brush² ▶ **n.** undergrowth, small trees, and shrubs. ■ land covered with such growth. ■ cut brushwood.
– ORIGIN Middle English: from Old French *broce*, perhaps based on Latin *bruscum*, denoting an excrescence on the maple.

brush·back /ˈbrəSHˌbak/ (also **brushback pitch**) ▶ **n.** Baseball a pitch aimed close to the body so that the batter must step back to avoid it.

brushed /brəSHt/ ▶ **adj.** having been treated with a brush, in particular: ■ (of fabric) having a soft raised nap: *brushed cotton.* ■ (of metal) finished with a nonreflective surface: *brushed aluminum.*

brush fire (also **brushfire**) ▶ **n.** **1** a fire in brush or scrub.
2 a conflict, esp. an armed conflict, that arises suddenly and is limited in scale or area: [as modifier] *fighting brush-fire wars.* ■ a minor crisis.

brush-off ▶ **n.** [in sing.] informal a rejection or dismissal in which someone is treated as unimportant: *he's been giving her the brush-off.*

brush·stroke /ˈbrəSHˌstrōk/ ▶ **n.** **1** the stroke of a brush, esp. a hair brush or paintbrush. ■ the mark or effect created by this: *an errant brushstroke doesn't necessarily destroy a painting.*
2 an individual action that contributes to an overall effect or work: *you write in broad, inaccurate brushstrokes, and seem incapable of grasping the meaning of your own words.*

brush tur·key ▶ **n.** a large mound-building bird of the megapode family, resembling a turkey and found mainly in New Guinea. ● Family Megapodiidae: several genera and species, including *Alectura lathami* of eastern Australia.

brush wolf ▶ **n.** another term for **COYOTE**.

brush·wood /ˈbrəSHˌwo͝od/ ▶ **n.** undergrowth, twigs, and small branches, typically used for firewood or kindling.

brush·work /ˈbrəSHˌwərk/ ▶ **n.** the way in which painters use their brush, as evident in their paintings: *canvases characterized by lively, flowing brushwork.*

brush·y /ˈbrəSHē/ ▶ **adj.** **1** covered in or consisting of brushwood: *a brushy hillside.*
2 Art relating to or displaying bold use of the brush in painting: *brushy outlining of form.*

brusque /brəsk/ ▶ **adj.** abrupt or offhand in speech or manner: *she could be brusque and impatient.*
– DERIVATIVES **brusque·ly adv.**, **brusque·ness n.**, **brus·que·rie** /ˌbrəskəˈrē, ˌbro͞o-/ **n.** (archaic).
– ORIGIN mid 17th cent.: from French, 'lively, fierce,' from Italian *brusco* 'sour.'

Brus·sels /ˈbrəsəlz/ the capital of Belgium, in the central part of the country; pop. 1,048,491 (2008). The headquarters of the European Commission is located here. Flemish name **Brussel**. French name **BRUXELLES**.

Brus·sels car·pet ▶ **n.** a carpet with a heavy woolen pile and a strong linen back.
– ORIGIN late 18th cent.: named after **BRUSSELS** in Belgium.

Brus·sels lace ▶ **n.** an elaborate kind of lace, typically with a raised design, made using a needle or lace pillow.

Brus·sels sprout (also **brussels sprout**) ▶ **n.** a vegetable consisting of the small compact bud of a variety of cabbage. ■ the plant that yields this vegetable, bearing many such buds along a tall single stem.

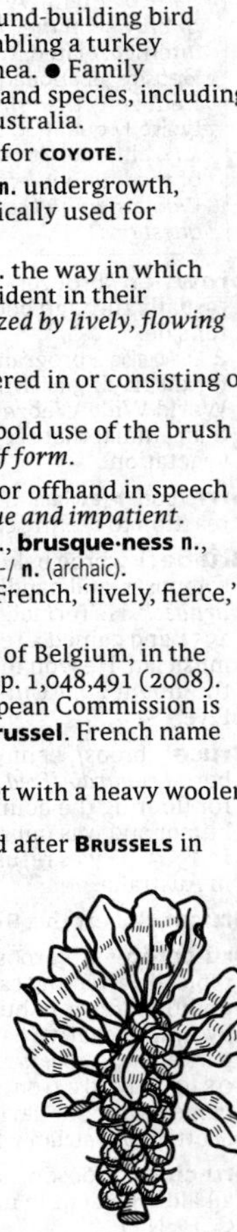

Brussels sprouts

brut /bro͞ot/ ▶ **adj.** (of sparkling wine) unsweetened; very dry.
– ORIGIN late 19th cent.: French, literally 'raw, rough.'

bru·tal /ˈbro͞otl/ ▶ **adj.** savagely violent: *a brutal murder.* ■ punishingly hard or uncomfortable: *the brutal winter wind.* ■ direct and lacking any attempt to disguise unpleasantness: *the brutal honesty of his observations.*
– DERIVATIVES **bru·tal·ly adv.**
– ORIGIN late 15th cent. (in the sense 'relating to the lower animals'): from Old French, or from medieval Latin *brutalis*, from *brutus* 'dull, stupid' (see **BRUTE**).

bru·tal·ism /ˈbro͞otlˌizəm/ ▶ **n.** a style of architecture or art characterized by a deliberate plainness, crudity, or violence of imagery. The term was first applied to functionalist buildings of the 1950s and 1960s that made much use of steel and concrete in starkly massive blocks.
– DERIVATIVES **bru·tal·ist n. & adj.**

bru·tal·i·ty /bro͞oˈtalitē/ ▶ **n.** savage physical violence; great cruelty: *brutality against civilians.*

bru·tal·ize /ˈbro͞otlˌīz/ ▶ **v.** [with obj.] attack (someone) in a savage and violent way: *they brutalize and torture persons in their custody.* ■ desensitize (someone) to the pain or suffering of others by exposing them to violent behavior or situations: *he had been brutalized in prison and became cynical* | (as adj. **brutalizing**) *the brutalizing effects of warfare.*
– DERIVATIVES **bru·tal·i·za·tion** /ˈbro͞otliˈzāSHən/ **n.**

brute /bro͞ot/ ▶ **n.** a savagely violent person or animal: *he was a cold-blooded brute.* ■ informal a cruel, unpleasant, or insensitive person: *what an unfeeling little brute you are.* ■ an animal as opposed to a human being. ■ something awkward, difficult, or unpleasant: *a great brute of a machine.*
▶ **adj.** [attrib.] unreasoning and animallike: *a brute struggle for social superiority.* ■ merely physical: *we achieve little by brute force.* ■ harsh, fundamental, or inescapable: *the brute necessities of basic subsistence.*
– ORIGIN late Middle English (as an adjective): from Old French *brut(e)*, from Latin *brutus* 'dull, stupid.'

brut·ish /ˈbro͞otiSH/ ▶ **adj.** resembling or characteristic of a brute: *brutish behavior.*
– DERIVATIVES **brut·ish·ly adv.**, **brut·ish·ness n.**

Bru·tus¹ /ˈbro͞otəs/, Lucius Junius, (6th century BC), legendary founder of the Roman Republic. Traditionally, he led a popular uprising, after the rape of Lucretia, against his uncle, the king, and drove him from Rome.

Bru·tus², Marcus Junius (85–42 BC), Roman senator. With Cassius he led the conspirators who assassinated Julius Caesar in 44. They were defeated by Caesar's supporters, Antony and Octavian, at the battle of Philippi in 42, after which he committed suicide.

Brux·elles /bryˈsel/ French name for **BRUSSELS**.

brux·ism /ˈbrəksizəm/ ▶ **n.** the involuntary or habitual grinding of the teeth, typically during sleep.
– ORIGIN 1930s: from Greek *brukhein* 'gnash the teeth' + **-ISM**.

Bry·an /ˈbrīən/ a city in east central Texas; pop. 72,357 (est. 2008).

Bry·ansk /brēˈänsk/ (also **Briansk**) an industrial city in western Russia, southwest of Moscow, on the Desna River; pop. 413,900 (est. 2008).

Bry·ant /ˈbrīənt/, William Cullen (1794–1878), US poet and editor. He was co-owner and editor of the New York Evening Post 1829–78; his poems "Thanatopsis" (1811) and "To a Waterfowl" (1821) established him as the leading poet of his time.

Bryce Can·yon /brīs/ a region in south central Utah, site of a national park noted for spectacular rock formations.

Bryl·creem /ˈbrilˌkrēm/ ▶ **n.** trademark a cream used on men's hair to give it a smooth, shiny appearance.
– DERIVATIVES **Bryl·creemed adj.**

bry·ol·o·gy /brīˈäləjē/ ▶ **n.** the study of mosses and liverworts.
– DERIVATIVES **bry·o·log·i·cal** /ˌbrīəˈläjikəl/ **adj.**, **bry·ol·o·gist** /-jist/ **n.**
– ORIGIN mid 19th cent.: from Greek *bruon* 'moss' + **-LOGY**.

bry·o·ny /ˈbrīənē/ ▶ **n.** (pl. **bryonies**) **1** (also **white bryony**) a climbing plant that has greenish-white flowers, red berries, and springlike tendrils. Native to Eurasia, it is the only British member of the gourd family. ● *Bryonia dioica*, family Cucurbitaceae.
2 (**black bryony**) a climbing plant with broad glossy leaves, poisonous red berries, and black tubers. Native to Europe, it is the only British member of the yam family. ● *Tamus communis*, family Dioscoreaceae.
– ORIGIN Old English, via Latin from Greek *bruōnia*.

Bry·oph·y·ta /brīˈäfitə/ Botany a division of small, simple plants that comprises the mosses and liverworts. They lack flowers and roots, reproduce by spores released from a stalked capsule, and are

anchored to the soil by specialized hairs. ● Division Bryophyta: classes Musci (mosses) and Hepaticae (liverworts).
– ORIGIN modern Latin (plural), from Greek *bruon* 'moss' + *phuta* 'plants.'

bry·o·phyte /ˈbrīəˌfīt/ ▶ **n.** Botany a small flowerless green plant of the division Bryophyta, which comprises the mosses and liverworts.

Bry·o·zo·a /ˌbrīəˈzōə/ Zoology a phylum of sedentary aquatic invertebrates that comprises the moss animals.
– ORIGIN modern Latin (plural), from Greek *bruon* 'moss' + *zōia* 'animals.'

bry·o·zo·an /ˌbrīəˈzōən/ Zoology ▶ **n.** a sedentary aquatic invertebrate of the phylum Bryozoa, which comprises the moss animals.
▶ **adj.** relating to or denoting bryozoans.

Bry·thon·ic /briˈᴛʜänik/ (also **Brittonic** /briˈtänik/) ▶ **adj.** denoting, relating to, or belonging to the southern group of Celtic languages, consisting of Welsh, Cornish, and Breton. Compare with **GOIDELIC**. Also called **P-CELTIC**.
▶ **n.** these languages collectively.
– ORIGIN from Welsh *Brython* 'Britons' + **-IC**.

Brześć nad Bu·giem /bəˈzʜescʜ näd ˈbo͞ogˌyem/ Polish name for **BREST** (sense 2).

BS ▶ **abbr.** ■ Bachelor of Science. ■ balance sheet. ■ Blessed Sacrament. ■ vulgar slang used as a euphemism for "bullshit."

BSA ▶ **abbr.** Boy Scouts of America.

BSc ▶ **abbr.** Bachelor of Science.

B-school /ˈbē ˌsko͞ol/ ▶ **abbr.** business school.

BSE ▶ **abbr.** bovine spongiform encephalopathy, a usually fatal disease of cattle affecting the central nervous system, causing agitation and staggering. It is thought to be caused by an agent such as a prion or a virino, and its possible connection with Creutzfeldt–Jakob disease in humans is still much debated. Also (popularly) called **MAD COW DISEASE**.

B-side ▶ **n.** the less important side of a pop single record.

BST ▶ **abbr.** bovine somatotropin, esp. as a hormone injected in cattle.

Bt. ▶ **abbr.** Baronet.

B2B ▶ **abbr.** business-to-business, denoting trade conducted via the Internet between businesses.

B2C ▶ **abbr.** business-to-consumer, denoting trade conducted via the Internet between businesses and consumers.

B-tree ▶ **n.** Computing an organizational structure for information storage and retrieval in the form of a tree in which all terminal nodes are the same distance from the base, and all nonterminal nodes have between *n* and 2*n* subtrees or pointers (where *n* is an integer).

Btu (also **BTU**) ▶ **abbr.** British thermal unit(s).

BTW ▶ **abbr.** by the way.

bu. ▶ **abbr.** ■ bureau. ■ bushel(s).

Bual /bwäl, bo͞oˈäl/ ▶ **n.** a variety of wine grape grown chiefly in Madeira. ■ a Madeira wine of a medium sweet type made from such grapes.
– ORIGIN from Portuguese *boal*.

bub /bəb/ ▶ **n.** informal an aggressive or rude way of addressing a boy or man: *hey, bub, I'm looking for someone.*
– ORIGIN mid 19th cent.

bu·bal /ˈbyo͞obəl/ ▶ **n.** a hartebeest, esp. one of an extinct race that was formerly found in North Africa. ● *Alcelaphus buselaphus buselaphus*, family Bovidae.
– ORIGIN late 18th cent.: from French *bubale*, via Latin from Greek *boubalos* 'wild ox, antelope.'

bub·ba /ˈbəbə/ ▶ **n.** informal **1** used as an informal or affectionate form of address to a brother: *my sister has always called me bubba.*
2 derogatory a working-class white male of the rural South.
– ORIGIN late 19th cent.: alteration of **BROTHER**.

bub·bie /ˈbo͝obē, ˈbəbē/ ▶ **n.** informal (chiefly Jewish) one's grandmother.
– ORIGIN from Yiddish *bubeleh* 'grandmother.'

bub·ble /ˈbəbəl/ ▶ **n. 1** a thin sphere of liquid enclosing air or another gas. ■ an air- or gas-filled spherical cavity in a liquid or a solidified liquid such as glass or amber.
2 used to refer to a state or feeling that is unstable and unlikely to last: *many companies enjoyed rapid expansion before the bubble burst* | *he said the plan was a bubble.*
3 a transparent domed cover or enclosure: *piglets born into a sterile bubble.* ■ a place or position that is protected from danger or unpleasant reality: *they are not on tour packages seeing foreign ports from a bubble.*
4 (also **bubble shell**) a marine mollusk that typically has a thin scroll-like shell. ● Bullidae and other families, order Cephalaspidea, class Gastropoda.
▶ **v.** [no obj.] (of a liquid) contain bubbles of air or gas rising to the surface: *a pot of soup bubbled away on the stove.* ■ (often as adj. **bubbling**) make a sound resembling this: *a bubbling fountain.* ■ (**bubble with or over with**) (of a person) be exuberantly filled with an irrepressible positive feeling: *Ellen was bubbling with such enthusiasm.* ■ (**bubble up**) (esp. of a negative feeling) become more intense and approach the point of being vehemently expressed: *the fury bubbling up inside her.*
– PHRASES **burst someone's bubble** shatter someone's illusions about something or destroy someone's sense of well-being. **on the bubble** informal (of a sports player or team) last or among the last awaiting news about qualifying for the final place in a competition. [from *sit on the bubble*, with the implication that the bubble may burst.]
– ORIGIN Middle English: partly imitative, partly an alteration of **BURBLE**.

bub·ble and squeak ▶ **n.** Brit. cooked cabbage fried with cooked potatoes and often meat.
– ORIGIN late 18th cent.: from the sounds of the mixture cooking.

bub·ble bath ▶ **n.** liquid, crystals, or powder added to bath water to make it foam and have a fragrant smell. ■ a bath of water with such a substance added.

bub·ble can·o·py ▶ **n.** a transparent domed canopy on an aircraft or bubble car.

bub·ble car ▶ **n.** a small car with a transparent domed canopy and typically three wheels.

bub·ble cham·ber ▶ **n.** Physics an apparatus designed to make the tracks of ionizing particles visible as a row of bubbles in a liquid.

bub·ble e·con·o·my ▶ **n.** an unstable expanding economy; in particular, a period of heightened prosperity and increased commercial activity in Japan in the late 1980s brought about by artificially adjusted interest rates.

bub·ble·gum /ˈbəbəlˌgəm/ ▶ **n. 1** chewing gum that can be blown into bubbles. ■ (also **bubblegum pink**) the bright pink color of such gum: [as modifier] *bubblegum capri pants.*
2 [usu. as modifier] a thing considered to be insipid, simplistic, or adolescent in taste or style: *rockers hate bubblegum pop.*

bub·ble·head /ˈbəbəlˌhed/ ▶ **n.** informal a foolish or empty-headed person.

bub·ble·jet print·er /ˈbəbəlˌjet/ ▶ **n.** a kind of inkjet printer which the ink is heated, producing bubbles which force droplets of ink onto the paper.

bub·ble lev·el ▶ **n.** another term for **LEVEL** (sense 3 of the noun).

bub·ble lift (also **bubble**) ▶ **n.** informal a ski lift with enclosed cabins.

bub·ble mem·o·ry ▶ **n.** Computing a type of memory in which data is stored as a pattern of magnetized regions in a thin layer of magnetic material.

bub·ble pack ▶ **n.** another term for **BUBBLE WRAP**.

bub·bler /ˈbəbələr/ ▶ **n.** a drinking fountain.

bub·ble tea ▶ **n.** a cold, frothy drink made with iced tea, sweetened milk or other flavorings, and usually with sweet black balls or "pearls" made from tapioca. Also called **BOBA TEA, PEARL TEA**.

bub·ble wrap (trademark **Bubble Wrap**) ▶ **n.** plastic packaging material in sheets containing numerous small air cushions designed to protect fragile goods.

bub·bly /ˈbəb(ə)lē/ ▶ **adj.** (**bubblier**, **bubbliest**)
1 containing bubbles: *bake until the top is crisp and bubbly.*
2 (of a person) full of cheerful high spirits: *a bright and bubbly personality.*
▶ **n.** informal champagne.

Bu·ber /ˈbo͞obər/, Martin (1878–1965), Israeli religious philosopher, born in Austria. In his existentialist work *I and Thou* (1923), he argued that religious experience involves reciprocal relationships with a personal subject, rather than knowledge of some "thing."

bu·bo /ˈb(y)o͞obō/ ▶ **n.** (pl. **buboes**) a swollen, inflamed lymph node in the armpit or groin.
– DERIVATIVES **bu·bon·ic** /b(y)o͞oˈbänik/ **adj.**
– ORIGIN late Middle English: from Latin, from Greek *boubōn* 'groin or swelling in the groin.'

bu·bon·ic plague ▶ **n.** the most common form of plague in humans, characterized by fever, delirium, and the formation of buboes.

The plague bacterium, *Yersinia pestis* is transmitted by rat fleas. Epidemics occurred in Europe throughout the Middle Ages (notably as the Black Death and the Great Plague of 1665–66); the disease is still endemic in parts of Asia.

bucatini /ˌbo͞okəˈtēnē/ ▶ **n.** pasta in the shape of small tubes.
– ORIGIN Italian.

buc·cal /ˈbəkəl/ ▶ **adj.** technical of or relating to the mouth: *the buccal cavity.* ■ of or relating to the cheek: *the buccal side of the molars.*
– ORIGIN early 19th cent.: from Latin *bucca* 'cheek' + **-AL**.

buc·ca·neer /ˌbəkəˈni(ə)r/ ▶ **n.** historical a pirate, originally off the Spanish-American coasts. ■ a daring, adventurous, and sometimes reckless person, esp. in business: [as modifier] *a shrewd and buccaneering businessman.*
– ORIGIN mid 17th cent. (originally denoting European hunters in the Caribbean): from French *boucanier*, from *boucan* 'a frame on which to cook or cure meat,' from Tupi *mukem*.

buc·ca·neer·ing /ˌbəkəˈniriɴɢ/ ▶ **adj.** daring and adventurous (often used in a business context): *the buccaneering nature of the oil-transport industry.*

buc·ci·na·tor /ˈbəksəˌnātər/ ▶ **n.** Anatomy a flat, thin muscle in the wall of the cheek.
– ORIGIN late 17th cent.: from Latin, from *buccinare* 'blow a trumpet,' from *buccina*, denoting a kind of trumpet.

Bu·ceph·a·lus /byo͞oˈsefələs/ the favorite horse of Alexander the Great, who tamed the horse as a boy and took it with him on his campaigns until its death, after a battle, in 326 BC.

Bu·chan·an /byo͞oˈkanən/, James (1791–1868), 15th president of the US 1857–61. A Pennsylvania Democrat, he served as US congressman 1821–31, minister to Russia 1832–33, US senator 1834–45, US secretary of state 1845–49, and minister to Great Britain 1853–56. As president, his leanings toward the pro-slavery side in the developing dispute over slavery made the issue more fraught. He retired from politics in 1861.

James Buchanan

Bu·cha·rest /ˈbo͞okəˌrest/ the capital of Romania, in the southeastern part of the country; pop. 1,931,236 (2006). Romanian name **BUCUREŞTI**.

Bu·chen·wald /ˈbo͞okənˌwôld/ a Nazi concentration camp in World War II, near the village of Buchenwald in central Germany.

Buch·ner /ˈbo͞oknər, ˈbo͝ok-/, Eduard (1860–1917), German organic chemist. He studied the chemistry of alcoholic fermentation and identified several enzymes, notably zymase. Nobel Prize for Chemistry (1907).

Buck /bək/, Pearl S. (1892–1973), US writer; full name *Pearl Sydenstricker Buck*. Her upbringing and work in China inspired her earliest novels, including *The Good Earth* (1931) and *Dragon Seed* (1942). Nobel Prize for Literature (1938).

buck¹ /bək/ ▶ **n. 1** the male of some antlered animals, esp. the fallow deer, roe deer, reindeer, and antelopes. Compare with **DOE**. ■ a male hare, rabbit, ferret, rat, or kangaroo.
2 a vaulting horse.
3 a vertical jump performed by a horse, with the head lowered, back arched, and back legs thrown out behind.
4 dated a fashionable and typically high-spirited young man.
5 informal, offensive a black or American Indian man.

b

6 (**bucks**) an oxford shoe made of buckskin.
▶ **v. 1** [no obj.] (of a horse) to perform a buck: *he's got to get his head down to buck* | [with obj.] *she **bucked** them off if they tried to get on her back*. ■ (of a vehicle) make sudden jerky movements: *the boat began to buck in the water*.
2 [with obj.] oppose or resist (something that seems oppressive or inevitable): *the shares bucked the market trend*.
3 [with obj.] informal make (someone) more cheerful: *Bella and Jim need me to **buck** them **up*** | [no obj.] (**buck up**) *buck up, kid, it's not the end of the world*.
▶ **adj.** military slang lowest of a particular rank: *a buck private*.
– ORIGIN Old English, partly from *buc* 'male deer' (of Germanic origin, related to Dutch *bok* and German *Bock*); reinforced by *bucca* 'male goat,' of the same ultimate origin.

buck[2] ▶ **n.** informal a dollar: *a run-down hotel room for five bucks a night*.
– PHRASES **big bucks** a lot of money. **a fast** (or **quick**) **buck** easily and quickly earned money: *the pursuit of a fast buck is the cause of most losses*.
– ORIGIN mid 19th cent.: of unknown origin.

buck[3] ▶ **n.** an article placed as a reminder before a player whose turn it is to deal at poker.
– PHRASES **the buck stops here** (or **with someone**) informal the responsibility for something cannot or should not be passed to someone else. **pass the buck** informal shift the responsibility for something to someone else.
– ORIGIN mid 19th cent.: from the use of a buck-handled knife to indicate the dealer in a poker game.

buck-and-wing ▶ **n.** chiefly historical a lively solo tap dance, typically done in wooden-soled shoes.

buck·a·roo /ˌbəkəˈro͞o/ ▶ **n.** a cowboy.
– ORIGIN early 19th cent.: alteration of VAQUERO.

buck·bean /ˈbəkˌbēn/ ▶ **n.** a plant of bogs and shallow water with creeping rhizomes, beanlike leaves that consist of three leaflets, and white or pinkish hairy flowers. Formerly used as a substitute for hops, it is now cultivated as an ornamental aquatic plant. Also called BOGBEAN. ● *Menyanthes trifoliata*, family Menyanthaceae.
– ORIGIN late 16th cent.: from Flemish *bocks boonen* 'goat's beans.'

buck·board /ˈbəkˌbôrd/ ▶ **n.** an open, four-wheeled, horse-drawn carriage with seating that is attached to a plank stretching between the front and rear axles.
– ORIGIN mid 19th cent.: from *buck* 'body of a cart' (perhaps a variant of obsolete *bouk* 'belly, body') + BOARD.

buck·brush /ˈbəkˌbrəsн/ ▶ **n.** coarse vegetation on which wild deer browse.

buck·e·roo /ˌbəkəˈro͞o/ ▶ **n.** variant spelling of BUCKAROO.

buck·et /ˈbəkit/ ▶ **n. 1** a roughly cylindrical open container, typically made of metal or plastic, with a handle, used to hold and carry liquids or other material. ■ the contents of such a container or the amount it can contain: *she emptied a bucket of water over them*. ■ (**buckets**) informal large quantities of liquid, typically rain or tears: *I wept buckets*. ■ Basketball informal a basket. ■ a compartment on the outer edge of a waterwheel. ■ the scoop of a dredger or grain elevator. ■ a scoop attached to the front of a loader, digger, or tractor.
2 Computing a unit of data that can be transferred from secondary storage in a single operation.
▶ **v.** (**buckets, bucketed, bucketing**) [no obj.] **1** (**it buckets, it is bucketing**, etc.) informal rain heavily: *it was still **bucketing down***.
2 [with adverbial of direction] (of a vehicle) move quickly and jerkily: *the car came bucketing out of a side road*.
– PHRASES **a drop in the bucket** see DROP. **kick the bucket** see KICK[1].
– DERIVATIVES **buck·et·ful** /-ˌfo͝ol/ **n.** (pl. **bucketfuls**).
– ORIGIN Middle English: from Anglo-Norman French *buquet* 'tub, pail,' perhaps from Old English *būc* 'belly, pitcher.'

buck·et bri·gade ▶ **n.** a line of people who pass buckets of water from one to another to put out a fire.

buck·et hat ▶ **n.** a simple soft cloth hat with a brim.

buck·et·load /ˈbəkitˌlōd/ ▶ **n.** as much as can be held by a bucket. ■ informal a large quantity: *he scoops up business donations by the bucketload*.

buck·et seat ▶ **n.** a seat in a car or aircraft with a rounded back to fit one person.

buck·et shop ▶ **n.** informal, derogatory an unauthorized office for speculating in stocks or currency using the funds of unwitting investors.

buck·et·wheel /ˈbəkit,(h)wēl/ ▶ **n.** a machine with a series of scoops or buckets on a rotating belt, used to excavate or move material.

buck·eye /ˈbəkˌī/ ▶ **n. 1** a North American tree or shrub related to the horse chestnut, with showy yellow, red, or white flowers. ● Genus *Aesculus*, family Hippocastanaceae: several species, including the **Ohio buckeye** (*A. glabra*), with yellow flowers and prickly fruit husks.
2 (also **buckeye butterfly**) an orange and brown New World butterfly with conspicuous eyespots on the wings. ● *Junonia coenia*, subfamily Nymphalinae, family Nymphalidae.
3 (**Buckeye**) informal a native of the state of Ohio. [from the name given to the state, with reference to the abundance of buckeye trees.]
4 (also **buckeye coupling**) a kind of automatic coupling for railroad rolling stock. [named after the *Buckeye* Steel Castings Company, Columbus, Ohio.]

buckeye butterfly

Buck·eye State a nickname for the state of OHIO.

buck fe·ver ▶ **n.** nervousness felt by novice hunters when they first sight game.

buck·horn /ˈbəkˌhôrn/ ▶ **n.** a horn of a deer. ■ such horn, used typically for knife handles, small containers, or rifle sights.

buckhound ▶ **n.** a staghound of a small breed.

buck·jump /ˈbəkˌjəmp/ Austral. ▶ **v.** [no obj.] (of a horse) jump vertically with the head lowered, back arched, and legs drawn together in an attempt to unseat the rider.
▶ **n.** [often as modifier] an act or display of buckjumping: *a buckjump rider*.
– DERIVATIVES **buck·jump·er n.**

buck·jump·ing /ˈbəkˌjəmpiNG/ ▶ **n.** a rodeo event in which a rider attempts to stay in the saddle of a bucking horse for a period of eight seconds: [as modifier] *a buckjumping event*.

buck·le /ˈbəkəl/ ▶ **n.** a flat, typically rectangular frame with a hinged pin, used for joining the ends of a belt or strap. ■ a similarly shaped ornament, esp. on a shoe.
▶ **v. 1** [with obj.] fasten or decorate with a buckle: *he buckled his belt*. ■ [no obj.] (**buckle up**) fasten one's seat belt in a car or aircraft.
2 [no obj.] bend and give way under pressure or strain: *the earth **buckled** under the titanic stress*. [from French *boucler* 'to bulge.'] ■ [with obj.] bend (something) out of shape: *a giant oak buckles the sidewalk*. ■ (of a person) yield or collapse under pressure: *a weaker person might have **buckled** under the strain*.
– PHRASAL VERBS **buckle down** tackle a task with determination: *they will **buckle down** to negotiations over the next few months*.
– ORIGIN Middle English: from Old French *bocle*, from Latin *buccula* 'cheek strap of a helmet,' from *bucca* 'cheek.'

buck·ler /ˈbəklər/ ▶ **n.** historical a small, round shield held by a handle or worn on the forearm.
– ORIGIN Middle English: from Old French (*escu*) *bocler*, literally '(shield) with a boss,' from *bocle* 'buckle, boss' (see BUCKLE).

Buck·ley /ˈbəklē/, William F., Jr. (1925–2008), US journalist and writer; full name *William Frank Buckley, Jr.* Founder of the politically conservative *National Review* magazine (1955), he hosted the television discussion program "Firing Line" 1966–99.

buck·min·ster·ful·ler·ene /ˌbəkminstərˈfo͝oləˌrēn/ ▶ **n.** Chemistry a form of carbon having molecules of 60 atoms arranged in a polyhedron resembling a geodesic sphere. See also FULLERENE.
– ORIGIN 1980s: named after Richard *Buckminster Fuller* (see FULLER[2]).

buck na·ked ▶ **adj.** informal completely naked.

buck·o /ˈbəkō/ ▶ **n.** (pl. **buckoes** or **buckos**) informal a young man (often as a form of address): *now hold on a minute, bucko*.
– ORIGIN late 19th cent. (originally nautical slang): from BUCK[1] + -O.

buck-pass·ing ▶ **n.** the practice of shifting the responsibility for something to someone else.

buck·ra /ˈbəkrə/ ▶ **n.** (pl. **same** or **buckras**) informal, offensive a white person, typically a man.
– ORIGIN mid 18th cent.: from Ibibio and Efik (*m*)*bakara* 'European, master.'

buck·ram /ˈbəkrəm/ ▶ **n.** coarse linen or other cloth stiffened with gum or paste and used typically as interfacing and in bookbinding.
– ORIGIN Middle English (denoting a kind of fine linen or cotton cloth): from Old French *boquerant*, perhaps from BUKHARA in central Asia.

buck·saw /ˈbəkˌsô/ ▶ **n.** a type of saw typically set in an H-shaped frame and used with both hands.

Bucks Coun·ty /ˌbəks ˈkountē/ a county in southeastern Pennsylvania, on the Delaware River, noted for its affluent Philadelphia suburbs and its artists' colonies; pop. 621,643 (est. 2008). Its seat is Doylestown.

buck·shee /bəkˈsнē, ˈbəksнē/ ▶ **adj.** informal, chiefly Brit. free of charge: *a buckshee brandy*.
– ORIGIN World War I (originally soldiers' slang): alteration of BAKSHEESH.

buck·shot /ˈbəkˌsнät/ ▶ **n.** coarse lead shot used in shotgun shells.

buck·skin /ˈbəkˌskin/ ▶ **n. 1** the skin of a male deer. ■ grayish leather with a suede finish, traditionally made from such skin but now more commonly made from sheepskin: [as modifier] *a pair of buckskin moccasins*. ■ (**buckskins**) clothes or shoes made from such leather. ■ thick, smooth cotton or woolen fabric.
2 a horse of a grayish-yellow color.
– DERIVATIVES **buck·skinned adj.**

buck·thorn /ˈbəkˌтнôrn/ ▶ **n. 1** a shrub or small tree of the buckthorn family, typically bearing thorns. Some kinds yield dyes, and others have been used medicinally. ● Genus *Rhamnus*, family Rhamnaceae: several species, including the European **common buckthorn** (*R. cathartica*), now established in the northeastern and central US, and the **Carolina buckthorn** (*R. caroliniana*) of the southern US.
2 (also **buckthorn bumelia**) a shrub or small tree of the sapodilla family, with sharp thorns and clusters of small white flowers, commonly found in moist soils of the southern and central US. ● *Bumelia lycioides*, family Sapotaceae.
– ORIGIN late 16th cent.: from BUCK[1] in the sense 'deer' + THORN, translating modern Latin *spina cervina*.

buck tooth ▶ **n.** an upper tooth that projects over the lower lip.
– DERIVATIVES **buck-toothed adj.**

buck·wheat /ˈbəkˌ(h)wēt/ ▶ **n. 1** an Asian plant of the dock family that produces starchy seeds. The seeds are used for fodder and are also milled into flour that is widely used in the US. ● *Fagopyrum esculentum*, family Polygonaceae.
2 (in full **buckwheat tree**) see TITI[2].
– ORIGIN mid 16th cent.: from Middle Dutch *boecweite* 'beech wheat,' its grains being shaped like beech mast.

buck·y·balls /ˈbəkēˌbôlz/ ▶ **plural n.** Chemistry, informal spherical molecules of a fullerene, esp. buckminsterfullerene. Related cylindrical molecules are termed **buckytubes**.

buck·y·tube /ˈbəkēˌt(y)o͞ob/ ▶ **n.** informal a carbon nanotube.

bu·col·ic /byo͞oˈkälik/ ▶ **adj.** of or relating to the pleasant aspects of the countryside and country life: *the church is lovely for its bucolic setting*.
▶ **n.** (usu. **bucolics**) a pastoral poem.
– ORIGIN early 16th cent. (denoting a pastoral poem): via Latin from Greek *boukolikos*, from *boukolos* 'herdsman,' from *bous* 'ox.'

Bu·cu·reşti /ˌbo͞okəˈresнt(y), -ˈresнtē/ Romanian name for BUCHAREST.

bud[1] /bəd/ ▶ **n.** a compact knoblike growth on a plant that develops into a leaf, flower, or shoot. ■ Biology an outgrowth from an organism (e.g., a yeast cell) that separates to form a new individual without sexual reproduction taking place. ■ [with modifier] Zoology (of an animal) a rudimentary leg or other appendage that has not yet grown, or never will grow, to full size.
▶ **v.** (**buds, budding, budded**) [no obj.] Biology (of a plant or animal) form a bud: *new blood vessels bud out from the vascular bed* | [with obj.] *tapeworms **bud** off egg-bearing sections from their tail end*. ■ [with obj.] graft a bud of (a plant) onto another plant.
– PHRASES **in bud** (of a plant) having newly formed buds.
– ORIGIN late Middle English: of unknown origin.

bud[2] ▶ **n.** informal a form of address, usually to a boy or man, used esp. when the name of the one being addressed is not known: *listen, bud, I saw you there with my own eyes*.
– ORIGIN mid 19th cent.: abbreviation of BUDDY.

Bu·da·pest /ˈbo͞odəˌpest, -ˌpesнt/ the capital of Hungary, in the northern central part of the country; pop. 1,712,210 (2009). It was formed in

1873 by the union of the city of Buda on the right bank of the Danube River with the city of Pest on the left.

Bud·dha /ˈbo͞odə, ˈbo͝odə/ (often **the Buddha**) a title given to the founder of Buddhism, Siddartha Gautama (*c.*563–*c.*460 BC). Born an Indian prince in what is now Nepal, he renounced wealth and family to become an ascetic, and after achieving enlightenment while meditating, taught all who came to learn from him. ■ (as noun **a buddha**) Buddhism a person who has attained full enlightenment. ■ a statue or picture of the Buddha.
–ORIGIN Sanskrit, literally 'enlightened,' past participle of *budh* 'know.'

Bud·dhism /ˈbo͞odizəm, ˈbo͝od-/ **n.** a widespread Asian religion or philosophy, founded by Siddartha Gautama in northeastern India in the 5th century BC.

Buddhism has no creator god and gives a central role to the doctrine of karma. The 'four noble truths' of Buddhism state that all existence is suffering, that the cause of suffering is desire, that freedom from suffering is nirvana, and that this is attained through the 'eightfold' path of ethical conduct, wisdom, and mental discipline (including meditation). There are two major traditions, Theravada and Mahayana.

–DERIVATIVES **Bud·dhist n. & adj.**, **Bud·dhis·tic** /bo͞oˈdistik, bo͝od-/ **adj.**, **Bud·dhis·ti·cal** /bo͞oˈdistikəl, bo͝od-/ **adj.**

bud·ding /ˈbədiNG/ ▶ **adj.** [attrib.] (of a plant) having or developing buds: *a budding chrysanthemum*. ■ (of a part of the body) becoming larger as part of the process of normal growth. ■ (of a person) beginning and showing signs of promise in a particular career or field: *budding young actors*. ■ just beginning and showing promising signs of continuing: *their budding relationship*.

bud·dle /ˈbədl/ ▶ **n.** a shallow inclined container in which ore is washed.
–ORIGIN mid 16th cent.: of unknown origin.

bud·dle·ia /ˈbədlēə, bədˈlēə/ ▶ **n.** a widely cultivated shrub with fragrant lilac, white, or yellow flowers. ● Genus *Buddleia* (or *Buddleja*), family Loganiaceae: several species, esp. the butterfly bush.
–ORIGIN modern Latin; named in honor of the English botanist Adam *Buddle* (died 1715), by Linnaeus, at the suggestion of Sir William Houston who introduced the plant to Europe from South America.

bud·dy /ˈbədē/ informal ▶ **n.** (pl. **buddies**) a close friend. ■ a working companion with whom close cooperation is required.
▶ **v.** (**buddies, buddying, buddied**) [no obj.] become friendly and spend time with: *I decided to **buddy up** to them.*
–ORIGIN mid 19th cent.: perhaps an alteration of **BROTHER**.

bud·dy-bud·dy ▶ **adj.** informal, chiefly derogatory very friendly: *he's buddy-buddy with the ambassador.*

bud·dy mov·ie ▶ **n.** informal a movie portraying a close friendship between two people, esp. between two men.

bud·dy sys·tem ▶ **n.** a cooperative arrangement whereby individuals are paired or teamed up and assume responsibility for one another's instruction, productivity, welfare, or safety.

Budge /bəj/, Don (1915–2000), US tennis player; full name *John Donald Budge*. He was the first to win all four Grand Slam singles titles in the same year (1938).

budge /bəj/ ▶ **v.** [usu. with negative] make or cause to make the slightest movement: [no obj.] *the line in the bank hasn't budged* | [with obj.] *I couldn't budge the door.* ■ [no obj.] (**budge over**) informal make room for another person by moving: *budge over, boys, make room for your uncle.* ■ [usu. with modal] change or make (someone) change an opinion: [no obj.] *I tried to persuade him, but he wouldn't budge* | [with obj.] *neither bribe nor threat will budge him.*
–ORIGIN late 16th cent.: from French *bouger* 'to stir,' based on Latin *bullire* 'to boil.'

budg·er·i·gar /ˈbəjərēˌgär/ ▶ **n.** a small gregarious Australian parakeet that in the wild is green with a yellow head. It is popular as a pet bird and has been bred in a variety of colors. ● *Melopsittacus undulatus*, family Psittacidae.
–ORIGIN mid 19th cent.: of Aboriginal origin, perhaps an alteration of Kamilaroi *gijirrigaa* (also in related languages).

budg·et /ˈbəjit/ ▶ **n. 1** an estimate of income and expenditure for a set period of time: *keep within the household budget* | [as modifier] *a budget deficit.* ■ an annual or other regular estimate of national revenue and expenditure put forward by the government, often including details of changes in taxation. ■ the amount of money needed or available for a purpose: *they have a limited budget.* **2** archaic a quantity of material, typically that which is written or printed.
▶ **v.** (**budgets, budgeting, budgeted**) [no obj.] allow or provide a particular amount of money in a budget: *the university is **budgeting for** a deficit* | (as noun **budgeting**) *corporate planning and budgeting.* ■ [with obj.] provide (a sum of money) for a particular purpose from a budget: *the council proposes to budget $100,000 to provide grants* | (as adj. **budgeted**) *a budgeted figure of $31,000.*
▶ **adj.** [attrib.] inexpensive: *a budget guitar.*
–PHRASES **on a budget** with a restricted amount of money: *we're traveling on a budget.*
–DERIVATIVES **budg·et·ar·y** /-ˌterē/ **adj.**
–ORIGIN late Middle English: from Old French *bougette*, diminutive of *bouge* 'leather bag,' from Latin *bulga* 'leather bag, knapsack,' of Gaulish origin. Compare with **BULGE**. The word originally meant a pouch or wallet, and later its contents. In the mid 18th cent., the Chancellor of the Exchequer in the UK, in presenting his annual statement, was said "to open the budget." In the late 19th cent. the use of the term was extended from governmental to private or commercial finances.

budg·ie /ˈbəjē/ ▶ **n.** (pl. **budgies**) informal term for **BUDGERIGAR**.

bud·graft ▶ **v.** [with obj.] graft a bud of (a plant) onto another plant.
▶ **n.** a plant grown by this method.

Bud·weis /ˈbo͞otˌvīs/ German name for **ČESKÉ BUDEJOVICE**.

bud·wood /ˈbədˌwo͝od/ ▶ **n.** short lengths of young branches with buds prepared for grafting onto the rootstock of another plant.

bud·worm /ˈbədˌwərm/ ▶ **n.** a moth caterpillar that is destructive to buds. See **SPRUCE BUDWORM**.

Bue·na Park /ˈbwānə, ˈbyo͞o-/ a city in southern California, southeast of Los Angeles; pop. 79,379 (est. 2008). Its tourist attractions include Knott's Berry Farm, a theme park.

Bue·na·ven·tu·ra /ˌbwānəvenˈt(y)o͝orə, ˌbwenə-/ the chief Pacific Ocean port of Colombia; pop. 324,207 (2005).

Bue·na Vis·ta a village in northern Mexico, in Coahuila state, near Saltillo, where US forces under Zachary Taylor won a major battle against Mexican forces under Santa Anna in February 1847.

Bue·nos Ai·res /ˌbwānəs ˈe(ə)rēz, ˈīriz/ the capital city and chief port of Argentina, in the eastern central part of the country, on the Plata River; pop. 3,042,600 (est. 2008).

Buer·ger's dis·ease /ˈbərgərz/ ▶ **n.** inflammation and thrombosis in small and medium-sized blood vessels, typically in the legs and leading to gangrene. It has been associated with smoking.
–ORIGIN early 20th cent.: named after L. *Buerger* (1879–1943), American surgeon.

buff[1] /bəf/ ▶ **n. 1** a yellowish-beige color: [as modifier] *a buff envelope.* **2** a stout, dull yellow leather with a velvety surface. ■ a stick, wheel, or pad used for polishing or smoothing.
▶ **v.** [with obj.] polish (something): *he buffed the glass until it gleamed.* ■ give (leather) a velvety finish by removing the surface of the grain.
▶ **adj.** informal being in good physical shape with fine muscle tone.
–PHRASES **in the buff** informal naked.
–ORIGIN mid 16th cent.: probably from French *buffle*, from Italian *bufalo*, from late Latin *bufalus* (see **BUFFALO**). The original sense in English was 'buffalo,' later 'oxhide' or 'color of oxhide.'

buff[2] ▶ **n.** [with modifier] informal a person who is enthusiastically interested in and very knowledgeable about a particular subject: *a computer buff.*
–ORIGIN early 20th cent.: from **BUFF**[1], originally applied to enthusiastic fire-watchers, because of the buff uniforms formerly worn by New York volunteer firemen.

Buf·fa·lo /ˈbəfəˌlō/ an industrial city in the northwestern part of the state of New York; pop. 270,919 (est. 2008). Located at the eastern end of Lake Erie, it is a major port on the St. Lawrence Seaway.

buf·fa·lo /ˈbəfəˌlō/ ▶ **n.** (pl. **same, buffaloes** or **buffalos**) **1** a heavily built wild ox with backswept horns, found mainly in the Old World tropics. ● four species native to southern Asia (genus *Bubalus*, family Bovidae). See also **WATER BUFFALO**, **ANOA** ● see **AFRICAN BUFFALO**. ■ the North American bison. **2** (also **buffalo fish**) a large grayish-olive freshwater fish with thick lips, common in North America. ● Genus *Ictiobus*, family Catostomidae: several species.
▶ **v.** (**buffaloes, buffaloing, buffaloed**) [with obj.] informal overawe or intimidate (someone): *she didn't like being buffaloed.* ■ baffle (someone): *the problem has buffaloed the advertising staff.*
–ORIGIN mid 16th cent.: probably from Spanish or Portuguese *búfalo*, from late Latin *bufalus*, from earlier *bubalus*, from Greek *boubalos* 'antelope, wild ox.'

b

buf·fa·lo ber·ry ▶ **n.** a North American shrub with silvery twigs and leaves and edible berries. See also **SOAPBERRY**. ● Genus *Shepherdia*, family Elaeagnaceae: two species, the western **silver buffalo berry** (*S. argentea*), with bright red berries, and the northern **Canada buffalo berry** (*S. canadensis*), with reddish or yellow berries. ■ the berry of this shrub.

Buf·fa·lo Bill (1846–1917), US showman; born *William Frederick Cody*. He gained his nickname for killing 4,280 buffalo in 8 months to feed the Union Pacific Railroad workers. He subsequently devoted his life to his traveling Wild West Show.

Buffalo Bill

buf·fa·lo gnat ▶ **n.** another term for **BLACK FLY** (sense 2).

buf·fa·lo grass ▶ **n.** any of a number of grasses, in particular: ● a creeping grass of the North American plains, which is sometimes used for erosion control (*Buchloe dactyloides*, family Gramineae). ● a grass native to Australia and New Zealand (*Stenotaphrum secundatum*, family Gramineae).

buf·fa·lo moz·za·rel·la ▶ **n.** mozzarella cheese made in the traditional way, from the milk of the water buffalo.

Buf·fa·lo Riv·er a river that flows for 132 miles (213 km) through the Ozark Plateau in northwestern Arkansas and is a designated national preserve.

buf·fa·lo robe ▶ **n.** a rug, cloak, or blanket made from the dressed hide of a North American bison.

buf·fa·lo sol·dier ▶ **n.** (in US history) an African-American cavalry soldier.

Buf·fa·lo wings (also **buffalo wings** or **Buffalo chicken wings**) ▶ **plural n.** deep-fried chicken wings coated in a spicy sauce and usually served with blue cheese dressing.

buff·er /ˈbəfər/ ▶ **n. 1** a person or thing that prevents incompatible or antagonistic people or things from coming into contact with or harming each other: *family and friends can provide a buffer against stress.* **2** (also **buffer solution**) Chemistry a solution that resists changes in pH when acid or alkali is added to it. Buffers typically involve a weak acid or alkali together with one of its salts. **3** Computing a temporary memory area or queue used when transferring data between devices or programs operating at different speeds.
▶ **v.** [with obj.] **1** lessen or moderate the impact of (something): *the massage helped to buffer the strain.* **2** treat with a chemical buffer: *add organic matter to buffer the resulting alkalinity.*
–ORIGIN mid 19th cent.: probably from obsolete *buff* (verb), imitative of the sound of a blow to a soft body.

buff·er state ▶ **n.** a small neutral country, situated between two larger hostile countries, serving to prevent the outbreak of regional conflict.

buff·er zone ▶ **n.** a neutral area serving to separate hostile forces or nations. ■ an area of land

b

designated for environmental protection: *oyster harvesters are not allowed in certain buffer zones.*

buf·fet[1] /bəˈfā/ ▶ **n. 1** a meal consisting of several dishes from which guests serve themselves: [as modifier] *a cold buffet lunch.*
2 a room or counter in a station, hotel, or other public building selling light meals or snacks.
3 a cabinet with shelves and drawers for keeping dinnerware and table linens.
– ORIGIN early 18th cent. (sense 3): from French, from Old French *bufet* 'stool,' of unknown origin.

buf·fet[2] /ˈbəfit/ ▶ **v.** (**buffets, buffeting, buffeted**) [with obj.] (esp. of wind or waves) strike repeatedly and violently; batter: *the rough seas buffeted the coast* | [no obj.] *the wind was* **buffeting at** *their bodies.* ■ knock (someone) over or off course: *he was buffeted from side to side.* ■ (of misfortunes or difficulties) afflict or harm (someone) repeatedly or over a long period: *they were buffeted by a major recession.*
▶ **n. 1** dated a blow, typically of the hand or fist. ■ a shock or misfortune: *the daily buffets of urban civilization.*
2 Aeronautics another term for **BUFFETING**.
– ORIGIN Middle English: from Old French *buffeter* (verb), *buffet* (noun), diminutive of *bufe* 'a blow.'

buf·fet·ing /ˈbəfitiNG/ ▶ **n. 1** the action of striking someone or something repeatedly and violently: *the roofs have survived the buffeting of worse winds than this.* ■ the action or result of afflicting or harming someone, typically repeatedly or over a long period: *the buffeting that people are taking in lost job status.*
2 Aeronautics irregular oscillation of part of an aircraft, caused by turbulence.

Buf·fett /ˈbəfit/, Warren Edward (1930–), US businessman and financier, noted for his philanthropic activities.

buf·fle·head /ˈbəfəlˌhed/ ▶ **n.** a small North American diving duck related to the goldeneye, with a large puffy head. The male has white plumage with a black back. ● *Bucephala albeola*, family Anatidae.
– ORIGIN mid 17th cent. (in the sense 'simpleton'): from obsolete *buffle* 'buffalo' + **HEAD**. The current sense (mid 18th cent.) may be an independent formation because of the duck's large square-shaped head.

buf·fo /ˈbo͞ofō/ ▶ **n.** (pl. **buffos**) a comic actor in Italian opera or a person resembling such an actor.
▶ **adj.** of or typical of Italian comic opera: *a buffo character.*
– ORIGIN mid 18th cent.: Italian, 'puff of wind, buffoon,' from *buffare* 'to puff,' of imitative origin.

Buf·fon /byˈfôN/, Georges-Louis Leclerc, Comte de (1707–88), French naturalist. A founder of paleontology, he emphasized the unity of all living species, minimizing the apparent differences between animals and plants. His compilation of the animal kingdom, the *Histoire Naturelle*, reached 36 volumes by the time of his death.

buf·foon /bəˈfo͞on/ ▶ **n.** a ridiculous but amusing person; a clown.
– DERIVATIVES **buf·foon·ish** adj.
– ORIGIN mid 16th cent.: from French *bouffon*, from Italian *buffone*, from medieval Latin *buffo* 'clown.' Originally recorded as a rare Scots word for a kind of pantomime dance, the term later (late 16th cent.) denoted a professional jester.

buf·foon·er·y /bəˈfo͞onərē/ ▶ **n.** (pl. **buffooneries**) behavior that is ridiculous but amusing.

bug /bəg/ ▶ **n. 1** a small insect. ■ informal a harmful microorganism, as a bacterium or virus. ■ an illness caused by such a microorganism: *suffering from a flu bug.* ■ [with modifier] informal an enthusiastic, almost obsessive, interest in something: *they* **caught the sailing bug** | *Joe* **was bitten by the showbiz bug**.
2 (also **true bug**) Entomology an insect of a large order distinguished by having mouthparts that are modified for piercing and sucking. ● Order Hemiptera: see **HEMIPTERA**.
3 a miniature microphone, typically concealed in a room or telephone, used for surveillance.
4 an error in a computer program or system.
▶ **v.** (**bugs, bugging, bugged**) [with obj.] **1** conceal a miniature microphone in (a room or telephone) in order to monitor or record someone's conversations: *the telephones in the presidential palace were bugged.* ■ record or monitor (a conversation) in this way.
2 informal annoy or bother (someone): *a persistent reporter was bugging me.*
– PHRASAL VERBS **bug off** informal go away. **bug out** informal **1** leave quickly: *if you see enemy troops, bug out.* **2** bulge outward: *he did a double take and his eyes bugged out.*
– ORIGIN early 17th cent.: of unknown origin. Current verb senses date from the early 20th cent.

bug·a·boo /ˈbəgəˌbo͞o/ ▶ **n.** an object of fear or alarm; a bugbear.
– ORIGIN mid 18th cent.: probably of Celtic origin and related to Welsh *bwci bo* 'bogey, the Devil,' *bwci* 'hobgoblin' and Cornish *bucca*.

bug·bane /ˈbəgˌbān/ ▶ **n.** a tall plant with wandlike spikes of cream or yellow flowers. A member of the buttercup family, it is native to north temperate regions. ● Genus *Cimicifuga*, family Ranunculaceae: several species, in particular the **American bugbane** (*C. americana*) of the eastern US and the **black cohosh** (*C. racemosa*).
– ORIGIN early 19th cent.: from **BUG** + **BANE**, with reference to the former use of the species *C. foetida* to drive away bedbugs.

bug·bear /ˈbəgˌbe(ə)r/ ▶ **n.** a cause of obsessive fear, irritation, or loathing. ■ archaic an imaginary being invoked to frighten children, typically a sort of hobgoblin supposed to devour them.
– ORIGIN late 16th cent.: probably from obsolete *bug* 'bogey' (of unknown origin) + **BEAR[2]**.

bug-eyed ▶ **adj. & adv.** with bulging eyes: [as adj.] *bug-eyed monsters* | [as adv.] *he stared bug-eyed at John.*

bug·ger /ˈbəgər, ˈbo͝og-/ vulgar slang, chiefly Brit. ▶ **n.**
1 a contemptible or pitied person, typically a man. ■ used as a term of affection or respect, typically grudgingly: *all right, let the* **little buggers** *come in.*
2 derogatory a person who commits buggery.
▶ **v.** [with obj.] penetrate the anus of (someone) during sexual intercourse; sodomize.
▶ **exclam.** used to express annoyance or anger.
– PHRASAL VERBS **bugger off** [usu. in imperative] go away.
– ORIGIN Middle English (originally denoting a heretic, specifically an Albigensian): from Middle Dutch, from Old French *bougre*, originally in the sense 'heretic,' from medieval Latin *Bulgarus* 'Bulgarian,' particularly one belonging to the Orthodox Church and therefore regarded as a heretic by the Roman Church. The sense 'sodomite' (16th cent.) arose from an association of heresy with forbidden sexual practices; its use as a general insult dates from the early 18th cent. Compare with **BULGAR**.

bug·ger·y /ˈbəgərē, ˈbo͝og-/ ▶ **n.** anal intercourse.
– ORIGIN Middle English (in the sense 'heresy'): from Middle Dutch *buggerie*, from Old French *bougrerie*, from *bougre* (see **BUGGER**).

bug·gy[1] /ˈbəgē/ ▶ **n.** (pl. **buggies**) a small or light vehicle, in particular: ■ a small motor vehicle, typically one with an open top: *a golf buggy.* ■ short for **BABY BUGGY**. ■ historical a light, horse-drawn vehicle for one or two people, with two or four wheels.
– ORIGIN mid 18th cent.: of unknown origin.

bug·gy[2] ▶ **adj.** (**buggier, buggiest**) **1** infested with bugs. ■ (of a computer program or system) faulty in operation.
2 informal crazy; insane.

bug·house /ˈbəgˌhous/ informal ▶ **n.** offensive a mental hospital or asylum.
▶ **adj.** crazy; insane.

bug juice ▶ **n. 1** whisky or other liquor, esp. when of poor quality.
2 a sweet, artificially colored, non-carbonated soft drink.

bu·gle[1] /ˈbyo͞ogəl/ ▶ **n.** a brass instrument like a small trumpet, typically without valves or keys and used for military signals. ■ a loud sound resembling that of a bugle, as the mating call of a bull elk: *the piercing bugle of adult bulls.*
▶ **v.** [no obj.] sound a bugle. ■ [with obj.] sound (a note or call) on a bugle: *he bugled a warning.* ■ issue a loud sound resembling that of a bugle, particularly the mating call of a bull elk.
– DERIVATIVES **bu·gler** /ˈbyo͞og(ə)lər/ **n.**
– ORIGIN Middle English: via Old French from Latin *buculus*, diminutive of *bos* 'ox.' The early English sense was 'wild ox,' hence the compound *bugle-horn*, being originally the horn of an ox used to give signals in hunting.

bu·gle[2] ▶ **n.** a creeping plant of the mint family with blue flowers held on upright stems. Also called **BUGLEWEED**. ● Genus *Ajuga*, family Labiatae: several species, esp. the common *A. reptans*.
– ORIGIN Middle English: from late Latin *bugula*.

bu·gle[3] ▶ **n.** (also **bugle bead**) an ornamental tube-shaped glass or plastic bead used in beadwork for clothing and fashion accessories.
– ORIGIN late 16th cent.: of unknown origin.

bu·gle·weed /ˈbyo͞ogəlˌwēd/ ▶ **n.** another term for **BUGLE[2]**.

bu·gloss /ˈbyo͞oglôs, -läs/ ▶ **n.** a bristly plant of the borage family, with bright blue flowers. ● *Anchusa*, *Lycopsis*, and other genera, family Boraginaceae: several species, including the **small bugloss** (*L. arvensis*) and the widespread **viper's bugloss**.
– ORIGIN late Middle English: from Old French *buglosse* or Latin *buglossus*, from Greek *bouglōssos* 'ox-tongued,' from *bous* 'ox' + *glōssa* 'tongue.'

buhl /bo͞ol/ ▶ **n.** brass, tortoiseshell, or other material cut to make a pattern and used for inlaying furniture: [as modifier] *buhl cabinets.* ■ work inlaid in such a way.
– ORIGIN early 19th cent.: from French *boule*, from the name of André Charles *Boulle* (1642–1732), French cabinetmaker. The variant *buhl*, apparently a modern Germanized spelling, is standard in the US.

buhr·stone /ˈbərˌstōn/ (also **burstone** or **burrstone**) ▶ **n.** a porous limestone formerly much used for millstones.

build /bild/ ▶ **v.** (past and past participle **built** /bilt/) [with obj.] construct (something, typically something large) by putting parts or material together over a period of time: *the factory was built in 1936.* ■ commission, finance, and oversee the building of (something): *the city council plans to build a bridge.* ■ (**build something in/into**) incorporate (something) and make it a permanent part of a structure, system, or situation: *engineers want to build in extra traction.* ■ Computing compile (a program, database, index, etc.). ■ establish and develop (a business, relationship, or situation) over a period of time: *he'd built up the store from nothing.* ■ [no obj.] (**build on**) use as a basis for further progress or development: *the nation should build on the talents of its workforce.* ■ increase the size, intensity, or extent of: *we built up confidence in our abilities* | [no obj.] *the air of excited anticipation builds.*
▶ **n. 1** the dimensions or proportions of a person's or animal's body: *she was of medium height and slim build* | [in sing.] *he has the ideal build for a sprinter.* ■ the style or form of construction of something, typically a vehicle.
2 Computing a compiled version of a program. ■ the process of compiling a program.
– PHRASES **build one's hopes up** become ever more hopeful or optimistic about something. **built upon/on sand** without reliable foundations or any real substance: *what more could you expect from a relationship built upon sand?*
– ORIGIN Old English *byldan*, from *bold*, *botl* 'dwelling,' of Germanic origin; related to **BOWER[1]**.

build·down /ˈbildˌdoun/ ▶ **n.** a gradual, systematic reduction in numbers, esp. of nuclear weapons.

build·er /ˈbildər/ ▶ **n.** a person who constructs something by putting parts or material together over a period of time: *a boat builder.* ■ a person whose job is to construct or repair houses, or to contract for their construction and repair. ■ [usu. in combination] a person or thing that creates or develops a particular thing: *breaking the record was a real confidence builder.*

build·ing /ˈbildiNG/ (abbr.: **bldg.**) ▶ **n. 1** a structure with a roof and walls, such as a house, school, store, or factory.
2 the process or business of constructing something: *the building of highways* | [as modifier] *building materials.* ■ the process of commissioning, financing, or overseeing the construction of something. ■ the process of creating or developing something, typically a system or situation, over a period of time: *the building of democracy in Guatemala.*

-building ▶ **comb. form** the process of constructing, shaping, developing, or forming a particular thing: *boat-building.* ■ the process of promoting something: *bridge-building (between the nations).* ■ able to build: *reef-building coral.*

build·ing block ▶ **n. 1** a child's toy brick, typically made of wood or plastic.
2 a basic unit from which something is built up: *sounds are the building blocks of language.*

build·ing site ▶ **n.** an area where a structure is being constructed or repaired.

build·out /ˈbildˌout/ ▶ **n.** the growth, development, or expansion of something: *the rapid buildout of digital technology.* ■ the state of maximum development as permitted by a plan or regulations: *Pueblo West will need a source for new water as the community approaches its buildout.* ■ the execution of a building or community development plan: *we are working on Phase I Engineering and don't know if we'll even get the buildout.*

build·up /ˈbildˌəp/ ▶ **n.** [usu. in sing.] **1** a gradual accumulation or increase, typically of something negative and typically leading to a problem or crisis: *the buildup of carbon dioxide in the atmosphere.*
2 a period of excitement and preparation in advance of a significant event: *the buildup to Christmas.* ■ a favorable description in advance; publicity: *a showbiz buildup before the album release.*

built /bilt/ past and past participle of **BUILD**.
▶ **adj.** (of a person) having a specified physical size or build: *a slightly built woman.*

built-in ▶ **adj.** [attrib.] forming an integral part of a structure or device: *a camera with a built-in zoom* *lens.* ■ (of a characteristic) inherent; innate: *the system has a built-in resistance to change.*

built-up ▶ **adj. 1** (of an area) densely covered by houses or other buildings.
2 increased in height by the addition of parts: *shoes with built-up heels.* ■ (of a feeling) increasing in intensity over a period of time: *built-up frustration.*

Bu·jum·bu·ra /bo͞o,jəm'bo͝orə/ the capital of Burundi, at the northeastern end of Lake Tanganyika; pop. 429,000 (est. 2007). It was known as Usumbura until 1962.

Bu·kha·ra /bo͞o'KHärə/ (also **Bukhoro** /bo͞o'KHôrō/, **Bokhara**) a city in southeastern Uzbekistan; pop. 249,000 (est. 2007). It is one of the oldest trade centers in central Asia, and is noted for the production of karakul fleeces.

Bu·la·wa·yo /,bo͞olə'wā-ō, -'wī-ō/ an industrial city in western Zimbabwe; pop. 740,100 (est. 2009).

bulb /bəlb/ ▶ **n. 1** a rounded underground storage organ present in some plants, notably those of the lily family, consisting of a short stem surrounded by fleshy scale leaves or leaf bases and resting over winter. Compare with CORM, RHIZOME. ■ a plant grown from an organ of this kind. ■ a similar underground organ such as a corm or a rhizome.
2 an object with a rounded or teardrop shape like a bulb, in particular: ■ a light bulb. ■ an expanded part of a glass tube such as that forming the reservoir of a thermometer. ■ a hollow flexible container with an opening through which the air can be expelled by squeezing, such as that used to fill a syringe. ■ a spheroidal dilated part at the end of an anatomical structure.
– ORIGIN late Middle English: via Latin from Greek *bolbos* 'onion, bulbous root.'

bul·bar /'bəlbər, -,bär/ ▶ **adj.** of or relating to an anatomical bulb, esp. the medulla oblongata.

bul·bil /'bəlbil/ ▶ **n.** Botany a small bulblike structure, esp. in the axil of a leaf or at the base of a stem, that may form a new plant.
– ORIGIN mid 19th cent.: from modern Latin *bulbillus*, diminutive of *bulbus* 'onion, bulbous root.'

bul·bous /'bəlbəs/ ▶ **adj. 1** fat, round, or bulging: *a bulbous nose.*
2 (of a plant) growing from a bulb.

bul·bul /'bo͝ol,bo͝ol/ ▶ **n.** a tropical African and Asian songbird that typically has a melodious voice and drab plumage. Many kinds have a crest. ● Family Pycnonotidae: several genera and numerous species.
– ORIGIN mid 17th cent.: from Persian, of imitative origin.

Bul·gar /'bəlgär, 'bo͝ol-/ ▶ **n.** a member of a Slavic people who settled in what is now Bulgaria in the 7th century.
– ORIGIN from medieval Latin *Bulgarus*, from Old Church Slavic *Blŭgarinŭ*. Compare with BUGGER.

bul·gar /'bəlgər/ (also **bulgur, bulgar wheat**) ▶ **n.** a cereal food made from whole wheat partially boiled then dried: [as modifier] *bulgar wheat.*
– ORIGIN 1930s: from Turkish *bulgur* 'bruised grain.'

Bul·gar·i·a /,bəl'ge(ə)rēə/ a country in southeastern Europe, on the western shores of the Black Sea; pop. 7,204,700 (est. 2009); capital, Sofia; official language, Bulgarian.

> Part of the Ottoman Empire from the 14th century, Bulgaria remained under Turkish rule until the late 19th century, becoming independent in 1908. A communist state was set up by the former Soviet Union after World War II, and a multiparty democratic system was introduced in 1989. Bulgaria joined NATO in 2004 and became a member of the EU in 2007.

– ORIGIN named after the Bulgars (see BULGAR).

Bul·gar·i·an /,bəl'ge(ə)rēən, ,bo͝ol-/ ▶ **n. 1** a native or inhabitant of Bulgaria.
2 the South Slavic language spoken in Bulgaria.
▶ **adj.** of or relating to Bulgaria, its people, or their language.

bulge /bəlj/ ▶ **n.** a rounded swelling or protuberance that distorts a flat surface. ■ (esp. in a military context) a piece of land that projects outward from an otherwise regular line: *the advance created an eastward-facing bulge in the line.* ■ [in sing.] informal a temporary unusual increase in number or size: *a bulge in the birth rate.*
▶ **v.** [no obj.] swell or protrude to an unnatural or incongruous extent: *the veins in his neck bulged* | (as adj. **bulging**) *he stared with bulging eyes.* ■ be full of and distended with: *a briefcase **bulging with** documents.*
– DERIVATIVES **bulg·y adj.**
– ORIGIN Middle English: from Old French *boulge*, from Latin *bulga* (see BUDGET). The original meaning was 'wallet or bag,' later 'a ship's bilge' (early 17th cent.); other senses presumably derived from association with the shape of a full bag.

bul·go·gi /bo͝ol'gōgē/ ▶ **n.** a Korean dish of thin beef slices marinated and grilled on a barbecue.

bul·gur /'bəlgər/ ▶ **n.** variant spelling of BULGAR.

bu·lim·a·rex·i·a /,bo͞olēmə'reksēə/ ▶ **n.** another term for BULIMIA NERVOSA (see BULIMIA).
– DERIVATIVES **bu·lim·a·rex·ic** /-'reksik/ **adj. & n.**
– ORIGIN 1970s: blend of BULIMIA and ANOREXIA.

bu·lim·i·a /bo͞o'limēə, 'lē-/ ▶ **n.** insatiable overeating as a medical condition, in particular: ■ (also **bulimia nervosa** /nər'vōsə/) an emotional disorder involving distortion of body image and an obsessive desire to lose weight, in which bouts of extreme overeating are followed by depression and self-induced vomiting, purging, or fasting. Also called BINGE-PURGE SYNDROME. ■ an eating disorder in which a large quantity of food is consumed in a short period of time, often followed by feelings of guilt or shame. Also called BINGE-EATING SYNDROME.
– DERIVATIVES **bu·lim·ic** /-'limik, 'lē-/ **adj. & n.**
– ORIGIN late Middle English (as *bolisme*, later *bulimy*): modern Latin, or from medieval Latin *bolismos*, from Greek *boulimia* 'ravenous hunger,' from *bous* 'ox' + *limos* 'hunger.'

bulk /bəlk/ ▶ **n.** the mass or magnitude of something large: *the sheer bulk of the bags.* ■ a large mass or shape, for example of a building or a heavy body: *he moved quickly in spite of his bulk.* ■ [as modifier] large in quantity or amount: *bulk orders of more than 100 copies.* ■ (**the bulk**) the majority or greater part of something: *the bulk of the traffic had passed.* ■ roughage in food: *bread and potatoes supply energy, essential protein, and bulk.* ■ cargo that is an unpackaged mass such as grain, oil, or milk.
▶ **v. 1** [no obj.] be or seem to be of great size or importance: *territorial questions **bulked large** in diplomatic relations.*
2 [with obj.] treat (a product) so that its quantity appears greater than it in fact is: *traders were **bulking up** their flour with chalk.* ■ [no obj.] (**bulk up**) build up body mass, typically in training for athletic events.
– PHRASES **in bulk 1** (esp. of goods) in large quantities, usually at a reduced price: *buying tomatoes in bulk from a local farmer.* **2** (of a cargo or commodity) loose; not packaged: *sugar is imported in bulk and bagged on the island.*
– ORIGIN Middle English: the senses 'cargo as a whole' and 'heap, large quantity' (the earliest recorded) are probably from Old Norse *búlki* 'cargo'; the origin of other senses remains uncertain, perhaps arising by alteration of obsolete *bouk* 'belly, body.' The original senses are also reflected in the phrases *break bulk* and *in bulk*.

bulk buy·ing ▶ **n.** the purchase of goods in large amounts, typically at a discount.
– DERIVATIVES **bulk-buy v.**

bulk car·ri·er ▶ **n.** a ship that carries nonliquid cargoes such as grain or ore in bulk.

bulk·er /'bəlkər/ ▶ **n.** informal another term for BULK CARRIER.

bulk·head /'bəlk,hed/ ▶ **n.** a dividing wall or barrier between compartments in a ship, aircraft, or other vehicle.
– ORIGIN late 15th cent.: from Old Norse *bálkr* 'partition' + HEAD.

bulk mail ▶ **n.** a class of mail for sending out large numbers of identical items at a reduced rate.

bulk·y /'bəlkē/ ▶ **adj.** (**bulkier, bulkiest**) taking up much space, typically inconveniently; large and unwieldy: *a bulky piece of luggage.* ■ (of a person) heavily built. ■ (of clothing) made of a thick yarn or fabric: *a bulky sweater.*
– DERIVATIVES **bulk·i·ly** /-kəlē/ **adv.**, **bulk·i·ness n.**

bull[1] /bo͝ol/ ▶ **n. 1** an uncastrated male bovine animal: [as modifier] *bull calves.* ■ a large male animal, esp. a whale or elephant. ■ (**the Bull**) the zodiacal sign or constellation Taurus.
2 Stock Market a person who buys shares hoping to sell them at a higher price later. Often contrasted with BEAR[2].
▶ **adj.** [attrib.] (of a part of the body, esp. the neck) resembling the corresponding part of a male bovine animal in build and strength: *his bull neck and broad shoulders.*
▶ **v. 1** [with obj.] push or drive powerfully or violently: *he bulled the motorcycle clear of the tunnel* | [no obj.] *he was **bulling his way** through a mob of admirers.*
2 [no obj.] (**be bulling**) (of a cow) behave in a manner characteristic of being in heat.
– PHRASES **like a bull in a china shop** behaving recklessly and clumsily in a place or situation where one is likely to cause damage or injury. (**like**) **a red rag to a bull** see RED. **take the bull by the horns** deal bravely and decisively with a difficult, dangerous, or unpleasant situation.
– ORIGIN late Old English *bula* (recorded in place names), from Old Norse *boli*. Compare with BULLOCK.

bull[2] ▶ **n.** a papal edict.
– ORIGIN Middle English: from Old French *bulle*, from Latin *bulla* 'bubble, rounded object' (in medieval Latin 'seal or sealed document').

bull[3] ▶ **n.** informal stupid or untrue talk or writing; nonsense: *much of what he says is sheer bull.*
– ORIGIN early 17th cent.: of unknown origin.

bul·la /'bo͝olə/ ▶ **n.** (pl. **bullae** /'bo͝olē/) **1** Medicine a bubblelike cavity filled with air or fluid, in particular: ■ a large blister containing serous fluid. ■ an abnormal air-filled cavity in the lung. [early 19th cent.]
2 Anatomy a rounded prominence. [mid 19th cent.]
3 a round seal attached to a papal bull, typically made of lead. [Middle English.]
– ORIGIN Latin, literally 'bubble.'

bul·lace /'bo͝olis/ ▶ **n.** a thorny shrub or small tree of the rose family that bears purple-black fruits. It is a wild plum, of which the damson is the cultivated form. ● *Prunus insititia* (or *Prunus domesticus* subsp. *insititia*), family Rosaceae.
– ORIGIN Middle English: from Old French *buloce* 'sloe': of unknown origin.

bul·late /'bo͝olāt/ ▶ **adj.** Botany covered with rounded swellings like blisters.
– ORIGIN mid 18th cent.: from Latin *bullatus*, from *bulla* 'bubble.'

bull·bait·ing /'bo͝ol,bātiNG/ ▶ **n.** historical the practice of setting dogs to harass and attack a tethered bull, popular as a sport in medieval Europe.

bull·bat /'bo͝ol,bat/ ▶ **n.** another term for NIGHTHAWK (sense 1).

bull·dog /'bo͝ol,dôg/ ▶ **n.** a dog of a sturdy smooth-haired breed with a large head and powerful protruding lower jaw, a flat wrinkled face, and a broad chest. ■ a person noted for courageous or stubborn tenacity: [as modifier] *the bulldog spirit.* ■ informal (at Oxford and Cambridge Universities) an official who assists the proctors, esp. in disciplinary matters.
▶ **v.** (**bulldogs, bulldogging, bulldogged**) [with obj.] wrestle (a steer) to the ground by holding its horns and twisting its neck: (as noun **bulldogging**) *cowboys compete in bulldogging and bareback riding.*
– DERIVATIVES **bull·dog·ger n.**

bulldog

bull·doze /'bo͝ol,dōz/ ▶ **v.** [with obj.] clear (ground) or destroy (buildings, trees, etc.) with a bulldozer: *developers are bulldozing the site.* ■ use insensitive force when dealing with (someone or something): *she believes that to build status you need to bulldoze everyone else.*
– ORIGIN late 19th cent. (in the sense 'intimidate'): from BULL[1] + *-doze*, alteration of the noun DOSE.

bull·doz·er /'bo͝ol,dōzər/ ▶ **n.** a powerful tractor with a broad upright blade at the front for clearing ground. ■ a person or group exercising irresistible power, esp. in disposing of obstacles or opposition: *he was a political bulldozer* | *as president of the board, she was an insufferable bulldozer.*

bulldozer

bull·dyke /'bo͝ol,dīk/ (also **bulldike** or **bulldyker**) ▶ **n.** informal, derogatory a particularly masculine lesbian.

bul·let /'bo͝olit/ ▶ **n. 1** a projectile for firing from a rifle, revolver, or other small firearm, typically made of metal, cylindrical and pointed, and sometimes

PRONUNCIATION KEY ə *ago, up;* ər *over, fur;* a *hat;* ā *ate;* ä *car;* e *let;* ē *see;* i *fit;* ī *by;* NG *sing;* ō *go;* ô *law, for;* oi *toy;* o͝o *good;* o͞o *goo;* ou *out;* TH *thin;* T͟H *then;* ZH *vision*

b

containing an explosive. ■ used in similes and comparisons to refer to someone or something that moves very fast: *the ball sped across the grass like a bullet.* ■ (in a sporting context) a very fast ball.
2 Printing a small symbol, such as a solid circle, printed just before a line of type, such as an item in a list, to emphasize it.
– ORIGIN early 16th cent. (denoting a cannonball): from French *boulet, boulette* 'small ball,' diminutive of *boule*, from Latin *bulla* 'bubble.'

bul·let·ed /ˈbo͝olitid/ ▶ **adj.** (of items in a list) preceded by a printed bullet.

bul·let·head /ˈbo͝olit,hed/ ▶ **n.** derogatory a person's head that is small and round. ■ a person with this type of head. ■ a stupid, self-important, or obstinate person.
– DERIVATIVES **bul·let·head·ed** adj.

bul·le·tin /ˈbo͝olitn, -,tin/ ▶ **n.** a short official statement or broadcast summary of news. ■ a regular newsletter or printed report issued by an organization or society.
– ORIGIN mid 17th cent. (denoting an official warrant in some European countries): from French, from Italian *bullettino*, diminutive of *bulletta* 'passport,' diminutive of *bulla* 'seal, bull.'

bul·le·tin board ▶ **n.** a board for displaying notices. ■ Computing (also **bulletin board system**) an information storage system designed to permit any authorized computer user to access and add to it from a remote terminal.

bul·let point ▶ **n.** each of several items in a list, typically the ideas or arguments in an article or presentation and typically printed with a bullet before each for emphasis.

bul·let·proof /ˈbo͝olit,pro͞of/ ▶ **adj.** designed to resist the penetration of bullets: *a bulletproof vest.*

bul·let train ▶ **n.** informal a high-speed passenger train: *a bullet train that would whisk passengers at speeds of 150-250 mph along a Tampa-Miami route.*

bull fid·dle ▶ **n.** informal a double bass.

bull·fight /ˈbo͝ol,fīt/ ▶ **n.** a public spectacle, particularly in Spain, Portugal, and Latin America, at which a bull is baited in a highly stylized manner and then usually killed.
– DERIVATIVES **bull·fight·er** n.

bull·fight·ing /ˈbo͝ol,fītiNG/ ▶ **n.** the sport of baiting and killing a bull as a public spectacle in an outdoor arena.

> Bullfighting is the national spectator sport of Spain, and is found also in Latin America and Portugal. Typically, the bull is tormented with darts stuck into its neck, and the matador then baits it with a red cape and attempts to kill it with a sword-blow beneath the shoulder blade.

bull·finch /ˈbo͝ol,finCH/ ▶ **n.** a stocky Eurasian finch with a short, thick bill, and typically with gray or pinkish plumage, dark wings, and a white rump. ● Genus *Pyrrhula*, family Fringillidae: several species, in particular the common *P. pyrrhula*, the male of which has a black face and pink breast.

bull·frog /ˈbo͝ol,frôg, -,fräg/ ▶ **n.** a very large frog that has a deep booming croak and is often a predator of smaller vertebrates. ● Genera *Rana* and *Pyxicephalus*, family Ranidae: the **North American bullfrog** (*R. catesbeiana*), the **Asian bullfrog** (*R. tigrina*), and the **African bullfrog** (*P. adspersus*).

bull·head /ˈbo͝ol,hed/ ▶ **n. 1** (also **bullhead catfish**) an American freshwater catfish with four pairs of barbels around the mouth. ● Family Ictaluridae: several genera and numerous species, including the **black bullhead** (*Ameiurus melas*).
2 a small, mainly freshwater Eurasian fish of the sculpin family, with a broad flattened head and spiny fins. ● Genera *Cottus* and *Taurulus*, family Cottidae: three species.
3 (also **bullhead lily**) a North American water lily with globular yellow flowers. ● *Nuphar variegatum*, family Nymphaeaceae.

Bull·head Cit·y /ˈbo͝ol,hed/ a city in northwestern Arizona, on the Colorado River, a resort and casino center; pop. 40,868 (est. 2008).

bull·head·ed /ˈbo͝ol,hedid/ ▶ **adj.** determined in an obstinate or unthinking way: *a bullheaded belief that she is right.*
– DERIVATIVES **bull·head·ed·ly** adv., **bull·head·ed·ness** n.

bull·horn /ˈbo͝ol,hôrn/ ▶ **n.** an electronic device for amplifying the sound of the voice so it can be heard at a distance.

bul·lion /ˈbo͝olyən/ ▶ **n. 1** gold or silver in bulk before coining, or valued by weight.
2 (also **bullion fringe**) ornamental braid or trimming made with twists of gold or silver thread.
– ORIGIN Middle English: from Anglo-Norman French, in the sense 'a mint,' variant of Old French *bouillon*, based on Latin *bullire* 'to boil.'

bul·lion knot ▶ **n.** a decorative stitch in embroidery made by winding the thread several times around the needle before sewing a backstitch.

bull·ish /ˈbo͝olisH/ ▶ **adj. 1** resembling a bull: *a sketch of his round, bullish head.* ■ stupid or oafish; bullheaded: *it's impossible to reason with such a bullish man.* ■ assertively masculine; macho: *surrounded by girls and the aura of bullish manhood.* ■ chiefly Brit. aggressively confident and self-assertive: *the team is at its most bullish.*
2 Stock Market characterized by rising share prices: *the market was bullish.* ■ (of a dealer) inclined to buy because of an anticipated rise in prices.
3 confident or optimistic about something: *those who are bullish on the nation's economic prospects.*
– DERIVATIVES **bull·ish·ly** adv., **bull·ish·ness** n.

bull kelp ▶ **n.** a very large brown seaweed found in Pacific and Antarctic waters, growing up to 165 feet (50 m) in length off the northwestern coasts of North America. ● *Nereocystis* and other genera, class Phaeophyceae.

bull mar·ket ▶ **n.** Stock Market a market in which share prices are rising, encouraging buying.

bull·mas·tiff /ˈbo͝olˈmastif/ ▶ **n.** a dog of a crossbreed of bulldog and mastiff.

Bull Moose ▶ **n.** a supporter or member of the Progressive Party.

Bull Moose Par·ty ▶ **n.** another term for the **Progressive Party**.

bull-necked ▶ **adj.** having a short, thick neck: *a bull-necked man.*

bull·nose /ˈbo͝ol,nōz/ technical ▶ **adj.** (also **bullnosed**) [attrib.] (of the edge of a surface) rounded. ■ (of a surface or object) having a rounded edge or edges: *a bullnose tile.*
▶ **n.** a rounded edge of this type.

bul·lock ▶ **n.** another term for **steer²**.
– ORIGIN late Old English *bulluc*, diminutive of *bula* (see **bull¹**).

bull of the woods ▶ **n. 1** a sexually mature male of a large wild species, such as moose or elk.
2 the supervisor of a logging camp.

bul·lous /ˈbo͝oləs/ ▶ **adj.** Medicine characterized by blisters or bullae on the skin.

bull·pen /ˈbo͝ol,pen/ ▶ **n.** (also **bull pen**) an enclosure for bulls. ■ an exercise area for baseball pitchers. ■ the relief pitchers of a baseball team. ■ an open-plan office area. ■ a large cell in which prisoners are held before a court hearing.

bull·ring /ˈbo͝ol,riNG/ ▶ **n.** an arena where bullfights are held.

Bull Run a small river in eastern Virginia that was the scene of two Confederate victories—1861 and 1862—during the Civil War.

bull·rush ▶ **n.** variant spelling of **bulrush**.

bull ses·sion ▶ **n.** an informal, typically impromptu discussion, esp. among a small group.
– ORIGIN 1920s: *bull* from **bull³**.

bulls·eye /ˈbo͝olz,ī/ ▶ **n. 1** the center of a target in sports such as archery, shooting, and darts. ■ a shot that hits such a target center. ■ used to refer to something that achieves exactly the intended effect: *the silence told him he'd scored a bullseye.*
2 a large, round, hard peppermint-flavored candy.
3 dated a hemisphere or thick disk of glass forming a small window in a ship or the glass of a lamp: [as modifier] *a bullseye lantern.* ■ a thick knob or boss of glass at the center of a blown glass sheet.

bull shark ▶ **n.** a large, stout-bodied aggressive shark. Its widespread distribution, its habits of feeding close to shore, and its tendency to venture far into estuaries and rivers makes it a species particularly dangerous to humans. ● *Carcharhinus leucas*, family Carcharhinidae.

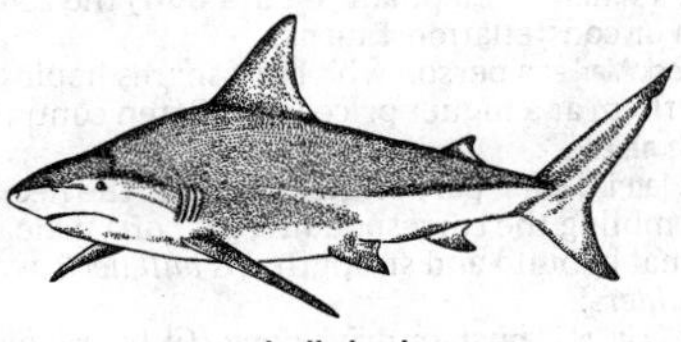

bull shark

bull·shit /ˈbo͝ol,SHit/ vulgar slang ▶ **n.** stupid or untrue talk or writing; nonsense.
▶ **v.** (**bullshits, bullshitting, bullshitted**) [with obj.] talk nonsense to (someone), typically to be misleading or deceptive.
– DERIVATIVES **bull·shit·ter** n.
– ORIGIN early 20th cent.: from **bull³** + **shit**.

bull·shot /ˈbo͝ol,SHät/ ▶ **n.** a cocktail made with vodka, beef bouillon, and Worcestershire sauce.

bull snake ▶ **n.** (also **bullsnake**) a constrictor found commonly on the plains and prairies of North America. ● Family Colubridae and genus *Pituophis*: several species, including the gopher snake *P. catenifer sayi*.

bull ter·ri·er ▶ **n.** a short-haired dog of a breed that is a cross between a bulldog and a terrier.

bull trout ▶ **n.** a North American trout that resembles the Dolly Varden, found in cold rivers and lakes. ● *Salvelinus confluentus*, family Salmonidae.

bull·whip /ˈbo͝ol,(h)wip/ ▶ **n.** a whip with a long heavy lash.
▶ **v.** (**bullwhips, bullwhipping, bullwhipped**) [with obj.] strike or thrash with such a whip.

bul·ly¹ /ˈbo͝olē/ ▶ **n.** (pl. **bullies**) a person who uses strength or power to harm or intimidate those who are weaker.
▶ **v.** (**bullies, bullying, bullied**) [with obj.] use superior strength or influence to intimidate (someone), typically to force him or her to do what one wants: *a local man was bullied into helping them.*
– ORIGIN mid 16th cent.: probably from Middle Dutch *boele* 'lover.' The original usage was as a term of endearment applied to either sex; later becoming a familiar form of address to a male friend. The current sense dates from the late 17th cent.

bul·ly² informal ▶ **adj.** very good; first-rate: *the statue really looked bully.*
▶ **exclam.** (**bully for**) an expression of admiration or approval: *he got away—bully for him.*
– ORIGIN late 16th cent. (originally of a person meaning 'admirable, gallant, jolly'): from **bully¹**. The current sense dates from the mid 19th cent.

bul·ly³ (also **bully beef**) informal ▶ **n.** corned beef.
– ORIGIN mid 18th cent.: from French *bouilli*, literally 'boiled.'

bul·ly boy ▶ **n.** a tough or aggressive man: [as modifier] *bully-boy tactics.*

bul·ly pul·pit ▶ **n.** [in sing.] a public office or position of authority that provides its occupant with an outstanding opportunity to speak out on any issue: *he could use the presidency as a bully pulpit to bring out the best in civic life.*
– ORIGIN early 20th cent.: apparently originally used by President Theodore Roosevelt, explaining his personal view of the presidency.

bul·ly·rag /ˈbo͝olē,rag/ ▶ **v.** (**bullyrags, bully-ragging, bullyragged**) [with obj.] informal treat (someone) in a scolding or intimidating way: *he would bullyrag his staff around but then kiss up to his superiors.*
– ORIGIN late 18th cent.: of unknown origin.

bul·rush /ˈbo͝ol,rəsH/ (also **bullrush**) ▶ **n. 1** another term for **cattail**.
2 a tall rushlike water plant of the sedge family. Native to temperate regions of the northern hemisphere, it has been widely used for weaving and is grown as an aid to water purification in some areas. ● *Scirpus lacustris*, family Cyperaceae.
3 (in biblical use) a papyrus plant.
– ORIGIN late Middle English: probably from **bull¹** in the sense 'large or coarse,' as in words such as *bullfrog*.

bul·wark /ˈbo͝ol,wərk/ ▶ **n. 1** a defensive wall. ■ a person, institution, or principle that acts as a defense: *the security forces are a bulwark against the breakdown of society.*
2 (usu. **bulwarks**) an extension of a ship's sides above the level of the deck.
– ORIGIN late Middle English: from Middle Low German and Middle Dutch *bolwerk*; related to **bole¹** and **work**.

Bul·wer-Lyt·ton /,bo͝olwər ˈlitn/ see **Lytton**.

bum¹ /bəm/ informal ▶ **n. 1** a vagrant. ■ a lazy or worthless person: *you ungrateful bum.*
2 [in combination] a person who devotes a great deal of time to a specified activity: *a ski bum | a poker bum.*
▶ **v.** (**bums, bumming, bummed**) **1** [no obj.] travel, with no particular purpose or destination: *he bummed around Florida for a few months.* ■ pass one's time idly: *we spent most of the summer just bumming around.*
2 [with obj.] get by asking or begging: *they tried to bum money off us.*
3 [with obj.] make (someone) feel upset or disappointed: *it really bummed me out when he forgot my birthday.*
▶ **adj.** [attrib.] of poor quality; bad or wrong: *not one bum note was played.*
– PHRASES **give someone** (or **get**) **the bum's rush** forcibly eject someone (or be forcibly ejected) from a place or gathering. ■ abruptly dismiss someone (or be abruptly dismissed) for a poor idea or performance. **on the bum** traveling with rough provisions and with no fixed home; living as a vagrant.
– ORIGIN mid 19th cent.: probably from **bummer**.

bum² ▶ **n.** Brit. informal buttocks.
– ORIGIN late Middle English: of unknown origin.

bum·bag /ˈbəmˌbag/ ▶ **n.** British term for FANNY PACK.

bum-bail·iff ▶ **n.** historical, derogatory a bailiff empowered to collect debts or arrest debtors for nonpayment.
– ORIGIN early 17th cent.: from BUM², so named because of the association of an approach from behind.

bum·ber·shoot /ˈbəmbərˌSHo͞ot/ ▶ **n.** informal an umbrella.

bum·ble /ˈbəmbəl/ ▶ **v. 1** [no obj.] move or act in an awkward or confused manner: *they bumbled around the house.*
2 [no obj.] speak in a confused or indistinct way: *the succeeding speakers bumbled.* ■ [with adverbial] (of an insect) buzz or hum: *she watched a bee bumble among the flowers.*
– DERIVATIVES **bum·bler** /-b(ə)lər/ **n.**
– ORIGIN late Middle English (in the sense 'hum, drone'): from BOOM¹ + -LE⁴.

bum·ble·bee /ˈbəmbəlˌbē/ ▶ **n.** a large hairy bee with a loud hum, living in small colonies in holes underground. ● Genus *Bombus*, family Apidae: many species.

bum·bling /ˈbəmb(ə)liNG/ ▶ **adj.** acting in a confused or ineffectual way; incompetent: *he's a bumbling fool.*

bum·boat /ˈbəmˌbōt/ ▶ **n.** a small vessel carrying provisions for sale to ships in port.
– ORIGIN late 17th cent.: from BUM¹ + BOAT. The term originally denoted a scavenger's boat removing refuse, etc., from ships, often also bringing produce for sale.

bumf /bəmf/ (also **bumph**) ▶ **n.** informal, chiefly Brit. useless or tedious printed information or documents.
– ORIGIN late 19th cent.: abbreviation of slang *bum-fodder*, in the same sense.

bum·ma·lo /ˈbəməˌlō/ ▶ **n.** (pl. **same**) a small elongated fish of southern Asian coasts that is dried and used as food. Also called BOMBAY DUCK. ● *Harpodon nehereus*, family Harpadontidae.
– ORIGIN late 17th cent.: perhaps from Marathi *bombīl*.

bum·mer /ˈbəmər/ ▶ **n.** informal **1** (**a bummer**) a thing that is annoying or disappointing: *the party was a real bummer.* ■ an unpleasant reaction to a hallucinogenic drug.
2 a loafer or vagrant.
▶ **exclam.** informal used to express frustration or disappointment, typically sympathetically: *You lost your wallet? Bummer!*
– ORIGIN mid 19th cent.: perhaps from German *Bummler*, from *bummeln* 'stroll, loaf around.'

bump /bəmp/ ▶ **n. 1** a light blow or a jolting collision: *a nasty bump on the head.* ■ the dull sound of such a blow or collision. ■ Aeronautics a rising air current causing an irregularity in an aircraft's motion.
2 a protuberance on a level surface: *bumps in the road.* ■ a swelling on the skin, esp. one caused by illness or injury. ■ dated or humorous a prominence on a person's skull, formerly thought to indicate a particular mental faculty; such a faculty: *he was making the most of his bump of direction.*
3 informal an increase: *a slight bump in sales.*
4 a loosely woven fleeced cotton fabric used in upholstery and as lining material.
▶ **v. 1** [no obj.] knock or run into someone or something, typically with a jolt: *I almost **bumped into** him* | [with obj.] *she bumped the girl with her hip.* ■ (**bump into**) meet by chance: *we might just bump into each other.* ■ [with obj.] hurt or damage (something) by striking or knocking it against something else: *she **bumped** her head **on** the sink.* ■ [with obj.] cause to collide with something: *she went through the door, **bumping** the bag **against** it.*
2 [no obj.] move or travel with much jolting and jarring: *the car **bumped along** the rutted track.* ■ [with obj.] push (something) jerkily in a specified direction: *she had to bump the wheelchair down the steps.*
3 [with obj.] refuse (a passenger) a reserved place on an airline flight, typically because of deliberate overbooking. ■ cause to move from a job or position, typically in favor of someone else; displace: *she was bumped for a youthful model.*
– PHRASES **a bump in the road** informal a problem or setback: *their relationship has **hit another bump in the road.***
– PHRASAL VERBS **bump someone off** informal murder someone. **bump someone up** informal move someone to a higher level or status; promote: *he was a writer for nine years before he was bumped up to editor.* **bump something up** informal **1** make larger, greater, or more numerous; increase: *they finally agreed to bump up her salary.* **2** make, complete, or release earlier than planned or expected: *the date of publication was bumped up.*
– ORIGIN mid 16th cent. (as a verb): imitative, perhaps of Scandinavian origin.

bump·er /ˈbəmpər/ ▶ **n. 1** a horizontal bar fixed across the front or back of a motor vehicle to reduce damage in a collision or as a trim.
2 archaic a generous glassful of an alcoholic drink, typically one drunk as a toast.
▶ **adj.** exceptionally large, fine, or successful: *a bumper crop.*
– PHRASES **bumper-to-bumper** very close together, as cars in a traffic jam.

bump·er car ▶ **n.** a small electrically powered car with rubber bumpers all around, driven in an enclosure at an amusement park with the aim of bumping into other such cars.

bump·er stick·er ▶ **n.** a label carrying a slogan or advertisement fixed to a vehicle's bumper.

bump·kin /ˈbəmpkin/ ▶ **n.** informal an unsophisticated or socially awkward person from the countryside: *she thought Tom a bit of a country bumpkin.*
– DERIVATIVES **bump·kin·ish adj.**
– ORIGIN late 16th cent.

bump-out ▶ **n.** an extension of a room or building that creates a projection in a wall: *a rear bump-out provided an ample extension to the master bedroom.*

bump run ▶ **n.** a ski run with many small mounds on it, caused by skiers turning in the same places.

bump·tious /ˈbəmpSHəs/ ▶ **adj.** self-assertive or proud to an irritating degree: *these bumptious young boys today.*
– DERIVATIVES **bump·tious·ly adv.**, **bump·tious·ness n.**
– ORIGIN early 19th cent.: humorously from BUMP, on the pattern of *fractious*.

bump·y /ˈbəmpē/ ▶ **adj.** (**bumpier**, **bumpiest**) (of a surface) uneven, with many patches raised above the rest: *the bumpy road.* ■ (of a journey or other movement) involving sudden jolts and jerks: *she took us all on a bumpy ride* | figurative *bumpy market conditions.*
– DERIVATIVES **bump·i·ly** /-pəlē/ **adv.**, **bump·i·ness n.**

bum rap ▶ **n.** [in sing.] informal a false charge, typically one leading to imprisonment: *he's been handed a bum rap for handling stolen goods.* ■ an unfair punishment or scolding.

bum-rush ▶ **v.** [with obj.] suddenly force or barge one's way into: *fans bum-rushed record stores.*

bum steer ▶ **n.** informal a piece of false information or guidance: *apparently, those who recommended your good service gave us a bum steer.*
– ORIGIN 1920s: from BUM² + STEER¹ in the sense 'advice, guidance.'

bun /bən/ ▶ **n. 1** a bread roll of various shapes and flavorings, typically sweetened and often containing dried fruit.
2 a hairstyle in which the hair is drawn back into a tight coil at the back of the head.
3 (**buns**) informal a person's buttocks.
– PHRASES **have a bun in the oven** informal be pregnant.
– ORIGIN late Middle English: of unknown origin.

bunch /bənCH/ ▶ **n.** a number of things, typically of the same kind, growing or fastened together: *a **bunch of** grapes.* ■ [in sing.] informal a group of people. ■ informal a large number or quantity; a lot: *I had to turn down a **bunch of** well-paid jobs.*
▶ **v.** [with obj.] collect or fasten into a compact group: *she bunched the carnations together.* ■ form or cause to form tight folds: [no obj.] *his pants bunched around his ankles* | [with obj.] *hold the fabric in both hands and gently **bunch** it **up**.* ■ [no obj.] form into a tight group or crowd: *he halted, forcing the rest of the field to **bunch up** behind him.* ■ [no obj.] (of muscles) flex or bulge.
– PHRASES **the best** (or **the pick**) **of the bunch** the best in a particular group.
– DERIVATIVES **bunch·y adj.**
– ORIGIN late Middle English: of unknown origin.

bunch·ber·ry /ˈbənCHˌberē/ ▶ **n.** (pl. **bunchberries**) a low-growing plant of the dogwood family that produces white flowers followed by red berries and bright red autumn foliage. It is native to North America, eastern Asia, and Greenland. ● *Cornus canadensis*, family Cornaceae.

Bunche /bənCH/, Ralph Johnson (1904–71), US diplomat and statesman. Instrumental in the settlement of the Israeli-Arab conflict in 1948, he was the first African American to receive a Nobel Prize. Nobel Peace Prize (1950).

bunch·flow·er /ˈbənCHˌflou(-ə)r/ ▶ **n.** a North American plant of the lily family that is sometimes cultivated for its yellowish-green flowers. ● *Melanthium virginicum*, family Liliaceae.

bunch grass (also **bunchgrass**) ▶ **n.** a grass that grows in clumps. ● *Schizachyrium* and other genera, family Gramineae: several species, esp. *S. scoparium*, used for grazing and in erosion control, esp. on the Great Plains.

bun·co /ˈbəNGkō/ (also **bunko**) informal ▶ **n.** (pl. **buncos**) [often as modifier] a swindle or confidence trick: *a bunco artist* | *he was out to make a buck using fraud or bunco.*
▶ **v.** (**buncoes**, **buncoing**, **buncoed**) [with obj.] dated swindle or cheat: *he didn't propose to be buncoed without a fight.*
– ORIGIN late 19th cent.: perhaps from Spanish *banca*, the name of a card game.

bun·combe ▶ **n.** variant spelling of BUNKUM.

bund¹ /bənd/ ▶ **n.** an embankment or causeway. ■ a wall surrounding an industrial fuel tank.
– ORIGIN early 19th cent.: from Urdu *band*, from Persian.

bund² /bo͝ond, bənd/ ▶ **n.** an association, esp. a political one. ■ (**Bund**) a pro-Nazi German-American organization of the 1930s. ■ (**Bund**) an Ashkenazi Jewish socialist movement founded in Russia in 1897.

Bun·des·tag /ˈbo͝ondəsˌtäg/ the Lower House of Parliament in Germany.
– ORIGIN German, from *Bund* 'federation' + *tagen* 'confer.'

bun·dle /ˈbəndl/ ▶ **n.** a collection of things, or a quantity of material, tied or wrapped up together: *a thick bundle of envelopes.* ■ a set of nerve, muscle, or other fibers running close together in parallel. ■ a set of software or hardware sold together. ■ (**a bundle**) informal a large amount of money: *the new printer **cost a bundle**.*
▶ **v. 1** [with obj.] tie or roll up (a number of things) together as though into a parcel: *she quickly **bundled up** her clothes.* ■ (usu. **be bundled up**) dress (someone) in many clothes to keep warm: *they were bundled up in thick sweaters* | [no obj.] *I bundled up in my parka.* ■ sell (items of hardware and software) as a package.
2 [with obj.] informal push or carry forcibly: *he was bundled into a van.* ■ send (someone) away hurriedly or unceremoniously: *the old man was **bundled off** into exile.* ■ [no obj.] (esp. of a group of people) move clumsily or in a disorganized way: *they bundled out into the corridor.*
3 [no obj.] dated sleep fully clothed with another person, particularly during courtship, as a former local custom in New England and Wales: *he would dance at country frolics and bundle with the Yankee lasses.*
– PHRASES **a bundle of fun** (or **laughs**) [often with negative] informal something extremely amusing or pleasant: *the last year hasn't been a bundle of fun.* **bundle of joy** informal a newborn baby. **a bundle of nerves** informal a person who is extremely timid or tense.
– ORIGIN Middle English: perhaps originally from Old English *byndelle* 'a binding,' reinforced by Low German and Dutch *bundel* (to which *byndelle* is related).

Bundt cake /ˈbənt/ ▶ **n.** trademark a ring-shaped cake made in a fluted tube pan, called a **Bundt pan**.

bun·fight /ˈbənˌfīt/ ▶ **n.** Brit. informal or humorous a tea party or other function, typically of a grand or official kind. ■ a heated argument or exchange.

bun foot ▶ **n.** (pl. **bun feet**) a foot in the shape of a flattened sphere, used for chairs, tables, or other furniture in the late 17th century.

bung /bəNG/ ▶ **n.** a stopper for closing a hole in a container.
▶ **v.** [with obj.] close with a stopper: *the casks are bunged before delivery.* ■ (**bung something up**) block (something), typically by overfilling it: *you let vegetable peelings bung up the sink.*
– ORIGIN late Middle English: from Middle Dutch *bonghe* (noun).

bun·ga·low /ˈbəNGgəˌlō/ ▶ **n.** a low house, with a broad front porch, having either no upper floor or upper rooms set in the roof, typically with dormer windows.
– ORIGIN late 17th cent.: from Hindi *baṅglā* 'belonging to Bengal.'

bun·ga·ro·tox·in /ˌbəNGgərəˈtäksin/ ▶ **n.** Biochemistry a powerful neurotoxin found in the venom of the krait.
– ORIGIN 1960s: from the modern Latin genus name *Bungarus* (perhaps from Sanskrit *bhaṅgura* 'bent') + TOXIN.

bun·gee /ˈbənjē/ ▶ **n.** (also **bungee cord**) a long nylon-cased rubber band, used typically in bungee jumping or for securing luggage.

▶ v. [no obj.] (as a sport) leap from a great height, typically a bridge or crane, while secured by such a band around the ankles.
– ORIGIN 1930s (denoting an elastic cord for launching a glider): of unknown origin.

b

bun·gee jump·ing ▶ n. the sport of leaping from a height while secured by a long nylon-cased rubber band from the ankles.
– DERIVATIVES **bun·gee jump** n., **bun·gee-jump·er** n.

bung·hole /ˈbəNGˌhōl/ ▶ n. an aperture through which a cask can be filled or emptied. ■ vulgar slang the anus.

bun·gle /ˈbəNGgəl/ ▶ v. [with obj.] carry out (a task) clumsily or incompetently, leading to failure or an unsatisfactory outcome: *she had bungled every attempt to help* | (as adj. **bungled**) *a bungled bank raid.* ■ [no obj.] (usu. as adj. **bungling**) make or be prone to making many mistakes: *the work of a bungling amateur.*
▶ n. a mistake or failure, typically one resulting from mismanagement or confusion.
– ORIGIN mid 16th cent.: of unknown origin; compare with **BUMBLE**.

bun·gler /ˈbəNG(g)(ə)lər/ ▶ n. a person who habitually bungles things; an amateur: *the Los Angeles Times this morning called them bunglers.*

Bu·nin /ˈbo͞onyin/, Ivan (Alekseevich) (1870–1953), Russian poet and writer. An opponent of modernism, he concentrated on the themes of peasant life and love. Nobel Prize for Literature (1933).

bun·ion /ˈbənyən/ ▶ n. a painful swelling on the first joint of the big toe.
– ORIGIN early 18th cent.: from Old French *buignon*, from *buigne* 'bump on the head.'

bunk[1] /bəNGk/ ▶ n. a narrow shelflike bed, typically one of two or more arranged one on top of the other.
▶ v. [no obj.] sleep in a narrow berth or improvised bed, typically in shared quarters as a temporary arrangement: *they bunk together in the dormitory.*
– ORIGIN mid 18th cent.: of unknown origin; perhaps related to **BUNKER**.

bunk[2] ▶ n. informal nonsense: *anyone with a brain cell would never believe such bunk.*
– ORIGIN early 20th cent.: abbreviation of **BUNKUM**.

bunk bed ▶ n. a piece of furniture consisting of two beds, one above the other, that form a unit.

bun·ker /ˈbəNGkər/ ▶ n. **1** a large container or compartment for storing fuel: *a coal bunker.* ■ (**bunkers**) fuel for a ship.
2 a reinforced underground shelter, typically for use in wartime.
3 a hollow filled with sand, used as an obstacle on a golf course.
▶ v. [with obj.] **1** fuel (a ship).
2 (**be bunkered**) Golf (of a player) have one's ball lodged in a bunker: *he was bunkered at the fifth hole.*
– ORIGIN mid 16th cent. (originally Scots, denoting a seat or bench): perhaps related to **BUNK**[1].

bun·ker bust·er ▶ n. a bomb designed to penetrate deep into the ground or rock before exploding.

Bun·ker Hill /ˈbəNGkər/ a hill in the Charlestown section of northern Boston in Massachusetts. It gave its name to the first pitched battle (1775) of the American Revolution, which was actually fought on nearby Breed's Hill. Although the British won, the good performance of the untrained Americans gave considerable impetus to the Revolution.

bunk·house /ˈbəNGkˌhous/ ▶ n. a building offering basic sleeping accommodations for workers, visitors, or campers.

bunk·mate /ˈbəNGkˌmāt/ ▶ n. a person who sleeps in an adjoining bunk or who shares one's sleeping quarters.

bun·ko ▶ n. variant spelling of **BUNCO**.

bun·kum /ˈbəNGkəm/ (also **buncombe**) ▶ n. informal, dated nonsense: *they talk a lot of bunkum about their products.*
– ORIGIN mid 19th cent. (originally *buncombe*): named after *Buncombe* County in North Carolina, mentioned in an inconsequential speech made by its congressman solely to please his constituents (*c.*1820).

bun·ny /ˈbənē/ ▶ n. (pl. **bunnies**) informal (also **bunny rabbit**) a rabbit, esp. a young one. ■ [with adj.] informal a person of a specified type or in a specified mood: *ski slopes crawling with snow bunnies* | *that dumb bunny actually thought I was a famous writer.*
– ORIGIN early 17th cent. (originally used as a term of endearment to a person, later as a pet name for a rabbit): from dialect *bun* 'squirrel, rabbit,' also used as a term of endearment, of unknown origin.

bun·ny boil·er ▶ n. informal a woman who acts vengefully after having been spurned by her lover.
– ORIGIN with reference to the movie *Fatal Attraction* (1987), in which a rejected woman boils her lover's pet rabbit.

bun·ny-hop ▶ v. [no obj.] jump forward in a crouched position: *he bunny-hopped around the stage.* ■ [with obj.] move (a vehicle) forward jerkily. ■ move a bicycle forward by jumping in the air while standing on the pedals. ■ [with obj.] jump (an obstacle) on a bicycle in this way.
▶ n. (usu. **bunny hop**) **1** a jump in a crouched position. ■ a short jump forward on a bicycle. ■ an obstacle on a cycling course that is usually cleared by jumping the bicycle over it.
2 a dance of hopping steps in which the participants face the same direction and form a line by placing their hands on the waist or shoulders of the person in front of them.

bun·ny hug·ger ▶ n. informal, derogatory an animal lover; a conservationist.

bun·ny slope ▶ n. Skiing a gentle slope suitable for beginners.

Bun·sen /ˈbənsən/, Robert Wilhelm Eberhard (1811–99), German chemist. With Gustav Kirchhoff, he pioneered spectroscopy, detecting new elements (cesium and rubidium) and determining the composition of many substances and of the sun and stars. He also designed some chemical apparatuses, most notably the Bunsen burner (1855).

Bunsen burner

Bun·sen burn·er ▶ n. a small adjustable gas burner used in laboratories.

Bun·shaft /ˈbənˌSHaft/, Gordon (1909–90), US architect. He is best known for his use of the International style in corporate architecture. He designed the Pepsi-Cola building 1960 in New York City and the Hirshhorn Museum and Sculpture Garden 1974 in Washington, DC.

bunt[1] /bənt/ ▶ v. [with obj.] **1** Baseball (of a batter) gently tap (a pitched ball) without swinging in an attempt to make it more difficult to field: *the batter tried to bunt the ball down the first baseline* | [no obj.] *Phil bunted and got to first.* ■ (of a batter) help (a base runner) to progress to a further base by tapping a ball in such a way: *he bunted Davis to third.*
2 (of a person or animal) butt with the head or horns: *he bunted her with his head.*
▶ n. **1** Baseball an act or result of tapping a pitched ball in such a way.
2 an act of flying an aircraft in part of an outside loop.
– ORIGIN mid 18th cent.: probably related to the noun **BUTT**[1] (the original sense). The usage in aeronautics dates from the 1930s.

bunt[2] ▶ n. the baggy center of a fishing net or a sail.
– ORIGIN late 16th cent.: of unknown origin.

bunt[3] ▶ n. a disease of wheat caused by a smut fungus, the spores of which give off a smell of rotten fish. Also called **STINKING SMUT**. ● This disease is caused by *Tilletia caries*, class Teliomycetes.
– ORIGIN early 17th cent. (denoting the puffball fungus): of unknown origin.

bunt·ing[1] /ˈbəntiNG/ ▶ n. **1** an Old World seed-eating songbird related to the finches, typically with brown streaked plumage and a boldly marked head. ● Family Emberizidae, subfamily Emberizinae (the **bunting family** and **subfamily**): several genera, in particular *Emberiza*, and numerous species.
2 a small New World songbird of the cardinal subfamily, the male of which is brightly colored. ● Family Emberizidae, subfamily Cardinalinae: genera *Passerina* and *Cyanocompsa*, and several species, in particular the deep blue **indigo bunting** (*P. cyanea*) and the **painted bunting** (*P. ciris*). The painted bunting, with its violet head, red body, and green back, is the only such multicolored songbird in North America.
– ORIGIN Middle English: of unknown origin.

bunt·ing[2] ▶ n. flags and other colorful festive decorations. ■ a loosely woven fabric used for such decoration.
– ORIGIN early 18th cent.: of unknown origin.

bunt·line /ˈbəntˌlīn/ ▶ n. a line for restraining the loose center of a sail while it is furled.

Bu·ñuel /bo͞onˈwel/, Luis (1900–83), Spanish movie director. Influenced by surrealism, he wrote and directed his first movie *Un Chien andalou* (1928) jointly with Salvador Dalí. Other notable movies: *Belle de jour* (1967) and *The Discreet Charm of the Bourgeoisie* (1972).

bun·ya /ˈbənyə/ (also **bunya pine** or **bunya-bunya**) ▶ n. a tall coniferous Australian tree of the monkey puzzle family that bears large cones containing edible seeds. ● *Araucaria bidwillii*, family Araucariaceae.
– ORIGIN mid 19th cent.: from Wiradhuri.

Bun·yan /ˈbənyən/, John (1628–88), English writer. His major work, *The Pilgrim's Progress* (1678–84), is an allegory recounting the spiritual journey of its hero Pilgrim.
– DERIVATIVES **Bun·yan·esque** /ˌbənyəˈnesk/ adj.

bun·yan·ize /ˈbənyəˌnīz/ ▶ v. [with obj.] cause (someone) to appear heroic or larger than life: *How are you going to allow teachers to finish their work if you keep bunyanizing them?*
– ORIGIN late 20th cent.: after Paul *Bunyan*, legendary American giant lumberjack.

bun·yip /ˈbənyip/ ▶ n. Austral. **1** a mythical amphibious monster inhabiting inland waterways.
2 [often as modifier] an impostor or pretender: *Australia's bunyip aristocracy.*
– ORIGIN from Wemba-Wemba *banib*.

Buo·na·par·te /ˌbwōnäˈpärtā/ see **BONAPARTE**.

Buo·nar·ro·ti /ˌbwänəˈrôtē/, Michelangelo, see **MICHELANGELO**.

bu·oy /ˈbo͞o-ē, boi/ ▶ n. an anchored float serving as a navigation mark, to show reefs or other hazards, or for mooring.
▶ v. [with obj.] **1** keep (someone or something) afloat: *I let the water buoy up my weight.* ■ cause to become cheerful or confident: *the party was buoyed by an election victory.* ■ cause (a price) to rise to or remain at a high level: *the price is buoyed up by investors.*
2 mark with a buoy: (as adj. **buoyed**) *a buoyed channel.*
– ORIGIN Middle English: probably from Middle Dutch *boye, boeie*, from a Germanic base meaning 'signal.'

buoy·an·cy /ˈboi-ənsē, ˈbo͞oyənsē/ ▶ n. **1** the ability or tendency to float in water or air or some other fluid. ■ the power of a liquid to keep something afloat.
2 an optimistic and cheerful disposition: *the happiness and buoyancy of his nature.*
3 a high level of activity in an economy or stock market: *there is renewed buoyancy in the demand for steel.*

buoy·ant /ˈboi-ənt, ˈbo͞oyənt/ ▶ adj. **1** able or apt to stay afloat or rise to the top of a liquid or gas. ■ (of a liquid or gas) able to keep something afloat.
2 cheerful and optimistic: *the conference ended with the party in a buoyant mood.*
3 (of an economy, business, or market) involving or engaged in much activity: *car sales were not buoyant.*
– DERIVATIVES **buoy·ant·ly** adv.
– ORIGIN late 16th cent.: from French *bouyant* or Spanish *boyante*, present participle of *boyar* 'to float' (see **BUOY**).

bup·kis /ˈbo͞opkis, ˈbəp-/ ▶ n. informal nothing at all: *you know bupkis about fundraising.*
– ORIGIN from Yiddish.

bup·pie /ˈbəpē/ ▶ n. (pl. **buppies**) informal a young urban black professional; a black yuppie.

bu·pro·pi·on /byo͞oˈprōpēən/ ▶ n. an antidepressant drug ($C_{13}H_{18}ClNO$) that is also given to relieve the symptoms of nicotine withdrawal. Also called **ZYBAN** (trademark).
– ORIGIN 1970s: from *butane* + *propionic*.

bur /bər/ (also **burr**) ▶ n. **1** a prickly seed case or flower head that clings to animals and clothes. [Middle English.] ■ [usu. as modifier] a plant that produces burs, e.g., bur reed.
2 [as modifier] denoting wood containing knots or other growths that show a pattern of dense swirls in the grain when sawn, used for veneers and other decorative woodwork: *bur walnut.* [late 19th cent.]
3 variant spelling of **BURR** (sense 2 of the noun, sense 3 of the noun, sense 5 of the noun).
– ORIGIN possibly of Scandinavian origin, identical or related to Danish *burre* 'bur,' 'burdock.' See also **BURR**.

bur. ▶ abbr. bureau.

burb /bərb/ ▶ n. (usu. **the burbs**) informal short for **SUBURB**: *the leafy burbs of Connecticut.*

Bur·bank[1] /ˈbərˌbaNGk/ a city in southern California, a northern suburb of Los Angeles; pop. 102,968 (est. 2008). It is a center of the movie and television industries.

Bur·bank[2], Luther (1849–1926), US horticulturist. His experiments in cross-breeding led to new types and improved varieties of plants, esp. the Shasta daisy and the potato.

Bur·ber·ry /ˈbərbərē, -ˌberē/ ▶ n. (pl. **Burberries**) trademark a kind of lightweight belted raincoat,

typically beige in color, with a distinctive tartan lining.
– ORIGIN early 20th cent.: from *Burberrys*, the name of the manufacturer.

bur·ble /ˈbərbəl/ ▶ **v.** [no obj.] make a continuous murmuring noise: *the wind burbled at his ear.* ■ speak in an unintelligible or silly way, typically at unnecessary length: *he burbled on about annuities* | [with obj.] *he was burbling inanities.* ■ Aeronautics (often as noun **burbling**) (of an airflow) break up into turbulence.
▶ **n.** continuous murmuring noise. ■ rambling speech: *an hour of boring burble.*
– ORIGIN Middle English (in the sense 'to bubble'): imitative. Current senses date from the late 19th cent.

bur·bot /ˈbərbət/ ▶ **n.** an elongated bottom-dwelling fish that is the only member of the cod family that lives in fresh water. It occurs in Eurasia and North America, but is almost extinct in Britain. ● *Lota lota*, family Gadidae.
– ORIGIN Middle English: from Old French *borbete*, probably from *borbe* 'mud, slime.'

bur·den /ˈbərdn/ ▶ **n. 1** a load, esp. a heavy one. ■ a duty or misfortune that causes hardship, anxiety, or grief; a nuisance: *the burden of mental illness.* ■ the main responsibility for achieving a specified aim or task: *the burden of establishing that the cost was unreasonable.* ■ a ship's carrying capacity; tonnage: *the schooner Wyoming, of about 6,000 tons burden.* **2** (**the burden**) the main theme or gist of a speech, book, or argument: *the burden of his views.* ■ the refrain or chorus of a song.
▶ **v.** [with obj.] load heavily: *she walked forward* ***burdened with*** *a wooden box.* ■ cause (someone) hardship or distress: *they were not yet burdened with adult responsibility.*
– PHRASES **burden of proof** the obligation to prove one's assertion.
– ORIGIN Old English *byrthen*; related to **BEAR**[1].

bur·den·some /ˈbərdnsəm/ ▶ **adj.** difficult to carry out or fulfill; taxing: *the burdensome responsibilities of professional life.* ■ undesirably restrictive: *bureaucratically burdensome assessment procedures.*

bur·dock /ˈbərdäk/ ▶ **n.** a large herbaceous Old World plant of the daisy family. The hook-bearing flowers become woody burrs after fertilization and cling to animals' coats for seed dispersal. ● Genus *Arctium*, family Compositae: several species, including the large-leaved **great burdock** (*A. lappa*), which has edible roots and is used in herbal medicine.
– ORIGIN late 16th cent.: from **BUR** + **DOCK**[3].

bu·reau /ˈbyo͝orō/ ▶ **n.** (pl. **bureaus** or **bureaux** /ˈbyo͝orōz/) **1** a chest of drawers. ■ Brit. a writing desk with drawers and typically an angled top opening downward to form a writing surface. **2** (abbr.: **bur.**) an office or department for transacting particular business: *a news bureau* | *the London bureau of the Washington Post.* ■ a government department: *the intelligence bureau.*
– ORIGIN late 17th cent.: from French, originally 'baize' (used to cover writing desks), from Old French *burel*, probably from *bure* 'dark brown.'

bu·reauc·ra·cy /byo͝oˈräkrəsē/ ▶ **n.** (pl. **bureaucracies**) a system of government in which most of the important decisions are made by state officials rather than by elected representatives. ■ a state or organization governed or managed according to such a system. ■ the officials in such a system, considered as a group or hierarchy. ■ excessively complicated administrative procedure, seen as characteristic of such a system: *the unnecessary bureaucracy in local government.*
– ORIGIN early 19th cent.: from French *bureaucratie*, from *bureau* (see **BUREAU**, **-CRACY**).

bu·reau·crat /ˈbyo͝orəˌkrat/ ▶ **n.** an official in a government department, in particular one perceived as being concerned with procedural correctness at the expense of people's needs.
– ORIGIN mid 19th cent.: from French *bureaucrate*, from *bureaucratie* (see **BUREAUCRACY**).

bu·reau·crat·ese /byo͝oˌräkrəˈtēz, -ˈtēs/ ▶ **n.** a style of speech or writing characterized by jargon, euphemism, and abstractions, held to be typical of bureaucrats.

bu·reau·crat·ic /ˌbyo͝orəˈkratik/ ▶ **adj.** relating to the business of running an organization, or government: *well-established bureaucratic procedures.* ■ overly concerned with procedure at the expense of efficiency or common sense: *the plan is overly bureaucratic and complex.*
– DERIVATIVES **bu·reau·crat·i·cal·ly** /ˌbyo͝orəˈkratik(ə)lē/ **adv.**

bu·reauc·ra·tize /byo͝oˈräkrəˌtīz/ ▶ **v.** [with obj.] (usu. as adj. **bureaucratized**) endue (someone or something) with the characteristics of a bureaucracy: *impersonal and bureaucratized welfare systems.*
– DERIVATIVES **bu·reauc·ra·ti·za·tion** /-ˌräkrətiˈzāshən/ **n.**

bu·reau de change /ˈbyo͝orō də ˈSHänZH/ ▶ **n.** (pl. **bureaux de change** pronunc. **same**) an establishment at which customers can exchange foreign money.
– ORIGIN 1950s: French, literally 'office of exchange.'

bu·rette /byo͝oˈret/ (also **buret**) ▶ **n.** a graduated glass tube with a tap at one end, for delivering known volumes of a liquid, esp. in titrations.
– ORIGIN mid 19th cent.: from French, from *buire* 'jug,' of Germanic origin; related to German *Bauch* 'stomach.'

burg /bərg/ ▶ **n.** an ancient or medieval fortress or walled town. [from late Latin *burgus* (see **BURGESS**).] ■ informal a town or city. [mid 19th cent.: from German *Burg* 'castle, city'; related to **BOROUGH**.]

bur·gage /ˈbərgij/ ▶ **n.** historical (in England and Scotland) tenure of land in a town held in return for service or annual rent. ■ a house or other property held by such tenure.
– ORIGIN late Middle English: from medieval Latin *burgagium*, from *burgus* 'fortified town,' of Germanic origin and related to **BOROUGH**.

Bur·gas /ˈbərgəs/ an industrial port and resort in eastern Bulgaria, on the coast of the Black Sea; pop. 188,861 (2008).

bur·gee /bərˈjē, ˈbərjē/ ▶ **n.** a flag bearing the colors or emblem of a sailing club, typically triangular.
– ORIGIN mid 18th cent.: perhaps from French *bourgeois* (see **BURGESS**) in the sense 'owner, master.'

bur·geon /ˈbərjən/ ▶ **v.** [no obj.] (often as adj. **burgeoning**) begin to grow or increase rapidly; flourish: *manufacturers are keen to cash in on the burgeoning demand.* ■ put forth young shoots; bud.
– ORIGIN Middle English: from Old French *bourgeonner* 'put out buds,' from *borjon* 'bud,' based on late Latin *burra* 'wool.'

Bur·ger /ˈbərgər/, Warren Earl (1907–95), US chief justice 1969–86. Appointed to head the US Supreme Court by President Richard Nixon, he was a conservative, except in matters of civil rights, and an advocate of judicial restraint.

burg·er /ˈbərgər/ ▶ **n.** short for **HAMBURGER**. ■ [with modifier] a particular variation of a hamburger with additional or substitute ingredients: *a veggie burger.*
– ORIGIN 1930s (originally US): abbreviation.

Bur·gess[1] /ˈbərjəs/, Anthony (1917–93), English novelist and critic; pseudonym of *John Anthony Burgess Wilson*. He wrote *A Clockwork Orange* (1962), a disturbing, futuristic vision of juvenile delinquency, violence, and high technology. Other notable works: *The Malayan Trilogy* (1956–59) and *Earthly Powers* (1980).

Bur·gess[2], Guy (Francis de Moncy) (1911–63), British foreign office official and spy. Acting as a Soviet agent from the 1930s, he was charged with espionage in 1951 and fled to the former Soviet Union with Donald Maclean.

bur·gess /ˈbərjis/ ▶ **n.** a person with municipal authority or privileges, in particular: ■ Brit. archaic an inhabitant of a town or borough with full rights of citizenship. ■ Brit. historical a member of Parliament for a borough, corporate town, or university. ■ (in the US and also historically in the UK) a magistrate or member of the governing body of a town. ■ historical a member of the assembly of colonial Maryland or Virginia.
– ORIGIN Middle English: from Anglo-Norman French *burgeis*, from late Latin *burgus* 'castle, fort' (in medieval Latin 'fortified town'); related to **BOROUGH**.

Bur·gess Shale /ˈbərjis/ a bed of shale exposed in the Rocky Mountains in British Columbia, Canada. The bed, dated to the Cambrian period (about 530 million years ago), is rich in well-preserved fossils of early marine invertebrates, many of which represent evolutionary lineages unknown in later times.
– ORIGIN named after the *Burgess* Pass, British Colombia, where the shale crops out.

burgh /bərg, ˈbərə/ ▶ **n.** historical or Scottish a borough or chartered town.
– DERIVATIVES **burgh·al** /ˈbərgəl/ **adj.**
– ORIGIN late Middle English: Scots form of **BOROUGH**.

burgh·er /ˈbərgər/ ▶ **n.** archaic or humorous a citizen of a town or city, typically a member of the wealthy bourgeoisie.
– ORIGIN Middle English: from **BURGH**, reinforced by Dutch *burger*, from *burg* 'castle' (see **BOROUGH**).

bur·glar /ˈbərglər/ ▶ **n.** a person who commits burglary.
– DERIVATIVES **bur·glar·i·ous** /bərˈgle(ə)rēəs/ **adj.** (archaic).
– ORIGIN mid 16th cent.: from legal French *burgler* or Anglo-Latin *burgulator, burglator*; related to Old French *burgier* 'pillage.'

bur·glar·ize /ˈbərgləˌrīz/ ▶ **v.** [with obj.] enter (a building) illegally with intent to commit a crime, esp. theft: *our summer house has been burglarized.*

bur·glar·proof /ˈbərglərˌpro͞of/ ▶ **adj.** protected against or providing protection against burglary.

bur·gla·ry /ˈbərglərē/ ▶ **n.** (pl. **burglaries**) entry into a building illegally with intent to commit a crime, esp. theft: *a two-year sentence for burglary* | *a series of burglaries.*
– ORIGIN early 16th cent.: from legal French *burglarie*, from *burgler* (see **BURGLAR**).

bur·gle /ˈbərgəl/ ▶ **v.** another term for **BURGLARIZE**.
– ORIGIN late 19th cent.: originally a humorous and colloquial back-formation from **BURGLAR**.

bur·go·mas·ter /ˈbərgəˌmastər/ ▶ **n.** the mayor of a Dutch, Flemish, German, Austrian, or Swiss town.
– ORIGIN late 16th cent.: from Dutch *burgemeester*, from *burg* 'castle, citadel' (see **BOROUGH**) + *meester* 'master.' The change in the final element was due to association with **MASTER**[1].

bur·go·net /ˈbərgəˌnet, ˌbərgəˈnet/ ▶ **n.** historical a kind of visored helmet.
– ORIGIN late 16th cent.: from French *bourguignotte*, perhaps a use of the feminine of *bourguignot* 'Burgundian,' the ending being assimilated to **-ET**[1].

burgonet

bur·goo /bərˈgo͞o/ ▶ **n.** a stew or thick soup, typically made for an outdoor meal. ■ an outdoor meal at which such food is served. ■ chiefly Nautical a thick porridge.
– ORIGIN from Arabic *burgul*.

Bur·gos /ˈbo͝orgōs/ a town in northern Spain; pop. 177,879 (2008).

Bur·goyne /ˈbərˌgoin, bərˈgoin/, John (1722–92), English general and playwright; known as **Gentleman Johnny**. He surrendered to the Americans at Saratoga (1777) during the American Revolution. His plays include *The Maid of the Oaks* (1774) and *The Heiress* (1786).

bur·grave /ˈbərgrāv/ ▶ **n.** historical the governor or hereditary ruler of a German town or castle.
– ORIGIN mid 16th cent.: from German *Burggraf*, from *Burg* 'castle' (see **BOROUGH**) + *Graf* 'count, noble.'

Bur·gun·di·an /bərˈgəndēən/ ▶ **n.** a native or inhabitant of Burgundy. ■ historical a member of a Germanic people that invaded Gaul from the east and established the kingdom of Burgundy in the 5th century AD.
▶ **adj.** of or relating to Burgundy or the Burgundians.

Bur·gun·dy /ˈbərgəndē/ a region and former duchy of eastern central France, the center of which is Dijon. The region is noted for its wine. French name **BOURGOGNE**.

bur·gun·dy /ˈbərgəndē/ (also **Burgundy**) ▶ **n.** (pl. **burgundies**) a wine from Burgundy (usually taken to be red unless otherwise specified): *a glass of Burgundy* | *elegant red burgundies.* ■ a deep red color like that of burgundy wine: *warm shades of brown and burgundy* | [as modifier] *burgundy leather.*

bur·i·al /ˈberēəl/ ▶ **n.** the action or practice of interring a dead body: *his remains were shipped home for burial.* ■ a ceremony at which someone's body is interred; a funeral: [as modifier] *burial rites.* ■ Archaeology a grave or the remains found in it: [as modifier] *burial mounds.*
– ORIGIN Old English *byrgels* 'place of burial, grave' (interpreted as plural in Middle English, hence the loss of the final *-s*), of Germanic origin; related to **BURY**.

bur·i·al ground ▶ **n.** (often as **burial grounds**) an area of ground set aside for the burying of human bodies. ■ a site at which the remains of once-living specimens can be found: *coral reefs are the burial grounds of untold organisms.*

bu·rin /ˈbyo͝orin/ ▶ **n.** a steel tool used for engraving in copper or wood. ■ Archaeology a flint tool with a chisel point.
– ORIGIN mid 17th cent.: from French; perhaps related to Old High German *bora* 'boring tool.'

bur·ka /ˈbo͝orkə/ (also **burkha**, **burqa**) ▶ **n.** a long, loose garment covering the whole body from head to feet, worn in public by many Muslim women.
– ORIGIN Urdu and Persian *burḳa'*, from Arabic *burḳu'*.

Burke, John (1787–1848), Irish genealogical and heraldic writer. In 1826, he compiled the first edition of *Burke's Peerage*, still regarded as the authoritative guide to the British aristocracy.

Bur·ki·na Fa·so /bər'kēnə 'fäsō/ a landlocked country in western Africa, in the Sahel; pop. 15,746,200 (est. 2009); capital, Ouagadougou; languages, French (official), indigenous languages. Former name (until 1984) **Upper Volta**.

> A French protectorate from 1898, it became an autonomous republic within the French Community in 1958 and a fully independent republic in 1960.

– DERIVATIVES **Bur·ki·nan** /-'kēnən/ **adj. & n.**

Bur·kitt's lym·pho·ma /'bərkits/ ▶ **n.** Medicine cancer of the lymphatic system, caused by the Epstein–Barr virus, chiefly affecting children in central Africa.
– ORIGIN 1960s: named after D. P. *Burkitt* (1911–93), the British surgeon who described it.

burl /bərl/ ▶ **n.** a slub or lump in wool or cloth. ■ a rounded knotty growth on a tree, giving an attractive figure when polished and used esp. for handcrafted objects and veneers: *she used warty burls to construct her pieces* | *wooden coin banks made of elm burl* | [as modifier] *a burl bowl.*
– ORIGIN late Middle English: from Old French *bourle* 'tuft of wool,' diminutive of *bourre* 'coarse wool,' from late Latin *burra* 'wool.'

bur·lap /'bərlap/ ▶ **n.** coarse canvas woven from jute, hemp, or a similar fiber, used esp. for sacking. ■ lighter material of a similar kind used in dressmaking and furnishing: [as modifier] *a burlap shirt* | *fabrics ranging from hessians to burlaps.*
– ORIGIN late 17th cent.: of unknown origin.

bur·lesque /bər'lesk/ ▶ **n. 1** an absurd or comically exaggerated imitation of something, esp. in a literary or dramatic work; a parody: *the funniest burlesque of opera* | [as modifier] *burlesque Shakespearean stanzas.* ■ humor that depends on comic imitation and exaggeration; absurdity: *the argument descends into burlesque.*
2 a variety show, typically including striptease: [as modifier] *burlesque clubs.*
▶ **v.** (**burlesques, burlesquing, burlesqued**) [with obj.] cause to appear absurd by parodying or copying in an exaggerated form: *she struck a ridiculous pose that burlesqued her own vanity.*
– ORIGIN mid 17th cent.: from French, from Italian *burlesco*, from *burla* 'mockery,' of unknown origin.

bur·ley /'bərlē/ ▶ **n.** (also **burley tobacco**) a tobacco of a light-colored variety grown mainly in Kentucky.
– ORIGIN late 19th cent.: of unknown origin.

Bur·ling·ton /'bərliNGtən/ **1** a city in southern Canada, on Lake Ontario, southwest of Toronto; pop. 164,415 (2006).
2 a city in north central North Carolina, noted as a textile center; pop. 50,857 (est. 2008).
3 a city in northwestern Vermont, the largest in the state, on Lake Champlain; pop. 38,897 (est. 2008).

bur·ly /'bərlē/ ▶ **adj.** (**burlier, burliest**) (of a person) large and strong; heavily built.
– DERIVATIVES **bur·li·ness n.**
– ORIGIN Middle English (in the sense 'dignified, imposing'): probably from an unrecorded Old English word meaning 'stately, fit for the bower' (see **bower**[1], **-ly**[1]).

Bur·ma /'bərmə/ a country in Southeast Asia, on the Bay of Bengal; pop. 48,137,700 (est. 2009); capital, Naypyidaw; official language, Burmese. Official name (since 1989) **Union of Myanmar**.

> Annexed by the British during the 19th century, the country was occupied by the Japanese from 1942 to 1945 and became an independent republic in 1948. In 1962, an army coup led by Ne Win overthrew the government and established an authoritarian state. The National League for Democracy (NLD) won the election held in May 1990, even though its leader Aung San Suu Kyi was under house arrest; however, the military regime did not relinquish power.

> **USAGE** The military authorities in Burma have promoted the name **Myanmar** as the name for their state since 1989, yet the name **Burma** continues to be used by various opposition groups within the country, as well as by certain foreign countries that do not recognize the current military government. Even US newscasters are not in agreement on the proper terminology: on one news program, you may hear a report about 'Myanmar, formerly Burma'; from another, the news may be about 'Burma, also known as Myanmar.'

bur mar·i·gold ▶ **n.** another term for **beggarticks**.

Bur·ma Road a route that links Lashio in Burma (Myanmar) to Kunming in China and covers 717 miles (1,154 km). Completed in 1939, it was built by the Chinese to serve as a supply route to the interior in response to the Japanese occupation of the Chinese coast.

Bur·mese /bər'mēz, -'mēs/ ▶ **n.** (pl. **same**) **1** a member of the largest ethnic group of Burma (Myanmar) in Southeast Asia.
2 a native or inhabitant of Burma.
3 the Tibeto-Burman language of the Burmese people, written in an alphabet derived from that of Pali and the official language of Burma.
4 (also **Burmese cat**) a cat of a short-haired breed originating in Asia.
▶ **adj.** of or relating to Burma, its people, or their language.

burn[1] /bərn/ ▶ **v.** (past and past participle **burned** or chiefly Brit. **burnt** /bərnt/) **1** [no obj.] (of a fire) flame or glow while consuming a material such as coal or wood: *a fire burned and crackled cheerfully in the grate.* ■ (of a candle or other source of light) be alight: *a light was burning in the hall.* ■ be or cause to be destroyed by fire: *he watched his restaurant* ***burn to the ground.*** ■ [with obj.] damage or injure by heat or fire: *I* ***burned myself*** *on the stove.*
2 [no obj.] (of a person, the skin, or a part of the body) become red and painful through exposure to the sun: *my skin tans easily but sometimes burns.* ■ feel or cause to feel sore, hot, or inflamed, typically as a result of illness or injury. ■ (**be burning with**) be possessed by (a desire or an emotion): *Martha was burning with curiosity.*
3 [with obj.] use (a type of fuel) as a source of heat or energy: *a diesel engine converted to burn natural gas.* ■ (of a person) convert (calories) to energy: *the speed at which your body burns calories.*
4 [with obj.] produce (a compact disc or DVD) by copying from an original or master copy.
5 [no obj., with adverbial of direction] informal drive very fast: *he burned past us like a maniac.*
▶ **n. 1** an injury caused by exposure to heat or flame: *he was treated in the hospital for* ***burns to*** *his hands.* ■ a mark left on something as a result of being burned: *the carpet was covered with cigarette burns.* ■ [with modifier] a feeling of heat and discomfort on the skin caused by friction, typically by a rope or razor: *a smooth shave without razor burn.*
2 consumption of a type of fuel as an energy source: *natural gas produces the cleanest burn of the lot.* ■ a firing of a rocket engine in flight.
3 an act of clearing vegetation by burning, intentionally or by accident. ■ an area of land cleared in this way.
4 a hot, painful sensation in the muscles experienced as a result of sustained vigorous exercise: *work up a burn.*
5 short for **burn rate**.
– PHRASES **be burned at the stake** historical be executed by being burned alive in public, typically for heresy or witchcraft. **burn one's bridges** do something that makes it impossible to return to an earlier state. **burn the candle at both ends** go to bed late and get up early, esp. to get work done. **burn the midnight oil** read, study, or work late into the night. **burn** (or **lay**) **rubber** informal drive very fast. **go for the burn** informal push one's body to the extremes when doing physical exercise. **money burns a hole in someone's pocket** someone has a strong urge to spend money as soon as they receive it. **slow burn** informal a state of slowly mounting anger or annoyance: *the medical community's shrugging acceptance is fueling a slow burn among women.*
– PHRASAL VERBS **burn something down** (or **burn down**) (of a building or structure) destroy or be destroyed completely by fire. **burn something in/into** brand or imprint by burning: *designs are burned into the skin* | figurative *a childhood incident that was burned into her memory.* ■ Photography expose one area of a print more than the rest: *the sky and bottom of the picture needed substantial burning in.* **burn something off** remove (a substance) using a flame: *using a blowtorch to burn off the paint.* **burn out** be completely consumed and thus no longer aflame: *the candle in the saucer had burned out* | figurative *his political ambitions had* ***burned themselves out.*** ■ cease to function as a result of excessive heat or friction: *the clutch had burned out.* **burn** (**oneself**) **out** ruin one's health or become completely exhausted through overwork. **burn someone out** make someone homeless by destroying their home by fire: *they were* ***burned out*** *of their homes.* **burn something out** completely destroy a building or vehicle by fire, so that only a shell remains. **burn up 1** (of a fire) produce brighter and stronger flames. **2** (of an object entering the earth's atmosphere) be destroyed by heat. **burn someone up** informal make someone angry: *his thoughtless remarks really burn me up.* **burn something up** ■ use up the calories or energy provided by food, rather than converting these to fat: *in the typical Western diet, all the energy in protein is burned up daily.*
– ORIGIN Old English *birnan* 'be on fire' and *bærnan* 'consume by fire,' both from the same Germanic base; related to German *brennen.*

burn[2] ▶ **n.** chiefly Scottish & N. English a small stream; a brook.
– ORIGIN Old English *burna, burn(e)*, of Germanic origin; related to Dutch *bron* and German *Brunnen* 'well.'

burned /bərnd/ (also **burnt**) past and past participle of **burn**[1].
▶ **adj.** [attrib.] having been burned: *burned wood* | *burned shoulders and peeling noses.* ■ (of a taste) like that of food that has been charred in cooking. ■ (of sugar) cooked or heated until caramelized. ■ (usu. **burnt**) (of a warm color) dark or deep: *burnt orange.*

burned-out (also **burnt-out**) ▶ **adj.** (of a vehicle or building) destroyed or badly damaged by fire; gutted. ■ (of an electrical device or component) having failed through overheating. ■ (of a person) in a state of physical or mental collapse caused by overwork or stress: *she felt burned out, an empty shell* | *a burned-out undercover cop.* ■ informal (of a teenager or other person) having dropped out; drug-using.

Burne-Jones /ˌbərn 'jōnz/, Sir Edward (Coley) (1833–98), English painter and designer. Notable paintings: *The Golden Stairs* (1880) and *The Mirror of Venus* (1898–99).

burn·er /'bərnər/ ▶ **n.** a thing that burns something or is burned, in particular: ■ a part of a stove, lamp, etc., that emits and shapes a flame. ■ an apparatus in which a fuel is used or an aromatic substance is heated. ■ [with adj.] an activity that uses something of a specified kind as energy: *uphill walking is a great calorie burner.* ■ short for **CD burner**. ■ informal a handgun.
– PHRASES **on the back** (or **front**) **burner** informal having low (or high) priority: *he wants the matter to* ***be put on the back burner.***

bur·net /bər'net, 'bərnit/ ▶ **n. 1** a herbaceous plant of the rose family, with globular pinkish flower heads and leaves composed of many small leaflets. ● Genus *Sanguisorba*, family Rosaceae: several species, including the edible **salad burnet** (*S. minor*), which is often cultivated, and the spiny shrublike **thorny burnet** (*S. spinosum*), common in the eastern Mediterranean.
2 a day-flying moth that typically has greenish-black wings marked with crimson spots. ● *Zygaena* and other genera, family Zygaenidae.
– ORIGIN Middle English (denoting a kind of dark brown woolen cloth): from Old French *brunete, burnete* (denoting brown cloth or a plant with brown flowers), diminutives of *brun* 'brown.'

Bur·nett, Frances (Eliza) Hodgson (1849–1924), US novelist; born in Britain. She is noted for her children's novels, which include *Little Lord Fauntleroy* (1886), *A Little Princess* (1905), and *The Secret Garden* (1911).

burn-in ▶ **n.** damage to a computer or television screen, caused by being left on too long. ■ a reliability test in which a device is switched on for a long time.

burn·ing /'bərniNG/ ▶ **adj.** [attrib.] on fire: *a burning building.* ■ very hot or bright: *burning desert sands.* ■ very keenly or deeply felt; intense: *he had a* ***burning ambition*** *to climb to the upper reaches of management.* ■ of urgent interest and importance; exciting or calling for debate: *democracy remains a* ***burning issue*** | *the* ***burning question*** *of independence.*
– DERIVATIVES **burn·ing·ly adv.**

burn·ing bush ▶ **n. 1** any of a number of shrubs noted for their bright red autumn foliage, in particular: ● the kochia. ● the smoke tree.
2 any of a number of shrubs or trees with bright red leaves or fruits. ● Several plants, in particular the purple-flowered North American *Euonymus atropurpurea* (family Celastraceae), a relative of the spindle tree.
3 another term for **gas plant**.
– ORIGIN mid 19th cent.: with biblical allusion to Exod. 3:2.

burn·ing glass ▶ **n.** a lens for concentrating the sun's rays on an object so as to set fire to it.

bur·nish /'bərniSH/ ▶ **v.** [with obj.] (usu. as adj. **burnished**) polish (something, esp. metal) by rubbing: *highly burnished armor.* ■ enhance or perfect (something such as a reputation or a skill).
▶ **n.** [in sing.] the shine on a highly polished surface.
– DERIVATIVES **bur·nish·er n.**
– ORIGIN Middle English: from Old French *burniss-*, lengthened stem of *burnir*, variant of *brunir* 'make brown,' from *brun* 'brown.'

bur·noose /bərˈno͞os/ (also **burnous**) ▶ **n.** a long, loose hooded cloak worn by Arabs.
– ORIGIN late 16th cent.: French, from Arabic *burnus*, from Greek *birros* 'cloak.'

burnoose

burn·out /ˈbərnˌout/ ▶ **n. 1** the reduction of a fuel or substance to nothing through use or combustion: *good carbon burnout* | [as modifier] *a burnout furnace.*
2 physical or mental collapse caused by overwork or stress: *high levels of professionalism that may result in burnout* | *you'll suffer a burnout.* ■ informal a dropout or drug abuser.
3 failure of an electrical device or component through overheating: *an antistall mechanism prevents motor burnout.*

burn rate ▶ **n.** the rate at which an enterprise spends money, esp. venture capital, in excess of income: *the corporation lays off workers to cut burn rate.*

Burns[1] /bərnz/, George (1896–1996), US comedian and movie actor; born *Nathan Birnbaum*. In 1922, he paired up with comedienne **Gracie Allen** (1902–64), whom he married in 1926. They had shows in vaudeville, on radio, and later on television. Notable movies: *The Sunshine Boys* (1975) and *Oh God!* (1977).

George Burns

Burns[2], Robert (1759–96), Scottish poet, noted for poems such as "The Jolly Beggars" (1786) and "Tam o' Shanter" (1791), and for old Scottish songs that he collected, including "Auld Lang Syne."

Burn·side /ˈbərnˌsīd/, Ambrose Everett (1824–81), US army officer. He was appointed General of the Army of the Potomac in 1862, but his incompetence at the Battle of Fredericksburg that same year led to his transfer to Ohio.

burn·side /ˈbərnˌsīd/ ▶ **n.** (usu. **burnsides**) a mustache in combination with whiskers on the cheeks but no beard on the chin.
– ORIGIN late 19th cent.: named after General Ambrose **Burnside**.

Burns·ville /ˈbərnzˌvil/ a city in southeastern Minnesota, south of Minneapolis; pop. 59,139 (est. 2008).

burnsides

burnt /bərnt/ ▶ **adj.** variant spelling of **burned**.

burnt o·cher ▶ **n.** a pigment made from ocher that has been darkened by heating, or resembling this in color. ■ the deep yellow-brown color of this pigment.

burnt of·fer·ing ▶ **n. 1** an offering burned on an altar as a religious sacrifice.
2 (usu. **burnt offerings**) humorous overcooked or charred food.

burnt si·en·na ▶ **n.** a deep reddish-brown pigment made from sienna that has been darkened by heating, or resembling this in color. ■ the color of this pigment.

burnt um·ber ▶ **n.** see **umber** (sense 1).

bur oak ▶ **n.** a North American oak, with large fringed acorn cups. Its timber was formerly important in shipbuilding. Also called **mossycup oak**. ● *Quercus macrocarpa*, family Fagaceae.

burp /bərp/ informal ▶ **v.** [no obj.] noisily release air from the stomach through the mouth; belch. ■ [with obj.] make (a baby) belch after feeding, typically by patting its back.
▶ **n.** a noise made by air released from the stomach through the mouth; a belch.
– ORIGIN 1930s: imitative.

burp gun ▶ **n.** informal a lightweight submachine gun.

bur·qa /ˈbo͝orkə/ ▶ **n.** variant spelling of **burka**.

Burr /bər/, Aaron (1756–1836), US statesman. In 1804, while US vice-president, he killed Alexander Hamilton, his rival, in a duel. He then plotted to form an independent administration in Mexico and was tried for treason but was acquitted.

burr /bər/ ▶ **n. 1** [in sing.] a rough sounding of the sound *r*, esp. with a uvular trill (a "French *r*") as in certain Northern England accents. [mid 18th cent.] ■ (loosely) a regional accent characterized by such a trill: *a soft Scottish burr.* ■ a whirring sound, such as a telephone ringing tone or the sound of cogs turning. [early 19th cent.]
2 (also **bur**) a rough edge or ridge left on an object (esp. of metal) by the action of a tool or machine. [early 17th cent.]
3 (also **bur**) a small rotary cutting tool with a shaped end, used chiefly in woodworking and dentistry. [mid 19th cent.] ■ a small surgical drill for making holes in bone, esp. in the skull.
4 a siliceous rock used for millstones. [mid 17th cent.] ■ a whetstone.
5 (also **bur**) a ring of bone at the base of a deer's antler. Also called **coronet**. [late 16th cent.: possibly from French *bourre* 'vine bud' or related to **burl**.]
6 variant spelling of **bur**.
▶ **v. 1** [no obj.] speak with an accent in which the sound *r* is trilled: [with direct speech] *"I like to have a purrrpose," she burrs.* [early 19th cent.] ■ make a whirring sound such as a telephone ringing tone or the sound of cogs turning. [late 18th cent.]
2 [with obj.] form a rough edge on (metal): *the handles were fixed by rivets **burred over** on the shield's front.* [late 19th cent.]
– PHRASES **a burr under one's saddle** informal a persistent source of irritation: *he had been a burr under the saddle of the government in his time.*
– ORIGIN Sense 1 of the noun of the noun and verb is probably imitative, the word *burr* incorporating the uvular *r*, but it is also possibly a figurative use borrowed from sense 2 of the noun, sense 3 of the noun, and sense 4 of the noun and sense 2 of the verb, the *r* being a 'rough' sound. See also **bur**.

bur·ra·wang /ˈbərəˌwaNG/ (also **burrawong**) ▶ **n.** an Australian cycad with palmlike leaves and a sunken underground trunk. ● *Macrozamia spiralis*, family Zamiaceae. ■ the poisonous nut of this tree, which loses its toxicity after prolonged soaking and becomes edible.
– ORIGIN early 19th cent.: from Dharuk.

bur reed ▶ **n.** an aquatic reedlike plant with rounded flower heads. Its oily seeds are an important source of winter food for wildfowl. ● Genus *Sparganium*, family Sparganiaceae.

burr·fish /ˈbərˌfiSH/ ▶ **n.** (pl. **same** or **burrfishes**) a porcupine fish with spines that are permanently erected, occurring in tropical waters of the Atlantic and Pacific. ● Genus *Chilomycterus*, family Diodontidae: several species, including the common **striped burrfish** (*C. schoepfi*) of the western Atlantic.

bur·ri·to /bəˈrētō/ ▶ **n.** (pl. **burritos**) a Mexican dish consisting of a tortilla rolled around a filling, typically of beans or ground or shredded beef.
– ORIGIN Latin American Spanish, diminutive of Spanish *burro*, literally 'donkey' (see **burro**).

bur·ro /ˈbərō, ˈbo͝orō/ ▶ **n.** (pl. **burros**) a small donkey used as a pack animal.
– ORIGIN early 19th cent.: from Spanish.

Bur·roughs[1] /ˈbərōz/, Edgar Rice (1875–1950), US novelist and science fiction writer. Although he began his writing career with science fiction stories, he was most successful with an adventure series that began with *Tarzan of the Apes* (1914).

Bur·roughs[2], John (1837–1921), US naturalist and author. At his home near the Hudson River at West Park, New York, he entertained friends such as John Muir, Theodore Roosevelt, and Walt Whitman. Among his works are *Wake-Robin* (1871), *Locusts and Wild Honey* (1879), and *The Summit of the Years* (1913).

Bur·roughs[3], William (Seward) (1914–97), US novelist. In the 1940s, he became addicted to heroin, and his best-known writing, such as *Junkie* (1953) and *The Naked Lunch* (1959), deals in a unique, surreal style with life as a drug addict.

bur·row /ˈbərō/ ▶ **n.** a hole or tunnel dug by a small animal, esp. a rabbit, as a dwelling.
▶ **v.** [no obj.] (of an animal) make a hole or tunnel, esp. to use as a dwelling: *moles burrowing away underground* | (as adj. **burrowing**) *burrowing earthworms* | [with obj.] *the fish can burrow a hiding place.* ■ [with adverbial of direction] advance into or through something solid by digging or making a hole: *worms that burrow through dead wood.* ■ [with adverbial of direction] move underneath or press close to something in order to hide oneself or in search of comfort: *the child **burrowed** deeper into the bed.* ■ [with obj.] move (something) in this way: *she **burrowed** her face into the pillow.* ■ make a thorough inquiry; investigate: *journalists are burrowing into the president's business affairs.*
– DERIVATIVES **bur·row·er** n.
– ORIGIN Middle English.

bur·ry /ˈbərē/ ▶ **adj. 1** having or containing burs; prickly.
2 (of speech) having a burr.

Bur·sa /ˈbərsə/ a city in northwestern Turkey; pop. 1,431,200 (est. 2007). It was the capital of the Ottoman Empire 1326–1402.

bur·sa /ˈbərsə/ ▶ **n.** (pl. **bursae** /-sē/ or **bursas**) Anatomy a fluid-filled sac or saclike cavity, esp. one countering friction at a joint.
– DERIVATIVES **bur·sal** adj.
– ORIGIN early 19th cent.: from medieval Latin, 'bag, purse,' from Greek *bursa* 'leather.'

bur·sa of Fa·bri·ci·us /faˈbrēSHəs/ ▶ **n.** Zoology a glandular sac opening into the cloaca of a bird, producing B cells.
– ORIGIN mid 19th cent. (in the Latin form *bursa Fabricii*): from **bursa**, and a Latinized form of the name of Girolama *Fabrici* (1533–1619), Italian anatomist.

bur·sar /ˈbərsər/ ▶ **n. 1** a person who manages the financial affairs of a college or university.
2 chiefly Scottish a student attending a college or university on a scholarship.
– ORIGIN late Middle English: from French *boursier* or (sense 1) medieval Latin *bursarius*, from *bursa* 'bag, purse' (see **bursa**).

bur·sa·ry /ˈbərsərē/ ▶ **n.** (pl. **bursaries**) **1** chiefly Brit. a scholarship to attend a college or university.
2 the treasury of an institution, esp. a religious one.
– ORIGIN late 17th cent. (sense 2): from medieval Latin *bursaria*, from *bursa* 'bag, purse' (see **bursa**).

burse /bərs/ ▶ **n.** a flat, square, fabric-covered case in which a folded corporal is carried to and from an altar in church.

bur·si·tis /bərˈsītis/ ▶ **n.** Medicine inflammation of a bursa, typically one in the knee, elbow or shoulder.

burst /bərst/ ▶ **v.** (past and past participle **burst**) [no obj.] (of a container) break suddenly and violently apart, spilling the contents, typically as a result of an impact or internal pressure: *we inflated dozens of balloons and only one burst.* ■ [with obj.] cause to break, esp. by puncturing: *he burst the balloon in my face.* ■ [with obj.] (of contents) break open (a container) from the inside by growing too large to be held: *the swollen river was expected to burst its banks.* ■ [with obj.] suffer from the sudden breaking of (a bodily organ or vessel): *he burst a blood vessel during a fit of coughing.* ■ be so full as almost to break open: *the drawers were **bursting with** clothes.* ■ feel a very strong or irrepressible emotion or impulse: *he was **bursting with** joy and excitement* | [with infinitive] *she was bursting to say something.* ■ suddenly begin doing something as an expression of a strong feeling: *if anyone said anything to upset me, I'd **burst out** crying* | *she **burst into** a fresh flood of tears.* ■ issue suddenly and uncontrollably, as though from a splitting container: *the words **burst from** him in an angry rush* | *an aircraft crashed and **burst into** flames.* ■ be opened suddenly and forcibly: *a door burst open and a girl raced out.* ■ [with adverbial of direction] make one's way suddenly and typically violently: *he burst into the room without knocking.* ■ [with obj.] separate (continuous stationery) into single sheets.
▶ **n.** an instance of breaking or splitting as a result of internal pressure or puncturing; an explosion. ■ a sudden issuing forth: *her breath was coming in short bursts.* ■ a sudden outbreak, typically short and often violent or noisy: *a sudden burst of activity* | *he heard a burst of gunfire.* ■ a short, sudden, and intense effort: *he sailed 474 miles in one 24-hour burst.*
– PHRASES **burst someone's bubble** see **bubble**.
– ORIGIN Old English *berstan*, of Germanic origin; related to Dutch *bersten, barsten.*

burst·er /ˈbərstər/ ▶ **n.** a thing that bursts, in particular: ■ Astronomy a cosmic source of powerful short-lived bursts of X-rays or other radiation. ■ a violent gale. ■ a machine that separates continuous stationery into single sheets.

burst·y /ˈbərstē/ ▶ **adj.** informal or technical occurring at intervals in short sudden episodes or groups.

PRONUNCIATION KEY ə *ago, up*; ər *over, fur*; a *hat*; ā *ate*; ä *car*; e *let*; ē *see*; i *fit*; ī *by*; NG *sing*; ō *go*; ô *law, for*; oi *toy*; o͝o *good*; o͞o *goo*; ou *out*; TH *thin*; T͟H *then*; ZH *vision*

b

■ relating to or denoting the transmission of data in short separate bursts of signals.

bur·then /ˈbərT͟Hən/ ▶ **n.** archaic form of BURDEN.

Bur·ton[1] /ˈbərtn/, Harold Hitz (1888–1964), US Supreme Court associate justice 1945–58. He was the mayor of Cleveland, Ohio 1935–40 and a US senator 1941–45 before being appointed to the Court by President Truman. He held strongly to a constructionist view of the US Constitution.

Bur·ton[2], Richard (1925–84), Welsh actor; born *Richard Jenkins*. He played a number of Shakespearean roles on stage before appearing in movies such as *The Spy Who Came in from the Cold* (1966) and *Who's Afraid of Virginia Woolf?* (1966). He often costarred with Elizabeth Taylor, whom he married twice.

Bur·ton[3], Sir Richard (Francis) (1821–90), English explorer, anthropologist, and translator. In 1858, he and John Hanning Speke were the first Europeans to see Lake Tanganyika. Notable translations: *Arabian Nights* (1885–88), *Kama Sutra* (1883), and *The Perfumed Garden* (1886).

bur·ton /ˈbərtn/ (also **burton-tackle**) ▶ **n.** chiefly historical a light two-block tackle for hoisting.
– ORIGIN early 18th cent.: alteration of Middle English *Breton tackle*, a nautical term in the same sense (see BRETON[1]).

Bu·run·di /bəˈro͝ondē/ a central African country on the northeastern side of Lake Tanganyika, south of Rwanda; pop. 9,511,300 (est. 2009); official languages, French and Kirundi; capital, Bujumbura.

Inhabited mainly by Hutu and Tutsi peoples, the area formed part of German East Africa from the 1890s until World War I, after which it was administered by Belgium. The country became an independent monarchy in 1962 and a republic in 1966. Multiparty elections in 1993 resulted in the country's being led for the first time by a member of the Hutu majority rather than the traditionally dominant Tutsis; the assassination of the president within months, and the death in 1994 of the country's next leader, sparked large-scale ethnic violence.

– DERIVATIVES **Bu·run·di·an** /-dēən/ **adj. & n.**

bur·y /ˈberē/ ▶ **v.** (**buries, burying, buried**) **1** [with obj.] put or hide under ground: *he buried the box in the back garden* | (as adj. **buried**) *buried treasure.* ■ (usu. **be buried**) place (a dead body) in the earth, in a tomb, or in the sea, typically with funeral rites: *he was buried in Arlington National Cemetery.* ■ lose (someone, typically a relative) through death: *she buried her sixty-year-old husband.*
2 completely cover; cause to disappear or become inconspicuous: *the countryside has been buried under layers of concrete* | figurative *the warehouse was buried in the faceless sprawl of the city.* ■ move or put out of sight: *she buried her face in her hands* | *with his hands buried in the pockets of his overcoat.* ■ deliberately forget; conceal from oneself: *they had buried their feelings of embarrassment and fear.* ■ overwhelm (an opponent) beyond hope of recovery: *losses that would bury multiple businesses.* ■ (**bury oneself**) involve oneself deeply in something to the exclusion of other concerns: *he buried himself in work.*
– PHRASES **bury the hatchet** end a quarrel or conflict and become friendly. **bury one's head in the sand** ignore unpleasant realities.
– ORIGIN Old English *byrgan*; related to the verb BORROW and to BOROUGH.

Bur·yat·ia /bo͝orˈyätēə/ (also **Buryat Republic** /bo͝orˈyät, ˈbo͝orˌyät/) an autonomous republic in southeastern Russia, between Lake Baikal and the Mongolian border; pop. 951,000 (est. 2009); capital, Ulan-Ude.

bur·y·ing bee·tle ▶ **n.** a black beetle that typically has broad orange bands on its wing cases. It buries small animal carcasses to provide a food store for its larvae. Also called SEXTON BEETLE. ● *Nicrophorus* and other genera, family Silphidae.

bus /bəs/ ▶ **n.** (pl. **buses** or **busses**) **1** a large motor vehicle carrying passengers by road, esp. one serving the public on a fixed route and for a fare: [as modifier] *a bus service.*
2 Computing a distinct set of conductors carrying data and control signals within a computer system, to which pieces of equipment may be connected in parallel.
▶ **v.** (**buses, bused, busing** or **busses, bussed, bussing**) **1** [with obj.] transport in a communal road vehicle: *managerial staff was bused in and out of the factory.* ■ transport (a child of one race) to a school where another race is predominant, in an attempt to promote racial integration.
2 [with obj.] remove (dirty tableware) from a table in a restaurant or cafeteria: *I'd never bused so many dishes in one night.* ■ remove dirty tableware from (a table): *Chad buses tables on weekends.*
– ORIGIN early 19th cent.: shortening of OMNIBUS.

bus. ▶ **abbr.** business.

bus·bar /ˈbəsˌbär/ (also **bus bar**) ▶ **n.** a system of electrical conductors in a generating or receiving station on which power is concentrated for distribution.

bus·boy /ˈbəsˌboi/ ▶ **n.** a young man who clears tables in a restaurant or cafeteria.
– ORIGIN late 19th cent.: shortening of OMNIBUS + BOY.

bus·by /ˈbəzbē/ ▶ **n.** (pl. **busbies**) a tall fur hat with a colored cloth flap hanging down on the right-hand side and often a plume on the top, worn by soldiers of certain regiments of hussars and artillerymen. ■ popular term for BEARSKIN (the cap).
– ORIGIN mid 18th cent. (denoting a large bushy wig): of unknown origin.

busby

Bush[1] /bo͝osH/, George (Herbert Walker) (1924–), 41st president of the US 1989–93. A Texas Republican, he served in the US House of Representatives 1967–71 and as director of the CIA 1976–77. His presidency was preceded by two terms as Ronald Reagan's vice president 1981–89. As president, Bush negotiated further arms reductions with the former Soviet Union and organized international action to expel the Iraqis from Kuwait following the invasion in 1990.

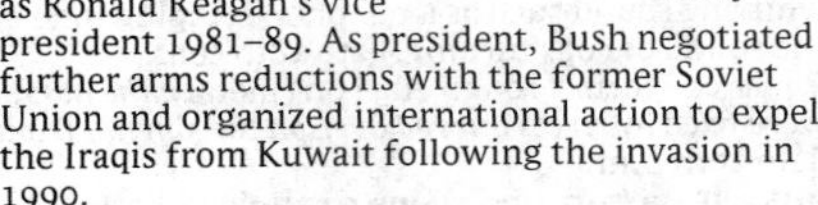

George Herbert Walker Bush

Bush[2], George Walker (1946–), 43rd president of the US 2001–2009. He is the son of President George Bush. A conservative Texas Republican, he served as governor of Texas 1995–2000 before he became president in one of the closest and most controversial presidential elections in US history, when the accuracy of the vote count in the state of Florida was challenged by Democratic nominee Al Gore. One of his early acts as president was to launch a 'War on Terror' against the Taliban regime in Afghanistan following the September 11 attacks on the World Trade Center and Pentagon; he also ordered the invasion of Iraq in March 2003, maintaining that Saddam Hussein was developing chemical, biological, and nuclear weapons.
– DERIVATIVES **Bush·ism** **n.**

George Walker Bush

bush /bo͝osH/ ▶ **n.** a shrub or clump of shrubs with stems of moderate length: *a rose bush* | *the plant will develop into a dense bush.* ■ a thing resembling such a shrub, esp. a clump of thick hair or fur: *a childish face with a bush of bright hair.* ■ vulgar slang a woman's pubic hair. ■ (**the bush**) (esp. in Australia, Africa, and Canada) wild or uncultivated country: *they have to spend a night camping in the bush.* ■ the vegetation growing in such a district: *the lowland country was covered in thick bush.*
▶ **adj.** informal short for BUSH LEAGUE.
▶ **v.** [no obj.] spread out into a thick clump: *her hair bushed out like a halo.*
– ORIGIN Middle English: from Old French *bos, bosc*, variants of *bois* 'wood,' reinforced by Old Norse *buski*, of Germanic origin and related to obsolete Dutch *bosch* (now *bos*) and German *Busch*. The sense 'uncultivated country' is probably directly from Dutch *bos*.

bush ba·by (also **bushbaby**) ▶ **n.** (pl. **bush babies**) a small nocturnal tree-dwelling African primate with very large eyes. Also called GALAGO. ● Genus *Galago*, family Lorisidae, suborder Prosimii: several species.

bush bean ▶ **n.** a variety of bean plant whose bushy growth requires no support. Compare with POLE BEAN. ■ the edible bean from such a plant.

bush·buck /ˈbo͝osHˌbək/ ▶ **n.** a small antelope with a reddish-brown coat with white markings, found in southern Africa. ● *Tragelaphus scriptus*, family Bovidae.
– ORIGIN mid 19th cent.: from BUSH + BUCK[1], influenced by obsolete Dutch *boshbok* (now *bosbok*).

bush·craft /ˈbo͝osHˌkraft/ ▶ **n.** skill at living in the bush.

bush dog ▶ **n.** a small, stocky carnivorous mammal of the dog family, with short legs and small ears. It is native to the forests of Central and South America. ● *Speothus venaticus*, family Canidae.

bushed /bo͝osHt/ ▶ **adj.** informal tired out: *after three days of training, the rookies were totally bushed.*

bush·el /ˈbo͝osHəl/ (abbr.: **bu.**) ▶ **n.** **1** a measure of capacity equal to 64 US pints (equivalent to 35.2 liters), used for dry goods. ■ informal a large amount: *we sold it for a bushel of money.*
2 Brit. a measure of capacity equal to 8 imperial gallons (equivalent to 36.4 liters), used for dry goods and liquids.
3 a container with the capacity of a bushel: [as modifier] *packing oysters into bushel baskets.*
– PHRASES **hide one's light under a bushel** see HIDE[1].
– DERIVATIVES **bush·el·ful** /-ˌfo͝ol/ **n.** (pl. **bushelfuls**).
– ORIGIN Middle English: from Old French *boissel*, perhaps of Gaulish origin.

bush fire (also **bushfire**) ▶ **n.** a fire in scrub or a forest, esp. one that spreads rapidly: figurative *news of discontent igniting a bush fire of revolt.*

bu·shi·do /ˈbo͞osHēdō/ ▶ **n.** the code of honor and morals developed by the Japanese samurai.
– ORIGIN Japanese, from *bushi* 'samurai' + *dō* 'way.'

bush·ing /ˈbo͝osHiNG/ ▶ **n.** **1** a metal lining for a round hole, esp. one in which an axle revolves. ■ a bearing for a revolving shaft.
2 a sleeve that and protects an electric cable where it passes through a panel.

bush jack·et ▶ **n.** a belted cotton jacket with patch pockets.

bush league ▶ **n.** a minor league of a professional sport, esp. baseball: [as modifier] *their bush league image.*
▶ **adj.** (**bush-league**) informal not of the highest quality or sophistication; second-rate.
– DERIVATIVES **bush lea·guer** **n.**

Bush·man /ˈbo͝osHmən/ ▶ **n.** (pl. **Bushmen**) **1** a member of any of several aboriginal peoples of southern Africa, esp. of the Kalahari Desert. They are traditionally nomadic hunter-gatherers. Also called SAN. [influenced by Dutch *boschjesman*.]
2 the language of these peoples. Now usually called SAN.
3 (**bushman**) a person who lives, works, or travels in the Australian bush.

bush·mas·ter /ˈbo͝osHˌmastər/ ▶ **n.** a pit viper that is the largest venomous snake in the New World, found in Central and South America. ● *Lachesis muta*, family Viperidae.
– ORIGIN early 19th cent.: perhaps from obsolete Dutch *boschmeester* (now *bosmeester*), from *bos* 'bush' + *meester* 'master.'

bush·meat /ˈbo͝osHˌmēt/ ▶ **n.** the meat of African wild animals.

bush pig (also **African bush pig**) ▶ **n.** a wild pig native to the forests and savannas of Africa and Madagascar. ● *Potamochoerus porcus* and *P. larvatus*, family Suidae.

bush pi·lot ▶ **n.** one who flies small aircraft into remote areas.

bush·rang·er /ˈbo͝osʜˌrānjər/ ▶ **n.** a person living far from civilization. ■ Austral. historical an outlaw living in the bush.

bush tea ▶ **n.** a tea made from dried leaves and twigs of various shrubs, esp. in tropical countries.

bush tel·e·graph ▶ **n.** [in sing.] a rapid informal network by which information or gossip is spread.

bush·tit /ˈbo͝osʜˌtit/ (also **bush tit**) ▶ **n.** a small American songbird of the long-tailed tit family, with mainly pale gray plumage and sometimes a black mask. ● *Psaltriparus minimus*, family Aegithalidae (formerly Paridae); formerly regarded as two species.

bush·wa /ˈbo͝osʜwä/ (also **bushwah**) ▶ **n.** informal rubbish; nonsense.
– ORIGIN early 20th cent.: from French *bourgeois*, now used as a euphemism for BULLSHIT.

bush·walk·ing /ˈbo͝osʜˌwôkiɴɢ/ ▶ **n.** chiefly Austral./NZ hiking or backpacking.
– DERIVATIVES **bush·walk·er** /-ˌwôkər/ **n.**

bush·whack /ˈbo͝osʜˌ(h)wak/ ▶ **v. 1** [no obj.] (often as noun **bushwhacking**) live or travel in wild or uncultivated country: *I have not seen a bear yet after seven days of bushwhacking.* ■ [with adverbial of direction] cut or push one's way in a specified direction through dense vegetation: *he'd bushwhacked down the steep slopes.*
2 [no obj.] fight as a guerrilla in the bush. ■ [with obj.] make a surprise attack on (someone) from a hidden place; ambush.

bush·whack·er /ˈbo͝osʜˌ(h)wakər/ ▶ **n. 1** a person who clears woods and bush country. ■ a person who lives or travels in bush country.
2 a guerrilla fighter (originally in the American Civil War).

bush·y /ˈbo͝osʜē/ ▶ **adj.** (**bushier**, **bushiest**)
1 growing thickly into or so as to resemble a bush: *a dense, bushy plant | his eyebrows were thick and bushy.*
2 covered with bush or bushes: *bushy desert areas.*
– DERIVATIVES **bush·i·ly** /ˈbo͝osʜəlē/ **adv.**, **bush·i·ness n.**

bus·i·ly /ˈbizəlē/ ▶ **adv.** in a very active way: *he was busily engaged in other activities.* ■ while giving all one's attention to something: *he was busily writing away.*

busi·ness /ˈbiznis/ ▶ **n. 1** a person's regular occupation, profession, or trade: *she had to do a lot of smiling in her business | are you here* **on business**? ■ an activity that someone is engaged in: *what is your business here?* ■ a person's concern: *this is none of your business | the neighbors make it their business to know all about you.* ■ work that has to be done or matters that have to be attended to: *government business | let's get down to business.*
2 the practice of making one's living by engaging in commerce: *whom do you* **do business with** *in Manila? | the jewelry business |* [as modifier] *the business community.* ■ trade considered in terms of its volume or profitability: *how's business?* ■ a commercial house or firm: *a catering business.*
3 [in sing.] informal an affair or series of events, typically a scandalous or discreditable one: *they must be told about this blackmailing business.* ■ informal a group of related or previously mentioned things: *use carrots, cauliflower, and broccoli, and serve the whole business hot.*
4 Theater actions other than dialogue performed by actors: *a piece of business.*
5 informal a scolding; harsh verbal criticism: *the supervisor really gave him the business.*
– PHRASES **business as usual** an unchanging state of affairs despite difficulties or disturbances: *apart from being under new management, it's business as usual in the department.* **have no business** have no right to do something or be somewhere: *he had no business tampering with social services.* **in business** operating, esp. in commerce: *they will have to import from overseas to remain in business.* ■ informal able to begin operations: *if you'll contact the right people, I think we'll be in business.* **in the business of** engaged in or prepared to engage in: *I am not in the business of making accusations.* **like nobody's business** informal to an extraordinarily high degree or standard: *these weeds spread like nobody's business.* **mean business** be in earnest. **mind one's own business** refrain from meddling in other people's affairs: *he was yelling at her to get out and mind her own business.* **send someone about his/her business** dated tell someone to go away.
– ORIGIN Old English *bisignis*(see BUSY, -NESS). The sense in Old English was 'anxiety'; the sense 'the state of being busy' was used from Middle English down to the 18th cent., but is now differentiated as *busyness*. The sense 'an appointed task' dates from late Middle English, and from it all the other current senses have developed.

busi·ness card ▶ **n.** a small card printed with one's name, professional occupation, company position, business address, and other contact information.

busi·ness ca·su·al ▶ **adj.** relating to or denoting a style of clothing that is less formal than traditional business wear, but is still intended to give a professional and businesslike impression.
▶ **n.** business casual clothing.

busi·ness cy·cle ▶ **n.** a cycle or series of cycles of economic expansion and contraction.

busi·ness day ▶ **n.** another term for WORKDAY.

busi·ness dou·ble ▶ **n.** Bridge a double made with the intention of increasing the penalty points scored by a partnership if they defeat their opponents' contract. Often contrasted with TAKEOUT DOUBLE.

busi·ness end ▶ **n.** informal (**the business end**) the functional part of a tool, device, or weapon: *he found himself facing the business end of six lethal-looking weapons.* ■ the essential or basic part of a process or operation: *the rigs are the business end of the oil industry.*

busi·ness hours ▶ **plural n.** another term for OFFICE HOURS.

busi·ness·like /ˈbiznisˌlīk/ ▶ **adj.** (of a person) carrying out tasks efficiently without wasting time or being distracted by personal or other concerns; systematic and practical: *his brisk, businesslike tone.* ■ (of clothing, furniture, etc.) designed or appearing to be practical rather than decorative.

busi·ness·man /ˈbiznisˌman, -mən/ ▶ **n.** (pl. **businessmen**) a man who works in business or commerce, esp. at an executive level. ■ [with adj.] a person with a specified level of skill in financial matters: *his knowledge and talent were never in question, but he was a poor businessman.*

busi·ness mod·el ▶ **n.** a design for the successful operation of a business, identifying revenue sources, customer base, products, and details of financing.

busi·ness park ▶ **n.** an area where company offices and light industrial premises are built.

busi·ness per·son (also **businessperson**) ▶ **n.** a man or woman who works in business or commerce, esp. at an executive level.

busi·ness proc·ess re·en·gi·neer·ing (abbr.: **BPR**) ▶ **n.** the process or activity of restructuring a company's organization and methods, esp. to exploit the capabilities of computers.

busi·ness stud·ies ▶ **plural n.** [treated as sing.] the study of economics and management, esp. as an educational topic.

busi·ness·wom·an /ˈbiznisˌwo͝omən/ ▶ **n.** a woman who works in business or commerce, esp. at an executive level. ■ [with adj.] a woman with a specified level of skill in financial affairs: *she has become quite the savvy businesswoman.*

busk[1] /bəsk/ ▶ **v.** [no obj.] play music or otherwise perform for voluntary donations in the street or in subways: *the group began by busking on Philadelphia sidewalks |* (as noun **busking**) *busking was a real means of living.* ■ (**busk it**) informal improvise.
– DERIVATIVES **busk·er n.**
– ORIGIN mid 17th cent.: from obsolete French *busquer* 'seek,' from Italian *buscare* or Spanish *buscar*, of Germanic origin. Originally in nautical use in the sense 'cruise about, tack,' the term later meant 'go around selling,' hence 'go around performing' (mid 19th cent).

busk[2] ▶ **n.** historical a stay or stiffening strip for a corset.
– ORIGIN late 16th cent.: from French *busc*, from Italian *busco* 'splinter' (related to French *bûche* 'log'), of Germanic origin.

bus·kin /ˈbəskin/ ▶ **n.** chiefly historical a calf-high or knee-high boot of cloth or leather. ■ a thick-soled laced boot worn by an ancient Athenian tragic actor to gain height. ■ (**the buskin**) the style or spirit of tragic drama.
– DERIVATIVES **bus·kined adj.**
– ORIGIN early 16th cent. (designating a calf-length boot): probably from Old French *bouzequin*, variant of *brousequin*, from Middle Dutch *broseken*, of unknown ultimate origin.

bus lane /ˈbəs ˌlān/ ▶ **n.** a division of a road marked off with painted lines for use by buses.

bus·man /ˈbəsmən/ ▶ **n.** (pl. **busmen**) a driver of a bus.
– PHRASES **a busman's holiday** a vacation or form of recreation that involves doing the same thing that one does at work.

buss /bəs/ archaic or informal ▶ **n.** a kiss.
▶ **v.** [with obj.] kiss.
– ORIGIN late 16th cent.: alteration of late Middle English *bass* (noun and verb), probably from French *baiser*, from Latin *basiare*.

bus·ser /ˈbəsər/ ▶ **n.** a person who clears tables in a restaurant or cafeteria.

bus shel·ter ▶ **n.** a roofed structure for people to wait under at a bus stop.

bus sta·tion ▶ **n.** a terminal where buses arrive and depart.

bus stop ▶ **n.** a place where a bus regularly stops, typically marked by a sign.

bust[1] /bəst/ ▶ **n. 1** a woman's chest as measured around her breasts: *a 36-inch bust.* ■ a woman's breasts, esp. considered in terms of their size: *selecting clothes that would minimize her big bust.*
2 a sculpture of a person's head, shoulders, and chest.
– ORIGIN mid 17th cent. (denoting the upper part or torso of a large sculpture): from French *buste*, from Italian *busto*, from Latin *bustum* 'tomb, sepulchral monument.'

bust[2] informal ▶ **v.** (past and past participle **busted** or **bust**) [with obj.] **1** break, split, or burst (something): *they bust the tunnel wide open |* figurative *the film busts every box-office record.* ■ [no obj.] come apart or split open: *he was laughing fit to bust.* ■ cause to collapse; defeat utterly: *he promised to bust the mafia.* ■ [no obj.] (**bust up**) (esp. of a married couple) separate, typically after a quarrel. ■ (**bust something up**) cause (something) to break up: *men hired to bust up union rallies.* ■ strike violently: *they wanted to bust me on the mouth.* ■ [no obj.] (**bust out**) break out; escape: *she* **busted out of** *prison.* ■ [no obj.] (in blackjack and similar card games) exceed the score of 21, losing one's stake.
2 raid or search (premises where illegal activity is suspected): *their house got busted.* ■ arrest: *he was busted for drugs.* ■ (**be/get busted**) be caught in the act of doing something wrong: *I sneaked up on them and told them they were busted.* ■ reduce (a soldier) to a lower rank; demote: *he was* **busted to** *private.*
▶ **n. 1** a period of economic difficulty or depression: *the boom was followed by the present bust.*
2 a raid or arrest by the police: *a drug bust.*
3 a worthless thing: *as a show it was a bust.*
▶ **adj.** bankrupt: *firms will* **go bust**.
– ORIGIN mid 18th cent. (originally as a noun in the sense 'an act of bursting or splitting'): variant of BURST.

bus·tard /ˈbəstərd/ ▶ **n.** a large, heavily built, swift-running bird, found in open country in the Old World. The males of most bustards have a spectacular courtship display. ● Family Otididae: several genera and species, including the **great bustard** (*Otis tarda*), which is the heaviest flying land bird.
– ORIGIN late 15th cent.: perhaps an Anglo-Norman French blend of Old French *bistarde* and *oustarde*, both from Latin *avis tarda* 'slow bird': the name is unexplained, as the bustards are fast runners.

bus·tard quail ▶ **n.** the barred button quail (see BUTTON QUAIL).

bust·ed flush ▶ **n. 1** (in poker) a hand containing four cards of the same suit and one of a different suit.
2 informal a promising person or thing that turns out to be unsuccessful: *her leadership is already a busted flush.*

bus·tee /ˈbəstē/ ▶ **n.** Indian a slum area or shanty town.
– ORIGIN from Hindi *bastī* 'dwelling.'

bust·er /ˈbəstər/ ▶ **n.** chiefly informal **1** a person or thing that breaks, destroys, or overpowers something: [in combination] *the drug's reputation as a flu-buster.* ■ short for BRONCOBUSTER.
2 informal used as a mildly disrespectful or humorous form of address, esp. to a man or boy: *your parents' decisions affect you, like it or not, buster.*

bus·tier /ˈbo͞ostyā/ ▶ **n.** a close-fitting strapless top worn by women.
– ORIGIN 1970s: from French, from *buste* (see BUST[1]).

bus·tle[1] /ˈbəsəl/ ▶ **v.** [no obj.] move in an energetic or noisy manner: *people clutching clipboards bustled about.* ■ [with obj.] make (someone) move hurriedly in a particular direction: *she bustled us into the kitchen.* ■ (of a place) be full of activity: *the small harbor bustled with boats |* (as adj. **bustling**) *the bustling little town.*
▶ **n.** excited activity and movement: *all the noise and the traffic and the bustle.*
– ORIGIN late Middle English: perhaps a variant of obsolete *buskle*, frequentative of *busk* 'prepare,' from Old Norse.

bus·tle[2] ▶ **n.** historical a pad or frame worn under a skirt and puffing it out behind.
– ORIGIN late 18th cent.: of unknown origin.

bust·y /ˈbəstē/ ▶ **adj.** (**bustier**, **bustiest**) informal (of a woman) having large breasts.
– DERIVATIVES **bust·i·ness n.**

bus·way /ˈbəsˌwā/ ▶ **n.** a road, or section of a road, set apart exclusively for buses, typically with tracks or grooves for guiding them.

bus·y /ˈbizē/ ▶ **adj.** (**busier**, **busiest**) having a great deal to do: *he had been too busy to enjoy himself* | *there was enough work to keep two people busy.* ■ occupied with or concentrating on a particular activity or object of attention: *the team members are busy raising money* | *he was* ***busy with*** *preparations.* ■ (of a place) full of activity. ■ excessively detailed or decorated; fussy: *they papered the bedroom with a busy pattern of satyrs and dryads.* ■ (of a telephone line) engaged.
▶ **v.** (**busies**, **busying**, **busied**) [with obj.] (**busy oneself**) keep occupied: *she* ***busied herself with*** *her new home.*
– DERIVATIVES **bus·y·ness n.**
– ORIGIN Old English *bisgian* (verb), *bisig* (noun); related to Dutch *bezig*.

bus·y bee ▶ **n.** informal an industrious person.

bus·y·bod·y /ˈbizēˌbädē/ ▶ **n.** (pl. **busybodies**) a meddling or prying person.

bus·y sig·nal ▶ **n.** a sound indicating that a telephone line is engaged, typically a repeated single bleep.

bus·y·work /ˈbizēˌwərk/ ▶ **n.** work that keeps a person busy but has little value in itself.

but /bət/ ▶ **conj. 1** used to introduce something contrasting with what has already been mentioned. ■ nevertheless; however: *he stumbled but didn't fall* | *this is one principle, but it is not the only one.* ■ on the contrary; in contrast: *I am clean but you are dirty* | *the problem is not that they are cutting down trees, but that they are doing it in a predatory way.*
2 [with negative or in questions] used to indicate the impossibility of anything other than what is being stated: *one* ***cannot but*** *sympathize* | *there was nothing they could do but swallow their pride* | *they had no alternative but to follow.*
3 used to introduce a response expressing a feeling such as surprise or anger: *but that's an incredible saving!* | *but why?*
4 used after an expression of apology for what one is about to say: *I'm sorry, but I can't pay you.*
5 [with negative] archaic without its being the case that: *it never rains but it pours.*
▶ **prep.** except; apart from; other than: *in Texas, we were never anything but poor* | *I trusted no one but him* | *the last but one.* ■ used with repetition of certain words to give emphasis: *nobody, but nobody, was going to stop her.*
▶ **adv.** no more than; only: *he is but a shadow of his former self* | *choose from a colorful array of oranges, cherries, and raspberries, to name but a few.*
▶ **n.** an argument against something; an objection: ***no buts****—just get out of here* | *as with all these proposals,* ***ifs and buts*** *abound.*
– PHRASES **all but** see ALL. **anything but** see ANYTHING. **but for** except for: *I walked along Broadway, deserted but for the occasional cab.* ■ if it were not for: *the game could be over but for you.* **but that** archaic other than that; except that: *who knows but that the pictures painted on air are eternal.* **but then** on the other hand; that being so: *it's a very hard exam, but then they all are.*
– ORIGIN Old English *be-ūtan, būtan, būta* 'outside, without, except' (see BY, OUT).

> **USAGE** For advice about using **but** and other conjunctions to begin a sentence, see usage at **AND**.

bu·ta·di·ene /ˌbyo͞otəˈdīēn/ ▶ **n.** Chemistry a colorless gaseous hydrocarbon made by catalytic dehydrogenation of butane and used in the manufacture of synthetic rubber. ● Chem. formula: $CH_2{=}CHCH{=}CH_2$.
– ORIGIN early 20th cent.: from BUTANE + DI-[1] + -ENE.

bu·tane /ˈbyo͞oˌtān/ ▶ **n.** Chemistry a flammable hydrocarbon gas that is a constituent of petroleum and is used in bottled form as a fuel. It is a member of the alkane series. See also ISOBUTANE. ● Chem. formula: $CH_3CH_2CH_2CH_3$.
– ORIGIN late 19th cent.: from BUTYL + -ANE[2].

bu·ta·no·ic ac·id /ˌbyo͞otnˈōik/ ▶ **n.** systematic chemical name for BUTYRIC ACID.

bu·ta·nol /ˈbyo͞otnˌôl, -ˌäl/ ▶ **n.** Chemistry each of two isomeric liquid alcohols used as solvents; butyl alcohol. ● Chem. formula: $CH_3CH_2CH_2CH_2OH$ (**1-butanol, butan-1-ol**) and $CH_3CH_2CH(OH)CH_3$ (**2-butanol, butan-2-ol**).

Bu·ta·zo·li·din /ˌbyo͞otəˈzälidin/ ▶ **n.** trademark a preparation of phenylbutazone used to reduce pain and inflammation.

butch /bo͝och/ informal ▶ **adj.** manlike or masculine in appearance or behavior, typically aggressively or ostentatiously so.
▶ **n.** a mannish lesbian, often contrasted with a more feminine partner. Compare with FEMME.
– DERIVATIVES **butch·y adj.**
– ORIGIN 1940s: perhaps an abbreviation of BUTCHER.

butch·er /ˈbo͝ochər/ ▶ **n. 1** a person whose trade is cutting up and selling meat in a shop. ■ a person who slaughters and cuts up animals for food: *a pork butcher.* ■ a person who kills or has people killed indiscriminately or brutally: *a callous butcher of men.*
2 informal a person selling refreshments, newspapers, and other items on a train or in a stadium or theater.
▶ **v.** [with obj.] slaughter or cut up (an animal) for food: *the meat will be butchered for the local market.* ■ kill (someone) brutally: *they butchered 250 people.* ■ ruin (something) deliberately or through incompetence: *the film was butchered by the studio that released it.*
– ORIGIN Middle English: from an Anglo-Norman French variant of Old French *bochier*, from *boc* 'he-goat,' probably of the same ultimate origin as BUCK[1].

butch·er·bird /ˈbo͝ochərˌbərd/ ▶ **n. 1** a shrike (family Laniidae) that impales its prey on thorns.
2 a crowlike predacious Australasian songbird, with a heavy hook-tipped bill. Compare with MAGPIE (sense 2). ● Family Cracticidae: three genera, in particular *Cracticus*, and several species.
– ORIGIN mid 17th cent.: from its habit of impaling its prey on thorns.

butch·er block ▶ **n.** a material used to make kitchen countertops and tables, consisting of strips of hardwood glued together: *a slab of butcher block* | [as modifier] *a butcher-block table.*

butch·er knife ▶ **n.** a large, broad-bladed knife used for cutting meat.

butch·er's block /ˈbo͝ochərz ˌbläk/ ▶ **n.** a sturdy wooden kitchen table with a square top on which food may be chopped.

butch·er's broom ▶ **n.** a low evergreen Eurasian shrub of the lily family, with flat shoots that give the appearance of stiff, spine-tipped leaves. ● *Ruscus aculeatus*, family Liliaceae.

butch·er·y /ˈbo͝ochərē/ ▶ **n.** (pl. **butcheries**) the savage killing of large numbers of people. ■ the work of slaughtering animals and preparing them for sale as meat.
– ORIGIN Middle English (denoting a slaughterhouse or meat market): from Old French *boucherie*, from *bouchier* 'butcher.'

bute /byo͞ot/ ▶ **n.** informal term for PHENYLBUTAZONE.

bu·te·o /ˈbyo͞otēō/ ▶ **n.** (pl. **buteos**) a bird of prey of a group distinguished by broad wings that are used for soaring. ● *Buteo* and related genera, family Accipitridae; many species, including the buzzards and the red-tailed and Harris's hawks.
– ORIGIN from Latin *buteo* 'buzzard, hawk.'

Bu·tey·ko meth·od /bo͞oˈtākō/ ▶ **n.** a technique of controlled breathing that is claimed to alleviate asthma.
– ORIGIN 1990s: named after Ukrainian physiologist Konstantin *Buteyko* (1923–2003), who devised the technique.

Bu·the·le·zi /ˌbo͞otlˈāzē/, Chief Mangosuthu (Gatsha) (1928–), South African politician; minister of home affairs 1994–2004. He has been president of the Inkatha Freedom Party since 1975.

But·ler[1] /ˈbətlər/, Pierce (1866–1939), US Supreme Court associate justice 1922–39. A conservative, he was appointed to the Court by President Harding.

But·ler[2], Samuel (1612–80), English poet, most notable for his three-part satirical poem *Hudibras* (1663–78).

But·ler[3], Samuel (1835–1902), English novelist. Notable works: *Erewhon* (1872), *Erewhon Revisited* (1901), and *The Way of All Flesh* (1903).

but·ler /ˈbətlər/ ▶ **n.** the chief manservant of a house.
– ORIGIN Middle English: from Old French *bouteillier* 'cupbearer,' from *bouteille* 'bottle.'

but·ler's pan·try ▶ **n.** a small service and storage room between a kitchen and a dining room.

bu·toh /ˈbo͞otō/ ▶ **n.** a style of Japanese modern dance featuring dancers covered in white body paint.
– ORIGIN Japanese, literally 'dance.'

butt[1] /bət/ ▶ **v.** [with obj.] (of a person or animal) hit (someone or something) with the head or horns: *she* ***butted*** *him* ***in the chest*** *with her head.* ■ strike (the head) against something: *he* ***butts*** *his head* ***against*** *a wall.*
▶ **n.** a push or blow, typically given with the head: *he would follow up with a butt from his head.*
– PHRASES **butt heads** engage in conflict or be in strong disagreement: *the residents continue to butt heads with the mall developers.*
– PHRASAL VERBS **butt in** take part in a conversation or activity, or enter somewhere, without being invited or expected: *sorry to* ***butt in*** *on you.* **butt out** informal stop interfering: *anyone who tries to cut across our policies should butt out.*
– ORIGIN Middle English: from Old French *boter*, of Germanic origin.

butt[2] ▶ **n.** the person or thing at which criticism or humor, typically unkind, is directed: *his singing is the butt of dozens of jokes.* ■ (usu. **butts**) an archery or shooting target or range. ■ a mound on or in front of which a target is set up for archery or shooting.
– ORIGIN Middle English (in the archery sense): from Old French *but*, of unknown origin; perhaps influenced by French *butte* 'rising ground.'

butt[3] ▶ **n. 1** (also **butt end**) the thicker end, esp. of a tool or a weapon: *a rifle butt.* ■ the square end of a plank or plate meeting the end or side of another, as in the side of a ship. ■ the thicker or hinder end of a hide used for leather.
2 (also **butt end**) the stub of a cigar or a cigarette: *the ashtray was crammed with cigarette butts.*
3 informal the buttocks or anus.
4 the trunk of a tree, esp. the part just above the ground.
▶ **v.** [no obj.] adjoin or meet end to end: *the church* ***butted up against*** *the row of houses* | *a garden that* ***butted up to*** *the neighbor's.* ■ [with obj.] join (pieces of stone, lumber, and other building materials) with the ends or sides flat against each other: *the floorboards will be* ***butted up against*** *each other to make tight seams.*
– ORIGIN late Middle English: the noun apparently related to Dutch *bot* 'stumpy,' also to BUTTOCK; the verb partly from BUTT[2], reinforced by ABUT.

butt[4] ▶ **n.** a cask, typically used for wine, ale, or water. ■ a liquid measure equal to 2 hogsheads (equivalent to 126 US gallons).
– ORIGIN late Middle English: from Old French *bot*, from late Latin *buttis*.

Butte /byo͞ot/ a city in southwestern Montana, noted as a mining center; pop. 32,119 (est. 2008).

butte /byo͞ot/ ▶ **n.** technical an isolated hill with steep sides and a flat top (similar to but narrower than a mesa).
– ORIGIN mid 19th cent.: from French, 'mound,' from Old French *but*, of unknown origin (compare with BUTT[2]).

but·ter /ˈbətər/ ▶ **n.** a pale yellow edible fatty substance made by churning cream and used as a spread or in cooking.
▶ **v.** [with obj.] spread (something) with butter: *she buttered the toast* | (as adj. **buttered**) *lavishly buttered bread.*
– PHRASES **look as if butter wouldn't melt in one's mouth** informal appear gentle or innocent while typically being the opposite.
– PHRASAL VERBS **butter someone up** informal flatter or otherwise ingratiate oneself with someone.
– ORIGIN Old English *butere*, of West Germanic origin; related to Dutch *boter* and German *Butter*, based on Latin *butyrum*, from Greek *bouturon* 'cow cheese.'

but·ter-and-eggs ▶ **n.** see TOADFLAX.

but·ter·ball /ˈbətərˌbôl/ ▶ **n.** informal derogatory a fat person. ■ a plump bird, esp. a turkey or bufflehead.

but·ter bean ▶ **n.** a lima bean, esp. one of a variety with large flat white seeds that are usually dried.

but·ter·bur /ˈbətərˌbər/ ▶ **n.** a Eurasian waterside plant of the daisy family, the rounded flower heads of which are produced before the leaves. The large soft leaves were formerly used to wrap butter, and extracts of the plant have long been used medicinally as a powerful anticonvulsant. ● Genus *Petasites*, family Compositae: several species, in particular the common *P. hybridus*.

but·ter·cream /ˈbətərˌkrēm/ ▶ **n.** a soft mixture of butter and powdered sugar used as a filling or topping for a cake.

but·ter·cup /ˈbətərˌkəp/ ▶ **n.** a herbaceous plant with bright yellow cup-shaped flowers, common in grassland and as a garden weed. All kinds are poisonous and generally avoided by livestock. ● Genus *Ranunculus*, family Ranunculaceae (the **buttercup family**): numerous species, including the very familiar **common buttercup** (*R. acris*). This large family also includes anemones, celandines, aconites, clematises, and hellebores, many of which have poisonous seeds.

but·ter·cup squash ▶ **n.** a winter squash of a variety with dark green skin and orange flesh.

but·ter·fat /ˈbətərˌfat/ ▶ **n.** the natural fat contained in milk and dairy products.

but·ter·fin·gers /ˈbətərˌfiNGgərz/ ▶ **n.** (pl. **same**) informal a clumsy person, esp. one who fails to hold a catch. ■ clumsiness in handling something: *fumbling for the ball with butterfingers.*
– DERIVATIVES **but·ter·fin·gered adj.**

but·ter·fish /ˈbətərˌfiSH/ ▶ **n.** (pl. **same** or **butterfishes**) any of a number of fishes with oily flesh or slippery skin, in particular: ● a deep-bodied edible fish of temperate and tropical seas (family Stromateidae), in particular *Peprilus triacanthus* of eastern North America. ● another term for **GUNNEL**[1] ● an Australasian reef fish (family Odacidae), in particular the edible *Odax pullus* of New Zealand, which has green bones and feeds on kelp. ● a tropical freshwater or marine fish that is popular in aquariums (several families, including Scatophagidae).

but·ter·fly /ˈbətərˌflī/ ▶ **n.** (pl. **butterflies**) an insect with two pairs of large wings that are covered with tiny scales, usually brightly colored, and typically held erect when at rest. Butterflies fly by day, have clubbed or dilated antennae, and usually feed on nectar. ● Superfamilies Papilionoidea and Hesperioidea, order Lepidoptera: several families. Formerly placed in a grouping known as the Rhopalocera. Compare with **MOTH**. ■ a showy or frivolous person: *a social butterfly.* ■ (**butterflies**) informal a fluttering and nauseated sensation felt in the stomach when one is nervous. ■ (in full **butterfly stroke**) [in sing.] a stroke in swimming in which both arms are raised out of the water and lifted forward together. ■ [as modifier] having a two-lobed shape resembling the spread wings of a butterfly: *a butterfly clip.*
▶ **v.** (**butterflies, butterflying, butterflied**) [with obj.] split (a piece of meat) almost in two and spread it out flat: (as adj. **butterflied**) *butterflied shrimp.*
– ORIGIN Old English, from **BUTTER** + **FLY**[2]; perhaps from the cream or yellow color of common species, or from an old belief that the insects stole butter.

but·ter·fly bush ▶ **n.** a Chinese buddleia that is cultivated in the West for its large spikes of fragrant purplish-lilac or white flowers, which are highly attractive to butterflies. ● *Buddleia davidii*, family Loganiaceae.

but·ter·fly ef·fect ▶ **n.** (with reference to chaos theory) the phenomenon whereby a minute localized change in a complex system can have large effects elsewhere.
– ORIGIN 1980s: from the notion that a butterfly fluttering in Rio de Janeiro could change the weather in Chicago.

but·ter·fly·fish ▶ **n. 1** any of a number of typically brightly colored or boldly marked fish of warm waters, in particular: ● a reef-dwelling fish that is popular in marine aquariums (*Chaetodon* and other genera, family Chaetodontidae). ● a predatory marine fish that bears long venomous spines (genus *Pterois*, family Scorpaenidae).
2 a West African freshwater fish with large pectoral fins used in leaping out of the water and long fin rays used as stilts. ● *Pantodon buchholzi*, the only member of the family Pantodontidae.

but·ter·fly knife ▶ **n.** a long broad knife used in pairs in some forms of kung fu.

but·ter·fly net ▶ **n.** a fine-meshed bag supported on a frame at the end of a handle for catching butterflies. ■ humorous such a net supposedly dropped over a person in order to take the person away to a mental hospital: *the men with the butterfly nets will be sitting on the foot of my bed.*

but·ter·fly nut ▶ **n.** another term for **WING NUT**.

but·ter·fly or·chid ▶ **n.** an epiphytic wild orchid of South America with large yellow and red flowers that somewhat resemble a butterfly in shape. ● *Oncidium papilio*, family Orchidaceae.

but·ter·fly stroke ▶ **n.** another term for **BUTTERFLY** (in swimming).

but·ter·fly valve ▶ **n. 1** a valve consisting of a disk rotating on an axis across the diameter of a pipe to regulate the flow, as in the throttles of many engines.
2 a valve consisting of a pair of semicircular plates that are attached to a spindle across a pipe and hinged to allow flow only one way.

but·ter·fly weed ▶ **n.** a North American milkweed with bright orange flowers that are attractive to butterflies. ● *Asclepias tuberosa*, family Asclepiadaceae.

but·ter·head let·tuce /ˈbətərˌhed ˈletəs/ ▶ **n.** a class of lettuce varieties having soft leaves that grow in a loose head.

but·ter ic·ing ▶ **n.** another term for **BUTTERCREAM**.

but·ter knife ▶ **n.** a blunt knife used for cutting or spreading butter or other similar spreads.

but·ter·milk /ˈbətərˌmilk/ ▶ **n.** the slightly sour liquid left after butter has been churned, used in baking or consumed as a drink. ■ a pale yellow color (used esp. to describe paint or wallpaper): [as modifier] *buttermilk paintwork.*

but·ter·nut /ˈbətərˌnət/ ▶ **n. 1** a North American walnut tree that bears oblong sticky fruits. Its light-colored, soft timber is useful primarily for making furniture and cabinetry. Also called **WHITE WALNUT**. ● *Juglans cinerea*, family Juglandaceae. ■ the edible oily nut of this tree.
2 historical, informal a Confederate soldier or supporter (so called because the fabric of the Confederate uniform was typically homespun and dyed with butternut extract).

but·ter·nut squash ▶ **n.** a popular winter squash of a variety that has a bell-shaped fruit with sweet orange-yellow flesh.

but·ter·scotch /ˈbətərˌskäCH/ ▶ **n.** a flavor created originally by combining melted butter with brown sugar: [as modifier] *butterscotch syrup.* ■ a candy with this flavor.

but·ter tart ▶ **n.** Canadian a tart with a filling of butter, eggs, brown sugar, and, typically, raisins.

but·ter·weed /ˈbətərˌwēd/ ▶ **n.** a yellow-flowered plant of the daisy family, closely related to ragwort. ● Genus *Senecio*, family Compositae: several species, including the **common butterweed** (*S. vulgaris*) of the Pacific states and **Bolander's butterweed** (*S. bolanderi*), found esp. along the Pacific coast of North America.

but·ter·wort /ˈbətərˌwərt, -ˌwôrt/ ▶ **n.** a carnivorous bog plant that has violet flowers borne above a rosette of yellowish-green greasy leaves that trap and digest small insects. It is native to both Eurasia and North America. ● Genus *Pinguicula*, family Lentibulariaceae: several species, in particular the **common butterwort** (*P. vulgaris*).
– ORIGIN late 16th cent.

but·ter·y[1] /ˈbətərē/ ▶ **adj.** containing or tasting like butter: *layers of flaky buttery pastry.* ■ covered with butter: *buttery fingers.*
– DERIVATIVES **but·ter·i·ness n.**

but·ter·y[2] ▶ **n.** (pl. **butteries**) a pantry, or a room for storing wine and liquor. ■ Brit. a room, esp. in a college, where food is kept and sold to students.
– ORIGIN Middle English: from Anglo-Norman French *boterie* 'storeroom for casks,' from Old French *bot* (see **BUTT**[4]).

butt·head /ˈbətˌhed/ ▶ **n.** informal a stupid or stubborn person: *only a butthead would drive a car like that.*

butt hinge ▶ **n.** a hinge attached to the abutting surfaces of a door and a door jamb.

butt·in·sky /bətˈinskē/ ▶ **n.** (pl. **buttinskies**) a person who habitually butts in; an intruder or meddler.

butt joint ▶ **n.** (of wood, metal, etc.) a joint formed by two surfaces abutting at right angles.

but·tle /ˈbətl/ ▶ **v.** [no obj.] humorous work as a butler: *there is no one today worth buttling for.*
– ORIGIN mid 19th cent.: back-formation from **BUTLER**.

but·tock /ˈbətək/ ▶ **n.** either of the two round fleshy parts that form the lower rear area of a human trunk. ■ (**buttocks**) the rump of an animal.
– ORIGIN Old English *buttuc*, probably from the base of **BUTT**[3] + **-OCK**.

but·ton /ˈbətn/ ▶ **n.** a small disk or knob sewn onto a garment, either to fasten it by being pushed through a slit made for the purpose, or for decoration: *a blouse with five buttons in front* | [as modifier] *button thread.* ■ a knob on a piece of electrical or electronic equipment that is pressed to operate it. ■ a badge bearing a design or slogan and pinned to the clothing. ■ a small, round object resembling a button: *chocolate buttons.* ■ Fencing a knob fitted to the point of a foil to make it harmless.
▶ **v.** [with obj.] fasten (clothing) with buttons: *he buttoned up his jacket.* ■ (**button someone into**) fasten the buttons of a garment being worn by (someone): *he buttoned himself into the raincoat.* ■ [no obj.] (of a garment) be fastened with buttons: *a dress that buttons down the front.* ■ (**button it**) [often in imperative] informal stop talking.
– PHRASES **button one's lip** informal stop or refrain from talking. **on the button** informal punctually: *it was nearly visiting hours and she would arrive on the button.* ■ exactly right: *his prediction was right on the button in terms of actual rainfall.* **press the button** informal initiate an action or train of events, esp. nuclear war. **push** (or **press**) **someone's buttons** informal arouse or provoke a reaction in someone: *stay cool and don't allow them to push your buttons.*
– PHRASAL VERBS **button something up 1** informal complete or conclude something satisfactorily: *trying to button up a deal.* **2** repress or contain something: *it was repressive enough to keep public opinion buttoned up.*
– DERIVATIVES **but·ton·less adj., but·toned adj.** [in combination] *a gold-buttoned blazer.*
– ORIGIN Middle English: from Old French *bouton*, of Germanic origin and related to **BUTT**[1].

but·ton·ball tree /ˈbətnˌbôl/ ▶ **n.** another term for **SYCAMORE** (sense 1).

but·ton·bush /ˈbətnˌbo͝oSH/ ▶ **n.** a low-growing North American aquatic shrub of the bedstraw family, with small tubular flowers that form globular flower heads. ● *Cephalanthus occidentalis*, family Rubiaceae.

but·ton-down ▶ **adj.** [attrib.] (of a collar) having points that are buttoned to the garment. ■ (of a shirt) having such a collar. ■ (of a person) conservative or unimaginative.
▶ **n.** a shirt with a button-down collar.

but·toned-up ▶ **adj. 1** reserved and not inclined to reveal information: *Fleischer's buttoned-up style.*
2 secured to the maximum degree against attack: *the tank had been buttoned up and had not been seriously damaged.*

but·ton·hole /ˈbətnˌhōl/ ▶ **n.** a slit made in a garment to receive a button for fastening. ■ Brit. a boutonnière.
▶ **v.** [with obj.] **1** informal attract the attention of and detain (someone) in conversation, typically against his or her will.
2 make slits for receiving buttons in (a garment).

but·ton·hol·er /ˈbətnˌhōlər/ ▶ **n.** an attachment for a sewing machine used to make buttonholes.

but·ton·hole stitch ▶ **n.** a looped stitch used for edging buttonholes or pieces of material: *the edges are worked in buttonhole stitch.*

but·ton·hook /ˈbətnˌho͝ok/ ▶ **n. 1** a small hook with a long handle for fastening tight buttons (often formerly on buttoned boots or gloves).
2 Football a play in which a pass receiver runs straight downfield and then doubles back sharply toward the line of scrimmage.

but·ton man ▶ **n.** informal a hired killer.

but·ton mush·room ▶ **n.** a young unopened mushroom.

but·ton quail ▶ **n.** a small quaillike Old World bird related to the rails, with only three toes. ● Family Turnicidae and genus *Turnix*: several species, including the widespread **barred button quail** (*T. suscitator*) of Asia.

But·tons /ˈbətnz/ ▶ **n.** Brit. informal a nickname for a liveried pageboy, esp. in pantomimes.
– ORIGIN mid 19th cent.: from the rows of buttons on his jacket.

but·ton·wood /ˈbətnˌwo͝od/ ▶ **n. 1** (also **buttonwood tree**) another term for **SYCAMORE** (sense 1).
2 either of two mangroves native mainly to tropical America, used in the production of tanbark and for charcoal. ● *Conocarpus erectus* (the **button mangrove**) and *Laguncularia racemosa*, family Combretaceae.

but·tress /ˈbətris/ ▶ **n. 1** a projecting support of stone or brick built against a wall. ■ a projecting portion of a hill or mountain.
2 a source of defense or support: *there was a demand for a new stable order as a buttress against social collapse.*
▶ **v.** [with obj.] **1** provide (a building or structure) with projecting supports built against its walls: (as adj. **buttressed**) *a buttressed wall.*
2 increase the strength of or justification for; reinforce: *authority was buttressed by religious belief.*
– ORIGIN Middle English: from Old French (*ars*) *bouterez* 'thrusting (arch),' from *boter* 'to strike, thrust' (see **BUTT**[1]).

but·tress root ▶ **n.** a tree root whose upper, exposed parts project from the trunk like a buttress.

butt ug·ly ▶ **adj.** informal extremely unattractive.

bu·tut /ˈbo͞oˌto͞ot/ ▶ **n.** (pl. **same** or **bututs**) a monetary unit of Gambia, equal to one hundredth of a dalasi.

bu·tyl /ˈbyo͞otl/ ▶ **n.** [as modifier] Chemistry an alkyl radical $-C_4H_9$, derived from butane: *butyl acetate.* ■ short for **BUTYL RUBBER**.
– ORIGIN mid 19th cent.: from **BUTYRIC ACID** + **-YL**.

bu·tyl al·co·hol ▶ **n.** any of four isomeric alcohols used as solvents and in organic synthesis.

bu·tyl·ate /'byo͞otl,āt/ ▶ **v.** [with obj.] Chemistry combine with a butyl group.
– DERIVATIVES **bu·tyl·a·tion** /,byo͞otl'āsHən/ **n.**

bu·tyl·at·ed hy·drox·y·an·i·sole /'byo͞otl,ātid hī,dräksē'anə,sōl/ (abbr.: **BHA**) ▶ **n.** a synthetic antioxidant used to preserve fats and oils in food. ● Chem. formula: $C_{11}H_{16}O_2$.

bu·tyl·at·ed hy·drox·y·tol·u·ene /hī,dräksē'tälyo͞o,ēn/ (abbr. **BHT**) ▶ **n.** a synthetic antioxidant used to preserve fats and oils in foods, medicinal drugs, and cosmetics. ● Chem. formula: $C_{15}H_{24}O$.

bu·tyl·ene /'byo͞otl,ēn/ ▶ **n.** any of several isomeric hydrocarbons obtained from petroleum and used to make polymers and in organic synthesis. ● Chem. formula: C_4H_8.

bu·tyl rub·ber ▶ **n.** a synthetic rubber made by polymerizing isobutylene and isoprene.

bu·tyr·a·ceous /,byo͞otə'rāsHəs/ ▶ **adj.** of or like butter.

bu·tyr·ic ac·id /byo͞o'tirik/ ▶ **n.** Chemistry a colorless, syrupy liquid organic acid found in rancid butter and in arnica oil. ● Alternative name: **butanoic acid**; chem. formula: C_3H_7COOH.
– DERIVATIVES **bu·tyr·ate** /'byo͞otə,rāt/ **n.**
– ORIGIN mid 19th cent.: *butyric* from Latin *butyrum* (see **BUTTER**) + **-IC**.

bu·ty·rin /'byo͞otərin/ ▶ **n.** any of three glyceryl esters of butyric acid found naturally in butter. ● Chem. formula: $C_3H_5(C_3H_4O_2)_3$.

bux·om /'bəksəm/ ▶ **adj.** (of a woman) plump, esp. with large breasts.
– DERIVATIVES **bux·om·ness n.**
– ORIGIN Middle English: from the stem of Old English *būgan* 'to bend' (see **BOW**[2]) + **-SOME**[1]. The original sense was 'compliant, obliging,' later 'lively and good-tempered,' influenced by the traditional association of plumpness and good health with an easygoing nature.

buy /bī/ ▶ **v.** (**buys, buying**; past and past participle **bought** /bôt/) [with obj.] **1** obtain in exchange for payment: *we had to find some money to buy a house* | *he had been able to* **buy up** *hundreds of acres* | [with two objs.] *he bought me a new dress* | [no obj.] *had no interest in* **buying into** *an entertainment company.* ■ (**buy someone out**) pay someone to give up an ownership, interest, or share. ■ procure the loyalty and support of (someone) by bribery: *here was a man who could not be bought* | *I'll* **buy off** *the investigators.* ■ [often with negative] be a means of obtaining (something) through exchange or payment: *money can't buy happiness.* ■ get by sacrifice or great effort: *greatness is* **dearly bought**. ■ [no obj.] make a profession of purchasing goods for a store or firm.
2 informal accept the truth of: *I am not prepared to buy the claim that the ends justify the means* | [no obj.] *I hate to* **buy into** *stereotypes.*
3 (**bought it**) informal used to say that someone has died: *his friends had bought it in the jungle.*
▶ **n.** informal a purchase: *the wine is a good buy at $3.49.* ■ an act of purchasing something: *out on a produce buy for the restaurant.*
– PHRASES **buy the farm** informal die: *I refused to admit to my recklessness, even when I nearly bought the farm.* **buy time** delay an event temporarily so as to have longer to improve one's own position.
– ORIGIN Old English *bycgan*, of Germanic origin.

buy·back ▶ **n.** the buying back of goods by the original seller. ■ the buying back by a company of its own shares. ■ a form of borrowing in which shares or bonds are sold with an agreement to repurchase them at a later date: *a share buy-back.*

buy·er /'bīər/ ▶ **n.** a person who makes a purchase. ■ a person employed to select and purchase stock or materials for a large retail or manufacturing business, etc.
– PHRASES **a buyer's market** an economic situation in which goods or shares are plentiful and buyers can keep prices down.

buy-in ▶ **n. 1** a purchase of shares by a broker after a seller has failed to deliver similar shares, the original seller being charged any difference in cost.
2 (also **management buy-in**) a purchase of shares in a company by managers who are not employed by it.
3 the buying back by a company of its own shares.
4 informal agreement to support a decision: *the CEO got a buy-in from all his vice presidents to launch the new product.*

buy·out /'bī,out/ ▶ **n.** the purchase of a controlling share in a company, esp. by its own managers.

buz·ka·shi /bo͞osH'kəsHē/ ▶ **n.** a sport in which teams on horseback compete to gain possession of a headless animal carcass and bring it to a scoring area. It is the national sport of Afghanistan.

buzz /bəz/ ▶ **n.** [in sing.] a low, continuous humming or murmuring sound, made by or similar to that made by an insect: *the buzz of the bees* | *a buzz of conversation.* ■ the sound of a buzzer or telephone. ■ informal a telephone call: *I'll give you a buzz.* ■ informal a rumor: *the buzz is that he's in big trouble.* ■ an atmosphere of excitement and activity: *there is a real buzz about the place.* ■ informal a feeling of excitement or euphoria: *I got such a buzz out of seeing the kids' faces.*
▶ **v.** [no obj.] **1** make a humming sound: *mosquitoes were buzzing all around us.* ■ (often as noun **buzzing**) (of the ears) be filled with a humming sound: *I remember a buzzing in my ears.* ■ signal with a buzzer: *the electric bell began to buzz for closing time* | [with obj.] *he buzzed the stewardesses every five minutes.* ■ [with obj.] informal make a telephone call to (someone).
2 [with adverbial of direction] move quickly or busily: *she buzzed along the highway back into town.* ■ [with obj.] Aeronautics, informal fly very close to (another aircraft, the ground, etc.) at a high speed.
3 (of a place) have an air of excitement or purposeful activity: *the club is* **buzzing with** *excitement.* ■ (of a person's mind or head) be filled with excited or confused thoughts: *her mind was buzzing with ideas.*
– PHRASAL VERBS **buzz off** [often in imperative] informal go away.
– ORIGIN late Middle English: imitative.

buz·zard /'bəzərd/ ▶ **n.** a large hawklike bird of prey with broad wings and a rounded tail, typically seen soaring in wide circles. ● Family Accipitridae: several genera, in particular *Buteo*, and including the common (**Eurasian**) **buzzard** (*B. buteo*). ■ a North American vulture, esp. a turkey vulture.
– ORIGIN late Middle English: from Old French *busard*, based on Latin *buteo* 'falcon.'

Buz·zards Bay /'bəzərdz/ an inlet of the Atlantic Ocean in southeastern Massachusetts, just west of Cape Cod.

buzz bomb ▶ **n.** informal a robot bomb, esp. the German V-1 used during World War II.

buzz cut ▶ **n.** a haircut in which all the hair is cut very close to the scalp.

buzz·er /'bəzər/ ▶ **n.** an electrical device, similar to a bell, that makes a buzzing noise and is used for signaling.
– PHRASES **at the buzzer** Sports at the end of a game or period of play: *Smith missed another 3-pointer at the buzzer.*

buzz·kill /'bəzkil/ ▶ **n.** informal a person or thing that has a depressing or dispiriting effect: *if you think bad weather at the zoo sounds like a buzzkill, you're right.*

buzz saw ▶ **n.** another term for **CIRCULAR SAW**.

buzz·word /'bəz,wərd/ (also **buzz phrase**) ▶ **n.** informal a technical word or phrase that has become fashionable, typically as a slogan.

buzz·y /'bəzē/ ▶ **adj.** (**buzzier, buzziest**) informal (esp. of a place or atmosphere) lively and exciting: *a buzzy bar with live music.*

BVDs ▶ **plural n.** trademark a type of boxer shorts.
– ORIGIN late 19th cent.: abbreviation from the name of the manufacturers; the mistaken full form in folk etymology is *babies' ventilated diapers.*

BVM ▶ **abbr.** Blessed Virgin Mary.

b/w ▶ **abbr.** black and white (used esp. to describe printing, movies, photographs, or television pictures).

bwa·na /'bwänə/ ▶ **n.** (in East Africa) a boss or master (often used as a title or form of address): *he can't hear you, bwana.*
– ORIGIN Kiswahili.

BWI ▶ **abbr.** historical British West Indies.

BWR ▶ **abbr.** boiling-water reactor.

by /bī/ ▶ **prep. 1** identifying the agent performing an action. ■ after a passive verb: *the door was opened by my cousin Annie* | *damage caused by fire.* ■ after a noun denoting an action: *further attacks by the mob* | *a clear decision by the electorate.* ■ identifying the author of a text, idea, or work of art: *a book by Ernest Hemingway.*
2 [often with verbal noun] indicating the means of achieving something: *malaria can be controlled by attacking the parasite* | *they plan to provide further working capital* **by means of** *borrowing.* ■ indicating a term to which an interpretation is to be assigned: *what is meant by "fair?"* ■ indicating a name according to which a person is known: *she mostly calls me by my last name.* ■ indicating the means of transport selected for a journey: *traveling by train to Boston.* ■ indicating the other parent of someone's child or children: *Richard is his son by his third wife.* ■ indicating the sire of a pedigree animal, esp. a horse: *a black filly by Goldfuerst.* ■ (followed by a noun without an adjective) in various phrases indicating how something happens: *I heard by chance that she has married again* | *Anderson, by contrast, rejects this view* | *she ate by candlelight.*
3 indicating the amount or size of a margin: *the shot missed her by miles* | *the raising of taxes by 2.5%.* ■ indicating a unit of measurement: *billing is by the minute.* ■ in phrases indicating something happening repeatedly or progressively, typically with repetition of a unit of time: *colors changing minute by minute* | *the risk becomes worse by the day.* ■ identifying a parameter: *a breakdown of employment figures by age and occupation.* ■ expressing multiplication, often in dimensions: *a map measuring 24 by 36 inches* | *she multiplied it by 89.*
4 indicating a deadline or the end of a particular time period: *I've got to do this report by Monday* | *by now Kelly needed extensive physiotherapy.*
5 indicating location of a physical object beside a place or object: *remains were discovered by the roadside* | *the lamp was by the door.* ■ past; beyond: *I drove by our house.*
6 indicating the period in which something happens: *this animal always hunts* **by night**.
7 concerning; according to: *anything you do is all right by me* | *she had done her duty by him.*
8 used in mild oaths: *it was the least he could do, by God.* [partly translating French *par* 'through the medium or agency of.']
▶ **adv.** so as to go past: *a car flashed by on the other side of the road* | *he let only a moment go by.*
▶ **n.** (pl. **byes**) variant spelling of **BYE**[1].
– PHRASES **by and by** before long; eventually. **by the by** (or **bye**) incidentally; parenthetically: *where's Hector, by the by?* **by and large** on the whole; everything considered: *mammals have, by and large, bigger brains than reptiles.* [originally in nautical use, describing the handling of a ship both with the wind and against it.] **by oneself 1** alone: *living in that big house by himself.* **2** unaided: *the patient often learns to undress by himself.* **by way of** see **WAY**.
– ORIGIN Old English *bī, bi, be*, of Germanic origin; related to Dutch *bij* and German *bei*.

by- ▶ **prefix** subordinate; incidental; secondary: *by-form* | *byproduct.*

By·att /'bīət/, A. S. (1936–), English novelist and literary critic; full name *Antonia Susan Byatt*. She is the sister of Margaret Drabble. Notable novels: *The Virgin in the Garden* (1978) and *Possession* (Booker Prize, 1990).

Byb·los /'bibləs/ an ancient Mediterranean seaport, located on the site of modern Jebeil, north of Beirut in Lebanon. It was a thriving Phoenician city in the 2nd millennium BC.

by-blow ▶ **n.** Brit. **1** a side-blow not at the main target.
2 a man's illegitimate child.

by-catch ▶ **n.** the unwanted fish and other marine creatures caught during commercial fishing for a different species.

Byd·goszcz /'bid,gôsH(cH)/ an industrial river port in northern central Poland; pop. 362,397 (2007). Twenty thousand of its citizens were massacred by Nazis in September 1939. German name **BROMBERG**.

bye[1] /bī/ ▶ **n. 1** the transfer of a competitor directly to the next round of a competition in the absence of an assigned opponent.
2 Golf one or more holes remaining unplayed after the match has been decided.
– PHRASES **by the bye** variant spelling of **BY THE BY** (see **BY**).
– ORIGIN mid 16th cent. (denoting a side issue or incidental matter): from the noun **BY**.

bye[2] ▶ **exclam.** informal short for **GOODBYE**.

bye-bye ▶ **exclam.** informal way of saying **GOODBYE**.
– ORIGIN early 18th cent.: child's reduplication.

by-e·lec·tion ▶ **n.** chiefly Brit. an election to fill a vacancy arising during a term of office.

Bye·lo·rus·sia variant spelling of **BELORUSSIA**.

Bye·lo·rus·sian ▶ **adj. & n.** variant spelling of **BELORUSSIAN**.

by-form ▶ **n.** a secondary form of a word: *historically, "inquire" is a by-form of "enquire."*

by·gone /'bī,gôn/ ▶ **adj.** belonging to an earlier time: *relics of a bygone society.*
▶ **n.** (usu. **bygones**) a thing dating from an earlier time.
– PHRASES **let bygones be bygones** forget past offenses or causes of conflict and be reconciled.

by·law /'bī,lô/ ▶ **n. 1** a rule made by a company or society to control the actions of its members.
2 a regulation made by a local authority; an ordinance.
– ORIGIN Middle English: probably from obsolete *byrlaw* 'local law or custom,' from Old Norse *býjar*,

genitive singular of *býr* 'town,' but associated with **BY**.

by·line /ˈbī,līn/ ▶ **n.** a line in a newspaper naming the writer of an article.

by·name /ˈbī,nām/ ▶ **n.** (also **by-name**) a sobriquet or nickname, esp. one given to distinguish people with the same given name.

BYOB ▶ **abbr.** bring your own bottle (or booze, or beer).

by·pass /ˈbī,pas/ ▶ **n.** a road passing around a town or its center to provide an alternative route for through traffic. ■ a secondary channel, pipe, or connection to allow a flow when the main one is closed or blocked. ■ an alternative passage made by surgery, typically to aid the circulation of blood. ■ a surgical operation to make such a passage: *a heart bypass.*
▶ **v.** [with obj.] go past or around: *bypass the farm and continue to the road.* ■ provide (a town) with a route diverting traffic from its center: *the town has been bypassed.* ■ avoid or circumvent (an obstacle or problem): *a manager might bypass formal channels of communication.*

by·path /ˈbī,paTH/ ▶ **n.** (also **by-path**) an indirect route.

by·play /ˈbī,plā/ ▶ **n.** (also **by-play**) secondary or subsidiary action or involvement in a play or movie.

by·prod·uct ▶ **n.** (also **by-product**) an incidental or secondary product made in the manufacture or synthesis of something else: *zinc is a byproduct of the glazing process.* ■ a secondary result, unintended but inevitably produced in doing or producing something else: *he saw poverty as the byproduct of colonial prosperity.*

Byrd[1] /bərd/, Charlie (Lee) (1925–99), US guitarist. He was responsible for introducing and applying acoustic classical guitar techniques to jazz and popular music and for launching the samba and bossa nova movements of the 1960s in the US with his album *Jazz Samba* (1962) with Stan Getz.

Byrd[2], Richard (Evelyn) (1888–1957), US explorer, naval officer, and aviator. He claimed to have made the first aircraft flight over the North Pole 1926, although his actual course has been disputed. He was the first to fly over the South Pole 1929 and led further scientific expeditions to the Antarctic in 1933–34 and 1939–41.

Byrd[3], Robert Carlyle (1917–), US politician. A West Virginia Democrat, he is the longest-serving member of the US Senate (1950–52, 1959–).

byre /bīr/ ▶ **n.** chiefly Brit. a cowshed.
– ORIGIN Old English *býre*; perhaps related to **BOWER**[1].

Byrnes /bərnz/, James Francis (1879–1972), US Supreme Court associate justice 1941–42. A Democrat from South Carolina, he was a member of the US House of Representatives 1911–25 and the US Senate 1931–41 before being appointed to the Court by President Franklin D. Roosevelt. He resigned from the Court a year later to take several federal positions in the war effort.

by·road /ˈbī,rōd/ ▶ **n.** (also **by-road**) a minor road.

By·ron /ˈbīrən/, George Gordon, 6th Baron (1788–1824), English poet. His poetry exerted considerable influence on the romantic movement, particularly on the Continent. Having joined the fight for Greek independence, he died of malaria before seeing serious action. Notable works: *Childe Harold's Pilgrimage* (1812–18) and *Don Juan* (1819–24).

By·ron·ic /bīˈränik/ ▶ **adj.** characteristic of Lord Byron or his poetry. ■ (of a man) alluringly dark, mysterious, or moody.

bys·si·no·sis /,bisəˈnōsis/ ▶ **n.** a lung disease caused by prolonged inhalation of textile fiber dust.
– ORIGIN late 19th cent.: from Latin *byssinus* 'made of byssus' (from Greek *bussinos*) + **-OSIS**.

bys·sus /ˈbisəs/ ▶ **n.** (pl. **byssuses** or **byssi** /ˈbisī/)
1 historical a fine textile fiber and fabric of flax.
2 Zoology a tuft of tough silky filaments by which mussels and some other bivalves adhere to rocks and other objects: [as modifier] *byssus threads.*
– DERIVATIVES **bys·sal** /-səl/ **adj.**
– ORIGIN late Middle English: from Latin, from Greek *bussos*, of Semitic origin.

by·stand·er /ˈbī,standər/ ▶ **n.** a person who is present at an event or incident but does not take part.

by·street /ˈbī,strēt/ ▶ **n.** a side street off the main thoroughfare.

byte /bīt/ ▶ **n.** Computing a group of binary digits or bits (usually eight) operated on as a unit. Compare with **BIT**[4]. ■ such a group as a unit of memory size.
– ORIGIN 1960s: an arbitrary formation based on **BIT**[4] and **BITE**.

By·tom /ˈbi,tôm/ a city in southern Poland, northwest of Katowice; pop. 185,793 (2007). German name **BEUTHEN**.

by·town·ite /bīˈtounīt/ ▶ **n.** a calcium-rich plagioclase present in many basic igneous rocks.
– ORIGIN mid 19th cent.: from *Bytown*, the former name of Ottawa, Canada, + **-ITE**[1].

by·way /ˈbī,wā/ ▶ **n.** a road or track not following a main route; a minor road or path. ■ a little-known area or detail: *byways of Russian music.*

by·word /ˈbī,wərd/ ▶ **n.** a person or thing cited as a notorious and outstanding example or embodiment of something: *his name became a* **byword** *for luxury.* ■ a word or expression summarizing a thing's characteristics or a person's principles: *"Small is beautiful" may be the byword for most couturiers.*

by-your-leave ▶ **n.** request for permission: *he borrowed my car without so much as a by-your-leave.* See also **LEAVE**[2].

Byz·an·tine /ˈbizən,tēn, bəˈzan-, -,tīn/ ▶ **adj.** of or relating to Byzantium, the Byzantine Empire, or the Eastern Orthodox Church. ■ of an ornate artistic and architectural style that developed in the Byzantine Empire and spread esp. to Italy and Russia. The art is generally rich and stylized (as in religious icons) and the architecture typified by many-domed, highly decorated churches. ■ (of a system or situation) excessively complicated, typically involving a great deal of administrative detail: *Byzantine insurance regulations.* ■ characterized by deviousness or underhanded procedure: *Byzantine intrigues | he has the most Byzantine mind in politics.*
▶ **n.** a citizen of Byzantium or the Byzantine Empire.
– DERIVATIVES **By·zan·tin·ism** /bəˈzantə,nizəm, bī-/ **n.**
– ORIGIN late 16th cent. (denoting a **BEZANT**, a Byzantine coin): from Latin *Byzantinus*, from **BYZANTIUM**.

Byz·an·tine Em·pire the empire in southeastern Europe and Asia Minor formed from the eastern part of the Roman Empire. It ended with the loss of Constantinople to the Ottoman Turks in 1453.

Byz·an·tin·ist /bəˈzantənist, bī-/ ▶ **n.** a historian or other scholar specializing in the study of the Byzantine Empire.

Byz·an·ti·um /bəˈzantēəm, -ˈzanCHēəm/ an ancient Greek city, founded in the 7th century BC, at the southern end of the Bosporus, site of the modern city of Istanbul. It was rebuilt by Constantine the Great in AD 324–330 as Constantinople.

BZP ▶ **abbr.** benzylpiperazine, a drug that has stimulant and euphoric properties similar to those of amphetamine. ● Chem. formula: $C_{11}H_{16}N_2$.

b

PRONUNCIATION KEY ə *ago, up*; ər *over, fur*; a *hat*; ā *ate*; ä *car*; e *let*; ē *see*; i *fit*; ī *by*; NG *sing*; ō *go*; ô *law, for*; oi *toy*; o͝o *good*; o͞o *goo*; ou *out*; TH *thin*; T͟H *then*; ZH *vision*

Cc

C[1] /sē/ (also **c**) ▶ **n.** (pl. **Cs** or **C's**) **1** the third letter of the alphabet. ■ denoting the third in a set of items, categories, sizes, etc. ■ denoting the third of three or more hypothetical people or things. ■ the third highest class of academic grades. ■ (**c**) Chess denoting the third file from the left of a chessboard, as viewed from White's side of the board. ■ (usu. **c**) the third fixed constant to appear in an algebraic expression, or a known constant. ■ denoting the lowest soil horizon, comprising parent materials.
2 a shape like that of a letter C: [in combination] *C-springs.*
3 (usu. **C**) Music the first note of the diatonic scale of C major, the major scale having no sharps or flats. ■ a key based on a scale with C as its keynote.
4 the Roman numeral for 100. [abbreviation of Latin *centum* 'hundred.']
5 (**C**) a high-level computer programming language originally developed for implementing the UNIX operating system. [formerly known as *B*, abbreviation of *BCPL*.]

C[2] ▶ **abbr.** ■ (**C.**) Cape (chiefly on maps): *C. Hatteras.* ■ Celsius or centigrade: *it was 29°C at noon.* ■ (©) copyright. ■ (in personal ads) Christian. ■ a 1.5 volt dry cell battery size. ■ Physics coulomb(s). ▶ **symbol** ■ Physics capacitance. ■ the chemical element carbon.
– PHRASES **the Big C** informal cancer.

c ▶ **abbr.** ■ cent(s). ■ [in combination] (in units of measurement) centi-: *centistokes (cS).* ■ (**c.**) century or centuries: *a watch case, 19th c.* ■ (also **c.**) (preceding a date or amount) circa; approximately: *Isabella was born c. 1759.* ■ (of water) cold: *all cabins have h & c.* ■ colt. ▶ **symbol** Physics the speed of light in a vacuum: $E = mc^2$.

CA ▶ **abbr.** ■ California (in official postal use). ■ Central America. ■ chief accountant. ■ Canadian & Scottish chartered accountant.

Ca ▶ **symbol** the chemical element calcium.

ca (also **ca.**) ▶ **abbr.** (preceding a date or amount) circa.

Caa·ba variant spelling of **KAABA**.

CAB ▶ **abbr.** Civil Aeronautics Board.

cab[1] /kab/ ▶ **n. 1** short for **TAXICAB**. ■ historical a horse-drawn vehicle for public hire.
2 the driver's compartment in a truck, bus, or train.
▶ **v.** (**cabs, cabbing, cabbed**) [no obj.] travel in a taxi: *Roger cabbed home.*
– ORIGIN early 19th cent.: abbreviation of **CABRIOLET**.

cab[2] ▶ **n.** informal a cabinet containing a speaker or speakers for a guitar amplifier.
– ORIGIN late 20th cent.: abbreviation.

ca·bal /kə'bäl, -'bal/ ▶ **n.** a secret political clique or faction: *a cabal of dissidents.*
– ORIGIN late 16th cent. (denoting the cabbala): from French *cabale*, from medieval Latin *cabala* (see **KABBALAH**).

Cab·a·la ▶ **n.** variant spelling of **KABBALAH**.

ca·ba·let·ta /,kabə'letə, ,käbə-/ ▶ **n.** (pl. **cabalettas** or **cabalette** /-'le,tā/) a simple aria with a repetitive rhythm. ■ the uniformly quick final section of an aria.
– ORIGIN mid 19th cent.: from Italian, variant of *coboletta* 'short stanza,' diminutive of *cobola*, from Old Provençal *cobla*, from Latin *copula* 'connection.'

cab·a·lis·tic /,kabə'listik/ ▶ **adj.** relating to or associated with mystical interpretation or esoteric doctrine. See also **KABBALAH**.
– DERIVATIVES **cab·a·lism** /'kabə,lizəm/ **n.**, **cab·a·list** /'kabəlist/ **n.**
– ORIGIN variant of *Kabbalistic*: see **KABBALAH**.

ca·bal·le·ro /,kabə(l)'ye(ə)rō, -'le(ə)rō/ ▶ **n.** (pl. **caballeros**) **1** a Spanish or Mexican gentleman.
2 (in the southwestern US) a horseman.
– ORIGIN mid 19th cent.: Spanish 'gentleman, horseman,' based on Latin *caballus* 'horse.' Compare with **CAVALIER, CHEVALIER**.

ca·ban·a /kə'ban(y)ə/ ▶ **n.** a cabin, hut, or shelter, esp. one at a beach or swimming pool.
– ORIGIN late 19th cent.: from Spanish *cabaña*, from late Latin *capana, cavana* 'cabin.'

cab·a·ret /,kabə'rā, 'kabə,rā/ ▶ **n.** entertainment held in a nightclub or restaurant while the audience eats or drinks at tables: *she was seen recently in cabaret* | [as modifier] *a cabaret act.* ■ a nightclub or restaurant where such entertainment is performed.
– ORIGIN mid-17th cent. (denoting a French inn): from Old French, literally 'wooden structure,' via Middle Dutch from Old Picard *camberet* 'little room.' Current senses date from the early 20th cent.

cab·bage /'kabij/ ▶ **n.** a cultivated plant eaten as a vegetable, having thick green or purple leaves surrounding a spherical heart or head of young leaves. ● *Brassica oleracea*, family Brassicaceae (the **cabbage family**). As well as the brassicas, the members of this family (known as crucifers) include the mustards and cresses together with many ornamentals (candytuft, alyssum, stocks, nasturtiums, wallflowers). ■ the leaves of this plant, eaten as a vegetable. ■ informal paper money: *I'd have cabbage galore in the bank if I were more frugal.*
– DERIVATIVES **cab·bage·y adj.**
– ORIGIN late Middle English: from Old French (Picard) *caboche* 'head,' variant of Old French *caboce*, of unknown origin.

cab·bage mag·got ▶ **n.** a small fly whose larvae feed on the roots and stems of cabbages and related plants and can be a serious pest. ● *Delia radicum*, family Anthomyiidae.

cab·bage moth ▶ **n.** a brown moth whose caterpillars are pests of cabbages and related plants. ● *Mamestra brassicae*, family Noctuidae.

cab·bage palm ▶ **n.** any of a number of palms or palmlike plants that resemble a cabbage in some way, in particular: ● a Caribbean palm with edible buds that resemble a cabbage (*Roystonea oleraceae*, family Palmae). ● an evergreen plant occurring in warm regions and grown elsewhere as a greenhouse or indoor plant (genus *Cordyline*, family Agavaceae).

cab·bage pal·met·to ▶ **n.** see **PALMETTO**.

cab·bage rose ▶ **n.** a kind of rose with a large, round, compact double flower.

cab·bage white ▶ **n.** a mainly white butterfly that has caterpillars that are pests of cabbages and related plants. ● Genus *Pieris*, family Pieridae: several species, in particular the imported cabbageworm *P. rapae.*

cab·bage·worm /'kabij,wərm/ ▶ **n.** any caterpillar that is a pest of cabbages, esp. that of the cabbage white butterfly.

Cab·ba·la ▶ **n.** variant spelling of **KABBALAH**.

cab·bie /'kabē/ (also **cabby**) ▶ **n.** (pl. **cabbies**) informal a taxicab driver.

ca·ber /'kābər, 'käbər/ ▶ **n.** a roughly trimmed tree trunk used in the Scottish Highland sport of **tossing the caber**. This involves holding the caber upright and running forward to toss it so that it lands on the opposite end.
– ORIGIN early 16th cent.: from Scottish Gaelic *cabar* 'pole.'

Ca·ber·net /,kabər'nā/ ▶ **n.** short for **CABERNET FRANC** or **CABERNET SAUVIGNON**.

Ca·ber·net Franc /'fräNGk/ ▶ **n.** a variety of black wine grape grown chiefly in parts of the Loire valley and northeastern Italy. ■ a red wine made from this grape.
– ORIGIN French.

Ca·ber·net Sau·vi·gnon /,sōvin'yôN, -vē'nyôN/ ▶ **n.** a variety of black wine grape from the Bordeaux area of France, now grown throughout the world. ■ a red wine made from this grape.
– ORIGIN French.

Ca·be·za Pri·e·ta /kə'bāzə prē'ātə/ a national wildlife refuge in southwestern Arizona, in the Sonoran Desert. The Cabeza Prieta Mountains give their name to the preserve, which is home to bighorn sheep and other species.

cab·e·zon /'kabə,zän, -,zōn/ ▶ **n.** a heavy-bodied fish with a broad tentacle above each eye and a green-brown body with white patches, found on the west coast of North America. ● *Scorpaenichthys marmoratus*, family Cottidae.
– ORIGIN Spanish.

cab-for·ward ▶ **adj.** [attrib.] (of the design of a car or truck) having the driver's or passenger compartment placed so as to extend further forward than the standard position.

ca·bil·do /kə'bildō/ ▶ **n.** (pl. **cabildos**) (in Spain and Spanish-speaking countries) a town council or local government council. ■ a town hall.
– ORIGIN Spanish, from late Latin *capitulum* 'chapter house.'

cab·in /'kabən/ ▶ **n. 1** a private room or compartment on a ship. ■ the area for passengers in an aircraft.
2 a small shelter or house, made of wood and situated in a wild or remote area.
▶ **v.** (**cabins, cabining, cabined**) [with obj.] (often as adj. **cabined**) dated confine in a small place.
– ORIGIN Middle English: from Old French *cabane*, from Provençal *cabana*, from late Latin *capanna, cavanna.*

cab·in boy ▶ **n.** chiefly historical a boy employed to wait on a ship's officers or passengers.

cab·in class ▶ **n.** the intermediate class of accommodations on a passenger ship.

cab·in crew ▶ **n.** [treated as sing. or pl.] the members of an aircraft crew who attend to passengers.

cab·in cruis·er ▶ **n.** a recreational motorboat with sleeping accommodations.

Ca·bin·da /kə'bində/ an exclave of Angola at the mouth of the Congo River, separated from the rest of Angola by a wedge of the Democratic Republic of the Congo (formerly Zaire). ■ the capital of this area; pop. 287,000 (est. 2004).

cab·i·net /'kabənit/ ▶ **n. 1** a cupboard with drawers or shelves for storing or displaying articles: *a medicine cabinet.* ■ a wooden box, container, or piece of furniture housing a radio, television set, or speaker.
2 (in the US) a body of advisers to the president, composed of the heads of the executive departments of the government: [as modifier] *a cabinet meeting.* ■ (also **Cabinet**) (in the UK, Canada, and other Commonwealth countries) the committee of senior ministers responsible for controlling government policy.
3 archaic a small private room.
– ORIGIN mid 16th cent.: from **CABIN** + **-ET**[1], influenced by French *cabinet.*

cab·i·net·mak·er /'kabənit,mākər/ ▶ **n.** a skilled joiner who makes furniture or similar high-quality woodwork.
– DERIVATIVES **cab·i·net·mak·ing** /-,mākiNG/ **n.**

cab·i·net min·is·ter ▶ **n.** (in the UK, Canada, and other Commonwealth countries) a member of a parliamentary cabinet.

cab·i·net·ry /'kabənitrē/ ▶ **n.** cabinets collectively.

cab·in fe·ver ▶ **n.** informal irritability, listlessness, and similar symptoms resulting from long confinement or isolation indoors during the winter.

ca·ble /'kābəl/ ▶ **n.** **1** a thick rope of wire or nonmetallic fiber, typically used for construction, mooring ships, and towing vehicles. ■ the chain of a ship's anchor. ■ Nautical a length of 200 yards (182.9 m) or (in the US) 240 yards (219.4 m). ■ short for CABLE STITCH. ■ (also **cable molding**) Architecture a molding resembling twisted rope. **2** an insulated wire or wires having a protective casing and used for transmitting electricity or telecommunication signals: *an underground cable | transatlantic phone calls went by cable.* ■ a cablegram. ■ short for CABLE TELEVISION.
▶ **v.** [with obj.] **1** contact or send a message to (someone) by cablegram. ■ transmit (a message) by cablegram. ■ [no obj.] send a cablegram: *we cabled to a boat at sea, asking it to stop.* **2** provide (an area or community) with power lines or with the equipment necessary for cable television. **3** Architecture decorate (a structure) with rope-shaped moldings.
– ORIGIN Middle English: from an Anglo-Norman French variant of Old French *chable*, from late Latin *capulum* 'halter.'

ca·ble car ▶ **n.** **1** a transportation system, typically one traveling up and down a mountain, in which cabins are suspended on a continuous moving cable driven by a motor at one end of the route. ■ a cabin on such a system. **2** a car on a cable railroad.

ca·ble·gram /'kābəl,gram/ ▶ **n.** historical a telegraph message sent by cable: *Walter shot off a cablegram | we received the word of his death by cablegram.*

ca·ble-laid ▶ **adj.** (of rope) made of three right-handed triple strands (or smaller ropes) twisted together left-handed, used originally of a very large rope of the type used for anchor cables.

ca·ble mo·dem ▶ **n.** a type of modem that connects a computer or local network to broadband Internet service through the same cable that supplies cable television service: [as modifier] *a cable-modem connection.*

ca·ble rail·road ▶ **n.** a railroad along which cars are drawn by a continuous cable.

ca·ble-read·y ▶ **adj.** [attrib.] adapted for cable television.

ca·ble re·lease ▶ **n.** Photography a cable attached to the shutter release of a camera, allowing the photographer to open the shutter without touching or moving the camera.

ca·ble-stayed bridge ▶ **n.** a bridge in which the weight of the deck is supported by a number of cables running directly to one or more towers.

ca·ble stitch ▶ **n.** a combination of knitted stitches done to resemble twisted rope.

ca·ble tel·e·vi·sion ▶ **n.** a system in which television programs are transmitted to the sets of subscribers by cable rather than by a broadcast signal.

ca·ble tier ▶ **n.** Nautical, historical a place in a ship for stowing a coiled cable.

ca·ble·way /'kābəl,wā/ ▶ **n.** a transportation system in which goods are carried suspended from a continuous moving cable.

cab·man /'kabmən/ ▶ **n.** (pl. **cabmen**) a taxicab driver. ■ historical the driver of a horse-drawn hackney carriage.

ca·boched ▶ **adj.** variant spelling of CABOSHED.

cab·o·chon /'kabə,SHän/ ▶ **n.** a gem polished but not faceted: [as modifier] *a necklace of cabochon rubies.*
– PHRASES **en cabochon** /än/ (of a gem) treated in this way.
– ORIGIN mid 16th cent.: from French, diminutive of *caboche* 'head.'

ca·bo·clo /kə'bôkloo, -klō/ ▶ **n.** (pl. **caboclos**) (in Brazil) an American Indian. ■ a Brazilian of mixed white and Indian or Indian and black ancestry.
– ORIGIN Brazilian Portuguese, perhaps from Tupi *Kaa-boc* 'person having copper-colored skin.'

ca·boo·dle /kə'boodl/ (also **kaboodle**) ▶ **n.** (in phrase **the whole caboodle** or **the whole kit and caboodle**) informal the whole number or quantity of people or things in question.
– ORIGIN mid 19th cent. (originally US): perhaps from the phrase *kit and boodle*, in the same sense (see KIT[1], BOODLE).

ca·boose /kə'boos/ ▶ **n.** **1** a railroad car with accommodations for the train crew, typically attached to the end of the train. ■ informal (typically referring to a woman) buttocks: *she's got a sexy caboose.* **2** archaic a kitchen on a ship's deck.
– ORIGIN mid 18th cent.: from Dutch *kabuis*, *kombuis*, of unknown origin.

Ca·bo·ra Bas·sa /kə,bôrə 'bäsə/ a lake on the Zambezi River in western Mozambique. Its waters are impounded by a dam and massive hydroelectric complex.

ca·boshed /kə'bäsHt/ (also **caboched** or **cabossed** /-'bäst/) ▶ **adj.** [usu. postpositive] Heraldry (of the head of a stag, bull, etc.) shown full face with no neck visible.
– ORIGIN late 16th cent.: from French *caboché*, in the same sense.

Cab·ot /'kabət/ the name of two Italian explorers and navigators. ■ **John** (*c.*1450–*c.*1498); Italian name *Giovanni Caboto*. An Italian in the service of England, he sailed from Bristol in 1497 in search of Asia, but in fact discovered the mainland of North America. ■ **Sebastian** (*c.*1475–*c.*1557), son of John. It is thought that he accompanied his father on his voyage in 1497 and that he made further voyages after the latter's death, most notably to explore the coast of Brazil and the Plate River in 1526.

cab·o·tage /'kabə,täzH, -bətij/ ▶ **n.** the right to operate sea, air, or other transport services within a particular territory. ■ restriction of the operation of sea, air, or other transport services within or into a particular country to that country's own transport services.
– ORIGIN mid 19th cent.: from French, from *caboter* 'sail along a coast,' perhaps from Spanish *cabo* 'cape, headland.'

Cab·ot Strait /'kabət/ an ocean passage between Newfoundland and Nova Scotia that links the Gulf of St. Lawrence with the Atlantic Ocean.

cab·o·ver /'kab,ōvər/ ▶ **n.** a truck where the driver's cab is mounted directly above the engine.

Ca·bra·les /kä'brälās/ ▶ **n.** a pungent blue cheese from Spain.
– ORIGIN Spanish, from *cabra* 'goat.'

Ca·bri·ni /kə'brēnē/, St. Frances Xavier (1850–1917), US religious leader, born in Italy; born *Maria Francesca Cabrini*; known as **Mother Cabrini**. She founded the Missionary Sisters of the Sacred Heart in 1880 and was responsible for the establishment of many schools, hospitals, and orphanages in the US and South America. She became the first American saint in 1946.

cab·ri·ole /'kabrē,ōl/ ▶ **n.** Ballet a jump in which one leg is extended into the air forward or backward, the other is brought up to meet it, and the dancer lands on the second foot.
– ORIGIN French, literally 'light leap,' from *cabrioler* (earlier *caprioler*), from Italian *capriolare* 'to leap in the air' (see CAPRIOLE).

cab·ri·ole leg ▶ **n.** a kind of curved leg characteristic of Chippendale and Queen Anne furniture.
– ORIGIN late 18th cent.: so named from the resemblance to the front leg of a leaping animal (see CABRIOLE).

cabriole leg

cab·ri·o·let /'kabrēə,lā/ ▶ **n.** **1** a car with a roof that folds down. **2** a light, two-wheeled carriage with a hood, drawn by one horse.
– ORIGIN mid 18th cent.: from French, from *cabriole* 'goat's leap,' from *cabrioler* 'to leap in the air' (see CABRIOLE); so named because of the carriage's motion.

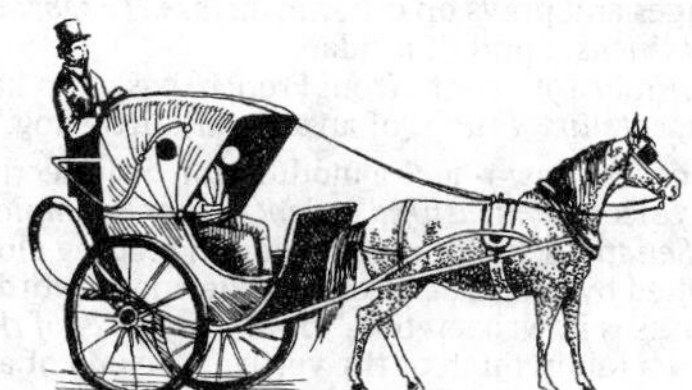

cabriolet 2

cab·stand /'kab,stand/ ▶ **n.** a place for taxis to wait for passengers.

ca·ca /'käkə/ ▶ **n.** informal excrement.
– ORIGIN late 19th cent.: from *cack* 'excrement,' or directly from Latin *cacare* 'defecate.'

ca'can·ny /kä'kanē/ ▶ **n.** Brit. dated the policy of deliberately limiting output at work.
– ORIGIN late 19th cent. (originally Scots in the sense 'proceed warily'): from *ca'* (variant of the verb CALL) and CANNY.

ca·ca·o /kə'kou, kə'kāō/ ▶ **n.** (pl. **cacaos**) **1** beanlike seeds from which cocoa, cocoa butter, and chocolate are made. **2** the small tropical American evergreen tree that bears these seeds, which are contained in large, oval pods that grow on the trunk. The tree is now cultivated mainly in West Africa. ● *Theobroma cacao*, family Sterculiaceae.
– ORIGIN mid 16th cent.: via Spanish from Nahuatl *cacaua*.

cac·cia·to·re /,käcHə'tôrē, ,kacH-/ (also **cacciatora** /-,tôrə/) ▶ **adj.** [postpositive] prepared in a spicy tomato sauce with mushrooms and herbs: *chicken cacciatore.*
– ORIGIN Italian, literally 'hunter' (because of the use of ingredients that a hunter might have at hand).

ca·cha·ca /kə'sHäkə, -'sHäsə/ (also **cachaça**) ▶ **n.** a Brazilian white rum made from sugar cane.
– ORIGIN mid 19th cent.: Brazilian Portuguese, from Portuguese *cacaça* '(white) rum.'

cach·a·lot /'kasHə,lät, -,lō/ ▶ **n.** another term for SPERM WHALE.
– ORIGIN mid 18th cent.: from French, from Spanish and Portuguese *cachalote*, from *cachola* 'big head.'

cache /kasH/ ▶ **n.** a collection of items of the same type stored in a hidden or inaccessible place: *an arms cache | a cache of gold coins.* ■ a hidden or inaccessible storage place for valuables, provisions, or ammunition. ■ (also **cache memory**) Computing an auxiliary memory from which high-speed retrieval is possible.
▶ **v.** [with obj.] store away in hiding or for future use. ■ Computing store (data) in a cache memory. ■ Computing provide (hardware) with a cache memory.
– ORIGIN late 18th cent.: from French, from *cacher* 'to hide.'

ca·chec·tic /kə'kektik/ ▶ **adj.** Medicine relating to or having the symptoms of cachexia.

cache·pot /'kasH,pät, 'kasH(ə),pō/ ▶ **n.** (pl. pronunc. **same**) an ornamental holder for a flowerpot.
– ORIGIN late 19th cent.: from French *cache-pot*, from *cacher* 'to hide' + *pot* 'pot.'

cache-sexe /'kasH,seks/ ▶ **n.** (pl. **cache-sexes** pronunc. **same**) a covering for a person's genitals, typically worn by erotic dancers or tribal peoples.
– ORIGIN 1920s: from French, from *cacher* 'to hide' and *sexe* 'genitals.'

ca·chet /ka'sHā/ ▶ **n.** **1** the state of being respected or admired; prestige: *no other shipping company had quite the cachet of Cunard.* **2** a distinguishing mark or seal. ■ Philately a printed design added to an envelope to commemorate a special event. **3** a flat capsule enclosing a dose of unpleasant-tasting medicine.
– ORIGIN early 17th cent.: from French, from *cacher* in the sense 'to press,' based on Latin *coactare* 'constrain.'

ca·chex·i·a /kə'keksēə/ ▶ **n.** Medicine weakness and wasting of the body due to severe chronic illness.
– ORIGIN mid 16th cent.: via late Latin from Greek *kakhexia*, from *kakos* 'bad' + *hexis* 'habit.'

cach·in·nate /'kakə,nāt/ ▶ **v.** [no obj.] literary laugh loudly.
– DERIVATIVES **cach·in·na·tion** /,kakə'nāsHən/ **n.**
– ORIGIN early 19th cent.: from Latin *cachinnat-* 'laughed loudly,' from the verb *cachinnare*, of imitative origin.

ca·chou /ka'sHoo, 'kasHoo/ ▶ **n.** (pl. **cachous**) **1** dated a pleasant-smelling lozenge sucked to mask bad breath. **2** var. of CATECHU.
– ORIGIN late 16th cent. (in the sense 'catechu'): from French, from Portuguese *cachu*, from Malay *kacu*. The 'lozenge' sense dates from the early 18th cent.

ca·chu·cha /kə'cHoocHə/ ▶ **n.** a lively Spanish solo dance in triple time, accompanied by castanets.
– ORIGIN Spanish.

ca·cique /kə'sēk/ ▶ **n.** **1** (in Latin America or the Spanish-speaking Caribbean) a native chief. **2** (in Spain or Latin America) a local political boss.
– ORIGIN mid 16th cent.: from Spanish or French, from Taino.

cack·le /'kakəl/ ▶ **v.** [no obj.] (of a bird, typically a hen or goose) give a raucous, clucking cry: *the hen was cackling as if demented* | (as adj. **cackling**) *cackling, whooping cries.* ■ make a harsh sound resembling such a cry when laughing: *she cackled with laughter* | [with direct speech] *"Ah ha!" he cackled.*

PRONUNCIATION KEY ə *ago, up*; ər *over, fur*; a *hat*; ā *ate*; ä *car*; e *let*; ē *see*; i *fit*; ī *by*; NG *sing*; ō *go*; ô *law, for*; oi *toy*; oo *good*; oo *goo*; ou *out*; TH *thin*; TH *then*; ZH *vision*

C

▶ n. the raucous clucking cry of a bird such as a hen or a goose. ■ a harsh laugh resembling such a cry: *her delighted cackle.*
– ORIGIN Middle English: probably from Middle Low German *kākelen*, partly imitative, reinforced by *kāke* 'jaw, cheek.'

cac·o·de·mon /ˌkakəˈdēmən/ ▶ n. a malevolent spirit or person.
– ORIGIN late 16th cent.: from Greek *kakodaimōn*, from *kakos* 'bad' + *daimōn* 'spirit.'

C

cac·o·dyl /ˈkakəˌdil/ ▶ n. Chemistry a malodorous, toxic, spontaneously flammable liquid compound containing arsenic. ● Chem. formula: $((CH_3)_2As)_2$. ■ [as modifier] of or denoting the radical $-As(CH_3)_2$, derived from this.
– ORIGIN mid 19th cent.: from Greek *kakōdēs* 'stinking' (from *kakos* 'bad') + -YL.

cac·o·dyl·ic ac·id /ˌkakəˈdilik/ ▶ n. Chemistry a toxic crystalline acid containing arsenic, used as a herbicide. ● Chem. formula: $(CH_3)_2AsO(OH)$.
– DERIVATIVES **cac·o·dyl·ate** /ˌkakəˈdilˌāt/ n.

cac·o·e·thes /ˌkakōˈwēTHēz/ ▶ n. [in sing.] rare an irresistible urge to do something inadvisable.
– ORIGIN mid 16th cent.: via Latin from Greek *kakoēthes* 'ill-disposed,' from *kakos* 'bad' + *ēthos* 'disposition.'

ca·cog·ra·phy /kəˈkägrəfē/ ▶ n. archaic bad handwriting or spelling.
– DERIVATIVES **ca·cog·ra·pher** /-fər/ n.
– ORIGIN late 16th cent.: from Greek *kakos* 'bad,' on the pattern of *orthography*.

ca·col·o·gy /kəˈkäləjē/ ▶ n. archaic bad choice of words or poor pronunciation.
– ORIGIN late 18th cent.: via late Latin from Greek *kakologia* 'vituperation,' from *kakos* 'bad.'

cac·o·mis·tle /ˈkakəˌmisəl/ ▶ n. a nocturnal raccoonlike animal with a dark-ringed tail, found in North and Central America. ● Genus *Bassariscus*, family Procyonidae: two species, in particular *B. sumichrasti* of Central America. See also RING-TAILED CAT.
– ORIGIN mid 19th cent.: from Latin American Spanish *cacomixtle*, from Nahuatl *tlacomiztli*.

ca·coph·o·nous /kəˈkäfənəs/ ▶ adj. involving or producing a harsh, discordant mixture of sounds: *the cacophonous sound of slot machines.*

ca·coph·o·ny /kəˈkäfənē/ ▶ n. (pl. **cacophonies**) a harsh, discordant mixture of sounds: *a cacophony of deafening alarm bells* | figurative *a cacophony of architectural styles* | *songs of unrelieved cacophony.*
– ORIGIN mid 17th cent.: from French *cacophonie*, from Greek *kakophōnia*, from *kakophōnos* 'ill-sounding,' from *kakos* 'bad' + *phōnē* 'sound.'

cac·tus /ˈkaktəs/ ▶ n. (pl. **cacti** /-tī, -tē/ or **cactuses**) a succulent plant with a thick, fleshy stem that typically bears spines, lacks leaves, and has brilliantly colored flowers. Cacti are native to arid regions of the New World and are cultivated elsewhere, esp. as houseplants. ● Family Cactaceae: numerous genera and species.
– DERIVATIVES **cac·ta·ceous** /kakˈtāSHəs/ adj.
– ORIGIN early 17th cent. (in the sense 'cardoon'): from Latin, from Greek *kaktos* 'cardoon.'

cac·tus dahl·ia ▶ n. a dahlia of a variety that has rolled petals, giving the flower a prickly appearance.

cac·tus wren ▶ n. the largest North American wren, with a distinct white eyestripe and spotted tail feathers, found in the southwestern US and Mexico. ● *Campylorhynchus brunneicapillus*, family Troglodytidae.

cactus wren

ca·cu·mi·nal /kəˈkyōōmənl/ ▶ adj. Phonetics another term for RETROFLEX.
– ORIGIN mid 19th cent.: from Latin *cacuminare* 'make pointed' (from *cacumen, cacumin-* 'top, summit') + -AL.

CAD /kad/ ▶ abbr. computer-aided design.

cad /kad/ ▶ n. dated or humorous a man who behaves dishonorably, esp. toward a woman: *her adulterous cad of a husband.*
– DERIVATIVES **cad·dish** adj., **cad·dish·ly** adv., **cad·dish·ness** n.
– ORIGIN late 18th cent. (denoting a passenger picked up by the driver of a horse-drawn coach for personal profit): abbreviation of CADDIE or CADET.

ca·das·tral /kəˈdastrəl/ ▶ adj. (of a map or survey) showing the extent, value, and ownership of land, esp. for taxation.
– ORIGIN mid 19th cent.: from French, from *cadastre* 'register of property,' from Provençal *cadastro*, from Italian *catastro* (earlier *catastico*), from late Greek *katastikhon* 'list, register,' from *kata stikhon* 'line by line.'

ca·das·tre /kəˈdas,tər/ ▶ n. a register of property showing the extent, value, and ownership of land for taxation.

ca·dav·er /kəˈdavər/ ▶ n. Medicine or literary a corpse.
– DERIVATIVES **ca·dav·er·ic** /-rik/ adj.
– ORIGIN late Middle English: from Latin, from *cadere* 'to fall.'

ca·dav·er·ine /kəˈdavəˌrēn/ ▶ n. a toxic liquid base, 1,5-diaminopentane, formed by the putrefaction of proteins. ● Chem. formula: $H_2N(CH_2)_5NH_2$.

ca·dav·er·ous /kəˈdavərəs/ ▶ adj. resembling a corpse in being very pale, thin, or bony: *he had a cadaverous appearance.*
– ORIGIN late Middle English: from Latin *cadaverosus*, from *cadaver* 'corpse.'

CADCAM /ˈkadˌkam/ (also **CAD/CAM**) ▶ abbr. computer-aided design, computer-aided manufacturing.

cad·die /ˈkadē/ (also **caddy**) ▶ n. (pl. **caddies**) a person who carries a golfer's clubs and provides other assistance during a match.
▶ v. (**caddied, caddying**) [no obj.] work as a caddie.
– ORIGIN mid 17th cent. (originally Scots): from French CADET. The original term denoted a gentleman who joined the army without a commission, intending to learn the profession and follow a military career, later coming to mean 'odd-job man' The current sense dates from the late 18th cent.

cad·dis·fly /ˈkadis,flī/ (also **caddis fly**) ▶ n. (pl. **caddisflies**) a small, mothlike insect with an aquatic larva that typically builds a protective, portable case of sticks, stones, and other particles. Some kinds have been traditionally used as bait by fishermen. ● Order Trichoptera: several families.
– ORIGIN mid 17th cent.: of unknown origin.

cad·dis worm /ˈkadis/ ▶ n. the soft-bodied, aquatic larva of a caddisfly, often used as fishing bait.

Cad·do·an /ˈkadō-ən/ ▶ adj. relating to or denoting a group of American Indian peoples formerly inhabiting the Midwest, or their languages.
▶ n. **1** a member of any of these peoples.
2 the family of languages spoken by these peoples, which includes Pawnee and may be related to Siouan and Iroquoian.
– ORIGIN from Caddo (a language of this family) *kaduhdacu*, denoting a band belonging to this group, + -AN.

cad·dy¹ /ˈkadē/ ▶ n. (pl. **caddies**) [usu. with modifier] a small storage container, typically one with divisions: *a tool caddy.* See also TEA CADDY.
– ORIGIN late 18th cent.: from earlier *catty*, denoting a unit of weight of $1^1/_3$ lb. (0.61 kg.), from Malay *kati*.

cad·dy² ▶ n. & v. variant spelling of CADDIE.

Cade /kād/, Jack (died 1450), Irish rebel; full name *John Cade*. In 1450, he assumed the name of Mortimer and led the Kentish rebels against Henry VI. They occupied London for three days and executed the treasurer of England and the sheriff of Kent.

ca·delle /kəˈdel/ ▶ n. a small, dark beetle that is frequently found in food storage, where it scavenges and preys on other insects. ● *Tenebroides mauritanicus*, family Cleridae.
– ORIGIN mid 19th cent.: from French, based on Latin *catella, catellus* 'young (of an animal), little dog.'

ca·dence /ˈkādns/ ▶ n. **1** a modulation or inflection of the voice: *the measured cadences that he employed in the Senate.* ■ such a modulation in reading aloud as implied by the structure and ordering of words and phrases in written text: *the dry cadences of the essay.* ■ a fall in pitch of the voice at the end of a phrase or sentence. ■ rhythm: *the thumping cadence of the engines* | *try to vary your cadence during a run.*
2 Music a sequence of notes or chords comprising the close of a musical phrase: *the final cadences of the Prelude.*
– DERIVATIVES **ca·denced** adj.
– ORIGIN late Middle English (in the sense 'rhythm or metrical beat'): via Old French from Italian *cadenza*, based on Latin *cadere* 'to fall.'

ca·den·cy /ˈkādnsē/ ▶ n. chiefly Heraldry the status of a younger branch of a family.
– ORIGIN early 17th cent. (in the sense 'rhythm or metrical beat'): based on Latin *cadent-* 'falling,' from the verb *cadere*. The current sense is apparently by association with CADET.

ca·den·tial /kāˈdenCHəl/ ▶ adj. of or relating to a cadenza or cadence.
– ORIGIN mid 19th cent.: from CADENCE, on the pattern of pairs such as *essence, essential*.

ca·den·za /kəˈdenzə/ ▶ n. Music a virtuoso solo passage inserted into a movement in a concerto or other work, typically near the end.
– ORIGIN mid 18th cent.: from Italian (see CADENCE).

ca·det /kəˈdet/ ▶ n. **1** a young trainee in the armed services or police force: *an air force cadet.* ■ a student in training at a military school.
2 formal or archaic a younger son or daughter. ■ [usu. as modifier] a junior branch of a family: *a cadet branch of the family.*
– DERIVATIVES **ca·det·ship** /-ˌSHip/ n.
– ORIGIN early 17th cent. (sense 2): from French, from Gascon dialect *capdet*, a diminutive based on Latin *caput* 'head.' The notion "little head" or "inferior head" gave rise to that of 'younger, junior.'

cadge /kaj/ ▶ v. [with obj.] informal ask for or obtain (something to which one is not strictly entitled): *he eats whenever he can cadge a meal* | [no obj.] *they cadge, but timidly.*
▶ n. Falconry a padded wooden frame on which hooded hawks are carried to the field. [apparently an alteration of CAGE, perhaps confused with the dialect verb *cadge* 'carry around.']
– PHRASES **on the cadge** Brit. informal looking for an opportunity to obtain something without paying for it.
– DERIVATIVES **cadg·er** n.
– ORIGIN early 17th cent. (in the dialect sense 'carry around'): back-formation from the noun *cadger*, which dates from the late 15th cent., denoting (in northern English and Scots) an itinerant dealer, whence the verb sense 'hawk, peddle,' giving rise to the current verb senses from the early 19th cent.

ca·di /ˈkädē, ˈkā-/ (also **kadi**) ▶ n. (pl. **cadis**) (in Islamic countries) a judge.
– ORIGIN late 16th cent.: from Arabic *ḳāḍī*, from *ḳaḍā* 'to judge.'

Ca·dil·lac¹ /ˈkädēˈyäk, ˈkadlˌak/, Antoine Laumet de La Mothe (1658–1730), French soldier and colonialist. He founded military posts at Mackinac 1694 and Detroit 1701; from 1713 to about 1716 or 1717 he served as governor of Louisiana.

Ca·dil·lac² ▶ n. **1** trademark a large luxury car that is the most prestigious brand of General Motors.
2 something that is an outstanding example of its kind, esp. in terms of luxury, quality, or size: *the aircraft is widely regarded as the Cadillac of commuter planes.*
– ORIGIN from Antoine Laumet de La Mothe CADILLAC¹.

Cad·il·lac Moun·tain /ˈkadlˌak/ a peak on Mount Desert Island in southeastern Maine, within Acadia National Park. At 1,532 feet (467 m), it is the highest point on the US east coast.

Ca·diz /kəˈdiz, ˈkādiz, ˈkä-/ a city and port on the southwestern coast of Spain; pop. 127,200 (2008). Spanish name **Cádiz**.

Cad·me·an /kadˈmēən, ˈkadmēən/ ▶ adj. of or relating to Cadmus.

cad·mi·um /ˈkadmēəm/ ▶ n. the chemical element of atomic number 48, a silvery-white metal. (Symbol: **Cd**)

> Cadmium occurs naturally in zinc ores and is obtained as a byproduct of zinc smelting. It is used as a component in low melting point alloys and as a corrosion-resistant coating on other metals.

– ORIGIN early 19th cent.: from Latin *cadmia* 'calamine,' so named because it is found with calamine in zinc ore. Compare with CALAMINE.

cad·mi·um cell ▶ n. a primary electric cell with a cathode of cadmium amalgam and an electrolyte of saturated cadmium sulfate solution, used in laboratories as a standard of electromotive force.

cad·mi·um yel·low ▶ n. a bright yellow pigment containing cadmium sulfide. Deeper versions are called **cadmium orange**; the addition of cadmium selenide gives **cadmium red**. ■ a bright yellow color.

Cad·mus /ˈkadməs/ Greek Mythology the brother of Europa and traditional founder of Thebes in Boeotia. He killed a dragon that guarded a spring, and when (on Athena's advice) he sowed the dragon's teeth, there came up a harvest of armed men; he disposed of the majority by setting them to fight one another, and the survivors formed the ancestors of the Theban nobility.

ca·dre /ˈkadrē, ˈkäd-, -ˌrā/ ▶ n. a small group of people specially trained for a particular purpose or profession: *a small cadre of scientists.* ■ a group of activists in a communist or other revolutionary organization. ■ a member of such a group.

– ORIGIN mid 19th cent.: from French, from Italian *quadro*, from Latin *quadrus* 'square.'

ca·du·ce·us /kə'd(y)o͞osēəs, -SHəs/ ▶ **n.** (pl. **caducei** /-sē,ī, -SHē,ī/) an ancient Greek or Roman herald's wand, typically one with two serpents twined around it, carried by the messenger god Hermes or Mercury. ■ a representation of this, traditionally associated with healing.
– ORIGIN Latin, from Doric Greek *karukeion*, from Greek *kērux* 'herald.'

caduceus

ca·du·ci·ty /kə'd(y)o͞ositē/ ▶ **n.** archaic the infirmity of old age; senility. ■ literary frailty or transitory nature: *read these books and reflect on their caducity.*
– ORIGIN mid 18th cent.: from French *caducité*, from *caduc*, from Latin *caducus* 'liable to fall,' from *cadere* 'to fall.'

ca·du·cous /kə'd(y)o͞okəs/ ▶ **adj.** chiefly Botany (of an organ or part) easily detached and shed at an early stage.
– ORIGIN late 17th cent. (in the sense 'epileptic'): from Latin *caducus* 'liable to fall' (from *cadere* 'to fall') + **-OUS**.

CAE ▶ **abbr.** computer-aided engineering.

cae·cil·i·an /si'silyən/ (also **coecilian**) ▶ **n.** Zoology a burrowing wormlike amphibian of a tropical order distinguished by poorly developed eyes and the lack of limbs. ● Order Gymnophiona (or Apoda): five families.
– ORIGIN from modern Latin *Caecilia* (genus name), from Latin *caecilia* 'slow-worm' + **-AN**.

cae·cum ▶ **n.** (pl. **caeca**) /-kə/ British spelling of **CECUM**.

Caed·mon /'kadmən/ (7th century), Anglo-Saxon monk and poet. He is said to have been an illiterate herdsman who was inspired in a vision to compose poetry on biblical themes.

Cae·lum /'sēləm/ Astronomy a small and faint southern constellation (the Chisel), next to Eridanus. ■ (as genitive **Caeli** /'sēlī, -lē/) used with a preceding letter or numeral to designate a star in this constellation: *the star Beta Caeli.*
– ORIGIN Latin.

Caen /kän/ an industrial city and river port in northern France, in Normandy, on the Orne River, capital of the region of Basse-Normandie; pop. 113,249 (2006).

Caer·dydd /kär'dēT͟H/ Welsh name for **CARDIFF**.

Caer·phil·ly /kär'filē/ ▶ **n.** a kind of mild white cheese, originally made in Caerphilly in Wales.

Cae·sar[1] /'sēzər/, Gaius Julius (100–44 BC), Roman general and statesman. He established the First Triumvirate with Pompey and Crassus in 60 and became consul in 59. Between 58 and 51 he fought the Gallic Wars, invaded Britain 55–54, and acquired immense power. After civil war with Pompey, which ended in Pompey's defeat at Pharsalus in 48, Caesar became dictator of the Roman Empire. He was murdered on the Ides (15th) of March in a conspiracy led by Brutus and Cassius.

Cae·sar[2], Sid (1922–), US comedian and actor; full name *Isaac Sidney Caesar*. He costarred in the live television sketch comedy *Your Show of Shows* (1950–54) with comedienne **Imogene Coca** (1908–2001).

Cae·sar[3] ▶ **n. 1** a title used by Roman emperors, esp. those from Augustus to Hadrian. ■ an autocrat.
2 Medicine, informal a Caesarean section.
– PHRASES **Caesar's wife** a person who is required to be above suspicion. [with reference to Plutarch's *Caesar* (x. 6) 'I thought my wife ought not even to be under suspicion.']
– ORIGIN Middle English: from Latin *Caesar*, family name of the Roman statesman Gaius Julius **CAESAR**[1].

Caes·a·re·a /,sēzə'rēə, ,ses-, ,sez-/ an ancient port on the Mediterranean coast of Israel, one of the principal cities of Roman Palestine.

Caes·a·re·a Maz·a·ca /'mazəkə/ former name for **KAYSERI**.

cae·sar·e·an /si'ze(ə)rēən/ ▶ **adj. & n. 1** (also **Caesarean**) variant spelling of **CESAREAN**.
2 (**Caesarean**) of or connected with Julius Caesar or the Caesars.

Caes·a·re·a Phi·lip·pi /'filə,pī, fə'lip,ī/ a city in ancient Palestine, on the site of the present-day village of Baniyas in the Golan Heights.

Cae·sar sal·ad ▶ **n.** a salad consisting of romaine lettuce and croutons served with a dressing of olive oil, lemon juice, raw egg, Worcestershire sauce, and seasoning.

– ORIGIN named after *Caesar* Cardini, the Mexican restaurateur who invented it in 1924.

cae·si·um ▶ **n.** British spelling of **CESIUM**.

cae·su·ra /si'ZHo͝orə, -'zo͝orə/ ▶ **n.** (in Greek and Latin verse) a break between words within a metrical foot. ■ (in modern verse) a pause near the middle of a line. ■ any interruption or break: *an unaccountable caesura: no deaths were reported in the newspapers.*
– DERIVATIVES **cae·su·ral** **adj.**
– ORIGIN mid 16th cent.: from Latin, from *caes-* 'cut, hewn,' from the verb *caedere*.

CAF ▶ **abbr.** cost and freight.

ca·fard /ka'fär/ ▶ **n.** depression; melancholia.
– ORIGIN from French.

CAFE ▶ **abbr.** Corporate Average Fuel Economy.

ca·fe /ka'fā, kə-/ (also **café**) ▶ **n. 1** a small restaurant selling light meals and drinks.
2 a bar or nightclub.
3 (**café**) a serving of coffee, esp. prepared European-style: [in combination] *an assortment of cappuccinos and café mochas.*
– ORIGIN early 19th cent.: French, 'coffee or coffeehouse.'

ca·fé A·mer·i·ca·no ▶ **n.** see **AMERICANO**.

ca·fé au lait /,ka,fā ō 'lā/ ▶ **n.** coffee with milk. ■ the light brown color of this: [as modifier] *smooth café au lait skin.*
– ORIGIN French.

ca·fé con le·che /'kafā kän 'leCHā, ka'fā-, kə'fā-/ ▶ **n.** coffee with milk.
– ORIGIN Spanish.

ca·fé noir /'ka,fā 'nwär/ ▶ **n.** black coffee.
– ORIGIN French.

caf·e·te·ri·a /,kafi'ti(ə)rēə/ ▶ **n.** a restaurant or dining room in a school or a business in which customers serve themselves or are served from a counter and pay before eating.
– ORIGIN mid 19th cent.: from Latin American Spanish *cafetería* 'coffee shop.'

caf·e·te·ri·a ben·e·fit ▶ **n.** an employee benefit selected from a variety of offerings under a fringe-benefit plan that can be tailored to fit individual needs.

ca·fet·i·ère /,kafə'tye(ə)r/ ▶ **n.** a coffee pot containing a plunger made of fine mesh with which the grounds are pushed to the bottom when the coffee is ready to be poured.
– ORIGIN mid 19th cent.: from French, from *café* 'coffee.'

caf·fein·at·ed /'kafə,nātid/ ▶ **adj.** (of coffee or tea) containing the natural amount of caffeine, or with caffeine added.

caf·feine /ka'fēn, 'kaf,ēn/ ▶ **n.** a crystalline compound that is found esp. in tea and coffee plants and is a stimulant of the central nervous system. ● An alkaloid, 1,3,7-trimethylxanthine; chem. formula: $C_8H_{10}N_4O_2$.
– ORIGIN mid 19th cent.: from French *caféine*, from *café* 'coffee.'

caf·tan ▶ **n.** variant spelling of **KAFTAN**.

Ca·ga·yan Is·lands /,kägə'yän/ a group of seven small islands in the western Philippines, in the Sulu Sea.

Cage /kāj/, John (Milton) (1912–92), US composer, pianist, and writer. He was noted for his experimental approach, which included the use of aleatory music and periods of silence. He also experimented with musical instruments.

cage /kāj/ ▶ **n.** a structure of bars or wires in which birds or other animals are confined: *she kept a canary in a cage* | figurative *his cage of loneliness.* ■ a prison cell or camp. ■ an open framework forming the compartment in an elevator. ■ a structure of crossing bars or wires designed to hold or support something. ■ Baseball a portable backstop situated behind the batter during batting practice. ■ (in hockey and other games) a goal made from a network frame. ■ an indoor athletic facility with areas fenced off for security.
▶ **v.** [with obj.] (usu. **be caged**) confine in or as in a cage: *the parrot screamed, furious at being caged* | (as adj. **caged**) *a caged bird.* ■ informal put in prison.
– ORIGIN Middle English: via Old French from Latin *cavea*.

cag·ey /'kājē/ (also **cagy**) ▶ **adj.** informal reluctant to give information owing to caution or suspicion: *manufacturers are cagey about the recipes they use to create a wine.*
– DERIVATIVES **cag·i·ly** /'kājilē/ **adv.**, **cag·i·ness** (also **cageyness**) **n.**
– ORIGIN early 20th cent. (originally US): of unknown origin.

Ca·glia·ri /,käl'yärē/ the capital of the Italian island of Sardinia, a port on the southern coast; pop. 157,297 (2008).

Cag·ney /'kagnē/, James (1899–1986), US actor. He is noted for playing gangster roles in movies such as *The Public Enemy* (1931) and *Angels with Dirty Faces* (1938). He was also a skilled dancer and comedian who received an Academy Award for his lead role in the musical *Yankee Doodle Dandy* (1942).

ca·goule /kə'go͞ol/ ▶ **n.** a lightweight, hooded, thigh-length waterproof jacket.
– ORIGIN 1950s: from French, literally 'cowl.'

ca·hier /kä'yā/ ▶ **n.** (pl. **same**) an exercise book or notebook.
– ORIGIN mid 19th cent.: from French; compare with **QUIRE**.

Ca·ho·kia /kə'hōkēə/ a village in southwestern Illinois, across the Mississippi River from St. Louis in Missouri; pop. 15,103 (est. 2008). The Cahokia Mounds, major pre-Columbian earthworks, are to the northeast.

ca·hoots /kə'ho͞ots/ ▶ **plural n.** (in phrase **in cahoots**) informal colluding or conspiring together secretly: *the area is dominated by guerrillas in cahoots with drug traffickers.*
– ORIGIN early 19th cent. (originally US): of unknown origin.

ca·houn ▶ **n.** variant spelling of **COHUNE**.

ca·how /kə'hou/ ▶ **n.** a large Atlantic petrel that breeds in Bermuda. It is an endangered species. ● *Pterodroma cahow*, family Procellariidae.
– ORIGIN early 17th cent.: imitative of its call.

CAI ▶ **abbr.** computer-assisted (or -aided) instruction.

cai·man /'kāmən/ (also **cayman**) ▶ **n.** a semiaquatic reptile similar to the alligator but with a heavily armored belly, native to tropical America. ● *Caiman* and other genera, family Alligatoridae: three species, in particular the **spectacled caiman** (*C. sclerops*).
– ORIGIN late 16th cent.: from Spanish *caimán*, Portuguese *caimão*, from Carib *acayuman*.

Cain /kān/ (in the Bible) the eldest son of Adam and Eve and murderer of his brother Abel.
– PHRASES **raise Cain** informal create trouble or a commotion.

Caine /kān/, Sir Michael (1933–), English actor; born *Maurice Micklewhite*. Notable movies: *The Ipcress File* (1965), *Educating Rita* (1983), *Hannah and Her Sisters* (1986), and *The Cider House Rules* (1999).

Cai·no·zo·ic /,kānə'zō-ik/ ▶ **adj.** variant spelling of **CENOZOIC**.

cai·pi·ri·nha /,kīpē'rēnyä, ,kīpə'rinyə/ ▶ **n.** a Brazilian cocktail made with cachaca, lime or lemon juice, sugar, and crushed ice.
– ORIGIN Brazilian Portuguese, from *caipira* 'yokel.'

ca·ique /kä'ēk, kīk/ ▶ **n. 1** a light rowboat used on the Bosporus.
2 a small eastern Mediterranean sailing ship.
– ORIGIN early 17th cent.: from French *caïque*, from Italian *caicco*, from Turkish *kayık*.

cairn /ke(ə)rn/ ▶ **n. 1** a mound of rough stones built as a memorial or landmark, typically on a hilltop or skyline. ■ a prehistoric burial mound made of stones.
2 (also **cairn terrier**) a small terrier of a breed with short legs, a longish body, and a shaggy coat. [perhaps so named from being used to hunt among cairns.]
– ORIGIN late Middle English: from Scottish Gaelic *carn*.

cairn·gorm /'ke(ə)rn'gôrm, kern'gôrm/ ▶ **n.** another term for **SMOKY QUARTZ**.
– ORIGIN late 18th cent.: named after the **CAIRNGORM MOUNTAINS**.

Cairn·gorm Moun·tains /'ke(ə)rn'gôrm, kern'gôrm/ (also **the Cairngorms**) a mountain range in northern Scotland.
– ORIGIN from Scottish Gaelic *carn gorm* 'blue cairn.'

Cai·ro /'kīrō/ the capital of Egypt, a port on the Nile River near the head of its delta; pop. 6,758,600 (est. 2006). Arabic name **AL-QAHIRA**.
– DERIVATIVES **Cai·rene** /kī'rēn/ **adj. & n.**

cais·son /'kā,sän, 'kāsən/ ▶ **n. 1** a large watertight chamber, open at the bottom from which the water is kept out by air pressure and in which construction work may be carried out under water. ■ a floating vessel or watertight structure used as a gate across the entrance of a dry dock or basin.
2 historical a chest or wagon for holding or conveying ammunition.
– ORIGIN late 17th cent.: from French, literally 'large chest,' from Italian *cassone*, the spelling having been altered in French by association with *caisse* 'case.'

cais·son dis·ease ▶ **n.** another term for **DECOMPRESSION SICKNESS**.

C

cai·tiff /ˈkātif/ ▶ **n.** archaic a contemptible or cowardly person: [as modifier] *a caitiff knight.*
– ORIGIN Middle English (denoting a captive or prisoner): from Old French *caitif* 'captive,' based on Latin *captivus* '(person) taken captive' (see **CAPTIVE**).

ca·jole /kəˈjōl/ ▶ **v.** [with obj.] (often **cajole someone into doing something**) persuade someone to do something by sustained coaxing or flattery: *he hoped to cajole her into selling the house* | [no obj.] *she pleaded and cajoled as she tried to win his support.*
– DERIVATIVES **ca·jole·ment n.**
– ORIGIN mid 17th cent.: from French *cajoler.*

ca·jol·er·y /kəˈjōl(ə)rē/ ▶ **n.** coaxing or flattery intended to persuade someone to do something: *she uses cajolery, deception, and manipulation to get what she wants.*

Ca·jun /ˈkājən/ ▶ **n.** a member of any of the largely self-contained communities in the bayou areas of southern Louisiana formed by descendants of French Canadians, speaking an archaic form of French.
▶ **adj.** of or relating to the Cajuns, esp. with reference to their folk music (typically featuring the concertina, accordion, and fiddle) or spicy cuisine.
– ORIGIN alteration of **ACADIAN**.

Ca·jun Coun·try a region of southern Louisiana that is inhabited largely by Cajuns, who are descendants of 18th-century exiles from Acadia, now Nova Scotia.

caj·u·put /ˈkajəpət, -ˌpo͝ot/ (also **cajeput**) ▶ **n. 1** (also **cajuput oil**) an aromatic medicinal oil that is similar to eucalyptus oil, obtained from a tree of the myrtle family.
2 a chiefly Australasian tree related to the bottlebrushes, having papery bark and yielding this aromatic oil. Also called **PAPERBARK**. ● Genus *Melaleuca*, family Myrtaceae: *M. cajuputi*, which produces cajuput oil, and *M. quinquenervia.*
– ORIGIN late 18th cent.: from Malay *kayu putih*, literally 'white tree.'

cake /kāk/ ▶ **n.** an item of soft, sweet food made from a mixture of flour, shortening, eggs, sugar, and other ingredients, baked and often decorated: *a carrot cake* | [as modifier] *cake pans* | *a mouthful of cake.* ■ an item of savory food formed into a flat, round shape, and typically baked or fried: *crab cakes.* ■ a pancake: *buckwheat cakes.* ■ a flattish, compact mass of something, esp. soap: ***a cake of soap.***
▶ **v.** [with obj.] (of a thick or sticky substance that hardens when dry) cover and become encrusted on (the surface of an object): *a pair of boots caked with mud.* ■ [no obj.] (of a thick or sticky substance) dry or harden into a solid mass: *the blood under his nose was beginning to cake.*
– PHRASES **cakes and ale** dated merrymaking. **a piece of cake** informal something easily achieved: *I never said that training him would be a piece of cake.* **take the cake** surpass or exceed all others: *of all the hard-hearted women, she takes the cake.* **you can't have your cake and eat it (too)** proverb you can't enjoy both of two desirable but mutually exclusive alternatives.
– ORIGIN Middle English (denoting a small flat bread roll): of Scandinavian origin; related to Swedish *kaka* and Danish *kage.*

cake·walk /ˈkākˌwôk/ ▶ **n. 1** informal an absurdly or surprisingly easy task: *winning the game won't be a cakewalk.*
2 a strutting dance popular at the end of the 19th century, developed from a black-American contest in graceful walking that had a cake as a prize.
▶ **v.** [no obj.] **1** informal achieve or win something easily: *he cakewalked to a 5-1 triumph.*
2 walk or dance in the manner of a cakewalk: *a troupe of clowns cakewalked by.*

CAL ▶ **abbr.** computer-assisted (or -aided) learning.

Cal ▶ **abbr.** large calorie(s).

cal (also **cal.**) ▶ **abbr.** ■ calendar. ■ caliber. ■ calorie. ■ small calorie(s).

Cal. ▶ **abbr.** California.

Cal·a·bar /ˈkaləˌbär, ˌkaləˈbär/ a seaport in southeastern Nigeria; pop. 429,700 (est. 2005).

Cal·a·bar bean ▶ **n.** the poisonous seed of a tropical West African climbing plant, containing physostigmine and formerly used for tribal ordeals. ● The plant is *Physostigma venosum*, family Leguminosae.
– ORIGIN late 19th cent.: named after **CALABAR**.

cal·a·bash /ˈkaləˌbasн/ ▶ **n.** (also **calabash tree**) an evergreen tropical American tree that bears fruit in the form of large woody gourds. ● *Crescentia cujete*, family Bignoniaceae. ■ a gourd from this tree. ■ a water container, tobacco pipe, or other object made from the dried shell of this or a similar gourd.
– ORIGIN mid 17th cent.: from French *calebasse*, from Spanish *calabaza*, perhaps from Persian *ḵarbuz* 'melon.'

ca·la·ba·za /ˌkaləˈbäzə/ ▶ **n.** another term for **CALABASH**.

cal·a·boose /ˈkaləˌbo͞os/ ▶ **n.** informal a prison.
– ORIGIN late 18th cent.: from black French *calabouse*, from Spanish *calabozo* 'dungeon.'

Ca·la·bri·a /kəˈläbrēə, -ˈlā-/ a region of southwestern Italy, forming the "toe" of the Italian peninsula; capital, Catanzaro.
– DERIVATIVES **Ca·la·bri·an adj. & n.**

ca·la·di·um /kəˈlādēəm/ ▶ **n.** (pl. **caladiums**) a tropical South American plant of the arum family that is cultivated for its brilliantly colored ornamental foliage. ● Genus *Caladium*, family Araceae.
– ORIGIN modern Latin, from Malay *keladi.*

Cal·ais /kaˈlā, ˈkalā/ a ferry port in northern France; pop. 75,790 (2006).

cal·a·man·co /ˌkaləˈmaNGkō/ ▶ **n.** (pl. **calamancoes**) historical a glossy woolen cloth checkered on one side only.
– ORIGIN late 16th cent.: of unknown origin.

cal·a·man·der /ˈkaləˌmandər/ (also **calamander wood**) ▶ **n.** another term for **COROMANDEL**.
– ORIGIN early 19th cent.: from Sinhalese *kalu-madīriya*, perhaps from *Coromandel ebony* (see **COROMANDEL**), changed by association with Sinhalese *kalu* 'black.'

ca·la·ma·ri /ˌkäləˈmärē, ˌkalə-/ (also **calamares** /ˌkäləˈmārēs, ˌkalə-/) ▶ **n.** squid served as food.
– ORIGIN Italian, plural of *calamaro*, from medieval Latin *calamarium* 'pen case,' from Greek *kalamos* 'pen' (with reference to the squid's long tapering internal shell and its ink). The variant *calamares* is Spanish.

cal·a·mi /ˈkaləˌmī, -ˌmē/ plural form of **CALAMUS**.

cal·a·mine /ˈkaləˌmīn/ ▶ **n.** a pink powder consisting of zinc carbonate and ferric oxide, used to make a soothing lotion or ointment. ■ dated smithsonite or a similar zinc ore.
– ORIGIN late Middle English: via Old French from medieval Latin *calamina*, alteration of Latin *cadmia* 'calamine,' from Greek *kadmeia (gē)* 'Cadmean (earth),' from *Kadmos* 'Cadmus' (see **CADMUS**).

cal·a·mint /ˈkaləˌmint/ ▶ **n.** an aromatic Eurasian herbaceous plant or shrub with blue or lilac flowers. ● Genus *Calamintha*, family Labiatae.
– ORIGIN Middle English: from Old French *calament*, from medieval Latin *calamentum*, from late Latin *calaminthe*, from Greek *kalaminthē.*

cal·a·mite /ˈkaləˌmīt/ ▶ **n.** a jointed-stemmed swamp plant of an extinct group related to the horsetails, growing to a height of 60 feet (18 m). Calamites are characteristic fossils of the Carboniferous coal measures. ● *Calamites* and other genera, family Calamitaceae, class Sphenopsida.
– ORIGIN modern Latin, from **CALAMUS**.

ca·lam·i·tous /kəˈlamitəs/ ▶ **adj.** involving calamity; catastrophic; disastrous: *such calamitous events as fires, hurricanes, and floods.*
– DERIVATIVES **ca·lam·i·tous·ly adv.**

ca·lam·i·ty /kəˈlamitē/ ▶ **n.** (pl. **calamities**) an event causing great and often sudden damage or distress; a disaster: *the fire was the latest calamity to strike the area* | *the journey had led to calamity and ruin.*
– ORIGIN late Middle English (in the sense 'disaster and distress'): from Old French *calamite*, from Latin *calamitas.*

Ca·lam·i·ty Jane /ˈjān/ (c.1852–1903), US frontierswoman; noted for her skill at shooting and riding; born *Martha Jane Cannary.* She dressed as a man and was known for her wild behavior and heavy drinking. She later joined Buffalo Bill's Wild West Show.

Calamity Jane

cal·a·mon·din /ˌkaləˈmändən/ (also **calamondin orange**) ▶ **n.** a small hybrid citrus plant that bears fragrant white flowers followed by small orange-yellow fruit, native to the Philippines and widely grown as a houseplant. ● × *Citrofortunella microcarpa* (formerly *Citrus mitis*), family Rutaceae.
– ORIGIN early 20th cent.: from Tagalog *kalamunding.*

cal·a·mus /ˈkaləməs/ ▶ **n.** (pl. **calami** /-ˌmī, -ˌmē/)
1 another term for **SWEET FLAG**. ■ (also **calamus root**) a preparation of the aromatic root of the sweet flag.
2 Zoology the hollow lower part of the shaft of a feather, which lacks barbs; a quill.
– ORIGIN late Middle English (denoting a reed or an aromatic plant mentioned in the Bible): from Latin, from Greek *kalamos.* Sense 1 dates from the mid 17th cent.

ca·lan·do /käˈländō/ ▶ **adv.** Music (esp. as a direction) gradually decreasing in tempo and volume of sound.
– ORIGIN Italian, literally 'slackening.'

ca·lan·dra /kəˈlandrə/ (also **calandra lark**) ▶ **n.** a large Eurasian lark with a stout bill and a black patch on each side of the neck. ● Genus *Melanocorypha*, family Alaudidae: two species, in particular *M. calandra.*
– ORIGIN late 16th cent.: from Old French *calandre*, via medieval Latin from Greek *kalandros.*

ca·lash /kəˈlasн/ ▶ **n.** another term for **CALÈCHE**.

cal·a·the·a /ˌkaləˈTHēə/ ▶ **n.** a tropical American plant that typically has variegated and ornamental leaves, widely grown as a greenhouse or indoor plant. ● Genus *Calathea*, family Marantaceae: many species.
– ORIGIN modern Latin, from Greek *kalathos* 'basket.'

Ca·la·ver·as Coun·ty /ˌkaləˈve(ə)rəs/ a largely rural county in east central California, in the Sierra Nevada, associated with the 1840s gold rush and the writings of Mark Twain.

calc- ▶ **comb. form** (used chiefly in geological terms) of lime or calcium: *calcalkaline.*
– ORIGIN from German *Kalk* 'lime,' with spelling influenced by Latin *calx* 'lime' (see **CALX**).

cal·cal·ka·line /kalˈkalkəlin, -ˌlīn/ ▶ **adj.** Geology (chiefly of rocks) relatively rich in both calcium and alkali metals.

cal·ca·ne·us /kalˈkānēəs/ (also **calcaneum** /-nēəm/) ▶ **n.** (pl. **calcanei** /-nēˌī, -nēˌē/ or **calcanea** /-nēə/) Anatomy the large bone forming the heel. It articulates with the cuboid bone of the foot and the talus bone of the ankle, and the Achilles tendon (or *tendo calcaneus*) is attached to it.
– DERIVATIVES **cal·ca·ne·al adj.**
– ORIGIN mid 18th cent.: from Latin.

cal·car·e·ous /kalˈke(ə)rēəs/ ▶ **adj.** containing calcium carbonate; chalky. ■ Ecology (of vegetation) occurring on chalk or limestone.
– ORIGIN late 17th cent.: from Latin *calcarius* (from *calx, calc-* 'lime') + **-EOUS**.

cal·ce·o·lar·i·a /ˌkalsēəˈle(ə)rēə/ ▶ **n.** a South American plant of the figwort family that is cultivated for its brightly colored slipper- or pouch-shaped flowers. Also called **POCKETBOOK PLANT**. ● Genus *Calceolaria*, family Scrophulariaceae.
– ORIGIN late 18th cent.: modern Latin, from Latin *calceolus*, diminutive of *calceus* 'shoe.'

cal·ces /ˈkalˌsēz/ plural form of **CALX**.

calci- ▶ **comb. form** relating to calcium or its compounds: *calcifuge.*
– ORIGIN from Latin *calx, calc-* 'lime.'

cal·cic /ˈkalsik/ ▶ **adj.** (chiefly of minerals) containing or relatively rich in calcium.

cal·ci·cole /ˈkalsiˌkōl/ ▶ **n.** Botany a plant that grows best in calcareous soil, occurring chiefly on chalk and limestone: [as modifier] *a rich calcicole flora.*
– DERIVATIVES **cal·cic·o·lous** /kalˈsikələs/ **adj.**
– ORIGIN late 19th cent.: from **CALCI-** + Latin *colere* 'inhabit.'

cal·cif·er·ol /kalˈsifəˌrôl, -ˌrōl/ ▶ **n.** Biochemistry one of the D vitamins, a sterol that is formed when its isomer ergosterol is exposed to ultraviolet light, and that is routinely added to dairy products. Also called **ERGOCALCIFEROL**, **VITAMIN D2** (see **VITAMIN D**).
– ORIGIN 1930s: from **CALCIFEROUS** + **-OL**.

cal·cif·er·ous /kalˈsifərəs/ ▶ **adj.** containing or producing calcium salts, esp. calcium carbonate.

cal·ci·fuge /ˈkalsəˌfyo͞oj/ ▶ **n.** Botany a plant that is not suited to calcareous soil: [as modifier] *calcifuge plants such as heathers.*

cal·ci·fy /ˈkalsəˌfī/ ▶ **v.** (**calcifies**, **calcifying**, **calcified**) [with obj.] (usu. as adj. **calcified**) harden by deposition of or conversion into calcium carbonate or some other insoluble calcium compounds: *calcified cartilage.*
– DERIVATIVES **cal·cif·ic** /kalˈsifik/ **adj.**, **cal·ci·fi·ca·tion** /ˌkalsəfiˈkāsнən/ **n.**

cal·ci·mine /ˈkalsəˌmīn/ (also **kalsomine**) ▶ **n.** a kind of white or pale blue wash for walls and ceilings.
▶ **v.** [with obj.] whitewash with calcimine.
– ORIGIN mid 19th cent.: of unknown origin.

cal·cine /ˈkalˌsīn/ ▶ **v.** [with obj.] (usu. as adj. **calcined**) reduce, oxidize, or desiccate by roasting or strong heat: *calcined bone ash.*
– DERIVATIVES **cal·ci·na·tion** /kalsəˈnāsHən/ **n.**
– ORIGIN late Middle English: from medieval Latin *calcinare*, from late Latin *calcina* 'lime,' from Latin *calx, calc-* 'lime' (see CALX).

cal·cite /ˈkalˌsīt/ ▶ **n.** a white or colorless mineral consisting of calcium carbonate. It is a major constituent of sedimentary rocks such as limestone, marble, and chalk, can occur in crystalline form (as in Iceland spar), and may be deposited in caves to form stalactites and stalagmites.
– DERIVATIVES **cal·cit·ic** /kalˈsitik/ **adj.**
– ORIGIN mid 19th cent.: coined in German from Latin *calx, calc-* 'lime' (see CALX).

cal·ci·to·nin /ˌkalsəˈtōnən/ ▶ **n.** Biochemistry a hormone secreted by the thyroid that has the effect of lowering blood calcium.
– ORIGIN 1960s: from CALCI- + TONIC + -IN¹.

cal·ci·um /ˈkalsēəm/ ▶ **n.** the chemical element of atomic number 20, a soft gray metal. (Symbol: **Ca**)

> Calcium is one of the alkaline earth metals. Its compounds occur naturally in limestone, fluorite, gypsum, and other minerals. Many physiological processes involve calcium ions, and calcium salts are an essential constituent of bone, teeth, and shells.

– ORIGIN early 19th cent.: from Latin *calx, calc-* 'lime' (see CALX) + -IUM.

cal·ci·um an·tag·o·nist ▶ **n.** Medicine a compound of a type that reduces the influx of calcium into the cells of cardiac and smooth muscle, reducing the strength of contractions. Such drugs are used to treat angina and high blood pressure.

cal·ci·um car·bide ▶ **n.** see CARBIDE.

cal·ci·um car·bon·ate ▶ **n.** a white, insoluble solid occurring naturally as chalk, limestone, marble, and calcite, and forming mollusk shells and stony corals. • Chem. formula: $CaCO_3$.

cal·ci·um chlo·ride ▶ **n.** a white crystalline salt used to de-ice roads and as a drying agent. • Chem. formula: $CaCl_2$.

cal·ci·um hy·drox·ide ▶ **n.** a soluble white crystalline solid commonly produced in the form of slaked lime. • Chem. formula: $Ca(OH)_2$.

cal·ci·um ox·ide ▶ **n.** a white caustic alkaline solid, commonly produced in the form of quicklime. • Chem. formula: CaO.

cal·cu·la·ble /ˈkalkyələbəl/ ▶ **adj.** able to be measured or assessed.
– DERIVATIVES **cal·cu·la·bil·i·ty** /ˌkalkyələˈbilətē/ **n.**, **cal·cu·la·bly** /-blē/ **adv.**

cal·cu·late /ˈkalkyəˌlāt/ ▶ **v.** [with obj.] **1** determine (the amount or number of something) mathematically: *Japanese land value was calculated at 2.5 times that of the U.S* | [with clause] *he calculated that Texas would gain four new seats in the House of Representatives.* ■ determine by reasoning, experience, or common sense; reckon or judge: *I was bright enough to calculate that she had been on vacation.* ■ [no obj.] (**calculate on**) include as an essential element in one's plans: *he may have calculated on maximizing pressure for policy revision.*
2 (usu. **be calculated to do something**) intend (an action) to have a particular effect: *his last words were calculated to wound her.*
3 [with clause] dialect suppose; believe.
– DERIVATIVES **cal·cu·la·tive** /-ˌlātiv/ **adj.**
– ORIGIN late Middle English: from late Latin *calculat-* 'counted,' from the verb *calculare*, from *calculus* 'a small pebble (as used on an abacus).'

cal·cu·lat·ed /ˈkalkyəˌlātid/ ▶ **adj.** (of an action) done with full awareness of the likely consequences: *a calculated decision* | *victims of vicious and calculated assaults.*
– DERIVATIVES **cal·cu·lat·ed·ly adv.**

cal·cu·lat·ing /ˈkalkyəˌlātiNG/ ▶ **adj.** acting in a scheming and ruthlessly determined way: *he was a coolly calculating, ruthless man.*
– DERIVATIVES **cal·cu·lat·ing·ly adv.**

cal·cu·la·tion /ˌkalkyəˈlāsHən/ ▶ **n.** a mathematical determination of the size or number of something: *finding ways of saving money involves complicated calculations* | *calculation of depreciation.* ■ (often **calculations**) an assessment of the risks, possibilities, or effects of a situation or course of action: *decisions are shaped by political calculations.*
– ORIGIN late Middle English: via Old French from late Latin *calculatio(n-)*, from the verb *calculare* (see CALCULATE).

cal·cu·la·tor /ˈkalkyəˌlātər/ ▶ **n.** something used for making mathematical calculations, in particular a small electronic device with a keyboard and a visual display.

cal·cu·lus /ˈkalkyələs/ ▶ **n.** **1** (pl. **calculuses**) (also **infinitesimal calculus**) the branch of mathematics that deals with the finding and properties of derivatives and integrals of functions, by methods originally based on the summation of infinitesimal differences. The two main types are **differential calculus** and **integral calculus**.
2 (pl. **calculuses**) Mathematics & Logic a particular method or system of calculation or reasoning.
3 (pl. **calculi** /-ˌlī, -ˌlē/) Medicine a concretion of minerals formed within the body, esp. in the kidney or gallbladder. ■ another term for TARTAR.
– ORIGIN mid 17th cent.: from Latin, literally 'small pebble (as used on an abacus).'

cal·cu·lus of var·i·a·tions ▶ **n.** a form of calculus applied to expressions or functions in which the law relating the quantities is liable to variation, esp. to find what relation between the variables makes an integral a maximum or a minimum.

Cal·cut·ta /kalˈkətə/ former name (until 2000) for KOLKATA.
– DERIVATIVES **Cal·cut·tan** /-ˈkətn/ **n. & adj.**

Cal·de·cott /ˈkôldikət, -ˌkät/, Randolph (1846–86), English graphic artist and watercolor painter. He is noted for his illustrations for children's books. A medal awarded annually for the illustration of US children's books is named for him.

Cal·der /ˈkôldər/, Alexander (1898–1976), US sculptor and painter. He was one of the first artists to introduce movement into sculpture, making mobiles incorporating abstract forms. His static sculptures are known as stabiles.

cal·de·ra /kalˈderə, kôl-, -ˈdi(ə)rə/ ▶ **n.** a large volcanic crater, typically one formed by a major eruption leading to the collapse of the mouth of the volcano.
– ORIGIN late 17th cent.: from Spanish, from late Latin *caldaria* 'boiling pot.'

Cal·de·rón /ˌkäldəˈrōn/, Felipe (1962–), Mexican statesman; president since 2006; full name *Felipe de Jesús Calderón Hinojosa.* A member of the National Action Party (PAN), he is a social conservative who advocates free trade.

Cal·de·rón de la Bar·ca /ˌkäldəˈrōn dā lä ˈbärkä/, Pedro (1600–81), Spanish playwright and poet. He wrote about 120 plays, more than 70 of them religious dramas.

cal·dron ▶ **n.** variant spelling of CAULDRON.

Cald·well /ˈkôldˌwel/, Erskine (Preston) (1903–87), US novelist and short-story writer. Caldwell reproduced the dialect of the poor whites in his realistic, earthy, and popular novels. Notable works: *Tobacco Road* (1932) and *God's Little Acre* (1933).

ca·lèche /kəˈlesH, -ˈlasH/ (also **caleche** or **calash**) ▶ **n.** historical **1** a light low-wheeled carriage with a removable folding hood.
2 Canadian a two-wheeled one-horse vehicle with a seat for the driver on the splashboard.
3 a woman's hooped silk hood.
– ORIGIN mid 17th cent.: French, from German *Kalesche*, from Polish *kołasa*, from *koło* 'wheel.'

Cal·e·do·ni·an /ˌkaləˈdōnēən/ ▶ **adj.** **1** (chiefly in names or geographical terms) of or relating to Scotland or the Scottish Highlands: *the Caledonian Railway.*
2 Geology relating to or denoting a mountain-forming (orogenic) period in northwestern Europe and Greenland during the Early Paleozoic era, esp. the late Silurian.
▶ **n.** **1** humorous or literary a person from Scotland.
2 (**the Caledonian**) Geology the Caledonian orogeny.
– ORIGIN from *Caledonia*, the Latin name for northern Britain, + -AN.

Cal·e·do·ni·an Ca·nal a system of lochs and canals that cross Scotland from east to west.

cal·e·fa·cient /ˌkaləˈfāsHənt/ ▶ **n.** Medicine, archaic a drug or other agent causing a sensation of warmth.
– ORIGIN mid 17th cent.: from Latin *calefacient-* 'making warm,' from the verb *calefacere*, from *calere* 'be warm' + *facere* 'make.'

cal·en·dar /ˈkaləndər/ (abbr.: **cal** or **cal.**) ▶ **n.** a chart or series of pages showing the days, weeks, and months of a particular year, or giving particular seasonal information. ■ a datebook. ■ a system by which the beginning, length, and subdivisions of the year are fixed. See also JEWISH CALENDAR, JULIAN CALENDAR, GREGORIAN CALENDAR. ■ a timetable of special days or events of a specified kind or involving a specified group: *the college calendar.*
▶ **v.** [with obj.] enter (something) in a calendar or timetable.
– DERIVATIVES **cal·en·dar·ize** /ˈkaləndəˌrīz/ **v.**, **ca·len·dric** /kəˈlendrik/ **adj.**, **ca·len·dri·cal** /kəˈlendrikəl/ **adj.**
– ORIGIN Middle English: from Old French *calendier*, from Latin *kalendarium* 'account book,' from *kalendae* (see CALENDS).

cal·en·dar·ize /ˈkaləndəˌrīz/ ▶ **v.** [with obj.] (usu. as adj. **calendarized**) schedule, allocate, or record (something) on a month-by-month basis: *a calendarized budget.*

cal·en·dar month ▶ **n.** see MONTH.

cal·en·dar year ▶ **n.** see YEAR (sense 2).

cal·en·der /ˈkaləndər/ ▶ **n.** a machine in which cloth or paper is pressed by rollers to glaze or smooth it.
▶ **v.** [with obj.] press in such a machine.
– ORIGIN late 15th cent. (as a verb): from French *calendre* (noun), *calendrer* (verb), of unknown origin.

cal·ends /ˈkaləndz, ˈkā-/ (also **kalends**) ▶ **plural n.** the first day of the month in the ancient Roman calendar.
– ORIGIN Old English (denoting an appointed time): from Old French *calendes*, from Latin *kalendae*, *calendae* 'first day of the month' (when accounts were due and the order of days was proclaimed); related to Latin *calare* and Greek *kalein* 'call, proclaim.'

ca·len·du·la /kəˈlenjələ, kəˈlendyōōlə/ ▶ **n.** a Mediterranean plant of a genus that includes the common (or pot) marigold. • Genus *Calendula*, family Compositae.
– ORIGIN modern Latin, diminutive of *calendae* (see CALENDS); perhaps because it flowers for most of the year.

cal·en·ture /ˈkalənˌCHŏŏr/ ▶ **n.** feverish delirium supposedly caused by the heat in the tropics.
– ORIGIN late 16th cent.: from French, from Spanish *calentura* 'fever,' from *calentar* 'be hot,' based on Latin *calere* 'be warm.'

calf¹ /kaf/ ▶ **n.** (pl. **calves** /kavz/) **1** a young bovine animal, esp. a domestic cow or bull in its first year. ■ the young of some other large mammals, such as elephants, rhinoceroses, large deer and antelopes, and whales. ■ short for CALFSKIN.
2 a floating piece of ice detached from an iceberg.
– PHRASES **in** (or **with**) **calf** (of a cow) pregnant. **kill the fatted calf** see FAT.
– DERIVATIVES **calf·like** /-ˌlīk/ **adj.**
– ORIGIN Old English *cælf*, of Germanic origin; related to Dutch *kalf* and German *Kalb*.

calf² ▶ **n.** (pl. **calves** /kavz/) the fleshy part at the back of a person's leg below the knee.
– ORIGIN Middle English: from Old Norse *kálfi*, of unknown origin.

calf-length ▶ **adj.** (of footwear or an item of clothing) reaching the calves: *a calf-length skirt.*

calf·skin /ˈkafˌskin/ ▶ **n.** leather made from the hide or skin of a calf, used chiefly in bookbinding and shoemaking.

Cal·ga·ry /ˈkalgərē/ a city in southern Alberta, in southwestern Canada; pop. 988,193 (2006).

Cal·houn /kalˈhōōn/, John Caldwell (1782–1850) US politician. A South Carolina Democrat, he served as US vice president 1825–32 and in the US Senate 1832–43, 1845–50. He was noted as a champion of states' rights and of slavery.

Ca·li /ˈkälē/ an industrial city in western Colombia; pop. 2,075,525 (2005).

cal·i·ber /ˈkaləbər/ (Brit. **calibre**) (abbr.: **cal** or **cal.**) ▶ **n.** **1** the quality of someone's character or the level of someone's ability: *they could ill afford to lose a man of his caliber.* ■ the standard reached by something: *educational facilities of a very high caliber.*
2 the internal diameter or bore of a gun barrel: [in combination] *a .22 caliber repeater rifle.* ■ the diameter of a bullet, shell, or rocket. ■ the diameter of a circular body, such as a tube, blood vessel, or fiber.
– DERIVATIVES **cal·i·bered adj.** [also in combination].
– ORIGIN mid 16th cent. (in the sense 'social standing or importance'): from French *calibre*, from Italian *calibro*, perhaps from Arabic *kālib* 'mold,' based on Greek *kalapous* 'shoemaker's last.'

cal·i·brate /ˈkaləˌbrāt/ ▶ **v.** [with obj.] mark (a gauge or instrument) with a standard scale of readings. ■ correlate the readings of (an instrument) with those of a standard in order to check the instrument's accuracy. ■ adjust (experimental results) to take external factors into account or to allow comparison with other data. ■ carefully

C

C

assess, set, or adjust (something abstract): *the regulators cannot properly calibrate the risks involved* | (as adj. **calibrated**) *their carefully calibrated economic policies*.
– DERIVATIVES **cal·i·bra·tor** /-brātər/ **n.**
– ORIGIN mid 19th cent.: from **CALIBER** + **-ATE**³.

cal·i·bra·tion /kaləˈbrāSHən/ ▶ **n.** the action or process of calibrating an instrument or experimental readings: *the measuring devices require calibration* | *calibrations in the field of electronic measurements*. ■ each of a set of graduations on an instrument.

ca·li·che /kəˈlēCHē/ ▶ **n.** a mineral deposit of gravel, sand, and nitrates, found esp. in dry areas of South America. ■ an area of calcium carbonate formed in the soils of semiarid regions.
– ORIGIN mid 19th cent.: from Latin American Spanish.

cal·i·co /ˈkaliˌkō/ ▶ **n.** (pl. **calicoes** or **calicos**) printed cotton fabric: [as modifier] *a calico dress*. ■ Brit. a type of cotton cloth, typically plain white or unbleached. ▶ **adj.** (of an animal, typically a cat) multicolored or mottled.
– ORIGIN mid 16th cent. (originally also *calicut*): alteration of **CALICUT**, where the fabric originated.

Cal·i·cut /ˈkalikət/ former name for **KOZHIKODE**.

Calif. ▶ **abbr.** California.

Cal·i·for·nia /ˌkaləˈfôrnyə, -nēə/ a state in the western US, on the coast of the Pacific Ocean; pop. 36,756,666 (est. 2008); capital, Sacramento; statehood, Sept. 9, 1850 (31). Formerly part of Mexico, it was ceded to the US in 1847, having briefly been an independent republic. Large numbers of settlers were attracted to California in the 19th century, esp. during the gold rushes of the 1840s; it is now the most populous state.
– DERIVATIVES **Cal·i·for·nian adj. & n.**

Cal·i·for·nia, Gulf of an arm of the Pacific Ocean that separates the Baja California peninsula from mainland Mexico.

Cal·i·for·nia Cur·rent a cold ocean current of the eastern Pacific Ocean that flows south along the western coast of North America.

Cal·i·for·nia pop·py ▶ **n.** an annual poppy native to western North America that is cultivated for its brilliant yellow or orange flowers. ● *Eschscholzia californica*, family Papaveraceae.

California poppy

Cal·i·for·nia sheeps·head ▶ **n.** see **SHEEPSHEAD**.

cal·i·for·ni·um /ˌkaləˈfôrnēəm/ ▶ **n.** the chemical element of atomic number 98, a radioactive metal of the actinide series, first produced by bombarding curium with helium ions. (Symbol: **Cf**)
– ORIGIN 1950s: named after *University of California at Berkeley* (where it was first made) + **-IUM**.

ca·lig·i·nous /kəˈlijənəs/ ▶ **adj.** archaic misty, dim; obscure, dark.
– DERIVATIVES **ca·lig·i·nos·i·ty** /kəˌlijəˈnäsitē/ **n.**

Ca·lig·u·la /kəˈligyələ/ (AD 12–41), Roman emperor 37–41; born *Gaius Julius Caesar Germanicus*. His reign was notorious for its tyrannical excesses.

cal·i·per /ˈkaləpər/ (also **calliper**) ▶ **n. 1** (**calipers**) an instrument for measuring external or internal dimensions, having two hinged legs resembling a pair of compasses and in-turned or out-turned points. ■ (also **caliper rule**) an instrument performing a similar function but having one linear component sliding along another, with two parallel jaws and a vernier scale. ■ (also **brake caliper**) a motor-vehicle or bicycle brake consisting of two or more hinged components.
2 (also **caliper splint**) a metal support for a person's leg.
– ORIGIN late 16th cent.: apparently an alteration of **CALIBER**.

ca·liph /ˈkālif, ˈkal-/ ▶ **n.** historical the chief Muslim civil and religious ruler, regarded as the successor of Muhammad. The caliph ruled in Baghdad until 1258 and then in Egypt until the Ottoman conquest of 1517; the title was then held by the Ottoman sultans until it was abolished in 1924 by Atatürk.
– DERIVATIVES **cal·iph·ate** /ˈkāləˌfāt, ˈkal-, -fit/ **n.**
– ORIGIN late Middle English: from Old French *caliphe*, from Arabic *ḵalīfa* meaning 'deputy (of God)' (from the title *ḵalīfat Allāh*), or meaning 'successor (of Muhammad)' (from the title *ḵalīfat rasūl Allāh* 'of the Messenger of God'), from *ḵalafa* 'succeed.'

cal·is·then·ics /ˌkaləsˈTHeniks/ (Brit. **callisthenics**) ▶ **plural n.** [treated as sing. or pl.] gymnastic exercises to achieve bodily fitness and grace of movement.
– DERIVATIVES **cal·is·then·ic adj.**
– ORIGIN early 19th cent.: from Greek *kallos* 'beauty' + *sthenos* 'strength' + **-ICS**.

ca·lix ▶ **n.** variant spelling of **CALYX**.

calk ▶ **n. & v.** variant spelling of **CAULK**.

call /kôl/ ▶ **v. 1** [with obj.] cry out to (someone) in order to summon them or attract their attention: *she heard Terry calling her* | [no obj.] *I distinctly heard you call*. ■ cry out (a word or words): *he heard an insistent voice calling his name* | *Meredith was already calling out a greeting*. ■ [no obj.] (of an animal, esp. a bird) make its characteristic cry. ■ shout out or chant (the steps and figures) to people performing a square dance or country dance. ■ telephone (a person or telephone number): *could I call you back?* ■ summon (something, esp. an emergency service or a taxicab) by telephone: *if you are suspicious, call the police*. ■ bring (a witness) into court to give evidence. ■ [with obj. and infinitive] archaic inspire or urge (someone) to do something: *I am called to preach the Gospel*. ■ fix a date or time for (a meeting, strike, or election). ■ [no obj.] guess the outcome of tossing a coin: *"You call," he said. "Heads or tails?"* ■ predict the result of (a future event, esp. an election or a vote): *in the Northeast, the race remains too close to call*. ■ Computing cause the execution of (a subroutine).
2 [with obj. and complement] give (an infant or animal) a specified name: *they called their daughter Hannah*. ■ (**be called**) have a specified name: *she is called Eva* | *a 1942 mystery called Time To Kill*. ■ address or refer to (someone) by a specified name, title, endearment, or term of abuse: *please call me Lucy*. ■ refer to, consider, or describe (someone or something) as being: *he's the only person I would call a friend*. ■ (of an umpire or other official in a game) pronounce (a ball, stroke, or other action) to be the thing specified: *the linesman called the ball wide*.
3 [no obj.] (of a person) pay a brief visit: *he called around last night looking for you*. ■ (**call for**) stop to pick up (someone) at the place where they are living or working: *I'll call for you around seven*.
▶ **n. 1** a cry made as a summons or to attract someone's attention: *in response to the call, a figure appeared*. ■ the characteristic cry of a bird or other animal. ■ [with modifier] a series of notes sounded on a brass instrument as a signal to do something: *a bugle call to rise at 5:30*. ■ a telephone communication or conversation: *I'll give you a call at around five*. ■ (**a call for**) an appeal or demand for: *the call for action was welcomed*. ■ a summons: *a messenger arrived bringing news of his call to the throne*. ■ [in sing.] a vocation: *his call to be a disciple*. ■ [in sing.] a powerful force of attraction: *hikers can't resist the call of the Sierras*. ■ [usu. with negative] (**a call for**) a demand or need for (goods or services): *there was little call for work as sophisticated as his*. ■ Computing a command to execute a subroutine. ■ a shout by an official in a game indicating whether the ball has gone out of play, a rule has been breached, etc.; the decision or ruling so made: *the replay shows that the umpire made a bad call*. ■ Bridge a bid, response, or double. ■ a direction in a square dance given by the caller. ■ a demand for payment of lent or unpaid capital. ■ Stock Market short for **CALL OPTION**. ■ a player's right or turn to make a bid in a card game.
2 a brief visit: *we paid a call on Howard*. ■ a visit or journey made in response to an emergency appeal for help: *the doctor was out on a call*.
– PHRASES **call attention to** cause people to notice: *he is seeking to call attention to himself by his crimes*. **call someone's bluff** see **BLUFF**¹. **call collect** make a telephone call reversing the charges. **call something into play** cause or require something to start working so that one can make use of it: *our active participation as spectators is called into play*. **call something into** (or **in**) **question** cast doubt on something: *these findings call into question the legitimacy of the proceedings*. **call it a day** see **DAY**. **call someone names** see **NAME**. **call of nature** see **NATURE**. **call the shots** (or **tune**) take the initiative in deciding how something should be done. **call a spade a spade** see **SPADE**¹. **call someone to account** see **ACCOUNT**. **call someone/something to mind** cause one to think of someone or something, esp. through similarity: *the still lifes call to mind certain of Cézanne's works*. ■ [with negative] remember someone or something: [with clause] *I cannot call to mind where I have seen you*. **call someone/something to order** ask those present at a meeting to be silent so that business may proceed. **don't call us, we'll call you** informal used as a dismissive way of saying that someone has not been successful in an audition or a job application. **good call** (or **bad call**) informal used to express approval (or criticism) of a person's decision or suggestion. [with reference to decisions made by referees or umpires.] **on call 1** (of a person) able to be contacted in order to provide a professional service if necessary, but not formally on duty: *our technicians are on call around the clock*. **2** (of money lent) repayable on demand. **to call one's own** used to describe something that one can genuinely feel belongs to one: *I had not an item to call my own*. **within call** near enough to be summoned by calling: *she moved into the guest room, within call of her father's room*.
– PHRASAL VERBS **call for** make necessary: *desperate times call for desperate measures*. ■ publicly ask for or demand: *the report calls for an audit of endangered species*. **call something forth** elicit a response: *few things call forth more compassion*. **call someone/something down 1** cause or provoke someone or something to appear or occur: *nothing called down the wrath of Nemesis quicker*. **2** dated reprimand someone. **call someone in** enlist someone's aid or services. **call something in** require payment of a loan or promise of money. **call someone/something off** order a person or dog to stop attacking someone. **call something off** cancel an event or agreement. **call on 1** pay a visit to (someone): *he's planning to call on Katherine today*. **2** (also **call upon**) have recourse to: *we are able to call on academic staff with a wide variety of expertise*. ■ [with infinitive] demand that (someone) do something: *he called on the government to hold a plebiscite*. **call someone out 1** summon someone, esp. to deal with an emergency or to do repairs. **2** order or advise workers to strike. **3** archaic challenge someone to a duel. **call something over** dated read out a list of names to determine those present. **call someone up 1** informal telephone someone. **2** summon someone to serve in the army: *they have called up more than 20,000 reservists*. ■ select someone to play in a team: *he was called up from Columbus to finish the season with the Yankees*. **call something up** summon for use something that is stored or kept available: *icons that allow you to call up a graphic*. ■ evoke something: *the special effects that called up the Mars landscape were impressive*.
– ORIGIN late Old English *ceallian*, from Old Norse *kalla* 'summon loudly.'

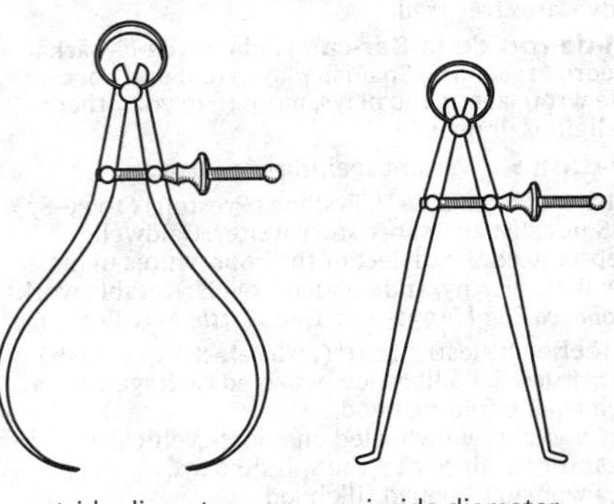
outside diameter caliper

inside diameter caliper

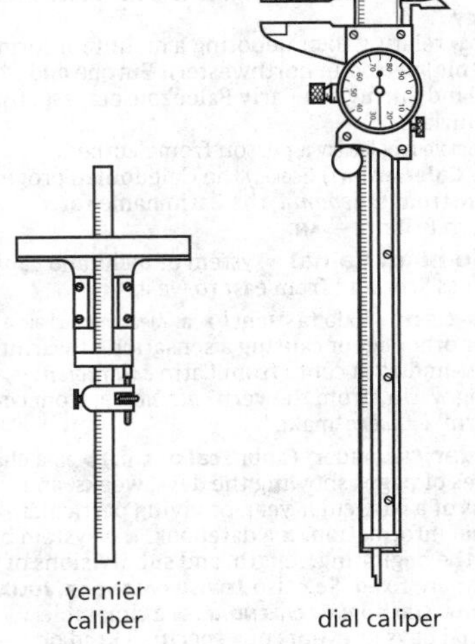
vernier caliper

dial caliper

calipers

cal·la /ˈkalə/ ▶ **n.** either of two plants of the arum family. ● (usu. **calla lily**) Genus *Zantedeschia*, family Araceae: several species, in particular *Z. aethiopica*. ● (also **wild calla**) another term for **WATER ARUM**.
– ORIGIN early 19th cent.: modern Latin.

call·a·ble /ˈkôləbəl/ ▶ **adj.** Finance designating a bond that can be paid off earlier than the maturity date.

Cal·la·ghan /ˈkalə,han/, James (1912–2005), British Labour statesman; full name *Leonard James Callaghan, Baron Callaghan of Cardiff*; prime minister 1976–79.

cal·la·loo /,kaləˈlo͞o, ˈkalə,lo͞o/ (also **callalou**) ▶ **n.** **1** the spinachlike leaves of a tropical American plant, widely used in Caribbean cooking. ■ a soup or stew made with such leaves.
2 the plant of the arum family from which these leaves are obtained. ● Genus *Xanthosoma*, family Araceae.
– ORIGIN mid 18th cent.: from American Spanish *calalú*.

Cal·la·net·ics /kaləˈnetiks/ ▶ **plural n.** [treated as sing. or pl.] trademark a system of physical exercises based on small repeated movements.
– ORIGIN late 20th cent.: named after *Callan* Pinckney (born 1939), American deviser of the system, perhaps on the pattern of *athletics*.

Ca·llao /kəˈyä-ō, kəˈyou/ the principal seaport of Peru, west of Lima; pop. 415,900 (est. 2007).

Cal·las /ˈkaləs/, Maria (1923–77), US opera singer; born *Maria Cecilia Anna Kalageropoulos*. She was a coloratura soprano whose bel canto style of singing was especially suited to early Italian opera.

call·back /ˈkôl,bak/ ▶ **n.** **1** an invitation to return for a second audition or interview.
2 a telephone call made to return a call received.
3 a recall of a defective product: *ask which products have the most callbacks*.
4 an emergency call summoning an employee to work after hours: *uncontrolled air leakage results in increased callbacks*.
5 Computing a security feature used by systems accessed by telephone, in which a remote user must log on using a previously registered phone number, to which the system then places a return call.

call-board ▶ **n.** a bulletin board in a theater on which announcements for the cast and crew are posted.

call box ▶ **n.** **1** a roadside telephone for use only in an emergency.
2 Brit. a public telephone booth.

call boy ▶ **n.** **1** a person in a theater who summons actors when they are due on stage.
2 a male prostitute who accepts appointments by telephone.

call cen·ter ▶ **n.** an office set up to handle a large volume of telephone calls, esp. for taking orders and providing customer service.

call·er /ˈkôlər/ ▶ **n.** **1** a person who makes a telephone call or pays a brief visit.
2 a person who calls out numbers in a game of bingo or directions in a dance.

call·er ID ▶ **n.** a facility that identifies and displays the telephone numbers of incoming calls made to a particular line.

call for·ward·ing ▶ **n.** a telephone feature that allows calls made to one number to be forwarded to another specified number.

call girl ▶ **n.** a female prostitute who accepts appointments by telephone.

Cal·lic·ra·tes /kəˈlikrə,tēz/ (5th century BC), Greek architect. He was the leading architect in Periclean Athens and, with Ictinus, designed the Parthenon (447–438 BC).

cal·li·graph /ˈkali,graf/ ▶ **v.** [with obj.] (usu. **be calligraphed**) write in calligraphic style: *invitations meticulously calligraphed in black ink*.
– ORIGIN mid 19th cent. (as a noun): from French *calligraphe*, via medieval Latin from Greek *kalligraphos* (see CALLIGRAPHY). The verb dates from the late 19th cent.

cal·li·graph·ic /,kaliˈgrafik/ ▶ **adj.** of or relating to calligraphy: *a calligraphic pen | calligraphic script*.

cal·lig·ra·phy /kəˈligrəfē/ ▶ **n.** decorative handwriting or handwritten lettering. ■ the art of producing decorative handwriting or lettering with a pen or brush.
– DERIVATIVES **cal·lig·ra·pher** /-fər/ **n.**, **cal·lig·ra·phist** /-fist/ **n.**
– ORIGIN early 17th cent.: from Greek *kalligraphia*, from *kalligraphos* 'person who writes beautifully,' from *kallos* 'beauty' + *graphein* 'write.'

Cal·lim·a·chus /kəˈliməkəs/ (*c.*305–*c.*240 BC), Greek poet and scholar. He wrote hymns and epigrams and was head of the library at Alexandria.

call-in ▶ **n.** chiefly US a radio or television program during which the listeners or viewers telephone the studio and participate. ■ [as modifier] denoting something conducted by people leaving answers or messages by telephone: *a call-in poll*.

call·ing /ˈkôliNG/ ▶ **n.** **1** the loud cries or shouts of an animal or person: *the calling of a cuckoo*.
2 [in sing.] a strong urge toward a particular way of life or career; a vocation: *those who have a special calling to minister to others' needs*. ■ a profession or occupation: *he considered engineering one of the highest possible callings*.

call·ing card ▶ **n.** **1** a card bearing a person's name and address, sent or left in lieu of a formal social or business visit. ■ an action by which someone or something can be identified: *a dog whose calling card is a savage nip at the nearest ankles*.
2 a card that allows the user to make telephone calls from any phone and charge the cost to their home telephone number. ■ a prepaid card that allows the user to make telephone calls up to a specified value.

Cal·li·o·pe /kəˈlīəpē/ Greek & Roman Mythology the Muse of epic poetry.
– ORIGIN from Greek *Kalliopē*, literally 'having a beautiful voice.'

cal·li·o·pe /kəˈlīəpē/ ▶ **n.** chiefly historical a keyboard instrument resembling an organ but with the notes produced by steam whistles, used chiefly on showboats and in traveling fairs.
– ORIGIN mid 19th cent.: from the Greek name *Kalliopē* (see CALLIOPE).

cal·li·per ▶ **n.** variant spelling of CALIPER.

cal·li·pyg·i·an /,kaləˈpijēən/ (also **callipygean**) ▶ **adj.** having well-shaped buttocks.
– DERIVATIVES **cal·li·py·gous** /-ˈpīgəs/ **adj.**
– ORIGIN late 18th cent.: from Greek *kallipūgos* (used to describe a famous statue of Venus), from *kallos* 'beauty' + *pūgē* 'buttocks,' + -IAN.

cal·lis·then·ics ▶ **plural n.** British spelling of CALISTHENICS.

Cal·lis·to /kəˈlistō/ **1** Greek Mythology a nymph who was changed into a bear by Zeus. See also URSA MAJOR.
2 Astronomy one of the Galilean moons of Jupiter, the eighth closest satellite to the planet. Icy with a dark, cratered surface, it has a diameter of 2,938 miles (4,800 km).

cal·li·tri·chid /,kaliˈtrikid, -ˈtrī-/ ▶ **n.** Zoology a primate of a family (Callitrichidae or Callithricidae) that comprises the marmosets and tamarins.
– ORIGIN late 18th cent.: from modern Latin *Callitrichidae* (plural), from Greek *kallitrikhos* 'beautiful-haired.'

call let·ters ▶ **plural n.** a sequence of letters used by a television or radio station as an identifying code.

call mon·ey ▶ **n.** money lent by a bank or other institution that is repayable on demand.

call num·ber ▶ **n.** a mark, esp. a number, on the spine of a library book, or listed in the library's catalog, indicating the book's location in the library.

call op·tion ▶ **n.** Stock Market an option to buy assets at an agreed price on or before a particular date.

cal·los·i·ty /kəˈläsitē/ ▶ **n.** (pl. **callosities**) technical a thickened and hardened part of the skin; a callus.
– ORIGIN late Middle English: from French *callosité*, from Latin *callositas*, from *callosus* 'hard-skinned,' from *callum*, *callus* 'hardened skin.'

cal·lous /ˈkaləs/ ▶ **adj.** showing or having an insensitive and cruel disregard for others: *his callous comments about the murder made me shiver*.
▶ **n.** variant spelling of CALLUS.
– DERIVATIVES **cal·lous·ly adv.**, **cal·lous·ness n.**
– ORIGIN late Middle English (in the Latin sense): from Latin *callosus* 'hard-skinned.'

cal·loused /ˈkaləst/ ▶ **adj.** variant spelling of CALLUSED.

call-out ▶ **n.** **1** an instance of being summoned, esp. in order to deal with an emergency or to do repairs: [as modifier] *a call-out charge*.
2 Printing a letter, word, number, or symbol identifying an illustration or a specific part of one. ■ a short piece of text set in larger type than the rest of the page and intended to attract attention.

cal·low /ˈkalō/ ▶ **adj.** (esp. of a young person) inexperienced and immature: *earnest and callow undergraduates*.
– DERIVATIVES **cal·low·ly adv.**, **cal·low·ness n.**
– ORIGIN Old English *calu* 'bald'; probably from Latin *calvus* 'bald.' This was extended to mean 'unfledged,' which led to the present sense 'immature.'

Cal·lo·way /ˈkalə,wā/, Cab (1907–94), US jazz singer and bandleader; full name *Cabell Calloway*. He was known for his style of scat singing and for his flamboyant appearance. He is associated with songs such as "Minnie the Moocher" (1931) and "Jumpin' Jive" (1939) and led a succession of outstanding big bands 1928–53.

call sign (also **call signal**) ▶ **n.** a message, code, or tune that is broadcast by radio to identify the broadcaster or transmitter.

call to quar·ters ▶ **n.** a bugle call summoning soldiers to their barracks.

call-up ▶ **n.** [in sing.] an act of summoning someone or of being summoned to serve in the armed forces or on a sports team: [as modifier] *my call-up papers*.

cal·lus /ˈkaləs/ (also **callous**) ▶ **n.** a thickened and hardened part of the skin or soft tissue, esp. in an area that has been subjected to friction. ■ Medicine the bony healing tissue that forms around the ends of broken bone. ■ Botany a hard formation of tissue, esp. new tissue formed over a wound.
– ORIGIN mid 16th cent.: from Latin *callus* (more commonly *callum*) 'hardened skin.'

cal·lused /ˈkaləst/ (also **calloused**) ▶ **adj.** (of a part of the body) having an area of hardened skin: *a callused palm*.

call wait·ing ▶ **n.** a service whereby someone making a telephone call is notified of an incoming call and is able to place the first call on hold while answering the second.

calm /kä(l)m/ ▶ **adj.** **1** (of a person, action, or manner) not showing or feeling nervousness, anger, or other emotions: *keep calm, she told herself | his voice was calm*. ■ (of a place) peaceful, esp. in contrast to recent violent activity: *the city was reported to be calm, but army patrols remained*.
2 (of the weather) pleasantly free from wind: *the night was clear and calm*. ■ (of the sea) not disturbed by large waves.
▶ **n.** **1** the absence of violent or confrontational activity within a place or group: *the elections proceeded in an atmosphere of relative calm* | [in sing.] *an edgy calm reigned in the capital*. ■ the absence of nervousness, agitation, or excitement in a person: *his usual calm deserted him*.
2 the absence of wind: *in the center of the storm calm prevailed*. ■ still air represented by force 0 on the Beaufort scale (less than 1 knot). ■ (often **calms**) an area of the sea without wind.
▶ **v.** [with obj.] make (someone) tranquil and quiet; soothe: *I took him inside and tried to calm him down | he lit a cigarette to calm his nerves* | (as adj. **calming**) *a cup of tea will have a calming effect*. ■ [no obj.] (**calm down**) (of a person) become tranquil and quiet: *gradually I calmed down and lost my anxiety*.
– PHRASES **the calm before the storm** see STORM.
– DERIVATIVES **calm·ly adv.**, **calm·ness n.**
– ORIGIN late Middle English: via one of the Romance languages from Greek *kauma* 'heat (of the day).'

calm·a·tive /ˈkä(l)mətiv/ ▶ **adj.** (of a drug) having a sedative effect.
▶ **n.** a calmative drug.

cal·mod·u·lin /kalˈmäjələn/ ▶ **n.** Biochemistry a protein that binds calcium and is involved in regulating a variety of activities in cells.
– ORIGIN 1970s: from *cal(cium)* + *modul(ate)* + -IN¹.

cal·o·mel /ˈkaləməl, -,mel/ ▶ **n.** a white powder used as a purgative and a fungicide. Also called MERCURIC CHLORIDE. ● Chem. formula: Hg_2Cl_2.
– ORIGIN late 17th cent.: modern Latin, perhaps from Greek *kalos* 'beautiful' + *melas* 'black' (perhaps because it was originally obtained from a black mixture of mercury and mercuric chloride).

Ca·lo·o·can /,kaləˈōkän/ (also **Kalookan**) a city in the Philippines, on southern Luzon, northwest of Manila; pop. 1,378,900 (est. 2007).

ca·lor·ic /kəˈlôrik, -ˈlär-/ ▶ **adj.** technical of or relating to heat; calorific: *a caloric value of 7 calories per gram*.
▶ **n.** Physics, historical (in the late 18th and early 19th centuries) a hypothetical fluid substance that was thought to be responsible for the phenomena of heat.
– DERIVATIVES **ca·lor·i·cal·ly adv.**
– ORIGIN late 18th cent. (as a noun): from French *calorique*, from Latin *calor* 'heat.'

cal·o·rie /ˈkal(ə)rē/ (abbr.: **cal.**) ▶ **n.** (pl. **calories**) either of two units of heat energy. ■ (also **small calorie**) (abbr.: **cal**) the energy needed to raise the temperature of 1 gram of water through 1 °C (now usually defined as 4.1868 joules). ■ (also **large calorie**) (abbr.: **Cal**) the energy needed to raise the temperature of 1 kilogram of water through 1 °C, equal to one thousand small calories and often used to measure the energy value of foods.
– ORIGIN mid 19th cent.: from French, from Latin *calor* 'heat' + French suffix *-ie* (see -Y³).

cal·o·rif·ic /,kaləˈrifik/ ▶ **adj.** chiefly Brit. relating to the amount of energy contained in food or fuel: *she knew the calorific contents of every morsel*. ■ (of food or drink) containing many calories and so likely to be fattening: *there is fruit salad for those who can resist the more calorific concoctions*.
– DERIVATIVES **cal·o·rif·i·cal·ly** /-ik(ə)lē/ **adv.**

– ORIGIN late 17th cent.: from Latin *calorificus*, from *calor* 'heat.'

cal·o·rif·ic val·ue ▶ **n.** the energy contained in a fuel or food, determined by measuring the heat produced by the complete combustion of a specified quantity of it. This is now usually expressed in joules per kilogram.

cal·o·rim·e·ter /ˌkaləˈrimitər/ ▶ **n.** an apparatus for measuring the amount of heat involved in a chemical reaction or other process.
– DERIVATIVES **cal·o·ri·met·ric** /ˌkalərəˈmetrik/ **adj.**, **cal·o·rim·e·try** /-ˈrimitrē/ **n.**
– ORIGIN late 18th cent.: from Latin *calor* 'heat' + **-METER**.

C

cal·o·type /ˈkaləˌtīp/ (also **calotype process**) ▶ **n.** historical an early photographic process in which negatives were made using paper coated with silver iodide.
– ORIGIN mid 19th cent.: from Greek *kalos* 'beautiful' + **TYPE**.

calque /kalk/ Linguistics ▶ **n.** another term for **LOAN TRANSLATION**.
▶ **v.** (**be calqued on**) originate or function as a loan translation of.
– ORIGIN 1930s: from French, literally 'copy, tracing,' from *calquer* 'to trace,' via Italian from Latin *calcare* 'to tread.'

cal·trop /ˈkaltrəp, ˈkôl-/ ▶ **n. 1** a spiked metal device thrown on the ground to impede wheeled vehicles or (formerly) cavalry horses.
2 a creeping plant with woody carpels that typically have hard spines and resemble military caltrops.
● Genus *Tribulus*, family Zygophyllaceae.
3 (also **water caltrop**) another term for **WATER CHESTNUT** (sense 3).
– ORIGIN Old English *calcatrippe*, denoting any plant that tended to catch the feet, from medieval Latin *calcatrippa*, from *calx* 'heel' or *calcare* 'to tread' + a word related to **TRAP**[1]. Sense 1 was probably adopted from French.

cal·u·met /ˈkalyəˌmet, -mit, ˌkalyəˈmet/ ▶ **n.** a North American Indian peace pipe.
– ORIGIN late 17th cent.: from French, from late Latin *calamellus* 'little reed,' diminutive of Latin *calamus* (referring to the pipe's reed stem).

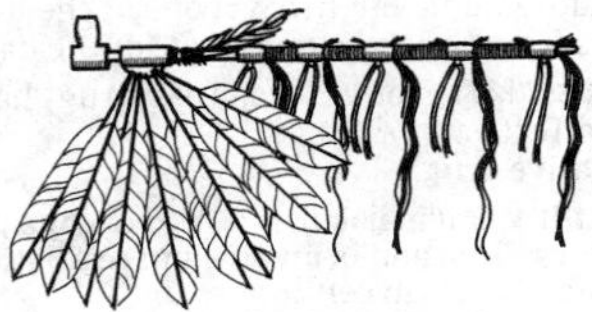
calumet

Cal·u·met Cit·y /ˈkalyəˌmet/ a city in northeastern Illinois, south of Chicago, on the Indiana border; pop. 36,800 (est. 2008). The surrounding industrial region, in both states, is called the Calumet.

ca·lum·ni·ate /kəˈləmnēˌāt/ ▶ **v.** [with obj.] formal make false and defamatory statements about: *foes were calumniating him in the US press.*
– DERIVATIVES **ca·lum·ni·a·tion** /kəˌləmnēˈāSHən/ **n.**, **ca·lum·ni·a·tor** /-ˌātər/ **n.**
– ORIGIN mid 16th cent.: from Latin *calumniari*, from *calumnia* (see **CALUMNY**).

cal·um·ny /ˈkaləmnē/ ▶ **n.** (pl. **calumnies**) the making of false and defamatory statements in order to damage someone's reputation; slander. ■ a false and slanderous statement.
– DERIVATIVES **ca·lum·ni·ous** /kəˈləmnēəs/ **adj.**
– ORIGIN late Middle English: from Latin *calumnia*.

cal·u·tron /ˈkalyəˌträn/ ▶ **n.** a device that uses large electromagnets to separate uranium isotopes from uranium ore. It was developed in the 1940s to produce highly enriched weapons-grade uranium.
– ORIGIN from *Cal(ifornia) U(niversity) (cyclo)tron*.

Cal·va·dos /ˌkalvəˈdōs/ (also **calvados**) ▶ **n.** apple brandy, traditionally made in the Calvados region of Normandy.

Cal·va·ry /ˈkalv(ə)rē/ the hill outside Jerusalem on which Jesus was crucified. ■ (as noun **a calvary**) a sculpture or picture representing the scene of the Crucifixion.
– ORIGIN from late Latin *calvaria* 'skull,' translation of Greek *golgotha* 'place of a skull' (Matt. 27:33) (see **GOLGOTHA**).

calve /kav/ ▶ **v. 1** [no obj.] (of cows and certain other large animals) give birth to a calf. ■ [with obj.] (of a person) help (a cow) give birth to a calf.
2 [with obj.] (of an iceberg or glacier) split and shed (a smaller mass of ice). ■ [no obj.] (of a mass of ice) split off from an iceberg or glacier.
– ORIGIN Old English *calfian*, from *cælf* 'calf.'

calves /kavz/ plural form of **CALF**[1], **CALF**[2].

Cal·vin[1] /ˈkalvin/, John (1509–64), French theologian and reformer. On becoming a Protestant, he fled to Switzerland, where he attempted to reorder society on reformed Christian principles. His *Institutes of the Christian Religion* (1536) was the first systematic account of reformed Christian doctrine.

Cal·vin[2], Melvin Ellis (1911–97), US biochemist. He investigated photosynthesis and discovered the cycle of reactions (the **Calvin cycle**) that constitutes the dark reaction. Nobel Prize for Chemistry (1961).

Cal·vin·ism /ˈkalvəˌnizəm/ ▶ **n.** the Protestant theological system of John Calvin and his successors, which develops Luther's doctrine of justification by faith alone and emphasizes the grace of God and the doctrine of predestination.
– DERIVATIVES **Cal·vin·ist n.**, **Cal·vin·is·tic** /ˌkalvəˈnistik/ **adj.**, **Cal·vin·is·ti·cal adj.**

Cal·vi·no /kälˈvēnō, kal-/, Italo (1923–87), Italian novelist and short-story writer; born in Cuba. Notable works: *The Path to the Nest of Spiders* (1947) and *If on a winter's night a traveler* (1979).

calx /kalks/ ▶ **n.** (pl. **calces** /ˈkalˌsēz/) Chemistry, archaic a powdery metallic oxide formed when an ore or mineral has been heated.
– ORIGIN late Middle English: from Latin, 'lime,' probably from Greek *khalix* 'pebble, limestone.'

Ca·lyp·so /kəˈlipsō/ Greek Mythology a nymph who kept Odysseus on her island, Ogygia, for seven years.
– ORIGIN Greek, literally 'she who conceals.'

ca·lyp·so /kəˈlipsō/ ▶ **n.** (pl. **calypsos**) a kind of West Indian (originally Trinidadian) music in syncopated African rhythm, typically with words improvised on a topical theme. ■ a song in this style.
– DERIVATIVES **ca·lyp·so·ni·an** /kəˌlipˈsōnēən, ˌkalip-/ **adj. & n.**
– ORIGIN 1930s: of unknown origin.

ca·lyx /ˈkāliks, ˈkal-/ (also **calix**) ▶ **n.** (pl. **calyces** /ˈkāləˌsēz, ˈkal-/ or **calyxes**) **1** Botany the sepals of a flower, typically forming a whorl that encloses the petals and forms a protective layer around a flower in bud. Compare with **COROLLA**.
2 Zoology a cuplike cavity or structure, in particular: ■ a portion of the pelvis of a mammalian kidney. ■ the cavity in a calcareous coral skeleton that surrounds the polyp. ■ the plated body of a crinoid, excluding the stalk and arms.
– ORIGIN late 17th cent.: from Latin, from Greek *kalux* 'case of a bud, husk,' related to *kaluptein* 'to hide.'

cal·zo·ne /kalˈzōn(ē)/ ▶ **n.** (pl. **calzoni** /-ˈzōnē/ or **calzones** /-ˈzōn(ē)z/) a type of pizza that is folded in half before cooking to contain a filling.
– ORIGIN Italian dialect, probably a special use of *calzone* 'trouser leg,' with reference to the shape of the pizza.

CAM /kam/ ▶ **abbr.** computer-aided manufacturing.

cam /kam/ ▶ **n.** a projection on a rotating part in machinery, designed to make sliding contact with another part while rotating and to impart reciprocal or variable motion to it. ■ short for **CAMSHAFT**. ■ short for **CAMERA**[1].
– ORIGIN late 18th cent.: from Dutch *kam* 'comb,' as in *kamrad* 'cogwheel.'

ca·ma /ˈkämə, ˈkamə/ ▶ **n.** a hybrid animal produced by crossing a camel with a llama.

ca·ma·ra·de·rie /ˌkäm(ə)ˈrädərē, ˌkam-, -ˈrad-/ ▶ **n.** mutual trust and friendship among people who spend a lot of time together: *a genuine camaraderie on the hockey team.*
– ORIGIN mid 19th cent.: from French, from *camarade* 'comrade.'

cam·a·ril·la /ˌkaməˈrilə, -ˈrēə/ ▶ **n.** a small group of people, esp. a group of advisers to a ruler or politician, with a shared, typically nefarious, purpose: *a military camarilla that has lost any sense of political reality.*
– ORIGIN mid 19th cent.: from Spanish, diminutive of *camara* 'chamber.'

Cam·a·ril·lo /ˌkaməˈrilō, -ˈrēyō/ a city in southwestern California, west of Los Angeles; pop. 63,324 (est. 2008).

cam·as /ˈkaməs/ (also **camass** or **quamash**) ▶ **n.** a North American plant of the lily family, cultivated for its starry blue or purple flowers. ● Genera *Camassia* and *Zigadenus*, family Liliaceae: several species, including *C. quamash*, the large bulbs of which are edible.
– ORIGIN mid 19th cent.: from Chinook Jargon *qamas*, *qawas*, perhaps from Nootka.

Cam·bay, Gulf of /kamˈbā/ an inlet of the Arabian Sea on the Gujarat coast of western India, north of Mumbai (Bombay). Also called **GULF OF KHAMBAT**.

cam·ber /ˈkambər/ ▶ **n.** a slightly convex or arched shape of a road or other horizontal surface: *the deck beams are curved for the camber of the deck.* ■ Brit. a tilt built into a road at a bend or curve, enabling vehicles to maintain speed. ■ the slight sideways inclination of the front wheels of a motor vehicle. ■ the extent of curvature of a section of an airfoil.
– DERIVATIVES **cam·bered adj.**
– ORIGIN late Middle English: from Old French *cambre*, dialect variant of *chambre* 'arched,' from Latin *camurus* 'curved inward.'

cam·bi·um /ˈkambēəm/ ▶ **n.** (pl. **cambia** /-bēə/ or **cambiums**) Botany a cellular plant tissue from which phloem, xylem, or cork grows by division, resulting (in woody plants) in secondary thickening.
– DERIVATIVES **cam·bi·al** /-bēəl/ **adj.**
– ORIGIN late 16th cent. (denoting one of the alimentary humors once supposed to nourish the body): from medieval Latin, 'change, exchange.'

Cam·bo·di·a /kamˈbōdēə/ a country in Southeast Asia between Thailand and southern Vietnam; pop. 14,494,300 (est. 2009); capital, Phnom Penh; official language, Khmer. Also officially called the **KHMER REPUBLIC** (1970–75) and **KAMPUCHEA** (1976–89).

> The country was made a French protectorate in 1863 and remained under French influence until it became fully independent in 1953. During the Vietnam War, it was the scene of fighting between the North Vietnamese army and South Vietnamese and US forces. Following a civil war 1970–75, Cambodia came under the control of the Khmer Rouge led by Pol Pot; more than 2 million Cambodians died before the regime was toppled by a Vietnamese invasion in 1979. The Vietnamese withdrew in 1989, and the monarchy was restored in 1993. Elections were held in 1998 and again in 2003.

Cam·bo·di·an /kamˈbōdēən/ ▶ **adj.** of or relating to Cambodia, its people, or their language.
▶ **n. 1** a native or inhabitant of Cambodia, or a person of Cambodian descent.
2 another term for **KHMER** (the language).

cam·bo·zo·la /ˌkambəˈzōlə/ (also **cambazola**) ▶ **n.** trademark a type of German blue soft cheese with a rind like Camembert, produced using Gorgonzola blue mold.
– ORIGIN an invented name, blend of **CAMEMBERT** and **GORGONZOLA**, with the insertion of *-bo-*.

Cam·brelle /kamˈbrel/ ▶ **n.** trademark a synthetic fabric that absorbs perspiration, used as a lining material for climbing and hiking boots.

Cam·bri·an /ˈkambrēən, ˈkām-/ ▶ **adj. 1** (chiefly in names or geographical terms) Welsh: *the Cambrian Railway.*
2 Geology of, relating to, or denoting the first period in the Paleozoic era, between the end of the Precambrian eon and the beginning of the Ordovician period. ■ (as noun **the Cambrian**) the Cambrian period or the system of rocks deposited during it.

> The Cambrian lasted from about 570 million to 510 million years ago and was a time of widespread seas. It is the earliest period in which fossils, notably trilobites, can be used in geological dating.

– ORIGIN mid 17th cent.: from Latin *Cambria* 'Wales,' variant of *Cumbria*, from Welsh *Cymry* 'Welshman' or *Cymru* 'Wales.'

cam·bric /ˈkāmbrik/ ▶ **n.** a lightweight, closely woven white linen or cotton fabric.
– ORIGIN late Middle English: from *Kamerijk*, Flemish form of *Cambrai*, a town in northern France, where it was originally made. Compare with **CHAMBRAY**.

Cam·bridge /ˈkāmbrij/ **1** a city in eastern England; pop. 116,900 (est. 2009). Cambridge University is located here.
2 a city in eastern Massachusetts, across the Charles River from Boston; pop. 105,596 (est. 2008). Harvard University and the Massachusetts Institute of Technology are located here.

Cam·bridge·shire /ˈkāmbrijsHər, -ˌSHi(ə)r/ a county in eastern England; county town, Cambridge.

Cam·by·ses /kamˈbīˌsēz/ (died 522 BC), king of Persia 529–522 BC, son of Cyrus. He is chiefly remembered for his conquest of Egypt in 525 BC.

cam·cord·er /ˈkamˌkôrdər/ ▶ **n.** a portable combined video camera and video recorder.
– ORIGIN 1980s: blend of **CAMERA**[1] and **RECORDER**.

Cam·den /ˈkamdən/ an industrial city in southwestern New Jersey, across the Delaware River from Philadelphia in Pennsylvania; pop. 79,383 (est. 2008).

came /kām/ past tense of **COME**.

cam·el /ˈkaməl/ ▶ **n. 1** a large, long-necked ungulate mammal of arid country, with long slender legs, broad cushioned feet, and either one or two humps on the back. Camels can survive for long periods without food or drink, chiefly by using up the fat reserves in their humps. ● Genus *Camelus*, family Camelidae (the **camel family**): two species (see **ARABIAN CAMEL**, **BACTRIAN CAMEL**). The camel family

also includes the llama and its relatives. ■ a fabric made from camel hair. ■ a light yellowish-brown color like that of camel hair.
2 an apparatus for raising a sunken ship, consisting of one or more watertight chests to provide buoyancy. ■ a large floating fender used to keep a vessel off the dock.
– ORIGIN Old English, from Latin *camelus*, from Greek *kamēlos*, of Semitic origin.

cam·el·back /ˈkaməlˌbak/ ▶ **n.** a back with a hump-shaped curve on a sofa or other piece of furniture: [as modifier] *a camelback sofa.*

cam·el crick·et ▶ **n.** a wingless humpbacked insect related to the grasshoppers, typically living in caves or holes. Also called CAVE CRICKET. ● Family Raphidophoridae: several genera.

cam·el·eer /ˌkaməˈli(ə)r/ ▶ **n.** a person who controls or rides a camel.

cam·el hair (also **camel's hair**) ▶ **n. 1** a fabric made from the hair of a camel: [as modifier] *a camel-hair coat.*
2 [usu. as modifier] fine, soft hair from a squirrel's tail, used in artists' brushes.

cam·e·lid /kəˈmēlid, ˈkaməlid/ ▶ **n.** Zoology a mammal of the camel family (Camelidae).
– ORIGIN late 20th cent.: from modern Latin *Camelidae* (plural), from Latin *camelus* 'camel,' from Greek *kamēlos*.

ca·mel·lia /kəˈmēlyə/ ▶ **n.** an evergreen eastern Asian shrub related to the tea plant, grown for its showy flowers and shiny leaves. ● Genus *Camellia*, family Theaceae: several species, in particular the **common camellia** (*C. japonica*), which has numerous cultivars and hybrids.
– ORIGIN modern Latin, named by Linnaeus after Joseph *Kamel* (Latinized as *Camellus*), Moravian botanist (1661–1706), who described the flora of Luzon, an island in the Philippines.

Ca·mel·lia State a nickname for the state of ALABAMA.

ca·mel·o·pard /kəˈmeləˌpärd/ ▶ **n.** archaic a giraffe.
– ORIGIN late Middle English: via Latin from Greek *kamēlopardalis*, from *kamēlos* 'camel' + *pardalis* (see PARD).

Ca·mel·o·par·da·lis /kəˌmeləˈpärdl-is/ Astronomy a large but inconspicuous northern constellation (the Giraffe), between Polaris and Perseus. ■ (as genitive **Camelopardalis**) used with a preceding letter or numeral to designate a star in this constellation: *the star Alpha Camelopardalis.*
– ORIGIN via Latin from Greek *kamēlopardalis* (see CAMELOPARD).

Cam·e·lot /ˈkaməˌlät/ (in Arthurian legend) the place where King Arthur held his court. ■ (as noun **a Camelot**) a place associated with glittering romance and optimism.

cam·el spi·der ▶ **n.** another term for SUN SPIDER.

Cam·em·bert /ˈkaməmˌbe(ə)r/ ▶ **n.** a kind of rich, soft, creamy cheese with a whitish rind, originally made near Camembert in Normandy.

cam·e·o /ˈkamēˌō/ ▶ **n.** (pl. **cameos**) **1** a piece of jewelry, typically oval in shape, consisting of a portrait in profile carved in relief on a background of a different color.
2 a short descriptive literary sketch that neatly encapsulates someone or something: *cameos of street life.* ■ a small character part in a play or movie, played by a distinguished actor or a celebrity: [as modifier] *he played numerous cameo roles.*
– ORIGIN late Middle English: from Old French *camahieu*, *cama(h)u*; later influenced by Italian *cam(m)eo*, from medieval Latin *cammaeus*, related to the Old French word.

cam·er·a[1] /ˈkam(ə)rə/ ▶ **n.** a device for recording visual images in the form of photographs, movie film, or video signals.
– PHRASES **on** (or **off**) **camera** while being filmed or televised (or not being filmed or televised): *on camera, she was error-prone and nervous.*
– ORIGIN mid 19th cent.: from Latin (see CAMERA[2], CAMERA OBSCURA).

cam·er·a[2] ▶ **n.** [in names] a chamber or round building: *the Radcliffe Camera.*
– PHRASES **in camera** chiefly Law in private, in particular taking place in the private chambers of a judge, with the press and public excluded: *judges assess the merits of such claims in camera.* [late Latin, 'in the chamber.']

cam·er·a lu·ci·da /ˈlo͞osidə/ ▶ **n.** an instrument in which rays of light are reflected by a prism to produce on a sheet of paper an image, from which a drawing can be made.
– ORIGIN mid 18th cent.: from Latin, 'bright chamber,' on the pattern of *camera obscura*.

cam·er·a·man /ˈkam(ə)rəmən, -ˌman/ (or **camerawoman**) ▶ **n.** (pl. **cameramen** or **camerawomen**) a person whose profession involves operating a television or movie camera.

cam·er·a ob·scu·ra /əbˈskyo͝orə/ ▶ **n.** a darkened box with a convex lens or aperture for projecting the image of an external object onto a screen inside. It is important historically in the development of photography. ■ a small round building with a rotating angled mirror at the apex of the roof, projecting an image of the landscape onto a horizontal surface inside.
– ORIGIN early 18th cent.: from Latin, 'dark chamber.'

cam·er·a·per·son /ˈkam(ə)rəˌpərsən/ ▶ **n.** a cameraman or camerawoman (used as a neutral alternative).

cam·er·a phone ▶ **n.** a cellular phone incorporating a digital camera.

cam·er·a-read·y ▶ **adj.** Printing (of matter to be printed) in the right form and of good enough quality to be reproduced photographically onto a printing plate: *camera-ready copy.*

cam·er·a·work /ˈkam(ə)rəˌwərk/ ▶ **n.** the way in which cameras are used in a movie or television program: *discreet camerawork and underplayed acting.*

Cam·er·on /ˈkamərən/, David (William Donald) (1966–), British Conservative statesman; prime minister since 2010.

Cam·e·roon /ˌkaməˈro͞on/ a country on the western coast of Africa, between Nigeria and Gabon; pop. 18,879,300 (est. 2009); capital, Yaoundé; languages, French and English (official), many local languages, pidgin. French name **Cameroun**.

> A German protectorate from 1884 until 1916, it was subsequently administered by France and then by Britain as a League of Nations (later United Nations) trusteeship. In 1960, the French part became an independent republic and was joined in 1961 by part of British Cameroon; the remainder became part of Nigeria. Cameroon became a member of the Commonwealth of Nations in 1995.

– DERIVATIVES **Cam·e·roon·i·an adj. & n.**

cam fol·low·er ▶ **n.** the part of a machine in sliding or rolling contact with a rotating cam and given motion by it.

cam·i /ˈkamē/ ▶ **n.** (pl. **camis**) informal a camisole.

Cam·i·sard /ˌkaməˈzär(d)/ ▶ **n.** a member of the French Protestant insurgents who rebelled against the persecution that followed the revocation of the Edict of Nantes.
– ORIGIN French, from Provençal *camisa*, from late Latin *camisia* 'shirt,' because of the white shirts worn by the insurgents over their clothing for ease of recognition.

cam·i·sole /ˈkaməˌsōl/ ▶ **n.** a woman's loose-fitting undergarment for the upper body, typically held up by shoulder straps and having decorative trimming.
– ORIGIN early 19th cent.: from French, either from Italian *camiciola*, diminutive of *camicia*, or from Spanish *camisola*, diminutive of *camisa*, both from late Latin *camisia* 'shirt or nightgown.'

cam·lock /ˈkamˌläk/ ▶ **n.** a fastening mechanism that incorporates a cam or tab that is turned to engage a catch or slot.

cam·o /ˈkamō/ ▶ **n.** informal short for CAMOUFLAGE: [as modifier] *a camo jacket.*

Ca·mõ·es /kəˈmoinsh/ (also **Camoëns** /ˈkamōˌens/), Luis (Vaz) de (*c.*1524–80), Portuguese poet. His most noted work, *The Lusiads* (1572), describes Vasco da Gama's discovery of the sea route to India.

cam·o·mile ▶ **n.** variant spelling of CHAMOMILE.

Ca·mor·ra /kəˈmôrə/ (**the Camorra**) a secret criminal society originating in Naples and Neapolitan emigrant communities in the 19th century. Some members later moved to the US and formed links with the Mafia.
– ORIGIN Italian, perhaps from Spanish *camorra* 'dispute, quarrel.'

cam·ou·flage /ˈkaməˌfläzh, -ˌfläj/ ▶ **n.** the disguising of military personnel, equipment, and installations by painting or covering them to make them blend in with their surroundings: *on the trenches were pieces of turf, which served for camouflage* | [as modifier] *camouflage nets.* ■ the clothing or materials used for such a purpose: *figures dressed in army camouflage.* ■ an animal's natural coloring or form that enables it to blend in with its surroundings: *the whiteness of polar bears provides camouflage.* ■ actions or devices intended to disguise or mislead: *much of my apparent indifference was merely protective camouflage.*
▶ **v.** [with obj.] hide or disguise the presence of (a person, animal, or object) by means of camouflage: *the war area had to be camouflaged with mud.* ■ conceal the existence of (something undesirable): *grievances should be discussed, not camouflaged.*
– ORIGIN World War I: from French, from *camoufler* 'to disguise' (originally thieves' slang), from Italian *camuffare* 'disguise, deceive,' perhaps by association with French *camouflet* 'whiff of smoke in the face.'

Camp /kamp/, Walter Chauncey (1859–1925), US football coach. One of the first to play US football, he coached at Yale 1888–92 and was influential in shaping the rules of the sport. In 1889, he and a colleague initiated the annual selection of an All-American football team.

camp[1] /kamp/ ▶ **n. 1** a place with temporary accommodations of huts, tents, or other structures, typically used by soldiers, refugees, prisoners, or travelers: *the enemy camp* | *a detention camp* | *the shot woke the whole camp.* ■ a recreational institution providing facilities for outdoor activities, sports, crafts, and other special interests and typically featuring rustic overnight accommodations: *a summer camp for children* | *drama camp.* ■ temporary overnight lodging out of doors, typically in tents: *we **made camp** at a bend in the creek* | *we **pitched camp** at a fine spot.* ■ a facility at which athletes train during the off-season: *football tryout camps.*
2 the supporters of a particular party or doctrine regarded collectively: *his views were firmly rooted in the conservative camp.*
▶ **v.** [no obj.] live for a time in a camp, tent, or camper, as when on vacation: *parks in which you can camp or stay in a chalet* | (as noun **camping**) *camping attracts people of all ages.* ■ lodge temporarily, esp. in an inappropriate or uncomfortable place: *we **camped out** for the night in a mission schoolroom.* ■ remain persistently in one place: *the press will be camping on your doorstep once they get onto this story.*
– PHRASES **break camp** take down a tent or the tents of an encampment when ready to leave.
– ORIGIN early 16th cent.: from French *camp*, *champ*, from Italian *campo*, from Latin *campus* 'level ground,' specifically applied to the *Campus Martius* in Rome, used for games, athletic practice, and military drill.

camp[2] informal ▶ **adj.** deliberately exaggerated and theatrical in style, typically for humorous effect: *the movie seems more camp than shocking or gruesome.* ■ (of a man or his manner) ostentatiously and extravagantly effeminate: *a heavily made-up and highly camp actor.*
▶ **n.** deliberately exaggerated and theatrical behavior or style: *Hollywood camp.*
▶ **v.** [no obj.] (of a man) behave in an ostentatiously effeminate way: *he **camped it up** a bit for the cameras.*
– DERIVATIVES **camp·i·ly** /ˈkampəlē/ **adv.**, **camp·i·ness n.**, **camp·y adj.**
– ORIGIN early 20th cent.: of unknown origin.

cam·paign /kamˈpān/ ▶ **n.** a series of military operations intended to achieve a particular objective, confined to a particular area, or involving a specified type of fighting: *a desert campaign* | *the air campaign* | *the army set off **on campaign**.* ■ an organized course of action to achieve a particular goal: *an advertising campaign* | *the campaign for a full inquiry into the regime* | [with infinitive] *his campaign to win the heart of a new woman.*
▶ **v.** [no obj.] work in an organized and active way toward a particular goal, typically a political or social one: *people who campaigned against child labor* | [with infinitive] *the services he had campaigned to protect.*
– ORIGIN early 17th cent. (denoting a tract of open country): from French *campagne* 'open country,' via Italian from late Latin *campania*, from *campus* 'level ground' (see CAMP[1]). The change in sense arose from an army's practice of "taking the field" (i.e., moving from a fortress or town to open country) at the onset of summer.

cam·paign·er /kamˈpānər/ ▶ **n.** a person who actively promotes the goals of a cause: *human rights campaigners are furious at the government's decision.*

Cam·pa·nel·la /ˌkampəˈnelə/, Roy (1921–93), US baseball player; known as **Campy**. He was a catcher for the Brooklyn Dodgers 1948–58. Baseball Hall of Fame (1969).

cam·pa·ni·le /ˌkampəˈnēlē, -ˈnēl/ ▶ **n.** an Italian bell tower, esp. a freestanding one.
– ORIGIN mid 17th cent.: from Italian, from *campana* 'bell.'

cam·pa·nol·o·gy /ˌkampəˈnäləjē/ ▶ **n.** the art or practice of bell-ringing.
– DERIVATIVES **cam·pa·no·log·i·cal** /ˌkampənlˈäjikəl/ **adj.**, **cam·pa·nol·o·gist** /-jist/ **n.**

C

– ORIGIN mid 19th cent.: from modern Latin *campanologia*, from late Latin *campana* 'bell.'

cam·pan·u·la /kam'panyələ/ ▶ n. another term for BELLFLOWER.
– ORIGIN modern Latin, diminutive of late Latin *campana* 'bell.'

cam·pan·u·late /kam'panyəlit, -ˌlāt/ ▶ adj. Botany (of a flower) bell-shaped, as in a campanula.

Cam·pa·ri /käm'pärē/ ▶ n. trademark a pinkish aperitif flavored with bitters.
– ORIGIN named after the manufacturer.

Camp·bell[1] /'kam(b)əl/, John Archibald (1811–89), US Supreme Court associate justice 1853–61. Appointed to the Court by President Pierce, he resigned to serve as assistant secretary of war in the Confederate cabinet 1862–65.

Camp·bell[2], Kim (1947–), Canadian Progressive Conservative statesman; prime minister 1993; full name *Avril Phaedra Douglas Campbell*. She was Canada's first female prime minister.

Camp·bell-Ban·ner·man /'banərmən/, Sir Henry (1836–1908), British statesman; prime minister 1905–08.

Camp Da·vid the country retreat of the President, in the Catoctin Mountains (part of the Blue Ridge Mountains) in northeastern Maryland. President Carter hosted talks there between the leaders of Israel and Egypt which resulted in the Camp David agreements (1978) and the Egypt–Israel peace treaty of 1979.

Cam·pe·che /käm'päcHā, kam'pēcHē/ a state in southeastern Mexico, on the Yucatán Peninsula. ■ its capital, a seaport on the Gulf of Mexico; pop. 238,850 (2005).

camp·er /'kampər/ ▶ n. **1** a person who spends a vacation in a tent or camp.
2 a large motor vehicle with facilities for sleeping and cooking while camping.
– PHRASES **happy camper** a comfortable, contented person: *when I'm onstage, I'm really a happy camper.*

cam·pe·si·no /ˌkampə'sēnō, ˌkäm-/ ▶ n. (pl. **campesinos**) (in Spanish-speaking regions) a peasant farmer.
– ORIGIN Spanish.

camp·fire /'kampˌfī(ə)r/ ▶ n. an open-air fire in a camp, used for cooking and as a focal point for social activity.

camp fol·low·er ▶ n. a civilian who works in or is attached to a military camp. ■ a person who is nominally attached to a group but is not fully committed or does not make a substantial contribution to its activities: *cynical opportunists and camp followers.*

camp·ground /'kampˌground/ ▶ n. a place used for camping, esp. one equipped with cooking grills, water, and bathrooms. ■ a place where a camp meeting is held.

cam·phor /'kamfər/ ▶ n. a white, volatile, crystalline substance with an aromatic smell and bitter taste, occurring in certain essential oils. ● A terpenoid ketone; chem. formula: $C_{10}H_{16}O$.
– ORIGIN Middle English: from Old French *camphore* or medieval Latin *camphora*, from Arabic *kāfūr*, via Malay from Sanskrit *karpūra*.

cam·phor·ate /'kamfəˌrāt/ ▶ v. [with obj.] (usu. as adj. **camphorated**) impregnate or treat with camphor.

cam·phor tree ▶ n. an eastern Asian tree that belongs to the laurel family and serves as the chief natural source of camphor. ● *Cinnamomum camphora*, family Lauraceae.

Cam·pi·nas /käm'pēnəs, kän-/ a city in southeastern Brazil, northwest of São Paulo; pop. 1,039,297 (2007).

Cam·pi·on /'kampēən/ St. Edmund (1540–81), English Jesuit priest and martyr. Feast day, December 1.

cam·pi·on /'kampēən/ ▶ n. a plant of the pink family, typically having pink or white flowers with notched petals, found in both Eurasia and North America. ● Genera *Silene* and *Lychnis*, family Caryophyllaceae.
– ORIGIN mid 16th cent.: perhaps related to CHAMPION. The name was originally used for the rose campion, whose name in Latin (*Lychnis coronaria*) and Greek (*lukhnis stephanōmatikē*) means 'campion fit for a crown,' and which was said in classical times to have been used for victors' garlands.

camp meet·ing ▶ n. a religious meeting held in the open air or in a tent, often lasting several days.

cam·po /'kampō, 'kämpō/ ▶ n. (pl. **campos**) **1** (usu. **the campo**) (in South America, esp. Brazil), a grass plain with occasional stunted trees.
2 a square in an Italian or Spanish town.
– ORIGIN from Spanish, Portuguese, and Italian *campo*, literally 'field.'

Cam·po·bel·lo Is·land /ˌkampə'belō/ a resort island in southwestern New Brunswick, off Eastport in Maine, noted as the vacation home of Franklin D. Roosevelt.

Cam·po Gran·de /'käN(m)pōō 'gräN(n)də/ a city in southwestern Brazil; pop. 724,524 (2007).

camp·o·ree /ˌkampə'rē/ ▶ n. a local or regional camping event for Girl Scouts or Boy Scouts.
– ORIGIN late 20th cent.: blend of CAMP[1] and JAMBOREE.

camp·site /'kampˌsīt/ ▶ n. a place used for camping.

cam·pus /'kampəs/ ▶ n. (pl. **campuses**) the grounds and buildings of a university or college: *for the first year I had a room **on campus**.* ■ the grounds of a school, hospital, or other institution.
– ORIGIN late 18th cent. (originally US): from Latin *campus* 'field' (see CAMP[1]).

cam·py·lo·bac·ter /'kampələˌbaktər, kam'pilə-/ ▶ n. Medicine a bacterium that sometimes causes abortion in animals and food poisoning in humans. ● Genus *Campylobacter*: several species, in particular *C. jejuni*; curved or spiral Gram-negative bacteria.
– ORIGIN 1970s: modern Latin, from Greek *kampulos* 'bent' + BACTERIUM.

Cam Ranh Bay /'kam 'rän/ an inlet of the South China Sea, in south central Vietnam. It has been a major base for France, Japan, the former Soviet Union, and the US, which had a major installation here during the Vietnam War.

cam·shaft /'kamˌsHaft/ ▶ n. a shaft with one or more cams attached to it, esp. one operating the valves in an internal combustion engine.

Ca·mus /ka'mōō/, Albert (1913–60), French novelist, playwright, and essayist; closely aligned with existentialism. Notable works: *The Stranger* (1942), *The Plague* (1947), and *The Rebel* (1951). Nobel Prize for Literature (1957).

can[1] /kan/ ▶ modal v. (3rd sing. present **can**; past **could** /ko͝od/) **1** be able to: *they can run fast | I could hear footsteps | he can't afford it.* ■ be able to through acquired knowledge or skill: *I can speak Italian.* ■ have the opportunity or possibility to: *there are many ways vacationers can take money abroad.* ■ [with negative or in questions] used to express doubt or surprise about the possibility of something's being the case: *he can't have finished | where can she have gone?*
2 be permitted to: *you can use the phone if you want to | nobody could legally drink on the premises.* ■ used to ask someone to do something: *can you open the window? | can't you leave me alone?* ■ used to make a suggestion or offer: *we can have another drink if you like.*
3 used to indicate that something is typically the case: *antique clocks can seem out of place in modern homes | he could be very moody.*
– ORIGIN Old English *cunnan* 'know' (in Middle English 'know how to'), related to Dutch *kunnen* and German *können*; from an Indo-European root shared by Latin *gnoscere* 'know' and Greek *gignōskein* 'know.'

> **USAGE** Is there any difference between **can** and **may** when used to request or express permission, as in ***may** I ask you a few questions?* or ***can** I ask you a few questions?* Many people feel that **can** should be reserved for expressions denoting capability, as in ***can** you swim?*, rather than for those relating to permission. **May** is, generally speaking, a politer and more formal way of asking for something, and is the better choice in more formal contexts. See also usage at MAY[1].

can[2] ▶ n. **1** a cylindrical metal container: *a garbage can | a can of paint.* ■ a small steel or aluminum container in which food or drink is hermetically sealed for storage over long periods: *soup cans.* ■ the quantity of food or drink held by such a container: *he drank two cans of beer.*
2 (**the can**) informal prison.
3 (**the can**) informal the toilet.
▶ v. (**cans, canning, canned**) [with obj.] **1** preserve (food) in a can.
2 informal dismiss (someone) from their job: *he was canned because of a fight over promotion.* ■ reject (something) as inadequate: *the editorial team was so disappointed that they canned the project.*
– PHRASES **a can of worms** a complicated matter likely to prove awkward or embarrassing: *to question the traditional model of education **opens up a can of worms**.* **in the can** informal on tape or film and ready to be broadcast or released.
– DERIVATIVES **can·ner** n.
– ORIGIN Old English *canne*, related to Dutch *kan* and German *Kanne*; either of Germanic origin or from late Latin *canna*.

Can. ▶ abbr. Canada or Canadian.

Ca·na /'kānə/ an ancient small town in Galilee where Christ is said to have performed his first miracle by changing water into wine during a marriage feast (John 2:1–11).

Ca·naan /'kānən/ the biblical name for the area of ancient Palestine west of the Jordan River, the Promised Land of the Israelites, who conquered and occupied it during the latter part of the 2nd millennium BC.
– DERIVATIVES **Ca·naan·ite** /-ˌnīt/ n. & adj.
– ORIGIN early 17th cent.: via ecclesiastical Latin from ecclesiastical Greek *Khanaan*, from Hebrew *kĕna ʿan*.

Can·a·da /'kanədə/ a country in northern North America, the second largest country in the world; pop. 33,487,200 (est. 2009); capital, Ottawa; official languages, English and French.

> Eastern Canada was colonized by the French in the 17th century, but the British emerged as the ruling colonial power in 1763 after the Seven Years War. Canada became a federation of provinces with dominion status in 1867. The signing of the Constitution Act of 1982 was the final step in attaining legal independence from the UK; however, Canada remains a member of the Commonwealth of Nations. French-speakers are largely concentrated in Quebec, the focal point for the French-Canadian separatist movement.

– DERIVATIVES **Ca·na·di·an** /kə'nādēən/ n. & adj.

Can·a·da bal·sam ▶ n. a yellowish resin obtained from the balsam fir and used for mounting preparations on microscope slides.

Can·a·da goose ▶ n. a common North American goose with a black head and neck, a white chinstrap, and a loud, trumpeting call. ● *Branta canadensis*, family Anatidae.

Can·a·da jay ▶ n. another term for GRAY JAY.

Can·a·darm /'kanəˌdärm/ ▶ n. the popular name for a robotic manipulation system designed for use in zero gravity. It has accompanied numerous space missions as a component on space shuttles.
– ORIGIN 1970s: blend of *Canada* (where it was manufactured) and *arm*.

Can·a·da this·tle ▶ n. the European creeping or field thistle, which has become naturalized as a serious weed in North America. ● *Cirsium arvense*, family Compositae.

Ca·na·di·an foot·ball /kə'nādēən/ ▶ n. a form of football played in Canada, derived from rugby but now resembling American football. There are twelve players on a side.

Ca·na·di·an French ▶ n. the form of the French language written and spoken by French Canadians.

Ca·na·di·an goose ▶ n. another term for CANADA GOOSE.

Ca·na·di·an Riv·er (also **South Canadian River**) a river that flows for 900 miles (1,450 km) from eastern New Mexico across the Texas Panhandle and Oklahoma. Oklahoma City lies on it.

Ca·na·di·an Shield a large plateau that occupies more than two fifths of the land area of Canada and is drained by rivers flowing into Hudson Bay. Also called LAURENTIAN PLATEAU.

ca·naille /kə'nī, -'nāl/ ▶ n. (**the canaille**) derogatory the common people; the masses: *the haughty contempt of a grandee sneering at the canaille.*
– ORIGIN French, from Italian *canaglia* 'pack of dogs,' from *cane* 'dog.'

ca·nal /kə'nal/ ▶ n. an artificial waterway constructed to allow the passage of boats or ships inland or to convey water for irrigation. ■ a tubular duct in a plant or animal, serving to convey or contain food, liquid, or air: *the ear canal.* ■ Astronomy any of a number of linear markings formerly reported as seen by telescope on the planet Mars. [named *canali* ('channels') by G. V. Schiaparelli (1835–1910); the markings are now thought to have arisen from eye or lens defects.]
– ORIGIN late Middle English: from Old French, alteration of *chanel* 'channel,' from Latin *canalis* 'pipe, groove, channel,' from *canna* 'cane.'

ca·nal boat ▶ n. a long, narrow boat used on canals.

Ca·na·let·to /ˌkanl'etō/ (1697–1768), Italian painter; born *Giovanni Antonio Canal*. He is noted for his paintings of Venetian festivals and scenery.

can·a·lic·u·lus /ˌkanl'ikyələs/ ▶ n. (pl. **canaliculi** /-ˌlī/) Anatomy a small channel or duct.
– DERIVATIVES **can·a·lic·u·lar** /-'ikyələr/ adj.

can·al·ize /'kanəlˌīz/ ▶ v. [with obj.] convert (a river) into a navigable canal. ■ convey (something) through a duct or channel. ■ give a direction or purpose to (something): *his strategy was to canalize the enthusiasm of the diehards into party channels.*
– DERIVATIVES **can·al·i·za·tion** /ˌkanl-ə'zāsHən/ n.
– ORIGIN mid 19th cent.: from French *canaliser*, from *canal* 'channel' (see CANAL).

Ca·nal Zone see PANAMA CANAL.

can·a·pé /ˈkanəˌpā, -ˌpē/ ▶ **n.** **1** a small piece of bread or pastry with a savory topping, often served with drinks at a reception or formal party.
2 a sofa, esp. a decorative French antique.
– ORIGIN French, sense 1 being a figurative extension of the sense 'sofa' (as a "couch" on which to place toppings). See also CANOPY.

ca·nard /kəˈnär(d)/ ▶ **n.** **1** an unfounded rumor or story: *the old canard that LA is a cultural wasteland.*
2 a small winglike projection attached to an aircraft forward of the main wing to provide extra stability or control, sometimes replacing the tail.
– ORIGIN mid 19th cent.: from French, literally 'duck,' also 'hoax,' from Old French *caner* 'to quack.'

Ca·nar·sie /kəˈnärsē/ a residential section of southeastern Brooklyn in New York City, along Jamaica Bay.
– ORIGIN named after the American Indian tribe who originally inhabited the area.

ca·nar·y /kəˈne(ə)rē/ ▶ **n.** (pl. **canaries**) **1** a mainly African finch with a melodious song, typically having yellowish-green plumage. One kind is popular as a pet bird and has been bred in a variety of colors, esp. bright yellow. ● Genus *Serinus*, family Fringillidae: several species, esp. the **island canary** (*S. canaria*), which is native to the Canary Islands, the Azores, and Madeira, and from which the domestic canary was developed.
2 (also **canary yellow**) a bright yellow color resembling the plumage of a canary.
3 (also **canary wine**) historical a sweet wine from the Canary Islands, similar to Madeira.
– ORIGIN late 16th cent.: from French *canari*, from Spanish *canario* 'canary' or 'person from the Canary Islands' (see CANARY ISLANDS).

ca·nar·y grass ▶ **n.** a tall grass of northwestern Africa and the Canary Islands, grown for its seeds, which are fed to canaries and other caged finches. ● Genus *Phalaris*, family Gramineae: several species, in particular *P. canariensis*.

Ca·nar·y Is·lands /kəˈne(ə)rē/ (also **the Canaries**) a group of islands in the Atlantic Ocean, off the northwestern coast of Africa, that forms an autonomous region of Spain; capital, Las Palmas; pop. 2,098,593 (2009).
– ORIGIN from French *Canarie*, via Spanish from Latin *Canaria* (*insula*) '(island) of dogs,' from *canis* 'dog,' one of the islands being noted in Roman times for large dogs.

ca·nas·ta /kəˈnastə/ ▶ **n.** a card game resembling rummy, using two packs. It is usually played by two pairs of partners, and the aim is to collect sets (or melds) of cards. ■ a meld of seven cards in this game.
– ORIGIN 1940s: from Spanish (of Uruguayan origin), literally 'basket,' based on Latin *canistrum* 'basket' (see CANISTER).

Ca·nav·er·al, Cape /kəˈnav(ə)rəl/ a cape on the eastern coast of Florida, known as Cape Kennedy from 1963 until 1973. It is the site of the John F. Kennedy Space Center.

Can·ber·ra /ˈkanb(ə)rə, -ˌberə/ the capital of Australia and seat of the federal government, in the Australian Capital Territory; it is an enclave within New South Wales; pop. 345,257 (2008).

can·can /ˈkanˌkan/ ▶ **n.** a lively, high-kicking stage dance originating in 19th-century Parisian music halls and performed by women in long skirts and petticoats.
– ORIGIN mid 19th cent.: from French, child's word for *canard* 'duck,' from Old French *caner* 'to quack.'

can·cel /ˈkansəl/ ▶ **v.** (**cancels, canceling, canceled**; Brit. **cancels, cancelling, cancelled**) [with obj.] **1** decide or announce that (an arranged or planned event) will not take place: *he was forced to cancel his visit.* ■ annul or revoke (a formal arrangement which is in effect): *his visa had been canceled.* ■ abolish or make void (a financial obligation): *I intend to cancel your debt to me.* ■ mark, pierce, or tear (a ticket, check, or postage stamp) to show that it has been used or invalidated: [as adj.] *canceled checks.*
2 (of a factor or circumstance) neutralize or negate the force or effect of (another): *the electric fields may cancel each other out.* ■ Mathematics delete (an equal factor) from both sides of an equation or from the numerator and denominator of a fraction.
▶ **n.** **1** a mark made on a postage stamp to show that it has been used.
2 Printing a new page or section inserted in a book to replace the original text, typically to correct an error: [as modifier] *a cancel title page.*
– ORIGIN late Middle English (in the sense 'obliterate or delete writing by drawing or stamping lines across it'): from Old French *canceller*, from Latin *cancellare*, from *cancelli* 'crossbars.'

can·cel·er /ˈkansələr/ (also **canceller**) ▶ **n.** a device used to cancel something, esp. one that makes a cancellation on a postage stamp.

can·cel·la·tion /ˌkansəˈlāSHən/ ▶ **n.** the action of canceling something that has been arranged or planned: *train services are subject to cancellation at short notice | the project was threatened with cancellation by the government | the cancellation of the performance.* ■ a crossing out of something written: *all cancellations on documents must be made indelibly.* ■ a visible or electronic mark placed on a postage stamp to show that it has been used. ■ Law the annulling of a legal document: *the debtor can procure cancellation if satisfied within one month.*

can·cel·lous /ˈkansələs/ ▶ **adj.** Anatomy of or denoting bone tissue with a meshlike structure containing many pores, typical of the interior of mature bones.
– ORIGIN mid 19th cent.: from Latin *cancelli* 'crossbars' + -OUS.

Can·cer /ˈkansər/ **1** Astronomy a constellation (the Crab), said to represent a crab crushed under the foot of Hercules. It is most noted for the globular star cluster of Praesepe (the Beehive cluster). ■ (as genitive **Cancri** /ˈkaNGkrē/) used with a preceding letter or numeral to designate a star in this constellation: *the star Delta Cancri.*
2 Astrology the fourth sign of the zodiac, which the sun enters at the northern summer solstice (about June 21). ■ (**a Cancer**) a person born when the sun is in this sign.
– PHRASES **tropic of Cancer** see TROPIC¹.
– DERIVATIVES **Can·cer·i·an** /kanˈsərēən, -ˈsi(ə)r-/ **n. & adj.** (sense 2).
– ORIGIN Latin.

can·cer /ˈkansər/ ▶ **n.** the disease caused by an uncontrolled division of abnormal cells in a part of the body: *he's got cancer | smoking is the major cause of lung cancer.* ■ a malignant growth or tumor resulting from such a division of cells: *most skin cancers are curable.* ■ a practice or phenomenon perceived to be evil or destructive and hard to contain or eradicate: *racism is a cancer sweeping across Europe.*
– DERIVATIVES **can·cer·ous** /ˈkansərəs/ **adj.**
– ORIGIN Old English, from Latin, 'crab or creeping ulcer,' translating Greek *karkinos*, said to have been applied to such tumors because the swollen veins around them resembled the limbs of a crab. CANKER was the usual form until the 17th cent. Compare with CANCER.

can·cer clus·ter ▶ **n.** a geographic area with a statistically higher than average occurrence of cancer among its residents.

can·cer stick ▶ **n.** informal, humorous a cigarette.

can·croid /ˈkaNGˌkroid/ ▶ **adj.** **1** Zoology like a crab, esp. in structure.
2 Medicine (of a growth) resembling cancer.

Can·cún /kaNGˈkōōn, kan-/ a resort town in southeastern Mexico, on the northeastern coast of the Yucatán Peninsula; pop. 526,701 (2005).

can·de·la /kanˈdēlə, -ˈdelə/ (abbr.: **cd**) ▶ **n.** Physics the SI unit of luminous intensity. One candela is the luminous intensity, in a given direction, of a source that emits monochromatic radiation of frequency 540×10^{12} Hz and has a radiant intensity in that direction of $^1/_{683}$ watt per steradian.
– ORIGIN 1950s: from Latin, 'candle.'

can·de·la·brum /ˌkandəˈläbrəm, -ˈlab-/ ▶ **n.** (pl. **candelabra** /-ˈläbrə, -ˈlabrə/) a large branched candlestick or holder for several candles or lamps.
– ORIGIN early 19th cent.: from Latin, from *candela* (see CANDLE).

> **USAGE** Based on the Latin forms, the correct singular is **candelabrum** and the plural is **candelabra**. In practice, however, **candelabra** is increasingly used as the singular form, with the plural as **candelabras**. In the Oxford English Corpus, these forms are more common than the traditional ones and are coming to be regarded as part of standard English.

can·des·cent /kanˈdesənt/ ▶ **adj.** glowing with, or as with, heat.
– DERIVATIVES **can·des·cence n., can·des·cent·ly adv.**

can·did /ˈkandid/ ▶ **adj.** **1** truthful and straightforward; frank: *his responses were remarkably candid | a candid discussion.*
2 (of a photograph of a person) taken informally, esp. without the subject's knowledge.
– DERIVATIVES **can·did·ly adv., can·did·ness n.**
– ORIGIN mid 17th cent. (in the Latin sense): from Latin *candidus* 'white.' Subsequent early senses were 'pure, innocent,' 'unbiased,' and 'free from malice,' hence 'frank' (late 17th cent). Compare with CANDOR.

can·di·da /ˈkandidə/ ▶ **n.** a yeastlike, parasitic fungus that can sometimes cause thrush. ● Genus *Candida*, phylum Ascomycota, esp. *C. albicans*.
– ORIGIN modern Latin, feminine of Latin *candidus* 'white.'

can·di·date /ˈkandiˌdāt, -dit/ ▶ **n.** a person who applies for a job or is nominated for election: *candidates applying for this position should be computer-literate | the Republican candidate.* ■ a person taking an examination: *doctoral candidates in literature.* ■ a person or thing regarded as suitable for or likely to receive a particular fate, treatment, or position: *she was the perfect candidate for a biography | a leading candidate for the title of New York's ugliest building.*
– DERIVATIVES **can·di·da·cy** /ˈkandidəsē/ **n.**, **can·di·da·ture** /-ˌCHo͝or, -CHər/ **n.** (Brit.).
– ORIGIN early 17th cent.: from Latin *candidatus* 'white-robed,' also denoting a candidate for office (who traditionally wore a white toga), from *candidus* 'white.'

can·di·di·a·sis /ˌkandiˈdīəsis/ ▶ **n.** infection with candida, esp. as causing oral or vaginal thrush.

can·di·ru /ˌkandəˈro͞o/ ▶ **n.** a minute, slender catfish of the Amazon region that feeds by sucking blood from other fishes and sometimes enters the body orifices of mammals. It is notorious for its occasional habit of entering the urethra of human swimmers. ● *Vandellia cirrhosa*, family Trichomycteridae.
– ORIGIN mid 19th cent.: via Portuguese from Tupi *candirú*.

can·dle /ˈkandl/ ▶ **n.** a cylinder or block of wax or tallow with a central wick that is lit to produce light as it burns. ■ (also **international candle**) Physics a unit of luminous intensity, superseded by the candela.
▶ **v.** [with obj.] (of a poultry breeder) test (an egg) for freshness or fertility by holding it to the light.
– PHRASES **be unable to hold a candle to** informal be not nearly as good as: *nobody in the final could hold a candle to her.*
– DERIVATIVES **can·dler** /ˈkandlər, -dl-ər/ **n.**
– ORIGIN Old English *candel*, from Latin *candela*, from *candere* 'be white or glisten.'

can·dle·ber·ry /ˈkandlˌberē/ ▶ **n.** (pl. **candleberries**) any of a number of trees or shrubs whose berries or seeds yield a wax or oil that can be used for making candles, in particular: ● a bayberry or related North American shrub (genus *Myrica*, family Myricaceae). ● the candlenut.

can·dle·fish /ˈkandlˌfiSH/ ▶ **n.** (pl. **same** or **candlefishes**) a small, edible marine fish with oily flesh, occurring on the west coast of North America. Also called EULACHON. ● *Thaleichthys pacificus*, family Osmeridae.
– ORIGIN so named because the Chinook Indians formerly burned the oily bodies of these fish as candles.

can·dle·hold·er /ˈkandlˌhōldər/ ▶ **n.** a holder or support for a candle, typically one that is small or sturdy.

can·dle·light /ˈkandlˌlīt/ ▶ **n.** dim light provided by a candle or candles: *we dined by candlelight.*

can·dle·lit /ˈkandlˌlit/ ▶ **adj.** lit by a candle or candles: *a romantic candlelit dinner.*

Can·dle·mas /ˈkandlməs/ ▶ **n.** a Christian festival held on February 2 to commemorate the purification of the Virgin Mary (after childbirth, according to Jewish law) and the presentation of Christ in the Temple. Candles were traditionally blessed at this festival.
– ORIGIN Old English *Candelmæsse* (see CANDLE, MASS).

can·dle·nut /ˈkandlˌnət/ ▶ **n.** an evergreen tree of the spurge family, with large seeds that yield an oil used for lighting and other purposes, native to Southeast Asia and the South Pacific islands. Also called CANDLEBERRY. ● *Aleurites moluccana*, family Euphorbiaceae.

can·dle·pow·er /ˈkandlˌpou(ə)r/ ▶ **n.** illuminating power expressed in candelas or candles: [as modifier] *a 16-candlepower lamp.*

can·dle·snuff·er /ˈkandlˌsnəfər/ ▶ **n.** see SNUFFER.

can·dle·stick /ˈkandlˌstik/ ▶ **n.** a support or holder for one or more candles, typically one that is tall and thin.

can·dle·wick /ˈkandlˌwik/ ▶ **n.** a thick, soft cotton fabric with a raised, tufted pattern: [as modifier] *a candlewick dressing gown.* ■ the yarn used to make such a fabric. ■ tufted embroidery work made with heavy cotton yarn similar to that used to make wicks for candles.

can-do /ˌkan ˈdo͞o/ ▶ **adj.** [attrib.] informal characterized by or exhibiting a determination or willingness to take action and achieve results: *I like his can-do attitude.*

can·dom·blé /ˌkan,dōmˈblā/ ▶ **n.** Brazilian sect of the macumba cult.
– ORIGIN Brazilian Portuguese.

C

can·dor /ˈkandər, -ˌdôr/ (Brit. **candour**) ▶ n. the quality of being open and honest in expression; frankness: *a man of refreshing candor.*
– ORIGIN late Middle English (in the Latin sense): from Latin *candor* 'whiteness.' The current sense dates from the mid 18th cent.; the development of the senses paralleled that of CANDID.

CANDU /ˈkanˌdo͞o, -ˈdo͞o/ (also **Candu**) ▶ n. a nuclear reactor of a Canadian design in which the fuel is unenriched uranium oxide clad in zircaloy and the coolant and moderator is heavy water.
– ORIGIN from *Can(ada)* + the initial letters of DEUTERIUM and URANIUM.

C & W ▶ abbr. country and western (music).

can·dy /ˈkandē/ ▶ n. (pl. **candies**) a sweet food made with sugar or syrup combined with fruit, chocolate, or nuts: [as modifier] *a candy bar* | *pink and yellow candies.* ■ sugar crystallized by repeated boiling and slow evaporation.
▶ v. (**candies, candying, candied**) [with obj.] (often as adj. **candied**) preserve (fruit) by coating and impregnating it with a sugar syrup: *candied fruit.*
– ORIGIN mid 17th cent. (as a verb): the noun use is from late Middle English *sugar-candy*, from French *sucre candi* 'crystallized sugar,' from Arabic *sukkar* 'sugar' + *qandī* 'candied,' based on Sanskrit *khaṇḍa* 'fragment.'

can·dy ap·ple ▶ n. an apple coated with a thin layer of cooked sugar or caramel and fixed on a stick. ■ (also **candy-apple red**) a bright red color.

can·dy-ass ▶ n. informal a timid, cowardly, or despicable person.
– DERIVATIVES **can·dy-assed** adj.

can·dy cane ▶ n. a cylindrical stick of striped, sweet candy with a curved end, resembling a walking stick.

can·dy corn ▶ n. a form of chewy candy shaped like a large kernel of corn.

can·dy·man /ˈkandēˌman/ ▶ n. (pl. **candymen**) informal a person who sells illegal drugs.
– ORIGIN mid 19th cent.: from CANDY + MAN, an earlier sense denoting a ragman who gave toffee in exchange for goods.

can·dy-striped ▶ adj. (of material or a garment) patterned with alternating stripes of white and another color, typically pink.
– DERIVATIVES **can·dy-stripe** adj. & n.

can·dy-strip·er /ˈstrīpər/ ▶ n. informal a teenage girl who does volunteer nursing in a hospital.
– ORIGIN so named because of the candy-striped uniforms of such nurses.

can·dy·tuft /ˈkandēˌtəft/ ▶ n. a European plant with small heads of white, pink, or purple flowers, often cultivated as a garden plant. ● Genus *Iberis*, family Brassicaceae.
– ORIGIN early 17th cent.: from *Candy* (obsolete form of *Candia*, former name of Crete) + TUFT.

cane /kān/ ▶ n. **1** the hollow, jointed stem of a tall grass, esp. bamboo or sugar cane, or the stem of a slender palm such as rattan. ■ any plant that produces such stems. ■ stems of bamboo, rattan, or wicker used as a material for making furniture or baskets: [as modifier] *a cane coffee table.* ■ short for SUGAR CANE. ■ a flexible, woody stem of the raspberry plant or any of its relatives.
2 a length of cane or a slender stick, esp. one used as a support for plants, as a walking stick, or as an instrument of punishment. ■ (**the cane**) chiefly Brit. a form of corporal punishment used in certain schools, involving beating with a cane: *wrong answers were rewarded by the cane.*
▶ v. [with obj.] **1** beat with a cane as a punishment.
2 (usu. as adj. **caned**) make or repair (furniture) with cane: *armchairs with caned seats.*
– DERIVATIVES **can·er** n.
– ORIGIN late Middle English: from Old French, via Latin from Greek *kanna, kannē*, of Semitic origin.

cane·brake /ˈkānˌbrāk/ ▶ n. a piece of ground covered with a dense growth of canes.

cane chair ▶ n. a chair with a seat made of woven cane strips.

cane rat ▶ n. a large, ratlike, African rodent found in wetlands south of the Sahara. It is often a pest of sugar plantations. ● Family Thryonomyidae and genus *Thryonomys*: two species.

cane sug·ar ▶ n. sugar obtained from sugar cane.

Ca·nes Ve·nat·i·ci /ˈkānēz vəˈnatəsē, -ˌsī/ Astronomy a small northern constellation (the Hunting Dogs), said to represent two dogs (Asterion and Chara) held on a leash by Boötes. ■ (as genitive **Canum Venaticorum** /ˈkānəm veˌnatiˈkôrəm/) used with a preceding letter or numeral to designate a star in this constellation: *the star Beta Canum Venaticorum.*
– ORIGIN Latin.

cane toad ▶ n. a large brown toad native to tropical America. It has been introduced elsewhere as a pest control agent but can become a serious pest itself, partly because animals eating it are killed by its toxins. Also called MARINE TOAD, GIANT TOAD. ● *Bufo marinus*, family Bufonidae.

Ca·net·ti /kəˈnetē/, Elias (1905–94), British writer; born in Bulgaria. Notable works: *Auto-da-Fé* (1936) and *Crowds and Power* (1960). Nobel Prize for Literature (1981).

Can·field /ˈkanˌfēld/ ▶ n. a form of the card game solitaire.
– ORIGIN early 20th cent.: named after Richard A. *Canfield* (1855–1914), an American gambler.

ca·nic·u·lar /kəˈnikyələr/ ▶ adj. pertaining to a dog, in particular: ■ of or pertaining to the Dog Star, Sirius. ■ of or pertaining to the dog days.

can·id /ˈkanid, ˈkā-/ ▶ n. Zoology a mammal of the dog family (Canidae).
– ORIGIN late 19th cent.: from modern Latin *Canidae* (plural), from Latin *canis* 'dog.'

ca·nine /ˈkāˌnīn/ ▶ adj. of, relating to, or resembling a dog or dogs: *canine distemper virus.* ■ Zoology of or relating to animals of the dog family.
▶ n. **1** a dog. ■ Zoology another term for CANID.
2 (also **canine tooth**) a pointed tooth between the incisors and premolars of a mammal, often greatly enlarged in carnivores.
– ORIGIN late Middle English (sense 2 of the noun): from French, from Latin *caninus*, from *canis* 'dog.'

ca·nine dis·tem·per ▶ n. see DISTEMPER[1] (sense 1).

Ca·nis Ma·jor /ˈkānis, ˈkan-/ Astronomy a small constellation (the Great Dog), said to represent one of the dogs following Orion. It is just south of the celestial equator and contains the brightest star, Sirius. ■ (as genitive **Canis Majoris** /məˈjôris/) used with a preceding letter or numeral to designate a star in this constellation: *the star Eta Canis Majoris.*
– ORIGIN Latin.

Ca·nis Mi·nor Astronomy a small constellation (the Little Dog), said to represent one of the dogs following Orion. It is close to the celestial equator and contains the bright star Procyon. ■ (as genitive **Canis Minoris** /mīˈnôris/) used with a preceding letter or numeral to designate a star in this constellation: *the star Beta Canis Minoris.*
– ORIGIN Latin.

can·is·ter /ˈkanəstər/ ▶ n. a round or cylindrical container, typically one made of metal, used for storing such things as food, chemicals, or rolls of film. ■ a cylinder of pressurized gas, typically one that explodes when thrown or fired from a gun: *riot police fired tear-gas canisters into the crowd.* ■ historical small bullets packed in cases that fit the bore of an artillery piece or gun: *another deadly volley of canister.*
– ORIGIN late 15th cent. (denoting a basket): from Latin *canistrum*, from Greek *kanastron* 'wicker basket,' from *kanna* 'cane, reed' (see CANE).

can·ker /ˈkaNGkər/ ▶ n. **1** a necrotic, fungal disease of apple and other trees that results in damage to the bark. ■ an open lesion in plant tissue caused by infection or injury. ■ fungal rot in some fruits and vegetables, e.g., parsnips and tomatoes.
2 Medicine an ulcerous condition or disease, in particular: ■ (also **canker sore**) a small ulcer of the mouth or lips. ■ another term for THRUSH[2] (sense 2). ■ ulceration of the throat and other orifices of birds, typically caused by a protozoal infection. ■ (also **ear canker**) inflammation of the ear of a dog, cat, or rabbit, typically caused by a mite infestation. ■ a malign and corrupting influence that is difficult to eradicate: [in sing.] *racism remains a canker at the heart of the nation.*
▶ v. **1** [no obj.] (of woody plant tissue) become infected with canker: (as noun **cankering**) *we found some cankering of the wood.*
2 [with obj.] (usu. as adj. **cankered**) infect with a pervasive and corrupting bitterness: *he hated her with a cankered, shameful abhorrence.*
– DERIVATIVES **can·ker·ous** /-kərəs/ adj.
– ORIGIN Middle English (denoting a tumor): from Old French *chancre*, from Latin *cancer* 'crab' (see CANCER).

can·ker·worm /ˈkaNGkərˌwərm/ ▶ n. the caterpillar of a North American moth that has wingless females. Cankerworms consume the buds and leaves of trees and can be a major pest. ● Several species in the family Geometridae, in particular *Paleacrita vernata* and *Alsophila pometaria*.

can·kle /ˈkaNGkəl/ ▶ n. informal an unusually thick or stout ankle.
– ORIGIN blend of *calf* and *ankle*.

Can·more /ˈkanˌmôr/ the nickname of Malcolm III of Scotland (see MALCOLM).

can·na /ˈkanə/ (also **canna lily**) ▶ n. a lilylike, tropical American plant with bright flowers and ornamental straplike leaves. ● Genus *Canna*, family Cannaceae: several species, in particular forms of Indian shot (*C. indica*), which are widely naturalized.
– ORIGIN from modern Latin, from Latin *canna* 'cane, reed' (see CANE).

can·na·bin /ˈkanəbən/ ▶ n. a poisonous resin extracted from cannabis.

can·nab·i·noid /ˈkanəbəˌnoid, kəˈnabə-/ ▶ n. Chemistry any of a group of closely related compounds that include cannabinol and the active constituents of cannabis.

can·nab·i·nol /ˈkanəbəˌnôl, kəˈnabə-, -ˌnōl/ ▶ n. Chemistry a crystalline compound whose derivatives, esp. THC, are the active constituents of cannabis. ● A polycyclic phenol; chem. formula: $C_{21}H_{26}O_2$.
– ORIGIN late 19th cent.: from CANNABIS + -OL.

can·na·bis /ˈkanəbəs/ ▶ n. a tall plant with a stiff upright stem, divided serrated leaves, and glandular hairs. It is used to produce hemp fiber and as a psychotropic drug. Also called INDIAN HEMP, MARIJUANA. ● *Cannabis sativa*, family Cannabaceae (or Cannabidaceae): two subspecies (sometimes considered two species), *C. s. sativa*, which is chiefly used for hemp, and *C. s. indica*, from which the drug is usually obtained. ■ a dried preparation of the flowering tops or other parts of this plant, or a resinous extract of it (**cannabis resin**), used (generally illegally) as a psychotropic drug, chiefly in cigarettes.
– ORIGIN from Latin, from Greek *kannabis*.

canned /kand/ ▶ adj. **1** (of food or drink) preserved or supplied in a sealed can: *canned beans.*
2 informal, often derogatory (of music, laughter, or applause) prerecorded and therefore considered to be lacking in freshness and spontaneity.

can·nel coal /ˈkanl/ ▶ n. a hard, compact kind of bituminous coal.
– ORIGIN mid 16th cent. (originally a northern English usage): of unknown origin.

can·nel·li·ni bean /ˌkanlˈēnē/ ▶ n. a kidney-shaped bean of a medium-sized, creamy-white variety.
– ORIGIN Italian *cannellini*, literally 'small tubes.'

can·nel·lo·ni /ˌkanlˈōnē/ ▶ n. rolls of pasta stuffed with a meat or vegetable mixture. ■ [treated as sing.] an Italian dish consisting of such rolls of pasta cooked in a cheese sauce.
– ORIGIN Italian, literally 'large tubes,' from *cannello* 'tube.'

can·ne·lure /ˈkanlˌ(y)o͝or/ ▶ n. a groove around the cylindrical part of a bullet.
– ORIGIN mid 18th cent.: from French, from *canneler* 'provide with a channel,' from *canne* 'reed, cane.'

can·ner·y /ˈkanərē/ ▶ n. (pl. **canneries**) a factory where food is canned.

Cannes /kan, kän/ a resort on the Mediterranean coast of France; pop. 71,526 (2006). An international film festival is held here annually.

can·ni·bal /ˈkanəbəl/ ▶ n. a person who eats the flesh of other human beings: [as modifier] *cannibal tribes.* ■ an animal that feeds on flesh of its own species.
– DERIVATIVES **can·ni·bal·ism** /-ˌlizəm/ n., **can·ni·bal·is·tic** /ˌkanəbəˈlistik/ adj., **can·ni·bal·is·ti·cal·ly** /ˌkanəbəˈlistik(ə)lē/ adv.
– ORIGIN mid 16th cent.: from Spanish *Canibales* (plural), variant (recorded by Columbus) of *Caribes*, the name of a West Indian people reputed to eat humans (see CARIB).

can·ni·bal·ize /ˈkanəbəˌlīz/ ▶ v. [with obj.] **1** use (a machine) as a source of spare parts for another, similar machine. ■ (of a company) reduce the sales of (one of its products) by introducing another similar product.
2 (of an animal) eat (an animal of its own kind): *female spiders cannibalize courting males.*
– DERIVATIVES **can·ni·bal·i·za·tion** /ˌkanəbələˈzāSHən/ n.

Can·niz·za·ro /ˌkänēdˈzärō/, Stanislao (1826–1910), Italian chemist. He revived Avogadro's law and used it to distinguish clearly between atoms and molecules and to introduce the unified system of atomic and molecular weights.

can·no·li /kəˈnōlē/ ▶ plural n. Italian pastries in the form of hard tubular shells filled with sweetened ricotta cheese and often containing nuts, citron, or chocolate bits.
– ORIGIN Italian, plural of *cannolo*, from *canna* 'reed,' from Greek *kanna*, of Semitic origin.

can·non /ˈkanən/ ▶ n. **1** (pl. usu. **same**) a large, heavy piece of artillery, typically mounted on wheels, formerly used in warfare. ■ an automatic heavy gun that fires shells from an aircraft or tank.
2 Billiards chiefly Brit. a carom. [early 19th cent.: alteration of CAROM.]

cannon 1

3 Engineering a heavy cylinder or hollow drum that is able to rotate independently on a shaft.
▶ **v.** [no obj.] Billiards & Snooker make a cannon shot.
– ORIGIN late Middle English: from French *canon,* from Italian *cannone* 'large tube,' from *canna* 'cane, reed' (see CANE).

can·non·ade /ˌkanəˈnād/ ▶ **n.** a period of continuous, heavy gunfire.
▶ **v.** [no obj.] discharge heavy guns continuously: (as noun **cannonading**) *the daily cannonading continued.*
– ORIGIN mid 16th cent.: from French, from Italian *cannonata,* from *cannone* (see CANNON).

can·non·ball /ˈkanənˌbôl/ ▶ **n.** a round metal or stone projectile fired from a cannon in former times. ■ (also **cannonball dive**) a jump into water performed upright with the knees clasped to the chest.

can·non bone ▶ **n.** a long, tube-shaped bone in the lower leg of a horse or other large quadruped, between the fetlock and the knee or hock.

can·non·eer /ˌkanəˈni(ə)r/ ▶ **n.** historical an artilleryman who positioned and fired a cannon.

can·non fod·der ▶ **n.** soldiers regarded merely as material to be expended in war.

can·non·ry /ˈkanənrē/ ▶ **n.** (pl. **cannonries**) the use or discharge of cannon; artillery.

can·not /kəˈnät, ˈkanˌät/ ▶ **contraction** can not.

USAGE Both the one-word form **cannot** and the two-word form **can not** are acceptable, but **cannot** is more common (in the Oxford English Corpus, three times as common). The two-word form is better only in a construction in which **not** is part of a set phrase, such as 'not only ... but (also)': *Paul can not only sing well, but he also paints brilliantly.*

can·nu·la /ˈkanyələ/ ▶ **n.** (pl. **cannulae** /-lē, -lī/ or **cannulas**) Surgery a thin tube inserted into a vein or body cavity to administer medicine, drain off fluid, or insert a surgical instrument.
– ORIGIN late 17th cent.: from Latin, 'small reed,' diminutive of *canna* (see CANE).

can·nu·late /ˈkanyəˌlāt/ ▶ **v.** [with obj.] Surgery introduce a cannula or thin tube into (a vein or body cavity).
– DERIVATIVES **can·nu·la·tion** /ˌkanyəˈlāSHən/ **n.**

can·ny /ˈkanē/ ▶ **adj.** (**cannier, canniest**) **1** having or showing shrewdness and good judgment, esp. in money or business matters: *canny shoppers came early for a bargain.*
2 Scottish & N. English pleasant; nice: *she's a canny lass.*
– DERIVATIVES **can·ni·ly** /ˈkanl-ē/ **adv.**, **can·ni·ness n.**
– ORIGIN late 16th cent. (originally Scots): from CAN[1] (in the obsolete sense 'know') + -Y[1].

ca·noe /kəˈnoo/ ▶ **n.** a narrow, keelless boat with pointed ends, propelled by a paddle or paddles.
▶ **v.** (**canoes, canoeing, canoed**) [no obj.] travel in or paddle a canoe: *he had once canoed down the Nile.*
– DERIVATIVES **ca·noe·ist** /-ˈnooist/ **n.**
– ORIGIN mid 16th cent.: from Spanish *canoa,* from Arawak, from Carib *canaoua.*

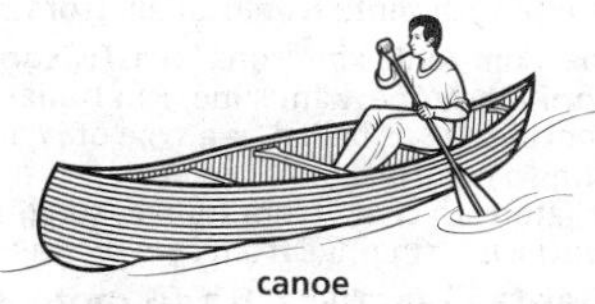
canoe

ca·noe·ing /kəˈnooiNG/ ▶ **n.** the sport or activity of traveling in or paddling a canoe.

can·o·la /kəˈnōlə/ ▶ **n.** oilseed rape of a variety developed in Canada and grown in North America. It yields a valuable culinary oil.
– ORIGIN 1970s: from CANADA + *-ola* (based on Latin *oleum* 'oil').

can·on[1] /ˈkanən/ ▶ **n. 1** a general law, rule, principle, or criterion by which something is judged: *the appointment violated the canons of fair play and equal opportunity.* ■ a church decree or law: *a set of ecclesiastical canons.*
2 a collection or list of sacred books accepted as genuine: *the formation of the biblical canon.* ■ the works of a particular author or artist that are recognized as genuine: *the Shakespeare canon.* ■ the list of works considered to be permanently established as being of the highest quality: *Hopkins was firmly established in the canon of English poetry.*
3 (also **canon of the Mass**) (in the Roman Catholic Church) the part of the Mass containing the words of consecration.
4 Music a piece in which the same melody is begun in different parts successively, so that the imitations overlap.
– PHRASES **in canon** Music with different parts successively beginning the same melody.
– ORIGIN Old English: from Latin, from Greek *kanōn* 'rule,' reinforced in Middle English by Old French *canon.*

can·on[2] ▶ **n.** a member of the clergy who is on the staff of a cathedral, esp. one who is a member of the chapter. The position is frequently conferred as an honorary one. ■ (also **canon regular** or **regular canon**) (in the Roman Catholic Church) a member of certain orders of clergy that live communally according to an ecclesiastical rule in the same way as monks.
– ORIGIN Middle English (in the sense 'canon regular'): from Old French *canonie,* from Latin *canonicus* 'according to rule' (see CANONIC). The other sense dates from the mid 16th cent.

ca·ñon /ˈkanyən/ ▶ **n.** archaic spelling of CANYON.

can·on can·cri·zans /ˈkaNGkrəˌzanz/ ▶ **n.** Music a canon in which the theme or subject is repeated backward in the second part. Also called CRAB CANON.
– ORIGIN late 19th cent.: from CANON[1] + medieval Latin *cancrizans* 'walking backward' (from *cancer* 'crab').

can·on·ess /ˈkanənəs/ ▶ **n.** (in the Roman Catholic Church) a member of certain religious orders of women living communally according to an ecclesiastical rule in the same way as nuns.

ca·non·ic /kəˈnänik/ ▶ **adj. 1** Music in canon form.
2 another term for CANONICAL.
– ORIGIN Old English (as a noun): from Old French *canonique* or Latin *canonicus* 'canonical,' from Greek *kanonikos,* from *kanon* 'rule' (see CANON[1]). The adjective dates from the late 15th cent.

ca·non·i·cal /kəˈnänikəl/ ▶ **adj. 1** according to or ordered by canon law: *the canonical rites of the Roman Church.*
2 included in the list of sacred books officially accepted as genuine: *the canonical Gospels of the New Testament.* ■ accepted as being accurate and authoritative: *the canonical method of comparative linguistics.* ■ (of an artist or work) belonging to the literary or artistic canon: *canonical writers like Jane Austen.* ■ according to recognized rules or scientific laws: *canonical nucleotide sequences.* ■ Mathematics of or relating to a general rule or standard formula.
3 of or relating to a cathedral chapter or a member of it.
▶ **plural n.** (**canonicals**) the prescribed official dress of the clergy: *Cardinal Bea in full canonicals.*
– DERIVATIVES **ca·non·i·cal·ly** /-ik(ə)lē/ **adv.**
– ORIGIN late Middle English: from medieval Latin *canonicalis,* from Latin *canonicus* (see CANONIC).

ca·non·i·cal hours ▶ **plural n.** the times of daily Christian prayer appointed in the breviary. ■ the offices set for these times, namely matins with lauds, prime, terce, sext, nones, vespers, and compline.

can·on·ic·i·ty /ˌkanəˈnisitē/ ▶ **n.** the fact or status of being canonical: *established standards of canonicity.*

can·on·ist /ˈkanənist/ ▶ **n.** an expert in canon law.
– DERIVATIVES **can·on·is·tic** /ˌkanəˈnistik/ **adj.**
– ORIGIN mid 16th cent.: from French *canoniste* or medieval Latin *canonista,* from Latin *canon* (see CANON[1]).

can·on·ize /ˈkanəˌnīz/ ▶ **v.** [with obj.] (in the Roman Catholic Church) officially declare (a dead person) to be a saint: *he was the last English saint to be canonized prior to the Reformation.* ■ regard as being above reproach or of great significance: *we have canonized freedom of speech as an absolute value overriding all others.* ■ accept into the literary or artistic canon: [as adj.] *a familiar, canonized writer.* ■ sanction by Church authority.
– DERIVATIVES **can·on·i·za·tion** /ˌkanənəˈzāSHən/ **n.**
– ORIGIN late Middle English: from late Latin *canonizare* 'admit as authoritative' (in medieval Latin 'admit to the list of recognized saints'), from Latin *canon* (see CANON[1]).

can·on law ▶ **n.** ecclesiastical law, esp. (in the Roman Catholic Church) that laid down by papal pronouncements.

can·on reg·u·lar ▶ **n.** see CANON[2].

can·on·ry /ˈkanənrē/ ▶ **n.** (pl. **canonries**) the office or benefice of a canon.

ca·noo·dle /kəˈnoodl/ ▶ **v.** [no obj.] informal kiss and cuddle amorously: *she was caught canoodling with her boyfriend.*
– ORIGIN mid 19th cent. of unknown origin.

Ca·no·pic jar /kəˈnōpik, -ˈnäpik/ (also **Canopic vase**) ▶ **n.** a covered urn used in ancient Egyptian burials to hold the entrails from an embalmed body.
– ORIGIN late 19th cent.: *Canopic* from Latin *Canopicus,* from *Canopus,* the name of a town in ancient Egypt.

Ca·no·pus /kəˈnōpəs/ Astronomy the second brightest star in the sky, and the brightest in the constellation Carina. It is a supergiant, visible only to observers in the southern hemisphere.
– ORIGIN Latin, from Greek *Kanōpus,* the name of the pilot of the fleet of King Menelaus in the Trojan War.

can·o·py /ˈkanəpē/ ▶ **n.** (pl. **canopies**) an ornamental cloth covering hung or held up over something, esp. a throne or bed: *a romantic four-poster bed complete with drapes and a canopy* | figurative *a full moon and a canopy of stars.* ■ Architecture a rooflike projection or shelter: *they mounted the station steps under the concrete canopy.* ■ the transparent plastic or glass cover of an aircraft's cockpit. ■ the expanding, umbrellalike part of a parachute, made of silk or nylon. ■ [in sing.] the uppermost trees or branches of the trees in a forest, forming a more or less continuous layer of foliage: *monkeys spend hours every day sitting high in the canopy.*
▶ **v.** (**canopies, canopying, canopied**) [with obj.] (usu. as adj. **canopied**) cover or provide with a canopy: *a canopied bed* | *the river was canopied by overhanging trees.*
– ORIGIN late Middle English: from medieval Latin *canopeum* 'ceremonial canopy,' alteration of Latin *conopeum* 'mosquito net over a bed,' from Greek *kōnōpeion* 'couch with mosquito curtains,' from *kōnōps* 'mosquito.'

ca·no·rous /kəˈnôrəs, ˈkanərəs/ ▶ **adj.** rare (of song or speech) melodious or resonant.
– ORIGIN mid 17th cent.: from Latin *canorus* (from *canere* 'sing') + -OUS.

canst /kanst/ archaic second person singular present of CAN[1].

cant[1] /kant/ ▶ **n. 1** hypocritical and sanctimonious talk, typically of a moral, religious, or political nature: *the liberal case against all censorship is often cant.*
2 [as modifier] denoting a phrase or catchword temporarily current or in fashion: *they are misrepresented as, in the cant word of our day, uncaring.* ■ language peculiar to a specified group or profession and regarded with disparagement: *thieves' cant.*
▶ **v.** [no obj.] dated talk hypocritically and sanctimoniously about something: *if they'd stop canting about "honest work," they might get somewhere.*
– ORIGIN early 16th cent.: probably from Latin *cantare* 'to sing' (see CHANT). The early meaning was 'musical sound, singing'; in the mid 17th cent. this gave rise to the senses 'whining manner of speaking' and 'form of words repeated mechanically in such a manner' (for example a beggar's plea), hence 'jargon' (of beggars and other such groups).

cant[2] ▶ **v.** [with obj.] cause (something) to be in a slanting or oblique position; tilt: *he canted his head to look at the screen.* ■ [no obj.] take or have a slanting position: *mismatched slate roofs canted at all angles.*
▶ **n. 1** [in sing.] a slope or tilt: *the outward cant of the curving walls.*
2 a wedge-shaped block of wood, esp. one remaining after the better-quality pieces have been cut off.
– ORIGIN Middle English (denoting an edge or brink): from Middle Low German *kant, kante,* Middle Dutch *cant* 'point, side, edge,' based on a Romance word related to medieval Latin *cantus* 'corner, side.'

Cant. ▶ **abbr.** Bible Canticles.

can't /kant/ ▶ **contraction** cannot.

can·ta·bi·le /känˈtäbəˌlā/ Music ▶ **adv. & adj.** in a smooth singing style.
▶ **n.** a cantabile passage or movement.
– ORIGIN Italian, literally 'singable.'

Can·ta·brig·i·an /ˈkantəˌbrijēən/ ▶ **adj.** of or relating to Cambridge (in England) or Cambridge University.
▶ **n.** a student or faculty member of Cambridge University.
– ORIGIN mid 16th cent.: from Latin *Cantabrigia* (see CAMBRIDGE) + -IAN.

can·tal /ˈkanˈtäl, känˈ-/ ▶ **n.** a hard, strong cheese made chiefly in the Auvergne.
– ORIGIN named after *Cantal,* a department of Auvergne, France.

can·ta·loupe /ˈkantlˌōp/ (also **cantaloupe melon**) ▶ **n.** a small, round melon of a variety with orange flesh and ribbed skin.
– ORIGIN late 18th cent.: from French *cantaloup,* from *Cantaluppi* near Rome, where it was first grown in Europe after being introduced from Armenia.

can·tan·ker·ous /kanˈtaNGkərəs/ ▶ **adj.** bad-tempered, argumentative, and uncooperative: *a crusty, cantankerous old man.*

PRONUNCIATION KEY ə *ago, up;* ər *over, fur;* a *hat;* ā *ate;* ä *car;* e *let;* ē *see;* i *fit;* ī *by;* NG *sing;* ō *go;* ô *law, for;* oi *toy;* o͝o *good;* o͞o *goo;* ou *out;* TH *thin;* T͟H *then;* ZH *vision*

– DERIVATIVES **can·tan·ker·ous·ly** adv., **can·tan·ker·ous·ness** n.
– ORIGIN mid 18th cent.: of unknown origin; perhaps a blend of Anglo-Irish *cant* 'auction' and *rancorous* (see RANCOR).

can·ta·ta /kən'tätə/ ▶ n. a medium-length narrative piece of music for voices with instrumental accompaniment, typically with solos, chorus, and orchestra.
– ORIGIN early 18th cent.: from Italian *cantata (aria)* 'sung (air),' from *cantare* 'sing.'

C

cant dog ▶ n. another term for CANT HOOK.

can·teen /kan'tēn/ ▶ n. **1** a restaurant provided by an organization such as a military camp, college, factory, or company for its soldiers, students, staff, etc.
2 a small water bottle, as used by soldiers or campers.
– ORIGIN mid 18th cent. (originally denoting a type of shop in a barracks or garrison town): from French *cantine*, from Italian *cantina* 'cellar.'

can·ter /'kantər/ ▶ n. [in sing.] a three-beat gait of a horse or other quadruped between a trot and a gallop: *he kicked his horse into a canter* | *I rode away at a canter*. ■ a ride on a horse at such a speed: *we came back from one of our canters*.
▶ v. [no obj.] (of a horse) move at a canter in a particular direction: *they cantered down into the village*. ■ [with obj.] make (a horse) move at a canter: *Katharine cantered Benji in a smaller and smaller circle*.
– ORIGIN early 18th cent. (as a verb): short for *Canterbury pace* or *Canterbury gallop*, from the supposed easy pace of medieval pilgrims to CANTERBURY.

Can·ter·bur·y /'kantər,berē, -bərē/ a city in Kent, in southeastern England, the seat of the archbishop of Canterbury; pop. 41,900 (est. 2009).

Can·ter·bur·y, Arch·bish·op of ▶ n. the archbishop of the southern province of the Church of England, who is Primate of All England and plays a leading role in the worldwide Anglican Church.

Can·ter·bur·y bell ▶ n. a tall, sturdy cultivated bellflower with large blue, pink, or white flowers. ● *Campanula medium*, family Campanulaceae.
– ORIGIN late 16th cent.: named after the bells on Canterbury pilgrims' horses (see CANTER).

can·thar·i·des /kan'THari,dēz/ ▶ plural n. see SPANISH FLY.
– ORIGIN late Middle English: from Latin, plural of *cantharis*, from Greek *kantharis* 'Spanish fly.'

can·tha·rus /'kanTHərəs/ ▶ n. (pl. **canthari** /-,rī, -rē/) (in ancient Greece and Rome) a large, two-handled drinking cup.
– ORIGIN Latin, from Greek *kantharos*.

cant hook ▶ n. a hinged metal hook at the end of a long handle, used for gripping and rolling logs.

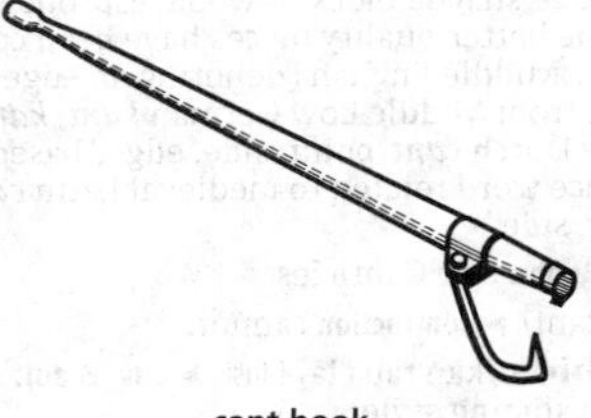
cant hook

can·thus /'kanTHəs/ ▶ n. (pl. **canthi** /-,THī, -,THē/) the outer or inner corner of the eye, where the upper and lower lids meet.
– DERIVATIVES **can·thic** /'kanTHik/ adj.
– ORIGIN mid 17th cent.: from Latin, from Greek *kanthos*.

can·ti·cle /'kantikəl/ ▶ n. **1** a hymn or chant, typically with a biblical text, forming a regular part of a church service.
2 (**Canticles** or **Canticle of Canticles**) another name for SONG OF SONGS (esp. in the Vulgate Bible).
– ORIGIN Middle English: from Latin *canticulum* 'little song,' diminutive of *canticum*, from *canere* 'sing.'

can·ti·le·na /,kantl'ēnə/ ▶ n. Music a lyrical vocal or instrumental melody in a composition.
– ORIGIN mid 18th cent.: from Italian, from Latin, 'song.'

can·ti·le·ver /'kantl,ēvər, -,evər/ ▶ n. a long projecting beam or girder fixed at only one end, used chiefly in bridge construction. ■ a long bracket or beam projecting from a wall to support a balcony, cornice, or similar structure.
▶ v. [with obj.] (usu. as adj. **cantilevered**) support by a cantilever or cantilevers: *a cantilevered deck*. ■ [no obj.] project as or like a cantilever: *a conveyor cantilevered out over the river*.
– ORIGIN mid 17th cent.: of unknown origin.

can·ti·le·ver bridge ▶ n. a bridge in which each span is constructed from cantilevers built out sideways from piers.

can·til·late /'kantl,āt/ ▶ v. [with obj.] rare chant or intone (a passage of religious text).
– DERIVATIVES **can·til·la·tion** /,kantl'āSHən/ n.
– ORIGIN mid 19th cent.: from Latin *cantillat-* 'hummed,' from the verb *cantillare*, from *cantare* (see CHANT).

can·ti·na /kan'tēnə/ ▶ n. (esp. in a Spanish-speaking country or the southwestern US) a bar. ■ (in Italy) a wine shop.
– ORIGIN late 19th cent.: from Spanish and Italian.

cant·ing arms ▶ plural n. Heraldry arms containing an allusion to the name of the bearer.
– ORIGIN early 17th cent.: *canting* from CANT[1], in the obsolete sense 'speak, say (in a particular way).'

can·tle /'kantl/ ▶ n. the raised, curved part at the back of a horse's saddle.
– ORIGIN Middle English (in the sense 'a corner'): from Anglo-Norman French *cantel*, variant of Old French *chantel*, from medieval Latin *cantellus*, from *cantus* 'corner, side.'

can·to /'kan,tō/ ▶ n. (pl. **cantos**) one of the sections into which certain long poems are divided.
– ORIGIN late 16th cent.: from Italian, literally 'song,' from Latin *cantus*.

Can·ton[1] /kan'tän/ another name for GUANGZHOU.

Can·ton[2] /'kantn/ an industrial city in northeastern Ohio; pop. 78,362 (est. 2008). The Professional Football Hall of Fame is here.

can·ton /'kantn, 'kan,tän/ ▶ n. **1** a subdivision of a country established for political or administrative purposes. ■ a state of the Swiss Confederation.
2 Heraldry a square charge smaller than a quarter and positioned in the upper (usually dexter) corner of a shield.
– DERIVATIVES **can·ton·al** /kan'tänl, 'kantnl/ adj.
– ORIGIN early 16th cent.: from Old French, literally 'corner,' from Provençal, based on a Romance word related to medieval Latin *cantus* (see CANT[2]).

Can·ton·ese /,kantn'ēz, -'ēs/ ▶ adj. of or relating to Canton (Guangzhou), its inhabitants, their dialect, or their cuisine.
▶ n. (pl. **same**) **1** a native or inhabitant of Canton.
2 a form of Chinese spoken mainly in southeastern China (including Hong Kong). Also called YUE.

can·ton·ment /kan'tōnmənt, -'tän-/ ▶ n. a military garrison or camp. ■ historical a permanent military station in British India.
– ORIGIN mid 18th cent.: from French *cantonnement*, from *cantonner* 'to quarter' (see CANTON).

Can·tor /'kantər/, Georg (1845–1918), German mathematician; born in Russia. His work on numbers laid the foundations for the theory of sets and stimulated 20th-century exploration of number theory.

can·tor /'kantər/ ▶ n. **1** an official who sings liturgical music and leads prayer in a synagogue. Also called HAZZAN.
2 (in formal Christian worship) a person who sings solo verses or passages to which the choir or congregation responds.
– ORIGIN mid 16th cent.: from Latin, 'singer,' from *canere* 'sing.'

can·to·ri·al /kan'tôrēəl/ ▶ adj. of or relating to a cantor. ■ relating to or denoting the north side of the choir of a church, the side on which the cantor sits. The opposite of DECANAL.

can·trip /'kantrip/ ▶ n. Scottish archaic a mischievous or playful act; a trick.
– ORIGIN late 16th cent. (also in the sense 'witch's trick'): of unknown origin.

can·tus /'kantəs/ ▶ n. the highest voice in polyphonic choral music.
– ORIGIN late 16th cent.: from Latin.

can·tus fir·mus /'fərməs/ ▶ n. (pl. **cantus firmi** /'fər,mī, -mē/) Music an existing melody used as the basis for a polyphonic composition.
– ORIGIN mid 19th cent.: from Latin, literally 'firm song.'

Ca·nuck /kə'nək/ ▶ n. informal a Canadian, esp. a French Canadian (chiefly used by Canadians themselves and often derogatory in the US).
– ORIGIN apparently from CANADA.

Ca·nute /kə'n(y)o͞ot/ (also **Cnut** or **Knut**) (died 1035), Danish king of England 1017–35, Denmark 1018–35, and Norway 1028–35; son of Sweyn I.

can·vas /'kanvəs/ ▶ n. a strong, coarse unbleached cloth made from hemp, flax, cotton, or a similar yarn, used to make items such as sails and tents and as a surface for oil painting: [as modifier] *a canvas bag*. ■ a piece of such cloth prepared for use as the surface for an oil painting. ■ an oil painting: *Turner's late canvases*. ■ a variety of canvas with an open weave, used as a basis for tapestry and embroidery. ■ (**the canvas**) the floor of a boxing or wrestling ring, having a canvas covering. ■ either of a racing boat's tapering ends, originally covered with canvas.
▶ v. (**canvases, canvasing, canvased**) [with obj.] (usu. **be canvased**) cover with canvas: *the door had been canvased over*.
– PHRASES **by a canvas** (in boat racing) by a small margin. [referring to the tapered front end of a racing boat (see above).] **under canvas 1** in a tent or tents: *the family will be living under canvas*. **2** with sails spread.
– ORIGIN late Middle English: from Old Northern French *canevas*, based on Latin *cannabis* 'hemp,' from Greek *kannabis*.

can·vas·back /'kanvəs,bak/ ▶ n. a North American diving duck with a long, sloping black bill, related (and with similar coloring) to the pochard, common in Eurasia. ● *Aythya valisineria*, family Anatidae.
– ORIGIN late 16th cent.: so named because of the white back of the male.

can·vas duck ▶ n. a lightweight cotton or linen fabric.

can·vass /'kanvəs/ ▶ v. **1** [with obj.] solicit votes from (electors in a constituency): *in each ward, two workers canvassed some 2,000 voters* | [no obj.] *she canvassed for votes*. ■ question (someone) in order to ascertain their opinion on something: *they promised to canvass all member clubs for their views*. ■ ascertain (someone's opinion) through questioning: *opinions on the merger were canvassed*. ■ try to obtain; request: *they're canvassing support among shareholders*.
2 [with obj.] discuss thoroughly: *the issues that were canvassed are still unresolved*.
▶ n. [usu. in sing.] an act or process of attempting to secure votes or ascertain opinions: *a house-to-house canvass*.
– DERIVATIVES **can·vass·er** n.
– ORIGIN early 16th cent. (in the sense 'toss in a canvas sheet' (as a sport or punishment)): from CANVAS. Later extended senses include 'criticize, discuss' (mid 16th cent.) and 'propose for discussion'; hence 'seek support for.'

can·yon /'kanyən/ ▶ n. a deep gorge, typically one with a river flowing through it.
– ORIGIN mid 19th cent.: from Spanish *cañón* 'tube,' based on Latin *canna* 'reed, cane.'

Can·yon de Chel·ly /də 'SHā(lē)/ a national monument in northeastern Arizona, on the Navajo Indian Reservation, noted for cliff dwellings and other ruins.

can·yon·ing /'kanyəniNG/ (also **canyoneering** /,kanyə'ni(ə)riNG/) ▶ n. the sport of exploring a canyon by engaging in such activities as rappelling, rafting, and waterfall jumping.

Can·yon·lands /'kanyən,landz/ a region in southeastern Utah, many of whose rock formations, carved by the Colorado and Green Rivers, are preserved in the Canyonlands National Park.

can·zo·na /kan'zōnə, kant'sōnə/ ▶ n. Music an instrumental arrangement of a French or Flemish song, typical of 16th-century Italy.
– ORIGIN late 19th cent.: from Italian, from CANZONE.

can·zo·ne /kan'zōnē, känt'sōnā/ ▶ n. (pl. **canzones** or **canzoni** /kan'zōnē, känt'sōnē/) an Italian or Provençal song or ballad. ■ a type of lyric resembling a madrigal.
– ORIGIN late 16th cent.: from Italian, 'song,' from Latin *cantio(n-)* 'singing,' from *canere* 'sing.'

can·zo·net·ta /,kanzə'netə/ ▶ n. (pl. **canzonettas** or **canzonette** /-'netē/) a short, light vocal piece, esp. in the Italian style of the 17th century.
– ORIGIN late 16th cent.: from Italian, 'little song,' diminutive of *canzone*, from Latin *cantio(n-)* 'singing,' from *canere* 'sing.'

caou·tchouc /'kou,CHo͝ok, -,CHo͞o(k)/ ▶ n. unvulcanized natural rubber.
– ORIGIN late 18th cent.: from French, from obsolete Spanish *cauchuc*, from Quechua *kauchuk*.

CAP ▶ abbr. Civil Air Patrol.

cap[1] /kap/ ▶ n. **1** a kind of soft, flat hat without a brim, and sometimes having a visor. ■ [with adj. or noun modifier] a kind of soft, close-fitting head covering worn for a particular purpose or as a mark of a particular profession or status: *a nurse's cap* | *a bathing cap*. ■ an academic mortarboard: *graduates in cap and gown*.
2 a protective lid or cover for an object such as a bottle, the point of a pen, or a camera lens. ■ Dentistry an artificial protective covering for a tooth. ■ the top of a bird's head when distinctively colored. ■ the broad upper part of the fruiting body of most mushrooms and toadstools, at the top of a stem and bearing gills or pores.
3 an upper limit imposed on spending or other activities: *a cap on government purchases*.
4 short for PERCUSSION CAP.

▶ **v.** (**caps**, **capped**, **capping**) [with obj.] **1** put a lid or cover on: *he capped his pen.* ■ form a covering layer or top part of: *several towers were capped by domes* | [as adj., in combination] (**-capped**) *snow-capped mountains.* ■ put an artificial protective covering on (a tooth). ■ provide a fitting climax or conclusion to: *he capped a memorable season by becoming champion.* ■ follow or reply to (a story, remark, or joke) by producing a better or more apposite one: *they capped each other's stories.*
2 place a limit or restriction on (prices, expenditure, or other activity): *council budgets will be capped.*
– PHRASES **cap** (or **hat**) **in hand** humbly asking for a favor: *we have to go cap in hand begging for funds.* **set one's cap for** (or **at**) dated (of a woman) try to attract (a particular man) as a suitor.
– DERIVATIVES **cap·ful** /-ˌfo͝ol/ **n.** (pl. **capfuls**).
– ORIGIN Old English *cæppe* 'hood,' from late Latin *cappa*, perhaps from Latin *caput* 'head.'

cap[2] /kap/ ▶ **n.** Finance short for capitalization: [as modifier] *mid-cap companies* | *small-cap stocks.*

cap. ▶ **abbr.** ■ capacity. ■ capital (city). ■ capital letter.

ca·pa·bil·i·ty /ˌkāpəˈbilitē/ ▶ **n.** (pl. **capabilities**) (often **capability of doing** (or **to do**) **something**) power or ability: *he had an intuitive capability of bringing the best out in people* | *the capability to increase productivity.* ■ (often **capabilities**) the extent of someone's or something's ability: *the job is beyond my capabilities.* ■ a facility on a computer for performing a specified task: *a graphics capability.* ■ forces or resources giving a country or state the ability to undertake a particular kind of military action: *their nuclear weapons capability.*

Ca·pa·bil·i·ty Brown see **BROWN**[5].

ca·pa·ble /ˈkāpəbəl/ ▶ **adj. 1** (**capable of doing something**) having the ability, fitness, or quality necessary to do or achieve a specified thing: *I'm quite capable of taking care of myself* | *the aircraft is capable of flying 5,000 miles nonstop.* ■ open to or admitting of something: *the strange events are capable of rational explanation.*
2 able to achieve efficiently whatever one has to do; competent: *she looked enthusiastic and capable* | *a highly capable man.*
– DERIVATIVES **ca·pa·bly** /-blē/ **adv.**
– ORIGIN mid 16th cent. (in the sense 'able to take in,' physically or mentally): from French, from late Latin *capabilis*, from Latin *capere* 'take or hold.'

ca·pa·cious /kəˈpāsнəs/ ▶ **adj.** having a lot of space inside; roomy: *she rummaged in her capacious handbag.*
– DERIVATIVES **ca·pa·cious·ly adv.**, **ca·pa·cious·ness n.**
– ORIGIN early 17th cent.: from Latin *capax, capac-* 'capable' + **-IOUS**.

ca·pac·i·tance /kəˈpasitəns/ ▶ **n.** Physics the ability of a system to store an electric charge. ■ the ratio of the change in an electric charge in a system to the corresponding change in its electric potential. (Symbol: **C**)
– ORIGIN late 19th cent.: from **CAPACITY** + **-ANCE**.

ca·pac·i·tate /kəˈpasiˌtāt/ ▶ **v.** [with obj.] formal or archaic make (someone) capable of a particular action or legally competent to act in a particular way. ■ (**be capacitated**) Physiology (of spermatozoa) undergo changes inside the female reproductive tract enabling them to penetrate and fertilize an ovum.
– DERIVATIVES **ca·pac·i·ta·tion** /kəˌpasiˈtāsнən/ **n.**

ca·pac·i·tor /kəˈpasitər/ ▶ **n.** a device used to store an electric charge, consisting of one or more pairs of conductors separated by an insulator.

ca·pac·i·ty /kəˈpasitē/ ▶ **n.** (pl. **capacities**) **1** [in sing.] the maximum amount that something can contain: *the capacity of the freezer is 1.1 cubic feet* | *the stadium's seating capacity* | *the room was filled to capacity.* ■ [as modifier] fully occupying the available area or space: *they played to a capacity crowd.* ■ the amount that something can produce: *the company aimed to double its electricity-generating capacity* | *when running at full capacity, the factory will employ 450 people.* ■ the total cylinder volume that is swept by the pistons in an internal combustion engine. ■ former term for **CAPACITANCE**.
2 the ability or power to do, experience, or understand something: *I was impressed by her capacity for hard work* | [with infinitive] *his capacity to inspire trust in others* | *their intellectual capacities.* ■ [in sing.] a person's legal competence: *cases where a patient's testamentary capacity is in doubt.*
3 [in sing.] a specified role or position: *I was engaged in a voluntary capacity* | *writing in his capacity as legal correspondent.*
– DERIVATIVES **ca·pac·i·tive** /-ətiv/ (also **ca·pac·i·ta·tive**) **adj.** (chiefly Physics).
– ORIGIN late Middle English: from French *capacité*, from Latin *capacitas*, from *capax, capac-* 'that can contain,' from *capere* 'take or hold.'

cap and bells ▶ **plural n.** historical the insignia of the professional jester.

ca·par·i·son /kəˈparəsən/ ▶ **n.** an ornamental covering spread over a horse's saddle or harness.
▶ **v.** (**be caparisoned**) (of a horse) be decked out in rich decorative coverings.
– ORIGIN early 16th cent.: from obsolete French *caparasson*, from Spanish *caparazón* 'saddlecloth,' from *capa* 'hood.'

cape[1] /kāp/ ▶ **n.** a sleeveless cloak, typically a short one. ■ a part of a longer coat or cloak that falls loosely over the shoulders from the neckband. ■ the pelt from the head and neck of an animal, for preparation as a hunting trophy.
▶ **v.** [with obj.] skin the head and neck of (an animal) to prepare a hunting trophy.
– DERIVATIVES **caped adj.**
– ORIGIN mid 16th cent.: from French, from Provençal *capa*, from late Latin *cappa* 'covering for the head.'

cape[2] ▶ **n. 1** a headland or promontory. ■ (**the Cape**) Cape Cod, Massachusetts. ■ (**the Cape**) the Cape of Good Hope. ■ (**the Cape**) the former Cape Province of South Africa.
2 (**Cape**) short for **CAPE COD** (the style of house).
– ORIGIN late Middle English: from Old French *cap*, from Provençal, based on Latin *caput* 'head.'

Cape A·gul·has, Cape Bon, etc. see **AGULHAS, CAPE**; **BON, CAPE**, etc.

Cape Bar·ren goose ▶ **n.** a pale gray Australian goose related to the shelducks, with a short black bill that is almost covered by a waxy yellow cere, and a black tail. Also called **CEREOPSIS GOOSE**. ● *Cereopsis novaehollandiae*, family Anatidae.
– ORIGIN mid 19th cent.: named after *Cape Barren*, an island in the Bass Strait, Australia.

Cape Bret·on Is·land /ˌbretn/ an island that forms the northeastern part of the province of Nova Scotia in eastern Canada.

Cape buf·fa·lo ▶ **n.** see **AFRICAN BUFFALO**.

Cape Cod /ˈkäd/ (abbr.: **CC**) **1** a sandy peninsula in southeastern Massachusetts that forms a wide curve enclosing Cape Cod Bay. The Pilgrims landed on the northern tip of Cape Cod in November 1620.
2 (also **Cape**) a type of rectangular house with a deeply gabled roof.

Cape Col·o·ny early name (1814–1910) for the former **CAPE PROVINCE**.

Cape col·ored ▶ **n.** (pl. **same** or **Cape coloreds**) (in South Africa) a person of mixed ethnic descent resident in the Western Cape Province, speaking Afrikaans or English as their first language, and typically not a Muslim. Compare with **CAPE MALAY**.
▶ **adj.** of or relating to Cape colored people.

Cape Cor·al a resort city in southwestern Florida, near the mouth of the Caloosahatchee River, southwest of Fort Myers; pop. 156,835 (est. 2008).

ca·peesh /kəˈpēsh/ ▶ **exclam.** informal do you understand?: *Upstairs is off limits. Capeesh?*
– ORIGIN 1940s: from Italian *capisce*, third person singular present tense of *capire* 'understand.'

Cape Fear Riv·er a river that flows for 200 miles (320 km) across eastern North Carolina to enter the Atlantic Ocean near Wilmington at Cape Fear.

cape goose·ber·ry ▶ **n. 1** a soft, edible, yellow berry enclosed in a husk that resembles a lantern in shape.
2 the tropical South American plant that has heart-shaped leaves and that bears this fruit. ● *Physalis peruviana*, family Solanaceae.

Cape hunt·ing dog ▶ **n.** see **HUNTING DOG** (sense 2).

Cape jas·mine (also **Cape jessamine**) ▶ **n.** a fragrant Chinese gardenia, some kinds of which have flowers that are used to perfume tea. ● Genus *Gardenia*, family Rubiaceae: several species, in particular *G. jasminoides*.

Ča·pek /ˈcнäpek/, Karel (1890–1938), Czech novelist and playwright. He is known for *R.U.R.* (*Rossum's Universal Robots*) (1920), which introduced the word *robot* to the English language, and for *The Insect Play* (1921), written with his brother **Josef** (1887–1945).

cap·e·lin /ˈkap(ə)lən/ (also **caplin** /ˈkaplən/) ▶ **n.** a small fish of the North Atlantic, resembling a smelt. It is abundant in coastal waters and provides a staple food for humans and many animals. ● *Mallotus villosus*, family *Osmeridae*.
– ORIGIN early 17th cent.: from French, from Provençal *capelan*, from medieval Latin *cappellanus* 'custodian' (see **CHAPLAIN**).

Ca·pel·la /kəˈpelə/ Astronomy the sixth brightest star in the sky, and the brightest in the constellation Auriga. It is a yellow giant.
– ORIGIN Latin, 'she-goat,' diminutive of *caper* 'goat.'

cap·el·li·ni /ˌkapəˈlēnē/ ▶ **plural n.** pasta in the form of long, thin round strands, only slightly thicker than angel hair.
– ORIGIN 1950s: Italian, diminutive of *capello* 'hair.'

Cape Ma·lay (also **Cape Muslim**) ▶ **n.** (in South Africa) a member of a predominantly Afrikaans-speaking and Muslim group resident mainly in the Western Cape Province. Compare with **CAPE COLORED**.
▶ **adj.** of or relating to the Cape Malay people.

Cape May a resort city in extreme southern New Jersey, on the Atlantic Ocean; pop. 3,686 (est. 2008).

Cape of Good Hope a mountainous promontory south of Cape Town, South Africa, near the southern extremity of Africa. Sighted toward the end of the 15th century by Bartolomeu Dias, it was sailed around for the first time by Vasco da Gama in 1497.

Cape pi·geon (also **Cape petrel**) ▶ **n.** a common petrel of southern oceans that has black plumage with white markings. Also called **PINTADO PETREL**. ● *Daption capense*, family Procellariidae.

Cape Prov·ince a former province of South Africa, containing the Cape of Good Hope. The area became a British colony in 1814; it was known as Cape Colony from then until 1910, when it joined the Union of South Africa. In 1994 it was divided into the provinces of Northern Cape, Western Cape, and Eastern Cape.

ca·per[1] /ˈkāpər/ ▶ **v.** [no obj.] skip or dance about in a lively or playful way: *children were capering about the room.*
▶ **n. 1** a playful skipping movement: *she did a little caper.*
2 informal an activity or escapade, typically one that is illicit or ridiculous. ■ an amusing or far-fetched story, esp. one presented on film or stage: *a cop caper about intergalactic drug dealers.*
– PHRASES **cut a caper** make a playful, skipping movement.
– DERIVATIVES **ca·per·er** /ˈkāpərər/ **n.**
– ORIGIN late 16th cent.: abbreviation of **CAPRIOLE**.

ca·per[2] ▶ **n. 1** (usu. **capers**) the cooked and pickled flower buds of a bramblelike southern European shrub, used to flavor food.
2 the shrub from which these buds are taken. ● *Capparis spinosa*, family Capparidaceae.
– ORIGIN late Middle English: from French *câpres* or Latin *capparis*, from Greek *kapparis*; later interpreted as plural, hence the loss of the final *-s* in the 16th cent.

cap·er·cail·lie /ˌkapərˈkāl(y)ē/ (Scottish also **capercailzie** /-ˈkālyē, -zē/) ▶ **n.** (pl. **capercaillies**) a large, turkeylike Eurasian grouse of mature pine forests. The male has a courtship display in which it fans the tail and makes an extraordinary succession of sounds. ● Genus *Tetrao*, family Tetraonidae (or Phasianidae): two species, in particular *T. urogallus*, which has been re-established in the Scottish Highlands.
– ORIGIN mid 16th cent.: from Scottish Gaelic *capull coille*, literally 'horse of the wood.'

cape·skin /ˈkāpˌskin/ ▶ **n.** a soft leather made from South African sheepskin.

Ca·pet /ˈkäˌpe, käˈpā, ˈkāpit/, Hugh (938–996), king of France 987–996; founder of the Capetian dynasty.

Ca·pe·tian /kəˈpēsнən/ ▶ **adj.** relating to or denoting the dynasty ruling France 987–1328.
▶ **n.** a member of this dynasty.

Cape Town a city in southwestern South Africa at the foot of Table Mountain, the legislative capital of the country and the administrative capital of the province of Western Cape; pop. 3,569,400 (est. 2009).

Cape Verde /ˈvərd/ (also **Cape Verde Islands**) a country in Africa that consists of a group of islands in the Atlantic Ocean off the coast of Senegal, named after the most western cape in Africa; pop. 429,500 (est. 2009); capital, Praia; languages, Portuguese (official) and Creole.

> Previously uninhabited, the islands were settled by the Portuguese from the 15th century and later served as a trading center for African slaves. They remained a Portuguese colony until 1975, when an independent republic was established.

– DERIVATIVES **Cape Ver·de·an** /ˈvərdēən/ **adj. & n.**

Cape York /ˈyôrk/ the northernmost point of Australia, on Torres Strait, at the tip of **Cape York Peninsula** in Queensland.

Cap-Ha·ï·tien /käp ˈhāsнən, ä-ēˈsyaN/ a historic port city in northern Haiti; pop. 127,800 (est. 2009). It is the former capital of Haiti and the second-largest city in the country.

ca·pi·as /ˈkāpēəs/ ▶ **n.** (pl. **capiases**) Law a writ ordering the arrest of a named person.

– ORIGIN late Middle English: from Latin *capias (ad respondendum)*, literally 'you are to seize (until reply is made),' from *capere* 'take.'

cap·il·lar·i·ty /ˌkapəˈlaritē/ ▶ **n.** the tendency of a liquid in a capillary tube or absorbent material to rise or fall as a result of surface tension. Also called CAPILLARY ACTION.
– ORIGIN mid 19th cent.: from French *capillarité*, from Latin *capillaris* 'like a hair' (see CAPILLARY).

C

cap·il·lar·y /ˈkapəˌlerē/ ▶ **n. 1** Anatomy any of the fine branching blood vessels that form a network between the arterioles and venules.
2 (also **capillary tube**) a tube that has an internal diameter of hairlike thinness.
▶ **adj.** [attrib.] of or relating to capillaries or capillarity.
– ORIGIN mid 17th cent.: from Latin *capillaris*, from *capillus* 'hair,' influenced by Old French *capillaire*.

cap·il·lar·y ac·tion ▶ **n.** another term for CAPILLARITY.

cap·il·lar·y at·trac·tion ▶ **n.** the tendency of a liquid in a capillary tube to rise as a result of surface forces.

cap·i·tal[1] /ˈkapitl/ ▶ **n. 1** (also **capital city** or **town**) the most important city or town of a country or region, usually its seat of government and administrative center. ■ [with modifier] a place associated more than any other with a specified activity or product: *Milan is the fashion capital of the world.*
2 wealth in the form of money or other assets owned by a person or organization or available or contributed for a particular purpose such as starting a company or investing: *the senior partner would provide the initial capital* | *rates of return on invested capital were high.* ■ the excess of a company's assets over its liabilities. ■ people who possess wealth and use it to control a society's economic activity, considered collectively: *a conflict of interest between capital and labor.* ■ [with modifier] a valuable resource of a particular kind: *there is insufficient investment in human capital.*
3 (also **capital letter**) a letter of the size and form used to begin sentences and names: *he wrote the name in capitals.*
▶ **adj. 1** [attrib.] (of an offense or charge) liable to the death penalty: *murder was a capital crime.*
2 [attrib.] (of a letter of the alphabet) large in size and of the form used to begin sentences and names.
3 informal, dated excellent: *he's a really capital fellow.*
▶ **exclam.** Brit. informal, dated used to express approval, satisfaction, or delight: *That's splendid! Capital!*
– PHRASES **make capital out of** use to one's own advantage: *trying to make political capital out of the weakness of his rival.* **with a capital —** used to give emphasis to the word or concept in question: *he's trouble with a capital T.*
– DERIVATIVES **cap·i·tal·ly adv.** (sense 3 of the adjective).
– ORIGIN Middle English (as an adjective in the sense 'relating to the head or top,' later 'standing at the head or beginning'): via Old French from Latin *capitalis*, from *caput* 'head.'

cap·i·tal[2] ▶ **n.** Architecture the distinct, typically broader section at the head of a pillar or column.
– ORIGIN Middle English: from Old French *capitel*, from late Latin *capitellum* 'little head,' diminutive of Latin *caput*.

Doric

Corinthian

Ionic

capital[2]

cap·i·tal gain ▶ **n.** (often **capital gains**) a profit from the sale of property or of an investment.

cap·i·tal gains tax ▶ **n.** a tax levied on profit from the sale of property or of an investment.

cap·i·tal goods ▶ **plural n.** goods that are used in producing other goods, rather than being bought by consumers. Often contrasted with CONSUMER GOODS.

cap·i·tal-in·ten·sive ▶ **adj.** (of a business or industrial process) requiring the investment of large sums of money.

cap·i·tal·ism /ˈkapətlˌizəm/ ▶ **n.** an economic and political system in which a country's trade and industry are controlled by private owners for profit, rather than by the state.

cap·i·tal·ist /ˈkapətlist/ ▶ **n.** a wealthy person who uses money to invest in trade and industry for profit in accordance with the principles of capitalism: *the creation of the factory system by nineteenth-century capitalists.*
▶ **adj.** practicing, supporting, or based on the principles of capitalism: *capitalist countries* | *the global economy is essentially capitalist.*
– DERIVATIVES **cap·i·tal·is·tic** /ˌkapətlˈistik/ **adj.**, **cap·i·tal·is·ti·cal·ly** /ˌkapətlˈistik(ə)lē/ **adv.**

cap·i·tal·ize /ˈkapətlˌīz/ ▶ **v. 1** [no obj.] (**capitalize on**) take the chance to gain advantage from: *an attempt by the opposition to capitalize on the government's embarrassment.*
2 [with obj.] provide (a company or industry) with capital: (as adj. **capitalized**) *a highly capitalized industry.*
3 realize (the present value of an income); convert into capital. ■ reckon (the value of an asset) by setting future benefits against the cost of maintenance: *a trader will want to capitalize repairs expenditure.*
4 [with obj.] write or print (a word or letter) in capital letters. ■ begin (a word) with a capital letter.
– DERIVATIVES **cap·i·tal·i·za·tion** /ˌkapətl-əˈzāSHən/ **n.**

cap·i·tal mar·ket ▶ **n.** the part of a financial system concerned with raising capital by dealing in shares, bonds, and other long-term investments.

cap·i·tal pun·ish·ment ▶ **n.** the legally authorized killing of someone as punishment for a crime.

cap·i·tal ship ▶ **n.** a large warship such as a battleship or aircraft carrier.

cap·i·tal sum ▶ **n.** a lump sum of money payable to an insured person or paid as an initial fee or investment.

cap·i·tal ter·ri·to·ry ▶ **n.** a territory containing the capital city of a country, in Australia, Nigeria, Pakistan, and elsewhere.

ca·pi·ta·no /ˌkapiˈtänō/ ▶ **n.** (pl. **capitanos**) (in Italy or among Italian speakers) a captain or chief (used chiefly as a form of address).
– ORIGIN Italian.

cap·i·tate /ˈkapiˌtāt/ ▶ **adj.** Botany & Zoology ending in a distinct compact head.
▶ **n.** (also **capitate bone**) Anatomy the largest of the carpal bones, situated at the base of the palm of the hand and articulating with the third metacarpal.
– ORIGIN mid 17th cent.: from Latin *capitatus*, from *caput*, *capit-* 'head.'

cap·i·ta·tion /ˌkapiˈtāSHən/ ▶ **n.** the payment of a fee or grant to a doctor, school, or other person or body providing services to a number of people, such that the amount paid is determined by the number of patients, students, or customers: *the increased capitation enabled schools to offer students an enhanced curriculum* | [as modifier] *income capitation fees.*
– ORIGIN early 17th cent. (denoting the counting of heads): from late Latin *capitatio* 'poll tax,' from *caput* 'head.'

Cap·i·tol /ˈkapitl/ (usu. **the Capitol**) **1** the seat of the US Congress in Washington, DC. ■ (**capitol**) a building housing a legislative assembly: *50,000 people marched on New Jersey's state capitol.*
2 the temple of Jupiter on the Capitoline Hill in ancient Rome.
– ORIGIN from Old French *capitolie*, *capitoile*, later assimilated to Latin *Capitolium* (from *caput*, *capit-* 'head').

US Capitol

Cap·i·tol Hill the region around the Capitol building in Washington, DC (often used as an allusive reference to the US Congress itself).

Cap·i·tol Reef Na·tion·al Park a preserve in south central Utah, noted for its fossils and rock formations.

ca·pit·u·lar /kəˈpiCHələr/ ▶ **adj. 1** of or relating to a cathedral chapter.
2 Anatomy & Biology of or relating to a capitulum.
– ORIGIN early 16th cent.: from late Latin *capitularis*, from Latin *capitulum* 'small head.'

ca·pit·u·lar·y /kəˈpiCHəˌlerē/ ▶ **n.** (pl. **capitularies**) historical a royal ordinance under the Merovingian dynasty.
– ORIGIN mid 17th cent.: from late Latin *capitularius*, from Latin *capitulum* in the sense 'section of a law.'

ca·pit·u·late /kəˈpiCHəˌlāt/ ▶ **v.** [no obj.] cease to resist an opponent or an unwelcome demand; surrender: *the patriots had to capitulate to the enemy forces.*
– DERIVATIVES **ca·pit·u·la·tor** /-ˌlātər/ **n.**
– ORIGIN mid 16th cent. (in the sense 'parley, draw up terms'): from French *capituler*, from medieval Latin *capitulare* 'draw up under headings,' from Latin *capitulum*, diminutive of *caput* 'head.'

ca·pit·u·la·tion /kəˌpiCHəˈlāSHən/ ▶ **n.** the action of surrendering or ceasing to resist an opponent or demand: *the victor sees it as a sign of capitulation* | *a capitulation to wage demands.* ■ (**capitulations**) historical an agreement or set of conditions.
– ORIGIN mid 16th cent.: from late Latin *capitulatio(n-)*, from the verb *capitulare* (see CAPITULATE).

ca·pit·u·lum /kəˈpiCHələm/ ▶ **n.** (pl. **capitula** /-lə/) Anatomy & Biology a compact head of a structure, in particular a dense, flat cluster of small flowers or florets, as in plants of the daisy family.
– ORIGIN early 18th cent.: from Latin, diminutive of *caput* 'head.'

cap·let /ˈkaplit/ (trademark **Caplet**) ▶ **n.** a coated oral medicinal tablet.
– ORIGIN 1930s: blend of CAPSULE and TABLET.

cap·lin /ˈkaplən/ ▶ **n.** variant spelling of CAPELIN.

cap'n /ˈkapn/ ▶ **n.** informal contraction of CAPTAIN, used in representing speech.

ca·po[1] /ˈkāpō, ˈkäpō/ (also **capo tasto**) ▶ **n.** (pl. **capos**) a clamp fastened across all the strings of a fretted musical instrument to raise their tuning by a chosen amount.
– ORIGIN late 19th cent.: from Italian *capo tasto*, literally 'head stop.'

ca·po[2] ▶ **n.** (pl. **capos**) the head of a crime syndicate, esp. the Mafia, or a branch of one.
– ORIGIN 1950s: from Italian, from Latin *caput* 'head.'

ca·po·ei·ra /ˌkäpōōˈārə/ ▶ **n.** a system of physical discipline and movement originating among Brazilian slaves, treated as a martial art and dance form.
– ORIGIN Portuguese.

capo[1]

cap of lib·er·ty ▶ **n.** a soft conical cap given to Roman slaves on their emancipation and often used as a republican symbol in more recent times.

ca·pon /ˈkāˌpän, -pən/ ▶ **n.** a castrated domestic cock fattened for eating.
– DERIVATIVES **ca·pon·ize** /ˈkāpəˌnīz/ **v.**
– ORIGIN late Old English: from Old French, based on Latin *capo*, *capon-*.

ca·po·na·ta /ˌkäpəˈnätə/ ▶ **n.** a dish of eggplant, olives, and onions seasoned with herbs, typically served as an appetizer.
– ORIGIN Italian.

Ca·pone /kəˈpōn/, Al (1899–1947), US gangster; full name *Alphonse Capone*. He was notorious for his domination of organized crime in Chicago in the 1920s. Although he was believed responsible for many murders, including the St. Valentine's Day Massacre, it was for federal income tax evasion that he was eventually imprisoned in 1931.

ca·po tas·to /ˌkäpō ˈtästō/ ▶ **n.** (pl. **capo tastos**) another term for CAPO[1].

Ca·po·te /kəˈpōtē/, Truman (1924–84), US writer; born *Truman Streckfus Persons*. Notable works: *Breakfast at Tiffany's* (1958) and *In Cold Blood* (1966).

Truman Capote

ca·pote /kəˈpōt/ ▶ **n.** historical a long cloak or coat with a hood, typically part of an army or company uniform.
– ORIGIN early 19th cent.: from French, diminutive of *cape* (see CAPE[1]).

Capp /kap/, Al (1909–79), US cartoonist; born *Alfred Gerald Caplin*. He was noted for his satirical comic strip "Li'l Abner," which appeared in North American newspapers from 1934 to 1977.

Cap·pa·do·cia /ˌkapəˈdōshə/ an ancient region of central Asia Minor, between Lake Tuz and the Euphrates River, north of Cilicia. It was an important center of early Christianity.
– DERIVATIVES **Cap·pa·do·cian adj. & n.**

cap·pel·let·ti /ˌkapəˈletē/ ▶ **n.** small pieces of pasta folded and stuffed with meat or cheese.
– ORIGIN Italian, literally 'little hats.'

cap·per /ˈkapər/ ▶ **n.** informal a more surprising, upsetting, or entertaining event or situation than all others that have gone before: *the capper was him accusing her of ripping off his car.*

cap·puc·ci·no /ˌkäpəˈchēnō, ˌkap-/ ▶ **n.** (pl. **cappuccinos**) coffee made with milk that has been frothed up with pressurized steam.
– ORIGIN 1940s: from Italian, literally 'Capuchin,' because its color resembles that of a Capuchin's habit.

Ca·pra /ˈkaprə/, Frank (1897–1991), US movie director; born in Italy. He is known for movies such as *It Happened One Night* (1934), *Mr. Deeds Goes to Town* (1936), *You Can't Take It with You* (1938), *Arsenic and Old Lace* (1944), and *It's a Wonderful Life* (1946).

Ca·pri /kəˈprē, ˈkaprē, ˈkäprē/ an island off the western coast of Italy, south of Naples.

ca·pric·ci·o /kəˈprēchēˌō, -chō/ ▶ **n.** (pl. **capriccios**) a lively piece of music, typically one that is short and free in form. ■ a painting or other work of art representing a fantasy or a mixture of real and imaginary features.
– ORIGIN early 17th cent. (denoting a sudden change of mind): from Italian, literally 'head with the hair standing on end,' hence 'horror,' later 'a sudden start' (influenced by *capra* 'goat,' associated with frisky movement), from *capo* 'head' + *riccio* 'hedgehog.'

ca·pric·ci·o·so /kəˌprēchēˈōsō, -ˈōzō/ ▶ **adv. & adj.** Music (esp. as a direction) in a free, playful, impulsive style.
– ORIGIN Italian, literally 'capricious,' from CAPRICCIO.

ca·price /kəˈprēs/ ▶ **n. 1** a sudden and unaccountable change of mood or behavior: *her caprices had made his life impossible | a land where men were ruled by law and not by caprice.*
2 Music another term for CAPRICCIO.
– ORIGIN mid 17th cent.: from French, from Italian (see CAPRICCIO).

ca·pri·cious /kəˈprishəs, -ˈprē-/ ▶ **adj.** given to sudden and unaccountable changes of mood or behavior: *a capricious and often brutal administration | a capricious climate.*
– DERIVATIVES **ca·pri·cious·ly adv.**, **ca·pri·cious·ness n.**
– ORIGIN early 17th cent.: from French *capricieux*, from Italian (see CAPRICCIOSO).

Cap·ri·corn /ˈkapriˌkôrn/ Astrology the tenth sign of the zodiac (the Goat), which the sun enters at the northern winter solstice (about December 21). Compare with CAPRICORNUS. ■ (**a Capricorn**) a person born when the sun is in this sign.
– PHRASES **tropic of Capricorn** see TROPIC[1].
– DERIVATIVES **Cap·ri·corn·i·an** /ˌkapriˈkôrnēən/ **n. & adj.**
– ORIGIN Old English, from Latin *capricornus*, from *caper, capr-* 'goat' + *cornu* 'horn,' on the pattern of Greek *aigokerōs* 'goat-horned, Capricorn.'

Cap·ri·cor·nus /ˌkapriˈkôrnəs/ Astronomy a constellation (the Goat), said to represent a goat with a fish's tail. It has few bright stars. Compare with CAPRICORN. ■ (as genitive **Capricorni** /ˌkapriˈkôrnē/) used with a preceding letter or numeral to designate a star in this constellation: *the star 41 Capricorni.*
– ORIGIN Latin (see CAPRICORN).

cap·rine /ˈkapˌrīn/ ▶ **adj.** of, relating to, or resembling goats.
– ORIGIN late Middle English: from Latin *caprinus*, from *caper, capr-* 'goat.'

cap·ri·ole /ˈkaprēˌōl/ ▶ **n.** a movement performed in classical riding, in which the horse leaps from the ground and kicks out with its hind legs. ■ a leap or caper in dancing, esp. a cabriole.
– ORIGIN late 16th cent.: from obsolete French (now *cabriole*), from Italian *capriola* 'leap,' from *capriolo* 'roebuck,' from Latin *capreolus*, diminutive of *caper, capr-* 'goat.'

ca·pri pants /kəˈprē/ (also **capris**) ▶ **plural n.** close-fitting calf-length tapered trousers, usually worn by women and girls.
– ORIGIN 1950s (originally US): named after the island of CAPRI.

Ca·pri·vi Strip /kəˈprēvē/ a narrow strip in Namibia that extends toward Zambia from the northeastern corner of Namibia and reaches the Zambezi River.
– ORIGIN named after Leo Graf von *Caprivi*, German imperial Chancellor 1890–94 at the time when this region became part of the colony of German Southwest Africa.

cap rock ▶ **n.** a layer of hard, impervious rock overlying and often sealing in a deposit of oil, gas, or coal.

ca·pro·ic ac·id /kəˈprō-ik/ ▶ **n.** Chemistry a liquid fatty acid present in milk fat and coconut and palm oils. ● Alternative name: **hexanoic acid**; chem. formula: $CH_3(CH_2)_4COOH$.
– ORIGIN mid 19th cent.: *caproic* from Latin *caper, capr-* 'goat' (because of its smell) + -IC.

cap·ro·lac·tam /ˌkaprōˈlakˌtam/ ▶ **n.** Chemistry a synthetic crystalline compound that is an intermediate in nylon manufacture. ● A lactam; chem. formula: $C_6H_{11}NO$.
– ORIGIN 1940s: from CAPROIC ACID + LACTAM.

ca·pryl·ic ac·id /kəˈprilik/ ▶ **n.** Chemistry a liquid fatty acid present in butter and other fats. ● Alternative name: **n-octanoic acid**; chem. formula: $CH_3(CH_2)_6COOH$.
– DERIVATIVES **cap·ry·late** /ˈkapraˌlāt/ **n.**
– ORIGIN mid 19th cent.: from Latin *caper, capr-* 'goat' + -YL + -IC.

caps /kaps/ ▶ **abbr.** capital letters.

cap·sa·i·cin /kapˈsāəsin/ ▶ **n.** Chemistry a compound that is responsible for the pungency of capsicums. ● A cyclic amide; chem. formula: $C_{18}H_{27}NO_3$.
– ORIGIN late 19th cent.: alteration of *capsicine*, the name of a substance formerly thought to have the same property.

Cap·si·an /ˈkapsēən/ ▶ **adj.** Archaeology of, relating to, or denoting a Paleolithic culture of North Africa and southern Europe, noted for its microliths. It is dated to *c.*8000–4500 BC. ■ (as noun **the Capsian**) the Capsian culture or period.
– ORIGIN early 20th cent.: from Latin *Capsa* (now *Gafsa* in Tunisia), where objects from this culture were found, + -IAN.

cap·si·cum /ˈkapsikəm/ ▶ **n.** (pl. **capsicums**) a tropical American pepper plant of the nightshade family with fruits containing many seeds. Many cultivated varieties with edible, pungent fruits have been developed. ● Genus *Capsicum*, family Solanaceae: several species and varieties, in particular *C. annuum* var. *annuum*, the cultivated forms of which include the 'grossum' group (sweet peppers) and the 'longum' group (chili peppers). ■ the fruit of any of these plants, varying in size, color, and pungency.
– ORIGIN late 16th cent.: modern Latin, perhaps from Latin *capsa* (see CASE[2]).

cap·sid[1] /ˈkapsid/ ▶ **n.** another term for MIRID.
– ORIGIN late 19th cent.: from modern Latin *Capsidae* (plural), from *Capsus* (genus name).

cap·sid[2] ▶ **n.** Microbiology the protein coat or shell of a virus particle, surrounding the nucleic acid or nucleoprotein core.
– ORIGIN 1960s: coined in French from Latin *capsa* (see CASE[2]).

cap·size /ˈkapˌsīz, kapˈsīz/ ▶ **v.** (of a boat) overturn in the water: [no obj.] *the craft capsized in heavy seas* | (as adj. **capsized**) *a capsized dinghy* | [with obj.] *gale-force gusts capsized the dinghies.*
▶ **n.** [in sing.] an instance of capsizing.
– ORIGIN late 18th cent.: perhaps based on Spanish *capuzar* 'sink (a ship) by the head,' from *cabo* 'head' + *chapuzar* 'to dive or duck.'

cap sleeve ▶ **n.** a sleeve extending only a short distance from the shoulder and tapering to nothing under the arm.

cap·stan /ˈkapstən/ ▶ **n.** a revolving cylinder with a vertical axis used for winding a rope or cable, powered by a motor or pushed around by levers. ■ the motor-driven spindle on a tape recorder that makes the tape travel past the head at constant speed.

capstan

– ORIGIN late Middle English: from Provençal *cabestan*, from *cabestre* 'halter,' from Latin *capistrum*, from *capere* 'seize.'

cap·stone /ˈkapˌstōn/ ▶ **n.** a stone fixed on top of something, typically a wall. ■ Archaeology a large, flat stone forming a roof over the chamber of a megalithic tomb.

cap·sule /ˈkapsəl, ˈkapˌso͞ol/ ▶ **n. 1** a small case or container, esp. a round or cylindrical one. ■ a small, soluble case of gelatin containing a dose of medicine, swallowed whole. ■ short for SPACE CAPSULE.
2 Anatomy a tough sheath or membrane that encloses something in the body, such as a kidney, a lens, or a synovial joint. ■ Biology a gelatinous layer forming the outer surface of some bacterial cells.
3 the foil or plastic covering the cork of a wine bottle.
4 Botany a dry fruit that releases its seeds by bursting open when ripe, such as a pea pod.
5 Botany the spore-producing structure of mosses and liverworts, typically borne on a stalk.
6 [as modifier] (of a piece of writing) shortened but retaining the essence of the original; condensed: *a capsule review of the movie.* ■ (of a collection of clothing) consisting of a relatively small set of key items.
– DERIVATIVES **cap·su·lar** /ˈkapsələr/ **adj.**, **cap·su·late** /ˈkapsələt, -ˌlāt/ **adj.**
– ORIGIN late Middle English (in the general sense 'small container'): via French from Latin *capsula*, diminutive of *capsa* (see CASE[2]).

cap·sul·ize /ˈkapsəˌlīz/ ▶ **v.** [with obj.] put (information) in compact form; summarize.

Capt. ▶ **abbr.** Captain.

cap·tain /ˈkaptən/ ▶ **n.** the person in command of a ship. ■ the pilot in command of a civil aircraft. ■ a naval officer of high rank, in particular (in the US Navy or Coast Guard) an officer ranking above commander and below commodore. ■ an army officer of high rank, in particular (in the US Army, Marine Corps, or Air Force) an officer ranking above first lieutenant and below major. ■ a police officer in charge of a precinct, ranking below a chief: *captain of the 20th precinct.* ■ the head of a precinct's fire department. ■ the leader of a team, esp. in sports. ■ a powerful or influential person in a particular field: *a captain of industry.* ■ a political party leader in a local district. ■ a supervisor of waiters or bellboys.
▶ **v.** [with obj.] be the captain of (a ship, aircraft, or sports team).
– DERIVATIVES **cap·tain·cy** /-tənsē/ **n.**
– ORIGIN late Middle English (in the general sense 'chief or leader'): from Old French *capitain* (superseding earlier *chevetaigne* 'chieftain'), from late Latin *capitaneus* 'chief,' from Latin *caput, capit-* 'head.'

cap·tain gen·er·al ▶ **n.** an honorary rank of senior officer in the British army, most commonly in an artillery regiment.

cap·tain's chair ▶ **n.** a wooden chair with a row of vertical spindles supporting a bar that forms the back and armrests.

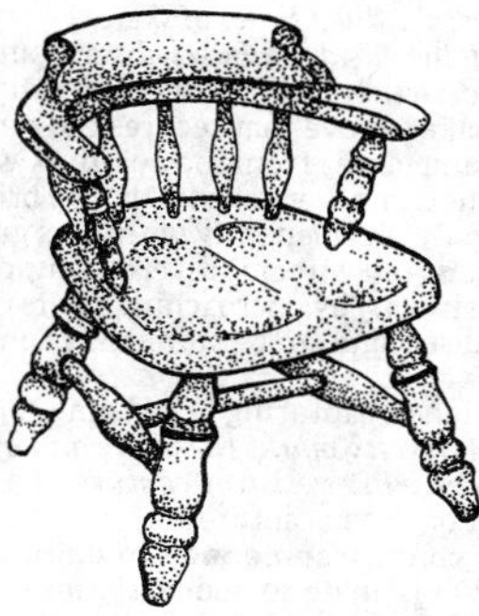

captain's chair

cap·tain's mast ▶ **n.** see MAST[1].

cap·tan /ˈkapˌtan/ ▶ **n.** a synthetic fungicide derived from a mercaptan.

captcha /ˈkapchə/ (also **CAPTCHA**) ▶ **n.** a program or system intended to distinguish human from machine input, typically as a way of thwarting spam and automated extraction of data from websites.
– ORIGIN early 21st cent.: acronym from *completely automated public Turing test to tell computers and humans apart.*

cap·tion /ˈkapshən/ ▶ **n.** a title or brief explanation appended to an article, illustration, cartoon, or poster. ■ a piece of text appearing on a movie or television screen as part of a movie or broadcast. ■ Law the heading of a legal document.
▶ **v.** [with obj.] (usu. **be captioned**) provide (an illustration) with a title or explanation: *the drawings*

C

were captioned with humorous texts | [with two objs.] *the photograph was captioned "Three little maids."*
– ORIGIN late Middle English (in the sense 'seizing, capture'): from Latin *caption-*, from *capere* 'take, seize.' Early senses 'arrest' and 'warrant for arrest' gave rise to 'statement of where, when, and by whose authority a warrant was issued' (late 17th cent.): this was usually appended to a legal document, hence the sense 'heading or appended wording' (late 18th cent.).

cap·tious /ˈkapSHəs/ ▶ **adj.** formal (of a person) tending to find fault or raise petty objections.
– DERIVATIVES **cap·tious·ly** adv., **cap·tious·ness** n.
– ORIGIN late Middle English (also in the sense 'intended to deceive someone'): from Old French *captieux* or Latin *captiosus*, from *captio(n-)* 'seizing,' (figuratively) 'deceiving' (see CAPTION).

cap·ti·vate /ˈkaptəˌvāt/ ▶ v. [with obj.] attract and hold the interest and attention of; charm: *he was captivated by her beauty.*
– DERIVATIVES **cap·ti·va·tion** /ˌkaptəˈvāSHən/ n.
– ORIGIN early 16th cent.: from late Latin *captivat-* 'taken captive,' from the verb *captivare*, from *captivus* (see CAPTIVE).

cap·ti·vat·ing /ˈkaptəˌvātiNG/ ▶ **adj.** capable of attracting and holding interest; charming: *a captivating smile.*
– DERIVATIVES **cap·ti·vat·ing·ly** /-ˌvātiNGlē/ adv.

cap·tive /ˈkaptiv/ ▶ **n.** a person who has been taken prisoner or an animal that has been confined.
▶ **adj.** imprisoned or confined: *the farm was used to hold prisoners of war captive* | *a captive animal.* ■ [attrib.] having no freedom to choose alternatives or to avoid something: *advertisements at the movie theater reach a captive audience.* ■ (of a facility or service) controlled by, and typically for the sole use of, an establishment or company: *a captive power plant.*
– ORIGIN late Middle English: from Latin *captivus*, from *capere* 'seize, take.'

cap·tive bal·loon ▶ **n.** a lighter-than-air balloon secured by a rope to the ground, used to carry radar equipment or for parachute jumps.

cap·tiv·i·ty /kapˈtivitē/ ▶ **n.** (pl. **captivities**) the condition of being imprisoned or confined: *he was released after 865 days in captivity* | *the third month of their captivity.* ■ **(the Captivity)** short for BABYLONIAN CAPTIVITY.
– ORIGIN late Middle English: from Latin *captivitas*, from *captivus* 'taken captive' (see CAPTIVE).

cap·tor /ˈkaptər, -ˌtôr/ ▶ **n.** a person or animal that catches or confines another.
– ORIGIN mid 16th cent.: from Latin, from *capt-* 'seized, taken,' from the verb *capere*.

cap·ture /ˈkapCHər/ ▶ v. [with obj.] take into one's possession or control by force: *the Russians captured 13,000 men.* ■ record or express accurately in words or pictures: *she did a series of sketches, trying to capture all his moods.* ■ Physics absorb (an atomic or subatomic particle). ■ (in chess and other board games) make a move that secures the removal of (an opposing piece) from the board. ■ Astronomy (of a star, planet, or other celestial body) bring (a less massive body) permanently within its gravitational influence. ■ (of a stream) divert the upper course of (another stream) by encroaching on its catchment area. ■ cause (data) to be stored in a computer or in a digital format.
▶ **n.** the action of capturing or of being captured: *the capture of the city marks the high point of his career* | *he was killed while resisting capture.* ■ a person or thing that has been captured.
– PHRASES **capture someone's imagination** (or **attention**) fascinate someone: *the project has captured the imagination of the local public.*
– DERIVATIVES **cap·tur·er** n.
– ORIGIN mid 16th cent. (as a noun): from French, from Latin *captura*, from *capt-* 'seized, taken,' from the verb *capere*.

Cap·u·chin /ˈkap(y)əSHən, kəˈp(y)o͞o-/ ▶ **n.** **1** a friar belonging to a branch of the Franciscan order that observes a strict rule drawn up in 1529.
2 (**capuchin**) a cloak and hood formerly worn by women.
3 (**capuchin** or **capuchin monkey**) a South American monkey with a cap of hair on the head that has the appearance of a cowl. ● Genus *Cebus*, family Cebidae: four species, including the **brown capuchin** (*C. apella*).
4 (**capuchin**) a pigeon of a breed with head and neck feathers resembling a cowl.
– ORIGIN late 16th cent.: from obsolete French, earlier form of *capucin*, from Italian *cappuccino*, from *cappuccio* 'hood, cowl,' from *cappa* (see CAPE[1]), the friars being so named because of their sharp-pointed hoods.

cap·y·ba·ra /ˌkapəˈberə, -ˈbärə/ ▶ **n.** (pl. **same** or **capybaras**) a South American mammal that resembles a giant, long-legged guinea pig. It lives in groups near water and is the largest living rodent. ● *Hydrochoerus hydrochaeris*, the only member of the family Hydrochaeridae.
– ORIGIN early 17th cent.: from Spanish *capibara* or Portuguese *capivara*, from Tupi *capiuára*, from *capí* 'grass' + *uára* 'eater.'

car /kär/ ▶ **n.** a road vehicle, typically with four wheels, powered by an internal combustion engine and able to carry a small number of people: *we're going by car* | [as modifier] *a car crash.* ■ a railroad vehicle for passengers or freight: *the first-class cars.* ■ the passenger compartment of an elevator, cableway, airship, or balloon. ■ literary a chariot.
– DERIVATIVES **car·ful** /-ˌfo͝ol/ n. (pl. **carfuls**).
– ORIGIN late Middle English (in the general sense 'wheeled vehicle'): from Old Northern French *carre*, based on Latin *carrum*, *carrus*, of Celtic origin.

ca·ra·ba·o /ˌkarəˈbou, ˌkär-/ ▶ **n.** (pl. **same** or **carabaos**) another term for WATER BUFFALO.
– ORIGIN early 20th cent.: from Spanish, from a local word in the Philippines.

car·a·bid /ˈkarəbid, kəˈrabid/ ▶ **n.** Entomology a fast-running beetle of a family (Carabidae) that comprises the predatory ground beetles.
– ORIGIN late 19th cent.: from modern Latin *Carabidae* (plural), from Latin *carabus*, denoting a kind of crab.

car·a·bi·neer /ˌkarəbəˈni(ə)r/ (also **carabinier**) ▶ **n.** historical a cavalry soldier whose principal weapon was a carbine.
– ORIGIN mid 17th cent.: from French *carabinier*, from *carabine* (see CARBINE).

car·a·bi·ner /ˌkarəˈbēnər/ (also **karabiner**) ▶ **n.** a coupling link with a safety closure, used by rock climbers.
– ORIGIN 1930s: shortened from German *Karabiner-haken* 'spring hook.'

ca·ra·bi·ne·ro /ˌkarəbəˈne(ə)rō, ˌkär-/ ▶ **n.** (pl. **carabineros**) a Spanish or South American frontier guard or customs officer.
– ORIGIN mid 19th cent.: Spanish, literally 'soldier armed with a carbine.'

ca·ra·bi·nie·re /ˌkarəbənˈye(ə)rē/ ▶ **n.** (pl. **carabinieri** pronunc. **same**) a member of the Italian paramilitary police.
– ORIGIN Italian, literally 'carabineer.'

car·a·cal /ˈkarəˌkal/ ▶ **n.** a long-legged lynxlike cat with black tufted ears and a uniform brown coat, native to Africa and western Asia. Also called AFRICAN LYNX. ● *Felis caracal*, family Felidae.
– ORIGIN mid 19th cent.: from French or Spanish, from Turkish *karakulak*, from *kara* 'black' + *kulak* 'ear' (because of its black ear tufts).

Car·a·cal·la /ˌkarəˈkalə/ (188–217), Roman emperor 211–217; born *Septimius Bassanius*; later called *Marcus Aurelius Severus Antoninus Augustus*. In 212, he granted Roman citizenship to all free inhabitants of the Roman Empire.

ca·ra·ca·ra /ˌkarəˈkarə, ˌkärəˈkärə/ ▶ **n.** (pl. **same** or **caracaras**) a large New World bird of prey of the falcon family, with a bare face and a deep bill, feeding largely on carrion. ● Family Falconidae: four genera and several species, in particular the **common caracara** (*Polyborus plancus*).
– ORIGIN mid 19th cent.: from Spanish or Portuguese *caracará*, from Tupi-Guarani, imitating its cry.

Ca·ra·cas /kəˈräkəs, kəˈrakəs/ the capital of Venezuela, in the northern part of the country near the Caribbean Sea; pop. 2,097,400 (est. 2009).

car·a·cole /ˈkarəˌkōl/ ▶ **n.** a half turn to the right or left by a horse.
▶ v. [no obj.] (of a horse) perform a caracole.
– ORIGIN early 17th cent.: from French *caracole*, *caracol* 'snail's shell, spiral.'

car·a·cul ▶ **n.** variant spelling of KARAKUL.

ca·rafe /kəˈraf, -ˈräf/ ▶ **n.** an open-topped glass flask typically used for serving wine or water.
– ORIGIN late 18th cent.: from French, from Italian *caraffa*, probably based on Arabic *garafa* 'draw water.'

car·a·ga·na /ˌkarəˈgänə, -ˈganə/ ▶ **n.** a leguminous shrub or small tree native to central Asia and Siberia, widely planted as an ornamental. ● Genus *Caragana*, family Leguminosae: several species, including the pea tree of Siberia.
– ORIGIN modern Latin, of Turkic origin.

Ca·ra·jás /ˌkäräˈZHäs/ a mining region in northern Brazil, the site of one of the world's richest deposits of iron ore.

ca·ram·ba /kəˈrämbə/ ▶ **exclam.** informal, often humorous an expression of surprise or dismay.
– ORIGIN mid 19th cent.: from Spanish.

ca·ram·bo·la /ˌkarəmˈbōlə/ ▶ **n.** **1** a golden-yellow juicy fruit with a star-shaped cross section. Also called STAR FRUIT.
2 the small tropical tree that bears this fruit. ● *Averrhoa carambola*, family Oxalidaceae.
– ORIGIN late 16th cent.: from Portuguese, probably from Marathi *karambal*.

car·a·mel /ˈkarəməl, -ˌmel, ˈkärməl/ ▶ **n.** sugar or syrup heated until it turns brown, used as a flavoring or coloring for food or drink: *an apple dipped in caramel* | [as modifier] *caramel ice cream.* ■ the light brown color of this substance: *the liquid turns a pale caramel* | [as modifier] *a caramel sweater.* ■ a soft candy made with sugar and butter that have been melted and further heated.
– ORIGIN early 18th cent.: from French, from Spanish *caramelo*.

car·a·mel·ize /ˈkarəməˌlīz, ˈkärmə-/ ▶ v. [no obj.] (of sugar or syrup) be converted into caramel. ■ [with obj.] (usu. as adj. **caramelized**) cook (food) with sugar so that it becomes coated with caramel.
– DERIVATIVES **car·a·mel·i·za·tion** /ˌkarəmələˈzāSHən/ n.
– ORIGIN mid 19th cent.: from French *caraméliser*, from *caramel* 'caramel.'

ca·ran·gid /kəˈranjid, -ˈraNGgid/ ▶ **n.** Zoology a marine fish of the jack family (Carangidae), whose members typically have a sloping forehead and two dorsal fins.
– ORIGIN late 19th cent.: from modern Latin *Carangidae* (plural), from the genus name *Caranx*.

car·a·pace /ˈkarəˌpās/ ▶ **n.** the hard upper shell of a turtle, crustacean, or arachnid.
– ORIGIN mid 19th cent.: from French, from Spanish *carapacho*, of unknown origin.

car·at /ˈkarət/ ▶ **n.** **1** a unit of weight for precious stones and pearls, now equivalent to 200 milligrams: *a half-carat diamond ring.*
2 chiefly British spelling of KARAT.
– ORIGIN late Middle English (sense 2): from French, from Italian *carato*, from Arabic *kīrāṭ* (a unit of weight), from Greek *keration* 'fruit of the carob' (also denoting a unit of weight), diminutive of *keras* 'horn,' with reference to the elongated seedpod of the carob.

Ca·ra·vag·gio /ˌkarəˈväjō/, Michelangelo Merisi da (*c.*1571–1610), Italian painter. He was an influential figure in the transition from late mannerism to baroque.

car·a·van /ˈkarəˌvan/ ▶ **n.** **1** Brit. a vehicle equipped for living in, typically towed by a car and used for vacations: [as modifier] *a caravan holiday.* ■ a covered horse-drawn wagon: *a gypsy caravan.* ■ a covered truck; a van.
2 historical a group of people, esp. traders or pilgrims, traveling together across a desert in Asia or North Africa. ■ any large group of people, typically with vehicles or animals traveling together, in single file: *a caravan of cars and trucks.*
– ORIGIN late 15th cent. (sense 2): from French *caravane*, from Persian *kārwān*. The sense 'covered horse-drawn wagon' dates from the early 19th cent.

car·a·van·sa·ry /ˌkarəˈvansərē/ (chiefly Brit. also **caravanserai** /-səˌrī/) ▶ **n.** (pl. **caravansaries** or **caravanserais** /-səˌrīz/) **1** historical an inn with a central courtyard for travelers in the desert regions of Asia or North Africa.
2 a group of people traveling together; a caravan.
– ORIGIN late 16th cent.: from Persian *kārwānsarāy*, from *kārwān* 'caravan' + *sarāy* 'palace.'

car·a·vel /ˈkarəˌvel, -vəl/ (also **carvel** /ˈkärvel/) ▶ **n.** historical a small, fast Spanish or Portuguese sailing ship of the 15th–17th centuries.
– ORIGIN early 16th cent.: from French *caravelle*, from Portuguese *caravela*, diminutive of *caravo*, via Latin from Greek *karabos* 'horned beetle' or 'light ship.'

car·a·way /ˈkarəˌwā/ ▶ **n.** **1** (also **caraway seed**) the seeds of a plant of the parsley family, used for flavoring and as a source of oil.
2 the white-flowered Mediterranean plant that bears these seeds. ● *Carum carvi*, family Umbelliferae.
– ORIGIN Middle English: from medieval Latin *carui*, from Arabic *alkarāwiyā*, probably from Greek *karon* 'cumin.'

carb[1] /kärb/ ▶ **n.** short for CARBURETOR.

carb[2] ▶ **n.** short for CARBOHYDRATE.

car·ba·mate /ˈkärbəˌmāt/ ▶ **n.** Chemistry a salt or ester containing the anion NH_2COO^- or the group $-OOCNH_2$, derived from the hypothetical compound **carbamic acid.**
– ORIGIN mid 19th cent.: from *carbamic* (from CARBO- + AMIDE + -IC) + -ATE[1].

car·ba·maz·e·pine /ˌkärbəˈmazəˌpēn/ ▶ **n.** Medicine a synthetic compound of the benzodiazepine class, used as an anticonvulsant and analgesic drug.
– ORIGIN 1990s: from CARBO- + AMIDE, on the pattern of *benzodiazepine*.

car·ban·i·on /kärˈbanˌīən, -ˌīˌän/ ▶ **n.** Chemistry an organic anion in which the negative charge is located on a carbon atom.

car·ba·ryl /ˈkärbəˌril/ ▶ **n.** Chemistry a synthetic insecticide used to protect crops and in the treatment of fleas and lice. ● Alternative name: **1-naphthyl-N-methylcarbamate**; chem. formula: $C_{12}H_{11}NO_2$.
– ORIGIN mid 20th cent.: from CARBAMATE + -YL.

car·ba·zole /ˈkärbəˌzōl/ ▶ **n.** Chemistry a colorless crystalline substance obtained from coal tar, used in dye production. ● A tricyclic heteroaromatic compound; chem. formula: $C_{12}H_9N$.
– ORIGIN late 19th cent.: from CARBO- + AZO- + -OLE.

car·bene /ˈkärˌbēn/ ▶ **n.** Chemistry a highly reactive molecule containing a divalent carbon atom, examples of which occur as intermediates in some organic reactions.

car·bide /ˈkärˌbīd/ ▶ **n.** Chemistry a binary compound of carbon with an element of lower or comparable electronegativity. ■ calcium carbide (CaC_2), used to generate acetylene by reaction with water and formerly used in portable lamps: [as modifier] *a carbide lamp*.

car·bine /ˈkärˌbīn, -ˌbēn/ ▶ **n.** a light automatic rifle. ■ historical a short rifle or musket used by cavalry.
– ORIGIN early 17th cent.: from French *carabine*, from *carabin* 'mounted musketeer,' of unknown origin.

carbo- ▶ **comb. form** representing CARBON.

car·bo·ca·tion /ˌkärbəˈkāsHən/ ▶ **n.** Chemistry another term for CARBONIUM ION.
– ORIGIN 1950s: from CARBO- + CATION.

car·bo·hy·drate /ˌkärbəˈhīˌdrāt/ ▶ **n.** Biochemistry any of a large group of organic compounds occurring in foods and living tissues and including sugars, starch, and cellulose. They contain hydrogen and oxygen in the same ratio as water (2:1) and typically can be broken down to release energy in the animal body.

car·bo·lat·ed /ˈkärbəˌlātid/ ▶ **adj.** impregnated with carbolic acid.

car·bol·ic /kärˈbälik/ ▶ **n.** short for CARBOLIC ACID or CARBOLIC SOAP.

car·bol·ic ac·id ▶ **n.** phenol, esp. when used as a disinfectant.

car·bol·ic soap ▶ **n.** disinfectant soap containing phenol.

car·bo-load /ˈkärbōˌlōd/ ▶ **v.** [no obj.] eat large amounts of carbohydrates, as in preparation for athletic endurance.

car·bo-load·ed /ˈkärbōˌlōdid/ ▶ **adj.** (of a food, beverage, or meal) containing a relatively high amount of carbohydrates.

car bomb ▶ **n.** a bomb concealed in or under a parked car, used esp. by terrorists.
▶ **v.** (**car-bomb**) [with obj.] attack with such a bomb.
– DERIVATIVES **car bomb·er n.**

car·bon /ˈkärbən/ ▶ **n.** **1** the chemical element of atomic number 6, a nonmetal that has two main forms (diamond and graphite) and that also occurs in impure form in charcoal, soot, and coal. (Symbol: **C**) ■ [usu. as modifier] carbon fiber: *a bike with a carbon frame*. ■ a rod of carbon in an arc lamp. ■ a piece of carbon paper or a carbon copy.
2 carbon dioxide or other gaseous carbon compounds released into the atmosphere, associated with climate change: *the level of carbon in the atmosphere has been consistently rising* | [as modifier] *fossil fuel consumption and carbon emissions continued to rise*.

> Compounds of carbon (organic compounds) form the physical basis of all living organisms. Carbon atoms are able to link with each other and with other atoms to form chains and rings, and an infinite variety of carbon compounds exist.

– DERIVATIVES **car·bon·less adj.**
– ORIGIN late 18th cent.: from French *carbone*, from Latin *carbo*, *carbon-* 'coal, charcoal.'

> **WORD TRENDS** No longer just a simple noun for a chemical element, **carbon** is now most commonly used as shorthand for carbon dioxide or other carbon compounds released into the atmosphere and associated with climate change. It was first recorded in this sense in 1977, in the phrase *carbon emissions*, which is still the second most common compound noun containing **carbon** in the Oxford English Corpus, after *carbon dioxide* itself. Other common compounds reflect concerns over the impact of humans on the environment, with *carbon tax*, *carbon footprint*, *carbon credit*, and *carbon trading* all frequently seen. Concern is also shifting from limiting the release of carbon to managing its levels in the atmosphere, as seen from the verbs regularly paired with the word—*store* is now twice as common as *release*, with *sequester*, *absorb*, and *capture* all close behind.

car·bon-12 ▶ **n.** the most common natural carbon isotope, of mass 12. It is the basis for the accepted scale of atomic mass units.

car·bon-14 ▶ **n.** a long-lived naturally occurring radioactive carbon isotope of mass 14, used in carbon dating and as a tracer in biochemistry.

car·bo·na·ceous /ˌkärbəˈnāsHəs/ ▶ **adj.** (chiefly of rocks or sediments) consisting of or containing carbon or its compounds.

car·bo·na·do /ˌkärbəˈnādō, -ˈnādō/ ▶ **n.** (pl. **carbonados**) a dark opaque diamond, used in abrasives and cutting tools. Compare with BORT.
– ORIGIN mid 19th cent.: from Portuguese.

car·bo·na·ra /ˌkärbəˈnärə, -ˈnarə/ ▶ **adj.** denoting a pasta sauce made with bacon or ham, egg, and cream: [postpositive] *spaghetti carbonara*.
– ORIGIN Italian, literally 'charcoal kiln,' perhaps influenced by *carbonata*, a dish of charcoal-grilled salt pork.

car·bo·nate /ˈkärbənət, -ˌnāt/ ▶ **n.** Chemistry a salt of the anion CO_3^{2-}, typically formed by reaction of carbon dioxide with bases.
▶ **v.** /ˈkärbəˌnāt/ [with obj.] dissolve carbon dioxide in (a liquid). ■ Chemistry convert into a carbonate, typically by reaction with carbon dioxide.
– DERIVATIVES **car·bo·na·tion** /ˌkärbəˈnāsHən/ **n.**

car·bo·nat·ed /ˈkärbənātid/ ▶ **adj.** (of a soft drink) effervescent on account of containing dissolved carbon dioxide.

car·bon black ▶ **n.** a fine carbon powder used as a pigment, made by burning hydrocarbons in insufficient air.

car·bon cap·ture and stor·age ▶ **n.** the process of trapping carbon dioxide produced by burning fossil fuels or any other chemical or biological process and storing it in such a way that it is unable to affect the atmosphere.

car·bon cop·y ▶ **n.** a copy of written or typed material made with carbon paper. ■ a person or thing identical or very similar to another: *Karl was a carbon copy of his father*.

car·bon cred·it ▶ **n.** a permit that allows a country or organization to produce a certain amount of carbon emissions and that can be traded if the full allowance is not used.

car·bon cy·cle ▶ **n.** Biochemistry **1** the series of processes by which carbon compounds are interconverted in the environment, chiefly involving the incorporation of carbon dioxide into living tissue by photosynthesis and its return to the atmosphere through respiration, the decay of dead organisms, and the burning of fossil fuels.
2 Astronomy the cycle of thermonuclear reactions believed to occur in stars, in which carbon nuclei are repeatedly formed and broken down in the conversion of hydrogen into helium.

Car·bon·dale /ˈkärbənˌdāl/ a city in south central Illinois, a coal center and home to Southern Illinois University; pop. 26,231 (est. 2008).

car·bon dat·ing ▶ **n.** the determination of the age of an organic object from the relative proportions of the carbon isotopes carbon-12 and carbon-14 that it contains. The ratio between them changes as radioactive carbon-14 decays and is not replaced by exchange with the atmosphere.

car·bon di·ox·ide ▶ **n.** a colorless, odorless gas produced by burning carbon and organic compounds and by respiration. It is naturally present in air (about 0.03 percent) and is absorbed by plants in photosynthesis. ● Chem. formula: CO_2.

car·bon di·sul·fide ▶ **n.** a colorless toxic flammable liquid used as a solvent, esp. for rubber and sulfur, and in the manufacture of viscose rayon, cellophane, and carbon tetrachloride. ● Chem. formula: CS_2.

car·bon fi·ber ▶ **n.** a material consisting of thin, strong crystalline filaments of carbon, used as a strengthening material, esp. in resins and ceramics: [as modifier] *a carbon-fiber chassis*.

car·bon foot·print ▶ **n.** the amount of carbon dioxide and other carbon compounds emitted due to the consumption of fossil fuels by a particular person, group, etc.

> **WORD TRENDS** See FOOTPRINT.

car·bon·ic /kärˈbänik/ ▶ **adj.** of or relating to carbon or its compounds, esp. carbon dioxide.

car·bon·ic ac·id ▶ **n.** Chemistry a very weak acid formed in solution when carbon dioxide dissolves in water. ● Chem. formula: H_2CO_3.

car·bon·ic ac·id gas ▶ **n.** archaic term for CARBON DIOXIDE.

car·bon·ic an·hy·drase /anˈhīˌdrās, -ˌdrāz/ ▶ **n.** Biochemistry an enzyme that catalyzes the interconversion of dissolved bicarbonates and carbon dioxide.

Car·bon·if·er·ous /ˌkärbəˈnifərəs/ ▶ **adj.** Geology of, relating to, or denoting the fifth period of the Paleozoic era, between the Devonian and Permian periods. ■ (**the Carboniferous**) [as noun] the Carboniferous period or the system of rocks deposited during it.

> The Carboniferous lasted from about 360 million to 286 million years ago. This period is subdivided into two periods, the **Older Carboniferous**, or **Mississippian Period** (about 360-320 million years ago), and the **Younger Carboniferous**, or **Pennsylvanian Period** (about 320-286 million years ago). During this time the first reptiles and seed-bearing plants appeared, and there were extensive coral reefs and coal-forming swamp forests.

car·bo·ni·um i·on /kärˈbōnēəm/ ▶ **n.** Chemistry an organic cation in which the positive charge is located on a carbon atom.
– ORIGIN early 20th cent.: *carbonium* from CARBO- 'carbon,' on the pattern of *ammonium*.

car·bon·ize /ˈkärbəˌnīz/ ▶ **v.** [with obj.] convert into carbon, typically by heating or burning, or during fossilization: *the steak was carbonized on the outside*. ■ (usu. as adj. **carbonized**) coat with carbon.
– DERIVATIVES **car·bon·i·za·tion** /ˌkärbənəˈzāsHən/ **n.**

car·bon mon·ox·ide ▶ **n.** a colorless, odorless toxic flammable gas formed by incomplete combustion of carbon. ● Chem. formula: CO.

car·bon·nade /ˌkärbəˈnäd/ ▶ **n.** a rich beef stew made with onions and beer.
– ORIGIN mid 17th cent. (denoting a piece of meat or fish cooked on hot coals): from French, from Latin *carbo, carbon-* 'coal, charcoal.'

car·bon-neu·tral ▶ **adj.** making no net release of carbon dioxide to the atmosphere, esp. through offsetting emissions by planting trees.

car·bon off·set·ting ▶ **n.** the counteracting of carbon dioxide emissions with an equivalent reduction of carbon dioxide in the atmosphere.

car·bon pa·per ▶ **n.** thin paper coated with carbon or another pigmented substance, used for making copies of written or typed documents.

car·bon proc·ess ▶ **n.** a method of making photographic prints that uses a pigment, esp. carbon, contained in a sensitized tissue of gelatin.

car·bon se·ques·tra·tion ▶ **n.** a natural or artificial process by which carbon dioxide is removed from the atmosphere and held in solid or liquid form.

car·bon sink ▶ **n.** Ecology a forest, ocean, or other natural environment viewed in terms of its ability to absorb carbon dioxide from the atmosphere.

car·bon steel ▶ **n.** steel in which the main alloying element is carbon, and whose properties are chiefly dependent on the percentage of carbon present.

car·bon tax ▶ **n.** a tax on fossil fuels, esp. those used by motor vehicles, intended to reduce the emission of carbon dioxide.

car·bon tet·ra·chlo·ride /ˌtetrəˈklôrˌīd/ ▶ **n.** Chemistry a colorless toxic volatile liquid used as a solvent, esp. for fats and oils. ● Chem. formula: CCl_4.

car·bon trad·ing ▶ **n.** another term for EMISSIONS TRADING.

car·bon·yl /ˈkärbəˌnil/ ▶ **n.** [as modifier] Chemistry of or denoting the divalent radical =C=O, present in such organic compounds as aldehydes, ketones, amides, and esters, and in organic acids as part of the carboxyl group: *carbonyl compounds*. ■ a coordination compound in which one or more carbon monoxide molecules are bonded as neutral ligands to a central metal atom: *nickel carbonyl*.

car·bon·yl chlo·ride ▶ **n.** another term for PHOSGENE.

car·bo·run·dum /ˌkärbəˈrəndəm/ ▶ **n.** a very hard black solid consisting of silicon carbide, used as an abrasive.
– ORIGIN late 19th cent. (originally US, as a trademark): blend of CARBON and CORUNDUM.

car·box·y·he·mo·glo·bin /kärˌbäksēˈhēməˌglōbən/ ▶ **n.** Biochemistry a compound formed in the blood by the binding of carbon monoxide to hemoglobin. It is stable and therefore cannot absorb or transport oxygen.

car·box·yl /kärˈbäksəl/ ▶ **n.** [as modifier] Chemistry of or denoting the acid radical –COOH, present in most organic acids: *the carboxyl group*.
– ORIGIN mid 19th cent.: from CARBO- + OX- 'oxygen' + -YL.

car·box·yl·ase /kärˈbäksəˌlās, -ˌlāz/ ▶ **n.** Biochemistry an enzyme that catalyzes the addition of a carboxyl group to a specified substrate.

car·box·yl·ate /kärˈbäksəˌlāt, -lit/ ▶ **n.** Chemistry a salt or ester of a carboxylic acid.

▶ v. [with obj.] add a carboxyl group to (a compound): (as adj. **carboxylated**) *carboxylated polysaccharides.*
– DERIVATIVES **car·box·yl·a·tion** /kärˌbäksəˈlāsʜən/ n.

car·box·yl·ic ac·id /ˈkärbäkˈsilik/ ▶ n. Chemistry an organic acid containing a carboxyl group. The simplest examples are methanoic (or formic) acid and ethanoic (or acetic) acid.

car·boy /ˈkärˌboi/ ▶ n. a large globular plastic bottle with a narrow neck, typically protected by a frame and used for holding acids or other corrosive liquids.
– ORIGIN mid 18th cent.: from Persian *ḳarāba* 'large glass flagon.'

car bra ▶ n. see BRA.

car·bun·cle /ˈkärˌbəNGkəl/ ▶ n. **1** a severe abscess or multiple boil in the skin, typically infected with staphylococcus bacteria.
2 a bright red gem, in particular a garnet cut en cabochon.
– DERIVATIVES **car·bun·cu·lar** /kärˈbəNGkyələr/ adj.
– ORIGIN Middle English (sense 2): from Old French *charbuncle*, from Latin *carbunculus* 'small coal,' from *carbo* 'coal, charcoal.'

car·bu·ret·ed /ˈkärb(y)əˌrātəd, -ˌretid/ (Brit. **carburetted**) ▶ adj. (of a vehicle or engine) having fuel supplied through a carburetor, rather than an injector.
– ORIGIN early 19th cent.: from archaic *carburet* 'carbide' + -ED².

car·bu·re·tor /ˈkärb(y)əˌrātər/ (also **carburator**, Brit. **carburettor** or **carburetter**) ▶ n. a device in an internal combustion engine for mixing air with a fine spray of liquid fuel.
– ORIGIN mid 19th cent.: from archaic *carburet* 'combine or charge with a hydrocarbon' + -OR¹.

car·bu·rize /ˈkärb(y)əˌrīz/ ▶ v. [with obj.] add carbon to (iron or steel), in particular by heating in the presence of carbon to harden the surface.
– DERIVATIVES **car·bu·ri·za·tion** /ˌkärb(y)ərəˈzāsʜən/ n.
– ORIGIN mid 19th cent.: from French *carbure* 'carbide' + -IZE.

car·ca·jou /ˈkärkəˌjo͞o, -ˌzʜo͞o/ ▶ n. another term for the North American WOLVERINE.
– ORIGIN early 18th cent.: from Canadian French, from Montagnais *kwāhkwāčēw* (compare with KINKAJOU).

car·cass /ˈkärkəs/ (Brit. also **carcase**) ▶ n. the dead body of an animal. ■ the trunk of an animal such as a cow, sheep, or pig, for cutting up as meat. ■ the remains of a cooked bird after all the edible parts have been removed. ■ derogatory or humorous a person's body, living or dead: *my obsession will last while there's life in this old carcass.* ■ the structural framework of a building, ship, or piece of furniture. ■ the remains of something being discarded, dismembered, or worthless: *the floor is littered with the carcasses of newspapers.*
– ORIGIN Middle English: from Anglo-Norman French *carcois*, variant of Old French *charcois*; in later use from French *carcasse*; of unknown ultimate origin.

car·cin·o·gen /kärˈsinəjən, ˈkärsənəˌjen/ ▶ n. a substance capable of causing cancer in living tissue.
– ORIGIN mid 19th cent.: from an abbreviation of CARCINOMA + -GEN.

car·cin·o·gen·e·sis /ˌkärsənəˈjenəsis/ ▶ n. the initiation of cancer formation.

car·cin·o·gen·ic /ˌkärsənəˈjenik/ ▶ adj. having the potential to cause cancer.
– DERIVATIVES **car·ci·no·ge·nic·i·ty** /-ˌnōjəˈnisitē/ n.

car·ci·noid /ˈkärsəˌnoid/ ▶ n. Medicine a tumor of a type occurring in the glands of the intestine (esp. the appendix) or in the bronchi, and abnormally secreting hormones.
– ORIGIN late 19th cent.: from an abbreviation of CARCINOMA + -OID.

car·ci·no·ma /ˌkärsəˈnōmə/ ▶ n. (pl. **carcinomas** or **carcinomata** /-ˈnōmətə/) a cancer arising in the epithelial tissue of the skin or of the lining of the internal organs.
– DERIVATIVES **car·ci·no·ma·tous** /-ˈnōmətəs/ adj.
– ORIGIN early 18th cent.: via Latin from Greek *karkinōma*, from *karkinos* 'crab' (compare with CANCER).

car coat ▶ n. a short, square-cut style of coat designed to be worn when driving a car.

card¹ /kärd/ ▶ n. **1** a piece of thick, stiff paper or thin pasteboard, in particular one used for writing or printing on: *some notes jotted down on a card.* ■ such a piece of thick paper printed with a picture and used to send a message or greeting: *a birthday card.* ■ a small piece of such paper with a person's name and other details printed on it for purposes of identification, for example a business card.
2 a small rectangular piece of plastic issued by a bank, containing personal data in a machine-readable form and used chiefly to obtain cash or credit. ■ a similar piece of plastic used for other purposes such as paying for a telephone call or gaining entry to a room or building.
3 a playing card: *a deck of cards.* ■ (**cards**) a game played with playing cards.
4 Computing short for EXPANSION CARD.
5 informal a person regarded as odd or amusing: *He laughed, "You're a card, you know."*
6 a program of events at a racetrack. ■ a record of scores in a sporting event; a scorecard.
▶ v. [with obj.] **1** write (something) on a card, esp. for indexing.
2 check the identity card of (someone), in particular as evidence of legal drinking age.
3 informal (in golf and other sports) score (a certain number of points on a scorecard): *he carded 68 in the final round.*
– PHRASES **hold all the cards** be in a very strong or advantageous position. **in the cards** informal very possible or likely: *an overwhelming military triumph is in the cards.* **play the —— card** exploit the specified issue or idea mentioned, esp. for political advantage: *he saw an opportunity to play the peace card.* **play one's cards right** make the best use of one's assets and opportunities. **put** (or **lay**) **one's cards on the table** be completely open and honest in declaring one's resources, intentions, or attitude.
– ORIGIN late Middle English(sense 3 of the noun): from Old French *carte*, from Latin *carta, charta*, from Greek *khartēs* 'papyrus leaf.'

card² ▶ v. [with obj.] comb and clean (raw wool, hemp fibers, or similar material) with a sharp-toothed instrument in order to disentangle the fibers before spinning.
▶ n. a toothed implement or machine for this purpose.
– DERIVATIVES **card·er** n.
– ORIGIN late Middle English: from Old French *carde*, from Provençal *carda*, from *cardar* 'tease, comb,' based on Latin *carere* 'to card.'

Card. ▶ abbr. Cardinal.

car·da·mom /ˈkärdəməm/ (also **cardamon** /-mən/) ▶ n. **1** the aromatic seeds of a plant of the ginger family, used as a spice and also medicinally.
2 the Southeast Asian plant that bears these seeds. ● *Elettaria cardamomum*, family Zingiberaceae.
– ORIGIN late Middle English: from Old French *cardamome* or Latin *cardamomum*, from Greek *kardamōmon*, from *kardamon* 'cress' + *amōmon*, the name of a kind of spice plant.

Car·da·mom Moun·tains /ˈkärdəməm/ a range of mountains in western Cambodia.

card·board /ˈkärdˌbôrd/ ▶ n. pasteboard or stiff paper: [as modifier] *a cardboard box.* ■ [as modifier] (of a character in a literary work) lacking depth and realism; artificial: *with its superficial, cardboard characters, the novel was typical of her work.*

card-car·ry·ing ▶ adj. [attrib.] registered as a member of a political party or labor union. ■ often humorous confirmed in or dedicated to a specified pursuit or outlook: *a card-carrying pessimist.*

Cár·de·nas /ˈkärˈdāˌnäs, ˈkärdn-əs/ an industrial port in north central Cuba, east of Havana; pop. 98,200 (est. 2009).

card·hold·er /ˈkärdˌhōldər/ ▶ n. a person who has a credit card or debit card.

car·di·a /ˈkärdēə/ ▶ n. Anatomy the upper opening of the stomach, where the esophagus enters.
– ORIGIN late 18th cent.: from Greek *kardia.*

car·di·ac /ˈkärdēˌak/ ▶ adj. **1** of or relating to the heart: *a cardiac arrest.*
2 of or relating to the part of the stomach nearest the esophagus.
▶ n. Medicine, informal a person with heart disease.
– ORIGIN late Middle English (as a noun denoting heart disease): from French *cardiaque* or Latin *cardiacus*, from Greek *kardiakos*, from *kardia* 'heart or upper opening of the stomach.' The adjective dates from the early 17th cent.

car·di·ac ar·rest ▶ n. a sudden, sometimes temporary, cessation of function of the heart.

car·di·ac mas·sage ▶ n. a procedure to resuscitate a patient suffering cardiac arrest or fibrillation by rhythmically compressing the chest and heart to restore circulation. Also called HEART MASSAGE.

car·di·ac mus·cle ▶ n. another term for MYOCARDIUM.

car·di·ac tam·pon·ade ▶ n. see TAMPONADE (sense 1).

car·di·al·gi·a /ˌkärdēˈalj(ē)ə/ ▶ n. **1** heartburn.
2 another term for CARDIODYNIA.

Car·diff /ˈkärdif/ the capital of Wales, a seaport on the Bristol Channel, in the southern part of the country; pop. 314,100 (est. 2009). Welsh name CAERDYDD.

car·di·gan /ˈkärdigən/ ▶ n. a knitted sweater fastening down the front, typically with long sleeves.
– ORIGIN mid 19th cent. (Crimean War): named after James Thomas Brudenel, 7th Earl of *Cardigan* (1797–1868), leader of the Charge of the Light Brigade, whose troops first wore such garments.

Car·din /kärˈdan, -ˈdan/, Pierre (1922–), French couturier, the first designer in the field of haute couture to show a collection of clothes for men as well as for women.

car·di·nal /ˈkärd-nl, ˈkärdn-əl/ ▶ n. **1** a leading dignitary of the Roman Catholic Church. Cardinals are nominated by the pope and form the Sacred College, which elects succeeding popes (now invariably from among their own number). ■ (also **cardinal red**) a deep scarlet color like that of a cardinal's cassock.
2 a New World songbird of the bunting family, with a stout bill and typically with a conspicuous crest. The male is partly or mostly red in color. ● Family Emberizidae, subfamily Cardinalinae (the **cardinal grosbeak subfamily**): four genera and several species, esp. the **northern** (or **common**) **cardinal** (*Cardinalis cardinalis*), the male of which is scarlet with a black face. This subfamily also includes American grosbeaks, buntings, and saltators.
▶ adj. [attrib.] of the greatest importance; fundamental: *two cardinal points must be borne in mind.*
– DERIVATIVES **car·di·nal·ate** /ˈkärd-nl-it, ˈkärdn-əlit, -ˌlāt/ n. (sense 1 of the noun), **car·di·nal·ly** adv., **car·di·nal·ship** /-ˌsʜip/ n. (sense 1 of the noun).
– ORIGIN Old English, from Latin *cardinalis*, from *cardo, cardin-* 'hinge.' Sense 1 of the noun has arisen through the notion of the important function of such priests as "pivots" of church life.

northern cardinal

car·di·nal bee·tle ▶ n. a mainly bright red beetle with feathery or comblike antennae. It typically lives under loose bark. ● Family Pyrochroidae: several genera.

car·di·nal fish ▶ n. a small brightly colored fish found in shallow tropical seas around reefs. The male often broods the eggs in his mouth. ● Family Apogonidae: several genera, in particular *Apogon*, and numerous species.

car·di·nal flow·er ▶ n. a tall scarlet-flowered lobelia found in North America. ● *Lobelia cardinalis*, family Campanulaceae.

car·di·nal hu·mor ▶ n. see HUMOR (sense 3 of the noun).

car·di·nal·i·ty /ˌkärdnˈalitē/ ▶ n. (pl. **cardinalities**) Mathematics the number of elements in a set or other grouping, as a property of that grouping.

car·di·nal num·ber ▶ n. a number denoting quantity (one, two, three, etc.), as opposed to an ordinal number (first, second, third, etc.).

car·di·nal point ▶ n. each of the four main points of the compass (north, south, east, and west).

car·di·nal sin ▶ n. **1** another name for DEADLY SIN.
2 chiefly humorous a serious error of judgment: *the program was canceled for the biggest cardinal sin of them all—it dared to be intelligent.*

car·di·nal vir·tue ▶ n. each of the chief natural virtues of justice, prudence, temperance, and fortitude, as defined by Plato and Aristotle and adopted by the Church Fathers. Compare with THEOLOGICAL VIRTUE.

card in·dex ▶ n. a catalog or similar collection of information in which each item is entered on a separate card, and the cards are arranged in a particular order, typically alphabetical.

card·ing wool ▶ n. short-stapled pieces of wool that result from the carding process, spun and woven to make standard-quality fabrics. Compare with COMBING WOOL.

cardio- ▶ comb. form of or relating to the heart: *cardiograph | cardiopulmonary.*
– ORIGIN from Greek *kardia* 'heart.'

car·di·o·dyn·i·a /ˌkärdēōˈdinēə/ ▶ n. pain in the region of the heart.

car·di·o·gram /ˈkärdēəˌgram/ ▶ n. a record of muscle activity within the heart made by a cardiograph.

car·di·o·graph /ˈkärdēəˌgraf/ ▶ n. an instrument for recording heart muscle activity, such as an electrocardiograph.
– DERIVATIVES **car·di·og·ra·pher** /ˌkärdēˈägrəfər/ n., **car·di·og·ra·phy** /-ˈägrəfē/ n.

car·di·oid /ˈkärdēˌoid/ ▶ n. Mathematics a heart-shaped curve traced by a point on the circumference of

a circle as it rolls around another identical circle. ■ (also **cardioid microphone**) a directional microphone with a pattern of sensitivity of this shape.
▶ **adj.** of the shape of a cardioid.
– ORIGIN mid 18th cent.: from Greek *kardioeidēs* 'heart-shaped,' from *kardia* 'heart' + *eidos* 'form.'

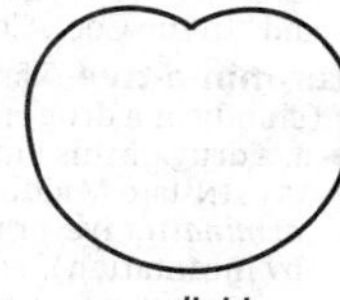
cardioid

car·di·ol·o·gy /ˌkärdēˈäləjē/ ▶ **n.** the branch of medicine that deals with diseases and abnormalities of the heart.
– DERIVATIVES **car·di·o·log·i·cal** /ˌkärdēəˈläjikəl/ **adj.**, **car·di·ol·o·gist** /-jist/ **n.**

car·di·o·meg·a·ly /ˌkärdēōˈmegəlē/ ▶ **n.** Medicine abnormal enlargement of the heart.
– ORIGIN 1960s: from CARDIO- + Greek *megas, megal-* 'great.'

car·di·o·my·op·a·thy /ˌkärdēˌōˌmīˈäpəTHē/ ▶ **n.** Medicine chronic disease of the heart muscle.

car·di·op·a·thy /ˌkärdēˈäpəTHē/ ▶ **n.** heart disease.

car·di·o·pul·mo·nar·y /ˌkärdēōˈpo͝olməˌnerē, -ˈpəl-/ ▶ **adj.** Medicine of or relating to the heart and the lungs.

car·di·o·pul·mo·nar·y re·sus·ci·ta·tion ▶ **n.** emergency medical procedures for restoring normal heartbeat and breathing to victims of heart failure, drowning, etc.

car·di·o·res·pi·ra·to·ry /ˌkärdēōˈresp(ə)rəˌtôrē, -rəˈspīrə-/ ▶ **adj.** Medicine relating to the action of both heart and lungs.

car·di·o·vas·cu·lar /ˌkärdēōˈvaskyələr/ ▶ **adj.** Medicine of or relating to the heart and blood vessels.

car·di·o·vas·cu·lar sys·tem ▶ **n.** another term for CIRCULATORY SYSTEM.

car·di·tis /kärˈdītəs/ ▶ **n.** Medicine inflammation of the heart.

card key ▶ **n.** another term for KEY CARD.

card·mem·ber /ˈkärdˌmembər/ ▶ **n.** a holder of a particular credit or charge card.

car·doon /kärˈdo͞on/ ▶ **n.** a tall thistlelike southern European plant related to the globe artichoke, with leaves and roots that may be used as vegetables. ● *Cynaracardunculus*, family Compositae.
– ORIGIN early 17th cent.: from French *cardon*, from *carde* 'edible part of an artichoke,' from modern Provençal *cardo*, based on Latin *carduus, cardus* 'thistle, artichoke.'

Car·do·zo /kärˈdōzō/, Benjamin Nathan (1870–1938), US Supreme Court associate justice 1932–38. Considered a liberal, he championed court involvement in the making of public policy.

card read·er ▶ **n. 1** an electronic sensor that reads a magnetic strip or bar code on a credit card, membership card, etc.
2 an electronic device that reads and transfers data from various portable memory storage devices.

card sharp (also **card sharper** or **card shark**) ▶ **n.** a person who cheats at cards in order to win money.

card ta·ble ▶ **n.** a square table for playing cards on, typically having legs that fold flat for storage.

CARE /ke(ə)r/ ▶ **abbr.** Cooperative for American Relief Everywhere, a large private organization that provides emergency and long-term assistance to people in need throughout the world.

care /ke(ə)r/ ▶ **n. 1** the provision of what is necessary for the health, welfare, maintenance, and protection of someone or something: *the care of the elderly | the child is safe* ***in the care of*** *her grandparents | health care.*
2 serious attention or consideration applied to doing something correctly or to avoid damage or risk: *he planned his departure with great care.* ■ an object of concern or attention: *the cares of family life.* ■ a feeling of or occasion for anxiety: *she was driving along without a care in the world.*
▶ **v.** [no obj.] **1** [often with negative] feel concern or interest; attach importance to something: *they don't care about human life* | [with clause] *I don't care what she says.* ■ feel affection or liking: *you care very deeply for him.* ■ (**care for something/care to do something**) like or be willing to do or have something: *would you care for some tea? | I don't care to listen to him.*
2 (**care for**) look after and provide for the needs of: *he has numerous animals to care for.*
– PHRASES **care of** at the address of: *write to me care of Anne.* **I** (or **he, she,** etc.) **couldn't** (or informal also **could**) **care less** informal used to express complete indifference: *he couldn't care less about football.* **for all you care** (or **he, she,** etc., **cares**) informal used to indicate that someone feels no interest or concern: *I could drown for all you care.* **have a care** [often in imperative] dated be cautious: *"Have a care!" she warned.* **take care 1** [often in imperative] be cautious; keep oneself safe: *take care if you're planning to go out tonight.* ■ said to someone on leaving them: *take care, see you soon.* **2** [with infinitive] make sure of doing something: *he would take care to provide himself with an escape clause.* **take care of 1** keep (someone or something) safe and provided for: *I can take care of myself.* **2** deal with (something): *he has the tools to take care of the electrical problem.*
– ORIGIN Old English *caru* (noun), *carian* (verb), of Germanic origin; related to Old High German *chara* 'grief, lament,' *charon* 'grieve,' and Old Norse *kǫr* 'sickbed.'

ca·reen /kəˈrēn/ ▶ **v. 1** [with obj.] turn (a ship) on its side for cleaning, caulking, or repair. ■ [no obj.] (of a ship) tilt; lean over: *a heavy flood tide caused my vessel to careen dizzily.*
2 [no obj.] move swiftly and in an uncontrolled way in a specified direction: *an electric golf cart careened around the corner.* [influenced by the verb CAREER.]
– ORIGIN late 16th cent. (as a noun denoting the position of a careened ship): from French *carène*, from Italian *carena*, from Latin *carina* 'a keel.'

ca·reer /kəˈri(ə)r/ ▶ **n.** an occupation undertaken for a significant period of a person's life and with opportunities for progress. ■ the time spent by a person in such an occupation or profession: *the end of a distinguished career in the navy.* ■ the progress through history of an institution or organization: *the court has had a checkered career.* ■ [as modifier] working permanently in or committed to a particular profession: *a career diplomat.* ■ [as modifier] (of a woman) pursuing a profession outside of the home.
▶ **v.** [no obj.] move swiftly and in an uncontrolled way in a specified direction: *the car careered across the road and went through a hedge.*
– PHRASES **in full career** archaic at full speed.
– ORIGIN mid 16th cent. (denoting a road or racecourse): from French *carrière*, from Italian *carriera*, based on Latin *carrus* 'wheeled vehicle.'

ca·reer·ist /kəˈri(ə)rist/ ▶ **n.** a person whose main concern is for professional advancement, esp. one willing to achieve this by any means: [as modifier] *a careerist politician.*
– DERIVATIVES **ca·reer·ism** /-ˌizəm/ **n.**

care·free /ˈke(ə)rˌfrē/ ▶ **adj.** free from anxiety or responsibility: *she changed from a carefree girl into a woman | the carefree days of summer.*
– DERIVATIVES **care·free·ness n.**

care·ful /ˈke(ə)rfəl/ ▶ **adj. 1** making sure of avoiding potential danger, mishap, or harm; cautious: *I begged him to be more careful | be careful not to lose her address* | [as exclamation] *Careful! That stuff's worth a fortune!* ■ (**careful of/about**) anxious to protect (something) from harm or loss; solicitous: *he was very careful of his reputation.* ■ prudent in the use of something, esp. money: *he had always been careful with money.*
2 done with or showing thought and attention: *a careful consideration of the facts.*
– DERIVATIVES **care·ful·ly adv.**, **care·ful·ness n.**
– ORIGIN Old English *carful* (see CARE, -FUL).

care·giv·er /ˈke(ə)rˌgivər/ ▶ **n.** a family member or paid helper who regularly looks after a child or a sick, elderly, or disabled person.
– DERIVATIVES **care·giv·ing n. & adj.**

care·less /ˈke(ə)rlis/ ▶ **adj.** not giving sufficient attention or thought to avoiding harm or errors: *she had been careless and had left the window unlocked.* ■ (of an action or its result) showing or caused by a lack of attention: *he admitted to careless driving | a careless error.* ■ [predic.] (**careless of/about**) not concerned or worried about: *he was careless about his own safety.* ■ showing no interest or effort; casual: *she gave a careless shrug.*
– DERIVATIVES **care·less·ly adv.**
– ORIGIN Old English *carlēas* 'free from care' (see CARE, -LESS).

care·less·ness /ˈke(ə)rlisnis/ ▶ **n.** failure to give sufficient attention to avoiding harm or errors; negligence: *most road accidents are caused by carelessness on the part of motorists.*

care pack·age ▶ **n.** a parcel of food, money, or luxury items sent to a loved one who is away.
– ORIGIN probably from the CARE Packages originally distributed by the humanitarian organization *Cooperative for American Remittances to Europe* after World War II.

ca·ress /kəˈres/ ▶ **v.** [with obj.] touch or stroke gently or lovingly: *she caressed the girl's forehead* | figurative *a gentle breeze caressed his skin* | (as adj. **caressing**) *his caressing touch.*
▶ **n.** a gentle or loving touch.
– DERIVATIVES **ca·ress·ing·ly adv.**
– ORIGIN mid 17th cent.: from French *caresser* (verb), *caresse* (noun), from Italian *carezza*, based on Latin *carus* 'dear.'

car·et /ˈkarit/ ▶ **n.** a mark (‸, ʌ) placed below the line to indicate a proposed insertion in a printed or written text.
– ORIGIN late 17th cent.: from Latin, 'is lacking.'

care·tak·er /ˈke(ə)rˌtākər/ ▶ **n. 1** a person employed to look after a public building or a house in the owner's absence. ■ [as modifier] holding power temporarily: *his was a caretaker regime.*
2 a person employed to look after people or animals.
– DERIVATIVES **care·take v.**

C

Ca·rew /kəˈro͞o/, Rod (1945–), US baseball player; born in Panama; full name *Rodney Cline Carew*. An infielder for the Minnesota Twins 1967–79 and the California Angels 1979–85, he was a seven-time American League batting champion 1969, 1972–75, 1977–78. Baseball Hall of Fame (1991).

care work·er ▶ **n.** Brit. a person employed to support and supervise vulnerable, infirm, or disadvantaged people, or those under the care of the state.

care·worn /ˈke(ə)rˌwôrn/ ▶ **adj.** tired and unhappy because of prolonged worry: *a careworn expression.*

Car·ey /ˈke(ə)rē/, George (Leonard) (1935–), English Anglican churchman; archbishop of Canterbury 1991–2002.

car·fare /ˈkärˌfe(ə)r/ ▶ **n.** the fare for travel on a bus, subway, or similar mode of public transportation.

car·go /ˈkärgō/ ▶ **n.** (pl. **cargoes** or **cargos**) goods carried on a ship, aircraft, or motor vehicle: *transportation of bulk cargo | a cargo of oil.*
– ORIGIN mid 17th cent.: from Spanish *cargo, carga*, from late Latin *carricare, carcare* 'to load,' from Latin *carrus* 'wheeled vehicle.'

car·go cult ▶ **n.** (in the Melanesian Islands) a system of belief based around the expected arrival of ancestral spirits in ships bringing cargoes of food and other goods.

car·go pants ▶ **n.** loose-fitting casual slacks with large patch pockets on the thighs.

car·hop /ˈkärˌhäp/ ▶ **n.** informal, dated a waiter or waitress at a drive-in restaurant.

Car·i·a /ˈke(ə)rēə/ an ancient region of southwestern Asia Minor, south of the Maeander River and northwest of Lycia.
– DERIVATIVES **Car·i·an adj. & n.**

car·i·am·a /ˌkarēˈämə/ ▶ **n.** former term for SERIEMA.

Car·ib /ˈkarib/ ▶ **n. 1** a member of an indigenous South American people living mainly in coastal regions of French Guiana, Suriname, Guyana, and Venezuela.
2 the Cariban language of this people. Also called GALIBI.

> The Caribs were in the process of colonizing the Lesser Antilles from the mainland, displacing Arawak peoples, when their expansion was halted by the arrival of the Spaniards, who all but wiped them out; a few hundred remain on Dominica. Carib is now spoken by around 20,000 people in parts of northern South America. **Island Carib** is an extinct language of the entirely distinct Arawakan group, formerly used in the Lesser Antilles; **Black Carib**, spoken in parts of Central America, is derived from this.

▶ **adj.** of or relating to the Caribs or their language. ■ of or relating to Island Carib or Black Carib.
– ORIGIN from Spanish *caribe*, from Haitian Creole. Compare with CANNIBAL.

Car·i·ban /ˈkarəbən, kəˈrē-/ ▶ **adj.** of, belonging to, or denoting a family of South American languages scattered widely throughout Brazil, Suriname, Guyana, Venezuela, and Colombia. With the exception of Carib, they are all extinct or nearly so.
▶ **n.** this family of languages.

Car·ib·be·an /ˌkarəˈbēən, kəˈribēən/ (**the Caribbean**) the region consisting of the Caribbean Sea, its islands (including the West Indies), and the surrounding coasts.
▶ **adj.** of or relating to this region.

> **USAGE** There are two possible pronunciations of the word **Caribbean**, and both are used widely and acceptably in the US. In the Caribbean itself, the preferred pronunciation puts the stress on the **-rib-**. In Britain, speakers more often put the stress on the **-be-**, although in recent years, the other pronunciation has gained ground in Britain as the more 'up-to-date' and, to some, the more 'correct' pronunciation.

Car·ib·be·an Sea the part of the Atlantic Ocean that lies between the Antilles and the mainland of Central and South America.

C

ca·ri·be /kə'rēbē/ ▶ **n.** another term for **PIRANHA**.
– ORIGIN Spanish: see **CARIB**.

Car·i·boo Moun·tains /'karə,bo͞o/ a range in east central British Columbia, part of the Rocky Mountains. It was the site of an 1860s gold rush.

car·i·bou /'karə,bo͞o/ ▶ **n.** (pl. **same** or **caribous**) a large North American reindeer. ● Genus *Rangifer*: several species, in particular the **woodland caribou** (*R. caribou*) and the **barren ground caribou** (*R. tarandus*).
– ORIGIN mid 17th cent.: from Canadian French, from Micmac *ɣalipu*, literally 'snowshoveler' (because the caribou scrapes away snow to feed on the vegetation underneath).

barren ground caribou

car·i·ca·ture /'karikəCHər, -,CHo͝or/ ▶ **n.** a picture, description, or imitation of a person or thing in which certain striking characteristics are exaggerated in order to create a comic or grotesque effect. ■ the art or style of such exaggerated representation: *there are elements of caricature in the portrayal of the hero.* ■ a ludicrous or grotesque version of someone or something: *he looked like a caricature of his normal self.*
▶ **v.** [with obj.] (usu. **be caricatured**) make or give a comically or grotesquely exaggerated representation of (someone or something): *he was caricatured on the cover of TV Guide | a play that caricatures the legal profession.*
– DERIVATIVES **car·i·ca·tur·al** /,karikə'CHo͝orəl/ **adj.**, **car·i·ca·tur·ist** /-,CHo͝orist/ **n.**
– ORIGIN mid 18th cent.: from French, from Italian *caricatura*, from *caricare* 'load, exaggerate,' from Latin *carricare* (see **CHARGE**).

car·ies /'kerēz/ ▶ **n.** decay and crumbling of a tooth or bone.
– ORIGIN late 16th cent.: from Latin.

car·il·lon /'karə,län, -lən/ ▶ **n.** a set of bells in a tower, played using a keyboard or by an automatic mechanism similar to a piano roll. ■ a tune played on such bells.
– DERIVATIVES **car·il·lon·neur** /,karələ'nər/ **n.**
– ORIGIN late 18th cent.: from French, from Old French *quarregnon* 'peal of four bells,' based on Latin *quattuor* 'four.'

Ca·ri·na /kə'rīnə/ Astronomy a southern constellation (the Keel) partly in the Milky Way, originally part of Argo. It contains the second brightest star in the sky, Canopus. ■ (as genitive **Carinae** /kə'rīnē/) used with a preceding letter or numeral to designate a star in this constellation: *the star Beta Carinae.*
– ORIGIN Latin.

ca·ri·na /kə'rēnə, -'rī-/ ▶ **n.** (pl. **carinae** /-,nē/ or **carinas**) chiefly Biology a keel-shaped structure, in particular: ■ Zoology the ridge of a bird's breastbone, to which the main flight muscles are attached. ■ Anatomy cartilage situated at the point where the trachea divides into the two bronchi.
– DERIVATIVES **ca·ri·nal adj.**
– ORIGIN early 18th cent.: from Latin, 'keel.'

car·i·nate /'karə,nāt, -nit/ ▶ **adj.** having a keellike ridge. ■ (of a bird) having a deep ridge on the breastbone for the attachment of flight muscles. Contrasted with **RATITE**.
– DERIVATIVES **car·i·nat·ed** /-,nātid/ **adj.**, **car·i·na·tion** /,karə'nāSHən/ **n.**
– ORIGIN late 18th cent.: from Latin *carinatus* 'having a keel,' from *carina* 'keel.'

car·ing /'ke(ə)riNG/ ▶ **adj.** displaying kindness and concern for others: *a caring and invaluable friend.*
▶ **n.** the work or practice of looking after those unable to care for themselves, esp. sick and elderly people: [as modifier] *the caring professions.*

car·ing pro·fes·sion ▶ **n.** a job that involves taking care of other people, such as nursing, teaching, or social work.

Car·i·o·ca /,karē'ōkə/ ▶ **n. 1** a native of Rio de Janeiro.
2 (**carioca**) a Brazilian dance resembling the samba.
– ORIGIN mid 19th cent.: from Portuguese, from Tupi *kari'oka* 'house of the white man.'

car·i·o·gen·ic /,karēə'jenik/ ▶ **adj.** technical causing tooth decay.

car·i·ole ▶ **n.** variant spelling of **CARRIOLE**.

car·i·ous /'karēəs/ ▶ **adj.** (of bones or teeth) decayed.
– ORIGIN mid 16th cent.: from Latin *cariosus* (see **CARIES**).

ca·ri·tas /'kari,tas, 'käri,täs/ ▶ **n.** Christian love of humankind; charity.
– ORIGIN mid 19th cent.: Latin.

car·jack·ing /'kär,jakiNG/ ▶ **n.** the action of violently stealing an occupied car.
– DERIVATIVES **car·jack v.**, **car·jack·er** /-,jakər/ **n.**
– ORIGIN 1990s: blend of **CAR** and *hijacking* (see **HIJACK**).

cark·ing /'kärkiNG/ ▶ **adj.** [attrib.] archaic causing distress or worry: *her carking doubts.*
– ORIGIN mid 16th cent.: present participle of Middle English *cark* 'worry, burden,' from Old Northern French *carkier*, based on late Latin *carcare* (see **CHARGE**).

carl /kärl/ ▶ **n.** archaic a peasant or man of low birth.
– ORIGIN Old English (denoting a peasant or villein): from Old Norse *karl* 'man, freeman,' of Germanic origin; related to **CHURL**.

car·line /'kär,lən/ (also **carline thistle**) ▶ **n.** a thistlelike European plant with flower heads that bear shiny persistent straw-colored bracts. ● Genus *Carlina*, family Compositae: several species, in particular *C. vulgaris*.
– ORIGIN late 16th cent.: from French, from medieval Latin *carlina*, perhaps an alteration of *cardina* (from Latin *carduus* 'thistle'), by association with *Carolus Magnus* (see **CHARLEMAGNE**), to whom its medicinal properties were said to have been revealed.

Car·lisle /kär'līl, 'kär,līl/ a historic borough in southern Pennsylvania, southwest of Harrisburg; pop. 18,379 (est. 2008). It is home to the Army War College.

Car·lism /'kär,lizəm/ ▶ **n.** historical a Spanish conservative political movement originating in support of Don Carlos, brother of Fernando VII (died 1833), who claimed the throne in place of Fernando's daughter Isabella. The movement supported the Catholic Church and opposed centralized government; it was revived in support of the Nationalist side during the Spanish Civil War.
– DERIVATIVES **Car·list adj. & n.**

car·load /'kär,lōd/ ▶ **n.** the number of people that can travel in an automobile: ***a carload of** passengers.* ■ the quantity of goods that can be carried in a railroad freight car.

Car·lo·vin·gi·an /,kärlə'vinj(ē)ən/ ▶ **adj. & n.** another term for **CAROLINGIAN**.
– ORIGIN from French *carlovingien*, from *Karl* 'Charles,' on the pattern of *mérovingien* 'Merovingian.'

Car·low /'kärlō/ a county in the Republic of Ireland, in the province of Leinster.

Carls·bad /'kärlz,bad/ **1** a city in southwestern California, on the Pacific coast, north of San Diego; pop. 96,374 (est. 2008).
2 a city in southeastern New Mexico, on the Pecos River; pop. 25,629 (est. 2008). To the southwest is Carlsbad Caverns, a vast cave complex.

Carls·bad plum ▶ **n.** a dessert plum of a blue-black variety, that is often crystallized.
– ORIGIN late 19th cent.: named after *Karlsbad* (now Karlovy Vary).

Car·lyle /kär'līl, 'kär,līl/, Thomas (1795–1881), Scottish historian and political philosopher. He wrote *History of the French Revolution* (1837).

car·mak·er /'kär,mākər/ ▶ **n.** a manufacturer of automobiles.

car·man /'kärmən/ ▶ **n.** (pl. **carmen**) dated a driver of a streetcar or horse-drawn carriage.

Car·mel /kär'mel/ a city in west central California, a resort on the Pacific Ocean, south of Monterey; pop. 3,886 (est. 2008).

Car·mel, Mount /'kärməl/ a group of mountains near the Mediterranean coast in northwestern Israel that shelter the port of Haifa. In the Bible it is the site of the defeat of the priests of Baal by the prophet Elijah (I Kings 18).

Car·mel·ite /'kärmə,līt/ ▶ **n.** a friar or nun of a contemplative Catholic order founded at Mount Carmel during the Crusades.
▶ **adj.** of or relating to the Carmelites.

Car·mi·chael[1] /'kär,mīkəl/ a community in north central California, northeast of Sacramento; pop. 49,742 (2000).

Car·mi·chael[2], Hoagy (1899–1981), US jazz pianist, composer, and singer; full name *Howard Hoagland Carmichael*. His best-known songs include "Stardust" (1929), "Georgia on My Mind" (1930), and "In the Cool, Cool, Cool of the Evening" (1951).

car·min·a·tive /kär'minətiv, 'kärmə,nātiv/ ▶ **adj.** (chiefly of a drug) relieving flatulence.
▶ **n.** a drug of this kind.
– ORIGIN late Middle English: from Old French *carminatif, -ive*, or medieval Latin *carminat-* 'healed (by incantation),' from the verb *carminare*, from Latin *carmen* (see **CHARM**).

car·mine /'kärmən, -,mīn/ ▶ **n.** a vivid crimson color: [as modifier] *carmine roses.* ■ a vivid crimson pigment made from cochineal.
– ORIGIN early 18th cent.: from French *carmin*, based on Arabic *ḳirmiz* (see **KERMES**). Compare with **CRIMSON**.

Car·nac /'kär,nak/ the site in Brittany of nearly 3,000 megalithic stones dating from the Neolithic period.

car·nage /'kärnij/ ▶ **n.** the killing of a large number of people.
– ORIGIN early 17th cent.: from French, from Italian *carnaggio*, from medieval Latin *carnaticum*, from Latin *caro, carn-* 'flesh.'

car·nal /'kärnl/ ▶ **adj.** relating to physical, esp. sexual, needs and activities: *carnal desire.*
– DERIVATIVES **car·nal·i·ty** /kär'nalitē/ **n.**, **car·nal·ly adv.**
– ORIGIN late Middle English: from Christian Latin *carnalis*, from *caro, carn-* 'flesh.'

car·nal know·ledge ▶ **n.** dated, chiefly Law sexual intercourse.

car·nall·ite /'kärnl,īt/ ▶ **n.** a white or reddish mineral consisting of a hydrated chloride of potassium and magnesium.
– ORIGIN mid 19th cent.: named after Rudolf von *Carnall* (1804–74), German mining engineer, + **-ITE**[1].

Car·nap /'kär,nap/, Rudolf (1891–1970), US philosopher; born in Germany; a founding member of the logical positivist Vienna Circle. Notable works: *The Logical Structure of the World* (1928) and *The Logical Foundations of Probability* (1950).

car·nas·si·al /kär'nasēəl/ ▶ **adj.** Zoology denoting the large upper premolar and lower molar teeth of a carnivore, adapted for shearing flesh.
▶ **n.** a tooth of this type.
– ORIGIN mid 19th cent.: from French *carnassier* 'carnivorous,' based on Latin *caro, carn-* 'flesh.'

Car·nat·ic /kär'natik/ ▶ **adj.** of or denoting the main style of classical music in southern India, as distinct from the Hindustani music of the north: *Carnatic music.*
– ORIGIN Anglicization of **KARNATAKA** in southwestern India.

car·na·tion[1] /kär'nāSHən/ ▶ **n.** a double-flowered cultivated variety of clove pink, with gray-green leaves and showy pink, white, or red flowers. ● *Dianthus caryophyllus*, family Caryophyllaceae: many cultivars.
– ORIGIN late 16th cent.: perhaps based on a misreading of Arabic *ḳaranful* 'clove or clove pink,' from Greek *karyophullon*. The early forms suggest confusion with *carnation* 'rosy pink color,' with *incarnation*, and with *coronation*.

car·na·tion[2] ▶ **n.** a rosy pink color: [as modifier] *sage and carnation throw pillows.*
– ORIGIN early 16th cent.: from French *carnation* 'color of one's flesh,' based on Latin *carn-* 'flesh.'

car·nau·ba /kär'nôbə, -'noubə/ ▶ **n.** a northeastern Brazilian fan palm, the leaves of which exude a yellowish wax. Also called **WAX PALM**. ● *Copernicia cerifera*, family Palmae. ■ (also **carnauba wax**) wax from this palm, formerly used as a polish and for making candles.
– ORIGIN mid 19th cent.: from Portuguese, from Tupi.

Car·ne·gie /'kärnigē, kär'nāgē/, Andrew (1835–1919), US industrialist and philanthropist; born in Scotland. After building up a fortune in the steel industry, he retired in 1901 and devoted his wealth to charitable purposes, in particular to libraries, education, and the arts. He established the Carnegie Institute of Technology in 1900.

car·nel·ian /kär'nēlyən/ (also **cornelian** /kôr-/) ▶ **n.** a semiprecious stone consisting of an orange or orange-red variety of chalcedony.
– ORIGIN late Middle English: from Old French *corneline*; the prefix *car-* being suggested by Latin *caro, carn-* 'flesh.'

car·net /kär'nā/ ▶ **n. 1** a book of tickets for use on public transport in some countries.
2 a customs permit allowing a motor vehicle to be taken across an international border for a limited period.
– ORIGIN 1920s: from French, 'notebook.'

Car·nic Alps /'kärnik/ (German name **Karnische Alpen**) a range of the Alps on the border of southern Austria and northeastern Italy that reaches 9,124 feet (2,781 m) at Monte Coglians (Hohe Warte).

car·ni·val /ˈkärnəvəl/ ▶ **n. 1** a period of public revelry at a regular time each year, typically during the week before Lent in Roman Catholic countries, involving processions, music, dancing, and the use of masquerade: *the culmination of the week-long carnival* | *Mardi Gras is the last day of carnival* | [as modifier] *a carnival parade.* ■ an exciting or riotous mixture of something: *the whole evening was a carnival of fun.*
2 a traveling amusement show or circus.
– DERIVATIVES **car·ni·val·esque** /ˌkärnəvəˈlesk/ **adj.**
– ORIGIN mid 16th cent.: from Italian *carnevale, carnovale,* from medieval Latin *carnelevamen, carnelevarium* 'Shrovetide,' from Latin *caro, carn-* 'flesh' + *levare* 'put away.'

Car·niv·o·ra /kärˈnivərə/ Zoology an order of mammals that comprises the cats, dogs, bears, hyenas, weasels, civets, raccoons, and mongooses. They are distinguished by having powerful jaws and teeth adapted for stabbing, tearing, and eating flesh.

car·ni·vore /ˈkärnəˌvôr/ ▶ **n.** an animal that feeds on flesh. ■ Zoology a mammal of the order Carnivora.
– ORIGIN mid 19th cent.: from French, from Latin *carnivorus* (see CARNIVOROUS).

car·niv·o·rous /kärˈnivərəs/ ▶ **adj.** (of an animal) feeding on other animals. ■ (of a plant) able to trap and digest small animals, esp. insects.
– DERIVATIVES **car·niv·o·rous·ly adv., car·niv·o·rous·ness n.**
– ORIGIN late 16th cent.: from Latin *carnivorus,* from *caro, carn-* 'flesh' + *-vorus* (see -VOROUS).

car·no·saur /ˈkärnəˌsôr/ (also **carnosaurus** /ˌkärnəˈsôrəs/) ▶ **n.** a large bipedal carnivorous dinosaur, typically one with greatly reduced forelimbs. ● Infraorder Carnosauria, suborder Theropoda, order Saurischia; includes tyrannosaurus, allosaurus, and megalosaurus.
– DERIVATIVES **car·no·sau·ri·an adj.**
– ORIGIN 1930s: from modern Latin, from Latin *caro, carn-* 'flesh' + Greek *sauros* 'lizard.'

Car·not /kärˈnō/, Nicolas Léonard Sadi (1796–1832), French scientist. His work in analyzing the efficiency of steam engines was of crucial importance to the theory of thermodynamics.

car·no·tite /ˈkärnəˌtīt/ ▶ **n.** a lemon-yellow radioactive mineral consisting of hydrated vanadate of uranium and potassium, often found near petrified trees.
– ORIGIN late 19th cent.: named after Marie Adolphe *Carnot* (1839–1920), French inspector of mines, + -ITE[1].

car·ny[1] /ˈkärnē/ (also **carnie** or **carney**) ▶ **n.** [usu. as modifier] informal a carnival or amusement show: *a carny atmosphere.* ■ a person who works in a carnival or amusement show.

car·ny[2] (also **carney**) ▶ **adj.** (**carnier, carniest**) Brit. informal artful; sly: *Finley's carny approach to baseball.*
– ORIGIN late 19th cent.: of unknown origin.

car·ob /ˈkarəb/ ▶ **n. 1** a brown floury powder extracted from the carob bean, used as a substitute for chocolate.
2 (also **carob tree**) a small evergreen Arabian tree that bears long brownish-purple edible pods. Also called LOCUST TREE (see LOCUST (sense 3)). ● *Ceratonia siliqua,* family Leguminosae. ■ (also **carob bean**) the edible pod of this tree. Also called LOCUST BEAN (see LOCUST (sense 2)).
– ORIGIN late Middle English (denoting the carob bean): from Old French *carobe,* from medieval Latin *carrubia,* from Arabic *ḵarrūba.*

car·ol /ˈkarəl/ ▶ **n.** a religious folk song or popular hymn, particularly one associated with Christmas: *singing Christmas carols around the tree* | [as modifier] *a carol service.*
▶ **v.** (**carols, caroling, caroled**; chiefly Brit. **carols, carolling, carolled**) [no obj.] **1** (often as noun **caroling**) sing Christmas songs or hymns, esp. in a group: *a night of Christmas caroling was traditional* | *we caroled from door to door.*
2 [with obj.] sing or say (something) happily: *she was cheerfully caroling the words of the song.*
– DERIVATIVES **car·ol·er n.**
– ORIGIN Middle English: from Old French *carole* (noun), *caroler* (verb), of unknown origin.

Car·ol Cit·y /ˈkarəl/ a suburban community in southeastern Florida, north of Miami; pop. 59,443 (2000).

Car·o·li·na /ˌkarəˈlīnə/ a commercial and residential suburb in Puerto Rico, east of San Juan; pop. 167,000 (est. 2009).

Car·o·li·na all·spice ▶ **n.** see ALLSPICE.

Car·o·li·na duck ▶ **n.** another term for WOOD DUCK.

Car·o·li·na par·a·keet ▶ **n.** a small long-tailed parakeet with mainly green plumage and a yellow and orange head. It was formerly common in the eastern US but was exterminated by about 1920.
● *Conuropsis* (or *Aratinga*) *carolinensis,* family Psittacidae.

Car·o·li·na rose ▶ **n.** another term for PASTURE ROSE.

Car·o·line /ˈkarəˌlīn, -lin/ ▶ **adj. 1** (also **Carolean** /ˌkarəˈlēən, ˌker-/) of or relating to the reigns of Charles I and II of England: *a Caroline poet.*
2 another term for CAROLINGIAN.
– ORIGIN early 17th cent.: from medieval Latin *Carolus* 'Charles.'

Car·o·line Is·lands /ˈkarəˌlin/ (also **the Carolines**) a group of islands in the western Pacific Ocean, north of the equator, divided between the Federated States of Micronesia and Palau.

Car·o·lin·gi·an /ˌkarəˈlinj(ē)ən/ (also **Carlovingian**) ▶ **adj.** of or relating to the Frankish dynasty, founded by Charlemagne's father (Pepin III), that ruled in western Europe from 750 to 987. ■ denoting or relating to a style of minuscule script developed in France during the time of Charlemagne, on which modern lower-case letters are largely based.
▶ **n.** a member of the Carolingian dynasty.
– ORIGIN alteration of earlier CARLOVINGIAN, by association with medieval Latin *Carolus* 'Charles.'

Car·o·lin·gi·an Ren·ais·sance a period during the reign of Charlemagne and his successors that was marked by achievements in art, architecture, learning, and music.

Car·ol Stream a village in northeastern Illinois, west of Chicago; pop. 40,004 (est. 2008).

car·om /ˈkarəm/ ▶ **n.** Billiards another term for BILLIARD (sense 2). ■ (also **carom billiards**) any of the billiard games played on a table without pockets.
▶ **v.** [no obj.] make a carom; strike and rebound.
– ORIGIN late 18th cent.: abbreviation of *carambole,* from Spanish *carambola,* apparently from *bola* 'ball.'

car·o·tene /ˈkarəˌtēn/ ▶ **n.** Chemistry an orange or red plant pigment found in carrots and many other plant structures. It is a terpenoid hydrocarbon with several isomers, of which one (**beta carotene**) is important in the diet as a precursor of vitamin A.
– ORIGIN mid 19th cent.: coined in German from Latin *carota* (see CARROT).

ca·rot·e·noid /kəˈrätnˌoid/ ▶ **n.** Chemistry any of a class of mainly yellow, orange, or red fat-soluble pigments, including carotene, which give color to plant parts such as ripe tomatoes and autumn leaves. They are terpenoids based on a structure having the formula $C_{40}H_{56}$.

Ca·roth·ers /kəˈrəT͟Hərz/, Wallace Hume (1896–1937), US industrial chemist. He developed neoprene, the first successful synthetic rubber and also Nylon 6.6, a synthetic fiber.

ca·rot·id /kəˈrätid/ ▶ **adj.** of, relating to, or denoting the two main arteries that carry blood to the head and neck, and their two main branches.
▶ **n.** each of these arteries.
– ORIGIN early 17th cent.: from French *carotide* or modern Latin *carotides,* from Greek *karōtides,* plural of *karōtis* 'drowsiness,' from *karoun* 'stupefy' (because compression of these arteries was thought to cause stupor).

ca·rot·id bod·y ▶ **n.** a small mass of receptors in the carotid artery sensitive to chemical change in the blood.

ca·rouse /kəˈrouz/ ▶ **v.** [no obj.] drink plentiful amounts of alcohol and enjoy oneself with others in a noisy, lively way: *they danced and caroused until the drink ran out* | (as noun **carousing**) *a night of carousing.*
▶ **n.** a noisy, lively drinking party: *corporate carouses.*
– DERIVATIVES **ca·rous·al** /-zəl/ **n., ca·rous·er n.**
– ORIGIN mid 16th cent.: originally as an adverb meaning 'all out, completely' in the phrase *drink carouse,* from German *gar aus trinken*; hence 'drink heavily, have a drinking bout.'

car·ou·sel /ˌkarəˈsel, ˈkarəˌsel/ (also **carrousel**) ▶ **n. 1** a merry-go-round. ■ a rotating machine or device, in particular a conveyor system at an airport from which arriving passengers collect their luggage.
2 historical a tournament in which groups of knights took part in chariot races and other demonstrations of equestrian skills.
– ORIGIN mid 17th cent.: from French *carrousel,* from Italian *carosello.*

carp[1] /kärp/ ▶ **n.** (pl. **same**) a deep-bodied freshwater fish, typically with barbels around the mouth. Carp are farmed for food in some parts of the world and are widely kept in large ponds. ● Family Cyprinidae (the **minnow family**): several genera and species, including the **common carp** (*Cyprinus carpio*) and **silver carp** (*Hypophthalmichthys molitrix*). The family includes the majority of freshwater fishes in Eurasia, Africa, and North and Central America.
– ORIGIN late Middle English: from Old French *carpe,* from late Latin *carpa.*

carp[2] ▶ **v.** [no obj.] complain or find fault continually, typically about trivial matters: *I don't want to carp about the way you did it* | *he was constantly carping at me.*
– DERIVATIVES **carp·er n.**
– ORIGIN Middle English (in the sense 'talk, chatter'): from Old Norse *karpa* 'brag'; later influenced by Latin *carpere* 'pluck at, slander.'

Car·pac·cio /kärˈpäCH(ē)ō/, Vittore (*c.*1455–1525), Italian painter.

car·pac·cio /kärˈpäCH(ē)ō/ ▶ **n.** an Italian hors d'oeuvre consisting of thin slices of raw beef or fish served with a sauce.
– ORIGIN Italian, named after Vittore CARPACCIO (from his use of red pigments, resembling raw meat).

car·pal /ˈkärpəl/ ▶ **n.** any of the eight small bones forming the wrist. See CARPUS.
▶ **adj.** of or relating to these bones.
– ORIGIN mid 18th cent.: from CARPUS + -AL.

car·pal tun·nel syn·drome ▶ **n.** a painful condition of the hand and fingers caused by compression of a major nerve where it passes over the carpal bones through a passage at the front of the wrist, alongside the flexor tendons of the hand. It may be caused by repetitive movements over a long period, or by fluid retention, and is characterized by sensations of tingling, numbness, or burning.

car park ▶ **n.** Brit. a parking lot or parking garage.

Car·pa·thi·an Moun·tains /kärˈpāTHēən/ (also **the Carpathians**) a mountain system that extends southeast from southern Poland and the Czech Republic into Romania.

car·pe di·em /ˌkärpā ˈdēˌem/ ▶ **exclam.** used to urge someone to make the most of the present time and give little thought to the future.
– ORIGIN early 19th cent.: Latin, 'seize the day!,' a quotation from Horace (*Odes* I.xi).

car·pel /ˈkärpəl/ ▶ **n.** Botany the female reproductive organ of a flower, consisting of an ovary, a stigma, and usually a style. It may occur singly or as one of a group.
– DERIVATIVES **car·pel·lar·y** /-ˌlerē/ **adj.**
– ORIGIN mid 19th cent.: from French *carpelle* or modern Latin *carpellum,* from Greek *karpos* 'fruit.'

Car·pen·tar·i·a, Gulf of /ˌkärpənˈte(ə)rēə/ a large bay on the northern coast of Australia, between Arnhem Land and the Cape York Peninsula.

car·pen·ter /ˈkärpəntər/ ▶ **n.** a person who makes and repairs wooden objects and structures.
▶ **v.** [with obj.] (usu. **be carpentered**) make by shaping wood: *the rails were carpentered very skillfully.* ■ [no obj.] do the work of a carpenter.
– ORIGIN Middle English: from Anglo-Norman French, from Old French *carpentier, charpentier,* from late Latin *carpentarius* (*artifex*) 'carriage (maker),' from *carpentum* 'wagon,' of Gaulish origin; related to CAR.

car·pen·ter ant ▶ **n.** a large ant that burrows into wood to nest. ● Genus *Camponotus,* family Formicidae: numerous species.

car·pen·ter bee ▶ **n.** a large solitary bee with purplish wings that nests in tunnels bored in dead wood or plant stems. ● Genus *Xylocopa,* family Apidae: several species.

car·pen·ter pants ▶ **plural n.** loose-fitting pants with many pockets of various sizes and loops for tools at the tops or sides of the legs.

car·pen·try /ˈkärpəntrē/ ▶ **n.** the activity or occupation of making or repairing things in wood. ■ the work made or done by a carpenter: *the superb carpentry of the mahogany desk.*
– ORIGIN late Middle English: from Anglo-Norman French *carpentrie,* Old French *charpenterie,* from *charpentier* (see CARPENTER).

car·pet /ˈkärpit/ ▶ **n.** a floor or stair covering made from thick woven fabric, typically shaped to fit a particular room: *the house has wall-to-wall carpets throughout* | *the floor was covered with carpet.* ■ a large rug, typically an oriental one: *priceless Persian carpets.* ■ a thick or soft expanse or layer of something: *carpets of snowdrops and crocuses.* ■ informal a carpetlike artificial playing surface on a tennis court or an athletic field.
▶ **v.** (**carpets, carpeting, carpeted**) [with obj.] **1** cover (a floor or stairs) with a carpet: *the stairs were carpeted in a lovely shade of red.* ■ cover with a thick or soft expanse or layer of something: *the meadows are carpeted with flowers.*
2 Brit. informal reprimand severely.

PRONUNCIATION KEY ə *ago, up*; ər *over, fur*; a *hat*; ā *ate*; ä *car*; e *let*; ē *see*; i *fit*; ī *by*; NG *sing*; ō *go*; ô *law, for*; oi *toy*; o͝o *good*; o͞o *goo*; ou *out*; TH *thin*; T͟H *then*; ZH *vision*

– PHRASES **call someone on the carpet** informal severely reprimand someone: *she might have called the accused person on the carpet.* [from *carpet* in the sense 'table covering,' referring to 'the carpet of the council table,' before which one would be summoned for reprimand; or simply referring to the carpet in front of a superior's desk.]
– ORIGIN Middle English (denoting a thick fabric used as a cover for a table or bed): from Old French *carpite* or medieval Latin *carpita,* from obsolete Italian *carpita* 'woolen bedspread,' based on Latin *carpere* 'pluck, pull to pieces.'

C

car·pet·bag /ˈkärpit,bag/ ▶ **n.** a traveling bag of a kind originally made of carpeting or carpetlike material.
▶ **v.** [no obj.] act as a carpetbagger: (as adj. **carpetbagging**) *rich, carpetbagging developers.*

car·pet·bag·ger /ˈkärpit,bagər/ ▶ **n.** derogatory a political candidate who seeks election in an area where they have no local connections. ■ historical (in the US) a person from the northern states who went to the South after the Civil War to profit from the Reconstruction. ■ a person perceived as an unscrupulous opportunist: *the organization is rife with carpetbaggers.*

car·pet bee·tle ▶ **n.** a small beetle whose larva (a woolly bear) is destructive to carpets, fabrics, and other materials. ● Genus *Anthrenus,* family Dermestidae.

car·pet-bomb ▶ **v.** [with obj.] (often as noun **carpet-bombing**) bomb (an area) intensively.

car·pet·ing /ˈkärpitiNG/ ▶ **n.** carpets collectively: *offices with wall-to-wall carpeting.* ■ the fabric from which carpets are made.

car·pet moth ▶ **n.** a drab moth related to the clothes moth, the larvae of which feed on coarse textiles and animal hair. ● *Trichophaga tapetzella,* family Tineidae.

car·pet shark ▶ **n.** a relatively small shallow-water shark with barbels around the nose or mouth and typically with a conspicuous color pattern. It is found in the Indo-Pacific region and the Red Sea. ● Family Orectolobidae: *Orectolobus* and other genera, and several species.

car·pet shell ▶ **n.** a burrowing bivalve mollusk of temperate and warm seas, with concentric growth rings and irregular colored markings. ● Genus *Venerupis,* family Veneriidae.

car·pet slip·per ▶ **n.** a soft slipper whose upper part is made of wool or thick cloth.

car·pet sweep·er ▶ **n.** a manual household implement used for sweeping carpets, having a revolving brush or brushes and a receptacle for dust and dirt.

car·pet·weed /ˈkärpit,wēd/ ▶ **n.** any of various dicotyledonous, usually succulent plants that typically grow in warm, sandy regions. ● Family Aizoaceae, order Caryophyllales: several genera and species, in particular *Mollugo verticillata,* a North American weed with small whitish flowers; like many of the carpetweeds, it is prostrate and forms a dense mat on the ground.

car·phol·o·gy /kärˈfäləjē/ ▶ **n.** rare plucking at the bedclothes by a delirious patient.
– ORIGIN mid 19th cent.: from Greek *karphologia,* from *karphos* 'straw' + *legein* 'collect.'

car phone ▶ **n.** a cellular phone designed for use in a motor vehicle.

carp·ing /ˈkärpiNG/ ▶ **adj.** difficult to please; critical: *she has silenced the carping critics with a successful debut tour.*

carpo- ▶ **comb. form** fruit: *carpology* | *carpophore.*

car·pol·o·gy /kärˈpäləjē/ ▶ **n.** rare the study of fruits and seeds.
– DERIVATIVES **car·po·log·i·cal** /,kärpəˈläjikəl/ **adj.**
– ORIGIN early 19th cent.: from Greek *karpos* 'fruit' + **-LOGY.**

car·pool /ˈkär,po͞ol/ ▶ **n.** an arrangement between people to make a regular journey in a single vehicle, typically with each person taking turns to drive the others. ■ a group of people with such an arrangement.
▶ **v.** [no obj.] form or participate in a carpool.
– DERIVATIVES **car·pool·er n.**

car·po·phore /ˈkärpə,fôr/ ▶ **n.** Botany (in a flower) an elongated axis that raises the stem of the pistil above the stamens. ■ (in a fungus) the stem of the fruiting body.
– ORIGIN late 19th cent.: from Greek *karpos* 'fruit' + **-PHORE.**

car·port /ˈkär,pôrt/ ▶ **n.** a shelter for a car consisting of a roof supported on posts, built beside a house.

car·pus /ˈkärpəs/ ▶ **n.** (pl. **carpi** /-,pī, -,pē/) the group of small bones between the main part of the forelimb and the metacarpus in terrestrial vertebrates. The eight bones of the human carpus form the wrist and part of the hand, and are arranged in two rows.
– ORIGIN late Middle English: from modern Latin, from Greek *karpos* 'wrist.'

Car·rac·ci /kärˈäCHē/ the name of a family of Italian painters comprised of brothers **Annibale** (1560–1609) and **Agostino** (1557–1602) and their cousin **Ludovico** (1555–1619). Together they established a teaching academy at Bologna. Annibale is famed for his frescoes on the ceiling of the Farnese Gallery in Rome and for his invention of the caricature.

car·rack /ˈkarək/ ▶ **n.** a large merchant ship of a kind operating in European waters in the 14th to the 17th century.
– ORIGIN late Middle English: from Old French *caraque;* perhaps from Spanish *carraca,* from Arabic, perhaps from *ḳarāḳir,* plural of *ḳurḳūra,* a type of merchant ship.

car·ra·geen /ˈkarə,gēn/ (also **carragheen** or **carrageen moss**) ▶ **n.** an edible red shoreline seaweed with flattened branching fronds, found in both Eurasia and North America and used to produce carrageenan. Also called **IRISH MOSS.** ● *Chondrus crispus,* phylum Rhodophyta.
– ORIGIN early 19th cent.: from Irish *carraigín.*

car·ra·gee·nan /,karəˈgēnən/ ▶ **n.** a substance extracted from red and purple seaweeds, consisting of a mixture of polysaccharides. It is used as a thickening or emulsifying agent in food products.
– ORIGIN 1960s: from **CARRAGEEN** + **-AN.**

Car·ra·ra /kəˈrärə, -ˈre(ə)rə/ a town in northwestern Italy, in Tuscany, known for the white marble quarried here since Roman times; pop. 65,760 (2008).

car·re·four /ˈkarə,fo͝or, ,karəˈfo͝or/ ▶ **n.** a crossroads. ■ a public square, plaza, or marketplace where roads converge.

Car·rel /käˈrel/, Alexis (1873–1944), French surgeon and biologist. He developed improved techniques for suturing arteries and veins and carried out some of the first organ transplants. Nobel Prize for Physiology or Medicine (1912).

car·rel /ˈkarəl/ ▶ **n.** a small cubicle with a desk for the use of a reader or student in a library. ■ historical a small enclosure or study in a cloister.
– ORIGIN late 16th cent.: apparently related to **CAROL** in the old sense 'ring.'

Car·re·ras /kəˈre(ə)rəs/, José (1946–), Spanish opera singer, noted for his work in operas by Verdi and Puccini. He was one of the Three Tenors, along with Luciano Pavarotti and Placido Domingo.

car·riage /ˈkarij/ ▶ **n. 1** a means of conveyance, in particular: ■ a four-wheeled passenger vehicle pulled by two or more horses: *a horse-drawn carriage.* ■ a baby carriage. ■ a shopping cart. ■ a wheeled support for moving a heavy object such as a gun. ■ Brit. a passenger car of a train: *the first-class carriages.*
2 the transporting of items or merchandise from one place to another.
3 a moving part of a machine that carries other parts into the required position: *a typewriter carriage.*
4 [in sing.] a person's bearing or deportment: *her carriage was graceful, her movements quick and deft.*
5 the harboring of a potentially disease-causing organism by a person or animal that does not contract the disease.
– ORIGIN late Middle English: from Old Northern French *cariage,* from *carier* (see **CARRY**).

car·riage bolt ▶ **n.** a large bolt with a round head, used chiefly for fixing wooden panels to masonry or to one another.

car·riage dog ▶ **n.** archaic term for **DALMATIAN.**
– ORIGIN early 19th cent.: because Dalmatians were formerly trained to run behind a carriage as a guard dog.

car·riage house ▶ **n.** a building for housing a horse-drawn carriage, typically such a building that has been converted into a dwelling.

car·riage re·lease ▶ **n.** a function or lever that enables the carriage on a manual or electric typewriter to move freely, instead of only in one direction when the keys are pressed.

car·riage re·turn ▶ **n.** another term for **RETURN** (sense 5 of the noun).

car·riage trade ▶ **n.** informal, humorous the wealthy clientele of a business.
– ORIGIN with reference to people who formerly would have been wealthy enough to maintain a private carriage.

car·riage·way /ˈkarij,wā/ ▶ **n.** Brit. each of the two sides of a divided highway or expressway, each of which usually have two or more lanes. ■ the part of a road intended for vehicles rather than pedestrians.

car·rick bend /ˈkarik/ ▶ **n.** a kind of knot used to join ropes, esp. hawsers, end to end, esp. so that they can go around a capstan without jamming.
– ORIGIN early 19th cent.: from **BEND**[2]: *carrick* perhaps an alteration of **CARRACK.**

car·ri·er /ˈkarēər/ ▶ **n. 1** a person or thing that carries, holds, or conveys something: *water carriers.*
2 a person or company that undertakes the professional conveyance of goods or people: *Pan Am was the third US carrier to cease operations in 1991.* ■ a vessel or vehicle for transporting people or things, esp. goods in bulk: *the largest timber carrier ever to dock at a Malaysian port.* ■ an aircraft carrier. ■ a company that provides facilities for conveying telecommunications messages.
3 a person or animal that transmits a disease-causing organism to others. Typically, the carrier suffers no symptoms of the disease: *the black rat, best known as carrier of bubonic plague.* ■ a person or other organism that possesses a particular gene, esp. as a single copy whose effect is masked by a dominant allele, so that the associated characteristic (such as a hereditary disease) is not displayed but may be passed to offspring.
4 a substance used to support or convey another substance such as a pigment, catalyst, or radioactive material. ■ Physics short for **CHARGE CARRIER.** ■ Biochemistry a molecule that transfers a specified molecule or ion within the body, esp. across a cell membrane.

car·ri·er pig·eon ▶ **n.** a homing pigeon trained to carry messages tied to its neck or leg.

car·ri·er wave ▶ **n.** a high-frequency electromagnetic wave modulated in amplitude or frequency to convey a signal.

car·ri·ole /ˈkarē,ōl/ (also **cariole**) ▶ **n. 1** historical a small open horse-drawn carriage for one person. ■ a light covered cart.
2 (in Canada) a kind of sled pulled by a horse or dogs and with space for one or more passengers.
– ORIGIN mid 18th cent.: from French, from Italian *carriuola,* diminutive of *carro,* from Latin *carrum* (see **CAR**).

car·ri·on /ˈkarēən/ ▶ **n.** the decaying flesh of dead animals.
– ORIGIN Middle English: from Anglo-Norman French and Old Northern French *caroine, caroigne,* Old French *charoigne,* based on Latin *caro* 'flesh.'

car·ri·on bee·tle ▶ **n.** a beetle that feeds on decaying animal and plant matter and insect larvae. ● Family Silphidae: many species, including the burying beetles.

car·ri·on crow ▶ **n. 1** a medium-sized, typically all-black crow that is common throughout much of Eurasia. ● *Corvus corone,* family Corvidae. See also **HOODED CROW.**
2 another name for **BLACK VULTURE** (sense 1).

car·ri·on flow·er ▶ **n. 1** a North American climbing plant with small white flowers that smell of decaying flesh. ● Genus *Smilax:* several species, in particular *S. herbacea.*
2 another term for **STAPELIA.**

Car·roll /ˈkarəl/, Lewis (1832–98), English writer; pseudonym of *Charles Lutwidge Dodgson.* He wrote the children's classics *Alice's Adventures in Wonderland* (1865) and *Through the Looking Glass* (1871), which were inspired by **Alice Liddell,** the young daughter of the dean at the Oxford college where Carroll was a mathematics lecturer.

Car·roll·ton /ˈkarəltən/ a city in northeastern Texas, north of Dallas; pop. 125,595 (est. 2008).

car·ron·ade /,karəˈnād/ ▶ **n.** historical a short large-caliber cannon, formerly in naval use.
– ORIGIN late 18th cent.: from *Carron,* Scotland, where this kind of cannon was first made.

car·rot /ˈkarət/ ▶ **n. 1** a tapering orange-colored root eaten as a vegetable.
2 the cultivated feathery-leaved plant that yields this vegetable. ● *Daucus carota,* family Umbelliferae: two subspecies and many varieties; wild forms lack the swollen root.
3 an offer of something enticing as a means of persuasion (often contrasted with the threat of something punitive or unwelcome): *carrots will promote cooperation over the environment far more effectively than sticks.* [with allusion to the proverbial encouragement of a donkey to move by enticing it with a carrot.]
– ORIGIN late 15th cent.: from French *carotte,* from Latin *carota,* from Greek *karōton.*

car·rot-and-stick ▶ **adj.** characterized by both the offer of reward and the threat of punishment: *carrot-and-stick reforms intended to break long-term dependency on state and federal handouts.*

car·rot·wood /ˈkarət,wo͝od/ ▶ **n.** a tree of the soapberry family, native to southeast Asia, that threatens mangrove swamps and other habitats in the US because of its invasive habit. ● *Cupaniopsis anacardioides*, family Sapindaceae.

car·rot·y /ˈkarətē/ ▶ adj. (of a person's hair or whiskers) orange-red in color.

car·rou·sel ▶ n. variant spelling of CAROUSEL.

car·ry /ˈkarē/ ▶ v. (**carries, carrying, carried**) [with obj.] **1** support and move (someone or something) from one place to another: *medics were carrying a wounded man on a stretcher.* ■ transport, conduct, or transmit: *the train service carries 20,000 passengers daily | nerves carry visual information from the eyes.* ■ have on one's person and take with one wherever one goes: *the money he was carrying was not enough to pay the fine* | figurative *she had carried the secret all her life.* ■ be infected with (a disease) and liable to transmit it to others: *ticks can carry Lyme disease.*
2 support the weight of: *the bridge is capable of carrying even the heaviest loads.* ■ be pregnant with: *she was carrying twins.* ■ (**carry oneself**) stand and move in a specified way: *she carried herself straight and with assurance.* ■ assume or accept (responsibility or blame): *they must carry the responsibility for the mess they have gotten the company into.* ■ be responsible for the effectiveness or success of: *they relied on dialogue to carry the plot.*
3 have as a feature or consequence: *being a combat sport, karate* **carries with it** *the risk of injury | each bike carries a ten-year guarantee.*
4 [no obj.] (of a sound, ball, missile, etc.) reach a certain point: *his voice carried clearly across the room | the balls seem to carry well in that ballpark.* ■ (of a gun or similar weapon) propel (a missile) to a specified distance. ■ Golf hit the ball over and beyond (a particular point). ■ take or develop (an idea or activity) to a specified point: *he carried the criticism much further.*
5 approve (a proposed measure) by a majority of votes: *the resolution was carried by a two-to-one majority.* ■ persuade (colleagues or followers) to support one's policy: *he could not carry the cabinet.* ■ gain (a state or district) in an election.
6 (of a newspaper or a television or radio station) publish or broadcast: *the paper carried a detailed account of the current crisis.* ■ (of a retail outlet) keep a regular stock of (particular goods for sale): *this store no longer carries phonograph equipment.* ■ have visible on the surface: *the product does not carry the "UL" symbol.* ■ be known by (a name): *some products carry the same names as overseas beers.*
7 transfer (a figure) to an adjacent column during an arithmetical operation (e.g., when a column of digits adds up to more than ten).
▶ n. (pl. **carries**) [usu. in sing.] **1** an act of lifting and transporting something from one place to another: *we did a carry of equipment from the camp.* ■ Football an act of running with the ball from scrimmage. ■ the action of keeping something, esp. a gun, on one's person: *this pistol is the right choice for on-duty or off-duty carry.* ■ historical a place or route between navigable waters over which boats or supplies had to be carried. ■ the transfer of a figure into an adjacent column (or the equivalent part of a computer memory) during an arithmetical operation. ■ Finance the maintenance of an investment position in a securities market, esp. with regard to the costs or profits accruing.
2 (in golf) the distance a ball travels before reaching the ground. ■ the range of a gun or similar weapon. ■ (in golf) the distance a ball must travel to reach a certain destination.
– PHRASES **carry conviction** be convincing. **carry the day** be victorious or successful. **carry weight** be influential or important: *the report is expected to carry considerable weight with the administration.*
– PHRASAL VERBS **be/get carried away** lose self-control: *I got a bit carried away when describing the final game.* **carry something away** Nautical lose (a mast or other part of a ship) through breakage. **carry something forward** transfer figures to a new page or account. ■ keep something to use or deal with at a later time: *we carried forward a reserve, which allowed us to meet demands.* **carry someone/something off** take someone or something away by force: *bandits carried off his mule.* ■ (of a disease) kill someone: *Parkinson's disease carried him off in September.* **carry something off** win a prize: *she failed to carry off the gold medal.* ■ succeed in doing something difficult: *he could not have carried it off without government help.* **carry on 1** continue an activity or task: *carry on with what you were doing.* ■ chiefly Brit. continue to move in the same direction: *I knew I was going the wrong way, but I just carried on.* **2** informal behave, esp. speak, in an excited or bad-tempered way: *she carries on about television programming.* **3** informal be engaged in a love affair, typically one of which the speaker disapproves: *she was carrying on with young Adam.* **carry something on** engage in an activity: *he could not carry on a logical conversation.* **carry something out** perform a task or planned operation: *we're carrying out a market-research survey.* **carry over** extend beyond the normal or original area of application: *his artistic practice is clearly carrying over into his social thought.* **carry something over** retain something and apply or deal with it in a new context: *much of the wartime economic planning was carried over into the next decade.* ■ postpone an event: *the match had to be carried over till Sunday.* ■ another way of saying CARRY SOMETHING FORWARD. **carry something through** bring a project to completion: *policy blueprints are rarely carried through perfectly.* ■ bring something safely out of difficulties: *he was the only person who could carry the country through.*
– ORIGIN late Middle English: from Anglo-Norman French and Old Northern French *carier*, based on Latin *carrus* 'wheeled vehicle.'

car·ry·all /ˈkarēˌôl/ ▶ n. **1** a large bag or case.
2 historical a light carriage. [early 18th cent.: apparently altered by folk etymology from French *carriole*, denoting a small covered carriage.] ■ a large car or truck with seats facing each other along the sides.

car·ry·back note /ˈkarēˌbak/ ▶ n. Finance a negotiable promissory note representing the value of real estate when the seller has provided the financing.

car·ry·ing ca·pac·i·ty ▶ n. the number or quantity of people or things that can be conveyed or held by a vehicle or container. ■ Ecology the number of people, other living organisms, or crops that a region can support without environmental degradation.

car·ry·ing charge ▶ n. **1** Finance an expense or effective cost arising from unproductive assets such as stored goods or unoccupied premises.
2 a sum payable for the conveying of goods.

car·ry·ing-on ▶ n. (pl. **carryings-on**) excited or overwrought behavior: *I'm fed up with your incessant carrying-on.* ■ salacious, improper, or immoral behavior: *the couple's public carrying-on embarrassed passersby.*

car·ry-on ▶ adj. (of a bag or suitcase) suitable for taking onto an aircraft as handheld luggage.

car·ry-out ▶ adj. & n. another term for TAKEOUT (sense 1).

car·ry·o·ver ▶ n. [usu. in sing.] something transferred or resulting from a previous situation or context: *the slow trading was a carryover from the big losses of last week.*

car·sick /ˈkärˌsik/ ▶ adj. affected with nausea caused by the motion of a car or other vehicle in which one is traveling.
– DERIVATIVES **car·sick·ness** n.

Car·son[1] /ˈkärsən/ a city in southwestern California, south of Los Angeles; pop. 92,366 (est. 2008).

Car·son[2] /ˈkärsən/, Johnny (1925–2005), US television personality and comedian; full name *John William Carson*. He hosted *The Tonight Show* 1962–92.

Car·son[3], Kit (1809–68), US frontiersman and scout; full name *Christopher Carson*. He was a US Indian agent in the Southwest 1853–61 and organized Union scouts in the West during the Civil War.

Car·son[4], Rachel Louise (1907–64), US biologist and environmentalist. Her works include *The Sea Around Us* (1951) and *Silent Spring* (1962).

Car·son Cit·y the capital of Nevada, in the western part of the state, southeast of Reno; pop. 54,867 (est. 2008).

cart /kärt/ ▶ n. a strong open vehicle with two or four wheels, typically used for carrying loads and pulled by a horse. ■ a shallow open container on wheels that may be pulled or pushed by hand. ■ a shopping cart.
▶ v. [with obj.] **1** convey or put in a cart or similar vehicle: *the produce was packed in crates and carted to Kansas City.*
2 informal carry (a heavy or cumbersome object) somewhere with difficulty: *they carted the piano down three flights of stairs.* ■ remove or convey (someone) somewhere unceremoniously: *they carted off the refugees in the middle of the night.*
– PHRASES **put the cart before the horse** reverse the proper order or procedure of something.
– DERIVATIVES **cart·er** n., **cart·ful** /-ˌfo͝ol/ n. (pl. **cartfuls**).
– ORIGIN Middle English: from Old Norse *kartr*, probably influenced by Anglo-Norman French and Old Northern French *carete*, diminutive of *carre* (see CAR).

cart·age /ˈkärtij/ ▶ n. the transporting of something in a cart or other vehicle.

Car·ta·ge·na /ˌkärtəˈhānə, -ˈgānə/ **1** a port in southeastern Spain; pop. 210,376 (2008). Originally named Mastia, it was refounded as Carthago Nova (New Carthage) in *c.*225 BC as a base for the Carthaginian conquest of Spain.
2 a port, resort, and oil-refining center in northwestern Colombia, on the Caribbean Sea; pop. 885,400 (2005).

carte blanche /ˈkärt ˈblänsh, ˈblänch/ ▶ n. complete freedom to act as one wishes or thinks best: *we were given carte blanche.*
– ORIGIN late 17th cent.: French, literally 'blank paper' (i.e., a blank sheet on which to write whatever one wishes, particularly one's own terms for an agreement).

C

carte de vi·site /ˌkärt də viˈzēt/ ▶ n. (pl. **cartes de visite** pronunc. **same**) historical a small photographic portrait of someone, mounted on a piece of card.
– ORIGIN mid 19th cent.: French, 'visiting card.'

car·tel /kärˈtel/ ▶ n. an association of manufacturers or suppliers with the purpose of maintaining prices at a high level and restricting competition: *the Colombian drug cartels.* ■ chiefly historical a coalition or cooperative arrangement between political parties intended to promote a mutual interest.
– ORIGIN late 19th cent.: from German *Kartell*, from French *cartel*, from Italian *cartello*, diminutive of *carta*, from Latin *carta* (see CARD[1]). It was originally used to refer to the coalition of the Conservatives and National Liberal parties in Germany (1887), and hence any political combination; later to denote a trade agreement (early 20th cent).

car·tel·ize /kärˈtelˌīz, ˈkärtl-/ ▶ v. [with obj.] (of manufacturers or suppliers) form a cartel in (an industry or trade).

Car·ter[1] /ˈkärtər/, Angela (1940–92), English novelist and short-story writer. Notable works: *The Magic Toyshop* (1967) and *Nights at the Circus* (1984).

Car·ter[2], Elliott (Cook) (1908–), US composer. He is noted for his innovative approach to meter and his choice of sources, which are as diverse as modern jazz and Renaissance madrigals.

Car·ter[3], Howard (1874–1939), English archaeologist. In 1922, while excavating in the Valley of the Kings at Thebes, he discovered the tomb of Tutankhamen.

Car·ter[4], Jimmy (1924–), 39th president of the US 1977–81; full name *James Earl Carter, Jr.* A Georgia Democrat, he served as a state senator 1962–66 and as governor 1971–74. As president, he hosted the talks that led to the Camp David agreements of 1978. The accomplishments of his administration were marred by the crisis caused by the seizure of 52 American hostages in Iran in 1979. After losing a bid for re-election, Carter remained politically active in world affairs, dedicated to the causes of peace and human rights. Nobel Peace Prize (2002).

Jimmy Carter

Car·te·sian /kärˈtēzhən/ ▶ adj. of or relating to Descartes and his ideas.
▶ n. a follower of Descartes.
– DERIVATIVES **Car·te·sian·ism** /-ˌnizəm/ n.
– ORIGIN mid 17th cent.: from modern Latin *Cartesianus*, from *Cartesius*, Latinized form of the name of *Descartes*.

Car·te·sian co·or·di·nates ▶ plural n. Mathematics numbers that indicate the location of a point relative to a fixed reference point (the origin), being its shortest (perpendicular) distances from two fixed axes (or three planes defined by three fixed axes) that intersect at right angles at the origin.

Car·te·sian prod·uct ▶ n. Mathematics the product of two sets: the product of set X and set Y is the set that contains all ordered pairs (x, y) for which x belongs to X and y belongs to Y.

Car·thage /ˈkärthij/ an ancient city on the coast of North Africa near present-day Tunis. Founded by

the Phoenicians *c.*814 BC, it became a major force in the Mediterranean Sea area and fought with Rome during the Punic Wars. It was finally destroyed by the Romans in 146 BC.
– DERIVATIVES **Car·tha·gin·i·an** /ˌkärTHəˈjinēən/ **n. & adj.**

cart horse ▶ **n.** Brit. a large, strong horse suitable for heavy work.

C

Car·thu·sian /kärˈTH(y)o͞oZHən/ ▶ **n.** a monk or nun of an austere contemplative order founded by St. Bruno in 1084.
▶ **adj.** of or relating to this order.
– ORIGIN from medieval Latin *Carthusianus*, from *Cart(h)usia*, Latin name of *Chartreuse*, near Grenoble, France, where the order was founded.

Car·tier /kärˈtyā, ˈkärtēˌā/, Jacques (1491–1557), French explorer. The first to establish France's claim to North America, he made three voyages to Canada between 1534 and 1541.

Car·tier-Bres·son /ˌkärtyā brāˈsôN/, Henri (1908–2004), French photographer and movie director. He is known for his collection of photographs, *The Decisive Moment* (1952), and for his documentary about the Spanish Civil War, *Return to Life* (1937).

Car·tier Is·lands /ˈkärtēˌā/ see **ASHMORE AND CARTIER ISLANDS**.

car·ti·lage /ˈkärtl-ij/ ▶ **n.** firm, whitish, flexible connective tissue found in various forms in the larynx and respiratory tract, in structures such as the external ear, and in the articulating surfaces of joints. It is more widespread in the infant skeleton, being replaced by bone during growth. ■ a particular structure made of this tissue.
– DERIVATIVES **car·ti·lag·i·noid** /ˌkärtlˈajəˌnoid/ **adj.**
– ORIGIN late Middle English: from French, from Latin *cartilago, cartilagin-*.

car·ti·lag·i·nous /ˌkärtlˈajənəs/ ▶ **adj.** Anatomy (of a structure) made of cartilage. ■ Zoology (of a vertebrate animal) having a skeleton of cartilage.
– ORIGIN late Middle English: from Old French, or from Latin *cartilaginosus*, from *cartilago, cartilagin-* 'cartilage.'

car·ti·lag·i·nous fish ▶ **n.** a fish of a class distinguished by having a skeleton of cartilage rather than bone, including the sharks, rays, and chimeras. Compare with **BONY FISH**. ● Class Chondrichthyes: subclasses Elasmobranchii (sharks and rays) and Holocephali (chimeras).

Cart·land /ˈkärtlənd/, Dame Barbara (1901–2000), English author of light romantic fiction; full name *Dame Mary Barbara Hamilton Cartland McCorquodale*.

cart·load /ˈkärtˌlōd/ ▶ **n.** the amount held by a cart.

car·to·gram /ˈkärtəˌgram/ ▶ **n.** a map on which statistical information is shown in diagrammatic form.
– ORIGIN late 19th cent.: from French *cartogramme*, from *carte* 'map or card' + *-gramme* (from Greek *gramma* 'thing written').

car·tog·ra·phy /kärˈtägrəfē/ ▶ **n.** the science or practice of drawing maps.
– DERIVATIVES **car·tog·ra·pher** /-fər/ **n.**, **car·to·graph·ic** /ˌkärtəˈgrafik/ **adj.**, **car·to·graph·i·cal** /ˌkärtəˈgrafikəl/ **adj.**, **car·to·graph·i·cal·ly** /ˌkärtəˈgrafik(ə)lē/ **adv.**
– ORIGIN mid 19th cent.: from French *cartographie*, from *carte* 'map, card' (see **CARD**[1]) + *-graphie* (see **-GRAPHY**).

car·to·man·cy /ˈkärtəˌmansē/ ▶ **n.** fortune-telling by interpreting a random selection of playing cards.
– ORIGIN late 19th cent.: from French *cartomancie*, from *carte* 'card' + *-mancie* (see **-MANCY**).

car·ton /ˈkärtn/ ▶ **n.** a light box or container, typically one made of waxed cardboard or plastic in which drinks or foodstuffs are packaged.
– ORIGIN early 19th cent.: from French, from Italian *cartone* (see **CARTOON**).

car·toon /kärˈto͞on/ ▶ **n. 1** a simple drawing showing the features of its subjects in a humorously exaggerated way, esp. a satirical one in a newspaper or magazine. ■ a comic strip. ■ a simplified or exaggerated version or interpretation of something: *this movie is a cartoon of rural life in America* | [as modifier] *Dolores becomes a cartoon housewife, reading glossy magazines in a bathrobe.*
2 a motion picture using animation techniques to photograph a sequence of drawings rather than real people or objects.
3 a full-size drawing made by an artist as a preliminary design for a painting or other work of art.
▶ **v.** [with obj.] make a drawing of (someone) in a simplified or exaggerated way: *she has a face with enough character to be cartooned.*
– DERIVATIVES **car·toon·ish adj.**, **car·toon·ist** /-ist/ **n.**, **car·toon·y adj.**
– ORIGIN late 16th cent. (sense 3 of the noun): from Italian *cartone*, from *carta*, from Latin *carta, charta* (see **CARD**[1]). Sense 1 of the noun dates from the mid 19th cent.

car·toon·ing /kärˈto͞oniNG/ ▶ **n.** the activity or occupation of drawing cartoons for newspapers or magazines.

car·touche /kärˈto͞oSH/ ▶ **n.** a carved tablet or drawing representing a scroll with rolled-up ends, used ornamentally or bearing an inscription. ■ Archaeology an oval or oblong enclosing a group of Egyptian hieroglyphs, typically representing the name and title of a monarch.
– ORIGIN early 17th cent.: from French *cartouche* (masculine noun), earlier *cartoche*, from Italian *cartoccio*, from *carta*, from Latin *carta, charta* (see **CARD**[1]).

car·tridge /ˈkärtrij/ ▶ **n.** a container holding a spool of photographic film, a quantity of ink, or other item or substance, designed for insertion into a mechanism. ■ a casing containing a charge and a bullet or shot for small arms or an explosive charge for blasting. ■ a component carrying the stylus on the pickup head of a record player.
– ORIGIN late 16th cent.: from French *cartouche* (feminine noun), from Italian *cartoccio* (see **CARTOUCHE**).

car·tridge belt ▶ **n.** a belt with pockets or loops for cartridges of ammunition, typically worn over the shoulder.

car·tridge clip ▶ **n.** a metal frame or container that holds cartridges for loading into an automatic rifle or pistol.

cart·wheel /ˈkärtˌ(h)wēl/ ▶ **n. 1** the wheel of a cart.
2 a circular sideways handspring with the arms and legs extended.
▶ **v.** [no obj.] perform such a handspring or handsprings: *he cartwheeled across the room.*

Cart·wright /ˈkärtˌrīt/, Edmund (1743–1823), English engineer. He invented the power loom.

car·un·cle /kəˈrəNGkəl, ˈkarˌəNG-/ ▶ **n. 1** a wattle of a bird such as a turkey.
2 the red prominence at the inner corner of the eye.
3 Botany an outgrowth from a seed near the micropyle, attractive to ants that aid the seed's dispersal.
– DERIVATIVES **ca·run·cu·lar** /kəˈrəNGkyələr/ **adj.**
– ORIGIN late 16th cent.: obsolete French, from Latin *caruncula*, from *caro, carn-* 'flesh.'

Ca·ru·so /kəˈro͞osō, -zō/, Enrico (1873–1921), Italian opera singer. He was the first major tenor to be recorded on phonograph records.

carve /kärv/ ▶ **v.** [with obj.] **1** cut (a hard material) in order to produce an aesthetically pleasing object or design: *the wood was carved with runes* | (as adj. **carved**) *bookcases of carved oak.* ■ produce (an object) by cutting and shaping a hard material: *the altar was carved from a block of solid jade.* ■ produce (an inscription or design) by cutting into hard material: *an inscription was carved over the doorway* | figurative *the river carved a series of gorges into the plain.*
2 cut (cooked meat) into slices for eating. ■ cut (a slice of meat) from a larger piece.
3 Skiing make (a turn) by tilting one's skis on to their edges and using one's weight to bend them so that they slide into an arc.
– PHRASAL VERBS **carve something out 1** take something from a larger whole, esp. with difficulty: *carving out a 5 percent share of the overall vote.* **2** establish or create something through painstaking effort: *he managed to carve out a successful photographic career for himself.* **carve someone up** informal slash someone with a knife or other sharp object. **carve something up** divide something ruthlessly into separate areas or domains: *West Africa was carved up by the Europeans.*
– ORIGIN Old English *ceorfan* 'cut, carve'; related to Dutch *kerven*.

car·vel /ˈkärvəl/ ▶ **n.** variant spelling of **CARAVEL**.

car·vel-built ▶ **adj.** (of a boat or ship) having hull planks that do not overlap. Compare with **LAPSTRAKE**.

carv·en /ˈkärvən/ archaic past participle of **CARVE**.

carve·out /ˈkärvˌout/ ▶ **n. 1** a small company created from a larger one: *companies that are breaking up—through spin-offs, split-offs, and carveouts.* ■ a class of medical procedures treated separately with regard to insurance coverage. ■ a class of employees treated separately with regard to benefits.
2 the activity of effecting such a separation.

Car·ver /ˈkärvər/, George Washington (*c.*1864–1943), US botanist. Born into slavery, he later became the director of agricultural research at Tuskegee Institute in 1896 and developed many products from soybeans, sweet potatoes, and peanuts.

George Washington Carver

car·ver /ˈkärvər/ ▶ **n. 1** a person who carves wood, stone, ivory, coral, etc., esp. professionally: *we watched a decoy carver at work.*
2 a knife designed for slicing meat.
3 a person who cuts and serves the meat at a meal.

carv·ing /ˈkärviNG/ ▶ **n.** an object or design cut from a hard material as an artistic work.

carv·ing knife ▶ **n.** a knife with a long blade used for carving cooked meat into slices.

car wash ▶ **n. 1** a building containing equipment for washing motor vehicles automatically.
2 an event, typically a fundraiser, in which motor vehicles are washed: *the Teen Center will hold its third annual car wash on Saturday.*

Cary /ˈkarē, ˈke(ə)rē/ a town in east central North Carolina, a commercial and research center; pop. 129,545 (est. 2008).

car·y·at·id /ˌkarēˈatid, ˈkarēəˌtid/ ▶ **n.** (pl. **caryatids** or **caryatides** /ˌkarēˈatəˌdēz/) Architecture a stone carving of a draped female figure, used as a pillar to support the entablature of a Greek or Greek-style building.
– ORIGIN mid 16th cent.: via French and Italian from Latin *caryatides*, from Greek *karuatides*, plural of *karuatis* 'priestess of Artemis at Caryae,' from *Karuai* (Caryae) in Laconia.

caryatid

car·y·o·phyl·la·ceous /ˌkarēōfəˈlāSHəs/ ▶ **adj.** Botany of, relating to, or denoting plants of the pink family (Caryophyllaceae).
– ORIGIN mid 19th cent.: from modern Latin *Caryophyllaceae* (plural), based on Greek *karuophullon* 'clove pink,' + **-OUS**.

car·y·op·sis /ˌkarēˈäpsis/ ▶ **n.** (pl. **caryopses** /-ˌsēz/) Botany a dry one-seeded fruit in which the ovary wall is united with the seed coat, typical of grasses and cereals.
– ORIGIN early 19th cent.: from modern Latin, from Greek *karuon* 'nut' + *opsis* 'appearance.'

ca·sa·ba /kəˈsäbə/ (also **cassaba**) ▶ **n.** a winter melon of a variety with a wrinkled yellow rind and sweet flesh.
– ORIGIN early 20th cent.: named after *Kasaba* (now Turgutlu) in Turkey, from which the melons were first exported.

Ca·sa·blan·ca /ˌkäsəˈbläNGkə, ˌkasəˈblaNGkə/ the largest city in Morocco, a seaport on the Atlantic coast; pop. 2,949,805 (2004).

Ca·sals /kəˈsälz/, Pablo (1876–1973), Spanish cellist, conductor, and composer.

Cas·a·no·va /ˌkazəˈnōvə, ˌkasə-/, Giovanni Jacopo (1725–98), Italian adventurer; full name *Giovanni Jacopo Casanova de Seingalt*. He is known for his memoirs that describe his sexual encounters and other exploits.

cas·bah /ˈkazˌbä/ (also **kasbah**) ▶ **n.** the citadel of a North African city. ■ (**the casbah**) the area surrounding such a citadel, typically the old part of a city.
– ORIGIN mid 18th cent.: French, from Arabic *kaṣaba* 'citadel.'

cas·ca·bel /ˈkaskəˌbel/ ▶ **n.** a small red chile pepper of a mild-flavored variety.
– ORIGIN mid 17th cent.: from Spanish, from Catalan *cascavel*, from medieval Latin *cascabellus* 'little bell.'

cas·cade /kas'kād/ ▶ **n. 1** a small waterfall, typically one of several that fall in stages down a steep rocky slope. ■ a mass of something that falls or hangs in copious or luxuriant quantities: *a cascade of pink bougainvillea.* ■ a large number or amount of something occurring or arriving in rapid succession: *a cascade of antiwar literature.*
2 a process whereby something, typically information or knowledge, is successively passed on: [as modifier] *the greater the number of people who are well briefed, the wider the cascade effect.* ■ a succession of devices or stages in a process, each of which triggers or initiates the next.
▶ **v. 1** [no obj.] (of water) pour downward rapidly and in large quantities: *water was cascading down the stairs.* ■ fall or hang in copious or luxuriant quantities: *blonde hair cascaded down her back.*
2 [with obj.] arrange (a number of devices or objects) in a series or sequence.
– ORIGIN mid 17th cent.: from French, from Italian *cascata*, from *cascare* 'to fall,' based on Latin *casus* (see CASE[1]).

Cas·cade Range a range of volcanic mountains in western North America that extends from southern British Columbia through Washington and Oregon to northern California. Its highest peak is Mount Rainier. The range also includes an active volcano, Mount St. Helens.

cas·car·a /kas'karə/ (also **cascara sagrada** /sə'grädə/) ▶ **n. 1** a purgative made from the dried bark of an American buckthorn.
2 (also **cascara buckthorn**) the tree from which this bark is obtained, native to the Pacific Northwest. ● *Rhamnus purshiana*, family Rhamnaceae.
– ORIGIN late 19th cent.: from Spanish *cáscara (sagrada)*, literally '(sacred) bark.'

Cas·co Bay /'kaskō/ an inlet of the Atlantic in southern Maine, known for its hundreds of islands and protected anchorages. Portland lies on it.

case[1] /kās/ ▶ **n. 1** an instance of a particular situation; an example of something occurring: *a case of mistaken identity | in many cases, valid statistics are not available.* ■ [usu. in sing.] the situation affecting or relating to a particular person or thing; one's circumstances or position: *I'll make an exception in your case.* ■ an incident or set of circumstances under police investigation: *a murder case.*
2 an instance of a disease or problem: *200,000 cases of hepatitis B.* ■ a person or their particular problem requiring or receiving medical or welfare attention: *most breast cancer cases were older women | the welfare office discussed Gerald's case.* ■ [with adj. or noun modifier] informal a person whose situation is regarded as pitiable or as having no chance of improvement: *Vicky was a very sad case.* ■ informal, dated an amusing or eccentric person.
3 a legal action, esp. one to be decided in a court of law: *a libel case | a former employee brought the case against the council.* ■ a set of facts or arguments supporting one side in such a legal action: *the case for the defense.* ■ a legal action that has been decided and may be cited as a precedent. ■ a set of facts or arguments supporting one side of a debate or controversy: *the case against tobacco advertising.*
4 Grammar any of the inflected forms of a noun, adjective, or pronoun that express the semantic relation of the word to other words in the sentence: *the accusative case.* ■ such a relation whether indicated by inflection or not: *English normally expresses case by the use of prepositions.*
– PHRASES **as the case may be** according to the circumstances (used when referring to two or more possible alternatives): *the authorities will decide if they are satisfied or not satisfied, as the case may be.* **be the case** be so. **in any case** whatever happens or may have happened. ■ used to confirm or support a point or idea just mentioned: *he wasn't allowed out yet, and in any case he wasn't well enough.* **(just) in case 1** as a provision against something happening or being true: *we put on thick sweaters, in case it was cold.* **2** if it is true that: *in case you haven't figured it out, let me explain.* **in case of** in the event of (a particular situation): *instructions about what to do in case of fire.* **in no case** under no circumstances. **in that case** if that happens or has happened; if that is the situation: *"I'm free this evening." "In that case, why not have dinner with me?"* **on** (or **off**) **someone's case** informal continually (or no longer) criticizing or harassing someone: *the teacher will get on your case if you keep forgetting your homework.*
– ORIGIN Middle English: from Old French *cas*, from Latin *casus* 'fall,' related to *cadere* 'to fall'; sense 4 directly from Latin, translating Greek *ptōsis*, literally 'fall.'

case[2] ▶ **n. 1** a container designed to hold or protect something: *he placed the trumpet safely in its velvet-lined case.* ■ the outer protective covering of a natural or manufactured object: *a seed case.* ■ Brit. an item of luggage; a suitcase. ■ a box containing bottles or cans of a beverage, sold as a unit: *there are twelve bottles of champagne in a case.*
2 each of the two forms, capital or minuscule, in which a letter of the alphabet may be written or printed. See also UPPERCASE, LOWERCASE. [from the use in printing to mean 'partitioned container for loose metal type.']
▶ **v.** [with obj.] **1** surround in a material or substance: *the towers are of steel cased in granite.* ■ enclose in a protective container: (as adj. **cased**) *a cased pair of pistols.*
2 informal reconnoiter (a place) before carrying out a robbery: *I was casing the joint.*
– ORIGIN late Middle English: from Old French *casse, chasse* (modern *caisse* 'trunk, chest,' *châsse* 'reliquary, frame'), from Latin *capsa*, related to *capere* 'to hold.'

ca·se·a·tion /,kāsē'āsHən/ ▶ **n.** Medicine a form of necrosis characteristic of tuberculosis, in which diseased tissue forms a firm, dry mass like cheese in appearance.
– ORIGIN mid 19th cent.: from medieval Latin *caseatio(n-)*, from Latin *caseus* 'cheese.'

case·book /'kās,bo͝ok/ ▶ **n.** a book containing a selection of source materials on a particular subject, esp. one used as a reference work or in teaching.

case·bound /'kās,bound/ ▶ **adj.** (of a book) in a hard cover.

case gram·mar ▶ **n.** Linguistics a form of grammar in which the structure of sentences is analyzed in terms of the semantic roles of nouns in relation to predicates.

case-hard·en ▶ **v.** [with obj.] (often as adj. **case-hardened**) harden the surface of (a material): *case-hardened sandstones.* ■ give a hard surface to (iron or steel) by carburizing it: *a case-hardened steel anvil.* ■ make (someone) callous or tough: *a case-hardened politician.*

case his·to·ry ▶ **n.** a record of a person's background or medical history kept by a doctor or social worker.

ca·sein /kā'sēn, 'kāsēən/ ▶ **n.** the main protein present in milk and (in coagulated form) in cheese. It is used in processed foods and in adhesives, paints, and other industrial products.
– ORIGIN mid 19th cent.: from Latin *caseus* 'cheese.'

case knife ▶ **n.** a type of dagger carried in a sheath.

case law ▶ **n.** the law as established by the outcome of former cases. Compare with COMMON LAW, STATUTE LAW.

case·load /'kās,lōd/ ▶ **n.** the amount of work (in terms of number of cases) with which a doctor, lawyer, or social worker is concerned at one time.

case·mate /'kās,māt/ ▶ **n.** historical a small room in the thickness of the wall of a fortress, with embrasures from which guns or missiles can be fired. ■ an armored enclosure for guns on a warship.
– ORIGIN mid 16th cent.: from French, from Italian *casamatta*, perhaps from Greek *khasma, khasmat-* (see CHASM).

case·ment /'kāsmənt/ ▶ **n.** a window or part of a window set on a hinge so that it opens like a door: [as modifier] *casement windows.* ■ chiefly literary a window. ■ the sash of a sash window.
– ORIGIN late Middle English (as an architectural term denoting a hollow molding): from Anglo-Latin *cassimentum*, from *cassa*, from Latin *capsa* (see CASE[2]).

ca·se·ous /'kāsēəs/ ▶ **adj.** Medicine characterized by caseation.
– ORIGIN mid 17th cent.: from Latin *caseus* 'cheese' + -OUS.

case-sen·si·tive ▶ **adj.** Computing (of a program or function) differentiating between capital and lowercase letters. ■ (of input) treated differently depending on whether it is in capitals or lowercase text.

case shot ▶ **n.** historical bullets or pieces of metal in an iron case fired from a cannon.

case stud·y ▶ **n. 1** a process or record of research in which detailed consideration is given to the development of a particular person, group, or situation over a period of time.
2 a particular instance of something used or analyzed in order to illustrate a thesis or principle: *airline deregulation provides a case study of the effects of the internal market.*

case·work[1] /'kās,wərk/ ▶ **n.** social work directly concerned with individuals, esp. that involving a study of a person's family history and personal circumstances.
– DERIVATIVES **case·work·er n.**

case·work[2] ▶ **n.** the decorative outer case protecting the workings of a complex mechanism such as an organ or harpsichord.

Cash /kasH/, Johnny (1932–2003), US country music singer and songwriter. Notable songs: "I Walk the Line" (1956), "Ring of Fire" (1963), and "A Boy Named Sue" (1969).

cash[1] /kasH/ ▶ **n.** money in coins or notes, as distinct from checks, money orders, or credit: *the staff were paid in cash | a discount for cash.* ■ money in any form, esp. that which is immediately available: *she was always short of cash.*
▶ **v.** [with obj.] give or obtain notes or coins for (a check or money order). ■ Bridge lead (a high card) so as to take the opportunity to win a trick.
– PHRASES **cash in one's chips** informal die. [with reference to gambling in a casino.]
– PHRASAL VERBS **cash in** informal take advantage of or exploit (a situation): *the breweries were cashing in on the rediscovered taste for real ales.* **cash something in** convert an insurance policy, savings account, or other investment into money. **cash out** cost: *juicy baked chicken cashed out at $7.* **cash something out** another way of saying CASH SOMETHING IN.
– DERIVATIVES **cash·a·ble adj.**
– ORIGIN late 16th cent. (denoting a box for money): from Old French *casse* or Italian *cassa* 'box,' from Latin *capsa* (see CASE[2]).

cash[2] ▶ **n.** (pl. **same**) historical a coin of low value from China, southern India, or Southeast Asia.
– ORIGIN late 16th cent.: from Portuguese *caixa*, from Tamil *kāsu*, influenced by CASH[1].

cash and car·ry ▶ **n.** a system of wholesale trading whereby goods are paid for in full at the time of purchase and taken away by the purchaser. ■ a wholesale store operating this system.

cash-back ▶ **adj.** denoting a form of incentive offered to buyers of certain products whereby they receive a cash refund after making their purchase.

cash bar ▶ **n.** a bar at a social function at which guests buy drinks rather than having them provided free.

cash·box /'kasH,bäks/ ▶ **n.** a lockable metal box for keeping cash in.

cash cow ▶ **n.** informal a business, investment, or product that provides a steady income or profit: *traditional cash cows like cars and VCRs.*

cash crop ▶ **n.** a crop produced for its commercial value rather than for use by the grower.
– DERIVATIVES **cash crop·ping n.**

cash·ew /'kasH,o͞o, kə'sHo͞o/ ▶ **n. 1** (also **cashew nut**) an edible kidney-shaped nut, rich in oil and protein, which is roasted and shelled before it can be eaten. Oil is extracted from the shells and used as a lubricant and insecticide and in the production of plastics.
2 (also **cashew tree**) a bushy tropical American tree related to the mango, bearing cashew nuts singly at the tip of each swollen fruit. Also called ACAJOU. ● *Anacardium occidentale*, family Anacardiaceae (the **cashew family**).
– ORIGIN late 16th cent.: from Portuguese, from Tupi *acajú, cajú.*

cash·ew ap·ple ▶ **n.** the swollen edible fruit of the cashew tree, from which the cashew nut hangs, sometimes used to make wine.

cash flow ▶ **n.** the total amount of money being transferred into and out of a business, esp. as affecting liquidity.

cash·ier[1] /ka'sHi(ə)r/ ▶ **n.** a person handling payments and receipts in a store, bank, or other business.
– ORIGIN late 16th cent.: from Dutch *cassier* or French *caissier*, from *caisse* 'cash.'

cash·ier[2] ▶ **v.** [with obj.] dismiss (someone) from the armed forces in disgrace because of a serious misdemeanor: *he was found guilty and cashiered |* (as adj. **cashiered**) *a cashiered National Guard major.* ■ informal suspend or dismiss from an office or position: *the team owner had been cashiered for consorting with a gambler.*
– ORIGIN late 16th cent. (in the sense 'dismiss or disband troops'): from Flemish *kasseren* 'disband (troops)' or 'revoke (a will),' from French *casser* 'revoke, dismiss,' from Latin *quassare* (see QUASH).

cash·less /'kasHləs/ ▶ **adj.** characterized by the exchange of funds by check, debit or credit card, or various electronic methods rather than the use of cash: *the cashless society.*

cash ma·chine ▶ **n.** another term for AUTOMATED TELLER MACHINE.

cash·mere /'kasH,mi(ə)r, 'kazH-/ ▶ **n.** fine soft wool, originally that from the Kashmir goat. ■ woolen

C

material made from or resembling such wool: [as modifier] *a cashmere sweater.*
– ORIGIN late 17th cent.: an early spelling of KASHMIR.

cash·mere goat ▶ n. variant spelling of KASHMIR GOAT.

cash nex·us ▶ n. the relationship constituted by monetary transactions.

cash on de·liv·er·y (abbr.: COD) ▶ n. the system of paying for goods when they are delivered.

C

cash·point /ˈkasʜ,point/ ▶ n. Brit. another term for AUTOMATED TELLER MACHINE.

cash reg·is·ter ▶ n. a machine used in places of business for regulating money transactions with customers. It typically has a compartmental drawer for cash, and it totals, displays, and records the amount of each sale.

cas·ing /ˈkāsiɴɢ/ ▶ n. **1** a cover or shell that protects or encloses something: *a waterproof casing.* **2** the frame around a door or window.

ca·si·no /kəˈsēnō/ ▶ n. (pl. **casinos**) a public room or building where gambling games are played.
– ORIGIN mid 18th cent.: from Italian, diminutive of *casa* 'house,' from Latin *casa* 'cottage.'

ca·si·ta /kəˈsētə/ ▶ n. (esp. in the US Southwest) a small house or other building.
– ORIGIN early 19th cent.: from Spanish, diminutive of *casa* 'house.'

cask /kask/ ▶ n. a large barrellike container made of wood, metal, or plastic, used for storing liquids, typically alcoholic drinks. ■ the quantity of liquid held in such a container: *a cask of cider.*
– ORIGIN early 16th cent.: from French *casque* or Spanish *casco* 'helmet.' The current senses appear only in English; from the late 16th to the late 18th centuries the word also denoted a helmet (compare with CASQUE).

cas·ket /ˈkaskit/ ▶ n. a small ornamental box or chest for holding jewels, letters, or other valuable objects. ■ a coffin.
– ORIGIN late Middle English: perhaps an Anglo-Norman French form of Old French *cassette,* diminutive of *casse* (see CASE²).

Cas·lon /ˈkaz,län, -lən/ ▶ n. a kind of roman typeface first introduced in the 18th century.
– ORIGIN mid 19th cent.: named after William *Caslon* (1692–1766), English type founder.

Cas·ne·wydd /käsˈne-wiᴛʜ/ Welsh name for NEWPORT.

Cas·par /ˈkaspər/ one of the three Magi.

Cas·per¹ /ˈkaspər/ a city in east central Wyoming, on the North Platte River; pop. 54,047 (est. 2008). Oil is central to its economy.

Cas·per², Billy (1931–), US golfer; full name *William Earl Casper, Jr.* His 68 professional wins include 51 PGA Tour wins, two US Open championships (1959, 1966), and a Masters Tournament championship (1970).

Cas·pi·an Sea /ˈkaspēən/ a large landlocked salt lake, bounded by Russia, Kazakhstan, Turkmenistan, Azerbaijan, and Iran. The world's largest body of inland water, its surface lies 92 feet (28 m) below sea level.

casque /kask/ ▶ n. **1** historical a helmet. **2** Zoology a helmetlike structure, such as that on the bill of a hornbill or the head of a cassowary.
– ORIGIN late 17th cent.: from French, from Spanish *casco.* Compare with CASK.

cas·sa·ba ▶ n. variant spelling of CASABA.

Cas·san·dra /kəˈsandrə, -ˈsän-/ Greek Mythology a daughter of the Trojan king Priam, who was given the gift of prophecy by Apollo. When she cheated him, however, he turned this into a curse by causing her prophecies, though true, to be disbelieved. ■ (as noun **a Cassandra**) a prophet of disaster, esp. one who is disregarded.

cas·sa·reep /ˈkasə,rēp/ (also **casareep**) ▶ n. W. Indian a thick brown syrup made by boiling down the juice of grated cassava with sugar and spices, and typically used as a flavoring for pepper pot (see PEPPER POT (sense 2)).
– ORIGIN from Arawak *casiripe.*

cas·sa·ta /kəˈsätə/ ▶ n. a Neapolitan ice cream containing candied fruit and nuts.
– ORIGIN from Italian, literally 'little case.'

cas·sa·tion /kaˈsāsʜən/ ▶ n. Music an informal instrumental composition of the 18th century, similar to a divertimento and originally often for outdoor performance.
– ORIGIN late 19th cent.: from German *Kassation* 'serenade,' from Italian *cassazione.*

Cas·satt /kəˈsat/, Mary (1844–1926), US painter. Known for her draftsmanship, etching, and drypoint studies, she was persuaded by Edgar Degas to exhibit with the Impressionists. She worked mostly in Paris, and her paintings, including *Lady at the Tea Table* (1885), display a close interest in everyday subject matter.

cas·sa·va /kəˈsävə/ ▶ n. **1** the starchy tuberous root of a tropical tree, used as food in tropical countries but requiring careful preparation to remove traces of cyanide from the flesh. Also called MANIOC. ■ a starch or flour obtained from such a root. **2** the shrubby tree from which this root is obtained, native to tropical America and cultivated throughout the tropics. ● Genus *Manihot,* family Euphorbiaceae: several species, in particular **bitter cassava** (*M. esculenta*) and **sweet cassava** (*M. dulcis*).
– ORIGIN mid 16th cent.: from Taino *casávi, cazábbi,* influenced by French *cassave.*

Cas·se·grain tel·e·scope /ˈkasə,grān/ ▶ n. a reflecting telescope in which light reflected from a convex secondary mirror passes through a hole in the primary mirror.
– ORIGIN late 19th cent.: named after N. *Cassegrain* (1625–1712), the French astronomer who devised it.

cas·se·role /ˈkasə,rōl/ ▶ n. a kind of stew that is cooked slowly in an oven: *a chicken casserole.* ■ a large covered dish, typically of earthenware or glass, used for cooking such stews.
▶ v. [with obj.] cook (food) slowly in such a dish: (as adj. **casseroled**) *casseroled chicken.*
– ORIGIN early 18th cent.: from French, diminutive of *casse* 'spoonlike container,' from Old Provençal *casa,* from late Latin *cattia* 'ladle, pan,' from Greek *kuathion,* diminutive of *kuathos* 'cup.'

cas·sette /kəˈset/ ▶ n. a sealed plastic unit containing a length of audiotape, videotape, film, etc. wound on a pair of spools, for insertion into a recorder or playback device.
– ORIGIN late 18th cent.: from French, diminutive of *casse* (see CASE²).

cas·sette tape ▶ n. a cassette of audiotape or videotape.

cas·sia /ˈkasʜə/ ▶ n. **1** a tree, shrub, or herbaceous plant of the pea family, native to warm climates. Cassias yield a variety of products, including fodder, timber, and medicinal drugs, and many are cultivated as ornamentals. [modern Latin.] ● Genus *Cassia,* family Leguminosae: many species, including *C. fistula,* which provides much of the commercially produced senna. **2** (also **cassia bark**) the aromatic bark of an eastern Asian tree, yielding an inferior kind of cinnamon that is sometimes used to adulterate true cinnamon. [from Latin, probably denoting the wild cinnamon, via Greek from Hebrew *qeṣīʿāh.*] ● *Cinnamomum aromaticum,* family Lauraceae.

Cas·si·ni /kaˈsēnē/, Giovanni Domenico (1625–1712), French astronomer; born in Italy. He discovered the gap in the rings of Saturn known as Cassini's division.

Cas·si·o·pe·ia /,kasēəˈpēə/ **1** Greek Mythology the wife of Cepheus, king of Ethiopia, and mother of Andromeda. **2** Astronomy a constellation near the north celestial pole, recognizable by the conspicuous "W" pattern of its brightest stars. ■ (as genitive **Cassiopeiae** /,kasēəˈpē-ē/) used with a preceding letter or numeral to designate a star in this constellation: *the star Delta Cassiopeiae.*

cas·sis¹ /kaˈsēs/ (also **crème de cassis** /,krem də kaˈsēs/) ▶ n. a syrupy liqueur flavored with black currants and produced mainly in Burgundy.
– ORIGIN late 19th cent.: French, literally 'black currant,' apparently from Latin *cassia* (see CASSIA).

cas·sis² ▶ n. a wine produced in the region of Cassis, a small town near Marseilles.

cas·sit·er·ite /kəˈsitə,rīt/ ▶ n. a reddish, brownish, or yellowish mineral consisting of tin dioxide. It is the main ore of tin.
– ORIGIN mid 19th cent.: from Greek *kassiteros* 'tin' + -ITE¹.

Cas·sius /ˈkasēəs, ˈkasʜəs/, Gaius (died 42 BC), Roman general; full name *Gaius Cassius Longinus.* He was one of the leaders of the conspiracy in 44 BC to assassinate Julius Caesar.

cas·sock /ˈkasək/ ▶ n. a full-length garment of a single color worn by certain Christian clergy, members of church choirs, acolytes, and others having some particular office or role in a church.

cassock

– DERIVATIVES **cas·socked** adj.
– ORIGIN mid 16th cent.: from French *casaque* 'long coat,' from Italian *casacca* 'riding coat,' probably from Turkic *kazak* 'vagabond.' Compare with COSSACK.

cas·sou·let /ˈkasə,lā/ ▶ n. a stew made with meat and beans.
– ORIGIN French, diminutive of dialect *cassolo* 'stewpan,' from Old Provençal *cassa* 'pan'; related to CASSEROLE.

cas·so·war·y /ˈkasə,werē/ ▶ n. (pl. **cassowaries**) a very large flightless bird related to the emu, with a bare head and neck, a tall horny crest, and one or two colored wattles. It is native mainly to the forests of New Guinea. ● Family Casuariidae and genus *Casuarius:* three species, in particular the **double-wattled** (or **Australian**) **cassowary** (*C. casuarius*).
– ORIGIN early 17th cent.: from Malay *kesuari.*

double-wattled cassowary

cast¹ /kast/ ▶ v. (past and past participle **cast** /kast/) **1** [with obj.] throw (something) forcefully in a specified direction: *lemmings cast themselves off the cliff* | figurative *individuals who do not accept the norms are cast out from the group.* ■ throw (something) so as to cause it to spread over an area: *the fishermen cast a large net around a school of tuna* | figurative *he cast his net far and wide in search of evidence.* ■ direct (one's eyes or a look) at something: *she cast down her eyes* | [with two objs.] *she cast him a desperate glance.* ■ throw the hooked and baited end of (a fishing line) out into the water. ■ register (a vote): *residents turned out in record numbers to cast their votes.* ■ Hunting let loose (hounds) on a scent. ■ [no obj.] Hunting (of a dog) search in different directions for a lost scent: *the dog cast furiously for the vanished rabbit.* ■ let down (an anchor or sounding line). **2** [with obj.] cause (light or shadow) to appear on a surface: *the moon cast a pale light over the cottages* | figurative *running costs were already casting a shadow over the program.* ■ cause (uncertainty or disparagement) to be associated with something: *journalists cast doubt on the government's version of events* | *I do not wish to cast aspersions on your honesty.* ■ cause (a magic spell) to take effect: *the witch cast a spell on her to turn her into a beast* | figurative *the city casts a spell on the visitor.* **3** [with obj.] discard: *the issue was cast from the list of concerns.* ■ shed (skin or horns) in the process of growth: *the antlers are cast each year.* ■ (of a horse) lose (a shoe). **4** [with obj.] shape (metal or other material) by pouring it into a mold while molten. ■ make (a molded object) in this way: *a bell was cast for the church.* ■ arrange and present in a specified form or style: *he issued statements cast in tones of reason.* ■ calculate and record details of (a horoscope). **5** [no obj.] (in country dancing) change one's position by moving a certain number of places in a certain direction along the outside of the line in which one is dancing.
▶ n. **1** an object made by shaping molten metal or similar material in a mold: *bronze casts of the sculpture.* ■ (also **plaster cast**) a mold used to make such an object. ■ (also **plaster cast**) a bandage stiffened with plaster of Paris, molded to the shape of a limb that is broken, and used to support and protect it. **2** an act of throwing something forcefully: *he grabbed a spear for a third cast.* ■ archaic at dice, a throw or a number thrown. ■ Fishing a throw of a fishing line. **3** [with adj.] the form or appearance of something, esp. someone's features or complexion: *she had a somewhat masculine cast of countenance* | *the colors he wore emphasized the olive cast of his skin.* ■ the character of something: *this question is for minds of a more philosophical cast than mine.* **4** a slight squint: *he had a cast in one eye.* **5** a convoluted mass of earth or sand ejected onto the surface by a burrowing worm. ■ a pellet regurgitated by a hawk or owl. **6** a search made by a hound or pack of hounds over a wide area to find a trail.
– PHRASES **be cast in a —— mold** (of a person) be of the type specified: *he was cast in a cautious mold.* **cast adrift** see ADRIFT. **cast one's bread upon the waters** see BREAD. **cast one's eyes over** have a quick appraising look at: *he was invited to cast his eyes over the exhibition.* **cast light on** see LIGHT¹. **cast lots** see LOT. **cast one's mind back** think back to a

particular event or time: *he cast his mind back to the fatal evening.*
– PHRASAL VERBS **cast about** (or **around**) search far and wide (physically or mentally): *he is restlessly casting about for novelties.* [from a hunting term meaning '(of a hound) go in all directions looking for game or a lost scent.'] **cast aside** discard or reject: *they cast aside the principles of their youth.* **be cast away** be stranded after a shipwreck. **be cast down** feel depressed: *she was greatly cast down by abusive criticism of her novels.* **cast off** (or **cast something off**) **1** Knitting take the stitches off the needle by looping each over the next to finish the edge. **2** set a boat or ship free from its moorings: *the boatmen cast off and rowed downriver | Jack cast off our moorings.* ■ (**cast off**) (of a boat or ship) be set free from its moorings: *the ferry cast off and made a beeline for the pier.* **3** let loose a hunting hound or hawk. **4** Printing estimate the space that will be taken in print by manuscript copy. **cast someone off** exclude someone from a relationship. **cast on** (or **cast something on**) Knitting make the first row of a specified number of loops on the needle: *cast on and knit a few rows of stockinette stitch.* **cast something up 1** (of the sea) deposit something on the shore. **2** dated add up figures.
– ORIGIN Middle English: from Old Norse *kasta* 'to cast or throw.'

cast[2] ▶ **n.** the actors taking part in a play, movie, or other production: *he draws sensitive performances from his inexperienced cast.*
▶ **v.** (past and past participle **cast**) [with obj.] assign a part in a play, movie, or other production to (an actor): *he was cast as the Spanish dancer* | figurative *a campaign for good nutrition, in which red meat is cast as the enemy.* ■ allocate parts in (a play, movie, or other production): *assembling a great baseball team is as tricky as casting a play.*
– ORIGIN mid 17th cent.: a special use of CAST[1].

cas·ta·nets /ˌkastəˈnets/ ▶ **plural n.** small concave pieces of wood, ivory, or plastic, joined in pairs by a cord and clicked together by the fingers as a rhythmic accompaniment to Spanish dancing.
– ORIGIN early 17th cent.: from Spanish *castañeta,* diminutive of *castaña,* from Latin *castanea* 'chestnut.'

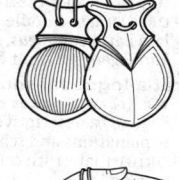

castanets

cast·a·way /ˈkastəˌwā/ ▶ **n.** a person who has been shipwrecked and stranded in an isolated place.

caste /kast/ ▶ **n.** each of the hereditary classes of Hindu society, distinguished by relative degrees of ritual purity or pollution and of social status: *members of the lower castes | a man of high caste.* ■ the system of dividing society into such classes. ■ any class or group of people who inherit exclusive privileges or are perceived as socially distinct: *those educated in private schools belong to a privileged caste.* ■ Entomology (in some social insects) a physically distinct individual with a particular function in the society.

> There are four basic classes, or varnas, in Hindu society: Brahman (priest), Kshatriya (warrior), Vaishya (merchant or farmer), and Shudra (laborer).

– ORIGIN mid 16th cent. (in the general sense 'race, breed'): from Spanish and Portuguese *casta* 'lineage, race, breed,' feminine of *casto* 'pure, unmixed,' from Latin *castus* 'chaste.'

caste Hin·du ▶ **n.** a Hindu who belongs to one of the four main castes.

caste·ism /ˈkastˌizəm/ ▶ **n. 1** adherence to a caste system.
2 prejudice or antagonism directed against someone of a different caste.
– DERIVATIVES **caste·ist adj.**

Cas·tel Gan·dol·fo /ˈkäsˌtel gänˈdôlfō, -ˈdälfō/ the summer residence of the pope, located on the edge of Lake Albano near Rome.

cas·tel·lan /ˈkastələn/ ▶ **n.** historical the governor of a castle.
– ORIGIN late Middle English: from Old Northern French *castelain,* from medieval Latin *castellanus,* from Latin *castellum* (see CASTLE).

cas·tel·lat·ed /ˈkastəˌlātid/ ▶ **adj.** having battlements: *a castellated tower.* ■ (of a nut or other mechanical part) having grooves or slots on its upper face.
– ORIGIN late 17th cent.: from medieval Latin *castellatus,* from Latin *castellum* (see CASTLE).

cas·tel·la·tions /ˌkastəˈlāsHənz/ ▶ **plural n.** defensive or decorative parapets with regularly spaced notches; battlements. ■ (**castellation**) the use or building of such parapets.
– ORIGIN early 19th cent.: based on medieval Latin *castellare* 'to build castles,' from *castellum* (see CASTLE).

caste mark ▶ **n.** a symbol on the forehead denoting membership of a particular Hindu caste.

cast·er /ˈkastər/ ▶ **n. 1** a person who casts something or a machine for casting something.
2 Fishing a fly pupa used as bait.
3 each of a set of small wheels, free to swivel in any direction, fixed to the legs or base of a heavy piece of furniture so that it can be moved easily. ■ the angular inclination of a steering pivot or kingpin, esp. that of the front wheel of a vehicle.
4 a small container with holes in the top, esp. one used for sprinkling sugar or pepper.

cas·ti·gate /ˈkastəˌgāt/ ▶ **v.** [with obj.] formal reprimand (someone) severely: *he was castigated for not setting a good example.*
– DERIVATIVES **cas·ti·ga·tion** /ˌkastəˈgāsHən/ **n., cas·ti·ga·tor** /-ˌgātər/ **n., cas·ti·ga·to·ry** /-gəˌtôrē/ **adj.**
– ORIGIN early 17th cent.: from Latin *castigare* 'reprove,' from *castus* 'pure, chaste.'

Cas·tile /kaˈstēl/ a region in central Spain, on the central plateau of the Iberian peninsula, formerly an independent Spanish kingdom.
– ORIGIN from French *Castille,* from Spanish *Castilla.*

Cas·tile soap ▶ **n.** fine, hard white or mottled soap made with olive oil and sodium hydroxide.
– ORIGIN late Middle English: named after CASTILE in Spain, where it was originally made.

Cas·til·ian /kəˈstilyən/ ▶ **n. 1** a native of Castile.
2 the dialect of Spanish spoken in Castile, which is standard Spanish.
▶ **adj.** of or relating to Castile, Castilians, or the Castilian form of Spanish.

Cas·til·la-La Man·cha /käˌstē(l)yä lä ˈmänCHə/ an autonomous region in central Spain; capital, Toledo.

Cas·til·la-Le·ón /käˌstē(l)yä läˈōn/ an autonomous region in northern Spain; capital, Valladolid.

cast·ing /ˈkastiNG/ ▶ **n.** an object made by pouring molten metal or other material into a mold.

cast·ing couch ▶ **n.** informal used in reference to the supposed practice whereby actors or actresses are awarded parts in movies, plays, or other productions in return for granting sexual favors to the casting director: *she was no stranger to the casting couch.*

cast·ing di·rec·tor ▶ **n.** the person responsible for assigning roles in a movie, play, or other production.

cast·ing vote ▶ **n.** an extra vote given by a chairperson to decide an issue when the votes on each side are equal.
– ORIGIN early 17th cent.: from an obsolete sense of *cast* 'turn the scale.'

cast i·ron ▶ **n. 1** a hard, relatively brittle alloy of iron and carbon that can be readily cast in a mold and contains a higher proportion of carbon than steel (typically 2.0–4.3 percent).
2 [as modifier] firm and unchangeable: *there are no cast-iron guarantees.*

Cas·tle /ˈkasəl/, Vernon Blythe (1887–1918), British dancer; born *Vernon Blythe.* With his wife **Irene** (1893–1969), he originated the one-step, the turkey trot, the Castle walk, and the hesitation waltz. He also served as an aviator 1916–18 during World War I.

cas·tle /ˈkasəl/ ▶ **n.** a large building or group of buildings fortified against attack with thick walls, battlements, towers, and in many cases a moat. ■ a magnificent and imposing mansion, esp. one that is the home or former home of a member of the nobility: [in names] *Castle Howard.* ■ Chess, informal old-fashioned term for ROOK[2].
▶ **v.** [no obj.] (often as noun **castling**) Chess make a special move (no more than once in a game by each player) in which the king is transferred from its original square two squares along the back rank toward the corner square of a rook, which is then transferred to the square passed over by the king. ■ [with obj.] move (the king) in this way.
– PHRASES **castles in the air** (or **in Spain**) visionary unattainable schemes; daydreams: *my father built castles in the air about owning a boat.*
– DERIVATIVES **cas·tled** /ˈkasəld/ **adj.** (archaic).
– ORIGIN late Old English: from Anglo-Norman French and Old Northern French *castel,* from Latin *castellum,* diminutive of *castrum* 'fort.'

cast net ▶ **n.** Fishing a net that is thrown out and immediately drawn in again, as opposed to one that is set up and left.

cast·off /ˈkastˌôf/ ▶ **adj.** no longer wanted; abandoned or discarded: *a pile of castoff clothes.*
▶ **n.** (usu. **castoffs**) something, esp. a garment, that is no longer wanted: *I'm not going out in her castoffs!*

Cas·tor /ˈkastər/ **1** Greek Mythology the twin brother of Pollux. See DIOSCURI.
2 Astronomy the second brightest star in the constellation Gemini, close to Pollux. It is a multiple star system, the three components visible in a moderate telescope being close binaries.

cas·tor /ˈkastər/ ▶ **n.** a reddish-brown oily substance secreted by beavers, used in medicine and perfumes.
– ORIGIN late Middle English (in the sense 'beaver'): from Old French or Latin, from Greek *kastōr.*

cas·tor bean ▶ **n.** the seed of the castor-oil plant. It contains a number of poisonous compounds, esp. ricin, as well as castor oil. ■ the castor-oil plant.

cas·tor oil ▶ **n.** a pale yellow oil obtained from castor beans, used as a purgative and a lubricant and in manufacturing oil-based products.
– ORIGIN mid 18th cent.: perhaps so named because it succeeded CASTOR in medicinal use.

cas·tor-oil plant ▶ **n.** an African shrub with lobed serrated leaves, yielding the seeds from which castor oil is obtained and widely naturalized in warm countries. ● *Ricinus communis,* family Euphorbiaceae.

cas·trate /ˈkasˌtrāt/ ▶ **v.** [with obj.] remove the testicles of (a male animal or man). ■ deprive of power, vitality, or vigor: (as adj. **castrated**) *the nation is a castrated giant, afraid to really punish subversives.*
▶ **n.** a man or male animal whose testicles have been removed.
– DERIVATIVES **cas·tra·tion** /kaˈstrāsHən/ **n., cas·tra·tor** /-ˌtrātər/ **n.**
– ORIGIN mid 16th cent.: from Latin *castrare.*

cas·tra·tion com·plex ▶ **n.** Psychoanalysis (in Freudian theory) an unconscious anxiety arising during psychosexual development, represented in males as a fear that the penis will be removed by the father in response to sexual interest in the mother, and in females as a compulsion to demonstrate that they have an adequate symbolic equivalent to the penis, whose absence is blamed on the mother.

cas·tra·to /kasˈträˌtō/ ▶ **n.** (pl. **castrati** /-tē/) historical a male singer castrated in boyhood so as to retain a soprano or alto voice. The practice of castration was banned in 1903.
– ORIGIN mid 18th cent.: from Italian, past participle of *castrare* (see CASTRATE).

Cas·tries /kasˈtrē, ˈkästrēs, -trēz/ the capital of the Caribbean island nation of St. Lucia, a seaport on the northwestern coast; pop. 14,000 (est. 2007).

Cas·tro /ˈkastrō/ the name of a family of Cuban political leaders, including: ■ **Fidel** (1927–), prime minister 1959–76 and president 1976–2008; full name *Fidel Alejandro Castro Ruz.* After overthrowing President Batista, he set up a communist regime that survived the abortive Bay of Pigs invasion, the Cuban Missile Crisis, and the collapse of the Soviet bloc. In 2008, he stood down in favor of his brother Raúl. ■ **Raúl** (1931–), president since 2008; full name *Raúl Modesto Castro Ruz.* He was Cuba's vice president 1976–2008, an office created for him by his brother Fidel.

Fidel Castro

Cas·tro·ism /ˈkastrōˌizəm/ ▶ **n.** the political principles or actions of Fidel Castro or his adherents or imitators.
– DERIVATIVES **Cas·tro·ist n. & adj., Cas·tro·ite** /-ˌīt/ **n. & adj.**

ca·su·al /ˈkaZHo͞oəl/ ▶ **adj. 1** relaxed and unconcerned: *she regarded his affairs with a*

PRONUNCIATION KEY ə *ago, up;* ər *over, fur;* a *hat;* ā *ate;* ä *car;* e *let;* ē *see;* i *fit;* ī *by;* NG *sing;* ō *go;* ô *law, for;* oi *toy;* o͝o *good;* o͞o *goo;* ou *out;* TH *thin;* T͟H *then;* ZH *vision*

C

casual indulgence | he tried to make his voice sound casual. ■ made or done without much thought or premeditation: *a casual remark.* ■ done or acting in a desultory way: *to the casual observer, rugby looks something like soccer.* ■ done or acting without sufficient care or thoroughness: *the casual way in which victims were treated.*
2 not regular or permanent, in particular: ■ employed or established on a temporary or irregular basis: *casual staff | casual jobs.* ■ (of a sexual relationship or encounter) occurring between people who are not regular or established sexual partners.
3 [attrib.] happening by chance; accidental: *he pretended it was a casual meeting.*
4 without formality of style or manner, in particular (of clothing) suitable for everyday wear rather than formal occasions: *a casual short-sleeved shirt | an ideal coat for casual occasions | the inn's casual atmosphere.*
▶ **n. 1** a person who does something irregularly: *a number of casuals became regular customers.* ■ a worker employed on an irregular or temporary basis.
2 (**casuals**) clothes or shoes suitable for everyday wear rather than formal occasions.
– DERIVATIVES **cas·u·al·ly adv., cas·u·al·ness n.**
– ORIGIN late Middle English (in sense 2 of the adjective and sense 3 of the adjective): from Old French *casuel* and Latin *casualis*, from *casus* 'fall' (compare with CASE[1]).

cas·u·al Fri·day ▶ **n.** Friday as a day when office workers are allowed to dress more casually than usual.

cas·u·al·ty /ˈkazH(o͞o)əltē/ ▶ **n.** (pl. **casualties**) a person killed or injured in a war or accident. ■ a person or thing badly affected by an event or situation: *the building industry has been one of the casualties of the recession.* ■ (chiefly in insurance) an accident, mishap, or disaster.
– ORIGIN late Middle English (in the sense 'chance, a chance occurrence'): from medieval Latin *casualitas*, from *casualis* (see CASUAL), on the pattern of words such as *penalty*.

cas·u·al wa·ter ▶ **n.** Golf water that has accumulated temporarily and does not constitute a recognized hazard of the course. A player may move a ball from casual water without penalty.

cas·u·a·ri·na /ˌkazHo͞oəˈrēnə/ ▶ **n.** a tree with slender, jointed, drooping twigs that resemble horsetails and bear tiny scalelike leaves. It is native to Australia and Southeast Asia, and is a valuable source of timber and firewood. ● Genus *Casuarina*, family Casuarinaceae.
– ORIGIN from modern Latin *casuarius* 'cassowary' (from the resemblance of the branches to the bird's feathers).

cas·u·ist /ˈkazHo͞oist/ ▶ **n.** a person who uses clever but unsound reasoning, esp. in relation to moral questions; a sophist. ■ a person who resolves moral problems by the application of theoretical rules to particular instances.
– DERIVATIVES **cas·u·is·tic** /ˌkazHo͞oˈistik/ **adj., cas·u·is·ti·cal** /ˌkazHo͞oˈistikəl/ **adj., cas·u·is·ti·cal·ly adv.**
– ORIGIN early 17th cent.: from French *casuiste*, from Spanish *casuista*, from Latin *casus* (see CASE[1]).

cas·u·ist·ry /ˈkazHo͞oəstrē/ ▶ **n.** the use of clever but unsound reasoning, esp. in relation to moral questions; sophistry. ■ the resolving of moral problems by the application of theoretical rules to particular instances.

ca·sus bel·li /ˈkäsəs ˈbelē, ˈkāsəs ˈbelˌī/ ▶ **n.** (pl. **same**) an act or situation provoking or justifying war.
– ORIGIN Latin, from *casus* (see CASE[1]) and *belli*, genitive of *bellum* 'war.'

CAT /kat/ ▶ **abbr.** ■ clear air turbulence. ■ computer-assisted (or -aided) testing. ■ Medicine computerized axial tomography: [as adj.] *a CAT scan.*

cat[1] /kat/ ▶ **n. 1** a small domesticated carnivorous mammal with soft fur, a short snout, and retractile claws. It is widely kept as a pet or for catching mice, and many breeds have been developed. ● *Felis catus*, family Felidae (the **cat family**); probably domesticated in ancient Egypt from the local race of wildcat, and held in great reverence there. The cat family also includes the ocelot, serval, margay, lynx, and the big cats. ■ a wild animal of the cat family: *a marbled cat.* See also BIG CAT. ■ used in names of catlike animals of other families, e.g., **ring-tailed cat.** ■ historical short for CAT-O'-NINE-TAILS. ■ short for CATFISH. ■ short for CATHEAD. ■ short for CATBOAT.
2 informal (particularly among jazz enthusiasts) a person, esp. a man.
▶ **v.** (**cats, catting, catted**) [with obj.] Nautical raise (an anchor) from the surface of the water to the cathead.
– PHRASES **cat and mouse** a series of cunning maneuvers designed to thwart an opponent: *their elite fighters are* ***playing cat and mouse*** *with US troops.* **a cat may look at a king** proverb even a person of low status or importance has rights. **has the cat got your tongue?** said to someone who, when expected to speak, remains silent. **let the cat out of the bag** informal reveal a secret carelessly or by mistake. **like a cat on a hot tin roof** informal very agitated or anxious. **like herding cats** informal used to refer to a difficult or impossible task, typically an attempt to organize a group of people: *controlling the members of this expedition is like herding cats.* **look like something the cat dragged in** (or **brought in**) informal (of a person) look very dirty or disheveled. **when** (or **while**) **the cat's away, the mice will play** proverb people will naturally take advantage of the absence of someone in authority to do as they like.
– ORIGIN Old English *catt, catte*, of Germanic origin; related to Dutch *kat* and German *Katze*; reinforced in Middle English by forms from late Latin *cattus*.

cat[2] ▶ **n.** short for CATALYTIC CONVERTER.

cat[3] ▶ **n.** short for CATAMARAN.

cata- (also **cat-**) ▶ **prefix 1** down; downward: *catadromous | cataract.*
2 wrongly; badly: *catachresis | catastrophe.*
3 completely; thoroughly: *catechize.*
4 against: *catapult.*
– ORIGIN from Greek *kata* 'down.'

ca·tab·o·lism /kəˈtabəˌlizəm/ ▶ **n.** Biology the breakdown of complex molecules in living organisms to form simpler ones, together with the release of energy; destructive metabolism.
– DERIVATIVES **cat·a·bol·ic** /ˌkatəˈbälik/ **adj., ca·tab·o·lize** /-ˌlīz/ **v.**
– ORIGIN late 19th cent.: from Greek *katabolē* 'throwing down,' from *kata-* 'down' + *ballein* 'to throw.'

ca·tab·o·lite /kəˈtabəˌlīt/ ▶ **n.** Biochemistry a product of catabolism.

cat·a·chre·sis /ˌkatəˈkrēsis/ ▶ **n.** (pl. **catachreses** /-sēz/) the use of a word in a way that is not correct, for example, the use of *mitigate* for *militate.*
– DERIVATIVES **cat·a·chres·tic** /-ˈkrestik/ **adj.**
– ORIGIN mid 16th cent.: from Latin, from Greek *katakhrēsis*, from *katakhrēsthai* 'misuse,' from *kata-* 'down' (expressing the sense 'wrongly') + *khrēsthai* 'use.'

cat·a·clysm /ˈkatəˌklizəm/ ▶ **n.** a large-scale and violent event in the natural world. ■ a sudden violent upheaval, esp. in a political or social context: *the cataclysm of the First World War.*
– ORIGIN early 17th cent. (originally denoting the biblical Flood described in Genesis): from French *cataclysme*, via Latin from Greek *kataklusmos* 'deluge,' from *kata-* 'down' + *kluzein* 'to wash.'

cat·a·clys·mic /ˌkatəˈklizmik/ ▶ **adj.** relating to or denoting a violent natural event. ■ informal denoting something unpleasant or unsuccessful on an enormous scale: *the concert was a cataclysmic failure.*
– DERIVATIVES **cat·a·clys·mi·cal·ly** /-mik(ə)lē/ **adv.**

cat·a·comb /ˈkatəˌkōm/ ▶ **n.** (usu. **catacombs**) an underground cemetery consisting of a subterranean gallery with recesses for tombs, as constructed by the ancient Romans. ■ an underground construction resembling or compared to such a cemetery.
– ORIGIN Old English, from late Latin *catacumbas*, the name of the subterranean cemetery of St. Sebastian near Rome.

cat·a·di·op·tric /ˌkatəˌdīˈäptrik/ ▶ **adj.** Optics denoting an optical system that involves both the reflecting and refracting of light, in order to reduce aberration.

ca·tad·ro·mous /kəˈtadrəməs/ ▶ **adj.** Zoology (of a fish such as the eel) migrating down rivers to the sea to spawn. The opposite of ANADROMOUS.
– ORIGIN late 19th cent.: from CATA- 'down' + Greek *dromos* 'running,' on the pattern of *anadromous.*

cat·a·falque /ˈkatəˌfô(l)k, -ˌfalk/ ▶ **n.** a decorated wooden framework supporting the coffin of a distinguished person during a funeral or while lying in state.
– ORIGIN mid 17th cent.: from French, from Italian *catafalco*, of unknown origin. Compare with SCAFFOLD.

Cat·a·lan /ˈkatlˌan, ˈkatl-ən/ ▶ **n. 1** a native of Catalonia.
2 a Romance language closely related to Castilian Spanish and Provençal, widely spoken in Catalonia (where it has official status alongside Castilian Spanish) and in Andorra, the Balearic Islands, and parts of southern France.
▶ **adj.** of or relating to Catalonia, its people, or its language.
– ORIGIN from French, from Spanish *catalán*, related to Catalan *català* 'Catalan,' *Catalunya* 'Catalonia.'

cat·a·lase /ˈkatlˌās, -ˌāz/ ▶ **n.** Biochemistry an enzyme that catalyzes the reduction of hydrogen peroxide.
– ORIGIN early 20th cent.: from CATALYSIS + -ASE.

cat·a·lec·tic /ˌkatlˈektik/ Prosody ▶ **adj.** (of a metrical line of verse) lacking one syllable in the last foot.
▶ **n.** a line lacking a syllable in the last foot.
– ORIGIN late 16th cent.: from late Latin *catalecticus*, from Greek *katalēktikos*, from *katalēgein* 'leave off.'

cat·a·lep·sy /ˈkatlˌepsē/ ▶ **n.** a medical condition characterized by a trance or seizure with a loss of sensation and consciousness accompanied by rigidity of the body.
– DERIVATIVES **cat·a·lep·tic** /ˌkatlˈeptik/ **adj. & n.**
– ORIGIN late Middle English: from French *catalepsie* or late Latin *catalepsia*, from Greek *katalēpsis*, from *katalambanein* 'seize upon.'

Cat·a·li·na /ˌkatlˈēnə/ another name for SANTA CATALINA.

cat·a·log /ˈkatlˌôg, -ˌäg/ (also **catalogue**) ▶ **n.** a complete list of items, typically one in alphabetical or other systematic order, in particular: ■ a list of all the books or resources in a library. ■ a publication containing details and often photographs of items for sale, esp. one produced by a mail-order company. ■ a descriptive list of works of art in an exhibition or collection giving detailed comments and explanations. ■ a list of courses offered by a university or college. ■ [in sing.] a series of unfortunate or bad things: *his life was a catalog of dismal failures.*
▶ **v.** (**catalogs, cataloged, cataloging**; also **catalogues, catalogued, cataloguing**) [with obj.] make a systematic list of (items of the same type). ■ enter (an item) in such a list: *the picture was withdrawn before being cataloged.* ■ list (similar situations, qualities, or events) in succession: *the report catalogs dangerous work practices in the company.*
– DERIVATIVES **cat·a·log·er** (also **cataloguer**) **n.**
– ORIGIN late Middle English: via Old French from late Latin *catalogus*, from Greek *katalogos*, from *katalegein* 'pick out or enroll.'

cat·a·logue rai·son·né /katlˌôg ˌrāzəˈnā, -ˌäg/ ▶ **n.** (pl. **catalogues raisonnés** /ˈkatlˌôg(z) ˌrāzəˈnā, -ˌäg(z)/) a descriptive catalog of works of art with explanations and scholarly comments.
– ORIGIN late 18th cent.: French, literally 'explained catalog.'

Cat·a·lo·ni·a /ˌkatlˈōnēə/ an autonomous region in northeastern Spain; capital, Barcelona. The region has a strong separatist tradition; the normal language for everyday purposes is Catalan, which has also won acceptance in recent years for various official purposes. Catalan name **Catalunya**; Spanish name **Cataluña**.

ca·tal·pa /kəˈtalpə/ ▶ **n.** a tree with large heart-shaped leaves, clusters of trumpet-shaped flowers, and long, slender beanlike seedpods, native to North America and eastern Asia and cultivated as an ornamental. ● Genus *Catalpa*, family Bignoniaceae: several species, including the **southern** (or **common**) **catalpa** (*C. bignonioides*).
– ORIGIN from Creek.

cat·a·lu·fa /ˌkatlˈo͞ofə/ ▶ **n.** another term for BIGEYE (sense 2).
– ORIGIN from Spanish.

ca·tal·y·sis /kəˈtaləsis/ ▶ **n.** Chemistry & Biochemistry the acceleration of a chemical reaction by a catalyst.
– ORIGIN mid 19th cent.: from modern Latin, from Greek *katalusis*, from *kataluein* 'dissolve,' from *kata-* 'down' + *luein* 'loosen.'

cat·a·lyst /ˈkatl-ist/ ▶ **n.** a substance that increases the rate of a chemical reaction without itself undergoing any permanent chemical change. ■ a person or thing that precipitates an event: *the governor's speech acted as a catalyst for debate.*
– ORIGIN early 20th cent.: from CATALYSIS, on the pattern of *analyst.*

cat·a·lyt·ic /ˌkatlˈitik/ ▶ **adj.** relating to or involving the action of a catalyst.
– DERIVATIVES **cat·a·lyt·i·cal·ly** /-ik(ə)lē/ **adv.**
– ORIGIN mid 19th cent.: from CATALYSIS, on the pattern of pairs such as *analysis, analytic.*

cat·a·lyt·ic con·vert·er ▶ **n.** a device incorporated in the exhaust system of a motor vehicle, containing a catalyst for converting pollutant gases into less harmful ones.

cat·a·lyze /ˈkatlˌīz/ (Brit. **catalyse**) ▶ **v.** [with obj.] cause or accelerate (a reaction) by acting as a catalyst. ■ cause (an action or process) to begin: *the tragic event helped to catalyze the already growing popular anger.*
– ORIGIN late 19th cent.: from CATALYSIS, on the pattern of *analyze.*

cat·a·ma·ran /ˌkatəməˈran, ˈkatəməˌran/ ▶ **n.** a yacht or other boat with twin hulls in parallel.
– ORIGIN early 17th cent.: from Tamil *kaṭṭumaram*, literally 'tied wood.'

catamaran

Cat·a·mar·ca /ˌkätäˈmärkä, ˌkatəˈmärkə/ a mining and commercial town in northwestern Argentina, the capital of Catamarca province; pop. 153,200 (est. 2005).

cat·a·mite /ˈkatəˌmīt/ ▶ **n.** archaic a boy kept for homosexual practices.
– ORIGIN late 16th cent.: from Latin *catamitus*, via Etruscan from Greek *Ganumēdēs* (see **GANYMEDE**).

cat·a·mount /ˈkatəˌmount/ (also **catamountain** /-ˌmountən/) ▶ **n.** a medium-sized or large wild cat, esp. a cougar.
– ORIGIN late Middle English (as *catamountain*): from the phrase *cat of the mountain*.

Ca·ta·nia /kəˈtänyə, -ˈtän-, -ˈtänēə/ a seaport on the east coast of Sicily, in southern Italy, at the foot of Mount Etna; pop. 296,469 (2008).

Ca·tan·za·ro /ˌkätän(d)ˈzärō/ the chief town of the Calabria region of southern Italy; pop. 93,519 (2008).

cat·a·phat·ic /ˌkatəˈfatik/ ▶ **adj.** Theology (of knowledge of God) obtained through affirmation. The opposite of **APOPHATIC**.
– ORIGIN mid 19th cent.: from Greek *kataphatikos* 'affirmative,' from *kataphasis* 'affirmation,' from *kata-* (as an intensifier) + *phanai* 'speak.'

cat·a·phor /ˈkatəfər, -ˌfôr/ ▶ **n.** Grammar a word or phrase that refers to or stands for a later word or phrase (e.g., in *when they saw Ruth, the men looked slightly abashed*, the word *they* is used as a cataphor for *the men*).
– ORIGIN late 20th cent.: back-formation from **CATAPHORA**.

ca·taph·o·ra /kəˈtafərə/ ▶ **n.** Grammar the use of a word or phrase that refers to or stands for a later word or phrase (e.g., the pronoun *he* in *he may be 37, but Jeff behaves like a teenager*). Compare with **ANAPHORA**.
– DERIVATIVES **cat·a·phor·ic** /ˌkatəˈfôrik/ **adj.**, **cat·a·phor·i·cal·ly** /ˌkatəˈfôrik(ə)lē/ **adv.**
– ORIGIN 1970s: from **CATA-** on the pattern of *anaphora*.

cat·a·phract /ˈkatəˌfrakt/ ▶ **n.** archaic a soldier in full armor.
– ORIGIN late 17th cent.: via Latin from Greek *kataphraktos* 'clothed in full armor.'

cat·a·plasm /ˈkatəˌplazəm/ ▶ **n.** another term for **POULTICE**.

cat·a·plex·y /ˈkatəˌpleksē/ ▶ **n.** a medical condition in which strong emotion or laughter causes a person to suffer sudden physical collapse though remaining conscious.
– DERIVATIVES **cat·a·plec·tic** /ˌkatəˈplektik/ **adj.**
– ORIGIN late 19th cent.: from Greek *kataplēxis* 'stupefaction,' from *kataplessein*, from *kata-* 'down' + *plēssein* 'strike.'

cat·a·pult /ˈkatəˌpəlt, -ˌpo͝olt/ ▶ **n.** a device in which accumulated tension is suddenly released to hurl an object some distance, in particular: ■ historical a military machine worked by a lever and ropes for hurling large stones or other missiles. ■ a mechanical device for launching a glider or other aircraft, esp. from the deck of a ship. ■ chiefly Brit. a slingshot.
▶ **v.** [with obj.] hurl or launch (something) in a specified direction with or as if with a catapult: *the plane was refueled and catapulted back into the air again* | *the explosion catapulted the car 30 yards along the road* | figurative *their music catapulted them to the top of the charts*. ■ [no obj.] move suddenly or at great speed as though hurled by a catapult: *the horse catapulted away from the fence*.
– ORIGIN late 16th cent.: from French *catapulte* or Latin *catapulta*, from Greek *katapeltēs*, from *kata-* 'down' + *pallein* 'hurl.'

cat·a·ract /ˈkatəˌrakt/ ▶ **n. 1** a large waterfall. ■ a sudden rush of water; a downpour: *the rain enveloped us in a deafening cataract*.
2 a medical condition in which the lens of the eye becomes progressively opaque, resulting in blurred vision: *she had cataracts in both eyes*.
– ORIGIN late Middle English: from Latin *cataracta* 'waterfall, floodgate,' also 'portcullis' (medical sense 2 probably being a figurative use of this), from Greek *kataraktēs* 'down-rushing,' from *katarassein*, from *kata-* 'down' + *arassein* 'strike, smash.'

ca·tarrh /kəˈtär/ ▶ **n.** excessive discharge or buildup of mucus in the nose or throat, associated with inflammation of the mucous membrane.
– DERIVATIVES **ca·tarrh·al** /kəˈtärəl/ **adj.**
– ORIGIN early 16th cent.: from French *catarrhe*, from late Latin *catarrhus*, from Greek *katarrhous*, from *katarrhein* 'flow down,' from *kata-* 'down' + *rhein* 'flow.'

cat·ar·rhine /ˈkatəˌrīn/ Zoology ▶ **adj.** of or relating to primates of a group that comprises the Old World monkeys, gibbons, great apes, and humans. They are distinguished by having nostrils that are close together and directed downward. Compare with **PLATYRRHINE**.
▶ **n.** a catarrhine primate. ● Infraorder Catarrhini, order Primates: four families.
– ORIGIN mid 19th cent.: from **CATA-** 'down' + Greek *rhis, rhin-* 'nose.'

ca·tas·tro·phe /kəˈtastrəfē/ ▶ **n.** an event causing great and often sudden damage or suffering; a disaster: *a national economic catastrophe* | *leading the world to catastrophe*. ■ the denouement of a drama, esp. a classical tragedy.
– ORIGIN mid 16th cent. (in the sense 'denouement'): from Latin *catastropha*, from Greek *katastrophē* 'overturning, sudden turn,' from *kata-* 'down' + *strophē* 'turning' (from *strephein* 'to turn').

ca·tas·tro·phe the·o·ry ▶ **n.** a branch of mathematics concerned with systems displaying abrupt discontinuous change.

cat·a·stroph·ic /ˌkatəˈsträfik/ ▶ **adj. 1** involving or causing sudden great damage or suffering: *a catastrophic earthquake*. ■ involving a sudden and large-scale alteration in the state of something: *the body undergoes catastrophic collapse toward the state of a black hole*. ■ of or relating to geological catastrophism.
2 extremely unfortunate or unsuccessful: *catastrophic mismanagement of the economy*.
– DERIVATIVES **cat·a·stroph·i·cal·ly** /-ik(ə)lē/ **adv.**

ca·tas·tro·phism /kəˈtastrəˌfizəm/ ▶ **n.** Geology the theory that changes in the earth's crust during geological history have resulted chiefly from sudden violent and unusual events. Often contrasted with **UNIFORMITARIANISM**.
– DERIVATIVES **ca·tas·tro·phist n. & adj.**

cat·a·to·ni·a /ˌkatəˈtōnēə/ ▶ **n.** Psychiatry abnormality of movement and behavior arising from a disturbed mental state (typically schizophrenia). It may involve repetitive or purposeless overactivity, or catalepsy, resistance to passive movement, and negativism. ■ informal a state of immobility and stupor.
– ORIGIN late 19th cent.: from **CATA-** 'badly' + Greek *tonos* 'tone or tension.'

cat·a·ton·ic /ˌkatəˈtänik/ ▶ **adj.** Psychiatry of, relating to, or characterized by catatonia: *catatonic schizophrenia*. ■ informal of or in an immobile or unresponsive stupor.

Ca·taw·ba /kəˈtôbə, -ˈtäbə/ ▶ **n.** a North American variety of grape. ■ a white wine made from this grape.
– ORIGIN named after the **CATAWBA RIVER**.

Ca·taw·ba Riv·er /kəˈtôbə/ a river that flows for 300 miles (480 km) from the Blue Ridge Mountains in North Carolina across much of South Carolina.

cat·bird /ˈkatˌbərd/ ▶ **n. 1** a long-tailed American songbird of the mockingbird family, with mainly dark gray or black plumage and catlike calls. ● Two genera and species, family Mimidae, in particular the **gray catbird** (*Dumetella carolinensis*) of North America.
2 a thickset Australasian bird of the bowerbird family, typically with a loud call like a yowling cat. It does not generally construct bowers. ● Genus *Ailuroedus* (and *Scenopoeetes*), family Ptilonorhynchidae: several species, in particular the **green catbird** (*A. crassirostris*).
– PHRASES **in the catbird seat** informal in a superior or advantageous position. [said to be an allusion to a baseball player in the fortunate position of having no strikes and therefore three balls still to play (a reference made in James Thurber's short story "The Catbird Seat").]

cat·boat /ˈkatˌbōt/ ▶ **n.** a sailboat with a single mast placed well forward and carrying only one sail.
– ORIGIN mid 19th cent.: perhaps from *cat* (denoting a type of merchant ship formerly used in the coal and timber trades in northeastern England) + **BOAT**.

cat·bri·er /ˈkatˌbrī(ə)r/ (also **catbriar**) ▶ **n.** another term for **GREENBRIER**.

cat bur·glar ▶ **n.** a thief who enters a building by climbing to an upper story.

cat·call /ˈkatˌkôl/ ▶ **n.** a shrill whistle or shout of disapproval, typically one made at a public meeting or performance. ■ a loud whistle or a comment of a sexual nature made by a man to a passing woman.
▶ **v.** [no obj.] make such a whistle, shout, or comment: *they were fired for catcalling at women*.
– ORIGIN mid 17th cent.: from **CAT**[1] + **CALL**, originally denoting a kind of whistle or squeaking instrument used to express disapproval at a theater.

C

catch /kacH, kecH/ ▶ **v.** (past and past participle **caught** /kôt/) [with obj.] **1** intercept and hold (something that has been thrown, propelled, or dropped): *she threw the bottle into the air and caught it again*. ■ intercept the fall of (someone). ■ seize or take hold of: *he* ***caught hold of*** *her arm as she tried to push past him*. ■ [no obj.] (**catch at**) grasp or try to grasp: *his hands caught at her arms as she tried to turn away*.
2 capture (a person or animal that tries or would try to escape): *we hadn't caught a single rabbit*. ■ [no obj.] (of an object) accidentally become entangled or trapped in something: *the charm bracelet always caught on her clothing*. ■ (of a person) have (a part of one's body or clothing) become entangled or trapped in something: *she caught her foot in the bedspread* | figurative *companies face increased risks of being caught in a downward spiral*. ■ fix or fasten in place: *her hair was caught back in a scrunchie*.
3 reach in time and board (a train, bus, or aircraft): *they caught the 12:15 from Chicago*. ■ reach or be in a place in time to see (a person, performance, program, etc.): *she was hurrying downstairs to catch the news*. ■ come upon (someone) unexpectedly: *unexpected snow* ***caught us by surprise***. ■ (**be caught in**) (of a person) unexpectedly find oneself in (an unwelcome situation): *my sister was caught in a thunderstorm*. ■ (**catch it**) informal be punished or told off. ■ surprise (someone) in an incriminating situation or in the act of doing something wrong: *he was caught with bomb-making equipment in his home*.
4 engage (a person's interest or imagination). ■ perceive fleetingly: *she* ***caught a glimpse of*** *herself in the mirror*. ■ hear or understand (something said), esp. with effort: *he bellowed something Jess couldn't catch*. ■ succeed in evoking or representing: *the program caught something of the flavor of Minoan culture*.
5 [with obj.] strike (someone) on a part of the body: *Ben caught him on the chin with an uppercut*. ■ accidentally strike (a part of one's body) against something: *she fell and caught her head on the corner of the hearth*.
6 contract (an illness) through infection or contagion.
7 [no obj.] become ignited, due to contact with flame, and start burning: *the rafters have caught*. ■ (of an engine) fire and start running.
▶ **n. 1** an act of catching something, typically a ball. ■ an amount of fish caught: *a record catch of 6.9 billion pounds of fish*. ■ [in sing.] informal a person considered attractive, successful, or prestigious and so desirable as a partner or spouse: *I mistakenly thought he would be a good catch*.
2 a device for securing something such as a door, window, or box: *the window catch was rusty*.
3 a hidden problem or disadvantage in an apparently ideal situation: *there's a catch in it somewhere*.
4 [in sing.] an unevenness in a person's voice caused by emotion: *there was a catch in Anne's voice*.
5 Music a round, typically one with words arranged to produce a humorous effect.
– PHRASES **catch someone napping** see **NAP**[1]. **be caught short** see **SHORT**. **catch at straws** see **STRAW**. **catch one's breath 1** draw one's breath in sharply as a reaction to an emotion. **2** recover one's breath after exertion. **catch one's death (of cold)** see **DEATH**. **catch someone's eye 1** be noticed by someone: *a vase on a side table caught his eye*. **2** attract someone's attention by making eye contact: *I caught Rhoda's eye and gave her a friendly wave*. **catch fire** become ignited and burn. **catch someone in the act** see **ACT**. **catch the light** shine or glint in the light. **catch sight of** suddenly notice; glimpse. **you wouldn't catch —— doing something** informal used to indicate that there is no possibility of the person mentioned doing what is specified: *you wouldn't catch me walking back to the house alone at night*.
– PHRASAL VERBS **catch on** informal **1** (of a practice or fashion) become popular: *his music never caught*

C

on in the South. **2** understand what is meant or how to do something: *I caught on to what it was the guy was saying.* **catch up** succeed in reaching a person who is ahead of one. ■ do work or other tasks that one should have done earlier: *he normally used the afternoons to catch up on paperwork.* **catch up with 1** succeed in reaching a person who is ahead of one: *you go with Stasia and Katie, and I'll catch up with you.* **2** talk to (someone) whom one has not seen for some time in order to find out what he or she has been doing in the interim: *a chance to catch up with old friends.* **3** begin to have a damaging effect on: *the physical exertions began to catch up with Sue.* **be/get caught up in** become involved in (something that one had not intended to become involved in): *he had no desire to be caught up in political activities.*
– DERIVATIVES **catch·a·ble** adj.
– ORIGIN Middle English (also in the sense 'chase'): from Anglo-Norman French and Old Northern French *cachier*, variant of Old French *chacier*, based on Latin *captare* 'try to catch,' from *capere* 'take.'

catch-22 ▶ n. a dilemma or difficult circumstance from which there is no escape because of mutually conflicting or dependent conditions: [as modifier] *a catch-22 situation.*
– ORIGIN 1970s: title of a novel by Joseph Heller (1961), in which the main character feigns madness in order to avoid dangerous combat missions, but his desire to avoid them is taken to prove his sanity.

catch-all ▶ n. [usu. as modifier] a term or category that includes a variety of different possibilities: *the stigmatizing catch-all term "schizophrenia."*

catch-as-catch-can ▶ n. archaic wrestling in which all holds are permitted.
▶ adj. [attrib.] using whatever methods or materials are available: *our catch-as-catch-can repair of fences.*

catch·er /ˈkaCHər, ˈkeCH-/ ▶ n. a person or thing that catches something. ■ Baseball a fielder positioned behind home plate to catch pitches not hit by the batter and to execute other defensive plays.

catch·fly /ˈkaCH,flī, ˈkeCH-/ ▶ n. (pl. **catchflies**) a campion or similar plant of the pink family, with a sticky stem. ● *Silene, Lychnis*, and other genera, family Caryophyllaceae.

catch·ing /ˈkaCHiNG, ˈkeCH-/ ▶ adj. [predic.] (of a disease) infectious: *Huntington's chorea isn't catching.* ■ (of a person's emotion or mood) likely to spread to other people: *her enthusiasm is catching.*

catch·light /ˈkaCH,līt, ˈkeCH-/ ▶ n. a gleam of reflected light in the eye of a person or animal in a photograph.

catch·line /ˈkaCH,līn, ˈkeCH-/ ▶ n. Printing a short, eye-catching line of type, typically one at the top of a page such as a running head. ■ Brit. an advertising slogan.

catch·ment /ˈkaCHmənt, ˈkeCH-/ ▶ n. **1** the action of collecting water, esp. the collection of rainfall over a natural drainage area.
2 short for CATCHMENT AREA.

catch·ment ar·e·a ▶ n. **1** the area from which rainfall flows into a river, lake, or reservoir.
2 chiefly Brit. the area of a city, town, etc., from which a hospital's patients or school's students are drawn.

catch·pen·ny /ˈkaCH,penē, ˈkeCH-/ ▶ adj. [attrib.] having a cheap superficial attractiveness designed to encourage quick sales.

catch·phrase /ˈkaCH,frāz, ˈkeCH-/ ▶ n. a well-known sentence or phrase, typically one that is associated with a particular famous person. ■ an advertising slogan.

catch-up (also **catchup**) ▶ n. informal an act of catching someone up in a particular activity.
– PHRASES **play catch-up 1** fall behind continually with work or financial matters: *I'm always playing catch-up with my homework.* **2** try to equal a competitor in a sport or game.

catch·weight /ˈkaCH,wāt, ˈkeCH-/ ▶ n. [usu. as modifier] chiefly historical unrestricted weight in a wrestling match or other sporting contest: *a catchweight contest.*

catch·word /ˈkaCH,wərd, ˈkeCH-/ ▶ n. **1** a briefly popular or fashionable word or phrase used to encapsulate a particular concept: *"motivation" is a great catchword.*
2 a word printed or placed so as to attract attention. ■ Printing, chiefly historical the first word of a page given at the foot of the previous one.

catch·y /ˈkaCHē, ˈkeCHē/ ▶ adj. (**catchier, catchiest**) (of a tune or phrase) instantly appealing and memorable: *a catchy recruiting slogan.*
– DERIVATIVES **catch·i·ly** /ˈkaCHəlē, ˈkeCH-/ adv., **catch·i·ness** n.

cate /kāt/ ▶ n. (usu. **cates**) archaic a choice food; a delicacy.
– ORIGIN late Middle English (in the sense 'selling, a bargain'): from obsolete *acate* 'purchasing, things purchased,' from Old French *acat, achat*, from *acater, achater* 'buy,' based on Latin *captare* 'seize,' from *capere* 'take.'

cat·e·che·sis /ˌkatəˈkēsis/ ▶ n. religious instruction given to a person in preparation for Christian baptism or confirmation, typically using a catechism.
– ORIGIN mid 18th cent.: via ecclesiastical Latin from Greek *katēkhēsis* 'oral instruction.'

cat·e·chet·i·cal /ˌkatəˈketikəl/ ▶ adj. of or relating to religious instruction given to a person in preparation for Christian baptism or confirmation. ■ of or relating to religious teaching by means of questions and answers.
– DERIVATIVES **cat·e·chet·ic** adj., **cat·e·chet·i·cal·ly** /-ik(ə)lē/ adv.
– ORIGIN early 17th cent.: from ecclesiastical Greek *katēkhētikos*, from *katēkhētēs* 'catechist,' from *katēkhein* 'instruct orally' (see CATECHIZE).

cat·e·chet·ics /ˌkatəˈketiks/ ▶ plural n. [treated as sing.] the branch of theology that deals with the instruction given to Christians before baptism or confirmation. ■ religious teaching in general, typically that given to children in the Roman Catholic Church.

cat·e·chin /ˈkatə,kin/ ▶ n. Chemistry a crystalline compound that is the major constituent of catechu. ● A phenol; chem. formula: $C_{15}H_{14}O_6$; several isomers.
– ORIGIN mid 19th cent.: from CATECHU + -IN[1].

cat·e·chism /ˈkatə,kizəm/ ▶ n. a summary of the principles of Christian religion in the form of questions and answers, used for the instruction of Christians. ■ a series of fixed questions, answers, or precepts used for instruction in other situations.
– DERIVATIVES **cat·e·chis·mal** /ˌkatəˈkizməl/ adj.
– ORIGIN early 16th cent.: from ecclesiastical Latin *catechismus*, from ecclesiastical Greek, from *katēkhizein* (see CATECHIZE).

cat·e·chist /ˈkatəkist/ ▶ n. a teacher of the principles of Christian religion, esp. one using a catechism.
– ORIGIN mid 16th cent.: via ecclesiastical Latin from ecclesiastical Greek *katēkhistēs*, from *katēkhein* 'instruct orally.'

cat·e·chize /ˈkatə,kīz/ ▶ v. [with obj.] instruct (someone) in the principles of Christian religion by means of question and answer, typically by using a catechism. ■ put questions to or interrogate (someone).
– DERIVATIVES **cat·e·chiz·er** n.
– ORIGIN late Middle English: via late Latin from ecclesiastical Greek *katēkhizein*, from *katēkhein* 'instruct orally, make hear.'

cat·e·chol /ˈkatə,kôl, -,kōl/ ▶ n. Chemistry a crystalline compound obtained by distilling catechu. ● Alternative name: **benzene-1,2-diol**; chem. formula: $C_6H_4(OH)_2$.
– ORIGIN late 19th cent.: from CATECHU + -OL.

cat·e·chol·a·mine /katəˈkōlə,mēn, -ˈkôlə-/ ▶ n. Biochemistry any of a class of aromatic amines that includes a number of neurotransmitters such as epinephrine and dopamine.

cat·e·chu /ˈkatə,CHoo, -,SHoo/ (also **cachou**) ▶ n. a vegetable extract containing tannin, esp. one (also called CUTCH) obtained from the heartwood of an Indian acacia tree, used chiefly for tanning and dyeing. ● The chief source of this is *Acacia catechu*, family Leguminosae.
– ORIGIN late 17th cent.: modern Latin, from Malay *kacu*. Compare with CACHOU.

cat·e·chu·men /ˌkatəˈkyoomən/ ▶ n. a Christian convert under instruction before baptism. ■ a young Christian preparing for confirmation.
– ORIGIN late Middle English: via ecclesiastical Latin from Greek *katēkhoumenos* 'being instructed,' present participle of *katēkhein* 'instruct orally' (see CATECHIZE).

cat·e·go·ri·cal /ˌkatəˈgôrikəl/ ▶ adj. unambiguously explicit and direct: *a categorical assurance.*
– DERIVATIVES **cat·e·gor·ic** adj., **cat·e·gor·i·cal·ly** /-ik(ə)lē/ adv.
– ORIGIN late 16th cent.: from late Latin *categoricus* (from Greek *katēgorikos*, from *katēgoria* 'statement': see CATEGORY) + -AL.

cat·e·go·ri·cal im·per·a·tive ▶ n. Philosophy (in Kantian ethics) an unconditional moral obligation that is binding in all circumstances and is not dependent on a person's inclination or purpose.

cat·e·go·rize /ˈkatəgə,rīz/ ▶ v. [with obj.] place in a particular class or group: *odors have been categorized into only seven basic groups.*
– DERIVATIVES **cat·e·go·ri·za·tion** /ˌkatəgərəˈzāSHən/ n.

cat·e·go·ry /ˈkatə,gôrē/ ▶ n. (pl. **categories**) **1** a class or division of people or things regarded as having particular shared characteristics: *five categories of intelligence.*
2 Philosophy one of a possibly exhaustive set of classes among which all things might be distributed. ■ one of the a priori conceptions applied by the mind to sense impressions.
– DERIVATIVES **cat·e·go·ri·al** /ˌkatəˈgôrēəl/ adj.
– ORIGIN late Middle English (sense 2): from French *catégorie* or late Latin *categoria*, from Greek *katēgoria* 'statement, accusation,' from *katēgoros* 'accuser.'

cat·e·go·ry kill·er ▶ n. a large store, typically one of a chain, that specializes in a particular type of discounted merchandise and becomes the dominant retailer in that category.

cat·e·go·ry mis·take (also **category error**) ▶ n. Logic the error of assigning to something a quality or action that can properly be assigned to things only of another category, for example, treating abstract concepts as though they had a physical location.

ca·te·na /kəˈtēnə/ ▶ n. (pl. **catenae** /-nē, -,nī/ or **catenas**) technical a connected series or chain. ■ a connected series of texts written by early Christian theologians.
– ORIGIN mid 17th cent.: from Latin, 'chain,' originally in *catena patrum* 'chain of the (Church) Fathers.'

cat·e·nar·y /ˈkatə,nerē, ˈkatn,erē/ ▶ n. (pl. **catenaries**) a curve formed by a wire, rope, or chain hanging freely from two points that are not in the same vertical line: [as modifier] *a catenary wire.* ■ a wire, rope, or chain forming such a curve.
– ORIGIN mid 18th cent.: from Latin *catenarius* 'relating to a chain,' from *catena* 'chain.'

cat·e·nat·ed /ˈkatə,nātid, ˈkatn,ātid/ ▶ adj. technical connected in a chain or series: *catenated molecules.*
– DERIVATIVES **cat·e·na·tion** /ˌkatəˈnāSHən, ˌkatnˈāSHən/ n.
– ORIGIN late 19th cent.: past participle of the rare verb *catenate*, from Latin *catenat-* 'chained, fettered,' from the verb *catenare*, from *catena* 'chain.'

cat·e·na·tive /ˈkatə,nātiv, ˈkatn,ātiv/ Grammar ▶ adj. denoting a verb that governs a nonfinite form of another verb, for example, *like* in *I like swimming.*
▶ n. a catenative verb.
– ORIGIN late 20th cent.: from Latin *catena* 'chain' + -ATIVE.

cat·e·noid /ˈkatə,noid, ˈkatn,oid/ ▶ n. Geometry the surface generated by rotating a catenary about its horizontal axis.
– ORIGIN late 19th cent.: from Latin *catena* 'chain' + -OID.

ca·ter /ˈkātər/ ▶ v. [with obj.] provide food and drink, typically at social events and in a professional capacity: *he catered a lunch for 20 people* | (as adj. **catered**) *planning another catered affair.* ■ [no obj.] (**cater for**) chiefly Brit. provide with food and drink, in this way: *my mother helped to cater for the party.* ■ [no obj.] (**cater to**) provide with what is needed or required: *the school caters to children with learning difficulties.* ■ [no obj.] (**cater to**) try to satisfy (a particular need or demand): *he catered to her every whim.*
– DERIVATIVES **ca·ter·er** n.
– ORIGIN late 16th cent.: from obsolete *cater* 'caterer,' from Old French *acateor* 'buyer,' from *acater* 'buy' (see CATE).

cat·er·an /ˈkatərən/ ▶ n. historical a warrior or raider from the Scottish Highlands.
– ORIGIN Middle English (originally in the plural or as a collective singular denoting the peasantry as fighters): from Scottish Gaelic *ceathairne* 'peasantry.'

cat·er-cor·nered /ˈkatē ˌkôrnərd, ˈkatər/ (also **cater-corner** or **catty-cornered** or **kitty-corner**) ▶ adj. & adv. situated diagonally opposite someone or something: [as adj.] *a restaurant cater-cornered from the movie theater* | [as adv.] *motorcyclists cut cater-cornered across his yard.*
– ORIGIN mid 19th cent.: from dialect *cater* 'diagonally,' from *cater* denoting the four on dice, from French *quatre* 'four,' from Latin *quattuor*.

cat·er·pil·lar /ˈkatə(r) ˌpilər/ ▶ n. **1** the larva of a butterfly or moth, having a segmented wormlike body with three pairs of true legs and several pairs of leglike appendages. Caterpillars may be hairy, have warning coloration, or be colored to resemble their surroundings. ■ (in general use) any similar larva of various insects, esp. sawflies.

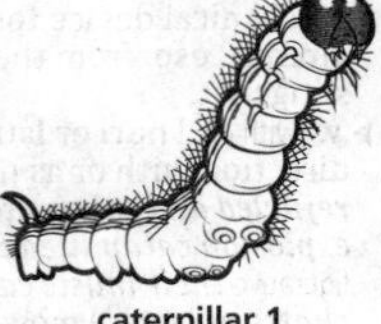
caterpillar 1

2 (also **caterpillar track** or **tread**) trademark an articulated steel band passing around the wheels of a vehicle for travel on rough ground. ■ a vehicle with such tracks.
– ORIGIN late Middle English: perhaps from a variant of Old French *chatepelose*, literally 'hairy

cat,' influenced by obsolete *piller* 'ravager.' The association with "cat" is found in other languages, e.g., Swiss German *Teufelskatz* (literally 'devil's cat'), Lombard *gatta* (literally 'cat'). Compare with French *chaton*, English CATKIN, resembling hairy caterpillars.

cat·er·waul /'katər,wôl/ ▶ **v.** [no obj.] (often as noun **caterwauling**) (of a cat) make a shrill howling or wailing noise: *the caterwauling of a pair of bobcats* | (as adj. **caterwauling**) figurative *a caterwauling guitar*.
▶ **n.** a shrill howling or wailing noise.
– ORIGIN late Middle English: from CAT[1] + imitative WAUL.

cat·fight /'kat,fīt/ ▶ **n.** informal a fight between women.
– DERIVATIVES **cat·fight·ing n.**

cat·fish /'kat,fisH/ ▶ **n.** (pl. **same** or **catfishes**) **1** a freshwater or marine fish with whiskerlike barbels around the mouth, typically bottom-dwelling. ● Order Siluriformes: many families, including the Eurasian family Siluridae and the large North American family Ictaluridae.
2 another term for WOLFFISH.

cat·gut /'kat,gət/ ▶ **n.** a material used for the strings of some musical instruments, made of the dried twisted intestines of sheep or horses (but not cats).
– ORIGIN late 16th cent.: the association with CAT[1] remains unexplained.

Cath. ▶ **abbr.** ■ Cathedral. ■ Catholic.

Cath·ar /'kaTH,är/ ▶ **n.** (pl. **Cathars** or **Cathari** /'kaTHə,rī, -,rē/) a member of a heretical medieval Christian sect that professed a form of Manichaean dualism and sought to achieve great spiritual purity.
– DERIVATIVES **Cath·a·rism** /'kaTHə,rizəm/ **n.**, **Cath·a·rist** /'kaTHərist/ **n. & adj.**
– ORIGIN mid 17th cent.: from medieval Latin *Cathari* (plural), from Greek *katharoi* 'the pure.'

ca·thar·sis /kə'THärsis/ ▶ **n.** (pl. **catharses** /-sēz/) **1** the process of releasing, and thereby providing relief from, strong or repressed emotions.
2 Medicine, rare purgation.
– ORIGIN early 19th cent. (sense 2): from Greek *katharsis*, from *kathairein* 'cleanse,' from *katharos* 'pure.' The notion of "release" through drama (sense 1) derives from Aristotle's *Poetics*.

ca·thar·tic /kə'THärtik/ ▶ **adj. 1** providing psychological relief through the open expression of strong emotions; causing catharsis: *crying is a cathartic release*.
2 Medicine (chiefly of a drug) purgative.
▶ **n.** Medicine a purgative drug.
– DERIVATIVES **ca·thar·ti·cal·ly adv.**
– ORIGIN early 17th cent. (in medical use): via late Latin from Greek *kathartikos*, from *katharsis* 'cleansing' (see CATHARSIS).

Ca·thay /kə'THā, ka-/ the name by which China was known to medieval Europe. Also called KHITAI.
– ORIGIN from medieval Latin *Cataya*, *Cathaya*, from Turkic *Khitāy*.

cat·head /'kat,hed/ ▶ **n.** a horizontal beam extending from each side of a ship's bow, used for raising and carrying an anchor.

ca·thec·tic /kə'THektik/ ▶ **adj.** Psychoanalysis of or relating to cathexis.
– ORIGIN 1920s: from Greek *kathektikos* 'capable of holding.'

ca·the·dra /kə'THēdrə/ ▶ **n.** (pl. **cathedrae** /-drē/) **1** a seat, specifically the chair of a bishop in his church.
2 a bishop's see. See also EX CATHEDRA.

ca·the·dral /kə'THēdrəl/ ▶ **n.** the principal church of a diocese, with which the bishop is officially associated: [in names] *St. Paul's Cathedral*.
– ORIGIN Middle English (as an adjective, the noun being short for *cathedral church* 'the church that contains the bishop's throne'): from late Latin *cathedralis*, from Latin *cathedra* 'seat,' from Greek *kathedra*.

ca·the·dral ceil·ing ▶ **n.** a pointed or slanting ceiling of a room that rises through more than one floor.

Ca·the·dral Cit·y a city in southern California, southeast of Palm Springs; pop. 52,095 (est. 2008).

Cath·er /'kaTHər/, Willa (Sibert) (1876–1974), US novelist and short-story writer. Her home state of Nebraska provides the setting for some of her best writing. Notable works: *O Pioneers!* (1913), *My Antonia* (1918), and *Death Comes for the Archbishop* (1927).

Cath·er·ine II /'kaTH(ə)rən/ (1729–96), empress of Russia; reigned 1762–96; known as **Catherine the Great**. She became empress after her husband, **Peter III**, was deposed. She formed alliances with Prussia and Austria and made territorial advances at the expense of the Turks and Tartars.

Cath·er·ine, St. (died *c.*307), early Christian martyr; known as **St. Catherine of Alexandria**. According to tradition, she opposed the persecution of Christians under the emperor **Maxentius** and refused to recant or to marry the emperor. Feast day, November 25.

Cath·er·ine de Mé·di·cis /də 'medəcHē/ (1519–89), queen of France; wife of Henry II; Italian name **Catherine de' Medici**. She ruled as regent 1560–74 during the minority reigns of her three sons: Francis II, Charles IX, and Henry III.

Cath·er·ine of Ar·a·gon (1485–1536), first wife of Henry VIII; youngest daughter of Ferdinand and Isabella of Castile; mother of Mary I. Henry's wish to annul his marriage to Catherine (due to her failure to produce a male heir) led eventually to England's break with the Roman Catholic Church.

Cath·er·ine wheel ▶ **n.** a firework in the form of a flat coil that spins when fixed to something solid and lit. ■ Heraldry a wheel with curved spikes projecting around the circumference.
– ORIGIN late 16th cent. (as a heraldic term): named after St. *Catherine* (see CATHERINE, ST.), with reference to her martyrdom.

cath·e·ter /'kaTHətər/ ▶ **n.** Medicine a flexible tube inserted through a narrow opening into a body cavity, particularly the bladder, for removing fluid.
– ORIGIN early 17th cent.: from late Latin, from Greek *kathetēr*, from *kathienai* 'send or let down.'

cath·e·ter·ize /'kaTHətə,rīz/ ▶ **v.** [with obj.] Medicine insert a catheter into (a patient or body cavity).
– DERIVATIVES **cath·e·ter·i·za·tion** /,kaTHətərə'zāsHən/ **n.**

ca·thex·is /kə'THeksis/ ▶ **n.** Psychoanalysis the concentration of mental energy on one particular person, idea, or object (esp. to an unhealthy degree).
– ORIGIN 1920s: from Greek *kathexis* 'retention,' translating German *Libidobesetzung*, coined by Freud.

cath·ode /'kaTH,ōd/ ▶ **n.** the negatively charged electrode by which electrons enter an electrical device. The opposite of ANODE. ■ the positively charged electrode of an electrical device, such as a primary cell, that supplies current.
– DERIVATIVES **cath·o·dal** /'kaTH,ōdl/ **adj.**, **ca·thod·ic** /ka'THädik/ **adj.**
– ORIGIN mid 19th cent.: from Greek *kathodos* 'way down,' from *kata-* 'down' + *hodos* 'way.'

cath·ode ray ▶ **n.** a beam of electrons emitted from the cathode of a high-vacuum tube.

cath·ode ray tube (abbr.: **CRT**) (also **cathode-ray tube**) ▶ **n.** a high-vacuum tube in which cathode rays produce a luminous image on a fluorescent screen, used chiefly in televisions and computer terminals.

cath·o·lic /'kaTH(ə)lik/ ▶ **adj. 1** (esp. of a person's tastes) including a wide variety of things; all-embracing.
2 (**Catholic**) of the Roman Catholic faith. ■ of or including all Christians. ■ of or relating to the historic doctrine and practice of the Western Church.
▶ **n.** (**Catholic**) a member of the Roman Catholic Church.
– DERIVATIVES **cath·o·lic·i·ty** /,kaTH(ə)'lisətē/ **n.**
– ORIGIN late Middle English (sense 2 of the adjective): from Old French *catholique* or late Latin *catholicus*, from Greek *katholikos* 'universal,' from *kata* 'with respect to' + *holos* 'whole.'

Cath·o·lic Church ▶ **n.** short for ROMAN CATHOLIC CHURCH.

Ca·thol·i·cism /kə'THälə,sizəm/ ▶ **n.** the faith, practice, and church order of the Roman Catholic Church. ■ adherence to the forms of Christian doctrine and practice that are generally regarded as Catholic rather than Protestant or Eastern Orthodox.

Ca·thol·i·cize /kə'THälə,sīz/ ▶ **v.** [with obj.] make Roman Catholic; convert to Catholicism.

Cath·o·lic League see HOLY LEAGUE.

Ca·thol·i·cos /kə'THäləkəs, -,käs/ ▶ **n.** (pl. **Catholicoses** /kə,THälə'kō,sēz/ or **Catholicoi** /kə'THälə,koi/) the Patriarch of the Armenian or the Nestorian Church.
– ORIGIN early 17th cent.: from medieval Greek *katholikos* 'universal' (see CATHOLIC).

cat·house /'kat,hous/ ▶ **n.** informal a brothel.

cat·i·on /'kat,īən, -,ī,än/ ▶ **n.** Chemistry a positively charged ion, i.e., one that would be attracted to the cathode in electrolysis. The opposite of ANION.
– DERIVATIVES **cat·i·on·ic** /,katī'änik/ **adj.**
– ORIGIN mid 19th cent.: from CATA- 'alongside' or from CATHODE, + ION.

cat·kin /'katkin/ ▶ **n.** a flowering spike of trees such as willow and hazel. Catkins are typically downy, pendulous, composed of flowers of a single sex, and wind-pollinated.
– ORIGIN late 16th cent.: from obsolete Dutch *katteken* 'kitten.'

cat·like /'kat,līk/ ▶ **adj.** resembling a cat in appearance, action, or character, esp. by moving gracefully or stealthily.

cat·lin·ite /'katlə,nīt/ ▶ **n.** a red clay of the Upper Missouri region, the sacred pipestone of the American Indians.
– ORIGIN mid 19th cent.: from the name of George *Catlin* (1796–1872), American artist, + -ITE[1].

C

cat lit·ter ▶ **n.** see LITTER (sense 3 of the noun).

cat·mint /'kat,mint/ ▶ **n.** another term for CATNIP.

cat·nap /'kat,nap/ ▶ **n.** a short, light sleep; a doze.
▶ **v.** (**catnaps, catnapping, catnapped**) [no obj.] have such a sleep.

cat·nip /'kat,nip/ ▶ **n.** a plant of the mint family, with downy leaves, purple-spotted white flowers, and a pungent smell attractive to cats. Also called CATMINT. ● Genus *Nepeta*, family Labiatae: several species, including the Eurasian *N. cataria*.
– ORIGIN late 18th cent. (originally US): from CAT[1] + *nip*, variant of dialect *nep*, *nept*, from medieval Latin *nepta*, from Latin *nepeta* 'catmint.'

Ca·to /'kātō/, Marcus Porcius (234–149 BC), Roman statesman, orator, and writer; known as **Cato the Elder** or **Cato the Censor**. As censor, he initiated a vigorous program of reform and attempted to stem the growing influence of Greek culture.

cat-o'-nine-tails ▶ **n.** historical a rope whip with nine knotted cords, formerly used (esp. at sea) to flog offenders.

Ca·tons·ville /'kātnz,vil/ a community in central Maryland, southwest of Baltimore; pop. 39,820 (2000).

ca·top·tric /kə'täptrik/ ▶ **adj.** Physics of or relating to a mirror, a reflector, or reflection.
– ORIGIN early 18th cent.: from Greek *katoptrikos*, from *katoptron* 'mirror.'

ca·top·trics /kə'täptriks/ ▶ **plural n.** [treated as sing.] Physics the branch of optics that deals with reflection.
– ORIGIN mid 16th cent. (originally *catoptric*): from Greek *katoptrikos* 'reflecting,' from *katoptron* 'mirror.'

cat rig ▶ **n.** the rig of a catboat with the single mast placed far forward.

Ca·tron /'kātrən/, John (c.1786–1865), US Supreme Court associate justice 1837–65. Appointed to the Court by President Jackson, he was an advocate of states' rights.

CAT scan ▶ **n.** an X-ray image made using computerized axial tomography.
– DERIVATIVES **CAT scan·ner n.**

cat's cra·dle ▶ **n.** a child's game in which a loop of string is put around and between the fingers and complex patterns are formed.

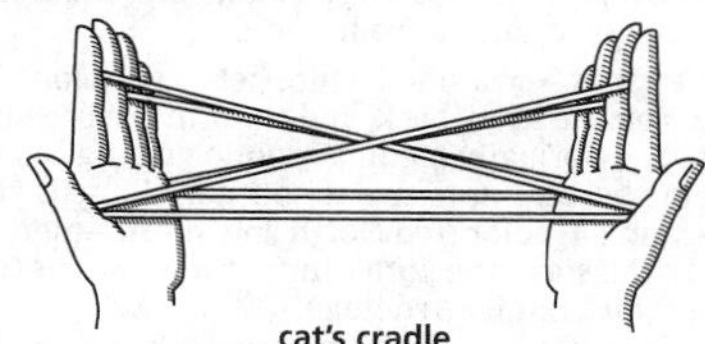

cat's cradle

cat scratch fe·ver (also **cat scratch disease**) ▶ **n.** an infectious disease occurring after a scratch by a cat's claw, a splinter, or a thorn. Symptoms include mild fever and inflammation of the injury site and of the lymph glands.

cat's ear (also **cat's ears**) ▶ **n.** a plant that resembles the dandelion, with yellow flowers and rosettes of leaves. ● Genus *Hypochaeris*, family Compositae: several species, in particular the Old World *H. radicata*, naturalized in North America.

cat's-eye ▶ **n.** a semiprecious stone, esp. chalcedony or chrysoberyl, with a chatoyant luster.

cat shark ▶ **n.** a small bottom-dwelling shark that has catlike eyes and small dorsal fins set well back. It is typically strikingly marked and lives in warmer waters. ● *Apristurus* and other genera, family Scyliorhinidae: several species, including the **brown cat shark** (*A. brunneus*).

Cats·kill Moun·tains /'kat,skil/ (also **the Catskills**) a range of mountains in the state of New York, part of the Appalachian system.

cat's me·ow ▶ **n.** (**the cat's meow**) informal, dated another term for THE CAT'S PAJAMAS (see CAT'S PAJAMAS).

cat's pa·ja·mas ▶ **n.** (**the cat's pajamas**) informal, dated an excellent person or thing: *this car is the cat's pajamas.*

cat's-paw ▶ **n.** a person who is used by another, typically to carry out an unpleasant or dangerous task.

cat·suit /ˈkatˌso͞ot/ ▶ **n.** a woman's jumpsuit, typically close-fitting and covering the body from the neck to the feet.

cat·sup /ˈkeCHəp, ˈkaCHəp, ˈkatsəp/ ▶ **n.** variant spelling of **KETCHUP**.

cat's whisk·er ▶ **n.** a fine adjustable wire in a crystal radio receiver.
– PHRASES **the cat's whiskers** informal another term for **THE CAT'S PAJAMAS** (see **CAT'S PAJAMAS**).

Catt /kat/, Carrie Clinton Chapman Lane (1859–1947), US suffragist. As president of the National American Woman Suffrage Association 1900–04, 1915–47 and of the International Woman Suffrage Alliance 1904–23, she was instrumental in the adoption of the 19th amendment to the Constitution in 1920.

cat·tail /ˈkatˌtāl/ ▶ **n.** a tall, reedlike marsh plant with straplike leaves and a dark brown, velvety cylindrical head of numerous tiny flowers. Also called **REED MACE, BULRUSH**. ● Genus *Typha*, family Typhaceae: several species, in particular the **common cattail** (*T. latifolia*).

common cattail

cat·te·ry /ˈkatərē/ ▶ **n.** (pl. **catteries**) a boarding or breeding establishment for cats.

cat·tish /ˈkatiSH/ ▶ **adj.** another term for **CATTY**.
– DERIVATIVES **cat·tish·ly adv.**, **cat·tish·ness n.**

cat·tle /ˈkatl/ ▶ **plural n. 1** large ruminant animals with horns and cloven hoofs, domesticated for meat or milk, or as beasts of burden; cows. ● *Bos taurus* (including the zebu, *B. indicus*), family Bovidae; descended from the extinct aurochs.
2 similar animals of a group related to domestic cattle, including yak, bison, and buffalo. ● Tribe Bovini, family Bovidae (the **cattle family**): four genera, in particular *Bos*. The cattle family also includes the sheep, goats, goat-antelopes, and antelopes.
– ORIGIN Middle English (also denoting personal property or wealth): from Anglo-Norman French *catel*, variant of Old French *chatel* (see **CHATTEL**).

cat·tle call ▶ **n.** informal an open audition for parts in a play, movie, or other production.

cat·tle e·gret ▶ **n.** a small white heron with long buff feathers on the head, back, and chest in the breeding season, and normally feeding around grazing cattle and game herds. It is native to southern Eurasia and Africa, and has colonized North and South America and Australasia in the 20th century. ● *Bubulcus* (or *Ardeola*) *ibis*, family Ardeidae.

cat·tle guard ▶ **n.** a metal grid covering a ditch, allowing vehicles and pedestrians to pass over but not cattle and other animals.

cat·tle·man /ˈkatlmən, -ˌman/ ▶ **n.** (pl. **cattlemen**) a person who tends or rears cattle.

catt·ley·a /ˈkatlēə, katˈlāə, katˈlēə/ ▶ **n.** a tropical American orchid with brightly colored showy flowers and thick leaves, typically growing as an epiphyte. It is a popular greenhouse plant, with many hybrids. ● Genus *Cattleya*, family Orchidaceae.
– ORIGIN early 19th cent.: modern Latin, named after William *Cattley* (died 1832), English patron of botany.

cat train ▶ **n.** Canadian a crawler tractor pulling a train of sleighs across snow or ice.
– ORIGIN *cat* from **CATERPILLAR**.

cat·ty /ˈkatē/ ▶ **adj.** (**cattier, cattiest**) **1** deliberately hurtful in one's remarks; spiteful.
2 of or relating to cats; catlike.
– DERIVATIVES **cat·ti·ly** /ˈkatl-ē/ **adv.**, **cat·ti·ness n.**

cat·ty-cor·nered ▶ **adj.** another term for **CATER-CORNERED**.

Ca·tul·lus /kəˈtələs/, Gaius Valerius (*c.*84–*c.*54 BC), Roman poet, known for his love poems.

CATV ▶ **abbr.** community antenna television (i.e., cable television).

cat·walk /ˈkatˌwôk/ ▶ **n. 1** a platform extending into an auditorium, along which models walk to display clothes in fashion shows; a runway.
2 a narrow walkway or open bridge, esp. in an industrial installation.

Cau·ca Riv·er /ˈloukə/ a river in western Colombia that flows north for 800 miles (1,300 km) from the Andes to the Magdalena River.

Cau·ca·sian /kôˈkāZHən/ ▶ **adj. 1** often offensive of or relating to one of the traditional divisions of humankind, covering a broad group of peoples from Europe, western Asia, and parts of India and North Africa. [so named because the German physiologist Blumenbach believed that it originated in the Caucasus region of southeastern Europe.] ■ white-skinned; of European origin.
2 of or relating to the Caucasus.
3 of or relating to a group of languages spoken in the region of the Caucasus, of which thirty-eight are known, many not committed to writing. The most widely spoken is Georgian, of the small **South Caucasian** family, not related to the three **North Caucasian** families.
▶ **n.** often offensive a Caucasian person. ■ a white person; a person of European origin.

> **USAGE** In the racial classification as developed by anthropologists in the 19th century, **Caucasian** (or **Caucasoid**) included peoples whose skin color ranged from light (in northern Europe) to dark (in parts of North Africa and India). Although the classification is outdated and the categories are now not generally accepted as scientific (see usage at **AUSTRALOID** and **MONGOLOID**), the term **Caucasian** has acquired a more restricted meaning. It is now used as a synonym for 'white or of European origin,' as in the following citation: *the police are looking for a **Caucasian** male in his forties.*

Cau·ca·soid /ˈkôkəˌsoid/ ▶ **adj.** often offensive of or relating to the Caucasian division of humankind.

Cau·ca·sus /ˈkôkəsəs/ (also **Caucasia** /kôˈkāZHə/) a mountainous region in southeastern Europe and southwestern Asia that lies between the Black and Caspian seas in Georgia, Armenia, Azerbaijan, and southeastern Russia.

Cau·chy /kôˈSHē/, Augustin Louis, Baron (1789–1857), French mathematician. He transformed the theory of complex functions, founded the modern theory of elasticity, and contributed substantially to the founding of group theory and analysis.

cau·cus /ˈkôkəs/ ▶ **n.** (pl. **caucuses**) **1** a meeting of the members of a legislative body who are members of a particular political party, to select candidates or decide policy. ■ the members of such a body.
2 a group of people with shared concerns within a political party or larger organization.
▶ **v.** (**caucuses, caucusing, caucused**) [no obj.] hold or form such a group or meeting.
– ORIGIN mid 18th cent. (originally US): perhaps from Algonquian *cau'-cau'-as'u* 'adviser.'

cau·dal /ˈkôdl/ ▶ **adj.** of or like a tail. ■ at or near the tail or the posterior part of the body.
– DERIVATIVES **cau·dal·ly adv.**
– ORIGIN mid 17th cent.: from modern Latin *caudalis*, from Latin *cauda* 'tail.'

cau·dal fin ▶ **n.** Zoology another term for **TAIL FIN**.

Cau·da·ta /kôˈdātə, kouˈdātə/ Zoology another term for **URODELA**.
– ORIGIN modern Latin (plural), from Latin *cauda* 'tail.'

cau·date /ˈkôˌdāt/ ▶ **adj. 1** Anatomy relating to or denoting the caudate nucleus.
2 Zoology (of an animal) having a tail.
▶ **n.** short for **CAUDATE NUCLEUS**.
– ORIGIN early 17th cent.: from medieval Latin *caudatus*, from *cauda* 'tail.'

cau·date nu·cle·us ▶ **n.** Anatomy the upper of the two gray nuclei of the corpus striatum in the cerebrum of the brain.

cau·dex /ˈkôˌdeks/ ▶ **n.** (pl. **caudices** /-dəˌsēz/ or **caudexes**) Botany the axis of a woody plant, esp. a palm or tree fern, comprising the stem and root.
– ORIGIN late 18th cent.: from Latin, earlier form of **CODEX**.

cau·dil·lo /kôˈdē(y)ō, kouˈdēˌ(y)ō/ ▶ **n.** (pl. **caudillos**) (in Spanish-speaking regions) a military or political leader.
– ORIGIN Spanish, from late Latin *capitellum*, diminutive of *caput* 'head.' The title *El Caudillo* 'the leader' was assumed by General Franco of Spain in 1938.

caught /kôt/ past and past participle of **CATCH**.

caul /kôl/ ▶ **n. 1** the amniotic membrane enclosing a fetus. ■ part of this membrane occasionally found on a child's head at birth, thought to bring good luck.
2 historical a woman's close-fitting indoor headdress or hairnet.
3 Anatomy the omentum.
– ORIGIN Middle English: perhaps from Old French *cale* 'head covering,' but recorded earlier.

caul·dron /ˈkôldrən/ (also **caldron**) ▶ **n.** a large metal pot with a lid and handle, used for cooking over an open fire. ■ a situation characterized by instability and strong emotions: *a cauldron of repressed anger.*
– ORIGIN Middle English: from Anglo-Norman French *caudron*, based on Latin *caldarium*, *calidarium* 'cooking pot,' from *calidus* 'hot.'

cau·li·flow·er /ˈkôliˌflou(-ə)r, ˈkäli-, -lē-/ ▶ **n.** a cabbage of a variety that bears a large immature flower head of small creamy-white flower buds. ■ the flower head of this plant eaten as a vegetable.
– ORIGIN late 16th cent.: from obsolete French *chou fleuri* 'flowered cabbage,' probably from Italian *cavolfiore* or modern Latin *cauliflora*. The original English form *colieflorie* or *cole-flory* had its first element influenced by **COLE**; the second element was influenced by **FLOWER** during the 17th cent.

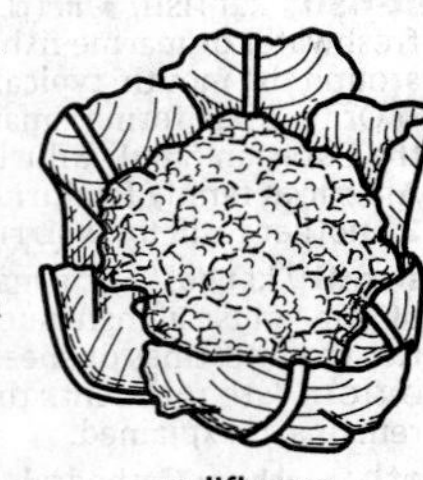
cauliflower

cau·li·flow·er ear ▶ **n.** an ear that has become thickened or deformed as a result of repeated blows, typically in boxing.

cau·li·flow·er fun·gus (also **cauliflower mushroom**) ▶ **n.** an edible fungus that forms a distinctive fruiting body with a yellowish lobed surface, growing on wood and other plant debris in both Eurasia and North America. ● Genus *Sparassis* and family Sparassidaceae, class Basidiomycetes: several species, in particular *S. crispa*.

caulk /kôk/ (also **calk**) ▶ **n.** (also **caulking**) a waterproof filler and sealant, used in building work and repairs.
▶ **v.** [with obj.] seal (a gap or seam) with such a substance. ■ stop up (the seams of a boat) with oakum and waterproofing material, or by driving plate-junctions together; make (a boat) watertight by this method.
– DERIVATIVES **caulk·er n.**
– ORIGIN late Middle English (in the sense 'copulate,' used of birds): from Old Northern French *cauquer*, *caukier*, variant of *cauchier* 'tread, press with force,' from Latin *calcare* 'tread,' from *calx, calc-* 'heel.'

caus·al /ˈkôzəl/ ▶ **adj.** of, relating to, or acting as a cause: *the causal factors associated with illness.* ■ Grammar & Logic expressing or indicating a cause: *a causal conjunction.*
– DERIVATIVES **caus·al·ly adv.**
– ORIGIN late Middle English (as a noun denoting a causal conjunction or particle): from late Latin *causalis*, from Latin *causa* 'cause.'

cau·sal·gi·a /kôˈzalj(ē)ə, -ˈsal-/ ▶ **n.** severe burning pain in a limb caused by injury to a peripheral nerve.
– ORIGIN mid 19th cent.: from Greek *kausos* 'heat, fever' + **-ALGIA**.

cau·sal·i·ty /kôˈzalətē/ ▶ **n. 1** the relationship between cause and effect.
2 the principle that everything has a cause.
– ORIGIN late 15th cent.: from French *causalité* or medieval Latin *causalitas*, from Latin *causa* 'cause.'

cau·sa·tion /kôˈzāSHən/ ▶ **n.** the action of causing something: *investigating the role of nitrate in the causation of cancer.* ■ the relationship between cause and effect; causality.
– ORIGIN late 15th cent.: from Latin *causatio(n-)* 'pretext' (in medieval Latin 'the action of causing'), from *causare* 'to cause.'

caus·a·tive /ˈkôzətiv/ ▶ **adj.** acting as a cause: *a causative factor.* ■ Grammar expressing causation: *a causative verb.*
▶ **n.** a causative verb.
– ORIGIN late Middle English: from Old French *causatif, -ive*, or late Latin *causativus*, from *causare* 'to cause.'

cause /kôz/ ▶ **n. 1** a person or thing that gives rise to an action, phenomenon, or condition: *the cause of the accident is not clear.* ■ reasonable grounds for doing, thinking, or feeling something: *Faye's condition had given no cause for concern* | [with infinitive] *the government had good cause to avoid war* | *class size is a cause for complaint in some schools.*
2 a principle, aim, or movement that, because of a deep commitment, one is prepared to defend or advocate: *she devoted her life to the cause of deaf people* | *I'm raising money for a good cause.*
3 a matter to be resolved in a court of law. ■ an individual's case offered at law.

▶ **v.** [with obj.] make (something, typically something bad) happen: *this disease can cause blindness* | [with obj. and infinitive] *we have no idea what has happened to cause people to stay away.*
– PHRASES **cause and effect** the principle of causation. ■ the operation or relation of a cause and its effect. **cause of action** Law a fact or facts that enable a person to bring an action against another. **in the cause of** so as to support, promote, or defend something. **make common cause** unite in order to achieve a shared aim: *nationalist movements **made common cause** with the reformers.* **a rebel without a cause** a person who is dissatisfied with society but does not have a specific aim to fight for. [from the title of a US film, released in 1955.]
– DERIVATIVES **cause·less** adj., **caus·er** n.
– ORIGIN Middle English: from Old French, from Latin *causa* (noun), *causare* (verb).

'cause /kəz/ ▶ **conj.** informal short for BECAUSE.

cause cé·lè·bre /ˌkôz səˈleb(rə), ˌkōz/ ▶ **n.** (pl. **causes célèbres** pronunc. **same**) a controversial issue that attracts a great deal of public attention.
– ORIGIN mid 18th cent.: French, literally 'famous case.'

cau·se·rie /ˌkōz(ə)ˈrē/ ▶ **n.** (pl. **causeries** pronunc. **same**) an informal article or talk, typically one on a literary subject.
– ORIGIN French, from *causer* 'to talk.'

cause·way /ˈkôzˌwā/ ▶ **n.** a raised road or track across low or wet ground.
– ORIGIN late Middle English: from *causey* (from Anglo-Norman French *causee*, based on Latin *calx* 'lime, limestone' (used for paving roads)) + WAY.

caus·tic /ˈkôstik/ ▶ **adj. 1** able to burn or corrode organic tissue by chemical action: *a caustic cleaner.* **2** sarcastic in a scathing and bitter way: *the players were making caustic comments about the refereeing.* **3** Physics formed by the intersection of reflected or refracted parallel rays from a curved surface.
▶ **n. 1** a caustic substance.
2 Physics a caustic surface or curve.
– DERIVATIVES **caus·ti·cal·ly** /-ik(ə)lē/ adv., **caus·tic·i·ty** /kôˈstisətē/ n.
– ORIGIN late Middle English: via Latin from Greek *kaustikos*, from *kaustos* 'combustible,' from *kaiein* 'to burn.'

caus·tic pot·ash ▶ **n.** another term for POTASSIUM HYDROXIDE.

caus·tic so·da ▶ **n.** another term for SODIUM HYDROXIDE.

cau·ter·ize /ˈkôtəˌrīz/ ▶ **v.** [with obj.] Medicine burn the skin or flesh of (a wound) with a heated instrument or caustic substance, typically to stop bleeding or prevent the wound from becoming infected.
– DERIVATIVES **cau·ter·i·za·tion** /ˌkôtərəˈzāSHən/ n.
– ORIGIN late Middle English: from Old French *cauteriser*, from late Latin *cauterizare*, from Greek *kautēriazein*, from *kautērion* 'branding iron,' from *kaiein* 'to burn.'

cau·ter·y /ˈkôtərē/ ▶ **n.** (pl. **cauteries**) Medicine an instrument or a caustic substance used for cauterizing. ■ the action of cauterizing something.
– ORIGIN late Middle English: via Latin from Greek *kautērion* 'branding iron' (see CAUTERIZE).

Cau·then /ˈkôTHən, ˈkä-/, Steve (1960–), US jockey. In 1978, riding Affirmed, he became the youngest jockey to win the Triple Crown. He retired in 1992 with a total of 2,794 career victories. Horse Racing Hall of Fame (1994).

cau·tion /ˈkôSHən/ ▶ **n. 1** care taken to avoid danger or mistakes: *anyone receiving a suspect package should exercise extreme caution.* ■ warning: *business advisers have sounded a note of caution.*
2 informal, dated an amusing or surprising person.
▶ **v.** [reporting verb] say something as a warning: [with clause] *the secretary cautioned that economic uncertainties remained* | [with direct speech] *"Be careful now," I cautioned.* ■ [no obj.] (**caution against**) warn or advise against (doing something): *advisers have cautioned against tax increases.*
– ORIGIN Middle English (denoting bail or a guarantee): from Latin *caution-*, from *cavere* 'take heed.'

cau·tion·ar·y /ˈkôSHəˌnerē/ ▶ **adj.** serving as a warning: *a cautionary tale.*

cau·tious /ˈkôSHəs/ ▶ **adj.** (of a person) careful to avoid potential problems or dangers: *a cautious driver.* ■ (of an action) characterized by such an attitude: *the plan received a cautious welcome.*
– DERIVATIVES **cau·tious·ly** adv., **cau·tious·ness** n.
– ORIGIN mid 17th cent.: from CAUTION, on the pattern of pairs such as *ambition, ambitious.*

Cau·ver·y /ˈkôvərē/ (also **Kaveri** /ˈkôvərē, ˈkä-/) a river in southern India that rises in northern Kerala and flows east for 475 miles (765 km) to the Bay of Bengal, south of Pondicherry. It is held sacred by Hindus.

ca·va /ˈkävə/ ▶ **n.** a Spanish sparkling wine made in the same way as champagne.
– ORIGIN Spanish.

cav·al·cade /ˌkavəlˈkād/ ▶ **n.** a formal procession of people walking, on horseback, or riding in vehicles.
– ORIGIN late 16th cent. (denoting a ride or raid on horseback): from French, from Italian *cavalcata*, from *cavalcare* 'to ride,' based on Latin *caballus* 'horse.'

cav·a·lier /ˌkavəˈli(ə)r/ ▶ **n. 1** (**Cavalier**) historical a supporter of King Charles I in the English Civil War. ■ archaic or literary a courtly gentleman, esp. one acting as a lady's escort. ■ archaic a horseman, esp. a cavalryman.
2 (also **Cavalier King Charles**) a small spaniel of a breed with a moderately long, noncurly, silky coat.
▶ **adj.** showing a lack of proper concern; offhand: *Anne was irritated by his cavalier attitude.*
– DERIVATIVES **cav·a·lier·ly** adv.
– ORIGIN mid 16th cent.: from French, from Italian *cavaliere*, based on Latin *caballus* 'horse.' Compare with CABALLERO and CHEVALIER.

cav·al·ry /ˈkavəlrē/ ▶ **n.** (pl. **cavalries**) [usu. treated as pl.] (in the past) soldiers who fought on horseback. ■ modern soldiers who fight in armored vehicles.
– DERIVATIVES **cav·al·ry·man** /-mən/ n. (pl. **cavalrymen**).
– ORIGIN mid 16th cent.: from French *cavallerie*, from Italian *cavalleria*, from *cavallo* 'horse,' from Latin *caballus.*

cav·al·ry twill ▶ **n.** strong woolen twill used typically for making pants and sportswear.

Cav·an /ˈkavən/ a county in the Republic of Ireland, part of the old province of Ulster.

ca·va·quin·ho /ˌkävəˈkēnyō/ ▶ **n.** (pl. **cavaquinhos**) a small, four-stringed guitar resembling a ukulele, popular in Brazil and Portugal.
– ORIGIN Portuguese.

cav·a·ti·na /ˌkavəˈtēnə/ ▶ **n.** (pl. **cavatine** /-ˈtēnā/) Music a short operatic aria in simple style without repeated sections. ■ a similar piece of lyrical instrumental music.
– ORIGIN early 19th cent.: from Italian.

cave /kāv/ ▶ **n.** a large underground chamber, typically of natural origin, in a hillside or cliff.
▶ **v.** [no obj.] **1** explore caves as a sport.
2 short for CAVE IN below.
– PHRASAL VERBS **cave in** (or **cave something in**) (with reference to a roof or similar structure) subside or collapse or cause something to do this: *the tunnel walls caved in* | *storms caved the roof in.* ■ yield or submit under pressure: *the manager caved in to his demands.*
– DERIVATIVES **cave·like** /-ˌlīk/ adj., **cav·er** n.
– ORIGIN Middle English: from Old French, from Latin *cava*, from *cavus* 'hollow' (compare with CAVERN). The usage *cave in* may be from the synonymous dialect expression *calve in*, influenced by obsolete *cave* 'excavate, hollow out.'

ca·ve·at /ˈkavēˌät, ˈkäv-/ ▶ **n.** a warning or proviso of specific stipulations, conditions, or limitations. ■ Law a notice, esp. in a probate, that certain actions may not be taken without informing the person who gave the notice.
– ORIGIN mid 16th cent.: from Latin, literally 'let a person beware.'

ca·ve·at emp·tor /ˈempˌtôr/ ▶ **n.** the principle that the buyer alone is responsible for checking the quality and suitability of goods before a purchase is made.
– ORIGIN early 16th cent.: Latin, literally 'let the buyer beware.'

cave bear ▶ **n.** a large extinct bear of the Pleistocene epoch, whose remains are found commonly in caves throughout Europe. ● *Ursus spelaeus*, family Ursidae.

cave crick·et ▶ **n.** another term for CAMEL CRICKET.

cave dwell·er ▶ **n.** a caveman or cavewoman.

cave·fish /ˈkāvˌfiSH/ ▶ **n.** (pl. **same** or **cavefishes**) a small colorless fish that lives only in limestone caves in North America. It has reduced or absent eyes, and the head and body are covered with papillae that are sensitive to vibration. Also called BLINDFISH. ● Family Amblyopsidae: four genera, in particular *Amblyopsis* and *Typhlichthys.*

cave-in ▶ **n.** a collapse of a roof or similar structure, typically underground: *a mine cave-in.* ■ [in sing.] an instance of yielding or submitting under pressure: *the government's cave-in to industry pressure.*

cave·man /ˈkāvˌman/ ▶ **n.** (pl. **cavemen**) a prehistoric man who lived in caves. ■ a man whose behavior is uncivilized or violent: [as modifier] *you can't change my mind by caveman tactics.*

Cav·en·dish /ˈkavəndiSH/, Henry (1731–1810), English chemist and physicist. He identified hydrogen, studied carbon dioxide, and determined their densities relative to atmospheric air.

cav·en·dish /ˈkavədiSH/ ▶ **n.** tobacco softened, sweetened, and formed into cakes.
– ORIGIN mid 19th cent.: probably from the surname *Cavendish.*

cave paint·ing ▶ **n.** a prehistoric picture on the interior of a cave, often depicting animals.

cav·ern /ˈkavərn/ ▶ **n.** a cave, or a chamber in a cave, typically a large one. ■ used in similes and comparisons to refer to a vast, dark space: *the dark cavern of the main performance hall* | *rouses me from the cavern of sleep.*
– ORIGIN late Middle English: from Old French *caverne* or from Latin *caverna*, from *cavus* 'hollow.' Compare with CAVE.

C

cav·ern·ous /ˈkavərnəs/ ▶ **adj.** like a cavern in size, shape, or atmosphere: *a cavernous warehouse.* ■ giving the impression of vast, dark depths: *his cavernous eyes.*
– DERIVATIVES **cav·ern·ous·ly** adv.
– ORIGIN late Middle English: from Old French *caverneux* or Latin *cavernosus* (from *caverna* 'cavern').

cave sal·a·man·der ▶ **n.** a cave-dwelling salamander with pinkish to brown skin. ● Several genera and species in the family Plethodontidae, including the North American *Eurycea lucifuga* and the European genus *Hydromantes.*

cav·es·son /ˈkavəsən/ ▶ **n.** (also **lunging cavesson**) a type of heavy bridle, which lacks a bit and has a thick noseband fitted with rings to which a lunge rein may be attached.
– ORIGIN late 16th cent.: from French *caveçon*, Italian *cavezzone*, based on Latin *caput* 'head.'

cave·wom·an /ˈkāvˌwo͝omən/ ▶ **n.** (pl. **cavewomen**) a prehistoric woman who lived in caves.

cav·i·ar /ˈkavēˌär/ (also **caviare**) ▶ **n.** the pickled roe of sturgeon or other large fish, eaten as a delicacy.
– ORIGIN mid 16th cent.: from Italian *caviale* (earlier *caviaro*) or French *caviar*, probably from medieval Greek *khaviari.*

cav·il /ˈkavəl/ ▶ **v.** [no obj.] make petty or unnecessary objections: *they caviled at the cost.*
▶ **n.** an objection of this kind.
– DERIVATIVES **cav·il·er** n.
– ORIGIN mid 16th cent.: from French *caviller*, from Latin *cavillari*, from *cavilla* 'mockery.'

cav·ing /ˈkāviNG/ ▶ **n.** another term for SPELUNKING.

cav·i·ta·tion /ˌkavəˈtāSHən/ ▶ **n.** Physics the formation of an empty space within a solid object or body. ■ the formation of bubbles in a liquid, typically by the movement of a propeller through it.

cav·i·ty /ˈkavitē/ ▶ **n.** (pl. **cavities**) an empty space within a solid object, in particular the human body: *the abdominal cavity* | *a body cavity.* ■ a decayed part of a tooth.
– DERIVATIVES **cav·i·tar·y** /-iˌterē/ adj.
– ORIGIN mid 16th cent.: from French *cavité* or late Latin *cavitas*, from Latin *cavus* 'hollow.'

cav·i·ty wall ▶ **n.** a wall formed from two thicknesses of masonry with a space between them.

cav·o·lo ne·ro /ˈkävəˌlō ˈne(ə)rō/ ▶ **n.** an Italian variety of kale with very dark-colored leaves.
– ORIGIN Italian, from *cavolo* 'cabbage' + *nero* 'black.'

cav·ort /kəˈvôrt/ ▶ **v.** [no obj.] jump or dance around excitedly: *spider monkeys leap and cavort in the branches.* ■ informal apply oneself enthusiastically to sexual or disreputable pursuits: *he spent his nights cavorting with the glitterati.*
– ORIGIN late 18th cent. (originally US): perhaps an alteration of CURVET.

Ca·vour /kəˈvo͝or/, Camillo Benso, Conte di (1810–61), Italian statesman. In 1861, he became the first premier of a unified Italy.

ca·vy /ˈkāvē/ ▶ **n.** (pl. **cavies**) a South American rodent with a sturdy body and vestigial tail. ● Family Caviidae: five genera and several species, in particular the guinea pig.
– ORIGIN late 18th cent.: from modern Latin *cavia*, from Galibi *cabiai.*

caw /kô/ ▶ **n.** the harsh cry of a crow or similar bird.
▶ **v.** [no obj.] utter such a cry.
– ORIGIN late 16th cent.: imitative.

Caw·ley /ˈkôlē/, Evonne Goolagong (1951–), Australian tennis player; born *Evonne Fay Goolagong.* During 1971–80, she won the women's singles title at two Wimbledon, one French Open, and four Australian Open tournaments.

Cawn·pore /kônˈpôr/ former name for KANPUR.

Cax·ton /ˈkakstən/, William (*c.*1422–91), English printer. He printed the first book in English in 1474.

cay /kē, kā/ ▶ **n.** a low bank or reef of coral, rock, or sand. Compare with **KEY**[2].
– ORIGIN late 17th cent.: from Spanish *cayo* 'shoal, reef,' from French *quai* 'quay.'

Cay·enne /kī'en, kā'en/ the capital and chief port of French Guiana; pop. 63,000 (est. 2007).

cay·enne /kī'en, kā-/ (also **cayenne pepper**) ▶ **n.** a pungent hot-tasting red powder prepared from ground dried chili peppers.
– ORIGIN early 18th cent.: from Tupi *kyynha, quiynha*, later associated with **CAYENNE**.

Cay·ley /'kālē/, Arthur (1821–95), English mathematician and attorney. The **Cayley numbers**, a generalization of complex numbers, are named after him.

cay·man ▶ **n.** variant spelling of **CAIMAN**.

Cay·man Is·lands /'kāmən/ (also **the Caymans**) a group of three islands in the Caribbean Sea, south of Cuba; pop. 49,000 (est. 2009); capital, George Town. The Cayman Islands are a British overseas territory.

Ca·yu·ga /kā'(y)o͞ogə, kī-/ ▶ **n.** (pl. **same** or **Cayugas**) **1** a member of an American Indian people, one of the Five Nations, formerly inhabiting New York. **2** the Iroquoian language of this people.
▶ **adj.** of or relating to this people or their language.
– ORIGIN from an Iroquoian place name.

Cay·u·ga, Lake /kə'yo͞ogə, kā'(y)o͞o-/ one of the Finger Lakes, in west central New York. Ithaca lies at its southern end.

Cay·use /'kī,(y)o͞os, kī'(y)o͞os/ ▶ **n.** (pl. **same** or **Cayuses**) **1** a member of an American Indian people of Washington State and Oregon. **2** the language of this people, of unknown affinity. **3** (**cayuse**) an American Indian pony. ■ informal a horse.
▶ **adj.** of or relating to this people or their language.
– ORIGIN probably from Chinook Jargon from Spanish *caballos*, 'horses,' for which the Cayuse were especially known.

CB ▶ **abbr.** Citizens' Band (radio frequencies).

CBC ▶ **abbr.** Canadian Broadcasting Corporation.

CBS ▶ **abbr.** Columbia Broadcasting System.

CBT ▶ **abbr.** cognitive behavioral therapy.

CC ▶ **abbr.** ■ closed-captioned. ■ Cape Cod.

cc (also **c.c.**) ▶ **abbr.** ■ carbon copy (used as an indication that a duplicate has been or should be sent to another person). ■ cubic centimeter(s).

CCD ▶ **abbr.** ■ Electronics charge-coupled device, a high-speed semiconductor used chiefly in image detection. ■ Confraternity of Christian Doctrine.

CCK ▶ **abbr.** Biochemistry cholecystokinin.

C clef ▶ **n.** the soprano, alto, or tenor clef.

CCS ▶ **abbr.** Ecology carbon capture and storage.

CCTV ▶ **abbr.** closed-circuit television.

CCU ▶ **abbr.** ■ cardiac care unit. ■ coronary care unit. ■ critical care unit.

CD[1] ▶ **n.** (pl. **CDs**) a compact disc.

CD[2] ▶ **abbr.** ■ certificate of deposit. ■ civil defense. ■ corps diplomatique.

Cd ▶ **symbol** the chemical element cadmium.

cd ▶ **abbr.** ■ candela. ■ cord.

CD burn·er ▶ **n.** a device for producing a compact disc by copying from an original or master copy.

CDC ▶ **abbr.** Centers for Disease Control.

CDM ▶ **abbr.** cold dark matter.

CDMA ▶ **abbr.** Electronics Code Division Multiple Access, a generic term denoting a wireless interface based on code division multiple access technology.

cDNA ▶ **abbr.** complementary DNA.

Cdr. (also **CDR**) ▶ **abbr.** Commander.

CD-R ▶ **n.** a blank compact disc which can be recorded on once only.
– ORIGIN 1980s: abbreviation of *compact disc recordable*.

Cdre. (also **CDRE**) ▶ **abbr.** Commodore.

CD-ROM /,sē,dē-'räm/ ▶ **n.** a compact disc used as a read-only optical memory device for a computer system.
– ORIGIN 1980s: acronym from *compact disc read-only memory*.

CD-RW ▶ **n.** a blank compact disc that can be recorded, erased, and rerecorded many times.
– ORIGIN 1980s: abbreviation of *compact disc rewritable*.

CDT ▶ **abbr.** Central Daylight Time (see **CENTRAL TIME**).

CE ▶ **abbr.** ■ Chemical Engineer. ■ Church of England. ■ civil engineer. ■ Common Era. ■ Corps of Engineers.

Ce ▶ **symbol** the chemical element cerium.

ce·a·no·thus /,sēə'nōTHəs/ ▶ **n.** a North American shrub of the buckthorn family, cultivated for its dense clusters of small blue or white flowers. ● Genus *Ceanothus*, family Rhamnaceae: numerous species, esp. in the western US, including the **blueblossom ceanothus** of the Pacific coast.
– ORIGIN modern Latin, from Greek *keanōthos*, denoting a kind of thistle.

Ce·a·rá /,sāə'rä/ a state in northeastern Brazil, on the Atlantic coast; capital, Fortaleza.

cease /sēs/ ▶ **v.** [no obj.] bring or come to an end: *the hostilities had ceased and normal life was resumed* | [with infinitive] *on his retirement the job will cease to exist* | [with obj.] *they were asked to cease all military activity*.
– PHRASES **never cease to** (in hyperbolic use) do something very frequently: *her exploits never cease to amaze me*. **without cease** without stopping.
– ORIGIN Middle English: from Old French *cesser*, from Latin *cessare* 'stop,' from *cedere* 'to yield.'

cease·fire /'sēsfīr/ ▶ **n.** a temporary suspension of fighting, typically one during which peace talks take place; a truce. ■ an order or signal to stop fighting.

cease·less /'sēslis/ ▶ **adj.** constant and unending: *the fort was subjected to ceaseless bombardment*.
– DERIVATIVES **cease·less·ly adv.**

Ceau·șes·cu /CHou'SHeskoo/, Nicolae (1918–89), Romanian communist statesman; first president of the Socialist Republic of Romania 1974–89. His regime became increasingly totalitarian and corrupt; a popular uprising in December 1989 resulted in its downfall and in his execution.

Ce·bu /sā'bo͞o/ an island in southern central Philippines. ■ its chief city and port; pop. 798,800 (est. 2007).

Ce·cil·ia, St. /sə'silyə, -'sēlyə/ (2nd or 3rd century), Roman martyr. According to legend, she took a vow of celibacy, but, when forced to marry, converted her husband to Christianity and both were martyred. She is the patron saint of church music. Feast day, November 22.

ce·cro·pi·a /si'krōpēə/ ▶ **n. 1** a fast-growing tropical American tree, typically among the first to colonize a cleared area. Many cecropias have a symbiotic relationship with ants. ● Genus *Cecropia*, family Cecropiaceae.
2 (also **cecropia moth**) a very large North American silkworm moth with boldly marked reddish-brown wings. The caterpillars feed on a variety of forest trees. ● *Hyalophora cecropia*, family Saturniidae.
– ORIGIN early 19th cent.: modern Latin, from the name *Cecrops*, a king of Attica.

cecropia moth

ce·cum /'sēkəm/ (Brit. **caecum**) ▶ **n.** (pl. **ceca** /-kə/) Anatomy a pouch connected to the junction of the small and large intestines.
– DERIVATIVES **ce·cal** /-kəl/ **adj.**
– ORIGIN late Middle English: from Latin (*intestinum*) *caecum* 'blind (gut),' translation of Greek *tuphlon enteron*.

ce·dar /'sēdər/ ▶ **n.** any of a number of conifers that typically yield fragrant, durable timber, in particular: ● a large tree of the pine family (genus *Cedrus*, family Pinaceae), in particular the **cedar of Lebanon** (*C. libani*), with spreading branches, and the deodar. ● a tall slender North American or Asian tree (genus *Thuja*, family Cupressaceae), in particular the **western red cedar** (*T. plicata*) and the **northern white cedar** (*T. occidentalis*).
– DERIVATIVES **ce·darn** /-dərn/ **adj.** (literary).
– ORIGIN Old English, from Old French *cedre* or Latin *cedrus*, from Greek *kedros*.

Ce·dar Ra·pids an industrial and commercial city in east central Iowa, on the Cedar River; pop. 128,056 (est. 2008).

ce·dar wax·wing ▶ **n.** a North American waxwing. ● *Bombycilla cedrorum*.

cedar waxwing

cede /sēd/ ▶ **v.** [with obj.] give up (power or territory): *they have had to cede control of the schools to the government*.
– ORIGIN early 16th cent.: from French *céder* or Latin *cedere* 'to yield.'

ce·di /'sādē/ ▶ **n.** (pl. **same** or **cedis**) the basic monetary unit of Ghana, equal to 100 pesewas.
– ORIGIN of Ghanaian origin, perhaps an alteration of **SHILLING**.

ce·dil·la /sə'dilə/ ▶ **n.** a mark (̧) written under the letter *c*, esp. in French, to show that it is pronounced like an *s* rather than a *k* (e.g., *façade*). ■ a similar mark under *s* in Turkish and other oriental languages.
– ORIGIN late 16th cent.: from obsolete Spanish, earlier form of *zedilla*, diminutive of *zeda* (the letter Z), from Greek *zēta*.

cei·ba /'sābə/ ▶ **n.** a very tall tropical American tree from which kapok is obtained, with lightweight yellowish or pinkish timber. It is pollinated by bats and was held sacred by the Maya. Also called **KAPOK**. ● *Ceiba pentandra*, family Bombacaceae.
– ORIGIN early 19th cent.: via Spanish from Taino, literally 'giant tree.'

ceil /sēl/ ▶ **v.** [with obj.] (usu. **be ceiled**) archaic line or plaster the roof of (a building).
– ORIGIN late Middle English (in the sense 'line (the interior of a room) with plaster or paneling'): perhaps related to Latin *celare*, French *céler* 'conceal.'

cei·lidh /'kālē/ ▶ **n.** a social event at which there is Scottish or Irish folk music and singing, traditional dancing, and storytelling.
– ORIGIN late 19th cent.: from Scottish Gaelic *ceilidh* and Irish *céilidhe* (earlier form of *céilí*), from Old Irish *céilide* 'visit, visiting,' from *céile* 'companion.'

ceil·ing /'sēliNG/ ▶ **n. 1** the upper interior surface of a room or other similar compartment. ■ an upper limit, typically one set on prices, wages, or expenditure. See also **GLASS CEILING**. ■ the maximum altitude that a particular aircraft can reach. ■ the altitude of the base of a cloud layer.
2 the inside planking of a ship's bottom and sides.
– ORIGIN Middle English (denoting the action of lining the interior of a room with plaster or paneling): from **CEIL** + **-ING**[1]. Sense 1 dates from the mid 16th cent.

cel /sel/ ▶ **n.** a transparent sheet of celluloid or similar film material that can be drawn on, used in the production of cartoons.
– ORIGIN mid 20th cent.: abbreviation of **CELLULOID**.

cel·a·don /'selə,dän/ ▶ **n.** a willow-green color: [as modifier] *paneling painted in celadon green*. ■ a gray-green glaze used on pottery, esp. that from China. ■ pottery made with this glaze.
– ORIGIN mid 18th cent.: from French *céladon*, a color named after the hero in d'Urfé's pastoral romance *L'Astrée* (1607–27).

cel·an·dine /'selən,dīn, -,dēn/ (also **lesser celandine**) ▶ **n.** a common plant of the buttercup family that produces yellow flowers in the early spring, reproducing either by seed or by bulbils at the base of the stems. See also **GREATER CELANDINE**. ● *Ranunculus ficaria*, family Ranunculaceae.
– ORIGIN Middle English, from Old French *celidoine*, from medieval Latin *celidonia*, based on Greek *khelidōn* 'swallow' (the flowering of the plant being associated with the arrival of swallows).

-cele ▶ **comb. form** variant spelling of **-COELE**.

ce·leb /sə'leb/ ▶ **n.** informal a celebrity: *a TV celeb*.
– ORIGIN early 20th cent. (originally US): abbreviation.

WORD TRENDS Has the culture of the celeb begun to decline? The Oxford English Corpus shows that use of **celebrity** has risen steadily since 2000, but that of the abbreviation **celeb** has dropped since 2006, suggesting that the public may be starting to tire of these *trashy, wannabe, Z-list* individuals (all words regularly found attached to **celeb** in the Corpus). Although it seems very much a product of the 21st century, with its glut of reality TV and promises of instant fame, the abbreviation of **celebrity** was first seen almost a hundred years ago. Since then, **celeb** has taken on strong associations of a very particular type of fame and its attendant lifestyle, with celebs often famous simply for being famous, rather than for any particular skill or talent.

Cel·e·bes /'selə,bēz, sə'lēbēz/ former name of **SULAWESI**.

Cel·e·bes sail·fish ▶ **n.** see **SAILFISH**.

Cel·e·bes Sea a part of the western Pacific Ocean between the Philippines and the island of Sulawesi, and bounded on the west by Borneo. It is linked to the Java Sea by the Makassar Strait.

Ce·leb·ra /sə'lebrə/ ▶ **n.** trademark a synthetic drug (a COX-2 inhibitor) used in the management of arthritic pain.
– ORIGIN 1990s: an invented word.

cel·e·brant /ˈseləbrənt/ ▶ **n.** **1** a person who performs a rite, esp. a priest at the Eucharist. **2** a person who celebrates something.
– ORIGIN mid 19th cent.: from French *célébrant* or Latin *celebrant-* 'celebrating,' from the verb *celebrare* (see CELEBRATE).

cel·e·brate /ˈseləˌbrāt/ ▶ **v.** [with obj.] **1** publicly acknowledge (a significant or happy day or event) with a social gathering or enjoyable activity: *they were celebrating their wedding anniversary at a restaurant* | [no obj.] *she celebrated with a glass of champagne.* ■ reach (a birthday or anniversary).
2 perform (a religious ceremony) publicly and duly, in particular officiate at (the Eucharist): *he celebrated holy communion.*
3 honor or praise publicly: *a film celebrating the actor's career.*
– DERIVATIVES **cel·e·bra·tor** /-ˌbrātər/ **n.**, **cel·e·bra·to·ry** /səˈlebrəˌtôrē, ˈseləbrə-/ **adj.**
– ORIGIN late Middle English (sense 2): from Latin *celebrat-* 'celebrated,' from the verb *celebrare*, from *celeber, celebr-* 'frequented or honored.'

cel·e·bra·ted /ˈseləˌbrātəd/ ▶ **adj.** greatly admired; renowned: *a celebrated mathematician.*

cel·e·bra·tion /ˌseləˈbrāsHən/ ▶ **n.** the action of marking one's pleasure at an important event or occasion by engaging in enjoyable, typically social, activity: *the birth of his son was a cause for celebration* | *a birthday celebration.*
– ORIGIN early 16th cent.: from Latin *celebratio(n-)*, from the verb *celebrare* (see CELEBRATE).

ce·leb·ri·ty /səˈlebrətē/ ▶ **n.** (pl. **celebrities**) a famous person. ■ the state of being well known: *his prestige and celebrity grew.*
– ORIGIN late Middle English (in the sense 'solemn ceremony'): from Old French *celebrite* or Latin *celebritas*, from *celeber, celebr-* 'frequented or honored.'

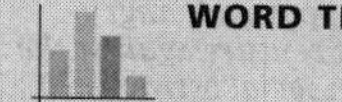
WORD TRENDS See CELEB.

ce·leb·u·tante /səˈlebyo͝oˌtänt, -yə-/ ▶ **n.** a celebrity who is well known in fashionable society.
– ORIGIN 1930s: blend of CELEBRITY and DEBUTANTE.

ce·ler·i·ac /səˈlerēˌak/ ▶ **n.** celery of a variety that forms a large swollen turniplike root that can be eaten cooked or raw. Also called CELERY ROOT. ● *Apium graveolens rapaceum.*
– ORIGIN mid 18th cent.: from CELERY + an arbitrary use of -AC.

ce·ler·i·ty /səˈleritē/ ▶ **n.** archaic or literary swiftness of movement.
– ORIGIN late 15th cent.: from Old French *celerite*, from Latin *celeritas*, from *celer* 'swift.'

cel·er·y /ˈsel(ə)rē/ ▶ **n.** a cultivated plant of the parsley family, with closely packed succulent leafstalks that are eaten raw or cooked. ● *Apium graveolens* var. *dulce*, family Umbelliferae.
– ORIGIN mid 17th cent.: from French *céleri*, from Italian dialect *selleri*, based on Greek *selinon* 'parsley.'

cel·er·y root ▶ **n.** another term for CELERIAC.

cel·er·y salt ▶ **n.** a mixture of salt and ground celery seed used for seasoning.

cel·er·y seed ▶ **n.** the seed of a plant related to the celery plant, with a celerylike flavor and aroma.

ce·les·ta /səˈlestə/ ▶ **n.** (also **celeste**) a small keyboard instrument in which felted hammers strike a row of steel plates suspended over wooden resonators, giving an ethereal bell-like sound.
– ORIGIN late 19th cent.: pseudo-Latin, based on French *céleste* 'heavenly.'

celesta

ce·les·tial /səˈlesCHəl/ ▶ **adj.** [attrib.] positioned in or relating to the sky, or outer space as observed in astronomy: *a celestial body.* ■ belonging or relating to heaven: *the celestial city.* ■ supremely good: *the celestial beauty of music.*
– DERIVATIVES **ce·les·tial·ly** **adv.**
– ORIGIN late Middle English: via Old French from medieval Latin *caelestialis*, from Latin *caelestis*, from *caelum* 'heaven.'

ce·les·tial bam·boo ▶ **n.** another term for NANDINA.

ce·les·tial e·qua·tor ▶ **n.** the projection into space of the earth's equator; an imaginary circle equidistant from the celestial poles.

ce·les·tial globe ▶ **n.** a spherical representation of the sky showing the constellations.

ce·les·tial ho·ri·zon ▶ **n.** see HORIZON (sense 1).

ce·les·tial lat·i·tude ▶ **n.** Astronomy the angular distance of a point north or south of the ecliptic. Compare with DECLINATION (sense 1).

ce·les·tial lon·gi·tude ▶ **n.** Astronomy the angular distance of a point east of the vernal equinox, measured along the ecliptic. Compare with RIGHT ASCENSION.

ce·les·tial me·chan·ics ▶ **plural n.** [treated as sing.] the branch of theoretical astronomy that deals with the calculation of the motions of celestial objects such as planets.

ce·les·tial me·rid·i·an ▶ **n.** see MERIDIAN (sense 1 of the noun).

ce·les·tial nav·i·ga·tion ▶ **n.** the action of finding one's way by observing the sun, moon, and stars.

ce·les·tial pole ▶ **n.** Astronomy the point on the celestial sphere directly above either of the earth's geographic poles, around which the stars and planets appear to rotate during the course of the night. The north celestial pole is currently within one degree of the star Polaris.

ce·les·tial sphere ▶ **n.** an imaginary sphere of which the observer is the center and on which all celestial objects are considered to lie.

ce·li·ac /ˈsēlēˌak/ (Brit. **coeliac**) ▶ **adj.** **1** Anatomy of or relating to the abdomen.
2 Medicine of, relating to, or affected by celiac disease: *a celiac child.*
▶ **n.** a person with celiac disease.
– ORIGIN mid 17th cent.: from Latin *coeliacus*, from Greek *koiliakos*, from *koilia* 'belly.'

ce·li·ac dis·ease ▶ **n.** a disease in which the small intestine is hypersensitive to gluten, leading to difficulty in digesting food.

cel·i·ba·cy /ˈseləbəsē/ ▶ **n.** the state of abstaining from marriage and sexual relations: *his brother's priestly vow of celibacy.*

cel·i·bate /ˈseləbət/ ▶ **adj.** abstaining from marriage and sexual relations, typically for religious reasons: *a celibate priest.* ■ having or involving no sexual relations: *I'd rather stay single and celibate.*
▶ **n.** a person who abstains from marriage and sexual relations.
– ORIGIN early 19th cent.: from *celibacy*, on the pattern of pairs such as *magistracy, magistrate.*

cell /sel/ ▶ **n.** **1** a small room in which a prisoner is locked up or in which a monk or nun sleeps. ■ historical a small monastery or nunnery dependent on a larger one.
2 Biology the smallest structural and functional unit of an organism, typically microscopic and consisting of cytoplasm and a nucleus enclosed in a membrane. Microscopic organisms typically consist of a single cell, which is either eukaryotic or prokaryotic. ■ an enclosed cavity in an organism. ■ a small compartment in a larger structure such as a honeycomb.
3 a small group forming a nucleus of political activity, typically a secret, subversive one: *the weapons may be used to arm terrorist cells.*
4 the local area covered by one of the short-range transmitters in a cellular telephone system. ■ a cellular phone: *I'll just call him on his cell.*
5 a device containing electrodes immersed in an electrolyte, used for current-generation or electrolysis. ■ a unit in a device for converting chemical or solar energy into electricity.
– DERIVATIVES **celled** **adj.** [in combination] *a single-celled organism*, **cell-like** /-ˌlīk/ **adj.**
– ORIGIN Old English, from Old French *celle* or Latin *cella* 'storeroom or chamber.'

cel·la /ˈselə/ ▶ **n.** (pl. **cellae** /ˈselē/) the inner area of an ancient temple, esp. one housing the hidden cult image in a Greek or Roman temple.
– ORIGIN late 17th cent.: Latin, literally 'storeroom, shrine,' from *celare* 'hide.' (See CONCEAL).

cel·lar /ˈselər/ ▶ **n.** a room below ground level in a house, typically one used for storing wine or coal. ■ a stock of wine.
▶ **v.** [with obj.] store (wine) in a cellar.
– ORIGIN Middle English (in the general sense 'storeroom'): from Old French *celier*, from late Latin *cellarium* 'storehouse,' from *cella* 'storeroom or chamber.'

cel·lar·age /ˈselərij/ ▶ **n.** cellars collectively. ■ money charged for the use of a cellar or storehouse.

cel·lar·er /ˈselərər/ ▶ **n.** the person in a monastery who is responsible for the provisioning of food and drink.

cel·lar·et /ˌseləˈret/ (also **cellarette**) ▶ **n.** historical a cabinet for keeping bottles of wine and liquor.

cell block ▶ **n.** a large single building or part of a complex subdivided into separate prison cells.

cell di·vi·sion ▶ **n.** Biology the division of a cell into two daughter cells with the same genetic material.

Cel·li·ni /CHəˈlēnē/, Benvenuto (1500–71), Italian goldsmith and sculptor.

cell line ▶ **n.** Biology a cell culture developed from a single cell and therefore consisting of cells with a uniform genetic makeup.

cell·mate /ˈselmāt/ ▶ **n.** a person with whom one shares a cell.

cell-me·di·at·ed ▶ **adj.** Physiology denoting the aspect of an immune response involving the action of white blood cells, rather than that of circulating antibodies. Often contrasted with HUMORAL.

cell mem·brane ▶ **n.** the semipermeable membrane surrounding the cytoplasm of a cell. Also called CYTOMEMBRANE.

cel·lo /ˈCHelō/ ▶ **n.** (pl. **cellos**) a bass instrument of the violin family, held upright on the floor between the legs of the seated player.
– DERIVATIVES **cel·list** /ˈCHelist/ **n.**
– ORIGIN late 19th cent.: shortening of VIOLONCELLO.

cello

cel·lo·phane /ˈseləˌfān/ ▶ **n.** a thin transparent wrapping material made from viscose.
– ORIGIN early 20th cent.: originally a trademark.

cell phone (also **cellphone**) ▶ **n.** short for CELLULAR PHONE.

cel·lu·lar /ˈselyələr/ ▶ **adj.** **1** of, relating to, or consisting of living cells: *cellular proliferation.*
2 denoting or relating to a mobile telephone system that uses a number of short-range radio stations to cover the area that it serves, the signal being automatically switched from one station to another as the user travels about.
3 (of a fabric item, such as a blanket or vest) knitted so as to form holes or hollows that trap air and provide extra insulation.
4 consisting of small compartments or rooms: *cellular accommodations.*
– DERIVATIVES **cel·lu·lar·i·ty** /ˌselyəˈlaritē/ **n.**
– ORIGIN mid 18th cent.: from French *cellulaire*, from modern Latin *cellularis*, from *cellula* 'little chamber,' diminutive of *cella*.

cel·lu·lar au·tom·a·ton ▶ **n.** (pl. **cellular automata**) Computing one of a set of units in a mathematical model that have simple rules governing their replication and destruction. They are used to model complex systems composed of simple units such as living things or parallel processors.

cel·lu·lar blind ▶ **n.** a window blind with a single or double layer of collapsible voids that provide insulation when the blind is extended.

cel·lu·lar phone (also **cellular telephone**) ▶ **n.** a telephone with access to a cellular radio system so it can be used over a wide area, without a physical connection to a network.

cel·lu·lase /ˈselyəˌlās, -ˌlāz/ ▶ **n.** Biochemistry an enzyme that converts cellulose into glucose or a disaccharide.
– ORIGIN early 20th cent.: from CELLULOSE + -ASE.

cel·lu·lite /ˈselyəˌlīt/ ▶ **n.** persistent subcutaneous fat causing dimpling of the skin, esp. on women's hips and thighs. Not in technical use.
– ORIGIN 1960s: from French, from *cellule* 'small cell.'

cel·lu·li·tis /ˌselyəˈlītis/ ▶ **n.** Medicine inflammation of subcutaneous connective tissue.

cel·lu·loid /ˈselyəˌloid/ ▶ **n.** a transparent flammable plastic made in sheets from camphor and nitrocellulose, formerly used for cinematographic film. ■ motion pictures as a genre: *having made the leap from theater to celluloid, she can now make more money.*
– ORIGIN mid 19th cent.: from CELLULOSE + -OID.

cel·lu·lose /ˈselyəˌlōs, -ˌlōz/ ▶ **n.** **1** an insoluble substance that is the main constituent of plant cell

walls and of vegetable fibers such as cotton. It is a polysaccharide consisting of chains of glucose monomers.
2 paint or lacquer consisting principally of cellulose acetate or nitrate in solution.
– DERIVATIVES **cel·lu·lo·sic** /ˌselyəˈlōsik, -ˈlōzik/ **adj.**
– ORIGIN mid 19th cent.: from French, from *cellule* 'small cell' + **-OSE²**.

cel·lu·lose ac·e·tate ▶ **n.** Chemistry a nonflammable thermoplastic polymer made by acetylating cellulose, used as the basis of artificial fibers and plastic.

cel·lu·lose ni·trate ▶ **n.** another term for **NITROCELLULOSE**.

cel·lu·lose tri·ac·e·tate ▶ **n.** see **TRIACETATE**.

cell wall ▶ **n.** Biology a rigid layer of polysaccharides lying outside the plasma membrane of the cells of plants, fungi, and bacteria. In the algae and higher plants, it consists mainly of cellulose.

ce·lom ▶ **n.** variant spelling of **COELOM**.

ce·lo·sia /siˈlōzн(ē)ə/ ▶ **n.** a plant of a genus that includes cockscomb. ● Genus *Celosia*, family Amarantaceae.
– ORIGIN modern Latin, from Greek *kēlos* 'burned or dry' (from the burned appearance of the flowers in some species).

Cel·si·us¹ /ˈselsēəs, ˈselsнəs/, Anders (1701–44), Swedish astronomer; best known for his temperature scale.

Cel·si·us² (abbr.: **C**) ▶ **adj.** [postpositive when used with a numeral] of or denoting a scale of temperature on which water freezes at 0° and boils at 100° under standard conditions.
▶ **n.** (also **Celsius scale**) this scale of temperature.

> **USAGE** **Celsius**, rather than **centigrade**, is the standard accepted term when giving temperatures: use *25° Celsius* rather than *25° centigrade*.

Celt /kelt, selt/ ▶ **n.** a member of a group of peoples inhabiting much of Europe and Asia Minor in pre-Roman times. Their culture developed in the late Bronze Age around the upper Danube, and reached its height in the La Tène culture (5th to 1st centuries BC) before being overrun by the Romans and various Germanic peoples. ■ a native of any of the modern nations or regions in which Celtic languages are (or were until recently) spoken; a person of Irish, Highland Scottish, Manx, Welsh, or Cornish descent.
– ORIGIN from Latin *Celtae* (plural), from Greek *Keltoi*; in later use from French *Celte* 'Breton' (taken as representing the ancient Gauls).

> **USAGE** See usage at **CELTIC**.

celt /selt/ ▶ **n.** Archaeology a prehistoric stone or metal implement with a beveled cutting edge, probably used as a tool or weapon.
– ORIGIN early 18th cent.: from medieval Latin *celtis* 'chisel.'

Celt·i·ber·i·an /ˌkeltīˈbirēən, ˌsel-/ ▶ **n.** another term for **IBERIAN** (sense 3 of the noun).

Celt·ic /ˈkeltik, ˈsel-/ ▶ **adj.** of or relating to the Celts or their languages, which constitute a branch of the Indo-European family and include Irish, Scottish Gaelic, Welsh, Breton, Manx, Cornish, and several extinct pre-Roman languages such as Gaulish.
▶ **n.** the Celtic language group. See also **P-CELTIC**, **Q-CELTIC**.
– DERIVATIVES **Celt·i·cism** /ˈkeltəˌsizəm, ˈsel-/ **n.**, **Celt·i·cist** /ˈkeltəˌsist, ˈsel-/ **n.**
– ORIGIN late 16th cent.: from Latin *Celticus* (from *Celtae* 'Celts'), or from French *Celtique* (from *Celte* 'Breton').

> **USAGE** Although **Celt** and **Celtic** can be pronounced with either an initial **k-** or an initial **s-** sound, in standard English the normal pronunciation is with the **k-** sound. A notable exception is the name of Boston's professional basketball team, the Celtics, which is always pronounced with the **s-** sound.

Celt·ic Church the Christian Church in the British Isles from its foundation in the 2nd or 3rd century until its assimilation into the Roman Catholic Church (664 in England; 12th century in Wales, Scotland, and Ireland).

Celt·ic cross ▶ **n.** a Latin cross with a circle around the center.

Celt·ic fringe ▶ **n.** the Highland Scots, Irish, Welsh, and Cornish in relation to the rest of Britain.

Celt·ic harp ▶ **n.** a small harp with wire strings, used in the folk and early music of Scotland and Ireland.

Celt·ic Sea the part of the Atlantic Ocean that is between southern Ireland and southwestern England.

cem·ba·lo /ˈcнembəˌlō/ ▶ **n.** (pl. **cembalos**) another term for **HARPSICHORD**.
– DERIVATIVES **cem·ba·list** /-bəlist/ **n.**
– ORIGIN mid 19th cent.: from Italian, shortening of *clavicembalo*, from medieval Latin *clavicymbalum*, from Latin *clavis* 'key' + *cymbalum* 'cymbal.'

ce·ment /siˈment/ ▶ **n.** a powdery substance made with calcined lime and clay. It is mixed with water to form mortar or mixed with sand, gravel, and water to make concrete. ■ a soft glue that hardens on setting: *rubber cement.* ■ an element that unites a group of people: ***traditional entertainment was a form of community cement.*** ■ another term for **CONCRETE**. ■ a substance for filling cavities in teeth. ■ (also **cementum**) Anatomy a thin layer of bony material that fixes teeth to the jaw. ■ Geology the material that binds particles together in sedimentary rock.
▶ **v.** [with obj.] attach with cement: *wooden posts were cemented into the ground.* ■ settle or establish firmly: ***the two firms are expected to cement an agreement soon.*** ■ Geology (of a material) bind (particles) together in sedimentary rock.
– DERIVATIVES **ce·ment·er n.**
– ORIGIN Middle English: from Old French *ciment* (noun), *cimenter* (verb), from Latin *caementum* 'quarry stone,' from *caedere* 'hew.'

ce·men·ta·tion /ˌsēˌmenˈtāsнən/ ▶ **n. 1** chiefly Geology the binding together of particles or other things by cement.
2 Metallurgy a process of altering a metal by heating it in contact with a powdered solid, esp. a former method of making steel by heating iron in contact with charcoal.

ce·ment·ite /siˈmenˌtīt/ ▶ **n.** Metallurgy a hard, brittle iron carbide present in cast iron and most steels. ● Chem. formula: Fe_3C.
– ORIGIN late 19th cent.: from **CEMENT** + **-ITE¹**.

ce·men·ti·tious /ˌsēˌmenˈtisнəs/ ▶ **adj.** of the nature of cement.

ce·ment mix·er (also **concrete mixer**) ▶ **n.** a machine with a revolving drum used for mixing cement with sand, gravel, and water to make concrete.

cem·e·ter·y /ˈseməˌterē/ ▶ **n.** (pl. **cemeteries**) a burial ground; a graveyard.
– ORIGIN late Middle English: via late Latin from Greek *koimētērion* 'dormitory,' from *koiman* 'put to sleep.'

cen·a·cle /ˈsenikəl/ ▶ **n. 1** a group of people, such as a discussion group or literary clique.
2 the room in which the Last Supper was held.
– ORIGIN late Middle English: from Old French *cenacle*, from Latin *cenaculum*, from *cena* 'dinner.'

ce·no·bite /ˈsenəˌbīt/ (also **coenobite**) ▶ **n.** a member of a monastic community.
– DERIVATIVES **ce·no·bit·ic** /ˌsenəˈbitik/ **adj.**, **ce·no·bit·i·cal** /ˌsenəˈbitikəl/ **adj.**
– ORIGIN late Middle English: from Old French *cenobite* or ecclesiastical Latin *coenobita*, via late Latin from Greek *koinobion* 'convent,' from *koinos* 'common' + *bios* 'life.'

ce·no·spe·cies /ˈsēnəˌspēsēz, -ˌspēsнēz/ ▶ **n.** a group of species whose members produce partially fertile hybrids when crossbred.

ce·no·taph /ˈsenəˌtaf/ ▶ **n.** a tomblike monument to someone buried elsewhere, esp. one commemorating people who died in a war.
– ORIGIN early 17th cent.: from French *cénotaphe*, from late Latin *cenotaphium*, from Greek *kenos* 'empty' + *taphos* 'tomb.'

Ce·no·zo·ic /ˌsenəˈzōik/ (also **Cainozoic** /ˌkīnə-/) ▶ **adj.** Geology relating to or denoting the most recent era, following the Mesozoic era and comprising the Tertiary and Quaternary periods. ■ (as noun **the Cenozoic**) the Cenozoic era, or the system of rocks deposited during it.

> The Cenozoic has lasted from about 65 million years ago to the present day. It has seen the rapid evolution and rise to dominance of mammals, birds, and flowering plants.

– ORIGIN mid 19th cent.: from Greek *kainos* 'new' + *zōion* 'animal' + **-IC**.

cense /sens/ ▶ **v.** [with obj.] perfume (something) ritually with the odor of burning incense.
– ORIGIN late Middle English: from Old French *encenser*.

cen·ser /ˈsensər/ ▶ **n.** a container in which incense is burned, typically during a religious ceremony.
– ORIGIN Middle English: from Old French *censier*, from *encensier*, from *encens* (see **INCENSE¹**).

cen·sor /ˈsensər/ ▶ **n. 1** an official who examines material that is about to be released, such as books, movies, news, and art, and suppresses any parts that are considered obscene, politically unacceptable, or a threat to security. ■ Psychoanalysis an aspect of the superego that is said to prevent certain ideas and memories from emerging into consciousness. [from a mistranslation of German *Zensur* 'censorship,' coined by Freud.]
2 (in ancient Rome) either of two magistrates who held censuses and supervised public morals.
▶ **v.** [with obj.] examine (a book, movie, etc.) officially and suppress unacceptable parts of it: *my mail was being censored.*
– DERIVATIVES **cen·so·ri·al** /senˈsôrēəl/ **adj.**
– ORIGIN mid 16th cent. (sense 2 of the noun): from Latin, from *censere* 'assess.'

> **USAGE** Both **censor** and **censure** are used as both verbs and nouns, but **censor** means 'scrutinize, revise, or cut unacceptable parts from (a book, movie, etc.)' or 'a person who does this,' while **censure** means 'criticize harshly' or 'harsh criticism': *the inmates received their mail only after prison officials had censored all the contents; some senators considered a resolution of censure to express strong disapproval of the president's behavior.*

cen·so·ri·ous /senˈsôrēəs/ ▶ **adj.** severely critical of others: *modest, charitable in his judgments, never censorious, Jim carried tolerance almost too far.*
– DERIVATIVES **cen·so·ri·ous·ly adv.**, **cen·so·ri·ous·ness n.**
– ORIGIN mid 16th cent.: from Latin *censorius* (from *censor* 'magistrate') + **-IOUS**.

cen·sor·ship /ˈsensərˌsнip/ ▶ **n.** the practice of officially examining books, movies, etc., and suppressing unacceptable parts: ***details of the visit were subject to military censorship.***

cen·sure /ˈsensнər/ ▶ **v.** [with obj.] express severe disapproval of (someone or something), typically in a formal statement: ***a judge was censured in 1983 for a variety of types of injudicious conduct.***
▶ **n.** the expression of formal disapproval: ***angry delegates offered a resolution of censure against the offenders | they paid the price in social ostracism and family censure.***
– DERIVATIVES **cen·sur·a·ble adj.**
– ORIGIN late Middle English (in the sense 'judicial sentence'): from Old French *censurer* (verb), *censure* (noun), from Latin *censura* 'judgment, assessment,' from *censere* 'assess.'

> **USAGE** On the difference in meaning between **censure** and **censor**, see usage at **CENSOR**.

cen·sus /ˈsensəs/ ▶ **n.** (pl. **censuses**) an official count or survey of a population, typically recording various details of individuals: ***population estimates extrapolated from the 1981 census*** | [as modifier] ***census data.***
– ORIGIN early 17th cent. (denoting a poll tax): from Latin, applied to the registration of citizens and property in ancient Rome, usually for taxation, from *censere* 'assess.' The current sense dates from the mid 18th cent.

cent /sent/ ▶ **n. 1** a monetary unit of the US, Canada, and various other countries, equal to one hundredth of a dollar, euro, or other decimal currency unit. ■ informal a small sum of money: *she saved every cent possible.* ■ [in sing. with negative] informal used for emphasis to denote any money at all: *he hadn't yet earned a cent.*
2 Music one hundredth of a half step.
– PHRASES **one's two cents' worth** informal one's unsolicited opinion.
– ORIGIN late Middle English (in the sense 'a hundred'): from French *cent*, Italian *cento*, or Latin *centum* 'hundred.'

cent. ▶ **abbr.** ■ centigrade. ■ century.

cen·tas /ˈsenˌtäs/ ▶ **n.** (pl. **same**) a monetary unit of Lithuania, equal to one hundredth of a litas.
– ORIGIN Lithuanian.

cen·taur /ˈsenˌtôr/ ▶ **n.** Greek Mythology a creature with the head, arms, and torso of a man and the body and legs of a horse.
– ORIGIN via Latin from Greek *kentauros*, the Greek name for a Thessalonian tribe of expert horsemen; of unknown ultimate origin.

centaur

cen·tau·re·a /senˈtôrēə/ ▶ **n.** a plant of a Eurasian genus that includes the cornflower and knapweed. Several kinds are cultivated for their bright flowers. ● Genus *Centaurea*, family Compositae.
– ORIGIN modern Latin based on Greek *kentauros* 'centaur' (see **CENTAURY**).

Cen·tau·rus /senˈtôrəs/ Astronomy a large southern constellation (the Centaur). It lies in the Milky Way

and contains the stars Alpha and Proxima Centauri. ■ (as genitive **Centauri** /sen'tôrē/) used with a preceding letter or numeral to designate a star in this constellation: *the star Lambda Centauri*.
– ORIGIN Latin.

cen·tau·ry /'sen,tôrē/ ▶ **n.** (pl. **centauries**) a widely distributed herbaceous plant of the gentian family, typically having pink petals atop long calyx tubes. ● *Centaurium* and related genera, family Gentianaceae: many species, including the wild *C. pulchellum* and the cultivated ornamental *C. scilloides*.
– ORIGIN late Middle English: from late Latin *centaurea*, based on Greek *kentauros* 'centaur' (because its medicinal properties were said to have been discovered by the centaur Chiron).

cen·ta·vo /sen'tävō/ ▶ **n.** (pl. **centavos**) a monetary unit of Mexico, Brazil, and certain other countries (including Portugal until the introduction of the euro), equal to one hundredth of the basic unit.
– ORIGIN Spanish and Portuguese, from Latin *centum* 'a hundred.'

CENTCOM (also **CentCom**) ▶ **abbr.** the unified armed forces command organization that oversees US military operations in the Middle East.
– ORIGIN acronym from *Central Command*.

cen·te·nar·i·an /,sentn'e(ə)rēən/ ▶ **n.** a person who is one hundred or more years old.
▶ **adj.** [attrib.] one hundred or more years old.

cen·ten·ar·y /sen'tenərē, 'sentn,erē/ chiefly Brit. ▶ **n.** (pl. **centenaries**) the hundredth anniversary of a significant event; a centennial.
▶ **adj.** of or relating to a hundredth anniversary; centennial.
– ORIGIN early 17th cent. (denoting a century): from Latin *centenarius* 'containing a hundred,' based on Latin *centum* 'a hundred.'

Cen·ten·ni·al /sen'tenēəl/ a city in north-central Colorado, governed by home rule; pop. 99,680 (est. 2008).

cen·ten·ni·al /sen'tenēəl/ ▶ **adj.** of or relating to a hundredth anniversary: *centennial celebrations*.
▶ **n.** a hundredth anniversary: *the museum's centennial*.
– ORIGIN late 18th cent.: from Latin *centum* 'a hundred,' on the pattern of *biennial*.

Cen·ten·ni·al State a nickname for the state of **COLORADO**.

cen·ter /'sentər/ (Brit. **centre**) ▶ **n.** **1** the middle point of a circle or sphere, equidistant from every point on the circumference or surface. ■ a point or part that is equally distant from all sides, ends, or surfaces of something; the middle: *the center of the ceiling | the center of a vast territory*. ■ a pivot or axis of rotation: *the galactic rotation of the solar system around the galactic center*. ■ a political party or group holding moderate opinions. ■ Sports the middle player in a line or group in many games: *Terry played center on the basketball team*. ■ Baseball short for **CENTER FIELD**: *he flied out to center*. ■ a core, such as the filling in a piece of chocolate: *truffles with liqueur centers*. ■ a conical adjustable support for a workpiece in a lathe or similar machine.
2 the point from which an activity or process is directed, or on which it is focused: *the city was* **a** *center of discontent | two issues* **at the center of** *the health-care debate*. ■ the most important place in the respect specified: *Geneva was then the center of the international world*.
3 a place or group of buildings where a specified activity is concentrated: *a center for medical research | a shopping center*.
▶ **v.** **1** [no obj.] (**center around/on** or **center something around/on**) have or cause to have something as (a major concern or theme): *the case centers around the couple's adopted children | the plot centers on two young men* | [with obj.] *he is centering his discussion on an analysis of patterns of mortality*. ■ (**be centered in**) (of an activity) occur mainly in or around (a specified place): *the mercantile association was centered in northern Germany*.
2 [with obj.] place in the middle: *to center the needle, turn the knob*. ■ Football pass the ball back from the ground to another player to begin a down; snap.
– DERIVATIVES **cen·ter·most** /-,mōst/ **adj.**
– ORIGIN late Middle English *centre*, from Old French, or from Latin *centrum*, from Greek *kentron* 'sharp point, stationary point of a pair of compasses,' related to *kentein* 'to prick.'

> **USAGE** The construction **center around** (as opposed to *center on*, or *revolve around*) has been denounced as incorrect and illogical since it first appeared in the mid 19th century. Although the phrase is common, it defies geometry by confusing the orbit with the fixed point: *the earth revolves around* (or *its revolution centers on*) *the sun*. A careful writer will use a precise expression, such as *centers on, revolves around, concerns*, or *involves*.

cen·ter back ▶ **n.** Sports a player in the middle of the back line in some sports, such as volleyball.

cen·ter bit ▶ **n.** a tool for boring cylindrical holes.

cen·ter·board /'sentər,bôrd/ ▶ **n.** a pivoted board that can be lowered through the keel of a sailboat to reduce sideways movement. Compare with **DAGGERBOARD**.

cen·tered /'sentərd/ (Brit. **centred**) ▶ **adj.** **1** placed or situated in the center.
2 [in combination] having the specified subject as the focal element: *a computer-centered industry*.
3 (of a person) well balanced and confident or serene.
4 [in combination] having a center or filling of a specified type: *a soft-centered chocolate*.
– DERIVATIVES **cen·tered·ness** **n.**

cen·ter field (also **centerfield**) ▶ **n.** Baseball the central part of the outfield, behind second base: *a single to center field*. ■ the position of an outfielder in this area: *Amaro played some center field when Dykstra went on the disabled list*.
– DERIVATIVES **cen·ter field·er** **n.**

cen·ter·fire /'sentər,fīr/ ▶ **adj.** [attrib.] (of a gun cartridge) having the primer in the center of the base. ■ (of a gun) using such cartridges.
▶ **n.** a gun using such a cartridge.

cen·ter·fold /'sentər,fōld/ ▶ **n.** the two middle pages of a magazine, typically taken up by a single illustration or feature. ■ an illustration on such pages, typically a picture of a naked or scantily clad model.

cen·ter for·ward ▶ **n.** Sports an attacker who plays in the middle of the field.

cen·ter half·back ▶ **n.** Sports another term for **CENTER BACK**.

cen·ter·ing /'sentəriNG/ ▶ **n.** Architecture framing used to support an arch or dome while it is under construction.

cen·ter·line /'sentər,līn/ (also **center line**) ▶ **n.** a real or imaginary line through the center of something, esp. one following an axis of symmetry. ■ a painted line running down the middle of a road, dividing traffic traveling in opposite directions.

cen·ter of at·ten·tion ▶ **n.** a person or thing that draws general attention.

cen·ter of at·trac·tion ▶ **n.** **1** Physics the point to which bodies tend by gravity.
2 another term for **CENTER OF ATTENTION**.

cen·ter of buoy·an·cy ▶ **n.** Physics the centroid of the immersed part of a ship or other floating body.

cen·ter of cur·va·ture ▶ **n.** Mathematics the center of a circle that passes through a curve at a given point and has the same tangent and curvature at that point.

cen·ter of grav·i·ty ▶ **n.** a point from which the weight of a body or system may be considered to act. In uniform gravity it is the same as the center of mass.

cen·ter of mass ▶ **n.** a point representing the mean position of the matter in a body or system.

cen·ter·piece /'sentər,pēs/ ▶ **n.** a decorative piece or display placed in the middle of a dining or serving table. ■ an item or issue intended to be a focus of attention: *the tower is the centerpiece of the park*.

cen·ter punch ▶ **n.** a tool with a conical point for making an indentation in an object, to allow a drill to make a hole at the same spot without slipping.

cen·ter spread ▶ **n.** the two facing middle pages of a newspaper or magazine.

cen·ter stage ▶ **n.** [in sing.] the center of a stage. ■ the most prominent position: *oil remains at center stage, with demands for expanded drilling*.
▶ **adv.** at or toward the middle of a stage: *at the play's opening she stands center stage*. ■ in or toward a prominent position: *Asian countries have moved center stage for world business*.

cen·tes·i·mal /sen'tesəməl/ ▶ **adj.** of or relating to division into hundredths.
– DERIVATIVES **cen·tes·i·mal·ly** **adv.**
– ORIGIN early 19th cent.: from Latin *centesimus* 'hundredth,' from *centum* 'a hundred.'

cen·tes·i·mo /sen'tesə,mō, CHen'tez-/ ▶ **n.** (pl. **centesimos** or **centesimi** /-mē/) a monetary unit of Italy until the introduction of the euro, worth one hundredth of a lira (used only in calculations).
– ORIGIN Italian.

cen·té·si·mo /sen'tesə,mō/ ▶ **n.** (pl. **centésimos**) a monetary unit of Uruguay and Panama, equal to one hundredth of a peso in Uruguay and one hundredth of a balboa in Panama.
– ORIGIN Spanish.

centi- ▶ **comb. form** used commonly in units of measurement. **1** one hundredth: *centiliter*.
2 hundred: *centigrade | centipede*.
– ORIGIN from Latin *centum* 'hundred.'

cen·ti·grade /'sentə,grād/ ▶ **adj.** [postpositive when used with a numeral] another term for **CELSIUS²**.
– ORIGIN early 19th cent.: from French, from Latin *centum* 'a hundred' + *gradus* 'step.'

> **USAGE** See usage at **CELSIUS²**.

cen·ti·gram /'sentə,gram/ (abbr.: **cg**) ▶ **n.** a metric unit of mass, equal to one hundredth of a gram.

cen·ti·li·ter /'sentə,lētər/ (Brit. **centilitre**) (abbr.: **cl**) ▶ **n.** a metric unit of capacity, equal to one hundredth of a liter.

cen·time /'sän,tēm, 'sent-/ ▶ **n.** a monetary unit of Switzerland and certain other countries (including France, Belgium, and Luxembourg until the introduction of the euro), equal to one hundredth of a franc or other decimal currency unit.
– ORIGIN French, from Latin *centesimus* 'hundredth,' from *centum* 'a hundred.'

cen·ti·me·ter /'sentə,mētər, 'sän-/ (Brit. **centimetre**) (abbr.: **cm**) ▶ **n.** a metric unit of length, equal to one hundredth of a meter.

cen·ti·me·ter-gram-sec·ond sys·tem ▶ **n.** a system of measurement using the centimeter, the gram, and the second as basic units of length, mass, and time.

cen·ti·mo /'sentəmō/ ▶ **n.** (pl. **centimos**) a monetary unit of Spain (until the introduction of the euro) and a number of Latin American countries, equal to one hundredth of the basic unit.
– ORIGIN Spanish.

cen·ti·pede /'sentə,pēd/ ▶ **n.** a predatory myriapod invertebrate with a flattened elongated body composed of many segments. Most segments bear a single pair of legs. ● Class Chilopoda: several orders.
– ORIGIN mid 17th cent.: from French *centipède* or Latin *centipeda*, from *centum* 'a hundred' + *pes, ped-* 'foot.'

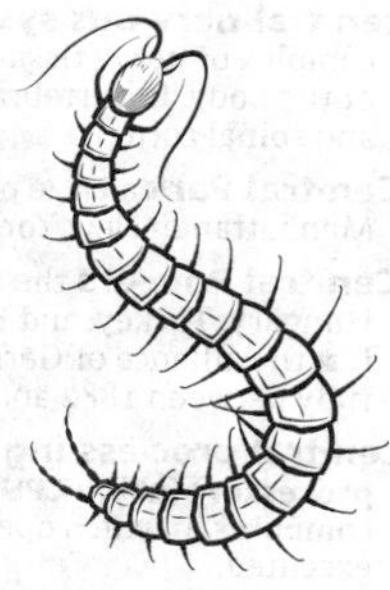
centipede

cen·to /'sentō/ ▶ **n.** (pl. **centos**) rare a literary work made up of quotations from other works.
– ORIGIN early 17th cent.: Latin, 'patchwork garment,' the original sense in English.

cen·tra /'sentrə/ a plural form of **CENTRUM**.

cen·tral /'sentrəl/ ▶ **adj.** **1** of, at, or forming the center: *the station has a central courtyard*. ■ accessible from a variety of places: *coaches met at a central location*. ■ Phonetics (of a vowel) articulated in the center of the mouth.
2 of the greatest importance; principal or essential: *his preoccupation with American history is* **central to** *his work | the rising crime rate remained the central campaign issue*. ■ [attrib.] (of a group or organization) having controlling power over a country or another organization: *central government | the central office*.
▶ **n.** informal a place with a high concentration of a specified type of person or thing: *you're in workaholic central here*.
– DERIVATIVES **cen·tral·i·ty** /sen'tralətē/ **n.**, **cen·tral·ly** **adv.**
– ORIGIN mid 17th cent.: from French, or from Latin *centralis*, from *centrum* (see **CENTER**).

Cen·tral Af·ri·can Re·pub·lic a country in central Africa; pop. 4,511,500 (est. 2009); capital, Bangui; languages, French (official) and Sango. Former name (until 1958) **UBANGHI SHARI**.

> Formerly a French colony, it became a republic within the French Community in 1958 and a fully independent state in 1960. Some stability was achieved when a civilian government was elected in 1993.

Cen·tral A·mer·i·ca the southernmost part of North America that links the continent to South America and consists of the countries of Guatemala, Belize, Honduras, El Salvador, Nicaragua, Costa Rica, and Panama.
– DERIVATIVES **Cen·tral A·mer·i·can** **adj.** & **n.**

cen·tral bank ▶ **n.** a national bank that provides financial and banking services for its country's government and commercial banking system, as well as implementing the government's monetary policy and issuing currency.

C

cen·tral cast·ing ▶ **n.** an agency or department that supplies actors for minor, usually stereotypical or generic film roles: figurative *Lynch is a mild, methodical guy, a bureaucrat from central casting.*
– ORIGIN 1920s: from the name of the organization *Central Casting Corporation.*

Cen·tral Com·mand (abbr.: **Centcom**) a military strike force consisting of units from the US Army, Air Force, and Navy, established in 1979 (as the Rapid Deployment Force) to operate in the Middle East and North Africa.

cen·tral heat·ing ▶ **n.** a system for warming a building by heating water or air in one place and circulating it through pipes and radiators or vents.

Cen·tral In·tel·li·gence A·gen·cy (abbr.: **CIA**) a US federal agency responsible for coordinating government intelligence activities.

cen·tral·ism /ˈsentrəˌlizəm/ ▶ **n.** a system that centralizes, esp. an administration.
– DERIVATIVES **cen·tral·ist n. & adj.**

cen·tral·ize /ˈsentrəˌlīz/ ▶ **v.** [with obj.] (often as adj. **centralized**) concentrate (control of an activity or organization) under a single authority: *a vast superstructure of centralized control.* ■ bring (activities) together in one place: *the ultimate goal is to centralize boxing under one umbrella.*
– DERIVATIVES **cen·tral·i·za·tion** /ˌsentrələˈzāsʜən/ **n.**

cen·tral lock·ing ▶ **n.** a locking system in a motor vehicle that enables the locks of all doors to be operated simultaneously by a single person.

cen·tral nerv·ous sys·tem ▶ **n.** Anatomy the complex of nerve tissues that controls the activities of the body. In vertebrates it comprises the brain and spinal cord.

Cen·tral Park a large public park in the center of Manhattan in New York City.

Cen·tral Pow·ers the alliance of Germany, Austria–Hungary, Turkey, and Bulgaria during World War I. ■ the alliance of Germany, Austria–Hungary, and Italy between 1882 and 1914.

cen·tral proc·ess·ing u·nit (also **central processor**) (abbr.: **CPU**) ▶ **n.** Computing the part of a computer in which operations are controlled and executed.

Cen·tral time the standard time in a zone that includes the central states of the US and parts of central Canada, specifically. ● (**Central Standard Time** abbr.: **CST**) standard time based on the mean solar time at longitude 90° W, six hours behind GMT. ● (**Central Daylight Time** abbr.: **CDT**) Central time during daylight saving, five hours behind GMT.

Cen·tral Val·ley a lowland in central California that is drained in the north by the Sacramento River and also is called the Sacramento Valley. In the south, it is called the San Joaquin Valley.

cen·tre ▶ **n.** British spelling of CENTER.

cen·trex /ˈsenˌtreks/ (trademark **Centrex**) ▶ **n.** a telephone service in which a group of phone lines can be joined by part of the local exchange acting as a private exchange.
– ORIGIN late 20th cent.: blend of CENTRAL and EXCHANGE.

cen·tric /ˈsentrik/ ▶ **adj. 1** in or at the center; central: *centric and peripheral forces.*
2 Botany (of a diatom) radially symmetrical. Compare with PENNATE.
– DERIVATIVES **cen·tri·cal** /-trikəl/ **adj.**, **cen·tric·i·ty** /senˈtrisətē/ **n.**
– ORIGIN late 16th cent.: from Greek *kentrikos*, from *kentron* 'sharp point' (see CENTER).

-centric ▶ **comb. form** having a specified center: *geocentric.* ■ forming an opinion or evaluation originating from a specified viewpoint: *Eurocentric | ethnocentric.*
– ORIGIN from Greek *kentrikos*, on the pattern of words such as *(con)centric.*

-centricity ▶ **comb. form** in nouns corresponding to adjectives ending in *-centric* (such as *ethnocentricity* corresponding to *ethnocentric*).

cen·trif·u·gal /senˈtrif(y)əgəl/ ▶ **adj.** Physics moving or tending to move away from a center. The opposite of CENTRIPETAL.
– DERIVATIVES **cen·trif·u·gal·ly adv.**
– ORIGIN early 18th cent.: from modern Latin *centrifugus*, from Latin *centrum* (see CENTER) + *-fugus* 'fleeing' (from *fugere* 'flee').

cen·trif·u·gal force ▶ **n.** Physics an apparent force that acts outward on a body moving around a center, arising from the body's inertia.

cen·trif·u·gal pump ▶ **n.** a pump that uses an impeller to move water or other fluids.

cen·tri·fuge /ˈsentrəˌfyo͞oj/ ▶ **n.** a machine with a rapidly rotating container that applies centrifugal force to its contents, typically to separate fluids of different densities (e.g., cream from milk) or liquids from solids.
▶ **v.** [with obj.] (usu. **be centrifuged**) subject to the action of a centrifuge. ■ separate by centrifuge: *the black liquid is centrifuged into oil and water.*
– DERIVATIVES **cen·trif·u·ga·tion** /ˌsentrəˌfyo͞oˈgāsʜən, senˌtrif(y)ə-/ **n.**

cen·tri·ole /ˈsentrēˌōl/ ▶ **n.** Biology a minute cylindrical organelle near the nucleus in animal cells, occurring in pairs and involved in the development of spindle fibers in cell division.
– ORIGIN late 19th cent.: from modern Latin *centriolum*, diminutive of *centrum* (see CENTER).

cen·trip·e·tal /senˈtripətl/ ▶ **adj.** Physics moving or tending to move toward a center. The opposite of CENTRIFUGAL.
– DERIVATIVES **cen·trip·e·tal·ly adv.**
– ORIGIN early 18th cent.: from modern Latin *centripetus*, from Latin *centrum* (see CENTER) + *-petus* 'seeking' (from *petere* 'seek').

cen·trip·e·tal force ▶ **n.** Physics a force that acts on a body moving in a circular path and is directed toward the center around which the body is moving.

cen·trist /ˈsentrist/ ▶ **adj.** having moderate political views or policies.
▶ **n.** a person who holds moderate political views.
– DERIVATIVES **cen·trism** /-ˌtrizəm/ **n.**
– ORIGIN late 19th cent.: from French *centriste*, from Latin *centrum* (see CENTER).

cen·troid /ˈsenˌtroid/ ▶ **n.** Mathematics the center of mass of a geometric object of uniform density.

cen·tro·mere /ˈsentrəˌmi(ə)r/ ▶ **n.** Biology the point on a chromosome by which it is attached to a spindle fiber during cell division.
– DERIVATIVES **cen·tro·mer·ic** /ˌsentrəˈmi(ə)rik, -ˈmerik/ **adj.**
– ORIGIN 1920s: from Latin *centrum* (see CENTER) + Greek *meros* 'part.'

cen·tro·some /ˈsentrəˌsōm/ ▶ **n.** Biology an organelle near the nucleus of a cell that contains the centrioles (in animal cells) and from which the spindle fibers develop in cell division.
– ORIGIN late 19th cent.: from Latin *centrum* (see CENTER) + Greek *sōma* 'body.'

cen·trum /ˈsentrəm/ ▶ **n.** (pl. **centrums** or **centra** /-trə/) Anatomy the solid central part of a vertebra, to which the arches and processes are attached.
– ORIGIN mid 19th cent.: from Latin.

cen·tu·ple /senˈt(y)o͞opəl, ˈsenˌt(y)o͞opəl/ ▶ **v.** [with obj.] multiply by a hundred or by a large amount: *they were centupling the national debt.*
– ORIGIN early 17th cent.: from French, or from ecclesiastical Latin *centuplus*, alteration of Latin *centuplex*, from *centum* 'hundred.'

cen·tu·ri·on /senˈt(y)o͝orēən/ ▶ **n.** the commander of a century in the ancient Roman army.
– ORIGIN Middle English: from Latin *centurion-*, from *centuria* (see CENTURY).

cen·tu·ry /ˈsenсʜ(ə)rē/ ▶ **n.** (pl. **centuries**) **1** a period of one hundred years: *a century ago most people walked to work.* ■ a period of one hundred years reckoned from the traditional date of the birth of Jesus Christ: *the fifteenth century* | [as modifier, in combination] (**-century**) *a twentieth-century lifestyle.*
2 a company in the ancient Roman army, originally of one hundred men. ■ an ancient Roman political division for voting.
3 a bicycle race of one hundred miles: [as modifier] *the nation's largest single-day century ride.* ■ a score of one hundred in a sporting event, such as a cricket match.
– DERIVATIVES **cen·tu·ri·al** /senˈt(y)o͝orēəl/ **adj.**
– ORIGIN late Middle English (sense 2): from Latin *centuria*, from *centum* 'hundred.' Sense 1 dates from the early 17th cent.

> **USAGE** **1** In contemporary use, a **century** is popularly calculated as beginning in a year that ends with '00,' whereas the traditional system designates the '00' year as the final year of a century. This discrepancy was particularly apparent on January 1, 2000, which was commercially celebrated worldwide as the first day of the 21st century, even though January 1, 2001, was regarded as the more proper date for this milestone. **2** Since the 1st century ran from the year 1 to the year 100, the ordinal number (i.e., second, third, fourth, etc.) used to denote the century will always be one digit higher than the corresponding cardinal digit(s). Thus, 1492 is a date in the 15th century, 1776 is in the 18th century, and so on.

cen·tu·ry plant ▶ **n.** a stemless agave with long spiny leaves, which produces a tall flowering stem after many years of growth and then dies. Also called AMERICAN ALOE. ● *Agave americana*, family Agavaceae.

century plant

CEO ▶ **abbr.** chief executive officer.

cep /sep/ (also **cèpe**) ▶ **n.** an edible European and North American mushroom with a smooth brown cap, a stout white stalk, and pores rather than gills, growing in dry woodland and much sought after as a delicacy. Also called KING BOLETE, PORCINI. ● *Boletus edulis*, family Boletaceae, class Basidiomycetes.
– ORIGIN mid 19th cent.: from French *cèpe*, from Gascon *cep* 'tree trunk, mushroom,' from Latin *cippus* 'stake.'

ce·phal·ic /səˈfalik/ ▶ **adj.** technical of, in, or relating to the head.
– ORIGIN late Middle English: from Old French *cephalique*, from Latin *cephalicus*, from Greek *kephalikos*, from *kephalē* 'head.'

-cephalic ▶ **comb. form** equivalent to -CEPHALOUS.

ce·phal·ic in·dex ▶ **n.** Anthropology a number expressing the ratio of the maximum breadth of a skull to its maximum length.

ceph·a·lin /ˈsefəlin/ ▶ **n.** Biochemistry any of a group of phospholipids present in cell membranes, esp. in the brain.
– ORIGIN late 19th cent.: from Greek *kephalē* 'brain' + -IN¹.

ceph·a·li·za·tion /ˌsefələˈzāsʜən/ ▶ **n.** Zoology the concentration of sense organs, nervous control, etc., at the anterior end of the body, forming a head and brain, both during evolution and in the course of an embryo's development.

cephalo- ▶ **comb. form** relating to the head or skull: *cephalometry.*
– ORIGIN from Greek *kephalē* 'head.'

Ceph·a·lo·chor·da·ta /ˌsefəlōˌkôrˈdātə, -ˈdätə/ Zoology a small group of marine invertebrates comprising the lancelets. ● Subphylum Cephalochordata, phylum Chordata.
– DERIVATIVES **ceph·a·lo·chor·date** /-ˈkôrˌdāt/ **n. & adj.**
– ORIGIN modern Latin (plural), from CEPHALO- 'head' + Latin *khorda* 'cord.'

ceph·a·lom·e·try /ˌsefəˈlämətrē/ ▶ **n.** Medicine measurement and study of the proportions of the head and face, esp. during development and growth.
– DERIVATIVES **ceph·a·lo·met·ric** /-lōˈmetrik/ **adj.**

ceph·a·lon /ˈsefəˌlän, -lən/ ▶ **n.** Zoology (in some arthropods, esp. trilobites) the region of the head, composed of fused segments.
– ORIGIN late 19th cent.: from Greek *kephalē* 'head.'

ceph·a·lo·pod /ˈsefələˌpäd/ ▶ **n.** Zoology an active predatory mollusk of the large class Cephalopoda, such as an octopus or squid.

Ceph·a·lop·o·da /ˌsefəˈläpədə/ Zoology a class of active predatory mollusks comprising octopuses, squids, and cuttlefish. They have a distinct head with large eyes and a ring of tentacles around a beaked mouth and are able to release a cloud of inky fluid to confuse predators.
– ORIGIN modern Latin (plural), from Greek *kephalē* 'head' + *pous, pod-* 'foot.'

ceph·a·lo·spo·rin /ˌsefələˈspôrən/ ▶ **n.** any of a group of semisynthetic broad-spectrum antibiotics resembling penicillin.
– ORIGIN 1950s: from modern Latin *Cephalosporium* (genus providing molds for this) + -IN¹.

ceph·a·lo·tho·rax /ˌsefələˈᴛʜôraks/ ▶ **n.** (pl. **cephalothoraces** /-ˈᴛʜôrəˌsēz/ or **cephalothoraxes**) Zoology the fused head and thorax of spiders and other chelicerate arthropods.

-cephalous ▶ **comb. form** -headed (used commonly in medical, zoological, and botanical terms): *macrocephalous.*
– ORIGIN based on Greek *kephalē* 'head' + -OUS.

ce·phe·id /ˈsēfēəd, ˈsef-/ (also **cepheid variable**) ▶ **n.** Astronomy a variable star having a regular cycle of brightness with a frequency related to its luminosity, so allowing estimation of its distance from the earth.
– ORIGIN early 20th cent.: from the name of the variable star *Delta Cephei*, which typifies this class of stars.

Ce·phe·us /ˈsēfēəs, ˈsēˌfyo͞os/ Astronomy a constellation near the north celestial pole. ■ (as genitive **Cephei** /ˈsēfēˌī/) used with a preceding letter or numeral to designate a star in this constellation: *the star Beta Cephei.*
– ORIGIN from the name of a king of Ethiopia, the husband of Cassiopeia.

'cept /sep(t)/ ▶ **prep., conj., & v.** nonstandard contraction of EXCEPT used in representing speech: *everyone else had visitors—'cept for Captain.*

ce·ram·ic /səˈramik/ ▶ **adj.** made of clay and hardened by heat: *a ceramic bowl.* ■ of or relating to the manufacture of such articles.
▶ **n.** (**ceramics**) pots and other articles made from clay hardened by heat: *handmade pottery and imaginative ceramics for the table.* ■ [usu. treated as sing.] the art of making such articles: *sculpting, drawing, ceramics, and fiber art.* ■ (**ceramic**) the material from which such articles are made: *tableware in ceramic.* ■ (**ceramic**) any nonmetallic solid that remains hard when heated.
– DERIVATIVES **ce·ram·i·cist** /səˈraməsist/ **n.**
– ORIGIN early 19th cent.: from Greek *keramikos*, from *keramos* 'pottery.'

Ce·ram Sea /ˈsāˌräm/ (also **Seram Sea**) the part of the western Pacific Ocean that is at the center of the Molucca Islands in Indonesia.

ce·ras·tes /səˈrasˌtēz/ ▶ **n.** a North African viper that has a spike over each eye. ● Genus *Cerastes*, family Viperidae: two species, in particular the horned viper.
– ORIGIN late Middle English: from Latin, from Greek *kerastēs* 'horned,' from *keras* 'horn.'

ce·rat·ed /ˈsi(ə)rˌātid/ ▶ **adj. 1** covered with wax or resin.
2 Ornithology having a cere.

cer·a·tite /ˈserəˌtīt/ ▶ **n.** an ammonoid fossil of an intermediate type found chiefly in the Permian and Triassic periods, typically with partly frilled and partly lobed suture lines. Compare with AMMONITE and GONIATITE. ● Typified by the genus *Ceratites*, order Ceratida.
– ORIGIN mid 19th cent.: from modern Latin *Ceratites* (from Greek *keras, kerat-* 'horn') + -ITE[1].

cer·a·top·si·an /ˌserəˈtäpsēən/ ▶ **n.** Paleontology a gregarious quadrupedal herbivorous dinosaur of a group found in the Cretaceous period, including triceratops. It had a large beaked and horned head and a bony frill protecting the neck. ● Infraorder Ceratopsia, order Ornithischia.
– ORIGIN early 20th cent.: from modern Latin *Ceratopsia* (plural) (from Greek *keras, kerat-* 'horn' + *ops* 'face') + -AN.

Cer·ber·us /ˈsərbərəs/ Greek Mythology a monstrous watchdog with three (or in some accounts fifty) heads that guarded the entrance to Hades.

cer·car·i·a /sərˈke(ə)rēə/ ▶ **n.** (pl. **cercariae** /-ˈke(ə)rēˌē/) Zoology a free-swimming larval stage in which a parasitic fluke passes from an intermediate host (typically a snail) to another intermediate host or to the final vertebrate host.
– ORIGIN mid 19th cent.: modern Latin, formed irregularly from Greek *kerkos* 'tail.'

cer·clage /sərˈkläZH/ ▶ **n.** Medicine the use of a ring or loop to bind together the ends of an obliquely fractured bone or to encircle the opening of a malfunctioning cervix.
– ORIGIN early 20th cent.: from French, literally 'encirclement.'

cer·co·pi·the·cine /ˌsərkōˈpiTHəˌsīn, -ˌsēn/ ▶ **n.** Zoology an Old World monkey of a group that includes the macaques, mangabeys, baboons, and guenons. ● Subfamily Cercopithecinae, family Cercopithecidae.
– ORIGIN from modern Latin *Cercopithecinae* (plural), based on Greek *kerkopithēkos* 'long-tailed monkey,' from *kerkos* 'tail' + *pithēkos* 'ape.'

cer·co·pi·the·coid /ˌsərkəˈpiTHəˌkoid/ Zoology ▶ **n.** a primate of a group that comprises the Old World monkeys. ● Superfamily Cercopithecoidea, family Cercopithecidae.
▶ **adj.** of or relating to monkeys of this group.
– ORIGIN late 19th cent.: from modern Latin *Cercopithecoidea*, based on Greek *kerkopithēkos* (see CERCOPITHECINE).

cer·cus /ˈsərkəs/ ▶ **n.** (pl. **cerci** /ˈsərˌsī, -ˌkī/) Zoology a small appendage at the end of the abdomen of some insects and other arthropods, occurring in pairs.
– ORIGIN early 19th cent.: from modern Latin, from Greek *kerkos* 'tail.'

cere /si(ə)r/ ▶ **n.** Ornithology a waxy, fleshy covering at the base of the upper beak in some birds.
– ORIGIN late 15th cent.: from Latin *cera* 'wax.'

ce·re·al /ˈsi(ə)rēəl/ ▶ **n.** a grain used for food, such as wheat, oats, or corn. ■ (usu. **cereals**) a grass producing such grain, grown as an agricultural crop: [as modifier] *low yields for cereal crops.* ■ a breakfast food made from roasted grain, typically eaten with milk: *a bowl of cereal* | [as modifier] *a cereal box.*
– ORIGIN early 19th cent. (as an adjective): from Latin *cerealis*, from *Ceres*, the name of the Roman goddess of agriculture.

ce·re·al bar ▶ **n.** a prepackaged food item similar in shape to a candy bar, made of breakfast cereal and, typically, fruit.

cer·e·bel·lum /ˌserəˈbeləm/ ▶ **n.** (pl. **cerebellums** or **cerebella** /-ˈbelə/) Anatomy the part of the brain at the back of the skull in vertebrates. Its function is to coordinate and regulate muscular activity.
– DERIVATIVES **cer·e·bel·lar adj.**
– ORIGIN mid 16th cent.: from Latin, diminutive of CEREBRUM.

ce·re·bral /səˈrēbrəl, ˈserəbrəl/ ▶ **adj. 1** of the cerebrum of the brain: *a cerebral hemorrhage* | *the cerebral cortex.* ■ intellectual rather than emotional or physical: *photography is a cerebral process.*
2 Phonetics another term for RETROFLEX.
– DERIVATIVES **ce·re·bral·ly adv.**
– ORIGIN early 19th cent.: from Latin *cerebrum* 'brain' + -AL.

ce·re·bral aq·ue·duct ▶ **n.** Anatomy a fluid-filled canal that runs through the midbrain connecting the third and fourth ventricles.

ce·re·bral dom·i·nance ▶ **n.** the normal tendency for one side of the brain to control particular functions, such as handedness and speech.

ce·re·bral e·de·ma ▶ **n.** Medicine a swelling in the brain caused by the presence of excessive fluid.

ce·re·bral pal·sy ▶ **n.** a condition marked by impaired muscle coordination (spastic paralysis) and/or other disabilities, typically caused by damage to the brain before or at birth. See also SPASTIC.

cer·e·bra·tion /ˌserəˈbrāSHən/ ▶ **n.** technical or formal the working of the brain; thinking.
– DERIVATIVES **cer·e·brate** /ˈserəˌbrāt/ **v.**

cerebro- ▶ **comb. form** of or relating to the brain: *cerebrospinal.*
– ORIGIN from Latin *cerebrum* 'brain.'

ce·re·bro·side /səˈrēbrəˌsīd, ˈserəbrə-/ ▶ **n.** Biochemistry any of a group of complex lipids present in the sheaths of nerve fibers.
– ORIGIN late 19th cent.: from Latin *cerebrum* 'brain' + -OSE[2] + -IDE.

ce·re·bro·spi·nal /səˌrēbrōˈspīnl, ˌserəbrō-/ ▶ **adj.** Anatomy of or relating to the brain and spine.

ce·re·bro·spi·nal flu·id ▶ **n.** Anatomy clear watery fluid that fills the space between the arachnoid membrane and the pia mater.

ce·re·bro·vas·cu·lar /səˌrēbrōˈvaskyələr, ˌserəbrō-/ ▶ **adj.** Anatomy of or relating to the brain and its blood vessels.

ce·re·brum /səˈrēbrəm, ˈserə-/ ▶ **n.** (pl. **cerebra** /-brə/) Anatomy the principal and most anterior part of the brain in vertebrates, located in the front area of the skull and consisting of two hemispheres, left and right, separated by a fissure. It is responsible for the integration of complex sensory and neural functions and the initiation and coordination of voluntary activity in the body. See also TELENCEPHALON.
– ORIGIN early 17th cent.: from Latin, 'brain.'

cere·cloth /ˈsi(ə)rˌklôTH/ ▶ **n.** historical waxed cloth typically used for wrapping a corpse.
– ORIGIN late Middle English: from earlier *cered cloth*, from *cere* 'to wax,' from Latin *cerare*, from *cera* 'wax.'

cere·ment /ˈserəmənt, ˈsi(ə)rmənt/ ▶ **n.** (usu. **cerements**) historical waxed cloth for wrapping a corpse.
– ORIGIN early 17th cent. (first used by Shakespeare in *Hamlet*, 1602): from *cere* (see CERECLOTH).

cer·e·mo·ni·al /ˌserəˈmōnēəl/ ▶ **adj. 1** relating to or used for formal events of a religious or public nature: *ceremonial robes* | *the solemn, ceremonial air of a procession of monks* | *presented at ceremonial occasions.*
2 (of a position or role) involving only nominal authority or power: *originally a ceremonial post, it is now a position with executive power.*
▶ **n.** the system of rules and procedures to be observed at a formal or religious occasion: *the procedure was conducted with all due ceremonial.* ■ a rite or ceremony: *a ceremonial called the ghost dance.*
– DERIVATIVES **cer·e·mo·ni·al·ism n.**, **cer·e·mo·ni·al·ist n.**, **cer·e·mo·ni·al·ly adv.**
– ORIGIN late Middle English: from late Latin *caerimonialis*, from *caerimonia* 'religious worship' (see CEREMONY).

cer·e·mo·ni·ous /ˌserəˈmōnēəs/ ▶ **adj.** relating or appropriate to grand and formal occasions: *a Great Hall where ceremonious and public appearances were made.* ■ excessively polite; punctilious: *he accepted the gifts with ceremonious dignity.*
– DERIVATIVES **cer·e·mo·ni·ous·ly adv.**, **cer·e·mo·ni·ous·ness n.**
– ORIGIN mid 16th cent.: from French *cérémonieux* or late Latin *caerimoniosus*, from *caerimonia* (see CEREMONY).

cer·e·mo·ny /ˈserəˌmōnē/ ▶ **n.** (pl. **ceremonies**)
1 a formal religious or public occasion, typically one celebrating a particular event or anniversary. ■ an act or series of acts performed according to a traditional or prescribed form.
2 the ritual observances and procedures performed at grand and formal occasions: *the new Queen was proclaimed with due ceremony.* ■ formal polite behavior: *he showed them to their table with great ceremony.*
– PHRASES **stand on ceremony** [usu. with negative] insist on the observance of formalities: *we don't stand on ceremony in this house.* **without ceremony** without preamble or politeness: *he was pushed without ceremony into the bathroom.*
– ORIGIN late Middle English: from Old French *ceremonie* or Latin *caerimonia* 'religious worship,' (plural) 'ritual observances.'

Ce·ren·kov /CHəˈreNGˌkôv, -ˌkôf, -kəf/, Pavel, see CHERENKOV.

Ce·ren·kov ra·di·a·tion (also **Cherenkov radiation**) ▶ **n.** Physics electromagnetic radiation emitted by particles moving through a medium at speeds greater than that of light in the same medium.

ce·re·ol·o·gy /ˌsi(ə)rēˈäləjē/ ▶ **n.** the study or investigation of crop circles.
– DERIVATIVES **ce·re·ol·o·gist** /-jist/ **n.**
– ORIGIN late 20th cent.: from CERES + -LOGY.

ce·re·op·sis goose /ˌsi(ə)rēˈäpsəs/ ▶ **n.** another term for CAPE BARREN GOOSE.
– ORIGIN late 19th cent.: from modern Latin *Cereopsis* (genus name), from Greek *kerinos* 'waxen' + *opsis* 'face' (because of its cere).

Ce·res /ˈsi(ə)rēz/ **1** Roman Mythology the goddess of grain and agriculture. Greek equivalent DEMETER.
2 Astronomy the first asteroid to be discovered, found by G. Piazzi of Palermo in 1801. It is also the largest, with a diameter of 567 miles (913 km).

cer·e·sin /ˈserəsin/ ▶ **n.** a hard whitish paraffin wax used with or instead of beeswax.
– ORIGIN late 19th cent.: from modern Latin *ceres* (from Latin *cera* 'wax') + -IN[1].

ce·ric /ˈsi(ə)rik/ ▶ **adj.** of cerium in its higher valency (4).

ce·rise /səˈrēs, -ˈrēz/ ▶ **n.** a bright or deep red color: *a shade of vivid cerise.*
– ORIGIN mid 19th cent.: from French, literally 'cherry.'

ce·ri·um /ˈsi(ə)rēəm/ ▶ **n.** the chemical element of atomic number 58, a silvery white metal. It is the most abundant of the lanthanide elements and is the main component of the alloy misch metal. (Symbol: **Ce**)
– ORIGIN early 19th cent.: named after the asteroid CERES, discovered shortly before.

cer·met /ˈsərˌmet/ ▶ **n.** any of a class of heat-resistant materials made of ceramic and sintered metal.
– ORIGIN 1950s: blend of CERAMIC and METAL.

CERN /sərn/ ▶ **abbr.** European Organization for Nuclear Research.
– ORIGIN initial letters of French *Conseil Européen pour la Recherche Nucléaire*, its former title.

ce·ro /ˈsi(ə)rō/ ▶ **n.** (pl. **same** or **ceros**) a large fish of the mackerel family, serving as an important food fish in the tropical western Atlantic. ● *Scomberomorus regalis*, family Scombridae.
– ORIGIN late 19th cent.: from Spanish *sierra* 'saw or sawfish.'

cero- ▶ **comb. form** of or relating to wax: *ceroplastic.*
– ORIGIN from Latin *cera* or Greek *kēros* 'wax.'

ce·roc /səˈräk/ ▶ **n.** chiefly Brit. a type of modern social dance having elements of rock and roll, jive, and salsa.
– ORIGIN 1990s: invented word, apparently coined in English from French *ce* 'this' + *roc* 'rock.'

ce·ro·plas·tic /ˌsi(ə)rōˈplastik, ˌserō-/ ▶ **adj.** of or relating to modeling in wax.

ce·rous /ˈsi(ə)rəs/ ▶ **adj.** of cerium in its lower valency (3).

Cer·ri·tos /səˈrētəs/ a city in southwestern California, southeast of Los Angeles; pop. 51,326 (est. 2008).

C

Cer·ro Gor·do /ˈserō ˈgôrdō/ a mountain pass in eastern Mexico, between Veracruz and Jalapa, scene of an 1847 victory by US forces in the Mexican War.

cert. ▶ **abbr.** ■ certificate. ■ certified.

cer·tain /ˈsərtn/ ▶ **adj. 1** known for sure; established beyond doubt: *it's certain that more changes are in the offing | she looks certain to win an Oscar.* ■ having complete conviction about something; confident: *are you absolutely* ***certain about*** *this? | true and certain knowledge of the essence of existence.*
2 [attrib.] specific but not explicitly named or stated: *he raised certain personal problems with me | the exercise was causing him a certain amount of pain.* ■ used when mentioning the name of someone not known to the reader or hearer: *a certain General Percy captured the town.*
▶ **pron.** (**certain of**) some but not all: *certain of his works have been edited.*
–PHRASES **for certain** without any doubt: *I don't know for certain.* **make certain** [with clause] take action to ensure that something happens or is the case: *I made certain that our paths would never cross again.* ■ establish whether something is definitely correct or true: *he probably knew her, but it didn't do any harm to make certain.*
–ORIGIN Middle English: from Old French, based on Latin *certus* 'settled, sure.'

cer·tain·ly /ˈsərtnlē/ ▶ **adv.** [sentence adverb] undoubtedly; definitely; surely: *the prestigious address certainly adds to the firm's appeal | it certainly isn't worth risking your life.* ■ (in answer to a question or command) yes; by all means: *"A good idea," she agreed. "Certainly!"*

cer·tain·ty /ˈsərtntē/ ▶ **n.** (pl. **certainties**) firm conviction that something is the case: *she knew with absolute* ***certainty*** *that they were dead.* ■ the quality of being reliably true: *there is a bewildering lack of certainty and clarity in the law.* ■ a fact that is definitely true or an event that is definitely going to take place: *an immediate transfer would be a certainty.* ■ a person or thing that may be relied on: *he was expected to be a certainty for a gold medal.*
–PHRASES **for a certainty** beyond the possibility of doubt.
–ORIGIN Middle English: from Old French *certainete,* from *certain* (see CERTAIN).

cer·tes /ˈsərtēz, sərts/ ▶ **adv.** archaic assuredly; I assure you.
–ORIGIN Middle English: from Old French, based on Latin *certus* 'settled, sure.'

cer·ti·fi·a·ble /ˈsərtəˌfīəbəl/ ▶ **adj. 1** able or needing to be certified: *encephalitis was a certifiable condition | little hope for certifiable progress.*
2 officially recognized as needing treatment for a mental disorder. ■ informal mad; crazy: *the world of fashion is almost entirely insane, the people who work in it mainly certifiable.*
–DERIVATIVES **cer·ti·fi·a·bly** /-blē/ **adj.**

cer·tif·i·cate /sərˈtifikit/ ▶ **n.** an official document attesting a certain fact, in particular: ■ a document recording a person's birth, marriage, or death. ■ a document attesting a level of achievement in a course of study or training: *graduate certificate in information technology.* ■ a document attesting ownership of a certain item: *a stock certificate.*
▶ **v.** /-ˈtifəkāt/ [with obj.] Brit. provide with or attest in an official document.
–DERIVATIVES **cer·ti·fi·ca·tion** /ˌsərtəfiˈkāsʜən/ **n.**
–ORIGIN late Middle English (in the sense 'certification, attestation'): from French *certificat* or medieval Latin *certificatum,* from *certificare* (see CERTIFY).

cer·tif·i·cate of de·pos·it (abbr.: **CD**) ▶ **n.** a certificate issued by a bank to a person depositing money for a specified length of time.

cer·ti·fied check ▶ **n.** a check that is guaranteed by a bank.

cer·ti·fied mail ▶ **n.** a postal service in which the sending and receipt of a letter or package are recorded.

cer·ti·fied milk ▶ **n.** historical milk guaranteed free from the tubercle bacillus.

cer·ti·fied pub·lic ac·count·ant (abbr.: **CPA**) ▶ **n.** a member of an officially accredited professional body of accountants.

cer·ti·fy /ˈsərtəˌfī/ ▶ **v.** (**certifies, certifying, certified**) [with obj.] attest or confirm in a formal statement: *the profits for the year had been certified by the auditors |* [with clause] *the medical witness certified that death was due to cerebral hemorrhage.* ■ (often as adj. **certified**) officially recognize (someone or something) as possessing certain qualifications or meeting certain standards: *a certified scuba instructor |* ***board certified*** *in obstetrics and gynecology.* ■ officially declare insane.
–ORIGIN Middle English: from Old French *certifier,* from late Latin *certificare,* from Latin *certus* 'certain.'

cer·ti·o·ra·ri /ˌsərsʜ(ē)əˈrärē, -ˈre(ə)rī/ ▶ **n.** Law a writ or order by which a higher court reviews a decision of a lower court: *an order of certiorari.*
–ORIGIN late Middle English: from Law Latin, 'to be informed,' a phrase originally occurring at the start of the writ, from *certiorare* 'inform,' from *certior,* comparative of *certus* 'certain.'

cer·ti·tude /ˈsərtəˌt(y)o͞od/ ▶ **n.** absolute certainty or conviction that something is the case: *the question may never be answered with certitude.* ■ something that someone firmly believes is true: *his certitude that "we're number one."*
–ORIGIN late Middle English: from late Latin *certitudo,* from *certus* 'certain.'

ce·ru·le·an /səˈro͞olēən/ ▶ **adj.** literary deep blue in color like a clear sky: *cerulean waters and golden sands.*
▶ **n.** a deep sky-blue color.
–ORIGIN mid 17th cent.: from Latin *caeruleus* 'sky blue,' from *caelum* 'sky.'

ce·ru·men /səˈro͞omən/ ▶ **n.** technical term for EARWAX.
–ORIGIN late 17th cent.: modern Latin, from Latin *cera* 'wax.'

ce·ruse /səˈro͞os, ˈsi(ə)rˌo͞os/ ▶ **n.** archaic term for WHITE LEAD.
–ORIGIN late Middle English: via Old French from Latin *cerussa,* perhaps from Greek *kēros* 'wax.'

Cer·van·tes /sərˈvantēz, serˈväntās/, Miguel de (1547–1616), Spanish novelist and playwright; full name *Miguel de Cervantes Saavedra.* His most well-known work is *Don Quixote* (1605–15), a satire on chivalric romances that greatly influenced the development of the novel.

cer·vi·cal /ˈsərvikəl/ ▶ **adj.** Anatomy **1** of or relating to the narrow necklike passage forming the lower end of the uterus: *cervical cancer.*
2 of or relating to the neck: *the fifth cervical vertebra.*
–ORIGIN late 17th cent.: from French, or from modern Latin *cervicalis,* from Latin *cervix, cervic-* 'neck.'

cer·vi·ci·tis /sərvəˈsītis/ ▶ **n.** Medicine inflammation of the cervix.

cer·vid /ˈsərvəd/ ▶ **n.** Zoology a mammal of the deer family (Cervidae).
–ORIGIN late 19th cent.: from modern Latin *Cervidae* (plural), from Latin *cervus* 'deer.'

cer·vine /ˈsərˌvīn, -vin/ ▶ **adj.** of or relating to deer; deerlike.
–ORIGIN mid 19th cent.: from Latin *cervinus,* from *cervus* 'deer.'

cer·vix /ˈsərviks/ ▶ **n.** (pl. **cervices** /-vəˌsēz/) the narrow necklike passage forming the lower end of the uterus. ■ technical the neck. ■ a part of other bodily organs resembling a neck.
–ORIGIN mid 18th cent.: Latin.

ce·sar·e·an /siˈze(ə)rēən/ (also **caesarean** or chiefly Brit. **caesarian**) ▶ **adj.** of or effected by cesarean section: *a cesarean delivery.*
▶ **n.** a cesarean section: *I had to have a cesarean | two sons both born by cesarean.*
–ORIGIN early 16th cent. (as a noun denoting a supporter of an emperor or imperial system): from Latin *Caesareus* 'of Caesar' + -AN.

ce·sar·e·an sec·tion ▶ **n.** a surgical operation for delivering a child by cutting through the wall of the mother's abdomen.
–ORIGIN early 17th cent.: *cesarean* from the story that Julius Caesar was delivered by this method.

ce·si·um /ˈsēzēəm/ (Brit. **caesium**) ▶ **n.** the chemical element of atomic number 55, a soft, silvery, extremely reactive metal. It belongs to the alkali metal group and occurs as a trace element in some rocks and minerals. (Symbol: **Cs**)
–ORIGIN mid 19th cent.: from Latin *caesius* 'grayish-blue' (because it has characteristic lines in the blue part of the spectrum).

České Bu·dě·jo·vi·ce /ˈcʜeske ˈbo͝odyəˌyôvitse/ a city in the southern Czech Republic, on the Vltava River; pop. 94,925 (2007). It is noted for the production of lager. German name **BUDWEIS**.

ces·pi·tose /ˈsespiˌtōs/ ▶ **adj.** Botany forming mats or growing in dense tufts or clumps.
–ORIGIN mid 19th cent.: from modern Latin *caespitosus,* from *caespes* 'turf': see -OSE[1].

cess[1] /ses/ (also **sess**) ▶ **n.** (in Scotland, Ireland, and India) a tax or levy.
–ORIGIN late 15th cent. (denoting the obligation placed on the Irish to supply the Lord Deputy's household and garrison with provisions at prices "assessed" by the government): shortened from the obsolete noun *assess* 'assessment.'

cess[2] ▶ **n.** (in phrase **bad cess to**) chiefly Irish a curse on: *bad cess to the day I joined that band!*
–ORIGIN mid 19th cent. (originally Anglo-Irish): perhaps from CESS[1].

ces·sa·tion /seˈsāsʜən/ ▶ **n.** the fact or process of ending or being brought to an end: *the cessation of hostilities | a cessation of animal testing of cosmetics.*
–ORIGIN late Middle English: from Latin *cessatio(n-),* from *cessare* 'cease.'

ces·ser /ˈsesər/ ▶ **n.** Law termination or cessation, esp. of a period of tenure or legal liability.
–ORIGIN mid 16th cent.: from Old French *cesser* 'cease,' used as a noun.

ces·sion /ˈsesʜən/ ▶ **n.** the formal giving up of rights, property, or territory, esp. by a state: *the cession of twenty important towns.*
–ORIGIN late Middle English: from Latin *cession-,* from *cedere* 'cede.'

cess·pit /ˈsesˌpit/ ▶ **n.** a pit for the disposal of liquid waste and sewage. ■ a disgusting or corrupt place or situation: *the affair threatened to be a cesspit of scandal.*
–ORIGIN mid 19th cent.: from *cess* (the supposed base of CESSPOOL) + PIT[1].

cess·pool /ˈsesˌpo͞ol/ ▶ **n.** an underground container for the temporary storage of liquid waste and sewage. ■ a disgusting or corrupt place: *they should clean out their own political cesspool.*
–ORIGIN late 17th cent. (denoting a trap under a drain to catch solids): probably an alteration, influenced by POOL[1], of archaic *suspiral* 'vent, water pipe, settling tank,' from Old French *souspirail* 'air hole,' based on Latin *sub-* 'from below' + *spirare* 'breathe.'

ces·ta /ˈsestə/ ▶ **n.** a wicker basket used in the game of jai alai to catch and throw the ball.
–ORIGIN Spanish.

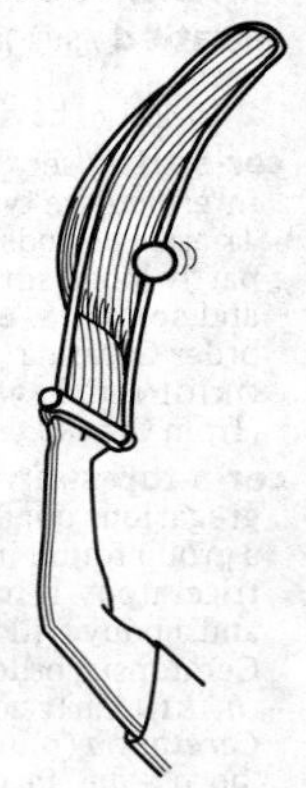
cesta

c'est la vie /ˌsā lä ˈvē/ ▶ **exclam.** that's life; such is life: *if you get thwarted, c'est la vie.*
–ORIGIN early 20th cent.: French.

Ces·to·da /sesˈtōdə/ (also **Cestoidea** /-ˈtoidēə/) Zoology a class of parasitic flatworms that comprises the tapeworms.
–ORIGIN modern Latin (plural), from Latin *cestus,* from Greek *kestos,* literally 'stitched,' used as a noun in the sense 'girdle.'

ces·tode /ˈsesˌtōd/ ▶ **n.** Zoology a parasitic flatworm of the class Cestoda; a tapeworm.

Ce·ta·cea /siˈtāsʜ(ē)ə/ Zoology an order of marine mammals that comprises the whales, dolphins, and porpoises. These have a streamlined hairless body, no hind limbs, a horizontal tail fin, and a blowhole on top of the head for breathing. See also MYSTICETI, ODONTOCETI.
–ORIGIN modern Latin (plural), from Latin *cetus,* from Greek *kētos* 'whale.'

ce·ta·cean /siˈtāsʜən/ ▶ **n.** a marine mammal of the order Cetacea; a whale, dolphin, or porpoise.
▶ **adj.** relating to or denoting cetaceans.

ce·tane /ˈsēˌtān/ ▶ **n.** Chemistry a colorless liquid hydrocarbon of the alkane series, used as a solvent. ● Alternative name: **n-hexadecane**; chem. formula: $C_{16}H_{34}$.
–ORIGIN late 19th cent.: from Latin *cetus* 'whale,' from Greek *kētos* (because related compounds were first derived from spermaceti) + -ANE[2].

ce·tane num·ber ▶ **n.** a measure of the ignition properties of diesel fuel relative to cetane as a standard.

ce·te·ris pa·ri·bus /ˌkātəris ˈparəbəs/ ▶ **adv.** formal with other conditions remaining the same: *shorter hours of labor will, ceteris paribus, reduce the volume of output.*
–ORIGIN early 17th cent.: modern Latin.

ce·tol·o·gy /sēˈtäləjē/ ▶ **n.** the branch of zoology that deals with whales, dolphins, and porpoises.
–DERIVATIVES **ce·tol·o·gist n.**
–ORIGIN mid 19th cent.: from Latin *cetus* 'whale' (see CETACEA) + -LOGY.

Cetsh·wa·yo /keCHˈwī-ō/ (also **Cetewayo** /ˌsetəˈwī-ō/) (*c.*1826–84), Zulu king. He became ruler of Zululand in 1873 and was involved in a series of battles with the Afrikaners and British; he was deposed as leader after the capture of his capital by the British in 1879.

Ce·tus /ˈsētəs/ Astronomy a large northern constellation (the Whale), said to represent the sea monster that threatened Andromeda. It contains the variable star Mira. ■ (as genitive **Ceti** /ˈsētē/) used with a preceding letter or numeral to designate a star in this constellation: *the star Tau Ceti.*
–ORIGIN Latin.

Ceu·ta /'THā,ōōtə, 'sā-/ a Spanish enclave, consisting of a port and a military post, on the coast of Morocco in northern Africa; pop. 77,389 (2008). It overlooks the Mediterranean approach to the Strait of Gibraltar and with Melilla forms a community of Spain.

Cé·vennes /sā'ven/ a mountain range in France, on the southeastern edge of the Massif Central.

ce·vi·che /sə'vēCHā, -CHē/ (also **seviche**) ▶ **n.** a South American dish of marinated raw fish or seafood, typically garnished and served as an appetizer.
– ORIGIN South American Spanish.

Cey·lon /si'län, sā'län/ former name (until 1972) of **SRI LANKA**.

Cey·lon moss ▶ **n.** a red seaweed of southern Asia, the main source of agar. ● *Gracilaria lichenoides*, phylum Rhodophyta.

Cey·lon sat·in·wood ▶ **n.** see **SATINWOOD** (sense 2).

Cé·zanne /sā'zän/, Paul (1839–1906), French painter. He is closely identified with post-Impressionism, and his later work had an important influence on cubism. Notable works: *Still Life with Cupid* (1895) and *Bathers* (sequence of paintings, 1890–1905).

CF ▶ **abbr.** ■ (also **c.f.**) carried forward (used to refer to figures transferred to a new page or account). ■ cost and freight. ■ cystic fibrosis.

Cf ▶ **symbol** the chemical element californium.

cf. ▶ **abbr.** compare with (used to refer a reader to another written work or another part of the same written work).
– ORIGIN from Latin *confer* 'compare.'

CFA¹ (also **CFA franc**) ▶ **n.** the basic monetary unit of Cameroon, Congo, Gabon, and the Central African Republic, equal to 100 centimes.
– ORIGIN from French *Communauté Financière Africaine* 'African Financial Community.'

CFA² ▶ **abbr.** chartered financial analyst.

CFC ▶ **n.** short for **CHLOROFLUOROCARBON**.

CFL ▶ **abbr.** compact fluorescent light (or lamp).

cfm ▶ **abbr.** cubic feet per minute.

CFO ▶ **abbr.** chief financial officer.

CFS ▶ **abbr.** chronic fatigue syndrome.

cfs ▶ **abbr.** cubic feet per second.

CG ▶ **abbr.** ■ Coast Guard. ■ commanding general.

cg ▶ **abbr.** centigram(s).

CGI ▶ **abbr.** **1** computer-generated imagery. **2** Computing common gateway interface, a script standard for writing interactive programs generated by visitors to web pages.

cGMP ▶ **abbr.** cyclic GMP.

cgs ▶ **abbr.** centimeter-gram-second.

CGT ▶ **abbr.** capital gains tax.

CH ▶ **abbr.** ■ courthouse. ■ custom house.

ch. ▶ **abbr.** ■ chaplain. ■ chapter. ■ (of a horse) chestnut in color. ■ church.

c.h. (also **C.H.**) ▶ **abbr.** clearinghouse.

chab·a·zite /'kabə,zīt/ ▶ **n.** a colorless, pink, or yellow zeolite mineral, typically occurring as rhombohedral crystals.
– ORIGIN early 19th cent.: from French *chabazie*, from Greek *khabazie*, a misreading of *khalazie*, vocative form of *khalazios* 'hailstone' (from *khalaza* 'hail,' because of its form and color), + **-ITE¹**.

Cha·blis /'SHablē, 'SHä-/ ▶ **n.** a dry white burgundy wine from Chablis in eastern France.

Cha·brol /SHä'brōl/, Claude (1930–), French movie director; a member of the *nouvelle vague*.

cha-cha /'CHä ,CHä/ (also **cha-cha-cha** /-'CHä/) ▶ **n.** a ballroom dance with small steps and swaying hip movements, performed to a Latin American rhythm. ■ music for or in the rhythm of such a dance.
▶ **v.** (**cha-chas**, **cha-chaing**, **cha-cha'd** or **cha-chaed**) [no obj.] dance the cha-cha.
– ORIGIN 1950s: Latin American Spanish.

cha·cha·la·ca /,CHäCHə'läkə/ ▶ **n.** a pheasantlike tree-dwelling bird of the guan family, with a loud harsh call. It is found mainly in the forests of tropical America. ● Genus *Ortalis*, family Cracidae: several species, in particular the **plain chachalaca** (*O. vetula*).
– ORIGIN late 19th cent.: via South American Spanish from Nahuatl, of imitative origin.

cha·cham /KHä'KHäm/ (also **haham** /'häham/) ▶ **n.** a spiritual leader among Sephardic Jews, or, more generally, a person learned in Jewish law.
– ORIGIN from Hebrew *ḥākām* 'wise.'

chac·ma ba·boon /'CHäkmə/ ▶ **n.** a dark gray baboon that lives on the savanna of southern Africa. ● *Papio ursinus*, family Cercopithecidae.
– ORIGIN mid 19th cent.: from Khoikhoi.

Cha·co /'CHäkō/ another name for **GRAN CHACO**.

cha·conne /SHä'kôn, -'kän, -'kən/ ▶ **n.** Music a composition in a series of varying sections in slow triple time, typically over a short repeated bass theme. Compare with **PASSACAGLIA**. ■ a stately dance performed to such music, popular in the 18th century.
– ORIGIN late 17th cent.: from French, from Spanish *chacona*.

Cha·co War a boundary dispute in 1932–35 between Bolivia and Paraguay, in which Paraguay eventually gained most of the disputed territory.

cha·cun à son goût /SHä,kœN nä sôN 'gōō/ ▶ **exclam.** each to one's own taste.
– ORIGIN late 19th cent.: French.

Chad /CHad/ a landlocked country in northern central Africa; pop. 10,329,200 (est. 2009); capital, N'Djamena; official languages, French and Arabic.

> Much of the country lies in the Sahel, as well as the Sahara Desert in the north. A French colony from 1913, Chad became autonomous within the French Community in 1958 and fully independent as a republic in 1960. The country has been troubled by rebellions in the north since 1998.

– DERIVATIVES **Chad·i·an** adj. & n.

chad /CHad/ ▶ **n.** a piece of waste material removed from card or tape by punching.
– ORIGIN 1930s: possibly from Scots *chad* 'gravel, small stones' or dialect *chat* 'chip of wood.' It is not, as suggested, from the name of Mr. Chadless, inventor of a *Chadless Keypunch*: no such person has been found. Nor is it formed as an acronym from 'card hole aggregate debris.'

Chad, Lake a shallow lake on the borders of Chad, Niger, and Nigeria in north central Africa. Its size varies seasonally from about 4,000 square miles (10,360 sq km) to about 10,000 square miles (25,900 sq km).

Chad·ic /'CHadik/ ▶ **n.** a group of Afro-Asiatic languages spoken in the region of Lake Chad, of which the most important is Hausa.
▶ **adj.** of or relating to this group of languages.

chad·or /'CHədər, 'CHäd,ôr/ (also **chadar** or **chuddar**) ▶ **n.** a large piece of cloth that is wrapped around the head and upper body leaving only the face exposed, worn esp. by Muslim women.
– ORIGIN early 17th cent.: from Urdu *chādar*, *chaddar*, from Persian *čādar* 'sheet or veil.'

Chad·wick /'CHadwik/, Sir James (1891–1974), English physicist who discovered the neutron. Nobel Prize for Physics (1935).

chae·bol /'kī,bäl, -,bôl/ ▶ **n.** (pl. **same** or **chaebols**) (in South Korea) a large business conglomerate, typically a family-owned one.
– ORIGIN 1980s: Korean, literally 'money clan.'

chae·ta /'kētə/ ▶ **n.** (pl. **chaetae** /-tē/) Zoology a stiff bristle made of chitin, esp. in an annelid worm.
– ORIGIN mid 19th cent.: modern Latin, from Greek *khaitē* 'long hair.'

Chae·tog·na·tha /kē'tägnəTHə/ Zoology a small phylum of marine invertebrates that comprises the arrow worms.
– DERIVATIVES **chae·tog·nath** /'kētäg,naTH/ **n.**
– ORIGIN modern Latin (plural), from Greek *khaitē* 'long hair' + *gnathos* 'jaw.'

chafe /CHāf/ ▶ **v.** **1** [with obj.] (of something restrictive or too tight) make (a part of the body) sore by rubbing against it: *the collar chafed his neck*. ■ [no obj.] (of a part of the body) be or become sore as a result of such rubbing. ■ [no obj.] (of an object) rub abrasively against another object: *the grommet stops the cable from chafing on the metal*.
2 [with obj.] rub (a part of the body) to restore warmth or sensation.
3 become or make annoyed or impatient because of a restriction or inconvenience: [no obj.] *the bank chafed at the restrictions imposed upon it* | [with obj.] *it chafed him to be confined like this*.
▶ **n.** **1** wear or damage caused by rubbing: *to prevent chafe the ropes should lie flat*.
2 archaic a state of annoyance.
– PHRASES **chafe at the bit** see **CHOMP AT THE BIT** at **CHOMP**.
– ORIGIN late Middle English (in the sense 'make warm'): from Old French *chaufer* 'make hot,' based on Latin *calefacere*, from *calere* 'be hot' + *facere* 'make.'

chaf·er /'CHāfər/ ▶ **n.** a flying beetle, the adult and larva of which can be very destructive to foliage and plant roots respectively. ● Several subfamilies of the family Scarabaeidae. See also **COCKCHAFER**.
– ORIGIN Old English *ceafor*, *cefer*, of Germanic origin; related to Dutch *kever*.

chaff¹ /CHaf/ ▶ **n.** the husks of corn or other seed separated by winnowing or threshing. ■ chopped hay and straw used as fodder. ■ worthless things; trash. ■ strips of metal foil or metal filings released in the atmosphere from aircraft, or deployed as missiles, to obstruct radar detection or confuse radar-tracking missiles.
– PHRASES **separate the wheat from the chaff** distinguish valuable people or things from worthless ones.
– DERIVATIVES **chaff·y adj.**
– ORIGIN Old English *cæf*, *ceaf*, probably from a Germanic base meaning 'gnaw'; related to Dutch *kaf*, also to **CHAFER**.

chaff² ▶ **n.** lighthearted joking; banter.
▶ **v.** [with obj.] tease.
– ORIGIN early 19th cent.: perhaps from **CHAFE**.

chaff-cut·ter ▶ **n.** chiefly historical a machine for chopping hay and straw for use as fodder.

Chaf·fee /'CHafē/, Roger B. see **GRISSOM**.

chaf·fer /'CHafər/ ▶ **v.** [no obj.] haggle about the terms of an agreement or price of something.
▶ **n.** archaic haggling about the price of something.
– DERIVATIVES **chaff·er·er n.**
– ORIGIN Middle English (in the sense 'trade or trading'): from Old English *cēap* 'a bargain' + *faru* 'journey'; probably influenced by Old Norse *kaupfọr*.

chaf·finch /'CHaf,inCH/ ▶ **n.** a Eurasian and North African finch, typically with a bluish top to the head and dark wings and tail. ● Genus *Fringilla*, family Fringillidae: two species, in particular *F. coelebs*, which (in the male of the typical European form) has a pinkish face and breast.
– ORIGIN Old English *ceaffinc* 'chaff finch' (because it forages around barns, picking seeds out of the chaff).

chaff·weed /'CHaf,wēd/ ▶ **n.** a tiny European pimpernel with pink or white flowers. ● *Anagallis minima*, family Primulaceae.
– ORIGIN mid 16th cent.: probably from the verb **CHAFE** + **WEED**.

chaf·ing dish /'CHāfiNG/ ▶ **n.** a metal pan with an outer pan of hot water, used for keeping food warm. ■ a metal pan, typically one containing an alcohol lamp, used for cooking at the table.
– ORIGIN late 15th cent.: from the original (now obsolete) sense of **CHAFE** 'become warm, warm up.'

Cha·gall /SHə'gäl/, Marc (1887–1985), French painter and graphic artist; born in Russia. His work was characterized by the use of rich emotive color and dream imagery and had a significant influence on surrealism.

Cha·gas' dis·ease /'SHägəs/ ▶ **n.** a disease caused by trypanosomes transmitted by bloodsucking bugs, endemic in South America and causing damage to the heart and central nervous system.
– ORIGIN early 20th cent.: named after Carlos *Chagas* (1879–1934), the Brazilian physician who first described it.

Cha·gos Ar·chi·pel·a·go /'CHägəs/ an island group in the Indian Ocean that forms the British Indian Ocean Territory.

cha·grin /SHə'grin/ ▶ **n.** distress or embarrassment at having failed or been humiliated: *Jeff, much to his chagrin, wasn't invited*.
▶ **v.** (**be chagrined**) feel distressed or humiliated: *he was chagrined when his friend poured scorn on him*.
– ORIGIN mid 17th cent. (in the sense 'melancholy'): from French *chagrin* (noun), literally 'rough skin, shagreen,' *chagriner* (verb), of unknown origin.

chai /CHī/ ▶ **n.** a type of Indian tea, made esp. by boiling the tea leaves with milk, sugar, and cardamom.
– ORIGIN a term in various Indian languages.

Chain /CHān/, Sir Ernst Boris (1906–79), British biochemist; born in Germany. With Howard Florey, he isolated and purified penicillin. Nobel Prize for Physiology or Medicine (1945), shared with Florey and Alexander Fleming.

chain /CHān/ ▶ **n.** **1** a connected flexible series of metal links used for fastening or securing objects and pulling or supporting loads. ■ (**chains**) such a series of links, or a set of them, used to confine a prisoner: *the drug dealer is being kept in chains*. ■ such a series of links worn as a decoration; a necklace. ■ (**chains**) short for **SNOW CHAINS**. ■ (**chains**) a force or factor that binds or restricts someone: *the chains of illness*.
2 a sequence of items of the same type forming a line: *he kept the chain of buckets supplied with water*. ■ a sequence or series of connected elements: *a chain of events* | *the food chain*. ■ a group of establishments, such as hotels, stores, or restaurants, owned by the same company: *the*

nation's largest hotel chain. ■ a range of mountains: *a chain of volcanic ridges.* ■ a part of a molecule consisting of a number of atoms (typically carbon) bonded together in a linear sequence. ■ a figure in a quadrille or similar dance, in which dancers meet and pass each other in a continuous sequence.
3 a jointed measuring line consisting of linked metal rods. ■ the length of such a measuring line (66 ft.). ■ Football a measuring chain of ten yards, used in the determination of first downs.
4 (**chains**) a structure of planks projecting horizontally from a sailing ship's sides abreast of the masts, used to widen the basis for the shrouds. [formed earlier of iron plates.]
▶ **v.** [with obj.] fasten or secure with a chain: *she chained her bicycle to the railing.* ■ confine with a chain: *he had been chained up* | figurative *as an actuary you will not be chained to a desk.*
– PHRASES **pull** (or **yank**) **someone's chain** informal tease someone, typically by leading them to believe something untrue.
– ORIGIN Middle English: from Old French *chaine, chaeine*, from Latin *catena* 'a chain.'

chain bridge ▶ **n.** a suspension bridge supported by chains rather than cables.

chain drive ▶ **n.** a mechanism in which power is transmitted from an engine, typically to the wheels of a vehicle or a boat's propeller, by means of a moving endless chain.
– DERIVATIVES **chain-driv·en adj.**

chain gang ▶ **n.** a group of convicts chained together while working outside the prison.

chain gear ▶ **n.** a gear transmitting motion by means of a moving endless chain, esp. on a bicycle.

chain har·row ▶ **n.** a harrow consisting of a net made of chains in a metal frame.

chain let·ter ▶ **n.** one of a sequence of letters, each recipient in the sequence being requested to send copies to a specific number of other people.

chain-link ▶ **adj.** [attrib.] made of wire in a diamond-shaped mesh: *a chain-link fence.*

chain mail ▶ **n.** historical armor made of small metal rings linked together.

chain·plate /ˈCHān,plāt/ ▶ **n.** a strong link or plate on the hull of a sailboat or sailing ship, to which a shroud is secured.

chain re·ac·tion ▶ **n.** a chemical reaction or other process in which the products themselves promote or spread the reaction, which under certain conditions may accelerate dramatically. ■ the self-sustaining fission reaction spread by neutrons that occurs in nuclear reactors and bombs. ■ a series of events, each caused by the previous one: *an article in one publication sets off a chain reaction in the media.*

chain·ring /ˈCHān,riNG/ ▶ **n.** a large cog carrying the chain on a bicycle, which is attached to the crank.

chain·saw /ˈCHān,sô/ ▶ **n.** a mechanical power-driven cutting tool with teeth set on a chain that moves around the edge of a blade.

chain shot ▶ **n.** historical pairs of cannonballs or half balls joined by a chain, fired from cannons in sea battles in order to damage masts and rigging.

chain-smoke ▶ **v.** [no obj.] smoke continually, esp. by lighting a new cigarette from the butt of the last one smoked.
– DERIVATIVES **chain-smok·er n.**

chain stitch ▶ **n.** an ornamental stitch in which loops are crocheted or embroidered in a chain.

chain store ▶ **n.** one of a series of stores owned by one company and selling the same merchandise.

chain wheel ▶ **n.** a toothed wheel transmitting power by means of a chain fitted to its edges.

chair /CHe(ə)r/ ▶ **n. 1** a separate seat for one person, typically with a back and four legs. ■ short for CHAIRLIFT. ■ (**the chair**) short for ELECTRIC CHAIR.
2 the person in charge of a meeting or organization (used as a neutral alternative to chairman or chairwoman): *a three-year term as the board's deputy chair.* ■ an official position of authority, for example on a board of directors: *the editorial chair.* ■ (also **chair umpire**) Tennis another term for UMPIRE.
3 a professorship: *he held a chair in physics.*
4 a particular seat in an orchestra: [as modifier, in combination] *she was fourth-chair trumpet.*
5 chiefly Brit. a metal socket holding a railroad rail in place.
▶ **v.** [with obj.] **1** act as chairperson of or preside over (an organization, meeting, or public event).
2 Brit. carry (someone) aloft in a chair or in a sitting position to celebrate a victory.
– PHRASES **take the chair** act as chairperson.
– ORIGIN Middle English: from Old French *chaiere* (modern *chaire* 'bishop's throne, etc.,' *chaise* 'chair'), from Latin *cathedra* 'seat,' from Greek *kathedra*. Compare with CATHEDRAL.

chair·borne /ˈCHe(ə)r,bôrn/ ▶ **adj.** military slang assigned to a desk job rather than field duty.

chair car ▶ **n.** a railroad car with individual seats instead of long benches; a parlor car.

chair·la·dy /ˈCHe(ə)r,lādē/ ▶ **n.** (pl. **chairladies**) another term for CHAIRWOMAN.

chair·lift /ˈCHe(ə)r,lift/ ▶ **n. 1** a series of chairs hung from a moving cable, typically used for carrying passengers up and down a mountain.
2 a device for carrying people in wheelchairs from one floor of a building to another.

chair·man /ˈCHe(ə)rmən/ ▶ **n.** (pl. **chairmen**) **1** a person, esp. a man, designated to preside over a meeting. ■ the permanent or long-term president of a committee, company, or other organization. ■ (**Chairman**) (since 1949) the leading figure in the Chinese Communist Party.
2 a person, esp. a man, who is the administrative head of a department of instruction at a college or university.
3 historical a sedan-bearer.
– DERIVATIVES **chair·man·ship** /-,SHip/ **n.**

chair·per·son /ˈCHe(ə)r,pərsən/ ▶ **n.** (pl. **chairpersons**) a chairman or chairwoman (used as a neutral alternative).

chair·wom·an /ˈCHe(ə)r,wo͝omən/ ▶ **n.** (pl. **chairwomen**) **1** a woman designated to preside over committee or board meetings.
2 a woman who is the administrative head of a department of instruction at a college or university.

chaise /SHāz/ ▶ **n. 1** chiefly historical a horse-drawn carriage for one or two people, typically one with an open top and two wheels. ■ another term for POST-CHAISE.
2 short for CHAISE LONGUE.
– ORIGIN mid 17th cent.: from French, variant of *chaire* (see CHAIR).

chaise longue /SHāz ˈlôNG/ ▶ **n.** (pl. **chaises longues** /ˈSHāz ˈlôNG(z)/) a reclining chair with a lengthened seat forming a leg rest.
– ORIGIN early 19th cent.: French, literally 'long chair.'

chaise lounge /SHāz ˈlounj, CHās/ ▶ **n.** variant of CHAISE LONGUE.
– ORIGIN early 20th cent.: alteration by association with LOUNGE.

Cha·ka variant spelling of SHAKA.

chak·ra /ˈCHäkrə/ ▶ **n.** (in Indian thought) each of the centers of spiritual power in the human body, usually considered to be seven in number.
– ORIGIN from Sanskrit *cakra* 'wheel or circle,' from an Indo-European base meaning 'turn,' shared by WHEEL.

cha·la·za /kəˈlāzə, -ˈlazə/ ▶ **n.** (pl. **chalazae** /-ˈlāzē, -ˈlazē, -,zī/) Zoology (in a bird's egg) each of two twisted membranous strips joining the yolk to the ends of the shell.
– DERIVATIVES **cha·la·zal adj.**
– ORIGIN early 18th cent.: modern Latin, from Greek *khalaza* 'small knot.'

Chal·ce·don /ˈkalsə,dän, kalˈsēdn/ a former city on the Bosporus in Asia Minor, now part of Istanbul. Turkish name KADIKÖY.

Chal·ce·don, Coun·cil of the fourth ecumenical council of the Christian Church, held at Chalcedon in 451. It condemned the Monophysite position and affirmed the dual but united nature of Christ as god and man.
– DERIVATIVES **Chal·ce·do·ni·an** /,kalsəˈdōnēən/ **n. & adj.**

chal·ced·o·ny /kalˈsednˌē, CHal-, ˈkalsə,dōnē, ˈCHalsə-/ ▶ **n.** (pl. **chalcedonies**) a microcrystalline type of quartz occurring in several different forms, including onyx, agate, and jasper.
– DERIVATIVES **chal·ce·don·ic** /,kalsəˈdänik/ **adj.**
– ORIGIN late Middle English: from Latin *calcedonius, chalcedonius* (often believed to mean 'stone of Chalcedon,' but this is doubtful), from Greek *khalkēdōn*.

chal·cid /ˈkalsid/ (also **chalcid wasp**) ▶ **n.** a minute parasitic wasp of a large group whose members lay eggs inside the eggs of other insects. They typically have bright metallic coloration. ● Superfamily Chalcidoidea, order Hymenoptera.
– ORIGIN late 19th cent.: from modern Latin *Chalcis* (genus name), from Greek *khalkos* 'copper, brass,' + -ID[3].

chal·co·cite /ˈkalkə,sīt/ ▶ **n.** cuprous sulfide, an ore of copper, usu. occurring as black, fine-grained masses. ● Chem. formula: Cu_2S.

chal·co·py·rite /,kalkəˈpī,rīt/ ▶ **n.** a yellow crystalline mineral consisting of a sulfide of copper and iron. It is the principal ore of copper. ● Chem. formula $CuFeS_2$.
– ORIGIN mid 19th cent.: from modern Latin *chalcopyrites*, from Greek *khalkos* 'copper' + *purītēs* (see PYRITE).

Chal·de·a /kalˈdēə/ an ancient country in what is now southern Iraq, inhabited by the Chaldeans.
– ORIGIN from Greek *Khaldaia*, from Akkadian *Kaldû*, the name of a Babylonian tribal group.

Chal·de·an /kalˈdēən/ ▶ **n. 1** a member of an ancient people who lived in Chaldea *c.*800 BC and ruled Babylonia 625–539 BC. They were renowned as astronomers and astrologers.
2 the Semitic language of the ancient Chaldeans. ■ a language related to Aramaic and spoken in parts of Iraq.
3 a member of a Syrian Uniate (formerly Nestorian) Church based mainly in Iran and Iraq.
▶ **adj. 1** of or relating to ancient Chaldea or its people or language.
2 of or relating to the East Syrian Uniate Church.

Chal·dee /ˈkal,dē/ ▶ **n. 1** the Semitic language of the ancient Chaldeans. ■ dated the Aramaic language as used in some books of the Old Testament.
2 a native of ancient Chaldea.
– ORIGIN from Latin *Chaldaei* 'Chaldeans,' from Greek *Khaldaioi*, from *Khaldaia* (see CHALDEA).

cha·let /SHaˈlā, ˈSHa,lā/ ▶ **n.** a wooden house or cottage with overhanging eaves, typically found in the Swiss Alps.
– ORIGIN late 18th cent.: from Swiss French, diminutive of Old French *chasel* 'farmstead,' based on Latin *casa* 'hut, cottage.'

chalet

chal·ice /ˈCHaləs/ ▶ **n.** historical a large cup or goblet, typically used for drinking wine. ■ the wine cup used in the Christian Eucharist.
– ORIGIN Middle English: via Old French from Latin *calix, calic-* 'cup.'

chal·i·co·there /ˈkalikō,THir/ ▶ **n.** a horselike fossil mammal of the late Tertiary period, with stout claws on the toes instead of hooves. ● Family Chalicotheriidae, order Perissodactyla: several genera, in particular *Moropus*.
– ORIGIN early 20th cent.: from modern Latin *Chalicotherium* (genus name), from Greek *khalix, khalik-* 'gravel' + *thērion* 'wild animal.'

chalk /CHôk/ ▶ **n. 1** a soft white limestone (calcium carbonate) formed from the skeletal remains of sea creatures. ■ a similar substance (calcium sulfate), made into white or colored sticks used for drawing or writing. ■ Geology a series of strata consisting mainly of chalk.
2 short for FRENCH CHALK.
▶ **v.** [with obj.] **1** draw or write with chalk. ■ draw or write on (a surface) with chalk: *blackboards chalked with Japanese phrases.*
2 rub (something, esp. a pool cue) with chalk.
3 Brit. charge (drinks bought in a bar) to a person's account.
– PHRASES **as different as** (or **like**) **chalk and cheese** Brit. fundamentally different or incompatible. **by a long chalk** Brit. by far.
– PHRASAL VERBS **chalk something out** sketch or plan something: *we have already chalked out the strategy for conducting raids* . **chalk something up 1** achieve something noteworthy: *he has chalked up a box-office success.* **2** ascribe something to a particular cause: *I chalked my sleeplessness up to nerves.*
– ORIGIN Old English *cealc* (also denoting lime), related to Dutch *kalk* and German *Kalk*, from Latin *calx* (see CALX).

chalk·board /ˈCHôk,bôrd/ ▶ **n.** another term for BLACKBOARD.

chalk·face /ˈCHôk,fās/ ▶ **n.** [in sing.] Brit. the day-to-day work of teaching in a school: *teachers at the chalkface.*

chalk·stone /ˈCHôk,stōn/ ▶ **n.** Medicine. dated a chalky deposit of sodium urate formed in the hands and feet of sufferers from severe gout.

chalk-stripe ▶ **adj.** [attrib.] (of a garment or material) having a pattern of thin white stripes on a dark background.
▶ **n.** (**chalk stripe**) a pattern of this kind.
– DERIVATIVES **chalk-striped adj.**

chalk talk ▶ **n.** a talk or lecture in which the speaker uses blackboard and chalk.

chalk·y /'CHôkē/ ▶ **adj.** (**chalkier, chalkiest**) **1** consisting of or rich in chalk: *a chalky, powdery soil.* **2** resembling chalk in texture or paleness of color: *patches of creamy or chalky white.*
– DERIVATIVES **chalk·i·ness n.**

chal·lah /'hälə, 'KHälə/ ▶ **n.** (pl. **challahs** /'häləz, 'KHäləz/ or **chalot(h)** /hä'lōt, KHä-, -'lōs/) a loaf of white leavened bread, typically plaited in form, traditionally baked to celebrate the Jewish sabbath.
– ORIGIN 1920s: from Hebrew *ḥallah.*

chal·lenge /'CHalənj/ ▶ **n. 1** a call to take part in a contest or competition, esp. a duel: *he accepted the challenge.* ■ a task or situation that tests someone's abilities: *the ridge is a challenge for experienced climbers.* ■ an attempt to win a contest or championship in a sport: *a world title challenge.* **2** an objection or query as to the truth of something, often with an implicit demand for proof: *a challenge to the legality of the order.* ■ a sentry's call for a password or other proof of identity. ■ Law an objection regarding the eligibility or suitability of a jury member. **3** Medicine exposure of the immune system to pathogenic organisms or antigens: *recently vaccinated calves should be protected from challenge.*
▶ **v.** [with obj.] **1** invite (someone) to engage in a contest: *he challenged one of my men to a duel.* ■ enter into competition with or opposition against: *incumbent Democrats are being challenged in the 29th district.* ■ make a rival claim to or threaten someone's hold on (a position): *they were challenging his leadership.* ■ [with obj. and infinitive] invite (someone) to do something that one thinks will be difficult or impossible; dare: *I challenged them to make up their own minds.* ■ test the abilities of: *he needed something both to challenge his skills and to regain his crown as the king of the thriller.* **2** dispute the truth or validity of: *employees challenged the company's requirement.* ■ Law object to (a jury member). ■ (of a sentry) call on (someone) for proof of identity. **3** Medicine expose (the immune system) to pathogenic organisms or antigens.
– DERIVATIVES **chal·lenge·a·ble adj.**, **chal·leng·er n.**
– ORIGIN Middle English (in the senses 'accusation' and 'accuse'): from Old French *chalenge* (noun), *chalenger* (verb), from Latin *calumnia* 'calumny,' *calumniari* 'calumniate.'

chal·lenged /'CHalənjd/ ▶ **adj.** [with submodifier or in combination] (used euphemistically) impaired or disabled in a specified respect: *physically challenged.* ■ informal lacking or deficient in a specified respect: *vertically challenged | today's attention-challenged teens.*

> **USAGE** The use with a preceding adverb, e.g., **physically challenged**, originally intended to give a more positive tone than such terms as **disabled** or **handicapped**, arose in the US in the 1980s. Despite the originally serious intention, the term rapidly became stalled by uses whose intention was to make fun of the attempts at euphemism and whose tone was usually clearly ironic: examples include **cerebrally challenged** (not very smart), **follicularly challenged** (bald or balding), **vertically challenged** (short), etc.

Chal·leng·er /'CHalənjər/ a US space shuttle that exploded 1.5 minutes after launch on January 28, 1986, killing its crew of seven.

Chal·leng·er Deep /'CHalənjər/ the deepest part (36,201 feet, 11,034 m) of the Mariana Trench in the North Pacific, discovered by HMS *Challenger II* in 1948.

chal·leng·ing /'CHalənjiNG/ ▶ **adj.** testing one's abilities; demanding: *challenging and rewarding employment.* ■ inviting competition; provocative: *there was a challenging glint in his eyes.*
– DERIVATIVES **chal·leng·ing·ly adv.**

> **WORD TRENDS** A fear of offending people has led to the replacement of many negative expressions with more positive alternatives, with the adjective **challenging** being a prime example. The Oxford English Corpus shows that it is used euphemistically for *difficult* or *trying* and applied to unpleasant situations (*a challenging period of slowing growth and rising unemployment*), troublesome individuals (*it's surprising how common it is for parents to encounter challenging behavior with their teenagers*), and even avant-garde music (*the opera's challenging atonal score*). See also **ISSUE**.

chal·lis /'SHalē/ ▶ **n.** a soft lightweight clothing fabric made from silk and worsted.
– ORIGIN mid 19th cent.: origin uncertain; perhaps from the surname *Challis.*

chal·u·meau /,SHalə'mō/ ▶ **n.** (pl. **chalumeaux** /-'mō(z)/) a reed instrument of the early 18th century from which the clarinet was developed. ■ (also **chalumeau register**) the lowest octave of the clarinet's range.
– ORIGIN early 18th cent.: from French, from Latin *calamellus* 'little reed,' diminutive of *calamus.*

cha·lu·pa /chə'lo͞opə/ ▶ **n.** a fried tortilla in the shape of a boat, with a spicy filling.
– ORIGIN late 19th cent.: Spanish, ultimately related to Dutch *sloep* 'sloop.'

cha·lyb·e·ate /kə'lēbēət, -'lib-/ ▶ **adj.** [attrib.] of or denoting natural mineral springs containing iron salts.
– ORIGIN mid 17th cent.: from modern Latin *chalybeatus*, from Latin *chalybs*, from Greek *khalups, khalub-* 'steel.'

Cham /kam/ ▶ **n.** (pl. **same** or **Chams**) **1** a member of an indigenous people of Vietnam and Cambodia, who formed an independent kingdom from the 2nd to 17th centuries AD, and whose culture is strongly influenced by that of India. **2** either of two Austronesian languages of this people.
▶ **adj.** of or relating to this people, their culture, or their language.

Cha·mae·le·on /kə'mēlyən, -lēən/ Astronomy a small and faint southern constellation (the Chameleon), close to the south celestial pole. ■ (as genitive **Chamaeleontis** /kə,mēlē'äntis/) used with a preceding letter or numeral to designate a star in this constellation: *the star Delta Chamaeleontis.*
– ORIGIN from Greek.

cha·mae·le·on ▶ **n.** chiefly Brit. variant spelling of **CHAMELEON.**

cham·ae·phyte /'kamə,fīt/ ▶ **n.** Botany a woody plant whose resting buds are on or near the ground.
– ORIGIN early 20th cent.: from Greek *khamai* 'on the ground' + **-PHYTE.**

cham·ber /'CHāmbər/ ▶ **n. 1** a large room used for formal or public events. ■ any of the houses of a legislature: *the Senate chamber.* **2** literary or archaic a private room, typically a bedroom: *he had his meals brought to his chamber.* ■ (**chambers**) Law a judge's room used for official proceedings not required to be held in open court. ■ (**chambers**) Brit. Law rooms used by a lawyer or lawyers. **3** an enclosed space or cavity: *an echo chamber.* ■ a large underground cavern. ■ the part of a gun bore that contains the charge or bullet. ■ Biology a cavity in a plant, animal body, or organ: *the four chambers of the heart.* **4** [as modifier] Music of or for a small group of instruments: *a chamber concert.*
▶ **v.** [with obj.] place (a bullet) into the chamber of a gun.
– DERIVATIVES **cham·bered adj.**
– ORIGIN Middle English (in the sense 'private room'): from Old French *chambre*, from Latin *camera* 'vault, arched chamber,' from Greek *kamara* 'object with an arched cover.'

cham·bered nau·ti·lus ▶ **n.** see **NAUTILUS.**

Cham·ber·lain[1] /'CHāmbərlən/, Neville (1869–1940), British statesman; prime minister 1937–40; full name *Arthur Neville Chamberlain.* He pursued a policy of appeasement with Nazi Germany and signed the Munich Agreement in 1938, but was forced to abandon this policy following Hitler's invasion of Czechoslovakia in 1939.

Cham·ber·lain[2], Owen (1920–2006), US physicist. He investigated subatomic particles and in 1955 discovered the antiproton with E. G. Segrè (1905–89). Nobel Prize for Physics (1959), shared with Segrè.

Cham·ber·lain[3], Wilt (1936–99), US basketball player; full name *Wilton Norman Chamberlain*; known as **Wilt the Stilt.** He played for the Philadelphia Warriors (later the Golden State Warriors), the Philadelphia 76ers, and the Los Angeles Lakers from 1959 until 1973. Basketball Hall of Fame (1978).

cham·ber·lain /'CHāmbərlən/ ▶ **n.** historical an officer who manages the household of a monarch or noble. ■ Brit. the treasurer of a corporation or public body.
– DERIVATIVES **cham·ber·lain·ship** /-,SHip/ **n.**
– ORIGIN Middle English (denoting a servant in a bedchamber): via Old French from Old Saxon *kamera*, from Latin *camera* 'vault' (see **CHAMBER**).

cham·ber·maid /'CHāmbər,mād/ ▶ **n.** a maid who cleans bedrooms and bathrooms, esp. in a hotel.

cham·ber mu·sic ▶ **n.** instrumental music played by a small ensemble, with one player to a part, the most important form being the string quartet which developed in the 18th century.

cham·ber of com·merce (abbr.: **C. of C.**) ▶ **n.** a local association to promote and protect the interests of the business community in a particular place.

Cham·ber of Dep·u·ties ▶ **n.** the lower legislative assembly in some parliaments.

cham·ber of hor·rors ▶ **n.** an exhibit containing such gruesome displays as instruments or scenes of torture or execution.
– ORIGIN mid 19th cent.: from the name given to a room in Madame Tussaud's waxworks exhibition in London.

cham·ber or·ches·tra ▶ **n.** a small orchestra.

cham·ber pot ▶ **n.** a bowl kept in a bedroom and used as a toilet, esp. at night.

Cham·bers /'CHāmbərz/, Whittaker (1901–61), US journalist; born *Jay Vivian Chambers.* In 1948, he accused Alger Hiss of Communist party membership and of passing State Department documents to Soviet agents.

Cham·ber·tin /,SHänber'taN/ ▶ **n.** a dry red burgundy wine of high quality from Gevrey Chambertin in eastern France.

cham·bray /'SHam,brā, -brē/ ▶ **n.** a linen-finished gingham cloth with a white weft and a colored warp, producing a mottled appearance.
– ORIGIN early 19th cent. (originally US): formed irregularly from *Cambrai*, the name of a town in northern France, where it was originally made. Compare with **CAMBRIC.**

cham·bré /'SHam,brā, SHam'brā/ ▶ **adj.** [predic.] (of red wine) at room temperature: *Cabernet tastes best chambré.*
– ORIGIN 1950s: French, past participle of *chambrer* 'bring to room temperature,' from *chambre* 'room' (see **CHAMBER**).

cha·me·le·on /kə'mēlyən, -lēən/ (chiefly Brit. also **chamaeleon**) ▶ **n.** a small slow-moving Old World lizard with a prehensile tail, long extensible tongue, protruding eyes that rotate independently, and a highly developed ability to change color. ● Family Chamaeleonidae: four genera, in particular *Chamaeleo*, and numerous species, including the **European chameleon** (*C. vulgaris*) and the **common chameleon** (*C. chamaeleon*). ■ (also **American chameleon**) an anole. ■ a person who changes their opinions or behavior according to the situation.

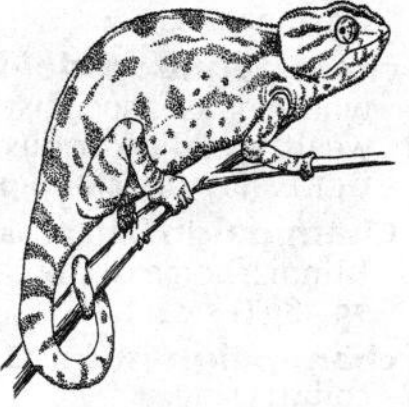
common chameleon

– DERIVATIVES **cha·me·le·on·ic** /kə,mēlē'änik/ **adj.**
– ORIGIN Middle English: via Latin *chamaeleon* from Greek *khamaileōn*, from *khamai* 'on the ground' + *leōn* 'lion.'

cha·metz /KHô'mäts, 'KHô,mets/ (also **chometz**) ▶ **n.** Judaism leaven, or food mixed with leaven, prohibited during Passover.
– ORIGIN mid 19th cent.: from Hebrew *ḥāmēṣ.*

cham·fer /'CHamfər/ ▶ **v.** [with obj.] in carpentry, cut away (a right-angled edge or corner) to make a symmetrical sloping edge.
▶ **n.** a symmetrical sloping surface at an edge or corner.
– ORIGIN mid 16th cent. (in the sense 'flute or furrow'): back-formation from *chamfering*, from French *chamfrain*, from *chant* 'edge' (see **CANT[2]**) + *fraint* 'broken' (from Old French *fraindre* 'break,' from Latin *frangere*).

cha·mise /SHə'mēz, CHə-, -mēs/ ▶ **n.** an evergreen shrub with small narrow leaves, common in the chaparral of California. Also called **GREASEWOOD.** ● *Adenostoma fasciculatum*, family Rosaceae.
– ORIGIN mid 19th cent.: from Mexican Spanish *chamiso.*

cham·ois /'SHamē/ ▶ **n.** (pl. **same** /'SHamēz/) **1** an agile goat-antelope with short hooked horns, found in mountainous areas of Europe from Spain to the Caucasus. ● Genus *Rupicapra*, family Bovidae: *R. rupicapra* (of the Alps, East, and southeastern Europe), and *R. pyrenaica* (of the Pyrenees and Apennines, also called **IZARD**). **2** (also **chamois leather**) a type of soft pliable leather now made from sheepskin or lambskin. ■ a piece of such leather, used typically for washing windows or cars.
– ORIGIN mid 16th cent.: from French, of unknown ultimate origin.

cham·o·mile /'kamə,mēl, -,mīl/ (also **camomile**) ▶ **n.** an aromatic European plant of the daisy

family, with white and yellow daisylike flowers. • The perennial **sweet** (or **Roman**) **chamomile** (*Chamaemelum nobile* (or *Anthemis nobilis*), family Compositae), used, esp. formerly, for lawns and herbal medicine, the annual **German chamomile** (*Matricaria recutita*), used medicinally, and the yellow-flowered **dyer's chamomile** (*Anthemis tinctoria*), used to produce a yellow-brown dye.
– ORIGIN Middle English: from Old French *camomille*, from late Latin *chamomilla*, from Greek *khamaimēlon* 'earth apple' (because of the applelike smell of its flowers).

C

cham·o·mile tea (also **camomile**) ▶ n. an infusion of dried flowers of sweet chamomile.

Cha·mor·ro /CHə'môrō/ ▶ n. **1** a member of the indigenous people of the Mariana Islands (including Guam).
2 the Austronesian language of this people.

champ[1] /CHamp/ ▶ v. another term for CHOMP.
– ORIGIN late Middle English: imitative.

champ[2] ▶ n. informal a champion.
– ORIGIN mid 19th cent.: abbreviation.

Cham·pagne /SHän'pänyə, SHam'pān/ a region and former province in northeastern France that now corresponds to the Champagne-Ardenne administrative region. It is noted for the white sparkling wine first produced here in about 1700.

cham·pagne /SHam'pān/ ▶ n. a white sparkling wine associated with celebration and regarded as a symbol of luxury, typically that made in the Champagne region of France. ■ a pale cream or straw color.

Cham·pagne-Ar·denne /SHän,pän är'den/ a region of northeastern France that consists of part of the Ardennes forest and the vine-growing area of Champagne.

cham·pagne so·cial·ist ▶ n. Brit. derogatory a person who espouses socialist ideals while enjoying a wealthy and luxurious lifestyle.
– DERIVATIVES **cham·pagne so·cial·ism** n.

Cham·paign /SHam'pān/ a city in east central Illinois, home to the University of Illinois; pop. 79,389 (est. 2008).

cham·paign /SHam'pān/ ▶ n. literary open level countryside.
– ORIGIN late Middle English: from Old French *champagne*, from late Latin *campania*, based on Latin *campus* 'level ground.' Compare with CAMPAIGN.

cham·pak /'CHəmpək, 'CHam-/ ▶ n. an Asian evergreen tree of the magnolia family, bearing fragrant orange flowers and sacred to Hindus and Buddhists. • *Michelia champaca*, family Magnoliaceae.
– ORIGIN from Sanskrit *campaka*.

cham·per·ty /'CHampərtē/ ▶ n. Law an illegal agreement in which a person with no previous interest in a lawsuit finances it with a view to sharing the disputed property if the suit succeeds.
– DERIVATIVES **cham·per·tous** /-təs/ adj.
– ORIGIN late Middle English: from Anglo-Norman French *champartie*, from Old French *champart* 'feudal lord's share of produce,' from Latin *campus* 'field' + *pars* 'part.'

cham·pi·gnon /SHam'pinyən, ,SHampē'nyōn/ ▶ n. a small edible mushroom with a light brown cap, growing in short grass in both Eurasia and North America and widely grown commercially. Also called MEADOW MUSHROOM, FIELD MUSHROOM. • *Agaricus campestris*, family Agaricaceae, class Basidiomycetes.
– ORIGIN late 16th cent.: from French, diminutive of Old French *champagne* 'open country' (see CHAMPAIGN).

Cham·pi·on /'CHampēən/, Gower (Carlyle) (1921–80), US choreographer, dancer, and director. He danced with his wife **Marge** (1919–) on stage and in movies such as *Jupiter's Darling* (1955), and he choreographed Broadway musicals such as *42nd Street* (1980).

cham·pi·on /'CHampēən/ ▶ n. **1** a person who has defeated or surpassed all rivals in a competition, esp. in sports: [as modifier] *a champion hurdler*.
2 a person who fights or argues for a cause or on behalf of someone else: *a champion of women's rights*. ■ historical a knight who fought in single combat on behalf of the monarch.
▶ v. [with obj.] support the cause of; defend: *priests who championed human rights*.
– ORIGIN Middle English (denoting a fighting man): from Old French, from medieval Latin *campio(n-)* 'fighter,' from Latin *campus* (see CAMP[1]).

cham·pi·on·ship /'CHampēən,SHip/ ▶ n. **1** a contest for the position of champion in a sport, often involving a series of games or matches. ■ the position or title of the winner of such a contest.
2 the vigorous support or defense of someone or something: *Alan's championship of his estranged wife*.

Cham·plain /SHam'plān/, Samuel de (1567–1635), French explorer and colonial statesman. He established a settlement at Quebec in Canada in 1608 and developed alliances with the indigenous peoples. He was appointed lieutenant governor in 1612.

Cham·plain, Lake /SHam'plān/ a lake in North America, east of the Adirondack Mountains. It forms part of the border between the states of New York and Vermont, and its northern tip extends into Quebec, Canada.
– ORIGIN named after Samuel de CHAMPLAIN, who reached it in 1609.

champ·le·vé /,SHänlə'vā/ ▶ n. enamelwork in which hollows made in a metal surface are filled with colored enamel.
– ORIGIN French, from *champ* 'field' + *levé* 'raised.'

Cham·pol·lion /,SHänpôl'yôn/, Jean-François (1790–1832), French Egyptologist. He is noted for his success in deciphering some of the hieroglyphic inscriptions on the Rosetta Stone in 1822.

Champs-É·ly·sées /,SHänz ,ālē'zā/ an avenue in Paris, France, that extends from the Place de la Concorde to the Arc de Triomphe.

chance /CHans/ ▶ n. **1** a possibility of something happening: *a chance of victory | there is little chance of his finding a job*. ■ (**chances**) the probability of something happening: *he played down his chances of becoming chairman*. ■ [in sing.] an opportunity to do or achieve something: *I gave her a chance to answer*. ■ a ticket in a raffle or lottery. ■ Baseball an opportunity to make a defensive play, which if missed counts as an error: *541 straight chances without an error*.
2 the occurrence and development of events in the absence of any obvious design: *he met his brother by chance | what a lucky chance that you are here*.
▶ adj. [attrib.] fortuitous; accidental: *a chance meeting*.
▶ v. **1** [no obj.] do something by accident or without design: *if they chanced to meet*. ■ (**chance upon/on**) find or see by accident: *he chanced upon an interesting advertisement*.
2 [with obj.] informal do (something) despite its being dangerous or of uncertain outcome: *she waited a few seconds and chanced another look*.
– PHRASES **by any chance** possibly (used in tentative inquiries or suggestions): *were you looking for me by any chance?* **no chance** informal there is no possibility of that: *I asked if we could leave early and she said, "No chance."* **on the (off) chance** just in case: *Joan phoned at noon on the off chance that he'd be home*. **stand a chance** [usu. with negative] have a prospect of success or survival: *his rivals don't stand a chance*. **take a chance** (or **chances**) behave in a way that leaves one vulnerable to danger or failure. ■ (**take a chance on**) put one's trust in (something or someone) knowing that it may not be safe or certain. **take one's chances** do something risky with the hope of success.
– ORIGIN Middle English: from Old French *cheance*, from *cheoir* 'fall, befall,' based on Latin *cadere*.

chan·cel /'CHansəl/ ▶ n. the part of a church near the altar, reserved for the clergy and choir, and typically separated from the nave by steps or a screen.
– ORIGIN Middle English: from Old French, from Latin *cancelli* 'crossbars.'

chan·cel·ler·y /'CHans(ə)lərē/ ▶ n. (pl. **chancelleries**) **1** the position, office, or department of a chancellor. ■ the official residence of a chancellor.
2 an office attached to an embassy or consulate.
– ORIGIN Middle English: from Old French *chancellerie*, from *chancelier* 'secretary' (see CHANCELLOR).

chan·cel·lor /'CHans(ə)lər/ ▶ n. a senior state or legal official. ■ the head of the government in some European countries, such as Germany. ■ the presiding judge of a chancery court. ■ the president or chief administrative officer of a college or university. ■ chiefly Brit. the nonresident honorary head of a college or university. ■ a bishop's law officer. ■ (**Chancellor**) short for CHANCELLOR OF THE EXCHEQUER.
– DERIVATIVES **chan·cel·lor·ship** /-,SHip/ n.
– ORIGIN late Old English, from Old French *cancelier*, from late Latin *cancellarius* 'porter, secretary' (originally a court official stationed at the grating separating public from judges), from *cancelli* 'crossbars.'

Chan·cel·lor of the Ex·cheq·uer ▶ n. the finance minister of the United Kingdom, responsible for preparing the nation's annual budgets.

Chan·cel·lors·ville /'CHans(ə)lərz,vil/ a historic locality in east central Virginia, west of Fredericksburg, site of a Civil War battle in May 1863.

chance-med·ley ▶ n. Law, rare the killing of a person accidentally in self-defense in a fight.
– ORIGIN late 15th cent.: from Anglo-Norman French *chance medlee*, literally 'mixed chance,' from *chance* 'luck' + *medlee*, feminine past participle of *medler* 'to mix' (based on Latin *miscere*).

chan·cer·y /'CHans(ə)rē/ ▶ n. (pl. **chanceries**) **1** a court of equity. ■ equity. ■ historical the court of a bishop's chancellor. ■ (**Chancery**) Brit. Law the Lord Chancellor's court, a division of the High Court of Justice.
2 chiefly Brit. an office attached to an embassy or consulate.
3 a public records office.
– ORIGIN late Middle English: contraction of CHANCELLERY.

Chan·chi·ang /'jän jē'äNG/ variant of ZHANJIANG.

chan·cre /'kaNGkər, 'SHaNG-/ ▶ n. Medicine a painless ulcer, particularly one developing on the genitals as a result of venereal disease.
– ORIGIN late 16th cent.: from French, from Latin *cancer* 'creeping ulcer.'

chan·croid /'kaNG,kroid, 'SHaNG-/ ▶ n. a venereal infection causing ulceration of the lymph nodes in the groin. Also called SOFT CHANCRE.

chanc·y /'CHansē/ ▶ adj. (**chancier, chanciest**) informal subject to unpredictable changes and circumstances: *the screening process was likely to be chancy and unreliable*.
– DERIVATIVES **chanc·i·ly** /-səlē/ adv., **chanc·i·ness** n.

chan·de·lier /,SHandə'li(ə)r/ ▶ n. a decorative hanging light with branches for several light bulbs or candles.
– ORIGIN mid 18th cent.: from French, from *chandelle* 'candle,' from Latin *candela*, from *candere* 'be white, glisten.'

chan·delle /SHan'del, SHän-/ ▶ n. a steep climbing turn executed in an aircraft to gain height while changing the direction of flight.
– ORIGIN 1970s: from French, literally 'candle.'

Chan·di·garh /,CHəndē'gär/ **1** a Union Territory in northwestern India, created in 1966.
2 a city in this territory; pop. 1,033,700 (est. 2009). The present city was designed in 1950 by Le Corbusier as a new capital for the Punjab and is now the capital of the states of Punjab and Haryana.

Chan·dler[1] /'CHandlər/ a city in south central Arizona, a suburb and resort southeast of Phoenix; pop. 247,140 (est. 2008).

Chan·dler[2], Raymond (Thornton) (1888–1959), US novelist; the creator of private detective Philip Marlowe. Many of his novels, written in a tough and realistic style, were made into movies. Notable novels: *The Big Sleep* (1939), *Farewell, My Lovely* (1940), and *The Long Goodbye* (1953).

chan·dler /'CHan(d)lər/ ▶ n. **1** (also **ship chandler**) a dealer in supplies and equipment for ships and boats.
2 historical a dealer in household items such as oil, soap, paint, and groceries. ■ a person who makes and sells candles.
– ORIGIN Middle English (denoting a candlemaker or candle seller): from Old French *chandelier*, from *chandelle* 'candle' (see CHANDELIER).

chan·dler·y /'CHan(d)lərē/ ▶ n. (pl. **chandleries**) the warehouse or store of a chandler. ■ goods sold by a chandler.

Chan·dra·gup·ta Mau·ry·a /,CHəndrə'gooptə 'mourēə/ (c.325–297 BC), Indian emperor. He founded the Mauryan empire and annexed provinces in Afghanistan from Alexander's Greek successors.

Chan·dra·se·khar /,CHəndrə'sākər/, Subrahmanyan (1910–95), US astronomer; born in India. He suggested that some stars could eventually collapse to form a dense white dwarf, provided that their mass does not exceed an upper limit (the **Chandrasekhar limit**).

Cha·nel /SHə'nel/, Coco (1883–1971), French couturière; born *Gabrielle Bonheur Chanel*. Her simple but sophisticated garments were a radical departure from the stiff corseted styles of the day.

Cha·ney /'CHānē/ the name of a family of US actors, notably: ■ **Lon** (1883–1930); full name *Alonso Chaney*. A silent film star known as **the Man of a Thousand Faces**, he played a wide variety of deformed villains and macabre characters in more than 150 movies, including *The Hunchback of Notre Dame* (1923) and *The Phantom of the Opera* (1925). ■ **Lon, Jr.** (1906–1973), Lon's son; born *Creighton Tull Chaney*. He played the lead in a number of horror movies, such as *The Wolf Man* (1941) and *Son of Dracula* (1943).

Chang·an /'CHäNG'än/ former name of XIAN.

Chang·chia·kow /ˌCHäNG jē'ä'kou/ variant of ZHANGJIAKOU.

Chang·chun /'CHäNG'CHŏŏn/ an industrial city in northeastern China, capital of Jilin province; pop. 2,455,900 (est. 2006).

change /CHānj/ ▶ v. **1** make or become different: [with obj.] *a proposal to change the law* | [no obj.] *a Virginia creeper just beginning to **change from** green **to** gold.* ■ make or become a different substance entirely; transform: [with obj.] *filters **change** the ammonia **into** nitrate* | [no obj.] *computer graphics can show cars changing into cheetahs.* ■ [no obj., with complement] alter in terms of: *the ferns began to change shape.* ■ [no obj.] (of traffic lights) move from one color of signal to another. ■ [no obj.] (of the moon) arrive at a fresh phase; become new.
2 [with obj.] take or use another instead of: *she decided to change her name.* ■ move from one to another: *she changed jobs incessantly* | *change sides.* ■ [no obj.] move to a different train, airplane, or subway line. ■ give up (something) in exchange for something else: *we **changed** the shades **for** vertical blinds.* ■ remove (something dirty or faulty) and replace it with another of the same kind: *change a light bulb.* ■ put a clean diaper on (a baby or young child). ■ engage a different gear in a motor vehicle: *wait for a gap and then change gears* | figurative *with business concluded, the convention changes gear and a gigantic circus takes over the town.* ■ exchange (a sum of money) for the same amount in smaller denominations or in coins, or for different currency. ■ [no obj.] put different clothes on: *he changed for dinner.*
▶ n. **1** the act or instance of making or becoming different: *the **change from** a nomadic **to** an agricultural society* | *environmental change.* ■ the substitution of one thing for another: *a change of venue.* ■ an alteration or modification: *a change came over Eddie's face.* ■ a new or refreshingly different experience: *couscous makes an interesting **change from** rice.* ■ [in sing.] a clean garment or garments as a replacement for clothes one is wearing: *a **change of** socks.* ■ (**the change** or **the change of life**) informal menopause. ■ the moon's arrival at a fresh phase, typically at the new moon. ■ Baseball another term for CHANGE-UP.
2 coins as opposed to paper currency: *a handful of loose change.* ■ money given in exchange for the same amount in larger denominations. ■ money returned to someone as the balance of the amount paid for something: *I watched him pocket the change.*
3 (usu. **changes**) an order in which a peal of bells can be rung.
4 (**Change** or **'Change**) Brit. historical a place where merchants met to do business.
– PHRASES **change color** blanch or flush. **change hands** (of a business or building) pass to a different owner. ■ (of money or a marketable commodity) pass to another person during a business transaction: *no money has changed hands.* **change one's mind** adopt a different opinion or plan. **a change of heart** a move to a different opinion or attitude. **change places** exchange places or roles: *under the bishop's plan, he and I were to change places.* **change step** (in marching) alter one's step so that the opposite leg marks time. **change the subject** begin talking about something different, esp. to avoid embarrassment or the divulgence of confidences. **change one's tune** express a different opinion or behave in a different way. **for a change** contrary to how things usually happen; for variety: *it's nice to be pampered for a change.* **ring the changes** vary the ways of expressing, arranging, or doing something. [with allusion to bell-ringing and the different orders in which a peal of bells may be rung.]
– PHRASAL VERBS **change off** take turns. **change over** move from one system or situation to another: *crop farmers have to **change over** to dairy farming.*
– DERIVATIVES **change·ful** /'CHānjfəl/ **adj.**
– ORIGIN Middle English: from Old French *change* (noun), *changer* (verb), from late Latin *cambiare*, from Latin *cambire* 'barter,' probably of Celtic origin.

change·a·ble /'CHānjəbəl/ ▶ **adj. 1** irregular; inconstant: *the weather will be changeable, with rain at times.*
2 able to change or be changed.
– DERIVATIVES **change·a·bil·i·ty** /ˌCHānjə'bilətē/ **n.**, **change·a·ble·ness n.**, **change·a·bly** /-blē/ **adv.**

change·less /'CHānjlis/ ▶ **adj.** remaining the same.
– DERIVATIVES **change·less·ly adv.**, **change·less·ness n.**

change·ling /'CHānjliNG/ ▶ **n.** a child believed to have been secretly substituted by fairies for the parents' real child in infancy.

change man·age·ment ▶ **n. 1** the management of change and development within a business or similar organization.
2 the controlled identification and implementation of required changes within a computer system.

change-out /'CHānjˌout/ ▶ **n.** the replacement of a spent, used, dysfunctional or otherwise inferior part or object with a new one.

change·o·ver /'CHānjˌōvər/ ▶ **n.** a change from one system or situation to another.

change purse ▶ **n.** a small strapless purse used for carrying money.

chang·er /'CHānjər/ ▶ **n.** a person or thing that changes something. ■ a device that holds several computer disks or compact discs and is able to switch between them.

change-ring·ing ▶ **n.** the ringing of sets of church bells or handbells in a constantly varying order.
– DERIVATIVES **change-ring·er n.**

change-up ▶ **n.** Baseball a deceptively slow pitch intended to throw off the batter's timing.

Chang Jiang /'CHäNG jē'äNG/ another name for YANGTZE.

Chang·sha /'CHäNG'SHä/ the capital of Hunan province in eastern central China; pop. 1,731,900 (est. 2006).

Chang·zhou /'CHäNG'jō/ a city in Jiangsu province in eastern China, on the Grand Canal, north of Shanghai; pop. 1,103,900 (est. 2006).

chan·nel /'CHanl/ ▶ **n. 1** a length of water wider than a strait, joining two larger areas of water, esp. two seas. ■ the navigable part of a waterway: *buoys marked the safe limits of the channel.* ■ a hollow bed for a natural or artificial waterway. ■ (**the Channel**) the English Channel. ■ a tubular passage or duct for liquid. ■ an electric circuit that acts as a path for a signal: *an audio channel.* ■ Electronics the semiconductor region in a field-effect transistor that forms the main current path between the source and the drain.
2 a band of frequencies used in radio and television transmission, esp. as used by a particular station. ■ a service or station using such a band: *a shopping channel.*
3 a medium for communication or the passage of information: *they didn't apply through the proper channels.*
▶ v. (**channels, channeling, channeled**; Brit. **channels, channelling, channelled**) [with obj.] **1** direct toward a particular end or object: *advertisers channel money into radio.* ■ guide along a particular route or through a specified medium: *many countries **channel** their aid **through** charities.* ■ (of a person) serve as a medium for (a spirit). ■ emulate or seem to be inspired by: *Meg Ryan plays Avery as if she's channeling Nicole Kidman.*
2 (usu. as adj. **channeled**) form channels or grooves in: *the lower jawbone is deeply channeled.*
– ORIGIN Middle English: from Old French *chanel*, from Latin *canalis* 'pipe, groove, channel,' from *canna* 'reed' (see CANE). Compare with CANAL.

> **WORD TRENDS** Mediums claim that they can **channel** the dead, allowing spirits to enter their bodies and communicate through them. This concept has been extended metaphorically to describe actors or musicians whose performances are strongly influenced by a predecessor, or just to comment on the style adopted by a noteworthy person. The path from the original psychic use can be clearly traced in some examples: *middle-aged white guys in acid-washed jeans think they can channel the ghost of Muddy Waters.* However, the sense is now commonly expressed without any reference to spirits or ghosts, with the object not necessarily being dead: *Griffiths, as Morris's wife, seems to be channeling the mid-'80s Debra Winger.* The word can suggest a level of falseness or artifice in stealing someone else's ideas or image, and is often applied to politicians: *the presidential hopeful channeled his old idol, John F. Kennedy.*

chan·nel cat (also **channel catfish**) ▶ **n.** a common North American freshwater catfish that has a pale blue to olive back with dark spots. ● *Ictalurus punctatus*, family Ictaluridae.

chan·nel-hop ▶ **v.** [no obj.] informal **1** another term for CHANNEL-SURF.
2 travel across the English Channel and back frequently or for only a brief trip.
– DERIVATIVES **chan·nel-hop·per n.**

Chan·nel Is·lands 1 a group of islands in the English Channel off the northwestern coast of France, a British Crown colony; pop. 200,000 (est. 2007). The largest are Jersey, Guernsey, and Alderney.
2 another name for the SANTA BARBARA ISLANDS in California.

chan·nel·ize /'CHanlˌīz/ ▶ **v.** [with obj.] another term for CHANNEL (verb).

chan·nel-surf ▶ **v.** informal change frequently from one television channel to another, using a remote control device.
– DERIVATIVES **chan·nel-surf·er n.**, **chan·nel-surf·ing n.**

Chan·nel Tun·nel a railroad tunnel under the English Channel that extends for 31 miles (49 km) and links England and France. The tunnel (popularly called the Chunnel) opened in 1994 after eight years of construction to link Holywell, near Folkestone, England, and Sangatte, near Calais, France.

chan·son /SHäN'sôn/ ▶ **n.** a French song.
– ORIGIN French, from Latin *cantio(n-)* 'singing,' from *canere* 'sing.'

chan·son de geste /SHäN'sôn də 'ZHest/ ▶ **n.** (pl. **chansons de geste** /SHäN'sôN(z)/) a medieval historical romance in French verse, typically one connected with Charlemagne.
– ORIGIN mid 19th cent.: French, literally 'song of heroic deeds,' from *chanson* 'song' (see CHANSON) and *geste* from Latin *gesta* 'actions, exploits.'

chant /CHant/ ▶ **n. 1** a repeated rhythmic phrase, typically one shouted or sung in unison by a crowd. ■ a monotonous or repetitive song, typically an incantation or part of a ritual.
2 Music a short musical passage in two or more phrases used for singing unmetrical words; a psalm or canticle sung to such music. ■ the style of music consisting of such passages: *Gregorian chant.*
▶ **v.** [with obj.] say or shout repeatedly in a singsong tone: *protesters were chanting slogans* | [with direct speech] *the crowd chanted, "No violence!"* ■ sing or intone (a psalm, canticle, or sacred text).
– ORIGIN late Middle English (in the sense 'sing'): from Old French *chanter* 'sing,' from Latin *cantare*, frequentative of *canere* 'sing.'

chant·er /'CHantər/ ▶ **n. 1** a person who chants something.
2 Music the pipe of a bagpipe with finger holes, on which the melody is played.
– ORIGIN late Middle English: from Old French *chanteor*, from Latin *cantator*, from *cantare* (see CHANT).

chan·te·relle /ˌSHantə'rel, ˌSHän-/ ▶ **n.** an edible woodland mushroom with a yellow funnel-shaped cap and a faint smell of apricots, found in both Eurasia and North America. ● *Cantharellus cibarius*, family Cantharellaceae, class Basidiomycetes.
– ORIGIN late 18th cent.: from French, from modern Latin *cantharellus*, diminutive of *cantharus*, from Greek *kantharos*, denoting a kind of drinking container.

chan·teuse /ˌSHän'tŏŏz, -'tœz/ ▶ **n.** a female singer of popular songs, esp. in a nightclub.
– ORIGIN French, from *chanter* 'sing.'

chant·ey /'SHantē/ (also **chanty**, **shanty**, or **sea chantey**) ▶ **n.** a song with alternating solo and chorus, of a kind originally sung by sailors while performing physical labor together.
– ORIGIN mid 19th. cent.: probably from French *chantez!* 'sing!,' imperative plural of *chanter*.

chan·ti·cleer /'CHantəˌkli(ə)r, 'SHant-/ ▶ **n.** literary a name given to a rooster, esp. in fairy tales.
– ORIGIN Middle English: from Old French *Chantecler*, the name of the cock in the fable *Reynard the Fox*, from *chanter* 'sing, crow' (see CHANT) + *cler* 'clear.'

Chan·til·ly lace /SHan'tilē/ ▶ **n.** a delicate kind of bobbin lace.
– ORIGIN mid 19th cent.: named after *Chantilly*, a town near Paris.

chant·ing gos·hawk ▶ **n.** a long-legged African hawk with pale gray upper parts, throat, and breast, noted for its prolonged musical fluting call delivered from a treetop perch. ● Genus *Melierax*, family Accipitridae: three species.

chan·try /'CHantrē/ ▶ **n.** (pl. **chantries**) an endowment for a priest or priests to celebrate masses for the founder's soul. ■ a chapel, altar, or other part of a church endowed for such a purpose.
– ORIGIN late Middle English: from Old French *chanterie*, from *chanter* 'to sing.'

chant·y ▶ **n.** (pl. **chanties**) variant spelling of CHANTEY.

Cha·nu·kah ▶ **n.** variant spelling of HANUKKAH.

Cha·nute /SHə'nōōt/, Octave (1832–1910), US aviation pioneer; born in France. From 1898, he produced a number of gliders, including a biplane that made over 700 flights. He assisted the Wright brothers in making the world's first controlled powered flight.

Chao Phra·ya /CHou 'prīə/ a major waterway in central Thailand that is formed by the junction of the Ping and Nan rivers.

cha·os /'kā,äs/ ▶ **n.** complete disorder and confusion: *snow caused chaos in the region.* ■ Physics behavior so unpredictable as to appear random, owing to great sensitivity to small changes in conditions. ■ the formless matter supposed to have existed before the creation of the universe. ■ (**Chaos**) Greek Mythology the first created being, from which came the primeval deities Gaia, Tartarus, Erebus, and Nyx.
– ORIGIN late 15th cent. (denoting a gaping void or chasm, later formless primordial matter): via French and Latin from Greek *khaos* 'vast chasm, void.'

cha·os the·o·ry ▶ **n.** the branch of mathematics that deals with complex systems whose behavior is highly sensitive to slight changes in conditions, so that small alterations can give rise to strikingly great consequences.

cha·ot·ic /kā'ätik/ ▶ **adj.** in a state of complete confusion and disorder: *a chaotic jumble of spools, tapes, and books.* ■ Physics of or relating to systems that exhibit chaos.
– DERIVATIVES **cha·ot·i·cal·ly** /-ik(ə)lē/ **adv.**
– ORIGIN early 18th cent.: from **CHAOS**, on the pattern of words such as *hypnotic*.

cha·ot·ic at·trac·tor ▶ **n.** Mathematics another term for **STRANGE ATTRACTOR**.

chap[1] /CHap/ ▶ **v.** (**chaps, chapping, chapped**) [no obj.] (of the skin) become cracked, rough, or sore, typically through exposure to cold weather. ■ [with obj.] (usu. as adj. **chapped**) (of the wind or cold) cause (skin) to crack in this way: *chapped lips.*
▶ **n.** a cracked or sore patch on the skin.
– ORIGIN late Middle English: of unknown origin.

chap[2] ▶ **n.** informal, chiefly Brit. a man or a boy. ■ dated a friendly form of address between men and boys: *best of luck, old chap.*
– ORIGIN late 16th cent. (denoting a buyer or customer): abbreviation of **CHAPMAN**. The current sense dates from the early 18th cent.

chap[3] ▶ **n.** (usu. **chaps**) the lower jaw or half of the cheek, esp. that of a pig used as food.
– ORIGIN mid 16th cent.: of unknown origin. Compare with **CHOPS**.

chap. ▶ **abbr.** chapter.

cha·pa·ra·jos /,SHapə'rā-ōs, -'räəs/ (also **chaparejos**) ▶ **plural n.** full form of **CHAPS**.
– ORIGIN mid 19th cent.: from Mexican Spanish *chaparreras*, from *chaparra* (with reference to protection from thorny vegetation: see **CHAPARRAL**); probably influenced by Spanish *aparejo* 'equipment.'

chap·ar·ral /,SHapə'ral/ ▶ **n.** vegetation consisting chiefly of tangled shrubs and thorny bushes.
– ORIGIN mid 19th cent.: from Spanish, from *chaparra* 'dwarf evergreen oak.'

cha·pa·ti /CHə'pätē/ (also **chapatti**) ▶ **n.** (pl. **chapatis**) (in Indian cooking) a thin pancake of unleavened whole-grain bread cooked on a griddle.
– ORIGIN from Hindi *capātī*, from *capānā* 'flatten, roll out.'

chap·book /'CHap,bo͝ok/ ▶ **n.** historical a small pamphlet containing tales, ballads, or tracts, sold by peddlers. ■ a small paperback booklet, typically containing poems or fiction.
– ORIGIN early 19th cent.: from **CHAPMAN** + **BOOK**.

chape /CHāp/ ▶ **n.** 1 historical the metal point of a scabbard.
2 the metal pin of a buckle.
– ORIGIN Middle English (in the general sense 'plate of metal overlaying or trimming something'): from Old French, literally 'cape, hood,' from late Latin *cappa* 'cap.'

cha·peau /SHa'pō/ ▶ **n.** (pl. **chapeaux** /-'pō(z)/) a hat or cap.
– ORIGIN late 15th cent.: from French, from Latin *cappellum*, diminutive of *cappa* 'cap.'

chap·el /'CHapəl/ ▶ **n.** 1 a small building for Christian worship, typically one attached to an institution or private house: *a service in the chapel | attendance at chapel was compulsory.* ■ a part of a large church or cathedral with its own altar and dedication. ■ a room or building in which funeral services are held. ■ Brit. a place of worship for certain Protestant denominations.
2 Brit. Printing the members or branch of a labor union at a particular place of work.
– ORIGIN Middle English: from Old French *chapele*, from medieval Latin *cappella*, diminutive of *cappa* 'cap or cape' (the first chapel being a sanctuary in which St. Martin's cloak was preserved).

Chap·el Hill a town in north central North Carolina, home to the University of North Carolina as well as many research facilities; pop. 52,542 (est. 2008).

chap·el of ease ▶ **n.** a chapel situated for the convenience of parishioners living a long distance from the parish church.

chap·er·one /'SHapə,rōn/ (also **chaperon**) ▶ **n.** a person who accompanies and looks after another person or group of people. ■ dated an older woman responsible for the decorous behavior of a young unmarried girl at social occasions.
▶ **v.** [with obj.] accompany and look after or supervise.
– DERIVATIVES **chap·er·on·age** /-,rōnij, ,SHapə'rōnij/ **n.**
– ORIGIN late Middle English (denoting a hood or cap, regarded as giving protection): from French, feminine of *chaperon* 'hood,' diminutive of *chape* (see **CHAPE**). The current sense dates from the early 18th cent.

chap·er·o·nin /,SHapə'rōnin/ ▶ **n.** Biochemistry a protein that aids the assembly and folding of other protein molecules in living cells.
– ORIGIN late 20th cent.: from **CHAPERONE** + **-IN**[1].

chap·fall·en /'CHap,fôlən/ (also **chopfallen** /'CHäp-/) ▶ **adj.** archaic with one's lower jaw hanging due to extreme exhaustion or dejection.
– ORIGIN late 16th cent.: from **CHAP**[3].

chap·lain /'CHaplən/ ▶ **n.** a member of the clergy attached to a private chapel, institution, ship, branch of the armed forces, etc.
– DERIVATIVES **chap·lain·cy** /'CHaplənsē/ **n.**
– ORIGIN Middle English: from Old French *chapelain*, from medieval Latin *cappellanus*, originally denoting a custodian of the cloak of St. Martin, from *cappella*, originally 'little cloak' (see **CHAPEL**).

chap·let /'CHaplət/ ▶ **n.** 1 a garland or wreath for a person's head.
2 a string of 55 beads (one third of the rosary number) for counting prayers, or as a necklace.
3 a metal support for the core of a hollow casting mold.
– DERIVATIVES **chap·let·ed** **adj.**
– ORIGIN late Middle English: from Old French *chapelet*, diminutive of *chapel* 'hat,' based on late Latin *cappa* 'cap.'

Chap·lin /'CHaplən/, Charlie (1889–1977), English movie actor and director; full name *Sir Charles Spencer Chaplin*. He directed and starred in many short silent comedies, mostly playing a bowler-hatted tramp, a character that was his trademark for more than 25 years. Notable movies: *The Kid* (1921) and *The Gold Rush* (1925).

Charlie Chaplin

chap·man /'CHapmən/ ▶ **n.** (pl. **chapmen**) archaic a peddler.
– ORIGIN Old English *cēapman*, from *cēap* 'bargaining, trade' (see **CHEAP**) + **MAN**.

Chap·pa·quid·dick Is·land /,CHapə'kwidik/ a small island in southern Massachusetts, just off the southeastern coast of Martha's Vineyard, the scene of a car accident in 1969 that involved Senator Edward Kennedy in which his assistant **Mary Jo Kopechne** drowned.

chap·pie /'CHapē/ ▶ **n.** (pl. **chappies**) Brit. informal another term for **CHAP**[2].

chaps /CHaps, SHaps/ ▶ **plural n.** leather pants without a seat, worn by a cowboy over ordinary pants to protect the legs.
– ORIGIN mid 19th cent.: short for **CHAPARAJOS**.

chaps

Chap Stick ▶ **n.** trademark a small stick of a cosmetic substance used to prevent chapping of the lips.

chap·tal·i·za·tion /,SHaptələ'zāSHən/ ▶ **n.** (in winemaking) the correction or improvement of must by the addition of calcium carbonate to neutralize acid, or of sugar to increase alcoholic strength.
– DERIVATIVES **chap·tal·ize** /'SHaptə,līz/ **v.**
– ORIGIN late 19th cent.: from the name of Jean A. *Chaptal* (1756–1832), the French chemist who invented the process, + *-ization* (see **-IZE**).

chap·ter /'CHaptər/ ▶ **n.** 1 a main division of a book, typically with a number or title.
2 a local branch of a society: *the local chapter of the American Cancer Society.*
3 the governing body of a religious community, esp. a cathedral or a knightly order.
4 a period of time or an episode in a person's life, a nation's history, etc.: *a tragic chapter in European history.* ■ a series or sequence: *the latest episode in a chapter of problems.*
– PHRASES **chapter and verse** an exact reference or authority: *she can give chapter and verse on current legislation.*
– ORIGIN Middle English: from Old French *chapitre*, from Latin *capitulum*, diminutive of *caput* 'head.'

Chap·ter 7 ▶ **n.** protection from creditors granted to individuals or companies who legally file for bankruptcy, providing for liquidation of certain assets to pay debts.
– ORIGIN with allusion to Chapter 7 of the US bankruptcy code.

Chap·ter 11 ▶ **n.** protection from creditors given to a company in financial difficulties for a limited period to allow it to reorganize.
– ORIGIN with allusion to Chapter 11 of the US bankruptcy code.

Chap·ter 13 ▶ **n.** protection from creditors granted to individuals who legally file for bankruptcy, providing for repayment of debts by a court-approved plan.
– ORIGIN with allusion to Chapter 13 of the US bankruptcy code.

chap·ter house ▶ **n.** a building used for the meetings of the canons of a cathedral or other religious community. ■ a place where a college fraternity or sorority meets.

Cha·pul·te·pec /CHə'po͞oltə,pek/ a hill ("Grasshopper Hill") in the major park of Mexico City in Mexico. It is the ancient seat of Aztec emperors and is surmounted by a castle that was captured by US forces in September 1847.

char[1] /CHär/ ▶ **v.** (**chars, charring, charred**) [with obj.] partially burn (an object) so as to blacken its surface: *their bodies were badly charred in the fire* | (as adj. **charred**) *charred remains.* ■ [no obj.] (of an object) become burned and discolored in such a way.
▶ **n.** material that has been charred.
– ORIGIN late 17th cent.: apparently a back-formation from **CHARCOAL**.

char[2] Brit. informal ▶ **n.** a charwoman.
▶ **v.** (**chars, charring, charred**) [no obj.] work as a charwoman.

char[3] (also **cha** /CHä/ or **chai** /CHī/) ▶ **n.** Brit. informal tea.
– ORIGIN late 16th cent. (as *cha*; rare before the early 20th cent.): from Chinese (Mandarin dialect) *chá*.

char[4] (also **charr**) ▶ **n.** (pl. **same**) a troutlike freshwater or marine fish of northern countries, widely valued as a food and game fish. ● Genus *Salvelinus*, family Salmonidae: several species, in particular the North American **brook trout** (*S. fontinalis*), which has been introduced widely elsewhere, and the red-bellied **Arctic char** (*S. alpinus*), which occurs in Arctic waters as well as landlocked lakes.

char·a·banc /'SHarə,baNG, -,baNGk/ ▶ **n.** Brit. an early form of bus, used typically for pleasure trips.
– ORIGIN early 19th cent.: from French *char-à-bancs* 'carriage with benches' (the original horse-drawn charabancs having rows of bench seats).

char·a·cin /'karəsən/ ▶ **n.** a small and brightly colored freshwater fish native to Africa and tropical America. ● Family Characidae: numerous species, including the piranhas and popular aquarium fishes such as the tetras.
– ORIGIN late 19th cent.: from modern Latin *Characinus* (genus name), from Greek *kharax*, literally 'pointed stake,' denoting a kind of fish.

char·ac·ter /'kariktər/ ▶ **n.** 1 the mental and moral qualities distinctive to an individual: *running away was not in keeping with her character.* ■ the distinctive nature of something: *gas lamps give the area its character.* ■ the quality of being individual, typically in an interesting or unusual way: *the island is full of character.* ■ strength and originality in a person's nature: *she had character as well as beauty.* ■ a person's good reputation: *to what do I owe this attack on my character?* ■ dated a written statement of someone's good qualities; a recommendation.
2 a person in a novel, play, or movie. ■ a part played by an actor. ■ [with adj.] a person seen in terms of a particular aspect of character: *he was a larger-*

than-life character | shady characters. ■ informal an interesting or amusing individual: *he's a real character.*
3 a printed or written letter or symbol. ■ Computing a symbol representing a letter or number.
4 chiefly Biology a characteristic, esp. one that assists in the identification of a species.
▶ **v.** [with obj.] archaic inscribe; engrave. ■ describe; characterize: *you have well charactered him.*
– PHRASES **in** (or **out of**) **character** in keeping (or not in keeping) with someone's usual pattern of behavior.
– DERIVATIVES **char·ac·ter·ful** /-fəl/ **adj.**, **char·ac·ter·ful·ly adv.**, **char·ac·ter·less adj.**
– ORIGIN Middle English: from Old French *caractere*, via Latin from Greek *kharaktēr* 'a stamping tool.' From the early sense 'distinctive mark' arose 'token, feature, or trait' (early 16th cent.), and from this 'a description, esp. of a person's qualities,' giving rise to 'distinguishing qualities.'

char·ac·ter ac·tor ▶ **n.** an actor who specializes in playing eccentric or unusual people rather than leading roles.

char·ac·ter as·sas·si·na·tion ▶ **n.** the malicious and unjustified harming of a person's good reputation.

char·ac·ter code ▶ **n.** Computing the binary code used to represent a letter or number.

char·ac·ter dance ▶ **n.** a style of ballet deriving inspiration from national or folk dances, or interpreting and representing a particular profession, mode of living, or personality. The movements used tend to be less stylized than in classical ballet, allowing greater individual expression and diversity.
– DERIVATIVES **char·ac·ter danc·er n.**

char·ac·ter·is·tic /ˌkariktəˈristik/ ▶ **adj.** typical of a particular person, place, or thing: *large farms are characteristic of this area.*
▶ **n. 1** a feature or quality belonging typically to a person, place, or thing and serving to identify it: *inherited characteristics such as blood groups.*
2 Mathematics the whole number or integral part of a logarithm, which gives the order of magnitude of the original number.
– DERIVATIVES **char·ac·ter·is·ti·cal·ly adv.**
– ORIGIN mid 17th cent.: from French *caractéristique* or medieval Latin *characteristicus*, from Greek *kharaktēristikos*, from *kharaktēr* 'a stamping tool.'

char·ac·ter·is·tic curve ▶ **n.** a graph showing the relationship between two variable but interdependent quantities.

char·ac·ter·is·tic func·tion ▶ **n.** Mathematics a function whose result is one for the members of a given set and zero for all nonmembers.

char·ac·ter·ize /ˈkariktəˌrīz/ ▶ **v.** [with obj.] **1** describe the distinctive nature or features of: *the historian characterized the period as the decade of revolution.*
2 (of a feature or quality) be typical or characteristic of: *the disease is **characterized by** weakening of the immune system.*
– DERIVATIVES **char·ac·ter·i·za·tion** /ˌkariktərəˈzāsHən/ **n.**
– ORIGIN late 16th cent. (in the sense 'engrave, inscribe'): from French *caractériser* or medieval Latin *characterizare*, from Greek *kharaktērizein*, from *kharaktēr* 'a stamping tool.'

char·ac·ter part ▶ **n.** a part played by a character actor.

char·ac·ter rec·og·ni·tion ▶ **n.** the identification by electronic means of printed or written characters.

char·ac·ter string ▶ **n.** a linear sequence of characters, typically one stored in or processed by a computer.

char·ac·ter wit·ness ▶ **n.** a person who attests to another's moral conduct and good reputation in a court of law.

cha·rade /sHəˈrād/ ▶ **n.** an absurd pretense intended to create a pleasant or respectable appearance: *talk of unity was nothing more than a charade.* ■ (**charades**) a game in which players guess a word or phrase from pantomimed clues.
– ORIGIN late 18th cent.: from French, from modern Provençal *charrado* 'conversation,' from *charra* 'chatter,' perhaps of imitative origin.

cha·ran·go /cHəˈraNGgō/ ▶ **n.** (pl. **charangos**) a small Andean guitar, traditionally made from an armadillo shell.
– ORIGIN 1920s: from South American Spanish.

cha·ras /ˈcHärəs/ ▶ **n.** a psychoactive resin from the flower heads of hemp; cannabis resin.
– ORIGIN from Hindi *caras.*

char·broil /ˈcHärˌbroil/ ▶ **v.** [with obj.] (usu. as adj. **charbroiled**) grill (food, esp. meat) on a rack over charcoal: *charbroiled steak.*
– ORIGIN 1950s: blend of CHARCOAL and BROIL[1].

char·coal /ˈcHärˌkōl/ ▶ **n.** a porous black solid, consisting of an amorphous form of carbon, obtained as a residue when wood, bone, or other organic matter is heated in the absence of air. ■ briquettes of charcoal used for barbecuing: *lamb grilled on charcoal.* ■ a drawing made using charcoal. ■ a dark gray color: *his charcoal sweater* | [as modifier] *charcoal gray.*
▶ **v.** (usu. as adj. **charcoaled**) cook over charcoal: *charcoaled lobster.*
– ORIGIN late Middle English: probably related to COAL in the early sense 'charcoal.'

char·coal burn·er ▶ **n. 1** a small stove using charcoal as fuel.
2 a person who makes charcoal.

char·coal fil·ter ▶ **n.** a filter containing charcoal to absorb impurities.

Char·cot /sHärˈkō/, Jean-Martin (1825–93), French neurologist; regarded as one of the founders of modern neurology. His work on hysteria was adopted by his student Sigmund Freud.

char·cu·te·rie /ˌsHärˈko͞otərē/ ▶ **n.** (pl. **charcuteries**) cold cooked meats collectively. ■ a store selling such meats.
– ORIGIN French, from obsolete *char* (earlier form of *chair*) 'flesh' + *cuite* 'cooked.'

chard /cHärd/ ▶ **n.** (also **Swiss chard**) a beet of a variety with broad white leaf stalks that may be prepared and eaten separately from the green parts of the leaf. ■ the blanched shoots of other plants, eaten as a vegetable, e.g., globe artichoke.
– ORIGIN mid 17th cent.: from French *carde*, perhaps influenced by *chardon* 'thistle.'

Char·don·nay /ˌsHärdnˈā/ ▶ **n.** a variety of white wine grape used for making champagne and other wines. ■ a wine made from this grape.
– ORIGIN French.

Char·en·tais /ˌsHärənˈtā/ (also **Charentais melon**) ▶ **n.** a small melon with a pale green rind and orange flesh.
– ORIGIN French, literally 'from the Charentes region.'

Cha·rente /sHäˈränt/ a river in western France that rises in the Massif Central and flows west for 225 miles (360 km) to the Bay of Biscay at Rochefort.

charge /cHärj/ ▶ **v.** [with obj.] **1** demand (an amount) as a price from someone for a service rendered or for goods supplied: *the restaurant charged $15 for dinner* | [with two objs.] *he charged me 2 euros for the postcard* | [no obj.] *museums should **charge for** admission.* ■ (**charge something to**) record the cost of something as an amount payable by (someone) or on (an account): *they charge the calls to their credit-card accounts.*
2 accuse (someone) of something, esp. an offense under law: *they were **charged with** assault.* ■ [with clause] make an accusation or assertion that: *opponents **charged that** below-cost pricing would reduce safety.* ■ Law accuse someone of (an offense).
3 entrust (someone) with a task as a duty or responsibility: *the committee was **charged with** reshaping the educational system.*
4 store electrical energy in (a battery or battery-operated device): *the shaver can be **charged up** and used while traveling.* ■ [no obj.] (of a battery or battery-operated device) receive and store electrical energy. ■ load or fill (a container, gun, etc.) to the full or proper extent: *will you see to it that your glasses are charged?* ■ fill or pervade (something) with a quality or emotion: *the air was **charged with** menace.*
5 [no obj.] rush forward in attack: *the plan is to charge headlong at the enemy.* ■ rush aggressively toward (someone or something) in attack. ■ [with adverbial of direction] move quickly and with impetus: *Henry charged up the staircase.*
6 Heraldry place a heraldic bearing on: *a pennant argent, charged with a cross gules.*
▶ **n. 1** a price asked for goods or services: *an admission charge.* ■ a financial liability or commitment: *an asset of $550,000 should have been taken **as a charge on** earnings.*
2 an accusation, typically one formally made against a prisoner brought to trial: *he appeared in court **on a charge of** attempted murder* | *three people were arrested but released **without charge.***
3 the responsibility of taking care or control of someone or something: *the people **in her charge** are pupils and not experimental subjects.* ■ a person or thing entrusted to the care of someone: *the babysitter watched over her charges.* ■ dated a responsibility or onerous duty assigned to someone. ■ an official instruction, esp. one given by a judge to a jury regarding points of law.
4 the property of matter that is responsible for electrical phenomena, existing in a positive or negative form. ■ the quantity of this carried by a body. ■ energy stored chemically for conversion into electricity. ■ an act or process of storing electrical energy in a battery. ■ [in sing.] informal a thrill: *I get a real **charge out of** working hard.*
5 a quantity of explosive to be detonated, typically in order to fire a gun or similar weapon.
6 a headlong rush forward, typically one made by attacking soldiers in battle: *a cavalry charge.*
7 Heraldry a device or bearing placed on a shield or crest.
– PHRASES **free of charge** without any payment due. **in charge** in control or with overall responsibility: *he was **in charge of** civil aviation matters.* **press** (or **prefer**) **charges** accuse someone formally of a crime so that they can be brought to trial. **take charge** assume control or responsibility: *the candidate must **take charge of** an actual flight.*
– DERIVATIVES **charge·a·ble adj.**, **charg·ee n.**
– ORIGIN Middle English (in the general senses 'to load' and 'a load'): from Old French *charger* (verb), *charge* (noun), from late Latin *carricare*, *carcare* 'to load,' from Latin *carrus* 'wheeled vehicle.'

C

charge ac·count ▶ **n.** an account to which goods and services may be charged on credit.

charge·back /ˈcHärjˌbak/ ▶ **n.** a demand by a credit-card provider for a retailer to make good the loss on a fraudulent or disputed transaction. ■ (in business use) an act or policy of allocating the cost of an organization's centrally located resources to the individuals or departments that use them.

charge card ▶ **n.** a credit card for use with an account that must be paid when a statement is issued.

charge car·ri·er ▶ **n.** Physics a particle that carries an electric charge. ■ a mobile electron or hole by which an electric charge passes through a semiconductor.

charge con·ju·ga·tion ▶ **n.** Physics the operation of changing every particle into its antiparticle.

charge-cou·pled de·vice ▶ **n.** see **CCD**.

charged /cHärjd/ ▶ **adj.** having an electric charge. ■ filled with excitement, tension, or emotion: *the highly charged atmosphere created by the boycott.*

char·gé d'af·faires /sHärˌZHā däˈfer/ (also **chargé**) ▶ **n.** (pl. **chargés d'affaires** /sHärˈzā(z)/) a diplomatic official who temporarily takes the place of an ambassador. ■ a state's diplomatic representative in a minor country.
– ORIGIN mid 18th cent.: French, '(a person) in charge of affairs.'

charge den·si·ty ▶ **n.** Physics the electric charge per unit area of a surface, or per unit volume of a field or body.

charge nurse ▶ **n.** Brit. a nurse in charge of a ward in a hospital.

Charge of the Light Bri·gade a British cavalry charge in 1854 during the Battle of Balaclava in the Crimean War. A misunderstanding between the commander of the Light Brigade and his superiors led to the British cavalry being destroyed. The charge was immortalized in verse by Tennyson.

charg·er[1] /ˈcHärjər/ ▶ **n. 1** a horse trained for battle; a cavalry horse.
2 a device for charging a battery or battery-powered equipment.
3 a person who charges forward.

charg·er[2] (also **charger plate**) ▶ **n.** a large, flat dish; a platter.
– ORIGIN Middle English: from Anglo-Norman French *chargeour*, from *chargier* 'to load,' from late Latin *carricare*, *carcare* 'to load' (see CHARGE).

charge sheet ▶ **n.** Brit. a record made in a police station of the charges against a person.

char·grill /ˈcHärˌgril/ ▶ **v.** (usu. as adj. **chargrilled**) grill (food, typically meat or fish) quickly at a high heat.
– ORIGIN late 20th cent.: on the pattern of *charbroil.*

char·i·ot /ˈcHarēət/ ▶ **n.** historical a two-wheeled horse-drawn vehicle used in ancient warfare and racing. ■ historical a four-wheeled carriage with back seats and a coachman's seat. ■ literary a stately or triumphal carriage.
▶ **v.** [with obj.] literary convey in or as in a chariot.
– ORIGIN late Middle English: from Old French, augmentative of *char* 'cart,' based on Latin *carrus* 'wheeled vehicle.'

two-wheeled chariot

char·i·ot·eer /ˌCHarēəˈti(ə)r/ ▶ **n.** a chariot driver. ■ (**the Charioteer**) the constellation Auriga.
– ORIGIN Middle English: from Old French *charieter*, from *chariot* 'large cart' (see CHARIOT). The sense in astronomy dates from the early 20th cent.

Cha·ri Riv·er /ˈSHärē/ (also **Shari**) a river that flows for 660 miles (1,060 km) through the Central African Republic, Chad, and Cameroon. Emptying into Lake Chad, it is the longest river in the African continent that drains internally.

C

char·ism /ˈkarˌizəm/ ▶ **n.** Theology another term for CHARISMA (sense 2).

cha·ris·ma /kəˈrizmə/ ▶ **n. 1** compelling attractiveness or charm that can inspire devotion in others: *she enchanted guests with her charisma.*
2 (pl. **charismata** /-ˌmətə/) (also **charism** /ˈkarˌizəm/) a divinely conferred power or talent.
– ORIGIN mid 17th cent. (sense 2): via ecclesiastical Latin from Greek *kharisma*, from *kharis* 'favor, grace.'

char·is·mat·ic /ˌkarizˈmatik/ ▶ **adj. 1** exercising a compelling charm that inspires devotion in others: *a charismatic leader.*
2 of or relating to the charismatic movement in the Christian Church. ■ (of a power or talent) divinely conferred: *charismatic prophecy.*
▶ **n.** an adherent of the charismatic movement. ■ a person who claims divine inspiration.
– DERIVATIVES **char·is·mat·i·cal·ly adv.**
– ORIGIN late 19th cent.: from Greek *kharisma, kharismat-* 'charisma' + -IC.

char·is·mat·ic move·ment ▶ **n.** a movement within some Christian churches that emphasizes gifts believed to be conferred by the Holy Spirit, such as speaking in tongues and healing of the sick.

char·i·ta·ble /ˈCHaritəbəl/ ▶ **adj. 1** of or relating to the assistance of those in need: *charitable works such as care of the sick.* ■ (of an organization or activity) officially recognized as devoted to the assistance of those in need. ■ generous in giving to those in need.
2 apt to judge others leniently or favorably: *those who were less charitable called for his resignation.*
– DERIVATIVES **char·i·ta·ble·ness n., char·i·ta·bly adv.**
– ORIGIN Middle English (in the sense 'showing Christian love to God and man'): from Old French, from *charite* (see CHARITY).

char·i·ty /ˈCHaritē/ ▶ **n.** (pl. **charities**) **1** the voluntary giving of help, typically in the form of money, to those in need. ■ help or money given in this way: *an unemployed teacher living on charity.*
2 an organization set up to provide help and raise money for those in need. ■ such organizations viewed collectively as the object of fundraising or donations: *the proceeds of the sale will go to charity.*
3 kindness and tolerance in judging others: *she found it hard to look on her mother with much charity.* ■ archaic love of humankind, typically in a Christian context: *faith, hope, and charity.*
– PHRASES **charity begins at home** proverb one's first responsibility is for the needs of one's own family and friends.
– ORIGIN late Old English (in the sense 'Christian love of one's fellows'): from Old French *charite*, from Latin *caritas*, from *carus* 'dear.'

char·i·ty school ▶ **n.** historical a school supported by charitable contributions.

chari·va·ri /ˌSHivəˈrē, ˈSHivəˌrē/ (also **shivaree**) ▶ **n.** (pl. **charivaris**) chiefly historical a cacophonous mock serenade, typically performed by a group of people in derision of an unpopular person or in celebration of a marriage. ■ a series of discordant noises.
– ORIGIN mid 17th cent.: from French, of unknown origin.

char·kha /ˈCHərkə, ˈCHär-/ (also **charka**) ▶ **n.** (in South Asia) a domestic spinning wheel used chiefly for cotton.
– ORIGIN from Urdu *charka* 'spinning wheel,' from Persian; related to Sanskrit *cakra* 'wheel.'

char·la·dy /ˈCHärˌlādē/ ▶ **n.** (pl. **charladies**) Brit. a charwoman.

char·la·tan /ˈSHärlətən, ˈSHärlətn/ ▶ **n.** a person falsely claiming to have a special knowledge or skill; a fraud.
– DERIVATIVES **char·la·tan·ism** /-ləṭəˌnizəm, -lətnˌizəm/ **n., char·la·tan·ry** /ˈSHärlətənrē, -lətnrē/ **n.**
– ORIGIN early 17th cent. (denoting an itinerant seller of supposed remedies): from French, from Italian *ciarlatano*, from *ciarlare* 'to babble.'

Char·le·magne /ˈSHärləˌmān/ (742–814), king of the Franks 768–814 and Holy Roman Emperor (as Charles I) 800–814; Latin name *Carolus Magnus*; known as **Charles the Great**. As the first Holy Roman emperor, Charlemagne promoted the arts and education, and his court became the cultural center of the Carolingian Renaissance.

Char·le·roi /ˌSHärləˈrwä, -ˈroi/ an industrial city in southwestern Belgium; pop. 201,593 (2008).

Charles[1] /CHärlz/ the name of two kings of England, Scotland, and Ireland. ■ **Charles I** (1600–49), son of James I; reigned 1625–49. His reign was dominated by the deepening religious and constitutional crisis that resulted in the English Civil War 1642–49. After the battle of Naseby, Charles tried to regain power in alliance with the Scots, but his forces were defeated in 1648; he was tried by a special Parliamentary court and beheaded. ■ **Charles II** (1630–85), son of Charles I; reigned 1660–85. Charles was restored to the throne after the collapse of Oliver Cromwell's regime. Although he displayed considerable adroitness in handling the difficult constitutional situation, religious and political strife continued during his reign.

Charles[2] the name of four kings of Spain. ■ **Charles I** (1500–58), son of Philip I; reigned 1516–56; Holy Roman Emperor (as Charles V) 1519–56. His reign was characterized by the struggle against Protestantism in Germany, rebellion in Castile, and war with France 1521–44. Exhausted by these struggles, Charles handed Naples, the Netherlands, and Spain over to his son Philip II and the imperial Crown to his brother Ferdinand before retiring to a monastery. ■ **Charles II** (1661–1700), reigned 1665–1700. He inherited a kingdom already in a decline that he was unable to halt. His choice of Philip of Anjou, grandson of Louis XIV of France, as his successor gave rise to the War of the Spanish Succession. ■ **Charles III** (1716–88), reigned 1759–88. He improved Spain's position as an international power by increasing foreign trade, and he brought a brief cultural and economic revival to Spain. ■ **Charles IV** (1748–1819), reigned 1788–1808. During the Napoleonic Wars he suffered the loss of the Spanish fleet, destroyed along with that of France at Trafalgar in 1805. Following the French invasion of Spain in 1807, he was forced to abdicate.

Charles[3] the name of two European kings. ■ **Charles VII** (1403–61), king of France 1422–61. At the time of his accession, much of northern France was under English occupation. After the intervention of Joan of Arc, however, the French experienced a dramatic military revival, and the defeat of the English ended the Hundred Years War. ■ **Charles XII** (also **Karl XII** /kärl/) (1682–1718), king of Sweden 1697–1718. In 1700, he initiated a war against Denmark, Poland-Saxony, and Russia. Initially successful, he embarked on an expedition into Russia in 1709 that ended in the destruction of his army and his internment.

Charles[4] the name of seven Holy Roman Emperors. ■ **Charles I** see CHARLEMAGNE. ■ **Charles II** (823–877), reigned 875–877. ■ **Charles III** (839–888), reigned 881–887. ■ **Charles IV** (1316–78), reigned 1355–78. ■ **Charles V** Charles I of Spain (see CHARLES[2]). ■ **Charles VI** (1685–1740), reigned 1711–40. His claim to the Spanish throne instigated the War of the Spanish Succession, but he was ultimately unsuccessful. He drafted the Pragmatic Sanction in an attempt to ensure that his daughter Maria Theresa succeeded to the Habsburg dominions; this triggered the War of the Austrian Succession after his death. ■ **Charles VII** (1697–1745), reigned 1742–45.

Charles[5], Ray (1930–2004), US pianist and singer; born *Ray Charles Robinson*. Totally blind from the age of six, he drew on blues, jazz, and country music for songs such as "What'd I Say" (1959), "Georgia On My Mind" (1960), and "Busted" (1963).

Charles, Prince, (1948–), son of Elizabeth II; full name *Charles Philip Arthur George, Prince of Wales*; heir apparent to Elizabeth II. He married Lady Diana Spencer in 1981; the couple had two children, **Prince William Arthur Philip Louis** (1982–) and **Prince Henry Charles Albert David** (known as Prince Harry, 1984–), and were divorced in 1996.

Charles' law (also **Charles's law**) Chemistry a law stating that the volume of an ideal gas at constant pressure is directly proportional to the absolute temperature.
– ORIGIN late 19th cent.: named after Jacques A. C. *Charles* (1746–1823), the French physicist who first formulated it.

Charles Mar·tel /ˈCHärlz märˈtel/ (*c.*688–741), Frankish ruler of the eastern part of the Frankish kingdom from 715 and the whole kingdom from 719; grandfather of Charlemagne. His rule marked the beginning of Carolingian power.

Charles Riv·er /CHärlz/ a river that flows for 60 miles (100 km) through eastern Massachusetts, between Cambridge and Boston, to Boston Harbor.

Charles's Wain archaic, chiefly Brit. the Big Dipper.
– ORIGIN Old English *Carles wægn* 'the wain of Carl (Charlemagne),' perhaps because the star Arcturus was associated with King Arthur, with whom Charlemagne was connected in legend.

Charles·ton[1] /ˈCHärlstən/ **1** the capital of West Virginia, in the southwestern part of the state; pop. 50,302 (est. 2008).
2 a city and port in South Carolina; pop. 111,978 (est. 2008). The bombardment of Fort Sumter in 1861 by Confederate troops marked the beginning of the Civil War.

Charles·ton[2] (also **charleston**) ▶ **n.** a lively dance of the 1920s that involved turning the knees inward and kicking out the lower legs.
▶ **v.** [no obj.] dance the Charleston.
– ORIGIN 1920s: named after CHARLESTON[1] in South Carolina.

Charles·town /ˈCHärlzˌtoun/ a neighborhood in northern Boston in Massachusetts, north of the Charles River. Bunker Hill is here.

char·ley horse /ˈCHärlē/ ▶ **n.** [in sing.] informal a cramp or feeling of stiffness in an arm or leg.
– ORIGIN late 19th cent.: of unknown origin.

Char·lie /ˈCHärlē/ ▶ **n. 1** a code word representing the letter C, used in radio communication.
2 informal cocaine.
3 historical military slang a member of the Vietcong or the Vietcong collectively. [shortening of *Victor Charlie*, radio code for *VC*, representing *Vietcong*.]
– ORIGIN late 19th cent.: diminutive of the male given name *Charles*.

char·lock /ˈCHärˌläk, -lək/ ▶ **n.** a wild mustard with yellow flowers, commonly found as a weed in fields and along roadsides. ● *Brassica kaber* (or *Sinapis arvensis*), family Brassicaceae.
– ORIGIN Old English *cerlic, cyrlic*, of unknown origin.

Char·lotte /ˈSHärlət/ a commercial city and transportation center in southern North Carolina; pop. 687,456 (est. 2008).

char·lotte /ˈSHärlət/ ▶ **n.** a dessert made of stewed fruit or mousse with a casing or covering of bread, sponge cake, ladyfingers, or breadcrumbs.
– ORIGIN French, from the female given name *Charlotte*.

Char·lotte A·ma·li·e /əˈmälyə, ˈamələ/ the capital of the US Virgin Islands, a resort on the island of St. Thomas; pop. 10,100 (est. 2009).
– ORIGIN named after the wife of King Christian V of Denmark.

char·lotte russe /ˈro͞os/ ▶ **n.** a dessert consisting of custard enclosed in sponge cake or a casing of ladyfingers.
– ORIGIN mid 19th cent.: French, literally 'Russian charlotte.'

Char·lottes·ville /ˈSHärləts,vil/ a city in central Virginia, in the Blue Ridge Mountains, home to the University of Virginia; pop. 41,487 (est. 2008). Monticello, the home of Thomas Jefferson, is nearby.

Char·lotte·town /ˈSHärlətˌtoun/ the capital and chief port of Prince Edward Island, in eastern Canada; pop. 32,174 (2006).

charm /CHärm/ ▶ **n. 1** the power or quality of giving delight or arousing admiration: *he was captivated by her youthful charm.* ■ (usu. **charms**) an attractive or alluring characteristic: *the hidden charms of the city.*
2 a small ornament worn on a necklace or bracelet.
3 an object, act, or saying believed to have magic power: *the dreamcatcher is a charm used to prevent bad dreams.* ■ an object kept or worn to ward off evil and bring good luck: *a good luck charm.*
4 Physics one of six flavors of quark.
▶ **v.** [with obj.] **1** delight greatly: *the books have charmed children the world over.* ■ gain or influence by charm: *he charmed her into going out.*
2 control or achieve by or as if by magic: *pretending to charm a cobra* | [with adverbial] *she will charm your warts away.*
– PHRASES **turn on the charm** use one's ability to charm in order to influence someone. **work like a charm** be completely successful or effective.
– ORIGIN Middle English (in the senses 'incantation or magic spell' and 'to use spells'): from Old French *charme* (noun), *charmer* (verb), from Latin *carmen* 'song, verse, incantation.'

charm brace·let ▶ **n.** a bracelet hung with small trinkets or ornaments.

charmed /CHärmd/ ▶ **adj. 1** (of a person's life) unusually lucky or happy as though protected by magic: *I felt that I had a charmed life.*
2 Physics (of a particle) possessing the property charm: *a charmed quark.*
▶ **exclam.** dated expressing polite pleasure at an introduction: *charmed, I'm sure.*

charm·er /ˈCHärmər/ ▶ **n.** a person with an attractive and engaging personality, typically one who uses this to impress or manipulate others.

char·meuse /SHärˈm(y)o͞oz, -ˈm(y)o͞os/ ▶ **n.** a soft, silky dress fabric.
– ORIGIN early 20th cent.: from French, feminine of *charmeur* 'charmer,' from *charmer* 'to charm.'

charm·ing /ˈCHärmiNG/ ▶ **adj.** pleasant or attractive: *a charming country cottage.* ■ (of a person or

manner) polite, friendly, and likable: *he was a charming, affectionate colleague.*
– DERIVATIVES **charm·ing·ly** adv.

charm·less /ˈCHärmlis/ ▶ adj. unattractive or unpleasant.
– DERIVATIVES **charm·less·ly** adv., **charm·less·ness** n.

charm of·fen·sive ▶ n. a campaign of flattery and friendliness designed to achieve the support or agreement of others: *a charm offensive aimed at winning the confidence of Russia.*

char·mo·ni·um /CHärˈmōnēəm/ ▶ n. (pl. **charmonia** /-nēə/) Physics a combination of a charmed quark and an antiquark.
– ORIGIN 1970s: from CHARM (sense 4 of the noun).

charm school ▶ n. dated or humorous a school offering tuition in social graces such as etiquette.

char·nel /ˈCHärnl/ ▶ n. short for CHARNEL HOUSE.
▶ adj. associated with death: *I gagged on the charnel stench of the place.*
– ORIGIN late Middle English: from Old French, from medieval Latin *carnale*, neuter (used as a noun) of *carnalis* 'relating to flesh' (see CARNAL).

char·nel house ▶ n. historical a building or vault in which corpses or bones are piled. ■ a place associated with violent death: *Europe in the immediate postwar period had become a charnel house.*
– ORIGIN mid 16th cent.: from Middle English *charnel* 'burying place,' from Old French, from medieval Latin *carnale*, from late Latin *carnalis* 'relating to flesh,' from *caro, carn-* 'flesh.'

Cha·ro·lais /ˌSHarəˈlā/ ▶ n. (pl. **same**) one of a breed of large white beef cattle.
– ORIGIN late 19th cent.: named after the *Monts du Charollais*, hills in eastern France where the breed originated.

Char·on /ˈkarən, ˈke(ə)r-/ **1** Greek Mythology an old man who ferried the souls of the dead across the Styx and Acheron rivers to Hades.
2 Astronomy the largest satellite of Pluto, discovered in 1978. Its diameter of 789 miles (1,270 km) is more than half that of Pluto.

Cha·roph·y·ta /kəˈräfitə/ Botany a phylum that includes the stoneworts, which are frequently treated as a class (Charophyceae) of the green algae.
– ORIGIN modern Latin (plural), former name of the family Characeae, from *Chara* (genus name) + Greek *phuton* 'a plant.'

char·o·phyte /ˈkarəˌfīt/ ▶ n. Botany a lower plant of the division Charophyta, such as a stonewort.

charr /CHär/ (also **char**) ▶ n. variant spelling of CHAR[4].
– ORIGIN mid 17th cent.: perhaps of Celtic origin.

char·rette /SHəˈret/ (also **charette**) ▶ n. a meeting in which all stakeholders in a project attempt to resolve conflicts and map solutions.
– ORIGIN late Middle English (denoting a cart or wagon): from French *charrette*, literally 'cart'; current sense dates from the mid 20th cent., possibly with reference to the use of a cart in 19th-cent. Paris to collect architecture students' work on the day of an exhibition.

char·ro /ˈCHärō/ ▶ n. (pl. **charros**) a Mexican horseman or cowboy, typically one in elaborate traditional dress.
– ORIGIN early 20th cent.: Mexican Spanish, from Spanish, literally 'rustic.'

chart /CHärt/ ▶ n. a sheet of information in the form of a table, graph, or diagram: *a chart showing how much do-it-yourself costs compared with retail.* ■ (usu. **the charts**) a weekly listing of the current best-selling pop records: *she topped the charts for eight weeks.* ■ a geographical map or plan, esp. one used for navigation by sea or air. ■ Medicine a written record of information about a patient: *scribbled on a patient's chart.* ■ (also **birth chart** or **natal chart**) Astrology a map showing the positions of the planets at the time of someone's birth, from which astrologers are said to be able to deduce character or potential.
▶ v. **1** [with obj.] make a map of (an area). ■ plot (a course) on a chart: *the pilot found his craft taking a route he had not charted.* ■ record the progress or development of: *the poems chart his descent into madness | a major series charting the history of country music.*
2 [no obj.] (of a record) enter the weekly music charts at a particular position: *the record will probably chart at about No. 74.*
– ORIGIN late 16th cent.: from French *charte*, from Latin *charta* 'paper, papyrus leaf' (see CARD[1]).

chart·bust·er /ˈCHärtˌbəstər/ ▶ n. informal a popular singer or group that makes a best-selling recording. ■ a best-selling recording.

char·ter /ˈCHärtər/ ▶ n. **1** a written grant by a country's legislative or sovereign power, by which an institution such as a company, college, or city is created and its rights and privileges defined. ■ a written constitution or description of an organization's functions.
2 the reservation of an aircraft, boat, or bus for private use: *a plane on charter to a multinational company.* ■ an aircraft, boat, or bus that is reserved for private use. ■ a trip made by an aircraft, boat, or bus under charter: *he liked to see the boat sparkling clean before each charter.*
▶ v. [with obj.] **1** grant a charter to (a city, college, or other institution): *the company was chartered in 1553.*
2 reserve (an aircraft, boat, or bus) for private use: *he chartered a plane to take him to Paris.*
– ORIGIN Middle English: from Old French *chartre*, from Latin *chartula*, diminutive of *charta* 'paper' (see CARD[1]).

char·tered /ˈCHärtərd/ ▶ adj. [attrib.] Brit. (of an accountant, engineer, librarian, etc.) qualified as a member of a professional body that has a royal charter.

char·ter·er /ˈCHärtərər/ ▶ n. a person or organization that charters an aircraft, boat, or bus.

char·ter flight ▶ n. a flight by an aircraft chartered for a specific trip, not part of an airline's regular schedule.

char·ter mem·ber ▶ n. an original or founding member of an organization.

char·ter school ▶ n. (in North America) a publicly funded independent school established by teachers, parents, or community groups under the terms of a charter with a local or national authority.

Chart·ism /ˈCHärtˌizəm/ ▶ n. a UK parliamentary reform movement of 1837–48, the principles of which were set out in a manifesto called *The People's Charter.*
– DERIVATIVES **Chart·ist** n. & adj.

chart·ist /ˈCHärtəst/ ▶ n. a person who uses charts of financial data to predict future trends and to guide investment strategies.
– DERIVATIVES **char·tism** /ˈCHärtˌizəm/ n.

Char·tres /ˈSHärt(rə)/ a city in northern France, noted for its Gothic cathedral; pop. 41,588 (2006).

Chartres Cathedral

char·treuse /SHärˈtro͞oz, -ˈtro͞os/ ▶ n. **1** a pale green or yellow liqueur made from brandy and aromatic herbs. ■ a pale yellow or green color resembling this liqueur.
2 a dish made in a mold using pieces of meat, vegetables, or (now most often) fruit in jelly.
– ORIGIN named after *La Grande Chartreuse*, the Carthusian monastery near Grenoble, France, where the liqueur (sense 1) was first made; sense 2 is an extended use.

chart-top·ping ▶ adj. informal (of a popular singer, group, or recording) having reached the top of the music charts.
– DERIVATIVES **chart-top·per** n.

char·wom·an /ˈCHärˌwo͝omən/ ▶ n. (pl. **charwomen**) Brit. dated a woman employed to clean houses or offices.
– ORIGIN late 16th cent.: from obsolete *char* or *chare* 'a turn of work, an odd job, chore' (obscurely related to CHORE) + WOMAN.

char·y /ˈCHe(ə)rē/ ▶ adj. (**charier, chariest**) cautiously or suspiciously reluctant to do something: *most people are chary of allowing themselves to be photographed.*
– DERIVATIVES **char·i·ly** /ˈCHe(ə)rəlē/ adv.
– ORIGIN Old English *cearig* 'sorrowful, anxious'; related to CARE. The current sense arose in the mid 16th cent.

Cha·ryb·dis /kəˈribdis, CHə-/ Greek Mythology a dangerous whirlpool in a narrow channel of the sea, opposite the cave of the sea monster Scylla.

Chas. ▶ abbr. Charles.

Chase[1] /CHās/, Salmon Portland (1808–73), US chief justice 1864–73. He served in the US Senate 1849–55, as governor of Ohio 1855–59, and as US secretary of the treasury 1861–64, during which time he established the national banking system and issued the first "greenbacks."

Chase[2], Samuel (1741–1811), US Supreme Court associate justice 1796–1811. A delegate to the Continental Congresses 1774–78, 1784, 1785 and a signer of the Declaration of Independence, he stressed national supremacy.

chase[1] /CHās/ ▶ v. [with obj.] **1** pursue in order to catch or catch up with: *police chased the stolen car through the city* | [no obj.] *the dog **chased after** the stick.* ■ seek to attain: *seventy candidates chasing a single job.* ■ seek the company of (a member of the opposite sex) in an obvious way: *playing football by day and chasing women by night.* ■ drive or cause to go in a specified direction: *she **chased** him **out of** the house.*
2 try to make contact with (someone) in order to get something owed or required: *chasing customers who had not paid their bills.* ■ make further investigation of (an unresolved matter): *investigators got a warrant, but they didn't have time to **chase down** the case.*
▶ n. an act of pursuing someone or something: *they captured the youths after a brief chase | a chase for limited supplies of hard currency | a car chase.* ■ (**the chase**) hunting as a sport: *she was an ardent follower of the chase.* ■ short for STEEPLECHASE. ■ Brit. an area of unenclosed land formerly reserved for hunting. ■ archaic a hunted animal.
– PHRASES **give chase** go in pursuit: *a patrol car gave chase and finally overtook him.*
– ORIGIN Middle English: from Old French *chacier* (verb), *chace* (noun), based on Latin *captare* 'continue to take,' from *capere* 'take.'

chase[2] ▶ v. [with obj.] (usu. as adj. **chased**) engrave (metal, or a design on metal): *a miniature container with a delicately chased floral design.*
– ORIGIN late Middle English: apparently from earlier *enchase*, from Old French *enchasser.*

chase[3] ▶ n. (in letterpress printing) a metal frame for holding the composed type and blocks being printed at one time.
– ORIGIN late 16th cent.: from French *châsse*, from Latin *capsa* 'box' (see CASE[2]).

chase[4] ▶ n. **1** the part of a gun enclosing the bore.
2 a groove or furrow cut in the face of a wall or other surface to receive a pipe.
– ORIGIN early 17th cent.: from French *chas* 'enclosed space,' from Provençal *cas, caus*, from medieval Latin *capsum* 'thorax or nave of a church.'

chas·er /ˈCHāsər/ ▶ n. **1** a person or thing that chases: [in combination] *promotion-chasers.*
2 informal a drink taken after another of a different kind, typically a weak alcoholic drink after a stronger one: *bourbon on the rocks with a beer chaser.*
3 a horse for steeplechasing.

Cha·sid ▶ n. variant spelling of HASID.

Cha·sid·ism ▶ n. variant spelling of HASIDISM.

chasm /ˈkazəm/ ▶ n. a deep fissure in the earth, rock, or another surface. ■ a profound difference between people, viewpoints, feelings, etc.: *the chasm between rich and poor.*
– DERIVATIVES **chas·mic** /ˈkazmik/ adj. (rare).
– ORIGIN late 16th cent. (denoting an opening up of the sea or land, as in an earthquake): from Latin *chasma*, from Greek *khasma* 'gaping hollow.'

chas·sé /SHaˈsā/ ▶ n. a gliding step in dancing in which one foot displaces the other.
▶ v. (**chassés, chasséing, chasséd**) [no obj.] make such a step.
– ORIGIN early 19th cent.: French, literally 'chased.'

chas·seur /SHaˈsər/ ▶ n. (pl. **same**) historical a soldier, usually in the light cavalry, equipped and trained for rapid movement, esp. in the French army.
– ORIGIN mid 18th cent.: French, from *chasser* 'to chase.'

Chas·sid ▶ n. variant spelling of HASID.

Chas·sid·ism ▶ n. variant spelling of HASIDISM.

chas·sis /ˈCHasē, ˈSHasē/ ▶ n. (pl. **same**) the base frame of a motor vehicle or other wheeled conveyance. ■ the outer structural framework of a piece of audio, radio, or computer equipment.
– ORIGIN early 20th cent.: from French *châssis* 'frame,' based on Latin *capsa* 'box' (see CASE[2]).

chaste /CHāst/ ▶ adj. abstaining from extramarital, or from all, sexual intercourse. ■ not having any sexual nature or intention: *a chaste, consoling embrace.* ■ without unnecessary ornamentation; simple or restrained: *the dark, chaste interior was lightened by tilework.*
– DERIVATIVES **chaste·ly** adv., **chaste·ness** n.
– ORIGIN Middle English: from Old French, from Latin *castus.*

chas·ten /ˈCHāsən/ ▶ v. [with obj.] (usu. **be chastened**) (of a reproof or misfortune) have a restraining or moderating effect on: *the director was somewhat chastened by his recent flops* | (as adj. **chastening**)

a chastening experience. ■ archaic (esp. of God) discipline; punish.
– DERIVATIVES **chas·ten·er** /ˈCHās(ə)nər/ **n.**
– ORIGIN early 16th cent.: from an obsolete verb *chaste*, from Old French *chastier*, from Latin *castigare* 'castigate,' from *castus* 'morally pure, chaste.'

chaste tree ▶ **n.** a southern European shrub with blue or white flowers, grown as an ornamental. It is also highly valued for its dark purple berries, which yield medicinal preparations used to treat gynecological conditions. Also called VITEX. ● *Vitex agnus-castus*, family Verbenaceae.
– ORIGIN mid 16th cent.: so named because of its association with chastity in sacrifices to Ceres.

C

chas·tise /CHasˈtīz/ ▶ **v.** [with obj.] rebuke or reprimand severely: *he chastised his colleagues for their laziness.* ■ dated punish, esp. by beating.
– DERIVATIVES **chas·tise·ment** /CHasˈtīzmənt, ˈCHastəz-/ **n.**, **chas·tis·er** /ˈCHas,tīzər/ **n.**
– ORIGIN Middle English: apparently formed irregularly from the obsolete verb *chaste* (see CHASTEN).

chas·ti·ty /ˈCHastətē/ ▶ **n.** the state or practice of refraining from extramarital, or esp. from all, sexual intercourse: *vows of chastity.*
– ORIGIN Middle English: from Old French *chastete*, from Latin *castitas*, from *castus* 'morally pure' (see CHASTE).

chas·ti·ty belt ▶ **n.** historical a garment or device designed to prevent a woman from having sexual intercourse.

chas·u·ble /ˈCHazəbəl, ˈCHaZH-, ˈCHas-/ ▶ **n.** a sleeveless outer vestment worn by a Catholic or High Anglican priest when celebrating Mass, typically ornate and having a simple hole for the head.
– ORIGIN Middle English: from Old French *chesible*, later *chasuble*, from late Latin *casubla*, alteration of Latin *casula* 'hooded cloak or little cottage,' diminutive of *casa* 'house.'

chasuble

chat¹ /CHat/ ▶ **v.** (**chats, chatting, chatted**) [no obj.] talk in a friendly and informal way: *she chatted to her mother on the phone every day.* ■ exchange messages online in real time with one or more simultaneous users of a computer network: *I keep getting messages popping up on my screen from people wanting to chat.*
▶ **n.** an informal conversation: *he dropped in for a chat | the perfect place for loads of cocktails and plenty of chat.* ■ the online exchange of messages in real time with one or more simultaneous users of a computer network: *join me for a live online chat Wednesday at 1400 hours.*
– PHRASAL VERBS **chat someone up** informal engage someone in flirtatious conversation. ■ talk persuasively to someone, esp. with a particular motive: *I chatted up the editor at the press club.*
– ORIGIN Middle English: shortening of CHATTER.

WORD TRENDS It seems that the Internet has taken over from the kitchen table as the favorite place for a **chat**. The Oxford English Corpus shows that the most common collocates of both the noun and the verb are computer-related, such as *online, Internet,* and *Web*, with *chatting on the Internet* nearly twice as common as *chatting on the phone* (an *Internet chat* beats out a *phone chat* by 12 to 1!). Although webcams and microphones are widely available, most people still choose to conduct their online chatting via keyboard, meaning that the word has shifted from a completely verbal method of communication to one that encompasses typing. People who regularly chat together online may never actually hear each other's voices.

chat² ▶ **n. 1** [often in combination] a small Old World songbird of the thrush subfamily, with a harsh call and typically with bold black, white, and buff or chestnut coloration. ● *Saxicola* and other genera, subfamily Turdinae, family Muscicapidae: numerous species. See also STONECHAT, WHINCHAT.
2 [with modifier] any of a number of small songbirds with harsh calls. ● a New World warbler that typically has a yellow or pink breast (genera *Icteria* and *Granatellus*, subfamily Parulinae, family Emberizidae). ● an Australian songbird related to the honeyeaters, the male of which is either mainly yellow or boldly marked (genera *Ephthianura* and *Ashbyia*, family Ephthianuridae).
– ORIGIN late 17th cent.: probably imitative of its call.

cha·teau /SHaˈtō/ (also **château**) ▶ **n.** (pl. **chateaux** /-ˈtō(z)/) a large French country house or castle often giving its name to wine made in its neighborhood: [in names] *Château Margaux.*
– ORIGIN mid 18th cent.: French, from Old French *chastel* (see CASTLE).

Cha·teau·bri·and /SHa,tōbrēˈän/, François-René, Vicomte de (1768–1848), French writer and diplomat. Notable works: *Le Génie du Christianisme* (1802) and *Mémoires d'outre-tombe* (autobiography, 1849–50).

cha·teau·bri·and /SHa,tōbrēˈōn/ ▶ **n.** a thick tenderloin of beef, typically served with Béarnaise sauce.
– ORIGIN late 19th cent.: named after François-René, Vicomte de CHATEAUBRIAND, whose chef is said to have created the dish.

Cha·teau-Thierr·y /SHa,tō tyeˈrē/ a town in the Picardy region of northern France, on the Marne River; pop. 15,359 (2007). It was a major battlefield during World War I; there is a monument to the US soldiers who took the town from German occupiers in 1918 and a military cemetery.

chat·e·lain /ˈSHatl,ān/ ▶ **n.** another term for CASTELLAN.
– ORIGIN late Middle English: from Old French *chastelain*, from medieval Latin *castellanus* 'castellan,' from Latin *castellum* (see CASTLE).

chat·e·laine /ˈSHatl,ān/ ▶ **n.** dated a woman in charge of a large house. ■ historical a set of short chains attached to a woman's belt, used for carrying keys or other items.
– ORIGIN mid 19th cent.: from French *châtelaine*, feminine of *châtelain* 'castellan,' from medieval Latin *castellanus* (see CHATELAIN).

Chat·ham /ˈCHatəm/, 1st Earl of, see PITT.

Chat·ham Is·lands /ˈCHatəm/ two islands, Pitt and Chatham, in the southwestern Pacific Ocean, east of New Zealand.

chat line (also **chatline**) ▶ **n.** a telephone service that allows conversation among a number of people who call into it separately. ■ the access to, or connection with, a chat room.

cha·toy·ant /SHəˈtoi-ənt/ ▶ **adj.** (of a gem, esp. when cut en cabochon) showing a band of bright reflected light caused by aligned inclusions in the stone.
– DERIVATIVES **cha·toy·ance n.**, **cha·toy·an·cy** /-ənsē/ **n.**
– ORIGIN late 18th cent.: French, present participle of *chatoyer* 'to shimmer.'

chat room ▶ **n.** an area on the Internet or other computer network where users can communicate, typically limiting communication to a particular topic.

chat show ▶ **n.** British term for TALK SHOW.

Chat·ta·hoo·chee Riv·er /,CHatəˈhōōCHē/ a river that flows for 435 miles (700 km) through Georgia to the Florida border, where it continues as the Apalachicola River into the Gulf of Mexico.

Chat·ta·noo·ga /,CHatnˈōōgə/ a city in southeastern Tennessee, on the Tennessee River, near the Georgia border, a rail and industrial center; pop. 170,880 (est. 2008).

chat·tel /ˈCHatl/ ▶ **n.** (in general use) a personal possession. ■ Law an item of property other than real estate. See also GOODS AND CHATTELS.
– ORIGIN Middle English: from Old French *chatel*, from medieval Latin *capitale*, from Latin *capitalis*, from *caput* 'head.' Compare with CAPITAL¹ and CATTLE.

chat·ter /ˈCHatər/ ▶ **v.** [no obj.] talk rapidly or incessantly about trivial matters: *the kids chattered and splashed at the edge of the lagoon.* ■ (of a bird, monkey, or machine) make a series of quick high-pitched sounds. ■ (of a person's teeth) click repeatedly together, typically from cold or fear.
▶ **n.** incessant trivial talk: *a stream of idle chatter.* ■ a series of quick high-pitched sounds: *the chatter of a typewriter.* ■ undesirable vibration in a mechanism: *the wipers should operate without chatter.*
– PHRASES **the chattering classes** derogatory educated people, esp. those in academic, artistic, or media circles.
– DERIVATIVES **chat·ter·y adj.**
– ORIGIN Middle English: imitative.

chat·ter·bot /ˈCHatər,bät/ ▶ **n.** a computer program designed to interact with people by simulating human conversation.
– ORIGIN 1990s: blend of *chatter* and *(ro)bot*.

chat·ter·box /ˈCHatər,bäks/ ▶ **n.** informal a person who talks at length about trivial matters.

chat·ter·er /ˈCHatərər/ ▶ **n. 1** another term for CHATTERBOX.
2 informal any of a number of birds with chattering calls, esp. a babbler, a waxwing, or a cotinga.

Chat·tis·garh /,CHətēsˈgär/ a state in central India, formed in 2000 from the southeastern part of Madhya Pradesh; capital, Raipur.

chat·ty /ˈCHatē/ ▶ **adj.** (**chattier, chattiest**) (of a person) fond of talking in an easy, informal way. ■ (of a conversation, letter, etc.) informal and lively.
– DERIVATIVES **chat·ti·ly** /ˈCHatl-ē/ **adv.**, **chat·ti·ness n.**

Chau·bu·na·gun·ga·maug, Lake /CHô,bənəˈgəNGgə,môg/ a small lake in southern Massachusetts, south of Worcester, in the town of Webster. The full form of its name, Chargoggagoggmanchaugagoggchaubunagungamaugg, is said to be the longest American place name.

Chau·cer /ˈCHôsər/, Geoffrey (*c.*1342–1400), English poet. His *Canterbury Tales* (*c.*1387–1400) is a cycle of linked tales told by a group of pilgrims. His skills of characterization, humor, and versatility established him as the first great English poet. Chaucer also wrote *Troilus and Criseyde* (*c.*1385).

Chau·ce·ri·an /CHôˈsi(ə)rēən/ ▶ **adj.** of or relating to Chaucer or his style.
▶ **n.** an admirer, imitator, or student of Chaucer or his writing.

Chau·diere Riv·er /SHōˈdyer/ a river that flows north for 120 miles (190 km) from the Maine border through Quebec and empties into the St. Lawrence River opposite Quebec City.

chauf·feur /ˈSHōfər, SHōˈfər/ ▶ **n.** a person employed to drive a private or rented automobile.
▶ **v.** [with obj.] drive (a car or a passenger in a car), typically as part of one's job: *she insisted on being chauffeured around.*
– ORIGIN late 19th cent. (in the general sense 'motorist'): from French, literally 'stoker' (by association with steam engines), from *chauffer* 'to heat.'

chauf·feuse /SHōˈfə(r)z/ ▶ **n.** rare a female chauffeur.

chaul·moo·gra /CHôlˈmōōgrə/ ▶ **n.** a tropical Asian evergreen tree with narrow leathery leaves and oil-rich seeds. ● Genus *Hydnocarpus*, family Flacourtiaceae: several species, in particular *H. kurzii*, a principal source of the oil. ■ (also **chaulmoogra oil**) the oil obtained from the seeds of this tree. It is used medically and as a preservative, and was formerly used in the treatment of leprosy.
– ORIGIN early 19th cent.: from Bengali *cāul-mugrā*.

chausses /SHōs/ ▶ **plural n.** historical pantaloons or close-fitting coverings for the legs and feet, in particular those forming part of a knight's armor.
– ORIGIN late 15th cent.: French, literally 'clothing for the legs.'

Chau·tau·qua /SHəˈtôkwə/ a resort town in southwestern New York, on Chautauqua Lake, noted as the birthplace of a 19th-century popular education movement; pop. 4,510 (est. 2008). ■ [as noun] (also **chautauqua**) an institution offering popular adult education courses and entertainment, typically held outdoors in the summer in the late 19th and early 20th centuries.

chau·vin·ism /ˈSHōvə,nizəm/ ▶ **n.** exaggerated or aggressive patriotism: *public opinion was easily moved to chauvinism and nationalism.* ■ excessive or prejudiced loyalty or support for one's own cause, group, or gender: *a bastion of male chauvinism.*
– ORIGIN late 19th cent.: named after Nicolas *Chauvin*, a Napoleonic veteran noted for his extreme patriotism, popularized as a character by the Cogniard brothers in *Cocarde Tricolore* (1831).

chau·vin·ist /ˈSHōvənist/ ▶ **n.** a person displaying aggressive or exaggerated patriotism. ■ a person displaying excessive or prejudiced loyalty or support for a particular cause, group, or gender: *what a male chauvinist that man is.*
▶ **adj.** showing or relating to such excessive or prejudiced support or loyalty: *a chauvinist slur.*

chau·vin·is·tic /,SHōvəˈnistik/ ▶ **adj.** feeling or displaying aggressive or exaggerated patriotism. ■ displaying excessive or prejudiced support for one's own cause, group, or sex.
– DERIVATIVES **chau·vin·is·ti·cal·ly** /,SHōvəˈnistik(ə)lē/ **adv.**

Cha·vez /ˈCHävez, ˈSHä-/, Cesar Estrada (1927–93), US labor leader. In 1962, he founded the organization that became the United Farm Workers, and he used nonviolent tactics to gain union contracts with California vineyard owners in 1970.

chaw /CHô/ informal ▶ **n.** an act of chewing something, esp. something not intended to be swallowed: *enjoying a good chaw.* ■ something chewed, esp. a wad of tobacco: *a chaw of tobacco.*
▶ **v.** [with obj.] chew (something, esp. tobacco).
– ORIGIN late Middle English (as a verb): variant of CHEW.

Cha·yef·sky /CHīˈefskē, -ˈev-/, Paddy (1923–81), US writer; born *Sidney Aaron Chayefsky*. He wrote television dramas, movie screenplays, stage plays, and a science fiction novel, *Altered States* (1978). His screenplays include *Marty* (1955), *Hospital* (1971), and *Network* (1976).

cha·yo·te /CHäˈyōtē/ ▶ **n. 1** a green pear-shaped tropical fruit that resembles cucumber in flavor.
2 the tropical American vine that yields this fruit, also producing an edible yamlike tuberous root.
● *Sechium edule*, family Cucurbitaceae.

–ORIGIN late 19th cent.: from Spanish, from Nahuatl *chayotli*.

CHD ▶ **abbr.** coronary heart disease.

Ch.E. ▶ **abbr.** Chemical Engineer.

cheap /CHēp/ ▶ **adj.** (of an item for sale) low in price; worth more than its cost: *they bought some cheap fruit | local buses were reliable and cheap.* ■ charging low prices: *a cheap restaurant.* ■ inexpensive because of inferior quality: *cheap, shoddy goods.* ■ informal miserly; stingy: *she's too cheap to send me a postcard.* ■ of little worth because achieved in a discreditable way requiring little effort: *her moment of cheap triumph.* ■ deserving of contempt: *a cheap trick.*
▶ **adv.** at or for a low price: *a house that was going cheap.*
–PHRASES **on the cheap** informal at a low cost: *in search of symbols of prestige, but on the cheap.*
–DERIVATIVES **cheap·ish adj.**, **cheap·ly adv.**, **cheap·ness n.**
–ORIGIN late 15th cent.: from an obsolete phrase *good cheap* 'a good bargain,' from Old English *cēap* 'bargaining, trade,' based on Latin *caupo* 'small trader, innkeeper.'

cheap·en /ˈCHēpən/ ▶ **v.** [with obj.] reduce the price of: *the depreciation of the dollar would cheapen U.S. exports.* ■ degrade: *the mass media simplify and cheapen the experience of art.*

cheap·jack /ˈCHēpˌjak/ ▶ **n.** a seller of cheap inferior goods, typically a hawker at a fair or market.
▶ **adj.** of inferior quality.
–ORIGIN mid 19th cent.: from CHEAP + JACK[1].

cheap·o /ˈCHēpō/ (also **cheapie**) informal ▶ **adj.** [attrib.] inexpensive and of poor quality: *a cheapo guitar.*
▶ **n.** (pl. **cheapos**) an inexpensive thing of poor quality.

cheap·skate /ˈCHēpˌskāt/ ▶ **n.** informal a stingy person.
–ORIGIN late 19th cent. (originally US): from CHEAP + *skate* 'a worn-out horse' or 'a mean, contemptible, or dishonest person,' of unknown origin.

cheat /CHēt/ ▶ **v. 1** [no obj.] act dishonestly or unfairly in order to gain an advantage, esp. in a game or examination: *she always cheats at cards.* ■ [with obj.] deceive or trick: *he had cheated her out of everything she had.* ■ informal be sexually unfaithful: *his wife was cheating on him.*
2 [with obj.] avoid (something undesirable) by luck or skill: *she cheated death in a spectacular crash.* ■ archaic help (time) pass: *the tuneless rhyme with which the warder cheats the time.*
▶ **n.** a person who behaves dishonestly in order to gain an advantage: *a liar and a cheat.* ■ an act of cheating; a fraud or deception.
–ORIGIN late Middle English: shortening of ESCHEAT (the original sense).

cheat·er /ˈCHētər/ ▶ **n. 1** a person who acts dishonestly in order to gain an advantage. ■ a person who cheats on a sexual partner.
2 (**cheaters**) informal a pair of glasses or sunglasses.

cheat grass (also **cheatgrass**) ▶ **n.** a tough wild grass of open land, sometimes growing as a weed among cereal crops and in pasture. ● Genus *Bromus*, family Gramineae: several species, in particular *B. tectorum*.
–ORIGIN late 18th cent.: a local word for various wild plants, perhaps from their resemblance to the cereals among which they grew.

cheat sheet ▶ **n.** informal a piece of paper bearing written notes intended to aid one's memory, typically one used surreptitiously in an examination.

Che·bok·sa·ry /ˌCHebäkˈsär(y)ē/ a city in western central Russia, on the Volga River, west of Kazan, capital of the autonomous republic of Chuvashia; pop. 441,600 (est. 2008).

Che·chen /ˈCHeCHən/ ▶ **n.** (pl. **same** or **Chechens**)
1 a member of the largely Muslim people inhabiting Chechnya.
2 the North Caucasian language of this people.
▶ **adj.** of or relating to this people or their language.
–ORIGIN from obsolete Russian *chechen* (earlier form of *chechenets*).

Chech·nya /ˈCHeCHnēə, CHeCHˈnyä/ (also **Chechenia** /CHeCHəˈnyə/) an autonomous republic in the Caucasus in southwestern Russia, on the border with Georgia; pop. 1,205,800 (est. 2009); capital, Grozny. The republic declared itself independent of Russia in 1991 and was invaded by Russian forces (1994). A peace treaty called for the withdrawal of troops, but the Russians invaded again in 1999. Also called **Chechen Republic**.

check[1] /CHek/ ▶ **v.** [with obj.] **1** examine (something) in order to determine its accuracy, quality, or condition, or to detect the presence of something: *customs officers have the right to check all luggage* | [no obj.] *a simple blood test to check for anemia.* ■ verify or establish to one's satisfaction: *check the expiration date on your passport* | [with clause] *she glanced over her shoulder to check that the door was shut.* ■ (**check against**) verify the accuracy of something by comparing it with (something else): *keep your receipt to check against your statement.* ■ another way of saying CHECK SOMETHING OFF. ■ another way of saying CHECK SOMETHING IN. ■ [no obj.] agree or correspond when compared. ■ informal look at; take notice of: *check the remix.*
2 stop or slow down the progress of (something undesirable): *efforts were made to check the disease.* ■ curb or restrain (a feeling or emotion): *he learned to check his excitement.* ■ Hockey hamper or neutralize (an opponent) with one's body or stick. ■ [no obj.] (**check against**) provide a means of preventing: *processes to check against deterioration in the quality of the data held.* ■ [no obj.] (of a hound) pause to make sure of or regain a scent. ■ [no obj.] (of a trained hawk) abandon the intended quarry and fly after other prey.
3 [with obj.] Chess move a piece or pawn so that (the opposing king) is under attack.
4 [no obj.] (in poker) choose not to make a bet when called upon, allowing the action to move to another player.
▶ **n. 1** an examination to test or ascertain accuracy, quality, or satisfactory condition: *a campaign calling for regular checks on gas appliances | a health check.*
2 a stopping or slowing of progress: *there was no check to the expansion of the market.* ■ a means of control or restraint: *a permanent check upon the growth or abuse of central authority.* ■ Hockey an act of hampering or neutralizing an opponent with one's body or stick. ■ a temporary loss of the scent in hunting. ■ Falconry a false stoop when a hawk abandons its intended quarry and pursues other prey. ■ a part of a piano that catches the hammer and prevents it from retouching the strings.
3 Chess a move by which a piece or pawn directly attacks the opponent's king. If the defending player cannot counter the attack, the king is checkmated.
4 the bill in a restaurant. ■ (also **baggage/luggage check**) a token of identification for left luggage. ■ a counter used as a stake in a gambling game.
5 short for CHECK MARK.
6 a crack or flaw in timber.
▶ **exclam. 1** informal expressing assent or agreement.
2 used by a chess player to announce that the opponent's king has been placed in check.
–PHRASES **in check 1** under control: *a way of keeping inflation in check.* **2** Chess (of a king) directly attacked by an opponent's piece or pawn; (of a player) having the king in this position. **keep a check on** monitor: *keep a regular check on your score.*
–PHRASAL VERBS **check in** (or **check someone in**) arrive and register at a hotel or airport: *you must check in at least one hour before takeoff | they check in the passengers.* **check something in** have one's baggage weighed and put aside for consignment to the hold of an aircraft on which one is booked to travel. ■ register and leave baggage in a left-luggage department. **check into** register one's arrival at (a hotel). **check something off** tick or otherwise mark an item on a list to show that it has been dealt with. **check on 1** verify, ascertain, or monitor the state or condition of: *the doctor had come to check on his patient.* **2** another way of saying CHECK UP ON. **check out** settle one's hotel bill before leaving. ■ informal die. **check someone/something out 1** establish the truth or inform oneself about someone or something: *they decided to go and check out a local restaurant.* **2** (**check something out**) enter the price of goods in a supermarket into a cash machine for addition and payment by a customer. ■ register something as having been borrowed. **check something over** inspect or examine something thoroughly. **check through** inspect or examine thoroughly. **check up on** investigate in order to establish the truth about or accuracy of.
–DERIVATIVES **check·a·ble adj.**
–ORIGIN Middle English (originally as used in the game of chess): the noun and exclamation from Old French *eschec*, from medieval Latin *scaccus*, via Arabic from Persian *šāh* 'king'; the verb from Old French *eschequier* 'play chess, put in check.' The sense 'stop, restrain, or control' arose from the use in chess, and led (in the late 17th cent.) to 'examine the accuracy of, verify.'

check[2] (Brit. **cheque**) ▶ **n.** a written order to a bank to pay a stated sum from the drawer's account: *he was awarded a check for $1,000.*
–ORIGIN early 18th cent. (originally denoting a check stub): variant of CHECK[1], in the sense 'device for checking the amount of an item.'

check[3] ▶ **n.** a pattern of small squares: *a fine black-and-white check.* ■ a garment or fabric with such a pattern.
▶ **adj.** [attrib.] having such a pattern: *a blue check T-shirt.*
–ORIGIN late Middle English: probably from CHECKER[2].

check·book /ˈCHekˌbo͝ok/ ▶ **n.** a book of blank checks with a register for recording checks written.

check·book jour·nal·ism ▶ **n.** chiefly derogatory the practice of paying large amounts of money for exclusive rights to material for newspaper stories, esp. personal ones.

check·box /ˈCHekˌbäks/ ▶ **n.** Computing a small box on a computer screen that, when selected by the user, is filled with a ✓ to show that the feature described alongside it has been enabled.

checked /CHekt/ ▶ **adj. 1** (of clothes or fabric) having a pattern of small squares: *a checked shirt.*
2 Phonetics (of a vowel) followed by one or more consonants in the same syllable.

check·er[1] /ˈCHekər/ ▶ **n. 1** a person or thing that verifies or examines something: *a spelling checker.*
2 a cashier in a supermarket.

check·er[2] (Brit. **chequer**) ▶ **n. 1** (often **checkers**) a pattern of squares, typically alternately colored: *a geometric shape bordered by checkers* | (as modifier **checker**) *a checker design.*
2 (**checkers**) [treated as sing.] a game for two players, with twelve pieces each, played on a checkerboard. ■ (**checker**) a round flat piece, usually red or black, used to play checkers.
–ORIGIN Middle English: from EXCHEQUER. The original sense 'chessboard' gave rise to *checkered* meaning 'marked like a chessboard'; hence sense 1 (early 16th cent).

check·er·ber·ry /ˈCHekərˌberē/ ▶ **n.** (pl. **checkerberries**) a creeping evergreen North American shrub of the heath family, with spiny scented leaves and waxy white flowers. Also called WINTERGREEN. ● *Gaultheria procumbens*, family Ericaceae. ■ the edible red fruit of this plant.
–ORIGIN late 18th cent.: from *checkers* or *chequers* 'berries of the service tree' (so named from their color) + BERRY.

check·er·board /ˈCHekərˌbôrd/ ▶ **n.** a board for playing checkers and certain other games, with a regular pattern of squares in alternating colors, typically black and white. ■ a pattern resembling such a board.

check·ered /ˈCHekərd/ ▶ **adj.** having a pattern of alternating squares of different colors. ■ marked by periods of varied fortune or discreditable incidents: *his checkered past might hurt his electability.*

check·ered flag ▶ **n.** Auto Racing a flag with a black-and-white checkered pattern, displayed to drivers as they finish a race.
–PHRASES **take the checkered flag** finish first in a race: *Unser took the checkered flag four times this spring.*

check·er·spot /ˈCHekərˌspät/ ▶ **n.** a North American butterfly with pale markings on the wings that typically form a checkered pattern. ● *Euphydryas* and other genera, subfamily Melitaeinae, family Nymphalidae: several species, in particular the **Baltimore checkerspot** (*E. phaeton*).

Baltimore checkerspot

check-in ▶ **n.** [often as modifier] the act of reporting one's presence and registering, typically at an airport or hotel: *the check-in counter.* ■ the point at which such registration takes place.

check·ing ac·count (Canadian **chequing account**) ▶ **n.** an account at a bank against which checks can be drawn by the account depositor.
–ORIGIN 1920s: from CHECK[2].

check·list /ˈCHekˌlist/ ▶ **n.** a list of items required, things to be done, or points to be considered, used as a reminder.

check mark ▶ **n.** a mark (✓) used to indicate that a textual item is correct or has been chosen or verified.

check·mate /ˈCHekˌmāt/ ▶ **n.** Chess a check from which a king cannot escape. ■ [as exclamation] (by a player) announcing that the opponent's king is in such a position. ■ a final defeat or deadlock: *if the rebel forces succeed in cutting off the road, they will have achieved checkmate.*

PRONUNCIATION KEY ə *ago, up;* ər *over, fur;* a *hat;* ā *ate;* ä *car;* e *let;* ē *see;* i *fit;* ī *by;* NG *sing;* ō *go;* ô *law, for;* oi *toy;* o͝o *good;* o͞o *goo;* ou *out;* TH *thin;* TH *then;* ZH *vision*

▶ v. [with obj.] Chess put into checkmate. ■ defeat or frustrate totally: *the use of technology to checkmate present missile technology.*
– ORIGIN Middle English: from Old French *eschec mat*, from Arabic *šāh māta*, from Persian *šāh manad* 'the king is helpless.'

check·out /ˈCHek,out/ ▶ n. **1** a point at which goods are paid for in a supermarket or other store: [as modifier] *packaging that is scanned at the checkout counter.*
2 the administrative procedure followed when a guest leaves a hotel at the end of a stay: [as modifier] *checkout time.*

check·point /ˈCHek,point/ ▶ n. a barrier or manned entrance, typically at a border, where travelers are subject to security checks. ■ a place along the route of a long-distance race where the time for each competitor is recorded. ■ a location whose exact position can be verified visually or electronically, used by pilots to aid navigation.

check rein ▶ n. a bearing rein.

check·room /ˈCHek,ro͝om, -,ro͞om/ ▶ n. a room in a public building where coats, hats, luggage, etc., may be left temporarily.

checks and bal·anc·es ▶ plural n. counterbalancing influences by which an organization or system is regulated, typically those ensuring that political power is not concentrated in the hands of individuals or groups.

check·sum /ˈCHek,səm/ ▶ n. a digit representing the sum of the correct digits in a piece of stored or transmitted digital data, against which later comparisons can be made to detect errors in the data.

check·up /ˈCHek,əp/ ▶ n. a thorough examination, esp. a medical or dental one.

check valve ▶ n. a valve that closes to prevent backward flow of liquid.

ched·dar /ˈCHedər/ ▶ n. a kind of firm smooth cheese, originally made in Cheddar in southern England.

che·der /ˈKHedər, ˈKHā-/ (also **heder**) ▶ n. (pl. **chedarim** /KHeˈdärim/, **cheders**) a school for Jewish children in which Hebrew and religious knowledge are taught.
– ORIGIN late 19th cent.: from Hebrew *ḥeder* 'room.'

chee·cha·ko /CHiˈCHäkō, -ˈCHôkō, CHē-/ ▶ n. (pl. **cheechakos**) informal a person newly arrived in the mining districts of Alaska or northwestern Canada.
– ORIGIN late 19th cent.: Chinook Jargon, 'newcomer.'

cheek /CHēk/ ▶ n. **1** either side of the face below the eye: *tears rolled down her cheeks.* ■ either of the inner sides of the mouth: *Sam had to bite his cheeks to keep from laughing.* ■ informal either of the buttocks. ■ either of two side pieces or parts in a structure.
2 [in sing.] impertinent talk or behavior: *he **had the cheek** to complain | that's enough of your cheek!*
– PHRASES **cheek by jowl** close together; side by side: *the houses were packed cheek by jowl along the coast.* [from a use of *jowl* in the sense 'cheek'; the phrase was originally *cheek by cheek*.] **cheek to cheek** (of two people dancing) with their heads close together in an intimate way. **turn the other cheek** refrain from retaliating when one has been attacked or insulted. [with biblical allusion to Matt. 5:39.]
– DERIVATIVES **cheeked** adj. [in combination] *rosy-cheeked.*
– ORIGIN Old English *cē(a)ce, cēoce* 'cheek, jaw'; related to Dutch *kaak.*

cheek·bone /ˈCHēk,bōn/ ▶ n. the bone below the eye.

cheek·piece /ˈCHēk,pēs/ ▶ n. a part of an object that covers or rests on the cheek, in particular: ■ the portion of the stock of a rifle or shotgun that rests against the face when aiming from the shoulder. ■ either of the two straps of a horse's bridle joining the bit and the headpiece. ■ a bar on a horse's bit that lies outside the mouth.

cheek pouch ▶ n. a saclike fold of skin on either side of the mouth, esp. in squirrels, monkeys, and gophers, used for carrying food.

Cheek·to·wa·ga /,CHēktəˈwägə/ a town in western New York, an industrial suburb east of Buffalo; pop. 87,788 (est. 2008).

cheek·y /ˈCHēkē/ ▶ adj. (**cheekier**, **cheekiest**) impudent or irreverent, typically in an endearing or amusing way: *a cheeky grin.*
– DERIVATIVES **cheek·i·ly** /-kəlē/ adv., **cheek·i·ness** n.

cheep /CHēp/ ▶ n. a shrill squeaky cry made by a bird, typically a young one. ■ a sound resembling such a cry: *an electronic cheep from the alarm.*
▶ v. [no obj.] make a shrill squeaky sound.
– ORIGIN early 16th cent. (originally Scots): imitative (compare with PEEP[2]).

cheer /CHi(ə)r/ ▶ v. **1** [no obj.] shout for joy or in praise or encouragement: *she cheered from the sidelines.* ■ [with obj.] praise or encourage with shouts: *they cheered his emotional speech | the cyclists were **cheered on** by the crowds.*
2 [with obj.] give comfort or support to: *he seemed greatly cheered by my arrival.* ■ (**cheer someone up** or **cheer up**) make or become less miserable: [with obj.] *I asked her out to lunch to cheer her up* | [no obj.] *he cheered up at the sight of the food.*
▶ n. **1** a shout of encouragement, praise, or joy: *a tremendous cheer from the audience.* ■ a brief phrase shouted in unison by a crowd, typically led by cheerleaders, in support of an athletic team.
2 (also **good cheer**) cheerfulness, optimism, or confidence: *an attempt to inject a little cheer into this gloomy season.* ■ food and drink provided for a festive occasion: *they had partaken heartily of the Christmas cheer.*
– PHRASES **of good cheer** archaic cheerful; optimistic. **three cheers** three successive hurrahs shouted to express appreciation or congratulation: ***three cheers** for the winners!* **what cheer?** archaic how are you?
– ORIGIN Middle English: from Old French *chiere* 'face,' from late Latin *cara*, from Greek *kara* 'head.' The original sense was 'face,' hence 'expression, mood,' later specifically 'a good mood.'

cheer·ful /ˈCHi(ə)rfəl/ ▶ adj. noticeably happy and optimistic: *how can she be so cheerful at six o'clock in the morning? | a cheerful voice.* ■ causing happiness by its nature or appearance: *a chatty, cheerful letter | the room was painted in cheerful colors.*
– DERIVATIVES **cheer·ful·ness** n.

cheer·ful·ly /ˈCHi(ə)rfəlē/ ▶ adv. in a way that displays happiness or optimism: *he was whistling cheerfully.* ■ in a way that inspires feelings of happiness: *cheerfully decorated rooms.* ■ readily and willingly: *I could cheerfully have strangled her.*

cheer·i·o /,CHi(ə)rēˈō/ ▶ exclam. Brit. informal used as an expression of good wishes on parting; goodbye. ■ dated used as a toast.

cheer·lead·er /ˈCHi(ə)r,lēdər/ ▶ n. a person who leads cheers and applause, esp. at a sports event. ■ an enthusiastic and vocal supporter: *he was a cheerleader for individual initiative.*
– DERIVATIVES **cheer·lead** v. (past and past participle **cheerled**).

cheer·less /ˈCHi(ə)rlis/ ▶ adj. gloomy; depressing: *the corridors were ill-lit and cheerless.*
– DERIVATIVES **cheer·less·ly** adv., **cheer·less·ness** n.

cheer·ly /ˈCHi(ə)rlē/ ▶ adv. archaic heartily (used as a cry of encouragement among sailors).

cheers /CHi(ə)rz/ ▶ exclam. informal expressing good wishes, in particular: ■ good wishes before drinking: *"Cheers," she said, raising her glass.* ■ chiefly Brit. good wishes on parting or ending a conversation: *"Cheers, Jack, see you later."* ■ chiefly Brit. gratitude or acknowledgment for something: *Billy tossed him the key. "Cheers, pal."*

cheer·y /ˈCHi(ə)rē/ ▶ adj. (**cheerier**, **cheeriest**) happy and optimistic: *a cheery smile.*
– DERIVATIVES **cheer·i·ly** /ˈCHi(ə)rəlē/ adv., **cheer·i·ness** n.

cheese[1] /CHēz/ ▶ n. **1** a food made from the pressed curds of milk: *grated cheese | a slice of cheese* | [as modifier] *a cheese sandwich.* ■ a molded mass of such food with its rind, often in a round flat shape: *a 50-pound, muslin-wrapped cheese.* ■ a round flat object resembling a cheese.
2 informal the quality of being too obviously sentimental: *the conversations tend too far toward cheese.*
– PHRASES **hard cheese** Brit. informal used to express sympathy over a petty matter. **say cheese** said by a photographer to encourage the subject to smile.
– ORIGIN Old English *cēse, cȳse*; related to Dutch *kaas* and German *Käse*; from Latin *caseus.*

cheese[2] (also **big cheese**) ▶ n. informal an important person: *he was a big cheese in the business world.*
– ORIGIN early 19th cent. (originally in the sense 'the right thing or something excellent'): probably from Urdu, from Persian *čīz* 'thing.' The current sense dates from the 1920s.

cheese[3] ▶ v. informal, chiefly Brit. exasperate, frustrate, or bore: *that really cheesed off Ricky.*
– PHRASES **cheese it 1** Brit. archaic look out. **2** dated run away: *cheese it, here comes Mr. Madigan!*
– ORIGIN early 19th cent. (CHEESE[1] (sense 1) of *cheese it*): of unknown origin.

cheese·ball /ˈCHēz,bôl/ informal ▶ adj. lacking taste, style, or originality: *I'll admit to watching some of those cheeseball daytime talk shows.*
▶ n. a person who lacks taste, style, or originality.

cheese·board /ˈCHēz,bôrd/ ▶ n. a board on which cheese is served and cut. ■ a selection of cheeses.

cheese·burg·er /ˈCHēz,bərgər/ ▶ n. a hamburger with a slice of cheese on it.

cheese·cake /ˈCHēz,kāk/ ▶ n. **1** a kind of rich dessert cake made with cream and soft cheese on a graham cracker, cookie, or pastry crust, typically topped with a fruit sauce.
2 informal photography, a movie, or art that portrays women in a manner emphasizing stereotypical sexual attractiveness: [as modifier] *a cheesecake photo of herself wearing a silly hat and little else.*

cheese·cloth /ˈCHēz,klôTH/ ▶ n. thin, loosely woven cloth of cotton, used originally for making and wrapping cheese.

cheese-cut·ter ▶ n. **1** an implement for cutting cheese, esp. by means of a wire that can be pulled through the cheese.
2 (also **cheese-cutter cap**) informal a cap with a broad, square brim.

cheese fly ▶ n. another term for CHEESE-SKIPPER.

cheese·head /ˈCHēz,hed/ ▶ n. **1** informal a resident of Wisconsin, esp. a fan of the Green Bay Packers football team. [so called because Wisconsin is noted for the production of cheese.]
2 informal a blockhead; an idiot.

cheese·mak·er /ˈCHēz,mākər/ ▶ n. a person who makes cheese.
– DERIVATIVES **cheese·mak·ing** n.

cheese·mon·ger /ˈCHēz,mäNGgər, -,məNGgər/ ▶ n. Brit. a person who sells cheese, butter, and other dairy products.

cheese·par·ing /ˈCHēz,pe(ə)riNG/ ▶ adj. careful or stingy with money.
▶ n. stinginess.

cheese-skip·per ▶ n. a small shiny black fly whose larvae frequently infest cheese. Also called CHEESE FLY. ● *Piophila casei*, family Piophilidae.

cheese·steak /ˈCHēz,stāk/ ▶ n. (also **Philly cheesesteak**) a sandwich containing thin-sliced sautéed beef, melted cheese, and typically sautéed onions, served in a long roll.

cheese straw ▶ n. a thin strip of pastry, flavored with cheese and eaten as a snack.

chees·y /ˈCHēzē/ ▶ adj. (**cheesier**, **cheesiest**) **1** like cheese in taste, smell, or consistency: *a pungent, cheesy sauce.*
2 informal cheap, unpleasant, or blatantly inauthentic: *a big cheesy grin | cheesy motel rooms.*
– DERIVATIVES **chees·i·ness** n.

chee·tah /ˈCHētə/ ▶ n. a large spotted cat found in Africa and parts of Asia. It is the fastest animal on land. ● *Acinonyx jubatus*, family Felidae.
– ORIGIN late 18th cent.: from Hindi *cītā*, perhaps from Sanskrit *citraka* 'leopard.'

Chee·ver /ˈCHēvər/, John (1912–82), US novelist and short-story writer. His stories frequently satirize affluent residents of the suburbs of Westchester County and New England. Notable works: *The Wapshot Chronicle* (1957), *The Wapshot Scandal* (1964), *Falconer* (1977), and *The Stories of John Cheever* (1978).

chef /SHef/ ▶ n. a professional cook, typically the chief cook in a restaurant or hotel.
▶ v. (**chefs, cheffing, cheffed**) [no obj.] informal work as a chef: *when they finish cheffing, they gather themselves together and they drink their owners' best wines.*
– ORIGIN early 19th cent.: French, literally 'head.'

chef-d'œu·vre /SHā ˈdœv(rə), ˈdə(r)v/ ▶ n. (pl. **chefs-d'œuvre** /SHāz ˈdœv(rə), ˈdə(r)v/) a masterpiece.
– ORIGIN early 17th cent.: French, literally 'chief work.'

Che·foo /ˈjəˈfo͞o/ former name of YANTAI.

chef's sal·ad ▶ n. a large salad of lettuce topped with strips of meat (usu. turkey and ham) and cheese, and large pieces of tomato and hard-boiled egg, typically served as a main course.

cheiro- ▶ comb. form variant spelling of CHIRO-.

Che·ka /ˈCHekə/ an organization under the Soviet regime for the investigation of counterrevolutionary activities. It executed many real and alleged enemies of Lenin's regime from its formation in 1917 until 1922 when it was replaced by the OGPU.
– ORIGIN Russian, from *che, ka*, the initial letters of *Chrezvychaĭnaya komissiya* 'Extraordinary Commission (for combating Counterrevolution, Sabotage, and Speculation).'

Che·khov /ˈCHek,ôv, ˈCHek,ôf/, Anton (Pavlovich) (1860–1904), Russian playwright and short-story writer. His work, which portrays upper-class life in prerevolutionary Russia with a blend of naturalism and symbolism, had a considerable influence on 20th-century drama. Notable plays: *The Seagull* (1895), *Uncle Vanya* (1900), *Three Sisters* (1901), and *The Cherry Orchard* (1904).

Che·kiang /ˈjəkēˈäNG/ variant of ZHEJIANG.

che·la¹ /ˈkēlə/ ▶ **n.** (pl. **chelae** /-lē, -lī/) Zoology a pincerlike claw, esp. of a crab or other crustacean. Compare with CHELICERA.
– ORIGIN mid 17th cent.: modern Latin, from Latin *chele* or Greek *khēlē* 'claw.'

che·la² /ˈCHālä/ ▶ **n.** a follower and student of a guru.
– ORIGIN from Hindi *celā*.

che·late /ˈkēˌlāt/ ▶ **n.** Chemistry a compound containing a ligand (typically organic) bonded to a central metal atom at two or more points.
▶ **adj.** Zoology (of an appendage) bearing chelae.
▶ **v.** [with obj.] Chemistry form a chelate with.
– DERIVATIVES **che·la·tion** /kēˈlāSHən/ **n.**, **che·la·tor** /-ˌlātər/ **n.**

che·la·tion ther·a·py ▶ **n.** a therapy for mercury or lead poisoning that binds the toxins in the bloodstream by circulating a chelating solution. ■ a form of complementary therapy involving the intravenous infusion of substances intended to remove calcium from hardened arteries.

che·lic·er·a /kəˈlisərə/ ▶ **n.** (pl. **chelicerae** /-ˈlisəˌrē/) Zoology either of a pair of appendages in front of the mouth in arachnids and some other arthropods, usually modified as pincerlike claws. Compare with CHELA¹.
– DERIVATIVES **che·lic·er·al** **adj.**
– ORIGIN mid 19th cent.: modern Latin, from Greek *khēlē* 'claw' + *keras* 'horn.'

Che·lic·er·at·a /kəˌlisəˈrätə/ Zoology a large group of arthropods that comprises the arachnids, sea spiders, and horseshoe crabs. They lack antennae, but possess a pair of chelicerae, a pair of pedipalps, and (typically) four pairs of legs. ● Subphylum Chelicerata, phylum Arthropoda.
– ORIGIN modern Latin (plural), from Greek *khēlē* 'claw' + *keras* 'horn.'

che·lic·er·ate /kəˈlisəˌrāt, -rət/ Zoology ▶ **n.** an arthropod of the large group Chelicerata; an arachnid, sea spider, or horseshoe crab.
▶ **adj.** relating to or denoting chelicerates.

Chel·le·an /ˈSHelēən/ ▶ **adj.** & **n.** former term for ABBEVILLIAN.
– ORIGIN late 19th cent.: from French *Chelléen*, from *Chelles*, near Paris, where tools from this period were discovered.

Chelms·ford /ˈCHelmsfərd/ a city in southeastern England, noted for its cathedral; the county town of Essex; pop. 107,800 (est. 2009).

Che·lo·ni·a /kəˈlōnēə/ Zoology former term for TESTUDINES.
– ORIGIN modern Latin (plural), from Greek *khelōnē* 'tortoise.'

che·lo·ni·an /kəˈlōnēən/ Zoology ▶ **n.** a reptile of the order Testudines (formerly Chelonia); a turtle, terrapin, or tortoise.
▶ **adj.** relating to or denoting chelonians.

Chel·sea /ˈCHelsē/ **1** an industrial and commercial city in northeastern Massachusetts, just north of Boston; pop. 41,577 (est. 2008).
2 a residential district of London, on the northern bank of the Thames River.
3 a fashionable residential section of southern Manhattan in New York City, on the west side of the city.

Chel·sea boot ▶ **n.** an elastic-sided, ankle-high boot.

Chel·ya·binsk /CHelˈyäbinsk/ an industrial city in southern Russia, on the eastern slopes of the Ural Mountains; pop. 1,092,500 (est. 2008).

chem. ▶ **abbr.** ■ chemical. ■ chemist. ■ chemistry.

chemi- ▶ **comb. form** representing CHEMICAL. See also CHEMO-.

chem·i·cal /ˈkemikəl/ (abbr.: **chem.**) ▶ **adj.** of or relating to chemistry or the interactions of substances as studied in chemistry: *the chemical composition of the atmosphere.* ■ of or relating to chemicals: *chemical treatments for killing fungi.* ■ relating to, involving, or denoting the use of poison gas or other chemicals as weapons of war: *the manufacture of chemical weapons.*
▶ **n.** a compound or substance that has been purified or prepared, esp. artificially: *never mix disinfectant with other chemicals | controversy arose over treatment of apples with this chemical.*
– DERIVATIVES **chem·i·cal·ly** /-ik(ə)lē/ **adv.**
– ORIGIN late 16th cent.: from French *chimique* or modern Latin *chimicus*, *chymicus*, from medieval Latin *alchymicus*, from *alchimia* (see ALCHEMY).

chem·i·cal a·buse ▶ **n.** another term for SUBSTANCE ABUSE.

chem·i·cal bond ▶ **n.** see BOND (sense 3 of the noun).

chem·i·cal com·pound ▶ **n.** see COMPOUND¹.

chem·i·cal de·pend·en·cy ▶ **n.** addiction to a mood- or mind-altering drug, such as alcohol or cocaine.

chem·i·cal el·e·ment ▶ **n.** see ELEMENT (sense 2).

chem·i·cal en·gi·neer·ing ▶ **n.** the branch of engineering concerned with the design and operation of industrial chemical plants.
– DERIVATIVES **chem·i·cal en·gi·neer** **n.**

chem·i·cal for·mu·la ▶ **n.** see FORMULA (sense 1).

chem·i·cal po·ten·tial ▶ **n.** the change in Gibbs free energy with respect to change in amount of the component, with pressure, temperature, and amounts of other components being constant. Components are in equilibrium if their chemical potentials are equal.

chem·i·cal re·ac·tion ▶ **n.** a process that involves rearrangement of the molecular or ionic structure of a substance, as opposed to a change in physical form or a nuclear reaction.

chem·i·cal weath·er·ing ▶ **n.** the erosion or disintegration of rocks, building materials, etc., caused by chemical reactions (chiefly with water and substances dissolved in it) rather than by mechanical processes.

chemico- ▶ **comb. form** representing CHEMICAL.

chem·i·lum·i·nes·cence /ˌkemiˌlo͞oməˈnesəns/ ▶ **n.** the emission of light during a chemical reaction that does not produce significant quantities of heat.
– DERIVATIVES **chem·i·lum·i·nes·cent** **adj.**

chem·in de fer /SHəˌman də ˈfe(ə)r/ ▶ **n.** a form of the card game baccarat.
– ORIGIN late 19th cent.: French, literally 'railroad.'

che·mise /SHəˈmēz, -ˈmēs/ ▶ **n.** a dress hanging straight from the shoulders and giving the figure a uniform shape, popular in the 1920s. ■ a woman's loose-fitting undergarment or nightdress, typically of silk or satin with a lace trim. ■ a priest's alb or surplice. ■ historical a smock.
– ORIGIN Middle English: from Old French, from late Latin *camisia* 'shirt or nightgown.'

chem·i·sette /ˌSHemiˈzet/ ▶ **n.** a woman's undergarment similar to a camisole, typically worn so as to be visible beneath an open-necked blouse or dress.
– ORIGIN early 19th cent.: French, diminutive of *chemise*.

chem·i·sorp·tion /ˌkemiˈsôrpSHən, -ˈzôrp-/ ▶ **n.** Chemistry adsorption in which the adsorbed substance is held by chemical bonds.
– DERIVATIVES **chem·i·sorbed** /ˈkemiˌsôrbd/ **adj.**
– ORIGIN 1930s: from CHEMI- + a shortened form of ADSORPTION (see ADSORB).

chem·ist /ˈkemist/ (abbr.: **chem.**) ▶ **n. 1** an expert in chemistry; a person engaged in chemical research or experiments.
2 Brit. a drugstore. ■ a pharmacist.
– ORIGIN late Middle English (denoting an alchemist): from French *chimiste*, from modern Latin *chimista*, from *alchimista* 'alchemist,' from *alchimia* (see ALCHEMY).

chem·is·try /ˈkemistrē/ (abbr.: **chem.**) ▶ **n.** (pl. **chemistries**) **1** the branch of science that deals with the identification of the substances of which matter is composed; the investigation of their properties and the ways in which they interact, combine, and change; and the use of these processes to form new substances. ■ the chemical composition and properties of a substance or body: *the chemistry of soil.*
2 the complex emotional or psychological interaction between two people: *their affair was triggered by intense sexual chemistry.*

Chem·nitz /ˈKHemnits/ an industrial city in eastern Germany, on the Chemnitz River; pop. 245,700 (est. 2006). Former name (1953–90) KARL-MARX-STADT.

che·mo /ˈkēmō/ ▶ **n.** informal chemotherapy.

chemo- ▶ **comb. form** representing CHEMICAL. See also CHEMI-.

che·mo·at·tract·ant /ˌkēmōəˈtraktənt, ˌkemō-/ ▶ **n.** Biology a substance that attracts motile cells of a particular type: *a fibroblast chemoattractant.*

che·mo·au·to·troph /ˌkēmōˈôtəˌtrōf, ˌkemō-/ ▶ **n.** Biology an organism, typically a bacterium, that derives energy from the oxidation of inorganic compounds.
– DERIVATIVES **che·mo·au·to·tro·phic** /-ˌôtəˈtrōfik/ **adj.**, **che·mo·au·tot·ro·phy** /-ˈôtəˌtrōfē/ **n.**

che·mo·kine /ˈkēmōˌkīn, ˈkemō-/ ▶ **n.** Physiology any of a class of cytokines with functions that include attracting white blood cells to sites of infection.

che·mo·pro·phy·lax·is /ˌkēmōˌprōfəˈlaksis, ˌkemō-/ ▶ **n.** the use of drugs to prevent disease.
– DERIVATIVES **che·mo·pro·phy·lac·tic** **adj.**

che·mo·re·cep·tor /ˈkēmōriˌseptər/ ▶ **n.** Physiology a sensory cell or organ responsive to chemical stimuli.
– DERIVATIVES **che·mo·re·cep·tion** /-riˈsepSHən/ **n.**

che·mo·sen·so·ry /ˌkēmōˈsensərē/ ▶ **adj.** Physiology (of a sense organ or receptor) responsive to chemical stimuli. ■ of or relating to such organs or their action: *patients with chemosensory impairment.*

che·mo·stat /ˈkēmōˌstat, ˈkemō-/ ▶ **n.** a system in which the chemical composition is kept at a controlled level, esp. for the culture of microorganisms.

che·mo·syn·the·sis /ˌkēmōˈsinTHəsəs, ˌkemō-/ ▶ **n.** Biology the synthesis of organic compounds by bacteria or other living organisms using energy derived from reactions involving inorganic chemicals, typically in the absence of sunlight. Compare with PHOTOSYNTHESIS.
– DERIVATIVES **che·mo·syn·thet·ic** /-sinˈTHetik/ **adj.**

che·mo·tax·is /ˌkēmōˈtaksis, ˌkemō-/ ▶ **n.** Biology movement of a motile cell or organism, or part of one, in a direction corresponding to a gradient of increasing or decreasing concentration of a particular substance.
– DERIVATIVES **che·mo·tac·tic** /-ˈtaktik/ **adj.**

che·mo·ther·a·py /ˌkēmōˈTHerəpē, ˌkemō-/ ▶ **n.** the treatment of disease by the use of chemical substances, esp. the treatment of cancer by cytotoxic and other drugs.
– DERIVATIVES **che·mo·ther·a·pist** /-pist/ **n.**

che·mot·ro·pism /kiˈmätrəˌpizəm/ ▶ **n.** a tropism, esp. of a plant, in response to a particular substance.
– DERIVATIVES **che·mo·trop·ic** /ˌkēmōˈträpik, ˌkemō-, -ˈtrō-/ **adj.**, **che·mo·trop·i·cal·ly** /-ik(ə)lē/ **adv.**

chempaka ▶ **n.** variant spelling of CHAMPAK.

chem·ur·gy /ˈkemərjē/ ▶ **n.** the chemical and industrial use of organic raw materials.
– DERIVATIVES **chem·ur·gic** /kəˈmərjik, ke-/ **adj.**
– ORIGIN 1930s: from CHEMO-, on the pattern of *metallurgy*.

Che·nab /CHəˈnäb/ a river in northern India and Pakistan that rises in the Himalayas and flows through Himachal Pradesh and Jammu and Kashmir to join the Sutlej River in Punjab. It is one of the five rivers that gave Punjab its name.

che·nar ▶ **n.** variant spelling of CHINAR.

Chen-chiang /ˌjən jēˈäNG/ variant of ZHENJIANG.

Cheng·chow /ˈjəNGˈjō/ variant of ZHENGZHOU.

Cheng·du /ˈCHəNGˈdo͞o/ the capital of Sichuan province in western central China; pop. 3,582,000 (est. 2006).

che·nille /SHəˈnēl/ ▶ **n.** a tufted velvety cord or yarn, used for trimming furniture and making carpets and clothing.
– ORIGIN mid 18th cent.: French, literally 'hairy caterpillar.'

Chennai /ˈCHinˌī/ a seaport on the eastern coast of India, capital of Tamil Nadu; pop. 4,590,300 (est. 2009). Former name (until 1995) MADRAS.

Chen·nault /SHəˈnôlt/, Claire Lee (1890–1958), US military pilot and officer. During World War II, he formed the "Flying Tigers," a US volunteer group, to aid China.

cheong·sam /ˈCHÔNGˌsäm/ ▶ **n.** a straight, close-fitting silk dress with a high neck, short sleeves, and a slit skirt, worn traditionally by Chinese and Indonesian women.
– ORIGIN Chinese (Cantonese dialect).

cheongsam

Che·ops /ˈkēˌäps/ (*fl.* early 26th century BC), Egyptian pharaoh of the 4th dynasty; Egyptian name **Khufu**. He commissioned the building of the Great Pyramid at Giza.

cheque ▶ **n.** British spelling of CHECK³.

cheq·uer ▶ **n.** & **v.** British spelling of CHECKER².

cheq·uer·board ▶ **n.** British spelling of CHECKERBOARD.

Cher /SHe(ə)r/ a river in central France that rises in the Massif Central and flows north for 220 miles (350 km) to meet the Loire River near Tours.

Cher·bourg /ˈSHerˌbo͝or(g), ˈSHər-/ a seaport and naval base in Normandy, in northern France; pop. 42,113 (2006).

Che·ren·kov /CHəˈreNGˌkôv, -ˌkôf, -kəf/ (also **Cerenkov**), Pavel (Alekseevich) (1904–90), Soviet physicist. He investigated the effects of high-energy particles and discovered the cause of blue light (now called **Cerenkov radiation**) emitted by radioactive substances underwater. He shared the 1958 Nobel Prize for Physics with Ilja Mikhailovich Frank (1908–90) and Igor Yevgenyevich Tamm (1895–1971).

Che·ren·kov ra·di·a·tion ▶ **n.** variant spelling of **Cerenkov radiation**.

Che·re·po·vets /ˌCHerəpə'v(y)ets/ a city in northwestern Russia, on the Rybinsk Reservoir; pop. 308,000 (est. 2008).

C

cher·i·moy·a /ˌCHerə'moiə, ˌCHir-/ (also **chirimoya**) ▶ **n. 1** a tropical American fruit with a flavor like pineapple and scaly green skin.
2 the small tree that bears this fruit, native to the Andes of Peru and Ecuador. ● *Annona cherimola*, family Annonaceae.
– ORIGIN mid 18th cent.: from Spanish, from Quechua, from *chiri* 'cold or refreshing' + *muya* 'circle.'

cher·ish /'CHeriSH/ ▶ **v.** [with obj.] protect and care for (someone) lovingly: *he cared for me beyond measure and cherished me in his heart.* ■ hold (something) dear: *I cherish the letters she wrote* | (as adj. **cherished**) *cherished possessions.* ■ keep (a hope or ambition) in one's mind: *he had long cherished a secret fantasy about his future.*
– ORIGIN Middle English (in the sense 'treat with affection'): from Old French *cheriss-*, lengthened stem of *cherir*, from *cher* 'dear,' from Latin *carus*.

Cher·kas·sy /CHir'käsē/ Russian for **Cherkasy**.

Cher·ka·sy /CHir'käsē/ a port in central Ukraine, on the Dnieper River; pop. 288,600 (est. 2009). Russian name **Cherkassy**.

Cher·kessk /CHir'k(y)esk/ a city in the Caucasus in southern Russia, capital of the republic of Karachai-Cherkessia; pop 113,000.

Cher·nen·ko /CHə'reNGkō/, Konstantin (Ustinovich) (1911–85), Soviet statesman, general secretary of the Communist Party of the former Soviet Union and president 1984–85. He died after only thirteen months in office and was succeeded by Mikhail Gorbachev.

Cher·ni·gov /CHi(ə)r'n(y)ēgəf/ Russian for **Chernihiv**.

Cher·ni·hiv /CHir'n(y)ēhəf/ a port in northern Ukraine, on the Desna River; pop. 297,800 (est. 2009). Russian name **Chernigov**.

Cher·niv·tsi /ˌCHirnift'sē/ a city in western Ukraine, in the foothills of the Carpathian Mountains, close to the border with Romania; pop. 249,500 (est. 2009). It was part of Romania between 1918 and 1940. Russian name **Chernovtsy**.

Cher·no·byl /CHir'nōbil, CHər'nōbəl/ a town near Kiev in Ukraine where an accident at a nuclear power station in April 1986 resulted in serious radioactive contamination in Ukraine, Belarus, and other parts of Europe.

Cher·no·rech·ye /ˌCHərnə'reCHə/ former name (until 1919) for **Dzerzhinsk**.

cher·no·zem /'CHernəˌZHôm, -ˌzem/ ▶ **n.** Soil Science a fertile black soil rich in humus, with a lighter lime-rich layer beneath. Such soils typically occur in temperate grasslands such as the Russian steppes and North American prairies.
– ORIGIN mid 19th cent.: from Russian, from *chërnyĭ* 'black' + *zemlya* 'earth.'

Cher·o·kee /'CHerəkē/ ▶ **n.** (pl. **same** or **Cherokees**) **1** a member of an American Indian people of the southeastern US, now living on reservations in Oklahoma and North Carolina.
2 the Iroquoian language of this people, which has had its own script since 1820.
▶ **adj.** of or relating to this people or their language.
– ORIGIN from Cherokee *tsaraki*.

Cher·o·kee rose ▶ **n.** a climbing rose with fragrant white flowers, native to China and naturalized in the southern US. ● *Rosa laevigata*, family Rosaceae.

che·root /SHə'ro͞ot/ ▶ **n.** a cigar with both ends open and untapered.
– ORIGIN late 17th cent.: from French *cheroute*, from Tamil *curuṭṭu* 'roll of tobacco.'

cher·ry /'CHerē/ ▶ **n.** (pl. **cherries**) **1** a small, round stone fruit that is typically bright or dark red. See also **maraschino cherry**.
2 (also **cherry tree**) the tree that bears such fruit. ● Genus *Prunus*, family Rosaceae: several species, the edible fruits being derived from the **mazzard** (or **sweet**) **cherry** (*P. avium*) and the **morello** (or **sour**) **cherry** (*P. cerasus*). ■ the wood of this tree. ■ used in names of unrelated plants with similar fruits, e.g., **cornelian cherry**.
3 a bright or deep red color: [as modifier] *her mouth was a bright cherry red.*
4 [in sing.] vulgar slang the hymen, as representing a woman's virginity.
– PHRASES **a bowl of cherries** [usu. with negative] a pleasant or enjoyable situation or experience: *being in the band isn't a bowl of cherries.* **pop someone's cherry** vulgar slang have sexual intercourse with a girl or woman who is a virgin.
– ORIGIN Middle English: from Old Northern French *cherise*, from medieval Latin *ceresia*, based on Greek *kerasos* 'cherry tree, cherry.' The final *-s* was lost because *cherise* was interpreted as plural (compare with **caper**[2] and **pea**).

Cher·ry Hill a township in southwestern New Jersey, southeast of Philadelphia in Pennsylvania; pop. 70,846 (est. 2008).

cher·ry lau·rel ▶ **n.** an evergreen shrub or small tree of the rose family, with leathery leaves, white flowers, and cherrylike fruits, native to the Balkans and widely cultivated. ● *Prunus laurocerasus*, family Rosaceae.

cher·ry-pick ▶ **v. 1** [with obj.] selectively choose (the most beneficial items) from what is available: *the company should buy the whole airline and not just cherry-pick its best assets.*
2 [no obj.] Sports in a game such as basketball, wait near the goal for a pass, which can be converted to an easy score.
– DERIVATIVES **cher·ry-pick·ing n.**

cher·ry pick·er ▶ **n.** informal **1** a hydraulic crane with a railed platform at the end for raising and lowering people, for instance to work on overhead cables.
2 a person who cherry-picks.

cher·ry to·ma·to ▶ **n.** a spherical miniature tomato. The fruit is glossy red, or occasionally yellow, and typically eaten in salad. ● Many varieties, in particular *Lycopersicon lycopersicum cerasiforme*.

Cher·so·nese /'kərsəˌnēz, ˌkərsəˌnēz/ ancient name for the Gallipoli peninsula.
– ORIGIN from Latin *chersonesus*, from Greek *khersonēsos*, from *khersos* 'dry' + *nēsos* 'island.'

chert /CHərt, CHat/ ▶ **n.** a hard, dark, opaque rock composed of silica (chalcedony) with an amorphous or microscopically fine-grained texture. It occurs as nodules (flint) or, less often, in massive beds.
– DERIVATIVES **chert·y adj.**
– ORIGIN late 17th cent. (originally dialect): of unknown origin.

cher·ub /'CHerəb/ ▶ **n.** (pl. **cherubim**) /'CHer(y)əbim/ a winged angelic being described in biblical tradition as attending on God. It is represented in ancient Middle Eastern art as a lion or bull with eagles' wings and a human face, and regarded in traditional Christian angelology as an angel of the second highest order of the ninefold celestial hierarchy. ■ (pl. **cherubim** or **cherubs**) a representation of a cherub in art, depicted as a chubby, healthy-looking child with wings. ■ (pl. **cherubs**) a beautiful or innocent-looking child.
– ORIGIN Old English *cherubin*, ultimately (via Latin and Greek) from Hebrew *kĕrūb*, plural *kĕrūbīm*. A rabbinic folk etymology, which explains the Hebrew singular form as representing Aramaic *kĕ-rabyā* 'like a child,' led to the representation of the cherub as a child.

che·ru·bic /CHə'ro͞obik/ ▶ **adj.** having the childlike innocence or plump prettiness of a cherub: *a round, cherubic face.*
– DERIVATIVES **che·ru·bi·cal·ly** /-bik(ə)lē/ **adv.**

Che·ru·bi·ni /ˌkerōō'bēnē/, (Maria) Luigi (Carlo Zenobio Salvatore) (1760–1842), Italian composer. He is principally known for his church music and operas.

cher·vil /'CHərvəl/ ▶ **n.** a plant of the parsley family, with small white flowers and delicate fernlike leaves that are used as a culinary herb. ● *Anthriscus cerefolium*, family Umbelliferae.
– ORIGIN Old English, from Latin *chaerephylla*, from Greek *khairephullon*.

Ches·a·peake /'CHesəˌpēk/ a port city in central Virginia, in the Hampton Roads area; pop. 220,111 (est. 2008).

Ches·a·peake Bay /'CHesəˌpēk/ a large inlet of the North Atlantic Ocean on the US coast that extends north for 200 miles (320 km) through the states of Virginia and Maryland.

che·sed /'KHesəd/ ▶ **n.** Judaism the attribute of grace, benevolence, or compassion, esp. (in Kabbalism) as one of the sephiroth.
– ORIGIN Hebrew *ḥesed* 'grace, loving kindness.'

Chesh·ire[1] /'CHeSHər, 'CHeSHˌir/ a county in western central England; county town, Chester.

Chesh·ire[2] /'CHeSHər/ (also **Cheshire cheese**) ▶ **n.** a kind of firm crumbly cheese, originally made in Cheshire, England.

Chesh·ire cat ▶ **n.** a cat depicted with a broad fixed grin, as popularized through Lewis Carroll's *Alice's Adventures in Wonderland* (1865).
– ORIGIN late 18th cent.: of unknown origin, but it is said that cheeses made in *Cheshire*, England, used to be marked with the face of a smiling cat.

chess /CHes/ ▶ **n.** a board game of strategic skill for two players, played on a checkered board. Each player begins the game with sixteen pieces that are moved and used to capture opposing pieces according to precise rules. The object is to put the opponent's king under a direct attack from which escape is impossible (*checkmate*).
– ORIGIN Middle English: from Old French *esches*, plural of *eschec* 'a check' (see **check**[1]).

chess·board /'CHesˌbôrd/ ▶ **n.** a square board divided into sixty-four alternating dark and light squares, used for playing chess or checkers.

chessboard and pieces

chess·man /'CHesˌman, -mən/ ▶ **n.** (pl. **chessmen**) a solid figure used as a chess piece.

chess pie ▶ **n.** a type of pie filled with a mixture of eggs, butter, and sugar, to which nuts and fruits may be added.

chess set ▶ **n.** a chessboard and a set of chessmen.

chest /CHest/ ▶ **n. 1** the front surface of a person's or animal's body between the neck and the abdomen. ■ the whole of a person's upper trunk, esp. with reference to physical size: *a 42-inch chest.*
2 a large strong box, typically made of wood and used for storage or shipping: *an oak chest.* ■ a small cabinet for medicines, toiletries, etc.: *the medicine chest.* ■ short for **chest of drawers**. ■ Brit. the treasury or financial resources of some institutions: *the university chest.*
– PHRASES **get something off one's chest** informal say something that one has wanted to say for a long time, resulting in a feeling of relief. **play** (or **keep**) **one's cards close to one's chest** (or **vest**) informal be secretive and cautious about one's intentions.
– DERIVATIVES **chest·ed adj.** [in combination] *a bare-chested youth.*
– ORIGIN Old English *cest, cyst*, related to Dutch *kist* and German *Kiste*, based on Greek *kistē* 'box.'

Ches·ter /'CHestər/ a town in western England, the county town of Cheshire; pop. 80,600 (est. 2009).

Ches·ter·field /'CHestərˌfēld/ a city in eastern Missouri, on the Missouri River, a suburb of St. Louis; pop. 46,064 (est. 2008).

ches·ter·field /'CHestərˌfēld/ ▶ **n. 1** a sofa with padded arms and a back of the same height and curved outward at the top. ■ chiefly Canadian any sofa or couch.
2 a man's plain straight overcoat, typically with a velvet collar.
– ORIGIN mid 19th cent. (sense 2): named after a 19th-cent. Earl of Chesterfield.

Ches·ter·ton /'CHestərtən/, G. K. (1874–1936), English essayist, novelist, and critic; full name *Gilbert Keith Chesterton*. His novels include *The Napoleon of Notting Hill* (1904) and a series of detective stories featuring Father Brown, a priest with a talent for crime detection.

Ches·ter White ▶ **n.** a pig of a prolific white breed with drooping ears, developed in Pennsylvania.

chest freez·er ▶ **n.** a freezer with a hinged lid that opens from the top, rather than a front-opening door.

chest·nut /'CHes(t)ˌnət/ ▶ **n. 1** (also **sweet chestnut**) a glossy brown nut that may be roasted and eaten.
2 (also **chestnut tree**, **sweet chestnut**, or **Spanish chestnut**) the large European tree that produces the edible chestnut, which develops within a bristly case, with serrated leaves and heavy timber. ● *Castanea sativa*, family Fagaceae. ■ (also **American chestnut**) a related tree (*C. dentata*), which succumbed to a fungus bark disease in the early 1900s. Once prolific in the eastern US, very few large specimens survived. ■ (also **Chinese chestnut**) a related tree (*C. mollissima*) native to China and Korea, cultivated elsewhere for its edible nut. The flowers have a putrid odor. ■ short for **horse chestnut**. ■ used in names of trees and

plants that are related to the sweet chestnut or that produce similar nuts, e.g., **water chestnut**.
3 a deep reddish-brown color: [as modifier] *chestnut hair*. ■ a horse of a reddish-brown color, with a brown mane and tail.
4 a small horny patch on the inside of each of a horse's legs.
– PHRASES **an old chestnut** a joke or story that has become tedious because of its age and constant repetition. **pull someone's chestnuts out of the fire** succeed in a hazardous undertaking for someone else's benefit. [with reference to the fable of a monkey using a cat's paw to extract roasting chestnuts from a fire.]
– ORIGIN early 16th cent.: from Old English *chesten* (from Old French *chastaine*, via Latin from Greek *kastanea*) + NUT.

Chest·nut Hill 1 an affluent suburban area west of Boston in Massachusetts, partly in Brookline and partly in Newton.
2 an affluent residential section in northern Philadelphia in Pennsylvania.

chest·nut oak ▶ **n.** a North American oak that has leaves resembling those of the chestnut.
● Genus *Quercus*, family Fagaceae: several species, in particular *Q. montana* (or *Q. prinus*) of the eastern US.

chest of drawers ▶ **n.** a piece of furniture consisting of a set of drawers in a frame, typically used for storing clothes.

chest pro·tec·tor ▶ **n.** Baseball a padded covering worn over the chest by a catcher or umpire as protection against fouled-off or errant pitches.

chest voice ▶ **n.** [in sing.] the lowest register of the voice in singing or speaking.

chest·y /ˈCHestē/ ▶ **adj.** informal **1** (of a woman) having large or prominent breasts.
2 conceited and arrogant.
3 having a lot of mucus in the lungs: *a chesty cough*.
– DERIVATIVES **chest·i·ly** /ˈCHestəlē/ **adv.**, **chest·i·ness n.**

Ches·van variant spelling of HESVAN.

Chet·nik /ˈCHetnik/ ▶ **n.** a member of a Slavic nationalist guerrilla force in the Balkans, esp. one active during World War II.
– ORIGIN early 20th cent.: from Serbian *četnik*, from *četa* 'band, troop.'

che·trum /ˈCHētrəm, ˈCHe-/ ▶ **n.** (pl. **same** or **chetrums**) a monetary unit of Bhutan, equal to one hundredth of a ngultrum.
– ORIGIN Dzongkha.

che·val-de-frise /SHəˈval də ˌfrēz/ ▶ **n. 1** a portable obstacle, consisting of a wooden frame covered with spikes or barbed wire, used by the military to close off a passage or block enemy advancement.
2 shards of glass or spikes set into masonry along the top of a wall.

che·val glass /SHəˈval/ (also **cheval mirror**) ▶ **n.** a tall mirror fitted at its middle to an upright frame so that it can be tilted.
– ORIGIN mid 19th cent.: *cheval* from French, in the sense 'frame.'

chev·a·lier /ˌSHevəˈli(ə)r/ ▶ **n.** historical a knight. ■ a chivalrous man. ■ a member of certain orders of knighthood or of modern French orders such as the Legion of Honor. ■ (**Chevalier**) Brit. historical the title of James and Charles Stuart, pretenders to the British throne.
– ORIGIN late Middle English (denoting a horseman or mounted knight): from Old French, from medieval Latin *caballarius*, from Latin *caballus* 'horse.' Compare with CABALLERO and CAVALIER.

Chev·i·ot /ˈSHevēət/ ▶ **n.** a sheep of a breed with short thick wool. ■ (**cheviot**) the wool or tweed cloth obtained from this breed.

Chev·i·ot Hills /ˈCHēvēət, ˈCHev-, ˈCHiv-, ˈSHev-/ (also **the Cheviots**) a range of hills on the border between England and Scotland.

chev·on /ˈSHevən/ ▶ **n.** the flesh of goats as food; goat meat: *the entree was crisp-on-the-outside, succulent-inside haunch of spring chevon*.
– ORIGIN from French *chèvre*, 'goat,' on the pattern of *mutton*.

chè·vre /ˈSHev(rə)/ ▶ **n.** cheese made with goat's milk.
– ORIGIN French, literally 'goat, she-goat,' from Latin *capra*.

chev·ron /ˈSHevrən/ ▶ **n.** a line or stripe in the shape of a V or an inverted V, esp. one on the sleeve of a uniform indicating rank or length of service. ■ Heraldry an ordinary in the form of a broad inverted V-shape.
– ORIGIN late Middle English (in heraldic use): from Old French, based on Latin *caper* 'goat'; compare with Latin *capreoli* (diminutive of *caper*) used to mean 'pair of rafters.'

chevron

chev·ro·tain /ˈSHevrəˌtān/ ▶ **n.** a small deerlike mammal with short tusks, typically nocturnal and found in the tropical rain forests of Africa and southern Asia. Also called MOUSE DEER. ● Family Tragulidae: genera *Moschiola* (one Asian species), *Tragulus* (two Asian species), and *Hyemoschus* (one African species).
– ORIGIN late 18th cent.: from French, diminutive of Old French *chevrot*, diminutive of *chèvre* 'goat.'

Chev·y /ˈSHevē/ ▶ **n.** (pl. **chevys**) informal a Chevrolet car.

chev·y /ˈCHivē/ ▶ **v.** variant spelling of CHIVVY.

Chevy Chase /ˈCHevē ˈCHās/ a fashionable suburb north of Washington, DC, in Montgomery County in Maryland; pop. 9,381 (2000).

chew /CHo͞o/ ▶ **v.** [with obj.] bite and work (food) in the mouth with the teeth, esp. to make it easier to swallow: *he was chewing a mouthful of toast* | [no obj.] *he chewed for a moment, then swallowed*. ■ gnaw at (something) persistently, typically as a result of worry or anxiety: *he chewed his lip reflectively* | [no obj.] *she chewed at a fingernail*.
▶ **n.** a repeated biting or gnawing of something. ■ something other than food that is meant for chewing: *a dog chew* | *a chew of tobacco*.
– PHRASES **chew the cud** see CUD. **chew the fat** (or **rag**) informal chat in a leisurely way, esp. at length.
– PHRASAL VERBS **chew someone out** informal reprimand someone severely: *he chewed me out for being late*. **chew something over** discuss or consider something at length: *executives met to chew over the company's future*. **chew something up** chew food until it is soft or in small pieces. ■ damage or destroy something as if by chewing: *the bikes were chewing up the paths*.
– DERIVATIVES **chew·a·ble adj.**, **chew·er n.** [usu. in combination] *a tobacco-chewer*.
– ORIGIN Old English *cēowan*; related to Dutch *kauwen* and German *kauen*.

chew·ing gum ▶ **n.** flavored gum for chewing, typically sold in packets of individually wrapped thin strips.

chew·y /ˈCHo͞oē/ ▶ **adj.** (**chewier**, **chewiest**) (of food) needing to be chewed hard or for some time: *the bread was never quite fresh, always pretty chewy*.
– DERIVATIVES **chew·i·ness n.**

Chey·enne[1] /SHīˈan, SHīˈen/ the capital of Wyoming, in the southeastern part of the state; pop. 56,915 (est. 2008).

Chey·enne[2] ▶ **n.** (pl. **same** or **Cheyennes**) **1** a member of an American Indian people formerly living between the Missouri and Arkansas rivers but now on reservations in Montana and Oklahoma.
2 the Algonquian language of this people.
▶ **adj.** of or relating to the Cheyenne or their language.
– ORIGIN Canadian French, from Dakota *šahíyena*, 'little Cree.'

Chey·enne Riv·er a river that flows for 530 miles (850 km) from northeastern Wyoming into western South Dakota to join the Missouri River at Lake Oahe.

Cheyne–Stokes breath·ing /ˈCHān ˈstōks ˈbrēT͟HiNG, ˈCHānē/ ▶ **n.** Medicine a cyclical pattern of breathing in which movement gradually decreases to a complete stop and then returns to normal. It occurs in various medical conditions, and at high altitudes.
– ORIGIN late 19th cent.: named after John *Cheyne* (1777–1836), Scottish physician, and William *Stokes* (1804–78), Irish physician.

chez /SHā/ ▶ **prep.** at the home of (used in imitation of French, often humorously): *I spent one summer chez Grandma*.
– ORIGIN mid 18th cent.: French, from Old French *chiese*, from Latin *casa* 'cottage.'

chi[1] /kī/ ▶ **n.** the twenty-second letter of the Greek alphabet (Χ, χ), transliterated in the traditional Latin style as 'ch' (as in *Christ*) or in the modern style as 'kh' (as in *Khaniá* and in the etymologies of this dictionary). ■ (**Chi**) [followed by Latin genitive] Astronomy the twenty-second star in a constellation: *Chi Ophiuchi*.

chi[2] /CHē/ (also **qi** or **ki**) ▶ **n.** variant spelling of QI.

chi·a /ˈCHēə/ ▶ **n.** a plant of the mint family with clusters of small two-lipped purple flowers. Chia is common throughout California and the Great Basin.
● *Salvia columbariae*, family Labiatae.

Chiang Kai-shek /ˌCHANG ˌkīˈSHek/ (also **Jiang Jie Shi** /jēˈäNG jēˈe ˈSHē/) (1887–1975), Chinese statesman and general; president of China 1928–31 and 1943–49, and of Taiwan 1950–75. He tried to unite China by military means in the 1930s but was defeated by the Communists. Forced to abandon mainland China in 1949, he set up a separate Nationalist Chinese State in Taiwan.

Chiang Kai-shek

Chiang·mai /tSHēˌäNGˈmī/ a city in northwestern Thailand; pop. 148,800 (est. 2007).

Chi·a·ni·na /ˌkēəˈnēnə/ ▶ **n.** an animal of a large white breed of cattle, raised for its lean meat.
– ORIGIN from Italian.

Chi·an·ti /kēˈäntē, -ˈantē/ (also **chianti**) ▶ **n.** (pl. **Chiantis**) a dry red wine, originally produced in Tuscany, Italy.
– ORIGIN named after the *Chianti* Mountains, Italy.

Chi·a·pas /CHēˈäpəs, ˈCHäpəs/ a state in southern Mexico that borders on Guatemala; capital, Tuxtla Gutiérrez.

chi·a·ro·scu·ro /kēˌärəˈsk(y)o͝orō, kēˌarə-/ ▶ **n.** the treatment of light and shade in drawing and painting. ■ an effect of contrasted light and shadow created by light falling unevenly or from a particular direction on something: *the chiaroscuro of cobbled streets*.
– ORIGIN mid 17th cent.: from Italian, from *chiaro* 'clear, bright' (from Latin *clarus*) + *oscuro* 'dark, obscure' (from Latin *obscurus*).

chi·as·ma /kīˈazmə/ ▶ **n.** (pl. **chiasmata** /-mətə/) Biology a point at which paired chromosomes remain in contact during the first metaphase of meiosis, and at which crossing over and exchange of genetic material occur between the strands. See also OPTIC CHIASMA.
– ORIGIN mid 19th cent.: modern Latin, from Greek *chiasma* 'crosspiece, cross-shaped mark,' from *khiazein* 'mark with the letter chi.'

chi·as·mus /kīˈazməs/ ▶ **n.** a rhetorical or literary figure in which words, grammatical constructions, or concepts are repeated in reverse order, in the same or a modified form; e.g. 'Poetry is the record of the best and happiest moments of the happiest and best minds.'
– DERIVATIVES **chi·as·tic** /kīˈastik/ **adj.**
– ORIGIN mid 17th cent. (in the general sense 'crosswise arrangement'): modern Latin, from Greek *khiasmos* 'crosswise arrangement,' from *khiazein* 'mark with the letter chi,' from *khi* 'chi.'

chi·as·to·lite /kīˈastəˌlīt/ ▶ **n.** a form of the mineral andalusite containing carbonaceous inclusions that cause some sections of the mineral to show the figure of a cross.
– ORIGIN early 19th cent.: from Greek *khiastos* 'arranged crosswise' + -LITE.

Chi·ba /ˈCHēbə/ a city in Japan, on the island of Honshu, east of Tokyo; pop. 910,142 (2007).

Chib·cha /ˈCHibCHä/ ▶ **n.** (pl. **same**) **1** a member of an indigenous people of Colombia whose well-developed political structure was destroyed by Europeans.
2 the Chibchan language of this people.
▶ **adj.** of or relating to the Chibcha or their language.
– ORIGIN American Spanish, from Chibcha *zipa* 'chief, hereditary leader.'

Chib·chan /ˈCHibCHən/ ▶ **n.** a language family of Colombia and Central America, most members of which are extinct or nearly so.

▶ **adj.** of or relating to this language family.

chi·bouk /CHə'bo͝ok, SHə-/ (also **chibouque**) ▶ **n.** a long Turkish tobacco pipe.
– ORIGIN early 19th cent.: French *chibouque*, from Turkish *çubuk*, literally 'tube.'

chic /SHēk/ ▶ **adj.** (**chicer**, **chicest**) elegantly and stylishly fashionable.
▶ **n.** stylishness and elegance, typically of a specified kind: *French chic | biker chic.*
– DERIVATIVES **chic·ly adv.**
– ORIGIN mid 19th cent.: from French, probably from German *Schick* 'skill.'

C

Chi·ca·go /SHi'kôgō, -'kägō/ a city in northeastern Illinois, on Lake Michigan; pop. 2,853,114 (est. 2008). Chicago developed during the 19th century as a major grain market and food-processing center.
– DERIVATIVES **Chi·ca·go·an** /-'kôgō-ən, -'käg-/ **n. & adj.**

Chi·ca·go Board of Trade ▶ **n.** see BOARD OF TRADE (sense 1).

Chi·ca·go·land /SHi'kägō,land/ ▶ **n.** Chicago and its suburbs, considered as a unit: [often as modifier] *a thoughtful unpretentious matchmaking service for Chicagoland singles.*

Chi·ca·na /CHi'känə, SHi-/ ▶ **n.** (in North America) a girl or woman of Mexican origin or descent.
– ORIGIN Mexican Spanish, alteration of Spanish *mejicana* (feminine) 'Mexican.'

> **USAGE** See usage at **CHICANO**.

chi·cane /SHi'kān, CHi-/ ▶ **n.** **1** an artificial narrowing or turn on a road or auto-racing course. **2** dated (in card games) a hand without cards of one particular suit; a void. **3** archaic chicanery.
▶ **v.** archaic employ trickery or chicanery. ■ [with obj.] deceive or trick (someone).
– ORIGIN late 17th cent. (in the senses 'chicanery' and 'use chicanery'): from French *chicane* (noun), *chicaner* (verb) 'quibble,' of unknown origin.

chi·can·er·y /SHi'kānərē, CHi-/ ▶ **n.** the use of trickery to achieve a political, financial, or legal purpose: *an underhanded person who schemes corruption and political chicanery behind closed doors.*
– ORIGIN late 16th cent.: from French *chicanerie*, from *chicaner* 'to quibble' (see CHICANE).

Chi·ca·no /CHi'känō, SHi-/ ▶ **n.** (pl. **Chicanos**) (in North America) a person, esp. male, of Mexican origin or descent. See also **CHICANA**.
– ORIGIN Mexican Spanish, alteration of Spanish *mejicano* (masculine) 'Mexican.'

> **USAGE** The term **Chicano** (derived from Mexican Spanish), and the feminine form **Chicana**, became current in the early 1960s, first used by politically active groups. **Chicano** and **Chicana** are still in frequent use and have become less politicized. However, Mexican-Americans with less militant political views might find the terms offensive. **Hispanic** is a more generic term denoting persons in the US of Latin-American or Spanish descent. See also usage at **HISPANIC**.

chi·cha·rron /,CHēCHə'rōn/ ▶ **n.** (pl. **chicharrones** /-'rōnēz/) (in Mexican cooking) a piece of fried pork crackling.
– ORIGIN from American Spanish *chicharrón*.

Chi·chén It·zá /CHi,CHen 'itsä/ a site in northern Yucatán, Mexico, the center of the Mayan empire after AD 918 until about 1200. Its pyramids, temples, and other structures have been partly restored.

Chi·ches·ter /'CHiCHəstər/, Sir Francis (Charles) (1901–72), English sailor. He was the first person to sail alone around the world 1966–67 with only one stop.

Chi·che·wa /CHi'CHäwə/ ▶ **n.** another term for **NYANJA** (the language).

chi·chi[1] /'SHēSHē, 'CHēCHē/ ▶ **adj.** attempting stylish elegance but achieving only an overelaborate pretentiousness: *the chichi world of Manhattan cultural privilege.*
▶ **n.** pretentious and overelaborate refinement: *the relentless chichi of late-eighties dining.*
– ORIGIN early 20th cent. (in the sense 'showiness or pretentious object'): from French, of imitative origin.

chi·chi[2] /'CHē,CHē/ ▶ **n.** informal a woman's breast.
– ORIGIN late 20th cent.: military slang, of Japanese origin.

Chi·chi·mec /'CHēCHə,mek/ ▶ **n.** (pl. **same** or **Chichimecs**) **1** a member of a group of indigenous peoples, including the Toltecs and the Aztecs, dominant in central Mexico from the 10th to the 16th centuries. **2** the Uto-Aztecan language of these peoples.
– ORIGIN Spanish, from Nahuatl.

chick /CHik/ ▶ **n.** **1** a young bird, esp. one newly hatched. ■ a newly hatched domestic fowl. **2** informal a young woman: *she's a great-looking chick.*
– PHRASES **neither chick nor child** dialect no children at all.
– ORIGIN Middle English: abbreviation of **CHICKEN**.

chick·a·dee /'CHikədē/ ▶ **n.** a North American titmouse, in particular: the **black-capped chickadee** (*Parus atricapillus*), with distinctive black cap and throat, and the similar but smaller **Carolina chickadee** (*P. carolinensis*).
– ORIGIN mid 19th cent.: imitative of its call.

black-capped chickadee

Chick·a·mau·ga Creek /,CHikə'môgə/ a stream that flows from northwestern Georgia into the Tennessee River, near Chattanooga in Tennessee. A brutal Civil War battle was fought along it in September 1863.

chick·a·ree /'CHikə,rē/ ▶ **n.** a squirrel with red fur, found in the coniferous forests of North America.
● Genus *Tamiasciurus*, family Sciuridae: three species, including the American red squirrel (*T. hudsonicus*).
– ORIGIN early 19th cent.: imitative of its call.

Chick·a·saw /'CHikə,sô/ ▶ **n.** (pl. **same** or **Chickasaws**) **1** a member of an American Indian people formerly resident in Mississippi and Alabama, and now in Oklahoma. **2** the Muskogean language of this people.
▶ **adj.** of or relating to this people or their language.
– ORIGIN the name in Chickasaw.

chick·ee /CHi'kē, 'CHikē/ ▶ **n.** a rough, open structure consisting of palm or palmetto thatching on a log frame with a raised floor, adapted for beach use from the original Seminole design.

chick·en /'CHikən/ ▶ **n.** **1** a domestic fowl kept for its eggs or meat, esp. a young one. ■ meat from such a bird: *roast chicken.* **2** informal a game in which the first person to lose nerve and withdraw from a dangerous situation is the loser. ■ a coward. **3** informal (among homosexuals) an adolescent male.
▶ **adj.** [predic.] informal cowardly: *they were too chicken to follow the murderers into the mountains.*
▶ **v.** [no obj.] (**chicken out**) informal withdraw from or fail in something through lack of nerve: *the referee **chickened out of** giving a penalty.*
– PHRASES **don't count your chickens before they're hatched** see COUNT[1].
– ORIGIN Old English *cicen*, *cycen*, of Germanic origin; related to Dutch *kieken* and German *Küchlein*, and probably also to COCK[1].

chick·en à la king ▶ **n.** cooked breast of chicken in a cream sauce with mushrooms and peppers.
– ORIGIN said to be named after E. Clark *King*, proprietor of a New York hotel.

chick·en-and-egg ▶ **adj.** [attrib.] denoting a situation in which each of two things appears to be necessary to the other, making it impossible to say which came first.

chick·en breast ▶ **n.** Medicine another term for **PIGEON BREAST**.
– DERIVATIVES **chick·en-breast·ed** (also **chicken-chested**) **adj.**

chick·en feed ▶ **n.** food for poultry. ■ informal an insignificant amount of money: *the pay was chicken feed for the work I put in.*

chick·en-fried steak ▶ **n.** a thin piece of beef that is lightly battered and fried until crisp.

chick·en hawk (also **chickenhawk**) ▶ **n.** a hawk of a type that is reputed to prey on domestic fowl. ■ informal a person who speaks out in support of war, yet has avoided active military service. ■ informal an older man who seeks younger men or boys as sexual partners.

chick·en-heart·ed (also **chicken-livered**) ▶ **adj.** easily frightened; cowardly.

Chick·en Lit·tle ▶ **n.** an alarmist or doomsayer: *my beloved capital sounds more and more these days like a barnyard filled with Chicken Littles.*
– ORIGIN 1990s: from the name of a character in a children's story who repeatedly warns that the sky is falling.

chick·en·pox /'CHikən,päks/ (also **chicken pox**) ▶ **n.** an infectious disease causing a mild fever and a rash of itchy inflamed blisters. It is caused by the herpes zoster virus and mainly affects children, who are afterward usually immune. Also called **VARICELLA**.
– ORIGIN early 18th cent.: probably so named because of its mildness, as compared to smallpox.

chick·en·shit /'CHikən,SHit/ vulgar slang ▶ **adj.** worthless or contemptible (used as a general term of deprecation): *no more chickenshit excuses.* ■ cowardly.
▶ **n.** a worthless or contemptible person. ■ something worthless or petty: *names are chickenshit; they didn't need any names.*

chick·en wire ▶ **n.** light wire netting with a hexagonal mesh.

chick flick ▶ **n.** informal a movie that appeals mainly to women.

chick·ling pea /'CHikliNG/ (also **chickling vetch**) ▶ **n.** another term for **GRASS PEA**.
– ORIGIN mid 16th cent.: based on obsolete *chich* 'chickpea.'

chick lit ▶ **n.** informal, chiefly derogatory literature that appeals mainly to women.

chick·pea /'CHik,pē/ ▶ **n.** **1** a round yellowish seed, used widely as food. Also called **GARBANZO**. **2** the leguminous Old World plant that bears these seeds. ● *Cicer arietinum*, family Leguminosae.
– ORIGIN early 18th cent. (earlier as *chiche-pease*): from late Middle English *chiche* (from Old French *chiche*, *cice*, from Latin *cicer* 'chickpea') + **PEASE**.

chick·weed /'CHik,wēd/ ▶ **n.** a small plant of the pink family with deeply cleft white petals, often growing as a garden weed and sometimes eaten by poultry. ● *Stellaria*, *Cerastium*, and other genera, family Caryophyllaceae: several species, including **common chickweed** (*S. media*), with smooth leaves and stems, and **mouse-ear chickweed** (*C. vulgatum*), with hairy leaves and stems.

chic·le /'CHikəl, 'CHiklē/ ▶ **n.** the milky latex of the sapodilla tree, used to make chewing gum. ■ another term for **SAPODILLA**.
– ORIGIN via Latin American Spanish, from Nahuatl *tzictli*.

Chi·co /'CHēkō/ a city in northern California, at the north end of the Sacramento Valley; pop. 83,791 (est. 2008).

Chic·o·pee /'CHikə,pē/ a city in south central Massachusetts, an industrial center on the northern side of Springfield; pop. 54,941 (est. 2008).

chic·o·ry /'CHikərē/ ▶ **n.** (pl. **chicories**) **1** a blue-flowered Mediterranean plant of the daisy family, cultivated for its edible salad leaves and carrot-shaped root. ● *Cichorium intybus*, family Compositae. ■ the root of this plant, which is roasted and ground for use as an additive to or substitute for coffee. **2** another term for **ENDIVE**.
– ORIGIN late Middle English: from obsolete French *cicorée* (earlier form of *chicorée*) 'endive,' via Latin from Greek *kikhorion*.

chicory 1

chide /CHīd/ ▶ **v.** (past **chided** or archaic **chid** /CHid/; past participle **chided** or archaic **chidden** /'CHidn/) [with obj.] scold or rebuke: *she chided him for not replying to her letters* | [with direct speech] *"You mustn't speak like that," she chided gently.*
– DERIVATIVES **chid·er n.**, **chid·ing·ly adv.**
– ORIGIN Old English *cīdan*, of unknown origin.

chief /CHēf/ ▶ **n.** **1** a leader or ruler of a people or clan: *the chief of the village | the Tlingit chief* | [as title] *an island where Chief Seattle was born.* ■ the person with the highest rank in an organization: *a bureau chief | the chief of police.* ■ an informal form of address, esp. to someone of superior rank or status: *it's quite simple, chief.* **2** Heraldry an ordinary consisting of a broad horizontal band across the top of the shield. ■ the upper third of the field.
▶ **adj.** most important: *the chief reason for the spending cuts | chief among her concerns is working alone at night.* ■ having or denoting the highest rank or authority: *the government's chief adviser.*
– PHRASES **chief cook and bottle-washer** informal a person who performs a variety of important but routine tasks. **in chief** Heraldry at the top; in the upper part. **too many chiefs and not enough Indians** too many people giving orders and not enough people to carry them out.
– DERIVATIVES **chief·dom** /-dəm/ **n.**, **chief·ship** /-,SHip/ **n.**
– ORIGIN Middle English: from Old French *chief*, *chef*, based on Latin *caput* 'head.'

chief jus·tice ▶ **n.** (the title of) the presiding judge in a supreme court. ■ (**Chief Justice of the United States**) (the formal title of) the chief justice of the US Supreme Court.

chief·ly /ˈCHēflē/ ▶ **adv.** above all; mainly: *he is remembered chiefly for his sonatas.* ■ for the most part; mostly: *this group has consisted chiefly of conservatives.*

chief mas·ter ser·geant ▶ **n.** a noncommissioned officer in the US Air Force ranking above senior master sergeant and below warrant officer.

chief of staff ▶ **n.** the senior staff officer of a service or command.

chief of state ▶ **n.** the titular head of a nation as distinct from the head of the government.

chief pet·ty of·fi·cer ▶ **n.** a senior noncommissioned officer in a navy, in particular an NCO in the US Navy or Coast Guard ranking above petty officer and below senior chief petty officer.

chief rab·bi ▶ **n.** (in the UK and some other countries) the preeminent rabbi of a national Jewish community.

chief·tain /ˈCHēftən/ ▶ **n.** the leader of a people or clan. ■ informal a powerful member of an organization.
– DERIVATIVES **chief·tain·cy** /-sē/ **n.** (pl. **chief·tain·cies**), **chief·tain·ship** /-ˌSHip/ **n.**
– ORIGIN Middle English and Old French *chevetaine*, from late Latin *capitaneus* (see CAPTAIN). The spelling was altered by association with CHIEF.

chief war·rant of·fi·cer ▶ **n.** a member of the US armed forces ranking above warrant officer and below the lowest-ranking commissioned officer.

chiff·chaff /ˈCHifˌCHaf/ ▶ **n.** a migratory Eurasian and North African leaf warbler with drab plumage. ● Genus *Phylloscopus*, family Sylviidae: two species, in particular the common *P. collybita*.
– ORIGIN late 18th cent.: imitative of its call.

chif·fon /SHiˈfän, ˈSHifˌän/ ▶ **n.** a light, sheer fabric typically made of silk or nylon: [as modifier] *a chiffon blouse.* ■ [as modifier] (of a cake or dessert) made with beaten egg whites to give a light consistency: *chiffon cake.*
– ORIGIN mid 18th cent. (originally plural, denoting trimmings or ornaments on a woman's dress): from French, from *chiffe* 'rag.'

chif·fo·nade /ˌSHifəˈnäd, -ˈnäd/ (also **chiffonnade**) ▶ **n.** a preparation of shredded or finely cut leaf vegetables, used as a garnish for soup.
– ORIGIN French, from *chiffonner* 'to crumple.'

chif·fo·nier /ˌSHifəˈni(ə)r/ ▶ **n. 1** a tall chest of drawers, often with a mirror on top.
2 Brit. a low cupboard, sometimes with a raised bookshelf on top.
– ORIGIN mid 18th cent.: from French *chiffonnier*, *chiffonnière*, literally 'ragpicker,' also denoting a chest of drawers for odds and ends.

chif·fo·robe /ˈSHifəˌrōb/ ▶ **n.** a piece of furniture with drawers on one side and hanging space on the other.
– ORIGIN early 20th cent.: blend of CHIFFONIER and WARDROBE.

chig·ger /ˈCHigər/ (also **jigger**) ▶ **n. 1** a tiny mite whose parasitic larvae live on or under the skin of warm-blooded animals, where they cause irritation and dermatitis and sometimes transmit scrub typhus. Also called HARVEST MITE. ● Genus *Trombicula*, family Trombiculidae: many species.
2 another term for CHIGOE.
– ORIGIN mid 18th cent.: variant of CHIGOE.

chigger 1

chi·gnon /ˈSHēnˌyän, SHēnˈyän/ ▶ **n.** a knot or coil of hair arranged on the back of a woman's head.
– ORIGIN late 18th cent.: from French, originally 'nape of the neck,' based on Latin *catena* 'chain.'

chig·oe /ˈCHigō, ˈCHē-/ ▶ **n.** a tropical flea, the female of which burrows and lays eggs beneath the host's skin, causing painful sores. Also called CHIGGER, SAND FLEA. ● *Tunga penetrans*, family Tungidae.
– ORIGIN mid 17th cent.: from French *chique*, from a West African language.

Chih·li, Gulf of /ˈjirˈlē, ˈCHēˈlē/ another name for BO HAI.

Chi·hua·hua /CHəˈwäwə, SHə-/ a state in northern Mexico. ■ its capital, the principal city of northern central Mexico; pop. 748,518 (2005).

chi·hua·hua /CHəˈwäwä, SHə-, -wə/ ▶ **n.** a small dog of a smooth-haired, large-eyed breed originating in Mexico.
– ORIGIN early 19th cent.: named after CHIHUAHUA.

chi·la·qui·les /ˌCHēläˈkēläs/ ▶ **n.** (in Mexican cooking) a dish of fried tortilla strips typically topped with a spicy tomato sauce and cheese.
– ORIGIN from Nahuatl.

chil·blain /ˈCHilˌblān/ ▶ **n.** a painful, itching swelling on the skin, typically on a hand or foot, caused by poor circulation in the skin when exposed to cold.
– DERIVATIVES **chil·blained adj.**
– ORIGIN mid 16th cent.: from CHILL + BLAIN.

Child[1] /CHīld/, Julia (1912–2004), US chef and cookbook author. Her cookbooks, beginning with *Mastering the Art of French Cooking* (written in 1961 with Simone Beck and Louisette Bertholle), and her television cooking show *The French Chef*, which began on PBS in 1963, revolutionized American cooking.

Child[2] /CHīld/, Lydia Marie (1802–80), US abolitionist and writer; born *Lydia Marie Francis*. She was editor of the National Anti-Slavery Standard 1841–43 and the author of novels, children's books, and the poem "Thanksgiving Day," which begins "Over the river and through the woods."

child /CHīld/ ▶ **n.** (pl. **children** /ˈCHildrən/) a young human being below the age of puberty or below the legal age of majority. ■ a son or daughter of any age. ■ an immature or irresponsible person: *she's such a child!* ■ a person who has little or no experience in a particular area: *he's a child in financial matters.* ■ (**children**) the descendants of a family or people: *the children of Abraham.* ■ (**child of**) a person or thing influenced by a specified environment: *a child of the sixties* | *OPEC was in a sense a child of the Cold War.*
– PHRASES **child's play** a task that is easily accomplished. **from a child** since childhood. **with child** formal pregnant.
– DERIVATIVES **child·less adj.**, **child·less·ness n.**
– ORIGIN Old English *cild*, of Germanic origin. The Middle English plural *childer* or *childre* became *childeren* or *children* by association with plurals ending in *-en*, such as *brethren*.

child a·buse ▶ **n.** physical maltreatment or sexual molestation of a child.

child·bear·ing /ˈCHīldˌbe(ə)riNG/ ▶ **n.** the process of giving birth to children: [as modifier] *women of childbearing age.*

child·bed /ˈCHīldˌbed/ ▶ **n.** archaic term for CHILDBIRTH.

child·bed fe·ver ▶ **n.** another term for PUERPERAL FEVER.

child·birth /ˈCHīldˌbərTH/ ▶ **n.** the action of giving birth to a child: *she died in childbirth.*

child care ▶ **n.** the action or skill of looking after children. ■ the care of children by a day-care center, babysitter, or other provider while parents are working.

child-cen·tered ▶ **adj.** giving priority to the interests and needs of children: *child-centered teaching methods.*

Childe /CHīld/ ▶ **n.** [in names] archaic or literary a youth of noble birth: *Childe Harold.*
– ORIGIN late Old English, variant of CHILD.

Chil·der·mas /ˈCHildərˌmas/ ▶ **n.** archaic the feast of the Holy Innocents, December 28.
– ORIGIN Old English *cildramæsse*, from *cildra* 'of children,' genitive plural of *cild* (see CHILD) + *mæsse* (see MASS).

child·free /ˈCHīldˈfrē/ ▶ **adj.** pertaining to adults who do not have or live with children: *I'm interested in finding a childfree computer geek-girl with a worldview similar to mine.*

child·hood /ˈCHīldˌho͝od/ ▶ **n.** the state of being a child: *the idealized world of childhood.* ■ the period during which a person is a child: *she spent her childhood in Pennsylvania* | [as modifier] *a childhood friend.*
– ORIGIN Old English *cildhād* (see CHILD, -HOOD).

child·ish /ˈCHīldiSH/ ▶ **adj.** of, like, or appropriate to a child: *childish enthusiasm.* ■ silly and immature: *a childish outburst.*
– DERIVATIVES **child·ish·ly adv.**, **child·ish·ness n.**

child la·bor ▶ **n.** the use of children in industry or business, esp. when illegal or considered inhumane.

child·like /ˈCHīldˌlīk/ ▶ **adj.** (of an adult) having good qualities associated with a child: *she speaks with a childlike directness.*

child·mind·er /ˈCHīldˌmīndər/ ▶ **n.** Brit. a child-care worker or babysitter.
– DERIVATIVES **child·mind·ing n.**

child·proof /ˈCHīldˌpro͞of/ ▶ **adj.** designed to prevent children from injuring themselves or doing damage: *disinfectants that are fitted with childproof caps.*
▶ **v.** [with obj.] make inaccessible to children: *childproof those cabinets with safety latches.*

child·rear·ing /ˈCHīldˌri(ə)riNG/ ▶ **n.** the process of bringing up a child or children: *modern ideas about childrearing* | [as modifier] *childrearing costs.*

chil·dren /ˈCHildrən/ plural form of CHILD.

chil·dren of Is·ra·el see ISRAEL[1] (sense 1).

Chil·dren's Cru·sade a crusade to the Holy Land in 1212 by tens of thousands of children, chiefly from France and Germany. Most of the children never reached their destination, and were sold into slavery.

child re·straint ▶ **n.** a device used to control and protect a child in a motor vehicle.

child sup·port ▶ **n.** court-ordered payments, typically made by a noncustodial divorced parent, to support one's minor child or children.

Chil·e /ˈCHilē/ a country in South America that occupies a long coastal strip that runs down the western coast of Bolivia and Argentina, on the Pacific Ocean; pop. 16,601,700 (est. 2009); capital, Santiago; official language, Spanish.

> Most of Chile was part of the Inca empire and became part of Spanish Peru after Pizarro's conquest. Independence was achieved in 1818 with help from Argentina. After the overthrow of the Marxist democrat Salvador Allende in 1973, Chile was ruled by the right-wing military dictatorship of General Pinochet until a democratically elected president took office in 1990.

– DERIVATIVES **Chil·e·an** /ˈCHilēən, CHəˈlāən/ **adj. & n.**

chil·e[1] /ˈCHilē/ ▶ **n.** variant spelling of CHILI.

chile[2] /CHīl/ ▶ **n.** nonstandard spelling of CHILD, used in representing chiefly southern US dialect: *where you been, honey chile?*

Chil·e·an sea bass /bas/ ▶ **n.** see PATAGONIAN TOOTHFISH.

Chil·e·an wine palm ▶ **n.** another term for COQUITO.

chil·e re·lle·no /rə(l)ˈyānō/ ▶ **n.** (pl. **chiles rellenos**) (in Mexican cuisine) a stuffed chili pepper, typically battered and deep-fried.
– ORIGIN early 20th cent.: Spanish, literally 'stuffed chili.'

Chil·e salt·pe·ter ▶ **n.** another term for SODIUM NITRATE, esp. as a commercial product mined in Chile and other arid parts of the world.

chil·i /ˈCHilē/ (also **chili pepper** or **chile** or Brit. **chilli**) ▶ **n.** (pl. **chilies** or **chiles** or Brit. **chillies**) a small hot-tasting pod of a variety of capsicum, used chopped (and often dried) in sauces, relishes, and spice powders. There are various forms with pods of differing size, color, and strength of flavor, such as cascabels and jalapeños. ● *Capsicum annuum* var. *annuum*, 'longum' group (or var. *longum*). ■ short for CHILI POWDER. ■ short for CHILI CON CARNE.
– ORIGIN early 17th cent.: from Spanish *chile*, from Nahuatl *chilli*.

chil·i·ast /ˈkilēˌast/ ▶ **n.** another term for MILLENARIAN.
– DERIVATIVES **chil·i·asm** /-ˌazəm/ **n.**, **chil·i·as·tic** /ˌkilēˈastik/ **adj.**
– ORIGIN late 16th cent.: via late Latin from Greek *khiliastēs*, from *khilias* 'a thousand years,' from *khilioi* 'thousand.'

chil·i·burg·er /ˈCHilēˌbərgər/ ▶ **n.** a hamburger with a topping of chili con carne.

chil·i con car·ne /kän ˈkärnē, kən/ ▶ **n.** a spicy stew of beef and red chilies or chili powder, often with beans and tomatoes.
– ORIGIN mid 19th cent.: from Spanish *chile con carne*, literally 'chili pepper with meat.'

chil·i dog ▶ **n.** a hot dog garnished with chili con carne.

chil·i pow·der ▶ **n.** a hot-tasting mixture of ground dried red chilies and other spices.

chil·i sauce ▶ **n.** a hot sauce made with tomatoes, chilies, and spices.

chill /CHil/ ▶ **n. 1** an unpleasant feeling of coldness in the atmosphere, one's surroundings, or the body: *there was a chill in the air* | *the disease begins with chills, headaches, and dizziness.* ■ a feverish cold: *we had better return before you catch a chill.* ■ a coldness of manner: *a chill in relations.* ■ a depressing influence: *his statements have **cast a chill** over this whole country.* ■ a sudden and powerful feeling of fear: *a chill ran down my spine.*
2 a metal mold or part of a mold, often cooled, designed to ensure rapid or even cooling of metal during casting.
▶ **v.** [with obj.] **1** make (someone) cold: *I'm chilled to the bone.* ■ cool (food or drink) in a refrigerator: (as adj. **chilled**) *chilled white wine.*
2 horrify or frighten (someone): *the city was chilled by the violence* | (as adj. **chilling**) *a chilling account of the prisoners' fate.*
3 (also **chill out**) [no obj.] informal calm down and relax: *I can lean back and chill* | *chill out, okay?* ■ pass time

without a particular aim or purpose, esp. with other people: *we had a week at home and we chilled out.* ▶ adj. chilly: *the chill gray dawn* | figurative *the chill winds of public censure.*
– PHRASES **chill someone's blood** horrify or terrify someone. **take the chill off** warm slightly.
– DERIVATIVES **chill·ing·ly** adv., **chill·ness** n., **chill·some** /-səm/ adj. (literary).
– ORIGIN Old English *cele, ciele* 'cold, coldness,' of Germanic origin; related to COLD.

C

chill·ax /ˈCHilaks/ ▶ v. [no obj.] informal calm down and relax: *you can dance to your favorite tune, chillax, or have friends over.*
– ORIGIN early 21st cent.: blend of CHILL and RELAX.

chill·er /ˈCHilər/ ▶ n. **1** a machine for cooling something, esp. a cold cabinet or refrigerator for keeping stored food a few degrees above freezing. **2** short for SPINE-CHILLER.

chill fac·tor ▶ n. another term for WINDCHILL.

chil·li ▶ n. (pl. **chillies**) British spelling of CHILI.

Chil·li·cothe /ˌCHiləˈkäTHē, -ˈkôTHē/ a historic city in south central Ohio, an early capital of the state; pop. 22,296 (est. 2008).

chill pill ▶ n. informal a notional pill taken to make a person calm down or relax: *is Tom right to get so uptight, or should he just take a chill pill?*

chil·lum /ˈCHiləm/ ▶ n. (pl. **chillums**) a hookah. ■ a pipe used for smoking marijuana.
– ORIGIN from Hindi *cilam*.

chill·y /ˈCHilē/ ▶ adj. (**chillier**, **chilliest**) uncomfortably cool or cold: *it had turned chilly* | *a chilly day.* ■ (of a person) feeling cold: *I felt a bit chilly.* ■ unfriendly: *a chilly reception.*
– DERIVATIVES **chill·i·ness** n.

Chi·lop·o·da /kīˈläpədə/ Zoology a class of myriapod arthropods that comprises the centipedes.
– DERIVATIVES **chi·lo·pod** /ˈkīləˌpäd/ n.
– ORIGIN modern Latin (plural), from Greek *kheilos* 'lip' + *pous, pod-* 'foot.'

Chil·pan·cin·go /ˌCHēlpänˈsiNGgō/ a city in southwestern Mexico, capital of the state of Guerrero; pop. 166,796 (2005).

Chil·tern Hun·dreds /ˈCHiltərn ˈhəndrədz/ (in the UK) a Crown manor, whose administration is a nominal office for which a member of Parliament applies as a way of resigning from the House of Commons.
– ORIGIN from the *Chiltern Hills* in southern England and *Hundreds* (see the noun HUNDRED).

Chi·lu·ba /CHəˈlo͞obə/ ▶ n. another term for LUBA (the language).

Chi·lung /ˈjēˈlo͝oNG/ (also **Chi-lung**, **Keelung**) a chief port and naval base in Taiwan, at the northern tip of the island; pop. 390,400 (est. 2007).

chi·mae·ra ▶ n. variant spelling of CHIMERA.

chim·bley ▶ n. (pl. **chimbleys**) dialect form of CHIMNEY.

Chim·bo·ra·zo /ˌCHimbəˈräzō, ˌSHim-/ the highest peak in the Andes in Ecuador. It rises to 20,487 feet (6,310 m).

Chim·bo·te /CHēmˈbōˌtā/ an industrial port city in west central Peru, on the Pacific Ocean north of Lima; pop. 334,600 (est. 2007).

chime[1] /CHīm/ ▶ n. (often **chimes**) a bell or a metal bar or tube, typically one of a set tuned to produce a melodious series of ringing sounds when struck. ■ a sound made by such an instrument: *I hear the chimes of the hour from the courthouse.* ■ (**chimes**) a set of tuned metal rods used as an orchestral instrument. ■ (**chimes**) a set of tuned bells used as a doorbell. ■ Bell-ringing a stroke of the clapper against one or both sides of a scarcely moving bell. ▶ v. [no obj.] **1** (of a bell or clock) make melodious ringing sounds, typically to indicate the time: [with complement] *the clock chimed eight.* **2** be in agreement; harmonize: *his poem chimes with our modern experience of loss.*
– PHRASAL VERBS **chime in 1** interject a remark: *"Yes, you do that," Doreen chimed in eagerly.* **2** join in harmoniously.
– DERIVATIVES **chim·er** n.
– ORIGIN Middle English (in the senses 'cymbal' and 'ring out'): probably from Old English *cimbal* (see CYMBAL), later interpreted as *chime bell*.

chime[2] (also **chimb**) ▶ n. the projecting rim at the end of a cask.
– ORIGIN late Middle English: probably from an Old English word related to Dutch *kim* and German *Kimme*. Compare with CHINE[3].

chi·me·ne·a /CHiməˈnēə/ (also **chiminea**) ▶ n. an earthenware

chimenea

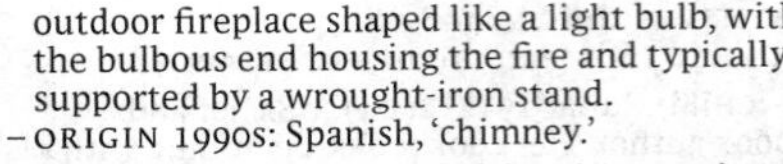

outdoor fireplace shaped like a light bulb, with the bulbous end housing the fire and typically supported by a wrought-iron stand.
– ORIGIN 1990s: Spanish, 'chimney.'

chi·me·ra /kīˈmi(ə)rə, kə-/ (also **chimaera**) ▶ n. **1** (**Chimera**) (in Greek mythology) a fire-breathing female monster with a lion's head, a goat's body, and a serpent's tail. ■ any mythical animal with parts taken from various animals. **2** a thing that is hoped or wished for but in fact is illusory or impossible to achieve: *the economic sovereignty you claim to defend is a chimera.* **3** Biology an organism containing a mixture of genetically different tissues, formed by processes such as fusion of early embryos, grafting, or mutation: *the sheeplike goat chimera.* ■ a DNA molecule with sequences derived from two or more different organisms, formed by laboratory manipulation. **4** (usu. **chimaera**) a cartilaginous marine fish with a long tail, an erect spine before the first dorsal fin, and typically a forward projection from the snout. ● Subclass Hoplocephali: three families, in particular Chimaeridae. See also RABBITFISH, RATFISH.
– DERIVATIVES **chi·mer·ic** /kīˈmi(ə)rik, kə-, -ˈmerik/ adj., **chi·mer·i·cal** adj., **chi·mer·i·cal·ly** adv.
– ORIGIN late Middle English: via Latin from Greek *khimaira* 'she-goat or chimera.'

chi·mer·ism /kīˈmi(ə)rˌizəm, ˈkīməˌrizəm/ ▶ n. Biology the state of being a genetic chimera.

chi·mi·chan·ga /ˌCHimiˈCHäNGgə, -ˈCHaNGgə/ ▶ n. a tortilla wrapped around a filling, typically of meat, and deep-fried.
– ORIGIN Mexican Spanish, literally 'trinket.'

chim·ney /ˈCHimnē/ ▶ n. (pl. **chimneys**) a vertical channel or pipe that conducts smoke and combustion gases up from a fire or furnace and typically through the roof of a building. ■ the part of such a structure that extends above the roof. ■ a glass tube that protects the flame of a lamp. ■ a steep narrow cleft by which a rock face may be climbed.
– ORIGIN Middle English (denoting a fireplace or furnace): from Old French *cheminee* 'chimney, fireplace,' from late Latin *caminata*, perhaps from *camera caminata* 'room with a fireplace,' from Latin *caminus* 'forge, furnace,' from Greek *kaminos* 'oven.'

chim·ney breast ▶ n. a part of an interior wall that projects to surround a chimney.

chim·ney cor·ner ▶ n. a warm seat at the side of an old-fashioned fireplace.

chim·ney piece ▶ n. Brit. a mantelpiece.

chim·ney pot ▶ n. an earthenware or metal pipe at the top of a chimney, narrowing the aperture and increasing the updraft.

chim·ney stack ▶ n. the part of a chimney that projects above a roof.

chim·ney sweep ▶ n. a person whose job is cleaning out the soot from chimneys.

chim·ney swift ▶ n. the common swift found over the eastern part of North America, with mainly dark gray plumage. ● *Chaetura pelagica*, family Apodidae.

chimney swift

chimp /CHimp/ ▶ n. informal term for CHIMPANZEE.

chim·pan·zee /ˌCHimˌpanˈzē, -panˈzē, -ˈpanzē/ ▶ n. a great ape with large ears, mainly black coloration, and lighter skin on the face, native to the forests of western and central Africa. Chimpanzees show advanced behavior such as the making and using of tools. ● Genus *Pan*, family Pongidae: the **common chimpanzee** (*P. troglodytes*) and the bonobo.
– ORIGIN mid 18th cent.: from French *chimpanzé*, from Kikongo.

Chin variant spelling of JIN.

chin /CHin/ ▶ n. the protruding part of the face below the mouth, formed by the apex of the lower jaw. ▶ v. [with obj.] draw one's body up so as to bring one's chin level with or above (a horizontal bar) with one's feet off the ground, as an exercise.
– PHRASES **keep one's chin up** informal remain cheerful in difficult circumstances: *keep your chin up, we're not lost yet.* **take it on the chin** endure or accept misfortune courageously or stoically.
– DERIVATIVES **chinned** adj. [in combination] *square-chinned.*
– ORIGIN Old English *cin, cinn*, of Germanic origin; related to Dutch *kin*, from an Indo-European root shared by Latin *gena* 'cheek' and Greek *genus* 'jaw.'

Ch'in variant spelling of QIN.

Chi·na /ˈCHīnə/ a country in eastern Asia, the third largest and most populous in the world; pop. 1,338,613,000 (est. 2009); capital, Beijing; language, Chinese (Mandarin is the official form). Official name PEOPLE'S REPUBLIC OF CHINA.

> Chinese civilization stretches back until at least the 3rd millennium BC, the country being ruled by a series of dynasties until the Qing (or Manchu) dynasty was overthrown by Sun Yat-sen in 1911; China was proclaimed a republic the following year. After World War II, the Kuomintang government of Chiang Kai-shek was overthrown by the Communists under Mao Zedong, and the People's Republic of China was declared in 1949. Market-oriented reforms were introduced in the last quarter of the twentieth century.

chi·na /ˈCHīnə/ ▶ n. a fine white or translucent vitrified ceramic material: *a plate made of china* | [as modifier] *a china cup.* Also called PORCELAIN. ■ household tableware or other objects made from this or a similar material: *the breakfast china.*
– ORIGIN late 16th cent. (as an adjective): from Persian *chīnī* used attributively relating to China, where it was originally made.

Chi·na, Republic of official name for TAIWAN.

Chi·na as·ter ▶ n. a Chinese plant of the daisy family, cultivated for its bright showy flowers. ● *Callistephus chinensis*, family Compositae.

chi·na·ber·ry /ˈCHīnəˌberē/ (also **Chinaberry**) ▶ n. (pl. **chinaberries**) a tall tree of the mahogany family native to Asia and Australasia, bearing fragrant lilac flowers and yellow berries. It has become naturalized in parts of North America. ● *Melia azedarach*, family Meliaceae. ■ the fruit of this tree, used as beads and to make insecticides: *a rosary made of chinaberries.*

chi·na blue ▶ n. a pale grayish blue.

chi·na clay ▶ n. another term for KAOLIN.

Chi·na·man /ˈCHīnəmən/ ▶ n. (pl. **Chinamen**) informal, dated, offensive a native of China.

chi·na mark·er ▶ n. a waxy pencil used to write on china, glass, or other hard surfaces.

chi·nar /CHiˈnär/ (also **chinar tree**) ▶ n. the oriental plane tree, native from southeastern Europe to northern Iran. ● *Platanus orientalis*, family Platanaceae.
– ORIGIN from Persian *chinār*.

Chi·na rose ▶ n. **1** a Chinese rose that was introduced into Europe in the 19th century. ● *Rosa chinensis*, family Rosaceae. ■ any of a number of garden rose varieties derived from crosses of this plant. **2** a tropical shrubby evergreen hibiscus, cultivated for its large showy flowers. ● *Hibiscus rosa-sinensis*, family Malvaceae.

Chi·na Sea the part of the Pacific Ocean off the coast of China, divided by the island of Taiwan into the **East China Sea** in the north and the **South China Sea** in the south.

chi·na stone ▶ n. partly kaolinized granite containing plagioclase feldspar, ground and mixed with kaolin to make porcelain.

Chi·na syn·drome ▶ n. a hypothetical sequence of events following the meltdown of a nuclear reactor, in which the core melts through its containment structure and deep into the earth.
– ORIGIN 1970s: from CHINA (as being on the opposite side of the earth from a reactor in the US).

Chi·na tea ▶ n. tea made from a small-leaved type of tea plant grown in China, typically flavored by smoke curing or the addition of flower petals.

Chi·na·town /ˈCHīnəˌtoun/ ▶ n. a district of any non-Chinese town, esp. a city or seaport, in which the population is predominantly of Chinese origin.

chi·na tree (also **China tree**) ▶ n. another term for CHINABERRY.

chi·na·ware /ˈCHīnəˌwer/ ▶ n. dishes made of china.

chinch /CHinCH/ (also **chinch bug**) ▶ n. a plant-eating ground bug that forms large swarms on grasses and rushes. ● Two species in the family Lygaeidae, suborder Heteroptera: the American *Blissus leucopterus*, which is a major pest of cereal crops, and the European *Ischnodemus sabuleti*.
– ORIGIN early 17th cent. (in the sense 'bedbug'): from Spanish *chinche*, from Latin *cimex, cimic-*.

chin·che·rin·chee /ˌCHinCHəˈrinCHē, -rinˈCHē/ ▶ n. a white-flowered South African lily. ● *Ornithogalum thyrsoides*, family Liliaceae.
– ORIGIN early 20th cent.: imitative of the squeaky sound made by rubbing its stalks together.

chin·chil·la /CHinˈCHilə/ ▶ n. a small South American rodent with soft gray fur and a long bushy tail. ● Genus *Chinchilla*, family Chinchillidae: two species, in particular *C. lanigera*. ■ a cat or rabbit

of a breed with silver-gray or gray fur. ■ the highly valued fur of the chinchilla, or of the chinchilla rabbit.
– ORIGIN early 17th cent.: from Spanish, from Aymara or Quechua.

chinchilla

Chin·co·teague Is·land /ˌSHINGkəˈtēg, ˌCHING-/ an island in eastern Virginia, west of Assateague Island, noted for its wild horses.

Chin·co·teague po·ny ▶ **n.** a small, hardy horse found running wild on the islands of Chincoteague and Assateague off the Virginia and Maryland coasts.

Chin·dit /ˈCHindit/ ▶ **n.** a member of the Allied forces behind the Japanese lines in Burma in 1943–45.
– ORIGIN World War II: from Burmese *chinthé*, a mythical creature.

Chin·dwin /ˈCHinˈdwin/ a river that rises in northern Burma (Myanmar) and flows south for 550 miles (885 km) to meet the Irrawaddy River.

chine[1] /CHīn/ ▶ **n.** a backbone, esp. that of an animal as it appears in a cut of meat. ■ a cut of meat containing all or part of this. ■ a mountain ridge or arête.
▶ **v.** [with obj.] cut (meat) across or along the backbone.
– ORIGIN Middle English: from Old French *eschine*, based on a blend of Latin *spina* 'spine' and a Germanic word meaning 'narrow piece,' related to SHIN.

chine[2] ▶ **n.** Brit. a deep, narrow ravine formed by running water.
– ORIGIN Old English *cinu* 'cleft, chink,' of Germanic origin; related to Dutch *keen*, also to CHINK[1].

chine[3] ▶ **n.** the angle where the bottom of a boat or ship meets the side.
– ORIGIN late Middle English: variant of CHIME[2] (the original sense).

Chi·nese /CHīˈnēz, -ˈnēs/ ▶ **adj.** of or relating to China or its language, culture, or people. ■ belonging to or relating to the people forming the dominant ethnic group of China and widely dispersed elsewhere. Also called **HAN**.
▶ **n.** (pl. **same**) **1** the Chinese language.
2 a native or inhabitant of China, or a person of Chinese descent.

> Chinese, a member of the Sino-Tibetan language family, is the world's most commonly spoken first language, with an estimated 1.2 billion native speakers worldwide. The script is logographic, using characters that originated as stylized pictographs but now also represent abstract concepts and the sounds of syllables. Though complex, it permits written communication between speakers of the many dialects, most of which are mutually incomprehensible in speech. About 8,000 characters are in everyday use, some having been simplified during the 20th century. For transliteration into the Roman alphabet, the Pinyin system is now usually used.

Chi·nese an·ise ▶ **n.** another term for STAR ANISE.

Chi·nese ar·ti·choke ▶ **n.** an Asian plant of the mint family, cultivated for its edible tubers. ● Genus *Stachys*, family Labiatae: several species, esp. *S. sieboldii* and *S. affinis*.

Chi·nese black mush·room ▶ **n.** another term for SHIITAKE.

Chi·nese box ▶ **n.** each of a series of nested boxes.

Chi·nese cab·bage ▶ **n.** an oriental cabbage that does not form a firm heart. ● Genus *Brassica*, family Brassicaceae: two species, bok choy (*B. chinensis*), which has smooth tapering leaves, and pe-tsai (*B. pekinenis*), which resembles lettuce; they are often treated as varieties of *B. rapa*.

Chi·nese check·ers ▶ **plural n.** [usu. treated as sing.] a board game for two to six players who attempt to move marbles or counters from one corner to the opposite one on a star-shaped board.

Chi·nese chest·nut ▶ **n.** see CHESTNUT.

Chi·nese chives ▶ **plural n.** an Asian relative of chives, with a garliclike flavor. Also called GARLIC CHIVES. ● *Allium tuberosum*, family Liliaceae (or Alliaceae).

Chi·nese date ▶ **n.** another term for JUJUBE.

Chi·nese fire drill ▶ **n.** informal, often offensive a state of disorder or confusion.

Chi·nese goose·ber·ry ▶ **n.** another term for KIWI FRUIT.

Chi·nese kale ▶ **n.** a leafy green Asian plant of the cabbage family, closely related to broccoli but with more leaf and stem and much smaller florettes. It is commonly used in Asian cooking. ● *Brassica alboglabra*, family Brassicaceae.

Chi·nese lan·tern ▶ **n.**
1 a collapsible paper lantern.
2 a Eurasian plant with white flowers and globular orange fruits enclosed in an orange-red papery calyx. The stems bearing these are dried and used for decoration. ● *Physalis alkekengi*, family Solanaceae.

Chinese lantern 2

Chi·nese pars·ley ▶ **n.** another term for CORIANDER.

Chi·nese pear ▶ **n.** another term for ASIAN PEAR.

Chi·nese puz·zle ▶ **n.** an intricate puzzle consisting of many interlocking pieces. ■ a very complicated or perplexing situation.

Chi·nese rad·ish ▶ **n.** another term for DAIKON.

Chi·nese red ▶ **n.** a vivid orange-red.

Chi·nese res·tau·rant syn·drome ▶ **n.** an illness marked by short attacks of weakness, numbness, palpitations, and headaches, often attributed to overconsumption of monosodium glutamate (commonly used as a seasoning in Chinese cooking).

Chi·nese rhu·barb ▶ **n.** a tall perennial plant with palmate leaves, whitish flowers, and winged fruits. The dried rhizomes and roots are used medicinally. ● *Rheum longifolia*, family Polygonaceae.

Chi·nese wall ▶ **n.** an insurmountable barrier, esp. to the passage of information or communication.
– ORIGIN early 20th cent.: with allusion to the GREAT WALL OF CHINA.

Chi·nese whis·pers ▶ **plural n.** [treated as sing.] another term for the game of telephone.

Chi·nese white ▶ **n.** white pigment made from zinc oxide.

Chi·nese wind·lass ▶ **n.** another term for DIFFERENTIAL WINDLASS.

ching /CHiNG/ ▶ **n.** an abrupt high-pitched ringing sound, typically one made by a cash register.
– ORIGIN imitative.

Ch'ing variant spelling of QING.

Chink /CHiNGk/ ▶ **n.** informal, offensive a Chinese person.
– ORIGIN late 19th cent.: irregular formation from CHINA.

chink[1] /CHiNGk/ ▶ **n.** a narrow opening or crack, typically one that admits light: *a chink in the curtains*. ■ a narrow beam or patch of light admitted by such an opening: *I noticed a chink of light under the door*.
– PHRASES **a chink in someone's armor** a weak point in someone's character, arguments, or ideas, making them vulnerable to attack or criticism.
– ORIGIN mid 16th cent.: related to CHINE[2].

chink[2] ▶ **v.** make or cause to make a light and high-pitched ringing sound, as of glasses or coins striking together: [no obj.] *the chain joining the handcuffs chinked* | [with obj.] *they chinked glasses and kissed*.
▶ **n.** a high-pitched ringing sound: *the chink of glasses*.
– ORIGIN late 16th cent.: imitative.

chin·ka·pin ▶ **n.** variant spelling of CHINQUAPIN.

chin·ka·ra /CHiNGˈkärə, CHin-/ ▶ **n.** (pl. **same**) (in South Asia) the Indian gazelle, which occurs from Iran to central India. ● *Gazella bennettii*, family Bovidae.
– ORIGIN mid 19th cent.: from Hindi *cikārā*, from Sanskrit *chikkāra*.

Chin·kiang /ˈjinjēˈäNG/ variant of ZHENJIANG.

Chink·y /ˈCHiNGkē/ informal, offensive ▶ **n.** (pl. **Chinkies**) a Chinese person.
▶ **adj.** Chinese.

chin·less /ˈCHinlis/ ▶ **adj.** (of a person) lacking a well-defined chin. ■ informal lacking strength of character; ineffectual.

chin mu·sic ▶ **n.** informal **1** idle chatter.
2 Baseball used to refer to a pitched ball that passes very close to the batter's chin: *Clemens delivered some wicked chin music to Hernandez*.

Chi·no /ˈCHēnō/ a city in southwestern California, east of Los Angeles; pop. 83,031 (est. 2008).

chi·no /ˈCHēnō/ ▶ **n.** (pl. **chinos**) a cotton twill fabric, typically khaki-colored. ■ (**chinos**) casual pants made from chino or a similar fabric.
– ORIGIN 1940s: from Latin American Spanish, literally 'toasted' (referring to the typical color).

Chino- ▶ **comb. form** equivalent to SINO-.

chi·nois /SHinˈwä, SHēn-/ ▶ **n.** a cone-shaped sieve with a closely woven mesh for straining sauces.

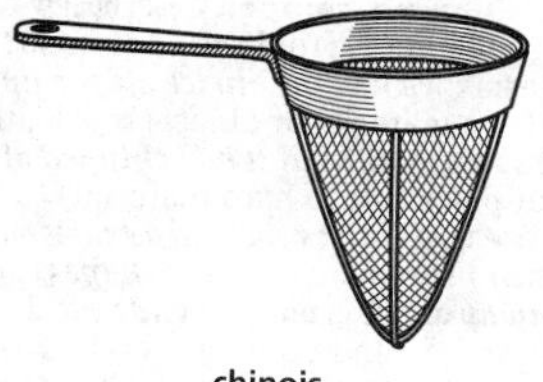
chinois

chi·noi·se·rie /ˌSHēnˌwäz(ə)ˈrē, ˌSHēnˈwäzərē/ ▶ **n.** (pl. **chinoiseries**) the imitation or evocation of Chinese motifs and techniques in Western art, furniture, and architecture, esp. in the 18th century. ■ objects or decorations in this style: *a piece of chinoiserie* | *one room has red velvet and chinoiseries*.
– ORIGIN late 19th cent.: from French, from *chinois* 'Chinese.'

Chi·nook /SHəˈno͝ok, CHə-/ ▶ **n.** (pl. **same** or **Chinooks**) **1** a member of an American Indian people originally inhabiting the region around the lower Columbia River in Oregon and Washington.
2 the language of this people.
▶ **adj.** of or relating to the Chinook or their language.
– ORIGIN from *c'inúk*, a Salishan word for the name of a Chinook village.

chi·nook /SHəˈno͝ok, CHə-/ ▶ **n. 1** (also **chinook wind**) a warm dry wind that blows down the east side of the Rocky Mountains at the end of winter.
2 (also **chinook salmon**) a large North Pacific salmon that is an important commercial food fish. ● *Oncorhynchus tshawytscha*, family Salmonidae.
– ORIGIN mid 19th cent.: from attributive use of CHINOOK.

Chi·nook Jar·gon ▶ **n.** an extinct pidgin composed of elements from Chinook, Nootka, English, French, and other languages, formerly used in the Pacific Northwest.

chin·qua·pin /ˈCHiNGkiˌpin/ (also **chinkapin**) ▶ **n.** a North American chestnut tree. ● Several species in the family Fagaceae, in particular the **Allegheny** (or **eastern**) **chinquapin** (*Castanea pumila*). ■ the edible nut of one of these trees.
– ORIGIN early 17th cent.: from Virginia Algonquian.

chin·strap /ˈCHinˌstrap/ ▶ **n.** a strap attached to a hat, helmet, or other headgear, designed to hold it in place by fitting under the wearer's chin.

chintz /CHints/ ▶ **n.** printed multicolored cotton fabric with a glazed finish, used esp. for curtains and upholstery: *a sofa upholstered in chintz* | [as modifier] *floral chintz curtains*.
– ORIGIN early 17th cent. (as *chints*, plural of *chint*, denoting a stained or painted calico cloth imported from India): from Hindi *chīṃṭ* 'spattering, stain.'

chintz·y /ˈCHintsē/ ▶ **adj.** (**chintzier**, **chintziest**) **1** Brit. of, like, or decorated with chintz: *brighten the room with fresh paint and chintzy fabrics*. ■ brightly colorful but gaudy and tasteless.
2 informal cheap and of poor quality. ■ miserly: *a chintzy salary increase*.
– DERIVATIVES **chintz·i·ly** /ˈCHintsəlē/ **adv.**, **chintz·i·ness n.**

chin-up ▶ **n.** another term for PULL-UP (sense 1).

chin·wag /ˈCHinˌwag/ (also **chin wag**) informal ▶ **n.** a chat.
▶ **v.** (**chinwags**, **chinwagging**, **chinwagged**) [no obj.] have a chat.

Chi·os /ˈkēˌäs, ˈkī-, -ˌôs/ a Greek island in the Aegean Sea; pop. 53,100 (2008). Greek name **KHIOS**.
– DERIVATIVES **Chi·an** /ˈkēən, ˈkī-/ **n. & adj.**

chip /CHip/ ▶ **n. 1** a small piece of something removed in the course of chopping, cutting, or breaking something, esp. a hard material such as wood or stone: *mulch the shrubs with cedar chips*. ■ a hole or flaw left by the removal of such a piece: *a chip on his tooth*. ■ Brit. wood or woody fiber split into thin strips and used for weaving hats or baskets.
2 a thin slice of food made crisp by being fried, baked, or dried and typically eaten as a snack: *tortilla chips dipped in salsa* | *banana chips*. ■ a small chunk of candy added to desserts or sweet snacks, esp. of chocolate. ■ (**chips**) chiefly Brit. French fries: *an order of fish and chips*.
3 short for MICROCHIP.

C

4 a counter used in certain gambling games to represent money: *a poker chip.*
5 (in golf, soccer, and other sports) a short lofted kick or shot with the ball. ■ Tennis a softly sliced return intended to land between the net and the opponent's service line.
▶ v. (**chips, chipping, chipped**) [with obj.] **1** cut or break (a small piece) from the edge or surface of a hard material: *we had to chip ice off the upper deck.* ■ [no obj.] (of a material or object) break at the edge or on the surface: *the paint had chipped off the gate.* ■ cut pieces off (a hard material) to alter its shape or break it up: *it required a craftsman to chip the blocks of flint to the required shape* | [no obj.] *she chipped away at the ground outside the door.*
2 (in golf, soccer, and other sports) kick or strike (a ball or shot) to produce a short lobbed shot or pass: *he chipped a superb shot.*
– PHRASES **a chip off the old block** informal someone who resembles his or her parent, esp. in character. **a chip on one's shoulder** informal a deeply ingrained grievance, typically about a particular thing. **when the chips are down** informal when a very serious and difficult situation arises.
– PHRASAL VERBS **chip away** gradually and relentlessly make something smaller or weaker: *rivals may chip away at one's profits by undercutting product prices.* **chip in** (or **chip something in**) contribute something as one's share of a joint activity, cost, etc.: *the rookie pitcher chipped in with nine saves and five wins* | *the council will chip in a further $30,000 a year.*
– ORIGIN Middle English: related to Old English *forcippian* 'cut off.'

chip·board /ˈCHipˌbôrd/ ▶ n. another term for PARTICLEBOARD.

Chip·e·wy·an /ˌCHipəˈwīən/ ▶ n. (pl. **same** or **Chipewyans**) **1** a member of a Dene people of northwestern Canada. Do not confuse with CHIPPEWA.
2 the Athabaskan language of this people.
▶ adj. of or relating to this people or their language.
– ORIGIN from Cree *čīpwayān*, literally '(wearing) pointed-skin (garments).'

chip·mak·er /ˈCHipˌmākər/ ▶ n. a company that manufactures microchips.

chip·munk /ˈCHipˌməNGk/ ▶ n. a burrowing ground squirrel with cheek pouches and light and dark stripes running down the body, found in North America and northern Eurasia. ● Genus *Tamias*, family Sciuridae: many species, including the **eastern chipmunk** (*T. striatus*), common in the eastern US.
– ORIGIN mid 19th cent.: from Ojibwa.

eastern chipmunk

chi·pot·le /CHiˈpōtlā/ ▶ n. a smoked hot chili pepper used esp. in Mexican cooking.
– ORIGIN Mexican Spanish, from Nahuatl.

Chip·pen·dale[1] /ˈCHipənˌdāl/, Thomas (1718–79), English furniture-maker and designer. He produced furniture in a neoclassical vein, with elements of the French rococo, chinoiserie, and Gothic revival styles.

Chip·pen·dale[2] ▶ adj. (of furniture) designed, made by, or in the style of Thomas Chippendale.

chip·per[1] /ˈCHipər/ ▶ adj. informal cheerful and lively.
– ORIGIN mid 19th cent.: perhaps from northern English dialect *kipper* 'lively.'

chip·per[2] ▶ n. a person or thing that turns something into chips. ■ a machine for chipping the trunks and limbs of trees.

Chip·pe·wa /ˈCHipəˌwä, -ˌwā, -wə/ (also **Chippeway** /-ˌwā/) ▶ n. (pl. **same**) another term for OJIBWA. Do not confuse with CHIPEWYAN.
– ORIGIN alteration of OJIBWA.

chip·pie /ˈCHipē/ ▶ n. (pl. **chippies**) variant spelling of CHIPPY.

chip·ping spar·row ▶ n. a common American songbird related to the buntings, with a chestnut crown and a white stripe over the eye. ● *Spizella passerina*, family Emberizidae (subfamily Emberizinae).
– ORIGIN early 19th cent.: *chipping* from *chip* 'chirp,' with reference to the bird's repetitive chirping song.

chip·py /ˈCHipē/ informal ▶ n. (also **chippie**) (pl. **chippies**) **1** a promiscuous young woman, esp. a prostitute.
2 Brit. a fish-and-chip shop.
3 Brit. a carpenter.
▶ adj. touchy and irritable. ■ (of an ice-hockey game or player) rough and belligerent, with or incurring numerous penalties.

chip·set /ˈCHipˌset/ ▶ n. a collection of integrated circuits that form the set needed to make an electronic device such as a computer motherboard or portable telephone.

chip shot ▶ n. Golf a stroke at which the ball is or must be chipped into the air.

Chi·rac /SHēˈräk/, Jacques (René) (1932–), French statesman; prime minister 1974–76 and 1986–88; president 1995–2007.

chi·ral /ˈkīrəl/ ▶ adj. Chemistry asymmetric in such a way that the structure and its mirror image are not superimposable. Chiral compounds are typically optically active; large organic molecules often have one or more **chiral centers** where four different groups are attached to a carbon atom.
– DERIVATIVES **chi·ral·i·ty** /kīˈralitē/ n.
– ORIGIN late 19th cent.: from Greek *kheir* 'hand' + -AL.

chi-rho /ˈkī ˌrō/ ▶ n. a monogram of chi (X) and rho (P) as the first two letters of Greek *Khristos* Christ, used as a Christian symbol.

Chir·i·ca·hua /ˌCHi-riˈkä-wə/ ▶ n. **1** a member of an Apache people, formerly located in southern New Mexico, southeastern Arizona, and northern Mexico, now living primarily in Oklahoma and New Mexico.
2 the Athabaskan language of this people.
▶ adj. of or relating to this people or their language.

Chi·ri·ca·hua Moun·tains a range in southeastern Arizona, on the Mexican border, controlled by Cochise and other Apache leaders during the 19th century.

chir·i·moy·a /ˌCHirəˈmoiə/ ▶ n. variant spelling of CHERIMOYA.

chiro- (also **cheiro-**) ▶ comb. form of the hand or hands: *chiromancy.*
– ORIGIN from Greek *kheir* 'hand.'

chi·rog·ra·phy /kīˈrägrəfē/ ▶ n. handwriting, esp. as distinct from typography.
– DERIVATIVES **chi·ro·graph·ic** /ˌkīrəˈgrafik/ adj.

chi·ro·man·cy /ˈkīrəˌmansē/ ▶ n. the prediction of a person's future from the lines on the palms of his or her hands; palmistry.

Chi·ron /ˈkīrən/ **1** Greek Mythology a learned centaur who acted as teacher to Jason, Achilles, and many other heroes.
2 Astronomy asteroid 2060, discovered in 1977, which is notable for having an orbit lying mainly between the orbits of Saturn and Uranus. It is believed to have a diameter of 370 km.

chi·ron·o·mid /kīˈränəmid/ ▶ n. Entomology an insect of a family (Chironomidae) that comprises the nonbiting midges.
– ORIGIN late 19th cent.: from modern Latin *Chironomidae* (plural), from the genus name *Chironomus*, from Greek *kheironomos* 'pantomime dancer.'

chi·rop·o·dy /kəˈräpədē, SHə-/ ▶ n. another term for PODIATRY.
– DERIVATIVES **chi·rop·o·dist** /kəˈräpədist/ n.
– ORIGIN late 19th cent.: from CHIRO- 'hand' + Greek *pous, pod-* 'foot.'

chi·ro·prac·tic /ˌkīrəˈpraktik/ ▶ n. a system of complementary medicine based on the diagnosis and manipulative treatment of misalignments of the joints, esp. those of the spinal column, which are held to cause other disorders by affecting the nerves, muscles, and organs.
– DERIVATIVES **chi·ro·prac·tor** /ˈkīrəˌpraktər/ n.
– ORIGIN late 19th cent.: from CHIRO- 'hand' + Greek *praktikos* 'practical,' from *prattein* 'do.'

Chi·rop·ter·a /kīˈräptərə/ Zoology an order of mammals that comprises the bats. There are over 900 living species of bats, and they are found on every continent except Antarctica. See also MEGACHIROPTERA, MICROCHIROPTERA.
– ORIGIN modern Latin (plural), from CHIRO- 'hand' + Greek *pteron* 'wing.'

chi·rop·ter·an /kīˈräptərən/ Zoology ▶ n. a mammal of the order Chiroptera; a bat.
▶ adj. relating to or denoting chiropterans.

chirp /CHərp/ ▶ v. [no obj.] (typically of a small bird or an insect) utter a short, sharp, high-pitched sound: *outside, the crickets chirped monotonously.* ■ [with direct speech] (of a person) say something in a lively and cheerful way: *"Good morning!" chirped Alex.*
▶ n. a short, sharp, high-pitched sound.
– DERIVATIVES **chirp·er** n.
– ORIGIN late Middle English: imitative.

chirp·y /ˈCHərpē/ ▶ adj. (**chirpier, chirpiest**) informal cheerful and lively.
– DERIVATIVES **chirp·i·ly** /ˈCHərpəlē/ adv., **chirp·i·ness** n.

chirr /CHər/ (also **churr**) ▶ v. [no obj.] (esp. of an insect) make a prolonged low trilling sound.
▶ n. a low trilling sound.
– ORIGIN early 17th cent.: imitative.

chir·rup /ˈCHi(ə)rəp, ˈCHərəp/ ▶ v. (**chirrups, chirruping, chirruped**) [no obj.] (esp. of a small bird) make repeated short high-pitched sounds; twitter. ■ [with direct speech] (of a person) say something in a high-pitched voice: *"Yes, Miss Honey," chirruped eighteen voices.*
▶ n. a short, high-pitched sound.
– DERIVATIVES **chir·rup·y** adj.
– ORIGIN late 16th cent.: alteration of CHIRP, by trilling the *-r-*.

chir·u /ˈCHirˌo͞o/ ▶ n. (pl. **same**) a sandy-colored gazelle with black horns, found on the Tibetan plateau. Also called TIBETAN ANTELOPE. ● *Pantholops hodgsoni*, family Bovidae.
– ORIGIN late 19th cent.: probably from Tibetan.

chis·el /ˈCHizəl/ ▶ n. a long-bladed hand tool with a beveled cutting edge and a plain handle that is struck with a hammer or mallet, used to cut or shape wood, stone, metal, or other hard materials.
▶ v. (**chisels, chiseling, chiseled**; Brit. **chisels, chiselling, chiselled**) [with obj.] **1** cut or shape (something) with a chisel: *carefully chisel out a groove for the hinge.*
2 informal cheat or swindle (someone) out of something: *he's chiseled me out of my dues.*
– DERIVATIVES **chis·el·er** /ˈCHiz(ə)lər/ n.
– ORIGIN late Middle English: from Old Northern French, based on Latin *cis-* (as in late Latin *cisorium*), variant of *caes-*, stem of *caedere* 'to cut.' Compare with SCISSORS.

chis·eled /ˈCHizəld/ ▶ adj. (of wood or stone) shaped or cut with a chisel. ■ (of a facial feature, typically a man's) strongly and clearly defined: *the chiseled features of a male model.*

Chis·holm /ˈCHizəm/, Shirley Anita St. Hill (1924–2005), US politician, social activist, and educator. The first African-American woman elected to Congress, she was a member of the House of Representatives from New York 1968–83.

Chis·holm Trail a historic route over which 19th-century cowboys drove cattle for 1,500 miles (2,400 km) north from Texas to Abilene and other Kansas cities that had been reached by developing railroads.

Chi·şi·nău /ˌkēSHəˈnou/ the capital of Moldova; pop. 630,300 (est. 2008). Russian name KISHINYOV.

chi-square /kī/ ▶ n. [as modifier] relating to or denoting a statistical method assessing the goodness of fit between observed values and those expected theoretically. (Symbol: χ^2)

chit[1] /CHit/ ▶ n. a short official note, memorandum, or voucher, typically recording a sum owed.
– ORIGIN late 18th cent.: Anglo-Indian, from Hindi *ciṭṭhī* 'note, pass.'

chit[2] ▶ n. a young woman regarded with disapproval for her immaturity or lack of respect: *a mere chit of a girl.*
– ORIGIN late Middle English (denoting a whelp, cub, or kitten): perhaps related to dialect *chit* 'sprout.'

Chi·ta /CHiˈtä/ a city in southeastern Siberia in Russia, on the Trans-Siberian Railway; pop. 306,100 (est. 2008).

chi·tal /ˈCHētl/ ▶ n. (pl. **same**) another term for AXIS DEER.
– ORIGIN late 19th cent.: from Hindi *cītal*, from Sanskrit *citrala* 'spotted,' from *citra* 'spot, mark.'

chit·chat /ˈCHitˌCHat/ informal ▶ n. inconsequential conversation.
▶ v. [no obj.] talk about trivial matters: *I can't stand around chitchatting.*
– ORIGIN late 17th cent.: reduplication of CHAT[1].

chi·tin /ˈkītn/ ▶ n. Biochemistry a fibrous substance consisting of polysaccharides and forming the major constituent in the exoskeleton of arthropods and the cell walls of fungi.
– DERIVATIVES **chi·tin·ous** /ˈkītn-əs/ adj.
– ORIGIN mid 19th cent.: from French *chitine*, formed irregularly from Greek *khitōn* (see CHITON).

chit·lin cir·cuit /ˈCHitˌlin/ ▶ n. chiefly historical (during the era of US racial segregation) a network of clubs, theaters, and other venues where black entertainers were allowed to perform.
– ORIGIN see CHITLINS.

chit·lins /ˈCHitˌlinz/ ▶ plural n. informal chitterlings.
– ORIGIN a dialect form of CHITTERLINGS (a food stereotypically associated with black people and poor southerners).

chi·ton /ˈkītn, ˈkīˌtän/ ▶ n. **1** a long woolen tunic worn in ancient Greece. [from Greek *khitōn* 'tunic.']

2 a marine mollusk that has an oval flattened body with a shell of overlapping plates. [modern Latin (genus name).] ● Class Polyplacophora.

Chit·ta·gong /ˈCHitəˌgäNG, -ˌgôNG/ a seaport in southeastern Bangladesh, on the Bay of Bengal; pop. 2,579,107 (2008).

chit·ter /ˈCHitər/ ▶ **v.** [no obj.] make a twittering or chattering sound.
– ORIGIN Middle English: imitative; compare with CHATTER.

chit·ter·lings /ˈCHitlənz/ ▶ **plural n.** the smaller intestines of a pig, cooked for food.
– ORIGIN Middle English: perhaps related to synonymous German *Kutteln*.

chiv·al·rous /ˈSHivəlrəs/ ▶ **adj.** (of a man or his behavior) courteous and gallant, esp. toward women. ■ of or relating to the historical notion of chivalry.
– DERIVATIVES **chiv·al·rous·ly adv.**
– ORIGIN late Middle English (in the sense 'characteristic of a medieval knight'): from Old French *chevalerous*, from *chevalier* (see CHEVALIER).

chiv·al·ry /ˈSHivəlrē/ ▶ **n.** the medieval knightly system with its religious, moral, and social code. ■ historical knights, noblemen, and horsemen collectively: *I fought against the cream of French chivalry*. ■ the combination of qualities expected of an ideal knight, esp. courage, honor, courtesy, justice, and a readiness to help the weak. ■ courteous behavior, esp. that of a man toward women: *their relations with women were models of chivalry and restraint*.
– DERIVATIVES **chi·val·ric** /SHəˈvalrik/ **adj.**
– ORIGIN Middle English: from Old French *chevalerie*, from medieval Latin *caballerius*, from late Latin *caballarius* 'horseman' (see CHEVALIER).

chives /CHīvz/ ▶ **plural n.** a widely cultivated small Eurasian plant related to the onion, with purple-pink flowers and dense tufts of long tubular leaves that are used as a culinary herb. ● *Allium schoenoprasum*, family Liliaceae (or Alliaceae). ■ the leaves from this plant: *freshly chopped chives* | (as modifier **chive**) *chive and garlic dressing*.
– ORIGIN Middle English: from Old French, dialect variant of *cive*, from Latin *cepa* 'onion.'

chiv·vy /ˈCHivē/ (also **chivy** or **chevy** /ˈCHevē/) ▶ **v.** (**chivvies, chivvying, chivvied**) [with obj.] tell (someone) repeatedly to do something: *an association that chivvies government into action*.
– ORIGIN late 18th cent.: probably from the ballad *Chevy Chase*, celebrating a skirmish (probably the battle of Otterburn, 1388) on the Scottish border (but often mistakenly thought to be a place name). Originally a noun denoting a hunting cry, the term later meant 'a pursuit,' hence the verb 'to chase, worry' (mid 19th cent).

Chka·lov /CHəˈkäləf/ former name (1938–57) for ORENBURG.

Chlad·ni fig·ures /ˈklädnē, ˈkladnē/ (also **Chladni patterns** or **Chladni's figures**) ▶ **plural n.** the patterns formed when a sand-covered surface is made to vibrate. The sand collects in the regions of least motion.
– ORIGIN early 19th cent.: named after Ernst *Chladni* (1756–1827), German physicist.

chlam·y·date /ˈklamiˌdāt/ ▶ **adj.** Zoology having a mantle or pallium like that of a mollusk.

chla·myd·e·ous kləˈmidēəs ▶ **adj.** Botany having or pertaining to a perianth or floral envelope.

chla·myd·i·a /kləˈmidēə/ ▶ **n.** (pl. **same** or **chlamydiae** /-ˈmidēˌē/) a very small parasitic bacterium that, like a virus, requires the biochemical mechanisms of another cell in order to reproduce. Bacteria of this type cause various diseases including trachoma, psittacosis, and nonspecific urethritis. ● Genus *Chlamydia* and order Chlamydiales.
– DERIVATIVES **chla·myd·i·al adj.**
– ORIGIN 1960s: modern Latin (plural), from Greek *khlamus, khlamud-* 'cloak.'

chlam·y·dom·o·nas /ˌklaməˈdämənəs/ ▶ **n.** Biology a common single-celled green alga that lives in water and moist soil and typically has two flagella for swimming. ● Genus *Chlamydomonas*, phylum Chlorophyta, kingdom Plantae (or Protista).
– ORIGIN late 19th cent.: modern Latin, from Greek *khlamus, khlamud-* 'cloak' + *monas* (see MONAD).

chla·myd·o·spore /kləˈmidəˌspôr/ ▶ **n.** Botany (in certain fungi) a thick-walled hyphal cell that functions as a spore.
– ORIGIN late 19th cent.: from Greek *khlamus, khlamud-* 'mantle' + SPORE.

chla·mys /ˈklaməs, ˈklā-/ ▶ **n.** (pl. **chlamyses** or **chlamydes** /ˈkləməˌdēz/) a short cloak worn by men in ancient Greece.
– ORIGIN late 17th cent.: from Greek *khlamus* 'mantle.'

chlo·as·ma /klōˈazmə/ ▶ **n.** a temporary condition, typically caused by hormonal changes, in which large brown patches form on the skin, mainly on the face.
– ORIGIN mid 19th cent.: from Greek *khloazein* 'become green.'

chlor- ▶ **comb. form** variant spelling of CHLORO- before a vowel (as in *chloracne*).

chlor·ac·ne /klôrˈaknē/ ▶ **n.** Medicine a skin disease resembling severe acne, caused by exposure to chlorinated chemicals.

chlo·ral /ˈklôrəl/ ▶ **n.** Chemistry a colorless, viscous liquid made by chlorinating acetaldehyde. ● Alternative name: **trichloroethanal**; chem. formula: CCl_3CHO. ■ short for CHLORAL HYDRATE.
– ORIGIN mid 19th cent.: from French, blend of *chlore* 'chlorine' and *alcool* 'alcohol.'

chlo·ral hy·drate ▶ **n.** Chemistry a colorless crystalline solid made from chloral and used as a sedative. ● Chem. formula: $CCl_3CH(OH)_2$.

chlo·ram·bu·cil /klôrˈambyəˌsil/ ▶ **n.** Medicine a cytotoxic drug used in the treatment of cancer. It belongs to the class of nitrogen mustards.
– ORIGIN 1950s: from *chlor(oethyl)am(inophenyl) bu(tyric acid)*, the systematic name, + *-cil*.

chlo·ra·mine /ˈklôrəˌmēn/ ▶ **n.** Chemistry an organic compound containing a chlorine atom bonded to nitrogen, esp. any of a group of sulfonamide derivatives used as antiseptics and disinfectants.

chlo·ram·phen·i·col /ˌklôrˌamˈfenəˌkôl, -ˌkōl/ ▶ **n.** Medicine an antibiotic used against serious infections such as typhoid fever. ● This antibiotic is obtained from the bacterium *Streptomyces venezuelae* or produced synthetically.
– ORIGIN 1940s: from CHLORO- (representing CHLORINE) + *am(ide)* + PHENO- + *ni(tro-)* + *(gly)col*.

chlor·dane /ˈklôrˌdān/ ▶ **n.** a synthetic viscous toxic compound used as an insecticide. ● A chlorinated derivative of indene; chem. formula: $C_{10}H_6Cl_8$.
– ORIGIN 1940s: from *chlor-* (representing CHLORINE) + *(in)dene* + -ANE[2].

chlor·di·az·e·pox·ide /ˌklôrdīˌazəˈpäkˌsīd/ ▶ **n.** Medicine a tranquilizer of the benzodiazepine group, used chiefly to treat anxiety and alcoholism. Also called LIBRIUM (trademark).

chlo·rel·la /kləˈrelə/ ▶ **n.** Biology a common single-celled green alga of both terrestrial and aquatic habitats, frequently turning stagnant water an opaque green. ● Genus *Chlorella*, phylum Chlorophyta, kingdom Plantae (or Protista).
– ORIGIN modern Latin, diminutive of Greek *khlōros* 'green.'

chlo·ric /ˈklôrik/ ▶ **adj.** of, relating to, or containing chlorine in the pentavalent state.

chlo·ric ac·id ▶ **n.** Chemistry a colorless liquid acid with strong oxidizing properties. ● Chem. formula: $HClO_3$. ■ any acid containing chlorine and oxygen.
– ORIGIN early 19th cent.: *chloric* from CHLORINE + -IC.

chlo·ride /ˈklôrˌīd/ ▶ **n.** Chemistry a compound of chlorine with another element or group, esp. a salt of the anion Cl^- or an organic compound with chlorine bonded to an alkyl group.
– ORIGIN early 19th cent.: from CHLORINE + -IDE.

chlo·ri·nate /ˈklôrəˌnāt/ ▶ **v.** [with obj.] (usu. as adj. **chlorinated**) impregnate or treat with chlorine: *chlorinated water*. ■ Chemistry introduce chlorine into (a compound).
– DERIVATIVES **chlo·ri·na·tion** /ˌklôrəˈnāSHən/ **n.**, **chlo·ri·na·tor** /-ˌnātər/ **n.**

chlo·rine /ˈklôrˌēn/ ▶ **n.** the chemical element of atomic number 17, a toxic, irritant, pale green gas. (Symbol: **Cl**)

> A member of the halogen group, chlorine occurs in nature mainly as sodium chloride in seawater and salt deposits. The gas was used as a poison gas in World War I. Chlorine is added to water supplies as a disinfectant.

– ORIGIN early 19th cent.: named by Sir Humphrey Davy, from Greek *khlōros* 'green' + -INE[4].

chlo·rite[1] /ˈklôrˌīt/ ▶ **n.** a dark green mineral consisting of a basic hydrated aluminosilicate of magnesium and iron. It occurs as a constituent of many metamorphic rocks, typically forming flat crystals resembling mica.
– DERIVATIVES **chlo·rit·ic** /klôrˈitik/ **adj.**
– ORIGIN late 18th cent.: via Latin from Greek *khlōritis*, a green precious stone.

chlo·rite[2] ▶ **n.** Chemistry a salt of chlorous acid, containing the anion ClO_2^-.
– ORIGIN mid 19th cent.: from CHLORINE + -ITE[1].

chlo·ri·toid /ˈklôrəˌtoid/ ▶ **n.** a greenish-gray or black mineral resembling chlorite, found in metamorphosed clay sediments. It consists of a basic aluminosilicate of iron, often with magnesium.

chloro- (usu. **chlor-** before a vowel) ▶ **comb. form**
1 Biology & Mineralogy green.
2 Chemistry representing CHLORINE: *chloroquine*.
– ORIGIN from Greek *khlōros* 'green.'

chlo·ro·car·bon /ˈklôrōˌkärbən/ ▶ **n.** a chemical compound that contains carbon and chlorine or carbon, chlorine, and hydrogen.

chlo·ro·fluor·o·car·bon /ˌklôrōˌflo͝orōˈkärbən/ (abbr.: **CFC**) ▶ **n.** any of a class of compounds of carbon, hydrogen, chlorine, and fluorine, typically gases used in refrigerants and aerosol propellants. They are harmful to the ozone layer in the earth's atmosphere owing to the release of chlorine atoms upon exposure to ultraviolet radiation.

chlo·ro·form /ˈklôrəˌfôrm/ ▶ **n.** a colorless, volatile, sweet-smelling liquid used as a solvent and formerly as a general anesthetic. ● Alternative name: **trichloromethane**; chem. formula: $CHCl_3$.
▶ **v.** [with obj.] render (someone) unconscious with this substance.
– ORIGIN mid 19th cent.: from CHLORO- (representing CHLORINE) + *form-* from FORMIC ACID.

chlo·ro·mel·a·nite /ˌklôrōˈmeləˌnīt/ ▶ **n.** a greenish-black variety of jadeite containing a high proportion of iron.

chlo·ro·my·ce·tin /ˌklôrōmīˈsētn/ ▶ **n.** trademark for CHLORAMPHENICOL.
– ORIGIN 1940s: from CHLORO- 'green' + Greek *mukēs, mukēt-* 'fungus' + -IN[1].

chlo·ro·phyll /ˈklôrəˌfil/ ▶ **n.** a green pigment, present in all green plants and in cyanobacteria, responsible for the absorption of light to provide energy for photosynthesis. Its molecule contains a magnesium atom held in a porphyrin ring.
– DERIVATIVES **chlo·ro·phyl·lous** /ˌklôrəˈfiləs/ **adj.**
– ORIGIN early 19th cent.: coined in French from Greek *khlōros* 'green' + *phullon* 'leaf.'

Chlo·roph·y·ta /klôrˈäfətə/ Botany a phylum that comprises the green algae. They are more recently treated as a phylum of the kingdom Protista.
– ORIGIN modern Latin (plural), from Greek *khlōros* 'green' + *phuton* 'plant.'

chlo·ro·phyte /ˈklôrəfīt/ ▶ **n.** Botany a lower plant of the division Chlorophyta, which comprises the green algae.

chlo·ro·plast /ˈklôrəˌplast/ ▶ **n.** Botany (in green plant cells) a plastid that contains chlorophyll and in which photosynthesis takes place.
– ORIGIN late 19th cent.: coined in German from Greek *khlōros* 'green' + *plastos* 'formed.'

chlo·ro·prene /ˈklôrəˌprēn/ ▶ **n.** Chemistry a colorless liquid made from acetylene and hydrochloric acid and polymerized to form neoprene. ● Chem. formula: $CH_2=CClCH=CH_2$.
– ORIGIN 1930s: from CHLORO- + a shortened form of ISOPRENE.

chlo·ro·quine /ˈklôrəˌkwēn/ ▶ **n.** Medicine a synthetic drug related to quinoline, chiefly used against malaria.
– ORIGIN 1940s: from CHLORO- + *quin(olin)e*.

chlo·ro·sis /klôˈrōsəs/ ▶ **n.** 1 Botany abnormal reduction or loss of the normal green coloration of leaves of plants, typically caused by iron deficiency in lime-rich soils, or by disease or lack of light.
2 Medicine anemia caused by iron deficiency, esp. in adolescent girls, causing a pale, faintly greenish complexion. It was a common diagnosis in the 19th century.
– DERIVATIVES **chlo·rot·ic** /klôrˈätik/ **adj.**

chlo·ro·thi·a·zide /ˌklôrōˈTHīəˌzīd/ ▶ **n.** Medicine a synthetic drug used to treat fluid retention and high blood pressure. It is one of the thiazide diuretics.

chlo·rous ac·id /ˈklôrəs/ ▶ **n.** Chemistry a weak acid with oxidizing properties, formed when chlorine dioxide dissolves in water. ● Chem. formula: $HClO_2$.

chlor·prom·a·zine /ˌklôrˈpräməˌzēn/ ▶ **n.** Medicine a synthetic drug used as a tranquilizer, sedative, and antiemetic. It is a phenothiazine derivative.
– ORIGIN 1950s: from CHLORO- + *prom(eth)azine*.

chlor·tet·ra·cy·cline /ˌklôrˌtetrəˈsīˌklēn/ ▶ **n.** Medicine an antibiotic of the tetracycline group, active against many bacterial and fungal infections. ● This antibiotic is obtained from the bacterium *Streptomyces aureofaciens* or produced synthetically.

cho·a·no·cyte /kōˈanəˌsīt/ ▶ **n.** Zoology a flagellated cell with a collar of protoplasm at the base of the flagellum, numbers of which line the internal chambers of sponges.
– ORIGIN late 19th cent.: from Greek *khoanē* 'funnel' + -CYTE.

C

choc·a·hol·ic ▶ **n.** variant spelling of CHOCOHOLIC.

chock /CHäk/ ▶ **n. 1** a wedge or block placed against a wheel or rounded object, to prevent it from moving. ■ a support on which a rounded structure, such as a cask or the hull of a boat, may be placed to keep it steady.
2 a fitting with a gap at the top, through which a rope or line is run.
▶ **v.** [with obj.] prevent the forward movement of (a wheel or vehicle) with a chock. ■ support (a boat, cask, etc.) on chocks.
– ORIGIN Middle English: probably from an Old Northern French variant of Old French *çouche, çoche* 'block, log,' of unknown ultimate origin.

chock·a·block /ˈCHäkəˌbläk/ ▶ **adj.** [predic.] informal crammed full of people or things: *the manual is* ***chockablock with information.***
– ORIGIN mid 19th cent. (originally in nautical use, with reference to tackle having the two blocks run close together): from *chock* (in CHOCK-FULL) and BLOCK.

chock-full /ˈCHäkˌfo͝ol, ˈCHək-/ ▶ **adj.** [predic.] informal filled to overflowing: *my briefcase is chock-full of notes.*
– ORIGIN late Middle English: of unknown origin; later associated with CHOCK.

chock·stone /ˈCHäkˌstōn/ ▶ **n.** Climbing a stone that has become wedged in a vertical cleft.

choc·o·hol·ic /ˌCHäkəˈhôlik, ˌCHô-, -ˈhälik/ (also **chocaholic**) ▶ **n.** informal a person who is addicted to or excessively fond of chocolate.

choc·o·late /ˈCHäk(ə)lit, ˈCHôk-/ ▶ **n.** a food preparation in the form of a paste or solid block made from roasted and ground cacao seeds, typically sweetened: *a bar of chocolate* | [as modifier] *a chocolate cookie.* ■ a candy made of or covered with this: *a box of chocolates.* ■ a drink made by mixing milk with chocolate: ***sipping on hot chocolate.*** ■ a deep brown color: [as modifier] ***huge spiders, yellow and chocolate brown.***
– DERIVATIVES **choc·o·lat·y** (also **chocolatey**) **adj.**
– ORIGIN early 17th cent. (in the sense 'a drink made with chocolate'): from French *chocolat* or Spanish *chocolate*, from Nahuatl *chocolatl* 'food made from cacao seeds,' influenced by unrelated *cacaua-atl* 'drink made from cacao.'

choc·o·late chip ▶ **n.** [usu. as modifier] a small piece of chocolate used in making cookies and other sweet foods: *chocolate-chip ice cream.*

choc·o·late mousse ▶ **n.** see MOUSSE.

choc·o·late spot ▶ **n.** a fungal disease affecting field and broad beans, characterized by dark brown spots on all parts of the plant. ● This is caused by the fungus *Botrytis fabae* (sometimes the gray mold *B. cinerea*), phylum Ascomycota.

choc·o·late vine ▶ **n.** a fast-growing, shade-tolerant woody twining vine, native to Asia and introduced as an ornamental in the US. It has escaped cultivation and threatens native plants in some woodland habitats. ● *Akebia quinata*, family Lardizabalaceae.

cho·co·la·tier /ˌCHôk(ə)ləˈti(ə)r, SHôkəläˈtyā/ ▶ **n.** a maker or seller of chocolate.
– ORIGIN late 19th cent.: French.

Choc·taw /ˈCHäkˌtô/ ▶ **n.** (pl. **same** or **Choctaws**) **1** a member of an indigenous people now living mainly in Mississippi.
2 the Muskogean language of this people, closely related to Chickasaw.
3 Figure Skating a step from one edge of a skate to the other edge of the other skate in the opposite direction.
▶ **adj.** of or relating to the Choctaw or their language.
– ORIGIN from Choctaw *čahta*.

choice /CHois/ ▶ **n.** an act of selecting or making a decision when faced with two or more possibilities: *the choice between good and evil.* ■ the right or ability to make, or possibility of making, such a selection: *I had to do it, I had no choice.* ■ a range of possibilities from which one or more may be selected: *you can have a sofa made to order in a choice of over forty fabrics.* ■ a course of action, thing, or person that is selected or decided upon: *this CD drive is the perfect choice for your computer.*
▶ **adj. 1** (esp. of food) of very good quality: *he picked some choice early plums.*
2 (of words, phrases, or language) rude and abusive: *he had a few choice words at his command.*
– PHRASES **by choice** of one's own volition. **of choice** selected as one's favorite or the best: *champagne was his drink of choice.* **of one's choice** that one chooses or has chosen: *the college of her choice.*
– DERIVATIVES **choice·ly adv.**, **choice·ness n.**
– ORIGIN Middle English: from Old French *chois*, from *choisir* 'choose,' of Germanic origin and related to CHOOSE.

choil /CHoil/ ▶ **n.** the end of a knife's cutting edge that is nearer to the handle.
– ORIGIN late 19th cent.: of unknown origin.

choir /ˈkwīr/ ▶ **n.** an organized group of singers, typically one that takes part in church services or performs regularly in public: *a church choir.* ■ one of two or more subdivisions of such a group performing together: *his famous* Spem in alium *for eight five-part choirs.* ■ the part of a cathedral or large church between the altar and the nave, used by the choir and clergy. ■ a group of instruments of one family playing together: *a clarinet choir.*
– ORIGIN Middle English *quer, quere*, from Old French *quer*, from Latin *chorus* (see CHORUS). The spelling change in the 17th cent. was due to association with Latin *chorus* and modern French *choeur*.

choir·boy /ˈkwīrˌboi/ ▶ **n.** a boy who sings in a church or cathedral choir.

choir·girl /ˈkwīrˌgərl/ ▶ **n.** a girl who sings in a church or cathedral choir.

choir·mas·ter /ˈkwīrˌmastər/ ▶ **n.** the conductor of a choir.

choir or·gan ▶ **n.** a separate division of many large organs, played using a third manual (keyboard), and typically having distinctively toned stops.

choir stall ▶ **n.** (usu. **choir stalls**) a fixed seat for one or more people in the choir of a church or chapel.

choi sum /CHoi ˈsəm/ (also **choy sum**) ▶ **n.** a small Chinese cabbage of a variety with mild-tasting leaves and small edible yellow flowers. ● *Brassica rapa* (var. *parachinensis*), family Cruciferae.
– ORIGIN Chinese (Cantonese dialect), literally 'vegetable heart.'

choi·sy·a /ˈCHoiˌzēə/ ▶ **n.** an evergreen Mexican shrub with sweet-scented white flowers, widely grown as an ornamental. ● *Choisya ternata*, family Rutaceae.
– ORIGIN named after Jacques D. *Choisy* (1799–1859), Swiss botanist.

choke[1] /CHōk/ ▶ **v. 1** [no obj.] (of a person or animal) have severe difficulty in breathing because of a constricted or obstructed throat or a lack of air: ***Willie choked on a mouthful of soda.*** ■ [with obj.] hinder or obstruct the breathing of (a person or animal) in such a way. ■ [with obj.] prevent (a plant) from growing by depriving it of light, air, or nourishment: *the bracken will choke the wild gladiolus.* ■ (**choke something down**) swallow something with difficulty: *I attempted to choke down supper.* ■ [with obj.] prevent or suppress (the occurrence of something): *higher rates of interest* ***choke off*** *investment demand.* ■ [no obj.] informal (in sports) fail to perform at a crucial point of a game or contest owing to a failure of nerve: *we were the only team not to choke when it came to the crunch.*
2 [with obj.] (often **be choked with**) fill (a passage or space), esp. so as to make movement difficult or impossible: *the roads were choked with traffic.*
3 [with obj.] overwhelm and make (someone) speechless with a strong and typically negative feeling or emotion: *she was choked with angry emotion.* ■ become or cause to become tearful or extremely upset: [no obj.] *I just* ***choked up*** *reading it.* ■ suppress a strong emotion or the expression of such an emotion: *Liz was* ***choking back*** *her anger.*
4 [with obj.] enrich the fuel mixture in (a gasoline engine) by reducing the intake of air.
▶ **n. 1** a valve in the carburetor of a gasoline engine that is used to reduce the amount of air in the fuel mixture when the engine is started. ■ a knob that controls such a valve. ■ a narrowed part of a shotgun bore, typically near the muzzle and serving to restrict the spread of the shot. ■ informal an electrical inductor, esp. an inductance coil used to smooth the variations of an alternating current or to alter its phase.
2 an action or sound of a person or animal having or seeming to have difficulty in breathing: *a little choke of laughter.*
– PHRASAL VERBS **choke up** (in sports) grip (a bat, racket, etc.) further from the narrow end than is usual: *he* ***choked up on*** *the bat a few inches.*
– ORIGIN Middle English: from Old English *āceōcian* (verb), from *cēoce* (see CHEEK).

choke[2] ▶ **n.** the inedible mass of silky fibers at the center of a globe artichoke.
– ORIGIN late 17th cent.: probably a confusion of the ending of *artichoke* with CHOKE[1].

choke·ber·ry /ˈCHōkˌberē/ ▶ **n.** (pl. **chokeberries**) a North American shrub of the rose family, with white flowers and red autumn foliage, cultivated as an ornamental. ● Genus *Aronia*, family Rosaceae: several species, esp. the **red chokeberry** (*A. arbutifolia*), **purple chokeberry** (*A. floribunda*), and **black chokeberry** (*A. melanocarpa*), each named for the color of its fruits. ■ the berrylike fruit of this shrub, which is bitter and unpalatable.

choke chain ▶ **n.** a chain formed into a loop by passing one end through a ring on the other, placed around a dog's neck to exert control by causing pressure on the windpipe when the dog pulls.

choke·cher·ry /ˈCHōkˌCHerē/ ▶ **n.** a North American cherry with an edible astringent fruit that is more palatable when cooked. ● *Prunus virginiana*, family Rosaceae.

choke·damp /ˈCHōkˌdamp/ ▶ **n.** another term for BLACKDAMP.

choke·hold /ˈCHōkˌhōld/ ▶ **n.** a tight grip around a person's neck, used to restrain him or her by restricting breathing: *the police have banned chokeholds* | figurative *the southern delegates had the convention in a chokehold.*

choke point ▶ **n.** a point of congestion or blockage: *the tunnel is a choke point at rush hour.*

chok·er /ˈCHōkər/ ▶ **n. 1** a necklace or ornamental band of fabric that fits closely around the neck. ■ a clerical or other high collar.
2 a cable looped around a log to drag it.

cho·ki·dar /ˈCHōkiˌdär/ ▶ **n.** variant spelling of CHOWKIDAR.

Chok·we /ˈCHäkwē/ ▶ **n.** (pl. **same**) **1** a member of a people living in the Democratic Republic of the Congo (formerly Zaire) and northern Angola.
2 the Bantu language of this people.
▶ **adj.** of or relating to this people or their language.

chok·y /ˈCHōkē/ ▶ **adj.** (**chokier, chokiest**) having or causing difficulty in breathing: *the whole place was choky with tear gas.* ■ breathless and overwhelmed with emotion: *"Nick," she said, suddenly choky.*

cho·la /ˈCHōlə/ ▶ **n.** a Latin American woman or girl with Indian blood; a mestiza: [as modifier] *a couple of chola girls.*
– ORIGIN mid 19th cent.: American Spanish (see CHOLO).

cho·lan·gi·og·ra·phy /kəˌlanjēˈägrəfē/ ▶ **n.** Medicine X-ray examination of the bile ducts, used to locate and identify an obstruction.
– DERIVATIVES **cho·lan·gi·o·gram** /kəˈlanjēəˌgram/ **n.**
– ORIGIN 1930s: coined in Spanish from Greek *kholē* 'bile' + *angeion* 'vessel' + *-graphia* (see -GRAPHY).

chole- (also **chol-** before a vowel) ▶ **comb. form** Medicine & Chemistry relating to bile or the bile ducts: *cholelithiasis* | *cholesterol.*
– ORIGIN from Greek *kholē* 'gall, bile.'

cho·le·cal·cif·er·ol /ˌkōləˌkalˈsifəˌrôl, -ˌrōl/ ▶ **n.** Biochemistry one of the D vitamins, a sterol that is formed by the action of sunlight on dehydrocholesterol in the skin. Deficiency of this vitamin affects calcium levels, causing rickets in children and osteomalacia in adults. Also called VITAMIN D3 (see VITAMIN D).

cholecyst- ▶ **comb. form** relating to the gallbladder: *cholecystectomy.*
– ORIGIN from modern Latin *cholecystis* 'gallbladder.'

cho·le·cys·tec·to·my /ˌkōləˌsisˈtektəmē/ ▶ **n.** (pl. **cholecystectomies**) surgical removal of the gallbladder.

cho·le·cys·ti·tis /kōləˌsisˈtītis/ ▶ **n.** Medicine inflammation of the gallbladder.

cho·le·cys·tog·ra·phy /ˌkōləˌsisˈtägrəfē/ ▶ **n.** Medicine X-ray examination of the gallbladder, esp. used to detect the presence of gallstones.

cho·le·cys·to·ki·nin /ˌkōləˌsistōˈkīnən/ ▶ **n.** Biochemistry a hormone that is secreted by cells in the duodenum and stimulates the release of bile into the intestine and the secretion of enzymes by the pancreas.

cho·le·li·thi·a·sis /ˌkōləˌləˈTHīəsəs/ ▶ **n.** Medicine the formation of gallstones.

cho·lent /ˈCHôlənt, ˈCHəl-/ ▶ **n.** a Jewish Sabbath dish of slowly baked meat and vegetables, prepared on a Friday and cooked overnight.
– ORIGIN from Yiddish *tsholnt*.

chol·er /ˈkälər/ ▶ **n.** (in medieval science and medicine) one of the four bodily humors, identified with bile, believed to be associated with a peevish or irascible temperament. Also called YELLOW BILE. ■ literary or archaic anger or irascibility.
– ORIGIN late Middle English (also denoting diarrhea): from Old French *colere* 'bile, anger,' from Latin *cholera* 'diarrhea' (from Greek *kholera*), which in late Latin acquired the senses 'bile or anger,' from Greek *kholē* 'bile.'

chol·er·a /ˈkälərə/ ▶ **n.** an infectious and often fatal bacterial disease of the small intestine, typically contracted from infected water supplies and causing severe vomiting and diarrhea. ● The disease is caused by the bacterium *Vibrio cholerae*. See VIBRIO.
– ORIGIN late Middle English (originally denoting bile and later applied to various ailments involving vomiting and diarrhea): from Latin (see CHOLER). The current sense dates from the early 19th cent.

chol·e·ra·ic /ˌkäləˈrā-ik/ ▶ **adj.** archaic infected with cholera.

chol·er·ic /ˈkälərik, kəˈlerik/ ▶ **adj.** bad-tempered or irritable. ■ historical influenced by or predominating in the humor called choler: *a choleric disposition.*
– DERIVATIVES **chol·er·i·cal·ly adv.**
– ORIGIN Middle English (in the sense 'bilious'): from Old French *cholerique*, via Latin from Greek *kholerikos*, from *kholera* (see CHOLER).

cho·les·ter·ol /kəˈlestəˌrôl, -ˌrōl/ ▶ **n.** a compound of the sterol type found in most body tissues, including the blood and the nerves. Cholesterol and its derivatives are important constituents of cell membranes and precursors of other steroid compounds, but high concentrations in the blood (mainly derived from animal fats in the diet) are thought to promote atherosclerosis. ● Chem. formula: $C_{27}H_{45}OH$.
– ORIGIN late 19th cent.: from Greek *kholē* 'bile' + *stereos* 'stiff' + -OL.

cho·lic ac·id /ˈkōlik/ ▶ **n.** Biochemistry a compound produced by oxidation of cholesterol. It is a steroidal fatty acid and its salts are present in bile.
– ORIGIN mid 19th cent.: from Greek *kholikos*, from *kholē* 'bile.'

cho·line /ˈkōˌlēn/ ▶ **n.** Biochemistry a strongly basic compound occurring widely in living tissues and important in the synthesis and transport of lipids. ● Chem. formula: $HON(CH_3)_3CH_2CH_2OH$.
– ORIGIN mid 19th cent.: coined in German from Greek *kholē* 'bile.'

cho·lin·er·gic /ˌkōləˈnərjik/ ▶ **adj.** Physiology **1** relating to or denoting nerve cells in which acetylcholine acts as a neurotransmitter. Contrasted with ADRENERGIC.
2 releasing or responding to acetylcholine.
– ORIGIN 1930s: from CHOLINE + Greek *ergon* 'work' + -IC.

cho·lin·es·ter·ase /ˌkōləˈnestəˌrās, -ˌrāz/ ▶ **n.** Biochemistry an enzyme, esp. acetylcholinesterase, that hydrolyzes esters of choline.

chol·la /ˈCHoi(y)ə/ ▶ **n.** a cactus with a cylindrical stem, native to Mexico and the southwestern US. ● Genus *Cylindropuntia*, family Cactaceae: several species, including the densely spiny **teddy-bear cholla** (*C. bigelovii*) and the treelike **cane cholla** (*C. spinosior*).
– ORIGIN mid 19th cent.: Mexican Spanish use of Spanish *cholla* 'skull, head,' of unknown origin.

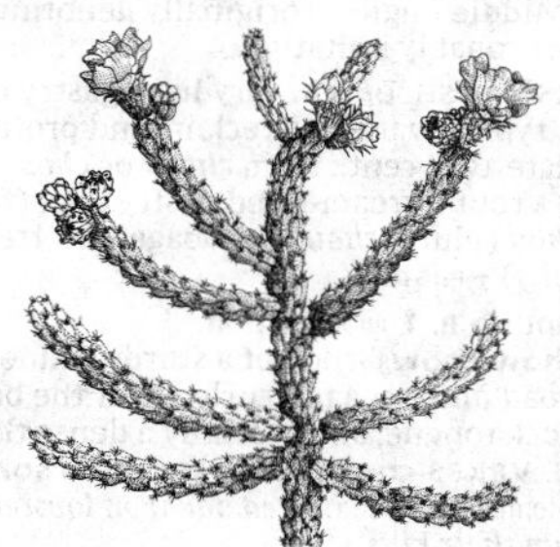
cane cholla

cho·lo /ˈCHōlō/ ▶ **n.** (pl. **cholos**) a Latin American with Indian blood; a mestizo. ■ informal, offensive a lower-class Mexican, esp. in an urban area. ■ a teenage boy, esp. in a Mexican-American community, who is a member of a street gang.
– ORIGIN mid 19th cent.: American Spanish, from *Chollolán* (now *Cholula*), in Mexico.

cho·metz ▶ **n.** variant spelling of CHAMETZ.

Chom·o·lung·ma variant form of QOMOLUNGMA.

chomp /CHämp, CHômp/ ▶ **v.** [no obj.] **1** munch or chew vigorously and noisily: *he chomped on his sandwich.* ■ (of a horse) make a noisy biting or chewing action.
2 fret impatiently: *he waited, chomping at her nonappearance.*
▶ **n.** [in sing.] a chewing noise or action.
– PHRASES **chomp** (or **champ** or **chafe**) **at the bit** be restless and impatient to start doing something.
– ORIGIN mid 17th cent.: probably imitative.

Chom·sky /ˈCHäm(p)skē/, Noam (1928–), US theoretical linguist; full name *Avram Noam Chomsky.* Noted for expounding the theory of generative grammar, he also theorized that linguistic behavior is innate, not learned, and that all languages share the same underlying grammatical base. Notable works: *Syntactic Structures* (1957) and *Aspects of the Theory of Syntax* (1965).

Chon·drich·thy·es /känˈdrikTHēˌēz/ Zoology a class of fishes that includes those with a cartilaginous skeleton. Compare with OSTEICHTHYES.
– ORIGIN modern Latin, from Greek *khondros* 'cartilage' + *ikhthus* 'fish.'

chon·drite /ˈkänˌdrīt/ ▶ **n.** a stony meteorite containing small mineral granules (chondrules).
– DERIVATIVES **chon·drit·ic** /känˈdritik/ **adj.**
– ORIGIN mid 19th cent.: from Greek *khondros* 'granule' + -ITE[1].

chondro- ▶ **comb. form** of or relating to cartilage: *chondrocyte.*
– ORIGIN from Greek *khondros* 'grain or cartilage.'

chon·dro·cra·ni·um /ˌkändrōˈkrānēəm/ ▶ **n.** Zoology & Embryology the primary skull of vertebrates, composed of cartilage, which in humans and most other vertebrates is replaced by bone during development.

chon·dro·cyte /ˈkändrəˌsīt/ ▶ **n.** Biology a cell that has secreted the matrix of cartilage and become embedded in it.

chon·dro·i·tin /känˈdroitn, -ˈdrōətn/ ▶ **n.** Biochemistry a compound that is a major constituent of cartilage and other connective tissue. It is a glycosaminoglycan and occurs mainly in the form of sulfate esters.
– ORIGIN late 19th cent.: from CHONDRO- + -ITE[1] + -IN[1].

chon·drule /ˈkändro͞ol/ ▶ **n.** a spheroidal mineral grain present in large numbers in some stony meteorites.

Chong·jin /ˈCHəNGˈjēn/ a port on the northeastern coast of North Korea; pop. 582,500 (est. 2005).

Chong·qing /ˈCHəNGˈkiNG/ (also **Chungking**) a city in Sichuan province, in central China, on the Yangtze River; pop. 4,776,000 (est. 2006). It was the capital of China from 1938 to 1946.

choo-choo /ˈCHo͞o ˌCHo͞o/ (also **choo-choo train**) ▶ **n.** a child's word for a railroad train or locomotive, esp. a steam engine.
– ORIGIN early 20th cent.: imitative.

choose /CHo͞oz/ ▶ **v.** (past **chose** /CHōz/; past participle **chosen** /ˈCHōzən/) [with obj.] pick out or select (someone or something) as being the best or most appropriate of two or more alternatives: *he chose a seat facing the door* | [no obj.] *now it's my turn to choose.* ■ [no obj.] decide on a course of action, typically after rejecting alternatives: [with infinitive] *he chose to go* | *I'll stay as long as I choose.*
– PHRASES **cannot choose but do something** formal have no alternative to doing something. **there is little** (or **nothing**) **to choose between** there is little or no difference between.
– DERIVATIVES **choos·er n.**
– ORIGIN Old English *cēosan*, of Germanic origin; related to Dutch *kiezen.*

choos·y /ˈCHo͞ozē/ ▶ **adj.** (**choosier**, **choosiest**) informal overly fastidious in making a choice.
– DERIVATIVES **choos·i·ly** /-zəlē/ **adv.**, **choos·i·ness n.**

chop /CHäp/ ▶ **v.** (**chops**, **chopping**, **chopped**) [with obj.] cut (something) into small pieces with repeated sharp blows using an ax or knife: *they chopped up the pulpit for firewood* | *finely chop the parsley.* ■ (**chop something off**) remove by cutting: *they chopped off all her hair.* ■ cut through the base of (something, esp. a tree) with blows from an ax or similar implement, in order to fell it: *the boy chopped down eight trees* | [no obj.] *the men were chopping at the undergrowth with machetes.* ■ strike (a ball) with a short heavy blow, as if cutting at something. ■ (usu. **be chopped**) abolish or reduce the size or extent of (something) in a way regarded as brutally sudden: *their training courses are to be chopped.*
▶ **n. 1** a downward cutting blow or movement, typically with the hand: *an effective chop to the back of the neck.*
2 a thick slice of meat, esp. pork or lamb, adjacent to, and typically including, a rib.
3 crushed or ground grain used as animal feed.
4 [in sing.] the broken motion of water, typically due to the action of the wind against the tide: *we started our run into a two-foot chop.*
– PHRASES **chop logic** argue in a tiresomely pedantic way; quibble. [mid 16th cent.: from a dialect use of *chop* meaning 'bandy words.']
– ORIGIN late Middle English: variant of CHAP[1].

chop-chop /ˌCHäp ˈCHäp/ ▶ **adv. & exclam.** quickly; quick: *"Two beers, chop-chop," Jimmy called.*
– ORIGIN mid 19th cent.: pidgin English, based on Chinese dialect *kuài-kuài.* Compare with CHOPSTICK.

chop·fall·en /ˈCHäpˌfôlən/ ▶ **adj.** variant spelling of CHAPFALLEN.

chop·house /ˈCHäpˌhous/ ▶ **n.** a restaurant that specializes in steaks, chops, and similar fare.

Cho·pin[1] /ˈSHōˌpan, SHōˈpaN/, Frédéric (François) (1810–49), French composer and pianist; born in Poland; Polish name *Fryderyk Franciszek Szopen.* Writing almost exclusively for the piano, he composed numerous mazurkas and polonaises inspired by Polish folk music, as well as nocturnes, preludes, and two piano concertos (1829; 1830).

Cho·pin[2] /ˈSHōˌpan, SHōˈpan/, Kate (O'Flaherty) (1851–1904), US novelist and short-story writer. Notable works: *Bayou Folk* (1894), *A Night in Acadie* (1897), and *The Awakening* (1899).

chopped liv·er ▶ **n. 1** a savory spread made from sautéed liver and onions.
2 informal, humorous a person or thing regarded as insignificant: *remember the three kings showed up with gold, frankincense, and myrrh, none of which were chopped liver back then.*

C

chop·per /ˈCHäpər/ ▶ **n. 1** a short ax with a large blade. ■ a butcher's cleaver. ■ a device for regularly interrupting an electric current or a beam of light or particles. ■ (**choppers**) informal teeth.
2 informal a helicopter.
3 informal a motorcycle, esp. one with high handlebars and the front-wheel fork extended forward.
4 Baseball a batted ball that makes a high bounce after hitting the ground in fair territory: *Bell followed with a high chopper to the third baseman.*

chop·ping block ▶ **n.** a block for chopping something on, in particular: ■ a block for chopping wood. ■ a block for chopping food such as meat, vegetables, and herbs. ■ historical an executioner's block.
– PHRASES **on the chopping block** likely to be abolished or drastically reduced.

chop·py /ˈCHäpē/ ▶ **adj.** (**choppier**, **choppiest**) (of a sea or river) having many small waves.
– DERIVATIVES **chop·pi·ly** /ˈCHäpəlē/ **adv.**, **chop·pi·ness n.**
– ORIGIN early 17th cent. (in the sense 'full of chaps or clefts'): from CHOP + -Y[1].

chops /CHäps/ ▶ **plural n.** informal **1** a person's or animal's mouth or jaws: *a smack in the chops.* ■ a person's cheeks; jowls.
2 the technical skill of a musician, esp. one who plays jazz: *when I'm on tour, my chops go down.*
– PHRASES **bust one's chops** informal exert oneself. **bust someone's chops** informal nag or criticize someone.
– ORIGIN late Middle English: variant of CHAP[3].

chop shop ▶ **n.** informal a place where stolen vehicles are dismantled so that the parts can be sold or used to repair other stolen vehicles.

chop·sock·y /ˌCHäpˈsäkē/ ▶ **n.** [usu. as modifier] informal kung fu or a similar martial art, esp. as depicted in violent action movies: *chopsocky epics from Hong Kong.*
– ORIGIN 1970s: perhaps humorously, suggested by CHOP SUEY.

chop·stick /ˈCHäpˌstik/ ▶ **n.** (usu. **chopsticks**) each of a pair of small, thin, tapered sticks of wood, ivory, or plastic, held together in one hand and used as eating utensils, esp. by the Chinese, the Japanese, and other people in eastern Asia.
– ORIGIN late 17th cent.: pidgin English, from *chop* 'quick' + STICK[1], translating Chinese dialect *kuàizi*, literally 'nimble ones.' Compare with CHOP-CHOP.

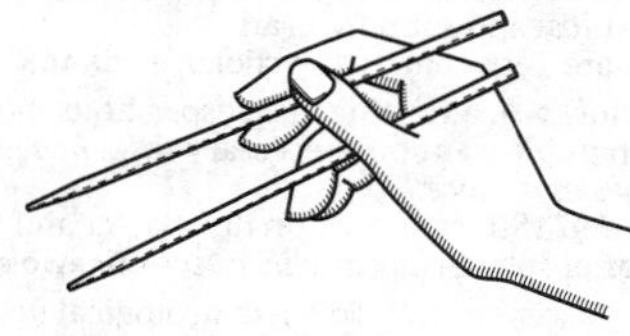
chopsticks

chop su·ey /ˌCHäp ˈso͞oē/ ▶ **n.** a Chinese-style dish of meat stewed and fried with bean sprouts, bamboo shoots, and onions, and often served with rice.
– ORIGIN late 19th cent.: from Chinese (Cantonese dialect) *tsaâp suì* 'mixed bits.'

cho·ral /ˈkôrəl/ ▶ **adj.** composed for or sung by a choir or chorus: *a choral work* | *choral singing.* ■ engaged in or concerned with singing: *a choral scholar.*
– DERIVATIVES **cho·ral·ly adv.**
– ORIGIN late 16th cent.: from medieval Latin *choralis*, from Latin *chorus* (see CHORUS).

cho·rale /kəˈral, -ˈräl/ ▶ **n. 1** a musical composition (or part of one) consisting of or resembling a harmonized version of a simple, stately hymn tune.
2 a choir or choral society.
– ORIGIN mid 19th cent.: from German *Choral* (*gesang*), translating medieval Latin *cantus choralis.*

PRONUNCIATION KEY ə *ago, up*; ər *over, fur*; a *hat*; ā *ate*; ä *car*; e *let*; ē *see*; i *fit*; ī *by*; NG *sing*; ō *go*; ô *law, for*; oi *toy*; o͝o *good*; o͞o *goo*; ou *out*; TH *thin*; TH *then*; ZH *vision*

cho·rale pre·lude ▶ **n.** an organ piece based on a chorale.

cho·ral speak·ing ▶ **n.** the recitation of poetry or prose by a chorus or ensemble.

chord¹ /kôrd/ ▶ **n.** a group of (typically three or more) notes sounded together, as a basis of harmony: *the triumphal opening chords* | *a G major chord.*
▶ **v.** [no obj.] (usu. as noun **chording**) play, sing, or arrange notes in chords.
– DERIVATIVES **chord·al** /ˈkôrdl/ **adj.**
– ORIGIN Middle English *cord*, from ACCORD. The spelling change in the 18th cent. was due to confusion with CHORD². The original sense was 'agreement, reconciliation,' later 'a musical concord or harmonious sound'; the current sense dates from the mid 18th cent.

chord² ▶ **n. 1** Mathematics a straight line joining the ends of an arc. ■ Aeronautics the width of an airfoil from leading to trailing edge. ■ Engineering each of the two principal members of a truss.
2 Anatomy variant spelling of CORD: *spinal chord.*
3 literary a string on a harp or other instrument.
– PHRASES **strike** (or **touch**) **a chord** affect or stir someone's emotions: *the issue of food safety strikes a chord with almost everyone.* [with figurative reference to the emotions being the 'strings' of the mind visualized as a musical instrument.] **strike** (or **touch**) **the right chord** skillfully appeal to or arouse a particular emotion in others: *Dickens knew how to strike the right chord in the hearts of his readers.*
– ORIGIN mid 16th cent. (in the anatomical sense): a later spelling (influenced by Latin *chorda* 'rope') of CORD.

> **USAGE** In modern English there are two words spelled **chord**: the first is the musical term meaning 'a group of notes sounded together,' and the second is a technical term in mathematics, aeronautics, and engineering. **Cord** meaning 'string or rope made from twisted strands' is etymologically related to the second **chord**, but is now regarded as a distinct word. The anatomical term generally uses the spelling **cord** (as in **spinal cord** and **vocal cord**), although **chord** is an acceptable variant.

Chor·da·ta /kôrˈdätə, -ˈdātə/ Zoology a large phylum of animals that includes the vertebrates together with the sea squirts and lancelets. They are distinguished by the possession of a notochord at some stage during their development.
– ORIGIN modern Latin (plural), from Latin *chorda* (see CHORD²), on the pattern of words such as *Vertebrata.*

chor·date /ˈkôrdət, -ˌdāt/ Zoology ▶ **n.** an animal of the large phylum Chordata, comprising the vertebrates together with the sea squirts and lancelets.
▶ **adj.** relating to or denoting chordates.

chor·do·phone /ˈkôrdəˌfōn/ ▶ **n.** Music, technical a stringed instrument.

chor·do·to·nal /ˌkôrdəˈtōnl/ ▶ **adj.** Entomology (in insects) denoting sense organs that are responsive to mechanical and sound vibrations.
– ORIGIN late 19th cent.: from CHORD² + TONAL.

chore /CHôr/ ▶ **n.** a routine task, esp. a household one. ■ an unpleasant but necessary task: *he sees interviews as a chore.*
– ORIGIN mid 18th cent. (originally dialect and US): variant of obsolete *char* or *chare* (see CHARWOMAN).

cho·re·a /kəˈrēə/ ▶ **n.** Medicine a neurological disorder characterized by jerky involuntary movements affecting esp. the shoulders, hips, and face. See also HUNTINGTON'S CHOREA, SYDENHAM'S CHOREA.
– ORIGIN late 17th cent.: via Latin from Greek *khoreia* 'dancing in unison,' from *khoros* 'chorus.'

cho·re·o·graph /ˈkôrēəˌgraf/ ▶ **v.** [with obj.] compose the sequence of steps and moves for (a performance of dance or ice skating): *he is now choreographing a ballet.* ■ plan and control (an event or operation): *the committee choreographs the movement of troops.*
– DERIVATIVES **cho·re·og·ra·pher** /ˌkôrēˈägrəfər/ **n.**
– ORIGIN 1940s: back-formation from CHOREOGRAPHY.

cho·re·og·ra·phy /ˌkôrēˈägrəfē/ ▶ **n.** the sequence of steps and movements in dance or figure skating, esp. in a ballet or other staged dance: *the lively choreography reflects the themes of the original play.* ■ the art or practice of designing such sequences. ■ the written notation for such a sequence.
– DERIVATIVES **cho·re·o·graph·ic** /ˌkôrēəˈgrafik/ **adj.**, **cho·re·o·graph·i·cal·ly** /ˌkôrēəˈgrafik(ə)lē/ **adv.**
– ORIGIN late 18th cent. (in the sense 'written notation of dancing'): from Greek *khoreia* 'dancing in unison' (from *khoros* 'chorus') + -GRAPHY.

cho·re·ol·o·gy /ˌkôrēˈäləjē/ ▶ **n.** the notation of dance movement.
– DERIVATIVES **cho·re·ol·o·gist** /-jist/ **n.**
– ORIGIN 1960s: from Greek *khoreia* 'dancing in unison' (from *khoros* 'chorus') + -LOGY.

cho·ri·am·bus /ˌkôrēˈambəs/ (also **choriamb** /ˈkôrēˌam(b)/) ▶ **n.** (pl. **choriambi** /-bī, -bē/) a metrical foot consisting of two short (or unstressed) syllables between two long (or stressed) ones.
– DERIVATIVES **cho·ri·am·bic** /-ˈambik/ **adj.**
– ORIGIN late 18th cent.: via late Latin from Greek *khoriambos*, from *khoreios* 'of the dance' + *iambos* (see IAMBUS).

cho·ric /ˈkôrik/ ▶ **adj.** belonging to, spoken by, or resembling a chorus in drama or recitation.
– ORIGIN mid 19th cent.: via late Latin from Greek *khorikos*, from *khoros* 'chorus.'

cho·rine /ˈkôrˌēn/ ▶ **n.** a chorus girl.
– ORIGIN 1920s (originally US): from CHORUS + -INE³.

chorio- ▶ **comb. form** representing CHORION or CHOROID.

cho·ri·o·al·lan·to·ic /ˌkôrēōˌalənˈtō-ik/ ▶ **adj.** Embryology relating to or denoting fused chorionic and allantoic membranes around a fetus.

cho·ri·o·car·ci·no·ma /ˌkôrēōˌkärsəˈnōmə/ ▶ **n.** (pl. **choriocarcinomas** or **choriocarcinomata** /-ˈnōmətə/) Medicine a malignant tumor of the uterus that originates in the cells of the chorion of a fetus.

cho·ri·oid /ˈkôrēˌoid/ ▶ **adj.** another term for CHOROID.

cho·ri·on /ˈkôrēˌän/ ▶ **n.** Embryology the outermost membrane surrounding an embryo of a reptile, bird, or mammal. In mammals (including humans), it contributes to the formation of the placenta.
– DERIVATIVES **cho·ri·on·ic** /ˌkôrēˈänik/ **adj.**
– ORIGIN mid 16th cent.: from Greek *khorion.*

cho·ri·on·ic vil·lus sam·pling (abbr.: **CVS**) ▶ **n.** Medicine a test made in early pregnancy to detect congenital abnormalities in the fetus. A tiny tissue sample is taken from the villi of the chorion, which forms the fetal part of the placenta.

chor·is·ter /ˈkôrəstər, ˈkär-/ ▶ **n. 1** a member of a choir, esp. a child or young person singing the treble part in a church choir.
2 a person who leads the singing of a church choir or congregation.
– ORIGIN late Middle English *queristre*, from an Anglo-Norman French variant of Old French *cueriste*, from *quer* (see CHOIR). The change in the first syllable in the 16th cent. was due to association with obsolete *chorist* 'member of a choir or chorus,' but the older form *quirister* long survived.

cho·ri·zo /CHəˈrēzō, -sō/ ▶ **n.** (pl. **chorizos**) a spicy Spanish pork sausage.
– ORIGIN Spanish.

cho·rog·ra·phy /kəˈrägrəfē/ ▶ **n.** chiefly historical the systematic description and mapping of regions or districts.
– DERIVATIVES **cho·rog·ra·pher** /-fər/ **n.**, **cho·ro·graph·ic** /ˌkôrəˈgrafik/ **adj.**
– ORIGIN mid 16th cent.: via Latin from Greek *khōrographia*, from *khōra* or *khōros* 'region.'

cho·roid /ˈkôrˌoid/ (also **chorioid** /ˈkôrēˌoid/) ▶ **adj.** resembling the chorion, particularly in containing many blood vessels.
▶ **n.** (also **choroid coat**) the pigmented vascular layer of the eyeball between the retina and the sclera.
– DERIVATIVES **cho·roi·dal** /kəˈroidl/ **adj.**
– ORIGIN mid 17th cent.: from Greek *khoroeidēs* (adjective), alteration of *khorioeidēs*, from *khorion* (see CHORION).

cho·roid plex·us ▶ **n.** (pl. **same** or **plexuses**) a network of blood vessels in each ventricle of the brain. It is derived from the pia mater and produces the cerebrospinal fluid.

chor·o·pleth map /ˈkôrəˌpleTH/ ▶ **n.** a map that uses differences in shading, coloring, or the placing of symbols within predefined areas to indicate the average values of a property or quantity in those areas. Compare with ISOPLETH.
– ORIGIN 1930s: *choropleth* from Greek *khōra* 'region' + *plēthos* 'multitude.'

Chor·ril·los /CHōˈrē(y)ōs/ a town in west central Peru, a resort and suburb south of Lima; pop. 262,525 (2005).

chor·tle /ˈCHôrtl/ ▶ **v.** [no obj.] laugh in a breathy, gleeful way; chuckle: *he chortled at his own pun.*
▶ **n.** a breathy, gleeful laugh: *Thomas gave a chortle.*
– ORIGIN 1871: coined by Lewis Carroll in *Through the Looking Glass*; probably a blend of CHUCKLE and SNORT.

cho·rus /ˈkôrəs/ ▶ **n.** (pl. **choruses**) **1** a large organized group of singers, esp. one that performs together with an orchestra or opera company. ■ a group of singers or dancers performing together in a supporting role in a stage musical or opera. ■ a piece of choral music, esp. one forming part of a larger work such as an opera or oratorio. ■ a part of a song that is repeated after each verse, typically by more than one singer. ■ a simple song for group singing, esp. in informal Christian worship.
2 (in ancient Greek tragedy) a group of performers who comment on the main action, typically speaking and moving together. ■ a simultaneous utterance of something by many people: *a growing chorus of complaint* | *"Good morning," we replied in chorus.* ■ a single character who speaks the prologue and other linking parts of the play, esp. in Elizabethan drama. ■ a section of text spoken by the chorus in drama. ■ a device used with an amplified musical instrument to give the impression that more than one instrument is being played: [as modifier] *a chorus pedal.*
▶ **v.** (**chorused, chorusing**) [with obj.] (of a group of people) say the same thing at the same time: *they chorused a noisy amen* | [with direct speech] *"Morning, Father," the children chorused.*
– ORIGIN mid 16th cent. (denoting a character speaking the prologue and epilogue in a play and serving to comment on events): from Latin, from Greek *khoros.*

cho·rus girl ▶ **n.** a young woman who sings or dances in the chorus of a musical.

chose /CHōz/ past of CHOOSE.

cho·sen /ˈCHōzən/ past participle of CHOOSE.
▶ **adj.** [attrib.] having been selected as the best or most appropriate: *music is his chosen vocation.*
– PHRASES **chosen few** a group of people who are special or different, typically in a way thought to be unfair: *why have they kept this secret to themselves, the chosen few?* **chosen people** the Jewish people considered (in Jewish and Christian tradition) as having been selected by God for a special relationship with him. ■ (in Christian use) those destined for salvation; believing Christians.

Chou variant spelling of ZHOU.

chou·croute /SHo͞oˈkro͝ot/ ▶ **n.** pickled cabbage; sauerkraut.
– ORIGIN French, from German dialect *Surkrut* 'sauerkraut,' influenced by French *chou* 'cabbage.'

Chou En-lai /ˌjō en ˈlī/ variant of ZHOU ENLAI.

chough /CHəf/ ▶ **n.** a black Eurasian and North African bird of the crow family, with a down-curved bill and broad rounded wings, typically frequenting mountains and sea cliffs. ● Genus *Pyrrhocorax*, family Corvidae: three species, esp. the **red-billed chough** (*P. pyrrhocorax*), with a long red bill, and the **alpine chough** (*P. graculus*), with a shorter yellow bill.
– ORIGIN Middle English (originally denoting the jackdaw): probably imitative.

choux pastry /SHo͞o/ ▶ **n.** very light pastry made with egg, typically used for eclairs and profiteroles.
– ORIGIN late 19th cent.: from *choux* or *chou*, denoting a round cream-filled pastry cake (from French *chou* (plural *choux*) 'cabbage, rosette,' from Latin *caulis*) + PASTRY.

chow /CHou/ ▶ **n. 1** informal food.
2 (also **chow chow**) a dog of a sturdy Chinese breed with a broad muzzle, a tail curled over the back, a bluish-black tongue, and typically a dense thick coat.
– PHRASAL VERBS **chow down** (or **chow something down**) informal eat: *he chowed down on lobster* | *lions chow down their kills.*
– ORIGIN late 19th cent.: shortened from CHOW CHOW.

chow 2

chow chow /ˈCHou ˌCHou/ ▶ **n. 1** another term for CHOW (sense 2).
2 (also **chow-chow**) a Chinese preserve of ginger, orange peel, and other ingredients, in syrup.
3 (also **chow-chow**) a mixed vegetable pickle.
– ORIGIN late 18th cent.: pidgin English, of unknown ultimate origin.

chow·der /ˈCHoudər/ ▶ **n.** a rich soup typically containing fish, clams, or corn with potatoes and onions: *clam chowder.*
– ORIGIN mid 18th cent.: perhaps from French *chaudière* 'stew pot,' related to Old Northern French *caudron* (see CAULDRON).

chow·der·head /ˈCHoudərˌhed/ ▶ **n.** informal a stupid person.

–DERIVATIVES **chow·der·head·ed** adj.
–ORIGIN mid 19th cent.: probably a variant form of early 17th-cent. *jolter-head* 'thick-headed person.'

chow·ki·dar /'CHôki,där/ (also **chokidar**) ▶ n. (in India) a watchman or gatekeeper.
–ORIGIN from Urdu *caukīdār*, from *caukī* 'toll house' + *-dār* 'keeper.'

chow mein /'CHou 'mān/ ▶ n. a Chinese-style dish of fried noodles with shredded meat or seafood and vegetables.
–ORIGIN late 19th cent.: from Chinese *chǎo miàn* 'fried noodles.'

choy sum ▶ n. variant spelling of CHOI SUM.

CHP ▶ abbr. combined heat and power, a system in which steam produced in a power station as a byproduct of electricity generation is used to heat nearby buildings.

Chr. ▶ abbr. Bible Chronicles.

chres·tom·a·thy /kre'stäməTHē/ ▶ n. (pl. **chrestomathies**) formal a selection of passages from an author or authors, designed to help in learning a language.
–ORIGIN mid 19th cent.: from Greek *khrēstomatheia*, from *khrēstos* 'useful' + *-matheia* 'learning.'

Chré·tien /krā'tyeN -'tyen/, Jean (1934–), Canadian Liberal statesman; prime minister 1993–2003; full name *Joseph-Jacques Jean Chrétien*.

Chré·tien de Troyes /krā'tyeN də 'trwä/ (12th century), French poet. His courtly romances on Arthurian themes include *Lancelot* (c.1177–81) and *Perceval* (c.1181–90, unfinished).

chrism /'krizəm/ ▶ n. a mixture of oil and balsam, consecrated and used for anointing at baptism and in other rites of Catholic, Orthodox, and Anglican Churches.
–ORIGIN Old English, from medieval Latin *crisma*, ecclesiastical Latin *chrisma*, from Greek *khrisma* 'anointing,' from *khriein* 'anoint.'

Chris·ma·tion /kriz'māSHən/ ▶ n. a rite in the Orthodox and Eastern Catholic churches that is comparable and similar to confirmation in the Roman Catholic Church.
–ORIGIN *chrism* (holy oil) + *-ation*.

chris·om /'krizəm/ ▶ n. historical a white robe put on a child at baptism.
–ORIGIN Middle English: alteration of CHRISM, representing a popular pronunciation with two syllables.

Chris·sake /krī(s)'sāk/ (also **Chrissakes**) ▶ n. (in phrase **for Chrissake**) informal for Christ's sake (used as an exclamation, typically of annoyance or exasperation): *for Chrissake, listen to me!*
–ORIGIN 1920s: representing a pronunciation.

Christ /krīst/ ▶ n. the title, also treated as a name, given to Jesus of Nazareth (see JESUS).
▶ exclam. an oath used to express irritation, dismay, or surprise.
–PHRASES **before Christ** full form of **BC**.
–DERIVATIVES **Christ·hood** /-,ho͝od/ n., **Christ·like** /-,līk/ adj., **Christ·ly** adj.
–ORIGIN Old English *Crīst*, from Latin *Christus*, from Greek *Khristos*, noun use of an adjective meaning 'anointed,' from *khriein* 'anoint,' translating Hebrew *māšīaḥ* 'Messiah.'

Chris·ta·del·phi·an /,kristə'delfēən/ ▶ n. a member of a Christian sect, founded in the US in 1848, that claims to return to the beliefs and practices of the earliest disciples and holds that Christ will return in power to set up a worldwide theocracy beginning at Jerusalem.
▶ adj. of or adhering to this sect and its beliefs.
–ORIGIN from late Greek *Khristadelphos* 'in brotherhood with Christ' (from *Khristos* 'Christ' + *adelphos* 'brother') + -IAN.

Christ·church /'krīs(t),CHərCH/ a city in New Zealand, on the eastern coast of South Island; pop. 348,435 (2006).

chris·ten /'krisən/ ▶ v. [with obj.] give (a baby) a Christian name at baptism as a sign of admission to a Christian Church: [with obj. and complement] *their second daughter was christened Jeanette*. ■ give to (someone or something) a name that reflects a notable quality or characteristic: [with obj. and complement] *a person so creepy that his colleagues christened him "Millipede."* ■ dedicate (a vessel, building, etc.) ceremonially: *their first garbage truck was christened with a bottle of champagne*. ■ informal use for the first time: *let's get steaks and christen the new grill*.
–DERIVATIVES **chris·ten·er** /'kris(ə)nər/ n.
–ORIGIN Old English *crīstnian* 'make Christian,' from *crīsten* 'Christian,' from Latin *Christianus*, from *Christus* 'Christ.'

Chris·ten·dom /'krisəndəm/ ▶ n. dated the worldwide body or society of Christians. ■ the Christian world: *the greatest church in Christendom*.
–ORIGIN Old English *crīstendōm*, from *crīsten* (see CHRISTEN) + *-dōm* (see -DOM).

Christ·er /'krīstər/ ▶ n. informal a sanctimonious or ostentatiously pious Christian.

Chris·tian[1] /'krisCHən/ ▶ adj. of, relating to, or professing Christianity or its teachings: *the Christian Church*. ■ informal having or showing qualities associated with Christians, esp. those of decency, kindness, and fairness.
▶ n. a person who has received Christian baptism or is a believer in Jesus Christ and his teachings.
–DERIVATIVES **Chris·tian·i·za·tion** /,krisCHənə'zāSHən/ n., **Chris·tian·ize** /-,nīz/ v., **Chris·tian·ly** adv.
–ORIGIN late Middle English: from Latin *Christianus*, from Greek *Christianos* (see CHRIST).

Chris·tian[2] Fletcher (c.1764–93), English seaman and mutineer. In April 1789, as first mate under Captain Bligh on the HMS *Bounty*, he seized the ship and cast Bligh and others adrift. In 1790, the mutineers settled on Pitcairn Island, where Christian was probably killed by Tahitians.

Chris·tian Broth·ers a Roman Catholic lay teaching order founded in France in 1684.

Chris·tian e·ra ▶ n. (**the Christian era**) the period of time that begins with the traditional date of Christ's birth.

Chris·ti·an·i·a /,kristē'anēə, ,krisCHē-/ (also **Kristiania**) former name (1624–1924) of OSLO.

Chris·ti·an·i·ty /,krisCHē'anitē/ ▶ n. the religion based on the person and teachings of Jesus of Nazareth, or its beliefs and practices. ■ Christian quality or character: *his Christianity sustained him*.

> Christianity is today the world's most widespread religion, with more than a billion members, mainly divided between the Roman Catholic, Protestant, and Eastern Orthodox Churches. It originated among the Jewish followers of Jesus of Nazareth, who believed that he was the promised Messiah (or 'Christ'), but the Christian Church soon became an independent organization, largely through the missionary efforts of St. Paul. In 313 Constantine ended official persecution in the Roman Empire and in 380 Theodosius I recognized it as the state religion. Most Christians believe in one God in three Persons (the Father, the Son, and the Holy Spirit) and that Jesus is the Son of God who rose from the dead after being crucified; a Christian hopes to attain eternal life after death through faith in Jesus Christ and tries to live by his teachings as recorded in the New Testament.

–ORIGIN Middle English: from Old French *crestiente*, from *crestien* 'Christian,' influenced by late Latin *christianitas*, from Latin *Christianus*, from *Christus* 'Christ.'

Chris·tian name ▶ n. a name given to an individual that distinguishes him or her from other members of the same family and is used as an address of familiarity; a forename, esp. one given at baptism.

> **USAGE** In recognition of the fact that English-speaking societies have many religions and cultures, not just Christian ones, the term **Christian name** has largely given way, at least in official contexts, to alternative terms such as **given name**, **first name**, or **forename**.

Chris·tian Sci·ence ▶ n. the beliefs and practices of the Church of Christ Scientist, a Christian sect founded by Mary Baker Eddy in 1879. Members hold that only God and the mind have ultimate reality, and that sin and illness are illusions that can be overcome by prayer and faith.
–DERIVATIVES **Chris·tian Sci·en·tist** n.

Chris·tian·sted /'krisCHən,sted/ a resort town on Saint Croix Island in the US Virgin Islands, once the capital of the Danish West Indies; pop. 2,700 (est. 2009).

Chris·tie[1] /'kristē/, Dame Agatha (1890–1976), English writer of detective fiction and plays. Many of her novels feature the Belgian detective Hercule Poirot or the resourceful Miss Marple. Her play *The Mousetrap* (1952) has run continuously since 1952 on the London stage. Other notable works: *Murder on the Orient Express* (1934) and *Death on the Nile* (1937).

Chris·tie[2] ▶ n. (pl. **Christies**) Skiing, dated a sudden turn in which the skis are kept parallel, used for changing direction fast or stopping short.
–ORIGIN 1920s (earlier as *Christiania*): named after CHRISTIANIA in Norway.

Chris·tin·gle /'kristiNGgəl/ ▶ n. a lighted candle symbolizing Christ as the light of the world, held by children esp. at a special Advent service originating in the Moravian Church.
–ORIGIN 1950s: probably from German dialect *Christkindl* 'Christ child, Christmas gift.'

Christ·mas /'krisməs/ ▶ n. (pl. **Christmases**) the annual Christian festival celebrating Christ's birth, held on December 25 in the Western Church. ■ the period immediately before and after December 25: *we had guests over Christmas*.
▶ exclam. informal expressing surprise, dismay, or despair.
–DERIVATIVES **Christ·mas·sy** /-məsē/ adj.
–ORIGIN Old English *Crīstes mæsse* (see CHRIST, MASS).

Christ·mas cac·tus ▶ n. a Brazilian cactus with branching stems of glossy green, flat, broad, tooth-edged sections, the tips of which bear long flowers, typically red or pink, with recurved outer petals. Christmas cacti are widely cultivated as houseplants. ● *Schlumbergera bridgesii* (or *Zygocactus bridgesii*), family Cactaceae.

Christ·mas card ▶ n. a greeting card sent at Christmas.

Christ·mas Day ▶ n. the day on which the festival of Christmas is celebrated, December 25.

Christ·mas Eve ▶ n. the day or the evening before Christmas Day, December 24.

Christ·mas fern ▶ n. an evergreen fern with dark green leathery fronds that grow in circular clumps from a central rootstock. ● *Polystichum acrostichoides*, family Polypodiaceae.

Christ·mas Is·land 1 an island in the Indian Ocean, 200 miles (350 km) south of Java, administered as an external territory of Australia since 1958; pop. 1,400 (est. 2009).
2 former name (until 1981) of KIRITIMATI.

Christ·mas stock·ing ▶ n. a long sock or similar receptacle hung up by children on Christmas Eve for Santa Claus to fill with presents.

Christ·mas tree ▶ n. a real or artificial evergreen tree set up and decorated with lights and ornaments as part of Christmas celebrations.

Christo- ▶ comb. form of or relating to Christ: *Christocentric* | *Christology*.
–ORIGIN from Latin *Christus* or Greek *Khristos* 'Christ.'

Chris·to·cen·tric /'kristə'sentrik, ,krī-/ ▶ adj. having Christ as its center: *a thoroughly Christocentric theology*.

Chris·to·gram /'kristə,gram/ ▶ n. a symbol for Christ, consisting of the Greek letters chi (X) and rho (P).

Chris·tol·o·gy /kris'täləjē/ ▶ n. the branch of Christian theology relating to the person, nature, and role of Christ.
–DERIVATIVES **Chris·to·log·i·cal** /,kristl'äjikəl/ adj., **Chris·to·log·i·cal·ly** /,kristl'äjik(ə)lē/ adv.

Chris·to·pher, St. /'kristəfər/ a legendary Christian martyr, adopted as the patron saint of travelers, since it is said that he once carried Christ in the form of a child across a river.

chris·to·phine /'kristə,fēn/ (also **christophene**) ▶ n. another term for CHAYOTE (sense 1).
–ORIGIN probably based on the French given name *Christophe*.

Christ's thorn ▶ n. a thorny shrub popularly supposed to have formed Christ's crown of thorns, in particular: ● either of two shrubs related to the buckthorn: *Paliurus spina-christi* (also called JERUSALEM THORN) and *Ziziphus spina-christi* (also called CROWN OF THORNS), family Rhamnaceae.

chro·ma /'krōmə/ ▶ n. purity or intensity of color.
–ORIGIN late 19th cent.: from Greek *khrōma* 'color.'

chro·maf·fin /krō'mafin/ ▶ adj. [attrib.] Physiology denoting granules or vesicles containing epinephrine and norepinephrine, and the secretory cells of the adrenal medulla in which they are found.
–ORIGIN early 20th cent.: from CHROMO-[1] 'chromium' + Latin *affinis* 'akin' (because readily stained brown by chromates).

chro·ma·key /'krōməkē/ ▶ n. a technique by which a block of a particular color (often blue or green) in a video image can be replaced either by another color or image, enabling, for example, a weather forecaster to appear against a background of a computer-generated weather map.
▶ v. (**chromakeys**, **chromakeying**, **chromakeyed**) [with obj.] manipulate (an image) using this technique.

chro·mate /'krō,māt/ ▶ n. Chemistry a salt in which the anion contains both chromium and oxygen, esp. one of the anion CrO_4^{2-}.
–ORIGIN early 19th cent.: from CHROMIC + -ATE[1].

PRONUNCIATION KEY ə ago, up; ər over, fur; a hat; ā ate; ä car; e let; ē see; i fit; ī by; NG sing; ō go; ô law, for; oi toy; o͝o good; o͞o goo; ou out; TH thin; T͟H then; ZH vision

chro·mat·ic /krō'matik/ ▶ **adj. 1** Music relating to or using notes not belonging to the diatonic scale of the key in which a passage is written. ■ (of a scale) ascending or descending by semitones. ■ (of an instrument) able to play all the notes of the chromatic scale.
2 of, relating to, or produced by color.
– DERIVATIVES **chro·mat·i·cal·ly** /-ik(ə)lē/ **adv.**, **chro·mat·i·cism** /-ə,sizəm/ **n.**
– ORIGIN early 17th cent.: from French *chromatique* or Latin *chromaticus*, from Greek *khrōmatikos*, from *khrōma, khrōmat-* 'color, chromatic scale.'

C

chro·mat·ic ab·er·ra·tion ▶ **n.** Optics the material effect produced by the refraction of different wavelengths of electromagnetic radiation through slightly different angles, resulting in a failure to focus. It causes colored fringes in the images produced by uncorrected lenses.

chro·ma·tic·i·ty /,krōmə'tisətē/ ▶ **n.** the quality of color, independent of brightness.

chro·ma·tid /'krōmə,tid/ ▶ **n.** Biology each of the two threadlike strands into which a chromosome divides longitudinally during cell division. Each contains a double helix of DNA.
– ORIGIN early 20th cent.: from Greek *khrōma, khrōmat-* 'color' + **-ID**[2].

chro·ma·tin /'krōmətən/ ▶ **n.** Biology the material of which the chromosomes of organisms other than bacteria (i.e., eukaryotes) are composed. It consists of protein, RNA, and DNA.
– ORIGIN late 19th cent.: coined in German from Greek *khrōma, khrōmat-* 'color.'

chromato- (also **chromo-**) ▶ **comb. form** color; of or in colors: *chromatopsia* | *chromosome*.
– ORIGIN from Greek *khrōma, khrōmat-* 'color.'

chro·mat·o·gram /krō'matə,gram/ ▶ **n.** a visible record (such as a series of colored bands, or a graph) showing the result of separation of the components of a mixture by chromatography.

chro·mat·o·graph /krō'matə,graf/ ▶ **n.** an apparatus for performing chromatography. ■ another term for **CHROMATOGRAM**.

chro·ma·tog·ra·phy /,krōmə'tägrəfē/ ▶ **n.** Chemistry the separation of a mixture by passing it in solution or suspension or as a vapor (as in gas chromatography) through a medium in which the components move at different rates.
– DERIVATIVES **chro·mat·o·graph·ic** /krō,matə'grafik/ **adj.**
– ORIGIN 1930s: from German *Chromatographie* (see **CHROMATO-**, **-GRAPHY**). The name alludes to the earliest separations when the result was displayed as a number of colored bands or spots.

chro·mat·o·phore /krə'matə,fôr, 'krōmətə-/ ▶ **n.** a cell or plastid that contains pigment.
– DERIVATIVES **chro·mat·o·phor·ic** /krə,matə'fôrik, ,krōmətə-/ **adj.**

chro·ma·top·si·a /,krōmə'täpsēə/ ▶ **n.** Medicine abnormally colored vision, a rare symptom of varied cause.
– ORIGIN mid 19th cent.: from **CHROMATO-** 'color' + Greek *-opsia* 'seeing.'

chrome /krōm/ ▶ **n.** chromium plate as a decorative or protective finish on motor-vehicle fittings and other objects: [as modifier] *a chrome bumper*. ■ [as modifier] denoting compounds or alloys of chromium: *chrome dyes*. ■ short for **CHROME YELLOW**.
– ORIGIN early 19th cent.: from French, from Greek *khrōma* 'color' (because of the brilliant colors of chromium compounds).

chrome al·um ▶ **n.** a reddish-purple crystalline compound used in solution in photographic processing and as a mordant in dyeing. ● Chem. formula: $K_2SO_4Cr_2(SO_4)_3{\cdot}24H_2O$.

chromed /krōmd/ ▶ **adj.** chromium-plated.

chrome leath·er ▶ **n.** leather tanned with chromium salts.

chrome-mol·y /,krōm 'mōlē/ (also **chromoly**) ▶ **n.** a strong steel alloy made principally of chromium and molybdenum: *the bicycle is made lighter and stronger with chrome-moly tubing*.
– ORIGIN 1980s: blend of **CHROMIUM** and **MOLYBDENUM**.

chrome red ▶ **n.** a bright red pigment consisting of lead chromate with varying amounts of lead oxide.

chrome steel ▶ **n.** a hard fine-grained steel containing chromium, used for making tools.

chrome yel·low ▶ **n.** a bright yellow pigment made from lead chromate, now little used.

chro·mic /'krōmik/ ▶ **adj.** Chemistry of chromium with a higher valence, usually three. Compare with **CHROMOUS**.

chro·mic ac·id ▶ **n.** Chemistry a corrosive and strongly oxidizing acid existing only in solutions of chromium trioxide. ● Chem. formula: H_2CrO_4.

chro·mi·nance /'krōmənəns/ ▶ **n.** the colorimetric difference between a given color in a television picture and a standard color of equal luminance.
– ORIGIN 1950s: from Greek *khrōma* 'color,' on the pattern of *luminance*.

chro·mite /'krō,mīt/ ▶ **n.** a brownish-black mineral that consists of a mixed oxide of chromium and iron and is the principal ore of chromium.
– ORIGIN mid 19th cent.: from **CHROME** or **CHROMIUM** + **-ITE**[1].

chro·mi·um /'krōmēəm/ ▶ **n.** the chemical element of atomic number 24, a hard white metal used in stainless steel and other alloys. (Symbol: **Cr**)
– ORIGIN early 19th cent.: from **CHROME** + **-IUM**.

chro·mi·um plate ▶ **n.** a decorative or protective coating of metallic chromium. ■ metal with such a coating.
▶ **v.** (**chromium-plate**) [with obj.] coat with chromium, typically by electrolytic deposition.

chro·mi·um steel ▶ **n.** another term for **CHROME STEEL**.

chro·mo /'krōmō/ ▶ **n.** (pl. **chromos**) **1** shortened form of **CHROMOLITHOGRAPH**.
2 informal chrome-moly.

chromo-[1] ▶ **comb. form** Chemistry representing **CHROMIUM**.

chromo-[2] ▶ **comb. form** variant spelling of **CHROMATO-**.

chro·mo·dy·nam·ics /,krōmōdī'namiks/ ▶ **plural n.** see **QUANTUM CHROMODYNAMICS**.

chro·mo·gen /'krōməjən/ ▶ **n.** a substance that can be readily converted into a dye or other colored compound.

chro·mo·gen·ic /,krōmə'jenik/ ▶ **adj.** involving the production of color or pigments, in particular: ■ Photography denoting a modern process of film developing that uses couplers to produce black-and-white or color images of very high definition. ■ Photography denoting any of a number of similar developing processes. ■ Microbiology (of a bacterium) producing a pigment.

chro·mo·lith·o·graph /,krōmō'liTHə,graf/ historical ▶ **n.** a colored picture printed by lithography, esp. in the late 19th and early 20th centuries.
▶ **v.** [with obj.] print or produce (a picture) by this process.
– DERIVATIVES **chro·mo·li·thog·ra·pher** /-li'THägrəfər/ **n.**, **chro·mo·lith·o·graph·ic** /-,liTHə'grafik/ **adj.**, **chro·mo·li·thog·ra·phy** /-li'THägrəfē/ **n.**

chro·mo·ly /krō'mälē/ variant spelling of **CHROME-MOLY**.

chro·mo·phore /'krōmə,fôr/ ▶ **n.** Chemistry an atom or group whose presence is responsible for the color of a compound.
– DERIVATIVES **chro·mo·phor·ic** /,krōmə'fôrik/ **adj.**

chro·mo·plast /'krōmə,plast/ ▶ **n.** Botany a colored plastid other than a chloroplast, typically containing a yellow or orange pigment.
– ORIGIN late 19th cent.: from **CHROMO-**[2] 'color' + Greek *plastos* 'formed.'

chro·mo·some /'krōmə,sōm/ ▶ **n.** Biology a threadlike structure of nucleic acids and protein found in the nucleus of most living cells, carrying genetic information in the form of genes.

> Each chromosome consists of a DNA double helix bearing a linear sequence of genes, coiled and recoiled around aggregated proteins (histones). Their number varies from species to species: humans have 22 pairs plus the two sex chromosomes (two X chromosomes in females, one X and one Y in males). During cell division, each DNA strand is duplicated, and the chromosomes condense to become visible as distinct pairs of chromatids joined at the centromere. Bacteria and viruses lack a nucleus and have a single chromosome without histones.

– DERIVATIVES **chro·mo·so·mal** /,krōmə'sōməl/ **adj.**
– ORIGIN late 19th cent.: coined in German from Greek *khrōma* 'color' + *sōma* 'body.'

chro·mo·some map ▶ **n.** Genetics a diagram showing the relative positions of genes along the length of a chromosome.

chro·mo·some num·ber ▶ **n.** Genetics the characteristic number of chromosomes found in the cell nuclei of organisms of a particular species.

chro·mo·sphere /'krōmə,sfi(ə)r/ ▶ **n.** Astronomy a reddish gaseous layer immediately above the photosphere of the sun or another star. Together with the corona, it constitutes the star's outer atmosphere.
– DERIVATIVES **chro·mo·spher·ic** /,krōmə'sfi(ə)rik, -'sferik/ **adj.**
– ORIGIN mid 19th cent.: from **CHROMO-**[2] 'color' + **SPHERE**.

chro·mo·ther·a·py /,krōmə'THerəpē/ ▶ **n.** another term for **COLOR THERAPY**.
– DERIVATIVES **chro·mo·ther·a·pist** **n.**

chro·mous /'krōməs/ ▶ **adj.** Chemistry of chromium with a valence of two; of chromium(II). Compare with **CHROMIC**.

Chron. ▶ **abbr.** Bible Chronicles.

chro·nax·ie /'krō,naksē, 'krä-/ ▶ **n.** Physiology the minimum amount of time needed to stimulate a muscle or nerve fiber, using an electric current twice the strength required to elicit a threshold response.

chron·ic /'kränik/ ▶ **adj.** (of an illness) persisting for a long time or constantly recurring: *chronic bronchitis*. Often contrasted with **ACUTE**. ■ (of a person) having such an illness: *a chronic asthmatic*. ■ (of a problem) long-lasting and difficult to eradicate: *the school suffers from chronic overcrowding*. ■ (of a person) having a particular bad habit: *a chronic liar*.
– DERIVATIVES **chron·i·cal·ly** /-ik(ə)lē/ **adv.**, **chro·nic·i·ty** /krä'nisətē/ **n.**
– ORIGIN late Middle English: from French *chronique*, via Latin from Greek *khronikos* 'of time,' from *khronos* 'time.'

> **USAGE** Chronic is often used to mean 'habitual, inveterate,' e.g., *a chronic liar*. Some consider this use incorrect. The precise meaning of **chronic** is 'persisting for a long time,' and it is used chiefly of illnesses or other problems: *more than one million people in the US have chronic bronchitis*.

chron·ic fa·tigue syn·drome (abbr.: **CFS**) ▶ **n.** a medical condition of unknown cause, with fever, aching, and prolonged tiredness and depression, typically occurring after a viral infection.

chron·i·cle /'kränikəl/ ▶ **n.** a factual written account of important or historical events in the order of their occurrence. ■ a work of fiction or nonfiction that describes a particular series of events.
▶ **v.** [with obj.] record (a related series of events) in a factual and detailed way: *his work chronicles 20th-century displacement and migration*.
– ORIGIN Middle English: from Anglo-Norman French *cronicle*, variant of Old French *cronique*, via Latin from Greek *khronika* 'annals,' from *khronikos* (see **CHRONIC**).

chron·i·cle play (also **chronicle history**) ▶ **n.** a historical drama consisting of a series of short episodes arranged chronologically.

chron·i·cler /'kräniklər/ ▶ **n.** a person who writes accounts of important or historical events: *a chronicler of 18th-century American life*.

Chron·i·cles /'kränikəlz/ the name of two books of the Bible, recording the history of Israel and Judah until the return from Exile (536 BC). See also **PARALIPOMENA**.

chrono- ▶ **comb. form** relating to time: *chronometry*.
– ORIGIN from Greek *khronos* 'time.'

chron·o·bi·ol·o·gy /,kränō,bī'äləjē, ,krō-/ ▶ **n.** the branch of biology concerned with natural physiological rhythms and other cyclical phenomena.
– DERIVATIVES **chron·o·bi·ol·o·gist** /-,bī'äləjist/ **n.**

chron·o·graph /'kränə,graf, 'krō-/ ▶ **n.** an instrument for recording time with great accuracy. ■ a stopwatch.
– DERIVATIVES **chron·o·graph·ic** /,kränə'grafik, ,krō-/ **adj.**

chron·o·log·i·cal /,kränl'äjikəl/ ▶ **adj.** (of a record of events) starting with the earliest and following the order in which they occurred: *the entries are in chronological order*. ■ relating to the establishment of dates and time sequences: *the diary provided a chronological framework for the events*. ■ calculated in terms of the passage of time rather than some other criterion: *ratings are calculated by dividing a child's mental age by his or her chronological age*.
– DERIVATIVES **chron·o·log·i·cal·ly** /-ik(ə)lē/ **adv.**

chro·nol·o·gy /krə'näləjē/ ▶ **n.** (pl. **chronologies**) the arrangement of events or dates in the order of their occurrence: *the novel abandons the conventions of normal chronology* | *a diary recording a chronology of events*. ■ a table or document displaying such an arrangement. ■ the study of historical records to establish the dates of past events.
– DERIVATIVES **chro·nol·o·gist** /-jist/ **n.**
– ORIGIN late 16th cent.: from modern Latin *chronologia*, from Greek *khronos* 'time' + *-logia* (see **-LOGY**).

chro·nom·e·ter /krə'nämətər/ ▶ **n.** an instrument for measuring time, esp. one designed to keep accurate time in spite of motion or variations in temperature, humidity, and air pressure. Chronometers were first developed for marine navigation, being used in conjunction with astronomical observation to determine longitude.

chro·nom·e·try /krəˈnämətrē/ ▶ **n.** the science of accurate time measurement.
– DERIVATIVES **chron·o·met·ric** /ˌkränəˈmetrik, ˌkrō-/ **adj.**, **chron·o·met·ri·cal** /ˌkränəˈmetrikəl, ˌkrō-/ **adj.**, **chron·o·met·ri·cal·ly** /ˌkränəˈmetrik(ə)lē/ **adv.**

chron·o·scope /ˈkränəˌskōp/ ▶ **n.** a device for measuring short time intervals, esp. in determining the velocity of projectiles, or a person's reaction time.

chron·o·stra·tig·ra·phy /ˌkränəˌstrəˈtigrəfē, ˌkrō-/ ▶ **n.** the branch of geology concerned with establishing the absolute ages of strata.
– DERIVATIVES **chron·o·strat·i·graph·ic** /-ˌstratəˈgrafik/ **adj.**

chron·o·ther·a·py /ˌkränəˈTHerəpē/ ▶ **n.** treatment of an illness or disorder that takes into account the body's natural rhythms and cycles.

chrys·a·lis /ˈkrisələs/ (also **chrysalid** /ˈkrisəˌlid/) ▶ **n.** (pl. **chrysalises**) a quiescent insect pupa, esp. of a butterfly or moth. ■ the hard outer case of this, esp. after being discarded. ■ a preparatory or transitional state: *she emerged from the chrysalis of self-conscious adolescence.*
– ORIGIN early 17th cent.: from Latin *chrysal(l)is, chrysal(l)id-*, from Greek *khrusallis*, from *khrusos* 'gold' (because of the gold color or metallic sheen of the pupae of some species).

chry·san·the·mum /kriˈsanTHəməm/ ▶ **n.** (pl. **chrysanthemums**) a popular plant of the daisy family, having brightly colored ornamental flowers and existing in many cultivated varieties. ● Genera *Chrysanthemum* or (most cultivated species) *Dendranthema*, family Compositae. ■ a flower or flowering stem of this plant.
– ORIGIN (originally denoting the corn marigold): from Latin, from Greek *khrusanthemon*, from *khrusos* 'gold' + *anthemon* 'flower.'

chrys·el·e·phan·tine /ˌkrisˌeləˈfanˌtēn, -ˈeləfənˌtēn, -ˌtīn/ ▶ **adj.** (of ancient Greek sculpture) overlaid with gold and ivory.
– ORIGIN early 19th cent.: from Greek *khruselephantinos*, from *khrusos* 'gold' + *elephas, elephant-* 'elephant' or 'ivory.'

Chrys·ler /ˈkrīslər/, Walter Percy (1875–1940), US automobile manufacturer. He was president and general manager of Buick Motor Company 1916–21 and introduced the Chrysler automobile in 1924.

chrys·o·ber·yl /ˈkrisəˌberəl/ ▶ **n.** a greenish or yellowish-green mineral consisting of an oxide of beryllium and aluminum. It occurs as tabular crystals, sometimes of gem quality.
– ORIGIN mid 17th cent.: from Latin *chrysoberyllus*, from Greek *khrusos* 'gold' + *bērullos* 'beryl.'

chrys·o·col·la /ˌkrisəˈkälə/ ▶ **n.** a greenish-blue mineral consisting of hydrated copper silicate, typically occurring as opaline crusts and masses.
– ORIGIN late 16th cent. (in the Greek sense): from Latin, from Greek *khrusokolla*, denoting a mineral used in ancient times for soldering gold.

chrys·o·lite /ˈkrisəˌlīt/ ▶ **n.** a yellowish-green or brownish variety of olivine, used as a gemstone.
– ORIGIN late Middle English: from Old French *crisolite*, from medieval Latin *crisolitus*, from Latin *chrysolithus*, based on Greek *khrusos* 'gold' + *lithos* 'stone.'

chrys·o·mel·id /ˌkrisəˈmelid, -ˈmēlid/ ▶ **n.** Entomology a beetle of a family (Chrysomelidae) that comprises the leaf beetles and their relatives.
– ORIGIN late 19th cent.: from modern Latin *Chrysomelidae* (plural), from *Chrysomela* (genus name), from Greek *khrusomēlon*, literally 'golden apple,' influenced by *khrusomēlolonthion* 'little golden chafer.'

chrys·o·prase /ˈkrisəˌprāz/ ▶ **n.** an apple-green variety of chalcedony containing nickel, used as a gemstone. ■ (in the New Testament) a golden-green precious stone, perhaps a variety of beryl.
– ORIGIN Middle English (in the New Testament sense): from Old French *crisopace*, via Latin from Greek *khrusoprasos*, from *khrusos* 'gold' + *prason* 'leek.'

Chrys·os·tom, St. John /ˈkrisəstəm, krisˈästəm/ (*c.*347–407), doctor of the Church; bishop of Constantinople. His attempts to reform the corrupt state of the court, clergy, and people caused him to be banished in 403. Feast day, January 27.

chrys·o·tile /ˈkrisəˌtīl/ ▶ **n.** a fibrous form of the mineral serpentine. Also called WHITE ASBESTOS (see ASBESTOS).
– ORIGIN mid 19th cent.: from Greek *khrusos* 'gold' + *tilos* 'fiber.'

chthon·ic /ˈTHänik/ (also **chthonian** /ˈTHōnēən/) ▶ **adj.** concerning, belonging to, or inhabiting the underworld: *a chthonic deity.*
– ORIGIN late 19th cent.: from Greek *khthōn* 'earth' + -IC.

chub /CHəb/ ▶ **n.** a thick-bodied European river fish with a gray-green back and white underparts, popular with anglers. ● *Leuciscus cephalus*, family Cyprinidae.
– ORIGIN late Middle English: of unknown origin.

chub·by /ˈCHəbē/ ▶ **adj.** (**chubbier, chubbiest**) plump and rounded: *a pretty child with chubby cheeks.*
– DERIVATIVES **chub·bi·ly** /ˈCHəbəlē/ **adv.**, **chub·bi·ness n.**
– ORIGIN early 17th cent. (in the sense 'short and thickset, like a chub'): from CHUB.

chuck[1] /CHək/ informal ▶ **v.** [with obj.] throw (something) carelessly or casually: *someone chucked a brick through the window* | figurative *chucking money at the problem won't solve it.* ■ throw (something) away: *they make a living out of stuff people chuck out.* ■ give up (a job or activity) suddenly: *Richard chucked his cultural studies course.* ■ break off a relationship with (a partner): *Mary chucked him for another guy.*
– PHRASES **chuck it all in** abandon a course of action or way of life, esp. for another that is radically different.
– PHRASAL VERBS **chuck someone out** force someone to leave a building: *the tenants have been chucked out of the cottages.*
– DERIVATIVES **chuck·er n.**
– ORIGIN late 17th cent. (as a verb): from CHUCK[2].

chuck[2] ▶ **v.** [with obj.] touch (someone) playfully or gently under the chin.
▶ **n.** a playful touch under the chin.
– ORIGIN early 17th cent. (as a noun): probably from Old French *chuquer*, later *choquer* 'to knock, bump,' of unknown ultimate origin.

chuck[3] ▶ **n. 1** a device for holding a workpiece in a lathe or a tool in a drill, typically having three or four jaws that move radially in and out.
2 a cut of beef that extends from the neck to the ribs, typically used for stewing.
– ORIGIN late 17th cent., as a variant of CHOCK; see also CHUNK[1].

chuck[4] ▶ **n.** US informal food or provisions.
– ORIGIN mid 19th cent.: perhaps the same word as CHUCK[3].

chuck[5] ▶ **n.** short for WOODCHUCK.

chuck-a-luck /ˈCHək əˌlək/ ▶ **n.** a gambling game played with three dice.

chuck·hole /ˈCHəkˌhōl/ ▶ **n.** a hole or rut in a road or track.

chuck key ▶ **n.** a small metal device for tightening the chuck of a drill so that it holds the drill bit securely.

chuck·le /ˈCHəkəl/ ▶ **v.** [no obj.] laugh quietly or inwardly: *I chuckled at the astonishment on her face* | [with direct speech] *"That's a bit strong, isn't it?" he chuckled.*
▶ **n.** [in sing.] a quiet or suppressed laugh.
– DERIVATIVES **chuck·ler** /ˈCHəklər/ **n.**
– ORIGIN late 16th cent. (in the sense 'laugh convulsively'): from *chuck* meaning 'to cluck' in late Middle English.

chuck·le·head /ˈCHəkəlˌhed/ ▶ **n.** informal a stupid person.
– DERIVATIVES **chuck·le·head·ed adj.**
– ORIGIN mid 18th cent.: from early 18th-cent. *chuckle* 'big and clumsy,' probably related to CHUCK[3].

chuck wag·on ▶ **n.** a wagon with cooking facilities providing food on a ranch, worksite, or campsite.
– ORIGIN late 19th cent.: *chuck*, colloquial in the sense 'food, provisions.'

chuck·wal·la /ˈCHəkˌwälə/ ▶ **n.** a large dark-bodied lizard, the male of which has a light yellow tail, native to the deserts of the southwestern US and Mexico. When threatened, it inflates itself with air to wedge itself into a crevice. ● *Sauromalus obesus*, family Iguanidae.
– ORIGIN late 19th cent.: from Mexican Spanish *chacahuala*, from American Indian.

chuck-will's-wid·ow /ˌCHək ˌwilz ˈwidō, ˈwidə/ ▶ **n.** a large nightjar native to eastern North America. ● *Caprimulgus carolinensis*, family Caprimulgidae.
– ORIGIN late 18th cent.: imitative of its call.

chud·dar /ˈCHədər/ ▶ **n.** variant spelling of CHADOR.

chu·fa /ˈCHōōfə/ ▶ **n.** an Old World sedge that yields an edible tuber. It is cultivated on a small scale, particularly in some marshy regions of Spain and Italy. Also called EARTH ALMOND. ● *Cyperus esculentus* var. *sativus*, family Cyperaceae. ■ the tuber of this plant, which may be roasted, made into flour, or turned into juice.
– ORIGIN mid 19th cent.: from Spanish.

chuff /CHəf/ ▶ **v.** [no obj.] (of a steam engine) move with a regular sharp puffing sound.
– ORIGIN early 20th cent.: imitative.

chuffed /CHəft/ ▶ **adj.** [predic.] Brit. informal very pleased: *I'm dead chuffed to have won.*
– ORIGIN 1950s: from dialect *chuff* 'plump or pleased.'

chug[1] /CHəg/ ▶ **v.** (**chugs, chugging, chugged**) [no obj.] emit a series of regular muffled explosive sounds, as of an engine running slowly: *he could hear the pipes chugging.* ■ (of a vehicle or boat) move slowly making such sounds: *a cabin cruiser was chugging down the river.*
▶ **n.** a muffled explosive sound or a series of such sounds: *the chug of a motorboat.*
– ORIGIN mid 19th cent. (as a noun): imitative.

chug[2] (also **chugalug** or **chug-a-lug** /ˈCHəgəˌləg/) informal ▶ **v.** (**chugs, chugging, chugged**) [with obj.] consume (a drink) in large gulps without pausing: *Avery chugged a cup of coffee.*
▶ **n.** a large gulp of a drink: *Chris took a long chug of his beer.*
– ORIGIN 1950s: imitative.

Chu·gach Moun·tains /ˈCHōōˌgaCH, -ˌgaSH/ a range of mountains, part of the Coast Ranges, in southern Alaska. Anchorage lies at its base, and it is noted for glaciers that flow south into the Gulf of Alaska.

chu·kar /ˈCHōōkˌär, CHōōkˈär/ (also **chukar partridge**) ▶ **n.** a Eurasian partridge similar to the red-legged partridge, but with a call like a clucking domestic hen. ● Genus *Alectoris*, family Phasianidae: two species, in particular *A. chukar.*
– ORIGIN early 19th cent.: from Sanskrit *cakora.*

Chuk·chi /ˈCHōōkCHē, ˈCHək-/ (also **Chukchee**) ▶ **n.** (pl. **same** or **Chukchis**) **1** a member of an indigenous people of extreme northeastern Siberia.
2 the language of this people, which belongs to a small, isolated language family.
▶ **adj.** of or relating to this people or their language.
– ORIGIN Russian (plural).

Chuk·chi Sea part of the Arctic Ocean that lies between North America and Asia and north of the Bering Strait.

chuk·ker /ˈCHəkər/ (also **chukka**) ▶ **n.** each of a number of periods (typically six) into which play in a game of polo is divided. A chukker lasts $7\frac{1}{2}$ minutes.
– ORIGIN late 19th cent.: from Hindi *cakkar*, from Sanskrit *cakra* 'circle or wheel.'

Chu·la Vis·ta /ˌCHōōlə ˈvistə/ a city in southwestern California, south of San Diego, near the Mexican border; pop. 219,318 (est. 2008).

chum[1] /CHəm/ informal ▶ **n.** a close friend. ■ a form of address expressing familiarity or friendliness: *it's your own fault, chum.*
▶ **v.** (**chums, chumming, chummed**) [no obj.] be friendly to or form a friendship with someone: *they started chumming around in high school.*
– ORIGIN late 17th cent. (originally Oxford University slang, denoting a roommate): probably short for *chamber-fellow.* Compare with COMRADE and CRONY.

chum[2] ▶ **n.** chopped fish, fish fluids, and other material thrown overboard as angling bait. ■ refuse from fish, esp. that remaining after expressing oil.
▶ **v.** (**chums, chumming, chummed**) [no obj.] use chum as bait when fishing.
– ORIGIN mid 19th cent.: of unknown origin.

chum[3] (also **chum salmon**) ▶ **n.** (pl. **same** or **chums**) a large North Pacific salmon that is commercially important as a food fish. ● *Oncorhyncus keta*, family Salmonidae.
– ORIGIN early 20th cent.: from Chinook Jargon *tzum (samun)*, literally 'spotted (salmon).'

Chu·mash /ˈCHōōˌmaSH/ ▶ **n.** (pl. **same** or **Chumashes**) **1** a member of an American Indian people inhabiting coastal parts of southern California.
2 the Hokan language of this people.
▶ **adj.** of or relating to this people or their language.
– ORIGIN Chumash, literally 'islander.'

chum·my /ˈCHəmē/ ▶ **adj.** (**chummier, chummiest**) on friendly terms; friendly: *she's become pretty chummy with Ted lately.*
– DERIVATIVES **chum·mi·ly** /ˈCHəməlē/ **adv.**, **chum·mi·ness n.**

chump /CHəmp/ ▶ **n.** informal a foolish or easily deceived person: *how can this chump be a detective?*
– ORIGIN early 18th cent. (in the sense 'thick lump of wood'): probably a blend of CHUNK[1] and LUMP[1] or STUMP.

chump change ▶ **n.** informal a small or insignificant amount of money.
– ORIGIN 1960s: originally black English.

Chün /jōōn, jYn, CHōōn/ ▶ **n.** a type of thickly glazed, typically bluish or purplish gray stoneware originally made at Chün Chou in Honan province, China, during the Song dynasty.

Chun·chon /ˈCHōōnˈCHən/ an industrial city in northeastern South Korea, the capital of Kangwon province; pop. 264,600 (est. 2008).

PRONUNCIATION KEY ə *ago, up*; ər *over, fur*; a *hat*; ā *ate*; ä *car*; e *let*; ē *see*; i *fit*; ī *by*; NG *sing*; ō *go*; ô *law, for*; oi *toy*; ŏŏ *good*; ōō *goo*; ou *out*; TH *thin*; TH *then*; ZH *vision*

Chung·king /ˈCHŏŏNGˈkiNG/ variant of **Chongqing**.

Chung·shan /ˌCHŏŏNG ˈSHän/ variant of **Zhongshan**.

chunk[1] /CHəNGk/ ▶ **n.** a thick, solid piece of something: *huge chunks of masonry littered the street.* ■ [in sing.] an amount or part of something: *fuel takes a large chunk of their small income.*
▶ **v.** [with obj.] divide (something) into chunks: *chunk four pounds of pears.* ■ (in psychology or linguistic analysis) group together (connected items or words) so that they can be stored or processed as single concepts.
– ORIGIN late 17th cent.: apparently an alteration of **chuck**[3].

chunk[2] ▶ **v.** [no obj.] move with or make a muffled, metallic sound: *the door chunked behind them.*
– ORIGIN late 19th cent.: imitative.

chunk·y /ˈCHəNGkē/ ▶ **adj.** (**chunkier**, **chunkiest**) **1** bulky and solid: *a chunky bracelet.* ■ (of a person) short and sturdy.
2 (of food) containing chunks: *fresh chunky salsa* | *a chunky soup.*
– DERIVATIVES **chunk·i·ly** /-kəlē/ **adv.**, **chunk·i·ness n.**

Chun·nel /ˈCHənl/ ▶ **n.** informal short for **Channel Tunnel**.
– ORIGIN 1920s (but rare before the 1950s): blend.

chu·pa·ca·bra /ˌCHōōpəˈkäbrə/ ▶ **n.** an animal said to exist in parts of Latin America, where it supposedly attacks animals, esp. goats.
– ORIGIN Spanish, literally 'goatsucker,' from *chupar* 'suck' + *cabra* 'goat.'

chup·pah /ˈKHŏŏpə/ (also **chuppa**) ▶ **n.** (pl. **chuppot** /ˈKHŏŏpōt, -ōs/) a canopy beneath which Jewish marriage ceremonies are performed.
– ORIGIN late 19th cent.: from Hebrew *ḥuppāh* 'cover, canopy.'

Chu·qui·sa·ca /ˌCHŏŏkēˈsäkə/ former name (1539–1840) of **Sucre**[1].

Church /CHərCH/, Frederick Edwin (1826–1900), US painter. A student of Thomas Cole and a leader of the Hudson River School, he was known for his landscapes.

church /CHərCH/ ▶ **n.** a building used for public Christian worship: *they came to church with me.* ■ (usu. **Church**) a particular Christian organization, typically one with its own clergy, buildings, and distinctive doctrines: *the Church of England.* ■ (**the Church**) the hierarchy of clergy of such an organization, esp. the Roman Catholic Church or the Church of England. ■ institutionalized religion as a political or social force: *the separation of church and state.*
▶ **v.** [with obj.] archaic take (a woman who has recently given birth) to church for a service of thanksgiving.
– ORIGIN Old English *cir(i)ce*, *cyr(i)ce*, related to Dutch *kerk* and German *Kirche*, based on medieval Greek *kurikon*, from Greek *kuriakon* (*dōma*) 'Lord's (house),' from *kurios* 'master or lord.' Compare with **kirk**.

Church·es of Christ a number of Protestant denominations, chiefly in the US, originating in the Disciples of Christ but later separated over doctrinal issues.

Church Fa·thers ▶ **n.** see **father** (sense 3).

church·go·er /ˈCHərCHˌgōər/ ▶ **n.** a person who goes to church, esp. one who does so regularly.
– DERIVATIVES **church·go·ing** /-ˌgō-iNG/ **n. & adj.**

Church·ill /ˈCHərˌCHil, ˈCHərCHˌhil/, Sir Winston (Leonard Spencer) (1874–1965), British statesman; prime minister 1940–45 and 1951–55. A consistent opponent of appeasement during the 1930s, he replaced Neville Chamberlain as British prime minister in 1940 and led Britain throughout World War II. Notable works: *The Second World War* (1948–53) and *A History of the English-Speaking Peoples* (1956–58). Nobel Prize for Literature (1953).

Winston Churchill

Church·ill Downs a horse-racing facility in Louisville in Kentucky, the site of the annual Kentucky Derby.

Church·ill Riv·er[1] a river that flows for 1,000 miles (1,600 km) from northern Saskatchewan across Manitoba to Hudson Bay at Churchill.

Church·ill Riv·er[2] a river that flows for 600 miles (1,000 km) from the Canadian Shield across eastern Labrador to the Labrador Sea. Its high falls generate hydroelectric power. Formerly called the **Hamilton River**.

church key ▶ **n.** a small metal device with a triangular point at one end for punching holes in cans and a rounded edge at the other end for removing bottle caps.

church·man /ˈCHərCHmən/ ▶ **n.** (pl. **churchmen**) a male member of the Christian clergy or of a church.

Church Mil·i·tant ▶ **n.** (**the Church Militant**) the whole body of living Christian believers.
– ORIGIN mid 16th cent.: contrasted with the *Church Triumphant* in heaven.

Church of Christ, Sci·en·tist the Christian Science Church.

Church of Eng·land the English branch of the Western Christian Church, which combines Catholic and Protestant traditions, rejects the pope's authority, and has the monarch as its titular head.

Church of Je·sus Christ of Lat·ter-Day Saints the church of the Mormons.

Church of Rome another term for **Roman Catholic Church**.

Church of Scot·land the national Christian Church in Scotland, established as Presbyterian in 1690.

church plant·ing ▶ **n.** the practice of establishing a core of Christian worshipers in a parish, with the intention that they should develop into a thriving congregation.

Church Slav·ic (also **Church Slavonic**) ▶ **n.** the liturgical language used in the Orthodox Church in Russia, Serbia, and some other countries. It is a modified form of Old Church Slavic.

church·ward·en /ˈCHərCHˌwôrdn/ ▶ **n. 1** either of the two elected lay representatives in an Anglican parish, formally responsible for movable church property and for keeping order in church. ■ a church administrator.
2 chiefly Brit. a long-stemmed clay pipe.

church·wom·an /ˈCHərCHˌwŏŏmən/ ▶ **n.** (pl. **churchwomen**) a female member of the Christian clergy or of a church.

church·y /ˈCHərCHē/ ▶ **adj. 1** (of a person) excessively pious and consequently narrow-minded or intolerant.
2 resembling a church: *Gothic design looks too churchy.*
– DERIVATIVES **church·i·ness n.**

church·yard /ˈCHərCHˌyärd/ ▶ **n.** an enclosed area surrounding a church, esp. as used for burials.

churl /CHərl/ ▶ **n.** an impolite and mean-spirited person. ■ archaic a miser. ■ archaic a person of low birth; a peasant.
– ORIGIN Old English *ceorl*; related to Dutch *kerel* and German *Kerl* 'fellow,' also to **carl**.

churl·ish /ˈCHərliSH/ ▶ **adj.** rude in a mean-spirited and surly way: *it seems churlish to complain.*
– DERIVATIVES **churl·ish·ly adv.**, **churl·ish·ness n.**
– ORIGIN Old English *cierlisc*, *ceorlisc* (see **churl**, **-ish**[1]).

churn /CHərn/ ▶ **n. 1** a machine or container in which butter is made by agitating milk or cream.
2 short for **churn rate**.
▶ **v. 1** [with obj.] agitate or turn (milk or cream) in a machine in order to produce butter: *the cream is ripened before it is churned.* ■ produce (butter) in such a way.
2 [no obj.] (of liquid) move about vigorously: *the seas churned* | figurative *her stomach was churning at the thought of the ordeal.* ■ [with obj.] cause (liquid) to move in this way: *in high winds most of the lake is churned up.* ■ [with obj.] break up the surface of (an area of ground): *the earth had been churned up where vehicles had passed through.*
3 [with obj.] (of a broker) encourage frequent turnover of (investments) in order to generate commission.
– PHRASAL VERBS **churn something out** produce something routinely or mechanically, esp. in large quantities: *artists continued to churn out insipid works.*
– ORIGIN Old English *cyrin*, of Germanic origin; related to Middle Low German *kerne* and Old Norse *kirna*.

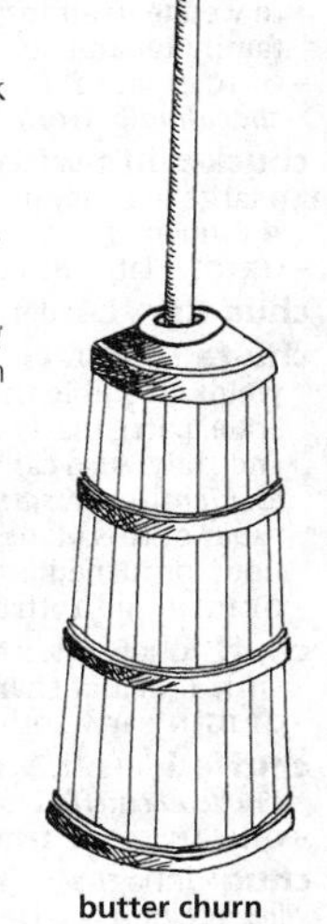
butter churn

churn rate ▶ **n.** the annual percentage rate at which customers discontinue using a service, in particular cable and satellite television.

churr ▶ **v. & n.** variant spelling of **chirr**.

Chur·ri·gue·resque /ˌCHŏŏrigəˈresk/ (also **churrigueresque**) ▶ **adj.** Architecture of or relating to the lavishly ornamented late Spanish baroque style: *a Churrigueresque church.*
– ORIGIN mid 19th cent.: from the name José Benito de *Churriguera* (1665–1725), a Spanish architect who worked in this style.

chur·ro /ˈCHŏŏrō/ ▶ **n.** (pl. **churros**) a Latin American snack consisting of a strip of fried dough, very similar to funnel cake.
– ORIGIN Spanish, of uncertain origin; perhaps related to *churro* 'coarse, rough.'

chute[1] /SHōōt/ (also **shoot**) ▶ **n.** a sloping channel or slide for conveying things to a lower level. ■ a water slide into a swimming pool. ■ short for **chute-the-chute**.
– ORIGIN early 19th cent.: from French, 'fall' (of water or rocks), from Old French *cheoite*, feminine past participle of *cheoir* 'to fall,' from Latin *cadere*; influenced by **shoot**.

chute[2] ▶ **n.** informal a parachute. ■ Sailing informal term for **spinnaker**.
– DERIVATIVES **chut·ist** /ˈSHōōtist/ **n.**
– ORIGIN 1920s: shortened form.

chute-the-chute (also **chute-the-chutes**) ▶ **n.** a steep slide or roller coaster, esp. with water at the foot.
▶ **v.** (**chute the chute** or **chute the chutes**) slide down or ride on a chute-the-chute.

chut·ney /ˈCHətnē/ ▶ **n.** (pl. **chutneys**) a spicy condiment made of fruits or vegetables with vinegar, spices, and sugar, originating in India.
– ORIGIN early 19th cent.: from Hindi *caṭnī*.

chutz·pah /ˈhŏŏtspə, ˈKHŏŏtspə, -spä/ (also **chutzpa** or **hutzpah** or **hutzpa**) ▶ **n.** informal shameless audacity; impudence.
– ORIGIN late 19th cent.: Yiddish, from Aramaic *ḥu**ṣpā*.

Chuuk Is·lands /CHŏŏk/ a group of 14 volcanic islands and numerous atolls in the western Pacific Ocean, in the Caroline Islands group, that forms part of the Federated States of Micronesia; pop. 53,300 (est. 2008). Former name **Truk Islands**.

Chu·vash /ˈCHōōˌväSH, CHōōˈväSH/ ▶ **n.** (pl. **same**) **1** a member of a people living mainly in Chuvashia.
2 the language of this people, usually classified as Turkic.
▶ **adj.** of or relating to this people or their language.

Chu·vash·i·a /CHōōˈväSHēə/ an autonomous republic in Russia, in Europe east of Nizhni Novgorod; pop. 1,278,600 (est. 2009); capital, Cheboksary.

chyle /kīl/ ▶ **n.** Physiology a milky fluid consisting of fat droplets and lymph. It drains from the lacteals of the small intestine into the lymphatic system during digestion.
– DERIVATIVES **chy·lous** /ˈkīləs/ **adj.**
– ORIGIN late Middle English: from late Latin *chylus*, from Greek *khūlos* 'juice' (see **chyme**).

chy·lo·mi·cron /ˌkīlōˈmīˌkrän/ ▶ **n.** Physiology a droplet of fat present in the blood or lymph after absorption from the small intestine.
– ORIGIN 1920s: from *chylo-* (combining form of **chyle**) + **micron**.

chyme /kīm/ ▶ **n.** Physiology the pulpy acidic fluid that passes from the stomach to the small intestine, consisting of gastric juices and partly digested food.
– DERIVATIVES **chy·mous** /ˈkīməs/ **adj.**
– ORIGIN late Middle English: from late Latin *chymus*, from Greek *khūmos* 'juice' (compare with **chyle**). The Greek words *khūlos* and *khūmos* are from the same root and more or less identical in sense; however, *khūlos* came to be used for juice in a raw or natural state, *khūmos* for juice produced by decoction or digestion.

chy·mo·tryp·sin /ˌkīmōˈtripsən/ ▶ **n.** Biochemistry a digestive enzyme that breaks down proteins in the small intestine. It is secreted by the pancreas and converted into an active form by trypsin.
– ORIGIN 1930s: from *chymo-* (combining form of **chyme**) + **trypsin**.

chy·ron /ˈkīˌrän/ ▶ **n.** trademark an electronically generated caption superimposed on a television or movie screen.
– ORIGIN 1970s: from *Chyron* Corporation, its manufacturer.

CI ▶ **abbr.** ■ certificate of insurance. ■ Channel Islands. ■ cost and insurance.

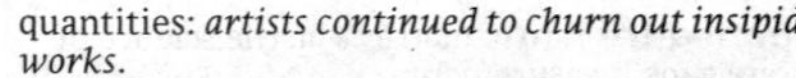

Ci ▶ **abbr.** ■ cirrus. ■ curie.

CIA ▶ **abbr.** Central Intelligence Agency.

cia·bat·ta /CHəˈbätə/ (also **ciabatta bread**) ▶ **n.** a type of flattish, open-textured Italian bread with a floury crust, made with olive oil.
– ORIGIN Italian, literally 'slipper' (from its shape).

ciao /CHou/ ▶ **exclam.** informal used as a greeting at meeting or parting.
– ORIGIN 1920s: Italian, dialect alteration of *schiavo* '(I am your) slave,' from medieval Latin *sclavus* 'slave.'

ci·bo·ri·um /səˈbôrēəm/ ▶ **n.** (pl. **ciboria** /-ˈbôrēə/) **1** a receptacle shaped like a shrine or a cup with an arched cover, used in the Christian Church for the reservation of the Eucharist.
2 a canopy over an altar in a church, standing on four pillars.
– ORIGIN mid 16th cent.: via medieval Latin from Greek *kibōrion* 'seed vessel of the water lily or a cup made from it.' Sense 1 is probably influenced by Latin *cibus* 'food.'

ci·ca·da /səˈkādə, səˈkädə/ ▶ **n.** a large homopterous insect with long transparent wings, occurring chiefly in warm countries. The male cicada makes a loud shrill droning noise by vibrating two membranes on its abdomen. ● Family Cicadidae, suborder Homoptera: many genera.
– ORIGIN late Middle English: from Latin *cicada, cicala.*

cicada

cic·a·trix /ˈsikəˌtriks/ (also **cicatrice** /-ˌtris/) ▶ **n.** (pl. **cicatrices** /ˌsikəˈtrīsēz, səˈkātrəˌsēz/) the scar of a healed wound. ■ a scar on the bark of a tree. ■ Botany a mark on a stem left after a leaf or other part has become detached.
– DERIVATIVES **cic·a·tri·cial** /ˌsikəˈtrisHəl/ **adj.**
– ORIGIN late Middle English (as *cicatrice*): from Latin *cicatrix* or Old French *cicatrice.*

cic·a·trize /ˈsikəˌtrīz/ ▶ **v.** (with reference to a wound) heal by scar formation: [with obj.] *it was used to cicatrize certain types of wounds* | [no obj.] *his wound had cicatrized.*
– DERIVATIVES **cic·a·tri·za·tion** /ˌsikətrəˈzāsHən/ **n.**
– ORIGIN late Middle English: from Old French *cicatriser*, from *cicatrice* 'scar' (see CICATRIX).

cic·e·ly /ˈsisilē/ (also **sweet cicely**) ▶ **n.** (pl. **cicelies**) an aromatic white-flowered plant of the parsley family, with fernlike leaves. ● Genera *Myrrhis* and *Osmorhiza*, family Umbelliferae: several species, in particular the European *M. odorata*, grown as a pot herb and used in herbal medicine, and the North American *O. claytoni.*
– ORIGIN late 16th cent.: from Latin *seselis*, from Greek. The spelling change was due to association with the given name *Cicely.*

Cic·e·ro[1] /ˈsisəˌrō/ a town in northeastern Illinois, just west of Chicago; pop. 80,414 (est. 2008).

Cic·e·ro[2] Marcus Tullius (106–43 BC), Roman statesman, orator, and writer. He established a model for Latin prose. A supporter of Pompey against Julius Caesar, he attacked Mark Antony in the *Philippics* (43 BC). For this offense, Mark Antony had him put to death.

cic·e·ro·ne /ˌsisəˈrōnē, ˌCHēCHə-/ ▶ **n.** (pl. **ciceroni** pronunc. **same**) a guide who gives information about antiquities and places of interest to sightseers.
– ORIGIN early 18th cent.: from Italian, from Latin *Cicero, Ciceron-* (see CICERO[2]), apparently alluding humorously to his eloquence and learning.

Cic·e·ro·ni·an /ˌsisəˈrōnēən/ ▶ **adj.** characteristic of the work and thought of Cicero. ■ (of a piece of speech or writing) in an eloquent and rhythmic style similar to that of Cicero.

cich·lid /ˈsiklid/ ▶ **n.** Zoology a perchlike freshwater fish of a family (Cichlidae) that is widely distributed in tropical countries. Cichlids provide a valuable source of food in some areas, and many are popular in aquariums.
– ORIGIN late 19th cent.: from modern Latin *Cichlidae* (plural), from Greek *kikhlē*, denoting a kind of fish.

CID ▶ **abbr.** (in the UK) Criminal Investigation Department.

-cide ▶ **comb. form 1** denoting a person or substance that kills: *insecticide* | *regicide.*
2 denoting an act of killing: *homicide* | *suicide.*
– ORIGIN via French; sense 1 from Latin *-cida*; sense 2 from Latin *-cidium*, both from *caedere* 'kill.'

Cid, El /sid/ (also **the Cid**), Count of Bivar (*c.*1043–99), Spanish soldier; born *Rodrigo Díaz de Vivar*. He captured Valencia from the Moors in 1094 and went on to rule it. He is immortalized in *Poema del Cid* (12th century) and in Pierre Corneille's play *Le Cid* (1637).

ci·der /ˈsīdər/ ▶ **n.** (also **sweet cider**) an unfermented drink made by crushing fruit, typically apples. ■ (also **hard cider**) an alcoholic drink made from fermented crushed fruit, typically apples.
– ORIGIN Middle English: from Old French *sidre*, via ecclesiastical Latin from ecclesiastical Greek *sikera*, from Hebrew *šēḵār* 'strong drink.'

ci·der press ▶ **n.** a press for crushing fruit, typically apples, to make cider.

ci·der vin·e·gar ▶ **n.** a vinegar made from fermented cider.

ci-de·vant /ˌsē dəˈväN/ ▶ **adj.** [attrib.] from or in an earlier time (used to indicate that someone or something once possessed a specified characteristic but no longer does so): *her ci-devant student, now her lover.*
– ORIGIN early 18th cent.: French, literally 'heretofore.'

Cien·fue·gos /sē-enˈfwāgōs/ a port city in south central Cuba, on Cienfuegos Bay in the Caribbean Sea, the capital of Cienfuegos province; pop. 143,356 (2008).

CIF (also **C.I.F.**) ▶ **abbr.** cost, insurance, freight (as included in a price).

cig /sig/ ▶ **n.** informal a cigarette.
– ORIGIN late 19th cent.: abbreviation.

ci·gar /siˈgär/ ▶ **n.** a cylinder of tobacco rolled in tobacco leaves for smoking.
– PHRASES **close, but no cigar** informal (of an attempt) almost, but not quite successful. [referring to a cigar received in congratulation.]
– ORIGIN early 18th cent.: from French *cigare*, or from Spanish *cigarro*, probably from Mayan *sik'ar* 'smoking.'

cig·a·rette /ˌsigəˈret, ˈsigəˌret/ (also **cigaret**) ▶ **n.** a thin cylinder of finely cut tobacco rolled in paper for smoking. ■ a similar cylinder containing a narcotic, herbs, or a medicated substance.
– ORIGIN mid 19th cent.: from French, diminutive of *cigare* (see CIGAR).

cig·a·rette pants ▶ **plural n.** women's pants with straight, very narrow legs.

cig·a·rette pa·per ▶ **n.** a piece of thin paper with a gummed edge in which tobacco can be rolled to make a cigarette.

cig·a·ril·lo /ˌsigəˈrilō, -ˈrē(y)ō/ ▶ **n.** (pl. **cigarillos**) a small cigar.
– ORIGIN mid 19th cent.: from Spanish, diminutive of *cigarro* (see CIGAR).

ci·gua·te·ra /ˌsēgwəˈterə/ ▶ **n.** poisoning by neurotoxins as a result of eating the flesh of a tropical marine fish that carries a toxic dinoflagellate. ● This is caused by *Gambierdiscus toxicus*, phylum Dinophyta.
– ORIGIN mid 19th cent.: from American Spanish, from *cigua* 'sea snail.'

ci·lan·tro /siˈlanˌtrō, -ˈlän-/ ▶ **n.** another term for CORIANDER (esp. the leaves).
– ORIGIN 1920s: from Spanish, from Latin *coliandrum* 'coriander.'

cil·i·a /ˈsilēə/ plural form of CILIUM.

cil·i·ar·y /ˈsilēˌerē/ ▶ **adj. 1** Biology of, relating to, or involving cilia: *ciliary action.*
2 Anatomy of or relating to the eyelashes or eyelids. ■ of or relating to the ciliary body of the eye.

cil·i·ar·y bod·y ▶ **n.** Anatomy the part of the eye that connects the iris to the choroid. It consists of the **ciliary muscle** (which alters the curvature of the lens), a series of radial **ciliary processes** (from which the lens is suspended by ligaments), and the **ciliary ring** (which adjoins the choroid).

cil·i·ate /ˈsilēˌāt, -ēət/ ▶ **n.** Zoology a single-celled animal of a phylum distinguished by the possession of cilia or ciliary structures. The ciliates are a large and diverse group of advanced protozoans. ● Phylum Ciliophora, kingdom Protista (formerly class Ciliata, phylum Protozoa).
▶ **adj.** Zoology (of an organism, cell, or surface) bearing cilia. ■ Botany (of a margin) having a fringe of hairs.
– DERIVATIVES **cil·i·at·ed** /ˈsilēˌātid/ **adj.**, **cil·i·a·tion** /ˌsilēˈāsHən/ **n.**

cil·ice /ˈsiləs/ ▶ **n.** a hair shirt. ■ a spiked garter or other device worn by penitents and ascetics.
– ORIGIN late 16th cent.: from French, from Latin *cilicium*, from Greek *kilikion*, from *Kilikia*, the Greek name for CILICIA in Asia Minor (because hair shirts were originally made of Cilician goats' hair).

Ci·li·cia /səˈlisHə/ an ancient region on the coast of southeastern Asia Minor.
– DERIVATIVES **Ci·li·cian adj. & n.**

Ci·li·cian Gates /səˈlisHən/ a mountain pass in the Taurus Mountains in southern Turkey. Historically, it forms part of a route that linked Anatolia with the Mediterranean coast.

cil·i·o·late /ˈsilēəlit, -ˌlāt/ ▶ **adj.** having cilia.

cil·i·um /ˈsilēəm/ ▶ **n.** (usu. in pl. **cilia** /ˈsilēə/) Biology & Anatomy a short, microscopic, hairlike vibrating structure. Cilia occur in large numbers on the surface of certain cells, either causing currents in the surrounding fluid, or, in some protozoans and other small organisms, providing propulsion. ■ an eyelash, or a delicate hairlike structure that resembles one.
– ORIGIN early 18th cent. (in the sense 'eyelash'): from Latin.

Cim·ar·ron Riv·er /ˈsiməˌrän, -ˌrōn/ a river that flows for 600 miles (1,000 km) from New Mexico across Oklahoma to the Arkansas River near Tulsa. The western part of Oklahoma's panhandle was once known as the Territory of Cimarron.

ci·met·i·dine /sīˈmetəˌdēn/ ▶ **n.** Medicine an antihistamine drug used to treat stomach acidity and peptic ulcers. It is a sulfur-containing derivative of imidazole.
– ORIGIN 1970s: from *ci-* (alteration of *cy-* in *cyano-*) + *met(hyl)* + -IDE + -INE[4].

Cim·me·ri·an /səˈmi(ə)rēən, -ˈmer-/ ▶ **adj.**
1 relating to or denoting members of an ancient nomadic people who overran Asia Minor in the 7th century BC.
2 Greek Mythology relating to or denoting members of a mythical people who lived in perpetual mist and darkness near the land of the dead.
▶ **n.** a member of the historical or mythological Cimmerian people.
– ORIGIN via Latin from Greek *Kimmerios* + -AN.

CINC /siNGk/ ▶ **abbr.** Commander in Chief.

cinch /sinCH/ ▶ **n. 1** informal an extremely easy task: *the program was a cinch to use.* ■ a sure thing; a certainty: *he was a cinch to take a prize.*
2 a girth for a Western saddle or pack.
▶ **v.** [with obj.] **1** secure (a garment) with a belt. ■ fix (a saddle) securely by means of a girth; girth up (a horse).
2 informal make certain of: *his advice cinched her decision to accept the offer.*
– ORIGIN mid 19th cent. (sense 2 of the noun): from Spanish *cincha* 'girth.'

cinch bug ▶ **n.** another term for CHINCH.

cin·cho·na /siNGˈkōnə, sinˈCHōnə/ ▶ **n.** an evergreen South American tree or shrub of the bedstraw family, with fragrant flowers and cultivated for its bark. ● Genus *Cinchona*, family Rubiaceae: several species. ■ (also **cinchona bark**) the dried bark of this tree, which is a source of quinine and other medicinal alkaloids.
– ORIGIN mid 18th cent.: modern Latin, named after the Countess of *Chinchón* (died 1641), who was treated with a similar drug in South America.

cin·cho·nine /ˈsiNGkəˌnēn, ˈsinCHə-/ ▶ **n.** Chemistry a compound with antipyretic properties, derived from cinchona bark and used as a substitute for quinine. ● An alkaloid; chem. formula: $C_{19}H_{22}ON_2$.

cin·chon·ism /ˈsiNGkəˌnizəm, ˈsinCHə-/ ▶ **n.** poisoning due to excessive ingestion of cinchona alkaloids.

Cin·cin·nat·i /ˌsinsəˈnatē/ an industrial city in southwestern Ohio, on the Ohio River; pop. 333,336 (est. 2008).

cinc·ture /ˈsiNGkCHər/ ▶ **n. 1** literary a girdle or belt.
2 Architecture a ring at either end of a column shaft.
– ORIGIN late 16th cent. (in the sense 'encircling or enclosure'): from Latin *cinctura*, from *cinct-* 'encircled,' from the verb *cingere.*

cin·der /ˈsindər/ ▶ **n.** a small piece of partly burned coal or wood that has stopped giving off flames but still has combustible matter in it.
– DERIVATIVES **cin·der·y adj.**
– ORIGIN Old English *sinder* 'slag,' of Germanic origin; related to German *Sinter*. The similar but unconnected French *cendre* (from Latin *cinis* 'ashes') has influenced both the sense development and the spelling. Compare with SINTER.

cin·der block ▶ **n.** a lightweight building brick made from small cinders mixed with sand and cement.

cin·der cone ▶ **n.** a cone formed around a volcanic vent by fragments of lava thrown out during eruptions.

Cin·der·el·la /ˌsindəˈrelə/ a girl in various traditional European fairy tales. In the version by Charles Perrault she is exploited as a servant by

her family but enabled by a fairy godmother to attend a royal ball. She meets and captivates Prince Charming but has to flee at midnight, leaving the prince to identify her by the glass slipper that she leaves behind. ■ [as noun] a person or thing of unrecognized or disregarded merit or beauty. ■ [as noun] a neglected aspect of something: *is research into breast cancer to remain the Cinderella of medicine?* ■ Philately any stamplike label that is not valid as postage.
– ORIGIN from CINDER + the diminutive suffix *-ella*, on the pattern of French *Cendrillon*, from *cendre* 'cinders.'

cin·der track (also **cinder path**) ▶ **n.** a footpath or running track laid with fine cinders.

cin·e /ˈsinē/ ▶ **adj.** chiefly Brit. cinematographic: *a cine camera.*

cine- ▶ **comb. form** representing CINEMATOGRAPHIC (see CINEMATOGRAPHY).

cin·e·aste /ˈsinē,ast/ (also **cineast**) ▶ **n.** a filmmaker. ■ an enthusiast for or devotee of movies or filmmaking.
– ORIGIN 1920s: from French *cinéaste*, from *ciné* (from *cinéma*), on the pattern of *enthousiaste* 'enthusiast.'

cin·e·ma /ˈsinəmə/ ▶ **n.** a movie theater. ■ the production of movies as an art or industry: *the history of American cinema.*
– ORIGIN early 20th cent.: from French *cinéma*, abbreviation of *cinématographe* (see CINEMATOGRAPH).

Cin·e·ma·Scope /ˈsinəmə,skōp/ ▶ **n.** trademark a cinematographic process in which special lenses are used to compress a wide image into a standard frame and then expand it again during projection. It results in an image that is almost two and a half times as wide as it is high.
– DERIVATIVES **Cin·e·ma·Scop·ic** /,sinəməˈskäpik/ **adj.**

cin·e·ma·theque /ˈsinəmə,tek/ ▶ **n. 1** a motion-picture library or archive.
2 a small movie theater, esp. one that shows avant-garde or classic movies.
– ORIGIN 1960s: from French *cinémathèque*, from *cinéma* 'cinema,' on the pattern of *bibliothèque* 'library.'

cin·e·mat·ic /,sinəˈmatik/ ▶ **adj.** of or relating to motion pictures: *cinematic output.* ■ having qualities characteristic of motion pictures: *the cinematic feel of their video.*
– DERIVATIVES **cin·e·mat·i·cal·ly** /-ik(ə)lē/ **adv.**

cin·e·ma·tize /ˈsinəmə,tīz/ ▶ **v.** [with obj.] adapt (a play, story, etc.) to the cinema; make a movie of.

cin·e·mat·o·graph /,sinəˈmatəgraf/ (also **kinematograph** /,kinə-/) ▶ **n.** chiefly Brit. historical an early motion-picture projector.
– ORIGIN late 19th cent.: from French *cinématographe*, from Greek *kinēma, kinēmat-* 'movement,' from *kinein* 'to move.'

cin·e·ma·tog·ra·phy /,sinəməˈtägrəfē/ ▶ **n.** the art of making motion pictures.
– DERIVATIVES **cin·e·ma·tog·ra·pher** /-fər/ **n.**, **cin·e·mat·o·graph·ic** /-,matəˈgrafik/ **adj.**, **cin·e·mat·o·graph·i·cal·ly** /-,matəˈgrafik(ə)lē/ **adv.**

ci·né·ma vé·ri·té /,sinəmə ,veriˈtā/ ▶ **n.** a style of filmmaking characterized by realistic, typically documentary motion pictures that avoid artificiality and artistic effect and are generally made with simple equipment. ■ motion pictures of this style collectively.
– ORIGIN mid 20th cent.: French, literally 'cinema truth.'

cin·e·phile /ˈsini,fīl/ ▶ **n.** a person who is fond of motion pictures.

cin·e·plex /ˈsini,pleks/ (also **Cineplex**) ▶ **n.** trademark a movie theater with several separate screens; a multiplex.
– ORIGIN 1970s: blend of CINEMA and COMPLEX.

cin·e·rar·i·a /,sinəˈre(ə)rēə/ ▶ **n.** a plant of the daisy family with compact masses of bright flowers, often cultivated as a houseplant. ● Genus *Pericallis* (formerly *Senecio* or *Cineraria*), family Compositae.
– ORIGIN modern Latin, feminine of Latin *cinerarius* 'of ashes,' from *cinis, ciner-* 'ashes' (because of the ash-colored down on the leaves).

cin·e·rar·i·um /,sinəˈre(ə)rēəm/ ▶ **n.** (pl. **cinerariums**) a place where the ashes of the cremated dead are kept.
– DERIVATIVES **cin·e·rar·y** /ˈsinə,rerē/ **adj.**
– ORIGIN late 19th cent.: from late Latin, neuter (used as a noun) of *cinerarius* 'of ashes.'

ci·ne·re·ous /səˈni(ə)rēəs/ ▶ **adj.** (esp. of hair or feathers) ash-gray.
– ORIGIN late Middle English: from Latin *cinereus* 'similar to ashes' (from *cinis, ciner-* 'ashes') + -OUS.

ci·ne·re·ous vul·ture ▶ **n.** another term for BLACK VULTURE (sense 2).

ci·né·vé·ri·té /,sinə ,veriˈtā, siˈnā/ ▶ **n.** another term for CINÉMA-VÉRITÉ.

cin·gu·lum /ˈsiNGgyələm/ ▶ **n.** (pl. **cingula** /-lə/) Anatomy **1** a curved bundle of nerve fibers in each hemisphere of the brain.
2 a ridge of enamel on the base or margin of the crown of a tooth.
– DERIVATIVES **cin·gu·late** /-lit/ **adj.**
– ORIGIN mid 19th cent.: from Latin, 'belt,' from *cingere* 'gird.'

cin·na·bar /ˈsinə,bär/ ▶ **n.** a bright red mineral consisting of mercury sulfide. It is the only important ore of mercury and is sometimes used as a pigment. ■ the bright red color of this; vermilion: [as modifier] *the blood coagulated in cinnabar threads.*
– ORIGIN Middle English: from Latin *cinnabaris*, from Greek *kinnabari*, of obscure origin.

cin·nam·ic /səˈnamik/ ▶ **adj.** of cinnamon. ■ denoting an acidic crystalline powder (**cinnamic acid**), $C_9H_8O_2$, derived from cinnamon or produced synthetically and used in medicine and perfumery.

cin·na·mon /ˈsinəmən/ ▶ **n. 1** an aromatic spice made from the peeled, dried, and rolled bark of a Southeast Asian tree. ■ a reddish- or yellowish-brown color resembling that of cinnamon.
2 (also **cinnamon tree**) the tree that yields this spice. ● Genus *Cinnamomum*, family Lauraceae: several species, in particular *C. zeylanicum*, native to southern India and Sri Lanka.
– ORIGIN late Middle English: from Old French *cinnamome* (from Greek *kinnamōmon*), and Latin *cinnamon* (from Greek *kinnamon*), both from a Semitic language and perhaps based on Malay.

cin·na·mon bear ▶ **n.** a North American black bear of a variety with reddish-brown hair.

cin·na·mon fern ▶ **n.** a large North American fern whose fertile fronds are cinnamon-colored in spring. ● *Osmunda cinnamomea*, family Osmundaceae.

cin·na·mon stick ▶ **n.** a piece, typically several inches long, of the peeled, dried, and rolled bark of a cinnamon tree, used decoratively or to flavor mulled drinks.

cin·quain /siNGˈkān/ ▶ **n.** (in verse) a five-line stanza.
– ORIGIN late 19th cent.: French, from *cinq* 'five.'

cinque /siNGk, saNGk/ (also **cinq**) ▶ **n.** the five on dice.
– ORIGIN late Middle English: from Old French *cinc, cink*, from Latin *quinque* 'five.'

cin·que·cen·to /,CHiNGkwiˈCHentō/ ▶ **n.** (**the cinquecento**) the 16th century as a period of Italian art, architecture, or literature, with a reversion to classical forms.
– ORIGIN Italian, literally '500' (shortened from *milcinquecento* '1500') used with reference to the years 1500–99.

cinque·foil /ˈsiNGk,foil, ˈsaNGk-/ ▶ **n. 1** a widely distributed herbaceous plant of the rose family, with compound leaves of five leaflets and five-petaled yellow flowers. ● Genus *Potentilla*, family Rosaceae: numerous species, including the small-flowered creeping **common cinquefoil** (*P. simplex*) and the larger-flowered erect **rough-fruited cinquefoil** (*P. recta*).
2 Art an ornamental design of five lobes arranged in a circle, e.g., in architectural tracery or heraldry.
– ORIGIN Middle English: from Latin *quinquefolium*, from *quinque* 'five' + *folium* 'leaf.'

rough-fruited cinquefoil

Cin·za·no /CHinˈzänō, sin-/ ▶ **n.** (pl. **Cinzanos**) trademark a type of vermouth produced in Italy.
– ORIGIN from the name of the producers.

CIO ▶ **abbr.** Congress of Industrial Organizations.

ci·on ▶ **n.** variant spelling of SCION (sense 1).

ci·pher /ˈsīfər/ (also **cypher**) ▶ **n. 1** a secret or disguised way of writing; a code: *he was writing cryptic notes in a cipher | the information may be given in cipher.* ■ a thing written in such a code. ■ a key to such a code.
2 dated a zero; a figure 0. ■ a person or thing of no importance, esp. a person who does the bidding of others and seems to have no will of their own.
3 a monogram.
4 a continuous sounding of an organ pipe, caused by a mechanical defect.
▶ **v. 1** [with obj.] put (a message) into secret writing; encode.
2 [no obj.] archaic do arithmetic.
– ORIGIN late Middle English (in the senses 'symbol for zero' and 'Arabic numeral'): from Old French *cifre*, based on Arabic *ṣifr* 'zero.' Sense 4 of the noun is perhaps a different word.

cir. (also **circ.**) ▶ **abbr.** ■ circle. ■ circuit. ■ circular. ■ circulation. ■ circumference.

cir·ca /ˈsərkə/ ▶ **prep.** (often preceding a date) approximately: *built circa 1935.*
– ORIGIN mid 19th cent.: Latin.

cir·ca·di·an /sərˈkādēən/ ▶ **adj.** Physiology (of biological processes) recurring naturally on a twenty-four-hour cycle, even in the absence of light fluctuations: *a circadian rhythm.*
– ORIGIN 1950s: formed irregularly from Latin *circa* 'around' + *dies* 'day.'

Cir·cas·sian /sərˈkasHən/ ▶ **adj.** relating to or denoting a group of mainly Sunni Muslim peoples of the northwest Caucasus.
▶ **n. 1** a member of this people.
2 either of two North Caucasian languages of these peoples.
– ORIGIN from *Circassia*, Latinized form of Russian *Cherkes*, denoting a district in the northern Caucasus.

Cir·ce /ˈsərsē/ Greek Mythology an enchantress who lived with her wild animals on the island of Aeaea. When Odysseus visited the island, his companions were changed into pigs by her potions, but he protected himself with the mythical herb *moly* and forced her to restore his men into human form.
– ORIGIN via Latin from Greek *Kirkē*.

cir·ci·nate /ˈsərsə,nāt/ ▶ **adj.** Botany rolled up with the tip in the center, for example the young frond of a fern. ■ Medicine circular in appearance.
– ORIGIN early 19th cent.: from Latin *circinatus*, past participle of *circinare* 'make round,' from *circinus* 'pair of compasses.'

Cir·ci·nus /ˈsərsənəs/ Astronomy a small and faint southern constellation (the Compasses), in the Milky Way next to Centaurus. ■ (as genitive **Circini** /ˈsərsənē/) used with a preceding letter or numeral to designate a star in this constellation: *the star Alpha Circini.*
– ORIGIN Latin.

cir·cle /ˈsərkəl/ (abbr.: **cir.** or **circ.**) ▶ **n. 1** a round plane figure whose boundary (the circumference) consists of points equidistant from a fixed point (the center). ■ something in the shape of such a figure: *the lamp spread a circle of light | they all sat around in a circle.* ■ a dark circular mark below each eye, typically caused by illness or tiredness. ■ a curved upper tier of seats in a theater. See also DRESS CIRCLE.
2 a group of people with shared professions, interests, or acquaintances: *she did not normally move in such exalted circles.*
▶ **v.** [with obj.] move all the way around (someone or something), esp. more than once: *the two dogs circle each other with hackles raised* | [no obj.] *we circled around the island.* ■ [no obj.] (**circle back**) move in a wide loop back toward one's starting point. ■ form a ring around: *the monastery was circled by a huge wall.* ■ draw a line around: *circle the correct answers.*
– PHRASES **circle the wagons** informal (of a group) unite in defense of a common interest. [with reference to the defensive position of a wagon train under attack.] **come** (or **turn**) **full circle** return to a past position or situation, esp. in a way considered to be inevitable. **go around** (or **around and around**) **in circles** informal do something for a long time without achieving anything but purposeless repetition: *the discussion went around and around in circles.* **run around in circles** informal be fussily busy with little result. **the wheel has turned** (or **come**) **full circle** the situation has returned to what it was in the past, as if completing a cycle. [with reference to Shakespeare's *King Lear*, by association with the wheel fabled to be turned by Fortune and representing mutability.]
– ORIGIN Old English, from Old French *cercle*, from Latin *circulus* 'small ring,' diminutive of *circus* 'ring.'

cir·cle dance ▶ **n.** a country dance or folk dance, typically following a traditional set of steps, in which dancers form a circle.

cir·cle graph ▶ **n.** another term for PIE CHART.

cir·clet /ˈsərklət/ ▶ **n.** a circular band, typically one made of precious metal, worn on the head as an ornament. ■ a small circular arrangement or object.
– ORIGIN late Middle English: from CIRCLE + -ET¹, perhaps reinforced by archaic French *cerclet*.

cir·cuit /ˈsərkət/ (abbr.: **cir.** or **circ.**) ▶ **n. 1** a roughly circular line, route, or movement that starts and finishes at the same place: *I ran a circuit of the village.*

2 an established itinerary of events or venues used for a particular activity, typically involving public performance: *the alternative cabaret circuit.* ■ a series of athletic exercises performed consecutively in one training session: [as modifier] *circuit training.* ■ a regular journey made by a judge around a particular district to hear cases in court: [as modifier] *a circuit judge.* ■ a district administered or formerly administered by traveling judges. ■ a group of local Methodist churches forming an administrative unit. ■ a chain of theaters or nightclubs under a single management.
3 a complete and closed path around which a circulating electric current can flow. ■ a system of electrical conductors and components forming such a path.
▶ v. [with obj.] move all the way around (a place or thing): *the trains will follow the northern line, circuiting the capital.*
– ORIGIN late Middle English: via Old French from Latin *circuitus*, from *circuire*, variant of *circumire* 'go around,' from *circum* 'around' + *ire* 'go.'

cir·cuit board ▶ n. a thin rigid board containing an electric circuit; a printed circuit.

cir·cuit break·er ▶ n. an automatic device for stopping the flow of current in an electric circuit as a safety measure.

cir·cu·i·tous /sər'kyo͞oətəs/ ▶ adj. (of a route or journey) longer than the most direct way: *the canal followed a circuitous route* | figurative *a circuitous line of reasoning.*
– DERIVATIVES **cir·cu·i·tous·ly** adv., **cir·cu·i·tous·ness** n.
– ORIGIN mid 17th cent.: from medieval Latin *circuitosus*, from *circuitus* 'a way around' (see CIRCUIT).

cir·cuit rid·er ▶ n. historical a clergyman who traveled on horseback from church to church, esp. within a rural Methodist circuit.

cir·cuit·ry /'sərkətrē/ ▶ n. (pl. **circuitries**) electric circuits collectively: *solid state circuitry.* ■ a circuit or system of circuits performing a particular function in an electronic device: *switching circuitry.*

cir·cu·lar /'sərkyələr/ (abbr.: **cir.** or **circ.**) ▶ adj.
1 having the form of a circle: *the building features a circular atrium.* ■ (of a movement or journey) starting and finishing at the same place and often following roughly the circumference of an imaginary circle: *a circular walk.*
2 Logic (of an argument) already containing an assumption of what is to be proved, and therefore fallacious.
3 [attrib.] (of a letter or advertisement) for distribution to a large number of people.
▶ n. a letter or advertisement that is distributed to a large number of people.
– DERIVATIVES **cir·cu·lar·i·ty** /,sərkyə'laritē/ n., **cir·cu·lar·ly** adv.
– ORIGIN late Middle English: from Old French *circulier*, from late Latin *circularis*, from Latin *circulus* 'small ring' (see CIRCLE).

cir·cu·lar breath·ing ▶ n. a technique of inhaling through the nose while blowing air through the lips from the cheeks, used to maintain constant exhalation esp. by players of certain wind instruments.

cir·cu·lar func·tion ▶ n. Mathematics another term for TRIGONOMETRIC FUNCTION.

cir·cu·lar·ize /'sərkyələ,rīz/ ▶ v. [with obj.] 1 distribute a large number of letters, leaflets, or questionnaires to (a group of people) in order to advertise something or canvas opinion.
2 Biochemistry make (a stretch of DNA) into a circular loop.
– DERIVATIVES **cir·cu·lar·i·za·tion** /,sərkyələrə'zāsHən/ n.

cir·cu·lar po·lar·i·za·tion ▶ n. Physics polarization of an electromagnetic wave in which either the electric or the magnetic vector executes a circle perpendicular to the path of propagation with a frequency equal to that of the wave. It is frequently used in satellite communications.

cir·cu·lar saw ▶ n. a power saw with a rapidly rotating toothed disk.

cir·cu·late /'sərkyə,lāt/ ▶ v. 1 move or cause to move continuously or freely through a closed system or area: [no obj.] *antibodies circulate in the bloodstream* | [with obj.] *the fan circulates hot air around the oven.* ■ [no obj.] move around a social function in order to talk to many different people.
2 pass or cause to pass from place to place or person to person: [no obj.] *rumors of his arrest circulated* | [with obj.] *they were circulating the list to conservation groups.*
– DERIVATIVES **cir·cu·la·tive** /-,lātiv, -lətiv/ adj., **cir·cu·la·tor** /-,lātər/ n.
– ORIGIN late 15th cent. (as an alchemical term meaning 'distill something in a closed container, allowing condensed vapor to return to the original liquid'): from Latin *circulat-* 'moved in a circular path,' from the verb *circulare*, from *circulus* 'small ring' (see CIRCLE). Sense 1 dates from the mid 17th cent.

cir·cu·lat·ing li·brar·y ▶ n. historical a small library with books lent for a small fee to subscribers.

cir·cu·la·tion /,sərkyə'lāsHən/ (abbr.: **cir.** or **circ.**) ▶ n. 1 movement to and fro or around something, esp. that of fluid in a closed system: *an extra pump for good water circulation.* ■ the continuous motion by which the blood travels through all parts of the body under the action of the heart. ■ the movement of sap through a plant.
2 the public availability or knowledge of something: *his music has achieved wide circulation.* ■ the movement, exchange, or availability of money in a country: *the new coins go into circulation today.* ■ [in sing.] the number of copies sold of a newspaper or magazine: *the magazine had a large circulation.*
– PHRASES **in** (or **out of**) **circulation** available (or unavailable) to the public; in (or not in) general use: *there is a huge volume of video material in circulation.* ■ used of a person who is seen (or not seen) in public: *Anne had made a good recovery and was back in circulation.*
– ORIGIN late Middle English (denoting continuous distillation of a liquid): from Latin *circulatio(n-)*, from the verb *circulare* (see CIRCULATE).

cir·cu·la·to·ry /'sərkyələ,tôrē/ ▶ adj. of or relating to the circulation of blood or sap.

cir·cu·la·to·ry sys·tem ▶ n. the system that circulates blood and lymph through the body, consisting of the heart, blood vessels, blood, lymph, and the lymphatic vessels and glands. Also called CARDIOVASCULAR SYSTEM.

circum. ▶ abbr. circumference.

circum- ▶ prefix about; around: *circumambulate* | *circumpolar.*
– ORIGIN from Latin *circum* 'around.'

cir·cum·am·bi·ent /,sərkəm'ambēənt/ ▶ adj. chiefly literary surrounding: *he could not see them clearly by reason of the circumambient water.*
– DERIVATIVES **cir·cum·am·bi·ence** n., **cir·cum·am·bi·en·cy** n.

cir·cum·am·bu·late /,sərkəm'ambyə,lāt/ ▶ v. [with obj.] formal walk all the way around (something): *they used to circumambulate the perimeter wall.*
– DERIVATIVES **cir·cum·am·bu·la·tion** /-,ambyə'lāsHən/ n., **cir·cum·am·bu·la·to·ry** /-'ambyələ,tôrē/ adj.

cir·cum·cise /'sərkəm,sīz/ ▶ v. [with obj.] cut off the foreskin of (a young boy or man, esp. a baby) as a religious rite, esp. in Judaism and Islam, or as a medical treatment. ■ cut off the clitoris, and sometimes the labia, of (a girl or young woman) as a traditional practice among some peoples.
– ORIGIN Middle English: from Old French *circonciser*, or from Latin *circumcis-* 'cut around,' from the verb *circumcidere*, from *circum* 'around, about' + *caedere* 'to cut.'

cir·cum·ci·sion /,sərkəm'sizHən, 'sərkəm,sizHən/ ▶ n. the action or practice of circumcising a young boy or man. See also FEMALE CIRCUMCISION. ■ (**Circumcision**) (in church use) the feast of the Circumcision of Jesus, January 1.
– ORIGIN Middle English: from late Latin *circumcisio(n-)*, from the verb *circumcidere* (see CIRCUMCISE).

cir·cum·fer·ence /sər'kəmf(ə)rəns/ (abbr.: **cir.**, **circ.**, or **circum.**) ▶ n. the enclosing boundary of a curved geometric figure, esp. a circle. ■ the distance around something: *babies who have small head circumferences* | *two inches in circumference.*
– DERIVATIVES **cir·cum·fer·en·tial** /sər,kəmfə'renCHəl/ adj., **cir·cum·fer·en·tial·ly** adv.
– ORIGIN late Middle English: from Old French *circonference*, from Latin *circumferentia*, from *circum* 'around, about' + *ferre* 'carry, bear.'

cir·cum·flex /'sərkəm,fleks/ ▶ n. (also **circumflex accent**) a mark (^) placed over a vowel in some languages to indicate contraction, length, or pitch or tone.
▶ adj. Anatomy bending around something else; curved: *circumflex coronary arteries.*
– ORIGIN late 16th cent.: from Latin *circumflexus* (from *circum* 'around, about' + *flectere* 'to bend'), translating Greek *perispōmenos* 'drawn around.'

cir·cum·flu·ent /sər'kəmflo͞oənt, ,sərkəm'flo͞oənt/ ▶ adj. flowing around; surrounding.
– DERIVATIVES **cir·cum·flu·ence** n.
– ORIGIN late 16th cent.: from Latin *circumfluent-* 'flowing around,' from the verb *circumfluere*, from *circum* 'around, about' + *fluere* 'to flow.'

cir·cum·fuse /,sərkəm'fyo͞oz/ ▶ v. [with obj.] (usu. **be circumfused**) archaic pour (a liquid) so as to cause it to surround something: *Earth with her nether Ocean circumfused.*
– ORIGIN late 16th cent.: from Latin *circumfus-* 'poured around,' from the verb *circumfundere*, from *circum* 'around' + *fundere* 'pour.'

cir·cum·ja·cent /,sərkəm'jāsənt/ ▶ adj. archaic surrounding: *the circumjacent parts of the mouth.*
– ORIGIN late 15th cent.: from Latin *circumjacent-* 'lying around, bordering upon,' from the verb *circumjacere*, from *circum* 'around' + *jacere* 'to lie.'

cir·cum·lo·cu·tion /,sərkəm,lō'kyo͞osHən/ ▶ n. the use of many words where fewer would do, esp. in a deliberate attempt to be vague or evasive: *his admission came after years of circumlocution* | *he used a number of poetic circumlocutions.*
– ORIGIN late Middle English: from Latin *circumlocutio(n-)* (translating Greek *periphrasis*), from *circum* 'around' + *locutio(n-)*, from *loqui* 'speak.'

cir·cum·loc·u·to·ry /,sərkəm'läkyə,tôrē/ ▶ adj. using many words where fewer would do, esp. in a deliberate attempt to be vague or evasive; long-winded: *he has a meandering, circumlocutory speaking style.*

cir·cum·lu·nar /,sərkəm'lo͞onər/ ▶ adj. moving or situated around the moon: *a circumlunar flight.*

cir·cum·nav·i·gate /,sərkəm'navə,gāt/ ▶ v. [with obj.] sail all the way around (something, esp. the world). ■ humorous go around or across (something): *he helped her to circumnavigate a frozen puddle.*
– DERIVATIVES **cir·cum·nav·i·ga·tion** /-,navə'gāsHən/ n., **cir·cum·nav·i·ga·tor** /-,gātər/ n.

cir·cum·po·lar /,sərkəm'pōlər/ ▶ adj. situated around or inhabiting one of the earth's poles: *the eight circumpolar countries met in 1991.* ■ Astronomy (of a star or motion) above the horizon at all times in a given latitude: *the Big Dipper is circumpolar at Mediterranean latitudes.*

cir·cum·ro·tate /,sərkəm'rōtāt/ ▶ v. [no obj.] revolve or turn like a wheel.

cir·cum·scribe /'sərkəm,skrīb/ ▶ v. [with obj.]
1 restrict (something) within limits: *their movements were strictly monitored and circumscribed.*
2 Geometry draw (a figure) around another, touching it at points but not cutting it. Compare with INSCRIBE.
– DERIVATIVES **cir·cum·scrib·er** n., **cir·cum·scrip·tion** /,sərkəm'skripsHən/ n.
– ORIGIN late Middle English: from Latin *circumscribere*, from *circum* 'around' + *scribere* 'write.'

cir·cum·so·lar /,sərkəm'sōlər/ ▶ adj. moving or situated around the sun.

cir·cum·spect /'sərkəm,spekt/ ▶ adj. wary and unwilling to take risks: *the officials were very circumspect in their statements.*
– DERIVATIVES **cir·cum·spect·ly** adv.
– ORIGIN late Middle English: from Latin *circumspectus*, from *circumspicere* 'look around,' from *circum* 'around, about' + *specere* 'look.'

cir·cum·spec·tion /,sərkəm'speksHən/ ▶ n. the quality of being wary and unwilling to take risks; prudence: *circumspection is required in the day-to-day exercise of administrative powers.*

cir·cum·stance /'sərkəm,stans, -stəns/ ▶ n. 1 (usu. **circumstances**) a fact or condition connected with or relevant to an event or action: *we wanted to marry but circumstances didn't permit.* ■ an event or fact that causes or helps to cause something to happen, typically something undesirable: *he was found dead but there were no suspicious circumstances* | *they were thrown together by circumstance.*
2 one's state of financial or material welfare: *the artists are living in reduced circumstances.*
– PHRASES **under no circumstances** never, whatever the situation is or might be: *under no circumstances may the child be identified.* **under** (or **in**) **the circumstances** given the difficult nature of the situation: *she had every right to be angry under the circumstances.*
– DERIVATIVES **cir·cum·stanced** adj.
– ORIGIN Middle English: from Old French *circonstance* or Latin *circumstantia*, from *circumstare* 'encircle, encompass,' from *circum* 'around' + *stare* 'stand.'

cir·cum·stan·tial /,sərkəm'stanCHəl/ ▶ adj. 1 (of evidence or a legal case) pointing indirectly toward someone's guilt but not conclusively proving it.
2 (of a description) containing full details: *the picture was circumstantial and therefore convincing.*

PRONUNCIATION KEY ə ago, up; ər over, fur; a hat; ā ate; ä car; e let; ē see; i fit; ī by; NG sing; ō go; ô law, for; oi toy; o͝o good; o͞o goo; ou out; TH thin; TH then; ZH vision

– DERIVATIVES **cir·cum·stan·ti·al·i·ty** /-ˌstanCHēˈalətē/ **n.**, **cir·cum·stan·tial·ly adv.**
– ORIGIN late 16th cent.: from Latin *circumstantia* (see **CIRCUMSTANCE**) + **-AL**.

cir·cum·stan·ti·ate /ˌsərkəmˈstanSHēˌāt/ ▶ **v.** [with obj.] rare set forth or support with circumstances or details.
– DERIVATIVES **cir·cum·stan·ti·a·tion** /ˌsərkəmˌstanSHēˈāSHən/ **n.**

C

cir·cum·ter·res·tri·al /ˌsərkəmtəˈrestrēəl, -təˈresCHəl/ ▶ **adj.** moving or situated around the earth: *circumterrestrial space.*

cir·cum·val·late /ˌsərkəmˈvalˌāt/ ▶ **v.** [with obj.] literary surround with or as if with a rampart: *the walls were circumvallated with a ditch.*
▶ **adj.** literary surrounded as if by a rampart: *we looked at the circumvallate mountains.* ■ Anatomy denoting certain papillae near the back of the tongue, surrounded by taste receptors.
– ORIGIN mid 17th cent. (as an adjective): from Latin *circumvallat-* 'surrounded with a rampart,' from the verb *circumvallare*, from *circum* 'around' + *vallare*, from *vallum* 'rampart.' The verb dates from the early 19th cent.

cir·cum·vent /ˌsərkəmˈvent/ ▶ **v.** [with obj.] find a way around (an obstacle). ■ overcome (a problem or difficulty), typically in a clever and surreptitious way: *I found it quite easy to circumvent security.* ■ archaic deceive; outwit: *he's circumvented her with some of his stories.*
– DERIVATIVES **cir·cum·ven·tion** /-ˈvenCHən/ **n.**
– ORIGIN late Middle English: from Latin *circumvent-* 'skirted around,' from the verb *circumvenire*, from *circum* 'around' + *venire* 'come.'

cir·cum·vo·lu·tion /ˌsərkəmvəˈlo͞oSHən, sərˌkəm-/ ▶ **n.** a winding movement, esp. of one thing around another.
– ORIGIN late Middle English: from Latin *circumvolut-* 'rolled around,' from the verb *circumvolvere*, from *circum* 'around' + *volvere* 'roll.'

cir·cum·volve /ˈsərkəmˌvälv/ ▶ **v.** rare rotate; revolve. ■ wind, fold, or twist around; enwrap.

cir·cus /ˈsərkəs/ ▶ **n.** (pl. **circuses**) **1** a traveling company of acrobats, trained animals, and clowns that gives performances, typically in a large tent, in a series of different places: [as modifier] *a circus elephant.* ■ (in ancient Rome) a rounded or oblong arena lined with tiers of seats, used for equestrian and other sports and games. ■ informal a group of people involved in a particular sport who travel around to compete against one another in a series of different places: *the Formula One circus.* ■ informal a public scene of frenetic and noisily intrusive activity: *a media circus.*
2 Brit. (in place names) a rounded open space in a city where several streets converge: *Piccadilly Circus.*
– ORIGIN late Middle English (with reference to the arena of Roman antiquity): from Latin, 'ring or circus.' The sense 'traveling company of performers' dates from the late 18th cent.

ci·ré /səˈrā/ (also **cire**) ▶ **n.** a fabric with a smooth shiny surface obtained by waxing and heating.
– ORIGIN 1920s: French, literally 'waxed.'

cire per·due /ˈsi(ə)r perˈd(y)o͞o/ ▶ **n.** another term for **LOST WAX**.
– ORIGIN late 19th cent.: French, literally 'lost wax.'

cirque /sərk/ ▶ **n. 1** Geology a half-open steep-sided hollow at the head of a valley or on a mountainside, formed by glacial erosion. Also called **CORRIE**, **CWM**.
2 literary a ring, circlet, or circle.
– ORIGIN late 17th cent. (sense 2): from French, from Latin *circus*.

cir·rho·sis /səˈrōsəs/ ▶ **n.** a chronic disease of the liver marked by degeneration of cells, inflammation, and fibrous thickening of tissue. It is typically a result of alcoholism or hepatitis.
– DERIVATIVES **cir·rhot·ic** /səˈrätik/ **adj.**
– ORIGIN early 19th cent.: modern Latin, from Greek *kirrhos* 'tawny' (because this is the color of the liver in many cases).

cir·ri·ped /ˈsirəˌped/ (also **cirripede** /ˈsirəˌpēd/) ▶ **n.** Zoology a crustacean of the class Cirripedia; a barnacle.

Cir·ri·pe·di·a /ˌsirəˈpēdēə, -ˈpedēə/ Zoology a class of crustaceans that comprises the barnacles.
– ORIGIN modern Latin (plural), from Latin *cirrus* 'a curl' (because of the form of the legs) + *pes*, *ped-* 'foot.'

cir·ro·cu·mu·lus /ˌsirōˈkyo͞omyələs/ ▶ **n.** cloud forming a broken layer of small fleecy clouds at high altitude, usually 16,500–45,000 feet (5–13 km), typically with a rippled or granulated appearance (as in a mackerel sky).

cir·ro·stra·tus /ˌsirōˈstratəs, -ˈstrātəs/ ▶ **n.** cloud forming a thin, more or less uniform, semitranslucent layer at high altitude, usually 16,500–45,000 feet (5–13 km).

cir·rus /ˈsirəs/ ▶ **n.** (pl. **cirri** /ˈsirˌī, ˈsirē/) **1** cloud forming wispy filamentous tufted streaks ("mare's tails") at high altitude, usually 16,500–45,000 feet (5–13 km).
2 Zoology a slender tendril or hairlike filament, such as the appendage of a barnacle, the barbel of a fish, or the intromittent organ of an earthworm. ■ Botany a tendril.
– ORIGIN early 18th cent. (in the sense 'tendril'): from Latin, literally 'a curl.'

CIS ▶ **abbr.** Commonwealth of Independent States.

cis /sis/ ▶ **adj.** Chemistry denoting or relating to a molecular structure in which two particular atoms or groups lie on the same side of a given plane in the molecule, in particular denoting an isomer in which substituents at opposite ends of a carbon–carbon double bond are on the same side of the bond: *the cis isomer of stilbene.* Compare with **TRANS**.
– ORIGIN independent usage of **CIS-**.

cis- ▶ **prefix 1** on this side of; on the side nearer to the speaker: *cisatlantic* | *cislunar.* ■ historical on the side nearer to Rome: *cisalpine.* ■ (of time) closer to the present: *cis-Elizabethan.* Often contrasted with **TRANS-** or **ULTRA-**.
2 Chemistry (usu. *cis-*) denoting molecules with cis arrangements of substituents: *cis-1,2-dichloroethylene.*
– ORIGIN from Latin *cis* 'on this side of.'

cis·al·pine /sisˈalpīn/ ▶ **adj.** on the southern side of the Alps.
– ORIGIN mid 16th cent.: from Latin *cisalpinus*.

Cis·al·pine Gaul /sisˈalˌpīn/ see **GAUL**[1].

cis·at·lan·tic /ˌsisətˈlantik/ ▶ **adj.** on the same side of the Atlantic as the speaker.

cis·co /ˈsiskō/ ▶ **n.** (pl. **ciscoes**) a freshwater whitefish of northern countries. Most species are migratory and are important food fishes. ● Genus *Coregonus*, family Salmonidae: several species, including the **lake cisco** (*C. artedii*) of North America, and the **Arctic cisco** (*C. autumnalis*) of northern Eurasia and northern North America.
– ORIGIN mid 19th cent.: of unknown origin.

cis·lu·nar /sisˈlo͞onər/ ▶ **adj.** between the earth and the moon: *the darkness of cislunar space.*

cis·mon·tane /sisˈmänˌtān/ ▶ **adj.** on this side of the mountains, esp. the Alps. Compare with **CISALPINE**.

cis·plat·in /sisˈplatn/ ▶ **n.** Medicine a cytotoxic drug used in cancer chemotherapy. ● A coordination compound of platinum; chem. formula: $Pt(NH_3)_2Cl_2$.
– ORIGIN late 20th cent.: from **CIS-** + **PLATINUM**.

cis·sus /ˈsisəs/ ▶ **n.** a woody climbing vine of the grape family, with trifoliate leaves that are sometimes evergreen. ● Genus *Cissus*, family Vitaceae: several species, esp. *C. incisa* of the central and southeastern US.
– ORIGIN modern Latin: from Greek *kissos* 'ivy.'

cist /sist, kist/ (also **kist**) ▶ **n. 1** Archaeology an ancient coffin or burial chamber made from stone or a hollowed tree.
2 a box used in ancient Greece for sacred utensils.
– ORIGIN early 19th cent.: from Latin *cista*, from Greek *kistē* 'basket'; sense 1 via Welsh.

Cis·ter·cian /sisˈtərSHən/ ▶ **n.** a monk or nun of an order founded in 1098 as a stricter branch of the Benedictines. The monks are now divided into two observances, the strict observance, whose adherents are known popularly as Trappists, and the common observance, which has certain relaxations.
▶ **adj.** of or relating to this order: *a Cistercian abbey.*
– ORIGIN from French *cistercien*, from *Cistercium*, the Latin name of *Cîteaux* near Dijon in France, where the order was founded.

cis·tern /ˈsistərn/ ▶ **n.** a tank for storing water, esp. one supplying taps or as part of a flushing toilet. ■ an underground reservoir for rainwater.
– ORIGIN Middle English: from Old French *cisterne*, from Latin *cisterna*, from *cista* 'box.'

cis·tron /ˈsisˌträn/ ▶ **n.** Biochemistry a section of a DNA or RNA molecule that codes for a specific polypeptide in protein synthesis.
– ORIGIN 1950s: from **CIS-** + **TRANS-** (because of the possibility of two genes being on the same or different chromosomes) + **-ON**.

cit. ▶ **abbr.** ■ citation. ■ cited. ■ citizen.

cit·a·del /ˈsitədl, -ˌdel/ ▶ **n.** a fortress, typically on high ground, protecting or dominating a city.
– ORIGIN mid 16th cent.: from French *citadelle*, or from Italian *cittadella*, based on Latin *civitas* 'city' (see **CITY**).

ci·ta·tion /sīˈtāSHən/ (abbr.: **cit.**) ▶ **n. 1** a quotation from or reference to a book, paper, or author, esp. in a scholarly work: *there were dozens of citations from the works of Byron* | *recognition through citation is one of the principal rewards in science.* ■ a mention of a praiseworthy act or achievement in an official report, esp. that of a member of the armed forces in wartime. ■ a note accompanying an award, describing the reasons for it: *the Nobel citation noted that his discovery would be useful for energy conversion technology.* ■ Law a reference to a former tried case, used as guidance in the trying of comparable cases or in support of an argument.
2 Law a summons: *a traffic citation.*
– ORIGIN Middle English (sense 2): from Old French, from Latin *citation-*, from *citare* 'cite.'

cite /sīt/ ▶ **v.** [with obj.] **1** quote (a passage, book, or author) as evidence for or justification of an argument or statement, esp. in a scholarly work. ■ mention as an example: *medics have been cited as a key example of a modern breed of technical expert.* ■ praise (someone, typically a member of the armed forces) for a courageous act in an official dispatch. ■ Law adduce a former tried case as a guide to deciding a comparable case or in support of an argument.
2 Law summon (someone) to appear in a court of law: *the summons cited four of the defendants.*
▶ **n.** a citation.
– DERIVATIVES **cit·a·ble adj.**
– ORIGIN late Middle English (sense 2 of the verb): from Old French *citer*, from Latin *citare*, from *ciere*, *cire* 'to call.'

CITES /ˈsītˌēz/ ▶ **abbr.** Convention on International Trade in Endangered Species.

cith·a·ra /ˈsiTHərə, ˈkiTH-/ (also **kithara** /ˈkiTH-/) ▶ **n.** an ancient Greek and Roman stringed musical instrument similar to the lyre.
– ORIGIN late 18th cent.: Latin, from Greek *kithara*. Compare with **CITTERN**.

cith·ern /ˈsiTHərn, ˈsiT͟H-/ ▶ **n.** variant spelling of **CITTERN**.

cit·ied /ˈsitēd/ ▶ **adj.** made into or like a city; occupied by a city or cities.

cit·i·fied /ˈsitiˌfīd/ (also **cityfied**) ▶ **adj.** often derogatory characteristic of or adjusted to an urban environment: *black-hatted, citified cowboys.*
– DERIVATIVES **cit·i·fi·ca·tion** /ˌsitifiˈkāSHən/ **n.**, **cit·i·fy** /-fī/ **v.** (**citifies, citifying, citified**).

cit·i·zen /ˈsitizən, -sən/ (abbr.: **cit.**) ▶ **n.** a legally recognized subject or national of a state or commonwealth, either native or naturalized: *a Polish citizen* | *the rights of every citizen.* ■ an inhabitant of a particular town or city: *the citizens of Los Angeles.*
– PHRASES **citizen of the world** a person who is at home in any country.
– DERIVATIVES **cit·i·zen·ry** /-rē/ **n.**, **cit·i·zen·ship** /-ˌSHip/ **n.**
– ORIGIN Middle English: from Anglo-Norman French *citezein*, alteration (probably influenced by *deinzein* 'denizen') of Old French *citeain*, based on Latin *civitas* 'city' (see **CITY**).

cit·i·zen jour·nal·ism ▶ **n.** the collection, dissemination, and analysis of news and information by the general public, esp. by means of the Internet.
– DERIVATIVES **cit·i·zen jour·nal·ist n.**

cit·i·zen's ar·rest ▶ **n.** an arrest by an ordinary person without a warrant, allowable in certain cases.

Cit·i·zens' Band (abbr.: **CB**) ▶ **n.** a range of radio frequencies that are allocated for local communication by private individuals, esp. by handheld or vehicle radio.

Ci·tlal·té·petl /sētˌlälˈtāˌpetl/ the highest peak in Mexico, in the eastern part of the country, north of Orizaba. It is 18,503 feet (5,699 m) high and is an extinct volcano. Spanish name **PICO DE ORIZABA**.
– ORIGIN Aztec, literally 'star mountain.'

cit·ral /ˈsitrəl/ ▶ **n.** Chemistry a fragrant liquid occurring in citrus and lemongrass oils and used in flavorings and perfumes. ● A terpene; chem. formula: $C_{10}H_{16}O$.

cit·rate /ˈsiˌtrāt/ ▶ **n.** a salt or ester of citric acid.

cit·ric /ˈsitrik/ ▶ **adj.** derived from or related to citrus fruit: *lemongrass gives a slightly sweet citric flavor.*
– ORIGIN late 18th cent.: from Latin *citrus* 'citron tree' + **-IC**.

cit·ric ac·id ▶ **n.** Chemistry a sharp-tasting crystalline acid present in the juice of lemons and other sour fruits. It is made commercially by the fermentation of sugar and used as a flavoring and setting agent. ● A tribasic acid; chem. formula: $C_6H_8O_7$.

cit·ric ac·id cy·cle ▶ **n.** another term for **KREBS CYCLE**.

cit·ri·cul·ture /ˈsitriˌkəlCHər/ ▶ **n.** the cultivation of citrus fruit trees.

cit·rin /ˈsitrən/ ▶ **n.** another term for **BIOFLAVONOID**.

cit·rine /ˈsiˈtrēn, ˈsiˌtrēn/ ▶ **n.** (also **citrine quartz**) a glassy yellow variety of quartz. Also called **FALSE TOPAZ**. ■ a light greenish-yellow.
– ORIGIN late Middle English: from Old French *citrin* 'lemon-colored,' from medieval Latin *citrinus*, from Latin *citrus* 'citron tree.'

cit·ron /ˈsitrən/ ▶ **n.** a shrubby Asian tree that bears large fruits similar to lemons, but with flesh that is less acid and peels that are thicker and more fragrant. ● *Citrus medica*, family Rutaceae; one of the ancestors of modern commercial citrus fruits. ■ the fruit of this tree.
– ORIGIN early 16th cent. (denoting the fruit): from French, from Latin *citrus* 'citron tree,' on the pattern of *limon* 'lemon.'

cit·ron·el·la /ˌsitrəˈnelə/ ▶ **n. 1** (also **citronella oil**) a fragrant natural oil used as an insect repellent and in perfume and soap manufacture.
2 the southern Asian grass from which this oil is obtained. ● *Cymbopogon nardus*, family Gramineae.
– ORIGIN mid 19th cent.: modern Latin, from CITRON + the diminutive suffix *-ella*.

cit·rus /ˈsitrəs/ ▶ **n.** (pl. **citruses**) a tree of a genus that includes citron, lemon, lime, orange, and grapefruit. Native to Asia, citrus trees are widely cultivated in warm countries for their fruit, which has juicy flesh and a pulpy rind. ● Genus *Citrus*, family Rutaceae. ■ (also **citrus fruit**) a fruit from such a tree: [as modifier] *citrus extracts*.
– DERIVATIVES **cit·rous adj.**, **cit·rus·y adj.**
– ORIGIN early 19th cent.: Latin, literally 'citron tree, thuja.'

Cit·rus Heights a city in north central California, northeast of Sacramento; pop. 84,432 (est. 2008).

cit·tern /ˈsitərn/ (also **cithern** /ˈsiᴛʜərn, ˈsi<u>ᴛʜ</u>-/) ▶ **n.** a stringed instrument similar to a lute, with a flattened back and wire strings, used in 16th- and 17th-century Europe.
– ORIGIN mid 16th cent.: from Latin *cithara*, from Greek *kithara*, denoting a kind of harp. The spelling has been influenced by GITTERN.

cit·y /ˈsitē/ ▶ **n.** (pl. **cities**) **1** a large town: [as modifier] *the city center*. ■ an incorporated municipal center.
2 [with modifier] informal a place or situation characterized by a specified attribute: *panic city*.
3 (**the City**) the financial and commercial district of London, England.
– DERIVATIVES **cit·y·ward** /-wərd/ **adj. & adv.**, **cit·y·wards** /-wərdz/ **adv.**, **cit·y·wide** /-ˌwīd/ **adj.**
– ORIGIN Middle English: from Old French *cite*, from Latin *civitas*, from *civis* 'citizen.' Originally denoting a town, and often used as a Latin equivalent to Old English *burh* 'borough,' the term was later applied to foreign and ancient cities and to the more important English boroughs.

cit·y desk ▶ **n.** the department of a newspaper dealing with local news.

cit·y ed·i·tor ▶ **n.** an editor dealing with local news in a newspaper or magazine.

cit·y fa·ther ▶ **n.** (usu. **city fathers**) a person concerned with or experienced in the administration of a city: *the city fathers decided to build a museum*.

cit·y·fied ▶ **adj.** variant spelling of CITIFIED.

cit·y hall (often **City Hall**) ▶ **n.** the administration building of a municipal government. ■ [treated as sing.] municipal offices or officers collectively: *they cultivated close ties with City Hall*.

cit·y man·ag·er ▶ **n.** an appointed official who directs the administration of a city.

Cit·y of God Paradise, perceived as an ideal community in Heaven. ■ the Christian Church. [from *The City of God* by St. Augustine.]

Cit·y of Lon·don the part of London that is within the ancient boundaries and governed by the Lord Mayor and the Corporation.

cit·y plan·ning ▶ **n.** the planning and control of the construction, growth, and development of a city or town. Also called TOWN PLANNING.
– DERIVATIVES **cit·y plan·ner n.**

cit·y·scape /ˈsitēˌskāp/ ▶ **n.** the visual appearance of a city or urban area; a city landscape: *shades of red brick which once colored the cityscape*. ■ a picture of a city.

cit·y slick·er ▶ **n.** chiefly derogatory a person with the sophistication and tastes or values generally associated with urban dwellers, typically regarded as unprincipled and untrustworthy.

cit·y state ▶ **n.** chiefly historical a city that with its surrounding territory forms an independent state.

Ciu·dad Bo·lí·var /syo͞oˈdä(d) bōˈlēvär/ a city in southeastern Venezuela, on the Orinoco River; pop. 355,800 (est. 2009). Formerly called **Angostura**, its name was changed in 1846 to honor Simón Bolívar, the country's liberator.

Ciu·dad del Es·te /syo͞oˈdäd del ˈestā/ a port city in southeastern Paraguay, on the Paraná River, near the Itaipu Dam; pop. 320,782 (2008). Called (before 1989) **Puerto Presidente Stroessner**.

Ciu·dad Gua·ya·na /syo͞oˈdäd gīˈänə/ an industrial city in eastern Venezuela, at the junction of the Caroní and Orinoco rivers; pop. 789,500 (est. 2009).

Ciu·dad Juá·rez /syo͞oˈdäd ˈhwäres/ a commercial and industrial city in Chihuahua state, in northern Mexico, across the Rio Grande from El Paso in Texas; pop. 1,216,608 (2005).

Ciu·dad Re·al /syo͞oˈdäd räˈäl/ an agricultural market town in central Spain, between the Guadiana and Jablón rivers, capital of Ciudad Real province; pop. 72,200 (est. 2008).

Ciu·dad Tru·jil·lo /syo͞oˈdä(d) tro͞oˈhē(y)ō/ former name (1936–61) for SANTO DOMINGO.

Ciu·dad Vic·to·ri·a /syo͞oˈdä(d) vēkˈtôryə/ a city in northeastern Mexico, capital of the state of Tamaulipas; pop. 278,455 (2005).

civ·et /ˈsivət/ ▶ **n.** (also **civet cat**) **1** a slender nocturnal carnivorous mammal with a barred and spotted coat and well-developed anal scent glands, native to Africa and Asia. ● Family Viverridae (the **civet family**): several genera and species, in particular the **African civet** (*Viverra civetta*). The civet family also includes the genets, linsang, and fossa, and formerly included the mongooses. ■ a strong musky perfume obtained from the secretions of the civet's scent glands.
2 another term for CACOMISTLE. ■ the fur of the cacomistle.
– ORIGIN mid 16th cent.: from French *civette*, from Italian *zibetto*, from medieval Latin *zibethum*, from Arabic *zabād*, denoting the perfume.

civ·ic /ˈsivik/ ▶ **adj.** [attrib.] of or relating to a city or town, esp. its administration; municipal: *civic and business leaders*. ■ of or relating to the duties or activities of people in relation to their town, city, or local area: *they could not be denied access to education, the vote, and other civic rights*.
– DERIVATIVES **civ·i·cal·ly** /-ik(ə)lē/ **adv.**
– ORIGIN mid 16th cent.: from French *civique* or Latin *civicus*, from *civis* 'citizen.' The original use was in *civic garland, crown*, etc., translating Latin *corona civica*, denoting a garland of oak leaves and acorns given in ancient Rome to a person who saved a fellow citizen's life.

civ·ic cen·ter ▶ **n.** a municipal building or building complex, often publicly financed, with space for conventions, sports events, and theatrical entertainment.

civ·ics /ˈsiviks/ ▶ **plural n.** [usu. treated as sing.] the study of the rights and duties of citizenship.

civ·ies ▶ **plural n.** variant spelling of CIVVIES.

civ·il /ˈsivəl/ ▶ **adj. 1** [attrib.] of or relating to ordinary citizens and their concerns, as distinct from military or ecclesiastical matters: *civil aviation*. ■ (of disorder or conflict) occurring between citizens of the same country. ■ Law relating to private relations between members of a community; noncriminal: *a civil action*. ■ Law of or relating to civil law.
2 courteous and polite: *we tried to be civil to him*.
3 (of time measurement or a point in time) fixed by custom or law rather than being natural or astronomical: *civil twilight starts at sunset*.
– DERIVATIVES **civ·il·ly adv.**
– ORIGIN late Middle English: via Old French from Latin *civilis*, from *civis* 'citizen.'

civ·il com·mit·ment ▶ **n.** post-sentence institutional detention of an offender with the intention of preventing further offenses: *a 75-year-old convicted sex offender being held in civil commitment*.

civ·il con·vic·tion ▶ **n.** (in military use) a current or former criminal conviction, under civil law, of an enlisted person.

civ·il court ▶ **n.** a court dealing with noncriminal cases.

civ·il death ▶ **n.** rare or chiefly historical the loss of a citizen's privileges through life imprisonment, banishment, etc.

civ·il de·fense ▶ **n.** the organization and training of civilians for the protection of lives and property during and after attacks in wartime.

civ·il dis·o·be·di·ence ▶ **n.** the refusal to comply with certain laws or to pay taxes and fines, as a peaceful form of political protest.

civ·il en·gi·neer ▶ **n.** an engineer who designs and maintains roads, bridges, dams, and similar structures.
– DERIVATIVES **civ·il en·gi·neer·ing n.**

ci·vil·ian /səˈvilyən/ ▶ **n.** a person not in the armed services or the police force.
▶ **adj.** of, denoting, or relating to a person not belonging to the armed services or police: *military agents in civilian clothes*.
– ORIGIN late Middle English (denoting a practitioner of civil law): from Old French *civilien*, in the phrase *droit civilien* 'civil law.' The current sense arose in the early 19th cent.

ci·vil·ian·ize /səˈvilyəˌnīz/ ▶ **v.** [with obj.] make (something) nonmilitary in character or function.
– DERIVATIVES **ci·vil·ian·i·za·tion** /səˌvilyənəˈzāsʜən/ **n.**

ci·vil·i·ty /səˈvilətē/ ▶ **n.** (pl. **civilities**) formal politeness and courtesy in behavior or speech: *I hope we can treat each other with civility and respect*. ■ (**civilities**) polite remarks used in formal conversation: *she was exchanging civilities with his mother*.
– ORIGIN late Middle English: from Old French *civilite*, from Latin *civilitas*, from *civilis* 'relating to citizens' (see CIVIL). In early use the term denoted the state of being a citizen and hence good citizenship or orderly behavior. The sense 'politeness' arose in the mid 16th cent.

civ·i·li·za·tion /ˌsivələˈzāsʜən/ ▶ **n.** the stage of human social development and organization that is considered most advanced: *they equated the railroad with progress and civilization*. ■ the process by which a society or place reaches this stage. ■ the society, culture, and way of life of a particular area: *the great books of Western civilization | the early civilizations of Mesopotamia and Egypt*. ■ the comfort and convenience of modern life, regarded as available only in towns and cities: *the fur traders moved further and further from civilization*.

civ·i·lize /ˈsivəˌlīz/ ▶ **v.** [with obj.] (usu. as adj. **civilized**) bring (a place or people) to a stage of social, cultural, and moral development considered to be more advanced: *a civilized society*. ■ (as adj. **civilized**) polite and well-mannered: *such an affront to civilized behavior will no longer be tolerated*.
– DERIVATIVES **civ·i·liz·a·ble adj.**, **civ·i·liz·er n.**
– ORIGIN early 17th cent.: from French *civiliser*, from *civil* 'civil.'

civ·il law ▶ **n.** the system of law concerned with private relations between members of a community rather than criminal, military, or religious affairs. Contrasted with CRIMINAL LAW. ■ the system of law predominant on the European continent and of which a form is in force in Louisiana, historically influenced by the codes of ancient Rome. Compare with COMMON LAW.

civ·il lib·er·ty ▶ **n.** the state of being subject only to laws established for the good of the community, esp. with regard to freedom of action and speech. ■ (**civil liberties**) individual rights protected by law from unjust governmental or other interference.
– DERIVATIVES **civ·il lib·er·tar·i·an n.**

civ·il mar·riage ▶ **n.** a marriage solemnized as a civil contract without religious ceremony.

civ·il rights ▶ **plural n.** the rights of citizens to political and social freedom and equality.

civ·il serv·ant ▶ **n.** a member of the civil service.

civ·il serv·ice ▶ **n.** the permanent professional branches of a government's administration, excluding military and judicial branches and elected politicians.
– ORIGIN late 18th cent.: originally applied to the part of the service of the British East India Company conducted by staff who did not belong to the army or navy.

civil un·ion ▶ **n.** a legally recognized union of a same-sex couple, with rights similar to those of marriage.

civ·il war ▶ **n.** a war between citizens of the same country. See also AMERICAN CIVIL WAR, ENGLISH CIVIL WAR, SPANISH CIVIL WAR.

civ·il wrong ▶ **n.** Law an infringement of a person's rights, such as a tort or breach of contract.

civ·il year ▶ **n.** see YEAR (sense 2).

civ·vies /ˈsivēz/ informal ▶ **plural n.** civilian clothes, as opposed to a uniform: *he showered and changed into civvies*.
▶ **adj.** [attrib.] (**civvy**) of or relating to civilians: *I learned a good trade for civvy life*.
– ORIGIN late 19th cent.: abbreviation.

CJ ▶ **abbr.** chief justice.

CJD ▶ **abbr.** Creutzfeldt–Jakob disease.

CL ▶ **abbr.** chemiluminescence.

Cl ▶ **symbol** the chemical element chlorine.

cl ▶ **abbr.** centiliter: *70 cl bottles*.

clab·ber /ˈklabər/ ▶ **n.** milk that has naturally clotted on souring.
▶ **v.** curdle or cause to curdle.
– ORIGIN early 19th cent.: shortening of BONNY CLABBER.

cla·chan /ˈklaᴋʜən/ ▶ **n.** (in Scotland or Northern Ireland) a small village or hamlet.
– ORIGIN late Middle English: from Scottish Gaelic and Irish *clachán*.

C

PRONUNCIATION KEY ə *ago, up*; ər *over, fur*; a *hat*; ā *ate*; ä *car*; e *let*; ē *see*; i *fit*; ī *by*; NG *sing*; ō *go*; ô *law, for*; oi *toy*; o͝o *good*; o͞o *goo*; ou *out*; TH *thin*; <u>TH</u> *then*; ZH *vision*

C

clack /klak/ ▶ **v.** make or cause to make a sharp sound or series of such sounds as a result of a hard object striking another: [no obj.] *he heard the sound of her heels clacking across flagstones* | [with obj.] *he clacked the castanets in fine syncopation.* ■ [no obj.] archaic chatter loudly: *he will sit clacking for hours.*
▶ **n.** a sharp sound or series of sounds made in such a way: *the clack of her high heels.* ■ archaic loud chatter: *her clack would go all day.*
– DERIVATIVES **clack·er** **n.**
– ORIGIN Middle English: imitative.

Clac·to·ni·an /klak'tōnēən/ ▶ **adj.** Archaeology of, relating to, or denoting a Lower Paleolithic culture represented by flint implements found at Clacton-on-Sea in southeastern England, dated to about 250,000–200,000 years ago. ■ (as noun **the Clactonian**) the Clactonian culture or period.

clad[1] /klad/ past participle of **CLOTHE**.
▶ **adj. 1** clothed: *they were clad in T-shirts and shorts* | [in combination] *a leotard-clad instructor.*
2 provided with cladding: [in combination] *copper-clad boards.*

clad[2] ▶ **v.** (**clads, cladding**; past and past participle **cladded** or **clad**) [with obj.] provide or encase with a covering or coating: *he cladded the concrete-frame structure in stainless steel.*
– ORIGIN mid 16th cent. (in the sense 'clothe'): apparently from **CLAD**[1].

clad·ding /'kladiNG/ ▶ **n.** a covering or coating on a structure or material: [as modifier] *a range of roofing and cladding products.*

clade /klād/ ▶ **n.** Biology a group of organisms believed to have evolved from a common ancestor, according to the principles of cladistics.
– ORIGIN 1950s: from Greek *klados* 'branch.'

cla·dis·tics /klə'distiks/ ▶ **plural n.** [treated as sing.] Biology a method of classification of animals and plants according to the proportion of measurable characteristics that they have in common. It is assumed that the higher the proportion of characteristics that two organisms share, the more recently they diverged from a common ancestor.
– DERIVATIVES **clad·ism** /'klād,izəm/ **n.**, **cla·dis·tic** **adj.**
– ORIGIN 1960s: from **CLADE** + **-IST** + **-ICS**.

clado- ▶ **comb. form** relating to a branch or branching: *cladogram.*
– ORIGIN from Greek *klados* 'branch or shoot.'

Cla·doc·er·a /klə'däsərə/ Zoology an order of minute branchiopod crustaceans that includes the water fleas. They typically have a transparent shell enclosing the trunk, and large antennae that are used for swimming.
– ORIGIN modern Latin (plural), from Greek *klados* 'branch or root' + *keras* 'horn' (because of the branched antennae).

cla·doc·er·an /klə'däsərən/ Zoology ▶ **n.** a minute branchiopod crustacean of the order Cladocera, which includes the water fleas.
▶ **adj.** relating to or denoting cladocerans.

clad·ode /'klad,ōd/ (also **cladophyll** /'kladə,fil/) ▶ **n.** Botany a flattened leaflike stem.
– ORIGIN late 19th cent.: from Greek *kladōdēs* 'with many shoots,' from *klados* 'shoot.'

clad·o·gen·e·sis /,kladə'jenəsəs/ ▶ **n.** Biology the formation of a new group of organisms or higher taxon by evolutionary divergence from an ancestral form. Compare with **ANAGENESIS**.
– DERIVATIVES **clad·o·ge·net·ic** /,kladōjə'netik/ **adj.**

clad·o·gram /'kladə,gram/ ▶ **n.** Biology a branching diagram showing the cladistic relationship between a number of species.

cla·fou·tis /kla'fo͞otē/ ▶ **n.** (pl. **same**) a tart made of fruit, typically cherries, baked in a sweet batter.
– ORIGIN French, from dialect *clafir* 'to stuff.'

Clai·borne /'klābôrn/, Craig (1920–2000), US food editor and critic. He was the food editor for *The New York Times* 1957–70, 1974–88. He wrote *The New York Times Cookbook* (1961), *Classic French Cuisine* (1970), and *Elements of Etiquette* (1992).

claim /klām/ ▶ **v.** [reporting verb] state or assert that something is the case, typically without providing evidence or proof: [with clause] *he claimed that he came from a wealthy, educated family* | [with direct speech] *"I'm entitled to be conceited," he claimed* | [with obj.] *these sunblocks claim protection factors as high as 34.* ■ [with obj.] assert that one has gained or achieved (something): *his supporters claimed victory in the presidential elections.* ■ [with obj.] formally request or demand; say that one owns or has earned (something): *if no one claims the items, they will become government property.* ■ [with obj.] make a demand for (money) under the terms of an insurance policy: *she could have claimed the cost through her insurance.* ■ call for (someone's notice and thought): *a most unwelcome event claimed his attention.* ■ cause the loss of (someone's life).
▶ **n. 1** an assertion of the truth of something, typically one that is disputed or in doubt: [with clause] *he was dogged by the claim that he had CIA links* | *history belies statesmen's claims to be in charge of events.*
2 a demand or request for something considered one's due: *the court had denied their claims to asylum.* ■ an application for compensation under the terms of an insurance policy. ■ a right or title to something: *they have first claim on the assets of the trust.* ■ (also **mining claim**) a piece of land allotted to or taken by someone in order to be mined.
– PHRASES **claim to fame** a reason for being regarded as unusual or noteworthy: *his claim to fame was bringing Garbo to Hollywood.*
– DERIVATIVES **claim·a·ble** **adj.**
– ORIGIN Middle English: from Old French *claime* (noun), *clamer* (verb), from Latin *clamare* 'call out.'

claim·ant /'klāmənt/ ▶ **n.** a person making a claim, esp. in a lawsuit or for a government-sponsored benefit.

claims ad·just·er ▶ **n.** an insurance agent who assesses the amount of compensation that should be paid after a person has made a claim on their insurance policy.

clair·au·di·ence /kle(ə)r'ôdēəns/ ▶ **n.** the supposed faculty of perceiving, as if by hearing, what is inaudible.
– DERIVATIVES **clair·au·di·ent** **adj. & n.**
– ORIGIN mid 19th cent.: from French *clair* 'clear' + **AUDIENCE**, on the pattern of *clairvoyance.*

clair de lune /,kle(ə)r dl'o͞on, -də 'lo͞on/ ▶ **n.** a pale blue-gray or pale green color. ■ a Chinese porcelain glaze of this color.
– ORIGIN late 19th cent.: French, literally 'moonlight.'

clair·voy·ance /kle(ə)r'voiəns/ ▶ **n.** the supposed faculty of perceiving things or events in the future or beyond normal sensory contact: *she stared at the card as if she could contact its writer by clairvoyance.*
– ORIGIN mid 19th cent.: from French, from *clair* 'clear' + *voir* 'to see.'

clair·voy·ant /kle(ə)r'voiənt/ ▶ **n.** a person who claims to have a supernatural ability to perceive events in the future or beyond normal sensory contact.
▶ **adj.** having or exhibiting such an ability: *he didn't tell me about it and I'm not clairvoyant.*
– DERIVATIVES **clair·voy·ant·ly** **adv.**
– ORIGIN late 17th cent. (in the sense 'clear-sighted, perceptive'): from French, from *clair* 'clear' + *voyant* 'seeing' (from *voir* 'to see'). The current sense dates from the mid 19th cent.

clam /klam/ ▶ **n. 1** a marine bivalve mollusk with shells of equal size. ● Subclass Heterodonta: several families and numerous species, including the edible North American **hard-shell clam** (see **QUAHOG**) and **soft-shell clam**. See also **GIANT CLAM**. ■ informal any of a number of edible bivalve mollusks, e.g., a scallop.

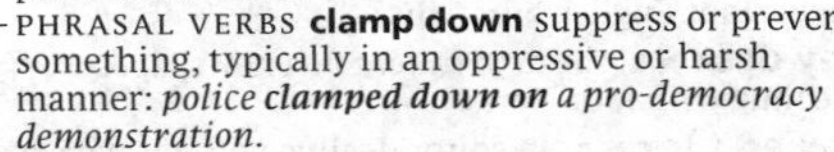
common Washington clam

2 informal a dollar: *all I got for the job was 50 lousy clams.*
3 informal a shy or withdrawn person.
▶ **v.** (**clams, clamming, clammed**) [no obj.] **1** dig for or collect clams: (as noun **clamming**) *it was one of the worst times for clamming.*
2 (**clam up**) informal abruptly stop talking, either for fear of revealing a secret or from shyness.
– ORIGIN early 16th cent.: apparently from earlier *clam* 'a clamp,' from Old English *clam, clamm* 'a bond or bondage,' of Germanic origin; related to Dutch *klemme*, German *Klemme*, also to **CLAMP**.

cla·mant /'klāmənt, 'klam-/ ▶ **adj.** forcing itself urgently on the attention: *the proper use of biotechnology has become a clamant question.*
– DERIVATIVES **cla·mant·ly** **adv.**
– ORIGIN mid 17th cent.: from Latin *clamant-* 'crying out,' from the verb *clamare.*

clam·bake /'klam,bāk/ ▶ **n.** an outdoor social gathering at which clams and other seafood (and often chicken, potatoes, and sweet corn) are baked or steamed, traditionally in a pit, over heated stones and under a bed of seaweed.

clam·ber /'klambər, 'klamər/ ▶ **v.** [no obj.] climb, move, or get in or out of something in an awkward and laborious way, typically using both hands and feet: *I clambered out of the trench.*
▶ **n.** [in sing.] a difficult climb or movement of this sort: *a clamber up the cliff path.*
– ORIGIN Middle English: probably from *clamb*, obsolete past tense of **CLIMB**.

clam·dig·gers /'klam,digərz/ ▶ **plural n.** close-fitting women's casual pants hemmed at mid-calf.

clam·my /'klamē/ ▶ **adj.** (**clammier, clammiest**) unpleasantly damp and sticky or slimy to touch: *his skin felt cold and clammy.* ■ (of air or atmosphere) damp and unpleasant: *the clammy atmosphere of the cave.*
– DERIVATIVES **clam·mi·ly** /'klaməlē/ **adv.**, **clam·mi·ness** **n.**
– ORIGIN late Middle English: from dialect *clam* 'to be sticky or adhere,' of Germanic origin; related to **CLAY**.

clam·or /'klamər/ (Brit. **clamour**) ▶ **n.** [in sing.] a loud and confused noise, esp. that of people shouting vehemently: *the questions rose to a clamor.* ■ a strongly expressed protest or demand, typically from a large number of people: *the growing public clamor for more policemen on the beat.*
▶ **v.** [no obj.] (of a group of people) shout loudly and insistently: *the surging crowds clamored for attention.* ■ make a vehement protest or demand: *scientists are clamoring for a ban on all chlorine substances.*
– ORIGIN late Middle English: via Old French from Latin *clamor*, from *clamare* 'cry out.'

clam·or·ous /'klamərəs/ ▶ **adj.** making a loud and confused noise: *a jostling, clamorous mob.* ■ expressing or characterized by vehement protests or demands: *the clamorous radical wing of the party.*
– DERIVATIVES **clam·or·ous·ly** /-ərəslē/ **adv.**, **clam·or·ous·ness** /-ərəsnəs/ **n.**

clamp /klamp/ ▶ **n.** a brace, band, or clasp used for strengthening or holding things together. ■ an electric circuit that serves to maintain the voltage limits of a signal at prescribed levels.
▶ **v.** [with obj.] fasten (something) in place with a clamp: *the sander is clamped onto the edge of a workbench.* ■ fasten (two things) firmly together: *the two frames are clamped together.* ■ hold (something) tightly against or in another thing: *Maggie had to clamp a hand over her mouth to stop herself from laughing.* ■ maintain the voltage limits of (an electrical signal) at prescribed values.

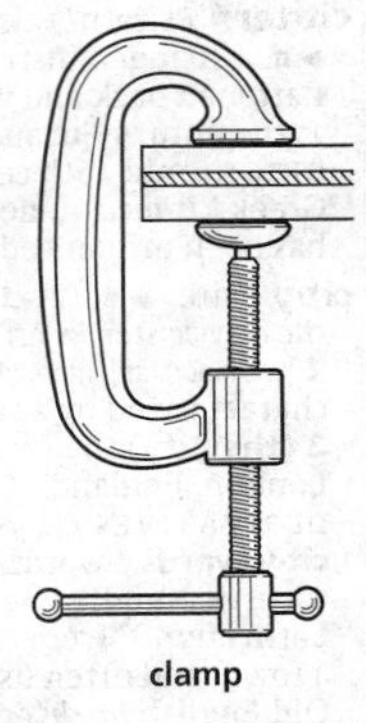
clamp

– PHRASAL VERBS **clamp down** suppress or prevent something, typically in an oppressive or harsh manner: *police clamped down on a pro-democracy demonstration.*
– DERIVATIVES **clamp·er** **n.**
– ORIGIN Middle English: probably of Dutch or Low German origin and related to **CLAM**.

clamp·down /'klamp,doun/ ▶ **n.** informal a severe or concerted attempt to suppress something: *a clampdown on crime.*

clam·shell /'klam,SHel/ ▶ **n.** the shell of a clam, formed of two roughly equal valves with a hinge. ■ a thing with hinged parts that open and shut in a manner resembling the parts of such a shell, such as a kind of mechanical digger, a portable computer, or a box for takeout food: *some clamshells offer full desktop power* | [as modifier] *a clamshell lid.*

clan /klan/ ▶ **n.** a group of close-knit and interrelated families (esp. associated with families in the Scottish Highlands). ■ often informal a family, esp. a large one: *the Kennedy clan gathered for the celebration.* ■ a group of people with a strong common interest: *New York's garrulous clan of artists.*
– ORIGIN late Middle English: from Scottish Gaelic *clann* 'offspring, family,' from Old Irish *cland*, from Latin *planta* 'sprout.'

Clan·cy /'klansē/, Tom (1947–), US novelist. His works, usually techno-military thrillers, include *The Hunt for Red October* (1984), *Patriot Games* (1987), *Rainbow Six* (1998), and *The Teeth of the Tiger* (2003).

clan·des·tine /klan'destən, -,tīn, -,tēn, 'klandəs-/ ▶ **adj.** kept secret or done secretively, esp. because illicit: *she deserved better than these clandestine meetings.*
– DERIVATIVES **clan·des·tine·ly** **adv.**, **clan·des·tin·i·ty** /,klandes'tinitē/ **n.**
– ORIGIN mid 16th cent.: from French *clandestin* or Latin *clandestinus*, from *clam* 'secretly.'

clang /klaNG/ ▶ **n.** a loud, resonant metallic sound or series of sounds: *the steel door slammed shut with a clang.*
▶ **v.** make or cause to make such a sound: [no obj.] *she turned the faucet on and the plumbing clanged* | [with obj.] *the belfry still clangs its bell at 9 p.m.*
– ORIGIN late 16th cent.: imitative, influenced by Latin *clangere* 'resound.'

clang·or /'klaNGər/ (Brit. **clangour**) ▶ **n.** [in sing.] a continuous loud banging or ringing sound: *he went deaf because of the clangor of the steam hammers.*

– DERIVATIVES **clang·or·ous** /ˈklaNGərəs/ **adj.**, **clang·or·ous·ly** /ˈklaNGərəslē/ **adv.**
– ORIGIN late 16th cent.: from Latin *clangor*, from *clangere* 'resound.'

clank /klaNGk/ ▶ **n.** a loud, sharp sound or series of sounds, typically made by pieces of metal meeting or being struck together: *the groan and clank of a winch.*
▶ **v.** make or cause to make such a sound: [no obj.] *I could hear the chain clanking* | [with obj.] *Cassie bounced on the bed, clanking the springs.*
– DERIVATIVES **clank·ing·ly adv.**
– ORIGIN late Middle English (but rare before the mid 17th cent.): imitative.

clan·nish /ˈklanisH/ ▶ **adj.** chiefly derogatory (of a group or their activities) tending to exclude others outside the group.
– DERIVATIVES **clan·nish·ly adv.**, **clan·nish·ness n.**

clans·man /ˈklanzmən/ ▶ **n.** (pl. **clansmen**) a member of a clan, esp. a male member.

clans·wom·an /ˈklanz,wŏŏmən/ ▶ **n.** (pl. **clanswomen**) a female member of a clan.

clap[1] /klap/ ▶ **v.** (**claps, clapping, clapped**) [with obj.] strike the palms of (one's hands) together repeatedly, typically in order to applaud: *Agnes clapped her hands in glee* | [no obj.] *the crowd was clapping and cheering.* ■ show approval of (a person or action) in this way. ■ strike the palms of (one's hands) together once, esp. as a signal: *the designer clapped his hands and the other girls exited the room.* ■ slap (someone) encouragingly on the back or shoulder: *as they parted, he clapped Owen on the back.* ■ place (a hand) briefly against or over one's mouth or forehead as a gesture of dismay or regret: *he swore and clapped a hand to his forehead.* ■ (of a bird) flap (its wings) audibly.
▶ **n. 1** an act of striking together the palms of the hands, either once or repeatedly. ■ a friendly slap or pat on the back or shoulder.
2 an explosive sound, esp. of thunder: *a clap of thunder echoed through the valley.*
– PHRASES **clap eyes on** see **EYE**. **clap someone in jail** (or **irons**) put someone in prison (or in chains).
– PHRASAL VERBS **clap something on** abruptly impose a restrictive or punitive measure on: *most countries clapped on tariffs to protect their farmers.*
– ORIGIN Old English *clappan* 'throb, beat,' of imitative origin. Sense 1 of the noun dates from late Middle English.

clap[2] ▶ **n.** (usu. **the clap**) informal a venereal disease, esp. gonorrhea.
– ORIGIN late 16th cent.: from Old French *clapoir* 'venereal bubo.'

clap·board /ˈklabərd, ˈklap,bôrd/ ▶ **n.** a long, thin, flat piece of wood with edges horizontally overlapping in series, used to cover the outer walls of buildings: [as modifier] *neat clapboard houses.* ■ informal a house with outer walls covered in such pieces of wood.
– DERIVATIVES **clap·board·ed adj.**
– ORIGIN early 16th cent. (denoting a piece of oak used for barrel staves or wainscot): partial translation of Low German *klapholt* 'barrel stave,' from *klappen* 'to crack' + *holt* 'wood.'

clapped-out ▶ **adj.** informal, chiefly Brit. (of a vehicle, machine, or person) worn out from age or heavy use and unable to work or operate: *a clapped-out old van.*

clap·per /ˈklapər/ ▶ **n.** the free-swinging metal piece inside a bell that is made to strike the bell to produce the sound.

clap·per·board /ˈklapər,bôrd/ ▶ **n.** a device of hinged boards that are struck together before filming as a signal to synchronize the starting of picture and sound machinery.

clap·per rail ▶ **n.** a large grayish rail of American coastal marshes. It has a distinctive clattering rattlelike call. ● *Rallus longirostris*, family Rallidae.
– ORIGIN from *clapper*, denoting a device for making a loud clattering sound, with reference to the bird's cry.

clap·trap /ˈklap,trap/ ▶ **n.** absurd or nonsensical talk or ideas: *such sentiments are just pious claptrap.*
– ORIGIN mid 18th cent. (denoting something designed to elicit applause): from **CLAP**[1] + **TRAP**[1].

claque /klak/ ▶ **n.** a group of people hired to applaud (or heckle) a performer or public speaker. ■ a group of sycophantic followers: *the president was surrounded by a claque of scheming bureaucrats.*
– ORIGIN mid 19th cent.: French, from *claquer* 'to clap.' The practice of paying members of an audience for their support originated at the Paris opera.

cla·queur /klaˈkər/ ▶ **n.** a member of a claque.
– ORIGIN mid 19th cent.: French, from *claquer* 'to clap.'

clar·a·bel·la /,klarəˈbelə/ ▶ **n.** an organ stop with the quality of a flute.
– ORIGIN mid 19th cent.: from the feminine forms of Latin *clarus* 'clear' and *bellus* 'pretty.'

Clare /kle(ə)r/ a county in the Republic of Ireland, on the western coast in the province of Munster; county town, Ennis.

clar·ence /ˈklarəns/ (also **Clarence**) ▶ **n.** historical a closed horse-drawn carriage with four wheels, seating four inside and two outside next to the coachman.
– ORIGIN mid 19th cent.: named in honor of the Duke of *Clarence*, later William IV.

Clar·en·don /ˈklarəndən/, Edward Hyde, Earl of (1609–74), English statesman and historian; chief adviser to Charles II and chancellor of Oxford University 1660–67.

Clare of As·si·si, St. /kle(ə)r/ (1194–1253), Italian saint and abbess. With St. Francis, she founded the order of Poor Ladies of San Damiano ("Poor Clares"). Feast day, August 11 (formerly 12).

clar·et /ˈklarit/ ▶ **n.** a red wine from Bordeaux, or wine of a similar character made elsewhere. ■ a deep purplish-red color.
– ORIGIN late Middle English (originally denoting a light red or yellowish wine, as distinct from a red or white): from Old French (*vin*) *claret* and medieval Latin *claratum* (*vinum*) 'clarified (wine),' from Latin *clarus* 'clear.'

clar·i·fi·ca·tion /,klarəfiˈkāsHən/ ▶ **n.** the action of making a statement or situation less confused and more comprehensible: *please advise us if you require further clarification.* ■ a statement resulting from this: *the remaining changes are small clarifications.*
– DERIVATIVES **clar·i·fi·ca·to·ry adj.**

clar·i·fy /ˈklarə,fī/ ▶ **v.** (**clarifies, clarifying, clarified**) [with obj.] **1** make (a statement or situation) less confused and more clearly comprehensible: *the report managed to clarify the government's position.* **2** (often as adj. **clarified**) melt (butter) in order to separate out the impurities.
– DERIVATIVES **clar·i·fi·er n.**
– ORIGIN Middle English (in the senses 'set forth clearly' and 'make pure and clean'): from Old French *clarifier*, from late Latin *clarificare*, from Latin *clarus* 'clear.'

clar·i·net /,klarəˈnet/ ▶ **n.** a woodwind instrument with a single-reed mouthpiece, a cylindrical tube with a flared end, and holes stopped by keys. ■ an organ stop with a tone resembling that of a clarinet.
– DERIVATIVES **clar·i·net·ist** /-ˈnetist/ (Brit. **clarinettist**) **n.**
– ORIGIN mid 18th cent.: from French *clarinette*, diminutive of *clarine*, denoting a kind of bell; related to **CLARION**.

clarinet

clar·i·on /ˈklarēən/ ▶ **n.** chiefly historical a shrill, narrow-tubed war trumpet. ■ an organ stop with a quality resembling that of such a trumpet.
▶ **adj.** loud and clear: *clarion trumpeters.*
– PHRASES **clarion call** a strongly expressed demand or request for action: *he issued a clarion call to young people to join the party.*
– ORIGIN Middle English: from medieval Latin *clario(n-)*, from Latin *clarus* 'clear.'

clar·i·ty /ˈklaritē/ ▶ **n.** the quality of being clear, in particular: ■ the quality of coherence and intelligibility: ***for the sake of clarity**, each of these strategies is dealt with separately.* ■ the quality of being easy to see or hear; sharpness of image or sound: *the clarity of the picture.* ■ the quality of being certain or definite: *it was clarity of purpose that he needed.* ■ the quality of transparency or purity: *the crystal clarity of water.*
– ORIGIN Middle English (in the sense 'glory, divine splendor'): from Latin *claritas*, from *clarus* 'clear.' The current sense dates from the early 17th cent.

Clark[1] /klärk/, George Rogers (1752–1818), American military leader and frontiersman. He defended the Illinois frontier against the British during the American Revolution.

Clark[2], Joe (1939–), Canadian Progressive Conservative statesman; prime minister 1979–80; full name *Charles Joseph Clark*.

Clark[3], Mark Wayne (1896–1984), US army officer. He served as chief of staff of the US Army ground forces in 1942 and as UN commander and commander in chief of the US Far East command 1952–53. He signed the Korean armistice.

Clark[4], Tom Campbell (1899–1977), US Supreme Court associate justice 1949–67. He was US attorney general 1945–49 before being appointed to the Court by President Truman. Considered somewhat conservative, he tended to be more liberal regarding civil rights issues.

Clark[5], Wesley (1944–), US Army general and politician. A commander in the Vietnam War and the first Gulf War, he served as Commander in Chief, US European Command and Supreme Allied Commander Europe 1997–2000 during the Kosovo conflict. In 2004 he ran for the Democratic presidential nomination.

Clark[6], William (1770–1838), US explorer. With Meriwether Lewis, he commanded an expedition 1804–06 across the North American continent.

Clarke[1] /klärk/, Sir Arthur C. (1917–2008), English science fiction writer; full name *Arthur Charles Clarke*. He wrote, with Stanley Kubrick, the screenplay for the movie *2001: A Space Odyssey* (1968).

Clarke[2], John Hessin (1857–1945), US Supreme Court associate justice 1916–22. Appointed to the Court by President Wilson, he was considered a liberal. He later headed the League of Nations Non-Partisan Committee 1922–28.

Clark Fork Riv·er a river that flows for 360 miles (580 km) from western Montana into eastern Idaho into the Columbia River.

clark·i·a /ˈklärkēə/ ▶ **n.** a North American plant with showy white, pink, or purple flowers, cultivated as a border plant in gardens. ● Genus *Clarkia*, family Onagraceae.
– ORIGIN modern Latin, named after W. **CLARK**[6], who discovered it.

Clarks·ville /ˈklärks,vil, -vəl/ an industrial and commercial city in north central Tennessee, on the Cumberland River; pop. 119,735 (est. 2008).

clar·y /ˈkle(ə)rē/ ▶ **n.** an aromatic herbaceous plant of the mint family, some kinds of which are used as culinary and medicinal herbs. ● Genus *Salvia*, family Labiatae: several species, in particular the southern European *S. sclarea*, which is used in perfumery and from which an essential oil (**clary sage**) is obtained.
– ORIGIN late Middle English: from obsolete French *clarie*, from medieval Latin *sclarea*.

clash /klasH/ ▶ **n. 1** a violent confrontation: *there have been minor **clashes with** security forces.* ■ an incompatibility leading to disagreement: *a personality clash.*
2 a mismatch of colors: *a clash of tweeds and a striped shirt.* ■ an inconvenient coincidence of the timing of events or activities: *it is hoped that clashes of dates will be avoided.*
3 a loud jarring sound made by or resembling that made by metal objects being struck together: *a clash of cymbals.*
▶ **v. 1** [no obj.] meet and come into violent conflict: *protesters demanding self-rule **clashed with** police.* ■ have a forceful disagreement: *Clarke has frequently **clashed with** his colleagues.* ■ be incompatible or at odds: *his thriftiness **clashed with** Ross's largesse.*
2 [no obj.] (of colors) appear discordant or ugly when placed close to each other: (as adj. **clashing**) *suits in clashing colors.* ■ inconveniently occur at the same time: *the date of the wedding **clashes with** Sean's graduation.*
3 [with obj.] strike (cymbals) together, producing a loud discordant sound.
– DERIVATIVES **clash·er n.**
– ORIGIN early 16th cent.: imitative.

clasp /klasp/ ▶ **v.** [with obj.] **1** grasp (something) tightly with one's hand: *he clasped her arm.* ■ place (one's arms) around something so as to hold it tightly: *Kate's arms were **clasped around** her knees.* ■ hold (someone) tightly: *he clasped Joanne in his arms.* ■ (**clasp one's hands**) press one's hands together with the fingers interlaced: *he lay on his back with his hands clasped behind his head.*
2 archaic fasten (something) with a small device, typically a metal one: *one modest emerald clasped her robe.*
▶ **n. 1** a device with interlocking parts used for fastening things together: *a handbag with a golden clasp.* ■ a silver bar on a medal ribbon, inscribed with the name of the battle at which the wearer was present.
2 [in sing.] an embrace. ■ a grasp or handshake: *he took her hand in a firm clasp.*
– PHRASES **clasp hands** shake hands with fervor or affection.
– ORIGIN Middle English: of unknown origin.

clasp·ers /ˈklaspərz/ ▶ **plural n.** Zoology a pair of appendages under the abdomen of a male shark or ray, or at the end of the abdomen of a male insect, used to hold the female during copulation.
– ORIGIN mid 19th cent.: from **CLASP**.

clasp knife ▶ **n.** a knife with a blade that folds into the handle.

C

class /klas/ ▶ **n. 1** a set or category of things having some property or attribute in common and differentiated from others by kind, type, or quality: *the accommodations were good for a hotel of this class* | *a new class of heart drug.* ■ Biology a principal taxonomic grouping that ranks above order and below phylum or division, such as Mammalia or Insecta.
2 the system of ordering a society in which people are divided into sets based on perceived social or economic status: *people who are socially disenfranchised by class* | [as modifier] *the class system.* ■ a set in a society ordered in such a way: *the ruling class.* ■ (**the classes**) archaic the rich or educated. ■ informal impressive stylishness in appearance or behavior: *she's got class—she looks like a princess.*
3 a group of students who are taught together. ■ an occasion when students meet with their teacher for instruction; a lesson: *I was late for a class.* ■ a course of instruction: *I took classes in Indian music.* ■ all those graduating from a school or college in a particular year: *the class of 1907.*
▶ **v.** [with obj.] (often **be classed as**) assign or regard as belonging to a particular category: *conduct that is classed as criminal.*
▶ **adj.** [attrib.] informal showing stylish excellence: *he's a class player.*
– PHRASES **class act** a person or thing displaying impressive and stylish excellence. **in a class of** (or **on**) **its** (or **one's**) **own** unequaled, esp. in excellence or performance: *the delicacy of English roses puts them in a class of their own.*
– ORIGIN mid 16th cent. (sense 3 of the noun): from Latin *classis* 'a division of the Roman people, a grade, or a class of pupils.'

class ac·tion ▶ **n.** Law a lawsuit filed or defended by an individual or small group acting on behalf of a large group.

class con·scious·ness ▶ **n.** awareness of one's place in a system of social classes, esp. (in Marxist terms) as it relates to the class struggle.
– DERIVATIVES **class-con·scious adj.**

clas·sic /ˈklasik/ ▶ **adj.** judged over a period of time to be of the highest quality and outstanding of its kind: *a classic novel* | *a classic car.* ■ (of a garment or design) of a simple elegant style not greatly subject to changes in fashion: *this classic navy blazer.* ■ remarkably and instructively typical: *Hamlet is the classic example of a tragedy* | *I had all the classic symptoms of flu.*
▶ **n. 1** a work of art of recognized and established value: *his books have become classics.* ■ a garment of a simple, elegant, and long-lasting style. ■ a thing that is memorable and a very good example of its kind: *he's hoping that tomorrow's game will be a classic.*
2 (usu. **Classics**) a school subject that involves the study of ancient Greek and Latin literature, philosophy, and history. ■ (usu. **the classics**) the works of ancient Greek and Latin writers and philosophers. ■ dated a scholar of ancient Greek and Latin.
3 a major sports tournament or competition, as in golf or tennis: *dozens of celebrity golfers attended the Bob Hope Desert Classic.*
– ORIGIN early 17th cent.: from French *classique* or Latin *classicus* 'belonging to a class or division,' later 'of the highest class,' from *classis* (see CLASS).

USAGE Note that **classic** means 'typical, excellent as an example, timeless,' as in *John Ford directed many classic Westerns*, and **classical** means 'relating to Greek or Roman antiquity,' as in *the museum was built in the classical style.* Great art is considered **classic**, not **classical**, unless it is created in the forms of antiquity. **Classical music** is one exception to this rule, being formal music adhering to certain stylistic principles of the late 18th century. A **classical education** exposes a student to *classical* literature, history, and languages (especially Latin and Greek), but the study of Greek and Latin languages and their literatures is also referred to as **the classics**.

clas·si·cal /ˈklasikəl/ ▶ **adj. 1** of or relating to ancient Greek or Latin literature, art, or culture: *classical mythology.* ■ (of art or architecture) influenced by ancient Greek or Roman forms or principles.
2 (typically of a form of art) regarded as representing an exemplary standard; traditional and long-established in form or style: *a classical ballet.*
3 of or relating to the first significant period of an area of study: *classical mechanics.* ■ Physics relating to or based upon concepts and theories that preceded the theories of relativity and quantum mechanics; Newtonian: *classical physics.*
– DERIVATIVES **clas·si·cal·ism** /-ˌlizəm/ **n.**, **clas·si·cal·i·ty** /ˌklasəˈkalətē/ **n.**, **clas·si·cal·ly** /-ik(ə)lē/ **adv.**
– ORIGIN late 16th cent. (in the sense 'outstanding for its kind'): from Latin *classicus* 'belonging to a class' (see CLASSIC) + -AL.

USAGE See usage at CLASSIC.

clas·si·cal con·di·tion·ing ▶ **n.** Psychology a learning process that occurs when two stimuli are repeatedly paired; a response that is at first elicited by the second stimulus is eventually elicited by the first stimulus alone.

clas·si·cal mu·sic ▶ **n.** serious or conventional music following long-established principles rather than a folk, jazz, or popular tradition. ■ (more specifically) music written in the European tradition during a period lasting approximately from 1750 to 1830, when forms such as the symphony, concerto, and sonata were standardized. Often contrasted with BAROQUE and ROMANTIC.

clas·si·cism /ˈklasəˌsizəm/ ▶ **n.** the following of ancient Greek or Roman principles and style in art and literature, generally associated with harmony, restraint, and adherence to recognized standards of form and craftsmanship, esp. from the Renaissance to the 18th century. Often contrasted with ROMANTICISM. ■ the following of traditional and long-established theories or styles.

clas·si·cist /ˈklasəsist/ ▶ **n. 1** a person who studies Classics (ancient Greek and Latin).
2 a follower of classicism in the arts.

clas·si·cize /ˈklasəˌsīz/ ▶ **v.** [no obj.] (usu. as adj. **classicizing**) imitate a classical style: *the classicizing strains in Guercino's art.*

Clas·si·co /ˈklasikō/ ▶ **adj.** [postpositive] used in the classification of Italian wines to designate a wine produced in the region from which the type takes its name: *Chianti Classico.*
– ORIGIN Italian.

clas·si·fi·ca·tion /ˌklasəfəˈkāsHən/ ▶ **n.** the action or process of classifying something according to shared qualities or characteristics: *the classification of disease according to symptoms.* ■ another term for TAXONOMY. ■ a category into which something is put.

clas·si·fied /ˈklasəˌfīd/ ▶ **adj.** arranged in classes or categories: *a classified catalog of books.* ■ [attrib.] (of newspaper or magazine advertisements or the pages on which these appear) organized in categories according to what is being advertised. ■ (of information or documents) designated as officially secret and to which only authorized people may have access: *classified information on nuclear experiments.*
▶ **n.** (**classifieds**) small advertisements placed in a newspaper and organized in categories.

clas·si·fi·er /ˈklasəˌfīər/ ▶ **n.** a person or thing that classifies something. ■ Linguistics an affix or word that indicates the semantic class to which a noun belongs, typically used in numerals or other expressions of counting, esp. in Chinese and Japanese, e.g. *head* in *two head of cattle.*

clas·si·fy /ˈklasəˌfī/ ▶ **v.** (**classifies, classifying, classified**) [with obj.] arrange (a group of people or things) in classes or categories according to shared qualities or characteristics: *mountain peaks are classified according to their shape.* ■ assign (someone or something) to a particular class or category: *elements are usually classified as metals or nonmetals.* ■ designate (documents or information) as officially secret or to which only authorized people may have access: *government officials classified 6.3 million documents in 1992.*
– DERIVATIVES **clas·si·fi·a·ble** /ˌklasəˈfīəbəl/ **adj.**, **clas·si·fi·ca·to·ry** /-fikəˌtôrē/ **adj.**
– ORIGIN late 18th cent.: back-formation from CLASSIFICATION, from French, from *classe* 'class,' from Latin *classis* 'division.'

clas·si·fy·ing /ˈklasəˌfī-iNG/ ▶ **adj.** Grammar denoting an adjective that describes the class that a head noun belongs to and characterized by not having a comparative or superlative (for example *American, mortal*). Contrasted with GRADABLE, QUALITATIVE.

class in·ter·val ▶ **n.** Statistics the size of each class into which a range of a variable is divided, as represented by the divisions of a histogram or bar chart.

class·ism /ˈklasˌizəm/ ▶ **n.** prejudice against or in favor of people belonging to a particular social class.
– DERIVATIVES **class·ist adj. & n.**

class·less /ˈklasləs/ ▶ **adj.** (of a society) not divided into social classes. ■ not showing obvious signs of belonging to a particular social class: *his voice was classless.*
– DERIVATIVES **class·less·ness n.**

class·mate /ˈklasˌmāt/ ▶ **n.** a fellow member of a class at school or college.

class·room /ˈklasˌro͞om, -ˌro͝om/ ▶ **n.** a room, typically in a school, in which a class of students is taught.

class strug·gle ▶ **n.** (in Marxist ideology) the conflict of interests between the workers and the ruling class in a capitalist society, regarded as inevitably violent.

class war (also **class warfare**) ▶ **n.** another term for CLASS STRUGGLE.

class·work /ˈklasˌwərk/ ▶ **n.** schoolwork that is done in class.

class·y /ˈklasē/ ▶ **adj.** (**classier, classiest**) informal stylish and sophisticated: *the hotel is classy but relaxed.*
– DERIVATIVES **class·i·ly** /ˈklasəlē/ **adv.**, **class·i·ness n.**

clast /klast/ ▶ **n.** Geology a constituent fragment of a clastic rock.
– ORIGIN mid 20th cent.: back-formation from CLASTIC.

clas·tic /ˈklastik/ ▶ **adj.** Geology denoting rocks composed of broken pieces of older rocks.
– ORIGIN late 19th cent.: from French *clastique*, from Greek *klastos* 'broken in pieces.'

clath·rate /ˈklaTHˌrāt/ ▶ **n.** Chemistry a compound in which molecules of one component are physically trapped within the crystal structure of another.
– ORIGIN 1940s: from Latin *clathratus*, from *clathri* 'lattice bars,' from Greek *klēthra.*

clat·ter /ˈklatər/ ▶ **n.** [in sing.] a continuous rattling sound as of hard objects falling or striking each other: *the horse spun around with a clatter of hooves* | *she dropped her knife and fork with a clatter.*
▶ **v.** make or cause to make a continuous rattling sound: [no obj.] *her coffee cup clattered in the saucer* | [with obj.] *she clattered cups and saucers onto a tray.* ■ [no obj.] fall or move with such a sound: *the knife clattered to the floor.*
– ORIGIN Old English (as a verb), of imitative origin.

Claude Lor·rain /ˌklôd ləˈrān, ˌklōd ləˈren/ (also **Lorraine**) (1600–82), French painter; born *Claude Gellée.* He is noted for the use of light in his landscapes. His works include *Ascanius and the Stag* (1682).

clau·di·ca·tion /ˌklôdəˈkāsHən/ ▶ **n.** Medicine limping. ■ (also **intermittent claudication**) a condition in which cramping pain in the leg is induced by exercise, typically caused by obstruction of the arteries.
– ORIGIN late Middle English: from Latin *claudicatio(n-)*, from the verb *claudicare* 'to limp,' from *claudus* 'lame.'

Clau·di·us /ˈklôdēəs/ (10 BC–AD 54), Roman emperor 41–54; full name *Tiberius Claudius Drusus Nero Germanicus.* He restored order after Caligula's decadence and expanded the empire, in particular by invading Britain in AD 43.

clause /klôz/ ▶ **n. 1** a unit of grammatical organization next below the sentence in rank and in traditional grammar said to consist of a subject and predicate. See also MAIN CLAUSE, SUBORDINATE CLAUSE.
2 a particular and separate article, stipulation, or proviso in a treaty, bill, or contract.
– DERIVATIVES **claus·al** /ˈklôzəl/ **adj.**
– ORIGIN Middle English: via Old French *clause*, based on Latin *claus-* 'shut, closed,' from the verb *claudere.*

Clau·se·witz /ˈklouzəˌvits/, Karl von (1780–1831), Prussian general and military theorist. He wrote *On War* (1833), which had a marked influence on strategic studies in the 19th and 20th centuries.

Clau·si·us /ˈklouzēəs/, Rudolf (1822–88), German physicist. He was one of the founders of modern thermodynamics.

claus·tral /ˈklôstrəl/ ▶ **adj.** of or relating to a cloister or religious house: *claustral buildings.* ■ enveloping; confining: *this claustral heat.*
– ORIGIN late Middle English: from late Latin *claustralis*, from Latin *claustrum* 'lock, enclosed place' (see CLOISTER).

claus·tra·tion /klôˈstrāsHən/ ▶ **n.** confinement as if in a cloister.
– ORIGIN mid 19th cent.: from Latin *claustrum* 'lock, bolt' + -ATION.

claus·tro·pho·bi·a /ˌklôstrəˈfōbēə/ ▶ **n.** extreme or irrational fear of confined places.
– DERIVATIVES **claus·tro·phobe** /ˈklôstrəˌfōb/ **n.**
– ORIGIN late 19th cent.: modern Latin, from Latin *claustrum* 'lock, bolt' + -PHOBIA.

claus·tro·pho·bic /ˌklôstrəˈfōbik/ ▶ **adj.** (of a person) suffering from claustrophobia: *crowds made him feel claustrophobic.* ■ (of a place or situation) inducing claustrophobia: *the claustrophobic interior of the cruiser.*
▶ **n.** a person who suffers from claustrophobia.
– DERIVATIVES **claus·tro·pho·bi·cal·ly** /-ik(ə)lē/ **adv.**

claus·trum /'klôstrəm, 'kloustrəm/ ▶ **n.** (pl. **claustra** /-trə/) Anatomy a thin layer of gray matter in each cerebral hemisphere between the lentiform nucleus and the insula.
–ORIGIN mid 19th cent.: Latin.

cla·vate /'klā,vāt/ ▶ **adj.** Botany & Zoology club-shaped; thicker at the apex than at the base.
–ORIGIN mid 17th cent.: from modern Latin *clavatus*, from Latin *clava* 'club.'

clave[1] /klāv/ ▶ **n.** (usu. **claves**) Music one of a pair of hardwood sticks used to make a hollow sound when struck together.
–ORIGIN 1920s: from Latin American Spanish, from Spanish *clave* 'keystone,' from Latin *clavis* 'key.'

clave[2] archaic past of CLEAVE[2].

clav·i·chord /'klavə,kôrd/ ▶ **n.** a small, rectangular keyboard instrument producing a soft sound by means of metal blades attached to the ends of key levers that gently press the strings, popular from the early 15th to early 19th centuries.
–ORIGIN late Middle English: from medieval Latin *clavichordium*, from Latin *clavis* 'key' + *chorda* 'string.'

clav·i·cle /'klavikəl/ ▶ **n.** Anatomy technical term for COLLARBONE.
–DERIVATIVES **cla·vic·u·lar** /klə'vikyələr, klə-/ **adj.**
–ORIGIN early 17th cent.: from Latin *clavicula* 'small key,' diminutive of *clavis* (because of its shape).

cla·vier /klə'vi(ə)r, 'klāvēər, 'klavēər/ ▶ **n.** a keyboard instrument, esp. one with strings, such as the harpsichord.
–ORIGIN early 18th cent.: from German *Klavier*, from French *clavier*, from medieval Latin *claviarius* 'key bearer,' from Latin *clavis* 'key.'

clav·i·form /'klavə,fôrm/ ▶ **adj.** technical another term for CLAVATE.
–ORIGIN early 19th cent.: from Latin *clava* 'club' + -IFORM.

claw /klô/ ▶ **n.** a curved pointed horny nail on each digit of the foot in birds, lizards, and some mammals. ■ either of a pair of small hooked appendages on an insect's leg. ■ the pincer of a crab, scorpion, or other arthropod. ■ a mechanical device resembling a claw, used for gripping or lifting.
▶ **v. 1** [no obj.] (of an animal or person) scratch or tear something with the claws or the fingernails: *the kitten was clawing at Lowell's trouser leg* | figurative *bitter jealousy clawed at her* | [with obj.] *her hands clawed his shoulders*. ■ clutch at something with the hands: *his fingers clawed at the air*. ■ (**claw one's way**) make one's way with difficulty by hauling oneself forward with one's hands: *he clawed his way over a pile of bricks*. ■ [with obj.] (**claw something away**) try desperately to move or remove something with the hands: *rescuers clawed away rubble with their bare hands*.
2 [no obj.] (of a sailing ship) beat to windward: *the ability to claw off a lee shore*.
–PHRASES **get one's claws into** informal enter into a possessive relationship with.
–PHRASAL VERBS **claw something back** (of a government) recover money disbursed in the form of an allowance or benefit, typically by taxation.
–DERIVATIVES **clawed adj.** [often in combination] *a short-clawed otter*, **claw·less adj.**
–ORIGIN Old English *clawu* (noun), *clawian* (verb); related to Dutch *klauw* and German *Klaue*.

claw·back /'klô,bak/ ▶ **n.** the recovery of money already disbursed: *funds that are not subject to any clawback by the government*.

clawed frog ▶ **n.** a frog with a flattened body and claws on the hind toes. ● *Xenopus* and other genera, family Pipidae: several species. See also XENOPUS.

claw foot ▶ **n.** (pl. **claw feet**) **1** a foot on a piece of furniture or a standing fixture, shaped to resemble a claw.
2 Medicine an excessively arched foot with an unnaturally high instep. ■ a disease causing such a distortion of the foot.
–DERIVATIVES **claw-foot·ed adj.**

claw foot 1

claw ham·mer ▶ **n. 1** a hammer with one side of the head split and curved, used for extracting nails.
2 (**clawhammer**) a style of banjo playing in which the thumb and fingers strum or pluck the strings in a downward motion.

Clay[1] /klā/, Cassius, see ALI[2].

Clay[2], Henry (1777–1852), US politician, statesman, and orator; nicknamed **the Great Pacificator** and **the Great Compromiser**. He was a leader of the "War Hawks" 1811 and championed the Missouri Compromise 1820. He served as secretary of state 1825–29 and as a senator from Kentucky 1831–42.

clay /klā/ ▶ **n.** a stiff, sticky fine-grained earth, typically yellow, red, or bluish-gray in color and often forming an impermeable layer in the soil. It can be molded when wet, and is dried and baked to make bricks, pottery, and ceramics. ■ technical sediment with particles smaller than silt, typically less than 0.00016 inch (0.004 mm). ■ a hardened clay surface for a tennis court. ■ literary the substance of the human body: *this lifeless clay*.
–PHRASES **feet of clay** see FOOT.
–DERIVATIVES **clay·ey** /'klā-ē/ **adj.**, **clay·ish adj.**, **clay·like** /-,līk/ **adj.**
–ORIGIN Old English *clǣg*; related to Dutch *klei*, also to CLEAVE[2] and CLIMB.

clay·ma·tion /klā'māsHən/ (also trademark **Claymation**) ▶ **n.** a method of animation in which clay figures are filmed using stop-motion photography.
–ORIGIN 1980s: from CLAY + ANIMATION.

clay min·er·al ▶ **n.** any of a group of minerals that occur as minute sheetlike or fibrous crystals in clay. They are all hydrated aluminosilicates having layered crystal structures.

clay·more /'klā,môr/ ▶ **n. 1** historical a two-edged broadsword used by Scottish Highlanders. ■ a single-edged broadsword having a hilt with a basketwork design, introduced in Scotland in the 16th century.
2 a type of antipersonnel mine.
–ORIGIN early 18th cent.: from Scottish Gaelic *claidheamh* 'sword' + *mór* 'great.'

clay pig·eon ▶ **n.** a saucer-shaped piece of baked clay or other material thrown up in the air from a trap as a target for shooting.

-cle ▶ **suffix** forming nouns such as *article*, *particle*, which were originally diminutives.
–ORIGIN via French from Latin *-culus*, *-cula*, *-culum*.

clean /klēn/ ▶ **adj. 1** free from dirt, marks, or stains: *the room was spotlessly clean* | *keep the wound clean*. ■ having been washed since last worn or used: *a clean blouse*. ■ [attrib.] (of paper) not yet marked by writing or drawing: *he copied the directions onto a clean sheet of paper*. ■ (of a person) attentive to personal hygiene: *by nature he was clean and neat*. ■ free from pollutants or unpleasant substances: *we will create a cleaner, safer environment*. ■ free from or producing relatively little radioactive contamination.
2 morally uncontaminated; pure; innocent: *clean living*. ■ not sexually offensive or obscene: *it's all good clean fun* | *even when clean, his verses are very funny*. ■ showing or having no record of offenses or crimes: *a clean driving license is essential for the job*. ■ played or done according to the rules: *it was a good clean fight*. ■ [predic.] informal not possessing or containing anything illegal, esp. drugs or stolen goods: *I searched him and his luggage, and he was clean*. ■ [predic.] informal (of a person) not taking or having taken drugs or alcohol. ■ free from ceremonial defilement, according to Mosaic Law and similar religious codes.
3 free from irregularities; having a smooth edge or surface: *a clean fracture of the leg*. ■ having a simple, well-defined, and pleasing shape: *the clean lines and pared-down planes of modernism*. ■ (of an action) smoothly and skillfully done: *I still hadn't made a clean takeoff*. ■ (of a taste, sound, or smell) giving a clear and distinctive impression to the senses; sharp and fresh: *clean, fresh, natural flavors*. ■ (of timber) free from knots.
▶ **adv. 1** so as to be free from dirt, marks, or unwanted matter: *the room had been washed clean*.
2 informal used to emphasize the completeness of a reported action, condition, or experience: *he was knocked clean off his feet* | *I clean forgot her birthday*.
▶ **v.** [with obj.] make (something or someone) free of dirt, marks, or mess, esp. by washing, wiping, or brushing: *clean your teeth properly after meals* | *chair covers should be easy to clean* | *we cleaned Uncle Jim up and made him presentable* | [no obj.] *he always expected other people to* **clean up after** *him* | (as noun **cleaning**) *Anne will help with the cleaning*. ■ remove the innards of (fish or poultry) prior to cooking.
–PHRASES **(as) clean as a whistle** see WHISTLE. **clean bill of health** see BILL OF HEALTH. **clean someone's clock** informal give someone a beating: *he went wild and cleaned everybody's clock down there in the dugout*. ■ defeat or surpass someone decisively. **clean house** do housework. ■ eliminate corruption or inefficiency: *unless our organization cleans house, it will be difficult to raise funds*. **clean one's plate** eat up all the food put on one's plate. **a clean sweep 1** the removal of all unwanted people or things in order to start afresh: *the new leaders wanted to* **make a clean sweep of** *the discredited old order*. **2** the winning of all of a group of similar or related competitions, events, or matches: *he was in reach of the nomination after a clean sweep of Tuesday's primaries*. **clean up one's act** informal begin to behave in a better way, esp. by giving up alcohol, drugs, or illegal activities: *the casino industry is bent on cleaning up its act*. **come clean** informal be completely honest; keep nothing hidden: *the company has refused to come clean about its pollution record*. **have clean hands** be uninvolved and blameless with regard to an immoral act: *no one involved in the conflict has clean hands*. **keep one's hands clean** not involve oneself in an immoral act. **keep one's nose clean** see NOSE. **make a clean breast of something** (or **make a clean breast of it**) confess fully one's mistakes or wrongdoings. **make a clean job of something** informal do something thoroughly. **wipe the slate clean** see WIPE.
–PHRASAL VERBS **clean someone out** informal use up or take all someone's money: *they were cleaned out by the Englishman at the baccarat table*. **clean up** ■ make things or an area clean or neat: *he was in the kitchen, cleaning up*. ■ informal make a substantial gain or profit. ■ win all the prizes available in a sporting competition or series of events: *the Germans cleaned up at Wimbledon*. **clean something up** restore order or morality to: *the police chief was given the job of cleaning up a notorious district*.
–DERIVATIVES **clean·a·ble adj.**, **clean·ish adj.**, **clean·ness n.**
–ORIGIN Old English *clǣne*; related to Dutch and German *klein* 'small.'

C

clean and jerk ▶ **n.** [in sing.] a two-movement weightlifting exercise in which a weight is raised above the head following an initial lift to shoulder level.

clean-cut ▶ **adj.** sharply outlined: *the normally clean-cut edge between sea and land has become blurred*. ■ giving the appearance of neatness and respectability: *the ad featured two clean-cut teenagers*.

clean·er /'klēnər/ ▶ **n.** a person or thing that cleans something, in particular: ■ a person employed to clean the interior of a building. ■ (**the cleaners**) a place of business where clothes and fabrics are dry-cleaned: *my suit's at the cleaners*. ■ a device for cleaning, such as a vacuum cleaner. ■ a chemical substance used for cleaning: *an oven cleaner*.
–PHRASES **take someone to the cleaners** informal take all someone's money or possessions in a dishonest or unfair way. ■ inflict a crushing defeat on someone: *the Blue Jays went home and were taken to the cleaners by the Red Sox*.

clean·er fish ▶ **n.** a small fish, esp. a striped wrasse, that is permitted to remove parasites from the skin, gills, and mouth of larger fishes, to their mutual benefit. ● Genus *Labroides*, family Labridae: several species, in particular *L. dimidiatus*.

clean-limbed ▶ **adj.** (esp. of the human figure) slim; well formed and shapely.

clean·ly ▶ **adv.** /'klēnlē/ **1** in a way that produces no dirt, noxious gases, or other pollutants: *the engine burns very cleanly*.
2 without difficulty or impediment; smoothly and efficiently: *he vaulted cleanly through the open window*. [Old English *clǣnlīce* (see CLEAN, -LY[2]).]
▶ **adj.** /'klenlē/ (**cleanlier**, **cleanliest**) archaic (of a person or animal) habitually clean and careful to avoid dirt. [Old English *clǣnlīc* (see CLEAN, -LY[1]).]
–DERIVATIVES **clean·li·ness** /'klenlēnis/ **n.**

clean room ▶ **n.** an environment free from dust and other contaminants, used chiefly for the manufacture of electronic components.

cleanse /klenz/ ▶ **v.** [with obj.] make (something, esp. the skin) thoroughly clean: *this preparation will cleanse and tighten the skin* | (as adj. **cleansing**) *a cleansing cream*. ■ rid (a person, place, or thing) of something seen as unpleasant, unwanted, or defiling: *the mission to* **cleanse** *the nation* **of** *subversives*. ■ free (someone) from sin or guilt. ■ archaic (in biblical translations) cure (a leper).
–ORIGIN Old English *clǣnsian*, from *clǣne* (see CLEAN).

cleans·er /'klenzər/ ▶ **n.** a substance that cleanses something, in particular a cosmetic product for cleansing the skin.

clean-shav·en ▶ **adj.** (of a man) without a beard or mustache.

clean slate ▶ **n.** an absence of existing restraints or commitments: *no government starts with a clean slate*.

clean·up /'klēn,əp/ ▶ **n. 1** an act of making a place clean or tidy: *an environmental cleanup*. ■ an act of removing or putting an end to disorder, immorality, or crime.

2 [usu. as modifier] Baseball the fourth position in a team's batting order, typically reserved for a power hitter likely to clear the bases by enabling any runners to score: *L.A.'s cleanup hitter smacked a fastball over the left-field fence* | [as adv.] *he garnered a certain amount of attention while playing right field and batting cleanup.*

C

clear /kli(ə)r/ ▶ **adj. 1** easy to perceive, understand, or interpret: *the voice on the telephone was clear and strong* | *clear and precise directions* | *her handwriting was clear* | *am I making myself clear?* ■ leaving no doubt; obvious or unambiguous: *it was clear that they were in a trap* | *a clear case of poisoning.* ■ having or feeling no doubt or confusion: *every student must be clear about what is expected.*
2 (of a substance) transparent: *the clear glass of the French windows* | *a stream of clear water.* ■ free of cloud, mist, or rain: *the day was fine and clear.* ■ (of a person's skin) free from blemishes. ■ (of a person's eyes) unclouded; shining: *I looked into her clear gray eyes.* ■ (of a color) pure and intense: *clear blue delphiniums.* ■ archaic (of a fire) burning with little smoke: *a bright, clear flame.*
3 free of any obstructions or unwanted objects: *with a clear road ahead, he shifted into high gear* | *I had a clear view in both directions* | *his desktop was almost clear.* ■ (of a period of time) free of any appointments or commitments: *the following Saturday Mattie had a clear day.* ■ [predic.] (of a person) free of something undesirable or unpleasant: *after 18 months of treatment he was clear of TB.* ■ (of a person's mind) free of something that impairs logical thought: *in the morning, with a clear head, she would tackle all her problems.* ■ (of a person's conscience) free of guilt.
4 [predic.] (**clear of**) not touching; away from: *the truck was wedged in the ditch, one wheel clear of the ground.*
5 [attrib.] (of a sum of money) net: *a clear profit of $1,100.*
6 Phonetics denoting a palatalized form of *l* (as in *salad* or *willing*) in some southern US accents or as in *leaf* in Irish accents. Often contrasted with **DARK**.
▶ **adv. 1** so as to be out of the way of or away from: *he leapt clear of the car* | *stand clear, I'll start the plane up.* ■ so as not to be obstructed or cluttered: *the floor had been swept clear of litter.*
2 completely: *he had time to get clear away.* ■ (**clear to**) all the way to: *you could see clear to the bottom of the lagoon.*
▶ **v. 1** [no obj.] become clear, in particular: ■ (of the sky or weather) become free of cloud or rain: *we'll go out if the weather clears.* ■ (of a liquid) become transparent: *a wine that refuses to clear.* ■ become free of obstructions: *the boy's lungs cleared and he began to breathe more easily.* ■ gradually go away or disappear: *the fever clears in two to four weeks* | *the mist had cleared away.* ■ (of a person's face or expression) assume a happier aspect following previous confusion or distress: *for a moment, Sam was confused; then his expression cleared.* ■ (of a person's mind) regain the capacity for logical thought; become free of confusion: *his mind cleared and he began to reflect.*
2 [with obj.] make (something) clear, in particular: ■ remove an obstruction or unwanted item or items from: *the driveway had been cleared of snow* | *Carolyn cleared the table.* ■ free (land) for cultivation or building by removing vegetation or existing structures. ■ free (one's mind) of unpleasantness or confusion: *even the final clue failed to clear his mind.* ■ cause people to leave (a building or place): *the police shouted a warning and cleared the streets.*
3 [with obj.] remove (an obstruction or unwanted item) from somewhere: *snow was cleared from the storm drains* | *park staff cleared away dead trees.* ■ chiefly Soccer send (the ball) away from the area near one's goal. ■ discharge (a debt).
4 [with obj.] get past or over (something) safely or without touching it: *the plane rose high enough to clear the trees.* ■ jump (a specified height) in a competition: *she cleared 1.50 meters in the high jump.*
5 [with obj.] show or declare (someone) officially to be innocent: *the commission had cleared the weightlifter of cheating.*
6 [with obj.] give official approval or authorization to: *I cleared him to return to his squadron.* ■ get official approval for (something): *the press releases had to be cleared with the White House.* ■ (of a person or goods) satisfy the necessary requirements to pass through (customs): *I can help her to clear customs quickly.* ■ pass (a check) through a clearinghouse so that the money goes into the payee's account: *the check could not be cleared until Monday.* ■ [no obj.] (of a check) pass through a clearinghouse in such a way.
7 [with obj.] earn or gain (an amount of money) as a net profit: *I would hope to clear $50,000 profit.*
– PHRASES **as clear as mud** see **MUD**. **clear the air** make the air less sultry. ■ defuse or clarify an angry, tense, or confused situation by frank discussion: *it's time a few things were said to clear the air.* **(as) clear as a bell** see **BELL**[1]. **(as) clear as day** very easy to see or understand. **clear the decks** prepare for a particular event or goal by dealing with anything beforehand that might hinder progress. **clear the name of** show to be innocent: *the spokesman released a statement attempting to clear his client's name.* **clear one's throat** cough slightly so as to speak more clearly, attract attention, or to express hesitancy before saying something awkward. **clear the way** remove an obstacle or hindrance to allow progress: *the ruling could be enough to clear the way for impeachment proceedings.* ■ [in imperative] stand aside: *Stand back, there! Clear the way!* **in clear** not encrypted; not in code: *the Russian staff practice of sending radio messages and orders in clear.* **in the clear** no longer in danger or suspected of something: *the latest information put her in the clear.* **out of a** (or **the**) **clear blue sky** as a complete surprise: *his moods blew up suddenly out of a clear blue sky.*
– PHRASAL VERBS **clear off** [usu. in imperative] informal go away: *"Clear off!" he yelled.* **clear out** informal leave quickly. **clear something out** remove the contents from something so as to tidy it or free it for alternative use: *they told her to clear out her desk by the next day.* **clear up 1** (of an illness or other medical condition) become cured: *all my health problems cleared up.* **2** (of the weather) become brighter. ■ (of rain) stop. **clear something up 1** (also **clear up**) tidy something up by removing trash or other unwanted items: *he decided to clear up his garage* | *I keep meaning to come down here and clear up.* ■ remove trash or other unwanted items to leave something tidy: *he asked the boys to clear up their mess.* **2** solve or explain something: *he wanted to clear up some misconceptions.* **3** cure an illness or other medical condition: *folk customs prescribed sage tea to clear up measles.*
– DERIVATIVES **clear·a·ble** adj., **clear·ness** n.
– ORIGIN Middle English: from Old French *cler*, from Latin *clarus*.

clear·ance /ˈkli(ə)rəns/ ▶ **n. 1** the action or process of removing or getting rid of something or of something's dispersing: *cleaning of the machine should include clearance of blockages* | *there will be sunny intervals after clearance of any early mist.* ■ [often with modifier] the removal of buildings, people, or trees from land so as to free it for alternative uses: *slum clearance accelerated during the 1960s* | *forest clearances.* ■ (in soccer and other games) a kick or hit that sends the ball out of a defensive zone.
2 official authorization for something to proceed or take place: *getting diplomatic clearance to fly into or over a country is not always easy.* ■ (also **security clearance**) official permission for someone to have access to classified information: *these people don't have clearance.* ■ permission for an aircraft to take off or land at an airport: *he took off without air traffic clearance.* ■ the clearing of a person or ship by customs. ■ a certificate showing that such clearance has been granted. ■ the process of clearing checks through a clearinghouse.
3 clear space allowed for a thing to move past or under another: *always give cyclists plenty of clearance.*

clear·ance sale ▶ **n.** a sale of goods at reduced prices to get rid of superfluous stock or because the store is closing down.

clear-cut ▶ **adj. 1** sharply defined; easy to perceive or understand: *we now had a clear-cut objective.*
2 (of an area) from which every tree has been cut down and removed.
▶ **v.** [with obj.] cut down and remove every tree from (an area): *colonizers who clear-cut large jungle tracts.*

clear-eyed ▶ **adj.** having unclouded, bright eyes: *a handsome, clear-eyed young man.* ■ having a shrewd understanding and no illusions: *clear-eyed about human nature.*

clear·head·ed /ˈkli(ə)r,hedid/ ▶ **adj.** alert and thinking logically and coherently.
– DERIVATIVES **clear·head·ed·ly** adv., **clear·head·ed·ness** n.

clear·ing /ˈkli(ə)riNG/ ▶ **n.** an open space in a forest, esp. one cleared for cultivation.

clear·ing·house /ˈkli(ə)riNG,hous/ (also **clearing house**) (abbr.: **c.h.** or **C.H.**) ▶ **n.** a bankers' establishment where checks and bills from member banks are exchanged, so that only the balances need be paid in cash. ■ an agency or organization that collects and distributes something, esp. information.

clear·ly /ˈkli(ə)rlē/ ▶ **adv.** in such a way as to allow easy and accurate perception or interpretation: *the ability to write clearly* | [as submodifier] *on white paper, the seeds are clearly visible.* ■ [sentence adverb] without doubt; obviously: *clearly, there have been disasters and reversals here.*

clear-sight·ed ▶ **adj.** thinking clearly and sensibly; perspicacious and discerning: *a clear-sighted sense of what is possible and appropriate.*
– DERIVATIVES **clear-sight·ed·ly** adv., **clear-sight·ed·ness** n.

clear·sto·ry ▶ **n.** (pl. **clearstories**) variant spelling of **CLERESTORY**.

Clear·wa·ter /ˈkli(ə)r,wôtər, -,wätər/ a city in west central Florida, on the Gulf of Mexico, west of Tampa; pop. 105,774 (est. 2008).

Clear·wa·ter Moun·tains a range in northern Idaho, part of the Rocky Mountains.

clear·wing /ˈkli(ə)r,wiNG/ (also **clearwing moth**) ▶ **n.** a day-flying moth that has narrow mainly transparent wings and mimics a wasp or bee in appearance. ● Family Sesiidae: several genera and many species, including the hornet moth.

cleat /klēt/ ▶ **n.** a T-shaped piece of metal or wood, esp. on a boat or ship, to which ropes are attached. ■ one of a number of projecting pieces of metal, rubber, or other material on the sole of a shoe, designed to prevent the wearer from losing their footing. ■ (**cleats**) athletic shoes with a cleated sole, typically used when playing football. ■ a projection on a spar or other part of a ship, to prevent slipping. ■ a small wedge, esp. one on a plow or scythe.
– DERIVATIVES **cleat·ed** adj.
– ORIGIN Middle English (in the sense 'wedge'); related to Dutch *kloot* 'ball, sphere' and German *Kloss* 'clod, dumpling,' also to **CLOT** and **CLOUT**.

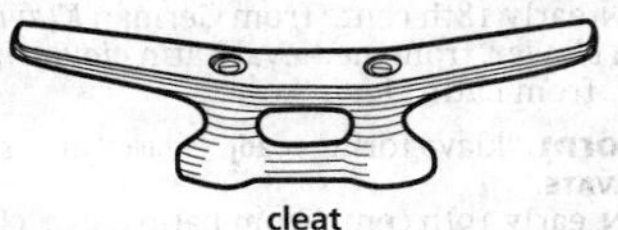
cleat

cleav·age /ˈklēvij/ ▶ **n.** a sharp division; a split: *a system dominated by the class cleavage.* ■ the hollow between a woman's breasts when supported, esp. as exposed by a low-cut garment. ■ Biology cell division, esp. of a fertilized egg cell. ■ the splitting of rocks or crystals in a preferred plane or direction.

cleave[1] /klēv/ ▶ **v.** (past **clove** /klōv/ or **cleft** /kleft/ or **cleaved** /klēvd/; past participle **cloven** /ˈklōvən/ or **cleft** or **cleaved**) [with obj.] split or sever (something), esp. along a natural line or grain: *the large ax his father used to cleave wood for the fire.* ■ split (a molecule) by breaking a particular chemical bond. ■ make a way through (something) forcefully, as if by splitting it apart: *they watched a coot cleave the smooth water* | *Stan was off, cleaving a path through the traffic* | [no obj.] *an unstoppable warrior clove through their ranks.* ■ [no obj.] Biology (of a cell) divide: *the egg cleaves to form a mulberry-shaped cluster of cells.*
– DERIVATIVES **cleav·a·ble** adj.
– ORIGIN Old English *clēofan*, of Germanic origin; related to Dutch *klieven* and German *klieben*.

cleave[2] ▶ **v.** [no obj.] (**cleave to**) literary stick fast to: *Rose's mouth was dry, her tongue cleaving to the roof of her mouth.* ■ adhere strongly to (a particular pursuit or belief): *part of why we cleave to sports is that excellence is so measurable.* ■ become very strongly involved with or emotionally attached to (someone): *it was his choice to cleave to the Brownings.*
– ORIGIN Old English *cleofian, clifian, clifan*; related to Dutch *kleven* and German *kleben*, also to **CLAY** and **CLIMB**.

Clea·ver /ˈklēvər/, Eldridge (1935–98), US civil rights activist. He converted to the Nation of Islam and wrote *Soul on Ice* (1968) about the black experience.

cleav·er /ˈklēvər/ ▶ **n.** a tool with a heavy broad blade, used by butchers for chopping meat.

cleav·ers /ˈklēvərz/ ▶ **plural n.** [treated as sing. or pl.] a widely distributed scrambling plant related to bedstraws, with hooked bristles on the stem, leaves, and seeds that cling to fur and clothing. Also called **GOOSEGRASS**. ● *Galium aparine*, family Rubiaceae.
– ORIGIN Old English *clīfe*, related to **CLEAVE**[2].

clef /klef/ ▶ **n.** Music any of several symbols placed at the left-hand end of a staff, indicating the pitch of the notes written on it.
– ORIGIN late 16th cent.: from French, from Latin *clavis* 'key.'

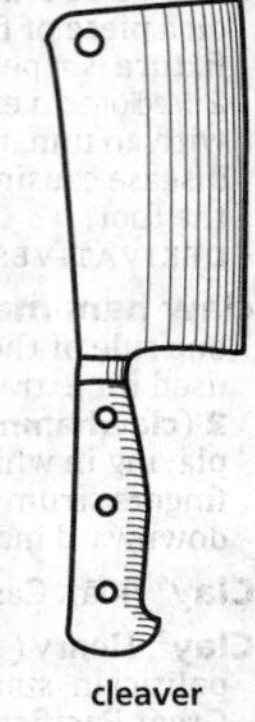
cleaver

cleft[1] /kleft/ past and past participle of **CLEAVE**[1].
▶ **adj.** split, divided, or partially divided into two: *a cleft chin.*

cleft[2] ▶ **n.** a fissure or split, esp. one in rock or the ground. ■ a vertical indentation in the middle of a person's forehead or chin. ■ a deep division between two parts of the body.
– ORIGIN Middle English *clift*: of Germanic origin; related to Dutch *kluft* and German *Kluft*, also to CLEAVE[1]. The form of the word was altered in the 16th cent. by association with CLEFT[1].

cleft lip ▶ **n.** a congenital split in the upper lip on one or both sides of the center, often associated with a cleft palate.

USAGE Cleft lip is the standard, accepted term and should be used instead of **harelip**, which can cause offense.

cleft pal·ate ▶ **n.** a congenital split in the roof of the mouth.

cleft sen·tence ▶ **n.** Grammar a sentence in which an element is emphasized by being put in a separate clause with the use of an empty introductory word such as *it* or *that*, e.g., *it's money we want*; *it was today that I saw him*; *that was the King you were talking to*.

cleg ▶ **n.** Brit. another term for HORSEFLY.
– ORIGIN late Middle English: from Old Norse *kleggi*.

cleis·tog·a·my /klīˈstägəmē/ ▶ **n.** Botany self-fertilization that occurs within a permanently closed flower.
– DERIVATIVES **cleis·tog·a·mous** /-əməs/ **adj.**
– ORIGIN late 19th cent.: from Greek *kleistos* 'closed' + *-gamy* (from *gamos* 'marriage').

clem·a·tis /ˈklemətəs, kləˈmatəs/ ▶ **n.** a climbing plant of the buttercup family that bears white, pink, or purple flowers and feathery seeds. Several kinds are cultivated as ornamentals. ● Genus *Clematis*, family Ranunculaceae.
– ORIGIN Latin (also denoting the periwinkle), from Greek *klēmatis*, from *klēma* 'vine branch.'

Cle·men·ceau /ˌklemənˈsō, ˌkläˌmänˈsō/, Georges (Eugène Benjamin) (1841–1929), French statesman, prime minister 1906–09 and 1917–20. At the Versailles peace talks he pushed hard for a punitive settlement with Germany, but failed to obtain all that he demanded.

clem·en·cy /ˈklemənsē/ ▶ **n.** mercy; lenience: *an appeal for clemency*.
– ORIGIN late Middle English: from Latin *clementia*, from *clemens, clement-* 'clement.'

Clem·ens[1] /ˈklemənz/, Roger (1962–), US baseball player; full name *William Roger Clemens*; known as **the Rocket**. In 2004, he became the first pitcher to have won seven Cy Young awards. He had previously set a major league record by twice (1986, 1996) striking out 20 batters during a nine-inning game. During his career 1984–2007, he played for the Boston Red Sox, Toronto Blue Jays, New York Yankees, and Houston Astros.

Clem·ens[2], Samuel Langhorne, see TWAIN.

clem·ent /ˈklemənt/ ▶ **adj. 1** (of weather) mild. **2** (of a person or a person's actions) merciful.
– ORIGIN late Middle English (sense 2): from Latin *clemens, clement-*.

Clem·ent, St. (1st century AD), pope (bishop of Rome) *c.*88–*c.*97, probably the third after St. Peter; known as **St. Clement of Rome**. Feast day, November 23.

Cle·men·te /kləˈmentā, -tē/, Roberto (1934–72), US baseball player; born in Puerto Rico; full name *Roberto Clemente Walker*. An outfielder for the Pittsburgh Pirates 1955–72, he was a four-time National League batting champion. He was killed in an airplane crash on his way to bring aid to Nicaraguan earthquake victims. Baseball Hall of Fame (1973).

clem·en·tine /ˈklemənˌtīn, -ˌtēn/ ▶ **n.** a tangerine of a deep orange-red North African variety that is grown around the Mediterranean and in South Africa.
– ORIGIN 1920s: from French *clémentine*, from the male given name *Clément*.

Clem·ent of Al·ex·an·dri·a, St. /ˈklemənt/ (*c.*150–*c.*215), Greek theologian; Latin name *Titus Flavius Clemens*. He related the ideas of Greek philosophy to the Christian faith. Feast day, December 5.

Clem·son /ˈklemsən/ a city in northwestern South Carolina, home to Clemson University; pop. 13,012 (est. 2008).

clen·bu·te·rol /klenˈbyo͞otəˌrôl, -ˌrōl/ ▶ **n.** Medicine a synthetic drug used in the treatment of asthma and other respiratory diseases and also in veterinary obstetrics. It also promotes the growth of muscle and has been used illegally by athletes to enhance performance.
– ORIGIN 1970s: from *c(h)l(oro-)* + *(ph)en(yl)* + *but(yl)* + *er* + *-OL*.

clench /klenCH/ ▶ **v.** (with reference to the fingers or hand) close into a tight ball, esp. when feeling extreme anger: [with obj.] *she clenched her fists, struggling for control* | [no obj.] *John's right hand clenched into a fist* | (as adj. **clenched**) *he struck the wall with his clenched fist*. ■ (with reference to the teeth) press or be pressed tightly together, esp. with anger or determination or so as to suppress a strong emotion: [no obj.] *her teeth clenched in anger*. ■ [with obj.] grasp (something) tightly, esp. with the hands or between the teeth: *he clenched the steering wheel so hard that the car wobbled*. ■ [no obj.] (of a muscular part of the body) tighten or contract sharply, esp. with strong emotion: *Mark felt his stomach clench in alarm*.
▶ **n.** [in sing.] a contraction or tightening of part of the body: *she saw the anger rise, saw the clench of his fists*.
– ORIGIN Old English (in the sense of *clinch* 'fix securely'): of Germanic origin; related to CLING.

cle·o·me /klēˈōmē/ ▶ **n.** a plant of a chiefly tropical genus that includes the spider flower. Cleomes are noted for their long stamens. ● Genus *Cleome*, family Capparidaceae.
– ORIGIN modern Latin, from Greek, denoting a different plant.

Cle·o·pa·tra /ˌklēəˈpatrə/ (69–30 BC), queen of Egypt 47–30; the last Ptolemaic (Macedonian dynasty) ruler; also known as **Cleopatra VII**. After a brief liaison with Julius Caesar, she formed a political and romantic alliance with Mark Antony. Their ambitions ultimately brought them into conflict with Rome, and they were defeated at the battle of Actium in 31. She is reputed to have committed suicide by allowing herself to be bitten by an asp.

cle·o·pa·tra /ˌklēəˈpatrə/ ▶ **n.** a European butterfly related to the brimstone, with wings that vary from pale cream to orange-yellow. ● *Gonepteryx cleopatra*, family Pieridae.

Cle·o·pa·tra's Nee·dles a pair of granite obelisks erected at Heliopolis by Tuthmosis III *c.*1475 BC. They were taken from Egypt in 1878, one being set up on the Thames Embankment in London and the other in Central Park, New York. They have no known historical connection with Cleopatra.

clep·sy·dra /ˈklepsədrə/ ▶ **n.** (pl. **clepsydras** or **clepsydrae** /-ˌdrē, -ˌdrī/) an ancient time-measuring device worked by a flow of water.
– ORIGIN late Middle English: via Latin from Greek *klepsudra*, based on *kleptein* 'steal' + *hudōr* 'water.'

clere·sto·ry /ˈkli(ə)rˌstôrē/ (also **clearstory**) ▶ **n.** (pl. **clerestories**) the upper part of the nave, choir, and transepts of a large church, containing a series of windows. It is clear of the roofs of the aisles and admits light to the central parts of the building. ■ such a series of windows in a church or similar windows in another building. ■ a raised section of roof running down the center of a railroad car, with small windows or ventilators.
– ORIGIN late Middle English: from CLEAR + STORY[2].

cler·gy /ˈklərjē/ ▶ **n.** (pl. **clergies**) [usu. treated as pl.] the body of all people ordained for religious duties, esp. in the Christian Church: *all marriages were to be solemnized by the clergy*.
– ORIGIN Middle English: from Old French, based on ecclesiastical Latin *clericus* 'clergyman' (see CLERIC).

cler·gy·man /ˈklərjēmən/ ▶ **n.** (pl. **clergymen**) a male priest or minister of a Christian church.

cler·gy·wom·an /ˈklərjēˌwo͝omən/ ▶ **n.** (pl. **clergywomen**) a female priest or minister of a Christian church.

cler·ic /ˈklerik/ ▶ **n.** a priest or religious leader, esp. a Christian or Muslim one.
– ORIGIN early 17th cent.: from ecclesiastical Latin *clericus* 'clergyman,' from Greek *klērikos* 'belonging to the Christian clergy,' from *klēros* 'lot, heritage' (Acts 1:26).

cler·i·cal /ˈklerikəl/ ▶ **adj. 1** (of a job or person) concerned with or relating to work in an office, esp. routine documentation and administrative tasks: *temps are always needed for clerical work*. **2** of or relating to the clergy: *he was still attired in his clerical outfit*.
– DERIVATIVES **cler·i·cal·ism n.** (sense 2), **cler·i·cal·ist n.** (sense 2), **cler·i·cal·ly adv.**
– ORIGIN late 15th cent. (sense 2): from ecclesiastical Latin *clericalis*, from *clericus* 'clergyman' (see CLERIC).

cler·i·cal col·lar ▶ **n.** a stiff upright white collar that fastens at the back, worn by the clergy in some churches.

cler·i·hew /ˈklerəˌhyo͞o/ ▶ **n.** a short comic or nonsensical verse, typically in two rhyming couplets with lines of unequal length and referring to a famous person.
– ORIGIN 1920s: named after Edmund *Clerihew* Bentley (1875–1956), the English writer who invented it.

cler·i·sy /ˈklerəsē/ ▶ **n.** [usu. treated as pl.] a distinct class of learned or literary people: *the clerisy are those who read for pleasure*.
– ORIGIN early 19th cent.: apparently influenced by German *Klerisei*, based on Greek *klēros* 'heritage' (see CLERIC).

clerk /klərk/ ▶ **n. 1** a person employed in an office or bank to keep records and accounts and to undertake other routine administrative duties: *a bank clerk*. ■ an official in charge of the records of a local council or court: *a clerk to the court*. ■ a lay officer of a cathedral, parish church, college chapel, etc.: *a chapter clerk*. **2** (also **desk clerk**) a receptionist in a hotel. ■ an assistant in a store; a salesclerk. **3** (also **clerk in holy orders**) formal a member of the clergy.
▶ **v.** [no obj.] work as a clerk: *eleven of those who left college this year are clerking in auction houses*.
– DERIVATIVES **clerk·ish adj.**
– ORIGIN Old English *cleric, clerc* (in the sense 'ordained minister, literate person'), from ecclesiastical Latin *clericus* 'clergyman' (see CLERIC); reinforced by Old French *clerc*, from the same source. Sense 1 of the noun dates from the early 16th cent.

clerk·ly /ˈklərklē/ ▶ **adj.** archaic of, relating to, or appropriate to a clerk: *a list drawn up in a clerkly hand*. ■ scholarly; learned.

clerk·ship /ˈklərkˌSHip/ ▶ **n.** the position or status of a clerk, esp. in the legal profession.

Cler·mont-Fer·rand /ˌklermôN fəˈräN/ an industrial city in central France, capital of the Auvergne region, at the center of the Massif Central; pop. 142,449 (2006).

C-lev·el (also **c-level**) ▶ **adj.** denoting the executive level of a corporation: *a c-level corporate officer*.
– ORIGIN early 2000s: from the fact that initialisms for jobs at this level begin with C (for *chief*).

Cleve·land[1] /ˈklēvlənd/ **1** a major port and industrial city in northeastern Ohio, on Lake Erie and the Cuyahoga River; pop. 433,748 (est. 2008). **2** a city in southeastern Tennessee, northeast of Chattanooga; pop. 39,753 (est. 2008).

Cleve·land[2], (Stephen) Grover (1837–1908), 22nd and 24th president of the US 1885–89 and 1893–97. A New York Democrat, he served as governor of his state 1883–85 before being elected to the presidency. During his first term, he championed civil service reform and revision of the tariff system. Although he was defeated for re-election by Benjamin Harrison in 1888, he was again elected in 1892. His second term was marked by his application of the Monroe Doctrine to Britain's border dispute with Venezuela in 1895.

Grover Cleveland

Cleve·land Heights a city in northeastern Ohio, northeast of Cleveland; pop. 45,827 (est. 2008).

clev·er /ˈklevər/ ▶ **adj.** (**cleverer**, **cleverest**) quick to understand, learn, and devise or apply ideas; intelligent: *a clever and studious young woman* | *how clever of him to think of this!* ■ skilled at doing or achieving something; talented: *he was clever at getting what he wanted* | *she is clever with her hands*. ■ showing intelligence or skill; ingenious: *a simple but clever idea for helping people learn computing*.

PRONUNCIATION KEY ə *ago, up*; ər *over, fur*; a *hat*; ā *ate*; ä *car*; e *let*; ē *see*; i *fit*; ī *by*; NG *sing*; ō *go*; ô *law, for*; oi *toy*; o͝o *good*; o͞o *goo*; ou *out*; TH *thin*; T͟H *then*; ZH *vision*

■ [usu. with negative] dated, informal sensible; well-advised: *it wasn't too clever, leaving Dolly alone.*
– PHRASES **too clever by half** informal annoyingly proud of one's intelligence or skill and in danger of overreaching oneself.
– DERIVATIVES **clev·er·ly** adv.
– ORIGIN Middle English (in the sense 'quick to catch hold,' only recorded in this period): perhaps of Dutch or Low German origin, and related to CLEAVE². In the late 16th cent. the term came to mean (probably through dialect use) 'manually skillful'; the sense 'possessing mental agility' dates from the early 18th cent.

C

clev·er·ness /ˈklevərnəs/ ▶ n. the quality of being clever; ingenuity or shrewdness: *people marveled at his cleverness | the cleverness of her strategy.*

clev·is /ˈklevəs/ ▶ n. a U-shaped or forked metal connector within which another part can be fastened by means of a bolt or pin passing through the ends of the connector.
– ORIGIN late 16th cent.: perhaps related to CLEAVE¹.

clew /klo͞o/ ▶ n. **1** Nautical the lower or after corner of a sail.
2 (**clews**) the cords by which a hammock is suspended. ■ (**clew**) a ball of thread (used esp. with reference to the thread supposedly used by Theseus to mark his way out of the Cretan labyrinth).
3 archaic variant of CLUE.
▶ v. [with obj.] (**clew a sail up**) haul up the clews of a sail to the yard or into the mast ready for furling. ■ (**clew a sail down**) lower an upper square sail by hauling down on the clew lines while slacking away on the halyard.
– ORIGIN Old English *cliwen, cleowen* (denoting a rounded mass, also a ball of thread), of Germanic origin; related to Dutch *kluwen.* All senses are also recorded for the form CLUE.

CLI ▶ abbr. short for COST-OF-LIVING INDEX.

cli·ché /klēˈSHā, kli-, ˈklē,SHā/ (also **cliche**) ▶ n. **1** a phrase or opinion that is overused and betrays a lack of original thought: *the old cliché "one man's meat is another man's poison."* ■ a very predictable or unoriginal thing or person: *each building is a mishmash of tired clichés.*
2 Printing chiefly Brit. a stereotype or electrotype.
– ORIGIN mid 19th cent.: French, past participle (used as a noun) of *clicher* 'to stereotype.'

cli·chéd /klēˈSHād, kli-, ˈklē,SHād/ (also **cliched**) ▶ adj. showing a lack of originality; based on frequently repeated phrases or opinions: *the clichéd storytelling lacks that vital spark.*

click /klik/ ▶ n. a short, sharp sound as of a switch being operated or of two hard objects coming quickly into contact: *she heard the click of the door.* ■ Phonetics an ingressive consonantal stop produced by sudden withdrawal of the tongue from the soft palate, front teeth, or back teeth and hard palate, occurring in some southern African and other languages. ■ Computing an act of pressing a button on a mouse or similar device.
▶ v. **1** make or cause to make a short, sharp sound: [no obj.] *the key clicked in the lock and the door opened* | [with obj.] *she clicked off the light | Martha clicked her tongue* | (as adj. **clicking**) *the clicking cameras outside the church.* ■ Computing press one of the buttons on a mouse to select a function or item on the screen: [no obj.] *click on the illustration for a larger version* | [with obj.] *click the left mouse button twice.*
2 [no obj.] informal become suddenly clear or understandable: *finally it clicked what all the fuss had been about.* ■ quickly become friendly or intimate: *we just clicked, and I found myself falling in love | I didn't meet a woman who I really clicked with until I was 40.* ■ become successful or popular: *I don't think this issue has clicked with the voters.*
– PHRASES **click into place** (of an object, esp. part of a mechanism) fall smoothly into its allotted position. ■ become suddenly clear and understandable: *everything has clicked into place for the organization.*
– ORIGIN late 16th cent. (as a verb): imitative.

click·a·ble /ˈklikəbəl/ ▶ adj. Computing (of text or images on a computer screen) such that clicking on them with a mouse will produce a reaction.

click bee·tle ▶ n. a long, narrow beetle that can spring up with a click as a means of startling predators and escaping. Its larva is the wireworm. Also called SKIPJACK. ● Family Elateridae: numerous genera.

click·er /ˈklikər/ ▶ n. a device that clicks. ■ a remote control keypad.

click·e·ty-clack /,klikətē ˈklak/ ▶ n. a repeated clicking sound as of shoe heels on a hard surface.
▶ v. [no obj., with adverbial of direction] move with such a sound: *the train clickety-clacked along the tracks.*

click lan·guage ▶ n. a language in which clicks are used.

clicks and mor·tar ▶ n. used to refer to a traditional business that has expanded its activities to operate also on the Internet: [as modifier] *a clicks-and-mortar strategy.* Compare with BRICKS AND MORTAR.

click stop ▶ n. a control for the aperture of a camera lens that clicks into position at certain standard settings.

click·stream /ˈklik,strēm/ ▶ n. a series of mouse clicks made while using a website or in linking to multiple websites.

click-through ▶ n. Computing the action or facility of following a hypertext link to a particular website, esp. a commercial one. ■ (also **click rate, click-through rate**) the ratio of clicks that an Internet advertisement receives to page views of the advertisement.

cli·ent /ˈklīənt/ ▶ n. **1** a person or organization using the services of a lawyer or other professional person or company: *insurance tailor-made to a client's specific requirements.* ■ a person receiving social or medical services: *a client referred for counseling.* ■ (also **client state**) a nation that is dependent on another, more powerful nation.
2 Computing (in a network) a desktop computer or workstation that is capable of obtaining information and applications from a server. ■ (also **client application** or **program**) a program that is capable of obtaining a service provided by another program.
3 (in ancient Rome) a plebeian under the protection of a patrician. ■ archaic a dependent; a hanger-on.
– DERIVATIVES **cli·ent·ship** /-,SHip/ n.
– ORIGIN late Middle English: from Latin *cliens, client-*, variant of *cluens* 'heeding,' from *cluere* 'hear or obey.' The term originally denoted a person under the protection and patronage of another, hence a person "protected" by a legal adviser (sense 1).

cli·en·tele /,klīənˈtel, ,klē-/ ▶ n. [treated as sing. or pl.] clients collectively: *an upscale clientele.* ■ the customers of a shop, bar, or place of entertainment: *the dancers don't mix with the clientele.*
– ORIGIN mid 16th cent. (in the sense 'clientship, patronage'): via French from Latin *clientela* 'clientship,' from *cliens, client-* (see CLIENT).

cli·en·tel·ism /,klīənˈtel,izəm, ,klē-/ (also **clientism** /ˈklīən,tizəm/) ▶ n. a social order that depends upon relations of patronage; in particular, a political approach that emphasizes or exploits such relations.
– DERIVATIVES **cli·en·tel·is·tic** /-telˈistik/ adj.
– ORIGIN 1970s: from Italian *clientelismo* 'patronage system.'

cli·ent-serv·er ▶ adj. Computing denoting a computer system in which a central server provides data to a number of networked workstations.

cliff /klif/ ▶ n. a steep rock face, esp. at the edge of the sea: *a path along the top of rugged cliffs* | [as modifier] *the cliff face.*
– DERIVATIVES **cliff·like** /-,līk/ adj., **cliff·y** adj.
– ORIGIN Old English *clif,* of Germanic origin; related to Dutch *klif.*

cliff·hang·er /ˈklif,haNGər/ ▶ n. an ending to an episode of a serial drama that leaves the audience in suspense. ■ a story or event with a strong element of suspense: *the game was a cliffhanger right up to the final buzzer.*
– DERIVATIVES **cliff·hang·ing** /-,haNGiNG/ adj.

Clif·ford¹ /ˈklifərd/, Clark McAdams (1906–98), US attorney and public official. A key adviser to four Democratic presidents, he helped draft the legislation that established the Central Intelligence Agency (CIA).

Clif·ford², Nathan (1803–81), US Supreme Court associate justice 1858–81. He was the US attorney general 1846–48 before being appointed to the Court by President Buchanan. He was an advocate of states' rights.

CliffsNotes /ˈklifs,nōts/ ▶ n. US trademark a brand name for a series of prepared notes used as study guides for literary works and other school and college subject matter.
– ORIGIN for *Cliff* Hillegass (1918–2001), US developer of the series.

cliff·top /ˈklif,täp/ ▶ n. an area of land at the top of a cliff: *the windswept clifftops* | [as modifier] *clifftop paths.*

Clift /klift/, Montgomery (1920–66), US actor; full name *Edward Montgomery Clift.* Notable movies: *A Place in the Sun* (1951), *From Here to Eternity* (1953), and *Judgment at Nuremberg* (1961).

Clif·ton /ˈkliftən/ an industrial city in northeastern New Jersey, immediately west of Passaic; pop. 78,219 (est. 2008).

cli·mac·ter·ic /klīˈmaktərik, ,klīmakˈterik/ ▶ n. a critical period or event: *the first major climacteric in twentieth-century poetry.* ■ Medicine the period of life when fertility and sexual activity are in decline; (in women) menopause. ■ Botany the ripening period of certain fruits such as apples, involving increased metabolism and only possible while still on the tree.
▶ adj. having extreme and far-reaching implications or results; critical: *Britain must possess so climacteric a weapon in order to deter an atomically armed enemy.* ■ Medicine occurring at, characteristic of, or undergoing the climacteric; (in women) menopausal. ■ Botany (of a fruit) undergoing a climacteric.
– ORIGIN mid 16th cent. (in the sense 'constituting a critical period in life'): from French *climactérique* or via Latin from Greek *klimaktērikos,* from *klimaktēr* 'critical period,' from *klimax* 'ladder, climax.'

cli·mac·tic /klīˈmaktik, klə-/ ▶ adj. (of an action, event, or scene) exciting or thrilling and acting as a climax to a series of events: *the film's climactic scenes.*
– DERIVATIVES **cli·mac·ti·cal·ly** /-ik(ə)lē/ adv.
– ORIGIN late 19th cent.: formed irregularly from CLIMAX + -IC, probably influenced by CLIMACTERIC.

> **USAGE** Climactic and climatic are very similar in spelling and are often confused. **Climactic** means 'forming a climax,' as in *the movie's climactic scene,* while **climatic** means 'relating to climate,' as in *prevailing climatic conditions.*

cli·mate /ˈklīmit/ ▶ n. the weather conditions prevailing in an area in general or over a long period: *our cold, wet climate | agricultural development is constrained by climate.* ■ a region with particular prevailing weather conditions: *vacationing in a warm climate.* ■ the prevailing trend of public opinion or of another aspect of public life: *the current economic climate.*
– ORIGIN late Middle English: from Old French *climat* or late Latin *clima, climat-*, from Greek *klima* 'slope, zone,' from *klinein* 'to slope.' The term originally denoted a zone of the earth between two lines of latitude, then any region of the earth, and later, a region considered with reference to its atmospheric conditions. Compare with CLIME.

cli·mate change ▶ n. the change in global climate patterns apparent from the mid to late 20th century onwards, attributed largely to the increased levels of atmospheric carbon dioxide produced by the use of fossil fuels.

> **WORD TRENDS** In the early 2000s, **global warming** was the buzzword of the environmentally minded, but it is apparently being overtaken by **climate change.** Although many people use the two terms interchangeably, there are important differences. **Global warming** describes a gradual heating up of the earth's atmosphere, whereas **climate change** can cover many other changes beyond an increase in temperature—such as alterations in precipitation patterns and sea level, and the increasing frequency of severe weather events. **Climate change** can also be seen as a less loaded and more politically neutral term, and is generally preferred by scientists, as many do not see rising temperature as the single most important effect of the changing climate. The Oxford English Corpus data from the year 2009 contains twice as many examples of **climate change** as **global warming.**

cli·mate con·trol ▶ n. another term for AIR CONDITIONING.

cli·mat·ic /klīˈmatik/ ▶ adj. relating to climate: *under certain climatic conditions, desert locusts increase in number.*
– DERIVATIVES **cli·mat·i·cal** /klīˈmatikəl/ adj., **cli·mat·i·cal·ly** /klīˈmatik(ə)lē/ adv.

> **USAGE** See usage at CLIMACTIC.

cli·ma·tol·o·gy /,klīməˈtäləjē/ ▶ n. the scientific study of climate.
– DERIVATIVES **cli·ma·to·log·i·cal** /,klīmətlˈäjikəl/ adj., **cli·ma·tol·o·gist** /-jist/ n.

cli·max /ˈklī,maks/ ▶ n. the most intense, exciting, or important point of something; a culmination or apex: *the climax of her speech | a thrilling climax to the game.* ■ an orgasm. ■ Ecology the final stage in a succession in a given environment, at which a plant community reaches a state of equilibrium: [as modifier] *a mixed hardwood climax forest.* ■ Rhetoric a sequence of propositions or ideas in order of increasing importance, force, or effectiveness of expression.
▶ v. [no obj.] culminate in an exciting or impressive event; reach a climax: *the day climaxed with a gala concert.* ■ [with obj.] bring (something) to a climax: *the sentencing climaxed a seven-month trial.* ■ have an orgasm.
– ORIGIN mid 16th cent. (in rhetoric): from late Latin, from Greek *klimax* 'ladder, climax.' The sense 'culmination' arose in the late 18th cent.

climb /klīm/ ▶ v. **1** [with obj.] go or come up (a slope, incline, or staircase), esp. by using the feet and sometimes the hands; ascend: *we began to climb the hill* | [no obj.] *the air became colder as they climbed*

higher | *he climbed up the steps slowly.* ■ [no obj.] (of an aircraft or the sun) go upward: *we decided to climb to 6,000 feet.* ■ [no obj.] (of a road or track) slope upward or up: *the track climbed steeply up a narrow, twisting valley.* ■ (of a plant) grow up (a wall, tree, or trellis) by clinging with tendrils or by twining: *when ivy climbs a wall, it infiltrates any crack* | [no obj.] *there were roses climbing up the walls.* ■ [no obj.] grow in scale, value, or power: *the stock market climbed 24 points* | *he climbed from a job as office messenger to president of the bank.* ■ move to a higher position in (a chart or table): *the song is climbing the adult-contemporary chart.*
2 [no obj., with adverbial of direction] move with effort, esp. into or out of a confined space; clamber: *Howard started to climb out of the front seat* | *I climbed down a narrow ladder* | *he climbed to a high bough.* ■ (**climb into**) put on (clothes): *he climbed into his suit.*
▶ **n.** an ascent, esp. of a mountain or hill, by climbing: *the rigorous climb up the mountain* | figurative *his long climb from poverty.* ■ a mountain, hill, or slope that is climbed or is to be climbed: *the mountain is no easy climb.* ■ a recognized route up a mountain or cliff: *this may be the hardest rock climb in the world.* ■ an aircraft's flight upward: *we leveled out from the climb at 600 feet* | *rate of climb.* ■ a rise or increase in value, rank, or power: *an above-average climb in prices.*
–PHRASES **be climbing the walls** informal feel frustrated, helpless, and trapped: *his job soon had him climbing the walls.*
–DERIVATIVES **climb·a·ble** adj.
–ORIGIN Old English *climban*; related to Dutch and German *klimmen*, also to CLAY and CLEAVE².

climb·er /ˈklīmər/ ▶ **n.** a person or animal that climbs: *leopards are great tree climbers.* ■ a mountaineer. ■ a climbing plant. ■ see SOCIAL CLIMBER.

climb·ing /ˈklīmiNG/ ▶ **n.** the sport or activity of ascending mountains or cliffs.

climb·ing eu·on·y·mus ▶ **n.** another name for WINTER CREEPER.

climb·ing i·rons ▶ **plural n.** a set of spikes attached to boots for climbing trees or ice slopes.

climb·ing perch ▶ **n.** a small, edible freshwater fish that is able to breathe air and move over land, native to Africa and Asia. ● Family Anabantidae: three genera and several species, including *Anabas testudinens.*

climb·ing wall ▶ **n.** a wall at a sports center or in a gymnasium fitted with attachments to simulate a rock face for climbing practice.

climb-out ▶ **n.** the part of a flight of an aircraft after takeoff and before it reaches a level altitude.

clime /klīm/ ▶ **n.** (usu. **climes**) chiefly literary a region considered with reference to its climate: *the Continent and its sunnier climes.*
–ORIGIN late Middle English: from late Latin *clima* 'zone' (see CLIMATE).

clin- ▶ **comb. form** CLINO- shortened before a vowel.

clinch /klinCH/ ▶ **v.** [with obj.] **1** confirm or settle (a contract or bargain): *to clinch a business deal.* ■ conclusively settle (an argument or debate): *these findings clinched the matter.* ■ confirm the winning or achievement of (a game, competition, or victory): *his team clinched the title.* ■ secure (a nail or rivet) by driving the point sideways when it has penetrated. ■ fasten (a rope or fishing line) with a clinch knot.
2 [no obj.] grapple at close quarters, esp. (of boxers) so as to be too closely engaged for full-arm blows. ■ (of two people) embrace.
▶ **n. 1** a struggle or scuffle at close quarters, esp. (in boxing) one in which the fighters become too closely engaged for full-arm blows. ■ an embrace, esp. an amorous one: *we went into a passionate clinch on the sofa.*
2 a knot used to fasten a rope to a ring or cringle, using a half hitch with the end seized back on its own part.
–ORIGIN late 16th cent. (in the senses 'something that grips' and 'fix securely'): variant of CLENCH.

clinch·er /ˈklinCHər/ ▶ **n. 1** a fact, argument, or event that settles a matter conclusively: *his two-run double was the clincher.*
2 (in full **clincher tire**) a bicycle or automobile tire that has flange beads that fit into the wheel rim.

Clinch Riv·er /klinCH/ a river that flows for 300 miles (480 km) from southwestern Virginia into Tennessee where it passes the Norris Dam and Oak Ridge before joining the Tennessee River.

cline /klīn/ ▶ **n.** a continuum with an infinite number of gradations from one extreme to the other: *a point along a cline of activity.* ■ Biology a gradation in one or more characteristics within a species or other taxon, esp. between different populations. See also ECOCLINE.
–DERIVATIVES **clin·al** /ˈklīnl/ **adj.**
–ORIGIN 1930s: from Greek *klinein* 'to slope.'

cling /kliNG/ ▶ **v.** (past and past participle **clung** /kləNG/) [no obj.] (**cling to/onto/on**) (of a person or animal) hold on tightly to: *she clung to Joe's arm* | *they clung together* | figurative *she clung onto life.* ■ (**cling to**) adhere or stick firmly or closely to; be hard to part or remove from: *the smell of smoke clung to their clothes* | *the fabric clung to her smooth skin.* ■ (**cling to**) remain very close to: *the fish cling to the line of the weed.* ■ remain persistently or stubbornly faithful to something: *she clung resolutely to her convictions.* ■ be overly dependent on someone emotionally: *you are clinging to him for security.*
▶ **n.** (also **cling peach**) a clingstone peach.
–DERIVATIVES **cling·er** n.
–ORIGIN Old English *clingan* 'stick together,' of Germanic origin; related to Middle Dutch *klingen* 'adhere,' Middle High German *klingen* 'climb,' also to CLENCH.

cling film ▶ **n.** British term for PLASTIC WRAP.

cling·fish /ˈkliNG,fiSH/ ▶ **n.** (pl. **same** or **clingfishes**) a small fish occurring mainly in shallow or intertidal water, with a sucker for attachment to rocks and other surfaces. ● Family Gobiesocidae: several genera and species, including the **shore clingfish** (*Lepadogaster lepadogaster*) of Europe and West Africa.

cling·ing /ˈkliNGiNG/ ▶ **adj. 1** (of a garment) fitting closely to the body and showing its shape: *she was wearing a clinging black dress.*
2 overly dependent on someone emotionally: *she wasn't the clinging type.*
–PHRASES **clinging vine** a person who is submissively dependent on another.

cling·stone /ˈkliNG,stōn/ ▶ **n.** a peach or nectarine of a variety in which the flesh adheres to the stone. Contrasted with FREESTONE (sense 2).

cling·y /ˈkliNGē/ ▶ **adj.** (**clingier, clingiest**) (of a person or garment) liable to cling; clinging: *at about 18 months my son became very clingy* | *clingy leggings.*
–DERIVATIVES **cling·i·ness** n.

clin·ic /ˈklinik/ ▶ **n. 1** a place or hospital department where outpatients are given medical treatment or advice, esp. of a specialist nature: *a mental health clinic.* ■ an occasion or time when such treatment or advice is given: *we're now holding regular clinics.* ■ a gathering at a hospital bedside for the teaching of medicine or surgery.
2 a conference or short course on a particular subject: *a ski clinic.*
–ORIGIN mid 19th cent. (in the sense 'teaching of medicine at the bedside'): from French *clinique*, from Greek *klinikē* (*tekhnē*) 'bedside (art),' from *klinē* 'bed.'

clin·i·cal /ˈklinikəl/ ▶ **adj. 1** of or relating to the observation and treatment of actual patients rather than theoretical or laboratory studies: *clinical medicine* | *clinical drug trials.* ■ (of a disease or condition) causing observable and recognizable symptoms: *clinical depression.*
2 efficient and unemotional; coldly detached: *the clinical detail of a textbook.* ■ (of a room or building) bare, functional, and clean.
–ORIGIN late 18th cent.: from Greek *klinikē* 'bedside' (see CLINIC) + -AL.

clin·i·cal death ▶ **n.** death as judged by the medical observation of cessation of vital functions. It is typically identified with the cessation of heartbeat and respiration, though modern resuscitation methods and life-support systems have required the introduction of the alternative concept of brain death.

clin·i·cal e·col·o·gy ▶ **n.** an earlier name for ENVIRONMENTAL MEDICINE.

clin·i·cal·ly /ˈklinik(ə)lē/ ▶ **adv. 1** as regards clinical medicine; in clinical terms: *the first clinically useful antibiotics* | *clinically dead.*
2 efficiently and without emotion: *he scrutinized her clinically.* ■ [usu. as submodifier] in a very functional and clean manner: *a clinically clean kitchen.*

clin·i·cal psy·chol·o·gy ▶ **n.** the branch of psychology concerned with the assessment and treatment of mental illness and disability.
–DERIVATIVES **clin·i·cal psy·chol·o·gist** n.

clin·i·cal ther·mom·e·ter ▶ **n.** a small medical thermometer with a short but finely calibrated range, for taking a person's temperature.

cli·ni·cian /kləˈnisHən/ ▶ **n.** a doctor having direct contact with and responsibility for patients, rather than one involved with theoretical or laboratory studies.

clink[1] /kliNGk/ ▶ **n.** a sharp ringing sound, such as that made when metal or glass are struck: *a clink of keys* | *the clink of ice in tall glasses.*
▶ **v.** make or cause to make such a sound: [no obj.] *his ring clinked against the crystal* | (as adj. **clinking**) *clinking chains* | [with obj.] *I heard Suzie clink a piece of crockery.* ■ [with obj.] strike (a glass or glasses) with another to express friendly feelings toward one's companions before drinking: *she clinked her glass on mine.*
–ORIGIN Middle English (as a verb): probably from Middle Dutch *klinken.*

clink[2] ▶ **n.** [in sing.] informal prison: *he was put in the clink for six days.*
–ORIGIN early 16th cent. (originally denoting a prison in Southwark, London): of unknown origin.

C

clink·er[1] /ˈkliNGkər/ ▶ **n.** the stony residue from burned coal or from a furnace. ■ (also **clinker brick**) a brick with a vitrified surface.
–ORIGIN mid 17th cent.: from obsolete Dutch *klinckaerd* (earlier form of *klinker*), from *klinken* 'to clink.'

clink·er[2] ▶ **n.** informal something that is unsatisfactory, of poor quality, or a failure: *marketing couldn't save such clinkers as these films.* ■ a wrong musical note.
–ORIGIN late 17th cent. (denoting a person or thing that clinks): from CLINK[1] + -ER[1]. The current sense (with depreciatory reference) dates from the 1930s.

clink·er-built ▶ **adj.** (of a boat) having external planks secured with clinched nails such that the bottom edge of an upper plank overlaps the upper edge of a lower plank. Compare with CARVEL-BUILT.
–ORIGIN mid 18th cent.: *clinker* from *clink* (northern English variant of CLINCH).

clino- (usu. **clin-** before a vowel) ▶ **comb. form** slant; slope: *clinometer.*

cli·nom·e·ter /klīˈnämətər/ ▶ **n.** Surveying an instrument used for measuring the angle or elevation of slopes.
–ORIGIN early 19th cent.: from Greek *klinein* 'to slope' + -METER.

cli·no·py·rox·ene /,klīnō,pīˈräk,sēn/ ▶ **n.** a mineral of the pyroxene group crystallizing in the monoclinic system.
–ORIGIN early 20th cent.: from *clino-* in the sense 'monoclinic' + PYROXENE.

clin·quant /ˈkliNGkənt/ ▶ **adj.** glittering with gold and silver; tinseled.
▶ **n.** imitation gold leaf. ■ literary or artistic tinsel; false glitter.

Clin·ton[1], Bill (1946–), 42nd president of the US 1993–2001; full name *William Jefferson Blythe Clinton.* An Arkansas Democrat, he served as governor of his state 1979–81, 1983–93 before becoming president. During his first term, he worked with a Republican-controlled Congress to balance the budget. His second term saw economic prosperity as well as international crises in the Middle East and Yugoslavia. Problems that included contested allegations of financial and sexual misconduct escalated, and in 1998 he became the second president ever to be impeached, in his case, on charges of perjury and obstruction of justice. He was acquitted by the Senate in 1999.

Bill Clinton

Clin·ton[2], DeWitt (1769–1828), US politician. Among his political positions, he was a member of the New York legislature 1798–1802, a US senator 1802–03, and mayor of New York City 1803–07, 1808–10, 1811–15. As governor of New York 1817–23, 1825–28, he was a champion of the Erie Canal.

Clin·ton[3], George (1739–1812), US politician. He was governor of New York 1777–95, 1801–04, and vice president of the US 1805–12.

Clin·ton[4], Hillary Rodham (1947–), US first lady and stateswoman; US secretary of state since 2009.

As first lady during Bill Clinton's administration 1993–2001, she worked on health care reform and wrote *It Takes a Village* (1996) about raising the children of the world. She served in the US Senate 2001–09 as a Democrat from New York.

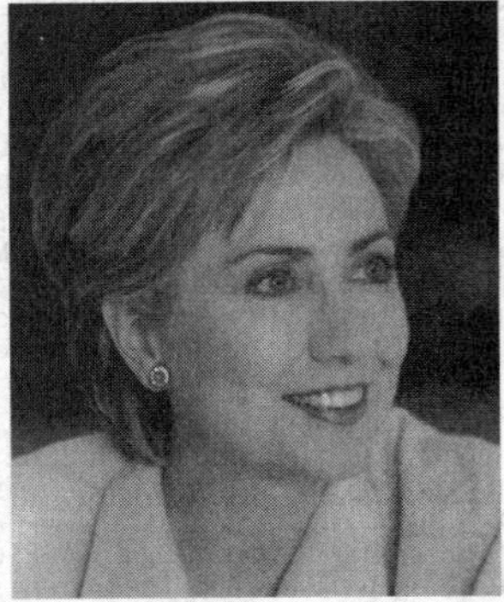
Hillary Rodham Clinton

Cli·o /ˈklīō, ˈklēō/ **1** Greek & Roman Mythology the Muse of history.
2 an award given annually for advertising achievement in television, radio, billboards, and other media.
– ORIGIN from Greek *kleiein* 'celebrate.'

cli·o·met·rics /ˌklīəˈmetriks/ ▶ **plural n.** [treated as sing.] a technique for the interpretation of economic history, based on the statistical analysis of large-scale numerical data from population censuses, parish registers, and similar sources.
– DERIVATIVES **cli·o·met·ric adj.**, **cli·o·me·tri·cian** /-meˈtrisHən/ **n.**
– ORIGIN 1960s (originally US): from **Clio**, on the pattern of words such as *econometrics*.

clip¹ /klip/ ▶ **n.** a device, typically flexible or worked by a spring, for holding an object or objects together or in place. ■ a device such as this used to hold paper currency. ■ a piece of jewelry fastened by a clip. ■ a metal holder containing cartridges for an automatic firearm.
▶ **v.** (**clips, clipping, clipped**) [with adverbial of place] fasten or be fastened with a clip or clips: [with obj.] *she clipped on a pair of diamond earrings* | [no obj.] *the panels simply clip onto the framework*.
– ORIGIN Old English *clyppan* (verb). The noun use dates from the late 15th cent.

clip² ▶ **v.** (**clips, clipping, clipped**) [with obj.] **1** cut short or trim (hair, wool, nails, or vegetation) with shears or scissors: *clipping the hedge*. ■ trim or remove the hair or wool of (an animal): *how to clip your horse*. ■ (**clip something off**) cut off a thing or part of a thing with shears or scissors: *he clipped off a piece of wire* | figurative *she clipped nearly two seconds off the world record*. ■ cut (a section) from a newspaper or magazine: *a photograph clipped from a magazine*. ■ pare the edge of (a coin), esp. illicitly: *they clipped the edges of gold coins and melted the clippings down*. ■ speak (words) in a quick, precise, staccato manner: *"Yes?" The word was clipped short* | (as adj. **clipped**) *cold, clipped tones*. ■ Computing process (an image) so as to remove the parts outside a certain area. ■ Electronics truncate the amplitude of (a signal) above or below predetermined levels.
2 strike briskly or with a glancing blow: *the steamroller clipped some parked cars* | *branches clipped his face*. ■ strike or kick (something, esp. a ball) briskly in a specified direction: *he clipped a right-field double*.
3 informal swindle or rob (someone): *in all the years he ran the place, he was clipped only three times*.
4 [no obj.] informal move quickly in a specified direction: *we clip down the track*.
▶ **n. 1** an act of clipping or trimming something: *I gave him a full clip*. ■ a short sequence taken from a movie or broadcast: *clips from earlier shows*. ■ (also **wool clip**) the quantity of wool clipped from a sheep or flock.
2 informal a quick or glancing blow: *you need a clip on the jaw*.
3 [in sing.] informal a specified speed or rate of movement, esp. when rapid: *we crossed the dance floor at a fast clip*.
– PHRASES **at a clip** informal at a time; all at once: *I spent several days with him, eight hours at a clip*. **clip the wings of** trim the feathers of (a bird) so as to disable it from flight. ■ prevent (someone) from acting freely; check the aspirations of: *he finally clipped the wings of his high-flying chief of staff*.
– ORIGIN Middle English: from Old Norse *klippa*, probably imitative.

clip art ▶ **n.** simple pictures and symbols made available for computer users to add to their documents.

clip·board /ˈklipˌbôrd/ ▶ **n.** a small board with a spring clip at the top, used for holding papers and providing support for writing. ■ Computing a temporary storage area where material cut or copied from a file is kept for pasting into another file.

clip-clop /ˈklip ˌkläp/ (also **clippety-clop**) ▶ **n.** [in sing.] the sound as of a horse's hoofs beating on a hard surface.
▶ **v.** [no obj.] move with such a sound: *the horses clip-clopped slowly along the street*.
– ORIGIN late 19th cent.: imitative.

clip joint ▶ **n.** informal a nightclub or bar that charges exorbitant prices.

clip-on ▶ **adj.** attached by a clip so as to be easy to fasten or remove: *a clip-on bow tie*.
▶ **n.** (usu. **clip-ons**) things, esp. sunglasses or earrings, that are attached by clips.

clip·per /ˈklipər/ ▶ **n. 1** (usu. **clippers**) an instrument for cutting or trimming small pieces off things: *hedge clippers*.
2 Electronics another term for LIMITER.
3 (also **clipper chip**) a microchip that inserts an identifying code into encrypted transmissions, allowing them to be deciphered by a third party having access to a government-held key.
4 (also **clipper ship**) a fast sailing ship, esp. one of 19th-century design with concave bows and raked masts.

clip·ping /ˈkliping/ ▶ **n.** (often **clippings**) a small piece trimmed from something: *hedge clippings and grass cuttings*. ■ an article cut from a newspaper or magazine.

clique /klēk, klik/ ▶ **n.** a small group of people, with shared interests or other features in common, who spend time together and do not readily allow others to join them.
– DERIVATIVES **cli·quish adj.**, **cli·quish·ness n.**
– ORIGIN early 18th cent.: from French, from Old French *cliquer* 'make a noise'; the modern sense is related to CLAQUE.

cli·quey /ˈklēkē, ˈklikē/ ▶ **adj.** (**cliquier, cliquiest**) (of a group or place) tending to form or hold exclusive groups and so not welcoming to outsiders: *a cliquey school*.

clit /klit/ ▶ **n.** vulgar slang short for CLITORIS.

cli·tel·lum /klīˈteləm/ ▶ **n.** (pl. **clitella** /-ˈtelə/) a raised band encircling the body of oligochaete worms and some leeches, made up of reproductive segments.

clit·ic /ˈklitik/ ▶ **n.** Grammar an unstressed word that normally occurs only in combination with another word, for example *'m* in *I'm*.
– DERIVATIVES **clit·i·ci·za·tion** /ˌklitəsəˈzāsHən/ **n.**
– ORIGIN 1940s: from *(en)clitic* and *(pro)clitic*.

clit·o·ri·dec·to·my /ˌklitərəˈdektəmē/ ▶ **n.** (pl. **clitoridectomies**) excision of the clitoris; female circumcision.

clit·o·ris /ˈklitərəs/ ▶ **n.** a small sensitive and erectile part of the female genitals at the anterior end of the vulva.
– DERIVATIVES **clit·o·ral** /ˈklitərəl/ **adj.**
– ORIGIN early 17th cent.: modern Latin, from Greek *kleitoris*.

clit·ter /ˈklitər/ ▶ **v.** [no obj.] make a thin, vibratory, rattling sound: *a coded message clittered over the radio speakers*.
– ORIGIN early 16th cent.: imitative.

cli·vi·a /ˈklīvēə, ˈklivēə/ ▶ **n.** a southern African plant of the lily family, with dark green, straplike leaves and trumpet-shaped orange, red, or yellow flowers. Also called KAFFIR LILY. ● Genus *Clivia*, family Liliaceae (or Amaryllidaceae).
– ORIGIN modern Latin, from *Clive*, the maiden name of Charlotte, Duchess of Northumberland (1787–1866).

clo·a·ca /klōˈākə/ ▶ **n.** (pl. **cloacae** /-ˌkē, -ˌsē/) Zoology a common cavity at the end of the digestive tract for the release of both excretory and genital products in vertebrates (except most mammals) and certain invertebrates. Specifically, the cloaca is present in birds, reptiles, amphibians, most fish, and monotremes. ■ archaic a sewer.
– DERIVATIVES **clo·a·cal adj.**
– ORIGIN late 16th cent. (in the sense 'sewer'): from Latin, related to *cluere* 'cleanse.' The current sense dates from the mid 19th cent.

cloak /klōk/ ▶ **n.** an outdoor overgarment, typically sleeveless, that hangs loosely from the shoulders. ■ something serving to hide or disguise something: *lifting the cloak of secrecy on the arms trade*.
▶ **v.** [with obj.] dress in a cloak: *she cloaked herself in black*. ■ hide, cover, or disguise (something): *the horror of war was cloaked in the trappings of chivalry*.
– ORIGIN Middle English: from Old French *cloke*, dialect variant of *cloche* 'bell, cloak' (from its bell shape), from medieval Latin *clocca* 'bell.' Compare with CLOCK¹.

cloak-and-dag·ger ▶ **adj.** involving or characteristic of mystery, intrigue, or espionage: *a cloak-and-dagger operation*.

cloak·room /ˈklōkˌro͞om, -ˌro͝om/ ▶ **n.** a room in a public building where coats and other belongings may be left temporarily.

clob·ber¹ /ˈkläbər/ ▶ **v.** [with obj.] informal hit (someone) hard: *if he does that I'll clobber him!* ■ treat or deal with harshly: *the recession clobbered other parts of the business*. ■ defeat heavily: [with obj.] *the Braves clobbered the Cubs 23–10*.
– ORIGIN World War II (apparently British air-force slang): of unknown origin.

clob·ber² ▶ **v.** [with obj.] add enameled decoration to (porcelain).
– ORIGIN late 19th cent.: of unknown origin.

clo·chard /ˈklōsHərd, klōˈsHär/ ▶ **n.** (pl. **same**) (in France) a beggar; a vagrant.
– ORIGIN French, from *clocher* 'to limp.'

cloche /klōsH/ ▶ **n.** a small translucent cover for protecting or forcing outdoor plants. ■ (also **cloche hat**) a woman's close-fitting, bell-shaped hat.
– ORIGIN late 19th cent.: from French, literally 'bell' (see CLOAK).

cloche hat

clock¹ /kläk/ ▶ **n.** a mechanical or electrical device for measuring time, indicating hours, minutes, and sometimes seconds, typically by hands on a round dial or by displayed figures. ■ (**the clock**) time taken as a factor in an activity, esp. in competitive sports: *they play against the clock* | *her life is ruled by the clock*. ■ informal a measuring device resembling a clock for recording things other than time, such as a speedometer, taximeter, or odometer. ■ see TIME CLOCK.
▶ **v.** [with obj.] **1** attain or register (a specified time, distance, or speed): *Thomas has clocked up forty years service* | [no obj.] *the book clocks in at 989 pages*. ■ achieve (a victory): *he clocked up his first win of the year*. ■ record as attaining a specified time or rate: *the tower operators clocked a gust of 185 mph*.
2 informal hit (someone), esp. on the head: *someone clocked him for no good reason*.
– PHRASES **around** (or **round**) **the clock** all day and all night: *working around the clock*. **run out the clock** Sports deliberately use as much time as possible in order to preserve one's own team's advantage: *facing a tie, he decided to run out the clock in the final moments*. **stop the clock** allow extra time by temporarily ceasing to count the time left before a deadline arrives: *he agreed to stop the clock as negotiations continued*. **turn** (or **put**) **back the clock** return to the past or to a previous way of doing things. **watch the clock** (of an employee) be overly strict or zealous about not working more than one's required hours.
– PHRASAL VERBS **clock in** (or **out**) (of an employee) punch in (or out).
– ORIGIN late Middle English: from Middle Low German and Middle Dutch *klocke*, based on medieval Latin *clocca* 'bell.'

clock² ▶ **n.** dated an ornamental pattern woven or embroidered on the side of a stocking or sock near the ankle.
– ORIGIN mid 16th cent.: of unknown origin.

clock·er /ˈkläkər/ ▶ **n.** informal a drug dealer, esp. one who sells cocaine or crack.

clock·mak·er /ˈkläkˌmākər/ ▶ **n.** a person who makes and repairs clocks and watches.
– DERIVATIVES **clock·mak·ing** /-ˌmākiNG/ **n.**

clock ra·di·o ▶ **n.** a combined radio and alarm clock that can be set so that the radio will come on at the desired time.

clock speed ▶ **n.** the operating speed of a computer or its microprocessor, defined as the rate at which it performs internal operations and expressed in cycles per second (megahertz).

clock tow·er ▶ **n.** a tower typically forming part of a church or civic building, with a large clock at the top.

clock·watch·er (also **clock watcher**) ▶ **n.** an employee who is overly strict or zealous about not working more than the required hours: *his lamp burned throughout the night; he was no clock-watcher*.
– DERIVATIVES **clock-watch v.**

clock·wise /ˈkläkˌwīz/ ▶ **adv. & adj.** in a curve corresponding in direction to the movement of the hands of a clock: [as adv.] *turn the knob clockwise* | [as adj.] *a clockwise direction.*

clock·work /ˈkläkˌwərk/ ▶ **n.** a mechanism with a spring and toothed gearwheels, used to drive a mechanical clock, toy, or other device.
▶ **adj.** [attrib.] driven by clockwork: *a clockwork motor* | *a clockwork toy.* ■ very smooth and regular: *the clockwork precision of the galaxy.* ■ repetitive and predictable: *it was a clockwork existence for the children.*
– PHRASES **as regular as clockwork** very regularly; repeatedly and predictably. **like clockwork** very smoothly and easily: *the event ran like clockwork.* ■ with mechanical regularity: *these hens lay like clockwork.*

clod /kläd/ ▶ **n.** **1** a lump of earth or clay.
2 informal a stupid person (often used as a general term of abuse).
– ORIGIN late Middle English: variant of CLOT.

clod·dish /ˈklädisн/ ▶ **adj.** foolish, awkward, or clumsy.
– DERIVATIVES **clod·dish·ly** **adv.**, **clod·dish·ness** **n.**

clod·hop·per /ˈklädˌhäpər/ ▶ **n.** **1** a large, heavy shoe.
2 informal a foolish, awkward, or clumsy person.

clod·hop·ping /ˈklädˌhäpiNG/ ▶ **adj.** informal foolish, awkward, or clumsy.

clog /kläg, klôg/ ▶ **n.** **1** a shoe with a thick wooden sole.
2 an encumbrance or impediment: *a clog in the system.*
▶ **v.** (**clogs, clogging, clogged**) block or become blocked with an accumulation of thick, wet matter: [with obj.] *the gutters were clogged up with leaves* | (as adj. **clogged**) *clogged drains* | [no obj.] *too much fatty food makes your arteries clog up.* ■ [with obj.] fill up or crowd (something) so as to obstruct passage: *tourists clog the roads in summer.*
– ORIGIN Middle English (in the sense 'block of wood to impede an animal's movement'): of unknown origin.

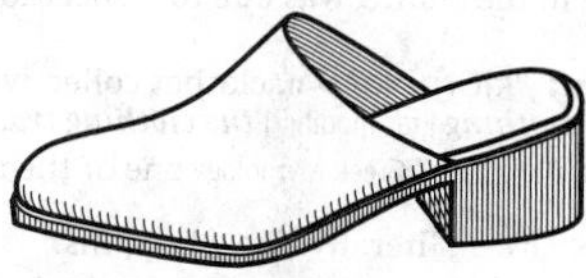
clog 1

clog dance ▶ **n.** a dance performed in clogs with rhythmic beating of the feet, esp. as a traditional dance in Ireland, Scotland, and the north of England. ■ a North American country tap dance of similar style.
– DERIVATIVES **clog danc·er** **n.**, **clog danc·ing** **n.**

clog·ger /ˈklägər, ˈklôgər/ ▶ **n.** **1** a person or thing that clogs something: *pore-cloggers.*
2 a person who performs a clog dance.

clog·ging /ˈkläging, ˈklôg-/ ▶ **n.** clog dancing.

cloi·son·né /ˌkloizəˈnā, ˌklwäz-/ ▶ **n.** decorative work in which enamel, glass, or gemstones are separated by strips of flattened wire placed edgeways on a metal backing.
– ORIGIN mid 19th cent.: French, literally 'partitioned,' past participle of *cloisonner*, from *cloison* 'a partition or division.'

clois·ter /ˈkloistər/ ▶ **n.** a covered walk in a convent, monastery, college, or cathedral, typically with a wall on one side and a colonnade open to a quadrangle on the other. ■ (**the cloister**) monastic life: *he was inclined more to the cloister than the sword.* ■ a convent or monastery.
▶ **v.** [with obj.] seclude or shut up in or as if in a convent or monastery: *the monastery was where the Brothers would cloister themselves to meditate* | *she cloisters herself at home.*
– DERIVATIVES **clois·tral** /ˈkloistrəl/ **adj.**
– ORIGIN Middle English (in the sense 'place of religious seclusion'): from Old French *cloistre*, from Latin *claustrum, clostrum* 'lock, enclosed place,' from *claudere* 'to close.'

cloister

clois·tered /ˈkloistərd/ ▶ **adj.** **1** kept away from the outside world; sheltered: *a cloistered upbringing.*
2 having or enclosed by a cloister, as in a monastery: *a cloistered walkway bordered the courtyard.*

clomb /klōm/ archaic past and past participle of CLIMB.

clom·i·phene /ˈkläməˌfēn, ˈklō-/ ▶ **n.** Medicine a synthetic nonsteroidal drug used to treat infertility in women by stimulating ovulation.

clomp /klämp, klômp/ ▶ **v.** [no obj.] walk with a heavy tread: *she clomped down the steps.*
– ORIGIN early 19th cent.: imitative; compare with CLUMP.

clon·al·i·ty /klōˈnalitē/ ▶ **n.** the fact or condition of being genetically identical, as to a parent, sibling, or other biological source: *the lack of genetic diversity may be a combination of both isolation and clonality.*

clone /klōn/ ▶ **n.** Biology an organism or cell, or group of organisms or cells, produced asexually from one ancestor or stock, to which they are genetically identical. ■ a person or thing regarded as identical to another: *successful women don't want to be male clones.* ■ a computer designed to simulate exactly the operation of another, typically more expensive, model: *an IBM PC clone.*
▶ **v.** [with obj.] propagate (an organism or cell) as a clone: *of the hundreds of new plants cloned, the best ones are selected.* ■ make an identical copy of. ■ Biochemistry replicate (a fragment of DNA placed in an organism) so that there is enough to analyze or use in protein production. ■ illegally copy the security codes from (a cellular phone) to one or more others as a way of obtaining free calls.
– DERIVATIVES **clon·al** /ˈklōnl/ **adj.**
– ORIGIN early 20th cent.: from Greek *klōn* 'twig.'

clonk /klängk, klôngk/ ▶ **n.** [in sing.] an abrupt, heavy sound of impact.
▶ **v.** **1** [no obj.] move with or make such a sound: *the horses clonked and snorted softly.*
2 [with obj.] informal hit: *I'll clonk you on the head.*
– DERIVATIVES **clonk·y** **adj.**
– ORIGIN mid 19th cent.: imitative.

clo·nus /ˈklōnəs/ ▶ **n.** Medicine muscular spasm involving repeated, often rhythmic, contractions.
– DERIVATIVES **clon·ic** /ˈklänik/ **adj.**
– ORIGIN early 19th cent.: from Greek *klonos* 'turmoil.'

clop /kläp/ ▶ **n.** [in sing.] a sound or series of sounds made by a horse's hooves on a hard surface.
▶ **v.** (**clops, clopping, clopped**) [no obj.] (of a horse) move with such a sound: *the animal clopped on at a steady pace.*
– ORIGIN mid 19th cent.: imitative.

clo·qué /klōˈkā/ ▶ **n.** a fabric with an irregularly raised or embossed surface.
– ORIGIN French, literally 'blistered.' It was first recorded (1920s) in the anglicized form *cloky*; use of the French form dates from the 1950s.

close¹ /klōs/ ▶ **adj.** **1** a short distance away or apart in space or time: *the hotel is **close to** the sea* | *her birthday and her wedding date were **close together*** | *the months of living **in close proximity to** her were taking their toll.* ■ with very little or no space in between; dense: *cloth with a closer weave* | *this work occupies over 1,300 pages of close print.* ■ narrowly enclosed: *animals in close confinement.* ■ [predic.] (**close to**) very near to (being or doing something): *on a good day the climate in LA is close to perfection* | *she was close to tears.* ■ (with reference to a competitive situation) won or likely to be won by only a small amount or distance: *the race will be a close contest* | *she finished a close second.* ■ Phonetics another term for HIGH (sense 7 of the adjective).
2 [attrib.] denoting a family member who is part of a person's immediate family, typically a parent or sibling: *the family history of cancer in close relatives.* ■ (of a person or relationship) on very affectionate or intimate terms: *they had always been very close, with no secrets at all.* ■ (of a connection or resemblance) strong: *the college has close links with many other institutions.*
3 (of observation, examination, etc.) done in a careful and thorough way: *we need to **keep a close eye on** this project* | ***pay close attention to** what your body is telling you about yourself.* ■ carefully guarded: *his whereabouts are a close secret.* ■ not willing to give away money or information; secretive: *you're very close about your work, aren't you?*
4 uncomfortably humid or airless: *a close, hazy day* | *it was very close in the dressing room.*
▶ **adv.** in a position so as to be very near to someone or something; with very little space between: *they stood close to the door* | *he was holding her close.*
– PHRASES **close by** very near; nearby: *her father lives quite close by.* **close to** (or **close on**) (of an amount) almost; very nearly: *he spent close to 30 years in jail.* **close to the bone** see BONE. **close to one's heart** see HEART. **close to home** see HOME. **close up** very near: *close up she was no less pretty.* **close to the wind** Sailing (of a sailing vessel) pointed as near as possible to the direction from which the wind is blowing while still making headway. **come close** almost achieve or do: *he came close to calling the President a liar.* **too close for comfort** dangerously or uncomfortably near: *the friendly stranger who suddenly comes too close for comfort.*
– DERIVATIVES **close·ly** **adv.**, **close·ness** **n.**, **clos·ish** **adj.**
– ORIGIN Middle English: from Old French *clos* (as noun and adjective), from Latin *clausum* 'enclosure' and *clausus* 'closed,' past participle of *claudere.*

close² /klōz/ ▶ **v.** **1** move or cause to move so as to cover an opening: [no obj.] *she jumped into the train just as the doors were closing* | [with obj.] *they had to close the window because of the insects.* ■ [with obj.] block up (a hole or opening): *glass doors close off the living room from the hall* | figurative *Stephen closed his ears to the sound.* ■ [with obj.] bring two parts of (something) together so as to block its opening or bring it into a folded state: *Loretta closed her mouth* | *Ron closed the book.* ■ [no obj.] gradually get nearer to someone or something: *they plotted a large group of aircraft about 130 miles away and closing fast.* ■ [no obj.] (**close around/over**) come into contact with (something) so as to encircle and hold it: *my fist closed around the weapon.* ■ [with obj.] make (an electric circuit) continuous: *this will cause a relay to operate and close the circuit.*
2 bring or come to an end: [with obj.] *the members were thanked for attending, and the meeting was closed* | [no obj.] *the concert closed with "Silent Night"* | (as adj. **closing**) *the closing stages of the election campaign.* ■ [no obj.] (of a business, organization, or institution) cease to be in operation or accessible to the public, either permanently or at the end of a working day or other period of time: *the factory is to close with the loss of 150 jobs* | [with obj.] *the country has been closed to outsiders for almost 50 years.* ■ [no obj.] finish speaking or writing: *we close with a point about truth* | (as adj. **closing**) *Nellie's closing words.* ■ [with obj.] bring (a business transaction) to a satisfactory conclusion: *he closed a deal with a metal dealer.* ■ [with obj.] remove all the funds from (a bank account) and cease to use it. ■ [with obj.] Computing make (a data file) inaccessible after use, so that it is securely stored until required again.
▶ **n.** [in sing.] **1** the end of an event or of a period of time or activity: *the afternoon drew to a close.* ■ (**the close**) the end of a day's trading on a stock market: *at the close the Dow Jones average was down 13.52 points.* ■ Music the conclusion of a phrase; a cadence.
2 the shutting of something, esp. a door: *the door jerked to a close behind them.*
– PHRASES **close the door on** (or **to**) see DOOR. **close one's eyes to** see EYE. **close one's mind to** see MIND. **close ranks** see RANK¹. **close up shop** see SHOP.
– PHRASAL VERBS **close something down** (or **close down**) cause to cease or cease business or operation, esp. permanently: *the government promised to close down the nuclear plants within twenty years.* **close in (on)** come nearer to someone being pursued: *the police were closing in on them.* ■ gradually surround, esp. with the effect of hindering movement or vision: *the weather has now closed in, so an attempt on the summit is unlikely.* ■ (of days) get successively shorter with the approach of the winter solstice: *November was closing in.* **close something out** bring something to an end: *Steve tried to close out the conversation.* **close up** (of a person's face) become blank and emotionless or hostile: *he didn't like her laughter and his face closed up angrily.* **close something up** (or **close up**) **1** cause to cease or cease operation or being used: *the broker advised me to close the house up for the time being.* **2** (**close up**) (of an opening) grow smaller or become blocked by something: *she felt her throat close up.* **close with** come near, esp. so as to engage with (an enemy force).
– DERIVATIVES **clos·a·ble** **adj.**, **clos·er** **n.**
– ORIGIN Middle English: from Old French *clos-*, stem of *clore*, from Latin *claudere* 'to shut.'

close call /klōs/ ▶ **n.** a narrow escape from danger or disaster.

close-cropped /klōs/ (also **closely cropped**) ▶ **adj.** (typically of hair or grass) cut very short.

closed /klōzd/ ▶ **adj.** not open: *rooms with closed doors lined the hallway* | *he sat with his eyes closed.* ■ (of a business) having ceased trading, esp. for a short period: *he put the "Closed" sign up on the door.* ■ (of a society or system) not communicating with or influenced by others; independent. ■ limited to certain people; not open or available to all: *the UN*

Security Council met in closed session. ■ unwilling to accept new ideas: *you're facing the situation with a closed mind.* ■ Mathematics (of a set) having the property that the result of a specified operation on any element of the set is itself a member of the set. ■ Mathematics (of a set) containing all its limit points. ■ Geometry of or pertaining to a curve whose ends are joined.

– PHRASES **behind closed doors** taking place secretly or without public knowledge. **closed book** a subject or person about which one knows nothing: *accounting has always been a closed book to me.*

closed cap·tion ▶ **n.** one of a series of subtitles to a television program, accessible through a decoder.
▶ **v.** (**closed-caption**) (with obj. usually as noun **closed-captioning**) provide (a program) with closed captions.

closed chain ▶ **n.** Chemistry a number of atoms bonded together to form a closed loop in a molecule.

closed-cir·cuit tel·e·vi·sion (abbr.: **CCTV**) ▶ **n.** a television system in which the video signals are transmitted from one or more cameras by cable to a restricted set of monitors.

closed cou·plet ▶ **n.** a rhyming couplet with end-stopped lines that is logically or grammatically complete, as "Instruct the planets in what orbs to run,/Correct old Time, and regulate the Sun."

closed-door ▶ **adj.** restricted; obstructive; secret: *the senior staff went into closed-door sessions.*

closed-end ▶ **adj.** having a predetermined and fixed extent: *a closed-end contract.* ■ denoting an investment trust or company that issues a fixed number of shares.

closed sea·son ▶ **n.** a period between specified dates when fishing or the killing of particular game is officially forbidden.

closed shop ▶ **n.** a place of work where membership in a union is a condition for being hired and for continued employment. Compare with OPEN SHOP, UNION SHOP. ■ [in sing.] a system whereby such an arrangement applies: *the outlawing of the closed shop.*

closed u·ni·verse ▶ **n.** Astronomy the condition in which there is sufficient matter in the universe to halt the expansion driven by the Big Bang and cause eventual recollapse. The amount of visible matter is only a tenth of the total required for closure, but there may be large quantities of dark matter.

close en·coun·ter /'klōs/ ▶ **n.** a supposed encounter with a UFO or with aliens.
– PHRASES **close encounter of the first** (or **second**, etc.) **kind** used to describe encounters involving increasing degrees of complexity and apparent exposure of the witness to aliens, with the first kind being a mere sighting and the fourth kind being abduction.

close-fist·ed /klōs/ ▶ **adj.** unwilling to spend money; stingy.

close-fit·ting /klōs/ ▶ **adj.** (of a garment) fitting tightly and showing the contours of the body.

close-grained /klōs/ ▶ **adj.** (of wood, stone, or other material) having tightly packed fibers, crystals, or other structural elements.

close har·mo·ny /klōs/ ▶ **n.** Music harmony in which the notes of the chord are close together, typically in vocal music.

close-hauled /klōs/ ▶ **adj. & adv.** Sailing (of a ship) close to the wind.

close-in /klōs/ ▶ **adj.** only a short distance away: *a close-in shot.* ■ near to the center of a town or city: *close-in parking.*

close-knit /klōs/ ▶ **adj.** (of a group of people) united or bound together by strong relationships and common interests: *a close-knit community.*

close-mouthed /klōs 'mouTHd, 'mouTHt, klōz-/ (also **close-lipped**) ▶ **adj.** reticent; discreet: *the candidates have been close-mouthed about their fund-raising goals.*

close·out /'klōzout/ ▶ **n.** [usu. as modifier] a sale of goods at reduced prices to get rid of superfluous stock: *a closeout sale | closeout prices.*

close quar·ters /klōs/ ▶ **plural n.** a situation of being very or uncomfortably close to someone or something: *living in close quarters with people | engaging the enemy at close quarters.*

clos·er /'klōzər/ ▶ **n.** Baseball a relief pitcher who specializes in pitching to the final batters of a game if the pitcher's team has the lead.

close range /klōs/ ▶ **n.** a short distance between someone or something and a target: *two bullets fired at close range | watching a bird at close range.*

close-ra·tio /klōs/ ▶ **adj.** (of a vehicle's gearbox) having gear ratios that are set at values not very different from each other.

close reach /klōs/ Sailing ▶ **n.** a point of sailing in which the wind blows from slightly forward of the beam: *we sailed on a close reach directly for Sharp's Island.*
▶ **v.** (**close-reach**) [no obj.] sail with the wind in this position.

close sea·son /klōz/ ▶ **n.** British term for CLOSED SEASON.

close-set /klōs/ ▶ **adj.** (of two or more things) placed or occurring with little space in between: *her eyes were too close-set for beauty.*

close shave /klōs/ ▶ **n. 1** a shave in which the hair is cut very short.
2 informal another term for CLOSE CALL.

clos·et /'kläzit/ ▶ **n. 1** a cupboard or wardrobe, esp. one tall enough to walk into. ■ a small room, esp. one used for storing things or for private study.
2 archaic a toilet.
3 (**the closet**) a state of secrecy or concealment, esp. about one's homosexuality: *lesbians who had come out of the closet.*
▶ **adj.** [attrib.] secret; covert: *a closet alcoholic.*
▶ **v.** (**closets, closeting, closeted**) [with obj.] shut (someone) away, esp. in private conference or study: *he was closeted with the king | he returned home and closeted himself in his room.*
– ORIGIN late Middle English (denoting a private or small room): from Old French, diminutive of *clos* 'closed' (see CLOSE[1]).

clos·et dra·ma (also **closet play**) ▶ **n.** a play to be read rather than acted.

close-up /'klōs,əp/ ▶ **n.** a photograph, movie, or video taken at close range and showing the subject on a large scale: *a close-up of her face | they see themselves in close-up* | [as modifier] *a close-up view.* ■ an intimate and detailed description or study: [as modifier] *the book's close-up account of the violence.*

clos·ing date ▶ **n.** the last date by which something must be submitted for consideration, esp. a job application.

clos·ing price ▶ **n.** the price of a security at the end of the day's business in a financial market.

clos·ing time ▶ **n.** the regular time at which a restaurant, store, or other place closes to the public each day.

clos·trid·i·um /klä'strideəm/ ▶ **n.** (pl. **clostridia** /klä'strideə/) Biology an anaerobic bacterium of a large genus that includes many pathogenic species, e.g., those causing tetanus, gas gangrene, botulism, and other forms of food poisoning. ● Genus *Clostridium*: typically rod-shaped and Gram-positive.
– DERIVATIVES **clos·trid·i·al** /-'stridēəl/ **adj.**
– ORIGIN modern Latin, based on Greek *klōstēr* 'spindle.'

clo·sure /'klōZHər/ ▶ **n. 1** the act or process of closing something, esp. an institution, thoroughfare, or frontier, or of being closed: *hospitals that face closure | road closures.* ■ a thing that closes or seals something, such as a cap or zipper.
2 a sense of resolution or conclusion at the end of an artistic work: *he brings modernistic closure to his narrative.* ■ a feeling that an emotional or traumatic experience has been resolved: *I am desperately trying to reach closure but I don't know how to do it without answers from him.*
– ORIGIN late Middle English: from Old French, from late Latin *clausura*, from *claus-* 'closed,' from the verb *claudere*.

clot /klät/ ▶ **n. 1** a thick mass of coagulated liquid, esp. blood, or of material stuck together: *a flat, wet clot of dead leaves* | figurative *a clot of people arguing in the doorway.*
2 Brit. informal a foolish or clumsy person: *"Watch where you're going, you clot!"*
▶ **v.** (**clots, clotting, clotted**) form or cause to form into clots: [no obj.] *drugs that help blood to clot* | [with obj.] *a blood protein known as factor VIII clots blood.* ■ [with obj.] cover (something) with sticky matter: *its nostrils were clotted with blood.*
– ORIGIN Old English *clott, clot*, of Germanic origin; related to German *Klotz*.

clot·bur /'klät,bər/ ▶ **n.** a herbaceous plant of the daisy family, with burred fruits. It originated in tropical America but is now cosmopolitan. See also COCKLEBUR. ● Genus *Xanthium*, family Compositae: two or three species, in particular **spiny clotbur** (*X. spinosum*). ■ a burdock.
– ORIGIN mid 16th cent.: from dialect *clote* 'burdock' + BURR.

cloth /klôTH/ ▶ **n.** (pl. **cloths** /klôTHz, klôTHs/)
1 woven or felted fabric made from wool, cotton, or a similar fiber: *shelves covered with bright red cloth* | [as modifier] *a cloth bag.* ■ a piece of cloth for a particular purpose, such as a dishcloth or a tablecloth: *wipe clean with a damp cloth.*
2 (**the cloth**) the clergy; the clerical profession: *a man of the cloth.*
– ORIGIN Old English *clāth*, related to Dutch *kleed* and German *Kleid*, of unknown ultimate origin.

clothe /klōTH/ ▶ **v.** (past and past participle **clothed** or **clad** /klad/) [with obj.] (often **be clothed in**) put clothes on (oneself or someone); dress: *she was clothed all in white | she lay down fully clothed* | [as adj., with submodifier] (**clothed**) *a partially clothed body.* ■ provide (someone) with clothes: *they already had eight children to feed and clothe.* ■ (usu. **be clothed with**) endow with a particular quality: *you have been clothed with power from on high.*
– ORIGIN Old English (only recorded in the past participle *geclāded*), from *clāth* (see CLOTH).

clothes /klō(TH)z/ ▶ **plural n. 1** items worn to cover the body: *he stripped off his clothes | baby clothes* | [as modifier] *a clothes shop.*
2 bedclothes.
– ORIGIN Old English *clāthas*, plural of *clāth* (see CLOTH).

clothes horse ▶ **n.** a frame on which washed clothes are hung to air indoors. ■ informal, often derogatory a person, typically a woman, who is excessively concerned with wearing fashionable clothes.

clothes·line /'klō(TH)z,līn/ ▶ **n.** a rope or wire on which washed clothes are hung to dry.
▶ **v.** [with obj.] (chiefly in football and other games) knock down (a runner) by placing one's outstretched arm in the runner's path at neck level.

clothes moth ▶ **n.** a small, drab moth whose larvae feed on a range of animal fibers and can be destructive to clothing and other domestic textiles. ● Family Tineidae: several species, in particular the **common clothes moth** (*Tineola bisselliella*).

clothes·pin /'klō(TH)z,pin/ (Brit. also **clothes peg**) ▶ **n.** a wooden or plastic clip for securing clothes to a clothes line.

cloth·ier /'klōTHyər, -THēər/ ▶ **n.** a person or company that makes, sells, or deals in clothes or cloth.
– ORIGIN Middle English *clother*, from CLOTH. The change in the ending was due to association with -IER.

cloth·ing /'klōTHiNG/ ▶ **n.** clothes collectively: *an item of clothing* | [as modifier] *the clothing trade.*

Clo·tho /'klōTHō/ Greek Mythology one of the three Fates.
– ORIGIN Greek, literally 'she who spins.'

cloth of gold ▶ **n.** fabric made of gold threads interwoven with silk or wool.

cloth yard ▶ **n.** a unit for measuring cloth, formerly 37 inches but now equivalent to a standard yard (36 inches).

clot·ted cream ▶ **n.** chiefly Brit. thick cream obtained by heating milk slowly and then allowing it to cool while the cream content rises to the top in coagulated lumps.

clot·ting fac·tor ▶ **n.** Physiology any of a number of substances in blood plasma that are involved in the clotting process, such as factor VIII.

clo·ture /'klōCHər/ ▶ **n.** (in a legislative assembly) a procedure for ending a debate and taking a vote: [as modifier] *a cloture motion.*
– ORIGIN late 19th cent.: from French *clôture*, from Old French *closure* (see CLOSURE).

cloud /kloud/ ▶ **n. 1** a visible mass of condensed water vapor floating in the atmosphere, typically high above the ground: *the sun had disappeared behind a cloud | the full moon, hidden by veils of cloud.* ■ an indistinct or billowing mass, esp. of smoke or dust: *a cloud of dust.* ■ a large number of insects or birds moving together: *clouds of orange butterflies.* ■ a vague patch of color in or on a liquid or transparent surface.
2 a state or cause of gloom, suspicion, trouble, or worry: *the only cloud to appear on the horizon was Leopold's unexpected illness | a black cloud hung over their lives.* ■ a frowning or depressed look: *a cloud passed over Jessica's face.*
▶ **v. 1** [no obj.] (of the sky) become overcast with clouds: *the blue skies clouded over abruptly.* ■ [with obj.] darken (the sky) with clouds: *the western sky was still clouded.*
2 make or become less clear or transparent: [with obj.] *blood pumped out, clouding the water* | [no obj.] *her eyes clouded with tears.* ■ [with obj.] make (a matter or mental process) unclear or uncertain; confuse: *don't allow your personal feelings to cloud your judgment.* ■ [with obj.] spoil or mar (something): *the general election was clouded by violence.*
3 [no obj.] (of someone's face or eyes) show worry, sorrow, or anger: *his expression clouded over.* ■ [with obj.] (of such an emotion) show in (someone's face): *suspicion clouded her face.*
– PHRASES **every cloud has a silver lining** see SILVER. **have one's head in the clouds** (of a person) be out of touch with reality; be daydreaming. **in the clouds** out of touch with reality: *this clergyman*

was in the clouds. **on cloud nine** extremely happy. [with reference to a ten-part classification of clouds in which "nine" was the next to the highest.] **under a cloud** under suspicion; discredited: *he left under something of a cloud, accused of misappropriating funds.*
– DERIVATIVES **cloud·less** adj., **cloud·less·ly** adv., **cloud·let** /-lət/ n.
– ORIGIN Old English *clūd* 'mass of rock or earth'; probably related to CLOT. Sense 1 of the noun dates from Middle English.

cloud base ▶ n. [in sing.] the level or altitude of the lowest part of a general mass of clouds.

cloud·ber·ry /ˈkloud,berē/ ▶ n. (pl. **cloudberries**) a dwarf bramble that has white flowers and edible orange fruit and that grows on the mountains and moorlands of northern Eurasia and northern North America. ● *Rubus chamaemorus*, family Rosaceae.
– ORIGIN late 16th cent.: apparently from the noun CLOUD in the obsolete sense 'hill' + BERRY.

cloud·burst /ˈkloud,bərst/ ▶ n. a sudden, violent rainstorm.

cloud cham·ber ▶ n. Physics a device that contains air or gas supersaturated with water vapor and that is used to detect charged particles, X-rays, and gamma rays by the condensation trails that they produce.

cloud com·put·ing ▶ n. the practice of using a network of remote servers hosted on the Internet to store, manage, and process data, rather than a local server or a personal computer.

cloud cov·er ▶ n. [in sing.] a mass of cloud covering all or most of the sky.

cloud deck ▶ n. Meteorology a bank of clouds of a particular type forming a layer at a certain altitude.

cloud·ed leop·ard ▶ n. a large spotted cat that hunts in trees at twilight and is found in forests in Southeast Asia. ● *Neofelis nebulosa*, family Felidae.

cloud hop·ping ▶ n. the flying of an aircraft from cloud to cloud, typically for concealment.

cloud·scape /ˈkloud,skāp/ ▶ n. a large cloud formation considered in terms of its visual effect.
– ORIGIN mid 19th cent.: from the noun CLOUD, on the pattern of words such as *landscape*.

cloud seed·ing ▶ n. the dropping of crystals into clouds to cause rain.

cloud·y /ˈkloudē/ ▶ adj. (**cloudier**, **cloudiest**) **1** (of the sky or weather) covered with or characterized by clouds; overcast: *next morning was cloudy.*
2 (of a liquid) not transparent or clear: *the pond water is slightly cloudy.* ■ (of a color) opaque; having white as a constituent: *cloudy reds and blues and greens.* ■ (of marble) variegated with cloudlike markings. ■ (of someone's eyes) misted with tears: *she stared at him, her eyes cloudy.* ■ uncertain; unclear: *the issue becomes more cloudy.*
– DERIVATIVES **cloud·i·ly** /ˈkloudl-ē/ adv., **cloud·i·ness** n.

Clou·et /klo͞oˈā, klo͞oˈe/ two French court portrait painters, **Jean** (*c.*1485–1541) and his son **François** (*c.*1516–72).

clout /klout/ ▶ n. **1** informal a heavy blow with the hand or a hard object: *a clout on the ear.*
2 informal influence or power, esp. in politics or business: *I knew he carried a lot of clout.*
3 archaic a piece of cloth or clothing, esp. one used as a patch.
4 Archery a target used in long-distance shooting, placed flat on the ground with a flag marking its center. ■ a shot that hits such a target.
▶ v. [with obj.] **1** informal hit hard with the hand or a hard object: *I clouted him on the head.*
2 archaic mend with a patch.
– ORIGIN Old English *clūt* (in the sense 'a patch or metal plate'); related to Dutch *kluit* 'lump, clod,' also to CLEAT and CLOT. The shift of sense to 'heavy blow,' which dates from late Middle English, is difficult to explain; possibly the change occurred first in the verb (from 'put a patch on' to 'hit hard').

clove[1] /klōv/ ▶ n. **1** the dried flower bud of a tropical tree, used as a pungent aromatic spice: *a teaspoon of ground cloves.* ■ (**oil of cloves**) aromatic analgesic oil extracted from these buds and used medicinally, esp. for the relief of dental pain.
2 the Indonesian tree from which these buds are obtained. ● *Syzygium aromaticum* (also called *Eugenia caryophyllus*), family Myrtaceae.
3 (also **clove pink**) a clove-scented pink that is the original type from which the carnation and other double pinks have been bred. ● *Dianthus caryophyllus*, family Caryophyllaceae.
– ORIGIN Middle English: from Old French *clou de girofle*, literally 'nail of gillyflower' (from its shape), GILLYFLOWER being originally the name of the spice and later applied to the similarly scented pink.

clove[2] ▶ n. any of the small bulbs making up a compound bulb of garlic, shallot, etc.
– ORIGIN Old English *clufu*, of Germanic origin, corresponding to the first element of German *Knoblauch* (altered from Old High German *klovolouh*), and the base of CLEAVE[1].

clove[3] past of CLEAVE[1].

clove hitch ▶ n. a knot by which a rope is secured by passing it twice around a spar or another rope that it crosses at right angles in such a way that both ends pass under the loop of rope at the front.
– ORIGIN mid 18th cent.: *clove*, past tense of CLEAVE[1] (because the rope appears as separate parallel lines at the back of the knot).

clo·ven /ˈklōvən/ past participle of CLEAVE[1].
▶ adj. split or divided in two.

clo·ven hoof (also **cloven foot**) ▶ n. the divided hoof or foot of ruminants such as cattle, sheep, goats, antelopes, and deer. ■ a similar foot ascribed to a satyr, the god Pan, or to the Devil, sometimes used as a symbol or mark of the Devil.
– DERIVATIVES **clo·ven-hoofed** adj., **clo·ven-foot·ed** adj.

clove pink ▶ n. see CLOVE[1] (sense 3).

clo·ver /ˈklōvər/ ▶ n. a herbaceous plant of the pea family that has dense, globular flower heads, and leaves that are typically three-lobed. It is an important and widely grown fodder and rotational crop. ● Genus *Trifolium*, family Leguminosae: many species, in particular **red clover** (*T. pratense*) and the creeping **white clover** (*T. repens*).
– PHRASES **in clover** in ease and luxury: *we'll be in clover down there, lying around in the sun and fishing on the lake.*
– ORIGIN Old English *clāfre*, of Germanic origin; related to Dutch *klaver* and German *Klee*.

clo·ver·leaf /ˈklōvər,lēf/ ▶ n. a shape or pattern resembling a leaf of clover: [as modifier] *cloverleaf rolls.* ■ a junction of roads intersecting at different levels with connecting sections forming the pattern of a four-leaf clover.

Clo·vis[1] /ˈklōvis/ **1** a city in central California, in the San Joaquin Valley, northeast of Fresno; pop. 92,318 (est. 2008).
2 an agricultural city in eastern New Mexico; pop. 32,352 (est. 2008). The Clovis culture of 11,000 years ago is named for artifacts found nearby.

Clo·vis[2] (465–511), king of the Franks 481–511. He extended Merovingian rule to Gaul and Germany, making Paris his capital. After his conversion to Christianity, he championed orthodoxy against the Arian Visigoths, finally defeating them in the battle of Poitiers 507.

Clo·vis[3] ▶ n. [usu. as modifier] Archaeology a Paleo-Indian culture of Central and North America, dated to about 11,500–11,000 years ago and earlier. The culture is distinguished by heavy, leaf-shaped stone spearheads. Compare with FOLSOM[2].
– ORIGIN first found near CLOVIS[1], New Mexico.

clown /kloun/ ▶ n. **1** a comic entertainer, esp. one in a circus, wearing a traditional costume and exaggerated makeup. ■ a comical, silly, playful person: *I was always the class clown.* ■ a foolish or incompetent person: *we need a serious government, not a bunch of clowns.*
2 archaic an unsophisticated country person; a rustic.
▶ v. [no obj.] behave in a comical way; act playfully: *Harvey **clowned around** pretending to be a dog.*
– DERIVATIVES **clown·ish** adj., **clown·ish·ly** adv., **clown·ish·ness** n.
– ORIGIN mid 16th cent. (sense 2 of the noun): perhaps of Low German origin.

clown·fish /ˈkloun,fisн/ ▶ n. (pl. **same** or **clownfishes**) a small, tropical marine fish with bold vertical stripes or other bright coloration. It lives in close association with anemones and is protected from their stings by mucus. Also called ANEMONE FISH. ● Genera *Amphiprion* and *Premnas*, family Pomacentridae: several species, including *A. percula*.

cloy /kloi/ ▶ v. [with obj.] (usu. as adj. **cloying**) disgust or sicken (someone) with an excess of sweetness, richness, or sentiment: *a romantic, rather cloying story* | *a curious bittersweetness that cloyed her senses* | [no obj.] *the first long sip gives a malty taste that never cloys.*
– DERIVATIVES **cloy·ing·ly** adv.
– ORIGIN late Middle English: shortening of obsolete *accloy* 'stop up, choke,' from Old French *encloyer* 'drive a nail into,' from medieval Latin *inclavare*, from *clavus* 'a nail.'

clo·za·pine /ˈklōzə,pēn/ ▶ n. Medicine a sedative drug of the benzodiazepine group, used to treat schizophrenia.
– ORIGIN mid 20th cent.: from *c(h)lo(ro)-* + elements of BENZODIAZEPINE.

cloze test /klōz/ ▶ n. a test in which one is asked to supply words that have been removed from a passage in order to measure one's ability to comprehend text.
– ORIGIN 1950s: *cloze* representing a spoken abbreviation of CLOSURE.

CLU ▶ abbr. Civil Liberties Union.

club[1] /kləb/ ▶ n. [treated as sing. or pl.] an association or organization dedicated to a particular interest or activity: *a photography club* | [as modifier] *the club secretary.* ■ the building or facilities used by such an association. ■ an organization or facility offering members social amenities, meals, and temporary residence: *we had dinner at his club.* ■ a nightclub, esp. one playing fashionable dance music. ■ [treated as sing. or pl.] an organization constituted to play games in a particular sport: *a football club* | [as modifier] *the club captain.* ■ [usu. with modifier] a commercial organization offering subscribers special benefits: *a shopping club.* ■ [with adj. or noun modifier] a group of people, organizations, or nations having something in common: *in cocktail lounges all over town convenes the daily meeting of the ain't-it-awful club.*
▶ v. (**clubs**, **clubbing**, **clubbed**) [no obj.] informal go out to nightclubs: *she enjoys **going clubbing** in Orlando.*
– PHRASES **join the club** [in imperative] informal, often humorous used as an observation that someone else is in a difficult or unwelcome situation similar to one's own: *if you're confused, join the club!*
– ORIGIN early 17th cent. (as a verb): formed obscurely from CLUB[2].

club[2] ▶ n. **1** a heavy stick with a thick end, esp. one used as a weapon. ■ short for GOLF CLUB.
2 (**clubs**) one of the four suits in a conventional pack of playing cards, denoted by a black trefoil. ■ a card of such a suit.
▶ v. (**clubs**, **clubbing**, **clubbed**) [with obj.] beat (a person or animal) with a club or similar implement: *the islanders clubbed whales to death.*
– ORIGIN Middle English: from Old Norse *clubba*, variant of *klumba*; related to CLUMP.

club·ba·ble /ˈkləbəbəl/ ▶ adj. suitable for membership of a club because of one's sociability or popularity.
– DERIVATIVES **club·ba·bil·i·ty** /,kləbəˈbilətē/ n.

club·by /ˈkləbē/ ▶ adj. (**clubbier**, **clubbiest**) informal friendly and sociable with fellow members of a group or organization but not with outsiders.

club car ▶ n. a railroad car equipped with a lounge and other amenities.

club chair ▶ n. a thickly upholstered armchair of the type often found in clubs.

club face ▶ n. the side of the head of a golf club that strikes the ball.

club foot ▶ n. **1** a deformed foot that is twisted so that the sole cannot be placed flat on the ground. It is typically congenital or a result of polio. Also called TALIPES.
2 a woodland toadstool with a grayish-brown cap, primrose-yellow gills, and a stem with a swollen woolly base, found in both Eurasia and North America. ● *Clitocybe clavipes*, family Tricholomataceae, class Basidiomycetes.
– DERIVATIVES **club-foot·ed** adj.

club·house /ˈkləb,hous/ ▶ n. a building having a bar and other facilities for the members of a club. ■ a building or part of a building used by a sports team, esp. a baseball team, as a locker room.

club·land /ˈkləb,land/ ▶ n. the world of nightclubs and of people who frequent them.

club·man /ˈkləbmən, -,man/ ▶ n. (pl. **clubmen**) a man who is a member of one or more clubs, esp. a member of a gentleman's club.

club moss (also **clubmoss**) ▶ n. a low-growing green plant that resembles a large moss, having branching stems with undivided leaves. Relatives of the club mosses were the first plants to colonize the land during the Silurian period. ● Class Lycopodiopsida, phylum Lycopodiophyta: one living family, Lycopodiaceae.

club·root /ˈkləb,ro͞ot, -,ro͝ot/ ▶ n. a fungal disease of cabbages, turnips, and related plants, in which the root becomes swollen and distorted by a single large gall or groups of smaller galls. ● The fungus is *Plasmodiophora brassicae*, phylum Plasmodiophoromycota.

club sand·wich ▶ n. a sandwich of meat (usually chicken and bacon), tomato, lettuce, and mayonnaise, with two layers of filling between three slices of toast or bread.

club so·da ▶ n. trademark another term for SODA (sense 1).

club steak ▶ n. another term for DELMONICO STEAK.

C

cluck /klək/ ▶ **n.** **1** the characteristic short, guttural sound made by a hen. ■ a similar sound made by a person to express annoyance: *Loretta gave a cluck of impatience.*
2 informal a stupid or foolish person: *a cluck too lazy to put up a clothesline.*
▶ **v.** (also **cluck-cluck**) [no obj.] (of a hen) make a short, guttural sound. ■ (of a person) make such a sound with one's tongue to express concern or disapproval: *the bystanders shook their heads and clucked sympathetically* | [with obj.] *Michael clucked his tongue irritably.* ■ [no obj.] (**cluck over/at/about**) express fussy concern about: *they were cluck-clucking over the dishonor he brought to the office.*
– ORIGIN late 15th cent. (as a verb): imitative, corresponding to Danish *klukke*, Swedish *klucka*.

clue /klo͞o/ ▶ **n.** **1** a piece of evidence or information used in the detection of a crime or solving of a mystery: *police officers are still searching for clues.* ■ a fact or idea that serves as a guide or aid in a task or problem: *archaeological evidence can give clues about the past.*
2 a verbal formula giving an indication as to what is to be inserted in a particular space in a crossword or other puzzle.
▶ **v.** (**clues, clueing, clued**) [with obj.] (**clue someone in**) informal inform someone about a particular matter: *Stella had clued her in about Peter.*
– PHRASES **not have a clue** informal know nothing about something or about how to do something.
– ORIGIN late Middle English: variant of CLEW. The original sense was 'a ball of thread'; hence one used to guide a person out of a labyrinth (literally or figuratively). Sense 1 of the noun dates from the early 17th cent.

clued-in ▶ **adj.** informal well-informed about a particular subject.

clue·ful /ˈklo͞ofəl/ ▶ **adj.** informal well-informed; competently intelligent: *clueful implementers are aware of the issues and are looking out for you.*

clue·less /ˈklo͞oləs/ ▶ **adj.** informal having no knowledge, understanding, or ability: *you're clueless about how to deal with the world.*
– DERIVATIVES **clue·less·ly** adv., **clue·less·ness** n.

Cluj–Na·po·ca /ˈklo͞ozʜ ˈnäpōkə, näˈpōkə/ a city in western central Romania; pop. 305,620 (2006). The name was changed from Cluj in the mid 1970s to incorporate the name of a nearby ancient settlement. Hungarian name KOLOZSVÁR; original name KLAUSENBURG.

Clum·ber span·iel /ˈkləmbər/ ▶ **n.** a spaniel of a slow, heavily built breed.
– ORIGIN mid 19th cent.: from the name of *Clumber* Park, an estate in Nottinghamshire, England.

clump /kləmp/ ▶ **n.** **1** a compacted mass or lump of something: ***clumps of** earth.* ■ a small, compact group of people: *they sat on the wall in **clumps of** two and three.* ■ a small group of trees or plants growing closely together: ***a clump of** ferns.* ■ Physiology an agglutinated mass of blood cells or bacteria, esp. as an indicator of the presence of an antibody to them.
2 a thick extra sole on a boot or shoe.
3 the sound of heavy footsteps.
▶ **v.** [no obj.] **1** form into a clump or mass: *the particles tend to **clump together**.*
2 (also **clomp**) walk with a heavy tread.
– ORIGIN Middle English (denoting a heap or lump): partly imitative, reinforced by Middle Low German *klumpe* and Middle Dutch *klompe*; related to CLUB[2].

clump·y /ˈkləmpē/ ▶ **adj.** (**clumpier, clumpiest**)
1 (of shoes or boots) heavy and inelegant.
2 forming or showing a tendency to form clumps.

clum·sy /ˈkləmzē/ ▶ **adj.** (**clumsier, clumsiest**) awkward in movement or in handling things: *a terribly clumsy fellow* | *the cold made his fingers clumsy.* ■ done awkwardly or without skill or elegance: *a clumsy attempt to park* | *a clumsy remake of an old movie.* ■ difficult to handle or use; unwieldy: *chairs with clumsy wooden armrests* | *the legal procedure is far too clumsy.* ■ lacking social skills and graces: *his choice of words was clumsy.*
– DERIVATIVES **clum·si·ly** /-zəlē/ adv., **clum·si·ness** n.
– ORIGIN late 16th cent.: from obsolete *clumse* 'make numb, be numb,' probably of Scandinavian origin and related to Swedish *klumsig.*

clung /kləNG/ past and past participle of CLING.

Clu·ni·ac /ˈklo͞onēˌak/ ▶ **adj.** of or relating to a reformed Benedictine monastic order founded at Cluny in eastern France in 910.
▶ **n.** a monk of this order.

clunk /kləNGk/ ▶ **n.** **1** a heavy, dull sound such as that made by thick pieces of metal striking together.
2 informal a stupid or foolish person.
▶ **v.** [no obj.] move with or make such a sound: *the machinery clunked into life.*
– ORIGIN late 18th cent. (originally Scots, as a verb): imitative; compare with CLANK, CLINK[1], and CLONK.

clunk·er /ˈkləNGkər/ ▶ **n.** informal an old, run-down vehicle or machine. ■ a thing that is totally unsuccessful: *novel after novel and not a clunker among them.*

clunk·y /ˈkləNGkē/ ▶ **adj.** (**clunkier, clunkiest**) informal
1 awkwardly solid, heavy, and outdated: *even last year's laptops look clunky* | *clunky brown shoes* | figurative *surprisingly clunky comedy.*
2 making a clunking sound: *clunky conveyor belts.*

clu·pe·oid /ˈklo͞opēˌoid/ Zoology ▶ **n.** a marine fish of a group that includes the herring family together with the anchovies and related fish. ● Order Clupeiformes or suborder Clupeoidei.
▶ **adj.** of or relating to fish of this group.
– ORIGIN mid 19th cent.: from modern Latin *Clupeoidei* (plural), from Latin *clupea*, the name of a river fish.

clus·ter /ˈkləstər/ ▶ **n.** a group of similar things or people positioned or occurring closely together: ***clusters of** creamy-white flowers* | ***a cluster of** antique shops.* ■ Astronomy a group of stars or galaxies forming a relatively close association. ■ Linguistics (also **consonant cluster**) a group of consonants pronounced in immediate succession, as *str* in *strong.* ■ a natural subgroup of a population, used for statistical sampling or analysis. ■ Chemistry a group of atoms of the same element, typically a metal, bonded closely together in a molecule.
▶ **v.** [no obj.] be or come into a cluster or close group; congregate: *the children **clustered around** her skirts.* ■ Statistics (of data points) have similar numerical values: *students tended to have scores clustering around 70 percent.*
– ORIGIN Old English *clyster*; probably related to CLOT.

clus·ter bean ▶ **n.** another term for GUAR.

clus·ter bomb ▶ **n.** a bomb that releases a number of projectiles on impact to injure or damage personnel and vehicles.

clus·tered /ˈkləstərd/ ▶ **adj.** [attrib.] growing or situated in a group: *the spires and clustered roofs of the old town.* ■ Architecture (of pillars, columns, or shafts) positioned close together, or disposed around or half-detached from a pier.

clus·ter fly ▶ **n.** a fly that often enters buildings in large numbers during the autumn while looking for a place to overwinter. ● *Pollenia rudis* (family Calliphoridae), whose larvae parasitize earthworms, and the smaller *Thaumatomyia notata* (family Chloropidae).

clus·ter head·ache ▶ **n.** a type of severe headache that tends to recur over a period of several weeks and in which the pain is usually limited to one side of the head.

clutch[1] /kləCH/ ▶ **v.** [with obj.] grasp or seize (something) tightly or eagerly: *he stood clutching a microphone* | [no obj.] figurative *Mrs. Longhill clutched at the idea.* ■ (also Brit. **clutch up**) become nervous and panicked: *doctors could clutch up and lose control as easily as anyone.*
▶ **n.** **1** a tight grasp or an act of grasping something: *she made a clutch at his body.* ■ (**someone's clutches**) a person's power or control, esp. when perceived as cruel or inescapable: *she escaped the clutches of her temperamental family.*
2 a slim, flat handbag without handles or a strap.
3 (**the clutch**) an emergency or critical moment: *he came through for us in the clutch* | [as modifier] *they were among the best clutch hitters in baseball.*
4 a mechanism for connecting and disconnecting a vehicle engine from its transmission system. ■ the pedal operating such a mechanism.
– PHRASES **clutch at straws** see STRAW.
– ORIGIN Middle English (in the sense 'bend, crook'): variant of obsolete *clitch* 'close the hand,' from Old English *clyccan* 'crook, clench,' of Germanic origin.

clutch[2] ▶ **n.** a group of eggs fertilized at the same time, typically laid in a single session and (in birds) incubated together. ■ a brood of chicks. ■ a small group of people or things: ***a clutch of** young girls on roller skates.*
– ORIGIN early 18th cent.: probably a southern variant of northern English dialect *cletch*, related to Middle English *cleck* 'to hatch,' from Old Norse *klekja.*

Clu·tha /ˈklo͞oTHə/ a gold-bearing river at the southern end of South Island, in New Zealand. It flows for 213 miles (338 km) to the Pacific Ocean.

clut·ter /ˈklətər/ ▶ **n.** a collection of things lying about in an untidy mass: *the attic is full of clutter.* ■ [in sing.] an untidy state: *the room was in a clutter of smelly untidiness.*
▶ **v.** [with obj.] crowd (something) untidily; fill with clutter: *his apartment was cluttered with paintings and antiques* | *luggage cluttered up the hallway.*
– ORIGIN late Middle English (as a verb): variant of dialect *clotter* 'to clot,' influenced by CLUSTER and CLATTER.

Clyde /klīd/ a river in western central Scotland that flows for 106 miles (170 km) from the southern uplands to the Firth of Clyde.

Clyde, Firth of the estuary of the Clyde River in western Scotland that separates southern Scotland on the east from the southern end of the Highlands on the northwest.

Clydes·dale /ˈklīdzˌdāl/ ▶ **n.** **1** a horse of a heavy, powerful breed, used for pulling heavy loads.
2 a dog of a small breed of terrier.
– ORIGIN from the name of the area around the river CLYDE in Scotland, where they were originally bred.

Clydesdale 1

clyp·e·us /ˈklipēəs/ ▶ **n.** (pl. **clypei** /ˈklipēˌī, -ēˌē/) Entomology a broad plate at the front of an insect's head.
– DERIVATIVES **clyp·e·al** /-pēəl/ adj.
– ORIGIN mid 19th cent.: from Latin, literally 'round shield.'

clys·ter /ˈklistər/ ▶ **n.** archaic term for ENEMA.
– ORIGIN late Middle English: from Old French *clystere* or Latin *clyster*, from Greek *klustēr* 'syringe,' from *kluzein* 'wash out.'

Cly·tem·nes·tra /ˌklītəmˈnestrə/ Greek Mythology wife of Agamemnon. She conspired with her lover Aegisthus to murder Agamemnon on his return from the Trojan War and was murdered in retribution by her son Orestes and her daughter Electra.

CM ▶ **abbr.** ■ command module. ■ common meter or measure.

Cm ▶ **symbol** the chemical element curium.

cm ▶ **abbr.** centimeter(s).

CMC ▶ **abbr.** computer-mediated communication (that is, communication by means of e-mail, instant messaging, social networking sites, etc.).

Cmdr. ▶ **abbr.** Commander.

Cmdre. ▶ **abbr.** Commodore.

CMEA ▶ **abbr.** Council for Mutual Economic Assistance.

c'mon /kəˈmän/ ▶ **contraction** come on: *C'mon, it'll be fun!*

CMOS ▶ **n.** [often as modifier] Electronics a technology for making low power integrated circuits. ■ a chip built using such technology.
– ORIGIN 1980s: from *Complementary Metal Oxide Semiconductor.*

CMSgt ▶ **abbr.** chief master sergeant.

CMV ▶ **abbr.** cytomegalovirus.

CMYK ▶ **abbr.** cyan, magenta, yellow, and black, the four colors used in most color printers, usually in two ink cartridges, one of black ink and the other containing cyan, magenta, and yellow inks in separate reservoirs.
– ORIGIN the final 'k' in *black* is used to differentiate black from blue; the color scheme RGB (red, green, blue) is used for color computer display screens.

cne·mi·al crest /ˈnēmēəl/ ▶ **n.** Zoology (in the legs of many mammals, birds, and dinosaurs) a ridge at the front of the head of the tibia or tibiotarsus to which the main extensor muscle of the thigh is attached. It is particularly well developed in running species.
– ORIGIN late 19th cent.: *cnemial*, from Greek *knēmē* 'tibia' + -AL.

CNG ▶ **abbr.** compressed natural gas.

Cni·dar·i·a /nīdˈe(ə)rēə/ Zoology a phylum of aquatic invertebrate animals that comprises the coelenterates.
– ORIGIN modern Latin (plural), from Greek *knidē* 'nettle.'

cni·dar·i·an /nīdˈe(ə)rēən/ Zoology ▶ **n.** an aquatic invertebrate animal of the phylum Cnidaria, which comprises the coelenterates.
▶ **adj.** relating to or denoting cnidarians.

CNN ▶ **abbr.** Cable News Network.

CNR ▶ **abbr.** historical Canadian National Railways.

CNS ▶ **abbr.** central nervous system.

Cnut /kəˈno͞ot/ variant of CANUTE.

CO ▶ **abbr.** ■ Colorado (in official postal use). ■ Commanding Officer. ■ conscientious objector.

Co ▶ **symbol** the chemical element cobalt.

Co. ▶ **abbr.** ■ company: *the Consett Iron Co.* ■ county: *Hudson Co.*
– PHRASES **and Co.** ■ used as part of the titles of commercial businesses to designate the partner or partners not named. ■ (also **and co.**) informal and the rest of them: *I got there at 12.30 and waited for Mark and Co. to arrive.*

c/o ▶ **abbr.** ■ care of. ■ carried over.

co- ▶ **prefix 1** (forming nouns) joint; mutual; common: *coeducation.*
2 (forming adjectives) jointly; mutually: *coequal.*
3 (forming verbs) together with another or others: *coproduce* | *co-own.*
4 Mathematics of the complement of an angle: *cosine.* ■ the complement of: *colatitude* | *coset.*
– ORIGIN from Latin, originally a form of COM-.

> **USAGE 1** In modern American English, the tendency increasingly is to write compound words beginning with **co-** without hyphenation, as in *costar, cosignatory,* and *coproduce.* British usage generally tends more often to show a preference for the older, hyphenated, spelling, but even in Britain the trend seems to be in favor of less hyphenation than in the past. In both the US and the UK, for example, the spellings of *coordinate* and *coed* are encountered with or without hyphenation, but the more common choice for either word in either country is without the hyphen. **2 Co-** with the hyphen is often used in compounds that are not yet standard (*co-golfer*), or to prevent ambiguity (*co-driver*—because *codriver* could be mistaken for *cod river*), or simply to avoid an awkward spelling (*co-own* is clearly preferable to *coown*). There are also some relatively less common terms, such as *co-respondent* (in a divorce suit), where the hyphenated spelling distinguishes the word's meaning and pronunciation from that of the more common *correspondent.*

CoA ▶ **abbr.** Biochemistry coenzyme A.

co·ac·er·vate /kō'asər,vāt/ ▶ **n.** Chemistry a colloid-rich viscous liquid phase that may separate from a colloidal solution on addition of a third component.
– ORIGIN early 20th cent.: back-formation from *coacervation,* based on Latin *cum* '(together) with' + *acervus* 'heap.'

coach[1] /kōCH/ ▶ **n. 1** a horse-drawn carriage, esp. a closed one.
2 a railroad car. ■ [as modifier] denoting economy class seating in an aircraft or train: *the cheapest coach-class fare.*
3 a bus, esp. one that is comfortably equipped and used for longer journeys.
▶ **v.** [no obj.] travel by coach: *they coached to Claude's dwelling.*
▶ **adv.** in economy class accommodations in an aircraft or train: *flying coach.*
– ORIGIN mid 16th cent. (sense 1 of the noun): from French *coche,* from Hungarian *kocsi* (*szekér*) '(wagon) from *Kocs,*' a town in Hungary.

coach[2] ▶ **n.** an athletic instructor or trainer. ■ a tutor who gives private or specialized teaching.
▶ **v.** [with obj.] train or instruct (a team or player): *he has coached Little League baseball.* ■ give (someone) extra or private teaching: *he was coached to speak more slowly and curb his hand gestures.* ■ teach (a subject or sport) as a coach: *a Washington realtor who coaches soccer.* ■ prompt or urge (someone) with instructions: *he had improperly coached the witness to testify more credibly.*
– ORIGIN early 18th cent. (as a verb): figuratively from COACH[1].

coach house ▶ **n.** an outbuilding in which a carriage is or was kept.

coach·man /'kōCHmən/ ▶ **n.** (pl. **coachmen**) a driver of a horse-drawn carriage.

coach·roof /'kōCH,ro͞of, -,ro͝of/ ▶ **n.** a raised part of the cabin roof of a yacht.

coach screw ▶ **n.** another term for LAG SCREW.

coach·whip /'kōCH,(h)wip/ ▶ **n.** (also **coachwhip snake**) a harmless, fast-moving North American snake. The pattern of scales on its slender body is said to resemble a braided whip. ● *Masticophis flagellum,* family Colubridae.

coach·wood /'kōCH,wo͝od/ ▶ **n.** a slender tree of the rain forests of Australia and New Guinea, with close-grained timber that has a characteristic caramel scent and is used for cabinetmaking and veneers. ● *Ceratopetalum apetalum,* family Cunoniaceae.

co·ac·tion /kō'akSHən/ ▶ **n. 1** compulsion; restraint; coercion.
2 concerted action; acting together.

co·a·dapt·ed /,kōə'daptid/ ▶ **adj.** Biology mutually adapted; mutually accommodating.
– DERIVATIVES **co·a·dap·ta·tion** /,kōadəp'tāSHən/ **n.**

co·ad·ju·tant /kō'ajətənt/ ▶ **adj.** helping another or others, or with another or others.
▶ **n.** a person who thus helps.

co·ad·ju·tor /,kōə'jo͞otər, kō'ajətər/ ▶ **n.** a bishop appointed to assist a diocesan bishop, and often also designated as his successor.
– ORIGIN late Middle English: via Old French from late Latin *coadjutor,* from *co-* (from Latin *cum* 'together with') + *adjutor* 'assistant' (from *adjuvare* 'to help').

co·ag·u·lant /kō'agyələnt/ ▶ **n.** a substance that causes blood or another liquid to coagulate.
– ORIGIN late 18th cent.: from Latin *coagulant-* 'curdling,' from the verb *coagulare* (see COAGULATE).

co·ag·u·lase /kō'agyə,lās, -,lāz/ ▶ **n.** Biochemistry a bacterial enzyme that brings about the coagulation of blood or plasma and is produced by disease-causing forms of staphylococcus.

co·ag·u·late /kō'agyə,lāt/ ▶ **v.** [no obj.] (of a fluid, esp. blood) change to a solid or semisolid state: *blood had coagulated around the edges of the wound.* ■ [with obj.] cause (a fluid) to change to a solid or semisolid state: *epinephrine coagulates the blood.*
– DERIVATIVES **co·ag·u·la·ble** /-ləbəl/ **adj.**, **co·ag·u·la·tion** /kō,agyə'lāSHən/ **n.**, **co·ag·u·la·tive** /-,lātiv, -lətiv/ **adj.**, **co·ag·u·la·tor** /-,lātər/ **n.**
– ORIGIN late Middle English: from Latin *coagulat-* 'curdled,' from the verb *coagulare,* from *coagulum* 'rennet.'

co·ag·u·lum /kō'agyələm/ ▶ **n.** (pl. **coagula** /-yələ/) a mass of coagulated matter.
– ORIGIN mid 16th cent. (denoting a coagulant): from Latin, literally 'rennet.'

Co·a·hui·la /,kōə'wēlə/ a state in northern Mexico, on the US border; capital, Saltillo.

coal /kōl/ ▶ **n.** a combustible black or dark brown rock consisting mainly of carbonized plant matter, found mainly in underground deposits and widely used as fuel: [as modifier] *a coal fire.* ■ a red-hot piece of coal or other material in a fire: *the glowing coals.*
▶ **v.** [with obj.] provide with a supply of coal: (as noun **coaling**) *the coaling and watering of the engine.*
– PHRASES **coals to Newcastle** something brought or sent to a place where it is already plentiful. **rake** (or **haul**) **someone over the coals** reprimand someone severely.
– DERIVATIVES **coal·y adj.**
– ORIGIN Old English *col* (in the senses 'glowing ember' and 'charred remnant'), of Germanic origin; related to Dutch *kool* and German *Kohle.* The sense 'combustible mineral used as fuel' dates from Middle English.

coal-black ▶ **adj.** as black as coal; utterly black.

coal·er /'kōlər/ ▶ **n. 1** a ship that transports coal.
2 a large mechanized structure for loading coal onto a ship, railroad car, or steam locomotive.

co·a·lesce /,kōə'les/ ▶ **v.** [no obj.] come together and form one mass or whole: *the puddles had coalesced into shallow streams* | *the separate details coalesce to form a single body of scientific thought.* ■ [with obj.] combine (elements) in a mass or whole: *to help coalesce the community, they established an office.*
– DERIVATIVES **co·a·les·cence** /-'lesəns/ **n.**, **co·a·les·cent** /-'lesənt/ **adj.**
– ORIGIN mid 16th cent. (in the sense 'bring together, unite'): from Latin *coalescere,* from *co-* (from *cum* 'with') + *alescere* 'grow up' (from *alere* 'nourish').

coal·field /'kōl,fēld/ ▶ **n.** an extensive area containing a number of underground coal deposits.

coal-fired ▶ **adj.** heated, driven, or produced by the burning of coal: *a coal-fired power station.*

coal gas ▶ **n.** a mixture of gases (chiefly hydrogen, methane, and carbon monoxide) obtained by the destructive distillation of coal and formerly used for lighting and heating.

coal·i·fi·ca·tion /,kōləfi'kāSHən/ ▶ **n.** the process by which plant remains become coal.

co·a·li·tion /,kōə'liSHən/ ▶ **n.** an alliance for combined action, esp. a temporary alliance of political parties forming a government or of states: *a coalition of conservatives and disaffected Democrats* | *the party was only able to govern in coalition with three or even four other parties* | [as modifier] *a coalition government.*
– DERIVATIVES **co·a·li·tion·ist** /-nist/ **n.**
– ORIGIN early 17th cent. (in the sense 'fusion'): from medieval Latin *coalitio(n-),* from the verb *coalescere* (see COALESCE). Usage in politics dates from the late 18th cent.

coal meas·ures ▶ **plural n.** Geology a series of strata of the Carboniferous period, including coal seams.

coal oil ▶ **n.** another term for KEROSENE.

Coal·port /'kōl,pôrt/ ▶ **n.** a kind of porcelain, frequently decorated with floral designs, produced at Coalport, England, from the late 18th century.

Coal·sack /'kōl,sak/ (**the Coalsack**) Astronomy a dark nebula of dust near the Southern Cross that gives the appearance of a gap in the stars of the Milky Way.

coal scut·tle ▶ **n.** see SCUTTLE[1].

coal tar ▶ **n.** a thick black liquid produced by the destructive distillation of bituminous coal. It contains benzene, naphthalene, phenols, aniline, and many other organic chemicals.

coam·ing /'kōmiNG/ (also **coamings**) ▶ **n.** a raised border around the cockpit or hatch of a yacht or other boat to keep out water.
– ORIGIN early 17th cent.: of unknown origin.

co·ap·ta·tion /,kō,ap'tāSHən/ ▶ **n.** the adaptation or adjustment of things, parts, or people to each other. ■ Medicine the drawing together of the separated tissue in a wound or fracture.
– ORIGIN mid 16th cent.: from late Latin *coaptatio(n-),* from the verb *coaptare,* from *co-* (from Latin *cum* 'with, together') + *aptare* (from *aptus* 'apt').

co·arc·tate /kō'ärk,tāt/ ▶ **adj.** chiefly Anatomy & Biology pressed close together; contracted; confined. ■ Entomology (of the pupa of certain flies) formed within and remaining concealed by the larval cuticle or puparium.
– ORIGIN late Middle English: from Latin *coarctatus,* past participle of *coarctare* 'press or draw together.'

co·arc·ta·tion /,kō,ärk'tāSHən/ ▶ **n.** Medicine congenital narrowing of a short section of the aorta.
– ORIGIN late Middle English: from Latin *coarctatio(n-),* from the verb *coarctare* (see COARCTATE).

coarse /kôrs/ ▶ **adj. 1** rough or loose in texture or grain: *a coarse woolen cloth.* ■ made of large grains or particles: *dry, coarse sand.* ■ (of grains or particles) large. ■ (of a person's features) not elegantly formed or proportioned. ■ (of food or drink) of inferior quality.
2 (of a person or their speech) rude, crude, or vulgar.
– DERIVATIVES **coarse·ly adv.**, **coars·ish adj.**
– ORIGIN late Middle English (in the sense 'ordinary or inferior'): origin uncertain; until the 17th cent. identical in spelling with COURSE, and possibly derived from the latter in the sense 'habitual or ordinary manner.'

coarse-grained ▶ **adj.** coarse in texture or grain: *a coarse-grained flour.* ■ (of photographic film) having a noticeably grainy appearance. ■ coarse in manner or speech: *a coarse-grained man.*

coars·en /'kôrsən/ ▶ **v.** make or become rough: [with obj.] *her hands were coarsened by outside work* | [no obj.] *his facial features appeared to coarsen with age.* ■ make or become crude, vulgar, or unpleasant: [with obj.] *her experience has not coarsened her or made her cynical* | [no obj.] *the voice coarsened.*

coarse·ness /kôrsnəs/ ▶ **n. 1** the quality of being rough or harsh: *the coarseness of her hair.* ■ the quality of being coarse in texture: *you can set the desired coarseness of your flour.*
2 rudeness; vulgarity: *he disliked the coarseness of the men around him.*

co·ar·tic·u·la·tion /,kō-är,tikyə'lāSHən/ ▶ **n.** Phonetics the articulation of two or more speech sounds together, so that one influences the other.

coast /kōst/ ▶ **n. 1** the part of the land near the sea; the edge of the land: *the west coast of Africa* | *they sailed further up the coast* | [as modifier] *the coast road.* ■ (**the Coast**) the Pacific coast of North America.
2 a run or movement in or on a vehicle without the use of power.
▶ **v. 1** [no obj.] (of a person or vehicle) move easily without using power: *the engines stopped, and the craft coasted along.* ■ act or make progress without making much effort: *he coasted to victory.* ■ slide down a snowy hill on a sled.
2 [no obj.] sail along the coast, esp. in order to carry cargo: (as adj. **coasting**) *a coasting schooner.*
– PHRASES **the coast is clear** there is no danger of being observed or caught.
– ORIGIN Middle English (in the sense 'side of the body'), from Old French *coste* (noun), *costeier* (verb), from Latin *costa* 'rib, flank, side.' Sense 1 of the noun arose from the phrase *coast of the sea* 'side of the sea.'

coast·al /'kōstəl/ ▶ **adj.** of, relating to, or near a coast: *coastal erosion* | *coastal waters.*

C

coast·eer·ing /ˌkōstˈi(ə)riNG/ ▸ **n.** chiefly Brit. the sport of exploring a shoreline that does not have a continuous pedestrian route.

coast·er /ˈkōstər/ ▸ **n. 1** a ship used to carry cargo along the coast. ■ [with adj.] a person who inhabits a specified coast: *a West coaster*.
2 a small tray or mat placed under a bottle or glass to protect the table underneath.
3 a toboggan. ■ short for ROLLER COASTER.

coast guard (also **coastguard**) ▸ **n.** (**Coast Guard**) a branch of the US armed forces, under the Department of Transportation since 1967, responsible for the enforcement of maritime law and for the protection of life and property at sea. In time of war, or at the direction of the president, the Coast Guard serves as part of the US Navy. ■ (**the coastguard**) a civilian or volunteer organization keeping watch on the sea near a coast in order to assist people or ships in danger and to prevent smuggling. ■ a member of such a federal or civilian organization.

coast·guards·man /ˈkōstˌgärdzmən/ ▸ **n.** a member of a coast guard, esp. the US Coast Guard.

coast·land /ˈkōstˌland/ ▸ **n.** (usu. **coastlands**) an expanse of land near the sea.

coast·line /ˈkōstˌlīn/ ▸ **n.** the outline of a coast, esp. with regard to its shape and appearance: *the hotel has wonderful views of the rugged coastline*.

Coast Moun·tains a range that curves northwest for 1,000 miles (1,600 km) from British Columbia to Alaska and extends the line of the Cascade Mountains. Mount Waddington at 13,104 feet (3,994 m) is the high point.

Coast Rang·es the name for various ranges that extend from southern California along the Pacific coast to Alaska. Parallel to and west of the Coast Mountains, they reach 19,524 feet (5,951 m) at Mount Logan in the Yukon Territory.

coast to coast ▸ **adj. & adv.** all the way across an island or continent: [as adv.] *retail stores from coast to coast* | (as adj. **coast-to-coast**) *a coast-to-coast journey*.

coast·ward /ˈkōstwərd/ (also **coastwards**) ▸ **adv. & adj.** toward the coast.

coast·wise /ˈkōstˌwīz/ ▸ **adj. & adv.** along, following, or connected with the coast: [as adj.] *a small coastwise steamer* | [as adv.] *the cargo was ferried coastwise*.

coat /kōt/ ▸ **n. 1** an outer garment worn outdoors, having sleeves and typically extending below the hips: *a winter coat* | [as modifier] *his coat pocket*. ■ a similar item worn indoors as a protective garment: *a laboratory coat*. ■ a man's jacket or tunic, esp. as worn when hunting or by soldiers. ■ a man's or woman's tailored jacket.
2 an animal's covering of fur or hair.
3 a structure, esp. a membrane, enclosing or lining an organ. ■ a skin, rind, or husk. ■ a layer of a plant bulb. ■ an outer layer or covering of a specified kind: *the protein coat of the virus*.
4 a covering of paint or similar material laid on a surface at one time: *a protective coat of varnish*.
▸ **v.** [with obj.] provide with a layer or covering of something; apply a coat to: *his boots were coated with mud* | *coat each part with a thin oil*. ■ (of a substance) form a covering to: *a film of dust coated the floor*.
– DERIVATIVES **coat·ed adj.** [in combination] *plastic-coated wire*.
– ORIGIN Middle English: from Old French *cote*, of unknown ultimate origin.

coat ar·mor ▸ **n.** heraldic arms.

coat check ▸ **n.** a cloakroom with an attendant.

coat check·er ▸ **n.** a cloakroom attendant.

coat dress ▸ **n.** a woman's tailored dress, typically fastening down the front and resembling a coat.

coat hang·er ▸ **n.** see HANGER (sense 2).

co·a·ti /kōˈätē/ ▸ **n.** (pl. **coatis**) a raccoonlike animal found mainly in Central and South America, with a long, flexible snout and a ringed tail. Also called COATIMUNDI. ● Genera *Nasua* and *Nasuella*, family Procyonidae: three or four species, in particular *Nasua nasua*, whose range reaches the southern US.
– ORIGIN early 17th cent.: from Spanish and Portuguese, from Tupi *kua'ti*, from *cua* 'belt' + *tim* 'nose.'

co·a·ti·mun·di /kōˌätiˈməndē/ ▸ **n.** (pl. **coatimundis**) another term for COATI.
– ORIGIN late 17th cent.: from Portuguese, from Tupi *kuatimu'ne*, from *kua'ti* (see COATI) + *mu'ne* 'snare or trick.' The *coatimundi* was originally thought to be a different species from the coati, but then discovered to be the male of the same species.

coat·ing /ˈkōtiNG/ ▸ **n.** a thin layer or covering of something: *a coating of paint*. ■ material used for making coats.

coat of arms ▸ **n.** the distinctive heraldic bearings or shield of a person, family, corporation, or country.

coat of mail ▸ **n.** historical a jacket covered with or composed of metal rings or plates, serving as armor.

coat·rack /ˈkōtˌrak/ ▸ **n.** a rack or stand with hooks on which to hang coats, hats, etc.

coat·room /ˈkōtˌro͞om, -ˌro͝om/ ▸ **n.** another term for CLOAKROOM.

Coats Land /ˈkōts/ a region of Antarctica, east of the Antarctic Peninsula.

coat stand ▸ **n.** another term for COATRACK.

coat·tail /ˈkōtˌtāl/ ▸ **n.** (usu. **coattails**) each of the flaps formed by the lower back of a coat, esp. a tailcoat.
– PHRASES **on someone's coattails** benefiting from another's success, sometimes undeservedly: *he was elected on the coattails of his predecessor*.

co·au·thor /kōˈôTHər/ ▸ **n.** a joint author.
▸ **v.** [with obj.] be a joint author of (a book, paper, or report).

coax¹ /kōks/ ▸ **v.** [with obj.] persuade (someone) gradually or by flattery to do something: *the trainees were **coaxed into** doing hard, boring work* | *"Come on now," I coaxed*. ■ (**coax something from/out of**) use such persuasion to obtain something from: *we coaxed money out of my father* | figurative *coaxing more speed from the car*. ■ manipulate (something) carefully into a particular shape or position: *her lovely hair had been coaxed into ringlets*.
– DERIVATIVES **coax·er n.**, **coax·ing·ly adv.**
– ORIGIN late 16th cent.: from obsolete *cokes* 'simpleton,' of unknown origin. The original sense was 'pet, fondle,' hence 'persuade by caresses or flattery,' the underlying sense being 'make a simpleton of.'

co·ax² /ˈkō-aks, kōˈaks/ informal ▸ **n.** coaxial cable.
▸ **adj.** coaxial: *coax connectors*.

co·ax·i·al /kōˈaksēəl/ ▸ **adj.** having a common axis. ■ (of a cable or line) consisting of two concentric conductors separated by an insulator.
– DERIVATIVES **co·ax·i·al·ly adv.**

COB ▸ **abbr.** close of business: *you have until COB today to show us why you should not be disconnected*.

cob¹ /käb/ ▸ **n. 1** (also **corncob**) the central, cylindrical, woody part of the corn ear to which the grains, or kernels, are attached.
2 (also **cobnut**) a hazelnut or filbert, esp. one of a large variety. ■ a hazel or filbert bush.
3 a powerfully built, short-legged horse.
4 a male swan.
5 Brit. a roundish lump of coal.
– ORIGIN late Middle English (denoting a strong man or leader): of unknown origin. The underlying general sense appears to be 'stout, rounded, sturdy.'

cob² ▸ **n.** Brit. a mixture of compressed clay and straw used, esp. in former times, for building walls: [as modifier] *cob and thatch cottages*.
– ORIGIN early 17th cent.: of unknown origin.

Co·bain, Kurt (Donald) (1967–94), US rock singer, guitarist, and songwriter. As leader of the Seattle band Nirvana, his style helped characterize the alternative music scene. His notoriety reached cult status, particularly after his suicide in April 1994.

co·bal·a·min /kōˈbaləmin/ ▸ **n.** Biochemistry any of a group of cobalt-containing substances including cyanocobalamin (vitamin B_{12}).
– ORIGIN 1950s: blend of COBALT and VITAMIN.

co·balt /ˈkōˌbôlt/ ▸ **n.** the chemical element of atomic number 27, a hard silvery-white magnetic metal. (Symbol: **Co**) ■ short for COBALT BLUE: [as modifier] *a cobalt sky*.

> Cobalt is chiefly obtained as a byproduct from nickel and copper ores. It is a transition metal similar in many respects to nickel. Its main use is as a component of magnetic alloys and those designed for use at high temperatures.

– DERIVATIVES **co·bal·tic** /kōˈbôltik/ **adj.**, **co·bal·tous** /kōˈbôltəs/ **adj.**
– ORIGIN late 17th cent.: from German *Kobalt* 'imp, demon' (because the presence of cobalt-bearing ore made it more difficult to extract silver, and miners believed that it was harmful to the silver ore with which it occurred).

co·balt blue ▸ **n.** a deep blue pigment containing cobalt and aluminum oxides. ■ the deep blue color of this.

Cobb /käb/, Ty (1886–1961), US baseball player; full name *Tyrus Raymond Cobb*; also known as **the Georgia Peach**. His lifetime batting average (.367) is the highest in baseball history. An outfielder, he played for the Detroit Tigers 1905–26 and the Philadelphia Athletics 1927–28. Baseball Hall of Fame (1936).

Cobb Coun·ty /käb/ a county in northwestern Georgia that contains many northwestern suburbs of Atlanta; pop. 698,158 (est. 2008). Its seat is Marietta.

cob·ble¹ /ˈkäbəl/ ▸ **n.** (usu. **cobbles**) a cobblestone. ■ (**cobbles**) Brit. coal in lumps of such a size.
– ORIGIN late Middle English: from COB¹ + -LE².

cob·ble² ▸ **v.** [with obj.] **1** dated repair (shoes).
2 (**cobble something together**) roughly assemble or put together something from available parts or elements: *the mayor cobbled together a budget*.
– ORIGIN late 15th cent.: back-formation from COBBLER.

cob·bled /ˈkäbəld/ ▸ **adj.** (of an area or roadway) paved with cobbles: *a cobbled courtyard*.

cob·bler /ˈkäblər/ ▸ **n. 1** a person who mends shoes as a job.
2 an iced drink made with wine or sherry, sugar, and lemon.
3 a fruit pie with a rich crust on top.
– PHRASES **let the cobbler stick to his last** proverb people should only concern themselves with things they know something about. [translating Latin *ne sutor ultra crepidam*.]
– ORIGIN Middle English: of unknown origin.

cob·ble·stone /ˈkäbəlˌstōn/ ▸ **n.** a small, round stone of a kind formerly used to cover road surfaces.

cob·by /ˈkäbē/ ▸ **adj.** (of horses, dogs, and other animals) shortish and thickset; stocky.

cob coal ▸ **n.** see COB¹ (sense 5).

COBE /ˈkōbē/ a NASA satellite launched in 1989 to map the background microwave radiation from space in a search for evidence of the Big Bang.
– ORIGIN abbreviation of *Cosmic Background Explorer*.

co-bel·lig·er·ent /kōbəˈlijərənt/ ▸ **n.** any of two or more nations engaged in war as allies.
– DERIVATIVES **co-bel·lig·er·ence n.**

co·bi·a /ˈkōbēə/ ▸ **n.** (pl. **same**) a large, edible game fish that lives in open waters of the Atlantic, Indian, and western Pacific oceans. Also called SERGEANT FISH. ● *Rachycentron canadum*, family Rachycentridae.
– ORIGIN mid 19th cent.: of unknown origin.

cob·nut /ˈkäbˌnət/ ▸ **n.** see COB¹ (sense 2).

COBOL /ˈkōˌbôl/ ▸ **n.** a computer programming language designed for use in commerce.
– ORIGIN 1960s: from *co(mmon) b(usiness) o(riented) l(anguage)*.

co·bra /ˈkōbrə/ ▸ **n.** a highly venomous snake native to Africa and Asia that spreads the skin of its neck into a hood when disturbed. ● *Naja* and two other genera, family Elapidae: several species, in particular the **king cobra** and the **spectacled cobra**.
– ORIGIN mid 17th cent.: from Portuguese *cobra de capello*, literally 'snake with hood,' based on Latin *colubra* 'snake.'

co-brand /ˈkōˌbrand/ ▸ **v.** [with obj.] designate (a product or service) with the brands of joint manufacturers or sponsors.
▸ **n.** a product or service jointly offered by two manufacturers or sponsors.
– DERIVATIVES **co-brand·ing n.**

cob·web /ˈkäbˌweb/ ▸ **n.** (usu. **cobwebs**) a spider's web, esp. when old and covered with dust. ■ Zoology a tangled three-dimensional spider's web. ■ something resembling a cobweb in delicacy or intricacy: *white cobwebs of frost*.
– PHRASES **blow** (or **clear**) **away the cobwebs** banish a state of sluggishness; enliven or refresh oneself.
– DERIVATIVES **cob·webbed adj.**, **cob·web·by adj.**
– ORIGIN Middle English *coppeweb*, *copweb*, from obsolete *coppe* 'spider' + WEB.

cob·web spi·der ▸ **n.** a spider that builds tangled three-dimensional webs. ● Family Theridiidae: many species, class Arachnida.

co·ca /ˈkōkə/ ▸ **n.** a tropical American shrub that is widely grown for its leaves, which are the source of cocaine. ● *Erythroxylum coca*, family Erythroxylaceae. ■ the dried leaves of this shrub, which are mixed with lime and chewed as a stimulant by the indigenous people of western South America.
– ORIGIN late 16th cent.: from Spanish, from Aymara *kuka* or Quechua *koka*.

co·caine /kōˈkān, ˈkōˌkān/ ▸ **n.** an addictive drug derived from coca or prepared synthetically, used as an illegal stimulant and sometimes medicinally as a local anesthetic. ● An alkaloid; chem. formula: $C_{17}H_{21}NO_4$.
– ORIGIN mid 19th cent.: from COCA + -INE⁴.

coc·cid /ˈkäksid/ ▸ **n.** a homopteran insect of the family Coccidae; a scale insect.

coc·cid·i·a /käkˈsidēə/ ▸ **plural n.** (sing. **coccidium** /-ˈsidēəm/) Biology parasitic protozoa of a group that includes those that cause diseases such as coccidiosis and toxoplasmosis. ● Suborder

Eimeriorina (formerly order or subclass Coccidia), phylum Sporozoa.
– DERIVATIVES **coc·cid·i·an** adj. & n.

coc·cid·i·oi·do·my·co·sis /käk,sidē,oidōmīˈkōsəs/ ▶ n. a serious fungal disease of the lungs and other tissues, endemic in the warmer, arid regions of America. ● The fungus is *Coccidioides immitis*, phylum Ascomycota.
– ORIGIN 1930s: from modern Latin *Coccidioides* (part of the binomial of the fungus) + MYCOSIS.

coc·cid·i·o·sis /käk,sidēˈōsəs/ ▶ n. a disease of birds and mammals that chiefly affects the intestines, caused by coccidia. ● The coccidia belong to the genera *Eimeria*, *Isopora*, and others.
– ORIGIN late 19th cent.: from *coccidium* (singular of modern Latin *Coccidia*, from Greek *kokkis*, diminutive of *kokkos* 'berry') + -OSIS.

coc·cid·i·o·stat /käkˈsidēō,stat/ ▶ n. Veterinary Medicine a substance administered to poultry, cattle, puppies, and kittens to retard the growth and reproduction of coccidian parasites.

coc·cid·i·um /käkˈsidēəm/ ▶ n. singular form of COCCIDIA.

coc·ci·nel·lid /,käksəˈnelid/ ▶ n. Entomology a beetle of a family (Coccinellidae) that includes the ladybugs.
– ORIGIN late 19th cent.: from modern Latin *Coccinellidae* (plural), from the genus name *Coccinella*, from Latin *coccineus* 'scarlet.'

coc·co·lith /ˈkäkə,liTH/ ▶ n. Biology a minute, rounded, calcareous platelet, numbers of which form the spherical shells of coccolithophores.
– ORIGIN mid 19th cent.: from Greek *kokkos* 'grain or berry' + *lithos* 'stone.'

coc·co·lith·o·phore /,käkəˈliTHə,fôr/ ▶ n. Biology a single-celled marine flagellate that secretes a calcareous shell, forming an important constituent of the phytoplankton. ● Order Coccolithophorida, phylum Haptophyta.
– DERIVATIVES **coc·co·lith·o·phor·id** /,käkəliˈTHäfərid/ n. & adj.

coc·cus /ˈkäkəs/ ▶ n. (pl. **cocci** /ˈkäk,(s)ī, ˈkäk,(s)ē/) Biology any spherical or roughly spherical bacterium.
– DERIVATIVES **coc·cal** /ˈkäkəl/ adj., **coc·coid** /ˈkäk,oid/ adj.
– ORIGIN mid 18th cent. (denoting a scale insect): modern Latin, from Greek *kokkos* 'berry.' Compare with COCHINEAL.

coc·cyx /ˈkäksiks/ ▶ n. (pl. **coccyges** /ˈkäksə,jēz/ or **coccyxes** /ˈkäksiksiz/) a small, triangular bone at the base of the spinal column in humans and some apes, formed of fused vestigial vertebrae.
– DERIVATIVES **coc·cyg·e·al** /käkˈsijēəl/ adj.
– ORIGIN late 16th cent.: via Latin from Greek *kokkux* 'cuckoo' (because the shape of the human bone resembles the cuckoo's bill).

Co·cha·bam·ba /,kōCHəˈbämbə/ a city in western central Bolivia, at the center of a rich agricultural region; pop. 611,056 (2009).

co·chair ▶ n. /ˈkō,CHe(ə)r/ a person who is in charge of a meeting or organization jointly with another or others.
▶ v. /,kōˈCHe(ə)r/ [with obj.] chair (a meeting) in this way.

Co·chin¹ /kōˈCHin/ former name for KOCHI.

Co·chin² /ˈkōCHin, ˈkäCHin/ (also **Cochin China**) ▶ n. a chicken of an Asian breed with feathery legs.

Co·chin-Chi·na /ˈkō,CHin/ the former name for the southern region of what is now Vietnam. Part of French Indo-China from 1862, it became a French overseas territory in 1946 and then merged officially with Vietnam in 1949.

coch·i·neal /ˈkäCHə,nēl, ˈkō-/ ▶ n. **1** a scarlet dye used chiefly for coloring food. ■ the dried bodies of a female scale insect, which are crushed to yield this dye. ■ a similar dye or preparation made from the oak kermes insect (see KERMES).
2 (**cochineal insect**) the scale insect that is used for cochineal, native to Mexico and formerly widely cultivated on cacti. ● *Dactylopius coccus*, family Dactylopiidae, suborder Homoptera.
– ORIGIN late 16th cent.: from French *cochenille* or Spanish *cochinilla*, from Latin *coccinus* 'scarlet,' from Greek *kokkos* 'berry' (because the insect bodies were originally mistaken for grains or berries). Compare with COCCUS and KERMES.

Co·chise /kōˈCHēs/ (c.1812–74), American Indian leader, chief of the Apache Indians. With a band of followers, he resisted white encroachment on Indian lands.

coch·le·a /ˈkōklēə, ˈkäk-/ ▶ n. (pl. **cochleae** /-lē,ē, -lē,ī/) the spiral cavity of the inner ear containing the organ of Corti, which produces nerve impulses in response to sound vibrations.
– DERIVATIVES **coch·le·ar** adj.
– ORIGIN mid 16th cent. (used to denote spiral objects such as a spiral staircase and an Archimedean screw): from Latin, 'snail shell or screw,' from Greek *kokhlias*. The current sense dates from the late 17th cent.

coch·le·ate /ˈkäklēit, -,āt/ (also **cochleated**) ▶ adj. chiefly Botany formed like a spiral shell; twisted.

Coch·ran¹ /ˈkäkrən/, Eddie (1938–60), US rock-and-roll singer and songwriter; born *Ray Edward Cochrane*. Notable songs: "Summertime Blues" (1958), "C'mon Everybody" (1959), and "Three Steps to Heaven" (1960).

Coch·ran², Jacqueline (c.1910–80), US aviator. The first woman to break the sound barrier 1953, she set many speed and altitude records.

cock¹ /käk/ ▶ n. **1** a male bird, esp. a rooster. ■ [in combination] used in names of birds, esp. game birds, e.g., **moorcock**. ■ Brit. a male lobster, crab, or salmon.
2 vulgar slang a penis.
3 Brit. informal nonsense: *that's all a lot of cock.*
4 a firing lever in a gun which can be raised to be released by the trigger.
5 a stopcock.
▶ v. [with obj.] **1** tilt (something) in a particular direction: *she cocked her head slightly to one side.* ■ bend a (limb or joint) at an angle: (as adj. **cocked**) *she listened, her little finger cocked as she held her coffee cup.* ■ (of a male dog) lift (a back leg) in order to urinate.
2 raise the cock of (a gun) in order to make it ready for firing.
– PHRASES **at full cock** (of a gun) with the cock lifted to the position at which the trigger will act. **cock one's ear** (of a dog) raise its ears to an erect position. ■ (of a person) listen attentively to or for something. **cock one's eye** (or **eyebrow**) glance in a quizzical or knowing manner with a raised eyebrow. **cock of the walk** someone who dominates others within a group. **cock a snook** see SNOOK².
– ORIGIN Old English *cocc*, from medieval Latin *coccus*; reinforced in Middle English by Old French *coq*.

cock² ▶ n. dated a small pile of hay, straw, or other material, with vertical sides and a rounded top.
▶ v. [with obj.] archaic pile (hay, straw, or other material) into such a shape.
– ORIGIN late Middle English: perhaps of Scandinavian origin and related to Norwegian *kok* 'heap, lump,' Danish *kok* 'haycock,' and Swedish *koka* 'clod.'

cock·ade /käˈkād/ ▶ n. a rosette or knot of ribbons worn in a hat as a badge of office or party, or as part of a livery.
– DERIVATIVES **cock·ad·ed** adj.
– ORIGIN mid 17th cent.: from French *cocarde*, originally in *bonnet à la coquarde*, from the feminine of obsolete *coquard* 'saucy.'

cock-a-doo·dle-doo /,käk ə ,do͞odl ˈdo͞o/ ▶ n. used to represent the sound made by a cock when it crows.

cock-a-hoop /,käk ə ˈho͝op, ˈho͞op/ ▶ adj. [predic.] extremely and obviously pleased, esp. about a triumph or success.
– ORIGIN mid 17th cent.: from the phrase *set cock a hoop*, of unknown origin, apparently denoting the action of turning on the tap and allowing liquor to flow (prior to a drinking session).

cock-a-leek·ie /,käk ə ˈlēkē/ ▶ n. a Scottish soup traditionally made with chicken and leeks.
– ORIGIN mid 18th cent.: from COCK¹ and LEEK.

cock·a·lo·rum /,käkəˈlôrəm/ ▶ n. (pl. **cockalorums**) informal, dated a self-important little man.
– ORIGIN early 18th cent.: an arbitrary formation from COCK¹.

cock·a·ma·mie /ˈkäkə,māmē, ,käkəˈmāmē/ (also **cockamamy**) ▶ adj. informal ridiculous; implausible: *a cockamamie theory.*
– ORIGIN 1940s (originally denoting a design left by a transfer): probably an alteration of DECALCOMANIA.

cock and bull sto·ry ▶ n. informal a ridiculous and implausible story.

cock·a·poo /ˈkäkə,po͞o/ ▶ n. a dog resulting from a cross between a cocker spaniel and a miniature poodle.

cock·a·tiel /ˈkäkə,tēl/ ▶ n. a slender, long-crested Australian parrot related to the cockatoos, with a mainly gray body, white shoulders, and a yellow and orange face. ● *Nymphicus hollandicus*, family Cacatuidae (or Psittacidae).
– ORIGIN late 19th cent.: from Dutch *kaketielje*, probably a diminutive of *kaketoe* 'cockatoo.'

cock·a·too /ˈkäkə,to͞o/ ▶ n. a parrot with an erectile crest, found in Australia, eastern Indonesia, and neighboring islands. ● Family Cacatuidae (or Psittacidae): several genera and numerous species, including the **sulfur-crested cockatoo** (*Cacatua galerita*).
– ORIGIN mid 17th cent.: from Dutch *kaketoe*, from Malay *kakatua*, the spelling influenced by COCK¹.

sulfur-crested cockatoo

cock·a·trice /ˈkäkətris, -,trīs/ ▶ n. another term for BASILISK (sense 1). ■ Heraldry a mythical animal depicted as a two-legged dragon (or wyvern) with a cock's head.
– ORIGIN late Middle English: from Old French *cocatris*, from Latin *calcatrix* 'tracker' (from *calcare* 'to tread or track'), translating Greek *ikhneueinōn* (see ICHNEUMON).

cock·bead /ˈkäk,bēd/ ▶ n. a projecting wooden molding used to decorate furniture.
– DERIVATIVES **cock·bead·ed** adj., **cock·bead·ing** n.

cock·chaf·er /ˈkäk,CHāfər/ ▶ n. a large brown European beetle that flies at dusk and often crashes into lighted windows. The adults are damaging to foliage and flowers, and the larvae are a pest of cereal and grass roots. ● *Melolontha melolontha*, family Scarabaeidae.
– ORIGIN early 18th cent.: from COCK¹ (expressing size or vigor) + CHAFER.

Cock·croft /ˈkäk,krôft/, Sir John Douglas (1897–1967), English physicist. In 1932, working with Ernest Walton, he succeeded in splitting the atom. Nobel Prize for Physics (1951), shared with Walton.

cock·crow /ˈkäk,krō/ ▶ n. literary dawn: *the hour of cockcrow was still far off.*

cocked hat ▶ n. a brimless triangular hat pointed at the front, back, and top. ■ historical a hat with a wide brim permanently turned up toward the crown, such as a tricorne.
– PHRASES **knock something into a cocked hat** utterly defeat or outdo something.

cock·er·el /ˈkäkərəl/ ▶ n. a young domestic cock.
– ORIGIN Middle English: diminutive of COCK¹.

cock·er span·iel /ˈkäkər/ (also **cocker**) ▶ n. a small spaniel of a breed with a silky coat.
– ORIGIN early 19th cent.: from COCK¹ + -ER¹ (because the dog was bred to flush game birds such as woodcock, for shooting).

cocker spaniel

cock·eye /ˈkäk,ī/ ▶ n. an eye that squints or is affected by strabismus.

cock·eyed /ˈkäkˈīd/ ▶ adj. informal crooked or askew; not level: *cockeyed camera angles.* ■ absurd; impractical: *do you expect us to believe a cockeyed story like that?* ■ drunk: *I got cockeyed.* ■ (of a person or a person's eyes) having a squint. ■ cross-eyed.
– ORIGIN early 19th cent.: apparently from the verb COCK¹ and EYE. The sense 'drunk' (originally US) dates from the 1920s.

cock·fight·ing /ˈkäk,fītiNG/ ▶ n. the sport (illegal in certain countries) of setting two cocks to fight each other. Fighting cocks often have had their legs fitted with metal spurs.
– DERIVATIVES **cock·fight** /ˈkäk,fīt/ n.

cock·le¹ /ˈkäkəl/ ▶ n. **1** an edible, burrowing bivalve mollusk with a strong ribbed shell. ● Genus *Cardium*, family Cardiidae.
2 (also **cockleshell**) literary a small shallow boat.
– PHRASES **warm the cockles of one's heart** give one a comforting feeling of pleasure or contentment.
– ORIGIN Middle English: from Old French *coquille* 'shell,' based on Greek *konkhulion*, from *konkhē* 'conch.'

cock·le² ▶ v. [no obj.] (of paper) bulge out in certain places so as to present a wrinkled or creased surface; pucker.
– ORIGIN mid 16th cent.: from French *coquiller* 'blister (bread in cooking),' from *coquille* 'shell' (see COCKLE¹).

cock·le·bur /ˈkäkəl,bər/ ▶ n. a herbaceous plant of the daisy family, with broad leaves and burred fruits. It originated in tropical America but is now cosmopolitan. See also CLOTBUR. ● Genus *Xanthium*, family Compositae: two or three species, in particular *X. strumarium*.
– ORIGIN mid 19th cent.: from COCKLE² + BURR.

PRONUNCIATION KEY ə *ago, up*; ər *over, fur*; a *hat*; ā *ate*; ä *car*; e *let*; ē *see*; i *fit*; ī *by*; NG *sing*; ō *go*; ô *law, for*; oi *toy*; o͝o *good*; o͞o *goo*; ou *out*; TH *thin*; T͟H *then*; ZH *vision*

C

cock·loft /ˈkäk,lôft/ ▶ **n.** a small loft or attic.

cock·ney /ˈkäknē/ ▶ **n.** (pl. **cockneys**) a native of East London, traditionally one born within hearing of Bow Bells. ■ the dialect or accent typical of such people.
▶ **adj.** of or characteristic of cockneys or their dialect or accent: *cockney humor.*
– ORIGIN early 17th cent.: originally in the sense 'a town dweller regarded as affected or puny.'

cock·ney·ism /ˈkäknē,izəm/ ▶ **n.** a feature or style of speech or idiom characteristic of cockneys.

cock-of-the-rock ▶ **n.** (pl. **cocks-of-the-rock**) a crested cotinga found in the tropical forests of South America. The male has brilliant orange or red plumage used in communal display. ● Genus *Rupicola*, family Cotingidae: two species.

cock·pit /ˈkäk,pit/ ▶ **n. 1** a compartment for the pilot and sometimes also the crew in an aircraft or spacecraft. ■ a similar compartment for the driver in a racing car. ■ a sunken area in the after deck of a boat providing space for members of the crew.
2 a place where a battle or other conflict takes place: *the cockpit of capitalist conflict in Europe.* ■ a place where cockfights are held.
– ORIGIN late 16th cent. (sense 2): from COCK[1] + PIT[1]. In the early 18th cent. the term was in nautical use, denoting an area in the aft lower deck of a man-of-war where the wounded were taken, later coming to mean 'the "pit" or well in a sailing yacht from which it was steered'; hence the place housing the controls of other vehicles (sense 1, early 20th cent).

cock·roach /ˈkäk,rōCH/ ▶ **n.** a beetlelike insect with long antennae and legs, feeding by scavenging. Several tropical species have become established worldwide as pests in homes and food service establishments. ● Suborder Blattodea, order Dictyoptera: many genera and species, including the **oriental cockroach** (*Blatta orientalis*) and the **American cockroach** (*Periplaneta americana*); some, esp. in the genus *Ectobius*, are small temperate species that live outdoors.
– ORIGIN early 17th cent. (as *cacaroch*): from Spanish *cucaracha*. The spelling change was due to association with COCK[1] and ROACH[2].

American cockroach

cocks·comb /ˈkäks,kōm/ ▶ **n. 1** the crest or comb of a domestic cock.
2 a tropical plant with a crest or plume of tiny yellow, orange, or red flowers, widely cultivated as a garden annual or a houseplant. ● *Celosia cristata*, family Amaranthaceae.
3 an orchid related to the coralroots but with more colorful flowers, native to southern North America. Also called CORALROOT. ● Genus *Hexalectris*, family Orchidaceae.

cockscomb 1

cocks·foot /ˈkäks,fo͝ot/ ▶ **n.** British term for ORCHARD GRASS.

cock·shy /ˈkäk,SHī/ ▶ **n.** (pl. **cockshies**) Brit. dated a target for throwing sticks or stones at as a game. ■ an act of throwing something at such a target. ■ an object of ridicule or criticism.
– ORIGIN from the original use of a cockerel, or a replica of a cockerel, as a target.

cocks·man /ˈkäksmən/ ▶ **n.** (pl. **cocksmen**) vulgar slang a man reputed to be extremely virile or sexually accomplished.
– DERIVATIVES **cocks·man·ship** /-,SHip/ **n.**

cock·spur thorn /ˈkäk,spər/ ▶ **n.** a North American hawthorn that is often cultivated for its rich orange autumn foliage. ● *Crataegus crus-galli*, family Rosaceae. ■ any of a number of trees bearing long spiny thorns.

cock·suck·er /ˈkäk,səkər/ ▶ **n.** vulgar slang a contemptible person (used as a generalized term of abuse).

cock·sure /ˈkäkˈSHo͝or/ ▶ **adj.** presumptuously or arrogantly confident.
– DERIVATIVES **cock·sure·ly adv.**, **cock·sure·ness n.**
– ORIGIN early 16th cent.: from archaic *cock* (a euphemism for *God*) + SURE; later associated with COCK[1].

cock·tail /ˈkäk,tāl/ ▶ **n. 1** an alcoholic drink consisting of a spirit or several spirits mixed with other ingredients, such as fruit juice, lemonade, or cream: [as modifier] *cocktail parties* | *a cocktail bar.* ■ a mixture of substances or factors, esp. when dangerous or unpleasant in its effects: *financial pressure plus isolation can be a deadly cocktail for some people* | *a cocktail of drugs that inhibits replication of HIV.*
2 a dish consisting of small pieces of seafood or fruits, typically served cold at the beginning of a meal as an hors d'oeuvre: *a shrimp cocktail.*
– ORIGIN early 17th cent.: from COCK[1] + TAIL[1]. The original use was as an adjective describing a creature with a tail like that of a cock, specifically a horse with a docked tail; hence (because hunters and coach horses were generally docked) a racehorse that was not a thoroughbred, having a cock-tailed horse in its pedigree (early 19th cent). Sense 1 (originally US, also early 19th cent.) is perhaps analogous, from the idea of an adulterated spirit.

cock·tail dress ▶ **n.** an elegant dress suitable for semiformal social occasions.

cock·tail lounge ▶ **n.** a bar, typically in a hotel, restaurant, or airport, where alcoholic drinks are served.

cock·tail nap·kin ▶ **n.** a small napkin designed to be placed under a drink when it is served.

cock·tail ta·ble ▶ **n.** another term for COFFEE TABLE.

cock·teas·er /ˈkäk,tēzər/ (also **cocktease**) ▶ **n.** vulgar slang a woman who leads a man to the mistaken belief that she is likely to have sexual intercourse with him.

cock-up ▶ **n.** Brit. informal something done badly or inefficiently: *we've made a total cock-up of it.*

cock·y /ˈkäkē/ ▶ **adj.** (**cockier**, **cockiest**) conceited or arrogant, esp. in a bold or impudent way.
– DERIVATIVES **cock·i·ly** /ˈkäkəlē/ **adv.**, **cock·i·ness n.**
– ORIGIN mid 16th cent. (in the sense 'lecherous'): from COCK[1] + -Y[1].

co·co /ˈkōkō/ ▶ **n.** (pl. **cocos**) **1** [usu. as modifier] coconut: *coco matting* | *coco palm.*
2 W. Indian the root of the taro.
– ORIGIN mid 16th cent. (originally denoting the nut): from Spanish and Portuguese, literally 'grinning face' (because of the appearance of the base of the coconut).

co·coa /ˈkōkō/ ▶ **n. 1** a chocolate powder made from roasted and ground cacao seeds. ■ a hot drink made from such a powder mixed with sugar and milk or water.
2 variant spelling of **coco**, usu. regarded as a misspelling.
– ORIGIN early 18th cent. (denoting cacao seed): alteration of CACAO.

co·coa bean ▶ **n.** a cacao seed.

co·coa but·ter ▶ **n.** a fatty substance obtained from cocoa beans and used esp. in the manufacture of confectionery and cosmetics.

co·co·bo·lo /,kōkōˈbōlō/ ▶ **n.** (pl. **cocobolos**) a tropical American tree with hard, reddish timber that is used chiefly to make cutlery handles. ● *Dalbergia retusa*, family Leguminosae.
– ORIGIN mid 19th cent.: via Spanish from Arawak *kakabali.*

co·co de mer /ˈkōkō də ˈmer/ ▶ **n.** a tall palm tree that is native to the Seychelles and has an immense, seaborne nut in a hard, woody shell, which is the largest known seed. ● *Lodoicea maldivica*, family Palmae. ■ the large nut of this palm.
– ORIGIN early 19th cent.: from French *coco-de-mer*, literally 'coco from the sea' (because the tree was first known from nuts found floating in the sea).

co·co·nut /ˈkōkə,nət/ (also **cocoanut**) ▶ **n. 1** the large, oval, brown seed of a tropical palm, consisting of a hard shell lined with edible white flesh and containing a clear liquid. It grows inside a woody husk, surrounded by fiber. ■ the flesh of a coconut, esp. when used as food.
2 (also **coconut palm** or **tree**) the tall palm tree that yields this nut, which grows mainly by coastal beaches and has become naturalized throughout the tropics. Many tropical economies are dependent upon its products, which include copra and coir. ● *Cocos nucifera*, family Palmae.

co·co·nut but·ter ▶ **n.** a solid fat obtained from the flesh of the coconut, and used in the manufacture of soap, candles, ointment, etc.

co·co·nut crab ▶ **n.** a large terrestrial crablike crustacean that climbs coconut palms to feed on the nuts, found on islands in the Indo-Pacific area. Also called ROBBER CRAB. ● *Birgus latro*, family Paguridae.
– ORIGIN so named because it climbs trees to reach coconuts.

Co·co·nut Creek a city in southeastern Florida, northwest of Fort Lauderdale; pop. 50,436 (est. 2008).

Co·co·nut Grove a district in southwestern Miami in Florida, noted as an arts colony and a thriving tourist destination.

co·co·nut mat·ting ▶ **n.** matting made of fiber from coconut husks.

co·co·nut milk ▶ **n.** the watery liquid found inside a coconut.

co·co·nut oil ▶ **n.** the fatty oil obtained from the coconut and used in candies and confections and in cosmetics.

co·co·nut palm ▶ **n.** see COCONUT (sense 2).

co·coon /kəˈko͞on/ ▶ **n.** a silky case spun by the larvae of many insects for protection in the pupal stage. ■ a covering that prevents the corrosion of metal equipment. ■ something that envelops or surrounds, esp. in a protective or comforting way: *the cocoon of her kimono* | figurative ***a warm cocoon of love.***
▶ **v.** [with obj.] envelop or surround in a protective or comforting way: *we began to feel cold even though we were* ***cocooned in*** *our sleeping bags.* ■ spray with a protective coating. ■ [no obj.] retreat from the stressful conditions of public life into the cozy private world of the family: *the movers and shakers are now cocooning.*
– DERIVATIVES **co·coon·er n.**
– ORIGIN late 17th cent.: from French *cocon*, from medieval Provençal *coucoun* 'eggshell, cocoon,' diminutive of *coca* 'shell.' The verb dates from the mid 19th cent.

Co·cos Is·lands /ˈkōkəs/ a group of 27 small coral islands in the Indian Ocean, administered as an external territory of Australia since 1955; pop. 600 (est. 2009). Also called KEELING ISLANDS.

co·cotte /kôˈkôt, kəˈkät/ ▶ **n. 1** (usu. **en cocotte**) a covered, heatproof dish or casserole in which food can be both cooked and served; a Dutch oven. [early 20th cent.: from French *cocasse*, from Latin *cucuma* 'cooking container.']
2 dated a fashionable prostitute. [mid 19th cent.: French, from a child's name for a hen.]

co·coun·sel·ing /ˈkō,kounsəliNG, kōˈkoun-/ (also **cocounseling**) ▶ **n.** a form of personal or psychological counseling in which two or more people alternate the roles of therapist and patient.

Coc·teau /käkˈtō/, Jean (1889–1963), French playwright, novelist, and movie director. His movies include *Beauty and the Beast* (1945) and *Orpheus* (1949).

co·cus wood /ˈkōkəs/ ▶ **n.** hard, heavy timber that blackens with age and is used for musical instruments. ● This timber is obtained from the Jamaican ebony (*Brya ebenus*, family Leguminosae).
– ORIGIN mid 17th cent.: *cocus*, of unknown origin.

COD ▶ **abbr.** ■ cash on delivery. ■ collect on delivery.

cod /käd/ (also **codfish** /ˈkäd,fiSH/) ▶ **n.** (pl. **same**) a large marine fish with a small barbel on the chin. ● Family Gadidae (the **cod family**): many genera and species, in particular the North Atlantic *Gadus morhua*, of great commercial importance as a food fish and as a source of cod liver oil. The cod family also includes the haddock, ling, pollack, whiting, and other food fishes. ■ used in names of similar or related fishes, e.g., **rock cod**, **tomcod**.
– ORIGIN Middle English: of unknown origin; one suggestion is that the word is the same as Old English *cod(d)* 'bag,' because of the fish's appearance.

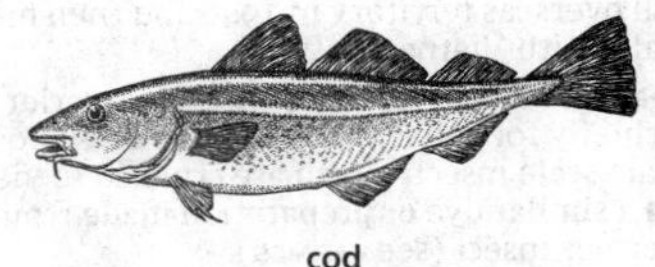
cod

co·da /ˈkōdə/ ▶ **n.** Music the concluding passage of a piece or movement, typically forming an addition to the basic structure. ■ the concluding section of a dance, esp. of a pas de deux, or the finale of a ballet in which the dancers parade before the audience. ■ a concluding event, remark, or section: *his new novel is a kind of coda to his previous books.*
– ORIGIN mid 18th cent.: Italian, from Latin *cauda* 'tail.'

cod·dle /ˈkädl/ ▶ **v.** [with obj.] **1** treat in an indulgent or overprotective way: *I was coddled and cosseted.*
2 cook (an egg) in water below the boiling point.
– DERIVATIVES **cod·dler** /ˈkädlər, ˈkädl-ər/ **n.**
– ORIGIN late 16th cent. (in the sense 'boil (fruit) gently'): origin uncertain; sense 1 is probably a dialect variant of obsolete *caudle* 'administer invalids' gruel,' based on Latin *caldum* 'hot drink,' from *calidus* 'warm.'

code /kōd/ ▶ **n. 1** a system of words, letters, figures, or other symbols substituted for other words, letters, etc., esp. for the purposes of secrecy: *the*

Americans cracked their diplomatic code | sending messages in code. ■ a system of signals, such as sounds, light flashes, or flags, used to send messages: *Morse code.* ■ a series of letters, numbers, or symbols assigned to something for the purposes of classification or identification: *the genetic code | calls with either code will work in the 201 area.*
2 Computing program instructions: *hundreds of lines of code | assembly code.*
3 a systematic collection of laws or regulations: *the criminal code.* ■ a set of conventions governing behavior or activity in a particular sphere: *a dress code.* ■ a set of rules and standards adhered to by a society, class, or individual: *a stern code of honor.*
▶ **v.** [with obj.] **1** convert (the words of a message) into a particular code in order to convey a secret meaning: *only Mitch knew how to read the message—even the name was coded.* ■ express the meaning of (a statement or communication) in an indirect or euphemistic way: (as adj. **coded**) *a national campaign against "playing by ear," a coded phrase that meant jazz.* ■ assign a code to (something) for purposes of classification, analysis, or identification: *she coded the samples and sent them down for dissection.*
2 write code for (a computer program).
3 [no obj.] (**code for**) Biochemistry specify the genetic sequence for (an amino acid or protein): *genes that code for human growth hormone.* ■ be the genetic determiner of (a characteristic): *one pair of homologous chromosomes that codes for eye color.*
– PHRASES **bring something up to code** renovate an old building or update its features in line with the latest building regulations.
– DERIVATIVES **cod·er n.**
– ORIGIN Middle English: via Old French from Latin *codex, codic-* (see CODEX). The term originally denoted a systematic collection of statutes made by one of the later Roman emperors, particularly that of Justinian; compare with sense 3 of the noun (mid 18th cent.), the earliest modern sense.

code·break·er /'kōd,brākər/ ▶ **n.** a person who solves a code or codes.
– DERIVATIVES **code·break·ing n.**

co·dec /'kō,dek/ ▶ **n.** a device or program that compresses data to enable faster transmission and decompresses received data.
– ORIGIN 1960s: blend of *coder* (see CODE) and DECODER.

co·de·fend·ant /,kōdi'fendənt/ ▶ **n.** a joint defendant.

co·deine /'kō,dēn/ ▶ **n.** Medicine a sleep-inducing and analgesic drug derived from morphine. ● An alkaloid; chem. formula: $C_{18}H_{21}NO_3$.
– ORIGIN mid 19th cent.: from Greek *kōdeia* 'poppy head' + -INE[4].

code mon·key ▶ **n.** informal a computer programmer, esp. an inexperienced or unskillful one.

code name ▶ **n.** a word used for secrecy or convenience instead of the usual name.
– DERIVATIVES **code-named adj.**

co·de·pend·en·cy /,kōdə'pendənsē/ ▶ **n.** excessive emotional or psychological reliance on a partner, typically a partner who requires support due to an illness or addiction.
– DERIVATIVES **co·de·pend·ence** /-dəns/ **n.**, **co·de·pend·ent** /-dənt/ **adj. & n.**

code-shar·ing ▶ **n.** agreement between two or more airlines to list certain flights in a reservation system under each other's names.
– DERIVATIVES **code-share v.**

co·de·ter·mi·na·tion /,kōdi,tərmə'nāsHən/ ▶ **n.** cooperation between management and workers in decision-making, esp. by the representation of workers on boards of directors.
– ORIGIN 1950s: from CO- 'together' + DETERMINATION (translating German *Mitbestimmung*).

co·dex /'kō,deks/ ▶ **n.** (pl. **codices** /'kōdə,sēz, 'käd-/ or **codexes**) an ancient manuscript text in book form. ■ an official list of medicines, chemicals, etc.
– ORIGIN late 16th cent. (denoting a collection of statutes or set of rules): from Latin, literally 'block of wood,' later denoting a block split into leaves or tablets for writing on, hence a book.

cod·fish /'käd,fisH/ ▶ **n.** (pl. **same** or **codfishes**) another term for COD.

codg·er /'käjər/ ▶ **n.** often derogatory an elderly man, esp. one who is old-fashioned or eccentric: *old codgers always harp on about yesteryear.*
– ORIGIN mid 18th cent.: perhaps a variant of *cadger* (see CADGE).

co·di·ces /'kōdə,sēz, 'käd-/ plural form of CODEX.

cod·i·cil /'kädəsəl, -,sil/ ▶ **n.** an addition or supplement that explains, modifies, or revokes a will or part of one.
– DERIVATIVES **cod·i·cil·la·ry** /,kädə'silərē/ **adj.**
– ORIGIN late Middle English: from Latin *codicillus*, diminutive of *codex, codic-* (see CODEX).

cod·i·fy /'kädə,fī, 'kōd-/ ▶ **v.** (**codifies, codifying, codified**) [with obj.] arrange (laws or rules) into a systematic code. ■ arrange according to a plan or system: *Verdi helped codify an international operatic culture.*
– DERIVATIVES **cod·i·fi·ca·tion** /,kädəfə'kāsHən, ,kōd-/ **n.**, **cod·i·fi·er** /'kädə,fīər, 'kōd-/ **n.**

cod·ing /'kōdiNG/ ▶ **n.** the process of assigning a code to something for the purposes of classification or identification. ■ a code assigned for such a purpose: *text type codings.* ■ Biochemistry the process of coding genetically for an amino acid, protein, or characteristic.

cod·ling /'kädliNG/ ▶ **n.** an immature cod.

cod·ling moth (also **codlin moth**) ▶ **n.** a small, grayish moth whose larva feeds on apples. ● *Cydia pomonella*, family Tortricidae.
– ORIGIN late Middle English: *codling* from Anglo-Norman French *quer de lion* 'lionheart.'

cod liv·er oil ▶ **n.** oil pressed from the fresh liver of cod, which is rich in vitamins D and A.

co·do·main /'kōdō,mān, ,kōdō'mān/ ▶ **n.** Mathematics a set that includes all the possible values of a given function.

co·don /'kō,dän/ ▶ **n.** Biochemistry a sequence of three nucleotides that together form a unit of genetic code in a DNA or RNA molecule.
– ORIGIN 1960s: from CODE + -ON.

cod·piece /'käd,pēs/ ▶ **n.** a pouch, esp. a conspicuous and decorative one, attached to a man's breeches or close-fitting hose to cover the genitals, worn in the 15th and 16th centuries.
– ORIGIN from earlier *cod* 'scrotum' (from Old English *codd* 'bag, pod') + PIECE.

cods·wal·lop /'kädz,wäləp/ ▶ **n.** Brit. informal nonsense.
– ORIGIN 1960s: sometimes said to be named after Hiram *Codd*, who invented a bottle for carbonated beverages (1875); the derivation remains unconfirmed.

Co·dy[1] /'kōdē/ a city in northwestern Wyoming, associated with Buffalo Bill Cody, who lived here; pop. 9,309 (est. 2008).

Co·dy[2], William Frederick, see BUFFALO BILL.

Coe /kō/, Sebastian (1956–), British middle-distance runner and politician. He won an Olympic gold medal in the 1,500 meters in 1980 and in 1984. After his retirement from athletics, he served as a member of Parliament 1992–97.

coe·cil·i·an ▶ **n.** variant spelling of CAECILIAN.

co·ed /'kō,ed/ informal ▶ **n.** dated a female student at a co-educational institution.
▶ **adj.** (of an institution or system) co-educational.
– ORIGIN late 19th cent.: abbreviation.

co·ed·u·ca·tion /,kō,ejə'kāsHən/ ▶ **n.** the education of students of both sexes together.
– DERIVATIVES **co·ed·u·ca·tion·al** /-sHənl/ **adj.**

co·ef·fi·cient /,kōə'fisHənt/ ▶ **n.** **1** Mathematics a numerical or constant quantity placed before and multiplying the variable in an algebraic expression (e.g., *4* in $4x^y$).
2 Physics a multiplier or factor that measures some property: *coefficients of elasticity | the drag coefficient.*
– ORIGIN mid 17th cent. (in the sense 'cooperating to produce a result'): from modern Latin *coefficient-*, from *com-* 'together' + *efficient-* 'accomplishing' (see EFFICIENT).

co·ef·fi·cient of fric·tion ▶ **n.** the ratio between the force necessary to move one surface horizontally over another and the pressure between the two surfaces.

co·ef·fi·cient of vis·cos·i·ty ▶ **n.** Physics the degree to which a fluid resists flow under an applied force, expressed as the ratio of the shearing stress to the velocity gradient. The coefficient of viscosity of liquids decreases as temperature increases because the bonds between molecules are weakened.

coe·la·canth /'sēlə,kanTH/ ▶ **n.** a large, bony marine fish with a three-lobed tail fin and fleshy pectoral fins. It is thought to be related to the ancestors of land vertebrates and was known only from fossils until one was found alive in 1938; since then others have been found near the Comoro Islands in the Indian Ocean and off Sulawesi, Indonesia. ● *Latimeria chalumnae*, family Latimeriidae (or Coelacanthidae), subclass Crossopterygii.
– ORIGIN mid 19th cent.: from modern Latin *Coelacanthus* (genus name), from Greek *koilos* 'hollow' + *akantha* 'spine' (because its fins have hollow spines).

-coele (also **-cele**) ▶ **comb. form** Medicine denoting a swelling or hernia in a specified part: *meningocele.*
– ORIGIN from Greek *kēlē* 'tumor.'

coe·len·ter·ate /si'lentə,rāt, -rət/ ▶ **n.** Zoology an aquatic invertebrate animal of a phylum that includes jellyfishes, corals, and sea anemones. They are distinguished by having a tube- or cup-shaped body and a single opening ringed with tentacles. Also called CNIDARIAN. ● Phylum Cnidaria (formerly Coelenterata): four classes.
– ORIGIN late 19th cent.: from modern Latin *Coelenterata*, from Greek *koilos* 'hollow' + *enteron* 'intestine.'

coe·len·ter·on /si'lentə,rän/ ▶ **n.** (pl. **coelentera** /-tərə/) the central gastric cavity of a coelenterate.

coe·li·ac ▶ **n.** British spelling of CELIAC.

coe·lom /'sēləm/ (also **celom**) ▶ **n.** (pl. **coeloms** or **coelomata** /si'lōmətə/) Zoology the body cavity in metazoans, located between the intestinal canal and the body wall.
– DERIVATIVES **coe·lo·mate** /'sēlə,māt/ **adj. & n.**, **coe·lom·ic adj.**
– ORIGIN late 19th cent.: from Greek *koilōma* 'cavity.'

coe·lo·stat /'sēlə,stat/ ▶ **n.** Astronomy an advanced version of a heliostat, having a rotating mirror that continuously reflects the light from the same area of sky, allowing the path of a celestial object to be monitored.
– ORIGIN late 19th cent.: formed irregularly from Latin *caelum* 'sky' + -STAT.

coe·lur·o·saur /si'lŏŏrə,sôr, sē-/ (also **coelurosaurus** /si,lŏŏrə'sôrəs, sē-/) ▶ **n.** a small, slender, bipedal, carnivorous dinosaur with long forelimbs, from which the birds are believed to have evolved. ● Infraorder Coelurosauria, suborder Theropoda, order Saurischia: many genera.
– DERIVATIVES **coe·lur·o·sau·ri·an** /-,lŏŏrə'sôrēən/ **adj.**
– ORIGIN 1950s: from Greek *koilos* 'hollow' + *oura* 'tail' + *sauros* 'lizard.'

coe·no·bite ▶ **n.** chiefly Brit. variant spelling of CENOBITE.

coe·no·cyte /'sēnə,sīt/ ▶ **n.** Botany a body of algal or fungal cytoplasm containing several nuclei enclosed in a single membrane.
– DERIVATIVES **coe·no·cyt·ic** /,sēnə'sitik/ **adj.**
– ORIGIN early 20th cent.: from Greek *koinos* 'common' + -CYTE.

co·en·zyme /kō'en,zīm/ ▶ **n.** Biochemistry a nonprotein compound that is necessary for the functioning of an enzyme.

co·en·zyme A ▶ **n.** Biochemistry a coenzyme derived from pantothenic acid, important in respiration and many other biochemical reactions.
– ORIGIN *A* from *acylation* (see ACYLATE).

co·en·zyme Q ▶ **n.** another term for UBIQUINONE.
– ORIGIN *Q* from QUINONE.

co·e·qual /kō'ēkwəl/ ▶ **adj.** equal with one another; having the same rank or importance: *coequal partners.*
▶ **n.** a person or thing equal with another.
– DERIVATIVES **co·e·qual·i·ty** /,kō-i'kwälitē/ **n.**
– ORIGIN late Middle English: from Latin *coaequalis* 'of the same age,' from *co-* 'jointly' + *aequalis* (see EQUAL).

co·erce /kō'ərs/ ▶ **v.** [with obj.] persuade (an unwilling person) to do something by using force or threats: *they were coerced into silence.* ■ obtain (something) by such means: *their confessions were allegedly coerced by torture.*
– DERIVATIVES **co·er·ci·ble adj.**
– ORIGIN late Middle English: from Latin *coercere* 'restrain,' from *co-* 'jointly, together' + *arcere* 'restrain.'

co·er·cion /kō'ərZHən, -SHən/ ▶ **n.** the practice of persuading someone to do something by using force or threats: *it wasn't slavery because no coercion was used.*

co·er·cive /kō'ərsiv/ ▶ **adj.** relating to or using force or threats: *coercive measures.*
– DERIVATIVES **co·er·cive·ly adv.**, **co·er·cive·ness n.**

co·er·cive force ▶ **n.** Physics another term for COERCIVITY.

co·er·civ·i·ty /,kōər'sivitē/ ▶ **n.** Physics the resistance of a magnetic material to changes in magnetization. ■ the field intensity necessary to demagnetize such material when fully magnetized.

co·es·sen·tial /,kōi'sencHəl/ ▶ **adj.** united or inseparable in essence or being. ■ having the same substance or essence.
– DERIVATIVES **co·es·sen·ti·al·i·ty** /kōi,sencHē'alitē/ **n.**, **co·es·sen·tial·ly adv.**, **co·es·sen·tial·ness n.**

co·e·ta·ne·ous /,kō-i'tānēəs/ ▶ **adj.** another term for COEVAL.

co·e·ter·nal /,kō-i'tərnl/ ▶ **adj.** equally eternal; existing with something else eternally: *the Deity is coeternal with Time and Space.*
– DERIVATIVES **co·e·ter·nal·ly adv.**

PRONUNCIATION KEY ə *ago, up*; ər *over, fur*; a *hat*; ā *ate*; ä *car*; e *let*; ē *see*; i *fit*; ī *by*; NG *sing*; ō *go*; ô *law, for*; oi *toy*; ŏŏ *good*; ōō *goo*; ou *out*; TH *thin*; TH *then*; ZH *vision*

C

C

Coet·zee /kōōt'sē/, J. M. (1940–), South African novelist; full name *John Maxwell Coetzee*. Notable works: *In the Heart of the Country* (1977), *Life & Times of Michael K* (1983), *White Writing* (1988), and *Age of Iron* (1990). Nobel Prize for Literature (2003).

Coeur d'Alene /,kôr dl'ān/ a commercial and resort city in northwestern Idaho, on Coeur d'Alene Lake, which is fed by the Coeur d'Alene River; pop. 43,360 (est. 2008).

co·e·val /kō'ēvəl/ ▶ **adj.** having the same age or date of origin; contemporary: *these lavas were coeval with the volcanic activity.*
▶ **n.** a person of roughly the same age as oneself; a contemporary: *like so many of his coevals, he yearned for stability.*
– DERIVATIVES **co·e·val·i·ty** /,kō-ē'valitē/ **n.**, **co·e·val·ly adv.**
– ORIGIN early 17th cent. (as a noun): from late Latin *coaevus*, from *co-* 'jointly, in common' + Latin *aevum* 'age.'

co·ev·o·lu·tion /,kōevə'lōōsHən, -ēvə-/ ▶ **n.** Biology the influence of closely associated species on each other in their evolution.
– DERIVATIVES **co·ev·o·lu·tion·ar·y** /-sHə,nerē/ **adj.**, **co·e·volve** /,kō-i'välv/ **v.**

co·ex·ist /,kō-ig'zist/ ▶ **v.** [no obj.] exist at the same time or in the same place: *traditional and modern values coexist in Africa.* ■ (of nations or peoples) exist in mutual tolerance despite different ideologies or interests: *the task of diplomacy was to help different states to coexist.*
– DERIVATIVES **co·ex·ist·ence** /-'zistəns/ **n.**, **co·ex·ist·ent** /-'zistənt/ **adj.**
– ORIGIN mid 17th cent.: from late Latin *coexistere*, from *co-* 'together' + *existere* 'exist,' from *ex-* 'out' + *sister* 'take a stand.'

co·ex·tend /,kō-ik'stend/ ▶ **v.** extend equally through the same space or period of time.

co·ex·ten·sive /,kō-ik'stensiv/ ▶ **adj.** extending over the same space or time; corresponding exactly in extent. ■ (of a term) denoting the same referent as another.

co·fac·tor /'kō,faktər/ ▶ **n. 1** a contributory cause of a disease.
2 Biochemistry a substance (other than the substrate) whose presence is essential for the activity of an enzyme.
3 Mathematics the quantity obtained from a determinant or a square matrix by removal of the row and column containing a specified element.

C. of C. ▶ **abbr.** Chamber of Commerce.

C. of E. ▶ **abbr.** Church of England.

cof·fee /'kôfē, 'käfē/ ▶ **n. 1** a drink made from the roasted and ground beanlike seeds of a tropical shrub, served hot or iced: *a cup of coffee* | [as modifier] *a coffee pot.* ■ a cup of this drink: *she'll buy you a coffee.* ■ these seeds raw, roasted and ground, or processed into a powder that dissolves in hot water: *a jar of instant coffee.* ■ a pale brown color like that of coffee mixed with milk. ■ a party or reception at which coffee is served: *going to coffees and answering questions.*
2 the shrub of the bedstraw family that yields these seeds, two of which are contained in each red berry. Native to the Old World tropics, most coffee is grown in tropical America. ● Genus *Coffea*, family Rubiaceae: several species. See also ARABICA and ROBUSTA.
– ORIGIN late 16th cent.: from Turkish *kahveh*, from Arabic *ḳahwa*, probably via Dutch *koffie*.

cof·fee bar ▶ **n.** a bar or cafe serving coffee and light refreshments.

cof·fee bean ▶ **n.** a beanlike seed of the coffee shrub.

cof·fee break ▶ **n.** a short break during the working day, during which people typically drink a cup of coffee or tea.

cof·fee cake ▶ **n.** a cake, often cinnamon-flavored, with a drizzled white icing or crumb topping, and usually eaten with coffee.

cof·fee grind·er ▶ **n.** a small machine for grinding roasted coffee beans.

cof·fee·house /'kôfē,hous, 'käfē-/ ▶ **n.** a place where coffee is served and people gather for conversation, music, poetry readings, and other informal entertainment.

cof·fee klatsch (also **coffee klatch**) ▶ **n.** variant spelling of KAFFEEKLATSCH.

cof·fee mak·er (also **coffeemaker**) ▶ **n.** a machine or pot for brewing coffee.

cof·fee mill ▶ **n.** another term for COFFEE GRINDER.

cof·fee pot ▶ **n.** a covered container with a spout, in which coffee is made or served.

cof·fee shop ▶ **n.** a small, informal restaurant, as found in a hotel. ■ a cafe serving coffee and light refreshments.

cof·fee ta·ble ▶ **n.** a low table, typically placed in front of a sofa.

cof·fee-ta·ble book ▶ **n.** a large, expensive, lavishly illustrated book, esp. one intended only for casual reading.

cof·fer /'kôfər, 'käfər/ ▶ **n. 1** a strongbox or small chest for holding valuables. ■ (**coffers**) the funds or financial reserves of a group or institution: *the federal government's empty coffers.*
2 a recessed panel in a ceiling.
– DERIVATIVES **cof·fered adj.** (sense 2).
– ORIGIN Middle English: from Old French *coffre* 'chest,' via Latin from Greek *kophinos* 'basket.'

cof·fer·dam /'kôfər,dam, 'käfər,dam/ ▶ **n.** a watertight enclosure pumped dry to permit construction work below the waterline, as when building bridges or repairing a ship.

Cof·fin /'kôfən, 'käf-/, William Sloan (1924–2006), US Presbyterian minister. As Yale University chaplain 1958–75, he was a leader of antiwar protests. He served as senior minister of Riverside Church in New York 1977–1987.

cof·fin /'kôfən, 'käfən/ ▶ **n.** a long, narrow box, typically of wood, in which a corpse is buried or cremated. ■ informal an old and unsafe aircraft or vessel.
▶ **v.** (**coffins, coffining, coffined**) [with obj.] put (a dead body) in a coffin.
– ORIGIN Middle English (in the general sense 'box, chest, casket'): from Old French *cofin* 'little basket or case,' from Latin *cophinus* (see COFFER).

cof·fin bone ▶ **n.** the terminal bone in a horse's hoof (the distal phalanx).

cof·fin joint ▶ **n.** the joint at the top of a horse's hoof.

cof·fin nail ▶ **n.** informal a cigarette.

cof·fle /'kôfəl, 'käfəl/ ▶ **n.** a line of animals or slaves fastened or driven along together.
– ORIGIN mid 18th cent.: from Arabic *ḳāfila* 'caravan.'

co·found·er /'kō'foundər, 'kō,foun-/ ▶ **n.** a joint founder.
– DERIVATIVES **co·found** /kō'found/ **v.**

co·func·tion /'kō,fəNGksHən/ ▶ **n.** Mathematics the trigonometric function of the complement of an angle or arc.

cog /käg/ ▶ **n.** a wheel or bar with a series of projections on its edge that transfers motion by engaging with projections on another wheel or bar. ■ each of such a series of projections.
– PHRASES **a cog in the** (or **a**) **machine** (or **wheel**) a small or insignificant member of a larger organization or system: *copywriters have been seen as just a cog in the big advertising machine.*
– DERIVATIVES **cogged adj.**
– ORIGIN Middle English: probably of Scandinavian origin and related to Swedish *kugge* and Norwegian *kug*.

co·gen·cy /'kōjənsē/ ▶ **n.** the quality of being clear, logical, and convincing; lucidity: *the cogency of this argument.*

co·gen·er·a·tion /,kō,jenə'rāsHən/ ▶ **n.** the generation of electricity and other energy jointly, esp. the utilization of the steam left over from electricity generation to produce heat.

co·gent /'kōjənt/ ▶ **adj.** (of an argument or case) clear, logical, and convincing.
– DERIVATIVES **co·gent·ly adv.**
– ORIGIN mid 17th cent.: from Latin *cogent-* 'compelling,' from the verb *cogere*, from *co-* 'together' + *agere* 'drive.'

cog·i·ta·ble /'käjətəbəl/ ▶ **adj.** rare able to be grasped by the mind; conceivable.
– ORIGIN late Middle English: from Latin *cogitabilis*, from the verb *cogitare* (see COGITATE).

cog·i·tate /'käjə,tāt/ ▶ **v.** [no obj.] formal or humorous think deeply about something; meditate or reflect: *he stroked his beard and retired to cogitate.*
– DERIVATIVES **cog·i·ta·tive** /-,tātiv/ **adj.**, **cog·i·ta·tor** /-,tātər/ **n.**
– ORIGIN late 16th cent.: from Latin *cogitat-* 'considered,' from the verb *cogitare*, from *co-* 'together' + *agitare* 'turn over, consider.'

cog·i·ta·tion /,käjə'tāsHən/ ▶ **n.** the action of thinking deeply about something; contemplation: *sorry, did I interrupt your cogitation?*

co·gi·to /'kägi,tō, 'käj-/ ▶ **n.** (usu. **the cogito**) Philosophy the principle establishing the existence of a being from the fact of its thinking or awareness.
– ORIGIN mid 19th cent.: Latin, literally 'I think,' in Descartes's formula (1641) *cogito, ergo sum* 'I think therefore I am.'

co·gnac /'kōn,yak, 'kän-, 'kôn-/ ▶ **n.** a high-quality brandy, properly that distilled in Cognac in western France.

cog·nate /'käg,nāt/ ▶ **adj. 1** Linguistics (of a word) having the same linguistic derivation as another; from the same original word or root (e.g., English *is*, German *ist*, Latin *est*, from Indo-European *esti*).
2 formal related; connected: *cognate subjects such as physics and chemistry.* ■ related to or descended from a common ancestor. Compare with AGNATE.
▶ **n. 1** Linguistics a cognate word.
2 Law a blood relative.
– DERIVATIVES **cog·nate·ly adv.**, **cog·nate·ness n.**
– ORIGIN early 17th cent.: from Latin *cognatus*, from *co-* 'together with' + *natus* 'born.'

cog·nate ob·ject ▶ **n.** Grammar a direct object that has the same linguistic derivation as the verb that governs it, as in "sing a song," "live a good life." ■ a direct object that makes explicit a semantic concept that is already wholly present in the semantics of the verb which governs it, as in "ask a question," "eat some food."

cog·ni·tion /,käg'nisHən/ ▶ **n.** the mental action or process of acquiring knowledge and understanding through thought, experience, and the senses. ■ a result of this; a perception, sensation, notion, or intuition.
– DERIVATIVES **cog·ni·tion·al** /-sHənl/ **adj.**
– ORIGIN late Middle English: from Latin *cognitio(n-)*, from *cognoscere* 'get to know.'

cog·ni·tive /'kägnətiv/ ▶ **adj.** of or relating to cognition.
– DERIVATIVES **cog·ni·tive·ly adv.**
– ORIGIN late 16th cent.: from medieval Latin *cognitivus*, from *cognit-* 'known,' from the verb *cognoscere*.

cog·ni·tive be·hav·ior·al ther·a·py ▶ **n.** see COGNITIVE THERAPY.

cog·ni·tive dis·so·nance ▶ **n.** Psychology the state of having inconsistent thoughts, beliefs, or attitudes, esp. as relating to behavioral decisions and attitude change.

cog·ni·tive gram·mar ▶ **n.** a theory of language that seeks to characterize knowledge of grammar in terms of symbolic conceptual and semantic categories and general cognitive processes.

cog·ni·tive map ▶ **n.** a mental representation of one's physical environment.

cog·ni·tive pros·the·sis ▶ **n.** an electronic computational device that extends the capability of human cognition or sense perception.

cog·ni·tive sci·ence ▶ **n.** the study of thought, learning, and mental organization, which draws on aspects of psychology, linguistics, philosophy, and computer modeling.
– DERIVATIVES **cog·ni·tive sci·en·tist n.**

cog·ni·tive ther·a·py (also **cognitive behavioral therapy**) ▶ **n.** a type of psychotherapy in which negative patterns of thought about the self and the world are challenged in order to alter unwanted behavior patterns or treat mood disorders such as depression.

cog·ni·tiv·ist /'kägnətivist/ ▶ **n.** a person who believes or works in cognitive grammar.
▶ **adj.** of or relating to cognitive grammar.
– DERIVATIVES **cog·ni·tiv·ism** /-,vizəm/ **n.**
– ORIGIN 1950s (in the sense 'believing that moral judgments are true or false statements about moral facts'): from COGNITIVE + -IST.

cog·ni·za·ble /'kägnəzəbəl, käg'nīz-/ ▶ **adj. 1** formal perceptible; clearly identifiable.
2 Law within the jurisdiction of a court.
– ORIGIN late 17th cent.: from COGNIZANCE + -ABLE.

cog·ni·zance /'kägnəzəns/ (also **cognisance**) ▶ **n.**
1 formal knowledge, awareness, or notice: *he was deputed to bring the affair to the cognizance of the board.* ■ Law the action of taking jurisdiction. ■ the action of taking judicial notice (of a fact beyond dispute).
2 Heraldry a distinctive device or mark, esp. an emblem or badge formerly worn by retainers of a noble house.
– PHRASES **take cognizance of** formal attend to; take account of.
– ORIGIN Middle English *conisance*, from Old French *conoisance*, based on Latin *cognoscere* 'get to know.' The spelling with *g*, influenced by Latin, arose in the 15th cent. and gradually affected the pronunciation.

cog·ni·zant /'kägnəzənt/ (also **cognisant**) ▶ **adj.** [predic.] formal having knowledge or being aware of: *statesmen must be cognizant of the political boundaries within which they work.*
– ORIGIN early 19th cent.: probably directly from COGNIZANCE.

cog·nize /käg'nīz, 'käg,nīz/ ▶ v. [with obj.] formal perceive, know, or become aware of: *what the novel cognizes, discerns, knows.*
– ORIGIN early 19th cent.: from COGNIZANCE, on the pattern of words such as *recognize.*

cog·no·men /käg'nōmən, 'kägnəmən/ ▶ n. an extra personal name given to an ancient Roman citizen, functioning rather like a nickname and typically passed down from father to son. ■ a name; a nickname.
– ORIGIN Latin, from *co-* 'together with' + *gnomen, nomen* 'name.'

co·gno·scen·te /,känyə'sHentē, ,kägnə-/ ▶ n. (pl. **cognoscenti** /-tē/) a connoisseur; a discerning expert.

co·gno·scen·ti /,känyō'sHentē, ,kägnə-/ ▶ plural n. people who are considered to be especially well informed about a particular subject: *it was hailed by the cognoscenti as one of the best golf courses in Europe.*
– ORIGIN late 18th cent.: from Italian *conoscenti,* literally 'people who know.' The *g* was added under the influence of Latin *cognoscent-* 'getting to know,' from the verb *cognoscere* (Italian *conoscere*).

co·gon grass /kō'gōn/ ▶ n. a perennial, rhizomatous grass of Asian origin, used for thatching and as a packing material; identified as a noxious weed in much of the southeastern US. ● *Imperata cylindrica,* family Poaceae.

cog rail·way ▶ n. a railroad with a toothed central rail between the bearing rails that engages with a cogwheel under the locomotive, providing traction for ascending very steep slopes.

cog·wheel /'käg,(h)wēl/ ▶ n. another term for COG.

co·hab·it /kō'habit/ ▶ v. (**cohabits, cohabiting, cohabited**) [no obj.] live together and have a sexual relationship without being married. ■ coexist: *animals that can cohabit with humans thrive.*
– DERIVATIVES **co·hab·it·ant** n., **co·hab·i·ta·tion** /kō,habə'tāsHən/ n., **co·hab·it·er** n.
– ORIGIN mid 16th cent.: from Latin *cohabitare,* from *co-* 'together' + *habitare* 'dwell.'

Co·han /'kō,han/, George Michael (1878–1942), US composer, playwright, actor, and producer. Among his best known songs are "Yankee Doodle Dandy" (1904) and "Give My Regards to Broadway" (1904).

co·heir /kō'e(ə)r/ ▶ n. a joint heir.

co·heir·ess /kō'e(ə)ris/ ▶ n. a joint heiress.

co·hen ▶ n. variant spelling of KOHEN.

co·here /kō'hi(ə)r/ ▶ v. [no obj.] **1** be united; form a whole: *our mixed physical and spiritual natures cohere and mature.*
2 (of an argument or theory) be logically consistent: *this view does not cohere with their other beliefs.*
– ORIGIN mid 16th cent.: from Latin *cohaerere,* from *co-* 'together' + *haerere* 'to stick.'

co·her·ence /kō'hi(ə)rəns/ ▶ n. **1** the quality of being logical and consistent: *this raises further questions on the coherence of state policy.*
2 the quality of forming a unified whole: *the group began to lose coherence and the artists took separate directions.*
– DERIVATIVES **co·her·en·cy** n.

co·her·ent /kō'hi(ə)rənt/ ▶ adj. **1** (of an argument, theory, or policy) logical and consistent: *they failed to develop a coherent economic strategy.* ■ (of a person) able to speak clearly and logically: *she was lucid and coherent and did not appear to be injured.*
2 united as or forming a whole: *divided into a number of geographically coherent kingdoms.*
3 Physics (of waves) having a constant phase relationship.
– DERIVATIVES **co·her·ent·ly** adv.
– ORIGIN mid 16th cent. (in the sense 'logically related to'): from Latin *cohaerent-* 'sticking together,' from the verb *cohaerere* (see COHERE).

co·he·sion /kō'hēzHən/ ▶ n. the action or fact of forming a united whole: *the work at present lacks cohesion.* ■ Physics the sticking together of particles of the same substance.
– ORIGIN mid 17th cent.: from Latin *cohaes-* 'cleaved together,' from the verb *cohaerere* (see COHERE), on the pattern of *adhesion.*

co·he·sive /kō'hēsiv, -ziv/ ▶ adj. characterized by or causing cohesion.
– DERIVATIVES **co·he·sive·ly** adv., **co·he·sive·ness** n.

Cohn /kōn/, Ferdinand Julius (1828–98), German botanist. A founder of bacteriology, he was the first to devise a systematic classification of bacteria into genera and species.

co·ho /'kōhō/ (also **coho salmon** or **cohoe**) ▶ n. (pl. **same, cohos,** or **cohoes**) a deep-bodied North Pacific salmon with small black spots. Also called SILVER SALMON. ● *Oncorhynchus kisutch,* family Salmonidae.
– ORIGIN mid 19th cent.: probably from Salish *k'wəxwəθ.*

co·hort /'kō,hôrt/ ▶ n. **1** [treated as sing. or pl.] an ancient Roman military unit, comprising six centuries, equal to one tenth of a legion.
2 [treated as sing. or pl.] a group of people banded together or treated as a group: ***a cohort of** civil servants patiently drafting legislation.* ■ a group of people with a common statistical characteristic: *the 1940–44 birth cohort of women.*
3 often derogatory a supporter or companion.
– ORIGIN late Middle English: from Old French *cohorte,* or from Latin *cohors, cohort-* 'yard, retinue.' Compare with COURT.

> **USAGE** The co- in **cohort** is not a prefix signifying a joint or auxiliary relationship (as in *coauthor* or *codependency*). The word derives from the Latin *cohors,* an ancient Roman military unit, and also 'band of people with a common interest.' In the mid 20th century, a new sense developed in the US, meaning 'a companion or colleague,' as in *young Jack arrived with three of his cohorts.* Although this use is well established, there are still some people who object to it on the grounds that **cohort** should be used only for groups of people, never for individuals.

co·hosh /'kō,häsH/ ▶ n. either of two medicinal plants native to North America. ● (also **black cohosh**) a plant of the buttercup family, with small white flowers (*Cimicifuga racemosa,* family Ranunculaceae). ● (also **blue cohosh**) a plant of the barberry family (*Caulophyllum thalictroides,* family Berberidaceae).
– ORIGIN late 18th cent.: from Eastern Abnaki.

co·host /'kō,hōst/ ▶ n. a joint host.
▶ v. [with obj.] act as a joint host.

co·hune /kə'hoon, kō-/ (also **cahoun**) ▶ n. a Central American palm that is a valuable source of oil. ● *Orbignya cohune,* family Palmae. ■ (also **cohune nut**) the oil-rich nut of this palm.
– ORIGIN mid 18th cent.: from Miskito.

coif ▶ n. **1** /koif/ a woman's close-fitting cap, now only worn under a veil by nuns. ■ historical a protective metal skullcap worn under armor.
2 /kwäf, koif/ informal short for COIFFURE.
▶ v. /kwäf, koif/ (**coifs, coiffing, coiffed;** also **coifs, coifing, coifed**) [with obj.] style or arrange (someone's hair), typically in an elaborate way: (as adj. **coiffed**) *her elaborately coiffed hair.* ■ style or arrange the hair of (someone): *she was sent to Paris to be groomed and coiffed.*
– ORIGIN Middle English: from Old French *coife* 'headdress,' from late Latin *cofia* 'helmet.'

coif·feur /kwä'fər/ ▶ n. a hairdresser.
– ORIGIN mid 19th cent.: French, from *coiffer* 'arrange the hair,' in Old French 'cover with a coif' (see COIF).

coif·feuse /kwä'f(y)ooz, -'fə(r)z/ ▶ n. a female hairdresser.

coif·fure /kwä'fyoor/ ▶ n. a person's hairstyle, typically an elaborate one.
– DERIVATIVES **coif·fured** adj.
– ORIGIN mid 17th cent.: French, from *coiffer* 'arrange the hair,' in Old French 'cover with a coif' (see COIF).

coign /koin/ ▶ n. a projecting corner or angle of a wall or building.
– PHRASES **coign of vantage** a favorable position for observation or action.
– ORIGIN late Middle English: variant of COIN. The phrase *coign of vantage* was first used by Shakespeare (*Macbeth* I. iv. 7), and later popularized by Sir Walter Scott.

coil[1] /koil/ ▶ n. a length of something wound or arranged in a spiral or sequence of rings: *a coil of rope.* ■ a single ring or loop in such a sequence: *the snake wrapped its coils around her.* ■ a roll of postage stamps, esp. one for use in a vending machine. ■ a slow-burning spiral made with the dried paste of pyrethrum powder, which produces a smoke that inhibits mosquitoes from biting. ■ (often **the coil**) an intrauterine contraceptive device in the form of a coil. ■ an electrical device consisting of a length of wire arranged in a coil for converting the level of a voltage, producing a magnetic field, or adding inductance to a circuit: *a relay coil.* ■ such a device used for transmitting high voltage to the spark plugs of an internal combustion engine.
▶ v. [with obj.] arrange or wind (something long and flexible) in a joined sequence of concentric circles or rings: *he began to coil up the heavy ropes* | *he coiled a lock of her hair around his finger.* ■ [no obj.] move or twist into such an arrangement or shape: *smoke coiled lazily toward the ceiling.*
– ORIGIN early 16th cent. (as a verb): from Old French *coillir,* from Latin *colligere* 'gather together' (see COLLECT[1]).

coil[2] ▶ n. archaic or dialect a confusion or turmoil.
– PHRASES **shuffle off this mortal coil** chiefly humorous die. [from Shakespeare's *Hamlet* (III. i. 67).]
– ORIGIN mid 16th cent.: of unknown origin.

coil spring ▶ n. a helical spring made from metal wire or a metal band.

Coim·ba·tore /'koimbə,toor/ a city in southern India, in the state of Tamil Nadu; pop. 1,008,300 (est. 2009).

coin /koin/ ▶ n. a flat, typically round piece of metal with an official stamp, used as money. ■ money in the form of coins: *large amounts of coin and precious metal.* ■ informal money: *he showed me how we could make a lot of coin.* ■ (**coins**) one of the suits in some tarot packs, corresponding to pentacles in others.
▶ v. [with obj.] **1** make (coins) by stamping metal. ■ make (metal) into coins.
2 invent or devise (a new word or phrase): *he coined the term "desktop publishing."*
– PHRASES **the other side of the coin** the opposite or contrasting aspect of a matter. **pay someone back in his or her own coin** retaliate with similar behavior. **to coin a phrase** said ironically when introducing a banal remark or cliché: *I had to find out the hard way—to coin a phrase.* ■ said when introducing a new expression or a variation on a familiar one.
– ORIGIN Middle English: from Old French *coin* 'wedge, corner, die,' *coigner* 'to mint,' from Latin *cuneus* 'wedge.' The original sense was 'cornerstone,' later 'angle or wedge' (senses now spelled QUOIN); in late Middle English the term denoted a die for stamping money, or a piece of money produced by such a die.

coin·age /'koinij/ ▶ n. **1** coins collectively: *the volume of coinage in circulation.* ■ the action or process of producing coins from metal. ■ a system or type of coins in use: *decimal coinage.*
2 the invention of a new word or phrase. ■ a newly invented word or phrase.
– ORIGIN late Middle English: from Old French *coigniage,* from *coignier* 'to mint' (see COIN).

co·in·cide /,kōən'sīd, 'kōən,sīd/ ▶ v. [no obj.] occur at or during the same time: *publication is timed **to coincide with** a major exhibition* | *the two events coincided.* ■ correspond in nature; tally: *the interests of employers and employees do not always coincide.* ■ correspond in position; meet or intersect: *the two long-distance walks briefly coincide here.* ■ be in agreement: *the members of the College **coincide in** this opinion.*
– ORIGIN early 18th cent. (in the sense 'occupy the same space'): from medieval Latin *coincidere,* from *co-* 'together with' + *incidere* 'fall upon or into.'

co·in·ci·dence /kō'insədəns, -,dens/ ▶ n. **1** a remarkable concurrence of events or circumstances without apparent causal connection: *it's no coincidence that this new burst of innovation has occurred in the free nations* | *they met **by coincidence.***
2 correspondence in nature or in time of occurrence: *the coincidence of interest between the mining companies and certain politicians.*
3 Physics the presence of ionizing particles or other objects in two or more detectors simultaneously, or of two or more signals simultaneously in a circuit.
– ORIGIN early 17th cent. (in the sense 'occupation of the same space'): from medieval Latin *coincidentia,* from *coincidere* 'coincide, agree' (see COINCIDE). Sense 3 dates from the 1930s.

co·in·ci·dent /kō'insədənt, -,dent/ ▶ adj. occurring together in space or time: *an increasing specialization of discourse **coincident with** the progress of the Industrial Revolution.* ■ in agreement or harmony: *the stake of defense attorneys is not always **coincident with** that of their clients.*
– DERIVATIVES **co·in·ci·dent·ly** /kō,insə'dentlē/ adv.
– ORIGIN mid 16th cent.: from medieval Latin *coincident-* 'coinciding, agreeing,' from the verb *coincidere* (see COINCIDE).

co·in·ci·den·tal /kō,insə'dentl/ ▶ adj. **1** resulting from a coincidence; done or happening by chance: *any resemblance between their reports is purely coincidental* | *it cannot be **coincidental that** these years were a time of important new developments.*
2 happening or existing at the same time: *it's convenient that his plan is **coincidental with** the group's closure.*
– DERIVATIVES **co·in·ci·den·tal·ly** /kō,insə'dentlē, -'dentl-ē/ adv. [sentence adverb] *coincidentally, we had both left our previous jobs on the same day.*

C

coin·er /ˈkoinər/ ▶ **n.** **1** historical a person who coins money, in particular a maker of counterfeit coins.
2 a person who invents or devises a new word, sense, or phrase.

coin-op·er·at·ed (also **coin-op**) ▶ **adj.** operated by inserting coins in a slot: *coin-operated telephones.*
▶ **n.** a machine that is coin-operated.

co·in·sur·ance ▶ **n.** a type of insurance in which the insured pays a share of the payment made against a claim.

Coin·treau /kwänˈtrō/ ▶ **n.** trademark a colorless orange-flavored liqueur.
– ORIGIN named after the *Cointreau* family, liqueur producers based in Angers, France.

coir /ˈkoi(ə)r/ ▶ **n.** fiber from the outer husk of the coconut, used for making ropes and matting.
– ORIGIN late 16th cent.: from Malayalam *kāyaṟu* 'cord, coir.'

co·i·tion /kōˈisHən/ ▶ **n.** another term for COITUS.
– ORIGIN mid 16th cent. (in the sense 'meeting or uniting'): from Latin *coitio(n-)*, from the verb *coire*, from *co-* 'together' + *ire* 'go.'

co·i·tus /ˈkōətəs, kōˈētəs/ ▶ **n.** formal sexual intercourse.
– DERIVATIVES **co·i·tal** /ˈkōətl, kōˈētl/ **adj.**
– ORIGIN mid 19th cent.: from Latin, from *coire* 'go together' (see COITION).

co·i·tus in·ter·rup·tus /intəˈrəptəs/ ▶ **n.** sexual intercourse in which the penis is withdrawn before ejaculation.
– ORIGIN from COITUS + Latin *interruptus* 'interrupted.'

co·i·tus re·ser·va·tus /ˌrezərˈvātəs, -ˈvätəs/ ▶ **n.** the postponement or avoidance of ejaculation, to prolong sexual intercourse.
– ORIGIN from COITUS + Latin *reservatus* 'reserved, kept.'

co·jo·nes /kəˈhōˌnāz, -ˌnās/ ▶ **plural n.** informal a man's testicles. ■ courage; guts: *he does not have the cojones to kill a flea.*
– ORIGIN Spanish.

coke[1] /kōk/ ▶ **n.** a solid fuel made by heating coal in the absence of air so that the volatile components are driven off. ■ carbon residue left after the incomplete combustion of gasoline or other fuels.
▶ **v.** [with obj.] (usu. as noun **coking**) convert (coal) into coke.
– ORIGIN late Middle English (in the sense 'charcoal'): of unknown origin. The current sense dates from the mid 17th cent.

coke[2] ▶ **n.** informal term for COCAINE.
– ORIGIN early 20th cent.: abbreviation.

Coke-bot·tle ▶ **n.** [as modifier] informal denoting very thick lenses for glasses or glasses with such lenses.

coked /kōkt/ ▶ **adj.** informal having taken a large amount of cocaine: *he was obviously drunk or coked up.*

col /käl/ ▶ **n.** the lowest point of a ridge or saddle between two peaks, typically affording a pass from one side of a mountain range to another.
■ Meteorology a region of slightly elevated pressure between two anticyclones.
– ORIGIN mid 19th cent.: from French, literally 'neck,' from Latin *collum*.

Col. ▶ **abbr.** ■ colonel. ■ Bible Colossians.

col. ▶ **abbr.** ■ collected. ■ college. ■ colony.
■ column.

col- ▶ **prefix** variant spelling of COM- assimilated before *l* (as in *collocate, collude*).

COLA ▶ **abbr.** cost-of-living adjustment, an increase made to wages or Social Security benefits to keep them in line with inflation.

co·la /ˈkōlə/ ▶ **n.** **1** a brown carbonated drink that is flavored with an extract of cola nuts, or with a similar flavoring. [shortening of *Coca-Cola*.]
2 (also **kola**) a small evergreen African tree that is cultivated in the tropics for its seeds (cola nuts). [from Temne *k'ola* 'cola nut.'] ● Genus *Cola*, family Sterculiaceae: several species, in particular *C. acuminata*.

col·an·der /ˈkələndər, ˈkäl-/ ▶ **n.** a perforated bowl used to strain off liquid from food, esp. after cooking.
– ORIGIN Middle English: based on Latin *colare* 'to strain.'

co·la nut (also **kola nut**) ▶ **n.** the seed of the cola tree, which contains caffeine and is chewed or made into a drink.

co·lat·i·tude /kōˈlatəˌt(y)o͞od/ ▶ **n.** Astronomy the complement of the latitude; the difference between latitude and 90°.

col·can·non /kälˈkanən/ ▶ **n.** an Irish and Scottish dish of cabbage and potatoes boiled and pounded.
– ORIGIN late 18th cent.: from COLE; the origin of the second element is uncertain but it is said that cannonballs were used to pound such vegetables as spinach.

col·chi·cine /ˈkälcHəˌsēn, ˈkälkə-/ ▶ **n.** Chemistry a yellow compound present in the corms of colchicums, used to relieve pain in cases of gout.
● An alkaloid; chem. formula: $C_{22}H_{25}NO_6$.

col·chi·cum /ˈkälcHikəm, ˈkälki-/ ▶ **n.** (pl. **colchicums**) a plant of a genus that includes the autumn crocuses. ● Genus *Colchicum*, family Liliaceae. ■ the dried corm or seed of meadow saffron, which has analgesic properties and is used medicinally, esp. as a tincture.
– ORIGIN from Latin, from Greek *kolkhikon* 'of Colchis' (see COLCHIS), alluding to the skills as a poisoner of the sorceress Medea of Colchis in classical mythology.

Col·chis /ˈkälkis/ an ancient region south of the Caucasus Mountains at the eastern end of the Black Sea. In classical mythology it was the goal of Jason's expedition for the Golden Fleece. Greek name KOLKHIS.

cold /kōld/ ▶ **adj.** **1** of or at a low or relatively low temperature, esp. when compared with the human body: *a freezing cold day | it's cold outside | a sharp, cold wind.* ■ (of food or drink) served or consumed without being heated or after cooling: *a cold drink | serve hot or cold.* ■ (of a person) feeling uncomfortably cold: *she was cold, and I put some more wood on the fire.* ■ feeling or characterized by fear or horror: *he suddenly went cold with a dreadful certainty | a cold shiver of fear.* ■ informal unconscious: *she was* **out cold**. ■ dead: *lying cold and stiff in a coffin.*
2 lacking affection or warmth of feeling; unemotional: *how cold and calculating he was | cold black eyes | cold politeness.* ■ not affected by emotion; objective: *cold statistics.* ■ sexually unresponsive; frigid. ■ depressing or dispiriting; not suggestive of warmth: *the cold, impersonal barrack-room | a cold light streamed through the window.* ■ (of a color) containing pale blue or gray. ■ ineffective in playing a game: *Butler capitalized on Xavier's cold shooting.*
3 (of the scent or trail of a hunted person or animal) no longer fresh and easy to follow: *the trail went cold.* ■ (in children's games) far from finding or guessing what is sought, as opposed to warm or nearing success.
4 without preparation or rehearsal; unawares: *going into the test cold.*
▶ **n.** **1** a low temperature, esp. in the atmosphere; cold weather; a cold environment: *my teeth chattered with the cold | they nearly died of cold.*
2 a common viral infection in which the mucous membrane of the nose and throat becomes inflamed, typically causing running at the nose, sneezing, a sore throat, and other similar symptoms.
▶ **adv.** informal completely; entirely: *she knew world capitals cold by age nine.*
– PHRASES **as cold as ice** (or **stone** or **the grave**, etc.) very cold. **catch** (or **take**) **cold** become infected with a cold. **cold comfort** poor or inadequate consolation: *another drop in the inflation rate was cold comfort for the 2.74 million jobless.* **cold feet** loss of nerve or confidence: *some investors* ***got cold feet*** *and backed out.* **the cold light of day** the objective realities of a situation: *in the cold light of day it all seemed so ridiculous.* **the cold shoulder** a show of intentional unfriendliness; rejection: *why is even his own family* ***giving him the cold shoulder***? **cold-shoulder someone** reject or be deliberately unfriendly to someone. **down cold** see DOWN[1]. **in cold blood** without feeling or mercy; ruthlessly: *the government forces killed them in cold blood.* **out in the cold** ignored; neglected: *the talks left the French out in the cold.* **throw** (or **pour**) **cold water on** be discouraging or negative about.
– DERIVATIVES **cold·ish** /ˈkōldisH/ **adj.**, **cold·ness** /ˈkōl(d)nəs/ **n.**
– ORIGIN Old English *cald*, of Germanic origin; related to Dutch *koud* and German *kalt*, also to Latin *gelu* 'frost.'

cold-blood·ed ▶ **adj.** **1** (of a kind of animal) having a body temperature varying with that of the environment; poikilothermic.
2 without emotion or pity; deliberately cruel or callous: *a cold-blooded murder.*
– DERIVATIVES **cold-blood·ed·ly** **adv.**, **cold-blood·ed·ness** **n.**

cold-call ▶ **v.** [with obj.] make an unsolicited call on (someone), by telephone or in person, in an attempt to sell goods or services: (as noun **cold-calling**) *severe new regulations against cold-calling.*
▶ **n.** (**cold call**) an unsolicited call of this kind.

cold cash ▶ **n.** another term for HARD CASH.

cold cath·ode ▶ **n.** Electronics a cathode that emits electrons without being heated.

cold chis·el ▶ **n.** a chisel used for cutting metal.

cold-cock ▶ **v.** [with obj.] informal knock (someone) out, typically with a blow to the head.

cold cream ▶ **n.** a cosmetic preparation used for cleansing and softening the skin.

cold cuts /ˈkōld ˌkəts/ ▶ **plural n.** slices of cold cooked or processed meats. See LUNCHMEAT.

cold dark mat·ter (abbr.: **CDM**) ▶ **n.** see DARK MATTER.

cold deck ▶ **n.** **1** informal a deck of cards that has been dishonestly arranged beforehand.
2 a pile of logs stored away from the immediate area where logging is taking place.

cold-drawn ▶ **adj.** (of metal) drawn out into a wire or bar while cold.
– DERIVATIVES **cold-draw·ing** **n.**

cold duck ▶ **n.** a type of sparkling wine made from red wine and champagne.

cold frame ▶ **n.** a four-sided frame of boards with a removable glass or plastic top. The frame is placed on the ground and is used to house, protect, and harden off seedlings and small plants, without artificial heat.

cold front ▶ **n.** Meteorology the boundary of an advancing mass of cold air, in particular the trailing edge of the warm sector of a low-pressure system.

cold fu·sion ▶ **n.** nuclear fusion occurring at or close to room temperature. Claims for its discovery in 1989 are generally held to have been mistaken.

cold-heart·ed ▶ **adj.** lacking affection or warmth; unfeeling.
– DERIVATIVES **cold-heart·ed·ly** **adv.**, **cold-heart·ed·ness** **n.**

cold light ▶ **n.** Physics light accompanied by little or no heat; luminescence.

cold·ly /ˈkōldlē/ ▶ **adv.** without affection or warmth of feeling; unemotionally: *Derek looked at her coldly | a coldly contemptuous tone.*

cold-mold·ed ▶ **adj.** (of an object) molded from a resin that hardens without being heated.
– DERIVATIVES **cold-mold·ing** **n.**

cold-rolled ▶ **adj.** Metallurgy (of metal) having been rolled into sheets while cold, resulting in a smooth hard finish.
– DERIVATIVES **cold-roll·ing** **n.**

cold snap ▶ **n.** a sudden, brief spell of cold weather.

cold sore ▶ **n.** an inflamed blister in or near the mouth, caused by infection with the herpes simplex virus.

Cold Spring Harbor a village on the north shore of Long Island in New York, in the town of Huntington, noted as a center for biological research; pop. 4,975 (2000).

cold stor·age ▶ **n.** the keeping of something in a refrigerator or other cold place for preservation.
■ the temporary postponement of something: *the project went into cold storage.*

cold store ▶ **n.** a large refrigerated room for preserving food stocks at very low temperatures.

cold sweat ▶ **n.** a state of sweating induced by fear, nervousness, or illness: *he used to* ***break into a cold sweat*** *when he was called on in class.*

cold tur·key informal ▶ **n.** the abrupt and complete cessation of taking a drug to which one is addicted: *cold turkey, with no medication, is not recommended for those with medical conditions.*
▶ **adv.** in a sudden and abrupt manner: *many banks have cut commercial builders off cold turkey.*

cold war ▶ **n.** a state of political hostility between countries characterized by threats, propaganda, and other measures short of open warfare, in particular:
■ (**the Cold War**) the state of political hostility that existed between the Soviet bloc countries and the US-led Western powers from 1945 to 1990.

cold wave ▶ **n.** **1** a spell of cold weather over a wide area.
2 a kind of permanent wave for the hair created by applying chemicals at room temperature.

cold-weld ▶ **v.** [with obj.] join (a piece of metal) to another without the use of heat, by forcing them together so hard that the surface oxide films are disrupted and adhesion occurs.

cold-work ▶ **v.** [with obj.] shape (metal) while it is cold.
▶ **n.** (**cold work**) the shaping of metal while it is cold.

Cole[1] /kōl/, Nat King (1919–65), US singer and pianist; born *Nathaniel Adams Coles*. He became the first African American to have his own series on radio (1948–49) and then television (1956–57).

Notable songs: "Mona Lisa" (1950) and "Ramblin' Rose" (1962).

Nat King Cole

Cole², Thomas (1801–48), US artist. He was one of the founders of the Hudson River School of painting.

cole /kōl/ ▶ n. chiefly archaic a brassica, esp. cabbage, kale, or rape.
– ORIGIN Old English *cāwel*, *caul*, related to Dutch *kool* and German *Kohl*, from Latin *caulis* 'stem, cabbage'; reinforced in Middle English by forms from Old Norse *kál*. Compare with KALE.

co·lec·to·my /kō'lektəmē/ ▶ n. (pl. **colectomies**) surgical removal of all or part of the colon.

Cole·man /'kōlmən/, Ornette (1930–), US jazz saxophonist, trumpeter, violinist, and composer. His music is noted for its lack of harmony and chordal structure.

cole·man·ite /'kōlmə,nīt/ ▶ n. a white crystalline mineral, typically occurring as glassy prisms, consisting of hydrated calcium borate.
– ORIGIN named after William T. *Coleman* (1824–93) + -ITE¹.

Cole·man lan·tern /'kōlmən/ (also **Coleman lamp**) ▶ n. trademark a type of bright gasoline lamp used by campers.

Co·le·op·ter·a /,kōlē'äptərə/ Entomology an order of insects that comprises the beetles (including weevils), forming the largest order of animals on the earth. ■ (as plural noun **coleoptera**) insects of this order; beetles.
– ORIGIN modern Latin (plural), from Greek *koleopteros*, from *koleos* 'sheath' + *pteron* 'wing.'

co·le·op·ter·an /,kōlē'äptərən/ Entomology ▶ n. an insect of the order Coleoptera; a beetle.
▶ adj. relating to or denoting coleopterans.
– DERIVATIVES **co·le·op·ter·ous** /-tərəs/ adj.

co·le·op·ter·ist /,kōlē'äptərist/ ▶ n. a person who studies or collects beetles.
– ORIGIN mid 19th cent.: from COLEOPTERA + -IST.

co·le·op·tile /,kōlē'äp,tīl/ ▶ n. Botany a sheath protecting a young shoot tip in a grass or cereal.
– ORIGIN mid 19th cent.: from Greek *koleon* 'sheath' + *ptilon* 'feather.'

co·le·o·rhi·za /,kōlēə'rīzə/ ▶ n. (pl. **coleorhizae** /-zē/) Botany a sheath protecting the root of a germinating grass or cereal grain.
– ORIGIN mid 19th cent.: from *koleos* 'sheath' + *rhiza* 'root.'

Cole·ridge /'kōl(ə)rij/, Samuel Taylor (1772–1834), English poet, critic, and philosopher. His *Lyrical Ballads* (1798), written with William Wordsworth, marked the start of English romanticism and included "The Rime of the Ancient Mariner." Other notable poems: "Christabel" and "Kubla Khan" (both 1816).

cole·seed /'kōl,sēd/ ▶ n. old-fashioned term for RAPE².
– ORIGIN late 17th cent.: from Dutch *koolzaad* 'cabbage or rape seed.'

cole·slaw /'kōl,slô/ ▶ n. sliced raw cabbage mixed with mayonnaise and other vegetables, eaten as a salad.
– ORIGIN late 18th cent. (originally US): from Dutch *koolsla*, from *kool* 'cabbage' + *sla* (see SLAW).

Co·lette /kə'let/ (1873–1954), French novelist; born *Sidonie Gabrielle Claudine*. Notable works *Chéri* (1920), *La Fin de Chéri* (1926), and *Gigi* (1945).

co·le·us /'kōlēəs/ ▶ n. a tropical Southeast Asian plant of the mint family that has brightly colored variegated leaves and is popular as a houseplant. ● Genus *Solenostemon* (formerly *Coleus*), family Labiatae.
– ORIGIN modern Latin, from Greek *koleos* 'sheath' (because of the way the stamens are joined together, resembling a sheath).

cole·wort /'kōl,wərt, -,wôrt/ ▶ n. chiefly archaic another term for COLE.

col·ic /'kälik/ ▶ n. severe, often fluctuating pain in the abdomen caused by intestinal gas or obstruction in the intestines and suffered esp. by babies.
– DERIVATIVES **col·ick·y** adj.
– ORIGIN late Middle English: from Old French *colique*, from late Latin *colicus*, from *colon* (see COLON²).

col·i·cin /'käləsin, -,sēn/ ▶ n. Biology a bacteriocin produced by a coliform bacterium.
– ORIGIN 1940s: from French *colicine* (from *coli*, denoting a bacterium) + -IN¹.

col·ic·root /'kälik,ro͞ot, -,ro͝ot/ ▶ n. a North American plant of the lily family, with a rosette of leaves and a spike of small goblet-shaped white or cream flowers. It was formerly used in the treatment of colic. ● *Aletris farinosa*, family Liliaceae.

col·i·form bac·te·ri·um /'kōlə,fôrm, 'käl-/ ▶ adj. a rod-shaped bacterium, esp. *Escherichia coli* and members of the genus *Aerobacter*, found in the intestinal tract of humans and other animals. Its presence in water indicates fecal contamination and can cause diarrhea and other dysenteric symptoms. Also called COLON BACILLUS.
– ORIGIN early 20th cent.: from modern Latin *coli*, specific epithet in the sense 'of the colon' + -IFORM + BACTERIUM.

Co·li·ma /kə'lēmə/ **1** a state in southwestern Mexico, on the Pacific coast.
2 the capital city of this state; pop. 123,587 (2005).

co·lin·e·ar /,kō'linēər/ (also **collinear**) ▶ adj. lying in the same straight line or linear sequence.

col·i·seum /,kälə'sēəm/ (also **colosseum**) ▶ n. [in names] a large theater or stadium: *the Charlotte Coliseum*.
– ORIGIN late 19th cent.: from medieval Latin, alteration of Latin *colosseum* (see COLOSSEUM).

co·li·tis /kə'lītis, kō-/ ▶ n. Medicine inflammation of the lining of the colon.

Coll /kôl/ an island in the Inner Hebrides, west of Mull.

Coll. ▶ abbr. ■ Collateral. ■ Collected or Collection (used in written references to published works or sources). ■ College. ■ Colloquial.

col·lab·o·rate /kə'labə,rāt/ ▶ v. [no obj.] work jointly on an activity, esp. to produce or create something: *he collaborated with a distinguished painter on the designs*. ■ cooperate traitorously with an enemy: *the indigenous elite who collaborated with the colonizers*.
– ORIGIN late 19th cent.: from Latin *collaborat-* 'worked with,' from the verb *collaborare*, from *col-* 'together' + *laborare* 'to work.'

col·lab·o·ra·tion /kə,labə'rāsʜən/ ▶ n. **1** the action of working with someone to produce or create something: *he wrote on art and architecture in collaboration with John Betjeman*. ■ something produced or created in this way: *his recent opera was a collaboration with Lessing*.
2 traitorous cooperation with an enemy: *he faces charges of collaboration*.
– DERIVATIVES **col·lab·o·ra·tion·ist** /-nist/ n. & adj. (sense 2).
– ORIGIN mid 19th cent.: from Latin *collaboratio(n-)*, from *collaborare* 'work together.'

col·lab·o·ra·tive /kə'labərətiv/ ▶ adj. produced or conducted by two or more parties working together: *collaborative research*.
– DERIVATIVES **col·lab·o·ra·tive·ly** adv.

col·lab·o·ra·tor /kə'labə,rātər/ ▶ n. **1** a person who works jointly on an activity or project; an associate: *his collaborator on the book*.
2 a person who cooperates traitorously with an enemy; a defector: *he was a collaborator during the occupation*.

col·lage /kə'läzʜ, kô-, kō-/ ▶ n. a form of art in which various materials such as photographs and pieces of paper or fabric are arranged and stuck to a backing. ■ a composition made in this way. ■ a combination or collection of various things.
– DERIVATIVES **col·lag·ist** /-läzʜist/ n.
– ORIGIN early 20th cent.: from French, literally 'gluing.'

col·la·gen /'käləjən/ ▶ n. Biochemistry the main structural protein found in animal connective tissue, yielding gelatin when boiled.
– ORIGIN mid 19th cent.: from French *collagène*, from Greek *kolla* 'glue' + French *-gène* (see -GEN).

col·lap·sar /kə'lap,sär/ ▶ n. Astronomy an old star that has collapsed under its own gravity to form a white dwarf, neutron star, or black hole.
– ORIGIN late 20th cent.: from COLLAPSE, on the pattern of words such as *pulsar*.

col·lapse /kə'laps/ ▶ v. [no obj.] **1** (of a structure) fall down or in; give way: *the roof collapsed on top of me*. ■ [with obj.] cause (something) to fall in or give way: *it feels as if the slightest pressure would collapse it* | figurative *many people tend to collapse the distinction between the two concepts*. ■ (of a lung or blood vessel) fall inward and become flat and empty: (as adj. **collapsed**) *a collapsed lung*. ■ [with obj.] cause (a lung or blood vessel) to do this.
2 (of a person) fall down and become unconscious, typically through illness or injury: *he collapsed from loss of blood*. ■ sit or lie down as a result of tiredness or amusement: *exhausted, he collapsed on the bed* | *the three of them collapsed with laughter*.
3 (of an institution or undertaking) fail suddenly and completely: *in the face of such resolve his opposition finally collapsed*. ■ (of a price or currency) drop suddenly in value.
4 fold or be folded to fit into a small space: [no obj.] *some cots collapse down to fit into a bag*. ■ [with obj.] compress a displayed part of (a spreadsheet or other electronic document): *tabulation programs can be used to collapse this list in various ways*.
▶ n. an instance of a structure falling down or in: *the collapse of a railroad bridge* | *the church roof is in danger of collapse*. ■ a sudden failure of an institution or undertaking: *the collapse of the Ottoman Empire*. ■ a physical or mental breakdown: *he suffered a collapse from overwork* | *she's lying there in a state of collapse*.
– ORIGIN early 17th cent. (as *collapsed*): from medical Latin *collapsus*, past participle of *collabi*, from *col-* 'together' + *labi* 'to slip.'

col·laps·i·ble /kə'lapsəbəl/ ▶ adj. (of an object) able to be folded into a small space: *a collapsible bed*.
– DERIVATIVES **col·laps·i·bil·i·ty** /kə,lapsə'bilitē/ n.

col·lar /'kälər/ ▶ n. **1** a band of material around the neck of a shirt, dress, coat, or jacket, either upright or turned over and generally an integral part of the garment: *we turned our collars up against the chill*. ■ short for CLERICAL COLLAR. ■ a band of leather or other material put around the neck of a domestic animal, esp. a dog or cat. ■ a colored marking resembling a collar around the neck of a bird or other animal. ■ a heavy rounded part of the harness worn by a draft animal, which rests at the base of its neck on the shoulders.
2 a restraining or connecting band, ring, or pipe in machinery.
3 Brit. a piece of meat rolled up and tied. ■ a cut of bacon taken from the neck of a pig.
4 Botany the part of a plant where the stem joins the roots.
▶ v. **1** [with obj.] put a collar on: *biologists who were collaring polar bears*.
2 [with obj.] informal seize, grasp, or apprehend (someone): *police collared the culprit*. ■ approach aggressively and talk to (someone who wishes to leave): *he collared a departing guest for some last words*.
– DERIVATIVES **col·lared** adj. [in combination] *a fur-collared jacket*, **col·lar·less** adj.
– ORIGIN Middle English: from Old French *colier*, from Latin *collare* 'band for the neck, collar,' from *collum* 'neck.'

col·lar beam ▶ n. a horizontal wooden joist or beam connecting two rafters and forming with them an A-shaped roof truss.

col·lar·bone /'kälər,bōn/ ▶ n. either of the pair of bones joining the breastbone to the shoulder blades. Also called CLAVICLE.

col·lards /'kälərdz/ (also **collard greens**) ▶ n. a cabbage of a variety that does not develop a heart.
– ORIGIN mid 18th cent.: reduced form of *colewort*, in the same sense, from COLE + WORT.

col·lared dove /dəv/ ▶ n. an Old World dove related to the ringed turtle dove, with buff, gray, or brown plumage and a narrow black band around the back of the neck. ● Genus *Streptopelia*, family Columbidae: several species, in particular the sandy gray *S. decaocto*, which originated in Asia, and has recently been found breeding widely in southeastern Florida.

col·lared liz·ard ▶ n. a lizard that is typically marked with spots and bands and has a distinctive black-and-white collar. It is found in dry rocky areas in the southern US and Mexico. ● *Crotaphytus collaris*, family Iguanidae.

col·lar stud ▶ n. a stud used to fasten a detachable collar to a shirt.

col·lar tie ▶ n. another term for COLLAR BEAM.

col·late /kə'lāt, 'kō,lāt, 'käl,āt/ ▶ v. [with obj.] **1** collect and combine (texts, information, or sets of figures) in proper order. ■ compare and analyze (texts or other data): *these accounts he collated with his own experience*. ■ Printing verify the order of (sheets of a book) by their signatures.
2 appoint (a clergyman) to a benefice.

PRONUNCIATION KEY ə *ago, up*; ər *over, fur*; a *hat*; ā *ate*; ä *car*; e *let*; ē *see*; i *fit*; ī *by*; NG *sing*; ō *go*; ô *law, for*; oi *toy*; o͝o *good*; o͞o *goo*; ou *out*; TH *thin*; T̲H̲ *then*; ZH *vision*

C

C

– ORIGIN mid 16th cent. (in the sense 'confer (a benefice) upon'): from Latin *collat-* 'brought together,' from the verb *conferre* (see CONFER).

col·lat·er·al /kə'latərəl, kə'latrəl/ ▶ n. **1** something pledged as security for repayment of a loan, to be forfeited in the event of a default.
2 a person having the same descent in a family as another but by a different line.
▶ adj. **1** additional but subordinate; secondary: *the collateral meanings of a word.* ■ used euphemistically to refer to inadvertent casualties among civilians and destruction in civilian areas in the course of military operations: *collateral damage to civilians | collateral casualties.*
2 descended from the same stock but by a different line: *a collateral descendant of George Washington.*
3 situated side by side; parallel: *collateral veins.*
– DERIVATIVES **col·lat·er·al·i·ty** /kə,latə'ralitē/ n., **col·lat·er·al·ly** adv.
– ORIGIN late Middle English (as an adjective): from medieval Latin *collateralis*, from *col-* 'together with' + *lateralis* (from *latus, later-* 'side'). Sense 1 of the noun (originally US) is from the phrase *collateral security*, denoting something pledged in addition to the main obligation of a contract.

col·lat·er·al con·tract ▶ n. Law a subsidiary contract that induces a person to enter into a main contract or that depends upon the main contract for its existence.

col·lat·er·al·ize /kə'latərə,līz, kə'latrə-/ ▶ v. [with obj.] provide something as collateral for (a loan): *these loans are collateralized by property.*

col·la·tion /kə'lāsHən, kō-, kä-/ ▶ n. **1** the action of collating something: *data management and collation.*
2 a light, informal meal. ■ (in the Roman Catholic Church) a light meal allowed during a fast.
– ORIGIN Middle English: via Old French from Latin *collation-*, from *conferre* (see CONFER). Originally (in the plural) the term denoted John Cassian's *Collationes Patrum in Scetica Eremo Commorantium* 'Conferences of, or with, the Egyptian Hermits' (AD 415–20), from which a reading would be given in Benedictine communities prior to a light meal (see sense 2).

col·la·tor /-tər/ ▶ n. a person or machine that collates.

col·league /'käl,ēg/ ▶ n. a person with whom one works, esp. in a profession or business.
– ORIGIN early 16th cent.: from French *collègue*, from Latin *collega* 'partner in office,' from *col-* 'together with' + *legare* 'depute.'

col·lect[1] /kə'lekt/ ▶ v. [with obj.] **1** bring or gather together (things, typically when scattered or widespread): *he went around the office collecting old coffee cups | he **collected up** all his clothing.* ■ accumulate and store over a period of time: *collect rainwater to use on the garden.* ■ systematically seek and acquire (items of a particular kind) as a hobby: *I've started collecting stamps* | [no obj.] *the urge to collect, to have the full set, is in us all.* ■ [no obj.] come together and form a group or mass: *worshipers **collected together** in a stadium | dust and dirt collect so quickly.*
2 call for and take away; fetch: *the children were collected from school.* ■ go somewhere and accept or receive (something), esp. as a right or due: *she went to Oxford to collect her honorary degree.* ■ solicit and receive (donations), esp. for charity: *collecting money for the war effort* | [no obj.] *we **collected for** the United Way.* ■ receive (money that is due); be paid: [with obj.] *they called to collect a debt* | [no obj.] *he'd come to collect.*
3 (**collect oneself**) regain control of oneself, typically after a shock. ■ bring together and concentrate (one's thoughts).
4 archaic conclude; infer: *by all best conjectures, I collect Thou art to be my fatal enemy.*
5 cause (a horse) to bring its hind legs further forward as it moves, thereby shortening the stride and increasing balance and impulsion.
▶ adv. & adj. (with reference to a telephone call) to be paid for by the person receiving it: [as adv.] *I called my mother collect* | [as adj.] *a collect call.*
– ORIGIN late Middle English: from Old French *collecter* or medieval Latin *collectare*, from Latin *collect-* 'gathered together,' from the verb *colligere*, from *col-* 'together' + *legere* 'choose or collect.'

col·lect[2] /'käl,ekt, -likt/ ▶ n. (in church use) a short prayer, esp. one assigned to a particular day or season.
– ORIGIN Middle English: from Old French *collecte*, from Latin *collecta* 'gathering,' feminine past participle of *colligere* 'gather together' (see COLLECT[1]).

col·lec·ta·ne·a /,käl,ek'tānēə/ ▶ plural n. [also treated as sing.] passages, remarks, and other pieces of text collected from various sources.
– ORIGIN mid 17th cent.: Latin, neuter plural of *collectaneus* 'gathered together,' used as an adjective in Caesar's *Dicta collectanea* and as a noun in Solinus' *Collectanea.*

col·lect·ed /kə'lektid/ ▶ adj. **1** (of a person) not perturbed or distracted: *outwardly they are cool, calm, and collected.*
2 (of individual works) brought together in one volume or edition: *the collected works of Edgar Allan Poe.* ■ (of a volume or edition) containing all the works of a particular person or category.
3 (of a horse) moving with a shortened stride and with its hind legs correctly placed to achieve balance and impulsion.
– DERIVATIVES **col·lect·ed·ly** adv. (sense 1).

col·lect·i·ble /kə'lektəbəl/ (also chiefly Brit. **collectable**) ▶ adj. **1** (of an item) worth collecting; of interest to a collector.
2 able to be collected: *a surplus collectible as rent by the landowner.*
▶ n. (usu. **collectibles**) an item valued and sought by collectors.
– DERIVATIVES **col·lect·i·bil·i·ty** /kə,lektə'bilitē/ n.

col·lec·tion /kə'leksHən/ ▶ n. **1** the action or process of collecting someone or something: *the collection of maple sap | tax collection.* ■ a regular removal of mail for dispatch or of trash for disposal. ■ an instance of collecting money in a church service or for a charitable cause: *when she died, they **took up a collection** for her burial.* ■ a sum collected in this way.
2 a group of things or people: *a rambling **collection** of houses.* ■ an assembly of items such as works of art, pieces of writing, or natural objects, esp. one systematically ordered: *paintings from the permanent collection | a record collection.* ■ (**collections**) an art museum's holdings organized by medium, such as sculpture, painting, or photography. ■ a book or recording containing various texts, poems, songs, etc.: *a collection of essays.* ■ a range of new clothes produced by a fashion house: *a preview of their autumn collection.*
– ORIGIN late Middle English: via Old French from Latin *collectio(n-)*, from *colligere* 'gather together' (see COLLECT[1]).

col·lec·tive /kə'lektiv/ ▶ adj. done by people acting as a group: *a collective protest.* ■ belonging or relating to all the members of a group: *ministers who share collective responsibility | a collective sigh of relief from parents.* ■ taken as a whole; aggregate: *the collective power of the workforce.*
▶ n. a cooperative enterprise. ■ a collective farm.
– DERIVATIVES **col·lec·tive·ly** adv., **col·lec·tive·ness** n., **col·lec·tiv·i·ty** /kə,lek'tivitē, ,käl,ek-/ n.
– ORIGIN late Middle English (in the sense 'representing many individuals'): from Old French *collectif, -ive* or Latin *collectivus*, from *collect-* 'gathered together,' from the verb *colligere* (see COLLECT[1]).

col·lec·tive bar·gain·ing ▶ n. negotiation of wages and other conditions of employment by an organized body of employees.

col·lec·tive farm ▶ n. a jointly operated amalgamation of several small farms, esp. one owned by the government.

col·lec·tive mark ▶ n. a trademark or service mark that identifies members of a union, cooperative, or other collective organization.

col·lec·tive mem·o·ry ▶ n. the memory of a group of people, typically passed from one generation to the next.

col·lec·tive noun ▶ n. Grammar a noun that denotes a group of individuals (e.g., *assembly, family, crew*).

> **USAGE** Examples of collective nouns include *group, crowd, family, committee, class, crew,* and the like. In the US, collective nouns are usually followed by a singular verb (*the crowd was nervous*), while in Britain it is more common to follow a collective noun with a plural verb (*the band were late for their own concert*). Notice that if the verb is singular, any following pronouns must also be singular: *the council is prepared to act, but not until it has taken a poll.* When preceded by the definite article *the*, the collective noun *number* is usually treated as a singular (*the number of applicants was beyond belief*), whereas it is treated as a plural when preceded by the indefinite article *a* (*a number of proposals were considered*). See also usage at NUMBER.

col·lec·tive se·cu·ri·ty ▶ n. the cooperation of several countries in an alliance to strengthen the security of each.

col·lec·tive un·con·scious ▶ n. (in Jungian psychology) the part of the unconscious mind that is derived from ancestral memory and experience and is common to all humankind, as distinct from the individual's unconscious.

col·lec·tiv·ism /kə'lektə,vizəm/ ▶ n. the practice or principle of giving a group priority over each individual in it. ■ the theory and practice of the ownership of land and the means of production by the people or the state.
– DERIVATIVES **col·lec·tiv·ist** adj. & n., **col·lec·tiv·is·tic** /-,lektə'vistik/ adj.

col·lec·ti·vize /kə'lektə,vīz/ ▶ v. [with obj.] (usu. as adj. **collectivized**) organize (something) on the basis of ownership by the people or the state, abolishing private ownership or involvement: *collectivized agriculture.*
– DERIVATIVES **col·lec·ti·vi·za·tion** /kə,lektəvə'zāsHən/ n.

col·lec·tor /kə'lektər/ ▶ n. **1** a person who collects things of a specified type, professionally or as a hobby: *an art collector.*
2 an official who is responsible for collecting money: *a tax collector.* ■ an official who collects tickets from bus or train passengers.
3 (in some South Asian countries) the chief administrative official of a district.
4 Electronics the region in a bipolar transistor that absorbs charge carriers.

col·lec·tor·ate /kə'lektərət/ ▶ n. (in some South Asian countries) a district under the jurisdiction of a collector. See COLLECTOR (sense 3).

col·lec·tor's i·tem ▶ n. an object of interest to collectors, esp. because it is rare, beautiful, or associated with someone famous.

col·leen /kə'lēn, 'käl,ēn/ ▶ n. an Irish term for a girl or young woman.
– ORIGIN early 19th cent.: from Irish *cailín*, diminutive of *caile* 'countrywoman.'

col·lege /'kälij/ ▶ n. **1** an educational institution or establishment, in particular: ■ one providing higher education or specialized professional or vocational training: *my brother wanted to go to college | I'm at college studying graphic design.* ■ (within a university) a school offering a general liberal arts curriculum leading only to a bachelor's degree. ■ (in Britain) any of a number of independent institutions within certain universities, each having its own teaching staff, students, and buildings. ■ Brit. a private secondary school: [in names] *Eton College.* ■ the teaching staff and students of a college considered collectively: *the college was shocked by his death.*
2 an organized group of professional people with particular aims, duties, and privileges: [in names] *the electoral college.*
– ORIGIN late Middle English: from Old French, from Latin *collegium* 'partnership, association,' from *collega* 'partner in office,' from *col-* 'together with' + *legare* 'depute.'

Col·lege Board ▶ n. an organization that prepares and administers standardized tests that are used in college admission and placement.

Col·lege of Arms (also **College of Heralds**) (in the UK) a corporation that officially records and grants armorial bearings. Formed in 1484, it comprises three Kings of Arms, six heralds, and four pursuivants. Also called HERALDS' COLLEGE.

Col·lege of Car·di·nals the body of cardinals of the Roman Catholic Church, founded in the 11th century and since 1179 responsible for the election of the pope. Also called SACRED COLLEGE.

Col·lege Park a city in central Maryland, just northeast of Washington, DC, home to the University of Maryland; pop. 26,925 (est. 2008).

Col·lege Station a city in east central Texas, home to Texas A&M University; pop. 84,128 (est. 2008).

col·lege try ▶ n. a sincere effort or attempt at performing a difficult, or seemingly impossible, task: *the chances of overturning this decision are slim, but the Democrats will **give it the old college try.***

col·le·gi·a /kə'lēgēə/ plural form of COLLEGIUM.

col·le·gi·al /kə'lēj(ē)əl/ ▶ adj. **1** relating to or involving shared responsibility, as among a group of colleagues.
2 another term for COLLEGIATE (sense 1).
– DERIVATIVES **col·le·gi·al·i·ty** /kə,lējē'alitē/ n.
– ORIGIN late Middle English: from Old French *collegial* or late Latin *collegialis*, from *collegium* 'partnership, association' (see COLLEGE).

col·le·gian /kə'lējən/ ▶ n. a member of a college, esp. within a university.
– ORIGIN late Middle English: from medieval Latin *collegianus*, from *collegium* 'partnership, association' (see COLLEGE).

col·le·giate /kə'lējət/ ▶ adj. **1** belonging or relating to a college or its students: *collegiate life.*
2 (of a university) composed of different colleges.
– ORIGIN late Middle English: from late Latin *collegiatus*, from *collegium* 'partnership, association' (see COLLEGE).

col·le·giate church ▶ n. a church endowed for a chapter of canons but without a bishop's see. ■ a church or group of churches established under two or more pastors.

col·le·giate Goth·ic ▶ n. a style of Gothic revival architecture used for many college and university buildings.
▶ adj. of or built in such a style.

col·le·gi·um /kəˈlējēəm/ ▶ n. (pl. **collegia** /-ˈlegēə/) **1** (in full **collegium musicum** /ˈm(y)o͞ozikəm/) (pl. **collegia musica** /ˈm(y)o͞ozikə/) a society of amateur musicians, esp. one attached to a German or US college.
2 historical an advisory or administrative board in Russia.
– ORIGIN late 19th cent.: from Latin, literally 'association.'

col le·gno /kō(l)ˈlānyō/ ▶ adv. (of a passage of music for a bowed instrument) played by hitting the strings with the back of the bow.
– ORIGIN Italian, 'with the wood (of the bow).'

Col·lem·bo·la /kəˈlembələ/ Entomology an order of insects that comprises the springtails. ■ (as plural noun **collembola**) insects of this order; springtails.
– DERIVATIVES **col·lem·bo·lan** /-bələn/ n. & adj.
– ORIGIN modern Latin (plural), from Greek *kolla* 'glue' + *embolon* 'peg, stopper' (with reference to the sticky substance secreted by the ventral tube of the insects).

col·len·chy·ma /kəˈleNGkəmə/ ▶ n. Botany tissue strengthened by the thickening of cell walls, as in young shoots.
– ORIGIN mid 19th cent.: from Greek *kolla* 'glue' + *enkhuma* 'infusion.'

Colles frac·ture /kälz/ ▶ n. Medicine a fracture of the lower end of the radius in the wrist with a characteristic backward displacement of the hand.
– ORIGIN late 19th cent.: named after Abraham *Colles* (1773–1843), Irish surgeon.

col·let /ˈkälət/ ▶ n. **1** a segmented band or sleeve put around a shaft or spindle and tightened so as to grip it. ■ a small collar in a clock to which the inner end of a balance spring is attached.
2 a flange or socket for setting a gem in jewelry.
– ORIGIN late Middle English (denoting a piece of armor to protect the neck): from Old French, diminutive of *col* 'neck,' from Latin *collum*.

col·lic·u·lus /kəˈlikyələs/ ▶ n. (pl. **colliculi** /-ˌlī, -ˌlē/) Anatomy a small protuberance, esp. one of two pairs in the roof of the midbrain, involved respectively in vision and hearing.
– DERIVATIVES **col·lic·u·lar** /-lər/ adj.
– ORIGIN mid 19th cent.: from Latin, diminutive of *collis* 'hill.'

col·lide /kəˈlīd/ ▶ v. [no obj.] hit with force when moving: *she **collided with** someone | two suburban trains collided.* ■ come into conflict or opposition: *in his work, politics and metaphysics collide.*
– ORIGIN early 17th cent. (in the sense 'cause to collide'): from Latin *collidere*, from *col-* 'together' + *laedere* 'to strike or damage.'

col·lid·er /kəˈlīdər/ ▶ n. Physics an accelerator in which two beams of particles are made to collide.

col·lie /ˈkälē/ ▶ n. (pl. **collies**) a sheepdog of a breed originating in Scotland, having a long, pointed nose and thick, long hair.
– ORIGIN mid 17th cent.: perhaps from COAL (the breed originally being black).

collie

col·lier /ˈkälyər/ ▶ n. chiefly Brit. **1** a coal miner.
2 a ship carrying coal.
– ORIGIN Middle English: from COAL + -IER. The original sense was 'maker of charcoal,' who usually brought it to market, hence 'person selling charcoal,' later 'person selling coal,' whence current senses.

col·lier·y /ˈkälyərē/ ▶ n. (pl. **colleries**) a coal mine and the buildings and equipment associated with it.

col·li·gate /ˈkäləˌgāt/ ▶ v. Linguistics be or cause to be juxtaposed or grouped in a syntactic relation: [no obj.] *the two grammatical items are said to colligate* | [with obj.] *pronouns are regularly colligated with verbal forms.*
– DERIVATIVES **col·li·ga·tion** /ˌkäləˈgāSHən/ n.
– ORIGIN mid 16th cent. (in the literal Latin sense): from Latin *colligat-* 'bound together,' from the verb *colligare*, from *col-* 'together' + *ligare* 'bind.' The current sense dates from the 1960s.

col·li·ga·tive /ˈkäləˌgātiv/ ▶ adj. Chemistry of or relating to the binding together of molecules: *the colligative properties of dilute solutions.*

col·li·mate /ˈkäləˌmāt/ ▶ v. [with obj.] make (rays of light or particles) accurately parallel: (as adj. **collimated**) *a collimated electron beam.* ■ accurately align (an optical or other system).
– DERIVATIVES **col·li·ma·tion** /ˌkäləˈmāSHən/ n.
– ORIGIN mid 19th cent.: from Latin *collimare*, an erroneous reading (in some editions of Cicero) of *collineare* 'align or aim,' from *col-* 'together with' + *linea* 'line.'

col·li·ma·tor /ˈkäləˌmātər/ ▶ n. a device for producing a parallel beam of rays or radiation. ■ a small fixed telescope used for adjusting the line of sight of an astronomical telescope.

col·lin·e·ar /kəˈlinēər, kä-/ ▶ adj. Geometry (of points) lying in the same straight line.
– DERIVATIVES **col·lin·e·ar·i·ty** /kəˌlinēˈaritē, kä-/ n.

Col·lins[1] /ˈkälənz/, Michael (1890–1922), Irish nationalist leader and politician. A member of Parliament for Sinn Fein, he was one of the negotiators of the Anglo-Irish Treaty of 1921. He commanded the Irish Free State forces in the civil war and became head of state but was assassinated ten days later.

Col·lins[2], Wilkie (1824–89), English novelist; full name *William Wilkie Collins*. He is noted for his detective stories *The Woman in White* (1860) and *The Moonstone* (1868).

Col·lins[3] ▶ n. short for TOM COLLINS.

col·li·sion /kəˈliZHən/ ▶ n. **1** an instance of one moving object or person striking violently against another: *a midair **collision between** two aircraft | the device increases the chances of collision.* ■ an instance of conflict between opposing ideas, interests, or factions: *a **collision between** experience and theory | cultures in collision.*
2 Computing an event of two or more records being assigned the same identifier or location in memory. ■ an instance of simultaneous transmission by more than one node of a network.
– PHRASES **on (a) collision course** going in a direction that will lead to a collision with another moving object or person. ■ adopting an approach that is certain to lead to conflict with another person or group: *the strikers are on a collision course with the government.*
– DERIVATIVES **col·li·sion·al** /-ZHənl/ adj.
– ORIGIN late Middle English: from late Latin *collisio(n-)*, from Latin *collidere* 'strike together' (see COLLIDE).

col·lo·cate /ˈkäləˌkāt/ ▶ v. **1** [no obj.] Linguistics (of a word) be habitually juxtaposed with another with a frequency greater than chance: *"maiden" collocates with "voyage."*
2 [with obj.] rare place side by side or in a particular relation: (as adj. **collocated**) *McAndrew was a collocated facility with Argentia Naval Station.*
▶ n. Linguistics a word that is habitually juxtaposed with another with a frequency greater than chance: *collocates for the word "mortgage" include "lend" and "property."*
– ORIGIN early 16th cent. (sense 2 of the verb): from Latin *collocat-* 'placed together,' from the verb *collocare*, from *col-* 'together' + *locare* 'to place.' Sense 1 of the verb dates from the 1950s.

col·lo·ca·tion /ˌkäləˈkāSHən/ ▶ n. **1** Linguistics the habitual juxtaposition of a particular word with another word or words with a frequency greater than chance: *the words have a similar range of collocation.* ■ a pair or group of words that are juxtaposed in such a way: *"strong coffee" and "heavy drinker" are typical English collocations.*
2 the action of placing things side by side or in position: *the collocation of the two pieces.*
– ORIGIN late Middle English: from Latin *collocatio(n-)*, from *collocare* 'place together' (see COLLOCATE).

col·lo·di·on /kəˈlōdēən/ ▶ n. a syrupy solution of nitrocellulose in a mixture of alcohol and ether, used for coating things, chiefly in surgery and in a former photographic process.
– ORIGIN mid 19th cent.: from Greek *kollōdēs* 'gluelike,' from *kolla* 'glue.'

col·logue /kəˈlōg/ ▶ v. (**collogues, colloguing, collogued**) [no obj.] archaic talk confidentially or conspiratorially.
– ORIGIN early 17th cent. (in the sense 'flatter, pretend to agree with or believe'): probably an alteration of obsolete *colleague* 'conspire,' by association with Latin *colloqui* 'to converse.'

col·loid /ˈkälˌoid/ ▶ n. a homogeneous, noncrystalline substance consisting of large molecules or ultramicroscopic particles of one substance dispersed through a second substance. Colloids include gels, sols, and emulsions; the particles do not settle and cannot be separated out by ordinary filtering or centrifuging like those in a suspension. ■ Anatomy & Medicine a substance of gelatinous consistency.
▶ adj. [attrib.] of the nature of, relating to, or characterized by a colloid or colloids.
– DERIVATIVES **col·loi·dal** /kəˈloidl/ adj.
– ORIGIN mid 19th cent.: from Greek *kolla* 'glue' + -OID.

C

col·lop /ˈkäləp/ dialect ▶ n. a slice of meat: *three collops of bacon.*
– ORIGIN late Middle English: of Scandinavian origin and related to Swedish *kalops* 'meat stew.'

col·lo·qui·al /kəˈlōkwēəl/ ▶ adj. (of language) used in ordinary or familiar conversation; not formal or literary.
– DERIVATIVES **col·lo·qui·al·ly** adv.
– ORIGIN mid 18th cent.: from Latin *colloquium* 'conversation' + -AL.

col·lo·qui·al·ism /kəˈlōkwēəˌlizəm/ ▶ n. a word or phrase that is not formal or literary, typically one used in ordinary or familiar conversation. ■ the use of such words or phrases.

col·lo·qui·um /kəˈlōkwēəm/ ▶ n. (pl. **colloquiums** or **colloquia** /-kwēə/) an academic conference or seminar.
– ORIGIN late 16th cent. (denoting a conversation or dialogue): from Latin, from *colloqui* 'to converse,' from *col-* 'together' + *loqui* 'to talk.'

col·lo·quy /ˈkäləkwē/ ▶ n. (pl. **colloquies**) **1** formal a conversation: *they broke off their colloquy at once | an evening of sophisticated colloquy.*
2 a gathering for discussion of theological questions.
– ORIGIN late Middle English: from Latin *colloquium* 'conversation.'

col·lo·type /ˈkäləˌtīp/ ▶ n. Printing a process for making high-quality prints from a sheet of light-sensitive gelatin exposed photographically to the image without using a screen: [as modifier] *collotype printing.* ■ a print made by such a process.
– ORIGIN late 19th cent.: from Greek *kolla* 'glue' + TYPE.

col·lude /kəˈlo͞od/ ▶ v. [no obj.] come to a secret understanding for a harmful purpose; conspire: *university leaders **colluded in** price-rigging | the president accused his opponents of **colluding with** foreigners.*
– DERIVATIVES **col·lud·er** n.
– ORIGIN early 16th cent.: from Latin *colludere* 'have a secret agreement,' from *col-* 'together' + *ludere* 'to play.'

col·lu·sion /kəˈlo͞oZHən/ ▶ n. secret or illegal cooperation or conspiracy, esp. in order to cheat or deceive others: *the armed forces were working **in collusion with** drug traffickers | **collusion between** media owners and political leaders.* ■ Law such cooperation or conspiracy, esp. between ostensible opponents in a lawsuit.
– DERIVATIVES **col·lu·sive** /-siv, -ziv/ adj., **col·lu·sive·ly** /-sivlē, -zivlē/ adv.
– ORIGIN late Middle English: from Latin *collusion-*, from *colludere* 'have a secret agreement' (see COLLUDE).

col·lu·vi·um /kəˈlo͞ovēəm/ ▶ n. Geology material that accumulates at the foot of a steep slope.
– DERIVATIVES **col·lu·vi·al** /-vēəl/ adj.
– ORIGIN mid 20th cent.: from Latin *colluvies* 'confluence or collection of matter,' from *colluere* 'to rinse,' from *col-* 'together' + *luere* 'to wash.'

col·lyr·i·um /kəˈli(ə)rēəm/ ▶ n. (pl. **collyria** /-ēə/) a medicated eyewash. ■ a kind of dark eyeshadow, used esp. in Eastern countries.
– ORIGIN late Middle English: Latin, from Greek *kollurion* 'poultice,' from *kollura* 'coarse bread roll.'

col·ly·wob·bles /ˈkälēˌwäbəlz/ ▶ plural n. informal, chiefly humorous stomach pain or queasiness: *an attack of collywobbles.* ■ intense anxiety or nervousness, esp. with such symptoms: *such organizations give him the collywobbles.*
– ORIGIN early 19th cent.: fanciful formation from COLIC and WOBBLE.

Colo. ▶ abbr. Colorado.

col·o·bine /ˈkäləˌbīn, -bin/ ▶ n. Zoology an Old World monkey of a mainly leaf-eating group that includes the colobus monkeys, langurs, and leaf monkeys.
● Subfamily Colobinae, family Cercopithecidae.
– ORIGIN 1950s: from modern Latin *Colobinae*, based on Greek *kolobos* 'curtailed.'

C

col·o·bo·ma /ˌkäləˈbōmə/ ▶ **n.** Medicine a congenital malformation of the eye causing defects in the lens, iris, or retina.
– ORIGIN mid 19th cent.: modern Latin, from Greek *kolobōma* 'part removed in mutilation,' from *kolobos* 'cut short.'

col·o·bus /ˈkäləbəs/ (also **colobus monkey**) ▶ **n.** (pl. **same**) a slender, leaf-eating African monkey with silky fur, a long tail, and very small or absent thumbs. ● Genera *Colobus* and *Procolobus*, family Cercopithecidae: several species.
– ORIGIN modern Latin, from Greek *kolobos* 'cut short.'

co·lo·cate /kōˈlōˌkāt, ˈkō-/ ▶ **v.** (**be colocated**) share a location or facility with someone (or something) else: *a woman officer can often be colocated with her husband.*

col·o·cynth /ˈkäləˌsinTH/ ▶ **n.** a tropical Old World climbing plant of the gourd family, which bears a pulpy fruit and has long been cultivated. Also called **BITTER APPLE**. ● *Citrullus colocynthis*, family Curcurbitaceae. ■ the fruit of this plant. ■ a bitter purgative drug obtained from this fruit.
– ORIGIN mid 16th cent.: via Latin from Greek *kolokunthis*.

Co·logne /kəˈlōn/ an industrial and university city in western Germany, in North Rhine–Westphalia, on the Rhine River; pop. 989,800 (est. 2006). German name **KÖLN**.

co·logne /kəˈlōn/ ▶ **n.** eau de cologne or scented toilet water.
– ORIGIN early 19th cent.: named after **COLOGNE** in Germany.

Co·lo·ma /kəˈlōmə/ a historic locality in northeastern California, on the American River, northeast of Sacramento, where gold was discovered in 1848 on John (Johann) Sutter's mill site that led to the California gold rush.

Co·lom·bi·a /kəˈləmbēə/ a country in extreme northwestern South America that has a coastline on both the Atlantic and the Pacific oceans; pop. 43,677,400 (est. 2009); capital, Bogotá; official language, Spanish.

> Colombia was conquered by the Spanish in the early 16th century and achieved independence in the early 19th century, although the resulting Republic of Great Colombia lasted only until 1830, when first Venezuela and then Ecuador broke away to become independent states in their own right. Since the civil war of 1949–53, the country has struggled with poverty and social problems. During the 1990s, guerrilla warfare, partly funded by the growing drug trade, dominated Colombia's countryside.

– DERIVATIVES **Co·lom·bi·an** **adj. & n.**

Co·lom·bo /kəˈləmbō/ the capital and chief port of Sri Lanka, on the southwestern coast of the country; pop. 672,700 (est. 2007).

co·lon[1] /ˈkōlən/ ▶ **n.** a punctuation mark (:) indicating: ■ that a writer is introducing a quotation or a list of items. ■ that a writer is separating two clauses of which the second expands or illustrates the first. ■ a statement of proportion between two numbers: *a ratio of 10:1.* ■ the separation of hours from minutes (and minutes from seconds) in a statement of time given in numbers: *4:30 p.m.* ■ the number of the chapter and verse respectively in biblical references: *Exodus 3:2.*
– ORIGIN mid 16th cent. (as a term in rhetoric denoting a section of a complex sentence, or a pause before it): via Latin from Greek *kōlon* 'limb, clause.'

co·lon[2] ▶ **n.** Anatomy the main part of the large intestine, which passes from the cecum to the rectum and absorbs water and electrolytes from food that has remained undigested. Its parts are called the ascending, transverse, descending, and sigmoid colon.
– ORIGIN late Middle English: via Latin from Greek *kolon*.

Co·lón /kəˈlōn/ the chief port of Panama, at the Caribbean Sea end of the Panama Canal; pop. 87,800 (est. 2009).

co·lón /kəˈlōn/ ▶ **n.** (pl. **colones** /-ˈlōˌnās/) the basic monetary unit of Costa Rica and El Salvador, equal to 100 centimos in Costa Rica and 100 centavos in El Salvador.
– ORIGIN from Cristóbal *Colón*, the Spanish name of Christopher Columbus (see **COLUMBUS**[2]).

co·lon ba·cil·lus ▶ **n.** another term for **COLIFORM BACTERIUM**.

colo·nel /ˈkərnl/ ▶ **n.** an army officer of high rank, in particular (in the US Army, Air Force, and Marine Corps) an officer above a lieutenant colonel and below a brigadier general. ■ informal short for **LIEUTENANT COLONEL**.
– DERIVATIVES **colo·nel·cy** /ˈkərnlsē/ **n.** (pl. **colonelcies**).
– ORIGIN mid 16th cent.: from obsolete French *coronel* (earlier form of *colonel*), from Italian *colonnello* 'column of soldiers,' from *colonna* 'column,' from Latin *columna*. The form *coronel*, source of the modern pronunciation, was usual until the mid 17th cent.

Colo·nel Blimp ▶ **n.** another term for **BLIMP** (sense 2).

colo·nel-in-chief ▶ **n.** (pl. **colonels-in-chief**) a title given to the honorary head of a regiment in the British army.

co·lo·ni·al /kəˈlōnyəl, -nēəl/ ▶ **adj.** **1** of, relating to, or characteristic of a colony or colonies: *British colonial rule* | *colonial expansion.* ■ relating to the period of the British colonies in America before independence. ■ (esp. of architecture or furniture) made during or in the style of this period.
2 (of animals or plants) living in colonies.
▶ **n.** **1** a native or inhabitant of a colony.
2 a house built in colonial style.
– DERIVATIVES **co·lo·ni·al·ly** **adv.**

co·lo·ni·al·ism /kəˈlōnēəˌlizəm, kəˈlōnyəˌlizəm/ ▶ **n.** the policy or practice of acquiring full or partial political control over another country, occupying it with settlers, and exploiting it economically.
– DERIVATIVES **co·lo·ni·al·ist** /-list/ **n. & adj.**

co·lon·ic /kōˈlänik, kə-/ ▶ **adj.** Anatomy of, relating to, or affecting the colon.
▶ **n.** informal an act or instance of colonic irrigation, performed for its supposed therapeutic benefits.

co·lon·ic ir·ri·ga·tion ▶ **n.** a water enema given to flush out the colon.

col·o·nist /ˈkälənist/ ▶ **n.** a settler in or inhabitant of a colony.

col·o·nize /ˈkäləˌnīz/ ▶ **v.** [with obj.] (of a country or its citizens) send a group of settlers to (a place) and establish political control over it: *the Greeks colonized Sicily and southern Italy.* ■ come to settle among and establish political control over (the indigenous people of an area): *a white family that tries to colonize a Caribbean island.* ■ appropriate (a place or domain) for one's own use. ■ Ecology (of a plant or animal) establish itself in an area: *mussels can colonize even the most inhospitable rock surfaces* | [no obj.] *insect borers colonize in rotted shoreline deadfalls.*
– DERIVATIVES **col·o·ni·za·tion** /ˌkälənəˈzāSHən/ **n.**, **col·o·niz·er** **n.**

col·on·nade /ˌkäləˈnād/ ▶ **n.** a row of columns supporting a roof, an entablature, or arcade. ■ a row of trees or other tall objects.
– DERIVATIVES **col·on·nad·ed** **adj.**
– ORIGIN early 18th cent.: from French, from *colonne* 'column,' from Latin *columna*.

co·lon·o·scope /kəˈlänəˌskōp/ ▶ **n.** Medicine a flexible fiber-optic instrument inserted through the anus in order to examine the colon.
– DERIVATIVES **co·lon·os·co·py** /ˌkōləˈnäskəpē/ **n.**

co·lon ther·a·py ▶ **n.** another term for **COLONIC IRRIGATION**.

col·o·ny /ˈkälənē/ ▶ **n.** (pl. **colonies**) **1** a country or area under the full or partial political control of another country, typically a distant one, and occupied by settlers from that country. ■ a group of people living in such a country or area, consisting of the original settlers and their descendants and successors. ■ (**the Colonies**) chiefly British term for **THIRTEEN COLONIES**. ■ (**the colonies**) all the foreign countries or areas formerly under British political control.
2 a group of people of one nationality or ethnic group living in a foreign city or country: *the British colony in New York.* ■ a place where a group of people with similar interests live together: *an artists' colony.*
3 Biology a community of animals or plants of one kind living close together or forming a physically connected structure: *a colony of seals.* ■ a group of fungi or bacteria grown from a single spore or cell on a culture medium.
– ORIGIN late Middle English (denoting a settlement formed mainly of retired soldiers, acting as a garrison in newly conquered territory in the Roman Empire): from Latin *colonia* 'settlement, farm,' from *colonus* 'settler, farmer,' from *colere* 'cultivate.'

col·o·ny-stim·u·lat·ing fac·tor ▶ **n.** Biochemistry a substance secreted by bone marrow that promotes the growth and differentiation of stem cells into colonies of specific blood cells.

col·o·phon /ˈkäləfən, -ˌfän/ ▶ **n.** a publisher's emblem or imprint, esp. one on the title page or spine of a book. ■ historical a statement at the end of a book, typically with a printer's emblem, giving information about its authorship and printing.
– ORIGIN early 17th cent. (denoting a finishing touch): via late Latin from Greek *kolophōn* 'summit or finishing touch.'

co·lo·pho·ny /kəˈläfənē, ˈkäləˌfōnē/ ▶ **n.** another term for **ROSIN**.
– ORIGIN Middle English: from Latin *colophonia* (*resina*) '(resin) from *Colophon*,' a town in Lydia, Asia Minor.

col·or /ˈkələr/ (Brit. **colour**) ▶ **n.** **1** the property possessed by an object of producing different sensations on the eye as a result of the way the object reflects or emits light: *the lights flickered and changed color.* ■ one, or any mixture, of the constituents into which light can be separated in a spectrum or rainbow, sometimes including (loosely) black and white: *a rich brown color* | *a range of bright colors.* ■ the use of all colors, not only black, white, and gray, in photography or television: *he has shot the whole film in color* | [as modifier] *color television.* ■ a substance used to give something a particular color: *lip color.* ■ Heraldry any of the major conventional colors used in coats of arms (gules, vert, sable, azure, purpure), esp. as opposed to the metals, furs, and stains.
2 pigmentation of the skin, esp. as an indication of someone's race: *discrimination on the basis of color.* ■ a group of people considered as being distinguished by skin pigmentation: *all colors and nationalities.* ■ rosiness of the complexion, esp. as an indication of someone's health: *there was some color back in his face.*
3 vividness of visual appearance resulting from the presence of brightly colored things: *for color, plant groups of winter-flowering pansies.* ■ picturesque or exciting features that lend a particularly interesting quality to something: *a town full of color and character.* ■ variety of musical tone or expression: *orchestral color.*
4 (**colors**) an item or items of a particular color or combination of colors worn to identify an individual or a member of a school, group, or organization. ■ the flag of a regiment or ship. ■ a national flag: *he was called to the colors during the war.*
5 a shade of meaning: *many events in her past had taken on a different color.* ■ character or general nature: *the hospitable color of his family.*
6 Physics a quantized property of quarks which can take three values (designated blue, green, and red) for each flavor.
7 Mining a particle of gold remaining in a mining pan after most of the mud and gravel have been washed away.
▶ **v.** **1** [with obj.] change the color of (something) by painting or dyeing it with crayons, paints, or dyes. ■ [no obj.] take on a different color: *the foliage will not color well if the soil is too rich.* ■ use crayons to fill (a particular shape or outline) with color: *color the head, eyes, and bill with crayons.* ■ make vivid or picturesque: *he has colored the dance with gestures from cabaret and vaudeville.*
2 [no obj.] (of a person or their skin) show embarrassment or shame by becoming red; blush: *everyone stared at him, and he colored slightly.* ■ [with obj.] cause (a person or their skin) to change in color: *rage colored his pale complexion.* ■ [with obj.] (of a particular color) imbue (a person's skin): *a faint pink flush colored her cheeks.* ■ [with obj.] (of an emotion) imbue (a person's voice) with a particular tone: *surprise colored her voice.*
3 [with obj.] influence, esp. in a negative way; distort: *the experiences had colored her whole existence.* ■ misrepresent by distortion or exaggeration: *witnesses might color evidence to make a story saleable.*
– PHRASES **lend** (or **give**) **color to** make something seem true or probable: *this lent color and credibility to his defense.* **—— of color** see **PERSON OF COLOR**. **show one's true colors** reveal one's real character or intentions, esp. when these are disreputable or dishonorable. **under color of** under the pretext of. **with flying colors** see **FLYING**.
– ORIGIN Middle English (as *colo(u)r*): from Old French *colour* (noun), *colourer* (verb), from Latin *color* (noun), *colorare* (verb).

col·or·a·ble /ˈkələrəbəl/ (Brit. **colourable**) ▶ **adj.**
1 apparently correct or justified: *a colorable legal claim.* ■ counterfeit.
2 capable of being colored: *colorable illustrations.*

Col·o·rad·o /ˌkäləˈrädō, -ˈradō/ **1** a river that rises in the Rocky Mountains of northern Colorado and flows southwest for 1,468 miles (2,333 km) to the Gulf of California. It passes through the Grand Canyon.
2 a river that flows east for 900 miles (1,450 km) across Texas, from the Llano Estacado to the Gulf of Mexico. Austin is situated on it.
3 a state in the central US; pop. 4,939,456 (est. 2008); capital, Denver; statehood, Aug. 1, 1876 (38). Part of Colorado was acquired by the US with the

Louisiana Purchase in 1803 and the rest was ceded by Mexico in 1848.
– DERIVATIVES **Col·o·rad·an** /-'rädn, -'radn/ **n. & adj.**

Col·o·rad·o blue spruce ▶ **n.** another term for BLUE SPRUCE.

Col·o·ra·do Desert a region in southern California and northern Baja California in Mexico. The Salton Sea, the Imperial Valley, and the city of Palm Springs are here.

Col·o·ra·do Plateau a region of arid uplands in the southwestern US; along the Colorado River in Colorado, Utah, New Mexico, and Arizona; noted for its scenery.

Col·o·rad·o po·ta·to bee·tle ▶ **n.** a yellow-and black-striped leaf beetle native to North America. The larvae are highly destructive to potato plants and have occurred in many countries. ● *Leptinotarsa decemlineata*, family Chrysomelidae.
– ORIGIN late 19th cent.: named after the state of COLORADO.

Colorado potato beetle

Col·o·ra·do Springs a city in central Colorado, south of Denver, at the foot of the Front Range of the Rocky Mountains, home to the US Air Force Academy; pop. 380,307 (est. 2008).

Col·o·rad·o spruce ▶ **n.** another term for BLUE SPRUCE.

col·or·ant /'kələrənt/ (Brit. **colourant**) ▶ **n.** a dye, pigment, or other substance that colors something.

col·or·a·tion /,kələ'rāSHən/ ▶ **n. 1** a visual appearance with regard to color: *some bacterial structures take on a purple coloration.* ■ the natural color or variegated markings of animals or plants: *the red coloration of many maples.* ■ a scheme or method of applying color: *the coloration of the drawing.*
2 a specified pervading character or tone of something: *the productions have taken on a political coloration.* ■ a variety of musical or vocal expression: *the subtle colorations of big-box speakers | a skillful singer can do much with coloration.*
– ORIGIN early 17th cent.: from late Latin *coloratio(n-)*, from *colorare* 'to color.'

col·o·ra·tu·ra /,kələrə'to͝orə, ,käl-/ ▶ **n.** elaborate ornamentation of a vocal melody, esp. in operatic singing by a soprano. ■ (also **coloratura soprano**) a soprano skilled in such singing.
– ORIGIN Italian, literally 'coloring,' from Latin *colorare* 'to color.'

col·or bar ▶ **n. 1** a social system in which a group of people (typically nonwhite) are denied access to the same rights, opportunities, and facilities as other people (typically white) on the basis of skin color.
2 a strip on printed material or a screen display showing a range of colors, used to ensure that all colors are printed or displayed correctly.

col·or-blind (also **colorblind**) ▶ **adj. 1** unable to distinguish certain colors, or (rarely in humans) any colors at all. See PROTANOPIA.
2 not influenced by racial prejudice: *a color-blind society.*
– DERIVATIVES **col·or-blind·ness n.**

col·or code ▶ **n.** a system of marking things with different colors as a means of identification.
▶ **v.** (**color-code**) [with obj.] (usu. **be color-coded**) mark (things) with different colors as a means of identification: *each unit is color-coded for clarity.* ■ mark different features of (something) with different colors: *the map is color-coded.*

co·lo·rec·tal /,kōlō'rektəl/ ▶ **adj.** relating to or affecting the colon and the rectum.

col·ored /'kələrd/ (Brit. **coloured**) ▶ **adj. 1** having or having been given a color or colors, esp. as opposed to being black, white, or neutral: *brightly colored birds are easier to see* | [in combination] *a peach-colored sofa.* ■ imbued with an emotive or exaggerated quality: *highly colored examples were used by both sides.*
2 (also **Colored**) wholly or partly of nonwhite descent (now considered offensive in the US). ■ (also **Coloured**) S. African used as an ethnic label for people of mixed ethnic origin, including African slave, Malay, Chinese, and white. ■ dated or offensive relating to people who are wholly or partly of nonwhite descent: *a colored club.*
▶ **n. 1** (also **Colored**) dated or offensive a person who is wholly or partly of nonwhite descent. ■ (also **Coloured**) S. African a person of mixed ethnic origin speaking Afrikaans or English as their mother tongue.
2 (**coloreds**) clothes, sheets, etc., that are any color but white (used esp. in the context of washing and color fastness).

> USAGE **1 Colored** referring to skin color is first recorded in the early 17th century and was adopted in the US by emancipated slaves as a term of racial pride after the end of the Civil War. In the US, and in Britain (as **coloured**), it was the accepted term until the 1960s, when it was superseded by **black**. The term **colored** lost favor among black people during this period and is now widely regarded as offensive except in historical contexts and in particular as part of the name of the NAACP (National Association for the Advancement of Colored People). **2** In South Africa, the term **coloured** (also written **Coloured**) has a different history. There it is used not as a synonym for **black**, but to refer to people of mixed-race parentage rather than to African peoples and their descendants. Under apartheid, it was imposed as an official racial designation. However, in modern use, the term is not generally considered offensive or derogatory.

col·or·fast /'kələr,fast/ ▶ **adj.** dyed in colors that will not fade or be washed out.
– DERIVATIVES **col·or·fast·ness n.**

col·or-field paint·ing (also **colorfield**) ▶ **n.** a style of American abstract painting prominent from the late 1940s to the 1960s that features large expanses of unmodulated color covering the greater part of the canvas. Barnett Newman and Mark Rothko were considered its chief exponents.

col·or fil·ter ▶ **n.** a photographic filter that absorbs light of certain colors.

col·or·ful /'kələrfəl/ (Brit. **colourful**) ▶ **adj. 1** having much or varied color; bright: *a colorful array of fruit.*
2 full of interest; lively and exciting: *a controversial and colorful character | a colorful account of the meeting.* ■ (of a person's life or background) involving variously disreputable activities: *he gained a playboy reputation during a colorful bachelorhood.* ■ (of language) vulgar or rude: *colorful words usually impolite in public meetings.*
– DERIVATIVES **col·or·ful·ly** /-f(ə)lē/ **adv.**, **col·or·ful·ness n.**

col·or guard ▶ **n.** a uniformed group, esp. of soldiers, police officers, or school representatives, who parade or present their institution's flag (and sometimes their national flag) on ceremonial occasions.

col·or·if·ic /,kələ'rifik/ ▶ **adj.** rare having much color: *the colorific radiance of costume.*
– ORIGIN late 17th cent.: from French *colorifique* or modern Latin *colorificus*, from Latin *color* 'color.'

col·or·im·e·ter /,kələ'rimitər/ ▶ **n.** an instrument for measuring the intensity of color.
– DERIVATIVES **col·or·i·met·ric** /,kələrə'metrik/ **adj.**, **col·or·im·e·try** /,kələ'rimitrē/ **n.**
– ORIGIN mid 19th cent.: from Latin *color* 'color' + -METER.

col·or·ing /'kələriNG/ (Brit. **colouring**) ▶ **n. 1** the process or skill of applying a substance to something so as to change its original color. ■ the process of filling in a particular shape or outline with crayons: [as modifier] *a coloring book.*
2 visual appearance with regard to color, in particular: ■ the arrangement of colors and markings on an animal. ■ the natural hues of a person's skin, hair, and eyes: *her fair coloring.* ■ the pervading character or tone of something: *the comments give a distinctly more ideological coloring to research conclusions.*
3 a substance used to give a particular color to something, esp. food.

col·or·ist /'kələrist/ (Brit. **colourist**) ▶ **n.** an artist or designer who uses color in a special or skillful way. ■ a person who tints black-and-white prints, photographs, or movies. ■ a hairdresser who specializes in dyeing people's hair.

col·or·is·tic /,kələ'ristik/ (Brit. **colouristic**) ▶ **adj.** showing or relating to a special use of color: *his great coloristic wallpapers.* ■ having or showing a variety of musical or vocal expression: *the choir's coloristic resources.*
– DERIVATIVES **col·or·is·ti·cal·ly** /-ik(ə)lē/ **adv.**

col·or·ize /'kələ,rīz/ (Brit. also **colourize**) ▶ **v.** [with obj.] add color to (a black-and-white movie) by means of computer technology.
– DERIVATIVES **col·or·i·za·tion** /,kələrə'zāSHən/ **n.** (trademark), **col·or·iz·er n.** (trademark).

col·or·less /'kələrləs/ (Brit. **colourless**) ▶ **adj. 1** (esp. of a gas or liquid) without color. ■ dull or pale in hue: *colorless cheeks.*
2 lacking distinctive character or interest; dull: *the book is rather colorless, like its author.*
– DERIVATIVES **col·or·less·ly adv.**

color line ▶ **n.** another term for COLOR BAR (sense 1).

col·or phase ▶ **n.** a genetic or seasonal variation in the color of the skin, pelt, or feathers of an animal.

col·or·point /'kələr,point/ (also **colourpoint**) ▶ **n.** chiefly British term for HIMALAYAN.

col·or re·ver·sal ▶ **n.** [usu. as modifier] Photography the process of producing a positive image directly from another positive: *color reversal films.*

col·or sat·u·ra·tion ▶ **n.** see SATURATION.

col·or scheme ▶ **n.** an arrangement or combination of colors, esp. as used in interior decoration: *a cool, simple color scheme.*

col·or sep·a·ra·tion ▶ **n.** Photography & Printing any of three negative images of the same subject taken through green, red, and blue filters and combined to reproduce the full color of the original. ■ the production of such images.

col·or tem·per·a·ture ▶ **n.** Astronomy & Physics the temperature at which a black body would emit radiation of the same color as a given object.

col·or ther·a·py ▶ **n.** a system of alternative medicine based on the use of color, esp. projected colored light.

col·or wash ▶ **n.** colored calcimine or tempera.
▶ **v.** (**color-wash**) [with obj.] paint (something) with colored calcimine or tempera.

col·or·way /'kələr,wā/ (Brit. **colourway**) ▶ **n.** any of a range of combinations of colors in which a style or design is available: *wallpaper books show coordinating patterns and colorways.*

col·or wheel ▶ **n.** a circle with different colored sectors used to show the relationship between colors.

co·los·sal /kə'läsəl/ ▶ **adj.** extremely large: *a colossal amount of mail | a colossal mistake.* ■ Architecture (of a giant order) having more than one story of columns. ■ Sculpture (of a statue) at least twice life size.
– DERIVATIVES **co·los·sal·ly adv.**
– ORIGIN early 18th cent.: from French, from *colosse*, from Latin *colossus* (see COLOSSUS).

Col·os·se·um /,kälə'sēəm/ the name since medieval times of the *Amphitheatrum Flavium*, a vast amphitheater in Rome, begun by Vespasian C.AD 75. It held 50,000 spectators, its sections connected by an elaborate network of stairs, and was the scene of various kinds of combat.
– ORIGIN from Latin, neuter of *colosseus* 'gigantic,' from *colossus* (see COLOSSUS).

the Colosseum

Co·los·sians /kə'läSHənz/ a book of the New Testament, an epistle of St. Paul to the Church at Colossae in Phrygia.

co·los·sus /kə'läsəs/ ▶ **n.** (pl. **colossi** /-'läs,ī/ or **colossuses**) a statue that is much bigger than life size. ■ a person or thing of enormous size, importance, or ability: *the Russian Empire was the colossus of European politics.*
– ORIGIN late Middle English: via Latin from Greek *kolossos* (applied by Herodotus to the statues of Egyptian temples).

Co·los·sus of Rhodes a huge bronze statue of the sun god Helios, one of the Seven Wonders of the World. Built c.292–280 BC, it stood beside the harbor entrance at Rhodes for about fifty years.

co·los·to·my /kə'lästəmē/ ▶ **n.** (pl. **colostomies**) a surgical operation in which a piece of the colon is diverted to an artificial opening in the abdominal wall so as to bypass a damaged part of the colon. ■ an opening so formed: [as modifier] *a colostomy bag.*
– ORIGIN late 19th cent.: from COLON[2] + Greek *stoma* 'mouth.'

co·los·trum /kə'lästrəm/ ▶ **n.** the first secretion from the mammary glands after giving birth, rich in antibodies.
– ORIGIN late 16th cent.: from Latin.

col·our ▶ **n. & v.** British spelling of COLOR.

col·por·teur /'käl,pôrtər, ,kälpôr'tər/ ▶ **n.** a peddler of books, newspapers, and similar literature. ■ someone employed by a religious society to distribute Bibles and other religious tracts.

PRONUNCIATION KEY ə *ago, up;* ər *over, fur;* a *hat;* ā *ate;* ä *car;* e *let;* ē *see;* i *fit;* ī *by;* NG *sing;* ō *go;* ô *law, for;* oi *toy;* o͝o *good;* o͞o *goo;* ou *out;* TH *thin;* T͟H *then;* ZH *vision*

C

– DERIVATIVES **col·por·tage** n.
– ORIGIN late 18th cent.: French, from the verb *colporter*, probably an alteration of *comporter*, from Latin *comportare* 'carry with one.'

col·po·scope /ˈkälpəˌskōp/ ▶ n. a surgical instrument used to examine the vagina and the cervix of the uterus.
– DERIVATIVES **col·pos·co·py** /kälˈpäskəpē/ n.
– ORIGIN 1940s: from Greek *kolpos* 'womb, uterus' + -SCOPE.

Colt[1] /kōlt/, Samuel (1814–62), US inventor. He is remembered chiefly for the revolver named after him, which he originally patented in 1836. It was adopted by the US Army in 1846. His armory at Hartford, Connecticut, advanced the manufacturing techniques of interchangeable parts and the production line.

Colt[2] ▶ n. trademark a type of revolver.

colt /kōlt/ ▶ n. a young, uncastrated male horse, in particular one less than four years old.
– ORIGIN Old English; perhaps related to Swedish *kult*, applied to boys or half-grown animals.

col·tan /ˈkältan/ ▶ n. a dull metallic mineral composed of columbite and tantalite, and refined to produce tantalum.
– ORIGIN early 21st cent.: from *col(umbite)* + *tan(talite)*.

col·ter /ˈkōltər/ ▶ n. variant spelling of COULTER.

colt·ish /ˈkōltisH/ ▶ adj. energetic but awkward in one's movements or behavior.
– DERIVATIVES **colt·ish·ly** adv., **colt·ish·ness** n.

Col·ton /ˈkōltn/ a city in southwestern California, just southwest of San Bernardino; pop. 50,517 (est. 2008).

Col·trane /ˈkōlˌtrān, kōlˈtrān/, John (William) (1926–67), US jazz saxophonist. He was a leading figure in avant-garde jazz, bridging the gap between the harmonically dense jazz of the 1950s and the free jazz that evolved in the 1960s.

colts·foot /ˈkōltsˌfo͝ot/ ▶ n. (pl. **coltsfoots**) a Eurasian plant of the daisy family, with yellow flowers that appear in early spring, followed by large, heart-shaped leaves. It is used in herbal medicine for the treatment of coughs and respiratory disorders. ● *Tussilago farfara*, family Compositae.
– ORIGIN mid 16th cent.: translating medieval Latin *pes pulli* 'foal's foot,' with reference to the shape of the leaves.

col·u·brid /ˈkäl(y)əbrid/ ▶ n. Zoology a snake of a very large family (Colubridae) that includes the majority of harmless species, such as grass snakes and garter snakes. The few venomous species have grooved fangs in the rear of the upper jaw.
– ORIGIN late 19th cent.: from modern Latin *Colubridae* (plural), from Latin *coluber* 'snake.'

col·u·brine /ˈkäl(y)əˌbrīn/ ▶ adj. of or belonging to a snake; snakelike: *he had played a game of subtle, colubrine misdirection.*
– ORIGIN early 16th cent.: from Latin *colubrinus*, from *coluber* 'snake.'

co·lu·go /kəˈlo͞ogō/ ▶ n. (pl. **colugos**) another term for FLYING LEMUR.
– ORIGIN late 18th cent.: of unknown origin.

Co·lum·ba /kəˈləmbə/ Astronomy a small and faint southern constellation (the Dove), near Canis Major. It is sometimes said to represent the dove that Noah sent out from the Ark. ■ (as genitive **Columbae** /kəˈləmbē, -ˌbī/) used with a preceding letter or numeral to designate a star in this constellation: *the star Beta Columbae.*
– ORIGIN Latin.

Co·lum·ba, St. (*c.*521–597), Irish abbot and missionary. He established a monastery at Iona *c.*563 and converted the Picts to Christianity. Feast day, June 9.

col·um·bar·i·um /ˌkäləmˈbe(ə)rēəm/ ▶ n. (pl. **columbaria** /-ˈbe(ə)rēə/) a room or building with niches for funeral urns to be stored. ■ a niche to hold a funeral urn.
– ORIGIN mid 18th cent.: from Latin, literally 'pigeon house.'

Co·lum·bi·a /kəˈləmbēə/ **1** a river in northwestern North America that rises in the Rocky Mountains of southeastern British Columbia, Canada, and flows for 1,230 miles (1,953 km), first south into the US and then west to enter the Pacific Ocean south of Seattle.
2 a residential community in central Maryland, between Baltimore and Washington, DC, planned and established in the 1960s; pop. 88,254 (2000).
3 a city in central Missouri, home to the University of Missouri; pop. 100,733 (est. 2008).
4 the capital of South Carolina, in the central part of the state; pop. 127,029 (est. 2008).

Co·lum·bi·a, District of see DISTRICT OF COLUMBIA.

Co·lum·bine /ˈkäləmˌbīn/ a character in Italian *commedia dell'arte*, the mistress of Harlequin.
– ORIGIN from French *Colombine*, from Italian *Colombina*, feminine of *colombino* 'dovelike,' from *colombo* 'dove.'

co·lum·bine /ˈkäləmˌbīn/ ▶ n. an aquilegia with long-spurred flowers. ● Genus *Aquilegia*, family Ranunculaceae: several species, including the white-flowered **Colorado blue columbine** (*A. coerulea*) with blue sepals, and the red-flowered *A. canadensis*.
– ORIGIN late Old Englis: from Old French *colombine*, from medieval Latin *colombina (herba)* 'dovelike (plant),' from Latin *columba* 'dove' (from the supposed resemblance of the flower to a cluster of five doves).

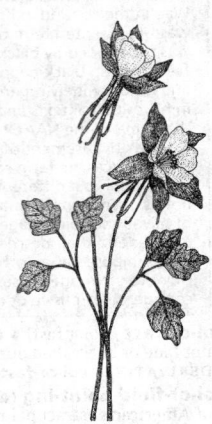

Colorado blue columbine

co·lum·bite /ˈkäləmˌbīt/ ▶ n. a black mineral, typically occurring as dense, tabular crystals, consisting of an oxide of iron, manganese, niobium, and tantalum. It is the chief ore of niobium.
– ORIGIN early 19th cent.: from COLUMBIUM + -ITE[1].

co·lum·bi·um /kəˈləmbēəm/ ▶ n. old-fashioned term for NIOBIUM.
– ORIGIN early 19th cent.: modern Latin, from *Columbia*, a poetic name for America from the name of Christopher *Columbus* (see COLUMBUS[2]).

Co·lum·bus[1] /kəˈləmbəs/ **1** an industrial city in western Georgia, on the Chattahoochee River, noted as a textile center; pop. 186,984 (est. 2008).
2 an industrial city in south central Indiana; pop. 40,001 (est. 2008).
3 the capital of Ohio, in the central part of the state; pop. 754,885 (est. 2008).

Co·lum·bus[2], Christopher (1451–1506), Spanish explorer; born in Italy; Italian name *Cristoforo Colombo*; Spanish name *Cristóbal Colón*. Columbus persuaded the Spanish monarchs, Ferdinand and Isabella, to sponsor an expedition to sail across the Atlantic in search of Asia and to prove that the world was round. In 1492, he set sail with three small ships (the *Niña*, the *Pinta*, the *Santa Maria*) and discovered the New World (in fact, various Caribbean islands). He made three further voyages between 1493 and 1504, landing on the South American mainland in 1498.

Co·lum·bus Day ▶ n. a legal holiday commemorating the discovery of the New World by Christopher Columbus in 1492. It is observed by most states on the second Monday of October.

col·u·mel·la /ˌkäl(y)əˈmelə/ ▶ n. (pl. **columellae** /-ˈmelˌī, -ˈmelē/) **1** Zoology an ossicle of the middle ear of birds, reptiles, and amphibians. ■ Anatomy the pillar around which the cochlea spirals.
2 Zoology the axis of a spiral shell.
3 Botany the axis of the spore-producing body of some lower plants.
– DERIVATIVES **col·u·mel·lar** /-ˈmelər/ adj.
– ORIGIN late 16th cent.: from Latin, 'small column.'

col·umn /ˈkäləm/ ▶ n. **1** an upright pillar, typically cylindrical and made of stone or concrete, supporting an entablature, arch, or other structure or standing alone as a monument. ■ a similar vertical, roughly cylindrical thing: *a great column of smoke.* ■ an upright shaft forming part of a machine and typically used for controlling it: *a Spitfire control column.*
2 a vertical division of a page or text. ■ a vertical arrangement of figures or other information. ■ a section of a newspaper or magazine regularly devoted to a particular subject or written by a particular person.
3 one or more lines of people or vehicles moving in the same direction: *a column of tanks moved northwest* | *we walked in a column.* ■ Military a narrow-fronted deep formation of troops in successive lines. ■ a military force deployed in such a formation.
– DERIVATIVES **co·lum·nar** /kəˈləmnər/ adj., **col·umned** /ˈkäləmd/ adj. [often in combination] *a four-columned portico.*
– ORIGIN late Middle English: partly from Old French *columpne*, reinforced by its source, Latin *columna* 'pillar.'

col·um·nat·ed /ˈkäləmˌnātid/ ▶ adj. Architecture supported on or having columns: *a columnated church interior.*

co·lum·ni·a·tion /kəˌləmnēˈāsHən/ ▶ n. Architecture the use or arrangement of columns.

col·umn inch ▶ n. a one-inch length of a column in a newspaper or magazine.

col·um·nist /ˈkäləmnist/ ▶ n. a journalist contributing regularly to a newspaper or magazine.

co·lure /kəˈlo͝or/ ▶ n. Astronomy either of two great circles intersecting at right angles at the celestial poles and passing through the ecliptic at either the equinoxes or the solstices.
– ORIGIN late Middle English: from late Latin *coluri* (plural), from Greek *kolourai (grammai)* 'truncated (lines),' from *kolouros* 'truncated,' so named because the lower part is permanently cut off from view.

co·ly /ˈkōlē/ ▶ n. (pl. **colies**) another term for MOUSEBIRD.
– ORIGIN mid 19th cent.: from modern Latin *Colius*, from Greek *kolios*, denoting a type of woodpecker.

col·za /ˈkälzə, ˈkōlzə/ ▶ n. another term for RAPE[2].
– ORIGIN early 18th cent.: from Walloon French *kolza*, from Low German *kōlsāt*, Dutch *koolzaad*, from *kool* 'cole' + *zaad* 'seed.'

COM /käm/ ▶ abbr. ■ computer output on microfilm or microfiche. ■ (also **Com.**) Commodore.

com- (also **co-**, **col-**, **con-**, or **cor-**) ▶ prefix with; together; jointly; altogether: *combine* | *command* | *collude.*
– ORIGIN from Latin *cum* 'with.'

co·ma[1] /ˈkōmə/ ▶ n. a state of deep unconsciousness that lasts for a prolonged or indefinite period, caused esp. by severe injury or illness: *a road crash left him in a coma* | figurative *a victim of a legislative coma.*
– ORIGIN mid 17th cent.: modern Latin, from Greek *kōma* 'deep sleep'; related to *koitē* 'bed' and *keisthai* 'lie down.'

co·ma[2] ▶ n. (pl. **comae** /ˈkōmē/) Astronomy a diffuse cloud of gas and dust surrounding the nucleus of a comet. ■ Optics aberration that causes the image of an off-axis point to be flared like a comet.
– ORIGIN early 17th cent. (as a botanical term): via Latin from Greek *komē* 'hair of the head.'

Co·ma Ber·e·ni·ces /ˈkōmə ˌberəˈnīsēz/ Astronomy an inconspicuous northern constellation (Berenice's Hair), said to represent the tresses of Queen Berenice. It contains a large number of galaxies. ■ (as genitive **Comae Berenices** /ˈkōmē/) used with a preceding letter or numeral to designate a star in this constellation: *the star Beta Comae Berenices.*
– ORIGIN Latin.

Co·man·che /kəˈmanCHē/ ▶ n. (pl. **same** or **Comanches**) **1** a member of an American Indian people of the southwestern US. The Comanche were among the first to acquire horses (from the Spanish) and resisted white settlers fiercely.
2 the Uto-Aztecan language of this people.
▶ adj. of or relating to this people or their language.
– ORIGIN Spanish, from Ute *kɨmmanči* 'strangers.'

Co·ma·ne·ci /ˌkōməˈnēCH, -ˈnäCH/, Nadia (1961–), Romanian gymnast; emigrated to the US in 1989. In 1976, she became the first Olympic gymnast to be awarded the maximum score of 10.00.

com·a·tose /ˈkōməˌtōs, ˈkämə-/ ▶ adj. of or in a state of deep unconsciousness for a prolonged or indefinite period, esp. as a result of severe injury or illness: *she had been comatose for seven months* | *lying in a comatose state.* ■ humorous (of a person or thing) extremely exhausted, lethargic, or sleepy: *the economy remains almost comatose.*
– ORIGIN late 17th cent.: from Greek *kōma, kōmat-* 'deep sleep' + -OSE[1].

comb /kōm/ ▶ n. **1** a strip of plastic, metal, or wood with a row of narrow teeth, used for untangling or arranging the hair. ■ [in sing.] an instance of untangling or arranging the hair with such a device: *she gave her hair a comb.* ■ a short curved device of this type, worn by women to hold hair in place or as an ornament.
2 something resembling a comb in function or structure, in particular: ■ a device for separating and dressing textile fibers. ■ a row of brass points for collecting the electricity in an electrostatic generator.
3 the red fleshy crest on the head of a domestic fowl, esp. a rooster.
4 short for HONEYCOMB (sense 1 of the noun).
▶ v. [with obj.] **1** untangle or arrange (the hair) by drawing a comb through it: (as adj. **combed**) *neatly combed hair.* ■ (**comb something out**) remove something from the hair by drawing a comb through it: *she combed the burrs out of the dog's coat.*
2 prepare (wool, flax, or cotton) for manufacture with a comb. ■ (usu. as adj. **combed**) treat (a fabric) in such a way: *the socks are made of soft combed cotton.*
3 search carefully and systematically: *police combed the area for the murder weapon* | [no obj.] *his mother combed through the cardboard boxes.*
– DERIVATIVES **comb·like** /-ˌlīk/ adj.

—ORIGIN Old English *camb*, of Germanic origin; related to Dutch *kam* and German *Kamm*.

com·bat ▶ **n.** /ˈkäm,bat/ fighting between armed forces: *men killed in combat* | *pilots re-enacted the aerial combats of yesteryear* | [as modifier] *a combat zone.* ■ nonviolent conflict or opposition: *intellectual combat.*
▶ **v.** /kəmˈbat, ˈkäm,bat/ (**combats, combating** or **combatting, combated** or **combatted**) [with obj.] take action to reduce, destroy, or prevent (something undesirable): *an effort to combat drug trafficking.* ■ archaic engage in a fight with; oppose in battle.
—ORIGIN mid 16th cent. (originally denoting a fight between two persons or parties): from French *combattre* (verb), from late Latin *combattere*, from *com-* 'together with' + *battere*, variant of Latin *batuere* 'to fight.'

com·bat·ant /kəmˈbatnt, ˈkämbətənt/ ▶ **n.** a person or nation engaged in fighting during a war. ■ a person engaged in conflict or competition with another.
▶ **adj.** engaged in fighting during a war: *all the combatant armies went to war with machine guns.*
—ORIGIN late Middle English (as an adjective used in heraldry to describe two lions facing one another with raised forepaws): from Old French, present participle of *combatre* 'to fight' (see COMBAT).

com·bat boots ▶ **plural n.** boots of a type worn by soldiers in combat, typically black with laces and thick rubber soles.

com·bat fa·tigue ▶ **n. 1** psychological disturbance caused by prolonged exposure to active warfare, esp. being under bombardment.
2 (**combat fatigues**) a uniform of a type to be worn into combat.

com·bat·ive /ˈkäm,bativ/ ▶ **adj.** ready or eager to fight; pugnacious: *he made some enemies with his combative style.*
—DERIVATIVES **com·bat·ive·ly adv.**, **com·bat·ive·ness n.**

com·bat jack·et ▶ **n.** a jacket of a type worn by soldiers in combat, typically having a camouflage pattern.

comb-back ▶ **n.** a high-backed Windsor chair with a straight top rail: [as modifier] *a comb-back rocker.*

combe /ko͞om, kōm/ (also **coomb** or **coombe**) ▶ **n.** Brit. a short valley or hollow on a hillside or coastline. ■ Geology a dry valley in a limestone or chalk escarpment.
—ORIGIN Old English *cumb*, occurring in charters in the names of places in southern England, many of which survive; of Celtic origin, related to CWM. The current general use dates from the late 16th cent.

comb·er /ˈkōmər/ ▶ **n. 1** a long curling sea wave.
2 a person or machine that separates and straightens the fibers of cotton or wool.

comb·fish /ˈkōm,fisн/ ▶ **n.** (pl. **same** or **combfishes**) a fish of the northeastern Pacific, with small rough scales and long spines in the comblike dorsal fin. ● Family Zaniolepididae and genus *Zaniolepis*: several species.

com·bi·na·tion /,kämbəˈnāsнən/ ▶ **n. 1** a joining or merging of different parts or qualities in which the component elements are individually distinct: *a combination of blackberries, raspberries, and rhubarb* | *this colour combination is stunningly effective.* ■ the state of being joined or united in such a way: *these four factors work together in combination.* ■ an arrangement of elements: *the canvases may be arranged in any number of combinations.* ■ (in various sports and games) a coordinated and effective sequence of moves: *a good uppercut/hook combination.* ■ [as modifier] uniting different uses, functions, or ingredients: *a combination garment bag and backpack.* ■ Chemistry the joining of substances in a compound with new properties.
2 a sequence of numbers or letters used to open a combination lock: [as modifier] *a combination briefcase.*
3 Mathematics a selection of a given number of elements from a larger number without regard to their arrangement.
—DERIVATIVES **com·bi·na·tion·al** /-sнənl/ **adj.**, **com·bi·na·tive** /ˈkämbə,nātiv, kəmˈbīnətiv/ **adj.**, **com·bi·na·to·ri·al** /,kämbənəˈtôrēəl, kəm,bīnə-/ **adj.** (Mathematics), **com·bi·na·to·ri·al·ly adv.** (Mathematics), **com·bi·na·to·ry** /kəmˈbīnə,tôre, ˈkämbənə-/ **adj.**
—ORIGIN late Middle English: from late Latin *combinatio(n-)*, from the verb *combinare* 'join two by two' (see COMBINE[1]).

com·bi·na·tion·al cir·cuit ▶ **n.** Electronics a circuit whose output depends only on the state of its inputs. Compare with SEQUENTIAL CIRCUIT.

com·bi·na·tion lock ▶ **n.** a lock that is opened by rotating a dial or set of dials, marked with letters or numbers, through a specific sequence.

com·bi·na·tion ov·en ▶ **n.** an oven operating by both conventional heating and microwaves.

com·bi·na·tion ther·a·py ▶ **n.** treatment in which a patient is given two or more drugs (or other therapeutic agents) for a single disease.

com·bi·na·tor·ics /,kämbənəˈtôriks, kəm,bīnə-/ ▶ **plural n.** [treated as sing.] the branch of mathematics dealing with combinations of objects belonging to a finite set in accordance with certain constraints, such as those of graph theory.
—ORIGIN 1940s: from *combinatorial* (see COMBINATION), influenced by German *Kombinatorik.*

com·bine[1] ▶ **v.** /kəmˈbīn/ [with obj.] unite; merge: *the band combines a variety of musical influences* | *combine the flour with the margarine and salt* | [no obj.] *high tides and winds combined to bring chaos to the East Coast.* ■ [no obj.] Chemistry unite to form a compound: *oxygen and hydrogen do not combine at room temperatures.* ■ [no obj.] unite for a common purpose: *groups of teachers combined to tackle a variety of problems.* ■ engage in simultaneously: *combine shopping and sightseeing.*
▶ **n.** /ˈkäm,bīn/ a group of people or companies acting together for a commercial purpose: *a powerful industrial combine.*
—DERIVATIVES **com·bin·a·ble** /kəmˈbīnəbəl/ **adj.**
—ORIGIN late Middle English: from Old French *combiner* or late Latin *combinare* 'join two by two,' from *com-* 'together' + Latin *bini* 'two together.'

com·bine[2] /ˈkäm,bīn/ ▶ **n.** (in full **combine harvester**) an agricultural machine that cuts, threshes, and cleans a grain crop in one operation.
▶ **v.** [with obj.] harvest (a crop) by means of a combine.

com·bin·er[1] /kəmˈbīnər/ ▶ **n.** any of various electronic devices that combine signals, in particular: ■ a device that couples different frequencies to a single antenna. ■ a component of a cipher that combines two data sources to encrypt text. ■ an electrical transformer comprising several smaller ones.

com·bin·er[2] /ˈkäm,bīnər/ ▶ **n.** an operator of a combine harvester.

comb·ings /ˈkōmiNGZ/ ▶ **plural n.** hairs or other material removed with a comb.

comb·ing wool ▶ **n.** long-stapled wool with straight, parallel fibers, suitable for combing and making into high-quality fabrics, in particular worsted. Compare with CARDING WOOL.

com·bin·ing form /kəmˈbīniNG/ ▶ **n.** Grammar a linguistic element used in combination with another element to form a word (e.g., *Anglo-* 'English' in *Anglo-American*, *bio-* 'life' in *biology*, *-graphy* 'writing' in *biography*).

> **USAGE** In this dictionary, **combining form** is used to denote an element that contributes to the particular sense of words (as with **bio-** and **-graphy** in **biography**), as distinct from a prefix or suffix that adjusts the sense of or determines the function of words (as with **un-**, **-able**, and **-ation**).

comb jel·ly ▶ **n.** a marine animal with a jellyfishlike body bearing rows of fused cilia for propulsion. They are typically small planktonic animals and are noted for their luminescence. ● Phylum Ctenophora: two classes.

com·bo /ˈkämbō/ ▶ **n.** (pl. **combos**) informal **1** a small jazz, rock, or pop band.
2 a combination, typically of different foods: [as modifier] *the combo platter.*
—ORIGIN 1920s (originally US): abbreviation of COMBINATION + -O.

com·bo box ▶ **n.** Computing, informal a type of dialogue box containing a combination of controls, such as sliders, text boxes, and drop-down lists.

com·bo drive ▶ **n.** Computing an optical disk drive that can read and record CDs and can also read DVDs.

comb·over /ˈkōm,ōvər/ ▶ **n.** hair that is combed over a bald spot in an attempt to cover it.

com·bust /kəmˈbəst/ ▶ **v.** [with obj.] consume by fire. ■ [no obj.] be consumed by fire.
—ORIGIN late 15th cent.: from obsolete *combust* 'burned, calcined,' from Latin *combustus*, past participle of *comburere* 'burn up.'

com·bus·ti·ble /kəmˈbəstəbəl/ ▶ **adj.** able to catch fire and burn easily: *highly combustible paint thinner.* ■ excitable; easily annoyed: *two combustible personalities.*
▶ **n.** a combustible substance.
—DERIVATIVES **com·bus·ti·bil·i·ty** /kəm,bəstəˈbilitē/ **n.**
—ORIGIN early 16th cent.: from Old French, from late Latin *combustibilis*, from Latin *combust-* 'burned up,' from the verb *comburere.*

com·bus·tion /kəmˈbəscнən/ ▶ **n.** the process of burning something: *the combustion of fossil fuels.* ■ Chemistry rapid chemical combination of a substance with oxygen, involving the production of heat and light.
—DERIVATIVES **com·bus·tive** /-ˈbəstiv/ **adj.**
—ORIGIN late Middle English: from late Latin *combustio(n-)*, from Latin *comburere* 'burn up.'

com·bus·tion cham·ber ▶ **n.** an enclosed space in which combustion takes place, esp. in an engine or furnace.

Comdr. ▶ **abbr.** commander.

come /kəm/ ▶ **v.** (past **came** /kām/; past participle **come**) [no obj.] **1** move or travel toward or into a place thought of as near or familiar to the speaker: *Jessica came into the kitchen* | *they came here as immigrants* | *he came rushing out.* ■ arrive at a specified place: *we walked along till we came to a stream* | *it was very late when she came back* | *my trunk hasn't come yet.* ■ (of a thing) reach or extend to a specified point: *women in slim dresses that came all the way to their shoes* | *the path comes straight down.* ■ (**be coming**) approach: *someone was coming* | *she heard the train coming.* ■ travel in order to be with a specified person, to do a specified thing, or to be present at an event: *the police came* | *come and live with me* | *the electrician came to fix the stove* | figurative *we have certainly come a long way since Aristotle.* ■ join someone in participating in a specified activity or course of action: *do you want to come fishing tomorrow?* ■ (**come along/on**) make progress; develop: *he's coming along nicely* | *she asked them how their garden was coming on.* ■ [in imperative] (also **come, come!**) said to someone when correcting, reassuring, or urging them on: *"Come, come, child, no need to thank me."*
2 occur; happen; take place: *twilight had not yet come* | *waiting for a crash that never came* | *a chance like this doesn't come along every day.* ■ be heard, perceived, or experienced: *a voice came from the kitchen* | *"No," came the reply* | *it came as a great shock.* ■ (of a quality) become apparent or noticeable through actions or performance: *as an actor your style and personality must come through.* ■ (**come across** or **off** or Brit. **over**) (of a person) appear or sound in a specified way; give a specified impression: *he'd always come across as a decent guy.* ■ (of a thought or memory) enter one's mind: *the basic idea came to me while reading an article* | *a passage from a novel came back to Adam.*
3 take or occupy a specified position in space, order, or priority: *prisons come far down the list of priorities* | *I make sure my kids come first.* ■ achieve a specified place in a race or contest: *she came second among sixty contestants.*
4 pass into a specified state, esp. one of separation or disunion: *his shirt had come undone.* ■ (**come to/into**) reach or be brought to a specified situation or result: *you will come to no harm* | *staff who come into contact with the public.* ■ reach eventually a certain condition or state of mind: *he had come to realize she was no puppet.*
5 be sold, available, or found in a specified form: *the cars come with a variety of extras* | *they come in three sizes.*
6 informal have an orgasm.
▶ **prep.** informal when a specified time is reached or event happens: *I don't think that they'll be far away from honors come the new season.*
▶ **n.** informal semen ejaculated at orgasm.
—PHRASES **as —— as they come** used to describe someone or something that is a supreme example of the quality specified: *Smith is as tough as they come.* **come again?** informal used to ask someone to repeat or explain something they have said. **come and go** arrive and then depart again; move around freely. ■ exist or be present for a limited time; be transitory: *health fads come and go.* **come from behind** win after lagging. **come off it** [in imperative] informal said when vigorously expressing disbelief. **come to nothing** have no significant or successful result in the end. **come to pass** chiefly literary happen; occur: *it came to pass that she had two sons.* **come to rest** eventually cease moving. **come to that** (or **if it comes to that**) informal in fact (said to introduce an additional point): *there isn't a clock on the mantelpiece—come to that, there isn't a mantelpiece!* **come to think of it** on reflection (said when an idea or point occurs to one while one is speaking). **come what may** no matter what happens. **have it coming** (**to one**) informal be due for retribution on account of something bad that one has done: *his uppity sister-in-law had it coming to her.* **how come?** informal said when asking how or why something happened or is the case: *how come you never married, Jimmy?* **to come** (following a noun) in the future: *films that would inspire generations to come* | *in years to come.*

C

where someone is coming from informal someone's meaning, motivation, or personality.
– PHRASAL VERBS **come about 1** happen; take place: *the relative speed with which emancipation came about.* **2** (of a ship) change direction. **come across 1** meet or find by chance: *I came across these old photos recently.* **2** informal hand over or provide what is wanted: *she has come across with some details.* ■ (of a woman) agree to have sexual intercourse with a man. **come after** pursue or hunt down (someone). **come along** [in imperative] said when encouraging someone or telling them to hurry up. **come around** (chiefly Brit. also **round**) **1** recover consciousness: *I'd just come around from a drunken stupor.* **2** be converted to another person's opinion: *I came around to her point of view.* **3** (of a date or regular occurrence) recur; be imminent again: *Friday had come around so quickly.* **come at** launch oneself at (someone); attack. **come away** be left with a specified feeling, impression, or result after doing something: *she came away feeling upset.* **come back 1** (in sports) recover from a deficit: *the Mets came back from a 3–0 deficit.* **2** reply or respond to someone, esp. vigorously: *he came back at Judy with a vengeance.* **come before** be dealt with by (a judge or court): *it is the most controversial issue to come before the Supreme Court.* **come between** interfere with or disturb the relationship of (two people): *I let my stupid pride come between us.* **come by 1** call casually and briefly as a visitor: *his friends came by* | *she came by the house.* **2** manage to acquire or obtain (something). **come down 1** (of a building or other structure) collapse or be demolished. ■ (of an aircraft) crash or crash-land. **2** be handed down by tradition or inheritance: *the name has come down from the last century.* **3** reach a decision or recommendation in favor of one side or another: *advisers and inspectors came down on our side.* **4** Brit. leave a university, esp. Oxford or Cambridge, after finishing one's studies. **5** informal experience the lessening of an excited or euphoric feeling, esp. one produced by a narcotic drug. **come down on** criticize or punish (someone) harshly: *she came down on me like a ton of bricks.* **come down to** (of a situation or outcome) be dependent on (a specified factor): *it came down to her word against Guy's.* **come down with** begin to suffer from (a specified illness): *I came down with influenza.* **come for** (of police or other officials) arrive to arrest or detain (someone). **come forward** volunteer oneself for a task or post or to give evidence about a crime. **come from** originate in; have as its source: *the word caviar comes from the Italian caviale.* ■ be the result of: *a dignity that comes from being in control.* ■ have as one's place of birth or residence: *I come from the Bronx.* ■ be descended from: *he comes from a family of artists.* **come in 1** join or become involved in an enterprise: *that's where Jack comes in* | *I agreed to come in on the project.* ■ have a useful role or function: *this is where grammar comes in.* ■ prove to have a specified good quality: *the money came in handy for treating his cronies at the tavern.* **2** finish a race in a specified position: *the favorite came in first.* **3** (of money) be earned or received regularly. **4** [in imperative] begin speaking or make contact, esp. in radio communication: *come in, London.* **5** (of a tide) rise; flow. **come in for** receive or be the object of (a reaction), typically a negative one: *he has come in for a lot of criticism.* **come into** suddenly receive (money or property), esp. by inheriting it. **come of** result from: *no good will come of it.* ■ be descended from: *she came of Neapolitan stock.* **come off 1** (of an action) succeed; be accomplished. ■ fare in a specified way in a contest: *Jeff always came off worse in an argument.* **2** become detached or be detachable from something. **come on 1** (of a state or condition) start to arrive or happen: *she felt a mild case of the sniffles coming on* | *it was coming on to rain.* **2** (also **come upon**) meet or find by chance. **3** [in imperative] said when encouraging someone to do something or to hurry up or when one feels that someone is wrong or foolish: *Come on! We must hurry!* ■ said or shouted to express support, for example for a sports team. **come on to** informal make sexual advances toward. **come out 1** (of a fact) emerge; become known: *it came out that the accused had illegally registered to vote.* ■ happen as a result: *something good can come out of something that went wrong.* ■ (of a photograph) be produced satisfactorily or in a specified way: *I hope my photographs come out all right.* ■ (of the result of a calculation or measurement) emerge at a specified figure: *rough cider usually comes out at about eight percent alcohol.* **2** (of a book or other work) appear; be released or published. **3** declare oneself as being for or against something: *residents have come out against the proposals.* **4** achieve a specified placing in an examination or contest: *he deservedly came out the winner on points* | *she came out victorious.* ■ acquit oneself in a specified way: *surprisingly, it's Penn who comes out best.* **5** (of a stain) be removed or able to be removed. **6** informal openly declare that one is homosexual. [from the phrase *come out of the closet* (see CLOSET (sense 3 of the noun)).] **7** dated (of a young upper-class woman) make one's debut in society. **come out in** Brit. (of a person's skin) break out in (pimples or a similar condition). **come out with** say (something) in a sudden, rude, or incautious way. **come over 1** (of a feeling or manner) begin to affect (someone). **2** change to another side or point of view. **come round** see COME AROUND. **come through 1** succeed in surviving or dealing with (an illness or ordeal): *she's come through the operation very well.* **2** (of a message) be sent and received. ■ (of an official decree) be processed and notified. **come to 1** (also **come to oneself**) recover consciousness. **2** (of an expense) reach in total; amount to: *he hasn't the least idea of how much it will come to.* **3** (of a ship) come to a stop. **come under 1** be classified as or among: *they all come under the general heading of opinion polls.* **2** be subject to (an influence or authority). ■ be subjected to (pressure or aggression): *his vehicle came under mortar fire.* **come up 1** (of an issue, situation, or problem) occur or present itself, esp. unexpectedly. ■ (of a specified time or event) approach or draw near: *she's got exams coming up.* ■ (of a legal case) reach the time when it is scheduled to be dealt with. **2** Brit. begin one's studies at a university, esp. Oxford or Cambridge. **come up against** be faced with or opposed by (something such as an enemy or problem). **come up with** produce (something), esp. when pressured or challenged. **come upon 1** attack by surprise. **2** see COME ON (sense 2).
– ORIGIN Old English *cuman*, of Germanic origin; related to Dutch *komen* and German *kommen*.

> **USAGE** The use of come followed by and, as in *come and see for yourself*, dates back to Old English, but is seen by some as incorrect or only suitable for informal English. For more details, see usage at AND.

come-a·long ▶ n. informal a hand-operated winch.

come·back /ˈkəmˌbak/ ▶ n. **1** a return by a well-known person, esp. an entertainer or sports player, to the activity in which they have formerly been successful: *the heavyweight champion is set to make his comeback* | [as modifier] *his career died after a couple of comeback attempts.* ■ a return to fashion of an item, activity, or style: *stirrup pants have made a comeback.*
2 informal a quick reply to a critical remark. ■ the opportunity to seek redress: *there's no comeback if he messes up your case.*

Com·e·con /ˈkäməˌkän/ an economic association of eastern European countries founded in 1949 and analogous to the European Economic Community. With the collapse of communism in eastern Europe, the association was dissolved in 1991.
– ORIGIN contraction of COUNCIL FOR MUTUAL ECONOMIC ASSISTANCE.

co·me·di·an /kəˈmēdēən/ ▶ n. an entertainer whose act is designed to make an audience laugh. ■ often ironic an amusing or entertaining person. ■ a comic actor.
– ORIGIN late 16th cent. (denoting a comic playwright): from French *comédien*, from Old French *comedie* (see COMEDY). The sense 'entertainer' dates from the late 19th cent.

Co·mé·die-Fran·çaise /ˌkômādē fränˈsez/ the French national theater (used for both comedy and tragedy), in Paris, founded in 1680 by Louis XIV.

co·me·di·enne /kəˌmēdēˈen/ ▶ n. a female comedian.
– ORIGIN mid 19th cent.: from French *comédienne*, feminine of *comédien* (see COMEDIAN).

com·e·do /ˈkäməˌdō/ ▶ n. (pl. **comedones** /ˌkäməˈdōnēz/) technical term for BLACKHEAD (sense 1).
– ORIGIN mid 19th cent.: from Latin, literally 'glutton,' from *comedere* 'eat up,' from *com-* 'altogether' + *edere* 'eat.' Used formerly as a name for parasitic worms, the term here alludes to the wormlike matter that can be squeezed from a blackhead.

com·e·do·gen·ic /ˌkäməˌdōˈjenik/ ▶ adj. tending to cause blackheads by blocking the pores of the skin.

come·down /ˈkəmˌdoun/ ▶ n. informal **1** a loss of status or importance: *patrol duty? A comedown for a sergeant.*
2 a feeling of disappointment or depression: *it's such a comedown after Christmas is over.* ■ [in sing.] a lessening of the sensations generated by a narcotic drug as its effects wear off.

com·e·dy /ˈkämədē/ ▶ n. (pl. **comedies**) professional entertainment consisting of jokes and satirical sketches, intended to make an audience laugh. ■ a movie, play, or broadcast program intended to make an audience laugh: *a rollicking new comedy.* ■ the style or genre of such types of entertainment. ■ the humorous or amusing aspects of something: *advertising people see the comedy in their work.* ■ a play characterized by its humorous or satirical tone and its depiction of amusing people or incidents, in which the characters ultimately triumph over adversity: *Shakespeare's comedies.* ■ the dramatic genre represented by such plays: *satiric comedy.* Compare with TRAGEDY (sense 2).
– PHRASES **comedy of errors** a situation made amusing by bungling and incompetence: *the comedy of errors that is Medicare's physician payment schedule.*
– DERIVATIVES **co·me·dic** /kəˈmēdik/ adj.
– ORIGIN late Middle English (as a genre of drama, also denoting a narrative poem with a happy ending, as in Dante's *Divine Comedy*): from Old French *comedie*, via Latin from Greek *kōmōidia*, from *kōmōidos* 'comic poet,' from *kōmos* 'revel' + *aoidos* 'singer.'

com·e·dy of man·ners ▶ n. a comedy that satirizes behavior in a particular social group, esp. the upper classes.

come-hith·er informal, dated ▶ adj. flirtatious; sexually inviting: *nymphs with come-hither looks.*

come·ly /ˈkəmlē/ ▶ adj. (**comelier**, **comeliest**) (typically of a woman) pleasant to look at; attractive. ■ agreeable; suitable.
– DERIVATIVES **come·li·ness** n.
– ORIGIN Middle English: probably shortened from *becomely* 'fitting, becoming,' from BECOME.

come-on ▶ n. informal a gesture or remark that is intended to attract someone sexually: *she was giving me the come-on.* ■ a marketing ploy, such as a free or cheap offer: [as modifier] *introductory come-on rates.*

come-out·er ▶ n. chiefly historical a person who dissociates himself or herself from an organization.

com·er /ˈkəmər/ ▶ n. **1** a person who arrives somewhere: *feeding every comer is still a sacred duty.* See also ALL COMERS at ALL; LATECOMER; NEWCOMER.
2 [in sing.] informal a person or thing likely to succeed: *many in the party see tax relief as a comer.*

co·mes·ti·ble /kəˈmestəbəl/ ▶ n. (usu. **comestibles**) an item of food: *a fridge groaning with comestibles.*
▶ adj. edible: *comestible plants.*
– ORIGIN late 15th cent.: from Old French, from medieval Latin *comestibilis*, from Latin *comest-* 'eaten up,' from the verb *comedere*, from *com-* 'altogether' + *edere* 'eat.'

com·et /ˈkämit/ ▶ n. a celestial object consisting of a nucleus of ice and dust and, when near the sun, a "tail" of gas and dust particles pointing away from the sun.

> Originating in the remotest regions of the solar system, most comets follow regular eccentric orbits and appear in the inner solar system as periodic comets, some of which break up and can be the origin of annual meteor showers. They were formerly considered to be supernatural omens.

– DERIVATIVES **com·et·ar·y** /ˈkämiˌterē/ adj.
– ORIGIN late Old English, from Latin *cometa*, from Greek *komētēs* 'long-haired (star),' from *komē* 'hair'; reinforced by Old French *comete*.

come·up·pance /kəˈməpəns/ ▶ n. [usu. in sing.] informal a punishment or fate that someone deserves: *he got his comeuppance.*

com·fit /ˈkəmfit, ˈkämfit/ ▶ n. dated a candy consisting of a nut, seed, or other center coated in sugar.
– ORIGIN Middle English: from Old French *confit*, from Latin *confectum* 'something prepared,' neuter past participle of *conficere* 'put together' (see CONFECT).

com·fort /ˈkəmfərt/ ▶ n. **1** a state of physical ease and freedom from pain or constraint: *room for four people to travel in comfort.* ■ (**comforts**) things that contribute to physical ease and well-being: *the low upholstered chair was one of the room's few comforts.* ■ prosperity and the pleasant lifestyle secured by it: *my father left us enough to live in comfort.*
2 consolation for grief or anxiety: *a few words of comfort.* ■ [in sing.] a person or thing that gives consolation: *his friendship was a great comfort.*
3 dialect a warm quilt.
▶ v. [with obj.] make (someone) feel less unhappy; console: *she broke down in tears and her friend tried to comfort her.* ■ help (someone) feel at ease; reassure: *her strength comforted and protected me.*
– PHRASES **too — for comfort** causing physical or mental unease by an excess of the specified quality: *it can be too hot for comfort in July and August.*
– ORIGIN Middle English (as a noun, in the senses 'strengthening, support, consolation'; as a verb, in the senses 'strengthen, give support, console'): from Old French *confort* (noun), *conforter* (verb), from late Latin *confortare* 'strengthen,' from *com-* (expressing intensive force) + Latin *fortis* 'strong.'

The sense 'something producing physical ease' arose in the mid 17th cent.

com·fort·a·ble /ˈkəmfərtəbəl, ˈkəmftərbəl/ ▶ **adj.** **1** (esp. of clothes or furnishings) providing physical ease and relaxation: *invitingly comfortable beds.* ■ (of a person) physically relaxed and free from constraint: *he would not be comfortable in any other clothes.* ■ not in pain (used esp. of a hospital patient). ■ free from stress or fear: *they appear very comfortable in each other's company | few of us are comfortable with confrontations.* ■ free from financial worry; having an adequate standard of living.
2 as large as is needed or wanted: *a comfortable income.* ■ with a wide margin: *a comfortable victory.*
▶ **n.** dialect a warm quilt.
– DERIVATIVES **com·fort·a·ble·ness** **n.**, **com·fort·a·bly** /-blē/ **adv.**
– ORIGIN Middle English (in the sense 'pleasant, pleasing'): from Anglo-Norman French *confortable*, from *conforter* 'to comfort' (see COMFORT).

com·fort eat·ing ▶ **n.** eating to make oneself feel happier, rather than to satisfy hunger.

com·fort·er /ˈkəmfərtər/ ▶ **n.** **1** a warm quilt.
2 a person or thing that provides consolation. ■ (**Comforter**) the Holy Spirit.
3 dated a woolen scarf.
– ORIGIN late Middle English: from Old French *comforteor*, from *conforter* 'to comfort' (see COMFORT).

com·fort food ▶ **n.** food that provides consolation or a feeling of well-being, typically any with a high sugar or other carbohydrate content and associated with childhood or home cooking.

com·fort·ing /ˈkəmfərtiNG/ ▶ **adj.** giving consolation for grief or anxiety; soothing: *his comforting presence.*
– DERIVATIVES **com·fort·ing·ly** **adv.**

com·fort·less /ˈkəmfərtlis/ ▶ **adj.** **1** offering no means of relaxation and pleasure: *a comfortless prison.*
2 having or offering no consolation: *he had left her comfortless.*

com·fort sta·tion ▶ **n.** a public restroom for travelers or campers.

com·fort zone ▶ **n.** a place or situation where one feels safe or at ease and without stress: *times when we must act beyond our comfort zones | if you stay within your comfort zone, you will never improve.*

com·frey /ˈkəmfrē/ ▶ **n.** (pl. **comfreys**) a Eurasian plant of the borage family, with large hairy leaves and clusters of purplish or white bell-shaped flowers. ● Genus *Symphytum*, family Boraginaceae: several species, in particular the **common comfrey** (*S. officinale*), which is used in herbal medicine (see BONESET).
– ORIGIN Middle English: from Anglo-Norman French *cumfirie*, based on Latin *conferva*, from *confervere* 'heal' (literally 'boil together,' referring to the plant's medicinal use).

com·fy /ˈkəmfē/ ▶ **adj.** (**comfier**, **comfiest**) informal comfortable.
– DERIVATIVES **com·fi·ly** /-fəlē/ **adv.**, **com·fi·ness** **n.**
– ORIGIN early 19th cent.: abbreviation.

com·ic /ˈkämik/ ▶ **adj.** causing or meant to cause laughter: *comic and fantastic exaggeration.* ■ relating to or in the style of comedy: *a comic actor | comic drama.*
▶ **n.** **1** a comedian, esp. a professional one: *a stand-up comic.*
2 (**comics**) comic strips.
– ORIGIN late 16th cent.: via Latin from Greek *kōmikos*, from *kōmos* 'revel.'

com·i·cal /ˈkämikəl/ ▶ **adj.** amusing: *a series of comical misunderstandings.*
– DERIVATIVES **com·i·cal·i·ty** /ˌkäməˈkalitē/ **n.**, **com·i·cal·ly** /-ik(ə)lē/ **adv.**
– ORIGIN late Middle English (in the sense 'relating to or in the style of comedy'): from Latin *comicus* (see COMIC) + -AL.

Co·mice /ˈkäməs/ (in full **Doyenne du Comice**) ▶ **n.** a large yellow dessert pear.
– ORIGIN mid 19th cent.: from French, literally 'association, cooperative,' referring to the *Comice Horticole* of Angers, France, where this variety was developed.

com·ic op·er·a ▶ **n.** an opera that portrays humorous situations and characters, enhanced by spoken dialogue.

com·ic re·lief ▶ **n.** comic episodes in a dramatic or literary work that offset more serious sections. ■ a character or characters providing this.

com·ic strip ▶ **n.** a sequence of drawings in boxes that tell an amusing story, typically printed in a newspaper or comic book.

com·ing /ˈkəmiNG/ ▶ **adj.** **1** due to happen or just beginning: *work is due to start in the coming year.*
2 likely to be important or successful in the future: *he was the coming man of French racing.*
▶ **n.** [in sing.] an arrival or an approach: *the coming of a new age.*
– PHRASES **comings and goings** the busy movements of a person or group of people, esp. in and out of a place. **not know if one is coming or going** informal be confused, esp. as a result of being very busy.

Co·mi·no /kəˈmēnō/ the smallest of the three main islands of Malta.

COMINT /ˈkämˌint/ ▶ **abbr.** communications intelligence.

Com·in·tern /ˈkäminˌtərn/ the Third International, a communist organization (1919–43). See INTERNATIONAL (sense 2 of the noun).
– ORIGIN from Russian *Komintern*, blend of *kom(munisticheskiĭ)* 'communist' and *intern(atsional)* 'international.'

com·i·tal /ˈkämətl/ ▶ **adj.** chiefly historical of or relating to a count or earl.
– ORIGIN mid 19th cent.: from medieval Latin *comitalis*, from *comes*, *comit-* 'a count.'

com·i·ty /ˈkämitē/ ▶ **n.** (pl. **comities**) **1** courtesy and considerate behavior toward others.
2 an association of nations for their mutual benefit. ■ (also **comity of nations**) the mutual recognition by nations of the laws and customs of others.
– ORIGIN mid 16th cent. (sense 1): from Latin *comitas*, from *comis* 'courteous.'

comm /käm/ ▶ **n.** short for COMMUNICATION: [as modifier] *a comm link.*

comm. ▶ **abbr.** ■ commerce. ■ commercial. ■ commission. ■ commissioner. ■ committee. ■ common.

com·ma /ˈkämə/ ▶ **n.** **1** a punctuation mark (,) indicating a pause between parts of a sentence. It is also used to separate items in a list and to mark the place of thousands in a large numeral.
2 Music a minute interval or difference of pitch.
3 (also **comma butterfly**) a butterfly that has wings with irregular, ragged edges and typically a white or silver comma-shaped mark on the underside of each hind wing. ● Genus *Polygonia*, subfamily Nymphalinae, family Nymphalidae: numerous species, in particular the common **eastern comma** (*P. comma*) of eastern North America.
– ORIGIN late 16th cent. (originally as a term in rhetoric denoting a group of words shorter than a colon; see COLON[1]): via Latin from Greek *komma* 'piece cut off, short clause,' from *koptein* 'cut.'

comma 3

Com·ma·ger /ˈkämijər/, Henry Steele (1902–98), US educator and writer. Among his notable works are *The Growth of the American Republic* (co-authored with Samuel Eliot Morison, 1931), *The American Mind* (1951), and *The Empire of Reason* (1977).

com·mand /kəˈmand/ ▶ **v.** **1** [reporting verb] give an authoritative order: [with obj. and infinitive] *a gruff voice commanded us to enter* | [with direct speech] *"Stop arguing!" he commanded* | [with clause] *he commanded that work should cease* | [with obj.] *my mother commands my presence.* ■ [with obj.] Military have authority over; be in charge of (a unit): *he commanded a battalion at Normandy.* ■ [with obj.] dominate (a strategic position) from a superior height: *the two castles commanded the harbor.* ■ [with obj.] archaic control or restrain (oneself or one's feelings): *he commanded himself with an effort.*
2 [with obj.] be in a strong enough position to have or secure (something): *no party commanded a majority | a moral force that commanded respect.*
▶ **n.** an authoritative order: *it's unlikely they'll obey your commands.* ■ Computing an instruction or signal that causes a computer to perform one of its basic functions. ■ authority, esp. over armed forces: *an officer took command | who's in command? | we will have nearly thirty thousand people under our command.* ■ [in sing.] the ability to use or control something: *he had a brilliant command of English.* ■ [treated as sing. or pl.] Military a group of officers exercising control over a particular group or operation. ■ Military a body of troops or a district under the control of a particular officer.
– PHRASES **at someone's command** at someone's disposal; available: *he had at his command a vast number of ready-made phrases.*
– ORIGIN Middle English: from Old French *comander* 'to command,' from late Latin *commandare*, from *com-* (expressing intensive force) + *mandare* 'commit, command.' Compare with COMMEND.

com·mand and con·trol ▶ **n.** [usu. as modifier] chiefly Military the running of an armed force or other organization: *a command-and-control bunker.*

com·man·dant /ˈkämənˌdant, -ˌdänt/ ▶ **n.** an officer in charge of a particular force or institution: *the West Point commandant of cadets.*
– ORIGIN late 17th cent.: from French *commandant*, or Italian or Spanish *comandante*, all from late Latin *commandare* 'to command' (see COMMAND).

com·mand-driv·en ▶ **adj.** Computing (of a program or computer) operated by means of commands keyed in by the user or issued by another program or computer.

com·mand e·con·o·my ▶ **n.** an economy in which production, investment, prices, and incomes are determined centrally by a government.

com·man·deer /ˌkämənˈdi(ə)r/ ▶ **v.** [with obj.] officially take possession or control of (something), esp. for military purposes: *telegraph and telephone lines were commandeered by the generals.* ■ take possession of (something) without authority: *he hoisted himself onto a table, commandeering it as a speaker's platform.* ■ enlist (someone) to help in a task, typically against the person's will: *he commandeered the men to find a table.*
– ORIGIN early 19th cent.: from Afrikaans *kommandeer*, from Dutch *commanderen*, from French *commander* 'to command' (see COMMAND).

com·mand·er /kəˈmandər/ (abbr.: **Comdr.**) ▶ **n.** **1** a person in authority, esp. over a body of troops or a military operation: *the commander of a paratroop regiment.* ■ a naval officer of high rank, in particular (in the US Navy or Coast Guard) an officer ranking above lieutenant commander and below captain. ■ (in certain metropolitan police departments) the officer in charge of a division, district, precinct, or squad.
2 a member of a higher class in some orders of knighthood.
– DERIVATIVES **com·mand·er·ship** /-ˌSHip/ **n.**
– ORIGIN Middle English: from Old French *comandeor*, from late Latin *commandare* 'to command' (see COMMAND).

com·mand·er in chief (also **Commander in Chief**) ▶ **n.** (pl. **commanders in chief**) a head of state or officer in supreme command of a country's armed forces. ■ an officer in charge of a major subdivision of a country's armed forces, or of its forces in a particular area.

Com·mand·er of the Faith·ful ▶ **n.** one of the titles of a caliph.

com·mand·ing /kəˈmandiNG/ ▶ **adj.** [attrib.] (in military contexts) having a position of authority: *a commanding officer.* ■ (of an advantage or position) controlling; superior: *a commanding 13-6 lead.* ■ indicating or expressing authority; imposing: *a man of commanding presence | her style is commanding.* ■ (of a place or position) dominating physically; giving a wide view: *a commanding position looking out over the sea.*
– DERIVATIVES **com·mand·ing·ly** **adv.**

com·mand lan·guage ▶ **n.** Computing a computer programming language composed chiefly of a set of commands or operators, used esp. for communicating with the operating system of a computer.

com·mand·ment /kəˈmandmənt/ ▶ **n.** a divine rule, esp. one of the Ten Commandments. ■ a rule to be observed as strictly as one of the Ten Commandments.
– ORIGIN Middle English: from Old French *comandement*, from *comander* 'to command' (see COMMAND).

com·mand mod·ule (abbr.: **CM**) ▶ **n.** the detachable control portion of a manned spacecraft.

com·man·do /kəˈmandō/ ▶ **n.** (pl. **commandos**) a soldier specially trained to carry out raids. ■ a unit of such troops.
– PHRASES **go commando** humorous wear no underpants.
– ORIGIN late 18th cent. (denoting a militia, originally consisting of Boers in South Africa): from Portuguese (earlier form of *comando*), from *commandar* 'to command,' from late Latin *commandare* (see COMMAND).

com·mand per·for·mance ▶ **n.** a presentation of a play, concert, opera, or other show at the request of royalty.

PRONUNCIATION KEY ə *ago, up*; ər *over, fur*; a *hat*; ā *ate*; ä *car*; e *let*; ē *see*; i *fit*; ī *by*; NG *sing*; ō *go*; ô *law, for*; oi *toy*; o͝o *good*; o͞o *goo*; ou *out*; TH *thin*; T͟H *then*; ZH *vision*

C

com·mand post ▶ **n.** the place from which a military unit is commanded.

com·mand ser·geant ma·jor ▶ **n.** a noncommissioned officer in the US Army ranking above first sergeant.

comme ci, comme ça /kôm ˈsē kôm'sä/ ▶ **adv. & adj.** (in answer to a question) neither very good nor very bad; so-so.
– ORIGIN French, literally 'like this, like that.'

com·me·dia dell'ar·te /kəˈmādēə dəl ˈärtē/ ▶ **n.** an improvised kind of popular comedy in Italian theaters in the 16th–18th centuries, based on stock characters. Actors adapted their comic dialogue and action according to a few basic plots (commonly love intrigues) and to topical issues.
– ORIGIN Italian,'comedy of art.'

comme il faut /ˌkôm ēl ˈfō/ ▶ **adj.** [predic.] correct in behavior or etiquette.
– ORIGIN mid 18th cent.: French, literally 'as is necessary.'

com·mem·o·rate /kəˈmeməˌrāt/ ▶ **v.** [with obj.] recall and show respect for (someone or something) in a ceremony: *a wreath-laying ceremony to commemorate the war dead.* ■ serve as a memorial to: *a stone commemorating a boy who died at sea.* ■ celebrate (an event, a person, or a situation) by doing or building something: *it was a night commemorated in a song.*
– DERIVATIVES **com·mem·o·ra·tor** /-ˌrātər/ **n.**
– ORIGIN late 16th cent.: from Latin *commemorat-* 'brought to remembrance,' from the verb *commemorare*, from *com-* 'altogether' + *memorare* 'relate' (from *memor* 'mindful').

com·mem·o·ra·tion /kəˌmeməˈrāsʜən/ ▶ **n.** remembrance, typically expressed in a ceremony: *solemn ceremonies of commemoration.* ■ a ceremony or celebration in which a person or event is remembered: *VJ-Day commemorations in August.*
– PHRASES **in commemoration** as a reminder, esp. a ritual or official one: *the window was ordered by the duchess in commemoration of her son.*
– ORIGIN late Middle English: from Latin *commemoratio(n-)*, from the verb *commemorare* 'bring to remembrance' (see COMMEMORATE).

com·mem·o·ra·tive /kəˈmem(ə)rətiv, kəˈmeməˌrātiv/ ▶ **adj.** acting as a memorial or mark of an event or person: *a commemorative plaque.*
▶ **n.** an object such as a stamp or coin made to mark an event or honor a person. Compare with DEFINITIVE.

com·mem·o·ra·to·ry /kəˈmemərəˌtôrē/ ▶ **adj.** serving to commemorate; commemorative.

com·mence /kəˈmens/ ▶ **v.** begin; start: [with obj.] *his design team commenced work* | [no obj.] *a public inquiry is due to commence on the 16th.*
– ORIGIN Middle English: from Old French *commencier, comencier*, based on Latin *com-* (expressing intensive force) + *initiare* 'begin.'

com·mence·ment /kəˈmensmənt/ ▶ **n. 1** [usu. in sing.] a beginning or start: *at the commencement of training.*
2 a ceremony in which degrees or diplomas are conferred on graduating students: [as modifier] *a commencement address.*
– ORIGIN Middle English: from Old French, from the verb *commencier* (see COMMENCE).

com·mend /kəˈmend/ ▶ **v.** [with obj.] **1** praise formally or officially: *he was commended by the judge for his courageous actions.* ■ present as suitable for approval or acceptance; recommend: *I commend her to you without reservation.* ■ cause to be acceptable or pleasing: *this recording has a lot to commend it.*
2 (**commend someone/something to**) entrust someone or something to: *I commend them to your care.*
– PHRASES **commend me to** archaic remember me kindly to (someone): *commend me to my son, and bid him rule better than I.*
– ORIGIN Middle English: from Latin *commendare*, from *com-* (expressing intensive force) + *mandare* 'commit, entrust.' Compare with COMMAND.

com·mend·a·ble /kəˈmendəbəl/ ▶ **adj.** deserving praise: *commendable restraint.*
– DERIVATIVES **com·mend·a·bly** /-blē/ **adv.**
– ORIGIN late Middle English: via Old French from Latin *commendabilis*, from *commendare* (see COMMEND).

com·men·da·tion /ˌkämənˈdāsʜən, -en-/ ▶ **n.** praise: *the film deserved the highest commendation* | *commendations for their kindness.* ■ an award involving special praise: *the detectives received commendations for bravery.*
– ORIGIN Middle English: from Old French, from Latin *commendatio(n-)*, from *commendare* 'commit to the care of' (see COMMEND). Originally (in the plural) the term denoted a liturgical office ending with a prayer commending the souls of the dead to God.

com·mend·a·to·ry /kəˈmendəˌtôrē/ ▶ **adj.** archaic serving to commend; recommending.
– ORIGIN mid 16th cent.: from late Latin *commendatorius*, from Latin *commendare* 'commit to the care of' (see COMMEND).

com·men·sal /kəˈmensəl/ ▶ **adj.** Biology of, relating to, or exhibiting commensalism.
▶ **n.** Biology a commensal organism, such as many bacteria.
– DERIVATIVES **com·men·sal·i·ty** /ˌkämenˈsalitē/ **n.**
– ORIGIN late 19th cent.: from medieval Latin *commensalis*, from *com-* 'sharing' + *mensa* 'a table.'

com·men·sal·ism /kəˈmensəˌlizəm/ ▶ **n.** Biology an association between two organisms in which one benefits and the other derives neither benefit nor harm.

com·men·su·ra·ble /kəˈmensərəbəl, kəˈmensʜərəbəl/ ▶ **adj. 1** measurable by the same standard: *the finite is not commensurable with the infinite.*
2 (**commensurable to**) rare proportionate to.
3 Mathematics (of numbers) in a ratio equal to a ratio of integers.
– DERIVATIVES **com·men·su·ra·bil·i·ty** /kəˌmensərəˈbilətē, -ˌmensʜə-/ **n.**, **com·men·su·ra·bly** /-blē/ **adv.**
– ORIGIN mid 16th cent.: from late Latin *commensurabilis*, from *com-* 'together' + *mensurabilis*, from *mensurare* 'to measure.'

com·men·su·rate /kəˈmensərət, -ˈmensʜə-/ ▶ **adj.** corresponding in size or degree; in proportion: *salary will be commensurate with experience* | *such heavy responsibility must receive commensurate reward.*
– DERIVATIVES **com·men·su·rate·ly** **adv.**
– ORIGIN mid 17th cent.: from late Latin *commensuratus*, from *com-* 'together' + *mensuratus*, past participle of *mensurare* 'to measure.'

com·ment /ˈkämˌent/ ▶ **n.** a verbal or written remark expressing an opinion or reaction: *you asked for comments on the new proposals.* ■ discussion, esp. of a critical nature, of an issue or event: *the plans were not sent to the council for comment.* ■ an indirect expression of the views of the creator of an artistic work: *their second single is a comment on the commercial nature of raves.* ■ an explanatory note in a book or other written text. ■ archaic a written explanation or commentary. ■ Computing a piece of specially tagged text placed within a program to help other users to understand it, which the computer ignores when running the program.
▶ **v.** [with obj.] express (an opinion or reaction): *the review commented that the book was agreeably written* | [no obj.] *the company would not comment on the venture* | *"He's an independent soul," she commented.* ■ [with obj.] Computing place a piece of specially tagged explanatory text within (a program) to assist other users. ■ Computing turn (part of a program) into a comment so that the computer ignores it when running the program: *you could try commenting out that line.*
– PHRASES **no comment** used in refusing to answer a question, esp. in a sensitive situation.
– DERIVATIVES **com·ment·er** **n.**
– ORIGIN late Middle English (in the senses 'expository treatise' and 'explanatory note'): from Latin *commentum* 'contrivance' (in late Latin also 'interpretation'), neuter past participle of *comminisci* 'devise.'

com·men·tar·i·at /ˌkämənˈte(ə)rēət/ ▶ **n.** members of the news media considered as a class.
– ORIGIN late 20th cent.: blend of *commentary* and *proletariat.*

com·men·tar·y /ˈkämənˌterē/ ▶ **n.** (pl. **commentaries**) an expression of opinions or offering of explanations explanations about an event or situation: *an editorial commentary* | *narrative overlaid with commentary.* ■ a descriptive spoken account (esp. on a broadcast) of an event or performance as it happens. ■ a set of explanatory or critical notes on a text: *a commentary on the Old Testament.*
– ORIGIN late Middle English: from Latin *commentarius, commentarium* (adjective, used as a noun), from *commentari*, frequentative of *comminisci* 'devise.'

com·men·tate /ˈkämənˌtāt/ ▶ **v.** [no obj.] report on an event as it occurs, esp. for a news or sports broadcast; provide a commentary.
– ORIGIN mid 19th cent.: back-formation from COMMENTATOR.

com·men·ta·tor /ˈkämənˌtātər/ ▶ **n.** a person who comments on events or on a text. ■ a person who delivers a live commentary on an event or performance.

com·merce /ˈkämərs/ (abbr.: **comm.**) ▶ **n. 1** the activity of buying and selling, esp. on a large scale: *the possible increase of commerce by a great railroad.*
2 dated social dealings between people: *outside the normal commerce of civilized life.*
3 archaic sexual intercourse.
– ORIGIN mid 16th cent. (sense 2): from French, or from Latin *commercium* 'trade, trading,' from *com-* 'together' + *mercium* (from *merx, merc-* 'merchandise').

com·mer·cial /kəˈmərsʜəl/ (abbr.: **comm.**) ▶ **adj. 1** concerned with or engaged in commerce: *a commercial agreement.*
2 making or intended to make a profit: *commercial products.* ■ having profit, rather than artistic or other value, as a primary aim: *their work is too commercial.*
3 (of television or radio) funded by the revenue from broadcast advertisements.
4 (of chemicals) supplied in bulk and not of the highest purity.
▶ **n.** a television or radio advertisement.
– DERIVATIVES **com·mer·ci·al·i·ty** /kəˌmərsʜēˈalitē/ **n.**, **com·mer·cial·ly** **adv.**

com·mer·cial art ▶ **n.** art used in advertising and selling.

com·mer·cial bank ▶ **n.** a bank that offers services to the general public and to companies.

com·mer·cial break ▶ **n.** an interruption in the transmission of broadcast programming during which advertisements are broadcast.

com·mer·cial·ism /kəˈmərsʜəˌlizəm/ ▶ **n.** emphasis on the maximizing of profit: *deficits prompted efforts for greater commercialism.* ■ derogatory practices and attitudes that are concerned with the making of profit at the expense of quality: *the issue of creeping commercialism in schools.*

com·mer·cial·ize /kəˈmərsʜəˌlīz/ ▶ **v.** [with obj.] manage or exploit (an organization, activity, etc.) in a way designed to make a profit: *the museum has been commercialized.*
– DERIVATIVES **com·mer·cial·i·za·tion** /kəˌmərsʜələˈzāsʜən/ **n.**

com·mer·cial·ized /kəˈmərsʜəˌlīzd/ ▶ **adj.** designed principally for financial gain; profit-oriented: *commercialized resort areas.*

com·mer·cial pa·per ▶ **n.** short-term unsecured promissory notes issued by companies.

com·mer·cial space ▶ **n.** see SPACE (sense 1 of the noun).

com·mer·cial trav·el·er ▶ **n.** dated a traveling sales representative.

com·mer·cial ve·hi·cle ▶ **n.** a vehicle used for carrying goods or fare-paying passengers.

com·mie /ˈkämē/ (also **Commie**) informal, derogatory ▶ **n.** (pl. **commies**) a communist.
▶ **adj.** communist.
– ORIGIN 1940s: abbreviation.

com·mi·na·tion /ˌkäməˈnāsʜən/ ▶ **n.** the action of threatening divine vengeance. ■ the recital of divine threats against sinners in the Anglican Liturgy for Ash Wednesday.
– ORIGIN late Middle English: from Latin *comminatio(n-)*, from the verb *comminari*, from *com-* (expressing intensive force) + *minari* 'threaten.'

com·min·a·to·ry /ˈkämənəˌtôrē, kəˈminə-/ ▶ **adj.** threatening, punitive, or vengeful.
– ORIGIN early 16th cent.: from medieval Latin *comminatorius*, from *comminat-* 'threatened,' from the verb *comminari* (see COMMINATION).

com·min·gle /kəˈmiNGgəl, kä-/ ▶ **v.** mix; blend: [no obj.] *the dust had commingled with the rain* | [with obj.] *publicly reproved for commingling funds.*
– ORIGIN early 17th cent.: from COM- 'together' + MINGLE.

com·mi·nut·ed /ˈkäməˌn(y)o͞otəd/ ▶ **adj.** technical reduced to minute particles or fragments. ■ Medicine (of a fracture) producing multiple bone splinters.
– ORIGIN early 17th cent.: past participle of *comminute*, from Latin *comminut-* 'broken into pieces,' from the verb *comminuere*, from *com-* 'together' + *minuere* 'lessen.'

com·mi·nu·tion /ˌkäməˈn(y)o͞osʜən/ ▶ **n.** technical the action of reducing a material, an ore, to minute particles or fragments.

com·mis /ˈkämē, kô-/ (also **commis chef**) ▶ **n.** (pl. **same**) a junior chef.
– ORIGIN 1930s: from French, 'deputy, clerk,' past participle of *commettre* 'entrust,' from Latin *committere* (see COMMIT).

com·mis·er·ate /kəˈmizəˌrāt/ ▶ **v.** [no obj.] express or feel sympathy or pity; sympathize: *she went over to commiserate with Rose on her unfortunate circumstances.* ■ [with obj.] archaic feel, show, or express pity for (someone): *she did not exult in her rival's fall, but, on the contrary, commiserated her.*
– DERIVATIVES **com·mis·er·a·tive** /-rətiv/ **adj.**

–ORIGIN late 16th cent.: from Latin *commiserat-* 'commiserated,' from the verb *commiserari*, from *com-* 'with' + *miserari* 'to lament' (from *miser* 'wretched').

com·mis·er·a·tion /kəˌmizəˈrāsнən/ ▶ **n.** sympathy and sorrow for the misfortunes of others; compassion: *the other actors offered him clumsy commiseration.* (**commiserations**) expressions of sympathy and sorrow for another: *our commiserations to those who didn't win.*

com·mish /kəˈmisн/ ▶ **n.** informal **1** short for COMMISSIONER.
2 short for COMMISSION: *out of commish.*

com·mis·saire /ˌkômiˈse(ə)r/ ▶ **n.** a senior police officer in France. ■ an official at a bicycle race or other sporting event.
–ORIGIN mid 18th cent.: French.

com·mis·sar /ˈkäməˌsär, ˌkäməˈsär/ ▶ **n.** an official of the Communist Party, esp. in the former Soviet Union or present-day China, responsible for political education and organization. ■ a head of a government department in the former Soviet Union before 1946. ■ a strict or prescriptive figure of authority: *our academic commissars.*
–ORIGIN early 20th cent. (Russian Revolution): from Russian *komissar*, from French *commissaire*, from medieval Latin *commissarius* (see COMMISSARY).

com·mis·sar·i·at /ˌkäməˈse(ə)rēit/ ▶ **n.** **1** chiefly Military a department for the supply of food and equipment.
2 a government department of the Soviet Union before 1946.
–ORIGIN late 16th cent. (as a Scots legal term denoting the jurisdiction of a commissary, often spelled *commissariot*): from French *commissariat*, reinforced by medieval Latin *commissariatus*, both from medieval Latin *commissarius* 'person in charge,' from Latin *committere* 'entrust.'

com·mis·sar·y /ˈkäməˌserē/ ▶ **n.** (pl. **commissaries**) **1** a restaurant in a movie studio, military base, prison, or other institution.
2 a deputy or delegate.
–DERIVATIVES **com·mis·sar·i·al** /ˌkäməˈse(ə)rēəl/ **adj.**
–ORIGIN late Middle English: from medieval Latin *commissarius* 'person in charge,' from Latin *commiss-* 'joined, entrusted,' from the verb *committere* (see COMMIT).

com·mis·sion /kəˈmisнən/ (abbr.: **comm.**) ▶ **n.** **1** an instruction, command, or duty given to a person or group of people: *his commission to redesign the building* | *he received a commission to act as an informer.* ■ an order for something, esp. a work of art, to be produced: *Mozart at last received a commission to write an opera.* ■ a work produced in response to such an order. ■ archaic the authority to perform a task or certain duties.
2 a group of people officially charged with a particular function: *the United Nations High Commission for Refugees.*
3 an amount of money, typically a set percentage of the value involved, paid to an agent in a commercial transaction: *foreign banks may charge a commission* | *he sold cosmetics on commission.*
4 a warrant conferring the rank of officer in an army, navy, or air force: *he has resigned his commission.*
5 the action of committing a crime or offense: *use of a deadly weapon in the commission of a felony.*
▶ **v.** [with obj.] **1** give an order for or authorize the production of (something such as a building, piece of equipment, or work of art). ■ order or authorize (a person or organization) to do or produce something: *they commissioned an architect to manage the building project.*
2 bring (something newly produced, such as a factory or machine) into working condition: *we had a few hiccups getting the heating equipment commissioned.* ■ bring (a warship) into readiness for active service: *the aircraft carrier Midway was commissioned in 1945.*
3 appoint (someone) to the rank of officer in the armed services: *he was commissioned after attending midshipman school* | (as adj. **commissioned**) *a commissioned officer.*
–PHRASES **in commission** (of a ship, vehicle, machine, etc.) in use or in service. **out of commission** not in service; not in working order. ■ (of a person) unable to work or function normally, esp. through illness or injury.
–DERIVATIVES **com·mis·sion·a·ble adj.**
–ORIGIN Middle English: via Old French from Latin *commissio(n-)*, from *committere* 'entrust' (see COMMIT).

com·mis·sion·aire /kəˌmisнəˈne(ə)r/ ▶ **n.** chiefly Brit. a uniformed door attendant at a hotel, theater, or other building.
–ORIGIN mid 17th cent.: from French, from medieval Latin *commissarius* 'person in charge,' from Latin *committere* 'entrust' (see COMMIT).

com·mis·sion·er /kəˈmisн(ə)nər/ (abbr.: **comm.**) ▶ **n.** a person appointed to a role on or by a commission: *the traffic commissioner* | *the New York State Health Commissioner.* ■ a person appointed to regulate a particular sport: *the baseball commissioner.* ■ a representative of the supreme authority in an area.
–DERIVATIVES **com·mis·sion·er·ship** /-ˌsнip/ **n.**
–ORIGIN late Middle English: from medieval Latin *commissionarius*, from Latin *commissio* (see COMMISSION).

com·mis·sure /ˈkäməˌsнŏŏr/ ▶ **n.** Anatomy **1** the joint between two bones.
2 a band of nerve tissue connecting the hemispheres of the brain, the two sides of the spinal cord, etc.
3 the line where the upper and lower lips or eyelids meet.
–DERIVATIVES **com·mis·su·ral** /ˌkäməˈsнŏŏrəl/ **adj.**
–ORIGIN late Middle English: from Latin *commissura* 'junction,' from *committere* 'join' (see COMMIT).

com·mit /kəˈmit/ ▶ **v.** (**commits, committing, committed**) [with obj.] **1** carry out or perpetrate (a mistake, crime, or immoral act): *he committed an uncharacteristic error.*
2 pledge or bind (a person or an organization) to a certain course or policy: *they were reluctant to **commit themselves to** an opinion* | *the treaty commits each party to defend the other* | *try it out before you commit to a purchase.* ■ pledge or set aside (resources) for future use: *manufacturers will have to **commit** substantial funds **to** developing new engines.* ■ (**be committed to**) be in a long-term emotional relationship with (someone). ■ (**be committed to**) be dedicated to (something): *we must be committed to peace.*
3 send, entrust, or consign, in particular: ■ consign (someone) officially to prison, esp. on remand: *he was **committed to** prison for contempt of court.* ■ send (a person or case) for trial. ■ send (someone) to be confined in a psychiatric hospital: *he had been committed for treatment.* ■ (**commit something to**) transfer something to (a state or place): *he composed a letter but didn't commit it to paper* | *she committed each tiny feature to memory* | *committed to the flames.* ■ refer (a legislative bill) to a committee.
–DERIVATIVES **com·mit·ta·ble adj.**, **com·mit·ter n.**
–ORIGIN late Middle English: from Latin *committere* 'join, entrust' (in medieval Latin 'put into custody'), from *com-* 'with' + *mittere* 'put or send.'

com·mit·ment /kəˈmitmənt/ ▶ **n.** **1** the state or quality of being dedicated to a cause, activity, etc.: *the company's **commitment to** quality.* ■ a pledge or undertaking: *I cannot make such a commitment at the moment.*
2 (usu. **commitments**) an engagement or obligation that restricts freedom of action: *business commitments* | *young people delay major commitments including marriage and children.*

com·mit·ment cer·e·mo·ny ▶ **n.** a ceremony to mark the spousal union of two people who are not legally allowed to marry, such as gay people.

com·mit·ment or·der ▶ **n.** an order authorizing the admission and detention of a patient in a psychiatric hospital.

com·mit·tal /kəˈmitl/ ▶ **n.** **1** the action of sending a person to an institution, esp. prison or a psychiatric hospital: *his **committal to** prison* | [as modifier] *committal proceedings.*
2 the burial of a corpse.

com·mit·ted /kəˈmitid/ ▶ **adj.** feeling dedication and loyalty to a cause, activity, or job; wholeheartedly dedicated: *a committed reformer.*

com·mit·tee /kəˈmitē/ ▶ **n.** **1** [treated as sing. or pl.] a group of people appointed for a specific function, typically consisting of members of a larger group: *the housing committee* | [as modifier] *a committee meeting.* ■ such a body appointed by a legislature to consider the details of proposed legislation: *there was much scrutiny **in committee**.*
2 Law a person who has been judicially committed to the charge of another because of insanity or mental retardation. ■ Brit. a person entrusted with the charge of another person or another person's property.
–ORIGIN late 15th cent. (in the general sense 'person to whom something has been entrusted'): from COMMIT + -EE.

com·mit·tee·man /kəˈmitēmən, -ˌman/ ▶ **n.** (pl. **committeemen**) (in the US) a male local political party leader.

com·mit·tee of the whole the entire membership of a legislative body when sitting as a committee.

com·mit·tee·wom·an /kəˈmitēˌwŏŏmən/ ▶ **n.** (pl. **committeewomen**) (in the US) a female local political party leader.

com·mix /kəˈmiks/ ▶ **v.** [with obj.] archaic mix; mingle: *beat them till they be thoroughly commixed.*
–DERIVATIVES **com·mix·ture** /kəˈmikscнər/ **n.**
–ORIGIN late Middle English (as the past participle *commixt*): from Latin *commixtus*, from *com-* 'together with' + *mixtus* 'mixed.'

com·mo /ˈkämō/ ▶ **n.** informal communication, esp. as a departmental function in an organization.

com·mode /kəˈmōd/ ▶ **n.** **1** a piece of furniture containing a concealed chamber pot. ■ a toilet. ■ historical a movable washstand.
2 a chest of drawers or chiffonier of a decorative type popular in the 18th century.
–ORIGIN mid 18th cent. (sense 2): from French, literally 'convenient, suitable,' from Latin *commodus*. Sense 1 dates from the early 19th cent.

com·mod·i·fy /kəˈmädəˌfī/ ▶ **v.** (**commodifies, commodifying, commodified**) [with obj.] turn into or treat as a commodity: (as adj. **commodified**) *art has become commodified.*
–DERIVATIVES **com·mod·i·fi·ca·tion** /kəˌmädəfəˈkāsнən/ **n.**
–ORIGIN 1980s: from COMMODITY + -FY.

com·mo·di·ous /kəˈmōdēəs/ ▶ **adj.** **1** formal (esp. of furniture or a building) roomy and comfortable.
2 archaic convenient.
–DERIVATIVES **com·mo·di·ous·ly adv.**, **com·mo·di·ous·ness n.**
–ORIGIN late Middle English (in the sense 'beneficial, useful'): from French *commodieux* or medieval Latin *commodiosus*, based on Latin *commodus* 'convenient.'

com·mod·i·tize /kəˈmädiˌtīz/ ▶ **v.** another term for COMMODIFY.
–DERIVATIVES **com·mod·i·ti·za·tion** /kəˌmäditəˈzāsнən/ **n.**

com·mod·i·ty /kəˈmäditē/ ▶ **n.** (pl. **commodities**) a raw material or primary agricultural product that can be bought and sold, such as copper or coffee. ■ a useful or valuable thing, such as water or time.
–ORIGIN late Middle English: from Old French *commodite* or Latin *commoditas*, from *commodus* (see COMMODIOUS).

com·mo·dore /ˈkäməˌdôr/ ▶ **n.** a naval officer of high rank, in particular an officer in the US Navy or Coast Guard ranking above captain and below rear admiral. ■ the president of a yacht club. ■ the senior captain of a shipping line.
–ORIGIN late 17th cent.: probably from Dutch *komandeur*, from French *commandeur* 'commander.'

com·mon /ˈkämən/ ▶ **adj.** (**commoner, commonest**) **1** occurring, found, or done often; prevalent: *salt and pepper are the two most common seasonings* | *it's **common for** a woman to be depressed after giving birth.* ■ (of an animal or plant) found or living in relatively large numbers; not rare. ■ ordinary; of ordinary qualities; without special rank or position: *the dwellings of common people* | *a common soldier.* ■ (of a quality) of a sort or level to be generally expected: *common decency.* ■ of the most familiar type: *the common or vernacular name.* ■ denoting the most widespread or typical species of an animal or plant: *the common blue spruce.*
2 showing a lack of taste and refinement; vulgar.
3 shared by, coming from, or done by more than one: *the two republics' common border* | *problems **common to** both communities.* ■ belonging to, open to, or affecting the whole of a community or the public: *common land.* ■ Mathematics belonging to two or more quantities.
4 Grammar (in Latin and certain other languages) of or denoting a gender of nouns that are conventionally regarded as masculine or feminine, contrasting with neuter. ■ (in English) denoting a noun that refers to individuals of either sex (e.g., *teacher*).
5 Prosody (of a syllable) able to be either short or long.
6 Law (of a crime) of relatively minor importance: *common assault.*
▶ **n.** **1** a piece of open land for public use, esp. in a village or town.
2 (in the Christian Church) a form of service used for each of a group of occasions.
–PHRASES **the common good** the benefit or interests of all: *it is time our elected officials stood up for the common good.* **common ground** opinions or interests shared by each of two or more parties: *artists from different cultural backgrounds found common ground.* **common knowledge** something known by most people. **common or garden** Brit. informal of the usual or ordinary type: *a yak is your basic common or garden cow, only bigger, hairier, and wilder.* **common property** a thing or things

held jointly. ■ something known by most people. **the common touch** the ability to get along with or appeal to ordinary people. **in common 1** in joint use or possession; shared: *car engines have nothing in common with aircraft engines.* **2** of joint interest: *the two men had little in common.* See also TENANCY IN COMMON. **in common with** in the same way as: *in common with other officers, I had to undertake guard duties.*
– DERIVATIVES **com·mon·ness** n.
– ORIGIN Middle English: from Old French *comun* (adjective), from Latin *communis.*

C

com·mon·a·ble /ˈkämənəbəl/ ▶ adj. Brit. chiefly historical (of land) allowed to be jointly used or owned. ■ (of an animal) allowed to be pastured on public land: *these Acts exclude the deer and commonable cattle.*
– ORIGIN early 17th cent.: from obsolete *common* 'to exercise right of common' + -ABLE.

com·mon·age /ˈkämənij/ ▶ n. **1** chiefly Brit. the right of pasturing animals on common land. ■ land held in common.
2 the common people; the commonalty.

Com·mon Ag·ri·cul·tur·al Pol·i·cy (abbr.: **CAP**) the system in the EU for establishing common prices for most agricultural products within the European Union, a single fund for price supports, and levies on imports.

com·mon·al·i·ty /ˌkämənˈalitē/ ▶ n. (pl. **commonalities**) **1** the state of sharing features or attributes: *a commonality of interest ensures cooperation.* ■ a shared feature or attribute: *we discern the commonalities between these writers.*
2 (**the commonality**) another term for COMMONALTY.
– ORIGIN late Middle English (in sense 2: variant of COMMONALTY. Sense 1 dates from the mid 16th cent., but was rarely used before the 1950s.

com·mon·al·ty /ˈkämənl-tē/ ▶ n. (treated as pl. **the commonalty**) chiefly historical people without special rank or position; common people: *a petition by the earls, barons, and commonalty of the realm.* ■ the general body of a group.
– ORIGIN Middle English: from Old French *comunalte,* from medieval Latin *communalitas,* from Latin *communis* 'common, general' (see COMMON).

com·mon car·ri·er ▶ n. a person or company that transports goods or passengers on regular routes at set rates. ■ a company providing public telecommunications facilities.

com·mon chord ▶ n. Music a triad containing a root, a major or minor third, and a perfect fifth.

com·mon cold ▶ n. (**the common cold**) another term for COLD (sense 2 of the noun).

com·mon coun·cil ▶ n. a town or city council in some parts of the US and Canada, and in London.

com·mon de·nom·i·na·tor ▶ n. Mathematics a shared multiple of the denominators of several fractions. See also LOWEST COMMON DENOMINATOR. ■ a feature shared by all members of a group: *the common denominator for the fevers was the bite of a tick.*

com·mon di·vi·sor ▶ n. Mathematics a number that can be divided into all of the other numbers of a given set without any remainder. Also called **common factor**.

com·mon·er /ˈkämənər/ ▶ n. **1** an ordinary person, without rank or title.
2 a person who has the right of common (commonage).
3 (at some British universities) an undergraduate who does not have a scholarship.
– ORIGIN Middle English (denoting a citizen or burgess): from medieval Latin *communarius,* from *communa, communia* 'community,' based on Latin *communis* (see COMMON).

Com·mon E·ra ▶ n. (**the Common Era**) another term for CHRISTIAN ERA.

com·mon frac·tion ▶ n. a fraction expressed by a numerator and a denominator, not decimally.

com·mon gen·der ▶ n. **1** the gender of those nouns in English that are not limited to either sex, such as cousin or spouse.
2 in some languages, such as Latin, the gender of those nouns that may be either masculine or feminine but not neuter.
3 in some languages, such as modern Danish, the gender of those nouns derived from the earlier masculine and feminine genders that do not belong to the neuter gender.

com·mon law ▶ n. the part of English law that is derived from custom and judicial precedent rather than statutes. Often contrasted with **statutory law**. ■ the body of English law as adopted and modified separately by the different states of the US and by the federal government. Compare with CIVIL LAW. ■ [as modifier] denoting a partner in a marriage by common law (which recognized unions created by mutual agreement and public behavior), not by a civil or ecclesiastical ceremony: *a common-law husband.* ■ [as modifier] denoting a partner in a long-term relationship of cohabitation.

com·mon log·a·rithm ▶ n. a logarithm to the base 10.

com·mon·ly /ˈkämənlē/ ▶ adv. very often; frequently: *BSE, commonly called mad cow disease | a commonly used industrial chemical.*

com·mon mar·ket ▶ n. a group of countries imposing few or no duties on trade with one another and a common tariff on trade with other countries. ■ (**the Common Market**) a name for the European Economic Community or European Union, used esp. in the 1960s and 1970s.

com·mon me·ter (also **common measure**) (abbr.: **CM**) ▶ n. a metrical pattern for hymns in which the stanzas have four lines containing eight and six syllables alternately rhyming *abcb* or *abab.*

com·mon mul·ti·ple ▶ n. Mathematics a number into which each number in a given set may be evenly divided.

com·mon noun ▶ n. Grammar a noun denoting a class of objects or a concept as opposed to a particular individual. Often contrasted with PROPER NOUN.

com·mon·place /ˈkämənˌplās/ ▶ adj. not unusual; ordinary: *unemployment was commonplace in his profession.* ■ not interesting or original; trite: *the usual commonplace remarks.*
▶ n. **1** a usual or ordinary thing: *bombing has become almost a commonplace of public life there.* ■ a trite saying or topic; a platitude: *it is a commonplace to talk of the young being alienated.*
2 a notable quotation copied into a commonplace book.
– DERIVATIVES **com·mon·place·ness** n.
– ORIGIN mid 16th cent. (originally *common place*): translation of Latin *locus communis,* rendering Greek *koinos topos* 'general theme.'

com·mon·place book ▶ n. a book into which notable extracts from other works are copied for personal use.

Com·mon Pleas (in full **Court of Common Pleas**) Law (in some jurisdictions) a court for hearing civil cases between citizens.

com·mon por·poise another term for HARBOR PORPOISE.

Com·mon Prayer the liturgy of the Anglican Communion, originally set forth in the *Book of Common Prayer* of Edward VI (1549).

com·mon rat ▶ n. another term for BROWN RAT.

com·mon room ▶ n. a room in a school, college, or other institution for use of students or staff outside teaching hours.

com·mons /ˈkämənz/ ▶ plural n. **1** a dining hall in a residential school or college.
2 [treated as sing.] land or resources belonging to or affecting the whole of a community.
3 (**the Commons**) short for HOUSE OF COMMONS. ■ historical the common people regarded as a part of a political system, esp. in Britain.
4 archaic provisions shared in common; rations.
– PHRASES **short commons** archaic insufficient allocation of food: *for two weeks we have been on short commons.*
– ORIGIN Middle English: plural of COMMON.

com·mon salt ▶ n. see SALT (sense 1 of the noun).

com·mon sense ▶ n. good sense and sound judgment in practical matters: *use your common sense | [as modifier] a common-sense approach.*
– DERIVATIVES **com·mon·sen·si·cal** /ˌkämənˈsensikəl/ adj.

com·mon sol·dier ▶ n. see SOLDIER (sense 1 of the noun).

com·mon stock ▶ plural n. (also **common stocks**) shares entitling their holder to dividends that vary in amount and may even be missed, depending on the fortunes of the company: *the company announced a public offering of 3.5 million shares of common stock.* Compare with PREFERRED STOCK.

com·mon time ▶ n. Music a rhythmic pattern in which there are four beats, esp. four quarter notes, in a measure. This pattern occurs often in classical music and is the norm in rock, jazz, country, and bluegrass.

com·mon·weal /ˈkämənˌwēl/ ▶ n. (**the commonweal**) the welfare of the public.

com·mon·wealth /ˈkämənˌwelTH/ ▶ n. **1** an independent country or community, esp. a democratic republic. ■ an aggregate or grouping of countries or other bodies. ■ a community or organization of shared interests in a nonpolitical field: *the Christian commonwealth | the commonwealth of letters.* ■ a self-governing unit voluntarily grouped with the US, such as Puerto Rico. ■ a formal title of some of the states of the US, esp. Kentucky, Massachusetts, Pennsylvania, and Virginia. ■ the title of the federated Australian states. ■ (**the Commonwealth**) the republican period of government in Britain between the execution of Charles I in 1649 and the Restoration of Charles II in 1660.
2 (**the Commonwealth**) (in full **the Commonwealth of Nations**) an international association consisting of the UK together with states that were previously part of the British Empire, and dependencies. The British monarch is the symbolic head of the Commonwealth.
3 (**the commonwealth**) archaic the general good.
– ORIGIN late Middle English (originally as two words, denoting public welfare; compare with COMMONWEAL): from COMMON + WEALTH.

Com·mon·wealth Games an amateur sports competition held every four years between member countries of the Commonwealth of Nations.

Com·mon·wealth of In·de·pend·ent States (abbr.: **CIS**) a confederation of independent states that were formerly constituent republics of the Soviet Union, established in 1991. Member states are Armenia, Belarus, Kazakhstan, Kyrgyzstan, Moldova, Russia, Tajikistan, Turkmenistan, and Uzbekistan.

com·mo·tion /kəˈmōSHən/ ▶ n. a state of confused and noisy disturbance: *she was distracted by a commotion across the street | figure out what all the commotion is about.* ■ civil insurrection: *damage caused by civil commotion.*
– ORIGIN late Middle English: from Latin *commotio(n-),* from *com-* 'altogether' + *motio* (see MOTION).

com·move /kəˈmo͞ov/ ▶ v. [with obj.] move violently; agitate or excite.

com·mu·nal /kəˈmyo͞onl, ˈkämyənəl/ ▶ adj. **1** shared by all members of a community; for common use: *a communal bathroom and kitchen.* ■ of, relating to, or done by a community: *communal achievement.* ■ involving the sharing of work and property: *communal living.*
2 (of conflict) between different communities, esp. those having different religions or ethnic origins: *violent communal riots.*
– DERIVATIVES **com·mu·nal·i·ty** /ˌkämyəˈnalitē/ n., **com·mu·nal·ly** adv.
– ORIGIN early 19th cent. (in the sense 'relating to a commune, esp. the Paris Commune'): from French, from late Latin *communalis,* from *communis* (see COMMON).

com·mu·nal·ism /kəˈmyo͞onlˌizəm, ˈkämyənəˌlizm/ ▶ n. **1** a principle of political organization based on federated communes. ■ the principle or practice of living together and sharing possessions and responsibilities.
2 allegiance to one's own ethnic group rather than to the wider society.
– DERIVATIVES **com·mu·nal·ist** adj. & n., **com·mu·nal·is·tic** /kəˌmyo͞onlˈistik/ adj.

com·mu·nal·ize /kəˈmyo͞onlˌīz/ ▶ v. [with obj.] rare organize (something) on the basis of shared ownership: *attempts to communalize farming.*
– DERIVATIVES **com·mu·nal·i·za·tion** /kəˌmyo͞onl-əˈzāSHən/ n.

com·mu·nard /ˌkämyəˈnär(d)/ ▶ n. a member of a commune. ■ (**Communard**) historical a supporter of the Paris Commune.
– ORIGIN late 19th cent.: from French, from COMMUNE[1].

com·mune[1] /ˈkämˌyo͞on/ ▶ n. **1** a group of people living together and sharing possessions and responsibilities. ■ a communal settlement in a communist country.
2 the smallest French territorial division for administrative purposes. ■ a similar division elsewhere.
3 (**the Commune**) the group that seized the municipal government of Paris in the French Revolution and played a leading part in the Reign of Terror until suppressed in 1794. ■ (also **the Paris Commune**) the municipal government organized on communalistic principles elected in Paris in 1871. It was soon brutally suppressed by government troops.
– ORIGIN late 17th cent. (sense 2): from French, from medieval Latin *communia,* neuter plural of Latin *communis* (see COMMON).

com·mune[2] /kəˈmyo͞on/ ▶ v. [no obj.] **1** (**commune with**) share one's intimate thoughts or feelings with (someone or something), esp. when the exchange is on a spiritual level: *the purpose of praying is to commune with God.* ■ feel in close spiritual contact with: *he spent an hour communing with nature on the bank of a stream.*
2 receive Holy Communion.
– ORIGIN Middle English: from Old French *comuner* 'to share,' from *comun* (see COMMON).

com·mu·ni·ca·ble /kəˈmyo͞onikəbəl/ ▶ adj. able to be communicated to others: *the value of the product*

must be communicable to the potential consumers. ■ (of a disease) able to be transmitted from one sufferer to another; contagious or infectious.
–DERIVATIVES **com·mu·ni·ca·bil·i·ty** /kə,myo͞onikə'bilitē/ **n.**, **com·mu·ni·ca·bly** /-blē/ **adv.**
–ORIGIN late Middle English (in the sense 'communicating, having communication'): from Old French, from late Latin *communicabilis*, from the verb *communicare* 'to share' (see COMMUNICATE).

com·mu·ni·cant /kə'myo͞onikənt/ ▶ **n. 1** Christian Church a person who receives Holy Communion. **2** archaic a person who imparts information.
–ORIGIN mid 16th cent.: from Latin *communicant-* 'sharing,' from the verb *communicare* (see COMMUNICATE).

com·mu·ni·cate /kə'myo͞onə,kāt/ ▶ **v. 1** [no obj.] share or exchange information, news, or ideas: *the prisoner was forbidden to communicate with his family.* ■ [with obj.] impart or pass on (information, news, or ideas): *he* ***communicated*** *his findings* ***to*** *the inspector.* ■ [with obj.] convey or transmit (an emotion or feeling) in a nonverbal way: *the ability of good teachers to communicate their own enthusiasm | his sudden fear* ***communicated itself.*** ■ succeed in conveying one's ideas or in evoking understanding in others: *a politician must have the ability to communicate.* ■ (of two people) be able to share and understand each other's thoughts and feelings. ■ [with obj.] (usu. **be communicated**) pass on (an infectious disease) to another person or animal. ■ [with obj.] transmit (heat or motion): *the heat is communicated through a small brass grating.* ■ (often as adj. **communicating**) (of two rooms) have a common connecting door: *he went into the communicating room to pick up the phone.* **2** [no obj.] Christian Church receive Holy Communion.
–DERIVATIVES **com·mu·ni·ca·tor** /-,kātər/ **n.**, **com·mu·ni·ca·to·ry** /-kə,tôrē/ **adj.**
–ORIGIN early 16th cent.: from Latin *communicat-* 'shared,' from the verb *communicare*, from *communis* (see COMMON).

com·mu·ni·ca·tion /kə,myo͞onə'kāsʜən/ ▶ **n. 1** the imparting or exchanging of information or news: *direct communication between the two countries will produce greater understanding | at the moment I am* ***in communication with*** *London.* ■ a letter or message containing such information or news. ■ the successful conveying or sharing of ideas and feelings: *there was a lack of* ***communication between*** *Pamela and her parents.* ■ social contact: *she gave him some hope of her return, or at least of their future communication.* **2** (**communications**) means of connection between people or places, in particular: ■ the means of sending or receiving information, such as telephone lines or computers: *satellite communications* | [as modifier] *a communications network.* ■ the means of traveling or of transporting goods, such as roads or railroads: *a city providing excellent road and rail communications.* ■ [treated as sing.] the field of study concerned with the transmission of information by various means.
–PHRASES **lines of communication** the connections between an army in the field and its bases. ■ any system for communicating information or ideas: *bureaucracies are characterized by established lines of communication.*
–DERIVATIVES **com·mu·ni·ca·tion·al** /-'kāsʜənl/ **adj.**
–ORIGIN late Middle English: from Old French *comunicacion*, from Latin *communicatio(n-)*, from the verb *communicare* 'to share' (see COMMUNICATE).

com·mu·ni·ca·tions sat·el·lite (also **communication satellite**) ▶ **n.** a satellite placed in orbit around the earth in order to relay television, radio, and telephone signals.

com·mu·ni·ca·tion the·o·ry (also **communications theory**) ▶ **n.** the branch of knowledge dealing with the principles and methods by which information is conveyed.

com·mu·ni·ca·tive /kə'myo͞onə,kātiv, -nikətiv/ ▶ **adj.** ready to talk or impart information: *the patient was alert and communicative.* ■ relating to the conveyance or exchange of information: *the communicative process in literary texts.*
–DERIVATIVES **com·mu·ni·ca·tive·ly adv.**
–ORIGIN late Middle English: from late Latin *communicativus*, from *communicat-* 'shared,' from the verb *communicare* (see COMMUNICATE).

com·mun·ion /kə'myo͞onyən/ ▶ **n. 1** the sharing or exchanging of intimate thoughts and feelings, esp. when the exchange is on a mental or spiritual level: *in this churchyard* ***communion with*** *the dead was almost palpable.* ■ common participation in a mental or emotional experience: *popular festivals where all take part in joyous communion.* **2** (often **Communion** or **Holy Communion**) the service of Christian worship at which bread and wine are consecrated and shared. See EUCHARIST. ■ the consecrated bread and wine so administered and received: *the priests gave him Holy Communion.* **3** a relationship of recognition and acceptance between Christian churches or denominations, or between individual Christians or Christian communities and a church (signified by a willingness to give or receive the Eucharist): *the Eastern Churches are not* ***in communion with*** *Rome.* ■ a group of Christian communities or churches that recognize one another's ministries or that of a central authority. See also ANGLICAN COMMUNION.
–PHRASES **make one's communion** receive bread and wine that has been consecrated at a Eucharist, as a sacramental, spiritual, or symbolic act of receiving the presence of Christ.
–ORIGIN late Middle English: from Latin *communio(n-)*, from *communis* (see COMMON).

com·mun·ion of saints ▶ **n.** [in sing.] a fellowship between Christians living and dead.

com·mu·ni·qué /kə,myo͞onə'kā, kə'myo͞onə,kā/ (also **communique**) ▶ **n.** an official announcement or statement, esp. one made to the media.
–ORIGIN mid 19th cent.: from French, past participle of *communiquer* 'communicate.'

com·mu·nism /'kämyə,nizəm/ (often **Communism**) ▶ **n.** a political theory derived from Karl Marx, advocating class war and leading to a society in which all property is publicly owned and each person works and is paid according to their abilities and needs. See also MARXISM.

> The most familiar form of communism is that established by the Bolsheviks after the Russian Revolution of 1917, and it has generally been understood in terms of the system practiced by the former Soviet Union and its allies in eastern Europe, in China since 1949, and in some developing countries such as Cuba, Vietnam, and North Korea. Communism embraced a revolutionary ideology in which the state would wither away after the overthrow of the capitalist system. In practice, however, the state grew to control all aspects of communist society. Communism in eastern Europe collapsed in the late 1980s and early 1990s against a background of failure to meet people's economic expectations, a shift to more democracy in political life, and increasing nationalism such as that which led to the breakup of the Soviet Union.

–ORIGIN mid 19th cent.: from French *communisme*, from *commun* (see COMMON).

Com·mu·nism Peak former name (1962–98) for ISMAIL SAMANI PEAK.

com·mu·nist /'kämyənist/ ▶ **n.** a person who supports or believes in the principles of communism: *I was very left-wing, but I was never a communist.*
▶ **adj.** adhering to or based on the principles of communism: *a French communist writer.*
–DERIVATIVES **com·mu·nis·tic** /,kämyə'nistik/ **adj.**

com·mu·ni·tar·i·an·ism /kə,myo͞oni'te(ə)rēə,nizəm/ ▶ **n.** a theory or system of social organization based on small self-governing communities. ■ an ideology that emphasizes the responsibility of the individual to the community and the social importance of the family unit.
–DERIVATIVES **com·mu·ni·tar·i·an adj. & .n.**
–ORIGIN mid 19th cent.: from COMMUNITY + -ARIAN, on the pattern of words such as *unitarian*.

com·mu·ni·ty /kə'myo͞onitē/ ▶ **n.** (pl. **communities**) **1** a group of people living in the same place or having a particular characteristic in common: *Rhode Island's Japanese community | the scientific community.* ■ a group of people living together in one place, esp. one practicing common ownership: *a community of nuns.* ■ a particular area or place considered together with its inhabitants: *a rural community.* ■ a body of nations or states unified by common interests: [in names] *the European Community | the African Economic Community.* ■ (**the community**) the people of a district or country considered collectively, esp. in the context of social values and responsibilities; society: *preparing prisoners for life back in the community.* ■ [as modifier] denoting a worker or resource designed to serve the people of a particular area: *community health services.* **2** a feeling of fellowship with others, as a result of sharing common attitudes, interests, and goals: *the sense of community that organized religion can provide.* ■ [in sing.] a similarity or identity: *writers who shared a community of interests.* ■ joint ownership or liability: *a commitment to the community of goods.* **3** Ecology a group of interdependent organisms of different species growing or living together in a specified habitat: *communities of insectivorous birds.*
–PHRASES **the international community** the countries of the world considered collectively.
–ORIGIN late Middle English: from Old French *comunete*, reinforced by its source, Latin *communitas*, from *communis* (see COMMON).

com·mu·ni·ty an·ten·na tel·e·vi·sion (abbr.: **CATV**) ▶ **n.** another term for CABLE TELEVISION.

com·mu·ni·ty ar·chi·tect ▶ **n.** an architect working in consultation with local inhabitants in designing housing and other amenities.
–DERIVATIVES **com·mu·ni·ty ar·chi·tec·ture n.**

com·mu·ni·ty bank ▶ **n.** a commercial bank that derives funds from and lends to the community where it operates, and is not affiliated with a multibank holding company.

com·mu·ni·ty cen·ter ▶ **n.** a place where people from a particular community can meet for social, educational, or recreational activities.

com·mu·ni·ty chest ▶ **n.** a fund for charitable activities among the people in a particular area.

com·mu·ni·ty col·lege ▶ **n.** a nonresidential junior college offering courses to people living in a particular area.

com·mu·ni·ty po·lic·ing ▶ **n.** the system of allocating police officers to particular areas so that they become familiar with the local inhabitants.

com·mu·ni·ty pro·per·ty ▶ **n.** property owned jointly by a husband and wife.

com·mu·ni·ty serv·ice ▶ **n.** voluntary work intended to help people in a particular area. ■ Law unpaid work, intended to be of social use, that an offender is required to do instead of going to prison: *sentenced to 600 hours of community service.*

com·mu·ni·ty-sup·port·ed ag·ri·cul·ture (also chiefly Canadian **community-shared agriculture**) ▶ **n.** a system in which a farm operation is supported by shareholders within the community who share both the benefits and risks of food production.

com·mu·ni·ver·si·ty /kə,myo͞onə'vərsitē/ ▶ **n.** an organization representing a liaison between a college or university and the community where it is located: [as modifier] *a communiversity theater.*
–ORIGIN 1990s: blend of *community* and *university*.

com·mu·nize /'kämyə,nīz/ ▶ **v.** [with obj.] cause (a country, people, or economic activity) to be organized on the principles of communism.
–DERIVATIVES **com·mu·ni·za·tion** /,kämyənə'zāsʜən/ **n.**
–ORIGIN late 19th cent.: from Latin *communis* (see COMMON) + -IZE.

com·mut·a·ble /kə'myo͞otəbəl/ ▶ **adj. 1** (of a place or journey) allowing regular commuting to and from work. **2** rare capable of being exchanged or converted.
–DERIVATIVES **com·mut·a·bil·i·ty** /kə,myo͞otə'bilitē/ **n.**

com·mu·tate /'kämyə,tāt/ ▶ **v.** [with obj.] regulate or reverse the direction of (an alternating electric current), esp. to make it a direct current.
–ORIGIN late 19th cent.: from Latin *commutat-* 'changed altogether, exchanged, interchanged,' from the verb *commutare* (see COMMUTE).

com·mu·ta·tion /,kämyə'tāsʜən/ ▶ **n. 1** action or the process of commuting a judicial sentence. ■ the conversion of a legal obligation or entitlement into another form, e.g., the replacement of an annuity or series of payments by a single payment. **2** the process of commutating an electric current. **3** Mathematics the property of having a commutative relation.
–ORIGIN late Middle English (in the sense 'exchange, barter,' later 'alteration'): from Latin *commutatio(n-)*, from *commutare* 'exchange, interchange' (see COMMUTE). Sense 1 dates from the late 16th cent.

com·mu·ta·tion tick·et ▶ **n.** a ticket issued at a reduced rate by a railroad or bus company, entitling the holder to travel a given route a fixed number of times or during a specified period.

com·mu·ta·tive /'kämyə,tātiv, kə'myo͞otətiv/ ▶ **adj.** Mathematics involving the condition that a group of quantities connected by operators gives the same result whatever the order of the quantities involved, e.g., $a \times b = b \times a$. ■ rare relating to or involving substitution or exchange.
–ORIGIN mid 16th cent. (in the sense 'relating to transactions between people'): from French *commutatif, -ive* or medieval Latin *commutativus*, from *commutat-* 'exchanged,' from the verb *commutare* (see COMMUTE).

com·mu·ta·tor /'kämyə,tātər/ ▶ **n.** an attachment, connected to the armature of a motor or generator, through which electrical connection is made and

C

which ensures that the current flows as direct current. ■ a device for reversing the direction of flow of electric current.

com·mute /kə'myo͞ot/ ▶ **v. 1** [no obj.] travel some distance between one's home and place of work on a regular basis: *she* **commuted from** *Westport in to Grand Central Station.*
2 [with obj.] reduce (a judicial sentence, esp. a sentence of death) to one less severe: *the governor recently commuted the sentences of dozens of women convicted of killing their husbands.* ■ (**commute something for/into**) change one kind of payment or obligation for (another). ■ replace (an annuity or other series of payments) with a single payment: *if he had commuted some of his pension, he would have received $330,000.*
3 [no obj.] Mathematics (of two operations or quantities) have a commutative relationship.
▶ **n.** a regular journey of some distance to and from one's place of work.
– ORIGIN late Middle English (in the sense 'interchange (two things)'): from Latin *commutare*, from *com-* 'altogether' + *mutare* 'to change.' Sense 1 of the verb originally meant to buy and use a *commutation ticket*, a dated term for 'a season ticket' (because the daily fare is commuted to a single payment).

com·mut·er /kə'myo͞otər/ ▶ **n.** a person who travels some distance to work on a regular basis.

com·mut·er belt ▶ **n.** the area surrounding a city from which a large number of people travel to work each day.

Co·mo, Lake /'kōmō/ a lake in the foothills of the Alps in northern Italy.

Co·mo·do·ro Ri·va·da·vi·a /,kōmō'dôrō ,rēvä'dävēə/ a port in southeastern Argentina, on the Atlantic coast of Patagonia; pop. 142,800 (est. 2005).

co·mon·o·mer /kō'mänəmər/ ▶ **n.** Chemistry one of the monomers that constitutes a copolymer.

co·mor·bid·i·ty /,kōmôr'biditē/ ▶ **n.** the simultaneous presence of two chronic diseases or conditions in a patient: *the comorbidity of anxiety and depression in Parkinson's disease.*
– DERIVATIVES **co·mor·bid adj.**

Com·o·ros /'kämə,rōz, kə'môrōz, -ōs/ a country in Africa that consists of a group of islands in the Indian Ocean, north of Madagascar; pop. 752,400 (est. 2009); capital, Moroni; languages, French (official), Arabic (official), and Shikomore (a blend of Swahili and Arabic).

> The islands were first visited by the English at the end of the 16th century. At that time and for long afterward, Arab influence was dominant. In the mid 19th century they came under French protection until 1974 when all but one of the four major islands voted for independence.

– DERIVATIVES **Com·o·ran** /'kämərən, kə'môrən/ **adj. & n.**

comp /kämp/ informal ▶ **n.** short for: ■ a composition. ■ a complimentary ticket or voucher. ■ compensation. ■ (also **comp time**) compensatory time. ■ a musical accompaniment. ■ a comprehensive examination.
▶ **v.** [with obj.] **1** play (music) as an accompaniment, esp. in jazz or blues: *if someone is comping chord changes, there are more textured harmonies* | [no obj.] *he comps with an open, jangly sound.*
2 give (something) away free, esp. as part of a promotion: *the management did graciously comp our wine selection.*
3 short for COMPOSITE.
▶ **adj.** [attrib.] **1** complimentary; free: *the average fan was unable to get comp press tickets.*
2 short for COMPENSATORY.

comp. ▶ **abbr.** ■ companion. ■ comparative. ■ compensation. ■ compilation. ■ compiled. ■ compiler. ■ complete. ■ composite. ■ composition. ■ compositor. ■ comprehensive.

com·pact[1] ▶ **adj.** /kəm'pakt, käm-, 'käm,pakt/
1 closely and neatly packed together; dense: *a compact cluster of houses.* ■ having all the necessary components or features neatly fitted into a small space: *a compact car.* ■ (of a person or animal) small, solid, and well-proportioned. ■ (of speech or writing) concise in expression: *a compact summary of the play.*
2 [predic.] (**compact of**) archaic composed or made up of: *towns compact of wooden houses.*
▶ **v.** /kəm'pakt, käm-/ [with obj.] exert force on (something) to make it more dense; compress: *the soil may be compacted by iron oxide* | (as adj. **compacted**) *compacted paper waste.* ■ [no obj.] (of a substance) become compressed in this way: *the snow hardened and compacted.* ■ archaic form (something) by pressing its component parts firmly together. ■ express in fewer words; condense: *the ideas are compacted into two sentences.*
▶ **n.** /'käm,pakt/ **1** a small flat case containing face powder, a mirror, and a powder puff.
2 something that is a small and conveniently shaped example of its kind, in particular: ■ short for COMPACT CAR.
3 Metallurgy a mass of powdered metal compacted together in preparation for sintering.
– DERIVATIVES **com·pac·tion** /kəm'pakSHən/ **n.**, **com·pact·ly adv.**, **com·pact·ness n.**, **com·pac·tor** /kəm'paktər, käm-, 'käm,paktər/ (also **compacter**) **n.**
– ORIGIN late Middle English: from Latin *compact-* 'closely put together, joined,' from the verb *compingere*, from *com-* 'together' + *pangere* 'fasten.'

com·pact[2] ▶ **n.** /'käm,pakt/ a formal agreement or contract between two or more parties.
▶ **v.** /kəm'pakt, käm-, 'käm,pakt/ [with obj.] make or enter into (a formal agreement) with another party or parties: *the Democratic Party compacted an alliance with dissident groups.*
– ORIGIN late 16th cent.: from Latin *compactum*, past participle of *compacisci*, from *com-* 'with' + *pacisci* 'make a covenant.' Compare with PACT.

com·pact car ▶ **n.** a medium-sized car.

com·pact disc (also **compact disk**) (abbr.: **CD**) ▶ **n.** a small plastic disc on which music or other digital information is stored, and from which the information can be read using reflected laser light. See also **CD-ROM**.

com·pact fluo·res·cent light bulb ▶ **n.** a low-wattage energy-efficient fluorescent light bulb designed for use in standard lighting equipment such as table lamps.

com·pa·dre /kəm'pädrā/ ▶ **n.** (pl. **compadres**) informal a way of addressing or referring to a friend or companion.
– ORIGIN mid 19th cent.: Spanish, literally 'godfather,' hence 'benefactor, friend.' Compare with COMPÈRE and GOSSIP.

com·pand /kəm'pand/ ▶ **v.** [with obj.] reduce the signal-to-noise ratio of (a signal) using a compander.
– ORIGIN 1950s: back-formation from COMPANDER.

com·pand·er /kəm'pandər/ (also **compandor**) ▶ **n.** a device that improves the signal-to-noise ratio of an electrical signal by compressing the range of amplitudes of the signal before transmission, and then expanding it on reproduction or reception.
– ORIGIN 1930s: blend of COMPRESSOR and *expander* (see EXPAND).

com·pan·ion[1] /kəm'panyən/ ▶ **n. 1** a person or animal with whom one spends a lot of time or with whom one travels: *his traveling companion* | figurative *fear became my constant companion.* ■ a person who shares the experiences of another, esp. when these are unpleasant or unwelcome: *my* **companions in** *misfortune.* ■ a person's long-term sexual partner outside marriage. ■ a person, esp. an unmarried or widowed woman, employed to live with and assist another. ■ Astronomy a star, galaxy, or other celestial object that is close to or associated with another.
2 one of a pair of things intended to complement or match each other: [as modifier] *a companion volume.* ■ [usu. in names] a book that provides information about a particular subject: *the Oxford Companion to English Literature.* ■ Brit. dated a piece of equipment containing objects used in a particular activity: *a traveler's companion.*
3 (**Companion**) a member of the lowest grade of certain orders of knighthood.
▶ **v.** [with obj.] formal accompany: *he is companioned by a pageboy.*
– ORIGIN Middle English: from Old French *compaignon*, literally 'one who breaks bread with another,' based on Latin *com-* 'together with' + *panis* 'bread.'

com·pan·ion[2] ▶ **n.** Nautical a covering over the hatchway leading below decks. ■ archaic a raised frame with windows on the quarterdeck of a ship to allow light into the decks below. ■ short for COMPANIONWAY.
– ORIGIN mid 18th cent.: from obsolete Dutch *kompanje* (earlier form of *kampanje*) 'quarterdeck,' from Old French *compagne*, from Italian (*camera della*) *compagna* '(storeroom for) provisions.'

com·pan·ion·a·ble /kəm'panyənəbəl/ ▶ **adj.** (of a person) friendly and sociable: *a companionable young man.* ■ (of a shared situation) relaxed and pleasant: *they walked in companionable silence.*
– DERIVATIVES **com·pan·ion·a·ble·ness n.**, **com·pan·ion·a·bly** /-blē/ **adv.**
– ORIGIN early 17th cent.: alteration of obsolete *companiable*, influenced by COMPANION[1].

com·pan·ion an·i·mal ▶ **n.** a pet or other domestic animal.

com·pan·ion·ate /kəm'panyənət/ ▶ **adj.** formal (of a marriage or relationship) between partners or spouses as equal companions. ■ (of a person) acting as a companion.

com·pan·ion plant·ing ▶ **n.** the close planting of different plants that enhance each other's growth or protect each other from pests.
– DERIVATIVES **com·pan·ion plant n.**, **com·pan·ion-plant v.**

com·pan·ion·ship /kəm'panyən,SHip/ ▶ **n.** a feeling of fellowship or friendship.

com·pan·ion·way /kəm'panyən,wā/ ▶ **n.** a set of steps leading from a ship's deck down to a cabin or lower deck.

com·pa·ny /'kəmpənē/ ▶ **n.** (pl. **companies**) **1** a commercial business: *a shipping company* | [in names] *the Ford Motor Company* | [as modifier] *a company director.*
2 the fact or condition of being with another or others, esp. in a way that provides friendship and enjoyment: *I could do with some company.* ■ a person or people seen as a source of such friendship and enjoyment: *she is excellent company.* ■ the person or group of people whose society someone is currently sharing: *he was silent among such distinguished company.* ■ a visiting person or group of people: *I'm expecting company.*
3 a number of individuals gathered together, esp. for a particular purpose: *the mayor addressed the assembled company.* ■ a body of soldiers, esp. the smallest subdivision of an infantry battalion, typically commanded by a major or captain: *the troops of C Company.* ■ a group of actors, singers, or dancers who perform together: *a touring opera company.*
4 (**the Company**) informal the Central Intelligence Agency.
▶ **v.** (**companies, companying, companied**) [no obj.] (**company with**) literary associate with; keep company with: *these men which have companied with us all this time.* ■ [with obj.] archaic accompany (someone): *the fair dame, companied by Statius and myself.*
– PHRASES **and company** used after a person's name to denote those people usually associated with them: *the psycholinguistics of Jacques Lacan and company.* ■ used in the name of a business to denote other unspecified partners: *Little, Brown and Company.* **be in good company** be in the same situation as someone important or respected: *if you spot the ghost, you are in good company: King George V saw it too.* **in company** with another person or a group of people: *you were never to mention in company your father's uncle.* **in company with** together with: *the U.S. dollar went through a bad patch in 1986, in company with the oil market.* **keep someone company** accompany or spend time with someone in order to prevent them from feeling lonely or bored. ■ engage in the same activity as someone else in order to be sociable: *I'll have a drink myself, just to keep you company.* **keep company with** associate with habitually: *we don't especially care for the people he's been keeping company with.* ■ have a social or romantic relationship with; date: *are you keeping company with anyone special these days?* **part company** see PART.
– ORIGIN Middle English (in sense 2 of the noun and sense 3 of the noun): from Old French *compainie*; related to *compaignon* (see COMPANION[1]).

com·pa·ny car ▶ **n.** a car provided by a company for the business and sometimes private use of an employee.

com·pa·ny of·fi·cer ▶ **n.** an army officer serving within an infantry company.

com·pa·ra·ble /'kämp(ə)rəbəl/ ▶ **adj.** (of a person or thing) able to be likened to another; similar: *flaked stone and bone tools* **comparable to** *Neanderthal man's tools.* ■ of equivalent quality; worthy of comparison: *nobody is comparable with this athlete.*
– DERIVATIVES **com·pa·ra·bil·i·ty** /,kämp(ə)rə'bilitē/ **n.**
– ORIGIN late Middle English: from Old French, from Latin *comparabilis*, from the verb *comparare* (see COMPARE).

> **USAGE** The correct pronunciation in standard English is with the stress on the first syllable rather than the second: comparable, not comparable.

com·pa·ra·bly /'kämp(ə)rəblē, kəm'parəblē/ ▶ **adv.** in a similar way or to a similar degree: *a comparably priced CD player.*

com·par·a·tist /kəm'parətist/ ▶ **n.** a person who carries out comparative study, esp. of language or literature.
– ORIGIN 1930s: from COMPARATIVE + -IST.

com·par·a·tive /kəm'parətiv/ ▶ **adj. 1** perceptible by comparison; relative: *he returned to the comparative comfort of his own home.*
2 of or involving comparison between two or more branches of science or subjects of study: *comparative religion.*

3 Grammar (of an adjective or adverb) expressing a higher degree of a quality, but not the highest possible (e.g., *braver; more fiercely*). Contrasted with **POSITIVE, SUPERLATIVE.** ■ (of a clause) involving comparison (e.g., *their memory is not as good as it used to be*).
▶ **n.** Grammar a comparative adjective or adverb. ■ (**the comparative**) the middle degree of comparison.
– ORIGIN late Middle English (sense 3 of the adjective): from Latin *comparativus*, from *comparare* 'to pair, match' (see **COMPARE**).

com·par·a·tive ad·van·tage ▶ **n.** the ability of an individual or group to carry out a particular economic activity (such as making a specific product) more efficiently than another activity.

com·par·a·tive lin·guis·tics ▶ **plural n.** [treated as sing.] the study of similarities and differences between languages, in particular the comparison of related languages with a view to reconstructing forms in their lost parent languages.

com·par·a·tive·ly /kəm'parətivlē/ ▶ **adv.** [as submodifier] to a moderate degree as compared to something else; relatively: *inflation was comparatively low*.

com·par·a·tor /kəm'parətər/ ▶ **n.** a device for comparing a measurable property or thing with a reference or standard. ■ an electronic circuit for comparing two electrical signals. ■ something used as a standard for comparison.
– ORIGIN late 19th cent.: from Latin *comparat-* 'paired, matched,' from the verb *comparare* (see **COMPARE**) + **-OR**[1].

com·pare /kəm'pe(ə)r/ ▶ **v.** [with obj.] **1** estimate, measure, or note the similarity or dissimilarity between: ***individual schools compared their facilities with** those of others in the area* | *the survey compares prices in different countries* | *total attendance figures were 28,000, **compared to** 40,000 at last year's event*. ■ (**compare something to**) point out the resemblances to; liken to: *her novel was compared to the work of Daniel Defoe*. ■ (**compare something to**) draw an analogy between one thing and (another) for the purposes of explanation or clarification: *he compared the religions to different paths toward the peak of the same mountain*. ■ [no obj.] have a specified relationship with another thing or person in terms of nature or quality: *salaries **compare favorably with** those of other professions*. ■ [no obj.] be of an equal or similar nature or quality: *sales were modest and cannot **compare with** the glory days of 1989*.
2 (usu. **be compared**) Grammar form the comparative and superlative degrees of (an adjective or an adverb): *words of one syllable are usually compared by "-er" and "-est."*
– PHRASES **beyond** (or **without**) **compare** of a quality or nature surpassing all others of the same kind: *a diamond beyond compare*. **compare notes** (of two or more people) exchange ideas, opinions, or information about a particular subject.
– ORIGIN late Middle English: from Old French *comparer*, from Latin *comparare*, from *compar* 'like, equal,' from *com-* 'with' + *par* 'equal.'

> **USAGE** Traditionally, **compare to** is used when similarities are noted in dissimilar things: *shall I compare thee to a summer's day?* To **compare with** is to look for either differences or similarities, usually in similar things: *compare the candidate's claims with his actual performance*. In practice, however, this distinction is rarely maintained. See also usage at **CONTRAST**.

com·par·i·son /kəm'parəsən/ ▶ **n.** **1** the act or instance of comparing: *they **drew a comparison between** Gandhi's teaching and that of other teachers* | *the two books invite comparison with one another*. ■ an analogy: *perhaps the best comparison is that of seasickness*. ■ the quality of being similar or equivalent: *if you want a thrill, there's no comparison to climbing on a truck and going out there on the expressway*.
2 Grammar the formation of the comparative and superlative forms of adjectives and adverbs.
– PHRASES **bear** (or **stand**) **comparison** be of sufficient quality to be likened favorably to someone or something of the same kind: *it **can stand comparison with** any publishing house*. **beyond comparison** another way of saying **BEYOND COMPARE** (see **COMPARE**). **by/in comparison** when compared: *computer-based communication is extremely fast **in comparison with** telephone or postal services*.
– ORIGIN Middle English: from Old French *comparesoun*, from Latin *comparatio(n-)*, from *comparare* 'to pair, match' (see **COMPARE**).

com·par·i·son shop·ping ▶ **n.** the practice of comparing the price of products or services from different vendors before buying.
– DERIVATIVES **com·par·i·son-shop v.**, **com·par·i·son shop·per n.**

com·part·ment /kəm'pärtmənt/ ▶ **n.** **1** a separate section or part of something, in particular: ■ a division of a railroad car marked by partitions: *a first-class compartment*. ■ a section of a container in which certain items can be kept separate from others: *there's some ice cream in the freezer compartment*. ■ a watertight section of a ship: *the aft cargo compartment*. ■ an area in which something can be considered in isolation from other things: *religion and politics should be kept in different compartments*.
2 Heraldry a grassy mound or other support depicted below a shield.
▶ **v.** [with obj.] (usu. **be compartmented**) divide (something) into separate parts or sections: *the buildings are to be compartmented by fire walls*.
– DERIVATIVES **com·part·men·ta·tion** /kəm,pärt,men'tāsʜən, -mən-/ **n.**
– ORIGIN mid 16th cent.: from French *compartiment*, from Italian *compartimento*, from *compartire*, from late Latin *compartiri* 'divide.'

com·part·men·tal /kəm,pärt'mentl/ ▶ **adj.** characterized by division into separate sections: *the compartmental interior of the church*.
– DERIVATIVES **com·part·men·tal·ly adv.**

com·part·men·tal·ize /kəm,pärt'mentl,īz/ ▶ **v.** [with obj.] divide into sections or categories: *he had the ability to compartmentalize his life*.
– DERIVATIVES **com·part·men·tal·ism** /-,izəm/ **n.**, **com·part·men·tal·i·za·tion** /kəm,pärt,mentl-ə'zāsʜən/ **n.**

com·part·ment syn·drome ▶ **n.** Medicine a condition resulting from increased pressure within a confined body space, esp. of the leg or forearm.

com·pass /'kəmpəs/ ▶ **n.** **1** (also **magnetic compass**) an instrument containing a magnetized pointer that shows the direction of magnetic north and bearings from it.

> The use of the compass for navigation at sea was reported from China c.1100, western Europe 1187, Arabia c.1220, and Scandinavia c.1300, although it probably dates from much earlier. Since the early 20th century the magnetic compass has been superseded by the gyrocompass as primary equipment for ships and aircraft.

2 (also **pair of compasses**) an instrument for drawing circles and arcs and measuring distances between points, consisting of two arms linked by a movable joint, one arm ending in a point and the other usually carrying a pencil or pen.
3 [in sing.] the range or scope of something: *the event had political repercussions that are **beyond the compass of** this book*. ■ the enclosing limits of an area: *this region had within its compass many types of agriculture*. ■ the range of notes that can be produced by a voice or a musical instrument: *the cellos were playing in a rather somber part of their compass*.
▶ **v.** [with obj.] archaic **1** go around (something) in a circular course: *the ship wherein Magellan compassed the world*. ■ surround or enclose on all sides: *they were compassed with numerous fierce and cruel tribes*.
2 contrive to accomplish (something): *he compassed his end only by the exercise of violence*.
– ORIGIN Middle English: from Old French *compas* (noun), *compasser* (verb), based on Latin *com-* 'together' + *passus* 'a step or pace.' Several senses ('measure,' 'artifice,' 'circumscribed area,' and 'pair of compasses') that appeared in Middle English are also found in Old French, but their development and origin are uncertain. The transference of sense to the magnetic compass is held to have occurred in the related Italian word *compasso*, from the circular shape of the compass box.

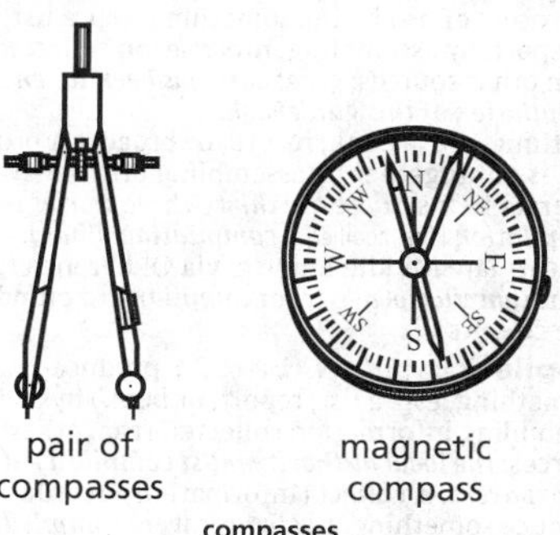

compasses

com·pass card ▶ **n.** a circular rotating card showing the 32 principal bearings, forming the indicator of a magnetic compass.

com·pas·sion /kəm'pasʜən/ ▶ **n.** sympathetic pity and concern for the sufferings or misfortunes of others: *the victims should be treated with compassion*.
– ORIGIN Middle English: via Old French from ecclesiastical Latin *compassio(n-)*, from *compati* 'suffer with.'

com·pas·sion·ate /kəm'pasʜənət/ ▶ **adj.** feeling or showing sympathy and concern for others.
– DERIVATIVES **com·pas·sion·ate·ly adv.**
– ORIGIN late 16th cent.: from **COMPASSION** + **-ATE**[2], influenced by archaic French *compassioné* 'feeling pity.'

com·pas·sion·ate leave ▶ **n.** a period of absence from work granted to someone as the result of particular personal circumstances, esp. the death of a close relative.

com·pas·sion fa·tigue ▶ **n.** indifference to charitable appeals on behalf of those who are suffering, experienced as a result of the frequency or number of such appeals.

com·pass rose ▶ **n.** a circle showing the principal directions printed on a map or chart.

com·pass saw ▶ **n.** a handsaw with a narrow blade for cutting curves.

com·pat·i·bil·i·ty /kəm,patə'bilitē/ ▶ **n.** a state in which two things are able to exist or occur together without problems or conflict: *he argues for the compatibility of science and religion*. ■ a feeling of sympathy and friendship; like-mindedness: *they felt the bond of true compatibility*. ■ Computing the ability of one computer, piece of software, etc., to work with another.

com·pat·i·ble /kəm'patəbəl/ ▶ **adj.** (of two things) able to exist or occur together without conflict: *the fruitiness of Beaujolais **is compatible with** a number of meat dishes*. ■ (of two people) able to have a harmonious relationship: well-suited: *it's a pity we're not compatible*. ■ (of one thing) consistent with another: *the symptoms were compatible with gastritis or a peptic ulcer*. ■ (of a computer, a piece of software, or other device) able to be used with a specified piece of equipment or software without special adaptation or modification: *the printer is fully compatible with all leading software*.
▶ **n.** a computer that can use software designed for another make or type.
– DERIVATIVES **com·pat·i·bly** /-blē/ **adv.**
– ORIGIN late Middle English: from French, from medieval Latin *compatibilis*, from *compati* 'suffer with.'

com·pa·tri·ot /kəm'pātrēət/ ▶ **n.** a fellow citizen or national of a country: *Stich defeated his compatriot Boris Becker in the quarterfinals*.
– ORIGIN late 16th cent.: from French *compatriote*, from late Latin *compatriota* (translating Greek *sumpatriōtēs*), from *com-* 'together with' + *patriota* (see **PATRIOT**).

com·peer /'käm,pi(ə)r, käm'pi(ə)r/ ▶ **n.** formal a person of equal rank, status, or ability: *he was better versed in his profession than his compeers*. ■ archaic a companion or associate.
– ORIGIN late Middle English: from Old French *comper*, from *com-* 'with' + *per*, from Latin *par* 'equal' (compare with **PEER**[2]).

com·pel /kəm'pel/ ▶ **v.** (**compels, compelling, compelled**) [with obj.] force or oblige (someone) to do something: [with obj. and infinitive] *a sense of duty compelled Harry to answer her questions*. ■ bring about (something) by the use of force or pressure: *they may compel a witness's attendance at court by issue of a summons*. ■ literary drive forcibly: *by heav'n's high will compell'd from shore to shore*.
– ORIGIN late Middle English: from Latin *compellere*, from *com-* 'together' + *pellere* 'drive.'

com·pel·la·ble /kəm'peləbəl/ ▶ **adj.** Law (of a witness) able to be made to attend court or testify.

com·pel·ling /kəm'peliNG/ ▶ **adj.** evoking interest, attention, or admiration in a powerfully irresistible way: *his eyes were strangely compelling* | *a compelling film*. ■ not able to be refuted; inspiring conviction: *compelling evidence* | *a compelling argument*. ■ not able to be resisted; overwhelming: *the temptation to give up was compelling*.
– DERIVATIVES **com·pel·ling·ly adv.**

com·pen·di·ous /kəm'pendēəs/ ▶ **adj.** formal containing or presenting the essential facts of something in a comprehensive but concise way: *a compendious study*.
– DERIVATIVES **com·pen·di·ous·ly adv.**, **com·pen·di·ous·ness n.**
– ORIGIN late Middle English: from Old French *compendieux*, from Latin *compendiosus*

C

'advantageous, brief,' from *compendium* 'profit, saving, abbreviation.'

com·pen·di·um /kəm'pendēəm/ ▶ **n.** (pl. **compendiums** or **compendia** /-dēə/) a collection of concise but detailed information about a particular subject, esp. in a book or other publication. ■ a collection of things, esp. one systematically gathered: *the program is a compendium of outtakes from our archives.*
– ORIGIN late 16th cent.: from Latin,'profit, saving' (literally 'what is weighed together'), from *compendere*, from *com-* 'together' + *pendere* 'weigh.'

com·pen·sa·ble /kəm'pensəbəl/ ▶ **adj.** (of a loss or hardship) for which compensation can be obtained.
– ORIGIN mid 17th cent.: French, from *compenser*, from Latin *compensare* 'weigh (something) against (another).'

com·pen·sate /'kämpən,sāt/ ▶ **v. 1** [with obj.] give (someone) something, typically money, in recognition of loss, suffering, or injury incurred; recompense: *payments were made to farmers to compensate them for cuts in subsidies.* ■ pay (someone) for work performed: *he will be richly compensated for his efforts.*
2 [no obj.] (**compensate for**) make up for (something unwelcome or unpleasant) by exerting an opposite force or effect: *officials have boosted levies to compensate for huge deficits.* ■ act to neutralize or correct (a deficiency or abnormality in a physical property or effect): *the output voltage rises, compensating for the original fall.* ■ Psychology attempt to conceal or offset (a disability or frustration) by development in another direction: *they identified with radical movements to compensate for their inability to relate to individual human beings.*
3 [with obj.] Mechanics provide (a pendulum) with extra or less weight to neutralize the effects of temperature, etc.
– DERIVATIVES **com·pen·sa·tive** /kəm'pensətiv, 'kämpən,sātiv/ **adj.**, **com·pen·sa·tor** /-,sātər/ **n.**
– ORIGIN mid 17th cent. (in the sense 'counterbalance'): from Latin *compensat-* 'weighed against,' from the verb *compensare*, from *com-* 'together' + *pensare* (frequentative of *pendere* 'weigh').

com·pen·sa·tion /,kämpən'sāsHən/ ▶ **n.** something, typically money, awarded to someone as a recompense for loss, injury, or suffering: *seeking compensation for injuries suffered at work* | [as modifier] *a compensation claim.* ■ the action or process of making such an award: *the compensation of victims.* ■ the money received by an employee from an employer as a salary or wages. ■ something that counterbalances or makes up for an undesirable or unwelcome state of affairs: *the gray streets of London were small compensation for the loss of her beloved Africa* | *getting older has some compensations.* ■ Psychology the process of concealing or offsetting a psychological difficulty by developing in another direction.
– DERIVATIVES **com·pen·sa·tion·al** /-sHənl/ **adj.**
– ORIGIN late Middle English: via Old French from Latin *compensatio(n-)*, from the verb *compensare* 'weigh against' (see COMPENSATE).

com·pen·sa·tion pen·du·lum ▶ **n.** Physics a pendulum constructed from metals with differing coefficients of expansion in order to neutralize the effects of temperature variation.

com·pen·sa·to·ry /kəm'pensə,tôrē/ ▶ **adj.** (of a payment) intended to recompense someone who has experienced loss, suffering, or injury: *$50 million in compensatory damages.* ■ reducing or offsetting the unpleasant or unwelcome effects of something: *the government is taking compensatory actions to keep the interest rate constant.*

com·pen·sa·to·ry time ▶ **n.** an arrangement by which eligible employees are entitled to time off in lieu of overtime pay.

com·père /'käm,pe(ə)r/ Brit. ▶ **n.** a person who introduces the performers or contestants in a variety show; host.
▶ **v.** [with obj.] act as a compère for (such a show).
– ORIGIN early 20th cent.: French, literally 'godfather.'

com·pete /kəm'pēt/ ▶ **v.** [no obj.] strive to gain or win something by defeating or establishing superiority over others who are trying to do the same: *universities are competing for applicants* | *he competed with a number of other candidates* | (as adj. **competing**) *competing political ideologies.* ■ take part in a contest: *he competed in numerous track meets as a child.*
– ORIGIN early 17th cent.: from Latin *competere*, in its late sense 'strive or contend for (something),' from *com-* 'together' + *petere* 'aim at, seek.'

com·pe·tence /'kämpətəns/ (also **competency** /-tənsē/) ▶ **n. 1** the ability to do something successfully or efficiently: *the players displayed varying degrees of competence.* ■ the legal authority of a court or other body to deal with a particular matter: *the court's competence has been accepted.* ■ the ability of a criminal defendant to stand trial, as gauged by their mental ability to understand the proceedings and to assist defense lawyers. ■ (also **linguistic** or **language competence**) Linguistics a speaker's subconscious, intuitive knowledge of the rules of their language. Often contrasted with PERFORMANCE. ■ Biology & Medicine effective performance of the normal function.
2 dated an income large enough to live on, typically unearned: *he found himself with an ample competence and no obligations.*

com·pe·tent /'kämpətənt/ ▶ **adj.** having the necessary ability, knowledge, or skill to do something successfully: *a highly competent surgeon* | *make sure the firm is* ***competent to*** *carry out the work.* ■ (of a person) efficient and capable: *an infinitely competent mother of three.* ■ acceptable and satisfactory, though not outstanding: *she spoke quite competent French.* ■ (chiefly of a court or other body) accepted as having legal authority to deal with a particular matter: *the governor was not the* ***competent authority*** *to deal with the matter.* ■ (of a criminal defendant) able to understand the charges and to aid in defending themselves. ■ Biology & Medicine capable of performing the normal function effectively.
– DERIVATIVES **com·pe·tent·ly** **adv.**
– ORIGIN late Middle English (in the sense 'suitable, adequate'): from Latin *competent-*, from the verb *competere* in its earlier sense 'be fit or proper' (see COMPETE).

com·pe·ti·tion /,kämpə'tisHən/ ▶ **n.** the activity or condition of competing: *there is fierce* ***competition between*** *banks* | *at this conservatory,* ***competition for*** *admissions is stiff.* ■ an event or contest in which people compete: *a beauty competition.* ■ [in sing.] the person or people with whom one is competing, esp. in a commercial or sporting arena; the opposition: *I walked around to check out the competition.* ■ Ecology interaction between organisms, populations, or species, in which birth, growth and death depend on gaining a share of a limited environmental resource.
– ORIGIN early 17th cent.: from late Latin *competitio(n-)* 'rivalry,' from *competere* 'strive for' (see COMPETE).

com·pet·i·tive /kəm'petətiv/ ▶ **adj. 1** of, relating to, or characterized by competition: *a competitive sport* | *the intensely competitive newspaper industry.* ■ having or displaying a strong desire to be more successful than others: *she had a competitive streak.*
2 as good as or better than others of a comparable nature: *a car industry competitive with any in the world.* ■ (of prices) low enough to compare well with those of rival merchants: *we offer prompt service at competitive rates.*
– DERIVATIVES **com·pet·i·tive·ness** **n.**
– ORIGIN early 19th cent.: from Latin *competit-* 'striven for,' from the verb *competere* (see COMPETE), + -IVE.

com·pet·i·tive ex·clu·sion ▶ **n.** Ecology the inevitable elimination from a habitat of one of two different species with identical needs for resources.

com·pet·i·tive·ly /kəm'petətivlē/ ▶ **adv. 1** in a way that strives to gain or win something by defeating others: *their father rowed competitively.*
2 (with reference to a product's pricing) in a way that compares favorably with others of the same nature: *our exports remained competitively priced.*

com·pet·i·tor /kəm'petətər/ ▶ **n.** an organization or country that is engaged in commercial or economic competition with others: *our main industrial competitors.* ■ a person who takes part in an athletic contest.

com·pi·la·tion /,kämpə'lāsHən/ ▶ **n. 1** the action or process of producing something, esp. a list, book, or report, by assembling information collected from other sources: *great care has been taken in the compilation of this guidebook.*
2 a thing, esp. a book, record, or broadcast program, that is put together by assembling previously separate items: *there are thirty-three stories in this compilation* | [as modifier] *a compilation album.*
– ORIGIN late Middle English: via Old French from Latin *compilatio(n-)*, from *compilare* 'to plunder' (see COMPILE).

com·pile /kəm'pīl/ ▶ **v.** [with obj.] **1** produce (something, esp. a list, report, or book) by assembling information collected from other sources: *the local authority must compile a list of taxpayers.* ■ collect (information) in order to produce something: *the figures were compiled from a survey of 2,000 schoolchildren.* ■ accumulate (a specified score): *the 49ers have compiled a league-leading 14–2 record.*
2 Computing (of a computer) convert (a program) into a machine-code or lower-level form in which the program can be executed.
– DERIVATIVES **com·pil·er** **n.**
– ORIGIN Middle English: from Old French *compiler* or its apparent source, Latin *compilare* 'plunder or plagiarize.'

comp·ing /'kämpiNG/ ▶ **n. 1** the process of making composite images, esp. electronically.
2 the action of playing a musical accompaniment, esp. in jazz or blues.
3 Brit. informal the practice of entering competitions, esp. those promoting consumer products.
– DERIVATIVES **comp·er** /-pər/ **n.** (Brit.) (sense 3).

com·pla·cen·cy /kəm'plāsənsē/ (also **complacence**) ▶ **n.** a feeling of smug or uncritical satisfaction with oneself or one's achievements: *the figures are better, but there are no grounds for complacency.*
– ORIGIN mid 17th cent.: from medieval Latin *complacentia*, from Latin *complacere* 'to please.'

com·pla·cent /kəm'plāsənt/ ▶ **adj.** showing smug or uncritical satisfaction with oneself or one's achievements: *you can't afford to be complacent about security.*
– DERIVATIVES **com·pla·cent·ly** **adv.**
– ORIGIN mid 17th cent. (in the sense 'pleasant'): from Latin *complacent-* 'pleasing,' from the verb *complacere.*

> **USAGE** **Complacent** and **complaisant** are two words that are similar in pronunciation and that both come from the Latin verb *complacere* 'to please,' but in English do not mean the same thing. **Complacent** is the more common word and means 'smug and self-satisfied': *after four consecutive championships, the team became complacent.* **Complaisant**, on the other hand, means 'willing to please': *the local people proved complaisant and cordial.*

com·plain /kəm'plān/ ▶ **v.** [with obj.] express dissatisfaction or annoyance about a state of affairs or an event: *local authorities complained that they lacked sufficient resources* | [no obj.] *"You never listen to me," Larry complained* | [no obj.] *we all* ***complained*** *bitterly* ***about*** *the food.* ■ [no obj.] (**complain of**) state that one is suffering from (a pain or other symptom of illness): *her husband began to complain of headaches.* ■ [no obj.] state a grievance: *they* ***complained to*** *the French government.* ■ [no obj.] literary make a mournful sound: *let the warbling flute complain.* ■ [no obj.] (of a structure or mechanism) groan or creak under strain.
– DERIVATIVES **com·plain·er** **n.**, **com·plain·ing·ly** **adv.**
– ORIGIN late Middle English: from Old French *complaindre*, from medieval Latin *complangere* 'bewail,' from *com-* (expressing intensive force) + *plangere* 'to lament.'

com·plain·ant /kəm'plānənt/ ▶ **n.** Law a plaintiff in certain lawsuits.
– ORIGIN late Middle English: from French *complaignant*, present participle of *complaindre* 'to lament' (see COMPLAIN).

com·plaint /kəm'plānt/ ▶ **n. 1** a statement that a situation is unsatisfactory or unacceptable: *I intend to make an official complaint* | *there were complaints that the building was an eyesore.* ■ a reason for dissatisfaction: *I have no complaints about the hotel.* ■ the expression of dissatisfaction: *a letter of complaint* | *he hasn't any cause for complaint.* ■ Law the plaintiff's reasons for proceeding in a civil action.
2 an illness or medical condition, esp. a relatively minor one: *she is receiving treatment for her skin complaint.*
– ORIGIN late Middle English: from Old French *complainte*, feminine past participle of *complaindre* 'to lament' (see COMPLAIN).

com·plai·sant /kəm'plāsənt/ ▶ **adj.** willing to please others; obliging; agreeable: *when unharnessed, Northern dogs are peaceful and complaisant.*
– DERIVATIVES **com·plai·sance** **n.**, **com·plai·sant·ly** **adv.**
– ORIGIN mid 17th cent.: French, from *complaire* 'acquiesce in order to please,' from Latin *complacere* 'to please.'

> **USAGE** See usage at COMPLACENT.

com·pleat /kəm'plēt/ ▶ **adj. & v.** archaic spelling of COMPLETE.

com·plect·ed /kəm'plektəd/ ▶ **adj.** [in combination] having a specified complexion: *lighter-complected invaders from the north.*
– ORIGIN early 19th cent.: apparently from COMPLEXION.

com·ple·ment ▶ **n.** /'kämpləmənt/ **1** a thing that completes or brings to perfection: *the libretto proved a perfect* ***complement to*** *the music.*
2 [in sing.] a number or quantity of something required to make a group complete: *at the moment we have* ***a full complement of*** *staff.* ■ the number of people required to crew a ship: *almost half the*

ship's complement of 322 were wounded. ■ Geometry the amount in degrees by which a given angle is less than 90°. ■ Mathematics the members of a set that are not members of a given subset.
3 Grammar one or more words, phrases, or clauses governed by a verb (or by a nominalization or a predicative adjective) that complete the meaning of the predicate. ■ (in systemic grammar) an adjective or noun that has the same reference as either the subject (as *mad* in *he is mad*) or the object (as *mad* in *he drove her mad*).
4 Physiology a group of proteins present in blood plasma and tissue fluid that combine with an antigen–antibody complex to bring about the lysis of foreign cells.
▶ **v.** /-ˌment, -mənt/ [with obj.] add to (something) in a way that enhances or improves it; make perfect: *a classic blazer complements a look that's stylish or casual.* ■ add to or make complete: *the proposals complement the incentives already available.*
– DERIVATIVES **com·ple·men·tal** /ˌkämpləˈmentl/ **adj.**
– ORIGIN late Middle English (in the sense 'completion'): from Latin *complementum*, from *complere* 'fill up' (see **COMPLETE**). Compare with **COMPLIMENT**.

> **USAGE** Complement and compliment (together with related words such as **complementary** and **complimentary**) are frequently confused. They are pronounced in the same way but have quite different meanings: as a verb, **complement** means 'add to something in a way that enhances or improves,' as in *a classic blazer* ***complements*** *a look that's smart or casual*, while **compliment** means 'admire and praise someone for something,' as in *he* ***complimented*** *her on her appearance*. **Complementary** means 'forming a complement or addition, completing,' as in *I purchased a suit with a complementary tie*. This is often confused with **complimentary**, for which one sense is 'given freely, as a courtesy': *honeymooners receive complimentary fruit and flowers*.

com·ple·men·tar·i·ty /ˌkämpləmenˈtaritē/ ▶ **n.** (pl. **complementarities**) a complementary relationship or situation: *a culture based on the complementarity of men and women.* ■ Physics the concept that two contrasted theories, such as the wave and particle theories of light, may be able to explain a set of phenomena, although each separately only accounts for some aspects. ■ Law the principle that jurisdictions will not overlap in legislation, administration, or prosecution of crime.

com·ple·men·ta·ry /ˌkämpləˈment(ə)rē/ ▶ **adj.** **1** combining in such a way as to enhance or emphasize the qualities of each other or another: *three guitarists playing interlocking, complementary parts | Internet technology is actually* ***complementary to*** *traditional technologies.* ■ Biochemistry (of gene sequences, nucleotides, etc.) related by the rules of base pairing.
2 [attrib.] of or relating to complementary medicine: *complementary therapies such as aromatherapy.*
– DERIVATIVES **com·ple·men·ta·ri·ly** /ˌkämpləˈmentrəlē, -menˈterəlē/ **adv.**, **com·ple·men·ta·ri·ness n.**

com·ple·men·ta·ry an·gle ▶ **n.** either of two angles whose sum is 90°.

com·ple·men·ta·ry col·ors ▶ **plural n.** colors directly opposite each other in the color spectrum, such as red and green or blue and orange, that when combined in the right proportions, produce white light.

com·ple·men·ta·ry dis·tri·bu·tion ▶ **n.** Linguistics the occurrence of speech sounds in mutually exclusive contexts.

com·ple·men·ta·ry DNA ▶ **n.** Biochemistry synthetic DNA in which the sequence of bases is complementary to that of a given example of DNA.

com·ple·men·ta·ry func·tion ▶ **n.** Mathematics the part of the general solution of a linear differential equation that is the general solution of the associated homogeneous equation obtained by substituting zero for the terms not containing the dependent variable.

com·ple·men·ta·ry med·i·cine ▶ **n.** any of a range of medical therapies that fall beyond the scope of scientific medicine but may be used alongside it in the treatment of disease and ill health. Examples include acupuncture and osteopathy. See also **ALTERNATIVE MEDICINE**.

com·ple·men·ta·tion /ˌkämplәmenˈtāsʜən/ ▶ **n.** the action of complementing something. ■ Grammar all the clause constituents that are governed by a verb, nominalization, or adjective. ■ Genetics the phenomenon by which the effects of two different nonallelic mutations in a gene are partly or entirely canceled out when they occur together.

com·ple·ment fix·a·tion test ▶ **n.** Medicine a test for infection with a microorganism that involves measuring the amount of complement available in serum to bind with an antibody–antigen complex.

com·ple·men·tiz·er /ˈkämpləˌmenˌtīzər, -mən-/ ▶ **n.** Grammar a word or morpheme that marks an embedded clause as functioning as a complement, typically a subordinating conjunction or infinitival *to*.

com·plete /kəmˈplēt/ ▶ **adj.** **1** having all the necessary or appropriate parts: *a complete list of courses offered by the college | no wardrobe is complete this year without culottes.* ■ entire; full: *I only managed one complete term at school.* ■ having run its full course; finished: *the restoration of the chapel is complete.*
2 (often used for emphasis) to the greatest extent or degree; total: *a complete ban on smoking | their marriage came as a complete surprise to me.* ■ (also **compleat**) chiefly humorous skilled at every aspect of a particular activity; consummate: *these articles are for the compleat mathematician.* [the spelling *compleat* is a revival of the 17th cent. use as in Walton's *The Compleat Angler*.]
▶ **v.** [with obj.] **1** finish making or doing: *he completed his Ph.D. in 1983.* ■ Football (esp. of a quarterback) successfully throw (a forward pass) to a receiver: *he completed 12 of 16 passes for 128 yards.* ■ [no obj.] Brit. conclude the sale of a property.
2 make (something) whole or perfect: *he only needed one thing to complete his happiness | more recent box cameras complete the collection.* ■ write the required information on (a form or questionnaire): *please complete the attached forms.*
– PHRASES **complete with** having something as an additional part or feature: *the detachable keyboard comes complete with numeric keypad.*
– DERIVATIVES **com·plete·ness n.**
– ORIGIN late Middle English: from Old French *complet* or Latin *completus*, past participle of *complere* 'fill up, finish, fulfill,' from *com-* (expressing intensive force) + *plere* 'fill.'

> **USAGE** On the use of adjectives like **complete**, **equal**, and **unique** with submodifiers such as **very** or **more**, see usage at **UNIQUE**.

com·plete game ▶ **n.** Baseball a game in which one pitcher pitches all innings without relief.

com·plete·ly /kəmˈplētlē/ ▶ **adv.** totally; utterly: *the fire completely destroyed the building* | [as submodifier] *no code can be completely secure.*

com·ple·tion /kəmˈplēsʜən/ ▶ **n.** the action or process of finishing something: *funds for the completion of the new building.* ■ the state of being finished: *work on the new golf course is nearing completion* | [as modifier] *the completion date is early next year.* ■ Football a successful forward pass: *21 completions in 26 attempts for 233 yards.* ■ Law the final stage in the sale of a property, at which point it legally changes ownership: *the risk stays with the seller until completion.*
– ORIGIN late 15th cent.: from Latin *completion-*, from *complere* 'fill up' (see **COMPLETE**).

com·ple·tist /kəmˈplētist/ ▶ **n.** an obsessive, typically indiscriminate, collector or fan of something.

com·ple·tive /kəmˈplētiv/ ▶ **n.** Grammar a word or morpheme that adds a sense of completeness to a word or phrase (e.g., *up* in the phrase *break up*).

com·plex ▶ **adj.** /kämˈpleks, kəmˈpleks, ˈkämˌpleks/ **1** consisting of many different and connected parts: *a complex network of water channels.* ■ not easy to analyze or understand; complicated or intricate: *a complex personality | the situation is more complex than it appears.*
2 Mathematics denoting or involving numbers or quantities containing both a real and an imaginary part.
3 Chemistry denoting an ion or molecule in which one or more groups are linked to a metal atom by coordinate bonds.
▶ **n.** /ˈkämˌpleks/ **1** a group of similar buildings or facilities on the same site: *a new apartment complex | a complex of hotels.* ■ a group or system of different things that are linked in a close or complicated way; a network: *a complex of mountain roads.*
2 Psychoanalysis a related group of emotionally significant ideas that are completely or partly repressed and that cause psychic conflict leading to abnormal mental states or behavior. ■ informal a disproportionate concern or anxiety about something: *there's no point having a* ***complex about*** *losing your hair.*
3 Chemistry an ion or molecule in which one or more groups are linked to a metal atom by coordinate bonds. ■ any loosely bonded species formed by the association of two molecules: *cross-linked protein-DNA complexes.*
▶ **v.** /kämˈpleks, kəmˈpleks, ˈkämˌpleks/ [with obj.] (usu. **be complexed**) Chemistry make (an atom or compound) form a complex with another: *the DNA* ***was complexed with*** *the nuclear extract* | (as adj. **complexed**) *the complexed metal ion.* ■ [no obj.] form a complex: *these proteins are capable of complexing with VP16.*
– DERIVATIVES **com·plex·a·tion** /ˌkämˌplekˈsāsʜən, kəm-/ **n.** (Chemistry), **com·plex·ly adv.**
– ORIGIN mid 17th cent. (in the sense 'group of related elements'): from Latin *complexus*, past participle (used as a noun) of *complectere* 'embrace, comprise,' later associated with *complexus* 'plaited'; the adjective is partly via French *complexe*.

com·plex con·ju·gate ▶ **n.** Mathematics each of two complex numbers having their real parts identical and their imaginary parts of equal magnitude but opposite sign.

com·plex·ion /kəmˈpleksʜən/ ▶ **n.** **1** the natural color, texture, and appearance of a person's skin, esp. of the face: *an attractive girl with a pale complexion.*
2 the general aspect or character of something: *Congress's new complexion became boldly apparent last summer | wind, rain, and road construction have gradually changed Baja's complexion.*
– DERIVATIVES **com·plex·ioned adj.** [often in combination] *they were both fair-complexioned.*
– ORIGIN Middle English: via Old French from Latin *complexio(n-)* 'combination' (in late Latin 'physical constitution'), from *complectere* 'embrace, comprise.' The term originally denoted physical constitution or temperament determined by the combination of the four bodily humors, hence sense 1 (late 16th cent.) as a visible sign of this.

com·plex·i·ty /kəmˈpleksitē/ ▶ **n.** (pl. **complexities**) the state or quality of being intricate or complicated: *an issue of great complexity.* ■ (usu. **complexities**) a factor involved in a complicated process or situation: *the complexities of family life.*

com·plex plane ▶ **n.** an infinite two-dimensional space representing the set of complex numbers, esp. one in which Cartesian coordinates represent the real and imaginary parts of the complex numbers.

com·plex sen·tence ▶ **n.** Grammar a sentence containing a subordinate clause or clauses.

com·pli·ance /kəmˈplīəns/ (also **compliancy** /-ˈplīənsē/) ▶ **n.** **1** the action or fact of complying with a wish or command: *they must secure each other's cooperation or compliance.* ■ the state or fact of according with or meeting rules or standards: *all imports of timber are* ***in compliance with*** *regulations* | [as modifier] *this paper estimates the compliance costs of such a policy change.* ■ unworthy or excessive acquiescence: *the appalling* ***compliance with*** *government views shown by the commission.*
2 Physics the property of a material of undergoing elastic deformation or (of a gas) change in volume when subjected to an applied force. It is equal to the reciprocal of stiffness. ■ Medicine the ability of an organ to distend in response to applied pressure.

com·pli·ant /kəmˈplīənt/ ▶ **adj.** **1** inclined to agree with others or obey rules, esp. to an excessive degree; acquiescent: *good-humored, eagerly compliant girls.* ■ meeting or in accordance with rules or standards: *the systems are Y2K compliant.*
2 Physics & Medicine having the property of compliance.
– DERIVATIVES **com·pli·ant·ly adv.**

com·pli·cate /ˈkämpləˌkāt/ ▶ **v.** [with obj.] make (something) more difficult or confusing by causing it to be more complex: *middlemen can complicate the process* | (as adj. **complicating**) *a complicating factor.* ■ Medicine introduce complications in (an existing condition): *smoking may complicate pregnancy.*
– ORIGIN early 17th cent. (in the sense 'combine, entangle, intertwine'): from Latin *complicat-* 'folded together,' from the verb *complicare*, from *com-* 'together' + *plicare* 'to fold.'

com·pli·cat·ed /ˈkämpləˌkātid/ ▶ **adj.** **1** consisting of many interconnecting parts or elements; intricate: *a complicated stereo system.* ■ involving many different and confusing aspects: *a long and complicated saga.*
2 Medicine involving complications: *complicated appendicitis.*
– DERIVATIVES **com·pli·cat·ed·ly adv.**

com·pli·ca·tion /ˌkämpləˈkāsʜən/ ▶ **n.** **1** a circumstance that complicates something; a difficulty: *there is a complication concerning ownership of the site.* ■ an involved or confused condition or state: *to add further complication, English speakers use a different name.*
2 Medicine a secondary disease or condition aggravating an already existing one: *she developed complications after the surgery.*

C

–ORIGIN late Middle English: from late Latin *complicatio(n-)*, from Latin *complicare* 'fold together' (see **COMPLICATE**).

com·plic·it /kəm'plisit/ ▶ **adj.** involved with others in an illegal activity or wrongdoing: *all of these people are* ***complicit in*** *some criminal conspiracy.*
–ORIGIN 1940s: back-formation from **COMPLICITY**.

com·plic·i·tous /kəm'plisitəs/ ▶ **adj.** another term for **COMPLICIT**: *the incident proves they were complicitous with Nazi authorities.*

com·plic·i·ty /kəm'plisitē/ ▶ **n.** the state of being involved with others in an illegal activity or wrongdoing: *they were accused of* ***complicity in*** *the attempt to overthrow the government.*
–ORIGIN mid 17th cent.: from Middle English *complice* 'an associate,' from Old French, from late Latin *complex, complic-* 'allied,' from Latin *complicare* 'fold together' (see **COMPLICATE**). Compare with **ACCOMPLICE**.

com·pli·ment ▶ **n.** /'kämpləmənt/ a polite expression of praise or admiration: *she paid me an enormous compliment.* ■ an act or circumstance that implies praise or respect: *it's a compliment to the bride to dress up on her special day.* ■ (**compliments**) congratulations or praise expressed to someone: ***my compliments on*** *your cooking.* ■ (**compliments**) greetings or regards, esp. when sent as a message: *carry my compliments to your kinsmen.*
▶ **v.** /'kämplə,ment/ [with obj.] politely congratulate or praise (someone) for something: *he* ***complimented*** *Erica* ***on*** *her appearance.* ■ praise (something) politely: *complimenting the other team's good play.* ■ (**compliment someone with**) archaic present someone with (something) as a mark of courtesy: *Prince George expected to be complimented with a seat in the royal coach.*
–PHRASES **compliments of the season** used as a seasonal greeting at Christmas or the New Year. **pay one's compliments** send or express formal greetings. **return the compliment** give a compliment in return for another. ■ retaliate or respond in kind. **with someone's compliments** (or **the compliments of**) used to express the fact that what one is giving is free: *all drinks will be supplied with our compliments.*
–ORIGIN mid 17th cent.: from French *compliment* (noun), *complimenter* (verb), from Italian *complimento* 'fulfillment of the requirements of courtesy,' from Latin *complementum* 'completion, fulfillment' (reflected in the earlier English spelling *complement*, gradually replaced by the French form between 1655 and 1715).

> **USAGE** **Compliment** (together with **complimentary**) is quite different in meaning from **complement** (and **complementary**). See usage at **COMPLEMENT**.

com·pli·men·ta·ry /,kämplə'mentərē, -'mentrē/ ▶ **adj. 1** expressing a compliment; praising or approving: *Jennie was very complimentary about Kathy's riding | complimentary remarks.*
2 given or supplied free of charge: *a complimentary bottle of wine.*

com·pli·men·tary close (also **complimentary closing**) ▶ **n.** the part of a letter that immediately precedes the writer's signature, consisting of words such as *Sincerely, Cordially, Very truly yours*, etc.

com·pline /'kämplin, -,plīn/ ▶ **n.** a service of evening prayers forming part of the Divine Office of the Western Christian Church, traditionally said (or chanted) before retiring for the night.
–ORIGIN Middle English: from Old French *complie*, feminine past participle of obsolete *complir* 'to complete,' from Latin *complere* 'fill up' (see **COMPLETE**). The ending *-ine* was probably influenced by Old French *matines* 'matins.'

com·ply /kəm'plī/ ▶ **v.** (**complies, complying, complied**) [no obj.] (of a person or group) act in accordance with a wish or command: *we are unable to* ***comply with*** *your request.* ■ (of an article) meet specified standards: *all secondhand furniture must* ***comply with*** *the new standards.*
–ORIGIN late 16th cent.: from Italian *complire*, Catalan *complir*, Spanish *cumplir*, from Latin *complere* 'fill up, fulfill' (see **COMPLETE**). The original sense was 'fulfill, accomplish,' later 'fulfill the requirements of courtesy,' hence 'to be agreeable, to oblige or obey.' Compare with **COMPLIMENT**.

com·po·nent /kəm'pōnənt/ ▶ **n.** a part or element of a larger whole, esp. a part of a machine or vehicle: *stereo components.* ■ Physics each of two or more forces, velocities, or other vectors acting in different directions that are together equivalent to a given vector.
▶ **adj.** constituting part of a larger whole; constituent: *light passed through a prism breaks up into its component colors.*
–ORIGIN mid 17th cent.: from Latin *component-* 'putting together,' from the verb *componere*, from *com-* 'together' + *ponere* 'put.' Compare with **COMPOUND**[1].

com·po·nen·tial a·nal·y·sis /,kämpə'nenCHəl/ ▶ **n.** Linguistics the analysis of the meaning of an expression into discrete semantic components.

com·po·ny /kəm'pōnē/ ▶ **adj.** [usu. postpositive] Heraldry divided into a single row of squares in alternating tinctures: *a bordure compony.*
–ORIGIN late 16th cent.: from French *compone*, from Old French *compondre*, from Latin *componere* 'put together.'

com·port[1] /kəm'pôrt/ ▶ **v. 1** (**comport oneself**) formal conduct oneself; behave: *articulate students who comported themselves well in television interviews.*
2 [no obj.] (**comport with**) accord with; agree with: *the actions that comport with her own liberal views.*
–ORIGIN late Middle English (in the sense 'tolerate'): from Latin *comportare*, from *com-* 'together' + *portare* 'carry, bear.'

com·port[2] /'käm,pôrt/ ▶ **n.** another term for **COMPOTE** (sense 2).
–ORIGIN late 19th cent.: apparently an abbreviation of French *comportier*, variant of *compotier* 'dessert dish.'

com·port·ment /kəm'pôrtmənt/ ▶ **n.** behavior; bearing: *he displayed the comportment expected of the rightful king.*
–ORIGIN late 16th cent.: from French *comportement*, from the verb *comporter*, from Latin *comportare* (see **COMPORT**[1]).

com·pose /kəm'pōz/ ▶ **v.** [with obj.] **1** write or create (a work of art, esp. music or poetry): *he composed the First Violin Sonata four years earlier.* ■ write or phrase (a letter or piece of writing) with care and thought: *the first sentence is so hard to compose.* ■ form (a whole) by ordering or arranging the parts, esp. in an artistic way: *compose and draw a still life.* ■ order or arrange (parts) to form a whole, esp. in an artistic way: *make an attempt to compose your images.*
2 (of elements) constitute or make up (a whole): *the system is* ***composed of*** *a group of machines.* ■ be (a specified number or amount) of a whole: *women compose 49 percent of that group.*
3 calm or settle (oneself or one's features or thoughts): *she tried to* ***compose herself.*** ■ archaic settle (a dispute): *the king, with some difficulty, composed this difference.*
4 prepare (a text) for printing by manually, mechanically, or electronically setting up the letters and other characters in the order to be printed. ■ set up (letters and characters) in this way.
–ORIGIN late Middle English (in the general sense 'put together, construct'): from Old French *composer*, from Latin *componere* (see **COMPONENT**), but influenced by Latin *compositus* 'composed' and Old French *poser* 'to place.'

com·posed /kəm'pōzd/ ▶ **adj.** having one's feelings and expression under control; calm.
–DERIVATIVES **com·pos·ed·ly** /-'pōzədlē/ **adv.**

com·pos·er /kəm'pōzər/ ▶ **n.** a person who writes music, esp. as a professional occupation.

com·pos·ite /kəm'päzət, käm-/ ▶ **adj. 1** made up of various parts or elements. ■ (esp. of a constructional material) made up of recognizable constituents: *a new composite material—a blend of plastic and ceramic resins.* ■ (of a railroad car) having compartments of more than one class or function. ■ Mathematics (of an integer) being the product of two or more factors greater than one; not prime.
2 (**Composite**) relating to or denoting a classical order of architecture consisting of elements of the Ionic and Corinthian orders.
3 Botany relating to or denoting plants of the daisy family (Compositae).
▶ **n. 1** a thing made up of several parts or elements: *the English legal system is a composite of legislation and judicial precedent.* ■ a composite constructional material.
2 Botany a plant of the daisy family (Compositae).
3 (**Composite**) the Composite order of architecture.
▶ **v.** [with obj.] (usu. as noun **compositing**) combine (two or more images) to make a single picture, esp. electronically: *photographic compositing by computer.*
–DERIVATIVES **com·pos·ite·ly adv.**, **com·pos·ite·ness n.**
–ORIGIN late Middle English (describing a number having more than one digit): via French from Latin *compositus*, past participle of *componere* 'put together.'

com·pos·ite pho·to·graph ▶ **n.** a photograph made by overlapping or juxtaposing two or more separate images.

com·po·si·tion /,kämpə'ziSHən/ ▶ **n. 1** the nature of something's ingredients or constituents; the way in which a whole or mixture is made up: *the social composition of villages.* ■ the action of putting things together; formation or construction: *the composition of a new government was announced.* ■ a thing composed of various elements: *a theory is a composition of interrelated facts.* ■ archaic mental constitution; character: *persons who have a touch of madness in their composition.* ■ [often as modifier] a compound artificial substance, esp. one serving the purpose of a natural one: *composition flooring.* ■ Linguistics the formation of words into a compound word. ■ Mathematics the successive application of functions to a variable, the value of the first function being the argument of the second, and so on: *composition of functions, when defined, is associative.* ■ Physics the process of finding the resultant of a number of forces.
2 a work of music, literature, or art: *Chopin's most romantic compositions.* ■ the action or art of producing such a work: *the technical aspects of composition.* ■ an essay, esp. one written by a school or college student. ■ the artistic arrangement of the parts of a picture: *spoiling the composition of many of the pictures.*
3 the preparing of text for printing by setting up the characters in order. See **COMPOSE** (sense 4).
4 a legal agreement to pay an amount of money in lieu of a larger debt or other obligation. ■ an amount of money paid in this way.
–DERIVATIVES **com·po·si·tion·al** /-SHənl/ **adj.**, **com·po·si·tion·al·ly** /-SHənl-ē/ **adv.**
–ORIGIN late Middle English: via Old French from Latin *composition-*, from *componere* 'put together.'

com·pos·i·tor /kəm'päzitər/ ▶ **n.** Printing a person who arranges type for printing or keys text into a composing machine.
–ORIGIN late Middle English (originally Scots, denoting an umpire or arbiter): from Anglo-Norman French *compositour*, from Latin *compositor*, from *composit-* 'put together,' from the verb *componere* (see **COMPOSITION**).

com·pos men·tis /,kämpəs 'mentəs/ ▶ **adj.** [predic.] having full control of one's mind; sane: *are you sure he was totally compos mentis?*
–ORIGIN early 17th cent.: Latin.

com·pos·si·ble /kəm'päsəbəl, käm-/ ▶ **adj.** rare (of one thing) compatible or possible in conjunction with another.
–ORIGIN mid 17th cent.: from Old French, from medieval Latin *compossibilis*, from *com-* 'together with' + *possibilis* (see **POSSIBLE**).

com·post /'käm,pōst/ ▶ **n.** decayed organic material used as a plant fertilizer. ■ a mixture of this with loam and/or other ingredients, used as a growing medium.
▶ **v.** [with obj.] make (vegetable matter or manure) into compost: *don't compost heavily infested plants.* ■ treat (soil) with compost: *we turned clay soil into almost workable soil by composting it.*
–DERIVATIVES **com·post·a·ble adj.**, **com·post·er n.**
–ORIGIN late Middle English: from Old French *composte*, from Latin *composita, compositum* 'something put together,' feminine and neuter past participle of *componere*.

com·post heap (also **compost pile**) ▶ **n.** a pile of garden and organic kitchen refuse that decomposes to produce compost.

com·po·sure /kəm'pōZHər/ ▶ **n.** the state or feeling of being calm and in control of oneself: *she was struggling to regain her composure.*
–ORIGIN late 16th cent. (in the sense 'composing, composition'): from **COMPOSE** + **-URE**.

com·pote /'käm,pōt/ ▶ **n. 1** fruit preserved or cooked in syrup. ■ a dish consisting of fruit salad or stewed fruit, often with syrup.
2 a bowl-shaped dessert dish with a stem.
–ORIGIN late 17th cent.: from French, from Old French *composte* 'mixture' (see **COMPOST**).

com·pound[1] ▶ **n.** /'käm,pound/ a thing that is composed of two or more separate elements; a mixture: *the air smelled like a compound of diesel and gasoline fumes.* ■ (also **chemical compound**) a substance formed from two or more elements chemically united in fixed proportions: *a compound of hydrogen and oxygen.* ■ a word made up of two or more existing words, such as *steamship*.
▶ **adj.** /'käm,pound, käm'pound, kəm'pound/ made up or consisting of several parts or elements, in particular: ■ (of a word) made up of two or more existing words or elements: *a compound noun.* ■ (of interest) payable on both capital and the accumulated interest: *compound interest*. Compare with **SIMPLE**. ■ Biology (esp. of a leaf, flower, or eye) consisting of two or more simple parts or individuals in combination.
▶ **v.** /kəm'pound, käm'pound, 'käm,pound/ [with obj.] **1** make up (a composite whole); constitute: *a dialect* ***compounded of*** *Spanish and Dutch.* ■ mix or combine (ingredients or constituents): *yellow pastas compounded with lemon zest or saffron.* ■ calculate

(interest) on previously accumulated interest: *the yield at which the interest is compounded.*
2 make (something bad) worse; intensify the negative aspects of: *I compounded the problem by trying to make wrong things right.*
3 Law, dated forbear from prosecuting (a felony) in exchange for money or other consideration. ■ settle (a debt or other matter) in this way: *he compounded the case with the defendant for a cash payment.*
– DERIVATIVES **com·pound·a·ble** /kəm'poundəbəl, käm-/ **adj.**
– ORIGIN late Middle English *compoune* (verb), from Old French *compoun-*, present tense stem of *compondre*, from Latin *componere* 'put together.' The final *-d* was added in the 16th cent. on the pattern of *expound* and *propound.*

> **USAGE** The sense of the verb **compound** that means 'worsen,' as in *this **compounds** their problems*, has an interesting history. It arose through a misinterpretation of the phrase **compound a felony**, which, strictly speaking, means 'forbear from prosecuting a felony in exchange for money or other consideration.' The 'incorrect' sense has become the usual one in legal uses and, by extension, in general senses too, and is now accepted as part of standard English.

com·pound² /'käm,pound/ ▶ **n.** an open area enclosed by a fence, for example around a factory or large house or within a prison.
– ORIGIN late 17th cent. (referring to such an area in Southeast Asia): from Portuguese *campon* or Dutch *kampoeng*, from Malay *kampong* 'enclosure, hamlet'; compare with KAMPONG.

com·pound-com·plex sen·tence ▶ **n.** a sentence having two or more coordinate independent clauses and one or more dependent clauses.

com·pound·er /käm'poundər, kəm'poundər, 'käm,poundər/ ▶ **n.** a person who mixes or combines ingredients in order to produce an animal feed, medicine, or other substance.

com·pound eye ▶ **n.** an eye consisting of an array of numerous small visual units, as found in insects and crustaceans. Contrasted with SIMPLE EYE.

com·pound frac·tion ▶ **n.** a fraction in which either the numerator or the denominator, or both, contain one or more fractions. Also called **complex fraction**.

com·pound frac·ture ▶ **n.** an injury in which a broken bone pierces the skin, causing a risk of infection. Compare with SIMPLE FRACTURE.

com·pound in·ter·val ▶ **n.** Music an interval greater than an octave.

com·pound leaf ▶ **n.** a leaf of a plant consisting of several or many distinct parts (leaflets) joined to a single stem.

com·pound num·ber ▶ **n.** a quantity expressed in terms of more than one unit or denomination, such as 5 feet 7 inches or 2 pounds 3 ounces.

com·pound sen·tence ▶ **n.** a sentence with more than one subject or predicate.

com·pound time ▶ **n.** Music musical rhythm or meter in which each beat in a bar is subdivided into three smaller units, so having the value of a dotted note. Compare with SIMPLE TIME.

com·pra·dor /,kämprə'dôr/ (also **compradore**) ▶ **n.** a person within a country who acts as an agent for foreign organizations engaged in investment, trade, or economic or political exploitation.
– ORIGIN early 17th cent. (denoting a local person employed in a European household in Southeast Asia or India to make small purchases and keep the household accounts): from Portuguese,'buyer,' from late Latin *comparator*, from Latin *comparare* 'to purchase,' from *com-* 'with' + *parare* 'provide.'

com·pre·hend /,kämpri'hend/ ▶ **v.** [with obj.] **1** grasp mentally; understand: *he couldn't comprehend her reasons for marrying Lovat | I simply couldn't comprehend what had happened.*
2 formal include, comprise, or encompass: *a divine order comprehending all men.*
– DERIVATIVES **com·pre·hend·er n.**
– ORIGIN Middle English: from Old French *comprehender*, or Latin *comprehendere*, from *com-* 'together' + *prehendere* 'grasp.'

com·pre·hen·si·ble /,kämpri'hensəbəl/ ▶ **adj.** able to be understood; intelligible: *clear and comprehensible English.*
– DERIVATIVES **com·pre·hen·si·bil·i·ty** /-,hensə'bilitē/ **n.**, **com·pre·hen·si·bly** /-blē/ **adv.**
– ORIGIN late 15th cent.: from French *compréhensible* or Latin *comprehensibilis*, from *comprehens-* 'seized, comprised,' from the verb *comprehendere* (see COMPREHEND).

com·pre·hen·sion /,kämpri'henCHən/ ▶ **n.** **1** the action or capability of understanding something: *some won't have the least comprehension of what I'm trying to do | the comprehension of spoken language.*
2 archaic inclusion.
– ORIGIN late Middle English: from French *compréhension* or Latin *comprehensio(n-)*, from the verb *comprehendere* 'seize, comprise' (see COMPREHEND).

com·pre·hen·sive /,kämpri'hensiv/ ▶ **adj.** **1** complete; including all or nearly all elements or aspects of something: *a comprehensive list of sources.* ■ of large content or scope; wide-ranging: *a comprehensive collection of photographs.* ■ (of automobile insurance) providing coverage for most risks, including damage to the policyholder's own vehicle: *comprehensive and collision insurance.* ■ (also **comprehensive examination** or **comp**) an examination testing a student's command of a special field of knowledge.
2 archaic of or relating to understanding.
▶ **n.** (in full **comprehensive school**) Brit. a secondary school catering to children of all abilities from a given area.
– DERIVATIVES **com·pre·hen·sive·ly adv.**, **com·pre·hen·sive·ness n.**
– ORIGIN early 17th cent.: from French *compréhensif, -ive*, from late Latin *comprehensivus*, from the verb *comprehendere* 'grasp mentally.'

com·press ▶ **v.** /kəm'pres/ [with obj.] flatten by pressure; squeeze; press: *the skirt can be folded and **compressed into** a small bag* | (as adj. **compressed**) *compressed gas.* ■ [no obj.] be squeezed or pressed together or into a smaller space: *the land is sinking as the soil compresses.* ■ squeeze or press (two things) together: *Violet compressed her lips together grimly.* ■ express in a shorter form; abridge: *in this chapter we **compress into** summary form the main findings.* ■ Computing alter the form of (data) to reduce the amount of storage necessary. ■ (as adj. **compressed**) chiefly Biology having a narrow shape as if flattened, esp. sideways: *most sea snakes have a compressed tail.*
▶ **n.** /'käm,pres/ a pad of absorbent material pressed onto part of the body to relieve inflammation or stop bleeding: *a cold compress.*
– DERIVATIVES **com·press·i·bil·i·ty** /kəm,presə'bilitē/ **n.**, **com·press·i·ble adj.**, **com·pres·sive** /-'presiv/ **adj.**
– ORIGIN late Middle English: from Old French *compresser* or late Latin *compressare*, frequentative of Latin *comprimere*, from *com-* 'together' + *premere* 'to press'; or directly from *compress-* 'pressed together,' from the verb *comprimere.*

com·pressed air ▶ **n.** air that has been compressed to a pressure higher than atmospheric pressure.

com·pres·sion /kəm'preSHən/ ▶ **n.** the action of compressing or being compressed. ■ the reduction in volume (causing an increase in pressure) of the fuel mixture in an internal combustion engine before ignition.
– DERIVATIVES **com·pres·sion·al** /-SHənl/ **adj.**
– ORIGIN late Middle English: via Old French from Latin *compressio(n-)*, from *comprimere* 'press together' (see COMPRESS).

com·pres·sion ra·tio ▶ **n.** the ratio of the maximum to minimum volume in the cylinder of an internal combustion engine.

com·pres·sive strength ▶ **n.** the resistance of a material to breaking under compression. Compare with TENSILE STRENGTH.

com·pres·sor /kəm'presər/ ▶ **n.** an instrument or device for compressing something. ■ a machine used to supply air or other gas at increased pressure, e.g., to power a gas turbine. ■ an electrical amplifier that reduces the dynamic range of a signal.

com·prise /kəm'prīz/ ▶ **v.** [with obj.] consist of; be made up of: *the country comprises twenty states.* ■ make up; constitute: *this single breed comprises 50 percent of the Swiss cattle population* | (**be comprised of**) *documents are comprised of words.*
– ORIGIN late Middle English: from French, 'comprised,' feminine past participle of *comprendre*, from Old French *comprehender* (see COMPREHEND).

> **USAGE** **1** **Comprise** primarily means 'consist of,' as in *the country **comprises** twenty states.* It can also mean 'constitute or make up a whole,' as in *this single breed **comprises** 50 percent of the Swiss cattle population.* When this sense is used in the passive (as in *the country **is comprised of** twenty states*), it is more or less synonymous with the first sense (*the country **comprises** twenty states*). This usage is part of standard English, but the construction **comprise of**, as in *the property **comprises of** bedroom, bathroom, and kitchen*, is regarded as incorrect.
> **2** On the differences between **comprise** and **include**, see usage at INCLUDE.

com·pro·mise /'kämprə,mīz/ ▶ **n.** an agreement or a settlement of a dispute that is reached by each side making concessions: *an ability to listen to two sides in a dispute, and devise a compromise acceptable to both | the secret of a happy marriage is compromise.* ■ a middle state between conflicting opinions or actions reached by mutual concession or modification: *a **compromise between** commercial appeal and historical interest.* ■ the acceptance of standards that are lower than is desirable: *sexism should be tackled without compromise.*
▶ **v.** **1** [no obj.] settle a dispute by mutual concession: *in the end we compromised and deferred the issue.* ■ [with obj.] archaic settle (a dispute) by mutual concession: *I should compromise the matter with my father.*
2 [with obj.] weaken (a reputation or principle) by accepting standards that are lower than is desirable: *commercial pressures could compromise safety.* ■ [no obj.] accept standards that are lower than is desirable: *we were not prepared to **compromise on** safety.* ■ bring into disrepute or danger by indiscreet, foolish, or reckless behavior: *situations in which his troops could be compromised.*
– DERIVATIVES **com·pro·mis·er n.**
– ORIGIN late Middle English (denoting mutual consent to arbitration): from Old French *compromis*, from late Latin *compromissum* 'a consent to arbitration,' neuter past participle of *compromittere*, from *com-* 'together' + *promittere* (see PROMISE).

com·pro·mis·ing /'kämprə,mīziNG/ ▶ **adj.** (of information or a situation) revealing an embarrassing or incriminating secret about someone: *to cover up compromising evidence of malpractice.*

compte ren·du /'kônt räN'dY, räN'd(y)o͞o/ ▶ **n.** (pl. **comptes rendus** pronunc. **same**) a formal report or review.
– ORIGIN early 19th cent.: French, literally 'account rendered.'

Comp·ton¹ /'kämptən/ an industrial city in southwestern California, just south of Los Angeles; pop. 93,851 (est. 2008).

Comp·ton², Arthur Holly (1892–1962), US physicist. He observed the Compton effect and thus demonstrated the dual particle and wave properties of electromagnetic radiation and matter, as predicted by quantum theory. Nobel Prize for Physics (1927), shared with C. T. R. Wilson.

Comp·ton ef·fect ▶ **n.** Physics an increase in wavelength of X-rays or gamma rays that occurs when they are scattered.
– ORIGIN early 20th cent.: named after A. H. *Compton* (see COMPTON²).

comp·trol·ler /kən'trōlər, ,käm(p)'trōlər, 'käm(p),trōlər/ ▶ **n.** a controller (used in the title of some financial officers).
– ORIGIN late 15th cent.: variant of CONTROLLER, by erroneous association with French *compte* 'calculation' or its source, late Latin *computus.*

com·pul·sion /kəm'pəlSHən/ ▶ **n.** **1** the action or state of forcing or being forced to do something; constraint: *the payment was made **under compulsion**.*
2 an irresistible urge to behave in a certain way, esp. against one's conscious wishes: *he felt a compulsion to babble on about what had happened.*
– ORIGIN late Middle English: via Old French from late Latin *compulsio(n-)*, from *compellere* 'to drive, force' (see COMPEL).

com·pul·sive /kəm'pəlsiv/ ▶ **adj.** **1** resulting from or relating to an irresistible urge, esp. one that is against one's conscious wishes: *compulsive eating.* ■ (of a person) acting as a result of such an urge: *a compulsive liar.*
2 irresistibly interesting or exciting; compelling: *this play is compulsive viewing.*
– DERIVATIVES **com·pul·sive·ly adv.**, **com·pul·sive·ness n.**
– ORIGIN late 16th cent. (in the sense 'compulsory'): from medieval Latin *compulsivus*, from *compuls-* 'driven, forced,' from the verb *compellere* (see COMPEL). Sense 1 (originally a term in psychology) dates from the early 20th cent.

com·pul·so·ry /kəm'pəlsərē/ ▶ **adj.** required by law or a rule; obligatory: *compulsory military service | it was compulsory to attend Mass.* ■ involving or exercising compulsion; coercive: *the abuse of compulsory powers.*
– DERIVATIVES **com·pul·so·ri·ly** /-sərəlē/ **adv.**, **com·pul·so·ri·ness n.**
– ORIGIN early 16th cent. (as a noun denoting a legal mandate that had to be obeyed): from medieval Latin *compulsorius*, from *compuls-* 'driven, forced,' from the verb *compellere* (see COMPEL).

C

com·punc·tion /kəm'pəNG(k)sHən/ ▶ **n.** [usu. with negative] a feeling of guilt or moral scruple that follows the doing of something bad: *spend the money without compunction.* ■ a pricking of the conscience: *he had no compunction about behaving blasphemously.*
– DERIVATIVES **com·punc·tion·less** adj., **com·punc·tious** /-sHəs/ adj., **com·punc·tious·ly** /-sHəslē/ adv.
– ORIGIN Middle English: from Old French *componction*, from ecclesiastical Latin *compunctio(n-)*, from Latin *compungere* 'prick sharply,' from *com-* (expressing intensive force) + *pungere* 'to prick.'

com·pur·ga·tion /,kämpər'gāsHən/ ▶ **n.** Law, historical acquittal from a charge or accusation, obtained by statements of innocence given by witnesses under oath.
– ORIGIN mid 17th cent.: from medieval Latin *compurgation-*, from Latin *compurgare*, from *com-* (expressing intensive force) + *purgare* 'purify' (from *purus* 'pure').

com·pur·ga·tor /'kämpər,gātər/ ▶ **n.** Law, historical a sworn witness to the innocence or good character of an accused person.
– ORIGIN mid 16th cent.: medieval Latin, from Latin *com-* 'together with' + *purgator*, from *purgare* 'purify' (see COMPURGATION).

com·pu·ta·tion /,kämpyōō'tāsHən/ ▶ **n.** the action of mathematical calculation: *months of computation carried out on 200 computers | statistical computations.* ■ the use of computers, esp. as a subject of research or study.
– ORIGIN late Middle English: from Latin *computatio(n-)*, from the verb *computare* (see COMPUTE).

com·pu·ta·tion·al /,kämpyōō'tāsHənl/ ▶ **adj.** of, relating to, or using computers: *the computational analysis of English | computational power.* ■ of or relating to the process of mathematical calculation.
– DERIVATIVES **com·pu·ta·tion·al·ly** /-sHənl-ē/ adv.

com·pu·ta·tion·al lin·guis·tics ▶ **plural n.** [treated as sing.] the branch of linguistics in which the techniques of computer science are applied to the analysis and synthesis of language and speech.

com·pute /kəm'pyōōt/ ▶ **v.** [with obj.] calculate or reckon (a figure or amount): *we can compute the exact increase | depreciation is computed by applying the straight-line method.* ■ [no obj.] make a calculation, esp. using a computer: *modern circuitry can compute faster than any chess player.* ■ [no obj., with negative] informal seem reasonable; make sense: *the idea just doesn't compute.* [from the phrase *does not compute*, once used as an error message in computing.]
– DERIVATIVES **com·put·a·bil·i·ty** /kəm,pyōōtə'bilitē/ n., **com·put·a·ble** adj., **com·put·a·bly** /-blē/ adv., **com·put·ist** /-'pyōōtist/ n.
– ORIGIN early 17th cent.: from French *computer* or Latin *computare*, from *com-* 'together' + *putare* 'to settle (an account).'

com·put·er /kəm'pyōōtər/ ▶ **n.** an electronic device for storing and processing data, typically in binary form, according to instructions given to it in a variable program. ■ a person who makes calculations, esp. with a calculating machine.

com·put·er an·i·ma·tion ▶ **n.** see ANIMATION.

com·put·er con·fer·enc·ing ▶ **n.** the use of computer and telecommunications technology to hold discussions between people operating computers in separate locations.

com·put·er dat·ing ▶ **n.** the use of computer databases to identify potentially compatible partners for people.

com·put·er-friend·ly ▶ **adj.** **1** suitable for use with computers; compatible with computers: *present the data in computer-friendly form.*
2 (of a person) well disposed toward computers: *a computer-friendly politician.*

com·put·er game ▶ **n.** a game played using a computer, typically a video game.

com·put·er graph·ics ▶ **plural n.** another term for GRAPHICS (sense 3).

com·put·er·ize /kəm'pyōōtə,rīz/ ▶ **v.** [with obj.] (often as adj. **computerized**) convert to a system that is operated or controlled by computer: *the advantages of computerized accounting.* ■ convert (information) to a form that is stored or processed by computer: *a computerized register of dogs.*
– DERIVATIVES **com·put·er·i·za·tion** /kəm,pyōōtərə'zāsHən/ n.

com·pu·ter·ized ax·i·al to·mog·ra·phy (abbr.: **CAT**) ▶ **n.** a form of tomography in which a computer controls the motion of the X-ray source and detectors, processes the data, and produces the image.

com·put·er-lit·er·ate ▶ **adj.** (of a person) having sufficient knowledge and skill to be able to use computers; familiar with the operation of computers.
– DERIVATIVES **com·put·er lit·er·a·cy** n.

com·put·er pro·gram·mer ▶ **n.** a person who writes programs for the operation of computers, esp. as an occupation.

com·put·er sci·ence ▶ **n.** the study of the principles and use of computers.

com·put·er vi·rus ▶ **n.** see VIRUS.

com·put·ing /kəm'pyōōtiNG/ ▶ **n.** the use or operation of computers: *developments in mathematics and computing | [as modifier] computing facilities.*

com·rade /'käm,rad, 'kämrəd/ ▶ **n.** a companion who shares one's activities or is a fellow member of an organization. ■ (also **comrade-in-arms**) a fellow soldier or serviceman. ■ a fellow socialist or communist (often as a form of address).
– DERIVATIVES **com·rade·ly** adj.
– ORIGIN mid 16th cent. (originally also *camerade*): from French *camerade, camarade* (originally feminine), from Spanish *camarada* 'roommate,' from Latin *camera* 'chamber.' Compare with CHUM[1].

com·rade·ship /'käm,rad,sHip, 'kämrəd,sHip/ ▶ **n.** the company and friendship of others with common aims: *his greatest joy came from comradeship with others in the team.*

Com·sat /'käm,sat/ ▶ **n.** trademark the Communications Satellite Corporation, a private corporation authorized by Congress to develop commercial communications satellite systems. ■ (**comsat**) informal a communications satellite.
– ORIGIN 1960s: blend.

Com·stock·er·y /'käm,stäkərē, 'kəm-/ ▶ **n.** excessive opposition to supposed immorality in the arts; prudery.
– ORIGIN named for Anthony Comstock (1844–1915), US author and reformer.

Com·stock Lode /'käm,stäk/ a historic gold and silver source in the Virginia Mountains of western Nevada, south of Reno, the basis of a boom that lasted from the 1850s through the late 19th century.

Comte /kônt/, Auguste (1798–1857), French philosopher; one of the founders of sociology. His positivist philosophy attempted to define the laws of social evolution and to found a genuine social science that could be used for social reconstruction.
– DERIVATIVES **Comt·ism** /'kôn,tizəm/ n.

con[1] /kän/ informal ▶ **v.** (**cons, conning, conned**) [with obj.] persuade (someone) to do or believe something, typically by use of a deception: *I conned him into giving me your home number | she was jailed for conning her aunt out of $500,000.*
▶ **n.** an instance of deceiving or tricking someone: *when depositors, realizing that the whole thing is a con, demand repayment | [as modifier] a con artist.*
– ORIGIN late 19th cent. (originally US): abbreviation of CONFIDENCE, as in *confidence trick.*

con[2] ▶ **n.** a disadvantage: *borrowers have to weigh up the pros and cons of each mortgage offer.*
– ORIGIN late 16th cent.: from Latin *contra* 'against.'

con[3] ▶ **n.** informal a convict.
– ORIGIN late 19th cent.: abbreviation.

con[4] variant spelling of CONN.

con[5] ▶ **v.** (**cons, conning, conned**) [with obj.] archaic study attentively or learn by heart (a piece of writing): *the girls conned their pages with a great show of industry.*
– ORIGIN Middle English *cunne, conne, con*, variants of CAN[1].

con[6] ▶ **n.** informal a convention, esp. one for science-fiction enthusiasts.
– ORIGIN 1940s: abbreviation.

con- ▶ **prefix** variant spelling of COM- assimilated before *c, d, f, g, j, n, q, s, t, v*, and sometimes before vowels (as in *concord, condescend, confide*, etc.).
– ORIGIN Latin variant of *com-*.

Co·na·kry /'kānəkrē/ the capital and chief port of Guinea, in the western part of the county, on the Atlantic coast; pop. 1,484,000 (est. 2007).

con a·mo·re /,kän ə'môrā, kōn/ ▶ **adv.** Music (esp. as a direction) with tenderness.
– ORIGIN Italian,'with love.'

Co·nan Doyle /'kōnən 'doil/ see DOYLE.

co·na·tion /kō'nāsHən/ ▶ **n.** Philosophy & Psychology the mental faculty of purpose, desire, or will to perform an action; volition.
– ORIGIN early 17th cent. (denoting an attempt or endeavor): from Latin *conatio(n-)*, from *conari* 'to try.'

con bri·o /kän 'brēō, kōn/ ▶ **adv.** Music (esp. as a direction) with vigor.
– ORIGIN Italian.

con·cat·e·nate /kən'katn,āt/ ▶ **v.** [with obj.] formal or technical link (things) together in a chain or series: *some words may be concatenated, such that certain sounds are omitted.*
– ORIGIN late 15th cent. (as an adjective): from late Latin *concatenat-* 'linked together,' from the verb *concatenare*, from *con-* 'together' + *catenare*, from *catena* 'chain.'

con·cat·e·na·tion /kən,katn'āsHən/ ▶ **n.** a series of interconnected things or events: *a singular concatenation of events unlikely to recur.* ■ the action of linking things together in a series.

con·cave /kän'kāv, 'kän,kāv/ ▶ **adj.** having an outline or surface that curves inward like the interior of a circle or sphere. Compare with CONVEX (sense 1).
– DERIVATIVES **con·cave·ly** adv.
– ORIGIN late Middle English: from Latin *concavus*, from *con-* 'together' + *cavus* 'hollow.'

con·cav·i·ty /kän'kavitē/ ▶ **n.** (pl. **concavities**) the state or quality of being concave. ■ a concave surface or thing.

con·ca·vo-con·cave /kän,kāvō,kän'kāv/ ▶ **adj.** another term for BICONCAVE.

con·ca·vo-con·vex /kän,kāvō,kän'veks/ ▶ **adj.** (of a lens) concave on one side and convex on the other and thickest at the periphery.

con·ceal /kən'sēl/ ▶ **v.** [with obj.] keep from sight; hide: *a line of sand dunes concealed the distant sea.* ■ keep (something) secret; prevent from being known or noticed: *love that they had to conceal from others.*
– DERIVATIVES **con·ceal·a·ble** adj.
– ORIGIN Middle English: from Old French *conceler*, from Latin *concelare*, from *con-* 'completely' + *celare* 'hide.'

con·cealed /kən'sēld/ ▶ **adj.** kept secret; hidden: *a concealed weapon | he spoke with barely concealed anger.*

con·ceal·er /kən'sēlər/ ▶ **n.** a flesh-toned cosmetic used to cover facial blemishes and dark circles under the eyes.

con·ceal·ment /kən'sēlmənt/ ▶ **n.** the action of hiding something or preventing it from being known: *the concealment of the body | the deliberate concealment of material facts.* ■ something that acts as a hiding place; cover: *he darted forward from the concealment of the bushes.*

con·cede /kən'sēd/ ▶ **v.** **1** [reporting verb] admit that something is true or valid after first denying or resisting it: [with clause] *I had to concede that I'd overreacted* | [with obj.] *that principle now seems to have been conceded.* ■ [with obj.] admit (defeat) in a contest: *he conceded defeat.* ■ [with obj.] admit defeat in (a contest): *ready to concede the gold medal.*
2 [with obj.] surrender or yield (something that one possesses): *to concede all the territory he'd won.* ■ grant (a right, privilege, or demand): *their rights to redress of grievances were conceded once more.* ■ (in sports) fail to prevent the scoring of (a goal or point) by an opponent: *the coach conceded three safeties rather than kick into the wind.* ■ allow (a lead or advantage) to slip: *he took an early lead that he never conceded.*
– DERIVATIVES **con·ced·er** n.
– ORIGIN late 15th cent.: from French *concéder* or Latin *concedere*, from *con-* 'completely' + *cedere* 'yield.'

con·ceit /kən'sēt/ ▶ **n.** **1** excessive pride in oneself: *he was puffed up with conceit.*
2 a fanciful expression in writing or speech; an elaborate metaphor: *the idea of the wind's singing is a prime romantic conceit.* ■ an artistic effect or device: *the director's brilliant conceit was to film this tale in black and white.* ■ a fanciful notion: *he is alarmed by the widespread conceit that he spent most of the 1980s drunk.*
– ORIGIN late Middle English (in the sense 'idea or notion,' also 'quaintly decorative article'): from CONCEIVE, on the pattern of pairs such as *deceive, deceit.*

con·ceit·ed /kən'sētid/ ▶ **adj.** excessively proud of oneself; vain.
– DERIVATIVES **con·ceit·ed·ly** adv., **con·ceit·ed·ness** n.

con·ceiv·a·ble /kən'sēvəbəl/ ▶ **adj.** capable of being imagined or grasped mentally: *a mass uprising was entirely conceivable | it was photographed from every conceivable angle.*
– DERIVATIVES **con·ceiv·a·bil·i·ty** /kən,sēvə'bilitē/ n.

con·ceiv·a·bly /kən'sēvəblē/ ▶ **adv.** [sentence adverb] it is conceivable or imaginable that: *it may conceivably cause liver disease.*

con·ceive /kən'sēv/ ▶ **v.** [with obj.] **1** become pregnant with (a child): *she was conceived when her father was 49.* ■ [no obj.] (of a woman) become pregnant: *five months ago Wendy conceived.*
2 form or devise (a plan or idea) in the mind: *the dam project was originally conceived in 1977 |* (as adj. **conceived**) *a brilliantly conceived and*

executed robbery. ■ form a mental representation of; imagine: *without society an individual cannot be conceived as having rights* | [no obj.] *we could not conceive of such things happening to us.* ■ become affected by (a feeling): *he conceived a passion for football.*
– ORIGIN Middle English: from Old French *concevoir*, from Latin *concipere*, from *com-* 'together' + *capere* 'take.'

con·cel·e·brate /kän'seləˌbrāt/ ▶ **v.** [with obj.] Christian Church officiate jointly at (a Mass): *to concelebrate a Mass with other priests.*
– DERIVATIVES **con·cel·e·brant** /-brənt/ **n.**, **con·cel·e·bra·tion** /känˌselə'brāsHən/ **n.**
– ORIGIN late 19th cent.: from Latin *concelebrat-* 'celebrated together,' from the verb *concelebrare*, from *con-* 'together' + *celebrare* (see CELEBRATE).

con·cen·ter /kən'sentər, kän-/ ▶ **v.** [with obj.] concentrate (something) in a small space or area. ■ [no obj.] come together or collect at a common center: *his thoughts concenter there monotonously.* ■ archaic bring or draw (two or more things) toward a common center.
– ORIGIN late 16th cent.: from French *concentrer*, from Latin *con-* 'together' + *centrum* 'center.'

con·cen·trate /'känsənˌtrāt/ ▶ **v. 1** [no obj.] focus one's attention or mental effort on a particular object or activity: *she couldn't concentrate on the movie.* ■ (**concentrate on/upon**) do or deal with (one particular thing) above all others: *Luke wants to concentrate on his film career.*
2 [with obj.] gather (people or things) together in numbers or in a mass: *wealth was concentrated in the hands of the governing elite.* ■ [no obj.] come together in this way: *troops were concentrating at the western front.* ■ increase the strength or proportion of (a substance or solution) by removing or reducing the water or any other diluting agent or by selective accumulation of atoms or molecules.
▶ **n.** a substance made by removing water or other diluting agent; a concentrated form of something, esp. food: *apple juice concentrate.*
– DERIVATIVES **con·cen·tra·tive** /-ˌtrātiv/ **adj.**, **con·cen·tra·tor** /-ˌtrātər/ **n.**
– ORIGIN mid 17th cent. (in the sense 'bring toward a center'): Latinized form of CONCENTER or from French *concentrer* 'to concentrate.' Sense 1 of the verb dates from the early 20th cent.

con·cen·trat·ed /'känsənˌtrātid/ ▶ **adj. 1** wholly directed to one thing; intense: *a concentrated campaign.*
2 (of a substance or solution) present in a high proportion relative to other substances; having had water or other diluting agent removed or reduced: *concentrated fruit juice.*
– DERIVATIVES **con·cen·trat·ed·ly adv.**

con·cen·tra·tion /ˌkänsən'trāsHən/ ▶ **n. 1** the action or power of focusing one's attention or mental effort: *frowning in concentration* | *the worker needs total concentration.* ■ (**concentration on/upon**) dealing with one particular thing above all others: *concentration on the needs of the young can mean that the elderly are forgotten.*
2 a close gathering of people or things: *the largest concentration of Canada geese on earth.* ■ the action of gathering together closely: *the concentration of power.*
3 the relative amount of a given substance contained within a solution or in a particular volume of space; the amount of solute per unit volume of solution: *the gas can collect in dangerous concentrations.* ■ the action of strengthening a solution by the removal of water or other diluting agent or by the selective accumulation of atoms or molecules.

con·cen·tra·tion camp ▶ **n.** a place where large numbers of people, esp. political prisoners or members of persecuted minorities, are deliberately imprisoned in a relatively small area with inadequate facilities, sometimes to provide forced labor or to await mass execution. The term is most strongly associated with the several hundred camps established by the Nazis in Germany and occupied Europe in 1933–45, among the most infamous being Dachau, Belsen, and Auschwitz.

con·cen·tric /kən'sentrik, kän-/ ▶ **adj.** of or denoting circles, arcs, or other shapes that share the same center, the larger often completely surrounding the smaller: *concentric circles indicate distances of 1 km, 2 km, and 3 km from the center.*
– DERIVATIVES **con·cen·tri·cal·ly** /-(ə)lē/ **adv.**, **con·cen·tric·i·ty** /ˌkänˌsen'trisitē/ **n.**

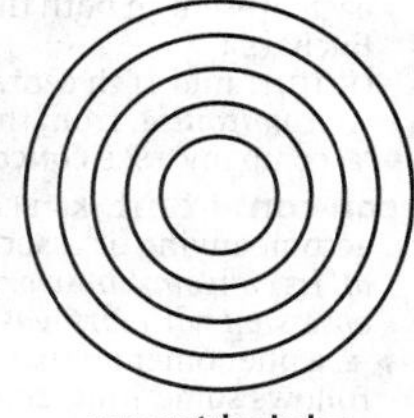
concentric circles

– ORIGIN late Middle English: from Old French *concentrique* or medieval Latin *concentricus*, from *con-* 'together' + *centrum* 'center.'

Con·cep·ción /ˌkänˌsepsē'ōn/ an industrial city in southern central Chile; pop. 220,000 (est. 2006).

con·cept /'känˌsept/ ▶ **n.** an abstract idea; a general notion: *structuralism is a difficult concept* | *the concept of justice.* ■ a plan or intention; a conception: *the center has kept firmly to its original concept.* ■ an idea or invention to help sell or publicize a commodity: *a new concept in corporate hospitality.* ■ Philosophy an idea or mental picture of a group or class of objects formed by combining all their aspects. ■ [as modifier] (of a car or other vehicle) produced as an experimental model to test the viability of new design features.
– ORIGIN mid 16th cent. (in the sense 'thought, frame of mind, imagination'): from Latin *conceptum* 'something conceived,' from *concept-* 'conceived,' from *concipere* (see CONCEIVE).

con·cept al·bum ▶ **n.** a rock album featuring a cycle of songs expressing a particular theme or idea.

con·cep·tion /kən'sepsHən/ ▶ **n. 1** the action of conceiving a child or of a child being conceived: *an unfertilized egg before conception* | *a rise in premarital conceptions.* ■ the forming or devising of a plan or idea: *the time between a product's conception and its launch.*
2 the way in which something is perceived or regarded: *our conception of how language relates to reality.* ■ a general notion; an abstract idea: *the conception of a balance of power.* ■ a plan or intention: *reconstructing Bach's original conceptions.* ■ understanding; ability to imagine: *he had no conception of politics.*
– DERIVATIVES **con·cep·tion·al** /-sHənl/ **adj.**
– ORIGIN Middle English: via Old French from Latin *conceptio(n-)*, from the verb *concipere* (see CONCEIVE).

con·cep·tu·al /kən'sepCHōōəl/ ▶ **adj.** of, relating to, or based on mental concepts: *philosophy deals with conceptual difficulties.*
– ORIGIN mid 17th cent.: from medieval Latin *conceptualis*, from Latin *concept-* 'conceived,' from the verb *concipere* (see CONCEPT).

con·cep·tu·al art (also **concept art**) ▶ **n.** art in which the idea presented by the artist is considered more important than the finished product, if there is one.

con·cep·tu·al·ism /kən'sepCHōōəˌlizəm/ ▶ **n.** Philosophy the theory that universals can be said to exist, but only as concepts in the mind.
– DERIVATIVES **con·cep·tu·al·ist n.**

con·cep·tu·al·ize /kən'sepCHōōəˌlīz/ ▶ **v.** [with obj.] form a concept or idea of (something): *we can more easily conceptualize speed in miles per hour.*
– DERIVATIVES **con·cep·tu·al·i·za·tion** /kənˌsepCHōōələ'zāsHən/ **n.**, **con·cep·tu·al·iz·er n.**

con·cep·tu·al·ly /kən'sepCHōōəlē/ ▶ **adv.** in terms of a concept or abstract idea: *a conceptually simple task* | *conceptually, this is a complex process.*

con·cep·tus /kən'septəs/ ▶ **n.** (pl. **conceptuses**) technical the embryo in the uterus, esp. during the early stages of pregnancy.
– ORIGIN mid 18th cent.: from Latin, literally 'conception, embryo.'

con·cern /kən'sərn/ ▶ **v.** [with obj.] **1** relate to; be about: *the story concerns a friend of mine* | (**be concerned with**) *this fable is concerned with forgiveness and redemption.* ■ be relevant or important to; affect or involve: *they should not pry into what does not concern them* | *many thanks to all concerned.* ■ (**be concerned with**) regard it as important or interesting to do something: *I was mainly concerned with making something that children could enjoy.* ■ (**be concerned in**) formal have a specific connection with or responsibility for: *the organs concerned in digestion and in blood-making.* ■ (**concern oneself with**) interest or involve oneself in: *we need not concern ourselves with the semantics of this language.*
2 worry (someone); make anxious: *the roof of the barn concerns me because eventually it will fall in* | *you must not concern yourself about me.*
▶ **n. 1** anxiety; worry: *such unsatisfactory work gives cause for concern.* ■ a cause of anxiety or worry: *the new techniques raise some safety concerns.*
2 a matter of interest or importance to someone: *oil reserves are the concern of the Energy Department* | *the survival of an endangered species is of concern to wildlife biologists.* ■ (**concerns**) affairs; issues: *public awareness of Aboriginal concerns.*
3 a business; a firm: *a small, debt-ridden concern.*
4 informal, dated a complicated or awkward object or structure.
– PHRASES **as** (or **so**) **far as —— is concerned** as regards the interests or case of ——: *the measures are irrelevant as far as inflation is concerned.* **have no concern with** formal have nothing to do with: *drama seemed to have no concern with "truth" at all.* **to whom it may concern** a formula placed at the beginning of a letter or document when the identity of the reader or readers is unknown.
– ORIGIN late Middle English: from French *concerner* or late Latin *concernere* (in medieval Latin 'be relevant to'), from *con-* (expressing intensive force) + *cernere* 'sift, discern.'

con·cerned /kən'sərnd/ ▶ **adj.** worried, troubled, or anxious: *the villagers are concerned about burglaries.*
– DERIVATIVES **con·cern·ed·ly** /-'sərnədlē/ **adv.**

con·cern·ing /kən'sərniNG/ ▶ **prep.** on the subject of or in connection with; about: *dreadful stories concerning a horrible beast.*

con·cern·ment /kən'sərnmənt/ ▶ **n.** archaic importance: *matters of great public concernment.* ■ a matter of interest or importance to someone; a concern: *a family or any absorbing concernment of that sort.*

con·cert ▶ **n.** /'känˌsərt, 'känsərt/ **1** a musical performance given in public, typically by several performers or of several separate compositions: *symphony concerts* | [as modifier] *a concert pianist.* ■ [as modifier] of, relating to, or denoting the performance of music written for opera, ballet, or theater on its own without the accompanying dramatic action: *the concert version of the fourth interlude from the opera.* See also CONCERT PERFORMANCE.
2 formal agreement, accordance, or harmony: *critics' inability to describe with any precision and concert the characteristics of literature.*
▶ **v.** /kən'sərt/ [with obj.] formal arrange (something) by mutual agreement or coordination: *they started meeting regularly to concert their tactics.*
– PHRASES **in concert 1** acting jointly: *he made his decision in concert with his son and son-in-law.* **2** (of music or a performer) giving a public performance; live: *they saw Pink Floyd in concert.*
– ORIGIN late 16th cent. (in the sense 'unite, cause to agree'): from French *concerter*, from Italian *concertare* 'harmonize.' The noun use, dating from the early 17th cent. (in the sense 'a combination of voices or sounds'), is from French *concert*, from Italian *concerto*, from *concertare*.

con·cer·tan·te /ˌkäsər'täntē, ˌkänCHər-, -ˌtā/ ▶ **adj. 1** denoting a piece of music containing one or more solo parts, typically of less prominence or weight than in a concerto. See also SINFONIA CONCERTANTE.
2 chiefly historical denoting prominent instrumental parts present throughout a piece of music, esp. in baroque and early classical compositions.
– ORIGIN Italian,'harmonizing,' from *concertare* 'harmonize.'

con·cert band ▶ **n.** a relatively large group of brass, woodwind, and percussion players that performs in a concert hall, as distinguished from a marching band.

con·cert·ed /kən'sərtəd/ ▶ **adj. 1** jointly arranged, planned, or carried out; coordinated: *determined to begin a concerted action against them.* ■ strenuously carried out; done with great effort: *it would take a concerted effort for a burglar to break into my home.*
2 (of music) arranged in several parts of equal importance: *concerted secular music for voices.*
– DERIVATIVES **con·cert·ed·ly adv.**

con·cert·go·er /'känsərtˌgōər/ ▶ **n.** a person who attends a concert, esp. one who does so regularly.

con·cert grand ▶ **n.** the largest size of grand piano, up to 12 feet (2.75 m) long, that produces enough sound to be used for concerts in large halls.

con·cert hall ▶ **n.** a large public building designed for the performance of concerts.

con·cer·ti·na /ˌkänsər'tēnə/ ▶ **n.** a small musical instrument, typically polygonal in form, played by stretching and squeezing between the hands, to work a central bellows that blows air over reeds, each note being sounded by a button. Compare with ACCORDION. ■ [as modifier] opening or closing in multiple folds: *concertina doors.*

concertina

▶ **v.** (**concertinas, concertinaing, concertinaed** /-'tēnəd/) [with obj.] extend, compress, or collapse

PRONUNCIATION KEY ə *ago, up*; ər *over, fur*; a *hat*; ā *ate*; ä *car*; e *let*; ē *see*; i *fit*; ī *by*; NG *sing*; ō *go*; ô *law, for*; oi *toy*; ŏŏ *good*; ōō *goo*; ou *out*; TH *thin*; TH *then*; ZH *vision*

in folds like those of a concertina: (as adj. **concertinaed**) *big rolls of concertinaed wire* | figurative *a request that the negotiations be concertinaed into a week-long session.*
– ORIGIN mid 19th cent.: from CONCERT + -INA.

con·cer·ti·no /ˌkänCHərˈtēnō/ ▶ n. (pl. **concertinos**)
1 a simple or short concerto.
2 a solo instrument or solo instruments playing with an orchestra.
– ORIGIN late 18th cent.: Italian, diminutive of *concerto* (see CONCERTO).

C

con·cert·ize /ˈkänsərˌtīz/ ▶ v. [no obj.] give a concert or concerts.

con·cert·mas·ter /ˈkänsərtˌmastər/ ▶ n. (fem. **concertmistress**) the leading first-violin player in some orchestras.

con·cer·to /kənˈCHertō/ ▶ n. (pl. **concertos** or **concerti** /-tē/) a musical composition for a solo instrument or instruments accompanied by an orchestra, esp. one conceived on a relatively large scale.
– ORIGIN early 18th cent.: Italian, from *concertare* 'harmonize.'

con·cer·to gros·so /ˈgrōsō, ˈgrôsō/ ▶ n. (pl. **concerti grossi** /ˈgrōsē, ˈgrôsē/) a musical composition for a group of solo instruments accompanied by an orchestra. The term is used mainly of baroque works.
– ORIGIN early 18th cent.: Italian, literally 'big concerto.'

con·cert o·ver·ture ▶ n. a piece of music in the style of an overture but intended for independent performance.

con·cert per·for·mance ▶ n. 1 a performance of a piece of music written for an opera, ballet, religious service, etc., at a concert without the accompanying dramatic action, dance, or liturgy.
2 a performance of a piece of music at a live concert.

con·cert pi·an·ist ▶ n. a classical pianist who regularly performs as a soloist in concert performances.

con·cert pitch ▶ n. Music a standard for the tuning of musical instruments, internationally agreed upon in 1960, in which the note A above middle C has a frequency of 440 Hz. ■ a state of readiness, efficiency, and keenness: *slightly unnerved by the contretemps, I was not at concert pitch.*

con·ces·sion /kənˈseSHən/ ▶ n. 1 a thing that is granted, esp. in response to demands; a thing conceded: *the strikers returned to work having won some concessions.* ■ the action of conceding, granting, or yielding something. ■ (**a concession to**) a gesture, esp. a token one, made in recognition of a demand or prevailing standard: *her only concession to fashion was her ornate silver ring.*
2 a preferential allowance or rate given by an organization: *tax concessions.*
3 the right to use land or other property for a specified purpose, granted by a government, company, or other controlling body: *new logging concessions.* ■ a commercial operation within the premises of a larger concern, typically selling refreshments: *operates the concessions at the stadium* | [as modifier] *public restrooms and concession stands.* ■ Canadian a piece of land into which surveyed land is divided, itself further divided into lots.
– ORIGIN late Middle English: from Latin *concessio(n-)*, from the verb *concedere* (see CONCEDE).

con·ces·sion·aire /kənˌseSHəˈne(ə)r/ (also **concessioner**) ▶ n. the holder of a concession or grant, esp. for the use of land or commercial premises.
– ORIGIN mid 19th cent.: from French *concessionnaire*, from Latin *concessio* (see CONCESSION).

con·ces·sion·al /kənˈseSHənl/ ▶ adj. [attrib.] (of a rate or allowance) constituting a concession: *concessional and commercial types of loans.*

con·ces·sion road (also **concession line**) ▶ n. Canadian a rural road separating concessions.

con·ces·sive /kənˈsesiv/ ▶ adj. 1 characterized by, or tending to concession: *we must look for a more concessive approach.*
2 Grammar (of a preposition or conjunction) introducing a phrase or clause denoting a circumstance that might be expected to preclude the action of the main clause, but does not (e.g., *in spite of*, *although*). ■ (of a phrase or clause) introduced by a concessive preposition or conjunction.
– ORIGIN early 18th cent. (sense 2): from late Latin *concessivus*, from *concess-* 'withdrawn, yielded' (see CONCESSION).

conch /käNGk, känCH, kôNGk/ ▶ n. (pl. **conchs** /käNGks, kôNGks/ or **conches** /ˈkänCHiz/) 1 (also **conch shell**) a tropical marine mollusk with a spiral shell that may bear long projections and have a flared lip. ● *Strombus* and other genera, family Strombidae, class Gastropoda. ■ a shell of this kind blown like a trumpet to produce a musical note, often depicted as played by Tritons and other mythological figures.
2 Architecture the roof of a semicircular apse, shaped like half a dome.
3 another term for CONCHA.
– ORIGIN late Middle English: from Latin *concha* 'shellfish, shell,' from Greek *konkhē* 'mussel, cockle, or shell-like cavity.'

con·cha /ˈkäNGkə/ ▶ n. (pl. **conchae** /-kē, -ˌkī/)
1 Anatomy & Zoology a body part that resembles a spiral shell, in particular: ■ the depression in the external ear leading to its central opening. ■ (also **nasal concha**) any of several thin, scroll-like (turbinate) bones in the sides of the nasal cavity.
2 a round or oval hammered metal disk used as decoration on jewelry, belts, harnesses, etc.
– ORIGIN late 16th cent.: from Latin (see CONCH).

con·chie /ˈkänCHē/ ▶ n. (pl. **conchies**) Brit. informal or derogatory a conscientious objector.
– ORIGIN World War I: abbreviation.

con·chif·er·ous /käNGˈkifərəs/ ▶ adj. producing, bearing, or characterized by the presence of shells.

con·chi·o·lin /käNGˈkīəlin/ ▶ n. Zoology a tough, insoluble protein secreted by mollusks, forming the organic matrix of the shell within which calcium carbonate is deposited.
– ORIGIN late 19th cent.: from Latin *concha* 'shell' + the diminutive suffix *-iola* + -IN¹.

conch·o belt /ˈkänCHō/ ▶ n. a belt decorated with conchas or representations of them.

con·choid /ˈkäNGˌkoid/ ▶ n. Mathematics a plane quartic curve consisting of two separate branches either side of and asymptotic to a central straight line (the asymptote), such that if a line is drawn from a fixed point (the pole) to intersect both branches, the part of the line falling between the two branches is of constant length and is exactly bisected by the asymptote. ● Such curves are represented by the general equation $(x - a)^2(x^2 + y^2) = b^2x^2$, where a is the distance between the pole and the asymptote, and b is the constant length. The branch on the same side of the asymptote as the pole typically has a cusp or loop.
– ORIGIN early 18th cent.: from CONCH + -OID.

con·choi·dal /käNGˈkoidl/ ▶ adj. chiefly Mineralogy denoting a type of fracture in a solid (such as flint or quartz) that results in a smooth rounded surface resembling the shape of a scallop shell.

con·chol·o·gy /käNGˈkäləjē/ ▶ n. the scientific study or collection of mollusk shells. Compare with MALACOLOGY.
– DERIVATIVES **con·cho·log·i·cal** /ˌkäNGkəˈläjikəl/ adj., **con·chol·o·gist** /-jist/ n.
– ORIGIN late 18th cent.: from Greek *konkhē* 'shell' + -LOGY.

con·cierge /kônˈsyerZH, ˌkänsēˈerZH/ ▶ n. 1 (esp. in France) a caretaker of an apartment complex or a small hotel, typically one living on the premises.
2 a hotel employee whose job is to assist guests by arranging tours, making theater and restaurant reservations, etc.
– ORIGIN mid 16th cent. (denoting the warden of a house, castle, prison, or royal palace): French, probably based on Latin *conservus* 'fellow slave.'

con·cil·i·ar /kənˈsilēər/ ▶ adj. of, relating to, or proceeding from a council, esp. an ecclesiastical one: *conciliar decrees.*
– ORIGIN late 17th cent.: from medieval Latin *consiliarius* 'counselor,' from Latin *concilium* (see COUNCIL).

con·cil·i·ate /kənˈsilēˌāt/ ▶ v. [with obj.] 1 stop (someone) from being angry or discontented; placate; pacify: *concessions were made to conciliate the peasantry.* ■ [no obj.] act as a mediator: *he sought to conciliate in the dispute.* ■ formal reconcile; make compatible: *all complaints about charges will be conciliated if possible.*
2 archaic gain (esteem or goodwill): *the arts which conciliate popularity.*
– DERIVATIVES **con·cil·i·a·tive** /-ˈsilēətiv, -ēˌātiv/ adj.
– ORIGIN mid 16th cent. (sense 2): from Latin *conciliat-* 'combined, gained,' from the verb *conciliare*, from *concilium* (see COUNCIL).

con·cil·i·a·tion /kənˌsilēˈāSHən/ ▶ n. the action of stopping someone from being angry; placation: *he held his hands up in a gesture of conciliation.* ■ the action of mediating between two disputing people or groups: *many disputes are settled through conciliation by the official body.*

con·cil·i·a·tor /kənˈsilēˌātər/ ▶ n. a person who acts as a mediator between two disputing people or groups: *he was seen as a conciliator, who would heal divisions in the party.*

con·cil·i·a·to·ry /kənˈsilēəˌtôrē/ ▶ adj. intended or likely to placate or pacify: *a conciliatory approach.*
– DERIVATIVES **con·cil·i·a·to·ri·ness** n.

con·cin·ni·ty /kənˈsinitē/ ▶ n. rare the skillful and harmonious arrangement or fitting together of the different parts of something. ■ studied elegance of literary or artistic style.
– ORIGIN mid 16th cent.: from Latin *concinnitas*, from *concinnus* 'skillfully put together.'

con·cise /kənˈsīs/ ▶ adj. giving a lot of information clearly and in a few words; brief but comprehensive: *a concise account of the country's history.*
– DERIVATIVES **con·cise·ly** adv., **con·cise·ness** n., **con·ci·sion** /-ˈsiZHən/ n.
– ORIGIN late 16th cent.: from French *concis* or Latin *concisus*, past participle of *concidere* 'cut up, cut down,' from *con-* 'completely' + *caedere* 'to cut.'

con·clave /ˈkänˌklāv/ ▶ n. a private meeting. ■ (in the Roman Catholic Church) the assembly of cardinals for the election of a pope. ■ the meeting place for such an assembly.
– ORIGIN late Middle English (denoting a private room): via French from Latin *conclave* 'lockable room,' from *con-* 'with' + *clavis* 'key.'

con·clude /kənˈklo͞od/ ▶ v. 1 [with obj.] bring (something) to an end: *they conclude their study with these words* | [no obj.] *we concluded by singing carols.* ■ [no obj.] come to an end: *the talk concluded with slides.* ■ formally and finally settle or arrange (a treaty or agreement): *an attempt to conclude a ceasefire.*
2 arrive at a judgment or opinion by reasoning: *the doctors **concluded that** Esther had suffered a stroke* | *what do you conclude from all this?* ■ say in conclusion: *"It's a wicked old world," she concluded.* ■ [with infinitive] dated decide to do something: *I concluded to go without his knowledge.*
– ORIGIN Middle English (in the sense 'convince'): from Latin *concludere*, from *con-* 'completely' + *claudere* 'to shut.'

con·clu·sion /kənˈklo͞oZHən/ ▶ n. 1 the end or finish of an event or process: *the conclusion of World War Two.* ■ the summing-up of an argument or text. ■ the settling or arrangement of a treaty or agreement: *the conclusion of a free-trade accord.*
2 a judgment or decision reached by reasoning: *each research group came to a similar conclusion.* ■ Logic a proposition that is reached from given premises.
– PHRASES **in conclusion** lastly; to sum up: *in conclusion it is clear that the market is maturing.* **jump** (or **leap**) **to conclusions** make a hasty judgment before learning or considering all the facts.
– ORIGIN late Middle English: from Latin *conclusio(n-)*, from the verb *concludere* (see CONCLUDE).

con·clu·sive /kənˈklo͞osiv, -ziv/ ▶ adj. (of evidence or argument) serving to prove a case; decisive or convincing: *conclusive evidence* | *the findings were by no means conclusive.* ■ (of a victory) achieved easily or by a large margin.
– DERIVATIVES **con·clu·sive·ly** adv., **con·clu·sive·ness** n.
– ORIGIN late 16th cent. (in the sense 'summing up, concluding'): from late Latin *conclusivus*, from Latin *conclus-* 'closed up,' from the verb *concludere* (see CONCLUSION).

con·coct /kənˈkäkt/ ▶ v. [with obj.] make (a dish or meal) by combining various ingredients: *they concoct relish from corn that is so naturally sweet no extra sugar is needed.* ■ create or devise (said esp. of a story or plan): *they concocted a preposterous but entertaining story.*
– DERIVATIVES **con·coct·er** n.
– ORIGIN mid 16th cent.: from Latin *concoct-*, literally 'cooked together,' from *concoquere*. The original sense was 'refine or purify metals or minerals by heating,' later 'cook.'

con·coc·tion /kənˈkäkSHən/ ▶ n. a mixture of various ingredients or elements: *a concoction of gables, shingles, stained glass, and towers inspired by English medieval houses.* ■ an elaborate story, esp. a fabrication: *her story is an improbable concoction.*

con·com·i·tance /kənˈkämitəns/ ▶ n. (also **concomitancy** /-tənsē/) the fact of existing or occurring together with something else. ■ Theology the doctrine that the body and blood of Christ are each present in both the bread and the wine of the Eucharist.
– ORIGIN mid 16th cent.: from medieval Latin *concomitantia*, from the verb *concomitari* 'accompany' (see CONCOMITANT).

con·com·i·tant /kənˈkämitənt/ formal ▶ adj. naturally accompanying or associated: *she loved travel, with all its concomitant worries* | ***concomitant with** his obsession with dirt was a desire for order.*
▶ n. a phenomenon that naturally accompanies or follows something: *some of us look on pain and illness as concomitants of the stresses of living.*

– DERIVATIVES **con·com·i·tant·ly** adv.
– ORIGIN early 17th cent.: from late Latin *concomitant-* 'accompanying,' from *concomitari*, from *con-* 'together with' + *comitari*, from Latin *comes* 'companion.'

Con·cord¹ /ˈkäNGkərd, -ˌkôrd/ **1** a city in north central California, northeast of Oakland; pop. 121,160 (est. 2008).
2 a town in northeastern Massachusetts; pop. 17,450 (est. 2008). Battles here and at Lexington in April 1775 marked the start of the American Revolution.
3 the capital of New Hampshire, in the southern part of the state, on the Merrimack River; pop. 42,255 (est. 2008).
4 an industrial city in south central North Carolina, a textile center; pop. 66,311 (est. 2008).

Con·cord² ▶ **n.** a variety of dessert grape developed at Concord, Massachusetts.

con·cord /ˈkäNG,kôrd, ˈkän-/ ▶ **n. 1** formal agreement or harmony between people or groups: *a pact of peace and concord.* ■ a treaty.
2 Grammar agreement between words in gender, number, case, person, or any other grammatical category that affects the forms of the words.
3 Music a chord that is pleasing or satisfactory in itself.
– ORIGIN Middle English: from Old French *concorde*, from Latin *concordia*, from *concors* 'of one mind,' from *con-* 'together' + *cor, cord-* 'heart.'

con·cord·ance /kənˈkôrdns/ ▶ **n. 1** an alphabetical list of the words (esp. the important ones) present in a text, usually with citations of the passages concerned: *a concordance to the Bible.*
2 formal agreement: *the concordance between the teams' research results.* ■ Medicine the inheritance by two related individuals (esp. twins) of the same genetic characteristic, such as susceptibility to a disease.
▶ **v.** [with obj.] (often as adj. **concordanced**) make a concordance of: *the value of concordanced information.*
– ORIGIN late Middle English: from Old French, from medieval Latin *concordantia*, from *concordant-* 'being of one mind' (see CONCORDANT).

con·cord·ant /kənˈkôrdnt/ ▶ **adj.** in agreement; consistent: *the answers were roughly concordant.* ■ Geology corresponding in direction with the planes of adjacent or underlying strata. ■ Medicine (of twins) inheriting the same genetic characteristic, such as susceptibility to a disease. ■ Music in harmony.
– DERIVATIVES **con·cord·ant·ly** adv.
– ORIGIN late 15th cent.: via Old French from Latin *concordant-* 'being of one mind,' from the verb *concordare* (see CONCORD).

con·cor·dat /kənˈkôr,dat/ ▶ **n.** an agreement or treaty, esp. one between the Vatican and a secular government relating to matters of mutual interest.
– ORIGIN early 17th cent.: from French, or from Latin *concordatum* 'something agreed upon,' neuter past participle of *concordare* 'be of one mind' (see CONCORD).

Con·corde /ˈkäNG,kôrd, ˈkän-/ a supersonic airliner able to cruise at twice the speed of sound. Produced through Anglo-French cooperation, it made its maiden flight in 1969 and its last in 2003.

Con·cord grape ▶ **n.** a cultivated variety of fox grape, used to make wine, juice, and jellies.

Con·cor·di·a /känˈkôrdēə/ a port city in northeastern Argentina, in a farming region of Entre Ríos province, on the Uruguay River and the border with Uruguay; pop. 144,900 (est. 2005).

con·cours /kôNˈko͝or/ (also **concours d'élégance** /dālāˈgäNs/) ▶ **n.** (pl. **same**) an exhibition or contest, esp. a parade of vintage or classic motor vehicles in which prizes are awarded for those in the best original condition.
– ORIGIN mid 20th cent.: French, literally 'contest (of elegance).'

con·course /ˈkän,kôrs, ˈkäNG-/ ▶ **n. 1** a large open area inside or in front of a public building, as in an airport or train station: *the domestic arrivals concourse.*
2 formal a crowd or assembly of people: *a vast concourse of learned men.* ■ the action of coming together or meeting: *the attracted concourse of the beauty and wealth of modern civilization.* ■ another term for CONCOURS.
– ORIGIN late Middle English (sense 2): from Old French *concours*, from Latin *concursus*, from *concurs-* 'run together, met,' from the verb *concurrere* (see CONCUR). Sense 1 (originally US) dates from the mid 19th cent.

con·cres·cence /kənˈkresəns/ ▶ **n.** Biology the coalescence or growing together of parts originally separate.
– DERIVATIVES **con·cres·cent** /-ˈkresənt/ **adj.**
– ORIGIN early 17th cent. (in the senses 'growth by assimilation' and 'a concretion'): from CON- 'together' + *-crescence*, on the pattern of words such as *excrescence*. The current sense dates from the late 19th cent.

con·crete ▶ **adj.** /känˈkrēt, ˈkän,krēt, kənˈkrēt/ existing in a material or physical form; real or solid; not abstract: *concrete objects like stones | it exists as a physically concrete form.* ■ specific; definite: *I haven't got any concrete proof.* ■ (of a noun) denoting a material object as opposed to an abstract quality, state, or action.
▶ **n.** /ˈkän,krēt, känˈkrēt/ a heavy, rough building material made from a mixture of broken stone or gravel, sand, cement, and water, that can be spread or poured into molds and that forms a stonelike mass on hardening: *slabs of concrete* | [as modifier] *the concrete sidewalk.*
▶ **v.** /ˈkän,krēt, känˈkrēt/ [with obj.] **1** cover (an area) with concrete: *the precious English countryside may soon be concreted over.* ■ [with obj.] fix in position with concrete: *the post is concreted into the ground.*
2 archaic form (something) into a mass; solidify: *the juices of the plants are concreted upon the surface.* ■ make real or concrete instead of abstract: *concreting God into actual form.*
– PHRASES **be set in concrete** (of a policy or idea) be fixed and unalterable: *I do not regard the Constitution as set in concrete.*
– DERIVATIVES **con·crete·ly** adv., **con·crete·ness** n.
– ORIGIN late Middle English (in the sense 'formed by cohesion, solidified'): from French *concret* or Latin *concretus*, past participle of *concrescere* 'grow together.' Early use was also as a grammatical term designating a quality belonging to a substance (usually expressed by an adjective such as *white* in *white paper*) as opposed to the quality itself (expressed by an abstract noun such as *whiteness*); later *concrete* came to be used to refer to nouns embodying attributes (e.g., *fool, hero*), as opposed to the attributes themselves (e.g., *foolishness, heroism*), and this is the basis of the modern use as the opposite of 'abstract' The noun sense 'building material' dates from the mid 19th cent.

con·crete jun·gle ▶ **n.** a city or area of a city that has a high density of large, unattractive, modern buildings and that is perceived as an unpleasant living environment.

con·crete mix·er ▶ **n.** a cement mixer.

con·crete mu·sic ▶ **n.** another term for MUSIQUE CONCRÈTE.

con·crete po·et·ry ▶ **n.** poetry in which the meaning or effect is conveyed partly or wholly by visual means, using patterns of words or letters and other typographical devices.

con·crete u·ni·ver·sal ▶ **n.** (in idealist philosophy) an abstraction that is manifest in a developing or organized set of instances, so having the qualities of both the universal and the particular.

con·cre·tion /kənˈkrēSHən, kän-/ ▶ **n.** a hard solid mass formed by the local accumulation of matter, esp. within the body or within a mass of sediment: *a mass of small concretions, each built up layer upon layer around some small nucleus.* ■ the formation of such a mass.
– DERIVATIVES **con·cre·tion·ar·y** /-SHə,nerē/ **adj.**
– ORIGIN mid 16th cent.: from Latin *concretio(n-)*, from *concrescere* 'grow together.'

con·cret·ism /känˈkrē,tizəm, ˈkänkrē-/ ▶ **n.** the theory or practice of concrete poetry, in which the visual arrangement of words in patterns or forms on the page takes precedence over the semantic or phonetic elements involved.

con·cre·tize /ˈkänkrə,tīz, känˈkrē,tīz/ ▶ **v.** [with obj.] make (an idea or concept) real; give specific or definite form to: *the theme park is an attempt to concretize our fantasies.*
– DERIVATIVES **con·cret·i·za·tion** /,kän,krētəˈzāSHən, ,käNGkrətə-/ **n.**

con·cu·bi·nage /kənˈkyo͞obənij, kän-/ ▶ **n.** chiefly historical the practice of keeping a concubine. ■ the state of being a concubine.
– ORIGIN late Middle English: from French, from Old French *concubine* (see CONCUBINE).

con·cu·bine /ˈkäNGkyo͞o,bīn/ ▶ **n.** chiefly historical (in polygamous societies) a woman who lives with a man but has lower status than his wife or wives. ■ archaic a mistress.
– DERIVATIVES **con·cu·bi·nar·y** /kənˈkyo͞obə,nerē, kän-/ **adj.**
– ORIGIN Middle English: from Old French, from Latin *concubina*, from *con-* 'with' + *cubare* 'to lie.'

con·cu·pis·cence /känˈkyo͞opisəns, kən-/ ▶ **n.** formal strong sexual desire; lust.
– ORIGIN Middle English: via Old French from late Latin *concupiscentia*, from Latin *concupiscent-* 'beginning to desire,' from the verb *concupiscere*, from *con-* (expressing intensive force) + *cupere* 'to desire.'

con·cu·pis·cent /känˈkyo͞opisənt, kən-/ ▶ **adj.** formal filled with sexual desire; lustful: *concupiscent dreams.*

con·cur /kənˈkər/ ▶ **v.** (**concurs, concurring, concurred**) [no obj.] **1** be of the same opinion; agree: *the authors concurred with the majority | they concurred in the creation of the disciplinary procedures | "That's right," the chairman concurred.* ■ (**concur with**) agree with (a decision, opinion, or finding): *we strongly concur with this recommendation.*
2 happen or occur at the same time; coincide: *in tests, cytogenetic determination has been found to concur with enzymatic determination.*
– ORIGIN late Middle English (also in the senses 'collide' and 'act in combination'): from Latin *concurrere* 'run together, assemble in crowds,' from *con-* 'together with' + *currere* 'to run.'

con·cur·rent /kənˈkərənt, -ˈkə-rənt/ ▶ **adj.** existing, happening, or done at the same time: *there are three concurrent art fairs around the city.* ■ (of two or more prison sentences) to be served at the same time. ■ Mathematics (of three or more lines) meeting at or tending toward one point.
– DERIVATIVES **con·cur·rence** /-ˈkərəns/ **n.**, **con·cur·ren·cy** /-ˈkərənsē/ **n.**, **con·cur·rent·ly** **adv.**
– ORIGIN late Middle English: from Latin *concurrent-* 'running together, meeting,' from the verb *concurrere* (see CONCUR).

con·cur·rent res·o·lu·tion ▶ **n.** a resolution adopted by both houses of a legislative assembly that does not require the signature of the chief executive and that does not have the force of law.

con·cuss /kənˈkəs/ ▶ **v.** [with obj.] (usu. as adj. **concussed**) hit the head of (a person or animal), causing temporary unconsciousness or confusion: *she was shaken, slightly concussed, and in no state to carry on.*
– DERIVATIVES **con·cus·sive** /-ˈkəsiv/ **adj.**
– ORIGIN late 16th cent. (in the sense 'shake violently'): from Latin *concuss-* 'dashed together, violently shaken,' from the verb *concutere*, from *con-* 'together' + *quatere* 'shake.'

con·cus·sion /kənˈkəSHən/ ▶ **n. 1** temporary unconsciousness caused by a blow to the head. The term is also used loosely of the aftereffects such as confusion or temporary incapacity.
2 a violent shock as from a heavy blow: *the ground shuddered with the concussion of the blast.*
– ORIGIN late Middle English: from Latin *concussio(n-)*, from the verb *concutere* 'dash together, shake' (see CONCUSS).

con·demn /kənˈdem/ ▶ **v.** [with obj.] **1** express complete disapproval of, typically in public; censure: *fair-minded people declined to condemn her on mere suspicion.*
2 sentence (someone) to a particular punishment, esp. death: *the rebels had been condemned to death* | (as adj. **condemned**) *the condemned men.* ■ officially declare (something, esp. a building) to be unfit for use: *the pool has been condemned as a health hazard.* ■ prove or show the guilt of: *she could see in his eyes that her stumble had condemned her.* ■ (of circumstances) force (someone) to endure something unpleasant or undesirable: *the physical ailments that condemned him to a lonely childhood.*
– DERIVATIVES **con·dem·na·ble** /-ˈdem(n)əbəl/ **adj.**
– ORIGIN Middle English (sense 2): from Old French *condemner*, from Latin *condemnare*, from *con-* (expressing intensive force) + *damnare* 'inflict loss on' (see DAMN).

con·dem·na·tion /,kändemˈnāSHən, -dəm-/ ▶ **n.** **1** the expression of very strong disapproval; censure: *there was strong international condemnation of the attack.*
2 the action of condemning someone to a punishment; sentencing.

con·dem·na·to·ry /kənˈdemnə,tôrē/ ▶ **adj.** expressing strong disapproval; censorious: *condemnatory statements.*

con·den·sate /ˈkändən,sāt, ˈkän,den-, kənˈden-/ ▶ **n.** liquid formed by condensation. ■ Chemistry a compound produced by a condensation reaction.

con·den·sa·tion /,kän,denˈsāSHən, -dən-/ ▶ **n.** **1** water that collects as droplets on a cold surface when humid air is in contact with it.
2 the conversion of a vapor or gas to a liquid. ■ (also **condensation reaction**) Chemistry a reaction in which two molecules combine to form a larger molecule, producing a small molecule such as H_2O as a byproduct. ■ Psychology the fusion of two or more

images, ideas, or symbolic meanings into a single composite or new image, as a primary process in unconscious thought exemplified in dreams.
3 a concise version of something, esp. a text: *a readable condensation of the recent literature.*
– ORIGIN early 17th cent.: from late Latin *condensatio(n-)*, from *condensare* 'press close together' (see CONDENSE).

C

con·dense /kən'dens/ ▶ v. **1** [with obj.] make (something) denser or more concentrated: *the limestones of the Jurassic age are condensed into a mere 11 feet.* ■ express (a piece of writing or speech) in fewer words; make concise: *he **condensed** the three plays **into** a three-hour drama.*
2 change or cause to change from a gas or vapor to a liquid: [no obj.] *the moisture vapor in the air **condenses into** droplets of water* | [with obj.] *the cold air was condensing his breath.*
– DERIVATIVES **con·den·sa·ble** adj.
– ORIGIN late Middle English: from Old French *condenser* or Latin *condensare*, from *condensus* 'very thick,' from *con-* 'completely' + *densus* 'dense.'

con·densed /kən'denst/ ▶ adj. made denser or more concise; compressed or concentrated: *a condensed version of the report.* ■ (of a liquid) concentrated by the removal of water: *condensed soup.*

con·densed milk ▶ n. canned milk that has been thickened by evaporation and sweetened.

con·densed tan·nin ▶ n. any of various tannins with antioxidant properties occurring naturally in plants, comprising polymers of flavonoids linked by a carbon-to-carbon bond.

con·dens·er /kən'densər/ ▶ n. **1** an apparatus or container for condensing vapor.
2 a lens or system of lenses for collecting and directing light.
3 another term for CAPACITOR.

con·de·scend /ˌkändə'send/ ▶ v. [no obj.] show feelings of superiority; be patronizing: *take care not to **condescend to** your reader.* ■ do something in a haughty way, as though it is below one's dignity or level of importance: *we'll be waiting for twenty minutes before she condescends to appear.*
– DERIVATIVES **con·de·scend·ence** /-'sendəns/ n. (rare).
– ORIGIN Middle English (in the sense 'give way, defer'): from Old French *condescendre*, from ecclesiastical Latin *condescendere*, from *con-* 'together' + *descendere* 'descend.'

con·de·scend·ing /ˌkändə'sendiNG/ ▶ adj. having or showing a feeling of patronizing superiority: *she thought the teachers were arrogant and condescending* | *a condescending smile.*
– DERIVATIVES **con·de·scend·ing·ly** adv.

con·de·scen·sion /ˌkändə'senCHən/ ▶ n. an attitude of patronizing superiority; disdain: *a tone of condescension* | *I'm treated with condescension.*

con·dign /kən'dīn/ ▶ adj. formal (of punishment or retribution) appropriate to the crime or wrongdoing; fitting and deserved.
– DERIVATIVES **con·dign·ly** adv.
– ORIGIN late Middle English (in the general sense 'worthy, appropriate'): from Old French *condigne*, from Latin *condignus*, from *con-* 'altogether' + *dignus* 'worthy.'

con·di·ment /'kändəmənt/ ▶ n. a substance such as salt or ketchup that is used to add flavor to food.
– ORIGIN late Middle English: from Latin *condimentum*, from *condire* 'to pickle.'

con·di·tion /kən'disHən/ ▶ n. **1** the state of something, esp. with regard to its appearance, quality, or working order: *the wiring is in good condition* | [in sing.] *the bridge is in an extremely dangerous condition.* ■ a person's or animal's state of health or physical fitness: *he is in fairly good condition considering what he has has been through* | [in sing.] *she was in a serious condition.* ■ an illness or other medical problem: *a heart condition.* ■ [in sing.] a particular state of existence: *a condition of misery.* ■ archaic social position or rank: *those of humbler condition.*
2 (**conditions**) the circumstances affecting the way in which people live or work, esp. with regard to their safety or well-being: *harsh working and living conditions.* ■ the factors or prevailing situation influencing the performance or the outcome of a process: *present market conditions.* ■ the prevailing state of the weather, ground, sea, or atmosphere at a particular time, esp. as it affects a sporting event: *the appalling conditions determined the style of play.*
3 a state of affairs that must exist or be brought about before something else is possible or permitted: *for a member to borrow money, three conditions have to be met* | *all personnel should comply with this policy **as a condition of** employment* | *I'll accept your offer **on one condition.***
▶ v. [with obj.] **1** have a significant influence on or determine (the manner or outcome of something): *national choices are conditioned by the international political economy.* ■ train or accustom (someone or something) to behave in a certain way or to accept certain circumstances: *we have all been conditioned to the conventional format of TV* | *the child is conditioned to dislike food* | (as noun **conditioning**) *the program examines aspects of social conditioning.*
2 bring (something) into the desired state for use: *a product for conditioning leather.* ■ (often as adj. **conditioned**) make (a person or animal) fit and healthy: *he was six feet two of perfectly conditioned muscle and bone.* ■ apply something to (the skin or hair) to give it a healthy or attractive look or feel: *I condition my hair regularly.* ■ (often as adj. **conditioned**) bring (beer or stout) to maturation after fermentation while the yeast is still present: *cask-conditioned real ales.* ■ [no obj.] (of a beer or stout) undergo such a process: *brews that are allowed to condition in the bottle.*
3 set prior requirements on (something) before it can occur or be done: *Congressmen have sought to limit and condition military and economic aid.*
– PHRASES **in** (or **out of**) **condition** in a fit (or unfit) physical state. **in no condition to do something** certainly not fit or well enough to do something: *you're in no condition to tackle the stairs.* **on condition that** with the stipulation that: *he proposed deep cuts in offensive forces, on condition that an agreement be reached.*
– ORIGIN Middle English: from Old French *condicion* (noun), *condicionner* (verb), from Latin *condicio(n-)* 'agreement,' from *condicere* 'agree upon,' from *con-* 'with' + *dicere* 'say.'

con·di·tion·al /kən'disHənl/ ▶ adj. **1** subject to one or more conditions or requirements being met; made or granted on certain terms: *Western aid was only granted conditional on further reform* | *the consortium has made a conditional offer.*
2 Grammar (of a clause, phrase, conjunction, or verb form) expressing a condition.
▶ n. **1** Grammar & Philosophy a conditional clause or conjunction. ■ a statement or sentence containing a conditional clause.
2 Grammar the conditional mood of a verb, for example *should die* in *if I should die.*
– DERIVATIVES **con·di·tion·al·i·ty** /kənˌdisHə'nalitē/ n., **con·di·tion·al·ly** adv.
– ORIGIN late Middle English: from Old French *condicionel* or late Latin *condicionalis*, from *condicio(n-)* 'agreement' (see CONDITION).

con·di·tion·al prob·a·bil·i·ty ▶ n. Statistics the probability of an event (*A*), given that another (*B*) has already occurred.

con·di·tion·al sale ▶ n. the sale of goods according to a contract containing conditions, typically that ownership does not pass to the buyer until after a set time, usually after payment of the last installment of the purchase price, although the buyer has possession and is committed to acquiring ownership.

con·di·tioned re·sponse (also **conditioned reflex**) ▶ n. Psychology an automatic response established by training to an ordinarily neutral stimulus. See also CLASSICAL CONDITIONING.

con·di·tion·er /kən'disH(ə)nər/ ▶ n. a substance or appliance used to improve or maintain something's condition: *add a water conditioner to neutralize chlorine.* ■ a liquid applied to the hair after shampooing to improve its condition: *conditioner will protect your hair from damage.*

con·do /'kändō/ ▶ n. (pl. **condos**) informal short for CONDOMINIUM (sense 1): *a high-rise condo.*

con·dole /kən'dōl/ ▶ v. [no obj.] (**condole with**) express sympathy for (someone); grieve with: *the priest came to condole with Madeleine.*
– ORIGIN late 16th cent.: from Christian Latin *condolere*, from *con-* 'with' + *dolere* 'grieve, suffer.'

con·do·lence /kən'dōləns/ ▶ n. (usu. **condolences**) an expression of sympathy, esp. on the occasion of a death: *we offer our sincere condolences to his widow* | *letters of condolence.*
– ORIGIN early 17th cent.: from CONDOLE, influenced by French *condoléance.*

con·dom /'kändəm, 'kən-/ ▶ n. a thin rubber sheath worn on a man's penis during sexual intercourse as a contraceptive or as protection against infection.
– ORIGIN early 18th cent.: of unknown origin; often said to be named after a physician who invented it, but no such person has been traced.

con·do·min·i·um /ˌkändə'minēəm/ ▶ n. (pl. **condominiums**) **1** a building or complex of buildings containing a number of individually owned apartments or houses. ■ each of the individual apartments or houses in such a building or complex. ■ the system of ownership by which these operate, in which owners have full title to the individual apartment or house and an undivided interest in the shared parts of the property.
2 the joint control of a country's or territory's affairs by other countries. ■ a state so governed.
– ORIGIN early 18th cent.: modern Latin, from *con-* 'together with' + *dominium* 'right of ownership' (see DOMINION). Sense 1 dates from the 1960s.

con·done /kən'dōn/ ▶ v. [with obj.] accept and allow (behavior that is considered morally wrong or offensive) to continue: *the college cannot condone any behavior that involves illicit drugs.* ■ approve or sanction (something), esp. with reluctance: *the practice is not officially condoned by any airline.*
– DERIVATIVES **con·don·a·ble** adj., **con·do·na·tion** /-'nāsHən, -dō-/ n., **con·don·er** n.
– ORIGIN mid 19th cent.: from Latin *condonare* 'refrain from punishing,' from *con-* 'altogether' + *donare* 'give.'

con·dor /'känˌdôr, -dər/ ▶ n. a large New World vulture with a bare head and mainly black plumage, living in mountainous country and spending much time soaring. ● Two species in the family Cathartidae: the **Andean condor** (*Vultur gryphus*) of South America, and the **California condor** (*Gymnogyps californianus*), which is close to extinction in the wild.
– ORIGIN early 17th cent.: from Spanish *cóndor*, from Quechua *kuntur.*

California condor

con·dot·tie·re /ˌkändätē'erē, ˌkändə'tyerē/ ▶ n. (pl. **condottieri** pronunc. **same**) historical a leader or a member of a troop of mercenaries, esp. in Italy.
– ORIGIN Italian, from *condotto* 'troop under contract,' from *condotta* 'a contract,' from *condurre* 'conduct,' from Latin *conducere* (see CONDUCT).

con·duce /kən'd(y)o͞os/ ▶ v. [no obj.] (**conduce to**) formal help to bring about (a particular situation or outcome): *every possible care was taken that could conduce to their health and comfort.*
– ORIGIN late Middle English (in the sense 'lead or bring'): from Latin *conducere* 'bring together' (see CONDUCT).

con·du·cive /kən'd(y)o͞osiv/ ▶ adj. making a certain situation or outcome likely or possible: *the harsh lights and cameras were hardly **conducive to** a relaxed atmosphere.*
– ORIGIN mid 17th cent.: from CONDUCE, on the pattern of words such as *conductive.*

con·duct ▶ n. /'känˌdəkt/ **1** the manner in which a person behaves, esp. on a particular occasion or in a particular context: *the conduct of the police during the riot* | *members are bound by a **code of conduct.***
2 the action or manner of managing an activity or organization: *his conduct of the campaign.* ■ archaic the action of leading; guidance: *traveling through the world under the conduct of chance.*
▶ v. /kən'dəkt/ [with obj.] **1** organize and carry out: *in the second trial he conducted his own defense* | *surveys conducted among students.* ■ direct the performance of (a piece of music or a musical ensemble): *my first attempt to conduct a great work* | [no obj.] *Toscanini is coming to conduct.* ■ lead or guide (someone) to or around a particular place: *he conducted us through his personal gallery of the Civil War.* ■ Physics transmit (a form of energy such as heat or electricity) by conduction: *heat is conducted to the surface.*
2 (**conduct oneself**) behave in a specified way: *he conducted himself with the utmost propriety.*
– DERIVATIVES **con·duct·i·ble** /kən'dəktəbəl/ adj., **con·duct·i·bil·i·ty** /kənˌdəktə'bilitē/ n.
– ORIGIN Middle English: from Old French, from Latin *conduct-* 'brought together,' from the verb *conducere*. The term originally denoted some provision for safe passage, such as an escort or pass, surviving in SAFE CONDUCT; later the verb sense 'lead, guide' arose, hence 'manage' and 'management' (late Middle English), later 'management of oneself, behavior' (mid 16th cent). The original form of the word was *conduit*, which was preserved only in the sense 'channel' (see CONDUIT); in all other uses the spelling was influenced by Latin.

con·duct·ance /kən'dəktəns/ ▶ n. the degree to which an object conducts electricity, calculated as the ratio of the current that flows to the potential difference present. This is the reciprocal of the resistance, and is measured in siemens or mhos. (Symbol: **G**).

con·duct dis·or·der ▶ n. a range of antisocial types of behavior displayed in childhood or adolescence.

con·duc·tion /kən'dəksHən/ ▶ n. the process by which heat or electricity is directly transmitted through a substance when there is a difference of temperature or of electrical potential between adjoining regions, without movement of the

material. ■ the process by which sound waves travel through a medium. ■ the transmission of impulses along nerves. ■ the conveying of fluid through a pipe or other channel.
– ORIGIN mid 16th cent. (in the senses 'provision for safe passage' and 'leadership'): from Latin *conductio(n-)*, from the verb *conducere* (see CONDUCT).

con·duc·tion band ▶ n. Physics a delocalized band of energy partly filled with electrons in a crystalline solid. These electrons have great mobility and are responsible for electrical conductivity.

con·duc·tive /kən'dəktiv/ ▶ adj. having the property of conducting something (esp. heat or electricity): *to induce currents in conductive coils.* ■ of or relating to conduction.
– DERIVATIVES **con·duc·tive·ly** adv.

con·duc·tiv·i·ty /ˌkänˌdəkˈtivitē, kən-/ ▶ n. (pl. **conductivities**) (also **electrical conductivity**) the degree to which a specified material conducts electricity, calculated as the ratio of the current density in the material to the electric field that causes the flow of current. It is the reciprocal of the resistivity. ■ (also **thermal conductivity**) the rate at which heat passes through a specified material, expressed as the amount of heat that flows per unit time through a unit area with a temperature gradient of one degree per unit distance.

con·duc·tor /kən'dəktər/ ▶ n. **1** a person who directs the performance of an orchestra or choir: *he was appointed principal conductor of the Berlin Philharmonic Orchestra.*
2 a person in charge of a train, streetcar, or other public conveyance, who collects fares and sells tickets.
3 Physics a material or device that conducts or transmits heat, electricity, or sound, esp. when regarded in terms of its capacity to do this: *graphite is a reasonably good conductor of electricity.* ■ another term for LIGHTNING ROD.
– DERIVATIVES **con·duc·to·ri·al** /ˌkänˌdəkˈtôrēəl, kən-/ adj., **con·duc·tor·ship** /-ˌSHip/ n. (sense 1).
– ORIGIN late Middle English (denoting a military leader): via Old French from Latin *conductor*, from *conducere* 'bring together' (see CONDUCT).

con·duc·tress /kən'dəktrəs/ ▶ n. a female conductor, esp. in a bus or other passenger vehicle.

con·duc·tus /kən'dəktəs/ ▶ n. (pl. **conducti** /-ˌtī, -ˌtē/) a musical setting of a metrical Latin text, of the 12th or 13th century.
– ORIGIN from medieval Latin, from Latin *conducere* 'bring together' (see CONDUCT).

con·duit /ˈkänˌd(y)o͞oət, ˈkänd(w)ət/ ▶ n. **1** a channel for conveying water or other fluid: *a conduit for conveying water to the power plant.* ■ a person or organization that acts as a channel for the transmission of something: *the office acts as a conduit for ideas to flow throughout the organization.*
2 a tube or trough for protecting electric wiring: *the gas pipe should not be close to any electrical conduit.*
– ORIGIN Middle English: from Old French, from medieval Latin *conductus*, from Latin *conducere* 'bring together' (see CONDUCT).

con·dy·larth /ˈkändəˌlärTH/ ▶ n. a fossil herbivorous mammal of the early Tertiary period, ancestral to the ungulates. ● Order Condylarthra: several families.
– ORIGIN late 19th cent.: from modern Latin *Condylarthra* (plural), from Greek *kondulos* 'knuckle' + *arthron* 'joint.'

con·dyle /ˈkänˌdīl/ ▶ n. Anatomy a rounded protuberance at the end of some bones, forming an articulation with another bone.
– DERIVATIVES **con·dy·lar** /ˈkändələr/ adj., **con·dy·loid** /ˈkändəˌloid/ adj.
– ORIGIN mid 17th cent.: from French, from Latin *condylus*, from Greek *kondulos* 'knuckle.'

con·dy·lo·ma /ˌkändəˈlōmə/ ▶ n. (pl. **condylomas** or **condylomata** /-mətə/) Medicine a raised growth on the skin resembling a wart, typically in the genital region, caused by viral infection or syphilis and transmissible by contact.
– DERIVATIVES **con·dy·lom·a·tous** /-mətəs/ adj.
– ORIGIN late Middle English: via Latin from Greek *kondulōma* 'callous lump,' from *kondulos* 'knuckle.'

cone /kōn/ ▶ n. **1** a solid or hollow object that tapers from a circular or roughly circular base to a point. ■ Mathematics a surface or solid figure generated by the straight lines that pass from a circle or other closed curve to a single point (the vertex) not in the same plane as the curve. A cone with the vertex perpendicularly over the center of a circular base is a **right circular cone**. ■ (also **traffic cone**) a plastic cone-shaped object that is used to separate off or close sections of a road. ■ an edible wafer container shaped like a cone in which ice cream is served. ■ a conical mountain or peak, esp. one of volcanic origin. ■ (also **pyrometric cone**) a ceramic pyramid that melts at a known temperature and is used to indicate the temperature of a kiln. ■ short for CONE SHELL.
2 the dry fruit of a conifer, typically tapering to a rounded end and formed of a tight array of overlapping scales on a central axis that separate to release the seeds. ■ a flower resembling a pine cone, esp. that of the hop plant.
3 Anatomy a light-sensitive cell of one of the two types present in the retina of the eye, responding mainly to bright light and responsible for sharpness of vision and color perception. Compare with ROD (sense 5).
– ORIGIN late Middle English (denoting an apex or vertex): from French *cône*, via Latin from Greek *kōnos*.

coned /kōnd/ ▶ adj. conical. ■ having cones: [in combination] *the big-coned southern California pine.*

cone·flow·er /ˈkōnˌflou(-ə)r/ ▶ n. a North American plant of the daisy family that has flowers with conelike disks that appear to consist of soft spines. ● *Rudbeckia, Echinacea*, and other genera, family Compositae: numerous species, including the yellow-flowered **sweet coneflower** (*R. subtomentosa*), the **purple coneflower** (*E. purpurea*) with swept-back reddish-purple petals, and the tall **green-headed coneflower** (*R. laciniata*) with yellow petals and greenish disks.

purple coneflower

cone of si·lence ▶ n. **1** an imaginary device that prevents eavesdropping on a private conversation. ■ an electronic device or isolated room intended for the same purpose.
2 a directive that prohibits oral communication about a specified subject. ■ an agreement or conspiracy to maintain secrecy about a subject.
– ORIGIN 1960s: originally a fantasy prop in the television series *Get Smart*.

cone shell ▶ n. shell a predatory mollusk of warm seas, with a conical shell that typically displays intricate patterns. It captures prey by injecting venom, which can be lethal to humans, and the shells are popular with collectors. ● Genus *Conus*, family Conidae, class Gastropoda: numerous species.

Con·es·to·ga wag·on /ˌkänəˈstōgə/ ▶ n. historical a large covered wagon used for long-distance travel, typically carrying pioneers in the westward migration.
– ORIGIN early 18th cent.: named after *Conestoga*, a town in Pennsylvania.

con·ex /ˈkänˌeks/ ▶ n. a large, steel-reinforced reusable container for shipping military cargo or, when modified, for use as temporary accommodations: *they told us we'd be staying in luxury air-conditioned conexes.*
– ORIGIN acronym from *container express*.

co·ney /ˈkōnē/ (also **cony**) ▶ n. (pl. **coneys**) **1** Brit. & Heraldry a pika. ■ a rabbit. ■ rabbit fur. ■ (in biblical use) a hyrax.
2 a small grouper (fish) found on the coasts of the tropical western Atlantic, with variable coloration. ● *Epinephelus fulvus*, family Serranidae.
– ORIGIN Middle English: from Old French *conin*, from Latin *cuniculus*.

Co·ney Is·land /ˈkōnē/ a resort and amusement park in the Brooklyn borough of New York City, on the southern shore of Long Island.

con·fab informal ▶ n. /ˈkänˌfab, kənˈfab/ an informal private conversation or discussion: *they wandered off to the woods for a private confab.* ■ a meeting or conference of members of a particular group: *this year's annual American Booksellers Association confab.*
▶ v. /kənˈfab, ˈkänˌfab/ (**confabs, confabbing, confabbed**) [no obj.] engage in informal private conversation: *Peter was confabbing with a curly-haired guy.*
– ORIGIN early 18th cent.: abbreviation of *confabulation* (see CONFABULATE).

con·fab·u·late /kənˈfabyəˌlāt/ ▶ v. [no obj.] **1** formal engage in conversation; talk: *she could be heard on the telephone confabulating with someone.*
2 Psychiatry fabricate imaginary experiences as compensation for loss of memory.
– DERIVATIVES **con·fab·u·la·tion** /-ˌfabyəˈlāSHən/ n., **con·fab·u·la·to·ry** /-ləˌtôrē/ adj.
– ORIGIN early 17th cent.: from Latin *confabulat-* 'chatted together,' from the verb *confabulari*, from *con-* 'together' + *fabulari* (from *fabula* 'fable').

con·fect /kənˈfekt/ ▶ v. [with obj.] literary make (something) by putting together various elements: *together they had confected a valiseful of show tunes.*
– ORIGIN late Middle English: from Latin *confect-* 'put together,' from the verb *conficere*, from *con-* 'together' + *facere* 'make.'

con·fec·tion /kənˈfekSHən/ ▶ n. **1** a dish or delicacy made with sweet ingredients: *a whipped chocolate and cream confection.* ■ an elaborately constructed thing, esp. a frivolous one: *the city is a classical confection of shimmering gold.* ■ a fashionable or elaborate article of women's dress: *she was wearing some white confection with an enormous satin bow.*
2 the action of mixing or compounding something.
– DERIVATIVES **con·fec·tion·ar·y** /-ˌnerē/ adj.
– ORIGIN Middle English (in the general sense 'something made by mixing,' esp. a medicinal preparation): via Old French from Latin *confectio(n-)*, from *conficere* 'put together' (see CONFECT).

con·fec·tion·er /kənˈfekSHənər/ ▶ n. a person whose occupation is making or selling candy and other sweets.

con·fec·tion·ers sug·ar (also **confectioner's sugar**) ▶ n. finely powdered sugar with cornstarch added, used for making icings and candy.

con·fec·tion·er·y /kənˈfekSHəˌnerē/ ▶ n. (pl. **confectioneries**) candy and other sweets considered collectively. ■ a shop that sells such items.

con·fed·er·a·cy /kənˈfedərəsē/ ▶ n. (pl. **confederacies**) a league or alliance, esp. of confederate states. ■ (**the Confederacy**) another term for CONFEDERATE STATES OF AMERICA. ■ an alliance of people or groups formed for an illicit purpose.
– ORIGIN late Middle English: from Old French *confederacie*, based on Latin *confoederare* 'join together in league' (see CONFEDERATION).

con·fed·er·al /kənˈfedərəl/ ▶ adj. relating to or denoting a confederation.
– ORIGIN late 18th cent.: from CONFEDERATION, on the pattern of *federal*.

con·fed·er·ate /kənˈfedərət/ ▶ adj. joined by an agreement or treaty: *some local groups united to form confederate councils.* ■ (**Confederate**) of or relating to the Confederate States of America: *the Confederate flag.*
▶ n. **1** a person one works with, esp. in something secret or illegal; an accomplice: *where was his confederate, the girl who had stolen Richard's wallet?*
2 (**Confederate**) a supporter of the Confederate States of America.
▶ v. /-ˌrāt/ [with obj.] (usu. as adj. **confederated**) bring (states or groups of people) into an alliance: *Switzerland is a model for the new confederated Europe.*
– ORIGIN late Middle English: from late (ecclesiastical) Latin *confoederatus*, from *con-* 'together' + *foederatus* (see FEDERATE).

Con·fed·er·ate States of A·mer·i·ca (also **the Confederacy**) the eleven southern states (Alabama, Arkansas, Florida, Georgia, Louisiana, Mississippi, North Carolina, South Carolina, Tennessee, Texas, and Virginia) that seceded from the US in 1860–61, thus precipitating the Civil War.

con·fed·er·a·tion /kənˌfedəˈrāSHən/ ▶ n. an organization that consists of a number of parties or groups united in an alliance or league: *a confederation of trade unions.* ■ a more or less permanent union of countries with some or most political power vested in a central authority: *Canada became a confederation in 1867.* ■ the action of confederating or the state of being confederated: *a referendum on confederation.*
– ORIGIN late Middle English: from Old French *confederacion* or late Latin *confederatio(n-)*, from Latin *confoederare*, from *con-* 'together' + *foederare* 'join in league with' (from *foedus* 'league, treaty').

con·fer /kənˈfər/ ▶ v. (**confers, conferring, conferred**) **1** [with obj.] grant or bestow (a title, degree, benefit, or right): *moves were made to confer an honorary degree on her.*
2 [no obj.] have discussions; exchange opinions: *the officials were conferring with allies.*
– DERIVATIVES **con·fer·ment** n. (sense 1), **con·fer·ra·ble** adj., **con·fer·ral** /-ˈfərəl/ n. (sense 1).
– ORIGIN late Middle English (in the general sense 'bring together,' also sense 2): from Latin *conferre*, from *con-* 'together' + *ferre* 'bring.'

C

con·fer·ee /ˌkänfəˈrē/ ▶ **n. 1** a person who attends a conference.
2 a person on whom something is conferred.

con·fer·ence /ˈkänf(ə)rəns/ ▶ **n. 1** a formal meeting for discussion: *he gathered all the men around the table for a conference.* ■ a formal meeting that typically takes place over a number of days and involves people with a shared interest, esp. one held regularly by an association or organization: *an international conference on the environment* | *the third annual National Wilderness Conference.* ■ [usu. as modifier] a linking of several telephones or computers, so that each user may communicate with the others simultaneously: *a conference call.*
2 an association of sports teams that play each other.
3 the governing body of some Christian churches, esp. the Methodist Church.
▶ **v.** [no obj.] (usu. as noun **conferencing**) take part in a conference or conference call: *video conferencing.*
– PHRASES **in conference** in a meeting; engaged in discussions.
– ORIGIN early 16th cent. (in the general sense 'conversation, talk'): from French *conférence* or medieval Latin *conferentia*, from Latin *conferre* 'bring together' (see CONFER).

Con·fer·ence on Dis·ar·ma·ment a committee of 65 member nations that seeks to negotiate multilateral disarmament.

con·fess /kənˈfes/ ▶ **v.** [reporting verb] admit or state that one has committed a crime or is at fault in some way: [with clause] *he confessed that he had attacked the old man* | [no obj.] *he wants to* **confess to** *Caroline's murder* | [with direct speech] *"I damaged your car," she confessed* | [with obj.] *once apprehended, they would confess their guilt.* ■ admit or acknowledge something reluctantly, typically because one feels slightly ashamed or embarrassed: [with clause] *I must confess that I was slightly surprised* | [no obj.] *he* **confessed to** *a lifelong passion for food* | [with direct speech] *"I needed to see you, too," he confessed.* ■ [with obj.] declare (one's religious faith): *150 people confessed faith in Christ.* ■ declare one's sins formally to a priest: [with obj.] *I could not confess all my sins to the priest* | [no obj.] *he gave himself up after confessing to a priest.* ■ [with obj.] (of a priest) hear the confession of (someone) in such a way: *St. Ambrose would weep bitter tears when confessing a sinner.*
– ORIGIN late Middle English: from Old French *confesser*, from Latin *confessus*, past participle of *confiteri* 'acknowledge,' from *con-* (expressing intensive force) + *fateri* 'declare, avow.'

con·fes·sant /kənˈfesənt/ ▶ **n.** a person who confesses to a priest; a penitent.

con·fess·ed·ly /kənˈfesədlē/ ▶ **adv.** by one's own admission: *many therapists have had clients who, confessedly or otherwise, have fallen in love with them.*

con·fes·sion /kənˈfesHən/ ▶ **n. 1** a formal statement admitting that one is guilty of a crime: *he signed a confession to the murders.* ■ an admission or acknowledgment that one has done something that one is ashamed or embarrassed about: *by his own confession, he had strayed perilously close to alcoholism.* ■ a formal admission of one's sins with repentance and desire of absolution, esp. privately to a priest as a religious duty: *she still had not been to confession.* See also SACRAMENT OF RECONCILIATION. ■ (**confessions**) often humorous intimate revelations about a person's private life or occupation, esp. as presented in a sensationalized form in a book, newspaper, or movie: *confessions of a driving instructor.*
2 (also **confession of faith**) a statement setting out essential religious doctrine. ■ (also **Confession**) the religious body or church sharing a confession of faith. ■ a statement of one's principles: *his words are a political confession of faith.*
– DERIVATIVES **con·fes·sion·ar·y** /-ˌnerē/ **adj.**
– ORIGIN late Middle English: via Old French from Latin *confessio(n-)*, from *confiteri* 'acknowledge' (see CONFESS).

con·fes·sion·al /kənˈfesHənl/ ▶ **n. 1** an enclosed stall in a church divided by a screen or curtain in which a priest sits to hear people confess their sins.
2 an admission or acknowledgment that one has done something that one is ashamed or embarrassed about; a confession.
▶ **adj. 1** (esp. of speech or writing) in which a person reveals or admits to private thoughts or past incidents, esp. ones that cause shame or embarrassment: *the autobiography is remarkably confessional* | *his confessional outpourings.* ■ of or relating to religious confession: *the priest leaned forward in his best confessional manner.*
2 of or relating to confessions of faith or doctrinal systems: *the confessional approach to religious education.*
– ORIGIN late Middle English (as an adjective): the adjective from CONFESSION + -AL; the noun via French from Italian *confessionale*, from medieval Latin, neuter of *confessionalis*, from Latin *confessio(n-)*, from *confiteri* 'acknowledge' (see CONFESS).

con·fes·sor /kənˈfesər/ ▶ **n. 1** /kōnˈfesər, ˈkänˌfesər, ˈkänfəˌsôr/ a priest who hears confessions and gives absolution and spiritual counsel. ■ a person to whom another confides personal problems.
2 /kənˈfesər, ˈkänˌfesər/ a person who avows religious faith in the face of opposition, but does not suffer martyrdom.
3 /kənˈfesər/ a person who makes a confession.
– ORIGIN Old English (sense 2): from Old French *confessour*, from ecclesiastical Latin *confessor*, from Latin *confess-* 'acknowledged' (see CONFESS).

con·fet·ti /kənˈfetē/ ▶ **n.** small pieces of colored paper thrown during a celebration such as a wedding.
– ORIGIN early 19th cent. (originally denoting the real or imitation sweets thrown during Italian carnivals): from Italian, literally 'sweets,' from Latin *confectum* 'something prepared,' neuter past participle of *conficere* 'put together' (see CONFECT).

con·fi·dant /ˈkänfəˌdant, -ˌdänt/ ▶ **n.** (fem. **confidante** pronunc. **same**) a person with whom one shares a secret or private matter, trusting them not to repeat it to others.
– ORIGIN mid 17th cent.: alteration of CONFIDENT (as a noun in the same sense in the early 17th cent.), probably to represent the pronunciation of French *confidente* 'having full trust.'

con·fide /kənˈfīd/ ▶ **v.** [with obj.] tell someone about a secret or private matter while trusting them not to repeat it to others: *he* **confided** *his fears to his mother* | *"I have been afraid," she confided* | *the judge confided that he had been swayed by the sister of the accused.* ■ [no obj.] (**confide in**) trust (someone) enough to tell them of such a secret or private matter: *he confided in friends that he and his wife planned to separate.* ■ (**confide something to**) dated entrust something to (someone) for safekeeping: *the property of others confided to their care was unjustifiably risked.*
– DERIVATIVES **con·fid·ing·ly adv.**
– ORIGIN late Middle English (in the sense 'place trust (in)'): from Latin *confidere* 'have full trust.' The sense 'impart as a secret' dates from the mid 18th cent.

con·fi·dence /ˈkänfədəns, -fəˌdens/ ▶ **n.** the feeling or belief that one can rely on someone or something; firm trust: *we had every* **confidence in** *the staff* | *he had gained the young man's confidence.* ■ the state of feeling certain about the truth of something: *it is not possible to say with confidence how much of the increase in sea levels is due to melting glaciers.* ■ a feeling of self-assurance arising from one's appreciation of one's own abilities or qualities: *she's brimming with confidence* | [in sing.] *he would walk up those steps with a confidence he didn't feel.* ■ the telling of private matters or secrets with mutual trust: *someone with whom you may raise your suspicions* **in confidence.** ■ (often **confidences**) a secret or private matter told to someone under such a condition of trust: *the girls exchanged confidences about their parents.*
– PHRASES **in someone's confidence** in a position of trust with someone. **take someone into one's confidence** tell someone one's secrets.
– ORIGIN late Middle English: from Latin *confidentia*, from *confidere* 'have full trust' (see CONFIDENT).

con·fi·dence game (Brit. also **confidence trick**) ▶ **n.** a swindle in which the victim is persuaded to trust the swindler in some way.
– DERIVATIVES **con·fi·dence trick·ster n.** Brit.

con·fi·dence in·ter·val ▶ **n.** Statistics a range of values so defined that there is a specified probability that the value of a parameter lies within it.

con·fi·dence lev·el ▶ **n.** Statistics the probability that the value of a parameter falls within a specified range of values.

con·fi·dence lim·it ▶ **n.** Statistics either of the extreme values of a confidence interval.

con·fi·dence man ▶ **n.** old-fashioned term for CON MAN.

con·fi·dent /ˈkänfədənt, -fəˌdent/ ▶ **adj.** feeling or showing confidence in oneself; self-assured: *she was a confident, outgoing girl* | *a confident smile.* ■ feeling or showing certainty about something: *this time they're* **confident of** *a happy ending* | *I am not very* **confident about** *tonight's game.*
▶ **n.** archaic a confidant.
– DERIVATIVES **con·fi·dent·ly adv.**
– ORIGIN late 16th cent.: from French *confident(e)*, from Italian *confidente*, from Latin *confident-* 'having full trust,' from the verb *confidere*, from *con-* (expressing intensive force) + *fidere* 'trust.'

con·fi·den·tial /ˌkänfəˈdencHəl/ ▶ **adj.** intended to be kept secret: *confidential information* | *knowledge that was privileged and confidential.* ■ (of a person's tone of voice) indicating that what one says is private or secret: *he dropped his voice to a confidential whisper.* ■ entrusted with private or restricted information: *a confidential secretary.*
– DERIVATIVES **con·fi·den·ti·al·i·ty** /-ˌdencHēˈalitē/ **n.**

con·fi·den·tial·ly /ˌkänfəˈdensHəlē/ ▶ **adv.** in a way that is intended to be private or secret; privately: *all queries will be treated confidentially.*

con·fig·u·ra·tion /kənˌfig(y)əˈrāsHən/ ▶ **n.** an arrangement of elements in a particular form, figure, or combination: *the broad configuration of the economy remains capitalist* | *the arena is equipped to stage indoor sports with various configurations of seating.* ■ Chemistry the fixed three-dimensional relationship of the atoms in a molecule, defined by the bonds between them. Compare with CONFORMATION. ■ Computing the arrangement in which items of computer hardware or software are interconnected: *it comes with a removable hard disk drive as part of the standard configuration.* ■ Psychology another term for GESTALT.
– DERIVATIVES **con·fig·u·ra·tion·al** /-sHənl/ **adj.**, **con·fig·u·ra·tion·al·ly** /-sHənl-ē/ **adv.**, **con·fig·u·ra·tive** /-ˈfig(y)ərətiv/ **adj.**
– ORIGIN mid 16th cent. (denoting the relative position of celestial objects): from late Latin *configuratio(n-)*, from Latin *configurare* 'shape after a pattern' (see CONFIGURE).

con·fig·ure /kənˈfigyər/ ▶ **v.** [with obj.] shape or put together in a particular form or configuration: *two of the aircraft will be configured as VIP transports.* ■ Computing arrange or order (a computer system or an element of it) so as to fit it for a designated task: *expanded memory can be configured as a virtual drive.*
– DERIVATIVES **con·fig·ur·a·ble adj.**
– ORIGIN late Middle English (in the Latin sense): from Latin *configurare* 'shape after a pattern,' from *con-* 'together' + *figurare* 'to shape' (from *figura* 'shape or figure').

con·fine ▶ **v.** /kənˈfīn/ [with obj.] (**confine someone/something to**) keep or restrict someone or something within certain limits of (space, scope, quantity, or time): *he does not confine his message to politics* | *your boating will mostly be confined to a few hours at weekends* | *you've* **confined yourself** *to what you know.* ■ (**confine someone to/in**) restrain or forbid someone from leaving (a place): *the troops were confined to their barracks.* ■ (**be confined to**) (of a person) be unable to leave (one's bed, home, or a wheelchair) because of illness or disability: *he was confined to bed for four days with a bad dose of flu.* ■ (**be confined**) dated (of a woman) remain in bed for a period before, during, and after the birth of a child: *she was confined for nearly a month.*
▶ **n.** /ˈkänˌfīn/ (**confines**) the borders or boundaries of a place, esp. with regard to their restricting freedom of movement: *they were cramped within* **the confines of** *a little cabin* | figurative *the narrow confines of political life.*
– ORIGIN late Middle English (as a noun): from French *confins* (plural noun), from Latin *confinia*, from *confinis* 'bordering,' from *con-* 'together' + *finis* 'end, limit' (plural *fines* 'territory'). The verb senses are from French *confiner*, based on Latin *confinis*.

con·fined /kənˈfīnd/ ▶ **adj.** (of a space) restricted in area or volume; cramped: *wear a dust mask and goggles when soldering in confined spaces.*

con·fine·ment /kənˈfīnmənt/ ▶ **n. 1** the action of confining, or the state of being confined: *he was immediately released from his confinement.*
2 dated the condition of being in childbirth: *the pros and cons of home versus hospital confinement* | *my grandmother's last six confinements.*

con·firm /kənˈfərm/ ▶ **v.** [with obj.] **1** establish the truth or correctness of (something previously believed, suspected, or feared to be the case): *if these fears are confirmed, the outlook for the economy will be dire* | *the report confirms that a diet rich in vitamin C can help to prevent cataracts.* ■ state with assurance that a report or fact is true: *he confirmed that the general was in the hands of the rebels* | *"It is indeed real coffee," I confirmed.* ■ (**confirm someone in**) reinforce someone in (an opinion, belief, or feeling): *he fueled his misogyny by cultivating women who confirmed him in this view.* ■ make (a provisional arrangement or appointment) definite: *Mr. Baker's assistant telephoned to confirm his appointment with the chairman.* ■ make (something, esp. a person's appointment to a position or an agreement) formally valid; ratify: *the organization has confirmed the appointment of Mr. Collins as managing director.* ■ formally declare (someone) to be appointed to a particular position: *he was* **confirmed as** *the new peace envoy.*
2 administer the religious rite of confirmation to: *he had been baptized and confirmed.*

– DERIVATIVES **con·firm·a·tive** /-mətiv/ **adj.**, **con·firm·a·to·ry** /-məˌtôrē/ **adj.**
– ORIGIN Middle English: from Old French *confermer*, from Latin *confirmare*, from *con-* 'together' + *firmare* 'strengthen' (from *firmus* 'firm').

con·fir·mand /ˈkänfərˌmand, ˌkänfərˈmand/ ▶ **n.** a person who is to undergo the religious rite of confirmation.

con·fir·ma·tion /ˌkänfərˈmāSHən/ ▶ **n.** **1** the action of confirming something or the state of being confirmed: *Sylvia received official confirmation of the instructorship.*
2 (in the Christian Church) the rite at which a baptized person, esp. one baptized as an infant, affirms Christian belief and is admitted as a full member of the church. ■ the Jewish ceremony of bar mitzvah or bat mitzvah.
– ORIGIN Middle English: via Old French from Latin *confirmatio(n-)*, from *confirmare* 'make firm, establish' (see CONFIRM).

con·firmed /kənˈfərmd/ ▶ **adj.** (of a person) firmly established in a particular habit, belief, or way of life and unlikely to change: *a confirmed bachelor | a confirmed teetotaler.*

con·fis·cate /ˈkänfəˌskāt/ ▶ **v.** [with obj.] take or seize (someone's property) with authority: *the guards confiscated his camera* | (as adj. **confiscated**) *confiscated equipment.* ■ take (a possession, esp. land) as a penalty and give it to the public treasury: *the government confiscated his property.*
– DERIVATIVES **con·fis·ca·tor** /-ˌskātər/ **n.**, **con·fis·ca·to·ry** /kənˈfiskəˌtôrē/ **adj.**
– ORIGIN mid 16th cent.: from Latin *confiscat-* 'put away in a chest, consigned to the public treasury,' from the verb *confiscare*, based on *con-* 'together' + *fiscus* 'chest, treasury.'

con·fis·ca·tion /ˌkänfəˈskāSHən/ ▶ **n.** the action of taking or seizing someone's property with authority; seizure: *a court ordered the confiscation of her property.*

con·fit /kônˈfē/ ▶ **n.** duck or other meat cooked slowly in its own fat.
– ORIGIN French,'conserved,' from *confire* 'prepare.'

Con·fit·e·or /känˈfitēˌôr/ ▶ **n.** a form of prayer confessing sins, used in the Roman Catholic Mass and some other sacraments.
– ORIGIN Middle English: Latin, literally 'I confess,' from the formula *Confiteor Deo Omnipotenti* 'I confess to Almighty God.'

con·fi·ture /ˈkänfiˌCHo͝or/ ▶ **n.** a preparation of preserved fruit. ■ a confection.

con·fla·grant /kənˈflāgrənt/ ▶ **adj.** on fire; blazing.

con·fla·gra·tion /ˌkänfləˈgrāSHən/ ▶ **n.** an extensive fire that destroys a great deal of land or property.
– ORIGIN late 15th cent. (denoting consumption by fire): from Latin *conflagratio(n-)*, from the verb *conflagrare*, from *con-* (expressing intensive force) + *flagrare* 'to blaze.'

con·flate /kənˈflāt/ ▶ **v.** [with obj.] combine (two or more texts, ideas, etc.) into one: *the urban crisis conflates a number of different economic and social issues.*
– DERIVATIVES **con·fla·tion** /-ˈflāSHən/ **n.**
– ORIGIN late Middle English (in the sense 'fuse or melt down metal'): from Latin *conflat-* 'kindled, fused,' from the verb *conflare*, from *con-* 'together' + *flare* 'to blow.'

con·flict ▶ **n.** /ˈkänˌflikt/ a serious disagreement or argument, typically a protracted one: *the eternal **conflict between** the sexes | doctors often **come into conflict with** politicians.* ■ a prolonged armed struggle: *overseas conflicts.* ■ an incompatibility between two or more opinions, principles, or interests: *there was a **conflict between** his business and domestic life.* ■ Psychology a condition in which a person experiences a clash of opposing wishes or needs.
▶ **v.** /kənˈflikt, ˈkänˌflikt/ [no obj.] be incompatible or at variance; clash: *parents' and children's interests sometimes conflict | those tournament dates would have **conflicted with** Memorial Day.* ■ (as adj. **conflicted**) having or showing confused and mutually inconsistent feelings: *my feelings are so conflicted that I hardly know how to answer.*
– DERIVATIVES **con·flic·tive** /kənˈfliktiv, ˈkänˌflik-/ **adj.**, **con·flic·tu·al** /kənˈflikCHo͞oəl/ **adj.**
– ORIGIN late Middle English: from Latin *conflict-* 'struck together, fought,' from the verb *confligere*, from *con-* 'together' + *fligere* 'to strike'; the noun is via Latin *conflictus* 'a contest.'

con·flict dia·mond ▶ **n.** a rough diamond mined in an area controlled by insurgent forces whose sale is used to finance antigovernment military action.

con·flict·ing /kənˈfliktiNG/ ▶ **adj.** incompatible or at variance; contradictory: *there are conflicting accounts of what occurred.*

con·flu·ence /ˈkänˌflo͞oəns, kənˈflo͞oəns/ ▶ **n.** the junction of two rivers, esp. rivers of approximately equal width: *here at **the confluence of** the Laramie and North Platte Rivers.* ■ an act or process of merging: *a major confluence of the world's financial markets.*
– ORIGIN late Middle English: from late Latin *confluentia*, from Latin *confluere* 'flow together' (see CONFLUENT).

con·flu·ent /ˈkänˌflo͞oənt, kənˈflo͞oənt/ ▶ **adj.** flowing together or merging: *warm confluent smells.*
– ORIGIN late 15th cent.: from Latin *confluent-* 'flowing together,' from *confluere*, from *con-* 'together' + *fluere* 'to flow.'

con·flux /ˈkänˌfləks/ ▶ **n.** another term for CONFLUENCE.
– ORIGIN early 17th cent.: from late Latin *confluxus*, from *con-* 'together' + *fluxus* (see FLUX).

con·fo·cal /känˈfōkəl/ ▶ **adj.** having a common focus or foci: *confocal ellipses.* ■ denoting or using a microscope whose imaging system only collects light from a small spot on the specimen, giving greater resolution.

con·form /kənˈfôrm/ ▶ **v.** [no obj.] comply with rules, standards, or laws: *the kitchen does not **conform to** hygiene regulations | the changes were introduced to **conform with** international classifications.* ■ (of a person) behave according to socially acceptable conventions or standards: *the pressure to conform.* ■ be similar in form or type; agree: *the countryside should **conform to** a certain idea of the picturesque.*
– ORIGIN Middle English (in the sense 'make (something) like another thing'): from Old French *conformer*, from Latin *conformare*, from *con-* 'together' + *formare* 'to form.'

con·form·a·ble /kənˈfôrməbəl/ ▶ **adj.** (usu. **conformable to**) (of a person) disposed or accustomed to conform to what is acceptable or expected. ■ similar in form or nature; consistent: *this proposition might be conformable to the original conjecture.* ■ Geology (of strata in contact) deposited in a continuous sequence, and typically having the same direction of stratification.
– DERIVATIVES **con·form·a·bil·i·ty** /-ˌfôrməˈbilitē/ **n.**, **con·form·a·bly** /-blē/ **adv.**
– ORIGIN late 15th cent. (in the sense 'compliant (to) or tractable'): from medieval Latin *conformabilis*, from Latin *conformare* 'to form, fashion' (see CONFORM).

con·for·mal /kənˈfôrməl/ ▶ **adj.** (of a map projection or a mathematical mapping) preserving the correct angles between directions within small areas, though distorting distances. Also called ORTHOMORPHIC.
– DERIVATIVES **con·for·mal·ly** **adv.**
– ORIGIN mid 17th cent. (in the sense 'conformable'): from late Latin *conformalis*, from *con-* 'together' + *formalis* 'formal.' The current sense was coined in German.

con·form·ance /kənˈfôrməns/ ▶ **n.** another term for CONFORMITY.

con·for·ma·tion /ˌkänfôrˈmāSHən, -fər-/ ▶ **n.** the shape or structure of something, esp. an animal: *the judges run their hands over the dog's body and legs, checking its conformation.* ■ Chemistry any of the spatial arrangements that the atoms in a molecule may adopt and freely convert between, esp. by rotation about individual single bonds. Compare with CONFIGURATION.
– DERIVATIVES **con·for·ma·tion·al** /-SHənl/ **adj.**
– ORIGIN early 16th cent. (in the sense 'conforming, adaptation'): from Latin *conformatio(n-)*, from *conformare* 'to shape, fashion' (see CONFORM).

con·form·er /kənˈfôrmər/ ▶ **n.** Chemistry a form of a compound having a particular molecular conformation: *changing the temperature alters the relative proportions of the conformers.*
– ORIGIN 1960s: blend of *conformational* (see CONFORMATION) and ISOMER.

con·form·ist /kənˈfôrmist/ ▶ **n.** a person who conforms to accepted behavior or established practices. ■ Brit. chiefly historical a person who conforms to the practices of the Church of England.
▶ **adj.** (of a person or activity) conforming to accepted behavior or established practices; conventional.
– DERIVATIVES **con·form·ism** /-ˌmizəm/ **n.**

con·form·i·ty /kənˈfôrmitē/ ▶ **n.** compliance with standards, rules, or laws: ***conformity to** regulations | the goods were **in conformity with** the contract.* ■ behavior in accordance with socially accepted conventions or standards: *loyalty to one's party need not imply unquestioning conformity.* ■ Brit., chiefly historical compliance with the practices of the Church of England. ■ similarity in form or type; agreement in character: *these changes are intended to ensure **conformity between** all schemes.* ■ Geology (of strata in contact) a continuous sequence of deposits, typically in parallel strata.

– ORIGIN late Middle English: from Old French *conformite* or late Latin *conformitas*, from *conformare* 'to form, fashion' (see CONFORM).

con·found /kənˈfound/ ▶ **v.** [with obj.] **1** cause surprise or confusion in (someone), esp. by acting against their expectations: *the inflation figure confounded economic analysts.* ■ prove (a theory, expectation, or prediction) wrong: *the rise in prices confounded expectations.* ■ defeat (a plan, aim, or hope): *we will confound these tactics by the pressure groups.* ■ archaic overthrow (an enemy).
2 (often **be confounded with**) mix up (something) with something else so that the individual elements become difficult to distinguish: *'nuke' is now a cooking technique, as microwave radiation is confounded with nuclear radiation.*
▶ **exclam.** dated used to express anger or annoyance: *oh, confound it, where is the thing?*
– ORIGIN Middle English: from Old French *confondre*, from Latin *confundere* 'pour together, mix up.' Compare with CONFUSE.

con·found·ed /kənˈfoundəd, kän-/ ▶ **adj.** informal, dated used for emphasis, esp. to express anger or annoyance: *he was a confounded nuisance.*
– DERIVATIVES **con·found·ed·ly** **adv.**

con·fra·ter·ni·ty /ˌkänfrəˈtərnitē/ ▶ **n.** (pl. **confraternities**) a brotherhood, esp. with a charitable or religious purpose.
– ORIGIN late Middle English: from Old French *confraternite*, from medieval Latin *confraternitas*, from *confrater* (see CONFRÈRE).

con·frère /ˈkänˌfrer, känˈfrer, kônˈfrer/ (also **confrere**) ▶ **n.** a fellow member of a profession; a colleague: *executives from the four broadcast television networks, along with their cable confreres.*
– ORIGIN mid 18th cent.: French, from medieval Latin *confrater*, from *con-* 'together with' + *frater* 'brother.'

con·front /kənˈfrənt/ ▶ **v.** [with obj.] meet (someone) face to face with hostile or argumentative intent: *300 policemen confronted an equal number of union supporters.* ■ face up to and deal with (a problem or difficult situation): *we knew we couldn't ignore the race issue and decided we'd confront it head on.* ■ compel (someone) to face or consider something, esp. by way of accusation: *Tricia **confronted** him **with** her suspicions.* ■ (of a problem, difficulty, etc.) present itself to (someone) so that dealing with it cannot be avoided: *post-czarist Russia was **confronted with** a Ukrainian national movement.* ■ (usu. **be confronted**) appear or be placed in front of (someone) so as to unsettle or threaten: *we were confronted with pictures of moving skeletons.*
– ORIGIN mid 16th cent.: from French *confronter*, from medieval Latin *confrontare*, from Latin *con-* 'with' + *frons, front-* 'face.'

con·fron·ta·tion /ˌkänfrənˈtāSHən/ ▶ **n.** a hostile or argumentative meeting or situation between opposing parties: *a confrontation with the legislature | four months of violent confrontation between government and opposition forces.*

con·fron·ta·tion·al /känfrənˈtāSHənl/ ▶ **adj.** tending to deal with situations in an aggressive way; hostile or argumentative: *he distanced himself from the confrontational approach adopted by his predecessor.*
– DERIVATIVES **confrontationally** **adv.**

Con·fu·cian /kənˈfyo͞oSHən/ ▶ **adj.** of or relating to Confucius or Confucianism.
▶ **n.** an adherent of Confucianism.

Con·fu·cian·ism /kənˈfyo͞oSHəˌnizəm/ ▶ **n.** a system of philosophical and ethical teachings founded by Confucius and developed by Mencius.
– DERIVATIVES **Con·fu·cian·ist** **n. & adj.**

Con·fu·cius /kənˈfyo͞oSHəs/ (551–479 BC), Chinese philosopher; Latinized name of *Kongfuzi* (*K'ung Fu-tzu*) "Kong the master." His ideas about the importance of practical moral values, collected by his disciples in the *Analects*, formed the basis of the philosophy known as Confucianism.

con·fus·a·ble /kənˈfyo͞ozəbəl/ ▶ **adj.** able or liable to be confused with something else.
▶ **n.** a word or phrase that is easily confused with another in meaning or usage, such as *mitigate*, which is often confused with *militate*.
– DERIVATIVES **con·fus·a·bil·i·ty** /kənˌfyo͞ozəˈbilitē/ **n.**

con·fuse /kənˈfyo͞oz/ ▶ **v.** [with obj.] cause (someone) to become bewildered or perplexed: *past and present blurred together, confusing her still further.* ■ make (something) more complex or less easy to understand: *the points made by the authors confuse rather than clarify the issue.* ■ identify wrongly;

mistake: *a lot of people **confuse** a stroke **with** a heart attack | purchasers might confuse the two products.*
–ORIGIN Middle English (in the sense 'rout, bring to ruin'): from Old French *confus*, from Latin *confusus*, past participle of *confundere* 'mingle together' (see CONFOUND). Originally all senses of the verb were passive, and therefore appeared only as the past participle *confused*; the active voice occurred rarely until the 19th cent. when it began to replace *confound*.

con·fused /kən'fyo͞ozd/ ▶ **adj.** (of a person) unable to think clearly; bewildered: *she was utterly **confused about** what had just happened | a very confused and unhappy boy.* ■ showing bewilderment: *a confused expression crossed her face.* ■ not in possession of all one's mental faculties, esp. because of old age: *interviewing confused old people does take longer.* ■ lacking order and thus difficult to understand: *the confused information supplied by authorities | reports about the incident were rather confused.* ■ lacking clear distinction of elements; jumbled: *the sound of a sort of confused hammering and shouting.*
–DERIVATIVES **con·fus·ed·ly** /-'fyo͞ozədlē/ **adv.**

con·fus·ing /kən'fyo͞oziNG/ ▶ **adj.** bewildering or perplexing: *he found being in Egypt very confusing.*
–DERIVATIVES **con·fus·ing·ly adv.**

con·fu·sion /kən'fyo͞ozHən/ ▶ **n. 1** lack of understanding; uncertainty: *there seems to be some **confusion about** which system does what | he cleared up the **confusion over** the party's policy.* ■ a situation of panic; a breakdown of order: *the shaken survivors retreated **in confusion**.* ■ a disorderly jumble: *all I can see is a **confusion of** brown cardboard boxes.*
2 the state of being bewildered or unclear in one's mind about something: *she looked about her **in confusion**.* ■ the mistaking of one person or thing for another: *there is some confusion between "unlawful" and "illegal" | most of the errors are reasonable confusions between similar words or sequences of words.*
–ORIGIN Middle English: from Latin *confusio(n-)*, from the verb *confundere* 'mingle together' (see CONFUSE).

con·fute /kən'fyo͞ot/ ▶ **v.** [with obj.] formal prove (a person or an assertion) to be wrong: *restorers who sought to confute this view were accused of ignorance.*
–DERIVATIVES **con·fu·ta·tion** /ˌkänfyo͝o'tāsHən/ **n.**
–ORIGIN early 16th cent.: from Latin *confutare* 'restrain, answer conclusively,' from *con-* 'altogether' + the base of *refutare* 'refute.'

Cong. ▶ **abbr.** ■ Congress. ■ Congressional. ■ Congregational.

con·ga /'käNGgə/ ▶ **n. 1** a Latin American dance of African origin, usually with several people in a single line, one behind the other.
2 (also **conga drum**) a tall, narrow, low-toned drum beaten with the hands.
▶ **v.** (**congas**, **congaing** /-gə-iNG/, **congaed** /-gəd/ or **conga'd**) [no obj.] dance the conga.
–ORIGIN 1930s: from Latin American Spanish, from Spanish, feminine of *congo* 'Congolese.'

conga drum

con game ▶ **n.** informal term for CONFIDENCE GAME.

con·gé /kôN'ZHā, 'känˌjā/ ▶ **n.** [in sing.] an unceremonious dismissal or rejection of someone: *the woman who gave you your congé when she wanted to marry Mr. Sugar.*
–ORIGIN late Middle English (in the general sense 'permission to do something'): from Old French *congie*, from Latin *commeatus* 'leave of absence,' from *commeare* 'go and come.' The word is now usually treated as equivalent to modern French.

con·geal /kən'jēl/ ▶ **v.** [no obj.] solidify or coagulate, esp. by cooling: *the blood had **congealed into blobs** |* (as adj. **congealed**) *congealed egg white.* ■ take shape or coalesce, esp. to form a satisfying whole: *the ballet failed to congeal as a single oeuvre.*
–DERIVATIVES **con·geal·a·ble adj.**, **con·geal·ment n.** (archaic).
–ORIGIN late Middle English: from Old French *congeler*, from Latin *congelare*, from *con-* 'together' + *gelare* 'freeze' (from *gelu* 'frost').

con·gee /'känjē/ ▶ **n.** (in Chinese cooking) broth or porridge made from rice.
–ORIGIN from Tamil *kañci*.

con·ge·la·tion /ˌkänjə'lāsHən/ ▶ **n.** the process of congealing or the state of being congealed: *the component of metals that causes their congelation.*
–ORIGIN late Middle English: from Latin *congelatio(n-)*, from the verb *congelare* 'freeze together' (see CONGEAL).

con·ge·ner /'känjənər, kən'jēnər/ ▶ **n. 1** a thing or person of the same kind or category as another. ■ an animal or plant of the same genus as another: *these birds or their congeners may be found in East Africa.*
2 a minor chemical constituent, esp. one that gives a distinctive character to a wine or liquor or is responsible for some of its physiological effects.
–ORIGIN mid 18th cent.: from Latin, from *con-* 'together with' + *genus, gener-* 'race, stock.'

con·ge·ner·ic /ˌkänjə'nerik/ ▶ **adj.** Biology (of an animal or plant species) belonging to the same genus: *this animal is **congeneric with** the later species.* ■ of a related nature or origin: *the two sets were congeneric.*
–DERIVATIVES **con·gen·er·ous** /kən'jenərəs, kän-, -'jēnərəs/ **adj.**
–ORIGIN mid 17th cent.: from Latin *congener* (see CONGENER) + -IC.

con·gen·ial /kən'jēnyəl/ ▶ **adj.** (of a person) pleasant because of a personality, qualities, or interests that are similar to one's own: *his need for some congenial company.* ■ (of a thing) pleasant or agreeable because suited to one's taste or inclination: *he went back to a climate more **congenial to** his cold stony soul.*
–DERIVATIVES **con·ge·ni·al·i·ty** /-ˌjēnē'alitē/ **n.**, **con·gen·ial·ly adv.**

con·gen·i·tal /kən'jenətl/ ▶ **adj.** (esp. of a disease or physical abnormality) present from birth: *a congenital malformation of the heart.* ■ (of a person) having a particular trait from birth or by firmly established habit: *a congenital liar.*
–DERIVATIVES **con·gen·i·tal·ly adv.**
–ORIGIN late 18th cent.: from Latin *congenitus*, from *con-* 'together' + *genitus* (past participle of *gignere* 'beget') + -AL.

con·ger /'käNGgər/ (also **conger eel**) ▶ **n.** a large edible predatory eel of shallow coastal waters.
● *Conger* and other genera, family Congridae: several species, in particular the European *C. conger* and the American *C. oceanicus*.
–ORIGIN Middle English: from Old French *congre*, via Latin from Greek *gongros*.

con·ge·ries /'känjərēz/ ▶ **n.** (pl. **same**) a disorderly collection; a jumble: *whiffs of ground coffee and a congeries of smells.*
–ORIGIN mid 16th cent.: from Latin *congeries* 'heap, pile,' from *congerere* 'heap up.'

con·gest·ed /kən'jestid/ ▶ **adj.** blocked up with or too full of something, in particular: ■ (of a road or place) so crowded with traffic or people as to hinder freedom of movement: *one of the most congested airports in the world | the streets are often heavily **congested with** traffic.* ■ (of the respiratory tract) blocked with mucus so as to hinder breathing: *his nose was congested.* ■ (of a part of the body) abnormally full of blood: *congested arteries.*
–ORIGIN mid 19th cent.: past participle of *congest*, from Latin *congest-* 'heaped up,' from the verb *congerere*, from *con-* 'together' + *gerere* 'bring.'

con·ges·tion /kən'jescHən/ ▶ **n.** the state of being congested: *the new bridge should ease congestion in the area.*
–ORIGIN late Middle English: via Old French from Latin *congestio(n-)*, from *congere* 'heap up,' from *con-* 'together' + *gerere* 'bring.'

con·ges·tive /kən'jestiv/ ▶ **adj.** Medicine involving or produced by congestion of a part of the body.
–ORIGIN mid 19th cent.: from *congest* (see CONGESTED) + -IVE.

con·ges·tive heart fail·ure ▶ **n.** a weakness of the heart that leads to a buildup of fluid in the lungs and surrounding body tissues.

con·gi·us /'känjēəs/ ▶ **n.** (pl. **congii** /-jēˌī/) an ancient Roman liquid measure of one eighth of an amphora, equal in modern terms to about 6.4 pints (3.6 liters).
–ORIGIN late Middle English: Latin, from Greek *konkhion, konkhē* (see CONCH).

con·glob·u·late /kən'gläbyələt/ ▶ **v.** [no obj.] rare join closely together: *a group of tourists conglobulating in a close mass.*
–ORIGIN mid 18th cent.: from Latin *globulus* 'globule,' on the pattern of earlier *conglobate* 'make into a ball.'

con·glom·er·ate ▶ **n.** /kən'glämərət/ **1** a number of different things or parts that are put or grouped together to form a whole but remain distinct entities: *the Earth is a specialized conglomerate of organisms.* ■ a large corporation formed by the merging of separate and diverse firms: *a media conglomerate.*
2 Geology a coarse-grained sedimentary rock composed of rounded fragments (> 2 mm) within a matrix of finer grained material: *the sediments vary from coarse conglomerate to fine silt and clay.*
▶ **adj.** of or relating to a conglomerate, esp. a large corporation: *conglomerate businesses.*
▶ **v.** /-ˌrāt/ [no obj.] gather together into a compact mass: *atoms that conglomerate at the center.* ■ form a conglomerate by merging diverse businesses.
–ORIGIN late Middle English (as an adjective describing something gathered up into a rounded mass): from Latin *conglomeratus*, past participle of *conglomerare*, from *con-* 'together' + *glomus, glomer-* 'ball.' The geological sense dates from the early 19th cent.; the other noun senses are later.

con·glom·er·a·tion /kənˌglämə'rāsHən/ ▶ **n. 1** a number of different things, parts or items that are grouped together; collection: *a loose conglomeration of pieces.*
2 the process of forming a conglomerate: *the practice of media conglomeration.*

Con·go /'käNGgō/ **1** a major river in central Africa that rises as the Lualaba River south of Kisangani in northern Democratic Republic of the Congo (formerly Zaire). It flows for 2,880 miles (4,630 km) in a great curve to the west and then turns southwest to form the border between the Congo and the Democratic Republic of the Congo before emptying into the Atlantic Ocean. Also called ZAIRE RIVER.
2 an equatorial country in Africa, with a short Atlantic coastline; pop. 4,012,800 (est. 2009); languages, French (official), Kikongo, and other Bantu languages; capital, Brazzaville. Also called **the Congo**, **Republic of the Congo**, **Congo-Brazzaville**.

> The region was colonized in the 19th century by France, and as Middle Congo formed part of the larger territory of French Congo (later, French Equatorial Africa). The country became independent in 1960.

Con·go, Dem·o·crat·ic Re·pub·lic of the a large country in central Africa with a short coastline on the Atlantic Ocean; pop. 68,692,500 (est. 2009); capital, Kinshasa; languages, French (official), Kongo, Lingala, Swahili, and others. Also called **Congo-Kinshasa**. Formerly called (until 1997) ZAIRE.

> The Democratic Republic of the Congo was a Belgian colony known as the Congo Free State 1885–1908 and the Belgian Congo 1908–60. Independence in 1960 was followed by civil war and UN intervention. General Mobutu seized control in a coup in 1965 and changed the name of the country from the Republic of the Congo to Zaire in 1971. The country experienced a huge influx of refugees following the violence in Rwanda in 1994, and the first of three destructive civil wars broke out in 1996. Mobutu was overthrown in 1997 by Laurent Kabila, who changed the country's name to the Democratic Republic of the Congo.

Con·go·lese /ˌkäNGgə'lēz, -'lēs/ ▶ **adj.** of or relating to the Congo or the Democratic Republic of the Congo (formerly Zaire).
▶ **n.** (pl. **same**) **1** a native or inhabitant of the Congo or the Democratic Republic of the Congo.
2 any of the Bantu languages spoken in the Congo region, in particular Kikongo.
–ORIGIN from French *Congolais*.

Con·go red ▶ **n.** a red-brown azo dye that becomes blue in acidic conditions, used as a chemical indicator and as a stain in histology.

con·grats /kən'grats/ ▶ **plural n.** informal congratulations: [as exclamation] *"Congrats on your promotion, Cal!"*
–ORIGIN late 19th cent.: abbreviation.

con·grat·u·late /kən'gracHəˌlāt, -'grajə-/ ▶ **v.** [with obj.] give (someone) one's good wishes when something special or pleasant has happened to them: *I went into the living room to **congratulate** Bill **on** his marriage.* ■ praise (someone) for a particular achievement: *the operators are to be **congratulated for** the excellent service that they now provide.* ■ (**congratulate oneself**) feel pride or satisfaction: *she **congratulated herself on** her powers of deduction | the Director was congratulating himself that nothing could go wrong.*
–DERIVATIVES **con·grat·u·la·tor** /-ˌlātər/ **n.**, **con·grat·u·la·to·ry** /-ləˌtôrē/ **adj.**
–ORIGIN mid 16th cent.: from Latin *congratulat-* 'congratulated,' from the verb *congratulari*, from *con-* 'with' + *gratulari* 'show joy' (from *gratus* 'pleasing').

con·grat·u·la·tion /kənˌgracHə'lāsHən, -ˌgrajə-/ ▶ **n.** an expression of praise for an achievement or good wishes on a special occasion; the act of congratulating: *he began pumping the hand of his son in congratulation.* ■ (**congratulations**) words expressing congratulation: *our congratulations to the winners |* [as exclamation] *congratulations on a job well done!*

–ORIGIN late Middle English: from Latin *congratulatio(n-)*, from the verb *congratulari* (see CONGRATULATE).

con·gre·gant /ˈkäNGgrəgənt/ ▶ n. a member of a congregation, esp. that of a church or synagogue.
–ORIGIN late 19th cent.: from Latin *congregant-* 'collecting (into a flock), uniting,' from the verb *congregare* (see CONGREGATE).

con·gre·gate ▶ v. /ˈkäNGgrəˌgāt/ [no obj.] gather into a crowd or mass: *some 4000 demonstrators had congregated at a border point.*
▶ adj. /-gət, -ˌgāt/ communal: *nursing homes and adult congregate living facilities.*
–ORIGIN late Middle English: from Latin *congregat-* 'collected (into a flock), united,' from the verb *congregare*, from *con-* 'together' + *gregare* (from *grex, greg-* 'a flock').

con·gre·ga·tion /ˌkäNGgrəˈgāSHən/ ▶ n. **1** a group of people assembled for religious worship. ■ a group of people regularly attending a particular place of worship: *that church took the place of the storefront the congregation had used before the war.*
2 a gathering or collection of people, animals, or things: *large congregations of birds may cause public harm.* ■ the action of gathering together in a crowd: *drought conditions lead to congregation of animals around watering points.*
3 (often **Congregation**) (in the Roman Catholic Church) a permanent committee of the College of Cardinals: *the Congregation for the Doctrine of the Faith.* ■ Brit. (in some universities) a general assembly of resident senior members.
4 a group of people obeying a common religious rule but under less solemn vows than members of the older religious orders: *the sisters of the Congregation of Our Lady.* ■ a group of communities within a religious order sharing particular historical or regional links.
–ORIGIN late Middle English: from Latin *congregatio(n-)*, from *congregare* 'collect (into a flock)' (see CONGREGATE).

con·gre·ga·tion·al /ˌkäNGgrəˈgāSHənl/ ▶ adj. **1** of or relating to a congregation: *congregational singing.*
2 (**Congregational**) of or adhering to Congregationalism: *the Congregational Church.*

Con·gre·ga·tion·al·ism /ˌkäNGgrəˈgāSHənlˌizəm/ ▶ n. a system of organization among Christian churches whereby individual local churches are largely self-governing.
–DERIVATIVES **Con·gre·ga·tion·al·ist** n. & adj.

con·gress /ˈkäNGgrəs, ˈkän-/ ▶ n. **1** the national legislative body of a country. ■ (**Congress**) the national legislative body of the US, meeting at the Capitol in Washington, DC. It was established by the Constitution of 1787 and is composed of the Senate and the House of Representatives: *changes in taxation required the approval of Congress.* ■ a particular session of the US Congress: *the 104th Congress.*
2 a formal meeting or series of meetings for discussion between delegates, esp. those from a political party or labor union or from within a particular discipline: *an international congress of mathematicians.*
3 a society or organization, esp. a political one: *the National Congress of American Indians.*
4 the action of coming together: *sexual congress.*
–DERIVATIVES **con·gres·sion·al** /kənˈgreSHənl/ adj.
–ORIGIN late Middle English (denoting an encounter during battle): from Latin *congressus*, from *congredi* 'meet,' from *con-* 'together' + *gradi* 'walk.'

con·gress boot ▶ n. dated a high boot with elastic sides.

Con·gres·sion·al Med·al of Hon·or ▶ n. see MEDAL OF HONOR.

con·gress·man /ˈkäNGgrəsmən, ˈkän-/ ▶ n. (pl. **congressmen**) a member of the US Congress (also used as a form of address), usually specifically a member of the US House of Representatives.

Con·gress of In·dus·tri·al Or·gan·i·za·tions (abbr.: **CIO**) a federation of North American labor unions, organized largely by industry rather than craft. In 1955 it merged with the American Federation of Labor to form the AFL-CIO.

con·gress·per·son /ˈkäNGgrəsˌpərsən, ˈkän-/ ▶ n. (pl. **congresspeople** or **congresspersons**) a member of a legislative congress, esp. the US House of Representatives.

con·gress·wom·an /ˈkäNGgrəsˌwŏŏmən, ˈkän-/ ▶ n. (pl. **congresswomen**) a female member of the US Congress (also used as a form of address).

Con·greve /ˈkäNGˌgrēv, ˈkänˌgrēv/, William (1670–1729), English playwright. His plays, such as *Love for Love* (1695) and *The Way of the World* (1700), epitomize the wit and satire of Restoration comedy.

con·gru·ence /kənˈgrŏŏəns, ˈkäNGgrŏŏəns/ ▶ n. agreement or harmony; compatibility: *the results show quite good congruence with recent studies.*
–DERIVATIVES **con·gru·en·cy** n.

con·gru·ent /kənˈgrŏŏənt, ˈkäNGgrŏŏənt/ ▶ adj. **1** in agreement or harmony: *institutional and departmental objectives are largely congruent | the rules may not be congruent with the requirements of the law.*
2 Geometry (of figures) identical in form; coinciding exactly when superimposed.
–DERIVATIVES **con·gru·ent·ly** adv.
–ORIGIN late Middle English: from Latin *congruent-* 'agreeing, meeting together,' from the verb *congruere*, from *con-* 'together' + *ruere* 'fall or rush.'

con·gru·ous /ˈkäNGgrŏŏəs/ ▶ adj. in agreement or harmony: *this explanation is congruous with earlier observations.*
–DERIVATIVES **con·gru·i·ty** /kənˈgrŏŏitē/ n., **con·gru·ous·ly** adv.
–ORIGIN late 16th cent.: from Latin *congruus*, from *congruere* 'agree' (see CONGRUENT), + -OUS.

con·ic /ˈkänik/ chiefly Mathematics ▶ adj. of or like a cone.
▶ n. short for CONIC SECTION. See also CONICS.
–ORIGIN late 16th cent.: from modern Latin *conicus*, from Greek *kōnikos*, from *kōnos* 'cone.'

con·i·cal /ˈkänikəl/ ▶ adj. having the shape of a cone.
–DERIVATIVES **con·i·cal·ly** /-ik(ə)lē/ adv.

con·i·cal pro·jec·tion (also **conic projection**) ▶ n. a map projection in which an area of the earth is projected onto a cone whose vertex is usually above one of the poles, then unrolled onto a flat surface.

con·ics /ˈkäniks/ ▶ plural n. [treated as sing.] the branch of mathematics concerned with conic sections.

con·ic sec·tion ▶ n. a figure formed by the intersection of a plane and a right circular cone. Depending on the angle of the plane with respect to the cone, a conic section may be a circle, an ellipse, a parabola, or a hyperbola.

co·nid·i·o·phore /kəˈnidēəˌfôr/ ▶ n. Botany (in certain fungi) a conidium-bearing hypha or filament.
–ORIGIN late 19th cent.: from *conidio-* (combining form of CONIDIUM) + -PHORE.

co·nid·i·um /kəˈnidēəm/ ▶ n. (pl. **conidia** /-ˈnidēə/) Botany a spore produced asexually by various fungi at the tip of a specialized hypha.
–ORIGIN late 19th cent.: modern Latin, from Greek *konis* 'dust' + the diminutive suffix *-idium*.

co·ni·fer /ˈkänəfər, kō-/ ▶ n. a tree that bears cones and evergreen needlelike or scalelike leaves. Conifers are of major importance as the source of softwood, and also supply resins and turpentine.
● Order Coniferales, class Coniferopsida, subdivision Gymnospermae: several families, including the pines and firs (Pinaceae) and the cypresses (Cupressaceae).
–DERIVATIVES **co·nif·er·ous** /kəˈnifərəs/ adj.
–ORIGIN mid 19th cent.: from Latin, literally 'cone-bearing,' from *conus* (see CONE).

co·ni·form /ˈkōnəˌfôrm, ˈkänə-/ ▶ adj. rare having the shape of a cone.
–ORIGIN late 18th cent.: from Latin *conus* 'cone' + -IFORM.

co·ni·ine /ˈkōnēˌēn, kōˈnē-in/ ▶ n. Chemistry a volatile poisonous compound found in hemlock and other plants. It affects the motor nerves, causing paralysis and asphyxia. ● An alkaloid, 2-propylpiperidine; chem. formula: $C_8H_{17}N$.
–ORIGIN mid 19th cent.: from Latin *conium* (from Greek *kōneion* 'hemlock') + -INE[4].

conj. ▶ abbr. conjunction.

con·jec·tur·al /kənˈjekCHərəl/ ▶ adj. based on or involving conjecture: *much of the racial history of Madagascar remains conjectural.*
–DERIVATIVES **con·jec·tur·al·ly** adv.
–ORIGIN mid 16th cent.: via French from Latin *conjecturalis*, from *conjectura* 'inference' (see CONJECTURE).

con·jec·ture /kənˈjekCHər/ ▶ n. an opinion or conclusion formed on the basis of incomplete information: *conjectures about the newcomer were many and varied | the purpose of the opening in the wall is open to conjecture.* ■ an unproven mathematical or scientific theorem: *the Goldbach conjecture.* ■ (in textual criticism) the suggestion or reconstruction of a reading of a text not present in the original source.
▶ v. [with obj.] form an opinion or supposition about (something) on the basis of incomplete information: *he conjectured the existence of an otherwise unknown feature | many conjectured that she had a second husband in mind.* ■ (in textual criticism) propose (a reading).
–DERIVATIVES **con·jec·tur·a·ble** adj.
–ORIGIN late Middle English (in the senses 'to divine' and 'divination'): from Old French, or from Latin *conjectura*, from *conicere* 'put together in thought,' from *con-* 'together' + *jacere* 'throw.'

con·join /kənˈjoin, kän-/ ▶ v. [with obj.] formal join; combine: *an approach that conjoins theory and method.*
–ORIGIN late Middle English: from Old French *conjoindre*, from Latin *conjungere*, from *con-* 'together' + *jungere* 'to join.'

con·joined twin ▶ n. either of a pair of twins who are physically joined at birth, sometimes sharing organs, and sometimes separable by surgery (depending on the degree of fusion).

> **USAGE** The term **conjoined twin** has supplanted Siamese twin in all contexts other than informal conversation.

con·joint /kənˈjoint, kän-/ ▶ adj. [attrib.] combining all or both people or things involved: *conjoint family therapy.*
–DERIVATIVES **con·joint·ly** adv.
–ORIGIN Middle English: from Old French, past participle of *conjoindre* (see CONJOIN).

con·ju·gal /ˈkänjəgəl/ ▶ adj. of or relating to marriage or the relationship between husband and wife: *conjugal loyalty.*
–DERIVATIVES **con·ju·gal·i·ty** /ˌkänjəˈgalitē/ n., **con·ju·gal·ly** adv.
–ORIGIN early 16th cent.: from Latin *conjugalis*, from *conjux, conjug-* 'spouse,' from *con-* 'together' + *jugum* 'a yoke.'

con·ju·gal rights ▶ plural n. the rights, esp. to sexual relations, regarded as exercisable in law by each partner in a marriage.

con·ju·gal vis·it ▶ n. Law a visit to a prisoner, by the spouse of the prisoner, esp. for sexual relations.

con·ju·gate ▶ v. /ˈkänjəˌgāt/ **1** [with obj.] Grammar give the different forms of (a verb in an inflected language) as they vary according to voice, mood, tense, number, and person.
2 [no obj.] Biology (of bacteria or unicellular organisms) become temporarily united in order to exchange genetic material: *E. coli only conjugate when one of the cells possesses fertility genes.* ■ (of gametes) become fused.
3 [with obj.] Chemistry be combined with or joined to reversibly: *bilirubin is then conjugated by liver enzymes and excreted in the bile.*
▶ adj. /ˈkänjigət, -jəˌgāt/ coupled, connected, or related, in particular: ■ Chemistry (of an acid or base) related to the corresponding base or acid by loss or gain of a proton. ■ Mathematics joined in a reciprocal relation, esp. having the same real parts and equal magnitudes but opposite signs of imaginary parts. Short for COMPLEX CONJUGATE. ■ Geometry (of angles) adding up to 360°; (of arcs) combining to form a complete circle. ■ Biology (esp. of gametes) fused.
▶ n. /ˈkänjigət, -jəˌgāt/ a thing that is conjugate or conjugated, in particular: ■ chiefly Biochemistry a substance formed by the reversible combination of two or more others. ■ a mathematical value or entity having a reciprocal relation with another. See also COMPLEX CONJUGATE.
–DERIVATIVES **con·ju·ga·cy** /ˈkänjəgəsē/ n., **con·ju·ga·tive** /ˈkänjəˌgātiv/ adj.
–ORIGIN late 15th cent. (as an adjective): from Latin *conjugat-* 'yoked together,' from the verb *conjugare*, from *con-* 'together' + *jugum* 'yoke.'

con·ju·gat·ed /ˈkänjəˌgātid/ ▶ adj. [attrib.] another term for CONJUGATE, in particular. ■ Chemistry relating to or denoting double or triple bonds in a molecule that are separated by a single bond, across which some sharing of electrons occurs. ■ (of a substance) reversibly combined with another: *conjugated bile salts.*

con·ju·gate di·am·e·ter ▶ n. Anatomy the distance between the front and rear of the pelvis.

con·ju·ga·ted pro·tein ▶ n. a complex protein, such as hemoglobin, consisting of amino acids combined with other substances.

con·ju·ga·tion /ˌkänjəˈgāSHən/ ▶ n. **1** the formation or existence of a link or connection between things, in particular: ■ Biology the temporary union of two bacteria or unicellular organisms for the exchange of genetic material. ■ Biology the fusion of two gametes, esp. when they are of a similar size. ■ chiefly Biochemistry the combination of two substances: *toxic compounds eliminated from the body by conjugation with glutathione.* ■ Chemistry the sharing of electron density between nearby multiple bonds in a molecule. ■ Mathematics the solution of a problem by transforming it into an equivalent problem of a different form, solving this, and then reversing the transformation.

2 Grammar the variation of the form of a verb in an inflected language such as Latin, by which are identified the voice, mood, tense, number, and person. ■ the class in which a verb is put according to the manner of this variation: *a past participle of the first conjugation.*
– DERIVATIVES **con·ju·ga·tion·al** /-sHənl/ **adj.**
– ORIGIN late Middle English (sense 2): from Latin *conjugatio(n-)*, from *conjugare* 'join together' (see CONJUGATE).

C

con·junct ▶ **adj.** /kən'jəNGkt, kän-/ joined together, combined, or associated. ■ Music of or relating to the movement of a melody between adjacent notes of the scale. ■ Astrology in conjunction with: *Moon conjunct Jupiter.*
▶ **n.** /'känjəNGkt/ each of two or more things that are joined or associated. ■ Logic each of the terms of a conjunctive proposition. ■ Grammar an adverbial whose function is to join two sentences or other discourse units (e.g., *however, anyway, in the first place*).
– ORIGIN late Middle English: from Latin *conjunctus*, past participle of *conjungere* 'join together' (see CONJOIN).

con·junc·tion /kən'jəNGksHən/ ▶ **n. 1** the action or an instance of two or more events or things occurring at the same point in time or space: *a conjunction of favorable political and economic circumstances | he postulated that the Americas were formed by the conjunction of floating islands.* ■ Astronomy & Astrology an alignment of two planets or other celestial objects so that they appear to be in the same, or nearly the same, place in the sky.
2 Grammar a word used to connect clauses or sentences or to coordinate words in the same clause (e.g., *and, but, if*).
– PHRASES **in conjunction** together: *herbal medicine was used **in conjunction with** acupuncture and massage.*
– DERIVATIVES **con·junc·tion·al** /-sHənl/ **adj.**
– ORIGIN late Middle English: via Old French from Latin *conjunctio(n-)*, from the verb *conjungere* (see CONJOIN).

con·junc·ti·va /,kän,jəNG(k)'tīvə, kən-/ ▶ **n.** (pl. **conjunctivae** /-'tīvē/) Anatomy the mucous membrane that covers the front of the eye and lines the inside of the eyelids.
– DERIVATIVES **con·junc·ti·val** **adj.**
– ORIGIN late Middle English: from medieval Latin *(membrana) conjunctiva* 'conjunctive (membrane),' from late Latin *conjunctivus*, from *conjungere* 'join together' (see CONJOIN).

con·junc·tive /kən'jəNG(k)tiv/ ▶ **adj.** serving to join; connective: *the conjunctive tissue.* ■ involving the combination or co-occurrence of two or more conditions or properties: *conjunctive hypotheses are simpler to process than negative or disjunctive ones.* ■ Grammar of the nature of or relating to a conjunction.
▶ **n.** Grammar a word or expression acting as a conjunction.
– DERIVATIVES **con·junc·tive·ly** **adv.**
– ORIGIN late Middle English: from late Latin *conjunctivus*, from *conjungere* 'join together' (see CONJUNCT).

con·junc·ti·vi·tis /kən,jəNG(k)tə'vītis/ ▶ **n.** Medicine inflammation of the conjunctiva of the eye. Also called PINKEYE.

con·junc·ture /kən'jəNGkCHər/ ▶ **n.** a combination of events: *the peculiar political conjunctures that led to war.* ■ a state of affairs: *the wider political conjuncture.*
– ORIGIN early 17th cent.: from CONJUNCTION, by substitution of the suffix; influenced by obsolete French *conjuncture*, from Italian *congiuntura*, based on Latin *conjungere* 'join together' (see CONJOIN).

con·jun·to /kän'hŏŏntō, -'həntō, kōn-/ ▶ **n.** (pl. **conjuntos**) (in Latin America or Hispanic communities) a small musical group or band: [as modifier] *Texas' leading female conjunto accordionist.*
– ORIGIN Spanish, literally 'an ensemble, group.'

con·jur·a·tion /,känjŏŏr'āsHən/ ▶ **n.** a magic incantation or spell. ■ the performance of something supernatural by means of a magic incantation or spell.
– ORIGIN late Middle English (also in the sense 'conspiracy, the swearing of an oath together'): via Old French from Latin *conjuratio(n-)*, from *conjurare* (see CONJURE).

con·jure ▶ **v. 1** /'känjər, 'kən-/ [with obj.] make (something) appear unexpectedly or seemingly from nowhere as if by magic: *Anne **conjured up** a most delicious homemade stew.* ■ call (an image) to mind: *she had forgotten how to **conjure up** the image of her mother's face.* ■ (of a word, sound, smell, etc.) cause someone to feel or think of (something): *one scent can **conjure up** a childhood summer beside a lake.* ■ call upon (a spirit or ghost) to appear, by means of a magic ritual: *they hoped to **conjure up** the spirit of their dead friend.*
2 /kən'jŏŏr/ [with obj.] archaic implore (someone) to do something.
– PHRASES **a name to conjure with** the name of an important person within a particular sphere of activity: *on the merger scene his is a name to conjure with.*
– ORIGIN Middle English (also in the sense 'oblige by oath'): from Old French *conjurer* 'to plot or exorcize,' from Latin *conjurare* 'band together by an oath, conspire' (in medieval Latin 'invoke'), from *con-* 'together' + *jurare* 'swear.'

con·jure wom·an /'känjər, 'kən-/ ▶ **n.** (masc. **conjure man**) a sorceress, esp. one who practices voodoo.

con·jur·ing /'känjəriNG, 'kən-/ ▶ **n.** [often as modifier] the performance of tricks that are seemingly magical, typically involving sleight of hand: *a conjuring trick.*

con·ju·ror /'känjərər, 'kən-/ (also **conjurer**) ▶ **n.** a person who conjures. ■ chiefly Brit. a performer of conjuring tricks; a magician.
– ORIGIN Middle English: partly from CONJURE, partly from Old French *conjureor, conjurere*, from medieval Latin *conjurator*, from Latin *conjurare* 'conspire' (see CONJURE).

conk[1] /käNGk, kôNGk/ ▶ **v.** [no obj.] (**conk out**) informal (of a machine) break down: *my car conked out.* ■ (of a person) faint or go to sleep: *he conked out on the rear seat.* ■ die.
– ORIGIN World War I: of unknown origin.

conk[2] informal ▶ **v.** [with obj.] hit (someone) on the head: *the clown conked him and sent him to the hospital with a concussion.*
▶ **n. 1** dated a person's head.
2 Brit. a person's nose.
– ORIGIN early 19th cent.: perhaps an alteration of CONCH.

conk[3] ▶ **n.** a hairstyle in which curly or kinky hair is straightened.
▶ **v.** [with obj.] straighten curly or kinky hair.

conk·er /'käNGkər/ ▶ **n.** Brit. the hard shiny dark brown nut of a horse chestnut tree. ■ (**conkers**) [treated as sing.] a children's game in which each child has a conker on the end of a string and takes turns trying to break another's with it.
– ORIGIN mid 19th cent. (a dialect word denoting a snail shell, with which the game, or a similar form of it, was originally played): perhaps from CONCH, but associated with (and frequently spelled) CONQUER in the 19th and early 20th centuries: an alternative name was *conquerors.*

con man (also **con artist**) ▶ **n.** informal a man who cheats or tricks someone by means of a confidence game.

con mo·to /kän 'mōtō, kōn/ ▶ **adv.** Music (esp. as a direction) with movement: *andante con moto.*
– ORIGIN Italian.

conn /kän/ (also **con**) Nautical ▶ **v.** [with obj.] direct the steering of (a ship): *he hadn't conned anything bigger than a Boston whaler.*
▶ **n.** (**the conn**) the action or post of conning a ship: *I quickly took the conn and restored the channel course.*
– ORIGIN early 17th cent.: apparently a weakened form of obsolete *cond* 'conduct, guide,' from Old French *conduire*, from Latin *conducere* (see CONDUCE).

Conn. ▶ **abbr.** Connecticut.

Con·nacht /'känôt, kə'nôt/ (also **Connaught**) a province in southwestern Republic of Ireland.

con·nate /'kän,āt, kä'nāt/ ▶ **adj. 1** (esp. of ideas or principles) existing in a person or thing from birth; innate: *are our ethical values connate?*
2 Biology (of parts) united so as to form a single part.
3 Geology (of water) trapped in sedimentary rock during its deposition.
– ORIGIN mid 17th cent.: from late Latin *connatus*, past participle of *connasci*, from *con-* 'together' + *nasci* 'be born.'

con·nat·u·ral /kə'naCH(ə)rəl, kä-/ ▶ **adj.** belonging naturally; innate: *religion is connatural with man.*
– DERIVATIVES **con·nat·u·ral·ly** **adv.**
– ORIGIN late 16th cent.: from late Latin *connaturalis*, from *con-* 'together' + Latin *naturalis* 'natural.'

Con·naught variant spelling of CONNACHT.

con·nect /kə'nekt/ ▶ **v.** [with obj.] bring together or into contact so that a real or notional link is established: *the electrodes **were connected to** a recording device | a modem connects computers over a telephone line.* ■ join together so as to provide access and communication: *all the buildings are connected by underground passages* | [no obj.] *the highway **connects with** major routes from all parts of the country.* ■ link to a power or water supply: *your house **is connected to** the main cable TV network.* ■ put (someone) into contact by telephone: *I was quickly **connected to** the police.* ■ [no obj.] (of a train, bus, aircraft, etc.) be timed to arrive at its destination before another train, aircraft, etc., departs so that passengers can transfer from one to the other: *the bus **connects with** trains from Union Station.* ■ associate or relate in some respect: *employees are rewarded with bonuses **connected to** their firm's performance | a variety of physical complaints **connected with** stress.* ■ think of as being linked or related: *I didn't **connect** the two incidents at the time.* ■ (of a thing) provide or have a link or relationship with (someone or something): *there was no evidence to **connect** Jeff **with** the theft.* ■ [no obj.] form a relationship or feel an affinity: *I taught in a reading program and I **connected with** kids individually.* ■ [no obj.] informal (of a blow) hit the intended target: *the blow connected and he felt a burst of pain.*
– DERIVATIVES **con·nect·a·ble** **adj.**, **con·nect·ed·ly** **adv.**, **con·nect·ed·ness** **n.**
– ORIGIN late Middle English (in the sense 'be united physically'; rare before the 18th cent.): from Latin *connectere*, from *con-* 'together' + *nectere* 'bind.'

Con·nect·i·cut /kə'netəkət/ a state in the northeastern US, on the coast of the Atlantic Ocean's Long Island Sound, one of the six New England states; pop. 3,501,252 (est. 2008); capital, Hartford; statehood, Jan. 9, 1788 (5). One of the original thirteen states. The Fundamental Orders, adopted by the Connecticut Colony in 1639, is often considered the first democratic constitution in America.

Con·nect·i·cut Riv·er the longest river in New England, flows south for 407 miles (655 km), from northern New Hampshire on the Quebec border, between New Hampshire and Vermont, through western Massachusetts and central Connecticut to Long Island Sound.

con·nect·ing rod ▶ **n.** a rod connecting two moving parts in a mechanism, esp. that between the piston and the crankpin (or equivalent parts) in an engine or pump.

con·nec·tion /kə'neksHən/ (Brit. also **connexion**) ▶ **n. 1** a relationship in which a person, thing, or idea is linked or associated with something else: *the connections between social attitudes and productivity | sufferers deny that their problems have any connection with drugs.* ■ the action of linking one thing with another: *connection to the Internet.* ■ the placing of parts of an electric circuit in contact so that a current may flow. ■ a link between pipes or electrical components: *it is important to ensure that all connections between the wires are properly made.* ■ a link between two telephones: *she replaced the receiver before the connection was made.* ■ an arrangement or opportunity for catching a connecting train, bus, aircraft, etc.: *ferry connections are sporadic in the off season.* ■ such a train, bus, etc.: *we had to wait for our connection to Frankfurt.* ■ (**connections**) people with whom one has social or professional contact or to whom one is related, esp. those with influence and able to offer one help: *he had connections with the music industry.*
2 informal a supplier of narcotics: *she introduced Jean to a number of her male drug connections.* ■ a narcotics sale or purchase.
3 chiefly historical an association of Methodist churches.
– PHRASES **in connection with** with reference to; concerning: *detectives are questioning two men in connection with alleged criminal damage.* **in this** (or **that**) **connection** with reference to this (or that): *of value in this connection was the work done by the state police.*
– DERIVATIVES **con·nec·tion·al** /-sHənl/ **adj.**
– ORIGIN late Middle English: from Latin *connexio(n-)*, from *connectere* (see CONNECT). The spelling *-ct* (18th cent.) is from *connect*, on the pattern of pairs such as *collect, collection.*

con·nec·tion·ism /kə'neksHə,nizəm/ ▶ **n.** an artificial intelligence approach to cognition in which multiple connections between nodes (equivalent to brain cells) form a massive interactive network in which many processes take place simultaneously. Certain processes in this network, operating in parallel, are grouped together in hierarchies that bring about results such as thought or action. Also called PARALLEL DISTRIBUTED PROCESSING.

con·nec·tive /kə'nektiv/ ▶ **adj.** connecting: *connective words and phrases.*
▶ **n.** something that connects, in particular: ■ Grammar a word or phrase whose function is to link linguistic units together. ■ Zoology a bundle of nerve fibers connecting two nerve centers or ganglia, esp. in invertebrate animals.

con·nec·tive tis·sue ▶ **n.** Anatomy tissue that connects, supports, binds, or separates other tissues or organs, typically having relatively few cells embedded in an amorphous matrix, often with collagen or other fibers, and including cartilaginous, fatty, and elastic tissues.

con·nec·tiv·i·ty /kəˌnekˈtivitē, ˈkänəkˌtivitē/ ▶ **n.** the state or extent of being connected or interconnected. ■ Computing capacity for the interconnection of platforms, systems, and applications: *connectivity between Sun and Mac platforms.*

con·nect·or /kəˈnektər/ ▶ **n.** a thing that links two or more things together: *a pipe connector.* ■ a device for keeping two parts of an electric circuit in contact. ■ a short road or highway that connects two longer roads or highways.

Con·ne·ma·ra /ˌkänəˈmärə, -ˈmarə/ a mountainous coastal region in Galway, in western Republic of Ireland.

Con·ne·ma·ra po·ny (also **Connemara**) ▶ **n.** a pony of a hardy breed originally from Ireland, typically gray.

Con·ner /ˈkänər/, Dennis (1942–), US yachtsman. Four-time winner of the America's Cup (1974, 1980, 1987, 1988), he is also the first US skipper to lose the cup (1983).

Con·ne·ry /ˈkänərē/, Sir Sean (1930–), Scottish movie actor; born *Thomas Connery*. He is best known for his portrayal of British agent James Bond in several movies. His other movies include *Marnie* (1964), *The Untouchables* (1987), and *The Hunt for Red October* (1990).

con·nex·ion /kəˈnekSHən/ ▶ **n.** British spelling of **CONNECTION**.

conn·ing tow·er ▶ **n.** the superstructure of a submarine, from which it can be commanded when on the surface, and containing the periscope.

con·nip·tion /kəˈnipSHən/ ▶ **n.** informal a fit of rage or hysterics: *the casting choice gave the writers a conniption.*
– ORIGIN mid 19th cent.: probably an invented word.

con·niv·ance /kəˈnīvəns/ ▶ **n.** willingness to secretly allow or be involved in wrongdoing, esp. an immoral or illegal act: *this infringement of the law had taken place with the connivance of officials.*
– ORIGIN late 16th cent. (also in the Latin sense 'winking'): from French *connivence* or Latin *conniventia*, from *connivere* 'shut the eyes (to)' (see **CONNIVE**).

con·nive /kəˈnīv/ ▶ **v.** [no obj.] (**connive at/in**) secretly allow (something considered immoral, illegal, wrong, or harmful) to occur: *you have it in your power to connive at my escape.* ■ (usu. **connive to do something**) conspire to do something considered immoral, illegal, or harmful: *the government had connived with security forces in permitting murder.*
– DERIVATIVES **con·niv·er** **n.**
– ORIGIN early 17th cent.: from French *conniver* or Latin *connivere* 'shut the eyes (to),' from *con-* 'together' + an unrecorded word related to *nictare* 'to wink.'

con·niv·ent /kəˈnīvənt/ ▶ **adj.** Botany coming into contact; converging and touching but not fused together.

con·niv·ing /kəˈnīviNG/ ▶ **adj.** given to or involved in conspiring to do something immoral, illegal, or harmful: *a heartless and conniving woman.*

con·nois·seur /ˌkänəˈsər, -ˈso͝or/ ▶ **n.** an expert judge in matters of taste: *a connoisseur of music.*
– DERIVATIVES **con·nois·seur·ship** /-ˌSHip/ **n.**
– ORIGIN early 18th cent.: from obsolete French, from *conoistre* 'know.'

Con·nol·ly /ˈkän(ə)lē/, Maureen Catherine (1934–69), US tennis player; known as **Little Mo**. She was the first woman to win all four Grand Slam singles titles in the same year (1953).

Con·nors /ˈkänərz/, Jimmy (1952–), US tennis player; full name *James Scott Connors*. Between 1974 and 1983, he won the men's singles title at two Wimbledon, one Australian Open, and five US Open tournaments.

con·no·ta·tion /ˌkänəˈtāSHən/ ▶ **n.** an idea or feeling that a word invokes in addition to its literal or primary meaning: *the word "discipline" has unhappy connotations of punishment and repression.* ■ the implication of such ideas or feelings: *the work functions both by analogy and by connotation.* ■ Philosophy the abstract meaning or intension of a term, which forms a principle determining which objects or concepts it applies to. Often contrasted with **DENOTATION**.
– ORIGIN mid 16th cent.: from medieval Latin *connotatio(n-)*, from *connotare* 'mark in addition' (see **CONNOTE**).

con·note /kəˈnōt/ ▶ **v.** [with obj.] (of a word) imply or suggest (an idea or feeling) in addition to the literal or primary meaning: *the term "modern science" usually connotes a complete openness to empirical testing.* ■ (of a fact) imply as a consequence or condition: *in that period a log cabin connoted hard luck.*
– DERIVATIVES **con·no·ta·tive** /ˈkänəˌtātiv/ **adj.**
– ORIGIN mid 17th cent.: from medieval Latin *connotare* 'mark in addition,' from *con-* 'together with' + *notare* 'to note' (from *nota* 'a mark').

> **USAGE** **Connote** does not mean the same as **denote**. **Denote** refers to the literal, primary meaning of something; **connote** refers to other characteristics suggested or implied by that thing. Thus, one might say that the word 'mother' **denotes** 'a woman who is a parent' but **connotes** qualities such as 'protection' and 'affection.'

con·nu·bi·al /kəˈn(y)o͞obēəl/ ▶ **adj.** literary of or relating to marriage or the relationship of husband and wife; conjugal: *their connubial bed.*
– DERIVATIVES **con·nu·bi·al·i·ty** /kəˌn(y)o͞obēˈalitē/ **n.**, **con·nu·bi·al·ly** **adv.**
– ORIGIN mid 17th cent.: from Latin *connubialis*, from *connubium* 'marriage,' from *con-* 'with' + *nubere* 'marry.'

co·no·dont /ˈkōnəˌdänt/ ▶ **n.** (also **conodont animal**) an extinct marine animal of the Cambrian to Triassic periods, having a long wormlike body, numerous small teeth, and a pair of eyes. It is now believed to be the earliest vertebrate. ● Class Conodonta, phylum Chordata: numerous families. ■ (also **conodont element**) a tooth of this animal, often found as a fossil.
– ORIGIN mid 19th cent.: from modern Latin *Conodonta* (plural), from Greek *kōnos* 'cone' + *odous*, *odont-* 'tooth.'

co·noid /ˈkōˌnoid/ ▶ **adj.** (also **conoidal** /kōˈnoidl/) chiefly Zoology approximately conical in shape.
▶ **n.** a conoid object.

con·quer /ˈkäNGkər/ ▶ **v.** [with obj.] overcome and take control of (a place or people) by use of military force: *the Magyars conquered Hungary in the Middle Ages.* ■ successfully overcome (a problem or weakness): *a fear she never managed to conquer.* ■ climb (a mountain) successfully: *the second American to conquer Everest.* ■ gain the love, admiration, or respect of (a person or group of people): *the Beatles were to leave Liverpool and conquer the world.*
– DERIVATIVES **con·quer·a·ble** /-k(ə)rəbəl/ **adj.**
– ORIGIN Middle English (also in the general sense 'acquire, attain'): from Old French *conquerre*, based on Latin *conquirere* 'gain, win,' from *con-* (expressing completion) + *quaerere* 'seek.'

con·quer·or /ˈkäNGkərər/ ▶ **n.** a person who conquers a place or people: *a people ruled over by a foreign conqueror* | figurative *a chance for revenge against his Olympic conqueror.*

con·quest /ˈkänˌkwest, ˈkäNG-/ ▶ **n.** the subjugation and assumption of control of a place or people by use of military force: *the conquest of the Aztecs by the Spanish.* ■ a territory that has been gained in such a way: *colonial conquests.* ■ (**the Conquest**) the invasion and assumption of control of England by William of Normandy in 1066. See also **NORMAN CONQUEST**. ■ the overcoming of a problem or weakness: *the conquest of inflation.* ■ a person whose affection or favor has been won: *someone he could display before his friends as his latest conquest.*
– ORIGIN Middle English: from Old French *conquest(e)*, based on Latin *conquirere* (see **CONQUER**).

con·quis·ta·dor /kôNGˈkēstəˌdôr, känˈk(w)istə-, kən-/ ▶ **n.** (pl. **conquistadores** /-ˌkēstəˈdôrēz, -ās, -ˌk(w)istə-/ or **conquistadors**) a conqueror, esp. one of the Spanish conquerors of Mexico and Peru in the 16th century.
– ORIGIN mid 19th cent.: Spanish.

Con·rad[1] /ˈkänˌrad/, Charles, Jr. (1930–99), US astronaut 1962–73; nickname **Pete**. He commanded the *Apollo 12* lunar mission in 1969, becoming the third man to set foot on the Moon. He was one of a few astronauts who flew four space missions (*Gemini V*, 1965; *Gemini XI*, 1966; *Apollo 12*; and *Skylab*, 1973).

Con·rad[2], Joseph (1857–1924), British novelist; born in Poland; born *Józef Teodor Konrad Korzeniowski*. Much of his work, including his novella *Heart of Darkness* (1902) and the novel *Nostromo* (1904), explores the darkness within human nature. Other notable works include *Lord Jim* (1900) and *Chance* (1913).

Con·roe /ˈkänrō/ a city in eastern Texas, north of Houston; pop. 55,429 (est. 2008).

con·san·guine /känˈsaNGgwin/ ▶ **adj.** another term for **CONSANGUINEOUS**.
– DERIVATIVES **con·san·guin·e·al** /ˌkänsaNGˈgwinēəl/ **adj.**

con·san·guin·e·ous /ˌkänˌsaNGˈgwinēəs/ ▶ **adj.** relating to or denoting people descended from the same ancestor: *consanguineous marriages.*
– DERIVATIVES **con·san·guin·i·ty** /-ˈgwinitē/ **n.**
– ORIGIN early 17th cent.: from Latin *consanguineus* 'of the same blood' (from *con-* 'together' + *sanguis* 'blood') + **-OUS**.

con·science /ˈkänCHəns/ ▶ **n.** an inner feeling or voice viewed as acting as a guide to the rightness or wrongness of one's behavior: *he had a guilty conscience about his desires* | *Ben was suffering a pang of conscience.*
– PHRASES **in (good) conscience** by any reasonable standard; by all that is fair: *they have in conscience done all they could.* **on one's conscience** weighing heavily and guiltily on one's mind: *an act of providence had prevented him from having a death on his conscience.*
– DERIVATIVES **con·science·less** **adj.**
– ORIGIN Middle English (also in the sense 'inner thoughts or knowledge'): via Old French from Latin *conscientia*, from *conscient-* 'being privy to,' from the verb *conscire*, from *con-* 'with' + *scire* 'know.'

con·science clause ▶ **n.** a clause that makes concessions to the consciences of those affected by a law: *Congress passed a "conscience clause" bill, which permitted any individual opposed to abortion to refuse to perform the procedure.*

con·science mon·ey ▶ **n.** money paid because of feelings of guilt, esp. about a payment that one has evaded.

con·science-strick·en ▶ **adj.** made uneasy by a guilty conscience: *she was still conscience-stricken over her outburst.*

con·sci·en·tious /ˌkänCHēˈenCHəs/ ▶ **adj.** **1** (of a person) wishing to do what is right, esp. to do one's work or duty well and thoroughly: *a conscientious and hardworking clerk.*
2 relating to a person's conscience: *the act does not provide exemption from service on the basis of personal conscientious beliefs.*
– DERIVATIVES **con·sci·en·tious·ly** **adv.**, **con·sci·en·tious·ness** **n.**
– ORIGIN early 17th cent.: from French *consciencieux*, from medieval Latin *conscientiosus*, from Latin *conscientia* (see **CONSCIENCE**).

con·sci·en·tious ob·jec·tor ▶ **n.** a person who for reasons of conscience objects to serving in the armed forces.
– DERIVATIVES **con·sci·en·tious ob·jec·tion** **n.**

con·scious /ˈkänCHəs/ ▶ **adj.** aware of and responding to one's surroundings; awake. ■ having knowledge of something; aware: *we are conscious of the extent of the problem.* ■ (**conscious of**) painfully aware of; sensitive to: *he was very conscious of his appearance.* ■ concerned with or worried about a particular matter: *they were growing increasingly security-conscious.* ■ (of an action or feeling) deliberate and intentional: *a conscious effort to walk properly.* ■ (of the mind or a thought) directly perceptible to and under the control of the person concerned.
– DERIVATIVES **con·scious·ly** **adv.**
– ORIGIN late 16th cent. (in the sense 'being aware of wrongdoing'): from Latin *conscius* 'knowing with others or in oneself' (from *conscire* 'be privy to') + **-OUS**.

con·scious·ness /ˈkänCHəsnəs/ ▶ **n.** the state of being awake and aware of one's surroundings: *she failed to regain consciousness and died two days later.* ■ the awareness or perception of something by a person: *her acute consciousness of Mike's presence.* ■ the fact of awareness by the mind of itself and the world: *consciousness emerges from the operations of the brain.*

con·scious·ness-rais·ing ▶ **n.** the activity of seeking to make people more aware of personal, social, or political issues: [as modifier] *a consciousness-raising group.*

con·script ▶ **v.** /kənˈskript/ [with obj.] enlist (someone) compulsorily, typically into the armed services: *they were conscripted into the army.*
▶ **n.** /ˈkänˌskript/ a person enlisted compulsorily.
– ORIGIN late 18th cent. (as a noun): from French *conscrit*, from Latin *conscriptus*, past participle of *conscribere* 'enroll.' The verb is a back-formation from **CONSCRIPTION**.

con·scrip·tion /kənˈskripSHən/ ▶ **n.** compulsory enlistment for state service, typically into the armed forces.
– ORIGIN early 19th cent.: via French (conscription was introduced in France in 1798), from late Latin *conscriptio(n-)* 'levying of troops,' from Latin *conscribere* 'write down together, enroll,' from *con-* 'together' + *scribere* 'write.'

con·se·crate /ˈkänsiˌkrāt/ ▶ **v.** [with obj.] (usu **be consecrated**) make or declare (something, typically

PRONUNCIATION KEY ə *ago, up*; ər *over, fur*; a *hat*; ā *ate*; ä *car*; e *let*; ē *see*; i *fit*; ī *by*; NG *sing*; ō *go*; ô *law, for*; oi *toy*; o͝o *good*; o͞o *goo*; ou *out*; TH *thin*; T̲H̲ *then*; ZH *vision*

C

C

a church) sacred; dedicate formally to a religious or divine purpose: *the present Holy Trinity church was consecrated in 1845* | (as adj. **consecrated**) *consecrated ground.* ■ (in Christian belief) make (bread or wine) into the body or blood of Christ: (as adj. **consecrated**) *they received the host but not the consecrated wine.* ■ ordain (someone) to a sacred office, typically that of bishop: [with obj. and complement] *in 1969 he was consecrated bishop of Northern Uganda.* ■ informal devote (something) exclusively to a particular purpose: *they'd decided to consecrate all their energies to this purposeful act.*
– DERIVATIVES **con·se·cra·tion** /ˌkänsiˈkrāsHən/ **n.**, **con·se·cra·tor** /-ˌkrātər/ **n.**, **con·se·cra·to·ry** /-krəˌtôrē/ **adj.**
– ORIGIN late Middle English: from Latin *consecrat-* 'dedicated, devoted as sacred,' from the verb *consecrare*, from *con-* (expressing intensive force) + *sacrare* 'dedicate,' from *sacer* 'sacred.'

con·sec·u·tive /kənˈsekyətiv/ ▶ **adj.** following continuously: *five consecutive months of serious decline.* ■ in unbroken or logical sequence. ■ Grammar expressing consequence or result: *a consecutive clause.* ■ Music denoting intervals of the same kind (esp. fifths or octaves) occurring in succession between two parts or voices.
– DERIVATIVES **con·sec·u·tive·ly adv.**, **con·sec·u·tive·ness n.**
– ORIGIN early 17th cent.: from French *consécutif, -ive*, from medieval Latin *consecutivus*, from Latin *consecut-* 'followed closely,' from the verb *consequi*.

con·sen·su·al /kənˈsencHōōəl/ ▶ **adj.** relating to or involving consent, esp. mutual consent: *he admitted to having consensual sex with two women.* ■ relating to or involving consensus: *decision-making was consensual.*
– DERIVATIVES **con·sen·su·al·ly adv.**
– ORIGIN mid 18th cent.: from Latin *consensus* 'agreement' (from *consens-* 'felt together, agreed,' from the verb *consentire*) + **-AL**.

con·sen·sus /kənˈsensəs/ ▶ **n.** [usu. in sing.] general agreement: *a consensus of opinion among judges* | [as modifier] *a consensus view.*
– ORIGIN mid 17th cent.: from Latin,'agreement,' from *consens-* 'agreed,' from the verb *consentire*.

con·sen·sus se·quence ▶ **n.** Biochemistry a sequence of DNA having similar structure and function in different organisms.

con·sent /kənˈsent/ ▶ **n.** permission for something to happen or agreement to do something: *no change may be made without the consent of all the partners.*
▶ **v.** [no obj.] give permission for something to happen: *he consented to a search by a detective.* ■ agree to do something: *he had consented to serve on the panel.*
– PHRASES **by common consent** with the agreement of all: *it was, by common consent, our finest performance.* **informed consent** permission granted in the knowledge of the possible consequences, typically that which is given by a patient to a doctor for treatment with full knowledge of the possible risks and benefits.
– ORIGIN Middle English: from Old French *consente* (noun), *consentir* (verb), from Latin *consentire*, from *con-* 'together' + *sentire* 'feel.'

con·sen·tient /kənˈsencHənt/ ▶ **adj.** archaic of the same opinion in a matter; in agreement.
– ORIGIN early 17th cent.: from Latin *consentient-* 'agreeing,' from the verb *consentire* (see **CONSENT**).

con·sent·ing a·dult ▶ **n.** an adult who willingly agrees to engage in an act, esp. a sexual act.

con·se·quence /ˈkänsikwəns, -ˌkwens/ ▶ **n. 1** a result or effect of an action or condition: *many have been laid off from work as a consequence of the administration's policies.*
2 [often with negative] importance or relevance: *the past is of no consequence* | *he didn't say anything of great consequence.* ■ dated social distinction: *a woman of consequence.*
– PHRASES **in consequence** as a result. **take the consequences** accept responsibility for the negative results of one's action.
– ORIGIN late Middle English: via Old French from Latin *consequentia*, from *consequent-* 'following closely,' from the verb *consequi*.

con·se·quent /ˈkänsikwənt, -ˌkwent/ ▶ **adj.** following as a result or effect: *labor shortages would be created with a consequent increase in wages.* ■ Geology (of a stream or valley) having a direction or character determined by the original slope of the land before erosion. ■ archaic logically consistent.
▶ **n.** a thing that follows another. ■ Logic the second part of a conditional proposition, whose truth is stated to be conditional upon that of the antecedent. ■ Mathematics the second term of a ratio.
– ORIGIN late Middle English: via Old French from Latin *consequent-* 'overtaking, following closely,' from the verb *consequi*.

con·se·quen·tial /ˌkänsəˈkwencHəl/ ▶ **adj.**
1 following as a result or effect: *a loss of confidence and a consequential withdrawal of funds.* ■ Law resulting from an act, but not immediately and directly: *consequential damages.*
2 important; significant: *perhaps the most consequential discovery of the eighteenth century.*
– DERIVATIVES **con·se·quen·ti·al·i·ty** /ˌkänsəˌkwencHēˈalitē/ **n.**, **con·se·quen·tial·ly adv.**
– ORIGIN early 17th cent.: from Latin *consequentia* (see **CONSEQUENCE**) + **-AL**.

con·se·quen·tial·ism /ˌkänsəˈkwencHəlizəm/ ▶ **n.** Philosophy the doctrine that the morality of an action is to be judged solely by its consequences.
– DERIVATIVES **con·se·quen·tial·ist adj. & n.**

con·se·quent·ly /ˈkänsikwəntlē, -ˌkwentlē/ ▶ **adv.** as a result: *flexible workers find themselves in great demand, and consequently earn high salaries.*

con·serv·an·cy /kənˈsərvənsē/ ▶ **n.** (pl. **conservancies**) **1** [in names] a body concerned with the preservation of nature, specific species, or natural resources: *the Nature Conservancy.* ■ Brit. a commission or group of officials controlling a port, river, or drainage basin.
2 the conservation of something, esp. wildlife and the environment.
– ORIGIN mid 18th cent.: alteration of obsolete *conservacy*, from Anglo-Norman French *conservacie*, via Anglo-Latin from Latin *conservation-* (see **CONSERVATION**).

con·ser·va·tion /ˌkänsərˈvāsHən/ ▶ **n.** the action of conserving something, in particular: ■ preservation, protection, or restoration of the natural environment, natural ecosystems, vegetation, and wildlife. ■ preservation, repair, and prevention of deterioration of archaeological, historical, and cultural sites and artifacts. ■ prevention of excessive or wasteful use of a resource. ■ Physics the principle by which the total value of a physical quantity (such as energy, mass, or linear or angular momentum) remains constant in a system.
– DERIVATIVES **con·ser·va·tion·al** /-sHənl/ **adj.**
– ORIGIN late Middle English (in the general sense 'conserving, preservation'): from Latin *conservatio(n-)*, from the verb *conservare* (see **CONSERVE**).

con·ser·va·tion·ist /ˌkänsərˈvāsHənist/ ▶ **n.** a person who advocates or acts for the protection and preservation of the environment and wildlife.

con·ser·va·tion of charge ▶ **n.** a principle stating that the total electric charge of an isolated system is fixed.

con·ser·va·tion of en·er·gy ▶ **n.** a principle stating that energy cannot be created or destroyed, but can be altered from one form to another.

con·ser·va·tion of mass ▶ **n.** a principle stating that mass cannot be created or destroyed.

con·serv·a·tive /kənˈsərvətiv/ ▶ **adj.** holding to traditional attitudes and values and cautious about change or innovation, typically in relation to politics or religion. ■ (of dress or taste) sober and conventional: *a conservative suit.* ■ (of an estimate) purposely low for the sake of caution: *the film was not cheap—$30,000 is a conservative estimate.* ■ (of surgery or medical treatment) intended to control rather than eliminate a condition, with existing tissue preserved as far as possible. ■ (**Conservative**) of or relating to the Conservative Party of Great Britain or a similar party in another country.
▶ **n.** a person who is averse to change and holds to traditional values and attitudes, typically in relation to politics. ■ (**Conservative**) a supporter or member of the Conservative Party of Great Britain or a similar party in another country.
– DERIVATIVES **con·serv·a·tism** /kənˈsərvəˌtizəm/ **n.**, **con·serv·a·tive·ly adv.**, **con·serv·a·tive·ness n.**
– ORIGIN late Middle English (in the sense 'aiming to preserve'): from late Latin *conservativus*, from *conservat-* 'conserved,' from the verb *conservare* (see **CONSERVE**). Current senses date from the mid 19th century onward.

Con·serv·a·tive Ju·da·ism ▶ **n.** a form of Judaism, particularly prevalent in North America, that seeks to preserve Jewish tradition and ritual but has a more flexible approach to the interpretation of the law than Orthodox Judaism.

Con·serv·a·tive Par·ty ▶ **n.** a political party promoting free enterprise and private ownership, in particular a major British party that emerged from the old Tory Party in the 1830s and 1840s.

con·ser·va·toire /kənˈsərvəˌtwär/ ▶ **n.** another term for **CONSERVATORY** (sense 1).
– ORIGIN late 18th cent.: French, from Italian *conservatorio*, from late Latin *conservatorium*, from *conservare* 'to preserve' (see **CONSERVE**). Compare with **CONSERVATORY**.

con·ser·va·tor /kənˈsərvətər, -ˌtôr, ˈkänsərˌvātər/ ▶ **n.** a person responsible for the repair and preservation of works of art, buildings, or other things of cultural or environmental interest. ■ a guardian or protector: *the court does not need to appoint a conservator to handle an incapacitated person's affairs.*
– DERIVATIVES **con·ser·va·tor·ship n.**

con·serv·a·to·ry /kənˈsərvəˌtôrē/ ▶ **n.** (pl. **conservatories**) **1** a college for the study of classical music or other arts.
2 a room with a glass roof and walls, attached to a house at one side and used as a greenhouse or a sun parlor.
– ORIGIN mid 16th cent. (denoting something that preserves): from late Latin *conservatorium*, from *conservare* 'to preserve' (see **CONSERVE**).

con·serve ▶ **v.** /kənˈsərv/ [with obj.] protect (something, esp. an environmentally or culturally important place or thing) from harm or destruction: *the funds raised will help conserve endangered meadowlands.* ■ prevent the wasteful or harmful overuse of (a resource): *industry should conserve more water.* ■ Physics maintain (a quantity such as energy or mass) at a constant overall total. ■ (usu. **be conserved**) Biochemistry retain (a particular amino acid, nucleotide, or sequence of these) unchanged in different protein or DNA molecules. ■ preserve (food, typically fruit) with sugar.
▶ **n.** /ˈkänˌsərv/ a sweet food made by preserving fruit with sugar; jam.
– ORIGIN late Middle English: from Old French *conserver* (verb), *conserve* (noun), from Latin *conservare* 'to preserve,' from *con-* 'together' + *servare* 'to keep.'

con·sid·er /kənˈsidər/ ▶ **v.** [with obj.] think carefully about (something), typically before making a decision: *each application is considered on its merits* | (as adj. **considered**) *it is my considered opinion that we should await further developments.* ■ think about and be drawn toward (a course of action): *he had considered giving up his job.* ■ regard (someone or something) as having a specified quality: [with obj. and complement] *I consider him irresponsible.* ■ believe; think: *at first women were considered to be at low risk from HIV* | *I don't consider that I'm to blame.* ■ take (something) into account when making an assessment or judgment: *one service area is not enough when you consider the number of cars using this highway.* ■ look attentively at: *he considered the women around the table with wariness.*
– PHRASES **all things considered** taking everything into account.
– ORIGIN late Middle English: from Old French *considerer*, from Latin *considerare* 'examine,' perhaps based on *sidus, sider-* 'star.'

con·sid·er·a·ble /kənˈsidər(ə)bəl, -ˈsidrəbəl/ ▶ **adj.** notably large in size, amount, or extent: *a position of considerable influence.* ■ (of a person) having merit or distinction: *he was a limited, but still considerable, novelist.*
– ORIGIN late Middle English (in the sense 'capable of being considered'): from medieval Latin *considerabilis* 'worthy of consideration,' from Latin *considerare* (see **CONSIDER**).

con·sid·er·a·bly /kənˈsidər(ə)blē, -ˈsidrəblē/ ▶ **adv.** by a notably large amount or to a notably large extent; greatly: *things have improved considerably over the last few years* | [as submodifier] *a considerably higher density.*

con·sid·er·ate /kənˈsidərət/ ▶ **adj.** careful not to cause inconvenience or hurt to others: *the quietest and most considerate tenants possible.* ■ archaic showing careful thought: *be considerate over your handwriting.*
– DERIVATIVES **con·sid·er·ate·ly adv.**, **con·sid·er·ate·ness n.**
– ORIGIN late 16th cent. (in the sense 'showing careful thought'): from Latin *consideratus*, past participle of *considerare* 'examine' (see **CONSIDER**).

con·sid·er·a·tion /kənˌsidəˈrāsHən/ ▶ **n. 1** careful thought, typically over a period of time: *a long process involving a great deal of careful consideration.* ■ a fact or a motive taken into account in deciding or judging something: *the idea was motivated by political considerations.* ■ thoughtfulness and sensitivity toward others: *companies should show more consideration for their employees.*
2 a payment or reward: *you can buy the books for a small consideration.* ■ Law (in a contractual agreement) anything given or promised or forborne by one party in exchange for the promise or undertaking of another.
3 archaic importance; consequence.
– PHRASES **in consideration of** on account of; taking into account: *a nightlight burned in consideration of Ernie's phobia.* ■ in return for: *he paid them in consideration of their services.* **take into consideration** take into account. **under consideration** being thought about: *a bird under consideration for being listed as endangered.*
– ORIGIN late Middle English: via Old French from Latin *consideration-*, from *considerare* 'examine.'

con·sid·er·ing /kənˈsidəriNG/ ▶ **prep. & conj.** taking into consideration: [as prep.] *considering the conditions, it's very good* | [as conjunction] *considering that he was the youngest on the field, he played well.*
▶ **adv.** informal taking everything into account: *they weren't feeling too bad, considering.*

con·si·glie·re /ˌkônsēˈlye-re, kənsiglēˈerē/ ▶ **n.** (pl. **consiglieri** /-rē/) an adviser, esp. to a crime boss.

con·sign /kənˈsīn/ ▶ **v.** [with obj.] deliver (something) to a person's custody, typically in order for it to be sold: *he consigned three paintings to Sotheby's.* ■ send (goods) by a public carrier. ■ (**consign someone/something to**) assign; commit decisively or permanently: *she consigned the letter to the wastebasket.*
– DERIVATIVES **con·sign·ee** /ˌkänsəˈnē, ˌkänˌsīˈnē, kənˌsīˈnē/ **n.**, **con·sign·or** /kənˈsīnər/ **n.**
– ORIGIN late Middle English (in the sense 'mark with the sign of the cross,' esp. at baptism or confirmation, as a sign of dedication to God): from French *consigner* or Latin *consignare* 'mark with a seal.'

con·sign·ment /kənˈsīnmənt/ ▶ **n.** a batch of goods destined for or delivered to someone: *a consignment of beef.* ■ the action of consigning or delivering something. ■ agreement to pay a supplier of goods after the goods are sold: *new and used children's clothing on consignment.*

con·sign·ment shop (or **consignment store**) ▶ **n.** a store that sells secondhand items (typically clothing and accessories) on behalf of the original owner, who receives a percentage of the selling price.

con·sil·i·ence /kənˈsilēəns/ ▶ **n.** agreement between the approaches to a topic of different academic subjects, esp. science and the humanities.
– DERIVATIVES **con·sil·i·ent adj.**
– ORIGIN mid 19th cent.: from *con*(*current*) + Latin *-silient-*, *-siliens* 'jumping' (as in *resilience*).

con·sist ▶ **v.** /kənˈsist/ [no obj.] **1** (**consist of**) be composed or made up of: *the exhibition consists of 180 drawings.* ■ (**consist in**) have as an essential feature: *his duties consist in taking the condition of the barometer.*
2 (**consist with**) archaic be consistent with: *the information perfectly consists with our friend's account.*
▶ **n.** Railroad the set of vehicles forming a complete train.
– ORIGIN late Middle English (in the sense 'be located or inherent in'): from Latin *consistere* 'stand firm or still, exist,' from *con-* 'together' + *sistere* 'stand (still).'

con·sist·ence /kənˈsistəns/ ▶ **n.** another term for **CONSISTENCY**.

con·sist·en·cy /kənˈsistənsē/ (also **consistence** /-təns/) ▶ **n.** (pl. **consistencies**) **1** conformity in the application of something, typically that which is necessary for the sake of logic, accuracy, or fairness: *the grading system is to be streamlined to ensure greater consistency.* ■ the achievement of a level of performance that does not vary greatly in quality over time: *his principal problem in tennis has been consistency.*
2 the way in which a substance, typically a liquid, holds together; thickness or viscosity: *the sauce has the consistency of creamed butter.*
– ORIGIN late 16th cent. (denoting permanence of form): from late Latin *consistentia*, from *consistent-* 'standing firm' (see **CONSISTENT**).

con·sist·ent /kənˈsistənt/ ▶ **adj.** (of a person, behavior, or process) unchanging in achievement or effect over a period of time: *manufacturing processes require a consistent approach.*
■ compatible or in agreement with something: *the injuries are consistent with falling from a great height.* ■ (of an argument or set of ideas) not containing any logical contradictions: *a consistent explanation.*
– DERIVATIVES **con·sist·ent·ly adv.**
– ORIGIN late 16th cent. (in the sense 'consisting or composed of'): from Latin *consistent-* 'standing firm or still, existing,' from the verb *consistere* (see **CONSIST**).

con·sis·to·ry /kənˈsistərē/ ▶ **n.** (pl. **consistories**) a church council or court, in particular: ■ (in the Roman Catholic Church) the council of cardinals, with or without the pope. ■ (also **consistory court**) (in the Church of England) a court presided over by a bishop, for the administration of ecclesiastical law in a diocese. ■ (in other churches) a local administrative body.
– DERIVATIVES **con·sis·to·ri·al** /ˌkänˌsisˈtôrēəl, kən-/ **adj.**
– ORIGIN Middle English (originally denoting a nonecclesiastical council): from Anglo-Norman French *consistorie*, from late Latin *consistorium*, from *consistere* 'stand firm' (see **CONSIST**).

con·so·ci·a·tion /ˌkänˌsōSHēˈāSHən, -ˌsōsē-, ˌkən-/ ▶ **n. 1** a group or association of a distinctive type, in particular: ■ a political system formed by the cooperation of different, esp. antagonistic, social groups on the basis of shared power. ■ Zoology a group of animals of the same species that interact more or less equally with each other. ■ dated an association of Congregational Churches.
2 dated close association or fellowship.
– DERIVATIVES **con·so·ci·a·tion·al** /-SHənl/ **adj.**, **con·so·ci·a·tion·al·ism** /-SHənlˌizəm/ **n.**
– ORIGIN late 16th cent. (in the sense 'associating, combination'): from Latin *consociatio(n-)*, from the verb *consociare*, from *con-* 'together' + *sociare* 'to associate' (from *socius* 'fellow').

con·so·la·tion /ˌkänsəˈlāSHən/ ▶ **n.** comfort received by a person after a loss or disappointment: *there was consolation in knowing that others were worse off.* ■ a person or thing providing such comfort: *the church was the main consolation in a short and hard life.* ■ Sports a round or contest for tournament entrants who have been eliminated before the finals, often to determine third and fourth place.
– DERIVATIVES **con·sol·a·to·ry** /kənˈsōləˌtôrē/ **adj.**
– ORIGIN late Middle English: via Old French from Latin *consolatio(n-)*, from the verb *consolari* (see **CONSOLE[1]**).

con·so·la·tion prize ▶ **n.** a prize given to a competitor who narrowly fails to win or who finishes last: *two hundred runners-up will get a consolation prize.*

con·sole[1] /kənˈsōl/ ▶ **v.** [with obj.] comfort (someone) at a time of grief or disappointment: *she tried to console him but he pushed her gently away* | *you can console yourself with the thought that you did your best.*
– DERIVATIVES **con·sol·a·ble adj.**, **con·sol·er n.**, **con·sol·ing·ly adv.**
– ORIGIN mid 17th cent. (replacing earlier *consolate*): from French *consoler*, from Latin *consolari*, from *con-* 'with' + *solari* 'soothe.'

con·sole[2] /ˈkänˌsōl/ ▶ **n. 1** a panel or unit accommodating a set of controls for electronic or mechanical equipment. ■ (also **games console**) a small electronic device for playing computerized video games. ■ a cabinet for television or radio equipment. ■ the cabinet or enclosure containing the keyboards, stops, pedals, etc., of an organ. ■ a monitor and keyboard in a multiuser computer system.
2 an ornamented bracket with scrolls or corbel supporting a cornice, shelf, or tabletop.
3 a support between the seats of an automobile that has indentations for holding small items.
– ORIGIN mid 17th cent. (sense 2): from French, perhaps from *consolider*, from Latin *consolidare* (see **CONSOLIDATE**).

con·sole ta·ble /ˈkänˌsōl/ ▶ **n.** a table supported by ornamented brackets, either movable or fixed against a wall.

con·sol·i·date /kənˈsäləˌdāt/ ▶ **v.** [with obj.] **1** make (something) physically stronger or more solid: *the first phase of the project is to consolidate the outside walls.* ■ reinforce or strengthen (one's position or power): *the company consolidated its position in the international market.*
2 combine (a number of things) into a single more effective or coherent whole: *all manufacturing activities have been consolidated in new premises.* ■ combine (a number of financial accounts or funds) into a single overall account or set of accounts. ■ combine (two or more legal actions involving similar questions) into one for action by a court.
– DERIVATIVES **con·sol·i·da·tion** /-ˌsäləˈdāSHən/ **n.**, **con·sol·i·da·tor** /-ˌdātər/ **n.**
– ORIGIN early 16th cent. (in the sense 'combine into a single whole'): from Latin *consolidare*, from *con-* 'together' + *solidare* 'make firm' (from *solidus* 'solid').

con·som·mé /ˌkänsəˈmā/ ▶ **n.** a clear soup made with concentrated stock.
– ORIGIN French, past participle of *consommer* 'consume or consummate,' from Latin *consummare* 'make complete' (see **CONSUMMATE**).

con·so·nance /ˈkänsənəns/ ▶ **n.** agreement or compatibility between opinions or actions: *consonance between conservation measures and existing agricultural practice.* ■ the recurrence of similar sounds, esp. consonants, in close proximity (chiefly as used in prosody). ■ Music the combination of notes that are in harmony with each other due to the relationship between their frequencies.
– ORIGIN late Middle English: from Old French, or from Latin *consonantia*, from *consonant-* 'sounding together,' from the verb *consonare* (see **CONSONANT**).

con·so·nant /ˈkänsənənt/ ▶ **n.** a basic speech sound in which the breath is at least partly obstructed and which can be combined with a vowel to form a syllable. Contrasted with **VOWEL**. ■ a letter representing such a sound.
▶ **adj. 1** denoting or relating to such a sound or letter: *a consonant phoneme.*
2 (**consonant with**) in agreement or harmony with: *the findings are consonant with other research.* ■ Music making a harmonious interval or chord: *the bass is consonant with all the upper notes.*
– DERIVATIVES **con·so·nan·tal** /ˌkänsəˈnantl/ **adj.**, **con·so·nant·ly adv.**
– ORIGIN Middle English (in the sense 'letter representing a consonantal sound'): via Old French from Latin *consonare* 'sound together,' from *con-* 'with' + *sonare* 'to sound' (from *sonus* 'sound').

con sor·di·no /kän ˌsôrˈdēnō, kōn/ ▶ **adv.** Music (esp. as a direction) with the use of a mute.
– ORIGIN Italian.

con·sort[1] ▶ **n.** /ˈkänˌsôrt/ a wife, husband, or companion, in particular the spouse of a reigning monarch. ■ a ship sailing in company with another.
▶ **v.** /kənˈsôrt, ˈkänˌsôrt/ [no obj.] (**consort with**) habitually associate with (someone), typically with the disapproval of others: *you chose to consort with the enemy.* ■ (**consort with/to**) archaic agree or be in harmony with.
– ORIGIN late Middle English (denoting a companion or colleague): via French from Latin *consors* 'sharing, partner,' from *con-* 'together with' + *sors, sort-* 'lot, destiny.' The verb senses are probably influenced by similar senses (now obsolete) of the verb *sort*.

con·sort[2] /ˈkänˌsôrt/ ▶ **n.** a small group of musicians performing together, typically playing instrumental music of the Renaissance period: *a consort of viols.*
– ORIGIN late 16th cent.: earlier form of **CONCERT**.

con·sor·ti·um /kənˈsôrSH(ē)əm, -ˈsôrtēəm/ ▶ **n.** (pl. **consortia** /-tēə, -SH(ē)ə/ or **consortiums**) **1** an association, typically of several business companies.
2 Law the right of association and companionship with one's husband or wife.
– ORIGIN early 19th cent. (in the sense 'partnership'): from Latin, from *consors* 'sharing, partner' (see **CONSORT[1]**).

con·spe·cif·ic /ˌkänspəˈsifik/ Biology ▶ **adj.** (of animals or plants) belonging to the same species.
▶ **n.** (usu. **conspecifics**) a member of the same species: *the rabbit was isolated from male conspecifics.*
– DERIVATIVES **con·spec·i·fic·i·ty** /ˌkänˌspesəˈfisitē/ **n.**

con·spec·tus /kənˈspektəs/ ▶ **n.** a summary or overview of a subject: *five of his works give a rich conspectus of his art.*
– ORIGIN mid 19th cent.: from Latin, past participle (used as a noun) of *conspicere* 'look at attentively.'

con·spic·u·ous /kənˈspikyo͞oəs/ ▶ **adj.** standing out so as to be clearly visible: *he was very thin, with a conspicuous Adam's apple.* ■ attracting notice or attention: *he showed conspicuous bravery.*
– PHRASES **conspicuous by one's absence** obviously not present in a place where one should be. [from a speech made by Lord John Russell in an address to electors (1859): taken from Tacitus (*Annals* iii. 76).]
– DERIVATIVES **con·spi·cu·i·ty** /ˌkänspiˈkyo͞oitē/ **n.**, **con·spic·u·ous·ly adv.**, **con·spic·u·ous·ness n.**
– ORIGIN mid 16th cent.: from Latin *conspicuus* (from *conspicere* 'look at attentively,' from *con-* (expressing intensive force) + *specere* 'look at') + **-OUS**.

con·spir·a·cist /kənˈspirəsist/ ▶ **n.** a person who supports a conspiracy theory.

con·spir·a·cy /kənˈspirəsē/ ▶ **n.** (pl. **conspiracies**) a secret plan by a group to do something unlawful or harmful: *a conspiracy to destroy the government.* ■ the action of plotting or conspiring: *they were cleared of conspiracy to pervert the course of justice.*
– PHRASES **a conspiracy of silence** an agreement to say nothing about an issue that should be generally known.
– ORIGIN late Middle English: from Anglo-Norman French *conspiracie*, alteration of Old French *conspiration*, based on Latin *conspirare* 'agree, plot' (see **CONSPIRE**).

con·spir·a·cy the·o·ry ▶ **n.** a belief that some covert but influential organization is responsible for an event.

con·spir·a·tor /kənˈspirətər/ ▶ **n.** a person who takes part in a conspiracy.
– DERIVATIVES **con·spir·a·to·ri·al** /kənˌspirəˈtôrēəl/ **adj.**, **con·spir·a·to·ri·al·ly** /kənˌspirəˈtôrēəlē/ **adv.**
– ORIGIN late Middle English: from Old French *conspirateur*, from Latin *conspirator*, from *conspirat-* 'agreed, plotted,' from the verb *conspirare* (see **CONSPIRE**).

PRONUNCIATION KEY ə *ago, up*; ər *over, fur*; a *hat*; ā *ate*; ä *car*; e *let*; ē *see*; i *fit*; ī *by*; NG *sing*; ō *go*; ô *law, for*; oi *toy*; o͝o *good*; o͞o *goo*; ou *out*; TH *thin*; T͟H *then*; ZH *vision*

C

con·spire /kən'spīr/ ▶ **v.** [no obj.] make secret plans jointly to commit an unlawful or harmful act: *they conspired against him* | *they deny conspiring to defraud the Internal Revenue Service.* ■ (of events or circumstances) seem to be working together to bring about a particular result, typically to someone's detriment: *everything conspires to exacerbate the situation.*
– ORIGIN late Middle English: from Old French *conspirer*, from Latin *conspirare* 'agree, plot,' from *con-* 'together with' + *spirare* 'breathe.'

C

con spi·ri·to /kän 'spiri,tō, 'kōn-/ ▶ **adv.** Music (as a direction) vigorously; in a spirited manner.

Con·sta·ble /'känstəbəl/, John (1776–1837), English painter. His early paintings were inspired by the landscape of his native Suffolk.

con·sta·ble /'känstəbəl/ ▶ **n. 1** a peace officer with limited policing authority, typically in a small town. ■ Brit. a police officer.
2 the governor of a royal castle. ■ historical the highest-ranking official in a royal household.
– ORIGIN Middle English (sense 2): from Old French *conestable*, from late Latin *comes stabuli* 'count (head officer) of the stable.'

con·stab·u·lar·y /kən'stabyə,lerē/ ▶ **n.** (pl. **constabularies**) the constables of a district, collectively. ■ an armed police force organized as a military unit. ■ Brit. a police force covering a particular area or city.
▶ **adj.** of or relating to a constabulary.
– ORIGIN late 15th cent. (denoting the district under the charge of a constable): from medieval Latin *constabularia (dignitas)* '(rank) of constable,' from *constabulus*, based on Latin *comes stabuli* (see CONSTABLE).

Con·stance, Lake /'känstəns/ a lake in southeastern Germany, on the northern side of the Swiss Alps where Germany, Switzerland, and Austria meet. It forms part of the course of the Rhine River. German name **BODENSEE**.

con·stan·cy /'känstənsē/ ▶ **n.** the quality of being faithful and dependable. ■ the quality of being enduring and unchanging: *the trade winds are noted for constancy in speed and direction.*
– ORIGIN late 15th cent.: from Latin *constantia*, from *constant-* 'standing firm' (see CONSTANT).

con·stant /'känstənt/ ▶ **adj.** occurring continuously over a period of time: *the pain is constant.* ■ remaining the same over a period of time: *the company has kept its prices fairly constant.* ■ (of a person) unchangingly faithful and dependable.
▶ **n.** a situation or state of affairs that does not change: *the condition of struggle remained a constant.* ■ Mathematics a quantity or parameter that does not change its value whatever the value of the variables, under a given set of conditions. ■ Physics a number expressing a relation or property that remains the same in all circumstances, or for the same substance under the same conditions.
– ORIGIN late Middle English (in the sense 'staying resolute or faithful'): from Old French, from Latin *constant-* 'standing firm,' from the verb *constare*, from *con-* 'with' + *stare* 'stand.' The noun senses date from the mid 19th cent.

Con·stan·ța /kōn'stäntsə, kôn-/ (also **Constanza**) the chief port of Romania, in the southeastern part of the country, on the Black Sea; pop. 305,550 (2006). Formerly called Tomis, it was renamed for Constantine I in the 4th century.

con·stant·an /'känstən,tan/ ▶ **n.** a copper–nickel alloy used in electrical work for its high resistance.
– ORIGIN early 20th cent.: from CONSTANT + -AN.

Con·stan·tine[1] /'känstən,tēn/ a city in northeastern Algeria; pop. 462,800 (est. 2009). Formerly called Cirta, it was the capital of the Roman province of Numidia. It was destroyed in 311 but was rebuilt by Constantine the Great and given his name.

Con·stan·tine[2] /'känstən,tēn, -,tīn/ (c.274–337), Roman emperor 306–37; known as **Constantine the Great**. He was the first Roman emperor to be converted to Christianity and in 324 made Christianity the empire's state religion. In 330, he moved his capital from Rome to Byzantium, renaming it Constantinopolis (Constantinople). He is venerated as a saint in the Orthodox Church.

Con·stan·ti·no·ple /,kän,stantn'ōpəl/ the former name of Istanbul from AD 330 (when it was given its name by Constantine the Great) until the early 20th century.

con·stant·ly /'känstəntlē/ ▶ **adv.** continuously over a period of time; always: *the world is constantly changing* | *he was constantly on her mind.*

con·sta·tive /'känstətiv, kən'stātiv/ Linguistics ▶ **adj.** denoting a speech act or sentence that is a statement declaring something to be the case. Often contrasted with **PERFORMATIVE**.
▶ **n.** a constative speech act or sentence.
– ORIGIN early 20th cent.: from Latin *constat-* 'established' (from the verb *constare*) + -IVE.

con·stel·late /'känstəlāt/ ▶ **v.** literary form or cause to form into a cluster or group; gather together: [no obj.] *the towns and valleys where people constellate* | [with obj.] *their stories were never constellated.*
– ORIGIN mid 17th cent.: from late Latin *constellatus*, from *con-* 'together' + *stellatus* 'arranged like a star.'

con·stel·la·tion /,känstə'lāsHən/ ▶ **n.** a group of stars forming a recognizable pattern that is traditionally named after its apparent form or identified with a mythological figure. Modern astronomers divide the sky into eighty-eight constellations with defined boundaries. ■ a group or cluster of related things: *no two patients ever show exactly the same constellation of symptoms.*
– ORIGIN Middle English (as an astrological term denoting the relative positions of the "stars" (planets), supposed to influence events): via Old French from late Latin *constellatio(n-)*, based on Latin *stella* 'star.'

con·ster·nate /'känstər,nāt/ ▶ **v.** [with obj.] fill (someone) with anxiety: (as adj. **consternated**) *you'll probably be consternated by all this talk.*
– ORIGIN mid 17th cent.: from Latin *consternat-* 'terrified, prostrated,' from the verb *consternare*.

con·ster·na·tion /,känstər'nāsHən/ ▶ **n.** feelings of anxiety or dismay, typically at something unexpected: *I always welcomed clover, much to the consternation of the neighbors.*
– ORIGIN early 17th cent.: from Latin *consternatio(n-)*, from the verb *consternare* 'lay prostrate, terrify' (see CONSTERNATE).

con·sti·pat·ed /'känstə,pātid/ ▶ **adj.** (of a person or animal) affected with constipation. ■ slow-moving; restricted or inhibited in some way: *spontaneous girls like Ellen are never going to be intimate with constipated deadpan fellows like me.*
– DERIVATIVES **con·sti·pate** /-,pāt/ **v.**
– ORIGIN mid 16th cent.: from Latin *constipat-* 'crowded or pressed together,' from the verb *constipare*, from *con-* 'together' + *stipare* 'press, cram.'

con·sti·pa·tion /,känstə'pāsHən/ ▶ **n.** a condition in which there is difficulty in emptying the bowels, usually associated with hardened feces. ■ a high level of constraint or restriction; a pronounced lack of ease: *literary constipation.*
– ORIGIN late Middle English (in the sense 'contraction of body tissues'): from late Latin *constipatio(n-)*, from the verb *constipare* (see CONSTIPATED).

con·stit·u·en·cy /kən'sticHōōənsē/ ▶ **n.** (pl. **constituencies**) a body of voters in a specified area who elect a representative to a legislative body: *the politician who wishes to remain in the good graces of his constituency.* ■ chiefly Brit. the area represented in this way. ■ a body of customers or supporters: *a constituency of racing fans.*

con·stit·u·ent /kən'sticHōōənt/ ▶ **adj. 1** being a part of a whole: *the constituent minerals of the rock.*
2 being a voting member of a community or organization and having the power to appoint or elect: *the constituent body has a right of veto.* ■ able to make or change a political constitution: *a constituent assembly.*
▶ **n. 1** a member of a constituency.
2 a component part of something: *the essential constituents of the human diet.* ■ Linguistics the common part of two or several more complex forms, e.g., *gentle* in *gentleman, gentlemanly, ungentlemanly.* ■ Linguistics a word or construction that is part of a larger construction.
– ORIGIN late 15th cent. (in the legal sense of the noun): from Latin *constituent-* (partly via French *constituant*) 'establishing, appointing,' from the verb *constituere* (see CONSTITUTE).

con·sti·tute /'känstə,t(y)ōōt/ ▶ **v.** [with obj.] **1** be (a part) of a whole: *single parents constitute a great proportion of the poor.* ■ (of people or things) combine to form (a whole): *there were enough members present to constitute a quorum.* ■ be or be equivalent to (something): *his failure to act constituted a breach of duty.*
2 (usu. **be constituted**) give legal or constitutional form to (an institution); establish by law.
– ORIGIN late Middle English: from Latin *constitut-* 'established, appointed,' from the verb *constituere*, from *con-* 'together' + *statuere* 'set up.'

con·sti·tu·tion /,känstə't(y)ōōsHən/ ▶ **n. 1** a body of fundamental principles or established precedents according to which a state or other organization is acknowledged to be governed. ■ (**the Constitution**) the basic written set of principles and precedents of federal government in the US, which came into operation in 1789 and has since been modified by twenty-seven amendments.
2 the composition of something: *the genetic constitution of a species.* ■ the forming or establishing of something: *the constitution of a police authority.*
3 a person's physical state with regard to vitality, health, and strength: *pregnancy had weakened her constitution.* ■ a person's mental or psychological makeup.
– ORIGIN Middle English (denoting a law, or a body of laws or customs): from Latin *constitutio(n-)*, from *constituere* 'establish, appoint' (see CONSTITUTE).

con·sti·tu·tion·al /,känstə't(y)ōōsHənl/ ▶ **adj. 1** of or relating to an established set of principles governing a state: *a constitutional amendment.* ■ in accordance with or allowed by such principles: *a constitutional monarchy.*
2 of or relating to someone's physical or mental condition: *a constitutional weakness.*
▶ **n.** dated a walk, typically one taken regularly to maintain or restore good health.
– DERIVATIVES **con·sti·tu·tion·al·i·ty** /-,t(y)ōōsHə'nalitē/ **n.**, **con·sti·tu·tion·al·ly adv.**

con·sti·tu·tion·al·ism /,känstə't(y)ōōsHənl-izəm/ ▶ **n.** constitutional government. ■ adherence to such a system of government.
– DERIVATIVES **con·sti·tu·tion·al·ist n.**

con·sti·tu·tion·al·ize /,känstə't(y)ōōsHənl-īz/ ▶ **v.** [with obj.] make subject to explicit provisions of a country's constitution: *divorce is not constitutionalized.*

Con·sti·tu·tion State a nickname for the state of **CONNECTICUT**.

con·sti·tu·tive /'känstə,t(y)ōōtiv, kən'sticHətiv/ ▶ **adj. 1** having the power to establish or give organized existence to something: *the state began to exercise a new and constitutive function.*
2 forming a part or constituent of something; component: *poverty is a constitutive element of a particular form of economic growth.* ■ forming an essential element of something: *language is constitutive of thought.*
3 Biochemistry relating to an enzyme or enzyme system that is continuously produced in an organism, regardless of the needs of cells.
– DERIVATIVES **con·sti·tu·tive·ly adv.**

con·strain /kən'strān/ ▶ **v.** [with obj.] severely restrict the scope, extent, or activity of: *agricultural development is considerably constrained by climate* | *we can constrain data access.* ■ compel or force (someone) toward a particular course of action: *children are constrained to work in the way the book dictates.* ■ (usu. as adj. **constrained**) cause to appear unnaturally forced, typically because of embarrassment: *he was acting in a constrained manner.* ■ literary confine forcibly; imprison. ■ archaic bring about (something) by compulsion: *Calypso in her caves constrained his stay.*
– DERIVATIVES **con·strain·ed·ly** /-nədlē/ **adv.**
– ORIGIN Middle English: from Old French *constraindre*, from Latin *constringere* 'bind tightly together.'

con·straint /kən'strānt/ ▶ **n.** a limitation or restriction: *the availability of water is the main constraint on food production* | *time constraints make it impossible to do everything.* ■ stiffness of manner and inhibition in relations between people: *they would be able to talk without constraint.*
– ORIGIN late Middle English (in the sense 'coercion'): from Old French *constreinte*, feminine past participle of *constraindre* (see CONSTRAIN).

con·strict /kən'strikt/ ▶ **v.** [with obj.] make narrower, esp. by encircling pressure: *chemicals that constrict the blood vessels* | (as adj. **constricted**) *constricted air passages.* ■ [no obj.] become narrower: *he felt his throat constrict.* ■ (of a snake) coil around (prey) in order to asphyxiate it. ■ inhibit or restrict: *the fear and the reality of crime constrict many people's lives.*
– DERIVATIVES **con·stric·tive** /-tiv/ **adj.**
– ORIGIN mid 18th cent.: from Latin *constrict-* 'bound tightly together,' from the verb *constringere* (see CONSTRAIN).

con·stric·tion /kən'striksHən/ ▶ **n.** the action of making something narrower by pressure or of becoming narrower; tightening: *asthma is a constriction of the airways.* ■ a place where something has become tighter or narrower; an obstruction: *flow was impeded at bends and constrictions.*

con·stric·tor /kən'striktər/ ▶ **n. 1** a snake that kills by coiling around its prey and asphyxiating it. ● Families Boidae and Pythonidae, and some members of other families (in particular Colubridae).
2 (also **constrictor muscle**) Anatomy a muscle whose contraction narrows a vessel or passage. ■ each of the muscles that constrict the pharynx.
– ORIGIN early 18th cent.: modern Latin, from *constrict-* 'bound tightly together,' from the verb *constringere* (see CONSTRAIN).

con·struct ▶ **v.** /kən'strəkt/ [with obj.] build or erect (something, typically a building, road, or machine):

a company that constructs oil rigs. ■ form (an idea or theory) by bringing together various conceptual elements, typically over a period of time: *Ptolemy combined his interests to construct a theory in support of Aristotle.* ■ Grammar form (a sentence) according to grammatical rules. ■ Geometry draw or delineate (a geometric figure) accurately to given conditions.
▶ **n.** /ˈkänˌstrəkt/ an idea or theory containing various conceptual elements, typically one considered to be subjective and not based on empirical evidence: *history is largely an ideological construct.* ■ Linguistics a group of words forming a phrase. ■ a physical thing that is deliberately built or formed.
– DERIVATIVES **con·struct·i·ble adj., con·struc·tor** /-tər/ **n.**
– ORIGIN late Middle English: from Latin *construct-* 'heaped together, built,' from the verb *construere,* from *con-* 'together' + *struere* 'pile, build.'

con·struc·tion /kənˈstrəksʜən/ ▶ **n.** the building of something, typically a large structure: *there was a skyscraper **under construction**.* ■ such activity considered as an industry. ■ the style or method used in the building of something: *the mill is of brick construction.* ■ a building or other structure. ■ the creation or formation of an abstract entity: *language plays a large part in our construction of reality.* ■ an interpretation or explanation: *you could **put an honest construction upon** their conduct.* ■ Grammar the arrangement of words according to syntactical rules: *sentence construction.*
– DERIVATIVES **con·struc·tion·al** /-sʜənl/ **adj., con·struc·tion·al·ly** /-sʜənl-ē/ **adv.**
– ORIGIN late Middle English: via Old French from Latin *constructio(n-),* from *construere* 'heap together' (see CONSTRUCT).

con·struc·tion·ism /kənˈstrəksʜəˌnizəm/ ▶ **n.** another term for CONSTRUCTIVISM.

con·struc·tion·ist /kənˈstrəksʜənist/ ▶ **n. 1** another term for CONSTRUCTIVIST (see CONSTRUCTIVISM).
2 a person who puts a particular construction upon a legal document, esp. the US Constitution.

con·struc·tion pa·per ▶ **n.** a type of thick colored paper used for making models, designs, and other crafts.

con·struc·tive /kənˈstrəktiv/ ▶ **adj. 1** serving a useful purpose; tending to build up: *constructive criticism.*
2 Law derived by inference; implied by operation of law; not obvious or explicit: *constructive liability.*
3 Mathematics relating to, based on, or denoting mathematical proofs that show how an entity may in principle be constructed or arrived at in a finite number of steps.
– DERIVATIVES **con·struc·tive·ly adv., con·struc·tive·ness n.**
– ORIGIN mid 17th cent. (sense 2): from late Latin *constructivus,* from Latin *construct-* 'heaped together,' from the verb *construere* (see CONSTRUCT).

con·struc·tiv·ism /kənˈstrəktiˌvizəm/ ▶ **n. 1** Art a style or movement in which assorted mechanical objects are combined into abstract mobile structural forms. The movement originated in Russia in the 1920s and has influenced many aspects of modern architecture and design. [transliterating Russian *konstruktivizm.*]
2 Mathematics a view which admits as valid only constructive proofs and entities demonstrable by them, implying that the latter have no independent existence.
– DERIVATIVES **con·struc·tiv·ist n.**

con·strue /kənˈstro͞o/ ▶ **v.** (**construes, construing, construed**) [with obj.] interpret (a word or action) in a particular way: *his words could hardly **be construed as** an apology.* ■ dated analyze the syntax of (a text, sentence, or word): *both verbs can be construed **with** either infinitive.* ■ dated translate (a passage or author) word for word, typically aloud.
– DERIVATIVES **con·stru·a·ble adj., con·stru·al** /-ˈstro͞oəl/ **n.**
– ORIGIN late Middle English: from Latin *construere* (see CONSTRUCT), in late Latin 'analyze the construction of a sentence.'

con·sub·stan·tial /ˌkänsəbˈstancʜəl/ ▶ **adj.** of the same substance or essence (used esp. of the three persons of the Trinity in Christian theology): *Christ is **consubstantial with** the Father.*
– DERIVATIVES **con·sub·stan·ti·al·i·ty** /-ˌstancʜēˈalətē/ **n.**
– ORIGIN late Middle English: from ecclesiastical Latin *consubstantialis* (translating Greek *homoousios* 'of one substance'), from *con-* 'with' + *substantialis* (see SUBSTANTIAL).

con·sub·stan·ti·a·tion /ˌkänsəbˌstancʜēˈāsʜən/ ▶ **n.** Christian Theology the doctrine, esp. in Lutheran belief, that the substance of the bread and wine coexists with the body and blood of Christ in the Eucharist. Compare with TRANSUBSTANTIATION.
– ORIGIN late 16th cent.: from modern Latin *consubstantiatio(n-),* from *con-* 'together,' on the pattern of *transubstantiatio-* 'transubstantiation.'

con·sue·tude /ˈkänswiˌt(y)o͞od/ ▶ **n.** an established custom, esp. one having legal force.
– DERIVATIVES **con·sue·tu·di·nar·y** /ˌkänswiˈt(y)o͞odnˌerē/ **adj.**
– ORIGIN late Middle English: from Old French, or from Latin *consuetudo* (see CUSTOM).

con·sul /ˈkänsəl/ ▶ **n. 1** an official appointed by a government to live in a foreign city and protect and promote the government's citizens and interests there.
2 (in ancient Rome) one of the two annually elected chief magistrates who jointly ruled the republic. ■ any of the three chief magistrates of the first French republic (1799–1804).
– DERIVATIVES **con·su·lar** /ˈkäns(y)ələr/ **adj., con·sul·ship** /-ˌsʜip/ **n.**
– ORIGIN late Middle English (denoting an ancient Roman magistrate): from Latin, related to *consulere* 'take counsel.'

con·su·late /ˈkänsələt/ ▶ **n. 1** the place or building in which a consul's duties are carried out. ■ the office or position of a consul.
2 historical the period of office of a Roman consul. ■ (**the consulate**) the system of government by consuls in ancient Rome.
3 (**the Consulate**) the government of the first French republic (1799–1804) by three consuls.
– ORIGIN late Middle English (denoting the government of Rome by consuls, or their office or dignity): from Latin *consulatus,* from *consul* (see CONSUL).

con·sul gen·er·al ▶ **n.** (pl. **consuls general**) a consul of the highest status, stationed in a major city and supervising other consuls in the district.

con·sult /kənˈsəlt/ ▶ **v.** [with obj.] seek information or advice from (someone with expertise in a particular area): *you should consult a financial advisor.* ■ have discussions or confer with (someone), typically before undertaking a course of action: *patients are entitled to be consulted about their treatment* | [no obj.] *they've got to **consult with** their board of directors.* ■ refer for information to (a book, watch, etc.) in order to ascertain something: *consult the index at the back of the brochure.*
– DERIVATIVES **con·sul·ta·tive** /-ˈsəltətiv/ **adj.**
– ORIGIN early 16th cent. (in the sense 'deliberate together, confer'): from French *consulter,* from Latin *consultare,* frequentative of *consulere* 'take counsel.'

con·sult·an·cy /kənˈsəltnsē/ ▶ **n.** (pl. **consultancies**) a professional practice that gives expert advice within a particular field, esp. business: *a management consultancy firm.* ■ the work of giving such advice.

con·sult·ant /kənˈsəltnt/ ▶ **n. 1** a person who provides expert advice professionally.
2 [usu. as modifier] Brit. a hospital doctor of senior rank within a specific field: *a consultant pediatrician.*
– ORIGIN late 17th cent. (in the sense 'a person who consults'): probably from French, from Latin *consultare* (see CONSULT).

con·sul·ta·tion /ˌkänsəlˈtāsʜən/ ▶ **n.** the action or process of formally consulting or discussing: *they improved standards **in consultation with** consumer representatives* | *consultations between the two governments.* ■ a meeting with an expert or professional, such as a medical doctor, in order to seek advice.
– ORIGIN late Middle English: from Latin *consultatio(n-),* from the verb *consultare* (see CONSULT).

con·sult·ing /kənˈsəltiɴɢ/ ▶ **adj.** engaged in the business of giving expert advice to people working in a professional or technical field: *a consulting engineer* | *an environmental consulting company.*
▶ **n.** the business of giving expert advice to other professionals, typically in financial and business matters.

con·sult·ing room ▶ **n.** a room in which a doctor or other therapeutic practitioner examines patients.

con·sum·a·ble /kənˈso͞oməbəl/ ▶ **adj.** (of an item for sale) intended to be used up and then replaced.
▶ **n.** (usu. **consumables**) a commodity that is intended to be used up relatively quickly: *drugs and other medical consumables.*

con·sume /kənˈso͞om/ ▶ **v.** [with obj.] eat, drink, or ingest (food or drink): *people consume a good deal of sugar in drinks.* ■ buy (goods or services). ■ use up (a resource): *these machines consume 5 percent of the natural gas in the U.S.* ■ (esp. of a fire) completely destroy: *the fire spread rapidly, consuming many homes.* ■ (usu. **be consumed**) (of a feeling) absorb all of the attention and energy of (someone): *Carolyn was consumed with guilt.*
– ORIGIN late Middle English: from Latin *consumere,* from *con-* 'altogether' + *sumere* 'take up'; reinforced by French *consumer.*

con·sum·er /kənˈso͞omər/ ▶ **n.** a person who purchases goods and services for personal use: [as modifier] *consumer demand.* ■ a person or thing that eats or uses something: *Scandinavians are the largest consumers of rye.*

con·sum·er goods ▶ **plural n.** goods bought and used by consumers, rather than by manufacturers for producing other goods. Often contrasted with CAPITAL GOODS.

con·sum·er·ism /kənˈso͞oməˌrizəm/ ▶ **n. 1** the protection or promotion of the interests of consumers.
2 often derogatory the preoccupation of society with the acquisition of consumer goods.
– DERIVATIVES **con·sum·er·ist adj. & n., con·sum·er·is·tic** /kənˌso͞oməˈristik/ **adj.**

con·sum·er price in·dex (abbr.: **CPI**) ▶ **n.** an index of the variation in prices paid by typical consumers for retail goods and other items.

con·sum·er re·search ▶ **n.** the investigation of the needs and opinions of consumers, esp. with regard to a particular product or service.

con·sum·er so·ci·e·ty ▶ **n.** often derogatory a society in which the buying and selling of goods and services is the most important social and economic activity.

con·sum·er sov·er·eign·ty ▶ **n.** Economics the situation in an economy where the desires and needs of consumers control the output of producers.

con·sum·ing /kənˈso͞omiɴɢ/ ▶ **adj.** (of a feeling) completely filling one's mind and attention; absorbing: *a consuming passion.*
– DERIVATIVES **con·sum·ing·ly adv.**

con·sum·mate ▶ **v.** /ˈkänsəˌmāt/ [with obj.] make (a marriage or relationship) complete by having sexual intercourse: *his first wife refused to consummate their marriage.* ■ complete (a transaction or attempt); make perfect: *his scheme of colonization was consummated through bloodshed.*
▶ **adj.** /ˈkänsəmət, kənˈsəmət/ showing a high degree of skill and flair; complete or perfect: *she dressed with consummate elegance.*
– DERIVATIVES **con·sum·mate·ly** /ˈkänsəmətlē, kənˈsəmətlē/ **adv., con·sum·ma·tor** /ˈkänsəˌmātər/ **n.**
– ORIGIN late Middle English (as an adjective in the sense 'completed, accomplished'): from Latin *consummat-* 'brought to completion,' from the verb *consummare,* from *con-* 'altogether' + *summa* 'sum total,' feminine of *summus* 'highest, supreme.'

con·sum·ma·tion /ˌkänsəˈmāsʜən/ ▶ **n.** the point at which something is complete or finalized: ***the consummation of** a sale.* ■ the action of making a marriage or relationship complete by having sexual intercourse: *the eager consummation that follows a long and passionate seduction.*
– ORIGIN late Middle English: from Latin *consummatio(n-),* from the verb *consummare* (see CONSUMMATE).

con·sump·tion /kənˈsəm(p)sʜən/ ▶ **n. 1** the using up of a resource: *industrialized countries should reduce their energy consumption.* ■ the eating, drinking, or ingesting of something: *liquor is sold for consumption off the premises.* ■ an amount of something that is used up or ingested: *a daily consumption of 15 cigarettes.* ■ the purchase and use of goods and services by the public: *an article for mass consumption.* ■ the reception of information or entertainment, esp. by a mass audience: *his confidential speech was not meant for public consumption.*
2 dated a wasting disease, esp. pulmonary tuberculosis.
– ORIGIN late Middle English: from Latin *consumptio(n-),* from the verb *consumere* (see CONSUME).

con·sump·tive /kənˈsəm(p)tiv/ ▶ **adj. 1** dated affected with a wasting disease, esp. pulmonary tuberculosis: *from birth he was sickly and consumptive.*
2 chiefly derogatory of or relating to the using up of resources: *tourism represents an insidious form of consumptive activity.*
▶ **n.** dated a person with a wasting disease, esp. pulmonary tuberculosis.
– DERIVATIVES **con·sump·tive·ly adv.**
– ORIGIN mid 17th cent.: from medieval Latin *consumptivus,* from Latin *consumpt-* 'consumed,' from the verb *consumere* (see CONSUME).

cont. ▶ **abbr.** ■ contents. ■ continued.

con·tact ▶ **n.** /ˈkänˌtakt/ **1** the state or condition of physical touching: *the tennis ball is in contact with the court surface for as little as 5 milliseconds.* ■ the state or condition of communicating or meeting: *Lewis and Clark **came into contact with** numerous river tribes | he **had lost contact with** his friends.* ■ [as modifier] activated by or operating through physical touch: *contact dermatitis.* ■ a connection for the passage of an electric current from one thing to another, or a part or device by which such a connection is made: *a one-way electrical contact between a metal and a semiconductor.* ■ (**contacts**) contact lenses.
2 a meeting, communication, or relationship with someone: *they have forged contacts with key people in business.* ■ a person who may be communicated with for information or assistance, esp. with regard to one's job: *Francie had good contacts.* ■ a person who has associated with a patient with a contagious disease (and so may carry the infection).
▶ **v.** /ˈkänˌtakt, kənˈtakt/ [with obj.] communicate with (someone), typically in order to give or receive specific information.
– DERIVATIVES **con·tact·a·ble** /ˈkänˌtaktəbəl, kənˈtak-/ **adj.**
– ORIGIN early 17th cent.: from Latin *contactus*, from *contact-* 'touched, grasped, bordered on,' from the verb *contingere*, from *con-* 'together with' + *tangere* 'to touch.'

con·tact cen·ter ▶ **n.** an integrated and usually automated communications system that coordinates all telephone and electronic contacts between an organization and the public.

con·tact·ee /ˌkänˌtakˈtē, kən-/ ▶ **n.** a person who claims to have been contacted by alien beings, esp. through an abduction.

con·tact flight (also **contact flying**) ▶ **n.** navigation of an aircraft by the observation of landmarks.

con·tact lens ▶ **n.** a thin plastic lens placed directly on the surface of the eye to correct visual defects.

con·tact·less /ˈkänˌtaktləs/ ▶ **adj.** denoting a smart card that uses radio signals to provide a wireless connection to a card reader, so that no physical contact is necessary.

con·tact met·a·mor·phism ▶ **n.** Geology metamorphism due to contact with or proximity to an igneous intrusion.

con·tac·tor /ˈkänˌtaktər, kənˈtak-/ ▶ **n.** a device for making and breaking an electric circuit.

con·tact per·son ▶ **n.** a person who provides a link for information or representation between two parties.

con·tact print ▶ **n.** a photographic print made by placing a negative directly onto sensitized paper, glass, or film and illuminating it.
▶ **v.** (**contact-print**) [with obj.] make a photograph from (a negative) in this way.

con·tact proc·ess ▶ **n.** the major industrial process used to make sulfuric acid, by oxidizing sulfur dioxide in the presence of a solid catalyst and absorbing the resulting sulfur trioxide in water.

con·tact sheet ▶ **n.** a piece of photographic paper onto which several or all of the negatives on a roll of film have been contact printed.

con·tact sport ▶ **n.** a sport in which the participants necessarily come into bodily contact with one another.

con·ta·di·na /ˌkäntəˈdēnə/ ▶ **n.** (pl. **contadine** /-ˈdēˌnā/ or **contadinas**) an Italian peasant girl or peasant woman.
– ORIGIN Italian.

con·ta·di·no /ˌkäntəˈdēnō/ ▶ **n.** (pl. **contadini** /-ˈdēnē/ or **contadinos**) an Italian peasant or rustic.
– ORIGIN Italian, from *contado*, denoting the peasant population around a city.

Con·ta·gem /ˌkōntəˈZHām/ a city in Minas Gerais state in southeastern Brazil, west of Belo Horizonte; pop. 608,700 (est. 2007).

con·ta·gion /kənˈtājən/ ▶ **n.** the communication of disease from one person to another by close contact: *the rooms held no risk of contagion.* ■ a disease spread in such a way. ■ the spreading of a harmful idea or practice: *the contagion of disgrace.*
– ORIGIN late Middle English (denoting a contagious disease): from Latin *contagio(n-)*, from *con-* 'together with' + the base of *tangere* 'to touch.'

con·ta·gious /kənˈtājəs/ ▶ **adj. 1** (of a disease) spread from one person or organism to another by direct or indirect contact: *a contagious infection.* ■ (of a person or animal) likely to transmit a disease by contact with other people or animals.
2 (of an emotion, feeling, or attitude) likely to spread to and affect others: *her enthusiasm is contagious.*
– DERIVATIVES **con·ta·gious·ly adv.**, **con·ta·gious·ness n.**
– ORIGIN late Middle English: from late Latin *contagiosus*, from *contagio* (see CONTAGION).

> **USAGE** Strictly, a **contagious** disease is one transmitted by physical contact, whereas an **infectious** one is transmitted via microorganisms in the air or water. In practice, there is little or no difference in meaning between **contagious** and **infectious** when applied to disease or its spread. In figurative senses, **contagious** may describe the spread of good things such as laughter and enthusiasm or bad ones such as violence or panic, whereas **infectious** usually refers to the spread of positive things, such as good humor or optimism.

con·ta·gium /kənˈtājəm, -jēəm/ ▶ **n.** (pl. **contagia** /-jə, -jēə/) a substance or agent, such as a virus, by which a contagious disease is transmitted.

con·tain /kənˈtān/ ▶ **v.** [with obj.] **1** have or hold (someone or something) within: *coffee cans that once contained a full pound of coffee.* ■ be made up of (a number of things); consist of: *borscht can contain mainly beets or a number of vegetables.* ■ (of a number) be divisible by (a factor) without a remainder.
2 control or restrain (oneself or a feeling): *she was scarcely able to contain herself as she waited to spill the beans.* ■ prevent (a severe problem) from increasing in extent or intensity: *a reassuring statement on efforts to contain the disaster.*
– DERIVATIVES **con·tain·a·ble adj.**
– ORIGIN Middle English: from Old French *contenir*, from Latin *continere*, from *con-* 'altogether' + *tenere* 'to hold.'

con·tain·er /kənˈtānər/ ▶ **n.** an object that can be used to hold or transport something: *a microwaveable glass container.* ■ a large metal box of a standard design and size used for the transportation of goods by road, rail, sea, or air: *a container ship.*

con·tain·er·ize /kənˈtānəˌrīz/ ▶ **v.** [with obj.] (usu. as adj. **containerized**) pack into or transport by container: *containerized cargo.*
– DERIVATIVES **con·tain·er·i·za·tion** /-ˌtānərəˈzāSHən/ **n.**

con·tain·er port ▶ **n.** a port that specializes in handling goods transported in containers.

con·tain·er ship ▶ **n.** a ship that is designed to carry goods stowed in containers.

con·tain·ment /kənˈtānmənt/ ▶ **n.** the action of keeping something harmful under control or within limits: *the containment of the AIDS epidemic.* ■ the action or policy of preventing the expansion of a hostile country or influence: *a policy of containment.*

con·tam·i·nate /kənˈtaməˌnāt/ ▶ **v.** [with obj.] make (something) impure by exposure to or addition of a poisonous or polluting substance: *the site was found to be contaminated by radioactivity* | figurative *celebrity has contaminated every aspect of public life* | (as adj. **contaminated**) *contaminated blood products.*
– DERIVATIVES **con·tam·i·nant** /-ˈtamənənt/ **n.**, **con·tam·i·na·tion** /-ˌtaməˈnāSHən/ **n.**, **con·tam·i·na·tor** /-ˌnātər/ **n.**
– ORIGIN late Middle English: from Latin *contaminat-* 'made impure,' from the verb *contaminare*, from *contamen* 'contact, pollution,' from *con-* 'together with' + the base of *tangere* 'to touch.'

con·te /kônt/ ▶ **n.** a short story as a form of literary composition. ■ a medieval narrative tale.
– ORIGIN French, based on Latin *computare* 'reckon, sum up.'

con·té /kônˈtā/ (also trademark **Conté**) ▶ **n.** a kind of hard, grease-free crayon used as a medium for artwork: *powerful drawings in rough red conté.*
– ORIGIN mid 19th cent.: named after Nicolas J. *Conté* (1755–1805), the French inventor who developed it.

con·temn /kənˈtem/ ▶ **v.** [with obj.] archaic treat or regard with contempt.
– DERIVATIVES **con·temn·er** /-ˈtem(n)ər/ **n.**
– ORIGIN late Middle English: from Latin *contemnere*, from *con-* (expressing intensive force) + *temnere* 'despise.'

con·tem·plate /ˈkäntəmˌplāt/ ▶ **v.** [with obj.] look thoughtfully for a long time at: *he sat on the carpet contemplating his image in the mirrors.* ■ think about: *the results of a trade war are too horrifying to contemplate.* ■ [no obj.] think profoundly and at length; meditate: *he sat morosely contemplating.* ■ have in mind as a probable though not certain intention: *she was contemplating a gold mining venture.*
– DERIVATIVES **con·tem·pla·tor** /-ˌplātər/ **n.**
– ORIGIN late 16th cent.: from Latin *contemplat-* 'surveyed, observed, contemplated,' from the verb *contemplari*, based on *templum* 'place for observation.'

con·tem·pla·tion /ˌkäntəmˈplāSHən/ ▶ **n.** the action of looking thoughtfully at something for a long time: *the road is too busy for leisurely contemplation of the scenery.* ■ deep reflective thought: *he would retire to his room for study or contemplation.* ■ the state of being thought about or planned. ■ religious meditation. ■ (in Christian spirituality) a form of prayer or meditation in which a person seeks to pass beyond mental images and concepts to a direct experience of the divine.
– ORIGIN Middle English: from Old French, from Latin *contemplatio(n-)*, from the verb *contemplari* (see CONTEMPLATE).

con·tem·pla·tive /kənˈtemplətiv/ ▶ **adj.** expressing or involving prolonged thought: *she regarded me with a contemplative eye.* ■ involving or given to deep silent prayer or religious meditation: *contemplative knowledge of God.*
▶ **n.** a person whose life is devoted primarily to prayer, esp. in a monastery or convent.
– DERIVATIVES **con·tem·pla·tive·ly adv.**

con·tem·po·ra·ne·ous /kənˌtempəˈrānēəs/ ▶ **adj.** existing or occurring in the same period of time: *Pythagoras was **contemporaneous with** Buddha.*
– DERIVATIVES **con·tem·po·ra·ne·i·ty** /-rəˈnēitē, -rəˈnāitē/ **n.**, **con·tem·po·ra·ne·ous·ly adv.**, **con·tem·po·ra·ne·ous·ness n.**
– ORIGIN mid 17th cent.: from Latin, from *con-* 'together with' + *temporaneus* (from *tempus*, *tempor-* 'time') + **-ous**.

con·tem·po·rar·y /kənˈtempəˌrerē/ ▶ **adj. 1** living or occurring at the same time: *the event was recorded by a contemporary historian.* ■ dating from the same time: *this series of paintings is **contemporary with** other works in an early style.*
2 belonging to or occurring in the present: *the tension and complexities of our contemporary society.* ■ following modern ideas or fashion in style or design: *contemporary art.*
▶ **n.** (pl. **contemporaries**) a person or thing living or existing at the same time as another: *he was a contemporary of Darwin.* ■ a person of roughly the same age as another: *my contemporaries at school.*
– DERIVATIVES **con·tem·po·rar·i·ly** /kənˌtempəˈre(ə)rəlē/ **adv.**, **con·tem·po·rar·i·ness n.**
– ORIGIN mid 17th cent.: from medieval Latin *contemporarius*, from *con-* 'together with' + *tempus*, *tempor-* 'time' (on the pattern of Latin *contemporaneus* and late Latin *contemporalis*).

con·tempt /kənˈtem(p)t/ ▶ **n.** the feeling that a person or a thing is beneath consideration, worthless, or deserving scorn: *he showed his contempt for his job by doing it very badly.* ■ disregard for something that should be taken into account: *this action displays an arrogant contempt for the wishes of the majority.* ■ (also **contempt of court**) the offense of being disobedient to or disrespectful of a court of law and its officers. ■ the offense of being similarly disobedient to or disrespectful of the lawful operation of a legislative body (e.g., its investigations).
– PHRASES **beneath contempt** utterly worthless or despicable. **hold someone in contempt** judge someone to have committed the offence of contempt of court. **hold someone/something in contempt** consider someone or something to be unworthy of respect or attention: *the speed limit is held in contempt by many drivers.*
– ORIGIN late Middle English: from Latin *contemptus*, from *contemnere* (see CONTEMN).

con·tempt·i·ble /kənˈtem(p)təbəl/ ▶ **adj.** deserving contempt; despicable: *a display of contemptible cowardice.*
– DERIVATIVES **con·tempt·i·bly** /-blē/ **adv.**
– ORIGIN late Middle English: from Old French, or from late Latin *contemptibilis*, from Latin *contemnere* (see CONTEMN).

con·temp·tu·ous /kənˈtem(p)CHo͞oəs/ ▶ **adj.** showing contempt; scornful: *she was intolerant and **contemptuous of** the majority of the human race.*
– DERIVATIVES **con·temp·tu·ous·ly adv.**, **con·temp·tu·ous·ness n.**
– ORIGIN mid 16th cent. (in the sense 'despising law and order'): from medieval Latin *contemptuosus*, from Latin *contemptus* 'contempt,' from *contemnere* (see CONTEMN).

con·tend /kənˈtend/ ▶ **v. 1** [no obj.] (**contend with/against**) struggle to surmount (a difficulty or danger): *she had to contend with his uncertain temper.* ■ (**contend for**) engage in a competition or campaign in order to win or achieve (something): *the local team should contend for a division championship* | (as adj. **contending**) *disputes continued between the contending parties.*
2 assert something as a position in an argument: *he contends that the judge was wrong.*
– DERIVATIVES **con·tend·er n.**
– ORIGIN late Middle English (in the sense 'compete for (something)'): from Old French *contendre* or

Latin *contendere*, from *con-* 'with' + *tendere* 'stretch, strive.'

con·tent¹ /kənˈtent/ ▶ **adj.** in a state of peaceful happiness: *he seemed more content, less bitter.* ■ satisfied with a certain level of achievement, good fortune, etc., and not wishing for more: *he had to be content with third place | the duke was content to act as Regent.*
▶ **v.** [with obj.] satisfy (someone): *nothing would content her.* ■ (**content oneself with**) accept as adequate despite wanting more or better: *we contented ourselves with a few small purchases.*
▶ **n. 1** a state of satisfaction: *the greater part of the century was a time of content.*
2 a member of the British House of Lords who votes for a particular motion.
– PHRASES **to one's heart's content** to the full extent of one's desires: *the children could run and play to their heart's content.*
– ORIGIN late Middle English: via Old French from Latin *contentus* 'satisfied,' past participle of *continere* (see CONTAIN).

con·tent² /ˈkänˌtent/ ▶ **n. 1** (usu. **contents**) the things that are held or included in something: *he unscrewed the top of the flask and drank the contents | he picked up the correspondence and scanned the contents.* ■ [usu. in sing.] the amount of a particular constituent occurring in a substance: *milk with a low-fat content.* ■ (**contents** or **table of contents**) a list of the titles of chapters or sections contained in a book or periodical: *the contents page.* ■ information made available by a website or other electronic medium: *online content providers.*
2 the substance or material dealt with in a speech, literary work, etc., as distinct from its form or style: *the outward form and precise content of the messages.*
– DERIVATIVES **con·tent·less** adj.
– ORIGIN late Middle English: from medieval Latin *contentum* (plural *contenta* 'things contained'), neuter past part. of *continere* (see CONTAIN).

con·tent·ed /kənˈtentəd/ ▶ **adj.** happy and at ease: *I felt warm and contented.* ■ willing to accept something; satisfied: *I was never contented with half measures.*
– DERIVATIVES **con·tent·ed·ly** adv., **con·tent·ed·ness** n.

con·ten·tion /kənˈtenCHən/ ▶ **n. 1** heated disagreement: *the captured territory was one of the main areas of contention between the two countries.*
2 an assertion, esp. one maintained in argument: *statistics bear out his contention that many runners are undertrained for this event.*
– PHRASES **in contention** having a good chance of success in a contest: *he was in contention for the batting title in September.*
– ORIGIN late Middle English: from Latin *contentio(n-)*, from *contendere* 'strive with' (see CONTEND).

con·ten·tious /kənˈtenCHəs/ ▶ **adj.** causing or likely to cause an argument; controversial: *a contentious issue.* ■ involving heated argument: *the socioeconomic plan had been the subject of contentious debate.* ■ (of a person) given to arguing or provoking argument: *a contentious amateur politician who has offended minority groups.* ■ Law relating to or involving differences between contending parties.
– DERIVATIVES **con·ten·tious·ly** adv., **con·ten·tious·ness** n.
– ORIGIN late Middle English: from Old French *contentieux*, from Latin *contentiosus*, from *content-* 'striven,' from the verb *contendere*.

con·tent·ment /kənˈtentmənt/ ▶ **n.** a state of happiness and satisfaction: *he found contentment in living a simple life in the country.*
– ORIGIN late Middle English (denoting the payment of a claim): from French *contentement*, from Latin *contentus* (see CONTENT¹).

con·tent pro·vid·er ▶ **n.** a person or organization who supplies information for use on a website: *the content provider for short law and practice news updates | he worked for an Internet content provider.*

con·ter·mi·nous /känˈtərmənəs, kən-/ ▶ **adj.** sharing a common boundary: *the forty-eight conterminous United States.* ■ having the same area, context, or meaning: *a genealogy conterminous with the history of the USA.*
– DERIVATIVES **con·ter·mi·nous·ly** adv.
– ORIGIN mid 17th cent.: from Latin *conterminus* (from *con-* 'with' + *terminus* 'boundary') + -OUS. Compare with COTERMINOUS.

con·tes·sa /kənˈtesə, kōn-/ ▶ **n.** an Italian countess.
– ORIGIN Italian, from late Latin *comitissa* (see COUNTESS).

con·test ▶ **n.** /ˈkänˌtest/ an event in which people compete for supremacy in a sport, activity, or particular quality: *a gigantic air rifle shooting contest | a beauty contest.* ■ a competition for a political position: *the presidential contest.* ■ a dispute or conflict: *a contest between traditional and liberal views.*
▶ **v.** /kənˈtest, ˈkänˌtest/ [with obj.] **1** engage in competition to attain (a position of power): *she declared her intention to contest the presidency.* ■ take part in (a competition or election): *a coalition was formed to contest the presidential elections.*
2 oppose (an action, decision, or theory) as mistaken or wrong: *the former chairman contests his dismissal.* ■ engage in dispute about: *the issues have been hotly contested.*
– PHRASES **no contest 1** another term for NOLO CONTENDERE: *he pleaded no contest to two misdemeanor counts.* **2** a competition, comparison, or choice of which the outcome is a foregone conclusion: *when the two teams faced each other it was no contest.* ■ a decision by the referee to declare a boxing match invalid on the grounds that one or both of the boxers are not making serious efforts.
– DERIVATIVES **con·test·a·ble** /kənˈtestəbəl/ adj., **con·test·er** /kənˈtestər, ˈkänˌtes-/ n.
– ORIGIN late 16th cent. (as a verb in the sense 'swear to, attest'): from Latin *contestari* 'call upon to witness, initiate an action (by calling witnesses),' from *con-* 'together' + *testare* 'to witness.' The senses 'wrangle, strive, struggle for' arose in the early 17th cent., whence the current noun and verb senses.

con·test·ant /kənˈtestənt/ ▶ **n.** a person who takes part in a contest or competition.
– ORIGIN mid 17th cent.: from French, present participle of *contester*, from Latin *contestari* 'call upon to witness' (see CONTEST).

con·tes·ta·tion /ˌkänˌtəsˈtāSHən/ ▶ **n.** formal the action or process of disputing or arguing.
– ORIGIN mid 16th cent. (in the sense 'solemn appeal or protest'): from Latin *contestatio(n-)*, from *contestari* 'call upon to witness' (see CONTEST); reinforced by French *contestation*.

con·text /ˈkänˌtekst/ ▶ **n.** the circumstances that form the setting for an event, statement, or idea, and in terms of which it can be fully understood and assessed: *the decision was taken within the context of planned cuts in spending.* ■ the parts of something written or spoken that immediately precede and follow a word or passage and clarify its meaning: *word processing is affected by the context in which words appear.*
– PHRASES **in context** considered together with the surrounding words or circumstances: *it is difficult now to view these masterpieces in context.* **out of context** without the surrounding words or circumstances and so not fully understandable: *comments that aides have long insisted were taken out of context.*
– DERIVATIVES **con·text·less** adj., **con·tex·tu·al** /kənˈteksCHo͞oəl/ adj., **con·tex·tu·al·ly** adv.
– ORIGIN late Middle English (denoting the construction of a text): from Latin *contextus*, from *con-* 'together' + *texere* 'to weave.'

con·tex·tu·al·ism /kənˈteksCHo͞oəˌlizəm/ ▶ **n.** Philosophy a doctrine that emphasizes the importance of the context of inquiry in a particular question.
– DERIVATIVES **con·tex·tu·al·ist** n.

con·tex·tu·al·ize /kənˈteksCHo͞oəˌlīz/ ▶ **v.** [with obj.] place or study in context: *the book contextualizes Melville's short fiction and poetry.*
– DERIVATIVES **con·tex·tu·al·i·za·tion** /kənˌteksCHo͞oələˈzāSHən/ n.

con·tex·ture /kənˈteksˌCHər/ ▶ **n.** the fact or manner of being woven or linked together to form a connected whole. ■ a mass of things interwoven together; a fabric. ■ the putting together of words and sentences in connected composition; the construction of a text. ■ a connected literary structure; a continuous text.

con·ti·gu·i·ty /ˌkäntəˈgyo͞oitē/ ▶ **n.** the state of bordering or being in direct contact with something: *nations bound together by geographical contiguity.* ■ Psychology the sequential occurrence or proximity of stimulus and response, causing their association in the mind.
– ORIGIN early 16th cent.: from late Latin *contiguitas*, from Latin *contiguus* 'touching' (see CONTIGUOUS).

con·tig·u·ous /kənˈtigyo͞oəs/ ▶ **adj.** sharing a common border; touching: *the 48 contiguous states.* ■ next or together in sequence: *five hundred contiguous dictionary entries.*
– DERIVATIVES **con·tig·u·ous·ly** adv.
– ORIGIN early 16th cent.: from Latin *contiguus* 'touching,' from the verb *contingere* 'be in contact, befall' (see CONTINGENT) + -OUS.

con·ti·nent¹ /ˈkäntnənt/ ▶ **n.** any of the world's main continuous expanses of land (Africa, Antarctica, Asia, Australia, Europe, North America, South America). ■ (also **the Continent**) the mainland of Europe as distinct from the British Isles. ■ a mainland contrasted with islands: *the maritime zone is richer in varieties of plant than the continent.*
– ORIGIN mid 16th cent. (denoting a continuous tract of land): from Latin *terra continens* 'continuous land.'

con·ti·nent² ▶ **adj. 1** able to control movements of the bowels and bladder.
2 exercising self-restraint, esp. sexually.
– DERIVATIVES **con·ti·nence** n., **con·ti·nent·ly** adv.
– ORIGIN late Middle English (in the sense 'characterized by self-restraint'): from Latin *continent-* 'holding together, restraining oneself,' from *continere* (see CONTAIN).

con·ti·nen·tal /ˌkäntnˈentl/ ▶ **adj. 1** forming or belonging to a continent: *continental Antarctica.*
2 coming from or characteristic of mainland Europe: *traditional continental cuisine.*
3 (also **Continental**) pertaining to the 13 original colonies of the US: *in 1783 the officers and men of the Continental forces had little to celebrate.*
▶ **n. 1** an inhabitant of mainland Europe.
2 (**Continental**) a member of the colonial army in the American Revolution: *22 Continentals were killed and scalped.*
3 (also **Continental**) a piece of paper currency used at the time of the American Revolution: *the redemption of Continentals by the government.*
– DERIVATIVES **con·ti·nen·tal·ly** adv.

Con·ti·nen·tal Ar·my the army raised by the Continental Congress of 1775, with George Washington as commander.

con·ti·nen·tal break·fast ▶ **n.** a light breakfast, typically consisting of coffee and rolls with butter and jam.

con·ti·nen·tal cli·mate ▶ **n.** a relatively dry climate with very hot summers and very cold winters, characteristic of the central parts of Asia and North America.

Con·ti·nen·tal Con·gress each of the three congresses held by the American colonies (in 1774, 1775, and 1776, respectively) in revolt against British rule. The second Congress, convened in the wake of the battles at Lexington and Concord, created a Continental Army, which fought and eventually won the American Revolution.

con·ti·nen·tal crust ▶ **n.** Geology the relatively thick part of the earth's crust that forms the large landmasses. It is generally older and more complex than the oceanic crust.

Con·ti·nen·tal Di·vide the main series of mountain ridges in North America, chiefly the crests of the Rocky Mountains that form a watershed that separates the rivers flowing east into the Atlantic Ocean or the Gulf of Mexico from those flowing west into the Pacific Ocean.

con·ti·nen·tal drift ▶ **n.** the gradual movement of the continents across the earth's surface through geological time.

> The theory of continental drift, proposed in 1912, suggested that continents and continental crust drifted over denser oceanic crust. The mechanisms by which the original theory explained the drift, however, could not be substantiated and were proven wrong. The theory of continental drift has been replaced by the theory of plate tectonics. It is believed that a single supercontinent called Pangaea broke up to form Gondwana and Laurasia, which further split to form the present-day continents. South America and Africa, for example, are moving apart at a rate of a few centimeters per year. See PLATE TECTONICS.

con·ti·nen·tal shelf ▶ **n.** the area of seabed around a large landmass where the sea is relatively shallow compared with the open ocean. The continental shelf is geologically part of the continental crust.

con·ti·nen·tal slope ▶ **n.** the slope between the outer edge of the continental shelf and the deep ocean floor.

con·tin·gence /kənˈtinjəns/ ▶ **n.** touching; contact. ■ connection; affinity.

con·tin·gen·cy /kənˈtinjənsē/ ▶ **n.** (pl. **contingencies**) a future event or circumstance that is possible but cannot be predicted with certainty: *a detailed contract that attempts to provide for all possible contingencies.* ■ a provision for such an events or circumstance: *a contingency reserve.* ■ an incidental expense: *allow an extra fifteen percent in the budget for contingencies.* ■ the absence of certainty in events: *the island's public affairs can be invaded by contingency.* ■ Philosophy the absence

C

of necessity; the fact of being so without having to be so.
–ORIGIN mid 16th cent. (in the philosophical sense): from late Latin *contingentia* (in its medieval Latin sense 'circumstance'), from *contingere* 'befall' (see CONTINGENT).

con·tin·gen·cy fee ▶ n. a sum of money that a lawyer receives as a fee only if the case is won.

con·tin·gen·cy fund ▶ n. a reserve of money set aside to cover possible unforeseen future expenses.

con·tin·gen·cy plan ▶ n. a plan designed to take a possible future event or circumstance into account: *contingency plans for dealing with oil spills.*

con·tin·gen·cy ta·ble ▶ n. Statistics a table showing the distribution of one variable in rows and another in columns, used to study the association between the two variables.

con·tin·gent /kən'tinjənt/ ▶ adj. **1** subject to chance: *the contingent nature of the job.* ■ (of losses, liabilities, etc.) that can be anticipated to arise if a particular event occurs: *businesses need to be aware of their liabilities, both actual and contingent.* ■ Philosophy true by virtue of the way things in fact are and not by logical necessity: *that men are living creatures is a contingent fact.*
2 (**contingent on/upon**) occurring or existing only if (certain other circumstances) are the case; dependent on: *resolution of the conflict was contingent on the signing of a ceasefire agreement.*
▶ n. a group of people united by some common feature, forming part of a larger group: *a contingent of Japanese businessmen attending a conference.* ■ a body of troops or police sent to join a larger force in an operation: *a contingent of 2,000 marines.*
–DERIVATIVES **con·tin·gent·ly** adv.
–ORIGIN late Middle English (in the sense 'of uncertain occurrence'): from Latin *contingere* 'befall,' from *con-* 'together with' + *tangere* 'to touch.' The noun sense was originally 'something happening by chance,' then 'a person's share resulting from a division, a quota'; the current sense dates from the early 18th cent.

con·tin·u·al /kən'tinyōōəl/ ▶ adj. frequently recurring; always happening: *his plane went down after continual attacks.* ■ having no interruptions: *some patients need continual safeguarding.*
–ORIGIN Middle English: from Old French *continuel*, from *continuer* 'continue,' from Latin *continuare*, from *continuus* (see CONTINUOUS).

> **USAGE** For an explanation of the difference between **continual** and **continuous**, see usage at CONTINUOUS.

con·tin·u·al·ly /kən'tinyōōəlē/ ▶ adv. **1** repeated frequently in the same way; regularly: *this information is continually updated.*
2 without interruption; constantly: *I was continually moving around.*

con·tin·u·ance /kən'tinyōōəns/ ▶ n. **1** formal the state of remaining in existence or operation: *his interests encouraged him to favor the continuance of war.* ■ the time for which a situation or action lasts: *the trademarks shall be used only during the continuance of this agreement.* ■ the state of remaining in a particular position or condition: *the king's ministers depended on his favor for their continuance in office.*
2 Law a postponement or adjournment: *if this man's testimony is important, I will grant a continuance.*
–ORIGIN late Middle English: from Old French, from *continuer* 'continue,' from Latin *continuare*, from *continuus* (see CONTINUOUS).

con·tin·u·ant /kən'tinyōōənt/ ▶ n. **1** Phonetics a consonant that is sounded with the vocal tract only partly closed, allowing the breath to pass through and the sound to be prolonged (as with *f, l, m, n, r, s, v*).
2 Philosophy & Psychology a thing that retains its identity even though its states and relations may change.
▶ adj. of, relating to, or denoting a continuant.
–ORIGIN early 17th cent. (as an adjective in the general sense 'continuing'): from French, from *continuer*, reinforced by Latin *continuant-* 'continuing,' from the verb *continuare*, from *continuus* (see CONTINUOUS). Current senses date from the 19th cent.

con·tin·u·a·tion /kən,tinyə'wāsʜən/ ▶ n. [usu. in sing.] the action of carrying something on over a period of time or the process of being carried on: *the continuation of discussions about a permanent peace.* ■ the state of remaining in a particular position or condition: *the administration's continuation in office.* ■ a part that is attached to and an extension of something else: *once a separate village, it is now a continuation of the suburbs.*
–ORIGIN late Middle English: via Old French from Latin *continuatio(n-)*, from *continuare* 'continue,' from *continuus* (see CONTINUOUS).

con·tin·u·a·tive /kən'tinyōōətiv, -,ātiv/ Linguistics ▶ adj. (of a word or phrase) having the function of moving a discourse or conversation forward.
▶ n. a word or phrase of this type (e.g., *yes, well, as I was saying*).
–ORIGIN mid 16th cent. (as a noun denoting something that brings about continuity): from late Latin *continuativus*, from *continuat-* 'continued,' from the verb *continuare* (see CONTINUE).

con·tin·u·a·tor /kən'tinyə,wātər/ ▶ n. a person or thing that continues something or maintains continuity. ■ a person who writes a continuation of another's work.

con·tin·ue /kən'tinyōō/ ▶ v. (**continues, continuing, continued**) **1** [no obj.] persist in an activity or process: *he was unable to continue with his job | prices continued to fall during April.* ■ remain in existence or operation: *discussions continued throughout the year.* ■ [with obj.] carry on with (something that one has begun): *I continued my stroll* | (as adj. **continued**) *he asked for their continued support.* ■ remain in a specified position or state: *they have indicated their willingness to continue in office | the weather continued warm and pleasant.* ■ carry on traveling in the same direction: *he hummed to himself as they continued northward.* ■ (of a road, river, etc.) extend farther in the same direction: *the main path continued through a tunnel.*
2 recommence or resume after interruption: [with obj.] *we continue the story from the point reached in Chapter 1* | [no obj.] *the trial continues tomorrow.* ■ [no obj.] carry on speaking after a pause or interruption: *I told him he was obstructing the inquiry and he let me continue.* ■ [with obj.] Law postpone or adjourn (a legal proceeding): *the case was continued without a finding until August 2.*
–DERIVATIVES **con·tin·u·er** n.
–ORIGIN Middle English: from Old French *continuer*, from Latin *continuare*, from *continuus* (see CONTINUOUS).

con·tin·ued frac·tion ▶ n. Mathematics a fraction of infinite length whose denominator is a quantity plus a fraction, which latter fraction has a similar denominator, and so on.

con·tin·u·ing ed·u·ca·tion ▶ n. education provided for adults after they have left the formal education system, consisting typically of short or part-time courses.

con·ti·nu·i·ty /,käntn'(y)ōōətē/ ▶ n. (pl. **continuities**) **1** the unbroken and consistent existence or operation of something over a period of time: *pension rights accruing through continuity of employment.* ■ a state of stability and the absence of disruption: *they have provided the country with a measure of continuity.* ■ (often **continuity between/with**) a connection or line of development with no sharp breaks: *they used the same style of masonry to provide continuity between new and old.*
2 the maintenance of continuous action and self-consistent detail in the various scenes of a movie or broadcast: [as modifier] *a continuity error.* ■ the linking of broadcast items, esp. by a spoken commentary.
–ORIGIN late Middle English: from Old French *continuite*, from Latin *continuitas*, from *continuare* 'continue,' from *continuus* (see CONTINUOUS).

con·tin·u·o /kən'tinyə,wō/ (also **basso continuo**) ▶ n. (pl. **continuos**) (in baroque music) an accompanying part that includes a bass line and harmonies, typically played on a keyboard instrument and with other instruments such as cello or bass viol.
–ORIGIN early 18th cent.: Italian *basso continuo* 'continuous bass.'

con·tin·u·ous /kən'tinyōōəs/ ▶ adj. **1** forming an unbroken whole; without interruption: *the whole performance is enacted in one continuous movement.* ■ forming a series with no exceptions or reversals: *there are continuous advances in design and production.* ■ Mathematics (of a function) of which the graph is a smooth unbroken curve, i.e., one such that as the value of x approaches any given value a, the value of $f(x)$ approaches that of $f(a)$ as a limit.
2 Grammar another term for PROGRESSIVE (sense 3 of the adjective).
–DERIVATIVES **con·tin·u·ous·ly** adv., **con·tin·u·ous·ness** n.
–ORIGIN mid 17th cent.: from Latin *continuus* 'uninterrupted,' from *continere* 'hang together' (from *con-* 'together with' + *tenere* 'hold') + **-ous**.

> **USAGE** There is some overlap in meaning between **continuous** and **continual**, but the two words are not wholly synonymous. Both can mean roughly 'without interruption' (*a long and **continual** war; five years of **continuous** warfare*), but **continuous** is much more prominent in this sense and, unlike **continual**, can be used to refer to space as well as time, as in *the development forms a **continuous** line along the coast.* **Continual**, on the other hand, typically means 'happening frequently, with intervals between,' as in *the bus service has been disrupted by **continual** breakdowns.* Overall, **continuous** occurs much more frequently than **continual** (almost five times more often in the Oxford English Corpus).

con·tin·u·ous cre·a·tion ▶ n. the creation of matter as a continuing process throughout time, esp. as postulated in steady state theories of the universe.

con·tin·u·ous spec·trum ▶ n. Physics an emission spectrum that consists of a continuum of wavelengths.

con·tin·u·ous wave ▶ n. an electromagnetic wave, esp. a radio wave, having a constant amplitude.

con·tin·u·um /kən'tinyōōəm/ ▶ n. (pl. **continua** /-yōōə/) [usu. in sing.] a continuous sequence in which adjacent elements are not perceptibly different from each other, although the extremes are quite distinct: *at the fast end of the fast-slow continuum.* ■ Mathematics the set of real numbers.
–ORIGIN mid 17th cent.: from Latin, neuter of *continuus* (see CONTINUOUS).

con·tin·u·um hy·poth·e·sis ▶ n. Mathematics the assertion that there is no transfinite cardinal between the cardinal of the set of positive integers and that of the set of real numbers.

con·tort /kən'tôrt/ ▶ v. twist or bend out of its normal shape: [with obj.] *a spasm of pain contorted his face* | [no obj.] *her face contorted with anger* | (as adj. **contorted**) *contorted limbs* | figurative *a contorted version of the truth.*
–DERIVATIVES **con·tor·tion** /kən'tôrsʜən/ n.
–ORIGIN late Middle English: from Latin *contort-* 'twisted around, brandished,' from the verb *contorquere*, from *con-* 'together' + *torquere* 'twist.'

con·tor·tion·ist /kən'tôrsʜənist/ ▶ n. an entertainer who twists and bends their body into strange and unnatural positions.

con·tour /'kän,tōōr/ ▶ n. (usu. **contours**) an outline, esp. one representing or bounding the shape or form of something: *she traced the contours of his face with her finger* | figurative *the contours of American life.* ■ an outline of a natural feature such as a hill or valley: *cliffs with grassy rounded contours.* ■ short for CONTOUR LINE. ■ a line joining points on a diagram at which some property has the same value: *the map shows contours of every 10-foot difference in elevation.* ■ a way in which something varies, esp. the pitch of music or the pattern of tones in an utterance: *the movement tends to place more emphasis on rhythm than melodic contour.*
▶ v. [with obj.] **1** (usu. **be contoured**) mold into a specific shape, typically one designed to fit into something else: *the compartment has been contoured with smooth rounded corners* | (as adj. **contoured**) *the contoured leather seats.*
2 mark (a map or diagram) with contour lines: (as adj. **contoured**) *a huge contoured map.*
3 (of a road or railroad) follow the outline of (a topographical feature), esp. along a contour line: *the road contours the hillside.*
–ORIGIN mid 17th cent.: from French, from Italian *contorno*, from *contornare* 'draw in outline,' from *con-* 'together' + *tornare* 'to turn.'

con·tour feath·er ▶ n. any of the mainly small feathers that form the outline of an adult bird's plumage.

con·tour line ▶ n. a line on a map joining points of equal height above or below sea level.

con·tour map ▶ n. a map marked with contour lines.

con·tour plow·ing ▶ n. plowing along the contours of the land in order to minimize soil erosion.

Con·tra /'käntrə/ ▶ n. a member of a guerrilla force in Nicaragua that opposed the left-wing Sandinista government 1979–90, and was supported by the US for much of that time. It was officially disbanded in 1990, after the Sandinistas' electoral defeat.
–ORIGIN abbreviation of Spanish *contrarrevolucionario* 'counterrevolutionary.'

contra- ▶ prefix **1** against; opposite; contrasting: *contradict | contraflow | contralateral.*
2 Music (of instruments or organ stops) pitched an octave below: *contralto | contrabass.*
–ORIGIN from Latin *contra* 'against.'

con·tra·band /'käntrə,band/ ▶ n. goods that have been imported or exported illegally: *the police looked for drugs, guns, and other contraband.* ■ trade in smuggled goods: *the government has declared a nationwide war on contraband.* ■ (also **contraband of war**) goods forbidden to be supplied by neutrals to those engaged in war. ■ (during the US Civil War) a black slave who escaped or was transported across Union lines.
▶ adj. imported or exported illegally, either in defiance of a total ban or without payment of duty:

contraband drug shipments. ■ relating to traffic in illegal goods: *the contraband market.*
– DERIVATIVES **con·tra·band·ist** /-ist/ **n.**
– ORIGIN late 16th cent.: from Spanish *contrabanda,* from Italian *contrabando,* from *contra-* 'against' + *bando* 'proclamation, ban.'

con·tra·bass /'käntrə,bās/ ▶ **n.** another term for DOUBLE BASS.
▶ **adj.** [attrib.] denoting a musical instrument with a range an octave lower than the normal bass range: *a contrabass clarinet.*
– ORIGIN late 18th cent.: from Italian *contrabasso,* from *contra-* 'pitched an octave below' + *basso* (see BASS[1]).

con·tra·bas·soon /,käntrəbə'so͞on, -ba-/ ▶ **n.** a bassoon that is larger and longer than the normal type and sounds an octave lower in pitch.

con·tra·cep·tion /,käntrə'sepsHən/ ▶ **n.** the deliberate use of artificial methods or other techniques to prevent pregnancy as a consequence of sexual intercourse. The major forms of artificial contraception are barrier methods, of which the most common is the condom; the contraceptive pill, which contains synthetic sex hormones that prevent ovulation in the female; intrauterine devices, such as the coil, which prevent the fertilized ovum from implanting in the uterus; and male or female sterilization.
– ORIGIN late 19th cent.: from CONTRA- 'against' + a shortened form of CONCEPTION.

con·tra·cep·tive /,käntrə'septiv/ ▶ **adj.** (of a method or device) serving to prevent pregnancy: *the contraceptive pill.* ■ of or relating to contraception: *a book popularizing contraceptive knowledge.*
▶ **n.** a device or drug serving to prevent pregnancy.

con·tract ▶ **n.** /'kän,trakt/ a written or spoken agreement, esp. one concerning employment, sales, or tenancy, that is intended to be enforceable by law: *both parties must sign employment contracts* | *a network of doctors and hospitals* ***under contract*** *to provide services.* ■ the branch of law concerned with the making and observation of such agreements. ■ informal an arrangement for someone to be killed by a hired assassin: *smuggling bosses routinely put out contracts on witnesses.* ■ Bridge the declarer's undertaking to win the number of tricks bid with a stated suit as trump: *South can make the contract with correct play.* ■ dated a formal agreement to marry.
▶ **v. 1** /kən'trakt/ [no obj.] decrease in size, number, or range: *glass contracts as it cools.* ■ (of a muscle) become shorter or tighter in order to effect movement of part of the body: *the heart is a muscle that contracts about seventy times a minute* | [with obj.] *then contract your lower abdominal muscles.* ■ [with obj.] shorten (a word or phrase) by combination or elision: *"quasistellar object" was soon contracted to "quasar."*
2 /'kän,trakt, kən'trakt/ [no obj.] enter into a formal and legally binding agreement: *the local authority will contract with a wide range of agencies to provide services.* ■ secure specified rights or undertake specified obligations in a formal and legally binding agreement: *a buyer may* ***contract for*** *the right to withhold payment* | *the paper had contracted to publish extracts from the diaries.* ■ impose an obligation on (someone) to do something by means of a formal agreement: *health authorities contract a hospital to treat a specific number of patients.* ■ [with obj.] (**contract something out**) arrange for work to be done by another organization: *local authorities will have to contract out waste management.* ■ [with obj.] formally enter into (a marriage): *before Fanny met him, he had contracted a disastrous liaison and marriage.* ■ [with obj.] enter into (a friendship or other relationship): *the patterns of social relationships contracted by men and women differ.*
3 /kən'trakt/ [with obj.] catch or develop (a disease or infectious agent): *three people contracted a killer virus.*
4 /kən'trakt/ [with obj.] become liable to pay (a debt): *he contracted a debt of $3,300.*
– DERIVATIVES **con·tract·ee** /,kän,trak'tē/ **n.**, **con·trac·tive** /kən'traktiv, 'kän,traktiv/ **adj.**
– ORIGIN Middle English: via Old French from Latin *contractus,* from *contract-* 'drawn together, tightened,' from the verb *contrahere,* from *con-* 'together' + *trahere* 'draw.'

con·tract·a·ble /kən'traktəbəl/ ▶ **adj.** (of a disease) able to be caught.

con·tract bridge /'kän,trakt/ ▶ **n.** the standard form of the card game bridge, in which only tricks bid and won count toward the game, as opposed to auction bridge.

con·tract·i·ble /kən'traktəbəl/ ▶ **adj.** able to be shrunk or capable of contracting.

con·trac·tile /kən'traktəl, -,tīl/ ▶ **adj.** Biology & Physiology capable of or producing contraction: *the contractile activity of the human colon.*
– DERIVATIVES **con·trac·til·i·ty** /,kän,trak'tilitē/ **n.**

con·trac·tile vac·u·ole ▶ **n.** Zoology a vacuole in some protozoans that expels excess liquid on contraction.

con·trac·tion /kən'traksHən/ ▶ **n.** the process of becoming smaller: *the general contraction of the industry did further damage to morale.* ■ the process in which a muscle becomes or is made shorter and tighter: *neurons control the contraction of muscles* | *repeat the exercise, holding each contraction for one second.* ■ (usu. **contractions**) a shortening of the uterine muscles occurring at intervals before and during childbirth. ■ a word or group of words resulting from shortening an original form: *"goodbye" is a contraction of "God be with you."* ■ the process of shortening a word by combination or elision.
– ORIGIN late Middle English: via Old French from Latin *contractio(n-),* from *contrahere* 'draw together' (see CONTRACT).

con·trac·tor /'kän,traktər, ,kən'traktər/ ▶ **n.** a person or company that undertakes a contract to provide materials or labor to perform a service or do a job.

con·trac·tu·al /kən'trakCHo͞oəl/ ▶ **adj.** agreed in a contract: *a contractual obligation.* ■ having similar characteristics to a contract: *the contractual nature of the shareholder's rights.*
– DERIVATIVES **con·trac·tu·al·ly adv.**

con·trac·ture /kən'trakCHər/ ▶ **n.** Medicine a condition of shortening and hardening of muscles, tendons, or other tissue, often leading to deformity and rigidity of joints.
– DERIVATIVES **con·trac·tur·al** /-CHərəl/ **adj.**
– ORIGIN mid 17th cent.: from French, or from Latin *contractura,* from Latin *contract-* 'drawn together,' from the verb *contrahere.*

con·tra·dance /'käntrə,dans/ ▶ **n.** a country dance in which the couples form lines facing each other.
– ORIGIN early 19th cent.: variant of CONTREDANSE.

con·tra·dict /,käntrə'dikt/ ▶ **v.** [with obj.] deny the truth of (a statement), esp. by asserting the opposite: *the survey appears to contradict the industry's claims* | *he did not contradict what he said last week.* ■ assert the opposite of a statement made by (someone): *he did not contradict her but just said nothing* | *within five minutes he had contradicted himself twice.* ■ be in conflict with: *that evaporation seems to contradict one of the most fundamental principles of physics.*
– DERIVATIVES **con·tra·dic·tor** /-'diktər/ **n.**
– ORIGIN late 16th cent.: from Latin *contradict-* 'spoken against,' from the verb *contradicere,* originally *contra dicere* 'speak against.'

con·tra·dic·tion /,käntrə'diksHən/ ▶ **n.** a combination of statements, ideas, or features of a situation that are opposed to one another: *the proposed new system suffers from a set of internal contradictions.* ■ a person, thing, or situation in which inconsistent elements are present: *the paradox of using force to overcome force is a real contradiction.* ■ the statement of a position opposite to one already made: *the second sentence appears to be in flat contradiction of the first* | *the experiment provides a contradiction of the hypothesis.*
– PHRASES **contradiction in terms** a statement or group of words associating objects or ideas that are incompatible: *"true fiction" is a contradiction in terms.*
– ORIGIN late Middle English: via Old French from Latin *contradictio(n-),* from the verb *contradicere* (see CONTRADICT).

con·tra·dic·to·ry /,käntrə'dikt(ə)rē/ ▶ **adj.** mutually opposed or inconsistent: *the two attitudes are contradictory.* ■ containing elements which are inconsistent or in conflict: *the committee rejected the policy as too vague and internally contradictory.* ■ Logic (of two propositions) so related that one and only one must be true. Compare with CONTRARY.
▶ **n.** (pl. **contradictories**) Logic a contradictory proposition.
– DERIVATIVES **con·tra·dic·to·ri·ly** /-'dikt(ə)rəlē/ **adv.**, **con·tra·dic·to·ri·ness n.**
– ORIGIN late Middle English (as a term in logic denoting a proposition or principle that contradicts another): from late Latin *contradictorius,* from Latin *contradict-* 'spoken against,' from the verb *contradicere* (see CONTRADICT).

con·tra·dis·tinc·tion /,käntrədə'stiNGksHən/ ▶ **n.** distinction made by contrasting the different qualities of two things: *the bacterium is termed "rough" in contradistinction to its ordinary smooth form.*

con·tra·dis·tin·guish /,käntrədə'stiNGgwisH/ ▶ **v.** [with obj.] archaic distinguish between (two things) by contrasting them.

con·tra·fac·tive /,käntrə'faktiv/ ▶ **adj.** Linguistics denoting a verb that assigns to its object (normally a clausal object) the status of not being true, e.g., *pretend* and *wish.* Contrasted with FACTIVE, NONFACTIVE.

con·tra·fac·tu·al /,käntrə'fakCHo͞oəl/ ▶ **adj.** another term for COUNTERFACTUAL.

con·trail /'kän,trāl/ ▶ **n.** a trail of condensed water from an aircraft or rocket at high altitude, seen as a white streak against the sky.
– ORIGIN 1940s: abbreviation of *condensation trail.*

con·tra·in·di·cate /,käntrə'ində,kāt/ ▶ **v.** [with obj.] (usu. **be contraindicated**) Medicine (of a condition or circumstance) suggest or indicate that (a particular technique or drug) should not be used in the case in question.
– DERIVATIVES **con·tra·in·di·ca·tion** /-,ində'kāsHən/ **n.**

con·tra·lat·er·al /,käntrə'latərəl, -'latrəl/ ▶ **adj.** Medicine relating to or denoting the side of the body opposite to that on which a particular structure or condition occurs: *the symptom develops in the hand contralateral to the lesion.*

con·tral·to /kən'traltō/ ▶ **n.** (pl. **contraltos**) the lowest female singing voice: *she sang in a high contralto.* ■ a singer with such a voice. ■ a part written for such a voice.
– ORIGIN mid 18th cent.: Italian, from *contra-* (in the sense 'counter to') + ALTO. Compare with COUNTERTENOR.

con·tra mun·dum /,käntrə 'mo͞ondəm, 'məndəm/ ▶ **adv.** defying or opposing everyone else.
– ORIGIN Latin, 'against the world.'

con·tra·po·si·tion /,käntrəpə'zisHən/ ▶ **n.** Logic conversion of a proposition from *all A is B* to *all not-B is not-A.*
– DERIVATIVES **con·tra·pos·i·tive** /-'päzətiv/ **adj. & n.**
– ORIGIN mid 16th cent.: from late Latin *contrapositio(n-),* from the verb *contraponere,* from *contra-* 'against' + *ponere* 'to place.'

con·trap·pos·to /,kōntrə'pästō/ ▶ **n.** (pl. **contrapposti** /-trə'pästē/) Sculpture an asymmetrical arrangement of the human figure in which the line of the arms and shoulders contrasts with while balancing those of the hips and legs.
– ORIGIN Italian, past participle of *contrapporre,* from Latin *contraponere* 'place against.'

con·trap·tion /kən'trapsHən/ ▶ **n.** a machine or device that appears strange or unnecessarily complicated, and often badly made or unsafe.
– ORIGIN early 19th cent.: perhaps from CONTRIVE (on the pattern of pairs such as *conceive, conception*), by association with TRAP[1].

con·tra·pun·tal /,käntrə'pəntl/ ▶ **adj.** Music of or in counterpoint. ■ (of a piece of music) with two or more independent melodic lines.
– DERIVATIVES **con·tra·pun·tal·ly adv.**, **con·tra·pun·tist** /-tist/ **n.**
– ORIGIN mid 19th cent.: from Italian *contrapunto* (see COUNTERPOINT) + -AL.

con·trar·i·an /kən'tre(ə)rēən, kän-/ ▶ **n.** a person who opposes or rejects popular opinion, esp. in stock exchange dealing.
▶ **adj.** opposing or rejecting popular opinion; going against current practice: *the comment came more from a contrarian disposition than moral conviction.*
– DERIVATIVES **con·trar·i·an·ism** /-,nizəm/ **n.**

con·tra·ri·e·ty /,käntrə'rīətē/ ▶ **n. 1** opposition or inconsistency between two or more things: *questions that involved much contrariety of opinion.*
2 Logic contrary opposition.
– ORIGIN late Middle English: from Old French *contrariete,* from late Latin *contrarietas,* from *contrarius* (see CONTRARY).

con·trar·i·ous /kən'tre(ə)rēəs/ ▶ **adj.** archaic
1 perverse; refractory.
2 opposed; unfavorable.

con·trar·i·wise /'kän,trerē,wīz, kən'tre(ə)rē-/ ▶ **adv.** in the opposite way or order. ■ in contrast to something that has just been stated or mentioned: *contrariwise, a registered person may vote, even if not entitled to be registered.*

con·trar·y ▶ **adj.** /'kän,tre(ə)rē/ **1** opposite in nature, direction, or meaning: *he ignored contrary advice and agreed on the deal.* ■ (of two or more statements, beliefs, etc.) opposed to one another: *his mother had given him contrary messages.* ■ (of a wind) blowing in the opposite direction to one's course; unfavorable. ■ Logic (of two propositions) so related that one or neither but not both must be true. Compare with CONTRADICTORY.
2 perversely inclined to disagree or to do the opposite of what is expected or desired: *she is sulky and contrary where her work is concerned.*

C

▶ **n.** /ˈkänˌtre(ə)rē/ (pl. **contraries**) **1** (**the contrary**) the opposite: *the magazine has proved that the contrary is true.*
2 Logic a contrary proposition.
– PHRASES **contrary to** conflicting with; counter to: *contrary to his expectations, he found the atmosphere exciting* | *the restrictions were not contrary to the public interest.* **on** (or **quite**) **the contrary** used to intensify a denial of what has just been implied or stated: *there was no malice in her; on the contrary, she was very kind.* **to the contrary** with the opposite meaning or implication: *he continued to drink despite medical advice to the contrary.*
– DERIVATIVES **con·trar·i·ly** /-əlē/ **adv.**, **con·trar·i·ness n.**
– ORIGIN Middle English: from Anglo-Norman French *contrarie*, from Latin *contrarius*, from *contra* 'against.'

con·trast ▶ **n.** /ˈkänˌtrast/ the state of being strikingly different from something else, typically something in juxtaposition or close association: *the day began cold and blustery, **in contrast to** almost two weeks of uninterrupted sunshine* | *a **contrast between** rural and urban trends.* ■ the degree of difference between tones in a television picture, photograph, or other image. ■ enhancement of the apparent brightness or clarity of a design provided by the juxtaposition of different colors or textures. ■ the action of calling attention to notable differences: *use knowledge of other languages for **contrast** and comparison with English.* ■ [in sing.] a thing or person having qualities noticeably different from another: *the castle is quite a **contrast to** other places where the singer has performed.*
▶ **v.** /ˈkänˌtrast, kənˈtrast/ [no obj.] differ strikingly: *his friend's success **contrasted with** his own failure* | (as adj. **contrasting**) *a contrasting view.* ■ [with obj.] compare in such a way as to emphasize differences: *people **contrasted** her **with** her sister.*
– DERIVATIVES **con·trast·ing·ly** /ˈkänˌtrastiNGlē, kənˈtras-/ **adv.**, **con·tras·tive** /kənˈtrastiv, ˈkänˌtras-/ **adj.**
– ORIGIN late 17th cent. (as a term in fine art, in the sense 'juxtapose so as to bring out differences in form and color'): from French *contraste* (noun), *contraster* (verb), via Italian from medieval Latin *contrastare*, from Latin *contra-* 'against' + *stare* 'stand.'

> **USAGE** Contrast means 'note the differences,' whereas **compare** means 'note the similarities' (or, in some cases, inconsistencies). See also usage at **COMPARE**.

con·trast me·di·um /ˈkänˌtrast/ ▶ **n.** Medicine a substance introduced into a part of the body in order to improve the visibility of internal structure during radiography.

con·trast·y /ˈkänˌtrastē/ ▶ **adj.** informal (of a photograph, movie, or television picture) showing a high degree of contrast.

con·tra·sug·gest·i·ble /ˌkäntrə səg(g)ˈjestəbəl/ ▶ **adj.** Psychology tending to respond to a suggestion by believing or doing the contrary.

con·tra·vene /ˌkäntrəˈvēn/ ▶ **v.** [with obj.] violate the prohibition or order of (a law, treaty, or code of conduct): *this would contravene the rule against hearsay.* ■ conflict with (a right, principle, etc.), esp. to its detriment: *this contravened Washington's commitment to its own proposal.*
– DERIVATIVES **con·tra·ven·er n.**
– ORIGIN mid 16th cent.: from late Latin *contravenire*, from Latin *contra-* 'against' + *venire* 'come.'

con·tra·ven·tion /ˌkäntrəˈvenCHən/ ▶ **n.** an action that violates a law, treaty, or other ruling: *young persons who commit offenses bear responsibility for their contraventions.*
– PHRASES **in contravention of** in a manner contrary and disobedient to (a law or other ruling).
– ORIGIN mid 16th cent.: via French from medieval Latin *contraventio(n-)*, from late Latin *contravenire* (see **CONTRAVENE**).

con·tre·coup /ˈkäntrəˌko͞o/ ▶ **n.** (pl. **contrecoups** /-ˌko͞oz/) a contusion resulting from the brain contacting the skull on the side opposite from where impact occurs. Compare with **COUP**.

con·tre·danse /ˈkäntrəˌdans, ˌkôNtrəˈdäNs/ ▶ **n.** (pl. pronunc. **same**) a French form of country dance, originating in the 18th century and related to the quadrille. ■ a piece of music for such a dance. ■ another term for **CONTRADANCE**.
– ORIGIN French, alteration of English **COUNTRY DANCE**, by association with *contre* 'against, opposite.'

con·tre-jour /ˌkôntrə ˈZHo͝or/ ▶ **adj. & adv.** Photography having or involving the sun or other light source behind the subject: [as adj.] *a glorious contre-jour effect* | [as adv.] *it is recommended not to use the film contre-jour.*
– ORIGIN early 20th cent.: French, from *contre* 'against' + *jour* 'daylight.'

con·tre·temps /ˈkäntrəˌtäN, ˌkôNtrəˈtäN/ ▶ **n.** (pl. **same** /-ˌtäN(z), -ˈtäN(z)/) an unexpected and unfortunate occurrence: *the hotel had to deal with more than one contretemps before the end of the night.* ■ a minor dispute or disagreement: *she had occasional contretemps with her staff.*
– ORIGIN late 17th cent. (originally as a fencing term, denoting a thrust made at an inopportune moment): French, originally 'motion out of time,' from *contre-* 'against' + *temps* 'time.'

con·trib·ute /kənˈtribyo͞ot, -byət/ ▶ **v.** [with obj.] give (something, esp. money) in order to help achieve or provide something: *he **contributed** more than $500,000 **to** the center* | [no obj.] *she contributed to a private pension.* ■ [no obj.] (**contribute to**) help to cause or bring about: *gases that contribute to global warming.* ■ supply (an article) for publication: *he **contributed** articles **to** the magazine* | [no obj.] *the staff who **contribute to** your sports pages are doing a splendid job.* ■ [no obj.] give one's views in a discussion: *he did not **contribute to** the meetings.*
– DERIVATIVES **con·trib·u·tive** /-yətiv/ **adj.**
– ORIGIN mid 16th cent.: from Latin *contribut-* 'brought together, added,' from the verb *contribuere*, from *con-* 'with' + *tribuere* 'bestow.'

con·tri·bu·tion /ˌkäntrəˈbyo͞oSHən/ ▶ **n.** a gift or payment to a common fund or collection: *charitable contributions.* ■ the part played by a person or thing in bringing about a result or helping something to advance: *he made a lasting contribution by designing the modern radio telescope.* ■ an article or other piece of writing submitted for publication in a collection.
– ORIGIN late Middle English (denoting a tax or levy): from late Latin *contributio(n-)*, from Latin *contribuere* 'bring together, add' (see **CONTRIBUTE**).

con·trib·u·tor /kənˈtribyətər/ ▶ **n.** a person or thing that contributes something, in particular: ■ a person who writes articles for a magazine or newspaper. ■ a person who donates money to a cause. ■ a causal factor in the existence or occurrence of something: *stress is a major **contributor to** most diseases.*

con·trib·u·to·ry /kənˈtribyəˌtôrē/ ▶ **adj. 1** playing a part in bringing something about: *smoking may be a contributory cause of lung cancer.*
2 (of or relating to a pension or insurance plan) operated by means of a fund into which people pay: *contributory benefits.*
– ORIGIN late Middle English (in the sense 'contributing to a fund'): from medieval Latin *contributorius*, from Latin *contribut-* 'added' (see **CONTRIBUTION**).

con·trib·u·to·ry neg·li·gence ▶ **n.** Law failure of an injured plaintiff to act prudently, considered to be a contributory factor in the injury suffered, and sometimes reducing the amount recovered from the defendant.

con·trite /kənˈtrīt, ˈkäntrīt/ ▶ **adj.** feeling or expressing remorse or penitence; affected by guilt: *a broken and a contrite heart.*
– DERIVATIVES **con·trite·ly adv.**, **con·trite·ness n.**
– ORIGIN Middle English: from Old French *contrit*, from Latin *contritus*, past participle of *conterere* 'grind down, wear away,' from *con-* 'together' + *terere* 'rub.'

con·tri·tion /kənˈtriSHən/ ▶ **n.** the state of feeling remorseful and penitent. ■ (in the Roman Catholic Church) the repentance of past sins during or after confession: *prayers of contrition.*
– ORIGIN Middle English: via Old French from late Latin *contritio(n-)*, from *contrit-* 'ground down,' from the verb *conterere* (see **CONTRITE**).

con·triv·ance /kənˈtrīvəns/ ▶ **n.** a thing that is created skillfully and inventively to serve a particular purpose: *an assortment of electronic equipment and mechanical contrivances.* ■ the use of skill to bring something about or create something: *the requirements of the system, by happy chance and some contrivance, can be summed up in an acronym.* ■ a device, esp. in literary or artistic composition, that gives a sense of artificiality.

con·trive /kənˈtrīv/ ▶ **v.** [with obj.] create or bring about (an object or a situation) by deliberate use of skill and artifice: *his opponents contrived a crisis* | *you contrived to be alone with me despite the supervision.* ■ manage to do something foolish or create an undesirable situation: *the poor guy in some way contrived to hang himself.*
– DERIVATIVES **con·triv·a·ble adj.**, **con·triv·er n.**
– ORIGIN Middle English: from Old French *contreuve-*, stressed stem of *controver* 'imagine, invent,' from medieval Latin *contropare* 'compare.'

con·trived /kənˈtrīvd/ ▶ **adj.** deliberately created rather than arising naturally or spontaneously. ■ created or arranged in a way that seems artificial and unrealistic: *the ending of the novel is too pat and contrived.*

con·trol /kənˈtrōl/ ▶ **n. 1** the power to influence or direct people's behavior or the course of events: *the whole operation is **under the control of** a production manager* | *the situation was slipping **out of** her **control**.* ■ the ability to manage a machine, vehicle, or other moving object: *he **lost control of** his car* | *improve your ball control.* ■ the restriction of an activity, tendency, or phenomenon: *pest control.* ■ the power to restrain something, esp. one's own emotions or actions: *give children time to get control of their emotions.* ■ (often **controls**) a means of limiting or regulating something: ***growing controls on** local spending.* ■ a switch or other device by which a machine is regulated: *the volume control.* ■ the place where a particular item is verified: *passport control.* ■ the base from which a system or activity is directed: *communications could be established with central control* | *mission control.* ■ Bridge a high card that will prevent opponents from establishing a particular suit. ■ Computing short for **CONTROL KEY**.
2 Statistics a group or individual used as a standard of comparison for checking the results of a survey or experiment: *they saw no difference between the cancer patients and the controls.*
3 a member of an intelligence organization who personally directs the activities of a spy.
▶ **v.** (**controls, controlling, controlled**) **1** [with obj.] determine the behavior or supervise the running of: *he was appointed to control the company's marketing strategy.* ■ maintain influence or authority over: *you shouldn't have dogs if you can't control them.* ■ limit the level, intensity, or numbers of: *he had to control his temper.* ■ (**control oneself**) remain calm and reasonable despite provocation: *he made an effort to control himself.* ■ regulate (a mechanical or scientific process): *the airflow is controlled by a fan.* ■ (as adj. **controlled**) (of a drug) restricted by law with respect to use and possession: *a sentence for possessing controlled substances.*
2 [no obj.] Statistics (**control for**) take into account (an extraneous factor that might affect results) when performing an experiment: *no attempt was made to control for variations* | (as adj. **controlled**) *a controlled trial.* ■ check; verify.
– PHRASES **in control** able to direct a situation, person, or activity: *I felt calm and in control.* **out of control** no longer possible to manage: *fires burning out of control.* **under control** (of a danger or emergency) being dealt with successfully and competently: *it took two hours to bring the blaze under control.*
– DERIVATIVES **con·trol·la·bil·i·ty** /kənˌtrōləˈbilitē/ **n.**, **con·trol·la·ble adj.**, **con·trol·la·bly** /-əblē/ **adv.**
– ORIGIN late Middle English (as a verb in the sense 'check or verify accounts,' esp. by referring to a duplicate register): from Anglo-Norman French *contreroller* 'keep a copy of a roll of accounts,' from medieval Latin *contrarotulare*, from *contrarotulus* 'copy of a roll,' from *contra-* 'against' + *rotulus* 'a roll.' The noun is perhaps via French *contrôle*.

con·trol ac·count ▶ **n.** an account used to record the balances on a number of subsidiary accounts and to provide a cross-check on them.

con·trol char·ac·ter ▶ **n.** Computing a character that does not represent a printable character but serves to initiate a particular action.

con·trol freak ▶ **n.** informal a person who feels an obsessive need to exercise control over themselves and others and to take command of any situation.

con·trol key ▶ **n.** Computing a key that alters the function of another key if both are pressed at the same time.

con·trol·ler /kənˈtrōlər/ ▶ **n.** a person or thing that directs or regulates something: *the power controller on a subway train.* ■ a person in charge of an organization's finances.
– DERIVATIVES **con·trol·ler·ship** /-ˌSHip/ **n.**
– ORIGIN Middle English (denoting a person who kept a duplicate register of accounts): from Anglo-Norman *contrerollour*, from *contreroller* 'keep a copy of a roll of accounts' (see **CONTROL**). Compare with **COMPTROLLER**.

con·trol·ling in·ter·est ▶ **n.** the holding by one person or group of a majority of the stock of a business, giving the holder a means of exercising control: *the purchase of a **controlling interest** in a company in California.*

con·trol rod ▶ **n.** a rod of a neutron-absorbing substance used to vary the output power of a nuclear reactor.

con·trol tow·er ▶ **n.** a tall building at an airport from which the movements of air and runway traffic are controlled.

con·tro·ver·sial /ˌkäntrəˈvərSHəl, -ˈvərsēəl/ ▶ **adj.** giving rise or likely to give rise to public disagreement: *years of wrangling over a controversial bypass.*

– DERIVATIVES **con·tro·ver·sial·ist** /-list/ **n.**, **con·tro·ver·sial·ly adv.**
– ORIGIN late 16th cent.: from late Latin *controversialis*, from *controversia* (see CONTROVERSY).

con·tro·ver·sy /ˈkäntrəˌvərsē/ ▶ **n.** (pl. **controversies**) disagreement, typically when prolonged, public, and heated: *he sometimes caused controversy because of his forceful views | the announcement ended a protracted controversy.*
– ORIGIN late Middle English: from Latin *controversia*, from *controversus* 'turned against, disputed,' from *contro-* (variant of *contra-* 'against') + *versus*, past participle of *vertere* 'to turn.'

con·tro·vert /ˈkäntrəˌvərt, ˌkäntrəˈvərt/ ▶ **v.** [with obj.] deny the truth of (something): *subsequent work from the same laboratory controverted these results.* ■ argue about (something): *the views in the article have been controverted.*
– DERIVATIVES **con·tro·vert·i·ble adj.**
– ORIGIN mid 16th cent.: from Latin *controversus* (see CONTROVERSY), on the pattern of pairs such as *adversus* (see ADVERSE), *advertere* (see ADVERT[2]).

con·tu·ma·cious /ˌkänt(y)əˈmāsHəs/ ▶ **adj.** archaic or Law (esp. of a defendant's behavior) stubbornly or willfully disobedient to authority.
– DERIVATIVES **con·tu·ma·cious·ly adv.**
– ORIGIN late 16th cent.: from Latin *contumax*, *contumac-* (perhaps from *con-* 'with' + *tumere* 'to swell') + -IOUS.

con·tu·ma·cy /kənˈt(y)o͞oməsē, ˈkänt(y)əməsē/ ▶ **n.** archaic or Law stubborn refusal to obey or comply with authority, esp. a court order or summons.
– ORIGIN Middle English: from Latin *contumacia* 'inflexibility,' from *contumax* (see CONTUMACIOUS).

con·tu·me·li·ous /ˌkänt(y)əˈmēlēəs/ ▶ **adj.** archaic (of behavior) scornful and insulting; insolent.
– DERIVATIVES **con·tu·me·li·ous·ly adv.**
– ORIGIN late Middle English: from Old French *contumelieus*, from Latin *contumeliosus*, from *contumelia* 'abuse, insult' (see CONTUMELY).

con·tu·me·ly /kənˈt(y)o͞omәlē, ˈkänt(y)əˌmēlē, ˈkänˌt(y)o͞omlē/ ▶ **n.** (pl. **contumelies**) insolent or insulting language or treatment: *the church should not be exposed to gossip and contumely.*
– ORIGIN late Middle English: from Old French *contumelie*, from Latin *contumelia*, perhaps from *con-* 'with' + *tumere* 'to swell.'

con·tuse /kənˈto͞oz/ ▶ **v.** [with obj.] (usu. **be contused**) injure (a part of the body) without breaking the skin, forming a bruise: *the whole region beneath the rib cage was contused.*
– ORIGIN late Middle English: from Latin *contus-* 'bruised, crushed,' from the verb *contundere*, from *con-* 'together' + *tundere* 'beat, thump.'

con·tu·sion /kənˈto͞ozHən/ ▶ **n.** a region of injured tissue or skin in which blood capillaries have been ruptured; a bruise.
– ORIGIN late Middle English: from French, from Latin *contusio(n-)*, from the verb *contundere* (see CONTUSE).

co·nun·drum /kəˈnəndrəm/ ▶ **n.** (pl. **conundrums**) a confusing and difficult problem or question: *one of the most difficult conundrums for the experts.* ■ a question asked for amusement, typically one with a pun in its answer; a riddle.
– ORIGIN late 16th cent.: of unknown origin, but first recorded in a work by Thomas Nashe, as a term of abuse for a crank or pedant, later coming to denote a whim or fancy, also a pun. Current senses date from the late 17th cent.

con·ur·ba·tion /ˌkänərˈbāsHən/ ▶ **n.** an extended urban area, typically consisting of several towns merging with the suburbs of one or more cities.
– ORIGIN early 20th cent.: from CON- 'together' + Latin *urbs, urb-* 'city' + -ATION.

con·ure /ˈkänyər, -ˌyo͝or/ ▶ **n.** a Central and South American parakeet that typically has green plumage with patches of other colors. ● *Aratinga, Pyrrhura*, and other genera, family Psittacidae: numerous species.
– ORIGIN mid 19th cent.: from modern Latin *conurus* (former genus name), from Greek *kōnos* 'cone' + *oura* 'tail.'

CO·NUS /ˈkōnəs/ ▶ **abbr.** chiefly Military the 48 contiguous states in the United States (that is, all the states except Alaska and Hawaii).
– ORIGIN acronym, from *con*tiguous *U*nited *S*tates.

co·nus /ˈkōnəs/ ▶ **n.** (pl. **coni** /ˈkōˌnī/) Anatomy **1** (in full **conus arteriosus** /ärˌti(ə)rēˈōsis/) the upper front part of the right ventricle of the heart. **2** (in full **conus medullaris** /ˌmedlˈe(ə)ris/) the conical lower extremity of the spinal cord.
– ORIGIN late 19th cent.: from Latin, literally 'cone.'

con·va·lesce /ˌkänvəˈles/ ▶ **v.** [no obj.] recover one's health and strength over a period of time after an illness or operation: *he spent eight months convalescing after the stroke.*
– ORIGIN late 15th cent.: from Latin *convalescere*, from *con-* 'altogether' + *valescere* 'grow strong' (from *valere* 'be well').

con·va·les·cence /ˌkänvəˈlesəns/ ▶ **n.** time spent recovering from an illness or medical treatment; recuperation: *a period of convalescence | I had a long convalescence ahead.*

con·va·les·cent /ˌkänvəˈlesənt/ ▶ **adj.** (of a person) recovering from an illness or operation. ■ relating to convalescence: *a convalescent home.*
▶ **n.** a person who is recovering after an illness or operation.
– ORIGIN mid 17th cent.: from Latin *convalescent-* 'growing strong, recovering,' from the verb *convalescere* (see CONVALESCE).

con·vect /kənˈvekt/ ▶ **v.** [with obj.] transport (heat or material) by convection: *this wood stove convects heat efficiently* | (as adj. **convected**) *convected warmth.* ■ [no obj.] (of a fluid or fluid body) undergo convection: *the fluid starts to convect* | (as adj. **convecting**) *the convecting layer.*
– ORIGIN late 19th cent.: back-formation from CONVECTION.

con·vec·tion /kənˈveksHən/ ▶ **n.** the movement caused within a fluid by the tendency of hotter and therefore less dense material to rise, and colder, denser material to sink under the influence of gravity, which consequently results in transfer of heat.
– DERIVATIVES **con·vec·tion·al** /-sHənl/ **adj.**, **con·vec·tive** /-ˈvektiv/ **adj.**
– ORIGIN mid 19th cent.: from late Latin *convectio(n-)*, from Latin *convehere*, from *con-* 'together' + *vehere* 'carry.'

con·vec·tion cell ▶ **n.** a self-contained convective zone in a fluid in which upward motion of warmer fluid in the center is balanced by downward motion of cooler fluid at the periphery.

con·vec·tion cur·rent ▶ **n.** a current in a fluid that results from convection.

con·vec·tion ov·en ▶ **n.** a cooking device that heats food by the circulation of hot air.

con·vec·tor /kənˈvektər/ ▶ **n.** a heating appliance that circulates warm air by convection.

con·ve·nance /ˈkänvənəns/ ▶ **n.** (also **convenances**) archaic conventional propriety.
– ORIGIN French, from *convenir* 'be fitting,' from Latin *convenire* (see CONVENE).

con·vene /kənˈvēn/ ▶ **v.** come or bring together for a meeting or activity; assemble: [with obj.] *he convened a group of well-known scientists and philosophers* | [no obj.] *the committee had convened for its final plenary session.*
– DERIVATIVES **con·ven·er n.**, **con·ve·nor** /-ˈvēnər/ **n.**
– ORIGIN late Middle English: from Latin *convenire* 'assemble, agree, fit,' from *con-* 'together' + *venire* 'come.'

con·ven·ience /kənˈvēnyəns/ ▶ **n. 1** the state of being able to proceed with something with little effort or difficulty: *the museum has a cafeteria for your convenience.* ■ the quality of contributing to such a state: *the convenience of a portable phone.* ■ a thing that contributes to an easy and effortless way of life: *voice mail was seen as one of the desktop conveniences of the electronic office.* **2** Brit. a public toilet.
– PHRASES **at one's convenience** at a time or place that suits one. **at one's earliest convenience** as soon as one can without difficulty.
– ORIGIN late Middle English: from Latin *convenientia*, from *convenient-* 'assembling, agreeing,' from the verb *convenire* (see CONVENE).

con·ven·ience food ▶ **n.** a food, typically a complete meal, that has been pre-prepared commercially and so requires little cooking by the consumer.

con·ven·ience store ▶ **n.** a store with extended opening hours and in a convenient location, stocking a limited range of household goods and groceries.

con·ven·ien·cy /kənˈvēnyənsē/ ▶ **n.** archaic term for CONVENIENCE (sense 1).

con·ven·ient /kənˈvēnyənt/ ▶ **adj.** fitting in well with a person's needs, activities, and plans: *I phoned your office to confirm that this date is convenient.* ■ involving little trouble or effort: *the new parking lot will make shopping much more convenient.* ■ (**convenient to**) situated so as to allow easy access to: *the 34-story building is convenient to downtown.* ■ occurring in a place or at a time that is useful: *put the blame on a convenient scapegoat.*
– DERIVATIVES **con·ven·ient·ly adv.** [sentence adverb] *he lived, conveniently, in Paris.*
– ORIGIN late Middle English (in the sense 'befitting, becoming, suitable'): from Latin *convenient-* 'assembling, agreeing, fitting,' from the verb *convenire* (see CONVENE).

con·vent /ˈkänˌvent/ ▶ **n.** a Christian community under monastic vows, esp. one of nuns. ■ (also **convent school**) a school, esp. one for girls, attached to and run by such a community. ■ the building or buildings occupied by such a community.
– ORIGIN Middle English: from Old French, from Latin *conventus* 'assembly, company,' from the verb *convenire* (see CONVENE). The original spelling was *covent* (surviving in the place name *Covent Garden*); the modern form dates from the 16th cent.

con·ven·ti·cle /kənˈventikəl/ ▶ **n.** historical a secret or unlawful religious meeting, typically of people with nonconformist views.
– ORIGIN late Middle English (in the general sense 'assembly, meeting,' particularly a clandestine or illegal one): from Latin *conventiculum* '(place of) assembly,' diminutive of *conventus* 'assembly, company,' from the verb *convenire* (see CONVENE).

con·ven·tion /kənˈvencHən/ ▶ **n. 1** a way in which something is usually done, esp. within a particular area or activity: *the woman who overturned so many conventions of children's literature.* ■ behavior that is considered acceptable or polite to most members of a society: *he was an upholder of convention and correct form | social conventions.* ■ Bridge an artificial bid by which a bidder tries to convey specific information about the hand to their partner. **2** an agreement between countries covering particular matters, esp. one less formal than a treaty. **3** a large meeting or conference, esp. of members of a political party or a particular profession: *a convention of retail merchants.* ■ (in the US) an assembly of the delegates of a political party to select candidates for office. ■ an organized meeting of enthusiasts for a television program, movie, or literary genre: *a Star Trek convention.* ■ a body set up by agreement to deal with a particular issue: *the convention is a UN body responsible for the regulation of sea dumping.*
– ORIGIN late Middle English (sense 3): via Old French from Latin *conventio(n-)* 'meeting, covenant,' from the verb *convenire* (see CONVENE). Sense 1 dates from the late 18th cent.

con·ven·tion·al /kənˈvencHənl/ ▶ **adj.** based on or in accordance with what is generally done or believed: *a conventional morality had dictated behavior.* ■ (of a person) concerned with what is generally held to be acceptable at the expense of individuality and sincerity. ■ (of a work of art or literature) following traditional forms and genres: *conventional love poetry.* ■ (of weapons or power) nonnuclear: *agreement on reducing conventional forces in Europe.* ■ Bridge (of a bid) intended to convey a particular meaning according to an agreed upon convention. Often contrasted with NATURAL.
– DERIVATIVES **con·ven·tion·al·ism** /-ˌizəm/ **n.**, **con·ven·tion·al·ist** /-ist/ **n.**, **con·ven·tion·al·i·ty** /-ˌvencHəˈnalitē/ **n.**, **con·ven·tion·al·ize** /-ˌīz/ **v.**, **con·ven·tion·al·ly adv.**
– ORIGIN late 15th cent. (in the sense 'relating to a formal agreement or convention'): from French *conventionnel* or late Latin *conventionalis*, from Latin *conventio(n-)* 'meeting, covenant,' from the verb *convenire* (see CONVENE).

con·ven·tion·al mem·o·ry ▶ **n.** Computing (in a computer running DOS) the first 640k of memory where programs to be run must be loaded.

con·ven·tion·eer /kənˌvencHəˈni(ə)r/ ▶ **n.** a person attending a convention.

con·ven·tu·al /kənˈvencHo͞oəl/ ▶ **adj.** relating or belonging to a convent: *the conventual life.* ■ relating to the less strict order of the Franciscans, living in large convents.
▶ **n.** a person who lives in or is a member of a convent.
– ORIGIN late Middle English: from medieval Latin *conventualis*, from Latin *conventus* 'assembly, company' (see CONVENT).

con·verge /kənˈvərj/ ▶ **v.** [no obj.] (of several people or things) come together from different directions so as eventually to meet: *convoys from America and the UK traversed thousands of miles to converge in the Atlantic* | figurative *two separate people whose lives converge briefly from time to time.* ■ (**converge on/upon**) come from different directions and meet at (a place): *half a million sports fans will converge on the capital.* ■ (of a number of things) gradually change so as to become similar or develop something in common: *two cultures converged as the French settled Vermont.* ■ (of lines) tend to meet at a point: *a pair of lines of longitude are parallel at the equator but converge toward the poles.* ■ Mathematics (of a series) approximate in the sum of its terms

C

toward a definite limit: *the powers of e therefore converge very slowly.*
– ORIGIN late 17th cent.: from late Latin *convergere*, from *con-* 'together' + Latin *vergere* 'incline.'

con·ver·gence /kənˈvərjəns/ (also **convergency** /-jənsē/) ▶ **n.** the process or state of converging: *the convergence of lines in the distance.* ■ Biology the tendency of unrelated animals and plants to evolve superficially similar characteristics under similar environmental conditions. ■ (also **convergence zone**) a location where airflows or ocean currents meet, characteristically marked by upwelling (of air) or downwelling (of water).

con·ver·gent /kənˈvərjənt/ ▶ **adj.** coming closer together, esp. in characteristics or ideas: *convergent changes in languages.* ■ relating to convergence: *a convergent boundary.* ■ Mathematics (of a series) approaching a definite limit as more of its terms are added. ■ Biology relating to or denoting evolutionary convergence. ■ (of thought) tending to follow well-established patterns.
– ORIGIN early 18th cent.: from late Latin *convergent-* 'inclining together,' from the verb *convergere* (see CONVERGE).

con·ver·sant /kənˈvərsənt/ ▶ **adj.** familiar with or knowledgeable about something: *many ladies are conversant with the merits of drill-eyed needles.*
– DERIVATIVES **con·ver·sance** **n.**, **con·ver·san·cy** /-sənsē/ **n.**
– ORIGIN Middle English: from Old French, present participle of *converser* (see CONVERSE[1]). The original sense was 'habitually spending time in a particular place or with a particular person.'

con·ver·sa·tion /ˌkänvərˈsāsʜən/ ▶ **n.** the informal exchange of ideas by spoken words: *the two men were deep in* **conversation**. ■ an instance of this: *she picked up the phone and* **held a conversation** *in French.*
– PHRASES **make conversation** talk for the sake of politeness without having anything to say.
– ORIGIN Middle English (in the sense 'living among, familiarity, intimacy'): via Old French from Latin *conversatio(n-)*, from the verb *conversari* (see CONVERSE[1]).

con·ver·sa·tion·al /ˌkänvərˈsāsʜənl/ ▶ **adj.** appropriate to an informal conversation: *his tone was casual and conversational.* ■ consisting of or relating to conversation: *conversational skills.*
– DERIVATIVES **con·ver·sa·tion·al·ly** **adv.**

con·ver·sa·tion·al·ist /ˌkänvərˈsāsʜənl-ist/ ▶ **n.** a person who is good at or fond of engaging in conversation.

con·ver·sa·tion piece ▶ **n.** **1** a type of genre painting in which a group of figures are posed in a landscape or domestic setting, popular esp. in the 18th century.
2 an object whose unusual quality makes it a topic of conversation.

con·ver·sa·tion-stop·per ▶ **n.** informal an unexpected or outrageous remark that cannot easily be answered.

con·ver·sa·zi·o·ne /ˌkänvərˌsätsēˈōnē, -ˈōˌnā/ ▶ **n.** (pl. **conversaziones** or **conversazioni** /-nē/) a scholarly social gathering held for discussion of literature and the arts.
– ORIGIN Italian, from Latin *conversatio* (see CONVERSATION).

con·verse[1] ▶ **v.** /kənˈvərs/ [no obj.] engage in conversation: *he fell in beside her and they began to converse amicably.*
▶ **n.** /ˈkänˌvərs/ archaic conversation.
– DERIVATIVES **con·vers·er** /kənˈvərsər/ **n.**
– ORIGIN late Middle English (in the sense 'live among, be familiar with'): from Old French *converser*, from Latin *conversari* 'keep company (with),' from *con-* 'with' + *versare*, frequentative of *vertere* 'to turn.' The current sense of the verb dates from the early 17th cent.

con·verse[2] /ˈkänˌvərs/ ▶ **n.** a situation, object, or statement that is the reverse of another, or that corresponds to it but with certain terms transposed: *if spirituality is properly political, the converse is also true: politics is properly spiritual.* ■ Mathematics a theorem whose hypothesis and conclusion are the conclusion and hypothesis of another.
▶ **adj.** /ˈkänˌvərs, kənˈvərs/ having characteristics that are the reverse of something else already mentioned: *the slow process of growth and the converse process of decay.*
– ORIGIN late Middle English: from Latin *conversus* 'turned around,' past participle of *convertere* (see CONVERT).

con·verse·ly /ˈkänˌvərslē, kənˈvərslē/ ▶ **adv.** introducing a statement or idea that reverses one that has just been made or referred to: *he would have preferred his wife not to work, although conversely he was also proud of what she did.*

con·ver·sion /kənˈvərzʜən/ ▶ **n.** **1** the act or an instance of converting or the process of being converted: *the conversion of food into body tissues.* ■ the fact of changing one's religion or beliefs or the action of persuading someone else to change theirs: *my conversion to the Catholic faith.* ■ Christian Theology repentance and change to a godly life. ■ the adaptation of a building for a new purpose: *the conversion of a house into apartments.* ■ Brit. a building or part of a building that has been adapted in this way. ■ Law the changing of real into personal property, or of joint into separate property, or vice versa. ■ Psychiatry the manifestation of a mental disturbance as a physical disorder or disease: [as modifier] *conversion disorders.* ■ Logic the transposition of the subject and predicate of a proposition according to certain rules to form a new proposition by inference.
2 Football the act of scoring an extra point or points after having scored a touchdown. ■ the act of gaining a first down.
3 Law the action of wrongfully dealing with goods in a manner inconsistent with the owner's rights: *he was found guilty of the fraudulent conversion of clients' monies.*
4 Physics the change in a quantity's numerical value as a result of using a different unit of measurement.
– ORIGIN Middle English (in the sense 'turning of sinners to God'): via Old French from Latin *conversio(n-)*, from *convers-* 'turned around,' from the verb *convertere* (see CONVERT).

con·ver·sion fac·tor ▶ **n.** **1** an arithmetical multiplier for converting a quantity expressed in one set of units into an equivalent expressed in another.
2 Economics the manufacturing cost of a product relative to the cost of raw materials.

con·ver·sion van ▶ **n.** a van in which the cargo space has been converted to a special purpose, such as a living space.

con·vert ▶ **v.** /kənˈvərt/ **1** [with obj.] cause to change in form, character, or function: *production processes that* **converted** *raw material* **into** *useful forms.* ■ [no obj.] change or be able to change from one form to another: *the seating* **converts to** *a double or two single beds.* ■ [no obj.] change one's religious faith or other beliefs: *at sixteen he* **converted to** *Catholicism.* ■ persuade (someone) to do this: *he was* **converted** *in his later years* **to** *the socialist cause.* ■ change (money, stocks, or units in which a quantity is expressed) into others of a different kind: *the figures have been converted at $0.545 to the Dutch guilder.* ■ adapt (a building) to make it suitable for a new purpose: *the space can be easily converted into a home office* | (as adj. **converted**) *they lived in a converted chicken house.* ■ Logic transpose the subject and predicate of (a proposition) according to certain rules to form a new proposition by inference.
2 [with obj.] score from (a penalty kick, pass, or other opportunity) in a sport or game. ■ [no obj.] Football score an extra point or points after having scored a touchdown by kicking a goal (one point) or running another play into the end zone (two points). ■ [no obj.] Football advance the ball far enough during a down to earn a first down: *the Oilers converted on over half of their third downs.*
▶ **n.** /ˈkänˌvərt/ a person who has been persuaded to change their religious faith or other beliefs: *he is a recent* **convert to** *the church.*
– PHRASES **convert something to one's own use** Law wrongfully make use of another's property.
– ORIGIN Middle English (in the sense 'turn around, send in a different direction'): from Old French *convertir*, based on Latin *convertere* 'turn around,' from *con-* 'altogether' + *vertere* 'turn.'

con·ver·ted rice ▶ **n.** trademark white rice prepared from brown rice that has been soaked, steamed under pressure, and then dried and milled.

con·vert·er /kənˈvərtər/ (also **convertor**) ▶ **n.** a person or thing that converts something: *the converter of a building to domestic use.* ■ a device for altering the nature of an electric current or signal, esp. from AC to DC or vice versa, or from analog to digital or vice versa. ■ a retort used in steelmaking. ■ short for CATALYTIC CONVERTER. ■ Computing a program that converts data from one format to another. ■ a camera lens that changes the focal length of another lens by a set amount: *a camera fitted with a x2 converter.*

con·vert·i·ble /kənˈvərtəbəl/ ▶ **adj.** able to be changed in form, function, or character: *a living room that is miraculously* **convertible into** *a bedroom.* ■ (of a car) having a folding or detachable roof: *his white convertible Mercedes.* ■ (of currency) able to be converted into other forms, esp. into gold or US dollars. ■ (of a bond or stock) able to be converted into ordinary or preference shares. ■ Logic (of terms) synonymous.
▶ **n.** **1** a car with a folding or detachable roof.
2 (usu. **convertibles**) a convertible security.
– DERIVATIVES **con·vert·i·bil·i·ty** /-ˌvərtəˈbilitē/ **n.**
– ORIGIN late Middle English (in the sense 'interchangeable'): from Old French, from Latin *convertibilis*, from *convertere* 'turn around' (see CONVERT).

con·vex /känˈveks, ˈkänˌveks, kənˈveks/ ▶ **adj.** **1** having an outline or surface curved like the exterior of a circle or sphere. Compare with CONCAVE.
2 (of a polygon) having only interior angles measuring less than 180°.
– DERIVATIVES **con·vex·i·ty** /känˈveksitē, kən-/ **n.**, **con·vex·ly** **adv.**
– ORIGIN late 16th cent.: from Latin *convexus* 'vaulted, arched.'

convex and concave

con·vex·o·con·cave /kənˌveksōˈkänˌkāv, -känˈkāv/ ▶ **adj.** (of a lens) convex on one side and concave on the other and thickest in the center.

con·vex·o·con·vex /kənˌveksōˈkänˌveks, -känˈveks/ ▶ **adj.** another term for BICONVEX.

con·vey /kənˈvā/ ▶ **v.** [with obj.] transport or carry to a place: *pipes were laid to convey water to the house.* ■ make (an idea, impression, or feeling) known or understandable to someone: *the real virtues and diversity of America had never been conveyed in the movies* | *it's impossible to convey how lost I felt.* ■ communicate (a message or information): *Mr. Harvey and his daughter have asked me to convey their very kind regards.* ■ Law transfer the title to (property).
– DERIVATIVES **con·vey·a·ble** **adj.**
– ORIGIN Middle English (in the sense 'escort'; compare with CONVOY): from Old French *conveier*, from medieval Latin *conviare*, from *con-* 'together' + Latin *via* 'way.'

con·vey·ance /kənˈvāəns/ ▶ **n.** **1** the action or process of transporting someone or something from one place to another: *he was building vessels for the conveyance of live cod.* ■ a means of transportation; a vehicle: *adventurers attempt the trail using all manner of conveyances, including mountain bikes and motorcycles.* ■ the action of making an idea, feeling, or impression known or understandable to someone: *art's conveyance of meaning is complicated.*
2 Law the legal process of transferring property from one owner to another: *protective measures that might be taken before the conveyance is concluded.* ■ a legal document effecting such a process.

con·vey·anc·ing /kənˈvāənsiɴɢ/ ▶ **n.** the branch of law concerned with the preparation of documents for the transferring of property. ■ the action of preparing documents for the transfer of property.
– DERIVATIVES **con·vey·anc·er** /-sər/ **n.**

con·vey·or /kənˈvāər/ (also **conveyer**) ▶ **n.** a person or thing that transports or communicates something: *a conveyor of information.* ■ a conveyor belt.

con·vey·or belt ▶ **n.** a continuous moving band of fabric, rubber, or metal used for moving objects from one place to another.

con·vict ▶ **v.** /kənˈvikt/ [with obj.] declare (someone) to be guilty of a criminal offense by the verdict of a jury or the decision of a judge in a court of law: *her former boyfriend was* **convicted of** *assaulting her* | (as adj. **convicted**) *a convicted murderer.*
▶ **n.** /ˈkänˌvikt/ a person found guilty of a criminal offense and serving a sentence of imprisonment.
– ORIGIN Middle English: from Latin *convict-* 'demonstrated, refuted, convicted,' from the verb *convincere* (see CONVINCE). The noun is from obsolete *convict* 'convicted.'

con·vic·tion /kənˈviksʜən/ ▶ **n.** **1** a formal declaration that someone is guilty of a criminal offense, made by the verdict of a jury or the decision of a judge in a court of law: *she had a previous conviction for a similar offense.*
2 a firmly held belief or opinion: *his conviction that the death was no accident* | *she takes pride in stating her political convictions.* ■ the quality of showing that one is firmly convinced of what one believes or says: *his voice lacked conviction.*
– ORIGIN late Middle English: from Latin *convictio(n-)*, from the verb *convincere* (see CONVINCE).

con·vince /kənˈvins/ ▶ **v.** [with obj.] cause (someone) to believe firmly in the truth of something: *Robert's expression had obviously convinced her of his innocence* | [with obj. and clause] *you couldn't convince him that a floppy disk was as good as a manuscript.* ■ persuade (someone) to do something: *she convinced my father to branch out on his own.*

– DERIVATIVES **con·vinc·er** n., **con·vin·ci·ble** adj.
– ORIGIN mid 16th cent. (in the sense 'overcome, defeat in argument'): from Latin *convincere*, from *con-* 'with' + *vincere* 'conquer.' Compare with CONVICT.

USAGE Although it is common to see **convince** and **persuade** used interchangeably, there are distinctions in meaning that careful writers and speakers try to preserve. **Convince** derives from a Latin word meaning 'conquer, overcome.' **Persuade** derives from a Latin word meaning 'advise, make appealing, sweeten.' One can **convince** or **persuade** someone with facts or arguments, but, in general, *convincing* is limited to the mind, while *persuasion* results in action (just as *dissuasion* results in nonaction): *the prime minister convinced the council that delay was pointless; the senator persuaded her colleagues to pass the legislation.*

con·vinced /kən'vinst/ ▶ **adj.** completely certain about something: *she was not entirely convinced of the soundness of his motives* | *I am convinced the war will be over in a matter of months.* ■ firm in one's belief, esp. with regard to a particular cause or issue: *a convinced pacifist.*

con·vinc·ing /kən'vinsiNG/ ▶ **adj.** capable of causing someone to believe that something is true or real: *there is no convincing evidence that advertising influences total alcohol consumption* | *to make the detective's character convincing, she did extensive research.* ■ (of a victory or a winner) leaving no margin of doubt; clear: *the team cruised to a convincing win.*
– DERIVATIVES **con·vinc·ing·ly** adv.

con·viv·i·al /kən'vivēəl, kən'vivyəl/ ▶ **adj.** (of an atmosphere or event) friendly, lively, and enjoyable. ■ (of a person) cheerful and friendly; jovial.
– DERIVATIVES **con·viv·i·al·ly** adv.
– ORIGIN mid 17th cent. (in the sense 'fit for a feast, festive'): from Latin *convivialis*, from *convivium* 'a feast,' from *con-* 'with' + *vivere* 'live.'

con·viv·i·al·i·ty /kən,vivē'alitē/ ▶ **n.** the quality of being friendly and lively; friendliness: *the conviviality of the evening.*

con·vo·ca·tion /,känvə'kāsHən/ ▶ **n. 1** a large formal assembly of people. ■ a formal ceremony at a college or university, as for the conferring of awards.
2 the action of calling people together for a large formal assembly.
– DERIVATIVES **con·vo·ca·tion·al** /-sHənl/ adj.
– ORIGIN late Middle English: from Latin *convocatio(n-)*, from the verb *convocare* (see CONVOKE).

con·voke /kən'vōk/ ▶ **v.** [with obj.] formal call together or summon (an assembly or meeting): *she sent messages convoking a Council of Ministers.*
– ORIGIN late 16th cent.: from Latin *convocare*, from *con-* 'together' + *vocare* 'call.'

con·vo·lute /'känvə,lo͞ot/ ▶ **v.** [with obj.] make (an argument, story, etc.) complex and difficult to follow.
▶ **adj.** Biology rolled longitudinally upon itself, as a leaf in the bud.

con·vo·lut·ed /'känvə,lo͞otid/ ▶ **adj. 1** (esp. of an argument, story, or sentence) extremely complex and difficult to follow: *its convoluted narrative encompasses all manner of digressions.*
2 chiefly technical intricately folded, twisted, or coiled: *walnuts come in hard and convoluted shells.*
– DERIVATIVES **con·vo·lut·ed·ly** adv.
– ORIGIN late 18th cent.: past participle of *convolute*, from Latin *convolutus*, past participle of *convolvere* 'roll together, intertwine' (see CONVOLVE).

con·vo·lu·tion /,känvə'lo͞osHən/ ▶ **n. 1** (often **convolutions**) a coil or twist, esp. one of many: *crosses adorned with elaborate convolutions.* ■ a thing that is complex and difficult to follow: *the convolutions of farm policy.* ■ a sinuous fold in the surface of the brain. ■ the state of being coiled or twisted, or the process of becoming so: *the flexibility of the polymer chain allows extensive convolution.*
2 (also **convolution integral**) Mathematics a function derived from two given functions by integration that expresses how the shape of one is modified by the other. ■ a method of determination of the sum of two random variables by integration or summation.
– DERIVATIVES **con·vo·lu·tion·al** /-sHənl/ adj.
– ORIGIN mid 16th cent.: from medieval Latin *convolutio(n-)*, from *convolvere* 'roll together' (see CONVOLVE).

con·volve /kən'välv, -'vôlv/ ▶ **v.** [with obj.] rare roll or coil together; entwine. ■ Mathematics combine (one function or series) with another by forming their convolution.
– ORIGIN late 16th cent. (in the sense 'enclose in folds'): from Latin *convolvere* 'roll together,' from *con-* 'together' + *volvere* 'roll.'

con·vol·vu·lus /kən'välvyələs, -'vôl-/ ▶ **n.** (pl. **convolvuluses**) a twining plant with trumpet-shaped flowers, some kinds of which are invasive weeds (see also BINDWEED), while others, esp. morning glories, are cultivated for their bright flowers. ● Genus *Convolvulus*, family Convolvulaceae.
– ORIGIN mid 16th cent.: Latin, literally 'bindweed,' from *convolvere* 'roll together' (see CONVOLVE).

con·voy /'kän,voi/ ▶ **n.** a group of ships or vehicles traveling together, typically accompanied by armed troops, warships, or other vehicles for protection.
▶ **v.** /'kän,voi, kən'voi/ [with obj.] (of a warship or armed troops) accompany (a group of ships or vehicles) for protection.
– PHRASES **in convoy** (of traveling vehicles) as a group; together: *the army trucks had passed through in convoy the previous evening.*
– ORIGIN late Middle English (originally Scots, as a verb in the senses 'convey,' 'conduct,' and 'act as escort'): from French *convoyer*, from medieval Latin *conviare* (see CONVEY).

con·vul·sant /kən'vəlsənt/ ▶ **adj.** (chiefly of drugs) producing sudden and involuntary muscle contractions.
▶ **n.** a convulsant drug.
– ORIGIN late 19th cent.: from French, from *convulser*, from Latin *convuls-* 'pulled violently, wrenched,' from the verb *convellere* (see CONVULSE).

con·vulse /kən'vəls/ ▶ **v. 1** [no obj.] (of a person) suffer violent involuntary contraction of the muscles, producing contortion of the body or limbs: *she convulsed, collapsing to the floor with the pain.* ■ [with obj.] (of an emotion, laughter, or physical stimulus) cause (someone) to make sudden, violent, uncontrollable movements: *Carlos was convulsed by a second bout of sneezing* | *she rocked backward and forward, convulsed with helpless mirth.*
2 [with obj.] throw (a country) into violent social or political upheaval: *a wave of mass strikes convulsed the Ruhr, Berlin, and central Germany.*
– ORIGIN mid 17th cent.: from Latin *convuls-* 'pulled violently, wrenched,' from the verb *convellere*, from *con-* 'together' + *vellere* 'to pull.'

con·vul·sion /kən'vəlsHən/ ▶ **n.** (often **convulsions**) **1** a sudden, violent, irregular movement of a limb or of the body, caused by involuntary contraction of muscles and associated esp. with brain disorders such as epilepsy, the presence of certain toxins or other agents in the blood, or fever in children. ■ (**convulsions**) uncontrollable laughter: *the audience collapsed in convulsions.* ■ an earthquake or other violent or major movement of the earth's crust: *the violent convulsions of tectonic plates.*
2 a violent social or political upheaval: *the convulsions of 1939–45.*
– ORIGIN mid 16th cent. (originally in the sense 'cramp, spasm'): from Latin *convulsio(n-)*, from the verb *convellere* (see CONVULSE).

con·vul·sive /kən'vəlsiv/ ▶ **adj.** producing or consisting of convulsions: *a convulsive disease* | *she gave a convulsive sob.*
– DERIVATIVES **con·vul·sive·ly** adv.

Con·way /'kän,wā/ a city in central Arkansas; pop. 57,544 (est. 2008).

co·ny ▶ **n.** (pl. **conies**) variant spelling of CONEY.

coo[1] /ko͞o/ ▶ **v.** (**coos, cooing, cooed**) [no obj.] (of a pigeon or dove) make a soft murmuring sound: *ringdoves cooed among the branches.* ■ (of a person) speak in a soft gentle voice: *I cruised the room, cooing at toddlers* | *"I knew I could count on you," she cooed.*
▶ **n.** a soft murmuring sound made by a dove or pigeon.
– PHRASES **bill and coo** see BILL[2].
– ORIGIN mid 17th cent.: imitative.

coo[2] ▶ **exclam.** Brit. informal used to express surprise: *"Coo, ain't it high!" Mary squeaked.*
– ORIGIN early 20th cent.: imitative.

co-oc·cur /,kōə'kər/ ▶ **v.** [no obj.] occur together or simultaneously.
– DERIVATIVES **co-oc·cur·rence** /,kōə'kərəns/ **n.**

Cook[1] /ko͝ok/, Captain James (1728–79), English explorer. On his first expedition to the Pacific 1768–71, he charted the coasts of New Zealand and New Guinea and explored the east coast of Australia, claiming it for Britain. He made two more voyages to the Pacific before being killed in a skirmish with the Hawaiians.

Cook[2], Thomas (1808–92), English founder of the travel agency, Thomas Cook. In 1841, he organized the first publicly advertised excursion train in England; the success of this venture led him to organize further excursions both in Britain and abroad, laying the foundations for the tourist and travel-agent industry.

cook /ko͝ok/ ▶ **v. 1** [with obj.] prepare (food, a dish, or a meal) by combining and heating the ingredients in various ways: *shall I cook dinner tonight?* | [no obj.] *I told you I could cook* | (as adj. **cooked**) *a cooked breakfast.* ■ [no obj.] (of food) be heated so that the condition required for eating is reached: *while the rice is cooking, add the saffron to the stock.* ■ (**cook something down**) heat food and cause it to thicken and reduce in volume: *cooking down the chutney can take up to 45 minutes.* ■ [no obj.] (**cook down**) (of food being cooked) be reduced in volume in this way. ■ (**be cooking**) informal be happening or planned: *what's cooking on the alternative fuels front?*
2 [with obj.] informal alter dishonestly; falsify: *a narcotics team who cooked the evidence.* ■ (**be cooked**) be in an inescapably bad situation: *if I can't talk to him, I'm cooked.*
3 [no obj.] informal perform or proceed vigorously or well: *the band used to get up on the bandstand and really cook.*
▶ **n.** a person who prepares and cooks food, esp. as a job or in a specified way: *a short order cook* | *I'm a good cook.*
– PHRASES **cook the books** informal alter facts or figures dishonestly or illegally. **cook someone's goose** informal cause someone's downfall: *I've got enough on you to cook your goose.* **too many cooks spoil the broth** proverb if too many people are involved in a task, it will not be done well.
– PHRASAL VERBS **cook something up** concoct a story, excuse, or plan, esp. an ingenious or devious one.
– DERIVATIVES **cook·a·ble** adj.
– ORIGIN Old English *cōc* (noun), from popular Latin *cocus*, from Latin *coquus*.

Cook, Mount the highest peak in New Zealand, in the Southern Alps on South Island, that rises to a height of 12,349 feet (3,764 m). It is named after **Captain James Cook.** Official name AORAKI/MOUNT COOK.

cook·book /'ko͝ok,bo͝ok/ ▶ **n.** a book containing recipes and other information about the preparation and cooking of food.

Cook Coun·ty /ko͝ok/ a county in northeastern Illinois that includes Chicago and most of its closer suburbs; pop. 5,294,664 (est. 2008).

Cooke[1] /ko͝ok/, Alastair (1908–2004), British journalist and broadcaster; in the US from 1937. His BBC broadcasts of "Letter from America" began in 1946 and continued until shortly before his death. He hosted *Omnibus* on CBS 1952–60 and *Masterpiece Theatre* on PBS 1971–92.

Cooke[2] /ko͝ok/, Jay (1821–1905), US financier. He was the founder of Jay Cooke and Company, a leading Philadelphia bank, in 1861; his sale of bonds helped to finance the Civil War, and his financing of western railroads precipitated the Panic of 1873.

cook·er /'ko͝okər/ ▶ **n.** chiefly Brit. an appliance used for cooking food.

cook·er·y /'ko͝okərē/ ▶ **n.** (pl. **cookeries**) **1** the practice or skill of preparing and cooking food.
2 a place in which food is cooked; a kitchen.

cook·house /'ko͝ok,hous/ ▶ **n. 1** a kitchen or dining hall in a military camp.
2 an outdoor kitchen in a warm country.

cook·ie /'ko͝okē/ ▶ **n.** (pl. **cookies**) **1** a small sweet cake, typically round, flat, and crisp.
2 informal a person of a specified kind: *a tough cookie with one eye on her bank account.*
3 Computing a packet of data sent by an Internet server to a browser, which is returned by the browser each time it subsequently accesses the same server, used to identify the user or track their access to the server.
– PHRASES **that's the way the cookie crumbles** informal that's how things turn out (often used of an undesirable but unalterable situation).
– ORIGIN early 18th cent.: from Dutch *koekje* 'little cake,' diminutive of *koek*.

cook·ie cut·ter ▶ **n.** a device with sharp edges for cutting cookie dough into a particular shape. ■ [as modifier] denoting something mass-produced or lacking any distinguishing characteristics: *a cookie-cutter apartment in a high-rise building.*

cook·ie jar ▶ **n.** a jar to hold cookies.
– PHRASES **with one's hand in the cookie jar** engaged in surreptitious theft from one's employer: *they got caught with their hands in the cookie jar.*

cook·ie sheet ▶ **n.** a flat metal tray on which cookies are baked.

C

cook·ing /ˈko͝okiNG/ ▶ **n.** the process of preparing food by heating it: *frozen food must be fully defrosted before cooking.* ■ food that has been prepared in a particular way: *authentic Italian cooking.* ■ [as modifier] suitable for or used in cooking: *cooking oil.*

Cook In·let an inlet of the Gulf of Alaska, west of the Kenai Peninsula in southern Alaska. Anchorage lies at its northern end.

Cook Is·lands a group of 15 islands in the southwestern Pacific Ocean between Tonga and French Polynesia that have the status of a self-governing territory in free association with New Zealand; pop. 11,900 (est. 2009); capital, Avarua, on Rarotonga.
– ORIGIN named after Captain J. Cook (see **Cook**[1]), who visited them in 1773.

cook·out /ˈko͝ok,out/ ▶ **n.** a party or gathering where a meal is cooked and eaten outdoors.

Cook·son /ˈko͝oksən/, Dame Catherine (Anne) (1906–98), English writer. A prolific author of light romantic fiction, she is best known for the Mary Ann series (1956–67), the Mallen trilogy (1973–74), and the Tilly Trotter series (1980–82).

Cook's tour ▶ **n.** informal a rapid tour of many places: figurative *he then took me on a Cook's tour of his neuroscientific theories.*
– ORIGIN early 20th cent.: from the name of the travel agent Thomas *Cook* (see **Cook**[2]).

Cook Strait the strait that separates North and South islands of New Zealand. It was named after **Captain James Cook**, who visited it in 1770.

cook·top /ˈko͝ok,täp/ ▶ **n.** a cooking unit, usually with hot plates or burners, built into or fixed on the top of a cabinet or other surface.

cook·ware /ˈko͝ok,we(ə)r/ ▶ **n.** pots, pans, or dishes for cooking food: *cast-iron cookware.*

cool /ko͞ol/ ▶ **adj. 1** of or at a fairly low temperature: *it'll be a cool afternoon* | *the wind kept them cool.* ■ soothing or refreshing because of its low temperature: *a cool drink in the leafy shade* | figurative *the bathroom was all glass and cool, muted blues.* ■ (esp. of clothing) keeping one from becoming too hot: *wear your cool, comfortable shirts.* ■ showing no friendliness toward a person or enthusiasm for an idea or project: *he gave a cool reception to the suggestion for a research center.* ■ free from excitement or anxiety: *he prided himself on* **keeping a cool head** | *she seems* **cool, calm, and collected.** ■ (of jazz, esp. modern jazz) restrained and relaxed.
2 informal fashionably attractive or impressive: *I always wore sunglasses to look cool.* ■ excellent: [as exclamation] *a computer you didn't even have to plug in. Cool!* ■ used to express acceptance or agreement: *if people want to freak out at our clubs, that's cool.*
3 (**a cool ——**) informal used to emphasize a specified quantity or amount, esp. of money: *a cool $15,000 to buy the franchise.*
▶ **n. 1** (**the cool**) a fairly low temperature: *the cool of the night air.* ■ a time or place at which the temperature is pleasantly low: *the cool of the evening.*
2 calmness; composure: *he recovered his cool and then started laughing at us.*
3 the quality of being fashionably attractive or impressive: *all the cool of high fashion.*
▶ **v.** become or cause to become less hot: [no obj.] *we dived into the river to* **cool off** | figurative *his feelings for her took a long time to cool* | [with obj.] *cool the pastry for five minutes.* ■ become or cause to become calm or less excited: [no obj.] *after I'd cooled off, I realized I was being irrational* | [with obj.] *George was trying to cool him down.* ■ (**cool down**) recover from strenuous physical exertion by doing gentle stretches and exercises; warm down. ■ [usu. in imperative] (**cool it**) informal behave in a less excitable manner: *"Cool it and tell me why you're so ecstatic."*
– PHRASES **cool one's heels** be kept waiting. **keep** (or **lose**) **one's cool** informal maintain (or fail to maintain) a calm and controlled attitude. **play it cool** see **play**.
– DERIVATIVES **cooled adj.** *a water-cooled engine,* **cool·ish adj., cool·ly adv., cool·ness n.**
– ORIGIN Old English *cōl* (noun), *cōlian* (verb), of Germanic origin; related to Dutch *koel*, also to **cold**.

> **WORD TRENDS** Cool has meant more than just 'chilly' since the 1920s, when it started being used, particularly by black Americans, to describe someone or something fashionable, stylish, and impressive. This sense became more widely known in the 1940s, with the popularity of jazz and the beatnik culture, and was then particularly 'cool' in the 1960s. As is often the fate of popular slang, the word itself became 'uncool' for a couple of decades, before reclaiming its place as a favorite way of expressing positive feelings (*there is some really cool stuff going on at some of these companies* | *winning awards is such a cool thing*) or agreement (*if you want to use mine, that's cool*). The Oxford English Corpus shows that this use is now just as common as the word's original sense of 'at a fairly low temperature.' See also **stuff**.

coo·la·bah /ˈko͞olə,bä/ ▶ **n.** variant spelling of **coolibah**.

cool·ant /ˈko͞olənt/ ▶ **n.** a liquid or gas that is used to remove heat from something.
– ORIGIN 1930s: from **cool**, on the pattern of *lubricant*.

cool·er /ˈko͞olər/ ▶ **n. 1** an insulated container for keeping food and drink cool. ■ a refrigerated room.
2 a tall drink, esp. a mixture of wine, fruit juice, and soda water.
3 (**the cooler**) informal prison or a prison cell.

Coo·ley's a·ne·mi·a /ˈko͞olēz/ ▶ **n.** another term for **thalassemia**.
– ORIGIN 1930s: named after Thomas B. *Cooley* (1871–1945), American pediatrician.

cool·head·ed /ˈko͞ol,hedəd/ ▶ **adj.** not easily worried or excited.

cool·hunt·er ▶ **n.** informal a person whose job is to make observations or predictions about new styles and trends.
– DERIVATIVES **cool·hunt·ing n.**

coo·li·bah /ˈko͞olə,bä/ (also **coolabah**) ▶ **n.** a northern Australian gum tree that typically grows near watercourses and yields strong, hard timber. ● *Eucalyptus microtheca*, family Myrtaceae.
– ORIGIN late 19th cent.: from Kamilaroi (and related languages) *gulubaa*.

Cool·idge /ˈko͞olij/, (John) Calvin (1872–1933), 30th president of the US 1923–29. A Republican, he served as Massachusetts's lieutenant governor 1916–18 and governor 1919–20. He became the US vice president in 1921, succeeding to the presidency upon the death of President Harding in 1923. Elected in 1924 to serve a full term, Coolidge was committed to reducing income taxes and the national debt, and was noted for his policy of noninterference in foreign affairs, which culminated in the Kellogg Pact in 1928.

Calvin Coolidge

coo·lie /ˈko͞olē/ ▶ **n.** (pl. **coolies**) offensive an unskilled native laborer in India, China, and some other Asian countries.
– ORIGIN mid 17th cent.: from Hindi and Telugu *kūlī* 'day-laborer,' probably associated with Urdu *ḳulī* 'slave.'

coo·lie hat ▶ **n.** a broad conical straw hat as worn by laborers in some Asian countries.

cool·ing-off pe·ri·od ▶ **n.** an interval during which two people or groups who are in disagreement can try to settle their differences before taking further action. ■ an interval after a sales contract is agreed upon during which the purchaser can decide to cancel without loss.

cool·ing tow·er ▶ **n.** a tall, open-topped, cylindrical concrete tower, used for cooling water or condensing steam from an industrial process.

Cool·Max /ˈko͞ol,maks/ ▶ **n.** trademark a polyester fabric that draws perspiration along its fibers away from the skin, used chiefly in sportswear.
– ORIGIN 1980s: an invented name, probably from *cool* + *max(imum)*.

coolth /ko͞olTH/ ▶ **n.** chiefly humorous **1** pleasantly low temperature: *the coolth of the evening.*
2 articles, activities, or people perceived as fashionable: *the pinnacle of 1960s coolth.*
– ORIGIN mid 16th cent. (but rare before the 20th cent.): from **cool** + **-th**[2].

coombe (also **coomb**) ▶ **n.** variant spelling of **combe**.

coon /ko͞on/ ▶ **n. 1** short for **raccoon**.
2 informal, offensive a black person. [Sense 1, from an earlier sense '(sly) fellow.']
– PHRASES **a coon's age** informal a long time: *I haven't seen you in a coon's age!*

coon·can /ˈko͞on,kan/ ▶ **n.** a card game for two players, originally from Mexico, similar to rummy.
– ORIGIN late 19th cent.: probably from Spanish *con quién* 'with whom?'

coon·hound /ˈko͞on,hound/ ▶ **n.** a dog of an American breed, used to hunt raccoons. There are several breeds, including the **black and tan coonhound** and the **bluetick coonhound**.

Coon Rap·ids a city in southeastern Minnesota, on the Mississippi River, north of Minneapolis; pop. 61,832 (est. 2008).

coon·skin /ˈko͞on,skin/ ▶ **n.** the pelt of a raccoon: *a coonskin hat.*

coop /ko͞op, ko͝op/ ▶ **n.** a cage or pen for confining poultry: *a chicken coop.*
▶ **v.** [with obj.] (usu. **be cooped up**) confine in a small space: *being cooped up indoors all day makes him fidgety.* ■ put or keep (a fowl) in a cage or pen.
– PHRASES **fly the coop** see **fly**[1].
– ORIGIN Middle English *cowpe*; related to Dutch *kuip* 'vat' and German *Kufe* 'cask,' based on Latin *cupa*. Compare with **cooper**.

co-op /ˈkō,äp, kōˈäp/ ▶ **n.** informal a cooperative society, business, or enterprise.
– ORIGIN mid 19th cent.: abbreviation.

Coop·er[1] /ˈko͞opər/, Gary (1901–61), US actor; born *Frank James Cooper*. He is noted for his Academy-Award–winning performances in *Sergeant York* (1941) and *High Noon* (1952). Other notable movies: *The Virginian* (1929) and *For Whom the Bell Tolls* (1943).

Coop·er[2], James Fenimore (1789–1851), US novelist. He is renowned for his tales of Native Americans and frontier life, in particular the Leatherstocking tales—*The Pioneers* (1823), *The Last of the Mohicans* (1826), and *The Prairie* (1827).

Coo·per[3], Leon N., see **Bardeen**.

coop·er /ˈko͞opər, ˈko͝opər/ ▶ **n.** a maker or repairer of casks and barrels.
▶ **v.** [with obj.] make or repair (a cask or barrel).
– ORIGIN Middle English *cowper*, from Middle Dutch, Middle Low German *kūper*, from *kūpe* 'tub, vat,' based on Latin *cupa*. Compare with **coop**.

coop·er·age /ˈko͞opərij, ˈko͝op-/ ▶ **n.** a cooper's business or premises. ■ the making of barrels and casks.

co·op·er·ate /kōˈäpə,rāt/ ▶ **v.** [no obj.] act jointly; work toward the same end: *the leaders promised to cooperate in ending the civil war.* ■ assist someone or comply with their requests: *I was the villain for not cooperating with the FBI.*
– DERIVATIVES **co·op·er·ant** /-rənt/ **n., co·op·er·a·tor** /-,rātər/ **n.**
– ORIGIN late 16th cent.: from ecclesiastical Latin *cooperat-* 'worked together,' from the verb *cooperari*, from *co-* 'together' + *operari* 'to work.'

co·op·er·a·tion /kō,äpəˈrāSHən/ ▶ **n.** the process of working together to the same end: *they worked in close cooperation with the AAA.* ■ assistance, esp. by ready compliance with requests: *we would like to ask for your cooperation in the survey.* ■ Economics the formation and operation of cooperatives.
– ORIGIN late Middle English: from Latin *cooperatio(n-)*, from the verb *cooperari* (see **cooperate**); later reinforced by French *coopération*.

co·op·er·a·tive /kōˈäp(ə)rətiv/ ▶ **adj.** involving mutual assistance in working toward a common goal: *every member has clearly defined tasks in a cooperative enterprise.* ■ willing to be of assistance: *they have been extremely considerate, polite, and cooperative.* ■ (of a farm, business, etc.) owned and run jointly by its members, with profits or benefits shared among them.
▶ **n.** a farm, business, or other organization that is owned and run jointly by its members, who share the profits or benefits.
– DERIVATIVES **co·op·er·a·tive·ly adv., co·op·er·a·tive·ness n.**
– ORIGIN early 17th cent.: from late Latin *cooperativus*, from Latin *cooperat-* 'worked together,' from the verb *cooperari* (see **cooperate**).

Co·op·er·a·tive Re·pub·lic of Guy·a·na official name for **Guyana**.

Coo·per pair /ˈko͞opər, ˈko͝opər/ ▶ **n.** Physics a loosely bound pair of electrons with opposite spins and moving with the same speed in opposite directions, held to be responsible for the phenomenon of superconductivity. ■ a similar bound pair of atoms in a superfluid.
– ORIGIN 1960s: named after Leon N. *Cooper* (born 1930), American physicist.

Coo·per's hawk ▶ **n.** a North American bird of prey resembling but smaller than the goshawk. ● *Accipiter cooperii*, family Accipitridae.

–ORIGIN early 19th cent.: named after William *Cooper* (1798–1864), American naturalist.

Coo·pers·town /ˈkōōpərz,toun, ˈkōōp-/ a resort village in central New York, on Otsego Lake, site of the Baseball Hall of Fame; pop. 1,898 (est. 2008).

coop·er·y /ˈkōōpərē, ˈkōōp-/ ▶ n. (pl. **cooperies**) another term for **cooperage**.

co·op·e·ti·tion /kō,äpiˈtisHən/ ▶ n. collaboration between business competitors, in the hope of mutually beneficial results.
–ORIGIN 1980s: blend of *cooperative* and *competition*.

co-opt /kōˈäpt, ˈkō,äpt/ ▶ v. [with obj.] appoint to membership of a committee or other body by invitation of the existing members. ■ divert to or use in a role different from the usual or original one: *social scientists were co-opted to work with the development agencies*. ■ adopt (an idea or policy) for one's own use: *the green parties have had most of their ideas co-opted by bigger parties*.
–DERIVATIVES **co-op·ta·tion** /kō,äpˈtāsHən/ n., **co-op·tion** /,kōˈäpsHən/ n., **co-op·tive** /-ˈäptiv/ adj.
–ORIGIN mid 17th cent.: from Latin *cooptare*, from *co-* 'together' + *optare* 'choose.'

co·or·di·nate ▶ v. /kōˈôrdə,nāt/ [with obj.] **1** bring the different elements of (a complex activity or organization) into a relationship that will ensure efficiency or harmony: *he had responsibility for coordinating Chicago's transportation services*. ■ [no obj.] negotiate with others in order to work together effectively: *you will coordinate with consultants and other departments on a variety of projects*. ■ [no obj.] match or harmonize attractively: *the stud fastenings are colored to coordinate with the shirt* | (as adj. **coordinating**) *a variety of coordinating colors*.
2 Chemistry form a coordinate bond to (an atom or molecule): *the sodium atom is coordinated to two oxygen atoms*.
▶ adj. /kōˈôrdn-ət/ **1** equal in rank or importance: *cross references in the catalog link subjects that may be coordinate*. ■ Grammar (of parts of a compound sentence) equal in rank and fulfilling identical functions.
2 Chemistry denoting a type of covalent bond in which one atom provides both the shared electrons.
▶ n. /kōˈôrdənət/ **1** Mathematics each of a group of numbers used to indicate the position of a point, line, or plane.
2 (**coordinates**) matching items of clothing.
–DERIVATIVES **co·or·di·na·tive** /kōˈôrdn-ətiv, ˈôrdn,ātiv/ adj., **co·or·di·na·tor** /-ˈôrdn,ātər/ n.
–ORIGIN mid 17th cent. (in the senses 'of the same rank' and 'place in the same rank'): from **co-** 'together' + Latin *ordinare* (from *ordo* 'order'), on the pattern of *subordinate*.

Co·or·di·nat·ed U·ni·ver·sal Time (abbr.: **UTC**) another term for **Greenwich Mean Time**.

co·or·di·nat·ing con·junc·tion ▶ n. a conjunction placed between words, phrases, clauses, or sentences of equal rank, e.g., *and, but, or*. Contrasted with **subordinating conjunction**.

co·or·di·na·tion /kō,ôrdnˈāsHən/ ▶ n. **1** the organization of the different elements of a complex body or activity so as to enable them to work together effectively: *both countries agreed to intensify efforts at economic policy coordination*. ■ cooperative effort resulting in an effective relationship: *action groups work* **in coordination with** *local groups to end rain forest destruction*.
2 the ability to use different parts of the body together smoothly and efficiently: *changing from one foot position to another requires coordination and balance*.
3 Chemistry the linking of atoms by coordinate bonds.
–ORIGIN mid 17th cent. (in the sense 'placing in the same rank'): from French or from late Latin *coordinatio(n-)*, based on Latin *ordo, ordin-* 'order.'

co·or·di·na·tion num·ber ▶ n. Chemistry the number of atoms or ions immediately surrounding a central atom in a complex or crystal.

coot /kōōt/ ▶ n. **1** (pl. **same**) an aquatic bird of the rail family, with blackish plumage, lobed feet, and a bill that extends back onto the forehead as a horny shield. ● Genus *Fulica*, family Rallidae: several species, in particular the widespread *F. atra*, which has a white bill and frontal shield.
2 informal a foolish or eccentric person, typically an old man.
–ORIGIN Middle English: probably of Dutch or Low German origin and related to Dutch *koet*.

coot·er /ˈkōōtər/ ▶ n. a North American river turtle with a dull brown shell and typically having yellow stripes on the head. ● Genus *Pseudemys*, family Emydidae: several species, in particular *P. concinna*, some races of which are known as sliders.
–ORIGIN early 19th cent.: of unknown origin.

coot·ie /ˈkōōtē/ ▶ n. informal a body louse. ■ a children's term for an imaginary germ or repellent quality transmitted by obnoxious or slovenly people.
–ORIGIN World War I: perhaps from Malay *kutu*, denoting a parasitic biting insect.

co-own /,kōˈōn/ ▶ v. [with obj.] own (something) jointly.
–DERIVATIVES **co-own·er** n., **co-own·er·ship** n.

cop[1] /käp/ informal ▶ n. a police officer.
▶ v. (**cops, copping, copped**) [with obj.] **1** catch or arrest (an offender): *he was copped for speeding*. ■ incur (something unwelcome): *the team's captain copped most of the blame*. ■ obtain (an illegal drug): *he copped some hash for me*. ■ steal: *he watched her cop a pair of earrings and then nabbed her at the door*. ■ receive or attain (something welcome): *she copped an award for her role in the film*.
2 strike (an attitude or pose): *I copped an attitude—I acted real tough*.
–PHRASES **cop a feel** informal fondle someone sexually, esp. in a surreptitious way or without their permission. **cop hold of** [usu. in imperative] Brit. take hold of: *cop hold of the suitcase, I'm off*. **cop a plea** engage in plea bargaining. **good cop, bad cop** used to refer to a police interrogation technique in which one officer feigns a sympathetic or protective attitude while another adopts an aggressive approach: *they'll bring you into the station and play good cop, bad cop with you* | figurative *a Jekyll and Hyde CEO is good cop, bad cop rolled into one expensive suit*. **it's a fair cop** see **fair[1]**.
–PHRASAL VERBS **cop out** avoid doing something that one ought to do: *he copped out at the last moment*. **cop to** accept or admit to: *there are a lot of people who don't cop to their past*.
–ORIGIN early 18th cent. (as a verb): perhaps from obsolete *cap* 'arrest,' from Old French *caper* 'seize,' from Latin *capere*. The noun is from **copper[2]**.

cop[2] ▶ n. a conical or cylindrical roll of thread wound onto a spindle.
–ORIGIN late 18th cent.: possibly from Old English *cop* 'summit, top.'

Co·pa·ca·ba·na Beach /,kōpəkəˈbanə/ a resort on the Atlantic coast of Brazil near Rio de Janeiro.

co·pa·cet·ic /,kōpəˈsetik/ (also **copasetic**) ▶ adj. informal in excellent order.
–ORIGIN early 20th cent.: of unknown origin.

co·pal /ˈkōpəl/ ▶ n. resin from any of a number of tropical trees, used to make varnish. ● The resin is obtained from trees in the families Leguminosae (genera *Guibourtia*, *Copaifera*, and *Trachylobium*) and Araucariaceae (genus *Agathis*).
–ORIGIN late 16th cent.: via Spanish from Nahuatl *copalli* 'incense.'

Co·pán /kōˈpän/ an ancient Mayan city, the ruins of which are in western Honduras near the Guatemalan frontier.

co-par·ent /kōˈpe(ə)rənt, -ˈpar-/ ▶ v. [with obj.] (often as noun **co-parenting**) (esp. of a separated or unmarried couple) share the duties of parenting (a child).
▶ n. a person who co-parents a child.

co·part·ner /ˈkō,pärtnər/ ▶ n. a partner or associate, esp. an equal partner in a business.
–DERIVATIVES **co·part·ner·ship** /-,SHip/ n.

co·pay·ment /kōˈpāmənt/ (also **copay**) ▶ n. a payment made by a beneficiary (esp. for health services) in addition to that made by an insurer.

COPD ▶ abbr. Medicine chronic obstructive pulmonary disease, involving constriction of the airways and difficulty or discomfort in breathing.

cope[1] /kōp/ ▶ v. [no obj.] (of a person) deal effectively with something difficult: *his ability* **to cope with** *stress* | *it all got too much for me and I couldn't cope*. ■ (of a machine or system) have the capacity to deal successfully with: *the roads are barely adequate to cope with the present traffic*.
–DERIVATIVES **cop·er** n.
–ORIGIN Middle English (in the sense 'meet in battle, come to blows'): from Old French *coper, colper*, from *cop, colp* 'a blow,' via Latin from Greek *kolaphos* 'blow with the fist.'

cope[2] ▶ n. a long, loose cloak worn by a priest or bishop on ceremonial occasions. ■ technical or literary a thing resembling or likened to a cloak: *the bay and the square were a seamless cope*.
▶ v. [with obj.] (usu. as adj. **coped**) (in building) cover (a joint or structure) with a coping.

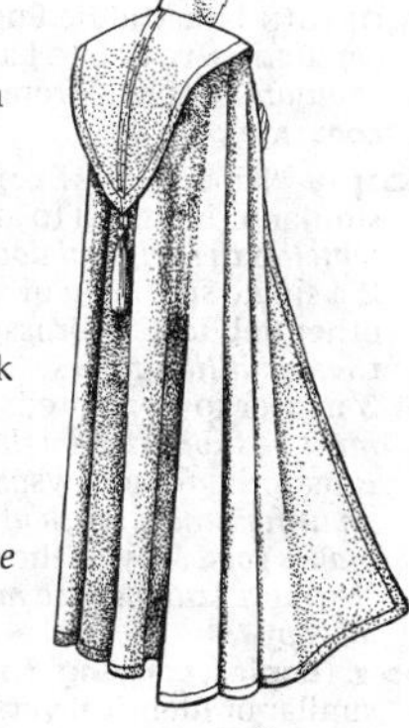
cope[2]

–ORIGIN Middle English (denoting a long outdoor cloak): from medieval Latin *capa*, variant of late Latin *cappa* (see **cap[1]** and **cape[1]**).

co·peck /ˈkō,pek/ ▶ n. chiefly British variant spelling of **kopek**.

Co·pen·ha·gen /ˈkōpən,hāgən, -,hägən/ the capital and chief port of Denmark, a city that occupies the eastern part of Zealand and northern part of the island of Amager; pop. 518,574 (2009). Danish name **København**.

C

co·pe·pod /ˈkōpə,päd/ ▶ n. Zoology a small or microscopic aquatic crustacean of the large class Copepoda.

Co·pep·o·da /kōˈpepədə/ Zoology a large class of small aquatic crustaceans, many of which occur in plankton and some of which are parasitic on larger aquatic animals.
–ORIGIN modern Latin, from Greek *kōpē* 'handle, oar' + *pous, pod-* 'foot' (because of its paddlelike feet).

Co·per·ni·can sys·tem /kəˈpərnikən/ (also **Copernican theory**) ▶ n. Astronomy the theory that the sun is the center of the solar system, with the planets (including the earth) orbiting around it. Compare with **Ptolemaic system**.
–ORIGIN mid 17th cent.: named after **Copernicus**.

Co·per·ni·cus /kəˈpərnikəs/, Nicolaus (1473–1543), Polish astronomer; Latinized name of *Mikołaj Kopernik*. He proposed a model of the solar system in which the planets orbit in perfect circles around the sun; his work ultimately led to rejection of the established geocentric cosmology.

cope·stone /ˈkōp,stōn/ ▶ n. a flat stone forming part of the coping of a wall. ■ the highest stone in a building, wall, or structure. ■ a finishing touch or crowning achievement.
–ORIGIN mid 16th cent.: from **cope[2]** + **stone**.

cop·i·a·ble /ˈkäpēəbəl/ ▶ adj. able to be copied, esp. legitimately photocopied.

cop·i·er /ˈkäpēər/ ▶ n. a machine that makes exact copies of something, esp. documents, video or audio recordings, or software.

co·pi·lot /ˈkō,pīlət/ ▶ n. a second pilot in an aircraft.
▶ v. [with obj.] act as the copilot of (an aircraft).

cop·ing /ˈkōpiNG/ ▶ n. the top, typically sloping, course of a brick or stone wall.
–ORIGIN mid 16th cent.: from the verb **cope[2]**, originally meaning 'dress in a cope,' hence 'to cover.'

cop·ing saw ▶ n. a saw with a very narrow blade stretched across a U-shaped frame, used for cutting curves in wood.
–ORIGIN 1920s: *coping* from **cope[2]**, used to describe likeness to a vault, arch, canopy, etc., based on Latin *cappa* 'cap or cape.'

cop·ing stone ▶ n. chiefly British term for **copestone**.

co·pi·ous /ˈkōpēəs/ ▶ adj. abundant in supply or quantity: *she took copious notes*. ■ archaic profuse in speech or ideas: *I had been a little too copious in talking of my country*.
–DERIVATIVES **co·pi·ous·ly** adv., **co·pi·ous·ness** n.
–ORIGIN late Middle English: from Old French *copieux* or Latin *copiosus*, from *copia* 'plenty.'

co·pla·nar /kōˈplānər, -,när/ ▶ adj. Geometry in the same plane.
–DERIVATIVES **co·pla·nar·i·ty** /,kō,plāˈne(ə)ritē/ n.

Cop·land /ˈkōplənd/, Aaron (1900–90), US composer, pianist, and conductor. He established a distinctive American style in his compositions, borrowing from jazz, folk, and other traditional music. Notable works: *Music for the Theater* (1925), *Appalachian Spring* (1944), and *Fanfare for the Common Man* (1942).

Cop·ley /ˈkäplē/, John Singleton (1738–1815), US painter. He is noted for his portraits and for paintings such as *The Death of Chatham* (1779–80), one of the first large-scale paintings of contemporary events.

co·pol·y·mer /kōˈpäləmər/ ▶ n. Chemistry a polymer made by reaction of two different monomers, with units of more than one kind.

co·pol·y·mer·ize /kōˈpäləmə,rīz/ ▶ v. [with obj.] Chemistry polymerize together to form a copolymer.
–DERIVATIVES **co·pol·y·mer·i·za·tion** /kō,päləmərəˈzāsHən/ n.

cop-out ▶ n. informal an instance of avoiding a commitment or responsibility: *being 'average' is the lazy person's cop-out*.

cop·per[1] /ˈkäpər/ ▶ n. **1** a red-brown metal, the chemical element of atomic number 29. (Symbol: **Cu**)

Copper was the earliest metal to be used by humans, first by itself and then later alloyed with tin to form bronze. A ductile, easily worked metal, it is a very good conductor of heat and electricity and is used esp. for electrical wiring.

C

2 dated a copper coin, esp. a penny: *you could hire a raft for a few coppers.* **3** a reddish-brown color like that of copper. **4** [with modifier] a small butterfly of North America and Eurasia. The upper surface of its wings is typically bright reddish-orange or purple. ● Genus *Lycaena*, family Lycaenidae: numerous species, including the **American copper** (*L. phlaeas*) of the eastern US and arctic North America.
▸ **v.** [with obj.] cover or coat (something) with copper.
– ORIGIN Old English *copor, coper* (related to Dutch *koper* and German *Kupfer*), based on late Latin *cuprum*, from Latin *cyprium aes* 'Cyprus metal' (so named because Cyprus was the chief source).

American copper

cop·per² ▸ **n.** informal a police officer.
– ORIGIN mid 19th cent.: from COP¹ + -ER¹.

cop·per·as /ˈkäpərəs/ ▸ **n.** green crystals of hydrated ferrous sulfate, esp. as an industrial product.
– ORIGIN late Middle English *coperose*, from Old French *couperose*, from medieval Latin *cuperosa*, literally 'flower of copper,' from late Latin *cuprum* (see COPPER¹) + *rosa* 'rose,' translating Greek *khalkanthon.*

cop·per beech ▸ **n.** a variety of European beech tree with purplish-brown leaves.

Cop·per·belt /ˈkäpərˌbelt/ a mining region in central Zambia that has rich deposits of copper, cobalt, and uranium; chief town, Ndola.

cop·per·head /ˈkäpərˌhed/ ▸ **n.** any of a number of stout-bodied venomous snakes with coppery-pink or reddish-brown coloration, in particular: ● a North American pit viper (*Agkistrodon contortrix*, family Viperidae). Also called HIGHLAND MOCCASIN ● an Australian snake of the cobra family (genus *Austrelaps*, family Elapidae, in particular *A. superbus*).

cop·per·plate /ˌkäpərˈplāt, ˈkäpərˌplāt/ ▸ **n. 1** a polished copper plate with a design engraved or etched into it. ■ a print made from such a plate. **2** a style of neat, round handwriting, usually slanted and looped, the thick and thin strokes being made by pressure with a flexible metal nib. [the copybooks for this round hand were originally printed from copperplates.]
▸ **adj.** of or in copperplate writing.

cop·per·smith /ˈkäpərˌsmiTH/ ▸ **n. 1** a person who makes things out of copper. **2** (also **coppersmith barbet**) the crimson-breasted barbet of Southeast Asia, which has a red breast band, a streaked belly, and a repetitive metallic call. ● *Megalaima haemacephala*, family Capitonidae.

cop·per sul·fate ▸ **n.** a blue crystalline solid used in electroplating and as a fungicide. ● Chem. formula: $CuSO_4.5H_2O$.

cop·per·y /ˈkäpərē/ ▸ **adj.** like copper, esp. in color: *his hair was fine and coppery.*

cop·pice /ˈkäpəs/ chiefly Brit. ▸ **n.** an area of woodland in which the trees or shrubs are, or formerly were, periodically cut back to ground level to stimulate growth and provide firewood or timber.
▸ **v.** [with obj.] cut back (a tree or shrub) to ground level periodically to stimulate growth: (as adj. **coppiced**) *coppiced timber.*
– ORIGIN late Middle English: from Old French *copeiz*, based on medieval Latin *colpus* 'a blow' (see COPE¹). Compare with COPSE.

Cop·po·la /ˈkäpələ/, Francis Ford (1939–), US movie director, writer, and producer. He is known for *The Godfather* (1972) and its two sequels, which chart the fortunes of a New York Mafia family over several generations. Other notable movies include *The Conversation* (1974) and *Apocalypse Now* (1979).

cop·ra /ˈkäprə/ ▸ **n.** dried coconut kernels, from which oil is obtained.
– ORIGIN late 16th cent.: via Portuguese and Spanish from Malayalam *koppara* 'coconut.'

copro- ▸ **comb. form** of or relating to dung or feces: *coprophagia* | *coprophilia.*
– ORIGIN from Greek *kopros* 'dung.'

co·proc·es·sor /kōˈpräˌsesər, ˌkōˈpräsəsər/ ▸ **n.** Computing a microprocessor designed to supplement the capabilities of the primary processor.

co·pro·duce /ˌkōprəˈd(y)o͞os/ ▸ **v.** [with obj.] produce (a theatrical work or a radio or television program) jointly.
– DERIVATIVES **co·pro·duc·er n.**, **co·pro·duc·tion** /-ˈdəkSHən/ **n.**

cop·ro·la·li·a /ˌkäprəˈlālēə/ ▸ **n.** Psychiatry the involuntary and repetitive use of obscene language, as a symptom of mental illness or organic brain disease.
– ORIGIN late 19th cent.: from Greek *kopros* 'dung' + *lalia* 'speech, chatter.'

cop·ro·lite /ˈkäprəˌlīt/ ▸ **n.** Paleontology a piece of fossilized dung.

cop·rol·o·gy /kəˈpräləjē/ ▸ **n.** another term for SCATOLOGY.

cop·roph·a·gy /kəˈpräfəjē/ (also **coprophagia** /ˌkäprəˈfāj(ē)ə/) ▸ **n.** Zoology the eating of feces or dung.
– DERIVATIVES **cop·ro·phag·ic** /ˌkäprəˈfajik/ **adj.**, **co·proph·a·gous** /-ˈpräfəgəs/ **adj.** (chiefly Zoology).

cop·ro·phil·i·a /ˌkäprəˈfilēə/ ▸ **n.** abnormal interest and pleasure in feces and defecation.

cops and rob·bers ▸ **plural n.** a children's game of hiding and chasing, in which the participants pretend to be police and criminals. ■ a simplistic polarization of the conflict between criminals and police, seen virtually as a game; a lifestyle centered around this: *to him this could be a lark, a bit of cops and robbers.*

copse /käps/ ▸ **n.** a small group of trees.
– ORIGIN late 16th cent.: shortened from COPPICE.

cop shop ▸ **n.** informal a police station.

Copt /käpt/ ▸ **n. 1** a native Egyptian in the Hellenistic and Roman periods. **2** a member of the Coptic Church.
– ORIGIN from French *Copte* or modern Latin *Coptus*, from Arabic *al-kibt, al-kubt* 'Copts,' from Coptic *Gyptios*, from Greek *Aiguptios* 'Egyptian.'

cop·ter /ˈkäptər/ ▸ **n.** informal term for HELICOPTER.

Cop·tic /ˈkäptik/ ▸ **n.** the language of the Copts, which represents the final stage of ancient Egyptian. It now survives only as the liturgical language of the Coptic Church.
▸ **adj.** of or relating to the Copts or their language.

Cop·tic Church the native Christian Church in Egypt, traditionally founded by St. Mark, and adhering to the Monophysite doctrine rejected by the Council of Chalcedon. Long persecuted after the Muslim Arab conquest of Egypt in the 7th century, the Coptic community now make up about 5 percent of Egypt's population.

cop·u·la /ˈkäpyələ/ ▸ **n.** Logic & Grammar a connecting word, in particular a form of the verb *be* connecting a subject and complement.
– DERIVATIVES **cop·u·lar** /ˈkäpyələr/ **adj.**
– ORIGIN early 17th cent.: from Latin,'connection, linking of words,' from *co-* 'together' + *apere* 'fasten.'

cop·u·late /ˈkäpyəˌlāt/ ▸ **v.** [no obj.] have sexual intercourse.
– DERIVATIVES **cop·u·la·to·ry** /-ləˌtôrē/ **adj.**
– ORIGIN late Middle English (in the sense 'join'): from Latin *copulat-* 'fastened together,' from the verb *copulare*, from *copula* (see COPULA).

cop·u·la·tion /ˌkäpyəˈlāsHən/ ▸ **n.** sexual intercourse: *males may seek copulation with the breeding female.*

cop·u·la·tive /ˈkäpyəˌlātiv, -lətiv/ ▸ **adj. 1** Grammar (of a word) connecting words or clauses linked in sense. Compare with DISJUNCTIVE. ■ connecting a subject and predicate. **2** of or relating to sexual intercourse.
– DERIVATIVES **cop·u·la·tive·ly adv.**
– ORIGIN late Middle English: from Old French *copulatif, -ive* or late Latin *copulativus*, from *copulat-* 'coupled,' from the verb *copulare* (see COPULATE).

cop·y /ˈkäpē/ ▸ **n.** (pl. **copies**) **1** a thing made to be similar or identical to another: *the problem is telling which is the original document and which the copy.* **2** a single specimen of a particular book, record, or other publication or issue: *the record has sold more than a million copies.* **3** matter to be printed: *copy for the next issue must be submitted by the beginning of the month.* ■ material for a newspaper or magazine article: *it is an unfortunate truth of today's media that bad news makes good copy.* ■ the text of an advertisement: *"No more stubble—no more trouble," trumpeted their ad copy.*
▸ **v.** (**copies, copying, copied**) [with obj.] **1** make a similar or identical version of; reproduce: *each form had to be copied and sent to a different department.* ■ Computing reproduce (data stored in one location) in another location: *the command will copy a file from one disc to another.* ■ write out information that one has read or heard: *he copied the details into his notebook* | *I began to copy out the addresses.* ■ (**copy something to**) send a copy of a letter to (a third party). ■ (**copy someone in**) send someone a copy of an e-mail that is addressed to a third party: *I attached the document and copied him in so he'd know it had been sent.* **2** imitate the style or behaviour of: *lifestyles that were copied from Miami and Fifth Avenue* | *she was such fun that everybody wanted to copy her* | [no obj.] *art students copied from approved old masters.* **3** [no obj.] hear or understand someone speaking on a radio transmitter: *this is Edwards, do you copy, over.*
– ORIGIN Middle English (denoting a transcript or copy of a document): from Old French *copie* (noun), *copier* (verb), from Latin *copia* 'abundance' (in medieval Latin 'transcript,' from such phrases as *copiam describendi facere* 'give permission to transcribe').

cop·y·book /ˈkäpēˌbo͝ok/ ▸ **n.** a book containing models of handwriting for learners to imitate.
▸ **adj.** exactly in accordance with established criteria; perfect. ■ tritely conventional: *out come the copybook maxims.*

cop·y·cat /ˈkäpēˌkat/ ▸ **n.** informal, derogatory (esp. in children's use) a person who copies another's behavior, dress, or ideas. ■ [as modifier] denoting an action, typically a crime, carried out in imitation of another: *copycat killings.*

cop·y·desk /ˈkäpēˌdesk/ ▸ **n.** a desk in a newspaper office at which copy is edited for printing.

cop·y·ed·it /ˈkäpēˌedit/ ▸ **v.** [with obj.] edit (text to be printed) by checking its consistency and accuracy.
– DERIVATIVES **cop·y·ed·i·tor** /-ˌedətər/ (also **copy editor**) **n.**

cop·y·hold /ˈkäpēˌhōld/ ▸ **n.** Brit. historical tenure of land based on manorial records.

cop·y·hold·er /ˈkäpēˌhōldər/ ▸ **n. 1** (also **copy holder**) a clasp or stand for holding sheets of text while it is keyed or typed. **2** Brit. historical a person who holds land in copyhold.

cop·y·ist /ˈkäpē-ist/ ▸ **n.** a person who makes copies, esp. of handwritten documents or music. ■ a person who imitates the styles of others, esp. in art.
– ORIGIN mid 17th cent.: from COPY + -IST; replacing earlier *copist*, from French *copiste* or medieval Latin *copista*, from *copiare* 'to copy,' from *copia* (see COPY).

cop·y·left /ˈkäpēˌleft/ ▸ **n.** an arrangement whereby software or artistic work may be used, modified, and distributed freely on condition that anything derived from it is bound by the same condition.
– DERIVATIVES **cop·y·left·ed adj.**
– ORIGIN 1980s: on the pattern of *copyright.*

cop·y·right /ˈkäpēˌrīt/ ▸ **n.** the exclusive legal right, given to an originator or an assignee to print, publish, perform, film, or record literary, artistic, or musical material, and to authorize others to do the same: *he issued a writ for breach of copyright* | *works whose copyrights had lapsed.* ■ a particular literary, artistic, or musical work that is covered by copyright.
▸ **adj.** protected by copyright: *permission to reproduce photographs and other copyright material.*
▸ **v.** [with obj.] secure copyright for (material).

cop·y·right li·brar·y ▸ **n.** Brit. a library entitled to receive one free copy of each book, pamphlet, map, music sheet or score, and periodical published in the UK. See also BODLEIAN LIBRARY.

cop·y·writ·er /ˈkäpiˌrītər/ ▸ **n.** a person who writes the text of advertisements or publicity material.
– DERIVATIVES **cop·y·writ·ing** /-ˌrītiNG/ **n.**

coq au vin /ˌkōk ō ˈvaN, ˌkäk/ ▸ **n.** a casserole of chicken pieces cooked in red wine.
– ORIGIN mid 20th cent.: French, literally 'cock in wine.'

co·quet /kōˈket/ ▸ **v.** flirt, or flirt with.
▸ **n.** dated a man who flirts.

co·quet·ry /ˈkōkətrē, kōˈketrē/ ▸ **n.** flirtatious behavior or a flirtatious manner.
– ORIGIN mid 17th cent.: from French *coquetterie*, from *coqueter* 'to flirt,' from *coquet* 'wanton' (see COQUETTE).

co·quette /kōˈket/ ▸ **n. 1** a woman who flirts. **2** a crested Central and South American hummingbird, typically with green plumage, a reddish crest, and elongated cheek feathers. ● *Lophornis* and two other genera, family Trochilidae: several species.
– ORIGIN mid 17th cent.: French, feminine of *coquet* 'wanton,' diminutive of *coq* 'cock.'

co·quet·tish /kōˈketisH/ ▸ **adj.** behaving in such a way as to suggest a playful sexual attraction; flirtatious: *a coquettish grin.*

–DERIVATIVES **co·quet·tish·ly** adv., **co·quet·tish·ness** n.

co·qui /ˈkōkē/ ▶ n. a singing tree frog (*Eleutherodactylus coqui*), native to Puerto Rico, that has become an invasive pest in Hawaii.
–ORIGIN imitative of the male's call.

co·qui·na /kōˈkēnə/ ▶ n. **1** a soft limestone of broken shells, used in road-making in the Caribbean and Florida.
2 (also **coquina clam**) a small bivalve mollusk with a wedge-shaped shell that has a wide variety of colors and patterns. ● Genus *Donax*, family Donacidae: several species, including the edible **American coquina** (*D. variabilis*).
–ORIGIN mid 19th cent.: from Spanish, literally 'cockle,' based on Latin *concha* (see CONCH).

co·qui·to /kōˈkētō/ ▶ n. (pl. **coquitos**) a thick-trunked Chilean palm tree that yields large amounts of sweet sap (palm honey) and fiber. Also called CHILEAN WINE PALM. ● *Jubaea chilensis*, family Palmae.
–ORIGIN mid 19th cent.: from Spanish, diminutive of *coco* 'coconut.'

cor /kôr/ ▶ exclam. Brit. informal expressing surprise, excitement, admiration, or alarm: *"Cor! That's a beautiful black eye you've got!"*
–PHRASES **cor blimey** /ˌkôr ˈblīmē/ see BLIMEY.
–ORIGIN 1930s: alteration of GOD.

Cor. ▶ abbr. ■ coroner. ■ Bible Corinthians.

cor- ▶ prefix variant spelling of COM- assimilated before *r* (as in *corrode, corrugate*).

Co·ra /ˈkôrə/ ▶ n. **1** a member of an American Indian people of western Mexico.
2 the Uto-Aztecan language of this people.
▶ adj. of or relating to this people or their language.

cor·a·cle /ˈkôrəkəl, ˈkär-/ ▶ n. (esp. in Wales and Ireland) a small, round boat made of wickerwork covered with a watertight material, propelled with a paddle.
–ORIGIN mid 16th cent.: from Welsh *corwgl, cwrwgl*, related to Scottish Gaelic and Irish *curach* 'small boat'; compare with CURRACH.

cor·a·coid /ˈkôrəˌkoid/ ▶ n. (also **coracoid process**) Anatomy a short projection from the shoulder blade in mammals, to which part of the biceps is attached.
–ORIGIN mid 18th cent.: from modern Latin *coracoides*, from Greek *korakoeidēs* 'ravenlike,' from *korax* 'raven' (because of the resemblance to a raven's beak).

cor·al /ˈkôrəl, ˈkär-/ ▶ n. **1** a hard stony substance secreted by certain marine coelenterates as an external skeleton, typically forming large reefs in warm seas: [as modifier] *a coral reef.* ■ precious red coral, used in jewelry. ■ the pinkish-red color of red coral.
2 a sedentary coelenterate of warm and tropical seas, with a calcareous, horny, or soft skeleton. Most corals are colonial and many rely on the presence of green algae in their tissues to obtain energy from sunlight. ● Several orders in the class Anthozoa, including the 'true' or **stony corals** (order Scleractinia or Madreporaria), which form reefs, the **soft corals** (order Alcyonacea), and the **horny corals** (order Gorgonacea).
3 the unfertilized roe of a lobster or scallop, which is used as food and becomes reddish when cooked.
–DERIVATIVES **cor·al·loid** /-ˌloid/ adj. (chiefly Biology & Zoology).
–ORIGIN Middle English: via Old French from Latin *corallum*, from Greek *korallion, kouralion*.

cor·al bells ▶ n. a red-flowered heuchera (*Heuchera sanguinea*) native to the southwestern US, but established elsewhere with many ornamental cultivars.

cor·al·ber·ry /ˈkôrəlˌberē, ˈkär-/ ▶ n. (pl. **coralberries**) an evergreen North American shrub of the honeysuckle family, which has fragrant white flowers followed by deep red berries. ● *Symphoricarpos orbiculatus*, family Caprifoliaceae.

cor·al fun·gus ▶ n. a widely distributed fungus that produces a fruiting body composed of upright branching fingerlike projections that resemble coral, found in both Eurasia and North America. ● *Clavulina, Ramaria*, and other genera, several families, class Basidiomycetes.

Cor·al Ga·bles a resort and commercial city in southeastern Florida, just southwest of Miami, on Biscayne Bay; pop. 42,781 (est. 2008).

cor·al·i·ta /ˌkôrəˈlētə, ˌkärə-/ ▶ n. a pink-flowered climbing vine native to Mexico and the Caribbean, grown as an ornamental. ● *Antigonon leptopus*, family Polygonaceae.
–ORIGIN late 19th cent.: from American Spanish *coralito*, diminutive of Spanish *coral* 'coral.'

cor·al·line /ˈkôrəˌlīn/ ▶ n. (also **coralline alga** or **coralline seaweed**) a branching reddish seaweed with a calcareous jointed stem. ● Family Corallinaceae, phylum Rhodophyta, in particular *Corallina officinalis*, which is common on the coasts of the North Atlantic. ■ (in general use) a sedentary colonial marine animal, esp. a bryozoan.
▶ adj. chiefly Geology derived or formed from coral: *the islands were volcanic rather than coralline in origin.* ■ of the pinkish-red color of precious red coral. ■ resembling coral: *coralline sponges.*
–ORIGIN mid 16th cent.: the noun from Italian *corallina*, diminutive of *corallo* 'coral,' the adjective (mid 17th cent.) from French *corallin* or late Latin *corallinus*, both based on Latin *corallum* 'coral.'

cor·al·lite /ˈkôrəˌlīt, ˈkär-/ ▶ n. Paleontology the cuplike calcareous skeleton of a single coral polyp. ■ a fossil coral.
–ORIGIN early 19th cent.: from Latin *corallum* 'coral' + -ITE[1].

cor·al·root /ˈkôrəlˌro͞ot, ˈkärəl-, -ˌro͝ot/ ▶ n. (also **coralroot orchid**) a leafless orchid that has inconspicuous flowers and lacks chlorophyll. It has a pale knobbly rhizome that obtains nourishment from decaying organic matter. ● Genus *Corallorhiza*, family Orchidaceae: several species, including the widespread *C. trifida*. ■ another term for COCKSCOMB (sense 3).

Cor·al Sea a part of the western Pacific Ocean that is surrounded by Australia, New Guinea, and Vanuatu, the scene of a naval battle between US and Japanese carriers in 1942 during World War II.

cor·al snake ▶ n. a brightly colored venomous snake of the cobra family, typically having conspicuous bands of red, yellow, white, and black. Compare with FALSE CORAL SNAKE. ● *Micrurus* and other genera in the family Elapidae: numerous species.

cor·al spot (also **coral spot disease**) ▶ n. a common fungal disease of trees and shrubs, appearing as numerous minute pink or dark red cushionlike bodies on the twigs and branches and causing dieback. ● *Nectria cinnabarina*, family Hypocreaceae, phylum Ascomycota.

Cor·al Springs a residential city in southeastern Florida; pop. 125,783 (est. 2008).

cor·al tree ▶ n. a tropical or subtropical thorny shrub or tree with showy red or orange flowers that are pollinated by birds. ● Genus *Erythrina*, family Leguminosae.

cor·beil /ˈkôrbəl, kôrˈbā/ ▶ n. Architecture a representation in stone of a basket of flowers.
–ORIGIN early 18th cent.: from French *corbeille* 'basket,' from late Latin *corbicula* 'small basket,' diminutive of *corbis*.

cor·beille /ˈkôrbəl, kôrˈbā/ ▶ n. an elegant basket of flowers or fruit.
–ORIGIN early 19th cent.: French,'basket' (see also CORBEIL).

cor·bel /ˈkôrbəl/ ▶ n. a projection jutting out from a wall to support a structure above it.
▶ v. (**corbels, corbeling, corbeled**; chiefly Brit. **corbels, corbelling, corbelled**) [with obj.] (often **be corbeled out**) support (a structure such as an arch or balcony) on corbels.
–ORIGIN late Middle English: from Old French, diminutive of *corp* 'crow,' from Latin *corvus* 'raven' (perhaps because of the shape of a corbel, resembling a crow's beak).

cor·bel ta·ble ▶ n. a projecting course of bricks or stones resting on corbels.

Cor·bett /ˈkôrbit/, James John (1866–1933), US boxer; known as **Gentleman Jim**. He won two world heavyweight championships 1892, 1897.

cor·bic·u·la /kôrˈbikyələ/ ▶ n. (pl. **corbiculae** /-yəˌlē, -yəˌlī/) Entomology another term for POLLEN BASKET.
–ORIGIN early 19th cent.: from late Latin.

cor·bie /ˈkôrbē/ ▶ n. (pl. **corbies**) Scottish a raven, crow, or rook.
–ORIGIN late Middle English: from Old French *corb*, variant of *corp* 'crow' (see CORBEL).

cor·bie·steps /ˈkôrbēˌsteps/ (also **corbie steps**) ▶ n. the steplike projections on the sloping part of a gable, common in Flemish architecture and 16- and 17th-century Scottish buildings. Also called CROW STEPS.

Cor·bin /ˈkôrbin/, Margaret (1751–1800), American Revolution heroine; born *Margaret Cochran*. After her husband's death in the attack on Fort Washington in 1776, she took his place at his cannon until becoming severely wounded. She was the first woman to be pensioned by the US government.

Cor·co·va·do /ˌkôrkōˈvädō/ a peak that rises to 2,310 feet (711 m) on the south side of Rio de Janeiro. A statue of Jesus Christ (named "Christ the Redeemer"), 131 feet (40 m) high, stands on its summit.

Cor·cy·ra /kôrˈsīrə/ ancient Greek name for CORFU.

cord /kôrd/ ▶ n. **1** long thin flexible string or rope made from several twisted strands: *hang the picture from a rail on a length of cord.* ■ a length of such material, typically one used to fasten or move a specified object: *a dressing-gown cord.* ■ an anatomical structure resembling a length of cord (e.g., the spinal cord, the umbilical cord): *the baby was still attached to its mother by the cord.* ■ a flexible insulated cable used for carrying electric current to an appliance.
2 ribbed fabric, esp. corduroy: [as modifier] *cord jackets.* ■ (**cords**) informal corduroy pants: *he was dressed in faded black cords.* ■ a cordlike rib on fabric.
3 a measure of cut wood, usually 128 cubic feet (3.62 cu m).
▶ v. [with obj.] attach a cord to.
–PHRASES **cut the** (**umbilical**) **cord** cease to rely on someone or something protective or supportive and begin to act independently.
–DERIVATIVES **cord·like** /-ˌlīk/ adj.
–ORIGIN Middle English: from Old French *corde*, from Latin *chorda*, from Greek *khordē* 'gut, string of a musical instrument.'

USAGE See usage at CHORD[2].

cord·age /ˈkôrdij/ ▶ n. cords or ropes, esp. in a ship's rigging.
–ORIGIN late 15th cent.: from Old French, from *corde* 'rope' (see CORD).

cor·date /ˈkôrˌdāt/ ▶ adj. Botany & Zoology heart-shaped.
–ORIGIN mid 17th cent. (in the sense 'wise, prudent'): from Latin *cordatus* 'wise' (in modern Latin 'heart-shaped'), from *cor, cord-* 'heart.'

Cor·day /kôrˈdā/, Charlotte (1768–93), French political assassin; full name *Marie Anne Charlotte Corday d'Armont*. In 1793, she assassinated revolutionary leader Jean Paul Marat in his bath; she was found guilty of treason and guillotined four days later.

cord blood ▶ n. blood from the human umbilical cord, a source of stem cells.

cord·ed /ˈkôrdəd/ ▶ adj. **1** (of cloth) ribbed. ■ (of a tensed muscle) standing out so as to resemble a piece of cord.
2 equipped with a cord: *a corded waistband | corded and cordless phones.*

cord·grass /ˈkôrdˌgras/ ▶ n. a coarse wiry coastal grass that is sometimes used to stabilize mudflats. ● Genus *Spartina*, family Gramineae.

cor·dial /ˈkôrjəl/ ▶ adj. warm and friendly: *the atmosphere was cordial and relaxed.* ■ strongly felt: *I earned his cordial loathing.*
▶ n. **1** another term for LIQUEUR.
2 a comforting or pleasant-tasting medicine.
–DERIVATIVES **cor·di·al·i·ty** /ˌkôrjēˈalitē/ n., **cor·dial·ly** adv.
–ORIGIN Middle English (also in the sense 'belonging to the heart'): from medieval Latin *cordialis*, from Latin *cor, cord-* 'heart.'

cor·di·er·ite /ˈkôrdēəˌrīt/ ▶ n. a dark blue mineral occurring chiefly in metamorphic rocks. It consists of an aluminosilicate of magnesium, and also occurs as a dichroic gem variety.
–ORIGIN early 19th cent.: named after Pierre L. A. *Cordier* (1777–1861), French geologist, + -ITE[1].

cor·di·form /ˈkôrdəˌfôrm/ ▶ adj. heart-shaped.

cor·dil·le·ra /ˌkôrdlˈ(y)erə/ ▶ n. a system or group of parallel mountain ranges together with the intervening plateaus and other features, esp. in the Andes or the Rockies.
–ORIGIN early 18th cent.: from Spanish, from *cordilla*, diminutive of *cuerda* 'cord,' from Latin *chorda* (see CORD).

cord·ing /ˈkôrdiNG/ ▶ n. cord or braid, esp. that used as a decorative fabric trimming.

cord·ite /ˈkôrˌdīt/ ▶ n. a smokeless explosive made from nitrocellulose, nitroglycerine, and petroleum jelly, used in ammunition.
–ORIGIN late 19th cent.: from CORD (because of its stringlike appearance) + -ITE[1].

cord·less /ˈkôrdləs/ ▶ adj. (of an electrical appliance or telephone) working without connection to a main supply or central unit.
▶ n. (usu. **the cordless**) a cordless telephone: *I keep the cordless with me at all times.*

Cor·do·ba /ˈkôrdəbə, -dəvə/ (also **Cordova**, Spanish name **Córdoba**) **1** a city in Andalusia, in southern Spain; pop. 325,453 (2008). Founded by the Carthaginians, it was under Moorish rule from

C

711 to 1236 and was renowned for its architecture, particularly the Great Mosque.
2 a city in central Argentina; pop. 1,319,000 (est. 2005).

cor·do·ba /ˈkôrdəbə, -dəvə/ ▶ n. the basic monetary unit of Nicaragua, equal to 100 centavos.
– ORIGIN named after F. Fernández de *Córdoba*, a 16th-cent. Spanish governor of Nicaragua.

C

cor·don /ˈkôrdn/ ▶ n. **1** a line or circle of police, soldiers, or guards preventing access to or from an area or building: *troops threw a cordon around the headquarters*.
2 an ornamental cord or braid.
3 Architecture another term for **STRINGCOURSE**.
▶ v. [with obj.] (**cordon off**) prevent access to or from (an area or building) by surrounding it with police or other guards: *the city center was cordoned off after fires were discovered in two stores*.
– ORIGIN late Middle English (denoting an ornamental braid worn on the person): from Italian *cordone*, augmentative of *corda*, and French *cordon*, diminutive of *corde*, both from Latin *chorda* 'string, rope' (see **CORD**). Sense 3 of the noun, the earliest of the current noun senses, dates from the early 18th cent.

cor·don bleu /ˌkôrdôN ˈblœ/ ▶ adj. Cooking of the highest class: *a cordon bleu chef*. ■ denoting a dish consisting of an escalope of veal or chicken rolled, filled with cheese and ham, and then fried in breadcrumbs.
▶ n. a cook of the highest class.
– ORIGIN mid 18th cent. (as a noun, often specifically denoting a first-class cook): French, literally 'blue ribbon.' The blue ribbon once signified the highest order of chivalry in the reign of the Bourbon kings.

cor·don sa·ni·taire /kôrdôN ˌsänēˈter/ ▶ n. (pl. **cordons sanitaires** pronunc. **same**) a guarded line preventing anyone from leaving an area infected by a disease and thus spreading it. ■ a measure designed to prevent communication or the spread of undesirable influences: *these rules help to reinforce the cordon sanitaire around the Pentagon*. ■ a series or chain of small neutral buffer states around a larger, potentially dangerous or hostile state.
– ORIGIN mid 19th cent.: French, from *cordon* 'line, border' (see **CORDON**) + *sanitaire* 'sanitary.'

Cor·do·va /ˈkôrdəvə/ English name for **CORDOBA**.

cor·do·van /ˈkôrdəvən/ ▶ n. a kind of soft leather made originally from goatskin and now from horsehide.
– ORIGIN late 16th cent.: from Spanish *cordován*, former spelling of *cordobán* 'of Cordoba' (see **CORDOBA** (sense 1)), where it was originally made.

Cor·du·ra /kôrˈd(y)o͝orə/ ▶ n. trademark a durable synthetic fabric.

cor·du·roy /ˈkôrdəˌroi/ ▶ n. a thick cotton fabric with velvety ribs. ■ (**corduroys**) pants made of corduroy.
– ORIGIN late 18th cent.: probably from **CORD** 'ribbed fabric' + *duroy*, denoting a kind of lightweight worsted formerly made in the West of England; of unknown origin.

cor·du·roy road ▶ n. historical a road made of tree trunks laid across a swamp.

cord·wood /ˈkôrdˌwo͝od/ ▶ n. wood that has been cut into uniform lengths, used esp. as firewood.

CORE /kôr/ ▶ abbr. Congress of Racial Equality.

core /kôr/ ▶ n. **1** the tough central part of various fruits, containing the seeds: *an apple core*.
2 the central or most important part of something, in particular: ■ [often as modifier] the part of something that is central to its existence or character: *managers can concentrate on their core activities | the plan has the interests of children at its core*. ■ an important or unchanging group of people forming the central part of a larger body. ■ the dense central region of a planet, esp. the nickel–iron inner part of the earth. ■ the central part of a nuclear reactor, which contains the fissile material. ■ a tiny ring of magnetic material used in a computer memory to store one bit of data, now superseded by semiconductor memories. ■ the inner strand of an electrical cable or rope. ■ a piece of soft iron forming the center of an electromagnet or an induction coil. ■ an internal mold filling a space to be left hollow in a casting. ■ a cylindrical sample of rock, ice, or other material obtained by boring with a hollow drill. ■ Archaeology a piece of flint from which flakes or blades have been removed.
▶ v. [with obj.] remove the tough central part and seeds from (a fruit): *peel and core the pears*.
– PHRASES **to the core** to the depths of one's being: *she was shaken to the core by his words*. ■ used to indicate that someone possesses a characteristic to a very high degree: *he is a politician to the core*.
– DERIVATIVES **cor·er** n.
– ORIGIN Middle English: of unknown origin.

-core ▶ comb. form (used as the second element of various compounds) denoting types of rock or dance music that have an aggressive presentation: *queercore*.
– ORIGIN from **CORE**, on the pattern of *hard-core*.

core as·set ▶ n. an asset of an enterprise considered to be essential to its success.

core com·pe·ten·cy ▶ n. a defining capability or advantage that distinguishes an enterprise from its competitors. ■ a defined level of competence in a particular job or academic program.

core dump ▶ n. Computing a dump of the contents of main memory, carried out typically as an aid to debugging.

co·ref·er·en·tial /ˌkōˌrefəˈrenCHəl/ ▶ adj. Linguistics (of two elements or units) having the same reference.
– DERIVATIVES **co·ref·er·ence** /kōˈref(ə)rəns, ˈkō-/ n.

co·re·li·gion·ist /ˌkō riˈlijənist/ ▶ n. an adherent of the same religion as another person.

co·rel·la /kəˈrelə/ ▶ n. a white Australasian cockatoo with some pink feathers on the face, bare blue skin around the eye, and typically a long bill. ● Genus *Cacatua*, family Cacatuidae (or Psittacidae): three species, in particular the widespread **little corella** (*C. sanguinea*).
– ORIGIN late 19th cent.: from Wiradhuri.

Co·rel·li /kəˈrelē/, Arcangelo (1653–1713), Italian violinist and composer, known for his concerti grossi and sonatas for violin.

co·re·op·sis /ˌkôrēˈäpsəs/ ▶ n. a plant of the daisy family, cultivated for its rayed, typically yellow, flowers. Also called **TICKSEED**. ● Genus *Coreopsis*, family Compositae.
– ORIGIN modern Latin, from Greek *koris* 'bug' + *opsis* 'appearance' (because of the shape of the seed).

co·re·spond·ent (also **corespondent**) ▶ n. a person cited in a divorce case as having committed adultery with the respondent.

Cor·fu /kôrˈfo͞o, ˈkôrf(y)o͞o/ a Greek island, one of the largest of the Ionian Islands, off the west coast of mainland Greece. It was known in ancient times as Corcyra; pop. 127,900 (est. 2009). Greek name **KÉRKIRA**.

cor·gi /ˈkôrgē/ ▶ n. (pl. **corgis**) short for **WELSH CORGI**.

co·ri·a·ceous /ˌkôrēˈāsHəs/ ▶ adj. technical resembling or having the texture of leather: *coriaceous leaves*.
– ORIGIN late 17th cent.: from late Latin *coriaceus* (from Latin *corium* 'leather') + **-OUS**.

co·ri·an·der /ˈkôrēˌandər, ˌkôrēˈandər/ ▶ n. an aromatic Mediterranean plant of the parsley family, the leaves and seeds of which are used as culinary herbs. ● *Coriandrum sativum*, family Umbelliferae.
– ORIGIN Middle English: from Old French *coriandre*, from Latin *coriandrum*, from Greek *koriannon*.

Cor·inth /ˈkôrinTH, ˈkär-/ a city on the northern coast of the Peloponnese, in Greece; pop. 27,600 (est. 2009). The modern city, built in 1858, is slightly northeast of the site of an ancient city of the same name that was a prominent city state in ancient Greece. Greek name **KÓRINTHOS**.

Cor·inth, Gulf of an inlet of the Ionian Sea that extends between the Peloponnese and central Greece. Also called **LEPANTO, GULF OF**.

Cor·inth, Isthmus of a narrow neck of land that links the Peloponnese with central Greece and separates the Gulf of Corinth from the Saronic Gulf.

Cor·inth Ca·nal a man-made shipping channel that crosses the narrowest part of the Isthmus of Corinth (a distance of 4 miles or 6.4 km). Opened in 1893, it links the Gulf of Corinth and the Saronic Gulf.

Co·rin·thi·an /kəˈrinTHēən/ ▶ adj. **1** belonging or relating to Corinth, esp. the ancient city. ■ relating to or denoting the lightest and most ornate of the classical orders of architecture (used esp. by the Romans), characterized by flared capitals with rows of acanthus leaves.
2 involving or displaying the highest standards of sportsmanship: *a club embodying the Corinthian spirit*.
▶ n. **1** a native of Corinth. ■ historical a wealthy amateur of sport.
2 the Corinthian order of architecture.

Co·rin·thi·ans /kəˈrinTHēənz/ either of two books of the New Testament, epistles of St. Paul to the Church at Corinth.

Cor·i·o·la·nus /ˌkôrēəˈlānəs/, Gaius (or Gnaeus) Marcius (5th century BC), Roman general who acquired his name from the capture of the Volscian town of Corioli.

Co·ri·o·lis ef·fect /ˌkôrēˈōləs/ ▶ n. Physics an effect whereby a mass moving in a rotating system experiences a force (the **Coriolis force**) acting perpendicular to the direction of motion and to the axis of rotation. On the earth, the effect tends to deflect moving objects to the right in the northern hemisphere and to the left in the southern and is important in the formation of cyclonic weather systems.
– ORIGIN early 20th cent.: named after Gaspard *Coriolis* (1792–1843), French engineer.

co·ri·um /ˈkôrēəm/ ▶ n. chiefly Zoology another term for **DERMIS**.
– ORIGIN early 19th cent.: from Latin, 'skin.'

Cork /kôrk/ a county in the Republic of Ireland, in the province of Munster, on the Celtic Sea. ■ its county town, a port on the Lee River; pop. 190,384 (2006).

cork /kôrk/ ▶ n. the buoyant, light brown substance obtained from the outer layer of the bark of the cork oak: [as modifier] *cork tiles*. ■ a bottle stopper, esp. one made of cork. ■ a piece of cork used as a float for a fishing line or net. ■ Botany a protective layer of dead cells immediately below the bark of woody plants.
▶ v. [with obj.] **1** close or seal (a bottle) with a cork. ■ (as adj. **corked**) (of wine) spoiled by tannin from the cork.
2 draw with burnt cork.
3 illicitly hollow out (a baseball bat) and fill it with cork to make it lighter.
– DERIVATIVES **cork·like** /-ˌlīk/ adj.
– ORIGIN Middle English: from Dutch and Low German *kork*, from Spanish *alcorque* 'cork-soled sandal,' from Arabic *al-* 'the' and (probably) Spanish Arabic *qurq, qorq*, based on Latin *quercus* 'oak, cork oak.'

cork·age /ˈkôrkij/ ▶ n. a charge made by a restaurant or hotel for serving wine that has been brought in by a customer.

cork cam·bi·um ▶ n. Botany tissue in the stem of a plant that gives rise to cork on its outer surface and a layer of cells containing chlorophyll on its inner surface.

cork·er /ˈkôrkər/ ▶ n. **1** an excellent or astonishing person or thing: *it was the season's first goal, and a corker*.
2 a device that places a cork into a bottle: *it's a great wine corker*.

cork oak ▶ n. an evergreen Mediterranean oak, the outer layer of the bark of which is the source of cork, which can be stripped without harming the tree. ● *Quercus suber*, family Fagaceae.

cork·screw /ˈkôrkˌskro͞o/ ▶ n. a device for pulling corks from bottles, consisting of a spiral metal rod that is inserted into the cork and a handle that extracts it. ■ [usu. as modifier] a thing with a spiral shape or movement: *a girl with corkscrew curls*.
▶ v. [no obj.] move or twist in a spiral motion: *the plane was corkscrewing toward the earth*.

cork tree (also **corktree**) ▶ n. **1** another term for **CORK OAK**.
2 an Asian citrus tree with a corky bark. ● Genus *Phellodendron*, family Rutaceae: several species, including *P. sachalinense*, often cultivated as an ornamental.

cork·wood /ˈkôrkˌwo͝od/ ▶ n. a shrub or tree that yields light porous timber, in particular: ● a small American tree that produces timber used for fishing floats (*Leitneria floridana*, family Leitneriaceae). ● a similar tree native to New Zealand (*Entelea arborescens*, family Tiliaceae).

cork·y /ˈkôrkē/ ▶ adj. (**corkier, corkiest**) **1** corklike.
2 (of wine) corked.

corm /kôrm/ ▶ n. a rounded underground storage organ present in plants such as crocuses, gladioli, and cyclamens, consisting of a swollen stem base covered with scale leaves. Compare with **BULB** (sense 1), **RHIZOME**.
– ORIGIN mid 19th cent.: from modern Latin *cormus*, from Greek *kormos* 'trunk stripped of its boughs.'

cor·mel /ˈkôrməl, kôrˈmel/ ▶ n. a small corm growing at the side of a mature corm.

corm·let /ˈkôrmlət/ ▶ n. a small corm growing at the base of a mature corm.

cor·mo·rant /ˈkôrmərənt/ ▶ n. a large diving bird with a long neck, long hooked bill, short legs, and mainly dark plumage. It typically breeds on coastal cliffs and is noted for its voracious appetite. ● Genus *Phalacrocorax* (and *Nannopterum*), family Phalacrocoracidae: numerous species, in particular the widespread **great** (or **European**) **cormorant** (*P. carbo*) and the North American **double-crested cormorant** (*P. auritus*).

double-crested cormorant

– ORIGIN Middle English: from Old French *cormaran*, from medieval Latin *corvus marinus* 'sea raven.' The final *-t* is on the pattern of words such as *peasant*.

corn[1] /kôrn/ ▶ **n. 1** a North American cereal plant that yields large grains, or kernels, set in rows on a cob. Its many varieties yield numerous products, highly valued for both human and livestock consumption. Also called **INDIAN CORN.** ● *Zea mays*, family Gramineae; it was domesticated before 5000 BC, although the wild ancestor is unidentified. ■ the grains of this: *creamed corn* | *two ears of corn.* ■ Brit. the chief cereal crop of a district, esp. (in England) wheat or (in Scotland) oats.
2 informal something banal or sentimental: *the movie is pure corn.*
– PHRASES **corn on the cob** corn when cooked and eaten straight from the cob; an ear of corn.
– ORIGIN Old English, of Germanic origin; related to Dutch *koren* and German *Korn.*

corn[1] 1

corn[2] ▶ **n.** a small, painful area of thickened skin on the foot, esp. on the toes, caused by pressure.
– ORIGIN late Middle English: via Anglo-Norman French from Latin *cornu* 'horn.'

Cor·na·ro Pis·co·pi·a /kôr'närō pis'kōpēə/, Elena Lucrezia (1646–1684), Venetian philosopher and mathematician. The first woman to be awarded a college degree, she received the doctorate of philosophy from the University of Padua on June 25, 1678.

corn·ball /'kôrn,bôl/ informal ▶ **adj.** trite and sentimental: *a cornball movie.*
▶ **n.** a person with trite or sentimental ideas.

corn beef ▶ **n.** corned beef.

Corn Belt name for parts of the US Midwest, esp. Illinois and Iowa, where corn is a major crop.

corn bor·er ▶ **n.** a moth whose larvae feed upon and bore into corn. ● Several species in the family Pyralidae, in particular the **European corn borer** (*Ostrinia nubilalis*), which was accidentally introduced into North America, and *Diatraea* (or *Zeadiatraea*) *grandiosella* of the southern US.

corn·bread /'kôrn,bred/ (also **corn bread**) ▶ **n.** a type of bread made from cornmeal and typically leavened without yeast.

corn cake (also **corncake**) ▶ **n.** cornbread made in the form of flat cakes.

corn·cob /'kôrn,käb/ (also **corn cob**) ▶ **n.** see **COB[1]** (sense 1).

corn·cob pipe ▶ **n.** a tobacco pipe with a bowl made from a dried corncob.

corn cock·le (also **corncockle**) ▶ **n.** a Mediterranean plant with bright pink or purple flowers and poisonous seeds, introduced into Britain and North America. If unchecked, it can be a prolific weed in fields of grain. It is often cultivated as a showy annual. ● *Agrostemma githago*, family Caryophyllaceae.
– ORIGIN early 18th cent.: from **CORN[1]** + *cockle* (from Old English *coccul* 'corn cockle,' perhaps via Latin from Greek *kokkos* 'berry').

corn·crake /'kôrn,krāk/ (also **corn crake**) ▶ **n.** a secretive Eurasian crake inhabiting coarse grasslands, with mainly brown streaked plumage and a distinctive double rasping call. Also called **LAND RAIL.** ● *Crex crex*, family Rallidae.

corn crib (also **corncrib**) ▶ **n.** a bin or ventilated building for storing unhusked ears of corn.

corn dodg·er ▶ **n.** a small, hard fried or baked cornmeal cake. ■ a boiled cornmeal dumpling.

corn dog ▶ **n.** a hot dog covered in cornmeal batter, fried, and served on a stick.

cor·ne·a /'kôrnēə/ ▶ **n.** the transparent layer forming the front of the eye.
– DERIVATIVES **cor·ne·al adj.**
– ORIGIN late Middle English: from medieval Latin *cornea tela* 'horny tissue,' from Latin *cornu* 'horn.'

corn ear·worm ▶ **n.** an American moth caterpillar that is a pest of corn, cotton, and tomatoes. Also called **BOLLWORM, COTTON BOLLWORM, TOMATO FRUITWORM.** ● *Heliothis zea*, family Noctuidae.

corned /kôrnd/ ▶ **adj.** (of food) preserved in salt water: *corned beef.*

corned beef (also **corn beef**) ▶ **n.** beef brisket cured in brine and boiled, served hot typically with cabbage, or cold, sliced for sandwiches.
– ORIGIN *corned*, in the sense 'preserved in salt water.'

Cor·neille /kôr'nā(l)/, Pierre (1606–84), French playwright; regarded as the founder of classical French tragedy. Notable plays: *Le Cid* (1637), *Cinna* (1641), and *Polyeucte* (1643).

cor·ne·i·tis /,kôrnē'ītis/ ▶ **n.** Medicine inflammation of the cornea.

cor·nel /'kôrnl, -,nel/ ▶ **n.** a dogwood, esp. of a dwarf variety. ● Genus *Cornus*, family Cornaceae: several species, including the dwarf *C. suecica*.
– ORIGIN late Middle English (denoting the wood of the cornelian cherry): from Old French *corneille*, from Latin *cornus*.

cor·nel·ian /kôr'nēlyən/ ▶ **n.** variant spelling of **CARNELIAN.**

cor·nel·ian cher·ry ▶ **n.** a Eurasian flowering shrub or small tree of the dogwood family, cultivated as an ornamental. ● *Cornus mas*, family Cornaceae. ■ the edible oval red berry of this plant.
– ORIGIN early 17th cent.: *cornelian* from **CORNEL** + **-IAN.**

cor·ne·ous /'kôrnēəs/ ▶ **adj.** formal hornlike; horny: *the skeleton is formed of a corneous substance.*
– ORIGIN mid 17th cent.: from Latin *corneus* (from *cornu* 'horn') + **-OUS.**

cor·ner /'kôrnər/ ▶ **n. 1** a place or angle where two or more sides or edges meet: *Jan sat at one corner of the table.* ■ an area inside a room, box, or square-shaped space, near the place where two or more edges or surfaces meet: *he drove the ball into the corner of the net.* ■ a place where two streets meet: *an apartment on the corner of 199th Street and Amsterdam Avenue* | [as modifier] *the corner house.* ■ a difficult or awkward situation: *he found himself* ***backed into a corner.*** ■ first or third base on a baseball diamond: *two outs, with runners on the corners.* ■ a sharp bend in a road: *serious racers want a car that is fast going into and out of the corners.*
2 a part, region, or area, esp. one regarded as secluded or remote: *they descended on the college* ***from all corners of the world*** | *his wisdom was disseminated to* ***the four corners of the earth*** | figurative *she couldn't bear journalists prying into every corner of her life.* ■ a position in which one dominates the supply of a particular commodity.
3 short for **CORNER KICK.**
4 Boxing & Wrestling each of the diagonally opposite ends of the ring, where a contestant rests between rounds. ■ a contestant's supporters or seconds: *Hodkinson was encouraged by his corner.*
5 Baseball each of the two parallel sides of home plate, which are perceived as defining the vertical edges of the strike zone.
▶ **v.** [with obj.] **1** force (a person or animal) into a place or situation from which it is hard to escape: *the man was eventually cornered by police dogs.* ■ detain (someone) in conversation, typically against their will: *I managed to corner Gary for fifteen minutes.*
2 control (a market) by dominating the supply of a particular commodity: *whether they will* ***corner the market*** *in graphics software remains to be seen.* ■ establish a corner in (a commodity): *you cornered vanadium and made a killing.*
3 [no obj.] (of a vehicle or driver) go around a bend in a road: *no squeal is evident from the tires when cornering fast.*
– PHRASES **(just) around** (or **round**) **the corner** very near: *there's a pharmacy around the corner.* **cut corners** see **CUT. in someone's corner** acting as a second, to a boxer. ■ on someone's side; giving someone support and encouragement. **on** (or **at** or **in**) **every corner** everywhere: *there were saloons on every corner* | *it's difficult to readjust when the past assaults you at every corner* | *young executives sprouted in every corner.* **see someone/something out of** (or **from**) **the corner of one's eye** see someone or something at the edge of one's field of vision. **turn the corner** see **TURN.**
– ORIGIN Middle English: from Anglo-Norman French, based on Latin *cornu* 'horn, tip, corner.'

cor·ner·back /'kôrnər,bak/ ▶ **n.** Football a defensive back positioned to the outside of the linebackers.

cor·nered /'kôrnərd/ ▶ **adj. 1** having a specified number of places or angles where the edges or sides meet: *young boys in six-cornered hats.* ■ having a specified number of parties involved: *a three-cornered meeting was being arranged in Hong Kong.*
2 (of a person or animal) forced into a place or situation from which it is hard to escape: *nothing is more dangerous than a cornered wild beast.*

cor·ner kick (also **corner**) ▶ **n.** Soccer a place kick taken by the attacking side from a corner of the field after the ball has been sent over the end line outside the goal by a defender: *Kavanagh lofted a corner kick.*

cor·ner·man /'kôrnər,man/ ▶ **n.** (pl. **cornermen**) a person whose job is to assist a boxer or wrestler at the corner between rounds.

cor·ner·stone /'kôrnər,stōn/ ▶ **n.** a stone that forms the base of a corner of a building, joining two walls. ■ an important quality or feature on which a particular thing depends or is based: *a national minimum wage remained the cornerstone of policy.*

cor·ner·wise /'kôrnər,wīz/ ▶ **adv.** at an angle of approximately 45°; diagonally: *he laid the cloth cornerwise on the polished table.*

cor·net /'kôrnət/ ▶ **n. 1** Music a brass instrument resembling a trumpet but shorter and wider, played chiefly in bands. ■ a compound organ stop with a powerful treble sound.
2 Brit. a cone-shaped wafer, esp. one filled with ice cream.
– DERIVATIVES **cor·net·ist** /-'netəst/ (also **cornettist**) **n.**
– ORIGIN late Middle English (originally denoting a wind instrument made of a horn): from Old French, diminutive of a variant of Latin *cornu* 'horn.'

cor·net·fish /kôr'net,fisн, 'kôrnət-/ ▶ **n.** (pl. **same** or **cornetfishes**) a large marine fish with a long, narrow, flutelike snout, an elongated body, and a whiplike extension to the tail. It is common in shallow tropical waters of the Atlantic and Indo-Pacific region. ● Family Fistularidae and genus *Fistularia*: several species.

cor·net·to /kôr'netō/ (also **cornett** /-'net/) ▶ **n.** (pl. **cornetti** /-'netē/ or **cornetts**) a woodwind instrument of the 16th and 17th centuries, typically curved, with finger holes and a cup-shaped mouthpiece.
– ORIGIN late 19th cent.: from Italian, diminutive of *corno* 'horn,' from Latin *cornu*. Compare with **CORNET.**

corn-fed (also **cornfed**) ▶ **adj.** fed on corn: *corn-fed chickens.* ■ informal plump; well fed. ■ informal provincial; unsophisticated: *a backward, corn-fed Heartland city.*

corn·field /'kôrn,fēld/ ▶ **n.** a field in which corn is grown.

corn·flakes /'kôrn,flāks/ ▶ **plural n.** a breakfast cereal consisting of toasted flakes made from corn.

corn flour ▶ **n.** flour made from corn: *the fish were coated with corn flour and fried.* ■ (usu. **cornflour**) British term for **CORNSTARCH.**

corn·flow·er /'kôrn,flouər/ ▶ **n.** a slender Eurasian plant related to the knapweeds, with flowers that are typically a deep, vivid blue. ● Genus *Centaurea*, family Compositae: several species, including the annual *Centaurea cyanus* (also called **BLUEBOTTLE**), formerly a common weed of cornfields, and the perennial *C. montana*, grown in gardens. ■ (also **cornflower blue**) a deep, vivid blue color.

Corn·husk·er State /'kôrn,həskər/ a nickname for the state of **NEBRASKA.**

corn·husk·ing /'kôrn,həskiNG/ ▶ **n.** the removal of husks from ears of corn. ■ the husking of corn by several people as a social event. Also called **HUSKING BEE.**
– DERIVATIVES **corn·husk·er n.**

cor·nice /'kôrnis/ ▶ **n. 1** an ornamental molding around the wall of a room just below the ceiling. ■ a horizontal molded projection crowning a building or structure, esp. the uppermost member of the entablature of an order, surmounting the frieze.
2 an overhanging mass of hardened snow at the edge of a mountain precipice.
– DERIVATIVES **cor·niced adj., cor·nic·ing n.**
– ORIGIN mid 16th cent.: from French *corniche*, from Italian *cornice*, perhaps from Latin *cornix* 'crow' (compare with **CORBEL**), but influenced by Greek *korōnis* 'copestone.'

cor·niche /'kôrnisн, kôr'nēsн/ ▶ **n.** a road cut into the edge of a cliff, esp. one running along a coast.
– ORIGIN mid 19th cent.: from French (see **CORNICE**).

Cor·nish /'kôrnisн/ ▶ **adj.** of or relating to Cornwall, or its people or language.
▶ **n. 1** (as plural noun **the Cornish**) the people of Cornwall collectively.
2 the extinct Brythonic language of Cornwall.
– DERIVATIVES **Cor·nish·man** /-mən/ **n.** (pl. **Cornishmen**), **Cor·nish·wom·an** /-,wo͝omən/ **n.** (pl. **Cornishwomen**).
– ORIGIN late Middle English: from the first element of **CORNWALL** + **-ISH[1]**.

Cor·nish hen (also **Cornish game hen**) ▶ **n.** another term for **ROCK CORNISH.**

Corn Laws (in the UK) a series of 19th-century laws introduced to protect British farmers from foreign competition. They were repealed in 1846.

corn mar·i·gold ▶ **n.** a daisylike yellow-flowered Eurasian plant. ● *Chrysanthemum segetum*, family Compositae.

C

corn·meal /ˈkôrnˌmēl/ ▶ **n.** meal made from ground, dried corn.

corn oil ▶ **n.** an oil obtained from the germ of corn, used in cooking and salad dressings.

corn pone ▶ **n.** see PONE.
▶ **adj.** (**corn-pone**) often derogatory rustic; unsophisticated: *corn-pone humor*.

corn roast ▶ **n.** Canadian an outdoor party at which fresh ears of sweet corn are roasted and eaten.

corn·rows /ˈkôrnˌrōz/ ▶ **plural n.** a style of braiding and plaiting the hair in narrow strips to form geometric patterns on the scalp.

corn sal·ad ▶ **n.** a small blue-flowered herbaceous plant of dry soils, native to Europe and the Mediterranean. Widely cultivated in North America, its narrow leaves are used in salad. Also called LAMB'S LETTUCE, MACHE. ● *Valerianella locusta*, family Valerianaceae.

corn·silk /ˈkôrnˌsilk/ ▶ **n.** the fine threadlike styles on an ear of corn.

corn snake ▶ **n.** a long North American rat snake with a spear-shaped mark between the eyes. ● *Elaphe guttata*, family Colubridae.
– ORIGIN late 17th cent.: so named because often found in cornfields.

corn snow ▶ **n.** snow with a rough granular surface resulting from alternate thawing and freezing.
– ORIGIN from *corn* in the dialect sense 'granule.'

corn spur·rey see SPURREY.

corn·stalk /ˈkôrnˌstôk/ ▶ **n.** the stem of a corn plant.

corn·starch /ˈkôrnˌstärCH/ ▶ **n.** finely ground corn flour, used as a thickener in cooking.

Corn State a nickname for the state of IOWA.

corn sug·ar ▶ **n.** dextrose, esp when made from cornstarch.

corn syr·up ▶ **n.** syrup made from cornstarch, consisting of dextrose, maltose, and dextrins.

cor·nu /ˈkôrn(y)o͞o/ ▶ **n.** (pl. **cornua** /-n(y)o͞oə/) Anatomy a structure with a shape likened to a horn, in particular: ■ a horn-shaped projection of the thyroid cartilage or of certain bones (such as the hyoid and the coccyx). ■ either of the two lateral cavities of the uterus, into which the Fallopian tubes pass. ■ each of three elongated parts of the lateral ventricles of the brain.
– DERIVATIVES **cor·nu·al** /-n(y)o͞oəl/ **adj.**
– ORIGIN late 17th cent.: from Latin, 'horn.'

cor·nu·co·pi·a /ˌkôrn(y)əˈkōpēə/ ▶ **n.** a symbol of plenty consisting of a goat's horn overflowing with flowers, fruit, and corn. ■ an ornamental container shaped like such a horn. ■ an abundant supply of good things of a specified kind: *the festival offers a cornucopia of pleasures*.
– DERIVATIVES **cor·nu·co·pi·an adj.**
– ORIGIN early 16th cent.: from late Latin, from Latin *cornu copiae* 'horn of plenty' (a mythical horn able to provide whatever is desired).

Corn·wall /ˈkôrnˌwôl, -wəl/ **1** a county occupying the extreme southwestern peninsula of England; county town, Truro.
2 a city in eastern Ontario in Canada, a port on the St. Lawrence River, across from Massena, New York; pop. 45,965 (2006).

Corn·wal·lis /kôrnˈwäləs/, Charles, 1st Marquis (1738–1805), English soldier. He surrendered the British forces at Yorktown in 1781, ending the fighting in the American Revolution.

corn·y /ˈkôrnē/ ▶ **adj.** (**cornier**, **corniest**) informal trite, banal, or mawkishly sentimental: *it sounds corny, but as soon as I saw her I knew she was the one*.
– DERIVATIVES **corn·i·ly** /ˈkôrnl-ē/ **adv.**, **corn·i·ness n.**
– ORIGIN 1930s: from an earlier sense 'rustic, appealing to country folk.'

co·rol·la /kəˈrälə, kəˈrōlə/ ▶ **n.** Botany the petals of a flower, typically forming a whorl within the sepals and enclosing the reproductive organs. Compare with CALYX.
– ORIGIN late 17th cent. (in the sense 'little crown'): from Latin, diminutive of *corona* 'wreath, crown, chaplet.'

cor·ol·lar·y /ˈkôrəˌlerē, ˈkärə-/ ▶ **n.** (pl. **corollaries**) a proposition that follows from (and is often appended to) one already proved. ■ a direct or natural consequence or result: *the huge increases in unemployment were the corollary of expenditure cuts*.
▶ **adj.** forming a proposition that follows from one already proved. ■ associated; supplementary.
– ORIGIN late Middle English: from Latin *corollarium* 'money paid for a garland or chaplet; gratuity' (in late Latin 'deduction'), from *corolla*, diminutive of *corona* 'wreath, crown, chaplet.'

cor·o·man·del /ˌkôrəˈmandəl, ˌkär-/ ▶ **n. 1** (also **coromandel wood** or **coromandel ebony**) a fine-grained, grayish-brown wood streaked with black, used in furniture. Also called CALAMANDER.
2 the Sri Lankan tree that yields this wood. ● *Diospyros quaesita*, family Ebenaceae.
▶ **adj.** denoting a form of Asian lacquerware with intaglio designs.
– ORIGIN from COROMANDEL COAST, from which Asian lacquerware was originally transshipped.

Cor·o·man·del Coast /ˌkôrəˈmandəl/ the southern part of the eastern coast of India, from Point Calimere to the mouth of the Krishna River.

Co·ro·na /kəˈrōnə/ a city in southwestern California, southwest of Riverside; pop. 149,923 (est. 2008).

co·ro·na¹ /kəˈrōnə/ ▶ **n.** (pl. **coronae** /-nē, -nī/)
1 Astronomy the rarefied gaseous envelope of the sun and other stars. The sun's corona is normally visible only during a total solar eclipse when it is seen as an irregularly shaped pearly glow surrounding the darkened disk of the moon. ■ (also **corona discharge**) Physics the glow around a conductor at high potential. ■ a small circle of light seen around the sun or moon, due to diffraction by water droplets.
2 Anatomy a crown or crownlike structure. ■ Botany the cup-shaped or trumpet-shaped outgrowth at the center of a daffodil or narcissus flower.
3 a circular chandelier in a church.
4 Architecture a part of a cornice having a broad vertical face.
– ORIGIN mid 16th cent. (sense 4): from Latin, 'wreath, crown.'

co·ro·na² ▶ **n.** a long, straight-sided cigar.
– ORIGIN late 19th cent.: from Spanish *La Corona*, literally 'the crown,' originally a proprietary name.

Co·ro·na Aus·tra·lis /kəˈrōnə ôˈstrāləs, äˈstrā-/ Astronomy a small southern constellation (the Southern Crown), with no bright stars. ■ (as genitive **Coronae Australis** /kəˈrōnē, -ˌnī/) used with a preceding letter or numeral to designate a star in this constellation: *the star Theta Coronae Australis*.
– ORIGIN Latin.

Co·ro·na Bo·re·al·is /bôrēˈalis/ Astronomy a northern constellation (the Northern Crown), in which the main stars form a small but prominent arc. ■ (as genitive **Coronae Borealis** /kəˈrōnē, -ˌnī/) used with a preceding letter or numeral to designate a star in this constellation: *the star R Coronae Borealis*.
– ORIGIN Latin.

cor·o·nach /ˈkôrənəKH, ˈkär-/ ▶ **n.** (in Scotland or Ireland) a funeral song.
– ORIGIN early 16th cent. (originally Scots, denoting the outcry of a crowd): from Scottish Gaelic *corranach* (Irish *coranach*), from *comh-* 'together' + *rànach* 'outcry.'

co·ro·na dis·charge ▶ **n.** see CORONA¹ (sense 1).

Co·ro·na·do /ˌkôrəˈnädō, ˌkär-/, Francisco Vásquez de (*c.*1510–54), Spanish explorer. His explorations into Arizona and New Mexico from Mexico opened the Southwest to Spanish colonization.

co·ro·na·graph /kəˈrōnəˌgraf/ ▶ **n.** an instrument that blocks out light emitted by the sun's actual surface so that the corona can be observed.

cor·o·nal¹ /ˈkôrənl, ˈkär-/ ▶ **adj. 1** of or relating to the crown or corona of something, in particular: ■ Astronomy of or relating to the corona of the sun or another star. ■ Anatomy of or relating to the crown of the head.
2 Anatomy of or in the coronal plane: *coronal imaging*.
3 Phonetics (of a consonant) formed by raising the tip or blade of the tongue toward the hard palate.
▶ **n.** Phonetics a coronal consonant.
– ORIGIN late Middle English (in the sense 'relating to the crown of the head'): from Latin *coronalis*, from *corona* 'crown.'

cor·o·nal² /ˈkôrənl, ˈkär-, kəˈrōnl/ ▶ **n.** a garland or wreath for the head: *her eyes sparkled beneath a coronal of flowers*. ■ literary a small crown; a coronet.
– ORIGIN Middle English: apparently from Anglo-Norman French, from *corune* 'crown, wreath' (see CROWN).

cor·o·nal plane ▶ **n.** Anatomy an imaginary plane dividing the body into dorsal and ventral parts.

cor·o·nal su·ture ▶ **n.** Anatomy the transverse suture in the skull separating the frontal bone from the parietal bones.

cor·o·nar·y /ˈkôrəˌnerē, ˈkär-/ ▶ **adj.** Anatomy relating to or denoting the arteries that surround and supply the heart. ■ relating to or denoting a structure that encircles a part of the body.
▶ **n.** (pl. **coronaries**) short for CORONARY THROMBOSIS.
– ORIGIN mid 17th cent. (in the sense 'resembling a crown'): from Latin *coronarius*, from *corona* 'wreath, crown.'

cor·o·nar·y ar·ter·y ▶ **n.** an artery supplying blood to the heart.

cor·o·nar·y care unit (abbr. **CCU**) ▶ **n.** a hospital department that provides special care and monitoring for heart patients.

cor·o·nar·y oc·clu·sion ▶ **n.** partial or total obstruction of a coronary artery, usually resulting in a myocardial infarction (heart attack).

cor·o·nar·y si·nus ▶ **n.** a wide venous channel about 2.25 centimeters in length that receives blood from the coronary veins and empties into the right atrium of the heart.

cor·o·nar·y throm·bo·sis ▶ **n.** a blockage of the flow of blood to the heart, caused by a blood clot in a coronary artery.

cor·o·nar·y vein ▶ **n.** any of several veins that drain blood from the heart wall and empty into the coronary sinus.

cor·o·na·tion /ˌkôrəˈnāSHən, ˌkär-/ ▶ **n.** the ceremony of crowning a sovereign or a sovereign's consort.
– ORIGIN late Middle English: via Old French from medieval Latin *coronatio(n-)*, from *coronare* 'to crown, adorn with a garland,' from *corona* (see CROWN).

co·ro·na·vi·rus /kəˈrōnəˌvīrəs/ ▶ **n.** Medicine any of a group of RNA viruses that cause a variety of diseases in humans and other animals.

cor·o·ner /ˈkôrənər, ˈkär-/ ▶ **n.** an official who investigates violent, sudden, or suspicious deaths. ■ historical in England, an official responsible for safeguarding the private property of the Crown.
– DERIVATIVES **cor·o·ner·ship** /-ˌSHip/ **n.**
– ORIGIN Middle English: from Anglo-Norman French *coruner*, from *corune* 'a crown' (see CROWN); reflecting the Latin title *custos placitorum coronae* 'guardian of the pleas of the crown.'

cor·o·net /ˌkôrəˈnet, ˌkär-/ ▶ **n. 1** a small or relatively simple crown, esp. as worn by lesser royalty and peers or peeresses. ■ a circular decoration for the head, esp. one made of flowers.
2 the band of tissue on the lowest part of a horse's pastern, containing the horn-producing cells from which the hoof grows. ■ another term for BURR (sense 5 of the noun).
– DERIVATIVES **cor·o·net·ed adj.**
– ORIGIN late Middle English: from Old French *coronete* 'small crown or garland,' diminutive of *corone* (see CROWN).

co·ro·ni·al /kəˈrōnēəl/ ▶ **adj.** Austral. relating to a coroner: *a coronial hearing*.

cor·o·noid /ˈkôrəˌnoid, ˈkär-/ ▶ **adj.** Anatomy relating to or denoting a hooked projection of bone. See CORONOID PROCESS.
▶ **n.** (also **coronoid bone**) Zoology a slender bone forming part of the lower jaw in primitive vertebrates.
– ORIGIN mid 18th cent.: from Greek *korōnē*, denoting something hooked, + -OID.

cor·o·noid proc·ess ▶ **n.** Anatomy **1** a flattened triangular projection above the angle of the jaw where the temporalis muscle is attached.
2 a projection from the front of the ulna forming part of the articulation of the elbow.
– ORIGIN mid 18th cent.: *coronoid* from Greek *korōnē* (denoting something hooked) + -OID.

Corp. ▶ **abbr.** ■ (**Corp**) informal corporal: *been abroad before, Corp?* ■ corporation: *IBM Corp.*

cor·po·ra /ˈkôrpərə/ plural form of CORPUS.

cor·po·ral¹ /ˈkôrp(ə)rəl/ ▶ **n.** a low-ranking noncommissioned officer in the armed forces, in particular (in the US Army) an NCO ranking above private first class and below sergeant or (in the US Marine Corps) an NCO ranking above lance corporal and below sergeant.
– ORIGIN mid 16th cent.: from French, obsolete variant of *caporal*, from Italian *caporale*, probably based on Latin *corpus, corpor-* 'body (of troops),' with a change of spelling in Italian due to association with *capo* 'head.'

cor·po·ral² ▶ **adj.** of or relating to the human body.
– DERIVATIVES **cor·po·ral·ly adv.**
– ORIGIN late Middle English: via Old French from Latin *corporalis*, from *corpus, corpor-* 'body.'

cor·po·ral³ ▶ **n.** a cloth on which the chalice and paten are placed during the celebration of the Eucharist.
– ORIGIN Middle English: from medieval Latin *corporale (pallium)* 'body (cloth),' from Latin *corpus, corpor-* 'body.'

cor·po·ral·i·ty /ˌkôrpəˈralitē/ ▶ **n.** rare material or corporeal existence.
– ORIGIN late Middle English: from late Latin *corporalitas*, from Latin *corporalis* 'relating to the body' (see CORPORAL²).

cor·po·ral pun·ish·ment ▶ **n.** physical punishment, such as caning or flogging. ■ punishment under law that includes imprisonment and death.

cor·po·rate /ˈkôrp(ə)rət/ ▶ **adj.** of or relating to a corporation, esp. a large company or group: *airlines are very keen on their corporate identity.* ■ Law (of a company or group of people) authorized to act as a single entity and recognized as such in law. ■ of or shared by all the members of a group: *the service emphasizes the corporate responsibility of the congregation.*
▶ **n.** a corporate company or group.
– DERIVATIVES **cor·po·rate·ly** adv.
– ORIGIN late 15th cent.: from Latin *corporatus*, past participle of *corporare* 'form into a body,' from *corpus, corpor-* 'body.'

cor·po·rate raid·er ▶ **n.** a financier who makes a practice of making hostile takeover bids for companies, either to control their policies or to resell them for a profit.

cor·po·rate wel·fare ▶ **n.** government support or subsidy of private business, such as by tax incentives.

cor·po·ra·tion /ˌkôrpəˈrāsHən/ ▶ **n.** a company or group of people authorized to act as a single entity (legally a person) and recognized as such in law. ■ (also **municipal corporation**) a group of people elected to govern a city, town, or borough. ■ dated, humorous a paunch.
– ORIGIN late Middle English: from late Latin *corporatio(n-)*, from Latin *corporare* 'combine in one body' (see CORPORATE).

cor·po·rat·ism /ˈkôrp(ə)rəˌtizəm/ ▶ **n.** the control of a state or organization by large interest groups.
– DERIVATIVES **cor·po·rat·ist** adj. & n.

cor·po·ra·tize /ˈkôrp(ə)rəˌtīz/ ▶ **v.** [with obj.] convert (a state organization) into an independent commercial company.

cor·po·re·al /kôrˈpôrēəl/ ▶ **adj.** of or relating to a person's body, esp. as opposed to their spirit: *he was frank about his corporeal appetites.* ■ having a body: *a corporeal God.* ■ Law consisting of material objects; tangible: *corporeal property.*
– DERIVATIVES **cor·po·re·al·i·ty** /kôrˌpôrēˈalitē/ n., **cor·po·re·al·ly** adv.
– ORIGIN late Middle English (in the sense 'material'): from late Latin *corporealis*, from Latin *corporeus* 'bodily, physical,' from *corpus, corpor-* 'body.'

cor·po·re·i·ty /ˌkôrpəˈrēitē, -ˈrāitē/ ▶ **n.** rare the quality of having a physical body or existence.
– ORIGIN early 17th cent.: from French *corporéité* or medieval Latin *corporeitas*, from Latin *corporeus* 'composed of flesh,' from *corpus, corpor-* 'body.'

cor·po·sant /ˈkôrpəˌsant, -zant/ ▶ **n.** archaic an appearance of St. Elmo's fire on a mast, rigging, or other structure.
– ORIGIN mid 16th cent.: from Old Spanish, Portuguese, and Italian *corpo santo* 'holy body.'

corps /kôr/ ▶ **n.** (pl. **corps** /kôrz/) a main subdivision of an armed force in the field, consisting of two or more divisions: *the 5th Army Corps.* ■ a branch of a military organization assigned to a particular kind of work: *the U.S. Army Medical Corps.* ■ a body of people engaged in a particular activity: *the press corps.* ■ short for CORPS DE BALLET.
– ORIGIN late 16th cent.: from French, from Latin *corpus* 'body.'

corps de bal·let /ˌkôr də baˈlā/ ▶ **n.** [treated as sing. or pl.] the members of a ballet company who dance together as a group. ■ the members of the lowest rank of dancers in a ballet company.
– ORIGIN early 19th cent.: French.

corpse /kôrps/ ▶ **n.** a dead body, esp. of a human being rather than an animal.
– ORIGIN Middle English (denoting the living body of a person or animal): alteration of CORSE by association with Latin *corpus*, a change that also took place in French (Old French *cors* becoming *corps*). The *p* was originally silent, as in French; the final *e* was rare before the 19th cent., but now distinguishes *corpse* from *corps*.

corps·man /ˈkôrmən/ ▶ **n.** an enlisted member of a military medical unit. ■ a member of a civilian corps, esp. a paramedical corps.

cor·pu·lence /ˈkôrpyələns/ ▶ **n.** the state of being fat; obesity: *her corpulence is the butt of every joke.*
– DERIVATIVES **cor·pu·len·cy** n.

cor·pu·lent /ˈkôrpyələnt/ ▶ **adj.** (of a person) fat.
– ORIGIN late Middle English: from Latin *corpulentus*, from *corpus* 'body.'

cor pul·mo·na·le /ˌkôr ˌpoŏlməˈnalē, -ˈnälē/ ▶ **n.** Medicine abnormal enlargement of the right side of the heart as a result of disease of the lungs or the pulmonary blood vessels.
– ORIGIN mid 19th cent.: from Latin *cor* 'heart' and modern Latin *pulmonalis* (from Latin *pulmo(n-)* 'lung').

cor·pus /ˈkôrpəs/ ▶ **n.** (pl. **corpora** /-pərə/ or **corpuses**) **1** a collection of written texts, esp. the entire works of a particular author or a body of writing on a particular subject: *the Darwinian corpus.* ■ a collection of written or spoken material in machine-readable form, assembled for the purpose of studying linguistic structures, frequencies, etc.
2 Anatomy the main body or mass of a structure. ■ the central part of the stomach, between the fundus and the antrum.
– ORIGIN late Middle English (denoting a human or animal body): from Latin, literally 'body.' Sense 1 dates from the early 18th cent.

cor·pus cal·lo·sum /kaˈlōsəm/ ▶ **n.** (pl. **corpora callosa** /ˈkôrpərə kaˈlōsə/) Anatomy a broad band of nerve fibers joining the two hemispheres of the brain.
– ORIGIN early 18th cent.: from CORPUS and Latin *callosum*, neuter of *callosus* 'tough.'

cor·pus ca·ver·no·sum /ˌkavərˈnōsəm/ ▶ **n.** (pl. **corpora cavernosa** /-ˈnōsə/) Anatomy either of two masses of erectile tissue forming the bulk of the penis and the clitoris.
– ORIGIN from CORPUS and Latin *cavernosum*, neuter of *cavernosus* 'containing hollows.'

Cor·pus Chris·ti[1] /ˌkôrpəs ˈkristē/ a city and port in southern Texas, on Corpus Christi Bay; pop. 286,462 (est. 2008).

Cor·pus Chris·ti[2] a feast of the Western Christian Church commemorating the institution of the Eucharist, observed on the Thursday after Trinity Sunday.
– ORIGIN Latin, literally 'body of Christ.'

cor·pus·cle /ˈkôrˌpəsəl/ ▶ **n.** Biology a minute body or cell in an organism, esp. a red or white cell in the blood of vertebrates. ■ historical a minute particle regarded as the basic constituent of matter or light.
– DERIVATIVES **cor·pus·cu·lar** /kôrˈpəskyələr/ adj.
– ORIGIN mid 17th cent.: from Latin *corpusculum* 'small body,' diminutive of *corpus*.

cor·pus de·lic·ti /dəˈlikˌtī, -tē/ ▶ **n.** Law the facts and circumstances constituting a breach of a law. ■ concrete evidence of a crime, such as a corpse.
– ORIGIN Latin, literally 'body of offense.'

cor·pus lu·te·um /ˈloōtēəm/ ▶ **n.** (pl. **corpora lutea** /ˈloōtēə/) Anatomy a hormone-secreting structure that develops in an ovary after an ovum has been discharged but degenerates after a few days unless pregnancy has begun.
– ORIGIN late 18th cent.: from CORPUS and Latin *luteum*, neuter of *luteus* 'yellow.'

cor·pus spon·gi·o·sum /ˌspənjēˈōsəm/ ▶ **n.** (pl. **corpora spongiosa** /ˌspənjēˈōsə/) Anatomy a mass of erectile tissue alongside the corpora cavernosa of the penis and terminating in the glans.
– ORIGIN from CORPUS and Latin *spongiosum*, neuter of *spongiosus* 'porous.'

cor·pus stri·a·tum /strīˈātəm/ ▶ **n.** (pl. **corpora striata** /strīˈātə/) Anatomy part of the basal ganglia of the brain, comprising the caudate and lentiform nuclei.
– ORIGIN from CORPUS and Latin *striatum*, neuter of *striatus* 'grooved.'

corr. ▶ **abbr.** ■ correction. ■ correspondence.

cor·ral /kəˈral/ ▶ **n.** a pen for livestock, esp. cattle or horses, on a farm or ranch. ■ historical a defensive enclosure of wagons in an encampment.
▶ **v.** (**corrals, corralling, corralled**) [with obj.] put or keep (livestock) in a corral. ■ gather (a group of people or things) together: *the organizers were corralling the crowd into marching formation.* ■ historical form (wagons) into a corral.
– ORIGIN late 16th cent.: from Spanish and Old Portuguese (now *curral*), perhaps based on Latin *currere* 'to run.' Compare with KRAAL.

cor·rect /kəˈrekt/ ▶ **adj.** free from error; in accordance with fact or truth: *make sure you have been given the correct information.* ■ not mistaken in one's opinion or judgment; right: *the government was correct to follow a course of defeating inflation.* ■ (of a thing or course of action) meeting the requirements of or most appropriate for a particular situation or activity: *cut the top and bottom tracks to the correct length with a hacksaw.* ■ (of a person or their appearance or behavior) conforming to accepted social standards; proper: *he was a polite man, invariably correct and pleasant with Mrs. Collins.* ■ conforming to a particular political or ideological orthodoxy. See also POLITICALLY CORRECT.
▶ **v.** [with obj.] put right (an error or fault): *the council issued a statement correcting some points in the press reports.* ■ mark the errors in (a written or printed text): *he corrected Dixon's writing for publication.* ■ tell (someone) that they are mistaken: *he had assumed she was married and she had not corrected him* | (as adj. **corrected**) *sorry, I stand corrected.* ■ counteract or rectify: *the problem of diminished sight can be reduced or corrected by wearing eyeglasses.* ■ adjust (an instrument) to function accurately or in accord with a standard: *motorists can have their headlights tested and corrected at a reduced price on Saturday.* ■ adjust (a numerical result or reading) to allow for departure from standard conditions: *data were* ***corrected for*** *radionuclide decay.*
– DERIVATIVES **cor·rect·a·ble** adj., **cor·rect·ness** n.
– ORIGIN Middle English (as a verb): from Latin *correct-* 'made straight, amended,' from the verb *corrigere*, from *cor-* 'together' + *regere* 'guide.' The adjective is via French.

cor·rec·tion /kəˈreksHən/ ▶ **n.** the action or process of correcting something: *I checked the typing for errors and sent it back for correction.* ■ a change that rectifies an error or inaccuracy: *he made a few corrections to my homework.* ■ used to introduce an amended version of something one has just said: *after today—correction, she thought grimly, after tonight—she'd never see him again.* ■ a quantity adjusting a numerical result to allow for a departure from standard conditions. ■ a temporary reversal in an overall trend of stock market prices, esp. a brief fall during an overall increase: *they're still looking for the market to go up and believe we are just going through a correction.* ■ punishment, esp. that of criminals in prison intended to rectify their behavior.
– ORIGIN Middle English: via Old French from Latin *correctio(n-)*, from *corrigere* 'make straight, bring into order' (see CORRECT).

cor·rec·tion·al /kəˈreksHənl/ ▶ **adj.** of or relating to the punishment of criminals in a way intended to rectify their behavior: *a correctional institution.*

cor·rec·tion flu·id ▶ **n.** an opaque liquid painted over a typed or written error so as to leave a blank space for the insertion of the correct character.

cor·rec·ti·tude /kəˈrektəˌt(y)oōd/ ▶ **n.** correctness, esp. conscious correctness in one's behavior.
– ORIGIN late 19th cent.: blend of CORRECT and RECTITUDE.

cor·rec·tive /kəˈrektiv/ ▶ **adj.** designed to correct or counteract something harmful or undesirable: *management was informed so that corrective action could be taken.*
▶ **n.** a thing intended to correct or counteract something else: *the move might be* ***a corrective to*** *some inefficient practices within hospitals.*
– DERIVATIVES **cor·rec·tive·ly** adv.
– ORIGIN mid 16th cent.: from French *correctif, -ive* or late Latin *correctivus*, from Latin *correct-* 'brought into order,' from the verb *corrigere* (see CORRECT).

cor·rect·ly /kəˈrektlē/ ▶ **adv.** in a way that is true, factual, or appropriate; accurately: *she correctly answered eight questions.* ■ in a way that is socially acceptable; properly: *she had acted correctly.*

cor·rec·tor /kəˈrektər/ ▶ **n.** a person or thing that corrects something, esp. a computer program or electronic device with a specified function: *a spelling corrector.*

Cor·reg·gio /kəˈrej(ē)ō/, Antonio Allegri da (c.1494–1534), Italian painter; born *Antonio Allegri*. The soft, sensual style of his devotional and mythological paintings influenced the rococo style of the 18th century.

Cor·reg·i·dor /kəˈregəˌdôr/ an island in the Philippines, just south of the Bataan Peninsula on Luzon Island, scene of World War II battles and now a national shrine.

cor·re·late ▶ **v.** /ˈkôrəˌlāt, ˈkär-/ [no obj.] have a mutual relationship or connection, in which one thing affects or depends on another: *the study found that success in the educational system* ***correlates*** *highly* ***with*** *class.* ■ [with obj.] establish such a relationship or connection between: *we should* ***correlate*** *general trends in public opinion* ***with*** *trends in the content of television news.*
▶ **n.** /-lət/ each of two or more related or complementary things: *strategies to promote health should pay greater attention to financial hardship and other correlates of poverty.*
– ORIGIN mid 17th cent. (as a noun): back-formation from CORRELATION and CORRELATIVE.

cor·re·la·tion /ˌkôrəˈlāsHən/ ▶ **n.** a mutual relationship or connection between two or more things: *research showed a clear* ***correlation between*** *recession and levels of property crime.* ■ Statistics interdependence of variable quantities. ■ Statistics a quantity measuring the extent of such interdependence. ■ the process of establishing a relationship or connection between two or more measures.
– DERIVATIVES **cor·re·la·tion·al** /-sHənl/ adj.

– ORIGIN mid 16th cent.: from medieval Latin *correlatio(n-)*, from *cor-* 'together' + *relatio* (see RELATION).

cor·re·la·tion co·ef·fi·cient ▶ n. Statistics a number between −1 and +1 calculated so as to represent the linear dependence of two variables or sets of data. (Symbol: **r**)

cor·rel·a·tive /kəˈrelətiv/ ▶ adj. having a mutual relationship; corresponding: *rights, whether moral or legal, can involve correlative duties.* ■ Grammar (of words such as *neither* and *nor*) corresponding to each other and regularly used together.
▶ n. a word or concept that has a mutual relationship with another word or concept: *the child's right to education is a correlative of the parent's duty to send the child to school.*
– DERIVATIVES **cor·rel·a·tive·ly** adv., **cor·rel·a·tiv·i·ty** /kəˌreləˈtivitē/ n.
– ORIGIN mid 16th cent.: from medieval Latin *correlativus*, from *cor-* 'together' + late Latin *relativus* (see RELATIVE).

C

cor·re·spond /ˌkôrəˈspänd, ˌkär-/ ▶ v. [no obj.] **1** have a close similarity; match or agree almost exactly: *the carved heads described in the poem* **correspond to** *those in the drawing | communication is successful when the ideas in the minds of the speaker and hearer correspond.* ■ be analogous or equivalent in character, form, or function: *the Inuit month* **corresponding to** *December was called Aagjulirvik.*
2 communicate by exchanging letters: *Margaret* **corresponded with** *him until his death | the doctor and I corresponded for more than two decades.*
– ORIGIN late Middle English: from Old French *correspondre*, from medieval Latin *correspondere*, from *cor-* 'together' + Latin *respondere* (see RESPOND).

cor·re·spond·ence /ˌkôrəˈspändəns, ˌkär-/ ▶ n. **1** a close similarity, connection, or equivalence: *there is a simple* **correspondence between** *the distance of a focused object from the eye and the size of its image on the retina.*
2 communication by exchanging letters with someone: *the organization engaged in detailed* **correspondence with** *local congressmen.* ■ letters sent or received: *his wife dealt with his private correspondence.*
– DERIVATIVES **cor·re·spond·en·cy** /-dənsē/ n. (rare).
– ORIGIN late Middle English: via Old French from medieval Latin *correspondentia*, from *correspondent-* 'corresponding' (see CORRESPONDENT).

cor·re·spond·ence course ▶ n. a course of study in which student and teachers communicate by mail.

cor·re·spond·ence prin·ci·ple ▶ n. Physics the principle that states that for very large quantum numbers the laws of quantum theory merge with those of classical physics.

cor·re·spond·ence school ▶ n. a school offering correspondence courses.

cor·re·spond·ence the·o·ry Philosophy ▶ n. the theory that states that the definition or criterion of truth is that true propositions correspond to the facts.

cor·re·spond·ent /ˌkôrəˈspändənt, ˌkär-/ ▶ n. a person who writes letters to a person or a newspaper, esp. on a regular basis: *she wasn't much of a correspondent.* ■ a person employed to report for a newspaper or broadcasting organization, typically on a particular subject or from a particular country: *a White House correspondent.*
▶ adj. corresponding.
– ORIGIN late Middle English (as an adjective): from Old French *correspondant* or medieval Latin *correspondent-* 'corresponding,' from the verb *correspondere* (see CORRESPOND).

cor·re·spond·ing /ˌkôrəˈspändiNG, ˌkär-/ ▶ adj. **1** similar in character, form, or function: *we discussed our corresponding viewpoints.* ■ able to be matched, joined, or interlocked: *he dovetailed the corresponding pieces.*
2 dealing with written communication; having this responsibility: *the corresponding secretary.* ■ having an honorary association with a group, esp. at a distance (from the group's headquarters).
– DERIVATIVES **cor·re·spond·ing·ly** adv.

cor·re·spond·ing an·gles ▶ plural n. Mathematics the angles that occupy the same relative position at each intersection where a straight line crosses two others. If the two lines are parallel, the corresponding angles are equal.

cor·ri·da /kôˈrēdə/ ▶ n. a bullfight.
– ORIGIN late 19th cent.: from Spanish *corrida de toros* 'running of bulls.'

cor·ri·dor /ˈkôrədər, ˈkär-, -ˌdôr/ ▶ n. a long passage in a building from which doors lead into rooms. ■ Brit. a passage along the side of a railroad car, from which doors lead into compartments. ■ a belt of land linking two other areas or following a road or river: *the valley provides the principal wildlife corridor between the uplands and the central urban area | the Boston-to-Washington corridor.*
– PHRASES **the corridors of power** the senior levels of government or administration, where covert influence is regarded as being exerted and significant decisions are made. [from the name of C. P. Snow's novel *The Corridors of Power* (1964).]
– ORIGIN late 16th cent. (as a military term denoting a strip of land along the outer edge of a ditch, protected by a parapet): from French, from Italian *corridore*, alteration (by association with *corridore* 'runner') of *corridoio* 'running place,' from *correre* 'to run,' from Latin *currere*. The current sense dates from the early 19th cent.

cor·rie /ˈkôrē, ˈkärē/ ▶ n. (pl. **corries**) a cirque, esp. one in the mountains of Scotland.
– ORIGIN mid 16th cent.: from Scottish Gaelic and Irish *coire* 'cauldron, hollow.'

Cor·rie·dale /ˈkôrēˌdāl, ˈkär-/ ▶ n. a sheep of a New Zealand breed kept for both wool and meat.
– ORIGIN early 20th cent.: named after an estate in New Zealand.

cor·ri·gen·dum /ˌkôriˈjendəm, ˌkär-/ ▶ n. (pl. **corrigenda** /-ˈjendə/) a thing to be corrected, typically an error in a printed book.
– ORIGIN early 19th cent.: Latin, neuter gerundive of *corrigere* 'bring into order' (see CORRECT).

cor·ri·gi·ble /ˈkôrijəbəl, ˈkär-/ ▶ adj. capable of being corrected, rectified, or reformed.
– DERIVATIVES **cor·ri·gi·bil·i·ty** /ˌkôrijəˈbilitē, ˌkär-/ n.
– ORIGIN late Middle English (in the sense 'liable to or deserving punishment'): via French from medieval Latin *corrigibilis*, from Latin *corrigere* 'to correct.'

cor·rob·o·rant /kəˈräbərənt/ ▶ adj. **1** corroborating; confirming.
2 archaic (of a medicine) invigorating; producing strength.
▶ n. **1** something that corroborates.
2 archaic an invigorating medicine.

cor·rob·o·rate /kəˈräbəˌrāt/ ▶ v. [with obj.] confirm or give support to (a statement, theory, or finding): *the witness had corroborated the boy's account of the attack.*
– DERIVATIVES **cor·rob·o·ra·tive** /-ˈräb(ə)rətiv/ adj., **cor·rob·o·ra·tor** /-ˌrātər/ n., **cor·rob·o·ra·to·ry** /-ˈräb(ə)rəˌtôrē/ adj.
– ORIGIN mid 16th cent. (in the sense 'make physically stronger'): from Latin *corroborat-* 'strengthened,' from the verb *corroborare*, from *cor-* 'together' + *roborare*, from *robur* 'strength.'

cor·rob·o·ra·tion /kəˌräbəˈrāsHən/ ▶ n. evidence that confirms or supports a statement, theory, or finding; confirmation: *there is no independent corroboration for this.*

cor·rob·o·ree /kəˈräbərē/ ▶ n. an Australian Aboriginal dance ceremony that may take the form of a sacred ritual or an informal gathering. ■ chiefly Austral. a party or other social gathering, esp. a lively one.
– ORIGIN from Dharuk *garaabara*, denoting a style of dancing.

cor·rode /kəˈrōd/ ▶ v. [with obj.] **1** destroy or damage (metal, stone, or other materials) slowly by chemical action: *acid rain poisons fish and corrodes buildings.* ■ [no obj.] (of metal or other materials) be destroyed or damaged in this way: *over the years copper tubing corrodes.*
2 destroy or weaken (something) gradually: *the self-centered climate corrodes ideals and concerns about social justice.*
– DERIVATIVES **cor·rod·i·ble** adj.
– ORIGIN late Middle English: from Latin *corrodere*, from *cor-* (expressing intensive force) + *rodere* 'gnaw.'

cor·ro·sion /kəˈrōZHən/ ▶ n. the process of corroding metal, stone, or other materials: *each aircraft part is sprayed with oil to prevent corrosion.* ■ damage caused by such a process: *engineers found the corrosion when checking the bridge.*
– ORIGIN late Middle English: from Old French, or from late Latin *corrosio(n-)*, from Latin *corrodere* 'gnaw through' (see CORRODE).

cor·ro·sive /kəˈrōsiv, -ziv/ ▶ adj. tending to cause corrosion.
▶ n. a corrosive substance.
– DERIVATIVES **cor·ro·sive·ly** adv., **cor·ro·sive·ness** n.
– ORIGIN late Middle English: from Old French *corosif, -ive*, from medieval Latin *corrosivus*, from Latin *corros-* 'gnawed through,' from the verb *corrodere* (see CORRODE).

cor·ro·sive sub·li·mate ▶ n. rare another term for MERCURIC CHLORIDE.

cor·ru·gate /ˈkôrəˌgāt, ˈkär-/ ▶ v. contract or cause to contract into wrinkles or folds: [no obj.] *Micky's brow corrugated in a simian frown.*
– ORIGIN late Middle English: from Latin *corrugat-* 'wrinkled,' from the verb *corrugare*, from *cor-* (expressing intensive force) + *rugare* (from *ruga* 'a wrinkle').

cor·ru·gat·ed /ˈkôrəˌgātid, ˈkär-/ ▶ adj. (of a material, surface, or structure) shaped into alternate ridges and grooves: *the roof was made of corrugated iron.*
– DERIVATIVES **cor·ru·ga·tion** /ˌkôrəˈgāsHən, ˌkär-/ n.

cor·ru·gat·ed i·ron ▶ n. a building material consisting of iron or steel sheeting bent into a corrugated form.

cor·ru·gat·ed pa·per ▶ n. packaging material made from layers of thick paper, the top layer of which is alternately grooved and ridged for added strength and rigidity.

cor·rupt /kəˈrəpt/ ▶ adj. **1** having or showing a willingness to act dishonestly in return for money or personal gain: *unscrupulous logging companies assisted by corrupt officials.* ■ evil or morally depraved: *the play can do no harm since its audience is already corrupt.* ■ archaic (of organic or inorganic matter) in a state of decay; rotten or putrid: *a corrupt and rotting corpse.*
2 (of a text or a computer database or program) made unreliable by errors or alterations.
▶ v. [with obj.] **1** cause to act dishonestly in return for money or personal gain: *there is a continuing fear of firms corrupting politicians in the search for contracts.* ■ cause to become morally depraved: *he has corrupted the boy.* ■ archaic infect; contaminate: (as adj. **corrupting**) *the corrupting smell of death.*
2 change or debase by making errors or unintentional alterations: *Epicurus's teachings have since been much corrupted.* ■ cause errors to appear in (a computer program or database): *a program that has somehow corrupted your system files.*
– DERIVATIVES **cor·rupt·er** n., **cor·rupt·i·bil·i·ty** /kəˌrəptəˈbilitē/ n., **cor·rupt·i·ble** adj., **cor·rup·tive** /-tiv/ adj., **cor·rupt·ly** adv.
– ORIGIN Middle English: from Latin *corruptus*, past participle of *corrumpere* 'mar, bribe, destroy,' from *cor-* 'altogether' + *rumpere* 'to break.'

cor·rup·tion /kəˈrəpsHən/ ▶ n. **1** dishonest or fraudulent conduct by those in power, typically involving bribery: *the journalist who wants to expose corruption in high places.* ■ the action of making someone or something morally depraved or the state of being so: *the word "addict" conjures up evil and corruption.* ■ archaic decay; putrefaction: *the potato turned black and rotten with corruption.*
2 the process by which something, typically a word or expression, is changed from its original use or meaning to one that is regarded as erroneous or debased. ■ the process of causing errors to appear in a computer program or database.
– ORIGIN Middle English: via Old French from Latin *corruptio(n-)*, from *corrumpere* 'mar, bribe, destroy' (see CORRUPT).

cor·rup·tion·ist /kəˈrəpsHənist/ ▶ n. one who practices or endorses corruption, esp. in politics.

cor·rupt prac·tice ▶ n. (often **corrupt practices**) a fraudulent activity, esp. an attempt to rig an election.

cor·sage /kôrˈsäZH, -ˈsäj/ ▶ n. **1** a spray of flowers worn pinned to a woman's clothes.
2 the upper part of a woman's dress.
– ORIGIN early 19th cent. (sense 2): French, from Old French *cors* 'body,' from Latin *corpus*.

cor·sair /ˌkôrˈse(ə)r/ ▶ n. archaic a pirate. ■ a pirate ship. ■ a privateer, esp. one operating along the southern coast of the Mediterranean in the 16th–18th centuries.
– ORIGIN mid 16th cent.: from French *corsaire*, from medieval Latin *cursarius*, from *cursus* 'a raid, plunder,' special use of Latin *cursus* 'course,' from *currere* 'to run.'

Corse /kôrs/ French name for CORSICA.

corse /kôrs/ ▶ n. archaic a corpse.
– ORIGIN Middle English: from Old French *cors* 'body,' from Latin *corpus*. Compare with CORPSE.

cor·se·let /ˈkôrslət/ ▶ n. **1** historical a piece of armor covering the trunk.
2 variant spelling of CORSELETTE.
– ORIGIN late 15th cent.: from Old French *corslet*, diminutive of *cors* 'body.'

cor·se·lette /ˈkôrslət/ (also **corselet**) ▶ n. a woman's foundation garment combining corset and bra.
– ORIGIN 1920s: from *corselet* (see CORSELET).

cor·set /ˈkôrsət/ ▶ n. a woman's tightly fitting undergarment extending from below the chest to the hips, worn to shape the figure. ■ a similar garment worn by men or women to support a weak or injured back. ■ historical a tightly fitting laced or stiffened outer bodice or dress.
– DERIVATIVES **cor·set·ed** adj., **cor·set·ry** /-trē/ n.
– ORIGIN Middle English: from Old French, diminutive of *cors* 'body,' from Latin *corpus*. The sense 'close-fitting undergarment' dates from the

late 18th cent., by which time the sense 'bodice' had mainly historical reference.

cor·se·tière /ˌkôrsəˈti(ə)r, -ˈtyer/ ▶ **n.** a woman who makes or fits corsets.
– ORIGIN mid 19th cent.: French, feminine of *corsetier*, from *corset* (see CORSET).

Cor·si·ca /ˈkôrsikə/ a mountainous island off the western coast of Italy that forms an administrative region of France; pop. 273,000 (est. 2004); chief towns, Bastia (northern department) and Ajaccio (southern department). It was the birthplace of Napoleon I. French name **CORSE**.

Cor·si·can /ˈkôrsikən/ ▶ **adj.** of or relating to Corsica, its people, or their language.
▶ **n. 1** a native of Corsica.
2 the language of Corsica, which originated as a dialect of Italian.

cor·tège /kôrˈtezʜ, ˈkôrˌtezʜ/ ▶ **n.** a solemn procession, esp. for a funeral. ■ a person's entourage or retinue.
– ORIGIN mid 17th cent.: from French, from Italian *corteggio*, from *corteggiare* 'attend court,' from *corte* 'court,' from Latin *cohors, cohort-* 'retinue.'

Cor·tes /ˈkôrˌtes/ the legislative assembly of Spain and formerly of Portugal.
– ORIGIN Spanish and Portuguese, plural of *corte* 'court,' from Latin *cohors, cohort-* 'yard, retinue.'

Cor·tés /kôrˈtez/ (also **Cortez**), Hernando (1485–1547), first of the Spanish conquistadors. He overthrew the Aztec empire by conquering its capital, Tenochtitlán, in 1519 and by deposing its emperor, Montezuma. In 1521, he destroyed Tenochtitlán completely, established Mexico City as the capital of New Spain (now Mexico), and served briefly as its governor.

cor·tex /ˈkôrˌteks/ ▶ **n.** (pl. **cortices** /-təˌsēz/) Anatomy the outer layer of the cerebrum (the **cerebral cortex**), composed of folded gray matter and playing an important role in consciousness. ■ an outer layer of another organ or body part such as a kidney (the **renal cortex**), the cerebellum, or a hair. ■ Botany an outer layer of tissue immediately below the epidermis of a stem or root.
– DERIVATIVES **cor·ti·cal** /ˈkôrtikəl/ **adj.**
– ORIGIN late Middle English: from Latin, literally 'bark.'

cor·ti·cate /ˈkôrtəˌkāt, -ikət/ ▶ **adj.** Botany having a cortex, bark, or rind.
– DERIVATIVES **cor·ti·ca·tion** /ˌkôrtəˈkāsʜən/ **n.**
– ORIGIN mid 19th cent.: from Latin *corticatus*, from *cortex, cortic-* 'bark.'

cortico- ▶ **comb. form** representing CORTEX, esp. with reference to the adrenal and cerebral cortices: *corticosterone*.
– ORIGIN from Latin *cortex, cortic-* 'bark.'

cor·ti·co·fu·gal /ˌkôrtikōˈfyo͞ogəl/ (also **corticifugal** /-ˈsifyəgəl/) ▶ **adj.** Anatomy (of a nerve fiber) originating in and running from the cerebral cortex.
– ORIGIN late 19th cent.: from CORTICO- 'cortex' + Latin *fugere* 'run from.'

cor·ti·coid /ˈkôrtiˌkoid/ ▶ **n.** another term for CORTICOSTEROID.

cor·ti·co·ster·oid /ˌkôrtikōˈsterˌoid, -ˈsti(ə)rˌoid/ ▶ **n.** Biochemistry any of a group of steroid hormones produced in the adrenal cortex or made synthetically. There are two kinds: glucocorticoids and mineralocorticoids. They have various metabolic functions and some are used to treat inflammation.

cor·ti·cos·ter·one /ˌkôrtəˈkästəˌrōn/ ▶ **n.** Biochemistry a hormone secreted by the adrenal cortex, one of the glucocorticoids.

cor·ti·co·tro·pin /ˌkôrtikōˈtrōpin/ (also **corticotrophin** /-ˈtrāfən/) ▶ **n.** Biochemistry another term for ADRENOCORTICOTROPIC HORMONE.

cor·ti·le /kôrˈtēˌlā/ ▶ **n.** (pl. **cortili** /-ˈtēlē/ or **cortiles** /-ˈtēˌlāz/) (in Italy) an enclosed area, typically roofless and arcaded, within or attached to a building.
– ORIGIN Italian, derivative of *corte* 'court.'

cor·ti·na /kôrˈtīnə, -ˈtēnə/ ▶ **n.** (pl. **cortinae** /-ˈtīnē, -ˈtēˌnī/) Botany (in some toadstools) a thin weblike veil extending from the edge of the cap to the stalk.
– DERIVATIVES **cor·ti·nate** /ˈkôrtnˌāt/ **adj.**
– ORIGIN mid 19th cent.: from late Latin, literally 'curtain.'

cor·ti·sol /ˈkôrtəˌsôl, -ˌsōl/ ▶ **n.** Biochemistry another term for HYDROCORTISONE.

cor·ti·sone /ˈkôrtəˌsōn/ ▶ **n.** Biochemistry a hormone produced by the adrenal cortex. One of the glucocorticoids, it is also made synthetically for use as an anti-inflammatory and anti-allergy agent.
– ORIGIN 1940s: from elements of its chemical name *17-hydroxy-11-dehydrocorticosterone*.

co·run·dum /kəˈrəndəm/ ▶ **n.** extremely hard aluminum oxide, used as an abrasive. Ruby and sapphire are varieties of corundum.
– ORIGIN early 18th cent.: from Tamil *kuruntam* and Telugu *kuruvindam*.

Co·run·na /kəˈrənə/ a port in northwestern Spain; pop. 245,164 (2008). It was the point of departure for the armada in 1588. Spanish name **LA CORUÑA**.

co·rus·cant /kəˈrəskənt/ ▶ **adj.** literary glittering; sparkling.
– ORIGIN late 15th cent.: from Latin *coruscant-* 'vibrating, glittering,' from the verb *coruscare*.

cor·us·cate /ˈkôrəˌskāt, ˈkär-/ ▶ **v.** [no obj.] literary (of light) flash or sparkle: *the light was coruscating from the walls*.
– DERIVATIVES **cor·us·ca·tion** /ˌkôrəˈskāsʜən/ **n.**
– ORIGIN early 18th cent.: from Latin *coruscat-* 'glittered,' from the verb *coruscare*.

cor·us·cat·ing /ˈkôrəˌskātiɴɢ/ ▶ **adj.** flashing; sparkling: *a coruscating kaleidoscope of colors*. ■ brilliant or striking in content or style: *the play's coruscating wit*.

Cor·val·lis /kôrˈvalis/ a city in western Oregon, on the Willamette River, home to Oregon State University; pop. 51,110 (est. 2008).

cor·vée /ˈkôrˌvā, kôrˈvā/ ▶ **n.** historical a day's unpaid labor owed by a vassal to his feudal lord. ■ forced labor exacted in lieu of taxes, in particular that on public roads.
– ORIGIN Middle English: from Old French, based on Latin *corrogare* 'ask for, collect.' Rare in English before the late 18th cent.

cor·vette /kôrˈvet/ ▶ **n.** a small warship designed for convoy escort duty. ■ historical a sailing warship with one tier of guns.
– ORIGIN mid 17th cent.: from French, from Dutch *korf*, denoting a kind of ship, + the diminutive suffix *-ette*.

cor·vid /ˈkôrvid/ ▶ **n.** Ornithology a bird of the crow family (Corvidae); a crow.
– ORIGIN mid 20th cent.: from modern Latin *Corvidae* (plural), from Latin *corvus* 'raven.'

cor·vi·na[1] /kôrˈvēnə/ ▶ **n.** a variety of wine grape native to the Veneto region of northeastern Italy, used to make Valpolicella and Bardolino.
– ORIGIN Italian (feminine adjective), literally 'raven-black.'

cor·vi·na[2] ▶ **n.** a marine food and game fish of the drum family, found on the Pacific coasts of California and Mexico and sometimes living in fresh water. ● Genus *Cynoscion*, family Sciaenidae: two species, in particular the **shortfin corvina** (*C. parvipennis*).
– ORIGIN late 18th cent.: from Spanish and Portuguese.

cor·vine /ˈkôrˌvīn/ ▶ **adj.** of or like a raven or crow, esp. in color.
– ORIGIN mid 17th cent.: from Latin *corvinus*, from *corvus* 'raven.'

Cor·vus /ˈkôrvəs/ Astronomy a small southern constellation (the Crow or Raven), south of Virgo. ■ (**Corvi** /-vī/) used with a preceding letter or numeral to designate a star in this constellation: *the star Gamma Corvi*.
– ORIGIN Latin.

cor·y·ban·tic /ˌkôrəˈbantik/ ▶ **adj.** wild; frenzied.
– ORIGIN mid 17th cent.: from *Corybantes*, Latin name of the priests of Cybele, a Phrygian goddess of nature who performed wild dances, from Greek *Korubantes* + -IC.

co·ryd·a·lis /kəˈridl-əs/ ▶ **n.** a herbaceous plant of the poppy family with spurred tubular flowers, closely related to bleeding heart and found in north temperate regions. ● Genus *Corydalis*, family Fumariaceae: many species, including **yellow corydalis** (*C. flavula*) of the eastern US.
– ORIGIN modern Latin, from Greek *korudallis* 'crested lark,' alluding to a similarity between the flower and the bird's spur.

cor·ymb /ˈkôrˌim(b), ˈkär-/ ▶ **n.** Botany a flower cluster whose lower stalks are proportionally longer so that the flowers form a flat or slightly convex head.
– DERIVATIVES **co·rym·bose** /ˈkôrəmˌbōs, ˈkär-, -ˌbōz/ **adj.**
– ORIGIN early 18th cent.: from French *corymbe* or Latin *corymbus*, from Greek *korumbos* 'cluster.'

cor·y·ne·bac·te·ri·um /ˌkôrənēbakˈti(ə)rēəm, kəˌrinə-/ ▶ **n.** (pl. **corynebacteria** /-ˈti(ə)rēə/) a bacterium that sometimes causes disease in humans and other animals, including diphtheria. ● Genus *Corynebacterium*; Gram-positive nonmotile club-shaped rods.
– ORIGIN modern Latin, from Greek *korunē* 'club' + BACTERIUM.

cor·y·phée /ˌkôrəˈfā/ ▶ **n.** a leading dancer in a corps de ballet.
– ORIGIN French, via Latin from Greek *koruphaios* 'leader of a chorus,' from *koruphē* 'head.'

co·ry·za /kəˈrīzə/ ▶ **n.** Medicine catarrhal inflammation of the mucous membrane in the nose, caused esp. by a cold or by hay fever.
– ORIGIN early 16th cent.: from Latin, from Greek *koruza* 'nasal mucus.'

cos[1] /käs, kôs/ (also **cos lettuce**) ▶ **n.** another term for ROMAINE.
– ORIGIN late 17th cent.: named after the Aegean island of *Cos*, where it originated.

cos[2] ▶ **abbr.** cosine.

Co·sa Nos·tra /ˌkōsə ˈnōstrə, ˌkōzə/ a US criminal organization resembling and related to the Mafia.
– ORIGIN Italian, literally 'our affair.'

Cos·by /ˈkôzbē, ˈkäz-/, Bill (1937–), US comedian, actor, and writer; full name *William Henry Cosby, Jr.* He was the first African American to star in a weekly television drama (*I Spy*; 1965–68). His comedy series *The Cosby Show* 1984–92 was one of the most successful programs in television history. He wrote *Fatherhood* (1987) and *Love and Marriage* (1989).

cos·co·ro·ba swan /ˌkäskəˈrōbə/ ▶ **n.** a small South American swan with white plumage and bright pink legs and feet. ● *Coscoroba coscoroba*, family Anatidae.
– ORIGIN early 19th cent.: *coscoroba* from the modern Latin taxonomic name, of unknown origin.

co·sec /ˈkōsek/ ▶ **abbr.** cosecant.

co·se·cant /kōˈsēˌkant, -kənt/ ▶ **n.** Mathematics the ratio of the hypotenuse (in a right-angled triangle) to the side opposite an acute angle; the reciprocal of sine.
– ORIGIN early 18th cent.: from modern Latin *cosecant-*, from CO- 'mutually' + Latin *secant-* 'cutting' (from the verb *secare*). Compare with SECANT.

co·seis·mal /kōˈsīzməl, -ˈsīsməl/ ▶ **adj.** relating to points on the earth's surface affected by an earthquake simultaneously.
▶ **n.** a line on a map connecting such points.
– ORIGIN mid 19th cent.: from CO- 'jointly' + *seismal* (from Greek *seismos* 'earthquake,' from *seien* 'to shake').

co·set /ˈkōˌset/ ▶ **n.** Mathematics a set composed of all the products obtained by multiplying each element of a subgroup in turn by one particular element of the group containing the subgroup.

cosh[1] /käsʜ/ Brit. informal ▶ **n.** a thick heavy stick or bar used as a weapon; a bludgeon.
▶ **v.** [with obj.] hit (someone) on the head with a cosh.
– ORIGIN mid 19th cent.: of unknown origin.

cosh[2] ▶ **abbr.** Mathematics hyperbolic cosine.
– ORIGIN from COS[2] + *-h* for *hyperbolic*. Compare with COTH.

co·sign /ˈkōˌsīn/ ▶ **v. 1** sign (a document) in order to guarantee a loan or other obligation: [with obj.] *co-sign a loan* | [no obj.] *see if your parents will co-sign for you*. **2** [with obj.] designate with two different labels or signs: *original interchange numbers will be co-signed with new numbers for two years after the conversion* | *U.S. 400 is co-signed with U.S. 166 for about 8 miles*.

co·sig·na·to·ry /kōˈsignəˌtôrē/ ▶ **n.** a person or state signing a treaty or other document jointly with others.

Cos·i·mo de' Me·di·ci /ˈkôzēˌmō də ˈmedəcʜē/ (1389–1464), Italian statesman and banker; known as **Cosimo the Elder**. He laid the foundations for the Medici family's power in Florence, becoming the city's ruler in 1434 and using his considerable wealth to promote the arts and learning.

co·sine /ˈkōˌsīn/ ▶ **n.** Mathematics the trigonometric function that is equal to the ratio of the side adjacent to an acute angle (in a right-angled triangle) to the hypotenuse.

co-sleep·ing /ˌkōˈslēpiɴɢ/ ▶ **n.** the practice of sleeping in the same bed with one's infant or young child: *co-sleeping often facilitates a good breastfeeding relationship*.
– DERIVATIVES **co-sleep v.**

cos·me·ceu·ti·cal /ˌkäzməˈso͞otikəl/ ▶ **n.** a cosmetic that has or is claimed to have medicinal properties, esp. anti-aging ones.
– ORIGIN 1980s: blend of *cosmetic* and *pharmaceutical*.

cos·met·ic /käzˈmetik/ ▶ **adj.** involving or relating to treatment intended to restore or improve a person's appearance: *cosmetic surgery*. ■ designed or serving to improve the appearance of the body, esp. the face: *lens designs can improve the cosmetic effect*

C

of your glasses. ■ affecting only the appearance of something rather than its substance: *the reform package was merely a cosmetic exercise.*
▶ n. (usu. **cosmetics**) a product applied to the body, esp. the face, to improve its appearance.
– DERIVATIVES **cos·met·i·cal·ly** /-(ə)lē/ **adv.**
– ORIGIN early 17th cent. (as a noun denoting the art of beautifying the body): from French *cosmétique*, from Greek *kosmētikos*, from *kosmein* 'arrange or adorn,' from *kosmos* 'order or adornment.'

C

cos·me·ti·cian /ˌkäzməˈtisHən/ ▶ n. a person who sells or applies cosmetics as an occupation.

cos·me·tol·o·gy /ˌkäzməˈtäləjē/ ▶ n. the professional skill or practice of beautifying the face, hair, and skin.
– DERIVATIVES **cos·me·to·log·i·cal** /-təˈläjikəl/ **adj.**, **cos·me·tol·o·gist** /-jist/ **n.**

cos·mic /ˈkäzmik/ ▶ adj. of or relating to the universe or cosmos, esp. as distinct from the earth: *cosmic matter.* ■ inconceivably vast: *the song is a masterpiece of cosmic proportions.*
– DERIVATIVES **cos·mi·cal adj.**, **cos·mi·cal·ly** /-(ə)lē/ **adv.**

cos·mic dust ▶ n. small particles of matter distributed throughout space.

cos·mic ra·di·a·tion ▶ n. radiation consisting of cosmic rays.

cos·mic ray ▶ n. a highly energetic atomic nucleus or other particle traveling through space at a speed approaching that of light.

cos·mic string ▶ n. another term for STRING (sense 5 of the noun).

cosmo- ▶ comb. form of or relating to the world or the universe: *cosmodrome* | *cosmography.*
– ORIGIN from Greek *kosmos* 'order, world.'

cos·mo·drome /ˈkäzməˌdrōm/ ▶ n. (in the countries of the former Soviet Union) a launching site for spacecraft.
– ORIGIN 1950s: from COSMO- + -DROME, on the pattern of *aerodrome.*

cos·mo·gen·e·sis /ˌkäzməˈjenəsis/ ▶ n. the origin or evolution of the universe.
– DERIVATIVES **cos·mo·ge·net·ic** /-jəˈnetik/ **adj.**, **cos·mo·gen·ic** /-ˈjenik/ **adj.**

cos·mog·o·ny /käzˈmägənē/ ▶ n. (pl. **cosmogonies**) the branch of science that deals with the origin of the universe, esp. the solar system. ■ a theory regarding this: *in their cosmogony, the world was thought to be a square, flat surface.*
– DERIVATIVES **cos·mo·gon·ic** /ˌkäzməˈgänik/ **adj.**, **cos·mo·gon·i·cal** /ˌkäzməˈgänikəl/ **adj.**, **cos·mog·o·nist** /-nist/ **n.**
– ORIGIN late 17th cent.: from Greek *kosmogonia*, from *kosmos* 'order or world' + *-gonia* '-begetting.'

cos·mog·ra·phy /käzˈmägrəfē/ ▶ n. (pl. **cosmographies**) the science that deals with the general features of the universe, including the earth. The branches of cosmography include astronomy, geography, and geology. ■ a description or representation of the universe or the earth.
– DERIVATIVES **cos·mog·ra·pher** /-fər/ **n.**, **cos·mo·graph·ic** /ˌkäzməˈgrafik/ **adj.**, **cos·mo·graph·i·cal** /ˌkäzməˈgrafikəl/ **adj.**
– ORIGIN late Middle English: from French *cosmographie*, or via late Latin from Greek *kosmographia*, from *kosmos* (see COSMOS[1]) + *-graphia* 'writing.'

cos·mo·log·i·cal ar·gu·ment /ˌkäzməˈläjikəl/ ▶ n. Philosophy an argument for the existence of God that claims that all things in nature depend on something else for their existence (i.e., are contingent), and that the whole cosmos must therefore itself depend on a being that exists independently or necessarily. Compare with ONTOLOGICAL ARGUMENT and TELEOLOGICAL ARGUMENT.

cos·mo·log·i·cal con·stant ▶ n. Physics an arbitrary constant in the field equations of general relativity.

cos·mol·o·gy /käzˈmäləjē/ ▶ n. (pl. **cosmologies**) the science of the origin and development of the universe. Modern astronomy is dominated by the Big Bang theory, which brings together observational astronomy and particle physics. ■ an account or theory of the origin of the universe.
– DERIVATIVES **cos·mo·log·i·cal** /ˌkäzməˈläjikəl/ **adj.**, **cos·mol·o·gist** /-jist/ **n.**
– ORIGIN mid 17th cent.: from French *cosmologie* or modern Latin *cosmologia*, from Greek *kosmos* 'order, world' + *-logia* 'discourse.'

cos·mo·naut /ˈkäzməˌnôt, -ˌnät/ ▶ n. a Russian astronaut.
– ORIGIN 1950s: from COSMOS[1], on the pattern of *astronaut* and Russian *kosmonavt.*

cos·mop·o·lis /käzˈmäpələs/ ▶ n. a city inhabited by people from many different countries.
– ORIGIN mid 19th cent.: from Greek *kosmos* 'world' + *polis* 'city.'

cos·mo·pol·i·tan /ˌkäzməˈpälitn/ ▶ adj. familiar with and at ease in many different countries and cultures: *his knowledge of French, Italian, and Spanish made him genuinely cosmopolitan.* ■ including people from many different countries: *immigration transformed the city into a cosmopolitan metropolis.* ■ having an exciting and glamorous character associated with travel and a mixture of cultures: *their designs became a byword for cosmopolitan chic.* ■ (of a plant or animal) found all over the world.
▶ n. **1** a cosmopolitan person. ■ a cosmopolitan organism or species.
2 a cocktail typically made with vodka, Cointreau, cranberry juice, and lime juice.
– DERIVATIVES **cos·mo·pol·i·tan·ism** /-ˌizəm/ **n.**, **cos·mo·pol·i·tan·ize** /-ˌīz/ **v.**
– ORIGIN mid 17th cent. (as a noun): from COSMOPOLITE + -AN.

cos·mop·o·lite /käzˈmäpəˌlīt/ ▶ n. a cosmopolitan person.
– ORIGIN early 17th cent.: from French, from Greek *kosmopolitēs*, from *kosmos* 'world' + *politēs* 'citizen.'

cos·mos[1] /ˈkäzməs, -ˌmōs, -ˌmäs/ ▶ n. (**the cosmos**) the universe seen as a well-ordered whole: *he sat staring deep into the void, reminding himself of his place in the cosmos.* ■ a system of thought: *the new gender-free intellectual cosmos.*
– ORIGIN Middle English: from Greek *kosmos* 'order or world.'

cos·mos[2] ▶ n. an ornamental plant of the daisy family with single dahlialike flowers. Native to tropical America, it is widely grown as an ornamental. ● Genus *Cosmos*, family Compositae.
– ORIGIN from Greek *kosmos* in the sense 'ornament.'

COSPAR /ˈkōˌspär/ ▶ abbr. Committee on Space Research.

cos·play /ˈkäzˌplā/ ▶ n. the practice of dressing up as a character from a movie, book, or video game, esp. one from the Japanese genres of manga and anime.
▶ v. [no obj.] engage in cosplay.
– DERIVATIVES **cos·play·er** **n.**
– ORIGIN 1990s: blend of COSTUME and PLAY.

Cos·sack /ˈkäsˌak, -ək/ ▶ n. a member of a people of southern Russia, Ukraine, and Siberia, noted for their horsemanship and military skill. ■ a member of a Cossack military unit.

> The Cossacks had their origins in the 15th century when refugees from religious persecution, outlaws, adventurers, and escaped serfs banded together in settlements for protection. Under the tsars they were allowed considerable autonomy in return for protecting the frontiers; with the collapse of Soviet rule, Cossack groups have reasserted their identity in both Russia and Ukraine.

▶ adj. of, relating to, or characteristic of the Cossacks.
– ORIGIN late 16th cent.: from Russian *kazak* from Turkic,'vagabond, nomad'; later influenced by French *Cosaque* (see also KAZAKH).

cos·set /ˈkäsət/ ▶ v. (**cossets, cosseting, cosseted**) [with obj.] care for and protect in an overindulgent way: *all her life she'd been cosseted by her family.*
– ORIGIN mid 16th cent. (as a noun denoting a lamb brought up by hand, later a spoiled child): probably from Anglo-Norman French *coscet* 'cottager,' from Old English *cotsǣta* 'cottar.'

cost /kôst/ ▶ v. (past and past participle **cost**) [with obj.]
1 (of an object or an action) require the payment of (a specified sum of money) before it can be acquired or done: *each issue of the magazine costs $2.25.* ■ cause the loss of: *driving at more than double the speed limit cost the woman her driving license.* ■ informal be expensive for (someone): *if you want to own an island, it'll cost you.*
2 (past and past participle **costed**) estimate the price of: *it is their job to plan and cost a media schedule for the campaign.*
▶ n. an amount that has to be paid or spent to buy or obtain something: *we are able to cover the cost of the event* | *health care costs* | *the tunnel has been built at no cost to the state.* ■ the effort, loss, or sacrifice necessary to achieve or obtain something: *she averted a train accident at the cost of her life.*
– PHRASES **at all costs** (or **at any cost**) regardless of the price to be paid or the effort needed: *he was anxious to avoid war at all costs.* **at cost** at cost price; without profit to the seller. **cost an arm and a leg** see ARM[1]. **cost someone dearly** (or **dear**) involve someone in a serious loss or a heavy penalty: *they were really bad mistakes on my part and they cost us dearly.*
– ORIGIN Middle English: from Old French *couster* (noun), *couster* (verb), based on Latin *constare* 'stand firm, stand at a price.'

Cos·ta /ˈkôstə/, Lúcio (1902–63), Brazilian architect, town planner, and architectural historian; born in France. He designed Brasilia, the capital of Brazil, in 1956.

cos·ta /ˈkästə/ ▶ n. (pl. **costae** /-tē, -tī/) Botany & Zoology a rib, midrib, or riblike structure. ■ Entomology the main vein running along the leading edge of an insect's wing.
– ORIGIN mid 19th cent.: from Latin.

Cos·ta Blan·ca /ˌkôstə ˈbläNGkə/ a resort region on the Mediterranean coast of southeastern Spain.
– ORIGIN Spanish, literally 'white coast.'

Cos·ta Bra·va /ˌkôstə ˈbrävə/ a resort region on the Mediterranean coast of northeastern Spain, north of Barcelona.
– ORIGIN Spanish, literally 'wild coast.'

cost ac·count·ing ▶ n. the recording of all the costs incurred in a business in a way that can be used to improve its management.
– DERIVATIVES **cost ac·count·ant** **n.**

Cos·ta del Sol /ˌkōstə del ˈsōl/ a resort region on the Mediterranean coast of southern Spain.
– ORIGIN Spanish,'coast of the sun.'

cos·tal /ˈkästəl/ ▶ adj. of or relating to the ribs. ■ Anatomy & Zoology of or relating to a costa.
– ORIGIN mid 17th cent.: from French, from modern Latin *costalis*, from Latin *costa* 'rib.'

Cos·ta Me·sa /ˌkōstə ˈmāsə, ˌkästə/ a city in southwestern California, on the Pacific Ocean, south of Los Angeles; pop. 110,080 (est. 2008).

co·star /ˈkōˌstär, kōˈstär/ ▶ n. a leading actor or actress appearing in a movie, on stage, etc., with another or others of equal importance.
▶ v. [no obj.] appear in a production as a costar: *she costarred with Robert De Niro in the movie version.* ■ [with obj.] (of a production) include as a costar: *his latest movie costars Meryl Streep.*

cos·tard /ˈkästərd/ (also **Costard**) ▶ n. Brit. a cooking apple of a large ribbed variety. ■ archaic, humorous a person's head.
– ORIGIN Middle English: from Anglo-Norman French, from *coste* 'rib,' from Latin *costa.*

Cos·ta Ri·ca /ˌkōstə ˈrēkə, ˌkôstə, ˌkästə/ a republic in Central America on the Isthmus of Panama, with coastlines on the Pacific Ocean and the Caribbean Sea; pop. 4,253,900 (est. 2009); capital, San José; language, Spanish.

> Colonized by Spain in the early 16th century, Costa Rica achieved independence in 1823 and emerged as a separate country in 1838.

– DERIVATIVES **Cos·ta Ri·can** /ˈrēkən/ **adj. & n.**
– ORIGIN Spanish,'rich coast.'

cos·tate /ˈkäsˌtāt, ˈkästət/ ▶ adj. Botany & Zoology ribbed; possessing a costa.
– ORIGIN early 19th cent.: from Latin *costatus*, from *costa* 'rib.'

cost–ben·e·fit ▶ adj. relating to or denoting a process that assesses the relation between the cost of an undertaking and the value of the resulting benefits: *a cost–benefit analysis.*

cost cen·ter ▶ n. a department or other unit within an organization to which costs may be charged for accounting purposes.

cost-ef·fec·tive ▶ adj. effective or productive in relation to its cost: *the most cost-effective way to invest in the stock market.*
– DERIVATIVES **cost-ef·fec·tive·ly adv.**, **cost-ef·fec·tive·ness n.**

cost-ef·fi·cient ▶ adj. another term for COST-EFFECTIVE.
– DERIVATIVES **cost-ef·fi·cien·cy n.**

cos·ter·mon·ger /ˈkästərˌməNGgər, -ˌmäNGgər/ ▶ n. Brit. dated a person who sells goods, esp. fruit and vegetables, from a handcart in the street.
– ORIGIN early 16th cent. (denoting an apple seller): from COSTARD + -MONGER.

cos·tive /ˈkästiv, ˈkôstiv/ ▶ adj. constipated. ■ slow or reluctant in speech or action; unforthcoming: *if he did ask her she would become costive.*
– DERIVATIVES **cos·tive·ly adv.**, **cos·tive·ness n.**
– ORIGIN late Middle English: via Old French from Latin *constipatus* 'pressed together' (see CONSTIPATED).

cost·ly /ˈkôstlē/ ▶ adj. (**costlier, costliest**) costing a lot; expensive: *major problems requiring costly repairs.* ■ causing suffering, loss, or disadvantage: *the government's biggest and most costly mistake.*
– DERIVATIVES **cost·li·ness n.**

cost·mar·y /ˈkôstˌme(ə)rē, ˈkäst-/ ▶ n. (pl. **costmaries**) an aromatic plant of the daisy family, formerly used in medicine and for flavoring ale prior to the use of hops. ● *Balsamita major*, family Compositae.
– ORIGIN late Middle English: from obsolete *cost* (via Latin from Greek *kostos*, via Arabic from Sanskrit *kuṣṭha*, denoting an aromatic plant) + *Mary*, the mother of Jesus Christ (with whom it

was associated in medieval times because of its medicinal qualities).

cost of liv·ing ▶ **n.** the level of prices relating to a range of everyday items.

cost-of-liv·ing in·dex (abbr.: **CLI**) ▶ **n.** former term for **CONSUMER PRICE INDEX**.

cost-plus ▶ **adj.** relating to or denoting a method of pricing a service or product in which a fixed profit factor is added to the costs.

cos·tume ▶ **n.** /ˈkäsˌt(y)o͞om, -təm/ a set of clothes in a style typical of a particular country or historical period: *authentic Elizabethan costumes | children in national costume singing folk music.* ■ a set of clothes worn by an actor or other performer for a particular role or by someone attending a masquerade: *a nun's costume.* ■ a set of clothes, esp. a woman's ensemble, for a particular occasion or purpose; an outfit.
▶ **v.** /käsˈt(y)o͞om, ˈkäst(y)o͞om, ˈkästəm/ [with obj.] dress (someone) in a particular set of clothes: *an all-woman troupe elaborately costumed in clinging silver lamé.*
– ORIGIN early 18th cent.: from French, from Italian *custume* 'custom, fashion, habit,' from Latin *consuetudo* (see **CUSTOM**).

cos·tume dra·ma (also **costume play**) ▶ **n.** a television or film production set in a particular historical period, in which the actors wear costumes typical of that period.

cos·tume jew·el·ry ▶ **n.** jewelry made with inexpensive materials or imitation gems.

cos·tum·er /ˈkäsˌt(y)o͞omər, käsˈt(y)o͞o-/ (also chiefly Brit. **costumier** /käsˈt(y)o͞omēər/) ▶ **n.** a person or company that makes or supplies theatrical or fancy-dress costumes.
– ORIGIN mid 19th cent.: from French *costumier*, from *costumer* 'dress in a costume' (see **COSTUME**).

co·sy ▶ **adj.** British spelling of **COZY**.

cot[1] /kät/ ▶ **n.** a camp bed, particularly a portable, collapsible one. ■ a plain narrow bed. ■ Brit. a baby's crib.
– ORIGIN mid 17th cent. (originally Anglo-Indian, denoting a light bedstead): from Hindi *khāṭ* 'bedstead, hammock.'

cot[2] ▶ **n.** a small shelter for livestock. ■ archaic a small, simple cottage.
– ORIGIN Old English, of Germanic origin; compare with Old Norse *kytja* 'hovel'; related to **COTE**.

cot[3] ▶ **abbr.** Mathematics cotangent.

co·tan·gent /kōˈtanjənt/ ▶ **n.** Mathematics (in a right-angled triangle) the ratio of the side (other than the hypotenuse) adjacent to a particular acute angle to the side opposite the angle.

cot death ▶ **n.** Brit. informal term for **SUDDEN INFANT DEATH SYNDROME**.

cote /kōt, kät/ ▶ **n.** a shelter for mammals or birds, esp. pigeons.
– ORIGIN Old English (in the sense 'cottage'), of Germanic origin; related to **COT**[2].

Côte d'Azur /ˌkōtdäˈzyr, -dəˈzo͞or/ a coastal area of southeastern France, along the Mediterranean Sea, roughly coterminous with the French Riviera. It includes the towns of Cannes, Saint Tropez, Juan-les-Pins, and Antibes and the city of Nice, as well as the principality of Monaco.

Côte d'I·voire /ˌkōt dēvˈwär/ a country in West Africa, on the Gulf of Guinea; pop. 20,617,100 (est. 2009); capital, Yamoussoukro; languages, French (official) and West African languages. Also called **IVORY COAST**.

> The area was explored by the Portuguese in the late 15th century. Subsequently, it was disputed over by traders from various European countries, who mainly sought ivory and slaves. Made a French protectorate in 1842, it became a fully independent republic in 1960.

cote-har·die /ˌkōt ˈärdē, ˈhär-/ ▶ **n.** (pl. **cote-hardies**) historical a medieval close-fitting tunic with sleeves, worn by both sexes.
– ORIGIN Middle English: from Old French, from *cote* 'coat' + *hardie* (feminine) 'bold.'

co·te·rie /ˈkōtərē, ˌkōtəˈrē/ ▶ **n.** (pl. **coteries**) a small group of people with shared interests or tastes, esp. one that is exclusive of other people: *a coterie of friends and advisers.*
– ORIGIN early 18th cent.: from French, earlier denoting an association of tenants, based on Middle Low German *kote* 'cote.'

co·ter·mi·nous /kōˈtərmənəs/ ▶ **adj.** having the same boundaries or extent in space, time, or meaning: *the southern frontier was coterminous with the French Congo colony.*
– DERIVATIVES **co·ter·mi·nous·ly** adv.
– ORIGIN late 18th cent.: alteration of **CONTERMINOUS**.

coth /käTH/ ▶ **abbr.** hyperbolic cotangent.
– ORIGIN from **COT**[3] + *-h* for *hyperbolic*.

co·thur·nus /kōˈTHərnəs/ ▶ **n.** **1** a thick-soled boot or buskin worn by actors in Greek tragedy.
2 an elevated style of acting in classical tragic drama.

co·tid·al line /kōˈtīdl/ ▶ **n.** a line on a map connecting points at which a tidal level, esp. high tide, occurs simultaneously.

co·til·lion /kəˈtilyən/ ▶ **n.** **1** an 18th-century French dance based on the contredanse. ■ a quadrille.
2 a formal ball, esp. one at which debutantes are presented.
– ORIGIN early 18th cent.: from French *cotillon*, literally 'petticoat dance,' diminutive of *cotte*, from Old French *cote*.

co·tin·ga /kōˈtiNGgə, kə-/ ▶ **n.** a perching bird found in the forests of Central and South America, the male of which is frequently brilliantly colored. ● Family Cotingidae (the **cotinga family**): several genera, esp. *Cotinga*, and numerous species. The cotinga family also includes the bellbirds, umbrellabirds, and cocks-of-the-rock, and is sometimes placed within the family Tyrannidae.
– ORIGIN via French from Tupi *cutinga*.

co·to·ne·as·ter /kəˈtōnēˌastər, ˈkätnˌēstər/ ▶ **n.** a small-leaved shrub of the rose family, cultivated as a hedging plant or for its bright red berries, which often remain on the plant throughout the winter. ● Genus *Cotoneaster*, family Rosaceae.
– ORIGIN mid 18th cent.: modern Latin, from Latin *cotoneum* (see **QUINCE**) + **-ASTER**.

Co·to·nou /ˌkōtnˈo͞o/ the largest city, chief port, and commercial and political center of Benin, on the coast of West Africa; pop. 719,912 (2006).

Co·to·pax·i /ˌkōtəˈpäksē, -ˈpaksē/ the highest active volcano in the world, in the Andes in central Ecuador, that rises to 19,142 feet (5,896 m). Its name is Quechuan and means "shining peak."

co·tri·mox·a·zole /ˌkōˌtrīˈmäksəˌzōl/ ▶ **n.** Medicine a mixture of the drugs sulfamethoxazole and trimethoprim, used to treat bacterial infections synergistically.

Cots·wold /ˈkätˌswōld/ ▶ **n.** a sheep of a breed with fine wool, often used to produce crossbred lambs.
▶ **adj.** of or relating to the Cotswolds.

Cots·wold Hills /ˈkätswəld, -ˌswōld/ (also **the Cotswolds**) a range of limestone hills in southwestern England.

cot·ta /ˈkätə/ ▶ **n.** a short garment resembling a surplice, worn typically by Catholic priests and servers.
– ORIGIN mid 19th cent.: from Italian; ultimately related to **COAT**.

cot·tage /ˈkätij/ ▶ **n.** a small simple house, typically one near a lake or beach. ■ a dwelling forming part of a farm establishment, used by a worker: *farm cottages.*
– ORIGIN late Middle English: from Anglo-Norman French *cotage* and Anglo-Latin *cotagium*, from **COT**[2] or **COTE**.

cot·tage cheese ▶ **n.** soft, lumpy white cheese made from the curds of slightly soured milk.

cot·tage in·dus·try ▶ **n.** a business or manufacturing activity carried on in a person's home.

cot·tag·er /ˈkätijər/ ▶ **n.** a person living in a cottage. ■ a person vacationing in a cottage.

cot·tar /ˈkätər/ (also **cotter**) ▶ **n.** historical (in Scotland and Ireland) a farm laborer or tenant occupying a cottage in return for labor.
– ORIGIN late Old English, from **COT**[2] + **-AR**[4].

Cott·bus /ˈkätˌbo͝os/ an industrial city in southeastern Germany, in the state of Brandenburg, on the Spree River; pop. 103,800 (est. 2006).

cot·ter pin /ˈkätər/ (also **cotter**) ▶ **n.** a metal pin used to fasten two parts of a mechanism together. ■ a split pin that is opened out after being passed through a hole.
– ORIGIN mid 17th cent.: of unknown origin.

cot·ti·er /ˈkätēər/ ▶ **n.** **1** Brit. archaic a rural laborer living in a cottage.
2 historical an Irish peasant holding land by cottier tenure.
– ORIGIN Middle English: from Old French *cotier*, ultimately of Germanic origin and related to **COT**[2].

cot·ti·er ten·ure ▶ **n.** historical (in Ireland) the renting of land in small portions direct to the laborers, at a rent fixed by competition.

cot·tise /ˈkätis/ (also **cotise**) ▶ **n.** Heraldry a narrow band adjacent and parallel to an ordinary such as a bend or chevron.
– DERIVATIVES **cot·tised** adj.
– ORIGIN late 16th cent.: from French *cotice* 'leather thong.'

cot·ton /ˈkätn/ ▶ **n.** **1** a soft white fibrous substance that surrounds the seeds of a tropical and subtropical plant and is used as textile fiber and thread for sewing: *a cargo of cotton and wheat | a white cotton blouse | an Indian hammock woven in colored cottons.* ■ a thread of this fiber. ■ absorbent cotton.
2 (also **cotton plant**) the plant that is commercially grown for this product. Oil and a protein-rich flour are also obtained from the seeds. ● Genus *Gossypium*, family Malvaceae: many species and forms, including *G. barbadense*, which is grown in the southern US.
▶ **v.** [no obj.] informal **1** (**cotton on**) begin to understand: *he cottoned on to what I was trying to say.*
2 (**cotton to**) have a liking for: *his rivals didn't cotton to all the attention he was getting.*
– DERIVATIVES **cot·ton·y** adj.
– ORIGIN late Middle English: from Old French *coton*, from Arabic *ḳuṭn*.

cot·ton bat·ting ▶ **n.** light, soft cotton fibers formed into layers, used esp. for filling quilts, cushions, etc.

Cot·ton Belt ▶ **n.** (**the Cotton Belt**) informal a region of the US South where cotton is the historic main crop, esp. in parts of Georgia, Alabama, and Mississippi.

cot·ton cake ▶ **n.** compressed cotton seed, used as food for cattle.

cot·ton can·dy ▶ **n.** a mass of fluffy spun sugar, usually pink or white, wrapped around a stick or a paper cone.

cot·ton gin ▶ **n.** a machine for separating cotton from its seeds.

cot·ton grass ▶ **n.** a sedge that typically grows on swampy land in the northern hemisphere, producing tufts of long white silky hairs, which aid in the dispersal of the seeds. ● Genus *Eriophorum*, family Cyperaceae.

cot·ton lav·en·der ▶ **n.** chiefly British term for **LAVENDER COTTON**.

cot·ton-leaf worm ▶ **n.** the larva of a migratory tropical moth that feeds on the leaves of the cotton plant and was formerly a major pest in North America. ● *Alabama argillacea*, family Noctuidae.

cot·ton·mouth /ˈkätnˌmouTH/ ▶ **n.** **1** a large, dangerous semiaquatic pit viper that inhabits lowland swamps and waterways of the southeastern US. When threatening, it opens its mouth wide to display the white interior. Also called **WATER MOCCASIN**. ● *Agkistrodon piscivorus*, family Viperidae.
2 (also **cotton mouth**) informal dryness of the mouth: *I often have cotton mouth and a headache when I wake up.*

cot·ton-pick·ing (also **cotton-pickin'**) ▶ **adj.** informal used for emphasis, esp. with disapproval or reproach: *just a cotton-picking minute! | he's a cotton-pickin' liar!*

cot·ton rat ▶ **n.** a short-tailed rat found in grassland and scrub from North America to Guyana. ● Genus *Sigmodon*, family Muridae: several species.

cot·ton·seed /ˈkätnˌsēd/ ▶ **n.** the seed of the cotton plant, yielding cottonseed oil.

cot·ton stain·er ▶ **n.** a North American bug that feeds on cotton bolls, causing reddish staining of the fibers. ● Genus *Dysdercus*, family Pyrrhocoridae, suborder Heteroptera: several species, in particular *D. suturellus*.

Cot·ton State a nickname for the state of **ALABAMA**.

cot·ton swab ▶ **n.** a small wad of absorbent cotton on a short thin stick, used for cosmetic or hygienic purposes.

cot·ton·tail /ˈkätnˌtāl/ ▶ **n.** an American rabbit that has a speckled brownish coat and a white underside to the tail. ● Genus *Sylvilagus*, family Leporidae: several species.

cot·ton·wood /ˈkätnˌwo͝od/ ▶ **n.** a North American poplar with seeds covered in white cottony hairs. ● Genus *Populus*, family Salicaceae: several species, including *P. deltoides*.

cot·ton wool ▶ **n.** **1** raw cotton.
2 British term for **ABSORBENT COTTON**.

cot·y·le·don /ˌkätlˈēdn/ ▶ **n.** Botany an embryonic leaf in seed-bearing plants, one or more of which are the first leaves to appear from a germinating seed.
– DERIVATIVES **cot·y·le·don·ar·y** /-ˈēdnˌerē/ adj.
– ORIGIN mid 16th cent. (denoting a patch of villi on the placenta of mammals): from Latin,'navelwort' (which has cup-shaped leaves), from Greek *kotulēdōn* 'cup-shaped cavity,' from *kotulē* 'cup.'

cou·cal /ˈko͞okal/ ▶ **n.** an ungainly long-tailed Old World bird that is a large ground-dwelling

member of the cuckoo family. ● Genus *Centropus* (and *Coua*), family Cuculidae: numerous species, including the Australasian **pheasant coucal** (*Centropus phasianinus*).
– ORIGIN early 19th cent.: from French, perhaps a blend of *coucou* 'cuckoo' and *alouette* 'lark.'

couch /kouCH/ ▶ n. a long upholstered piece of furniture for several people to sit on. ■ a reclining seat with a headrest at one end on which a psychoanalyst's subject or doctor's patient lies while undergoing treatment.
▶ v. [with obj.] **1** (usu. **be couched in**) express (something) in language of a specified style: *many false claims are couched in scientific jargon.*
2 [no obj.] literary lie down: *two creatures couched side by side in the deep grass.*
3 archaic lower (a spear) to the position for attack.
4 (usu. as noun **couching**) chiefly historical treat (a cataract) by pushing the lens of the eye downward and backward, out of line with the pupil.
5 (in embroidery) fix (a thread) to a fabric by stitching it down flat with another thread: *gold and silver threads couched by hand.*
– PHRASES **on the couch** undergoing psychoanalysis or psychiatric treatment.
– ORIGIN Middle English (as a noun denoting something to sleep on; as a verb in the sense 'lay something down'): from Old French *couche* (noun), *coucher* (verb), from Latin *collocare* 'place together' (see COLLOCATE).

couch·ant /'kouCHənt/ ▶ adj. [usu. postpositive] Heraldry (of an animal) lying with the body resting on the legs and the head raised: *two lions couchant.*
– ORIGIN late Middle English: French, 'lying,' present participle of *coucher* (see COUCH).

cou·chette /kōō'sHet/ ▶ n. a European railroad car with seats convertible into sleeping berths. ■ a berth in such a car.
– ORIGIN 1920s: French, literally 'little bed,' diminutive of *couche* 'a couch.'

couch grass /kouCH, kōōCH/ ▶ n. a coarse grass with long creeping roots, which can be troublesome in lawns and gardens. ● Genera *Elymus* and *Agropyron*, family Gramineae: several species, in particular the **common couch** (*A. repens*).
– ORIGIN late 16th cent.: variant of QUITCH.

couch po·ta·to /'kouCH/ ▶ n. informal a person who spends little or no time exercising and a great deal of time watching television.

cou·dé /kōō'dā/ ▶ adj. relating to or denoting a telescope in which the rays are bent to a focus at a fixed point off the axis.
▶ n. a telescope constructed in this way.
– ORIGIN late 19th cent.: French, literally 'bent at right angles,' past participle of *couder*, from *coude* 'elbow,' from Latin *cubitum*.

cou·gar /'kōōgər/ ▶ n. **1** a large American wild cat with a plain tawny to grayish coat, found from Canada to Patagonia. Also called MOUNTAIN LION, PUMA, PANTHER, PAINTER[2], or CATAMOUNT. ● *Felis concolor*, family Felidae.
2 informal an older woman seeking a sexual relationship with a younger man.
– ORIGIN late 18th cent.: from French *couguar*, abbreviation of modern Latin *cuguarcarana*, from Guarani *guaçuarana*.

cough /kôf/ ▶ v. [no obj.] expel air from the lungs with a sudden sharp sound. ■ (of an engine) make a sudden harsh noise, esp. as a sign of malfunction. ■ [with obj.] force (something, esp. blood) out of the lungs or throat by coughing: *he coughed up bloodstained fluid.* ■ [with obj.] (**cough something out**) say something in a harsh, abrupt way: *he coughed out his orders.*
▶ n. an act or sound of coughing: *she gave a discreet cough.* ■ a condition of the respiratory organs causing coughing: *he looked feverish and had a bad cough.*
– PHRASAL VERBS **cough something up** (or **cough up**) informal give something reluctantly, esp. money or information that is due or required.
– ORIGIN Middle English: of imitative origin; related to Dutch *kuchen* 'to cough' and German *keuchen* 'to pant.'

cough drop ▶ n. a medicated lozenge sucked to relieve a cough or sore throat.

cough syr·up ▶ n. liquid medicine taken either to suppress or expectorate a cough.

could /kŏŏd/ ▶ modal v. past of CAN[1]. ■ used to indicate possibility: *they could be right* | *I would go if I could afford it.* ■ used in making polite requests: *could I use the phone?* ■ used to indicate annoyance because of something that has not been done: *they could have told me!* ■ used to indicate a strong inclination to do something: *he irritates me so much that I could scream.*

could·n't /'kŏŏdnt/ ▶ contraction could not.

couldst /kŏŏdst/ (also **couldest** /'kŏŏdist/) ▶ v. archaic second person singular of COULD.

cou·lee /'kōōlē/ ▶ n. **1** a deep ravine.
2 a lava flow.
– ORIGIN early 19th cent.: from French *coulée* '(lava) flow,' from *couler* 'to flow,' from Latin *colare* 'to strain or flow,' from *colum* 'strainer.'

cou·li·biac /kōō'lēbyäk/ ▶ n. a Russian fish pie typically made with salmon or sturgeon, hard-boiled eggs, mushrooms, and herbs, in a puff pastry shell.
– ORIGIN from Russian *kulebyaka*.

cou·lis /'kōōlē/ ▶ n. (pl. **same**) a thin fruit or vegetable purée, used as a sauce.
– ORIGIN French, from *couler* 'to flow.'

cou·lisse /kōō'lēs/ ▶ n. a flat piece of scenery at the side of the stage in a theater. ■ (**the coulisses**) the spaces between these pieces of scenery; the wings.
– ORIGIN early 19th cent.: French, feminine of *coulis* 'sliding,' based on Latin *colare* 'to flow.'

cou·loir /kōōl'wär/ ▶ n. a steep, narrow gully on a mountainside.
– ORIGIN early 19th cent.: French, 'gully or corridor,' from *couler* 'to flow.'

cou·lomb /'kōō,läm, -,lōm/ (abbr.: **C**) ▶ n. Physics the SI unit of electric charge, equal to the quantity of electricity conveyed in one second by a current of one ampere.
– ORIGIN late 19th cent.: named after Charles-Augustin de *Coulomb* (1736–1806), French military engineer.

Cou·lomb's law Physics a law stating that like charges repel and opposite charges attract, with a force proportional to the product of the charges and inversely proportional to the square of the distance between them.
– ORIGIN late 18th cent.: named after C.-A. de *Coulomb* (see COULOMB).

coul·ter /'kōltər/ (also **colter**) ▶ n. a vertical cutting blade fixed in front of a plowshare. ■ the part of a seed drill that makes the furrow for the seed.

cou·ma·rin /'kōōmərən/ ▶ n. Chemistry a vanilla-scented compound found in many plants, formerly used for flavoring food. ● A bicyclic lactone; chem. formula: $C_9H_6O_2$. ■ any derivative of this.
– ORIGIN mid 19th cent.: from French *coumarine*, from *coumarou*, via Portuguese and Spanish from Tupi *cumarú* 'tonka bean.'

cou·ma·rone /'kōōmə,rōn/ ▶ n. Chemistry an organic compound present in coal tar, used to make thermoplastic resins chiefly for paints and varnishes. ● A bicyclic compound with fused benzene and furan rings; chem. formula: C_8H_6O.
– ORIGIN late 19th cent.: from COUMARIN + -ONE.

coun·cil /'kounsəl/ ▶ n. an advisory, deliberative, or legislative body of people formally constituted and meeting regularly: *an official human rights council.* ■ a body of people elected to manage the affairs of a city, county, or other municipal district. ■ an ecclesiastical assembly. ■ an assembly or meeting for consultation or advice: *that evening, she held a family council.*
– ORIGIN Old English (in the sense 'ecclesiastical assembly'): from Anglo-Norman French *cuncile*, from Latin *concilium* 'convocation, assembly,' from *con-* 'together' + *calare* 'summon.' Compare with COUNSEL.

Coun·cil Bluffs an industrial and commercial city in southwestern Iowa, on the Missouri River, opposite Omaha in Nebraska; pop. 59,536 (est. 2008).

Coun·cil for Mu·tu·al Ec·o·nom·ic As·sis·tance historical fuller form of COMECON.
– ORIGIN translating Russian *Sovet ékonomicheskoĭ vzaimopomoshchi*.

coun·cil·man /'kounsəlmən/ ▶ n. (pl. **councilmen**) a person, esp. a man, who is a member of a council, esp. a municipal one.

Coun·cil of Chal·ce·don, Coun·cil of Eu·rope, etc. see CHALCEDON, COUNCIL OF; EUROPE, COUNCIL OF, etc.

coun·cil of min·is·ters ▶ n. an administrative body that advises the chief executive or head of state. ■ (**Council of Ministers**) the policymaking body of the European Economic Community.

coun·cil of war ▶ n. a gathering of military officers in wartime. ■ a meeting held to plan a response to an emergency.

coun·ci·lor /'kouns(ə)lər/ (also chiefly Brit. **councillor**) ▶ n. a member of a council.
– DERIVATIVES **coun·ci·lor·ship** /-,SHip/ n.
– ORIGIN late Middle English: alteration of COUNSELOR, by association with COUNCIL.

USAGE On the difference between councilor and counselor, see usage at COUNSELOR.

coun·cil·wom·an /'kounsəl,wŏŏmən/ ▶ n. (pl. **councilwomen**) a woman who is a member of a council, esp. a municipal one.

coun·sel /'kounsəl/ ▶ n. **1** advice, esp. that given formally. ■ consultation, esp. to seek or give advice.
2 (pl. **same**) the lawyer or lawyers conducting a case: *the counsel for the defense.*
▶ v. (**counsels, counseling, counseled**; chiefly Brit. **counsels, counselling, counselled**) [with obj.] give advice to (someone): *he was counseled by his supporters to return to Germany.* ■ give professional psychological help and advice to (someone): *he was being counseled for depression.* ■ recommend (a course of action): *the athlete's coach counseled caution.*
– PHRASES **keep one's own counsel** say nothing about what one believes, knows, or plans: *she doubted what he said but kept her own counsel.* **take counsel** discuss a problem: *the party leader and chairman took counsel together.*
– ORIGIN Middle English: via Old French *counseil* (noun), *conseiller* (verb), from Latin *consilium* 'consultation, advice,' related to *consulere* (see CONSULT). Compare with COUNCIL.

coun·sel·ing /'kouns(ə)liNG/ (also chiefly Brit. **counselling**) ▶ n. the provision of assistance and guidance in resolving personal, social, or psychological problems and difficulties, esp. by a professional: *bereavement counseling.*

coun·se·lor /'kouns(ə)lər/ (also chiefly Brit. **counsellor**) ▶ n. **1** a person trained to give guidance on personal, social, or psychological problems: *a marriage counselor.* ■ [often with adj.] a person who gives advice on a specified subject: *a debt counselor.*
2 a person who supervises children at a camp.
3 a trial lawyer.
4 a senior officer in the diplomatic service.
– ORIGIN Middle English (in the general sense 'adviser'): from Old French *conseiller*, from Latin *consiliarius*, and Old French *conseillour*, from Latin *consiliator*, both from *consilium* 'consultation or advice.'

USAGE A **counselor** is someone who gives advice or counsel, especially an attorney. A **councilor** is a member of a council, such as a town or city council. Confusion arises because many *counselors* sit on councils, and *councilors* are often called on to give counsel.

count[1] /kount/ ▶ v. **1** [with obj.] determine the total number of (a collection of items): *I started to count the stars I could see* | *they **counted up** their change.* ■ [no obj.] recite numbers in ascending order, usually starting at the number one: *hold the position as you count to five.* ■ [no obj.] (**count down**) recite or display numbers backward to zero to indicate the time remaining before the launch of a rocket or the start of an operation: *the floor manager pointed at the camera and counted down.* ■ [no obj.] (**count down**) prepare for a significant event in the short time remaining before it: *with more orders expected, the company is **counting down to** a bumper Christmas.*
2 [with obj.] take into account; include: *the staff has shrunk to four, or five if you count the summer intern.* ■ (**count someone in**) include someone in an activity or the plans for it: *if the project gets started, count me in.* ■ consider (someone or something) to possess a specified quality or fulfill a specified role: *she met some rebuffs from people she had **counted as** her friends* | [with obj. and complement] *I count myself fortunate to have known him.* ■ [no obj.] be regarded as possessing a specified quality or fulfilling a specified role: *the rebate **counts as** taxable income.*
3 [no obj.] be significant: *it did not matter what the audience thought—it was the critics that counted.* ■ (of a factor) play a part in influencing opinion for or against someone or something: *he hopes his sportsmanlike attitude will **count in his favor**.* ■ (**count for**) be worth (a specified amount): *he has no power base and his views count for little.* ■ (**count toward**) be included in an assessment of (a final result or amount): *reduced rate contributions do not count toward your pension.* ■ (**count on/upon**) rely on: *whatever you're doing, you can count on me.*
▶ n. **1** an act of determining the total number of something: ***at the last count**, fifteen applications were still outstanding* | *the party's only candidate was eliminated at the first count.* ■ the total determined by such an action: *there was a moderate increase in the white cell count in both patients.*
2 an act of reciting numbers in ascending order, up to the specified number: *hold the position for five counts* | *hold it for a count of seven.* ■ Boxing an act of reciting numbers up to ten by the referee when a boxer is knocked down, the boxer being considered knocked out if still down when ten is reached. ■ Baseball the number of balls and strikes that have

been charged to the batter, as recalculated with each pitch: *the count on Gwynn is 1 ball and 2 strikes.* **3** a point for discussion or consideration: *the program remained vulnerable **on a number of counts**.* ■ Law a separate charge in an indictment: *he pleaded guilty to five counts of murder.* **4** the measure of the fineness of a yarn expressed as the weight of a given length or the length of a given weight. ■ a measure of the fineness of a woven fabric expressed as the number of warp or weft threads in a given length.
– PHRASES **beat the count** (of a boxer who has been knocked down) get up before the referee counts to ten. **count one's blessings** be grateful for what one has. **count the cost** calculate the consequences of something, typically a careless or foolish action. **count the days** (or **hours**) be impatient for time to pass: *they counted the days until they came home on leave.* **count (something) on the fingers of one hand** used to emphasize the small number of a particular thing: *I could count on the fingers of one hand the men I know who are desperate to experience fatherhood.* **count (one's) pennies** see PENNY. **count sheep** see SHEEP. **don't count your chickens before they're hatched** proverb don't be too confident in anticipating success or good fortune before it is certain: *I wouldn't count your chickens—I've agreed to sign the contract but that's all I've agreed to.* **down** (or Brit. **out**) **for the count** Boxing defeated by being knocked to the canvas and unable to rise within ten seconds. ■ unconscious or soundly asleep. **keep count** (or **a count**) take note of the number or amount of something: *you can protect yourself by keeping a count of what you drink.* **lose count** forget how many of something there are, esp. because the number is so high: *I've lost count of the hundreds of miles I've covered.* **take the count** Boxing be knocked out.
– PHRASAL VERBS **count someone out 1** complete a count of ten seconds over a fallen boxer to indicate defeat. **2** not include someone in an activity: *if this is a guessing game, you can count me out.* **3** (in children's games) select a player for dismissal or a special role by using a counting rhyme. **count something out** take items one by one from a stock of something, esp. money, keeping a note of how many one takes: *opening the wallet, I counted out 19 dollars.*
– ORIGIN Middle English (as a noun): from Old French *counte* (noun), *counter* (verb), from the verb *computare* 'calculate' (see COMPUTE).

count² ▶ n. a European nobleman whose rank corresponds to that of an English earl.
– DERIVATIVES **count·ship** /-,SHip/ n.
– ORIGIN late Middle English: from Old French *conte*, from Latin *comes, comit-* 'companion, overseer, attendant' (in late Latin 'person holding a state office'), from *com-* 'together with' + *it-* 'gone' (from the verb *ire* 'go').

count·a·ble /ˈkountəbəl/ ▶ adj. able to be counted.

count·down /ˈkount,doun/ ▶ n. [usu. in sing.] an act of counting numerals in reverse order to zero, esp. to time the last seconds before the launching of a rocket or missile: *the launch crews would begin their final countdown.* ■ (often **countdown to**) the final moments before a significant event and the procedures carried out during this time: *it is hard to imagine the countdown to war continuing without an intensification of diplomacy.* ■ a digital display that counts down.

coun·te·nance /ˈkountn-əns/ ▶ n. **1** a person's face or facial expression: *his impenetrable eyes and inscrutable countenance give little away.* **2** support: *she was giving her specific countenance to the occasion.*
▶ v. [with obj.] admit as acceptable or possible: *he was reluctant to countenance the use of force.*
– PHRASES **keep one's countenance** maintain one's composure, esp. by refraining from laughter. **keep someone in countenance** help someone to remain calm and confident: *to keep herself in countenance she opened her notebook.* **out of countenance** disconcerted or unpleasantly surprised: *I put him clean out of countenance just by looking at him.*
– ORIGIN Middle English: from Old French *contenance* 'bearing, behavior,' from *contenir* (see CONTAIN). The early sense was 'bearing, demeanor,' also 'facial expression,' hence 'the face.'

coun·ter¹ /ˈkountər/ ▶ n. **1** a long flat-topped fixture in a store or bank across which business is conducted with customers. ■ a similar structure used for serving food and drinks in a cafeteria or bar. ■ a countertop. **2** an apparatus used for counting: *the counter tells you how many pictures you have taken.* ■ a person who counts something, for example votes in an election. ■ Physics an apparatus used for counting individual ionizing particles or events. **3** a small disk used as a place marker or for keeping the score in board games. ■ a token representing a coin.
– PHRASES **behind the counter** serving in a store or bank: *ask the young man behind the counter.* **over the counter** by ordinary retail purchase, with no need for a prescription or license: [as adj.] *over-the-counter medicines.* ■ (of share transactions) taking place outside the stock exchange system. **under the counter** (or **table**) (with reference to goods bought or sold) surreptitiously and typically illegally: *certain labs have been peddling this drug under the counter* | [as adj.] *an under-the-counter deal.*
– ORIGIN Middle English (sense 3): from Old French *conteor*, from medieval Latin *computatorium*, from Latin *computare* (see COMPUTE).

coun·ter² ▶ v. [with obj.] speak or act in opposition to: *the second argument is more difficult to counter.* ■ [no obj.] respond to hostile speech or action: *"What would you like me to do about it?" she countered.* ■ [no obj.] Boxing give a return blow while parrying: *he countered with a left hook.*
▶ adv. (**counter to**) in the opposite direction to or in conflict with: *some actions by the authorities **ran counter to** the call for leniency.*
▶ adj. responding to something of the same kind, esp. in opposition. See also COUNTER-.
▶ n. **1** [usu. in sing.] a thing that opposes or prevents something else: *the stimulus to employers' organization was partly **a counter to** growing union power.* ■ an answer to an argument or criticism: *he anticipates an objection and plans his counter.* ■ Boxing a blow given while parrying; a counterpunch. **2** the curved part of the stern of a ship projecting aft above the waterline. **3** Printing the white space enclosed by a letter such as *O* or *c*.
– ORIGIN late Middle English: from Old French *contre*, from Latin *contra* 'against,' or directly from COUNTER-.

coun·ter³ ▶ n. the back part of a shoe or boot, enclosing the heel.
– ORIGIN mid 19th cent.: abbreviation of *counterfort* 'buttress,' from French *contrefort*.

coun·ter- ▶ prefix denoting opposition, retaliation, or rivalry: *counterattack* | *counterespionage.* ■ denoting movement or effect in the opposite direction: *counterbalance* | *counterpoise.* ■ denoting correspondence, duplication, or substitution: *counterpart* | *counterpoint.*
– ORIGIN from Anglo-Norman French *countre-*, Old French *contre*, from Latin *contra* 'against.'

coun·ter·act /ˌkountərˈakt/ ▶ v. [with obj.] act against (something) in order to reduce its force or neutralize it: *should we deliberately intervene in the climate system to counteract global warming?*
– DERIVATIVES **coun·ter·ac·tion** /ˌkountərˈakSHən/ n., **coun·ter·ac·tive** /ˌkountərˈaktiv/ adj.

coun·ter·ar·gu·ment /ˈkountərˌärgyəmənt/ ▶ n. an argument or set of reasons put forward to oppose an idea or theory developed in another argument: *the obvious counterargument to that dire prediction is that the recession has depressed earnings.*

coun·ter·at·tack /ˈkountərə,tak/ ▶ n. an attack made in response to one by an enemy or opponent.
▶ v. [no obj.] attack in response: *as deputies tried to dislodge him, he counterattacked by forcing through elections.*
– DERIVATIVES **coun·ter·at·tack·er** n.

coun·ter·bal·ance ▶ n. /ˈkountər,baləns/ a weight that balances another weight. ■ a factor having the opposite effect to that of another and so preventing it from exercising a disproportionate influence: *his restoration to power was intended as **a counterbalance to** his rival's influence.*
▶ v. /ˌkountərˈbaləns/ [with obj.] (of a weight) balance (another weight). ■ neutralize or cancel by exerting an opposite influence: *the extra cost of mail order may be counterbalanced by its convenience.*

coun·ter·blow /ˈkountər,blō/ ▶ n. a blow given in return.

coun·ter·bore /ˈkountər,bôr/ ▶ n. a drilled hole that has a flat-bottomed enlargement at its mouth. ■ a drill whose bit has a uniform smaller diameter near the tip, for drilling counterbores in one operation.
▶ v. [with obj.] drill a counterbore in (an object).

coun·ter·change /ˈkountər,CHānj/ ▶ v. [with obj.] **1** change (places or parts); interchange. **2** literary checker with contrasting colors. ■ Heraldry interchange the tinctures of (a charge) with that of a divided field.
▶ n. change that is equivalent in degree but opposite in effect to a previous change.
– ORIGIN late Middle English (as a heraldic term): from French *contrechanger*, from *contre* (expressing substitution) + *changer* 'to change.'

coun·ter·charge /ˈkountər,CHärj/ ▶ n. an accusation made in turn by someone against their accuser: *charges and countercharges concerning producers, quotas, and affidavits.* ■ a charge by police or an armed force in response to one made against them.

count·er·check /ˈkountər,CHek/ ▶ n. **1** a second check for security or accuracy. **2** archaic a restraint.
▶ v. [with obj.] archaic stop (something) by acting to cancel or counteract it: *the king with his own hand wrote to countercheck his former decree.*

coun·ter·claim /ˈkountər,klām/ ▶ n. a claim made to rebut a previous claim. ■ Law a claim made by a defendant against the plaintiff.
▶ v. [no obj.] chiefly Law make a counterclaim for something.

coun·ter·clock·wise /ˌkountərˈkläk,wīz/ ▶ adv. & adj. in the opposite direction to the way in which the hands of a clock move around.

coun·ter·con·di·tion·ing /ˌkountərkənˈdiSH(ə)niNG/ ▶ n. a technique employed in animal training, and in the treatment of phobias and similar conditions in humans, in which behavior incompatible with a habitual undesirable pattern is induced. Compare with DECONDITION (sense 2).

coun·ter·cul·ture /ˈkountər,kəlCHər/ ▶ n. a way of life and set of attitudes opposed to or at variance with the prevailing social norm: *the idealists of the 60s counterculture.*

coun·ter·cur·rent ▶ n. /ˈkountər,kərənt/ a current flowing in an opposite direction to another.
▶ adv. /ˌkountərˈkərənt/ in or with opposite directions of flow.

coun·ter·dem·on·stra·tion /ˈkountər,demənˈstrāSHən/ ▶ n. a public demonstration organized in order to express opposition to the aims of another demonstration: *an effort by right-wing elements to organize a counterdemonstration failed.*

coun·ter·es·pi·o·nage /ˌkountərˈespēə,näZH, -,näj/ ▶ n. activities designed to prevent or thwart spying by an enemy.

coun·ter·fac·tu·al /ˌkountərˈfakCHōōəl/ Philosophy ▶ adj. relating to or expressing what has not happened or is not the case.
▶ n. a counterfactual conditional statement (e.g., *If kangaroos had no tails, they would topple over*).

coun·ter·feit /ˈkountər,fit/ ▶ adj. made in exact imitation of something valuable or important with the intention to deceive or defraud: *two men were remanded on bail on a charge of passing counterfeit $10 bills.* ■ pretended; sham: *a counterfeit image of reality.*
▶ n. a fraudulent imitation of something else; a forgery: *he knew the tapes to be counterfeits.*
▶ v. [with obj.] imitate fraudulently: *my signature is extremely hard to counterfeit.* ■ pretend to feel or possess (an emotion or quality): *no pretense could have counterfeited such terror.* ■ literary resemble closely: *sleep counterfeited Death so well.*
– DERIVATIVES **coun·ter·feit·er** n.
– ORIGIN Middle English (as a verb): from Anglo-Norman French *countrefeter*, from Old French *contrefait*, past participle of *contrefaire*, from Latin *contra-* 'in opposition' + *facere* 'make.'

coun·ter·foil /ˈkountər,foil/ ▶ n. chiefly Brit. the part of a check, receipt, ticket, or other document that is torn off and kept as a record by the person issuing it.

coun·ter·in·sur·gen·cy /ˌkountərinˈsərjənsē/ ▶ n. [usu. as modifier] military or political action taken against the activities of guerrillas or revolutionaries: *a counterinsurgency force.*

coun·ter·in·tel·li·gence /ˌkountərinˈteləjəns/ ▶ n. activities designed to prevent or thwart spying, intelligence gathering, and sabotage by an enemy or other foreign entity.

coun·ter·in·tu·i·tive /ˌkountərinˈt(y)ōōitiv/ ▶ adj. contrary to intuition or to common-sense expectation (but often nevertheless true).
– DERIVATIVES **coun·ter·in·tu·i·tive·ly** adv.

coun·ter·ir·ri·tant /ˌkountərˈiritənt/ ▶ n. something such as heat or an ointment that is used to produce surface irritation of the skin, thereby counteracting underlying pain or discomfort.
– DERIVATIVES **coun·ter·ir·ri·ta·tion** /-,iriˈtāSHən/ n.

coun·ter·mand /ˌkountərˈmand, ˈkountər,mand/ ▶ v. [with obj.] revoke (an order): *an order to arrest the strike leaders had been countermanded.* ■ revoke an order issued by (another person): *he was already countermanding her.* ■ declare (a vote or election) invalid.
▶ n. an order revoking a previous one.

PRONUNCIATION KEY ə ago, up; ər over, fur; a hat; ā ate; ä car; e let; ē see; i fit; ī by; NG sing; ō go; ô law, for; oi toy; ōō good; ōō goo; ou out; TH thin; TH then; ZH vision

C

– ORIGIN late Middle English: from Old French *contremander* (verb), *contremand* (noun), from medieval Latin *contramandare*, from *contra-* 'against' + *mandare* 'to order.'

coun·ter·march /ˈkountərˌmärCH/ ▶ **v.** [no obj.] march in the opposite direction or back along the same route.
▶ **n.** an act or instance of marching in this way.

coun·ter·mark /ˈkountərˌmärk/ ▶ **n.** chiefly Brit. an additional mark placed on something already marked, typically for increased security. ■ a second watermark.

coun·ter·meas·ure /ˈkountərˌmeZHər/ ▶ **n.** an action taken to counteract a danger or threat.

coun·ter·mel·o·dy /ˈkountərˌmelədē/ ▶ **n.** (pl. **countermelodies**) a subordinate melody accompanying a principal one.

coun·ter·mine /ˈkountərˌmīn/ Military ▶ **n.** an excavation dug to intercept another dug by an enemy.
▶ **v.** [with obj.] dig a countermine against.

coun·ter·move /ˈkountərˌmo͞ov/ ▶ **n.** a move or other action made in opposition to another.
– DERIVATIVES **coun·ter·move·ment n.**

coun·ter·nar·cot·ics /ˈkountərˌnärˈkätiks/ ▶ **n.** measures or activities designed to prevent the use or distrubution of iillegal narcotic drugs.

coun·ter·of·fen·sive /ˈkountərəˌfensiv/ ▶ **n.** an attack made in response to one from an enemy, typically on a large scale or for a prolonged period.

coun·ter·of·fer /ˈkountərˌôfər, -ˌäfər/ ▶ **n.** an offer made in response to another.

coun·ter·pane /ˈkountərˌpān/ ▶ **n.** dated a bedspread.
– ORIGIN early 17th cent.: alteration of **COUNTERPOINT**, from Old French *contrepointe*, based on medieval Latin *culcitra puncta* 'quilted mattress' (*puncta*, literally meaning 'pricked,' from the verb *pungere*). The change in the ending was due to association with **PANE** in an obsolete sense 'cloth.'

coun·ter·part /ˈkountərˌpärt/ ▶ **n. 1** a person or thing holding a position or performing a function that corresponds to that of another person or thing in another place: *the minister held talks with his French counterpart.*
2 Law one of two or more copies of a legal document.

coun·ter·plot /ˈkountərˌplät/ ▶ **n.** a plot intended to thwart another plot.
▶ **v.** (**counterplots, counterplotting, counterplotted**) [no obj.] devise a counterplot.

coun·ter·point /ˈkountərˌpoint/ ▶ **n. 1** Music the art or technique of setting, writing, or playing a melody or melodies in conjunction with another, according to fixed rules. ■ a melody played in conjunction with another.
2 an argument, idea, or theme used to create a contrast with the main element: *I have used my interviews with parents as a counterpoint to a professional judgment.*
▶ **v.** [with obj.] **1** Music add counterpoint to (a melody): *the orchestra counterpoints the vocal part.*
2 emphasize by contrast: *the cream walls and maple floors are counterpointed by black accents.* ■ compensate for: *the story's fanciful excesses are counterpointed with some sharp and unsentimental dialogue.*
– ORIGIN late Middle English: from Old French *contrepoint*, from medieval Latin *contrapunctum* '(song) pricked or marked over against (the original melody),' from *contra-* 'against' + *punctum*, from *pungere* 'to prick.'

coun·ter·poise /ˈkountərˌpoiz/ ▶ **n.** a factor, force, or influence that balances or neutralizes another: *they see the power of Brussels as* ***a counterpoise to*** *that of London.* ■ a counterbalancing weight. ■ a state of equilibrium.
▶ **v.** [with obj.] have an opposing and balancing effect on: *excess on one hand is counterpoised by fundamental lack on the other.* ■ bring into contrast: *the stories counterpoise a young recruit with an old-timer.*
– ORIGIN late Middle English: from Old French *contrepois*, from *contre* 'against' + *pois* from Latin *pensum* 'weight.' Compare with **POISE**[1]. The verb, originally *counterpeise*, from Old French *contrepeser*, was altered under the influence of the noun in the 16th cent.

coun·ter·pose /ˌkountərˈpōz/ ▶ **v.** [with obj.] set against or in opposition to.
– DERIVATIVES **coun·ter·po·si·tion** /-pəˈziSHən/ **n.**

coun·ter·pro·duc·tive /ˌkountərprəˈdəktiv/ ▶ **adj.** having the opposite of the desired effect: *the response to the disaster was unsuccessful and perhaps even counterproductive.*

coun·ter·pro·lif·er·a·tion /kountərprəˌlifəˈrāSHən/ ▶ **n.** action intended to prevent an increase or spread in the possession of nuclear weapons.

coun·ter·pro·pos·al /ˈkountərprəˈpōzəl/ ▶ **n.** an alternative proposal made in response to a previous proposal that is regarded as unacceptable or unsatisfactory: *the union rejected the airline's counterproposal.*

coun·ter·punch /ˈkountərˌpənCH/ Boxing ▶ **n.** a punch thrown in return for one received.
▶ **v.** [no obj.] throw a counterpunch.
– DERIVATIVES **coun·ter·punch·er n.**

Coun·ter-Ref·or·ma·tion the reform of the Church of Rome in the 16th and 17th centuries that was stimulated by the Protestant Reformation.

> Measures to oppose the spread of the Reformation were decided on at the Council of Trent (1545–63), and the Jesuit order became the spearhead of the Counter-Reformation, both within Europe and abroad. Although most of northern Europe remained Protestant, southern Germany and Poland were brought back to the Roman Catholic Church.

coun·ter·rev·o·lu·tion /ˌkountərˌrevəˈlo͞oSHən/ ▶ **n.** a revolution opposing a former one or reversing its results.
– DERIVATIVES **coun·ter·rev·o·lu·tion·ar·y** /-ˌnerē/ **adj. & n.**

coun·ter·ro·tate /ˌkountərˈrōˌtāt/ ▶ **v.** [no obj.] rotate in opposite directions, esp. about the same axis.
– DERIVATIVES **coun·ter·ro·ta·tion** /-rōˈtāSHən/ **n.**

coun·ter·scarp /ˈkountərˌskärp/ ▶ **n.** the outer wall of a ditch in a fortification. Compare with **SCARP**.
– ORIGIN late 16th cent.: from French *contrescarpe*, from Italian *controscarpa*; compare with **SCARP**.

coun·ter·shad·ing /ˈkountərˌSHādiNG/ ▶ **n.** Zoology protective coloration of some animals in which parts normally in shadow are light and those exposed to the sky are dark.
– DERIVATIVES **coun·ter·shad·ed** /-ˌSHādid/ **adj.**

coun·ter·shaft /ˈkountərˌSHaft/ ▶ **n.** a machine driveshaft that transmits motion from the main shaft to where it is required, such as the drive axle in a vehicle.

coun·ter·sign /ˈkountərˌsīn/ ▶ **v.** [with obj.] add a signature to (a document already signed by another person): *each check had to be signed and countersigned.*
▶ **n.** archaic a signal or password given in reply to a soldier on guard.
– DERIVATIVES **coun·ter·sig·na·ture** /ˌkountərˈsignəCHər, -ˌCHo͝or/ **n.**
– ORIGIN late 16th cent. (as a noun): from French *contresigner* (verb), *contresigne* (noun), from Italian *contrassegno*, based on Latin *signum* 'sign.'

coun·ter·sink /ˈkountərˌsiNGk/ ▶ **v.** (past and past participle **countersunk** /-ˌsəNGk/) [with obj.] enlarge and bevel the rim of (a drilled hole) so that a screw, nail, or bolt can be inserted flush with the surface. ■ drive (a screw, nail, or bolt) into such a hole.

coun·ter·spy /ˈkountərˌspī/ ▶ **n.** (pl. **counterspies**) a spy engaged in counterespionage.

coun·ter·stain /ˈkountərˌstān/ Biology ▶ **n.** an additional dye used in a microscopy specimen to produce a contrasting background or to make clearer the distinction between different kinds of tissue.
▶ **v.** [with obj.] treat (a specimen) with a counterstain.

coun·ter·sto·ry /ˈkountərˌstôrē/ ▶ **n.** an alternative or opposing narrative or explanation.

coun·ter·sub·ject /ˈkountərˌsəbjikt, -ˌjekt/ ▶ **n.** Music a second or subsidiary subject, esp. accompanying the subject or its answer in a fugue.

coun·ter·ten·or /ˈkountərˌtenər/ ▶ **n.** Music the highest male adult singing voice (sometimes distinguished from the male alto voice by its strong, pure tone). ■ a singer with such a voice.
– ORIGIN late Middle English: from French *contreteneur*, from obsolete Italian *contratenore*, based on Latin *tenor* (see **TENOR**[1]). Compare with **CONTRALTO**.

coun·ter·ter·ror·ism /ˌkountərˈterəˌrizəm/ ▶ **n.** political or military activities designed to prevent or thwart terrorism.
– DERIVATIVES **coun·ter·ter·ror·ist** /ˌkountərˈterərist/ **n. & adj.**

coun·ter·top /ˈkountərˌtäp/ ▶ **n.** a flat surface for working on, esp. in a kitchen.

coun·ter·trade /ˈkountərˌtrād/ ▶ **n.** international trade by exchange of goods rather than by currency purchase.

coun·ter·trans·fer·ence /ˌkountərˌtransˈfərəns, -ˌtranz-/ ▶ **n.** Psychoanalysis the emotional reaction of the analyst to the subject's contribution. Compare with **TRANSFERENCE**.

coun·ter·vail /ˌkountərˈvāl/ ▶ **v.** [with obj.] (usu. as adj. **countervailing**) offset the effect of (something) by countering it with something of equal force: *the dominance of the party was mediated by a number of countervailing factors.*
– ORIGIN late Middle English (in the sense 'be equivalent to in value, compensate for'): from Anglo-Norman French *contrevaloir*, from Latin *contra valere* 'be of worth against.'

coun·ter·vail·ing du·ty ▶ **n.** an import tax imposed on certain goods in order to prevent dumping or counter export subsidies.

coun·ter·weight /ˈkountərˌwāt/ ▶ **n.** another term for **COUNTERBALANCE**.

count·ess /ˈkountəs/ ▶ **n.** the wife or widow of a count or earl. ■ a woman holding the rank of count or earl in her own right.
– ORIGIN Middle English: from Old French *contesse*, from late Latin *comitissa*, feminine of *comes* (see **COUNT**[2]).

coun·ti·an /ˈkountēən/ ▶ **n.** an inhabitant of a particular county: *a Sussex Countian.*

count·ing /ˈkountiNG/ ▶ **prep.** taking account of when reaching a total; including: *there were three of us in the family, or four counting my pet rabbit* | *the college had 139 employees,* ***not counting*** *those engaged in routine clerical work.*

count·ing·house /ˈkountiNGˌhous/ ▶ **n.** historical an office or building in which the accounts and money of a person or company were kept.

count·less /ˈkountləs/ ▶ **adj.** too many to be counted; very many: *she'd apologized countless times before.*

count noun ▶ **n.** Grammar a noun that can form a plural and, in the singular, can be used with the indefinite article (e.g., *books, a book*). Contrasted with **MASS NOUN**.

count pal·a·tine ▶ **n.** (pl. **counts palatine**) historical a feudal lord having royal authority within a region of a kingdom. ■ a high official of the Holy Roman Empire with royal authority within his domain.
– ORIGIN see **PALATINE**[1].

coun·tri·fied /ˈkəntriˌfīd/ (also **countryfied**) ▶ **adj.** reminiscent or characteristic of the country, esp. in being unsophisticated: *a countrified cottage garden* | *her tweeds were far too countrified.*
– ORIGIN mid 17th cent.: past participle of *countrify* 'make rural.'

coun·try /ˈkəntrē/ ▶ **n.** (pl. **countries**) **1** a nation with its own government, occupying a particular territory: *the country's increasingly precarious economic position.* ■ (**the country**) the people of a nation: *the whole country took to the streets.*
2 (often **the country**) districts and small settlements outside large towns, cities, or the capital: *the airfield is right out in the country* | [as modifier] *a country lane.*
3 an area or region with regard to its physical features: *a tract of wild country.* ■ a region associated with a particular person, esp. a writer, or with a particular work: *Steinbeck country includes the Monterey Peninsula.*
4 short for **COUNTRY MUSIC**.
– PHRASES **across country** not keeping to roads: *their route was across country, through fields of corn.*
– ORIGIN Middle English: from Old French *cuntree*, from medieval Latin *contrata* (*terra*) '(land) lying opposite,' from Latin *contra* 'against, opposite.'

coun·try and west·ern ▶ **n.** another term for **COUNTRY MUSIC**: [as modifier] *country-and-western singer.*

coun·try blues ▶ **n.** a simple form of blues in which the singer is accompanied by an acoustic guitar.

coun·try club ▶ **n.** a club with sporting and social facilities, set in a suburban area.

coun·try cous·in ▶ **n.** a person with an unsophisticated and provincial appearance or manners.

coun·try dance ▶ **n.** a traditional type of social English dance, in particular one performed by couples facing each other in long lines.

coun·try·fied ▶ **adj.** variant spelling of **COUNTRIFIED**.

coun·try-fried ▶ **adj.** (of an item of food) covered in batter, flour, or breadcrumbs and fried: *country-fried steak.* ■ informal rural or unsophisticated: *country-fried tunes.*

coun·try gen·tle·man ▶ **n.** chiefly Brit. a rich man of good social standing who owns and lives on an estate in a rural area.

coun·try ham ▶ **n.** a ham that is dry-cured with salt before smoking.

coun·try house ▶ **n.** chiefly Brit. a large house in the country, typically the home of a wealthy or aristocratic family.

coun·try·man /ˈkəntrēmən/ ▶ **n.** (pl. **countrymen**) **1** Brit. a person living or born in a rural area, esp. one engaged in a typically rural occupation.

2 a person from the same country or region as someone else: *she followed in the tradition of her countrymen | they trust a fellow countryman.*

coun·try mile ▶ **n.** informal a very long way: *he hit the ball a country mile.*

coun·try mu·sic ▶ **n.** a form of popular music originating in the rural southern US. It is traditionally a mixture of ballads and dance tunes played characteristically on fiddle, guitar, steel guitar, drums, and keyboard. Also called COUNTRY AND WESTERN.

coun·try·pol·i·tan /ˌkəntriˈpälitn/ ▶ **n.** a type of country music that resembles pop music, usually characterized by orchestrated arrangements: [usu. as modifier] *a slick countrypolitan ballad.*
▶ **adj.** relating to or denoting an architectural style that combines country charm with sophistication.
– ORIGIN on the pattern of *cosmopolitan.*

coun·try rock[1] ▶ **n.** Geology the rock that encloses a mineral deposit, igneous intrusion, or other feature.

coun·try rock[2] ▶ **n.** a type of popular music that is a blend of rock and country music.

coun·try seat ▶ **n.** Brit. a large country house and estate belonging to an aristocratic family.

coun·try·side /ˈkəntrēˌsīd/ ▶ **n.** the land and scenery of a rural area: *they explored the surrounding countryside.* ■ the inhabitants of such an area: *the political influence of the countryside remains strong.*

coun·try·wide /ˈkəntrēˈwīd/ ▶ **adj. & adv.** extending throughout a nation: [as adj.] *a countrywide tour* | [as adv.] *traveling countrywide.*

coun·try·wom·an /ˈkəntrēˌwo͝omən/ ▶ **n.** (pl. **countrywomen**) **1** a woman living or born in a rural area, esp. one engaged in a typically rural occupation.
2 a woman from the same country or district as someone else: *a fellow countrywoman from Ohio.*

coun·ty /ˈkountē/ ▶ **n.** (pl. **counties**) (in the US) a political and administrative division of a state, providing certain local governmental services. ■ a territorial division of some countries, forming the chief unit of local administration.
– DERIVATIVES **coun·ty·wide adj. & adv.**
– ORIGIN Middle English: from Old French *conte,* from Latin *comitatus,* from *comes, comit-* (see COUNT[2]). The word seems earliest to have denoted a meeting held periodically to transact the business of a shire.

coun·ty bor·ough ▶ **n.** (in England, Wales, and Northern Ireland) a large town formerly having the administrative status of a county.

coun·ty clerk ▶ **n.** (in the US) an elected county official who is responsible for local elections and maintaining public records.

coun·ty court ▶ **n.** a court in some states with civil and criminal jurisdiction for a given county.

coun·ty crick·et ▶ **n.** first-class cricket played in the UK between the eighteen professional teams contesting the County Championship.

Coun·ty Pal·a·tine historical (in England and Ireland) a county in which royal privileges and exclusive rights of jurisdiction were held by its earl or lord.
– ORIGIN see PALATINE[1].

coun·ty seat ▶ **n.** the town that is the governmental center of a county.

coup /ko͞o/ ▶ **n.** (pl. **coups** /ko͞oz/) **1** (also **coup d'état**) a sudden, violent, and illegal seizure of power from a government: *he was overthrown in an army coup.*
2 a notable or successful stroke or move: *it was a major coup to get such a prestigious contract.* ■ an unusual or unexpected but successful tactic in card play.
3 a contusion caused by contact of the brain with the skull at the point of trauma. Compare with CONTRECOUP.
4 historical (among North American Indians) an act of touching an armed enemy in battle as a deed of bravery, or an act of first touching an item of the enemy's in order to claim it.
– ORIGIN late 18th cent.: from French, from medieval Latin *colpus* 'blow' (see COPE[1]).

coup de fou·dre /ˌko͞o də ˈfo͞od(rə)/ ▶ **n.** (pl. **coups de foudre** pronunc. **same**) a sudden unforeseen event, in particular an instance of love at first sight.
– ORIGIN late 18th cent.: French, literally 'stroke of lightning.'

coup de grâce /ˌko͞o də ˈgräs/ ▶ **n.** (pl. **coups de grâce** pronunc. **same**) a final blow or shot given to kill a wounded person or animal: *he administered the coup de grâce with a knife.* ■ an action or event that serves as the culmination of a bad or deteriorating situation: *the epidemic has been the coup de grâce for the airline crisis.*
– ORIGIN late 17th cent.: French, literally 'stroke of grace.'

coup de main /ˌko͞o də ˈmaN/ ▶ **n.** (pl. **coups de main** pronunc. **same**) a sudden surprise attack, esp. one made by an army during war.
– ORIGIN mid 18th cent.: French, literally 'stroke of hand.'

coup de maî·tre /ˌko͞o də ˈmet(rə)/ ▶ **n.** (pl. **coups de maître** pronunc. **same**) a master stroke.
– ORIGIN French.

coup d'é·tat /ˌko͞o dāˈtä/ ▶ **n.** (pl. **coups d'état** /ˌko͞o dā ˈtä(z)/) another term for COUP (sense 1).
– ORIGIN mid 17th cent.: French, literally 'blow of state.'

coup de thé·â·tre /ˌko͞o də tāˈät(rə)/ ▶ **n.** (pl. **coups de théâtre** pronunc. **same**) a sensational or dramatically sudden action or turn of events, esp. in a play.
– ORIGIN mid 18th cent.: French, literally 'blow of theater.'

coup d'œil /ˌko͞o ˈdœē/ ▶ **n.** (pl. **coups d'œil** pronunc. **same**) a glance that takes in a comprehensive view.
– ORIGIN mid 18th cent.: French, literally 'stroke of eye.'

coupe[1] /ko͞op/ (also **coupé** /ko͞oˈpā/) ▶ **n. 1** a car with a fixed roof and two doors.
2 historical a four-wheeled enclosed carriage for two passengers and a driver.
3 historical an end compartment in a railroad car, with seats on only one side.
– ORIGIN mid 19th cent. (sense 2): from French *carrosse coupé,* literally 'cut carriage.' Sense 1 dates from the early 20th cent.

coupe[2] ▶ **n.** a shallow glass or glass dish, typically with a stem, in which desserts or champagne are served. ■ a dessert served in such a dish.
– ORIGIN late 19th cent.: French, literally 'goblet.'

cou·ple /ˈkəpəl/ ▶ **n. 1** two individuals of the same sort considered together: *a couple of girls were playing marbles.* ■ informal an indefinite small number: *he hoped she'd be better in a couple of days* | [as pronoun] *we got some eggs—would you like a couple?* | [as modifier] *just a couple more questions* | *clean the stains with a couple squirts of dishwashing liquid.*
2 [treated as sing. or pl.] two people who are married, engaged, or otherwise closely associated romantically or sexually. ■ a pair of partners in a dance or game. ■ Mechanics a pair of equal and parallel forces acting in opposite directions, and tending to cause rotation about an axis perpendicular to the plane containing them.
▶ **v.** [with obj.] (often **be coupled to/with**) combine: *a sense of hope is coupled with a palpable sense of loss.* ■ connect (a railroad vehicle or a piece of equipment) to another: *a cable is coupled up to one of the wheels.* ■ [no obj.] (**couple up**) join to form a pair. ■ [no obj.] dated have sexual intercourse. ■ connect (two electrical components) using electromagnetic induction, electrostatic charge, or an optical link: (as adj. **coupled**) *networks of coupled oscillators.*
– DERIVATIVES **cou·ple·dom** /-dəm/ **n.**
– ORIGIN Middle English: from Old French *cople* (noun), *copler* (verb), from Latin *copula* (noun), *copulare* (verb), from *co-* 'together' + *apere* 'fasten.' Compare with COPULA and COPULATE.

cou·pler /ˈkəp(ə)lər/ ▶ **n.** something that connects two things, esp. mechanical components or systems: *a hydraulic coupler* | [as modifier] *coupler rod.* ■ Music a device in an organ for connecting two manuals, or a manual with pedals, so that they both sound when only one is played. ■ Music (also **octave coupler**) a similar device for connecting notes with their octaves above or below. ■ Photography a compound in a developer or an emulsion that combines with the products of development to form an insoluble dye, part of the image. ■ (also **acoustic coupler**) a modem that converts digital signals from a computer into audible sound signals and vice versa, so that the former can be transmitted and received over telephone lines.

cou·plet /ˈkəplət/ ▶ **n.** two lines of verse, usually in the same meter and joined by rhyme, that form a unit.
– ORIGIN late 16th cent.: from French, diminutive of *couple,* from Old French *cople* (see COUPLE).

cou·pling /ˈkəp(ə)liNG/ ▶ **n. 1** a device for connecting parts of machinery. ■ a fitting on the end of a railroad vehicle for connecting it to another.
2 the pairing of two items: *the coupling of coaching and personal training* | *this coupling of two of the greatest works of Haydn.* ■ sexual intercourse. ■ an interaction between two electrical components by electromagnetic induction, electrostatic charge, or optical link.

coupling 1

cou·pling con·stant ▶ **n.** Physics a measure of the strength of interaction between two particles, or between a particle and a field.

cou·pon /ˈk(y)o͞oˌpän/ ▶ **n. 1** a voucher entitling the holder to a discount for a particular product. ■ a detachable portion of a bond that is given up in return for a payment of interest.
2 a form in a newspaper or magazine that may be filled in and sent as an application for a purchase or information.
– ORIGIN early 19th cent. (denoting a detachable portion of a bond to be given up in return for payment of interest): from French, literally 'piece cut off,' from *couper* 'cut,' from Old French *colper* (see COPE[1]).

cou·pon bond ▶ **n.** an investment bond on which interest is paid by presenting coupons.

cou·pon clip·per ▶ **n.** informal a person with a large number of coupon bonds.

coup stick /ko͞o/ ▶ **n.** (among North American Indians) a decorated stick recording coups attained by the warrior.

cour·age /ˈkərij, ˈkə-rij/ ▶ **n.** the ability to do something that frightens one: *she called on all her courage to face the ordeal.* ■ strength in the face of pain or grief: *he fought his illness with great courage.*
– PHRASES **have the courage of one's convictions** act on one's beliefs despite danger or disapproval. **pluck up** (or **screw up** or **take**) **courage** make an effort to do something that frightens one. **take one's courage in both hands** nerve oneself to do something that frightens one.
– ORIGIN Middle English (denoting the heart, as the seat of feelings): from Old French *corage,* from Latin *cor* 'heart.'

cou·ra·geous /kəˈrājəs/ ▶ **adj.** not deterred by danger or pain; brave: *her courageous human rights work.*
– DERIVATIVES **cou·ra·geous·ly adv., cou·ra·geous·ness n.**
– ORIGIN Middle English: from Old French *corageus,* from *corage* (see COURAGE).

cou·rant /ˈko͞orənt, ko͞oˈrant, ko͞oˈränt/ ▶ **adj.** [usu. postpositive] Heraldry represented as running: *white horse courant.*
– ORIGIN early 17th cent.: French, 'running,' present participle of *courir.*

cou·rante /ko͞oˈränt, -ˈrant/ ▶ **n.** a 16th-century court dance consisting of short advances and retreats. ■ a piece of music written for or in the style of such a dance, typically one forming a movement of a suite.
– ORIGIN late 16th cent.: French, literally 'running,' feminine present participle of *courir.*

Cour·bet /ko͝orˈbā/, Gustave (1819–77), French painter. A leader of the 19th-century realist school of painting, his works include *Burial at Ornans* (1850) and *Painter in His Studio* (1855).

cou·reur de bois /ko͞oˌrər də ˈbwä/ ▶ **n.** (pl. **coureurs de bois** pronunc. **same**) historical (in Canada and the northern US) a woodsman or trader of French origin.
– ORIGIN early 18th cent.: French, literally 'wood runner.'

cour·gette /ˌko͝orˈZHet/ ▶ **n.** Brit. a zucchini.
– ORIGIN 1930s: from French, diminutive of *courge* 'gourd,' from Latin *cucurbita.*

cour·i·er /ˈko͝orēər, ˈkərēər/ ▶ **n. 1** a messenger who transports goods or documents, in particular: ■ a company or employee of a company that transports commercial packages and documents: *the check was dispatched by courier* | [as modifier] *a courier service.* ■ a messenger for an underground or espionage organization.
2 a person employed to guide and assist a group of tourists.
▶ **v.** [with obj.] send or transport (goods or documents) by courier.
– ORIGIN late Middle English (denoting a person sent to run with a message): originally from Old French *coreor;* later from French *courier* (now *courrier*), from Italian *corriere;* based on Latin *currere* 'to run.'

Cour·règes /ko͞orˈeZH/, André (1923–), French fashion designer. He is noted for his futuristic and youth-oriented styles, in particular, the use of plastic and metal, and for unisex fashion such as trouser suits for women.

course /kôrs/ ▶ **n. 1** [in sing.] the route or direction followed by a ship, aircraft, road, or river: *the road adopts a tortuous course along the coast* | *the new*

C

fleet changed course to join the other ships. ■ the way in which something progresses or develops: *the course of history.* ■ a procedure adopted to deal with a situation. ■ an area of land set aside and prepared for racing, golf, or another sport.
2 a dish, or a set of dishes served together, forming one of the successive parts of a meal: *guests are offered a choice of main course* | [in combination] *a four-course meal.*
3 a series of lectures or lessons in a particular subject, typically leading to a qualification: *a business studies course.* ■ Medicine a series of repeated treatments or doses of medication: *the doctor prescribed a course of antibiotics.*
4 Architecture a continuous horizontal layer of brick, stone, or other material in a building.
5 a pursuit of game (esp. hares) with greyhounds by sight rather than scent.
6 the lowest sail on a square-rigged mast.
7 a set of adjacent strings on a guitar, lute, etc., tuned to the same note.
▶ **v. 1** [no obj.] (of liquid) move without obstruction; flow: *tears were coursing down her cheeks* | figurative *exultation coursed through him.*
2 [with obj.] pursue (game, esp. hares) with greyhounds using sight rather than scent: *many of the hares coursed escaped unharmed* | [no obj.] *she would course for hares with her greyhounds.*
– PHRASES **course of action** a procedure adopted to deal with a situation: *the wisest course of action is to tackle the problem at its source.* **the course of nature** events or processes that are normal and to be expected: *each man would, in the course of nature, have his private opinions.* **in the course of — 1** undergoing the specified process: *a new text book was in the course of preparation.* **2** during the specified period: *he was a friend to many people in the course of his life.* ■ during and as a part of the specified activity: *they became friends in the course of their long walks.* **in the course of time** as time goes by. **in due course** see DUE. **a matter of course** see MATTER. **of course** used to introduce an idea or turn of events as being obvious or to be expected: *the point is, of course, that the puzzle itself is misleading.* ■ used to give or emphasize agreement or permission: *"Can I see you for a minute?" "Of course."* ■ introducing a qualification or admission: *of course we've been in touch by phone, but I wanted to see things for myself.* **off course** not following the intended route: *the car went careering off course.* **on course** following the intended route: *he battled to keep the ship on course* | figurative *we need to spend money to get the economy back on course.* **run** (or **take**) **its course** complete its natural development without interference: *his illness had to run its course.*
– ORIGIN Middle English: from Old French *cours*, from Latin *cursus*, from *curs-* 'run,' from the verb *currere*.

cours·er¹ /ˈkôrsər/ ▶ **n.** dated or literary a swift horse.
– ORIGIN Middle English: from Old French *corsier*, based on Latin *cursus* (see COURSE).

cours·er² ▶ **n.** a fast-running ploverlike bird related to the pratincoles, typically found in open country in Africa and Asia. ● Genera *Cursorius* and *Rhinoptilus*, family Glareolidae: several species, in particular the desert-dwelling **cream-colored courser** (*C. cursor*).
– ORIGIN mid 18th cent.: from modern Latin *Cursorius* 'adapted for running,' from *cursor* 'runner,' from the verb *currere* (see COURSE).

cours·er³ ▶ **n.** a person who hunts animals such as hares with greyhounds using sight rather than scent.
– ORIGIN early 17th cent.: from COURSER¹.

course·ware /ˈkôrs,we(ə)r/ ▶ **n.** computer programs or other material designed for use in an educational or training course.

course·work /ˈkôrs,wərk/ (also **course work**) ▶ **n.** written or practical work done by a student during a course of study, usually assessed in order to count toward a final mark or grade: *the graduate program combines coursework and internship.*

cours·ing /ˈkôrsiNG/ ▶ **n.** the sport of hunting game animals such as hares with greyhounds using sight rather than scent.

Court /kôrt/, Margaret Smith (1942–), Australian tennis player. She won more Grand Slam events (62) than any other player.

court /kôrt/ ▶ **n. 1** (also **court of law**) a tribunal presided over by a judge, judges, or a magistrate in civil and criminal cases: *a settlement was reached during the first sitting of the court* | *she will take the matter to court* | [as modifier] *a court case.* ■ the place where such a tribunal meets. ■ (**the court**) the judge or judges presiding at such a tribunal.
2 a quadrangular area, either open or covered, marked out for ball games such as tennis or basketball: *I prefer an indoor court.* ■ a quadrangular area surrounded by a building or group of buildings. ■ a subdivision of a building, usually a large hall extending to the ceiling with galleries and staircases.
3 the establishment, retinue, and courtiers of a sovereign: *the emperor is shown with his court.* ■ a sovereign and his or her councilors, constituting a ruling power: *relations between the king and the imperial court.* ■ a sovereign's residence.
▶ **v.** [with obj.] dated be involved with romantically, typically with the intention of marrying: *he was courting a girl from the neighboring farm* | [no obj.] *we went to the movies when we were courting.* ■ (of a male bird or other animal) try to attract (a mate). ■ pay special attention to (someone) in an attempt to win their support or favor: *Western politicians courted the leaders of the newly independent states.* ■ go to great lengths to win (favorable attention): *he never had to court the approval of the political elite.* ■ risk incurring (misfortune) because of the way one behaves: *he has often courted controversy.*
– PHRASES **go to court** take legal action. **hold court** see HOLD¹. **in court** appearing as a party or an attorney in a court of law. **out of court 1** before a legal hearing can take place: *they are trying to settle the squabble out of court* | [as adj.] *an out-of-court settlement.* **2** treated as impossible or not worthy of consideration: *the price would put it out of court for most private buyers.* **pay court to** pay flattering attention to someone in order to win favor.
– ORIGIN Middle English: from Old French *cort*, from Latin *cohors*, *cohort-* 'yard or retinue.' The verb is influenced by Old Italian *corteare*, Old French *courtoyer*. Compare with COHORT.

court bouil·lon /ˌko͝or ˈbo͞o(l)ˌyän, ˌko͝or bēˈôn/ ▶ **n.** a stock made from wine and vegetables, typically used in fish dishes.
– ORIGIN French, from *court* 'short' and BOUILLON.

court card ▶ **n.** British term for FACE CARD.
– ORIGIN mid 17th cent.: alteration of 16th-cent. *coat card*, so named because of the decorative dress of the figures depicted.

court costs ▶ **plural n.** legal expenses, esp. those allowed in favor of the winning party or against the losing party in a suit.

court dress ▶ **n.** historical formal clothing worn at a royal court.

cour·te·ous /ˈkərtēəs/ ▶ **adj.** polite, respectful, or considerate in manner.
– DERIVATIVES **cour·te·ous·ly** adv., **cour·te·ous·ness** n.
– ORIGIN Middle English (meaning 'having manners fit for a royal court'): from Old French *corteis*, based on Latin *cohors* 'yard, retinue' (see COURT). The change in the ending in the 16th cent. was due to association with words ending in -EOUS.

cour·te·san /ˈkôrtəzən, ˈkər-/ ▶ **n.** a prostitute, esp. one with wealthy or upper-class clients.
– ORIGIN mid 16th cent.: from French *courtisane*, from obsolete Italian *cortigiana*, feminine of *cortigiano* 'courtier,' from *corte* (see COURT).

cour·te·sy /ˈkərtəsē/ ▶ **n.** (pl. **courtesies**) the showing of politeness in one's attitude and behavior toward others: *he had been treated with a degree of courtesy not far short of deference.* ■ (often **courtesies**) a polite speech or action, esp. one required by convention: *the superficial courtesies of diplomatic exchanges.* ■ [as modifier] (esp. of transport) supplied free of charge to people who are already paying for another service: *he traveled from the hotel in a courtesy car.* ■ archaic a curtsy.
– PHRASES **by courtesy** as a favor rather than by right: *he was not at the conference only by courtesy.* **(by) courtesy of** given or allowed by: *photograph courtesy of the Evening Star.* ■ informal as a result of; thanks to.
– ORIGIN Middle English: from Old French *cortesie*, from *corteis* (see COURTEOUS).

cour·te·sy light ▶ **n.** a small light in a car, automatically switched on when one of the doors is opened.

cour·te·sy ti·tle ▶ **n.** a title given to someone, esp. the son or daughter of a peer, that has no legal validity.

court hand ▶ **n.** Brit. a notoriously illegible style of handwriting used in English courts of law until banned in 1731.

court·house /ˈkôrt,hous/ ▶ **n. 1** a building in which a judicial court is held.
2 a building containing the administrative offices of a county.

cour·ti·er /ˈkôrtēər, ˈkôrCHər/ ▶ **n.** a person who attends a royal court as a companion or adviser to the king or queen.
– ORIGIN Middle English: via Anglo-Norman French from Old French *cortoyer* 'be present at court,' from *cort* (see COURT).

court·ly /ˈkôrtlē/ ▶ **adj.** (**courtlier**, **courtliest**)
1 polished or refined, as befitting a royal court: *he gave a courtly bow.*
2 given to flattery; obsequious.
– DERIVATIVES **court·li·ness** n.

court·ly love ▶ **n.** a highly conventionalized medieval tradition of love between a knight and a married noblewoman, first developed by the troubadours of Southern France and extensively employed in European literature of the time. The love of the knight for his lady was regarded as an ennobling passion and the relationship was typically unconsummated.

court-mar·tial ▶ **n.** (pl. **courts-martial** or **court-martials**) a judicial court for trying members of the armed services accused of offenses against military law: *they appeared before a court-martial* | *he was found guilty by court-martial.*
▶ **v.** (**court-martials**, **court-martialing**, **court-martialed**; Brit. **court-martials**, **court-martialling**, **court-martialled**) [with obj.] try (someone) by such a court.

court of ap·peals ▶ **n.** a court to which appeals are taken in a federal circuit or a state.

court of claims ▶ **n.** a court in which claims against the government are adjudicated.

court of in·quir·y ▶ **n.** in the armed forces, a tribunal appointed to investigate a complaint against a member of the military to decide whether a court-martial is called for.

court of law ▶ **n.** see COURT (sense 1 of the noun).

court of rec·ord ▶ **n.** a court whose proceedings are recorded and available as evidence of fact.

Court of St. James's the British sovereign's court.

court or·der ▶ **n.** a direction issued by a court or a judge requiring a person to do or not do something.

court plas·ter ▶ **n.** historical sticking plaster made of silk or other cloth with an adhesive such as isinglass.
– ORIGIN late 18th cent.: so named because it was formerly used by ladies at court for beauty spots.

court rec·ord ▶ **n.** see RECORD (sense 1 of the noun).

court·room /ˈkôrt,ro͞om, -,ro͝om/ ▶ **n.** the place or room in which a court of law meets.

court·ship /ˈkôrt,SHip/ ▶ **n.** a period during which a couple develop a romantic relationship, esp. with a view to marriage. ■ behavior designed to persuade someone to marry or develop a romantic relationship with one: *he was eventually successful in his patient courtship of Dorothy.* ■ the behavior of male birds and other animals aimed at attracting a mate. ■ the process of attempting to win a person's favor or support: *the country's courtship of foreign investors.*

court ten·nis ▶ **n.** the original form of tennis, played with a solid ball on an enclosed court divided into equal but dissimilar halves, the service side (from which service is always delivered) and the hazard side (on which service is received).

court·yard /ˈkôrt,yärd/ ▶ **n.** an unroofed area that is completely or mostly enclosed by the walls of a large building.

cous·cous /ˈko͞o,sko͞os/ ▶ **n.** a type of North African semolina in granules made from crushed durum wheat. ■ a spicy dish made by steaming or soaking such granules and adding meat, vegetables, or fruit.
– ORIGIN early 17th cent.: from French, from Arabic *kuskus*, from *kaskasa* 'to pound,' probably of Berber origin.

cous·in /ˈkəzən/ ▶ **n.** (also **first cousin**) a child of one's uncle or aunt. ■ a person belonging to the same extended family. ■ a thing related or analogous to another: *the new motorbikes are not proving as popular as their four-wheeled cousins.* ■ (usu. **cousins**) a person of a kindred culture, race, or nation: *the Russians and their Slavic cousins.* ■ historical a title formerly used by a sovereign in addressing another sovereign or a noble of their own country.
– PHRASES **first cousin once removed 1** a child of one's first cousin. **2** one's parent's first cousin. **first cousin twice removed 1** a grandchild of one's first cousin. **2** one's grandparent's first cousin. **second cousin** a child of one's parent's first cousin. **second cousin once removed 1** a child of one's second cousin. **2** one's parent's second cousin. **third cousin** a child of one's parent's second cousin.
– DERIVATIVES **cous·in·hood** /-,ho͝od/ n., **cous·in·ly** adj., **cous·in·ship** /-,SHip/ n.
– ORIGIN Middle English: from Old French *cosin*, from Latin *consobrinus* 'mother's sister's child,' from *con-* 'with' + *sobrinus* 'second cousin' (from *soror* 'sister').

cous·in-ger·man ▶ **n.** (pl. **cousins-german**) old-fashioned term for COUSIN.
– ORIGIN Middle English: from French *cousin germain* (see COUSIN, GERMAN).

Cous·teau /ko͞oˈstō/, Jacques-Yves (1910–97), French oceanographer and documentary movie director. He devised the scuba apparatus, but is known primarily for several documentaries and television series on marine life.

Cou·sy /ˈko͞ozē/, Bob (1928–), US basketball player; full name *Robert Joseph Cousy*. He played for the Boston Celtics from 1950 until 1963. Basketball Hall of Fame (1970).

couth /ko͞oTH/ humorous ▶ **adj.** cultured, refined, and well mannered: *it is more couth to hold your shrimp by the tail.*
▶ **n.** good manners; refinement: *their hockey team had more talent but less couth.*
– ORIGIN late 19th cent.: back-formation from UNCOUTH.

cou·ture /ko͞oˈto͝or, -ˈtʏr/ ▶ **n.** the design and manufacture of fashionable clothes to a client's specific requirements and measurements. See also HAUTE COUTURE. ■ fashionable made-to-measure clothes: *they were dressed in size eight printed-silk couture.*
– ORIGIN 1920s: French,'sewing, dressmaking.'

cou·tu·ri·er /ko͞oˈto͝orēər, -ˈto͝orē,ā/ ▶ **n.** a fashion designer who manufactures and sells clothes that have been tailored to a client's specific requirements and measurements.
– ORIGIN late 19th cent.: French, from COUTURE.

cou·tu·ri·ère /ko͞oˈto͝orēər, -,to͝orēˈe(ə)r/ ▶ **n.** a female couturier.

cou·vade /ko͞oˈväd/ ▶ **n.** the custom in some cultures in which a man takes to his bed and goes through certain rituals when his child is being born, as though he were physically affected by the birth.
– ORIGIN mid 19th cent.: French, from *couver* 'to hatch,' from Latin *cubare* 'lie down.' The adoption of the term in French was due to a misunderstanding of the phrase *faire la couvade* 'sit doing nothing,' used by earlier writers.

cou·vert /ko͞oˈver/ ▶ **n. 1** another term for COVER (sense 4 of the noun).
2 another term for COVER CHARGE: *there is a $1.50 couvert weekdays and $2.00 Saturdays and holidays.*
– ORIGIN mid 18th cent.: French, past participle (used as a noun) of *couvrir* 'to cover.'

cou·ver·ture /,ko͞overˈt(y)o͝or/ ▶ **n.** chocolate made with extra cocoa butter to give a high gloss, used for covering sweets and cakes.
– ORIGIN 1930s: French, literally 'covering.'

co·va·lent /,kōˈvālənt/ ▶ **adj.** Chemistry of, relating to, or denoting chemical bonds formed by the sharing of electrons between atoms. Often contrasted with IONIC.
– DERIVATIVES **co·va·lence n.**, **co·va·lent·ly adv.**

co·var·i·ance /,kōˈve(ə)rēəns/ ▶ **n. 1** Mathematics the property of a function of retaining its form when the variables are linearly transformed.
2 Statistics the mean value of the product of the deviations of two variates from their respective means.

co·var·i·ant /kōˈve(ə)rēənt/ Mathematics ▶ **n.** a function of the coefficients and variables of a given function that is invariant under a linear transformation except for a factor equal to a power of the determinant of the transformation.
▶ **adj.** changing in such a way that mathematical interrelations with another simultaneously changing quantity or set of quantities remain unchanged. ■ of, having the properties of, or relating to a covariant.

co·var·i·a·tion /,kōve(ə)rēˈāSHən/ ▶ **n.** Mathematics correlated variation.

cove[1] /kōv/ ▶ **n. 1** a small sheltered bay. ■ dialect a sheltered recess, esp. in the side of a mountain.
2 Architecture a concave arched molding, esp. one formed at the junction of a wall with a ceiling.
▶ **v.** [with obj.] (usu. as adj. **coved**) Architecture provide (a room, ceiling, etc.) with a cove.
– ORIGIN Old English *cofa* 'chamber, cave,' of Germanic origin; related to German *Koben* 'pigpen, pen.' Sense 1 of the noun dates from the late 16th cent.

cove[2] ▶ **n.** Brit. informal, dated a man: *he is a perfectly amiable cove.*
– ORIGIN mid 16th cent.: perhaps from Romany *kova* 'thing or person.'

co·vel·lite /kōˈvel,īt, ˈkōvə,līt/ ▶ **n.** a blue mineral consisting of copper sulfide, typically occurring as a coating on other copper minerals.
– ORIGIN mid 19th cent.: named after Nicolò *Covelli* (1790–1829), Italian chemist, + -ITE[1].

cov·en /ˈkəvən/ ▶ **n.** a group or gathering of witches who meet regularly. ■ often derogatory a secret or close-knit group of associates: *covens of militants within the party.*
– ORIGIN mid 17th cent.: variant of COVIN.

cov·e·nant /ˈkəvənənt/ ▶ **n.** an agreement. ■ Law a contract drawn up by deed. ■ Law a clause in a contract. ■ Theology an agreement that brings about a relationship of commitment between God and his people. The Jewish faith is based on the biblical covenants made with Abraham, Moses, and David. See also ARK OF THE COVENANT.
▶ **v.** [no obj.] agree, esp. by lease, deed, or other legal contract: *the landlord covenants to repair the property.*
– PHRASES **Old Covenant** Christian Theology the covenant between God and Israel in the Old Testament. **New Covenant** Christian Theology the covenant between God and the followers of Jesus Christ.
– DERIVATIVES **cov·e·nan·tal** /,kəvəˈnantl/ **adj.**, **cov·e·nant·er** (also chiefly Law **covenantor**) **n.**
– ORIGIN Middle English: from Old French, present participle of *covenir* 'agree,' from Latin *convenire* (see CONVENE).

cov·e·nan·tee /,kəvənənˈtē, -nan-/ ▶ **n.** Law the person to whom a promise by covenant is made.

Cov·e·nant·er /ˈkəvənantər, -ənəntər/ ▶ **n.** an adherent of the National Covenant (1638) or of the Solemn League and Covenant (1643), upholding the organization of the Scottish Presbyterian Church.

cov·e·nant of grace ▶ **n.** (in Calvinist theology) the covenant between God and humanity that was established by Jesus Christ at the Atonement.

cov·e·nant of works ▶ **n.** (in Calvinist theology) the covenant between God and humanity that was broken by Adam's sin at the Fall.

Cov·ent Gar·den /ˈkəvənt/ a district in central London.

Cov·en·try /ˈkəvəntrē, ˈkäv-/ an industrial city in central England; pop. 271,100 (est. 2009).

cov·er /ˈkəvər/ ▶ **v.** [with obj.] **1** put something such as a cloth or lid on top of or in front of (something) in order to protect or conceal it: *the table had been covered with a checked tablecloth* | *she covered her face with a pillow.* ■ envelop in a layer of something, esp. dirt: *he was covered in mud* | figurative *she was covered in confusion.* ■ scatter a layer of loose material over (a surface, esp. a floor), leaving it completely obscured: *the barn floor was covered in straw.* ■ lie over or adhere to (a surface), as decoration or to conceal something: *masonry paint will cover hairline cracks.* ■ protect (someone) with a garment or hat: (as adj. **covered**) *keep children covered with T-shirts.* ■ extend over (an area): *the grounds covered eight acres.* ■ travel (a specified distance): *it took them four days to cover 150 miles.*
2 deal with (a subject) by describing or analyzing its most important aspects or events: *a sequence of novels that will cover the period from 1968 to the present.* ■ investigate, report on, or publish or broadcast pictures of (an event): *NBC is covering the Olympics.* ■ work in, have responsibility for, or provide services to (a particular area): *development officers whose work would cover a large area.* ■ (of a rule or law) apply to (a person or situation).
3 (of a sum of money) be enough to pay (a bill or cost): *there are grants to cover the cost of materials for loft insulation.* ■ (of insurance) protect against a liability, loss, or accident involving financial consequences: *your contents are now covered against accidental loss or damage in transit.* ■ (**cover oneself**) take precautionary measures so as to protect oneself against future blame or liability: *one reason doctors take temperatures is to cover themselves against negligence claims.*
4 disguise the sound or fact of (something) with another sound or action: *Louise laughed to cover her embarrassment.* ■ [no obj.] (**cover for**) disguise the illicit absence or wrongdoing of (someone) in order to spare them punishment: *if the sergeant wants to know where you are, I'll cover for you.* ■ [no obj.] (**cover for**) temporarily take over the job of (a colleague) in their absence: *during August ministers cover for other ministers.*
5 aim a gun at (someone) in order to prevent them from moving or escaping. ■ protect (an exposed person) by shooting at an enemy: (as adj. **covering**) *the jeeps retreated behind spurts of covering fire.* ■ (of a fortress, gun, or cannon) have (an area) within range. ■ (in team games) take up a position ready to defend against (an opposing player). ■ Baseball be in position at (a base) ready to catch a thrown ball.
6 Bridge play a higher card on (a high card) in a trick: *the ploy will fail if the ten is covered* | [no obj.] *East covered with his queen.*
7 record or perform a new version of (a song) originally performed by someone else: *other artists who have covered the song include U2.*
8 (of a male animal, esp. a stallion) copulate with (a female animal), esp. as part of a commercial transaction between the owners of the animals.
▶ **n. 1** a thing that lies on, over, or around something, esp. in order to protect or conceal it: *a seat cover.* ■ a thin solid object that seals a container or hole; a lid: *a manhole cover.* ■ a thick protective outer part or page of a book or magazine: *her life was captured between hard covers in her 1986 autobiography.* ■ Philately a card or envelope that has traveled through the mail or that contains postal markings. ■ (**the covers**) bedclothes: *she burrowed down beneath the covers.*
2 physical shelter or protection sought by people in danger: *the sirens wailed and people ran for cover* | *store seats under cover before the bad weather sets in.* ■ undergrowth, trees, or other vegetation used as a shelter by animals: *the standing crops of game cover* | *a landscape bare of woodland except for neat little fox covers.* See also COVERT (sense 1 of the noun). ■ an activity or organization used as a means of concealing an illegal or secret activity: *a restaurant is run as a cover for a money-laundering operation.* ■ [in sing.] an identity or activity adopted by a person, typically a spy, to conceal their true activities: *he was worried that their cover was blown.* ■ military support given when someone is in danger from or being attacked by an enemy: *they agreed to provide additional naval cover.* ■ Ecology the amount of ground covered by a vertical projection of the vegetation, usually expressed as a percentage.
3 short for COVER CHARGE.
4 a place setting at a table in a restaurant. [rendering French *couvert*.]
5 (also **cover version**) a recording or performance of a previously recorded song made esp. to take advantage of the original's success.
– PHRASES **break cover** suddenly leave a place of shelter, esp. vegetation, when being hunted or pursued. **cover one's ass** (or **back**) informal foresee and avoid the possibility of attack or criticism. **cover all bases** (or **cover all the bases**) deal with something thoroughly: *for the prospective homebuilder, this book covers all bases* | *if you meet these basic requirements, you 'll cover all bases.* **cover a multitude of sins** conceal or gloss over many problems or defects: *stucco could cover a multitude of sins, including poor brickwork.* **cover one's position** purchase securities in order to be able to fulfill a commitment to sell. **cover one's tracks** conceal evidence of what one has done. **cover the waterfront** informal include a wide range of things; cover every aspect of something: *while half the dishes are Italian, the kitchen covers the waterfront from Greece to Morocco.* **from cover to cover** from beginning to end of a book or magazine. **take cover** protect oneself from attack by ducking down into or under a shelter: *if the bombing starts, take cover in the basement.* **under cover of** concealed by: *the yacht made landfall under cover of darkness.* ■ while pretending to do something: *Moran watched every move under cover of reading the newspaper.* **under plain cover** in an envelope or parcel without any marks to identify the sender. **under separate cover** in a separate envelope.
– PHRASAL VERBS **cover something up** put something on, over, or around something, esp. in order to conceal or disguise it. ■ try to hide or deny the fact of an illegal or illicit action or activity.
– DERIVATIVES **cov·er·a·ble adj.**
– ORIGIN Middle English: from Old French *covrir*, from Latin *cooperire*, from *co-* (expressing intensive force) + *operire* 'to cover.' The noun is partly a variant of COVERT.

cov·er·age /ˈkəv(ə)rij/ ▶ **n.** the extent to which something deals with or applies to something else: *the grammar did not offer total coverage of the language.* ■ the treatment of an issue by the media: *the program won an award for its news coverage.* ■ the amount of protection given by an insurance policy. ■ the area reached by a particular broadcasting station or advertising medium: *a network of eighty transmitters would give nationwide coverage.* ■ Football the manner in which a defender or a defensive team covers a player, an area, or a play.

cov·er·all /ˈkəvər,ôl/ ▶ **n.** (usu. **coveralls**) a full-length protective outer garment often zipped up the front. ■ [as modifier] inclusive: *a coverall term.*

cov·er charge ▶ **n.** a flat fee paid for admission to a restaurant, bar, club, etc.

cov·er crop ▶ **n.** a crop grown for the protection and enrichment of the soil.

Cov·er·dale /ˈkəvər,dāl/, Miles (1488–1568), English biblical scholar. He translated the first complete printed English Bible in 1535.

cov·ered wag·on ▶ **n.** a horse- or mule-drawn wagon topped with a spacious. arched canvas-covered framework. Covered wagons were the common transport for the western-moving North

C

American pioneers of the 19th century. See also CONESTOGA WAGON, PRAIRIE SCHOONER.

covered wagon

cov·er girl ▶ n. a female model whose picture appears on magazine covers.

cov·er glass ▶ n. another term for COVERSLIP.

cov·er·ing /ˈkəv(ə)riNG/ ▶ n. a thing used to cover something else, typically in order to protect or conceal it: *a vinyl floor covering.* ■ [usu. in sing.] a layer of something that covers something else: *the sky was obscured by a covering of cloud.*

cov·er·ing let·ter ▶ n. British term for COVER LETTER.

cov·er·let /ˈkəvərlət/ ▶ n. a bedspread, typically less than floor-length.
– ORIGIN Middle English: from Anglo-Norman French *covrelet*, from Old French *covrir* 'to cover' + *lit* 'bed.'

cov·er let·ter ▶ n. a letter sent with, and explaining the contents of, another document or a parcel of goods.

cov·er sheet ▶ n. **1** a page sent as the first page of a fax transmission, identifying the sender, number of pages, etc.
2 a page placed before a manuscript or report, typically with the name of the author, title of the book or report, and date.

cov·er·slip /ˈkəvərˌslip/ (also **cover slip**) ▶ n. a small, thin piece of glass used to cover and protect a specimen on a microscope slide.

cov·er sto·ry ▶ n. **1** a magazine article that is illustrated or advertised on the front cover.
2 a fictitious account invented to conceal a person's identity or reasons for doing something.

co·vert ▶ adj. /ˈkōvərt, kōˈvərt, ˈkəvərt/ **1** not openly acknowledged or displayed: *covert operations against the dictatorship.*
2 Law (of a woman) married and under the authority and protection of her husband.
▶ n. /ˈkəvər(t), ˈkōvərt/ **1** a thicket in which game can hide.
2 Ornithology any of the feathers covering the bases of the main flight or tail feathers of a bird.
– DERIVATIVES **co·vert·ly** /ˈkōvərtlē, kōˈvərtlē, ˈkəvərtlē/ adv., **co·vert·ness** n.
– ORIGIN Middle English (in the general senses 'covered' and 'a cover'): from Old French, 'covered,' past participle of *covrir* (see COVER).

cov·er·ture /ˈkəvərˌCHo͝or, -CHər/ ▶ n. **1** literary protective or concealing covering.
2 Law, historical the legal status of a married woman, considered to be under her husband's protection and authority.
– ORIGIN Middle English: from Old French, from *covrir* 'to cover.' It originally denoted a coverlet or a garment, later various kinds of covering or shelter.

cov·er-up (also **coverup**) ▶ n. **1** an attempt to prevent people's discovering the truth about a serious mistake or crime.
2 a loose outer garment, as worn over a swimsuit or exercise outfit.

cov·er ver·sion ▶ n. see COVER (sense 5 of the noun).

cov·et /ˈkəvət/ ▶ v. (**covets, coveting, coveted**) [with obj.] yearn to possess or have (something): *the president-elect covets time for exercise and fishing* | (as adj. **coveted**) *he won the coveted Booker Prize for fiction.*
– DERIVATIVES **cov·et·a·ble** adj.
– ORIGIN Middle English: from Old French *cuveitier*, based on Latin *cupiditas* (see CUPIDITY).

cov·et·ous /ˈkəvətəs/ ▶ adj. having or showing a great desire to possess something, typically something belonging to someone else: *she fingered the linen with covetous hands.*
– DERIVATIVES **cov·et·ous·ly** adv., **cov·et·ous·ness** n.
– ORIGIN Middle English: from Old French *coveitous*, based on Latin *cupiditas* (see CUPIDITY).

cov·ey /ˈkəvē/ ▶ n. (pl. **coveys**) a small party or flock of birds, esp. partridge. ■ a small group of people or things: *coveys of actors rushed through the rooms.*
– ORIGIN Middle English: from Old French *covee*, feminine past participle of *cover*, from Latin *cubare* 'lie down.'

cov·in /ˈkəvən, ˈkō-/ (also **covine**) ▶ n. archaic fraud; deception.
– ORIGIN Middle English (denoting a company or band): from Old French, from medieval Latin *convenium*, from Latin *convenire* (see CONVENE). Compare with COVEN.

Co·vi·na /kōˈvēnə/ a city in southwestern California, east of Los Angeles; pop. 46,944 (est. 2008).

Cov·ing·ton a city in northern Kentucky, where the Licking River flows into the Ohio River; pop. 43,235 (est. 2008).

cow[1] /kou/ ▶ n. a fully grown female animal of a domesticated breed of ox, used as a source of milk or beef: *a dairy cow.* See CATTLE. ■ (loosely) a domestic bovine animal, regardless of sex or age. ■ (in farming) a female domestic bovine animal that has borne more than one calf. Compare with HEIFER. ■ the female of certain other large animals, for example elephant, rhinoceros, whale, seal, or reindeer. ■ informal, derogatory a woman, esp. a fat or stupid one: *what does he see in that cow?*
– PHRASES **have a cow** informal become angry, excited, or agitated: *don't have a cow—it's no big deal.* **till the cows come home** informal for an indefinitely long time: *those two could talk till the cows came home.*
– ORIGIN Old English *cū*, of Germanic origin; related to Dutch *koe* and German *Kuh*, from an Indo-European root shared by Latin *bos* and Greek *bous*.

cow[2] ▶ v. [with obj.] (usu. **be cowed**) cause (someone) to submit to one's wishes by intimidation: *the intellectuals had been cowed into silence.*
– ORIGIN late 16th cent.: probably from Old Norse *kúga* 'oppress.'

cow·a·bun·ga /ˌkou-əˈbəNGgə/ ▶ exclam. informal used to express delight or satisfaction: *Cowabunga! It's an actor's dream.*
– ORIGIN 1940s: originally *cowabonga*, an exclamation frequently used by the character Chief Thunderthud on the *Howdy Doody Show*.

cow·age /ˈkouij/ (also **cowhage**) ▶ n. a leguminous climbing plant, *Mucuna pruriens*, with hairy pods that cause stinging and itching.
– ORIGIN mid 17th cent.: from Hindi *kāuṅc*.

Cow·ard /ˈkou-ərd/, Sir Noël (Pierce) (1899–1973), English playwright, actor, and composer. He is remembered for witty, satirical plays, such as *Hay Fever* (1925) and *Private Lives* (1930), as well as for revues and musicals featuring songs such as "Mad Dogs and Englishmen" (1932).

cow·ard /ˈkou-ərd/ ▶ n. a person who lacks the courage to do or endure dangerous or unpleasant things.
▶ adj. **1** literary excessively afraid of danger or pain.
2 Heraldry (of an animal) depicted with the tail between the hind legs.
– ORIGIN Middle English: from Old French *couard*, based on Latin *cauda* 'tail,' possibly with reference to a frightened animal with its tail between its legs, reflected in sense 2 of the adjective (early 16th cent).

cow·ard·ice /ˈkou-ərdəs/ ▶ n. lack of bravery.
– ORIGIN Middle English: from Old French *couardise*, from *couard* (see COWARD).

cow·ard·ly /ˈkou-ərdlē/ ▶ adj. lacking courage. ■ (of an action) carried out against a person who is unable to retaliate: *a cowardly attack on a helpless victim.*
▶ adv. archaic in a way that shows a lack of courage.
– DERIVATIVES **cow·ard·li·ness** n.

cow·bane /ˈkouˌbān/ ▶ n. any of a number of tall poisonous plants of the parsley family, growing in swampy or wet habitats. ● another term for WATER HEMLOCK ● a North American plant (*Oxypolis rigidior*, family Umbelliferae).
– ORIGIN late 18th cent.: from COW[1] + BANE, because it is poisonous to grazing cattle.

cow·bell /ˈkouˌbel/ ▶ n. a bell hung around a cow's neck in order to help locate the animal by the noise it makes. ■ a similar bell used as a percussion instrument, typically without a clapper and struck with a stick.

cow·ber·ry /ˈkouˌberē/ ▶ n. (pl. **cowberries**) another term for MOUNTAIN CRANBERRY.

cow·bird /ˈkouˌbərd/ ▶ n. a New World songbird with dark plumage and a relatively short bill, typically laying its eggs in other birds' nests. ● Genus *Molothrus* (and *Scaphidura*), family Icteridae: several species, in particular the widespread **brown-headed** (or **common**) **cowbird** (*M. ater*).

cow·boy /ˈkouˌboi/ ▶ n. **1** a man, typically one on horseback, who herds and tends cattle, esp. in the western US and as represented in westerns and novels: *they are always playing cowboys and Indians.*
2 informal a person who is reckless or careless, esp. when driving an automobile.
▶ v. [no obj.] work as a cowboy: *Sonora, Mexico, where he learned to cowboy.*
– PHRASES **cowboy up** informal mount a brave effort to overcome a formidable obstacle: *Millar cowboyed up, but couldn't he have flipped the Enrique grounder to Pedro?*

cow·boy boot ▶ n. a style of boot with a pointed toe and a moderately high heel, extending to mid-calf.

Cow·boy State a nickname for the state of WYOMING.

cow camp ▶ n. a seasonal camp apart from the main buildings of a ranch, used during a cattle roundup.

cow·catch·er /ˈkouˌkaCHər, -ˌkeCHər/ ▶ n. a metal frame at the front of a locomotive for pushing aside cattle or other obstacles on the line.

cow chip ▶ n. informal a dried cowpat.

cow·er /ˈkou(-ə)r/ ▶ v. [no obj.] crouch down in fear: *children cowered in terror as the shoot-out erupted.*
– ORIGIN Middle English: from Middle Low German *kūren* 'lie in wait,' of unknown ultimate origin.

cow·fish /ˈkouˌfiSH/ ▶ n. (pl. **same** or **cowfishes**) a boxfish with spines that resemble horns on the head, and typically with other spines on the back and sides. ● Several genera and species in the family Ostraciontidae, in particular *Lactoria diaphana*.

cow flop (also **cowflop** or chiefly Canadian **cow flap** or **cowflap**) ▶ n. informal a cowpat.

cow·girl /ˈkouˌgərl/ ▶ n. a female equivalent of a cowboy, esp. as represented in westerns and novels.

cow·hage ▶ n. variant spelling of COWAGE.

cow·hand /ˈkouˌhand/ ▶ n. a person employed to tend or ranch cattle; a cowboy or cowgirl.

cow·herd /ˈkouˌhərd/ ▶ n. a person who tends grazing cattle.
– ORIGIN Old English, from COW[1] + obsolete *herd* 'herdsman.'

cow·hide /ˈkouˌhīd/ ▶ n. a cow's hide. ■ leather made from a cow's hide. ■ a whip made from such leather.

cowl /koul/ ▶ n. a large loose hood, esp. one forming part of a monk's habit. ■ a monk's hooded, sleeveless habit. ■ a cloak with wide sleeves worn by members of Benedictine orders. ■ the hood-shaped covering of a chimney or ventilation shaft. ■ the part of a motor vehicle that supports the windshield and houses the dashboard. ■ another term for COWLING.
– DERIVATIVES **cowled** adj.
– ORIGIN Old English *cugele*, *cūle*, from ecclesiastical Latin *cuculla*, from Latin *cucullus* 'hood of a cloak.'

cow·lick /ˈkouˌlik/ ▶ n. a lock of hair that grows in a direction different from the rest and that resists being combed flat: *a little sprig of a cowlick stood up on the back of her head.*

cowl·ing /ˈkouliNG/ ▶ n. the removable cover of a vehicle or aircraft engine.

cowl neck ▶ n. a neckline on a woman's garment that hangs in draped folds: [as modifier] *a cowl-neck sweater.*

cow·man /ˈkoumən, -ˌman/ ▶ n. (pl. **cowmen**) a person who owns or is in charge of a cattle ranch. ■ a cowboy.

co·work·er /ˈkōˌwərkər, kōˈwərkər/ ▶ n. a fellow worker.

cow pars·nip ▶ n. a very large, bad-smelling hogweed. Cow parsnips prefer moist ground and can reach a height of 10 feet (3 m). ● *Heracleum maximum*, family Umbelliferae.

cow·pat /ˈkouˌpat/ ▶ n. a flat, round piece of cow dung.

cow·pea /ˈkouˌpē/ ▶ n. a plant of the pea family native to the Old World tropics. It is an important pulse for animal feed and human consumption, both the pod and the seed being edible. ● *Vigna unguiculata*, family Leguminosae. ■ the seed of this plant as food.

Cow·per /ˈko͞opər, ˈko͝opər, ˈkoupər/, William (1731–1800), English poet, noted for the poem *The Task* (1785) and for the comic ballad *John Gilpin* (1782).

Cow·per's gland /ˈkoupərz, ˈko͞opərz, ˈko͝opərz/ ▶ n. Anatomy either of a pair of small glands that open into the urethra at the base of the penis and secrete a constituent of seminal fluid.
– ORIGIN mid 18th cent.: named after William *Cowper* (1666–1709), English anatomist.

cow pie ▶ n. informal a cowpat.

cow·poke /ˈkouˌpōk/ ▶ n. informal a cowboy.

cow po·ny ▶ n. a small horse trained for use in cattle ranching.

cow·pox /ˈkouˌpäks/ ▶ n. a viral disease of cows' udders which, when contracted by humans through contact, resembles mild smallpox, and was the basis of the first smallpox vaccines.

cow·punch·er /ˈkouˌpənCHər/ ▶ n. informal a cowboy.

C

cow·rie /ˈkourē/ (also **cowry**) ▸ **n.** (pl. **cowries**) a marine mollusk that has a smooth, glossy, domed shell with a long narrow opening, typically brightly patterned and popular with collectors. ● Genus *Cypraea*, family Cypraeidae, class Gastropoda: numerous species, including the small **money cowrie** (*C. moneta*). ■ the flattened yellowish shell of the money cowrie, formerly used as money in parts of Africa and the Indo-Pacific area.
– ORIGIN mid 17th cent.: from Hindi *kaurī*.

co·write /kōˈrīt, ˈkōˌrīt/ ▸ **v.** [with obj.] write (something) with another person: *the movie is based on a story he cowrote with his wife.*
– DERIVATIVES **co·writ·er n.**

cow shark ▸ **n.** a dull gray or brown shark that lives mainly in deep water, esp. in the North Atlantic and Mediterranean. ● *Hexanchus griseus*, family Hexanchidae.

cow·shed /ˈkouˌsʜed/ ▸ **n.** a farm building in which cattle are kept when not in a pasture, or in which they are milked.

cow·slip /ˈkouˌslip/ ▸ **n. 1** a European primula with clusters of drooping fragrant yellow flowers in spring, growing on dry grassy banks and in pasture. ● *Primula veris*, family Primulaceae.
2 any of a number of herbaceous plants, in particular: ● another term for MARSH MARIGOLD ● (also **Virginia bluebell**) a North American plant with blue flowers (*Mertensia virginica*, family Boraginaceae).
– ORIGIN Old English *cūslyppe*, from *cū* 'cow' + *slipa*, *slyppe* 'slime,' i.e., cow slobber or dung.

cow·town /ˈkouˌtoun/ (also **cow town**) ▸ **n.** a town or city in a cattle-raising area of western North America. ■ a small, isolated, or unsophisticated town.

cow wheat ▸ **n.** a yellowish-flowered plant of the figwort family, partly parasitic on the roots of other plants and found in both Eurasia and North America. ● Genus *Melampyrum*, family Scrophulariaceae: several species, including *M. lineare*.

COX /käks/ ▸ **n.** Biochemistry the enzyme cyclooxygenase, which is required for the formation of prostaglandins and is blocked by painkillers such as aspirin and ibuprofen.

cox /käks/ ▸ **n.** a coxswain, esp. of a racing boat.
▸ **v.** [with obj.] act as a coxswain for (a racing boat or crew): *the winning eight was coxed by a woman* | (as adj. **coxed**) *the coxed pairs* | [no obj.] *he once coxed for Harvard.*
– DERIVATIVES **cox·less adj.**
– ORIGIN mid 19th cent.: abbreviation.

COX-2 in·hib·i·tor ▸ **n.** a painkiller that works by inhibiting the enzyme cyclooxygenase-2 (COX-2), which triggers the release of prostaglandins.

cox·a /ˈkäksə/ ▸ **n.** (pl. **coxae** /ˈkäksē, -sī/) Anatomy the hipbone or hip joint. ■ Entomology the first or basal segment of the leg of an insect.
– DERIVATIVES **cox·al adj.**
– ORIGIN late 17th cent.: from Latin,'hip.'

cox·al·gi·a /käkˈsalj(ē)ə/ ▸ **n.** pain in the hip joint.

cox·comb /ˈkäksˌkōm/ ▸ **n. 1** dated a vain and conceited man; a dandy.
2 variant spelling of COCKSCOMB (sense 2).
– DERIVATIVES **cox·comb·ry n.** (pl. **coxcombries**) (sense 1), **cox·comb·er·y** /-ˌkōm(ə)rē/ **n.**
– ORIGIN mid 16th cent. (denoting a simpleton): variant of COCKSCOMB, in the sense 'jester's cap' (resembling a cock's comb), hence 'a jester, a fool.'

cox·op·o·dite /käkˈsäpəˌdīt/ ▸ **n.** Zoology the segment nearest the body in the leg of an arthropod, esp. a crustacean.
– ORIGIN late 19th cent.: from Latin *coxa* 'hip' + Greek *pous, pod-* 'foot' + -ITE[1].

Cox·sack·ie vi·rus /käkˈsakē, ko͝ok-/ (also **coxsackie virus** or **coxsackievirus**) ▸ **n.** Medicine any of a group of enteroviruses that cause various respiratory, neurological, and muscular diseases in humans.
– ORIGIN 1940s: named after *Coxsackie*, New York, where the first cases were diagnosed.

cox·swain /ˈkäksən/ ▸ **n.** the steersman of a ship's boat, lifeboat, racing boat, or other boat.
– DERIVATIVES **cox·swain·ship** /-ˌsʜip/ **n.**
– ORIGIN Middle English: from obsolete *cock* + SWAIN. Compare with BOATSWAIN.

coy /koi/ ▸ **adj.** (**coyer, coyest**) (esp. with reference to a woman) making a pretense of shyness or modesty that is intended to be alluring: *she treated him to a coy smile of invitation.* ■ reluctant to give details, esp. about something regarded as sensitive: *he is coy about his age.* ■ dated quiet and reserved; shy.
– DERIVATIVES **coy·ly adv.**
– ORIGIN Middle English: from Old French *coi, quei*, from Latin *quietus* (see QUIET). The original sense was 'quiet, still' (esp. in behavior), later 'modestly retiring,' and hence (of a woman) 'affecting to be unresponsive to advances.'

coy·dog /ˈkoiˌdôg/ ▸ **n.** the hybrid offspring of a coyote and a dog.

coy·ness /ˈkoinis/ ▸ **n. 1** (esp. in a woman) the quality of feigning shyness or modesty in an attempt to seem alluring.
2 the quality of being reluctant to give details about something regarded as sensitive; reticence: *the company's coyness about their spring offering.*

Co·yo·a·cán /ˌkoi-ōəˈkän/ a municipality within the Federal District of Mexico, a suburb of Mexico City; pop. 606,373 (2005).

coy·o·te /ˈkīˌōt, kīˈōtē/ ▸ **n. 1** (pl. **same** or **coyotes**) a wolflike wild dog native to North America. Also called BRUSH WOLF or PRAIRIE WOLF. ● *Canis latrans*, family Canidae.
2 informal a person who smuggles Latin Americans across the US border, typically for a high fee: *at the bus station, there were coyotes offering to drive us to Los Angeles.*
– ORIGIN mid 18th cent.: from Mexican Spanish, from Nahuatl *coyotl*.

Coy·o·te State a nickname for the state of SOUTH DAKOTA.

coy·pu /ˈkoiˌpo͞o/ ▸ **n.** (pl. **coypus**) another term for NUTRIA.
– ORIGIN late 18th cent.: from Araucanian.

coz /kəz/ ▸ **n.** an informal word for 'cousin,' used esp. as a term of address.
– ORIGIN mid 16th cent.: abbreviation.

coz·en /ˈkəzən/ ▸ **v.** [with obj.] trick or deceive: *do not think to cozen your contemporaries.* ■ obtain by deception: *he was able to cozen a profit.*
– DERIVATIVES **coz·en·age** /-nij/ **n.**, **coz·en·er n.**
– ORIGIN late 16th cent.: perhaps from obsolete Italian *cozzonare* 'to cheat,' from *cozzone* 'middleman, broker,' from Latin *cocio* 'dealer.'

Co·zu·mel /ˌkōzo͞oˈmel/ a resort island in the Caribbean Sea, off the northeastern coast of the Yucatán Peninsula in Mexico.

co·zy /ˈkōzē/ (Brit. **cosy**) ▸ **adj.** (**cozier, coziest**) giving a feeling of comfort, warmth, and relaxation: *a cozy cabin tucked away in the trees.* ■ (of a relationship or conversation) intimate and relaxed. ■ avoiding or not offering challenge or difficulty; complacent: *a rather cozy assumption among automakers that they would never actually go bust.* ■ (of a transaction or arrangement) working to the mutual advantage of those involved (used to convey a suspicion of corruption): *a cozy deal.*
▸ **n.** (pl. **cozies**) a cover to keep a teapot hot.
▸ **v.** (**cozies, cozying, cozied**) [with obj.] informal give (someone) a feeling of comfort or complacency: *she cozied him, pretending to find him irresistibly attractive.* ■ [no obj.] (**cozy up**) snuggle up to someone or something: *almost everyone loves to cozy up to a roaring fire* | *I shall have a certain lovely lady to cozy up with.* ■ [no obj.] (**cozy up to**) ingratiate oneself with: *he decided to resign rather than cozy up to hard-liners in the party.*
– DERIVATIVES **co·zi·ly** /-zəlē/ **adv.**, **co·zi·ness n.**
– ORIGIN early 18th cent. (originally Scots): of unknown origin.

CP ▸ **abbr.** ■ cerebral palsy. ■ Command Post. ■ Finance commercial paper. ■ Common Pleas. ■ Communist Party. ■ (also **cp**) candlepower.

cp. ▸ **abbr.** compare.

CPA ▸ **abbr.** certified public accountant.

cpd. ▸ **abbr.** compound.

CPI ▸ **abbr.** consumer price index.

Cpl. ▸ **abbr.** corporal.

CPO ▸ **abbr.** Chief Petty Officer.

CPR ▸ **abbr.** cardiopulmonary resuscitation.

cps (also **c.p.s.**) ▸ **abbr.** ■ Computing characters per second. ■ cycles per second.

Cpt. ▸ **abbr.** Captain.

CPU ▸ **abbr.** Computing central processing unit.

CPUSA ▸ **abbr.** Communist Party USA.

CPVC ▸ **abbr.** chlorinated polyvinyl chloride, a plastic material used to make water pipes.

CR ▸ **abbr.** ■ Conditioned reflex. ■ Conditioned response.

Cr ▸ **symbol** the chemical element chromium.

cr ▸ **abbr.** ■ credit. ■ creditor.

crab[1] /krab/ ▸ **n. 1** a crustacean with a broad carapace, stalked eyes, and five pairs of legs, the first pair of which are modified as pincers. Crabs are abundant on many shores, esp. in the tropics, where some have become adapted to life on land. ● Many families in the order Decapoda, class Malacostraca. ■ the flesh of a crab as food. ■ (**the Crab**) the zodiacal sign or constellation Cancer.
2 (also **crab louse**) a louse that infests human body hair, esp. in the genital region, causing extreme irritation. Also called PUBIC LOUSE. ● *Phthirus pubis*, family Pediculidae, order Anoplura. ■ (**crabs**) informal an infestation of crab lice.
3 a machine for picking up and lifting heavy weights.
▸ **v.** (**crabs, crabbing, crabbed**) **1** [no obj.] move sideways or obliquely: *he began crabbing sideways across the roof.* ■ [with obj.] steer (an aircraft or ship) slightly sideways to compensate for a crosswind or current.
2 [no obj.] fish for crabs.
– PHRASES **catch a crab** Rowing make a faulty stroke in which the oar is under water too long or misses the water altogether.
– DERIVATIVES **crab·ber n.**, **crab·like** /-ˌlīk/ **adj. & adv.**
– ORIGIN Old English *crabba*, of Germanic origin; related to Dutch *krabbe*, and more distantly to Dutch *kreeft* and German *Krebs*; also to CRAB[3].

crab[2] ▸ **n.** short for CRAB APPLE.

crab[3] ▸ **n.** informal an irritable person.
▸ **v.** (**crabs, crabbing, crabbed**) informal **1** [no obj.] grumble, typically about something petty: *on picnics, I would crab about sand in my food.*
2 [with obj.] act so as to spoil: *you're trying to crab my act.*
– ORIGIN late 16th cent. (referring to hawks, meaning 'claw or fight each other'): from Low German *krabben*; related to CRAB[1].

crab ap·ple (also **crabapple**) ▸ **n.** (also **crab**) **1** a small, sour apple.
2 (also **crab tree, crab-apple tree**, or **crabapple tree**) the small tree that bears this fruit. ● Genus *Malus*, family Rosaceae: several species and hybrids, in particular the wild **Eurasian crab apple** (*M. sylvestris*), which is one of the possible ancestors of cultivated apples.
– ORIGIN late Middle English: *crab* perhaps an alteration (influenced by CRAB[1] or CRABBED) of Scots and northern English *scrab*, in the same sense, probably of Scandinavian origin.

crab·bed /ˈkrabd/ ▸ **adj. 1** (of handwriting) ill-formed and hard to decipher. ■ (of style) contorted and difficult to understand: *crabbed legal language.*
2 ill-humored: *a crabbed, unhappy middle age.*
– DERIVATIVES **crab·bed·ly adv.**, **crab·bed·ness n.**
– ORIGIN Middle English (in the sense 'perverse, wayward'): from CRAB[1], because of the crab's sideways gait and habit of snapping, thought to suggest a perverse or irritable disposition.

crab·by /ˈkrabē/ ▸ **adj.** (**crabbier, crabbiest**) irritable.
– DERIVATIVES **crab·bi·ly** /ˈkrabəlē/ **adv.**, **crab·bi·ness n.**

crab can·on ▸ **n.** another term for CANON CANCRIZANS.

crab·eat·er seal /ˈkrabˌētər/ ▸ **n.** a slender, gray Antarctic seal that lives on the pack ice, feeding mainly on krill. ● *Lobodon carcinophagus*, family Phocidae.

crab·grass /ˈkrabˌgras/ ▸ **n.** a creeping grass that can become a serious weed. ● *Digitaria* and other genera, family Gramineae: several species, in particular *D. sanguinalis* and *D. ciliaris*.

crab louse ▸ **n.** see CRAB[1] (sense 2 of the noun).

crab·meat /ˈkrabˌmēt/ ▸ **n.** the flesh of a crab as food.

Crab Neb·u·la Astronomy an irregular patch of luminous gas in the constellation Taurus, believed to be the remnant of a supernova explosion seen by Chinese astronomers in 1054. At its center is the first pulsar to be observed visually, and the nebula is a strong source of high-energy radiation.

crab pot ▸ **n.** a wicker trap for crabs.

crab spi·der ▸ **n.** a spider with long front legs, moving with a crablike sideways motion and typically lying in wait in vegetation and flowers for passing prey. ● Family Thomisidae: several genera.

crab stick ▸ **n.** a rectangular stick of mixed, compressed fish pieces flavored with crab.

crab tree ▸ **n.** see CRAB APPLE (sense 2).

crab·wise /ˈkrabˌwīz/ ▸ **adv. & adj.** (of movement) sideways, typically in an awkward way: [as adv.] *supermarket carts that only go crabwise* | [as adj.] *crabwise steps.*

crack /krak/ ▸ **n. 1** a line on the surface of something along which it has split without breaking into separate parts: *a hairline crack down the middle of the glass.* ■ a narrow space between two surfaces, esp. ones that have broken or been moved apart:

he climbed into a crack between two rocks | the door opened a tiny crack. ■ a vulnerable point; a flaw: *the company spotted a crack in their rival's defenses.*
2 a sudden sharp or explosive noise: *a loud crack of thunder.* ■ a sharp blow, esp. one that makes a noise: *she gave the thief a crack over the head with her rolling pin.* ■ a sudden harshness or change in pitch in a person's voice: *the boy's voice had an uncertain crack in it.*
3 informal a joke, typically a critical or unkind one.
4 [in sing.] informal an attempt to gain or achieve something: *I thought I **had a crack at** winning.* ■ a chance to attack or compete with someone: *he wanted to **have a crack at** the enemy.*
5 (also **crack cocaine**) a hard, crystalline form of cocaine broken into small pieces and smoked.
▶ **v. 1** break or cause to break without a complete separation of the parts: [no obj.] *the ice all over the lake had cracked* | [with obj.] *a stone cracked the headlight glass on his car.* ■ break or cause to break open or apart: [no obj.] *you can see how the landmasses have **cracked up** and moved around* | figurative *his face cracked into a smile* | [with obj.] *she cracked an egg into the frying pan.* ■ [with obj.] break (wheat or corn) into coarse pieces. ■ [with obj.] open slightly: *gingerly, he cracks open his door.* ■ give way or cause to give way under torture, pressure, or strain: [no obj.] *the witnesses cracked and the truth came out* | [with obj.] *no one can crack them—they believe their story.*
2 make or cause to make a sudden sharp or explosive sound: [no obj.] *a shot cracked across the ridge* | [with obj.] *he **cracked** his whip and galloped away.* ■ [no obj.] knock against something, making a noise on impact: *she winced as her knees cracked against metal.* ■ [with obj.] hit (someone or something) hard, making a sharp noise: *she cracked him across the forehead.* ■ [no obj.] (of a person's voice, esp. that of an adolescent boy or a person under strain) suddenly change in pitch: *"I want to get away," she said, her voice cracking.*
3 [with obj.] informal find a solution to; decipher or interpret: *a hacker cracked the codes used in Internet software.* ■ break into (a safe).
4 [with obj.] tell (a joke): *he cracked jokes which she didn't find very funny.*
5 [with obj.] decompose (hydrocarbons) by heat and pressure with or without a catalyst to produce lighter hydrocarbons, esp. in oil refining: (as noun **cracking**) *catalytic cracking.*
▶ **adj.** [attrib.] very good, esp. at a specified activity or in a specified role: *he is a crack shot* | *crack troops.*
– PHRASES **crack a book** informal open a book and read it; study. **crack of dawn** a time very early in the morning; daybreak. **crack of doom** a thunder peal announcing the Day of Judgment. **be cracked up to be** [with negative] informal asserted to be (used to indicate that someone or something has been described too favorably): *life on tour is not as glamorous as it's cracked up to be.* **crack wise** informal make jokes; wisecrack. **fall** (or **slip**) **through the cracks** escape from or be missed by something organized to catch or deal with one: *fatherless kids were not allowed to fall through the cracks.* **get cracking** informal act quickly and energetically: *most tickets have been snapped up, so get cracking if you want one.*
– PHRASAL VERBS **crack down on** informal take severe measures against: *we need to crack down hard on workplaces that break safety regulations.* **crack on** (of a sailing vessel) sail in high winds with all sails unfurled. **crack up** informal **1** suffer an emotional breakdown under pressure. **2** (also **crack someone up**) burst or cause to burst into laughter.
– ORIGIN Old English *cracian* 'make an explosive noise'; of Germanic origin; related to Dutch *kraken* and German *krachen.*

crack·a·jack /ˈkrakəˌjak/ ▶ **adj.** variant spelling of CRACKERJACK.

crack·brained /ˈkrakˌbrānd/ ▶ **adj.** informal extremely foolish; crazy: *a crackbrained idea.*

crack·down /ˈkrakˌdoun/ ▶ **n.** [usu. in sing.] severe measures to restrict or discourage undesirable or illegal people or behavior: *a crackdown on crime and corruption.*

cracked /krakt/ ▶ **adj. 1** damaged and showing lines on the surface from having split without coming apart: *the old pipes were cracked and leaking.* ■ (of a person's voice) having an unusual harshness or pitch, often due to distress.
2 [predic.] informal crazy; insane: *you must think my family is cracked.*

cracked wheat ▶ **n.** grains of wheat that have been crushed into small pieces.

crack·er /ˈkrakər/ ▶ **n. 1** a thin, crisp wafer often eaten with cheese or other savory toppings.
2 a person or thing that cracks. ■ a person who breaks into a computer system, typically for an illegal purpose. ■ an installation for cracking hydrocarbons: *a catalytic cracker.*
3 often offensive another term for POOR WHITE.
4 Brit. informal a fine example of something: *don't miss this cracker of a CD.*
5 chiefly Brit. a paper cylinder that is pulled apart at Christmas or other celebrations, making a sharp noise and releasing a small toy or other novelty. ■ a firework that explodes with a sharp noise.

crack·er·bar·rel ▶ **adj.** [attrib.] (esp. of a philosophy) plain, simple, and unsophisticated: *his cracker-barrel fascism.*
– ORIGIN late 19th cent.: with reference to the barrels of soda crackers once found in country stores, around which informal discussions would take place between customers.

crack·er·jack /ˈkrakərˌjak/ informal ▶ **adj.** exceptionally good: *a crackerjack eye surgeon.*
▶ **n.** an exceptionally good person or thing.

crack·ers /ˈkrakərz/ ▶ **adj.** informal, chiefly Brit. insane: *if Luke wasn't here I'd go crackers.*

crack·head /ˈkrakˌhed/ ▶ **n.** informal a person who habitually takes crack cocaine.

crack house ▶ **n.** a place where crack cocaine is traded.

crack·ing /ˈkrakiNG/ Brit. informal ▶ **adj.** excellent: *he is in cracking form to win this race* | *a cracking good war story.*

crack·le /ˈkrakəl/ ▶ **v.** [no obj.] make a rapid succession of slight cracking noises: *the fire suddenly crackled and spat sparks.* ■ give a sense of great tension or animation: *attraction and antagonism were crackling between them.*
▶ **n. 1** a sound made up of a rapid succession of slight cracking sounds: *there was a crackle and a whine from the microphone.*
2 a pattern of minute surface cracks on painted or varnished surfaces, glazed ceramics, or glass.
– DERIVATIVES **crack·ly** /ˈkrak(ə)lē/ **adj.**
– ORIGIN late Middle English: from CRACK + -LE[4].

crack·ling /ˈkraklən, -liNG/ ▶ **n.** the crisp, fatty skin of roast pork.

crack·nel /ˈkraknəl/ ▶ **n. 1** a light, crisp, savory biscuit.
2 small pieces of crackling.
– ORIGIN late Middle English: alteration of Old French *craquelin,* from Middle Dutch *krākelinc,* from *krāken* 'to crack.'

crack·pot /ˈkrakˌpät/ informal ▶ **n.** an eccentric or foolish person.
▶ **adj.** eccentric; impractical: *his head's full of crackpot ideas.*

cracks·man /ˈkraksmən/ ▶ **n.** (pl. **cracksmen**) informal, dated a burglar, esp. a safecracker.

crack-up (also **crackup**) ▶ **n.** [usu. in sing.] informal **1** a collapse under strain: *he had a complete mental crack-up.*
2 an act of breaking up or splitting apart: *the crack-up of a political system.*
3 a car crash: *motorists were asked to report minor crack-ups later.*

crack wil·low ▶ **n.** a large Eurasian willow with long, glossy leaves, growing typically in damp or riverside habitats. The brittle branches break off easily, often taking root and producing new growth. ● *Salix fragilis,* family Salicaceae.

crack·y /ˈkrakē/ ▶ **n.** (in phrase **by cracky**) informal, dated an exclamation used for emphasis.

Crac·ow /ˈkräkˌou, ˈkräˌkoof/ an industrial and college city in southern Poland, on the Vistula River; pop 754,624 (2008). It was the capital of Poland from 1320 until it was replaced by Warsaw in 1609. Polish name **KRAKÓW**.

-cracy ▶ **comb. form** denoting a particular form of government, rule, or influence: *autocracy* | *democracy.*
– ORIGIN from French *-cratie,* via medieval Latin from Greek *-kratia* 'power, rule.'

cra·dle /ˈkrādl/ ▶ **n. 1** an infant's bed or crib, typically one mounted on rockers. ■ (**the cradle**) infancy: *a society that would secure the welfare of its citizens **from cradle to grave**.* ■ (**the cradle of**) a place, process, or event in which something originates or flourishes: *he saw Greek art as the cradle of European civilization.*
2 a framework resembling a cradle, in particular: ■ a framework on which a ship or boat rests during construction or repairs. ■ the part of a telephone on which the receiver rests when not in use. ■ Mining a trough on rockers in which auriferous earth or sand is shaken in water to separate the gold.
▶ **v.** [with obj.] **1** hold gently and protectively: *she cradled his head in her arms.* ■ be the place of origin of: *the northeastern states cradled an American industrial revolution.*
2 place (a telephone receiver) in its cradle.
– ORIGIN Old English *cradol,* of uncertain origin; perhaps related to German *Kratte* 'basket.'

cra·dle·board /ˈkrādlˌbôrd/ ▶ **n.** (among North American Indians) a board to which an infant is strapped.

cra·dle cap ▶ **n.** a skin condition sometimes seen in babies caused by excessive production of sebum, characterized by areas of yellowish or brownish scales on the top of the head.

cra·dle-rob·ber ▶ **n.** derogatory a person who marries or has a sexual relationship with a much younger person.

cra·dle song ▶ **n.** a lullaby.

cra·dling /ˈkrādliNG, ˈkrādl-iNG/ ▶ **n.** Architecture a wooden or iron framework, typically one used as a structural support in a ceiling.

craft /kraft/ ▶ **n. 1** an activity involving skill in making things by hand: *the craft of bookbinding* | *pewter craft.* ■ (**crafts**) work or objects made by hand: *the shop sells local crafts* | (as modifier **craft**) *a craft fair.* ■ skill in carrying out one's work: *a player with plenty of craft.* ■ skill used in deceiving others: *her cousin was not her equal in guile and evasive craft.* ■ the members of a skilled profession. ■ (**the Craft**) the brotherhood of Freemasons.
2 (pl. **same**) a boat or ship: *sailing craft.* ■ an airplane or spaceship.
▶ **v.** [with obj.] exercise skill in making (something): *he crafted the chair lovingly* | (as adj. **crafted**) *a beautifully crafted object.*
– DERIVATIVES **craft·er n.**
– ORIGIN Old English *cræft* 'strength, skill,' of Germanic origin; related to Dutch *kracht,* German *Kraft,* and Swedish *kraft* 'strength' (the change of sense to 'skill' occurring only in English). Sense 2 of the noun, originally in the expression *small craft* 'small trading vessels or lighters,' may be elliptical, referring to vessels requiring a small amount of "craft" or skill to handle, as opposed to large oceangoing ships.

craft brew (also **craft beer**) ▶ **n.** a beer with a distinctive flavor, produced in small quantities and distributed in a particular region.
– DERIVATIVES **craft-brewed adj., craft brew·er n., craft brew·ing n.**

craft guild ▶ **n.** historical an association of workers of the same trade for mutual benefit.

crafts·man /ˈkraf(t)smən/ ▶ **n.** (pl. **craftsmen**) a person who is skilled in a particular craft.

crafts·man·ship /ˈkraf(t)smənˌSHip/ ▶ **n.** skill in a particular craft: *I admire his engineering skills and craftsmanship.* ■ the quality of design and work shown in something made by hand; artistry: *a piece of fine craftsmanship.*

crafts·per·son /ˈkraf(t)sˌpərsən/ ▶ **n.** (pl. **craftspeople** /-ˌpēpəl/) a person who is skilled in a particular craft (used as a neutral alternative).

crafts·wom·an /ˈkraf(t)sˌwo͝omən/ ▶ **n.** (pl. **craftswomen**) a woman who is skilled in a particular craft.

craft un·ion ▶ **n.** a labor union of people of the same skilled craft.

craft·work /ˈkraftˌwərk/ ▶ **n.** chiefly Brit. the making of things, esp. decorative objects, by hand as a profession or leisure activity. ■ work produced in such a way.
– DERIVATIVES **craft·work·er n.**

craft·y /ˈkraftē/ ▶ **adj.** (**craftier, craftiest**) **1** clever at achieving one's aims by indirect or deceitful methods: *a crafty crook faked an injury to escape from prison.* ■ of, involving, or relating to indirect or deceitful methods: *a shameless and crafty trick to mislead public opinion.*
2 informal of, involving, or relating to the making of decorative objects and other things by hand: *a market full of crafty pots and interesting earrings.*
– DERIVATIVES **craft·i·ly** /-təlē/ **adv., craft·i·ness n.**
– ORIGIN Old English *cræftig* 'strong, powerful,' later 'skillful' (see CRAFT, -Y[1]).

crag /krag/ ▶ **n.** a steep or rugged cliff or rock face.
– ORIGIN Middle English: of Celtic origin.

crag·gy /ˈkragē/ ▶ **adj.** (**craggier, craggiest**) (of a landscape) having many crags: *a craggy coastline.* ■ (of a cliff or rock face) rough and uneven. ■ (of a person's face, typically a man's) rugged and rough-textured in an attractive way.
– DERIVATIVES **crag·gi·ly** /ˈkragəlē/ **adv., crag·gi·ness n.**

crags·man /ˈkragzmən/ ▶ **n.** (pl. **cragsmen**) a skilled rock climber.

Cra·io·va /krīˈōvə/ a city in southwestern Romania; pop. 300,587 (2006).

crake /krāk/ ▶ **n.** a bird of the rail family, esp. one with a short bill like the corncrake. ● Family Rallidae: several genera, in particular *Porzana,* and numerous species. ■ the rasping cry of the corn crake.

– ORIGIN Middle English (originally denoting a crow or raven): from Old Norse *kráka, krákr,* of imitative origin.

cram /kram/ ▶ v. (**crams, cramming, crammed**) **1** [with obj.] completely fill (a place or container) to the point that it appears to be overflowing: *the ashtray by the bed was crammed with cigarette butts.* ■ force (people or things) into a place or container that is or appears to be too small to contain them: *it's amazing how you've managed to cram everyone in | he crammed the sandwiches into his mouth |* figurative *he had crammed so much into his short life.* ■ [no obj.] (of a number of people) enter a place or space that is or seems to be too small to accommodate all of them: *they all crammed into the car.*
2 [no obj.] study intensively over a short period of time just before an examination: *lectures were called off so students could cram for finals.*
– ORIGIN Old English *crammian,* of Germanic origin; related to Dutch *krammen* 'to cramp or clamp.'

cram·bo /ˈkrambō/ ▶ n. a game in which a player gives a word or line of verse to which each of the other players must find a rhyme.
– ORIGIN early 17th cent. (denoting a particular fashion in drinking): from earlier *crambe* 'cabbage,' used figuratively to denote something distasteful that is repeated, apparently from Latin *crambe repetita* 'cabbage served up again,' applied by Juvenal to any distasteful repetition.

cram·mer /ˈkramər/ ▶ n. Brit. a person or institution that prepares pupils for an examination intensively over a short period of time.

cram·ming /ˈkramiNG/ ▶ n. the fraudulent practice of adding unauthorized charges to a customer's phone bill.

cramp /kramp/ ▶ n. **1** a painful, involuntary contraction of a muscle or muscles, typically caused by fatigue or strain: *he suffered severe cramps in his foot.* ■ (**cramps**) abdominal pain caused by menstruation.
2 a tool, typically shaped like a capital G, for clamping two objects together for gluing or other work. ■ (also **cramp-iron**) a metal bar with bent ends for holding masonry together.
▶ v. **1** [with obj.] restrict or inhibit the development of: *tighter rules will cramp economic growth.*
2 [with obj.] fasten with a cramp or cramps: *cramp the gates to the posts.*
3 [no obj.] suffer from sudden and painful contractions of a muscle or muscles.
– PHRASES **cramp someone's style** informal prevent a person from acting freely or naturally.
– ORIGIN late Middle English: from Middle Low German and Middle Dutch *krampe;* sense 1 of the noun is via Old French *crampe.*

cramped /kram(p)t/ ▶ adj. **1** feeling or causing someone to feel uncomfortably confined or hemmed in by lack of space: *the staff had to work in cramped conditions.* ■ restricting or inhibiting the development of someone or something: *he felt cramped in a large organization.* ■ (of handwriting) small and difficult to read.
2 suffering from a cramp: *cramped muscles.*

cram·pon /ˈkram,pän/ ▶ n. (usu. **crampons**) **1** a metal plate with spikes fixed to a boot for walking on ice or rock climbing.
2 archaic term for GRAPPLING HOOK.
– ORIGIN Middle English (sense 2): from Old French, of Germanic origin.

Cra·nach /ˈkränəKH, -äKH/ two German painters. **Lucas** (1472–1553), known as **Cranach the Elder**, was a member of the Danube School, noted for his early religious pictures. His son **Lucas** (1515–86), known as **Cranach the Younger**, continued working in the same tradition as his father.

cran·ber·ry /ˈkran,berē, -bərē/ ▶ n. (pl. **cranberries**) **1** a small, red, acid berry used in cooking.
2 the evergreen dwarf shrub of the heath family that yields this fruit. ● Genus *Vaccinium,* family Ericaceae: several species, in particular the North American *V. macrocarpon,* which thrives in boggy places and from which most commercial varieties originate.
– ORIGIN mid 17th cent. (originally North American): from German *Kranbeere* or Low German *kranebeere* 'crane-berry.'

cran·ber·ry sauce ▶ n. a jellied sauce made from cranberries, a traditional accompaniment to turkey.

Crane¹ /krān/, Hart (1899–1932), US poet; full name *Harold Hart Crane.* He published only two books—*White Buildings* (1926), a collection, and *The Bridge* (1930), a mystical epic poem concerned with American life and consciousness—before committing suicide by jumping from a ship.

Crane², Stephen (1871–1900), US writer. He is well known for the novel, *The Red Badge of Courage* (1895), a study of an inexperienced soldier during the Civil War. It was hailed as a masterpiece of psychological realism, even though Crane himself had no personal war experience.

crane¹ /krān/ ▶ n. a large, tall machine used for moving heavy objects, typically by suspending them from a projecting arm or beam. ■ a moving platform supporting a television or movie camera.
▶ v. **1** [no obj.] stretch out one's neck in order to see something: *she craned forward to look more clearly.* ■ [with obj.] stretch out (one's neck) in this way.
2 [with obj.] move (a heavy object) with a crane: *the wheelhouse module is craned into position on the hull.*

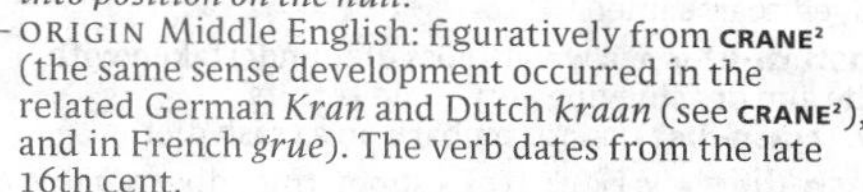
crane¹

– ORIGIN Middle English: figuratively from CRANE² (the same sense development occurred in the related German *Kran* and Dutch *kraan* (see CRANE²), and in French *grue*). The verb dates from the late 16th cent.

crane² ▶ n. a tall, long-legged, long-necked bird, typically with white or gray plumage and often with tail plumes and patches of bare red skin on the head. Cranes are noted for their elaborate courtship dances. ● Family Gruidae: four genera, in particular *Grus,* and several species, including the Eurasian **common crane** (*G. grus*).
– ORIGIN Old English, of Germanic origin; related to Dutch *kraan* and German *Kran,* from an Indo-European root shared by Latin *grus* and Greek *geranos.*

crane fly ▶ n. a slender, two-winged fly with very long legs. The larva of some kinds is the leatherjacket. ● Family Tipulidae: many genera and species, in particular the large and common *Tipula maxima.*

cranes·bill /ˈkrānz,bil/ ▶ n. a herbaceous plant that typically has lobed leaves and purple, violet, or pink five-petaled flowers. ● Genus *Geranium,* family Geraniaceae: several species, including the common **meadow cranesbill** (*G. pratense*), with deeply toothed leaves and bluish-purple flowers.
– ORIGIN mid 16th cent.: so named because of the long spur on the fruit, thought to resemble a crane's beak.

cra·ni·al /ˈkrānēəl/ ▶ adj. Anatomy of or relating to the skull or cranium.
– ORIGIN early 19th cent.: from CRANIUM + -AL.

cra·ni·al in·dex ▶ n. another term for CEPHALIC INDEX.

cra·ni·al nerve ▶ n. Anatomy each of twelve pairs of nerves that arise directly from the brain, not from the spinal cord, and pass through separate apertures in the skull.

> They are (with conventional roman numbering) the olfactory (I), optic (II), oculomotor (III), trochlear (IV), trigeminal (V), abducens (VI), facial (VII), vestibulocochlear (VIII), glossopharyngeal (IX), vagus (X), accessory (XI), and hypoglossal (XII) nerves.

cra·ni·ate /ˈkrānē,āt, -nēət/ Zoology ▶ n. an animal that possesses a skull. Compare with VERTEBRATE. ● Subphylum Craniata, phylum Chordata; used instead of Vertebrata in some classification schemes.
▶ adj. of or relating to the craniates.
– ORIGIN late 19th cent.: from modern Latin *craniatus,* from medieval Latin *cranium* (see CRANIUM).

cranio- ▶ comb. form relating to the skull: *craniotomy.*
– ORIGIN from Greek *kranion* 'skull.'

cra·ni·o·ce·re·bral /,krānēōsəˈrēbrəl, -ˈserəbrəl/ ▶ adj. relating to or involving both the cranium and the cerebrum.

cra·ni·o·fa·cial /,krānēōˈfāSHəl/ ▶ adj. Anatomy relating to the cranium and the face: *craniofacial surgery.*

cra·ni·ol·o·gy /,krānēˈäləjē/ ▶ n. historical the scientific study of the shape and size of the skulls of different human races. ■ another term for PHRENOLOGY.
– DERIVATIVES **cra·ni·o·log·i·cal** /-nēəˈläjikəl/ adj., **cra·ni·ol·o·gist** /-jist/ n.

cra·ni·om·e·ter /,krānēˈämitər/ ▶ n. a device for measuring the external dimensions of the skull.

cra·ni·om·e·try /,krānēˈämətrē/ ▶ n. historical the scientific measurement of skulls, esp. in relation to craniology.
– DERIVATIVES **cra·ni·o·met·ric** /,krānēəˈmetrik/ adj.

cra·ni·op·a·gus /,krānēˈäpəgəs/ ▶ n. (pl. **craniopagi**) (of conjoined twins) the condition of being joined at the head: [as modifier] *the first time that surgeons had tried to separate adult craniopagus twins.*
– ORIGIN based on *cranio-* 'skull' + Greek *pagos* 'something that has become solid.'

cra·ni·o·sa·cral ther·a·py /,krānēōˈsakrəl, -ˈsākrəl/ ▶ n. a system of alternative medicine intended to relieve pain and tension by gentle manipulations of the skull regarded as harmonizing with a natural rhythm in the central nervous system.

cra·ni·ot·o·my /,krānēˈätəmē/ ▶ n. surgical opening into the skull. ■ surgical perforation of the skull of a dead fetus to ease delivery.

cra·ni·um /ˈkrānēəm/ ▶ n. (pl. **craniums** or **crania** /-nēə/) Anatomy the skull, esp. the part enclosing the brain.
– ORIGIN late Middle English: via medieval Latin from Greek *kranion* 'skull.'

crank¹ /kraNGk/ ▶ v. [with obj.] **1** turn the crankshaft of (an internal combustion engine), typically in order to start the engine. ■ turn (a handle), typically in order to start an engine. ■ (**crank something up**) informal increase the intensity of something: *he cranked up the foghorn to full volume.* ■ (**crank something out**) informal produce something regularly and routinely: *an army of researchers cranked out worthy studies.*
2 (usu. as adj. **cranked**) give a bend to (a shaft, bar, etc.).
▶ n. **1** a part of an axle or shaft bent out at right angles, for converting reciprocal to circular motion and vice versa.
2 informal the drug methamphetamine.
– ORIGIN Old English *cranc* (recorded in *crancstæf,* denoting a weaver's implement), related to *crincan* (see CRINGE).

crank² ▶ n. **1** an eccentric person, esp. one who is obsessed by a particular subject or theory: *when he first started to air his views, they labeled him a crank |* [as modifier] *I am used to getting crank calls from conspiracy theorists.* ■ a bad-tempered person. [mid 19th cent.: back-formation from CRANKY.]
2 literary a fanciful turn of speech. [late 16th cent.: perhaps from a base meaning 'bent together, curled up,' shared by Old English *cranc* (see CRANK¹).]

crank³ ▶ adj. Nautical, archaic (of a sailing ship) easily keeled over, esp. by wind or sea through improper design or loading.
– ORIGIN early 17th cent.: perhaps from dialect *crank* 'weak, shaky' (compare with CRANKY or CRANK¹).

crank·case /ˈkraNGk,kās/ ▶ n. a case or covering enclosing a crankshaft.

crank·pin /ˈkraNGk,pin/ ▶ n. a pin by which a connecting rod is attached to a crank.

crank·shaft /ˈkraNGk,SHaft/ ▶ n. a shaft driven by a crank.

crank·y /ˈkraNGkē/ ▶ adj. (**crankier, crankiest**) informal ill-tempered; irritable: *he was bored and cranky after eight hours of working.* ■ eccentric or strange, typically because highly unorthodox: *a cranky scheme to pipe ground-level ozone into the stratosphere.* ■ (of a machine) working badly; shaky: *the cranky elevator breaks down periodically.*
– DERIVATIVES **crank·i·ly** /-kəlē/ adv., **crank·i·ness** n.
– ORIGIN late 18th cent. (in the sense 'sickly, in poor health'): perhaps from obsolete (*counterfeit*) *crank* 'a rogue feigning sickness,' from Dutch or German *krank* 'sick.'

Cran·mer /ˈkranmər/, Thomas (1489–1556), English cleric and martyr. A leader in the English Reformation, he was appointed the first Protestant archbishop of Canterbury in 1532 and was responsible for liturgical reform and the compilation of the Book of Common Prayer (1549). He was convicted of treason and heresy under Mary Tudor and burned at the stake.

cran·nog /ˈkran,ôg, -əg/ ▶ n. an ancient fortified dwelling constructed in a lake or marsh in Scotland or Ireland.
– ORIGIN early 17th cent.: from Irish *crannóg,* Scottish Gaelic *crannag* 'timber structure,' from *crann* 'tree, beam.'

cran·ny /ˈkranē/ ▶ n. (pl. **crannies**) a small, narrow space or opening.
– PHRASES **every nook and cranny** see NOOK.
– DERIVATIVES **cran·nied** /ˈkranēd/ adj.
– ORIGIN late Middle English: from Old French *crane* 'notched,' from *cran,* from popular Latin *crena* 'notch.'

Cran·ston /ˈkranstən/ an industrial city in central Rhode Island, south of Providence; pop. 79,980 (est. 2008).

PRONUNCIATION KEY ə *ago, up;* ər *over, fur;* a *hat;* ā *ate;* ä *car;* e *let;* ē *see;* i *fit;* ī *by;* NG *sing;* ō *go;* ô *law, for;* oi *toy;* o͝o *good;* o͞o *goo;* ou *out;* TH *thin;* T͟H *then;* ZH *vision*

C

crap[1] /krap/ vulgar slang ▶ **n. 1** something of extremely poor quality. ■ nonsense. ■ rubbish; junk. **2** excrement. ■ [in sing.] an act of defecation.
▶ **v.** (**craps, crapping, crapped**) [no obj.] defecate.
– ORIGIN Middle English: related to Dutch *krappe*, from *krappen* 'pluck or cut off,' and perhaps also to Old French *crappe* 'siftings,' Anglo-Latin *crappa* 'chaff.' The original sense was 'chaff,' later 'residue from rendering fat,' also 'dregs of beer.' Current senses date from the late 19th cent.

crap[2] ▶ **n.** a losing throw of 2, 3, or 12 in craps.
▶ **v.** [no obj.] (**crap out**) informal make a losing throw at craps. ■ withdraw from or give up on a game or activity because of fear or fatigue: *when entrepreneurs get to $1 billion they crap out and turn their companies over to others.* ■ fail in what one is attempting to do: *the Rams almost crapped out late in the game.* ■ (of a machine) break down: *his TelePrompTer crapped out.*
– ORIGIN early 20th cent.: from CRAPS.

crape /krāp/ ▶ **n.** archaic spelling of CREPE.
– DERIVATIVES **crap·y adj.**
– ORIGIN early 16th cent.: from French *crêpe* (see CREPE).

crape myr·tle (also **crepe myrtle**) ▶ **n.** an ornamental Asian shrub or small tree with pink, white, or purplish crinkled petals. ● Genus *Lagerstroemia*, family Lythraceae: several species, in particular **common crape myrtle** (*L. indica*) and **queen's crape myrtle** (*L. speciosa*).

crap game ▶ **n.** a game of craps.

crap·o·la /kra'pōlə/ ▶ **n.** vulgar slang nonsense; rubbish.
– ORIGIN from CRAP[1] and *-ola*, a suffix used humorously to extend standard words.

crap·per /'krapər/ ▶ **n.** vulgar slang a toilet.

crap·pie /'kräpē, 'krapē/ ▶ **n.** (pl. **crappies**) a North American freshwater fish of the sunfish family, the male of which builds a nest and guards the eggs and young. ● Genus *Pomoxis*, family Centrarchidae: several species, including the **black crappie** (*P. nigromaculatus*) and the **white crappie** (*P. annularis*).
– ORIGIN mid 19th cent.: of unknown origin.

crap·py /'krapē/ ▶ **adj.** (**crappier, crappiest**) vulgar slang of extremely poor quality: *crappy wine.* ■ ill; in poor physical condition: *I feel really crappy today.*

craps /kraps/ ▶ **plural n.** [treated as sing.] a gambling game played with two dice, chiefly in North America. A throw of 7 or 11 is a winning throw, 2, 3, or 12 is a losing throw; any other throw must be repeated. See also CRAP[2].
– ORIGIN early 19th cent.: perhaps from CRAB[1] or *crab's eyes*, denoting the lowest throw (two ones) at dice.

crap·shoot /'krap,SHōōt/ ▶ **n.** a crap game. ■ informal a risky or uncertain matter: *predicting any extreme weather event is a scientific crapshoot.*
– DERIVATIVES **crap·shoot·er n.**

crap·u·lent /'krapyələnt/ ▶ **adj.** literary of or relating to the drinking of alcohol or drunkenness.
– DERIVATIVES **crap·u·lence n., crap·u·lous** /-yələs/ **adj.**
– ORIGIN mid 17th cent.: from late Latin *crapulentus* 'very drunk,' from Latin *crapula* 'inebriation,' from Greek *kraipalē* 'drunken headache.'

cra·que·lure /kra'klŏŏr, 'krak,lŏŏr/ ▶ **n.** a network of fine cracks in the paint or varnish of a painting.
– ORIGIN early 20th cent.: French, from *craqueler* 'to crackle.'

crash[1] /krasH/ ▶ **v. 1** [no obj.] (of a vehicle) collide violently with an obstacle or another vehicle: *the stolen car she was riding in crashed into a tree.* ■ [with obj.] cause (a moving object) to collide in this way. ■ (of an aircraft) fall from the sky and violently hit the land or sea: *a jet crashed 200 yards from the school.* ■ [with obj.] cause (an aircraft) to fall from the sky in this way.
2 move or cause to move with force, speed, and sudden loud noise: [no obj.] *huge waves crashed down on us* | [with obj.] *she crashed down the telephone receiver.* ■ [no obj.] make a sudden loud, deep noise: *the thunder crashed.*
3 [no obj.] informal (of a business, a market, or a price) fall suddenly and disastrously in value: *silver prices crashed in early 1980.*
4 [no obj.] Computing (of a machine, system, or software) fail suddenly: *the project was postponed because the computer crashed.* ■ (of a patient) suffer a cardiac arrest.
5 [with obj.] informal enter (a party) without an invitation or permission.
6 [no obj.] informal go to sleep, esp. suddenly or in an improvised setting: *I'll crash in the back of the van for a couple of hours.*
▶ **n. 1** a violent collision, typically of one vehicle with another or with an obstacle: *a car crash.* ■ an instance of an aircraft falling from the sky to hit the land or sea.
2 a sudden loud noise as of something breaking or hitting another object: *he slammed the phone down with a crash.*
3 a sudden disastrous drop in the value or price of something, esp. shares of stock: *a stock market crash* | *the crash of 1987.* ■ the sudden collapse of a business.
4 Computing a sudden failure which puts a system out of action.
▶ **adj.** done rapidly or urgently and involving a concentrated effort: *a crash course in Italian.*
▶ **adv.** with a sudden loud sound: *crash went the bolt.*
– PHRASES **crash and burn** informal come to grief or fail spectacularly.
– ORIGIN late Middle English: imitative, perhaps partly suggested by CRAZE and DASH.

crash[2] ▶ **n.** dated a coarse plain linen, woolen, or cotton fabric, used for curtains and towels.
– ORIGIN early 19th cent.: from Russian *krashenina* 'dyed coarse linen.'

crash di·et ▶ **n.** a weight-loss diet undertaken with the aim of achieving very rapid results.
▶ **v.** (**crash-diet**) [no obj.] embark on a crash diet.

crash-dive ▶ **v.** [no obj.] (of a submarine) dive rapidly and steeply to a deeper level in an emergency. ■ (of an aircraft) plunge steeply downward into a crash.
▶ **n.** (**crash dive**) a steep dive of this kind by a submarine or aircraft.

crash hel·met ▶ **n.** a helmet worn by a motorcyclist or a race car driver to protect the head in case of a crash.

crash·ing /'krasHiNG/ ▶ **adj.** informal complete; total (used for emphasis): *a crashing bore.*
– DERIVATIVES **crash·ing·ly adv.**

crash-land ▶ **v.** [no obj.] (of an aircraft) land roughly in an emergency, typically without lowering the landing gear: (as noun **crash landing**) *a plane made a crash landing near the airport.*

crash pad ▶ **n. 1** informal a place to sleep, esp. for a single night or in an emergency.
2 a thick piece of shock-absorbing material for the protection of the occupants of an aircraft cockpit or motor vehicle.

crash-test ▶ **v.** [with obj.] deliberately crash (a new vehicle) under controlled conditions in order to evaluate and improve its ability to withstand impact.
▶ **n.** (**crash test**) a test of this kind.

crash·wor·thy /'krasH,wərT͟Hē/ ▶ **adj.** (of a vehicle or an aircraft) relatively well able to withstand a crash.
– DERIVATIVES **crash·wor·thi·ness n.**

crass /kras/ ▶ **adj.** lacking sensitivity, refinement, or intelligence: *the crass assumptions that men make about women.*
– DERIVATIVES **cras·si·tude** /'krasə,t(y)ōōd/ **n., crass·ly adv., crass·ness n.**
– ORIGIN late 15th cent. (in the sense 'dense or coarse (in constitution or texture)'): from Latin *crassus* 'solid, thick.'

Cras·sus /'krasəs/, Marcus Licinius (*c.*115–53 BC), Roman politician. After defeating Spartacus in 71 BC, he joined Caesar and Pompey in the First Triumvirate in 60.

-crat ▶ **comb. form** denoting a member or supporter of a particular form of government or rule: *plutocrat* | *technocrat.*
– ORIGIN from French *-crate*, from adjectives ending in *-cratique* (see -CRATIC).

crate /krāt/ ▶ **n. 1** a slatted wooden case used for transporting or storing goods: *a crate of bananas.* ■ a square metal or plastic container divided into small individual units, used for transporting or storing bottles: *a milk crate* | *a crate of beer.*
2 informal, dated an old and dilapidated vehicle.
▶ **v.** [with obj.] pack (something) in a crate for transportation.
– DERIVATIVES **crate·ful** /'krāt,fōōl/ **n.** (pl. **cratefuls**).
– ORIGIN late Middle English: perhaps related to Dutch *krat* 'tailboard of a wagon,' earlier 'box of a coach,' of unknown origin.

Cra·ter /'krātər/ Astronomy a small and faint southern constellation (the Cup), between Hydra and Leo, said to represent the goblet of Apollo. ■ (as genitive **Crateris** /krā'teris/) used with a preceding letter or numeral to designate a star in this constellation: *the star Delta Crateris.*
– ORIGIN Latin, from Greek,'mixing bowl.'

cra·ter /'krātər/ ▶ **n. 1** a large, bowl-shaped cavity in the ground or on the surface of a planet or the moon, typically one caused by an explosion or the impact of a meteorite or other celestial body. ■ a large pit or hollow forming the mouth of a volcano. ■ a cavity or hole in any surface.
2 a large bowl used in ancient Greece for mixing wine.
▶ **v.** [with obj.] form a crater in (the ground or a planet): *he has the offensive power to crater the enemy's runways* | (as adj. **cratered**) *the heavily cratered areas of the moon.*
– ORIGIN early 17th cent. (denoting the hollow forming the mouth of a volcano): via Latin from Greek *kratēr* 'mixing bowl,' from *krasis* 'mixture.'

Cra·ter Lake a lake that fills a volcanic crater in the Cascade Mountains in southwestern Oregon. With a depth of more than 1,968 feet (600 m), it is the deepest lake in the US.

-cratic ▶ **comb. form** relating to a particular kind of government or rule: *bureaucratic* | *democratic.*
– ORIGIN from French *-cratique*, from *-cratie* (see -CRACY).

-cratically ▶ **suffix** forming adverbs corresponding to adjectives ending in *-cratic*: *democratically.*
– ORIGIN from -CRATIC + -ALLY. (See -CRACY).

C rations ▶ **plural n.** a type of canned food formerly used by US soldiers.
– ORIGIN C for *combat.*

cra·ton /'krā,tän, 'kra-/ ▶ **n.** Geology a large, stable block of the earth's crust forming the nucleus of a continent.
– DERIVATIVES **cra·ton·ic** /krā'tänik, kra-, krə-/ **adj.**
– ORIGIN 1930s: alteration of *kratogen* in the same sense, from Greek *kratos* 'strength.'

cra·vat /krə'vat/ ▶ **n.** a short, wide strip of fabric worn by men around the neck and tucked inside an open-necked shirt. ■ a necktie.
– DERIVATIVES **cra·vat·ted adj.**
– ORIGIN mid 17th cent.: from French *cravate*, from *Cravate* 'Croat' (from German *Krabat*, from Serbian and Croatian *Hrvat*), because of the scarf worn by Croatian mercenaries in France.

crave /krāv/ ▶ **v.** [with obj.] feel a powerful desire for (something): *a program to give the infants the human touch they crave.* ■ dated beg for (something): *I must crave your indulgence.*
– DERIVATIVES **crav·er n.**
– ORIGIN Old English *crafian* (in the sense 'demand, claim as a right'), of Germanic origin; related to Swedish *kräva*, Danish *kræve* 'demand.' The current sense dates from late Middle English.

cra·ven /'krāvən/ ▶ **adj.** contemptibly lacking in courage; cowardly: *a craven abdication of his moral duty.*
▶ **n.** archaic a cowardly person.
– DERIVATIVES **cra·ven·ly adv., cra·ven·ness n.**
– ORIGIN Middle English *cravant* 'defeated,' perhaps via Anglo-Norman French from Old French *cravante*, past participle of *cravanter* 'crush, overwhelm,' based on Latin *crepare* 'burst.' The change in the ending in the 17th cent. was due to association with past participles ending in *-en* (see -EN[3]).

crav·ing /'krāviNG/ ▶ **n.** a powerful desire for something: *a craving for chocolate.*

craw /krô/ ▶ **n.** dated the crop of a bird or insect. ■ chiefly humorous the stomach of a person or animal.
– PHRASES **stick in one's craw** see STICK[2].
– ORIGIN late Middle English: from or related to Middle Dutch *crāghe* or Middle Low German *krage* 'neck, throat.'

craw·dad /'krô,dad/ ▶ **n.** a freshwater crayfish.
– ORIGIN early 20th cent.: fanciful alteration of CRAWFISH.

craw·fish /'krô,fisH/ ▶ **n.** (pl. **same** or **crawfishes**) a freshwater crayfish. ■ another term for SPINY LOBSTER.
▶ **v.** [no obj.] informal retreat from a position: *the three networks, intimidated by the public outcry, had begun to crawfish.*
– ORIGIN early 17th cent.: variant of CRAYFISH.

Craw·ford /'krôfərd/, Joan (1908–77), US actress; born *Lucille Le Sueur*. Notable movies: *The Women* (1939), *Mildred Pierce* (1945), *Johnny Guitar* (1954), and *Whatever Happened to Baby Jane?* (1962).

Joan Crawford

crawl /krôl/ ▶ **v.** [no obj.] **1** (of a person) move forward on the hands and knees or by dragging the body close to the ground: *they crawled out from under the table.* ■ (of an insect or small animal) move slowly along a surface: *the tiny spider was crawling up Nicky's arm.* ■ (of a vehicle) move at an unusually slow pace: *the traffic was crawling along.* ■ swim using the crawl. ■ informal behave obsequiously or ingratiatingly in the hope of gaining someone's favor: *don't come crawling back to me later when you realize your mistake.* ■ technical (of paint or other liquid) move after application to form an uneven layer over the surface below: *glazes can crawl away from a crack in the piece.*
2 (**be crawling with**) be covered or crowded with insects or people, to an extent that is disgusting or objectionable: *the place was crawling with soldiers.*
▶ **n.** [in sing.] **1** an act of moving on one's hands and knees or dragging one's body along the ground: *they began the crawl back to their own lines.* ■ a slow rate of movement, typically that of a vehicle: *he reduced his speed to a crawl.*
2 a swimming stroke involving alternate overarm movements and rapid kicks of the legs.
3 a strip or band running across the bottom of a computer or television screen, within which news headlines, public service announcements, and advertisements are continuously scrolled.
– PHRASES **make someone's skin crawl** see SKIN.
– DERIVATIVES **crawl·ing·ly** adv., **crawl·y** adj.
– ORIGIN Middle English: of unknown origin; possibly related to Swedish *kravla* and Danish *kravle.*

crawl·er /ˈkrôlər/ ▶ **n.** a thing that crawls or moves at a slow pace, esp. an insect. ■ (in full **crawler tractor**) a tractor or other vehicle moving on an endless caterpillar track. ■ Computing a program that searches the World Wide Web, typically in order to create an index of data.

crawl·ing peg ▶ **n.** a point on a scale of exchange rates in which a currency's value is allowed to go up or down frequently by small amounts within overall limits.

crawl space ▶ **n.** an area of limited height under a floor or roof, giving access to wiring and plumbing.

cray·fish /ˈkrāˌfisн/ ▶ **n.** (pl. **same** or **crayfishes**) (also **freshwater crayfish**) a nocturnal freshwater crustacean that resembles a small lobster and inhabits streams and rivers. ● Several genera in the infraorder Astacidea, class Malacostraca, including *Astacus* of Europe and *Cambarus* of North America. ■ (also **marine crayfish**) another term for SPINY LOBSTER.
– ORIGIN Middle English: from Old French *crevice,* of Germanic origin and related to German *Krebs* (see CRAB[1]). In the 16th cent. or earlier the second syllable was altered by association with FISH[1].

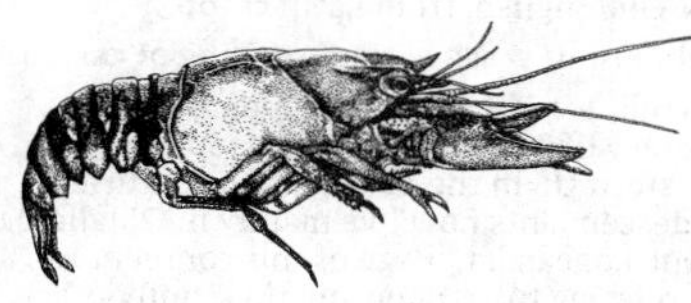

crayfish

cray·on /ˈkrāˌän, ˈkrāən/ ▶ **n.** a pencil or stick of colored chalk or wax, used for drawing.
▶ **v.** [with obj.] draw with a crayon or crayons: *Jeff crayoned a picture on a legal pad* | [no obj.] *a child crayoning in a coloring book.*
– ORIGIN mid 17th cent.: from French, from *craie* 'chalk,' from Latin *creta.*

craze /krāz/ ▶ **n.** an enthusiasm for a particular activity or object that typically appears suddenly and achieves widespread but short-lived popularity: *the latest craze for bungee jumping.*
▶ **v.** [with obj.] **1** (usu. as adj. **crazed**) wildly insane or excited: *a crazed killer* | *power-crazed tinpot dictators.*
2 produce a network of fine cracks on (a surface): *the lake was frozen over but crazed with cracks.* ■ [no obj.] develop such cracks.
– ORIGIN late Middle English (in the sense 'break, shatter, produce cracks'): perhaps of Scandinavian origin and related to Swedish *krasa* 'crunch.'

cra·zy /ˈkrāzē/ informal ▶ **adj.** (**crazier, craziest**) **1** mentally deranged, esp. as manifested in a wild or aggressive way: *Stella went crazy and assaulted a visitor* | *a crazy grin.* ■ extremely annoyed or angry: *the noise they made was* ***driving me crazy.*** ■ foolish: *it was crazy to hope that good might come out of this mess.*
2 extremely enthusiastic: *I'm* ***crazy about*** *Cindy* | *a football-crazy bunch of boys.*
3 (of an angle) appearing absurdly out of place or in an unlikely position: *the monument leaned at a crazy angle.* ■ archaic (of a ship or building) full of cracks or flaws; unsound or shaky.
▶ **n.** (pl. **crazies**) a mentally deranged person.
– PHRASES **like crazy** to a great degree: *I was laughing like crazy.*
– DERIVATIVES **cra·zi·ly** /-zilē/ adv., **cra·zi·ness** n.

cra·zy bone ▶ **n.** another term for FUNNY BONE.

Cra·zy Horse (*c.*1849–77), Sioux chief; Sioux name *Ta-Sunko-Witko.* A leading figure in the resistance to white settlement on Native American land, he was at the center of the confederation that defeated General Custer at Little Bighorn in 1876. He surrendered in 1877 and was killed while in custody.

cra·zy quilt ▶ **n.** a patchwork quilt of a type traditionally made in North America, with patches of randomly varying sizes, shapes, colors, and fabrics. ■ a disorganized collection of things: *colonial America was a crazy quilt of laws.*

CRC ▶ **abbr.** ■ Printing camera-ready copy. ■ Civil Rights Commission. ■ Computing cyclic redundancy check (or code).

creak /krēk/ ▶ **v.** [no obj.] **1** (of an object, typically a wooden one) make a harsh, high-pitched sound when being moved or when pressure or weight is applied: *the stairs creaked as she went up them* | *the garden gate creaked open.*
2 show weakness or frailty under strain: *stock prices creaked to a mixed finish today.*
▶ **n.** a harsh scraping or squeaking sound: *the creak of a floorboard broke the silence.*
– DERIVATIVES **creak·ing·ly** adv.
– ORIGIN Middle English (as a verb in the sense 'croak'): imitative.

creak·y /ˈkrēkē/ ▶ **adj.** (**creakier, creakiest**) **1** (of an object, typically a wooden one) making or liable to make a harsh, high-pitched sound when being moved or when pressure or weight is applied: *I climbed the creaky stairs.* ■ (of a voice) producing such a sound.
2 old-fashioned or decrepit: *the country's creaky legal system.*
– DERIVATIVES **creak·i·ly** /-kəlē/ adv., **creak·i·ness** n.

cream /krēm/ ▶ **n.** **1** the thick white or pale yellow fatty liquid that rises to the top when milk is left to stand and that can be eaten as an accompaniment to desserts or used as a cooking ingredient: *strawberries and cream* | [as modifier] *a cream sauce.* ■ the part of a liquid that gathers at the top. ■ a sauce, soup, dessert, or similar food containing cream or milk or having the consistency of cream: *a can of* ***cream of*** *mushroom soup.* ■ a candy of a specified flavor that is creamy in texture, typically covered with chocolate: *a peppermint cream.*
2 a thick liquid or semisolid cosmetic or medical preparation applied to the skin: *shaving cream* | *moisturizing creams.*
3 the very best of a group of people or things: *the paper's readership is* ***the cream of*** *American society.*
4 a very pale yellow or off-white color: *the dress is available in white or cream* | [as modifier] *a cream linen jacket.*
▶ **v.** [with obj.] **1** work (butter, typically with sugar) to form a smooth soft paste. ■ (usu. as adj. **creamed**) mash (a cooked vegetable) and mix with milk or cream: *creamed turnips.* ■ add cream to (coffee).
2 rub a cosmetic cream into (the skin): *Madge was creaming her face in front of the mirror.*
3 informal defeat (someone) heavily, esp. in a sports contest. ■ hit or collide heavily and violently with (someone), esp. in a car: *she got creamed by a speeding car.*
4 [no obj.] vulgar slang (of a person) be sexually aroused, esp. to the point of producing sexual secretions. ■ [with obj.] moisten (one's underpants) due to such arousal.
– PHRASAL VERBS **cream something off** take the best of a group of people or things, esp. in a way that is considered unfair: *the schools cream off some of the better students.* ■ make a disproportionate or excessive profit on a transaction.
– ORIGIN Middle English: from Old French *cresme,* from a blend of late Latin *cramum* (probably of Gaulish origin) and ecclesiastical Latin *chrisma* (see CHRISM).

cream cheese ▶ **n.** soft, rich cheese made from unskimmed milk and cream.

cream·er /ˈkrēmər/ ▶ **n.** **1** a cream or milk substitute for adding to coffee or tea.
2 a small jug for cream.
3 historical a flat dish used for skimming the cream off milk. ■ a machine used for separating cream from milk.

cream·er·y /ˈkrēm(ə)rē/ ▶ **n.** (pl. **creameries**) a place where butter and cheese are produced. ■ dated a shop where dairy products are sold.
– ORIGIN mid 19th cent.: from CREAM, on the pattern of French *crémerie.*

cream of tar·tar ▶ **n.** a white, crystalline, acidic compound obtained as a byproduct of wine fermentation and used chiefly in baking powder. ● Alternative name: **potassium hydrogen tartrate**; chem. formula: HOOC(CHOH)$_2$COOK.

cream puff ▶ **n.** **1** a cake made of light pastry filled with cream.
2 informal a weak or ineffectual person. ■ [as modifier] denoting something of little consequence or difficulty: *a cream-puff assignment.*
3 informal a secondhand car or other item maintained in excellent condition.

cream so·da ▶ **n.** a carbonated, vanilla-flavored soft drink.

cream·ware /ˈkrēmˌwe(ə)r/ ▶ **n.** glazed earthenware pottery of a rich cream color, developed by Josiah Wedgwood in about 1760.

cream·y /ˈkrēmē/ ▶ **adj.** (**creamier, creamiest**) resembling cream in consistency or color: *beat the sugar and egg yolks together until thick and creamy* | *creamy white flowers.* ■ containing a lot of cream: *a thick, creamy dressing.*
– DERIVATIVES **cream·i·ly** /-məlē/ adv., **cream·i·ness** n.

cre·ance /ˈkrēəns/ ▶ **n.** Falconry a long, fine cord attached to a hawk's leash to prevent escape during training.
– ORIGIN late 15th cent.: from French *créance* 'faith,' also denoting a cord to retain a bird of *peu de créance* ('of little faith,' i.e., which cannot yet be relied upon).

crease /krēs/ ▶ **n.** **1** a line or ridge produced on paper or cloth by folding, pressing, or crushing it: *khaki trousers with knife-edge creases.* ■ a wrinkle or furrow in the skin, typically of the face, caused by age or a particular facial expression.
2 (usu. **the crease**) an area around the goal in ice hockey or lacrosse that attacking players may not normally enter unless the puck or ball has already done so. ■ Cricket any of a number of lines marked on the pitch at specified places, esp. the position of a batsman.
▶ **v.** [with obj.] **1** make a crease in (cloth or paper): *he sank into the chair, careful not to crease his dinner jacket* | (as adj. **creased**) *a creased piece of paper.* ■ cause a crease to appear temporarily in (the face or its features), typically as a result of the expression of an emotion or feeling: *a small frown creased her forehead.*
2 (of a bullet) graze (someone or something), causing little damage: *a bullet creased his thigh.*
– ORIGIN late 16th cent.: probably a variant of CREST.

cre·ate /krēˈāt/ ▶ **v.** [with obj.] bring (something) into existence: *he created a thirty-acre lake* | *over 170 jobs were created.* ■ cause (something) to happen as a result of one's actions: *divorce only created problems for children.* ■ (of an actor) originate (a role) by playing a character for the first time. ■ [with obj. and complement] invest (someone) with a new rank or title: *he was created a baronet.*
– ORIGIN late Middle English (in the sense 'form out of nothing,' used of a divine or supernatural being): from Latin *creat-* 'produced,' from the verb *creare.*

cre·a·tine /ˈkrēəˌtēn, ˈkrēətn/ ▶ **n.** Biochemistry a compound formed in protein metabolism and present in much living tissue. It is involved in the supply of energy for muscular contraction. ● A guanidine derivative, usually present as a phosphate; chem. formula: $C_4H_9N_3O_2$.
– ORIGIN mid 19th cent.: formed irregularly from Greek *kreas* 'meat' + -INE[4].

cre·a·tine phos·phate ▶ **n.** another term for PHOSPHOCREATINE.

cre·at·i·nine /krēˈatnˌēn, -ˈatn-in/ ▶ **n.** Biochemistry a compound that is produced by metabolism of creatine and excreted in the urine. ● An anhydride of creatine; chem. formula: $C_7H_4N_3O$.

cre·a·tion /krēˈāsнən/ ▶ **n.** **1** the action or process of bringing something into existence: *the creation of a coalition government* | *job creation.* ■ a thing that has been made or invented, esp. something showing artistic talent: *she treats fictional creations as if they were real people.*
2 (**the Creation**) the bringing into of existence of the universe, esp. when regarded as an act of God. ■ everything so created; the universe: *our alienation from the rest of Creation.*
3 the action or process of investing someone with a new rank or title.
– ORIGIN late Middle English: via Old French from Latin *creatio(n-),* from the verb *creare* (see CREATE).

cre·a·tion·ism /krēˈāsнəˌnizəm/ ▶ **n.** the belief that the universe and living organisms originate from specific acts of divine creation, as in the biblical account, rather than by natural processes such as evolution. ■ another term for CREATION SCIENCE.
– DERIVATIVES **cre·a·tion·ist** n. & adj.

C

cre·a·tion sci·ence ▶ **n.** the interpretation of scientific knowledge in accord with belief in the literal truth of the Bible, esp. regarding the creation of matter, life, and humankind in six days.

cre·a·tive /krēˈātiv/ ▶ **adj.** relating to or involving the imagination or original ideas, esp. in the production of an artistic work: *change unleashes people's creative energy* | *creative writing*. ■ (of a person) having good imagination or original ideas: *Homer, the creative genius of Greek epic*.
▶ **n.** informal a person who is creative, typically in a professional context.
– DERIVATIVES **cre·a·tive·ly adv.**, **cre·a·tive·ness n.**

cre·a·tive ac·count·an·cy (also **creative accounting**) ▶ **n.** informal the exploitation of loopholes in financial regulation in order to gain advantage or present figures in a misleadingly favorable light.

cre·a·tiv·i·ty /ˌkrē-āˈtivitē/ ▶ **n.** the use of the imagination or original ideas, esp. in the production of an artistic work.

cre·a·tor /krēˈātər/ ▶ **n.** a person or thing that brings something into existence. ■ (**the Creator**) used as a name for God.

crea·ture /ˈkrēCHər/ ▶ **n.** an animal, as distinct from a human being: *night sounds of birds and other creatures*. ■ an animal or person: *as fellow creatures on this planet, animals deserve respect*. ■ a fictional or imaginary being, typically a frightening one: *a creature from outer space*. ■ archaic anything living or existing: *dress, jewels, and other transitory creatures*. ■ a person of a specified kind, typically one viewed with pity, contempt, or desire: *you heartless creature!* ■ a person or organization considered to be under the complete control of another: *the village teacher was expected to be the creature of his employer*.
– PHRASES **creature of habit** a person who follows an unvarying routine.
– DERIVATIVES **crea·ture·ly adj.**
– ORIGIN Middle English (in the sense 'something created'): via Old French from late Latin *creatura*, from the verb *creare* (see CREATE).

crea·ture com·forts ▶ **plural n.** material comforts that contribute to physical ease and well-being, such as good food and accommodations.

crèche /kresH/ ▶ **n. 1** a model or tableau representing the scene of Jesus Christ's birth, displayed in homes or public places at Christmas.
2 Brit. a nursery where babies and young children are cared for during the working day.
– ORIGIN late 18th cent. (sense 1): French.

Cré·cy, Battle of /krāˈsē/ a battle between the English and the French in 1346 near the village of Crécy-en-Ponthieu in Picardy, at which the forces of Edward III defeated those of Philip VI. It was the first major English victory of the Hundred Years War.

cred /kred/ ▶ **n.** informal term for STREET CREDIBILITY.

cred·al /ˈkrēdl/ (also **creedal**) ▶ **adj.** of or relating to a statement of Christian or other religious belief.

cre·dence /ˈkrēdns/ ▶ **n. 1** belief in or acceptance of something as true: *psychoanalysis finds little credence among laymen*. ■ the likelihood of something being true; plausibility: *being called upon by the media as an expert **lends credence to** one's opinions*.
2 [usu. as modifier] a small side table, shelf, or niche in a church for holding the elements of the Eucharist before they are consecrated: *a credence table*.
– PHRASES **give credence to** accept as true.
– ORIGIN Middle English: via Old French from medieval Latin *credentia*, from Latin *credent-* 'believing,' from the verb *credere*.

cre·den·tial /krəˈdenCHəl/ ▶ **n.** (usu. **credentials**) a qualification, achievement, personal quality, or aspect of a person's background, typically when used to indicate that they are suitable for something: *recruitment is based mainly on academic credentials*. ■ a document or certificate proving a person's identity or qualifications. ■ a letter of introduction given by a government to an ambassador before a new posting.
– ORIGIN late Middle English: from medieval Latin *credentialis*, from *credentia* (see CREDENCE). The original use was as an adjective in the sense 'giving credence to, recommending,' frequently in *credential letters* or *papers*, hence *credentials* (mid 17th cent).

cre·den·tialed /krəˈdensHəld/ ▶ **adj.** awarded or in possession of credentials: *impeccably credentialed professionals*.

cre·den·za /krəˈdenzə/ ▶ **n.** a sideboard or cupboard.
– ORIGIN late 19th cent.: Italian, from medieval Latin *credentia* (see CREDENCE).

cred·i·bil·i·ty /ˌkredəˈbilitē/ ▶ **n.** the quality of being trusted and believed in: *the government's loss of credibility*. ■ the quality of being convincing or believable: *the book's anecdotes have scant regard for credibility*. ■ another term for STREET CREDIBILITY.
– ORIGIN mid 16th cent.: from medieval Latin *credibilitas*, from Latin *credibilis* (see CREDIBLE).

cred·i·bil·i·ty gap ▶ **n.** an apparent difference between what is said or promised and what happens or is true.

cred·i·ble /ˈkredəbəl/ ▶ **adj.** able to be believed; convincing: *few people found his story credible* | *a credible witness*. ■ capable of persuading people that something will happen or be successful: *a credible threat*.
– DERIVATIVES **cred·i·bly** /-blē/ **adv.**
– ORIGIN late Middle English: from Latin *credibilis*, from *credere* 'believe.'

cred·it /ˈkredit/ ▶ **n. 1** the ability of a customer to obtain goods or services before payment, based on the trust that payment will be made in the future: *I've got unlimited credit*. ■ the money lent or made available under such an arrangement: *the bank refused to extend their credit* | [as modifier] *he was exceeding his credit limit*.
2 an entry recording a sum received, listed on the right-hand side or column of an account. The opposite of DEBIT. ■ a payment received: *you need to record debits or credits made to your account*.
3 public acknowledgment or praise, typically that given or received when a person's responsibility for an action or idea becomes or is made apparent: *the president claims credit for each accomplishment*. ■ [in sing.] a source of pride, typically someone or something that reflects well on another person or organization: *he's **a credit to** his mother*. ■ (usu. **credits**) an acknowledgment of a contributor's services to a movie or a television program, typically one of a list that is scrolled down the screen at the beginning or end of a movie or program: *the closing credits finished rolling*.
4 the acknowledgment of a student's completion of a course that counts toward a degree or diploma as maintained in a school's records: *a student can earn one unit of academic credit*. ■ a unit of study counting toward a degree or diploma: *in his first semester he earned 17 credits*. ■ acknowledgment of merit in an examination which is reflected in the grades awarded: *students will receive credit for accuracy and style*.
5 archaic the quality of being believed or credited: *the abstract philosophy of Cicero has lost its credit*. ■ favorable estimation; good reputation: *John Gilpin was a citizen of credit and renown*.
▶ **v.** (**credits, crediting, credited**) [with obj.] **1** publicly acknowledge someone as a participant in the production of (something published or broadcast): *the screenplay is **credited to** one American and two Japanese writers*. ■ (**credit someone with**) ascribe (an achievement or good quality) to someone: *he is credited with painting one hundred and twenty-five canvases*.
2 add (an amount of money) to an account: *this deferred tax can be **credited to** the profit and loss account*.
3 believe (something surprising or unlikely): *you would hardly credit it—but it was true*.
– PHRASES **credit where credit is due** praise given when it is deserved, even if one is reluctant to give it. **do someone credit** (or **do credit to someone**) make someone worthy of praise or respect: *your concern does you credit*. **give someone credit for** commend someone for (a quality or achievement), esp. with reluctance or surprise: *please give me credit for some sense*. **have something to one's credit** have achieved something notable: *he has 65 tournament wins to his credit*. **on credit** with an arrangement to pay later. **on the credit side** as a good aspect of the situation: *on the credit side, the text is highly readable*. **to one's credit** used to indicate that something praiseworthy has been achieved, esp. despite difficulties: *to her credit, she had never betrayed a confidence*.
– ORIGIN mid 16th cent. (originally in the senses 'belief,' 'credibility'): from French *crédit*, probably via Italian *credito* from Latin *creditum*, neuter past participle of *credere* 'believe, trust.'

cred·it·a·ble /ˈkreditəbəl/ ▶ **adj.** (of a performance, effort, or action) deserving public acknowledgment and praise but not necessarily outstanding or successful: *a very creditable 2–4 defeat*.
– DERIVATIVES **cred·it·a·bil·i·ty** /ˌkreditəˈbilitē/ **n.**, **cred·it·a·bly** /ˈkreditəblē/ **adv.**

cred·it an·a·lyst ▶ **n.** a person employed to assess the credit rating of people or companies.

cred·it bu·reau ▶ **n.** a company that collects information relating to the credit ratings of individuals and makes it available to credit card companies, financial institutions, etc.

cred·it card ▶ **n.** a small plastic card issued by a bank, business, etc., allowing the holder to purchase goods or services on credit.

cred·it crunch ▶ **n.** a sudden sharp reduction in the availability of money or credit from banks and other lenders: *the beleaguered company has become the latest victim of the credit crunch*.

cred·it line ▶ **n.** another term for LINE OF CREDIT (see LINE[1]).

cred·i·tor /ˈkreditər/ ▶ **n.** a person or company to whom money is owed.

cred·it rat·ing ▶ **n.** an estimate of the ability of a person or organization to fulfill their financial commitments, based on previous dealings. ■ the process of assessing this.

cred·it score ▶ **n.** Finance a number assigned to a person that indicates to lenders their capacity to repay a loan.

cred·it un·ion ▶ **n.** a nonprofit-making money cooperative whose members can borrow from pooled deposits at low interest rates.

cred·it·worth·y /ˈkreditˌwərT͟Hē/ ▶ **adj.** (of a person or company) considered suitable to receive credit, esp. because of being reliable in paying money back in the past.
– DERIVATIVES **cred·it·wor·thi·ness n.**

cre·do /ˈkrēdō, ˈkrādō/ ▶ **n.** (pl. **credos**) a statement of the beliefs or aims that guide someone's actions: *he announced his credo in his first editorial*. ■ (**Credo**) a creed of the Christian Church in Latin. ■ (**Credo**) a musical setting of the Nicene Creed, typically as part of a mass.
– ORIGIN Middle English: Latin, 'I believe.' Compare with CREED.

cre·du·li·ty /krəˈd(y)o͞olitē/ ▶ **n.** a tendency to be too ready to believe that something is real or true.

cred·u·lous /ˈkrejələs/ ▶ **adj.** having or showing too great a readiness to believe things.
– DERIVATIVES **cred·u·lous·ly adv.**, **cred·u·lous·ness n.**
– ORIGIN late 16th cent. (in the general sense 'inclined to believe'): from Latin *credulus* (from *credere* 'believe') + -OUS.

Cree /krē/ ▶ **n.** (pl. **same** or **Crees**) **1** a member of a American Indian people living in a vast area of central Canada.
2 the Algonquian language of this people, closely related to Montagnais.
▶ **adj.** of or relating to the Cree or their language.
– ORIGIN from Canadian French *Cris*, abbreviation of *Cristinaux*, from Algonquian *kiristinō*.

creed /krēd/ ▶ **n.** a system of Christian or other religious belief; a faith: *people of many creeds and cultures*. ■ (often **the Creed**) a formal statement of Christian beliefs, esp. the Apostles' Creed or the Nicene Creed. ■ a set of beliefs or aims that guide someone's actions: *liberalism was more than a political creed*.
– ORIGIN Old English, from Latin CREDO.

creed·al /ˈkrēdl/ ▶ **adj.** variant spelling of CREDAL.

Creek /krēk/ ▶ **n.** (pl. **same**) **1** a member of a confederacy of American Indian peoples of the southeastern US in the 16th to 19th centuries whose descendants now live mainly in Oklahoma.
2 the Muskogean language of this confederacy.
▶ **adj.** of, relating to, or denoting this confederacy.
– ORIGIN from CREEK, because they lived beside the waterways of the flatlands of Georgia and Alabama.

creek /krēk, krik/ ▶ **n.** a stream, brook, or minor tributary of a river. ■ an inlet in a shoreline, a channel in a marsh, or another narrow, sheltered waterway.
– PHRASES **be up the creek** (**without a paddle**) informal be in severe difficulty or trouble, esp. with no means of extricating oneself from it. **be up shit creek** see SHIT.
– ORIGIN Middle English: from Old French *crique* or from Old Norse *kriki* 'nook'; perhaps reinforced by Middle Dutch *krēke*; of unknown ultimate origin.

creel /krēl/ ▶ **n. 1** a wicker basket for carrying fish. ■ an angler's fishing basket.
2 a rack holding bobbins or spools for spinning.

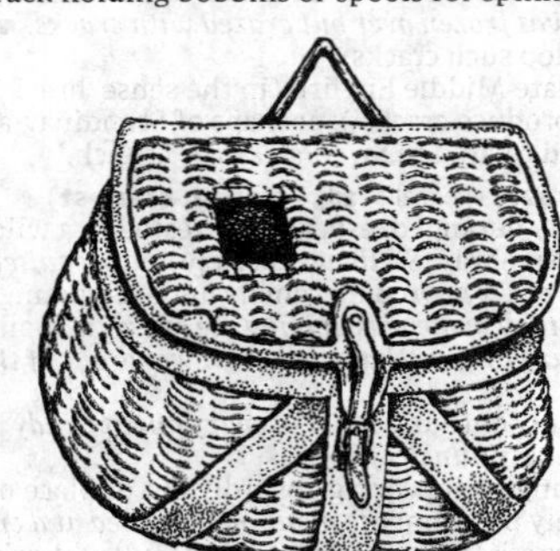

creel 1

–ORIGIN Middle English (sense 1; originally Scots and northern English): of unknown origin. Sense 2 (perhaps the same word) dates from the mid 19th cent.

creep /krēp/ ▶ v. (past and past participle **crept** /krept/) [no obj.] **1** move slowly and carefully, esp. in order to avoid being heard or noticed: *he crept downstairs, hardly making any noise* | *they were taught how to creep up on an enemy.* ■ (of a thing) move very slowly at an inexorably steady pace: *the fog was creeping up from the marsh.* ■ (of a plant) grow along the ground or other surface by means of extending stems or branches: (as adj. **creeping**) *tufts of fine leaves grow on creeping rhizomes.* ■ (of a plastic solid) undergo gradual deformation under stress.
2 (**creep in/into**) (of an unwanted and negative characteristic or fact) occur or develop gradually and almost imperceptibly: *errors crept into his game* | (as adj. **creeping**) *the creeping centralization of power.* ■ (**creep up**) increase slowly but steadily in number or amount: *interest rates have been creeping up in the past few weeks.*
▶ n. **1** informal a detestable person. ■ a person who behaves in an obsequious way in the hope of advancement.
2 slow movement, esp. at a steady but almost imperceptible pace: *an attempt to prevent this slow creep of costs.* ■ the tendency of a car with automatic transmission to move when in gear without the accelerator being pressed. ■ the gradual downward movement of disintegrated rock or soil due to gravitational forces: *stones and earth slowly slip down the slopes by soil creep.* ■ the gradual deformation of a plastic solid under stress. ■ gradual bulging of the floor of a mine owing to pressure on the pillars.
–PHRASES **give someone the creeps** informal induce a feeling of revulsion or fear in someone. **make one's flesh creep** feel disgust or revulsion and have a sensation like that of something crawling over the skin.
–PHRASAL VERBS **creep someone out** (past and past participle **creeped**) informal give someone an unpleasant feeling of fear or unease: *an anonymous note like that would creep me out.*
–ORIGIN Old English *crēopan* 'move with the body close to the ground,' of Germanic origin; related to Dutch *kruipen*. Sense 1 of the verb dates from Middle English.

creep·er /'krēpər/ ▶ n. **1** Botany any plant that grows along the ground, around another plant, or up a wall by means of extending stems or branches.
2 any of a number of small birds that creep around in trees, vegetation, etc. ● (**brown creeper**) the American treecreeper (*Certhia americana*, family Certhiidae). ● (**brown creeper**) NZ a New Zealand songbird (*Mohoua* (or *Finschia*) *novaeseelandiae*, family Pachycephalidae or Acanthizidae). ● a Philippine songbird (family Rhabdornithidae and genus *Rhabdornis*: two species). ● a Hawaiian honeycreeper (genus *Paroreomyza*, family Drepanididae: three species).
3 a low, wheeled platform on which a mechanic lies while working on the underside of a motor vehicle.

creep·ing Char·lie ▶ n. a creeping or trailing plant, in particular: ■ another term for MONEYWORT. ■ another term for GROUND IVY.

creep·ing Jen·ny ▶ n. another term for MONEYWORT.

creep·y /'krēpē/ ▶ adj. (**creepier, creepiest**) informal causing an unpleasant feeling of fear or unease: *the creepy feelings one often gets in a strange house.*
–DERIVATIVES **creep·i·ly** /-pəlē/ adv., **creep·i·ness** n.

creep·y-crawl·y /'krôlē/ informal ▶ n. (pl. **creepy-crawlies**) a spider, worm, or other small, flightless creature, esp. when considered unpleasant or frightening.
▶ adj. causing an unpleasant feeling of fear or unease: *creepy-crawly stories.*

creese ▶ n. archaic spelling of KRIS.

cre·ma /'krema/ ▶ n. a brownish foam that forms on the top of freshly made espresso.
–ORIGIN Italian, literally 'cream.'

cre·mains /kri'mānz/ ▶ plural n. a person's cremated remains.

cre·mas·ter /kri'mastər/ ▶ n. **1** (also **cremaster muscle**) Anatomy the muscle of the spermatic cord, by which the testicle can be partially raised.
2 Entomology the hooklike tip of a butterfly pupa, serving as an anchorage point.
–ORIGIN late 17th cent.: from Greek *kremastēr*, from *krema-* 'hang.'

cre·mate /'krē,māt, kri'māt/ ▶ v. [with obj.] dispose of (a dead person's body) by burning it to ashes, typically after a funeral ceremony. ■ informal burn (something), typically food.
–DERIVATIVES **cre·ma·tion** /kri'māSHən/ n., **cre·ma·tor** /-mātər/ n.
–ORIGIN late 19th cent. (as *cremation*): from Latin *cremare* 'burn.'

cre·ma·to·ri·um /,krēmə'tôrēəm, ,krem-/ ▶ n. (pl. **crematoria** /-'tôrēə/ or **crematoriums**) another term for CREMATORY.
–ORIGIN late 19th cent.: modern Latin, from *cremare* 'burn.'

cre·ma·to·ry /'krēmə,tôrē, 'krem-/ ▶ n. (pl. **crematories**) a place where a dead person's body is cremated.
▶ adj. of or relating to cremation.

crème an·glaise /,krem äNG'glez, -'glāz/ ▶ n. a rich egg custard.
–ORIGIN French, literally 'English cream.'

crème brû·lée /,krem brōō'lā/ ▶ n. (pl. **crèmes brûlées** pronunc. **same**, or **crème brûlées** /brōō'lāz/) a dessert of custard topped with caramelized sugar.
–ORIGIN late 19th cent.: French, literally 'burned cream.'

crème car·a·mel /,krem karə'mel, 'karə,mel/ ▶ n. (pl. **crèmes caramel** pronunc. **same**, or **crème caramels** /-'melz, -,melz/) a custard dessert made with whipped cream and eggs and topped with caramel.
–ORIGIN early 20th cent.: French, literally 'caramel custard.'

crème de ca·ca·o /,krem də kə'kou, 'kōkō/ ▶ n. a chocolate-flavored liqueur.
–ORIGIN mid 20th cent.: French, literally 'cream of cacao.'

crème de cas·sis /,krem də ka'sēs/ ▶ n. see CASSIS[1].
–ORIGIN French, literally 'cream of black currant.'

crème de la crème /,krem də lə 'krem/ ▶ n. the best person or thing of a particular kind: *the crème de la crème of the dancers have left the country.*
–ORIGIN mid 19th cent.: French, literally 'cream of the cream.'

crème de menthe /,krēm də 'menTH ,krēm, 'mint/ ▶ n. a peppermint-flavored liqueur.
–ORIGIN early 20th cent.: French, literally 'cream of mint.'

crème fraiche /,krem 'freSH/ ▶ n. a type of thick cream made from heavy cream with the addition of buttermilk, sour cream, or yogurt.
–ORIGIN from French *crème fraîche*, literally 'fresh cream.'

cre·mi·ni /krə'mēnī/ ▶ n. (pl. **same** or **creminis**) an immature portobello mushroom, eaten before the cap has opened.
–ORIGIN Italian.

Cre·mo·na /krə'mōnə/ a city in northern Italy, in Lombardy; pop. 72,267 (2008). Between the 16th and the 18th century the city was home to three renowned families of violin-makers: the Amati, the Guarneri, and the Stradivari.

cre·nate /'krē,nāt/ ▶ adj. Botany & Zoology (esp. of a leaf or shell) having a round-toothed or scalloped edge. Compare with CRENULATE.
–DERIVATIVES **cre·nat·ed** adj., **cre·na·tion** /kri'nāSHən/ n.
–ORIGIN late 18th cent. (earlier as *crenated*): from modern Latin *crenatus*, from popular Latin *crena* 'notch.'

cren·el /'krenl/ (also **crenelle** /krə'nel/) ▶ n. an indentation in the battlements of a fort or castle, used for shooting or firing missiles through.
–ORIGIN late 15th cent.: from Old French, based on popular Latin *crena* 'notch.'

cren·el·late /'krenl,āt/ (also **crenelate**) ▶ v. [with obj.] (usu. as adj. **crenellated**) chiefly historical provide (a wall of a building) with battlements.
–ORIGIN early 19th cent.: from French *créneler*, from Old French *crenel* (see CRENEL).

cren·el·la·tions /,krenl'āSHənz/ ▶ plural n. the battlements of a castle or other building.

cren·u·late /'krenyəlit, -yə,lāt/ ▶ adj. technical (esp. of a leaf, shell, or shoreline) having a finely scalloped or notched outline or edge. Compare with CRENATE.
–DERIVATIVES **cren·u·lat·ed** adj., **cren·u·la·tion** /,krenyə'lāSHən/ n.
–ORIGIN late 18th cent.: from modern Latin *crenulatus*, from *crenula*, diminutive of *crena* 'notch.'

cre·o·dont /'krēə,dänt/ ▶ n. an extinct carnivorous mammal of the early Tertiary period, ancestral to modern carnivores. ● Order Creodonta: several families.
–ORIGIN late 19th cent.: from modern Latin *Creodonta* (plural), from Greek *kreas* 'flesh' + *odous, odont-* 'tooth.'

Cre·ole /'krē,ōl/ (also **creole**) ▶ n. **1** a person of mixed European and black descent, esp. in the Caribbean. ■ a descendant of Spanish or other European settlers in the Caribbean or Central or South America. ■ a white descendant of French settlers in Louisiana and other parts of the southern US.
2 a mother tongue formed from the contact of two languages through an earlier pidgin stage: *a Portuguese-based Creole.*
▶ adj. of or relating to a Creole or Creoles.
–ORIGIN from French *créole, criole*, from Spanish *criollo*, probably from Portuguese *crioulo* 'black person born in Brazil, home-born slave,' from *criar* 'to breed,' from Latin *creare* 'produce, create.'

cre·o·lize /'krēə,līz/ ▶ v. [with obj.] form (a Creole language) from the contact of two languages: (as adj. **creolized**) *a creolized variety of French.*
–DERIVATIVES **cre·o·li·za·tion** /,krēələ'zāSHən/ n.

cre·o·sol /'krēə,sôl, -,sōl/ ▶ n. Chemistry a colorless liquid that is the chief constituent of wood-tar creosote. ● Alternative name: **2-methoxy-4-methylphenol**; chem. formula: $C_8H_{10}O_2$.
–ORIGIN mid 19th cent.: from CREOSOTE + -OL.

cre·o·sote /'krēə,sōt/ ▶ n. (also **creosote oil**) a dark brown oil distilled from coal tar and used as a wood preservative. It contains a number of phenols, cresols, and other organic compounds. ■ a colorless, pungent, oily liquid, containing creosol and other compounds, distilled from wood tar and used as an antiseptic.
▶ v. [with obj.] treat (wood) with creosote.
–ORIGIN mid 19th cent.: coined in German from Greek *kreas* 'flesh' + *sōtēr* 'preserver,' with reference to its antiseptic properties.

cre·o·sote bush ▶ n. a shrub native to arid parts of Mexico and the western US. Its leaves smell of creosote and when steeped in boiling water, they yield an antiseptic lotion. ● *Larrea tridentata*, family Zygophyllaceae.

crepe (also **crêpe**) ▶ n. **1** /krāp/ a light, thin fabric with a wrinkled surface: [as modifier] *a silk crepe blouse.* ■ (also **crepe rubber**) hard-wearing wrinkled rubber, used esp. for the soles of shoes.
2 /krāp/ black silk or imitation silk, formerly used for mourning clothes. ■ a band of such fabric formerly worn around a person's hat as a sign of mourning.
3 /krāp, krep/ a thin pancake.
–DERIVATIVES **crep·ey** adj.
–ORIGIN late 18th cent.: French, from Old French *crespe* 'curled, frizzed,' from Latin *crispus*.

crepe de chine /,krāp də 'SHēn/ (also **crepe de Chine**) ▶ n. a fine crepe of silk or similar fiber.
–ORIGIN late 19th cent.: French, literally 'crepe of China.'

crepe myr·tle ▶ n. variant spelling of CRAPE MYRTLE.

crepe pa·per ▶ n. thin, crinkled paper resembling crepe, used esp. for making decorations.

crêp·er·ie /,krep(ə)'rē, 'krāpərē/ ▶ n. (pl. **crêperies**) a small restaurant, typically one in France, in which a variety of crepes are served.
–ORIGIN French.

crêpe su·zette /,krāp sōō'zet/ ▶ n. (pl. **crêpes suzette** pronunc. **same**) a thin dessert pancake with a brandy and citrus sauce, usually set aflame when served.

crépinette /,krāpə'net, ,krep-/ ▶ n. a flat sausage consisting of minced meat and savory stuffing wrapped in pieces of pork caul.
–ORIGIN French, diminutive of *crépine* 'caul.'

crep·i·tate /'krepə,tāt/ ▶ v. [no obj.] make a crackling sound: *the night crepitates with an airy, whistling cacophony* | (as adj. **crepitating**) *spidery fingers of crepitating electricity.*
–DERIVATIVES **crep·i·tant** /'krepətənt/ adj.
–ORIGIN early 17th cent. (in the sense 'break wind'): from Latin *crepitat-* 'crackled, rustled,' from the verb *crepitare*, from *crepare* 'to rattle.'

crep·i·ta·tion /,krepə'tāSHən/ ▶ n. a crackling or rattling sound: *pistollike crepitations.* ■ Medicine a crackling sound made in breathing by a person with an inflamed lung, detected using a stethoscope. ■ Entomology the explosive ejection of irritant fluid from the abdomen of a bombardier beetle.
–ORIGIN mid 17th cent.: from French *crépitation* or Latin *crepitatio(n-)*, from the verb *crepitare* (see CREPITATE).

crep·i·tus /'krepətəs/ ▶ n. Medicine a grating sound or sensation produced by friction between bone and cartilage or the fractured parts of a bone. ■ the production of crepitations in the lungs; rale.
–ORIGIN early 19th cent.: from Latin, from *crepare* 'rattle.'

cré·pon /'krā,pän/ ▶ n. a fabric resembling crepe, but heavier and with a more pronounced crinkled effect.
–ORIGIN late 19th cent.: French.

crept /krept/ past and past participle of CREEP.

PRONUNCIATION KEY ə *ago, up*; ər *over, fur*; a *hat*; ā *ate*; ä *car*; e *let*; ē *see*; i *fit*; ī *by*; NG *sing*; ō *go*; ô *law, for*; oi *toy*; ōō *good*; ōō *goo*; ou *out*; TH *thin*; TH *then*; ZH *vision*

cre·pus·cu·lar /krə'pəskyələr/ ▶ **adj.** of, resembling, or relating to twilight. ■ Zoology (of an animal) appearing or active in twilight.
– ORIGIN mid 17th cent.: from Latin *crepusculum* 'twilight' + **-AR**[1].

cre·pus·cule /kri'pəs,kyōōl/ ▶ **n.** the period of partial darkness at the beginning or end of the day; twilight.

cresc. (also **cres.**) ▶ **abbr.** Music crescendo.

cre·scen·do /krə'sHendō/ ▶ **n.** (pl. **crescendos** or **crescendi** /-dē/) Music a gradual increase in loudness in a piece of music. ■ Music a passage of music marked to be performed in this way. ■ the loudest point reached in a gradually increasing sound: *Deborah's voice was rising to a crescendo.* ■ a progressive increase in force or intensity: *a crescendo of misery.* ■ the most intense point reached in this; a climax: *the negative reviews reached a crescendo in mid-February.*
▶ **adv. & adj.** Music with a gradual increase in loudness: [as adj.] *a short crescendo kettledrum roll.*
▶ **v.** (**crescendoes, crescendoing, crescendoed**) [no obj.] increase in loudness or intensity: *the reluctant cheers began to crescendo.*
– ORIGIN late 18th cent.: Italian, present participle of *crescere* 'to increase,' from Latin *crescere* 'grow.'

cres·cent /'kresənt/ ▶ **n. 1** the curved sickle shape of the waxing or waning moon. ■ a representation of such a shape used as an emblem of Islam or of Turkey. ■ (**the Crescent**) chiefly historical the political power of Islam or of the Ottoman Empire.
2 a thing that has has the shape of a single curve, esp. one that is broad in the center and tapers to a point at each end: *a three-mile crescent of golden sand | a crescent-shaped building.* ■ a street or row of houses forming an arc: *we lived at Westway Crescent.* ■ Heraldry a charge in the form of a crescent, typically with the points upward (also a mark of cadency for a second son).
3 a moth or butterfly that bears crescent-shaped markings on the wings, in particular: ● an orange or brown American butterfly with a silvery mark on the underside of the hind wing (genus *Phyciodes*, subfamily Melitaeinae, family Nymphalidae). ● a brownish European moth with a pale mark on the forewing (several species in the family Noctuidae, in particular *Celaena leucostigma*).
▶ **adj. 1** having the shape of a crescent: *a crescent moon.*
2 literary growing, increasing, or developing.
– DERIVATIVES **cres·cen·tic** /krə'sentik/ **adj.**
– ORIGIN late Middle English *cressant*, from Old French *creissant*, from Latin *crescere* 'grow.' The spelling change in the 17th century was due to the influence of the Latin.

cres·cent wrench ▶ **n.** an adjustable wrench designed to grip hexagonal nuts, with an adjusting screw fitted in the crescent-shaped head of the wrench.

cre·sol /'krē,sôl, -,sōl/ ▶ **n.** Chemistry each of three isomeric crystalline compounds present in coal-tar creosote, used as disinfectants. ● The *ortho-*, *meta-*, and *para-*methyl derivatives of phenol; chem. formula: $CH_3C_6H_4OH$.
– ORIGIN mid 19th cent.: from **CREOSOTE** + **-OL**.

cress /kres/ ▶ **n.** a plant of the cabbage family, typically having small white flowers and pungent leaves. Some kinds are edible and are eaten raw as salad. ● *Barbarea* and other genera, family Brassicaceae: several species, including **garden cress** and **watercress**.
– ORIGIN Old English *cresse, cærse*; related to Dutch *kers* and German *Kresse*.

cres·set /'kresit/ ▶ **n.** historical a metal container of oil, grease, wood, or coal burned as a torch and typically mounted on a pole.
– ORIGIN late Middle English: from Old French, from *craisse*, variant of *graisse* 'oil, grease.'

Cres·si·da /'kresədə/ (in medieval legends of the Trojan War) the daughter of Calchas, a priest. She was unfaithful to her lover Troilus, a son of Priam.

crest /krest/ ▶ **n. 1** a comb or tuft of feathers, fur, or skin on the head of a bird or other animal. ■ a thing resembling such a tuft, esp. a plume of feathers on a helmet.
2 the top of something, esp. a mountain or hill: *she reached the crest of the hill.* ■ the curling foamy top of a wave. ■ Anatomy a ridge along the surface of a bone. ■ the upper line of the neck of a horse or other mammal.
3 Heraldry a distinctive device borne above the shield of a coat of arms (originally as worn on a helmet), or separately reproduced, for example on writing paper or silverware, to represent a family or corporate body.
▶ **v.** [with obj.] reach the top of (something such as a hill or wave): *she crested a hill and saw the valley spread out before her.* ■ [no obj.] (of a river) rise to its highest level: *the river was expected to crest at eight feet above flood stage.* ■ [no obj.] (of a wave) form a curling foamy top. ■ (**be crested**) have attached or affixed at the top: *his helmet was crested with a fan of spikes.*
– DERIVATIVES **crest·less adj.**
– ORIGIN Middle English: from Old French *creste*, from Latin *crista* 'tuft, plume.'

crest·ed /'krestid/ ▶ **adj. 1** (of a bird or other animal) having a comb or tuft of feathers, fur, or skin on the head: *the crested drake mandarin duck | a plush-crested jay.*
2 emblazoned with a coat of arms or other emblem: *crested notepaper.*

crest·ed tit ▶ **n.** a small European tit (songbird) with a short crest, living chiefly in coniferous woodland. ● *Parus cristatus*, family Paridae.

crest·ed wood i·bis ▶ **n.** see **WOOD IBIS** (sense 2).

crest·fal·len /'krest,fôlən/ ▶ **adj.** sad and disappointed: *he came back empty-handed and crestfallen.*
– ORIGIN late 16th cent.: figuratively, from the original use referring to a mammal or bird having a fallen or drooping crest.

crest·fish /'krest,fisH/ ▶ **n.** (pl. **same** or **crestfishes**) a very elongated silvery marine fish with a crimson dorsal fin running the full length of its body and a forehead that projects forward into a long filament. ● *Lophotus lacepedei*, family Lophotidae.

crest·ing /'krestiNG/ ▶ **n.** an ornamental decoration at the ridge of a roof or top of a wall or screen.

cres·yl /'kresəl, 'krē,sil/ ▶ **n.** [as modifier] Chemistry of or denoting a radical $-OC_6H_4CH_3$, derived from a cresol.

Cre·ta·ceous /krə'tāsHəs/ ▶ **adj.** Geology of, relating to, or denoting the last period of the Mesozoic era, between the Jurassic and Tertiary periods. ■ (as noun **the Cretaceous**) the Cretaceous period or the system of rocks deposited during it.

> The Cretaceous lasted from about 146 million to 65 million years ago. The climate was warm, and the sea level rose; the period is characterized esp. in northwestern Europe and parts of North America by the deposition of chalk. The first flowering plants emerged, and the domination of the dinosaurs continued although they died out quite abruptly toward the end of it.

– ORIGIN late 17th cent.: from Latin *cretaceus* (from *creta* 'chalk') + **-OUS**.

Cre·ta·ceous–Ter·ti·ar·y bound·a·ry (also **K/T boundary**) Geology the division between the Cretaceous and Tertiary periods, about 65 million years ago.

> A widespread layer of sediment dating from this time has been shown since 1980 to be enriched in iridium and other elements and carbon deposits indicative of extensive fires. This appears to indicate the catastrophic impact of one or more large meteorites, and geologists have identified a formation at Chicxulub in the Yucatán Peninsula, Mexico, as a probable impact site. A resulting drastic climate change has been suggested as the cause of the extinction of dinosaurs and many other organisms at this time, but this remains controversial.

Crete /krēt/ a Greek island in the eastern Mediterranean Sea; pop. 630,000 (est. 2005); capital, Heraklion. It is noted for the remains of the Minoan civilization that flourished here in the 2nd millennium BC. Crete played an important role in the Greek struggle for independence from the Turks in the late 19th and early 20th centuries that resulted in it becoming administratively part of an independent Greece in 1913. Greek name **KRÍTI**.
– DERIVATIVES **Cre·tan** /'krētn/ **adj. & n.**

cre·tic /'krētik/ ▶ **n.** Prosody a metrical foot containing one short or unstressed syllable between two long or stressed ones.
– ORIGIN late 16th cent.: from Latin *Creticus*, from Greek *Krētikos*, from *Krētē* 'Crete.'

cre·tin /'krētn/ ▶ **n.** a stupid person (used as a general term of abuse). ■ Medicine, dated a person who is deformed and mentally handicapped because of congenital thyroid deficiency.
– DERIVATIVES **cre·tin·ism** /-,izəm/ **n.**, **cre·tin·ous** /-əs/ **adj.**
– ORIGIN late 18th cent.: from French *crétin*, from Swiss French *crestin* 'Christian' (from Latin *Christianus*), here used to mean 'human being,' apparently as a reminder that, though deformed, cretins were human and not beasts.

cre·tonne /'krē,tän, kri'tän/ ▶ **n.** a heavy cotton fabric, typically with a floral pattern printed on one or both sides, used for upholstery.
– ORIGIN late 19th cent.: from French, of unknown origin.

Creutz·feldt–Ja·kob dis·ease /'kroits,felt 'yäkôb/ ▶ **n.** a fatal degenerative disease affecting nerve cells in the brain, causing mental, physical, and sensory disturbances such as dementia and seizures. It is believed to be caused by prions and hence to be related to BSE and other spongiform encephalopathies such as kuru and scrapie.
– ORIGIN 1930s: named after H. G. *Creutzfeldt* (1885–1964) and A. *Jakob* (1882–1927), the German neurologists who first described cases of the disease in 1920–21. Creutzfeldt is credited with the first description of the disease in 1920, although the case is atypical by current diagnostic criteria; a year later Jakob described four cases, at least two of whom had clinical features suggestive of CJD as it is currently described.

cre·vasse /krə'vas/ ▶ **n.** a deep open crack, esp. one in a glacier. ■ a breach in the embankment of a river or canal.
– ORIGIN early 19th cent.: from French, from Old French *crevace* (see **CREVICE**).

crev·ice /'krevəs/ ▶ **n.** a narrow opening or fissure, esp. in a rock or wall.
– ORIGIN Middle English: from Old French *crevace*, from *crever* 'to burst,' from Latin *crepare* 'to rattle, crack.'

crew[1] /krōō/ ▶ **n.** [treated as sing. or pl.] **1** a group of people who work on and operate a ship, boat, aircraft, spacecraft, or train. ■ such a group other than the officers: *the ship's captain and crew may be brought to trial.* ■ the sport of rowing a racing shell.
2 a group of people who work closely together: *an ambulance crew | crews of firefighters from neighboring towns were called in.* ■ informal, often derogatory a group of people associated in some way: *a crew of assorted computer geeks.* ■ informal a group of rappers, breakdancers, or graffiti artists performing or operating together.
▶ **v.** [with obj.] provide (a craft or vehicle) with a group of people to operate it: *normally the boat is crewed by 5 people.* ■ [no obj.] act as a member of a crew, subordinate to a captain: *I've never crewed for a world-famous yachtsman before.*
– DERIVATIVES **crew·man** /'krōōmən/ **n.** (pl. **crewmen**).
– ORIGIN late Middle English: from Old French *creue* 'augmentation, increase,' feminine past participle of *croistre* 'grow,' from Latin *crescere*. The original sense was 'band of soldiers serving as reinforcements'; hence it came to denote any organized armed band or, generally, a company of people (late 16th cent).

crew[2] chiefly Brit. past of **CROW**[2].

crew cut ▶ **n.** a very short haircut for men and boys.
– ORIGIN 1940s: apparently first adopted as a style by boat crews of Harvard and Yale universities.

crew·el /'krōōəl/ ▶ **n.** a thin, loosely twisted, worsted yarn used for tapestry and embroidery.
– ORIGIN late 15th cent.: of unknown origin.

crew·el work ▶ **n.** embroidery or tapestry done with crewel yarn on linen cloth.

crew neck ▶ **n.** a close-fitting, round neckline, esp. on a sweater or T-shirt: [as modifier] *a crew-neck sweater.* ■ a sweater with such a neckline.

crib /krib/ ▶ **n. 1** a young child's bed with barred or latticed sides. ■ a barred container or rack for animal fodder; a manger.
2 Brit. informal a translation of a text for use by students, esp. in a surreptitious way: *an English crib of Caesar's Gallic Wars.* ■ a thing that has been plagiarized: *is the song a crib from Mozart's "Don Giovanni?"*
3 informal an apartment or house.
4 short for **CRIBBAGE**. ■ the cards discarded by the players at cribbage, counting to the dealer.
5 (also **cribwork**) a heavy timber framework used in foundations for a building or to line a mine shaft.
▶ **v.** (**cribs, cribbing, cribbed**) [with obj.] **1** informal copy (another person's work) illicitly or without acknowledgment: *he was doing an exam and didn't want anybody to crib the answers from him* | [no obj.] *he often cribbed from other researchers.* ■ archaic steal.
2 archaic restrain: *he had been so cabined, cribbed, and confined by office.*
– DERIVATIVES **crib·ber** /'kribər/ **n.**
– ORIGIN Old English (in the sense 'manger'), of Germanic origin; related to Dutch *krib, kribbe* and German *Krippe*.

crib·bage /'kribij/ ▶ **n.** a card game for two to four players, in which the objective is to play so that the value of one's cards played reaches exactly 15 or 31.
– ORIGIN mid 17th cent.: related to **CRIB**; the game is said to have been invented by the English poet Sir John Suckling (1609–42); it seems to have been developed from an older game called Noddy.

crib·bage board ▶ **n.** a board with pegs and holes, used for scoring at cribbage.

crib·bit·ing ▶ n. a repetitive habit of some horses that involves biting and chewing of wood, esp. that of doors and mangers, in the stable, causing excessive wear to the front teeth.

crib death ▶ n. informal term for SUDDEN INFANT DEATH SYNDROME.

cri·bel·lum /kri'beləm/ ▶ n. (pl. **cribella** /-'belə/) Zoology (in some spiders) an additional spinning organ with numerous fine pores, situated in front of the spinnerets.
– DERIVATIVES **cri·bel·late** /'kribələt, -ˌlāt/ **adj.**
– ORIGIN late 19th cent.: from late Latin, diminutive of *cribrum* 'sieve.'

cri·bo /'krēˌbō/ ▶ n. (pl. **cribos**) another term for INDIGO SNAKE.
– ORIGIN late 19th cent.: of unknown origin.

crib·ri·form /'kribrəˌfôrm/ ▶ adj. Anatomy denoting an anatomical structure that is pierced by numerous small holes, in particular the plate of the ethmoid bone through which the olfactory nerves pass.
– ORIGIN mid 18th cent.: from Latin *cribrum* 'sieve' + -IFORM.

crib·work /'kribˌwərk/ ▶ n. see CRIB (sense 5 of the noun).

Crich·ton[1] /'krītn/, James (1560–c.1585), Scottish adventurer; known as **the Admirable Crichton**. He was an accomplished swordsman, poet, and scholar and served in the French army.

Crich·ton[2] /'krītn/, Michael (1942–2008), US novelist; full name *John Michael Crichton*. Notable works: *The Andromeda Strain* (1969), *The Great Train Robbery* (1975), *Jurassic Park* (1990), and *Next* (2006).

Crick /krik/, Francis Harry Compton (1916–2004), English biophysicist. With James Watson, he proposed the double helix structure of the DNA molecule, thus broadly explaining how genetic information is carried in living organisms and how genes replicate. Nobel Prize for Physiology or Medicine (1962), shared with Watson and Maurice Wilkins.

crick[1] /krik/ ▶ n. a painful stiff feeling in the neck or back.
▶ v. [with obj.] twist or strain (one's neck or back), causing painful stiffness: (as adj. **cricked**) *he suffered a cricked neck during tackling practice.*
– ORIGIN late Middle English: of unknown origin.

crick[2] ▶ n. dialect a creek.

crick·et[1] /'krikit/ ▶ n. an insect related to the grasshoppers. The male produces a characteristic rhythmical chirping sound. ● Family Gryllidae: many genera and species, including the **field cricket** and the **house cricket**.
– ORIGIN Middle English: from Old French *criquet*, from *criquer* 'to crackle,' of imitative origin.

crick·et[2] ▶ n. an open-air game played on a large grass field with ball, bats, and two wickets, between teams of eleven players, the object of the game being to score more runs than the opposition.

> Cricket is played mainly in Britain and in territories formerly under British rule, including Australia, South Africa, the West Indies, New Zealand, and the Indian subcontinent. The full game with two innings per side can last several days; shorter matches are usual at the amateur level and have become popular at the professional level since the 1960s.

– PHRASES **not cricket** Brit. informal a thing contrary to traditional standards of fairness or rectitude.
– DERIVATIVES **crick·et·er** n., **crick·et·ing** adj.
– ORIGIN late 16th cent.: of unknown origin.

crick·et[3] ▶ n. a low stool, typically with a rectangular or oval seat and four legs splayed out.

cri·coid /'krīˌkoid/ ▶ n. (also **cricoid cartilage**) Anatomy the ring-shaped cartilage of the larynx.
– ORIGIN mid 18th cent.: from modern Latin *cricoides* 'ring-shaped,' from Greek *krikoeidēs*, from *krikos* 'ring.'

cri de cœur /ˌkrē də 'kər/ ▶ n. (pl. **cris de cœur** /ˌkrē(z)/) a passionate appeal, complaint, or protest.
– ORIGIN early 20th cent.: French, literally 'cry from the heart.'

cried /krīd/ past and past participle of CRY.

cri·er /'krīər/ ▶ n. an officer who makes public announcements in a court of justice. ■ short for TOWN CRIER.
– ORIGIN late Middle English: from Old French *criere*, from *crier* 'to shout.'

cri·key /'krīkē/ ▶ exclam. Brit. informal an expression of surprise: *Crikey! I never thought I'd see you again.*
– ORIGIN mid 19th cent.: euphemism for CHRIST.

crime /krīm/ ▶ n. an action or omission that constitutes an offense that may be prosecuted by the state and is punishable by law: *shoplifting was a serious crime.* ■ illegal activities: *the victims of crime.* ■ an action or activity that, although not illegal, is considered to be evil, shameful, or wrong: *they condemned apartheid as a crime against humanity | it's a crime to keep a creature like Willy in a tank.*
– ORIGIN Middle English (in the sense 'wickedness, sin'): via Old French from Latin *crimen* 'judgment, offense,' based on *cernere* 'to judge.'

Cri·me·a /krī'mēə/ (usu. **the Crimea**) a peninsula in Ukraine that lies between the Sea of Azov and the Black Sea. The Crimean War was fought here in the 1850s.
– DERIVATIVES **Cri·me·an** adj.

Cri·me·an War /krī'mēən/ a war (1853–56) between Russia and an alliance of Great Britain, France, Sardinia, and Turkey. Russian aggression against Turkey led to war, with Turkey's European allies intervening to destroy Russian naval power in the Black Sea in 1854; eventually the allies captured the fortress city of Sebastopol in 1855 after a lengthy siege.

crime-fight·ing ▶ n. the action of working to reduce the incidence of crime.
– DERIVATIVES **crime-fight·er** n.

crime pas·si·on·nel /ˌkrēm ˌpasyə'nel/ ▶ n. (pl. **crimes passionnels** pronunc. **same**) a crime, typically a murder, committed in a fit of sexual jealousy.
– ORIGIN early 20th cent.: French, literally 'crime of passion.'

crime wave ▶ n. a sudden increase in the number of crimes committed in a country or area.

crime writ·er ▶ n. a writer of detective stories or thrillers.

crim·i·nal /'krimənl/ ▶ n. a person who has committed a crime: *these men are dangerous criminals.*
▶ adj. of or relating to a crime: *he is charged with conspiracy to commit criminal damage.* ■ Law of or relating to crime as opposed to civil matters: *a criminal court.* ■ informal (of an action or situation) deplorable and shocking: *he may never fulfill his potential, and that would be a criminal waste.*
– DERIVATIVES **crim·i·nal·i·ty** /ˌkrimə'nalitē/ n., **crim·i·nal·ly** adv.
– ORIGIN late Middle English (as an adjective): from late Latin *criminalis*, from Latin *crimen, crimin-* (see CRIME).

crim·i·nal con·ver·sa·tion ▶ n. historical adultery, esp. as formerly constituting grounds for the recovery of legal damages by a husband from his adulterous wife's partner.

crim·i·nal·is·tics /ˌkrimənl'istiks/ ▶ plural n. [treated as sing.] another term for FORENSICS (see FORENSIC).
– DERIVATIVES **crim·i·nal·ist** n.

crim·i·nal·ize /'krimənlˌīz/ ▶ v. [with obj.] turn (an activity) into a criminal offense by making it illegal: *his view is that the state should not criminalize drug use but discourage it.* ■ turn (someone) into a criminal by making their activities illegal: *these punitive measures would further criminalize travelers for their way of life.*
– DERIVATIVES **crim·i·nal·i·za·tion** /ˌkrimənl-ə'zāSHən/ n.

crim·i·nal jus·tice sys·tem ▶ n. the system of law enforcement that is directly involved in apprehending, prosecuting, defending, sentencing, and punishing those who are suspected or convicted of criminal offenses.

crim·i·nal law ▶ n. a system of law concerned with the punishment of those who commit crimes. Contrasted with CIVIL LAW.

crim·i·nal li·bel ▶ n. Law a malicious, defamatory statement in a permanent form, rendering the maker liable to criminal prosecution.

crim·i·nal re·cord ▶ n. a history of being convicted for crime: *he admits he has a criminal record.* ■ a list of a person's previous criminal convictions: *the court said his criminal record would be expunged at the end of the year.*

crim·i·no·gen·ic /ˌkrimənə'jenik/ ▶ adj. (of a system, situation, or place) causing or likely to cause criminal behavior: *the criminogenic nature of homelessness.*

crim·i·nol·o·gy /ˌkrimə'näləjē/ ▶ n. the scientific study of crime and criminals.
– DERIVATIVES **crim·i·no·log·i·cal** /ˌkrimənl'äjikəl/ adj., **crim·i·nol·o·gist** /-jist/ n.
– ORIGIN late 19th cent.: from Latin *crimen, crimin-* 'crime' + -LOGY.

crim·i·ny /'krīmənē/ ▶ exclam. informal used to express surprise or disbelief: *criminy, what is this world coming to?*
– ORIGIN late 17th cent. (as *crimine*): origin uncertain; perhaps an alteration of *Christ*, perhaps from Italian *crimine* 'crime.'

crimp /krimp/ ▶ v. [with obj.] **1** compress (something) into small folds or ridges: *she crimped the edge of the pie.* ■ connect (a wire or cable) by squeezing the end or ends. ■ (often as adj. **crimped**) make waves in (someone's hair) with a curling iron: *crimped blond hair.*
2 informal have a limiting or adverse effect on (something): *farmers complain that the drought could crimp their income potential.*
▶ n. **1** a curl, wave, or folded or compressed edge: *this cascade of delicate crimps depends on a perm | the wool had too much crimp to be used in weaving.* ■ a small connecting piece for crimping wires or lines together.
2 informal a restriction or limitation: *the crimp on take-home pay has been even tighter since taxes were raised.*
– PHRASES **put a crimp in** informal have an adverse effect on: *well, that puts a crimp in my theory.*
– DERIVATIVES **crimp·er** n., **crimp·y** adj.
– ORIGIN Old English *gecrympan*, of Germanic origin; related to Dutch *krimpen* 'shrink, wrinkle.' Of rare occurrence before the 18th cent., the word was perhaps reintroduced from Low German or Dutch.

crim·son /'krimzən/ ▶ adj. of a rich deep red color inclining to purple: *she blushed crimson with embarrassment.*
▶ n. a rich deep red color inclining to purple.
▶ v. [no obj.] (of a person's face) become flushed, esp. through embarrassment: *my face crimsoned and my hands began to shake.*
– ORIGIN late Middle English: from obsolete French *cramoisin* or Old Spanish *cremesin*, based on Arabic *ḳirmizī*, from *ḳirmiz* (see KERMES). Compare with CARMINE.

cringe /krinj/ ▶ v. (**cringes, cringing, cringed**) [no obj.] bend one's head and body in fear or in a servile manner: *he cringed away from the blow* | (as adj. **cringing**) *we are surrounded by cringing yes-men and sycophants.* ■ experience an inward shiver of embarrassment or disgust: *I cringed at the fellow's stupidity.*
▶ n. an act of cringing.
– DERIVATIVES **cring·er** n.
– ORIGIN Middle English *crenge, crenche*, related to Old English *cringan, crincan* 'bend, yield, fall in battle,' of Germanic origin and related to Dutch *krengen* 'heel over' and German *krank* 'sick,' also to CRANK[1].

cringe-mak·ing ▶ adj. another term for CRINGEWORTHY.

cringe·wor·thy /'krinjˌwərT͟Hē/ ▶ adj. informal causing feelings of embarrassment or awkwardness: *the play's cast was excellent, but the dialogue was unforgivably cringeworthy.*

cring·ing·ly /'krinjiNGlē/ ▶ adv. in a servile or sycophantic way: *he shrank cringingly to one side.* ■ so as to make one feel embarrassed or disgusted: *their early performances were cringingly awkward.*

crin·gle /'kriNGgəl/ ▶ n. Sailing a ring of rope formed in the edge of a sail and containing a thimble, for another rope to pass through.
– ORIGIN early 17th cent.: from Low German *kringel*, diminutive of *kring* 'ring.'

crin·kle /'kriNGkəl/ ▶ v. form small creases or wrinkles in the surface of something, esp. the skin of the face as the result of a facial expression: [no obj.] *Rose's face crinkled in bewilderment* | [with obj.] *Burney crinkled his eyes in a smile* | (as adj. **crinkled**) *plants with crinkled foliage.* ■ [with obj.] cause (something) to make a crackling or rustling sound: *we tried hard not to crinkle the plastic as we unwrapped the pies.*
▶ n. a wrinkle or crease on the surface of something: *there was a crinkle of suspicion on her forehead.*
– ORIGIN late Middle English: related to Old English *crincan* (see CRINGE).

crin·kle-cut ▶ adj. (esp. of French fries) cut with wavy edges.

crin·kly /'kriNGk(ə)lē/ ▶ adj. (**crinklier, crinkliest**) full of creases or wrinkles; wrinkled: *brown crinkly paper.*

crin·kum-cran·kum /ˌkriNGkəm 'kraNGkəm/ ▶ n. archaic elaborate decoration or detail.
– ORIGIN mid 17th cent.: fanciful reduplication of the nouns CRANK[1] and CRANK[2].

cri·noid /'krīˌnoid/ Zoology ▶ n. an echinoderm of the class Crinoidea, which comprises the sea lilies and feather stars.
▶ adj. relating to or denoting crinoids.
– DERIVATIVES **cri·noi·dal** /'krīˌnoidl/ adj.

Cri·noid·e·a /krī'noidēə/ Zoology a class of echinoderms that comprises the sea lilies and feather stars. They have slender, feathery arms and (in some kinds) a stalk for attachment, and were abundant in the Paleozoic era.

–ORIGIN modern Latin (plural), from Greek *krinoeidēs* 'lilylike,' from *krinon* 'lily.'

crin·o·line /ˈkrinl-in/ ▶ n. 1 historical a stiffened or hooped petticoat worn to make a long skirt stand out.
2 a stiff fabric made of horsehair and cotton or linen thread, typically used for stiffening petticoats or as a lining.
–ORIGIN mid 19th cent. (sense 2, early crinolines being made of such material): from French, formed irregularly from Latin *crinis* 'hair' + *linum* 'thread.'

C

cri·ol·lo /krēˈō(l)yō/ (also **Criollo**) ▶ n. (pl. **criollos**) 1 a person from Spanish South or Central America, esp. one of pure Spanish descent. ■ a horse or other domestic animal of a South or Central American breed.
2 (also **criollo tree**) a cacao tree of a variety producing thin-shelled beans of high quality.
–ORIGIN late 19th cent.: Spanish, literally 'native to the locality' (see CREOLE).

crip /krip/ ▶ n. informal 1 derogatory a disabled person. [early 20th cent.: abbreviation of CRIPPLE.]
2 (usu. **Crip**) a member of a Los Angeles street gang.

cripes /krīps/ ▶ exclam. informal used as a euphemism for Christ.
–ORIGIN early 20th cent.: alteration of CHRIST.

crip·ple /ˈkripəl/ ▶ n. dated, offensive a person who is unable to walk or move properly because of disability or injury to their back or legs. ■ a person with a severe limitation of a specified kind: *an emotional cripple.*
▶ v. [with obj.] cause (someone) to become unable to move or walk properly: (as adj. **crippling**) *a crippling disease.* ■ cause severe and disabling damage to (a machine): *over-lubrication might well lead to piston seizure, crippling the engine.* ■ cause a severe and almost insuperable problem for: *developing countries are crippled by their debts.*
–DERIVATIVES **crip·pler** /ˈkrip(ə)lər/ n., **crip·pling·ly** adv.
–ORIGIN Old English: from two words, *crypel* and *crēopel*, both of Germanic origin and related to CREEP.

> **USAGE** The word **cripple** has long been in use to refer to 'a person unable to walk due to illness or disability' and is recorded as early as AD 950. In the 20th century, the term acquired offensive connotations and has now been largely replaced by broader terms such as 'disabled person.'

crip·pled /ˈkripəld/ ▶ adj. (of a person) unable to walk or move properly; disabled: *a crippled old man.* ■ (of a machine) severely damaged: *the pilot displayed skill and nerve in landing the crippled plane.*

> **USAGE** See usage at CRIPPLE.

crip·ple·ware /ˈkripəl,we(ə)r/ ▶ n. Computing, informal software distributed with reduced functionality with a view to attracting payment for a fully functional version.

cri·sis /ˈkrīsis/ ▶ n. (pl. **crises** /-,sēz/) a time of intense difficulty, trouble, or danger: *the current economic crisis | a family in crisis | a crisis of semiliteracy among high school graduates.* ■ a time when a difficult or important decision must be made: [as modifier] *a crisis point of history.* ■ the turning point of a disease when an important change takes place, indicating either recovery or death.
–ORIGIN late Middle English (denoting the turning point of a disease): medical Latin, from Greek *krisis* 'decision,' from *krinein* 'decide.' The general sense 'decisive point' dates from the early 17th cent.

cri·sis cen·ter ▶ n. a facility, telephone answering system, etc., where individuals going through personal crises can obtain help or advice. ■ an office or agency that serves as a clearinghouse for information and coordinates action during an emergency or disaster.

cri·sis man·age·ment ▶ n. the process by which a business or other organization deals with a sudden emergency situation.

crisp /krisp/ ▶ adj. 1 (of a substance) firm, dry, and brittle, esp. in a way considered pleasing or attractive: *crisp bacon | the snow is lovely and crisp.* ■ (of a fruit or vegetable) firm, indicating freshness: *crisp lettuce.* ■ (of the weather) cool, fresh, and invigorating: *a crisp autumn day.* ■ (of paper or cloth) smoothly and attractively stiff and uncreased: *a crisp $5 bill.* ■ (of hair) having tight curls, giving an impression of rigidity.
2 (of a way of speaking or writing) briskly decisive and matter-of-fact, without hesitation or unnecessary detail: *they were cut off with a crisp "Thank you."*
▶ n. 1 a dessert of fruit baked with a crunchy topping of brown sugar, butter, and flour: *rhubarb crisp.*
2 (also **potato crisp**) British term for POTATO CHIP.
▶ v. [with obj.] give (something, esp. food) a crisp surface by placing it in an oven or grill: *crisp the pita rounds in the oven.* ■ [no obj.] (of food) acquire a crisp surface in this way: *open the foil so that the bread browns and crisps.* ■ archaic curl into short, stiff, wavy folds or crinkles.
–PHRASES **burn something to a crisp** burn something completely, leaving only a charred remnant.
–DERIVATIVES **crisp·ly** adv., **crisp·ness** n.
–ORIGIN Old English (referring to hair in the sense 'curly'): from Latin *crispus* 'curled.' Other senses may result from symbolic interpretation of the sound of the word.

cris·pate /ˈkris,pāt, -pət/ ▶ adj. Botany (esp. of a leaf) having a wavy or curly edge.
–ORIGIN mid 19th cent.: from Latin *crispatus*, past participle of *crispare* 'to curl.'

crisp·er /ˈkrispər/ ▶ n. a compartment at the bottom of a refrigerator for storing fruit and vegetables.

crisp·y /ˈkrispē/ ▶ adj. (**crispier, crispiest**) (of food, typically cooked food) having a pleasingly firm, dry, and brittle surface or texture: *crispy fried bacon.*
–DERIVATIVES **crisp·i·ness** n.

cris·sal thrash·er /ˈkrisəl/ ▶ n. a large gray thrasher (songbird) with a red patch under the tail, found in the southwestern US and Mexico. ● *Toxostoma dorsale* (or *crissale*), family Mimidae.
–ORIGIN late 19th cent.: *crissal* from modern Latin *crissum* (denoting the vent region of a bird) + -AL.

criss·cross /ˈkris,krôs/ ▶ n. a pattern of intersecting straight lines or paths: *the crisscross of wrinkles on his face.*
▶ adj. (of a pattern) containing a number of straight lines or paths that intersect each other: *the streets ran in a regular crisscross pattern.*
▶ adv. in a pattern of intersecting straight lines: *the swords were strung crisscross on his back.*
▶ v. [with obj.] (usu. **be crisscrossed**) form a pattern of intersecting lines or paths on (a place): *the green hill was crisscrossed with a network of sheep tracks.* ■ [no obj.] (of straight lines or paths) intersect repeatedly: *the smaller streets crisscrossed in a grid pattern.* ■ move or travel around (a place) by going back and forth repeatedly: *the President crisscrossed America.*
–ORIGIN early 17th cent. (denoting a figure of a cross preceding the alphabet in a hornbook): from *Christ-cross* (in the same sense in late Middle English), from *Christ's cross*. The form was later treated as a reduplication of CROSS.

cris·ta /ˈkristə/ ▶ n. (pl. **cristae** /-tē, -tī/) 1 Anatomy & Zoology a ridge or crest.
2 Biology each of the partial partitions in a mitochondrion formed by infolding of the inner membrane.
–DERIVATIVES **cris·tate** /ˈkris,tāt/ adj.
–ORIGIN mid 19th cent.: from Latin,'tuft, plume, crest.'

cris·to·bal·ite /kriˈstōbə,līt/ ▶ n. a form of silica that is the main component of opal and also occurs as small octahedral crystals.
–ORIGIN late 19th cent.: named after *Cerro San Cristóbal* in Mexico, where it was discovered, + -ITE[1].

crit /krit/ ▶ n. informal short for CRITICISM or CRITIC.

cri·te·ri·on /krīˈti(ə)rēən/ ▶ n. (pl. **criteria** /-ˈti(ə)rēə/) a principle or standard by which something may be judged or decided: *the launch came too close to violating safety criteria.*
–DERIVATIVES **cri·te·ri·al** /-ˈti(ə)rēəl/ adj.
–ORIGIN early 17th cent.: from Greek *kritērion* 'means of judging,' from *kritēs* (see CRITIC).

> **USAGE** Strictly speaking, the singular form (following the original Greek) is **criterion** and the plural form is **criteria**. It is a common mistake, however, to use **criteria** as if it were a singular, as in *a further* ***criteria*** *needs to be considered.*

cri·te·ri·um /krīˈti(ə)rēəm/ ▶ n. a one-day bicycle race on a circuit road course.

crit·ic /ˈkritik/ ▶ n. 1 a person who expresses an unfavorable opinion of something: *critics say many schools are not prepared to handle the influx of foreign students.*
2 a person who judges the merits of literary, artistic, or musical works, esp. one who does so professionally: *a film critic.*
–ORIGIN late 16th cent.: from Latin *criticus*, from Greek *kritikos*, from *kritēs* 'a judge,' from *krinein* 'judge, decide.'

crit·i·cal /ˈkritikəl/ ▶ adj. 1 expressing adverse or disapproving comments or judgments: *he was* ***critical of*** *many U.S. welfare programs.*
2 expressing or involving an analysis of the merits and faults of a work of literature, music, or art: *she never won the critical acclaim she sought.* ■ (of a published literary or musical text) incorporating a detailed and scholarly analysis and commentary: *a critical edition of a Bach sonata.* ■ involving the objective analysis and evaluation of an issue in order to form a judgement: *professors often find it difficult to encourage critical thinking in their students.*
3 (of a situation or problem) having the potential to become disastrous; at a point of crisis: *the flood waters had not receded, and the situation was still critical.* ■ (of a person) extremely ill and at risk of death: *he had been* ***in critical condition*** *since undergoing surgery.* ■ having a decisive or crucial importance in the success or failure of something: *temperature is a critical factor in successful fruit storage.*
4 Mathematics & Physics relating to or denoting a point of transition from one state to another. ■ (of a nuclear reactor or fuel) maintaining a self-sustaining chain reaction: *the reactor is due to go critical in October.*
–DERIVATIVES **crit·i·cal·i·ty** /,kritəˈkalitē/ n. (sense 3, sense 4), **crit·i·cal·ly** /ˈkritik(ə)lē/ adv. [as submodifier] *he's critically ill*, **crit·i·cal·ness** n.
–ORIGIN mid 16th cent. (in the sense 'relating to the crisis of a disease'): from late Latin *criticus* (see CRITIC).

crit·i·cal an·gle ▶ n. Optics the angle of incidence beyond which rays of light passing through a denser medium to the surface of a less dense medium are no longer refracted but totally reflected.

crit·i·cal ap·pa·rat·us ▶ n. see APPARATUS (sense 3).

crit·i·cal damp·ing ▶ n. Physics damping just sufficient to prevent oscillations.

crit·i·cal list ▶ n. [in sing.] a list of those who are critically ill in the hospital.

crit·i·cal mass ▶ n. 1 Physics the minimum amount of fissile material needed to maintain a nuclear chain reaction.
2 the minimum size or amount of something required to start or maintain a venture: *a communication system is of no value unless there is a critical mass of users.*

crit·i·cal path ▶ n. the sequence of stages determining the minimum time needed for an operation, esp. when analyzed on a computer for a large organization.

crit·i·cal path a·nal·y·sis ▶ n. the mathematical network analysis technique of planning complex working procedures with reference to the critical path of each alternative system.

crit·i·cal pe·ri·od ▶ n. Psychology a period during someone's development in which a particular skill or characteristic is believed to be most readily acquired.

crit·i·cal point ▶ n. 1 Chemistry a point on a phase diagram at which both the liquid and gas phases of a substance have the same density, and are therefore indistinguishable.
2 Mathematics a point on a curve where the gradient is zero.

crit·i·cal pres·sure ▶ n. Chemistry the pressure of a gas or vapor in its critical state.

crit·i·cal state ▶ n. Chemistry the state of a substance when it is at the critical point, i.e., at critical temperature and pressure.

crit·i·cal tem·per·a·ture ▶ n. Chemistry the temperature of a gas or vapor in its critical state. Above this temperature, a gas cannot be liquefied by pressure alone.

crit·i·cal the·o·ry ▶ n. a philosophical approach to culture, and esp. to literature, that seeks to confront the social, historical, and ideological forces and structures that produce and constrain it. The term is applied particularly to the work of the Frankfurt School.

crit·i·cal vol·ume ▶ n. Chemistry the volume occupied by a unit mass of a gas or vapor in its critical state.

crit·ic·as·ter /ˈkritə,kastər/ ▶ n. rare a minor or inferior critic.
–ORIGIN late 17th cent.: from CRITIC + -ASTER.

crit·i·cism /ˈkritə,sizəm/ ▶ n. 1 the expression of disapproval of someone or something based on perceived faults or mistakes: *he received a lot of criticism | he ignored the criticisms of his friends.*
2 the analysis and judgment of the merits and faults of a literary or artistic work: *alternative methods of criticism supported by well-developed literary theories.* ■ the scholarly investigation of literary or historical texts to determine their origin or intended form.
–ORIGIN early 17th cent.: from CRITIC or Latin *criticus* + -ISM.

crit·i·cize /ˈkritə,sīz/ ▶ v. [with obj.] 1 indicate the faults of (someone or something) in a disapproving way: *states criticized the failure to provide an adequate and permanent compensation | technicians were criticized for defective workmanship.*

2 form and express a sophisticated judgment of (a literary or artistic work): *a literary text may be criticized on two grounds: the semantic and the expressive.*
– DERIVATIVES **crit·i·ciz·a·ble** adj., **crit·i·ciz·er** n.

cri·tique /kri'tēk/ ▶ n. a detailed analysis and assessment of something, esp. a literary, philosophical, or political theory.
▶ v. (**critiques, critiquing, critiqued**) [with obj.] evaluate (a theory or practice) in a detailed and analytical way: *the authors critique the methods and practices used in the research.*
– ORIGIN mid 17th cent. (as a noun): from French, based on Greek *kritikē tekhnē* 'critical art.'

crit·ter /'kritər/ ▶ n. informal or dialect a living creature; an animal. ■ a person of a particular kind: *the old critter used to live in a shack.*
– ORIGIN early 19th cent.: variant of CREATURE.

CRM ▶ abbr. customer relationship management, denoting strategies and software that enable a company to organize and optimize its customer relations.

croak /krōk/ ▶ n. a deep hoarse sound made by a frog or a crow. ■ a sound resembling this, esp. one made by a person: *Lorton tried to laugh—it came out as a croak.*
▶ v. [no obj.] **1** (of a frog or crow) make a characteristic deep hoarse sound. ■ (of a person) make a similar sound when speaking or laughing: *"Thank you," I croaked.* ■ archaic prophesy evil or misfortune, esp. unjustifiably and to the irritation of others: *without croaking, it may be observed that our government is upon a dangerous experiment.*
2 informal die: *the dog finally croaked in 1987.* ■ [with obj.] kill (someone): *Scissors Haggerty's mob croaked two messengers.*
– ORIGIN Middle English (as a verb): imitative.

croak·er /'krōkər/ ▶ n. a person or animal that croaks. ■ another term for DRUM[3].

croak·y /'krōkē/ ▶ adj. (**croakier, croakiest**) (of a person's voice) deep and hoarse.
– DERIVATIVES **croak·i·ly** /-kəlē/ adv.

Cro·at /'krō,at, 'krō,ät, krōt/ ▶ n. **1** a native or inhabitant of Croatia, or a person of Croatian descent.
2 the South Slavic language of the Croats, almost identical to Serbian but written in the Roman alphabet. See SERBO-CROAT.
▶ adj. of or relating to the Croats or their language.
– ORIGIN from modern Latin *Croatae* (plural), from Serbian and Croatian *Hrvat*.

Cro·a·tia /krō'āshə/ a country in southeastern Europe, formerly a constituent republic of Yugoslavia; pop. 4,489,400 (est. 2009); capital, Zagreb; language, Croatian. Croatian name HRVATSKA.

> Apart from a period of Turkish rule in the 16th–17th centuries, Croatia largely remained linked with Hungary until 1918, when it joined the Kingdom of the Serbs, Croats, and Slovenes (later Yugoslavia). After a period during World War II as a Nazi puppet state (1941–45), it became part of Yugoslavia once more and remained a constituent republic until it declared itself independent in 1991. The secession of Croatia led to war between Croats and the Serb minority, and with Serbia; a ceasefire was called in 1992.

Cro·a·tian /krō'āshən/ ▶ n. & adj. another term for CROAT.

croc /kräk/ ▶ n. informal a crocodile.
– ORIGIN late 19th cent.: abbreviation.

Cro·ce /'krōchā/, Benedetto (1866–1952), Italian philosopher and politician. In his "Philosophy of Spirit," he denied the physical reality of a work of art and identified philosophical endeavor with a methodological approach to history.

cro·chet /krō'shā/ ▶ n. a handicraft in which yarn is made up into a patterned fabric by looping yarn with a hooked needle: [as modifier] *a crochet hook.* ■ fabric or items made in such a way: *the bikini is tiny, three triangles of cotton crochet.*
▶ v. (**crochets, crocheting** /-'shāiNG/, **crocheted** /-'shād/) [with obj.] make (a garment or piece of fabric) in such a way: *she had crocheted the shawl herself* | [no obj.] *her mother had stopped crocheting.*
– DERIVATIVES **cro·chet·er** /-'shāər/ n.
– ORIGIN mid 19th cent.: from French, diminutive of *croc* 'hook,' from Old Norse *krókr*.

cro·ci /'krō,kī, -,sī/ plural form of CROCUS.

cro·cid·o·lite /krō'sidl,īt/ ▶ n. a fibrous blue or green mineral consisting of a silicate of iron and sodium. Also called BLUE ASBESTOS (see ASBESTOS).
– ORIGIN mid 19th cent.: from Greek *krokis, krokid-* 'nap of cloth' + -LITE.

crock[1] /kräk/ ▶ n. **1** an earthenware pot or jar. ■ a broken piece of earthenware.
2 (also vulgar slang **crock of shit**) a thing that is considered to be complete nonsense.
– ORIGIN Old English *croc, crocca*, of Germanic origin; related to Old Norse *krukka* and probably to Dutch *kruik* and German *Krug*.

crock[2] informal ▶ n. an old person who is feeble and useless.
▶ v. [with obj.] Brit. cause an injury to (a person or part of the body): *he crocked a shoulder.*
– ORIGIN late Middle English: perhaps from Flemish, and probably related to CRACK. Originally a Scots term for an old ewe, it came in the late 19th cent. to denote an old or broken-down horse.

crocked /kräkt/ ▶ adj. informal drunk: *his party guests were pretty crocked.*

crock·er·y /'kräkərē/ ▶ n. plates, dishes, cups, and other similar items, esp. ones made of earthenware or china.
– ORIGIN early 18th cent.: from obsolete *crocker* 'potter,' from CROCK[1].

crock·et /'kräkit/ ▶ n. (in Gothic architecture) a small carved ornament, typically a bud or curled leaf, on the inclined side of a pinnacle or gable.
– ORIGIN Middle English (denoting a curl or roll of hair): from Old Northern French, variant of Old French *crochet* (see CROTCHET). The current sense dates from the late 17th cent., but *crotchet* was used in the same sense from late Middle English until the 19th cent.

Crock·ett /'kräkit/, Davy (1786–1836), US frontiersman, soldier, and politician; full name *David Crockett*. While a member of the House of Representatives 1827–35, he cultivated the image of a rough backwoods legislator. When he left politics, he returned to the frontier, where he fought for the cause of Texan independence. He was killed at the siege of the Alamo.

Crock·pot /'kräk,pät/ ▶ trademark a large electric cooking pot used to cook stews and other dishes slowly.

croc·o·dile /'kräkə,dīl/ ▶ n. **1** a large predatory semiaquatic reptile with long jaws, long tail, short legs, and a horny textured skin, using submersion and stealth to approach prey unseen. The crocodile has been extensively hunted for its valuable skin. ● Family Crocodylidae: three genera, in particular *Crocodylus*, and several species. ■ leather made from crocodile skin, used esp. to make bags and shoes.
2 Brit. informal a line of schoolchildren walking in pairs.
– ORIGIN Middle English *cocodrille, cokadrill*, from Old French *cocodrille*, via medieval Latin from Latin *crocodilus*, from Greek *krokodilos* 'worm of the stones,' from *krokē* 'pebble' + *drilos* 'worm.' The spelling was changed in the 16th cent. to conform with the Latin and Greek forms.

croc·o·dile bird ▶ n. the Egyptian plover, which is said to feed on insects parasitic on crocodiles.

croc·o·dile clip ▶ n. British term for ALLIGATOR CLIP.

croc·o·dile tears ▶ plural n. tears or expressions of sorrow that are insincere.
– ORIGIN mid 16th cent.: said to be so named from a belief that crocodiles wept while devouring or luring their prey.

croc·o·dil·i·an /,kräkə'dilēən/ ▶ n. Zoology a large, predatory, semiaquatic reptile of an order that comprises the crocodiles, alligators, caimans, and gharial. Crocodilians are distinguished by long jaws, short legs, and a powerful tail. ● Order Crocodylia: three families.
▶ adj. of or relating to such reptiles.

cro·co·ite /'kräkə,wīt/ ▶ n. a rare, bright orange mineral consisting of lead chromate.
– ORIGIN mid 19th cent.: originally as French *crocoise*, from Greek *krokoeis* 'saffron-colored,' from *krokos* 'crocus.' The spelling was altered to *crocoisite*, then *crocoite*.

cro·cus /'krōkəs/ ▶ n. (pl. **crocuses** or **croci** /-kī, -sī/) a small, spring-flowering plant of the iris family, which grows from a corm and bears bright yellow, purple, or white flowers. See also AUTUMN CROCUS. ● Genus *Crocus*, family Iridaceae.
– ORIGIN late Middle English (also denoting saffron, obtained from a species of crocus): via Latin from Greek *krokos*, of Semitic origin and related to Hebrew *karkōm* and Arabic *kurkum*.

Croe·sus /'krēsəs/ (6th century BC), last king of Lydia c.560–546 BC. Renowned for his great wealth, he subjugated the Greek cities on the coast of Asia Minor before being overthrown by Cyrus the Great of Persia.

croft /krôft/ Brit. ▶ n. a small rented farm, esp. one in Scotland, comprising a plot of arable land attached to a house and with a right of pasturage held in common with other such farms. ■ an enclosed field used for tillage or pasture, typically attached to a house and worked by the occupier.
▶ v. [with obj.] farm (land) as a croft or crofts.
– DERIVATIVES **croft·er** n.
– ORIGIN Old English: of unknown origin.

Crohn's dis·ease /'krōnz/ ▶ n. a chronic inflammatory disease of the intestines, esp. the colon and ileum, associated with ulcers and fistulae.
– ORIGIN 1930s: named after Burrill B. Crohn (1884–1983), American pathologist, who was among the first to describe it.

C

crois·sant /k(r)wä'sänt, -'säN/ ▶ n. a French crescent-shaped roll made of sweet flaky pastry, often eaten for breakfast.
– ORIGIN late 19th cent.: French (see CRESCENT). The term had occasionally been recorded earlier as a variant of *crescent*.

Cro-Mag·non man /krō 'magnən, 'manyən/ ▶ n. the earliest form of modern human in Europe, associated with the Aurignacian flint industry. Their appearance c.35,000 years ago marked the beginning of the Upper Paleolithic and the apparent decline and disappearance of Neanderthal man; the group persisted at least into the Neolithic period.
– ORIGIN *Cro-Magnon*, the name of a hill in the Dordogne, France, where remains were found in 1868.

crom·bec /'kräm,bek/ ▶ n. a small African warbler with a very short tail, and gray or green upper parts with rufous or white underparts. ● Genus *Sylvietta*, family Sylviidae: several species, in particular the (**northern**) **crombec** (*S. brachyura*).
– ORIGIN early 20th cent.: from French, from Dutch *krom* 'crooked' + *bek* 'beak.'

Crome /krōm/, John (1768–1821), English painter; founder and leading member of the Norwich School.

crom·lech /'kräm,lek, -,lekH/ ▶ n. (in Wales) a megalithic tomb consisting of a large flat stone laid on upright ones. Also called DOLMEN. [Welsh, from *crom*, feminine of *crwm* 'arched' + *llech* 'flat stone.'] ■ (in Brittany) a circle of standing stones. [via French from Breton *krommlec'h*.]

Crom·well[1] /'krämwəl, -,wel/, Oliver (1599–1658), English general and statesman; lord protector of the Commonwealth 1653–58. He was the leader of the victorious Parliamentary forces (or Roundheads) in the English Civil War. As head of state, he instituted many puritan reforms in the Church of England. He was briefly succeeded by his son **Richard** (1626–1712), who was forced into exile in 1659.
– DERIVATIVES **Crom·well·i·an** adj.

Crom·well[2], Thomas (c.1485–1540), English statesman, chief minister to Henry VIII 1531–40. He presided over the king's divorce from Catherine of Aragon (1533) and his break with the Roman Catholic Church. Although untried, he was executed for treason.

crone /krōn/ ▶ n. an old woman who is thin and ugly.
– ORIGIN late Middle English: via Middle Dutch *croonje, caroonje* 'carcass, old ewe' from Old Northern French *caroigne* 'carrion, cantankerous woman' (see CARRION).

Cro·nin /'krōnən/, A. J. (1896–1981), Scottish novelist; full name *Archibald Joseph Cronin*. His novels, including *The Citadel* (1937), often reflect his early experiences as a doctor.

cron·ing /'krōniNG/ ▶ n. (esp. among feminists in the US and Australasia) a celebration or ceremony to honor older women.
– ORIGIN 1990s: blend of *crone* + *crowning*.

Cron·kite /'kräNG,kīt, 'krän-/, Walter Leland, Jr. (1916–2009), US television journalist. He anchored the *The CBS News with Walter Cronkite* 1962–81, ending each broadcast with "And that's the way it is."

Walter Cronkite

Cro·nus /'krōnəs/ (also **Kronos**) Greek Mythology the supreme god until dethroned by Zeus. The youngest son of Uranus (Heaven) and Gaia (Earth), Cronus overthrew and castrated his father and then married his sister Rhea. Because he was fated to be overcome by one of his male children, Cronus swallowed all of them as soon as they were born, but when Zeus was born, Rhea deceived him and hid the baby away. Roman equivalent **Saturn**.

cro·ny /'krōnē/ ▶ **n.** (pl. **cronies**) informal, often derogatory a close friend or companion: *he went gambling with his cronies.*
– ORIGIN mid 17th cent. (originally Cambridge University slang): from Greek *khronios* 'long-lasting' (here used to mean 'contemporary'), from *khronos* 'time.' Compare with **chum**¹.

cro·ny·ism /'krōnē,izəm/ ▶ **n.** derogatory the appointment of friends and associates to positions of authority, without proper regard to their qualifications.

Crook /kro͝ok/, George (1829–90), US army officer. He served during the Civil War and then fought against the Indians in the northwest. He was defeated by Crazy Horse in 1876 but went on to fight against the Apaches under Geronimo 1882–85.

crook /kro͝ok/ ▶ **n. 1** the hooked staff of a shepherd. ■ a bishop's crozier. ■ a bend in something, esp. at the elbow in a person's arm: *her head was cradled in the crook of Luke's left arm.* ■ a piece of extra tubing that can be fitted to a brass instrument to lower the pitch by a set interval. ■ a metal tube on which the reed of some wind instruments (such as the bassoon) is set.
2 informal a person who is dishonest or a criminal.
▶ **v.** [with obj.] bend (something, esp. a finger as a signal): *he crooked a finger for the waitress.*
▶ **adj.** Austral./NZ informal (esp. of a situation) bad, unpleasant, or unsatisfactory: *it was pretty crook on the land in the early 1970s.* ■ (of a person or a part of the body) unwell or injured: *a crook knee.* ■ dishonest; illegal: *some pretty crook things went on there.* [late 19th cent.: abbreviation of **crooked**.]
– DERIVATIVES **crook·er·y** /'kro͝okərē/ **n.**
– ORIGIN Middle English (in the sense 'hooked tool or weapon'): from Old Norse *krókr* 'hook.' A noun sense 'deceit, guile, trickery' (compare with **crooked**) was recorded in Middle English but was obsolete by the 17th cent.

crook·back /'kro͝ok,bak/ ▶ **n.** archaic a person with a hunchback.
– DERIVATIVES **crook·backed** /-,bakt/ **adj.**

crook·ed /'kro͝okəd/ ▶ **adj.** (**crookeder**, **crookedest**)
1 bent or twisted out of shape or out of place: *his teeth were yellow and crooked.*
2 informal dishonest or illegal: *a crooked business deal.*
– DERIVATIVES **crook·ed·ly adv.**, **crook·ed·ness n.**
– ORIGIN Middle English: from **crook**, probably modeled on Old Norse *krókóttr* 'crooked, cunning.'

crook·neck /'kro͝ok,nek/ (also **crookneck squash**) ▶ **n.** a squash of a club-shaped variety with a curved neck and warty skin.

croon /kro͞on/ ▶ **v.** [no obj.] hum or sing in a soft, low voice, esp. in a sentimental manner: *she was crooning to the child* | [with obj.] *the female vocalist crooned smoky blues into the microphone.* ■ say in a soft, low voice: *"Goodbye, you lovely darling," she crooned.*
▶ **n.** [in sing.] a soft, low voice or tone: *he sang in a gentle, highly expressive croon.*
– ORIGIN late 15th cent. (originally Scots and northern English): from Middle Low German and Middle Dutch *krōnen* 'groan, lament.' The use of *croon* in standard English was probably popularized by Robert Burns.

croon·er /'kro͞onər/ ▶ **n.** a singer, typically a male one, who sings sentimental songs in a soft, low voice.

crop /kräp/ ▶ **n. 1** a cultivated plant that is grown as food, esp. a grain, fruit, or vegetable: *the main crops were oats and barley.* ■ an amount of such plants or their produce harvested at one time: *a heavy crop of fruit.* ■ an abundance of something, esp. a person's hair: *he had a thick crop of wiry hair.* ■ the total number of young farm animals born in a particular year on one farm. ■ a group or amount of related people or things appearing or occurring at one time: *the current crop of politicians.* ■ the entire tanned hide of an animal.
2 a hairstyle in which the hair is cut very short.
3 short for **riding crop**.
4 a pouch in a bird's gullet where food is stored or prepared for digestion. ■ a similar organ in an insect or earthworm.
▶ **v.** (**crops**, **cropping**, **cropped**) [with obj.] **1** cut (something, esp. a person's hair) very short: (as adj. **cropped**) *cropped blond hair.* ■ (of an animal) bite off and eat the tops of (plants): *the horse was gratefully cropping the grass.* ■ cut the edges of (a photograph) in order to produce a better picture or to fit a given space.
2 harvest (plants or their produce) from a particular area: *hay would have been cropped several times through the summer.* ■ sow or plant (land) with plants that will produce food or fodder, esp. on a large commercial scale: *the southern areas are cropped in cotton* | (as adj. **cropped**) *intensively cropped areas.*
– PHRASAL VERBS **crop out** (of rock) appear or be exposed at the surface of the earth. **crop up** appear, occur, or come to one's notice unexpectedly: *some urgent business had cropped up.*
– ORIGIN Old English, of Germanic origin; related to German *Kropf*. From Old English to the late 18th cent. there existed a sense 'flower head, ear of corn,' giving rise to sense 1 of the noun and senses referring to the top of something, whence sense 3 of the noun.

crop cir·cle ▶ **n.** an area of standing crops that has been flattened in the form of a circle or more complex pattern. No general cause of crop circles has been identified although various natural and unorthodox explanations have been put forward; many of the circles are known to have been hoaxes.

crop dust·ing ▶ **n.** the spraying of powdered or liquid insecticide or fertilizer on crops, esp. from the air.

crop-eared ▶ **adj.** historical (esp. of an animal) having the tops of the ears cut off. ■ (esp. of a Roundhead in the English Civil War) having the hair cut very short.

crop·per /'kräpər/ ▶ **n. 1** a plant that yields a crop of a specified kind or in a specified way: *the white-fleshed varieties are the heaviest croppers.*
2 a machine or person that cuts or trims something, such as wool off a sheep or the pile of a carpet during manufacture.
3 a person who raises a crop, esp. as a sharecropper.
– PHRASES **come a cropper** informal fall heavily. ■ suffer a defeat or disaster: *the club's challenge for the championship has come a cropper.*

crop ro·ta·tion ▶ **n.** see **rotation**.

crop top ▶ **n.** a woman's casual garment or undergarment for the upper body, cut short so that it reveals the stomach.

cro·quem·bouche /,krôk,än'bo͞osH/ ▶ **n.** a decorative dessert consisting of cream puff pastry and crystallized fruit or other confectionery items arranged in a cone and held together by a caramel sauce.
– ORIGIN French, literally 'crunch in the mouth.'

cro·quet /krō'kā/ ▶ **n.** a game played on a lawn, in which colored wooden balls are driven through a series of wickets by means of mallets: [as modifier] *a croquet lawn.* ■ an act of croqueting a ball.
▶ **v.** (**croquets**, **croqueting** /-'kāiNG/, **croqueted** /-'kād/) [with obj.] drive away (an opponent's ball) by holding one's own ball against it and striking this with the mallet. A player is entitled to do this after their ball has struck an opponent's ball.
– ORIGIN mid 19th cent.: perhaps a dialect form of French *crochet* 'hook.'

cro·quette /krō'ket/ ▶ **n.** a small roll of chopped vegetables, meat, or fish, fried in breadcrumbs: *a potato croquette.*
– ORIGIN French, from *croquer* 'to crunch.'

crore /krôr/ ▶ **n.** Indian ten million; one hundred lakhs, esp. of rupees, units of measurement, or people.
– ORIGIN from Hindi *karoṛ*, based on Sanskrit *koṭi* 'ten million.'

Cros·by /'krôzbē/, Bing (1904–77), US singer and actor; born *Harry Lillis Crosby*. His songs include "Pennies from Heaven," "Blue Skies," and, in particular, "White Christmas" (introduced in the movie *Holiday Inn*, 1942), one of the best-selling songs of all time. He also starred in the series of *Road* movies from 1940 to 1962 with Bob Hope and Dorothy Lamour.

Bing Crosby

cro·sier ▶ **n.** variant spelling of **crozier**.

cross /krôs/ ▶ **n. 1** a mark, object, or figure formed by two short intersecting lines or pieces (+ or ×): *cut a cross in the bark with a sharp knife.* ■ Brit. a mark of this type (×) used to show that something is incorrect or unsatisfactory.
2 an upright post with a transverse bar, as used in antiquity for crucifixion. ■ (**the Cross**) the cross on which Jesus was crucified. ■ this, or a representation of it, as an emblem of Christianity: *she wore a cross around her neck.* ■ a thing that is unavoidable and has to be endured: *she's just a cross we have to bear.* ■ short for **sign of the cross** (see **sign**). ■ a staff surmounted by a cross carried in religious processions. ■ a cross-shaped decoration awarded for personal valor or indicating rank in some orders of knighthood: *the Military Cross.* ■ (**the Cross**) the constellation Southern Cross. Also called **crux**.
3 an animal or plant resulting from crossbreeding; a hybrid: *a Devon and Holstein cross.* ■ (**a cross between**) a mixture or compromise of two things: *the system is a cross between a monorail and a conventional railroad.*
4 a sideways or transverse movement or pass, in particular: ■ Soccer a pass of the ball across the field toward the center close to one's opponents' goal. ■ Boxing a blow delivered across and over the opponent's lead: *a right cross.*
▶ **v.** [with obj.] **1** go or extend across or to the other side of (a path, road, stretch of water, or area): *he has crossed the Atlantic twice* | *two paths crossed the field* | figurative *a shadow of apprehension crossed her face* | [no obj.] *we crossed over the bridge.* ■ go across or climb over (an obstacle or boundary): *he attempted to cross the border into Jordan* | [no obj.] *we crossed over a fence.* ■ [no obj.] (**cross over**) (esp. of an artist or an artistic style or work) begin to appeal to a different audience, esp. a wider one: *a talented animator who crossed over to live action.*
2 [no obj.] pass in an opposite or different direction; intersect: *the two lines cross at 90°.* ■ [with obj.] cause (two things) to intersect: *cross the cables in opposing directions.* ■ [with obj.] place (something) crosswise: *Michele sat back and crossed her arms.* ■ (of a letter) be sent before receipt of another from the person being written to: *our letters crossed.*
3 draw a line or lines across; mark with a cross: *cross the t's.* ■ Brit. mark or annotate (a check), typically by drawing a pair of parallel lines across it, to indicate that it must be paid into a named bank account. ■ (**cross someone/something off**) delete a name or item on a list as being no longer required or involved: *Liz crossed off the days on the calendar.* ■ (**cross something out**) delete an incorrect or inapplicable word or phrase by drawing a line through it.
4 (**cross oneself**) (of a person) make the sign of the cross in front of one's chest as a sign of Christian reverence or to invoke divine protection.
5 Soccer pass (the ball) across the field toward the center when attacking.
6 cause (an animal of one species, breed, or variety) to interbreed with one of another species, breed, or variety: *many animals of the breed were crossed with the closely related Guernsey* | figurative *he behaved like an old regular officer crossed with a mathematician.* ■ cross-fertilize (a plant): *a hybrid tea was crossed with a polyantha rose.*
7 oppose or stand in the way of (someone): *no one dared cross him.*

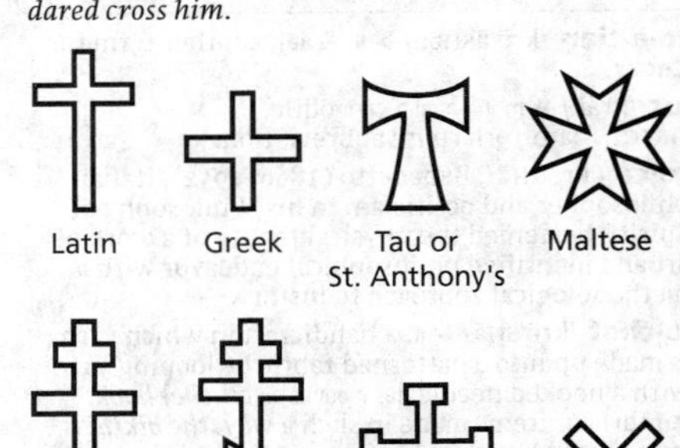

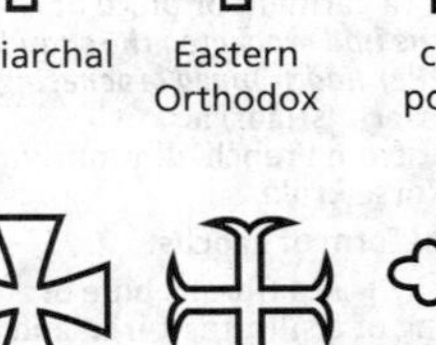

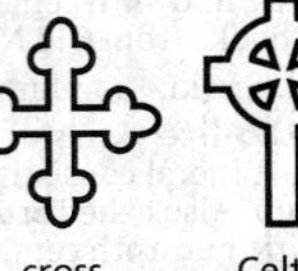
cross patée · cross moline · cross botonée · Celtic

types of cross

▶ **adj.** annoyed: *he seemed to be very cross about something.*
– PHRASES **at cross purposes** misunderstanding or having different aims from one another: *we had been talking at cross purposes.* **cross one's fingers** (or **keep one's fingers crossed**) put one finger across another as a sign of hoping for good luck. ■ hope that someone or something will be successful. **cross the floor** Brit. join the opposing side in Parliament. **cross my heart** (**and hope to die**) used to emphasize the truthfulness and sincerity of what one is saying, and sometimes reinforced by making a sign of the cross over one's chest. **cross one's mind** (of a thought) occur to one, esp. transiently: *it never crossed my mind to leave the tent and live in a house.* **cross someone's palm with silver** often humorous pay someone for a favor or service, esp. before having one's fortune told. **cross someone's path** meet or encounter someone. **cross swords** have an argument or dispute. **get one's wires** (or **lines**) **crossed** become wrongly connected by telephone. ■ have a misunderstanding. **the way of the Cross** see WAY.
– DERIVATIVES **cross·er** n., **cross·ly** adv., **cross·ness** n.
– ORIGIN late Old English (in the sense 'monument in the form of a cross'): from Old Norse *kross*, from Old Irish *cros*, from Latin *crux*.

cross- ▶ **comb. form 1** denoting movement or position across something: *cross-channel.* ■ denoting interaction: *cross-pollinate.* ■ passing from side to side; transverse: *crosspiece.*
2 describing the form or figure of a cross: *crossbones.*
– ORIGIN from CROSS.

cross-as·sem·bler ▶ **n.** Computing an assembler that can convert instructions into machine code for a computer other than that on which it is run.

cross·bar /ˈkrôsˌbär/ ▶ **n.** a horizontal bar fixed across another bar or between two upright bars, in particular: ■ (in sports) the bar between the two upright posts of a goal. ■ the horizontal metal bar between the handlebars and saddle on a man's or boy's bicycle.

cross·beam /ˈkrôsˌbēm/ ▶ **n.** a transverse beam.

cross-bed·ding ▶ **n.** Geology layering within a stratum and at an angle to the main bedding plane.

cross·bill /ˈkrôsˌbil/ ▶ **n.** a thickset finch with a crossed bill adapted for extracting seeds from the cones of conifers. The plumage is typically red in the male and olive green in the female. ● Genus *Loxia*, family Fringillidae: four species, in particular the widespread **red** (or **common**) **crossbill** (*L. curvirostra*).

cross·bones /ˈkrôsˌbōnz/ ▶ **n.** see SKULL AND CROSSBONES at SKULL.

cross-bor·der ▶ **adj.** passing, occurring, or performed across a border between two countries: *cross-border trade.*

cross·bow /ˈkrôsˌbō/ ▶ **n.** a medieval bow of a kind that is fixed across a wooden support and has a groove for the bolt and a mechanism for drawing and releasing the string.
– DERIVATIVES **cross·bow·man** /-ˌbōmən/ n. (pl. **crossbowmen**).

cross·breed /ˈkrôsˌbrēd/ ▶ **n.** an animal or plant produced by mating or hybridizing two different species, breeds, or varieties: [as modifier] *a crossbreed Labrador.*
▶ **v.** [with obj.] produce (an animal or plant) in this way: (as adj. **crossbred**) *a crossbred puppy.* ■ hybridize (a breed, species, or variety) with another. ■ [no obj.] (of an animal or plant) breed with a different breed, species, or variety.

cross-check ▶ **v.** [with obj.] **1** verify (figures or information) by using an alternative source or method: *always try to cross-check your bearings* | (as noun **cross-checking**) *no cross-checking has been done.*
2 Ice Hockey obstruct (an opponent) illegally with the stick held horizontally in both hands.
▶ **n. 1** an instance of verifying something by using an alternative source or method: *as a cross-check, they were also asked to give their date of birth.*
2 Ice Hockey an illegal obstruction using the stick held horizontally in both hands.

cross-claim ▶ **n.** Law a claim brought by one defendant against another in the same proceeding.

cross-col·or ▶ **n.** colored flashes of interference in a color television receiver caused by the misinterpretation of high-frequency luminance detail as color information.

cross-com·pil·er ▶ **n.** Computing a compiler that can convert instructions into machine code or low level code for a computer other than that on which it is run.

cross-con·nec·tion ▶ **n.** a connection made between two or more distinct things, typically parts of different networks or circuits.

cross-con·tam·i·na·tion ▶ **n.** the process by which bacteria or other microorganisms are unintentionally transferred from one substance or object to another, with harmful effect.
– DERIVATIVES **cross-con·tam·i·nate** v.

cross-cor·re·late ▶ **v.** [with obj.] compare (a sequence of data) against another.
– DERIVATIVES **cross-cor·re·la·tion** n.

cross-coun·try ▶ **adj. 1** across fields or countryside, as opposed to on roads or tracks: *cross-country walking.* ■ of, relating to, or denoting the sport of running, riding, or driving along a course in the countryside, as opposed to around a track. ■ of, relating to, or denoting skiing over relatively flat or mountainous terrain, as opposed to skiing only downhill.
2 across a region or country, in particular: ■ not keeping to main or direct roads, routes, or railroad lines: *mine shafts camouflaged by vegetation have swallowed up more than one cross-country hiker* | [as adv.] *if you are traveling cross-country, choose where you walk with care.* ■ traveling to many different parts of a country: *a whirlwind cross-country tour.*
▶ **n.** a cross-country race or competition. ■ the sport of cross-country running, riding, skiing, or driving: *skiing in the Rockies is a pleasant mix of downhill and cross-country.*

cross·court /ˈkrôsˌkôrt/ ▶ **adv. & adj.** (of a stroke in tennis and other racket sports) hit diagonally across the court: [as adj.] *a crosscourt volley.*
▶ **n.** a stroke of this type.

cross cous·ins ▶ **plural n.** first cousins who are children of a brother and sister. Compare with PARALLEL COUSINS.

cross-cul·tur·al ▶ **adj.** of or relating to different cultures or comparison between them: *cross-cultural understanding.*

cross·cur·rent /ˈkrôsˌkərənt/ ▶ **n. 1** a current in a river or sea that flows across another.
2 a process or tendency that is in conflict with another: *strong crosscurrents of debate.*

cross·cut /ˈkrôsˌkət/ ▶ **v.** [with obj.] **1** cut (wood or stone) across its main grain or axis.
2 alternate (one sequence) with another when editing a movie.
▶ **n. 1** a diagonal cut, esp. one across the main grain or axis of wood or stone. ■ short for CROSSCUT SAW. ■ Mining a cutting made across the course of a vein or the general direction of the workings.
2 an instance of alternating between two or more sequences when editing a movie.

cross·cut saw ▶ **n.** a saw with a handle at each end, used by two people for cutting across the grain of timber.

cross-dress ▶ **v.** [no obj.] wear clothing typical of the opposite sex.
– DERIVATIVES **cross-dress·er** n.

crosse /krôs/ ▶ **n.** the stick used in lacrosse.
– ORIGIN mid 19th cent.: from French, from Old French *croce* 'bishop's crook,' ultimately of Germanic origin and related to CRUTCH.

cross-ex·am·ine ▶ **v.** [with obj.] question (a witness called by the other party) in a court of law to discredit or undercut testimony already given. Compare with DIRECT EXAMINATION. ■ question (someone) aggressively or in great detail: *I was cross-examined over the breakfast table.*
– DERIVATIVES **cross-ex·am·i·na·tion** n., **cross-ex·am·in·er** n.

cross-eyed ▶ **adj.** having one or both eyes turned inward toward the nose, either from focusing on something very close, through temporary loss of control of focus, or as a permanent condition (convergent strabismus).

cross-fade ▶ **v.** [no obj.] (in sound or movie editing) make a picture or sound appear or be heard gradually as another disappears or becomes silent.
▶ **n.** an act or instance of cross-fading.

cross-fer·ti·lize ▶ **v.** [with obj.] **1** fertilize (a plant) using pollen from another plant of the same species. ■ [no obj.] (of two plants) fertilize each other.
2 stimulate the development of (something) with an exchange of ideas or information: *sessions between the two groups cross-fertilize ideas and provide insights.*
– DERIVATIVES **cross-fer·ti·li·za·tion** n.

cross·fire /ˈkrôsˌfīr/ ▶ **n.** gunfire from two or more directions passing through the same area: *a photographer was killed in the crossfire* | figurative *grape growers have been caught in the crossfire of the boycott.*

cross·flow /ˈkrôsˌflō/ ▶ **n.** a type of engine cylinder head where the intake ports are on the opposite side of the engine from the exhaust ports.

cross-grain ▶ **adj.** running across the regular grain in timber: *cross-grain swelling.*

cross-grained ▶ **adj.** (of timber) having a grain that runs across the regular grain. ■ stubbornly contrary or bad-tempered: *Bruce was a cross-grained and boastful individual.*

cross·hairs /ˈkrôsˌhe(ə)rz/ ▶ **plural n.** a pair of fine wires or lines crossing at right angles at the focus of an optical instrument or gun sight, for use in positioning, aiming, or measuring. ■ a representation of this on a computer screen.

cross·hatch /ˈkrôsˌhaCH/ ▶ **v.** [with obj.] (often as noun **crosshatching**) (in drawing or graphics) shade (an area) with intersecting sets of parallel lines.

cross·head /ˈkrôsˌhed/ ▶ **n.** a bar or block between the piston rod and connecting rod in a steam engine.

cross in·dex ▶ **n.** a note or cross reference in a book or list that refers the reader to other material.
▶ **v.** (**cross-index**) [with obj.] index (something) under another heading as a cross reference: [as adj.] *a cross-indexed file.*

cross in·fec·tion ▶ **n.** the transfer of infection, esp. to a hospital patient with a different infection or between different species of animal or plant.

cross·ing /ˈkrôsiNG/ ▶ **n. 1** a place where two roads, two railroad lines, or a road and a railroad line cross. ■ the action of moving across or over something: *the crossing of the Pyrenees.* ■ a journey across water in a ship: *a short ferry crossing.* ■ a place at which one may safely cross something, esp. a street. ■ a place at which one can cross a border between countries. ■ Architecture the intersection of a church nave and the transepts.
2 crossbreeding.

cross·ing guard ▶ **n.** a person whose job it is to help pedestrians, esp. schoolchildren, to cross intersections safely.

cross·ing o·ver ▶ **n.** Genetics the exchange of genes between homologous chromosomes, resulting in a mixture of parental characteristics in offspring.

cross-leg·ged /ˈleg(ə)d/ ▶ **adj. & adv.** (of a seated person) with the legs crossed at the ankles and the knees bent outward: [as adv.] *John sat cross-legged on the floor.*

cross-li·cense ▶ **v.** [with obj.] give one party a license to use (patented or copyright material) in return for a similar license: *the two companies have agreed to cross-license their intellectual property.*
▶ **adj.** involving or effected by cross-licensing: *a ten-year patent cross-license agreement.*

cross·light /ˈkrôsˌlīt/ ▶ **n.** a light positioned to illuminate the parts of a photographic subject that the main lighting leaves in shade.

cross-link ▶ **n.** a chemical bond between different chains of atoms in a polymer or other complex molecule.
▶ **v.** make or become linked with such a bond. ■ [with obj.] connect (something) by a series of transverse links.
– DERIVATIVES **cross-link·age** n.

cross·match /ˈkrôsˌmaCH/ Medicine ▶ **v.** [with obj.] (often as noun **crossmatching**) test the compatibility of (a donor's and a recipient's blood or tissue).
▶ **n.** an instance of such testing.

cross·mem·ber /ˈkrôsˌmembər/ ▶ **n.** a transverse structural piece that adds support to a motor-vehicle chassis or other construction.

cross of Lor·raine ▶ **n.** another term for LORRAINE CROSS.

cros·sop·te·ryg·i·an /ˌkrôˌsäptəˈrijēən/ Zoology ▶ **n.** a lobe-finned fish, such as the coelacanth.
▶ **adj.** of or relating to such fishes.
– ORIGIN mid 19th cent.: from modern Latin *Crossopterygii*, from Greek *krossos* 'tassel' + *pterux, pteryg-* 'fin.'

cross·o·ver /ˈkrôsˌōvər/ ▶ **n. 1** a point or place of crossing from one side to the other. ■ a short length of track joining two adjacent railroad lines.
2 the process of achieving success in a different field or style, esp. in popular music: [as modifier] *a jazz-classical crossover album.*
3 a person who votes for a candidate in a different political party than the one they usually support: [as modifier] *crossover votes.*

4 [as modifier] relating to or denoting trials of medical treatment in which experimental subjects and control groups are exchanged after a set period: *a crossover study*.

cross·o·ver dis·tor·tion ▶ **n.** Electronics distortion occurring where a signal changes from positive to negative or vice versa.

C

cross·o·ver net·work ▶ **n.** a filter in a loudspeaker unit that divides the signal and delivers different parts to bass and treble speakers.

cross own·er·ship ▶ **n.** the ownership by one corporation of different companies with related interests or commercial aims.

cross-par·ty ▶ **adj.** involving or relating to two or more political parties.

> **USAGE** Although it appears occasionally in American writing to denote cooperation between the two main political parties, the term **cross-party** does not compete very effectively with the default term **bipartisan**. **Cross-party** is far more common in other English dialects, and in American English to describe political cooperation in other countries.

cross·patch /ˈkrôs,pacн/ ▶ **n.** informal a bad-tempered person.
– ORIGIN early 18th cent.: from the adjective CROSS + obsolete *patch* 'fool, clown,' perhaps from Italian *pazzo* 'madman.'

cross peen (also **cross pein**) ▶ **n.** a hammer having a peen that lies crossways to the length of the shaft.

cross·piece /ˈkrôs,pēs/ ▶ **n.** a beam or bar fixed or placed across something else.

cross-plat·form ▶ **adj.** Computing able to be used on different types of computers or with different software packages: *a cross-platform game*.

cross-pol·li·nate ▶ **v.** [with obj.] pollinate (a flower or plant) with pollen from another flower or plant.
– DERIVATIVES **cross-pol·li·na·tion** **n.**

cross-post (also **crosspost**) Computing ▶ **v.** [with obj.] post a single message to multiple Internet newsgroups or message boards.
▶ **n.** a message posted to more than one newsgroup or message board.

cross-post·ing ▶ **n.** the simultaneous sending of a message to more than one newsgroup or other distribution system on the Internet in such a way that the receiving software at individual sites can detect and ignore duplicates.

cross-pres·sure ▶ **v.** [with obj.] expose (someone) to different, incompatible opinions: *the executive has been cross-pressured by the interests of the states and the electorate*.

cross prod·uct ▶ **n.** another term for VECTOR PRODUCT.

cross pro·mo·tion ▶ **n.** the cooperative marketing by two or more companies of one another's products.
– DERIVATIVES **cross-pro·mote** **v.**

cross-ques·tion ▶ **v.** [with obj.] question (someone) in great detail; cross-examine: *it seemed ungrateful to cross-question him* | (as noun **cross-questioning**) *the cross-questioning of Lopez*.

cross-rate ▶ **n.** Finance an exchange rate between two currencies computed by reference to a third currency, usually the US dollar.

cross-re·ac·tion ▶ **n.** Biochemistry the reaction of an antibody with an antigen other than the one that gave rise to it.
– DERIVATIVES **cross-re·act** **v.**, **cross-re·ac·tive** **adj.**, **cross-re·ac·tiv·i·ty** **n.**

cross-re·fer ▶ **v.** [no obj.] (of a text) refer to another text or part of a text, typically in order to elaborate on a point: *the database cross-refers to the printed book*. ■ [with obj.] refer (someone) to another text: *the entry cross-refers readers to "Style."* ■ (of a person) follow a cross reference from one part of a text to another, or one text to another: *students should be shown how to cross-refer between texts*.

cross ref·er·ence ▶ **n.** a reference to another text or part of a text, typically given in order to elaborate on a point.
▶ **v.** [with obj.] (usu. **be cross-referenced**) provide with cross references to another text or part of a text: *entries are fully cross-referenced*.

cross-rhythm ▶ **n.** Music a rhythm used simultaneously with another rhythm or rhythms. ■ the use of two or more rhythms simultaneously.

cross·roads /ˈkrôs,rōdz/ ▶ **n.** an intersection of two or more roads. ■ a point at which a crucial decision must be made that will have far-reaching consequences: *we stand again at a historic crossroads*. ■ (**crossroad**) a road that crosses a main road or joins two main roads.

cross·ruff /ˈkrôs,rəf, -ˈrəf/ ▶ **n.** a sequence of play in bridge or whist in which partners alternately trump each other's leads.
▶ **v.** [no obj.] alternately trump particular suits in such a way.

cross sec·tion ▶ **n.** a surface or shape that is or would be exposed by making a straight cut through something, esp. at right angles to an axis: *the cross section of an octahedron is a square* | *in cross section the sailfish's body looks like a tapering spear*. ■ a thin strip of organic tissue or other material removed by making two such cuts. ■ a diagram representing what such a cut would reveal. ■ a typical or representative sample of a larger group, esp. of people: *a cross section of our senior managers*. ■ Physics a quantity having the dimensions of an area which expresses the probability of a given interaction between particles.
▶ **v.** (**cross-section**) [with obj.] make a cross section of (something): (as noun **cross-sectioning**) *complex triangular terrain models for contour cross-sectioning*.
– DERIVATIVES **cross-sec·tion·al** **adj.**

cross-sell ▶ **v.** [with obj.] sell (a different product or service) to an existing customer: *their database is used to cross-sell financial services*.

cross-slide ▶ **n.** a sliding part on a lathe or planing machine that is supported by the saddle and carries the tool in a direction at right angles to the bed of the machine.

cross-stitch Needlework ▶ **n.** a stitch formed of two stitches crossing each other. ■ needlework done using such stitches.
▶ **v.** [with obj.] sew or embroider using such stitches: (as adj. **cross-stitched**) *a cross-stitched pillow*.

cross street ▶ **n.** a street crossing another or connecting two streets.

cross-sub·si·dize ▶ **v.** [with obj.] subsidize (a business or activity) out of the profits of another business or activity.
– DERIVATIVES **cross-sub·si·di·za·tion** **n.**, **cross-sub·si·dy** **n.**

cross·talk /ˈkrôs,tôk/ ▶ **n.** 1 unwanted transfer of signals between communication channels.
2 casual conversation.

cross·tie /ˈkrôs,tī/ ▶ **n.** a wooden or concrete beam laid transversely under the rails of a railroad track to support it.

cross-tol·er·ance ▶ **n.** resistance to the effects of a substance because of exposure to a pharmacologically similar substance: *cross-tolerance of barbiturates with alcohol was observed*.

cross·town /ˈkrôs,toun/ ▶ **adj. & adv.** running or leading across a town: [as adj.] *the crosstown traffic* | [as adv.] *she drove us crosstown*.

cross-train ▶ **v.** [no obj.] learn another skill, esp. one related to one's current job.

cross-train·ing ▶ **n.** training in two or more sports in order to improve fitness and performance, esp. in a main sport.

cross·trees /ˈkrôs,trēz/ ▶ **plural n.** a pair of horizontal struts attached to a sailing ship's mast to spread the rigging, esp. at the head of a topmast.

cross vault ▶ **n.** a vault formed by the intersection of two or more vaults.

cross·walk /ˈkrôs,wôk/ ▶ **n.** a marked part of a road where pedestrians have right of way to cross.

cross·ways /ˈkrôs,wāz/ ▶ **adv.** another term for CROSSWISE.

cross·wind /ˈkrôs,wind/ ▶ **n.** a wind blowing across one's direction of travel.

cross·wise /ˈkrôs,wīz/ ▶ **adv.** in the form of a cross: *their arms were held out crosswise*. ■ diagonally; transversely: *wash the potatoes and halve them crosswise*.

cross·word /ˈkrôswərd/ (also **crossword puzzle**) ▶ **n.** a puzzle consisting of a grid of squares and blanks into which words crossing vertically and horizontally are written according to clues.
– ORIGIN said to have been invented by the journalist Arthur Wynne, whose puzzle (called a "word-cross") appeared in a Sunday newspaper, the *New York World*, on December 21, 1913.

cros·ti·ni /krôˈstēnē/ ▶ **plural n.** small pieces of toasted or fried bread served with a topping as an appetizer or canapé.
– ORIGIN Italian, plural of *crostino* 'little crust.'

crot·al ▶ **n.** variant spelling of CROTTLE.

cro·tale /ˈkrō,täl, ˈkrōtl/ ▶ **n.** (usu. **crotales**) a small tuned cymbal.
– ORIGIN 1930s: French, from Latin *crotalum*, denoting an ancient type of castanet, from Greek *krotalon*.

crotch /krӓcн/ ▶ **n.** the part of the human body between the legs where they join the torso. ■ the part of a garment that passes between the legs. ■ a fork in a tree, road, or river.
– ORIGIN mid 16th cent. (denoting an agricultural or garden fork, also a crutch): perhaps related to Old French *croche* 'crozier, shepherd's crook,' based on Old Norse *krókr* 'hook'; partly also a variant of CRUTCH.

crotch·et /ˈkrӓcнət/ ▶ **n.** 1 Music chiefly Brit. a quarter note.
2 a perverse or unfounded belief or notion: *the natural crotchets of inveterate bachelors*.
– ORIGIN Middle English (in the sense 'hook'): from Old French *crochet*, diminutive of *croc* 'hook,' from Old Norse *krókr*.

crotch·et·y /ˈkrӓcнətē/ ▶ **adj.** irritable: *he was tired and crotchety*.
– DERIVATIVES **crotch·et·i·ness** **n.**
– ORIGIN early 19th cent.: from CROTCHET + -Y[1].

crotch·less /ˈkrӓcнləs/ ▶ **adj.** (of a garment) having a hole cut so as to leave the genitals uncovered.

cro·ton /ˈkrōtn/ ▶ **n.** 1 a strong-scented tree, shrub, or herbaceous plant of the spurge family, native to tropical and warm regions. Several kinds yield timber and other commercially important products. • Genus *Croton*, family Euphorbiaceae: numerous species, including *C. laccifer*, the host plant for the lac insect.
2 a small evergreen tree or shrub of the Indo-Pacific region, which is grown for its colorful ornamental foliage. • Genus *Codiaeum*, family Euphorbiaceae: several species, in particular *C. variegatum*, many varieties of which are popular houseplants.
– ORIGIN modern Latin, from Greek *krotōn* 'sheep tick' (from the shape of the seeds of the croton sense 1).

cro·ton oil ▶ **n.** a foul-smelling oil, formerly used as a purgative, obtained from the seeds of a tropical Asian croton tree. • The tree is *Croton tiglium* (family Euphorbiaceae).

Cro·ton Riv·er /ˈkrōtn/ a short river in eastern New York that flows into the Hudson River. It was dammed to form part of New York City's water system.

crot·tin /ˈkrӓtӓN/ ▶ **n.** (pl. pronunc. **same**) a small, round cheese made from goat's milk.
– ORIGIN French, literally 'piece of horse dung.'

crot·tle /ˈkrӓtl/ (also **crotal**) ▶ **n.** a common lichen found on rocks, used in Scotland to make a golden-brown or reddish-brown dye for staining wool for making tweed. • *Parmelia saxatilis* (order Parmeliales) and other species.
– ORIGIN mid 18th cent.: from Scottish Gaelic and Irish *crotal, crotan*.

crouch /kroucн/ ▶ **v.** [no obj.] adopt a position where the knees are bent and the upper body is brought forward and down, sometimes to avoid detection or to defend oneself: *we crouched down in the trench* | (**be crouched**) *Leo was crouched before the fire*. ■ (**crouch over**) bend over in this way so as to be close to (someone or something): *she was crouching over some flower bed*.
▶ **n.** [in sing.] a crouching stance or posture.
– ORIGIN late Middle English: perhaps from Old French *crochir* 'be bent,' from *croche* (see CROTCH).

croup[1] /kro͞op/ ▶ **n.** inflammation of the larynx and trachea in children, associated with infection and causing breathing difficulties.
– DERIVATIVES **croup·y** **adj.**
– ORIGIN mid 18th cent.: from dialect *croup* 'to croak,' of imitative origin.

croup[2] ▶ **n.** the rump or hindquarters, esp. of a horse.
– ORIGIN Middle English: from Old French *croupe*, ultimately of Germanic origin and related to CROP.

croup·i·er /ˈkro͞opē,ā, -pēər/ ▶ **n.** 1 the person in charge of a gaming table, gathering in and paying out money or tokens.
2 historical the assistant chairman at a public dinner, seated at the lower end of the table.
– ORIGIN early 18th cent. (denoting a person standing behind a gambler to give advice): French, from Old French *cropier* 'pillion rider, rider on the croup,' related to Old French *croupe* (see CROUP[2]). Compare with CRUPPER.

crous·tade /kro͞oˈstäd/ ▶ **n.** a crisp piece of bread or pastry hollowed to receive a savory filling.
– ORIGIN French, from Old French *crouste* or Italian *crostata* 'tart' (from *crosta* 'crust').

croute /kro͞ot/ ▶ **n.** a piece of toasted bread on which savory snacks can be served. See also EN CROUTE.
– ORIGIN French *croûte* (see CRUST).

crou·ton /'kro͞oˌtän, kro͞o'tän/ ▶ **n.** a small piece of fried or toasted bread served with soup or used as a garnish.
– ORIGIN from French *croûton*, from *croûte* (see CRUST).

Crow /krō/ ▶ **n.** (pl. **same** or **Crows**) **1** a member of an American Indian people inhabiting eastern Montana.
2 the Siouan language of this people.
▶ **adj.** of or relating to this people or their language.
– ORIGIN suggested by French (*gens des*) *corbeaux* '(people of the) crows,' translating Siouan *apsáaloke* 'crow people.'

crow[1] /krō/ ▶ **n. 1** a large perching bird with mostly glossy black plumage, a heavy bill, and a raucous voice. ● Genus *Corvus*, family Corvidae (the **crow family**): several species, including the **American crow** (*C. brachyrhynchos*) and the **carrion crow** (*C. corone*). The crow family also includes the ravens, jays, magpies, choughs, and nutcrackers.

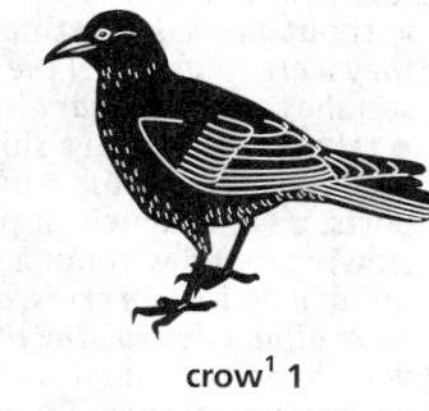
crow[1] 1

2 derogatory a woman, esp. an old or ugly one.
3 (**the Crow**) the constellation Corvus.
– PHRASES **as the crow flies** in a straight line: *Easingwold was 22 miles away as the crow flies.* **eat crow** informal be humiliated by having to admit one's defeats or mistakes.
– ORIGIN Old English *crāwe*; related to Dutch *kraai* and German *Krähe*, also to CROW[2].

crow[2] ▶ **v.** (past **crowed** or Brit. **crew** /kro͞o/) [no obj.] (of a cock) utter its characteristic loud cry. ■ (of a person) make a sound expressing a feeling of happiness or triumph: *Ruby crowed with delight.* ■ say something in a tone of gloating satisfaction: *avoid crowing about your success* | *"I knew you'd be back," she crowed.*
▶ **n.** [usu. in sing.] the cry of a cock. ■ a sound made by a person expressing triumph or happiness: *she gave a little crow of triumph.*
– ORIGIN Old English *crāwan*; related to German *krähen*, also to CROW[1]; ultimately imitative.

crow·bait /'krōˌbāt/ ▶ **n.** informal, derogatory an old horse.

crow·bar /'krōˌbär/ ▶ **n.** an iron bar with a flattened end, used as a lever.
▶ **v.** (**crowbars, crowbarring, crowbarred**) [with obj. and complement] use a crowbar to open (something): *he crowbarred the box open.*

crow·ber·ry /'krōˌberē/ ▶ **n.** (pl. **crowberries**) a creeping heatherlike dwarf shrub with small, needle-shaped leaves and black or reddish berries. ● Genus *Empetrum*, family Empetraceae: several species, in particular the **black crowberry** (*E. nigrum*), with pea-sized black berries. ■ the edible but flavorless berry of this plant.

crowd /kroud/ ▶ **n.** a large number of people gathered together, typically in a disorganized or unruly way: *a huge crowd gathered in the street outside.* ■ an audience: *a crowd of 500 filled the synagogue.* ■ informal, often derogatory a group of people who are linked by a common interest or activity: *I've broken away from that whole junkie crowd.* ■ (**the crowd**) the mass or multitude of people, esp. those considered to be drearily ordinary or anonymous: *make yourself stand out from the crowd.* ■ a large number of things regarded collectively: *the crowd of tall buildings.*
▶ **v.** [with obj.] **1** (of a number of people) fill (a space) almost completely, leaving little or no room for movement: *the dance floor was crowded with revelers.* ■ [no obj.] (**crowd into**) (of a number of people) move into (a space, esp. one that seems too small): *they crowded into the cockpit.* ■ [no obj.] (**crowd around**) (of a group of people) form a tightly packed mass around (someone or something): *photographers crowded around him.*
2 move too close to (someone): *don't crowd her, she needs air.* ■ Baseball (of a batter) stand very close to (the plate) when batting. ■ [no obj.] (**crowd in on**) overwhelm and preoccupy (someone): *as demands crowd in on you it becomes difficult to keep things in perspective.*
3 (**crowd someone/something out**) exclude someone or something by taking their place: *grass invading the canyon has crowded out native plants.*
– ORIGIN Old English *crūdan* 'press, hasten,' of Germanic origin; related to Dutch *kruien* 'push in a wheelbarrow.' In Middle English the senses 'move by pushing' and 'push one's way' arose, leading to the sense 'congregate,' and hence (mid 16th cent.) to the noun.

crowd·ed /'kroudid/ ▶ **adj.** (of a space) full of people, leaving little or no room for movement; packed: *a very crowded room* | *the crowded streets of Manhattan.*
– DERIVATIVES **crowd·ed·ness n.**

crowd·ie /'kroudē/ (also **crowdy**) ▶ **n.** a soft Scottish cheese made from buttermilk or sour milk.
– ORIGIN early 19th cent.: from CRUD + -IE.

crowd-pleas·er ▶ **n.** a person or thing with great popular appeal.
– DERIVATIVES **crowd-pleas·ing adj.**

crowd-pull·er ▶ **n.** informal an event, person, or thing that attracts a large audience.

crowd·sourc·ing /'kroudˌsôrsiNG/ ▶ **n.** the practice whereby an organization enlists a variety of freelancers, paid or unpaid, to work on a specific task or problem.

crowd-surf·ing ▶ **n.** the activity of being passed in a prone position over the heads of the audience at a rock concert, typically after having jumped from the stage.
– DERIVATIVES **crowd-surf v.**

crow·foot /'krōˌfo͝ot/ ▶ **n.** a herbaceous plant related to the buttercups, typically having lobed or divided leaves and white or yellow flowers. Many kinds are aquatic with flowers held above the water. ● Genus *Ranunculus*, family Ranunculaceae: many species, in particular the European **water crowfoot** (*R. aquatilis*).

crown /kroun/ ▶ **n. 1** a circular ornamental headdress worn by a monarch as a symbol of authority, usually made of or decorated with precious metals and jewels. ■ (**the Crown**) the reigning monarch, representing a country's government: *their loyalty to the Church came before their loyalty to the Crown.* ■ (usu. **the Crown**) the power or authority residing in the monarchy: *they claimed immunity on behalf of the Crown.* ■ an ornament, emblem, or badge shaped like a crown. ■ a wreath of leaves or flowers, esp. that worn as an emblem of victory in ancient Greece or Rome. ■ an award or distinction gained by a victory or achievement, esp. in sports: *the world heavyweight crown.*
2 the top or highest part of something: *the crown of the hill.* ■ the top part of a person's head or a hat. ■ the part of a plant just above and below the ground from which the roots and shoots branch out. ■ the upper branching or spreading part of a tree or other plant. ■ the upper part of a cut gem, above the girdle. ■ the part of a tooth projecting from the gum. ■ an artificial replacement or covering for the upper part of a tooth. ■ the point of an anchor at which the arms reach the shaft.
3 (also **crown piece**) a British coin with a face value of five shillings or 25 pence, now minted only for commemorative purposes. ■ a foreign coin with a name meaning 'crown,' esp. the krona or krone.
4 (in full **metric crown**) a paper size, now standardized at 384 × 504 mm. ■ (in full **crown octavo**) a book size, now standardized at 186 × 123 mm. ■ (in full **crown quarto**) a book size, now standardized at 246 × 189 mm.
▶ **v.** [with obj.] **1** (usu. **be crowned**) ceremonially place a crown on the head of (someone) in order to invest them as a monarch: *he went to Rome to be crowned* | [with complement] *she was crowned queen in 1953.* ■ [with obj and complement] declare or acknowledge (someone) as the best, esp. at a sport: *he was crowned world champion last September.* ■ (in checkers) promote (a piece) to king by placing another on top of it. ■ rest on or form the top of: *the distant knoll was crowned with trees.* ■ fit a crown to (a tooth). ■ informal hit on the head: *she contained the urge to crown him.*
2 be the triumphant culmination of (an effort or endeavor, esp. a prolonged one): *years of struggle were crowned by a state visit to Paris* | (as adj. **crowning**) *the crowning moment of a worthy career.*
3 [no obj.] (of a baby's head during labor) fully appear in the vaginal opening prior to emerging.
– PHRASES **crowning glory** the best and most notable aspect of something: *the scene is the crowning glory of this marvelously entertaining show.* ■ chiefly humorous a person's hair. **to crown it all** as the final event in a series of particularly fortunate or unfortunate events: *it was cold and raining, and, to crown it all, we had to walk home.*
– ORIGIN Middle English: from Anglo-Norman French *corune* (noun), *coruner* (verb), Old French *corone* (noun), *coroner* (verb), from Latin *corona* 'wreath, chaplet.'

Crown at·tor·ney ▶ **n.** In Canada, a government prosecutor in criminal cases.

Crown Col·o·ny a British colony whose legislature and administration is controlled by the Crown, represented by a governor.

Crown Der·by ▶ **n.** a kind of soft-paste porcelain made at Derby, England, and often marked with a crown above the letter "D."

crowned crane ▶ **n.** an African crane with a yellowish bristly crest, a mainly black or dark gray body, much white on the wings, and pink and white cheeks. ● Genus *Balearica*, family Gruidae: two species, in particular the (**black**) **crowned crane** (*B. pavonina*).

crowned head ▶ **n.** (usu. **crowned heads**) a king or queen.

crowned pi·geon ▶ **n.** the largest known pigeon, which has mainly bluish plumage and a tall, erect crest, and is found in New Guinea. ● Genus *Goura*, family Columbidae: three species, including the **Victoria crowned pigeon** (*G. victoria*).

crown e·ther ▶ **n.** Chemistry any of a class of organic compounds whose molecules are large rings containing a number of ether linkages.

crown fire ▶ **n.** a forest fire that spreads from treetop to treetop.

crown gall ▶ **n.** a bacterial disease of plants, esp. fruit bushes and trees, that is characterized by large tumorlike galls on the roots and lower trunk. ● This disease is caused by the soil bacterium *Agrobacterium tumefaciens.* ■ a gall of this type.

crown glass ▶ **n.** glass made without lead or iron, originally in a circular sheet. Formerly used in windows, it is now used as optical glass of low refractive index.

Crown Heights a neighborhood in northern Brooklyn in New York City, noted for its West Indian and Orthodox Jewish communities.

crown im·pe·ri·al ▶ **n.** an Asian fritillary (plant) with a cluster of bell-like flowers at the top of a tall, largely bare stem. ● *Fritillaria imperialis*, family Liliaceae.

Crown Jew·els ▶ **plural n.** the crown and other ornaments and jewelry worn or carried by the sovereign on certain state occasions. ■ (**crown jewel**) a prized asset, achievement, or person: *the new stadium will be the crown jewel of sporting arenas.*

Crown land ▶ **n.** (also **Crown lands**) land belonging to the British Crown. ■ land belonging to the state in some parts of the Commonwealth.

crown lens ▶ **n.** a lens made of crown glass and usu. forming one component of an achromatic lens.

crown mold·ing ▶ **n.** another term for CORNICE (sense 1).

crown of thorns ▶ **n. 1** (also **crown-of-thorns-starfish**) a large spiky starfish of the tropical Indo-Pacific, feeding on coral and sometimes causing great damage to reefs. ● *Acanthaster planci*, class Asteroidea.
2 a Madagascan shrub of the spurge family, with bright red flowers and many slender thorns. It is a popular houseplant and is sometimes used for hedges in the tropics. ● *Euphorbia milii*, family Euphorbiaceae. ■ any of a number of other thorny plants, esp. Christ's thorn.
– ORIGIN by association with Christ's crown of thorns.

crown piece ▶ **n.** see CROWN (sense 3 of the noun).

Crown Point a resort town in northeastern New York, on Lake Champlain, scene of much military action during the 18th century.

crown prince ▶ **n.** (in some countries) a male heir to a throne.

crown prin·cess ▶ **n.** the wife of a crown prince. ■ (in some countries) a female heir to a throne.

crown roast ▶ **n.** a roast of rib pieces of pork or lamb arranged like a crown in a circle with the bones pointing upward.

crown saw ▶ **n.** another term for HOLE SAW.

crown wheel ▶ **n.** a gearwheel or cogwheel with teeth that project from the face of the wheel at right angles, used esp. in the gears of motor vehicles.

crow-pheas·ant ▶ **n.** a coucal, esp. the greater coucal, which has black plumage with chestnut wings and back and is found in southern Asia. ● Genus *Centropus*, family Cuculidae, esp. *C. sinensis.*

C

crow's-foot ▶ n. (pl. **crow's-feet**) **1** (usu. **crow's-feet**) a branching wrinkle at the outer corner of a person's eye.
2 a mark, symbol, or design formed of lines diverging from a point, resembling a bird's footprint.
3 historical a caltrop.

crow's-nest ▶ n. a shelter or platform fixed near the top of the mast of a vessel as a place for a lookout to stand.

crow steps ▶ plural n. another term for CORBIESTEPS.
– DERIVATIVES **crow-stepped** adj.

croze /krōz/ ▶ n. a groove at the end of a cask or barrel to receive the edge of the head. ■ a cooper's tool for making such grooves.
– ORIGIN early 17th cent.: perhaps from French *creux*, *creuse* 'hollow.'

Cro·zet Is·lands /krō'zā/ a group of five small islands in the southern Indian Ocean, under French administration.

cro·zier /'krōZHər/ (also **crosier**) ▶ n. a hooked staff carried by a bishop as a symbol of pastoral office. ■ the curled top of a young fern.
– ORIGIN Middle English (originally denoting the person who carried a processional cross in front of an archbishop): partly from Old French *croisier* 'cross bearer,' from *crois* 'cross,' based on Latin *crux*; reinforced by Old French *crocier* 'bearer of a bishop's crook,' from *croce* (see CROSSE).

CRT ▶ abbr. cathode ray tube.

cru /kro͞o, krY/ ▶ n. (pl. **crus** pronunc. **same**) (in France) a vineyard or group of vineyards, esp. one of recognized quality. See also GRAND CRU, PREMIER CRU.
– ORIGIN French, from *crû*, literally 'growth,' past participle of *croître*.

cru·ces /'kro͞o,sēz/ plural form of CRUX.

cru·cial /'kro͞oSHəl/ ▶ adj. decisive or critical, esp. in the success or failure of something: *negotiations were at a crucial stage*. ■ of great importance: *this game is crucial to our survival*.
– DERIVATIVES **cru·ci·al·i·ty** /,kro͞oSHē'alitē/ n., **cru·cial·ly** adv.
– ORIGIN early 18th cent. (in the sense 'cross-shaped'): from French, from Latin *crux*, *cruc-* 'cross.' The sense 'decisive' is from Francis Bacon's Latin phrase *instantia crucis* 'crucial instance,' which he explained as a metaphor from a *crux* or fingerpost marking a fork at a crossroad; Newton and Boyle took up the metaphor in *experimentum crucis* 'crucial experiment.'

> **USAGE** Crucial is used in formal contexts to mean 'decisive, critical': *the testimony of the only eyewitness was crucial to the case*. Its broader use to mean 'very important' should be restricted to informal contexts: *it is crucial to get good light for your photographs*.

cru·cian /'kro͞oSHən/ (also **crucian carp**) ▶ n. a small olive-green to reddish-brown European carp of still or slow-moving waters, important as a farmed fish in eastern Europe. ● *Carassius carassius*, family Cyprinidae.
– ORIGIN mid 18th cent.: from Low German *karusse*, *karutze*, perhaps based on Latin *coracinus*, from Greek *korax* 'raven,' also denoting a black fish found in the Nile.

cru·ci·ate /'kro͞oSH(ē)ət, -SHē,āt/ ▶ adj. Anatomy & Botany cross-shaped.
– ORIGIN early 19th cent.: from Latin *cruciatus*, from *crux*, *cruc-* 'cross.'

cru·ci·ate lig·a·ment ▶ n. Anatomy either of a pair of ligaments in the knee that cross each other and connect the femur to the tibia.

cru·ci·ble /'kro͞osəbəl/ ▶ n. a ceramic or metal container in which metals or other substances may be melted or subjected to very high temperatures. ■ a place or occasion of severe test or trial: *the crucible of combat*. ■ a place or situation in which different elements interact to produce something new: *the crucible of the new Romantic movement*.
– ORIGIN late Middle English: from medieval Latin *crucibulum* 'night lamp, crucible' (perhaps originally a lamp hanging in front of a crucifix), from Latin *crux*, *cruc-* 'cross.'

cru·ci·fer /'kro͞osəfər/ ▶ n. **1** Botany a cruciferous plant, with four petals arranged in a cross.
2 a person carrying a cross or crucifix in a procession.
– ORIGIN mid 16th cent.: from Christian Latin, from Latin *crux*, *cruc-* 'cross.'

cru·cif·er·ous /kro͞o'sifərəs/ ▶ adj. Botany of, relating to, or denoting plants of the cabbage family (Brassicaceae, formerly Cruciferae).
– ORIGIN mid 19th cent.: from modern Latin *Cruciferae* (plural), from Latin *crux*, *cruc-* 'cross' + *-fer* 'bearing' (because the flowers have four equal petals arranged crosswise), + -OUS.

cru·ci·fix /'kro͞osə,fiks/ ▶ n. a representation of a cross with a figure of Jesus Christ on it.
– ORIGIN Middle English: via Old French from ecclesiastical Latin *crucifixus*, from Latin *cruci fixus* 'fixed to a cross.' Compare with CRUCIFY.

cru·ci·fix·ion /,kro͞osə'fikSHən/ ▶ n. chiefly historical the execution of a person by nailing or binding them to a cross. ■ (**the Crucifixion**) the killing of Jesus Christ in such a way. ■ (**Crucifixion**) [in sing.] an artistic representation or musical composition based on this event.
– ORIGIN late Middle English: from ecclesiastical Latin *crucifixio(n-)*, from the verb *crucifigere* (see CRUCIFY).

cru·ci·form /'kro͞osə,fôrm/ ▶ adj. having the shape of a cross: *a cruciform sword*. ■ of or denoting a church having a cross-shaped plan with a nave and transepts.
▶ n. a thing shaped like a cross.
– ORIGIN mid 17th cent.: from Latin *crux*, *cruc-* 'cross' + -IFORM.

cru·ci·fy /'kro͞osə,fī/ ▶ v. (**crucifies, crucifying, crucified**) [with obj.] **1** chiefly historical put (someone) to death by nailing or binding them to a cross: *two thieves were crucified with Jesus*. ■ cause anguish to (someone): *she'd been crucified by his departure*.
2 informal criticize (someone) severely and unrelentingly: *our fans would crucify us if we lost*.
– DERIVATIVES **cru·ci·fi·er** n.
– ORIGIN Middle English: from Old French *crucifier*, from late Latin *crucifigere*, from Latin *crux*, *cruc-* 'cross' + *figere* 'fix.' Compare with CRUCIFIX.

cruck /krək/ ▶ n. Brit. either of a pair of curved timbers extending to the ground in the roof framework of a type of medieval house: [as modifier] *a cruck barn*.
– ORIGIN late 16th cent.: variant of CROOK.

crud /krəd/ ▶ n. informal a substance that is disgusting or unpleasant, typically because of its dirtiness. ■ snow that is not packed down or groomed, on which it is difficult to ski. ■ nonsense: *they just want the simple truth without any religious crud*. ■ a contemptible person.
– DERIVATIVES **crud·dy** /'krədē/ adj.
– ORIGIN late Middle English: variant of CURD (the original sense). The earliest modern senses, 'filth' and 'nonsense' (originally US), date from the 1940s.

crude /kro͞od/ ▶ adj. **1** in a natural or raw state; not yet processed or refined: *crude oil*. ■ Statistics (of figures) not adjusted or corrected: *the crude mortality rate*. ■ (of an estimate or guess) likely to be only approximately accurate.
2 constructed in a rudimentary or makeshift way: *a relatively crude nuclear weapon*. ■ (of an action) showing little finesse or subtlety and as a result unlikely to succeed: *the measure was condemned by economists as crude and ill-conceived*.
3 (of language, behavior, or a person) offensively coarse or rude, esp. in relation to sexual matters: *a crude joke*.
▶ n. natural petroleum: *the ship was carrying 80,000 tons of crude*.
– DERIVATIVES **crude·ly** adv., **crude·ness** n.
– ORIGIN late Middle English: from Latin *crudus* 'raw, rough.'

crude tur·pen·tine ▶ n. see TURPENTINE (sense 1 of the noun).

cru·di·tés /,kro͞odə'tā/ ▶ plural n. assorted raw vegetables served as an hors d'oeuvre, typically with a sauce into which they may be dipped.
– ORIGIN plural of French *crudité* 'rawness, crudity,' from Latin *crudus* 'raw, rough.'

cru·di·ty /'kro͞oditē/ ▶ n. **1** the quality of being rudimentary or makeshift; primitiveness: *he criticizes the crudity of design*.
2 the quality of being offensively coarse or rude; vulgarity: *the crudity of the language*.

cru·el /'kro͞oəl/ ▶ adj. (**crueler, cruelest**; Brit. **crueller, cruellest**) ■ willfully causing pain or suffering to others, or feeling no concern about it: *people who are cruel to animals* | *a cruel remark*. causing pain or suffering: *the winters are long, hard, and cruel*.
– DERIVATIVES **cru·el·ly** adv.
– ORIGIN Middle English: via Old French from Latin *crudelis*, related to *crudus* (see CRUDE).

cru·el·ty /'kro͞oəltē/ ▶ n. (pl. **cruelties**) callous indifference to or pleasure in causing pain and suffering: *he has treated her with extreme cruelty*. ■ behavior that causes pain or suffering to a person or animal: *we can't stand cruelty to animals* | *the cruelties of forced assimilation and genocide*. ■ Law behavior that causes physical or mental harm to another, esp. a spouse, whether intentionally or not.
– ORIGIN Middle English: from Old French *crualte*, based on Latin *crudelitas*, from *crudelis* (see CRUEL).

cru·el·ty-free ▶ adj. (of cosmetics or other commercial products) manufactured or developed by methods that do not involve experimentation on animals.

cru·et /'kro͞oət/ ▶ n. **1** a small container for salt, pepper, oil, or vinegar for use at a dining table.
2 (in church use) a small container for the wine or water to be used in the celebration of the Eucharist.
– ORIGIN Middle English (sense 2): from Anglo-Norman French, diminutive of Old French *crue* 'pot,' from Old Saxon *krūka*; related to CROCK[2].

Cruik·shank /'kro͝ok,SHANGk/, George (1792–1878), English painter, illustrator, and caricaturist.

cruise /kro͞oz/ ▶ v. [no obj.] sail about in an area without a precise destination, esp. for pleasure: *they were cruising off the California coast* | [with obj.] *she cruised the canals of France in a barge*. ■ take a vacation on a ship or boat following a predetermined course, usually calling in at several ports. ■ (of a vehicle or person) travel or move slowly around without a specific destination in mind: *a police van cruised past us* | [with obj.] *teenagers were aimlessly cruising the mall*. ■ (of a motor vehicle or aircraft) travel smoothly at a moderate or economical speed. ■ achieve an objective with ease, esp. in sports: *he cruised to an easy victory in Tuesday's primary*. ■ [with obj.] informal wander about (a place) in search of a sexual partner: *he cruised the gay bars of Los Angeles*. ■ [with obj.] informal attempt to pick up (a sexual partner): *he was cruising a pair of sailors*.
▶ n. a voyage on a ship or boat taken for pleasure or as a holiday and usually calling in at several places: *a cruise down the Nile* | [as modifier] *a cruise liner*.
– PHRASES **cruising for a bruising** informal heading or looking for trouble.
– ORIGIN mid 17th cent. (as a verb): probably from Dutch *kruisen* 'to cross,' from *kruis* 'cross,' from Latin *crux*.

cruise con·trol ▶ n. an electronic device in a motor vehicle that can be switched on to maintain a selected constant speed without the use of the accelerator. ■ used in reference to actions performed with little effort: *the team went on cruise control during the second half*.

cruise mis·sile ▶ n. a low-flying missile that is guided to its target by an on-board computer.

cruis·er /'kro͞ozər/ ▶ n. **1** a relatively fast warship larger than a destroyer and less heavily armed than a battleship.
2 a yacht or motorboat with passenger accommodations, designed for leisure use. ■ a person who goes on a pleasure cruise.
3 an automobile that can be driven smoothly at high speed. ■ a police patrol car.
– ORIGIN late 17th cent.: from Dutch *kruiser*, from *kruisen* (see CRUISE).

cruis·er·weight /'kro͞ozər,wāt/ ▶ n. chiefly Brit. another term for LIGHT HEAVYWEIGHT. ■ in professional boxing, a weight between light heavyweight and heavyweight, ranging from 175 to 190 pounds (79 to 85 kg).

cruis·ing range ▶ n. the maximum distance a ship or aircraft can travel at a given speed without refueling.

cruis·ing speed ▶ n. a speed for a particular vehicle, ship, or aircraft, usually somewhat below maximum, that is comfortable and economical.

crul·ler /'krələr/ ▶ n. a small cake made of rich, sweetened dough twisted or curled and fried in deep fat.
– ORIGIN early 19th cent.: from Dutch *kruller*, from *krullen* 'to curl.'

crumb /krəm/ ▶ n. **1** a small fragment of bread, cake, or cracker. ■ a very small amount of something: *the budget provided few crumbs of comfort*. ■ the soft inner part of a loaf of bread. ■ a dessert topping made of brown sugar, butter, flour, and spices and crumbled over a pie or cake: [as modifier] *apple crumb pie*. ■ (usu. **crumb rubber**) granulated rubber, made from recycled tires.
2 informal an objectionable or contemptible person: *he's an absolute crumb*.
▶ v. [with obj.] cover (food) with breadcrumbs: (as adj. **crumbed**) *crispy crumbed mushrooms with garlic dip*.
– PHRASES **crumbs from someone's** (or **a rich man's**) **table** an unfair and inadequate or unsatisfactory share of something.
– ORIGIN Old English *cruma*, of Germanic origin; related to Dutch *kruim* and German *Krume*. The final *-b* was added in the 16th cent., perhaps from CRUMBLE but also influenced by words such as *dumb*,

where the original final *-b* is retained although no longer pronounced.

crum·ble /ˈkrəmbəl/ ▶ **v.** [no obj.] break or fall apart into small fragments, esp. over a period of time as part of a process of deterioration: *the plaster started to crumble* | (as adj. **crumbling**) *their crumbling ancestral home.* ■ [with obj.] cause (something) to break apart into small fragments: *the easiest way to crumble blue cheese.* ■ (of an organization, relationship, or structure) disintegrate gradually over a period of time: *the party's fragile unity began to crumble.*
▶ **n.** Brit. a mixture of flour and butter that is rubbed to the texture of breadcrumbs and cooked as a topping for fruit. ■ a dessert made with such a topping and a particular fruit: *rhubarb crumble.*
– ORIGIN late Middle English: probably from an Old English word related to CRUMB.

crum·bly /ˈkrəmblē/ ▶ **adj.** (**crumblier, crumbliest**) consisting of or easily breaking into small fragments: *the cheese is crumbly and moist.*
– DERIVATIVES **crum·bli·ness** n.

crumb struc·ture ▶ **n.** the porous structure or condition of soil when its particles are moderately aggregated.

crumb·y /ˈkrəmē/ ▶ **adj.** (**crumbier, crumbiest**)
1 like or covered in crumbs.
2 variant spelling of CRUMMY.

crum·horn ▶ **n.** variant spelling of KRUMMHORN.

crum·my /ˈkrəmē/ (also **crumby**) informal ▶ **adj.** (**crummier, crummiest**) dirty, unpleasant, or of poor quality: *a crummy little room.* ■ unwell; ill: *I'm feeling crummy and want to get better.*
▶ **n.** an old or converted truck used to transport loggers to and from work. ■ another term for CABOOSE (sense 1).
– DERIVATIVES **crum·mi·ly** /ˈkrəməlē/ adv., **crum·mi·ness** n.
– ORIGIN mid 19th cent. (earlier in the literal senses 'crumbly' and 'like or covered with crumbs'): variant of CRUMBY.

crump /krəmp/ ▶ **n.** a loud thudding sound, esp. one made by an exploding bomb or shell.
▶ **v.** [no obj.] make such a sound.
– ORIGIN mid 17th cent.: imitative. The original sense (as a verb) was 'munch, crunch,' later 'hit hard' (used initially as a term in the game of cricket), hence the military sense 'bombard' (World War I).

crum·pet /ˈkrəmpət/ ▶ **n.** a thick, flat, savory cake with a soft, porous texture, made from a yeast mixture cooked on a griddle and eaten toasted and buttered.
– ORIGIN late 17th cent.: of unknown origin.

crum·ple /ˈkrəmpəl/ ▶ **v.** [with obj.] crush (something, typically paper or cloth) so that it becomes creased and wrinkled: *he **crumpled up** the paper bag* | (as adj. **crumpled**) *a crumpled sheet.* ■ [no obj.] become bent, crooked, or creased: *they heard the jetliner crumple moments before it crashed.* ■ [no obj.] (of a person) suddenly flop down to the ground: *she crumpled to the floor in a dead faint.* ■ [no obj.] (of a person's face) suddenly sag and show an expression of desolation: *the child's face crumpled and he began to howl.*
▶ **n.** a crushed fold, crease, or wrinkle.
– DERIVATIVES **crum·ply** /ˈkrəmp(ə)lē/ adj.
– ORIGIN Middle English: from obsolete *crump* 'make or become curved,' from Old English *crump* 'bent, crooked'; related to German *krumm.*

crum·ple zone ▶ **n.** a part of a motor vehicle, esp. the extreme front and rear, designed to crumple easily in a crash and absorb the main force of an impact.

crunch /krənCH/ ▶ **v. 1** [with obj.] crush (a hard or brittle foodstuff) with the teeth, making a loud but muffled grinding sound: *she paused to crunch a ginger snap.* ■ [no obj.] make such a sound, esp. when walking or driving over gravel or an icy surface. ■ strike or crush noisily: *two cab drivers who had just crunched fenders.*
2 process large amounts of information or perform operations of great complexity, esp. by computer: *computers crunch data from real-world observations.*
▶ **n. 1** [usu. in sing.] a loud muffled grinding sound made when crushing, moving over, or hitting something: *Marco's fist struck Brian's nose with a crunch.*
2 (**the crunch**) informal a crucial point or situation, typically one at which a decision with important consequences must be made: *when it comes to the crunch, you chicken out.* ■ a severe shortage of money or credit: *the Fed would do what it could to ease America's credit crunch.*
3 a physical exercise designed to strengthen the abdominal muscles; a sit-up.
– ORIGIN early 19th cent. (as a verb): variant of 17th-cent. *cranch* (probably imitative), by association with CRUSH and MUNCH.

crunch·er /ˈkrənCHər/ ▶ **n.** informal **1** a critical or vital point; a crucial or difficult question.
2 a computer, system, or person able to perform operations of great complexity or to process large amounts of information: *a global information cruncher.* See also NUMBER CRUNCHER.

crunch·y /ˈkrənCHē/ ▶ **adj.** (**crunchier, crunchiest**)
1 making a sharp noise when bitten or crushed and (of food) pleasantly crisp: *bake until the topping is crunchy.*
2 informal politically and environmentally liberal: *a song that incorporates whale-singing seems pretty crunchy.*
– DERIVATIVES **crunch·i·ly** /-CHəlē/ adv., **crunch·i·ness** n.

crunk /krəNGk/ ▶ **n.** a type of hip-hop or rap music characterized by repeated shouted catchphrases and elements typical of electronic dance music, such as prominent bass.
▶ **adj.** chiefly black slang (of a person) very excited or full of energy: *get crunk with some raw hip hop.*
– ORIGIN 1990s: perhaps an altered past participle of CRANK[1] or a blend of CRAZY and DRUNK.

crup·per /ˈkrəpər/ ▶ **n.** a strap buckled to the back of a saddle and looped under the horse's tail to prevent the saddle or harness from slipping forward.
– ORIGIN Middle English: from Old French *cropiere,* related to *croupe* (see CROUP[2]). Compare with CROUPIER.

cru·ra /ˈkro͝orə/ plural form of CRUS.

cru·ra ce·re·bri /ˈkro͝orə ˈserəˌbrī, ˈkerəˌbrē/ plural form of CRUS CEREBRI.

cru·ral /ˈkro͝o(ə)rəl/ ▶ **adj.** Anatomy & Zoology of or relating to the leg or the thigh. ■ of or relating to any part called "crus," for example, the crura cerebri.
– ORIGIN late 16th cent.: from Latin *cruralis,* from *crus, crur-* 'leg.'

crus /kro͞os, krəs/ ▶ **n.** (pl. **crura** /ˈkro͝orə/) Anatomy an elongated part of an anatomical structure, esp. one that occurs in the body as a pair. See CRUS CEREBRI.
– ORIGIN early 18th cent.: Latin, literally 'leg.'

cru·sade /kro͞oˈsād/ ▶ **n.** (often **Crusade**) a medieval military expedition, one of a series made by Europeans to recover the Holy Land from the Muslims in the 11th, 12th, and 13th centuries. ■ a war instigated by the Church for alleged religious ends. ■ an organized campaign concerning a political, social, or religious issue, typically motivated by a fervent desire for change: *a **crusade against** crime.*
▶ **v.** [no obj.] lead or take part in an energetic and organized campaign concerning a social, political, or religious issue: *he crusaded against gambling in the 1950s.*
– ORIGIN late 16th cent. (originally as *croisade*): from French *croisade,* an alteration (influenced by Spanish *cruzado*) of earlier *croisée,* literally 'the state of being marked with the cross,' based on Latin *crux, cruc-* 'cross'; in the 17th cent. the form *crusado,* from Spanish *cruzado,* was introduced; the blending of these two forms led to the current spelling, first recorded in the early 18th cent.

cru·sad·er /kro͞oˈsādər/ ▶ **n. 1** (**Crusader**) a fighter in the medieval Crusades.
2 a person who campaigns vigorously for political, social, or religious change; a campaigner: ***crusaders for** early detection and treatment of mental illness.*

crus ce·re·bri /ˈserəˌbrī, ˈkerəˌbrē/ ▶ **n.** (pl. **crura cerebri** /ˈkro͝orə/) Anatomy either of two symmetrical tracts of nerve fibers at the base of the midbrain, linking the pons and the cerebral hemispheres.
– ORIGIN early 18th cent.: from Latin, literally 'leg of the brain.'

cruse /kro͞oz/ ▶ **n.** archaic an earthenware pot or jar.
– ORIGIN Old English *crūse,* of Germanic origin; related to Dutch *kroes* and German *Krause;* reinforced in Middle English by Low German *krūs.*

crush /krəSH/ ▶ **v.** [with obj.] deform, pulverize, or force inwards by compressing forcefully: *you can crush a pill between two spoons* | *he was crushed to death by a subway train* | (as adj. **crushed**) *the crushed remains of a Ford Bronco.* ■ crease or crumple (cloth or paper): (as adj. **crushed**) *crushed trousers and a crumpled jacket.* ■ (of a government or state) violently subdue (opposition or a rebellion): *the government had taken elaborate precautions to crush any resistance.* ■ bring about a feeling of overwhelming disappointment or embarrassment in (someone): *his defeat crushed a lot of left-wing supporters* | (as adj. **crushing**) *the news came as a crushing blow.*
▶ **n. 1** [usu. in sing.] a crowd of people pressed closely together, esp. in an enclosed space: *a number of youngsters fainted in the crush.*
2 informal a brief but intense infatuation for someone, esp. someone unattainable or inappropriate: *she did **have a crush on** Dr. Russell.*
3 a drink made from the juice of pressed fruit: *lemon crush.*
– DERIVATIVES **crush·a·ble** adj., **crush·er** n., **crush·ing·ly** adv.
– ORIGIN Middle English: from Old French *cruissir* 'gnash (teeth) or crack,' of unknown origin.

crushed vel·vet ▶ **n.** velvet that has its nap pointing in different directions in irregular patches.

crush space ▶ **n. 1** space in a motor vehicle between occupants and a point of impact that can absorb some of the shock of collision.
2 space in the common area of a performance venue that can accommodate the largest crowd expected.

crush zone ▶ **n.** another term for CRUMPLE ZONE.

crust /krəst/ ▶ **n.** the tough outer part of a loaf of bread: *a sandwich with the crusts cut off* | *I tore off several pieces of crust from the loaf.* ■ a hard, dry scrap of bread: *a kindly old woman might give her a crust.* ■ a layer of pastry covering a pie. ■ a hardened layer, coating, or deposit on the surface of something, esp. something soft: *a crust of snow.* ■ the outermost layer of rock of which a planet consists, esp. the part of the earth above the mantle: *the earth's crust* | *at the midocean ridge new crust is formed.* ■ a deposit of tartrates and other substances formed in wine aged in the bottle, esp. port.
▶ **v.** [no obj.] form into a hard outer layer: *the blisters eventually crust over.* ■ [with obj.] cover with a hard outer layer: *the burns crusted his cheek.*
– DERIVATIVES **crus·tal** /ˈkrəstəl/ adj. Geology.
– ORIGIN Middle English: from Old French *crouste,* from Latin *crusta* 'rind, shell, crust.'

Crus·ta·cea /krəˈstāSHə/ Zoology a large group of mainly aquatic arthropods that include crabs, lobsters, shrimps, wood lice, barnacles, and many minute forms. They are very diverse, but most have four or more pairs of limbs and several other appendages. ● Subphylum (or phylum) Crustacea. ■ (as plural noun **crustacea**) arthropods of this group.
– ORIGIN modern Latin (plural), from *crusta* (see CRUST).

crus·ta·cean /krəˈstāSHən/ Zoology ▶ **n.** an arthropod of the large, mainly aquatic group Crustacea, such as a crab, lobster, shrimp, or barnacle.
▶ **adj.** relating to or denoting crustaceans.
– DERIVATIVES **crus·ta·ceous** /-SHəs/ adj.

crust·ed /ˈkrəstəd/ ▶ **adj. 1** having or forming a hard top layer or covering: *she washed away the crusted blood.* ■ denoting a style of unfiltered, blended port that deposits a sediment in the bottle.
2 old-fashioned; venerable: *a crusted establishment figure.*

crus·tose /ˈkrəsˌtōs/ ▶ **adj.** Botany (of a lichen or alga) forming or resembling a crust.
– ORIGIN late 19th cent.: from Latin *crustosus,* from *crusta* (see CRUST).

crust·y /ˈkrəstē/ ▶ **adj.** (**crustier, crustiest**) **1** having a crisp or hard outer layer or covering: *crusty bread.* ■ (of a substance) acting as a hard outer layer or covering: *Lake Manyara was ringed by crusty salt deposits.*
2 (esp. of an old person) outspoken and irritable: *a crusty old grandfather.*
– DERIVATIVES **crust·i·ly** /ˈkrəstəlē/ adv., **crust·i·ness** n.

crutch /krəCH/ ▶ **n. 1** a long stick with a crosspiece at the top, used as a support under the armpit by a lame person. ■ [in sing.] a thing used for support or reassurance: *they use the Internet as a crutch for their loneliness.*
2 archaic another term for CROTCH (of the body or a garment).
– ORIGIN Old English *crycc, cryc,* of Germanic origin; related to Dutch *kruk* and German *Krücke.*

Crux /krəks, kro͝oks/ Astronomy another term for the SOUTHERN CROSS. ■ (as genitive **Crucis** /ˈkro͞osis/) used with a preceding letter or numeral to designate a star in this constellation: *the star Beta Crucis.*
– ORIGIN Latin.

crux /krəks, kro͝oks/ ▶ **n.** (pl. **cruxes** or **cruces** /ˈkro͞oˌsēz/) (**the crux**) the decisive or most important point at issue: *the crux of the matter is that attitudes have changed.* ■ a particular point of difficulty: *both cruces can be resolved by a consideration of the manuscripts.*

–ORIGIN mid 17th cent. (denoting a representation of a cross, chiefly in *crux ansata* 'ankh,' literally 'cross with a handle'): from Latin, literally 'cross.'

cru·za·do /kro͞o'zädō/ ▶ **n.** (pl. **cruzados**) the basic monetary unit of Brazil from 1988 to 1990, equal to 100 centavos.
–ORIGIN from Portuguese *cruzado, crusado* 'marked with the cross.'

C

cru·zei·ro /kro͞o'ze(ə)rō/ ▶ **n.** (pl. **cruzeiros**) the basic monetary unit of Brazil from 1990 to 1993, equal to 100 centavos.
–ORIGIN Portuguese, literally 'large cross.'

cry /krī/ ▶ **v.** (**cries, crying, cried**) [no obj.] shed tears, esp. as an expression of distress or pain: *don't cry—it'll be all right* | [with obj.] *you'll cry tears of joy.* ■ shout or scream, esp. to express one's fear, pain, or grief: *the little girl fell down and cried for her mommy.* ■ say something in an excited or anguished tone of voice: *"Where will it end?" he cried out.* ■ (of a bird or other animal) make a loud characteristic call: *the wild birds cried out over the water.* ■ [with obj.] (of a hawker) proclaim (wares) for sale in the street.
▶ **n.** (pl. **cries**) a spell of weeping: *I still have a cry, sometimes, when I realize that my mother is dead.* ■ a loud inarticulate shout or scream expressing a powerful feeling or emotion: *a cry of despair.* ■ a distinctive call of a bird or other animal. ■ a loud excited utterance of a word or words: *there was a cry of "Silence!"* ■ the call of a hawker selling wares on the street. ■ an urgent appeal or entreaty: *fund-raisers have issued a cry for help.* ■ a demand or opinion expressed by many people: *peace became the popular cry.*
–PHRASES **cry one's eyes** (or **heart**) **out** weep bitterly and at length. **cry for the moon** ask for what is unattainable or impossible. **cry foul** protest strongly about a real or imagined wrong or injustice. **cry from the heart** a passionate and honest appeal or protest. **cry wolf** see **WOLF**. **for crying out loud** informal used to express one's irritation or impatience: *why do you have to take everything so personally, for crying out loud?* **in full cry** used to describe hounds baying in keen pursuit. **it's no use crying over spilt** (or **spilled**) **milk** see **MILK**.
–PHRASAL VERBS **cry someone/something down** dated disparage or belittle someone or something. **cry off** informal go back on a promise or fail to keep to an arrangement: *we were going to Spain together and he cried off at the last moment.* **cry out for** demand as a self-evident requirement or solution: *the present system cries out for reform.* **cry someone/something up** dated praise or extol someone or something.
–ORIGIN Middle English (in the sense 'ask for earnestly or loudly'): from Old French *crier* (verb), *cri* (noun), from Latin *quiritare* 'raise a public outcry,' literally 'call on the *Quirites* (Roman citizens) for help.'

cry·ba·by /'krī,bābē/ ▶ **n.** (pl. **crybabies**) a person, esp. a child, who sheds tears frequently or readily.

cry·er /'krīər/ ▶ **n.** archaic spelling of **CRIER**.

cry·ing /'krī-iNG/ ▶ **adj.** very great: *it would be a crying shame to let some other woman have it.*

cryo- ▶ **comb. form** involving or producing cold, esp. extreme cold: *cryostat* | *cryosurgery.*
–ORIGIN from Greek *kruos* 'frost.'

cry·o·bi·ol·o·gy /,krīō,bī'äləjē/ ▶ **n.** the branch of biology that deals with the properties of organisms and tissues at low temperatures.
–DERIVATIVES **cry·o·bi·o·log·i·cal** /-,bīə'läjəkəl/ **adj.**, **cry·o·bi·ol·o·gist** /-jist/ **n.**

cry·o·gen /'krīəjən/ ▶ **n.** a substance used to produce very low temperatures.

cry·o·gen·ics /,krīə'jeniks/ ▶ **plural n.** [treated as sing.] the branch of physics dealing with the production and effects of very low temperatures. ■ another term for **CRYONICS**.
–DERIVATIVES **cry·o·gen·ic adj.**, **cry·o·gen·i·cal·ly** /-ik(ə)lē/ **adv.**

cry·og·e·ny /krī'äjənē/ ▶ **n.** another term for **CRYOGENICS**.

cry·o·glob·u·lin /,krīə'gläbyələn/ ▶ **n.** Biochemistry a protein that occurs in the blood in certain disorders. It can be precipitated out of solution below 10°C, causing obstruction in the fingers and toes.

cry·o·lite /'krīə,līt/ ▶ **n.** a white or colorless mineral consisting of a fluoride of sodium and aluminum. It is added to bauxite as a flux in aluminum smelting.
–ORIGIN early 19th cent.: from **CRYO-** 'cold, frost' (because the main deposits are found in Greenland) + **-LITE**.

cry·om·e·ter /krī'ämitər/ ▶ **n.** a thermometer for measuring very low temperatures.

cry·on·ics /krī'äniks/ ▶ **plural n.** [treated as sing.] the practice or technique of deep-freezing the bodies of those who have died of an incurable disease, in the hope of a future cure.
–DERIVATIVES **cry·on·ic adj.**
–ORIGIN 1960s: contraction of **CRYOGENICS**.

cry·o·pre·cip·i·tate /,krīōpri'sipətət, -'sipə,tāt/ ▶ **n.** chiefly Biochemistry a substance precipitated from a solution, esp. from the blood, at low temperatures. ■ Medicine an extract rich in a blood-clotting factor obtained as a residue when frozen blood plasma is thawed.

cry·o·pre·serve /,krīōpri'zərv/ ▶ **v.** [with obj.] Biology & Medicine preserve (cells or tissues) by cooling them below the freezing point of water.
–DERIVATIVES **cry·o·pres·er·va·tion** /-,prezər'vāSHən/ **n.**

cry·o·pro·tect·ant /,krīōprə'tektənt/ ▶ **n.** Physiology a substance that prevents the freezing of tissues, or prevents damage to cells during freezing.

cry·o·scope /'krīə,skōp/ ▶ **n.** an instrument used to determine the freezing point of a liquid or a solution.

cry·o·stat /'krīə,stat/ ▶ **n.** an apparatus for maintaining a very low temperature. ■ an apparatus for taking very fine slices of tissue while it is kept very cold.

cry·o·sur·ger·y /,krīō'sərjərē/ ▶ **n.** surgery using the local application of intense cold to destroy unwanted tissue.

cry·o·ther·a·py /,krīō'THerəpē/ ▶ **n.** the use of extreme cold in surgery or other medical treatment.

crypt /kript/ ▶ **n. 1** an underground room or vault beneath a church, used as a chapel or burial place.
2 Anatomy a small tubular gland, pit, or recess.
–ORIGIN late Middle English (in the sense 'cavern'): from Latin *crypta*, from Greek *kruptē* 'a vault,' from *kruptos* 'hidden.'

crypt·a·nal·y·sis /,kriptə'naləsəs/ ▶ **n.** the art or process of deciphering coded messages without being told the key.
–DERIVATIVES **crypt·an·a·lyst** /,krip'tanl-əst/ **n.**, **crypt·an·a·lyt·ic** /-,tanl'itik/ **adj.**, **crypt·an·a·lyt·i·cal** /-,tanl'itikəl/ **adj.**
–ORIGIN 1920s: from **CRYPTO-** + **ANALYSIS**.

cryp·tic /'kriptik/ ▶ **adj. 1** having a meaning that is mysterious or obscure: *he found his boss's utterances too cryptic.* ■ (of a crossword) having difficult clues that indicate the solutions indirectly.
2 Zoology (of coloration or markings) serving to camouflage an animal in its natural environment.
–DERIVATIVES **cryp·ti·cal·ly** /-ik(ə)lē/ **adv.**
–ORIGIN early 17th cent.: from late Latin *crypticus*, from Greek *kruptikos*, from *kruptos* 'hidden.' Sense 2 dates from the late 19th cent.

cryp·to /'kriptō/ ▶ **n. 1** short for **CRYPTOGRAPHY**.
2 (pl. **cryptos**) informal a person having a secret allegiance to a political creed, esp. communism.

crypto- ▶ **comb. form** concealed; secret: *cryptogram.*
–ORIGIN from Greek *kruptos* 'hidden.'

cryp·to·bi·ont /,kriptə'bī,änt/ ▶ **n.** Biology an organism capable of cryptobiosis.

cryp·to·bi·o·sis /,kriptə,bī'ōsis/ ▶ **n.** Biology a physiological state in which metabolic activity is reduced to an undetectable level without disappearing altogether. It is known in certain plant and animal groups adapted to survive periods of extremely dry conditions.

cryp·to·bi·ot·ic /,kriptə,bī'ätik/ ▶ **adj.** Biology **1** of, relating to, or capable of cryptobiosis.
2 of or denoting primitive organisms of the kind presumed to have existed in earlier geological periods but to have left no trace of their existence.

cryp·to·clas·tic /,kriptō'klastik/ ▶ **adj.** Geology composed of microscopic fragments.

cryp·to·coc·co·sis /,kriptəkä'kōsəs/ ▶ **n.** Medicine infestation with a yeastlike fungus, resulting in tumors in the lungs and sometimes spreading to the brain. ● The fungus is *Cryptococcus neoformans*, phylum Basidiomycota, class Basidiomycetes.
–DERIVATIVES **cryp·to·coc·cal** /-'käkəl/ **adj.**
–ORIGIN 1930s: from modern Latin *Cryptococcus* (part of the binomial of the fungus) + **-OSIS**.

cryp·to·crys·tal·line /,kriptō'kristə,lin, -,līn, -,lēn/ ▶ **adj.** having a crystalline structure visible only when magnified.

cryp·to·gam /'kriptə,gam/ ▶ **n.** Botany, dated a plant that has no true flowers or seeds, including ferns, mosses, liverworts, lichens, algae, and fungi.
–DERIVATIVES **cryptogamous** /krip'tägəməs/ **adj.**
–ORIGIN mid 19th cent.: from French *cryptogame*, from modern Latin *cryptogamae (plantae)*, denoting nonflowering plants, from Greek *kruptos* 'hidden' + *gamos* 'marriage' (because the means of reproduction was not apparent).

cryp·to·gam·ic /,kriptə'gamik/ ▶ **adj.** Botany of, relating to, or denoting cryptogams. ■ Ecology (of a desert soil or surface crust) covered with or consisting of a fragile black layer of cyanobacteria, mosses, and lichens, which is often important in preventing erosion.

cryp·to·gen·ic /,kriptə'jenik/ ▶ **adj.** (of a disease) of obscure or uncertain origin.

cryp·to·gram /'kriptə,gram/ ▶ **n. 1** a text written in code.
2 a symbol or figure with secret or occult significance.

cryp·tog·ra·phy /krip'tägrəfē/ ▶ **n.** the art of writing or solving codes.
–DERIVATIVES **cryp·tog·ra·pher** /-fər/ **n.**, **cryp·to·graph·ic** /,kriptə'grafik/ **adj.**, **cryp·to·graph·i·cal·ly** /,kriptə'grafik(ə)lē/ **adv.**

cryp·tol·o·gy /krip'täləjē/ ▶ **n.** the study of codes, or the art of writing and solving them.
–DERIVATIVES **cryp·to·log·i·cal** /,kriptə'läjikəl/ **adj.**, **cryp·tol·o·gist** /-jist/ **n.**

cryp·to·me·ri·a /,kriptə'mi(ə)rēə/ ▶ **n.** a tall, conical, coniferous tree with long, curved, spirally arranged leaves and short cones. Native to China and Japan, it is grown for timber in Japan. Also called **JAPANESE CEDAR**. ● *Cryptomeria japonica*, family Taxodiaceae.
–ORIGIN modern Latin, from **CRYPTO-** 'hidden' + Greek *meros* 'part' (because the seeds are concealed by scales).

cryp·to·nym /'kriptə,nim/ ▶ **n.** a code name.
–DERIVATIVES **cryp·ton·y·mous** /krip'tänəməs/ **adj.**
–ORIGIN late 19th cent.: from **CRYPTO-** 'hidden' + Greek *onuma* 'name.'

cryp·tor·chid /krip'tôrkid/ ▶ **n.** Medicine a person suffering from cryptorchidism.

cryp·tor·chi·dism /krip'tôrki,dizəm/ ▶ **n.** Medicine a condition in which one or both of the testes fail to descend from the abdomen into the scrotum.
–ORIGIN late 19th cent.: from **CRYPTO-** 'hidden' + Greek *orkhis, orkhid-* 'testicle' + **-ISM**.

cryp·to·spor·i·di·um /,kriptəspə'ridēəm/ ▶ **n.** a parasitic coccidian protozoan found in the intestinal tract of many vertebrates, where it sometimes causes disease. ● Genus *Cryptosporidium*, phylum Sporozoa.
–ORIGIN early 20th cent.: from **CRYPTO-** 'concealed' + modern Latin *sporidium* 'small spore.'

Cryp·to·zo·ic /,kriptə'zō-ik/ ▶ **adj.** Geology of, relating to, or denoting the period (the Precambrian) in which rocks contain no, or only slight, traces of living organisms. Compare with **PHANEROZOIC**.
–ORIGIN early 20th cent.: from Greek *kruptos* 'hidden' + *zōē* 'life' + **-IC**.

cryp·to·zo·ic /,kriptə'zō-ik/ ▶ **adj.** Ecology (of small invertebrates) living on the ground but hidden in the leaf litter, under stones or pieces of wood.
–DERIVATIVES **cryp·to·zo·a** /-'zōə/ **plural n.**
–ORIGIN late 19th cent.: from Greek *kruptos* 'hidden' + *zōē* 'life' + **-IC**.

cryp·to·zo·ol·o·gy /,kriptəzō'äləjē, -zo͞o-/ ▶ **n.** the search for and study of animals whose existence or survival is disputed or unsubstantiated, such as the Loch Ness monster and the yeti.
–DERIVATIVES **cryp·to·zo·o·log·i·cal** /-,zōə'läjikəl, -,zo͞oə-/ **adj.**, **cryp·to·zo·ol·o·gist** /-jist/ **n.**

crys·tal /'kristl/ ▶ **n. 1** a piece of a homogeneous solid substance having a natural geometrically regular form with symmetrically arranged plane faces. ■ Chemistry any solid consisting of a symmetrical, ordered, three-dimensional aggregation of atoms or molecules. ■ Electronics a crystalline piece of semiconductor used as an oscillator or transducer. ■ a clear transparent mineral, esp. quartz. ■ a piece of crystalline substance believed to have healing powers.
2 (also **crystal glass**) highly transparent glass with a high refractive index: [as modifier] *a crystal chandelier.* ■ articles made of such glass: *a collection of crystal.* ■ the glass over a watch face.
▶ **adj.** clear and transparent like crystal: *the clean crystal waters of the lake.*
–PHRASES **crystal clear** completely transparent and unclouded. ■ unambiguous; easily understood: *the house rules are crystal clear.*
–ORIGIN late Old English (denoting ice or a mineral resembling it), from Old French *cristal*, from Latin *crystallum*, from Greek *krustallos* 'ice, crystal.' The chemistry sense dates from the early 17th cent.

crys·tal ax·is ▶ **n.** each of three axes used to define the edges of the unit cell of a crystal.

crys·tal ball ▶ n. a solid globe of glass or rock crystal, used by fortune-tellers and clairvoyants for crystal-gazing.

crys·tal form ▶ n. a set of crystal faces defined according to their relationship to the crystal axes.

crys·tal-gaz·ing ▶ n. looking intently into a crystal ball with the aim of seeing images relating to future or distant events. ■ attempting to forecast the future.

crys·tal heal·ing (also **crystal therapy**) ▶ n. the use of the healing powers of crystals in alternative medicine.

crys·tal lat·tice ▶ n. the symmetrical three-dimensional arrangement of atoms inside a crystal.

crys·tal·lif·er·ous /ˌkristlˈifərəs/ (also **crystalligerous** /-ˈijərəs/) ▶ adj. bearing, containing, or producing crystals.

crys·tal·lin /ˈkristəlin/ ▶ n. Biochemistry a protein of the globulin class present in the lens of the eye.
– ORIGIN mid 19th cent.: from Latin *crystallum* 'crystal' + -IN¹.

crys·tal·line /ˈkristl-in, -tl-ˌīn, -tl-ˌēn/ ▶ adj. having the structure and form of a crystal; composed of crystals: *a crystalline rock*. ■ literary very clear: *he writes a crystalline prose.*
– DERIVATIVES **crys·tal·lin·i·ty** /ˌkristlˈinitē/ n.
– ORIGIN Middle English: from Old French *cristallin*, via Latin from Greek *krustallinos*, from *krustallos* (see CRYSTAL).

crys·tal·line lens ▶ n. the transparent elastic structure behind the iris by which light is focused onto the retina of the eye.

crys·tal·line sphere ▶ n. historical (in ancient and medieval astronomy) a transparent sphere of the heavens postulated to lie between the fixed stars and the *primum mobile* and to account for the precession of the equinox and other motions.

crys·tal·lite /ˈkristəˌlīt/ ▶ n. an individual perfect crystal or region of regular crystalline structure in the substance of a material, typically of a metal or a partly crystalline polymer. ■ a very small crystal.

crys·tal·lize /ˈkristəˌlīz/ ▶ v. form or cause to form crystals: [no obj.] *when most liquids freeze they crystallize.* ■ [no obj.] make or become definite and clear: *vague feelings of unrest crystallized into something more concrete* | [with obj.] *writing can help to crystallize your thoughts.* ■ (usu. as adj. **crystallized**) coat and impregnate (fruit or petals) with sugar as a means of preserving them: *a box of crystallized fruits.*
– DERIVATIVES **crys·tal·liz·a·ble** /ˈkristəˌlīzəbəl, ˌkristəˈlīzəbəl/ adj., **crys·tal·li·za·tion** /ˌkristələˈzāSHən/ n.

crys·tal·log·ra·phy /ˌkristəˈlägrəfē/ ▶ n. the branch of science concerned with the structure and properties of crystals.
– DERIVATIVES **crys·tal·log·ra·pher** /-fər/ n., **crys·tal·lo·graph·ic** /-ləˈgrafik/ adj., **crys·tal·lo·graph·i·cal·ly** /-ləˈgrafik(ə)lē/ adv.

crys·tal·loid /ˈkristəˌloid/ ▶ adj. resembling a crystal in shape or structure.
▶ n. **1** Botany a small, crystallike mass of protein in a plant cell.
2 Chemistry a substance that, when dissolved, forms a true solution rather than a colloid and is able to pass through a semipermeable membrane.

crys·tal meth ▶ n. see METH (sense 1).

Crys·tal Pal·ace a large building of prefabricated iron and glass resembling a giant greenhouse, designed by Joseph Paxton for the Great Exhibition of 1851 in Hyde Park, London, and re-erected at Sydenham near Croydon; it was accidentally burned down in 1936.

crys·tal set (also **crystal radio**) ▶ n. a simple early form of radio receiver with a crystal touching a metal wire as the rectifier (instead of a tube or transistor), and no amplifier or loudspeaker, necessitating headphones or an earphone.

crys·tal sys·tem ▶ n. each of seven categories of crystals (cubic, tetragonal, orthorhombic, trigonal, hexagonal, monoclinic, and triclinic) classified according to the possible relations of the crystal axes.

crys·tal ther·a·py ▶ n. another term for CRYSTAL HEALING.

crys·tal vi·o·let ▶ n. a synthetic violet dye, related to rosaniline, used as a stain in microscopy and as an antiseptic in the treatment of skin infections.

Cs ▶ symbol the chemical element cesium.

c/s ▶ abbr. cycles per second.

CSA ▶ abbr. ■ Confederate States of America. ■ community-supported agriculture. ■ chiefly Canadian community-shared agriculture.

csar·das /ˈCHärˌdäsH, -ˌdäs/ (also **czardas**) ▶ n. (pl. **same**) a Hungarian dance with a slow introduction and a fast, wild finish.
– ORIGIN mid 19th cent.: from Hungarian *csárdás*, from *csárda* 'inn.'

CSC ▶ abbr. Civil Service Commission.

CSF ▶ abbr. cerebrospinal fluid.

CS gas ▶ n. a powerful form of tear gas used particularly in the control of riots.
– ORIGIN 1960s: from the initials of Ben B. *Corson* (born 1896) and Roger W. *Stoughton* (1906–57), the American chemists who discovered the properties of the chemical in 1928.

CSM ▶ abbr. ■ command and service modules (see COMMAND MODULE). ■ command sergeant major.

CST ▶ abbr. Central Standard Time (see CENTRAL TIME).

CT ▶ abbr. ■ computerized (or computed) tomography. ■ Connecticut (in official postal use).

ct. ▶ abbr. ■ carat: *18 ct. gold.* ■ cent. ■ county. ■ court.

cte·nid·i·um /təˈnidēəm/ ▶ n. (pl. **ctenidia** /-ˈnidēə/) Zoology a comblike structure, esp. a respiratory organ or gill in a mollusk, consisting of an axis with a row of projecting filaments.
– ORIGIN late 19th cent.; modern Latin, from Greek *ktenidion*, diminutive of *kteis, kten-* 'comb.'

cte·noid /ˈtēˌnoid, ˈtenˌoid/ ▶ adj. Zoology (of fish scales) having many tiny projections on the edge like the teeth of a comb, as in many bony fishes. Compare with GANOID and PLACOID.
– ORIGIN mid 19th cent.: from Greek *kteis, kten-* 'comb' + -OID.

Cte·noph·o·ra /tiˈnäfərə/ Zoology a small phylum of aquatic invertebrates that comprises the comb jellies.
– ORIGIN modern Latin (plural), from Greek *kteis, kten-* 'comb' + *pherein* 'to bear.'

cten·o·phore /ˈtenəˌfôr/ ▶ n. Zoology an aquatic invertebrate of the phylum Ctenophora, which comprises the comb jellies.

ctn. ▶ abbr. ■ carton. ■ Mathematics cotangent.

C2C ▶ abbr. consumer-to-consumer, denoting transactions conducted via the Internet between consumers.

CTS ▶ abbr. carpal tunnel syndrome.

CT scan ▶ n. another term for CAT SCAN.
– DERIVATIVES **CT scan·ner** n.

CTT ▶ abbr. capital transfer tax.

Cu ▶ symbol the chemical element copper.
– ORIGIN from late Latin *cuprum*.

cu. ▶ abbr. cubic (in units of measurement: for example, cu. ft. = cubic feet).

cua·dril·la /kwäˈdrē(l)yə/ ▶ n. a matador's team of assistants, including picadors and banderilleros.
– ORIGIN mid 19th cent.: Spanish.

cua·tro /ˈkwätrō/ ▶ n. (pl. **cuatros**) a small guitar, typically with four (or five) single or paired strings, used in Latin American and Caribbean folk music, esp. in Puerto Rico.
– ORIGIN Latin American Spanish, literally 'four.'

cub /kəb/ ▶ n. the young of a fox, bear, lion, or other carnivorous mammal. ■ archaic a young man, esp. one who is awkward or ill-mannered.
▶ v. (**cubs, cubbing, cubbed**) [no obj.] give birth to cubs: *both share the same earth during the first ten days after cubbing.*
– ORIGIN mid 16th cent.: of unknown origin.

Cu·ba /ˈkyo͞obə/ a country in the western West Indies, the largest and furthest west of the islands, in the Caribbean Sea at the mouth of the Gulf of Mexico; pop. 11,451,700 (est. 2009); capital, Havana; official language, Spanish.

> A Spanish colony, Cuba became nominally independent after the Spanish–American War of 1898 and achieved full autonomy in 1934. Fidel Castro led a communist revolution in 1959, and held the presidency until replaced by his brother Raúl Castro in 2008. The country suffered under a US trade embargo and, after the collapse of the Soviet Union and the Eastern bloc in 1991, lost much of its trade.

– DERIVATIVES **Cu·ban** adj. & n.

cub·age /ˈkyo͞obij/ ▶ n. cubic content or capacity.

Cu·ba li·bre /ˌk(y)o͞obə ˈlēbrā/ ▶ n. (pl. **Cuba libres**) a cocktail typically containing cola, lime juice, rum, and a garnish of lime.
– ORIGIN late 19th cent.: American Spanish, literally 'free Cuba.'

Cu·ban·go /ko͞oˈbäNGgō/ another name for OKAVANGO.

Cu·ban heel /ˈkyo͞obən/ ▶ n. a moderately high, straight-sided heel on a shoe or boot.

Cu·ban Mis·sile Cri·sis an international crisis in October 1962, the closest approach to nuclear war at any time between the US and the Soviet Union. When the US discovered Soviet nuclear missiles on Cuba, President John F. Kennedy demanded their removal and announced a naval blockade of the island; the Soviet leader Khrushchev acceded to the US demands a week later.

Cu·ban sand·wich ▶ n. a type of submarine sandwich, typically grilled, esp. with ham, roast pork, Swiss cheese, mustard, and pickles.

cu·ba·ture /ˈkyo͞obəˌCHər/ ▶ n. the determination of the volume of a solid.
– ORIGIN late 17th cent.: from the verb CUBE, on the pattern of *quadrature*.

cub·by /ˈkəbē/ ▶ n. (pl. **cubbies**) a cubbyhole.
– ORIGIN mid 17th cent. (originally Scots, denoting a straw basket): related to dialect *cub* 'stall, pen, hutch,' of Low German origin.

cub·by·hole /ˈkəbēˌhōl/ ▶ n. a small, enclosed compartment or room.

cube /kyo͞ob/ ▶ n. a symmetrical three-dimensional shape, either solid or hollow, contained by six equal squares. ■ short for CUBICLE. ■ a block of something with six sides: *a sugar cube.* ■ Mathematics the product of a number multiplied by its square, represented by a superscript figure 3: *a body increasing in weight by the cube of its length.*
▶ v. [with obj.] **1** Mathematics raise (a number or value) to its cube.
2 cut (food) into small cubes: *I bought sirloin from the butcher and cubed it myself.*
3 tenderize (meat) by scoring a pattern of small squares into its surface: (as adj. **cubed**) *cubed steaks.*
– ORIGIN mid 16th cent.: from Old French, or via Latin from Greek *kubos*.

cu·beb /ˈkyo͞oˌbeb/ ▶ n. a tropical shrub of the pepper family that bears pungent berries. ● Genus *Piper*, family Piperaceae: several species, including the Asian *P. cubeba*. ■ the dried unripe berries of this shrub, used medicinally and to flavor cigarettes.
– ORIGIN Middle English: from Old French *cubebe*, from Spanish Arabic *kubēba*, from Arabic *kubāba*.

cube farm ▶ n. a large open-plan office divided into cubicles for individual workers.

cube root ▶ n. the number that produces a given number when cubed.

cu·bic /ˈkyo͞obik/ ▶ adj. having the shape of a cube: *a cubic room.* ■ denoting a unit of measurement equal to the volume of a cube whose side is one of the linear unit specified: *15 billion cubic meters of water.* ■ measured or expressed in such units. ■ involving the cube (and no higher power) of a quantity or variable: *a cubic equation.* ■ of or denoting a crystal system or three-dimensional geometric arrangement having three equal axes at right angles.
▶ n. Mathematics a cubic equation, or a curve described by one.
– DERIVATIVES **cu·bi·cal** adj., **cu·bi·cal·ly** /-ik(ə)lē/ adv.
– ORIGIN late 15th cent. (in the sense 'involving the cube (and no higher power)'): from Old French *cubique*, or via Latin from Greek *kubikos*, from *kubos* 'cube.'

cu·bic ca·pac·i·ty ▶ n. the volume contained by a hollow structure, expressed in liters, cubic centimeters, or other cubic units.

cu·bic con·tent ▶ n. the volume of a solid, often expressed in cubic meters.

cu·bi·cle /ˈkyo͞obikəl/ ▶ n. a small partitioned-off area of a room, for example one containing a bed in a dwelling or one containing a desk in an office: *each cubicle is equipped with a PC and printer, and there are two fax machines in the east alcove.*
– ORIGIN late Middle English (in the sense 'bedroom'): from Latin *cubiculum*, from *cubare* 'lie down.'

cu·bic zir·co·ni·a ▸ n. a colorless form of zirconia that is very similar to diamond in refractivity and appearance.

cu·bi·form /ˈkyo͞obiˌfôrm/ ▸ adj. technical cube-shaped: *the columns are thick and have cubiform capitals.*

cub·ism /ˈkyo͞oˌbizəm/ ▸ n. an early 20th-century style and movement in art, esp. painting, in which perspective with a single viewpoint was abandoned and use was made of simple geometric shapes, interlocking planes, and, later, collage.

> Cubism was a reaction against traditional modes of representation and Impressionist concerns with light and color. The style, created by Picasso and Braque and first named by the French critic Louis Vauxcelles in 1908, was inspired by the later work of Cézanne and by African sculpture.

– DERIVATIVES **cub·ist** n. & adj., **cub·is·tic** /kyo͞oˈbistik/ adj.
– ORIGIN early 20th cent.: from French *cubisme*, from *cube* (see CUBE).

cu·bit /ˈkyo͞obit/ ▸ n. an ancient measure of length, approximately equal to the length of a forearm. It was typically about 18 inches or 44 cm, though there was a **long cubit** of about 21 inches or 52 cm.
– ORIGIN Middle English: from Latin *cubitum* 'elbow, forearm, cubit.'

cu·bi·tal /ˈkyo͞obitl/ ▸ adj. **1** Anatomy of the forearm or the elbow: *the cubital vein.*
2 Entomology of the cubitus.
– ORIGIN late Middle English: from Latin *cubitalis*, from *cubitus* 'cubit.'

cu·bi·tus /ˈkyo͞obitəs/ ▸ n. Entomology the fifth longitudinal vein from the anterior edge of an insect's wing.
– ORIGIN early 19th cent.: from Latin.

cu·boid /ˈkyo͞oˌboid/ ▸ adj. more or less cubic in shape: *the school was a hideous cuboid erection of brick and glass.*
▸ n. **1** Geometry a solid that has six rectangular faces at right angles to each other.
2 (also **cuboid bone**) Anatomy a squat tarsal bone on the outer side of the foot, articulating with the heel bone and the fourth and fifth metatarsals.
– DERIVATIVES **cu·boi·dal** /-ˌboidl/ adj.
– ORIGIN early 19th cent.: from modern Latin *cuboides*, from Greek *kuboeidēs*, from *kubos* (see CUBE).

cub re·port·er ▸ n. informal a young or inexperienced newspaper reporter.

Cub Scout ▸ n. a member of the junior branch of the Boy Scouts, for boys aged about 8 to 10.

cuck·ing stool /ˈkəkiNG/ ▸ n. historical a chair to which a disorderly person was tied and then ducked into water or subjected to public ridicule as a punishment.
– ORIGIN Middle English: from obsolete *cuck* 'defecate,' of Scandinavian origin; so named because a stool containing a chamber pot was often used for the purpose.

cuck·old /ˈkəkəld, -ōld/ ▸ n. archaic the husband of an adulteress, often regarded as an object of derision.
▸ v. [with obj.] (of a man) make (another man) a cuckold by having a sexual relationship with his wife. ■ (of a man's wife) make (her husband) a cuckold.
– DERIVATIVES **cuck·old·ry** /-drē/ n.
– ORIGIN late Old English, from Old French *cucuault*, from *cucu* 'cuckoo' (from the cuckoo's habit of laying its egg in another bird's nest). The equivalent words in French and other languages applied to both the bird and the adulterer; *cuckold* has never been applied to the bird in English.

cuck·oo /ˈko͞okoo, ˈko͞okoo/ ▸ n. **1** a medium-sized long-tailed bird, typically with a gray or brown back and barred or pale underparts. Many cuckoos lay their eggs in the nests of small songbirds. ● Family Cuculidae (the **cuckoo family**): numerous genera and species, esp. the **(Eurasian) cuckoo** (*Cuculus canorus*), the male of which has a well-known two-note call. The cuckoo family also includes the coucals, roadrunners, and anis.
2 informal a mad person.
▸ adj. informal mad; crazy: *people think you're cuckoo.*
– PHRASES **cuckoo in the nest** an unwelcome intruder in a place or situation.
– ORIGIN Middle English: from Old French *cucu*, imitative of its call.

cuck·oo bee ▸ n. a bee that lays its eggs in the nest of another species of bee, the young being raised and fed by the host. ● *Nomada* and related genera (which parasitize solitary bees), and *Psithyrus* (which parasitize bumblebees), family Apidae.

cuck·oo clock ▸ n. a clock that strikes the hour with a sound like a cuckoo's call and typically has a mechanical cuckoo that emerges with each note.

cuck·oo·flow·er /ˈko͞oko͞oˌflou(-ə)r, ˈko͞oko͞o-/ ▸ n. a spring-flowering, herbaceous plant with pale lilac flowers, growing in damp meadows and by streams. ● *Cardamine pratensis*, family Brassicaceae.
– ORIGIN late 16th cent.: so named because it flowers at the time of year when the cuckoo is first heard calling.

cuck·oo·pint /ˈko͞oko͞oˌpint, ˈko͞oko͞o-/ ▸ n. the common European wild arum of woodland and hedgerows, with a pale spathe and a purple or green spadix followed by bright red berries. Also called LORDS-AND-LADIES or JACK-IN-THE-PULPIT. ● *Arum maculatum*, family Araceae.
– ORIGIN late Middle English: from earlier *cuckoo-pintle*, from PINTLE in the obsolete sense 'penis' (because of the shape of the spadix).

cuck·oo spit ▸ n. whitish froth found in compact masses on leaves and plant stems, exuded by the nymphs of froghoppers.

cuck·oo wasp ▸ n. a wasp that lays its eggs in the nest of a bee or another species of wasp, in particular: ● a true wasp lacking a worker caste, whose larvae are fed by the social wasp host (several species in the family Vespidae, including *Vespula austriaca*).

cu·cum·ber /ˈkyo͞oˌkəmbər/ ▸ n. **1** a long, green-skinned fruit with watery flesh, usually eaten raw in salads or pickled.
2 the climbing plant of the gourd family that yields this fruit, native to the Chinese Himalayan region. It is widely cultivated but very rare in the wild. ● *Cucumis sativus*, family Cucurbitaceae.
– PHRASES **(as) cool as a cucumber** untroubled by heat, stress, or exertion. ■ calm and relaxed.
– ORIGIN late Middle English: from Old French *cocombre, coucombre*, from Latin *cucumis, cucumer-*.

cu·cum·ber mo·sa·ic ▸ n. a viral disease affecting plants of the gourd family, spread by beetles and aphids and causing mottling and stunting.

cu·cur·bit /kyo͞oˈkərbət/ ▸ n. a plant of the gourd family (Cucurbitaceae), which includes melon, pumpkin, squash, and cucumber.
– DERIVATIVES **cu·cur·bi·ta·ceous** /kyo͞oˌkərbəˈtāSHəs/ adj.
– ORIGIN late Middle English: from Old French *cucurbite*, from Latin *cucurbita*.

Cú·cu·ta /ˈko͞oko͞oˌtä/ an industrial and commercial city in northern Colombia, near the Venezuelan border, in the Andes; pop. 603,800 (est. 2009).

cud /kəd/ ▸ n. partly digested food returned from the first stomach of ruminants to the mouth for further chewing.
– PHRASES **chew the cud 1** (of a ruminant animal) further chew partly digested food. **2** think or talk reflectively.
– ORIGIN Old English *cwidu, cudu*, of Germanic origin; related to German *Kitt* 'cement, putty' and Swedish *kåda* 'resin.'

cud·dle /ˈkədl/ ▸ v. [with obj.] hold close in one's arms as a way of showing love or affection: *he cuddles the baby close* | *they were cuddling each other in the back seat* | [no obj.] *the pair have been spotted kissing and cuddling.* ■ [no obj.] lie or sit close and snug: *I love cuddling up in front of a fire* | *they cuddled together to keep out the cold.*
▸ n. a prolonged and affectionate hug.
– DERIVATIVES **cud·dle·some** /-səm/ adj.
– ORIGIN early 16th cent. (rare before the 18th cent.): of unknown origin.

cud·dly /ˈkədlē, ˈkədl-ē/ ▸ adj. **(cuddlier, cuddliest)** endearing and pleasant to cuddle, esp. as a result of being soft or plump: *she was short and cuddly.*

cud·dy[1] /ˈkədē/ ▸ n. a small room or compartment, esp. on a boat.

cud·dy[2] ▸ n. (pl. **cuddies**) dialect, chiefly Scottish a donkey. ■ a stupid person: *you great soft cuddy!*
– ORIGIN early 18th cent.: perhaps a nickname for the given name *Cuthbert*, once popular in Scotland and northern England.

cudg·el /ˈkəjəl/ ▸ n. a short thick stick used as a weapon.
▸ v. **(cudgels, cudgeling, cudgeled**; Brit. **cudgels, cudgelling, cudgelled)** [with obj.] beat with a cudgel.
– PHRASES **cudgel one's brain** (or **brains**) think hard about a problem. **take up the cudgels** start to defend or support someone or something strongly: *there was no one else to take up the cudgels on their behalf.*
– ORIGIN Old English *cycgel*, of unknown origin.

cue[1] /kyo͞o/ ▸ n. a thing said or done that serves as a signal to an actor or other performer to enter or to begin their speech or performance. ■ a signal for action: *any conversational lull was my cue for asking a question.* ■ a piece of information or circumstance that aids the memory in retrieving details not recalled spontaneously. ■ Psychology a feature of something perceived that is used in the brain's interpretation of the perception: *expectancy is communicated both by auditory and visual cues.* ■ a hint or indication about how to behave in particular circumstances: *my teacher joked about such attitudes and I followed her cue.* ■ a facility for playing through an audio or video recording very rapidly until a desired starting point is reached.
▸ v. **(cues, cueing** or **cuing, cued)** [with obj.] give a cue to or for: *curious pedestrians are cued by the arrival of stretch limousines.* ■ act as a prompt or reminder: *have a list of needs and questions on paper to cue you.* ■ set a piece of audio or video equipment in readiness to play (a particular part of the recorded material): *features make it easier to cue up a tape for editing.*
– PHRASES **on cue** at the correct moment: *right on cue the door opened.* **take one's cue from** follow the example or advice of: *McGee did not move and Julia took her cue from him.*
– ORIGIN mid 16th cent.: of unknown origin.

cue[2] ▸ n. a long, straight, tapering wooden rod for striking the ball in pool, billiards, snooker, etc.
▸ v. **(cues, cueing** or **cuing, cued)** [no obj.] use such a rod to strike the ball.
– ORIGIN mid 18th cent. (denoting a long plait or pigtail): variant of QUEUE.

cue ball ▸ n. the ball, usually a white one, that is to be struck with the cue in pool, billiards, snooker, etc.

cue bid ▸ n. Bridge a bid intended to give specific information about the content of the hand to the bidder's partner, for example, possession of a control in the opponents' suit.

cue·ca /ˈkwākə/ ▸ n. a lively South American dance.
– ORIGIN early 20th cent.: American Spanish, from *zamacueca*, also denoting a dance performed esp. in Chile.

cue card ▸ n. a card held beside a camera for a television broadcaster to read from while appearing to look into the camera.

cued speech /kyo͞od/ ▸ n. a type of sign language that uses hand movements combined with mouth shapes to communicate to the hearing impaired.

Cuen·ca /ˈkweNGkə/ a city in the Andes in southern Ecuador; pop. 374,200 (est. 2008). Founded in 1557, it is known as the "marble city" because of its many fine buildings.

Cuer·na·va·ca /ˌkwernəˈväkə/ a resort town in central Mexico, at an altitude of 5,060 feet (1,542 m), capital of the state of Morelos; pop. 332,197 (2005).

cues·ta /ˈkwestə/ ▸ n. Geology a ridge with a gentle slope (dip) on one side and a steep slope (scarp) on the other.
– ORIGIN early 19th cent. (originally a US term for a steep slope at the edge of a plain): from Spanish, 'slope,' from Latin *costa* 'rib, flank.'

cuff[1] /kəf/ ▸ n. **1** the end part of a sleeve, where the material of the sleeve is turned back or a separate band is sewn on. ■ the part of a glove covering the wrist. ■ the turned-up end of a trouser leg. ■ the top part of a boot, typically padded or turned down. ■ an inflatable bag wrapped around the arm when blood pressure is measured.
2 **(cuffs)** informal handcuffs.
▸ v. [with obj.] informal secure with handcuffs: *the man's hands were cuffed behind his back.*
– PHRASES **off the cuff** informal without preparation: *they posed some difficult questions to answer off the cuff* | [as adj.] *an off-the-cuff remark.* [as if from impromptu notes made on one's shirt cuffs.]
– DERIVATIVES **cuffed** adj. [in combination] *a double-cuffed striped shirt.*
– ORIGIN late Middle English (denoting a glove or mitten): of unknown origin.

cuff[2] ▸ v. [with obj.] strike (someone) with an open hand, esp. on the head: *he cuffed him playfully on the ear.*
▸ n. [usu. in sing.] a blow given with an open hand.
– ORIGIN mid 16th cent.: of unknown origin.

cuff·link /ˈkəfˌliNGk/ ▸ n. (usu. **cufflinks**) a device for fastening together the sides of a shirt cuff, often decorative.

Cu·fic /ˈk(y)o͞ofik/ ▸ n. & adj. variant spelling of KUFIC.

Cu·ia·bá /ˌko͞oyəˈbä/ **1** a river port in west central Brazil, on the Cuiabá River; pop. 526,831 (2007).
2 a river in western Brazil that rises in the Mato Grosso plateau and flows for 300 miles (483 km) to

join the São Lourenço River near the border with Bolivia.

cui bo·no? /kwē ˈbōnō/ ▶ **exclam.** who stands, or stood, to gain (from a crime, and so might have been responsible for it)?
– ORIGIN early 17th cent.: Latin, literally 'to whom (is it) a benefit?'

cui·rass /kwiˈras, kyo͝orˈas/ ▶ **n. 1** historical a piece of armor consisting of breastplate and backplate fastened together. ■ a hard protective cover on an animal.
2 Medicine an artificial ventilator that encloses the body, leaving the limbs free, and forces air in and out of the lungs by changes in pressure.
– ORIGIN late Middle English: from Old French *cuirace*, based on late Latin *coriaceus* (adjective), from *corium* 'leather' (of which a cuirass was originally made).

cuirass 1

cui·ras·sier /ˌkwi(ə)rəˈsi(ə)r, ˌkyo͝or-/ ▶ **n.** historical a cavalry soldier wearing a cuirass.
– ORIGIN mid 16th cent.: French, from *cuirasse*, from Old French *cuirace* (see CUIRASS).

cui·sine /kwiˈzēn/ ▶ **n.** a style or method of cooking, esp. as characteristic of a particular country, region, or establishment: *much Venetian cuisine is based on seafood.* ■ food cooked in a certain way: *we spent the evening sampling the local cuisine.*
– ORIGIN late 18th cent.: French, literally 'kitchen.'

cuisse /kwis/ (also **cuish** /kwisH/) ▶ **n.** (usu. **cuisses** or **cuishes**) historical a piece of armor for the thigh.
– ORIGIN Middle English (originally in the plural): from Old French *cuisseaux*, plural of *cuissel*, from late Latin *coxale*, from *coxa* 'hip.'

cuke /kyo͞ok/ ▶ **n.** informal term for CUCUMBER.

Cul·bert·son /ˈkəlbərtsən/, Ely (1891–1955), US bridge player. He revolutionized the game of contract bridge by formalizing a system of bidding.

culch ▶ **n.** variant spelling of CULTCH.

Cul·dee /ˈkəlˌdē/ ▶ **n.** an Irish or Scottish monk of the 8th to 12th centuries, living as a recluse usually in a group of thirteen (on the analogy of Jesus Christ and his Apostles). The tradition ceased as the Celtic Church was brought under Roman Catholic rule.
– ORIGIN late Middle English: from medieval Latin *culdeus*, alteration, influenced by Latin *cultores Dei* 'worshipers of God,' of *kelledei* (plural, found in early Scottish records), from Old Irish *céle dé*, literally 'companion of God.'

cul-de-sac /ˈkəl di ˌsak/ ▶ **n.** (pl. **cul-de-sacs** or **culs-de-sac** /ˈkəl(z)/) a street or passage closed at one end. ■ a route or course leading nowhere: *the pro-democracy forces found themselves in a political cul-de-sac.* ■ Anatomy a vessel, tube, or sac, e.g., the cecum, open at only one end.
– ORIGIN mid 18th cent. (originally in anatomy): French, literally 'bottom of a sack.'

-cule ▶ **suffix** forming nouns such as *molecule*, *reticule*, which were originally diminutives.
– ORIGIN from French *-cule* or Latin *-culus*, *-cula*, *-culum*.

cu·lex /ˈkyo͞oˌleks/ (also **culex mosquito**) ▶ **n.** (pl. **culices** /-ləˌsēz/) a mosquito of a genus that includes a number of kinds commonly found in cooler regions. They do not transmit malaria, but can pass on a variety of other parasites including those causing filariasis. Compare with ANOPHELES. ● Genus *Culex*, subfamily Culicinae, family Culicidae.
– DERIVATIVES **cu·li·cine** /ˈkyo͞oləˌsīn/ **adj. & n.**
– ORIGIN late 19th cent.: Latin, literally 'gnat.'

Cu·lia·cán Ro·sa·les /ˌko͞olyəˈkän rōˈsäləs, rōˈzäləs/ a city in northwestern Mexico, capital of the state of Sinaloa; pop. 605,304 (2005).

cu·li·nar·y /ˈkələˌnerē, ˈkyo͞olə-/ ▶ **adj.** of or for cooking: *culinary skills | savor the culinary delights of the region.*
– DERIVATIVES **cu·li·nar·i·ly adv.**
– ORIGIN mid 17th cent.: from Latin *culinarius*, from *culina* 'kitchen.'

cull /kəl/ ▶ **v.** [with obj.] (usu. **be culled**) select from a large quantity; obtain from a variety of sources: *anecdotes culled from Greek and Roman history.* ■ reduce the population of (a wild animal) by selective slaughter: *he sees culling deer as a necessity* | (as noun **culling**) *kangaroo culling.* ■ send (an inferior or surplus animal on a farm) to be slaughtered. ■ literary pick (flowers or fruit): (as adj. **culled**) *fresh culled daffodils.*
▶ **n.** a selective slaughter of wild animals. ■ [usu. as modifier] an inferior or surplus livestock animal selected for killing: *a cull cow.*
– DERIVATIVES **cull·er n.**
– ORIGIN Middle English: from Old French *coillier*, based on Latin *colligere* (see COLLECT[1]).

Cul·len /ˈkələn/, Countee (1903–46), US poet and leader of the Harlem Renaissance. His works include *Color* (1925), *The Black Christ* (1929), and *The Medea and Some Poems* (1935).

cul·let /ˈkələt/ ▶ **n.** recycled broken or waste glass used in glassmaking.
– ORIGIN early 19th cent.: variant of COLLET, in the obsolete sense 'glass left on the blowing iron when the finished article is removed.'

Cul·lo·den, Battle of /kəˈlädn/ the final engagement of the Jacobite uprising of 1745–46, fought April 16 on a moor near Inverness, the last pitched battle on British soil. The Hanoverian army under the Duke of Cumberland crushed the small and poorly supplied Jacobite army of Charles Edward Stuart, and a ruthless pursuit after the battle effectively prevented any chance of saving the Jacobite cause.

cul·ly /ˈkəlē/ ▶ **n.** (pl. **cullies**) Brit. archaic, informal (often as a form of address) a man; a friend.
– ORIGIN mid 17th cent. (denoting a person who is imposed upon): of unknown origin.

Culm /kəlm/ ▶ **n.** Geology a series of Carboniferous strata in southwestern England, mainly shale and limestone with some thin coal seams. ■ (**culm**) archaic coal dust or slack.
– ORIGIN Middle English (in the sense 'soot, smut,' now only Scots): probably related to COAL.

culm /kəlm/ ▶ **n.** the hollow stem of a grass or cereal plant, esp. that bearing the flower.
– ORIGIN mid 17th cent.: from Latin *culmus* 'stalk.'

cul·men /ˈkəlmən/ ▶ **n.** (pl. **culmina** /-mənə/)
1 Ornithology the upper ridge of a bird's bill.
2 Anatomy a small region in the brain on the anterior surface of the cerebellum.
– ORIGIN mid 17th cent. (in the sense 'top, summit'): from Latin, contraction of *columen* 'top, summit.'

cul·mi·nant /ˈkəlmənənt/ ▶ **adj.** at or forming the top or highest point.

cul·mi·nate /ˈkəlməˌnāt/ ▶ **v.** [no obj.] reach a climax or point of highest development: *the tensions and disorders which **culminated in** World War II.* ■ [with obj.] be the climax or point of highest development of: *her book culminated a research project on the symmetry studies of Escher.* ■ Astronomy & Astrology (of a celestial body) reach the highest point at the meridian.
– ORIGIN mid 17th cent. (in astronomy and astrology): from late Latin *culminat-* 'exalted,' from the verb *culminare*, from *culmen* 'summit.'

cul·mi·na·tion /ˌkəlməˈnāsHən/ ▶ **n.** [in sing.] the highest or climactic point of something, esp. as attained after a long time: *the product was the culmination of 13 years of research.* ■ Astronomy & Astrology the reaching of the meridian by a celestial body.

cu·lottes /ˈk(y)o͞oˌläts, k(y)o͞oˈläts/ ▶ **plural n.** women's knee-length trousers, cut with very full legs to resemble a skirt.
– ORIGIN mid 19th cent.: French, 'breeches,' diminutive of *cul* 'rump,' from Latin *culus*.

cul·pa·bil·i·ty /ˌkəlpəˈbilitē/ ▶ **n.** responsibility for a fault or wrong; blame: *a level of moral culpability.*

cul·pa·ble /ˈkəlpəbəl/ ▶ **adj.** deserving blame: *sometimes you're just as culpable when you watch something as when you actually participate.*
– DERIVATIVES **cul·pa·bly** /-blē/ **adv.**
– ORIGIN Middle English (in the sense 'deserving punishment'): from Old French *coupable*, *culpable*, from Latin *culpabilis*, from *culpare* 'to blame,' from *culpa* 'fault, blame.'

cul·prit /ˈkəlprət, ˈkəlˌprit/ ▶ **n.** a person who is responsible for a crime or other misdeed. ■ the cause of a problem or defect: *viruses could turn out to be the culprit.*
– ORIGIN late 17th cent. (originally in the formula *Culprit, how will you be tried?*, said by the Clerk of the Crown in England to a prisoner pleading not guilty): perhaps from a misinterpretation of the written abbreviation *cul. prist*, for Anglo-Norman French *Culpable: prest d'averrer notre bille* '(You are) guilty: (We are) ready to prove our indictment'; in later use influenced by Latin *culpa* 'fault, blame.'

cult /kəlt/ ▶ **n.** a system of religious veneration and devotion directed toward a particular figure or object: *the cult of St. Olaf.* ■ a relatively small group of people having religious beliefs or practices regarded by others as strange or sinister: *a network of Satan-worshiping cults.* ■ a misplaced or excessive admiration for a particular person or thing: *a cult of **personality** surrounding the leaders.* ■ [usu. as modifier] a person or thing that is popular or fashionable, esp. among a particular section of society: *a cult film.*
– DERIVATIVES **cul·tic** /-tik/ **adj.**, **cult·ish adj.**, **cult·ish·ness n.**, **cult·ism** /-ˌtizəm/ **n.**, **cult·ist** /-tist/ **n.**
– ORIGIN early 17th cent. (originally denoting homage paid to a divinity): from French *culte* or Latin *cultus* 'worship,' from *cult-* 'inhabited, cultivated, worshiped,' from the verb *colere*.

C

cultch /kəlCH/ (also **culch**) ▶ **n.** the mass of stones, broken shells, and grit of which an oyster bed is formed.
– ORIGIN mid 17th cent.: of unknown origin.

cul·ti·gen /ˈkəltəjən/ ▶ **n.** Botany a plant species or variety known only in cultivation, esp. one with no known wild ancestor.
– ORIGIN early 20th cent.: from *cultivated* (past participle of CULTIVATE) + -GEN.

cul·ti·var /ˈkəltəˌvär/ ▶ **n.** Botany a plant variety that has been produced in cultivation by selective breeding. Cultivars are usually designated in the style *Taxus baccata* "Variegata." See also VARIETY (sense 2).
– ORIGIN 1920s: blend of CULTIVATE and VARIETY.

cul·ti·vate /ˈkəltəˌvāt/ ▶ **v.** [with obj.] **1** prepare and use (land) for crops or gardening. ■ break up (soil) in preparation for sowing or planting. ■ raise or grow (plants), esp. on a large scale for commercial purposes. ■ Biology grow or maintain (living cells or tissue) in culture.
2 try to acquire or develop (a quality, sentiment, or skill): *he cultivated an air of indifference.* ■ try to win the friendship or favor of (someone): *it helps if you go out of your way to cultivate the local people.* ■ apply oneself to improving or developing (one's mind or manners).
– DERIVATIVES **cul·ti·va·ble** /-vəbəl/ **adj.**, **cul·ti·vat·a·ble** /-ˌvātəbəl/ **adj.**
– ORIGIN mid 17th cent.: from medieval Latin *cultivat-* 'prepared for crops,' from the verb *cultivare*, from *cultiva (terra)* 'arable (land),' from *colere* 'cultivate, inhabit.'

cul·ti·vat·ed /ˈkəltəˌvātid/ ▶ **adj.** refined and well educated: *he was a remarkably cultivated and educated man.*

cul·ti·va·tion /ˌkəltəˈvāsHən/ ▶ **n. 1** the action of cultivating land, or the state of being cultivated: *the cultivation of crops | the economy was based largely on rice cultivation.*
2 the process of trying to acquire or develop a quality or skill: *the cultivation of good staff–management relations.*
3 refinement and good education: *a man of cultivation and taste.*

cul·ti·va·tor /ˈkəltəˌvātər/ ▶ **n.** a person or thing that cultivates something: *they were herders of cattle and cultivators of corn.* ■ a mechanical implement for breaking up the soil and uprooting weeds.

cul·tur·al /ˈkəlCHərəl/ ▶ **adj.** of or relating to the ideas, customs, and social behavior of a society: *the cultural diversity of the world's peoples.* ■ of or relating to the arts and to intellectual achievements: *a cultural festival.*
– DERIVATIVES **cul·tur·al·ly adv.**
– ORIGIN mid 19th cent.: from Latin *cultura* 'tillage' + -AL.

cul·tur·al an·thro·pol·o·gy ▶ **n.** see ANTHROPOLOGY.

cul·tur·al at·ta·ché ▶ **n.** an embassy official whose function is to promote cultural relations between the home country and the foreign country.

Cul·tur·al Rev·o·lu·tion a political upheaval in China 1966–76 intended to bring about a return to revolutionary Maoist beliefs. Largely carried forward by the Red Guard, it resulted in attacks on intellectuals, a large-scale purge in party posts, and the appearance of a personality cult around Mao Zedong. It led to considerable economic dislocation and was gradually brought to a halt by premier Zhou Enlai.

cul·tu·ra·ti /ˌkəlCHəˈrätē/ ▶ **plural n.** well-educated people who appreciate the arts.
– ORIGIN 1980s: blend of *culture* and *literati*.

cul·ture /ˈkəlCHər/ ▶ **n. 1** the arts and other manifestations of human intellectual achievement regarded collectively: *20th century popular culture.* ■ a refined understanding or appreciation of this: *men of culture.* ■ the customs, arts, social institutions, and achievements of a particular

nation, people, or other social group: *Caribbean culture | people from many different cultures.* ■ [with modifier] the attitudes and behavior characteristic of a particular social group: *the emerging drug culture.*
2 Biology the cultivation of bacteria, tissue cells, etc., in an artificial medium containing nutrients: *the cells proliferate readily in culture.* ■ a preparation of cells obtained in such a way: *the bacterium was isolated in two blood cultures.* ■ the cultivation of plants: *this variety of lettuce is popular for its ease of culture.*
▶ **v.** [with obj.] Biology maintain (tissue cells, bacteria, etc.) in conditions suitable for growth.
– ORIGIN Middle English (denoting a cultivated piece of land): the noun from French *culture* or directly from Latin *cultura* 'growing, cultivation'; the verb from obsolete French *culturer* or medieval Latin *culturare*, both based on Latin *colere* 'tend, cultivate' (see CULTIVATE). In late Middle English the sense was 'cultivation of the soil' and from this (early 16th cent.) arose 'cultivation (of the mind, faculties, or manners)'; sense 1 of the noun dates from the early 19th cent.

cul·ture-bound ▶ **adj.** restricted in character or outlook by belonging or referring to a particular culture.

cul·tured /ˈkəlCHərd/ ▶ **adj. 1** characterized by refined taste and manners and good education: *the development of a modern, cultured society.*
2 Biology (of tissue cells, bacteria, etc.) grown or propagated in an artificial medium. ■ (of a pearl) formed around a foreign body inserted into an oyster.

cul·ture shock ▶ **n.** the feeling of disorientation experienced by someone who is suddenly subjected to an unfamiliar culture, way of life, or set of attitudes.

cul·ture vul·ture ▶ **n.** informal a person who is very interested in the arts, esp. to an obsessive degree.

cul·ture war ▶ **n.** a conflict between groups with different ideals, beliefs, and philosophies: *a culture war between secular and religious activism.*

cul·tus /ˈkəltəs/ ▶ **n.** technical a system or variety of religious worship.
– ORIGIN mid 19th cent.: Latin (see CULT).

Cul·ver Cit·y /ˈkəlvər/ a city in southwestern California, west of Los Angeles, an industrial and filmmaking center; pop. 38,580 (est. 2008).

cul·ver·in /ˈkəlvərin/ ▶ **n. 1** a 16th- or 17th- century cannon with a relatively long barrel for its bore, typically about 10 to 13 feet long.
2 a kind of handgun of the 15th and 16th centuries.
– ORIGIN late 15th cent. (sense 2): from Old French *coulevrine*, from *couleuvre* 'snake,' based on Latin *colubra*.

cul·vert /ˈkəlvərt/ ▶ **n.** a tunnel carrying a stream or open drain under a road or railroad.
▶ **v.** [with obj.] (usu. **be culverted**) channel (a stream or drain) through a culvert.
– ORIGIN late 18th cent.: of unknown origin.

cum¹ /ko͝om, kəm/ ▶ **prep.** [usu. in combination] combined with; also used as (used to describe things with a dual nature or function): *a study-cum-bedroom.*
– ORIGIN late 19th cent.: Latin.

cum² ▶ **n.** informal variant spelling of COME.

cum. ▶ **abbr.** cumulative.

Cu·ma·ná /ˌko͞oməˈnä/ a historic port city in northeastern Venezuela, capital of Sucre state, on the Manzanares River; pop. 322,000 (est. 2009). It is said to be the oldest European settlement in South America.

cum·ber /ˈkəmbər/ ▶ **v.** [with obj.] dated hamper or hinder (someone or something): *they were cumbered with greatcoats and swords.* ■ obstruct (a path or space): *the road was clean and dry and not still cumbered by slush.*
▶ **n.** archaic a hindrance, obstruction, or burden: *a cumber of limestone rocks.*
– ORIGIN Middle English (in the sense 'overthrow, destroy'): probably from ENCUMBER.

Cum·ber·land /ˈkəmbərlənd/ a city in northeastern Rhode Island, north of Providence; pop. 34,209 (est. 2008).

Cum·ber·land Gap /ˈkəmbərlənd/ a historic pass through the Appalachian Mountains, from southwestern Virginia into southeastern Kentucky.

Cum·ber·land Riv·er a river that flows for 690 miles (1,110 km) from the Cumberland Plateau in southeastern Kentucky across northern Tennessee and back into Kentucky, where it joins the Ohio River near Paducah.

Cum·ber·land sauce ▶ **n.** a piquant sauce served as a relish with game and cold meats. It is typically made from red currant jelly flavored with orange, mustard, and port.

cum·ber·some /ˈkəmbərsəm/ ▶ **adj.** large or heavy and therefore difficult to carry or use; unwieldy: *cumbersome diving suits.* ■ slow or complicated and therefore inefficient: *organizations with cumbersome hierarchical structures.*
– DERIVATIVES **cum·ber·some·ly** adv., **cum·ber·some·ness** n.
– ORIGIN late Middle English (in the sense 'difficult to get through'): from CUMBER + -SOME¹.

cum·bi·a /ˈko͞ombēə/ ▶ **n.** a kind of dance music of Colombian origin, similar to salsa. ■ a dance performed to this music.
– ORIGIN 1940s: from Colombian Spanish, perhaps from Spanish *cumbé*.

Cum·bri·a /ˈkəmbrēə/ a county in northwestern England; county town, Carlisle. Cumbria was an ancient British kingdom, and the name continued to be used for the hilly northwestern region of England that contains the Lake District and much of the northern Pennines. The county of Cumbria was formed in 1974.
– DERIVATIVES **Cum·bri·an** adj. & n.
– ORIGIN from medieval Latin, from Welsh *Cymry* 'Welshman.'

cum·brous /ˈkəmbrəs/ ▶ **adj.** literary term for CUMBERSOME.
– DERIVATIVES **cum·brous·ly** adv., **cum·brous·ness** n.
– ORIGIN late Middle English (in the sense 'difficult to get through'): from CUMBER + -OUS.

cum div·i·dend ▶ **adv.** (of stocks) with a dividend.

cu·mec /ˈkyo͞oˌmek/ ▶ **n.** a unit of flow equal to one cubic meter of water per second: *minimum flows proposed would vary seasonally between 80 cumecs in winter and 140 cumecs in summer.*
– ORIGIN on the model of *cusec*.

cu·mene /ˈkyo͞oˌmēn/ ▶ **n.** Chemistry a liquid hydrocarbon made catalytically from benzene, chiefly as an intermediate in phenol synthesis.
● Alternative name: **isopropyl benzene**; chem. formula: $C_6H_5CH(CH_3)_2$.
– ORIGIN mid 19th cent.: from Latin *cuminum* 'cumin' + -ENE.

cum gra·no sal·is /ko͞om ˌgränō ˈsälis/ ▶ **adv.** (in phrase **take something cum grano salis**) another way of saying TAKE SOMETHING WITH A GRAIN OF SALT (see SALT).
– ORIGIN Latin, literally 'with a grain of salt.'

cum·in /ˈkəmən, ˈk(y)o͞o-/ (also **cummin**) ▶ **n. 1** the aromatic seeds of a plant of the parsley family, used as a spice, esp. ground and used in curry powder.
2 the small, slender plant that bears this fruit and grows from the Mediterranean to central Asia.
● *Cuminum cyminum*, family Umbelliferae.
– ORIGIN Old English *cymen*, from Latin *cuminum*, from Greek *kuminon*, probably of Semitic origin and related to Hebrew *kammōn* and Arabic *kammūn*; superseded in Middle English by forms from Old French *cumon, comin*, also from Latin.

cum lau·de /ko͝om ˈloudə, ˈloudē/ ▶ **adv. & adj.** with distinction (with reference to college degrees and diplomas).
– ORIGIN Latin, literally 'with praise.'

cum·mer·bund /ˈkəmərˌbənd/ ▶ **n.** a sash worn around the waist, esp. as part of a man's evening clothes.
– ORIGIN early 17th cent.: from Urdu and Persian *kamar-band*, from *kamar* 'waist, loins' and *-bandi* 'band.' The sash was formerly worn in the Indian subcontinent by domestic workers and low-status office workers.

cummerbund

Cum·mings /ˈkəmiNGz/, E. E. (1894–1962), US poet and novelist; full name *Edward Estlin Cummings*. His poems are characterized by their experimental typography (most notably by the avoidance of capital letters), technical skill, frank vocabulary, and sharp satire. Notable works: *The Enormous Room* (1922) and *95 Poems* (1956).

cum·ming·ton·ite /ˈkəmiNGtəˌnīt/ ▶ **n.** a mineral occurring typically as brownish fibrous crystals in some metamorphic rocks. It is a magnesium-rich iron silicate of the amphibole group.
– ORIGIN early 19th cent.: named after *Cummington*, a town in Massachusetts, + -ITE¹.

cum·quat /ˈkəmˌkwät/ ▶ **n.** variant spelling of KUMQUAT.

cu·mu·late ▶ **v.** /ˈkyo͞omyəˌlāt/ [with obj.] gather together and combine: *the systems cumulate data over a period of years.* ■ [no obj.] be gathered together and combined: *all unpaid dividend payments cumulate and are paid when earnings are sufficient.* ■ (as adj. **cumulated**) Chemistry denoting two double bonds attached to the same carbon atom.
▶ **n.** /ˈkyo͞omyəˌlit/ Geology an igneous rock formed by gravitational settling of particles in a magma.
– DERIVATIVES **cu·mu·la·tion** /ˌkyo͞omyəˈlāSHən/ n.
– ORIGIN mid 16th cent. (as a verb in the sense 'gather in a heap'): from Latin *cumulat-* 'heaped,' from the verb *cumulare*, from *cumulus* 'a heap.' Current senses date from the early 20th cent.

cu·mu·la·tive /ˈkyo͞omyələtiv, -ˌlātiv/ ▶ **adj.** increasing or increased in quantity, degree, or force by successive additions: *the cumulative effect of two years of drought.*
– DERIVATIVES **cu·mu·la·tive·ly** adv., **cu·mu·la·tive·ness** n.

cu·mu·la·tive dis·tri·bu·tion func·tion ▶ **n.** Statistics a function whose value is the probability that a corresponding continuous random variable has a value less than or equal to the argument of the function.

cu·mu·la·tive er·ror ▶ **n.** Statistics an error consistently in the same direction for all observations.

cu·mu·la·tive pre·ferred stock ▶ **n.** a preferred stock whose annual fixed-rate dividend, if it cannot be paid in any year, accrues until it can and is paid before common dividends.

cu·mu·la·tive vot·ing ▶ **n.** a system of voting in an election in which each voter is allowed as many votes as there are candidates and may give all to one candidate or varying numbers to several.

cu·mu·li·form /ˈkyo͞omyələˌfôrm/ ▶ **adj.** (of a cloud) developed in a predominantly vertical direction.

cu·mu·lo·nim·bus /ˌkyo͞omyəlōˈnimbəs/ ▶ **n.** (pl. **cumulonimbi** /-ˈnimbī, -bē/) Meteorology a cloud forming a towering mass with a flat base at fairly low altitude and often a flat top, as in thunderstorms.

cu·mu·lus /ˈkyo͞omyələs/ ▶ **n.** (pl. **cumuli** /-ˌlī, -lē/) Meteorology a cloud forming rounded masses heaped on each other above a flat base at fairly low altitude.
– DERIVATIVES **cu·mu·lous** /-ləs/ adj.
– ORIGIN mid 17th cent. (denoting a heap or an accumulation): from Latin,'heap.'

Cu·na ▶ **n. & adj.** variant spelling of KUNA.

Cu·nard /k(y)o͞oˈnärd/, Sir Samuel (1787–1865), British shipowner; born in Canada. He founded the steamship company that still bears his name with the aid of a contract that began in 1840 to carry the mail between Britain and Canada.

cunc·ta·tion /kəNGkˈtāSHən/ ▶ **n.** the action or an instance of delaying; tardy action.

cu·ne·ate /ˈkyo͞onēˌāt, -nēət/ ▶ **adj.** chiefly Anatomy & Botany wedge-shaped.
– ORIGIN early 19th cent.: from Latin *cuneus* 'wedge' + -ATE².

cu·ne·i·form /kyo͞oˈnēəˌfôrm, ˈkyo͞on(ē)ə-/ ▶ **adj.** denoting or relating to the wedge-shaped characters used in the ancient writing systems of Mesopotamia, Persia, and Ugarit, surviving mainly impressed on clay tablets: *a cuneiform inscription.* ■ Anatomy denoting three bones of the tarsus (ankle) between the navicular bone and the metatarsals. ■ chiefly Biology wedge-shaped: *the eggs are cuneiform.*
▶ **n.** cuneiform writing.
– ORIGIN late 17th cent.: from French *cunéiforme* or modern Latin *cuneiformis*, from Latin *cuneus* 'wedge.'

Cu·ne·ne /ko͞oˈnānə/ a river in Angola that rises near the city of Huambo and flows south and then west for 156 miles (250 km) to the Atlantic Ocean.

cun·ner /ˈkənər/ ▶ **n.** an edible greenish-gray wrasse (fish) that lives along the Atlantic coast of North America. ● *Tautogolabrus adspersus*, family Labridae.
– ORIGIN early 17th cent.: perhaps associated with archaic *conder*, denoting a lookout who alerts the crew of fishing boats to the direction taken by shoals of herring.

cun·nil·in·gus /ˌkənlˈiNGgəs/ ▶ **n.** stimulation of the female genitals using the tongue or lips.
– ORIGIN late 19th cent.: from Latin, from *cunnus* 'vulva' + *lingere* 'lick.'

cun·ning /ˈkəniNG/ ▶ **adj. 1** having or showing skill in achieving one's ends by deceit or evasion: *a cunning look came into his eyes.* ■ ingenious: *plants have evolved cunning defenses.*
2 attractive; quaint: *the baby will look cunning in that pink print.*

▸ n. skill in achieving one's ends by deceit: *a statesman to whom cunning had come as second nature.* ■ ingenuity: *what resources of energy and cunning it took just to survive.*
– DERIVATIVES **cun·ning·ly** adv., **cun·ning·ness** n.
– ORIGIN Middle English: perhaps from Old Norse *kunnandi* 'knowledge,' from *kunna* 'know' (related to CAN¹), or perhaps from Middle English *cunne,* an obsolete variant of CAN¹. The original sense was '(possessing) erudition or skill' and had no implication of deceit; the sense 'deceitfulness' dates from late Middle English.

Cun·ning·ham /ˈkəniNG,ham/, Merce (1919–2009), US dancer and choreographer. As a dancer with the Martha Graham dance company 1939–45, he experimented with choreography and collaborated with composer John Cage in solo performances in 1944. He formed his own company in 1953.

Cu·no·be·li·nus /,k(y)o͞onōbəˈlīnəs, -ˈlē-/ variant of CYMBELINE.

cunt /kənt/ ▸ n. vulgar slang a woman's genitals.
– ORIGIN Middle English: of Germanic origin; related to Norwegian and Swedish dialect *kunta,* and Middle Low German, Middle Dutch, and Danish dialect *kunte.*

cup /kəp/ ▸ n. **1** a small, bowl-shaped container for drinking from, typically having a handle. ■ the contents of such a container: *a strong cup of tea.* ■ a measure of capacity used in cooking, equal to half a pint—that is, 8 ounces (0.237 l): *one cup of butter.* ■ (in church use) a chalice used at the Eucharist. ■ an ornamental trophy in the form of a cup, usually made of gold or silver and having a stem and two handles, awarded as a prize in a contest. ■ (**Cup**) such a contest: *playing in the Cup is the best thing ever.* ■ (**cups**) one of the suits in a tarot pack.
2 a cup-shaped thing. ■ either of the two parts of a bra shaped to contain or support one breast. ■ a jockstrap having a protective reinforcement of rigid plastic or metal. ■ Golf the hole on a putting green or the metal container in it. ■ Canadian a receptacle forming part of a liquidizer.
3 a mixed drink served at parties, typically flavored with fruit juices and containing wine or cider.
▸ v. (**cups, cupping, cupped**) [with obj.] **1** form (one's hand or hands) into the curved shape of a cup: *"Hey!" Dad shouted, with his hands cupped around his mouth.* ■ place the curved hand or hands around: *he cupped her face in his hands.*
2 Medicine, historical bleed (someone) by using a glass in which a partial vacuum is formed by heating: *Dr. Ross ordered me to be cupped.*
– PHRASES **in one's cups** informal drunk. **not one's cup of tea** informal not what one likes or is interested in: *cats were not her cup of tea.*
– ORIGIN Old English: from popular Latin *cuppa,* probably from Latin *cupa* 'tub.'

cup-and-ring ▸ adj. denoting marks cut in megalithic monuments consisting of a circular depression surrounded by concentric rings.

cup·bear·er ▸ n. chiefly historical or literary a person who serves wine, esp. in a royal or noble household.

cup·board /ˈkəbərd/ ▸ n. a cabinet or closet, usually with a door and shelves, used for storage: *a kitchen cupboard.*
– PHRASES **the cupboard is bare** there are no resources or money available for a particular purpose.
– ORIGIN late Middle English (denoting a table or sideboard on which cups, plates, etc., were displayed): from CUP + BOARD.

cup·cake /ˈkəp,kāk/ ▸ n. **1** a small cake baked in a cup-shaped container and typically iced.
2 an attractive woman (often as a term of address). ■ a weak or effeminate man.

cup cor·al ▸ n. a small, brightly colored, solitary coral with tentacles that end in small knobs, sometimes found in colder seas. ● Genus *Caryophyllia,* order Scleractinia (or Madreporaria): several species, including the **Devonshire cup coral** (*C. smithi*), of European waters.

cu·pel /kyo͞oˈpel, ˈkyo͞opəl/ ▸ n. a shallow, porous container in which gold or silver can be refined or assayed by melting with a blast of hot air, which oxidizes lead or other base metals.
▸ v. (**cupels, cupeling, cupeled**; Brit. **cupels, cupelling, cupelled**) [with obj.] assay or refine (a metal) in such a container.
– DERIVATIVES **cu·pel·la·tion** /,kyo͞opəˈlāSHən/ n.
– ORIGIN early 17th cent. (as a noun): from French *coupelle,* diminutive of *coupe* 'goblet.'

Cu·per·ti·no /,ko͞opərˈtēnō/ a city in north central California, west of San Jose, part of the Silicon Valley complex; pop. 53,637 (est. 2008).

Cup Fi·nal ▸ n. the final match in a sports competition in which the winners are awarded a cup.

cup·ful /ˈkəp,fo͝ol/ ▸ n. (pl. **cupfuls**) the amount held by a cup: *a cupful of water.* ■ another term for CUP as a measure in cooking: *add 1 cupful of flour.*

cup fun·gus ▸ n. a fungus in which the spore-producing layer forms the lining of a shallow cup. ● Several families in the orders Helotiales and Pezizales, phylum Ascomycota.

cup·hold·er /ˈkəp,hōldər/ ▸ n. a device for holding a plastic cup or other drinking container, as in the console of a motor vehicle.

Cu·pid /ˈkyo͞opəd/ Roman Mythology the god of love. He is represented as a naked, winged boy with a bow and arrows, with which he wounds his victims. Greek equivalent EROS. ■ [as noun] (also **cupid**) a representation of a naked winged child, typically carrying a bow.
– ORIGIN from Latin *Cupido,* personification of *cupido* 'love, desire,' from *cupere* 'to desire.'

cu·pid·i·ty /kyo͞oˈpiditē/ ▸ n. greed for money or possessions.
– ORIGIN late Middle English: from Old French *cupidite* or Latin *cupiditas,* from *cupidus* 'desirous,' from *cupere* 'to desire.' Compare with COVET.

Cu·pid's bow ▸ n. a shape like that of the double-curved bow often shown carried by Cupid, esp. at the top edge of a person's upper lip.

cup li·chen ▸ n. a greenish-gray lichen that has small, cuplike structures arising from its spreading lobes and is found typically on heathland and moorland. ● Genus *Cladonia,* order Cladoniales: many species.

cu·po·la /ˈkyo͞opələ/ ▸ n. a small dome, esp. a small dome on a drum on top of a larger dome, adorning a roof or ceiling. ■ a gun turret; a small domed hatch above a gun turret on some tanks. ■ (also **cupola furnace**) a cylindrical furnace for refining metals, with openings at the bottom for blowing in air and originally with a dome leading to a chimney above.
– DERIVATIVES **cu·po·laed** adj.
– ORIGIN mid 16th cent.: Italian, from late Latin *cupula* 'small cask or burying vault,' diminutive of *cupa* 'cask.'

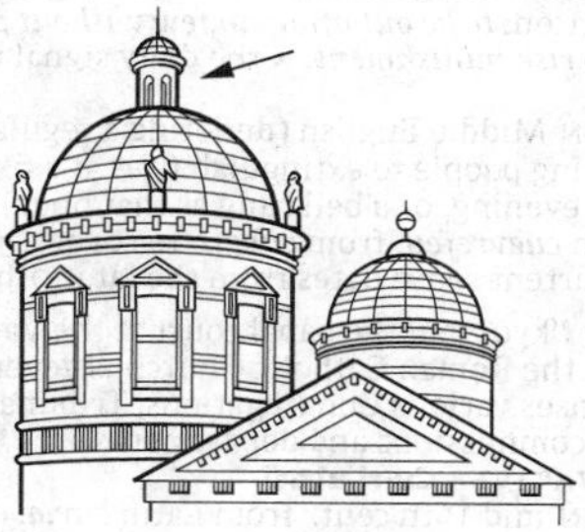
cupola

cup·pa /ˈkəpə/ Brit. informal ▸ n. a cup of tea: *a good strong cuppa.*
▸ contraction cup of: *let's have another cuppa coffee.*
– ORIGIN 1920s: alteration.

cup·ping /ˈkəpiNG/ ▸ n. (in Chinese medicine) a therapy in which heated glass cups are applied to the skin along the meridians of the body, creating suction as a way of stimulating the flow of energy.

cup·py /ˈkəpē/ ▸ adj. (**cuppier, cuppiest**) (of ground) full of shallow depressions.

cupr- ▸ comb. form variant spelling of CUPRO- shortened before a vowel (as in *cuprammonium*).

cu·pram·mo·ni·um /,k(y)o͞oprəˈmōnēəm/ ▸ n. [as modifier] Chemistry a complex ion, $Cu(NH_3)_4^{2+}$, formed in solution when ammonia is added to copper salts. The solution is deep blue and is used to dissolve cellulose.

cu·pre·ous /ˈk(y)o͞oprēəs/ ▸ adj. of or like copper.
– ORIGIN mid 17th cent.: from late Latin *cupreus* (from *cuprum* 'copper') + -OUS.

cu·pric /ˈk(y)o͞oprik/ ▸ adj. Chemistry of copper with a valence of two; of copper(II). Compare with CUPROUS.
– ORIGIN late 18th cent.: from late Latin *cuprum* 'copper' + -IC.

cu·prite /ˈk(y)o͞o,prīt/ ▸ n. a dark red or brownish black mineral consisting of cuprous oxide.

cu·pro /ˈk(y)o͞oprō/ ▸ n. a type of rayon made by dissolving cotton cellulose with cuprammonium salts and spinning the resulting solution into filaments.
– ORIGIN 1980s: an invented word, probably from *cuprammonium.*

cupro- (also **cupr-**) ▸ comb. form of or relating to copper: *cupronickel.*
– ORIGIN from late Latin *cuprum.*

cu·pro·nick·el /,k(y)o͞oprōˈnikəl/ ▸ n. an alloy of copper and nickel, esp. in the proportions 3:1 as used in "silver" coins.

cu·prous /ˈk(y)o͞oprəs/ ▸ adj. Chemistry of copper with a valence of one; of copper(I).
– ORIGIN mid 17th cent.: partly directly from late Latin *cuprum* 'copper' (reinforced by CUPRIC) + -OUS.

cu·pule /ˈkyo͞opyo͞ol/ ▸ n. Botany & Zoology a cup-shaped organ, structure, or receptacle in a plant or animal.
– ORIGIN late Middle English: from late Latin *cupula* (see CUPOLA).

cur /kər/ ▸ n. an aggressive dog or one that is in poor condition, esp. a mongrel. ■ informal a contemptible man.
– ORIGIN Middle English (in the general sense 'dog'): probably originally in *cur-dog,* perhaps from Old Norse *kurr* 'grumbling.'

cur. ▸ abbr. ■ currency. ■ current.

cur·a·ble /ˈkyo͝orəbəl/ ▸ adj. (of a disease or condition) able to be cured: *most skin cancers are completely curable.* ■ (of plastic, varnish, etc.) able to be hardened by some additive or other agent: *a radiation-curable coating.*
– DERIVATIVES **cur·a·bil·i·ty** /,kyo͝orəˈbilitē/ n.
– ORIGIN late Middle English: from Old French, or from late Latin *curabilis,* from Latin *curare* (see CURE).

Cu·ra·çao /,k(y)o͝orəˈsō, -ˈsou/ the largest island in the Netherlands Antilles, in the Caribbean Sea, 37 miles (60 km) north of the Venezuelan coast; pop.141,766 (2009); chief town, Willemstad.

cu·ra·çao /ˈkyo͝orə,sō, -,sou/ ▸ n. (pl. **curaçaos**) a liqueur flavored with the peel of bitter oranges.
– ORIGIN early 19th cent.: named after CURAÇAO, where the oranges are grown.

cu·ra·cy /ˈkyo͝orəsē/ ▸ n. (pl. **curacies**) the office, position, or work of a curate: *I was in England serving my curacy.*

cu·ran·de·ro /,kyo͞orənˈderō/ ▸ n. (pl. **curanderos**) (fem. **curandera** /-ˈderə/) (in Spain and Latin America) a healer who uses folk remedies.
– ORIGIN Spanish, from *curar* 'to cure,' from Latin *curare.*

cu·ra·re /k(y)o͝oˈrärē/ ▸ n. a bitter, resinous substance obtained from the bark and stems of some South American plants. It paralyzes the motor nerves and is traditionally used by some Indian peoples to poison their arrows and blowpipe darts. ● Curare is obtained from *Curarea* species and *Chondodendron tomentosum* (family Menispermaceae), and *Strychnos toxifera* (family Loganiaceae).
– ORIGIN late 18th cent.: from a Carib word, partly via Spanish and Portuguese.

cu·ras·sow /ˈk(y)o͝orə,sou, -,sō/ ▸ n. a large, crested, pheasantlike bird of the guan family, found in tropical American forests. The male is typically black in color. ● Genus *Crax* (and *Nothocrax*), family Cracidae: several species.
– ORIGIN late 17th cent.: anglicized form of CURAÇAO.

cu·rate¹ /ˈkyo͝orət, -,rāt/ ▸ n. (also **assistant curate**) a member of the clergy engaged as assistant to a vicar, rector, or parish priest. ■ archaic a minister with pastoral responsibility.
– ORIGIN Middle English: from medieval Latin *curatus,* from Latin *cura* 'care.'

cu·rate² /ˈkyo͝o,rāt/ ▸ v. [with obj.] select, organize, and look after the items in (a collection or exhibition): *both exhibitions are curated by the museum's director.* ■ select acts to perform at (a music festival): *in past years the festival has been curated by the likes of David Bowie.*
– DERIVATIVES **cu·ra·tion** /kyəˈrāSHən/ n.
– ORIGIN late 19th cent.: back-formation from CURATOR.

cu·rate's egg ▸ n. Brit. a thing that is partly good and partly bad: *this book is a bit of a curate's egg.*
– ORIGIN early 20th cent.: from a cartoon in *Punch* (1895) depicting a meek curate who, given a stale egg at the bishop's table, assures his host that "parts of it are excellent."

cur·a·tive /ˈkyo͝orətiv/ ▸ adj. able to cure something, typically disease: *the curative properties of herbs.*
▸ n. a medicine or remedy.
– DERIVATIVES **cur·a·tive·ly** adv.
– ORIGIN late Middle English (in the sense 'relating to cures'): from French *curatif, -ive,* from medieval Latin *curativus,* from Latin *curare* (see CURE).

C

cu·ra·tor /ˈkyo͝orˌātər, kyo͝oˈrātər, ˈkyo͝orətər/ ▶ **n.** a keeper or custodian of a museum or other collection. ■ a person who selects acts to perform at a music festival.
– DERIVATIVES **cu·ra·to·ri·al** /ˌkyo͝orəˈtôrēəl/ **adj.**, **cu·ra·tor·ship** /-ˌSHip/ **n.**
– ORIGIN late Middle English (denoting an ecclesiastical pastor, also (still a Scots legal term) the guardian of a minor): from Old French *curateur* or, in later use, directly from Latin *curator*, from *curare* (see **CURE**). The current sense dates from the mid 17th cent.

curb /kərb/ ▶ **n.** **1** a stone or concrete edging to a street or path.
2 a check or restraint on something: ***curbs** on the powers of labor unions.*
3 (also **curb bit**) a type of bit that is widely used in western riding. In English riding it is usually only used with a snaffle as part of a double bridle.
4 a swelling on the back of a horse's hock, caused by spraining a ligament.
▶ **v.** [with obj.] **1** restrain or keep in check: *she promised she would curb her temper.* ■ restrain (a horse) by means of a curb.
2 lead (a dog being walked) near the curb to urinate or defecate.
– ORIGIN late 15th cent. (denoting a strap fastened to the bit): from Old French *courber* 'bend, bow,' from Latin *curvare* (see **CURVE**).

curb chain ▶ **n.** a small chain which is attached to a curb bit and lies in the groove on a horse's chin.

curb·ing /ˈkərbiNG/ ▶ **n.** the concrete or stones collectively forming a curb.

curb mar·ket ▶ **n.** a market for selling shares not dealt with on the normal stock exchange.

curb roof ▶ **n.** another term for **GAMBREL**.

curb serv·ice ▶ **n.** service, esp. at a restaurant, extended to customers remaining in their parked vehicles.

curb·side /ˈkərbˌsīd/ ▶ **n.** [usu. as modifier] the side of a road or sidewalk that is nearer to the curb: *curbside collection of trash.*

curb·stone /ˈkərbˌstōn/ ▶ **n.** a long, narrow stone or concrete block, laid end to end with others to form a curb. ■ [as modifier] informal unqualified; amateur: *curbstone commentators.*

curb weight ▶ **n.** the weight of an automobile without occupants or baggage.

cur·cu·li·o /kərˈkyo͞olēˌō/ ▶ **n.** (pl. **curculios**) a beetle of the weevil family, esp. one that is a pest of fruit trees. ● Several genera and species in the family Curculionidae, including the **plum curculio** (*Conotrachelus nenuphar*).
– ORIGIN modern Latin, used as the genus name for weevils in the 18th cent., now restricted to the nut weevils.

cur·cu·ma /ˈkərkyəmə/ ▶ **n.** a tropical Asian plant of a genus that includes turmeric, zedoary, and other species that yield spices, dyes, and medicinal products. ● Genus *Curcuma*, family Zingiberaceae.
– ORIGIN modern Latin, from Arabic *kurkum* 'saffron,' from Sanskrit *kuṅkuma* (so named because the color of turmeric resembles that of saffron).

curd /kərd/ ▶ **n.** **1** (also **curds**) a soft, white substance formed when milk sours, used as the basis for cheese. ■ a fatty substance found between the flakes of poached salmon.
2 the edible head of a cauliflower or similar plant.
– DERIVATIVES **curd·y** **adj.**
– ORIGIN late Middle English: of unknown origin.

curd cheese ▶ **n.** chiefly Brit. a mild, soft, smooth cheese made from skimmed milk curd.

cur·dle /ˈkərdl/ ▶ **v.** separate or cause to separate into curds or lumps: [no obj.] *take care not to let the soup boil or it will curdle* | [with obj.] *making cheese by curdling milk.*
– PHRASES **make one's blood curdle** fill one with horror.
– DERIVATIVES **cur·dler** /ˈkərdlər, ˈkərdl-ər/ **n.**
– ORIGIN late 16th cent.: frequentative of obsolete *curd* 'congeal.'

cure /kyo͝or/ ▶ **v.** [with obj.] **1** relieve (a person or animal) of the symptoms of a disease or condition: *he was **cured of** the disease* | figurative *centuries of science have not **cured us of** our superstitions.* ■ eliminate (a disease, condition, or injury) with medical treatment: *this technology could be used to cure diabetes.* ■ solve (a problem): *stopping foreign investment is no way to cure the fundamental problem.*
2 preserve (meat, fish, tobacco, or an animal skin) by various methods such as salting, drying, or smoking: *some farmers cured their own bacon* | (as adj. **cured**) *home-cured ham.* ■ harden (rubber, plastic, concrete, etc.) after manufacture by a chemical process such as vulcanization. ■ [no obj.] undergo this process.
▶ **n.** **1** a substance or treatment that cures a disease or condition: *the search for a cure for the common cold.* ■ restoration to health: *he was beyond cure.* ■ a solution to a problem: *the cure is to improve the clutch operation.*
2 the process of curing rubber, plastic, or other material.
3 a Christian minister's pastoral charge or area of responsibility for spiritual ministry: *a benefice involving the **cure of souls**.* ■ a parish.
– DERIVATIVES **cur·er** **n.**
– ORIGIN Middle English (as a noun): from Old French *curer* (verb), *cure* (noun), both from Latin *curare* 'take care of,' from *cura* 'care.' The original noun senses were 'care, concern, responsibility,' in particular spiritual care (hence sense 3 of the noun). In late Middle English the senses 'medical care' and 'successful medical treatment' arose, and hence 'remedy.'

cu·ré /kyo͞oˈrā, ˈkyo͝orˌā/ ▶ **n.** a parish priest in a French-speaking country or region.
– ORIGIN French, from medieval Latin *curatus* (see **CURATE¹**).

cure-all ▶ **n.** a medicine or other remedy that will supposedly cure any ailment. ■ a solution to any problem: *unfortunately, the new output circuitry is not a cure-all.*

cu·ret·tage /ˌkyo͝orəˈtäZH/ ▶ **n.** Surgery the use of a curette, esp. on the lining of the uterus. See **DILATATION AND CURETTAGE**.
– ORIGIN late 19th cent.: from French, from **CURETTE**.

cu·rette /kyo͞oˈret/ ▶ **n.** a surgical instrument used to remove material by a scraping action, esp. from the uterus.
▶ **v.** [with obj.] clean or scrape with a curette.
– ORIGIN mid 18th cent. (as a noun): from French, from *curer* 'cleanse,' from Latin *curare* (see **CURE**).

cur·few /ˈkərˌfyo͞o/ ▶ **n.** a regulation requiring people to remain indoors between specified hours, typically at night: *a dusk-to-dawn curfew* | *the whole area was immediately placed **under curfew**.* ■ the hour designated as the beginning of such a restriction: *to be out after curfew without permission was to risk punishment.* ■ the daily signal indicating this.
– ORIGIN Middle English (denoting a regulation requiring people to extinguish fires at a fixed hour in the evening, or a bell rung at that hour): from Old French *cuevrefeu*, from *cuvrir* 'to cover' + *feu* 'fire.' The current sense dates from the late 19th cent.

Cu·ri·a /ˈkyo͝orēə/ the papal court at the Vatican, by which the Roman Catholic Church is governed. It comprises various Congregations, Tribunals, and other commissions and departments.
– DERIVATIVES **Cu·ri·al** **adj.**
– ORIGIN mid 19th cent.: from Latin *curia*, denoting a division of an ancient Roman tribe, also (by extension) the senate of cities other than Rome; later the term came to denote a feudal or Roman Catholic court of justice, whence the current sense.

Cu·rie /kyo͞oˈrē, ˈkyo͝orē/, Marie (1867–1934) and Pierre (1859–1906), French physicists (Marie was born *Maria Sklodowska* in Poland); pioneers in radioactivity. Working together on the mineral pitchblende, they discovered the elements polonium and radium. After her husband's accidental death, Marie isolated radium. She died of leukemia, caused by prolonged exposure to radioactive materials. She shared the 1903 Nobel Prize for Physics and the 1911 Nobel Prize for Chemistry with Becquerel.

Marie Curie

cu·rie /ˈkyo͝orē, kyo͞oˈrē/ (abbr.: **Ci**) ▶ **n.** (pl. **curies**) a unit of radioactivity, corresponding to 3.7×10^{10} disintegrations per second. ■ the quantity of radioactive substance that has this amount of activity.
– ORIGIN early 20th cent.: named after Pierre and Marie **CURIE**.

cu·ri·o /ˈkyo͝orēˌō/ ▶ **n.** (pl. **curios**) a rare, unusual, or intriguing object.
– ORIGIN mid 19th cent.: abbreviation of **CURIOSITY**.

cu·ri·o·sa /ˌkyo͝orēˈōsə, -ˈōzə/ ▶ **plural n.** curiosities, esp. erotic or pornographic books or articles.
– ORIGIN late 19th cent.: from Latin, neuter plural of *curiosus* (see **CURIOUS**).

cu·ri·os·i·ty /ˌkyo͝orēˈäsitē/ ▶ **n.** (pl. **curiosities**) **1** a strong desire to know or learn something: *filled with curiosity, she peered through the window* | ***curiosity** got the better of me, so I called him.*
2 a strange or unusual object or fact: *he showed them some of the curiosities of the house.*
– PHRASES **curiosity killed the cat** proverb being inquisitive about other people's affairs may get you into trouble.
– ORIGIN late Middle English: from Old French *curiousete*, from Latin *curiositas*, from *curiosus* (see **CURIOUS**).

cu·ri·ous /ˈkyo͝orēəs/ ▶ **adj.** **1** eager to know or learn something: *I began to be curious about the whereabouts of the bride and groom* | *she was **curious to know** what had happened.* ■ expressing curiosity: *a curious stare.*
2 strange; unusual: *a curious sensation overwhelmed her.*
– DERIVATIVES **cu·ri·ous·ly** **adv.** [sentence adverb] *curiously, I find snooker riveting*, **cu·ri·ous·ness** **n.**
– ORIGIN Middle English: from Old French *curios*, from Latin *curiosus* 'careful,' from *cura* 'care.' Sense 2 dates from the early 18th cent.

Cu·ri·ti·ba /ˌko͝orəˈtēbə/ a city in southern Brazil, capital of the state of Paraná; pop. 1,797,408 (2007).

cu·ri·um /ˈkyo͝orēəm/ ▶ **n.** the chemical element of atomic number 96, a radioactive metal of the actinide series. Curium does not occur naturally and was first made by bombarding plutonium with helium ions. (Symbol: **Cm**)
– ORIGIN 1940s: modern Latin, from the name of Marie and Pierre **CURIE**.

curl /kərl/ ▶ **v.** **1** form or cause to form into a curved or spiral shape: [no obj.] *her fingers curled around the microphone* | *a slice of ham had begun to **curl up** at the edges* | [with obj.] *she used to curl her hair with rags.* ■ [no obj.] (**curl up**) sit or lie with the knees drawn up: *she curled up and went to sleep.* ■ move or cause to move in a spiral or curved course: [no obj.] *a wisp of smoke curling across the sky.* ■ (with reference to one's mouth or upper lip) raise or cause to raise slightly on one side as an expression of contempt or disapproval: [no obj.] *Maria saw his lip curl sardonically.* ■ (in weight training) lift (a weight) using only the hands, wrists, and forearms.
2 [no obj.] play at the game of curling.
▶ **n.** **1** something having a spiral or inwardly curved form, esp. a lock of hair: *her blond hair was a mass of tangled curls* | *a curl of blue smoke.* ■ (with reference to a person's hair) a state or condition of being curled: *your hair has a natural curl* | *large perm rods give volume and control rather than lots of curl.* ■ a curling movement: *the sneering curl of his lip.* ■ see **LEAF CURL**. ■ a weightlifting exercise involving movement of only the hands, wrists, and forearms: *a dumbbell curl.*
2 Mathematics the vector product of the operator del and a given vector.
– PHRASES **make someone's hair curl** informal shock or horrify someone.
– ORIGIN late Middle English: from obsolete *crulle* 'curly,' from Middle Dutch *krul*.

curl·er /ˈkərlər/ ▶ **n.** **1** (usu. **curlers**) a roller or clasp around which a lock of hair is wrapped to curl it.
2 a player in the game of curling.

cur·lew /ˈkərˌlo͞o, ˈkərlˌyo͞o/ ▶ **n.** (pl. **same** or **curlews**) a large wading bird of the sandpiper family, with a long down-curved bill, brown streaked plumage, and frequently a distinctive ascending two-note call. See also **STONE CURLEW**. ● Genus *Numenius*, family Scolopacidae: several species, including the common Eurasian *N. arquata* and the North American **long-billed curlew** (*N. americanus*).

long-billed curlew

– ORIGIN Middle English: from Old French *courlieu*, alteration (by association with *courliu* 'courier,' from *courre* 'run' + *lieu* 'place') of imitative *courlis*.

Cur·ley /ˈkərlē/, James Michael (1874–1958), US politician. An urban political boss, he was a member of the US House of Representatives 1911–14 and 1943–47, mayor of Boston for four terms between

1914 and 1950, and governor of Massachusetts 1935–37.

curl·i·cue /ˈkərlē,kyo͞o/ (also **curlycue**) ▶ **n.** a decorative curl or twist in calligraphy or in the design of an object.
– ORIGIN mid 19th cent.: from CURLY + CUE² (in the sense 'pigtail'), or *-cue* representing the letter *q*.

curl·ing /ˈkərliNG/ ▶ **n.** a game played on ice, esp. in Scotland and Canada, in which large, round, flat stones are slid across the surface toward a mark. Members of a team use brooms to sweep the surface of the ice in the path of the stone to control its speed and direction.

curl·ing i·ron ▶ **n.** a heated rod used for rolling a person's hair into curls.

curl·ing stone ▶ **n.** a large, polished, circular stone with an iron handle on top, used in the game of curling.

curl·y /ˈkərlē/ ▶ **adj.** (**curlier**, **curliest**) made, growing, or arranged in curls or curves: *my hair is just naturally thick and curly.*
– DERIVATIVES **curl·i·ness** n.

cur·ly·cue ▶ **n.** variant spelling of CURLICUE.

curl·y en·dive ▶ **n.** see ENDIVE.

curl·y kale ▶ **n.** kale of a variety with dark green, tightly curled leaves.

cur·ly top (also **curly top disease**) ▶ **n.** a viral disease affecting plants, esp. beets and members of the gourd family, spread by beetles, particularly the beet leafhopper. Infected plants become dwarfed and have puckered, distorted foliage.

curl·y-wurl·y ▶ **adj.** informal twisting and curling.
– ORIGIN late 18th cent.: reduplication of CURLY.

cur·mudg·eon /kərˈməjən/ ▶ **n.** a bad-tempered or surly person.
– DERIVATIVES **cur·mudg·eon·li·ness** n., **cur·mudg·eon·ly** adj.
– ORIGIN late 16th cent.: of unknown origin.

cur·rach /ˈkərə(KH)/ (also **curragh**) ▶ **n.** Irish and Scottish term for CORACLE.
– ORIGIN late Middle English: from Irish and Scottish Gaelic *curach* 'small boat.' Compare with CORACLE.

cur·ragh ▶ **n.** variant spelling of CURRACH.

cur·ra·jong ▶ **n.** variant spelling of KURRAJONG.

cur·rant /ˈkərənt, ˈkə-rənt/ ▶ **n. 1** a small dried fruit made from a seedless variety of grape originally grown in the eastern Mediterranean region, now widely produced in California, and much used in cooking: [as modifier] *a currant bun.*
2 a Eurasian shrub that produces small edible black, red, or white berries. ● Genus *Ribes*, family Grossulariaceae: numerous species, including **black currant** and **red currant**. ■ a berry from such a shrub.
– ORIGIN Middle English *raisons of Corauntz*, translating Anglo-Norman French *raisins de Corauntz* 'grapes of Corinth' (the original source).

cur·rant gall ▶ **n.** a spherical red or purple gall that forms on the leaves or male catkins of oak trees in response to the developing larva of a gall wasp. It results from eggs laid in the spring and alternates with the spangle gall. ● The wasp is *Neuroterus quercusbaccarum*, family Cynipidae.

cur·rant to·ma·to ▶ **n.** a kind of tomato with tiny fruits, native to the Andes. ● *Lycopersicon pimpinellifolium*, family Solanaceae.

cur·ren·cy /ˈkərənsē, ˈkə-rənsē/ ▶ **n.** (pl. **currencies**) **1** a system of money in general use in a particular country: *the dollar was a strong currency* | *travelers checks in foreign currency* | figurative *he was rich in the currency of love.*
2 the fact or quality of being generally accepted or in use: *the term gained currency during the second half of the 20th century.* ■ the time during which something is in use or operation: *no claim had been made during the currency of the policy.*

cur·rent /ˈkərənt, ˈkə-rənt/ ▶ **adj.** belonging to the present time; happening or being used or done now: *keep abreast of current events* | *I started my current job last year.* ■ in common or general use: *the other meaning of the word is still current.*
▶ **n.** a body of water or air moving in a definite direction, esp. through a surrounding body of water or air in which there is less movement: *ocean currents.* ■ a flow of electricity which results from the ordered directional movement of electrically charged particles. ■ a quantity representing the rate of flow of electric charge, usually measured in amperes. ■ the general tendency or course of events or opinion: *the student movement formed a distinct current of protest.*
– ORIGIN Middle English (in the adjective sense 'running, flowing'): from Old French *corant* 'running,' from *courre* 'run,' from Latin *currere* 'run.'

cur·rent af·fairs ▶ **plural n.** events of political or social interest and importance happening in the world at the present time.

cur·rent as·sets ▶ **plural n.** cash and other assets that are expected to be converted to cash within a year. Compare with FIXED ASSETS.

cur·rent cost ac·count·ing ▶ **n.** a method of accounting in which assets are valued on the basis of their current replacement cost, and increases in their value as a result of inflation are excluded from calculations of profit.

cur·rent den·si·ty ▶ **n.** Physics the amount of electric current flowing per unit cross-sectional area of a material.

cur·rent li·a·bil·i·ties ▶ **plural n.** amounts due to be paid to creditors within twelve months.

cur·rent·ly /ˈkərəntlē, ˈkə-rəntlē/ ▶ **adv.** at the present time: *the price is currently at a premium.*

cur·ri·cle /ˈkərikəl/ ▶ **n.** historical a light, open, two-wheeled carriage pulled by two horses side by side.
– ORIGIN mid 18th cent.: from Latin *curriculum* 'course, racing chariot,' from *currere* 'to run.'

cur·ric·u·lum /kəˈrikyələm/ ▶ **n.** (pl. **curricula** /-lə/ or **curriculums**) the subjects comprising a course of study in a school or college.
– DERIVATIVES **cur·ric·u·lar** /-lər/ adj.
– ORIGIN early 19th cent.: from Latin (see CURRICLE).

cur·ric·u·lum vi·tae /kəˈrik(y)ələm ˈvēˌtī, ˈvītē/ (abbr.: **CV**) ▶ **n.** (pl. **curricula vitae** /kəˈrik(y)ələ/) a brief account of a person's education, qualifications, and previous experience, typically sent with a job application.
– ORIGIN early 20th cent.: Latin, literally 'course of life.'

Cur·ri·er /ˈkərēər, ˈkə-rēər/, Nathaniel (1813–88), US lithographer. He partnered with James Ives in 1857 to establish the company of Currier & Ives, which produced hand-colored prints of American scenes.

cur·ri·er /ˈkərēər, ˈkə-rēər/ ▶ **n.** a person who curries leather.
– ORIGIN late Middle English: from Old French *corier*, from Latin *coriarius*, from *corium* 'leather.'

cur·rish /ˈkəriSH/ ▶ **adj. 1** like a cur; snappish.
2 ignoble.
– DERIVATIVES **cur·rish·ly** adv., **cur·rish·ness** n.

cur·ry¹ /ˈkərē, ˈkə-rē/ ▶ **n.** (pl. **curries**) a dish of meat, vegetables, etc., cooked in an Indian-style sauce of strong spices and turmeric and typically served with rice.
▶ **v.** (**curries**, **currying**, **curried**) [with obj.] (usu. as adj. **curried**) prepare or flavor with a sauce of hot-tasting spices: *curried chicken.*
– ORIGIN late 16th cent.: from Tamil *kaṛi*.

cur·ry² ▶ **v.** (**curries**, **currying**, **curried**) [with obj.]
1 groom (a horse) with a rubber or plastic curry comb.
2 historical treat (tanned leather) to improve its properties. ■ archaic thrash; beat.
– PHRASES **curry favor** ingratiate oneself with someone through obsequious behavior: *a wimpish attempt to curry favor with the new bosses.* [alteration of Middle English *curry favel*, from the name (*Favel* or *Fauvel*) of a chestnut horse in a 14th-cent. French romance who became a symbol of cunning and duplicity; hence 'to rub down Favel' meant to use the cunning that he personified.]
– ORIGIN Middle English: from Old French *correier*, ultimately of Germanic origin.

cur·ry comb ▶ **n.** a handheld metal device with serrated ridges, used for removing dirt out of a horse's coat or for cleaning brushes with which a horse is being groomed. ■ (also **rubber curry comb**) a similar device of flexible rubber, used for grooming horses.

curry comb

cur·ry leaf ▶ **n.** a shrub or small tree native to India and Sri Lanka, the leaves of which are widely used in Indian cooking. ● *Murraya koenigii*, family Rutaceae.

cur·ry plant ▶ **n.** a small, shrubby plant of the daisy family, which has narrow, silver-gray leaves and small yellow flowers and emits a strong smell of curry. ● *Helichrysum angustifolium*, family Compositae.

cur·ry pow·der ▶ **n.** a mixture of finely ground spices, such as turmeric, ginger, and coriander, used for making curry.

curse /kərs/ ▶ **n. 1** a solemn utterance intended to invoke a supernatural power to inflict harm or punishment on someone or something: *she'd put a curse on him.* ■ [usu. in sing.] a cause of harm or misery: *impatience is the curse of our day and age.* ■ (**the curse**) informal menstruation.
2 an offensive word or phrase used to express anger or annoyance: *his mouth was spitting vile oaths and curses.*
▶ **v. 1** [with obj.] invoke or use a curse against: *it often seemed as if the family had been cursed.* ■ (**be cursed with**) be afflicted with: *many owners have been cursed with a series of bankruptcies.*
2 [no obj.] utter offensive words in anger or annoyance: *drivers were cursing and sounding their horns.* ■ [with obj.] address with such words: *I cursed myself for my carelessness.*
– DERIVATIVES **curs·er** n.
– ORIGIN Old English, of unknown origin.

curs·ed /ˈkərsid, kərst/ ▶ **adj.** informal, dated used to express annoyance or irritation: *he didn't whine about his cursed fate.*
– DERIVATIVES **curs·ed·ly** /ˈkərsidlē/ adv., **curs·ed·ness** /ˈkərsidnəs/ n.

cur·sil·lo /kərˈsē(l)yō/ ▶ **n.** (pl. **cursillos**) a short informal spiritual retreat by a group of Roman Catholics, organized mainly by lay people and originally developed in Spain.
– ORIGIN 1950s: Spanish, literally 'little course.'

cur·sive /ˈkərsiv/ ▶ **adj.** written with the characters joined: *cursive script.*
▶ **n.** writing with such a style.
– DERIVATIVES **cur·sive·ly** adv.
– ORIGIN late 18th cent.: from medieval Latin *cursivus*, from Latin *curs-* 'run,' from the verb *currere*.

cur·sor /ˈkərsər/ ▶ **n.** a movable indicator on a computer screen identifying the point that will be affected by input from the user, for example showing where typed text will be inserted. ■ chiefly historical the transparent slide engraved with a hairline that is part of a slide rule and is used for marking a point on the rule while bringing a point on the central sliding portion up to it.
– ORIGIN Middle English (denoting a runner or running messenger): from Latin, 'runner,' from *curs-* (see CURSIVE). The sense 'sliding part of an instrument' dates from the late 16th cent.

cur·so·ri·al /kərˌsôrēəl/ ▶ **adj.** Zoology having limbs adapted for running.
– ORIGIN mid 19th cent.: from Latin *cursor* (see CURSOR) + -IAL.

cur·so·ry /ˈkərsərē/ ▶ **adj.** hasty and therefore not thorough or detailed: *a cursory glance at the figures.*
– DERIVATIVES **cur·so·ri·ly** /ˈkərsərəlē/ adv., **cur·so·ri·ness** n.
– ORIGIN early 17th cent.: from Latin *cursorius* 'of a runner,' from *cursor* (see CURSOR).

curst /kərst/ ▶ **adj.** archaic spelling of CURSED.

curt /kərt/ ▶ **adj.** rudely brief: *his reply was curt.*
– DERIVATIVES **curt·ly** adv., **curt·ness** n.
– ORIGIN late Middle English (in the sense 'short, shortened'): from Latin *curtus* 'cut short, abridged.'

cur·tail /kərˈtāl/ ▶ **v.** [with obj.] reduce in extent or quantity; impose a restriction on: *civil liberties were further curtailed.* ■ (**curtail someone of**) archaic deprive someone of (something): *I that am curtailed of this fair proportion.*
– ORIGIN late 15th cent.: from obsolete *curtal* 'horse with a docked tail,' from French *courtault*, from *court* 'short,' from Latin *curtus*. The change in the ending was due to association with TAIL¹ and perhaps also with French *tailler* 'to cut.'

cur·tail·ment /kərˈtālmənt/ ▶ **n.** the action or fact of reducing or restricting something: *the curtailment of human rights.*

cur·tain /ˈkərtn/ ▶ **n.** a piece of material suspended at the top to form a covering or screen, typically one of a pair at a window: *she drew the curtains and lit the fire* | figurative *through the curtain of falling snow, she could just make out gravestones.* ■ (**the curtain**) a screen of heavy cloth or other material that can be raised or lowered at the front of a stage. ■ a raising or lowering of such a screen at the beginning or end of an act or scene: *the art is to hold your audience right from the opening curtain.* ■ (**curtains**) informal a disastrous outcome: *it looked like curtains for me.*
▶ **v.** [with obj.] (often as adj. **curtained**) provide with a curtain or curtains: *a curtained window.* ■ conceal or screen with a curtain: *a curtained-off side room* | figurative *her unbound hair curtaining her face.*

–PHRASES **bring down the curtain on** bring to an end: *her decision brought down the curtain on a glittering 30-year career.*
–ORIGIN Middle English: from Old French *cortine*, from late Latin *cortina*, translation of Greek *aulaia*, from *aulē* 'court.'

cur·tain call ▶ n. the appearance of one or more performers on stage after a performance to acknowledge the audience's applause.

C

cur·tain lec·ture ▶ n. dated an instance of a wife reprimanding her husband in private.
–ORIGIN mid 17th cent.: originally a reprimand given behind bed curtains.

cur·tain rais·er ▶ n. an entertainment or other arts event happening just before a longer or more important one: *Bach's Sinfonia in B flat was an ideal **curtain-raiser to** Mozart's last piano concerto.*
–ORIGIN late 19th cent.: originally used in the theater to denote a short opening piece performed before a play.

cur·tain speech ▶ n. a speech of thanks or appreciation to an audience, made after a performance by an actor playing a leading role, typically from the front of the stage with the curtains closed.

cur·tain time ▶ n. [in sing.] the beginning of a stage performance: *curtain time is at 8 p.m.*

cur·tain wall ▶ n. a fortified wall around a medieval castle, typically one linking towers together. ■ a wall that encloses the space within a building but does not support the roof, typically on a modern high-rise.

cur·tal /ˈkərtl/ ▶ adj. archaic shortened, abridged, or curtailed.
▶ n. historical a dulcian or bassoon of the late 16th to early 18th century.
–ORIGIN late 15th cent. (denoting a short-barreled cannon): from French *courtault*, from *court* 'short' + the pejorative suffix *-ault*. In both English and French the noun denoted various items characterized by something short, esp. an animal with a docked tail, which probably gave rise to the adjective sense.

cur·ta·na /kərˈtänə, -ˈtānə/ ▶ n. Brit. the unpointed sword carried in front of English sovereigns at their coronation to represent mercy.
–ORIGIN Middle English: from Anglo-Latin *curtana* (*spatha*) 'shortened (sword),' from Old French *cortain*, the name of the sword belonging to ROLAND (the point of which was damaged when it was thrust into a block of steel), from *cort* 'short,' from Latin *curtus* 'cut short.'

cur·te·sy /ˈkərtəsē/ ▶ n. (pl. **curtesies**) Law, historical a tenure by which a husband, after his wife's death, held certain kinds of property that she had inherited.

cur·ti·lage /ˈkərtl-ij/ ▶ n. Law an area of land attached to a house and forming one enclosure with it: *the roads **within the curtilage of** the development site.*
–ORIGIN Middle English: from Anglo-Norman French, variant of Old French *courtillage*, from *courtil* 'small court,' from *cort* 'court.'

Cur·tis /ˈkərtis/, Benjamin Robbins (1809–74), US Supreme Court associate justice 1851–57. He resigned in protest over the Court's handling of the Dred Scott case 1857. He served as chief counsel to Andrew Johnson during Johnson's impeachment in 1868. His brother, **George Ticknor Curtis** (1812–94), a lawyer and writer, argued for the plaintiff before the US Supreme Court in the Dred Scott case.

Cur·tiss /ˈkərtəs/, Glenn (Hammond) (1878–1930), US air pioneer and aircraft designer. In 1908, Curtiss made the first public US flight, traversing 0.6 miles (1.0 km). He built his first airplane in 1909 and invented the aileron and then demonstrated the first practical seaplane two years later.

curt·sy /ˈkərtsē/ (also **curtsey**) ▶ n. (pl. **curtsies** or **curtseys**) a woman's or girl's formal greeting made by bending the knees with one foot in front of the other: *she **bobbed a curtsy to** him.*
▶ v. (**curtsies**, **curtsying**, **curtsied** or **curtseys**, **curtseying**, **curtseyed**) [no obj.] perform such an action: *she curtsied onto the stage.*
–ORIGIN early 16th cent.: variant of COURTESY. Both forms were used to denote the expression of respect or courtesy by a gesture, esp. in phrases such as *do courtesy*, *make courtesy*, and from this arose the current use (late 16th cent).

cu·rule /ˈkyo͝orˌo͞ol/ ▶ adj. historical denoting or relating to the authority exercised by the senior magistrates in ancient Rome, chiefly the consul and praetor, who were entitled to use the *sella curulis* ('curule seat,' a kind of folding chair).
–ORIGIN early 17th cent.: from Latin *curulis*, from *currus* 'chariot' (in which the chief magistrate was conveyed to the seat of office), from *currere* 'to run.'

cur·va·ceous /kərˈvāsHəs/ ▶ adj. (esp. of a woman or a woman's figure) having an attractively curved shape.
–DERIVATIVES **cur·va·ceous·ness** n.

cur·va·ture /ˈkərvəCHər, -ˌCHo͝or/ ▶ n. the fact of being curved or the degree to which something is curved: *spinal curvature* | *the curvature of the earth* | *it has a distinct curvature near the middle.* ■ Geometry the degree to which a curve deviates from a straight line, or a curved surface deviates from a plane. ■ a numerical quantity expressing this.
–ORIGIN late Middle English: via Old French from Latin *curvatura*, from *curvare* (see CURVE).

curve /kərv/ ▶ n. a line or outline that gradually deviates from being straight for some or all of its length: *the parapet wall sweeps down in a bold curve.* ■ a place where a road deviates from a straight path: *the vehicle rounded a curve.* ■ (**curves**) a curving contour of a woman's figure. ■ a line on a graph (whether straight or curved) showing how one quantity varies with respect to another: *the population curve.* ■ a system in which grades are assigned to students based on their performance relative to other students, regardless of their actual knowledge of the subject: *grades were marked on a curve.* ■ Baseball another term for CURVEBALL.
▶ v. form or cause to form a curve: [no obj.] *her mouth curved in a smile* | [with obj.] *starting with arms outstretched, curve the body sideways.*
–PHRASES **ahead of** (or **behind**) **the curve** (esp. of a business or politician) ahead of (or lagging behind) current thinking or trends.
–ORIGIN late Middle English: from Latin *curvare* 'to bend,' from *curvus* 'bent.' The noun dates from the late 17th cent.

curve·ball /ˈkərvˌbôl/ ▶ n. Baseball a ball that is pitched with a snap of the wrist and a strong downward spin, which causes the ball to drop suddenly and deceptively veer away from home plate.

curved /kərvd/ ▶ adj. having the form of a curve; bent: *birds with long curved bills.*

cur·vet /kərˈvet/ ▶ v. (**curvets**, **curvetting**, **curvetted** or **curvets**, **curveting**, **curveted**) [no obj.] (of a horse) leap gracefully or energetically.
▶ n. a graceful or energetic leap.
–ORIGIN late 16th cent.: from Italian *corvetta*, diminutive of *corva*, earlier form of *curva* 'a curve,' from Latin *curvus* 'bent.'

cur·vi·lin·e·ar /ˌkərvəˈlinēər/ ▶ adj. contained by or consisting of a curved line or lines: *these designs employ flowing, curvilinear forms.*
–DERIVATIVES **cur·vi·lin·e·ar·ly** adv.
–ORIGIN early 18th cent.: from *curvi-* 'curved,' from Latin *curvus*, on the pattern of *rectilinear*.

cur·vi·ros·tral /ˌkərvəˈrästrəl/ ▶ adj. with a curved beak.

curv·y /ˈkərvē/ ▶ adj. (**curvier**, **curviest**) having many curves: *a curvy stretch of road.* ■ informal (esp. of a woman's figure) shapely and voluptuous.
–DERIVATIVES **curv·i·ness** n.

cus·cus /ˈkəskəs, ˈko͞osko͞os/ ▶ n. a tree-dwelling marsupial with a rounded head and prehensile tail, native to New Guinea and northern Australia. ● Four genera in the family Phalangeridae: several species, including the **spotted cuscus** (*Spilocuscus maculatus*) and the **grey cuscus** (*Phalanger orientalis*). See also PHALANGER.
–ORIGIN mid 17th cent.: via French and Dutch from a local name in the Molucca Islands.

cu·sec /ˈkyo͞oˌsek/ ▶ n. a unit of flow (esp. of water) equal to one cubic foot per second.
–ORIGIN early 20th cent.: abbreviation of *cubic foot per second.*

Cush /ko͝osH/ **1** (in the Bible) the eldest son of Ham and grandson of Noah (Gen. 10:6).
2 the southern part of ancient Nubia, first mentioned in Egyptian records of the Middle Kingdom. In the Bible it is the country of the descendants of Cush.

cush·at /ˈkəsHət/ ▶ n. dialect, chiefly Scottish a wood pigeon.
–ORIGIN Old English, of unknown origin.

cu·shaw /ko͞oˈsHô, ˈko͞oˌsHô/ (also **cushaw squash**) ▶ n. a large winter squash of a variety with a curved neck.
–ORIGIN late 16th cent.: of unknown origin.

cush-cush /ˈko͝osH ˌko͝osH/ (also **cush-cush yam**) ▶ n. a tropical American yam that produces a number of tubers on each plant. Also called YAMPEE. ● *Dioscorea trifida*, family Dioscoreaceae. ■ the edible tuber of this plant, eaten as a vegetable.
–ORIGIN late 19th cent.: perhaps ultimately of African origin.

Cush·ing /ˈko͝osHiNG/, William (1732–1810), US Supreme Court associate justice 1789–1810. After serving as chief justice of the Massachusetts Supreme Court 1780–89, he was the first person to be nominated by President Washington to serve as an associate justice on the US Supreme Court.

Cush·ing's dis·ease /ˈko͝osHiNGz/ ▶ n. Cushing's syndrome as caused by a tumor of the pituitary gland.

Cush·ing's syn·drome ▶ n. Medicine a metabolic disorder caused by overproduction of corticosteroid hormones by the adrenal cortex and often involving obesity and high blood pressure.
–ORIGIN 1930s: named after Harvey W. *Cushing* (1869–1939), American surgeon.

cush·ion /ˈko͝osHən/ ▶ n. a pillow or pad stuffed with a mass of soft material, used as a comfortable support for sitting or leaning on. ■ something providing support or protection against impact: *the pad forms a cushion between carpet and floor* | figurative *a poll showed the candidate with a 14-point cushion.* ■ the elastic lining of the sides of a billiard table, from which the ball rebounds. ■ the layer of air supporting a hovercraft or similar vehicle.
▶ v. [with obj.] soften the effect of an impact on: *the bag cushions equipment from inevitable knocks.* ■ mitigate the adverse effects of: *he called for federal assistance **to cushion the blow** for farmers.*
–DERIVATIVES **cush·ioned** adj., **cush·ion·y** adj.
–ORIGIN Middle English: from Old French *cuissin*, based on a Latin word meaning 'cushion for the hip,' from *coxa* 'hip, thigh.'

cush·ion cap·i·tal ▶ n. Architecture a capital resembling a cushion pressed down by a weight, seen particularly in Romanesque churches.

Cush·it·ic /ko͝osHˈitik, ˌkəsH-/ ▶ n. a group of East African languages of the Afro-Asiatic family spoken mainly in Ethiopia and Somalia, including Somali and Oromo.
▶ adj. of or relating to this group of languages.
–ORIGIN early 20th cent.: from CUSH + -ITIC.

cush·y /ˈko͝osHē/ ▶ adj. (**cushier**, **cushiest**) informal **1** (of a job, task, or situation) undemanding, easy, or secure: *cushy jobs that pay you to ski.*
2 (of furniture) comfortable.
–DERIVATIVES **cush·i·ness** n.
–ORIGIN World War I (originally Anglo-Indian): from Urdu *ḳushī* 'pleasure,' from Persian *ḳuš*.

cusk /kəsk/ ▶ n. another term for TORSK.
–ORIGIN early 17th cent.: of unknown origin.

cusk-eel ▶ n. a small, eellike fish with a tapering body and fins that form a pointed tail, typically found in deep water. ● Family Ophidiidae: numerous genera.

cusp /kəsp/ ▶ n. **1** a pointed end where two curves meet, in particular: ■ Architecture a projecting point between small arcs in Gothic tracery. ■ a cone-shaped prominence on the surface of a tooth, esp. of a molar or premolar. ■ Anatomy a pocket or fold in the wall of the heart or a major blood vessel that fills and distends if the blood flows backward, so forming part of a valve. ■ Mathematics a point at which the direction of a curve is abruptly reversed. ■ each of the pointed ends of a crescent, esp. of the moon.
2 Astrology the initial point of an astrological sign or house: *he was Aries **on the cusp** with Taurus.*
3 a point of transition between two different states: *those **on the cusp of** adulthood.*
–DERIVATIVES **cus·pate** /ˈkəspət, -ˌpāt/ adj., **cusped** adj., **cus·pi·date** /ˈkəspəˌdāt/ adj.
–ORIGIN late 16th cent. (sense 2): from Latin *cuspis* 'point or apex.'

cus·pid /ˈkəspid/ ▶ n. a tooth with a single cusp or point; a canine tooth.
–ORIGIN mid 18th cent.: from Latin *cuspis*, *cuspid-* 'point or apex.'

cus·pi·dor /ˈkəspəˌdôr/ ▶ n. a spittoon.
–ORIGIN mid 18th cent.: from Portuguese, literally 'spitter.'

cusp·ing /ˈkəspiNG/ ▶ n. **1** formation of a cusp or cusps: *if you use the incorrect pressure there will be serious cusping and uneven wear on the tire.*
2 Architecture a decorative feature consisting of cusps.

cuss /kəs/ informal ▶ n. **1** an annoying or stubborn person or animal: *he was certainly an unsociable cuss.*
2 another term for CURSE (sense 2 of the noun).
▶ v. another term for CURSE (sense 2 of the verb).

cuss·ed /ˈkəsəd/ ▶ adj. informal stubborn; annoying: *why do you have to be so cussed?*
–DERIVATIVES **cuss·ed·ly** adv., **cuss·ed·ness** n.
–ORIGIN mid 19th cent. (originally US): variant of CURSED.

cuss word ▶ **n.** informal a swear word.

cus·tard /ˈkəstərd/ ▶ **n.** a dessert or sweet sauce made with milk, eggs, and sugar.
– ORIGIN late Middle English *crustarde, custarde* (denoting an open pie containing meat or fruit in a spiced or sweetened sauce thickened with eggs), from Old French *crouste* (see CRUST).

cus·tard ap·ple ▶ **n. 1** a large, fleshy, tropical fruit with a sweet yellow pulp. See also CHERIMOYA and SWEETSOP.
2 the tree that bears this fruit, native to Central and South America. ● Genus *Annona*, family Annonaceae: several species.

Cus·ter /ˈkəstər/, George (Armstrong) (1839–76), US cavalry officer. He served with distinction during the Civil War. In 1876, he was killed, along with all of his men (266) in a clash (popularly known as Custer's Last Stand) with the Sioux Indians at Little Bighorn in Montana.

cus·to·di·an /kəsˈtōdēən/ ▶ **n.** a person who has responsibility for or looks after something: *the custodians of pension and insurance funds.* ■ a person employed to clean and maintain a building.
– DERIVATIVES **cus·to·di·an·ship** /-ˌSHip/ **n.**
– ORIGIN late 18th cent.: from CUSTODY, on the pattern of *guardian.*

cus·to·dy /ˈkəstədē/ ▶ **n.** the protective care or guardianship of someone or something: *the property was placed in the custody of a trustee.* ■ imprisonment: *my father was being* ***taken into custody.*** ■ Law parental responsibility, esp. as allocated to one of two divorcing parents: *he was trying to get* ***custody of*** *their child.*
– DERIVATIVES **cus·to·di·al** /ˌkəˈstōdēəl/ **adj.**
– ORIGIN late Middle English: from Latin *custodia,* from *custos* 'guardian.'

cus·tom /ˈkəstəm/ ▶ **n. 1** a traditional and widely accepted way of behaving or doing something that is specific to a particular society, place, or time: *the old English custom of dancing around the maypole | custom demanded that a person should have gifts for the child.* ■ [in sing.] a thing that one does habitually: *it was my custom to nap for an hour every day.* ■ Law established practice or usage having the force of law or right.
2 chiefly Brit. regular dealings with a shop or business by customers: *if you keep me waiting, I will take my custom elsewhere.*
▶ **adj.** made or done to order for a particular customer: *a custom guitar.*
– ORIGIN Middle English: from Old French *coustume,* based on Latin *consuetudo,* from *consuetus,* past participle of *consuescere* 'accustom,' from *con-* (expressing intensive force) + *suescere* 'become accustomed.'

cus·tom·al ▶ **n.** variant spelling of CUSTUMAL.

cus·tom·ar·i·ly /ˌkəstəˈme(ə)rəlē/ ▶ **adv.** in a way that follows customs or usual practices; usually: *the leaves are customarily used for animal fodder.*

cus·tom·ar·y /ˈkəstəˌmerē/ ▶ **adj.** according to the customs or usual practices associated with a particular society, place, or set of circumstances: *it is* ***customary to*** *mark an occasion like this with a toast.* ■ according to a person's habitual practice: *I put the kettle on for our customary cup of tea.* ■ Law established by or based on custom rather than common law or statute.
▶ **n.** (pl. **customaries**) historical another term for CUSTUMAL.
– DERIVATIVES **cus·tom·ar·i·ness n.**
– ORIGIN late Middle English (as a noun): from medieval Latin *custumarius,* from *custuma,* from Anglo-Norman French *custume* (see CUSTOM).

cus·tom-built ▶ **adj.** another term for CUSTOM-MADE.

cus·tom·er /ˈkəstəmər/ ▶ **n. 1** a person or organization that buys goods or services from a store or business: *Mr. Harrison was a regular customer at the Golden Lion* | [as modifier] *customer service.*
2 a person or thing of a specified kind that one has to deal with: *the fish is a slippery customer and very hard to catch | Jon won over Lucie's father, but her mother is a tough customer.*

cus·tom·er-fac·ing ▶ **adj.** dealing directly with customers: *the programs are particularly valuable in customer-facing environments such as call centers.*

cus·tom house (also **customs house**) ▶ **n.** chiefly historical the office at a port or frontier where customs duty is collected.

cus·tom·ize /ˈkəstəˌmīz/ ▶ **v.** [with obj.] modify (something) to suit a particular individual or task: *the suit can be customized for every skydiving need* | (as adj. **customized**) *many caterers offer private tastings and customized menus.*

cus·tom-made ▶ **adj.** made to a particular customer's order.

cus·toms /ˈkəstəmz/ ▶ **plural n.** the official department that administers and collects the duties levied by a government on imported goods: *cocaine seizures by customs have risen this year* | [as modifier] *a customs officer.* ■ the place at a port, airport, or frontier where officials check incoming goods, travelers, or luggage: *arriving refugees were whisked through customs.* ■ (usu. **customs duties**) the duties levied by a government on imported goods.
– ORIGIN late Middle English: originally in the singular, denoting a customary due paid to a ruler, later duty levied on goods on their way to market.

cus·toms un·ion ▶ **n.** a group of countries that have agreed to charge the same import duties as each other and usually to allow free trade between themselves.

cus·tu·mal /ˈkəstəməl, ˈkəsCHə-/ (also **customal**) ▶ **n.** historical a written account of the customs of a manor or other local community or large establishment.
– ORIGIN late 16th cent.: from medieval Latin *custumale* 'customs book,' neuter of *custumalis,* from *custuma* 'custom.'

cut /kət/ ▶ **v.** (**cuts, cutting**; past and past participle **cut**) [with obj.] **1** make an opening, incision, or wound in (something) with a sharp-edged tool or object: *he cut his big toe on a sharp stone | he* ***cut open*** *MacKay's face with the end of his hockey stick* | [no obj.] figurative *his scorn cut deeper than knives.*
2 remove (something) from something larger by using a sharp implement: *I cut his photograph out of the paper | some prisoners had their right hands* ***cut off.*** ■ informal castrate (an animal, esp. a horse). ■ remove the foreskin of a penis; circumcise. ■ (**cut something out**) make something by cutting: *I cut out some squares of paper.* ■ (**cut something out**) remove, exclude, or stop eating or doing something undesirable: *start today by cutting out fatty foods.* ■ (**cut something out**) separate an animal from the main herd.
3 divide into pieces with a knife or other sharp implement: ***cut*** *the beef* ***into*** *thin slices | he* ***cut*** *his food* ***up*** *into teeny pieces.* ■ make divisions in (something): *land that has been* ***cut up*** *by streams into forested areas.* ■ separate (something) into two; sever: *they cut the rope before he choked.* ■ (**cut something down**) make something, esp. a tree, fall by cutting it through at the base. ■ (**cut someone down**) (of a weapon, bullet, or disease) kill or injure someone: *Barker had been cut down by a sniper's bullet.*
4 make or form (something) by using a sharp tool to remove material: *workmen* ***cut a hole in*** *the pipe.* ■ make or design (a garment) in a particular way: (as adj. **cut**) *an impeccably cut chalk-stripe suit.* ■ make (a path, tunnel, or other route) by excavation, digging, or chopping: *plans to cut a road through a rain forest* | [no obj.] *investigators called for a machete to* ***cut through*** *the bush* | figurative *a large woman with a voice that* ***cut through*** *crowds.*
5 trim or reduce the length of (something, esp. grass or a person's hair or fingernails) by using a sharp implement: *cutting the lawn |* ***cut back*** *all the year's growth to about four leaves.*
6 reduce the amount or quantity of: *buyers will bargain hard to* ***cut the cost of*** *the house they want | I should* ***cut down*** *my sugar intake* | [no obj.] *they've* ***cut back on*** *costs | the state passed a law to cut* ***down on*** *drunk-driving | the paper glut cuts into profits.* ■ abridge (a text, movie, or performance) by removing material: *he had to cut unnecessary additions made to the opening scene.* ■ Computing delete (part of a text or other display) completely or so as to insert a copy of it elsewhere. See also CUT AND PASTE. ■ (in sports) remove (a player) from a team's roster. ■ end or interrupt the provision of (something, esp. power or food supplies): *we resolved to cut oil supplies to territories controlled by the rebels | if the pump develops a fault, the electrical supply is immediately* ***cut off.*** ■ (**cut something off**) block the usual means of access to a place: *the caves were* ***cut off from*** *the outside world by a landslide.* ■ absent oneself deliberately from (something one should normally attend, esp. school): *Robert was cutting class.* ■ switch off (an engine or a light).
7 (of a line) cross or intersect (another line): *the point where the line cuts the vertical axis.* ■ [no obj.] (**cut across**) pass or traverse, esp. so as to shorten one's route: *the following aircraft cut across to join him.* ■ [no obj.] (**cut across**) have an effect regardless of (divisions or boundaries between groups): *subcultures that cut across national and political boundaries.* ■ [no obj.] (**cut along**) informal, dated leave or move hurriedly: *you can cut along now.*
8 dated ignore or refuse to recognize (someone).
9 [no obj., often in imperative] stop filming or recording. ■ move to another shot in a movie: *cut to a dentist's surgery.* ■ [with obj.] make (a movie) into a coherent whole by removing parts or placing them in a different order.
10 make (a sound recording).
11 divide (a pack of playing cards) by lifting a portion from the top, either to reveal or draw a card at random or to place the top portion under the bottom portion.
12 Golf slice (the ball).
13 adulterate (a drug) or dilute (alcohol) by mixing it with another substance: *speed* ***cut with*** *rat poison.*
14 (**cut it**) informal come up to expectations; meet requirements: *this CD player doesn't quite cut it.* [shortened form of the idiom *cut the mustard.*]
▶ **n. 1** an act of cutting, in particular: ■ [in sing.] a haircut: *his hair was in need of a cut.* ■ a stroke or blow given by a sharp-edged implement or by a whip or cane: *he could skin an animal with a single cut of the knife.* ■ a wounding remark or act: *his unkindest cut at Elizabeth was to call her heartless.* ■ a reduction in amount or size: *she took a 20% pay cut | a* ***cut in*** *interest rates.* ■ (in sports) a removal of a player from a team's roster. ■ an act of removing part of a play, movie, or book, esp. to shorten the work or to delete offensive material: *they would not publish the book unless the author was willing to* ***make cuts.*** ■ an immediate transition from one scene to another in a movie. ■ Golf the halfway point of a golf tournament, where half of the players are eliminated. ■ Tennis a stroke made with a sharp horizontal or downward action of the racket, imparting spin.
2 a result of cutting something, in particular: ■ a long narrow incision in the skin made by something sharp. ■ a long narrow opening or incision made in a surface or piece of material: *make a single cut along the top of each potato.* ■ a piece of meat cut from a carcass: *a good lean cut of beef.* ■ [in sing.] informal a share of the profits from something: *the directors are demanding their cut.* ■ a recording of a piece of music: *a cut from his forthcoming album.* ■ a version of a movie after editing: *the director's cut.* ■ a passage cut or dug out, as a railroad cutting or a new channel made for a river or other waterway. ■ a woodcut.
3 [in sing.] the way or style in which something, esp. a garment or someone's hair, is cut: *the elegant cut of his dinner jacket.*
– PHRASES **be cut out for** (or **to be**) [usu. with negative] informal have exactly the right qualities for a particular role, task, or job: *I'm just not cut out to be a policeman.* **a cut above** informal noticeably superior to: *she's a cut above the rest.* **cut and dried** [often with negative] (of a situation) completely settled or decided: *the championship is not as cut and dried as everyone thinks.* [early 18th cent.: originally used to distinguish the herbs of herbalists' shops from growing herbs.] **cut and run** informal make a speedy or sudden departure from an awkward or hazardous situation rather than deal with it. [originally a nautical phrase, meaning 'cut the anchor cable because of some emergency and make sail immediately.'] **cut and thrust** Fencing the use of both the edge and the point of one's sword while fighting. ■ a spirited and rapid interchange of views: *the cut and thrust of political debate.* ■ a situation or sphere of activity regarded as carried out under adversarial conditions: *the ruthless cut and thrust of the business world.* **cut both ways** (of a point or statement) serve both sides of an argument. ■ (of an action or process) have both good and bad effects: *the triumphs of civilization cut both ways.* **cut the corner** take the shortest course by going across and not around a corner. **cut corners** undertake something in what appears to be the easiest, quickest, or cheapest way, esp. by omitting to do something important or ignoring rules. **cut the crap** [often in imperative] vulgar slang get to the point; state the real situation. **cut someone dead** completely ignore someone. **cut a deal** informal come to an arrangement, esp. in business; make a deal. **cut someone down to size** informal deflate someone's exaggerated sense of self-worth. **cut something down to size** reduce the size or power of something, for example an organization, that is regarded as having become too large or powerful. **cut a —— figure** present oneself or appear in a particular way: *David has cut a dashing figure on the international social scene.* **cut from the same cloth** of the same nature; similar: *don't assume all women are cut from the same cloth.* **cut in line** push into a line of people in order to be served or dealt with before one's turn. **cut it fine** see FINE[1]. **cut it out** [usu. in imperative] informal used to ask someone to stop doing or saying something that is annoying or offensive: *I'm sick of that joke; cut it out, can't you?* **cut loose** distance oneself from a person,

group, or system by which one is unduly influenced or on which one is overdependent: *they cut loose from from the factory and started their own.* ■ act without restraint: *consumers want to cut loose and have secret bacchanals.* **cut someone/something loose** (or **free**) free someone or something from something that holds or restricts them: *he'd cut loose the horses.* **cut one's losses** abandon an enterprise or course of action that is clearly going to be unprofitable or unsuccessful before one suffers too much loss or harm. **cut the mustard** informal come up to expectations; reach the required standard: *I didn't cut the mustard as a hockey player.* **cut no ice** informal have no influence or effect: *your holier-than-thou attitude cuts no ice with me.* **cut someone off** (or **down**) **in their prime** bring someone's life or career to an abrupt end while they are at the peak of their abilities. **cut someone/something short** interrupt someone or something; bring an abrupt or premature end to something said or done: *Peter cut him short rudely.* **cut someone to pieces** kill or severely injure someone. ■ totally defeat someone. **cut a** (or **the**) **rug** informal dance, typically in an energetic or accomplished way: *you can cut a rug when dance bands and singers take to the stage.* **cut one's teeth** acquire initial practice or experience of a particular sphere of activity or with a particular organization: *the brothers cut their professional teeth at Lusardi's before starting their own restaurant.* **cut a tooth** (usu. of a baby or child) have a tooth appear through the gum. **cut to the chase** informal come to the point: *cut to the chase—what is it you want us to do?* [*cut* in the sense 'move to another part of the movie,' expressing the notion of ignoring any preliminaries.] **cut your coat according to your cloth** proverb undertake only what you have the money or ability to do and no more. **have one's work cut out** see WORK. **make the cut** Golf equal or better a required score, thus avoiding elimination from the last two rounds of a four-round tournament. **miss the cut** Golf fail to equal or better a required score, thus being eliminated from the last two rounds of a four-round tournament.

– PHRASAL VERBS **cut in 1** interrupt someone while they are speaking: *"It's urgent," Raoul cut in.* ■ dated interrupt a dancing couple to take over from one partner. **2** pull in too closely in front of another vehicle after having overtaken it: *she cut in on a station wagon, forcing the driver to brake.* **3** (of a motor or other mechanical device) begin operating, esp. when triggered automatically by an electrical signal: *emergency generators cut in.* **cut someone in** informal include someone in a deal and give them a share of the profits. **cut into** interrupt the course of: *Victoria's words cut into her thoughts.* **cut someone off** interrupt someone while they are speaking. ■ interrupt someone during a telephone call by breaking the connection: *I listened to prerecorded messages for twenty-three minutes before being cut off.* ■ prevent someone from receiving or being provided with something, esp. power or water: *consumers cut off for nonpayment.* ■ reject someone as one's heir; disinherit someone: *Gabrielle's family cut her off without a penny.* ■ prevent someone from having access to somewhere or someone; isolate someone from something they previously had connections with: *we were cut off from reality.* ■ informal (of a driver) overtake someone and pull in too closely in front of them. **cut out 1** (of a motor or engine) suddenly stop operating. **2** informal (of a person) leave quickly, esp. so as to avoid a boring or awkward situation. **cut someone out** exclude someone: *his mother cut him out of her will.* **cut up 1** informal behave in a mischievous or unruly manner: *kids cutting up in a classroom.* **2** informal (of a horse race) have a particular selection of runners: *the race has cut up badly with no other opposition from England.* **cut someone up** informal criticize someone severely: *my kids cut him up about his appetite all the time.*

– ORIGIN Middle English (probably existing, although not recorded, in Old English); probably of Germanic origin and related to Norwegian *kutte* and Icelandic *kuta* 'cut with a small knife,' *kuti* 'small blunt knife.'

cut-and-come-a·gain ▶ **n.** [usu. as modifier] a garden plant, esp. a green vegetable or a flower, that can be repeatedly cut or harvested: *cut-and-come-again spinach.*

cut-and-cov·er ▶ **n.** a method of building a tunnel by making a cutting, which is then lined and covered over.

cut and paste ▶ **n.** Computing a process in which text or other data is moved from one part of a document and inserted elsewhere.
▶ **v.** [with obj.] move (text or other data) using this technique.

cu·ta·ne·ous /kyo͞oˈtānēəs/ ▶ **adj.** of, relating to, or affecting the skin: *cutaneous pigmentation.*
– ORIGIN late 16th cent.: from modern Latin *cutaneus* (from Latin *cutis* 'skin') + -OUS.

cut·a·way /ˈkətəˌwā/ ▶ **n.** [often as modifier] **1** a coat or jacket with the front cut away below the waist so as to curve back to the tails.
2 a diagram or drawing with some external parts left out to reveal the interior.
3 a shot in a movie that is of a different subject from those to which it is joined in editing.

cutaway jacket

cut·back /ˈkətˌbak/ ▶ **n.** an act or instance of reducing something, typically expenditures: *cutbacks in defense spending.*

cutch /kəCH/ ▶ **n.** see CATECHU.

cut·down /ˈkətˌdoun/ ▶ **n.**
1 a decrease or reduction: [as modifier] *left with a cutdown staff.*
2 Surgery a procedure of cutting into a vein in order to insert a needle or cannula.

cute /kyo͞ot/ ▶ **adj. 1** attractive in a pretty or endearing way: *a cute kitten.* ■ informal sexually attractive.
2 informal clever or cunning, esp. in a self-seeking or superficial way: *I don't want to be cute with you.*
– DERIVATIVES **cute·ly** adv., **cute·ness** n.
– ORIGIN early 18th cent. (in the sense 'clever, shrewd'): shortening of ACUTE.

cute·sy /ˈkyo͞otsē/ ▶ **adj.** informal cute to a sentimental or mawkish extent: *hair pulled back in cutesy little bows.*

cut·ey ▶ **n.** variant spelling of CUTIE.

cut glass ▶ **n.** glass that has been ornamented by having patterns cut into it by grinding and polishing: [as modifier] *a cut-glass vase.*

Cuth·bert, St. /ˈkəTHbərt/ (died 687), English monk. Feast day, March 20.

cu·ti·cle /ˈkyo͞otikəl/ ▶ **n. 1** the outer layer of living tissue, in particular: ■ Botany & Zoology a protective and waxy or hard layer covering the epidermis of a plant, invertebrate, or shell. ■ the outer cellular layer of a hair. ■ Zoology another term for EPIDERMIS.
2 the dead skin at the base of a fingernail or toenail.
– DERIVATIVES **cu·tic·u·lar** /kyo͞oˈtikyələr/ adj.
– ORIGIN late 15th cent. (denoting a membrane of the body): from Latin *cuticula*, diminutive of *cutis* 'skin.'

cut·ie /ˈkyo͞otē/ (also **cutie pie**) ▶ **n.** informal an attractive or endearing person.

cut·in /ˈkyo͞otn/ ▶ **n.** Biochemistry a waxy, water-repellent substance occurring in the cuticle of plants and consisting of highly polymerized esters of fatty acids.
– ORIGIN mid 19th cent.: from CUTIS + -IN[1].

cut-in ▶ **n.** a shot in a movie that is edited into another shot or scene.

cu·tis /ˈkyo͞otəs/ ▶ **n.** Anatomy the true skin or dermis.
– ORIGIN early 17th cent.: from Latin,'skin.'

cut·lass /ˈkətləs/ ▶ **n.** a short sword with a slightly curved blade, formerly used by sailors.
– ORIGIN late 16th cent.: from French *coutelas*, based on Latin *cultellus* 'small knife' (see CUTLER).

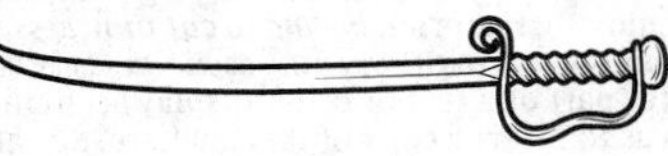

cutlass

cut·lass·fish /ˈkətləsˌfiSH/ ▶ **n.** (pl. **same** or **cutlassfishes**) a long, slender marine fish with sharp teeth and a dorsal fin running the length of the back. ● Family Trichiuridae: several species, including the Atlantic *Trichiurus lepturus* (also called SNAKEFISH), an important food fish in the tropics.

cut·ler /ˈkətlər/ ▶ **n.** a person who makes or sells cutlery.
– ORIGIN Middle English: from Old French *coutelier*, from *coutel* 'knife,' from Latin *cultellus*, diminutive of *culter* 'knife, plowshare.' Compare with COULTER.

cut·ler·y /ˈkətlərē/ ▶ **n. 1** cutting utensils, esp. knives for cutting food.
2 knives, forks, and spoons used for eating or serving food.
– ORIGIN Middle English: from Old French *coutellerie*, from *coutelier* (see CUTLER).

cut·let /ˈkətlət/ ▶ **n.** a portion of sliced meat breaded and served either grilled or fried. ■ a flat croquette of minced meat, nuts, or pulses, typically covered in breadcrumbs and fried.
– ORIGIN early 18th cent.: from French *côtelette*, earlier *costelette*, diminutive of *coste* 'rib,' from Latin *costa*.

cut·line /ˈkətˌlīn/ ▶ **n. 1** the caption to a photograph or other illustration.
2 (in squash) the line above which a served ball must strike the front wall.

cut·off /ˈkətˌôf/ ▶ **adj. 1** of or constituting a limit: *the cutoff date to register is July 2.*
2 (of a device) producing an interruption or cessation of a power or fuel supply: *a cutoff valve.*
3 (of an item of clothing) having been cut short: *a cutoff T-shirt.*
4 (of a person) isolated from or no longer having access to someone or something: *aid to the cutoff troops in the north.*
▶ **n. 1** a point or level that is a designated limit of something: *1 p.m. is the cutoff for being out of the woods.*
2 an act of stopping or interrupting the supply or provision of something: *a cutoff of aid would be a disaster.* ■ a device for producing an interruption or cessation of a power or fuel supply. ■ a sudden drop in amplification or responsiveness of an electric device at a certain frequency: [as modifier] *a cutoff frequency of 8 Hz.* ■ the stopping of the supply of steam to the cylinders of a steam engine when the piston has traveled a set percentage of its stroke.
3 (**cutoffs**) shorts made by cutting off the legs of a pair of jeans or other trousers above or at the knee and leaving the edges unhemmed.
4 a shortcut.
5 Geology a pattern of a meandering stream in which a channel cuts a new course to bypass a meander bend.

cut·out /ˈkətˌout/ ▶ **n. 1** a shape of a person or thing cut out of cardboard or another material. ■ a person perceived as characterless or as lacking in individuality: *this film's protagonists are cardboard cutouts.*
2 a hole cut in something for decoration or to allow the insertion of something else.
3 a device that automatically breaks an electric circuit for safety and either resets itself or can be reset.

cut·o·ver /ˈkətˌōvər/ ▶ **n.** a rapid transition from one phase of a business enterprise or project to another.
▶ **adj.** (of land) having had its saleable timber felled and removed.

cut·purse /ˈkətpərs/ ▶ **n.** archaic term for PICKPOCKET.
– ORIGIN late Middle English: with reference to stealing by cutting purses suspended from a waistband.

cut-rate (also **cut-price**) ▶ **adj.** for sale at a reduced or unusually low price: *cut-rate tickets.* ■ offering goods at such prices: *a cut-rate furniture store.*

cut·scene /ˈkətˌsēn/ ▶ **n.** (in computer games) a scene that develops the story line and is often shown on completion of a certain level, or when the player's character dies.

cut·ter /ˈkətər/ ▶ **n. 1** a person or thing that cuts something, in particular: ■ [often with adj. or modifier] a tool for cutting something, esp. one intended for cutting a particular thing or for producing a particular shape: *a glass cutter* | (**cutters**) *a pair of bolt cutters.* ■ a person who cuts or edits movies. ■ a person in a tailoring establishment who takes measurements and cuts the cloth. ■ a person who reduces or cuts down on something, esp. expenditures: *a determined cutter of costs.*
2 a light, fast coastal patrol boat. ■ a ship's boat used for carrying light stores or passengers. ■ historical a small fore-and-aft-rigged sailing ship with one mast, more than one headsail, and a running bowsprit, used as a fast auxiliary. ■ a yacht with a gaff-rigged mainsail and two foresails.
3 Baseball (also **cut fastball**) a fastball that breaks somewhat on being pitched.
4 a light horse-drawn sleigh.

cut·throat /ˈkətˌTHrōt/ ▶ **n. 1** dated a murderer or other violent criminal.
2 (also **cutthroat trout**) a trout of western North America, with red or orange markings under the jaw. ● *Salmo clarki*, family Salmonidae.
▶ **adj.** (of a competitive situation or activity) fierce and intense; involving the use of ruthless measures: *cutthroat competition led to a lot of bankruptcies* | *the cutthroat world of fashion.* ■ (of a person) using ruthless methods in a competitive situation: *the greedy cutthroat manufacturers he worked for.* ■ Sports relating to or being a game or contest in which each of three players scores individually against the other two. ■ denoting a form of whist (or other card game normally for four) played by three players.

cut·throat ra·zor ▶ **n.** British term for STRAIGHT RAZOR.

cut·throat weav·er (also **cutthroat** or **cutthroat finch**) ▶ **n.** a small, finchlike African bird of the waxbill family, with speckled brown plumage, a conspicuous crimson throat band, and a rufous belly. ● *Amadina fasciata*, family Estrildidae.

cut·ting /ˈkətiNG/ ▶ **n. 1** the action of someone or something that cuts: *the cutting of the cake | tax-cutting.*
2 (often **cuttings**) a piece cut off from something, esp. what remains when something is being trimmed or prepared: *grass cuttings.* ■ a piece cut from a plant for propagation. ■ Brit. a clipping from a newspaper or periodical.
3 an open passage excavated through higher ground for a railroad, road, or canal.
▶ **adj.** capable of cutting something: *the cutting blades of the hedge trimmer.* ■ (esp. of a comment) causing emotional pain; hurtful: *a cutting remark.* ■ (of the wind) bitterly cold.
– DERIVATIVES **cut·ting·ly adv.**

cut·ting edge ▶ **n. 1** the edge of a tool's blade.
2 [in sing.] the latest or most advanced stage in the development of something: *researchers at the cutting edge of molecular biology.*
3 [in sing.] a dynamic or invigorating quality: *the campaign began to lose its cutting edge.* ■ incisiveness and directness of expression: *his wit retains its cutting edge.*
▶ **adj.** (**cutting-edge**) at the latest or most advanced stage of development; innovative or pioneering: *cutting-edge technology.*

cut·ting horse ▶ **n.** a horse trained in separating cattle from a herd.

cut·ting room ▶ **n.** a room in a production studio where film or videotape is cut and edited: [as modifier] *such a scene would end up on the cutting-room floor.*

cut·tle /ˈkətl/ ▶ **n.** a cuttlefish.
– ORIGIN Old English *cudele* 'cuttlefish,' of Germanic origin; related to *codd* 'bag,' with reference to its ink bag.

cut·tle·bone /ˈkətl,bōn/ ▶ **n.** the flattened oval internal skeleton of the cuttlefish, which is made of white, lightweight, chalky material. It is used as a dietary supplement for caged birds and for making casts for precious metal items.

cut·tle·fish /ˈkətl,fisH/ ▶ **n.** (pl. **same** or **cuttlefishes**) a swimming marine mollusk that resembles a broad squid, having eight arms and two long tentacles that are used for grabbing prey. Its internal skeleton is cuttlebone, which it uses for adjusting buoyancy. ● Order Sepioidea, class Cephalopoda: *Sepia* and other genera.
– ORIGIN late 16th cent.: from **CUTTLE** + **FISH**[1].

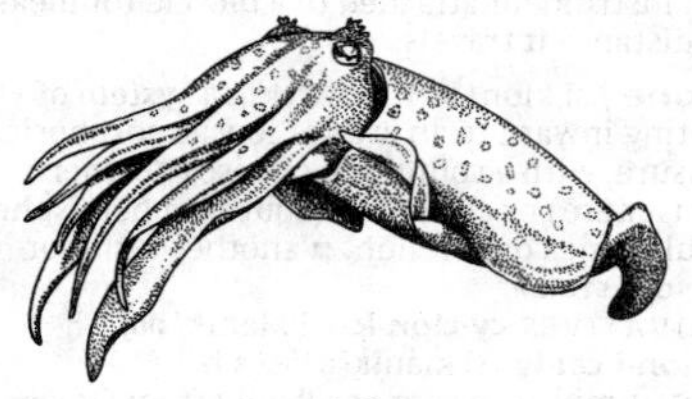

cuttlefish

Cut·ty Sark /särk/ the only survivor of the British tea clippers, launched in 1869 and now preserved as a museum ship at Greenwich, London.
– ORIGIN from Robert Burns's *Tam o' Shanter*, a poem about a Scottish farmer chased by a young witch who wore only her "cutty sark" (= short shift).

cut·ty-stool ▶ **n.** Scottish historical a stool on which an offender was publicly rebuked during a church service.

cut-up (also **cut up**) ▶ **adj. 1** divided into pieces by cutting: *cut-up vegetables.* ■ (of a soft piece of ground) having an uneven surface after the passage of heavy vehicles or animals: *the ground was deeply cut up where the cattle had strayed.*
2 informal (of a person) very distressed: *his girlfriend is dying and he's really cut up about it.*
▶ **n. 1** a film or sound recording made by cutting and editing material from preexisting recordings.
2 (**cutup**) informal a person who is fond of making jokes or playing pranks.

cut·wa·ter /ˈkət,wôtər, -,wätər/ ▶ **n. 1** the forward edge of a ship's prow.
2 a wedge-shaped projection on the pier of a bridge, which divides the flow of water and prevents debris from becoming trapped against the pier.

cut·work /ˈkət,wərk/ ▶ **n.** embroidery or lace with parts cut out and the edges oversewn or filled with needlework designs. ■ appliqué work in which the pattern is cut out and sewn on.

cut·worm /ˈkətwərm/ ▶ **n.** a moth caterpillar that lives in the upper layers of the soil and eats through the stems of young plants at ground level. ● Several species in the family Noctuidae.

cu·vée /k(y)o͞oˈvā/ ▶ **n.** a type, blend, or batch of wine, esp. champagne.
– ORIGIN mid 19th cent.: French,'vatful,' from *cuve* 'cask,' from Latin *cupa.*

cu·vette /kyo͞oˈvet/ ▶ **n.** Biochemistry a straight-sided, optically clear container for holding liquid samples in a spectrophotometer or other instrument.
– ORIGIN early 18th cent.: from French, diminutive of *cuve* 'cask,' from Latin *cupa.*

Cu·vi·er /ko͞oˈvyā/, Georges Léopold Chrétien Frédéric Dagobert, Baron (1769–1832), French naturalist. Cuvier founded the science of paleontology.

cuz /kəz/ (also **'cuz** or **coz**) ▶ **conj.** informal short for **BECAUSE**.

Cuz·co /ˈko͞oskō/ a city in the Andes in southern Peru; pop. 348,900 (est. 2007). It was the capital of the Inca empire until the Spanish conquest in 1533.

CV ▶ **abbr.** ■ cardiovascular. ■ curriculum vitae.

cv. ▶ **abbr.** cultivated variety.

CVS ▶ **abbr.** chorionic villus sampling.

CVT ▶ **abbr.** continuously variable transmission.

cwm /ko͝om, ko͞om/ ▶ **n.** a cirque, esp. one in the mountains of Wales.
– ORIGIN mid 19th cent.: Welsh; related to **COMBE**.

CWO ▶ **abbr.** Chief Warrant Officer.

c.w.o. ▶ **abbr.** cash with order.

cwr ▶ **abbr.** continuous welded rail; railroad track laid in long unbroken strips rather than as short fixed lengths with gaps.

cwt. ▶ **abbr.** hundredweight.

CY ▶ **abbr.** calendar year.

-cy ▶ **suffix 1** denoting state or condition: *bankruptcy.*
2 denoting rank or status: *baronetcy.*
– ORIGIN from Latin *-cia, -tia* and Greek *-k(e)ia, -t(e)ia.*

cy·an /ˈsī,an, ˈsīən/ ▶ **n.** a greenish-blue color, which is one of the primary subtractive colors, complementary to red.
– ORIGIN late 19th cent.: from Greek *kuaneos* 'dark blue.'

cy·an·a·mide /sīˈanəməd, -,mīd/ ▶ **n.** Chemistry a weakly acidic crystalline compound made as an intermediate in the industrial production of ammonia. ● Alternative name: **cyanogen amide**; chem. formula: CH_2N_2. ■ a salt of this containing the anion CN_2^{2-} esp. the calcium salt (**calcium cyanamide**) used as a fertilizer.
– ORIGIN mid 19th cent.: blend of **CYANOGEN** and **AMIDE**.

cy·an·ic /sīˈanik/ ▶ **adj.** rare blue; azure.
– ORIGIN early 19th cent.: from **CYAN** + **-IC**.

cy·an·ic ac·id ▶ **n.** Chemistry a colorless, poisonous, volatile, strongly acidic liquid. ● Chem. formula: HOCN. See also **FULMINIC ACID**.
– DERIVATIVES **cy·a·nate** /ˈsīə,nāt, -nət/ **n.**
– ORIGIN early 19th cent.: from **CYANOGEN**.

cy·a·nide /ˈsīə,nīd/ ▶ **n.** Chemistry a salt or ester of hydrocyanic acid, containing the anion CN^- or the group –CN. The salts are generally extremely toxic. Compare with **NITRILE**. ■ sodium or potassium cyanide used as a poison or in the extraction of gold and silver.
– ORIGIN early 19th cent.: from **CYANOGEN** + **-IDE**.

cy·a·nine /ˈsīə,nēn, -nin/ ▶ **n.** a blue pigment that is a mixture of cobalt blue and Prussian blue.

cy·a·nite /ˈsīə,nīt/ ▶ **n.** variant of **KYANITE**.

cyano- ▶ **comb. form 1** relating to the color blue, esp. dark blue: *cyanosis.*
2 representing **CYANIDE**.
– ORIGIN from Greek *kuan(e)os* 'dark blue.'

cy·a·no·ac·ry·late /,sīənōˈakrə,lāt, sī,anō-/ ▶ **n.** Chemistry any of a class of compounds that are cyanide derivatives of acrylates. They are easily polymerized and are used to make quick-setting adhesives.

Cy·a·no·bac·te·ri·a /,sīənōbakˈtirēə, sī,anō-/ Biology a division of microorganisms that are related to the bacteria but are capable of photosynthesis. They are prokaryotic and represent the earliest known form of life on the earth. ● Class Cyanophyceae, kingdom Eubacteria. ■ (as plural noun **cyanobacteria**) microorganisms of this division. Also called **BLUE-GREEN ALGAE**.
– ORIGIN modern Latin (plural), from Greek *kuaneos* 'dark blue' + plural of **BACTERIUM**.

cy·a·no·co·bal·a·min /,sīənō,kōˈbaləmin, sī,anō-/ ▶ **n.** a vitamin found in foods of animal origin such as liver, fish, and eggs, a deficiency of which can cause pernicious anemia. It contains a cyanide group bonded to the central cobalt atom of a cobalamin molecule. Also called **VITAMIN B12** (see **VITAMIN B**).
– ORIGIN 1950s: from **CYANOGEN** and *cobalamin* (blend of **COBALT** and **VITAMIN**).

cy·a·no·gen /sīˈanəjən/ ▶ **n.** Chemistry a colorless, flammable, highly poisonous gas made by oxidizing hydrogen cyanide. One of the pseudohalogens, cyanogen is an intermediate in fertilizer manufacture. ● Chem. formula: C_2N_2.
– ORIGIN early 19th cent.: from French *cyanogène*, from Greek *kuanos* 'dark blue mineral' + *-gène* (see **-GEN**), so named because it is a constituent of Prussian blue.

cy·a·no·gen·e·sis /,sīənōˈjenəsis, sī,anō-/ ▶ **n.** Botany the production of hydrogen cyanide by certain plants, such as cherry laurel, bracken, and some legumes, as a response to wounding or a deterrent to herbivores.

cy·a·no·gen·ic /,sīənōˈjenik, sī,anō-/ ▶ **adj.** Botany (of a plant) capable of cyanogenesis: *cyanogenic forms.* ■ Biochemistry containing a cyanide group in the molecule.

cy·a·no·hy·drin /,sīənōˈhīdrin, sī,anō-/ ▶ **n.** Chemistry an organic compound containing a carbon atom linked to both a cyanide group and a hydroxyl group.

cy·a·no·phyte /ˈsīənə,fīt, sīˈanə-/ ▶ **n.** Biology a microorganism of the division Cyanobacteria.

cy·a·no·sis /,sīəˈnōsəs/ ▶ **n.** Medicine a bluish discoloration of the skin resulting from poor circulation or inadequate oxygenation of the blood.
– DERIVATIVES **cy·a·not·ic** /,sīəˈnätik/ **adj.**
– ORIGIN mid 19th cent.: modern Latin, from Greek *kuanōsis* 'blueness,' from *kuaneos* 'dark blue.'

cy·an·o·type /ˈsīənə,tīp, sīˈanə-/ ▶ **n.** a photographic blueprint.

cy·ath·i·um /sīˈaTHēəm/ ▶ **n.** (pl. **cyathia** /-ˈaTHēə/) Botany the characteristic inflorescence of the spurges, resembling a single flower. It consists of a cup-shaped involucre of fused bracts enclosing several greatly reduced male flowers and a single female flower.
– ORIGIN late 19th cent.: modern Latin, from Greek *kuathion*, diminutive of *kuathos* 'cup.'

Cyb·e·le /ˈsibəlē/ Mythology a mother goddess worshiped esp. in Phrygia and later in Greece (where she was associated with Demeter), Rome, and the Roman provinces, with her consort Attis.

cy·ber /ˈsībər/ ▶ **adj.** of, relating to, or characteristic of the culture of computers, information technology, and virtual reality: *the cyber age.*
– ORIGIN 1980s: abbreviation of **CYBERNETICS**.

cyber- ▶ **comb. form** relating to electronic communication networks and virtual reality: *cyberpunk | cyberspace.*
– ORIGIN back-formation from **CYBERNETICS**.

WORD TRENDS Cyber- seems to be a thoroughly modern prefix, summoning up images of advanced technology, supercomputers, and virtual reality. However, in striving to be so very up to date it has developed a whiff of the old-fashioned. The word's rise in popularity is part of the problem—it seems to be added to almost anything to give a high-tech twist. The Oxford English Corpus contains examples of *cyberartist, cybertalk,cyberfiction, cyberculture, cyber-economy, cyber-activist, cyberpiracy, cybercriminal, cybercinema,* and so on. Using **cyber-** like this draws attention to the use of technology and the Internet, implying that such a notion is unusual or remarkable. As these resources become an ever more integral part of our lives, the use of computers in almost every aspect of life will be assumed, eventually making the addition of **cyber-** redundant.

cy·ber·at·tack /ˈsībərə,tak/ ▶ **n.** an attempt by hackers to damage or destroy a computer network or system.

cy·ber·ca·fe /ˈsībərka,fā/ (also **cybercafé**) ▶ **n.** a cafe that offers Internet access on computers that it owns, or via Wi-Fi on patrons' computers.

cy·ber·cash /ˈsībər,kasH/ ▶ **n. 1** funds used in electronic financial transactions, esp. over the Internet.
2 money stored on an electronic smart card or in an online credit account.

cy·ber·crime /ˈsībər,krīm/ ▶ **n.** crime conducted via the Internet or some other computer network.

C

C

cy·ber·law /ˈsībərˌlô/ ▶ **n.** laws, or a specific law, relating to Internet and computer offenses, esp. fraud or copyright infringement.

cy·ber·mall /ˈsībərˌmôl/ ▶ **n.** a commercial website through which a range of goods may be purchased; a virtual shopping mall on the Internet.

cy·ber·naut /ˈsībərˌnôt, -ˌnät/ ▶ **n.** Computing a person who wears sensory devices in order to experience virtual reality. ■ a person who uses the Internet.
–ORIGIN 1990s: from **CYBER-**, on the pattern of *astronaut* and *aeronaut*.

cy·ber·net·ics /ˌsībərˈnetiks/ ▶ **plural n.** [treated as sing.] the science of communications and automatic control systems in both machines and living things.
–DERIVATIVES **cy·ber·net·ic adj.**, **cy·ber·ne·ti·cian** /-nəˈtiSHən/ **n.**, **cy·ber·net·i·cist** /-ˈnetəsəst/ **n.**
–ORIGIN 1940s: from Greek *kubernētēs* 'steersman,' from *kubernan* 'to steer.'

cy·ber·pet /ˈsībərˌpet/ ▶ **n.** an electronic toy that simulates a real pet and with which human interaction is possible. Also called **DIGIPET** or **VIRTUAL PET**.

cy·ber·pho·bi·a /ˌsībərˈfōbēə/ ▶ **n.** extreme or irrational fear of computers or technology.
–DERIVATIVES **cy·ber·phobe** /ˈsībərˌfōb/ **n.**, **cy·ber·pho·bic** /-ˈfōbik/ **adj. & n.**

cy·ber·porn /ˈsībərˌpôrn/ ▶ **n.** pornography accessed via the Internet.

cy·ber·punk /ˈsībərˌpəNGk/ ▶ **n.** a genre of science fiction set in a lawless subculture of an oppressive society dominated by computer technology.

cy·ber·sex /ˈsībərˌseks/ ▶ **n.** sexual arousal using computer technology, esp. by wearing virtual reality equipment or by exchanging messages with another person via the Internet.

cy·ber·shop /ˈsībərˌSHäp/ ▶ **v.** (**cybershops**, **cybershopping**, **cybershopped**) [no obj.] (often as noun **cybershopping**) purchase or shop for goods and services on a website.
▶ **n.** (also **cyberstore**) a website that sells or provides information about retail goods or services.

cy·ber·space /ˈsībərˌspās/ ▶ **n.** the notional environment in which communication over computer networks occurs.

cy·ber·squat·ting /ˈsībərˌskwätiNG/ ▶ **n.** the practice of registering names, esp. well-known company or brand names, as Internet domains, in the hope of reselling them at a profit.
–DERIVATIVES **cy·ber·squat·ter n.**

cy·ber·stalk·ing /ˈsībərˌstôkiNG/ ▶ **n.** the repeated use of electronic communications to harass or frighten someone, for example by sending threatening e-mails.
–DERIVATIVES **cy·ber·stalk·er n.**

cy·ber·store /-ˌstôr/ ▶ **n.** another term for **CYBERSHOP**.

cy·ber·ter·ror·ism /ˌsībərˈterəˌrizəm/ ▶ **n.** the politically motivated use of computers and information technology to cause severe disruption or widespread fear in society: *a bill that would make it easier for law enforcement to wiretap computers and combat cyberterrorism*.
–DERIVATIVES **cy·ber·ter·ror·ist n.**

cy·ber·war /ˈsībərˌwôr/ ▶ **n.** the use of computers to disrupt the activities of an enemy country, esp. the deliberate attacking of communication systems.

cy·borg /ˈsīˌbôrg/ ▶ **n.** a fictional or hypothetical person whose physical abilities are extended beyond normal human limitations by mechanical elements built into the body.
–ORIGIN 1960s: blend of **CYBER-** and **ORGANISM**.

cy·brar·i·an /sīˈbre(ə)rēən/ ▶ **n.** a librarian or researcher who uses the Internet as an information resource.
–ORIGIN 1990s: blend of *cyber-* and *librarian*.

cy·cad /ˈsīkəd, ˈsīˌkad/ ▶ **n.** a palmlike plant of tropical and subtropical regions, bearing large male or female cones. Cycads were abundant during the Triassic and Jurassic eras, but have since been in decline. ● Class Cycadopsida, subdivision Gymnospermae: twenty species in the genus *Cycas* and family Cycadaceae.
–ORIGIN mid 19th cent.: from modern Latin *Cycas*, *Cycad-* (order name), from supposed Greek *kukas*, scribal error for *koikas*, plural of *koix* 'Egyptian palm.'

Cyc·la·des /ˈsikləˌdēz/ a large group of islands in the southern Aegean Sea, regarded in antiquity as circling around the sacred island of Delos. Greek name **KIKLÁDHES**.
–ORIGIN Latin, based on Greek *kuklos* 'circle.'

Cy·clad·ic /sīˈkladik, sə-/ ▶ **adj.** of or relating to the Cyclades. ■ Archaeology of, relating to, or denoting a Bronze Age civilization that flourished in the Cyclades, dated to *c.*3000–1050 BC. ■ (as noun **the Cycladic**) the Cycladic culture or period.

cy·cla·mate /ˈsīkləˌmāt, -mət/ ▶ **n.** Chemistry a salt of a synthetic acid which is a cyclohexyl derivative of sulfamic acid. Sodium and calcium cyclamates were formerly used as artificial sweeteners.
–ORIGIN 1950s: contraction of *cyclohexylsulphamate*.

cy·cla·men /ˈsīkləmən, ˈsik-/ ▶ **n.** (pl. **same** or **cyclamens**) a European plant of the primrose family, having pink, red, or white flowers with backward-curving petals and widely grown as a winter-flowering houseplant. ● Genus *Cyclamen*, family Primulaceae: several species. ■ a pinkish-purple color.
–ORIGIN modern Latin, from Latin *cyclaminos*, from Greek *kuklaminos*, perhaps from *kuklos* 'circle,' with reference to its bulbous roots.

cy·cle /ˈsīkəl/ ▶ **n. 1** [often with adj. or noun modifier] a series of events that are regularly repeated in the same order: *the boom and slump periods of a trade cycle*. ■ the period of time taken to complete a single sequence of such events: *the cells are shed over a cycle of twenty-eight days*. ■ technical a recurring series of successive operations or states, as in the working of an internal combustion engine, or in the alternation of an electric current or a wave: *the familiar four cycles of intake, combustion, ignition, and exhaust*. ■ Biology a recurring series of events or metabolic processes in the lifetime of a plant or animal: *the storks' breeding cycle*. ■ Biochemistry a series of successive metabolic reactions in which one of the products is regenerated and reused. ■ Ecology the movement of a simple substance through the soil, rocks, water, atmosphere, and living organisms of the earth. See **CARBON CYCLE, NITROGEN CYCLE**. ■ Computing a single set of hardware operations, esp. that by which memory is accessed and an item is transferred to or from it, to the point at which the memory may be accessed again. ■ Physics a cycle per second; one hertz.
2 a complete set or series: *the painting is one of a cycle of seven*. ■ a series of songs, stories, plays, or poems composed around a particular theme and usually intended to be performed or read in sequence: *Wagner's Ring Cycle*.
3 a bicycle or tricycle. ■ [in sing.] a ride on a bicycle: *a 112-mile cycle*.
▶ **v.** [no obj.] **1** ride a bicycle: *she cycled to work every day*.
2 move in or follow a regularly repeated sequence of events: *economies cycle regularly between boom and slump*.
–ORIGIN late Middle English: from Old French, from late Latin *cyclus*, from Greek *kuklos* 'circle.'

cy·cle of e·ro·sion ▶ **n.** Geology, dated an idealized course of landscape evolution, passing from youthful stages, which are marked by steep gradients, to old age, when the landscape is reduced to a peneplain.

cy·clic /ˈsīklik, ˈsik-/ ▶ **adj. 1** occurring in cycles; regularly repeated: *the cyclic pattern of the last two decades*. ■ Mathematics (of a group) having the property that each element of the group can be expressed as a power of one particular element. ■ relating to or denoting a musical or literary composition with a recurrent theme or structural device.
2 Mathematics of or relating to a circle or other closed curve. ■ Geometry (of a polygon) having all its vertices lying on a circle. ■ Chemistry (of a compound) having a molecular structure containing one or more closed rings of atoms. ■ Botany (of a flower) having its parts arranged in whorls.
–ORIGIN late 18th cent.: from French *cyclique* or Latin *cyclicus*, from Greek *kuklikos*, from *kuklos* 'circle.'

cy·cli·cal /ˈsīklik(ə)l, ˈsik-/ ▶ **adj.** occurring in cycles; recurrent: *the cyclical nature of the cement industry*.
–DERIVATIVES **cy·cli·cal·ly** /-ik(ə)lē/ **adv.**

cy·cli·cals /ˈsīklikəlz, ˈsik-/ ▶ **plural n.** stocks in cyclical companies (those whose success varies with the seasonal or economic cycle).

cy·clic AMP (abbr.: **cAMP**) ▶ **n.** Biochemistry a cyclic form of adenosine monophosphate (adenylic acid) that plays a major role in controlling many enzyme-catalyzed processes in living cells.

cy·clic GMP (abbr.: **cGMP**) ▶ **n.** a cyclic version of the nucleotide guanosine monophosphate. In cellular metabolism, it is a secondary messenger affecting cell growth and division.

cy·clic re·dun·dan·cy check (also **cyclic redundancy code**) (abbr.: **CRC**) ▶ **n.** Computing a code added to data that is used to detect errors occurring during transmission, storage, or retrieval.

cy·clin /ˈsīklən/ ▶ **n.** Biochemistry any of a number of proteins associated with the cycle of cell division that are thought to initiate certain processes of mitosis.
–ORIGIN 1980s: from **CYCLE** + **-IN**[1].

cy·cling /ˈsīk(ə)liNG/ ▶ **n.** the sport or activity of riding a bicycle. Bicycle racing has three main forms: road racing (typically over long distances), track racing (on an oval track), and cyclocross (over rough, open country).

Cy·cli·oph·o·ra /ˌsiklēˈäfərə, ˌsī-/ Zoology a phylum established for a minute marine invertebrate (*Symbion pandora*) discovered in the 1990s attached to the mouthparts of lobsters. It is related to the phyla Bryozoa and Entoprocta.
–ORIGIN modern Latin (plural), from Greek *kuklios* 'circular' + *pherein* 'to bear.'

cy·clist /ˈsīk(ə)list/ ▶ **n.** a person who rides a bicycle.

cy·clize /ˈsīk(ə)ˌlīz/ ▶ **v.** Chemistry undergo or cause to undergo a reaction in which one part of a molecule becomes linked to another to form a closed ring.
–DERIVATIVES **cy·cli·za·tion** /ˌsīk(ə)ləˈzāSHən/ **n.**

cyclo- ▶ **comb. form 1** circular: *cyclorama*.
2 relating to a cycle or cycling: *cyclocross*.
3 cyclic: *cycloparaffin*.
–ORIGIN from Greek *kuklos* 'circle,' or directly from **CYCLE** or **CYCLIC**.

cy·clo·ad·di·tion /ˌsīklōəˈdiSHən/ ▶ **n.** Chemistry an addition reaction in which a cyclic molecule is formed.

cy·clo·al·kane /ˌsīklōˈalˌkān/ ▶ **n.** Chemistry another term for **CYCLOPARAFFIN**.

cy·clo·cross /ˈsīkləˌkrôs/ ▶ **n.** cross-country racing on bicycles.

cy·clo·hex·ane /ˌsīklōˈhekˌsān/ ▶ **n.** Chemistry a colorless, flammable liquid cycloparaffin obtained from petroleum or by hydrogenating benzene, and used as a solvent and paint remover. ● Chem. formula: C_6H_{12}.

cy·clo·hex·yl /ˌsīkləˈheksəl/ ▶ **n.** [as modifier] Chemistry of or denoting the cyclic hydrocarbon radical $-C_6H_{11}$, derived from cyclohexane.

cy·cloid /ˈsīˌkloid/ ▶ **n.** Mathematics a curve (resembling a series of arches) traced by a point on a circle being rolled along a straight line.
–DERIVATIVES **cy·cloi·dal** /sīˈkloidl/ **adj.**
–ORIGIN mid 17th cent.: from Greek *kukloeidēs* 'circular,' from *kuklos* 'circle.'

cy·clom·e·ter /sīˈklämətər/ ▶ **n. 1** an instrument for measuring circular arcs.
2 an instrument attached to a bicycle for measuring the distance it travels.

cy·clone /ˈsīˌklōn/ ▶ **n.** Meteorology a system of winds rotating inward to an area of low atmospheric pressure, with a counterclockwise (northern hemisphere) or clockwise (southern hemisphere) circulation; a depression. ■ another term for **TROPICAL STORM**.
–DERIVATIVES **cy·clon·ic** /sīˈklänik/ **adj.**, **cy·clon·i·cal·ly** /sīˈklänik(ə)lē/ **adv.**
–ORIGIN mid 19th cent.: probably from Greek *kuklōma* 'wheel, coil of a snake,' from *kuklos* 'circle.' The change of spelling from *-m* to *-n* is unexplained.

cy·clo·par·af·fin /ˌsīklōˈparəfin/ ▶ **n.** Chemistry a hydrocarbon with a molecule containing a ring of carbon atoms joined by single bonds.

cy·clo·pe·an /ˌsīkləˈpēən, sīˈklōpēən/ (also **cyclopian**) ▶ **adj. 1** denoting a type of ancient masonry made with massive irregular blocks: *cyclopean stone walls*. [by association with the great size of the Cyclops.]
2 of or resembling a Cyclops: *a cyclopean eye*.

cy·clo·pe·di·a /ˌsīkləˈpēdēə/ (also **cyclopaedia**) ▶ **n.** archaic (except in book titles) an encyclopedia: *Bailey's Cyclopedia of Horticulture*.
–DERIVATIVES **cy·clo·pe·dic** /-ˈpēdik/ **adj.**
–ORIGIN late 17th cent.: shortening of **ENCYCLOPEDIA**.

cy·clo·pen·ta·di·ene /ˌsīkləˌpentəˈdīēn, ˌsiklə-/ ▶ **n.** a colorless toxic liquid derived from the distillation of coal tar, insoluble in water, soluble in alcohol, and used in the manufacture of insecticides and resins.

cy·clo·phos·pha·mide /ˌsīklōˈfäsfəˌmīd/ ▶ **n.** Medicine a synthetic cytotoxic drug used in treating leukemia and lymphoma and as an immunosuppressive agent.

cy·clo·ple·gia /ˌsīkləˈplēj(ē)ə/ ▶ **n.** paralysis of the ciliary muscle of the eye.

cy·clo·pro·pane /ˌsīklōˈprōˌpān/ ▶ **n.** Chemistry a flammable, gaseous synthetic compound whose molecule contains a ring of three carbon atoms. It has some use as a general anesthetic. ● Chem. formula: C_3H_6.

Cy·clops /ˈsīˌkläps/ ▶ **n. 1** (pl. **Cyclops** or **Cyclopes** /sīˈklōpēz/) Greek Mythology a member of a race of savage one-eyed giants. In the *Odyssey*, Odysseus escaped death by blinding the Cyclops Polyphemus. **2** (**cyclops**) a minute predatory freshwater crustacean which has a cylindrical body with a single central eye. ● Genus *Cyclops* and other genera, order Cyclopoida.
– ORIGIN via Latin from Greek *Kuklōps*, literally 'round-eyed,' from *kuklos* 'circle' + *ōps* 'eye.'

cy·clo·ram·a /ˌsīkləˈramə, -ˈrämə/ ▶ **n.** a circular picture of a 360° scene, viewed from inside. ■ a cloth stretched tight in an arc around the back of a stage set, often used to depict the sky.
– DERIVATIVES **cy·clo·ram·ic** /-ˈramik/ **adj.**
– ORIGIN mid 19th cent.: from CYCLO-, on the pattern of words such as *panorama*.

cy·clo·spo·rine /ˌsīkləˈspôrin, -ˌēn/ (also **cyclosporin A**, **cyclosporin**) ▶ **n.** Medicine a drug with immunosuppressive properties used to prevent the rejection of grafts and transplants. A cyclic peptide, it is obtained from a fungus. ● This drug is obtained from the fungus *Trichoderma polysporum*.
– ORIGIN 1970s: from CYCLO- + *-sporin* (from Latin *spora* 'spore') + -IN[1].

cy·clo·stome /ˈsīkləˌstōm/ ▶ **n.** Zoology an eellike, jawless vertebrate with a round sucking mouth, formerly included in a group with the lampreys and hagfishes. ● Subclass Cyclostomata, now incorporated in the superclass Agnatha.
– ORIGIN mid 19th cent.: from CYCLO- + Greek *stoma* 'mouth.'

cy·clo·style /ˈsīkləˌstīl/ ▶ **n.** an early device for duplicating handwriting, in which a pen with a small toothed wheel pricks holes in a sheet of waxed paper, which is then used as a stencil.
▶ **v.** [with obj.] (usu. as adj. **cyclostyled**) duplicate with such a device: *a cyclostyled leaflet*.
– ORIGIN late 19th cent.: from CYCLO- 'circular' + the noun STYLE.

cy·clo·thy·mi·a /ˌsīkləˈTHīmēə/ ▶ **n.** Psychiatry, dated a mental state characterized by marked swings of mood between depression and elation; manic-depressive tendency.
– DERIVATIVES **cy·clo·thy·mic** /-ˈTHīmik/ **adj.**
– ORIGIN 1920s: from CYCLO- + Greek *thumos* 'temper.'

cy·clo·tron /ˈsīkləˌträn/ ▶ **n.** Physics an apparatus in which charged atomic and subatomic particles are accelerated by an alternating electric field while following an outward spiral or circular path in a magnetic field.

cy·der ▶ **n.** archaic spelling of CIDER.

cyg·net /ˈsignət/ ▶ **n.** a young swan.
– ORIGIN late Middle English: from Anglo-Norman French *cignet*, diminutive of Old French *cigne* 'swan,' based on Latin *cycnus*, from Greek *kuknos*.

Cyg·nus /ˈsignəs/ Astronomy a prominent northern constellation (the Swan), said to represent a flying swan that was the form adopted by Zeus on one occasion. It contains the bright star Deneb. ■ (as genitive **Cygni** /ˈsignē/) used with a preceding letter or numeral to designate a star in this constellation: *the star Delta Cygni*.
– ORIGIN Latin.

cyl. ▶ **abbr.** cylinder.

cyl·in·der /ˈsiləndər/ ▶ **n.** a solid geometric figure with straight parallel sides and a circular or oval section. ■ a solid or hollow body, object, or part with such a shape. ■ a piston chamber in a steam or internal combustion engine. ■ a cylindrical container for liquefied gas under pressure. ■ a rotating metal roller in a printing press. ■ Archaeology a cylinder seal.
– DERIVATIVES **cy·lin·dric** /səˈlindrik/ **adj.**, **cy·lin·dri·cal** /səˈlindrikəl/ **adj.**, **cy·lin·dri·cal·ly** /səˈlindrik(ə)lē/ **adv.**
– ORIGIN late 16th cent.: from Latin *cylindrus*, from Greek *kulindros* 'roller,' from *kulindein* 'to roll.'

cyl·in·der block ▶ **n.** see BLOCK (sense 1 of the noun).

cyl·in·der head ▶ **n.** the end cover of a cylinder in an internal combustion engine, against which the piston compresses the cylinder's contents.

cyl·in·der lin·er ▶ **n.** see LINER[2].

cyl·in·der lock ▶ **n.** a lock with the keyhole and tumbler mechanism contained in a cylinder.

cyl·in·der seal ▶ **n.** Archaeology a small, barrel-shaped stone object with a hole down the center and an incised design or cuneiform inscription. It was originally rolled on clay when soft to indicate ownership or to authenticate a document and was used chiefly in Mesopotamia from the late 4th to the 1st millennium BC.

cyl·in·droid /ˈsilənˌdroid/ ▶ **n.** a figure or body resembling a cylinder.
▶ **adj.** resembling a cylinder in shape.

cy·ma /ˈsīmə/ ▶ **n.** (pl. **cymas** or **cymae** /-mē, -mī/) **1** Architecture a cornice molding with an S-shaped cross section. Compare with OGEE. **2** Botany variant spelling of CYME.
– ORIGIN mid 16th cent.: modern Latin, from Greek *kuma* 'wave or wavy molding.'

cym·bal /ˈsimbəl/ ▶ **n.** a musical instrument consisting of a slightly concave round brass plate that is either struck against another one or struck with a stick to make a ringing or clashing sound.
– DERIVATIVES **cym·bal·ist** /-ist/ **n.**
– ORIGIN Old English, from Latin *cymbalum*, from Greek *kumbalon*, from *kumbē* 'cup'; readopted in Middle English from Old French *cymbale*.

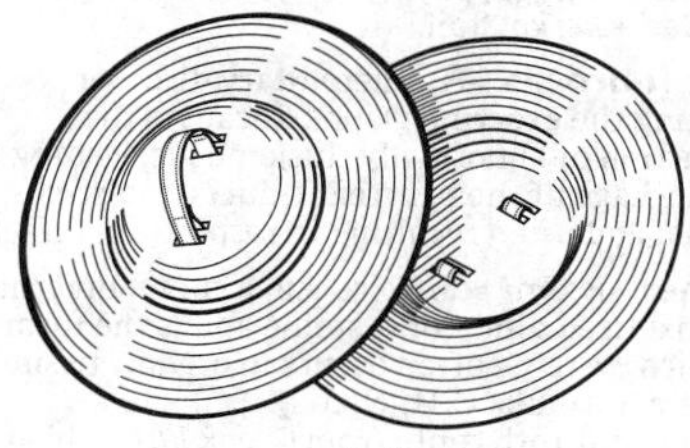
cymbals

cym·ba·lom /ˈsimbələm/ (also **cimbalom**) ▶ **n.** a large Hungarian dulcimer.
– ORIGIN late 19th cent.: from Hungarian, from Italian *cembalo*, *cimbalo*, from Latin *cymbalum* (see CYMBAL).

Cym·be·line /ˈsimbəˌlēn/ (also **Cunobelinus** /ˌk(y)o͞onōbəˈlīnəs/) (died *c.*AD 42), English chieftain. A powerful ruler, he made the town of Camulodunum (Colchester) his capital and established a mint.

cym·bid·i·um /ˌsimˈbidēəm/ ▶ **n.** (pl. **cymbidiums**) a tropical orchid with long, narrow leaves and arching stems bearing several flowers, growing chiefly as an epiphyte from Asia to Australasia and widely cultivated for boutonnières. ● Genus *Cymbidium*, family Orchidaceae.
– ORIGIN modern Latin, from Greek *kumbē* 'cup.'

cyme /sīm/ ▶ **n.** Botany a flower cluster with a central stem bearing a single terminal flower that develops first, the other flowers in the cluster developing as terminal buds of lateral stems. Compare with RACEME.
– DERIVATIVES **cy·mose** /ˈsīˌmōs/ **adj.**
– ORIGIN early 18th cent. (denoting the unopened head of a plant): from French, literally 'summit,' from a popular variant of Latin *cyma*.

cy·moid /ˈsīˌmoid/ ▶ **adj.** resembling a cyma or a cyme.

Cym·raeg /kəmˈrīg/ ▶ **n.** the Welsh language.
– ORIGIN Welsh.

Cym·ric /ˈkəmrik/ ▶ **adj.** Welsh in language or culture.
▶ **n.** the Welsh language.
– ORIGIN mid 19th cent.: from Welsh *Cymru* 'Wales,' *Cymry* 'the Welsh,' + -IC.

Cym·ru /ˈkəmrē/ Welsh name for WALES.

Cyn·e·wulf /ˈkinəˌwo͝olf, ˈko͞on-/ (late 8th–9th centuries), Anglo-Saxon poet. Four poems are attributed to him: *Juliana*, *Elene*, *The Fates of the Apostles*, and *Christ II*.

cyn·ic /ˈsinik/ ▶ **n. 1** a person who believes that people are motivated purely by self-interest rather than acting for honorable or unselfish reasons: *some cynics thought that the controversy was all a publicity stunt*. ■ a person who questions whether something will happen or whether it is worthwhile: *the cynics were silenced when the factory opened*. **2** (**Cynic**) a member of a school of ancient Greek philosophers founded by Antisthenes, marked by an ostentatious contempt for ease and pleasure. The movement flourished in the 3rd century BC and revived in the 1st century AD.
– ORIGIN mid 16th cent. (sense 2): from Latin *cynicus*, from Greek *kunikos*; probably originally from *Kunosarges*, the name of a gymnasium where Antisthenes taught, but popularly taken to mean 'doglike, churlish,' *kuōn*, *kun-* 'dog' becoming a nickname for a Cynic.

cyn·i·cal /ˈsinikəl/ ▶ **adj. 1** believing that people are motivated by self-interest; distrustful of human sincerity or integrity: *her cynical attitude*. ■ doubtful as to whether something will happen or whether it is worthwhile: *most residents are cynical about efforts to clean mobsters out of their city*. ■ contemptuous; mocking: *he gave a cynical laugh*. **2** concerned only with one's own interests and typically disregarding accepted or appropriate standards in order to achieve them: *a cynical manipulation of public opinion*.
– DERIVATIVES **cyn·i·cal·ly** /-ik(ə)lē/ **adv.**

cyn·i·cism /ˈsinəˌsizəm/ ▶ **n. 1** an inclination to believe that people are motivated purely by self-interest; skepticism: *public cynicism about politics*. ■ an inclination to question whether something will happen or whether it is worthwhile; pessimism: *cynicism about the future*. **2** (**Cynicism**) a school of ancient Greek philosophers, the Cynics.

cyno- ▶ **comb. form** of or relating to dogs: *cynodont*.
– ORIGIN from Greek *kuōn*, *kun-* 'dog.'

cyn·o·dont /ˈsīnəˌdänt/ ▶ **n.** a carnivorous, mammallike fossil reptile of the late Permian and Triassic periods, with well-developed, specialized teeth. ● Suborder Cynodontia, order Therapsida: several families.
– ORIGIN late 19th cent.: from Greek *kuōn*, *kun-* 'dog' + *odous*, *odont-* 'tooth.'

cy·no·sure /ˈsīnəˌSHo͝or, ˈsin-/ ▶ **n.** [in sing.] a person or thing that is the center of attention or admiration: *the Queen was the cynosure of all eyes*.
– ORIGIN late 16th cent.: from French, or from Latin *cynosura*, from Greek *kunosoura* 'dog's tail' (also 'Ursa Minor'), from *kuōn*, *kun-* 'dog' + *oura* 'tail.' The term originally denoted the constellation Ursa Minor, or the star Polaris that it contains, long used as a guide by navigators.

cy·pher ▶ **n.** variant spelling of CIPHER.

cy·pher·punk /ˈsīfərˌpəNGk/ ▶ **n.** a person who uses encryption when accessing a computer network in order to ensure privacy, esp. from government authorities.
– ORIGIN 1990s: on the pattern of *cyberpunk*.

cy·pres /sēˈprā/ ▶ **adv. & adj.** Law as near as possible to the testator's or donor's intentions when these cannot be precisely followed.
– ORIGIN early 19th cent.: from a late Anglo-Norman French variant of French *si près* 'so near.'

Cy·press /ˈsīprəs/ a city in south central California, southeast of Los Angeles; pop. 47,123 (est. 2008).

cy·press /ˈsīprəs/ ▶ **n.** (also **cypress tree**) an evergreen coniferous tree with small, rounded, woody cones and flattened shoots bearing small, scalelike leaves. ● *Cupressus*, *Chamaecyparis*, and other genera, family Cupressaceae: many species, including the columnar **Italian cypress** (*Cupressus sempervirens*), common throughout southern Europe. See also LAWSON CYPRESS. ■ a tree of this type, or branches from it, as a symbol of mourning. ■ used in names of similar coniferous trees of other families, e.g., **bald cypress**.
– ORIGIN Middle English: from Old French *cipres*, from late Latin *cypressus*, from Greek *kuparissos*.

cy·press knees ▶ **plural n.** the cone-shaped exposed growths on the buttress roots of a bald cypress.

Cyp·ri·an, St. /ˈsiprēən/ (died 258), Carthaginian bishop and martyr. Feast day, September 16 or 26.

cy·pri·nid /ˈsiprənid/ ▶ **n.** Zoology a fish of the minnow (or carp) family (Cyprinidae).
– ORIGIN late 19th cent.: from modern Latin *Cyprinidae* (plural), based on Greek *kuprinos* 'carp.'

cyp·ri·noid /ˈsiprəˌnoid/ Zoology ▶ **n.** a fish of a large group that includes the carps, suckers, and loaches, and (in some classification schemes) the characins. ● Order Cypriniformes or superfamily Cyprinoidea.
▶ **adj.** of or relating to fish of this group.
– ORIGIN mid 19th cent.: from modern Latin *Cyprinoidea*, based on Latin *cyprinus* 'carp' (from Greek *kuprinos*).

Cyp·ri·ot /ˈsiprēət, -ˌät/ ▶ **n. 1** a native or inhabitant of Cyprus. **2** the dialect of Greek used in Cyprus.
▶ **adj.** of or relating to Cyprus or its people or the Greek dialect used there.
– ORIGIN from Greek *Kupriōtes*, from *Kupros* 'Cyprus.'

cyp·ri·pe·di·um /ˌsiprəˈpēdēəm/ ▶ **n.** (pl. **cypripediums**) an orchid of a genus that comprises the lady's slippers. ● Genus *Cypripedium*, family Orchidaceae.
– ORIGIN modern Latin, from Greek *Kupris* 'Aphrodite' + *pedilon* 'slipper.'

Cy·prus /ˈsīprəs/ an island country in southeastern Europe, in the eastern Mediterranean Sea, about 50 miles (80 km) south of the Turkish coast; pop. 1,084,700 (est. 2009); capital, Nicosia; official languages, Greek and Turkish.

C

A Greek colony in ancient times, Cyprus was held by the Turks from 1571 until 1878, when it was placed under British administration. After virtual civil war between the Greek Cypriots (some of whom favor enosis or union with Greece) and the Turkish Cypriots, Cyprus became an independent Commonwealth of Nations republic in 1960.
In 1974, Turkish forces took over the northern part of the island, which proclaimed itself the independent Turkish Republic of Northern Cyprus in 1983 and effectively divided the island between the Greek and Turkish communities. The Greek Cypriot-controlled Republic of Cyprus joined the EU in May 2004.

cyp·se·la /ˈsipsələ/ ▶ **n.** (pl. **cypselae** /-lē/) Botany a dry, single-seeded fruit formed from a double ovary, of which only one develops into a seed, as in the daisy family.
– ORIGIN late 19th cent.: modern Latin, from Greek *kupselē* 'hollow vessel.'

Cyr·a·no de Ber·ge·rac /ˈsirənō də ˈbərZHəˌrak, ˈberZHˌrak/, Savinien (1619–55), French soldier, duelist, and writer. He is chiefly remembered for the large number of duels that he fought (many because of his proverbially large nose) as immortalized in *Cyrano de Bergerac* (1897), a play by Edmond Rostand.

Cyr·e·na·ic /ˌsirəˈnāik/ ▶ **adj.** of or denoting the hedonistic school of philosophy, which was founded *c.*400 BC by Aristippus the Elder of Cyrene and which holds that pleasure is the highest good and that virtue is to be equated with the ability to enjoy.
▶ **n.** a follower of this school of philosophy.
– DERIVATIVES **Cyr·e·na·i·cism** /-ˈnāəˌsizəm/ **n.**

Cyr·e·na·i·ca /ˌsirəˈnāəkə/ a region in northeastern Libya that borders on the Mediterranean Sea and was settled by the Greeks *c.*640 BC.

Cy·re·ne /sīˈrēnē/ an ancient Greek city in North Africa, near the coast in Cyrenaica.

Cyr·il, St. /ˈsirəl/ (826–869), Greek missionary. The invention of the Cyrillic alphabet is named for him. Feast day (in the Eastern Church) May 11; (in the Western Church) February 14.

Cy·ril·lic /səˈrilik/ ▶ **adj.** denoting the alphabet used by many Slavic peoples, chiefly those with a historical allegiance to the Orthodox Church. Ultimately derived from Greek uncials, it is now used for Russian, Bulgarian, Serbian, Ukrainian, and some other Slavic languages.
▶ **n.** the Cyrillic alphabet.
– ORIGIN early 19th cent.: named after St. *Cyril* (see CYRIL, ST.).

Cyr·il of Al·ex·an·dri·a, St. (died 444), doctor of the Church and patriarch of Alexandria. He is best known for his vehement opposition to the views of **Nestorius**, the patriarch of Constantinople. Feast day, February 9.

Cy·rus[1] /ˈsīrəs/ (died *c.*530 BC), king of Persia 559–530 BC; founder of the Achaemenid dynasty; father of Cambyses; known as **Cyrus the Great**. He defeated the Median empire in 550 BC and went on to conquer Asia Minor, Babylonia, Syria, Palestine, and most of the Iranian plateau. He is said to have ruled with wisdom and moderation, maintaining good relations with the Jews (whom he freed from the Babylonian Captivity) and the Phoenicians.

Cy·rus[2] (died 401 BC), Persian prince; known as **Cyrus the Younger**. On the death of his father, **Darius II**, in 405 BC, Cyrus led an army of mercenaries against his elder brother, who had succeeded to the throne as Artaxerxes II.

cyst /sist/ ▶ **n.** Biology in an animal or plant, a thin-walled, hollow organ or cavity containing a liquid secretion; a sac, vesicle, or bladder. ■ Medicine in the body, a membranous sac or cavity of abnormal character containing fluid. ■ a tough protective capsule enclosing the larva of a parasitic worm or the resting stage of an organism.
– ORIGIN early 18th cent.: from late Latin *cystis*, from Greek *kustis* 'bladder.'

cys·tec·to·my /sisˈtektəmē/ ▶ **n.** 1 (pl. **cystectomies**) a surgical operation to remove the urinary bladder.
2 a surgical operation to remove an abnormal cyst: *an ovarian cystectomy.*

cys·te·ine /ˈsistəˌēn, ˈsisˌtēn/ ▶ **n.** Biochemistry a sulfur-containing amino acid that occurs in keratins and other proteins, often in the form of cystine, and is a constituent of many enzymes. ● Chem. formula: $HSCH_2CH(NH_2)COOH$.
– ORIGIN late 19th cent.: from CYSTINE + *-eine* (variant of -INE[4]).

cys·tic /ˈsistik/ ▶ **adj.** 1 chiefly Medicine of, relating to, or characterized by cysts. ■ Zoology (of a parasite or other organism) enclosed in a cyst: *the cystic stage.*
2 of or relating to the urinary bladder or the gallbladder: *the cystic artery.*
– ORIGIN mid 17th cent. (originally referring to the gallbladder): from French *cystique* or modern Latin *cysticus*, from late Latin *cystis* (see CYST).

cys·ti·cer·cus /ˌsistəˈsərkəs, -ˈkərkəs/ ▶ **n.** (pl. **cysticerci** /-ˈsərˌsī, -ˈsərˌkī/) Zoology a larval tapeworm that is at a stage in which the scolex is inverted in a sac, and that is typically found encysted in the muscle tissue of the host.
– DERIVATIVES **cys·ti·cer·coid** /-ˈsərˌkoid/ **adj.** & **n.**
– ORIGIN mid 19th cent.: modern Latin (originally the name of a supposed genus), from Greek *kustis* 'bladder' + *kerkos* 'tail.'

cys·tic fi·bro·sis ▶ **n.** a hereditary disorder affecting the exocrine glands. It causes the production of abnormally thick mucus, leading to the blockage of the pancreatic ducts, intestines, and bronchi and often resulting in respiratory infection.

cys·tine /ˈsisˌtēn/ ▶ **n.** Biochemistry a compound that is an oxidized dimer of cysteine and is the form in which cysteine often occurs in organic tissue. ● Chem. formula: $C_6H_{12}N_2O_4S_2$.
– ORIGIN mid 19th cent.: from Greek *kustis* 'bladder' (because it was first isolated from urinary calculi) + -INE[4].

cys·ti·tis /sisˈtītis/ ▶ **n.** Medicine inflammation of the urinary bladder. It is often caused by infection and is usually accompanied by frequent, painful urination.

cysto- ▶ **comb. form** of or relating to the urinary bladder: *cystotomy.*
– ORIGIN from Greek *kustis* 'bladder.'

cyst·oid /ˈsistoid/ ▶ **adj.** of the nature of a cyst.
▶ **n.** a cystoid formation.

cys·to·scope /ˈsistəˌskōp/ ▶ **n.** Medicine an instrument inserted into the urethra for examining the urinary bladder.
– DERIVATIVES **cys·to·scop·ic** /ˌsistəˈskäpik/ **adj.**, **cys·tos·co·py** /sisˈtäskəpē/ **n.**

cys·tot·o·my /sisˈtätəmē/ ▶ **n.** (pl. **cystotomies**) a surgical incision into the urinary bladder.

-cyte ▶ **comb. form** Biology denoting a mature cell: *lymphocyte.* Compare with -BLAST.
– ORIGIN from Greek *kutos* 'vessel.'

Cyth·er·e·a /ˌsiTHəˈrēə/ ▶ **n.** another name for APHRODITE.
– ORIGIN from Latin *Cythera* 'Kithira,' the name of an Ionian island.

Cyth·er·ean /ˌsiTHəˈrēən/ ▶ **adj.** Astronomy of or relating to the planet Venus: *the Cytherean atmosphere.* ■ Mythology of or relating to the goddess Cytherea.

cyt·i·dine /ˈsitəˌdēn, ˈsīt-/ ▶ **n.** Biochemistry a nucleoside composed of cytosine linked to ribose, obtained from RNA by hydrolysis.
– ORIGIN early 20th cent.: from CYTO- + -IDE + -INE[4].

cyto- ▶ **comb. form** Biology of a cell or cells: *cytology* | *cytoplasm.*
– ORIGIN from Greek *kutos* 'vessel.'

cy·to·ar·chi·tec·ton·ics /ˌsītōˌärkəˌtekˈtäniks/ ▶ **plural n.** [treated as sing. or pl.] another term for CYTOARCHITECTURE.
– DERIVATIVES **cy·to·ar·chi·tec·ton·ic** **adj.**

cy·to·ar·chi·tec·ture /ˌsītōˈärkiˌtekCHər/ ▶ **n.** Anatomy the arrangement of cells in a tissue, esp. in specific areas of the cerebral cortex characterized by the arrangement of their cells and each associated with particular functions. Also called CYTOARCHITECTONICS. ■ the study of this.
– DERIVATIVES **cy·to·ar·chi·tec·tur·al** /-ˌärkiˈtekCHərəl/ **adj.**, **cy·to·ar·chi·tec·tur·al·ly** /-ˌärkiˈtekCHərəlē/ **adv.**

cy·to·cen·tri·fuge /ˌsītəˈsentrəˌfyoōj/ Biology ▶ **n.** a centrifuge used for depositing cells suspended in a liquid onto a slide for microscopic examination.
▶ **v.** [with obj.] deposit (cells) on a slide using such a centrifuge.

cy·to·cha·la·sin /ˌsītəkəˈlāsən/ ▶ **n.** Biochemistry any of a group of polycyclic compounds produced by fungi and used experimentally in research for their property of interfering with cell processes.
– ORIGIN 1960s: from CYTO- 'cell' + Greek *khalasis* 'dislocation.'

cy·to·chem·is·try /ˌsītəˈkeməstrē/ ▶ **n.** the chemistry of living cells, esp. as studied microscopically.
– DERIVATIVES **cy·to·chem·i·cal** /-ˈkemikəl/ **adj.**

cy·to·chrome /ˈsītəˌkrōm/ ▶ **n.** Biochemistry any of a number of compounds consisting of heme bonded to a protein. Cytochromes function as electron transfer agents in many metabolic pathways, esp. cellular respiration.

cy·to·gen·e·sis /ˌsītəˈjenəsis/ (also **cytogeny** /sīˈtäjənē/) ▶ **n.** the formation and development of cells.

cy·to·ge·net·ics /ˌsītōjəˈnetiks/ ▶ **plural n.** [treated as sing.] Biology the study of inheritance in relation to the structure and function of chromosomes.
– DERIVATIVES **cy·to·ge·net·ic** **adj.**, **cy·to·ge·net·i·cal** /-ikəl/ **adj.**, **cy·to·ge·net·i·cal·ly** /-ik(ə)lē/ **adv.**, **cy·to·ge·net·i·cist** /-jəˈnetəsist/ **n.**

cy·to·kine /ˈsītəˌkīn/ ▶ **n.** Physiology any of a number of substances, such as interferon, interleukin, and growth factors, that are secreted by certain cells of the immune system and have an effect on other cells.

cy·to·ki·ne·sis /ˌsītōkəˈnēsis, -kī-/ ▶ **n.** Biology the cytoplasmic division of a cell at the end of mitosis or meiosis, bringing about the separation into two daughter cells.

cy·to·ki·nin /ˌsītəˈkīnin/ ▶ **n.** another term for KININ (sense 2).

cy·tol·o·gy /sīˈtäləjē/ ▶ **n.** the branch of biology concerned with the structure and function of plant and animal cells.
– DERIVATIVES **cy·to·log·i·cal** /ˌsītlˈäjikəl/ **adj.**, **cy·to·log·i·cal·ly** /ˌsītlˈäjik(ə)lē/ **adv.**, **cy·tol·o·gist** /-jist/ **n.**

cy·tol·y·sis /sīˈtäləsəs/ ▶ **n.** Biology the dissolution or disruption of cells, esp. by an external agent.
– DERIVATIVES **cy·to·lyt·ic** /ˌsītlˈlitik/ **adj.**

cy·to·me·gal·ic /ˌsītəmiˈgalik/ ▶ **adj.** Medicine characterized by enlarged cells, esp. with reference to a disease caused by a cytomegalovirus.

cy·to·meg·a·lo·vi·rus /ˌsītəˈmegəlōˌvīrəs/ (abbr.: **CMV**) ▶ **n.** Medicine a kind of herpesvirus that usually produces very mild symptoms in an infected person but may cause severe neurological damage in people with weakened immune systems and in the newborn.

cy·to·mem·brane /ˌsītəˈmembrān/ ▶ **n.** another term for CELL MEMBRANE.

cy·to·path·ic /ˌsītəˈpaTHik/ (also **cytopathogenic** /ˌsītəˌpaTHəˈjenik/) ▶ **adj.** of, pertaining to, or producing damage to living cells.

cy·to·phil·ic /ˌsītəˈfilik/ ▶ **adj.** having an affinity for living cells.

cy·to·pho·tom·e·try /ˌsītəfōˈtämətrē/ ▶ **n.** Biology the investigation of the contents of cells by measuring the light they allow through after staining.
– DERIVATIVES **cy·to·pho·tom·e·ter** /-ˈtämətər/ **n.**, **cy·to·pho·to·met·ric** /-ˌfōtəˈmetrik/ **adj.**

cy·to·plasm /ˈsītəˌplazəm/ ▶ **n.** Biology the material or protoplasm within a living cell, excluding the nucleus.
– DERIVATIVES **cy·to·plas·mic** /ˌsītəˈplazmik/ **adj.**

cy·to·plast /ˈsītəˌplast/ ▶ **n.** the intact cytoplasmic content of a single cell.

cy·to·sine /ˈsītəˌsēn/ ▶ **n.** Biochemistry a compound found in living tissue as a constituent base of nucleic acids. It is paired with guanine in double-stranded DNA. ● A pyrimidine derivative; chem. formula: $C_4H_5N_3O$.

cy·to·skel·e·ton /ˌsītəˈskelitn/ ▶ **n.** Biology a microscopic network of protein filaments and tubules in the cytoplasm of many living cells, giving them shape and coherence.
– DERIVATIVES **cy·to·skel·e·tal** /-ˈskelitl/ **adj.**

cy·to·sol /ˈsītəˌsäl, -ˌsôl/ ▶ **n.** Biology the aqueous component of the cytoplasm of a cell, within which various organelles and particles are suspended.
– DERIVATIVES **cy·to·sol·ic** /ˌsītəˈsälik, -ˈsôlik/ **adj.**

cy·to·stat·ic /ˌsītəˈstatik/ ▶ **adj.** inhibiting cell growth and division.
▶ **n.** any substance that inhibits cell growth and division.

cy·to·tax·on·o·my /ˌsītəˌtakˈsänəmē/ ▶ **n.** taxonomy based on cytological (and esp. cytogenetic) study.

cy·to·tox·ic /ˌsītəˈtäksik/ ▶ **adj.** toxic to living cells.
– DERIVATIVES **cy·to·tox·ic·i·ty** /-täkˈsisətē/ **n.**

cy·to·tox·ic T cell ▶ **n.** another term for KILLER CELL.

cy·to·tox·in /ˌsītəˈtäksin/ ▶ **n.** a substance toxic to cells.

Cy Young A·ward ▶ **n.** Baseball an annual award to the outstanding pitcher in each of the major leagues.
– ORIGIN named in honor of Cy Young.

czar ▶ **n.** see TSAR.

czar·das ▶ **n.** variant spelling of CSARDAS.

czar·e·vich /ˈzärəˌviCH, ˈ(t)sär-/ variant spelling of TSAREVICH.

cza·rev·na /zäˈrevnə, (t)sä-/ variant spelling of TSAREVNA.

cza·ri·na /zäˈrēnə, (t)sä-/ variant spelling of TSARINA.

Czech /CHek/ ▶ **n. 1** a native or inhabitant of the Czech Republic or (formerly) Czechoslovakia, or a person of Czech descent.
2 the West Slavic language spoken in the Czech Republic, closely related to Slovak.
▶ **adj.** of or relating to the Czechs or their language.
– ORIGIN Polish spelling of Czech *Čech*.

Czech·o·slo·va·ki·a /ˌCHekəsləˈväkēə, -ˈvakēə/ a former country in central Europe, now divided between the Czech Republic and Slovakia; capital, Prague. Created out of the northern part of the Austro-Hungarian Empire at the end of World War I, it was crushed by the Nazi takeover of the Sudetenland in 1938 and the rest of the country in 1939. After World War II, it fell under Soviet domination. The two parts separated on January 1, 1993.
– DERIVATIVES **Czech·o·slo·vak** /-ˈslōˌväk, -ˌvak/ **n. & adj.**, **Czech·o·slo·va·ki·an adj. & n.**

Czech Re·pub·lic a country in central Europe; pop. 10,211,900 (est. 2009); capital, Prague; official language, Czech.

> The Czech Republic was formerly one of the two constituent republics of Czechoslovakia. When Czechoslovakia was partitioned on January 1, 1993, the Czech Republic became independent. It includes the former provinces of Bohemia, Silesia, and Moravia. In 2004 the Czech Republic joined both NATO and the EU.

Czę·sto·cho·wa /ˌCHenstəˈKHōvə/ an industrial city in south central Poland; pop. 244,137 (2007). It is known for the statue of the black Madonna in its church.

C

PRONUNCIATION KEY ə *ago, up*; ər *over, fur*; a *hat*; ā *ate*; ä *car*; e *let*; ē *see*; i *fit*; ī *by*; NG *sing*; ō *go*; ô *law, for*; oi *toy*; o͝o *good*; o͞o *goo*; ou *out*; TH *thin*; T͟H *then*; ZH *vision*

D[1] /dē/ (also **d**) ▶ **n.** (pl. **Ds** or **D's**) **1** the fourth letter of the alphabet. ■ denoting the fourth in a set of items, categories, sizes, etc. ■ the fourth highest category of academic mark. ■ (**d**) Chess denoting the fourth file from the left, as viewed from White's side of the board. ■ denoting the second-lowest-earning socioeconomic category for marketing purposes, including semiskilled and unskilled personnel.
2 (**D**) a shape like that of a capital D: [in combination] *the D-shaped handle*. ■ a loop or ring of this shape.
3 (usu. **D**) Music the second note of the diatonic scale of C major. ■ a key based on a scale with D as its keynote.
4 the Roman numeral for 500. [understood as half of CIↃ, an earlier form of M (= 1,000).]

D[2] ▶ **abbr.** ■ Democrat or Democratic. ■ depth (in the sense of the dimension of an object from front to back). ■ Chemistry dextrorotatory: *D-glucose*. ■ (with a numeral) dimension(s) or dimensional: *a 3-D model*. ■ (in tables of sports results) drawn. ■ (on an automatic gearshift) drive. ■ (in personal ads) divorced. ▶ **symbol** ■ Physics electric flux density. ■ Chemistry the hydrogen isotope deuterium.

d ▶ **abbr.** ■ date. ■ (in genealogies) daughter. ■ day(s): *orbital period (Mars): 687.0d*. ■ deceased. ■ deep. ■ [in combination] (in units of measurement) deci-. ■ (in travel timetables) departs. ■ (**d.**) died (used to indicate a date of death): *Barents, Willem (d.1597)*. ■ divorced. ■ Brit. penny or pence (of predecimal currency): *£20 10s 6d*. [from Latin *denarius* 'penny.'] ■ Chemistry denoting electrons and orbitals possessing two units of angular momentum: *d-electrons*. [*d* from *diffuse*, originally applied to lines in atomic spectra.] ▶ **symbol** ■ Mathematics diameter. ■ Mathematics denoting a small increment in a given variable: *dy/dx*.

'd ▶ **contraction** had: *they'd already gone*. ■ would: *I'd expect that*.

DA ▶ **abbr.** ■ district attorney. ■ Doctor of Arts. ■ informal duck's ass (a man's hairstyle of the 1950s).

da[1] ▶ **abbr.** [in combination] (in units of measurement) deca-.

da[2] /də/ ▶ **determiner** nonstandard spelling of *the*, used in representing informal speech.

D/A ▶ **abbr.** Electronics digital to analog.

DAB ▶ **abbr.** digital audio broadcasting.

dab[1] /dab/ ▶ **v.** (**dabs, dabbing, dabbed**) [with obj.] **1** press against (something) lightly with a piece of absorbent material in order to clean or dry it: *he dabbed his mouth with his napkin* | [no obj.] *she **dabbed at** her eyes with a handkerchief*. ■ apply (a substance) with light quick strokes: *she dabbed disinfectant **on** the cut*.
2 aim at or strike with a light blow.
▶ **n.** a small amount of something: *she licked **a dab of** chocolate from her finger*. ■ a brief application of cosmetic, paint, or the like to a surface: *apply concealer with light dabs*.
– ORIGIN Middle English: symbolic of a light striking movement; compare with **DABBLE** and **DIB**.

dab[2] ▶ **n.** a small, commercially important flatfish that is found chiefly in the North Atlantic. ● *Limanda* and other genera, family Pleuronectidae (several species, in particular the European *L. limanda*), and genus *Citharichthys*, family Bothidae (see also **SAND DAB**).
– ORIGIN late Middle English: of unknown origin.

dab·ber /'dabər/ ▶ **n.** a rounded pad used in printing to apply ink to a surface.

dab·ble /'dabəl/ ▶ **v. 1** [with obj.] immerse (one's hands or feet) partially in water and move them around gently: *they dabbled their feet in the rock pools*. ■ [no obj.] (of a duck or other waterbird) move the bill around in shallow water while feeding: *teal dabble in the shallows*.
2 [no obj.] take part in an activity in a casual or superficial way: *he **dabbled in** writing as a young man*.
– DERIVATIVES **dab·bler** /'dab(ə)lər/ **n.**
– ORIGIN mid 16th cent.: from obsolete Dutch *dabbelen*, or a frequentative of the verb **DAB**[1].

dab·bling duck /'dab(ə)liNG/ ▶ **n.** a freshwater duck that typically feeds in shallow water by dabbling and upending, such as the mallard, teal, shoveler, and pintail. Compare with **DIVING DUCK**. ● Tribe Anatini, family Anatidae: genus *Anas* (numerous species), and perhaps some other genera.

dab·chick /'dab,CHik/ ▶ **n.** a small grebe, esp. the little grebe. ● Genera *Tachybaptus* and *Podilymbus*, family Podicipedidae: several species.
– ORIGIN mid 16th cent. (as *dapchick* or *dopchick*): the first element is perhaps related to **DIP** and **DEEP**.

dab hand ▶ **n.** Brit. informal a person who is an expert at a particular activity: *Tony is **a dab hand at** golf*.
– ORIGIN early 19th cent.: of unknown origin.

DAC ▶ **abbr.** Electronics digital to analog converter.

da ca·po /dä 'käpō/ Music ▶ **adv.** (esp. as a direction) repeat from the beginning. Compare with **DAL SEGNO**.
▶ **adj.** [attrib.] including the repetition of a passage at the beginning: *da capo arias*.
– ORIGIN Italian, literally 'from the head.'

Dac·ca /'däkä/ variant spelling of **DHAKA**.

dace /dās/ ▶ **n.** (pl. **same**) a small freshwater fish of the minnow family, typically living in running water. ● *Leuciscus* and numerous other genera, family Cyprinidae: several species, including the **longfin dace** (*Agosia chrysogaster*) of western North America and the widely distributed *L. leuciscus* of northern Eurasia.
– ORIGIN late Middle English: from Old French *dars* (see **DART**).

da·cha /'däCHə/ ▶ **n.** a country house or cottage in Russia, typically used as a second or vacation home.
– ORIGIN mid 19th cent.: Russian, originally 'grant (of land).'

Da·chau /'dä,KHou/ a city in Bavaria in southwestern Germany, on the Amper River, near Munich, site of a Nazi concentration camp from 1933 until 1945; pop. 41,200 (est. 2007).

dachs·hund /'däksənd, 'däks,ho͝ont/ ▶ **n.** a dog of a short-legged, long-bodied breed.
– ORIGIN late 19th cent.: from German, literally 'badger dog' (the breed being originally used to dig badgers out of their setts).

Da·ci·a /'dāSH(ē)ə/ an ancient country in southeastern Europe in what is now northwestern Romania. It was annexed by Trajan in AD 106 as a province of the Roman Empire.
– DERIVATIVES **Da·ci·an** /'dāSH(ē)ən/ **adj. & n.**

da·cite /'dā,sīt/ ▶ **n.** Geology a volcanic rock resembling andesite but containing free quartz.
– DERIVATIVES **da·cit·ic** /dā'sitik/ **adj.**
– ORIGIN late 18th cent.: from the name of the Roman province of **DACIA** (as it was first found in the Carpathian Mountains) + **-ITE**[1].

da·coit /də'koit/ ▶ **n.** a member of a band of armed robbers in India or Burma (Myanmar).
– ORIGIN from Hindi *ḍakait*, from *ḍakaitī* 'robbery by a gang.'

da·coit·y /də'koitē/ ▶ **n.** (pl. **dacoities**) an act of armed robbery committed by a gang in India or Burma (Myanmar).
– ORIGIN from Hindi *ḍakaitī*.

Da·cron /'dā,krän, 'dak,rän/ ▶ **n.** trademark a synthetic polyester (polyethylene terephthalate) with tough, elastic properties, used as a textile fabric.
– ORIGIN 1950s: an invented name.

dac·tyl /'daktl/ ▶ **n.** Prosody a metrical foot consisting of one stressed syllable followed by two unstressed syllables or (in Greek and Latin) one long syllable followed by two short syllables.
– ORIGIN late Middle English: via Latin from Greek *daktulos*, literally 'finger' (the three bones of the finger corresponding to the three syllables).

dac·tyl·ic /dak'tilik/ Prosody ▶ **adj.** of or using dactyls: *dactylic rhythm*.
▶ **n.** (usu. **dactylics**) dactylic verse.
– ORIGIN late 16th cent.: via Latin from Greek *daktulikos*, from *daktulos*, literally 'finger' (see **DACTYL**).

dad /dad/ ▶ **n.** informal one's father: *his dad was with him* | *what are you making, Dad?*
– ORIGIN mid 16th cent.: perhaps imitative of a young child's first syllables *da, da*.

Da·da /'dädä/ ▶ **n.** an early-20th-century international movement in art, literature, music, and film, repudiating and mocking artistic and social conventions and emphasizing the illogical and absurd.

> Dada was launched in Zurich in 1916 by Tristan Tzara and others, soon merging with a similar group in New York. It favored montage, collage, and the ready-made. Leading figures: Jean Arp, André Breton, Max Ernst, Man Ray, and Marcel Duchamp.

– DERIVATIVES **Da·da·ism** /-,izəm/ **n.**, **Da·da·ist** /-ist/ **n. & adj.**, **Da·da·is·tic** /,dädä'istik/ **adj.**
– ORIGIN French, literally 'hobbyhorse,' the title of a review that appeared in Zurich in 1916.

da·da /'dada, -də/ ▶ **n.** informal one's father.
– ORIGIN late 17th cent.: perhaps imitative of a young child's first syllables (see **DAD**).

dad·dy /'dadē/ ▶ **n.** (pl. **daddies**) informal one's father. ■ the oldest, best, or biggest example of something: ***the daddy of** all potholes*.
– ORIGIN early 16th cent.: from **DAD** + **-Y**[2].

dad·dy long·legs ▶ **n.** (pl. **same**) **1** an arachnid with a globular body and long thin legs, typically living in leaf litter and on tree trunks. Also called **HARVESTMAN**. ● Order Phalangida: numerous genera and species, including the common *Phalangium opilio*.
2 Brit. a crane fly.

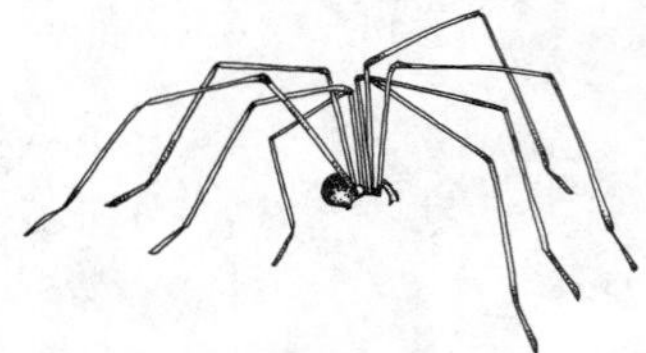

daddy longlegs 1

dad·dy's girl ▶ **n.** informal a girl or woman who is particularly attached to, and indulged by, her father.

Dade Coun·ty /dād/ a county in southeastern Florida, on the Atlantic coast, that includes Miami and many suburbs as well as much of the Everglades; pop. 2,398,245 (est. 2008). Formally ***Miami-Dade County***.

da·do /'dādō/ ▶ **n.** (pl. **dados**) the lower part of the wall of a room, below about waist height, if it is a different color or has a different covering than the upper part. ■ a groove cut in the face of a board, into which the edge of another board is fixed.

■ Architecture the part of a pedestal between the base and the cornice.
– ORIGIN mid 17th cent. (denoting the main part of a pedestal, above the base): from Italian, literally 'dice or cube,' from Latin *datum* 'something given, starting point' (see DATUM).

Da·dra and Na·gar Ha·ve·li /dəˈdrä and ˌnəgər əˈvelē/ a union territory in western India, on the Arabian Sea; pop. 303,200 (est. 2009); capital, Silvassa.

Daed·a·lus /ˈdedl-əs/ Greek Mythology a craftsman, considered the inventor of carpentry, who is said to have built the labyrinth for Minos, king of Crete. Minos imprisoned him and his son Icarus, but they escaped using wings that Daedalus made and fastened with wax. Icarus, however, flew too near the sun and was killed.

dae·mon[1] /ˈdēmən/ (also **daimon**) ▶ **n. 1** (in ancient Greek belief) a divinity or supernatural being of a nature between gods and humans. ■ an inner or attendant spirit or inspiring force.
2 archaic spelling of DEMON[1].
– DERIVATIVES **dae·mon·ic** /diˈmänik/ **adj.**
– ORIGIN mid 16th cent.: common spelling of DEMON[1] until the 19th cent.

dae·mon[2] (also **demon**) ▶ **n.** Computing a background process that handles requests for services such as print spooling and file transfers, and is dormant when not required.
– ORIGIN 1980s: perhaps from *d(isk) a(nd) e(xecution) mon(itor)* or from *de(vice) mon(itor)*, or merely a transferred use of DEMON[1].

daf·fo·dil /ˈdafəˌdil/ ▶ **n.** a bulbous plant that typically bears bright yellow flowers with a long trumpet-shaped center (corona). ● Genus *Narcissus*, family Liliaceae (or Amaryllidaceae): several species, in particular the common *N. pseudonarcissus* and its varieties. See also NARCISSUS.
– ORIGIN mid 16th cent.: from late Middle English *affodill*, from medieval Latin *affodilus*, variant of Latin *asphodilus* (see ASPHODEL). The initial *d-* is unexplained.

daffodil

daf·fy /ˈdafē/ ▶ **adj.** (**daffier, daffiest**) informal silly; mildly eccentric: *daffy anecdotes.*
– DERIVATIVES **daf·fi·ness n.**
– ORIGIN late 19th cent.: from northern English dialect *daff* 'simpleton' + -Y[1]; perhaps related to DAFT.

daft /daft/ ▶ **adj.** informal silly; foolish: *don't ask such daft questions.* ■ (**daft about**) infatuated with: *we were all daft about him.*
– DERIVATIVES **daft·ness n.**
– ORIGIN Old English *gedæfte* 'mild, meek,' of Germanic origin; related to Gothic *gadaban* 'become or be fitting.'

dag /dag/ ▶ **n.** Austral./NZ informal an unfashionable or socially conservative person.
– ORIGIN late Middle English (in the sense 'a hanging part of something'): of unknown origin.

da Ga·ma /də ˈgämə/, Vasco (*c.*1469–1524), Portuguese explorer. He led the first European expedition around the Cape of Good Hope in 1497, sighting and naming Natal on Christmas Day before crossing the Indian Ocean and arriving in Calicut (Kozhikode, in India) in 1498.

Da·ge·stan /ˌdägəˈstän, ˌdagəˈstan/ an autonomous republic in southwestern Russia, on the western shore of the Caspian Sea; pop. 2,707,900 (est. 2009); capital, Makhachkala.
– DERIVATIVES **Da·ge·stan·i n. & adj., Da·ge·stan·i·an n. & adj.**

dag·ga /ˈdägə/ ▶ **n.** chiefly S. African marijuana.
– ORIGIN late 17th cent.: from Afrikaans, from Khoikhoi *dachab.*

dag·ger /ˈdagər/ ▶ **n. 1** a short knife with a pointed and edged blade, used as a weapon. ■ Printing another term for OBELUS.
2 a moth with a dark dagger-shaped marking on the forewing. ● Genus *Acronicta*, family Noctuidae: several species.
– PHRASES **at daggers drawn** in bitter enmity. **look daggers at** glare angrily or venomously at.
– ORIGIN late Middle English: perhaps from obsolete *dag* 'pierce, stab,' influenced by Old French *dague* 'long dagger.'

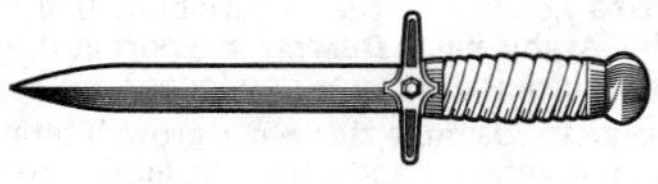

dagger 1

dag·ger·board /ˈdagərˌbôrd/ ▶ **n.** a board that slides vertically through the keel of a sailboat to reduce sideways movement. Compare with CENTERBOARD.

da·go /ˈdāgō/ ▶ **n.** (pl. **dagos** or **dagoes**) informal, offensive an Italian, Spanish, or Portuguese-speaking person.
– ORIGIN mid 19th cent.: from the Spanish given name *Diego* (equivalent to *James*).

Da·gon /ˈdāˌgän/ (in the Bible) a national deity of the ancient Philistines, represented as a fish-tailed man.
– ORIGIN via Latin and Greek from Hebrew *dāgōn*, perhaps from *dāgān* 'corn,' but said (according to folk etymology) to be from *dāg* 'fish.'

da·go red ▶ **n.** offensive cheap red wine, typically from Italy.

Da·guerre /dəˈge(ə)r, däˈger/, Louis-Jacques-Mandé (1789–1851), French physicist. He invented the first practical photographic process, which became known as the daguerreotype process.

da·guerre·o·type /dəˈge(ə)rəˌtīp/ (also **daguerrotype**) ▶ **n.** a photograph taken by an early photographic process employing an iodine-sensitized silvered plate and mercury vapor.
– ORIGIN mid 19th cent.: from French *daguerréotype*, named after L.-J.-M. DAGUERRE, its French inventor.

Dag·wood sand·wich /ˈdagˌwo͝od/ (also **Dagwood**) ▶ **n.** a thick sandwich with a variety of different fillings.
– ORIGIN 1970s: named after *Dagwood* Bumstead, a comic-strip character who makes and eats this type of sandwich.

dah /dä/ ▶ **n.** (in Morse code) another term for DASH.
– ORIGIN World War II: imitative.

da·ha·be·ah /ˌdähəˈbēə/ (also **dahabeeyah**) ▶ **n.** a passenger boat used on the Nile, typically with lateen sails.
– ORIGIN mid 19th cent.: from Arabic, literally 'golden,' denoting the gilded state barge formerly used by the Muslim rulers of Egypt.

Dahl /däl/, Roald (1916–90), British writer. His fiction and drama, such as the short-story collection *Tales of the Unexpected* (1979), typically include macabre plots and unexpected outcomes. Notable works for children include *James and the Giant Peach* (1961) and *Charlie and the Chocolate Factory* (1964).

dahl ▶ **n.** variant spelling of DAL[1].

dahl·ia /ˈdalyə, ˈdäl-/ ▶ **n.** a tuberous-rooted Mexican plant of the daisy family, cultivated for its brightly colored single or double flowers. ● Genus *Dahlia*, family Compositae.
– ORIGIN modern Latin, named in honor of Andreas *Dahl* (1751–89), Swedish botanist.

Da·ho·mey /dəˈhōmē/ former name (until 1975) of BENIN.

dai·kon /ˈdīˌkän, -kən/ ▶ **n.** a radish of a variety with a large slender white root that is typically eaten cooked, esp. in Eastern cuisine, and is also used for fodder.
– ORIGIN Japanese, from *dai* 'large' + *kon* 'root.'

dai·ly /ˈdālē/ ▶ **adj.** [attrib.] done, produced, or occurring every day or every weekday: *a daily newspaper | daily flights to Prague.* ■ relating to the period of a single day: *boats can be rented for a daily rate.*
▶ **adv.** every day: *the museum is open daily.*
▶ **n.** (pl. **dailies**) informal **1** a newspaper published every day except Sunday.
2 (**dailies**) the first prints from cinematographic takes, made rapidly for movie producers or editors; the rushes.
3 (also **daily help**) Brit. dated a woman who is employed to clean someone's house each day.
– PHRASES **daily life** the activities and experiences that constitute a person's normal existence.
– ORIGIN late Middle English: from DAY + -LY[1], -LY[2].

dai·ly dou·ble ▶ **n.** Horse Racing a single bet on the winners of two named races in a day.

dai·ly doz·en ▶ **n.** [in sing.] informal, dated regular exercises, esp. those done first thing in the morning.

Daim·ler /ˈdīmlər/, Gottlieb (1834–1900), German engineer and engine manufacturer. In 1884 he produced a small internal combustion engine using gasoline as a fuel and made it propel a bicycle. In 1890 he formed a company to produce these engines.

dai·mon /ˈdīˌmōn/ ▶ **n.** (pl. **daimons** or **daimones** /-məˌnēz/) variant spelling of DAEMON[1].
– DERIVATIVES **dai·mon·ic** /dīˈmänik/ **adj.**

dai·myo /ˈdīmyō/ (also **daimio**) ▶ **n.** (pl. **daimyos**) historical (in feudal Japan) one of the great lords who were vassals of the shogun.
– ORIGIN Japanese, from *dai* 'great' + *myō* 'name.'

dain·ty /ˈdāntē/ ▶ **adj.** (**daintier, daintiest**) **1** delicately small and pretty: *a dainty lace handkerchief.* ■ (of a person) delicate and graceful in build or movement. ■ (of food) particularly good to eat: *a dainty morsel.*
2 fastidious or difficult to please, typically concerning food: *a dainty appetite.*
▶ **n.** (pl. **dainties**) (usu. **dainties**) something good to eat; a delicacy.
– DERIVATIVES **dain·ti·ly** /ˈdāntəlē/ **adv., dain·ti·ness n.**
– ORIGIN Middle English (in the sense 'tidbit, [something] pleasing to the palate'): from Old French *daintie, deintie* 'choice morsel, pleasure,' from Latin *dignitas* 'worthiness or beauty,' from *dignus* 'worthy.'

dai·qui·ri /ˈdakərē, ˈdīkə-/ ▶ **n.** (pl. **daiquiris**) a cocktail containing rum and lime juice.
– ORIGIN named after *Daiquiri*, a rum-producing district in Cuba.

Dai·ren /ˈdīˈrən, -ˈren/ former name of DALIAN.

dair·y /ˈde(ə)rē/ ▶ **n.** (pl. **dairies**) a building, room, or establishment for the storage, processing, and distribution of milk and milk products. ■ a store where milk and milk products are sold. ■ food made from or containing milk.
▶ **adj.** [attrib.] containing or made from milk: *dairy products.* ■ concerned with or involved in the production of milk: *a dairy farmer.*
– ORIGIN Middle English *deierie*, from *deie* 'dairymaid' (in Old English *dǣge* 'female servant'), of Germanic origin; related to Old Norse *deigja*, also to DOUGH and to the second element of Old English *hlǣfdige* (see LADY).

dair·y·ing /ˈde(ə)rē-iNG/ ▶ **n.** the business of producing, storing, and distributing milk and its products.

dair·y·maid /ˈde(ə)rēˌmād/ ▶ **n.** archaic a woman employed in a dairy.

dair·y·man /ˈde(ə)rēmən, -ˌman/ ▶ **n.** (pl. **dairymen**) a man who is employed in a dairy or sells dairy products.

da·is /ˈdāis, ˈdī-/ ▶ **n.** a low platform for a lectern, seats of honor, or a throne.
– ORIGIN Middle English (originally denoting a raised table for distinguished guests): from Old French *deis*, from Latin *discus* 'disk or dish' (later 'table'). Little used after the Middle English period, the word was revived by antiquarians in the early 19th cent. with the disyllabic pronunciation.

dai·sy /ˈdāzē/ ▶ **n.** (pl. **daisies**) a small grassland plant that has flowers with a yellow disk and white rays. It has given rise to many ornamental garden varieties. ● *Bellis perennis*, family Compositae (or Asteraceae; the **daisy family**). The plants of this large family (known as composites) are distinguished by having composite flower heads consisting of numerous disk florets, ray florets, or both; they include many weeds (dandelions, thistles, ragworts) and garden flowers (asters, chrysanthemums, dahlias, marigolds). ■ used in names of other plants of this family with similar flowers, e.g., **Michaelmas daisy, Shasta daisy.**
– PHRASES **(as) fresh as a daisy** healthy and full of energy. **pushing up (the) daisies** informal dead and buried.
– ORIGIN Old English *dæges ēage* 'day's eye' (because the flower opens in the morning and closes at night).

dai·sy chain ▶ **n.** a string of daisies threaded together by their stems. ■ a string of associated people or things: *we can all make daisy chains of blame.* ■ informal a sexual activity in which participants serve as partners to different people simultaneously.
▶ **v.** (**daisy-chain**) [with obj.] Computing connect (several devices) together in a linear series.
– DERIVATIVES **dai·sy-chain·a·ble adj.**

dai·sy-cut·ter ▶ **n.** informal an immensely powerful aerial bomb that derives its destructive power from the mixture of ammonium nitrate and aluminum powder with air.
– ORIGIN early 20th cent.: so named because the bomb explodes just above ground level.

dai·sy wheel ▶ **n.** a device used as a printer in some word processors, consisting of a disc of spokes each terminating in a printing character.

Dak. ▶ **abbr.** Dakota.

Da·kar /däˈkär, ˈdakˌär/ the capital of Senegal, a port on the Atlantic coast of West Africa; pop. 2,604,000 (est. 2007).

PRONUNCIATION KEY ə *ago, up;* ər *over, fur;* a *hat;* ā *ate;* ä *car;* e *let;* ē *see;* i *fit;* ī *by;* NG *sing;* ō *go;* ô *law, for;* oi *toy;* o͝o *good;* o͞o *goo;* ou *out;* TH *thin;* TH *then;* ZH *vision*

d

Da·ko·ta¹ /də'kōtə/ a former territory of the US that was organized in 1889 into the states of North Dakota and South Dakota.
– DERIVATIVES **Da·ko·tan n. & adj.**

Da·ko·ta² ▶ **n.** (pl. **same** or **Dakotas**) **1** a member of a North American Indian people of the upper Mississippi valley and the surrounding plains. **2** the Siouan language of this people. Also called SIOUX.
▶ **adj.** of or relating to this people or their language.
– ORIGIN early 19th cent.: the name in Dakota, literally 'allies.'

Da·ko·ta Riv·er another name for JAMES RIVER (sense 1).

dal¹ /däl/ (also **dhal**) ▶ **n.** (in Indian cooking) split pulses, in particular lentils. ■ a dish made with these.
– ORIGIN from Hindi *dāl*.

dal² ▶ **abbr.** decaliter(s).

Da·lai La·ma /'dälī 'lämə/ ▶ **n.** the spiritual head of Tibetan Buddhism and, until the establishment of Chinese communist rule, the spiritual and temporal ruler of Tibet.

> Each Dalai Lama is believed to be the reincarnation of the bodhisattva Avalokiteshvara, reappearing in a child when the incumbent Dalai Lama dies. The present Dalai Lama, the fourteenth incarnation, escaped to India in 1959 following the invasion of Tibet by the Chinese and was awarded the Nobel Peace Prize in 1989.

– ORIGIN late 17th cent.: from Tibetan, literally 'ocean guru,' so named because he is regarded as "the ocean of compassion" (see LAMA).

da·la·si /də'läsē/ ▶ **n.** (pl. **same** or **dalasis** /-sēz/) the basic monetary unit of Gambia, equal to 100 butut.
– ORIGIN a local word.

Dal·croze /dal'krōz/ see JAQUES-DALCROZE.

Dale /dāl/, Sir Henry Hallett (1875–1968), English physiologist and pharmacologist. He investigated the role of histamine in anaphylactic shock and allergy and the role of acetylcholine as a natural neurotransmitter. Nobel Prize for Physiology or Medicine (1936), shared with Otto Loewi.

dale /dāl/ ▶ **n.** a valley, esp. a broad one.
– ORIGIN Old English *dæl*, of Germanic origin; related to Old Norse *dalr*, Dutch *dal*, and German *Tal*, also to DELL.

Da·lí /'dälē, dä'lē/, Salvador (1904–89), Spanish painter. A surrealist, he portrayed dream images with almost photographic realism against backgrounds of arid Catalan landscapes. Notable works: *The Persistence of Memory* (1931) and *Christ of St. John of the Cross* (1951).

Salvador Dali

Da·lian /'dä'lyan/ a port and shipbuilding center on the Liaodong Peninsula in northeastern China, now part of the urban complex of Luda. Former name DAIREN.

Da·lit /'dälit/ ▶ **n.** (in the traditional Indian caste system) a member of the lowest caste. See also UNTOUCHABLE, SCHEDULED CASTE.
– ORIGIN via Hindi from Sanskrit *dalita* 'oppressed.'

Dal·las /'daləs/ a city in northeastern Texas, noted as a center of the oil industry; pop. 1,279,910 (est. 2008). Pres. John F. Kennedy was assassinated here in November 1963.

dal·li·ance /'daleəns, 'dalyəns/ ▶ **n.** a casual romantic or sexual relationship. ■ brief or casual involvement with something: *Berkeley was my last **dalliance with** the education system.*
– ORIGIN Middle English (in the sense 'conversation'): from DALLY + -ANCE.

Dall sheep /dôl/ (also **Dall's sheep**) ▶ **n.** a wild North American sheep found in mountainous country from Alaska to British Columbia. ● *Ovis dalli*, family Bovidae.
– ORIGIN early 20th cent.: named after William H. *Dall* (1845–1927), US naturalist.

dal·ly /'dalē/ ▶ **v.** (**dallies, dallying, dallied**) [no obj.] **1** act or move slowly: *workers were loafing, dallying, or goofing off.*
2 have a casual romantic or sexual liaison with someone: *he should stop **dallying with** movie stars.* ■ show a casual interest in something, without committing oneself seriously: *the company has been **dallying with** the idea of opening a new office.*
– ORIGIN Middle English: from Old French *dalier* 'to chat' (commonly used in Anglo-Norman French), of unknown origin.

Dal·ma·tia /dal'māsH(ē)ə/ an ancient region in what is now southwestern Croatia that is composed of mountains and a narrow coastal plain along the Adriatic Sea, together with offshore islands. It once formed part of the Roman province of Illyricum.

Dal·ma·tian /dal'māsHən/ ▶ **n. 1** a dog of a white, short-haired breed with dark spots.
2 a native or inhabitant of Dalmatia.
– ORIGIN late 16th cent. (sense 2): the dog is believed to have originated in Dalmatia in the 18th cent.

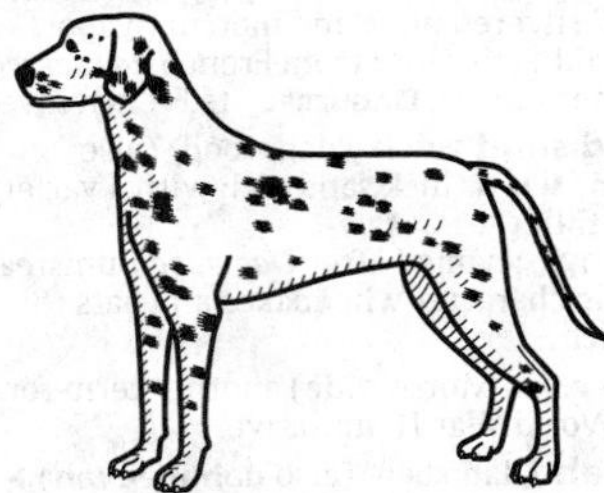

Dalmatian 1

dal·mat·ic /dal'matik/ ▶ **n.** a wide-sleeved, long, loose vestment open at the sides, worn by deacons and bishops, and by some monarchs at their coronation.
– ORIGIN late Middle English: from Old French *dalmatique* or late Latin *dalmatica*, from *dalmatica (vestis)* '(robe) of (white) Dalmatian wool,' from *Dalmaticus* 'of Dalmatia.'

dal se·gno /däl 'sānyō/ ▶ **adv.** Music (esp. as a direction) repeat from the point marked by a sign. Compare with DA CAPO.
– ORIGIN Italian, 'from the sign.'

Dal·ton, John (1766–1844), English chemist; father of the modern atomic theory. He defined an atom as the smallest part of a substance that could participate in a chemical reaction and argued that elements are composed of atoms. He produced the first table of comparative atomic weights.

dal·ton /'dôltn/ ▶ **n.** Chemistry a unit used in expressing the molecular weight of proteins, equivalent to atomic mass unit.
– ORIGIN 1930s: named after John DALTON.

dal·ton·ism /'dôltn,izəm, -tə,niz-/ ▶ **n.** another term for PROTANOPIA, a form of color-blindness.
– ORIGIN mid 19th cent.: from the name of J. DALTON + -ISM.

Dal·ton's law /'dôltnz/ Chemistry a law stating that the pressure exerted by a mixture of gases in a fixed volume is equal to the sum of the pressures that would be exerted by each gas alone in the same volume.

Da·ly Cit·y /'dālē/ a city in north central California, southwest of San Francisco; pop. 101,514 (est. 2008).

dam¹ ▶ **abbr.** decameter(s).

dam² /dam/ ▶ **n.** a barrier, typically of concrete, constructed to hold back water and raise its level, the resulting reservoir being used in the generation of electricity or as a water supply. ■ a barrier of branches in a stream, constructed by a beaver to provide a deep pool and a lodge. ■ a rubber sheet used to keep saliva from the teeth during dental operations, or as a prophylactic device during cunnilingus and anilingus.
▶ **v.** (**dams, damming, dammed**) [with obj.] build a dam across (a river or lake). ■ hold back or obstruct (something): *the closed lock gates **dammed up** the canal.*
– ORIGIN Middle English: from Middle Low German or Middle Dutch; related to Dutch *dam* and German *Damm*, also to Old English *fordemman* 'close up.'

dam³ ▶ **n.** the female parent of an animal, esp. a domestic mammal.
– ORIGIN late Middle English (denoting a human mother): alteration of DAME.

dam·age /'damij/ ▶ **n. 1** physical harm caused to something in such a way as to impair its value, usefulness, or normal function. ■ unwelcome and detrimental effects: *the damage to his reputation was considerable.*
2 (**damages**) a sum of money claimed or awarded in compensation for a loss or an injury: *she was awarded $284,000 in damages.*
▶ **v.** [with obj.] inflict physical harm on (something) so as to impair its value, usefulness, or normal function: *the car was badly damaged in the accident* | (as adj. **damaged**) *damaged ligaments.* ■ have a detrimental effect on: *the scandal could seriously damage his career.*
– PHRASES **what's the damage?** informal, humorous used to ask the cost of something.
– ORIGIN Middle English: from Old French, from *dam, damne* 'loss or damage,' from Latin *damnum* 'loss or hurt'; compare with DAMN.

dam·age con·trol (Brit. also **damage limitation**) ▶ **n.** action taken to limit the damaging effects of an accident or error: *the cost of doing damage control after problems reach the crisis stage.*

dam·aged goods ▶ **plural n.** a person regarded as inadequate or impaired in some way: *I was just damaged goods, another misfit.*

dam·ag·ing /'damijiNG/ ▶ **adj.** causing physical damage: *new cars are less **damaging to** the environment.* ■ having a detrimental effect on someone or something: *damaging allegations of corruption.*
– DERIVATIVES **dam·ag·ing·ly adv.**

Dam·an and Di·u /də'män and 'dē-ōō/ a union territory in India, on the western coast, north of Mumbai (Bombay); pop. 217,500 (est. 2009); capital, Daman.

dam·ar ▶ **n. & adj.** variant spelling of DAMMAR.

Dam·a·scene /'damə,sēn, ,damə'sēn/ ▶ **adj.** of or relating to the city of Damascus. ■ of, relating to, or resembling the conversion of St. Paul on the road to Damascus: *a transformation of Damascene proportions.* ■ historical of or relating to Damascus steel or its manufacture. ■ (often **damascene**) relating to or denoting a process of inlaying a metal object with gold or silver decoration.
▶ **n.** a native or inhabitant of Damascus.
– ORIGIN late Middle English (as a noun): via Latin from Greek *Damaskēnos* 'of Damascus.'

dam·a·scened /'damə,sēnd, ,damə'sēnd/ ▶ **adj.** (of iron or steel) given a wavy pattern by hammer-welding and repeated heating and forging. ■ (of a metal object) inlaid with gold or silver decoration.

Da·mas·cus /də'maskəs/ the capital of Syria since the country's independence in 1946; pop. 1,614,300 (est. 2009). It has existed as a city for over 4,000 years.

Da·mas·cus steel ▶ **n.** historical steel made with a wavy surface pattern produced by hammer-welding strips of steel and iron followed by repeated heating and forging, used chiefly for knife and sword blades. Such items were often marketed, but not necessarily made, in Damascus during the medieval period.

dam·ask /'daməsk/ ▶ **n. 1** a figured woven fabric with a pattern visible on both sides, typically used for table linen and upholstery.
2 short for DAMASK ROSE.
3 (also **damask steel**) historical another term for DAMASCUS STEEL.
▶ **adj.** made of or resembling damask: *the satinlike finish of these damask napkins.* ■ literary having the velvety pink or light red color of a damask rose.
▶ **v.** [with obj.] literary decorate with or as if with a variegated pattern.
– ORIGIN late Middle English: from *Damaske*, early form of the name of *Damascus*, where the fabric was first produced.

dam·ask rose ▶ **n.** a sweet-scented rose of an old variety (or hybrid) that is typically pink or light red in color. The petals are soft and velvety and are used to make attar. ● *Rosa damascena*, family Rosaceae.

dame /dām/ ▶ **n. 1** (**Dame**) (in the UK) the title given to a woman equivalent to the rank of knight.
2 informal a woman. ■ archaic or humorous an elderly or mature woman.
– ORIGIN Middle English (denoting a female ruler): via Old French from Latin *domina* 'mistress.'

dam·fool /'dam'fōōl/ informal, dated ▶ **adj.** (also **damfoolish**) [attrib.] (of a person) thoroughly foolish and stupid.
▶ **n.** a stupid or foolish person.

dam·i·an·a /,damē'anə/ ▶ **n.** a small shrub native to Mexico whose leaves are used in herbal medicine and in the production of a liqueur. It is reputed to possess aphrodisiac qualities. ● *Turnera diffusa*, family Turneraceae.
– ORIGIN American Spanish.

Dam·i·et·ta /,damē'etə/ the eastern branch of the Nile delta. Arabic name DUMYAT. ■ a port at the mouth of this delta; pop. 206,700 (2006).

da·min·o·zide /də'minə,zīd/ ▶ **n.** a growth retardant sprayed on vegetables and fruit, esp. apples, to enhance the quality of the crop. In the US, the application of daminozide is now restricted to ornamental plants owing to the potential health risks of consuming the chemical. ● Chem. formula: $C_6H_{12}N_2O_3$.

dam·mar /ˈdamər/ (also **damar**) ▶ **n.** resin obtained from any of a number of tropical and mainly Indo-Malaysian trees, used to make varnish. ● The resin is obtained from trees in the families Araucariaceae (genus *Agathis*), Dipterocarpaceae (genera *Hopea, Shorea,* and *Vatica*), and Burseraceae (genus *Canarium*).
– ORIGIN late 17th cent.: from Malay *damar* 'resin.'

dam·mit /ˈdamit/ ▶ **exclam.** informal used to express anger and frustration.
– ORIGIN mid 19th cent.: alteration of *damn it.*

damn /dam/ ▶ **v.** [with obj.] **1** (**be damned**) (in Christian belief) be condemned by God to suffer eternal punishment in hell: *be forever damned with Lucifer.* ■ be doomed to misfortune or failure: *the enterprise was damned.*
2 condemn, esp. by the public expression of disapproval: *intellectuals whom he damns as rigid doctrinaire idealists.* ■ curse (someone or something): *she cleared her throat, damning it for its huskiness | damn him for making this sound trivial.*
▶ **exclam.** informal expressing anger, surprise, or frustration: *Damn! I completely forgot!*
▶ **adj.** [attrib.] informal used for emphasis, esp. to express anger or frustration: *turn that damn thing off!* | [as submodifier] *don't be so damn silly!*
– PHRASES **—— be damned** used to express rejection of someone or something previously mentioned: *"Glory be damned!"* **damn all** Brit. informal nothing at all. **damn well** informal used to emphasize a statement, esp. when the speaker is angry: *this is your mess and you can damn well clear it up!* **damn someone/something with faint praise** praise someone or something so unenthusiastically as to imply condemnation. **I'll be** (or **I'm**) **damned if** informal used to express a strong negative: *I'll be damned if I'll call her.* **not be worth a damn** informal have no value or validity at all. **not give a damn** see GIVE. **well I'll be** (or **I'm**) **damned** informal used as an expression of surprise.
– ORIGIN Middle English: from Old French *dam(p)ner*, from Latin *dam(p)nare* 'inflict loss on,' from *damnum* 'loss, damage.'

dam·na·ble /ˈdamnəbəl/ ▶ **adj. 1** extremely bad or unpleasant: *leave this damnable place behind.*
2 subject to or worthy of divine condemnation: *suicide was thought damnable in the Middle Ages.*
– DERIVATIVES **dam·na·bly** /-blē/ **adv.**
– ORIGIN Middle English (in the sense 'worthy of condemnation'): from Old French *dam(p)nable*, from Latin *dam(p)nabilis*, from *dam(p)nare* 'inflict loss on' (see DAMN).

dam·na·tion /damˈnāsнən/ ▶ **n.** (in Christian belief) condemnation to eternal punishment in hell.
▶ **exclam.** expressing anger or frustration.
– ORIGIN Middle English: via Old French from Latin *dam(p)natio(n-)*, from the verb *dam(p)nare* 'inflict loss on' (see DAMN).

dam·na·to·ry /ˈdamnəˌtôrē/ ▶ **adj.** conveying or causing censure or damnation: *the case against you was most damnatory.*
– ORIGIN late 17th cent.: from Latin *damnatorius*, from *dam(p)nat-* 'caused to suffer loss,' from the verb *dam(p)nare* (see DAMN).

damned /damd/ ▶ **adj. 1** (in Christian belief) condemned by God to suffer eternal punishment in hell: (as plural noun **the damned**) *the spirits of the damned.*
2 [attrib.] informal used for emphasis, esp. to express anger or frustration: *it's none of your damned business* | [as submodifier] *she's too damned arrogant* | *you can damned well tell him yourself!* ■ (**damnedest**) used to emphasize the surprising nature of something: *the damnedest thing I ever saw.*
– PHRASES **do** (or **try**) **one's damnedest** do or try one's utmost.

dam·ni·fy /ˈdamnəˌfī/ ▶ **v.** (**damnifies, damnifying, damnified**) [with obj.] Law, rare cause injury to.
– DERIVATIVES **dam·ni·fi·ca·tion** /ˌdamnəfiˈkāsнən/ **n.**
– ORIGIN early 16th cent.: from Old French *damnefier, dam(p)nifier*, from late Latin *damnificare* 'injure, condemn,' from Latin *damnificus* 'hurtful,' from *damnus* 'loss, damage.'

damn·ing /ˈdamiNG/ ▶ **adj.** (of a circumstance or piece of evidence) strongly suggesting guilt or error: *presented with damning affidavits.* ■ extremely critical: *last year's damning report on the industry.*
– DERIVATIVES **damn·ing·ly adv.**

Dam·o·cles /ˈdaməˌklēz/ a legendary courtier who extravagantly praised the happiness of Dionysius I, ruler of Syracuse. To show him how precarious this happiness was, Dionysius seated him at a banquet with a sword hung by a single hair over his head.
– PHRASES **sword of Damocles** used to refer to a precarious situation.

Da·mon /ˈdāmən/ a legendary Syracusan of the 4th century BC whose friend Pythias was sentenced to death by Dionysius I. Damon stood bail for Pythias, who returned just in time to save him, and was himself reprieved.

damp /damp/ ▶ **adj.** slightly wet: *her hair was still damp from the shower.*
▶ **n. 1** moisture diffused through the air or a solid substance or condensed on a surface, typically with detrimental or unpleasant effects. ■ foul, stifling, or poisonous gas, esp. in a mine. ■ (**damps**) archaic damp air or atmosphere.
2 archaic a check or discouragement: *shame gave a damp to her triumph.*
▶ **v.** [with obj.] **1** make (something) slightly wet: *damp a small area with water.*
2 control or restrain (a feeling or a state of affairs): *she tried to damp down her feelings of despair.* ■ make (a fire) burn less strongly by reducing the flow of air to it.
3 restrict the amplitude of vibrations on (a piano or other musical instrument) so as to reduce the volume of sound: *rapidly damping the cymbals after repeatedly clashing them together.* ■ Physics progressively reduce the amplitude of (an oscillation or vibration): *concrete structures damp out any vibrations.*
– DERIVATIVES **damp·ish adj., damp·ly adv.**
– ORIGIN Middle English (in the noun sense 'noxious inhalation'); related to a Middle Low German word meaning 'vapor, steam, smoke.'

damp-dry ▶ **v.** [no obj.] dry (something) until it is only damp: *the machine automatically washes, rinses, and damp-dries.*

damp·en /ˈdampən/ ▶ **v.** [with obj.] **1** make slightly wet: *the fine rain dampened her face.*
2 make less strong or intense: *nothing could dampen her enthusiasm.* ■ reduce the amplitude of (a sound source): *slider switches on the mixers can dampen the drums.*
– DERIVATIVES **damp·en·er n.**

damp·er /ˈdampər/ ▶ **n.** a person or thing that has a depressing, subduing, or inhibiting effect: *another damper on reactor development was the problem of safeguards.* ■ Music a pad that silences a piano string except when removed by means of a pedal or by the note being struck. ■ a device for reducing mechanical vibration, in particular a shock absorber on a motor vehicle. ■ a conductor used to reduce hunting in an electric motor or generator. ■ a movable metal plate in a flue or chimney, used to regulate the draft and so control the rate of combustion.
– PHRASES **put a damper on** have a depressing, subduing, or inhibiting effect on: *he put a damper on her youthful excitement.*

damp·ing /ˈdampiNG/ ▶ **n. 1** technical a decrease in the amplitude of an oscillation as a result of energy being drained from the system to overcome frictional or other resistive forces. ■ a mechanism or system for bringing about such a decrease. ■ a method of bringing about a decrease in oscillatory peaks in an electric current or voltage using an energy-absorbing or resistance circuit.
2 short for DAMPING-OFF.

damp·ing-off ▶ **n.** a plant disease occurring in excessively damp conditions, in particular the collapse and death of young seedlings as a result of a fungal infection. ● The disease is commonly caused by fungi of the genera *Pythium* (phylum Oomycota) or *Fusarium* (phylum Ascomycota).

damp·ness /ˈdampnəs/ ▶ **n.** the state or condition of being slightly wet: *the dampness in the air.*

dam·sel /ˈdamzəl/ ▶ **n.** archaic or literary a young unmarried woman.
– PHRASES **damsel in distress** often humorous a young woman in trouble (with the implication that the woman needs to be rescued, as by a prince in a fairy tale).
– ORIGIN Middle English: from Old French *dameisele, damisele*, based on Latin *domina* 'mistress.'

dam·sel bug ▶ **n.** a slender long-legged bug that is a predator of other insects. ● Family Nabidae, suborder Heteroptera: several genera.

dam·sel·fish /ˈdamzəlˌfisн/ ▶ **n.** (pl. **same** or **damselfishes**) a small brightly colored tropical fish that lives in or near coral reefs. ● *Chromis* and other genera, family Pomacentridae: numerous species, in particular *C. chromis.*

dam·sel·fly /ˈdamzəlˌflī/ ▶ **n.** (pl. **damselflies**) a slender insect related to the dragonflies, having weak flight and typically resting with the wings folded back along the body. ● Suborder Zygoptera, order Odonata: several families.

dam·son /ˈdamzən, -sən/ ▶ **n. 1** a small purple-black plumlike fruit. ■ a dark purple color.
2 (also **damson tree**) the small deciduous tree that bears this fruit, probably derived from the bullace. ● *Prunus domestica* subsp. *insititia* (or *P. damascena*), family Rosaceae.
– ORIGIN late Middle English *damascene*, from Latin *damascenum (prunum)* '(plum) of Damascus.' Compare with DAMASCENE and DAMASK.

Dan /dan/ (in the Bible) a Hebrew patriarch, son of Jacob and Bilhah. ■ the tribe of Israel traditionally descended from him. ■ an ancient town in the north of Canaan, where the tribe of Dan settled. It marked the northern limit of the ancient Hebrew kingdom of Israel.

d

dan[1] /dän, dan/ ▶ **n.** any of ten degrees of advanced proficiency in judo or karate. ■ a person who has achieved such a degree.
– ORIGIN 1940s: from Japanese.

dan[2] /dan/ (also **dan buoy**) ▶ **n.** a small marker buoy with a lightweight flagpole.
– ORIGIN late 17th cent.: of unknown origin.

Dan. ▶ **abbr.** Bible Daniel.

Da·na[1] /ˈdānə/, Charles Anderson (1819–97), US newspaper editor. He was a resident of the Brook Farm commune near Boston 1841–46, an experimental community, and the owner and editor of the *New York Sun* 1868–97.

Da·na[2], James Dwight (1813–95), US naturalist, geologist, and mineralogist. He founded a classification of minerals based on chemistry and physics and viewed the earth as a unit.

Da·na[3], Richard Henry (1815–82), US adventurer, lawyer, and writer. An expert in maritime law and an editor of an international law journal, he is most noted for the account of his voyage from Boston around Cape Horn to California in *Two Years before the Mast* (1840).

Dan·a·e /ˈdanəˌē/ Greek Mythology the daughter of Acrisius, king of Argos. An oracle foretold that she would bear a son who would kill her father. Attempting to evade this, Acrisius imprisoned her, but Zeus visited her in the form of a shower of gold and she conceived Perseus, who killed Acrisius by accident.

da·na·id /ˈdanē-id, ˈdanā-/ ▶ **n.** a large strikingly marked butterfly of a group that includes the monarch, found chiefly in the tropics of Africa and East Asia. ● Subfamily Danainae, family Nymphalidae (formerly family Danaidae).
– ORIGIN late 19th cent.: from modern Latin *Danaidae*, arbitrary use of the Latin name of the daughters of Danaus.

Da·na·ids /dəˈnā-idz, ˈdanē-idz/ Greek Mythology the daughters of Danaus, king of Argos, who were compelled to marry the sons of his brother Aegyptus but murdered their husbands on the wedding night, except for one, Hypermnestra, who helped her husband to escape. The remaining Danaids were punished in Hades by being sent to fill a leaky jar with water.

Da Nang /ˈdä ˈnäNG, də ˈnaNG/ a port and city in central Vietnam, on the South China Sea; pop. 770,500 (est. 2009). It served as a US military base during the Vietnam War. Former name TOURANE.

Dan·bury /ˈdanˌberē, -b(ə)rē/ a city in west central Connecticut, formerly noted for its hat industry; pop. 79,256 (est. 2008).

dance /dans/ ▶ **v.** [no obj.] **1** move rhythmically to music, typically following a set sequence of steps: *their cheeks were pressed together as they danced.* ■ [with obj.] perform (a particular dance or a role in a ballet): *they danced a tango.* ■ [with obj.] lead (someone) in a particular direction while dancing: *I danced her out of the room.*
2 [with adverbial of direction] (of a person) move in a quick and lively way: *Sheila danced in gaily.* ■ [with adverbial of place] move up and down lightly and quickly: *midges danced over the stream.* ■ (of someone's eyes) sparkle brightly with pleasure or excitement.
▶ **n.** a series of movements that match the speed and rhythm of a piece of music. ■ a particular sequence of steps and movements constituting a particular form of dancing. ■ steps and movements of this type considered as an activity or art form: *she has studied dance with Martha Graham.* ■ a social gathering at which people dance: *she met her husband at a dance.* ■ a set of lively movements resembling a dance: *he gesticulated comically and did a little dance.* ■ a piece of music for dancing to: *the last dance had been played.* ■ (also **dance music**) music for dancing to, esp. in a nightclub.

– PHRASES **dance attendance on** do one's utmost to please someone by attending to all possible needs or requests. **dance to someone's tune** comply completely with someone's demands and wishes. **lead someone a dance** (or **a merry dance**) Brit. cause someone a great deal of trouble or worry.
– DERIVATIVES **dance·a·bil·i·ty** n., **dance·a·ble** adj., **dancey** (also **dancy**) adj.
– ORIGIN Middle English: from Old French *dancer* (verb), *dance* (noun), of unknown origin.

dance band ▶ n. a band that plays music suitable for dancing, esp. swing.

dance card ▶ n. dated a card bearing the names of a woman's prospective partners at a formal dance.

dance floor ▶ n. an area of floor in a nightclub, disco, or restaurant that is reserved for dancing. ■ [as modifier] denoting a recording or type of music particularly popular as an accompaniment to dancing: *a current dance-floor hit.*

dance hall ▶ n. **1** a large public hall or building where people pay to enter and dance.
2 (**dancehall**) an uptempo style of dance music originating in Jamaica and derived from reggae, in which a DJ improvises lyrics over a recorded instrumental backing track or to the accompaniment of live musicians.

dance of death ▶ n. a medieval allegorical representation in which a personified Death leads people to the grave, designed to emphasize the equality of all before death. Also called **DANSE MACABRE**.

danc·er /ˈdansər/ ▶ n. a person who dances or whose profession is dancing.

dan·cer·cise /ˈdansərˌsīz/ (also **dancercize**) ▶ n. a system of aerobic exercise using dance movements.
– ORIGIN 1960s: blend of **DANCE** and **EXERCISE**.

danc·ing girl ▶ n. a female professional dancer, esp. an erotic dancer or a member of the chorus in a musical.

D and C ▶ abbr. dilation and curettage.

dan·de·li·on /ˈdandlˌīən/ ▶ n. a widely distributed weed of the daisy family, with a rosette of leaves, bright yellow flowers followed by globular heads of seeds with downy tufts, and stems containing a milky latex. ● Genus *Taraxacum*, family Compositae: several species, in particular the common *T. officinale*, which has edible leaves.
– ORIGIN late Middle English: from French *dent-de-lion*, translation of medieval Latin *dens leonis* 'lion's tooth' (because of the jagged shape of the leaves).

dan·de·li·on greens ▶ plural n. fresh dandelion leaves used as a salad vegetable or herb.

dan·der[1] /ˈdandər/ ▶ n. (in phrase **get/have one's dander up**) informal lose one's temper.
– ORIGIN mid 19th cent.: of unknown origin.

dan·der[2] ▶ n. skin flakes in an animal's fur or hair.
– ORIGIN late 18th cent.: related to **DANDRUFF**.

dan·di·a·cal /danˈdīəkəl/ ▶ adj. dated, humorous relating to or characteristic of a dandy.
– ORIGIN mid 19th cent.: from **DANDY**, on the pattern of words such as *hypochondriacal*.

Dan·die Din·mont /ˈdandē ˈdinˌmänt/ ▶ n. a terrier of a breed with short legs, a long body, and a rough coat.
– ORIGIN early 19th cent.: named after a farmer who owned a special breed of terriers, portrayed in Sir Walter Scott's *Guy Mannering*.

dan·di·fied /ˈdandiˌfīd/ ▶ adj. (of a man) showing excessive concern about his clothes or appearance. ■ self-consciously sophisticated or elaborate: *he writes a dandified prose.*

dan·di·prat /ˈdandēˌprat/ ▶ n. archaic, informal a young or insignificant person.
– ORIGIN early 16th cent. (denoting a coin worth three halfpence): of unknown origin.

dan·dle /ˈdandl/ ▶ v. [with obj.] move (a baby or young child) up and down in a playful or affectionate way. ■ move (something) lightly up and down: *dandling the halter rope, he gently urged the pony's head up.*
– ORIGIN mid 16th cent.: of unknown origin.

Dan·dong /ˈdänˈdŏŏNG/ a port in Liaoning province, in northeastern China, near the mouth of the Yalu River, on the border with North Korea; pop. 597,900 (est. 2006). Former name **ANTUNG**.

dan·druff /ˈdandrəf/ ▶ n. small pieces of dead skin in a person's hair.
– DERIVATIVES **dan·druff·y** adj.
– ORIGIN mid 16th cent.: the first element is unknown; the second (*-ruff*) is perhaps related to Middle English *rove* 'scurfiness.'

D & X ▶ abbr. dilation and extraction. See **PARTIAL-BIRTH ABORTION**.

dan·dy /ˈdandē/ ▶ n. (pl. **dandies**) **1** a man unduly devoted to style, neatness, and fashion in dress and appearance.
2 informal, dated an excellent thing of its kind: *this umbrella is a dandy.*
▶ adj. (**dandier**, **dandiest**) **1** informal excellent: *upgrading seemed a dandy idea | things are all fine and dandy.*
2 relating to or characteristic of a dandy.
– DERIVATIVES **dan·dy·ish** adj., **dan·dy·ism** /-ˌizəm/ n.
– ORIGIN late 18th cent.: perhaps a shortened form of 17th-cent. *Jack-a-dandy* 'conceited fellow' (the last element representing *Dandy*, a nickname for the given name *Andrew*).

dan·dy brush ▶ n. a coarse brush used for grooming a horse.

dan·dy roll (also **dandy roller**) ▶ n. a roller that is used to solidify partly formed paper during its manufacture, and to impress the water mark.

Dane /dān/ ▶ n. a native or inhabitant of Denmark, or a person of Danish descent. ■ historical one of the Viking invaders of the British Isles in the 9th–11th centuries.
– ORIGIN Old English *Dene*; superseded in Middle English by forms influenced by Old Norse *Danir* and late Latin *Dani* (both plural).

Dane·geld /ˈdānˌgeld/ ▶ n. historical a land tax levied in medieval England, originally to raise funds for protection against Danish invaders.
– ORIGIN late Old English, from Old Norse *Danir* 'Danes' + *gjald* 'payment.'

Dan·forth an·chor /ˈdanˌfôrTH/ ▶ n. a type of stockless lightweight anchor with flat flukes.

dang /daNG/ ▶ adj. exclam., & v. informal euphemism for **DAMN**: [as adj.] *just get the dang car started!* | [as exclamation] *dang it, Phil, stop snoring!* | [as verb] *I'll be danged.*

dan·ger /ˈdānjər/ ▶ n. the possibility of suffering harm or injury: *his life was in danger.* ■ a person or thing that is likely to cause harm or injury: *infertile soils where drought is a danger.* ■ the possibility of something unwelcome or unpleasant: *there was no danger of the champagne running out.* ■ Brit. the status of a railroad signal indicating that the line is not clear and that a train should not proceed.
– PHRASES **in danger of** likely to incur or to suffer from: *the animal is in danger of extinction.* **out of danger** (of a person who has suffered a serious injury or illness) not expected to die.
– ORIGIN Middle English: from Old French *dangier*, based on Latin *dominus* 'lord.' The original sense was 'jurisdiction or power,' specifically 'power to harm,' hence the current meaning 'liability to be harmed.'

dan·ger·ous /ˈdānjərəs/ ▶ adj. able or likely to cause harm or injury: *a dangerous animal | ice was making the roads dangerous.* ■ *it is dangerous to underestimate an enemy.* ■ likely to cause problems or to have adverse consequences: *our most dangerous opponents in the playoffs | it is dangerous to underestimate an enemy.*
– DERIVATIVES **dan·ger·ous·ly** adv., **dan·ger·ous·ness** n.
– ORIGIN Middle English (in the senses 'arrogant,' 'fastidious,' and 'difficult to please'): from Old French *dangereus*, from *dangier* (see **DANGER**).

dan·ger sign ▶ n. an indication that a bad or dangerous situation is likely to develop: *parents of young addicts often miss the early danger signs.*

dan·gle /ˈdaNGgəl/ ▶ v. [no obj.] hang or swing loosely: *saucepans dangled from a rail* | [with obj.] *they were dangling their legs over the water.* ■ [with obj.] offer (an enticing incentive) to someone: *two rich commissions that had been dangling so sweetly in front of me.*
– PHRASES **keep someone dangling** keep someone in an uncertain position.
– DERIVATIVES **dan·gler** /-glər/ n., **dan·gly** /-glē/ adj.
– ORIGIN late 16th cent.: symbolic of something loose and pendulous, corresponding to Danish *dangle*, Swedish *dangla*, but the origin is not clear.

dan·gling /ˈdaNGgliNG/ ▶ adj. hanging or swinging loosely: *a pair of dangling earrings.*

dan·gling par·ti·ci·ple /ˈdaNGg(ə)liNG/ ▶ n. Grammar a participle intended to modify a noun that is not actually present in the text.

> **USAGE** A **participle** is a word formed as an inflection of the verb, such as *arriving* or *arrived*. A **dangling participle** is one left "hanging" because, in the grammar of the clause, it does not relate to the noun it should. In the sentence ***arriving at the station, she** picked up her case*, the construction is correct because the participle *arriving* and the subject *she* relate to each other (*she* is the one doing the *arriving*). But in the following sentence, a **dangling participle** has been created: ***arriving at the station, the sun** came out*. We know, logically, that it is not *the sun* that is *arriving*, but grammatically that is exactly the link that has been created. Such errors are frequent in written English and can give rise to confusion.

Dan·iel[1] /ˈdanyəl/ a Hebrew prophet (6th century BC), who spent his life as a captive at the court of Babylon. In the biblical account, he interpreted the dreams of Nebuchadnezzar and was delivered by God from the lions' den into which he had been thrown as the result of a trick; in the apocryphal book of Susanna he is portrayed as a wise judge. ■ a book of the Bible containing Daniel's prophecies. It was probably written at the outbreak of the persecution of the Jews under Seleucid rule c.167 BC.

Dan·iel[2], Peter Vivian (1784–1860), US Supreme Court associate justice 1841–60. Appointed to the Court by President Van Buren, he advocated states' rights.

dan·i·o /ˈdanēˌō/ ▶ n. (pl. **danios**) a small, typically brightly colored freshwater fish native to South and Southeast Asia. ● Genera *Danio* and *Brachydanio*, family Cyprinidae: several species.
– ORIGIN modern Latin (genus name).

Dan·ish /ˈdāniSH/ ▶ adj. of or relating to Denmark or its people or language.
▶ n. **1** the North Germanic language of Denmark, which is also the official language of Greenland and the Faroe Islands.
2 (as plural noun **the Danish**) the people of Denmark.
3 informal short for **DANISH PASTRY**.
– ORIGIN Old English *Denisc*, of Germanic origin; superseded in Middle English by forms influenced by Old French *daneis* and medieval Latin *Danensis* (from late Latin *Dani* 'Danes').

Dan·ish blue ▶ n. a soft, salty, strong-flavored white cheese with blue veins.

Dan·ish pas·try ▶ n. a pastry made of sweetened yeast dough with toppings or fillings such as fruit, nuts, or cheese.

dank /daNGk/ ▶ adj. disagreeably damp, musty, and typically cold.
– DERIVATIVES **dank·ly** adv., **dank·ness** n.
– ORIGIN Middle English: probably of Scandinavian origin and related to Swedish *dank* 'marshy spot.'

Dan·mark /ˈdänˌmärk/ Danish name for **DENMARK**.

Dan·ne·brog /ˈdanəˌbräg/ ▶ n. the Danish national flag.
– ORIGIN early 18th cent.: Danish, literally 'Danish cloth.'

Da·no-Nor·we·gian /ˌdānōnôrˈwējən/ ▶ n. another term for **BOKMÅL**.

Dan Riv·er /dan/ a river that flows for 180 miles (290 km) from southwestern Virginia into North Carolina to the Roanoke River.

danse ma·ca·bre /ˈdäns məˈkäbrə/ ▶ n. another term for **DANCE OF DEATH**.
– ORIGIN French, recorded from late Middle English in anglicized forms such as *dance of Machabray*, *dance of Macaber* (see also **MACABRE**).

dan·seur /dänˈsər/ ▶ n. a male ballet dancer.
– ORIGIN French, from *danser* 'to dance.'

dan·seuse /dänˈsōōz, -ˈsœz/ ▶ n. a female ballet dancer.
– ORIGIN early 19th cent.: French, literally 'female dancer.'

Dan·te /ˈdänˌtā, ˈdanˌtā, ˈdantē/ (1265–1321), Italian poet; full name *Dante Alighieri*. He wrote *The Divine Comedy* (c.1309–20), an epic poem that describes his spiritual journey through Hell and Purgatory and finally to Paradise. His love for **Beatrice Portinari** is described in *Vita nuova* (c.1290–94).

Dan·te·an /ˈdäntēən, ˈdan-/ ▶ adj. of or reminiscent of the poetry of Dante, esp. in invoking his vision of hell in *The Divine Comedy*.
▶ n. an admirer or student of Dante or his writing.

Dan·tesque /dänˈtesk/ (also **Dante-esque** /ˌdäntāˈesk/) ▶ adj. another term for **DANTEAN**.

Dan·ton /däNˈtôN/, Georges (Jacques) (1759–94), French revolutionary. Initially an ally of Robespierre, he later revolted against the severity of the Revolutionary Tribunal and was executed on Robespierre's orders.

Dan·ube /ˈdanyōōb/ a river that rises in the Black Forest in southwestern Germany and flows for about 1,770 miles (2,850 km) into the Black Sea. It is the second longest river in Europe (after the Volga); the cities of Vienna, Budapest, and Belgrade are situated on its banks. German name **DONAU**.
– DERIVATIVES **Dan·u·bi·an** /danˈyōōbēən/ adj.

Dan·ube School a group of landscape painters working in the Danube region in the early 16th century. Its members included Altdorfer and Cranach the Elder.

Dan·vers /ˈdanvərz/ a town in northeastern Massachusetts, northeast of Boston; pop. 26,762 (est. 2008).

Dan·ville /ˈdanˌvil/ a city in southern Virginia, on the Dan River; pop. 44,660 (est. 2008).

Dan·zig /ˈdäntsig, ˈdant-/ German name for **GDAŃSK**.

dap /dap/ ▶ **v.** (**daps, dapping, dapped**) [no obj.] fish by letting the fly bob lightly on the water without letting the line touch the water.
– ORIGIN mid 17th cent. (as a verb): symbolic of a flicking movement, similar to **DAB**[1].

Daph·ne /ˈdafnē/ Greek Mythology a nymph who was turned into a laurel bush to save her from the amorous pursuit of Apollo.

daph·ne /ˈdafnē/ ▶ **n.** a small Eurasian shrub with sweet-scented flowers and, typically, evergreen leaves. ● Genus *Daphne*, family Thymelaeaceae: several species, including mezereon and spurge laurel.
– ORIGIN late Middle English (denoting the laurel or bay tree): from Greek *daphnē*, from the name of the nymph **DAPHNE**.

daph·ni·a /ˈdafnēə/ ▶ **n.** (pl. **same**) a tiny and semitransparent freshwater crustacean with long antennae and prominent eyes, often used as food for aquarium fish. Also called **WATER FLEA**. ● Genus *Daphnia*, order Cladocera.
– ORIGIN modern Latin, from Greek *Daphnē*, from the name of the nymph **DAPHNE**.

Daph·nis /ˈdafnis/ Greek Mythology a Sicilian shepherd who, according to one version of the legend, was struck with blindness for his infidelity to the nymph Echenaïs. He consoled himself with pastoral poetry, of which he was the inventor.

dap·per /ˈdapər/ ▶ **adj.** (typically of a man) neat and trim in dress, appearance, or bearing.
– DERIVATIVES **dap·per·ly adv.**, **dap·per·ness n.**
– ORIGIN late Middle English: probably from a Middle Low German or Middle Dutch word meaning 'strong, stout.'

dap·ple /ˈdapəl/ ▶ **v.** [with obj.] (usu. **be dappled**) mark with spots or rounded patches: *the floor was dappled with pale moonlight*.
▶ **n.** a patch or spot of color or light. ■ an animal whose coat is marked with patches or spots.
– ORIGIN late 16th cent. (earlier as an adjective): perhaps related to Old Norse *depill* 'spot.'

dap·pled /ˈdapəld/ ▶ **adj.** marked with spots or rounded patches: *the horse's dappled flank*.

dap·ple gray ▶ **adj.** (of a horse) gray or white with darker ringlike markings.
▶ **n.** a horse of this type.

Dap·sang /däpˈsäNG/ another name for **K2**.

dap·sone /ˈdapˌsōn/ ▶ **n.** Medicine a sulfur compound with bacteriostatic action, used chiefly in the treatment of leprosy. ● Alternative name: **bis(4-aminophenyl)sulfone**; chem. formula: $(H_2NC_6H_4)_2SO_2$.
– ORIGIN 1950s: from elements of its alternative systematic name *dipara-aminophenyl sulfone*.

Da·qing /ˈdäˈCHiNG/ (also **Taching**) a major industrial city in northeastern China, in Heilongjiang province; pop. 976,200 (est. 2006).

DAR ▶ **abbr.** Daughters of the American Revolution.

Dard /därd/ ▶ **n. 1** a member of a group of peoples inhabiting eastern Afghanistan, northern Pakistan, and Kashmir.
2 a group of languages, including Kashmiri, usually classified as Indic but showing strong Iranian influence.
▶ **adj.** of or relating to the Dards or their languages.
– DERIVATIVES **Dard·ic** /ˈdärdik/ **n. & adj.**
– ORIGIN the name in Dard.

Dar·da·nelles /ˌdärdnˈelz/ a narrow strait between Europe and Asiatic Turkey (called the Hellespont in classical times) that links the Sea of Marmara with the Aegean Sea. It is 38 miles (60 km) long. In 1915, it was the scene of an unsuccessful attack on Turkey by Allied troops (see **GALLIPOLI**).

Dare /de(ə)r/, Virginia (1587–?), first English child born in North America. Born on Roanoke Island, Virginia, to Ananias Dare and Elinor White, she disappeared with the other 117 Roanoke colonists, as was discovered in 1591.

dare /de(ə)r/ ▶ **v.** (3rd sing. present usu. **dare** before an expressed or implied infinitive without **to**) **1** (usu. with infinitive with or without **to** often with negative) have the courage to do something: *a story he dare not write down* | *she leaned forward as far as she dared*.
2 [with obj. and infinitive] defy or challenge (someone) to do something: *she was daring him to disagree* | [with obj.] *swap with me, I dare you*.
3 [with obj.] literary take the risk of; brave: *few dared his wrath*.
▶ **n.** a challenge, esp. to prove courage: *athletes who eat ground glass on a dare*.
– PHRASES **don't you dare** used to order someone threateningly not to do something: *don't you dare touch me!* **how dare you** used to express indignation: *how dare you talk to me like that!* **I dare say** (or **daresay**) used to indicate that one believes something is probable: *I dare say you've heard about her*.
– DERIVATIVES **dar·er n.**
– ORIGIN Old English *durran*, of Germanic origin; related to Gothic *gadaursan*, from an Indo-European root shared by Greek *tharsein* and Sanskrit *dhṛṣ-* 'be bold.'

dare·dev·il /ˈde(ə)rˌdevəl/ ▶ **n.** a reckless person who enjoys doing dangerous things.
▶ **adj.** [attrib.] reckless and daring.
– DERIVATIVES **dare·dev·il·ry** /-rē/ **n.**

daresay /ˈde(ə)rˈsā/ ▶ **v.** see **DARE**.

Dar es Sa·laam /ˌdär ˌes səˈläm/ the chief port and former capital of Tanzania; pop. 2,930,000 (est. 2007). Its Arabic name means "haven of peace."

Dar·fur /därˈfo͝or/ a region in the west of Sudan, an independent kingdom until 1874. In 2003, a rebellion against the Sudanese government began, and many thousands died or were displaced in the subsequent conflict.

Da·ri /ˈdärē/ ▶ **n.** the form of Persian spoken in Afghanistan.

Dar·i·en /därˈyen, ˌde(ə)rēˈen/ a sparsely populated province in eastern Panama. The name was formerly applied to the whole of the Isthmus of Panama.

Dar·i·en, Gulf of part of the Caribbean Sea between Panama and Colombia.

dar·ing /ˈde(ə)riNG/ ▶ **adj.** (of a person or action) adventurous or audaciously bold: *a daring crime*. ■ boldly unconventional: *a pretty girl in daring clothes*.
▶ **n.** adventurous courage: *the zeal and daring of climbers*.
– DERIVATIVES **dar·ing·ly adv.**

dar·i·ole /ˈdarēˌōl/ (also **dariole mold**) ▶ **n.** (in French cooking) a small, round metal mold in which an individual sweet or savory dish is cooked and served.
– ORIGIN late Middle English: from Old French.

Da·ri·us I /ˈde(ə)rēəs, dəˈrīəs/ (c.550–486 BC), king of Persia 521–486 BC; known as **Darius the Great**. After a revolt by the Greek cities in Ionia (499–494 BC), he invaded Greece but was defeated at Marathon (490 BC).

Dar·jee·ling /därˈjēliNG/ ▶ **n.** a high-quality tea grown in the mountainous regions of northern India.

dark /därk/ ▶ **adj. 1** with little or no light: *it's too dark to see much*. ■ hidden from knowledge; mysterious: *a dark secret*. ■ archaic ignorant; unenlightened: *he is dark on certain points of scripture*. ■ (of a theater) closed; not in use: *on Tuesdays he'd wait tables because the theater was dark*.
2 (of a color or object) not reflecting much light; approaching black in shade: *dark green*. ■ (of someone's skin, hair, or eyes) brown or black in color. ■ (of a person) having such skin, hair, or eyes: *both my father and I are very dark*. ■ served or drunk with only a little or no milk or cream.
3 (of a period of time or situation) characterized by tragedy, unhappiness, or unpleasantness: *the dark days of the war*. ■ gloomily pessimistic: *a dark vision of the future*. ■ (of an expression) angry; threatening: *Matthew flashed a dark look at her*. ■ suggestive of or arising from evil characteristics or forces; sinister: *so many dark deeds had been committed*.
4 Phonetics denoting a velarized form of the sound of the letter *l* (as in *pull*).
▶ **n. 1** (**the dark**) the absence of light in a place: *Carolyn was sitting in the dark* | *he's scared of the dark*. ■ nightfall: *I'll be home before dark*.
2 a dark color or shade, esp. in a painting.
– PHRASES **the darkest hour is just before the dawn** proverb when things seem to be at their worst, they are about to start improving. **in the dark** in a state of ignorance about something: *we're clearly being kept in the dark about what's happening*. **keep something dark** keep something secret from other people: *I asked Ann to keep my identity dark*. **a shot** (or **stab**) **in the dark** an act whose outcome cannot be foreseen; a mere guess.
– DERIVATIVES **dark·ish adj.**, **dark·some** /-səm/ **adj.** (literary).
– ORIGIN Old English *deorc*, of Germanic origin, probably distantly related to German *tarnen* 'conceal.'

dark ad·ap·ta·tion ▶ **n.** the adjustment of the eye to low light intensities, involving reflex dilation of the pupil and activation of the rod cells in preference to the cone cells.
– DERIVATIVES **dark-a·dapt·ed adj.**

Dark Ag·es 1 the period in western Europe between the fall of the Roman Empire and the high Middle Ages, c.AD 500–1100, during which Germanic tribes swept through Europe and North Africa, often attacking and destroying towns and settlements. ■ a period of supposed unenlightenment: *the dark ages of racism*. ■ (**the dark ages**) humorous or derogatory an obscure or little-regarded period in the past, esp. as characterizing an outdated attitude or practice: *the judge is living in the dark ages*.
2 Archaeology a period in Greece and the Aegean from the end of the Bronze Age until the beginning of the archaic period. There was no building of palaces and fortresses, and the art of writing was apparently lost.

Dark and Blood·y Ground a nickname for the state of **KENTUCKY**.

dark choc·o·late ▶ **n.** slightly bitter chocolate, of a deep brown color, without added milk.

Dark Con·ti·nent historical a name given to Africa at a time when it was little known to Europeans.

dark cur·rent ▶ **n.** the residual electric current flowing in a photoelectric device when there is no incident illumination.

dark·en /ˈdärkən/ ▶ **v. 1** make or become dark or darker: [no obj.] *the sky was darkening rapidly* | [with obj.] *darken the eyebrows with black powder* | (as adj. **darkened**) *a darkened room*. ■ [with obj.] (of an unpleasant event or state of affairs) cast a shadow over something; spoil: *the abuse darkened the rest of their lives*.
2 make or become gloomy, angry, or unhappy: [no obj.] *his mood darkened* | [with obj.] *the abuse darkened the rest of their lives*. ■ [no obj.] (of someone's eyes or expression) show anger or another strong negative emotion: *his face darkened and he lunged away*. ■ [with obj.] (of such an emotion) show in (someone's eyes or expression): *misery darkened her gaze*.
– PHRASES **darken someone's door** [with negative] visit someone's home: *never darken my door again!*
– DERIVATIVES **dark·en·er n.**

dark en·er·gy ▶ **n.** Physics a theoretical repulsive force that counteracts gravity and causes the universe to expand at an accelerating rate.

dark-field mi·cros·co·py ▶ **n.** a type of light microscopy that produces brightly illuminated objects on a dark background.

dark glass·es ▶ **plural n.** glasses with tinted lenses, worn to protect or conceal a person's eyes.

dark horse ▶ **n.** a candidate or competitor about whom little is known but who unexpectedly wins or succeeds: [as modifier] *a dark-horse candidate*.
– ORIGIN early 19th cent.: originally racing slang.

dark·ie /ˈdärkē/ ▶ **n.** variant spelling of **DARKY**.

dark lan·tern ▶ **n.** a lantern with a movable panel that can be used to hide the light.

dark line ▶ **n.** Physics a line in an absorption spectrum, appearing as a black line at visible wavelengths.

dark·ling /ˈdärkliNG/ ▶ **adj.** literary of or relating to growing darkness: *the darkling sky*.
– ORIGIN Middle English: from **DARK** + *-ling*, a suffix denoting condition or situation. The verb *darkle* is a back-formation dating from the 15th century.

dark·ling bee·tle ▶ **n.** a dark-colored nocturnal beetle, typically with reduced or absent wings. ● Family Tenebrionidae: numerous genera and species.

dark·ly /ˈdärklē/ ▶ **adv. 1** in a threatening, mysterious, or ominous way: *"You can't trust him," said Jacob darkly*. ■ in a depressing or pessimistic way: *I wondered darkly if I was wasting my time*.
2 with a dark color: *a figure silhouetted darkly against the trees*.

dark mat·ter ▶ **n.** Astronomy (in some cosmological theories) nonluminous material that is postulated to exist in space and that could take any of several forms including weakly interacting particles (**cold dark matter**) or high-energy randomly moving particles created soon after the Big Bang (**hot dark matter**).

dark neb·u·la ▶ **n.** Astronomy a nonluminous nebula of dust and gas that is observable because it obscures light from other sources.

dark·ness /ˈdärknis/ ▶ **n. 1** the partial or total absence of light: *the office was in darkness*. ■ night: *they began to make camp before darkness fell*. ■ the quality of being dark in color: *the darkness of his jacket*.
2 wickedness or evil: *the forces of darkness*. ■ unhappiness, distress, or gloom: *moments of darkness were rare*. ■ secrecy or mystery: *they drew a veil of darkness across the proceedings*. ■ lack of

d

spiritual or intellectual enlightenment; ignorance: *his accomplishments shone in a world of darkness.*

dark·net /'därk,net/ ▶ **n.** Computing a computer network with restricted access that is used chiefly for illegal peer-to-peer file sharing.

dark night of the soul ▶ **n.** Christian Theology a period of spiritual desolation suffered by a mystic in which all sense of consolation is removed.
– ORIGIN mid 19th cent.: used to translate Spanish *Noche oscura*, the title of a poem by the mystic St. John of the Cross.

dark re·ac·tion ▶ **n.** Biochemistry the cycle of reactions (the Calvin cycle) that occurs in the second phase of photosynthesis and does not require the presence of light. It involves the fixation of carbon dioxide and its reduction to carbohydrate and the dissociation of water, using chemical energy stored in ATP.

dark·room /'därk,ro͞om, -,ro͝om/ ▶ **n.** a room from which normal light is excluded, used for developing photographs.

dark star ▶ **n.** Astronomy a starlike object that emits little or no visible light. Its existence is inferred from other evidence, such as the eclipsing of other stars.

dark·y /'därkē/ (also **darkie**) ▶ **n.** (pl. **darkies**) informal, offensive a person with black or dark skin.

dar·ling /'därliNG/ ▶ **n.** used as an affectionate form of address to a beloved person: *good night, my darling.* ■ a lovable or endearing person: *he's such a darling.* ■ a person who is particularly popular with a certain group: *she is **the darling of** the media.*
▶ **adj.** [attrib.] beloved: *his darling wife.* ■ (esp. in affected use) pretty; charming: *a darling little pillbox hat.*
– ORIGIN Old English *dēorling* (see DEAR, -LING).

Dar·ling Riv·er /'därliNG/ a river in southeastern Australia that flows southwest for 1,712 miles (2,757 km) to join the Murray River.

Darm·stadt /'därm,stat, -,SHtät/ an industrial town in western Germany, in the state of Hesse; pop. 141,300 (est. 2006).

darm·stadt·i·um /därm'statēəm, -'SHtät-/ ▶ **n.** the synthetic chemical element of atomic number 110. It is a superheavy metal that decays in thousandths of a second. (Symbol: **Ds**)
– ORIGIN early 21st cent.: after a laboratory in *Darmstadt*, Germany, where the element was first created.

darn[1] /därn/ ▶ **v.** [with obj.] mend (knitted material or a hole in this) by weaving yarn across the hole with a needle: *I don't expect you to darn my socks.* ■ embroider (material) with a large running stitch.
▶ **n.** a place in a garment that has been mended in such a way.
– ORIGIN early 17th cent.: perhaps from dialect *dern* 'to hide,' which is from Old English *diernan*; compare with Middle Dutch *dernen* 'stop holes in (a dike).'

darn[2] (also **durn**) ▶ **v., adj., & exclam.** informal euphemism for DAMN: [as verb] *darn it all, Poppa* | [as adj.] *the darn things were expensive.*

darned /därnd/ (also **durned** /dərnd/) ▶ **adj.** informal euphemism for DAMNED: *you have to work a darned sight harder* | [as submodifier] *they're darned good songwriters.*
– DERIVATIVES **darned·est** adj.

dar·nel /'därnl/ ▶ **n.** a Eurasian ryegrass. ● Genus *Lolium*, family Gramineae: several species, in particular the widespread *L. temulentum.*
– ORIGIN Middle English: of unknown origin; apparently related to French (Walloon dialect) *darnelle.*

darn·er /'därnər/ ▶ **n. 1** a darning needle.
2 a large slender-bodied dragonfly. Also called DARNING NEEDLE, DEVIL'S DARNING NEEDLE. [said to be so named because of the popular belief that the dragonfly sews up the lips and eyelids of people sleeping.] ● Family Aeshnidae: several genera.

darn·ing /'därniNG/ ▶ **n.** the skill or activity of one who darns: *long hours of tedious darning.* ■ articles being darned or needing to be darned: *Aunt Edie bent her head to her darning.*

darn·ing egg ▶ **n.** an egg-shaped piece of wood or other smooth hard material used to stretch and support material being darned.

darn·ing nee·dle ▶ **n.** a long sewing needle with a large eye, used in darning. ■ another term for DARNER (sense 2).

Darn·ley /'därnlē/, Henry Stewart (or Stuart), Lord (1545–67), Scottish nobleman; second husband of Mary, Queen of Scots; father of James I of England.

DARPA /'därpə/ ▶ **abbr.** Defense Advanced Research Projects Agency, the central research and development organization for the US Department of Defense.

Dar·row /'darō/, Clarence Seward (1857–1938), US lawyer. He served as defense counsel in several well-publicized trials, including that of John T. Scopes, a teacher in Dayton, Tennessee, who was charged with violating state law for teaching evolution in a public school in 1925.

dar·shan /'där,SHän, -SHən/ ▶ **n.** Hinduism an opportunity or occasion of seeing a holy person or the image of a deity.
– ORIGIN via Hindi from Sanskrit *darśana* 'sight or seeing.'

Dart /därt/, Raymond Arthur (1893–1988), South African anthropologist and anatomist; born in Australia. In 1925, he found the first specimen of the hominid species *Australopithecus africanus*, for which he coined the genus name.

dart /därt/ ▶ **n. 1** a small pointed missile that can be thrown or fired. ■ a small pointed missile with a feather or plastic tail, used in the game of darts. ■ Zoology a dartlike calcareous organ of a snail forming part of the reproductive system, exchanged during copulation.
2 an act of running somewhere suddenly and rapidly: *the cat made a dart for the door.* ■ a sudden, intense pang of a particular emotion: *a dart of panic.*
3 a tapered tuck stitched into a garment in order to shape it.
▶ **v.** [no obj.] move or run somewhere suddenly or rapidly: *she darted across the street.* ■ [with obj.] cast (a look or one's eyes) suddenly and rapidly in a particular direction: *she darted a glance across the table.* ■ [with obj.] archaic throw (a missile). ■ [with obj.] shoot (an animal) with a dart, typically in order to administer a drug.
– ORIGIN Middle English: from Old French, accusative of *darz, dars*, from a West Germanic word meaning 'spear, lance.'

dart·board /'därt,bôrd/ ▶ **n.** a circular board marked with numbered segments, used as a target in the game of darts.

dart·er /'därtər/ ▶ **n. 1** another term for ANHINGA.
2 a small North American freshwater fish, the male of which may develop bright coloration during the breeding season. ● Genera *Etheostoma* and *Percina*, family Percidae: numerous species.

darts /därts/ ▶ **plural n.** [usu. treated as sing.] an indoor game in which small pointed missiles with feather or plastic flights are thrown at a circular target marked with numbers in order to score points.

Dar·win /'därwin/, Charles (Robert) (1809–82), English natural historian and geologist; a proponent of the theory of evolution by natural selection. While the naturalist on HMS *Beagle* for her voyage around the Southern Hemisphere 1831–36, he collected the material that became the basis for his ideas on natural selection. Notable works: *On the Origin of Species* (1859) and *The Descent of Man* (1871).

Dar·win·i·an /där'winēən/ ▶ **adj.** of or relating to Darwinism.
▶ **n.** an adherent of Darwinism.

Dar·win·ism /'därwə,nizəm/ ▶ **n.** the theory of the evolution of species by natural selection advanced by Charles Darwin.

> Darwin argued that since offspring tend to vary slightly from their parents, mutations that make an organism better adapted to its environment will be encouraged and developed by the pressures of natural selection, leading to the evolution of new species differing widely from one another and from their common ancestors. Darwinism was later developed by the findings of Mendelian genetics (see NEO-DARWINIAN).

– DERIVATIVES **Dar·win·ist** n. & adj.

Dar·win's finch·es ▶ **plural n.** a group of songbirds related to the buntings and found on the Galapagos Islands, discovered by Charles Darwin and used by him to illustrate his theory of natural selection. They are believed to have evolved from a common ancestor and have developed a variety of bills to suit various modes of life. ● Family Emberizidae (subfamily Emberizinae): four to six genera, esp. *Geospiza* (the **ground finches**) and *Camarhynchus* (the **tree finches**).

Da·sein /'dä,zīn/ ▶ **n.** Philosophy (in Hegelianism) existence or determinate being; (in existentialism) human existence.
– ORIGIN mid 19th cent.: German, from *dasein* 'exist,' from *da* 'there' + *sein* 'be.'

dash /daSH/ ▶ **v. 1** [no obj.] run or travel somewhere in a great hurry: *I dashed into the garden* | *I must dash, I'm late.* ■ (often **dash about/around**) move about in a great hurry, esp. in the attempt to do several things in a short period of time: *I dash about for four days in a manic fit to straighten things up.*
2 [with obj.] strike or fling (something) somewhere with great force, esp. so as to have a destructive effect; hurl: *the ship was dashed upon the rocks.* ■ [no obj.] strike forcefully against something: *a gust of rain dashed against the bricks.* ■ destroy or frustrate (a person's hopes or expectations): *the budget dashed hopes of an increase in funding.* ■ cause (someone) to lose confidence; dispirit: *I won't tell Stuart—I think he'd be dashed.*
▶ **exclam.** Brit. informal, dated used to express mild annoyance: *"Dash it all, I am in charge."*
▶ **n. 1** [in sing.] an act of running somewhere suddenly and hastily: *she **made a dash for** the door.* ■ a journey or period of time characterized by urgency or eager haste: *a 20-mile dash to the airport.* ■ a short fast race run in one heat; a sprint: *the 100-yard dash.*
2 a small quantity of a substance, esp. a liquid, added to something else: *whiskey with **a dash of** soda.* ■ a small amount of a particular quality adding piquancy or distinctiveness to something else: *a casual atmosphere with a dash of sophistication.*
3 a horizontal stroke in writing or printing to mark a pause or break in sense, or to represent omitted letters or words. ■ the longer signal of the two used in Morse code. Compare with DOT[1]. ■ Music a short vertical mark placed above or beneath a note to indicate that it is to be performed in a very staccato manner.
4 impetuous or flamboyant vigor and confidence; panache: *he has youthful energy, dash, and charisma.*
5 short for DASHBOARD.
– PHRASAL VERBS **dash something off** write something hurriedly and without much premeditation.
– ORIGIN Middle English (in the sense 'strike forcibly against'): probably symbolic of forceful movement and related to Swedish *daska* and Danish *daske.*

dash·board /'daSH,bôrd/ ▶ **n. 1** the panel facing the driver of a vehicle or the pilot of an aircraft, containing instruments and controls.
2 historical a board of wood or leather in front of a carriage, to keep out mud.

dashed /daSHt/ ▶ **adj.** [attrib.] **1** Brit. informal, dated used for emphasis: *it's a dashed shame* | [as submodifier] *she was dashed rude.*
2 (of a line on a piece of paper) composed of dashes.

da·sheen /da'SHēn/ ▶ **n.** another term for TARO.
– ORIGIN late 19th cent. (originally West Indian): of unknown origin.

dash·er /'daSHər/ ▶ **n. 1** informal a person who dresses or acts flamboyantly or stylishly.
2 a plunger for agitating cream in a churn.
3 Hockey the ledge along the top of the boards of a rink.

da·shi /'däSHē/ ▶ **n.** stock made from fish and kelp, used in Japanese cooking.

da·shi·ki /'däSHēkē/ ▶ **n.** (pl. **dashikis**) a loose, brightly colored shirt or tunic, originally from West Africa.
– ORIGIN from Yoruba or Hausa.

dash·ing /'daSHiNG/ ▶ **adj.** (of a man) attractive in a romantic, adventurous way: *a dashing pirate on the high seas.* ■ stylish or fashionable: *a dashing S-type Jaguar.*
– DERIVATIVES **dash·ing·ly** adv.

dash·pot /'daSH,pät/ ▶ **n.** a device for damping shock or vibration.

das·sie /'dasē/ ▶ **n.** (pl. **dassies**) a hyrax, esp. the rock hyrax of southern Africa. ● Family Procaviidae, in particular *Procavia capensis.*
– ORIGIN late 18th cent.: from Afrikaans, from South African Dutch *dasje*, diminutive of Dutch *das* 'badger.'

das·tard /'dastərd/ ▶ **n.** dated, humorous a dishonorable or despicable person.
– ORIGIN late Middle English (in the sense 'stupid person'): probably from *dazed*, influenced by *dotard* and *bastard.*

das·tard·ly /'dastərdlē/ ▶ **adj.** dated, humorous wicked and cruel: *pirates and their dastardly deeds.*
– DERIVATIVES **das·tard·li·ness** n.
– ORIGIN mid 16th cent. (in the sense 'dull or stupid'): from DASTARD in the obsolete sense 'base coward.'

das·y·ure /'dasē,yo͝or/ ▶ **n.** another term for QUOLL.
– ORIGIN mid 19th cent.: from French, from modern Latin *dasyurus*, from Greek *dasus* 'rough, hairy' + *oura* 'tail.'

DAT /dat/ ▶ **abbr.** digital audiotape.

da·ta /'datə, 'dātə/ ▶ **n.** [treated as sing. or pl.] facts and statistics collected together for reference or analysis. See also DATUM. ■ Computing the quantities, characters, or symbols on which operations are performed by a computer, being stored and

transmitted in the form of electrical signals and recorded on magnetic, optical, or mechanical recording media. ■ Philosophy things known or assumed as facts, making the basis of reasoning or calculation.
– ORIGIN mid 17th cent. (as a term in philosophy): from Latin, plural of DATUM.

> **USAGE** In Latin, **data** is the plural of **datum** and, historically and in specialized scientific fields, it is also treated as a plural in English, taking a plural verb, as in *the data were collected and classified*. In modern nonscientific use, however, it is generally not treated as a plural. Instead, it is treated as a mass noun, similar to a word like **information**, which takes a singular verb. Sentences such as *data was collected over a number of years* are now widely accepted in standard English.

da·ta·bank /ˈdatəˌbaNGk, ˈdā-/ (also **data bank**) ▶ **n.** Computing a large repository of data on a particular topic, sometimes formed from more than one database, and accessible by many users.

da·ta·base /ˈdatəˌbās, ˈdā-/ ▶ **n.** a structured set of data held in a computer, esp. one that is accessible in various ways.

da·ta·base man·age·ment sys·tem (abbr.: **DBMS**) ▶ **n.** Computing software that handles the storage, retrieval, and updating of data in a computer system.

dat·a·ble /ˈdātəbəl/ (also **dateable**) ▶ **adj.** able to be dated to a particular time.

da·ta cen·ter ▶ **n.** a large group of networked computer servers typically used by organizations for the remote storage, processing, or distribution of large amounts of data.

da·ta com·mun·i·ca·tions ▶ **n.** the electronic transmission of encoded information to, from, or between computers.

da·ta dic·tion·ar·y ▶ **n.** Computing a set of information describing the contents, format, and structure of a database and the relationship between its elements, used to control access to and manipulation of the database.

da·ta·glove /ˈdatəˌgləv, ˈdā-/ ▶ **n.** Computing a device, worn like a glove, that allows the manual manipulation of images in virtual reality.

da·ta·link /ˈdatəˌlinGk, ˈdātə-/ ▶ **n.** an electronic connection for the exchange of information: *a datalink system that would allow aircraft controllers and pilots to exchange electronic messages.*

da·ta min·ing ▶ **n.** Computing the practice of examining large databases in order to generate new information.

da·ta·point /ˈdatəˌpoint, ˈdātə-/ ▶ **n.** an identifiable element in a data set: *software that can quickly process tens of thousands of datapoints.*

da·ta proc·ess·ing ▶ **n.** a series of operations on data, esp. by a computer, to retrieve, transform, or classify information.
– DERIVATIVES **da·ta proc·es·sor** **n.**

da·ta set ▶ **n.** Computing a collection of related sets of information that is composed of separate elements but can be manipulated as a unit by a computer.

da·ta smog ▶ **n.** informal an overwhelming excess of information, esp. from the Internet: *nowadays, people need help getting their intellectual bearings because cable has become a torrent of ideology, dueling experts and data smog.*

da·ta ter·mi·nal ▶ **n.** Computing a terminal at which a person can enter data into a computer-based system or receive data from one.

da·ta type ▶ **n.** Computing a particular kind of data item, as defined by the values it can take, the programming language used, or the operations that can be performed on it.

da·ta·veil·lance /ˌdatəˈvāləns, ˌdātə-/ ▶ **n.** the practice of monitoring the online activity of a person or group, from algorithmic study of the residue of their various electronic and digital transactions and activities.
– ORIGIN 1980s: blend of *data* and *surveillance*.

da·ta ware·house ▶ **n.** Computing a large store of data accumulated from a wide range of sources within a company and used to guide management decisions.
– DERIVATIVES **da·ta ware·hous·ing** **n.**

date[1] /dāt/ ▶ **n. 1** the day of the month or year as specified by a number: *what's the date today?* | *please give your name, address, and* **date of birth**. ■ a particular day or year when a given event occurred or will occur: *significant dates like 1776 and 1789* | *they've set a date for the wedding.* ■ (**dates**) the years of a person's birth and death or of the beginning and end of a period or event: *giving the dates of kings and queens.* ■ the period of time to which an artifact or structure belongs: *the church is the largest of its date.* ■ *these Roman coins bear an explicit date.*
2 a social or romantic appointment or engagement: *a college student* **on a date** *with someone he met in class.* ■ a person with whom one has such an engagement: *my date isn't going to show, it seems.* ■ a musical or theatrical engagement or performance, esp. as part of a tour: *possible live dates in the near future.*
▶ **v.** [with obj.] **1** establish or ascertain the date of (an object or event): *they date the paintings to 1460–70.* ■ mark with a date: *sign and date the document.* ■ [no obj.] have its origin at a particular time; have existed since: *the controversy* **dates back to** *1986.*
2 indicate or expose as being old-fashioned: *disco—that word alone dates me.* ■ [no obj.] seem old-fashioned: *a movie that will date quickly.*
3 go out with (someone in whom one is romantically or sexually interested): *my sister's pretty judgmental about the girls I date* | [no obj.] *they have been dating for more than a year.*
– PHRASES **to date** until now: *their finest work to date.*
– ORIGIN Middle English: via Old French from medieval Latin *data*, feminine past participle of *dare* 'give'; from the Latin formula used in dating letters, *data (epistola)* '(letter) given or delivered,' to record a particular time or place.

date[2] ▶ **n. 1** a sweet, dark brown, oval fruit containing a hard stone, often eaten dried.
2 (also **date palm**) the tall palm tree that bears clusters of this fruit, native to western Asia and North Africa. ● *Phoenix dactylifera*, family Palmae.
– ORIGIN Middle English: from Old French, via Latin from Greek *daktulos* 'finger' (because of the fingerlike shape of its leaves).

date·a·ble ▶ **adj.** variant spelling of DATABLE.

date·book /ˈdātˌbo͝ok/ ▶ **n.** a book with spaces for each day of the year in which one notes appointments or important information for each day.

dat·ed /ˈdātid/ ▶ **adj. 1** marked with a date: *a signed and dated painting.*
2 old-fashioned: *a dated expression.*

date·less /ˈdātlis/ ▶ **adj. 1** not clearly belonging to any particular period, therefore not likely to go out of date: *dateless dresses.* ■ (of a document or stamp) having no date mark.
2 not having, or incapable of having, social or romantic appointments or engagements: *dateless men reduce women to sex objects and dateless women become space-age scanners.*

date·line /ˈdātˌlīn/ ▶ **n.** a line at the head of a dispatch or special article in a newspaper showing the date and place of writing.
▶ **v.** [with obj.] mark (a dispatch or article) with a dateline.

Date Line (also **International Date Line**) an imaginary north–south line through the Pacific Ocean, adopted in 1884, to the east of which the date is a day earlier than it is to the west. It lies chiefly along the meridian farthest from Greenwich, England (i.e., longitude 180°), with diversions to pass around some island groups.

date palm ▶ **n.** see DATE[2].

date rape ▶ **n.** rape committed by the victim's escort.

date-rape drug ▶ **n.** a drug that causes temporary loss of memory or inhibition, surreptitiously given to a girl or a woman so that her date may sexually abuse or rape her.

date stamp ▶ **n.** a stamped mark indicating a date, typically used on food packaging or mailed envelopes. ■ an adjustable stamp used to make such a mark.
▶ **v.** (**date-stamp**) [with obj.] mark (something) with a date stamp.

dat·ing serv·ice ▶ **n.** an agency that arranges introductions for people seeking romantic partners or friends with similar interests.

da·tive /ˈdātiv/ Grammar ▶ **adj.** (in Latin, Greek, German, and other languages) denoting a case of nouns and pronouns, and words in grammatical agreement with them, indicating an indirect object or recipient.
▶ **n.** a noun or other word of this type. ■ (**the dative**) the dative case.
– ORIGIN late Middle English: from Latin *(casus) dativus* '(case) of giving,' from *dat-* 'given,' from the verb *dare*.

Da·tong /ˈdäˈto͝oNG/ a city in northern China, in Shanxi province; pop. 1,105,100 (est. 2006).

da·tum /ˈdātəm, ˈdatəm/ ▶ **n.** (pl. **data** /ˈdātə, ˈdatə/) **1** a piece of information. See also DATA. ■ an assumption or premise from which inferences may be drawn. See SENSE DATUM.
2 a fixed starting point of a scale or operation.
– ORIGIN mid 18th cent.: from Latin, literally 'something given,' neuter past participle of *dare* 'give.'

da·tum line (also **datum level**) ▶ **n.** a standard of comparison or point of reference. ■ Surveying an assumed surface used as a reference for the measurement of heights and depths. ■ a line to which dimensions are referred on engineering drawings, and from which measurements are calculated.

da·tu·ra /dəˈt(y)o͝orə/ ▶ **n.** a shrubby annual plant with large trumpet-shaped flowers, native to southern North America. Daturas contain toxic or narcotic alkaloids and are used as hallucinogens by some American Indian peoples. See also ANGEL'S TRUMPET. ● Genus *Datura*, family Solanaceae: several species, including the jimson weed.
– ORIGIN modern Latin, from Hindi *dhatūrā*.

daub /dôb/ ▶ **v.** [with obj.] coat or smear (a surface) with a thick or sticky substance in a carelessly rough or liberal way: *she* **daubed** *her face* **with** *night cream.* ■ spread (a thick or sticky substance) on a surface in such a way: *a canvas with paint* **daubed on** *it.* ■ paint (words or drawings) on a surface in such a way: *they daubed graffiti on the walls.*
▶ **n. 1** plaster, clay, or another substance used for coating a surface, esp. when mixed with straw and applied to laths or wattles to form a wall: *square huts, mostly daub and wattle.* ■ a patch or smear of a thick or sticky substance: *a daub of paint.*
2 a painting executed without much skill.
– ORIGIN late Middle English: from Old French *dauber*, from Latin *dealbare* 'whiten, whitewash,' based on *albus* 'white.'

daube /dōb/ ▶ **n.** a stew of meat, typically beef, braised slowly in wine.
– PHRASES **en daube** (of meat) cooked in this way.
– ORIGIN French; compare with Italian *addobbo* 'seasoning.'

daub·er /ˈdôbər/ ▶ **n.** a crude or inartistic painter. ■ an implement used for daubing.

Dau·bi·gny /ˌdôbēˈnyē/, Charles François (1817–78), French landscape painter. A member of the Barbizon School, he is often regarded as a linking figure between this group and the Impressionists.

daugh·ter /ˈdôtər, ˈdä-/ ▶ **n.** a girl or woman in relation to her parents. ■ a female offspring of an animal. ■ a female descendant: *we are the sons and daughters of Adam.* ■ a woman considered as the product of a particular person, influence, or environment: *a daughter of the dry savannas of Africa.* ■ archaic used as a term of affectionate address to a woman or girl, typically by an older person. ■ literary a thing personified as a daughter in relation to its origin or source: *Italian, the eldest daughter of ancient Latin.* ■ Physics a nuclide formed by the radioactive decay of another.
▶ **adj.** Biology originating through division or replication: *daughter cells.*
– DERIVATIVES **daugh·ter·hood** /-ˌho͝od/ **n.**, **daugh·ter·ly** **adj.**
– ORIGIN Old English *dohtor*, of Germanic origin; related to Dutch *dochter* and German *Tochter*, from an Indo-European root shared by Greek *thugatēr*.

daugh·ter·board /ˈdôtərˌbôrd, ˈdä-/ (also **daughtercard**) ▶ **n.** Electronics an expansion circuit card affixed to a motherboard that accesses memory and the CPU directly rather than through a bus.

daugh·ter-in-law ▶ **n.** (pl. **daughters-in-law**) the wife of one's son.

Daugh·ters of the A·mer·i·can Rev·o·lu·tion (abbr.: **DAR**) a patriotic society whose aims include encouraging education and the study of US history and that tends to be politically conservative. Membership is limited to female descendants of those who aided the cause of independence.

Dau·mier /dōˈmyā/, Honoré (1808–78), French painter and lithographer. Working as a cartoonist, he produced lithographs satirizing French society and politics.

daunt /dônt, dänt/ ▶ **v.** [with obj.] (usu. **be daunted**) make (someone) feel intimidated or apprehensive: *some people are daunted by technology.*
– PHRASES **nothing daunted** without having been made fearful or apprehensive: *nothing daunted, the committee set to work.*
– ORIGIN Middle English: from Old French *danter*, from Latin *domitare*, frequentative of *domare* 'to tame.'

PRONUNCIATION KEY ə *ago, up*; ər *over, fur*; a *hat*; ā *ate*; ä *car*; e *let*; ē *see*; i *fit*; ī *by*; NG *sing*; ō *go*; ô *law, for*; oi *toy*; o͝o *good*; o͞o *goo*; ou *out*; TH *thin*; T͟H *then*; ZH *vision*

daunt·ing /ˈdôntiNG, ˈdänt-/ ▶ **adj.** seeming difficult to deal with in anticipation; intimidating: *a daunting task.*
– DERIVATIVES **daunt·ing·ly** adv.

daunt·less /ˈdôntlis, ˈdänt-/ ▶ **adj.** showing fearlessness and determination: *dauntless bravery.*
– DERIVATIVES **daunt·less·ly** adv., **daunt·less·ness** n.

dau·phin /ˈdôfin/ ▶ **n.** historical the eldest son of the king of France.
– ORIGIN French, from the family name of the lords of the Dauphiné (first used in this way in the 14th cent.), ultimately a nickname meaning 'dolphin.'

d

dau·phi·nois /ˌdôfinˈwä/ (also **dauphinoise** /-ˈwäz/) ▶ **adj.** (of potatoes or other vegetables) sliced and cooked in milk, typically with a topping of cheese.
– ORIGIN French, 'from the province of Dauphiné.'

Da·vao /ˈdäˌvou, däˈvou/ a seaport in the southern Philippines, on the island of Mindanao; pop. 785,700 (est. 2007).

da·ven /ˈdävən/ ▶ **v.** (**davens, davening, davened**) [no obj.] (in Judaism) recite the prescribed liturgical prayers.
– ORIGIN Yiddish.

Dav·en·port /ˈdavənˌpôrt/ an industrial city in southeastern Iowa, on the Mississippi River, one of the Quad Cities; pop. 100,827 (est. 2008).

dav·en·port /ˈdavənˌpôrt/ ▶ **n. 1** a large upholstered sofa, typically able to be converted into a bed. [perhaps from a manufacturer's name.]
2 Brit. an ornamental writing desk with drawers and a sloping surface for writing. [probably named after Captain *Davenport*, for whom early examples of this type of desk were made in the late 18th cent.]

Da·vid[1] /ˈdāvid/ (died *c.*962 BC), king of Judah and Israel *c.*1000–*c.*962 BC. In the biblical account, he killed the Philistine Goliath and, on Saul's death, became king, making Jerusalem his capital. He is traditionally regarded as the author of the Psalms, although this has been disputed.

Da·vid[2] the name of two kings of Scotland. ■ **David I** (*c.*1084–1153), sixth son of Malcolm III; reigned 1124–53. In 1136, he invaded England in support of his niece Matilda's claim to the throne, but he was defeated at the Battle of the Standard in 1138. ■ **David II** (1324–71), son of Robert the Bruce; reigned 1329–71.

Da·vid[3] /däˈvēd/, Jacques-Louis (1748–1825), French painter. He is noted for neoclassical paintings such as *The Oath of the Horatii* (1784) and *The Intervention of the Sabine Women* (1799).

Da·vid, St. /ˈdāvid/ (6th century), Welsh monk; Welsh name **De·wi** /ˈde-wē/ . Since the 12th century he has been regarded as the patron saint of Wales. Feast day, March 1.

da Vin·ci, Leonardo /də ˈvinCHē/ see **LEONARDO DA VINCI.**

Da·vis[1] /ˈdāvis/ an academic and agricultural city in north central California, west of Sacramento; pop. 62,593 (est. 2008).

Da·vis[2], Angela Yvonne (1944–), US civil rights leader and writer. She wrote *Women, Race and Class* (1980).

Da·vis[3], Benjamin Oliver (1877–1970), US military leader. In 1940, he became the first African-American general in the US Army. His son, **Benjamin O. Davis, Jr.** (1912–2002), an aviator, became the first African-American Air Force general in 1953.

Bette Davis

Da·vis[4], Bette (1908–89), US actress; born *Ruth Elizabeth Davis.* She established her Hollywood career playing a number of strong, independent female characters in such movies as *Dangerous* (1935) and *Jezebel* (1938). Her flair for suggesting the macabre and menacing emerged in later movies, such as *Whatever Happened to Baby Jane?* (1962).

Da·vis[5], David (1815–86), US Supreme Court associate justice 1862–77 and a US senator from Illinois 1877–83.

Jefferson Davis

Da·vis[6], Jefferson (1808–89), US politician and president of the Confederate States of America (CSA). As a US senator from Mississippi 1847–51 and a defender of slavery, he withdrew from the Senate when Mississippi seceded from the Union and was elected president of CSA in 1862. He wrote *The Rise and Fall of the Confederate Government* (1881).

Da·vis[7], Miles (Dewey) (1926–91), US jazz trumpeter, composer, and bandleader. His influence on "cool jazz" is heard in his *Birth of the Cool* recordings (1948–49). His album *Kind of Blue* (1959) introduced "modal jazz." In the 1960s, he pioneered the fusion of jazz and rock.

Da·vis[8], Sammy, Jr. (1925–90), US actor, singer, and dancer. He appeared in *Ocean's Eleven* (1960) along with Frank Sinatra and other members of the "Rat Pack." His recording of "Candy Man" (1972) became his theme song.

Da·vis Cup an annual tennis championship for men, first held in 1900, between teams from different countries.
– ORIGIN named after Dwight F. *Davis* (1879–1945), the US doubles champion who donated the trophy.

Da·vis Moun·tains a range in southwestern Texas, site of the Mount Locke observatory and several resorts.

Da·vis·son /ˈdāvəsən/, Clinton Joseph (1881–1958), US physicist. With **L. H. Germer** (1896–1971), he discovered electron diffraction, thus confirming de Broglie's theory of the wave nature of electrons. He shared the 1937 Nobel Prize for Physics with George P. Thomson (1892–1975).

Da·vis Strait a sea passage 400 miles (645 km) long that separates Greenland from Baffin Island and connects Baffin Bay with the Atlantic Ocean.
– ORIGIN named after John *Davis* (*c.*1550–1605), the English explorer who sailed through it in 1587.

da·vit /ˈdavit, ˈdā-/ ▶ **n.** a small crane on board a ship, esp. one of a pair for suspending or lowering a lifeboat.
– ORIGIN late 15th cent.: from Old French *daviot*, diminutive of *david*, denoting a kind of carpenter's tool.

Da·vy /ˈdāvē/, Sir Humphry (1778–1829), English chemist; a pioneer of electrochemistry. He discovered nitrous oxide (laughing gas) and the elements sodium, potassium, magnesium, calcium, strontium, and barium. He also identified and named the element chlorine, determined the properties of iodine, and demonstrated that diamond was a form of carbon.

Da·vy Jones's lock·er /ˌdāvē ˈjōnz(əz)/ ▶ **n.** informal the bottom of the sea, esp. regarded as the grave of those drowned at sea.
– ORIGIN extension of early 18th-cent. nautical slang *Davy Jones*, denoting the evil spirit of the sea.

Da·vy lamp ▶ **n.** historical a miner's portable safety lamp with the flame enclosed by wire gauze to reduce the risk of an explosion of gas.

daw /dô/ ▶ **n.** another term for **JACKDAW.**
– ORIGIN late Middle English: of Germanic origin; related to German *Dohle.*

daw·dle /ˈdôdl/ ▶ **v.** [no obj.] waste time; be slow: *I couldn't dawdle over my coffee any longer.* ■ [with adverbial of direction] move slowly and idly: *Ruth dawdled back through the woods.*
– DERIVATIVES **daw·dler** /ˈdôd(ə)lər/ **n.**
– ORIGIN mid 17th cent.: related to dialect *daddle, doddle* 'dally.'

Dawes[1] /dôz/, Charles Gates (1865–1951), US politician, lawyer, and financier; US vice president 1925–29. He was instrumental in formulating the 1923 plan for restructuring post–World War I Germany's economy. Nobel Peace Prize (1925).

Dawes[2], William (1745–99), US patriot. With Paul Revere he rode from Lexington to Concord, Massachusetts, to warn of approaching British soldiers on April 18, 1775.

dawg /dôg/ ▶ **n.** nonstandard spelling of **DOG**, used esp. to represent American speech.

dawn /dôn, dän/ ▶ **n.** the first appearance of light in the sky before sunrise: *the rose-pink light of dawn.* ■ the beginning of a phenomenon or period of time, esp. one considered favorable: *the dawn of civilization.*
▶ **v.** [no obj.] **1** (of a day) begin: [with complement] *Thursday dawned bright and sunny.* ■ come into existence: *a new era of land-use policy was dawning.*
2 become evident to the mind; be perceived or understood: *the awful truth was beginning to* ***dawn on him*** | (as adj. **dawning**) *he smiled with dawning recognition.*
– PHRASES **from dawn to dusk** all day; ceaselessly: *day after day from dawn to dusk, they drove those loaded canoes.*
– ORIGIN late 15th cent. (as a verb): back-formation from Middle English **DAWNING.**

dawn cho·rus ▶ **n.** [in sing.] the singing of a large number of birds before dawn each day, particularly during the breeding season.

dawn·ing /ˈdôniNG, ˈdän-/ ▶ **n.** literary dawn. ■ the beginning or first appearance of something: *the dawning of civilization.*
– ORIGIN Middle English: alteration of earlier *dawing*, from Old English *dagian* 'to dawn,' of Germanic origin; related to Dutch *dagen* and German *tagen*, also to **DAY.**

dawn red·wood ▶ **n.** a coniferous tree with deciduous needles, known only as a fossil until it was found growing in southwestern China in 1941. Also called **METASEQUOIA.** ● *Metasequoia glyptostroboides*, family Taxodiaceae.

Daw·son /ˈdôsən/ a town in the west central Yukon Territory, on the Klondike and Yukon rivers, center of a gold rush after 1896.

DAX ▶ **abbr.** Deutscher Aktien Index, the German stock exchange index.

Day[1] /dā/, Doris (1924–), US actress and singer; born *Doris Kappelhoff.* She became a movie star in the 1950s with roles in lighthearted musicals, comedies, and romances, such as *Calamity Jane* (1953) and *Pillow Talk* (1959).

Day[2], Dorothy (1897–1980), US journalist and reformer. She founded the *Catholic Worker* newspaper with social activist Peter Maurin (1877–1949) in 1933.

Day[3], William Rufus (1849–1923), US Supreme Court associate justice 1903–22. He was appointed to the Court by President Theodore Roosevelt.

day /dā/ ▶ **n. 1** a period of twenty-four hours as a unit of time, reckoned from one midnight to the next, corresponding to a rotation of the earth on its axis. ■ the part of this period when it is light; the time between sunrise and sunset: *she sleeps all day and goes out at night* | *the animals hunt* ***by day.*** ■ the time spent working during such a period: *he works an eight-hour day.* ■ Astronomy a single rotation of a planet in relation to its primary. ■ Astronomy the period on a planet when its primary star is above the horizon. ■ archaic daylight: *by the time they had all gone it was broad day.*
2 (usu. **days**) a particular period of the past; an era: *the laws were very strict in those days.* ■ **(the day)** the present time: *the political issues of the day.* ■ [with adj.] a day associated with a particular event or purpose: *graduation day* | *Christmas Day.* ■ a day's endeavor, or the period of an endeavor, esp. as bringing success: *speed and surprise would win the day.* ■ [usu. with modifier] **(days)** a particular period in a person's life or career: *my student days.* ■ **(one's day)** the successful, fortunate, or influential period of a person's life or career: *he had been a matinée idol in his day.* ■ **(one's days)** the span of someone's life: *she cared for him for the rest of his days.*
▶ **adj.** [attrib.] carried out during the day as opposed to the evening or at night: *my day job.* ■ (of a person) working during the day as opposed to at night: *a day nurse.*
– PHRASES **all in a** (or **the**) **day's work** (of something unusual or difficult) accepted as part of someone's normal routine or as a matter of course: *dodging sharks is all in a day's work for these scientists.* **any day** informal at any time or under any circumstances (used to express a strong opinion or preference): *I'd rather live in a shack in the woods than a penthouse in the city, any day* | *you can take me dancing* ***any day of the week.*** ■ very soon: *she's expected to give birth any day.* **at the end of the day** see **END. by the day** gradually and steadily: *the campaign is growing by the day.* **call it a day** end a period of activity, esp. resting content that enough

has been done: *we were prepared to do another long march before calling it a day.* **day after day** on each successive day, esp. over a long period: *the rain poured down day after day.* **day and night** all the time: *they kept working, day and night.* **day by day** gradually and steadily: *day by day I grew worse.* **day in, day out** continuously or repeatedly over a long period of time. **day of reckoning** the time when past mistakes or misdeeds must be punished or paid for; a testing time when the degree of one's success or failure will be revealed. [with allusion to Judgment Day, on which (in some beliefs) the judgment of humankind is expected to take place.] **from day one** from the very beginning: *children need a firm hand from day one.* **have had one's** (or **its**) **day** be no longer popular, successful, or influential: *power dressing has had its day.* **if someone is a day** at least (added to a statement about a person's age): *he must be seventy if he's a day.* **in this day and age** at the present time; in the modern era: *it simplifies housekeeping, which is essential in this day and age.* **not someone's day** used to convey that someone has had a bad day. **—— of the day** a thing currently considered to be particularly interesting or important: *the big news story of the day.* **one day** (or **one of these days**) at some time in the future: *our wishes will come true one of these days.* **one of those days** a day when several things go wrong. **that will** (or **that'll**) **be the day** informal that will never happen. **these days** at present: *he is drinking far too much these days.* **those were the days** used to assert that a particular past time was better than the present. **to the day** exactly: *it's four years to the day since we won the lottery.* **to this day** up to the present time; still: *the tradition continues to this day.*
– ORIGIN Old English *dæg*, of Germanic origin; related to Dutch *dag* and German *Tag*.

Day·ak /ˈdīˌak/ (also **Dyak**) ▶ **n.** (pl. **same** or **Dayaks**) **1** a member of a group of indigenous peoples inhabiting parts of Borneo. **2** the group of Austronesian languages spoken by these peoples.
▶ **adj.** of or relating to these peoples or their languages.
– ORIGIN mid 19th cent.: Malay, literally 'up-country.'

Da·yan /däˈyän/, Moshe (1915–81), Israeli statesman and general. As minister of defense he oversaw Israel's victory in the Six Day War, and as foreign minister he played a prominent role in negotiations that led to the Camp David agreements of 1979.

day·bed /ˈdāˌbed/ ▶ **n.** a couch that can be made up into a bed.

day·book /ˈdāˌbo͝ok/ ▶ **n.** an account book in which a day's transactions are entered for later transfer to a ledger. ■ a diary.

day·break /ˈdāˌbrāk/ ▶ **n.** the time in the morning when daylight first appears; dawn: *she set off at daybreak.*

day care ▶ **n.** daytime care for the needs of people who cannot be fully independent, such as children or elderly people: *family issues such as day care* | [as modifier] *a day-care center for employees' children.*

day·dream /ˈdāˌdrēm/ ▶ **n.** a series of pleasant thoughts that distract one's attention from the present.
▶ **v.** [no obj.] indulge in such a series of thoughts: *stop daydreaming and pay attention.*
– DERIVATIVES **day·dream·er** **n.**, **day·dream·y** **adj.**

day·flow·er /ˈdāˌflou(-ə)r/ ▶ **n.** a plant related to the spiderwort, with short-lived flowers that are typically blue. ● Genus *Commelina*, family Commelinaceae.

Day-Glo /ˈdāˌglō/ ▶ **n.** trademark a fluorescent paint or other coloring.
▶ **adj.** (also **day-glo**) of or denoting very bright or fluorescent coloring: *wearing Day-Glo pink T-shirts.*
– ORIGIN 1950s: blend of DAY and GLOW.

day job ▶ **n.** a person's regular job and main source of income, usually performed during the normal business day, and either allowing them to practice an avocation or contrasting with a vocation they would rather pursue.

day la·bor ▶ **n.** unskilled labor paid by the day.
– DERIVATIVES **day la·bor·er** **n.**

Day Lew·is /dā ˈlo͞oəs/, C. (1904–72), English poet, novelist, and critic; full name *Cecil Day Lewis*. He served as Britain's poet laureate 1968–72 and also wrote detective novels under the name **Nicholas Blake**.

day·light /ˈdāˌlīt/ ▶ **n. 1** the natural light of the day: *there were two hours of daylight left* | [as modifier] *the daylight hours.* ■ the first appearance of light in the morning; dawn: *I returned at daylight.* ■ visible distance between one person or thing and another: figurative *their views on education are so close that it's difficult to see daylight between them.* **2** (**daylights**) used to emphasize the severity or thoroughness of an action: *my father beat the living daylights out of them.* [from *daylights* meaning 'eyes,' hence 'any vital organ.']
– PHRASES **see daylight** begin to understand what was previously puzzling or unclear.

day·light·ing /ˈdāˌlītiNG/ ▶ **n.** the illumination of buildings by natural light: *daylighting is achieved by using properly designed windows and skylights.*

day·light sav·ing time (also **daylight savings time**) ▶ **n.** time as adjusted to achieve longer evening daylight, esp. in summer, by setting the clocks an hour ahead of the standard time.

day·lil·y /ˈdāˌlilē/ (also **day lily**) ▶ **n.** a lily that bears large yellow, red, or orange flowers, each flower lasting only one day. ● Genus *Hemerocallis*, family Liliaceae.

day·long /ˈdāˈlôNG/ ▶ **adj.** of a day's duration; lasting all day: *a daylong deluge.*

day·mare /ˈdāˌme(ə)r/ ▶ **n.** a frightening or oppressive trance or hallucinatory condition experienced while awake.
– ORIGIN mid 17th cent.: from DAY, on the pattern of *nightmare*.

day nurs·er·y ▶ **n.** a place where young children are cared for during the working day.

Day of A·tone·ment another term for YOM KIPPUR.

day off ▶ **n.** (pl. **days off**) a day's vacation from work or school on what would normally be a working day.

Day of Judg·ment another term for JUDGMENT DAY.

day·pack /ˈdāˌpak/ ▶ **n.** a small backpack, used for day hikes or for carrying books, etc.

day room (also **dayroom**) ▶ **n.** a room used for daytime recreation, esp. a communal room in an institution.

day·sail /ˈdāˌsāl/ ▶ **v.** [no obj.] sail a yacht for a single day: (as noun **daysailing**) *an outstanding boat for daysailing.*

day·sail·er /ˈdāˌsālər/ ▶ **n.** a sailboat without a cabin, designed for day trips.

day school ▶ **n.** a nonresidential school, typically a private one.

day shift ▶ **n.** a period of time worked during the daylight hours in a hospital, factory, etc., as opposed to the night shift. ■ [treated as sing. or pl.] the employees who work during this period.

day·side /ˈdāˌsīd/ ▶ **n.** Astronomy the side of a planet that is facing its primary star.

Days of Awe ▶ **plural n.** another term for HIGH HOLIDAYS.

day·spring /ˈdāˌspriNG/ ▶ **n.** literary dawn.

day stu·dent ▶ **n.** a student who attends classes at a boarding school or college but who does not live at the school.

day·time /ˈdāˌtīm/ ▶ **n.** the time of the day between sunrise and sunset: *she was alone* ***in the daytime*** | [as modifier] *a daytime telephone number.*

day-to-day ▶ **adj.** [attrib.] happening regularly every day: *the day-to-day management of the classroom.* ■ ordinary; everyday: *our day-to-day domestic life.* ■ short-term; without consideration for the future: *the struggle for day-to-day survival.* ■ Sports (of an injured player) not playing owing to a minor injury that is being treated and evaluated on a daily basis: *their shortstop has an ankle sprain and is listed as day-to-day.*
▶ **n.** [in sing.] an ordinary, everyday routine: *they have come to escape the day-to-day.*
▶ **adv.** on a daily basis: *the information to be traded is determined day-to-day.*

Day·ton /ˈdātn/ a city in western Ohio; pop. 154,200 (est. 2008). It was the home of aviation pioneers Wilbur and Orville Wright and is still a center of aerospace research.

Day·to·na Beach /dāˈtōnə/ a resort city in northeastern Florida, on the Atlantic coast; pop. 64,211 (est. 2008).

day trad·ing ▶ **n.** the buying and selling of securities on the same day, often online, on the basis of small, short-term price fluctuations.
– DERIVATIVES **day-trade** **v.**, **day trad·er** **n.**

day trip ▶ **n.** a journey or excursion completed in one day.
– DERIVATIVES **day-trip·per** (or **day tripper**) **n.**

day·wear /ˈdāˌwe(ə)r/ ▶ **n.** articles of casual clothing suitable for informal or everyday occasions.

day·work /ˈdāˌwərk/ ▶ **n.** casual work paid for on a daily basis.
– DERIVATIVES **day·work·er** **n.**

daze /dāz/ ▶ **v.** [with obj.] (usu. **be dazed**) make (someone) unable to think or react properly; stupefy; bewilder: *she was dazed by his revelations* | (as adj. **dazed**) *he staggered home dazed and confused.*
▶ **n.** [in sing.] a state of stunned confusion or bewilderment: *he was walking around* ***in a daze.***
– DERIVATIVES **daz·ed·ly** /ˈdāzidlē/ **adv.**
– ORIGIN Middle English: back-formation from *dazed* (adjective), from Old Norse *dasathr* 'weary'; compare with Swedish *dasa* 'lie idle.'

da·zi·bao /ˌdädzēˈbou/ ▶ **n.** (pl. **same**) (in the People's Republic of China) a wall poster written in large characters.
– ORIGIN Chinese, from *dà* 'big' + *zì* 'character' + *bào* 'newspaper or poster.'

daz·zle /ˈdazəl/ ▶ **v.** [with obj.] (of a bright light) blind (a person) temporarily: *she was dazzled by the headlights.* ■ amaze or overwhelm (someone) with a particular impressive quality: *I was dazzled by the beauty and breadth of the exhibition.* ■ [no obj.] archaic (of the eyes) be affected by a bright light: *my eyes dazzled and I could not move.*
▶ **n.** brightness that confuses someone's vision temporarily: [in sing.] *a dazzle of green and red spotlights.*
– DERIVATIVES **daz·zle·ment** **n.**
– ORIGIN late 15th cent. (in the sense 'be dazzled'): frequentative of the verb DAZE.

daz·zler /ˈdaz(ə)lər/ ▶ **n.** a person or thing that dazzles, in particular a person who is overwhelmingly impressive or skillful.

daz·zling /ˈdaz(ə)liNG/ ▶ **adj.** extremely bright, esp. so as to blind the eyes temporarily: *the sunlight was dazzling* | figurative *a dazzling smile.* ■ extremely impressive, beautiful, or skillful: *a dazzling display of football.*
– DERIVATIVES **daz·zling·ly** **adv.**

Db ▶ **symbol** the chemical element dubnium.

dB ▶ **abbr.** decibel(s).

dba (also **d/b/a**) ▶ **abbr.** doing business as.

DBMS ▶ **abbr.** database management system.

DBS ▶ **abbr.** ■ direct broadcasting by satellite. ■ direct-broadcast satellite.

dbx ▶ **n.** trademark electronic circuitry designed to increase the dynamic range of reproduced sound and reduce noise in the system.
– ORIGIN 1970s: from DB 'decibel' + *x* (representing *expander*).

DC ▶ **abbr.** ■ Music da capo. ■ direct current. ■ District of Columbia: *Washington, DC.* ■ Doctor of Chiropractic.

DCL ▶ **abbr.** Doctor of Civil Law.

DCM ▶ **abbr.** (in the UK) Distinguished Conduct Medal, awarded for bravery.

DD ▶ **abbr.** ■ Department of Defense (on forms and documents): *a DD 214.* ■ Military dishonorable discharge. ■ Doctor of Divinity.

D-Day ▶ **n.** the day (June 6, 1944) in World War II on which Allied forces invaded northern France by means of beach landings in Normandy. ■ the day on which an important operation is to begin or a change to take effect: *it's D-day at the Websters', as Sally gives Kevin an ultimatum.*
– ORIGIN from *D* for *day* + DAY. Compare with H-HOUR.

DDC (also **ddC**) ▶ **abbr.** dideoxycytidine.

DDE ▶ **n.** Computing a standard allowing data to be shared between different programs.
– ORIGIN 1980s: abbreviation of *Dynamic Data Exchange*.

DDI (also **ddI**) ▶ **abbr.** dideoxyinosine.

DDoS (also **DDOS**) ▶ **abbr.** distributed denial of service, the intentional paralyzing of a computer network by flooding it with data sent simultaneously from many individual computers: [as modifier] *so-called zombies which are used to stage DDOS attacks.*

DDR ▶ **abbr.** German Democratic Republic.
– ORIGIN abbreviation of German *Deutsche Demokratische Republik*.

DDS ▶ **abbr.** ■ Doctor of Dental Science. ■ Doctor of Dental Surgery.

DDT ▶ **abbr.** dichlorodiphenyltrichloroethane, a synthetic organic compound introduced in the 1940s and used as an insecticide. Like other chlorinated aromatic hydrocarbons, DDT tends to persist in the environment and become concentrated in animals at the head of the food chain. Its use is now banned in many countries. ● Chem. formula: $CCl_3CH(C_6H_4Cl)_2$.

DE ▶ **abbr.** ■ Football defensive end. ■ Delaware (in official postal use).

de- ▶ **prefix 1** (forming verbs and their derivatives) down; away: *descend* | *deduct.* ■ completely: *denude* | *derelict.* **2** (added to verbs and their derivatives) denoting removal or reversal: *deaerate* | *de-ice.*

PRONUNCIATION KEY ə *ago, up*; ər *over, fur*; a *hat*; ā *ate*; ä *car*; e *let*; ē *see*; i *fit*; ī *by*; NG *sing*; ō *go*; ô *law, for*; oi *toy*; o͝o *good*; o͞o *goo*; ou *out*; TH *thin*; T͟H *then*; ZH *vision*

3 denoting formation from: *deverbal*.
– ORIGIN from Latin *de* 'off, from'; sense 2 via Old French *des-* from Latin *dis-*.

de·ac·ces·sion /ˌdēakˈsesHən/ ▶ v. [with obj.] officially remove (an item) from the listed holdings of a library, museum, or art gallery, typically in order to sell it to raise funds.
▶ n. the disposal of books, works of art, or other items in this way.

dea·con /ˈdēkən/ ▶ n. (in Catholic, Anglican, and Orthodox churches) an ordained minister of an order ranking below that of priest. ■ (in some Protestant churches) a lay officer appointed to assist a minister, esp. in secular affairs. ■ historical (in the early church) an appointed minister of charity.
▶ v. [with obj.] appoint or ordain as a deacon.
– DERIVATIVES **dea·con·ship** /-ˌSHip/ n.
– ORIGIN Old English *diacon*, via ecclesiastical Latin from Greek *diakonos* 'servant' (in ecclesiastical Greek 'Christian minister').

d

dea·con·ess /ˈdēkənis/ ▶ n. (in the early church and some modern churches) a woman with duties similar to those of a deacon.

de·ac·ti·vate /dēˈaktəvāt/ ▶ v. [with obj.] make (something, typically technical equipment or a virus) inactive by disconnecting or destroying it: *the switch deactivates the alarm*. ■ Military remove from active duty.
– DERIVATIVES **de·ac·ti·va·tion** /dēˌaktəˈvāsHən/ n., **de·ac·ti·va·tor** /-vātər/ n.

dead /ded/ ▶ adj. **1** no longer alive: *a dead body* | [as complement] *he was shot dead*. ■ (of a part of the body) having lost sensation; numb. ■ having or displaying no emotion, sympathy, or sensitivity: *a cold, dead voice*. ■ no longer current, relevant, or important: *pollution had become a dead issue*. ■ devoid of living things: *a dead planet*. ■ resembling death: *a dead faint*. ■ (of a place or time) characterized by a lack of activity or excitement: *Brussels isn't dead after dark, if you know where to look*. ■ (of money) not financially productive. ■ (of sound) without resonance; dull. ■ (of a color) not glossy or bright. ■ (of a piece of equipment) no longer functioning, esp. because of a fault: *the phone had gone dead*. ■ (of an electric circuit or conductor) carrying or transmitting no current: *the batteries are dead*. ■ no longer burning: *the fire had been dead for some days*. ■ (of air or water) not circulating; stagnant. ■ (of a glass or bottle) empty or no longer being used. ■ (of the ball in a game) out of play. See also DEAD BALL. ■ (of a playing field, ball, or other surface) lacking springiness or bounce.
2 [attrib.] complete; absolute: *we sat in dead silence*.
▶ adv. [often as submodifier] absolutely; completely: *you're dead right* | *he was dead against the idea*. ■ exactly: *they arrived dead on time*. ■ straight; directly: *red flares were seen dead ahead*. ■ Brit. informal very: *omelets are dead easy to prepare*.
▶ n. (as plural noun **the dead**) those who have died.
– PHRASES **dead and buried** over; finished: *the incident is dead and buried*. **(as) dead as a** (or **the**) **dodo** see DODO. **(as) dead as a doornail** see DOORNAIL. **dead from the neck up** informal stupid. **dead in the water** (of a ship) unable to move. ■ unable to function effectively: *the economy is dead in the water*. **dead meat** informal in serious trouble: *if anyone finds out, you're dead meat*. **the dead of night** the quietest, darkest part of the night. **the dead of winter** the coldest part of winter. **dead on** exactly right: *her judgment was dead on*. **dead on arrival** used to describe a person who is declared dead immediately upon arrival at a hospital. ■ (of an idea, etc.) declared ineffective without ever having been put into effect: *why are people pronouncing the plan dead on arrival in the legislature?* **dead on one's feet** informal extremely tired. **dead set against** informal strongly opposed to: *they were dead set against seeing any more open spaces divided up*. **dead to rights** informal in the act of doing something wrong; red-handed: *he had me dead to rights, so I meekly suffered the rebuke*. **dead to the world** informal fast asleep. **from the dead** from a state of death: *Christ rose from the dead*. ■ from a period of obscurity or inactivity: *the cartoon brought animation back from the dead*. **make a dead set at** see SET[2]. **over my dead body** see BODY. **wouldn't be seen** (or **caught**) **dead** informal used to express strong dislike for a particular thing: *James Bond wouldn't be caught dead wearing a paper napkin bib*.
– DERIVATIVES **dead·ness** n.
– ORIGIN Old English *dēad*, of Germanic origin: related to Dutch *dood* and German *tot*, also to DIE[1].

dead air ▶ n. an unintended interruption of the video or audio signal during a television or radio broadcast.

dead ball ▶ n. Sports a ball that has gone out of play or is declared to be out of play.

dead-ball line ▶ n. Soccer the part of the goal line to either side of the goal.

dead·beat /ˈdedˌbēt/ ▶ n. informal a person who tries to evade paying debts. ■ an idle, feckless, or disreputable person.
▶ adj. (of a clock escapement or other mechanism) without recoil.

dead·bolt /ˈdedˌbōlt/ ▶ n. a bolt engaged by turning a knob or key, rather than by spring action.

dead cat bounce ▶ n. Stock Market a temporary recovery in share prices after a substantial fall, caused by speculators buying in order to cover their positions.

dead cen·ter ▶ n. the position of a crank when it is in line with the connecting rod and not exerting torque.

dead duck ▶ n. informal a person or thing that is useless, unsuccessful, defunct, etc.: *totalitarianism is a dead duck, he says*.
– ORIGIN from the old saying "never waste powder on a dead duck."

dead·en /ˈdedn/ ▶ v. [with obj.] make (a noise or sensation) less intense: *ether was used to deaden the pain*. ■ deprive of the power of sensation: *diabetes can deaden the nerve endings*. ■ deprive of force or vitality; stultify: *the syllabus has deadened the teaching process* | (as adj. **deadening**) *a deadening routine*. ■ make (someone) insensitive to something: *laughter might deaden us to the moral issue*.
– DERIVATIVES **dead·en·er** n.

dead end ▶ n. an end of a road or passage from which no exit is possible; a cul-de-sac: *the path came to a dead end*. ■ a road or passage having such an end. ■ a situation offering no prospects of progress or development: [as modifier] *a dead-end job*.
▶ v. [no obj.] (**dead-end**) (of a road or passage) come to a dead end: *he kept walking, until the corridor dead-ended*.

dead·eye /ˈdedˌī/ ▶ n. **1** Sailing a circular wooden block with a groove around the circumference to take a lanyard, used singly or in pairs to tighten a shroud.
2 informal an expert marksman.

dead·fall /ˈdedˌfôl/ ▶ n. **1** a trap consisting of a heavy weight positioned to fall on an animal.
2 a tangled mass of fallen trees and brush. ■ a fallen tree.

dead hand ▶ n. an undesirable persisting influence: *the dead hand of government control*. ■ Law see MORTMAIN.

dead·head /ˈdedˌhed/ ▶ n. **1** (**Deadhead**) a fan and follower of the rock group the Grateful Dead.
2 informal a commercial carrier with no paying passengers or freight on a trip. ■ a passenger or member of an audience with a free ticket. ■ informal a boring or unenterprising person.
3 a sunken or partially submerged log.
▶ v. **1** [no obj.] informal (of a commercial driver, etc.) complete a trip without paying passengers or freight: *trucks deadheading into California to pick up outbound loads*. ■ ride (in a plane or other vehicle) without paying for a ticket: *he calls his airline and gets a seat on the red-eye to deadhead to Boston*.
2 [with obj.] remove dead flower heads from (a plant) to encourage further blooming.

dead heat ▶ n. a situation in or result of a race in which two or more competitors are exactly even.
▶ v. [no obj.] (**dead-heat**) run or finish a race exactly even.

dead lan·guage ▶ n. a language no longer in everyday spoken use, such as Latin.

dead let·ter ▶ n. **1** a letter that is undeliverable and unreturnable, typically one with an incorrect address.
2 a law or treaty that has not been repealed but is ineffectual or defunct in practice. ■ a thing that is impractical or obsolete: *theoretical reasoning is a dead letter to a child*.

dead lift ▶ n. Weightlifting a lift made from a standing position, without the use of a bench or other equipment.

dead·light /ˈdedˌlīt/ ▶ n. **1** a protective cover or shutter fitted over a porthole or window on a ship.
2 a skylight designed not to be opened.

dead·line /ˈdedˌlīn/ ▶ n. **1** the latest time or date by which something should be completed: *the deadline for submissions is February 5th*.
2 historical a line drawn around a prison beyond which prisoners were liable to be shot.

dead load ▶ n. the intrinsic weight of a structure or vehicle, excluding the weight of passengers or goods. Often contrasted with LIVE LOAD.

dead·lock /ˈdedˌläk/ ▶ n. **1** [in sing.] a situation, typically one involving opposing parties, in which no progress can be made: *an attempt to break the deadlock*. ■ a situation in a contest or game where the scores are equal: *Ashton broke the deadlock with a penalty after 15 minutes*.
2 British term for DEADBOLT.
▶ v. [with obj.] **1** [no obj.] cause (a situation or opposing parties) to come to a point where no progress can be made because of fundamental disagreement: *the jurors were deadlocked on six charges*. ■ (**be deadlocked**) (of a contest or game) be in a tie: *with the score still deadlocked at three-three*.
2 Brit. secure (a door) with a deadlock.

dead loss ▶ n. a venture or situation that produces no profit whatsoever. ■ informal, chiefly Brit. a person or thing that is completely useless.

dead·ly /ˈdedlē/ ▶ adj. (**deadlier, deadliest**) causing or able to cause death: *a deadly weapon*. ■ filled with hate: *his voice was cold and deadly*. ■ (typically in the context of shooting or sports) extremely accurate, effective, or skillful: *his aim is deadly*. ■ informal extremely boring: *he's well meaning, but so utterly deadly*. ■ [attrib.] complete; total: *she was in deadly earnest*.
▶ adv. [as submodifier] in a way resembling or suggesting death; as if dead: *her skin was deadly pale*. ■ extremely: *a deadly serious remark*.
– DERIVATIVES **dead·li·ness** n.
– ORIGIN Old English *dēadlīc* 'mortal, in danger of death' (see DEAD, -LY').

dead·ly night·shade ▶ n. a poisonous bushy Eurasian plant with drooping purple flowers and black cherrylike fruit. Also called BELLADONNA. ● *Atropa belladonna*, family Solanaceae.

dead·ly sin ▶ n. (in Christian tradition) a sin regarded as leading to damnation, esp. one of a traditional list of seven. See SEVEN DEADLY SINS.

dead·man /ˈdedˌman/ ▶ n. an object buried in or secured to the ground for the purpose of providing anchorage or leverage.

dead man's fin·gers ▶ plural n. **1** a soft coral that has spongy lobes stiffened by calcareous spines. When found washed up on the beach it is said to resemble the fingers of a corpse. ● *Alcyonium digitatum*, order Alcyonacea.
2 a fungus that produces clumps of dull black, irregular, fingerlike fruiting bodies at the bases of dead tree stumps in both Eurasia and North America. ● *Xylaria polymorpha*, family Xylariaceae, phylum Ascomycota.
3 informal the fingerlike divisions of a lobster's or crab's gills.

dead-man's float ▶ n. a floating position, often used by beginning swimmers, in which a person lies face down in the water with arms outstretched or extended forward and legs extended backward.

dead man's han·dle (also **dead man's pedal**) ▶ n. (esp. in a diesel or electric train) a lever that acts as a safety device by shutting off power when not held in place by the driver.

dead march ▶ n. a slow, solemn piece of music suitable to accompany a funeral procession.

dead-net·tle ▶ n. an Old World plant of the mint family, with leaves that resemble those of a nettle but lack stinging hairs. ● *Lamium* and related genera, family Labiatae: several species, including the common **white dead-nettle** (*L. album*).

dead·pan /ˈdedˌpan/ ▶ adj. deliberately impassive or expressionless: *answers his phone in a deadpan tone* | *deadpan humor*.
▶ adv. in a deadpan manner.
▶ v. (**deadpans, deadpanning, deadpanned**) [with direct speech] say something amusing while affecting a serious manner: *"I'm an undercover dentist," he deadpanned*.

dead reck·on·ing ▶ n. the process of calculating one's position, esp. at sea, by estimating the direction and distance traveled rather than by using landmarks, astronomical observations, or electronic navigation methods.

dead ring·er ▶ n. a person or thing that seems exactly like someone or something else: *he is a dead ringer for his late papa*.

dead·rise /ˈdedˌrīz/ ▶ n. the vertical distance between a line horizontal to the keel of a vessel and its chine.

Dead Sea a salt lake or inland sea in the Jordan valley, on the Israel–Jordan border. Its surface is 1,300 feet (400 m) below sea level.

Dead Sea scrolls a collection of Hebrew and Aramaic manuscripts discovered in pottery storage jars in caves near Qumran between 1947 and 1956. Thought to have been hidden by the Essenes or a similar Jewish sect shortly before the revolt against Roman rule AD 66–70, the scrolls include texts of many books of the Bible; they are some 1,000 years older than previously known versions.

dead set ▶ n. see SET[2] (sense 2).

dead·stick land·ing /ˈdedˌstik/ ▶ n. an unpowered landing of an aircraft.

dead time ▶ **n.** time in which someone or something is inactive or unable to act productively. ■ Physics the period after the recording of a particle or pulse when a detector is unable to record another.

dead weight (also **deadweight**) ▶ **n.** the weight of an inert person or thing: *the net was a dead weight on his shoulders.* ■ a heavy or oppressive burden: *the past was just so much dead weight, excess baggage.* ■ the total weight of cargo, stores, etc., that a ship carries or can carry at a particular draft. ■ another term for DEAD LOAD. ■ Farming animals sold by the estimated weight of salable meat that they will yield. ■ [usu. as modifier] Economics losses incurred because of the inefficient allocation of resources, esp. through taxation or restriction: *a dead-weight burden.*

dead white Eu·ro·pe·an male (also **dead white male**) ▶ **n.** informal a writer, philosopher, or other significant figure whose importance and talents may have been exaggerated by virtue of his belonging to a historically dominant gender and ethnic group.

Dead·wood /'ded,wo͝od/ a city in western South Dakota, in the Black Hills, known for its 1870s gold rush and Boot Hill cemetery; pop. 1,283 (est. 2008).

dead·wood /'ded,wo͝od/ ▶ **n.** a branch or part of a tree that is dead. ■ people or things that are no longer useful or productive.

dead zone ▶ **n.** **1** a place or period in which nothing happens or in which no life exists. ■ an area of the ocean that is depleted of oxygen, frequently due to pollution.
2 a place where it is not possible to receive a mobile-phone or radio signal.

de·aer·ate /dē'e(ə)rāt/ ▶ **v.** [with obj.] (usu. **be deaerated**) partially or completely remove dissolved air from (something): *the electrolyte was deaerated by purging it with argon.*
– DERIVATIVES **de·aer·a·tion** /,dē-er'āSHən/ **n.**

deaf /def/ ▶ **adj.** lacking the power of hearing or having impaired hearing: *I'm a bit deaf | deaf children.* ■ unwilling or unable to hear or pay attention to something: *she is deaf to all advice.*
– PHRASES **(as) deaf as a post** completely or extremely deaf. **fall on deaf ears** (of a statement or request) be ignored. **turn a deaf ear** refuse to listen or respond to a statement or request.
– DERIVATIVES **deaf·ness n.**
– ORIGIN Old English *dēaf*, of Germanic origin; related to Dutch *doof* and German *taub*, from an Indo-European root shared by Greek *tuphlos* 'blind.'

deaf aid ▶ **n.** Brit. a hearing aid.

deaf-blind ▶ **adj.** having a severe impairment of both hearing and vision.

deaf·en /'defən/ ▶ **v.** [with obj.] (usu. **be deafened**) cause (someone) to lose the power of hearing permanently or temporarily: *we were deafened by the explosion.* ■ (of a loud noise) overwhelm (someone) with sound: *the roar of the water deafened them.* ■ **(deafen someone to)** (of a sound) cause someone to be unaware of (other sounds): *the noise deafened him to Ron's approach.*

deaf·en·ing /'defəniNG/ ▶ **adj.** (of a noise) so loud as to make it impossible to hear anything else: *the music reached a deafening crescendo.*
– DERIVATIVES **deaf·en·ing·ly adv.**

de·af·fer·en·ta·tion /dē,afəren'tāSHən/ ▶ **n.** Biology the interruption or destruction of the afferent connections of nerve cells, performed esp. in animal experiments to demonstrate the spontaneity of locomotor movement.
– DERIVATIVES **de·af·fer·ent·ed** /dē'afə,rentid/ **adj.**

deaf-mute usu. offensive ▶ **n.** a person who is both deaf and unable to speak.
▶ **adj.** (of a person) both deaf and unable to speak.

> **USAGE** In modern use, **deaf-mute** has acquired offensive connotations (implying, wrongly, that such people are without the capacity for communication). It should be avoided in favor of other terms such as *profoundly deaf*. See also usage at MUTE.

deal¹ /dēl/ ▶ **v.** (past and past participle **dealt** /delt/)
1 [with obj.] distribute (cards) in an orderly rotation to the players for a game or round: *the cards were dealt for the last hand* | [with two objs.] figurative *fate dealt her a different hand.* ■ **(deal someone in)** include a new player in a card game by giving them cards. ■ distribute or mete out (something) to a person or group: *the funds raised were dealt out to the needy.*
2 [no obj.] take part in commercial trading of a particular commodity: *directors were prohibited from dealing in the company's shares.* ■ be concerned with: *a movie that deals in ideas and issues.* ■ informal buy and sell illegal drugs: [with obj.] *Frankie started dealing cocaine.*
3 [no obj.] **(deal with)** take measures concerning (someone or something), esp. with the intention of putting something right: *the government had been unable to deal with the economic crisis.* ■ cope with (a difficult person or situation): *you'll have to find a way of dealing with those feelings.* ■ [with adverbial] treat (someone) in a particular way: *life had dealt harshly with her.* ■ have relations with (a person or organization), esp. in a commercial context: *the bank deals directly with the private sector.* ■ take or have as a subject; discuss: *the novel deals with several different topics.*
4 [with two objs.] inflict (a blow) on (someone or something): *hopes of an economic recovery were dealt another blow.*
▶ **n. 1** an agreement entered into by two or more parties for their mutual benefit, esp. in a business or political context: *the band signed a major recording deal.* ■ an attractive price on a commodity for a purchaser; a bargain: *we've got great deals on the latest camcorders.* ■ [with adj.] a particular form of treatment given or received: *working mothers get a raw deal.*
2 a significant but unspecified amount of something: *he lost a great deal of blood.*
3 [in sing.] the process of distributing the cards to players in a card game. ■ a player's turn to distribute cards. ■ the round of play following this. ■ the set of hands dealt to the players.
– PHRASES **a big deal** [usu. with negative] informal a thing considered important: *they don't make a big deal out of minor irritations.* ■ an important person: *Sam Kinison became a big deal.* ■ **(big deal)** used to express one's contempt for something regarded as impressive or important by another person. **a good** (or **great**) **deal** a large amount: *I don't know a great deal about politics.* ■ to a considerable extent: *she had gotten to know him a good deal better.* **cut a deal** informal make an agreement: *he had gone to the board of directors with his new robot design and cut a deal.* **it's a deal** informal used to express one's assent to an agreement.
– ORIGIN Old English *dǣlan* 'divide,' 'participate,' of Germanic origin; related to Dutch *deel* and German *Teil* 'part' (noun), also to DOLE¹. The sense 'divide' gave rise to 'distribute,' hence sense 1 of the verb and sense 4 of the verb ; the sense 'participate' gave rise to 'have dealings with,' hence sense 2 of the verb and sense 3 of the verb.

deal² ▶ **n.** fir or pine wood, esp. when sawn into planks of a standard size. ■ a plank of such wood.
– ORIGIN Middle English: from Middle Low German and Middle Dutch *dele* 'plank.'

deal·break·er ▶ **n.** (in business and politics) a factor or issue that, if unresolved during negotiations, would cause one party to withdraw from a deal.

de·al·co·hol·ize /dē'alkəhô,līz/ ▶ **v.** [with obj.] (usu. as adj. **de-alcoholized**) remove the alcohol from (a normally alcoholic drink): *de-alcoholized beer.*

deal·er /'dēlər/ ▶ **n. 1** a person or business that buys and sells goods: *a car dealer.* ■ a person who buys and sells shares, securities, or other financial assets as a principal (rather than as a broker or agent). See also BROKER-DEALER. ■ informal a person who buys and sells drugs: *he posed as a dealer willing to buy heroin.*
2 the player who distributes the cards at the start of a game or hand.
– DERIVATIVES **deal·er·ship** /-,SHip/ **n.** (sense 1).

deal·fish /'dēl,fiSH/ ▶ **n.** (pl. **same** or **dealfishes**) a slender silvery fish with a dorsal fin running the length of the body, living in the northeastern Atlantic. ● *Trachipterus arcticus*, family Trachipteridae.
– ORIGIN mid 19th cent.: from DEAL² in the sense 'board' (with reference to its shape) + FISH¹.

de·a·lign /,dēə'līn/ ▶ **v.** [no obj.] (of a voter) withdraw allegiance to a political party.
– DERIVATIVES **de·a·lign·ment n.**

deal·ing /'dēliNG/ ▶ **n. 1** (usu. **dealings**) a business relation or transaction: *they had dealings with an insurance company.* ■ a personal connection or association with someone: *my dealings with David consisted of giving him his late-night formula.* ■ the activity of buying and selling a particular commodity: *car dealing | drug dealing.*
2 the particular way in which someone behaves toward others: *fair dealing came naturally to him.*

de·al·lo·cate /dē'alə,kāt/ ▶ **v.** [with obj.] Computing return (allocated memory) to the store of available RAM.
– DERIVATIVES **de·al·lo·ca·tion** /dē,alə'kāSHən/ **n.**

deal·mak·er /'dēl,mākər/ ▶ **n.** a person who is skilled at bringing commercial or political deals to a satisfactory conclusion.
– DERIVATIVES **deal·mak·ing n.**

dealt /delt/ past participle of DEAL¹.

de·am·i·na·tion /dē,ami'nāSHən/ ▶ **n.** Biochemistry the removal of an amino group from an amino acid or other compound.
– DERIVATIVES **de·am·i·nat·ed** /dē'amə,nātid/ **adj.**

Dean¹ /dēn/, Dizzy (1911–74), US baseball player and broadcaster; born *Jay Hanna Dean.* He pitched for the St. Louis Cardinals 1932–37 and the Chicago Cubs 1938–41. Baseball Hall of Fame (1953).

Dean², James (Byron) (1931–55), US actor. Although he starred in only three movies before dying in a car accident, he became a cult figure closely identified with the title role of *Rebel Without a Cause* (1955), symbolizing for many the disaffected youth of the postwar era. Other movies: *East of Eden* (1955) and *Giant* (1956).

James Dean

Dean³, John (Wesley III) (1938–), US political adviser. After serving as presidential counsel to Richard Nixon, he became the chief witness in the Watergate hearings 1973–74, was convicted of conspiracy, and served four months in prison. He wrote *Blind Ambition* (1976).

dean¹ /dēn/ ▶ **n. 1** the head of a college or university faculty or department: *the dean of the law school.* ■ a college or university official, esp. one with disciplinary and advisory functions: *the dean of students.* ■ the leader or senior member of a group: *the dean of California winemakers.*
2 the head of the chapter of a cathedral or collegiate church.
– ORIGIN Middle English: from Old French *deien*, from late Latin *decanus* 'chief of a group of ten,' from *decem* 'ten.' Compare with DOYEN.

dean² ▶ **n.** variant spelling of DENE¹.

dean·er·y /'dēnərē/ ▶ **n.** (pl. **deaneries**) **1** Brit. the group of parishes presided over by a rural dean.
2 the official residence of a dean. ■ the position or office of a dean.

dean's list ▶ **n.** a list of students recognized for academic achievement during a semester by the dean of the college they attend.

dear /di(ə)r/ ▶ **adj. 1** regarded with deep affection; cherished by someone: *a dear friend | he is very dear to me.* ■ used in speech as a way of addressing a person in a polite way: *Martin, my dear fellow.* ■ used as part of the polite introduction to a letter, esp. in a formula denoting the degree of formality involved: *Dear Sir or Madam.* ■ endearing; sweet: *a dear little puppy.*
2 expensive. ■ (of money) available as a loan only at a high rate of interest.
▶ **n.** used as an affectionate or friendly form of address: *don't you worry, dear.* ■ a sweet or endearing person.
▶ **adv.** at a high cost: *they buy property cheaply and sell dear.*
▶ **exclam.** used in expressions of surprise, dismay, or sympathy: *oh dear, I've upset you.*
– PHRASES **for dear life** see LIFE.
– DERIVATIVES **dear·ness n.**
– ORIGIN Old English *dēore*, of Germanic origin; related to Dutch *dier* 'beloved,' also to Dutch *duur* and German *teuer* 'expensive.'

Dear·born /'di(ə)r,bôrn, -bərn/ a city in southeastern Michigan, southwest of Detroit, home to the Ford Motor Company and to the Henry Ford Museum and Greenfield Village; pop. 86,477 (est. 2008).

dear·est /'di(ə)rist/ ▶ **adj. 1** most loved or cherished: *one of my dearest friends.*
2 Brit. most expensive: *beer is dearest in Germany.*
▶ **n.** used as an affectionate form of address to a much-loved person: *you make me so happy, dearest.* ■ *I was going to miss my dearest.*

dear·ie /'di(ə)rē/ ▶ **n.** (pl. **dearies**) informal, chiefly Brit. used as a friendly or condescending form of address.

Dear John let·ter (also **Dear John**) ▶ **n.** informal a letter from a woman to a man, esp. a serviceman, terminating a personal relationship: *a young officer gets his Dear John letter*.

dear·ly /ˈdi(ə)rlē/ ▶ **adv. 1** very much: *he loved his parents dearly*.
2 with much loss or suffering; at great cost: *freedom to worship our religion has been bought dearly*.

dearth /dərTH/ ▶ **n.** [in sing.] a scarcity or lack of something: *there is **a dearth of** evidence*.
– ORIGIN Middle English *derthe* (originally in the sense 'shortage and dearness of food') (see DEAR, -TH[2]).

death /deTH/ ▶ **n.** the action or fact of dying or being killed; the end of the life of a person or organism: *I don't believe in life after death | an increase in deaths from skin cancer* | [as modifier] *a death sentence*. ■ the state of being dead: *even in death, she was beautiful*. ■ the permanent ending of vital processes in a cell or tissue. ■ (**Death**) [in sing.] the personification of the power that destroys life, often represented in art and literature as a skeleton or an old man holding a scythe. ■ [in sing.] the destruction or permanent end of something: *the death of her hopes*. ■ informal a damaging or destructive state of affairs: *to be driven to a dance by one's father would be social death*.
– PHRASES **at death's door** (esp. in hyperbolic use) so ill that one might die. **be the death of** (often used hyperbolically or humorously) cause someone's death: *you'll be the death of me with all your questions*. **be in at the death** be present when a hunted animal is caught and killed. ■ be present when something fails or comes to an end. **catch one's death (of cold)** informal catch a severe cold or chill. **do someone to death** kill someone. **do something to death** perform or repeat something so frequently that it becomes tediously familiar: *a subject that has been done to death by generations of painters*. **a fate worse than death** a terrible experience, esp. that of seduction or rape. **like death warmed over** (or **up**) informal extremely tired or ill. **a matter of life and death** see LIFE. **put someone to death** kill someone, esp. with official sanction. **till** (or **until**) **death us do part** for as long as both people in a couple live. [from the marriage service in the *Book of Common Prayer*.] **to death** used of a particular action or process that results in someone's death: *he was stabbed to death*. ■ used to emphasize the extreme nature of a specific action, feeling, or state of mind: *I'm **sick to death of** you | the story **scared** me **to death***. **to the death** until dead: *a fight to the death*.
– DERIVATIVES **death·like** /-ˌlīk/ **adj.**
– ORIGIN Old English *dēath*, of Germanic origin; related to Dutch *dood* and German *Tod*, also to DIE[1].

death ad·der ▶ **n.** a venomous Australian snake that has a thin wormlike tail, which it uses to lure birds and other prey. ● Genus *Acanthophis*, family Elapidae: three species, in particular *A. antarcticus*.

death·bed /ˈdeTHˌbed/ ▶ **n.** the bed where someone is dying or has died. ■ used in reference to the time when someone is dying: *she visited him on his deathbed* | [as modifier] *a deathbed confession*.

death ben·e·fit ▶ **n.** the amount paid to a beneficiary upon the death of an insured person. Also called FACE AMOUNT.

death blow ▶ **n.** an impact or stroke that causes death. ■ an event, circumstance, or action that ends something abruptly: *it was Galileo Galilei who dealt **the death blow to** the geocentric theory*.

death camp ▶ **n.** a prison camp, esp. one for political prisoners or prisoners of war, in which many die from poor conditions and treatment or from mass execution.

death cer·tif·i·cate ▶ **n.** an official statement, signed by a physician, of the cause, date, and place of a person's death.

death-deal·ing ▶ **adj.** capable of causing death: *death-dealing drugs*.

death house ▶ **n.** informal the building in which prisoners are kept in preparation for execution.

death in·stinct ▶ **n.** Psychoanalysis an innate desire for self-annihilation, thought to be manifest in the conservative and regressive tendency of the psyche to reduce tension. Compare with LIFE INSTINCT.

death knell ▶ **n.** [in sing.] the tolling of a bell to mark someone's death. ■ used to refer to the imminent destruction or failure of something: *the chaos may **sound the death knell for** the peace plan*.

death·less /ˈdeTHlis/ ▶ **adj.** chiefly literary, humorous immortal: *deathless beauty | he died before his song could be recorded, but his compositions are deathless*.
– DERIVATIVES **death·less·ness n.**

death·ly /ˈdeTHlē/ ▶ **adj.** (**deathlier, deathliest**) resembling or suggestive of death: *a deathly hush fell over the breakfast table* | [as submodifier] *she felt deathly cold*. ■ archaic, literary of, relating to, or causing death: *an eagle carrying a snake in its deathly grasp*.

death mask ▶ **n.** a plaster cast taken of a dead person's face, used to make a mask or model.

death·match /ˈdeTHˌmaCH/ ▶ **n. 1** (in wrestling) a match in which many of the normal rules do not apply, typically leading to a more violent contest.
2 (in computer gaming) a mode of play in which the aim is to kill the characters controlled by other players.

death met·al ▶ **n.** a form of heavy metal music using lyrics preoccupied with death, suffering, and destruction.

death pen·al·ty ▶ **n.** the punishment of execution, administered to someone legally convicted of a capital crime.

death rate ▶ **n.** the ratio of deaths to the population of a particular area during a particular period of time, usually calculated as the number of deaths per one thousand people per year.

death rat·tle ▶ **n.** a gurgling sound heard in a dying person's throat.

death row /ˈrō/ ▶ **n.** a prison block or section for prisoners sentenced to death: *a convicted killer **on death row***.

death sen·tence ▶ **n.** Law a sentence to be put to death for a capital crime. ■ a disastrous result or outcome: *the market crash was a death sentence for many dot-coms*.

death's head ▶ **n.** a human skull as a symbol of mortality.

death's-head hawk moth ▶ **n.** a large dark European hawk moth with a skull-like marking on the thorax and a very large caterpillar. ● *Acherontia atropos*, family Sphingidae.

death song ▶ **n.** a song sung before or after someone's death or to commemorate the dead.

death squad ▶ **n.** an armed paramilitary group formed to kill particular people, esp. political opponents.

death tax ▶ **n.** another term for ESTATE TAX, INHERITANCE TAX.

death toll ▶ **n.** the number of deaths resulting from a particular cause, esp. an accident, battle, or natural disaster.

death trap (also **deathtrap**) ▶ **n.** a place, structure, or vehicle that is potentially dangerous: *the theaters were often death traps*.

Death Val·ley a deep arid desert basin below sea level in southeastern California and southwestern Nevada, the hottest and driest part of North America. It contains the lowest point in the US at Badwater, which is 282 feet (86 m) below sea level.

death war·rant ▶ **n.** an official order for the execution of a condemned person: figurative *in making his announcement he has signed his political death warrant*.

death·watch /ˈdeTHˌwäCH/ ▶ **n. 1** a vigil kept beside a dead or dying individual. ■ a guard set over a person due for execution.
2 (also **deathwatch beetle**) a small beetle with larvae that bore into dead wood and structural timbers, causing considerable damage. The adult makes a sound like a watch ticking that was formerly believed to portend death. ● *Xestobium rufovillosum*, family Anobiidae.

death wish ▶ **n.** a desire for someone's death, esp. an unconscious desire for one's own death. Compare with DEATH INSTINCT.

de·at·tri·bute /dē-əˈtriˌbyo͞ot/ ▶ **v.** [with obj.] cease to attribute (a work of art) to a particular artist.
– DERIVATIVES **de·at·tri·bu·tion** /dēˌatrəˈbyo͞oSHən/ **n.**

deb /deb/ ▶ **n.** informal short for DEBUTANTE.

de·ba·cle /diˈbakəl, -ˈbäkəl/ ▶ **n.** a sudden and ignominious failure; a fiasco: *the economic debacle that became known as the Great Depression*.
– ORIGIN early 19th cent.: from French *débâcle*, from *débâcler* 'unleash,' from *dé-* 'un-' + *bâcler* 'to bar' (from Latin *baculum* 'staff').

de·bag /dēˈbag/ ▶ **v.** (**debags, debagging, debagged**) [with obj.] Brit. informal remove the pants of (someone) as a joke or punishment.

de·bal·last /dēˈbaləst/ ▶ **v.** [with obj.] remove ballast from (a ship) in order to increase its buoyancy.

de·bar /dēˈbär/ ▶ **v.** (**debars, debarring, debarred**) [with obj.] (usu. **be debarred**) exclude or prohibit (someone) officially from doing something: *people declaring that they were HIV-positive could be debarred entry*.
– DERIVATIVES **de·bar·ment n.** /-mənt/.
– ORIGIN late Middle English: from French *débarrer*, from Old French *desbarrer* 'unbar,' from *des-* (expressing reversal) + *barrer* 'to bar.'

de·bark[1] /dēˈbärk/ ▶ **v.** [no obj.] leave a ship or aircraft. ■ [with obj.] unload (cargo or troops) from a ship or aircraft.
– DERIVATIVES **de·bar·ka·tion** /ˌdēbärˈkāSHən/ **n.**
– ORIGIN mid 17th cent.: from French *débarquer*.

de·bark[2] ▶ **v.** [with obj.] remove (the bark) from a tree.

de·base /diˈbās/ ▶ **v.** [with obj.] reduce (something) in quality or value; degrade: *the love episodes debase the dignity of the drama*. ■ lower the moral character of (someone): *war debases people*. ■ historical lower the value of (coinage) by reducing the content of precious metal.
– DERIVATIVES **de·base·ment n., de·bas·er n.**
– ORIGIN mid 16th cent. (in the sense 'humiliate, belittle'): from DE- 'down' + the obsolete verb *base* (compare with ABASE), expressing the notion 'bring down completely.'

de·based /diˈbāst/ ▶ **adj.** reduced in quality or value: *the debased traditions of sportsmanship*.

de·bat·a·ble /diˈbātəbəl/ ▶ **adj.** open to discussion or argument: *it is debatable whether the country is coming out of recession*. ■ historical (of land) on the border between two countries and claimed by each.
– DERIVATIVES **de·bat·a·bly** /-blē/ **adv.**

de·bate /diˈbāt/ ▶ **n.** a formal discussion on a particular topic in a public meeting or legislative assembly, in which opposing arguments are put forward. ■ an argument about a particular subject, esp. one in which many people are involved: *the national **debate on** abortion | there has been much debate about prices*.
▶ **v.** [with obj.] argue about (a subject), esp. in a formal manner: *the board debated his proposal | the date when people first entered America is hotly debated*. ■ [with clause] consider a possible course of action in one's mind before reaching a decision: *he debated whether he should leave the matter alone or speak to her*.
– PHRASES **be open to debate** be unproven; require further discussion. **under debate** being discussed or disputed.
– DERIVATIVES **de·bat·er n.**
– ORIGIN Middle English: via Old French from Latin *dis-* (expressing reversal) + *battere* 'to fight.'

de·bat·ing point ▶ **n.** an extraneous proposition or inessential piece of information used to gain advantage in a debate.

de·bauch /diˈbôCH/ ▶ **v.** [with obj.] destroy or debase the moral purity of; corrupt. ■ dated seduce (a woman): *he debauched sixteen schoolgirls*.
▶ **n.** a bout of excessive indulgence in sensual pleasures, esp. eating and drinking. ■ the habit or practice of such indulgence; debauchery: *his life had been spent in debauch*.
– DERIVATIVES **de·bauch·er n.**
– ORIGIN late 16th cent.: from French *débaucher* (verb) 'turn away from one's duty,' from Old French *desbaucher*, of uncertain ultimate origin.

de·bauched /diˈbôCHt/ ▶ **adj.** indulging in or characterized by sensual pleasures to a degree perceived to be morally harmful; dissolute: *a debauched lifestyle*.

deb·au·chee /ˌdibôˈCHē/ ▶ **n.** a person given to excessive indulgence in sensual pleasures.
– ORIGIN mid 17th cent.: from French *débauché* 'turned away from duty,' past participle of *débaucher* (see DEBAUCH).

de·bauch·er·y /diˈbôCHərē/ ▶ **n.** excessive indulgence in sensual pleasures.

de·beak /dēˈbēk/ ▶ **v.** [with obj.] remove the upper part of the beak of (a bird) to prevent it from injuring other birds: (as noun **debeaking**) *debeaking is thought to cause chickens chronic pain*.

de Beau·voir /də bōˈvwär, də ˈbōˌvwär/, Simone (1908–86), French existentialist philosopher, novelist, and feminist. Her best-known work is *The Second Sex* (1949), a central book of the "second wave" of feminism. She was closely associated with Jean-Paul Sartre.

de·ben·ture /diˈbenCHər/ ▶ **n.** (also **debenture bond**) an unsecured loan certificate issued by a company, backed by general credit rather than by specified assets. ■ Brit. a long-term security yielding a fixed rate of interest, issued by a company and secured against assets.
– ORIGIN late Middle English (denoting a voucher issued by a royal household, giving the right to claim payment for goods or services): from Latin *debentur* 'are owing' (from *debere* 'owe'), used as the first word of a certificate recording a debt. The current sense dates from the mid 19th cent.

de·bil·i·tate /diˈbiliˌtāt, dē-/ ▶ **v.** [with obj.] make (someone) weak and infirm: *a weakness that debilitates him despite his overwhelming physical might* | (as adj. **debilitated**) *a debilitated patient*. ■ hinder, delay, or weaken: *hard drugs destroy families and debilitate communities*.

– DERIVATIVES **de·bil·i·ta·tion** /di,bili'tāSHən/ **n.**, **de·bil·i·ta·tive** /di'bili,tātiv/ **adj.**
– ORIGIN mid 16th cent.: from Latin *debilitat-* 'weakened,' from the verb *debilitare*, from *debilitas* (see DEBILITY).

de·bil·i·tat·ing /di'bili,tātiNG/ ▶ **adj.** (of a disease or condition) making someone very weak and infirm: *debilitating back pain*. ■ tending to weaken something: *the debilitating effects of underinvestment*.
– DERIVATIVES **de·bil·i·tat·ing·ly** **adv.**

de·bil·i·ty /di'bilitē/ ▶ **n.** physical weakness, esp. as a result of illness.
– ORIGIN late Middle English: from Old French *debilite*, from Latin *debilitas*, from *debilis* 'weak.'

deb·it /'debit/ ▶ **n.** an entry recording an amount owed, listed on the left-hand side or column of an account. The opposite of CREDIT. ■ a payment made or owed.
▶ **v.** (**debits, debiting, debited**) [with obj.] (usu. **be debited**) (of a bank or other financial organization) remove (an amount of money) from a customer's account, typically as payment for services or goods: *$10,000 was debited from their account*. ■ remove an amount of money from (a bank account): *the tag on the rear window automatically activates the pump and debits any major credit card*.
– PHRASES **on the debit side** as an unsatisfactory aspect of the situation: *on the debit side, they predict a rise in book prices*.
– ORIGIN late Middle English (in the sense 'debt'): from French *débit*, from Latin *debitum* 'something owed' (see DEBT). The verb sense dates from the 17th cent.; the current noun sense from the late 18th cent.

deb·it card ▶ **n.** a card issued by a bank allowing the holder to transfer money electronically to another bank account when making a purchase.

deb·o·nair /,debə'ne(ə)r/ ▶ **adj.** (of a man) confident, stylish, and charming.
– DERIVATIVES **deb·o·nair·ly** **adv.**
– ORIGIN Middle English (in the sense 'meek or courteous'): from Old French *debonaire*, from *de bon aire* 'of good disposition.'

de·bone /dē'bōn/ ▶ **v.** remove the bones from (meat, poultry, or fish), esp. before cooking.

Deb·o·rah /'deb(ə)rə/ a biblical prophet and leader who inspired the Israelite army to defeat the Canaanites. The "Song of Deborah," a song of victory attributed to her, is thought to be one of the oldest sections of the Bible.

de·bouch /di'bouCH, -'bo͞osH/ ▶ **v.** [no obj.] emerge from a narrow or confined space into a wide, open area: *the soldiers debouched from their jeeps and dispersed among the trees* | *the stream finally debouches into a silent pool*.
– DERIVATIVES **de·bouch·ment** **n.**
– ORIGIN mid 18th cent.: from French *déboucher*, from *dé-* (expressing removal) + *bouche* 'mouth' (from Latin *bucca* 'cheek').

De·bre·cen /'debrət,sen/ an industrial and commercial city in eastern Hungary; pop. 206,225 (2009).

de·bride·ment /di'brēdmənt/ ▶ **n.** Medicine the removal of damaged tissue or foreign objects from a wound.
– DERIVATIVES **de·bride** **v.**
– ORIGIN mid 19th cent.: from French, from *débrider*, literally 'unbridle,' based on *bride* 'bridle' (of Germanic origin).

de·brief /dē'brēf/ ▶ **v.** [with obj.] question (someone, typically a soldier or spy) about a completed mission or undertaking: *together they debriefed their two colleagues* | (as noun **debriefing**) *during his debriefing, he exposed two Russian spies*.
▶ **n.** a series of questions about a completed mission or undertaking.
– DERIVATIVES **de·brief·er** **n.**

de·bris /də'brē, ,dā-/ ▶ **n.** scattered fragments, typically of something wrecked or destroyed: *the bomb hits it, showering debris from all sides*. ■ loose natural material consisting esp. of broken pieces of rock: *a stable arrangement of planets, comets, and debris orbiting the sun*. ■ dirt or refuse: *clean away any collected dust or debris*.
– ORIGIN early 18th cent.: from French *débris*, from obsolete *débriser* 'break down.'

de Bro·glie /də 'brôyə, də 'broi/, Louis-Victor, Prince (1892–1987), French physicist. He was the first to suggest that subatomic particles can also have the properties of waves, and his name is now applied to such a wave. Nobel Prize for Physics (1929).

debt /det/ ▶ **n.** something, typically money, that is owed or due: *I paid off my debts* | *a way to reduce Third World debt*. ■ the state of owing money: *the firm is heavily in debt*. ■ [usu. in sing.] a feeling of gratitude for a service or favor: *we owe them a debt of thanks*.
– PHRASES **be in someone's debt** owe gratitude to someone for a service or favor.
– ORIGIN Middle English *dette*: from Old French, based on Latin *debitum* 'something owed,' past participle of *debere* 'owe.' The spelling change in French and English was by association with the Latin word.

debt coun·se·lor ▶ **n.** a person who offers professional advice on methods of debt repayment.

debt of hon·or ▶ **n.** a debt that is not legally recoverable, esp. one incurred in gambling.

debt·or /'detər/ ▶ **n.** a person or institution that owes a sum of money.

debt re·lief ▶ **n.** the partial or total remission of debts, esp. those owed by developing countries to external creditors.

debt se·cu·ri·ty ▶ **n.** a negotiable or tradable liability or loan.

debt swap (also **debt-for-nature swap**) ▶ **n.** a transaction in which a foreign exchange debt owed by a developing country is transferred to another organization on the condition that the country use local currency for a designated purpose, usually environmental protection.

de·bug /dē'bəg/ ▶ **v.** (**debugs, debugging, debugged**) [with obj.] **1** identify and remove errors from (computer hardware or software): *games are the worst to debug* | (as noun **debugging**) *software debugging*.
2 detect and remove concealed microphones from (an area).
3 remove insects from (something), esp. with a pesticide.
▶ **n.** the process of identifying and removing errors from computer hardware or software.

de·bug·ger /dē'bəgər/ ▶ **n.** a computer program that assists in the detection and correction of errors in computer programs.

de·bunk /di'bəNGk/ ▶ **v.** [with obj.] expose the falseness or hollowness of (a myth, idea, or belief): *the magazine that debunks claims of the paranormal*. ■ reduce the inflated reputation of (someone), esp. by ridicule: *comedy takes delight in debunking heroes*.
– DERIVATIVES **de·bunk·er** **n.**, **de·bunk·er·y** **n.**

de·burr /dē'bər/ (also **debur**) ▶ **v.** (**deburrs, deburring, deburred**) [with obj.] neaten and smooth the rough edges or ridges of (an object, typically one made of metal): *hand tools for deburring holes in metal*.

De·bus·sy /,debyo͞o'sē, ,dā-/, Claude (1862–1918), French composer and critic; full name *Achille Claude Debussy*. He incorporated the ideas of impressionist art and symbolist poetry into music, using melodies based on the whole-tone scale and delicate harmonies that exploit overtones.

de·but /dā'byo͞o/ ▶ **n.** a person's first appearance or performance in a particular capacity or role: *the film marked his debut as a director*. ■ the first public appearance of a new product or presentation of a theatrical show: *the car makes its world debut*. ■ [as modifier] denoting the first recording or publication of a group, singer, or writer: *a debut album*. ■ dated the first appearance of a debutante in society.
▶ **v.** [no obj.] perform in public for the first time: *the Rolling Stones debuted at the Marquee*. ■ (of a new product) be launched: *the model is expected to debut at $19,000*. ■ [with obj.] (of a company) launch (a new product): *the company is to debut new software*.
– ORIGIN mid 18th cent.: from French *début*, from *débuter* 'lead off.'

deb·u·tant /'debyo͞o,tänt, 'debyə-/ ▶ **n.** a person making a first appearance in a career or in fashionable society.
– ORIGIN early 19th cent.: from French *débutant* 'leading off,' from the verb *débuter*.

deb·u·tante /'debyo͞o,tänt, 'debyə-/ ▶ **n.** an upper-class young woman making her first appearance in fashionable society.
– ORIGIN early 19th cent.: from French *débutante* (feminine) 'leading off,' from the verb *débuter*.

De·bye /də'bī/, Peter Joseph William (1884–1966), US chemical physicist; born in the Netherlands. He is noted for establishing the existence of permanent electric dipole moments in many molecules, for demonstrating the use of these to determine molecular size and shape, and for modifying Einstein's theory of specific heats as applied to solids. Nobel Prize for Chemistry (1936).

de·bye /di'bī/ (also **debye unit**) ▶ **n.** Chemistry a unit used to express electric dipole moments of molecules. One debye is equal to 3.336×10^{-30} coulomb meter.
– ORIGIN early 20th cent.: named after P. J. DEBYE.

Dec. ▶ **abbr.** December.

dec. ▶ **abbr.** deceased.

deca- (also **dec-** before a vowel) ▶ **comb. form** (used commonly in units of measurement) ten; having ten: *decahedron* | *decane*.
– ORIGIN from Greek *deka* 'ten.'

dec·ade /'dekād/ ▶ **n. 1** a period of ten years: *he taught at the university for nearly a decade*. ■ a period of ten years beginning with a year ending in 0 (or, by another reckoning, 1): *the fourth decade of the nineteenth century*.
2 a set, series, or group of ten, in particular: ■ /'dekid/ each of the five divisions of each chapter of the rosary.
– DERIVATIVES **dec·a·dal** /'dekədl/ **adj.**
– ORIGIN late Middle English (denoting each of ten parts of a literary work): via Old French and late Latin from Greek *deka* 'ten.' Sense 1 dates from the early 17th cent.

dec·a·dence /'dekədəns/ ▶ **n.** moral or cultural decline as characterized by excessive indulgence in pleasure or luxury: *he denounced Western decadence*. ■ luxurious self-indulgence: *"French" connotes richness and decadence, and that's the idea of this ice cream*.
– ORIGIN mid 16th cent.: from French *décadence*, from medieval Latin *decadentia*; related to DECAY.

dec·a·dent /'dekədənt/ ▶ **adj.** characterized by or reflecting a state of moral or cultural decline. ■ luxuriously self-indulgent: *a decadent soak in a scented bath*.
▶ **n.** a person who is luxuriously self-indulgent. ■ (often **Decadent**) a member of a group of late-19th-cent. French and English poets associated with the Aesthetic Movement.
– DERIVATIVES **dec·a·dent·ly** **adv.**
– ORIGIN mid 19th cent.: from French *décadent*, from medieval Latin *decadentia* (see DECADENCE).

de·caf /'dē,kaf/ ▶ **n.** informal decaffeinated coffee.
– ORIGIN 1960s: abbreviation.

de·caf·fein·ate /dē'kafə,nāt/ ▶ **v.** [with obj.] (usu. as adj. **decaffeinated**) remove most or all of the caffeine from (coffee or tea): *decaffeinated coffee*.
– DERIVATIVES **de·caf·fein·a·tion** /dē,kafə'nāSHən/ **n.**

dec·a·gon /'dekə,gän/ ▶ **n.** a plane figure with ten straight sides and angles.
– DERIVATIVES **de·cag·o·nal** /də'kagənl/ **adj.**
– ORIGIN mid 17th cent.: via medieval Latin from Greek *dekagōnon*, neuter (used as a noun) of *dekagōnos* 'ten-angled.'

dec·a·gram /'dekə,gram/ (also **dekagram**) ▶ **n.** a metric unit of mass or weight, equal to 10 grams.

dec·a·he·dron /,dekə'hēdrən/ ▶ **n.** (pl. **decahedrons** or **decahedra** /-drə/) a solid figure with ten plane faces.
– DERIVATIVES **dec·a·he·dral** /-drəl/ **adj.**
– ORIGIN early 19th cent.: from DECA- 'ten' + -HEDRON, on the pattern of words such as *polyhedron*.

de·cal /'dēkal/ ▶ **n.** a design prepared on special paper for transfer onto another surface such as glass, porcelain, or metal.
– ORIGIN 1950s: abbreviation of DECALCOMANIA.

de·cal·ci·fied /dē'kalsə,fīd/ ▶ **adj.** (of rock or bone) containing a reduced quantity of calcium salts: *decalcified chalk*.
– DERIVATIVES **de·cal·ci·fi·ca·tion** /dē,kalsəfi'kāSHən/ **n.**, **de·cal·ci·fi·er** /-,fīər/ **n.**

de·cal·co·ma·ni·a /dē,kalkə'mānēə/ ▶ **n.** the process of transferring designs from prepared paper onto glass or porcelain. ■ a technique used by some surrealist artists that involves pressing paint between sheets of paper.
– ORIGIN mid 19th cent.: from French *décalcomanie*, from *décalquer* 'transfer a tracing' + *-manie* '-mania' (with reference to the enthusiasm for the process in the 1860s).

dec·a·li·ter /'dekə,lētər/ (also **dekaliter**) (abbr.: **dal** or **dkl**) ▶ **n.** a metric unit of capacity, equal to 10 liters.

Dec·a·logue /'dekə,lôg, -,läg/ ▶ **n.** (usu. **the Decalogue**) the Ten Commandments.
– ORIGIN late Middle English: via French and ecclesiastical Latin from Greek *dekalogos* (*biblos*) '(book of) the Ten Commandments,' from *hoi deka logoi* 'the Ten Commandments' (literally 'the ten sayings').

De·cam·er·on /di'kamərən, -,rän/ a work by Boccaccio, written between 1348 and 1358, containing a hundred tales supposedly told in ten days by a party of ten young people who had fled from the Black Death in Florence. The work was influential on later writers such as Chaucer and Shakespeare.

dec·a·me·ter /ˈdekəˌmētər/ (also **dekameter**) (abbr.: **dam** or **dkm**) ▶ **n.** a metric unit of length, equal to 10 meters.
– DERIVATIVES **dec·a·met·ric** /ˌdekəˈmetrik/ **adj.**

de·camp /diˈkamp/ ▶ **v.** [no obj.] depart suddenly or secretly, esp. to relocate one's business or household in another area: *now he has decamped to Hollywood.* ■ archaic break up or leave a military camp: *the armies of both chiefs had decamped.*
– DERIVATIVES **de·camp·ment n.**
– ORIGIN late 17th cent.: from French *décamper*, from *dé-* (expressing removal) + *camp* 'camp.'

dec·an /ˈdekən/ ▶ **n.** Astrology each of three equal ten-degree divisions of a sign of the zodiac.
– ORIGIN late 16th cent.: from late Latin *decanus* 'chief of a group of ten' (see DEAN[1]).

dec·a·nal /ˈdekənl, diˈkānl/ ▶ **adj.** of or relating to a dean or deanery. ■ relating to or denoting the south side of the choir of a church, the side on which the dean sits. The opposite of CANTORIAL.
– ORIGIN early 18th cent.: from medieval Latin *decanalis*, from late Latin *decanus* (see DEAN[1]).

dec·ane /ˈdekān/ ▶ **n.** Chemistry a colorless liquid hydrocarbon of the alkane series, present in petroleum products such as kerosene. ● Chem. formula: $C_{10}H_{22}$; many isomers, esp. the straight-chain isomer (*n*-**decane**), which is used as a solvent and in jet fuel research.

de·cant /diˈkant/ ▶ **v.** [with obj.] gradually pour (liquid, typically wine or a solution) from one container into another, esp. without disturbing the sediment: *the wine was decanted about 40 minutes before being served.*
– ORIGIN mid 17th cent.: from medieval Latin *decanthare*, from Latin *de-* 'away from' + *canthus* 'edge, rim' (used to denote the angular lip of a beaker), from Greek *kanthos* 'corner of the eye.'

de·cant·er /diˈkantər/ ▶ **n.** a stoppered glass container into which wine is decanted.

de·cap·i·tate /diˈkapiˌtāt/ ▶ **v.** [with obj.] cut off the head of (a person or animal): (as adj. **decapitated**) *a decapitated body.* ■ attempt to undermine (a group or organization) by removing its leaders: *Italy's organized-crime network was decapitated when the godfather of the Sicilian Mafia was arrested.*
– DERIVATIVES **de·cap·i·ta·tion** /diˌkapiˈtāSHən/ **n.**, **de·cap·i·ta·tor** /-ˌtātər/ **n.**
– ORIGIN early 17th cent.: from late Latin *decapitat-* 'decapitated,' from the verb *decapitare*, from *de-* (expressing removal) + *caput, capit-* 'head.'

de·cap·i·ta·tion strike ▶ **n.** a debilitating military attack, esp. one aimed at the enemy's leadership.

dec·a·pod /ˈdekəˌpäd/ Zoology ▶ **n.** a crustacean of the order Decapoda, such as a shrimp, crab, or lobster.
▶ **adj.** relating to or denoting decapods.

De·cap·o·da /diˈkapədə/ Zoology **1** an order of crustaceans that includes shrimps, crabs, and lobsters. They have five pairs of walking legs and are typically marine.
2 a former order of cephalopod mollusks that includes squids and cuttlefishes, having eight arms and two long tentacles. Compare with OCTOPODA.
– ORIGIN modern Latin (plural), from DECA- 'ten' + Greek *pous, pod-* 'foot.'

de·cap·su·late /dēˈkapsŏŏˌlāt/ ▶ **v.** [with obj.] Surgery remove the capsule or covering from (a kidney or other encapsulated organ).
– DERIVATIVES **de·cap·su·la·tion** /dēˌkapsŏŏˈlāSHən/ **n.**

de·car·bon·ize /dēˈkärbəˌnīz/ ▶ **v.** [with obj.] remove carbon or carbonaceous deposits from (an engine or other metal object).
– DERIVATIVES **de·car·bon·i·za·tion** /dēˌkärbənəˈzāSHən/ **n.**, **de·car·bon·iz·er n.**

de·car·box·yl·ase /ˌdēkärˈbäksəˌlās, -ˌlāz/ ▶ **n.** Biochemistry an enzyme that catalyzes the decarboxylation of a particular organic molecule.

de·car·box·yl·ate /ˌdēkärˈbäksəˌlāt/ ▶ **v.** [with obj.] Chemistry eliminate a carboxylic acid group from (an organic compound). ■ [no obj.] undergo this process.
– DERIVATIVES **de·car·box·yl·a·tion** /ˌdēkärˌbäksəˈlāSHən/ **n.**

de·car·bu·rize /dēˈkärb(y)əˌrīz/ ▶ **v.** [with obj.] Metallurgy remove carbon from (iron or steel); decarbonize.
– DERIVATIVES **de·car·bu·ri·za·tion** /dēˌkärb(y)ərəˈzāSHən/ **n.**
– ORIGIN mid 19th cent.: from DE- (expressing removal) + CARBURIZE, on the pattern of French *décarburer*.

dec·a·syl·lab·ic /ˌdekəsiˈlabik/ Prosody ▶ **adj.** (of a metrical line) consisting of ten syllables.
▶ **n.** (also **decasyllable**) a metrical line of ten syllables.

de·cath·lon /diˈkaTH(ə)ˌlän/ ▶ **n.** an athletic event taking place over two days, in which each competitor takes part in the same prescribed ten events (100-meter dash, long jump, shot put, high jump, 400-meter dash, 110-meter hurdles, discus, pole vault, javelin, and 1,500-meter run).
– DERIVATIVES **de·cath·lete** /-ˈkaTH(ə)ˌlēt/ **n.**
– ORIGIN early 20th cent.: from DECA- 'ten' + Greek *athlon* 'contest.'

De·ca·tur[1] /diˈkātər/ **1** an industrial city in northern Alabama, on the Tennessee River; pop. 56,068 (est. 2008).
2 an industrial and commercial city in central Illinois; pop. 76,256 (est. 2008).

De·ca·tur[2], Stephen (1779–1820), US naval officer. He was a daring commander in the Tripolitan War and the War of 1812. He is noted for his well-known toast, "Our country! In her intercourse with foreign nations may she always be in the right; but our country, right or wrong!"

de·cay /diˈkā/ ▶ **v.** [no obj.] (of organic matter) rot or decompose through the action of bacteria and fungi: (as adj. **decayed**) *a decayed cabbage leaf* | (as adj. **decaying**) *the odor of decaying fish.* ■ [with obj.] cause to rot or decompose: *the fungus will decay soft timber.* ■ (of a building or area) fall into disrepair; deteriorate: *urban neighborhoods decay when elevated freeways replace surface roads.* ■ decline in quality, power, or vigor: *the moral authority of the party was decaying.* ■ Physics (of a radioactive substance, particle, etc.) undergo change to a different form by emitting radiation: *the trapped radiocarbon begins to decay at a known rate.* ■ technical (of a physical quantity) undergo a gradual decrease: *the time taken for the current to decay to zero.*
▶ **n.** the state or process of rotting or decomposition: *hardwood is more resistant to decay than softwood* | *tooth decay.* ■ structural or physical deterioration: *the old barn rapidly **fell into decay**.* ■ rotten matter or tissue: *fluoride heals small spots of decay.* ■ the process of declining in quality, power, or vigor: *preachers warning of moral decay.* ■ Physics the change of a radioactive substance, particle, etc., into another by the emission of radiation: *the gas radon is produced by the decay of uranium in rocks and soil.* ■ technical gradual decrease in the magnitude of a physical quantity: *the decay of electrical fields in the electromagnets.*
– ORIGIN late Middle English: from Old French *decair*, based on Latin *decidere* 'fall down or off,' from *de-* 'from' + *cadere* 'fall.'

Dec·can /ˈdekən, ˈdekˌan/ a triangular plateau in southern India, bounded by the Malabar Coast in the west, the Coromandel Coast in the east, and the Vindhaya mountains in the north.

de·cease /diˈsēs/ ▶ **n.** [in sing.] formal or Law death: *a doctor's sudden decease.*
▶ **v.** [no obj.] archaic die.
– ORIGIN Middle English: from Old French *deces*, from Latin *decessus* 'death,' past participle (used as a noun) of *decedere* 'to die.'

de·ceased /diˈsēst/ Law, formal ▶ **n.** (**the deceased**) a person who has died: *in memory of the deceased.*
▶ **adj.** dead; no longer living: *the cremation of a deceased person.*

de·ce·dent /diˈsēdnt/ ▶ **n.** Law a person who has died: *to make sure the decedent's property passes to his children.*
– ORIGIN late 16th cent.: from Latin *decedent-* 'dying,' from the verb *decedere* (see DECEASE).

de·ceit /diˈsēt/ ▶ **n.** the action or practice of deceiving someone by concealing or misrepresenting the truth: *a web of deceit* | *a series of lies and deceits.*
– ORIGIN Middle English: from Old French, past participle (used as a noun) of *deceveir* 'deceive.'

de·ceit·ful /diˈsētfəl/ ▶ **adj.** guilty of or involving deceit; deceiving or misleading others: *such an act would have been deceitful and irresponsible.*
– DERIVATIVES **de·ceit·ful·ly adv.**, **de·ceit·ful·ness n.**

de·ceive /diˈsēv/ ▶ **v.** [with obj.] (of a person) cause (someone) to believe something that is not true, typically in order to gain some personal advantage: *I didn't intend to **deceive** people **into** thinking it was French champagne.* ■ (of a thing) give a mistaken impression: *the area may seem to offer nothing of interest, but don't be deceived* | [no obj.] *everything about him was intended to deceive.* ■ (**deceive oneself**) fail to admit to oneself that something is true: *enabling the rulers to deceive themselves about the nature of their own rule.* ■ be sexually unfaithful to (one's regular partner).
– DERIVATIVES **de·ceiv·a·ble adj.**, **de·ceiv·er n.**
– ORIGIN Middle English: from Old French *deceivre*, from Latin *decipere* 'catch, ensnare, cheat.'

de·cel·er·ate /dēˈseləˌrāt/ ▶ **v.** [no obj.] (of a vehicle, machine, or process) reduce speed; slow down: *international growth rates decelerated in the early 1970s.* ■ [with obj.] cause to move more slowly: *gravity decelerates the cosmic expansion.*
– DERIVATIVES **de·cel·er·a·tion** /-ˌseləˈrāSHən/ **n.**, **de·cel·er·a·tor** /-ˌrātər/ **n.**, **de·cel·er·om·e·ter** /-ˌseləˈrämitər/ **n.**
– ORIGIN late 19th cent.: from DE- (expressing removal) + a shortened form of ACCELERATE.

De·cem·ber /diˈsembər/ ▶ **n.** the twelfth month of the year, in the northern hemisphere usually considered the first month of winter: *the fuel shortage worsened during December* | [as modifier] *a December day.*
– ORIGIN Middle English: from Latin, from *decem* 'ten' (being originally the tenth month of the Roman year).

De·cem·brist /diˈsembrist/ ▶ **n.** a member of a group of Russian revolutionaries who in December 1825 led an unsuccessful revolt against Tsar Nicholas I. The leaders were executed and later came to be regarded as martyrs by the Left.

de·cen·cy /ˈdēsənsē/ ▶ **n.** (pl. **decencies**) behavior that conforms to accepted standards of morality or respectability: *she **had the decency to** come and confess.* ■ modesty and propriety: *a loose dress, rather too low-cut for decency.* ■ (**decencies**) the requirements of accepted or respectable behavior: *an appeal to common decencies.* ■ (**decencies**) things required for a reasonable standard of life: *I can't afford any of the decencies of life.*

de·cen·ni·al /diˈsenēəl/ ▶ **adj.** recurring every ten years: *the decennial census.* ■ lasting for or relating to a period of ten years: *decennial insurance.*
– DERIVATIVES **de·cen·ni·al·ly adv.**
– ORIGIN mid 17th cent.: from Latin *decennium* 'a decade,' from *decennis* 'of ten years' (from *decem* 'ten' + *annus* 'year'), + -AL.

de·cen·ni·um /diˈsenēəm/ ▶ **n.** (pl. **decennia** /-ˈsenēə/ or **decenniums**) a decade.
– ORIGIN late 17th cent.: from Latin, from *decem* 'ten' + *annus* 'year.'

de·cent /ˈdēsənt/ ▶ **adj. 1** conforming with generally accepted standards of respectable or moral behavior: *the good name of such a decent and innocent person.* ■ appropriate; fitting: *they would meet again after a decent interval.* ■ not likely to shock or embarrass others: *a decent high-necked dress.* ■ informal sufficiently clothed to see visitors: *make yourself decent.*
2 [attrib.] of an acceptable standard; satisfactory: *find me a decent cup of coffee* | *people need decent homes.* ■ good: *the deer are small: a 14-inch spread is a pretty decent buck.* ■ kind, obliging, or generous: *that was pretty awfully decent of him.*
– PHRASES **do the decent thing** take the most honorable or appropriate course of action, even if is not necessarily in one's own interests: *after his defeat, he should do the decent thing and step down.*
– DERIVATIVES **de·cent·ly adv.**
– ORIGIN mid 16th cent. (in the sense 'suitable, appropriate'): from Latin *decent-* 'being fitting,' from the verb *decere*.

de·cen·ter /dēˈsentər/ (Brit. **decentre**) ▶ **v.** [with obj.] displace from the center or from a central position. ■ remove or displace (the individual human subject, such as the author of a text) from a primary place or central role: (as noun **decentering**) *the egocentric infant develops by a progressive decentering.*

de·cen·tral·ize /dēˈsentrəˌlīz/ ▶ **v.** [with obj.] (often as adj. **decentralized**) transfer (authority) from central to local government: *Canada has one of the most decentralized governments in the world* | [no obj.] *European countries were trying to decentralize.* ■ move departments of (a large organization) away from a single administrative center to other locations, usually granting them some degree of autonomy.
– DERIVATIVES **de·cen·tral·ist** /-list/ **n. & adj.**, **de·cen·tral·i·za·tion** /dēˌsentrəliˈzāSHən/ **n.**

de·cep·tion /diˈsepSHən/ ▶ **n.** the action of deceiving someone: *obtaining property by deception.* ■ a thing that deceives: *a range of elaborate deceptions.*
– ORIGIN late Middle English: from late Latin *deceptio(n-)*, from *decipere* 'deceive.'

de·cep·tive /diˈseptiv/ ▶ **adj.** giving an appearance or impression different from the true one; misleading: *he put the question with deceptive casualness.*
– DERIVATIVES **de·cep·tive·ness n.**

de·cep·tive·ly /diˈseptivlē/ ▶ **adv.** [usu. as submodifier] in a way or to an extent that gives a misleading impression. ■ to a lesser extent than appears the case: *the idea was deceptively simple.* ■ to a greater extent than appears the case: *the airy and deceptively spacious lounge.*

USAGE Deceptively belongs to a very small set of words whose meaning is genuinely ambiguous in that it can be used in similar contexts to mean both one thing and also its complete opposite. A *deceptively smooth surface* is one that appears smooth but in fact is not smooth at all, while a *deceptively spacious room* is one that does not look spacious but is in fact *more* spacious than it appears. But what is a *deceptively steep gradient*? Or a person who is described as *deceptively strong*? To avoid confusion, use with caution (or not at all), unless the context makes clear in what way the thing modified is not what it first appears to be.

de·cer·e·brate /dē'serə,brāt/ ▶ **v.** [with obj.] (usu. as adj. **decerebrated**) Biology remove the cerebrum from (a laboratory animal).
– DERIVATIVES **de·cer·e·bra·tion** /-,serə'brāsHən/ **n.**

de·cer·ti·fy /dē'sərtə,fī/ ▶ **v.** (**decertifies, decertifying, decertified**) [with obj.] remove a certificate or certification from (someone or something), typically for failure to comply with a regulating authority's rules or standards.
– DERIVATIVES **de·cer·ti·fi·ca·tion** /-,sərtəfi'kāsHən/ **n.**

de·chris·tian·i·za·tion /dē,krisCHənə'zāsHən/ ▶ **n.** the action or process or removing Christian influences or characteristics from something: *the dechristianization of modern society.*
– DERIVATIVES **de·chris·tian·ize** /-'krisCHə,nīz/ **v.**

deci- ▶ **comb. form** (used commonly in units of measurement) one tenth: *deciliter.*
– ORIGIN from Latin *decimus* 'tenth.'

dec·i·bel /'desə,bel, -bəl/ (abbr.: **dB**) ▶ **n.** a unit used to measure the intensity of a sound or the power level of an electrical signal by comparing it with a given level on a logarithmic scale. ■ (in general use) a degree of loudness: *his voice went up several decibels.*
– ORIGIN early 20th cent.: from DECI- 'ten' + BEL (the unit being one tenth of a bel).

de·cide /di'sīd/ ▶ **v.** [no obj.] come to a resolution in the mind as a result of consideration: [with infinitive] *they decided to appoint someone else* | [with clause] *you've decided that a hedge is what you want.* ■ [with obj.] cause to come to such a resolution: *this business about the letter decided me.* ■ make a choice from a number of alternatives: *she had decided **on** her plan of action* | *I've decided **against** having children.* ■ give a judgment concerning a matter or legal case: *the courts decided **in favor of** the New York claimants* | [with obj.] *the judge will decide the case.* ■ [with obj.] come to a decision about (something): *we must decide the fates of the people who headed the coup.* ■ [with obj.] resolve or settle (a question or contest): *an exciting game was decided in a sudden-death overtime.*
– DERIVATIVES **de·cid·a·ble adj., de·cid·er n.**
– ORIGIN late Middle English (in the sense 'bring to a settlement'): from French *décider*, from Latin *decidere* 'determine,' from *de-* 'off' + *caedere* 'cut.'

de·cid·ed /di'sīdid/ ▶ **adj.** [attrib.] (of a quality) definite; unquestionable: *the sunshine is a decided improvement.* ■ (of a person) having clear opinions; resolute. ■ [attrib.] (of a legal case) that has been resolved.
– DERIVATIVES **de·cid·ed·ness n.**

de·cid·ed·ly /di'sīdidlē/ ▶ **adv.** **1** [usu. as submodifier] undoubtedly; undeniably: *he looked decidedly uncomfortable.*
2 in a decisive and confident way: *"No," Donna said decidedly.*

de·cid·ing /di'sīdiNG/ ▶ **adj.** serving to resolve or settle something: *quality service is often the **deciding factor** for customers.*

de·cid·u·a /di'sijoōə/ ▶ **n.** Physiology the thick layer of modified mucous membrane that lines the uterus during pregnancy and is shed with the afterbirth.
– DERIVATIVES **de·cid·u·al** /-joōəl/ **adj.**
– ORIGIN late 18th cent.: from modern Latin *decidua (membrana)*, literally 'falling off (membrane).'

de·cid·u·ous /di'sijoōəs/ ▶ **adj.** (of a tree or shrub) shedding its leaves annually. Often contrasted with EVERGREEN. ■ informal (of a tree or shrub) broadleaved. ■ denoting the milk teeth of a mammal, which are shed after a time.
– DERIVATIVES **de·cid·u·ous·ly adv., de·cid·u·ous·ness n.**
– ORIGIN late 17th cent.: from Latin *deciduus* (from *decidere* 'fall down or off') + -OUS.

dec·ile /'des,īl, -əl/ ▶ **n.** Statistics each of ten equal groups into which a population can be divided according to the distribution of values of a particular variable: *the lowest income decile of the population.* ■ each of the nine values of the random variable that divide a population into ten such groups.
– ORIGIN late 17th cent.: from French *décile*, from a medieval Latin derivative of Latin *decem* 'ten.'

dec·i·li·ter /'desə,lētər/ (Brit. **decilitre**) (abbr.: **dl**) ▶ **n.** a metric unit of capacity, equal to one tenth of a liter.

dec·i·mal /'des(ə)məl/ ▶ **adj.** relating to or denoting a system of numbers and arithmetic based on the number ten, tenth parts, and powers of ten: *decimal arithmetic.* ■ relating to or denoting a system of currency, weights and measures, or other units in which the smaller units are related to the principal units as powers of ten: *decimal coinage.*
▶ **n.** (also **decimal fraction**) a fraction whose denominator is a power of ten and whose numerator is expressed by figures placed to the right of a decimal point. ■ the system of decimal numerical notation.
– DERIVATIVES **dec·i·mal·ly adv.**
– ORIGIN early 17th cent.: from modern Latin *decimalis* (adjective), from Latin *decimus* 'tenth.'

dec·i·mal·ize /'desəmə,līz/ ▶ **v.** [with obj.] convert (a system of coinage or weights and measures) to a decimal system.
– DERIVATIVES **dec·i·mal·i·za·tion** /,des(ə)mələ'zāsHən/ **n.**

dec·i·mal place ▶ **n.** the position of a digit to the right of a decimal point.

dec·i·mal point ▶ **n.** a dot placed after the figure representing units in a decimal fraction.

dec·i·mate /'desə,māt/ ▶ **v.** [with obj.] **1** kill, destroy, or remove a large percentage or part of: *the project would decimate the fragile wetland wilderness* | *the American chestnut, a species decimated by blight.* ■ drastically reduce the strength or effectiveness of (something): *plant viruses that can decimate yields.*
2 historical kill one in every ten of (a group of soldiers or others) as a punishment for the whole group.
– DERIVATIVES **dec·i·ma·tion** /,desə'māsHən/ **n., dec·i·ma·tor** /-,mātər/ **n.**
– ORIGIN late Middle English: from Latin *decimat-* 'taken as a tenth,' from the verb *decimare*, from *decimus* 'tenth.' In Middle English the term *decimation* denoted the levying of a tithe, and later the tax imposed in England by Cromwell on the Royalists (1655). The verb *decimate* originally alluded to the Roman punishment of executing one man in ten of a mutinous legion.

USAGE Historically, the meaning of the word **decimate** is 'kill one in every ten of (a group of people).' This sense has been superseded by the later, more general sense 'kill or destroy a large percentage or part of,' as in *the virus has **decimated** the population.* Some traditionalists argue that this and other later senses are incorrect, but it is clear that these extended senses are now part of standard English. It is sometimes also argued that **decimate** should refer to people and not to things or animals such as weeds or insects. It is generally agreed that **decimate** should not be used to mean 'defeat utterly.'

dec·i·me·ter /'desə,mētər/ (Brit. **decimetre**) (abbr.: **dm**) ▶ **n.** a metric unit of length, equal to one tenth of a meter.
– DERIVATIVES **dec·i·met·ric** /,desə'metrik/ **adj.**

de·ci·pher /di'sīfər/ ▶ **v.** [with obj.] convert (a text written in code, or a coded signal) into normal language: *enable the government to decipher coded computer transmissions.* ■ succeed in understanding, interpreting, or identifying (something): *an expression she could not decipher came and went upon his face.*
– DERIVATIVES **de·ci·pher·a·ble adj., de·ci·pher·ment n.**
– ORIGIN early 16th cent.: from DE- (expressing reversal) + CIPHER, on the pattern of French *déchiffrer.*

de·ci·sion /di'sizHən/ ▶ **n.** a conclusion or resolution reached after consideration: *I'll make the decision on my own* | *the editor's decision is final.* ■ the action or process of deciding something or of resolving a question: *the information was used as the basis for decision.* ■ a formal judgment: *last year's Supreme Court decision.* ■ the ability or tendency to make decisions quickly; decisiveness: *she was a woman **of decision**.* ■ Boxing the awarding of a fight, in the absence of a knockout or technical knockout, to the boxer with the most rounds won or with the most points. ■ Baseball a win or a loss assigned to a pitcher.
– ORIGIN late Middle English: from Latin *decisio(n-)*, from *decidere* 'determine' (see DECIDE).

de·ci·sion-mak·ing ▶ **n.** the action or process of making decisions, esp. important ones: *the system encourages workers' participation in corporate decision-making.*
– DERIVATIVES **de·ci·sion-mak·er n.**

de·ci·sion prob·lem ▶ **n.** Logic the problem of finding a way to decide whether a formula or class of formulas is true or provable within a given system of axioms.
– ORIGIN 1930s: translating German *Entscheidungsproblem.*

de·ci·sion sup·port sys·tem (abbr.: **DSS**) ▶ **n.** Computing a set of related computer programs and the data required to assist with analysis and decision-making within an organization.

de·ci·sion the·o·ry ▶ **n.** the mathematical study of strategies for optimal decision-making between options involving different risks or expectations of gain or loss depending on the outcome. Compare with GAME THEORY.

de·ci·sive /di'sīsiv/ ▶ **adj.** settling an issue; producing a definite result: *the Supreme Court voided the statute by a decisive 7–2 vote* | *decisive evidence.* ■ (of a person) having or showing the ability to make decisions quickly and effectively.
– DERIVATIVES **de·ci·sive·ly adv., de·ci·sive·ness n.**
– ORIGIN early 17th cent.: from French *décisif, -ive*, from medieval Latin *decisivus*, from *decis-* 'determined,' from the verb *decidere* (see DECIDE).

De·cius /'dēsH(ē)əs/, Gaius Messius Quintus Trajanus (*c.*201–251), Roman emperor 249–251. He was the first Roman emperor to promote systematic persecution of the Christians.

deck /dek/ ▶ **n.** **1** a structure of planks or plates, approximately horizontal, extending across a ship or boat at any of various levels, esp. one of those at the highest level and open to the weather: *he stood on the deck of his flagship.* ■ a floor or platform resembling or compared to a ship's deck, esp. the floor of a pier or a platform for sunbathing. ■ a platformlike structure, typically made of lumber and unroofed, attached to a house or other building: *they cooked hamburgers on the deck adjoining the living room.* ■ a level of a large, open building, esp. a sports stadium: *Jeter hit an enormous home run into the upper deck.* ■ (**the deck**) informal the ground or floor: *there was a big thud when I **hit the deck**.* ■ the flat part of a skateboard or snowboard.
2 a component or unit in sound-reproduction equipment that incorporates a playing or recording mechanism for discs or tapes: *the car has cruise control and a tape deck.*
3 a pack of cards: *shuffle the deck.* ■ informal a packet of narcotics.
▶ **v.** [with obj.] **1** (usu. **be decked**) decorate or adorn brightly or festively: *Ingrid **was decked out** in her Sunday best.*
2 informal knock (someone) to the ground with a punch.
– PHRASES **clear the decks** see CLEAR. **not playing with a full deck** informal mentally deficient. **on deck** on or onto a ship's main deck: *she stood on deck for hours.* ■ ready for action or work. ■ Baseball next to hit in the batting order.
– DERIVATIVES **decked adj.** [in combination] *a three-decked vessel.*
– ORIGIN late Middle English: from Middle Dutch *dec* 'covering, roof, cloak,' *dekken* 'to cover.' Originally denoting canvas used to make a covering (esp. on a ship), the term came to mean the covering itself, later denoting a solid surface serving as roof and floor.

deck chair ▶ **n.** a folding chair of wood and canvas, typically used near the sea or on the deck of passenger ships.

-decker ▶ **comb. form** having a specified number of decks or layers: *double-decker.*

deck·hand /'dek,hand/ ▶ **n.** a member of a ship's crew whose duties include maintenance of hull, decks, and superstructure and mooring and cargo handling.

deck·house /'dek,hous/ ▶ **n.** a superstructure on the deck of a ship or boat, used primarily to house equipment or for storage, or (formerly) for accommodations.

deck·ing /'dekiNG/ ▶ **n.** **1** the material of the deck of a ship, a floor, or a platform.
2 the action of ornamenting something.

deck·le /'dekəl/ ▶ **n.** (also **deckle strap**) a device in a papermaking machine for limiting the size of the sheet, consisting of a continuous belt on either side of the wire. ■ a frame on the mold used to shape the pulp when making paper by hand.
– ORIGIN mid 18th cent.: from German *Deckel*, diminutive of *Decke* 'covering.'

deck·le edge ▶ **n.** the rough uncut edge of a sheet of paper, formed by a deckle.
– DERIVATIVES **deck·le-edged adj.**

deck of·fi·cer ▶ **n.** an officer in charge of the above-deck workings and maneuvers at sea of a ship or boat.

deck pas·sen·ger ▶ **n.** a passenger on a ship who does not have a cabin.

d

deck shoe another term for BOAT SHOE.

de·claim /di'klām/ ▶ v. [reporting verb] utter or deliver words or a speech in a rhetorical or impassioned way, as if to an audience: [with obj.] *she declaimed her views* | [no obj.] *a preacher declaiming from the pulpit.* ■ [no obj.] (**declaim against**) forcefully protest against or criticize (something).
– DERIVATIVES **de·claim·er** n., **de·clam·a·to·ry** /-'klamə,tôrē/ adj.
– ORIGIN late Middle English: from French *déclamer* or Latin *declamare*, from *de-* (expressing thoroughness) + *clamare* 'to shout.'

dec·la·ma·tion /,dekləˈmāSHən/ ▶ n. the action or art of declaiming: *Shakespearean declamation* | *declamations of patriotism.* ■ a rhetorical exercise or set speech. ■ forthright or distinct projection of words set to music: *a soprano soloist with wonderfully clear declamation.*
– ORIGIN late Middle English (in the sense 'a set speech'): from Latin *declamatio(n-)*, from the verb *declamare* (see DECLAIM).

de·clar·ant /di'kle(ə)rənt/ chiefly Law ▶ n. a person or party who makes a formal declaration. ■ an alien who has signed a declaration of intent to become a US citizen.
▶ adj. making or having made a formal declaration.
– ORIGIN late 17th cent.: from French *déclarant*, present participle of *déclarer*, from Latin *declarare* 'make quite clear' (see DECLARE).

dec·la·ra·tion /,dekləˈrāSHən/ ▶ n. a formal or explicit statement or announcement: *they issued a declaration at the close of the talks* | *declarations of love.* ■ the formal announcement of the beginning of a state or condition: *the declaration of war* | *a declaration of independence.* ■ a listing of goods, property, income, etc., subject to duty or tax. ■ a written public announcement of intentions or of the terms of an agreement. ■ Law a plaintiff's statement of claims in proceedings. ■ Law an affirmation made instead of taking an oath. ■ the naming of trump in bridge, whist, or a similar card game.
– ORIGIN late Middle English: from Latin *declaratio(n-)*, from *declarare* 'make quite clear' (see DECLARE).

Dec·la·ra·tion of In·de·pen·dence a document declaring the US to be independent of the British Crown, signed on July 4, 1776, by the congressional representatives of the Thirteen Colonies, including Thomas Jefferson, Benjamin Franklin, and John Adams.

de·clar·a·tive /di'kle(ə)rətiv, -'klar-/ ▶ adj. **1** of the nature of or making a declaration: *declarative statements.* ■ Grammar (of a sentence or phrase) taking the form of a simple statement.
2 Computing denoting high-level programming languages that can be used to solve problems without requiring the programmer to specify an exact procedure to be followed.
▶ n. a statement in the form of a declaration. ■ Grammar a declarative sentence or phrase.
– DERIVATIVES **de·clar·a·tive·ly** adv.

de·clare /di'kle(ə)r/ ▶ v. **1** [reporting verb] say something in a solemn and emphatic manner: [with clause] *he declared that he never revises his prose* | [with direct speech] *"I was under too much pressure," he declared.* ■ [with obj.] formally announce the beginning of (a state or condition): *Spain declared war on Britain in 1796.* ■ [with obj. and complement] pronounce or assert (a person or thing) to be something specified: *the mansion was declared a fire hazard.* ■ [no obj.] (**declare for/against**) openly align oneself for or against (a party or position) in a dispute: *Mr. Roosevelt had declared for "a new deal."* ■ [no obj.] announce oneself as a candidate for an election: *he declared last April.* ■ (**declare oneself**) reveal one's intentions or identity. ■ (**declare oneself**) archaic express feelings of love to someone: *she waited in vain for him to declare himself.*
2 [with obj.] acknowledge possession of (taxable income or dutiable goods).
3 [with obj.] announce that one holds (certain combinations of cards) in a card game.
– PHRASES **well, I declare** (or **I do declare**) an exclamation of incredulity, surprise, or vexation.
– DERIVATIVES **de·clar·a·ble** adj., **de·clar·a·to·ry** /-'kle(ə)rə,tôrē/ adj., **de·clar·ed·ly** /-'kle(ə)ridlē/ adv.
– ORIGIN Middle English: from Latin *declarare*, from *de-* 'thoroughly' + *clarare* 'make clear' (from *clarus* 'clear').

de·clar·er /di'kle(ə)rər/ ▶ n. Bridge the player whose bid establishes the suit of the contract and who must therefore play both their own hand and the exposed hand of the dummy.

de·class /dē'klas/ ▶ v. [with obj.] (usu. **be declassed**) demote (someone) from their original social class to a lower one.

dé·clas·sé /,dāklä'sā/ (also **déclassée**) ▶ adj. having fallen in social status: *his parents were poor and déclassé.*
– ORIGIN late 19th cent.: French, 'removed from one's class, degraded,' past participle of *déclasser*.

de·clas·si·fy /dē'klasə,fī/ ▶ v. (**declassifies, declassifying, declassified**) [with obj.] officially declare (information or documents) to be no longer secret: *government documents were declassified.*
– DERIVATIVES **de·clas·si·fi·ca·tion** /dē,klasəfi'kāSHən/ n.

de·claw /dē'klô/ ▶ v. [with obj.] remove the claws from. ■ make harmless or less threatening: *the Grimms' fairy tales were declawed beyond recognition.*

de·clen·sion /di'klenSHən/ ▶ n. **1** (in the grammar of Latin, Greek, and other languages) the variation of the form of a noun, pronoun, or adjective, by which its grammatical case, number, and gender are identified. ■ the class to which a noun or adjective is assigned according to the manner of this variation.
2 literary a condition of decline or moral deterioration: *the declension of the new generation.*
– DERIVATIVES **de·clen·sion·al** /-SHənl/ adj.
– ORIGIN late Middle English *declinson*, from Old French *declinaison*, from *decliner* 'to decline.' The change in the ending was probably due to association with words such as *ascension*.

de Cle·ram·bault's syn·drome /də ,klerəm'bōz ,sindrōm/ ▶ n. Psychiatry another term for EROTOMANIA.
– ORIGIN from the name of French psychiatrist Gatin *de Clérambault* (1872–1934), who first described it.

dec·li·na·tion /,dekləˈnāSHən/ ▶ n. **1** Astronomy the angular distance of a point north or south of the celestial equator. Compare with RIGHT ASCENSION and CELESTIAL LATITUDE. ■ the angular deviation of a compass needle from true north (because the magnetic north pole and the geographic north pole do not coincide).
2 formal refusal: *in the face of this declination of the proposition.*
– DERIVATIVES **dec·li·na·tion·al** /-SHənl/ adj.
– ORIGIN late Middle English: from Latin *declinatio(n-)*, from the verb *declinare* (see DECLINE).

dec·li·na·tion ax·is ▶ n. Astronomy the axis of an equatorially mounted telescope that is at right angles to the polar axis, about which the telescope is turned in order to view points at different declinations but at a constant right ascension.

de·cline /di'klīn/ ▶ v. **1** [no obj.] (typically of something regarded as good) become smaller, fewer, or less; decrease: *the birth rate continued to decline.* ■ diminish in strength or quality; deteriorate: *her health began to decline* | (as adj. **declining**) *the victims of declining educational standards.*
2 [with obj.] politely refuse (an invitation or offer): *Caroline declined the coffee.* ■ [with infinitive] politely refuse to do something: *the company declined to comment.*
3 [no obj.] (esp. of the sun) move downward. ■ archaic bend down; droop.
4 [with obj.] (in the grammar of Latin, Greek, and certain other languages) state the forms of (a noun, pronoun, or adjective) corresponding to cases, number, and gender.
▶ n. [in sing.] a gradual and continuous loss of strength, numbers, quality, or value: *a serious decline in bird numbers* | *a civilization in decline.* ■ archaic the gradual setting of the sun. ■ archaic any disease in which bodily strength gradually fails, esp. tuberculosis.
– DERIVATIVES **de·clin·a·ble** adj., **de·clin·er** n.
– ORIGIN late Middle English: from Old French *decliner*, from Latin *declinare* 'bend down, turn aside,' from *de-* 'down' + *clinare* 'to bend.'

de·clin·ing years ▶ plural n. a person's old age, esp. when regarded as the time when health, vigor, and mental faculties deteriorate. ■ the period leading up to the end of an enterprise or institution: *the declining years of the Austro-Hungarian empire.*

de·cliv·i·ty /di'klivitē/ ▶ n. (pl. **declivities**) a downward slope: *a thickly wooded declivity.*
– DERIVATIVES **de·cliv·i·tous** /-təs/ adj.
– ORIGIN early 17th cent.: from Latin *declivitas*, from *declivis* 'sloping down,' from *de-* 'down' + *clivus* 'a slope.'

de·clut·ter /'dēklətər/ ▶ v. [with obj.] remove unnecessary items from (an untidy or overcrowded place): *there's no better time to declutter your home.*

dec·o /'dekō/ ▶ n. **1** short for ART DECO.
2 (in scuba diving) short for DECOMPRESSION.

de·coct /di'kākt/ ▶ v. [with obj.] archaic extract the essence from (something) by heating or boiling it.
– ORIGIN late Middle English (in the sense 'cook, heat up'): from Latin *decoct-* 'boiled down,' from the verb *decoquere*, from *de-* 'down' + *coquere* 'cook.'

de·coc·tion /di'kākSHən/ ▶ n. the liquor resulting from concentrating the essence of a substance by heating or boiling, esp. a medicinal preparation made from a plant: *a decoction of a root.* ■ the action or process of extracting the essence of something.
– ORIGIN late Middle English: from late Latin *decoctio(n-)*, from *decoquere* 'boil down' (see DECOCT).

de·code /di'kōd/ ▶ v. [with obj.] convert (a coded message) into intelligible language. ■ analyze and interpret (a verbal or nonverbal communication or image): *a handbook to help parents decode street language.* ■ convert (audio or video signals) into another form, e.g., to analog from digital in sound reproduction: *processors used to decode CD-quality digital audio signals.*
▶ n. informal a translation of a coded message.
– DERIVATIVES **de·cod·a·ble** adj.

de·cod·er /di'kōdər/ ▶ n. a person or thing that analyzes and interprets something, in particular: ■ an electronic device for analyzing the information components of an audio or visual signal and feeding them to separate amplifier channels. ■ an electronic device that converts a coded signal into one that can be used by other equipment, esp. a device to decode satellite television signals.

de·col·late[1] /di'kä,lāt/ ▶ v. [with obj.] archaic behead (someone).
– DERIVATIVES **de·col·la·tion** /,dekə'lāSHən/ n.
– ORIGIN late Middle English: from Latin *decollat-* 'beheaded,' from the verb *decollare*, from *de-* (expressing removal) + *collum* 'neck.'

de·col·late[2] /'dekə,lāt, 'dēkə-/ ▶ v. [no obj.] separate sheets of paper, such as multi-ply computer paper, into different piles.
– DERIVATIVES **de·col·la·tion** /,dekə'lāSHən, ,dēkə-/ n., **de·col·la·tor** /-,lātər/ n.
– ORIGIN 1960s: from DE- 'away from' + COLLATE.

dé·colle·tage /dā,kälə'täZH ,dekələ-/ ▶ n. a low neckline on a woman's dress or top. ■ a woman's cleavage as revealed by such a neckline.
– ORIGIN late 19th cent.: French, from *décolleter* 'expose the neck,' from *dé-* (expressing removal) + *collet* 'collar of a dress.'

dé·colle·té /dā,kälə'tā ,dekələ-/ ▶ adj. (also **décolletée**) (of a woman's dress or top) having a low neckline.
▶ n. a low neckline on a woman's dress or top.
– ORIGIN mid 19th cent.: French, past participle of *décolleter* 'expose the neck.'

de·col·o·nize /dē'kälə,nīz/ ▶ v. [with obj.] (of a country) withdraw from (a colony), leaving it independent: *they must decolonize French Polynesia.*
– DERIVATIVES **de·col·o·ni·za·tion** /-,kälənə'zāSHən/ n.

de·col·or·ize /dē'kələ,rīz/ ▶ v. [with obj.] remove the color from: *ethane decolorizes bromine water.*
– DERIVATIVES **de·col·or·i·za·tion** /-,kələrə'zāSHən/ n.

de·com·mis·sion /,dēkə'miSHən/ ▶ v. [with obj.] withdraw (someone or something) from service, in particular: ■ make (a nuclear reactor or weapon) inoperative, and dismantle and decontaminate it to make it safe. ■ take (a ship) out of service.

de·com·mu·nize /dē'kämyə,nīz/ ▶ v. [with obj.] remove the features or influence of communism from.
– DERIVATIVES **de·com·mu·ni·za·tion** /-,kämyə,nə'zāSHən/ n.

de·com·pen·sa·tion /dē,kämpən'sāSHən/ ▶ n. Medicine the failure of an organ (esp. the liver or heart) to compensate for the functional overload resulting from disease. ■ Psychiatry the failure to generate effective psychological coping mechanisms in response to stress, resulting in personality disturbance or disintegration, esp. that which causes relapse in schizophrenia.
– DERIVATIVES **de·com·pen·sat·ed** /-'kämpən,sātid/ adj.

de·com·pile /,dēkəm'pīl/ ▶ v. [with obj.] Computing produce source code from (compiled code).
– DERIVATIVES **de·com·pi·la·tion** /dē,kämpə'lāSHən, ,dēkäm-/ n., **de·com·pil·er** n.

de·com·pose /,dēkəm'pōz/ ▶ v. (with reference to a dead body or other organic matter) make or become rotten; decay or cause to decay: [no obj.] *leaves stuffed in plastic bags do not decompose* | (as adj. **decomposed**) *the body was badly decomposed* | [with obj.] *dead plant matter can be completely decomposed by microorganisms.* ■ (with reference to a chemical compound) break down or cause to break down into component elements or simpler constituents: [no obj.] *many chemicals decompose rapidly under high temperature.*
– DERIVATIVES **de·com·pos·a·ble** adj.
– ORIGIN mid 18th cent. (in the sense 'separate into simpler constituents'): from French *décomposer*, from *de-* (expressing reversal) + *composer*.

de·com·pos·er /,dēkəm'pōzər/ ▶ n. an organism, esp. a soil bacterium, fungus, or invertebrate, that decomposes organic material. ■ a device or installation that is used to break down a chemical substance.

de·com·po·si·tion /ˌdēˌkämpəˈzisʜən/ ▶ **n.** the state or process of rotting; decay: *the decomposition of organic waste.*

de·com·press /ˌdēkəmˈpres/ ▶ **v.** **1** [with obj.] relieve of compressing forces, in particular: ■ expand (compressed data) to its normal size so that it can be read and processed by a computer. ■ subject (a diver) to decompression.
2 [no obj.] informal calm down and relax: *Michael sits for a minute to decompress before walking home.*

de·com·pres·sion /ˌdēkəmˈpresʜən/ ▶ **n.** a release of compressing forces, in particular: ■ reduction in air pressure: *decompression of the aircraft cabin.* ■ a gradual reduction of air pressure on a person who has been experiencing high pressure while diving, in order to prevent decompression sickness. ■ the process of expanding computer data to its normal size so that it can be read by a computer. ■ a surgical procedure that relieves excessive pressure on an internal part of the body such as the cranium or spinal cord.

de·com·pres·sion cham·ber ▶ **n.** a small room in which the air pressure can be varied, used chiefly to allow deep-sea divers to adjust gradually to normal air pressure.

de·com·pres·sion sick·ness ▶ **n.** a condition that results when sudden decompression causes nitrogen bubbles to form in the tissues of the body. It is suffered particularly by divers (who often call it **the bends**), and can cause pain in the muscles and joints, cramps, numbness, nausea, and paralysis. Also called CAISSON DISEASE.

de·com·pres·sor /ˌdēkəmˈpresər/ ▶ **n.** an instrument or device for decompressing something. ■ a computer program that decompresses data by digitally expanding it to its original size and form.

de·con·di·tion /ˌdēkənˈdisʜən/ ▶ **v.** [with obj.]
1 (usu. as adj. **deconditioned**) cause to lose fitness or muscle tone, esp. through lack of exercise: *deconditioned muscles.*
2 (usu. as noun **deconditioning**) Psychiatry reform or reverse (previously conditioned behavior), esp. in the treatment of phobia and other anxiety disorders in which the fear response to certain stimuli is brought under control. Compare with COUNTERCONDITIONING. ■ informal persuade (someone) to abandon a habitual mode of thinking.

de·con·flict /ˌdēkənˈflikt/ ▶ **v.** [with obj.] Military reduce the risk of collision between (aircraft, airborne weaponry, etc.) in an area by coordinating their movements.
– DERIVATIVES **de·con·flic·tion** **n.**

de·con·gest /ˌdēkənˈjest/ ▶ **v.** [with obj.] relieve the congestion of (something).
– DERIVATIVES **de·con·ges·tion** /-ˈjesʜən/ **n.**

de·con·ges·tant /ˌdēkənˈjestənt/ ▶ **adj.** (chiefly of a medicine) used to relieve nasal congestion.
▶ **n.** a decongestant medicine.

de·con·se·crate /dēˈkänsiˌkrāt/ ▶ **v.** [with obj.] (usu. **be deconsecrated**) transfer (a building) from sacred to secular use: *the church was deconsecrated in the early nineteenth century.*
– DERIVATIVES **de·con·se·cra·tion** /-ˌkänsiˈkrāsʜən/ **n.**

de·con·struct /ˌdēkənˈstrəkt/ ▶ **v.** [with obj.] analyze (a text or a linguistic or conceptual system) by deconstruction, typically in order to expose its hidden internal assumptions and contradictions and subvert its apparent significance or unity. ■ reduce (something) to its constituent parts in order to reinterpret it: *do we need to deconstruct all the institutions that we've created in order to improve them?*
– DERIVATIVES **de·con·struc·tive** /-tiv/ **adj.**
– ORIGIN late 19th cent.: back-formation from DECONSTRUCTION.

de·con·struc·tion /ˌdēkənˈstrəksʜən/ ▶ **n.** a method of critical analysis of philosophical and literary language that emphasizes the internal workings of language and conceptual systems, the relational quality of meaning, and the assumptions implicit in forms of expression.

> Deconstruction focuses on a text as such rather than as an expression of the author's intention, stressing the limitlessness (or impossibility) of interpretation and rejecting the Western philosophical tradition of seeking certainty through reasoning by privileging certain types of interpretation and repressing others. It was effectively named and popularized by the French philosopher Jacques Derrida from the late 1960s and taken up particularly by US literary critics.

– DERIVATIVES **de·con·struc·tion·ism** /-ˌnizəm/ **n.**, **de·con·struc·tion·ist** /-ist/ **adj.** & **n.**
– ORIGIN late 19th cent. (originally in the general sense 'taking to pieces'): from DE- (expressing reversal) + CONSTRUCTION.

de·con·tam·i·nate /ˌdēkənˈtaməˌnāt/ ▶ **v.** [with obj.] neutralize or remove dangerous substances, radioactivity, or germs from (an area, object, or person): *they tried to decontaminate nearby villages.*
– DERIVATIVES **de·con·tam·i·na·tion** /-ˌtaməˈnāsʜən/ **n.**

de·con·tex·tu·al·ized /ˌdēkənˈteksʜo͞oəˌlīzd/ ▶ **adj.** considered in isolation from its context: *coffee-table photo books with their beautiful but decontextualized photographs.*
– DERIVATIVES **de·con·tex·tu·al·i·za·tion** /-ˌteksʜo͞oələˈzāsʜən/ **n.**, **de·con·tex·tu·al·ize** **v.**

de·con·trol /ˌdēkənˈtrōl/ ▶ **v.** (**decontrols, decontrolling, decontrolled**) [with obj.] release (a commodity, market, etc.) from controls or restrictions: *whether gas prices should be totally decontrolled.*
▶ **n.** the action of decontrolling something.

de·con·vo·lu·tion /dēˌkänvəˈlo͞osʜən/ ▶ **n.** a process of resolving something into its constituent elements or removing complication in order to clarify it: *the editor helped in the deconvolution of phrase and thought.* ■ Mathematics the resolution of a convolution function into the functions from which it was formed in order to separate their effects. ■ (also **deconvolution analysis**) the improvement of resolution of images or other data by a mathematical algorithm designed to separate the information from artifacts that result from the method of collecting it.

de·cor /dāˈkôr, di-/ ▶ **n.** the furnishing and decoration of a room. ■ the decoration and scenery of a stage.
– ORIGIN late 19th cent.: from French *décor*, from the verb *décorer*, from Latin *decorare* 'embellish' (see DECORATE).

dec·o·rate /ˈdekəˌrāt/ ▶ **v.** [with obj.] **1** make (something) look more attractive by adding extra items or images to it. ■ provide (a room or building) with a color scheme, paint, wallpaper, etc.: *the five bedrooms are individually decorated.*
2 confer an award or medal on (a member of the armed forces): *he was decorated for outstanding bravery.*
– ORIGIN mid 16th cent. (in the sense 'to grace or honor'): from Latin *decoratus* 'embellished' (past participle of *decorare*), from *decus, decor-* 'beauty, honor, or embellishment.'

Dec·o·rat·ed /ˈdekəˌrātid/ ▶ **adj.** denoting a stage of English Gothic church architecture typical of the 14th century (between Early English and Perpendicular), with increasing use of decoration and geometric, curvilinear, and reticulated tracery.

dec·o·ra·tion /ˌdekəˈrāsʜən/ ▶ **n.** **1** the process or art of decorating or adorning something: *the lavish decoration of cloth with gilt.* ■ ornamentation: *pearwood inlaid with floral decoration of stained woods.* ■ a thing that serves as an ornament: *Christmas tree decorations.* ■ paint or wallpaper applied when decorating a room: *an authority on English furniture and decoration.*
2 a medal or award conferred as an honor.

Dec·o·ra·tion Day ▶ **n.** another term for MEMORIAL DAY.

dec·o·ra·tive /ˈdek(ə)rətiv, ˈdekəˌrātiv/ ▶ **adj.** serving to make something look more attractive; ornamental: *the outside of the building is functional rather than decorative.* ■ relating to decoration: *a decorative artist.*
– DERIVATIVES **dec·o·ra·tive·ly** **adv.**, **dec·o·ra·tive·ness** **n.**

dec·o·ra·tive arts ▶ **plural n.** the arts concerned with the production of high-quality objects that are both useful and beautiful.

dec·o·ra·tor /ˈdekəˌrātər/ ▶ **n.** a person who decorates, in particular: ■ a person whose job is to design the interior of someone's home, by choosing colors, carpets, materials, and furnishings. ■ chiefly Brit. a person whose job is to decorate the interior of buildings by painting the walls and hanging wallpaper: *she became a painter and decorator.*

dec·o·rous /ˈdekərəs, diˈkôrəs/ ▶ **adj.** in keeping with good taste and propriety; polite and restrained: *dancing with decorous space between partners.*
– DERIVATIVES **dec·o·rous·ly** **adv.**, **dec·o·rous·ness** **n.**
– ORIGIN mid 17th cent. (in the sense 'appropriate, seemly'): from Latin *decorus* 'seemly' + -OUS.

de·cor·ti·cate /dēˈkôrtiˌkāt/ ▶ **v.** [with obj.] **1** (often as adj. **decorticated**) technical remove the bark, rind, or husk from: *decorticated peanuts.*
2 subject to surgical decortication.
▶ **adj.** Biology & Psychology of or relating to an animal that has had the cortex of the brain removed or separated.
– ORIGIN early 17th cent.: from Latin *decorticat-* 'stripped of its bark,' from the verb *decorticare*, from *de-* (expressing removal) + *cortex, cortic-* 'bark.'

de·cor·ti·ca·tion /dēˌkôrtiˈkāsʜən/ ▶ **n.** the removal of the outer layer or cortex from a structure, esp. the lung, brain, or other organ. ■ Medicine the operation of removing fibrous scar tissue that prevents expansion of the lung.
– ORIGIN early 17th cent.: from Latin *decorticatio(n-)*, from *decorticare* 'strip of bark' (see DECORTICATE).

de·co·rum /diˈkôrəm/ ▶ **n.** behavior in keeping with good taste and propriety: *you exhibit remarkable modesty and decorum.* ■ etiquette: *he had no idea of funeral decorum.* ■ (usu. **decorums**) archaic a particular requirement of good taste and propriety. ■ archaic suitability to the requirements of a person, rank, or occasion.
– ORIGIN mid 16th cent. (as a literary term, denoting suitability of style): from Latin, neuter of the adjective *decorus* 'seemly.'

de·cou·page /ˌdāko͞oˈpäzʜ/ ▶ **n.** the decoration of a surface with applied paper cut-outs, often finished with varnish or lacquer.
– ORIGIN 1960s: French, from *découper* 'cut out.'

de·cou·ple /dēˈkəpəl/ ▶ **v.** [with obj.] separate, disengage, or dissociate (something) from something else: *the mountings effectively **decouple** movements of the engine **from** those of the wheels.* ■ make the interaction between (electrical components) so weak that there is little transfer of energy between them, esp. to remove unwanted AC distortion or oscillations in circuits with a common power supply. ■ muffle the sound or shock of (a nuclear explosion) by causing it to take place in an underground cavity.

de·coy ▶ **n.** /ˈdēˌkoi/ **1** a bird or mammal, or an imitation of one, used by hunters to attract other birds or mammals: [as modifier] *a decoy duck.* ■ a person or thing used to mislead or lure an animal or person into a trap.■
2 a pond from which narrow netted channels lead, into which wild ducks may be enticed for capture.
▶ **v.** /diˈkoi/ [with obj.] lure or entice (a person or animal) away from an intended course, typically into a trap: *they would try to decoy the enemy toward the hidden group.*
– ORIGIN mid 16th cent. (earlier as *coy*): from Dutch *de kooi* 'the decoy,' from Middle Dutch *de kouw* 'the cage,' from Latin *cavea* 'cage.' Sense 2 of the noun is from the practice of using tamed ducks to lead wild ones along channels into captivity.

de·crease ▶ **v.** /diˈkrēs/ make or become smaller or fewer in size, amount, intensity, or degree: [no obj] *the population of the area has decreased radically* | [with obj] *in some cases vitamin E has decreased cholesterol levels.*
▶ **n.** /ˈdēˌkrēs, diˈkrēs/ an instance or example of becoming smaller or fewer: *a decrease in births* | *the rate of decrease became greater.*
– PHRASES **on the decrease** becoming less common or widespread; decreasing.
– DERIVATIVES **de·creas·ing·ly** /diˈkrēsiɴglē/ **adv.** [as submodifier] *voters have proved decreasingly willing to support the party.*
– ORIGIN late Middle English: from Old French *decreis* (noun), *decreistre* (verb), based on Latin *decrescere*, from *de-* 'down' + *crescere* 'grow.'

de·cree /diˈkrē/ ▶ **n.** an official order issued by a legal authority. ■ the issuing of such an order: *the king ruled by decree.* ■ a judgment or decision of certain law courts.
▶ **v.** (**decrees, decreeing, decreed**) [with obj.] order (something) by decree: *the government decreed a ban on any contact with the guerrillas* | [with clause] *the president decreed that the military was to be streamlined.*
– ORIGIN Middle English (denoting an edict issued by an ecclesiastical council to settle a point of doctrine or discipline): from Old French *decre, decret*, from Latin *decretum* 'something decided,' from *decernere* 'decide.'

dec·re·ment /ˈdekrəmənt/ ▶ **n.** a reduction or diminution: *relaxation produces a decrement in sympathetic nervous activity.* ■ an amount by which something is reduced or diminished: *the dose was reduced by 10 mg weekly decrements.* ■ Physics the ratio of the amplitudes in successive cycles of a damped oscillation.
▶ **v.** [with obj.] chiefly Computing cause a discrete reduction in (a numerical quantity): *the instruction decrements the accumulator by one.*
– ORIGIN early 17th cent. (as a noun): from Latin *decrementum* 'diminution,' from the stem of *decrescere* 'to decrease.'

de·cre·o·lize /dēˈkrēəˌlīz/ ▶ **v.** [with obj.] (usu. as adj. **decreolized**) modify (a Creole language) toward the local standard language.
– DERIVATIVES **de·cre·o·li·za·tion** /-ˌkrēələˈzāsʜən/ **n.**

de·crep·it /di'krepit/ ▶ **adj.** (of a person) elderly and infirm: *a decrepit old drunk.* ■ worn out or ruined because of age or neglect: *centuries-old buildings, now decrepit and black with soot.*
– ORIGIN late Middle English: from Latin *decrepitus*, from *de-* 'down' + *crepitus*, past participle of *crepare* 'rattle, creak.'

de·crep·i·tate /di'krəpi,tāt/ ▶ **v.** [no obj.] technical (of a crystal or an inclusion of something within a crystal) disintegrate audibly when heated.
– DERIVATIVES **de·crep·i·ta·tion** /-,krepi'tāsHən/ **n.**
– ORIGIN mid 17th cent.: from DE- 'away' + Latin *crepitat-* 'crackled,' from the verb *crepitare*, frequentative of *crepare* 'rattle' (see DECREPIT).

de·crep·i·tude /di'krepi,t(y)ōōd/ ▶ **n.** the state of being decrepit: *he had passed directly from middle age into decrepitude.*

de·cre·scen·do /,dēkrə'sHendō/ ▶ **n.** (pl. **decrescendos**), **adv.**, & **adj.** another term for DIMINUENDO: [as noun] *the decrescendo of distant thunder* | [as adj.] *a decrescendo heart murmur.*
– ORIGIN early 19th cent.: Italian, literally 'decreasing.'

de·cres·cent /di'kresənt/ ▶ **adj.** [attrib.] (of the moon) waning.
– ORIGIN early 17th cent.: from Latin *decrescent-* 'growing less,' from the verb *decrescere* (see DECREASE).

de·cre·tal /di'krētl/ ▶ **n.** a papal decree concerning a point of canon law.
▶ **adj.** of the nature of a decree.
– ORIGIN Middle English: from late Latin *decretale*, neuter of *decretalis* (adjective), from Latin *decret-* 'decided,' from the verb *decernere*.

De·cre·tum /di'krētəm/ ▶ **n.** a collection of decisions and judgments in canon law.
– ORIGIN Latin, literally 'something decreed.'

de·crim·i·nal·ize /dē'kriminl,īz/ ▶ **v.** [with obj.] cease by legislation to treat (something) as illegal: *a battle to decriminalize drugs.*
– DERIVATIVES **de·crim·i·nal·i·za·tion** /-,kriminl-i'zāsHən/ **n.**

de·cry /di'krī/ ▶ **v.** (**decries**, **decrying**, **decried**) [with obj.] publicly denounce: *they decried human rights abuses.*
– DERIVATIVES **de·cri·er** **n.**
– ORIGIN early 17th cent. (in the sense 'decrease the value of coins by royal proclamation'): from DE- 'down' + CRY, on the pattern of French *décrier* 'cry down.'

de·crypt /di'kript/ ▶ **v.** [with obj.] make (a coded or unclear message) intelligible: *the computer can be used to encrypt and decrypt sensitive transmissions.*
▶ **n.** a text that has been decoded.
– DERIVATIVES **de·cryp·tion** /-'kripsHən/ **n.**
– ORIGIN 1930s: from DE- (expressing reversal) + *crypt* as in *encrypt*.

de·cub·i·tus /di'kyōōbitəs/ ▶ **n.** chiefly Medicine the posture adopted by a person who is lying down: [as modifier] *lumbar puncture with the patient in the lateral decubitus position.*
– ORIGIN late 19th cent.: modern Latin, from Latin *decumbere* 'lie down,' on the pattern of words such as *accubitus* 'reclining at table.'

de·cub·i·tus ul·cer ▶ **n.** technical term for BEDSORE.

de·cum·bent /di'kəmbənt/ ▶ **adj.** Botany (of a plant or part of a plant) lying along the ground or along a surface, with the extremity curving upward.
– ORIGIN late 18th cent.: from Latin *decumbent-* 'lying down,' from the verb *decumbere*, based on *de-* 'down' + a verb related to *cubare* 'to lie.'

de·cur·rent /di'kərənt, -'kə-rənt/ ▶ **adj.** Botany (of a fungus gill, leaf, etc.) extending down the stem below the point of attachment. ■ (of a shrub or the crown of a tree) having several roughly equal branches.
– ORIGIN mid 18th cent.: from Latin *decurrent-* 'running down,' from the verb *decurrere*.

de·curved /dē'kərvd/ ▶ **adj.** Biology (esp. of a bird's bill) curved downward.

dec·us·sate /'dekə,sāt, di'kəsāt/ technical ▶ **v.** [reciprocal] (of two or more things) cross or intersect each other to form an X: *the fibers decussate in the collar.*
▶ **adj.** shaped like an X. ■ Botany (of leaves) arranged in opposite pairs, each pair being at right angles to the pair below.
– DERIVATIVES **dec·us·sa·tion** /,dekə'sāsHən/ **n.**
– ORIGIN mid 17th cent. (as a verb): from Latin *decussatus*, past participle of *decussare* 'divide crosswise,' from *decussis* (describing the figure X, i.e., the Roman numeral for the number 10), from *decem* 'ten.'

de·dans /də'dän/ ▶ **n.** (in court tennis) an open gallery for spectators at the service side of a court.
– ORIGIN early 18th cent.: French, literally 'inside.'

de·den·dum /di'dendəm/ ▶ **n.** Engineering the radial distance from the pitch circle of a cogwheel or worm wheel to the bottom of the tooth space or groove. Compare with ADDENDUM.
– ORIGIN early 20th cent.: from Latin, 'to be given up, surrendered.'

ded·i·cate /'dedi,kāt/ ▶ **v.** [with obj.] (often **dedicate something to**) devote (time, effort, or oneself) to a particular task or purpose: *Joan has dedicated her life to animals.* ■ devote (something) to a particular subject or purpose: *you should dedicate a telephone line to each modem you plan to install.* ■ cite (a book or other artistic work) as being issued or performed in someone's honor: *the novel is dedicated to the memory of my mother.* ■ formally open or unveil (a building or memorial): *the ex-president came to dedicate a $2.6 million recreation center.* ■ ceremonially assign (a church or other building) to a deity or saint: *the parish church is dedicated to St. Paul.*
– DERIVATIVES **ded·i·ca·tee** /,dedikā'tē/ **n.**, **ded·i·ca·tor** /-,kātər/ **n.**, **ded·i·ca·to·ry** /-kə,tôrē/ **adj.**
– ORIGIN late Middle English (in the sense 'devote to sacred use by solemn rites'): from Latin *dedicat-* 'devoted, consecrated,' from the verb *dedicare*.

ded·i·cat·ed /'dedi,kātid/ ▶ **adj.** (of a person) devoted to a task or purpose; having single-minded loyalty or integrity: *a team of dedicated doctors.* ■ (of a thing) exclusively allocated to or intended for a particular service or purpose: *investing in dedicated bike lanes will encourage more bicycle commuters.*
– DERIVATIVES **ded·i·cat·ed·ly** **adv.**

ded·i·ca·tion /,dedi'kāsHən/ ▶ **n. 1** the quality of being dedicated or committed to a task or purpose: *his **dedication to** his duties.*
2 the action of dedicating a church or other building: *the dedication and unveiling was attended by some 5,000 people.* ■ the words with which a book or other artistic work is dedicated: *the hardback edition contained a warm **dedication to** his wife.*
– ORIGIN late Middle English: from Latin *dedicatio(n-)*, from *dedicare* 'devote, consecrate' (see DEDICATE).

de dicto /dā 'diktō/ ▶ **adj.** Philosophy relating to the form of an assertion or expression itself, rather than any property of a thing it refers to. Compare with DE RE.
– ORIGIN Latin, 'from what is said.'

de·dif·fer·en·ti·ate /dē,difə'rensHē,āt/ ▶ **v.** [no obj.] Biology (of a cell or tissue) undergo a reversal of differentiation and lose specialized characteristics.
– DERIVATIVES **de·dif·fer·en·ti·a·tion** /-,rensHē'āsHən/ **n.**

de·duce /di'd(y)ōōs/ ▶ **v.** [with obj.] arrive at (a fact or a conclusion) by reasoning; draw as a logical conclusion: *little can be safely **deduced from** these figures* | [with clause] *they **deduced that** the fish died because of water pollution.* ■ archaic trace the course or derivation of: *he cannot deduce his descent wholly by heirs male.*
– DERIVATIVES **de·duc·i·ble** /-səbəl/ **adj.**
– ORIGIN late Middle English (in the sense 'lead or convey'): from Latin *deducere*, from *de-* 'down' + *ducere* 'lead.'

de·duct /di'dəkt/ ▶ **v.** [with obj.] subtract or take away (an amount or part) from a total: *tax has been **deducted from** the payments.*
– ORIGIN late Middle English: from Latin *deduct-* 'taken or led away,' from the verb *deducere*. *Deduct* and *deduce* were not distinguished in sense until the mid 17th cent.

de·duct·i·ble /di'dəktəbəl/ ▶ **adj.** able to be deducted, esp. from taxable income or tax to be paid: *child-care vouchers will be deductible expenses for employers.* See also TAX-DEDUCTIBLE.
▶ **n.** (in an insurance policy) a specified amount of money that the insured must pay before an insurance company will pay a claim: *a traditional insurance policy with a low deductible.*
– DERIVATIVES **de·duct·i·bil·i·ty** /-,dəktə'bilitē/ **n.**

de·duc·tion /di'dəksHən/ ▶ **n. 1** the action of deducting or subtracting something: *the dividend will be paid without deduction of tax.* ■ an amount that is or may be deducted from something, esp. from taxable income or tax to be paid: *tax deductions.*
2 the inference of particular instances by reference to a general law or principle: *the detective must uncover the murderer by deduction from facts* | *we do not yet know if these deductions are correct.* Often contrasted with INDUCTION.
– ORIGIN late Middle English: from Latin *deductio(n-)*, from the verb *deducere* (see DEDUCE).

de·duc·tive /di'dəktiv/ ▶ **adj.** characterized by the inference of particular instances from a general law: *deductive reasoning.* ■ based on reason and logical analysis of available facts: *I used my deductive powers.*
– DERIVATIVES **de·duc·tive·ly** **adv.**
– ORIGIN mid 17th cent.: from medieval Latin *deductivus*, from *deduct-* 'deduced,' from the verb *deducere* (see DEDUCE).

de Du·ve /də 'dōōv, də 'dʏv/, Christian René (1917–), Belgian biochemist; born in Britain. He was a pioneer in the study of cell biology. He shared the 1974 Nobel Prize for Physiology or Medicine with Albert Claude (1899–1983) and George Palade (1912–2008).

Dee /dē/ **1** a river in northeastern Scotland that rises in the Grampian Mountains and flows east to the North Sea at Aberdeen.
2 a river that rises in North Wales and flows into England, past Chester and on into the Irish Sea.

deed /dēd/ ▶ **n. 1** chiefly literary an action that is performed intentionally or consciously: *doing good deeds.* ■ a brave or noble act: *their deeds will live on in song.* ■ action or performance: *she had erred in both deed and manner.*
2 a legal document that is signed and delivered, esp. one regarding the ownership of property or legal rights. See also TITLE DEED.
▶ **v.** [with obj.] convey or transfer (property or rights) by legal deed: *they **deeded** their property **to** their children.*
– ORIGIN Old English *dēd*, *dǣd*, of Germanic origin; related to Dutch *daad* and German *Tat*, from an Indo-European root shared by DO¹.

dee·jay /'dē,jā/ informal ▶ **n.** a disc jockey.
▶ **v.** (**deejays**, **deejaying**, **deejayed**) [no obj.] act as, or hold a job as, a disc jockey.
– ORIGIN 1950s: representing the pronunciation of *DJ*.

deem /dēm/ ▶ **v.** [with obj. and complement] regard or consider in a specified way: *the event was deemed a great success* | [with obj. and infinitive] *the strike was deemed to be illegal.*
– ORIGIN Old English *dēman* (also in the sense 'act as judge'), of Germanic origin; related to Dutch *doeman*, also to DOOM.

de·em·pha·size /dē'emfə,sīz/ ▶ **v.** [with obj.] reduce the importance or prominence given to (something): *the reform de-emphasized central planning and placed more power in the association of socialized industries.*
– DERIVATIVES **de·em·pha·sis** /-fəsis/ **n.**

de·en·er·gize /dē'enər,jīz/ ▶ **v.** [with obj.] disconnect (an electric circuit) from a power supply. ■ [no obj.] undergo loss of electrical power: *the starter relay automatically de-energizes.*

deep /dēp/ ▶ **adj. 1** extending far down from the top or surface: *a deep gorge* | *the lake was deep and cold.* ■ extending or situated far in or down from the outer edge or surface: *a deep alcove* | *deep in the woods.* ■ [predic.] (after a measurement and in questions) extending a specified distance from the top, surface, or outer edge: *the well was 200 feet deep.* ■ [in combination] as far up or down as a specified point: *standing waist-deep in the river.* ■ [predic.] in a specified number of ranks one behind another: [in combination] *they were standing three-deep at the bar.* ■ taking in or giving out a lot of air: *she took a deep breath.* ■ Baseball far back in the outfield: *his first pitch was hit into deep left field.*
2 very intense or extreme: *she was in deep trouble* | *a deep sleep* | *a deep economic recession.* ■ (of an emotion or feeling) intensely felt: *deep disappointment.* ■ profound or penetrating in awareness or understanding: *a deep analysis.* ■ difficult to understand: *this is all getting too deep for me.* ■ [predic.] (**deep in**) fully absorbed or involved in (a state or activity): *they were deep in their own thoughts.* ■ (of a person) unpredictable and secretive: *that Thomas is a deep one.*
3 (of sound) low in pitch and full in tone; not shrill: *a deep, resonant voice.*
4 (of color) dark and intense: *a deep pink.*
▶ **n.** (**the deep**) literary the sea: *denizens of the deep.* ■ (usu. **deeps**) a deep part of the sea: *the dark and menacing deeps* | figurative *the deeps of her imagination.*
▶ **adv.** far down or in; deeply: *traveling deep into the countryside.* ■ (in sports) distant from the start of a play or the forward line of one's team: *the defense played deep.*
– PHRASES **the deep end** the end of a swimming pool where the water is deepest. **go off** (or **go in off**) **the deep end** informal give way immediately to an emotional outburst, esp. of anger. ■ go mad; behave extremely strangely: *they looked at me as if I had gone off the deep end.* **go** (or **run**) **deep** (of emotions, beliefs, etc.) be strongly and wholeheartedly felt or held: *his passion runs deep.* **in deep** informal inextricably involved in or committed to a situation: *he knew that he was in deep when his things began to proliferate in her apartment.* **in deep water** (or **waters**) informal in trouble or difficulty: *he landed in deep water when he began the affair.*

jump (or **be thrown**) **in at the deep end** informal face a difficult problem or undertaking with little experience of it.
– DERIVATIVES **deep·ness** n.
– ORIGIN Old English *dēop* (adjective), *diope, dēope* (adverb), of Germanic origin; related to Dutch *diep* and German *tief*, also to DIP.

deep brain stim·u·la·tion ▶ n. a nonsurgical treatment to reduce tremor and to block involuntary movements in patients with motion disorders. Small electric shocks are delivered to the thalamus (esp. in the treatment of multiple sclerosis) or the globus pallidus (esp. in the treatment of Parkinson's disease), rendering these parts of the brain inactive without surgically destroying them.

deep breath·ing ▶ n. breathing with long breaths, esp. as exercise or a method of relaxation.

deep-cy·cle ▶ adj. denoting a type of electric battery that can be totally discharged and recharged several times.

deep-dis·count ▶ adj. denoting financial securities carrying a low rate of interest relative to prevailing market rates and issued at a discount to their redemption value, thus mainly providing capital gain rather than income. ■ heavily discounted; greatly reduced in price: *deep-discount pricing has kept airfares affordable.*

deep-dish ▶ adj. **1** (of a pie) baked in a deep dish to allow for a large filling: *deep-dish apple pie.* ■ (of a pizza) baked in a deep dish and having a thick dough base.
2 informal extreme or thoroughgoing: *a deep-dish Catholic.*

deep-dyed ▶ adj. informal thoroughgoing; complete: *a deep-dyed Beatles fan.*

deep e·col·o·gy ▶ n. an environmental movement and philosophy that regards human life as just one of many equal components of a global ecosystem.

deep·en /ˈdēpən/ ▶ v. make or become deep or deeper: [no obj.] *the crisis deepened.* ■ (of a weather system) decrease in barometric pressure. Compare with FILL: (as adj. **deepening**) *a deepening depression.*

deep freeze ▶ n. (also **deep freezer**, trademark **deepfreeze**) a refrigerated cabinet or room in which food can be quickly frozen and kept for long periods at a low temperature: *plenty of garden space to keep our deep freezes supplied with fruit and vegetables.* ■ a place or situation in which progress or activity is suspended: *the nation is now beginning to resume its history after twenty years in the deep freeze.*
▶ v. (**deep-freeze**) [with obj.] (often as adj. **deep-frozen**) store (something) in a deep freeze.

deep-fry ▶ v. [with obj.] (as adj. **deep-fried**) fry (food) in an amount of fat or oil sufficient to cover it completely: *deep-fried onion rings.*

deep kiss ▶ n. dated a kiss involving insertion of the tongue into the partner's mouth.

deep-laid ▶ adj. (of a scheme) secret and elaborate: *a deep-laid plot.*

deep·ly /ˈdēplē/ ▶ adv. far down or in: *he breathed deeply | fragments of rock were deeply embedded within the wood.* ■ intensely: [as submodifier] *she was deeply hurt.*

deep mourn·ing ▶ n. a state of mourning, conventionally expressed by wearing only black clothing. ■ the black clothing worn by someone in deep mourning.

deep pock·ets ▶ n. abundant financial resources: *these companies have deep pockets and don't mind spending to get their projects off the ground.*

deep-root·ed ▶ adj. (of a plant) deeply implanted. ■ firmly embedded in thought, behavior, or culture, and so having a persistent influence: *deep-rooted concern about declining values.*
– DERIVATIVES **deep-root·ed·ness** n.

deep sea ▶ n. [usu. as modifier] the deeper parts of the ocean, esp. those beyond the edge of the continental shelf: *deep-sea diving.*

deep-seat·ed ▶ adj. firmly established at a deep or profound level: *deep-seated anxiety.*

deep-set ▶ adj. (of a person's eyes) positioned deeply in the head: *his deep-set black eyes are powerful, still, and unrelenting.* ■ embedded firmly: *the bees found only a few deep-set plants.* ■ long-established, ingrained, or profound: *a deep-set enmity.*

deep-six ▶ v. [with obj.] informal destroy or dispose of (something) irretrievably: *someone had deliberately deep-sixed evidence.*
– ORIGIN 1920s (as *the deep six* 'the grave'): perhaps from the custom of burial at a depth of six feet.

Deep South (**the Deep South**) the southeastern region of the US that is regarded as embodying traditional Southern culture and traditions.

deep space ▶ n. another term for OUTER SPACE.

deep struc·ture ▶ n. (in generative grammar) the abstract representation of the syntactic structure of a sentence. Contrasted with SURFACE STRUCTURE.

deep throat ▶ n. informal a person who anonymously supplies information about covert or illegal action in the organization where they work.
– ORIGIN 1970s: from the pseudonym used by a Watergate informant, the name having been taken from the title of a pornographic movie (1972).

deep time ▶ n. Geology the multimillion year time frame within which scientists believe the earth has existed, and which is supported by the observation of natural, mostly geological, phenomena.

deep-vein throm·bo·sis ▶ n. thrombosis in a vein lying deep below the skin, esp. in the legs. It is a particular hazard of long-haul flying.

deer /di(ə)r/ ▶ n. (pl. **same**) a hoofed grazing or browsing animal, with branched bony antlers that are shed annually and typically borne only by the male. See also MOUSE DEER, MUSK DEER. ● Family Cervidae: several genera and many species.
– ORIGIN Old English *dēor*, also originally denoting any quadruped, used in the (now archaic) phrase *small deer* meaning 'small creatures collectively'; of Germanic origin; related to Dutch *dier*, German *Tier.*

Deere /di(ə)r/, John (1804–86), US manufacturer. He founded John Deere & Co. in 1868, originally manufacturing steel plows.

Deer·field /ˈdi(ə)rˌfēld/ a historic town in northwestern Massachusetts, on the Connecticut River; pop. 4,694 (est. 2008). It suffered major Indian attacks in 1675 and 1704.

Deer·field Beach a resort city in southeastern Florida, north of Fort Lauderdale; pop. 74,584 (est. 2008).

deer·fly /ˈdi(ə)rˌflī/ ▶ n. **1** a bloodsucking horsefly that attacks humans and other large mammals. It can transmit various diseases, including tularemia. ● Genus *Chrysops*, family Tabanidae: several species, including *C. callidus*, widespread throughout North America.
2 a bloodsucking louse fly that is a parasite of deer. It loses its wings on finding a host, and the female gives birth to fully grown larvae. ● *Lipoptena cervi*, family Hippoboscidae.

deerfly 1

deer hair ▶ n. hair from a deer, particularly as used in making artificial fishing flies.

deer·hound /ˈdi(ə)rˌhound/ ▶ n. a large dog of a rough-haired breed resembling the greyhound.

deer lick ▶ n. a place where deer come to lick salt, either from a block of salt placed there or from a natural source.

deer mouse ▶ n. a mainly nocturnal mouse found in a wide range of habitats in North and Central America. ● Genus *Peromyscus*, family Muridae: numerous species, in particular *P. maniculatus*.

deer·skin /ˈdi(ə)rˌskin/ ▶ n. leather made from a deer's skin.

deer·stalk·er /ˈdi(ə)rˌstôkər/ ▶ n. **1** a soft cloth cap, originally worn for hunting, with bills in front and behind, and ear flaps that can be tied together over the top.
2 a person who stalks deer.

deerstalker 1

de-es·ca·late /dēˈeskəˌlāt/ ▶ v. [with obj.] reduce the intensity of (a conflict or potentially violent situation).
– DERIVATIVES **de-es·ca·la·tion** /-ˌeskəˈlāsʜən/ n.

Deet /dēt/ ▶ n. trademark a brand of diethyltoluamide, a colorless oily liquid with a mild odor, used as an insect repellent.

def /def/ ▶ adj. informal excellent: *a truly def tattoo.*
– ORIGIN 1980s: probably an alteration of DEATH (used in Jamaican English as an intensifier), or shortened from DEFINITIVE or DEFINITE.

de·face /diˈfās/ ▶ v. [with obj.] spoil the surface or appearance of (something), e.g., by drawing or writing on it; mar or disfigure: *he defaced library books | the canyon's spectacular limestone walls have been defaced by the reservoir.*
– DERIVATIVES **de·face·ment** n., **de·fac·er** n.
– ORIGIN Middle English: from Old French *desfacier*, from *des-* (expressing removal) + *face* 'face.'

de fac·to /di ˈfaktō, dā/ ▶ adv. in fact, or in effect, whether by right or not: *the island has been de facto divided into two countries.* Often contrasted with DE JURE.
▶ adj. [attrib.] denoting someone or something that is such in fact: *a de facto one-party system.*
– ORIGIN early 17th cent.: Latin, literally 'of fact.'

de·fal·cate /diˈfalkāt, -ˈfôl-/ ▶ v. [with obj.] formal embezzle (funds with which one has been entrusted): *the officials were charged with defalcating government money.*
– DERIVATIVES **de·fal·ca·tion** /ˌdēfalˈkāsʜən, -fôl-/ n., **de·fal·ca·tor** /-kātər/ n.
– ORIGIN mid 16th cent. (in the sense 'deduct, subtract'): from medieval Latin *defalcat-* 'lopped,' from the verb *defalcare*, from *de-* 'away from, off' + Latin *falx, falc-* 'sickle.'

d

def·a·ma·tion /ˌdefəˈmāsʜən/ ▶ n. the action of damaging the good reputation of someone; slander or libel: *she sued him for defamation.*

de·fam·a·to·ry /diˈfaməˌtôrē/ ▶ adj. (of remarks, writing, etc.) damaging the good reputation of someone; slanderous or libelous: *a defamatory allegation.*

de·fame /diˈfām/ ▶ v. [with obj.] damage the good reputation of (someone); slander or libel: *he claimed that the article defamed his family.*
– DERIVATIVES **de·fam·er** n.
– ORIGIN Middle English: from Old French *diffamer*, from Latin *diffamare* 'spread evil report,' from *dis-* (expressing removal) + *fama* 'report.'

de·fa·mil·iar·ize /ˌdēfəˈmilyərīz/ ▶ v. [with obj.] render unfamiliar or strange (used esp. in the context of art and literature): *art serves to defamiliarize our experience of our own present.*

de·fang /dēˈfaNG/ ▶ v. [with obj.] (often as adj. **defanged**) render harmless or ineffectual: *the military, demoralized and defanged, gave up their campaign.*

de·fat /dēˈfat/ ▶ v. (**defats, defatting, defatted**) [with obj.] (usu. as adj. **defatted**) remove fat from (food): *soup made with defatted chicken stock.*

de·fault /diˈfôlt/ ▶ n. **1** failure to fulfill an obligation, esp. to repay a loan or appear in a court of law: *it will have to restructure its debts to avoid default.*
2 a preselected option adopted by a computer program or other mechanism when no alternative is specified by the user or programmer: *the default is fifty lines* | [as modifier] *default settings.*
▶ v. [no obj.] **1** fail to fulfill an obligation, esp. to repay a loan or to appear in a court of law: *some had defaulted on student loans.* ■ [with obj.] declare (a party) in default and give judgment against that party: *the possibility that cases would be defaulted and defendants released.*
2 (**default to**) (of a computer program or other mechanism) revert automatically to (a preselected option): *when you start a fresh letter, the system will default to its own style.*
– PHRASES **by default** because of a lack of opposition: *they won the last election by default.* ■ through lack of positive action rather than conscious choice: *legislation dies by default if the governor fails to act on it.* **in default** guilty of failing to repay a loan or appear in a court of law: *the company is already in default on its loans.* **in default of** in the absence of: *in default of agreement, the rent was to be determined by a surveyor.*
– ORIGIN Middle English: from Old French *defaut*, from *defaillir* 'to fail,' based on Latin *fallere* 'disappoint, deceive.'

de·fault·er /diˈfôltər/ ▶ n. a person who fails to fulfill a duty, obligation, or undertaking, esp. to pay a debt. ■ a person who fails to complete a course of medical treatment.

de·fea·sance /diˈfēzəns/ ▶ n. Law the action or process of rendering something null and void. ■ a clause or condition which, if fulfilled, renders a deed or contract null and void.
– ORIGIN late Middle English (as a legal term): from Old French *defesance*, from *defaire, desfaire* 'undo' (see DEFEAT).

de·fea·si·ble /diˈfēzəbəl/ ▶ adj. chiefly Law & Philosophy open in principle to revision, valid objection, forfeiture, or annulment.
– DERIVATIVES **de·fea·si·bil·i·ty** /-ˌfēzəˈbilitē/ n., **de·fea·si·bly** /-blē/ adv.

– ORIGIN Middle English: via Anglo-Norman French from the stem of Old French *desfesant* 'undoing' (see also DEFEASANCE).

de·feat /di'fēt/ ▶ **v.** [with obj.] win a victory over (someone) in a battle or other contest; overcome or beat: *Arab armies defeated the Byzantine garrison.* ■ prevent (someone) from achieving an aim: *she was defeated by the last steep hill.* ■ prevent (an aim) from being achieved: *don't cheat by allowing your body to droop—this defeats the object of the exercise.* ■ reject or block (a motion or proposal): *the amendment was defeated.* ■ be impossible for (someone) to understand: *this line of reasoning defeats me, I must confess.* ■ Law render null and void; annul.
▶ **n.** an instance of defeating or being defeated: *the defeat of the Armada in 1588 | she had still not quite admitted defeat.*
– ORIGIN late Middle English (in the sense 'undo, destroy, annul'): from Old French *desfait* 'undone,' past participle of *desfaire*, from medieval Latin *disfacere* 'undo.'

de·feat·ed /di'fētid/ ▶ **adj.** having been beaten in a battle or other contest: *the defeated army.* ■ demoralized and overcome by adversity.
– DERIVATIVES **de·feat·ed·ly adv.**

de·feat·ist /di'fētist/ ▶ **n.** a person who expects or is excessively ready to accept failure.
▶ **adj.** demonstrating expectation or acceptance of failure: *we have a duty not to be so defeatist.*
– DERIVATIVES **de·feat·ism** /-tizəm/ **n.**
– ORIGIN early 20th cent.: from French *défaitiste*, from *défaite* 'defeat.'

def·e·cate /'defi,kāt/ ▶ **v.** [no obj.] discharge feces from the body.
– DERIVATIVES **def·e·ca·tor** /-,kātər/ **n.**, **def·e·ca·to·ry** /-kə,tôrē/ **adj.**
– ORIGIN late Middle English (in the sense 'clear of dregs, purify'): from Latin *defaecat-* 'cleared of dregs,' from the verb *defaecare*, from *de-* (expressing removal) + *faex, faec-* 'dregs.' The current sense dates from the mid 19th cent.

def·e·ca·tion /,defi'kāsHən/ ▶ **n.** the discharge of feces from the body.

de·fect[1] /'dē,fekt/ ▶ **n.** a shortcoming, imperfection, or lack: *genetic defects | the property is free from defect.*
– ORIGIN late Middle English (as a noun, influenced by Old French *defect* 'deficiency'): from Latin *defectus*, past participle of *deficere* 'desert or fail,' from *de-* (expressing reversal) + *facere* 'do.'

de·fect[2] /di'fekt/ ▶ **v.** [no obj.] abandon one's country or cause in favor of an opposing one: *he* **defected to** *the Soviet Union after the war.*
– DERIVATIVES **de·fec·tor** /-tər/ **n.**
– ORIGIN late 16th cent.: from Latin *defect-* 'failed,' from the verb *deficere* (see DEFECT[1]).

de·fec·tion /di'feksHən/ ▶ **n.** the desertion of one's country or cause in favor of an opposing one: *his defection from the Republican Party | a number of defections by leading ballet dancers.*

de·fec·tive /di'fektiv/ ▶ **adj.** imperfect or faulty: *complaints over defective goods.* ■ archaic or offensive mentally handicapped. ■ lacking or deficient: *dystrophin is commonly* **defective in** *muscle tissue.* ■ Grammar (of a word) not having all the inflections normal for the part of speech.
▶ **n.** archaic or offensive a mentally handicapped person.
– DERIVATIVES **de·fec·tive·ly adv.**, **de·fec·tive·ness n.**

de·fem·i·nize /dē'femə,nīz/ ▶ **v.** [with obj.] deprive of feminine characteristics.

de·fence ▶ **n.** British spelling of DEFENSE.

de·fend /di'fend/ ▶ **v.** [with obj.] resist an attack made on (someone or something); protect from harm or danger: *we shall defend our country, whatever the cost.* ■ speak or write in favor of (an action or person); attempt to justify: *he defended his policy of imposing high taxes.* ■ conduct the case for (the party being accused or sued) in a lawsuit: *the lawyer had defended anticommunist dissidents.* ■ compete to retain (a title or seat) in a contest or election: *he successfully defended his congressional seat in new elections* | (as adj. **defending**) *the defending champion.* ■ [no obj.] (in sports) protect one's goal rather than attempt to score against one's opponents.
– DERIVATIVES **de·fend·a·ble adj.**
– ORIGIN Middle English: from Old French *defendre*, from Latin *defendere*, from *de-* 'off' + *-fendere* 'to strike.' Compare with OFFEND.

de·fend·ant /di'fendənt/ ▶ **n.** an individual, company, or institution sued or accused in a court of law. Compare with PLAINTIFF.
– ORIGIN Middle English (as an adjective in the sense 'defending'): from Old French, 'warding off,' present participle of *defendre* (see DEFEND).

de·fend·er /di'fendər/ ▶ **n.** a person who defends someone or something: *a defender of family values.* ■ (in soccer, hockey, and other games) a player whose task it is to protect the team's goal. ■ Bridge either member of the partnership that did not win the auction. Compare with DECLARER.
– ORIGIN Middle English: from Old French *defendeor.*

De·fend·er of the Faith ▶ **n.** a title conferred on Henry VIII by Pope Leo X in 1521. It was recognized by Parliament as an official title of the English monarch in 1544 and has been borne by all subsequent sovereigns.
– ORIGIN translation of Latin *Fidei Defensor.*

de·fen·es·tra·tion /dē,fenə'strāsHən/ ▶ **n.** formal or humorous the action of throwing someone or something out of a window.
– DERIVATIVES **de·fen·es·trate** /-'fenə,strāt/ **v.**
– ORIGIN early 17th cent.: from modern Latin *defenestratio(n-)*, from *de-* 'down from' + Latin *fenestra* 'window.'

de·fense /di'fens, 'dē,fens/ (Brit. **defence**) ▶ **n. 1** the action of defending from or resisting attack: *they relied on missiles for the country's defense | she came* **to the defense of** *the eccentric professor.* ■ attempted justification or vindication of something: *he spoke* **in defense of** *a disciplined approach.* ■ an instance of defending a title or seat in a contest or election: *his first title defense against Jones.* ■ military measures or resources for protecting a country: *the minister of defense* | [as modifier] *defense policy.* ■ a means of protecting something from attack: *education is the best defense against tyranny.* ■ (**defenses**) fortifications or barriers against attack: *coastal defenses.* ■ (in sports) the action or role of defending one's goal against the opposition: *we played solid defense.* ■ (**the defense**) the players in a team who perform this role.
2 the case presented by or on behalf of the party being accused or sued in a lawsuit.
3 (usu. **the defense**) [treated as sing. or pl.] one or more defendants and the counsel in a trial: *the defense requested more time to prepare their case.*
– PHRASES **defense in depth** the practice of arranging defensive lines or fortifications so that they can defend each other, esp. in case of an enemy incursion.
– ORIGIN Middle English: from Old French *defens*, from late Latin *defensum* (neuter), *defensa* (feminine), past participles of *defendere* 'defend.'

de·fense·less /di'fenslis/ ▶ **adj.** without defense or protection; totally vulnerable: *attacks on defenseless civilians.*
– DERIVATIVES **de·fense·less·ness n.**

de·fense·man /di'fensmən/ ▶ **n.** (pl. **defensemen**) (in ice hockey and lacrosse) a player, other than the goaltender, in a defensive position.

de·fense mech·an·ism ▶ **n.** an automatic reaction of the body against disease-causing organisms. ■ a mental process (e.g., repression or projection) initiated, typically unconsciously, to avoid conscious conflict or anxiety.

de·fen·si·ble /di'fensəbəl/ ▶ **adj. 1** justifiable by argument: *a morally defensible penal system.*
2 able to be protected: *a fort with a defensible yard at its feet.*
– DERIVATIVES **de·fen·si·bil·i·ty** /di,fensə'bilitē/ **n.**, **de·fen·si·bly** /-blē/ **adv.**
– ORIGIN Middle English (used of a weapon, a fortified place, etc., in the sense 'capable of giving protective defense'): from late Latin *defensibilis*, from Latin *defendere* (see DEFEND).

de·fen·sive /di'fensiv/ ▶ **adj. 1** used or intended to defend or protect: *troops in defensive positions.* ■ [attrib.] (in sports) relating to or intended as defense.
2 very anxious to challenge or avoid criticism: *he was very defensive about that side of his life.*
– PHRASES **on the defensive** expecting or resisting criticism or attack: *the forces have remained on the defensive.*
– DERIVATIVES **de·fen·sive·ness n.**
– ORIGIN late Middle English: from Old French *défensif, -ive*, from medieval Latin *defensivus*, from Latin *defens-* 'warded off,' from the verb *defendere* (see DEFEND).

de·fen·sive end ▶ **n.** Football either of the two defensive players positioned at the end of the players who are linemen.

de·fen·sive·ly /di'fensivlē/ ▶ **adv.** in a defensive manner: *"No, I didn't," he replied defensively.* ■ (in sports) in terms of defense: *we must tighten up defensively.*

de·fer[1] /di'fər/ ▶ **v.** (**defers, deferring, deferred**) [with obj.] put off (an action or event) to a later time; postpone: *they deferred the decision until February.* ■ historical postpone the conscription of (someone): *he was no longer* **deferred from** *the draft.*
– DERIVATIVES **de·fer·ra·ble adj.**, **de·fer·ral** /-'fərəl/ **n.**
– ORIGIN late Middle English (also in the sense 'put on one side'): from Old French *differer* 'defer or differ,' from Latin *differre*, from *dis-* 'apart' + *ferre* 'bring, carry.' Compare with DEFER[2] and DIFFER.

de·fer[2] ▶ **v.** (**defers, deferring, deferred**) [no obj.] (**defer to**) submit humbly to (a person or a person's wishes or qualities): *he deferred to Tim's superior knowledge.*
– DERIVATIVES **de·fer·rer n.**
– ORIGIN late Middle English: from Old French *deferer*, from Latin *deferre* 'carry away, refer (a matter),' from *de-* 'away from' + *ferre* 'bring, carry.' Compare with DEFER[1].

def·er·ence /'defərəns/ ▶ **n.** humble submission and respect: *he addressed her with the deference due to age.*
– PHRASES **in deference to** out of respect for; in consideration of.
– ORIGIN mid 17th cent.: from French *déférence*, from *déférer* 'refer' (see DEFER[2]).

def·er·ent[1] /'defərənt/ ▶ **adj.** another term for DEFERENTIAL.
– ORIGIN early 19th cent.: from DEFER[2] and DEFERENCE.

def·er·ent[2] ▶ **n.** (in the Ptolemaic system of astronomy) the large circular orbit followed by the center of the small epicycle in which a planet was thought to move.
– ORIGIN late Middle English: from medieval Latin *deferent-* 'carrying away,' from the verb *deferre.*

def·er·en·tial /,defə'rencHəl/ ▶ **adj.** showing deference; respectful: *people were always* **deferential to** *him.*
– DERIVATIVES **def·er·en·tial·ly adv.**
– ORIGIN early 19th cent.: from DEFERENCE, on the pattern of pairs such as *prudence, prudential.*

de·fer·ment /di'fərmənt/ ▶ **n.** the action or fact of putting something off to a later time; postponement: *deferment of the decision.* ■ historical the postponement of a person's conscription: *he was granted five deferments from the draft.*

de·ferred an·nu·i·ty ▶ **n.** an annuity that commences only after a lapse of some specified time after the final purchase premium has been paid.

de·fer·ves·cence /,dēfər'vesəns, ,defər-/ ▶ **n.** Medicine the abatement of a fever as indicated by a decrease in bodily temperature.
– DERIVATIVES **de·fer·vesce** /-'ves/ **v.**
– ORIGIN early 18th cent.: from Latin *defervescent-* 'ceasing to boil,' from the verb *defervescere.*

de·fi·ance /di'fīəns/ ▶ **n.** open resistance; bold disobedience: *the demonstration was held* **in defiance of** *official warnings.*
– ORIGIN Middle English (denoting the renunciation of an allegiance or friendship): from Old French, from *defier* 'defy.'

de·fi·ant /di'fīənt/ ▶ **adj.** showing defiance: *she was in a defiant mood.*
– DERIVATIVES **de·fi·ant·ly adv.**
– ORIGIN late 16th cent.: from French *défiant* or directly from DEFIANCE.

de·fib·ril·la·tion /dē,fibrə'lāsHən/ ▶ **n.** Medicine the stopping of fibrillation of the heart by administering a controlled electric shock in order to allow restoration of the normal rhythm.
– DERIVATIVES **de·fib·ril·late** /dē'fibrə,lāt/ **v.**

de·fib·ril·la·tor /dē'fibrə,lātər/ ▶ **n.** Medicine an apparatus used to control heart fibrillation by application of an electric current to the chest wall or heart.

de·fi·cien·cy /di'fisHənsē/ ▶ **n.** (pl. **deficiencies**) a lack or shortage: *vitamin A deficiency in children.* ■ a failing or shortcoming: *they did not like having the deficiencies of their city pointed out to them.*

de·fi·cien·cy dis·ease ▶ **n.** a disease caused by the lack of some essential or important element in the diet, usually a particular vitamin or mineral. See also IMMUNODEFICIENCY.

de·fi·cien·cy pay·ment ▶ **n.** a payment made, typically by a government body, to cover a financial deficit incurred in the course of an activity such as farming or education.

de·fi·cient /di'fisHənt/ ▶ **adj.** [predic.] not having enough of a specified quality or ingredient: *this diet is* **deficient in** *vitamin B.* ■ insufficient or inadequate: *they trashed the legislation as deficient.* ■ (also **mentally deficient**) offensive having a mental handicap.
– ORIGIN late 16th cent. (originally in the theological phrase *deficient cause*, denoting a failure or deficiency that has a particular consequence): from Latin *deficient-* 'failing,' from the verb *deficere* (see DEFECT[1]).

def·i·cit /'defəsit/ ▶ **n.** the amount by which something, esp. a sum of money, is too small. ■ an excess of expenditure or liabilities over income or assets in a given period: *an annual operating deficit | the budget will remain* **in deficit.** ■ (in sports) the

amount or score by which a team or individual is losing: *came back from a 3–0 deficit.* ■ technical a deficiency or failing, esp. in a neurological or psychological function: ***deficits** in speech comprehension.*
– ORIGIN late 18th cent.: via French from Latin *deficit* 'it is lacking,' from the verb *deficere* (see DEFECT[1]).

def·i·cit fi·nanc·ing ▶ **n.** government funding of spending by borrowing.

def·i·cit spend·ing ▶ **n.** government spending, in excess of revenue, of funds raised by borrowing rather than from taxation.

def·i·lade /ˈdefəˌlād, ˌdefəˈlād/ Military ▶ **n.** the protection of a position, vehicle, or troops against enemy observation or gunfire.
▶ **v.** [with obj.] protect (a position, vehicle, or troops) against enemy observation or gunfire: (as adj. **defiladed**) *a defiladed tank.*
– ORIGIN early 19th cent.: from French *défiler* 'protect from the enemy' + -ADE[1].

de·file[1] /diˈfīl/ ▶ **v.** [with obj.] sully, mar, or spoil: *the land was defiled by a previous owner.* ■ desecrate or profane (something sacred): *the tomb had been defiled and looted.* ■ archaic violate the chastity of (a woman).
– DERIVATIVES **de·fil·er n.**
– ORIGIN late Middle English: alteration of obsolete *defoul*, from Old French *defouler* 'trample down,' influenced by obsolete *befile* 'befoul, defile.'

de·file[2] /diˈfīl, ˈdēˌfīl/ ▶ **n.** a steep-sided, narrow gorge or passage (originally one requiring troops to march in single file).
▶ **v.** [no obj.] archaic (of troops) march in single file: *we emerged after defiling through the mountainsides.*
– ORIGIN late 17th cent.: from French *défilé* (noun), *défiler* (verb), from *dé* 'away from' + *file* 'column, file.'

de·file·ment /diˈfīlmənt/ ▶ **n.** the action of defiling or the state of being defiled: *the heinous defilement of their most sacred site.*

de·fin·a·ble /diˈfīnəbl/ ▶ **adj.** able to be defined: *it may not serve a definable purpose.*

de·fine /diˈfīn/ ▶ **v.** [with obj.] **1** state or describe exactly the nature, scope, or meaning of: *the contract will seek to define the client's obligations.* ■ give the meaning of (a word or phrase), esp. in a dictionary. ■ make up or establish the character of: *for some, the football team defines their identity.*
2 mark out the boundary or limits of: (as adj. **defined**) *clearly defined boundaries.* ■ make clear the outline of; delineate: *she defined her eyes by applying eyeshadow.*
– DERIVATIVES **de·fin·er n.**
– ORIGIN late Middle English (also in the sense 'bring to an end'): from Old French *definer*, from a variant of Latin *definire*, from *de-* (expressing completion) + *finire* 'finish' (from *finis* 'end').

de·fined ben·e·fit plan (also **defined benefit pension plan**) ▶ **n.** a company pension plan in which an employee's pension payments are calculated according to length of service and the salary they earned at the time of retirement.

de·fin·i·en·dum /diˌfinēˈendəm/ ▶ **n.** (pl. **definienda** /-də/) a word, phrase, or symbol that is the subject of a definition, esp. in a dictionary entry, or that is introduced into a logical system by being defined. Contrasted with DEFINIENS.
– ORIGIN late 19th cent.: from Latin, 'that which is to be defined,' from the verb *definire* (see DEFINE).

de·fin·i·ens /diˈfinēənz/ ▶ **n.** (pl. **definientia** /diˌfinēˈensʜ(ē)ə/) a word, phrase, or symbolic expression used to define something, esp. in a dictionary entry, or introducing a word or symbol into a logical system by providing a statement of its meaning. Contrasted with DEFINIENDUM.
– ORIGIN late 19th cent.: from medieval Latin, 'defining,' present participle of *definire* (see DEFINE).

de·fin·ing mo·ment ▶ **n.** an event that typifies or determines all subsequent related occurrences.

def·i·nite /ˈdefənit/ ▶ **adj.** clearly stated or decided; not vague or doubtful: *we had no definite plans.* ■ clearly true or real; unambiguous: *no definite proof has emerged.* ■ [predic.] (of a person) certain or sure about something: *you're very definite about that!* ■ clear or undeniable (used for emphasis): *video is a definite asset in the classroom.* ■ having exact and discernible physical limits or form.
– DERIVATIVES **def·i·nite·ness n.**
– ORIGIN mid 16th cent.: from Latin *definitus* 'defined, set within limits,' past participle of *definire* (see DEFINE).

> **USAGE** For an explanation of the difference between **definite** and **definitive**, see usage at DEFINITIVE.

def·i·nite ar·ti·cle ▶ **n.** Grammar a determiner (*the* in English) that introduces a noun phrase and implies that the thing mentioned has already been mentioned, or is common knowledge, or is about to be defined (as in *the book on the table; the art of government; the famous poet and short story writer*). Compare with INDEFINITE ARTICLE.

def·i·nite de·scrip·tion ▶ **n.** chiefly Philosophy a noun phrase introduced by the definite article or its equivalent, and purporting to denote a particular entity or phenomenon.

def·i·nite in·te·gral ▶ **n.** Mathematics an integral expressed as the difference between the values of the integral at specified upper and lower limits of the independent variable.

def·i·nite·ly /ˈdefənitlē/ ▶ **adv.** without doubt (used for emphasis): *I will definitely be at the airport to meet you.* ■ in a definite manner; clearly: *we couldn't plan to go elsewhere until we had heard from you more definitely.*

def·i·ni·tion /ˌdefəˈnisʜən/ ▶ **n. 1** a statement of the exact meaning of a word, esp. in a dictionary. ■ an exact statement or description of the nature, scope, or meaning of something: *our definition of what constitutes poetry.* ■ the action or process of defining something.
2 the degree of distinctness in outline of an object, image, or sound, esp. of an image in a photograph or on a screen. ■ the capacity of an instrument or device for making images distinct in outline: [in combination] *high-definition television.*
– PHRASES **by definition** by its very nature; intrinsically: *underachievement, by definition, is not due to lack of talent.*
– DERIVATIVES **def·i·ni·tion·al** /-sʜənl/ **adj.**, **def·i·ni·tion·al·ly** /-sʜənl-ē/ **adv.**
– ORIGIN late Middle English: from Latin *definitio(n-)*, from the verb *definire* 'set bounds to' (see DEFINE).

de·fin·i·tive /diˈfinitiv/ ▶ **adj. 1** (of a conclusion or agreement) done or reached decisively and with authority: *a definitive diagnosis.* ■ (of a book or other text) the most authoritative of its kind: *the definitive biography of Harry Truman.*
2 (of a postage stamp) for general use and typically of standard design, not special or commemorative.
▶ **n.** a definitive postage stamp.
– DERIVATIVES **de·fin·i·tive·ly adv.**
– ORIGIN late Middle English: from Old French *definitif, -ive*, from Latin *definitivus*, from *definit-* 'set within limits,' from the verb *definire* (see DEFINE).

> **USAGE** **Definitive** in the sense 'decisive, unconditional, final' is sometimes confused with **definite**. **Definite** means 'clearly defined, precise, having fixed limits,' but **definitive** goes further, meaning 'most complete, satisfying all criteria, most authoritative': *although some critics found a few* **definite** *weak spots in the author's interpretations, his book was nonetheless widely regarded as the* **definitive** *history of the war.* A **definite** decision is simply one that has been made clearly and is without doubt, whereas a **definitive** decision is one that is not only conclusive but also carries the stamp of authority or is a benchmark for the future, as in a Supreme Court ruling. It is a common error to use **definitive** as though it were a more elegant way of saying **definite**.

de·fin·i·tive host ▶ **n.** Biology an organism that supports the adult or sexually reproductive form of a parasite. Compare with INTERMEDIATE HOST.

def·la·grate /ˈdefləˌgrāt/ ▶ **v.** Chemistry, dated burn away or cause (a substance) to burn away with a sudden flame and rapid, sharp combustion: [with obj.] *the current will deflagrate some of the particles.*
– DERIVATIVES **def·la·gra·tor** /-tər/ **n.**
– ORIGIN early 18th cent.: from Latin *deflagrat-* 'burned up,' from the verb *deflagrare*, from *de-* 'away, thoroughly' + *flagrare* 'to burn.'

def·la·gra·tion /ˌdefləˈgrāsʜən/ ▶ **n.** the action of heating a substance until it burns away rapidly. ■ technical combustion that propagates through a gas or across the surface of an explosive at subsonic speeds, driven by the transfer of heat. Compare with DETONATION.
– ORIGIN early 17th cent.: from Latin *deflagratio(n-)*, from the verb *deflagrare* (see DEFLAGRATE).

de·flate /diˈflāt/ ▶ **v. 1** [with obj.] let air or gas out of (a tire, balloon, or similar object): *he deflated one of the tires.* ■ [no obj.] be emptied of air or gas: *the balloon deflated.*
2 cause (someone) to suddenly lose confidence or feel less important: (as adj. **deflated**) *the news left him feeling utterly deflated.* ■ reduce the level of (an emotion or feeling): *her anger was deflated.*
3 Economics bring about a general reduction of price levels in (an economy).
– DERIVATIVES **de·fla·tor** /-tər/ **n.**
– ORIGIN late 19th cent.: from DE- (expressing reversal) + *-flate* (as in *inflate*).

de·fla·tion /diˈflāsʜən/ ▶ **n. 1** the action or process of deflating or being deflated: *deflation of the illusion that the 1960s were a perpetual party.*
2 Economics reduction of the general level of prices in an economy.
3 Geology the removal of particles of rock, sand, etc., by the wind.
– DERIVATIVES **de·fla·tion·ist** /-ist/ **n. & adj.**
– ORIGIN late 19th cent. (in the sense 'release of air from something inflated'): from DEFLATE; sense 3 via German from Latin *deflat-* 'blown away,' from the verb *deflare*.

de·fla·tion·ar·y /diˈflāsʜəˌnerē/ ▶ **adj.** of, characterized by, or tending to cause economic deflation.

de·flect /diˈflekt/ ▶ **v.** [with obj.] cause (something) to change direction by interposing something; turn aside from a straight course: *the bullet was deflected harmlessly into the ceiling* | figurative *he attempted to deflect attention away from his private life.* ■ [no obj.] (of an object) change direction after hitting something: *the ball **deflected off** his body.* ■ cause (someone) to deviate from an intended purpose: *she refused to be **deflected from** anything she had set her mind on.* ■ cause (something) to change orientation: *the compass needle is **deflected from** magnetic north by metal in the aircraft.*
– ORIGIN mid 16th cent.: from Latin *deflectere*, from *de-* 'away from' + *flectere* 'to bend.'

de·flec·tion /diˈfleksʜən/ (also **deflexion**) ▶ **n.** the action or process of deflecting or being deflected: *the deflection of the light beam.* ■ the amount by which something is deflected: *an 11-mile deflection of the river.*
– ORIGIN early 17th cent.: from late Latin *deflexio(n-)*, from *deflectere* 'bend away' (see DEFLECT).

de·flec·tor /diˈflektər/ ▶ **n.** a device that deflects something, in particular: ■ a plate or other attachment for deflecting a flow of air, water, heat, etc. ■ an electrode in a cathode ray tube whose magnetic field is used to deflect a beam of electrons onto a phosphor screen to form an image.

de·flexed /diˈflekst/ ▶ **adj.** technical (typically of plant or animal structures) bent or curving downward or backward: *a deflexed beak.*
– ORIGIN early 19th cent. (earlier as *deflex*): from Latin *deflexus* 'bent away' (past participle of *deflectere*) + -ED[1].

de·floc·cu·late /dēˈfläkyəˌlāt/ ▶ **v.** [with obj.] Chemistry break up the floccules (of a substance suspended in a liquid) into fine particles, producing a dispersion.
– DERIVATIVES **de·floc·cu·la·tion** /dēˌfläkyəˈlāsʜən/ **n.**

def·lo·ra·tion /ˌdefləˈrāsʜən/ ▶ **n.** literary the taking of a woman's virginity.
– ORIGIN late Middle English: from late Latin *defloratio(n-)*, from the verb *deflorare* (see DEFLOWER).

de·flow·er /dēˈflou(-ə)r/ ▶ **v.** [with obj.] **1** dated or literary deprive (a woman) of her virginity.
2 (usu. as adj. **deflowered**) strip (a plant or garden) of flowers: *deflowered rose bushes.*
– ORIGIN late Middle English: from Old French *desflourer*, from a variant of late Latin *deflorare*, from *de-* (expressing removal) + Latin *flos, flor-* 'a flower.'

de·fo·cus /dēˈfōkəs/ ▶ **v.** (**defocuses, defocusing, defocused** or **defocusses, defocussing, defocussed**) [with obj.] cause (an image, lens, or beam) to go out of focus: *the filter lets you defocus all or part of an image.* ■ [no obj.] go out of focus: *the view defocused, then resolved.* ■ take the focus of interest or activity away from (something): *defocusing the traditional contract approach in business.*

De·foe /dəˈfō/, Daniel (1660–1731), English novelist and journalist. His novel *Robinson Crusoe* (1719) is loosely based on the true story of shipwrecked sailor Alexander Selkirk and has a claim to being the first British novel. Other notable works: *Moll Flanders* (1722) and *A Journal of the Plague Year* (1722).

de·fog·ger /dēˈfôgər, -ˈfä-/ ▶ **n.** a device on a vehicle that removes condensation from the windshield by directing a jet of air onto it.
– DERIVATIVES **de·fog v.**

de·fo·li·ant /dēˈfōlēənt/ ▶ **n.** a chemical that removes the leaves from trees and plants and is often used in warfare.

de·fo·li·ate /dēˈfōlēˌāt/ ▶ **v.** [with obj.] remove leaves from (a tree, plant, or area of land), for agricultural

purposes or as a military tactic: *the area was defoliated and napalmed many times.*
– DERIVATIVES **de·fo·li·a·tion** /dēˌfōlēˈāsʜən/ **n.**
– ORIGIN late 18th cent.: from Late Latin *defoliat-* 'stripped of leaves,' from the verb *defoliare,* from *de-* (expressing removal) + *folium* 'leaf.'

de·fo·li·a·tor /dēˈfōlēˌātər/ ▶ **n.** an adult or larval insect that strips all the leaves from a tree or shrub. ■ a machine that removes the leaves from a root crop.

de·force /diˈfôrs/ ▶ **v.** [with obj.] Law withhold (land or other property) wrongfully or forcibly from the rightful owner. ■ deprive (someone) wrongfully or forcibly of rightful property.
– ORIGIN late Middle English: from Anglo-Norman French *deforcer,* from *de-* (expressing removal) + *forcer* 'to force.'

de·for·est /dēˈfôrist, -ˈfär-/ ▶ **v.** [with obj.] clear (an area) of forests or trees.
– DERIVATIVES **de·for·est·a·tion** /dēˌfôrəˈstāsʜən, -ˌfär-/ **n.**

De For·est /də ˈfôrəst, ˈfär-/, Lee (1873–1961), US physicist and electrical engineer. He designed a triode valve that was crucial to the development of radio communication, television, and computers. De Forest successfully transmitted a live broadcast in 1910.

de·form /diˈfôrm/ ▶ **v.** [with obj.] distort the shape or form of; make misshapen: *he was physically deformed by a rare bone disease.* ■ [no obj.] become distorted or misshapen; undergo deformation: *the suspension deforms slightly on corners.*
– DERIVATIVES **de·form·a·ble** **adj.**
– ORIGIN late Middle English: from Old French *desformer,* via medieval Latin from Latin *deformare,* from *de-* (expressing reversal) + *forma* 'a shape.'

de·for·ma·tion /ˌdēfôrˈmāsʜən, ˌdefər-/ ▶ **n.** the action or process of changing in shape or distorting, esp. through the application of pressure: *solid rock undergoing slow deformation.* ■ the result of such a process: *the deformation will be temporary.* ■ an altered form of a word, esp. one used to avoid overt profanity (e.g., *dang* for *damn*).
– DERIVATIVES **de·for·ma·tion·al** /-sʜənl/ **adj.**

de·formed /diˈfôrmd/ ▶ **adj.** (of a person or part of the body) not having the normal or natural shape or form; misshapen: *his deformed hands.*

de·form·i·ty /diˈfôrmitē/ ▶ **n.** (pl. **deformities**) a deformed part, esp. of the body; a malformation: *children born with deformities.* ■ the state of being deformed or misshapen: *respiratory problems caused by spinal deformity.*
– ORIGIN late Middle English: from Old French *desformite,* from Latin *deformitas,* from *deformis* 'misshapen.'

de·frag /dēˈfrag/ ▶ **v.** (**defrags, defragging, defragged**) [with obj.] Computing short for **DEFRAGMENT.**
▶ **n.** an instance of defragging a disk, or the utility that does this.

de·frag·ment /ˌdēfragˈment/ ▶ **v.** [with obj.] Computing (of software) reduce the fragmentation of (a file) by concatenating parts stored in separate locations on a disk: *the safe way to defragment your files.*
– DERIVATIVES **de·frag·men·ta·tion** /dēˌfragmənˈtāsʜən, -ˌmen-/ **n.**, **de·frag·ment·er** **n.**

de·fraud /diˈfrôd/ ▶ **v.** [with obj.] illegally obtain money from (someone) by deception: *he used a false identity to defraud the bank of thousands of dollars* | [no obj.] *conspiracy to defraud.*
– DERIVATIVES **de·fraud·er** **n.**
– ORIGIN late Middle English: from Old French *defrauder* or Latin *defraudare,* from *de-* 'from' + *fraudare* 'to cheat' (from *fraus, fraud-* 'fraud').

de·fray /diˈfrā/ ▶ **v.** [with obj.] provide money to pay (a cost or expense): *the proceeds from the raffle help to defray the expenses of the evening.*
– DERIVATIVES **de·fray·a·ble** **adj.**, **de·fray·al** /-ˈfrāəl/ **n.**, **de·fray·ment** **n.**
– ORIGIN late Middle English (in the general sense 'spend money'): from French *défrayer,* from *dé-* (expressing removal) + obsolete *frai* 'cost, expenses' (from medieval Latin *fredum* 'a fine for breach of the peace').

de·friend /ˌdiˈfrend/ ▶ **v.** another term for **UNFRIEND.**

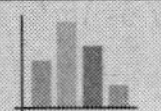
WORD TRENDS See **FRIEND.**

de·frock /dēˈfräk/ ▶ **v.** [with obj.] deprive (a person in holy orders) of ecclesiastical status. ■ (usu. as adj. **defrocked**) deprive (someone) of professional status or membership in a prestigious group: *a defrocked psychiatrist.*
– ORIGIN early 17th cent.: from French *défroquer,* from *dé-* (expressing removal) + *froc* 'frock.'

de·frost /diˈfrôst/ ▶ **v.** [with obj.] remove frost or ice from (the windshield of a motor vehicle). ■ thaw (frozen food) before cooking it: *defrost the turkey slowly.* ■ [no obj.] (of frozen food) thaw before being cooked: *make sure that it has thoroughly defrosted.* ■ free (the interior of a refrigerator) of accumulated ice, usually by turning it off for a period. ■ [no obj.] (of a refrigerator) become free of accumulated ice in this way: *she opened the door to let the fridge defrost.*
– DERIVATIVES **de·frost·er** **n.**

deft /deft/ ▶ **adj.** neatly skillful and quick in one's movements: *a deft piece of footwork.* ■ demonstrating skill and cleverness: *the script was both deft and literate.*
– DERIVATIVES **deft·ly** **adv.**, **deft·ness** **n.**
– ORIGIN Middle English: variant of **DAFT,** in the obsolete sense 'meek.'

de·funct /diˈfəɴɢkt/ ▶ **adj.** no longer existing or functioning: *a now defunct technology that only people over a certain age remember.*
– ORIGIN mid 16th cent. (in the sense 'deceased'): from Latin *defunctus* 'dead,' past participle of *defungi* 'carry out, finish,' from *de-* (expressing reversal) + *fungi* 'perform.'

de·fund /dēˈfənd/ ▶ **v.** [with obj.] prevent from continuing to receive funds: *the California legislature has defunded the Industrial Welfare Commission.*

de·fuse /diˈfyo͞oz/ ▶ **v.** [with obj.] remove the fuse from (an explosive device) in order to prevent it from exploding: *explosives specialists tried to defuse the grenade.* ■ reduce the danger or tension in (a difficult situation): *he had the ability to defuse tense moments with humor.*

USAGE On the difference between **defuse** and **diffuse,** see usage at **DIFFUSE.**

de·fy /diˈfī/ ▶ **v.** (**defies, defying, defied**) [with obj.] openly resist or refuse to obey: *a woman who defies convention.* ■ (of a thing) make (an action or quality) almost impossible: *his actions defy belief.* ■ [with obj. and infinitive] appear to be challenging (someone) to do or prove something: *he glowered at her, defying her to mock him.* ■ archaic challenge to combat: *go now, defy him to the combat.*
– DERIVATIVES **de·fi·er** **n.**
– ORIGIN Middle English (in the senses 'renounce an allegiance' and 'challenge to combat'): from Old French *desfier,* based on Latin *dis-* (expressing reversal) + *fidus* 'faithful.'

deg. ▶ **abbr.** degree(s).

dé·ga·gé /ˌdāgäˈzʜä/ ▶ **adj.** unconcerned or unconstrained; relaxed.
▶ **n.** (pl. **same**) Ballet pointing of the foot to an open position with an arched instep slightly off the floor.
– ORIGIN late 17th cent.: French, past participle of *dégager* 'set free.'

De·gas /dāˈgä/, Edgar (1834–1917), French painter and sculptor. Full name *Hilaire Germain Edgar Degas.* An Impressionist painter, he is known for his paintings of ballet dancers, such as *Dancer Lacing Her Shoe* (c.1878).

de·gas /dēˈgas/ ▶ **v.** (**degass, degassing, degassed**) make or become free of unwanted or excess gas: [with obj.] *the column has not been degassed* | [no obj.] *the summit craters were degassing freely.*

de Gaulle /də ˈgôl/, Charles (André Joseph Marie) (1890–1970), French general and statesman; head of government 1944–46; president 1959–69. A wartime organizer of the Free French movement, he is remembered particularly for his assertive foreign policy and for quelling the student uprisings and strikes of May 1968.

de·gauss /dēˈgous/ ▶ **v.** [with obj.] (often as noun **degaussing**) Electronics remove unwanted magnetism from (a television or monitor) in order to correct color disturbance. ■ historical neutralize the magnetic field of (a ship) by encircling it with a conductor carrying electric currents.
– DERIVATIVES **de·gauss·er** **n.**

de·gen·er·a·cy /diˈjenərəsē/ ▶ **n.** the state or property of being degenerate: *the ills of society, from sexual degeneracy to political corruption.*

de·gen·er·ate ▶ **adj.** /diˈjenərit/ **1** having lost the physical, mental, or moral qualities considered normal and desirable; showing evidence of decline: *a degenerate form of a higher civilization.* **2** technical lacking some property, order, or distinctness of structure previously or usually present, in particular: ■ Mathematics relating to or denoting an example of a particular type of equation, curve, or other entity that is equivalent to a simpler type, often occurring when a variable or parameter is set to zero. ■ Physics relating to or denoting an energy level that corresponds to more than one quantum state. ■ Physics relating to or denoting matter at densities so high that gravitational contraction is counteracted either by the Pauli exclusion principle or by an analogous quantum effect between closely packed neutrons. ■ Biology having reverted to a simpler form as a result of losing a complex or adaptive structure present in the ancestral form.
▶ **n.** /diˈjenərit/ an immoral or corrupt person.
▶ **v.** /diˈjenəˌrāt/ [no obj.] decline or deteriorate physically, mentally, or morally: *the quality of life had degenerated* | *the debate* **degenerated into** *a brawl.*
– DERIVATIVES **de·gen·er·ate·ly** /-ritlē/ **adv.**
– ORIGIN late 15th cent.: from Latin *degeneratus* 'no longer of its kind,' from the verb *degenerare,* from *degener* 'debased,' from *de-* 'away from' + *genus, gener-* 'race, kind.'

de·gen·er·a·tion /diˌjenəˈrāsʜən/ ▶ **n.** the state or process of being or becoming degenerate; decline or deterioration: *overgrazing has caused serious degeneration of grassland.* ■ Medicine deterioration and loss of function in the cells of a tissue or organ: *degeneration of the muscle fibers.*

de·gen·er·a·tive /diˈjenərətiv, -əˌrātiv/ ▶ **adj.** (of a disease or symptom) characterized by progressive, often irreversible deterioration, and loss of function in the organs or tissues: *degenerative diseases.* ■ of or tending to decline and deterioration: *the young generation had fallen into a degenerative backslide.*

de·gen·er·a·tive joint dis·ease ▶ **n.** another term for **OSTEOARTHRITIS.**

de·gen·er·es·cence /diˌjenəˈresəns/ ▶ **n.** another term for **DEGENERATION.**
– ORIGIN mid 19th cent.: from French *dégénérescence,* from *dégénérer* 'to degenerate.'

de·gla·ci·a·tion /dēˌglāsʜēˈāsʜən, -ˌglāsē-/ ▶ **n.** Geology the disappearance of ice from a previously glaciated region. ■ a period of geological time during which this takes place: *the last deglaciation.*

de·glam·or·ize /dēˈglaməˌrīz/ ▶ **v.** [with obj.] make (someone or something) less glamorous or attractive.
– DERIVATIVES **de·glam·or·i·za·tion** /dēˌglamərəˈzāsʜən/ **n.**

de·glaze /dēˈglāz/ ▶ **v.** [with obj.] dilute meat sediments in (a pan) in order to make a gravy or sauce, typically using wine: *deglaze the pan with the white wine.*
– ORIGIN late 19th cent.: from French *déglacer.*

de·glu·ti·tion /ˌdēglo͞oˈtisʜən/ ▶ **n.** technical the action or process of swallowing.
– DERIVATIVES **de·glu·ti·tive** /dēˈglo͞otətiv/ **adj.**
– ORIGIN mid 17th cent.: from French *déglutition* or modern Latin *deglutitio(n-),* from *deglutire* 'swallow down.'

deg·ra·da·tion /ˌdegrəˈdāsʜən/ ▶ **n.** the condition or process of degrading or being degraded: *a trail of human misery and degradation.* ■ Geology the wearing down of rock by disintegration.
– ORIGIN mid 16th cent. (in the sense 'deposition from an office or rank as a punishment'): from Old French, or from ecclesiastical Latin *degradatio(n-),* from the verb *degradare* (see **DEGRADE**).

de·grade /diˈgrād/ ▶ **v. 1** [with obj.] treat or regard (someone) with contempt or disrespect: *she thought that many supposedly erotic pictures degraded women.* ■ lower the character or quality of: *repeaters clean up and amplify the degraded signal.* ■ archaic reduce (someone) to a lower rank, esp. as a punishment: *he was degraded from his high estate.* **2** break down or deteriorate chemically: [no obj.] *when exposed to light, the materials will degrade* | [with obj.] *the bacteria will degrade hydrocarbons.* ■ [with obj.] Physics reduce (energy) to a less readily convertible form. ■ [with obj.] Geology wear down (rock) and cause it to disintegrate.
– DERIVATIVES **de·grad·a·bil·i·ty** /diˌgrādəˈbilitē/ **n.**, **de·grad·a·ble** **adj.**, **deg·ra·da·tive** /ˈdegrəˌdātiv/ **adj.**, **de·grad·er** **n.**
– ORIGIN late Middle English: from Old French *degrader,* from ecclesiastical Latin *degradare,* from *de-* 'down, away from' + Latin *gradus* 'step or grade.'

de·grad·ed /diˈgrādid/ ▶ **adj.** treated or regarded with contempt or disrespect: *she had felt cheap and degraded.* ■ reduced in quality; inferior: *it will grow successfully even on degraded land.*

de·grad·ing /diˈgrādiɴɢ/ ▶ **adj.** causing a loss of self-respect; humiliating: *cruel or degrading treatment.*
– DERIVATIVES **de·grad·ing·ly** **adv.**

de·gran·u·late /dēˈgranyəˌlāt/ ▶ **v.** [no obj.] Physiology (of a cell) lose or release granules of a substance, typically as part of an immune reaction: *the eosinophils degranulate, releasing the toxic contents of the granules.*
– DERIVATIVES **de·gran·u·la·tion** /dēˌgranyəˈlāsʜən/ **n.**

de·grease /dēˈgrēs/ ▶ **v.** [with obj.] (often as noun **degreasing**) remove excess grease or fat from (something).
– DERIVATIVES **de·greas·ant** /-sənt/ **n.**, **de·greas·er** **n.**

de·gree /diˈgrē/ ▶ **n.** **1** [in sing.] the amount, level, or extent to which something happens or is present: *a degree of caution is probably wise* | *a question of degree.*
2 a unit of measurement of angles, one three-hundred-and-sixtieth of the circumference of a circle: *set at an angle of 45 degrees.* (Symbol: °)
3 a stage in a scale or series, in particular: ■ a unit in any of various scales of temperature, intensity, or hardness: *water boils at 100 degrees Celsius.* (Symbol: °) ■ [in combination] each of a set of grades (usually three) used to classify burns according to their severity. See **FIRST-DEGREE, SECOND-DEGREE, THIRD-DEGREE.** ■ [in combination] a legal grade of crime or offense, esp. murder: *second-degree murder.* ■ [often in combination] a step in direct genealogical descent: *second-degree relatives.* ■ Music a position in a musical scale, counting upward from the tonic or fundamental note: *the lowered third degree of the scale.* ■ Mathematics the class into which an equation falls according to the highest power of unknowns or variables present: *an equation of the second degree.* ■ Grammar any of the three steps on the scale of comparison of gradable adjectives and adverbs, namely positive, comparative, and superlative. ■ archaic a thing placed like a step in a series; a tier or row.
4 an academic rank conferred by a college or university after examination or after completion of a course of study, or conferred as an honor on a distinguished person: *a degree in zoology.* ■ archaic social or official rank: *persons of unequal degree.* ■ a rank in an order of Freemasonry.
– PHRASES **by degrees** a little at a time; gradually: *rivalries and prejudice were by degrees fading out.* **to a degree** to some extent: *to a degree, it is possible to educate oneself.* ■ dated to a considerable extent: *the pressure you were put under must have been frustrating to a degree.*
– ORIGIN Middle English (in the senses 'step,' 'tier,' 'rank,' or 'relative state'): from Old French, based on Latin *de-* 'down' + *gradus* 'step or grade.'

de·gree day ▶ **n.** a unit used to determine the heating requirements of buildings, representing a fall of one degree below a specified average outdoor temperature (usually 18°C or 65°F) for one day.

de·gree of free·dom ▶ **n.** each of a number of independently variable factors affecting the range of states in which a system may exist, in particular: ■ Physics a direction in which independent motion can occur. ■ Chemistry each of a number of independent factors required to specify a system at equilibrium. ■ Statistics the number of independent values or quantities that can be assigned to a statistical distribution.

de·gres·sive /diˈgresiv/ ▶ **adj.** reducing by gradual amounts. ■ (of taxation) at successively lower rates on lower amounts.
– ORIGIN late 19th cent.: from Latin *degress-* 'descended' (from the verb *degredi,* from *de-* 'down' + *gradi* 'walk') + **-IVE.**

de·gu /ˈdāgo͞o/ ▶ **n.** a ratlike rodent with a long silky coat, found in southern South America. ● Genus *Octodon,* family Octodontidae: three species.
– ORIGIN mid 19th cent.: from American Spanish, from South American Indian *deuñ.*

de·gust /diˈgəst/ ▶ **v.** [with obj.] rare taste (something) carefully, so as to appreciate it fully.
– DERIVATIVES **de·gus·ta·tion** /ˌdēgəˈstāsʜən/ **n.**
– ORIGIN early 17th cent.: from Latin *degustare,* from *de-* 'completely' + *gustare* 'to taste.'

de haut en bas /də ˌōt än ˈbä, də ˌō tän ˈbä/ ▶ **adv. & adj.** in a condescending or superior manner: [as adv.] *he never addressed his students de haut en bas* | [as adj.] *he has a certain de haut en bas style.*
– ORIGIN late 17th cent.: French, literally 'from above to below.'

de Hav·il·land[1] /də ˈhavələnd/, Sir Geoffrey (1882–1965), English aircraft designer and manufacturer. He designed and built many aircraft, including the Mosquito used in World War II.

de Hav·il·land[2], Olivia (1916–), US actress; born in Japan; sister of Joan Fontaine. Notable movies: *Gone with the Wind* (1939), *Hold Back the Dawn* (1941), *To Each His Own* (1946), and *The Heiress* (1949).

de·hisce /diˈhis/ ▶ **v.** [no obj.] technical (of a pod or seed vessel, or of a cut or wound) gape or burst open: *after the anther lobes dehisce, the pollen is set free.*
– DERIVATIVES **de·his·cence** /-ˈhisəns/ **n.**, **de·his·cent** /-ˈhisənt/ **adj.**
– ORIGIN mid 17th cent.: from Latin *dehiscere,* from *de-* 'away' + *hiscere* 'begin to gape' (from *hiare* 'gape').

de Hooch /də ˈhōkʜ/ (also **de Hoogh**), Pieter (*c.*1629–*c.*1684), Dutch genre painter. He is noted for his depictions of domestic interior and courtyard scenes.

de·horn /dēˈhôrn/ ▶ **v.** [with obj.] remove the horns from (an animal).

de·hors /dəˈ(h)ôr/ ▶ **prep.** Law other than, not including, or outside the scope of: *the plea shows that no request, dehors the letter, existed.*
– ORIGIN early 18th cent.: from an Old French usage as a preposition (in modern French functioning as an adverb and noun).

Deh·ra Dun /ˈdārə ˈdo͞on/ (also **Dehradun**) a city in northern India, the capital of Uttarakhand state; pop. 551,300 (est. 2009).

de·hu·man·ize /dēˈ(h)yo͞oməˌnīz/ ▶ **v.** [with obj.] deprive of positive human qualities: (as adj. **dehumanizing**) *the dehumanizing effects of war.*
– DERIVATIVES **de·hu·man·i·za·tion** /dēˌ(h)yo͞oməniˈzāsʜən/ **n.**

de·hu·mid·i·fi·er /ˌdē(h)yo͞oˈmidəˌfīər/ ▶ **n.** a device that removes excess moisture from the air.

de·hu·mid·i·fy /ˌdē(h)yo͞oˈmidəˌfī/ ▶ **v.** (**dehumidifies, dehumidifying, dehumidified**) [with obj.] remove moisture from (the air or a gas).
– DERIVATIVES **de·hu·mid·i·fi·ca·tion** /-midəfiˈkāsʜən/ **n.**

de·hy·drate /dēˈhīdrāt/ ▶ **v.** [with obj.] (often as adj. **dehydrated**) cause (a person or a person's body) to lose a large amount of water: *his body temperature was high, and he had become dehydrated.* ■ [no obj.] lose a large amount of water from the body. ■ remove water from (food) in order to preserve and store it: *dehydrated mashed potatoes.*
– DERIVATIVES **de·hy·dra·tion** /ˌdēhīˈdrāsʜən/ **n.**, **de·hy·dra·tor** /-tər/ **n.**
– ORIGIN late 19th cent.: from **DE-** (expressing removal) + Greek *hudōr, hudr-* 'water.'

de·hy·dro·cho·les·ter·ol /dēˌhīdrōkəˈlestəˌrôl/ ▶ **n.** Biochemistry a derivative of cholesterol present in the skin. It can be converted to cholecalciferol (vitamin D_3) by the action of ultraviolet radiation. ● Chem. formula: $C_{27}H_{44}O$. The particular isomer involved in vitamin D_3 formation is **7-dehydrocholesterol.**
– ORIGIN 1930s: from *dehydro-* 'that has lost hydrogen' + **CHOLESTEROL.**

de·hy·dro·ep·i·an·dro·ste·rone (abbr.: **DHEA**) ▶ **n.** a naturally occurring weak androgenic steroid hormone produced by the adrenal glands with benefits such as the prevention of aging, the improvement of sexual function, the enhancement of athletic performance, and the treatment of osteoporosis.

de·hy·dro·gen·ase /ˌdēˈhīdrəjəˌnās, -ˌnāz/ ▶ **n.** Biochemistry an enzyme that catalyzes the removal of hydrogen atoms from a particular molecule, particularly in the electron transport chain reactions of cell respiration in conjunction with the coenzymes NAD and FAD.
– ORIGIN early 20th cent.: from **DE-** (expressing removal) + **HYDROGEN** + **-ASE.**

de·hy·dro·gen·ate /dēˈhīdrəjəˌnāt/ ▶ **v.** [with obj.] Chemistry remove a hydrogen atom or atoms from (a compound).
– DERIVATIVES **de·hy·dro·gen·a·tion** /dēˌhīdrəjəˈnāsʜən/ **n.**
– ORIGIN mid 19th cent.: from **DE-** (expressing removal) + **HYDROGEN** + **-ATE**[3].

De·ia·ni·ra /ˌdēyəˈnīrə/ Greek Mythology the wife of Hercules, who was tricked into smearing poison on a garment that caused his death.

de-ice /dēˈīs/ ▶ **v.** [with obj.] remove ice from: *airplanes are de-iced before takeoff.*
– DERIVATIVES **de-ic·er** **n.**

de·i·cide /ˈdēəˌsīd/ ▶ **n.** the killer of a god. ■ the killing of a god.
– DERIVATIVES **de·i·cid·al** /ˌdēəˈsīdl/ **adj.**
– ORIGIN early 17th cent.: from ecclesiastical Latin *deicida* 'killer of a god,' or directly from Latin *deus* 'god' + **-CIDE.**

deic·tic /ˈdīktik/ Linguistics ▶ **adj.** of, relating to, or denoting a word or expression whose meaning is dependent on the context in which it is used, e.g., *here, you, me, that one there,* or *next Tuesday.* Also called **INDEXICAL.**
▶ **n.** a deictic word or expression.
– DERIVATIVES **deic·ti·cal·ly** /-ik(ə)lē/ **adv.**
– ORIGIN early 19th cent.: from Greek *deiktikos, deiktos* 'demonstrative.'

de·i·fy /ˈdēəˌfī/ ▶ **v.** (**deifies, deifying, deified**) [with obj.] (usu. **be deified**) worship, regard, or treat (someone or something) as a god: *she was deified by the early Romans as a fertility goddess.*
– DERIVATIVES **de·i·fi·ca·tion** /ˌdēəfiˈkāsʜən/ **n.**
– ORIGIN Middle English (in the sense 'make godlike in character'): from Old French *deifier,* from ecclesiastical Latin *deificare,* from *deus* 'god.'

Deigh·ton /ˈdātn/, Len (1929–), English writer; full name *Leonard Cyril Deighton.* Several of his spy thrillers have been adapted as movies and for television. Notable works: *The Ipcress File* (1962) and the trilogy *Berlin Game, Mexico Set,* and *London Match* (1983–85).

deign /dān/ ▶ **v.** [no obj.] do something that one considers to be beneath one's dignity: *she did not deign to answer the maid's question.* ■ [with obj.] archaic condescend to give (something): *he had deigned an apology.*
– ORIGIN Middle English: from Old French *degnier,* from Latin *dignare, dignari* 'deem worthy,' from *dignus* 'worthy.'

De·i gra·ti·a /ˈdeē ˈgrätsēə/ ▶ **adv.** by the grace of God.
– ORIGIN early 17th cent.: Latin.

deil /dēl/ ▶ **n.** Scottish form of **DEVIL.**

Dei·mos /ˈdimäs/ Astronomy the outer, and smaller, of the two satellites of Mars, discovered in 1877. It is football-shaped and 10 miles (16 km) long. Compare with **PHOBOS.**
– ORIGIN named after one of the sons of Ares in Greek mythology, the name means literally 'fear, terror.'

de·in·dex /dēˈinˌdeks/ ▶ **v.** [with obj.] end the indexation to inflation of (pensions or other benefits).

de·in·dus·tri·al·i·za·tion /ˌdē-inˌdəstrēəliˈzāsʜən/ ▶ **n.** decline in industrial activity in a region or economy: *severe deindustrialization with substantial job losses.*
– DERIVATIVES **de·in·dus·tri·al·ize** /-ˈdəstrēəˌlīz/ **v.**

de-ink /dē-ˈiɴɢk/ ▶ **v.** [with obj.] remove ink from (paper being recycled).

dei·non·y·chus /dīˈnänikəs/ ▶ **n.** a dromaeosaurid dinosaur of the mid Cretaceous period, growing up to 11 feet (3.3 m) in length. ● Genus *Deinonychus,* family Dromaeosauridae, suborder Theropoda.
– ORIGIN modern Latin, from Greek *deinos* 'terrible' + *onux, onukh-* 'claw.'

dei·no·the·ri·um /ˌdīnəˈᴛʜi(ə)rēəm/ (also **deinothere** /ˈdīnəˌᴛʜi(ə)r/) ▶ **n.** (pl. **deinotheria** /-ᴛʜi(ə)rēə/ or **deinotheriums**) an elephantlike fossil mammal found mainly in the Pliocene epoch, the lower jaw having tusks that curve downward and backward. ● Genus *Deinotherium,* suborder Deinotherioidea, order Proboscidea.
– ORIGIN modern Latin, from Greek *deinos* 'terrible' + *thērion* 'wild beast.'

de·in·stall /ˌdē-inˈstôl/ (Brit. also **deinstal**) ▶ **v.** (**deinstalls** or Brit. **deinstals, deinstalling, deinstalled**) [with obj.] uninstall. ■ humorous dismiss from employment: *the company lost funding and I was deinstalled.*
– DERIVATIVES **de·in·stal·la·tion** /ˌdē-instəˈlāsʜən/ **n.**, **de·in·stall·er** **n.**

de·in·sti·tu·tion·al·ize /dēˌinstəˈt(y)o͞osʜənlˌīz/ ▶ **v.** [with obj.] discharge (a long-term inmate) from an institution such as a mental hospital or prison: *the changes aim to deinstitutionalize mentally ill people.*
– DERIVATIVES **de·in·sti·tu·tion·al·i·za·tion** /-ˌt(y)o͞osʜənl-əˈzāsʜən/ **n.**

de·i·on·ize /dēˈīəˌnīz/ ▶ **v.** [with obj.] (usu. as adj. **deionized**) remove the ions or ionic constituents from (a substance, esp. water).
– DERIVATIVES **de·i·on·i·za·tion** /dēˌīənəˈzāsʜən/ **n.**, **de·i·on·iz·er** **n.**

Deir·dre /ˈdi(ə)rdrə/ Irish Mythology a tragic heroine of whom it was prophesied that her beauty would bring banishment and death to heroes. King Conchobar of Ulster wanted to marry her, but she fell in love with Naoise, son of Usnach, who with his brothers carried her off to Scotland. They were lured back by Conchobar and treacherously slain, and Deirdre took her own life.

de·ism /ˈdēizəm/ ▶ **n.** belief in the existence of a supreme being, specifically of a creator who does not intervene in the universe. The term is used chiefly of an intellectual movement of the 17th and 18th centuries that accepted the existence of a creator on the basis of reason but rejected belief in a supernatural deity who interacts with humankind. Compare with **THEISM.**
– DERIVATIVES **de·ist** **n.**, **de·is·tic** /dēˈistik/ **adj.**, **de·is·ti·cal** /dēˈistikəl/ **adj.**
– ORIGIN late 17th cent.: from Latin *deus* 'god' + **-ISM.**

de·i·ty /ˈdēitē/ ▶ **n.** (pl. **deities**) a god or goddess (in a polytheistic religion): *a deity of ancient Greece.* ■ divine status, quality, or nature: *a ruler driven by delusions of deity.* ■ (usu. **the Deity**) the creator and supreme being (in a monotheistic religion such as Christianity). ■ a representation of a god or goddess, such as a statue or carving.
– ORIGIN Middle English (denoting the divine nature of God): from Old French *deite,* from ecclesiastical

PRONUNCIATION KEY ə *ago, up;* ər *over, fur;* a *hat;* ā *ate;* ä *car;* e *let;* ē *see;* i *fit;* ī *by;* ɴɢ *sing;* ō *go;* ô *law, for;* oi *toy;* o͝o *good;* o͞o *goo;* ou *out;* ᴛʜ *thin;* T͟H *then;* ᴢʜ *vision*

Latin *deitas* (translating Greek *theotēs*), from *deus* 'god.'

deix·is /'dīksis/ ▶ n. Linguistics the function or use of deictic words, forms, or expressions.
– ORIGIN 1940s: from Greek, literally 'demonstrative force, reference.'

dé·jà vu /ˌdāzhä 'vo͞o/ ▶ n. a feeling of having already experienced the present situation. ■ tedious familiarity: *to list the opponents of his policies is to invite boredom and a sense of déjà vu.*
– ORIGIN early 20th cent.: French, literally 'already seen.'

d

de·ject /di'jekt/ ▶ v. [with obj.] archaic make sad or dispirited; depress: *nothing dejects a trader like the interruption of his profits.*
– ORIGIN late Middle English (also in the sense 'overthrow, abase, degrade'): from Latin *deject-* 'thrown down,' from the verb *deicere*, from *de-* 'down' + *jacere* 'to throw.'

de·ject·ed /di'jektəd/ ▶ adj. sad and depressed; dispirited: *he stood in the street looking dejected.*
– DERIVATIVES **de·ject·ed·ly** adv.

de·jec·tion /di'jekshən/ ▶ n. a sad and depressed state; low spirits: *he was slumped in deep dejection.*
– ORIGIN late Middle English: from Latin *dejectio(n-)*, from *deicere* 'throw down' (see DEJECT).

de·junk /dē'jəngk/ ▶ v. [with obj.] informal clear (a room or other space) by disposing of clutter and unwanted possessions: *dejunk the house before you move.*

de ju·re /di 'jo͝orē, dā 'jo͝orā/ ▶ adv. according to rightful entitlement or claim; by right. Often contrasted with DE FACTO.
▶ adj. denoting something or someone that is rightfully such: *he had been de jure king since his father's death.*
– ORIGIN mid 16th cent.: Latin, literally 'of law.'

dek·a·gram ▶ n. variant spelling of DECAGRAM.

De Kalb /di'kalb/ an industrial city in north central Illinois; pop. 45,497 (est. 2008).

dek·a·li·ter ▶ n. variant spelling of DECALITER.

dek·a·me·ter ▶ n. variant spelling of DECAMETER.

deke /dēk/ Sports ▶ n. a deceptive movement or feint that induces an opponent to move out of position.
▶ v. [with obj.] draw (a player) out of position by such a movement.
– ORIGIN 1960s: shortened form of DECOY.

dek·ko /'dekō/ ▶ n. [in sing.] Brit. informal a quick look or glance: *come and have a dekko at this.*
– ORIGIN late 19th cent. (originally used by the British army in India): from Hindi *dekho* 'look!,' imperative of *dekhnā*.

de Klerk /də 'klerk/, F. W. (1936–), South African statesman; state president 1989–94; full name *Frederik Willem de Klerk*. As president, he freed Nelson Mandela in 1990, lifted the ban on membership in the African National Congress (ANC), and opened the negotiations that led to the first democratic elections in 1994. Nobel Peace Prize (1993), shared with Mandela.

de Koo·ning /də 'ko͞oning/, Willem (1904–97), US painter; born in the Netherlands; a leading exponent of abstract expressionism. He usually retained figurative elements in his work, either represented or merely hinted at, as in *Painting* (1948). The female form became a central theme in his later work, notably in the *Women* series (1950–53).

del /del/ ▶ n. Mathematics an operator used in vector analysis. (Symbol: ∇) ● del is defined as $\mathbf{i}\partial/\partial x + \mathbf{j}\partial/\partial y + \mathbf{k}\partial/\partial z$, where **i**, **j**, and **k** are vectors directed respectively along the Cartesian axes *x*, *y*, and *z*.
– ORIGIN early 20th cent.: abbreviation of DELTA[1], from the representation of the operator as an inverted capital delta.

Del. ▶ abbr. Delaware.

De·la·croix /ˌdelə'krwä/, (Ferdinand Victor) Eugène (1798–1863), French painter. The chief painter of the French romantic school, he is known for his use of vivid color, free drawing, and sometimes violent subject matter.

de la Mare /ˌdel ə 'me(ə)r/, Walter (John) (1873–1956), English poet. He is known for his children's poetry.

de·lam·i·nate /dē'laməˌnāt/ ▶ v. divide or become divided into layers: [with obj.] *delaminating the horn into thin sheets* | [no obj.] *the plywood was starting to delaminate.*
– ORIGIN late 19th cent.: from DE- 'away' + Latin *lamina* 'thin plate' + -ATE[3].

De·la·no /də'lānō/ an agricultural city in south central California; pop. 53,051 (est. 2008).

de·late /di'lāt/ ▶ v. [with obj.] archaic report (an offense or crime): *they may delate my slackness to my patron.* ■ inform against or denounce (someone): *they deliberated together on delating her as a witch.*
– DERIVATIVES **de·la·tion** /-'lāshən/ n., **de·la·tor** /-'lātər/ n.
– ORIGIN late 15th cent.: from Latin *delat-* 'referred, carried away,' from the verb *deferre* (see DEFER[2]).

De·lau·nay /dəlô'nā/, Robert (1885–1941), French painter. He painted some of the first purely abstract pictures and was one of the founding members of Orphism, together with his wife Sonia Delaunay-Terk.

De·lau·nay-Terk /dəlˌônā 'terk/, Sonia (1885–1979), French painter and textile designer; born in Russia; wife of Robert Delaunay. She created abstract paintings based on harmonies of form and color.

Del·a·ware[1] /'deləˌwe(ə)r/ **1** a river in the northeastern US that rises in the Catskill Mountains in New York and flows south for about 280 miles (450 km) to northern Delaware, where it meets the Atlantic Ocean at Delaware Bay. For much of its length it forms the eastern border of Pennsylvania. **2** a state in the eastern US, on the Atlantic coast;; pop. 873,092 (est. 2008); capital, Dover; statehood, Dec. 7, 1787 (1). One of the original thirteen states, it was the first to ratify the US Constitution.

Del·a·ware[2] ▶ n. (pl. **same** or **Delawares**) **1** a member of an American Indian people formerly inhabiting the Delaware River valley of New Jersey and eastern Pennsylvania.
2 either of two Algonquian languages (Munsi and Unami) spoken by this people.
▶ adj. of or relating to the Delaware or their languages.
– ORIGIN named after the *Delaware* River (see DELAWARE[1]).

de·lay /di'lā/ ▶ v. [with obj.] make (someone or something) late or slow: *the train was delayed.* ■ [no obj.] be late or slow; loiter: *time being of the essence, they delayed no longer.* ■ postpone or defer (an action): *he may decide to delay the next cut in interest rates.*
▶ n. a period of time by which something is late or postponed: *a two-hour delay* | *long* **delays in** *obtaining passports.* ■ the action of delaying or being delayed: *I set off without delay.* ■ Electronics the time interval between the propagation of an electrical signal and its reception. ■ an electronic device that introduces such an interval, esp. in an audio signal.
– DERIVATIVES **de·lay·er** n.
– ORIGIN Middle English: from Old French *delayer* (verb).

de·layed-ac·tion ▶ adj. [attrib.] operating or effective after a predetermined length of time: *delayed-action bombs.*
▶ n. (**delayed action**) the operation of something after a predetermined length of time.

de·lay·ing ac·tion ▶ n. action taken to gain time, esp. a military engagement that delays the advance of an enemy.

de·lay·ing tac·tics ▶ plural n. tactics designed to defer or postpone something in order to gain an advantage for oneself.

de·lay line ▶ n. a device producing a specific desired delay in the transmission of a signal. ■ a set of mirrors controlling the path lengths between outlying telescopes and a central receiver.

de·le /'dēlē/ ▶ v. (**deles, deleing, deled**) [with obj.] delete or mark (a part of a text) for deletion.
▶ n. a proofreader's sign indicating matter to be deleted.
– ORIGIN early 18th cent.: Latin, 'blot out! efface!,' imperative of *delere*.

de·lec·ta·ble /di'lektəbəl/ ▶ adj. (of food or drink) delicious: *delectable handmade chocolates.* ■ chiefly humorous extremely beautiful or attractive: *the delectable Ms. Davis.*
– DERIVATIVES **de·lec·ta·bil·i·ty** /-ˌlektə'bilitē/ n., **de·lec·ta·bly** /-blē/ adv.
– ORIGIN late Middle English: via Old French from Latin *delectabilis*, from *delectare* 'to charm' (see DELIGHT).

de·lec·ta·tion /ˌdēlek'tāshən/ ▶ n. formal or humorous pleasure and delight: *a box of chocolates* **for their delectation**.
– ORIGIN late Middle English: via Old French from Latin *delectatio(n-)*, from *delectare* 'to charm' (see DELIGHT).

del·e·ga·cy /'deligəsē/ ▶ n. (pl. **delegacies**) [treated as sing. or pl.] a body of delegates; a committee or delegation. ■ an appointment as a delegate.
– ORIGIN late Middle English: from DELEGATE, on the pattern of the pair *prelate, prelacy*.

del·e·gate ▶ n. /'deligit/ a person sent or authorized to represent others, in particular an elected representative sent to a conference. ■ a member of a committee.
▶ v. /'deləˌgāt/ [with obj.] entrust (a task or responsibility) to another person, typically one who is less senior than oneself: *he delegates routine tasks* | *the power* **delegated to** *him must never be misused.* ■ [with obj. and infinitive] send or authorize (someone) to do something as a representative: *Edward was delegated to meet new arrivals.*
– DERIVATIVES **del·e·ga·ble** /-gəbəl/ adj., **del·e·ga·tor** /-ˌgātər/ n.
– ORIGIN late Middle English: from Latin *delegatus* 'sent on a commission,' from the verb *delegare*, from *de-* 'down' + *legare* 'depute.'

del·e·ga·tion /ˌdeli'gāshən/ ▶ n. **1** [treated as sing. or pl.] a body of delegates or representatives; a deputation: *a delegation of teachers.*
2 the act or process of delegating or being delegated: *prioritizing tasks for delegation.*
– ORIGIN early 17th cent. (denoting the act or process of delegating; also in the sense 'delegated power'): from Latin *delegatio(n-)*, from *delegare* 'send on a commission' (see DELEGATE).

de·le·git·i·mate /ˌdēli'jitəˌmāt/ ▶ v. another term for DELEGITIMIZE.

de·le·git·i·ma·tize /ˌdēli'jitəməˌtīz/ ▶ v. another term for DELEGITIMIZE.

de·le·git·i·mize /ˌdēli'jitəˌmīz/ ▶ v. [with obj.] withdraw legitimate status or authority from (someone or something): *political efforts to delegitimize nuclear weapons.*
– DERIVATIVES **de·le·git·i·mi·za·tion** /-ˌjitəmə'zāshən/ n.

de·lete /di'lēt/ ▶ v. [with obj.] remove or obliterate (written or printed matter), esp. by drawing a line through it or marking it with a delete sign: *the passage was deleted.* ■ (usu. **be deleted**) remove (data) from a computer's memory. ■ (**be deleted**) Genetics (of a section of genetic code, or its product) be lost or excised from a nucleic acid or protein sequence: *if one important gene is deleted from an animal's DNA, other genes can stand in.* ■ remove (a product, esp. a recording) from the catalog of those available for purchase: *their EMI release has already been deleted.*
▶ n. a command or key on a computer that erases text.
– ORIGIN late Middle English (in the sense 'destroy'): from Latin *delet-* 'blotted out, effaced,' from the verb *delere*.

del·e·te·ri·ous /ˌdeli'ti(ə)rēəs/ ▶ adj. causing harm or damage: *divorce is assumed to have deleterious effects on children.*
– DERIVATIVES **del·e·te·ri·ous·ly** adv.
– ORIGIN mid 17th cent.: via medieval Latin from Greek *dēlētērios* 'noxious' + -OUS.

de·le·tion /di'lēshən/ ▶ n. **1** the action or process of deleting something: *deletion of a file.*
2 Genetics the loss or absence of a section from a nucleic acid molecule or chromosome.

de·lev·er·ag·ing /dē'levərijing, dē'lēv-/ ▶ n. Finance the process or practice of reducing the level of one's debt by rapidly selling one's assets.
– DERIVATIVES **de·lev·er·age** n. & v.

de·lex·i·cal /dē'leksikəl/ ▶ adj. Linguistics (of a verb) having little or no meaning in its own right, for example *take* in *take a photograph.*

Delft /delft/ a town in the Netherlands, in the province of South Holland; pop. 96,168 (2008). The home of painters Pieter de Hooch and Jan Vermeer, it also is noted for its pottery.
– ORIGIN originally *Delf*, from Dutch *delf* 'ditch,' still the name of the town's main canal.

delft /delft/ ▶ n. English or Dutch tin-glazed earthenware, typically decorated by hand in blue on a white background.
– DERIVATIVES **delft·ware** /-ˌwe(ə)r/ n.
– ORIGIN late 17th cent. (originally *Delf ware*): see DELFT, where the pottery originated.

Del·hi /'delē/ (also **Old Delhi**) a walled city on the River Jumna in north central India, which was made the capital of the Mogul empire in 1638 by Shah Jahan (1592–1666). See also NEW DELHI.

del·i /'delē/ ▶ n. (pl. **delis**) informal short for DELICATESSEN.

De·li·an /'dēlēən/ ▶ adj. of or relating to Delos.
▶ n. a native or inhabitant of Delos.

De·li·an League an alliance of ancient Greek city states, dominated by Athens, that joined in 478–447 BC against the Persians. The league was disbanded on the defeat of Athens in the Peloponnesian War (404 BC), but again united under Athens' leadership against Spartan aggression in 377–338 BC. Also called ATHENIAN EMPIRE.

de·lib·er·ate ▶ adj. /di'libərit/ done consciously and intentionally: *a deliberate attempt to provoke conflict.* ■ fully considered; not impulsive: *a deliberate decision.* ■ done or acting in a careful and unhurried way: *a careful and deliberate worker.*

▶ v. /-ˌrāt/ [no obj.] engage in long and careful consideration: *she deliberated over the menu.* ■ [with obj.] consider (a question) carefully: *jurors deliberated the fate of those charged* | [with clause] *deliberating what she should do.*
– DERIVATIVES **de·lib·er·ate·ness** /-ritnis/ n., **de·lib·er·a·tor** /-ˌrātər/ n.
– ORIGIN late Middle English (as an adjective): from Latin *deliberatus*, 'considered carefully,' past participle of *deliberare*, from *de-* 'down' + *librare* 'weigh' (from *libra* 'scales').

de·lib·er·ate·ly /diˈlibəritlē/ ▶ adv. **1** consciously and intentionally; on purpose: *the fire was started deliberately.*
2 in a careful and unhurried way: *slowly and deliberately he rose from the armchair.*

de·lib·er·a·tion /diˌlibəˈrāsHən/ ▶ n. **1** long and careful consideration or discussion: *after much deliberation, we arrived at a compromise* | *the commission's deliberations.*
2 slow and careful movement or thought: *he replaced the glass on the table with deliberation.*
– ORIGIN late Middle English: via Old French from Latin *deliberatio(n-)*, from *deliberare* 'consider carefully' (see DELIBERATE).

de·lib·er·a·tive /diˈlibərətiv, -əˌrātiv/ ▶ adj. relating to or intended for consideration or discussion: *a deliberative assembly.*
– DERIVATIVES **de·lib·er·a·tive·ly** adv.

del·i·ca·cy /ˈdelikəsē/ ▶ n. (pl. **delicacies**) **1** the quality of being delicate, in particular: ■ fineness or intricacy of texture or structure: *miniature pearls of exquisite delicacy.* ■ susceptibility to illness or adverse conditions; fragility. ■ the quality of requiring discretion or sensitivity: *the delicacy of the situation.* ■ tact and consideration: *I have to treat this matter with the utmost delicacy.* ■ accuracy of perception; sensitiveness.
2 a choice or expensive food: *asparagus was considered a delicacy by the ancient Greeks.*
– ORIGIN late Middle English (in the senses 'voluptuousness' and 'luxuriousness'): from DELICATE + -ACY.

del·i·cate /ˈdelikit/ ▶ adj. **1** very fine in texture or structure; of intricate workmanship or quality: *a spider's web, strong yet delicate.* ■ (of a color or a scent) subtle and subdued: *delicate pastel shades* | *a delicate fragrance.* ■ (of food or drink) subtly and pleasantly flavored: *a delicate cream sauce.*
2 easily broken or damaged; fragile: *delicate china.* ■ (of a person, animal, or plant) susceptible to illness or adverse conditions: *his delicate health.* ■ (of a state or condition) easily upset or damaged: *owls have a delicate balance with their habitat.*
3 requiring sensitive or careful handling: *delicate negotiations.* ■ (of a person or an action) tactful and considerate: *the most delicate tact was called for.* ■ skillful and finely judged; deft: *his delicate ball-playing skills.* ■ (of an instrument) highly sensitive.
▶ n. informal a delicate fabric or garment made of such fabric.
– PHRASES **in a delicate condition** archaic pregnant.
– DERIVATIVES **del·i·cate·ly** adv., **del·i·cate·ness** n.
– ORIGIN late Middle English (in the sense 'delightful, charming'): from French *délicat* or Latin *delicatus*, of unknown origin. Senses also expressed in Middle English (now obsolete) include 'voluptuous,' 'self-indulgent,' 'fastidious,' and 'effeminate.'

del·i·ca·tes·sen /ˌdelikəˈtesən/ ▶ n. a store selling cold cuts, cheeses, and a variety of salads, as well as a selection of unusual or foreign prepared foods.
– ORIGIN late 19th cent. (originally denoting prepared foods for sale): from German *Delikatessen* or Dutch *delicatessen*, from French *délicatesse* 'delicateness,' from *délicat* (see DELICATE).

de·li·cense /dēˈlīsəns/ ▶ v. [with obj.] deprive of a license or authority to operate: *physicians are being threatened, impoverished, delicensed, and imprisoned for prescribing in good faith with the intention of relieving pain.*

De·li·cious /diˈlisHəs/ ▶ n. a red or yellow variety of eating apple with a sweet flavor and a slightly elongated shape, originally cultivated in the US.

de·li·cious /diˈlisHəs/ ▶ adj. highly pleasant to the taste: *delicious home-baked brown bread.* ■ delightful: *a delicious irony.*
– DERIVATIVES **de·li·cious·ly** adv., **de·li·cious·ness** n.
– ORIGIN Middle English (also in the sense 'characterized by sensuous indulgence'): via Old French from late Latin *deliciosus*, from Latin *deliciae* (plural) 'delight, pleasure.'

de·lict /diˈlikt/ ▶ n. Law a violation of the law; a tort: *an international delict.*
– ORIGIN late Middle English: from Latin *delictum* 'something showing fault,' neuter past participle of *delinquere* (see DELINQUENT).

de·light /diˈlīt/ ▶ v. [with obj.] please (someone) greatly: *an experience guaranteed to delight both young and old.* ■ [no obj.] (**delight in**) take great pleasure in: *they delight in playing tricks.*
▶ n. great pleasure: *she took great delight in telling your story.* ■ a cause or source of great pleasure: *the trees here are a delight.*
– ORIGIN Middle English: from Old French *delitier* (verb), *delit* (noun), from Latin *delectare* 'to charm,' frequentative of *delicere*. The *-gh-* was added in the 16th cent. by association with LIGHT¹.

de·light·ed /diˈlītid/ ▶ adj. feeling or showing great pleasure: *a delighted smile* | [with infinitive] *we were delighted to see her.*
– DERIVATIVES **de·light·ed·ly** adv.

de·light·ful /diˈlītfəl/ ▶ adj. causing delight; charming: *a delightful secluded garden.*
– DERIVATIVES **de·light·ful·ly** adv., **de·light·ful·ness** n.

De·li·lah /diˈlīlə/ (in the Bible) a woman who betrayed Samson to the Philistines by revealing to them that the secret of his strength lay in his long hair. ■ (as noun **a Delilah**) a seductive and wily temptress.

de·lim·it /diˈlimit/ ▶ v. (**delimits, delimiting, delimited**) [with obj.] determine the limits or boundaries of: *agreements delimiting fishing zones.*
– DERIVATIVES **de·lim·i·ta·tion** /-ˌlimiˈtāsHən/ n., **de·lim·it·er** n.
– ORIGIN mid 19th cent.: from French *délimiter*, from Latin *delimitare*, from *de-* 'down, completely' + *limitare* (from *limes, limit-* 'boundary, limit').

de·lin·e·ate /diˈlinēˌāt/ ▶ v. [with obj.] describe or portray (something) precisely: *the law should delineate and prohibit behavior that is socially abhorrent.* ■ indicate the exact position of (a border or boundary).
– DERIVATIVES **de·lin·e·a·tor** /-ˌātər/ n.
– ORIGIN mid 16th cent. (in the sense 'trace the outline of something'): from Latin *delineat-* 'outlined,' from the verb *delineare*, from *de-* 'out, completely' + *lineare* (from *linea* 'line').

de·lin·e·a·tion /diˌlinēˈāsHən/ ▶ n. **1** the action of describing or portraying something precisely: *the artist's exquisite delineation of costume and jewelry.*
2 the action of indicating the exact position of a border or boundary.

de·link /dēˈlinGk/ ▶ v. [with obj.] break the connection between (something) and something else: *the country delinked its trade policy from international policy.*

de·lin·quen·cy /diˈlinGkwənsē/ ▶ n. (pl. **delinquencies**) minor crime, esp. that committed by young people: *social causes of crime and delinquency.* ■ formal neglect of one's duty: *he relayed this in such a manner as to imply grave delinquency on the host's part.* ■ a failure to pay an outstanding debt.
– ORIGIN mid 17th cent.: from ecclesiastical Latin *delinquentia*, from Latin *delinquent-* 'offending' (see DELINQUENT).

de·lin·quent /diˈlinGkwənt/ ▶ adj. (typically of a young person or that person's behavior) showing or characterized by a tendency to commit crime, particularly minor crime: *delinquent children.* ■ in arrears: *delinquent accounts.* ■ formal failing in one's duty.
▶ n. a delinquent person: *young delinquents.*
– DERIVATIVES **de·lin·quent·ly** adv.
– ORIGIN late 15th cent.: from Latin *delinquent-* 'offending,' from the verb *delinquere*, from *de-* 'away' + *linquere* 'to leave.'

del·i·quesce /ˌdeliˈkwes/ ▶ v. [no obj.] (of organic matter) become liquid, typically during decomposition. ■ Chemistry (of a solid) become liquid by absorbing moisture from the air.
– ORIGIN mid 18th cent.: from Latin *deliquescere* 'dissolve,' from *de-* 'down' + *liquescere* 'become liquid' (from *liquere* 'be liquid').

del·i·ques·cent /deliˈkwesənt/ ▶ adj. becoming liquid or having a tendency to become liquid. ■ Chemistry (of a solid) tending to absorb moisture from the air and dissolve in it.
– DERIVATIVES **del·i·ques·cence** n.
– ORIGIN late 18th cent.: from Latin *deliquescent-* 'dissolving,' from the verb *deliquescere* (see DELIQUESCE).

de·lir·i·ous /diˈli(ə)rēəs/ ▶ adj. in an acutely disturbed state of mind resulting from illness or intoxication and characterized by restlessness, illusions, and incoherence of thought and speech. ■ in a state of wild excitement or ecstasy: *there was a great roar from the delirious crowd.*
– DERIVATIVES **de·lir·i·ant** /-ənt/ adj., **de·lir·i·ous·ly** adv.

de·lir·i·um /diˈli(ə)rēəm/ ▶ n. an acutely disturbed state of mind that occurs in fever, intoxication, and other disorders and is characterized by restlessness, illusions, and incoherence of thought and speech. ■ wild excitement or ecstasy.
– ORIGIN mid 16th cent.: from Latin, from *delirare* 'deviate, be deranged' (literally 'deviate from the furrow'), from *de-* 'away' + *lira* 'ridge between furrows.'

de·lir·i·um tre·mens /diˈli(ə)rēəm ˈtrēmənz/ ▶ n. a psychotic condition typical of withdrawal in chronic alcoholics, involving tremors, hallucinations, anxiety, and disorientation.
– ORIGIN early 19th cent.: from Latin, 'trembling delirium.'

de·lish /diˈlisH/ ▶ adj. informal delicious.

de·list /dēˈlist/ ▶ v. [with obj.] remove (something) from a list, in particular: ■ remove (a security) from the official register of a stock exchange: *the stock collapsed and was delisted.* ■ remove (a product) from the list of those sold by a particular retailer.

d

de·liv·er /diˈlivər/ ▶ v. [with obj.] **1** bring and hand over (a letter, parcel, or ordered goods) to the proper recipient or address: *the products should be delivered on time* | [no obj.] *we'll deliver direct to your door.* ■ formally hand over (someone): *they would have **delivered him to the Germans** for vengeance.* ■ ■ launch or aim (a blow, a ball, or an attack): *the pitcher winds up to deliver the ball.* ■ provide (something promised or expected): *he had been able to deliver votes in huge numbers* | *she's waiting for him to **deliver on** his promise.* ■ (**deliver someone/something from**) save, rescue, or set free from: *deliver us from misery.* ■ (**deliver someone/something up**) surrender someone or something: *to deliver up to justice a member of his own family.* ■ Law acknowledge that one intends to be bound by (a deed), either explicitly by declaration or implicitly by formal handover.
2 state in a formal manner: *the President will deliver a speech* | *he **delivered himself of** a sermon.* ■ (of a judge or court) give (a judgment or verdict): *the judge delivered his verdict.*
3 assist in the birth of: *the village midwife delivered the baby.* ■ give birth to: *she will deliver a child.* ■ assist (a woman or animal) in giving birth: *she has never been delivered of a foal that lived.*
– PHRASES **deliver the goods** informal provide what is promised or expected.
– DERIVATIVES **de·liv·er·ee** /-ˌliv(ə)ˈrē/ n., **de·liv·er·er** n.
– ORIGIN Middle English: from Old French *delivrer*, based on Latin *de-* 'away' + *liberare* 'set free.'

de·liv·er·a·ble /diˈlivərəbəl/ ▶ adj. able to be delivered: *goods in a deliverable state.*
▶ n. (usu. **deliverables**) a thing able to be provided, esp. as a product of a development process.

de·liv·er·ance /diˈlivərəns/ ▶ n. **1** the action of being rescued or set free: *prayers for deliverance.*
2 a formal or authoritative utterance.
– ORIGIN Middle English: from Old French *delivrance*, from the verb *delivrer* (see DELIVER).

de·liv·er·y /diˈlivərē/ ▶ n. (pl. **deliveries**) **1** the action of delivering letters, packages, or ordered goods: *allow up to 28 days for delivery.* ■ a regular or scheduled occasion for this: *there will be around 15 deliveries a week.* ■ an item or items delivered on a particular occasion: *they are getting smaller deliveries.* ■ Law the formal or symbolic handing over of property, esp. a sealed deed, to a grantee or third party.
2 the process of giving birth: *injuries sustained during delivery* | *practically all deliveries take place in a hospital* | [as modifier] *the delivery room.*
3 an act of throwing or bowling a ball or striking a blow: *a quick, compact delivery that sent the ball zinging.*
4 the manner or style of giving a speech: *her delivery was stilted.*
5 the supply or provision of something: *delivery of electricity at a specified price.*
– PHRASES **take delivery of** receive (something purchased): *we took delivery of the software in February.*
– ORIGIN late Middle English: from Anglo-Norman French *delivree*, feminine past participle of *delivrer* (see DELIVER).

dell /del/ ▶ n. literary a small valley, usually among trees: *lush green valleys and wooded dells.*
– ORIGIN Old English, of Germanic origin; related to Dutch *del* and German dialect *Telle*, also to DALE.

Del·la Crus·can /ˌdelə ˈkrəskən/ ▶ adj. of or relating to the Academy della Crusca in Florence, an institution established in 1582, with the purity of the Italian language as its chief interest. ■ of or relating to a late-18th-century school of English poets with an artificial style modeled on that of purist Italian writers.

▶ **n.** a member of the Academy della Crusca. ■ a Della Cruscan poet.
– ORIGIN from Italian (*Accademia*) *della Crusca* '(Academy) of the bran' (with reference to "sifting" of the language).

del·la Quer·cia /ˌdelə ˈkwerCHə/, Jacopo (*c.*1374–1438), Italian sculptor. He is noted for the biblical reliefs on the portal of San Petronio in Bologna (1425–35).

del·la Rob·bia /ˌdelə ˈrōbēə, ˈräb-/, Luca (1400–82), Italian sculptor and ceramicist. He is best known for his relief panels in Florence Cathedral and his color-glazed terra-cotta figures.

Del·mar·va /delˈmärvə/ (also **Delmarva Peninsula**) a peninsular region 180 miles (290 km) long in the eastern US that includes Delaware, the Eastern Shore of Maryland, and a small strip of Virginia; it separates Chesapeake Bay from the Atlantic Ocean.
– ORIGIN acronym from *Del*aware, *Mar*yland, and *V*irgini*a*.

Del·mon·i·co steak /delˈmäniˌkō/ ▶ **n.** a small steak cut from the front section of the short loin of beef. Also called CLUB STEAK.
– ORIGIN named for Lorenzo Delmonico (1813–81), Swiss-born US restaurateur.

de·lo·cal·ize /dēˈlōkəˌlīz/ ▶ **v.** [with obj.] detach or remove (something) from a particular place or location, or from local limitations: (as adj. **delocalized**) *delocalized cortical activity* | (as noun **delocalizing**) *delocalizing of finance capital*. ■ (**be delocalized**) Chemistry (of electrons) be shared among more than two atoms in a molecule.
– DERIVATIVES **de·lo·cal·i·za·tion** /-ˌlōkələˈzāSHən/ **n.**

De·lors /dəˈlôr/, Jacques (Lucien Jean) (1925–), French socialist politician; president of the European Commission 1985–94. During his presidency, he pressed for closer European union and oversaw the introduction of a single market within the European Community, which came into effect on January 1, 1993.

De·los /ˈdēläs, ˈdelōs/ a small Greek island in the Aegean Sea, regarded as the center of the Cyclades. Although it is now virtually uninhabited, it was considered to be sacred to Apollo in classical times and, according to legend, was the birthplace of Apollo and Artemis.

de·louse /dēˈlous/ ▶ **v.** [with obj.] rid (a person or animal) of lice and other parasitic insects.

Del·phi /ˈdelˌfī/ one of the most important religious sanctuaries of the ancient Greek world, dedicated to Apollo, situated on the lower southern slopes of Mount Parnassus above the Gulf of Corinth. Thought of as the navel of the earth, it was the seat of the Delphic Oracle, whose riddling responses to a wide range of questions were delivered by the Pythia.

Del·phic /ˈdelfik/ (also **Delphian** /-fēən/) ▶ **adj.** of or relating to the ancient Greek oracle at Delphi. ■ (typically of a pronouncement) deliberately obscure or ambiguous.

del·phin·i·um /delˈfinēəm/ ▶ **n.** (pl. **delphiniums**) a popular garden plant of the buttercup family that bears tall spikes of blue flowers. ● Genus *Delphinium*, family Ranunculaceae.
– ORIGIN modern Latin, from Greek *delphinion* 'larkspur,' from *delphin* 'dolphin' (because of the shape of the spur, thought to resemble a dolphin's back).

Del·phi·nus /delˈfīnəs/ Astronomy a small constellation (the Dolphin), just north of the celestial equator near Cygnus. ■ (as genitive **Delphini** /delˈfīnē/) used with a preceding letter or numeral to designate a star in this constellation: *the star Alpha Delphini*.
– ORIGIN Latin.

Del·phi tech·nique ▶ **n.** a method of group decision-making and forecasting that involves successively collating the judgments of experts.
– ORIGIN in allusion to the ancient Greek oracle at *Delphi*.

Del·ray Beach /ˈdelˌrā/ a resort city in southeastern Florida, north of Fort Lauderdale; pop. 64,092 (est. 2008).

del Sar·to /del ˈsärtō/, Andrea, see SARTO.

del·ta[1] /ˈdeltə/ ▶ **n. 1** the fourth letter of the Greek alphabet (Δ, δ), transliterated as 'd.' ■ [as modifier] the fourth in a series of items, categories, etc.: *delta hepatitis*. ■ (**Delta**) [followed by Latin genitive] Astronomy the fourth (usually fourth-brightest) star in a constellation: *Delta Cephei*.
2 a code word representing the letter D, used in radio communication. ▶ **symbol** ■ (δ) Mathematics variation of a variable or function. ■ (Δ) Mathematics a finite increment. ■ (δ) Astronomy declination.

del·ta[2] ▶ **n.** a triangular tract of sediment deposited at the mouth of a river, typically where it diverges into several outlets. ■ (**the Delta**) a region in northern Mississippi that lies between the Yazoo and Mississippi rivers and is known for its cotton and for blues music. Also called **Yazoo Delta** or **Mississippi Delta**.
– DERIVATIVES **del·ta·ic** /delˈtāik/ **adj.**
– ORIGIN mid 16th cent.: originally specifically as *the Delta* (of the Nile River), from the shape of the Greek letter (see DELTA[1]).

del·ta con·nec·tion ▶ **n.** a triangular arrangement of electrical three-phase windings in series, each of the three wires of the circuit being connected to a junction of two windings.

Del·ta Force an elite US Army unit whose main responsibilities are rescue operations and special forces work.

del·ta rays ▶ **plural n.** Physics rays of low penetrative power consisting of slow electrons or other particles ejected from atoms by the impact of ionizing radiation.

del·ta rhythm ▶ **n.** electrical activity of the brain at a frequency of around 1–8 Hz, typical of sleep. The resulting oscillations, detected using an electroencephalograph, are called **delta waves**.

del·ta-v (also **delta-vee**) ▶ **n.** informal acceleration: *four hundred knots of delta-v*.
– ORIGIN late 20th cent.: from DELTA[1] (as a mathematical symbol denoting variation) + *v* for *velocity*.

del·ta wing ▶ **n.** a single triangular swept-back wing on some aircraft, typically military aircraft.
– DERIVATIVES **del·ta-winged adj.**

del·ti·ol·o·gist /ˌdeltēˈäləjist/ ▶ **n.** a person who collects postcards as a hobby.
– DERIVATIVES **del·ti·ol·o·gy** /-jē/ **n.**
– ORIGIN 1940s: from Greek *deltion* (diminutive of *deltos* 'writing tablet') + -LOGIST.

del·toid /ˈdeltoid/ ▶ **adj.** technical triangular: *a tree with large deltoid leaves*. ■ denoting a thick triangular muscle covering the shoulder joint and used for raising the arm away from the body.
▶ **n.** a deltoid muscle. ■ each of the three parts of a deltoid muscle, attached at the front, side, and rear of the shoulder: *the anterior deltoid*.
– ORIGIN mid 18th cent.: from French *deltoïde*, or via modern Latin from Greek *deltoeidēs*.

de·lude /diˈlo͞od/ ▶ **v.** [with obj.] impose a misleading belief upon (someone); deceive; fool: *too many theorists have deluded the public* | (as adj. **deluded**) *the poor deluded creature*.
– DERIVATIVES **de·lud·ed·ly adv.**, **de·lud·er n.**
– ORIGIN late Middle English: from Latin *deludere* 'to mock,' from *de-* (with pejorative force) + *ludere* 'to play.'

del·uge /ˈdel(y)o͞oj/ ▶ **n.** a severe flood. ■ (**the Deluge**) the biblical Flood (recorded in Genesis 6–8). ■ a heavy fall of rain: *a deluge of rain hit the plains*. ■ a great quantity of something arriving at the same time: *a deluge of complaints*.
▶ **v.** [with obj.] (usu. **be deluged**) inundate with a great quantity of something: *he has been deluged with offers of work*. ■ flood: *the country was deluged with rain*.
– ORIGIN late Middle English: from Old French, variant of *diluve*, from Latin *diluvium*, from *diluere* 'wash away.'

de·lu·sion /diˈlo͞oZHən/ ▶ **n.** an idiosyncratic belief or impression that is firmly maintained despite being contradicted by what is generally accepted as reality or rational argument, typically a symptom of mental disorder: *the delusion of being watched*. ■ the action of deluding someone or the state of being deluded: *what a capacity television has for delusion*.
– PHRASES **delusions of grandeur** a false impression of one's own importance.
– DERIVATIVES **de·lu·sion·al** /-ZHənl/ **adj.**
– ORIGIN late Middle English (in the sense 'act of deluding or of being deluded'): from late Latin *delusio(n-)*, from the verb *deludere* (see DELUDE).

de·lu·sive /diˈlo͞osiv/ ▶ **adj.** giving a false or misleading impression: *the delusive light of Venice*.
– DERIVATIVES **de·lu·sive·ly adv.**, **de·lu·sive·ness n.**

de·lu·so·ry /diˈlo͞osərē, -zərē/ ▶ **adj.** another term for DELUSIVE.
– ORIGIN late 15th cent.: from late Latin *delusorius*, from *delus-* 'mocked,' from the verb *deludere* (see DELUDE).

de·lust·er /dēˈləstər/ (Brit. **delustre**) ▶ **v.** [with obj.] remove the luster from (a textile), typically by chemical treatment.

de·luxe /diˈləks/ ▶ **adj.** luxurious or sumptuous; of a superior kind: *a deluxe hotel*.
– ORIGIN early 19th cent.: from French *de luxe*, literally 'of luxury.'

delve /delv/ ▶ **v.** [no obj.] reach inside a receptacle and search for something: *she delved in her pocket*. ■ research or make painstaking inquiries into something: *as we delve further into the atom's secrets*. ■ [with obj.] literary dig; excavate: (as adj. **delved**) *the approach from the surface above had awed her, so hugely delved were the tunnels*.
– DERIVATIVES **delv·er n.**
– ORIGIN Old English *delfan* 'dig'; related to Dutch *delven*.

Dem. ▶ **abbr.** Democrat.

de·mag·net·ize /dēˈmagniˌtīz/ ▶ **v.** [with obj.] remove magnetic properties from.
– DERIVATIVES **de·mag·net·i·za·tion** /-ˌmagnitəˈzāSHən/ **n.**, **de·mag·net·iz·er n.**

dem·a·gogue /ˈdeməˌgäg/ ▶ **n.** a political leader who seeks support by appealing to popular desires and prejudices rather than by using rational argument. ■ (in ancient Greece and Rome) a leader or orator who espoused the cause of the common people.
– DERIVATIVES **dem·a·gog·ic** /ˌdeməˈgäjik, -ˈgägik, -ˈgōjik/ **adj.**, **dem·a·gogu·er·y** /ˈdeməˌgägərē/ **n.**, **dem·a·go·gy** /ˈdeməˌgäjē, -ˌgōjē/ **n.**
– ORIGIN mid 17th cent.: from Greek *dēmagōgos*, from *dēmos* 'the people' + *agōgos* 'leading' (from *agein* 'to lead').

de Main·te·non /də manˈt(ə)nôN/ see MAINTENON.

de·mand /diˈmand/ ▶ **n.** an insistent and peremptory request, made as if by right: *a series of **demands for** far-reaching reforms*. ■ (**demands**) pressing requirements: *he's got enough **demands on** his time already*. ■ Economics the desire of purchasers, consumers, clients, employers, etc., for a particular commodity, service, or other item: *a recent slump in demand* | *a demand for specialists*.
▶ **v.** [reporting verb] ask authoritatively or brusquely: [with direct speech] *"Where is she?" he demanded* | [with clause] *the police demanded that he give them the names*. ■ [with obj.] insist on having: *an outraged public demanded retribution* | *too much was being **demanded of** the top players*. ■ require; need: *a complex activity demanding detailed knowledge*. ■ Law call into court; summon.
– PHRASES **in demand** sought after: *all these skills are much in demand*. **on demand** as soon as or whenever required: *he promised us endless coffee on demand* | [as modifier] *an on-demand movie service on broadband*.
– DERIVATIVES **de·mand·er n.**
– ORIGIN Middle English (as a noun): from Old French *demande* (noun), *demander* (verb), from Latin *demandare* 'hand over, entrust' (in medieval Latin 'demand'), from *de-* 'formally' + *mandare* 'to order.'

de·mand curve ▶ **n.** a graph showing how the demand for a commodity or service varies with changes in its price.

de·mand de·pos·it ▶ **n.** a deposit of money that can be withdrawn without prior notice.

de·mand draft ▶ **n.** a financial draft payable on demand.

de·mand feed·ing ▶ **n.** the practice of feeding a baby when it cries to be fed rather than at set times.

de·mand·ing /diˈmandiNG/ ▶ **adj.** (of a task) requiring much skill or effort: *she has a busy and demanding job*. ■ (of a person) making others work hard or meet high standards.
– DERIVATIVES **de·mand·ing·ly adv.**

de·mand-led (also **demand-driven**) ▶ **adj.** Economics caused or determined by demand from consumers or clients.

de·mand note ▶ **n.** a formal request for payment. ■ another term for DEMAND DRAFT.

de·mand pull ▶ **adj.** relating to or denoting inflation caused by an excess of demand over supply.

de·man·toid /diˈmantoid/ ▶ **n.** a lustrous green variety of andradite (garnet).
– ORIGIN late 19th cent.: from German, from *Demant* 'diamond.'

de·mar·cate /diˈmärˌkāt, ˈdēmärˌkāt/ (also **demarkate**) ▶ **v.** [with obj.] set the boundaries or limits of: *plots of land demarcated by barbed wire*. ■ separate or distinguish from: *art was being demarcated from the more objective science*.
– ORIGIN early 19th cent.: back-formation from DEMARCATION.

de·mar·ca·tion /ˌdēmärˈkāSHən/ ▶ **n.** the action of fixing the boundary or limits of something: *the demarcation of the maritime border*. ■ a dividing line: *a horizontal band that produces a distinct demarcation two inches from the top*.
– DERIVATIVES **de·mar·ca·tor** /diˈmärˌkātər/ **n.**
– ORIGIN early 18th cent.: from Spanish *demarcación*, from *demarcar* 'mark the bounds of,' ultimately of Germanic origin and related to MARK[1]. Originally used in the phrase *line of demarcation* (Spanish *linea de demarcación*, Portuguese *linha de demarcação*), the word denoted a line dividing the New World between the Spanish and Portuguese, laid down by the pope in 1493.

dé·marche /dā'märsн/ ▶ **n.** a political step or initiative: *foreign policy démarches.*
– ORIGIN mid 17th cent.: French, from *démarcher* 'take steps.'

de·mas·si·fy /dē'masi,fī/ ▶ **v.** (**demassifies, demassifying, demassified**) [with obj.] divide or break up (a social or political unit) into its component parts.
– DERIVATIVES **de·mas·si·fi·ca·tion** /-,masifi'kāsнən/ **n.**

de·ma·te·ri·al·ize /,dēmə'ti(ə)rēə,līz/ ▶ **v.** [no obj.] become free of physical substance; cease to have material character or qualities: *the kiss dematerializes into a kind of spiritual rebirth.* ■ (in science fiction) disappear or cease to be physically present through some imagined technological process: *he watched the time machine dematerialize.* ■ [with obj.] (usu. as adj. **dematerialized**) replace (physical records or certificates) with a paperless computerized system: *a dematerialized stock lending service.*
– DERIVATIVES **de·ma·te·ri·al·i·za·tion** /-,ti(ə)rēələ'zāsнən/ **n.**

de Mau·pas·sant /də ,mōpə'sänt, də mōpə'säɴ/, Guy, see MAUPASSANT.

deme /dēm/ ▶ **n. 1** a political division of Attica in ancient Greece. ■ an administrative division in modern Greece.
2 Biology a subdivision of a population consisting of closely related plants, animals, or people, typically breeding mainly within the group.
– ORIGIN from Greek *dēmos* 'township'; sense 2 is an extended use dating from the 1930s.

de·mean[1] /di'mēn/ ▶ **v.** [with obj.] cause a severe loss in the dignity of and respect for (someone or something): *I had demeaned the profession.* ■ (**demean oneself**) do something that is beneath one's dignity.
– ORIGIN early 17th cent.: from DE- 'away, down' + the adjective MEAN[2], on the pattern of *debase.*

de·mean[2] ▶ **v.** (**demean oneself**) archaic conduct oneself in a particular way: *no man demeaned himself so honorably.*
– ORIGIN Middle English (also in the sense 'manage, control'): from Old French *demener* 'to lead,' based on Latin *de-* 'away' + *minare* 'drive (animals), drive on with threats' (from *minari* 'threaten').

de·mean·ing /di'mēniɴɢ/ ▶ **adj.** causing someone to lose their dignity and the respect of others: *the poster was not demeaning to women.*
– DERIVATIVES **de·mean·ing·ly** **adv.**

de·mean·or /di'mēnər/ (Brit. **demeanour**) ▶ **n.** outward behavior or bearing: *a quiet, somber demeanor.*
– ORIGIN late 15th cent.: from DEMEAN[2], probably influenced by obsolete *havour* 'behavior.'

de' Med·i·ci[1], Catherine, see CATHERINE DE MÉDICIS.

de' Med·i·ci[2], Cosimo, see COSIMO DE' MEDICI.

de' Med·i·ci[3], Giovanni, the name of Pope Leo X (see LEO[1]).

de' Med·i·ci[4], Lorenzo, see LORENZO DE' MEDICI.

de Méd·i·cis, Marie, see MARIE DE MÉDICIS.

de·ment /di'ment/ ▶ **n.** archaic a person suffering from dementia.
– ORIGIN late 15th cent. (as an adjective in the sense 'demented'): from French *dément* or Latin *demens, dement-* 'insane.' The noun use dates from the late 19th cent.

de·ment·ed /di'mentid/ ▶ **adj.** suffering from dementia. ■ informal driven to behave irrationally due to anger, distress, or excitement: *a demented, dangerous, and sadistic Mafioso.*
– DERIVATIVES **de·ment·ed·ly** **adv.**, **de·ment·ed·ness** **n.**
– ORIGIN mid 17th cent.: past participle of earlier *dement* 'drive mad,' from Old French *dementer* or late Latin *dementare,* from *demens* 'out of one's mind.'

dé·men·ti /,dāmän'tē/ ▶ **n.** an official denial of a published statement.
– ORIGIN French, from *démentir* 'contradict or accuse of lying.'

de·men·tia /di'mensнə/ ▶ **n.** Medicine a chronic or persistent disorder of the mental processes caused by brain disease or injury and marked by memory disorders, personality changes, and impaired reasoning.
– ORIGIN late 18th cent.: from Latin, from *demens, dement-* 'out of one's mind.'

de·men·tia prae·cox /di'mensнə 'prē,käks/ ▶ **n.** dated term for SCHIZOPHRENIA.
– ORIGIN late 18th cent. Latin, literally 'early insanity.'

Dem·e·ra·ra /,demə're(ə)rə, -'rärə/ a river in northern Guyana. Rising in the Guiana Highlands, it flows north for about 200 miles (320 km) to the Atlantic Ocean.

dem·e·ra·ra /,demə're(ə)rə, -'rärə/ ▶ **n. 1** (also **demerara sugar**) light brown cane sugar coming originally and chiefly from Guyana.
2 (also **demerara rum**) a dark rum fermented from molasses, made in Guyana.
– ORIGIN mid 19th cent.: named after the region of DEMERARA.

de·mer·it /di'merit/ ▶ **n. 1** a feature or fact deserving censure: *the merits and demerits of these proposals.*
2 a mark awarded against someone for a fault or offense.
– DERIVATIVES **de·mer·i·to·ri·ous** /-,meri'tôrēəs/ **adj.**
– ORIGIN late Middle English (also in the sense 'merit'): from Old French *desmerite* or Latin *demeritum* 'something deserved,' neuter past participle of *demereri,* from *de-* 'thoroughly' (also understood in medieval Latin as denoting reversal) + *mereri* 'to merit.'

Dem·e·rol /'demə,rôl, -,räl/ ▶ **n.** trademark for MEPERIDINE.
– ORIGIN 1940s: of unknown origin.

de·mer·sal /di'mərsəl/ ▶ **adj.** (typically of fish) living close to the floor of the sea or a lake. Often contrasted with PELAGIC.
– ORIGIN late 19th cent.: from Latin *demersus* (past participle of *demergere* 'submerge, sink,' from *de-* 'down' + *mergere* 'plunge') + -AL.

de·mesne /di'mān/ ▶ **n.** historical **1** land attached to a manor and retained for the owner's own use. ■ the lands of an estate. ■ archaic a region or domain: *she may one day queen it over that fair demesne.*
2 Law possession of real property in one's own right.
– PHRASES **held in demesne** (of an estate) occupied by the owner, not by tenants.
– ORIGIN Middle English: from Old French *demeine* (later Anglo-Norman French *demesne*) 'belonging to a lord,' from Latin *dominicus,* from *dominus* 'lord, master.' Compare with DOMAIN.

De·me·ter /di'mētər/ Greek Mythology the goddess of cereal grains, daughter of Cronus and Rhea and mother of Persephone. She is associated with Cybele; her symbol is typically an ear of wheat. The Eleusinian mysteries were held in honor of her. Roman equivalent CERES. See also PERSEPHONE.

demi- ▶ **prefix 1** half; half-size: *demisemiquaver* | *demitasse.*
2 partially; in an inferior degree: *demigod* | *demimonde.*
– ORIGIN via French from medieval Latin *dimedius* 'half,' from earlier *dimidius.*

de·mi·ca·rac·tère /,demē,karək'te(ə)r/ ▶ **n.** (pl. **same**) a style of ballet having elements of character dance but executed with steps based on the classical technique. ■ a dancer specializing in this type of dance.
– ORIGIN late 18th cent.: French, literally 'half character.'

de·mi-glace /'demē,glas/ (also **demi-glaze** /,glāz/) ▶ **n.** a rich, glossy brown sauce from which the liquid has been partly evaporated, typically flavored with wine and served with meat.
– ORIGIN early 20th cent.: French, literally 'half glaze.'

dem·i·god /'demē,gäd/ ▶ **n.** (fem. **demigoddess** /'demē,gädis/) a being with partial or lesser divine status, such as a minor deity, the offspring of a god and a mortal, or a mortal raised to divine rank. ■ a person who is greatly admired or feared.
– ORIGIN mid 16th cent.: translating Latin *semideus.*

dem·i·john /'demē,jän/ ▶ **n.** a bulbous, narrow-necked bottle holding from 3 to 10 gallons of liquid, typically enclosed in a wicker cover.
– ORIGIN mid 18th cent.: probably an alteration of French *dame-jeanne* 'Lady Jane,' by association with DEMI- 'half-sized' and the given name *John.*

de·mil·i·ta·rize /dē'militə,rīz/ ▶ **v.** [with obj.] (usu. as adj. **demilitarized**) remove all military forces from (an area): *a demilitarized zone.*
– DERIVATIVES **de·mil·i·ta·ri·za·tion** /-,militərə'zāsнən/ **n.**

De Mille /də 'mil/, Cecil B. (1881–1959), US movie producer and director, noted for his spectacular epics; full name *Cecil Blount De Mille.* He founded the Jesse L. Lasky Feature Play Company (later Paramount) with Samuel Goldwyn in 1913 and chose the then little-known Los Angeles suburb of Hollywood as a location for their first movie, *The Squaw Man* (1914). Other notable movies: *The Ten Commandments* (1923; remade 1956) and *Samson and Delilah* (1949).

de Mille /də 'mil/, Agnes George (1905–93), US dancer and choreographer; the niece of movie director Cecil B. De Mille. Her style of dancing mixed classical ballet with folk dance. She choreographed the ballet *Rodeo* (1942) and the Broadway musicals *Oklahoma!* (1943), *Brigadoon* (1947), *Gentlemen Prefer Blondes* (1949), and *Paint Your Wagon* (1951), among others.

dem·i·mon·daine /,demēmän'dān/ ▶ **n.** a woman considered to belong to the demimonde.
– ORIGIN late 19th cent.: from French *demi-mondaine,* literally 'woman of the demimonde.'

dem·i·monde /'demē,mänd/ ▶ **n.** (in 19th-century France) the class of women considered to be of doubtful morality and social standing. ■ a group of people considered to be on the fringes of respectable society: *the demimonde of arms deals.*
– ORIGIN mid 19th cent.: from French *demi-monde,* literally 'half-world.'

de·mine /dē'mīn/ ▶ **v.** [with obj.] remove explosive mines from: *the country would now move to demine the 41 sites.*
– DERIVATIVES **de·min·er** **n.**

de·min·er·al·ize /dē'minərə,līz/ ▶ **v.** [with obj.] (often as adj. **demineralized**) remove salts from (water). ■ deprive (teeth or bones) of minerals, causing loss of tooth enamel or softening of the skeleton.
– DERIVATIVES **de·min·er·al·i·za·tion** /-,minərələ'zāsнən/ **n.**

de min·i·mis /dā 'mini,mēs/ ▶ **adj.** too trivial or minor to merit consideration, esp. in law: *de minimis fringe benefit rules.*
– ORIGIN from Latin *de minimis non curat lex* 'the law is not concerned with trivial matters.'

de·mi·pen·sion /,demēpäɴ'syôɴ/ ▶ **n.** hotel accommodations with bed, breakfast, and one main meal per day.
– ORIGIN French, literally 'half board.'

dem·i·rep /'demē,rep/ ▶ **n.** archaic a woman whose chastity is considered doubtful.
– ORIGIN mid 18th cent.: abbreviation of *demi-reputable.*

de·mise /di'mīz/ ▶ **n.** [in sing.] **1** a person's death: *Mr. Grisenthwaite's tragic demise.* ■ the end or failure of an enterprise or institution: *the demise of industry.*
2 Law conveyance or transfer of property or a title by demising.
▶ **v.** [with obj.] Law convey or grant (an estate) by will or lease. ■ transmit (a sovereign's title) by death or abdication.
– ORIGIN late Middle English (as a legal term): from Anglo-Norman French, past participle (used as a noun) of Old French *desmettre* 'dismiss,' (in reflexive) 'abdicate,' based on Latin *dimittere* (see DISMISS).

dem·i-sec /'demē,sek/ ▶ **adj.** (of wine) medium dry.
– ORIGIN mid 20th cent.: French, literally 'half-dry.'

dem·i·sem·i·qua·ver /,demē'semī,kwāvər/ ▶ **n.** chiefly Brit. Music a thirty-second note.

de·mit /di'mit/ ▶ **v.** (**demits, demitting, demitted**) [with obj.] formal resign from (an office or position): *arguments within his congregation led to his demitting his post.*
– DERIVATIVES **de·mis·sion** /-'misнən/ **n.**
– ORIGIN early 16th cent. (in the sense 'dismiss'): from French *démettre,* from *dé-* 'away from' + *mettre* 'put.'

dem·i·tasse /'demē,täs, -,tas/ ▶ **n.** a small coffee cup.
– ORIGIN mid 19th cent.: from French, literally 'half-cup.'

dem·i·urge /'demē,ərj/ ▶ **n.** a being responsible for the creation of the universe, in particular: ■ (in Platonic philosophy) the Maker or Creator of the world. ■ (in Gnosticism and other theological systems) a heavenly being, subordinate to the Supreme Being, that is considered to be the controller of the material world and antagonistic to all that is purely spiritual.
– DERIVATIVES **dem·i·ur·gic** /,demē'ərjik/ **adj.**, **dem·i·ur·gi·cal** /,demē'ərjikəl/ **adj.**
– ORIGIN early 17th cent. (denoting a magistrate in certain ancient Greek states): via ecclesiastical Latin from Greek *dēmiourgos* 'craftsman,' from *dēmios* 'public' (from *dēmos* 'people') + *-ergos* 'working.'

dem·o /'demō/ informal ▶ **n.** (pl. **demos**) a demonstration of the capabilities of something, typically computer software or a musical group: [as modifier] *a demo tape.*
▶ **v.** (**demos, demoing, demoed**) [with obj.] demonstrate the capabilities of (software or equipment). ■ record (a song) for demonstration purposes: *they've already demoed twelve new songs.*

de·mob /dē'mäb/ Brit. informal ▶ **v.** (**demobs, demobbing, demobbed**) [with obj.] demobilize.
▶ **n.** demobilization: *we were waiting for our demob.*
– ORIGIN 1920s (following World War I): abbreviation.

PRONUNCIATION KEY ə *ago, up*; ər *over, fur*; a *hat*; ā *ate*; ä *car*; e *let*; ē *see*; i *fit*; ī *by*; ɴɢ *sing*; ō *go*; ô *law, for*; oi *toy*; o͝o *good*; o͞o *goo*; ou *out*; тн *thin*; т̲н̲ *then*; zн *vision*

de·mo·bi·lize /dēˈmōbəˌlīz/ ▶ **v.** [with obj.] (usu. **be demobilized**) take (troops) out of active service, typically at the end of a war: *he was demobilized in February 1946.* ■ [no obj.] cease military operations: *Germany demanded that they demobilize within twelve hours.*
– DERIVATIVES **de·mo·bi·li·za·tion** /-ˌmōbəliˈzāshən/ **n.**
– ORIGIN late 19th cent.: from French *démobiliser,* from *dé-* (expressing reversal) + *mobiliser* 'mobilize.'

de·moc·ra·cy /diˈmäkrəsē/ ▶ **n.** (pl. **democracies**) a system of government by the whole population or all the eligible members of a state, typically through elected representatives: *capitalism and democracy are ascendant in the third world.* ■ a state governed in such a way: *a multiparty democracy.* ■ control of an organization or group by the majority of its members: *the intended extension of industrial democracy.* ■ the practice or principles of social equality: *demands for greater democracy.*
– ORIGIN late 16th cent.: from French *démocratie,* via late Latin from Greek *dēmokratia,* from *dēmos* 'the people' + *-kratia* 'power, rule.'

dem·o·crat /ˈdeməˌkrat/ ▶ **n. 1** an advocate or supporter of democracy.
2 (**Democrat**) a member of the Democratic Party.
– ORIGIN late 18th cent. (originally denoting an opponent of the aristocrats in the French Revolution of 1790): from French *démocrate,* on the pattern of *aristocrate* 'aristocrat.'

dem·o·crat·ic /ˌdeməˈkratik/ ▶ **adj. 1** of, relating to, or supporting democracy or its principles: *democratic reforms | democratic government.* ■ favoring or characterized by social equality; egalitarian: *cycling is a democratic activity that can be enjoyed by anyone.*
2 (**Democratic**) of or relating to the Democratic Party.
– DERIVATIVES **dem·o·crat·i·cal·ly** /-ik(ə)lē/ **adv.**
– ORIGIN early 17th cent.: from French *démocratique,* via medieval Latin from Greek *dēmokratikos,* from *dēmokratia* (see DEMOCRACY).

dem·o·crat·ic cen·tral·ism ▶ **n.** the Leninist organizational system in which policy is decided centrally and is binding on all members.

Dem·o·crat·ic Par·ty one of the two main US political parties (the other being the Republican Party), which follows a liberal program, tending to promote a strong central government and expansive social programs.

Dem·o·crat·ic-Re·pub·li·can Par·ty a US political party that was founded in 1792 by Thomas Jefferson and was a forerunner of the modern Democratic Party.

Dem·o·crat·ic Re·pub·lic of the Con·go see CONGO, DEMOCRATIC REPUBLIC OF THE.

de·moc·ra·tize /diˈmäkrəˌtīz/ ▶ **v.** [with obj.] introduce a democratic system or democratic principles to: *public institutions need to be democratized.* ■ make (something) accessible to everyone: *mass production has not democratized fashion.*
– DERIVATIVES **de·moc·ra·ti·za·tion** /-ˌmäkrətəˈzāshən/ **n.**
– ORIGIN late 18th cent.: from French *démocratiser.*

De·moc·ri·tus /dəˈmäkritəs, dē-/ (*c.*460–*c.*370 BC), Greek philosopher. He developed the atomic theory originated by his teacher **Leucippus** that explained natural phenomena in terms of the arrangement and rearrangement of atoms moving in a void.

dé·mo·dé /ˌdāmōˈdā/ ▶ **adj.** out of fashion.
– ORIGIN French, past participle of *démoder* 'go out of fashion.'

de·mo·dec·tic mange /ˌdēməˈdektik ˈmānj/ ▶ **n.** a form of mange caused by follicle mites and tending to affect chiefly the head and foreparts. Compare with SARCOPTIC MANGE.
– ORIGIN late 19th cent.: *demodectic* from modern Latin *Demodex* (from Greek *dēmos* 'fat' + *dēx* 'woodworm') + -IC.

de·mod·u·late /dēˈmäjəˌlāt/ ▶ **v.** [with obj.] Electronics extract (a modulating signal) from its carrier. ■ separate a modulating signal from (its carrier).
– DERIVATIVES **de·mod·u·la·tion** /-ˌmäjəˈlāshən/ **n.**, **de·mod·u·la·tor** /-ˌlātər/ **n.**

dem·o·graph·ic /ˌdeməˈgrafik/ ▶ **adj.** relating to the structure of populations: *the demographic trend is toward an older population.*
▶ **n.** a particular sector of a population: *the drink is popular with a young demographic.*
– DERIVATIVES **dem·o·graph·i·cal adj.**, **dem·o·graph·i·cal·ly** /-ik(ə)lē/ **adv.**

dem·o·graph·ics /ˌdeməˈgrafiks/ ▶ **plural n.** statistical data relating to the population and particular groups within it: *the demographics of book buyers.*

de·mog·ra·phy /diˈmägrəfē/ ▶ **n.** the study of statistics such as births, deaths, income, or the incidence of disease, which illustrate the changing structure of human populations. ■ the composition of a particular human population: *Europe's demography is changing.*
– DERIVATIVES **de·mog·ra·pher** /-fər/ **n.**
– ORIGIN late 19th cent.: from Greek *dēmos* 'the people' + -GRAPHY.

de·moi /ˈdēmoi/ plural form of DEMOS.

dem·oi·selle /ˌdem(w)əˈzel/ ▶ **n. 1** (also **demoiselle crane**) a small, graceful Old World crane with a black head and breast and white ear tufts, breeding in southeastern Europe and central Asia. ● *Anthropoides virgo,* family Gruidae.
2 a damselfly, esp. of the genus *Agrion.*
3 a damselfish.
4 archaic or literary a young woman.
– ORIGIN early 16th cent. (sense 4): from French, from Old French *dameisele* 'damsel.'

de Moi·vre's the·o·rem /də ˈmwäv(rə)z/ Mathematics a theorem that states that $(\cos\theta + i\sin\theta)n = \cos n\theta + i\sin n\theta$, where i is the square root of -1.
– ORIGIN early 18th cent.: named after Abraham *de Moivre* (1667–1754) French-born English mathematician, fellow of the Royal Society.

de·mol·ish /diˈmälish/ ▶ **v.** [with obj.] pull or knock down (a building). ■ comprehensively refute (an argument or its proponent): *I looked forward keenly to demolishing my opponent.* ■ informal overwhelmingly defeat (a player or team): *they demolished the Denver Broncos, 55-10.* ■ humorous eat up (food) quickly: *we demolished the potato pancakes.*
– DERIVATIVES **de·mol·ish·er n.**
– ORIGIN mid 16th cent.: from French *démoliss-,* lengthened stem of *démolir,* from Latin *demoliri,* from *de-* (expressing reversal) + *moliri* 'construct' (from *moles* 'mass').

dem·o·li·tion /ˌdeməˈlishən/ ▶ **n.** the action or process of demolishing or being demolished: *the monument was saved from demolition.* ■ informal an overwhelming defeat.
– ORIGIN mid 16th cent.: via French from Latin *demolitio(n-),* from the verb *demoliri* (see DEMOLISH).

dem·o·li·tion der·by ▶ **n.** a competition in which typically older cars are driven into each other until only one is left running.

de·mon[1] /ˈdēmən/ ▶ **n. 1** an evil spirit or devil, esp. one thought to possess a person or act as a tormentor in hell. ■ a cruel, evil, or destructive person or thing: *I was a little demon, I can tell you.* ■ [often as modifier] a forceful, fierce, or skillful performer of a specified activity: *a friend of mine is a demon cook | a demon for work.* ■ reckless mischief; devilry: *his eyes are bursting with pure demon.*
2 another term for DAEMON[1] (sense 1).
– PHRASES **like a demon** in a very forceful, fierce, or skillful way: *he worked like a demon.*
– ORIGIN Middle English: from medieval Latin, from Latin *daemon,* from Greek *daimōn* 'deity, genius'; sense 1 also from Latin *daemonium* 'lesser or evil spirit,' from Greek *daemonion,* diminutive of *daimōn.*

de·mon[2] ▶ **n.** variant spelling of DAEMON[2].

de·mon·e·tize /dēˈmäniˌtīz/ ▶ **v.** [with obj.] (usu. **be demonetized**) deprive (a coin or precious metal) of its status as money.
– DERIVATIVES **de·mon·e·ti·za·tion** /-ˌmänitəˈzāshən/ **n.**
– ORIGIN mid 19th cent.: from French *démonétiser,* from *dé-* (expressing reversal) + Latin *moneta* 'money.'

de·mo·ni·ac /diˈmōnēˌak/ ▶ **adj.** of, like, or characteristic of a demon or demons: *a goddess with both divine and demoniac qualities | demoniac rage.*
▶ **n.** a person believed to be possessed by an evil spirit.
– DERIVATIVES **de·mo·ni·a·cal** /ˌdēməˈnīəkəl/ **adj.**, **de·mo·ni·a·cal·ly** /ˌdēməˈnīək(ə)lē/ **adv.**
– ORIGIN late Middle English: from Old French *demoniaque,* from ecclesiastical Latin *daemoniacus,* from *daemonium* 'lesser or evil spirit' (see DEMON[1]).

de·mon·ic /diˈmänik/ ▶ **adj.** of, resembling, or characteristic of demons or evil spirits: *demonic possession | her laughter was demonic.* ■ fiercely energetic or frenzied: *in a demonic hurry.*
– DERIVATIVES **de·mon·i·cal·ly** /-ik(ə)lē/ **adv.**
– ORIGIN mid 17th cent.: via late Latin from Greek *daimonikos,* from *daimōn* (see DEMON[1]).

de·mon·ism /ˈdēməˌnizəm/ ▶ **n. 1** belief in the power of demons.
2 action or behavior that seems too cruel or wicked to be human: *the demonism of warfare.*

de·mon·ize /ˈdēməˌnīz/ ▶ **v.** [with obj.] portray as wicked and threatening: *seeking to demonize one side in the conflict.*
– DERIVATIVES **de·mon·i·za·tion** /ˌdēməniˈzāshən/ **n.**

demono- ▶ **comb. form** of or relating to demons: *demonolatry.*
– ORIGIN from Greek *daimōn* 'demon.'

de·mon·ol·a·try /ˌdēməˈnälətrē/ ▶ **n.** the worship of demons.

de·mon·ol·o·gy /ˌdēməˈnäləjē/ ▶ **n.** the study of demons or of demonic belief.
– DERIVATIVES **de·mon·o·log·i·cal** /-nəˈläjikəl/ **adj.**, **de·mon·ol·o·gist** /-jist/ **n.**

de·mo·nop·o·lize /ˌdēməˈnäpəˌlīz/ ▶ **v.** [with obj.] introduce competition into (a market or economy) by privatizing previously nationalized assets.
– DERIVATIVES **de·mo·nop·o·li·za·tion** /-ˌnäpələˈzāshən/ **n.**

de·mon·stra·ble /diˈmänstrəbəl/ ▶ **adj.** clearly apparent or capable of being logically proved: *the demonstrable injustices of racism.*
– DERIVATIVES **de·mon·stra·bil·i·ty** /-ˌmänstrəˈbilitē/ **n.**
– ORIGIN late Middle English: from Latin *demonstrabilis,* from *demonstrare* 'point out.'

de·mon·stra·bly /diˈmänstrəblē/ ▶ **adv.** clearly and undeniably: *the situation is demonstrably unfair.*

dem·on·strate /ˈdemənˌstrāt/ ▶ **v. 1** [with obj.] clearly show the existence or truth of (something) by giving proof or evidence: *their shameful silence demonstrates their ineptitude.* ■ give a practical exhibition and explanation of (how a machine, skill, or craft works or is performed): *computerized design methods will be demonstrated* | [with clause] *he demonstrated how to make his favorite hotdog.* ■ show or express (a feeling or quality) by one's actions: *she began to demonstrate a new-found confidence.*
2 [no obj.] take part in a public demonstration: *thousands demonstrated in favor of the government.*
– ORIGIN mid 16th cent. (in the sense 'point out'): from Latin *demonstrat-* 'pointed out,' from the verb *demonstrare.*

dem·on·stra·tion /ˌdemənˈstrāshən/ ▶ **n. 1** the action or process of showing the existence or truth of something by giving proof or evidence: *it is not capable of mathematical demonstration | Lind's demonstration that citrus fruits cure scurvy.* ■ the outward showing of feeling: *physical demonstrations of affection.* ■ a practical exhibition and explanation of how something works or is performed: *a microwave cooking demonstration.*
2 a public meeting or march protesting against something or expressing views on a political issue.
– ORIGIN late Middle English (also in the senses 'proof provided by logic' and 'sign, indication'): from Latin *demonstratio(n-),* from *demonstrare* 'point out' (see DEMONSTRATE). Sense 2 dates from the mid 19th cent.

de·mon·stra·tive /diˈmänstrətiv/ ▶ **adj. 1** (of a person) tending to show feelings, esp. of affection, openly.
2 serving as conclusive evidence of something; giving proof: *demonstrative evidence.* ■ involving demonstration, esp. by scientific means: *the possibility of a demonstrative science of ethics.*
3 Grammar (of a determiner or pronoun) indicating the person or thing referred to (e.g., *this, that, those*).
▶ **n.** Grammar a demonstrative determiner or pronoun.
– DERIVATIVES **de·mon·stra·tive·ly adv.**, **de·mon·stra·tive·ness n.**
– ORIGIN late Middle English (in the senses 'serving as conclusive evidence of' and 'making manifest'): from Old French *demonstratif, -ive,* from Latin *demonstrativus,* from *demonstrare* 'point out' (see DEMONSTRATE).

de·mon·stra·tive leg·a·cy ▶ **n.** Law a legacy that is directed to be paid from a specified fund or pool.

dem·on·stra·tor /ˈdemənˌstrātər/ ▶ **n. 1** a person who takes part in a public protest meeting or march.
2 a person who shows how a particular piece of equipment works or how a skill or craft is performed. ■ a person who teaches in this way, esp. in a laboratory. ■ a piece of merchandise that can be tested by potential buyers.

de Mon·tes·pan /də ˌmôNtəˈspäN/, Marquise de, see MONTESPAN.

de Mont·fort /də ˈmäntfərt, -ˌfôrt/, Simon, see MONTFORT[1].

de·mor·al·ize /diˈmôrəˌlīz/ ▶ **v.** [with obj.] **1** cause (someone) to lose confidence or hope; dispirit: *their rejection of the treaty has demoralized the diplomatic community.*
2 archaic corrupt the morals of (someone).
– DERIVATIVES **de·mor·al·i·za·tion** /-ˌmôrələˈzāshən/ **n.**, **de·mor·al·iz·ing adj.**, **de·mor·al·iz·ing·ly adv.**
– ORIGIN late 18th cent.: from French *démoraliser* (a word of the French Revolution), from *dé-* (expressing reversal) + *moral* 'moral,' from Latin *moralis.*

de·mor·al·ized /diˈmôrəˌlīzd/ ▶ **adj.** having lost confidence or hope; disheartened: *a weak and demoralized president.*

de Mor·gan's laws /di ˈmôrgənz/ Mathematics two laws in Boolean algebra and set theory that state that AND and OR, or union and intersection, are dual. They are used to simplify the design of electronic circuits. ● The laws can be expressed in Boolean logic as: NOT (*a* AND *b*) = NOT *a* OR NOT *b*; NOT (*a* OR *b*) = NOT *a* AND NOT *b*.
– ORIGIN early 20th cent.: named after Augustus *de Morgan* (1806–71), English mathematician, but already known (by logicians) as principles in the Middle Ages.

de·mos /ˈdēmäs/ ▶ **n.** (pl. **demoi** /-moi/) the common people of an ancient Greek state. ■ the populace as a political unit, esp. in a democracy.
– ORIGIN from Greek *dēmos.*

De·mos·the·nes /dəˈmäsᴛʜəˌnēz/ (384–322 BC), Athenian orator and statesman. He is known for his political speeches on the need to resist the aggressive tendencies of Philip II of Macedon (the *Philippics*).

de·mote /diˈmōt/ ▶ **v.** [with obj.] give (someone) a lower rank or less senior position, usually as a punishment: *the head of the army was demoted to deputy defense secretary.*
– ORIGIN late 19th cent.: from **DE-** 'down' + a shortened form of **PROMOTE.**

de·mot·ic /diˈmätik/ ▶ **adj.** denoting or relating to the kind of language used by ordinary people; popular or colloquial: *a demotic idiom.* ■ relating to or denoting the form of modern Greek used in everyday speech and writing. Compare with **KATHAREVOUSA.** ■ relating to or denoting a simplified, cursive form of ancient Egyptian script, dating from *c.*650 BC and replaced by Greek in the Ptolemaic period. Compare with **HIERATIC.**
▶ **n.** ordinary colloquial speech. ■ demotic Greek. ■ demotic Egyptian script.
– ORIGIN early 19th cent. (in the sense 'relating to the Egyptian demotic'): from Greek *dēmotikos* 'popular,' from *dēmotēs* 'one of the people,' from *dēmos* 'the people.'

de·mo·tion /diˈmōsʜən/ ▶ **n.** reduction in rank or status: *too many demotions would weaken morale.*
– ORIGIN early 20th cent.: from **DEMOTE,** on the pattern of *promotion.*

de·mo·ti·vate ▶ **v.** [with obj.] make (someone) less eager to work or study: *some children disrupt classes and demotivate pupils.*
– DERIVATIVES **de·mo·tiv·a·tion n.**

de·mount·a·ble /dēˈmountəbəl/ ▶ **adj.** able to be dismantled or removed from its setting and readily reassembled or repositioned.
– DERIVATIVES **de·mount v.**

Demp·sey /ˈdem(p)sē/, Jack (1895–1983), US boxer; full name *William Harrison Dempsey.* He was world heavyweight champion 1919–26.

de·mul·cent /diˈməlsənt/ Medicine ▶ **adj.** (of a substance) relieving inflammation or irritation.
▶ **n.** a substance that relieves irritation of the mucous membranes in the mouth by forming a protective film.
– ORIGIN mid 18th cent.: from Latin *demulcent-* 'stroking caressingly,' from the verb *demulcere,* from *de-* 'away' + *mulcere* 'soothe.'

de·mur /diˈmər/ ▶ **v.** (**demurs, demurring, demurred**) [no obj.] raise doubts or objections or show reluctance: *normally she would have accepted the challenge, but she demurred.* ■ Law, dated put forward a demurrer.
▶ **n.** [usu. with negative] the action or process of objecting to or hesitating over something: *they accepted this ruling without demur.*
– ORIGIN Middle English (in the sense 'linger, delay'): from Old French *demourer* (verb), *demeure* (noun), based on Latin *de-* 'away, completely' + *morari* 'delay.'

de·mure /diˈmyo͝or/ ▶ **adj.** (**demurer, demurest**) (of a woman or her behavior) reserved, modest, and shy: *a demure little wife who sits at home minding the house.* ■ (of clothing) lending such an appearance.
– DERIVATIVES **de·mure·ly adv., de·mure·ness n.**
– ORIGIN late Middle English (in the sense 'sober, serious, reserved'): perhaps from Old French *demoure,* past participle of *demourer* 'remain, stay' (see **DEMUR**); influenced by Old French *mur* 'grave,' from Latin *maturus* 'ripe or mature.' The sense 'reserved, shy' dates from the late 17th cent.

de·mur·ra·ble /diˈmərəbəl, -ˈmə-rə-/ ▶ **adj.** dated, chiefly Law open to demurrer.

de·mur·rage /diˈmərij, -ˈmə-rij/ ▶ **n.** Law a charge payable to the owner of a chartered ship in respect of failure to load or discharge the ship within the time agreed.
– ORIGIN mid 17th cent. (also in the general sense 'procrastination, delay'): from Old French *demourage,* from the verb *demourer* (see **DEMUR**).

de·mur·ral /diˈmərəl, -ˈmə-rəl/ ▶ **n.** the action of demurring: *words of demurral.*

de·mur·rer /diˈmərər, -ˈmə-rər/ ▶ **n.** an objection. ■ Law, dated an objection that an opponent's point is irrelevant or invalid, while granting the factual basis of the point: ***on demurrer*** *it was held that the plaintiff's claim succeeded.*
– ORIGIN early 16th cent.: from Anglo-Norman French (infinitive used as a noun), from Old French *demourer* 'remain, stay' (see **DEMUR**).

de·mu·tu·al·ize /dēˈmyo͞ocʜo͞oəˌlīz/ ▶ **v.** [with obj.] change (a mutual organization such as a savings and loan association) to one of a different kind.
– DERIVATIVES **de·mu·tu·al·i·za·tion** /-ˌmyo͞ocʜo͞oəliˈzāsʜən/ **n.**

de·my /diˈmī/ (in full **metric demy**) ▶ **n.** a paper size, now standardized at 564 × 444 mm. ■ (in full **demy octavo**) a book size, now standardized at 216 × 138 mm. ■ (in full **demy quarto**) a book size, now standardized at 276 × 219 mm.
– ORIGIN late Middle English (as an adjective in the sense 'half-sized'): from **DEMI-,** or from its source, French *demi* 'half.'

de·my·e·li·nate /dēˈmīələˌnāt/ ▶ **v.** [with obj.] (usu. as adj. **demyelinating**) Medicine cause the loss or destruction of myelin in (nerve tissue): *a chronic demyelinating disease.*
– DERIVATIVES **de·my·e·li·na·tion** /-ˌmīəliˈnāsʜən/ **n.**

de·mys·ti·fy /dēˈmistəˌfī/ ▶ **v.** (**demystifies, demystifying, demystified**) [with obj.] make (a difficult or esoteric subject) clearer and easier to understand: *this book attempts to demystify technology.*
– DERIVATIVES **de·mys·ti·fi·ca·tion** /-ˌmistəfiˈkāsʜən/ **n.**

de·my·thol·o·gize /ˌdēmiˈᴛʜäləˌjīz/ ▶ **v.** [with obj.] reinterpret (a subject or text) so that it is free of mythical or heroic elements: *he undertakes to demythologize the man who has been for many the modern counterpart of St. Augustine.* ■ reinterpret what are considered to be mythological elements of (the Bible).

den /den/ ▶ **n.** a wild animal's lair or habitation. ■ informal a small, comfortable room in a house where a person can pursue an activity in private. ■ a place where people meet in secret, typically to engage in some illicit activity: *an opium den | a den of iniquity.* ■ a small subdivision of a Cub Scout pack.
▶ **v.** (**dens, denning, denned**) [no obj.] (of a wild animal) live in or retreat to a den: *the cubs denned in the late autumn.*
– ORIGIN Old English *denn,* of Germanic origin; related to German *Tenne* 'threshing floor,' also to **DENE**[1].

De·na·li /dəˈnälē/ another name for Mount McKinley (see **MCKINLEY, MOUNT**).

de·nar /diˈnär/ ▶ **n.** the basic monetary unit of the former Yugoslav Republic of Macedonia.
– ORIGIN based on Latin *denarius*; compare with **DINAR.**

de·nar·i·us /diˈne(ə)rēəs/ ▶ **n.** (pl. **denarii** /-ˈne(ə)rēˌī/) an ancient Roman silver coin, originally worth ten asses. ■ a unit of weight equal to that of a silver denarius. ■ an ancient Roman gold coin worth 25 silver denarii.
– ORIGIN late Middle English: Latin, literally 'containing ten,' from the phrase *denarius nummus* 'coin worth ten asses' (see **AS**[2]), from *deni* 'in tens,' from *decem* 'ten.'

den·a·ry /ˈdenərē, ˈdē-/ ▶ **adj.** relating to or based on the number ten; less common term for **DECIMAL:** *denary numbers.*
– ORIGIN mid 19th cent.: from Latin *denarius* 'containing ten' (see **DENARIUS**).

de·na·tion·al·ize /dēˈnasʜənlˌīz/ ▶ **v.** [with obj.] **1** transfer (a nationalized industry or institution) from public to private ownership.
2 deprive (a country or person) of nationality or national characteristics.
– DERIVATIVES **de·na·tion·al·i·za·tion** /-ˌnasʜənləˈzāsʜən/ **n.**
– ORIGIN early 19th cent. (sense 2): from French *dénationaliser* (a word of the French Revolution), from *dé-* (expressing reversal) + *nationaliser* 'nationalize.'

de·nat·u·ral·ize /dēˈnacʜərəˌlīz/ ▶ **v.** [with obj.] **1** make (something) unnatural.
2 deprive (someone) of citizenship of a country.
– DERIVATIVES **de·nat·u·ral·i·za·tion** /-ˌnacʜərələˈzāsʜən/ **n.**

de·na·tur·ant /dēˈnācʜərənt/ ▶ **n.** a substance added to alcohol to make it unfit for drinking. ■ Biochemistry a substance that causes denaturation of proteins or other biological compounds.

de·na·ture /dēˈnācʜər/ ▶ **v.** [with obj.] (often as adj. **denatured**) take away or alter the natural qualities of: *empty verbalisms and denatured ceremonies.* ■ make (alcohol) unfit for drinking by the addition of toxic or foul-tasting substances. ■ Biochemistry destroy the characteristic properties of (a protein or other biological macromolecule) by heat, acidity, or other effects that disrupt its molecular conformation. ■ [no obj.] (of a substance) undergo this process.
– DERIVATIVES **de·na·tur·a·tion** /dēˌnācʜəˈrāsʜən/ **n.**
– ORIGIN late 17th cent. (in the sense 'make unnatural'): from French *dénaturer,* from *dé-* (expressing reversal) + *nature* 'nature.'

de·na·zi·fi·ca·tion /dēˌnätsəfiˈkāsʜən/ ▶ **n.** the process of bringing the leaders of the National Socialist regime in Germany to justice and of purging all elements of Nazism from public life, carried out esp. between 1945 and 1948.

de·na·zi·fy /dēˈnätsəˌfī/ ▶ **v.** (**denazifies, denazifying, denazified**) [with obj.] remove the Nazi (or figuratively, the fascist or repressive) influence from.

den·dri·form /ˈdendrəˌfôrm/ ▶ **adj.** having the shape or form of a tree.

den·dri·mer /ˈdendrəmər/ ▶ **n.** a synthetic polymer with a branching, treelike structure.
– ORIGIN 1990s: from Greek *dendron* 'tree' + *-i-* + *-mer.*

den·drite /ˈdendrīt/ ▶ **n. 1** Physiology a short branched extension of a nerve cell, along which impulses received from other cells at synapses are transmitted to the cell body. Compare with **AXON.**
2 a crystal or crystalline mass with a branching, treelike structure. ■ a natural treelike or mosslike marking on a piece of rock or mineral.

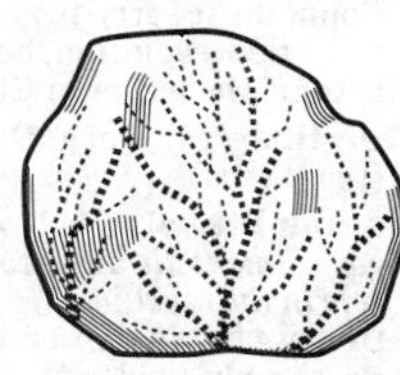
dendrite 2

– ORIGIN early 18th cent.: from French, from Greek *dendritēs* 'treelike,' from *dendron* 'tree.'

den·drit·ic /denˈdritik/ ▶ **adj.** technical having a branched form resembling a tree. ■ Physiology of or relating to a dendrite or dendrites. ■ (of a solid) consisting of crystalline dendrites: *dendritic salt.*
– DERIVATIVES **den·drit·i·cal·ly** /-ik(ə)lē/ **adv.**

dendro- ▶ **comb. form** of or relating to a tree or trees: *dendrology.*
– ORIGIN from Greek *dendron* 'tree.'

den·dro·chro·nol·o·gy /ˌdendrōkrəˈnäləjē/ ▶ **n.** the science or technique of dating events, environmental change, and archaeological artifacts by using the characteristic patterns of annual growth rings in timber and tree trunks.
– DERIVATIVES **den·dro·chron·o·log·i·cal** /-ˌkränlˈäjikəl/ **adj., den·dro·chro·nol·o·gist** /-jist/ **n.**

den·dro·gram /ˈdendrəˌgram/ ▶ **n.** a tree diagram, esp. one showing taxonomic relationships.

den·droid /ˈdendroid/ ▶ **adj.** Biology (of a plant, marine invertebrate, or structure) tree-shaped; arborescent; branching. ■ Paleontology denoting graptolites of a type that formed many-branched colonies, found chiefly in strata from the Ordovician and Silurian periods.
▶ **n.** Paleontology a graptolite of this type. ● Order Dendroidea, class Graptolithina.
– ORIGIN mid 19th cent.: from **DENDRO-** 'tree' + **-OID.**

den·drol·o·gy /denˈdräləjē/ ▶ **n.** the scientific study of trees.
– DERIVATIVES **den·dro·log·i·cal** /ˌdendrəˈläjikəl/ **adj., den·drol·o·gist** /-jist/ **n.**

den·dron /ˈdendrän/ ▶ **n.** another term for **DENDRITE** (sense 1).
– ORIGIN late 19th cent.: from **DENDRITE,** on the pattern of words such as *axon.*

De·ne /diˈnā/ ▶ **n.** (pl. **same**) **1** a member of a group of American Indian peoples of the Canadian Northwest and Alaska, traditionally speaking Athabaskan languages, and having collective representation in Canadian political life.
2 any of the languages of these peoples.
▶ **adj.** of or relating to these peoples or their languages.
– ORIGIN from French *Déné,* from an Athabaskan word meaning 'people.'

dene[1] /dēn/ (also **dean**) ▶ **n.** Brit. (usu. in place names) a vale, esp. the deep, narrow, wooded valley of a small river: *Rottingdean | Deepdene.*

– ORIGIN Old English *denu*, of Germanic origin; related to **DEN**.

dene² ▶ **n.** dialect a bare, sandy tract or low dune by the sea.
– ORIGIN Middle English: perhaps of Germanic origin and related to **DUNE**.

Den·eb /ˈdenˌeb/ Astronomy the brightest star in the constellation Cygnus, a yellow supergiant.
– ORIGIN from Arabic, literally 'tail' (i.e., of the "swan").

De·neb·o·la /dəˈnebələ/ Astronomy the second brightest star in the constellation Leo.
– ORIGIN from Arabic *dhanab al(-asad)* '(lion's) tail.'

d

de·ner·vate /dēˈnərvāt/ ▶ **v.** [with obj.] Medicine remove or cut off the nerve supply from (an organ or other body part): (as adj. **denervated**) *the denervated muscle fibers.*
– DERIVATIVES **de·ner·va·tion** /ˌdēnərˈvāSHən/ **n.**

den·gue /ˈdeNGgē, -gā/ (also **dengue fever**) ▶ **n.** a debilitating viral disease of the tropics, transmitted by mosquitoes, and causing sudden fever and acute pains in the joints.
– ORIGIN early 19th cent.: from West Indian Spanish, from Kiswahili *dinga* (in full *kidingapopo*), influenced by Spanish *dengue* 'fastidiousness' (with reference to the dislike of movement by affected patients).

Deng Xiao·ping /ˈdəNG ˈSHouˈpiNG/ (also **Teng Hsiao-p'ing**) (1904–97), Chinese communist statesman; vice-premier 1973–76 and 1977–80; vice-chairman of the Central Committee of the Chinese Communist Party 1977–80. Discredited during the Cultural Revolution, he was reinstated in 1977 and became the leader of China.

Den Haag /den ˈhäg/ Dutch name for The Hague (see **HAGUE**).

de·ni·a·ble /diˈnīəbəl/ ▶ **adj.** able to be denied: *the government did agree to play a limited and deniable role in the rebellion.*
– DERIVATIVES **de·ni·a·bil·i·ty** /-ˌnīəˈbilitē/ **n.**, **de·ni·a·bly** /-blē/ **adv.**

de·ni·al /diˈnīəl/ ▶ **n.** the action of declaring something to be untrue: *she shook her head in* ***denial.*** ■ the refusal of something requested or desired: *the denial of insurance to people with certain medical conditions.* ■ a statement that something is not true: *official denials | his* ***denial that*** *he was having an affair.* ■ Psychology failure to acknowledge an unacceptable truth or emotion or to admit it into consciousness, used as a defense mechanism: *you're living* ***in denial.*** ■ short for **SELF-DENIAL**. ■ disavowal of a person as one's leader.

> **WORD TRENDS** In 1991, the British historian David Irving was convicted in Germany of Holocaust **denial**—claiming that the mass murder of the Jews and other groups by the Nazis in World War II never happened. In 2006, he was imprisoned on a similar charge in Austria. *Holocaust denial* is not a crime under US or UK law, but in the 21st century, it is often considered taboo to deny the truth of certain concepts. After *Holocaust*, the most common modifiers of **denier** in the Oxford English Corpus reflect some highly contentious issues: *climate change, evolution,* and *global warming*. Refusal to acknowledge the existence of certain things is now seen as so dangerous that some green activists have called for *climate change denial* to be made illegal.

de·ni·al of ser·vice ▶ **n.** (abbr.: **DoS**) Computing an interruption in an authorized user's access to a computer network, typically one caused with malicious intent.

de·ni·er¹ ▶ **n. 1** /dəˈni(ə)r, ˈdenyər/ a unit of weight by which the fineness of silk, rayon, or nylon yarn is measured, equal to the weight in grams of 9000 meters of the yarn and often used to describe the thickness of hosiery: *840 denier nylon.*
2 /dəˈni(ə)r, dənˈyā/ historical a French coin, equal to one twelfth of a sou, which was withdrawn from use in the 19th century.
– ORIGIN late Middle English: via Old French from Latin *denarius* (see **DENARIUS**). Sense 1 dates from the mid 19th cent.

de·ni·er² /diˈnīər/ ▶ **n.** a person who denies something: *a prominent denier of global warming.*

den·i·grate /ˈdeniˌgrāt/ ▶ **v.** [with obj.] criticize unfairly; disparage: *there is a tendency to denigrate the poor.*
– DERIVATIVES **den·i·gra·tion** /ˌdeniˈgrāSHən/ **n.**, **den·i·gra·tor** /-ˌgrātər/ **n.**, **den·i·gra·to·ry** /-grəˌtôrē/ **adj.**
– ORIGIN late Middle English (in the sense 'blacken, make dark'): from Latin *denigrat-* 'blackened,' from the verb *denigrare*, from *de-* 'away, completely' + *nigrare* (from *niger* 'black').

den·im /ˈdenəm/ ▶ **n.** a sturdy cotton twill fabric, typically blue, used for jeans, overalls, and other clothing. ■ (**denims**) clothing made of such fabric: *a pair of denims.*
– ORIGIN late 17th cent. (as *serge denim*): from French *serge de Nimes*, denoting a kind of serge from the manufacturing town of **NîMES**.

De Ni·ro /də ˈni(ə)rō/, Robert (1943–), US actor. Notable movies: *Bang the Drum Slowly* (1973), *The Godfather Part II* (1974), *Taxi Driver* (1976), *Raging Bull* (1980), *A Bronx Tale* (1993; also directed), and *Meet the Fockers* (2004).

Robert De Niro

Den·is, St. /ˈdenis, dəˈnē/ (also **Denys**) (died c.250), French bishop; born in Italy; patron saint of France; Roman name *Dionysius*. According to tradition, he was one of a group of seven missionaries sent from Rome to convert Gaul; he became bishop of Paris and was martyred in the reign of the emperor Valerian. Feast day, October 9.

de·ni·tri·fy /dēˈnītrəˌfī/ ▶ **v.** (**denitrifies, denitrifying, denitrified**) [with obj.] (chiefly of bacteria) remove the nitrates or nitrites from (soil, air, or water) by chemical reduction.
– DERIVATIVES **de·ni·tri·fi·ca·tion** /-ˌnītrəfiˈkāSHən/ **n.**

den·i·zen /ˈdenəzən/ ▶ **n.** formal or humorous an inhabitant or occupant of a particular place: *denizens of field and forest.* ■ Brit. historical a foreigner allowed certain rights in the adopted country.
– DERIVATIVES **den·i·zen·ship** /-ˌSHip/ **n.**
– ORIGIN late Middle English *deynseyn*, via Anglo-Norman French from Old French *deinz* 'within' (from Latin *de* 'from' + *intus* 'within') + *-ein* (from Latin *-aneus* '-aneous'). The change in the form of the word was due to association with **CITIZEN**.

De·niz·li /ˌdenizˈlē/ a commercial city in southwestern Turkey, the site of ancient ruins; pop. 323,200 (est. 2007).

Den·mark /ˈdenˌmärk/ a country in northwestern Europe, on the Jutland peninsula and many islands, between the North and the Baltic seas; pop. 5,500,500 (est. 2009); capital, Copenhagen; official language, Danish. Danish name **DANMARK**.

> Denmark emerged as a separate country during the Viking period of the 10th and 11th centuries. In the 14th century Denmark and Norway were united under a Danish king; the union was joined between the late 1300s and 1523 by Sweden, and Norway was ceded to Sweden in 1814. Although neutral, Denmark was occupied by Germany for much of World War II. It joined the EC (now the EU) in 1973.

den moth·er ▶ **n.** the female leader of a den of Cub Scouts.

de·nom·i·nal /dēˈnämənl/ ▶ **adj.** [attrib.] (of a word) derived from a noun.
▶ **n.** a verb or other word that is derived from a noun.
– ORIGIN 1930s: from **DE-** + **NOMINAL**.

de·nom·i·nate /diˈnäməˌnāt/ ▶ **v. 1** (**be denominated**) (of sums of money) be expressed in a specified monetary unit: *the borrowings were* ***denominated in*** *U.S. dollars.*
2 [with obj. and complement] formal call; name: *the whole train was denominated a "bull-outfit."*
– ORIGIN late Middle English (in the sense 'give a name to'): from Latin *denominat-* 'named,' from the verb *denominare*, from *de-* 'away, formally' + *nominare* 'to name' (from *nomen, nomin-* 'name'). Sense 1 dates from the mid 20th cent.

de·nom·i·na·tion /diˌnäməˈnāSHən/ ▶ **n. 1** a recognized autonomous branch of the Christian Church. ■ a group or branch of any religion: *Jewish clergy of all denominations.*
2 the face value of a banknote, coin, or postage stamp: *a hundred dollars or so, in small denominations.* ■ the rank of a playing card within a suit, or of a suit relative to others: *two cards of the same denomination.*
3 formal a name or designation, esp. one serving to classify a set of things. ■ the action of naming or classifying something: *denomination of oneself as a fat woman.*
– ORIGIN late Middle English (sense 3): from Latin *denominatio(n-)*, from the verb *denominare* (see **DENOMINATE**). Sense 1 dates from the mid 17th cent.

de·nom·i·na·tion·al /diˌnäməˈnāSHənl/ ▶ **adj.** relating to or according to the principles of a particular religious denomination: *denominational relief agencies.*
– DERIVATIVES **de·nom·i·na·tion·al·ism** /-ˌizəm/ **n.**

de·nom·i·na·tive /diˈnäməˌnātiv, -nətiv/ ▶ **adj.** old-fashioned term for **DENOMINAL**.
– ORIGIN late 16th cent. (as a noun in the grammatical sense): from late Latin *denominativus*, from *denominat-* 'named,' from the verb *denominare* (see **DENOMINATE**).

de·nom·i·na·tor /diˈnäməˌnātər/ ▶ **n.** Mathematics the number below the line in a common fraction; a divisor. ■ a figure representing the total population in terms of which statistical values are expressed.
– ORIGIN mid 16th cent.: from French *dénominateur* or medieval Latin *denominator*, from *denominare* 'to name' (see **DENOMINATE**).

de·no·ta·tion /ˌdēnōˈtāSHən/ ▶ **n.** the literal or primary meaning of a word, in contrast to the feelings or ideas that the word suggests: *beyond their immediate denotation, the words have a connotative power.* ■ the action or process of indicating or referring to something by means of a word, symbol, etc. ■ Philosophy the object or concept to which a term refers, or the set of objects of which a predicate is true. Often contrasted with **CONNOTATION**.
– DERIVATIVES **de·no·ta·tion·al** /-SHənl/ **adj.**

de·note /diˈnōt/ ▶ **v.** [with obj.] be a sign of; indicate: *this mark denotes purity and quality.* ■ stand as a name or symbol for: *the level of output per firm, denoted by X.*
– DERIVATIVES **de·no·ta·tive** /ˈdēnōˌtātiv, diˈnōtətiv/ **adj.**
– ORIGIN late 16th cent. (in the sense 'be a sign of, mark out'): from French *dénoter* or Latin *denotare*, from *de-* 'away, thoroughly' + *notare* 'observe, note' (from *nota* 'a mark').

> **USAGE** For an explanation of the difference between **denote** and **connote**, see usage at **CONNOTE**.

de·noue·ment /ˌdānōōˈmäN/ ▶ **n.** the final part of a play, movie, or narrative in which the strands of the plot are drawn together and matters are explained or resolved. ■ the climax of a chain of events, usually when something is decided or made clear: *I waited by the eighteenth green to see the denouement.*
– ORIGIN mid 18th cent.: French *dénouement*, from *dénouer* 'unknot.'

de·nounce /diˈnouns/ ▶ **v.** [with obj.] publicly declare to be wrong or evil: *the Assembly denounced the use of violence | he was widely* ***denounced as*** *a traitor.* ■ inform against: *some of his own priests denounced him to the King for heresy.*
– DERIVATIVES **de·nounce·ment n.**, **de·nounc·er n.**
– ORIGIN Middle English (originally in the sense 'proclaim, announce,' also 'proclaim someone to be wicked, cursed, a rebel, etc'): from Old French *denoncier*, from Latin *denuntiare* 'give official information,' based on *nuntius* 'messenger.'

de nou·veau /ˌdə nōōˈvō/ ▶ **adv.** archaic starting again from the beginning; anew.
– ORIGIN late 18th cent.: French, literally 'from new.'

de no·vo /dā ˈnōvō, di/ ▶ **adv. & adj.** starting from the beginning; anew: [as adv.] *in a pure meritocracy, everyone must begin de novo* | [as adj.] *a general strategy for de novo protein design.*
– ORIGIN early 17th cent.: Latin, literally 'from new.'

Den·pa·sar /denˈpäˌsär/ the chief city of the island of Bali in Indonesia, a seaport on the southern coast; pop. 424,300 (est. 2009).

dense /dens/ ▶ **adj. 1** closely compacted in substance: *dense volcanic rock | swirling, dense smoke.* ■ having the constituent parts crowded closely together: *an estuary dense with marine life.*
2 informal (of a person) stupid.
3 (of a text) hard to understand because of complexity of ideas.
– DERIVATIVES **dense·ly adv.**, **dense·ness n.**
– ORIGIN late Middle English: from Latin *densus*.

den·si·fy /ˈdensəˌfī/ ▶ **v.** (**densifies, densifying, densified**) [with obj.] (often as adj. **densified**) make (something) more dense: *densified hardboard.*
– DERIVATIVES **den·si·fi·ca·tion** /ˌdensəfiˈkāSHən/ **n.**

den·sim·e·ter /denˈsimitər/ ▶ **n.** an instrument for measuring density, esp. of liquids.
– ORIGIN mid 19th cent.: from Latin *densus* 'dense' + **-METER**.

den·si·tom·e·ter /ˌdensiˈtämitər/ ▶ **n. 1** a device for measuring the density of a material.
2 an instrument for measuring the photographic density of an image on a film or photographic print.

– DERIVATIVES **den·si·to·met·ric** /-sitəˈmetrik/ **adj.**, **den·si·to·met·ri·cal·ly** /-sitəˈmetrik(ə)lē/ **adv.**, **den·si·tom·e·try** /-ˈtämətrē/ **n.**

den·si·ty /ˈdensitē/ ▶ **n.** (pl. **densities**) the degree of compactness of a substance: *a reduction in bone density.* ■ Computing a measure of the amount of information on a storage medium (tape or disk). For magnetic tape it is the amount of information recorded per unit length of tape (bits per inch or millimeter); for a disk, a fixed number of bits per sector, sectors per track, and tracks per disk: *chip density doubles every eighteen months* | [as modifier, in combination] *a **low-density** 5.25-inch floppy disk* | *a drive capable of handling **high-density** 1.44 megabyte disks.* ■ Physics degree of consistency measured by the quantity of mass per unit volume. ■ the opacity of a photographic image. ■ the quantity of people or things in a given area or space: *areas of low population density* | *a density of 10,000 per square mile.*
– ORIGIN early 17th cent.: from French *densité* or Latin *densitas*, from *densus* 'dense.'

den·si·ty func·tion ▶ **n.** short for PROBABILITY DENSITY FUNCTION.

dent /dent/ ▶ **n.** a slight hollow in a hard, even surface made by a blow or by the exertion of pressure. ■ a diminishing effect; a reduction: *a dent in profits.*
▶ **v.** [with obj.] mark with a dent: *the moose dropped a hind foot and dented the hood of the car.* ■ have an adverse effect on; diminish: *this neither deterred him nor dented his enthusiasm.*
– ORIGIN Middle English (as a noun designating a blow with a weapon): variant of DINT.

dent. ▶ **abbr.** ■ dental. ■ dentist. ■ dentistry.

den·tal /ˈdentl/ ▶ **adj. 1** [attrib.] of or relating to the teeth: *dental health.* ■ (abbr.: **dent.**) of or relating to dentistry: *dental councils.*
2 Phonetics (of a consonant) pronounced with the tip of the tongue against the upper front teeth (as *th*) or the alveolar ridge (as *n, d, t*).
▶ **n.** Phonetics a dental consonant.
– DERIVATIVES **den·tal·ize** /ˈdentlˌīz/ **v.** (Phonetics), **den·tal·ly** **adv.**
– ORIGIN late 16th cent.: from late Latin *dentalis*, from Latin *dens, dent-* 'tooth.'

den·tal dam ▶ **n.** a thin sheet of latex used by dentists to isolate a tooth being worked on, or as a prophylactic device during cunnilingus and anilingus.

den·tal floss ▶ **n.** a soft thread of floss silk or similar material used to clean between the teeth.

den·tal for·mu·la ▶ **n.** Zoology a formula expressing the number and kinds of teeth possessed by a mammal. A dental formula is usually written in the form of four "fractions," one for each type of tooth, with the upper and lower lines describing the upper and lower jaws respectively.

den·tal hy·gien·ist ▶ **n.** an ancillary dental worker specializing in scaling and polishing teeth and in giving advice on cleaning the teeth.
– DERIVATIVES **den·tal hy·giene** **n.**

den·ta·li·um /denˈtālēəm/ ▶ **n.** tooth shells used as ornaments or as a form of currency: *a white mare purchased with dentalium.*
– ORIGIN modern Latin, from late Latin *dentalis* (see DENTAL).

den·tal nurse ▶ **n.** a nurse who assists a dentist.

den·tal sur·geon ▶ **n.** a dentist.

den·tal tech·ni·cian ▶ **n.** a person who makes and repairs artificial teeth.

den·ta·ry /ˈdentərē/ ▶ **n.** (pl. **dentaries**) Zoology the anterior bone of the lower jaw, which bears the teeth. In mammals it forms the whole of the lower jaw (or mandible).
– ORIGIN mid 19th cent.: from late Latin *dentarius*, from Latin *dens, dent-* 'tooth.'

den·tate /ˈdenˌtāt/ ▶ **adj.** Botany & Zoology having a toothlike or serrated edge.
– ORIGIN late Middle English: from Latin *dentatus*, from *dens, dent-* 'tooth.'

den·telle /denˈtel/ ▶ **n.** (pl. or pronunc. **same**) ornamental tooling used in bookbinding, resembling lace edging.
– ORIGIN mid 19th cent.: from French, 'lace,' from *dent* 'tooth' + the diminutive suffix *-elle*.

den·tex /ˈdenˌteks/ ▶ **n.** (pl. **same** or **dentexes**) any of various sea breams of the genus *Dentex*, esp. *D. dentex* of the Mediterranean and the North African Atlantic coast. Many are important food fishes.
– ORIGIN modern Latin (genus name), from Latin.

den·ti·cle /ˈdentikəl/ ▶ **n.** Zoology a small tooth or toothlike projection.
– ORIGIN late Middle English (denoting a pointer on an astrolabe): from Latin *denticulus*, diminutive of *dens, dent-* 'tooth.'

den·tic·u·late /denˈtikyəlit/ ▶ **adj.** having small teeth or toothlike projections; finely toothed.
– DERIVATIVES **den·tic·u·lat·ed** /-ˌlātid/ **adj.**
– ORIGIN mid 17th cent.: from Latin *denticulatus*, from *denticulus* 'small tooth' (see DENTICLE).

den·ti·frice /ˈdentəfris/ ▶ **n.** a paste or powder for cleaning the teeth.
– ORIGIN late Middle English: from French, from Latin *dentifricium*, from *dens, dent-* 'tooth' + *fricare* 'to rub.'

den·til /ˈdentl, -til/ ▶ **n.** [often as modifier] (in classical architecture) one of a number of small, rectangular blocks resembling teeth and used as a decoration under the soffit of a cornice: *a dentil frieze.*
– ORIGIN late 16th cent.: from Italian *dentello* or obsolete French *dentille*, diminutive of *dent* 'tooth,' from Latin *dens, dent-*.

den·ti·lin·gual /ˌdentəˈliNGgwəl/ ▶ **adj.** Phonetics (of a consonant) pronounced with the teeth and the tongue; dental.
– ORIGIN late 19th cent.: from Latin *dens, dent-* 'tooth' + LINGUAL.

den·tin /ˈdentn, -tin/ (also **dentine** /ˈdenˌtēn/) ▶ **n.** hard, dense, bony tissue forming the bulk of a tooth beneath the enamel.
– DERIVATIVES **den·tin·al** /ˈdentn-əl/ **adj.**
– ORIGIN mid 19th cent.: from Latin *dens, dent-* 'tooth' + -IN[1].

den·tist /ˈdentist/ ▶ **n.** a person qualified to treat the diseases and conditions that affect the teeth and gums, esp. the repair and extraction of teeth and the insertion of artificial ones.
– DERIVATIVES **den·tist·ry** /-strē/ **n.**
– ORIGIN mid 18th cent.: from French *dentiste*, from *dent* 'tooth,' from Latin *dens, dent-*.

den·ti·tion /denˈtisHən/ ▶ **n.** the arrangement or condition of the teeth in a particular species or individual.
– ORIGIN late 16th cent. (denoting the process of developing of teeth): from Latin *dentitio(n-)*, from *dentire* 'teethe,' from *dens, dent-* 'tooth.'

Den·ton /ˈdentn/ a commercial city in northeastern Texas; pop. 119,454 (est. 2008).

den·ture /ˈdencHər/ ▶ **n.** (usu. **dentures**) a removable plate or frame holding one or more artificial teeth.
– ORIGIN late 19th cent.: from French, from *dent* 'tooth,' from Latin *dens, dent-*.

den·tur·ist /ˈdencHərist/ ▶ **n.** a person who makes dentures.

de·nu·cle·ar·ize /dēˈn(y)o͞oklēəˌrīz/ ▶ **v.** [with obj.] remove nuclear weapons from.
– DERIVATIVES **de·nu·cle·ar·i·za·tion** /-ˌn(y)o͞oklēərəˈzāsHən/ **n.**

de·nude /diˈn(y)o͞od/ ▶ **v.** [with obj.] strip (something) of its covering, possessions, or assets; make bare: *almost overnight the Arctic was **denuded of** animals.*
– DERIVATIVES **den·u·da·tion** /ˌden(y)o͞oˈdāsHən/ **n.**
– ORIGIN late Middle English: from Latin *denudare*, from *de-* 'completely' + *nudare* 'to bare' (from *nudus* 'naked').

de·nu·mer·a·ble /dēˈn(y)o͞omərəbəl/ ▶ **adj.** Mathematics able to be counted by a one-to-one correspondence with the infinite set of integers.
– DERIVATIVES **de·nu·mer·a·bil·i·ty** /-ˌn(y)o͞omərəˈbilitē/ **n.**, **de·nu·mer·a·bly** /-blē/ **adv.**
– ORIGIN early 20th cent.: from late Latin *denumerare* 'count out' + -ABLE.

de·nun·ci·a·tion /diˌnənsēˈāsHən/ ▶ **n.** public condemnation of someone or something. ■ the action of informing against someone.
– DERIVATIVES **de·nun·ci·a·tor** /-ˈnənsēˌātər/ **n.**, **de·nun·ci·a·to·ry** /-ˈnənsēəˌtôrē/ **adj.**
– ORIGIN late Middle English: from Latin *denuntiatio(n-)*, from the verb *denuntiare* (see DENOUNCE). The original sense was 'public announcement,' also 'formal accusation or charge'; the main sense dates from the mid 19th cent.

Den·ver /ˈdenvər/ the capital of Colorado, in the central part of the state, on the South Platte River; pop. 598,707 (est. 2008). It is situated at an altitude of 5,280 feet (1,608 m) on the eastern side of the Rocky Mountains.

Den·ver boot ▶ **n.** see BOOT[1] (sense 1 of the noun).
– ORIGIN mid 20th cent.: named after *Denver*, Colorado, where the boot was introduced in 1949.

de·ny /diˈnī/ ▶ **v.** (**denies, denying, denied**) [with obj.] refuse to admit the truth or existence of: *they deny any responsibility for the tragedy.* ■ [with two objs.] refuse to give or grant (something requested or desired) to (someone): *the inquiry was denied access to intelligence sources.* ■ (**deny oneself**) refrain from satisfying oneself: *he had denied himself sexually for years.* ■ archaic refuse access to (someone): *the servants are ordered to deny him.*
– ORIGIN Middle English: from Old French *deni-*, stressed stem of *deneier*, from Latin *denegare*, from *de-* 'formally' + *negare* 'say no.'

Den·ys, St. see DENIS, ST.

de·o·dar /ˈdēəˌdär/ ▶ **n.** a tall, broadly conical cedar that is native to the Himalayas and has drooping branches and large barrel-shaped cones. ● *Cedrus deodara*, family Pinaceae.
– ORIGIN early 19th cent.: from Hindi *deodār*, from Sanskrit *devadāru* 'divine tree.'

de·o·dor·ant /dēˈōdərənt/ ▶ **n.** a substance that removes or conceals unpleasant smells, esp. bodily odors.
– ORIGIN mid 19th cent.: from DE- (expressing removal) + Latin *odor* 'smell' + -ANT.

de·o·dor·ize /dēˈōdəˌrīz/ ▶ **v.** [with obj.] remove or conceal an unpleasant smell in: *people used dried flowers to deodorize their homes.*
– DERIVATIVES **de·o·dor·i·za·tion** /-ˌōdərəˈzāsHən/ **n.**, **de·o·dor·iz·er** **n.**
– ORIGIN mid 19th cent.: from DE- (expressing removal) + Latin *odor* 'smell' + -IZE.

De·o gra·ti·as /ˈdāō ˈgrätsēəs/ ▶ **exclam.** thanks be to God.
– ORIGIN late 16th cent.: Latin.

de·on·tic /dēˈäntik/ ▶ **adj.** Philosophy of or relating to duty and obligation as ethical concepts. ■ Linguistics expressing duty or obligation.
– ORIGIN mid 19th cent. (as noun *deontics*): from Greek *deont-* 'being right' (from *dei* 'it is right') + -IC.

de·on·tol·o·gy /ˌdēänˈtäləjē/ ▶ **n.** Philosophy the study of the nature of duty and obligation.
– DERIVATIVES **de·on·to·log·i·cal** /dēˌäntˈäjikəl/ **adj.**, **de·on·tol·o·gist** /-jist/ **n.**
– ORIGIN early 19th cent.: from Greek *deont-* 'being necessary' (from *dei* 'it is necessary') + -LOGY.

De·o vo·len·te /ˈdāō vəˈlentē/ ▶ **adv.** God willing; if nothing prevents it.
– ORIGIN mid 18th cent.: Latin.

de·ox·i·dize /dēˈäksiˌdīz/ ▶ **v.** [with obj.] remove combined oxygen from (a substance, usually a metal).
– DERIVATIVES **de·ox·i·da·tion** /-ˌäksiˈdāsHən/ **n.**, **de·ox·i·diz·er** **n.**

de·ox·y·cor·ti·cos·ter·one /dēˌäksēˌkôrtiˈkästəˌrōn/ ▶ **n.** Biochemistry a corticosteroid hormone involved in regulating the salt and water balance in the human body.

de·ox·y·gen·ate /dēˈäksijəˌnāt/ ▶ **v.** [with obj.] (usu. as adj. **deoxygenated**) remove oxygen from: *deoxygenated air.*
– DERIVATIVES **de·ox·y·gen·a·tion** /-ˌäksijəˈnāsHən/ **n.**

de·ox·y·ri·bo·nu·cle·ase /dēˌäksēˌrībōˈn(y)o͞oklēˌās, -ˌāz/ ▶ **n.** Biochemistry another term for DNASE.

de·ox·y·ri·bo·nu·cle·ic ac·id /dēˌäksēˌrībōn(y)o͞oˈklēik/ ▶ **n.** see **DNA**.
– ORIGIN 1930s: *deoxyribonucleic* from a blend of DEOXYRIBOSE and NUCLEIC ACID.

de·ox·y·ri·bose /dēˌäksēˈrībōs, -bōz/ ▶ **n.** Biochemistry a sugar derived from ribose by replacing a hydroxyl group with hydrogen. ● Chem. formula; $C_5H_{10}O_4$. There are several isomers; the isomer **2-deoxyribose** is a constituent of DNA.
– ORIGIN 1930s: from DE- (expressing reduction) + OXY-[2] + RIBOSE.

dep. ▶ **abbr.** ■ departs. ■ deputy.

de·part /diˈpärt/ ▶ **v.** [no obj.] leave, typically in order to start a journey: *they **departed for** Germany* | *a contingent was **departing from** Cairo.* ■ (**depart from**) deviate from (an accepted, prescribed, or traditional course of action): *he **departed from** the precedent set by many.*
– PHRASES **depart this life** archaic die.
– ORIGIN Middle English: from Old French *departir*, based on Latin *dispertire* 'to divide.' The original sense was 'separate,' also 'take leave of each other,' hence 'go away.'

de·part·ed /diˈpärtid/ ▶ **adj.** deceased: *a dear departed relative.*
▶ **n.** (**the departed**) a particular dead person or dead people: *the prayer for the departed.*

de·part·ment /diˈpärtmənt/ ▶ **n.** a division of a large organization such as a government, university, business, or shop, dealing with a specific subject, commodity, or area of activity: *the English department.* ■ an administrative district in France and other countries. ■ (**one's department**) informal an area of special expertise or responsibility: *that's not my department.* ■ [with modifier] informal a specified

aspect or quality: *I never thought of myself as above average in the looks department.*
– ORIGIN late Middle English: from Old French *departement*, from *departir* (see DEPART). The original sense was 'division or distribution,' later 'separation,' hence 'a separate part' (core sense, mid 18th cent).

de·part·men·tal /di,pärt'mentl, ,dēpärt-/ ▶ **adj.** concerned with or belonging to a department of an organization: *a departmental meeting.*
– DERIVATIVES **de·part·men·tal·ly** **adv.**

de·part·men·tal·ism /dipärt'mentl,izəm, ,dēpärt-/ ▶ **n.** adherence to departmental methods or structure.

de·part·men·tal·ize /dipärt'mentl,īz, ,dēpärt-/ ▶ **v.** [with obj.] (usu. **be departmentalized**) divide (an organization or its work) into departments.
– DERIVATIVES **de·part·men·tal·i·za·tion** /-,mentl-ə'zāsʜən/ **n.**

de·part·ment store ▶ **n.** a large store stocking many varieties of goods in different departments.

de·par·ture /di'pärcʜər/ ▶ **n.** the action of leaving, typically to start a journey: *the day of departure | she made a hasty departure.* ■ a deviation from an accepted, prescribed, or traditional course of action or thought: *a departure from their usual style.* ■ Nautical the east–west distance between two points, esp. as traveled by a ship or aircraft and expressed in miles.
– ORIGIN late Middle English: from Old French *departeure*, from the verb *departir* (see DEPART).

de·paup·er·ate /di'pôpərit/ ▶ **adj.** Biology (of a flora, fauna, or ecosystem) lacking in numbers or variety of species: *oceanic islands are generally depauperate in mayflies.* ■ (of a plant or animal) imperfectly developed.
– ORIGIN late Middle English (in the sense 'impoverished'): from medieval Latin *depauperatus*, past participle of *depauperare*, from *de-* 'completely' + *pauperare* 'make poor' (from *pauper* 'poor').

dé·pay·sé /,dāpā'zā/ (also **dépaysée**) ▶ **adj.** removed from one's habitual surroundings.
– ORIGIN early 20th cent.: French, literally '(removed) from one's own country.'

de·pend /di'pend/ ▶ **v.** [no obj.] **1** (**depend on/upon**) be controlled or determined by: *differences in earnings depended on a wide variety of factors.*
2 (**depend on/upon**) rely on: *the kind of person you could depend on.* ■ need or require for financial or other support: *a town that had depended heavily upon the wool industry.* ■ be grammatically dependent on.
3 archaic or literary hang down: *his tongue depended from open jaws.*
– PHRASES **depending on** being conditioned by; contingent on: *makes 8–10 burgers (depending on size)* | [with clause] *the article sneered or just condescended, depending on how you read it.* **it** (or **that**) (**all**) **depends** used to express uncertainty or qualification in answering a question: *How many people use each screen? It all depends.*
– ORIGIN late Middle English (sense 3; also in the sense 'wait or be in suspense'): from Old French *dependre*, from Latin *dependere*, from *de-* 'down' + *pendere* 'hang.'

> **USAGE** In informal use, it is quite common for the on to be dropped in sentences such as *it all depends how you look at it* (rather than *it all depends on how you look at it*), but in well-formed written English, the **on** should be retained. In more formal writing, and sometimes for sound, rhythm, or other rhetorical effect, **upon** is the preferred preposition: *You may depend upon it.*

de·pend·a·ble /di'pendəbəl/ ▶ **adj.** trustworthy and reliable.
– DERIVATIVES **de·pend·a·bil·i·ty** /-,pendə'bilitē/ **n.**, **de·pend·a·bly** /-blē/ **adv.**

de·pend·ence /di'pendəns/ ▶ **n.** the state of relying on or being controlled by someone or something else: *Japan's dependence on imported oil.* ■ reliance on someone or something for financial support: *the dependence of our medical schools on grant funds.* ■ addiction to drink or drugs: *alcohol dependence.*
– ORIGIN late Middle English (in the sense 'hanging down or something that hangs down'): from Old French *dependance*, from the verb *dependre* (see DEPEND).

de·pend·en·cy /di'pendənsē/ ▶ **n.** (pl. **dependencies**) **1** a dependent or subordinate thing, esp. a country or province controlled by another.
2 dependence: *the country's dependency on the oil industry.*

de·pend·ent /di'pendənt/ ▶ **adj.** **1** [predic.] (**dependent on/upon**) contingent on or determined by: *the various benefits will be dependent on length of service.*
2 requiring someone or something for financial, emotional, or other support: *an economy heavily dependent on oil exports | households with dependent children.* ■ unable to do without: *people dependent on drugs* | [in combination] *welfare-dependent families.* ■ Grammar (of a clause, phrase, or word) subordinate to another clause, phrase, or word.
▶ **n.** (Brit. also **dependant**) a person who relies on another, esp. a family member, for financial support: *a single man with no dependents.*
– DERIVATIVES **de·pend·ent·ly** **adv.**
– ORIGIN late Middle English *dependant* 'hanging down,' from Old French, present participle of *dependre* (see DEPEND). The spelling change in the 16th cent. was due to association with the Latin participial stem *dependent-*.

de·pend·ent var·i·a·ble ▶ **n.** Mathematics a variable (often denoted by y) whose value depends on that of another.

de·per·son·al·i·za·tion /dē,pərsənələ'zāsʜən/ ▶ **n.** the action of divesting someone or something of human characteristics or individuality. ■ Psychiatry a state in which one's thoughts and feelings seem unreal or not to belong to oneself, or in which one loses all sense of identity.

de·per·son·al·ize /dē'pərsənə,līz/ ▶ **v.** [with obj.] divest of human characteristics or individuality: *medical technology depersonalizes treatment.*

de·phlo·gis·ti·cat·ed /,dēflə'jisti,kātid/ ▶ **adj.** Chemistry, historical deprived of "phlogiston." Oxygen was originally called **dephlogisticated air** by Joseph Priestley.

de·pict /di'pikt/ ▶ **v.** [with obj.] show or represent by a drawing, painting, or other art form. ■ portray in words; describe: *youth is depicted as a time of vitality and good health.*
– DERIVATIVES **de·pict·er** **n.**
– ORIGIN late Middle English: from Latin *depict-* 'portrayed,' from the verb *depingere*, from *de-* 'completely' + *pingere* 'to paint.'

de·pic·tion /di'piksʜən/ ▶ **n.** the action or result of depicting something, esp. in art: *the painting's horrific depiction of war | Michelangelo's depictions of the male nude.*

de·pig·ment /dē'pigmənt/ ▶ **v.** [with obj.] (usu. as adj. **depigmented**) reduce or remove the pigmentation of (the skin).
– DERIVATIVES **de·pig·men·ta·tion** /-,pigmən'tāsʜən/ **n.**

dep·i·late /'depə,lāt/ ▶ **v.** [with obj.] remove the hair from: *they scrubbed and depilated her* | (as adj. **depilated**) *his permanently depilated and tattooed skull.*
– DERIVATIVES **dep·i·la·tion** /,depə'lāsʜən/ **n.**
– ORIGIN mid 16th cent. (earlier (late Middle English) as *depilation*): from Latin *depilat-* 'stripped of hair,' from the verb *depilare*, from *de-* (expressing removal) + *pilare* (from *pilus* 'hair').

dep·i·la·tor /'depə,lātər/ ▶ **n.** an instrument that removes unwanted bodily hair, typically by plucking it from the root.

de·pil·a·to·ry /di'pilə,tôrē/ ▶ **adj.** used to remove unwanted hair.
▶ **n.** (pl. **depilatories**) a cream or lotion for removing unwanted hair.
– ORIGIN early 17th cent.: from Latin *depilatorius*, from *depilat-* 'stripped of hair,' from the verb *depilare* (see DEPILATE).

de·plane /dē'plān/ ▶ **v.** [no obj.] disembark from an aircraft: *we landed and deplaned.*

de·plete /di'plēt/ ▶ **v.** (often as adj. **depleted**) use up the supply or resources of: *fish stocks are severely depleted.* ■ [no obj.] diminish in number or quantity: *supplies are depleting fast.*
– ORIGIN early 19th cent. (earlier (mid. 17th cent.) as *depletion*): from Latin *deplet-* 'emptied out,' from the verb *deplere*, from *de-* (expressing reversal) + *plere* 'fill' (from *plenus* 'full').

de·plet·ed u·ra·ni·um (abbr.: **DU**) ▶ **n.** uranium from which most of the fissile isotope uranium-235 has been removed.

de·ple·tion /di'plēsʜən/ ▶ **n.** reduction in the number or quantity of something: *the depletion of the ozone layer.*

de·ple·tion al·low·ance /di'plēsʜən/ ▶ **n.** a tax concession allowable to a company whose normal business activities (in particular oil extraction) reduce the value of its own assets.

de·plor·a·ble /di'plôrəbəl/ ▶ **adj.** deserving strong condemnation: *the deplorable conditions in which most prisoners are held.* ■ shockingly bad in quality: *her spelling was deplorable.*
– DERIVATIVES **de·plor·a·bly** /-blē/ **adv.**
– ORIGIN early 17th cent.: from French *déplorable* or late Latin *deplorabilis*, from the verb *deplorare* (see DEPLORE).

de·plore /di'plôr/ ▶ **v.** [with obj.] feel or express strong disapproval of (something): *we deplore this act of violence.*
– DERIVATIVES **de·plor·ing·ly** **adv.**
– ORIGIN mid 16th cent. (in the sense 'weep for, regret deeply'): from French *déplorer* or Italian *deplorare*, from Latin *deplorare*, from *de-* 'away, thoroughly' + *plorare* 'bewail.'

de·ploy /di'ploi/ ▶ **v.** [with obj.] move (troops) into position for military action: *forces were deployed at strategic locations.* ■ [no obj.] (of troops) move into position for such action: *the air force began to deploy forward.* ■ bring into effective action; utilize: *they are not always able to deploy this skill.*
– DERIVATIVES **de·ploy·ment** **n.**
– ORIGIN late 18th cent.: from French *déployer*, from Latin *displicare* and late Latin *deplicare* 'unfold or explain,' from *dis-*, *de-* 'un-' + *plicare* 'to fold.' Compare with DISPLAY.

de·plume /dē'plōōm/ ▶ **v.** [with obj.] deprive (a bird) of feathers. ■ archaic strip or deprive of honor, status, or wealth.
– ORIGIN late Middle English: from Old French *desplumer* or medieval Latin *deplumare*, from *des-*, *de-* (expressing reversal) + Latin *pluma* 'feather.'

de·po·lar·ize /dē'pōlə,rīz/ ▶ **v.** [with obj.] Physics reduce or remove the polarization of: *the threshold necessary to depolarize the membrane.*
– DERIVATIVES **de·po·lar·i·za·tion** /-,pōlərə'zāsʜən/ **n.**

de·po·lit·i·cize /,dēpə'liti,sīz/ ▶ **v.** [with obj.] remove from political activity or influence: *we have to depoliticize sex education.*
– DERIVATIVES **de·po·lit·i·ci·za·tion** /-,litisə'zāsʜən/ **n.**

de·po·lym·er·ize /dē'päləmə,rīz/ ▶ **v.** [with obj.] Chemistry break (a polymer) down into monomers or other smaller units. ■ [no obj.] undergo this process: *the ideal disposable polymer would depolymerize naturally.*
– DERIVATIVES **de·po·lym·er·i·za·tion** /-,päləmerə'zāsʜən/ **n.**

de·po·nent /di'pōnənt/ ▶ **adj.** Grammar (of a verb, esp. in Latin or Greek) passive or middle in form but active in meaning.
▶ **n.** **1** Grammar a deponent verb.
2 Law a person who makes a deposition or affidavit under oath.
– ORIGIN late Middle English: from Latin *deponent-* 'laying aside, putting down' (in medieval Latin 'testifying'), from the verb *deponere*, from *de-* 'down' + *ponere* 'place.' The use in grammar arose from the notion that the verb had "laid aside" the passive sense (although in fact these verbs were originally reflexive).

de·pop·u·late /dē'päpyə,lāt/ ▶ **v.** [with obj.] substantially reduce the population of (an area): *the disease could depopulate a city the size of New Haven.*
– DERIVATIVES **de·pop·u·la·tion** /-,päpyə'lāsʜən/ **n.**
– ORIGIN mid 16th cent. (in the sense 'ravage, lay waste'): from Latin *depopulat-* 'ravaged,' from the verb *depopulari*, from *de-* 'completely' + *populari* 'lay waste' (from *populus* 'people').

de·port /di'pôrt/ ▶ **v.** **1** [with obj.] expel (a foreigner) from a country, typically on the grounds of illegal status or for having committed a crime: *he was deported for violation of immigration laws.* ■ exile (a native) to another country.
2 (**deport oneself**) archaic conduct oneself in a specified manner: *he has deported himself with great dignity.*
– DERIVATIVES **de·port·a·ble** **adj.**
– ORIGIN late 16th cent. (sense 2): from French *déporter*, from Latin *deportare*, from *de-* 'away' + *portare* 'carry.'

de·por·ta·tion /,dēpôr'tāsʜən/ ▶ **n.** the action of deporting a foreigner from a country: *asylum seekers facing deportation* | [as modifier] *a deportation order.*

de·por·tee /,dēpôr'tē/ ▶ **n.** a person who has been or is being expelled from a country.

de·port·ment /di'pôrtmənt/ ▶ **n.** a person's behavior or manners: *there are team rules governing deportment on and off the field.*
– ORIGIN early 17th cent.: from French *déportement*, from the verb *déporter* (see DEPORT).

de·pose /di'pōz/ ▶ **v.** [with obj.] **1** remove from office suddenly and forcefully: *he had been deposed by a military coup.*
2 Law testify to or give (evidence) on oath, typically in a written statement: *every affidavit shall state which of the facts deposed to are within the deponent's knowledge.*
3 Law question (a witness) in deposition.

– ORIGIN Middle English: from Old French *deposer*, from Latin *deponere* (see DEPONENT), but influenced by Latin *depositus* and Old French *poser* 'to place.'

de·pos·it /di'päzit/ ▶ **n.** **1** a sum of money placed or kept in a bank account, usually to gain interest. ■ an act of placing money in a bank account: *I'd like to **make a deposit**.*
2 a sum payable as a first installment on the purchase of something or as a pledge for a contract, the balance being payable later: *we've saved enough for a **deposit on** a house.* ■ a returnable sum payable on the rental of something, to cover any possible loss or damage.
3 a layer or body of accumulated matter: *the deposits of salt on the chrome.* ■ a natural layer of sand, rock, coal, or other material.
▶ **v.** (**deposits, depositing, deposited**) **1** [with obj.] put or set down (something or someone) in a specific place, typically unceremoniously: *he deposited a pile of schoolbooks on the kitchen table.* ■ (usu. **be deposited**) (of water, the wind, or other natural agency) lay down (matter) gradually as a layer or covering: *beds where salt is deposited by the tide.* ■ lay (an egg): *the female deposits a line of eggs.*
2 [with obj.] store or entrust with someone for safekeeping. ■ pay (a sum of money) into a bank account: *the money is deposited with a bank.* ■ pay (a sum) as a first installment or as a pledge for a contract: *I had to deposit 10% of the price of the house.*
– ORIGIN late 16th cent. (esp. in the phrases *in deposit* or *on deposit*): from Latin *depositum* (noun), medieval Latin *depositare* (verb), both from Latin *deposit-* 'laid aside,' from the verb *deponere*.

de·pos·i·tar·y /di'päzi,terē/ (also **depository**) ▶ **n.** (pl. **depositaries**) a person to whom something is lodged in trust.
▶ **adj.** (of a share or receipt) representing a share in a foreign company. The depositary share or receipt is traded on the stock exchange of the investor's country rather than the actual share, which is deposited in a foreign bank.
– ORIGIN early 17th cent.: from late Latin *depositarius*, from the verb *deponere* (see DEPOSIT).

dep·o·si·tion /,depə'zisHən/ ▶ **n.** **1** the action of deposing someone, esp. a monarch: *Edward V's deposition.*
2 Law the process of giving sworn evidence: *the deposition of four expert witnesses.*
3 Law a formal, usually written, statement to be used as evidence.
4 the action of depositing something: *pebbles formed by the deposition of calcium in solution.*
5 (**the Deposition**) the taking down of the body of Jesus Christ from the Cross.
– ORIGIN late Middle English: from Latin *depositio(n-)*, from the verb *deponere* (see DEPOSIT).

de·pos·i·tor /di'päzitər/ ▶ **n.** a person who keeps money in a bank account.

de·pos·i·to·ry /di'päzi,tôrē/ ▶ **n.** (pl. **depositories**) **1** a place where things are stored.
2 variant spelling of DEPOSITARY.
– ORIGIN mid 17th cent. (denoting a depositary): from late Latin *depositorium*, from *deposit-* 'laid aside,' from the verb *deponere* (see DEPOSIT).

de·pot /'dēpō, 'de-/ ▶ **n.** a place for the storage of large quantities of equipment, food, or some other commodity: *an arms depot.* ■ a railroad or bus station. ■ a place where buses, trains, or other vehicles are housed and maintained and from which they are dispatched for service. ■ the headquarters of a regiment; a place where recruits or other troops are assembled.
– ORIGIN late 18th cent. (in the sense 'act of depositing'): from French *dépôt*, from Latin *depositum* 'something deposited' (see DEPOSIT).

de·prave /di'prāv/ ▶ **v.** [with obj.] make (someone) immoral or wicked: *this book would deprave and corrupt young children.*
– DERIVATIVES **dep·ra·va·tion** /,deprə'vāsHən/ **n.**
– ORIGIN late Middle English (in the sense 'pervert the meaning or intention of something'): from Old French *depraver* or Latin *depravare*, from *de-* 'down, thoroughly' + *pravus* 'crooked, perverse.'

de·praved /di'prāvd/ ▶ **adj.** morally corrupt; wicked: *a depraved indifference to human life.*

de·prav·i·ty /di'pravitē/ ▶ **n.** (pl. **depravities**) moral corruption; wickedness: *a tale of wickedness and depravity.* ■ a wicked or morally corrupt act. ■ Christian Theology the innate corruption of human nature, due to original sin.
– ORIGIN mid 17th cent.: alteration (influenced by DEPRAVE) of obsolete *pravity*, from Latin *pravitas*, from *pravus* 'crooked, perverse.'

dep·re·cate /'depri,kāt/ ▶ **v.** [with obj.] **1** express disapproval of: (as adj. **deprecating**) *he sniffed in a deprecating way.*
2 another term for DEPRECIATE (sense 2): *he deprecates the value of children's television.*
– DERIVATIVES **dep·re·cat·ing·ly** **adv.**, **dep·re·ca·tion** /,deprə'kāsHən/ **n.**, **dep·re·ca·tive** /-,kātiv/ **adj.**, **dep·re·ca·tor** /-,kātər/ **n.**
– ORIGIN early 17th cent. (in the sense 'pray against'): from Latin *deprecat-* 'prayed against (as being evil),' from the verb *deprecari*, from *de-* (expressing reversal) + *precari* 'pray.'

dep·re·ca·to·ry /'deprikə,tôrē/ ▶ **adj.** expressing disapproval; disapproving. ■ apologetic or appeasing: *a deprecatory smile.*

de·pre·ci·ate /di'prēsHē,āt/ ▶ **v.** **1** [no obj.] diminish in value over a period of time: *the pound is expected to **depreciate against** the dollar.* ■ reduce the recorded value in a company's books of (an asset) each year over a predetermined period: *the computers would be depreciated at 50 percent per annum.*
2 [with obj.] disparage or belittle (something): *she was already depreciating her own aesthetic taste.*
– DERIVATIVES **de·pre·ci·a·to·ry** /-sHēə,tôrē/ **adj.**
– ORIGIN late Middle English (sense 2): from late Latin *depreciat-* 'lowered in price, undervalued,' from the verb *depreciare*, from Latin *de-* 'down' + *pretium* 'price.'

de·pre·ci·a·tion /di,prēsHē'āsHən/ ▶ **n.** a reduction in the value of an asset with the passage of time, due in particular to wear and tear. ■ decrease in the value of a currency relative to other currencies: *depreciation leads to losses for non-dollar-based investors | a currency depreciation.*

dep·re·da·tion /,deprə'dāsHən/ ▶ **n.** (usu. **depredations**) an act of attacking or plundering: *protecting grain from the depredations of rats and mice.*
– ORIGIN late 15th cent. (in the sense 'plundering, robbery,' (plural) 'ravages'): from French *déprédation*, from late Latin *depraedatio(n-)*, from *depraedari* 'plunder.'

dep·re·da·tor /'deprə,dātər/ ▶ **n.** archaic a person or thing that makes depredations, esp. a predatory animal.
– DERIVATIVES **dep·re·da·to·ry** /di'predə,tôrē/ **adj.**

de·press /di'pres/ ▶ **v.** [with obj.] **1** make (someone) feel utterly dispirited or dejected: *that first day at school depressed me.* ■ reduce the level or strength of activity in (something, esp. an economic or biological system): *fear of inflation in America depressed bond markets | alcohol depresses the nervous system.*
2 push or pull (something) down into a lower position: *depress the lever.*
– DERIVATIVES **de·press·i·ble** **adj.**
– ORIGIN late Middle English: from Old French *depresser*, from late Latin *depressare*, frequentative of *deprimere* 'press down.'

de·pres·sant /di'presənt/ ▶ **adj.** (chiefly of a drug) reducing functional or nervous activity.
▶ **n.** a depressant drug. ■ an influence that depresses economic or other activity: *higher taxation is a depressant.*

de·pressed /di'prest/ ▶ **adj.** (of a person) in a state of general unhappiness or despondency. ■ (of a person) suffering from clinical depression. ■ (of a place or economic activity) suffering the damaging effects of a lack of demand or employment: *depressed urban areas.* ■ (of an object or part of an object) in a physically lower position, having been pushed or forced down: *a depressed fracture of the skull.*

de·press·ing /di'presiNG/ ▶ **adj.** causing or resulting in a feeling of miserable dejection: *that thought is too depressing for words.* ■ causing a damaging reduction in economic activity: *the mortgage rate increase will have a depressing effect on the housing market.*
– DERIVATIVES **de·press·ing·ly** **adv.**

de·pres·sion /di'presHən/ ▶ **n.** **1** severe despondency and dejection, typically felt over a period of time and accompanied by feelings of hopelessness and inadequacy. ■ Medicine a condition of mental disturbance characterized by such feelings to a greater degree than seems warranted by the external circumstances, typically with lack of energy and difficulty in maintaining concentration or interest in life: *clinical depression.* ■ a long and severe recession in an economy or market: *the depression in the housing market.* ■ (**the Depression** or **the Great Depression**) the financial and industrial slump of 1929 and subsequent years.
2 the act lowering something or pressing something down: *the depression of prices.* ■ a sunken place or hollow on a surface: *the original shallow depressions were slowly converted to creeks.* ■ Astronomy & Geography the angular distance of an object below the horizon or a horizontal plane. ■ Meteorology a region of lower atmospheric pressure, esp. a cyclonic weather system.
– ORIGIN late Middle English: from Latin *depressio(n-)*, from *deprimere* 'press down' (see DEPRESS).

De·pres·sion glass ▶ **n.** machine-pressed, tinted glassware that was mass-produced in the US from the late 1920s to the 1940s and often used as giveaways to persuade customers to purchase goods.

de·pres·sive /di'presiv/ ▶ **adj.** causing feelings of hopelessness, despondency, and dejection. ■ Medicine relating to or tending to suffer from clinical depression: *a depressive illness.* ■ causing a reduction in strength, effectiveness, or value: *steroids have a depressive effect on the immune system.*
▶ **n.** Medicine a person suffering from or with a tendency to suffer from depression.

de·pres·sor /di'presər/ ▶ **n.** **1** Anatomy (also **depressor muscle**) a muscle whose contraction pulls down the part of the body to which it is attached. ■ any of several specific muscles in the face: [followed by Latin genitive] *depressor anguli oris.*
2 Physiology a nerve whose stimulation results in a lowering of blood pressure.
3 an instrument for pressing something down.
– ORIGIN early 17th cent. (in the general sense 'someone or something that depresses'): from Latin, from *depress-* 'pressed down,' from the verb *deprimere* (see DEPRESS).

de·pres·sur·ize /dē'presHə,rīz/ ▶ **v.** [with obj.] release the pressure of the gas inside (a pressurized vehicle or container). ■ [no obj.] (of a pressurized vehicle or container) lose pressure.
– DERIVATIVES **de·pres·sur·i·za·tion** /-,presHərə'zāsHən/ **n.**

dep·ri·va·tion /,deprə'vāsHən/ ▶ **n.** the damaging lack of material benefits considered to be basic necessities in a society: *low wages mean that 3.75 million people suffer serious deprivation.* ■ the lack or denial of something considered to be a necessity: *sleep deprivation.* ■ archaic the action of depriving someone of office, esp. an ecclesiastical office.
– ORIGIN late Middle English (in the sense 'removal from office'): from medieval Latin *deprivatio(n-)*, from the verb *deprivare* (see DEPRIVE).

de·prive /di'prīv/ ▶ **v.** [with obj.] deny (a person or place) the possession or use of something: *the city was **deprived of** its water supplies.* ■ archaic depose (someone, esp. a clergyman) from office: *Archbishop Bancroft deprived a considerable number of puritan clergymen.*
– DERIVATIVES **de·priv·al** /-vəl/ **n.**
– ORIGIN Middle English (in the sense 'depose from office'): from Old French *depriver*, from medieval Latin *deprivare*, from *de-* 'away, completely' + *privare* (see PRIVATE).

de·prived /di'prīvd/ ▶ **adj.** suffering a severe and damaging lack of basic material and cultural benefits: *the charity cares for destitute and deprived children.* ■ (of a person) suffering a lack of a specified benefit that is considered important: *the men felt sexually deprived.*

de pro·fun·dis /,dā prə'fo͝ondis/ ▶ **n.** a heartfelt cry of appeal expressing one's deepest feelings of sorrow or anguish.
– ORIGIN late Middle English: Latin, literally 'from the depths,' the opening words of Psalm 130.

de·pro·gram /dē'prō,gram, -grəm/ ▶ **v.** (**deprograms, deprogramming, deprogrammed** or **deprograming, deprogramed**) [with obj.] release (someone) from apparent brainwashing, typically that of a religious cult, by the systematic reindoctrination of conventional values.

de·pro·tein·ize /dē'prōtē(ə),nīz/ ▶ **v.** [with obj.] remove the protein from (a substance), usually as a stage in chemical purification.
– DERIVATIVES **de·pro·tein·i·za·tion** /-,prōtē(ə)nə'zāsHən/ **n.**

Dept. ▶ **abbr.** Department.

depth /depTH/ ▶ **n.** **1** the distance from the top or surface of something to its bottom: *shallow water of no more than 12 feet **in depth**.* ■ distance from the nearest to the farthest point of something or from the front to the back: *the depth of the wardrobe.* ■ used to specify the distance below the top or surface of something to which someone or something percolates or at which something happens: [in sing.] *loosen the soil to **a depth of** 8 inches.* ■ the apparent existence of three dimensions in a picture, photograph, or other two-dimensional representation; perspective: *texture in a picture gives it depth.* ■ lowness of pitch: *my voice had not yet acquired husky depths.*

2 complexity and profundity of thought: *the book has unexpected depth.* ■ extensive and detailed study or knowledge: *third-year courses typically go into more depth.* ■ intensity of emotion, usually considered as a laudable quality: *a man of compassion and depth of feeling.* ■ intensity of color: *the wine shows good depth of color.*
3 (**the depths**) a point far below the surface: *he lifted the manhole cover and peered into the depths beneath.* ■ (also **the depth**) the worst or lowest part or state: *4 a.m. in the depths of winter | the putrid depths to which morality has sunk.* ■ a time when one's negative feelings are at their most intense: *she was in the depths of despair.* ■ a place that is remote and inaccessible: *a remote little village somewhere in the depths of Russia.*
4 Sports the strength of a team in its reserve of substitute players: *they have so much depth that they could afford the luxury of breaking in their players slowly.*
– PHRASES **hidden depths** usually admirable but previously unnoticed qualities of a person: *hidden depths and insights within children.* **in depth** in great detail; comprehensively and thoroughly: *research students pursue a specific aspect of a subject in depth.* See also IN-DEPTH. **out of one's depth** in water too deep to stand in. ■ beyond one's knowledge or ability to cope: *the governor is out of his depth, politically adrift.*
– ORIGIN late Middle English: from DEEP + -TH², on the pattern of pairs such as *long, length.*

depth charge ▶ n. an explosive charge designed to be dropped from a ship or aircraft and to explode under water at a preset depth, used for attacking submarines.

depth find·er ▶ n. an echo sounder or other device for measuring water depth, esp. for navigation and fishing.

depth gauge ▶ n. a device fitted to a drill bit to ensure that the hole drilled does not exceed the required depth.

depth·less /ˈdepTHlis/ ▶ adj. 1 unfathomably deep: *a depthless gorge.*
2 shallow and superficial.
– DERIVATIVES **depth·less·ly** adv.

depth of field ▶ n. the distance between the nearest and the farthest objects that give an image judged to be in focus in a camera.

depth of fo·cus ▶ n. the distance between the two extreme axial points behind a lens at which an image is judged to be in focus.

depth per·cep·tion ▶ n. the ability to perceive the relative distance of objects in one's visual field.

depth psy·chol·o·gy ▶ n. the study of unconscious mental processes and motives, esp. in psychoanalytic theory and practice.

depth sound·er ▶ n. another term for ECHO SOUNDER.

de·pub·li·ca·tion /dēˌpəbliˈkāSHən/ ▶ n. the act of depublishing: *the League of California cities had requested depublication of the Div. Seven ruling.*

de·pub·lish /dēˈpəblisH/ ▶ v. [with obj.] chiefly Law remove from an official record or publication: *the Supreme Court may also elect to depublish a case on its own motion.*

dep·u·ra·tion /ˌdepyəˈrāSHən/ ▶ n. technical the action or process of freeing something of impurities.
– DERIVATIVES **dep·u·rate** /ˈdepyəˌrāt/ v., **dep·u·ra·tive** /-ˌrātiv/ adj. & n., **dep·u·ra·tor** /-ˌrātər/ n.
– ORIGIN early 17th cent.: from Latin *depuratio(n-)*, from the verb *depurare*, from *de-* 'completely' + *purare* 'purify' (from *purus* 'pure').

dep·u·ta·tion /ˌdepyəˈtāSHən/ ▶ n. a group of people appointed to undertake a mission or take part in a formal process on behalf of a larger group: *he had been a member of a deputation to Napoleon III.*
– ORIGIN late Middle English (in the sense 'appointment to an office or function'): from late Latin *deputatio(n-)*, from the verb *deputare* (see DEPUTE).

de·pute /diˈpyo͞ot/ ▶ v. [with obj.] appoint or instruct (someone) to perform a task for which one is responsible: *she had been deputed to look after him while Clarissa was away.* ■ delegate (authority or a task).
– ORIGIN late Middle English: via Old French from Latin *deputare* 'consider to be, assign,' from *de-* 'away' + *putare* 'think over, consider.'

dep·u·tize /ˈdepyəˌtīz/ ▶ v. [with obj.] make (someone) a deputy: *some officers will be deputized as federal marshals.* ■ [no obj.] temporarily act or speak as a deputy.

dep·u·ty /ˈdepyətē/ ▶ n. (pl. **deputies**) a person whose immediate superior is a senior figure within an organization and who is empowered to act as a substitute for this superior. ■ a parliamentary representative in certain countries.
– PHRASES **by deputy** historical instructing another person to act in one's stead; by proxy: *the wardens of the forests performed important duties by deputy.*
– DERIVATIVES **dep·u·ty·ship** /-ˌSHip/ n.
– ORIGIN late Middle English: from Old French *depute*, from late Latin *deputatus*, past participle of *deputare* (see DEPUTE).

de·queue /dēˈkyo͞o/ ▶ v. (**dequeues, dequeuing** or **dequeueing, dequeued**) [with obj.] Computing remove (an item of data awaiting processing) from a queue of such items.

De Quin·cey /də ˈkwinsē/, Thomas (1785–1859), English essayist and critic. He was known for his *Confessions of an English Opium Eater* (1822), a study of his addiction to opium and its psychological effects.

de·rac·in·ate /diˈrasəˌnāt/ ▶ v. [with obj.] literary tear (something) up by the roots.
– DERIVATIVES **de·rac·i·na·tion** /-ˌrasəˈnāSHən/ n.
– ORIGIN late 16th cent.: from French *déraciner*, from *dé-* (expressing removal) + *racine* 'root' (based on Latin *radix*).

de·rac·i·nat·ed /diˈrasəˌnātid/ ▶ adj. another term for DÉRACINÉ.

dé·ra·ci·né /dāˌräsiˈnā/ ▶ adj. uprooted or displaced from one's geographical or social environment: *the self-consciousness of déraciné Americans.*
▶ n. a person who has been or feels displaced.
– ORIGIN early 20th cent.: French, literally 'uprooted.'

de·rail /dēˈrāl/ ▶ v. [with obj.] (usu. **be derailed**) cause (a train or trolley car) to leave its tracks accidentally: *a train was derailed after it collided with a herd of cattle.* ■ [no obj.] (of a train or trolley car) accidentally leave the tracks: *the trolley cars had a tendency to derail on sharp corners.* ■ [with obj.] obstruct (a process) by diverting it from its intended course: *the plot is seen by some as an attempt to derail the negotiations.*
– DERIVATIVES **de·rail·ment** n.
– ORIGIN mid 19th cent.: from French *dérailler*, from *dé-* (expressing removal) + *rail* 'rail.'

de·rail·leur /diˈrālər/ ▶ n. a bicycle mechanism that moves the chain out and up, allowing it to shift to different cogs.
– ORIGIN 1930s: from French, from *dérailler* 'derail.'

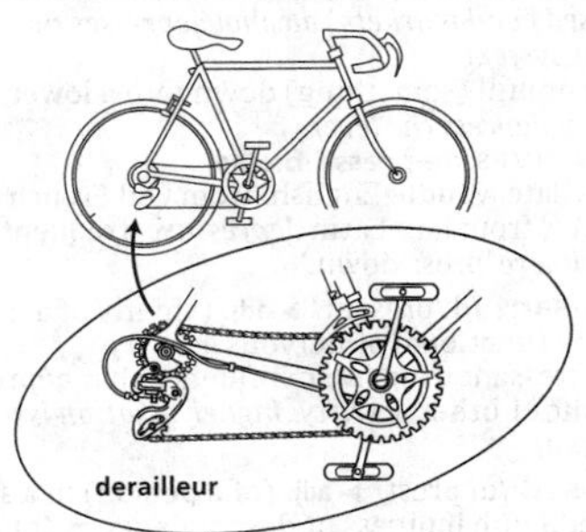

derailleur

De·rain /dəˈraN/, André (1880–1954), French painter; an exponent of Fauvism.

de·range /diˈrānj/ ▶ v. [with obj.] cause (someone) to become insane: *that business last month must have deranged him a bit.* ■ throw (something) into confusion; cause to act irregularly: *stress deranges the immune system.* ■ archaic intrude on; interrupt: *I am sorry to have deranged you for so small a matter.*
– DERIVATIVES **de·range·ment** n.
– ORIGIN late 18th cent.: from French *déranger*, from Old French *desrengier*, literally 'move from orderly rows.'

de·ranged /diˈrānjd/ ▶ adj. mad; insane: *a deranged gunman.*

de·rate /dēˈrāt/ ▶ v. [with obj.] reduce the power rating of (a component or device): *the engines were derated to 90 horse power.*

Der·by¹ /ˈdärbē/ a city in north central England, on the Derwent River; pop. 244,700 (est. 2009).

Der·by² /ˈdärbē/ Edward George Geoffrey Smith Stanley, 14th Earl of (1799–1869), British statesman; prime minister 1852, 1858–59, and 1866–68.

Der·by³ /ˈdərbē/ ▶ n. (pl. **Derbies**) 1 (Brit. /ˈdärbē/) an annual horse race for three-year-olds, founded in 1780 by the 12th Earl of Derby. The race is run on Epsom Downs in England in late May or early June. ■ a similar race elsewhere: *the Kentucky Derby.* ■ (**derby**) a sporting contest open to the general public: *sign up for the fishing derby.*
2 (**derby**, also **derby hat**) a bowler hat. [said to be from American demand for a hat of the type worn at the Epsom Derby.]
3 a boot or shoe having the eyelet tabs stitched on top of the vamp. [so named because originally a sports boot.]

Der·by⁴ /ˈdərbē/ ▶ n. a hard pressed cheese made from skimmed milk, chiefly in Derbyshire.

derby hat

Der·by Day ▶ n. the day on which the Epsom Derby is run. ■ the day on which the Kentucky Derby is run.

Der·by·shire /ˈdärbēSHər, -ˌSHi(ə)r/ a county in north central England; county town, Matlock.

de re /dā ˈrā/ ▶ adj. Philosophy relating to the properties of things mentioned in an assertion or expression, rather than to the assertion or expression itself. Compare with DE DICTO.
– ORIGIN Latin, literally 'about the thing.'

de·re·al·i·za·tion /dēˌrē(ə)ləˈzāSHən/ ▶ n. a feeling that one's surroundings are not real, esp. as a symptom of mental disturbance.
– DERIVATIVES **de·re·al·ized** /dēˈrē(ə)ˌlīzd/ adj.

de·re·cho /dāˈräˌCHō/ ▶ n. (pl. **derechos**) a line of intense, widespread, and fast-moving windstorms and sometimes thunderstorms that moves across a great distance and is characterized by damaging winds.
– ORIGIN Spanish, literally 'straight.'

de·ref·er·ence /dēˈref(ə)rəns/ ▶ v. [with obj.] Computing obtain from (a pointer) the address of a data item held in another location.

de·reg·u·late /dēˈregyəˌlāt/ ▶ v. [with obj.] remove regulations or restrictions from: *a law that would deregulate cable TV prices.*
– DERIVATIVES **de·reg·u·la·tion** /-ˌregyəˈlāSHən/ n., **de·reg·u·la·to·ry** /-ləˌtôrē/ adj.

der·e·lict /ˈderəˌlikt/ ▶ adj. in a very poor condition as a result of disuse and neglect: *the cities were derelict and dying.* ■ (of a person) shamefully negligent in not having done what one should have done: *he was derelict in his duty to his country.*
▶ n. a person without a home, job, or property: *derelicts who could fit all their possessions in a paper bag.* ■ a piece of property, esp. a ship, abandoned by the owner and in poor condition.
– ORIGIN mid 17th cent.: from Latin *derelictus* 'abandoned,' past participle of *derelinquere*, from *de-* 'completely' + *relinquere* 'forsake.'

der·e·lic·tion /ˌderəˈlikSHən/ ▶ n. the state of having been abandoned and become dilapidated: *every year valuable gardens start the slow slide to dereliction.*
■ (usu. **dereliction of duty**) the shameful failure to fulfill one's obligations.
– ORIGIN late 16th cent.: from Latin *derelictio(n-)*, from the verb *derelinquere* (see DERELICT).

de·re·press /ˌdēriˈpres/ ▶ v. [with obj.] Biochemistry & Genetics activate (enzymes, genes, etc.) from an inoperative or latent state.
– DERIVATIVES **de·re·pres·sion** /-ˈpreSHən/ n.

de·req·ui·si·tion /dēˌrekwəˈzisHən/ ▶ v. [with obj.] dated return (requisitioned property) to its former owner.

de·re·strict /ˌdēriˈstrikt/ ▶ v. [with obj.] remove restrictions from.
– DERIVATIVES **de·re·stric·tion** /-ˈstrikSHən/ n.

de·ride /diˈrīd/ ▶ v. [with obj.] express contempt for; ridicule: *critics derided the proposals as clumsy attempts to find a solution.*
– DERIVATIVES **de·rid·er** n.
– ORIGIN mid 16th cent.: from Latin *deridere* 'scoff at.'

de ri·gueur /də riˈgər, rēˈgœr/ ▶ adj. required by etiquette or current fashion: *it was de rigueur for bands to grow their hair long.*
– ORIGIN mid 19th cent.: French, literally 'in strictness.'

de·ri·sion /diˈriZHən/ ▶ n. contemptuous ridicule or mockery: *my stories were greeted with derision and disbelief.*
– PHRASES **hold** (or **have**) **in derision** archaic regard with mockery.
– DERIVATIVES **de·ris·i·ble** /-ˈrizəbəl/ adj.
– ORIGIN late Middle English: via Old French from late Latin *derisio(n-)*, from *deridere* 'scoff at.'

de·ri·sive /diˈrīsiv/ ▶ adj. expressing contempt or ridicule: *a harsh, derisive laugh.*
– DERIVATIVES **de·ri·sive·ly** adv., **de·ri·sive·ness** n.
– ORIGIN mid 17th cent.: from DERISION, on the pattern of the pair *decision, decisive.*

USAGE On the difference between **derisive** and **derisory**, see usage at DERISORY.

de·ri·so·ry /di'rīsərē, -'rī-/ ▶ **adj. 1** ridiculously small or inadequate: *they were given a derisory pay rise.*
2 another term for **DERISIVE**: *his derisory gaze swept over her.*
– ORIGIN early 17th cent. (in the sense 'derisive'): from late Latin *derisorius*, from *deris-* 'scoffed at,' from the verb *deridere* (see **DERISION**).

USAGE Although the words **derisory** and **derisive** share similar roots, they have different core meanings. **Derisory** usually means 'ridiculously small or inadequate,' as in *a* ***derisory*** *pay offer* or *the security arrangements were* ***derisory***. **Derisive**, on the other hand, is used to mean 'showing contempt,' as in *he gave a* ***derisive*** *laugh.*

der·i·vate /'derəvit/ ▶ **n.** something derived, esp. a product obtained chemically from a raw material.
– ORIGIN late Middle English: from Latin *derivat-* 'derived,' from the verb *derivare* (see **DERIVE**).

der·i·va·tion /ˌderə'vāSHən/ ▶ **n. 1** the obtaining or developing of something from a source or origin: *the* ***derivation*** *of scientific laws* ***from*** *observation.* ■ the formation of a word from another word or from a root in the same or another language. ■ origin; extraction: *music of primarily Turkish derivation.* ■ something derived; a derivative.
2 Linguistics in generative grammar, the set of stages that link the abstract underlying structure of an expression to its surface form.
3 Mathematics the process of deducing a new formula, theorem, etc., from previously accepted statements. ■ a sequence of statements showing that a formula, theorem, etc., is a consequence of previously accepted statements.
– DERIVATIVES **der·i·va·tion·al** /-SHənl/ **adj.**
– ORIGIN late Middle English (denoting the drawing of a fluid, specifically the drawing of pus or blood; also in the sense 'formation of a word from another word'): from Latin *derivatio(n-)*, from the verb *derivare* (see **DERIVE**).

de·riv·a·tive /di'rivətiv/ ▶ **adj.** (typically of an artist or work of art) imitative of the work of another person, and usually disapproved of for that reason: *an artist who is not in the slightest bit derivative.* ■ originating from, based on, or influenced by: *Darwin's work is* ***derivative of*** *the moral philosophers.* ■ [attrib.] (of a financial product) having a value deriving from an underlying variable asset: *equity-based derivative products.*
▶ **n.** something that is based on another source: *a derivative of the system was chosen for the Marine Corps' V-22 tilt rotor aircraft.* ■ (often **derivatives**) an arrangement or instrument (such as a future, option, or warrant) whose value derives from and is dependent on the value of an underlying asset: [as modifier] *the derivatives market.* ■ a word derived from another or from a root in the same or another language. ■ a substance that is derived chemically from a specified compound: *crack is a highly addictive cocaine derivative.* ■ Mathematics an expression representing the rate of change of a function with respect to an independent variable.
– DERIVATIVES **de·riv·a·tive·ly adv.**
– ORIGIN late Middle English (in the adjective sense 'having the power to draw off,' and in the noun sense 'a word derived from another'): from French *dérivatif, -ive*, from Latin *derivativus*, from *derivare* (see **DERIVE**).

de·rive /di'rīv/ ▶ **v.** [with obj.] (**derive something from**) obtain something from (a specified source): *they derived great comfort from this assurance.* ■ (**derive something from**) base a concept on a logical extension or modification of (another concept): *Eliot derived his poetics from the French Symbolists.* ■ [no obj.] (**derive from**) (of a word) have (a specified word, usually of another language) as a root or origin: *the word "punch" derives from the Hindustani "pancha"* | (**be derived from**) *the word "man" is derived from the Sanskrit "manu."* ■ [no obj.] (**derive from**) arise from or originate in (a specified source): *words whose spelling derives from Dr. Johnson's incorrect etymology.* ■ (**be derived from**) Linguistics (of an expression in a natural language) be linked by a set of stages to (its underlying abstract form). ■ (**be derived from**) (of a substance) be formed or prepared by (a chemical or physical process affecting another substance): *strong acids are derived from the combustion of fossil fuels.* ■ Mathematics obtain (a function or equation) from another by a sequence of logical steps, for example by differentiation.
– DERIVATIVES **de·riv·a·ble adj.**
– ORIGIN late Middle English (in the sense 'draw a fluid through or into a channel'): from Old French *deriver* or Latin *derivare*, from *de-* 'down, away' + *rivus* 'brook, stream.'

de·rived de·mand ▶ **n.** Economics a demand for a commodity, service, etc., that is a consequence of the demand for something else.

de·rived fos·sil ▶ **n.** a fossil redeposited in a sediment that is younger than the one in which it first occurred.

derm /dərm/ ▶ **n.** another term for **DERMIS**.

der·ma[1] /'dərmə/ ▶ **n.** another term for **DERMIS**.
– ORIGIN early 18th cent.: modern Latin, from Greek 'skin.'

der·ma[2] ▶ **n.** beef or chicken intestine, stuffed and cooked in dishes such as kishke.
– ORIGIN from Yiddish *derme*, plural of *darm* 'intestine'; related to Old English *tharm* 'intestine.'

der·ma- (also **dermo-**) ▶ **comb. form** skin: *dermabrasion.*
– ORIGIN from Greek, *derma* 'skin.'

derm·a·bra·sion /ˌdərmə'brāZHən/ ▶ **n.** the removal of superficial layers of skin with a rapidly revolving abrasive tool, as a technique in cosmetic surgery.
– ORIGIN 1950s: from Greek *derma* 'skin' + **ABRASION**.

Der·map·te·ra /dər'maptərə/ Entomology an order of insects that comprises the earwigs.
– DERIVATIVES **der·map·ter·an n. & adj.**, **der·map·ter·ous** /-rəs/ **adj.**
– ORIGIN modern Latin (plural), from Greek *derma* 'skin' + *pteron* 'wing.'

der·ma·ti·tis /ˌdərmə'tītis/ ▶ **n.** a condition of the skin in which it becomes red, swollen, and sore, sometimes with small blisters, resulting from direct irritation of the skin by an external agent or an allergic reaction to it. Compare with **ECZEMA**.
– ORIGIN late 19th cent.: from Greek *derma, dermat-* 'skin' + **-ITIS**.

dermato- ▶ **comb. form** of or relating to the skin: *dermatomycosis.*
– ORIGIN from Greek *derma, dermat-* 'skin, hide.'

der·mat·o·glyph·ics /ˌdərmətə'glifiks, dərˌmatə-/ ▶ **plural n.** [treated as sing.] the study of skin markings or patterns on fingers, hands, and feet, and its application, esp. in criminology.
– DERIVATIVES **der·mat·o·glyph** /dər'matəˌglif/ **n.**, **der·mat·o·glyph·ic adj.**, **der·mat·o·glyph·i·cal·ly** /-ik(ə)lē/ **adv.**
– ORIGIN 1920s: from **DERMATO-** 'skin' + Greek *gluphikos* 'carved' (from *gluphē* 'carving').

der·ma·tol·o·gy /ˌdərmə'täləjē/ ▶ **n.** the branch of medicine concerned with the diagnosis and treatment of skin disorders.
– DERIVATIVES **der·ma·to·log·i·cal** /-mətl'äjikəl/ **adj.**, **der·ma·to·log·i·cal·ly** /-mətl'äjik(ə)lē/ **adv.**, **der·ma·tol·o·gist** /-jist/ **n.**

der·ma·tome /'dərməˌtōm/ ▶ **n.** Embryology the lateral wall of each somite in a vertebrate embryo, giving rise to the connective tissue of the skin. Compare with **MYOTOME, SCLEROTOME**. ■ Physiology an area of the skin supplied by nerves from a single spinal root.

der·mat·o·my·co·sis /dərˌmatəˌmī'kōsis, 'dərmətō-/ ▶ **n.** (pl. **dermatomycoses** /-ˌsēz/) a fungal infection of the skin, esp. by a dermatophyte.

der·mat·o·my·o·si·tis /dərˌmatəˌmīə'sītis, 'dərmətō-/ ▶ **n.** Medicine inflammation of the skin and underlying muscle tissue, involving degeneration of collagen, discoloration, and swelling, typically occurring as an autoimmune condition or associated with internal cancer.

der·mat·o·phyte /dər'matəˌfīt, 'dərmətə-/ ▶ **n.** a pathogenic fungus that grows on skin, mucous membranes, hair, nails, feathers, and other body surfaces, causing ringworm and related diseases. ● *Trichophyton* and other genera, subdivision Deuteromycotina.
– DERIVATIVES **der·mat·o·phyt·ic** /dərˌmatə'fitik, ˌdərmətə-/ **adj.**

der·mat·o·phy·to·sis /dərˌmatəfī'tōsis/ ▶ **n.** (pl. **dermatophytoses** /-sēz/) another term for **DERMATOMYCOSIS**.

der·ma·to·sis /ˌdərmə'tōsis/ ▶ **n.** (pl. **dermatoses** /-sēz/) a disease of the skin, esp. one that does not cause inflammation.

der·mes·tid /dər'mestid/ ▶ **n.** Entomology a small beetle of a family (Dermestidae) that includes many kinds that are destructive (esp. as larvae) to hides, skin, fur, wool, and other animal substances.
– ORIGIN late 19th cent.: from modern Latin *Dermestidae* (plural), from the genus name *Dermestes*, formed irregularly from Greek *derma* 'skin' + *esthiein* 'eat.'

der·mis /'dərmis/ ▶ **n.** technical the skin. ■ Anatomy the thick layer of living tissue below the epidermis that forms the true skin, containing blood capillaries, nerve endings, sweat glands, hair follicles, and other structures.
– DERIVATIVES **der·mal** /-məl/ **adj.**, **der·mic** /-mik/ **adj.** (rare).
– ORIGIN mid 19th cent.: modern Latin, suggested by *epidermis*.

der·moid /'dərˌmoid/ ▶ **n.** short for **DERMOID CYST**.

der·moid cyst ▶ **n.** Medicine an abnormal growth (teratoma) containing epidermis, hair follicles, and sebaceous glands, derived from residual embryonic cells.

Der·mop·ter·a /dər'mäptərə/ Zoology a small order of mammals that comprises the flying lemurs or colugos.
– ORIGIN modern Latin (plural), from Greek *derma* 'skin' + *pteron* 'wing.'

der·nier cri /'dernyā 'krē/ ▶ **n.** (**the/le dernier cri**) the very latest fashion: *as soon as he was passé on the European scene, he became the dernier cri here.*
– ORIGIN late 19th cent.: French, literally 'last cry.'

der·o·gate /'derəˌgāt/ ▶ **v.** formal **1** [with obj.] disparage (someone or something): *it is typical of Pirandello to derogate the powers of reason.*
2 [no obj.] (**derogate from**) detract from: *this does not derogate from his duty to act honestly and faithfully.*
3 [no obj.] (**derogate from**) deviate from (a set of rules or agreed form of behavior): *one country has derogated from the Rome Convention.*
– DERIVATIVES **de·rog·a·tive** /di'rägətiv/ **adj.**
– ORIGIN late Middle English: from Latin *derogat-* 'abrogated,' from the verb *derogare*, from *de-* 'aside, away' + *rogare* 'ask.'

der·o·ga·tion /ˌderə'gāSHən/ ▶ **n. 1** an exemption from or relaxation of a rule or law: *the massive derogation of human rights.*
2 the perception or treatment of someone as being of little worth: *the derogation of women.*
– ORIGIN late Middle English (in the sense 'impairment of the force of'): from Latin *derogatio(n-)*, from the verb *derogare* (see **DEROGATE**).

de·rog·a·to·ry /di'rägəˌtôrē/ ▶ **adj.** showing a critical or disrespectful attitude: *she tells me I'm fat and is always making derogatory remarks.*
– DERIVATIVES **de·rog·a·to·ri·ly** /-ˌtôrəlē/ **adv.**
– ORIGIN early 16th cent. (in the sense 'impairing in force or effect'): from late Latin *derogatorius*, from *derogat-* 'abrogated,' from the verb *derogare* (see **DEROGATE**).

der·rick /'derik/ ▶ **n. 1** a kind of crane with a movable pivoted arm for moving or lifting heavy weights, esp. on a ship.
2 the framework over an oil well or similar boring that holds the drilling machinery.
– ORIGIN early 17th cent. (denoting a hangman, also the gallows): from *Derrick*, the surname of a hangman in London, England.

Der·ri·da /dəri'dä, ˌderi-/, Jacques (1930–2004), French philosopher and literary critic. He was an important figure in the theory of deconstructionism.

der·ri·ère /ˌderē'e(ə)r/ ▶ **n.** informal euphemistic term for a person's buttocks.
– ORIGIN late 18th cent.: French, literally 'behind.'

der·ring-do /ˌderiNG'do͞o/ ▶ **n.** dated, humorous action displaying heroic courage: *tales of derring-do.*
– ORIGIN late 16th cent.: from late Middle English *dorryng do* 'daring to do,' used by Chaucer, and, in a passage by Lydgate based on Chaucer's work, misprinted in 16th-cent. editions as *derrynge do*; this was misinterpreted by Spenser to mean 'manhood, chivalry,' and subsequently taken up and popularized by Sir Walter Scott.

der·rin·ger /'derinjər/ ▶ **n.** a small pistol that has a large bore and is very effective at close range.
– ORIGIN mid 19th cent.: named after Henry *Deringer* (1786–1868), the American gunsmith who invented it.

derringer

der·ris /'deris/ ▶ **n. 1** an insecticide made from the powdered roots of certain tropical plants containing rotenone. [late 19th cent.: originally used in Malaya to stupefy fish.]
2 a woody, climbing plant of the pea family that bears leathery pods and has tuberous roots from

which this insecticide is obtained. [modern Latin, from Greek, 'leather covering' (referring to its pod).] ● Genus *Derris*, family Leguminosae.

Der·ry /ˈderē/ **1** see **LONDONDERRY**.
2 a town in southeastern New Hampshire, southeast of Manchester; pop. 34,242 (est. 2008).

der·vish /ˈdərviSH/ ▶ **n.** a member of a Muslim (specifically Sufi) religious order who has taken vows of poverty and austerity. Dervishes first appeared in the 12th century; they were noted for their wild or ecstatic rituals and were known as **dancing**, **whirling**, or **howling dervishes** according to the practice of their order.
– ORIGIN from Turkish *derviş*, from Persian *darvīš* 'poor,' (as a noun) 'religious mendicant.'

DES ▶ **abbr.** ■ diethylstilbestrol. ■ Computing data encryption standard.

de·sa·cral·ize /dēˈsākrəˌlīz/ ▶ **v.** [with obj.] remove the religious or sacred status or significance from: *we have chosen to desacralize the world through modern science.*
– DERIVATIVES **de·sa·cral·i·za·tion** /-ˌsākrələˈzāSHən/ **n.**

de Sade /də ˈsäd/, Marquis, see **SADE**.

de·sal·i·nate /dēˈsaləˌnāt/ ▶ **v.** [with obj.] (usu. as adj. **desalinated**) remove salt from (seawater).
– DERIVATIVES **de·sal·i·na·tion** /-ˌsaləˈnāSHən/ **n.**, **de·sal·i·na·tor** /-ˌnātər/ **n.**

de·sal·in·ize /dēˈsaləˌnīz/ ▶ **v.** another term for **DESALINATE**.
– DERIVATIVES **de·sal·in·i·za·tion** /-ˌsalənəˈzāSHən/ **n.**

de·salt /dēˈsôlt/ ▶ **v.** another term for **DESALINATE**.

de·sa·pa·re·ci·do /ˌdesəˌpärəˈsēdō/ ▶ **n.** (pl. **desaparecidos**) (esp. in South America), a person who has disappeared, presumed killed by members of the armed services or the police.
– ORIGIN late 20th cent.: Spanish, literally 'disappeared.'

de·sat·u·rate /dēˈsaCHəˌrāt/ ▶ **v.** [with obj.] make less saturated; cause to become unsaturated.
– DERIVATIVES **de·sat·u·ra·tion** /-ˌsaCHəˈrāSHən/ **n.**

des·ca·mi·sa·do /ˌdeskaməˈsädō/ ▶ **n.** (pl. **descamisados**) (in Latin America) a very poor person.
– ORIGIN mid 19th cent.: Spanish, literally 'shirtless.'

des·cant ▶ **n.** /ˈdesˌkant/ Music an independent treble melody usually sung or played above a basic melody. ■ archaic or literary a melodious song. ■ a discourse on a theme or subject: *his descant of deprivation.*
▶ **v.** /desˈkant/ [no obj.] literary talk tediously or at length: *I have* **descanted on** *this subject before.*
– ORIGIN late Middle English: from Old French *deschant*, from medieval Latin *discantus* 'part-song, refrain.'

des·cant re·cord·er ▶ **n.** British term for **SOPRANO RECORDER**.

Des·cartes /dāˈkärt/, René (1596–1650), French philosopher, mathematician, and man of science. He concluded that everything was open to doubt except conscious experience and existence as a necessary condition of this: "*Cogito, ergo sum*" (I think, therefore I am). In mathematics, he developed the use of coordinates to locate a point in two or three dimensions.

de·scend /diˈsend/ ▶ **v.** [no obj.] **1** move or fall downward: *the aircraft began to descend.* ■ [with obj.] move down (a slope or stairs): *the vehicle descended a ramp.* ■ (of stairs, a road or path, or a piece of land) be on a slope or incline and extend downward: *a side road descended into the forest* | [with obj.] *a narrow flight of stairs descended a steep slope.* ■ come or go down a scale, esp. from the superior to the inferior: (as adj. **descending**) *the categories are listed in descending order of usefulness.* ■ Music (of sound) become lower in pitch: (as adj. **descending**) *a passage of descending chords.* ■ (**descend to**) act in a specified shameful way that is far below one's usual standards: *she descended to self-pity.* ■ (**descend into**) (of a situation or group of people) reach (a state considered undesirable or shameful): *the army had descended into chaos.*
2 (**descend on/upon**) make a sudden attack on: *the militia descended on Rye.* ■ make an unexpected and typically unwelcome visit to: *treasure-seekers descended upon the site.* ■ (of a feeling or atmosphere) develop suddenly and be felt throughout a place or by a person or group of people: *an air of gloom descended on the Democratic Party headquarters.* ■ (of night or darkness) begin to occur: *as the winter darkness descended, the fighting ceased.*
3 (**be descended from**) be a direct blood relative of (a specified, typically illustrious ancestor): *she is descended from Charles II.* ■ (of an asset) pass by inheritance, typically from parent to child: *his lands descended to his eldest son.*
– ORIGIN Middle English: from Old French *descendre*, from Latin *descendere*, from *de-* 'down' + *scandere* 'to climb.'

de·scend·ant /diˈsendənt/ ▶ **n.** a person, plant, or animal that is descended from a particular ancestor: *Shakespeare's last direct descendant.* ■ a machine, artifact, system, etc., that has developed from an earlier, more rudimentary version.
– ORIGIN late Middle English (as an adjective in the sense 'descending'): from French, present participle of *descendre* 'to descend' (see **DESCEND**). The noun dates from the early 17th cent.

> **USAGE** The correct spelling for the noun meaning 'person descended from a particular ancestor' is **descendant**, ending with the suffix **-ant**, not **-ent** (as in *she claims to be a* **descendant** *of Paul Revere*). The word **descendent** is an adjective, now used almost exlusively in scientific contexts, meaning 'descending from an ancestor' (as in *extinct species are replaced by* **descendent** *species*). Almost 15 percent of the citations for the noun in the Oxford English Corpus use the wrong spelling.

de·scend·ent /diˈsendənt/ ▶ **adj.** descending from an ancestor: *a peculiar genealogy that buds off numerous descendent species* | figurative *descendent theories.*

> **USAGE** On the difference between **descendent** and **descendant**, see usage at **DESCENDANT**.

de·scend·er /diˈsendər/ ▶ **n.** a part of a letter that extends below the level of the base of a letter such as *x* (as in *g* and *p*). ■ a letter having such a part.

de·scen·deur /diˈsendər/ ▶ **n.** Climbing a piece of metal around which a rope is passed and which makes use of friction to slow descent during rappelling.
– ORIGIN late 20th cent.: French, literally 'descender.'

de·scend·i·ble /diˈsendəbəl/ ▶ **adj.** Law (of property) able to be inherited by a descendant.

de·scend·ing co·lon ▶ **n.** Anatomy the part of the large intestine that passes downward on the left side of the abdomen toward the rectum.

de·scent /diˈsent/ ▶ **n.** **1** [usu. in sing.] an action of moving downward, dropping, or falling: *the plane had gone into a steep descent.* ■ a downward slope, esp. a path or track: *a steep, badly eroded descent.* ■ a moral, social, or psychological decline into a specified undesirable state: *the ancient empire's slow descent into barbarism.*
2 the origin or background of a person in terms of family or nationality: *American families of Hungarian descent.* ■ the transmission of qualities, property, or privileges by inheritance.
3 (**descent on**) a sudden, violent attack: *a descent on the enemy airstrip.*
– ORIGIN Middle English: from Old French *descente*, from *descendre* 'to descend' (see **DESCEND**).

de·scram·ble /dēˈskrambəl/ ▶ **v.** [with obj.] convert or restore (a signal) to intelligible form.
– DERIVATIVES **de·scram·bler** /-b(ə)lər/ **n.**

de·scribe /diˈskrīb/ ▶ **v.** [with obj.] **1** give an account in words of (someone or something), including all the relevant characteristics, qualities, or events: *the police said the man was* **described as** *white, 6 ft. tall, with mousy, cropped hair.*
2 mark out or draw (a geometric figure): *on the diameter of a circle an equilateral triangle is described.*
– DERIVATIVES **de·scrib·a·ble adj.**, **de·scrib·er n.**
– ORIGIN late Middle English: from Latin *describere*, from *de-* 'down' + *scribere* 'write.'

de·scrip·tion /diˈskripSHən/ ▶ **n.** **1** a spoken or written representation or account of a person, object, or event: *people who had seen him were able to give a description.* ■ the action of giving such a representation or account: *teaching by demonstration and description.*
2 a sort, kind, or class of people or things: *ships of every description.*
– PHRASES **beyond description** to a great and astonishing extent: *his face was swollen beyond description.* **defy description** be so unusual or remarkable as to be impossible to describe: *the sheer scale of the Requiem defies description.* **answers** (or **fits**) **the description** has the qualities specified.
– ORIGIN late Middle English: via Old French from Latin *descriptio(n-)*, from *describere* 'write down.'

de·scrip·tive /diˈskriptiv/ ▶ **adj.** **1** serving or seeking to describe. ■ Grammar (of an adjective) assigning a quality rather than restricting the application of the expression modified, e.g., *blue* as distinct from *few*.
2 describing or classifying without expressing feelings or judging. ■ Linguistics denoting or relating to an approach to language analysis that describes accents, forms, structures, and usage without making value judgments. Often contrasted with **PRESCRIPTIVE**.
– DERIVATIVES **de·scrip·tive·ly adv.**, **de·scrip·tive·ness n.**
– ORIGIN mid 18th cent.: from late Latin *descriptivus*, from *descript-* 'written down,' from the verb *describere* (see **DESCRIBE**).

de·scrip·tiv·ism /diˈskriptəˌvizəm/ ▶ **n.** Philosophy the doctrine that the meanings of ethical or aesthetic terms and statements are purely descriptive rather than prescriptive, evaluative, or emotive.
– DERIVATIVES **de·scrip·tiv·ist n. & adj.**

de·scrip·tor /diˈskriptər/ ▶ **n.** an element or term that has the function of describing, identifying, or indexing, in particular: ■ Linguistics a word or expression used to describe or identify something. ■ Computing a piece of stored data that indicates how other data is stored.

de·scry /diˈskrī/ ▶ **v.** (**descries**, **descrying**, **descried**) [with obj.] literary catch sight of: *she descried two figures.*
– ORIGIN Middle English: perhaps confused with obsolete *descry* 'describe,' variant of obsolete *descrive* (via Old French from Latin *describere* 'write down'), which also had the meaning 'perceive.'

des·e·crate /ˈdesiˌkrāt/ ▶ **v.** [with obj.] treat (a sacred place or thing) with violent disrespect; violate: *more than 300 graves were desecrated.*
– DERIVATIVES **des·e·cra·tor** /-ˌkrātər/ **n.**
– ORIGIN late 17th cent.: from **DE-** (expressing reversal) + a shortened form of **CONSECRATE**.

des·e·cra·tion /ˌdesiˈkrāSHən/ ▶ **n.** the action of desecrating something: *the desecration of a grave.*

de·seed /dēˈsēd/ ▶ **v.** [with obj.] (usu. as adj. **deseeded**) remove the seeds from (a plant, vegetable, or fruit).
– DERIVATIVES **de·seed·er n.**

de·seg·re·gate /dēˈsegriˌgāt/ ▶ **v.** [with obj.] end a policy of racial segregation in: *actions to desegregate schools.*
– DERIVATIVES **de·seg·re·ga·tion** /dēˌsegriˈgāSHən/ **n.**

de·se·lect /ˌdēsəˈlekt/ ▶ **v.** [with obj.] turn off (a selected feature) on a list of options on a computer menu.
– DERIVATIVES **de·se·lec·tion** /-ˈlekSHən/ **n.**

de·sen·si·tize /dēˈsensiˌtīz/ ▶ **v.** [with obj.] make less sensitive: *creams to desensitize the skin at the site of the injection.* ■ make (someone) less likely to feel shock or distress at scenes of cruelty, violence, or suffering by overexposure to such images: (as adj. **desensitized**) *people who view such movies become desensitized to violence.* ■ free (someone) from a phobia or neurosis by gradually exposing the person to the thing that is feared. See **SYSTEMATIC DESENSITIZATION**.
– DERIVATIVES **de·sen·si·ti·za·tion** /dēˌsensitəˈzāSHən/ **n.**, **de·sen·si·tiz·er n.**

Des·er·et /ˌdezəˈret/ the name proposed in the 1840s by Mormon settlers for what became Utah.

de·sert[1] /dəˈzərt/ ▶ **v.** [with obj.] abandon (a person, cause, or organization) in a way considered disloyal or treacherous: *he deserted his wife and daughter and went back to England.* ■ (of a number of people) leave (a place), causing it to appear empty: *good weather came after the summer hordes had deserted the beaches.* ■ (of a quality or ability) fail (someone), esp. at a crucial moment when most needed: *her luck deserted her.* ■ [no obj.] Military (of a soldier) illegally run away from military service.
– ORIGIN late Middle English: from Old French *deserter*, from late Latin *desertare*, from Latin *desertus* 'left waste' (see **DESERT**[2]).

des·ert[2] /ˈdezərt/ ▶ **n.** a dry, barren area of land, esp. one covered with sand, that is characteristically desolate, waterless, and without vegetation. ■ a situation or area considered dull and uninteresting: *a cultural desert.*
▶ **adj.** [attrib.] like a desert: *overgrazing has created desert conditions.* ■ uninhabited and desolate: *desert wastes.*
– DERIVATIVES **de·ser·tic adj.**
– ORIGIN Middle English: via Old French from late Latin *desertum* 'something left waste,' neuter past participle of *deserere* 'leave, forsake.'

de·sert[3] /diˈzərt/ ▶ **n.** (usu. **deserts**) a person's worthiness or entitlement to reward or punishment: *the penal system fails to punish offenders in accordance with their deserts.*
– PHRASES **get** (or **receive**) **one's just deserts** receive the appropriate reward or (more usually) punishment for one's actions: *those who caused great torment to others rarely got their just deserts.*
– ORIGIN Middle English: via Old French from *deservir* 'serve well' (see **DESERVE**).

> **USAGE** People who get their **just deserts** get what they deserve. **Deserts** here is related to **deserve**, and is spelled with one *-s-* in the middle. This usage has no relation to the **dessert** course of

a meal, yet the *-ss-* spelling (**just desserts**) is found in the Oxford English Corpus nearly as often as the correct spelling.

des·ert boot /ˈdezərt/ ▶ **n.** a lightweight boot with the upper made from suede.

de·sert·ed /dəˈzərtid/ ▶ **adj.** (of a place) empty of people: *deserted beaches of soft sand.*

de·sert·er /dəˈzərtər/ ▶ **n.** a member of the armed forces who deserts: *deserters from the army.*
– ORIGIN mid 17th cent.: from DESERT[1], on the pattern of French *déserteur.*

de·sert·i·fi·ca·tion /di,zərtəfiˈkāSHən/ ▶ **n.** the process by which fertile land becomes desert, typically as a result of drought, deforestation, or inappropriate agriculture.

de·ser·tion /dəˈzərSHən/ ▶ **n.** the action of deserting a person, cause, or organization: *her mother's desertion of her family.* ■ Military the action of illegally leaving the armed forces: *three officers were shot for desertion | the number of desertions was rising.*

des·ert is·land /ˈdezərt/ ▶ **n.** a remote uninhabited tropical island.

des·ert pave·ment /ˈdezərt/ ▶ **n.** Geology a surface layer of closely packed or cemented pebbles, rock fragments, etc., from which fine material has been removed by the wind in arid regions.

des·ert rat /ˈdezərt/ ▶ **n.** informal **1** a soldier of the 7th British armored division (with the jerboa as a badge) in the North African desert campaign of 1941–42.
2 a jerboa.

des·ert rose /ˈdezərt/ ▶ **n. 1** a flowerlike aggregate of crystals of a mineral occurring in arid areas.
2 a succulent plant with pink, tubular flowers and a swollen, woody stem containing toxic, milky sap that is sometimes used for arrow poison. It is native to East Africa and Arabia. ● *Adenium obesum,* family Apocynaceae.
3 (also **Sturt's desert rose**) a dense shrub with pinkish-lilac flowers and black spotted leaves and fruit. Native to arid regions of Australia, it is the floral emblem of the Northern Territory of Australia. ● *Gossypium sturtianum,* family Malvaceae.

des·ert var·nish /ˈdezərt/ ▶ **n.** Geology a dark, hard film of oxides formed on exposed rock surfaces in arid regions.

de·serve /dəˈzərv/ ▶ **v.** [with obj.] do something or have or show qualities worthy of (reward or punishment): *the referee deserves a pat on the back for his bravery* | [with infinitive] *people who park like that deserve to be towed away.*
– ORIGIN Middle English: from Old French *deservir,* from Latin *deservire* 'serve well or zealously.'

de·served /dəˈzərvd/ ▶ **adj.** rightfully earned because of something done or qualities shown; merited: *a deserved standing ovation.*

de·serv·ed·ly /dəˈzərvidlē/ ▶ **adv.** in the way that is deserved; rightfully: *a deservedly popular sitcom | they are top of the division, and deservedly so.*

de·serv·ing /dəˈzərviNG/ ▶ **adj.** worthy of being treated in a particular way, typically of being given assistance: *the deserving poor.*
– DERIVATIVES **de·serv·ing·ly adv., de·serv·ing·ness n.**

de·sex /dēˈseks/ ▶ **v.** [with obj.] (usu. as adj. **desexed**) **1** deprive (someone) of sexual qualities or attraction: *Lawrence portrays feminists as shrill, humorless, and desexed.*
2 castrate or spay (an animal).

de·sex·u·al·ize /dēˈsekSHo͞oə,līz/ ▶ **v.** [with obj.] deprive of sexual character or the distinctive qualities of a sex.
– DERIVATIVES **de·sex·u·al·i·za·tion** /-,sekSHo͞oələˈzāSHən/ **n.**

des·ha·bille /,dezəˈbēl, -ˈbē/ ▶ **n.** variant spelling of DISHABILLE.

de·si /ˈdāsē/ (also **deshi** /ˈdāSHē/) Indian ▶ **adj. 1** local; indigenous. ■ derogatory rustic; unsophisticated.
2 unadulterated or pure: *desi ghee.*
▶ **n.** a person of Indian, Pakistani, or Bangladeshi birth or descent who lives abroad.
– ORIGIN via Hindi from Sanskrit *deśa* 'country, land.'

De Si·ca /də ˈsēkə/, Vittorio (1901–74), Italian movie director and actor; a key figure in Italian neorealist cinema. His directorial work includes *The Bicycle Thief* (1948) and *Two Women* (1960).

des·ic·cant /ˈdesikənt/ ▶ **n.** a hygroscopic substance used as a drying agent.
– ORIGIN late 17th cent.: from Latin *desiccant-* 'making thoroughly dry,' from the verb *desiccare.*

des·ic·cate /ˈdesi,kāt/ ▶ **v.** [with obj.] **1** (usu. as adj. **desiccated**) remove the moisture from (something, esp. food), typically in order to preserve it: *desiccated coconut.*
2 (as adj. **desiccated**) lacking interest, passion, or energy: *a desiccated history of ideas.*
– DERIVATIVES **des·ic·ca·tion** /-ˈkāSHən/ **n., des·ic·ca·tive** /-,kātiv/ **adj.**
– ORIGIN late 16th cent.: from Latin *desiccat-* 'made thoroughly dry,' from the verb *desiccare.*

des·ic·ca·tor /ˈdesi,kātər/ ▶ **n.** a glass container or other apparatus holding a drying agent for removing moisture from specimens and protecting them from water vapor in the air.

de·sid·er·ate /diˈsidə,rāt/ ▶ **v.** [with obj.] archaic feel a keen desire for (something lacking or absent): *I desiderate the resources of a family.*
– ORIGIN mid 17th cent.: from Latin *desiderat-* 'desired,' from the verb *desiderare,* perhaps from *de-* 'down' + *sidus, sider-* 'star.' Compare with CONSIDER.

de·sid·er·a·tive /diˈsidərətiv, -,rātiv/ ▶ **adj.** Grammar (in Latin and other inflected languages) denoting a verb formed from another and expressing a desire to do the act denoted by the root verb (such as Latin *esurire* 'want to eat,' from *edere* 'eat'). ■ having, expressing, or relating to desire.
▶ **n.** Grammar a desiderative verb.
– ORIGIN mid 16th cent.: from late Latin *desiderativus,* from Latin *desiderat-* 'desired,' from the verb *desiderare* (see DESIDERATE).

de·sid·er·a·tum /di,sidəˈrätəm, -ˈrātəm, -,zidə-/ ▶ **n.** (pl. **desiderata** /-tə/) something that is needed or wanted: *integrity was a desideratum.*
– ORIGIN mid 17th cent.: from Latin, 'something desired,' neuter past participle of *desiderare* (see DESIDERATE).

de·sign /dəˈzīn/ ▶ **n. 1** a plan or drawing produced to show the look and function or workings of a building, garment, or other object before it is built or made: *he has just unveiled his design for the new museum.* ■ the art or action of conceiving of and producing such a plan or drawing: *good design can help the reader understand complicated information | the cloister is of late twelfth century design.* ■ an arrangement of lines or shapes created to form a pattern or decoration: *pottery with a lovely blue and white design.*
2 purpose, planning, or intention that exists or is thought to exist behind an action, fact, or material object: *the appearance of design in the universe.*
▶ **v.** [with obj.] decide upon the look and functioning of (a building, garment, or other object), typically by making a detailed drawing of it: *a number of architectural students were designing a factory* | [as adj. with submodifier] (**designed**) *specially designed buildings.* ■ do or plan (something) with a specific purpose or intention in mind: [with obj. and infinitive] *the tax changes were designed to stimulate economic growth.*
– PHRASES **by design** as a result of a plan; intentionally: *I became a presenter by default rather than by design.* **have designs on** aim to obtain (something desired), typically in a secret and dishonest way: *he suspected her of having designs on the family fortune.*
– ORIGIN late Middle English (as a verb in the sense 'to designate'): from Latin *designare* 'to designate,' reinforced by French *désigner.* The noun is via French from Italian.

des·ig·nate ▶ **v.** /ˈdezig,nāt/ [with obj.] appoint (someone) to a specified position: *he was designated as prime minister.* ■ officially assign a specified status or ascribe a specified name or quality to: [with obj. and complement] *certain schools are designated "science schools" | a personality disorder that Adler designates the Ruling Type.* ■ signify; indicate: *the term "brainstem" designates the medulla, pons, and mesencephalon.*
▶ **adj.** /-nit, -,nāt/ [postpositive] appointed to an office or position but not yet installed: *the Director designate.*
– DERIVATIVES **des·ig·na·tor** /-,nātər/ **n.**
– ORIGIN mid 17th cent. (as an adjective): from Latin *designatus* 'designated,' past participle of *designare,* based on *signum* 'a mark.' The verb dates from the late 18th cent.

des·ig·nat·ed driv·er ▶ **n.** a member of a group who abstains from alcohol in order to drive the others safely.

des·ig·nat·ed hit·ter ▶ **n.** Baseball a nonfielding player named before the start of a game to be in the batting order, typically in place of the pitcher.

des·ig·na·tion /,dezigˈnāSHən/ ▶ **n.** the choosing and naming of someone to be the holder of an official position: *a leader's designation of his own successor.* ■ the action of choosing a place for a special purpose or giving it a special status: *the designation of parts of Santa Ana as an enterprise zone.* ■ a name, description, or title, typically one that is officially bestowed: *a group of tribes banded together under the designation "Sheepeaters."*
– ORIGIN late Middle English (in the sense 'the action of marking'): from Latin *designatio(n-),* from the verb *designare* (see DESIGNATE).

de·sign·ed·ly /dəˈzīnidlē/ ▶ **adv.** deliberately in order to produce a specific effect: [as submodifier] *let me propose a designedly vague criterion.*

des·ig·nee /,dezigˈnē/ ▶ **n.** a person who has been designated.

de·sign·er /dəˈzīnər/ ▶ **n.** a person who plans the form, look, or workings of something before its being made or built, typically by drawing it in detail: *he's one of the world's leading car designers.* ■ [as modifier] made by or having the expensive sophistication of a famous and prestigious fashion designer: *a designer label.* ■ [as modifier] upscale and fashionable: *designer food.*

de·sign·er ba·by ▶ **n.** a baby whose genetic makeup has been selected in order to eradicate a particular defect, or to ensure that a particular gene is present.

de·sign·er drug ▶ **n.** a synthetic analog of a legally restricted or prohibited drug, devised to circumvent drug laws.

de·sign·er stub·ble ▶ **n.** beard stubble that is deliberately groomed to look fashionable or trendy.

de·sign·ing /dəˈzīniNG/ ▶ **adj.** [attrib.] acting in a calculating, deceitful way: *she was a designing little minx.*

de·sir·a·bil·i·ty /də,zī(ə)rəˈbilitē/ ▶ **n.** the quality of being desirable: *we agree on the desirability of a negotiated settlement.*

de·sir·a·ble /dəˈzī(ə)rəbəl/ ▶ **adj.** wanted or wished for as being an attractive, useful, or necessary course of action: [with infinitive] *it is desirable to exercise some social control over technology.* ■ (of a person) arousing sexual desire: *she had never looked more desirable.*
▶ **n.** a desirable person, thing, or quality.
– DERIVATIVES **de·sir·a·ble·ness n., de·sir·a·bly** /-blē/ **adv.**
– ORIGIN late Middle English: from Old French, suggested by Latin *desiderabilis,* from *desiderare* 'to desire' (see DESIDERATE).

de·sire /dəˈzī(ə)r/ ▶ **n.** a strong feeling of wanting to have something or wishing for something to happen: [with infinitive] *a desire to work in the dirt with your bare hands.* ■ strong sexual feeling or appetite: *they were clinging together in fierce mutual desire.*
▶ **v.** [with obj.] strongly wish for or want (something): *he never achieved the status he so desired* | (as adj. **desired**) *it failed to create the desired effect.* ■ want (someone) sexually: *there had been a time, years ago, when he had desired her.* ■ archaic express a wish to (someone); request or entreat.
– ORIGIN Middle English: from Old French *desir* (noun), *desirer* (verb), from Latin *desiderare* (see DESIDERATE).

De·si·ree /ˈdezə,rā/ ▶ **n.** a potato of a pink-skinned variety with yellow, waxy flesh.

de·sir·ous /diˈzīrəs/ ▶ **adj.** [predic.] having or characterized by desire: *the pope was desirous of peace in Europe.*
– ORIGIN Middle English: from Old French *desireus,* based on Latin *desiderare* 'to desire' (see DESIDERATE).

de·sist /diˈsist/ ▶ **v.** [no obj.] cease; abstain: *each pledged to* ***desist from*** *acts of sabotage.*
– ORIGIN late Middle English: from Old French *desister,* from Latin *desistere,* from *de-* 'down from' + *sistere* 'to stop' (reduplication of *stare* 'to stand').

desk /desk/ ▶ **n.** a piece of furniture with a flat or sloped surface and typically with drawers, at which one can read, write, or do other work. ■ Music a position in an orchestra at which two players share a music stand: *an extra desk of first and second violins.* ■ a counter in a hotel, bank, or airport at which a customer may check in or obtain information: *the reception desk.* ■ [with modifier] a specified section of a news organization, esp. a newspaper: *he landed a job on the sports desk.*
– ORIGIN late Middle English: from medieval Latin *desca,* probably based on Provençal *desca* 'basket' or Italian *desco* 'table, butcher's block,' both based on Latin *discus* (see DISCUS).

desk-bound ▶ **adj.** restricted to working in an office, rather than in an active, physical capacity: *he is no desk-bound theoretician.*

desk dic·tion·ar·y ▶ **n.** a one-volume dictionary of medium size.

de·skill /dēˈskil/ ▶ **v.** [with obj.] reduce the level of skill required to carry out (a job): *advances in technology had deskilled numerous working-class jobs.* ■ make the skills of (a worker) obsolete.

d

desk job ▶ **n.** a job based at a desk, esp. as opposed to one in active military or police service.

desk jock·ey ▶ **n.** informal, humorous a person who works at a desk; an office worker.
– ORIGIN on the pattern of *disc jockey*.

desk ser·geant ▶ **n.** a sergeant in administrative charge of a police station.

desk·top /ˈdeskˌtäp/ ▶ **n.** the working surface of a desk. ■ [as modifier] denoting a piece of equipment such as a computer that is suitable for use at an ordinary desk: *a desktop machine.* ■ a desktop computer. ■ the working area of a computer screen regarded as a representation of a notional desktop and containing icons representing items such as files and a wastebasket.

d

desk·top pub·lish·ing (abbr.: **DTP**) ▶ **n.** the production of printed matter by means of a printer linked to a desktop computer, with special software. The system enables reports, advertising matter, company magazines, etc., to be produced cheaply with a layout and print quality similar to that of typeset books, for xerographic or other reproduction.

des·man /ˈdesmən/ ▶ **n.** a small, semiaquatic European mammal related to the mole, with a long, tubular muzzle and webbed toes. ● Family Talpidae: the **Russian desman** (*Desmana moschata*) and the **Pyrenean desman** (*Galemys pyrenaicus*).
– ORIGIN late 18th cent.: via French and German from Swedish *desman-råtta* 'muskrat,' from *desman* 'musk.'

des·mid /ˈdezmid/ ▶ **n.** Biology a single-celled, freshwater alga that appears to be composed of two rigid cells with a shared nucleus. The presence of desmids is usually an indicator of unpolluted water. ● Family Desmidiaceae, division Chlorophyta (or phylum Gamophyta, kingdom Protista).
– ORIGIN mid 19th cent.: from modern Latin *Desmidium* (genus name), from Greek *desmos* 'band, chain' (because the algae are often found united in chains or masses).

des·moid /ˈdezmoid/ ▶ **adj.** Medicine denoting a type of fibrous tumor of muscle and connective tissue, typically in the abdomen.
– ORIGIN mid 19th cent.: from Greek *desmos* 'bond' or *desmē* 'bundle' + **-OID**.

Des Moines /di ˈmoin/ the capital of and the largest city in Iowa, in the southern central part of the state; pop. 197,052 (est. 2008).

des·mo·some /ˈdezməˌsōm/ ▶ **n.** Biology a structure by which two adjacent cells are attached, formed from protein plaques in the cell membranes linked by filaments.
– DERIVATIVES **des·mo·so·mal** /ˌdezməˈsōməl/ **adj.**
– ORIGIN 1930s: from Greek *desmos* 'bond, chain' + **-SOME³**.

Des·na Riv·er /dyisˈnä, dəˈsnä/ a river in western Russia and Ukraine that rises east of Smolensk and flows for 550 miles (885 km) to enter the Dnieper River near Kiev.

des·o·late ▶ **adj.** /ˈdesəlit/ (of a place) deserted of people and in a state of bleak and dismal emptiness: *a desolate moor.* ■ feeling or showing misery, unhappiness, or loneliness: *I suddenly felt desolate and bereft.*
▶ **v.** /ˈdesəˌlāt/ [with obj.] make (a place) bleakly and depressingly empty or bare: *the droughts that desolated the dry plains.* ■ (usu. **be desolated**) make (someone) feel utterly wretched and unhappy: *he was desolated by the deaths of his treasured friends.*
– DERIVATIVES **des·o·late·ly adv.**, **des·o·late·ness** /-litnis/ **n.**, **des·o·la·tor** /-ˌlātər/ **n.**
– ORIGIN late Middle English: from Latin *desolatus* 'abandoned,' past participle of *desolare*, from *de-* 'thoroughly' + *solus* 'alone.'

des·o·la·tion /ˌdesəˈlāshən/ ▶ **n.** a state of complete emptiness or destruction: *the stony desolation of the desert.* ■ anguished misery or loneliness: *in choked desolation, she watched him leave.*
– ORIGIN late Middle English: from late Latin *desolatio(n-)*, from Latin *desolare* 'to abandon' (see **DESOLATE**).

de·sol·der /dēˈsädər/ ▶ **v.** [with obj.] remove the solder from (electrical components), usually to effect separation: *cut the pins one by one on the component side, desolder the halves, then throw the chip out.*

de·sorb /dēˈsôrb, -ˈzôrb/ ▶ **v.** [with obj.] Chemistry cause the release of (an adsorbed substance) from a surface. ■ [no obj.] (of an adsorbed substance) become released.
– DERIVATIVES **de·sorb·ent** /-bənt/ **adj. & n.**, **de·sorb·er n.**, **de·sorp·tion** /-ˈzôrpshən, -ˈsôrp-/ **n.**
– ORIGIN 1920s: originally as *desorption* (from *de-* 'away' + *adsorption*), from which *desorb* is a back-formation.

De So·to /də ˈsōtō/ a city in northeastern Texas, south of Dallas; pop. 47,568 (est. 2008).

de So·to /də ˈsōtō/, Hernando (c.1496–1542), Spanish soldier and explorer. After serving as military commander of Nicaragua and of Peru, he landed in Florida in 1539 and explored much of what is now the southeastern US, as far west as Oklahoma. He died of a fever on the banks of the Mississippi River.

de·spair /diˈspe(ə)r/ ▶ **n.** the complete loss or absence of hope: ***driven to despair**, he throws himself under a train* | ***in despair**, I hit the bottle.*
▶ **v.** [no obj.] lose or be without hope: *we should not despair* | *he was beginning to **despair of** ever knowing.*
– PHRASES **be the despair of** be the cause of a feeling of hopelessness in (someone else): *my handwriting was the despair of my teachers.*
– ORIGIN Middle English: the noun via Anglo-Norman French from Old French *desespeir*; the verb from Old French *desperer*, from Latin *desperare*, from *de-* 'down from' + *sperare* 'to hope.'

des·pair·ing /diˈspe(ə)riNG/ ▶ **adj.** showing the loss of all hope: *he gave a despairing little shrug.*
– DERIVATIVES **des·pair·ing·ly adv.**

des·patch ▶ **v. & n.** variant spelling of **DISPATCH**.

des·per·a·do /ˌdespəˈrädō/ ▶ **n.** (pl. **desperadoes** or **desperados**) a desperate or reckless person, esp. a criminal.
– DERIVATIVES **des·per·a·do·ism** /-ˌizəm/ **n.**
– ORIGIN early 17th cent.: pseudo-Spanish alteration of the obsolete noun *desperate*. Both *desperate* and *desperado* originally denoted a person in despair or in a desperate situation, hence someone made reckless by despair.

des·per·ate /ˈdesp(ə)rit/ ▶ **adj.** feeling, showing, or involving a hopeless sense that a situation is so bad as to be impossible to deal with: *a desperate sadness enveloped Ruth.* ■ (of an act or attempt) tried in despair or when everything else has failed; having little hope of success: *drugs used in a desperate attempt to save his life.* ■ (of a situation) extremely bad, serious, or dangerous: *there is a desperate shortage of teachers.* ■ [predic.] (of a person) having a great need or desire for something: *I am desperate **for** a cigarette* | [with infinitive] *the government is desperate to clean up Rio's streets.* ■ (of a person or fight) violent or dangerous: *a desperate criminal* | *a desperate struggle.*
– PHRASES **desperate diseases must have desperate remedies** proverb extreme measures are justified as a response to a difficult or dangerous situation.
– DERIVATIVES **des·per·ate·ness n.**
– ORIGIN late Middle English (in the sense 'in despair'): from Latin *desperatus* 'deprived of hope,' past participle of *desperare* (see **DESPAIR**).

des·per·ate·ly /ˈdesp(ə)ritlē/ ▶ **adv.** in a way that shows despair: *he looked around desperately.* ■ used to emphasize the extreme degree of something: *he desperately needed a drink* | [as submodifier] *I am desperately disappointed.*

des·per·a·tion /ˌdespəˈrāshən/ ▶ **n.** a state of despair, typically one that results in rash or extreme behavior: *she wrote to him in desperation.*
– ORIGIN late Middle English: from Old French, from Latin *desperatio(n-)*, from the verb *desperare* (see **DESPAIR**).

des·pi·ca·ble /diˈspikəbəl/ ▶ **adj.** deserving hatred and contempt: *a despicable crime.*
– DERIVATIVES **des·pi·ca·bly** /-blē/ **adv.**
– ORIGIN mid 16th cent.: from late Latin *despicabilis*, from *despicari* 'look down on.'

de Spi·no·za /də spiˈnōzə/, Baruch, see **SPINOZA**.

de·spise /diˈspīz/ ▶ **v.** [with obj.] feel contempt or a deep repugnance for: *he despised himself for being selfish.*
– DERIVATIVES **de·spis·er n.**
– ORIGIN Middle English: from Old French *despire*, from Latin *despicere*, from *de-* 'down' + *specere* 'look at.'

de·spite /diˈspīt/ ▶ **prep.** without being affected by; in spite of: *he remains a great leader despite age and infirmity.*
▶ **n.** archaic or literary **1** outrage; injury: *the despite done by him to the holy relics.*
2 contempt; disdain: *the theater only earns my despite.*
– PHRASES **despite** (or **in despite**) **of** archaic in spite of. **despite oneself** used to indicate that one did not intend or expect to do the thing mentioned: *despite herself Fran felt a ripple of appreciation for his beauty.*
– DERIVATIVES **de·spite·ful** /-fəl/ **adj.** (archaic or literary).
– ORIGIN Middle English (originally used as a noun meaning 'contempt, scorn' in the phrase *in despite of*): from Old French *despit*, from Latin *despectus* 'looking down on,' past participle (used as a noun) of *despicere* (see **DESPISE**).

Des Plaines /des ˈplānz/ a city in northeastern Illinois, northwest of Chicago; pop. 57,062 (est. 2008).

de·spoil /diˈspoil/ ▶ **v.** [with obj.] steal or violently remove valuable or attractive possessions from; plunder: *the church was **despoiled of** its marble wall covering.*
– DERIVATIVES **de·spoil·er n.**, **de·spoil·ment n.**
– ORIGIN Middle English: from Old French *despoillier*, from Latin *despoliare* 'rob, plunder' (from *spolia* 'spoil').

de·spo·li·a·tion /diˌspōlēˈāshən/ ▶ **n.** the action of despoiling or the condition of being despoiled; plunder: *the despoliation of the resources of the natural world.*

de·spond /diˈspänd/ ▶ **v.** [no obj.] archaic become dejected and lose confidence.
▶ **n.** a state of unhappiness and low spirits.
– ORIGIN mid 17th cent.: from Latin *despondere* 'give up, abandon,' from *de-* 'away' + *spondere* 'to promise.' The word was originally used as a noun in **SLOUGH OF DESPOND**.

de·spond·en·cy /diˈspändənsē/ ▶ **n.** a state of low spirits caused by loss of hope or courage: *he hinted at his own deep despondency.*
– DERIVATIVES **de·spond·ence** /-dəns/ **n.**

de·spond·ent /diˈspändənt/ ▶ **adj.** in low spirits from loss of hope or courage.
– DERIVATIVES **de·spond·ent·ly adv.**

des·pot /ˈdespət/ ▶ **n.** a ruler or other person who holds absolute power, typically one who exercises it in a cruel or oppressive way.
– ORIGIN mid 16th cent.: from French *despote*, via medieval Latin from Greek *despotēs* 'master, absolute ruler.' Originally (after the Turkish conquest of Constantinople) the term denoted a petty Christian ruler under the Turkish empire. The current sense dates from the late 18th cent.

des·pot·ic /diˈspätik/ ▶ **adj.** of or typical of a despot; tyrannical: *a despotic regime.*
– DERIVATIVES **des·pot·i·cal·ly** /diˈspätik(ə)lē/ **adv.**

des·pot·ism /ˈdespəˌtizəm/ ▶ **n.** the exercise of absolute power, esp. in a cruel and oppressive way: *the King's arbitrary despotism.* ■ a country or political system where the ruler holds absolute power.
– ORIGIN early 18th cent.: from French *despotisme*, from *despote* (see **DESPOT**).

des·qua·mate /ˈdeskwəˌmāt/ ▶ **v.** [no obj.] (of a layer of cells, e.g., of the skin) come off in scales or flakes: (as adj. **desquamated**) *desquamated cells.*
– DERIVATIVES **des·qua·ma·tion** /ˌdeskwəˈmāshən/ **n.**, **des·qua·ma·tive** /-ˌmātiv/ **adj.**
– ORIGIN early 18th cent. (in the sense 'remove the scales from'): from Latin *desquamat-* 'scaled,' from the verb *desquamare*, from *de-* 'away from' + *squama* 'a scale.'

des·sert /diˈzərt/ ▶ **n.** the sweet course eaten at the end of a meal: *a dessert of chocolate mousse.*
– ORIGIN mid 16th cent.: from French, past participle of *desservir* 'clear the table,' from *des-* (expressing removal) + *servir* 'to serve.'

des·sert·spoon /diˈzərtˌspōōn/ ▶ **n.** a spoon used for dessert, smaller than a tablespoon and larger than a teaspoon. ■ the amount held by such a spoon.
– DERIVATIVES **des·sert·spoon·ful** /-fōōl/ **n.** (pl. **dessertspoonfuls**).

des·sert wine ▶ **n.** a sweet wine drunk with or following dessert.

de·sta·bi·lize /dēˈstābəˌlīz/ ▶ **v.** [with obj.] upset the stability of; cause unrest in: *the discovery of an affair can destabilize a relationship.*
– DERIVATIVES **de·sta·bi·li·za·tion** /-ˌstābələˈzāshən/ **n.**

de Staël /də ˈstäl/, Madame (1766–1817), French novelist and critic; a precursor of the French romantics; born *Anne Louise Germaine Necker*. Her critical work, *De l'Allemagne* (1810), introduced late-18th-century German writers and thinkers to France.

de·stain /dēˈstān/ ▶ **v.** [with obj.] Biology selectively remove stain from (a specimen for microscopy, a chromatography gel, etc.) after it has previously been stained.

de-Sta·lin·i·za·tion /dēˌstälənəˈzāshən/ ▶ **n.** (in communist countries) the policy of eradicating the memory or influence of Joseph Stalin and Stalinism, esp. after 1956.

De Stijl /də ˈstīl/ a 20th-century Dutch art movement founded in 1917 by **Theo van Doesburg** (1883–1931) and Piet Mondrian. The movement favored an abstract, economical style. It was influential on the Bauhaus and constructivist movements.
– ORIGIN Dutch, literally 'the style,' originally the name of the movement's periodical.

des·ti·na·tion /ˌdestəˈnāsʜən/ ▶ n. the place to which someone or something is going or being sent: *a popular destination for golfers.*
▶ adj. being a place that people will make a special trip to visit: *a destination restaurant.*
– ORIGIN late Middle English: from Latin *destinatio(n-)*, from *destinare* 'make firm, establish.' The original sense was 'the action of intending someone or something for a particular purpose,' later 'being destined for a particular place,' hence (from the early 19th cent.) the place itself.

des·ti·na·tion charge ▶ n. a fee added to the price of a new car to cover the cost of shipping the vehicle from the manufacturer to the dealer.

des·tine /ˈdestin/ ▶ v. [with obj.] intend or choose (someone or something) for a particular purpose or end.
– ORIGIN Middle English (in the sense 'predetermine, decree'): from Old French *destiner*, from Latin *destinare* 'make firm, establish.'

des·tined /ˈdestind/ ▶ adj. [predic.] (of a person's future) developing as though according to a plan: *she could see that he was destined for great things* | [with infinitive] *they were destined to become diplomats.* ■ (**destined to**) certain to meet (a particular fate): *she was destined to become a life-long friend.* ■ (**destined for**) intended for or traveling toward (a particular place): *agricultural exports destined for the United States.* ■ [attrib.] preordained: *your heroine will be united with her destined mate.*

des·ti·ny /ˈdestinē/ ▶ n. (pl. **destinies**) the events that will necessarily happen to a particular person or thing in the future: *she was unable to control her own destiny.* ■ the hidden power believed to control what will happen in the future; fate: *he believes in destiny.*
– ORIGIN Middle English: from Old French *destinee*, from Latin *destinata*, feminine past participle of *destinare* 'make firm, establish.'

des·ti·tute /ˈdestiˌt(y)o͞ot/ ▶ adj. without the basic necessities of life: *the charity cares for destitute children.* ■ [predic.] (**destitute of**) not having: *towns destitute of commerce.*
– ORIGIN late Middle English (in the sense 'deserted, abandoned, empty'): from Latin *destitutus*, past participle of *destituere* 'forsake,' from *de-* 'away from' + *statuere* 'to place.'

des·ti·tu·tion /ˌdestiˈt(y)o͞osʜən/ ▶ n. poverty so extreme that one lacks the means to provide for oneself: *the family faced eviction and destitution.*

de-stress /dēˈstres/ ▶ v. [no obj.] relax after a period of work or tension.

des·tri·er /ˈdestrēər/ ▶ n. a medieval knight's warhorse.
– ORIGIN Middle English: from Old French, based on Latin *dextera* 'the right hand,' from *dexter* 'on the right' (because the squire led the knight's horse with his right hand).

de·stroy /diˈstroi/ ▶ v. [with obj.] put an end to the existence of (something) by damaging or attacking it: *the room had been destroyed by fire.* ■ ruin (someone) emotionally or spiritually: *he has been determined to destroy her.* ■ defeat (someone) utterly: *the Tigers destroyed the Padres in five games.* ■ (usu. **be destroyed**) kill (a sick, savage, or unwanted animal) by humane means: *their terrier was destroyed after the attack.*
– ORIGIN Middle English: from Old French *destruire*, based on Latin *destruere*, from *de-* (expressing reversal) + *struere* 'build.'

de·stroy·er /diˈstroiər/ ▶ n. a small, fast warship, esp. one equipped for a defensive role against submarines and aircraft. ■ someone or something that destroys: *the greatest destroyer of love and peace.*

de·stroy·ing an·gel ▶ n. a deadly poisonous white toadstool that grows in woodlands and is native to both Eurasia and North America. ● Genus *Amanita*, family Amanitaceae, class Hymenomycetes: several species, including the North American *Amanita bisporigera* and the European *Amanita virosa.*

de·struct /diˈstrəkt/ ▶ v. [with obj.] cause deliberate, irreparable damage to (something, typically a rocket or missile).
▶ n. [in sing., usu. as modifier] the deliberate causing of terminal damage: *he had ordered him to go for the destruct button.*
– ORIGIN 1950s: back-formation from DESTRUCTION.

de·struct·i·ble /diˈstrəktəbəl/ ▶ adj. able to be destroyed.
– DERIVATIVES **de·struct·i·bil·i·ty** /-ˌstrəktəˈbilitē/ n.
– ORIGIN mid 18th cent. (earlier in *indestructible*): from French, from late Latin *destructibilis*, from Latin *destruct-* 'destroyed,' from the verb *destruere* (see DESTROY).

de·struc·tion /diˈstrəksʜən/ ▶ n. the action or process of causing so much damage to something that it no longer exists or cannot be repaired: *the destruction of the library in Alexandria* | *the avalanche left a trail of destruction.* ■ the action or process of killing or being killed: *the wanton destruction of human life.* ■ [in sing.] a cause of someone's ruin: *gambling was his destruction.*
– ORIGIN Middle English: from Latin *destructio(n-)*, from the verb *destruere* (see DESTROY).

de·struc·tive /diˈstrəktiv/ ▶ adj. causing great and irreparable harm or damage: *the destructive power of weapons.* ■ tending to refute or disparage; negative and unhelpful: *destructive criticism.*
– DERIVATIVES **de·struc·tive·ly** adv., **de·struc·tive·ness** n.

de·struc·tive dis·til·la·tion ▶ n. Chemistry decomposition of a solid by heating it in a closed container and collecting the volatile constituents given off.

des·ue·tude /ˈdeswiˌt(y)o͞od/ ▶ n. formal a state of disuse: *the docks **fell into desuetude**.*
– ORIGIN early 17th cent. (in the sense 'cessation'): from French, from Latin *desuetudo*, from *desuet-* 'made unaccustomed,' from the verb *desuescere*, from *de-* (expressing reversal) + *suescere* 'be accustomed.'

de·sul·fu·rize /dēˈsəlf(y)əˌrīz/ (also **desulphurize**) ▶ v. [with obj.] remove sulfur or sulfur compounds from (a substance).
– DERIVATIVES **de·sul·fu·ri·za·tion** n., **de·sul·fu·riz·er** n.

des·ul·to·ry /ˈdesəlˌtôrē/ ▶ adj. lacking a plan, purpose, or enthusiasm: *a few people were left, dancing in a desultory fashion.* ■ (of conversation or speech) going constantly from one subject to another in a halfhearted way; unfocused: *the desultory conversation faded.* ■ occurring randomly or occasionally: *desultory passengers were appearing.*
– DERIVATIVES **des·ul·to·ri·ly** /-ˌtôrəlē/ adv., **des·ul·to·ri·ness** n.
– ORIGIN late 16th cent. (also in the literal sense 'skipping around'): from Latin *desultorius* 'superficial' (literally 'relating to a vaulter'), from *desultor* 'vaulter,' from the verb *desilire.*

de·su·per·heat·er /dēˈso͞opərˌhētər/ ▶ n. a container for reducing the temperature of steam to make it less superheated.

de·syn·chro·nize /dēˈsiɴɢkrəˌnīz/ ▶ v. [with obj.] disturb the synchronization of; put out of step or phase.
– DERIVATIVES **de·syn·chro·ni·za·tion** /-ˌsiɴɢkrənəˈzāsʜən/ n.

Det. ▶ abbr. detective: *Det. Sgt. Eric Atkinson.*

de·tach /diˈtacʜ/ ▶ v. [with obj.] **1** disengage (something or part of something) and remove it: *he detached the front lamp from its bracket* | figurative *federal strings need to be detached to restore parental authority.* ■ [no obj.] be easily removable: *the screen detaches from the keyboard.* ■ (**detach oneself from**) leave or separate oneself from (a group or place): *a figure in brown detached itself from the shadows.* ■ (**detach oneself from**) avoid or put an end to any connection or association with: *the newspaper detached itself from the political parties.*
2 (usu. **be detached**) Military send (a group of soldiers or ships) on a separate mission: *our crew was detached to Puerto Rico for the exercise.*
– DERIVATIVES **de·tach·a·bil·i·ty** /-ˌtacʜəˈbilitē/ n., **de·tach·a·ble** adj.
– ORIGIN late 16th cent. (in the sense 'discharge a gun'): from French *détacher*, earlier *destacher*, from *des-* (expressing reversal) + *attacher* 'attach.'

de·tached /diˈtacʜt/ ▶ adj. separate or disconnected, in particular: ■ (of a house or other building) not joined to another on either side: *a four-bedroom detached house.* ■ aloof and objective: *he managed to remain detached from petty politics.*
– DERIVATIVES **de·tach·ed·ly** /-cʜidlē/ adv.

de·tached ret·i·na ▶ n. a retina that has become separated from the underlying choroid tissue at the back of the eye, causing loss of vision in the affected area.

de·tach·ment /diˈtacʜmənt/ ▶ n. **1** the state of being objective or aloof: *he felt a sense of detachment from what was going on.*
2 Military a group of troops, aircraft, or ships sent away on a separate mission: *a detachment of Marines* | *the battalion went **on detachment** to Florida.* ■ a party of people similarly separated from a larger group: *a truck containing a detachment of villagers.*
3 the action or process of detaching; separation: *structural problems resulted in cracking and detachment of the wall.*
– ORIGIN mid 17th cent.: from French *détachement*, from *détacher* 'to detach' (see DETACH).

de·tail /diˈtāl, ˈdētāl/ ▶ n. **1** an individual feature, fact, or item: *we shall consider every detail of the bill* | *her meticulous attention to detail.* ■ a minor or less significant item or feature: *he didn't want them to get sidetracked on a detail of policy.* ■ a minor decorative feature of a building or work of art: *a detail on Charlemagne's tomb.* ■ the style or treatment of such features: *the classical French detail of the building's facade.* ■ a small part of a picture or other work of art reproduced separately for close study: *detail of right eye showing marks on the lids.* ■ (**details**) Brit. itemized facts or information about someone; personal particulars: *the official asked for my father's details.*
2 a small detachment of troops or police officers given a special duty: *the candidate's security detail.* ■ [often with modifier] a special duty assigned to such a detachment.
▶ v. [with obj.] **1** describe item by item; give the full particulars of: *the report details the environmental and health costs of the car.*
2 [with obj. and infinitive] assign (someone) to undertake a particular task: *the ships were detailed to keep watch.*
3 clean (a motor vehicle) intensively and minutely: *the Buick dealer gave him a job washing and detailing cars.*
– PHRASES **go into detail** give a full account of something. **in detail** as regards every feature or aspect; fully: *we will have to examine the proposals in detail.*
– DERIVATIVES **de·tail·er** n.
– ORIGIN early 17th cent. (in the sense 'minor items or events regarded collectively'): from French *détail* (noun), *détailler* (verb), from *dé-* (expressing separation) + *tailler* 'to cut' (based on Latin *talea* 'twig, cutting').

de·tailed /diˈtāld, ˈdēˌtāld/ ▶ adj. having many details or facts; showing attention to detail: *more detailed information was needed.* ■ (of a work of art) executed with many minor decorative features: *an exquisitely detailed carving.*

de·tail·ing /ˈdētāliɴɢ/ ▶ n. small, decorative features on a building, garment, or work of art.

de·tain /diˈtān/ ▶ v. [with obj.] keep (someone) in official custody, typically for questioning about a crime or in politically sensitive situations: *she was detained without trial for two years.* ■ keep (someone) from proceeding; hold back: *she made to open the door, but he detained her.*
– DERIVATIVES **de·tain·ment** n.
– ORIGIN late Middle English (in the sense 'be afflicted with sickness or infirmity'): from Old French *detenir*, from a variant of Latin *detinere*, from *de-* 'away, aside' + *tenere* 'to hold.'

de·tain·ee /diˌtāˈnē, ˌdētāˈnē/ ▶ n. a person held in custody, esp. for political reasons.

de·tain·er /diˈtānər, dē-/ ▶ n. **1** Law the action of detaining or withholding property. ■ the detention of a person in custody. ■ an order authorizing the continued detention of a person in custody.
2 chiefly Law a person who detains someone or something.
– ORIGIN early 17th cent.: from Anglo-Norman French *detener* 'detain' (used as a noun), variant of Old French *detenir* (see DETAIN).

de·tan·gle /dēˈtaɴɢgəl/ ▶ v. [with obj.] remove tangles from (hair).

de·tect /diˈtekt/ ▶ v. [with obj.] discover or identify the presence or existence of: *cancer may soon be detected in its earliest stages.* ■ discover or investigate (a crime or its perpetrators): *the public can help the police to detect crime.* ■ discern (something intangible or barely perceptible): *Paul detected a faint note of weariness in his father's voice.*
– DERIVATIVES **de·tect·a·ble** adj., **de·tect·a·bly** /-əblē/ adv.
– ORIGIN late Middle English: from Latin *detect-* 'uncovered,' from the verb *detegere*, from *de-* (expressing reversal) + *tegere* 'to cover.' The original senses were 'uncover, expose' and 'give someone away,' later 'expose the real or hidden nature of something or someone'; hence the current senses (partly influenced by DETECTIVE).

de·tec·tion /diˈteksʜən/ ▶ n. the action or process of identifying the presence of something concealed: *the early detection of fetal abnormalities.* ■ the work of a detective in investigating a crime: [as modifier] *the detection rate for murder is over 90 percent.* ■ another term for DEMODULATION (see DEMODULATE).
– ORIGIN late 15th cent. (in the sense 'revelation of what is concealed'): from late Latin *detectio(n-)*, from Latin *detegere* 'uncover' (see DETECT).

de·tec·tive /diˈtektiv/ ▶ n. a person, esp. a police officer, whose occupation is to investigate and solve crimes. ■ [as modifier] denoting a particular rank of police officer: *Detective Sergeant Fox.* ■ [as modifier] concerning crime and its investigation: *detective work.*

PRONUNCIATION KEY ə *ago, up*; ər *over, fur*; a *hat*; ā *ate*; ä *car*; e *let*; ē *see*; i *fit*; ī *by*; ɴɢ *sing*; ō *go*; ô *law, for*; oi *toy*; o͝o *good*; o͞o *goo*; ou *out*; ᴛʜ *thin*; T͟H *then*; ᴢʜ *vision*

– ORIGIN mid 19th cent.: from **DETECT**, on the pattern of pairs such as *elect, elective*. The noun was originally short for *detective policeman*, from an adjectival use of the word in the sense 'serving to detect.'

de·tec·tive sto·ry (also **detective novel**) ▶ **n.** a story whose plot revolves around the investigation and solving of a crime.

de·tec·tor /diˈtektər/ ▶ **n.** [often with modifier] a device or instrument designed to detect the presence of a particular object or substance and to emit a signal in response: *methane detectors*. ■ another term for **DEMODULATOR** (see **DEMODULATE**).

de·tent /diˈtent/ ▶ **n.** a catch in a machine that prevents motion until released. ■ (in a clock) a catch that regulates striking.
– ORIGIN late 17th cent. (denoting a catch in clocks and watches): from French *détente*, from Old French *destente*, from *destendre* 'slacken,' from *des-* (expressing reversal) + Latin *tendere* 'to stretch.'

dé·tente /dāˈtänt/ (also **detente**) ▶ **n.** the easing of hostility or strained relations, esp. between countries: *a serious effort at détente with the eastern bloc.*
– ORIGIN early 20th cent.: French, literally 'loosening, relaxation.'

de·ten·tion /diˈtenCHən/ ▶ **n.** the action of detaining someone or the state of being detained in official custody, esp. as a political prisoner: *one of the effects of police detention is isolation from friends and family*. ■ the punishment of being kept in school after hours: *he has made students fear after-school detention | arbitrary after-school detentions.*
– ORIGIN late Middle English (in the sense 'withholding of what is claimed or due'): from late Latin *detentio(n-)*, from Latin *detinere* 'hold back' (see **DETAIN**).

de·ten·tion cen·ter ▶ **n.** an institution where people are held in detention for short periods, in particular illegal immigrants, refugees, people awaiting trial or sentence, or youthful offenders.

de·ter /diˈtər/ ▶ **v.** (**deters, deterring, deterred**) [with obj.] discourage (someone) from doing something, typically by instilling doubt or fear of the consequences: *only a health problem would* ***deter*** *him* ***from*** *seeking re-election*. ■ prevent the occurrence of: *strategists think not only about how to deter war, but about how war might occur.*
– ORIGIN mid 16th cent.: from Latin *deterrere*, from *de-* 'away from' + *terrere* 'frighten.'

de·terge /diˈtərj/ ▶ **v.** [with obj.] rare cleanse thoroughly.
– ORIGIN early 17th cent.: from French *déterger* or Latin *detergere* 'wipe away.'

de·ter·gent /diˈtərjənt/ ▶ **n.** a water-soluble cleansing agent that combines with impurities and dirt to make them more soluble and differs from soap in not forming a scum with the salts in hard water. ■ any additive with a similar action, e.g., an oil-soluble substance that holds dirt in suspension in lubricating oil.
▶ **adj.** of or relating to such compounds or their action: *staining that resists detergent action.*
– DERIVATIVES **de·ter·gence** n., **de·ter·gen·cy** n.
– ORIGIN early 17th cent. (as an adjective): from Latin *detergent-* 'wiping away,' from the verb *detergere*, from *de-* 'away from' + *tergere* 'to wipe.'

de·te·ri·o·rate /diˈti(ə)rēəˌrāt/ ▶ **v.** [no obj.] become progressively worse: *relations between the countries had deteriorated sharply* | (as adj. **deteriorating**) *deteriorating economic conditions.*
– DERIVATIVES **de·te·ri·o·ra·tive** /-ˌrātiv/ adj.
– ORIGIN late 16th cent. (used transitively in the sense 'make worse'): from late Latin *deteriorat-* 'worsened,' from the verb *deteriorare*, from Latin *deterior* 'worse.'

de·te·ri·o·ra·tion /diˌti(ə)rēəˈrāSHən/ ▶ **n.** the process of becoming progressively worse: *a deterioration in the condition of the patient.*

de·ter·mi·na·ble /diˈtərminəbəl/ ▶ **adj. 1** able to be firmly decided or definitely ascertained: *a readily determinable market value.*
2 Law capable of being brought to an end under given conditions; terminable.
– ORIGIN late Middle English: via Old French from late Latin *determinabilis* 'finite,' from the verb *determinare* (see **DETERMINE**).

de·ter·mi·nant /diˈtərminənt/ ▶ **n. 1** a factor that decisively affects the nature or outcome of something: *pure force of will was the main determinant of his success*. ■ Biology a gene or other factor that determines the character and development of a cell or group of cells in an organism, a set of which forms an individual's idiotype.
2 Mathematics a quantity obtained by the addition of products of the elements of a square matrix according to a given rule.
▶ **adj.** serving to determine or decide something.
– ORIGIN early 17th cent.: from Latin *determinant-* 'determining,' from the verb *determinare* (see **DETERMINE**).

de·ter·mi·nate /dəˈtərmənit/ ▶ **adj.** having exact and discernible limits or form: *the phrase has lost any determinate meaning*. ■ Botany (of a flowering shoot) having the main axis ending in a flower bud and therefore no longer extending in length, as in a cyme.
– DERIVATIVES **de·ter·mi·na·cy** /-minəsē/ n., **de·ter·mi·nate·ly** adv., **de·ter·mi·nate·ness** n.
– ORIGIN late Middle English: from Latin *determinatus* 'limited, determined,' past participle of *determinare* (see **DETERMINE**).

de·ter·mi·na·tion /diˌtərməˈnāSHən/ ▶ **n.**
1 firmness of purpose; resoluteness: *he advanced with an unflinching determination.*
2 the process of establishing something exactly, typically by calculation or research: *determination of molecular structures*. ■ Law the settlement of a dispute by the authoritative decision of a judge or arbitrator. ■ Law a judicial decision or sentence.
3 the controlling or deciding of something's nature or outcome: *genetic sex determination.*
4 Law the cessation of an estate or interest.
5 archaic a tendency to move in a fixed direction.
– ORIGIN late Middle English (in the senses 'settlement of a controversy by a judge or by reasoning' and 'authoritative opinion'): via Old French from Latin *determinatio(n-)*, from the verb *determinare* (see **DETERMINE**).

de·ter·mi·na·tive /dəˈtərməˌnātiv, -nətiv/ ▶ **adj.** [predic.] chiefly Law serving to define, qualify, or direct: *the employer's view is not determinative of the issue.*
▶ **n.** Grammar another term for **DETERMINER**.

de·ter·mine /diˈtərmin/ ▶ **v.** [with obj.] **1** cause (something) to occur in a particular way; be the decisive factor in: *it will be her mental attitude that determines her future.*
2 ascertain or establish exactly, typically as a result of research or calculation: *officials are working with state police to determine the cause of a deadly bus crash* | [with clause] *the point of our study was to* ***determine what*** *is true, not what is practicable*. ■ Mathematics specify the value, position, or form of (a mathematical or geometric object) uniquely.
3 [no obj.] firmly decide: *he* ***determined on*** *a withdrawal of his forces* | [with infinitive] *she determined to tackle Stephen the next day.*
4 Law, archaic bring or come to an end.
– DERIVATIVES **de·ter·min·ing** adj.
– ORIGIN late Middle English: from Old French *determiner*, from Latin *determinare* 'limit, fix,' from *de-* 'completely' + *terminare* 'terminate.'

de·ter·mined /diˈtərmind/ ▶ **adj.** having made a firm decision and being resolved not to change it: [with infinitive] *Alice was determined to be heard*. ■ processing or displaying resolve: *Helen was a determined little girl | a determined effort to reduce inflation.*
– DERIVATIVES **de·ter·mined·ly** adv., **de·ter·mined·ness** n.

de·ter·min·er /diˈtərminər/ ▶ **n. 1** a person or thing that determines or decides something.
2 Grammar a modifying word that determines the kind of reference a noun or noun group has, for example *a, the, every*. See also **DEFINITE ARTICLE, INDEFINITE ARTICLE**.

de·ter·min·ism /diˈtərməˌnizəm/ ▶ **n.** Philosophy the doctrine that all events, including human action, are ultimately determined by causes external to the will. Some philosophers have taken determinism to imply that individual human beings have no free will and cannot be held morally responsible for their actions.
– DERIVATIVES **de·ter·min·ist** n. & adj., **de·ter·min·is·tic** /-ˌtərməˈnistik/ adj., **de·ter·min·is·ti·cal·ly** /-ˌtərməˈnistik(ə)lē/ adv.

de·ter·rent /diˈtərənt/ ▶ **n.** a thing that discourages or is intended to discourage someone from doing something. ■ a nuclear weapon or weapons system regarded as deterring an enemy from attack.
▶ **adj.** able or intended to deter: *the deterrent effect of heavy prison sentences.*
– DERIVATIVES **de·ter·rence** n.
– ORIGIN early 19th cent.: from Latin *deterrent-* 'deterring,' from the verb *deterrere* (see **DETER**).

de·ter·ri·to·ri·al·i·za·tion /dēˌteriˌtôrēələˈzāSHən/ ▶ **n.** the severance of social, political, or cultural practices from their native places and populations.
– DERIVATIVES **de·ter·ri·to·ri·al·ize** v.

de·test /diˈtest/ ▶ **v.** [with obj.] dislike intensely: *of all birds the carrion crow is the most detested by gamekeepers.*
– DERIVATIVES **de·test·er** n.
– ORIGIN late 15th cent.: from Latin *detestari*, from *de-* 'down' + *testari* 'witness, call upon to witness' (from *testis* 'a witness').

de·test·a·ble /diˈtestəbəl/ ▶ **adj.** deserving intense dislike: *I found the film's violence detestable.*
– DERIVATIVES **de·test·a·bly** /-blē/ adv.
– ORIGIN late Middle English: from Old French, or from Latin *detestabilis*, from the verb *detestari* (see **DETEST**).

de·tes·ta·tion /ˌdēteˈstāSHən/ ▶ **n.** intense dislike: *Wordsworth's detestation of aristocracy*. ■ archaic a detested person or thing: *he is the detestation of the neighborhood.*
– ORIGIN late Middle English: via Old French from Latin *detestatio(n-)*, from the verb *detestari* (see **DETEST**).

de·throne /dēˈTHrōn/ ▶ **v.** [with obj.] remove (a ruler, esp. a monarch) from power. ■ remove from a position of authority or dominance: *he dethroned the defending titleholder.*
– DERIVATIVES **de·throne·ment** n.

det·i·nue /ˈdetnˌ(y)o͞o/ ▶ **n.** Law a legal claim to recover wrongfully detained goods or possessions.
– ORIGIN late Middle English: from Old French *detenue*, past participle (used as a noun) of *detenir* 'detain.'

det·o·nate /ˈdetnˌāt/ ▶ **v.** explode or cause to explode: [no obj.] *two other bombs failed to detonate* | [with obj.] *a trigger that can detonate nuclear weapons.*
– DERIVATIVES **det·o·na·tive** /-ˌātiv/ adj.
– ORIGIN early 18th cent.: from Latin *detonat-* 'thundered down or forth,' from the verb *detonare*, from *de-* 'down' + *tonare* 'to thunder.'

det·o·na·tion /ˌdetnˈāSHən/ ▶ **n.** the action of causing a bomb or explosive device to explode. ■ a loud explosion: *a series of deafening detonations was heard*. ■ technical combustion of a substance that is initiated suddenly and propagates extremely rapidly, giving rise to a shock wave. Compare with **DEFLAGRATION**. ■ the premature combustion of fuel in an internal combustion engine, causing knocking.
– ORIGIN late 17th cent.: from French *détonation*, from the verb *détoner*, from Latin *detonare* 'thunder down' (see **DETONATE**).

det·o·na·tor /ˈdetnˌātər/ ▶ **n.** a device or a small, sensitive charge used to detonate an explosive. ■ another term for **TORPEDO** (sense 1 of the noun).

de·tor·sion /diˈtôrSHən/ ▶ **n.** Zoology (in gastropod mollusks) the evolutionary reversal of a group to a primitive linear body plan. Compare with **TORSION**.

de·tour /ˈdēˌto͝or/ ▶ **n.** a long or roundabout route taken to avoid something or to visit somewhere along the way: *he had* ***made a detour to*** *a cafe*. ■ an alternative route for use by traffic when the usual road is temporarily closed.
▶ **v.** [no obj.] take a long or roundabout route: *he detoured around the walls*. ■ [with obj.] avoid or bypass (something) by taking such a route: *I would detour the endless stream of motor homes.*
– ORIGIN mid 18th cent. (as a noun): from French *détour* 'change of direction,' from *détourner* 'turn away.'

de·tox /ˈdētäks/ informal ▶ **n.** short for **DETOXIFICATION**: *he ended up* ***in detox*** *for three months.*
▶ **v.** short for **DETOXIFY**.

de·tox·i·cate /dēˈtäksiˌkāt/ ▶ **v.** another term for **DETOXIFY**.
– DERIVATIVES **de·tox·i·ca·tion** /-ˌtäksiˈkāSHən/ n.
– ORIGIN mid 19th cent.: from **DE-** (expressing removal) + Latin *toxicum* 'poison,' on the pattern of *intoxicate*.

de·tox·i·fi·ca·tion /dēˌtäksəfiˈkāSHən/ ▶ **n.** the process of removing toxic substances or qualities. ■ medical treatment of an alcoholic or drug addict involving abstention from drink or drugs until the bloodstream is free of toxins.

de·tox·i·fy /dēˈtäksəˌfī/ ▶ **v.** (**detoxifies, detoxifying, detoxified**) [with obj.] remove toxic substances or qualities from: *the process uses chemical reagents to detoxify the oil*. ■ (usu. **be detoxified**) treat (an alcoholic or drug addict) to remove the effects of drink or drugs in order to help them overcome addiction: *he was twice detoxified from heroin*. ■ [no obj.] abstain from drink and drugs until the bloodstream is free of toxins in order to overcome alcoholism or drug addiction. ■ [no obj.] become free of poisonous substances or qualities: *you can help your body detoxify by cutting down on coffee.*
– DERIVATIVES **de·tox·i·fi·er** n.
– ORIGIN early 20th cent.: from **DE-** (expressing removal) + Latin *toxicum* 'poison' + **-FY**.

de·tract /diˈtrakt/ ▶ **v. 1** [no obj.] (**detract from**) reduce or take away the worth or value of: *these quibbles in no way detract from her achievement*. ■ [with obj.] deny or take away (a quality or achievement) so as to make its subject seem less impressive: *it detracts not one iota from the credit due to them.*
2 [with obj.] (**detract someone/something from**) divert or distract (someone or something) away

from: *the complaint was timed to detract attention from the ethics issue.*
– DERIVATIVES **de·trac·tion** /-ˈtrakSHən/ **n.**, **de·trac·tive** /-ˈtraktiv/ **adj.**
– ORIGIN late Middle English: from Latin *detract-* 'drawn away,' from the verb *detrahere*, from *de-* 'away from' + *trahere* 'draw.'

de·trac·tor /diˈtraktər/ ▶ **n.** a person who disparages someone or something.

de·train /dēˈtrān/ ▶ **v.** [no obj.] leave a train. ■ [with obj.] cause or assist to leave a train: *passengers were detrained because the train was on fire.*
– DERIVATIVES **de·train·ment n.**

de·trib·al·ize /dēˈtrībəˌlīz/ ▶ **v.** [with obj.] (usu. as adj. **detribalized**) remove (someone) from a traditional tribal social structure: *the 250,000 Australian Aborigines include many detribalized urban people.* ■ remove a traditional tribal social structure from (a culture).
– DERIVATIVES **de·trib·al·i·za·tion** /-ˌtrībələˈzāSHən/ **n.**

det·ri·ment /ˈdetrəmənt/ ▶ **n.** the state of being harmed or damaged: *he is engrossed in his work **to the detriment of** his married life.* ■ a cause of harm or damage: *such tests are **a detriment to** good education.*
– ORIGIN late Middle English in the sense 'loss sustained by damage': from Old French, from Latin *detrimentum*, from *detri-*, stem of *deterere* 'wear away.'

det·ri·men·tal /ˌdetrəˈmentl/ ▶ **adj.** tending to cause harm: *releasing the documents would be detrimental to national security | moving her could have a detrimental effect on her health.*
– DERIVATIVES **det·ri·men·tal·ly adv.**

de·tri·tion /diˈtriSHən/ ▶ **n.** rare the action of wearing away by friction.
– ORIGIN late 17th cent.: from medieval Latin *detritio(n-)*, from *detri-*, stem of *deterere* 'wear away.'

de·tri·ti·vore /diˈtritəˌvôr/ ▶ **n.** Zoology an animal that feeds on dead organic material, esp. plant detritus.
– DERIVATIVES **det·ri·tiv·or·ous** /ˌdetrəˈtivərəs/ **adj.**
– ORIGIN 1960s: from DETRITUS + *-vore* 'eating' (see -VOROUS).

de·tri·tus /diˈtrītəs/ ▶ **n.** waste or debris of any kind: *streets filled with rubble and detritus.* ■ gravel, sand, silt, or other material produced by erosion. ■ organic matter produced by the decomposition of organisms.
– DERIVATIVES **de·tri·tal** /-təl/ **adj.**
– ORIGIN late 18th cent. (in the sense 'detrition'): from French *détritus*, from Latin *detritus*, from *deterere* 'wear away.'

De·troit /diˈtroit, ˈdēˌtroit/ a major industrial city and Great Lakes shipping center in southeastern Michigan; pop. 912,062 (est. 2008). It is the center of the US automobile industry. In the 1960s, it was also an important center for rock and soul music.

de trop /də ˈtrō/ ▶ **adj.** not wanted; unwelcome: *she had no grasp of the conversation and felt herself de trop.*
– ORIGIN mid 18th cent.: French, literally 'excessive.'

de Troyes /də ˈtrwä/, Chrétien, see CHRÉTIEN DE TROYES.

de·tru·sor /diˈtro͞ozər/ (also **detrusor muscle**) ▶ **n.** Anatomy a muscle that forms a layer of the wall of the bladder.
– ORIGIN mid 18th cent.: modern Latin, from Latin *detrus-* 'thrust down,' from the verb *detrudere.*

de·tu·mes·cence /ˌdēt(y)o͞oˈmesəns/ ▶ **n.** the process of subsiding from a state of tension, swelling, or (esp.) sexual arousal.
– DERIVATIVES **de·tu·mesce** /-ˈmes/ **v.**, **de·tu·mes·cent adj.**
– ORIGIN late 17th cent.: from Latin *detumescere*, from *de-* 'down, away' + *tumescere* 'to swell.'

de·tune /dēˈt(y)o͞on/ ▶ **v.** [with obj.] **1** cause (a musical instrument) to become out of tune.
2 (usu. as adj. **detuned**) reduce the performance or efficiency of (a motor vehicle or engine) by adjustment.
3 change the frequency of (an oscillatory system such as a laser) away from a state of resonance.

Deu·ca·li·on /d(y)o͞oˈkālēən/ Greek Mythology the son of Prometheus. With his wife Pyrrha he survived a flood sent by Zeus to punish human wickedness; they were then instructed to throw stones over their shoulders, and these turned into humans to repopulate the world.

deuce[1] /d(y)o͞os/ ▶ **n. 1** a thing representing, or represented by, the number two, in particular: ■ the two on dice or playing cards. ■ a throw of two at dice. ■ informal, dated a two-dollar bill.
2 Tennis the tie score of 40-all in a game, at which a player needs two consecutive points to win the game.
– ORIGIN late 15th cent.: from Old French *deus* 'two,' from Latin *duos.*

deuce[2] ▶ **n.** (**the deuce**) informal used as a euphemism for "devil" in expressions of annoyance, impatience, or surprise or for emphasis: ***how the deuce are we to** make a profit? | **what the deuce** are you trying to do?*
– PHRASES **a** (or **the**) **deuce of a ——** used to emphasize how bad, difficult, or serious something is.
– ORIGIN mid 17th cent.: from Low German *duus*, probably of the same origin as DEUCE[1] (two aces at dice being the worst throw).

deuc·ed /ˈd(y)o͞osid/ informal, dated ▶ **adj.** [attrib.] used for emphasis, esp. to express disapproval or frustration: *I know it's deuced awkward for you* | [as submodifier] *I'm so deuced fond of you.*
– DERIVATIVES **deuc·ed·ly adv.** [as submodifier] *they're deucedly hard to find.*

de·us ex ma·chi·na /ˈdāəs eks ˈmäkənə, -ˈmak-/ ▶ **n.** an unexpected power or event saving a seemingly hopeless situation, esp. as a contrived plot device in a play or novel.
– ORIGIN late 17th cent.: modern Latin, translation of Greek *theos ek mēkhanēs*, 'god from the machinery.' In Greek theater, actors representing gods were suspended above the stage, the denouement of the play being brought about by their intervention.

Deut. ▶ **abbr.** Bible Deuteronomy.

deu·ter·ag·o·nist /ˌd(y)o͞otəˈragənist/ ▶ **n.** the person second in importance to the protagonist in a drama.
– ORIGIN mid 19th cent.: from Greek *deuteragōnistēs*, from *deuteros* 'second' + *agōnistēs* 'actor.'

deu·ter·a·nope /ˈd(y)o͞otərəˌnōp/ ▶ **n.** a person suffering from deuteranopia.

deu·ter·a·no·pi·a /ˌd(y)o͞otərəˈnōpēə/ ▶ **n.** colorblindness resulting from insensitivity to green light, causing confusion of greens, reds, and yellows. Compare with PROTANOPIA.
– ORIGIN early 20th cent.: from DEUTERO- 'second' (the color green being regarded as the second component of color vision) + AN-[1] + -OPIA.

deu·ter·at·ed /ˈd(y)o͞otəˌrātid/ (also **deuteriated** /d(y)o͞oˈti(ə)rēˌātid/) ▶ **adj.** Chemistry (of a compound) in which the ordinary isotope of hydrogen has been replaced with deuterium.
– DERIVATIVES **deu·ter·a·tion** /ˌd(y)o͞otəˈrāSHən/ **n.**

deu·ter·ic /d(y)o͞oˈterik/ ▶ **n.** Geology relating to or denoting alteration of the minerals of an igneous rock during the later stages of consolidation.
– ORIGIN early 20th cent.: from DEUTERO- 'secondary' + -IC.

deu·te·ri·um /d(y)o͞oˈti(ə)rēəm/ ▶ **n.** Chemistry a stable isotope of hydrogen with a mass approximately twice that of the usual isotope. (Symbol: **D**)

> Deuterium atoms have a neutron as well as a proton in the nucleus, and the isotope is present to about 1 part in 6,000 in naturally occurring hydrogen. It is used as a fuel in thermonuclear bombs, and heavy water (D_2O) is used as a moderator in nuclear reactors.

– ORIGIN 1930s: modern Latin, from Greek *deuteros* 'second.'

deutero- ▶ **comb. form** second: *Deutero-Isaiah.* ■ secondary: *deuterocanonical.*
– ORIGIN from Greek *deuteros* 'second.'

deu·ter·o·ca·non·i·cal /ˌd(y)o͞otəˌrōkəˈnänikəl/ ▶ **adj.** (of sacred books or literary works) forming a secondary canon.

Deu·ter·o-I·sa·iah /ˌd(y)o͞otəˌrō ˌīˈzāə/ the supposed later author of Isaiah 40–55.

deu·ter·on /ˈd(y)o͞otəˌrän/ ▶ **n.** the nucleus of a deuterium atom, consisting of a proton and a neutron.
– ORIGIN 1930s: from Greek *deuteros* 'second,' on the pattern of *proton.*

Deu·ter·on·o·my /ˌd(y)o͞otəˈränəmē/ the fifth book of the Bible, containing a recapitulation of the Ten Commandments and much of the Mosaic law.

Deutsch·land /ˈdoiCHˌlänt/ German name for GERMANY.

Deutsch·mark /ˈdoiCHˌmärk/ (also **Deutsche Mark** /ˈdoiCHə/) ▶ **n.** the basic monetary unit of Germany (until the introduction of the euro), equal to 100 pfennigs.
– ORIGIN mid 20th cent.: from German *deutsche Mark* 'German mark.'

deut·zi·a /ˈd(y)o͞otsēə/ ▶ **n.** an ornamental shrub with white or pinkish flowers native to Asia and Central America. ● Genus *Deutzia*, family Hydrangeaceae.
– ORIGIN modern Latin, named after Johann van der *Deutz*, 18th-cent. Dutch patron of botany.

de·va /ˈdāvə/ ▶ **n.** a member of a class of divine beings in the Vedic period, which in Indian religion are benevolent and in Zoroastrianism are evil. Compare with ASURA. ■ Indian (in general use) a god.
– ORIGIN early 19th cent.: Sanskrit, literally 'shining one,' later 'god.'

de·va·da·si /ˌdävəˈdäsē/ ▶ **n.** (pl. **devadasis** /-sēz/) a hereditary female dancer and courtesan in a Hindu temple.
– ORIGIN from Sanskrit *devadāsī*, literally 'female servant of a god.'

de Va·le·ra /ˌdevəˈlerə, ˌdā-/, Eamon (1882–1975), Irish statesman; born in the US, taoiseach (prime minister) 1937–48, 1951–54, and 1957–59 and president of the Republic of Ireland 1959–73. He was the leader of Sinn Fein 1917–26 and the founder of the Fianna Fáil Party in 1926. As president of the Irish Free State from 1932, de Valera was largely responsible for the new constitution of 1937 that created the state of Eire.

de·val·or·ize /dēˈvaləˌrīz/ ▶ **v.** [with obj.] rare devalue.
– DERIVATIVES **de·val·or·i·za·tion** /-ˌvalərəˈzāSHən/ **n.**
– ORIGIN early 20th cent.: from French *dévaloriser.*

de·val·ue /dēˈvalyo͞o/ ▶ **v.** (**devalues, devaluing, devalued**) [with obj.] reduce or underestimate the worth or importance of: *I resent the way people seem to devalue my achievement.* ■ Economics reduce the official value of (a currency) in relation to other currencies: *the dinar was devalued by 20 percent.*
– DERIVATIVES **de·val·u·a·tion** /ˌdēvalyo͞oˈāSHən/ **n.**

De·va·na·ga·ri /ˌdävəˈnägərē/ ▶ **n.** the alphabet used for Sanskrit, Hindi, and other Indian languages.
– ORIGIN late 18th cent.: Sanskrit, literally 'divine town script,' from *deva* 'god' + *nāgarī* (from *nagara* 'town'), an earlier name of the script.

dev·as·tate /ˈdevəˌstāt/ ▶ **v.** [with obj.] destroy or ruin (something): *the city was devastated by a huge earthquake | bad weather has devastated the tourist industry.* ■ cause (someone) severe and overwhelming shock or grief: *she was devastated by the loss of Damian.*
– DERIVATIVES **dev·as·ta·tor** /-ˌstātər/ **n.**
– ORIGIN mid 17th cent.: from Latin *devastat-* 'laid waste,' from the verb *devastare*, from *de-* 'thoroughly' + *vastare* 'lay waste.'

dev·as·tat·ing /ˈdevəˌstātiNG/ ▶ **adj.** highly destructive or damaging: *a devastating cyclone struck Bangladesh.* ■ causing severe shock, distress, or grief: *the news came as a devastating blow.* ■ informal extremely impressive, effective, or attractive: *she had a devastating wit.*
– DERIVATIVES **dev·as·tat·ing·ly adv.** [as submodifier] *a devastatingly attractive man.*

dev·as·ta·tion /ˌdevəˈstāSHən/ ▶ **n. 1** great destruction or damage: *the floods caused widespread devastation.*
2 severe and overwhelming shock or grief: *she spoke of her devastation at his death.*

de·vein /dēˈvān/ ▶ **v.** [with obj.] remove the main central vein from (a shrimp or prawn).

de·vel·op /diˈveləp/ ▶ **v.** (**develops, developing, developed**) **1** grow or cause to grow and become more mature, advanced, or elaborate: [no obj.] *motion pictures developed into mass entertainment* | (as adj. **developing**) *this is a rapidly developing field* | [with obj.] *entrepreneurs develop their skills through trial and error.* ■ [no obj.] (often as adj. **developing**) (of a poor agricultural country) become more economically and socially advanced: *the developing world.* ■ [with obj.] convert (land) to a new purpose by constructing buildings or making other use of its resources. ■ construct or convert (a building) so as to improve existing resources. ■ [with obj.] elaborate (a musical theme) by modification of the melody, harmony, or rhythm. ■ [with obj.] Chess bring (a piece) into play from its initial position on a player's back rank. ■ [with obj.] Geometry convert (a curved surface) conceptually into a plane figure as if by unrolling. ■ [with obj.] Mathematics expand (a function, etc.) in the form of a series.
2 start to exist, experience, or possess: [no obj.] *a strange closeness developed* | [with obj.] *I developed an interest in law* | [with obj.] *AIDS patients often develop a rare type of cancer.*
3 [with obj.] treat (a photographic film) with chemicals to make a visible image.
– ORIGIN mid 17th cent. (in the sense 'unfold, unfurl'): from French *développer*, based on Latin *dis-* 'un-' + a second element of unknown origin found also in ENVELOP.

d

de·vel·op·a·ble /di'veləpəbəl/ ▶ **adj.** able to be developed, in particular: ■ (of land or property) able to be adapted or improved so as to become productive or profitable. ■ Geometry (of a curved surface) capable of being flattened into a plane without overlap or separation, as with a cylinder. ■ Mathematics (of a function or expression) capable of being expanded as a series.

de·vel·oped /di'veləpt/ ▶ **adj.** advanced or elaborated to a specified degree: *a fully developed system of public law.* ■ (of a person or part of the body) having specified physical proportions: *a strongman with well-developed muscles.* ■ (of a country or region) advanced economically and socially: *economic assistance to the less-developed countries | the developed world.*

de·vel·op·er /di'veləpər/ ▶ **n.** a person or thing that develops something: *a property developer | software developers.* ■ [with adj.] a person who grows or matures at a specified time or rate: *I was a slow developer.* ■ a chemical agent used for treating photographic film to make a visible image.

de·vel·op·ing coun·try ▶ **n.** a poor agricultural country that is seeking to become more advanced economically and socially.

de·vel·op·ment /di'veləpmənt/ ▶ **n. 1** the process of developing or being developed: *she traces the development of the novel | the development of less invasive treatment.* ■ a specified state of growth or advancement: *the wings attain their full development several hours after birth.* ■ a new and refined product or idea: *the latest developments in information technology.* ■ an event constituting a new stage in a changing situation: *I don't think there have been any new developments since yesterday.* ■ the process of converting land to a new purpose by constructing buildings or making use of its resources: *land suitable for development.* ■ an area of land with new buildings on it: *a major housing development in Chicago.* ■ Chess the process of bringing one's pieces into play in the opening phase of a game.
2 the process of starting to experience or suffer from an ailment or feeling: *the development of brittle bones.*
3 the process of treating photographic film with chemicals to make a visible image.

de·vel·op·men·tal /di,veləp'mentl/ ▶ **adj.** concerned with the development of someone or something: *developmental problems | developmental psychology.* ■ concerned with the evolution of animals and plants: *developmental biology.*
– DERIVATIVES **de·vel·op·men·tal·ly adv.**

de·vel·op·men·tal de·lay ▶ **n.** the condition of a child being less developed mentally or physically than is normal for its age: *mercury contributes to many known health problems, including neurological injury, developmental delay, and cerebral palsy.*

de·vel·op·ment sys·tem ▶ **n.** Computing a system of software and hardware designed to assist in the development of new software or products.

dé·vel·op·pé /də,velə'pā/ ▶ **n.** (pl. **développés** pronunc. **same**) Ballet a movement in which one leg is raised to the knee of the supporting leg, then unfolded and kept in a fully extended position.

de·verb·al /dē'vərbəl/ ▶ **adj.** (of a noun or adjective) derived from a verb.
▶ **n.** a deverbal noun or adjective.

De·vi /'dāvē/ Hinduism the supreme goddess, often identified with Parvati and Shakti. ■ (**devi**) Indian (in general use) a goddess. ■ Indian used after the first name of a Hindu woman as a form of respect: *Deval Devi.*

de·vi·ance /'dēvēəns/ ▶ **n.** the fact or state of departing from usual or accepted standards, esp. in social or sexual behavior.
– DERIVATIVES **de·vi·an·cy** /-ənsē/ **n.**

de·vi·ant /'dēvēənt/ ▶ **adj.** departing from usual or accepted standards, esp. in social or sexual behavior: *deviant behavior | a deviant ideology.* ■ derogatory homosexual.
▶ **n.** a deviant person or thing.
– ORIGIN late Middle English: from late Latin *deviant-* 'turning out of the way,' from the verb *deviare* (see **DEVIATE**).

de·vi·ate ▶ **v.** /'dēvē,āt/ [no obj.] depart from an established course: *you must not deviate from the agreed route.* ■ depart from usual or accepted standards: *those who deviate from society's values.*
▶ **n. & adj.** /'dēvē,it/ old-fashioned term for **DEVIANT**.
– DERIVATIVES **de·vi·a·tor** /-,ātər/ **n.**
– ORIGIN mid 16th cent. (as an adjective in the sense 'remote'): from late Latin *deviat-* 'turned out of the way,' from the verb *deviare*, from *de-* 'away from' + *via* 'way.' The verb dates from the mid 17th cent.

de·vi·a·tion /,dēvē'āsHən/ ▶ **n. 1** the action of departing from an established course or accepted standard: *deviation from a norm | sexual deviation | deviations from standard English.*
2 Statistics the amount by which a single measurement differs from a fixed value such as the mean.
3 the deflection of a vessel's compass needle caused by iron in the vessel, which varies with the vessel's heading.
– DERIVATIVES **de·vi·a·tion·ism** /-,izəm/ **n.**, **de·vi·a·tion·ist** /-ist/ **n.**
– ORIGIN late Middle English: via French from medieval Latin *deviatio(n-)*, from Latin *deviare* (see **DEVIATE**).

de·vice /di'vīs/ ▶ **n. 1** a thing made or adapted for a particular purpose, esp. a piece of mechanical or electronic equipment: *a measuring device.* ■ a bomb or other explosive weapon: *an incendiary device.* ■ archaic the design or look of something: *works of strange device.*
2 a plan, scheme, or trick with a particular aim: *writing a public letter is a traditional device for signaling dissent.* ■ a turn of phrase intended to produce a particular effect in speech or a literary work: *a rhetorical device.*
3 a drawing or design: *the decorative device on the invitations.* ■ an emblematic or heraldic design: *their shields bear the device of the Blazing Sun.*
– PHRASES **leave someone to their own devices** leave someone to do as they wish without supervision.
– ORIGIN Middle English: from Old French *devis*, based on Latin *divis-* 'divided,' from the verb *dividere*. The original sense was 'desire or intention,' found now only in *leave a person to his or her own devices* (which has become associated with sense 2).

dev·il /'devəl/ ▶ **n. 1** (usu. **the Devil**) (in Christian and Jewish belief) the chief evil spirit; Satan. ■ an evil spirit; a demon. ■ a very wicked or cruel person: *they prefer voting for devils rather than for decent men.* ■ a mischievously clever or self-willed person: *the cunning old devil is up to something.* ■ [with adj.] informal a person with specified characteristics: *the poor devil | a lucky devil.* ■ (**the devil**) fighting spirit; wildness: *he was dangerous when the devil was in him.* ■ (**the devil**) a thing that is very difficult or awkward to do or deal with: *it's going to be the very devil to disentangle.*
2 (**the devil**) expressing surprise or annoyance in various questions or exclamations: *"Where the devil is he?"*
3 an instrument or machine, esp. one fitted with sharp teeth or spikes, used for tearing or other destructive work.
4 informal, dated a junior assistant of a lawyer or other professional. See also **PRINTER'S DEVIL**.
▶ **v.** (**devils, deviling, deviled**; Brit. **devils, devilling, devilled**) **1** [no obj.] informal, dated act as a junior assistant for a lawyer or other professional.
2 [with obj.] harass or worry (someone): *he was deviled by a new-found fear.*
– PHRASES **between the devil and the deep (blue) sea** caught in a dilemma. [alluding to two equally dangerous alternatives.] **devil a ——** archaic not even one or any: *the devil a man of you stirred himself over it.* **the devil can quote scripture for his purpose** proverb people may conceal unworthy motives by reciting words that sound morally authoritative. [with allusion to Jesus' Temptation in Matt. 4.] **the devil finds work for idle hands to do** proverb someone who doesn't have enough work to do is liable to cause or get into trouble. **the devil looks after his own** proverb success or good fortune often seem to come to those who least deserve it. **a devil of a ——** informal used to emphasize great size or degree: *we are in a devil of a mess here.* **the devil is in the details** the details of a matter are its most problematic aspect. **the devil's own ——** informal used to emphasize the difficulty or seriousness of something: *he was in the devil's own hurry.* **(the) devil take the hindmost** proverb everyone should (or does) look after their own interests rather than considering those of others: *full speed ahead and the devil take the hindmost.* [with allusion to a chase by the Devil, in which the slowest will be caught.] **the devil to pay** serious trouble to be dealt with: *there was the devil to pay when we got home.* **give the devil his due** proverb acknowledge the good qualities of even a bad or undeserving person. **go to the devil 1** said in angry rejection or condemnation of someone. **2** fall into moral depravity: *he must go to the devil in his own way.* **like the devil** with great speed or energy: *he drove like the devil.* **play the devil with** have a damaging or disruptive effect on: *this brandy plays the devil with one's emotions!* **speak** (or **talk**) **of the devil** said when a person appears just after being mentioned. [from the superstition that the devil will appear if his name is spoken.]
– ORIGIN Old English *dēofol* (related to Dutch *duivel* and German *Teufel*), via late Latin from Greek *diabolos* 'accuser, slanderer' (used in the Septuagint to translate Hebrew *śāṭān* 'Satan'), from *diaballein* 'to slander,' from *dia* 'across' + *ballein* 'to throw.'

dev·iled /'devəld/ ▶ **adj.** (of food) cooked with hot seasoning: *deviled eggs.*

dev·il·fish /'devəl,fisH/ ▶ **n.** (pl. **same** or **devilfishes**) any of a number of marine creatures that are perceived as having a sinister appearance, in particular a devil ray, a stonefish, or an octopus or squid.

dev·il·ish /'devəlisH/ ▶ **adj.** of, like, or appropriate to a devil in evil and cruelty: *devilish tortures.* ■ mischievous and rakish: *a wide, devilish grin.* ■ very difficult to deal with or use: *it turned out to be a devilish job.*
▶ **adv.** [as submodifier] informal, dated very; extremely: *a devilish clever chap.*
– DERIVATIVES **dev·il·ish·ness n.**

dev·il·ish·ly /'devəlisHlē/ ▶ **adv.** in a devilish manner. ■ [as submodifier] informal very; extremely: *their music is devilishly difficult.*

dev·il-may-care ▶ **adj.** cheerful and reckless: *lighthearted, devil-may-care young pilots.*

dev·il·ment /'devəlmənt/ ▶ **n.** reckless mischief; wild spirits: *his eyes were blazing with devilment.*

dev·il ray ▶ **n.** a large, long-tailed ray that has a fleshy, hornlike projection on each side of the mouth. It occurs on or near the surface of warm seas and feeds on plankton. ● Family Mobulidae: two genera and several species, including the manta.

dev·il·ry /'devəlrē/ ▶ **n.** wicked activity: *some devilry was afoot.* ■ reckless mischief: *a perverse sense of devilry urged her to lead him on.* ■ black magic; dealings with the devil.

dev·il's ad·vo·cate ▶ **n.** a person who expresses a contentious opinion in order to provoke debate or test the strength of the opposing arguments: *the interviewer will need to* **play devil's advocate** *to put the other side's case forward.* ■ historical the popular title of the person appointed by the Roman Catholic Church to challenge a proposed beatification or canonization, or the verification of a miracle.

dev·il's bit ▶ **n.** a North American plant of the lily family bearing tightly packed spikes of white flowers. ● *Chamaelirium luteum*, family Liliaceae.

dev·il's claw ▶ **n.** a plant whose seedpods bear clawlike hooks that can harm livestock. ● Two genera in the family Pedaliaceae: genus *Proboscidea* of warm regions of America, used in basketry or grown for their fruit, and *Harpagophytum procumbens* of southern Africa and Madagascar, used in herbal medicine.

dev·il's club ▶ **n.** a very spiny, straggling shrub of western North America. ● *Oplopanax horridus*, family Araliaceae.

dev·il's darn·ing nee·dle ▶ **n.** another term for **DARNER** (sense 2).

dev·il's food cake ▶ **n.** a rich chocolate cake.

dev·il's grip ▶ **n.** informal term for **BORNHOLM DISEASE**.

Dev·il's Is·land a rocky island off the coast of French Guiana that was used from 1852 as a penal settlement, esp. for political prisoners. The last prisoner was released in 1953.

dev·il's paint·brush ▶ **n.** a deep orange European hawkweed, which has become naturalized in North America. ● *Hieracium aurantiacum*, family Compositae.

Dev·il's Tower /'devəlz/ a rock column that is 865 feet (264 m) high in northeastern Wyoming, a national monument on the Belle Fourche River.

dev·il's walk·ing stick ▶ **n.** See **HERCULES-CLUB**.

dev·il·try /'devəltrē/ ▶ **n.** archaic variant of **DEVILRY**.

de·vi·ous /'dēvēəs/ ▶ **adj. 1** showing a skillful use of underhanded tactics to achieve goals: *he's as devious as a politician needs to be | they have devious ways of making money.*
2 (of a route or journey) longer and less direct than the most straightforward way: *they arrived at the town by a devious route.*
– DERIVATIVES **de·vi·ous·ly adv.**, **de·vi·ous·ness n.**
– ORIGIN late 16th cent.: from Latin *devius* (from *de-* 'away from' + *via* 'way') + **-ous**. The original sense was 'remote or sequestered'; the later sense 'departing from the direct route' gave rise to the figurative sense 'deviating from the straight way' and hence 'skilled in underhanded tactics.'

de·vise /di'vīz/ ▶ **v.** [with obj.] **1** plan or invent (a complex procedure, system, or mechanism) by careful thought: *a training program should be devised | a complicated game of his own devising.*
2 Law leave (real estate) to someone by the terms of a will.
▶ **n.** Law a clause in a will leaving real estate to someone.
– DERIVATIVES **de·vis·a·ble adj.**, **de·vi·see** /di,vī'zē/ **n.** (sense 2 of the verb), **de·vis·er n.**, **de·vi·sor** /-'vīzər/ **n.** (sense 2 of the verb).

– ORIGIN Middle English: the verb from Old French *deviser,* from Latin *divis-* 'divided,' from the verb *dividere* (this sense being reflected in the original English sense of the verb); the noun is a variant of DEVICE (in the early sense 'will, desire').

de·vi·tal·ize /dē'vītl,īz/ ▶ **v.** [with obj.] (usu. as adj. **devitalized**) deprive of strength and vigor: *an effective product to treat devitalized skin.*
– DERIVATIVES **de·vi·tal·i·za·tion** /dē,vītlə'zāsHən/ **n.**

de·vit·ri·fy /dē'vitrə,fī/ ▶ **v.** (**devitrifies, devitrifying, devitrified**) [no obj.] (of glass or vitreous rock) become hard, opaque, and crystalline. ■ [with obj.] make hard, opaque, and crystalline.
– DERIVATIVES **de·vit·ri·fi·ca·tion** /-,vitrəfi'kāsHən/ **n.**

de·voice /dē'vois/ ▶ **v.** [with obj.] Phonetics make (a vowel or voiced consonant) voiceless.

de·void /di'void/ ▶ **adj.** [predic.] (**devoid of**) entirely lacking or free from: *Lisa kept her voice devoid of emotion.*
– ORIGIN late Middle English: past participle of obsolete *devoid* 'cast out,' from Old French *devoidier.*

de·voir /dəv'wär/ ▶ **n.** archaic a person's duty: *you have done your devoir right well.* ■ (**pay one's devoirs**) pay one's respects formally.
– ORIGIN Middle English: from Old French *deveir,* from Latin *debere* 'owe.' The spelling, and subsequently the pronunciation, was changed under the influence of modern French *devoir.*

dev·o·lu·tion /,devə'lo͞osHən/ ▶ **n.** the transfer or delegation of power to a lower level, esp. by central government to local or regional administration. ■ formal descent or degeneration to a lower or worse state: *the devolution of the gentlemanly ideal into a glorification of drunkenness.* ■ Law the legal transfer of property from one owner to another. ■ Biology evolutionary degeneration.
– DERIVATIVES **dev·o·lu·tion·ar·y** /-,nerē/ **adj.**, **dev·o·lu·tion·ist** /-ist/ **n.**
– ORIGIN late 15th cent. (in the sense 'transference by default'): from late Latin *devolutio(n-),* from Latin *devolvere* 'roll down' (see DEVOLVE).

de·volve /di'välv/ ▶ **v.** [with obj.] transfer or delegate (power) to a lower level, esp. from central government to local or regional administration: *measures to devolve power to the provinces* | (as adj. **devolved**) *devolved and decentralized government.* ■ [no obj.] (**devolve on/upon/to**) (of duties or responsibility) pass to (a body or person at a lower level): *his duties devolved on a comrade.* ■ [no obj.] (**devolve into**) formal degenerate or be split into: *the Empire devolved into separate warring states.*
– DERIVATIVES **de·volve·ment n.**
– ORIGIN late Middle English (in the sense 'roll down'): from Latin *devolvere,* from *de-* 'down' + *volvere* 'to roll.'

Dev·on[1] /'devən/ (also **Devonshire** /-sHər, -,sHi(ə)r/) a county in southwestern England; county town, Exeter.

Dev·on[2] ▶ **n.** an animal of a breed of red beef cattle.
– ORIGIN mid 19th cent.: named after the county of *Devon* (see DEVON[1]).

De·vo·ni·an /di'vōnēən/ ▶ **adj. 1** of or relating to Devon.
2 Geology of, relating to, or denoting the fourth period of the Paleozoic era, between the Silurian and Carboniferous periods.

> The Devonian period lasted from about 409 million to 363 million years ago. During this period fish became abundant; the first amphibians evolved, and the first forests appeared.

▶ **n. 1** a native or inhabitant of Devon.
2 (**the Devonian**) Geology the Devonian period or the system of rocks deposited during it.

Dev·on·shire cream /'devənsHər, -,sHi(ə)r/ ▶ **n.** clotted cream.

de·vo·ré /də'vôrā/ (also **devore**) ▶ **n.** a velvet fabric with a pattern formed by burning the pile away with acid: [as modifier] *a devoré top.*
– ORIGIN 1990s: from French *dévoré,* lit. 'devoured,' past part. of *dévorer.*

de·vote /di'vōt/ ▶ **v.** [with obj.] **1** (**devote something to**) give all or a large part of one's time or resources to (a person, activity, or cause): *I wanted to devote more time to my family* | *she devoted herself to fundraising.*
2 archaic invoke or pronounce a curse upon.
– ORIGIN late 16th cent. (in the sense 'dedicate formally, consecrate'): from Latin *devot-* 'consecrated,' from the verb *devovere,* from *de-* 'formally' + *vovere* 'to vow.'

de·vot·ed /di'vōtid/ ▶ **adj. 1** very loving or loyal: *he was a devoted husband* | *Leo was devoted to his job.*
2 [predic.] (**devoted to**) given over to the display, study, or discussion of: *there is a museum devoted to her work.*
– DERIVATIVES **de·vot·ed·ly adv.** (sense 1), **de·vot·ed·ness n.** (sense 1).

dev·o·tee /,devə'tē, -'tā/ ▶ **n.** a person who is very interested in and enthusiastic about someone or something: *a devotee of classical music.* ■ a strong believer in a particular religion or god: *devotees of Krishna* | *devotees thronged the temple.*

de·vo·tion /di'vōsHən/ ▶ **n.** love, loyalty, or enthusiasm for a person, activity, or cause: *Eleanor's devotion to her husband* | *his courage and devotion to duty never wavered.* ■ religious worship or observance: *the order's aim was to live a life of devotion.* ■ (**devotions**) prayers or religious observances.
– ORIGIN Middle English: from Latin *devotio(n-),* from *devovere* 'consecrate' (see DEVOTE).

de·vo·tion·al /di'vōsHənl/ ▶ **adj.** of or used in religious worship: *devotional books.*

de·vour /di'vou(ə)r/ ▶ **v.** [with obj.] eat (food or prey) hungrily or quickly: *he devoured half of his burger in one bite.* ■ (of fire, disease, or other forces) consume (someone or something) destructively: *the hungry flames devoured the old house.* ■ read (something) quickly and eagerly: *she spent her evenings devouring the classics.* ■ (**be devoured**) (of a person) be totally absorbed by an unpleasant feeling: *she was devoured by need.*
– DERIVATIVES **de·vour·er n.**, **de·vour·ing·ly adv.**
– ORIGIN Middle English: from Old French *devorer,* from Latin *devorare,* from *de-* 'down' + *vorare* 'to swallow.'

de·vout /di'vout/ ▶ **adj.** having or showing deep religious feeling or commitment: *she was a devout Catholic* | *a rabbi's devout prayers.* ■ totally committed to a cause or belief: *the most devout environmentalist.*
– DERIVATIVES **de·vout·ly adv.**, **de·vout·ness n.**
– ORIGIN Middle English: from Old French *devot,* from Latin *devotus* 'devoted,' past participle of *devovere* (see DEVOTE).

de Vries /də 'vrēz/, Hugo (1848–1935), Dutch plant physiologist and geneticist. He did much work on osmosis and water relations in plants, coining the term *plasmolysis.* His subsequent work on heredity contributed substantially to the chromosome theory of heredity.

DEW ▶ **abbr.** distant early warning.

dew /d(y)o͞o/ ▶ **n.** tiny drops of water that form on cool surfaces at night, when atmospheric vapor condenses: *the grass was wet with dew* | [in sing.] *a cold, heavy dew dripped from the leaves.* ■ [in sing.] a beaded or glistening liquid resembling such drops: *her body had broken out in a fine dew of perspiration.*
▶ **v.** [with obj.] wet (a part of someone's body) with a beaded or glistening liquid: *sweat dewed her lashes.*
– ORIGIN Old English *dēaw,* of Germanic origin; related to Dutch *dauw* and German *Tau* (noun), *tauen* (verb).

de·wan ▶ **n.** variant spelling of DIWAN.

Dew·ar /'d(y)o͞oər/, Sir James (1842–1923), Scottish chemist and physicist. He devised the vacuum flask, achieved temperatures close to absolute zero, and was the first to produce liquid oxygen and hydrogen in quantity.

dew·ar /'d(y)o͞oər/ ▶ **n.** a double-walled flask of metal or silvered glass with a vacuum between the walls, used to hold liquids at well below ambient temperature.
– ORIGIN late 19th cent.: named after Sir James DEWAR.

de·wa·ter /dē'wätər, -'wô-/ ▶ **v.** [with obj.] drain (a waterlogged or flooded area). ■ remove water from (sediment or waste materials).

dew·ber·ry /'d(y)o͞o,berē/ ▶ **n.** (pl. **dewberries**) a trailing European bramble with soft prickles and edible fruit which has a dewy white bloom on the skin. ● *Rubus caesius,* family Rosaceae. ■ any of a number of trailing brambles. ■ the blue-black fruit of any of these plants.

dew·claw /'d(y)o͞o,klô/ ▶ **n.** a rudimentary inner toe present in some dogs. ■ a false hoof on an animal such as a deer, which is formed by its rudimentary side toes.
– ORIGIN late 16th cent.: apparently from the nouns DEW and CLAW.

dewclaw

dew·drop /'d(y)o͞o,dräp/ ▶ **n.** a drop of dew.

Dew·ey[1] /'d(y)o͞o-ē/, George (1837–1917), US naval officer. Appointed commodore of the navy in 1896, he was the hero of the battle of Manila Bay in the Philippines in 1898 during the Spanish-American War.

Dew·ey[2], John (1859–1952), US philosopher and educational theorist. He defined knowledge as successful practice and espoused the educational theory that children learn best by doing.

Dew·ey[3], Melvil (1851–1931), US librarian. He devised a decimal system of classifying books that used ten main subject categories.

Dew·ey[4], Thomas Edmund (1902–71), US lawyer and politician. He served as governor of New York 1943–55 and was the Republican presidential candidate in 1944 and 1948.

Dew·ey dec·i·mal clas·si·fi·ca·tion (also **Dewey system**) ▶ **n.** an internationally applied decimal system of library classification that uses a three-figure code from 000 to 999 to represent the major branches of knowledge, and allows finer classification to be made by the addition of further figures after a decimal point.
– ORIGIN late 19th cent.: named after M. *Dewey.*

dew·fall /'d(y)o͞o,fôl/ ▶ **n.** literary the formation of dew, or the time of the evening when dew begins to form. ■ the film of dew covering an area.

De·wi /'däwē/ Welsh name for St. David (see DAVID, ST.).

dew·lap /'d(y)o͞o,lap/ ▶ **n.** a fold of loose skin hanging from the neck or throat of an animal or bird, esp. that present in many cattle.
– ORIGIN Middle English: from DEW and LAP[1], perhaps influenced by a Scandinavian word (compare with Danish *doglæp*).

dewlap

de·worm /dē'wərm/ ▶ **v.** [with obj.] treat (an animal) to free it of worms.
– DERIVATIVES **de·worm·er n.**

dew point ▶ **n.** the atmospheric temperature (varying according to pressure and humidity) below which water droplets begin to condense and dew can form.

dew worm ▶ **n.** an earthworm, in particular one used as fishing bait.
– ORIGIN Old English *deaw-wyrm* 'ringworm'; compare with East Frisian *dauworm,* denoting both ringworm and the earthworm.

dew·y /'d(y)o͞oē/ ▶ **adj.** (**dewier, dewiest**) wet with dew. ■ (of a person's skin) appearing soft and lustrous: *your skin will begin to feel revitalized and dewy.* ■ youthful and fresh: *the girls have yet to lose their dewy charm.*
– DERIVATIVES **dew·i·ly** /'d(y)o͞oəlē/ **adv.**, **dew·i·ness n.**
– ORIGIN Old English *dēawig* (see DEW, -Y[1]).

dew·y-eyed ▶ **adj.** having eyes that are moist with tears (used typically to indicate that a person is nostalgic, naive, or sentimental): *she gets slightly dewy-eyed as she talks about her family.*

dex /deks/ ▶ **n.** informal short for DEXEDRINE.

dex·a·meth·a·sone /,deksə'meTHə,zōn/ ▶ **n.** Medicine a synthetic drug of the corticosteroid type, used esp. as an anti-inflammatory agent.
– ORIGIN 1950s: from *dexa-* (blend of DECA- and HEXA-) + *meth(yl)* + *-a-* + *(cortis)one.*

Dex·e·drine /'deksə,drən, -,drin/ ▶ **n.** trademark for AMPHETAMINE SULFATE (see AMPHETAMINE).
– ORIGIN 1940s: probably from DEXTRO-, on the pattern of *Benzedrine.*

dex·ter[1] /'dekstər/ ▶ **adj.** [attrib.] archaic & Heraldry of, on, or toward the right-hand side (in a coat of arms, from the bearer's point of view, i.e., the left as it is depicted). The opposite of SINISTER.
– ORIGIN mid 16th cent.: from Latin, 'on the right.'

dex·ter[2] ▶ **n.** an animal of a small, hardy breed of Irish cattle.
– ORIGIN late 19th cent.: said to have been named after the breeder.

d

dex·ter·i·ty /dek'steritē/ ▶ n. skill in performing tasks, esp. with the hands: *her dexterity with chopsticks | his record testifies to a certain dexterity in politics*.
– ORIGIN early 16th cent. (in the sense 'mental adroitness'): from French *dextérité*, from Latin *dexteritas*, from *dexter* 'on the right.'

dex·ter·ous /'dekst(ə)rəs/ (also **dextrous**) ▶ adj. demonstrating neat skill, esp. with the hands: *dexterous accordion playing*. ■ mentally adroit; clever: *power users are dexterous at using software, rather than creating it*.
– DERIVATIVES **dex·ter·ous·ly** adv., **dex·ter·ous·ness** n.
– ORIGIN early 17th cent. (in the sense 'mentally adroit, clever'): from Latin *dexter* 'on the right' + -OUS.

dex·tral /'dekstrəl/ ▶ adj. of or on the right side or the right hand (the opposite of SINISTRAL), in particular: ■ right-handed. ■ Geology relating to or denoting a strike-slip fault in which the motion of the block on the farther side of the fault from an observer is toward the right. ■ Zoology (of a spiral mollusk shell) with whorls rising to the right and coiling in a counterclockwise direction.
▶ n. a right-handed person.
– DERIVATIVES **dex·tral·i·ty** /dek'stralitē/ n., **dex·tral·ly** adv.
– ORIGIN mid 17th cent.: from medieval Latin *dextralis*, from Latin *dextra* 'the right hand,' from *dexter* 'on the right.'

dex·tran /'dek,stran, -strən/ ▶ n. Chemistry a carbohydrate gum formed by the fermentation of sugars and consisting of polymers of glucose. ■ Medicine a solution containing a hydrolyzed form of this, used as a substitute for blood plasma.
– ORIGIN late 19th cent.: from DEXTRO- + -AN.

dex·trin /'dekstrin/ ▶ n. a soluble gummy substance obtained by hydrolysis of starch, used as a thickening agent and in adhesives and dietary supplements.
– ORIGIN mid 19th cent.: from DEXTRO- + -IN[1].

dextro- ▶ comb. form on or to the right: *dextrorotatory*.
– ORIGIN from Latin *dexter, dextr-* 'right.'

dex·tro·ro·ta·to·ry /,dekstrə'rōtə,tôrē/ ▶ adj. Chemistry (of a compound) having the property of rotating the plane of a polarized light ray to the right, i.e., clockwise facing the oncoming radiation. The opposite of LEVOROTATORY.
– DERIVATIVES **dex·tro·ro·ta·tion** /-,rō'tāSHən/ n.

dex·trose /'dekstrōs/ ▶ n. Chemistry the dextrorotatory form of glucose (and the predominant naturally occurring form).
– ORIGIN mid 19th cent.: from Latin *dexter, dextr-* 'on the right' + -OSE[2].

dex·trous ▶ adj. variant spelling of DEXTEROUS.

dex·y /'deksē/ ▶ n. (pl. **dexies**) informal Dexedrine. ■ a tablet of Dexedrine.
– ORIGIN 1950s: abbreviation.

de·zinc·i·fi·ca·tion /dē,ziNGkifi'kāSHən/ ▶ n. a form of corrosion and weakening of brass objects in which zinc is dissolved out of the brass alloy.

DF ▶ abbr. ■ Defender of the Faith. [from Latin *Defensor Fidei*.] ■ direction finder.

DFC ▶ abbr. Distinguished Flying Cross.

Dfl ▶ abbr. Dutch florins.

DFM ▶ abbr. (in the UK) Distinguished Flying Medal, a decoration awarded to RAF personnel for acts of courage or devotion to duty when not in action against an enemy, instituted in 1918.

DG ▶ abbr. ■ Dei gratia, by the grace of God. ■ Deo gratias, thanks be to God. ■ (in the UK) director general.

DH ▶ abbr. ■ Doctor of Humanities. ■ Baseball designated hitter.
▶ v. (**DH's, DHing, DH'd**) [no obj.] act as a designated hitter. ■ [with obj.] use (a player) as a designated hitter.

Dhah·ran /dä'rän, ,dähə'rän/ an oil town in eastern Saudi Arabia that was an Allied forces port and military base during the Persian Gulf War; pop. 110,800 (est. 2009).

Dha·ka /'däkə, 'dakə/ (also **Dacca**) the capital of Bangladesh, in the central part of the country, on the Ganges delta; pop. 7,000,940 (2008).
– DERIVATIVES **Dha·kai** /'däk,ī, 'dak,ī/ adj.

dhal ▶ n. variant spelling of DAL'.

dham·ma /'dämə/ ▶ n. another term for DHARMA, esp. among Theravada Buddhists.
– ORIGIN Pali, from Sanskrit *dharma* 'decree or custom.'

Dhan·bad /'dän,bäd/ a city in northeastern India, in Jharkand; pop. 241,800 (est. 2009).

dhan·sak /'dən,säk/ ▶ n. an Indian dish of meat or vegetables cooked with lentils and coriander: *chicken dhansak*.
– ORIGIN Gujarati.

dhar·ma /'därmə/ ▶ n. **1** Hinduism the principle of cosmic order. ■ virtue, righteousness, and duty, esp. social and caste duty in accord with the cosmic order.
2 Buddhism the teaching or religion of the Buddha. ■ one of the fundamental elements of which the world is composed.
– ORIGIN late 18th cent.: Sanskrit, literally 'decree or custom.'

dhar·ma·sha·la /,därmə'SHälə/ (also **dharmasala** /-'sälə/) ▶ n. (in South Asia) a building devoted to religious or charitable purposes, esp. a rest house for travelers.
– ORIGIN from Sanskrit *dharmaśālā*, from *dharma* 'virtue' + *śālā* 'house.'

dhar·na /'därnə/ ▶ n. Indian a mode of compelling payment or compliance, by sitting at the debtor's or offender's door without eating until the demand is complied with. ■ a peaceful demonstration.
– ORIGIN from Hindi *dharnā* 'sitting in restraint, placing.'

Dha·ruk /'də,ro͝ok/ ▶ n. an Aboriginal language of the area around Sydney, Australia, now extinct.

Dhar·war /där'wär/ a city in southern India, twinned with Hubli, in Karnataka state, noted for manufacturing textiles; pop. 905,000 (2009).

Dhau·la·gi·ri /,doulə'gi(ə)rē/ a mountain massif in Nepal, in the Himalayas, that has six peaks and rises to 26,810 feet (8,172 m) at its highest point.

DHEA ▶ abbr. dihydroepiandrosterone.

dhikr /'T͟Hikər/ (also **zikr** /'zēkər/) ▶ n. Islam a form of devotion, associated chiefly with Sufism, in which the worshiper is absorbed in the rhythmic repetition of the name of God or his attributes. ■ a Sufi ceremony in which this is practiced.

dho·bi /'dōbē/ ▶ n. (pl. **dhobis**) (in South Asia) a washerman or washerwoman.
– ORIGIN from Hindi *dhobī*, from *dhob* 'washing.'

dho·bi itch ▶ n. informal itching inflammation of the skin, esp. in the groin region, suffered particularly in the tropics and typically caused by certain types of ringworm infection or by allergic dermatitis.

Dho·far /dō'fär/ the fertile southern province of Oman.

dhol /dōl/ ▶ n. a large, barrel-shaped or cylindrical wooden drum, typically two-headed, used in South Asia.
– ORIGIN from Hindi *ḍhol*.

dho·lak /'dōlək/ ▶ n. a dhol, esp. a relatively small one.
– ORIGIN Hindi, from *ḍhol* (see DHOL) + the diminutive suffix *-ak*.

dhole /dōl/ ▶ n. an Asian wild dog that has a sandy coat and a black, bushy tail and lives in packs. ● *Cuon alpinus*, family Canidae.
– ORIGIN early 19th cent.: of unknown origin.

dho·ti /'dōtē/ ▶ n. (pl. **dhotis**) a garment worn by male Hindus, consisting of a piece of material tied around the waist and extending to cover most of the legs.
– ORIGIN Hindi *dhotī*.

dhow /dou/ ▶ n. a lateen-rigged ship with one or two masts, used in the Indian Ocean.
– ORIGIN late 18th cent.: from Arabic *dāwa*, probably related to Marathi *dāw*.

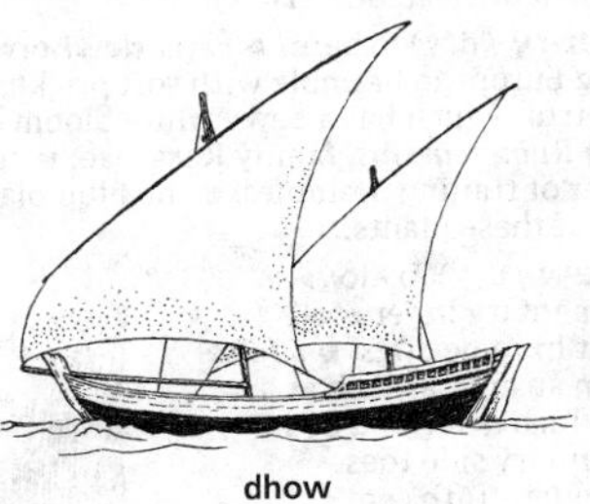
dhow

DHT ▶ abbr. dihydrotestosterone.

DHTML ▶ abbr. Computing dynamic HTML, a collection of browser enhancements that enable dynamic and interactive features on web pages.

dhur·rie /'do͝orē/ (also **durrie**) ▶ n. (pl. **dhurries**) a heavy cotton rug of Indian origin.
– ORIGIN from Hindi *darī*.

dhya·na /dī'yänə/ ▶ n. (in Hindu and Buddhist practice) profound meditation that is the penultimate stage of yoga.
– ORIGIN from Sanskrit *dhyāna*.

DI ▶ abbr. drill instructor.

di-[1] ▶ comb. form twice; two-; double: *dichromatic*. ■ Chemistry containing two atoms, molecules, or groups of a specified kind: *dioxide*.
– ORIGIN from Greek *dis* 'twice.'

di-[2] ▶ prefix variant spelling of DIS- before *l, m, n, r, s* (followed by a consonant), and *v*; also often before *g*, and sometimes before *j*.
– ORIGIN from Latin.

di-[3] ▶ prefix variant spelling of DIA- before a vowel (as in *dielectric*).

dia. ▶ abbr. diameter.

dia- (also **di-** before a vowel) ▶ prefix **1** through; across: *diameter | diaphanous | diuretic*.
2 apart: *diakinesis*.
– ORIGIN from Greek *dia* 'through.'

di·a·base /'dīə,bās/ ▶ n. Geology another term for DOLERITE.
– ORIGIN mid 19th cent. (originally denoting diorite): from French, formed irregularly as if from *di-* 'two' + *base* 'base' (thus 'rock with two bases,' referring to the base minerals of diorite), but associated later perhaps with Greek *diabasis* 'transition.'

di·a·be·tes /,dīə'bētēz, -tis/ ▶ n. a disorder of the metabolism causing excessive thirst and the production of large amounts of urine.
– ORIGIN mid 16th cent.: via Latin from Greek, literally 'siphon,' from *diabainein* 'go through.'

di·a·be·tes in·sip·i·dus /in'sipidəs/ ▶ n. a rare form of diabetes caused by a deficiency of the pituitary hormone vasopressin, which regulates kidney function.
– ORIGIN late 19th cent.: from DIABETES + Latin *insipidus* 'insipid.'

di·a·be·tes mel·li·tus /mə'lītəs, 'meli-/ ▶ n. the most common form of diabetes, caused by a deficiency of the pancreatic hormone insulin, which results in a failure to metabolize sugars and starch. Sugars accumulate in the blood and urine, and the byproducts of alternative fat metabolism disturb the acid–base balance of the blood, causing a risk of convulsions and coma.
– ORIGIN late 19th cent.: from DIABETES + Latin *mellitus* 'sweet.'

di·a·be·tic /,dīə'betik/ ▶ adj. having diabetes. ■ relating to or designed to relieve diabetes: *a diabetic clinic | a diabetic diet*.
▶ n. a person suffering from diabetes.

di·a·ble·rie /dē'äblərē/ ▶ n. reckless mischief; charismatic wildness: *the beauty and diablerie of the great actor*. ■ archaic sorcery supposedly assisted by the devil.
– ORIGIN mid 18th cent.: from French, from *diable*, from ecclesiastical Latin *diabolus* 'devil.'

di·a·bol·i·cal /,dīə'bälikəl/ (also **diabolic**) ▶ adj. belonging to or so evil as to recall the Devil: *his diabolical cunning*.
– DERIVATIVES **di·a·bol·i·cal·ly** /-ik(ə)lē/ adv. [as submodifier] *I am going to get diabolically drunk*.

di·ab·o·lism /dī'abə,lizəm/ ▶ n. worship of the Devil. ■ devilish or atrociously wicked conduct.
– DERIVATIVES **di·ab·o·list** n.
– ORIGIN early 17th cent.: from ecclesiastical Latin *diabolus* or Greek *diabolos* 'devil' + -ISM.

di·ab·o·lize /dī'abə,līz/ ▶ v. [with obj.] archaic represent as diabolical.

di·ab·o·lo /dē'abə,lō/ ▶ n. (pl. **diabolos**) a game in which a two-headed top is thrown up and caught with a string stretched between two sticks. ■ the wooden top used in this game.
– ORIGIN early 20th cent.: from Italian, from ecclesiastical Latin *diabolus* 'devil'; the game was formerly called *devil on two sticks*.

di·a·bu·lim·i·a /,dīəbo͞o'limēə, -'lē-/ ▶ n. the manipulation by diabetic patients of insulin treatments in order to lose weight.
– ORIGIN from DIABETES + BULIMIA.

di·a·ce·tyl·mor·phine /,dīə,sētl'môrfēn/ ▶ n. technical term for HEROIN.

di·a·chron·ic /,dīə'kränik/ ▶ adj. concerned with the way in which something, esp. language, has developed and evolved through time. Often contrasted with SYNCHRONIC.
– DERIVATIVES **di·a·chro·ne·i·ty** /-krə'nāitē/ n., **di·a·chron·i·cal·ly** /-ik(ə)lē/ adv., **di·a·chron·is·tic** /-,krə'nistik/ adj., **di·ach·ro·ny** /dī'akrənē/ n.
– ORIGIN mid 19th cent.: from DIA- 'through' + Greek *khronos* 'time' + -IC.

di·a·chron·ism /dī'akrə,nizəm/ ▶ n. Geology the occurrence of a feature or phenomenon in different geological periods.
– DERIVATIVES **di·ach·ro·nous** /-nəs/ adj., **di·ach·ro·nous·ly** /-nəslē/ adv.

di·ac·o·nal /dī'akənl/ ▶ adj. relating to a deacon, or to the role of a deacon.
– ORIGIN early 17th cent.: from ecclesiastical Latin *diaconalis*, from *diaconus* (see DEACON).

di·ac·o·nate /dīˈakənit, -ˌnāt/ ▶ **n.** the office of deacon, or a person's tenure in it. ■ a body of deacons collectively.
– ORIGIN early 18th cent.: from ecclesiastical Latin *diaconatus*, from *diaconus* (see DEACON).

di·a·crit·ic /ˌdīəˈkritik/ ▶ **n.** a sign, such as an accent or cedilla, which when written above or below a letter indicates a difference in pronunciation from the same letter when unmarked or differently marked.
▶ **adj.** (of a mark or sign) indicating a difference in pronunciation.
– ORIGIN late 17th cent.: from Greek *diakritikos*, from *diakrinein* 'distinguish,' from *dia-* 'through' + *krinein* 'to separate.'

di·a·crit·i·cal /ˌdīəˈkritikəl/ ▶ **adj.** (of a mark or sign) serving to indicate different pronunciations of a letter above or below which it is written.
– DERIVATIVES **di·a·crit·i·cal·ly** /-ik(ə)lē/ **adv.**

di·a·del·phous /ˌdīəˈdelfəs/ ▶ **adj.** Botany (of stamens) united by their filaments so as to form two groups.
– ORIGIN early 19th cent.: from DI-[1] 'two' + Greek *adelphos* 'brother' + -OUS.

di·a·dem /ˈdīəˌdem/ ▶ **n.** a jeweled crown or headband worn as a symbol of sovereignty. ■ (**the diadem**) archaic the authority or dignity symbolized by a diadem: *the princely diadem.*
– DERIVATIVES **di·a·demed adj.**
– ORIGIN Middle English: from Old French *diademe*, via Latin from Greek *diadēma* 'the regal headband of the Persian kings,' from *diadein* 'bind around.'

di·aer·e·sis ▶ **n.** variant spelling of DIERESIS.

diag. ▶ **abbr.** ■ diagonal. ■ diagram.

di·a·gen·e·sis /ˌdīəˈjenəsis/ ▶ **n.** Geology the physical and chemical changes occurring during the conversion of sediment to sedimentary rock.
– DERIVATIVES **di·a·ge·net·ic** /-jəˈnetik/ **adj.**, **di·a·ge·net·i·cal·ly** /-jəˈnetik(ə)lē/ **adv.**

Dia·ghi·lev /dēˈägəˌlef/, Sergei (Pavlovich) (1872–1929), Russian ballet impresario. In 1909, he formed the Ballets Russes, which he directed until his death.

di·ag·nose /ˌdīəgˈnōs/ ▶ **v.** [with obj.] identify the nature of (an illness or other problem) by examination of the symptoms: *doctors diagnosed a rare and fatal liver disease.* ■ (usu. **be diagnosed**) identify the nature of the medical condition of (someone): *she was finally* ***diagnosed as having*** *epilepsy* | *20,000 men are* ***diagnosed with*** *skin cancer every year.*
– DERIVATIVES **di·ag·nos·a·ble adj.**
– ORIGIN mid 19th cent.: back-formation from DIAGNOSIS.

di·ag·no·sis /ˌdīəgˈnōsis/ ▶ **n.** (pl. **diagnoses** /-ˌsēz/) **1** the identification of the nature of an illness or other problem by examination of the symptoms: *early diagnosis and treatment are essential* | *a diagnosis of Crohn's disease was made.*
2 the distinctive characterization in precise terms of a genus, species, or phenomenon.
– ORIGIN late 17th cent.: modern Latin, from Greek, from *diagignōskein* 'distinguish, discern,' from *dia* 'apart' + *gignōskein* 'recognize, know.'

di·ag·nos·tic /ˌdīəgˈnästik/ ▶ **adj. 1** concerned with the diagnosis of illness or other problems: *a diagnostic tool.* ■ (of a symptom) distinctive, and so indicating the nature of an illness: *there are fifteen infections that are* ***diagnostic of*** *AIDS.*
2 characteristic of a particular species, genus, or phenomenon: *the diagnostic character of having not one but two pairs of antennae.*
▶ **n. 1** a distinctive symptom or characteristic. ■ Computing a program or routine that helps a user to identify errors.
2 (**diagnostics**) the practice or techniques of diagnosis: *advanced medical diagnostics.*
– DERIVATIVES **di·ag·nos·ti·cal·ly** /-ik(ə)lē/ **adv.**, **di·ag·nos·ti·cian** /-ˌnäsˈtisHən/ **n.**
– ORIGIN early 17th cent.: from Greek *diagnōstikos* 'able to distinguish,' from *diagignōskein* 'distinguish'; the noun from *hē diagnōstikē tekhnē* 'the art of distinguishing (disease).'

di·ag·o·nal /dīˈagənl/ (abbr.: **diag.**) ▶ **adj.** (of a straight line) joining two opposite corners of a square, rectangle, or other straight-sided shape. ■ (of a line) straight and at an angle; slanting: *a tie with diagonal stripes.*
▶ **n.** a straight line joining two opposite corners of a square, rectangle, or other straight-sided shape. ■ Mathematics the set of elements of a matrix that lie on a line joining two opposite corners. ■ a slanting straight pattern or line: *the bars of light made diagonals across the entrance* | *tiles can be laid* ***on the diagonal.*** ■ Chess a slanting row of squares whose color is the same.
– ORIGIN mid 16th cent.: from Latin *diagonalis*, from Greek *diagōnios* 'from angle to angle,' from *dia* 'through' + *gōnia* 'angle.'

di·ag·o·nal·ly /dīˈagənlē/ ▶ **adv.** in a diagonal direction: *now walk diagonally across the field toward a farmhouse.*

di·ag·o·nal ma·trix ▶ **n.** Mathematics a matrix having nonzero elements only in the diagonal running from the upper left to the lower right.

di·a·gram /ˈdīəˌgram/ ▶ **n.** (abbr.: **diag.**) a simplified drawing showing the appearance, structure, or workings of something; a schematic representation: *a diagram of the living room.* ■ Geometry a figure composed of lines that is used to illustrate a definition or statement or to aid in the proof of a proposition.
▶ **v.** (**diagrams, diagraming, diagramed**; also **diagramming, diagrammed**) [with obj.] represent (something) in graphic form: *the experiment is diagramed on page fourteen.*
– ORIGIN early 17th cent.: from Latin *diagramma*, from Greek, from *diagraphein* 'mark out by lines,' from *dia* 'through' + *graphein* 'write.'

di·a·gram·mat·ic /ˌdīəgrəˈmatik/ ▶ **adj.** of or in the form of a diagram: *a diagrammatic representation of the system.*
– DERIVATIVES **di·a·gram·mat·i·cal·ly** /ˌdīəgrəˈmatik(ə)lē/ **adv.**

di·a·ki·ne·sis /ˌdīəkəˈnēsis/ ▶ **n.** (pl. **diakineses** /-sēz/) Biology the fifth and last stage of the prophase of meiosis, following diplotene, when the separation of homologous chromosomes is complete and crossing over has occurred.
– ORIGIN early 20th cent.: from DIA- 'through, across' + Greek *kinēsis* 'motion.'

di·al /ˈdī(ə)l/ ▶ **n.** a face of a clock, watch, or sundial that is marked to show units of time. ■ a similar face or flat plate with a scale and pointer for showing measurements of weight, volume, pressure, compass direction, etc. ■ a disk with numbered holes on a telephone, enabling someone to make a call by inserting a finger in each of the holes corresponding to the number to be called and turning the disk. ■ a plate or disk on a radio, stove, washing machine, or other piece of equipment that is tuned to select a wavelength or setting.
▶ **v.** (**dials, dialing, dialed**; Brit. **dials, dialling, dialled**) [with obj.] call (a telephone number) by turning a disk with numbered holes or pressing a set of buttons: *he dialed room service* | [no obj.] *company employees* ***dial out from*** *their office.* ■ (**dial something up**) gain access to a service using a telephone line: *plans to enable customers to dial up videos from their living room.* ■ indicate or regulate by means of a dial: *you're expected to* ***dial in*** *volume and tone settings.* ■ include or add: *the car has a lot of understeer* ***dialed into*** *the suspension.*
– ORIGIN Middle English (denoting a mariner's compass): from medieval Latin *diale* 'clock dial,' based on Latin *dies* 'day.'

dial-a- ▶ **comb. form** denoting a service available for booking by telephone: *dial-a-ride.*

di·al-a·round ▶ **adj.** used to describe a telephone service that requires callers to dial a special access code that enables them to bypass (or 'dial around') their chosen long-distance carrier in order to obtain a better rate.

di·a·lect /ˈdīəˌlekt/ ▶ **n.** a particular form of a language that is peculiar to a specific region or social group: *this novel is written in the dialect of Trinidad.* ■ Computing a particular version of a programming language.
– DERIVATIVES **di·a·lec·tal** /ˌdīəˈlektəl/ **adj.**
– ORIGIN mid 16th cent. (denoting the art of investigating the truth of opinions): from French *dialecte*, or via Latin from Greek *dialektos* 'discourse, way of speaking,' from *dialegesthai* 'converse with' (see DIALOGUE).

di·a·lec·tic /ˌdīəˈlektik/ Philosophy ▶ **n.** (also **dialectics**) [usu. treated as sing.] **1** the art of investigating or discussing the truth of opinions.
2 inquiry into metaphysical contradictions and their solutions. ■ the existence or action of opposing social forces, concepts, etc.

> The ancient Greeks used the term dialectic to refer to various methods of reasoning and discussion in order to discover the truth. More recently, Kant applied the term to the criticism of the contradictions that arise from supposing knowledge of objects beyond the limits of experience, e.g., the soul. Hegel applied the term to the process of thought by which apparent contradictions (which he termed thesis and antithesis) are seen to be part of a higher truth (synthesis).

▶ **adj.** of or relating to dialectic or dialectics; dialectical.
– ORIGIN late Middle English: from Old French *dialectique* or Latin *dialectica*, from Greek *dialektikē* (*tekhnē*) '(art) of debate,' from *dialegesthai* 'converse with' (see DIALOGUE).

di·a·lec·ti·cal /ˌdīəˈlektikəl/ ▶ **adj. 1** relating to the logical discussion of ideas and opinions: *dialectical ingenuity.*
2 concerned with or acting through opposing forces: *a dialectical opposition between social convention and individual libertarianism.*
– DERIVATIVES **di·a·lec·ti·cal·ly** /-ik(ə)lē/ **adv.**

di·a·lec·ti·cal ma·te·ri·al·ism ▶ **n.** the Marxist theory (adopted as the official philosophy of the Soviet communists) that political and historical events result from the conflict of social forces and are interpretable as a series of contradictions and their solutions. The conflict is believed to be caused by material needs.
– DERIVATIVES **di·a·lec·ti·cal ma·te·ri·al·ist n. & adj.**

di·a·lec·ti·cian /ˌdīəlekˈtisHən/ ▶ **n.** a person skilled in philosophical debate.
– ORIGIN mid 16th cent.: from French *dialecticien*, from Latin *dialecticus*, based on Greek *dialegesthai* 'converse with.'

di·a·lec·tics /ˌdīəˈlektiks/ ▶ **plural n. & adj.** see DIALECTIC.

di·a·lec·tol·o·gy /ˌdīəlekˈtäləjē/ ▶ **n.** the branch of linguistics concerned with the study of dialects.
– DERIVATIVES **di·a·lec·to·log·i·cal** /-təˈläjikəl/ **adj.**, **di·a·lec·tol·o·gist** /-jist/ **n.**

di·al·er /ˈdī(ə)lər/ ▶ **n.** a device or piece of software for calling telephone numbers automatically: *hackers can break in with speed dialers.*

di·al-in ▶ **adj.** another term for DIAL-UP.

di·a·log box /ˈdīəˌläg, -ˌlôg/ ▶ **n.** Computing a small area on screen, in which the user is prompted to provide information or select commands.

di·a·log·ic /ˌdīəˈläjik/ ▶ **adj.** relating to or in the form of dialogue.
– DERIVATIVES **di·a·log·i·cal adj.**
– ORIGIN mid 19th cent.: via late Latin from Greek *dialogikos*, from *dialogos* (see DIALOGUE).

di·al·o·gism /dīˈaləˌjizəm/ ▶ **n.** the use in a text of different tones or viewpoints, whose interaction or contradiction is important to the text's interpretation.
– ORIGIN mid 16th cent.: from late Latin *dialogismos*, from Greek *dialogizesthai* 'to converse,' from *dialogos* 'discourse' (see DIALOGUE).

di·a·logue /ˈdīəˌläg, -ˌlôg/ (also **dialog**) ▶ **n.** conversation between two or more people as a feature of a book, play, or movie: *the book consisted of a series of dialogues* | *passages of dialogue.* ■ a discussion between two or more people or groups, esp. one directed toward exploration of a particular subject or resolution of a problem: *the U.S. would enter into a direct dialogue with Vietnam* | *interfaith dialogue.*
▶ **v.** [no obj.] take part in a conversation or discussion to resolve a problem: *he stated that he wasn't going to dialogue with the guerrillas.* ■ [with obj.] provide (a movie or play) with a dialogue.
– PHRASES **dialogue of the deaf** a discussion in which each party is unresponsive to what the other says.
– ORIGIN Middle English: from Old French *dialoge*, via Latin from Greek *dialogos*, from *dialegesthai* 'converse with,' from *dia* 'through' + *legein* 'speak.'

di·al tone ▶ **n.** a sound that a telephone produces indicating that a caller may start to dial.

di·al-up ▶ **adj.** (of a computer system or service) used remotely via a telephone line.

di·al·y·sis /dīˈaləsis/ ▶ **n.** (pl. **dialyses** /-sēz/) Chemistry the separation of particles in a liquid on the basis of differences in their ability to pass through a membrane. ■ Medicine the clinical purification of blood by this technique, as a substitute for the normal function of the kidney.
– DERIVATIVES **di·a·lyt·ic** /ˌdīəˈlitik/ **adj.**
– ORIGIN mid 19th cent.: via Latin from Greek *dialusis*, from *dialuein* 'split, separate,' from *dia* 'apart' + *luein* 'set free.'

di·al·y·zate /dīˈaləˌzāt/ (also **dialysate**) ▶ **n.** the part of a mixture that passes through the membrane in dialysis. ■ the solution this forms with the fluid on the other side of the membrane. ■ the fluid used on the other side of the membrane during dialysis to remove impurities.
– ORIGIN late 19th cent.: from DIALYSIS + -ATE[1]; the term originally denoted the part of the mixture that does *not* pass through the membrane.

di·a·lyze /ˈdīəˌlīz/ (Brit. **dialyse**) ▶ **v.** [with obj.] purify (a mixture) by means of dialysis. ■ treat (a patient) by means of dialysis.
– ORIGIN mid 19th cent.: from DIALYSIS, on the pattern of *analyze*.

diam. ▶ **abbr.** diameter.

di·a·mag·net·ic /ˌdīəmagˈnetik/ ▶ **adj.** Physics (of a substance or body) tending to become magnetized in a direction at 180° to the applied magnetic field.
– DERIVATIVES **di·a·mag·net** /ˈdīəˌmagnit/ **n.**, **di·a·mag·net·i·cal·ly** /-ik(ə)lē/ **adv.**, **di·a·mag·net·ism** /-ˈmagnəˌtizəm/ **n.**
– ORIGIN 1846: coined by Faraday, from Greek *dia* 'through, across' + MAGNETIC.

di·a·man·té /ˌdēəmänˈtā/ ▶ **adj.** decorated with artificial jewels: *a diamanté brooch.*
▶ **n.** artificial jewels. ■ fabric or costume jewelry decorated with artificial jewels.
– ORIGIN early 20th cent.: French, literally 'set with diamonds,' past participle of *diamanter*, from *diamant* 'diamond.'

di·a·man·tif·er·ous /ˌdīəmənˈtifərəs/ ▶ **adj.** (of a rock formation, region, etc.) producing or yielding diamonds.
– ORIGIN late 19th cent.: from French *diamantifère*, from *diamant* 'diamond' + *-fère* 'producing.'

di·a·man·tine /ˌdīəˈmanˌtīn, ˈdīəˌman-, -ˌtēn/ ▶ **adj.** made from or reminiscent of diamonds.
– ORIGIN mid 16th cent. (in the sense 'hard as diamond'): from French *diamantin*, from *diamant* 'diamond.'

di·am·e·ter /dīˈamitər/ (abbr.: **diam.**) ▶ **n.** **1** a straight line passing from side to side through the center of a body or figure, esp. a circle or sphere. ■ the length of this line. ■ a transverse measurement of something; width or thickness.
2 a unit of linear measurement of magnifying power.
– DERIVATIVES **di·am·e·tral** /-trəl/ **adj.**
– ORIGIN late Middle English: from Old French *diametre*, via Latin from Greek *diametros* (*grammē*) '(line) measuring across,' from *dia* 'across' + *metron* 'measure.'

di·a·met·ri·cal /ˌdīəˈmetrikəl/ ▶ **adj.** **1** used to emphasize how completely different two or more things are: *he's the diametrical opposite of Gabriel.*
2 of or along a diameter.
– DERIVATIVES **di·a·met·ric** **adj.**
– ORIGIN mid 16th cent. (sense 2): from Greek *diametrikos* (from *diametros* 'measuring across': see DIAMETER) + -AL.

di·a·met·ri·cal·ly /ˌdīəˈmetrik(ə)lē/ ▶ **adv.** (with reference to opposition) completely; directly: [as submodifier] *two **diametrically opposed** viewpoints.*

di·am·ine /ˈdīəˌmēn, dīˈamin/ ▶ **n.** Chemistry a compound whose molecule contains two amino groups, esp. when not part of amide groups.

dia·mond /ˈdī(ə)mənd/ ▶ **n.** **1** a precious stone consisting of a clear and typically colorless crystalline form of pure carbon, the hardest naturally occurring substance. ■ a tool with a small stone of such a kind for cutting glass.

> Diamonds occur in some igneous rock formations (kimberlite) and alluvial deposits. They are typically octahedral in shape but can be cut in many ways to enhance the internal reflection and refraction of light, producing jewels of sparkling brilliance. Diamonds are also used in cutting tools and abrasives.

2 [often as modifier] a figure with four straight sides of equal length forming two opposite acute angles and two opposite obtuse angles; a rhombus: *decorative diamond shapes.* ■ (**diamonds**) one of the four suits in a conventional pack of playing cards, denoted by a red figure of such a shape. ■ a card of this suit: *she led a losing diamond.* ■ the area delimited by the four bases of a baseball field, forming a square shape. ■ a baseball field.
– PHRASES **diamond in the rough** a person who is generally of good character but lacks manners, education, or style.
– DERIVATIVES **dia·mond·if·er·ous** /ˌdī(ə)mənˈdifərəs/ **adj.**
– ORIGIN Middle English: from Old French *diamant*, from medieval Latin *diamas, diamant-*, variant of Latin *adamans* (see ADAMANT).

dia·mond·back /ˈdī(ə)mendˌbak/ ▶ **n.** **1** (also **diamondback rattlesnake**) a large, common North American rattlesnake with diamond-shaped markings. Also called DIAMOND RATTLESNAKE. ● Genus *Crotalus*, family Viperidae: two species.
2 another term for TERRAPIN (sense 1).

dia·mond·back moth ▶ **n.** a small, grayish moth that displays a pattern of diamonds along its back when the wings are folded. The caterpillar can be a pest of brassicas and other cultivated vegetables. ● *Plutella xylostella*, family Yponomeutidae.

dia·mond-cut ▶ **adj.** **1** cut with facets like a diamond.
2 cut into the shape of a diamond.

Dia·mond Head a volcanic crater that overlooks the port of Honolulu on the Hawaiian island of Oahu.

dia·mond ju·bi·lee ▶ **n.** the sixtieth anniversary of a notable event, esp. a sovereign's accession or the foundation of an organization.

dia·mond plate ▶ **n.** a diamond-shaped design that is stamped into metal to give it industrial strength.

dia·mond py·thon ▶ **n.** a carpet python of a race occurring in the coastal areas of New South Wales. ● *Morelia spilota spilota*, family Pythonidae.

dia·mond rat·tle·snake ▶ **n.** another term for DIAMONDBACK (sense 1).

Dia·mond State a nickname for the state of DELAWARE[1].

dia·mond wed·ding (also **diamond wedding anniversary**) ▶ **n.** the sixtieth (or seventy-fifth) anniversary of a wedding.

dia·mond wil·low ▶ **n.** a willow with diamond-shaped depressions on the trunk as a result of fungal attack, resulting in timber with a diamond-shaped pattern of pale sapwood and darker heartwood. ● Several species in the genus *Salix* are affected, in particular *S. bebbiana*.

di·a·mor·phine /ˌdīəˈmôrfēn/ ▶ **n.** short for DIACETYLMORPHINE (heroin).

Di·an·a /dīˈanə/ Roman Mythology an early Italian goddess associated with hunting, virginity, and, in later literature, with the moon. Greek equivalent ARTEMIS.

di·an·a /dīˈanə/ ▶ **n.** a North American fritillary (butterfly), the male of which is orange and black and the female blue and black. ● *Speyeria diana*, subfamily Argynninae, family Nymphalidae.
– ORIGIN modern Latin; associated with the goddess of the moon, because of the silvery crescents on the wings.

Di·an·a, Princess of Wales (1961–97), former wife of Prince Charles; title before marriage *Lady Diana Frances Spencer*. The daughter of the 8th Earl Spencer, she married Prince Charles in 1981; the couple were divorced in 1996. She became a popular figure through her charity work and glamorous media appearances, and her death in an automobile accident in Paris gave rise to intense international mourning.

Di·an·a mon·key ▶ **n.** a West African monkey that has a black face with a white crescent on the forehead. ● *Cercopithecus diana*, family Cercopithecidae.
– ORIGIN early 19th cent.: named after the Roman moon goddess DIANA.

Di·a·net·ics /ˌdīəˈnetiks/ ▶ **plural n.** [treated as sing.] a system developed by the founder of the Church of Scientology, L. Ron Hubbard, that aims to relieve psychosomatic disorder by cleansing the mind of harmful mental images.
– ORIGIN 1950s: from Greek *dianoētikos* 'relating to thought' + -ICS.

di·an·thus /dīˈanTHəs/ ▶ **n.** (pl. **dianthuses**) a flowering plant of a genus that includes the pinks and carnations. ● Genus *Dianthus*, family Caryophyllaceae.
– ORIGIN from Greek *Dios* 'of Zeus' + *anthos* 'a flower.'

di·a·pa·son /ˌdīəˈpāzən, -sən/ ▶ **n.** **1** (also **open diapason** or **stopped diapason**) an organ stop sounding a main register of flue pipes, typically of eight-foot pitch.
2 a grand swelling burst of harmony.
3 literary the entire compass, range, or scope of something.
– ORIGIN late Middle English (denoting the interval of an octave): via Latin from Greek *dia pasōn* (*khordōn*) 'through all (notes).'

di·a·pause /ˈdīəˌpôz/ Zoology ▶ **n.** a period of suspended development in an insect, other invertebrate, or mammal embryo, esp. during unfavorable environmental conditions.
▶ **v.** [no obj.] (usu. as adj. **diapausing**) (of an insect or other animal) undergo such a period of suspended development.
– ORIGIN late 19th cent.: from DIA- 'through' + the noun PAUSE.

di·a·pe·de·sis /ˌdīəpəˈdēsis/ ▶ **n.** Medicine the passage of blood cells through the intact walls of the capillaries, typically accompanying inflammation.
– ORIGIN early 17th cent.: modern Latin, based on Greek *dia* 'through' + *pēdan* 'throb or leap.'

dia·per /ˈdī(ə)pər/ ▶ **n.** **1** a piece of absorbent material wrapped around a baby's bottom and between its legs to absorb and retain urine and feces.
2 a linen or cotton fabric woven in a repeating pattern of small diamonds. ■ a repeating geometric or floral pattern used to decorate a surface.
▶ **v.** [with obj.] **1** put a diaper on (a baby).
2 decorate (a surface) with a repeating geometric or floral pattern.
– ORIGIN Middle English: from Old French *diapre*, from medieval Latin *diasprum*, from medieval Greek *diaspros* (adjective), from *dia* 'across' + *aspros* 'white.' The term seems originally to have denoted a costly fabric, but after the 15th cent. it was used in sense 2 of the noun; babies' diapers were originally made from pieces of this fabric, hence sense 1 of the noun (late 16th cent).

dia·per rash ▶ **n.** inflammation of a baby's skin caused by prolonged contact with a damp diaper.

di·aph·a·nous /dīˈafənəs/ ▶ **adj.** (esp. of fabric) light, delicate, and translucent: *a diaphanous dress of pale gold.*
– ORIGIN early 17th cent.: from medieval Latin *diaphanus*, from Greek *diaphanēs*, from *dia* 'through' + *phainein* 'to show.'

di·a·phone /ˈdīəˌfōn/ ▶ **n.** a low-pitched fog signal operated by compressed air, characterized by the "grunt" that ends each note.
– ORIGIN early 20th cent.: from Greek *dia* 'through' + *phōnē* 'sound.'

di·aph·o·rase /dīˈafəˌrās, -ˌrāz/ ▶ **n.** Biochemistry an enzyme of the flavoprotein type, able to oxidize a reduced form of the coenzyme NAD.
– ORIGIN 1930s: from Greek *diaphoros* 'different' + -ASE.

di·a·pho·re·sis /ˌdīəfəˈrēsis/ ▶ **n.** technical sweating, esp. to an unusual degree as a symptom of disease or a side effect of a drug.
– ORIGIN late 17th cent.: via late Latin from Greek, from *diaphorein* 'carry off, sweat out,' from *dia* 'through' + *phorein* 'carry.'

di·a·pho·ret·ic /ˌdīəfəˈretik/ ▶ **adj.** Medicine (chiefly of a drug) inducing perspiration. ■ (of a person) sweating heavily.
– ORIGIN late Middle English: via late Latin from Greek *diaphorētikos*, from *diaphorein* 'sweat out.'

di·a·phragm /ˈdīəˌfram/ ▶ **n.** **1** a dome-shaped, muscular partition separating the thorax from the abdomen in mammals. It plays a major role in breathing, as its contraction increases the volume of the thorax and so inflates the lungs.
2 a thin sheet of material forming a partition. ■ a taut, flexible membrane in mechanical or acoustic systems. ■ a thin contraceptive cap fitting over the cervix.
3 a device for varying the effective aperture of the lens in a camera or other optical system.
– DERIVATIVES **di·a·phrag·mat·ic** /ˌdīəfragˈmatik/ **adj.**
– ORIGIN late Middle English: from late Latin *diaphragma*, from Greek, from *dia* 'through, apart' + *phragma* 'a fence.'

di·a·phragm pump ▶ **n.** a pump using a flexible diaphragm in place of a piston.

di·aph·y·sis /dīˈafəsis/ ▶ **n.** (pl. **diaphyses** /-ˌsēz/) Anatomy the shaft or central part of a long bone. Compare with EPIPHYSIS.
– ORIGIN mid 19th cent.: from Greek *diaphusis* 'growing through,' from *dia* 'through' + *phusis* 'growth.'

di·a·pir /ˈdīəˌpir/ ▶ **n.** Geology a domed rock formation in which a core of rock has moved upward to pierce the overlying strata.
– DERIVATIVES **di·a·pir·ic** /ˌdīəˈpirik/ **adj.**, **di·a·pir·ism** /-ˌizəm/ **n.**
– ORIGIN early 20th cent.: from Greek *diapeirainein* 'pierce through,' from *dia* 'through' + *peirainein* (from *peran* 'pierce').

di·a·pos·i·tive /ˌdīəˈpäzitiv/ ▶ **n.** a positive photographic slide or transparency.

di·ap·sid /dīˈapsid/ ▶ **n.** Zoology a reptile of a large group characterized by the presence of two temporal openings in the skull, including the lizards, snakes, crocodiles, dinosaurs, and pterosaurs. ● Subclass Anapsida.
– ORIGIN early 20th cent.: from modern Latin *Diapsida*, from DI-[1] 'two' + Greek *apsis, apsid-* 'arch.'

di·ar·chy /ˈdīˌärkē/ (also **dyarchy**) ▶ **n.** (pl. **diarchies**) government by two independent authorities (esp. in India 1919–35).
– DERIVATIVES **di·ar·chal** /dīˈärkəl/ **adj.**, **di·ar·chic** /dīˈärkik/ **adj.**
– ORIGIN late 19th cent.: from DI-[1] 'two' + Greek *arkhia* 'rule,' on the pattern of *monarchy*.

di·a·rist /ˈdīərist/ ▶ **n.** a person who writes a diary.
– DERIVATIVES **di·a·ris·tic** /ˌdīəˈristik/ **adj.**

di·a·rize /ˈdīəˌrīz/ ▶ **v.** [no obj.] archaic keep a record of events in a diary.

di·ar·rhe·a /ˌdīəˈrēə/ (Brit. **diarrhoea**) ▶ **n.** a condition in which feces are discharged from the bowels frequently and in a liquid form.
– DERIVATIVES **di·ar·rhe·al** adj., **di·ar·rhe·ic** /-ˈrēik/ adj.
– ORIGIN late Middle English: via late Latin *diarrhoea* from Greek *diarrhoia*, from *diarrhein* 'flow through,' from *dia* 'through' + *rhein* 'to flow.'

di·a·ry /ˈdīərē/ ▶ **n.** (pl. **diaries**) a book in which one keeps a daily record of events and experiences: *I resolved to* ***keep a diary*** *of events during the war.* ■ a datebook.
– ORIGIN late 16th cent.: from Latin *diarium*, from *dies* 'day.'

Di·as /ˈdēəs, ˈdēˌäsн/ (also **Diaz** /ˈdēəsн/), Bartolomeu (*c.*1450–1500), Portuguese navigator and explorer. He was the first European to sail around the Cape of Good Hope 1488, thereby establishing a sea route from the Atlantic Ocean to Asia.

di·as·po·ra /dīˈaspərə/ ▶ **n.** (often **the Diaspora**) Jews living outside Israel. ■ the dispersion of the Jews beyond Israel. ■ the dispersion of any people from their original homeland: *the diaspora of boat people from Asia.* ■ the people so dispersed: *the Ukrainian diaspora flocked back to Kiev.*

> The main diaspora began in the 8th–6th centuries BC, and even before the sack of Jerusalem in AD 70, the number of Jews dispersed by the diaspora was greater than that living in Israel. Thereafter Jews were dispersed even more widely throughout the Roman world and beyond.

– ORIGIN Greek, from *diaspeirein* 'disperse,' from *dia* 'across' + *speirein* 'scatter.' The term originated in the Septuagint (Deuteronomy 28:25) in the phrase *esē diaspora en pasais basileiais tēs gēs* 'thou shalt be a dispersion in all kingdoms of the earth.'

di·a·spore /ˈdīəˌspôr/ ▶ **n.** Botany a spore, seed, or other structure that functions in plant dispersal; a propagule.

di·a·stase /ˈdīəˌstās, -ˌstāz/ ▶ **n.** Biochemistry another term for **AMYLASE**.
– ORIGIN mid 19th cent.: from Greek *diastasis* 'separation,' from *dia* 'apart' + *stasis* 'placing.'

di·a·ste·ma /ˌdīəˈstēmə/ ▶ **n.** (pl. **diastemata** /-mətə/) a gap between the teeth, in particular: ■ Zoology a space separating teeth of different functions, esp. that between the biting teeth (incisors and canines) and grinding teeth (premolars and molars) in rodents and ungulates. ■ a gap between a person's two upper front teeth.
– ORIGIN mid 19th cent.: via late Latin from Greek *diastēma* 'space between.'

di·a·ste·re·o·i·so·mer /ˌdīəˌsterēōˈīsəmər/ ▶ **n.** Chemistry each of a pair of stereoisomeric compounds that are not mirror images of one another.
– DERIVATIVES **di·a·ster·e·o·i·so·mer·ic** /-ˌīsəˈmerik/ adj.

di·as·to·le /dīˈastl-ē/ ▶ **n.** Physiology the phase of the heartbeat when the heart muscle relaxes and allows the chambers to fill with blood. Often contrasted with **SYSTOLE**.
– DERIVATIVES **di·as·tol·ic** /ˌdīəˈstälik/ adj.
– ORIGIN late 16th cent.: via late Latin from Greek, 'separation, expansion,' from *diastellein*, from *dia* 'apart' + *stellein* 'to place.'

di·a·tes·sa·ron /ˌdīəˈtesərən/ ▶ **n.** the four Gospels combined into a single narrative.

di·a·ther·my /ˈdīəˌтнərmē/ ▶ **n.** a medical and surgical technique involving the production of heat in a part of the body by high-frequency electric currents, to stimulate the circulation, relieve pain, destroy unhealthy tissue, or cause bleeding vessels to clot.
– ORIGIN early 20th cent.: from **DIA-** 'through' + *thermon* 'heat.'

di·ath·e·sis /dīˈaтнəsis/ ▶ **n. 1** [usu. with modifier] Medicine a tendency to suffer from a particular medical condition: *a bleeding diathesis.*
2 Linguistics another term for **VOICE** (sense 4 of the noun).
– ORIGIN mid 17th cent.: modern Latin, from Greek, 'disposition,' from *diatithenai* 'arrange.' Sense 2 dates from the mid 20th cent.

di·a·tom /ˈdīəˌtäm/ ▶ **n.** Biology a single-celled alga that has a cell wall of silica. Many kinds are planktonic, and extensive fossil deposits have been found. ● Class Bacillariophyceae, division Chromophycota or Heterokontophyta (or phylum Bacillariophyta, kingdom Protista).
– DERIVATIVES **di·a·to·ma·ceous** /ˌdīətəˈmāsнəs/ adj.
– ORIGIN mid 19th cent.: from modern Latin *Diatoma* (genus name), from Greek *diatomos* 'cut in two,' from *diatemnein* 'to cut through.'

di·a·to·ma·ceous earth ▶ **n.** a soft, crumbly, porous sedimentary deposit formed from the fossil remains of diatoms.

di·a·tom·ic /ˌdīəˈtämik/ ▶ **adj.** Chemistry consisting of two atoms.

di·at·o·mite /dīˈatəˌmīt/ ▶ **n.** Geology a fine-grained sedimentary rock formed from consolidated diatomaceous earth.
– ORIGIN late 19th cent.: from **DIATOM** + **-ITE**[1].

di·a·ton·ic /ˌdīəˈtänik/ ▶ **adj.** Music (of a scale, interval, etc.) involving only notes proper to the prevailing key without chromatic alteration. ■ (of a melody or harmony) constructed from such a scale.
– ORIGIN early 17th cent. (denoting a tetrachord divided into two tones and a lower semitone, or ancient Greek music based on this): from French *diatonique*, or via late Latin from Greek *diatonikos* 'at intervals of a tone,' from *dia* 'through' + *tonos* 'tone.'

di·a·treme /ˈdīəˌtrēm/ ▶ **n.** Geology a long, vertical pipe or plug formed when gas-filled magma forced its way up through overlying strata.
– ORIGIN early 20th cent.: from **DIA-** 'through' + Greek *trēma* 'perforation.'

di·a·tribe /ˈdīəˌtrīb/ ▶ **n.** a forceful and bitter verbal attack against someone or something: *a diatribe against the Roman Catholic Church.*
– ORIGIN late 16th cent. (denoting a disquisition): from French, via Latin from Greek *diatribē* 'spending of time, discourse,' from *dia* 'through' + *tribein* 'rub.'

Di·az /ˈdēəsн/ variant spelling of **DIAS**.

Dí·az /ˈdē-äs/, Porfirio (1830–1915), Mexican general and statesman; president 1877–80 and 1884–1911.

di·az·e·pam /dīˈazəˌpam/ ▶ **n.** a tranquilizing muscle-relaxant drug used chiefly to relieve anxiety. Also called **VALIUM** (trademark). ● A member of the benzodiazepine group; chem. formula: $C_{16}H_{13}N_2OCl$.
– ORIGIN 1960s: blend of **BENZODIAZEPINE** and **AMIDE**.

di·az·i·non /dīˈazəˌnän/ ▶ **n.** an organophosphorus insecticide derived from pyrimidine.
– ORIGIN mid 20th cent.: from *diazine* (see **DI-**[1], **AZINE**) + *-on* (suffix of unknown origin).

di·az·o /dīˈazō/ (also **diazotype**) ▶ **n.** a copying or coloring process using a diazo compound decomposed by ultraviolet light: [as modifier] *diazo printers.*

di·az·o com·pound ▶ **n.** Chemistry an organic compound containing two nitrogen atoms bonded together, esp. a diazonium compound.
– ORIGIN late 19th cent.: *diazo* from **DIAZONIUM**.

di·az·o·meth·ane /dīˌazōˈmeтнān/ ▶ **n.** Chemistry a poisonous, reactive yellow gas used as a methylating agent in chemical synthesis. ● Chem. formula: CH_2N_2.
– ORIGIN late 19th cent.: from *diazo-* (indicating the presence of two nitrogen atoms) + **METHANE**.

di·a·zo·ni·um /dīəˈzōnēəm/ ▶ **n.** [as modifier] Chemistry an organic cation containing the group $-N_2^+$ bonded to an organic group. Aromatic diazonium compounds are typically intensely colored and include many synthetic dyes.
– ORIGIN late 19th cent.: coined in German from *diazo-* (indicating the presence of two nitrogen atoms) + the suffix *-onium* (from **AMMONIUM**).

dib /dib/ ▶ **v.** (**dibs, dibbing, dibbed**) Fishing another term for **DAP**.
– ORIGIN late 17th cent.: related to **DAB**[1].

di·ba·sic /dīˈbāsik/ ▶ **adj.** Chemistry (of an acid) having two replaceable hydrogen atoms.
– ORIGIN mid 19th cent.: from **DI-**[1] 'two' + **BASIC**.

dib·ble /ˈdibəl/ ▶ **n.** a pointed hand tool for making holes in the ground for seeds or young plants.
▶ **v.** [with obj.] make (a hole) in soil with a dibble. ■ sow (a seed or plant) with a dibble.
– ORIGIN late Middle English: apparently related to **DIB** (also used in this sense in dialect).

dibble

di·bo·rane /dīˈbôrˌān/ ▶ **n.** Chemistry a poisonous, reactive gas made by the action of acids on some borides. It is the simplest of the boranes and is an example of electron-deficient bonding. ● Chem. formula: B_2H_6.

dibs /dibz/ ▶ **plural n.** informal money.
– PHRASES **have first dibs on** have the first right to or choice of: *they never got first dibs on great prospects.*
– ORIGIN mid 18th cent. (denoting pebbles used in a children's game): from earlier *dib-stones*, perhaps from **DIB**.

dice /dīs/ ▶ **n.** (pl. **same**) a small cube with each side having a different number of spots on it, ranging from one to six, thrown and used in gambling and other games involving chance. See also **DIE**[2]. ■ a game played with dice. ■ small cubes of food.
▶ **v. 1** [no obj.] play or gamble with dice: (as noun **dicing**) *prohibitions on all dancing and dicing.*
2 [with obj.] cut (food or other matter) into small cubes: *dice the peppers* | (as adj. **diced**) *add the diced onions.*
– PHRASES **dice with death** take serious risks. **no dice** informal used to refuse a request or indicate no chance of success. **roll** (or **throw**) **of the dice** a risky attempt to do or achieve something: *the merger was their last roll of the dice, and it failed miserably.*
– DERIVATIVES **dic·er** n.
– ORIGIN Middle English: from Old French *des*, plural of *de* (see **DIE**[2]).

> **USAGE** Historically, **dice** is the plural of **die**, but in modern standard English, **dice** is both the singular and the plural: *throw the* **dice** could mean a reference to two or more dice, or to just one. In fact, the singular **die** (rather than **dice**) is increasingly uncommon.

d

di·cen·tra /dīˈsentrə/ ▶ **n.** a plant of the genus *Dicentra* (family Fumariaceae), esp. (in gardening) a bleeding heart.
– ORIGIN modern Latin, from Greek *dikentros*, from *di-* 'two' + *kentron* 'spur, sharp point.'

di·cen·tric /dīˈsentrik/ Genetics ▶ **adj.** (of a chromosome) having two centromeres.
▶ **n.** a chromosome of this type.

dic·ey /ˈdīsē/ ▶ **adj.** (**dicier, diciest**) informal unpredictable and potentially dangerous: *the lot of a wanderer is always dicey.*

di·cha·si·um /dīˈkāzн(ē)əm, -zēəm/ ▶ **n.** (pl. **dichasia** /-zнēə, -zēə/) Botany a cyme in which each flowering branch gives rise to two or more branches symmetrically placed.
– ORIGIN late 19th cent.: modern Latin, from **DI-**[1] 'two' + Greek *khasis* 'separation.'

di·chlor·vos /dīˈklôrvəs/ ▶ **n.** Chemistry a pale yellow liquid used as an insecticide and veterinary anthelmintic. ● An organophosphorus compound; alternative name: **2,2-dichlorovinyl dimethyl phosphate**; chem. formula: $(CH_3O)_2PO_2CHCCl_2$.
– ORIGIN mid 20th cent.: from elements of the systematic name (see above).

di·chog·a·my /dīˈkägəmē/ ▶ **n.** Botany the ripening of the stamens and pistils of a flower at different times, so that self-fertilization is prevented. Compare with **HOMOGAMY** (sense 3).
– DERIVATIVES **di·chog·a·mous** /-məs/ adj.
– ORIGIN mid 19th cent.: from Greek *dikho-* 'apart, in two' + *gamos* 'marriage.'

di·chot·ic /dīˈkätik/ ▶ **adj.** involving or relating to the simultaneous stimulation of the right and left ear by different sounds.
– ORIGIN mid 20th cent.: from Greek *dikho-* 'apart' + *ous, ōt-* 'ear' + **-IC**.

di·chot·o·mize /dīˈkätəˌmīz/ ▶ **v.** [with obj.] regard or represent as divided or opposed: *these rules dichotomize love and sex.*

di·chot·o·mous /dīˈkätəməs/ ▶ **adj.** exhibiting or characterized by dichotomy: *a dichotomous view of the world.* ■ Botany (of branching) in which the axis is divided into two branches.
– DERIVATIVES **di·chot·o·mous·ly** adv.
– ORIGIN late 17th cent.: via late Latin from Greek *dikhotomos* (from *dikho-* 'in two' + *temnein* 'to cut') + **-OUS**.

di·chot·o·my /dīˈkätəmē/ ▶ **n.** (pl. **dichotomies**) [usu. in sing.] a division or contrast between two things that are or are represented as being opposed or entirely different: *a rigid* ***dichotomy between*** *science and mysticism.* ■ Botany repeated branching into two equal parts.
– ORIGIN late 16th cent.: via modern Latin from Greek *dikhotomia*, from *dikho-* 'in two, apart' + *-tomia* (see **-TOMY**).

di·chro·ic /dīˈkrō-ik/ ▶ **adj.** (of a crystal) showing different colors when viewed from different directions, or (more generally) having different absorption coefficients for light polarized in different directions.
– DERIVATIVES **di·chro·ism** /ˈdīkrōˌizəm/ n.
– ORIGIN mid 19th cent.: from Greek *dikhroos* (from *di-* 'twice' + *khrōs* 'color') + **-IC**.

di·chro·mate /dīˈkrōmāt/ ▶ **n.** Chemistry a salt, typically red or orange, containing the anion $Cr_2O_7^{2-}$.
– ORIGIN mid 19th cent.: from **DI-**[1] 'two' + **CHROMATE**.

di·chro·ma·tism /dīˈkrōməˌtizəm/ ▶ **n. 1** (typically in an animal species) the occurrence of two different kinds of coloring.
2 color-blindness in which only two of the three primary colors can be discerned.
– DERIVATIVES **di·chro·mat·ic** /ˌdīkrōˈmatik/ adj.

dick[1] /dik/ vulgar slang ▶ **n. 1** a penis.
2 [with negative] anything at all: *you don't know dick about this—you haven't a clue!*
3 short for DICKHEAD.
▶ **v. 1** [no obj.] handle something inexpertly; meddle: *he started* ***dicking around*** *with the controls.*
2 [with obj.] (of a man) have sexual intercourse with (someone).
– ORIGIN mid 16th cent. (in the general sense 'fellow'): nickname for the given name *Richard.* Sense 1 of the noun dates from the late 18th cent.

dick[2] ▶ **n.** dated, informal a detective.
– ORIGIN early 20th cent.: perhaps an arbitrary shortening of DETECTIVE, or from obsolete slang *dick* 'look,' from Romany.

d

dick·cis·sel /dik'sisəl, 'dik,sisəl/ ▶ **n.** a sparrowlike North American songbird related to the cardinals, with a black-and-white throat and bright yellow breast. ● *Spiza americana*, family Emberizidae (subfamily Cardinalinae).
– ORIGIN late 19th cent.: imitative of its call.

Dick·ens /'dikənz/, Charles (John Huffam) (1812–70), English novelist. His novels are notable for their satirical humor and treatment of contemporary social problems, including the plight of the urban poor and the corruption and inefficiency of the legal system. Notable works include *Oliver Twist* (1837–38), *A Christmas Carol* (1843), *David Copperfield* (1850), and *Great Expectations* (1860–61).

dick·ens /'dikinz/ ▶ **n.** [in sing.] informal, dated used for emphasis, euphemistically invoking the Devil: *they work like the dickens | she was in a dickens of a rush.* ■ (**the dickens**) used when asking questions to express annoyance or surprise: *what the dickens is going on?*
– ORIGIN late 16th cent.: probably a use of the surname *Dickens.*

Dick·en·si·an /di'kenzēən/ ▶ **adj.** of or reminiscent of the novels of Charles Dickens, esp. in suggesting the poor social conditions or comically repulsive characters that they portray: *the back streets of Dickensian London.*

dick·er /'dikər/ ▶ **v.** [no obj.] **1** engage in petty argument or bargaining: *she advised him not to dicker over the extra fee.*
2 treat something casually or irresponsibly; toy with something: (as noun **dickering**) *there was no dickering with the lyrics.*
– DERIVATIVES **dick·er·er n.**
– ORIGIN early 19th cent.: perhaps from obsolete *dicker* 'set of ten (hides),' used as a unit of trade, based on Latin *decem* 'ten.'

Dick·ey /'dikē/, James (Lafayette) (1923–97), US poet and writer. His works include the poetry in *Buckdancer's Choice* (1965) and the novel *Deliverance* (1970).

dick·ey /'dikē/ (also **dicky**) ▶ **n.** (pl. **dickeys** or **dickies**) informal **1** a false shirtfront.
2 dated, chiefly Brit. a folding outside seat at the back of a vehicle; a rumble seat. ■ historical chiefly Brit. a driver's seat in a carriage.
– ORIGIN mid 18th cent. (denoting a petticoat): each sense probably having different origins; perhaps partly from *Dicky*, nickname for the given name *Richard.*

dick·ey bird ▶ **n.** informal used by children to refer to a little bird. [late 18th cent.: probably from *Dicky*, nickname for the given name *Richard.*]

dick·head /'dik,hed/ ▶ **n.** vulgar slang a stupid, irritating, or ridiculous person, particularly a man.
– ORIGIN 1960s: from DICK[1] + HEAD.

Dick·in·son /'dikənsən/, Emily (Elizabeth) (1830–86), US poet. Her poems use an elliptical language and emphasize assonance and alliteration rather than rhyme. They reflect the struggles of her reclusive life. Although she wrote nearly 2,000 poems, only 7 were published during her lifetime.

Emily Dickinson

dick·wad /'dik,wäd/ ▶ **n.** vulgar slang a contemptible person.
– ORIGIN 1980s: from *dick* in the sense 'penis' + *wad.*

dick·y /'dikē/ ▶ **adj.** (**dickier, dickiest**) Brit. informal (of a part of the body, a structure, or a device) not strong, healthy, or functioning reliably: *a man with a dicky leg.*
– ORIGIN late 18th cent. (in the sense 'almost over'): perhaps from the given name *Dick*, in the old saying *as queer as Dick's hatband.*

di·cot /'dīkät/ ▶ **n.** short for DICOTYLEDON.

di·cot·y·le·don /dī,kätl'ēdn/ ▶ **n.** Botany a flowering plant with an embryo that bears two cotyledons (seed leaves). Dicotyledons constitute the larger of the two great divisions of flowering plants, and typically have broad, stalked leaves with netlike veins (e.g., daisies, hawthorns, oaks). Compare with MONOCOTYLEDON. ● Class Dicotyledoneae (or -donae, -dones; sometimes Magnoliopsida), subdivision Angiospermae.
– DERIVATIVES **di·cot·y·le·don·ous** /-əs/ **adj.**
– ORIGIN early 18th cent.: from modern Latin *dicotyledones* (plural), from *di-* 'two' + *cotyledon* (see COTYLEDON).

di·crot·ic /dī'krätik/ ▶ **adj.** Medicine denoting a pulse in which a double beat is detectable for each beat of the heart.
– ORIGIN early 19th cent.: from Greek *dikrotos* 'beating twice' + -IC.

dict. ▶ **abbr.** ■ dictation. ■ dictionary.

dic·ta /'diktə/ plural form of DICTUM.

dic·tam·nus /dik'tamnəs/ ▶ **n. 1** another term for DITTANY OF CRETE (see DITTANY).
2 another term for GAS PLANT.
– ORIGIN mid 16th cent.: from Latin.

Dic·ta·phone /'diktə,fōn/ (also **dictaphone**) ▶ **n.** trademark a small cassette recorder used to record speech for transcription at a later time.
– ORIGIN early 20th cent.: from DICTATE or DICTATION + -PHONE.

dic·tate /'dik,tāt/ ▶ **v.** [with obj.] **1** lay down authoritatively; prescribe: *the tsar's attempts to dictate policy* | [no obj.] *that doesn't give you the right to dictate to me.* ■ control or decisively affect; determine: *choice is often dictated by availability* | [no obj.] *a review process can be changed as circumstances dictate.*
2 say or read aloud (words to be typed, written down, or recorded on tape): *I have four letters to dictate.*
▶ **n.** (usu. **dictates**) an order or principle that must be obeyed: *the dictates of fashion.*
– ORIGIN late 16th cent. (sense 2 of the verb): from Latin *dictat-* 'dictated,' from the verb *dictare.*

dic·ta·tion /dik'tāshən/ ▶ **n. 1** (abbr.: **dict.**) the action of saying words aloud to be typed, written down, or recorded on tape: *the dictation of letters.* ■ the activity of taking down a passage that is read aloud by a teacher as a test of spelling, writing, or language skills: *passages for dictation.* ■ an utterance that is typed, written down, or recorded: *the person who writes the dictation down is his agent.*
2 the action of giving orders authoritatively or categorically.
– ORIGIN mid 17th cent. (sense 2): from late Latin *dictatio(n-)*, from the verb *dictare* (see DICTATE).

dic·ta·tor /'dik,tātər/ ▶ **n. 1** a ruler with total power over a country, typically one who has obtained power by force. ■ a person who tells people what to do in an autocratic way or who determines behavior in a particular sphere: *the prewar era was a period whose apple-cheeked dictator was Doris Day.* ■ (in ancient Rome) a chief magistrate with absolute power, appointed in an emergency.
2 a machine that records words spoken into it, used for personal or administrative purposes.
– ORIGIN late Middle English: from Latin, from *dictat-* 'dictated,' from the verb *dictare* (see DICTATE).

dic·ta·to·ri·al /,diktə'tôrēəl/ ▶ **adj.** of or typical of a ruler with total power: *a dictatorial regime.* ■ having or showing a tendency to tell people what to do in an autocratic way: *his dictatorial manner.*
– DERIVATIVES **dic·ta·to·ri·al·ly adv.**

dic·ta·tor·ship /dik'tātər,ship, 'diktātər-/ ▶ **n.** government by a dictator: *forty years of dictatorship.* ■ a country governed by a dictator. ■ absolute authority in any sphere.

dic·tion /'dikshən/ ▶ **n. 1** the choice and use of words and phrases in speech or writing: *Wordsworth campaigned against exaggerated poetic diction.*
2 the style of enunciation in speaking or singing: *she began imitating his careful diction.*
– ORIGIN mid 16th cent. (denoting a word or phrase): from Latin *dictio(n-)*, from *dicere* 'to say.'

dic·tion·ar·y /'dikshə,nerē/ (abbr.: **dict.**) ▶ **n.** (pl. **dictionaries**) a book that lists the words of a language in alphabetical order and gives their meaning, or that gives the equivalent words in a different language. ■ a reference book on any subject, the items of which are arranged in alphabetical order: *a dictionary of quotations.*
– PHRASES **have swallowed a dictionary** informal (of a person) use long and obscure words when speaking.
– ORIGIN early 16th cent.: from medieval Latin *dictionarium (manuale)* or *dictionarius (liber)* 'manual or book of words,' from Latin *dictio* (see DICTION).

dic·tion·ar·y at·tack ▶ **n.** an attempted illegal entry to a computer system that uses a dictionary headword list to generate possible passwords.

dic·tum /'diktəm/ ▶ **n.** (pl. **dicta** /-tə/ or **dictums**) a formal pronouncement from an authoritative source: *the First Amendment dictum that "Congress shall make no law ... abridging the freedom of speech"* ■ a short statement that expresses a general truth or principle: *the old dictum "might makes right."* ■ Law short for OBITER DICTUM.
– ORIGIN late 16th cent.: from Latin, literally 'something said,' neuter past participle of *dicere.*

dic·ty /'diktē/ ▶ **adj.** informal ostentatiously stylish; pretentious: *up there in their dicty Detroit suburb living the so-called good life.*
– ORIGIN early 20th cent.: of unknown origin.

Dic·ty·op·ter·a /,diktē'äptərə/ Entomology an order of insects that comprises the cockroaches and mantises. They have a somewhat flattened form, two pairs of wings, and long spiky legs.
– DERIVATIVES **dic·ty·op·ter·an n. & adj.**
– ORIGIN modern Latin (plural), from Greek *diktuon* 'net' + *pteron* 'wing.'

di·cyn·o·dont /dī'sinə,dänt/ ▶ **n.** a herbivorous, mammallike fossil reptile of the late Permian and Triassic periods, with beaked jaws and no teeth apart from two tusks in the upper jaw of the male. ● *Dicynodon* and other genera, infra-order Dicynodontia, order Therapsida.
– ORIGIN mid 19th cent.: from modern Latin *Dicynodontia* (plural), from Greek *di-* 'two' + *kuōn* 'dog' + *odous, odont-* 'tooth.'

did /did/ past of DO[1].

di·dac·tic /dī'daktik/ ▶ **adj.** intended to teach, particularly in having moral instruction as an ulterior motive: *a didactic novel that set out to expose social injustice.* ■ in the manner of a teacher, particularly so as to treat someone in a patronizing way: *slow-paced, didactic lecturing.*
– DERIVATIVES **di·dac·ti·cal·ly** /-ik(ə)lē/ **adv.**, **di·dac·ti·cism** /-tə,sizəm/ **n.**
– ORIGIN mid 17th cent.: from Greek *didaktikos*, from *didaskein* 'teach.'

di·dan·o·sine /dī'danə,sēn/ ▶ **n.** Medicine another term for DIDEOXYINOSINE.

did·dle /'didl/ ▶ **v.** informal **1** [with obj.] (usu. **be diddled**) cheat or swindle (someone) so as to deprive them of something: *he thought he'd been diddled out of his change.* ■ deliberately falsify (something): *he diddled his income tax returns.*
2 [no obj.] informal pass time aimlessly or unproductively: *why* ***diddle around*** *with slow costly tests?* ■ (**diddle with**) play or mess with: *he diddled with the graphics on his computer.*
3 [with obj.] vulgar slang have sexual intercourse with (someone). [originally in Scots dialect use in the sense 'jerk from side to side,' apparently corresponding to dialect *didder* 'tremble.']
– DERIVATIVES **did·dler n.**
– ORIGIN early 19th cent.: probably from the name of Jeremy *Diddler*, a character in the farce *Raising the Wind* (1803) by the Irish dramatist James Kenney (1780–1849). Diddler constantly borrowed and failed to repay small sums of money: the name may have been based on an earlier verb *diddle* 'walk unsteadily, swerve.'

did·dly-squat /'didlē ,skwät/ (also **diddly**) ▶ **pron.** [usu. with negative] informal anything: *she didn't care diddly-squat about what Darryl thought | they don't know diddly about softball.*
– ORIGIN mid 20th cent.: probably from slang *doodle* 'excrement' + SQUAT in the sense 'defecate.'

di·de·ox·y·cyt·i·dine /,dīdē,äksi'sītə,dēn/ (abbr.: **DDC** or **ddC**) ▶ **n.** Medicine a drug that inhibits the replication of HIV and is used in the treatment of AIDS, esp. in combination with zidovudine. It is a synthetic analog of a pyrimidine nucleoside.

di·de·ox·y·in·o·sine /,dīdē,äksē'inə,sēn/ (abbr.: **DDI** or **ddI**) ▶ **n.** Medicine a drug that inhibits the replication of HIV and is used in the treatment of AIDS, esp. in combination with zidovudine. It is a synthetic analog of a purine nucleoside.
– ORIGIN 1970s: from DI-[1] 'two' + *deoxy-* (in the sense 'that has lost oxygen') + INOSINE.

Di·de·rot /'dēdə,rō/, Denis (1713–84), French philosopher, writer, and critic. A leading figure of the Enlightenment in France, he was principal editor of the *Encyclopédie* (1751–76). Other notable works: *Le Rêve de D'Alembert* (1782) and *Le Neveu de Rameau* (1805).

didg·er·i·doo /ˌdijərēˈdo͞o/ (also **didjeridoo** or **didjeridu**) ▶ **n.** an Australian Aboriginal wind instrument in the form of a long wooden tube, traditionally made from a hollow branch, which is blown to produce a deep, resonant sound, varied by rhythmic accents of timbre and volume.
– ORIGIN 1920s: imitative; from an Aboriginal language of Arnhem Land, Northern Territory.

did·i·coi /ˈdidiˌkoi/ ▶ **n.** (pl. **didicois**) dialect a Gypsy or other nomadic person.
– ORIGIN mid 19th cent.: perhaps an alteration of Romany *dik akei* 'look here.'

did·n't /ˈdidnt/ ▶ **contraction** did not.

Di·do /ˈdīdō/ (in the *Aeneid*) the queen and founder of Carthage, who fell in love with the shipwrecked Aeneas and killed herself when he deserted her.

di·do /ˈdīˌdō/ ▶ **n.** (pl. **didoes** or **didos**) (in phrase **cut/cut up didoes**) informal perform mischievous tricks or deeds.
– ORIGIN early 19th cent.: of unknown origin.

Did·rik·son, Babe, see **ZAHARIAS**.

didst /didst/ archaic second person singular past of **DO**[1].

Did·y·ma /ˈdidimə/ an ancient sanctuary of Apollo, site of one of the most famous oracles of the Aegean region, close to the west coast of Asia Minor.

di·dym·i·um /dīˈdimēəm/ ▶ **n.** Chemistry a mixture containing the rare earth elements praseodymium and neodymium, used to color glass for optical filters. It was originally regarded as a single element.
– ORIGIN mid 19th cent.: from Greek *didumos* 'twin' (because it was closely associated with lanthanum) + *-ium* (used as a suffix for new metals).

die[1] /dī/ ▶ **v.** (**dies**, **dying** /ˈdīiNG/, **died**) [no obj.] **1** (of a person, animal, or plant) stop living: *she died of cancer* | *the sheep* ***died from*** *the heat* | [with obj.] *the king died a violent death.* ■ (**die for**) be killed for (a cause): *they were prepared to die for their country.* ■ [with complement] have a specified status at the time of one's death: *the inventor died a pauper.* ■ (**die out**) become extinct: *many species died out.* ■ be forgotten: *her genius has assured her name will never die.* ■ [with adverbial] become less loud or strong: *after a while, the noise* ***died down*** | *at last the storm* ***died away.*** ■ (**die back**) (of a plant) decay from the tip toward the root: *rhubarb dies back to a crown of buds each winter.* ■ (**die off**) die one after another until few or none are left: *the founders died off or retired.* ■ (of a fire or light) stop burning or gleaming. ■ informal (of a machine) stop functioning: *three toasters have* ***died on me.***
2 informal used to emphasize that one wants to do or have something very much: *they must be* ***dying for*** *a drink* | [with infinitive] *he's dying to meet you.*
3 informal used to emphasize feelings of shock, embarrassment, amusement, or misery: ***I nearly died*** *when I saw them* | *we nearly died laughing when he told us* | *I'm simply* ***dying of*** *thirst.*
4 archaic have an orgasm.
– PHRASES **die hard** disappear or change very slowly: *old habits die hard.* **die on the vine** be unsuccessful at an early stage. **never say die** used to encourage someone in a difficult situation. **to die for** informal extremely good or desirable: *the ice cream is to die for.*
– ORIGIN Middle English: from Old Norse *deyja*, of Germanic origin; related to **DEAD**.

die[2] ▶ **n. 1** singular form of **DICE**. ■ Architecture the cubical part of a pedestal between the base and the cornice; a dado or plinth.
2 (pl. **dies**) a device for cutting or molding metal into a particular shape. ■ an engraved device for stamping a design on coins or medals.
– PHRASES **the die is cast** an event has happened or a decision has been made that cannot be changed. **(as) straight as a die** absolutely straight.
– ORIGIN Middle English: from Old French *de*, from Latin *datum* 'something given or played,' neuter past participle of *dare*.

USAGE See usage at **DICE**.

die·back /ˈdīˌbak/ ▶ **n.** a condition in which a tree or shrub begins to die from the tip of its leaves or roots backward, owing to disease or an unfavorable environment.

die-cast ▶ **adj.** (of a metal object) formed by pouring molten metal into a reusable mold: *a die-cast aluminum loudspeaker chassis.*
▶ **v.** [with obj.] (usu. as noun **die-casting**) make (a metal object) in this way.

Dief·en·bak·er /ˈdēfənˌbākər/, John George (1895–1979), Canadian Progressive Conservative statesman; prime minister 1957–63.

dief·fen·bach·i·a /ˌdēfənˈbäkēə/ ▶ **n.** a plant of a genus that includes dumb cane and its relatives. ● Genus *Dieffenbachia*, family Araceae.
– ORIGIN modern Latin, named after Ernst *Dieffenbach* (1811–55), German horticulturalist.

di·e·ge·sis /ˌdīəˈjēsis/ ▶ **n.** (pl. **diegeses** /-sēz/) a narrative or plot, typically in a movie.
– DERIVATIVES **di·e·get·ic** /-ˈjetik/ **adj.**
– ORIGIN early 19th cent.: from Greek *diēgēsis* 'narrative.'

die·hard /ˈdīˌhärd/ ▶ **n.** [often as modifier] a person who strongly opposes change or who continues to support something in spite of opposition: *diehard traditionalists* | *she was a diehard Yankees fan.*
– ORIGIN mid 19th cent.: from *die hard* (see **DIE**[1]).

die-in ▶ **n.** informal a demonstration in which people lie down as if dead: *should it be a mass die-in on the campus main lawn?*

di·el /ˈdī(ə)l, ˈdē(ə)l/ ▶ **adj.** Biology denoting or involving a period of 24 hours: *tidal and diel cycles.*
– ORIGIN 1930s: from Latin *dies* 'day' + *-(a)l* (see **-AL**).

diel·drin /ˈdēldrin/ ▶ **n.** a toxic insecticide produced by the oxidation of aldrin, now largely banned because of its persistence in the environment. ● A chlorinated epoxide; chem. formula: $C_{12}H_8Cl_6O$.
– ORIGIN 1940s: blend of the name *Diels* (see **DIELS–ALDER REACTION**) + **ALDRIN**.

di·e·lec·tric /ˌdīəˈlektrik/ Physics ▶ **adj.** having the property of transmitting electric force without conduction; insulating.
▶ **n.** a medium or substance with such a property; an insulator.
– DERIVATIVES **di·e·lec·tri·cal·ly** /-ik(ə)lē/ **adv.**
– ORIGIN mid 19th cent.: from **DI-**[3] + **ELECTRIC**, literally 'across which electricity is transmitted (without conduction).'

di·e·lec·tric con·stant ▶ **n.** Physics a quantity measuring the ability of a substance to store electrical energy in an electric field.

di·e·lec·tro·pho·re·sis /ˌdīəˌlektrəfəˈrēsis/ ▶ **n.** Physics the migration of uncharged particles toward the position of maximum field strength in a nonuniform electric field.
– ORIGIN mid 20th cent.: blend of **DIELECTRIC** and **ELECTROPHORESIS**.

die link ▶ **n.** an established connection between coins struck from the same die.
▶ **v.** [with obj.] (**die-link**) establish a connection between (coins).

Diels-Al·der re·ac·tion /ˌdēlz ˈôldər/ ▶ **n.** Chemistry an addition reaction in which a conjugated diene reacts with a compound with a double or triple bond so as to form a six-membered ring.
– ORIGIN 1940s: named after Otto *Diels* (1876–1954), and Kurt *Alder* (1902–58), German chemists.

Dien Bien Phu /ˌdyen ˌbyen ˈfo͞o/ a village in northwestern Vietnam. It was the site of a French military post that was captured by the Vietminh after a 55-day siege in 1954.

di·en·ceph·a·lon /ˌdīenˈsefəˌlän/ ▶ **n.** Anatomy the caudal (posterior) part of the forebrain, containing the epithalamus, thalamus, hypothalamus, and ventral thalamus and the third ventricle. Compare with **TELENCEPHALON**.
– DERIVATIVES **di·en·ce·phal·ic** /-səˈfalik/ **adj.**
– ORIGIN late 19th cent.: from **DI-**[3] 'across' + Greek *enkephalos* 'brain.'

di·ene /ˈdīˌēn/ ▶ **n.** Chemistry an unsaturated hydrocarbon containing two double bonds between carbon atoms.
– ORIGIN early 20th cent.: from **DI-**[1] 'two' + **-ENE**.

die-off ▶ **n.** a period in which a significant proportion of a population dies naturally, usually within a short time. ■ a process causing this. ■ the death of a significant proportion of a population in this way.

di·er·e·sis /dīˈerəsis/ (also **diaeresis**) ▶ **n.** (pl. **diereses** /-ˌsēz/) **1** a mark (¨) placed over a vowel to indicate that it is sounded in a separate syllable, as in *naïve, Brontë.* ■ the division of a sound into two syllables, esp. by sounding a diphthong as two vowels.
2 Prosody a natural rhythmic break in a line of verse where the end of a metrical foot coincides with the end of a word.
– ORIGIN late 16th cent. (denoting the division of one syllable into two): via Latin from Greek *diairesis* 'separation,' from *diairein* 'take apart,' from *dia* 'apart' + *hairein* 'take.'

Die·sel /ˈdēzəl/, Rudolf (Christian Karl) (1858–1913), German engineer; born in France. He invented the diesel engine in the late 19th century.

die·sel /ˈdēzəl, -səl/ ▶ **n.** (also **diesel engine**) an internal combustion engine in which heat produced by the compression of air in the cylinder is used to ignite the fuel: [as modifier] *a diesel locomotive.* ■ a heavy petroleum fraction used as fuel in diesel engines: *eleven gallons of diesel.*
– DERIVATIVES **die·sel·ize** /-ˌlīz/ **v.**
– ORIGIN late 19th cent.: named after R. **DIESEL**.

die·sel-e·lec·tric ▶ **adj.** denoting or relating to a locomotive driven by the electric current produced by a diesel-engined generator.
▶ **n.** a locomotive of this type.

die·sel-hy·drau·lic ▶ **adj.** denoting or relating to a locomotive driven by a hydraulic transmission system powered by a diesel engine.
▶ **n.** a locomotive of this type.

die·sink·er ▶ **n.** a person who engraves dies used to stamp designs on coins or medals.

Di·es I·rae /ˈdēās ˈi(ə)rā/ ▶ **n.** a Latin hymn formerly sung in a Mass for the dead.
– ORIGIN Latin, literally 'day of wrath' (the opening words of the hymn).

di·e·sis /ˈdīəsis/ ▶ **n.** (pl. **dieses**) Printing the double dagger symbol ‡.
– ORIGIN late Middle English: Latin, from Greek *diēsis*, from *diienai* 'send through,' from *dia* 'through' + *ienai* 'send.'

di·es non /ˌdēāz ˈnän/ ▶ **n.** (pl. **same**) a day on which no legal business can be done, or which does not count for legal or other purposes.
– ORIGIN Latin, short for *dies non juridicus* 'nonjudicial day.'

die-stamp·ing ▶ **n.** a method of embossing paper or another surface using a die. ■ a method of printing using an inked die to produce raised print.

die·stock /ˈdīˌstäk/ ▶ **n.** a hand tool used in the cutting of external screw threads, consisting of a holder for the die that is turned using long handles.

di·es·trus /dīˈestrəs/ ▶ **n.** Zoology (in most female mammals) a period of sexual inactivity between recurrent periods of estrus.

di·et[1] /ˈdī-it/ ▶ **n. 1** the kinds of food that a person, animal, or community habitually eats: *a vegetarian diet* | *a specialist in diet.* ■ a regular occupation or series of activities in which one participates: *a healthy diet of classical music.*
2 a special course of food to which one restricts oneself, either to lose weight or for medical reasons: ***I'm going on a diet.*** ■ [as modifier] (of food or drink) with reduced fat or sugar content: *diet soft drinks.*
▶ **v.** (**diets**, **dieting**, **dieted**) [no obj.] restrict oneself to small amounts or special kinds of food in order to lose weight: *it's difficult to diet.*
– DERIVATIVES **di·et·er n.**
– ORIGIN Middle English: from Old French *diete* (noun), *dieter* (verb), via Latin from Greek *diaita* 'a way of life.'

di·et[2] ▶ **n.** a legislative assembly in certain countries. ■ historical a regular meeting of the states of a confederation. ■ Scots Law a meeting or session of a court.
– ORIGIN late Middle English: from medieval Latin *dieta* 'day's work, wages, etc.,' also 'meeting of councilors.'

die·tar·y /ˈdī-iˌterē/ ▶ **adj.** of or relating to diets or dieting: *dietary advice for healthy skin and hair.* ■ provided by one's diet: *the average dietary calcium intake was 140 milligrams per day.*
▶ **n.** (pl. **dietaries**) dated a regulated or restricted diet.
– ORIGIN late Middle English (as a noun): from medieval Latin *dietarium*, from Latin *diaeta* (see **DIET**[1]).

di·e·tet·ic /ˌdī-iˈtetik/ ▶ **adj.** concerned with diet and nutrition: *experienced dietetic advice.*
– DERIVATIVES **di·e·tet·i·cal·ly** /-ik(ə)lē/ **adv.**
– ORIGIN mid 16th cent. (as a noun in the sense 'dietetics'): via Latin from Greek *diaitētikos*, from *diaita* 'a way of life.'

di·e·tet·ics /ˌdī-iˈtetiks/ ▶ **plural n.** [treated as sing.] the branch of knowledge concerned with the diet and its effects on health, esp. with the practical application of a scientific understanding of nutrition.

di·eth·yl·ene gly·col /dīˈeTHəˌlēn ˈglīkôl/ ▶ **n.** Chemistry a colorless, soluble liquid used as a solvent and antifreeze. ● Chem. formula: $(C_2H_4OH)_2O$.

di·eth·yl e·ther /dīˈeTHəl ˈēTHər/ ▶ **n.** see **ETHER** (sense 1).

di·eth·yl·stil·bes·trol /dīˌeTHəlstilˈbestrôl/ ▶ **n.** another term for **STILBESTROL**.

di·e·ti·tian /ˌdī-iˈtiSHən/ (also **dietician**) ▶ **n.** an expert on diet and nutrition.

Di·et of Worms a meeting of the Holy Roman Emperor Charles V's imperial diet at Worms in 1521, at which Martin Luther was summoned to appear. Luther committed himself there to the cause of Protestant reform, and his teaching was formally condemned in the Edict of Worms.

Die·trich /ˈdētrik/, Marlene (1901–92), US actress and singer; born in Germany; born *Maria Magdelene Dietrich*. She became known for her part as Lola in *The Blue Angel* (1930), one of many movies that she made with Josef von Sternberg. From the 1950s, she was also successful as a cabaret performer.

Marlene Dietrich

Dieu et mon droit /ˈdyo͞o ā môn ˈdwä/ ▶ **n.** God and my right (the motto of the British monarch).
– ORIGIN French.

dif- ▶ **prefix 1** variant spelling of DIS-.
2 assimilated before *f* (as in *diffraction, diffuse.*).
– ORIGIN from Latin, variant of DIS-.

diff /dif/ ▶ **n.** informal short for DIFFERENCE.
▶ **v.** [with obj.] Computing compare (files) in order to determine how or whether they differ.

dif·fer /ˈdifər/ ▶ **v.** [no obj.] be unlike or dissimilar: *the second set of data **differed from** the first* | *tastes differ* | (as adj. **differing**) *widely differing circumstances.* ■ disagree: *he **differed from** his contemporaries in ethical matters.*
– PHRASES **agree to differ** cease to argue about something because neither party will compromise or be persuaded. **beg to differ** politely disagree: *that's your opinion—I beg to differ.*
– ORIGIN late Middle English (also in the sense 'put off, defer'): from Old French *differer* 'differ, defer,' from Latin *differre*, from *dis-* 'from, away' + *ferre* 'bring, carry.' Compare with DEFER¹.

dif·fer·ence /ˈdif(ə)rəns/ ▶ **n.** a point or way in which people or things are not the same: *the **differences between** men and women.* ■ the state or condition of being dissimilar or unlike: *their **difference from** one another.* ■ a disagreement, quarrel, or dispute: *the couple are patching up their differences.* ■ a quantity by which amounts differ; the remainder left after subtraction of one value from another: *the gross margin is the difference between the total cost of the goods and the final selling price.* ■ Heraldry an alteration in a coat of arms to distinguish members or branches of a family.
▶ **v.** [with obj.] Heraldry alter (a coat of arms) to distinguish members or branches of a family.
– PHRASES **make a** (or **no**) **difference** have a significant effect (or no effect) on a person or situation: *the law **will make no difference to** my business.* **with a difference** having a new or unusual feature or treatment: *a fashion show with a difference.*
– ORIGIN Middle English: via Old French from Latin *differentia* (see DIFFERENTIA).

dif·fer·ence thresh·old ▶ **n.** the smallest amount by which two sensory stimuli can differ in order for an individual to perceive them as different.

dif·fer·ent /ˈdif(ə)rənt/ ▶ **adj. 1** not the same as another or each other; unlike in nature, form, or quality: *you can play this game in different ways* | (**different from/than**) *the car is different from anything else on the market.* ■ informal novel and unusual: *try something deliciously different.*
2 distinct; separate: *on two different occasions.*
– PHRASES **different strokes for different folks** proverb different things appeal to different people.
– DERIVATIVES **dif·fer·ent·ly adv.**, **dif·fer·ent·ness n.**
– ORIGIN late Middle English: via Old French from Latin *different-* 'carrying away, differing,' from the verb *differre* (see DIFFER).

> **USAGE** **Different from, different than,** and **different to:** what are the distinctions between these three constructions, and is one more correct than the others? In practice, **different from** is both the most common structure and the most accepted. **Different than** is used chiefly in North America, although its use is increasing in British English. Because it can be followed by a clause, it is sometimes more concise than **different from** (compare *"things are **different than** they were a year ago"* with *"things are **different from the way** they were a year ago"*). **Different to,** although common in Britain, is disliked by traditionalists and sounds peculiar to American ears.

dif·fer·en·ti·a /ˌdifəˈrensн(ē)ə/ ▶ **n.** (pl. **differentiae** /-sнē,ē/) a distinguishing mark or characteristic. ■ chiefly Philosophy an attribute that distinguishes a species of thing from other species of the same genus.
– ORIGIN late 17th cent.: from Latin, literally 'difference,' from *different-* 'carrying away' (see DIFFERENT).

dif·fer·en·ti·a·ble /ˌdifəˈrensнəbəl/ ▶ **adj.** able to be differentiated.
– DERIVATIVES **dif·fer·en·ti·a·bil·i·ty** /-ˌrensнəˈbilitē/ **n.**
– ORIGIN mid 19th cent.: from DIFFERENTIATE, on the pattern of pairs such as *depreciate, depreciable.*

dif·fer·en·tial /ˌdifəˈrencнəl/ chiefly technical ▶ **adj.** [attrib.] of, showing, or depending on a difference; differing or varying according to circumstances or relevant factors: *the differential achievements of boys and girls.* ■ constituting a specific difference; distinctive: *the differential features between benign and malignant tumors.* ■ Mathematics relating to infinitesimal differences or to the derivatives of functions. ■ of or relating to a difference in a physical quantity: *a differential amplifier.*
▶ **n.** a difference between amounts of things: *the **differential between** gasoline and diesel prices.* ■ Mathematics an infinitesimal difference between successive values of a variable. ■ (also **differential gear**) a set of gears allowing a vehicle's driven wheels to revolve at different speeds when going around corners.
– DERIVATIVES **dif·fer·en·tial·ly adv.**
– ORIGIN mid 17th cent.: from medieval Latin *differentialis*, from Latin *differentia* 'difference' (see DIFFERENTIA).

dif·fer·en·tial cal·cu·lus ▶ **n.** a branch of mathematics concerned with the determination, properties, and application of derivatives and differentials. Compare with INTEGRAL CALCULUS.

dif·fer·en·tial co·ef·fi·cient ▶ **n.** Mathematics another term for DERIVATIVE.

dif·fer·en·tial di·ag·no·sis ▶ **n.** Medicine the process of differentiating between two or more conditions that share similar signs or symptoms.

dif·fer·en·tial e·qua·tion ▶ **n.** an equation involving derivatives of a function or functions.

dif·fer·en·tial lock ▶ **n.** a device that disables the differential of a motor vehicle in slippery conditions to improve grip.

dif·fer·en·tial op·er·a·tor ▶ **n.** Mathematics another term for DEL.

dif·fer·en·tial wind·lass ▶ **n.** a hoisting device consisting of two drums of different diameters on the same axis and turning at the same rate, so that a line wound on the larger drum and unwound from the smaller drum provides a mechanical advantage in lifting. Also called **Chinese windlass.**

dif·fer·en·ti·ate /ˌdifəˈrensнē,āt/ ▶ **v.** [with obj.]
1 recognize or ascertain what makes (someone or something) different: *children can **differentiate** the past **from** the present.* ■ [no obj.] (**differentiate between**) identify differences between (two or more things or people): *he is unable to differentiate between fantasy and reality.* ■ make (someone or something) appear different or distinct: *Twain was careful to **differentiate** Huck's speech **from** that of other white people.*
2 technical make or become different in the process of growth or development: [with obj.] *the receptors are developed and differentiated into sense organs* | [no obj.] *the cells differentiate into a wide variety of cell types.*
3 Mathematics transform (a function) into its derivative.
– DERIVATIVES **dif·fer·en·ti·a·tor** /-ˌātər/ **n.**
– ORIGIN early 19th cent.: from medieval Latin *differentiat-* 'carried away from,' from the verb *differentiare*, from *differentia* (see DIFFERENTIA).

dif·fer·en·ti·a·tion /ˌdifərensнēˈāsнən/ ▶ **n.** the action or process of differentiating: *packaging can be a source of product differentiation.*

dif·fer·ent·ly a·bled ▶ **adj.** disabled.

> **USAGE** **Differently abled** was first proposed (in the 1980s) as an alternative to **disabled, handicapped,** etc., on the grounds that it gave a more positive message and so avoided discrimination toward people with disabilities. The term has gained little currency, however, and can seem overeuphemistic and condescending. The accepted term in general use is still **disabled.**

dif·fi·cult /ˈdifikəlt/ ▶ **adj.** needing much effort or skill to accomplish, deal with, or understand: *she had a difficult decision to make* | *the questions are too **difficult for** the children.* ■ characterized by or causing hardships or problems: *a difficult economic climate.* ■ (of a person) not easy to please or satisfy: *Lily could be difficult.*
– DERIVATIVES **dif·fi·cult·ly adv.** (rare), **dif·fi·cult·ness n.**
– ORIGIN late Middle English: back-formation from DIFFICULTY.

dif·fi·cul·ty /ˈdifikəltē/ ▶ **n.** (pl. **difficulties**) the state or condition of being difficult: *Guy had **no difficulty in** making friends* | *she walks **with difficulty**.* ■ a thing that is hard to accomplish, deal with, or understand: *there is a practical difficulty* | *a club with financial difficulties.* ■ (often **difficulties**) a situation that is difficult or dangerous: *they went for a swim but **got into difficulties**.*
– ORIGIN late Middle English (in the senses 'requiring effort or skill' and 'something difficult'): from Latin *difficultas*, from *dis-* (expressing reversal) + *facultas* 'ability, opportunity.'

dif·fi·dence /ˈdifidəns/ ▶ **n.** modesty or shyness resulting from a lack of self-confidence: *I say this with some diffidence.*

dif·fi·dent /ˈdifidənt/ ▶ **adj.** modest or shy because of a lack of self-confidence: *a diffident youth.*
– DERIVATIVES **dif·fi·dent·ly adv.**
– ORIGIN late Middle English (in the sense 'lacking confidence or trust in someone or something'): from Latin *diffident-* 'failing in trust,' from the verb *diffidere*, from *dis-* (expressing reversal) + *fidere* 'to trust.'

dif·fract /diˈfrakt/ ▶ **v.** [with obj.] Physics cause to undergo diffraction.
– DERIVATIVES **dif·frac·tive** /-tiv/ **adj.**, **dif·frac·tive·ly** /-tivlē/ **adv.**
– ORIGIN early 19th cent.: from Latin *diffract-* 'broken in pieces,' from the verb *diffringere*, from *dis-* 'away, from' + *frangere* 'to break.'

dif·frac·tion /diˈfraksнən/ ▶ **n.** the process by which a beam of light or other system of waves is spread out as a result of passing through a narrow aperture or across an edge, typically accompanied by interference between the wave forms produced.

dif·frac·tion grat·ing ▶ **n.** a plate of glass or metal ruled with very close parallel lines, producing a spectrum by diffraction and interference of light.

dif·frac·tom·e·ter /ˌdifrakˈtämitər/ ▶ **n.** an instrument for measuring diffraction, chiefly used to determine the structure of a crystal by analysis of the diffraction of X-rays.

dif·fuse ▶ **v.** /diˈfyo͞oz/ spread or cause to spread over a wide area or among a large number of people: [no obj.] *technologies diffuse rapidly* | [with obj.] *the problem is how to diffuse power without creating anarchy.* ■ become or cause (a fluid, gas, individual atom, etc.) to become intermingled with a substance by movement, typically in a specified direction or at specified speed: [no obj.] *oxygen molecules **diffuse across** the membrane* | [with obj.] *gas is **diffused into** the bladder.* ■ [with obj.] cause (light) to glow faintly by dispersing it in many directions.
▶ **adj.** /diˈfyo͞os/ spread out over a large area; not concentrated: *the diffuse community centered on the church* | *the light is more diffuse.* ■ (of disease) not localized in the body: *diffuse hyperplasia.* ■ lacking clarity or conciseness: *the second argument is more diffuse.*
– DERIVATIVES **dif·fuse·ly** /-ˈfyo͞oslē/ **adv.**, **dif·fuse·ness** /-ˈfyo͞osnis/ **n.**
– ORIGIN late Middle English: from Latin *diffus-* 'poured out,' from the verb *diffundere*, from *dis-* 'away' + *fundere* 'pour'; the adjective via French *diffus* or Latin *diffusus* 'extensive,' from *diffundere*.

> **USAGE** The verbs **diffuse** and **defuse** sound similar but have different meanings. **Diffuse** means, broadly, 'disperse,' while the nonliteral meaning of **defuse** is 'reduce the danger or tension in.' Thus sentences such as *Cooper successfully **diffused** the situation* are regarded as incorrect, while *Cooper successfully **defused** the situation* would be correct. However, such uses of **diffuse** are widespread, and can make sense: the image in, for example, *only peaceful dialogue between the two countries could diffuse tension* is not of making a bomb safe but of reducing something dangerous to particles and dispersing them harmlessly.

dif·fus·er /diˈfyo͞ozər/ (also **diffusor**) ▶ **n.** a thing that diffuses something, in particular: ■ an attachment or duct for broadening an airflow and reducing its speed. ■ Photography a device that spreads the light from a light source evenly and reduces harsh shadows.

dif·fus·i·ble /diˈfyo͞ozəbəl/ ▶ **adj.** able to intermingle by diffusion: *diffusible factors in the cytoplasm.*

dif·fu·sion /diˈfyo͞oZHən/ ▶ **n.** the spreading of something more widely: *the diffusion of Duchamp's thought and art.* ■ the action of spreading the light from a light source evenly so as to reduce glare and harsh shadows. ■ Chemistry the intermingling of substances by the natural movement of their particles: *the rate of diffusion of a gas.* ■ Anthropology the dissemination of elements of culture to another region or people.
– DERIVATIVES **dif·fu·sive** /-siv/ **adj.** (Chemistry).
– ORIGIN late Middle English (in the sense 'pouring out, effusion'): from Latin *diffusion-*, from *diffundere* 'pour out.'

dif·fu·sion·ist /diˈfyo͞oZHənist/ Anthropology ▶ **adj.** advocating the theory of the dissemination of elements of culture to another region or people: *the rural sociological literature of the diffusionist school.*
▶ **n.** an advocate of such a theory.
– DERIVATIVES **dif·fu·sion·ism** /-ˌnizəm/ **n.**

dif·fu·siv·i·ty /ˌdifyo͞oˈsivitē/ ▶ **n.** (pl. **diffusivities**) Physics a measure of the capability of a substance or energy to be diffused or to allow something to pass by diffusion.

dig /dig/ ▶ **v.** (**digs, digging**; past and past participle **dug** /dəg/) **1** [no obj.] break up and move earth with a tool or machine, or with hands, paws, snout, etc.: *the boar had been digging for roots* | [with obj.] *she had to dig the garden* | *authorities cause chaos by digging* ***up*** *roads.* ■ [with obj.] make (a hole, grave, etc.) by breaking up and moving earth in such a way: *he took a spade and dug a hole* | (as adj. **dug**) *the newly dug grave.* ■ [with obj.] extract from the ground by breaking up and moving earth: *they* ***dug up*** *fossils of an animal about the size of a turkey.* ■ (**dig in**) (of a soldier) protect oneself by making a trench or similar ground defense. ■ [in imperative] (**dig in**) informal used to encourage someone to start eating with gusto and have as much as they want: *put the sausage on top of the polenta; then dig in.* ■ [with obj.] (**dig something in/into**) push or poke something in or into: *he dug his hands into his pockets.* ■ [with obj.] excavate (an archaeological site): *apart from digging a site, recording evidence is important.* ■ [with obj.] (**dig something out**) bring out something that is hidden or has been stored for a long time: *they dug out last year's notes.* ■ (**dig into**) informal find money from (somewhere): *members have to dig deep into their pockets.* ■ search or rummage in a specified place: *Catherine dug into her handbag and produced her card.* ■ engage in research; conduct an investigation: *a professional* ***digging for*** *information* | *he had no compunction about digging into her private affairs.* ■ [with obj.] (**dig something up/out**) discover information after a search or investigation: *have you* ***dug up*** *any information on the captain?*
2 [with obj.] informal like, appreciate, or understand: *I really dig heavy rock.*
▶ **n. 1** [in sing.] an act or spell of digging: *a thorough dig of the whole plot.* ■ an archaeological excavation.
2 a push or poke with one's elbow, finger, etc.: *Ginnie gave her sister* ***a dig in the ribs.*** ■ informal a remark intended to mock or criticize: *this was a cruel dig at Jenny.*
– PHRASES **dig up dirt** informal discover and reveal damaging information about someone. **dig oneself into a hole** (or **dig a hole for oneself**) get oneself into an awkward or restrictive situation. **dig in one's heels** resist stubbornly; refuse to give in: *he has dug in his heels and refuses to leave.* **dig's one's own grave** see **GRAVE**[1].
– ORIGIN Middle English: perhaps from Old English *dīc* 'ditch.'

Di·gam·ba·ra /diˈgəmbərə/ ▶ **n.** a member of one of two principal sects of Jainism, which was formed as a result of doctrinal schism in about AD 80 and continues today in parts of southern India. Male ascetic members of the sect traditionally reject property ownership and do not wear clothes. See also **SVETAMBARA**.
– ORIGIN from Sanskrit *Digāmbara*, literally 'sky-clad.'

di·gam·ma /dīˈgamə/ ▶ **n.** the sixth letter of the early Greek alphabet (Ϝ, ϝ), pronounced as "w." It became obsolete in many Greek dialects before the Classical period.
– ORIGIN late 17th cent.: via Latin from Greek, from *di-* 'twice' + **GAMMA** (because of the shape of the letter, resembling gamma (Γ) with an extra stroke).

di·gas·tric /dīˈgastrik/ (also **digastric muscle**) ▶ **n.** Anatomy each of a pair of muscles that run under the jaw and act to open it.
– ORIGIN late 17th cent.: from modern Latin *digastricus*, from *di-* 'twice' + Greek *gastēr* 'belly' (because the muscle has two fleshy parts or "bellies" at an angle, connected by a tendon).

di·ge·ne·an /dīˈjēnēən/ Zoology ▶ **adj.** of or relating to a group of flukes that are internal parasites needing two to four hosts to complete their life cycle. Compare with **MONOGENEAN**.
▶ **n.** a digenean fluke; a trematode. ● Subclass Digenea, class Trematoda.
– ORIGIN 1960s: from modern Latin *Digenea* (from Greek *di-* 'twice' + *genea* 'generation, race') + **-AN**.

di·ge·ra·ti /dijəˈrätē/ ▶ **plural n.** people with expertise or professional involvement in information technology.
– ORIGIN 1990s: blend of **DIGITAL** and **LITERATI**.

di·gest ▶ **v.** /diˈjest, dī-/ [with obj.] break down (food) in the alimentary canal and intestines into substances that can be used by the body. ■ understand or assimilate (new information or the significance of something) by a period of reflection. ■ arrange (something) in a systematic or convenient order, esp. by reduction: *the computer* ***digested*** *your labors into a form understandable by a program.* ■ Chemistry treat (a substance) with heat, enzymes, or a solvent in order to decompose it or extract essential components.
▶ **n.** /ˈdīˌjest/ **1** a compilation or summary of material or information: *a digest of their findings.* ■ a periodical consisting of condensed versions of pieces of writing or news published elsewhere. ■ a methodical summary of a body of laws. ■ (**the Digest**) the compendium of Roman law compiled in the reign of Justinian.
2 Chemistry a substance or mixture obtained by digestion: *a digest of cloned DNA.*
– ORIGIN late Middle English: from Latin *digest-* 'distributed, dissolved, digested,' from the verb *digerere*, from *di-* 'apart' + *gerere* 'carry'; the noun from Latin *digesta* 'matters methodically arranged,' from *digestus* 'divided,' from *digerere*.

di·gest·er /diˈjestər, dī-/ ▶ **n.** Chemistry a container in which substances are treated with heat, enzymes, or a solvent in order to promote decomposition or extract essential components.

di·gest·i·ble /diˈjestəbəl, dī-/ ▶ **adj.** (of food) able to be digested. ■ (of information) easy to understand or follow: *her books convey philosophical issues in digestible form.*
– DERIVATIVES **di·gest·i·bil·i·ty** /-ˌjestəˈbilitē/ **n.**
– ORIGIN late Middle English: via Old French from Latin *digestibilis*, from *digest-* 'digested,' from the verb *digerere* (see **DIGEST**).

di·ges·tif /ˌdējesˈtēf/ ▶ **n.** a drink or portion of food drunk or eaten in order to aid the digestion.
– ORIGIN early 20th cent.: French, literally 'digestive.'

di·ges·tion /diˈjesCHən, dī-/ ▶ **n.** the process of breaking down food by mechanical and enzymatic action in the stomach and intestines into substances that can be used by the body. ■ a person's capacity to break down food in such a way: *bouts of dysentery impaired his digestion.* ■ Chemistry the process of treating a substance by means of heat, enzymes, or a solvent to promote decomposition or extract essential components.
– ORIGIN late Middle English: via Old French from Latin *digestio(n-)*, from the verb *digerere* (see **DIGEST**).

di·ges·tive /diˈjestiv, dī-/ ▶ **adj.** of or relating to the process of digesting food: *stomach ulcers and other digestive disorders.* ■ (of food or medicine) aiding or promoting the process of digestion: *digestive mints.*
▶ **n.** a food or medicine that aids or promotes the digestion of food. ■ (also **digestive biscuit**) Brit. a round, semisweet cookie made of wholewheat flour.
– DERIVATIVES **di·ges·tive·ly** **adv.**
– ORIGIN late Middle English: from Old French *digestif, -ive* or Latin *digestivus*, from *digest-* 'digested,' from the verb *digerere* (see **DIGEST**).

di·ges·tive gland ▶ **n.** Zoology a glandular organ of digestion present in crustaceans, mollusks, and certain other invertebrates.

dig·ger /ˈdigər/ ▶ **n. 1** a person, animal, or large machine that digs earth: [in combination] *a grave-digger.* ■ (**Digger**, in full **Digger Indian**) offensive a North American Indian of any of several tribes that subsisted on roots dug from the ground.
2 Austral./NZ informal a man, esp. a private soldier (often used as a friendly form of address): *how are you, Digger?* [early 20th cent.: from *digger* 'miner,' reinforced by association with the digging of trenches on the battlefields.]

dig·ger wasp ▶ **n.** a solitary wasp that typically excavates a burrow in sandy soil, filling it with one or more paralyzed insects or spiders for its larvae to feed on. ● Families Sphecidae (which includes sand wasps) and Pompilidae (which includes spider-hunting wasps).

dig·gings /ˈdiGiNGz/ ▶ **plural n. 1** a site such as a mine or goldfield that has been excavated: *hills scarred with peat diggings.* ■ material that has been dug from the ground.
2 Brit. informal, dated lodgings.

dig·ging stick ▶ **n.** a primitive digging implement consisting of a pointed stick, sometimes weighted with a stone.

dight /dīt/ ▶ **adj.** archaic clothed or equipped.
▶ **v.** [with obj.] literary make ready for a use or purpose; prepare: *let the meal be dighted.*
– ORIGIN Middle English: past participle of archaic *dight* 'order, deal with,' based on Latin *dictare* 'compose (in language), order.' The wide and varied use of the word in Middle English is reflected dialectally.

dig·i·cam /ˈdijiˌkam/ ▶ **n.** a digital camera.
– ORIGIN blend.

dig·i·pak /ˈdijipak/ ▶ **n.** trademark a type of packaging for CDs or DVDs, typically made from cardboard with an internal plastic holder for one or more discs.
– ORIGIN 1980s: from **DIGITAL** and **PACK**[1].

d

dig·it /ˈdijit/ ▶ **n. 1** any of the numerals from 0 to 9, esp. when forming part of a number.
2 a finger (including the thumb) or toe. ■ Zoology an equivalent structure at the end of the limbs of many higher vertebrates.
– ORIGIN late Middle English: from Latin *digitus* 'finger, toe'; sense 1 arose from the practice of counting on the fingers.

dig·it·al /ˈdijitl/ ▶ **adj. 1** relating to or using signals or information represented by discrete values (digits) of a physical quantity, such as voltage or magnetic polarization, to represent arithmetic numbers or approximations to numbers from a continuum or logical expressions and variables: *digital TV*. Often contrasted with **ANALOG**. ■ involving or relating to the use of computer technology: *the digital revolution.*
2 ■ (of a clock or watch) showing the time by means of displayed digits rather than hands or a pointer.
3 of or relating to a finger or fingers.
– DERIVATIVES **dig·it·al·ly** **adv.**
– ORIGIN late 15th cent.: from Latin *digitalis*, from *digitus* 'finger, toe.'

dig·it·al au·di·o·tape (abbr.: **DAT**) ▶ **n.** magnetic tape used to make digital sound recordings of very high quality.

dig·it·al cam·er·a ▶ **n.** a camera that records and stores digital images.

dig·it·al cash (also **digital money**) ▶ **n.** money that may be transferred electronically from one party to another during a transaction.

dig·it·al com·press·ion ▶ **n.** a method of reducing the number of bits (zeros and ones) in a digital signal by using mathematical algorithms to eliminate redundant information.

dig·it·al di·vide ▶ **n.** the gulf between those who have ready access to computers and the Internet, and those who do not: *a worrying "digital divide" based on race, gender, educational attainment, and income.*

dig·i·tal·in /ˌdijiˈtalin/ ▶ **n.** a drug containing the active constituents of digitalis.
– ORIGIN mid 19th cent.: from **DIGITALIS** + **-IN**[1].

dig·i·tal·is /ˌdijiˈtalis/ ▶ **n.** a drug prepared from the dried leaves of foxglove and containing substances (notably digoxin and digitoxin) that stimulate the heart muscle.
– ORIGIN late 18th cent.: from the modern Latin genus name of the foxglove, from *digitalis* (*herba*) '(plant) relating to the finger,' from *digitus* 'finger, toe'; suggested by German *Fingerhut* 'thimble or foxglove.'

dig·i·tal·ize[1] /ˈdijitlˌīz/ ▶ **v.** another term for **DIGITIZE**.
– DERIVATIVES **dig·i·tal·i·za·tion** /ˌdijitl-əˈzāSHən/ **n.**

dig·i·tal·ize[2] ▶ **v.** [with obj.] Medicine administer digitalis or digoxin to (a patient with a heart complaint).
– DERIVATIVES **dig·i·tal·i·za·tion** /ˌdijitl-əˈzāSHən/ **n.**

dig·it·al lock·er ▶ **n.** Computing an Internet service that allows registered users to access music, movies, videos, photographs, games, and other multimedia files.

dig·it·al ob·ject i·den·ti·fi·er (abbr.: **DOI**) ▶ **n.** Computing a unique string of characters allocated to a website, file, or other piece of digital information.

dig·it·al sig·na·ture ▶ **n.** Computing a digital code (generated and authenticated by public key encryption) that is attached to an electronically transmitted document to verify its contents and the sender's identity.

dig·i·tal sub·scrib·er line ▶ **n.** Computing see **DSL**.

dig·it·al tel·e·vi·sion (abbr.: **DTV**) ▶ **n.** television broadcasting in which the pictures are transmitted as digital signals that are decoded by a device in or attached to the receiving television set.

dig·i·tal-to-an·a·log con·vert·er ▶ n. an electronic device for converting digital signals to analog form.

dig·i·tal ver·sa·tile disc ▶ n. Computing see **DVD**.

dig·i·tal vid·e·o re·cord·er ▶ n. (abbr. **DVR**) a programmable electronic device that writes audio and video input, typically from a television signal, to a rewritable hard disk.

dig·i·tate /ˈdijiˌtāt/ ▶ adj. technical shaped like a spread hand: *digitate leaves | a digitate delta.*
– ORIGIN mid 17th cent.: from Latin *digitatus*, from *digitus* 'finger, toe.'

dig·i·ta·tion /ˌdijiˈtāSHən/ ▶ n. Zoology & Botany a fingerlike protuberance or division.

dig·i·ti·grade /ˈdijitiˌgrād/ ▶ adj. Zoology (of a mammal) walking on its toes and not touching the ground with its heels, as a dog, cat, or rodent. Compare with **PLANTIGRADE**.
– ORIGIN mid 19th cent.: from Latin *digitus* 'finger, toe' + *-gradus* '-walking.'

dig·i·tize /ˈdijiˌtīz/ ▶ v. [with obj.] (usu. as adj. **digitized**) convert (pictures or sound) into a digital form that can be processed by a computer.
– DERIVATIVES **dig·i·ti·za·tion** /ˌdijitəˈzāSHən/ n., **dig·i·tiz·er** n.

dig·i·tox·in /ˌdijiˈtäksin/ ▶ n. Chemistry a compound with similar properties to digoxin and found with it in the foxglove and similar plants.

di·glos·si·a /dīˈglôsēə, -ˈglä-/ ▶ n. Linguistics a situation in which two languages (or two varieties of the same language) are used under different conditions within a community, often by the same speakers. The term is usually applied to languages with distinct "high" and "low" (colloquial) varieties, such as Arabic.
– DERIVATIVES **di·glos·sic** /-sik/ adj.
– ORIGIN 1950s: from Greek *diglōssos* 'bilingual,' on the pattern of French *diglossie*.

dig·ni·fied /ˈdigniˌfīd/ ▶ adj. having or showing a composed or serious manner that is worthy of respect: *she maintained a dignified silence | a dignified old lady.*
– DERIVATIVES **dig·ni·fied·ly** /-ˌfī(ə)dlē/ adv.

dig·ni·fy /ˈdignəˌfī/ ▶ v. (**dignifies, dignifying, dignified**) [with obj.] make (something) seem worthy and impressive: *the Americans had dignified their departure with a ceremony.* ■ give an impressive name to (someone or something that one considers worthless): *dumps are increasingly* **dignified** *as landfills.*
– ORIGIN late Middle English: from Old French *dignefier*, from late Latin *dignificare*, from Latin *dignus* 'worthy.'

dig·ni·tar·y /ˈdigniˌterē/ ▶ n. (pl. **dignitaries**) a person considered to be important because of high rank or office.
– ORIGIN late 17th cent.: from **DIGNITY**, on the pattern of the pairs *propriety, proprietary*.

dig·ni·ty /ˈdignitē/ ▶ n. (pl. **dignities**) the state or quality of being worthy of honor or respect: *a man of dignity and unbending principle | the dignity of labor.* ■ a composed or serious manner or style: *he bowed with great dignity.* ■ a sense of pride in oneself; self-respect: *it was* **beneath his dignity** *to shout.* ■ a high or honorable rank or position: *he promised dignities to the nobles in return for his rival's murder.*
– PHRASES **stand on one's dignity** insist on being treated with due respect.
– ORIGIN Middle English: from Old French *dignete*, from Latin *dignitas*, from *dignus* 'worthy.'

dig·ox·in /dijˈäksin/ ▶ n. Chemistry a poisonous compound present in the foxglove and other plants. It is a steroid glycoside and is used in small doses as a cardiac stimulant.
– ORIGIN 1930s: contraction of **DIGITOXIN**.

di·graph /ˈdīˌgraf/ ▶ n. a combination of two letters representing one sound, as in *ph* and *ey*. ■ Printing a character consisting of two joined letters; a ligature.
– DERIVATIVES **di·graph·ic** /dīˈgrafik/ adj.

di·gress /dīˈgres/ ▶ v. [no obj.] leave the main subject temporarily in speech or writing: *I have* **digressed** *a little from my original plan.*
– DERIVATIVES **di·gress·er** n., **di·gres·sive** /-ˈgresiv/ adj., **di·gres·sive·ly** /-ˈgresivlē/ adv., **di·gres·sive·ness** /-ˈgresivnis/ n.
– ORIGIN early 16th cent.: from Latin *digress-* 'stepped away,' from the verb *digredi*, from *di-* 'aside' + *gradi* 'to walk.'

di·gres·sion /dīˈgreSHən/ ▶ n. a temporary departure from the main subject in speech or writing: *let's return to the main topic after that brief digression.*

digs ▶ plural n. informal living quarters: *settled into new digs in Los Angeles.*
– ORIGIN late 19th cent.: short for *diggings*, used in the same sense, probably referring to the land where a farmer digs, i.e., works and, by extension, lives.

di·he·dral /dīˈhēdrəl/ ▶ adj. having or contained by two plane faces: *a dihedral angle.*
▶ n. an angle formed by two plane faces. ■ Aeronautics inclination of an aircraft's wing from the horizontal, esp. upward away from the fuselage. Compare with **ANHEDRAL**. ■ Climbing a place where two planes of rock meet at an angle of between 60° and 120°.
– ORIGIN late 18th cent.: from **DI-**[1] 'two' + *-hedral* (see **-HEDRON**).

di·hy·brid /dīˈhībrid/ ▶ n. Genetics a hybrid that is heterozygous for alleles of two different genes: [as modifier] *a dihybrid cross.*

di·hy·dric /dīˈhīdrik/ ▶ adj. Chemistry (of an alcohol) containing two hydroxyl groups.
– ORIGIN late 19th cent.: from **DI-**[1] 'two' + **HYDROGEN** + **-IC**.

di·hy·dro·tes·tos·ter·one /dīˌhīdrōtesˈtästəˌrōn/ ▶ n. Biochemistry a male sex hormone that is the active form of testosterone, formed from testosterone in bodily tissue.
– ORIGIN 1950s: from *dihydro-* (in the sense 'containing two hydrogen atoms in the molecule') + **TESTOSTERONE**.

di·hy·drox·y·ac·e·tone /ˌdīhīˌdräksēˈasiˌtōn/ ▶ n. Chemistry a synthetic compound with strong reducing properties, used in lotions for coloring the skin in sunlight. ● Chem. formula: $(CH_2OH)CO$.
– ORIGIN late 19th cent.: from *dihydroxy-* (in the sense 'containing two hydroxyl groups in the molecule') + **ACETONE**.

Di·jon /dēˈZHôN, dēˈZHän/ an industrial city in eastern central France, the former capital of Burgundy; pop. 155,340 (2006).

Di·jon mus·tard ▶ n. a medium-hot mustard, typically prepared with white wine and originally made in Dijon, France.

dik-dik /ˈdikˌdik/ ▶ n. (pl. **same** or **dik-diks**) a dwarf antelope found on the dry savanna of Africa, the female of which is larger than the male. ● Genus *Madoqua*, family Bovidae: several species.
– ORIGIN late 19th cent.: a local word in East Africa, imitative of its call.

dike[1] /dīk/ (also **dyke**) ▶ n. **1** a long wall or embankment built to prevent flooding from the sea. ■ (often in place names) a low wall or earthwork serving as a boundary or defense: *Offa's Dike.* ■ a causeway. ■ Geology an intrusion of igneous rock cutting across existing strata. Compare with **SILL**. **2** a ditch or watercourse.
▶ v. [with obj.] (often as adj. **diked**) provide (land) with a wall or embankment to prevent flooding.
– PHRASES **put one's finger in the dike** attempt to stem the advance of something undesirable. [from a story of a small Dutch boy who saved his community from a flood by placing his finger in a hole in a dike.]
– ORIGIN Middle English (denoting a trench or ditch): from Old Norse *dík*, related to **DITCH**. Sense 1 of the noun has been influenced by Middle Low German *dīk* 'dam' and Middle Dutch *dijc* 'ditch, dam.'

dike[2] ▶ n. variant spelling of **DYKE**[2].

dik·tat /dikˈtät/ ▶ n. an order or decree imposed by someone in power without popular consent: *a diktat from the Bundestag | he can disband the legislature and rule by diktat.*
– ORIGIN 1930s: from German, from Latin *dictatum* 'something dictated,' neuter past participle of *dictare*.

DIL ▶ abbr. Electronics dual in-line (package). See **DIP**.

Di·lan·tin /dīˈlantin/ ▶ n. Medicine trademark for **PHENYTOIN**.
– ORIGIN 1930s: from **DI-**[1] 'two' + *-l-* + *(hyd)ant(o)in*.

di·lap·i·date /diˈlapiˌdāt/ ▶ v. [with obj.] archaic cause (something) to fall into disrepair or ruin.
– DERIVATIVES **di·lap·i·da·tion** /diˌlapiˈdāSHən/ n.
– ORIGIN early 16th cent. (in the sense 'waste, squander'): from Latin *dilapidat-* 'demolished, squandered,' from the verb *dilapidare*, literally 'scatter as if throwing stones,' from *di-* 'apart, abroad' + *lapis, lapid-* 'stone.'

di·lap·i·dat·ed /diˈlapiˌdātid/ ▶ adj. (of a building or object) in a state of disrepair or ruin as a result of age or neglect.

di·lat·an·cy /dīˈlātnsē/ ▶ n. Chemistry the phenomenon exhibited by some fluids, sols, and gels in which they become more viscous or solid under pressure.

dil·a·ta·tion /ˌdiləˈtāSHən, ˌdī-/ ▶ n. chiefly Medicine & Physiology the action of dilating a vessel or opening or the process of becoming dilated. ■ a dilated part of a hollow organ or vessel.
– ORIGIN late Middle English: via Old French from late Latin *dilatatio(n-)*, from the verb *dilatare* (see **DILATE**).

di·late /dīˈlāt, dīˈlāt/ ▶ v. **1** make or become wider, larger, or more open: [no obj.] *her eyes dilated with horror* | [with obj.] *the woman dilated her nostrils.* **2** [no obj.] (**dilate on**) speak or write at length on (a subject).
– DERIVATIVES **di·lat·a·ble** adj., **di·la·tion** /dīˈlāSHən/ n.
– ORIGIN late Middle English: from Old French *dilater*, from Latin *dilatare* 'spread out,' from *di-* 'apart' + *latus* 'wide.'

di·la·tion and cu·ret·tage (also **dilatation and curettage**) (abbr.: **D and C**) ▶ n. Medicine a surgical procedure involving dilatation of the cervix and curettage of the uterus, performed after a miscarriage or for the removal of cysts or tumors.

di·la·tor /ˈdīˌlātər, dīˈlātər/ ▶ n. a thing that dilates something, in particular: ■ (also **dilator muscle**) Anatomy a muscle whose contraction dilates an organ or aperture, such as the pupil of the eye. ■ a surgical instrument for dilating a tube or cavity in the body. ■ a vasodilatory drug.

dil·a·to·ry /ˈdiləˌtôrē/ ▶ adj. slow to act: *he had been dilatory in appointing a solicitor.* ■ intended to cause delay: *they resorted to dilatory procedural tactics, forcing a postponement of peace talks.*
– DERIVATIVES **dil·a·to·ri·ly** /ˌdiləˈtôrəlē/ adv., **dil·a·to·ri·ness** n.
– ORIGIN late Middle English: from late Latin *dilatorius* 'delaying,' from Latin *dilator* 'delayer,' from *dilat-* 'deferred,' from the verb *differre*.

dil·do /ˈdildō/ ▶ n. (pl. **dildos**) an object shaped like an erect penis used for sexual stimulation. ■ vulgar slang a stupid or ridiculous person.
– ORIGIN late 16th cent.: of unknown origin.

di·lem·ma /diˈlemə/ ▶ n. a situation in which a difficult choice has to be made between two or more alternatives, esp. equally undesirable ones: *the people often face the dilemma of feeding themselves or their cattle.* ■ a difficult situation or problem: *the insoluble dilemma of adolescence.* ■ Logic an argument forcing an opponent to choose either of two unfavorable alternatives.
– ORIGIN early 16th cent. (denoting a form of argument involving a choice between equally unfavorable alternatives): via Latin from Greek *dilēmma*, from *di-* 'twice' + *lēmma* 'premise.'

> **USAGE** At its core, a **dilemma** is a situation in which a difficult choice has to be made between two or more alternatives (*this is my dilemma: do I stay here for the job security, or do I risk it all for the chance of a better career?*). More informally, **dilemma** can mean 'a difficult situation or problem' (as in *the insoluble dilemma of adolescence*). Some traditionalists object to this weakened use, but it is recorded as early as the first part of the 17th century, and is now widespread and generally acceptable.

dil·et·tante /ˌdiliˈtänt, -ˈtäntē/ ▶ n. (pl. **dilettanti** /-ˈtäntē/ or **dilettantes**) a person who cultivates an area of interest, such as the arts, without real commitment or knowledge: [as modifier] *a dilettante approach to science.* ■ archaic a person with an amateur interest in the arts.
– DERIVATIVES **dil·et·tan·tish** adj., **dil·et·tant·ism** /-ˌtizəm/ n.
– ORIGIN mid 18th cent.: from Italian, 'person loving the arts,' from *dilettare* 'to delight,' from Latin *delectare*.

Di·li /ˈdilē/ the capital and chief port of East Timor, on the northern coast of the island; pop. 171,400 (2009).

dil·i·gence[1] /ˈdiləjəns/ ▶ n. careful and persistent work or effort.
– ORIGIN Middle English (in the sense 'close attention, caution'): via Old French from Latin *diligentia*, from *diligent-* 'assiduous' (see **DILIGENT**).

dil·i·gence[2] ▶ n. historical a public stagecoach.
– ORIGIN late 17th cent.: from French, shortened from *carrosse de diligence* 'coach of speed.'

dil·i·gent /ˈdiləjənt/ ▶ adj. having or showing care and conscientiousness in one's work or duties: *many caves are located only after a diligent search.*
– DERIVATIVES **dil·i·gent·ly** adv.
– ORIGIN Middle English: via Old French from Latin *diligens, diligent-* 'assiduous,' from *diligere* 'love, take delight in.'

dill /dil/ ▶ n. an aromatic annual herb of the parsley family, with fine blue-green leaves and yellow flowers. The leaves and seeds of dill are used for flavoring and for medicinal purposes. ● *Anethum graveolens*, family Umbelliferae. ■ (also **dillweed** or **dill weed**) the fresh or dried leaves of this plant used to flavor food.
– ORIGIN Old English *dile, dyle*; related to Dutch *dille* and German *Dill*; of unknown ultimate origin.

Dil·lin·ger /ˈdilinjər/, John (1903–34), US criminal. He was a bank robber who made daring escapes from jail and was named "Public Enemy Number 1" by the Federal Bureau of Investigation (FBI). He was eventually betrayed by the "lady in red" in an ambush set up by the FBI.

dill pick·le ▶ **n.** pickled cucumber flavored with dill.

dill wa·ter ▶ **n.** an extract distilled from dill, used to relieve flatulence.

dil·ly /'dilē/ ▶ **n.** (pl. **dillies**) [usu. in sing.] informal an excellent example of a particular type of person or thing: *that's a dilly of a breakfast recipe.*
– ORIGIN late 19th cent. (as an adjective in the sense 'delightful'): alteration of the first syllable of DELIGHTFUL or DELICIOUS.

dil·ly-dal·ly ▶ **v.** (**dilly-dallies, dilly-dallying, dilly-dallied**) [no obj.] informal waste time through aimless wandering or indecision: *don't dilly-dally for too long.*
– ORIGIN early 17th cent.: reduplication of DALLY.

di·loph·o·saur /dī,läfə'sôr/ (also **dilophosaurus** /dī,läfə'sôrəs/) ▶ **n.** one of the earliest of the large bipedal dinosaurs, which had two long crests on the head and occurred in the early Jurassic period. ● Genus *Dilophosaurus*, infraorder Carnosauria, suborder Theropoda.
– DERIVATIVES **di·loph·o·sau·ri·an adj.**
– ORIGIN modern Latin, from Greek *dilophos* 'two-crested' + *sauros* 'lizard.'

dil·u·ent /'dilyoo͞ənt/ technical ▶ **n.** a substance used to dilute something.
▶ **adj.** acting to cause dilution.
– ORIGIN early 18th cent. (denoting a medicine used to increase the proportion of water in the blood): from Latin *diluent-* 'dissolving,' from the verb *diluere.*

di·lute /di'lo͞ot, dī-/ ▶ **v.** [with obj.] make (a liquid) thinner or weaker by adding water or another solvent to it: *bleach can be diluted with cold water.* ■ make (something) weaker in force, content, or value by modifying it or adding other elements to it: *the reforms have been diluted.* ■ reduce the value of (a shareholding) by issuing more shares in a company without increasing the values of its assets.
▶ **adj.** (of a liquid) made thinner or weaker by having had water or another solvent added to it. ■ Chemistry (of a solution) having a relatively low concentration of solute: *a dilute solution of potassium permanganate.* ■ (of color or light) weak or low in concentration: *a short measure of dilute sun.*
– DERIVATIVES **di·lut·er n.**
– ORIGIN mid 16th cent.: from Latin *dilut-* 'washed away, dissolved,' from the verb *diluere.*

di·lu·tion /di'lo͞osHən, dī-/ ▶ **n.** the action of making a liquid more dilute. ■ the action of making something weaker in force, content, or value: *he is resisting any dilution of dogma.* ■ a liquid that has been diluted. ■ the degree to which a solution has been diluted: *the antibody was applied at a dilution of 1:50.* ■ a reduction in the value of a shareholding due to the issue of additional shares in a company without an increase in assets.
– DERIVATIVES **di·lu·tive** /-'lo͞otiv/ **adj.** (chiefly Finance).

di·lu·vi·al /di'lo͞ovēəl/ ▶ **adj.** of or relating to a flood or floods, esp. the biblical Flood.
– ORIGIN mid 17th cent.: from late Latin *diluvialis,* from *diluvium* 'deluge,' from *diluere* 'wash away.'

di·lu·vi·an /di'lo͞ovēən/ ▶ **adj.** another term for DILUVIAL.

dim /dim/ ▶ **adj.** (**dimmer, dimmest**) **1** (of a light, color, or illuminated object) not shining brightly or clearly: *her face was softened by the dim light.* ■ (of an object or shape) made difficult to see by darkness, shade, or distance: *a dim figure in the dark kitchen.* ■ (of a room or space) made difficult to see in by darkness: *long dim corridors.* ■ (of the eyes) not able to see clearly: *his eyes became dim.* ■ (of a sound) indistinct or muffled: *the dim drone of their voices.* ■ (of prospects) not giving cause for hope or optimism: *their prospects for the future looked pretty dim.*
2 not clearly recalled or formulated in the mind: *she had dim memories of that time | the matter was in the dim and distant past.* ■ informal stupid or slow to understand: *you're just incredibly dim.*
▶ **v.** (**dims, dimming, dimmed**) make or become less bright or distinct: [with obj.] *a smoky inferno that dimmed the sun* | [no obj.] *the lights dimmed and the curtains parted.* ■ [with obj.] lower (a vehicle's headlights) from high to low beam: (as adj. **dimmed**) *the car moved slowly, its headlights dimmed.* ■ make or become less intense or favorable: [with obj.] *the difficulty in sleeping couldn't dim her happiness* | [no obj.] *the company's prospects have dimmed.* ■ make or become less able to see clearly: [with obj.] *your sight is dimmed* | [no obj.] *his eyes dimmed.*
– PHRASES **take a dim view of** regard with disapproval.
– DERIVATIVES **dim·ly adv., dim·mish adj., dim·ness n.**
– ORIGIN Old English *dim, dimm,* of Germanic origin; related to German dialect *timmer.*

dim. ▶ **abbr.** ■ dimension. ■ diminuendo. ■ diminutive.

Di·Mag·gi·o /də'majē,ō/, Joe (1914–99), US baseball player; full name *Joseph Paul DiMaggio*; called **Joltin' Joe** and the **Yankee Clipper**. Star of the New York Yankees 1936–51, he was renowned for his outstanding batting ability and for his outfield play. In 1941, he achieved a 56-game hitting streak, a record that has not been challenged. He was briefly married to Marilyn Monroe in 1954. Baseball Hall of Fame (1955).

Joe DiMaggio

dime /dīm/ ▶ **n.** a ten-cent coin. ■ informal a small amount of money: *he didn't have a dime.* ■ informal short for DIME BAG.
– PHRASES **a dime a dozen** informal very common and of no particular value: *experts in this field are a dime a dozen.* **drop a** (or **the**) **dime on someone** informal inform on someone. **get off the dime** informal be decisive and show initiative: *at some point you have to get off the dime and do something.* **on a dime** informal used to refer to a maneuver that can be performed by a moving vehicle or person within a small area or short distance: *boats that can turn on a dime.*
– ORIGIN late Middle English: from Old French *disme,* from Latin *decima pars* 'tenth part.' The word originally denoted a tithe or tenth part; the modern sense 'ten-cent coin' dates from the late 18th cent.

dime bag ▶ **n.** informal a specified amount of an illegal drug, packaged and sold for a fixed price.

dime nov·el ▶ **n.** historical a cheap, popular novel, typically a melodramatic romance or adventure story.

di·men·sion /di'mencHən/ ▶ **n. 1** an aspect or feature of a situation, problem, or thing: *sun-dried tomatoes add a new dimension to this sauce.*
2 (usu. **dimensions**) a measurable extent of some kind, such as length, breadth, depth, or height: *the final dimensions of the pond were 14 ft. x 8 ft | the drawing must be precise in dimension.* ■ a mode of linear extension of which there are three in space and two on a flat surface, which corresponds to one of a set of coordinates specifying the position of a point. ■ Physics an expression for a derived physical quantity in terms of fundamental quantities such as mass, length, or time, raised to the appropriate power (acceleration, for example, having the dimension of *length* × *time*$^{-2}$).
▶ **v.** [with obj.] cut or shape (something) to particular measurements. ■ mark (a diagram) with measurements: (as adj. **dimensioned**) *draw a dimensioned front elevation.*
– DERIVATIVES **di·men·sion·al** /-cHənl/ **adj.** [in combination] *multidimensional scaling,* **di·men·sion·al·i·ty** /di,mencHə'nalətē/ **n., di·men·sion·al·ly** /-cHənl-ē/ **adj., di·men·sion·less adj.**
– ORIGIN late Middle English (sense 2 of the noun): via Old French from Latin *dimensio(n-),* from *dimetiri* 'measure out.' Sense 1 of the noun dates from the 1920s.

di·men·sion·al a·nal·y·sis /də'mencHənl/ ▶ **n.** Mathematics analysis using the fact that physical quantities added to or equated with each other must be expressed in terms of the same fundamental quantities (such as mass, length, or time) for inferences to be made about the relations between them.

di·mer /'dīmər/ ▶ **n.** Chemistry a molecule or molecular complex consisting of two identical molecules linked together.
– DERIVATIVES **di·mer·ic** /dī'merik/ **adj.**
– ORIGIN 1930s: from DI-[1] 'two,' on the pattern of *polymer.*

di·mer·cap·rol /,dīmər'kaprôl/ ▶ **n.** Chemistry a colorless, oily liquid with an unpleasant smell, used as an antidote for poisoning by mercury, arsenic, lead, and other heavy metals. ● Alternative name: **2,3,-dimercapto-1-propanol**; chem. formula: $CH_2(SH)CH(SH)CH_2OH$.
– ORIGIN 1940s: from elements of the systematic name (see above).

di·mer·ize /'dīmə,rīz/ ▶ **v.** [no obj.] Chemistry combine with a similar molecule to form a dimer: *ClO dimerizes to form Cl_2O_2.*
– DERIVATIVES **di·mer·i·za·tion** /,dīmərə'zāsHən/ **n.**

dim·er·ous /'dimərəs/ ▶ **adj.** Botany & Zoology having parts arranged in groups of two. ■ consisting of two joints or parts.
– ORIGIN early 19th cent.: from modern Latin *dimerus* (from Greek *dimerēs* 'bipartite') + -OUS.

dime store ▶ **n.** a shop selling cheap merchandise (originally one where the maximum price was a dime). ■ [as modifier] cheap and inferior: *plastic dime-store toys.*

dim·e·ter /'dimitər/ ▶ **n.** Prosody a line of verse consisting of two metrical feet.
– ORIGIN late 16th cent.: via late Latin from Greek *dimetros* 'of two measures,' from *di-* 'twice' + *metron* 'a measure.'

di·meth·o·ate /dī'meTHō,āt/ ▶ **n.** a crystalline, synthetic, organophosphorus compound used in solution as an insecticide.
– ORIGIN 1960s: from DI-[1] 'two' + METHYL + THIO- + -ATE[1].

di·meth·yl sulf·ox·ide /dī'meTHəl səl'fäk,sīd/ (chiefly Brit. **dimethyl sulphoxide**) (abbr.: **DMSO**) ▶ **n.** Chemistry a colorless liquid used as a solvent and synthetic reagent. It is readily able to penetrate the skin and is used in medicinal preparations for skin application. ● Chem. formula: $(CH_3)_2SO$.

di·met·ric /dī'metrik/ ▶ **adj.** (in technical drawing) denoting or incorporating a method of showing projection or perspective using a set of three geometric axes, of which two are of the same scale or dimension but the third is of another.
– ORIGIN mid 19th cent.: from DI-[1] 'two' + Greek *metron* 'measure' + -IC.

di·met·ro·don /dī'metrə,dän/ ▶ **n.** a large, carnivorous, synapsid fossil reptile of the Permian period, with long spines on its back supporting a sail-like crest. ● Genus *Dimetrodon,* order Pelycosauria, subclass Synapsida.
– ORIGIN modern Latin, from *di-* 'twice' + Greek *metron* 'measure' + *odous, odont-* 'tooth' (taken in the sense 'two long teeth').

di·mid·i·ate /di'midē,āt/ ▶ **v.** [with obj.] Heraldry (of a coat of arms or charge) adjoin (another) so that only half of each is visible. ■ (as adj. **dimidiated**) (of a charge) having only one half depicted.
– ORIGIN late 16th cent.: from Latin *dimidiat-* 'halved,' from the verb *dimidiare,* from *dimidium* 'half.'

di·mid·i·a·tion /di,midē'āsHən/ ▶ **n.** Heraldry the combination of two coats of arms by juxtaposing the dexter half of one and the sinister half of the other on a single shield (a practice largely superseded by impalement).

di·min·ish /di'minisH/ ▶ **v.** make or become less: [with obj.] *a tax whose purpose is to diminish spending* | [no obj.] *the pain will gradually diminish.* ■ [with obj.] make (someone or something) seem less impressive or valuable: *the trial has aged and diminished him.*
– PHRASES **(the law of) diminishing returns** used to refer to a point at which the level of profits or benefits gained is less than the amount of money or energy invested.
– DERIVATIVES **di·min·ish·a·ble adj.**
– ORIGIN late Middle English: blend of archaic *minish* 'diminish' (based on Latin *minutia* 'smallness') and obsolete *diminue* 'speak disparagingly' (based on Latin *deminuere* 'lessen' (in late Latin *diminuere*), from *minuere* 'make small').

di·min·ished /di'minisHt/ ▶ **adj. 1** made smaller or less: *a diminished role for local government.* ■ [predic.] made to seem less impressive or valuable: *she felt diminished by the report.*
2 [attrib.] Music denoting or containing an interval that is one semitone less than the corresponding minor or perfect interval: *a diminished fifth.*

di·min·ished ca·pac·i·ty ▶ **n.** Law an unbalanced mental state that is considered to make a person less answerable for a crime and is recognized as grounds to reduce the charge.

di·min·ished sev·enth ▶ **n.** Music **1** the interval that is a semitone less than a minor seventh, e.g., from A to G flat (which in equal tuning sounds the same as a major sixth).
2 (also **diminished seventh chord**) a chord formed by a note together with those above it at intervals of a minor third, a diminished fifth, and a diminished

seventh. The resulting chord consists entirely of superimposed minor thirds, and is much used in modern music in modulating between keys.

di·min·u·en·do /di,minyōō'endō/ Music ▶ **n.** (pl. **diminuendos** or **diminuendi** /-dē/) a decrease in loudness: *the sudden diminuendos are brilliantly effective.* ■ a passage to be performed with such a decrease.
▶ **adv. & adj.** (esp. as a direction) with a decrease in loudness: [as adj.] *the diminuendo chorus before the final tumult.*
▶ **v.** (**diminuendos, diminuendoing, diminuendoed**) [no obj.] decrease in loudness or intensity: *the singers left and the buzz diminuendoed.*
– ORIGIN Italian, literally 'diminishing,' from *diminuire*, from Latin *deminuere* 'lessen' (see **DIMINISH**).

d

dim·i·nu·tion /,dimə'n(y)ōōSHən/ ▶ **n.** a reduction in the size, extent, or importance of something: *a permanent diminution in value | the disease shows no signs of diminution.* ■ Music the shortening of the time values of notes in a melodic part.
– ORIGIN Middle English: via Old French from Latin *deminutio(n-)*, from the verb *deminuere* (see **DIMINISH**).

di·min·u·tive /di'minyətiv/ ▶ **adj.** extremely or unusually small: *a diminutive figure dressed in black.* ■ (of a word, name, or suffix) implying smallness, either actual or imputed in token of affection, scorn, etc., (e.g., *teeny, -let, -kins*).
▶ **n.** a smaller or shorter thing, in particular: ■ a diminutive word or suffix. ■ a shortened form of a name, typically used informally: *"Nick" is a diminutive of "Nicholas."* ■ Heraldry a charge of the same form as an ordinary but of lesser size or width.
– DERIVATIVES **di·min·u·tive·ly adv.**, **di·min·u·tive·ness n.**
– ORIGIN late Middle English (as a grammatical term): from Old French *diminutif, -ive*, from late Latin *diminutivus*, from Latin *deminut-* 'diminished,' from the verb *deminuere* (see **DIMINISH**).

dim·i·ty /'dimitē/ ▶ **n.** a hard-wearing, sheer cotton fabric woven with raised stripes or checks.
– ORIGIN late Middle English: from Italian *dimito* or medieval Latin *dimitum*, from Greek *dimitos*, from *di-* 'twice' + *mitos* 'warp thread'; the origin of the final *-y* is unknown.

dim·mer /'dimər/ ▶ **n. 1** (also **dimmer switch**) a device for varying the brightness of an electric light. **2** a headlight with a low beam. ■ (**dimmers**) small parking lights on a motor vehicle.

di·mor·phic /dī'môrfik/ ▶ **adj.** chiefly Biology occurring in or representing two distinct forms: *in this sexually dimorphic species only the males have wings.*
– DERIVATIVES **di·mor·phism** /-fizəm/ **n.**
– ORIGIN mid 19th cent.: from Greek *dimorphos* (from *di-* 'twice' + *morphē* 'form') + **-IC**.

dim·ple /'dimpəl/ ▶ **n.** a small depression in the flesh, either one that exists permanently or one that forms in the cheeks when one smiles. ■ [often as modifier] a slight depression in the surface of something: *a sheet of dimple foam.*
▶ **v.** [with obj.] produce a dimple or dimples in the surface of (something): *a sucking swirl dimpled the water.* ■ [no obj.] form or show a dimple or dimples: *the water ruffled and dimpled* | (as adj. **dimpled**) *a dimpled smile.*
– DERIVATIVES **dim·ply** /'dimp(ə)lē/ **adj.**
– ORIGIN Middle English: of Germanic origin; related to German *Tümpel* 'pond.'

dim sum /'dim 'səm/ ▶ **n.** a Chinese dish of small steamed or fried savory dumplings containing various fillings, served as a snack or main course.
– ORIGIN from Chinese (Cantonese dialect) *tim sam*, from *tim* 'dot' and *sam* 'heart.'

dim·wit /'dim,wit/ ▶ **n.** informal a stupid or silly person.

dim·wit·ted /'dim,witid/ ▶ **adj.** informal stupid or silly: *a dimwitted waiter.*
– DERIVATIVES **dim·wit·ted·ly adv.**, **dim·wit·ted·ness n.**

DIN /din/ ▶ **n.** any of a series of technical standards originating in Germany and used internationally, esp. to designate electrical connections, film speeds, and paper sizes: [as modifier] *a DIN socket.*
– ORIGIN early 20th cent.: acronym from *Deutsche Industrie-Norm* 'German Industrial Standard' (as laid down by the *Deutsches Institut für Normung* 'German Institute for Standards').

din /din/ ▶ **n.** [in sing.] a loud, unpleasant, and prolonged noise: *the fans made an awful din.*
▶ **v.** (**dins, dinning, dinned**) **1** [with obj.] (**din something into**) make (someone) learn or remember something by constant repetition: *the doctrine that has been dinned into all our heads.* **2** [no obj.] make a loud, unpleasant, and prolonged noise: *the sound dinning in my ears was the telephone ringing.*
– ORIGIN Old English *dyne, dynn* (noun), *dynian* (verb), of Germanic origin; related to Old High German *tuni* (noun) and Old Norse *dynr* (noun), *dynja* 'come rumbling down.'

di·nar /'dēnär/ ▶ **n. 1** the basic monetary unit of Serbia, equal to 100 paras.
2 the basic monetary unit of certain countries of the Middle East and North Africa, equal to 1000 fils in Jordan, Bahrain, and Iraq, 1000 dirhams in Libya, and 100 centimes in Algeria.
3 a monetary unit of Iran, equal to one hundredth of a rial.
– ORIGIN from Arabic and Persian *dīnār*, Turkish and Serbian *dinar*, via late Greek from Latin *denarius* (see **DENARIUS**).

Di·nar·ic Alps /di'narik/ a mountain range in the Balkans that runs parallel to the Adriatic coast from Slovenia in the northwest, through Croatia, Bosnia, and Montenegro, to Albania in the southeast.

din-din /'din ,din/ ▶ **n.** a child's word for dinner.

dine /dīn/ ▶ **v.** [no obj.] eat dinner: *we dined at a restaurant* | (as noun **dining**) *a dining area.* ■ (**dine out**) eat dinner in a restaurant or the home of friends. ■ (**dine on**) eat (something) for dinner. ■ (**dine out on**) regularly entertain friends with (a humorous story or interesting piece of information): *it should have been one of those stories one dines out on afterward.* ■ [with obj.] take (someone) to dinner: *I'll dine you soon.*
– PHRASES **wine and dine** see **WINE**.
– ORIGIN Middle English: from Old French *disner*, probably from *desjëuner* 'to break fast,' from *des-* (expressing reversal) + *jëun* 'fasting' (from Latin *jejunus*).

din·er /'dīnər/ ▶ **n. 1** a person who is eating, typically a customer in a restaurant.
2 a dining car on a train. ■ a small roadside restaurant with a long counter and booths, originally one designed to resemble a dining car on a train.

di·ne·ro /di'ne(ə)rō/ ▶ **n.** informal money: *their pockets full of dinero.*
– ORIGIN mid 19th cent.: Spanish, 'coin, money.'

Din·e·sen /'dinəsən/, Isak, see **BLIXEN**.

di·nette /dī'net/ ▶ **n.** a small room or part of a room used for eating meals. ■ a set of table and chairs for such an area.
– ORIGIN 1930s: formed irregularly from **DINE** + **-ETTE**.

ding[1] /diNG/ ▶ **v.** [no obj.] make a ringing sound: *cash registers were dinging softly.*
▶ **exclam.** used to imitate a metallic ringing sound resembling a bell.
– ORIGIN early 17th cent.: imitative.

ding[2] informal ▶ **n.** a deliberate or accidental blow, esp. a mark or dent on the bodywork of a car, boat, or other vehicle.
▶ **v.** [with obj.] dent (something). ■ hit (someone), esp. on the head: *I dinged him one.* ■ criticize, injure, or penalize (someone): *agents who stayed on a call too long got dinged.*
– ORIGIN Middle English: probably of Scandinavian origin; compare with Danish *dænge* 'beat, bang.'

ding-a-ling /'diNG ə ,liNG/ ▶ **n. 1** [in sing.] the ringing sound of a bell.
2 informal an eccentric or stupid person.
– ORIGIN late 19th cent.: imitative.

Ding an sich /,diNG än 'siSH/ ▶ **n.** (in Kant's philosophy) a thing as it is in itself, not mediated through perception by the senses or conceptualization, and therefore unknowable.
– ORIGIN mid 19th cent.: German, literally 'thing in itself.'

ding·bat /'diNG,bat/ informal ▶ **n. 1** a stupid or eccentric person.
2 a typographical device other than a letter or numeral (such as an asterisk), used to signal divisions in text or to replace letters in a euphemistically presented vulgar word.
– ORIGIN mid 19th cent. (in early use applied to various vaguely specified objects): origin uncertain; perhaps based on obsolete *ding* 'to beat, deal heavy blows.' Sense 1 dates from the early 20th cent.

ding-dong /'diNG ,dôNG/ ▶ **n.** informal a silly or foolish person.
▶ **adv. & adj. 1** with the simple alternate chimes of or as of a bell: [as adv.] *the church bells go ding-dong* | [as adj.] *he heard the ding-dong tones.*
2 [as adj.] Brit. informal (of a contest) evenly matched and intensely waged: *the game was an exciting ding-dong battle.*
– ORIGIN mid 16th cent.: imitative.

ding·er /'diNGər/ ▶ **n.** informal a thing outstanding of its kind: *by God, ain't that a dinger!* ■ Baseball a home run: *he beat the Braves twice with extra-inning dingers.*
– ORIGIN late 19th cent.: shortening of **HUMDINGER**.

din·ghy /'diNGē/ ▶ **n.** (pl. **dinghies**) a small boat for recreation or racing, esp. an open boat with a mast and sails. ■ a small, inflatable rubber boat. ■ the smallest of a ship's boats.
– ORIGIN early 19th cent. (denoting a rowboat used on rivers in India): from Hindi *ḍiṅgī*.

din·gle /'diNGgəl/ ▶ **n.** literary or dialect a deep wooded valley or dell.
– ORIGIN Middle English (denoting a deep abyss): of unknown origin. The current sense dates from the mid 17th cent.

din·gle·ber·ry /'diNGəl,berē/ ▶ **n.** (pl. **dingleberries**) vulgar slang **1** a particle of fecal matter attached to the anal hair of an animal.
2 a foolish or inept person.
– ORIGIN 1950s: from *dingle* of unknown origin + **BERRY**.

din·go /'diNGgō/ ▶ **n.** (pl. **dingoes** or **dingos**) a wild or half-domesticated dog with a sandy-colored coat, found in Australia. It is believed to have been introduced by early Aboriginal immigrants. ● *Canis dingo*, family Canidae.
– ORIGIN late 18th cent.: from Dharuk *din-gu* 'domesticated dingo.'

ding·us /'diNGgəs/ ▶ **n.** (pl. **dinguses**) informal used to refer to something whose name the speaker cannot remember, is unsure of, or is humorously or euphemistically omitting: *here's a doohickey—and there's the dingus.*
– ORIGIN late 19th cent.: via Afrikaans from Dutch *ding* 'thing.'

din·gy /'dinjē/ ▶ **adj.** (**dingier, dingiest**) gloomy and drab: *a dingy room.*
– DERIVATIVES **din·gi·ly** /-əlē/ **adv.**, **din·gi·ness n.**
– ORIGIN mid 18th cent.: perhaps based on Old English *dynge* 'dung.'

din·ing car ▶ **n.** a railroad car equipped as a restaurant.

din·ing hall ▶ **n.** a large room, typically in a school or other institution, in which people eat meals together.

din·ing room ▶ **n.** a room in a house or hotel in which meals are eaten.

din·ing ta·ble ▶ **n.** a table on which meals are served in a dining room.

di·ni·tro·gen te·trox·ide /dī'nītrəjən te'träk,sīd/ ▶ **n.** see **NITROGEN DIOXIDE**.

dink[1] /diNGk/ ▶ **n.** informal a partner in a well-off working couple with no children.
– ORIGIN 1980s: acronym from *double income, no kids*.

dink[2] chiefly Tennis ▶ **n.** a drop shot.
▶ **v.** [with obj.] hit (the ball) with a drop shot.
– ORIGIN 1930s: symbolic of the light action.

Din·ka /'diNGkə/ ▶ **n.** (pl. **same** or **Dinkas**) **1** a member of a Sudanese people of the Nile basin.
2 the Nilotic language of this people, with about 1.4 million speakers.
▶ **adj.** of or relating to this people or their language.
– ORIGIN from the local word *Jieng* 'people.'

din·kum /'diNGkəm/ ▶ **adj.** Austral./NZ informal (of an article or person) genuine: *Andy's dinkum hat from Australia.*
– PHRASES **fair dinkum** used to emphasize that or query whether something is genuine or true: *it's a fair dinkum Aussie wedding.* ■ used to emphasize that behavior complies with accepted standards: *they were asking a lot for the car, but fair dinkum considering its list price.*
– ORIGIN late 19th cent.: of unknown origin.

dink·y /'diNGkē/ ▶ **adj.** (**dinkier, dinkiest**) informal small; insignificant: *I can't believe the dinky salaries they pay here.*
– ORIGIN late 18th cent.: from Scots and northern English dialect *dink* 'neat, trim,' of unknown origin.

din·ner /'dinər/ ▶ **n.** the main meal of the day, taken either around midday or in the evening. ■ a formal evening meal, typically one in honor of a person or event.
– ORIGIN Middle English: from Old French *disner* (infinitive used as a noun: see **DINE**).

din·ner dance ▶ **n.** a formal social event in which guests have dinner, followed by dancing.

din·ner jack·et ▶ **n.** a man's short jacket without tails, typically a black one, worn with a bow tie for formal occasions in the evening.

din·ner pail ▶ **n.** dated a pail in which a laborer's or schoolchild's dinner is carried and kept warm.
– PHRASES **hand in one's dinner pail** informal die.

din·ner par·ty ▶ **n.** a social occasion at which guests eat dinner together.

din·ner ring ▶ **n.** a woman's dress ring, usually with a large stone or an ornate setting, often worn on special occasions.

din·ner serv·ice (also **dinner set**) ▶ **n.** a set of matching dishes for serving a meal.

din·ner the·a·ter ▶ **n.** a theater in which a meal is included in the price of a ticket.

din·ner·ware /ˈdinər,we(ə)r/ ▶ **n.** tableware, including plates, glassware, and cutlery.

din·o·flag·el·late /ˌdīnōˈflajəlit, -ˌlāt/ ▶ **n.** Biology a single-celled organism with two flagella, occurring in large numbers in marine plankton and also found in fresh water. Some produce toxins that can accumulate in shellfish, resulting in poisoning when eaten. ● Division Dinophyta or class Dinophyceae, division Chromophycota (or phylum Dinophyta, kingdom Protista).
– ORIGIN late 19th cent. (as an adjective): from modern Latin *Dinoflagellata* (plural), from Greek *dinos* 'whirling' + Latin *flagellum* 'small whip' (see FLAGELLUM).

di·no·saur /ˈdīnə,sôr/ ▶ **n. 1** a fossil reptile of the Mesozoic era, often reaching an enormous size.

> The dinosaurs are placed, according to their hip structure, in two distantly related orders (see ORNITHISCHIAN and SAURISCHIAN). Some of them may have been warm-blooded, and their closest living relatives are the birds. Dinosaurs were all extinct by the end of the Cretaceous period (65 million years ago), a popular theory being that the extinctions were the result of the impact of a large meteorite.

2 a person or thing that is outdated or has become obsolete because of failure to adapt to changing circumstances.
– DERIVATIVES **di·no·sau·ri·an** /ˌdīnəˈsôrēən/ **adj. & n.**
– ORIGIN mid 19th cent.: from modern Latin *dinosaurus*, from Greek *deinos* 'terrible' + *sauros* 'lizard.'

pterodactyl
Jurassic and Cretaceous, 213–65 million years ago

velociraptor
Cretaceous, 144–65 million years ago

stegosaurus
Jurassic, 213–144 million years ago

tyrannosaurus
Cretaceous, 144–65 million years ago

triceratops
Cretaceous, 144–65 million years ago

apatosaurus
Jurassic, 213–144 million years ago

dinosaurs

dint /dint/ ▶ **n. 1** an impression or hollow in a surface: *the soft dints at the top of a coconut.* **2** archaic a blow or stroke, typically one made with a weapon in fighting. ■ force of attack; impact: *I perceive you feel the dint of pity.*
▶ **v.** [with obj.] mark (a surface) with impressions or hollows: (as adj. **dinted**) *the metal was dull and dinted.*
– PHRASES **by dint of** by means of: *he had gotten to where he was today by dint of sheer hard work.*
– ORIGIN Old English *dynt* 'stroke with a weapon,' reinforced in Middle English by the related Old Norse word *dyntr*; of unknown ultimate origin. Compare with DENT.

di·oc·e·san /dīˈäsisən/ ▶ **adj.** of or concerning a diocese.
▶ **n.** the bishop of a diocese.
– ORIGIN late Middle English: from French *diocésain*, from medieval Latin *diocesanus*, from Latin *dioecesis* (see DIOCESE).

di·o·cese /ˈdīəsis, -ˌsēz, -ˌsēs/ ▶ **n.** (pl. **dioceses**) a district under the pastoral care of a bishop in the Christian Church.
– ORIGIN Middle English: from Old French *diocise*, from late Latin *diocesis*, from Latin *dioecesis* 'governor's jurisdiction, diocese,' from Greek *dioikēsis* 'administration, diocese,' from *dioikein* 'keep house, administer.'

Di·o·cle·tian /ˌdīəˈklēSHən/ (245–313), Roman emperor 284–305; full name *Gaius Aurelius Valerius Diocletianus*. Faced with mounting military problems, in 286 he divided the empire between himself in the east and **Maximian** in the west. He launched the final persecution of the Christians 303.

di·ode /ˈdī,ōd/ ▶ **n.** Electronics a semiconductor device with two terminals, typically allowing the flow of current in one direction only. ■ a thermionic tube having two electrodes (an anode and a cathode).
– ORIGIN early 20th cent.: from DI-¹ 'two' + a shortened form of ELECTRODE.

di·oe·cious /dīˈēSHəs/ ▶ **adj.** Biology (of a plant or invertebrate animal) having the male and female reproductive organs in separate individuals. Compare with MONOECIOUS.
– DERIVATIVES **di·oe·cy** /ˈdi,ēsē/ **n.**
– ORIGIN mid 18th cent.: from modern Latin *Dioecia* (a class in Linnaeus's sexual system), from DI-¹ 'two' + Greek *-oikos* 'house.'

Di·og·e·nes /dīˈäjə,nēz/ (*c.*400–*c.*325 BC), Greek philosopher. The most noted of the Cynics, he emphasized self-sufficiency and the need for natural, uninhibited behavior, regardless of social conventions.

di·og·e·nite /dīˈäjə,nīt/ ▶ **n.** a stony meteorite of a kind consisting largely of pyroxenes and plagioclase.
– ORIGIN late 19th cent.: from Greek *Diogenēs* 'descended from Zeus' + -ITE¹.

di·ol /ˈdīôl/ ▶ **n.** Chemistry an alcohol containing two hydroxyl groups in its molecule.
– ORIGIN 1920s: from DI-¹ 'two' + -OL.

Di·o·mede Is·lands /ˈdīə,mēd/ two islands in the Bering Strait, separated by the International Date Line. Big Diomede belongs to Russia, and Little Diomede belongs to the US.

Di·o·ne /dīˈōnē/ Astronomy a satellite of Saturn, the twelfth closest to the planet, discovered by Cassini in 1684. Icy with a partly cratered and partly smooth surface, it has a diameter of 696 miles (1,120 km).
– ORIGIN named after a Titan, the mother of Aphrodite, in Greek mythology.

Di·o·ny·sian /ˌdīəˈniSHən, -ˈnisēən, -ˈnīsēən/ (also **Dionysiac** /-ˈnisē,ak, -ˈnīsē-/) ▶ **adj. 1** Greek Mythology of or relating to the god Dionysus. **2** of or relating to the sensual, spontaneous, and emotional aspects of human nature: *dark, grand Dionysian music.* Compare with APOLLONIAN.

Di·o·ny·si·us /ˌdīəˈnisēəs, -ˈnisHəs/ the name of two rulers of Syracuse. ■ **Dionysius I** (*c.*430–367 BC), ruled 405–367; known as **Dionysius the Elder**. A tyrannical ruler, he waged three wars against the Carthaginians for control of Sicily, the third of which resulted in his defeat at Cronium in 375. ■ **Dionysius II** (*c.*397–*c.*344 BC), son of Dionysius I; ruled 367–357 and 346–344; known as **Dionysius the Younger**. He lacked his father's military ambitions and signed a peace treaty with Carthage in 367.

Di·o·ny·si·us Ex·ig·u·us /egˈzigyo͞oəs/ (died *c.*556), Scythian-born monk and scholar. He is noted for developing in 505 the system of dates BC and AD that is still in use today. His calculation of Jesus Christ's incarnation being 753 years after the founding of Rome has since been shown to be mistaken by several years. He is said to have taken the nickname *Exiguus* ("little") as a sign of humility.

Di·o·ny·si·us of Hal·i·car·nas·sus /ˌhalikärˈnasəs/ (1st century BC), Greek historian, literary critic, and rhetorician. He lived in Rome from 30 BC and is best known for his detailed history of the city, written in Greek.

Di·o·ny·si·us the Ar·e·op·a·gite /ˌarēˈäpə,gīt, -,jīt/ (1st century AD), Greek churchman. His conversion by St. Paul is recorded in

PRONUNCIATION KEY ə *ago, up*; ər *over, fur*; a *hat*; ā *ate*; ä *car*; e *let*; ē *see*; i *fit*; ī *by*; NG *sing*; ō *go*; ô *law, for*; oi *toy*; o͝o *good*; o͞o *goo*; ou *out*; TH *thin*; T̲H̲ *then*; ZH *vision*

Acts 17:34, and according to tradition he went on to become the first bishop of Athens.

Di·o·ny·sus /ˌdīəˈnīsəs/ Greek Mythology a Greek god, son of Zeus and Semele. He was originally a god of the fertility of nature, associated with wild and ecstatic religious rites; in later traditions he is a god of wine who loosens inhibitions and inspires creativity in music and poetry. Also called **Bacchus**.

Di·o·phan·tine e·qua·tion /ˌdīəˈfanˌtin, -tīn/ ▶ **n.** Mathematics a polynomial equation with integral coefficients for which integral solutions are required.
– ORIGIN early 18th cent.: named after **Diophantus**.

d

Di·o·phan·tus /ˌdīəˈfantəs/ (*fl. c.* AD 250), Greek mathematician. He was the first to attempt an algebraical notation, showing in *Arithmetica* how to solve simple and quadratic equations.

di·op·side /dīˈäpˌsīd/ ▶ **n.** a mineral occurring as white to pale green crystals in metamorphic and basic igneous rocks. It consists of a calcium and magnesium silicate of the pyroxene group, often also containing iron and chromium.
– ORIGIN early 19th cent.: from French, formed irregularly from **di-**[3] 'through' + Greek *opsis* 'aspect,' later interpreted as derived from Greek *diopsis* 'a view through.'

di·op·tase /dīˈäptās, -tāz/ ▶ **n.** a rare mineral occurring as emerald green or blue-green crystals. It consists of a hydrated silicate of copper.
– ORIGIN early 19th cent.: from French, formed irregularly from Greek *dioptos* 'transparent.'

di·op·ter /dīˈäptər/ ▶ **n.** a unit of refractive power that is equal to the reciprocal of the focal length (in meters) of a given lens.
– ORIGIN late 16th cent. (originally denoting an alidade): from French, from Latin *dioptra*, from Greek, from *di-* 'through' + *optos* 'visible.' The term was used in the early 17th cent. to denote an ancient form of theodolite; the current sense dates from the late 19th cent.

di·op·tric /dīˈäptrik/ ▶ **adj.** of or relating to the refraction of light, esp. in the organs of sight or in devices that aid or improve the vision.
– ORIGIN mid 17th cent.: from Greek *dioptrikos*, from *dioptra*, a kind of theodolite (see **diopter**).

di·op·trics /dīˈäptriks/ ▶ **plural n.** [treated as sing.] the branch of optics that deals with refraction.

Di·or /dēˈôr/, Christian (1905–57), French couturier. His first collection 1947 featured the narrow-waisted New Look, with tightly fitted bodices and full pleated skirts. He later created the A-line style.

di·o·ram·a /ˌdīəˈramə, -ˈrä-/ ▶ **n.** a model representing a scene with three-dimensional figures, either in miniature or as a large-scale museum exhibit. ■ chiefly historical a scenic painting, viewed through a peephole, in which changes in color and direction of illumination simulate changes in the weather, time of day, etc. ■ a miniature movie set used for special effects or animation.
– ORIGIN early 19th cent.: coined in French from **dia-** 'through,' on the pattern of *panorama*.

di·o·rite /ˈdīəˌrīt/ ▶ **n.** Geology a speckled, coarse-grained igneous rock consisting essentially of plagioclase, feldspar, and hornblende or other mafic minerals.
– DERIVATIVES **di·o·rit·ic** /ˌdīəˈritik/ **adj.**
– ORIGIN early 19th cent.: coined in French, formed irregularly from Greek *diorizein* 'distinguish' + **-ite**[1].

Di·os·cu·ri /ˌdīəˈskyo͝orē/ Greek & Roman Mythology the twins Castor and Pollux, born to Leda after her seduction by Zeus. Castor was mortal, but Pollux was immortal; at Pollux's request they shared his immortality between them, spending half their time below the earth in Hades and the other half on Olympus. They are often identified with the constellation Gemini.
– ORIGIN from Greek *Dioskouroi* 'sons of Zeus.'

di·os·gen·in /ˌdī-äzˈjenin, dīˈäzjənin/ ▶ **n.** Chemistry a steroid compound obtained from Mexican yams and used in the synthesis of steroid hormones.
– ORIGIN 1930s: from *dios-* (from the modern Latin genus name *Dioscorea*) + *genin*, denoting steroids that occur as the nonsugar part of certain glycosides.

di·ox·ane /dīˈäkˌsān/ (also **dioxan** /-ˈäksän, -sən/) ▶ **n.** Chemistry a colorless, toxic liquid used as an organic solvent. ● A heterocyclic compound with a ring of four carbon and two oxygen atoms; chem. formula: $C_4H_8O_2$.
– ORIGIN early 20th cent.: from **di-**[1] 'two' + **ox-** 'oxygen' + **-an** (or **-ane**[2]).

di·ox·ide /dīˈäkˌsīd/ ▶ **n.** Chemistry an oxide containing two atoms of oxygen in its molecule or empirical formula.

di·ox·in /dīˈäksin/ ▶ **n.** a highly toxic compound produced as a byproduct in some manufacturing processes, notably herbicide production and paper bleaching. It is a serious and persistent environmental pollutant. ● A heterocyclic organochlorine compound; alternative name: 2,3,7,8-tetrachlorodibenzoparadioxin (abbr.: **TCDD**); chem. formula: $C_{12}H_4O_2Cl_4$. ■ any of the class of compounds to which this belongs.
– ORIGIN early 20th cent.: from **di-**[1] 'two' + **ox-** 'oxygen' + **-in**[1].

DIP /dip/ ▶ **abbr.** ■ Computing document image processing, a system for the digital storage and retrieval of documents as scanned images. ■ Electronics dual in-line package, a package for an integrated circuit consisting of a rectangular sealed unit with two parallel rows of downward-pointing pins.

dip /dip/ ▶ **v.** (**dips, dipping, dipped**) **1** [with obj.] (**dip something in/into**) put or let something down quickly or briefly in or into (liquid): *he dipped a brush in the paint*. ■ [no obj.] (**dip into**) put a hand or tool into (a bag or container) in order to take something out: *Ian dipped into his briefcase and pulled out a photograph*. ■ [no obj.] (**dip into**) spend from or make use of (one's financial resources): *you won't have to dip into your savings*. ■ [no obj.] (**dip into**) read only parts of (a publication) or explore (a subject) in a desultory manner. ■ take (snuff). ■ immerse (sheep) in a chemical solution that kills parasites. ■ make (a candle) by immersing a wick repeatedly in hot wax: (as adj. **dipped**) *dipped candles are made using simple equipment*. ■ informal, dated baptize (someone) by immersion in water. **2** [no obj.] sink, drop, or slope downward: *swallows dipped and soared | the sun had dipped below the horizon*. ■ (of a level or amount) become lower or smaller, typically temporarily: *the president's popularity has dipped | audiences dipped below 600,000 for the series*. ■ [with obj.] lower or move (something) downward: *the plane dipped its wings*.
▶ **n. 1** a brief swim: *she went for a dip in a pool*. ■ a brief immersion in liquid: *a dip in hot water is prescribed to destroy fruit flies*. ■ short for **sheep dip**. ■ a cursory read of a publication or a superficial exploration of a subject: *a quick dip into this document*.
2 a thick sauce in which pieces of food are dunked before eating: *tasty garlic dip*.
3 a brief downward slope followed by an upward one: *the road's precipitous dips and turns*. ■ an act of sinking or dropping briefly before rising again: *a dip in the share price*.
4 technical the extent to which something is angled downward from the horizontal, in particular: ■ (also **magnetic dip**) the angle made with the horizontal at any point by the earth's magnetic field, or by a magnetic needle in response to this. ■ Geology the angle a stratum makes with the horizontal: *the cliff profile tends to be dominated by the dip of the beds*. ■ Astronomy & Surveying the apparent depression of the horizon from the line of observation, due to the curvature of the earth.
5 informal, dated a pickpocket.
6 informal a stupid or foolish person.
7 archaic a candle made by immersing a wick repeatedly in hot wax.
– PHRASES **dip one's toe into** (or **in**) put one's toe briefly in (water), typically to check the temperature. ■ begin to do or test (something) cautiously: *the company has already dipped its toe into the market*.
– ORIGIN Old English *dyppan*, of Germanic origin; related to **deep**.

Dip. ▶ **abbr.** diploma.

dip-dye ▶ **v.** [with obj.] immerse (a yarn or fabric) in a special solution in order to color it.

di·pep·tide /dīˈpepˌtīd/ ▶ **n.** Biochemistry a peptide composed of two amino-acid residues.

di·phen·hy·dra·mine /ˌdīfenˈhīdrəˌmēn/ ▶ **n.** Medicine an antihistamine compound used for the symptomatic relief of allergies. ● A synthetic amine, usually used as a hydrochloride salt; chem. formula: $C_{17}H_{21}NO$.
– ORIGIN 1940s: from *diphen-* (denoting the presence of two phenyl groups) + **hydr-** + **amine**.

di·phen·yl·a·mine /dīˈfenl-əˌmēn, -ˈfē-/ ▶ **n.** Chemistry a synthetic crystalline compound with basic properties, used in making azo dyes and as an insecticide and larvicide. ● Chem. formula: $(C_6H_5)_2NH$.

diph·the·ri·a /difˈTHi(ə)rēə, dip-/ ▶ **n.** an acute, highly contagious bacterial disease causing inflammation of the mucous membranes, formation of a false membrane in the throat that hinders breathing and swallowing, and potentially fatal heart and nerve damage by a bacterial toxin in the blood. It is now rare in developed countries because of immunization. ● The disease is caused by *Corynebacterium diphtheriae*.
– DERIVATIVES **diph·the·ri·al** **adj.**, **diph·the·rit·ic** /ˌdifTHəˈritik, ˌdip-/ **adj.**
– ORIGIN mid 19th cent.: modern Latin, from French *diphthérie* (earlier *diphthérite*), from Greek *diphthera* 'skin, hide.'

> **USAGE** In the past, **diphtheria** was correctly pronounced with an **f** sound representing the two letters **ph** (as in *telephone*, *phantom*, and other **ph** words derived from Greek). In recent years, the pronunciation has shifted and today the more common pronunciation, no longer incorrect in standard English, is with a **p** sound. Nevertheless, the **f** sound remains the primary pronunciation.

diph·the·roid /ˈdifTHəˌroid, ˈdip-/ ▶ **n.** Microbiology any bacterium of a genus that includes the diphtheria bacillus, esp. one that does not cause disease. See **corynebacterium**.
▶ **adj.** [attrib.] Medicine similar to diphtheria.

diph·thong /ˈdifˌTHäNG, ˈdip-, -ˌTHôNG/ ▶ **n.** a sound formed by the combination of two vowels in a single syllable, in which the sound begins as one vowel and moves toward another (as in *coin*, *loud*, and *side*). Often contrasted with **monophthong**, **triphthong**. ■ a digraph representing the sound of a diphthong or single vowel (as in *feat*). ■ a compound vowel character; a ligature (such as æ).
– DERIVATIVES **diph·thon·gal** /difˈTHäNGgəl, dip-, -ˈTHôNG-/ **adj.**
– ORIGIN late Middle English: from French *diphtongue*, via late Latin from Greek *diphthongos*, from *di-* 'twice' + *phthongos* 'voice, sound.'

diph·thong·ize /ˈdifTHäNGˌgīz, dip-, -THôNG-/ ▶ **v.** [with obj.] change (a vowel) into a diphthong.
– DERIVATIVES **diph·thong·i·za·tion** /ˌdifTHäNGgəˈzāSHən, ˌdip-, -THôNG-/ **n.**

diph·y·cer·cal /difiˈsərkəl/ ▶ **adj.** Zoology (of a fish's tail) approximately symmetrical and with the vertebral column continuing to the tip, as in lampreys. Contrasted with **heterocercal**, **homocercal**.
– ORIGIN mid 19th cent.: from Greek *diphu-* 'of double form' + *kerkos* 'tail' + **-al**.

di·ple·gia /dīˈplēj(ē)ə/ ▶ **n.** Medicine paralysis of corresponding parts on both sides of the body, typically affecting the legs more severely than the arms.
– ORIGIN late 19th cent.: from **di-**[1] 'two,' on the pattern of *hemiplegia* and *paraplegia*.

diplo- ▶ **comb. form 1** double: *diplococcus*.
2 diploid: *diplohaplontic*.
– ORIGIN from Greek *diplous* 'double.'

dip·lo·blas·tic /diplōˈblastik/ ▶ **adj.** Zoology having a body derived from only two embryonic cell layers (ectoderm and endoderm, but no mesoderm), as in sponges and coelenterates.

dip·lo·coc·cus /ˌdiplōˈkäkəs/ ▶ **n.** (pl. **diplococci** /-ˈkäk(s)ī, -(s)ē/) a bacterium that occurs as pairs of cocci, e.g., pneumococcus.

di·plod·o·cus /diˈplädəkəs/ ▶ **n.** a huge, herbivorous dinosaur of the late Jurassic period, with a long, slender neck and tail. ● Genus *Diplodocus*, infraorder Sauropoda, order Saurischia.
– ORIGIN modern Latin, from **diplo-** 'double' + Greek *dokos* 'wooden beam.'

dip·lo·hap·lon·tic /ˌdiplōhapˈläntik/ ▶ **adj.** Genetics (of an alga or other lower plant) having a life cycle in which full-grown haploid and diploid forms alternate. Compare with **diplontic** and **haplontic**.

dip·loid /ˈdipˌloid/ Genetics ▶ **adj.** (of a cell or nucleus) containing two complete sets of chromosomes, one from each parent. Compare with **haploid**. ■ (of an organism or part) composed of diploid cells.
▶ **n.** a diploid cell, organism, or species.
– DERIVATIVES **dip·loi·dy** /-ˌloidē/ **n.**
– ORIGIN late 19th cent.: from Greek *diplous* 'double' + **-oid**.

dip·loid num·ber ▶ **n.** Genetics the number of chromosomes present in the body cells of a diploid organism.

di·plo·ma /diˈplōmə/ ▶ **n.** a certificate awarded by an educational establishment to show that someone has successfully completed a course of study. ■ an official document or charter.
– ORIGIN mid 17th cent. (in the sense 'state paper'): via Latin from Greek *diplōma* 'folded paper,' from *diploun* 'to fold,' from *diplous* 'double.'

di·plo·ma·cy /diˈplōməsē/ ▶ **n.** the profession, activity, or skill of managing international relations, typically by a country's representatives abroad: *the government should assign an ambassador-at-large to oversee diplomacy in the region*. ■ the art of dealing with people in a sensitive and effective way: *his genius for tact and diplomacy*.
– ORIGIN late 18th cent.: from French *diplomatie*, from *diplomatique* 'diplomatic,' on the pattern of *aristocratie* 'aristocracy.'

dip·lo·mat /ˈdipləˌmat/ ▶ **n.** an official representing a country abroad. ■ a person who can deal with people in a sensitive and effective way.
– ORIGIN early 19th cent.: from French *diplomate*, back-formation from *diplomatique* 'diplomatic,' from Latin *diploma* (see DIPLOMA).

dip·lo·mate /ˈdipləˌmāt/ ▶ **n.** a person who holds a diploma, esp. a doctor certified as a specialist by a board of examiners.

dip·lo·mat·ic /ˌdipləˈmatik/ ▶ **adj. 1** of or concerning the profession, activity, or skill of managing international relations: *diplomatic relations between the United States and Britain.* ■ having or showing an ability to deal with people in a sensitive and effective way: *that was a very diplomatic way of putting it.*
2 (of an edition or copy) exactly reproducing an original version: *a diplomatic transcription.*
– DERIVATIVES **dip·lo·mat·i·cal·ly** /-ik(ə)lē/ **adv.**
– ORIGIN early 18th cent. (in the sense 'relating to official documents'): from modern Latin *diplomaticus* and French *diplomatique*, from Latin *diploma* (see DIPLOMA). Sense 1 (late 18th cent.) is probably due to the publication of the *Codex Juris Gentium Diplomaticus* (1695), a collection of public documents, many of which dealt with international affairs.

dip·lo·mat·ic corps ▶ **n.** the body of diplomats residing in a particular country.

dip·lo·mat·ic im·mu·ni·ty ▶ **n.** the privilege of exemption from certain laws and taxes granted to diplomats by the country in which they are working.

dip·lo·mat·ic pouch ▶ **n.** a container in which official mail is sent to or from an embassy without being subject to customs inspection.

dip·lo·mat·ic serv·ice ▶ **n.** another term for FOREIGN SERVICE.

di·plo·ma·tist /diˈplōmətist/ ▶ **n.** old-fashioned term for DIPLOMAT.

dip·lont·ic /dipˈläntik/ ▶ **n.** Genetics (of an alga or other lower plant) having a life cycle in which the main form, except for the gametes, is diploid. Compare with HAPLONTIC and DIPLOHAPLONTIC.
– DERIVATIVES **dip·lont** /ˈdipˌlänt/ **n.**
– ORIGIN 1920s: from DIPLO- 'double' + Greek *ōn, ont-* 'being' (from *einai* 'be, exist') + -IC.

di·plo·pi·a /diˈplōpēə/ ▶ **n.** technical term for DOUBLE VISION.

Di·plop·o·da /dipləˈpōdə/ Zoology a class of myriapod arthropods that comprises the millipedes.
– DERIVATIVES **dip·lo·pod** /ˈdipləˌpäd/ **n.**
– ORIGIN modern Latin (plural), from Greek *diploos* 'double' + *pous, pod-* 'foot.'

dip·lo·tene /ˈdipləˌtēn/ ▶ **n.** Biology the fourth stage of the prophase of meiosis, following pachytene, during which the paired chromosomes begin to separate into two pairs of chromatids.
– ORIGIN 1920s: from DIPLO- 'double' + Greek *tainia* 'band.'

Di·plu·ra /dīˈplo͝orə/ Entomology an order of small, primitive, wingless insects that resemble the true bristletails but have two bristles at the end of the abdomen. ● Order Diplura, subclass Apterygota, class Insecta (or Hexapoda).
– DERIVATIVES **di·plu·ran** **n.** & **adj.**
– ORIGIN modern Latin (plural), from DI-[1] 'two' + Greek *pleura* 'side of the body.'

dip net ▶ **n.** a small fishing net with a long handle.
▶ **v.** (**dip-net**) [with obj.] catch (fish) using such a net.

di·pole /ˈdīˌpōl/ ▶ **n.** Physics a pair of equal and oppositely charged or magnetized poles separated by a distance. ■ an antenna consisting of a horizontal metal rod with a connecting wire at its center. ■ Chemistry a molecule in which a concentration of positive electric charge is separated from a concentration of negative charge.
– DERIVATIVES **di·po·lar** /dīˈpōlər/ **adj.**

di·pole mo·ment ▶ **n.** Physics & Chemistry the mathematical product of the separation of the ends of a dipole and the magnitude of the charges.

dip·per /ˈdipər/ ▶ **n. 1** a short-tailed songbird related to the wrens, frequenting fast-flowing streams and able to swim, dive, and walk under water to feed. ● Family Cinclidae and genus *Cinclus*: five species, in particular the Eurasian (**white-throated**) **dipper** (*C. cinclus*).
2 a ladle or scoop.
3 a person who immerses something in liquid. ■ archaic an informal term for a Baptist or Anabaptist.

dip·py /ˈdipē/ ▶ **adj.** (**dippier, dippiest**) informal stupid; foolish.
– ORIGIN early 20th cent.: of unknown origin.

dip·shit /ˈdipˌsHit/ ▶ **n.** vulgar slang a contemptible or inept person.
– ORIGIN 1970s: perhaps a blend of DIPPY and SHIT.

dip·so /ˈdipsō/ ▶ **n.** (pl. **dipsos**) informal a person suffering from dipsomania; an alcoholic.

dip·so·ma·ni·a /ˌdipsəˈmānēə/ ▶ **n.** alcoholism, specifically in a form characterized by intermittent bouts of craving for alcohol.
– DERIVATIVES **dip·so·ma·ni·ac** /-nēˌak/ **n.**, **dip·so·ma·ni·a·cal** /-məˈnīəkəl/ **adj.**
– ORIGIN mid 19th cent.: from Greek *dipso-* (from *dipsa* 'thirst') + -MANIA.

dip·stick /ˈdipˌstik/ ▶ **n. 1** a graduated rod for measuring the depth of a liquid, esp. oil in a vehicle's engine.
2 informal a stupid or inept person.

DIP switch ▶ **n.** Computing an arrangement of switches in a dual in-line package used to select the operating mode of a device such as a printer.

dip·sy-doo·dle /ˈdipsē ˌdo͞odl/ ▶ **n.** informal a quick dipping motion, such as that made by football players to avoid a tackle. ■ an act or movement designed to evade, confuse, or distract an opponent or competitor.
▶ **v.** [no obj.] follow a zigzag course.

Dip·ter·a /ˈdiptərə/ Entomology a large order of insects that comprises the two-winged or true flies, which have the hind wings reduced to form balancing organs (halteres). It includes many biting forms, such as mosquitoes and tsetse flies, that are vectors of disease. ■ (as plural noun **diptera**) insects of this order; flies.
– ORIGIN modern Latin (plural), from Greek *diptera*, neuter plural of *dipteros* 'two-winged,' from *di-* 'two' + *pteron* 'wing.'

dip·ter·al /ˈdiptərəl/ ▶ **adj.** Architecture having a double peristyle.
– ORIGIN early 19th cent.: from Latin *dipteros* (from Greek, from *di-* 'twice' + *pteron* 'wing') + -AL.

dip·ter·an /ˈdiptərən/ Entomology ▶ **n.** an insect of the large order Diptera; a fly.
▶ **adj.** relating to or denoting dipterans.

dip·ter·ist /ˈdiptərist/ ▶ **n.** a person who studies or collects flies.
– ORIGIN late 19th cent.: from DIPTERA + -IST.

dip·ter·o·carp /ˈdiptərəˌkärp/ ▶ **n.** a tall forest tree from which are obtained resins and timber for the export trade, occurring mainly in Southeast Asia. ● Family Dipterocarpaceae: numerous species.
– ORIGIN late 19th cent.: from modern Latin *Dipterocarpus*, from Greek *dipteros* 'two-winged' + *karpos* 'fruit.'

dip·ter·ous /ˈdiptərəs/ ▶ **adj. 1** Entomology of or relating to flies of the order Diptera.
2 Botany having two winglike appendages.
– ORIGIN late 18th cent.: from modern Latin *dipterus* (from Greek *dipteros* 'two-winged') + -OUS.

dip·tych /ˈdiptik/ ▶ **n. 1** a painting, esp. an altarpiece, on two hinged wooden panels that may be closed like a book.
2 an ancient writing tablet consisting of two hinged leaves with waxed inner sides.
– ORIGIN early 17th cent.: via late Latin from late Greek *diptukha* 'pair of writing tablets,' neuter plural of Greek *diptukhos* 'folded in two,' from *di-* 'twice' + *ptukhē* 'a fold.'

di·pyr·id·a·mole /dīˈpiridəˌmōl/ ▶ **n.** Medicine a synthetic drug used as a coronary vasodilator to treat angina and to reduce platelet aggregation and hence the chance of thrombosis.
– ORIGIN mid 20th cent.: from DI-[1] 'two' + *pyr(imidine)* + *(piper)id(ine)* + *am(ino-)* + -OL.

di·quat /ˈdīˌkwät/ ▶ **n.** a synthetic compound used in controlling plant growth, often as a nonpersistent contact herbicide. ● A bromide of a quaternary amine; chem. formula: $(C_5H_4NCH_2)_2Br_2$.
– ORIGIN 1960s: from DI-[1] 'two' + QUATERNARY.

dir. ▶ **abbr.** director.

Di·rac /dəˈräk/, Paul Adrian Maurice (1902–84), English theoretical physicist. He described the behavior of the electron, including its spin, and predicted the existence of the positron by applying Albert Einstein's theory of relativity to quantum mechanics. Nobel Prize for Physics (1933), shared with Erwin Schrödinger.

dire /dīr/ ▶ **adj.** (of a situation or event) extremely serious or urgent: *dire consequences.* ■ (of a warning or threat) presaging disaster: *dire warnings about breathing the fumes.*
– DERIVATIVES **dire·ly** **adv.**, **dire·ness** **n.**
– ORIGIN mid 16th cent.: from Latin *dirus* 'fearful, threatening.'

di·rect /diˈrekt, dī-/ ▶ **adj. 1** extending or moving from one place to another by the shortest way without changing direction or stopping: *there was no direct flight that day.* ■ Astronomy & Astrology (of apparent planetary motion) proceeding from west to east in accord with actual motion.
2 without intervening factors or intermediaries: *the complications are a direct result of bacteria spreading.* ■ (of light or heat) proceeding from a source without being reflected or blocked: *ferns like a bright position out of direct sunlight.* ■ (of genealogy) proceeding in continuous succession from parent to child. ■ (of a quotation) taken from someone's words without being changed. ■ (of taxation) levied on income or profits rather than on goods or services. ■ complete (used for emphasis): *nonviolence is the direct opposite of compulsion.*
3 (of a person or their behavior) going straight to the point; frank. ■ (of evidence or proof) bearing immediately and unambiguously upon the facts at issue: *there is no direct evidence that officials accepted bribes.*
4 perpendicular to a surface; not oblique: *a direct butt joint between surfaces of steel.*
▶ **adv.** with no one or nothing in between: *buy direct and save.* ■ by a straight route or without breaking a journey: *Austrian Airlines is flying direct to Innsbruck again.*
▶ **v.** [with obj.] **1** control the operations of; manage or govern: *an economic elite directed the nation's affairs.* ■ supervise and control (a movie, play, or other production, or the actors in it). ■ (usu. **be directed**) train and conduct (a group of musicians).
2 aim (something) in a particular direction or at a particular person: *heating ducts to direct warm air to rear-seat passengers | his smile was directed at Laura.* ■ tell or show (someone) how to get somewhere: *can you direct me to the railroad station, please?* ■ address or give instructions for the delivery of (a letter or parcel). ■ focus or concentrate (one's attention, efforts, or feelings) on: *we direct our anger and frustration at family.* ■ (**direct something at/to**) address a comment to or aim a criticism at: *he directed his criticism at media coverage of the Catholic Church | I suggest that he direct his remarks to the council.* ■ (**direct something at**) target a product specifically at (someone): *the book is directed at the younger reader.* ■ archaic guide or advise (someone or their judgment) in a course or decision: *the conscience of the credulous prince was directed by saints and bishops.*
3 [with obj. and infinitive] give (someone) an official order or authoritative instruction: *the judge directed him to perform community service* | [with clause] *he directed that no picture from his collection could be sold.*
– DERIVATIVES **di·rect·ness** **n.**
– ORIGIN late Middle English: from Latin *directus*, past participle of *dirigere*, from *di-* 'distinctly' or *de-* 'down' + *regere* 'put straight.'

di·rect ac·cess ▶ **n.** the facility of retrieving data immediately from any part of a computer file, without having to read the file from the beginning. Compare with RANDOM ACCESS and SEQUENTIAL ACCESS.

di·rect ac·tion ▶ **n.** the use of strikes, demonstrations, or other public forms of protest rather than negotiation to achieve one's demands.

di·rect cur·rent (abbr.: **DC**) ▶ **n.** an electric current flowing in one direction only. Compare with ALTERNATING CURRENT.

di·rect deb·it ▶ **n.** a payment system whereby creditors are authorized to debit a customer's bank account directly at regular intervals.

di·rect de·pos·it ▶ **n.** the electronic transfer of a payment directly from the account of the payer to the recipient's account.

di·rect di·al·ing ▶ **n.** the facility of making a telephone call without connection by the operator.
– DERIVATIVES **di·rect di·al** **adj.**

di·rect dis·course ▶ **n.** another term for DIRECT SPEECH.

di·rect-drive ▶ **adj.** [attrib.] denoting or relating to mechanical parts driven directly by a motor, without a belt or other device to transmit power.

di·rect ex·am·i·na·tion ▶ **n.** Law the questioning of a witness by the party that has called that witness to give evidence, in order to support the case that is being made. Also called EXAMINATION-IN-CHIEF. Compare with CROSS-EXAMINE.

di·rect in·jec·tion ▶ **n.** (in diesel engines) the use of a pump to spray fuel into the cylinder at high pressure, without the use of compressed air.

di·rec·tion /diˈreksHən, dī-/ ▶ **n. 1** a course along which someone or something moves: *she set off in the opposite direction | the storm was expected to take a more northwesterly direction.* ■ the course that must be taken in order to reach a destination: *he had a terrible sense of direction.* ■ a point to or from which a person or thing moves or faces: *a house with*

views in all directions | figurative *support came from an unexpected direction.* ■ a general way in which someone or something is developing: *new directions in painting and architecture | any dialogue between them is **a step in the right direction** | it is time to change direction and find a new job.* ■ general aim or purpose: *the campaign's lack of direction.*
2 the management or guidance of someone or something: *under his direction, the college has developed an international reputation.* ■ the work of supervising and controlling the actors and other staff in a movie, play, or other production.
■ **(directions)** instructions on how to reach a destination or about how to do something: *Preston gave him directions to a restaurant | directions for making puff pastry.* ■ an authoritative order or command: *to suggest that members of Congress would take direction on how to vote is an affront.*
– PHRASES **sense of direction** a person's ability to know without explicit guidance the direction in which they are or should be moving.
– ORIGIN late Middle English (sense 2): from Latin *directio(n-)*, from the verb *dirigere* (see DIRECT).

d

di·rec·tion·al /di'reksHənl/ ▶ **adj. 1** relating to or indicating the direction in which someone or something is situated, moving, or developing: *directional signs wherever two paths joined.*
2 having a particular direction of motion, progression, or orientation: *coiling the wire permits directional flow of the magnetic flux.* ■ relating to, denoting, or designed for the projection, transmission, or reception of light, radio, or sound waves in or from a particular direction or directions: *a directional microphone.*
– DERIVATIVES **di·rec·tion·al·i·ty** /di,reksHə'nalitē/ **n.**, **di·rec·tion·al·ly adv.**

di·rec·tion find·er ▶ **n.** a special radio receiver with a system of antennas for locating the source of radio signals, used as an aid to navigation.

di·rec·tion·less /di'reksHənlis/ ▶ **adj.** lacking in general aim or purpose: *I feel directionless and miserable.*

di·rec·tive /di'rektiv/ ▶ **n.** an official or authoritative instruction: *moral and ethical directives.*
▶ **adj.** involving the management or guidance of operations: *he is seeking a directive role in energy policy.*
– ORIGIN late Middle English (as an adjective): from medieval Latin *directivus*, from *direct-* 'guided, put straight,' from the verb *dirigere* (see DIRECT).

di·rect la·bor ▶ **n. 1** labor involved in production rather than administration, maintenance, and other support services.
2 labor employed by the authority commissioning the work, not by a contractor.

di·rect·ly /di'rektlē/ ▶ **adv. 1** without changing direction or stopping: *they went directly to the restaurant.* ■ at once; immediately: *I went directly after breakfast.* ■ dated in a little while; soon: *I'll be back directly.*
2 with nothing or no one in between: *the decisions directly affect people's health | the security forces were directly responsible for the massacre.* ■ exactly in a specified position: *the ceiling directly above the door | the houses directly opposite.*
3 in a frank way: *she spoke simply and directly.*
▶ **conj.** Brit. as soon as: *she fell asleep directly she got into bed.*

di·rect mail ▶ **n.** unsolicited advertising sent to prospective customers through the mail.
– DERIVATIVES **di·rect mail·ing n.**

di·rect mar·ket·ing ▶ **n.** the business of selling products or services directly to the public, e.g., by mail order or telephone selling, rather than through retailers.

di·rect ob·ject ▶ **n.** a noun phrase denoting a person or thing that is the recipient of the action of a transitive verb, for example *the dog* in *Jimmy fed the dog.* Compare with INDIRECT OBJECT.

Di·rec·toire /,direk'twär/ ▶ **adj.** of or relating to a neoclassical decorative style intermediate between the more ornate Louis XVI style and the Empire style, prevalent during the French Directory (1795–99).
– ORIGIN late 18th cent.: French, from Late Latin *directorius*, from *director* 'one who directs, director.'

Di·rec·toire draw·ers (also **Directoire knickers**) ▶ **plural n.** Brit. historical underpants that are straight, full, and knee-length.

di·rec·tor /di'rektər/ (abbr.: **dir.**) ▶ **n.** a person who is in charge of an activity, department, or organization: *he has been appointed finance director.* ■ a member of the board of people that manages or oversees the affairs of a business. ■ a person who supervises the actors, camera crew, and other staff for a movie, play, television program, or similar production. ■ short for MUSICAL DIRECTOR.
– DERIVATIVES **di·rec·to·ri·al** /di,rek'tôrēəl, ,dīrek-/ **adj.**, **di·rec·tor·ship** /-,sHip/ **n.**
– ORIGIN late Middle English: from Anglo-Norman French *directour*, from late Latin *director* 'governor,' from *dirigere* 'to guide.'

di·rec·to·rate /di'rektərit/ ▶ **n.** [treated as sing. or pl.] the board of directors of a company. ■ a section of a government department in charge of a particular activity: *the Directorate of Intelligence.*

di·rec·tor gen·er·al ▶ **n.** (also **director-general**) (pl. **directors general**) chiefly Brit. the chief executive of a large organization.

di·rec·tor's chair ▶ **n.** a folding armchair with crossed legs and a canvas seat and back piece.

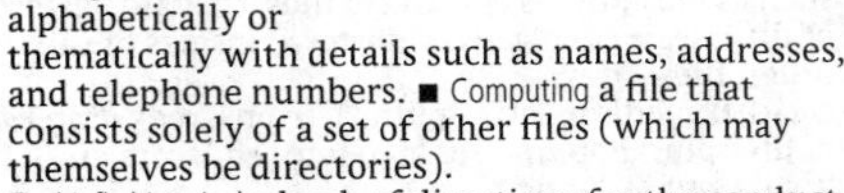
director's chair

di·rec·tor's cut ▶ **n.** a version of a movie that reflects the director's original intentions, released after the first studio version.

di·rec·to·ry /di'rektərē/ ▶ **n.** (pl. **directories**) **1** a book listing individuals or organizations alphabetically or thematically with details such as names, addresses, and telephone numbers. ■ Computing a file that consists solely of a set of other files (which may themselves be directories).
2 chiefly historical a book of directions for the conduct of Christian worship, esp. in Presbyterian and Roman Catholic churches.
3 **(the Directory)** the revolutionary government in France 1795–99, comprising two councils and a five-member executive. It maintained an aggressive foreign policy but could not control events at home and was overthrown by Napoleon Bonaparte.
– ORIGIN late Middle English (in the general sense 'something that directs'): from late Latin *directorium*, from *director* 'governor,' from *dirigere* 'to guide.'

di·rec·to·ry as·sis·tance ▶ **plural n.** a telephone service used to find out someone's telephone number.

di·rect pay·ment ▶ **n.** another term for DIRECT DEBIT.

di·rect pro·por·tion (also **direct ratio**) ▶ **n.** the relation between quantities whose ratio is constant: *sensors emit an electronic signal **in direct proportion to** the amount of light detected.*

di·rec·tress /di'rektris/ (also **directrice**) ▶ **n.** a female director.
– ORIGIN early 17th cent.: from DIRECTOR + -ESS[1]; the variant *directrice* is an adopted French form.

di·rec·trix /di'rektriks/ ▶ **n.** (pl. **directrices** /-trə,sēz/) Geometry a fixed line used in describing a curve or surface.
– ORIGIN early 18th cent.: from medieval Latin, literally 'directress,' based on Latin *dirigere* 'to guide.'

di·rect rule ▶ **n.** a system of government in which a province is controlled by a central government.

di·rect speech ▶ **n.** the reporting of speech by repeating the actual words of a speaker, for example *"I'm going," she said.* Contrasted with REPORTED SPEECH.

di·rect tax ▶ **n.** a tax, such as income tax, that is levied on the income or profits of the person who pays it, rather than on goods or services.

dire·ful /'dīrfəl/ ▶ **adj.** archaic or literary extremely bad; dreadful.
– DERIVATIVES **dire·ful·ly adv.**
– ORIGIN late 16th cent.: from DIRE + -FUL.

dire wolf ▶ **n.** a large extinct wolf of the Pleistocene epoch that preyed on large mammals. ● *Canis dirus*, family Canidae.
– ORIGIN *dire* in the sense 'threatening,' translating the modern Latin taxonomic name.

dirge /dərj/ ▶ **n.** a lament for the dead, esp. one forming part of a funeral rite. ■ a mournful song, piece of music, or poem: *singers chanted dirges |* figurative *the wind howled dirges around the chimney.*
– DERIVATIVES **dirge·ful** /-fəl/ **adj.**
– ORIGIN Middle English (denoting the Office for the Dead): from Latin *dirige!* (imperative) 'direct!,' the first word of an antiphon (Psalm 5:8) used in the Latin Office for the Dead.

dir·ham /də'ram/ ▶ **n. 1** the basic monetary unit of Morocco and the United Arab Emirates, equal to 100 centimes in Morocco and 100 fils in the United Arab Emirates.
2 a monetary unit of Libya and Qatar, equal to one thousandth of a dinar in Libya and one hundredth of a riyal in Qatar.
– ORIGIN from Arabic, from Greek *drakhmē*, denoting an Attic weight or coin. Compare with DRACHMA.

dir·i·gi·ble /'dirijəbəl, də'rijə-/ ▶ **adj.** capable of being steered, guided, or directed: *a dirigible spotlight.*
▶ **n.** a dirigible airship, esp. one with a rigid structure.
– ORIGIN late 16th cent.: from Latin *dirigere* 'to direct' + -IBLE.

di·ri·gisme /'diri,zHizəm, ,diri'zHizəm, ,dērē'zHēsm(ə)/ ▶ **n.** state control of economic and social matters.
– DERIVATIVES **di·ri·giste** /,diri'zHēst, ,dirē-/ **adj.**
– ORIGIN 1950s: from French, from the verb *diriger*, from Latin *dirigere* 'to direct.'

dir·i·ment im·ped·i·ment /'dirəmənt/ ▶ **n.** (in ecclesiastical law) a factor that invalidates a marriage, such as the existence of a prior marriage.
– ORIGIN mid 19th cent.: *diriment* from Latin *diriment-* 'interrupting,' from the verb *dirimere*.

dirk /dərk/ ▶ **n.** a short dagger of a kind formerly carried by Scottish Highlanders.
– ORIGIN mid 16th cent.: of unknown origin.

dirn·dl /'dərndl/ ▶ **n. 1** (also **dirndl skirt**) a full, wide skirt with a tight waistband.
2 a woman's dress in the style of Alpine peasant costume, with such a skirt and a close-fitting bodice.
– ORIGIN 1930s: from south German dialect, diminutive of *Dirne* 'girl.'

dirndl 2

dirt /dərt/ ▶ **n.** a substance, such as mud or dust, that soils someone or something: *his face was covered in dirt.* ■ loose soil or earth; the ground: *the soldier sagged to the dirt.* ■ [usu. as modifier] earth used to make a surface for a road, floor, or other area of ground: *a dirt road.* ■ short for DIRT TRACK. ■ informal excrement: *a lawn covered in dog dirt.* ■ a state or quality of uncleanliness: *Pittsburgh used to be renowned for the sweat and dirt of industry.*
■ informal gossip, esp. information about someone's activities or private life that could prove damaging if revealed: *is there any dirt on Desmond?* ■ informal a worthless or contemptible person or thing: *she treats him like dirt.*
– PHRASES **do someone dirt** (also **do dirt to someone**) informal harm someone's reputation maliciously. **drag the name of someone** (or **something**) **through the dirt** informal give someone or something a bad reputation through bad behavior or damaging revelations: *he condemned players for dragging the name of football through the dirt.* **eat dirt** informal suffer insults or humiliation: *the film bombed at the box office and the critics made it eat dirt.*
– ORIGIN Middle English: from Old Norse *drit* 'excrement,' an early sense in English.

dirt·bag /'dərt,bag/ ▶ **n.** informal a very unkempt or unpleasant person.

dirt bike ▶ **n.** a motorcycle designed for use on rough terrain, such as unsurfaced roads or tracks, and used esp. in scrambling.

dirt·board /'dərt,bôrd/ ▶ **n.** a long skateboard with larger-than-average wheels, designed for off-road use.
– DERIVATIVES **dirt·board·ing n.**

dirt cheap ▶ **adv. & adj.** informal extremely cheap: [as adv.] *the auctioneers let us have the stuff dirt cheap |* [as adj.] *a dirt-cheap price.*

dirt farm·er ▶ **n.** a farmer who ekes out a living from a farm or poor land, typically without the help of hired labor.
– DERIVATIVES **dirt farm n.**

dirt poor ▶ **adj.** extremely poor: *dirt-poor villages.*

dirt track ▶ **n.** a course made of rolled cinders for motorcycle racing or of earth for flat racing.
– DERIVATIVES **dirt track·er n.**

dirt·y /'dərtē/ ▶ **adj.** (**dirtier**, **dirtiest**) covered or marked with an unclean substance: *a tray of dirty cups and saucers | her boots were dirty.* ■ causing a person or environment to become unclean: *farming is a hard, dirty job.* ■ (of a nuclear weapon) producing considerable radioactive fallout. ■ (of a color) not bright, clear, or pure: *the sea was a waste of dirty gray.* ■ concerned with sex in an unpleasant or obscene way: *he told a stream of dirty jokes.* ■ [attrib.] informal used to emphasize one's disgust for someone or something: *you dirty rat!*
■ (of an activity) dishonest; dishonorable: *he had a reputation for dirty dealing.* ■ (of weather) rough, stormy, and unpleasant: *the yacht was ready for dirty*

weather. ■ (of popular music) having a distorted or rasping tone: *Nirvana's dirty guitar sound.*
▶ v. (**dirties, dirtying, dirtied**) [with obj.] make dirty: *she didn't like him dirtying her nice clean towels.*
– PHRASES **the dirty end of the stick** informal the difficult or unpleasant part of a task or situation. **get one's hands dirty** (or **dirty one's hands**) do manual, menial, or other hard work: *unlike most chairmen, he gets his hands dirty working alongside the other managers.* ■ informal become involved in dishonest or dishonorable activity: *they can make a lot of money, but fat cats don't get their hands dirty.* **play dirty** informal act in a dishonest or unfair way. **talk dirty** informal speak about sex in a coarse or obscene way. **wash one's dirty laundry in public** see WASH.
– DERIVATIVES **dirt·i·ly** /ˈdərtəlē/ adv., **dirt·i·ness** n.

dirt·y bomb ▶ n. a nuclear weapon improvised from radioactive nuclear waste material and conventional explosives.

dirt·y look ▶ n. informal a facial expression of disapproval, disgust, or anger: *they were giving me dirty looks for taking up so much room at the bar.*

dirt·y mon·ey ▶ n. money obtained unlawfully or immorally: *the bank was found to have been laundering dirty money.*

dirt·y old man ▶ n. informal an older man who is sexually interested in younger women or girls.

dirt·y pool ▶ n. informal dishonest, unfair, or unsportsmanlike conduct.

dirt·y rice ▶ n. a Cajun dish consisting of white rice cooked with onions, peppers, chicken livers, and herbs.

dirt·y trick ▶ n. a dishonest or unkind act. ■ (**dirty tricks**) underhanded political or commercial activity designed to discredit an opponent or competitor.

dir·ty week·end ▶ n. informal a weekend spent away, esp. in secret, with a lover.

dirt·y word ▶ n. an offensive or indecent word. ■ a thing regarded with dislike or disapproval: *people can talk about profit without it being a dirty word.*

dirt·y work ▶ n. activities or tasks that are unpleasant or dishonest and given to someone else to undertake.

dis /dis/ informal ▶ v. (also **diss**) (**diss, dissing, dissed**) [with obj.] speak disrespectfully to or criticize: *I don't like her dissing my friends | a campaign of forum postings and emails dissing the company.*
▶ n. disrespectful talk: *the airwaves bristle with the sexual dis of shock jocks.*
– ORIGIN 1980s: abbreviation of DISRESPECT.

dis- ▶ prefix **1** expressing negation: *dislike | disquiet.*
2 denoting reversal or absence of an action or state: *dishonor | disintegrate.* ■ denoting separation: *discharge | disengage.* ■ denoting expulsion: *disbar | disinherit.*
3 denoting removal of the thing specified: *disbud | dismember.*
4 expressing completeness or intensification of an unpleasant or unattractive action: *discombobulate | disgruntled.*
– ORIGIN from Latin, sometimes via Old French *des-*.

dis·a·bil·i·ty /ˌdisəˈbilitē/ ▶ n. (pl. **disabilities**) a physical or mental condition that limits a person's movements, senses, or activities. ■ a disadvantage or handicap, esp. one imposed or recognized by the law: *he had to quit his job and go on disability.*

dis·a·ble /disˈābəl/ ▶ v. [with obj.] (of a disease, injury, or accident) limit (someone) in their movements, senses, or activities: *it's an injury that could disable somebody for life* | (as adj. **disabling**) *a progressively disabling disease* | [no obj.] *anxiety can disrupt and disable.* ■ put out of action: *the raiders tried to disable the alarm system.*
– DERIVATIVES **dis·a·ble·ment** n.

dis·a·bled /disˈābəld/ ▶ adj. (of a person) having a physical or mental condition that limits movements, senses, or activities: *facilities for disabled people* | (as plural noun **the disabled**) *the needs of the disabled.* ■ (of an activity, organization, or facility) specifically designed for or relating to people with such a physical or mental condition.

USAGE See usage at HANDICAPPED and LEARNING DISABILITY.

dis·a·bled list (abbr.: **DL**) ▶ n. Sports a list of players who are not available for play, owing to injury.

dis·a·buse /ˌdisəˈbyo͞oz/ ▶ v. [with obj.] persuade (someone) that an idea or belief is mistaken: *he quickly **disabused me of** my fanciful notions.*

di·sac·cha·ride /dīˈsakəˌrīd/ ▶ n. Chemistry any of a class of sugars whose molecules contain two monosaccharide residues.

dis·ac·cord /ˌdisəˈkôrd/ ▶ n. rare lack of agreement or harmony: *the disaccord remains in effect.*
▶ v. [no obj.] archaic disagree; be at variance: *this disaccords with the precise date.*

dis·ad·van·tage /ˌdisədˈvantij/ ▶ n. an unfavorable circumstance or condition that reduces the chances of success or effectiveness: *a major disadvantage is the limited nature of the data | the impact of poverty and disadvantage on children.*
▶ v. [with obj.] place in an unfavorable position in relation to someone or something else: *we are disadvantaging the next generation.*
– PHRASES **at a disadvantage** in an unfavorable position relative to someone or someone else: *stringent regulations have **put** farmers **at a disadvantage**.* **to one's disadvantage** so as to cause harm to one's interests or standing: *his poor record inevitably worked to his disadvantage.*
– ORIGIN late Middle English: from Old French *desavantage*, from *des-* (expressing reversal) + *avantage* 'advantage.'

dis·ad·van·taged /ˌdisədˈvantijd/ ▶ adj. (of a person or area) in unfavorable circumstances, esp. with regard to financial or social opportunities: *disadvantaged groups such as the elderly and unemployed* | (as plural noun **the disadvantaged**) *we began to help the disadvantaged.*

dis·ad·van·ta·geous /disˌadvənˈtājəs/ ▶ adj. involving or creating unfavorable circumstances that reduce the chances of success or effectiveness: *the system was **disadvantageous to** the Connecticut merchants | the disadvantageous position in which some people are placed.*
– DERIVATIVES **dis·ad·van·ta·geous·ly** adv.

dis·af·fect·ed /ˌdisəˈfektid/ ▶ adj. dissatisfied with the people in authority and no longer willing to support them: *a military plot by disaffected elements in the army.*
– DERIVATIVES **dis·af·fect·ed·ly** adv.
– ORIGIN mid 17th cent.: past participle of *disaffect*, originally in the sense 'dislike or disorder,' from DIS- (expressing reversal) + AFFECT².

dis·af·fec·tion /ˌdisəˈfeksʜən/ ▶ n. a state or feeling of being dissatisfied with the people in authority and no longer willing to support them: *there is growing **disaffection with** large corporations.*

dis·af·fil·i·ate /ˌdisəˈfilēˌāt/ ▶ v. [with obj.] (of a group or organization) end its official connection with (a subsidiary group): *the executive disaffiliated the league.* ■ [no obj.] (of a subsidiary group) end such a connection: *a region may elect to **disaffiliate from** a dominant state.*
– DERIVATIVES **dis·af·fil·i·a·tion** /ˌdisəˌfilēˈāsʜən/ n.

dis·af·firm /ˌdisəˈfərm/ ▶ v. [with obj.] Law repudiate; declare void: *to disaffirm a contract is to say it never existed.*
– DERIVATIVES **dis·af·fir·ma·tion** /disˌafərˈmāsʜən/ n.

dis·ag·gre·gate /disˈagrigāt/ ▶ v. [with obj.] separate (something) into its component parts: *a method for disaggregating cells.*
– DERIVATIVES **dis·ag·gre·ga·tion** /-ˌagriˈgāsʜən/ n.

dis·a·gree /ˌdisəˈgrē/ ▶ v. (**disagrees, disagreeing, disagreed**) [no obj.] **1** have or express a different opinion: *no one was willing to **disagree with** him | historians often disagree.* ■ (**disagree with**) disapprove of: *she disagreed with the system of apartheid.*
2 (of statements or accounts) be inconsistent or fail to correspond: *results that disagree with the findings reported so far.* ■ (**disagree with**) (of food, climate, or an experience) have an adverse effect on (someone): *the North Sea crossing seemed to have disagreed with her.*
– ORIGIN late 15th cent. (sense 2, also in the sense 'refuse to agree to'): from Old French *desagreer*.

dis·a·gree·a·ble /ˌdisəˈgrēəbəl/ ▶ adj. not pleasant or enjoyable: *another disagreeable thought came to him | some aspects of his work are **disagreeable to** him.* ■ unfriendly and bad-tempered: *Henry was always a very disagreeable boy.*
– DERIVATIVES **dis·a·gree·a·ble·ness** n., **dis·a·gree·a·bly** /-blē/ adv.
– ORIGIN late Middle English (in the sense 'discordant, incongruous'): from Old French *desagreable*, based on *agreer* 'agree.'

dis·a·gree·ment /ˌdisəˈgrēmənt/ ▶ n. lack of consensus or approval: *there was some disagreement about the details | the meeting **ended in disagreement** | disagreements between parents and adolescents.* ■ lack of consistency or correspondence: *disagreement between the results of the two assessments.*

dis·al·low /ˌdisəˈlou/ ▶ v. [with obj.] (usu. **be disallowed**) refuse to declare valid: *the judge disallowed his evidence.*
– DERIVATIVES **dis·al·low·ance** /ˌdisəˈlouəns/ n.
– ORIGIN late Middle English (in the sense 'disown, refuse to accept'): from Old French *desalouer*.

dis·am·big·u·ate /ˌdisamˈbigyo͞oˌāt/ ▶ v. [with obj.] remove uncertainty of meaning from (an ambiguous sentence, phrase, or other linguistic unit).
– DERIVATIVES **dis·am·big·u·a·tion** /-ˌbigyo͞oˈāsʜən/ n.

dis·ap·pear /ˌdisəˈpi(ə)r/ ▶ v. **1** [no obj.] cease to be visible: *he **disappeared into** the trees | the sun had disappeared.* ■ cease to exist or be in use: *the tension had completely disappeared.* ■ (of a thing) be lost or impossible to find: *my wallet seems to have disappeared.* ■ (of a person) go missing or (in coded political language) be killed: *the family disappeared after being taken into custody.*
2 [with obj.] cause to disappear, as by consumption: *statistics show that the community disappears about 200 pounds of cabbage a year.*
– ORIGIN late Middle English: from DIS- (expressing reversal) + APPEAR, on the pattern of French *disparaître*.

dis·ap·pear·ance /ˌdisəˈpi(ə)rəns/ ▶ n. [usu. in sing.] an instance or fact of someone or something ceasing to be visible. ■ an instance or fact of someone going missing or (in coded political language) being killed: *the police were investigating her disappearance.* ■ the process or fact of something ceasing to exist or be in use: *the disappearance of grammar schools.*

dis·ap·pear·ing act ▶ n. informal an instance of someone being impossible to find, esp. when they are required to face something unpleasant.

dis·ap·point /ˌdisəˈpoint/ ▶ v. [with obj.] fail to fulfill the hopes or expectations of (someone): *I have no wish to disappoint everyone by postponing the visit.* ■ prevent (hopes or expectations) from being realized: *to disappoint the hopes that are now awakened could be very dangerous.*
– ORIGIN late Middle English (in the sense 'deprive of an office or position'): from Old French *desappointer*.

dis·ap·point·ed /ˌdisəˈpointid/ ▶ adj. (of a person) sad or displeased because someone or something has failed to fulfill one's hopes or expectations: *I'm **disappointed in** you, Mary | thousands of disappointed customers were kept waiting.* ■ (of hopes or expectations) prevented from being realized.
– DERIVATIVES **dis·ap·point·ed·ly** adv.

dis·ap·point·ing /ˌdisəˈpointiɴɢ/ ▶ adj. failing to fulfill someone's hopes or expectations: *the team made a disappointing start* | [with clause] *it's **disappointing that** the market hasn't gone higher.*
– DERIVATIVES **dis·ap·point·ing·ly** adv. [as submodifier] *there was disappointingly little change* | [sentence adverb] *disappointingly, my German failed to improve.*

dis·ap·point·ment /ˌdisəˈpointmənt/ ▶ n. the feeling of sadness or displeasure caused by the nonfulfillment of one's hopes or expectations: ***to her disappointment**, there was no chance to talk privately with Luke.* ■ a person, event, or thing that causes such a feeling: *the job proved a disappointment | I was a big **disappointment to** her.*

dis·ap·pro·ba·tion /disˌaprəˈbāsʜən/ ▶ n. strong disapproval, typically on moral grounds: *she braved her mother's disapprobation and slipped out to enjoy herself.*

dis·ap·prov·al /ˌdisəˈpro͞ovəl/ ▶ n. possession or expression of an unfavorable opinion: *Jill replied with a hint of disapproval in her voice.*

dis·ap·prove /ˌdisəˈpro͞ov/ ▶ v. [no obj.] have or express an unfavorable opinion about something: *Bob strongly **disapproved of** drinking and driving.* ■ [with obj.] officially refuse to agree to: *a company may take power to disapprove the transfer of shares.*
– DERIVATIVES **dis·ap·prov·er** n.

dis·ap·prov·ing /ˌdisəˈpro͞oviɴɢ/ ▶ adj. expressing an unfavorable opinion: *he shot a disapproving glance at her.*
– DERIVATIVES **dis·ap·prov·ing·ly** adv.

dis·arm /disˈärm/ ▶ v. [with obj.] **1** take a weapon or weapons away from (a person, force, or country): *guerrillas had completely disarmed and demobilized their forces.* ■ [no obj.] (of a country or force) give up or reduce its armed forces or weapons: *the other militias had disarmed by the agreed deadline.* ■ remove the fuse from (a bomb), making it safe.
2 allay the hostility or suspicions of: *his tact and political skills will disarm critics.* ■ deprive of the power to injure or hurt: *camp humor acts to provoke rather than disarm moral indignation.*
– ORIGIN late Middle English: from Old French *desarmer*.

dis·ar·ma·ment /disˈärməmənt/ ▶ n. the reduction or withdrawal of military forces and weapons.

PRONUNCIATION KEY ə *ago, up*; ər *over, fur*; a *hat*; ā *ate*; ä *car*; e *let*; ē *see*; i *fit*; ī *by*; ɴɢ *sing*; ō *go*; ô *law, for*; oi *toy*; o͝o *good*; o͞o *goo*; ou *out*; ᴛʜ *thin*; ᴛʜ *then*; ᴢʜ *vision*

dis·ar·mer ▶ **n.** a person who advocates or campaigns for the withdrawal of nuclear weapons.

dis·arm·ing /disˈärmiNG/ ▶ **adj.** (of manner or behavior) having the effect of allaying suspicion or hostility, esp. through charm: *he gave her a disarming smile.*
– DERIVATIVES **dis·arm·ing·ly adv.**

dis·ar·range /ˌdisəˈrānj/ ▶ **v.** [with obj.] make (something) untidy or disordered: *her hair was disarranged all around her face.*
– DERIVATIVES **dis·ar·range·ment n.**

d

dis·ar·ray /ˌdisəˈrā/ ▶ **n.** a state of disorganization or untidiness: *her gray hair was* ***in disarray*** | *his plans have been* ***thrown into disarray.***
▶ **v.** [with obj.] **1** throw (someone or something) into a state of disorganization or untidiness: *the inspection disarrayed the usual schedule.*
2 literary strip (someone) of clothing: *attendant damsels to help to disarray her.*
– ORIGIN late Middle English: from Anglo-Norman French *dissairay.*

dis·ar·tic·u·late /ˌdisärˈtikyəˌlāt/ ▶ **v.** [with obj.] separate (bones) at the joints: *the African egg-eating snake can disarticulate its lower jaw from its upper.* ■ break up and disrupt the logic of (an argument or opinion): *novels disarticulate theories.*
– DERIVATIVES **dis·ar·tic·u·la·tion** /-ˌtikyəˈlāSHən/ **n.**

dis·as·sem·ble /ˌdisəˈsembəl/ ▶ **v.** [with obj.] take (something) apart: *the piston can be disassembled for transport.* ■ Computing translate (a program) from machine code into a symbolic language.
– DERIVATIVES **dis·as·sem·bly** /-blē/ **n.**

dis·as·sem·bler /ˌdisəˈsemb(ə)lər/ ▶ **n.** Computing a program for converting machine code into a low-level symbolic language.

dis·as·so·ci·ate /ˌdisəˈsōSHēˌāt, -ˈsōsē-/ ▶ **v.** another term for DISSOCIATE.
– DERIVATIVES **dis·as·so·ci·a·tion** /ˌdisəˌsōSHēˈāSHən, -ˌsōsē-/ **n.**

dis·as·ter /diˈzastər/ ▶ **n.** a sudden event, such as an accident or a natural catastrophe, that causes great damage or loss of life: *159 people died in the disaster* | *disaster struck within minutes of takeoff.* ■ [as modifier] denoting a genre of films that use natural or accidental catastrophe as the mainspring of plot and setting: *a disaster movie.* ■ an event or fact that has unfortunate consequences: *a string of personal disasters* | *reduced legal aid could spell financial disaster.* ■ informal a person, act, or thing that is a failure: *my perm is a total disaster.*
– PHRASES **be a recipe for disaster** be extremely likely to have unfortunate consequences: *sky-high interest rates are a recipe for disaster.*
– ORIGIN late 16th cent.: from Italian *disastro* 'ill-starred event,' from *dis-* (expressing negation) + *astro* 'star' (from Latin *astrum*).

dis·as·ter ar·e·a ▶ **n.** an area in which a major disaster has recently occurred: *the vicinity of the explosion was declared a disaster area.* ■ [in sing.] informal a place, situation, person, or activity regarded as chaotic, ineffectual, or failing in some fundamental respect: *the room was a disaster area, stuff piled everywhere* | *she was a disaster area in fake leopard skin and stacked heels.*

dis·as·trous /diˈzastrəs/ ▶ **adj.** causing great damage: *a disastrous fire swept through the museum.* ■ informal highly unsuccessful: *the team made a disastrous start to the season.*
– DERIVATIVES **dis·as·trous·ly adv.**
– ORIGIN late 16th cent. (in the sense 'ill-fated'): from French *désastreux,* from Italian *disastroso,* from *disastro* 'disaster.'

dis·a·vow /ˌdisəˈvou/ ▶ **v.** [with obj.] deny any responsibility or support for: *he appears to be in denial of his own past, which he continually disavows.*
– ORIGIN late Middle English: from Old French *desavouer.*

dis·a·vow·al /ˌdisəˈvouəl/ ▶ **n.** denial of any responsibility or support for something; repudiation: *his disavowal of his previous writings* | *they know this, despite their disavowals.*

dis·band /disˈband/ ▶ **v.** (of an organized group) break up or cause to break up and stop functioning.
– DERIVATIVES **dis·band·ment n.**
– ORIGIN late 16th cent.: from obsolete French *desbander.*

dis·bar /disˈbär/ ▶ **v.** (**disbars, disbarring, disbarred**) [with obj.] **1** (usu. **be disbarred**) expel (a lawyer) from the Bar, so that they no longer have the right to practice law.
2 exclude (someone) from something: *competitors wearing rings will be* ***disbarred from*** *competition.*
– DERIVATIVES **dis·bar·ment** /-mənt/ **n.**
– ORIGIN mid 16th cent. (sense 2): from DIS- 'away' + BAR[1].

dis·be·lief /ˌdisbəˈlēf/ ▶ **n.** inability or refusal to accept that something is true or real: *Laura shook her head in disbelief.* ■ lack of faith in something: *I'll burn in hell for disbelief.*

dis·be·lieve /ˌdisbəˈlēv/ ▶ **v.** [with obj.] be unable to believe (someone or something): *he seemed to disbelieve her.* ■ [no obj.] have no faith in God, spiritual beings, or a religious system: *to disbelieve is as much an act of faith as belief.*

dis·be·liev·er /ˌdisbəˈlēvər/ ▶ **n.** a person who refuses to believe something or who lacks religious faith: *she intends to prove the disbelievers wrong.*

dis·be·liev·ing /ˌdisbəˈlēviNG/ ▶ **adj.** feeling or expressing disbelief: *the disbelieving look in her eyes.*
– DERIVATIVES **dis·be·liev·ing·ly adv.**

dis·bound /disˈbound/ ▶ **adj.** (of a portion of a book) removed from a bound volume.

dis·bud /disˈbəd/ ▶ **v.** (**disbuds, disbudding, disbudded**) [with obj.] remove superfluous or unwanted buds from (a plant). ■ Farming remove the horn buds from (a young animal).

dis·bur·den /disˈbərdn/ ▶ **v.** [with obj.] relieve (someone or something) of a burden or responsibility: *I decided to disburden myself of the task.* ■ archaic relieve (someone's mind) of worries and anxieties.

dis·burse /disˈbərs/ ▶ **v.** [with obj.] pay out (money from a fund): *$67 million of the pledged aid had already been disbursed.*
– DERIVATIVES **dis·bur·sal** /-səl/ **n., dis·burse·ment n., dis·burs·er n.**
– ORIGIN mid 16th cent.: from Old French *desbourser,* from *des-* (expressing removal) + *bourse* 'purse.'

disc ▶ **n.** variant spelling of DISK.

dis·calced /disˈkalst/ ▶ **adj.** denoting or belonging to one of several strict orders of Catholic friars or nuns who go barefoot or wear only sandals.
– ORIGIN mid 17th cent.: variant, influenced by French *déchaux,* of earlier *discalceated,* from Latin *discalceatus,* from *dis-* (expressing removal) + *calceatus* (from *calceus* 'shoe').

dis·card ▶ **v.** /disˈkärd/ [with obj.] get rid of (someone or something) as no longer useful or desirable: *Hilary bundled up the clothes she had discarded.* ■ (in bridge, whist, and similar card games) play (a card that is neither of the suit led nor a trump), when one is unable to follow suit.
▶ **n.** /ˈdisˌkärd/ a person or thing rejected as no longer useful or desirable. ■ (in bridge, whist, and similar card games) a card played which is neither of the suit led nor a trump, when one is unable to follow suit.
– DERIVATIVES **dis·card·a·ble** /disˈkärdəbəl/ **adj.**
– ORIGIN late 16th cent. (originally in the sense 'reject (a playing card)'): from DIS- (expressing removal) + the noun CARD[1].

dis·car·nate /disˈkärnit, -ˌnāt/ ▶ **adj.** (of a person or being) not having a physical body.
– ORIGIN late 19th cent.: from DIS- 'without' + Latin *caro, carn-* 'flesh' or late Latin *carnatus* 'fleshy.'

disc brake ▶ **n.** a type of vehicle brake employing the friction of pads against a disc that is attached to the wheel.

disc drive ▶ **n.** British spelling of DISK DRIVE.

disc·ec·to·my /disˈkektəmē/ ▶ **n.** surgical removal of the whole or a part of an intervertebral disc.

dis·cern /diˈsərn/ ▶ **v.** [with obj.] perceive or recognize (something): *I can discern no difference between the two policies* | [with clause] *students quickly discern what is acceptable to the teacher.* ■ distinguish (someone or something) with difficulty by sight or with the other senses: *she could faintly discern the shape of a skull.*
– DERIVATIVES **dis·cern·er n.**
– ORIGIN late Middle English: via Old French from Latin *discernere,* from *dis-* 'apart' + *cernere* 'to separate.'

dis·cern·i·ble /diˈsərnəbəl/ ▶ **adj.** able to be discerned; perceptible: *the scandal had no discernible effect on his career.*
– DERIVATIVES **dis·cern·i·bly** /-əblē/ **adv.**

dis·cern·ing /diˈsərniNG/ ▶ **adj.** having or showing good judgment: *the restaurant attracts discerning customers.*
– DERIVATIVES **dis·cern·ing·ly adv.**

dis·cern·ment /diˈsərnmənt/ ▶ **n. 1** the ability to judge well: *an astonishing lack of discernment.*
2 (in Christian contexts) perception in the absence of judgment with a view to obtaining spiritual direction and understanding: *without providing for a time of healing and discernment, there will be no hope of living through this present moment without a shattering of our common life.*

dis·cerp·tion /diˈsərpSHən/ ▶ **n.** archaic the action of pulling something apart. ■ a piece severed from something.
– DERIVATIVES **dis·cerp·ti·bil·i·ty** /-ˌsərptəˈbilitē/ **n., dis·cerp·ti·ble** /-təbəl/ **adj.**
– ORIGIN mid 17th cent.: from late Latin *discerptio(n-),* from Latin *discerpere* 'pluck to pieces.'

dis·charge ▶ **v.** /disˈCHärj/ [with obj.] **1** tell (someone) officially that they can or must leave, in particular: ■ send (a patient) out of the hospital because they are judged fit to go home. ■ dismiss or release (someone) from a job, esp. from service in the armed forces or police. ■ release (someone) from the custody or restraint of the law: *he ordered that 1,671 prisoners of war be* ***discharged from prison.*** ■ relieve (a juror or jury) from serving in a case. ■ Law relieve (a bankrupt) of liability. ■ release (a party) from a contract or obligation: *the insurer is discharged from liability from the day of breach.*
2 allow (a liquid, gas, or other substance) to flow out from where it has been confined: *industrial plants* ***discharge*** *highly toxic materials* ***into*** *rivers* | [no obj.] *the overflow should discharge in an obvious place.* ■ (of an orifice or diseased tissue) emit (pus, mucus, or other liquid): *the swelling will eventually break down and discharge pus* | [no obj.] *the eyes and nose began to discharge.* ■ Physics release or neutralize the electric charge of (an electric field, battery, or other object): *the electrostatic field that builds up on a monitor screen can be discharged* | [no obj.] *batteries have a tendency to discharge slowly.* ■ (of a person) fire (a gun or missile): *when you shoot you can discharge as many barrels as you wish.* ■ [no obj.] (of a firearm) be fired: *there was a dull thud as the gun discharged.* ■ (of a person) allow (an emotion) to be released: *he discharged his resentment in the harmless form of memoirs.* ■ unload (cargo or passengers) from a ship: *the ferry was discharging passengers* | [no obj.] *ninety ships were waiting to discharge.*
3 do all that is required to fulfill (a responsibility) or perform (a duty). ■ pay off (a debt or other financial claim).
4 Law (of a judge or court) cancel (an order of a court). ■ cancel (a contract) because of completion or breach: *an existing mortgage to be discharged on completion.*
▶ **n.** /ˈdisˌCHärj/ **1** the action of discharging someone from a hospital or from a job: *his discharge from the hospital* | *offending policemen receive a dishonorable discharge.* ■ Brit. an act of releasing someone from the custody or restraint of the law: *four days in jail and one year conditional discharge.* ■ Law the action of relieving a bankrupt from residual liability.
2 the action of discharging a liquid, gas, or other substance: *those germs might lead to vaginal discharge.* ■ a substance that has been discharged: *large volumes of sewage discharge* | *environmental damage from toxic chemical discharges.* ■ Physics the release of electricity from a charged object: *slow discharge of a condenser is fundamental to oscillatory circuits.* ■ a flow of electricity through air or other gas, esp. when accompanied by emission of light: *a sizzling discharge between sky and turret.* ■ the action of firing a gun or missile: *a police permit for discharge of an air gun* | *sounds like discharges of artillery.* ■ the action of unloading a ship of its cargo or passengers.
3 the action of doing all that is required to fulfill a responsibility or perform a duty: *directors must use skill in the discharge of their duties.* ■ the payment of a debt or other financial claim: *money paid in discharge of a claim.*
4 Law the action of canceling an order of a court.
– DERIVATIVES **dis·charge·a·ble** /disˈCHärjəbəl/ **adj., dis·charg·er** /disˈCHärjər/ **n.**
– ORIGIN Middle English (in the sense 'relieve of an obligation'): from Old French *descharger,* from late Latin *discarricare* 'unload,' from *dis-* (expressing reversal) + *carricare* 'to load' (see CHARGE).

dis·charge lamp /ˈdisˌCHärj/ ▶ **n.** a lamp in which the light is produced by a discharge tube.

dis·charge tube /ˈdisˌCHärj/ ▶ **n.** a tube containing charged electrodes and filled with a gas in which ionization is induced by an electric field. The gas molecules emit light as they return to the ground state.

dis·ci·ple /diˈsīpəl/ ▶ **n.** a personal follower of Jesus during his life, esp. one of the twelve Apostles. ■ a follower or student of a teacher, leader, or philosopher: *a disciple of Rousseau.*
– DERIVATIVES **dis·ci·ple·ship** /-ˌSHip/ **n., dis·cip·u·lar** /-ˈsipyələr/ **adj.**
– ORIGIN Old English, from Latin *discipulus* 'learner,' from *discere* 'learn'; reinforced by Old French *deciple.*

Dis·ci·ples of Christ a Protestant denomination, originating among American Presbyterians in the early 19th century and found chiefly in the US, which rejects creeds and regards the Bible as the only basis of faith.

dis·ci·pli·nar·i·an /ˌdisəpləˈnerēən/ ▶ **n.** a person who believes in or practices firm discipline.

dis·ci·pli·nar·y /ˈdisəpləˌnerē/ ▶ **adj.** concerning or enforcing discipline: *a soldier will face disciplinary action after going absent without leave.*
– ORIGIN late 15th cent. (originally with reference to ecclesiastical order): from medieval Latin *disciplinarius*, from Latin *disciplina*, from *discipulus* 'learner' (see DISCIPLE).

dis·ci·pline /ˈdisəplin/ ▶ **n. 1** the practice of training people to obey rules or a code of behavior, using punishment to correct disobedience: *a lack of proper parental and school discipline.* ■ the controlled behavior resulting from such training: *he was able to maintain discipline among his men.* ■ activity or experience that provides mental or physical training: *the tariqa offered spiritual discipline | Kung fu is a discipline open to old and young.* ■ a system of rules of conduct: *he doesn't have to submit to normal disciplines.*
2 a branch of knowledge, typically one studied in higher education: *sociology is a fairly new discipline.*
▶ **v.** [with obj.] train (someone) to obey rules or a code of behavior, using punishment to correct disobedience: *many parents have been afraid to discipline their children.* ■ punish or rebuke (someone) formally for an offense: *a member of the staff was to be disciplined by management.* ■ (**discipline oneself to do something**) train oneself to do something in a controlled and habitual way: *every month discipline yourself to go through the file.*
– DERIVATIVES **dis·ci·plin·a·ble** adj., **dis·ci·pli·nal** /-nəl/ adj.
– ORIGIN Middle English (in the sense 'mortification by scourging oneself'): via Old French from Latin *disciplina* 'instruction, knowledge,' from *discipulus* (see DISCIPLE).

dis·ci·plined /ˈdisəplind/ ▶ **adj.** showing a controlled form of behavior or way of working: *a disciplined approach to management.*

disc jock·ey (also **disk jockey**) ▶ **n.** a person who introduces and plays recorded popular music, esp. on radio or at a disco.

dis·claim /disˈklām/ ▶ **v.** [with obj.] refuse to acknowledge; deny: *the school disclaimed any responsibility for his death.* ■ Law renounce a legal claim to (a property or title).
– ORIGIN late Middle English (in legal contexts): from Anglo-Norman French *desclamer*, from *des-* (expressing reversal) + *clamer* 'to claim' (see CLAIM).

dis·claim·er /disˈklāmər/ ▶ **n.** a statement that denies something, esp. responsibility: *the novel carries the usual disclaimer about the characters bearing no relation to living persons.* ■ Law an act of repudiating another's claim or renouncing one's own.
– ORIGIN late Middle English (as a legal term): from Anglo-Norman French *desclamer* (infinitive used as noun: see DISCLAIM).

dis·close /disˈklōz/ ▶ **v.** [with obj.] make (secret or new information) known: *they disclosed her name to the press* | [with clause] *the magazine disclosed that he had served a prison sentence for fraud.* ■ allow (something) to be seen, esp. by uncovering it: *he cleared away the grass and disclosed a narrow opening descending into the darkness.*
– DERIVATIVES **dis·clos·er** n.
– ORIGIN late Middle English: from Old French *desclos-*, stem of *desclore*, based on Latin *claudere* 'to close.'

dis·clo·sure /disˈklōZHər/ ▶ **n.** the action of making new or secret information known: *a judge ordered the disclosure of the government documents.* ■ a fact, esp. a secret, that is made known: *the government's disclosures about missile programs.*
– ORIGIN late 16th cent.: from DISCLOSE, on the pattern of *closure*.

dis·co /ˈdiskō/ informal ▶ **n.** (pl. **discos**) **1** a club or party at which people dance to pop music.
2 pop music intended mainly for dancing to at discos, typically soul-influenced and melodic with a regular bass beat and popular particularly in the late 1970s.
▶ **v.** (**discoes, discoing, discoed**) [no obj.] attend or dance at such a club or party: *for the next three hours he discoed nonstop.*
– ORIGIN 1960s (originally US): abbreviation of DISCOTHEQUE.

dis·cog·ra·phy /disˈkägrəfē/ ▶ **n.** (pl. **discographies**) a descriptive catalog of musical recordings, particularly those of a particular performer or composer. ■ all of a performer's or composer's recordings considered as a body of work: *his discography is overwhelmingly classical.* ■ the study of musical recordings and compilation of descriptive catalogs.
– DERIVATIVES **dis·cog·ra·pher** /-fər/ n.
– ORIGIN 1930s: from DISC + -GRAPHY, on the pattern of *biography*.

dis·coid /ˈdisˌkoid/ ▶ **adj.** technical shaped like a disc.
▶ **n.** a thing that is shaped like a disc, particularly a type of ancient stone tool.
– DERIVATIVES **dis·coi·dal** /disˈkoidl/ adj.
– ORIGIN late 18th cent.: from Greek *diskoeidēs*, from *diskos* (see DISCUS).

dis·col·or /disˈkələr/ ▶ **v.** change or cause to change to a different, less attractive color: [no obj.] *do not overknead the dough while adding the fruit or it will discolor* | [with obj.] *too much aluminum can discolor water.*
– ORIGIN late Middle English: from Old French *descolorer* or medieval Latin *discolorare*, from *des-*, *dis-* (expressing reversal) + Latin *colorare* 'to color.'

dis·col·or·a·tion /disˌkələˈrāSHən/ ▶ **n.** the process of changing to a different, less attractive color: *a bluish* **discoloration** *of the skin.*

dis·col·ored /disˈkələrd/ ▶ **adj.** changed in color in a way that is less attractive: *her beauty was marred by discolored teeth.*

dis·com·bob·u·late /ˌdiskəmˈbäbyəˌlāt/ ▶ **v.** [with obj.] humorous disconcert or confuse (someone): *this attitude totally discombobulated Bruce* | (as adj. **discombobulated**) *he is looking a little pained and discombobulated.*
– DERIVATIVES **dis·com·bob·u·la·tion** n.
– ORIGIN mid 19th cent.: probably based on DISCOMPOSE or DISCOMFIT.

dis·com·fit /disˈkəmfit/ ▶ **v.** (**discomfits, discomfiting, discomfited**) [with obj.] make (someone) feel uneasy or embarrassed: *he was not noticeably discomfited by her tone.*
– DERIVATIVES **dis·com·fi·ture** /disˈkəmfiˌCHo͝or/ n.
– ORIGIN Middle English (in the sense 'defeat in battle'): from Old French *desconfit*, past participle of *desconfire*, based on Latin *dis-* (expressing reversal) + *conficere* 'put together' (see CONFECTION).

dis·com·fort /disˈkəmfərt/ ▶ **n.** lack of physical comfort: *the discomforts of too much sun in summer.* ■ slight pain: *the patient complained of discomfort in the left calf.* ■ a state of mental unease; worry or embarrassment: *his remarks caused her discomfort.*
▶ **v.** [with obj.] make (someone) feel uneasy, anxious, or embarrassed: *she liked to discomfort my mother by her remarks.* ■ (often as adj. **discomforting**) cause (someone) slight pain: *the patient's condition has discomforting symptoms.*
– ORIGIN Middle English (as a verb in the sense 'dishearten, distress'): from Old French *desconforter* (verb), *desconfort* (noun), from *des-* (expressing reversal) + *conforter* 'to comfort' (see COMFORT).

dis·com·mode /ˌdiskəˈmōd/ ▶ **v.** [with obj.] formal cause (someone) trouble or inconvenience: *I am sorry to have discommoded you.*
– DERIVATIVES **dis·com·mo·di·ous** /-ˈmōdēəs/ adj., **dis·com·mod·i·ty** /-ˈmäditē/ n.
– ORIGIN early 18th cent.: from obsolete French *discommoder*, variant of *incommoder* (see INCOMMODE).

dis·com·pose /ˌdiskəmˈpōz/ ▶ **v.** [with obj.] (often as adj. **discomposed**) disturb or agitate (someone): *she looked a little discomposed as she spoke.*

dis·com·po·sure /ˌdiskəmˈpōZHər/ ▶ **n.** the state or feeling of being disturbed or agitated; agitation: *he made the admission without the slightest discomposure.*

dis·con·cert /ˌdiskənˈsərt/ ▶ **v.** [with obj.] disturb the composure of; unsettle: *the abrupt change of subject disconcerted her* | (as adj. **disconcerted**) *she was amused to see a disconcerted expression on his face.*
– DERIVATIVES **dis·con·cert·ed·ly** adv., **dis·con·cer·tion** /-ˈsərSHən/ n., **dis·con·cert·ment** n. (rare).
– ORIGIN late 17th cent. (in the sense 'upset the progress of'): from obsolete French *desconcerter*, from *des-* (expressing reversal) + *concerter* 'bring together.'

dis·con·cert·ing /ˌdiskənˈsərtiNG/ ▶ **adj.** causing one to feel unsettled: *he had a disconcerting habit of offering jobs to people he met at dinner parties.*
– DERIVATIVES **dis·con·cert·ing·ly** adv.

dis·con·firm /ˌdiskənˈfərm/ ▶ **v.** [with obj.] show that (a belief or hypothesis) is not or may not be true.
– DERIVATIVES **dis·con·fir·ma·tion** /disˌkänfərˈmāSHən/ n., **dis·con·fir·ma·to·ry** /-məˌtôrē/ adj.

dis·con·form·i·ty /ˌdiskənˈfôrmitē/ ▶ **n.** (pl. **disconformities**) **1** lack of conformity.
2 Geology a break in a sedimentary sequence that does not involve a difference of inclination between the strata on each side of the break. Compare with UNCONFORMITY.

dis·con·nect /ˌdiskəˈnekt/ ▶ **v.** [with obj.] break the connection of or between: *take all violence out of television drama and you disconnect it from reality.* ■ take (an electrical device) out of action by detaching it from a power supply. ■ interrupt or terminate (a telephone conversation) by breaking the connection: *that might explain why her call got disconnected mid-expletive.* ■ terminate the connection of (a household) to water, electricity, gas, or telephone, typically because of nonpayment of bills.
▶ **n.** a discrepancy or lack of connection: *there can be a disconnect between boardrooms and IT departments when it comes to technology.*
– DERIVATIVES **dis·con·nec·tion** /-ˈnekSHən/ n.

dis·con·nect·ed /ˌdiskəˈnektid/ ▶ **adj.** having a connection broken: *he expected the disconnected phone to start ringing.* ■ [predic.] (of a person) lacking contact with reality: *I drove away, feeling* **disconnected from** *the real world.* ■ (of speech, writing, or thought) lacking a logical sequence; incoherent: *a disconnected narrative.*
– DERIVATIVES **dis·con·nect·ed·ly** adv., **dis·con·nect·ed·ness** n.

dis·con·so·late /disˈkänsəlit/ ▶ **adj.** without consolation or comfort; unhappy: *he'd met the man's disconsolate widow.* ■ (of a place or thing) causing or showing a complete lack of comfort; cheerless: *solitary, disconsolate clumps of cattails.*
– DERIVATIVES **dis·con·so·late·ly** adv., **dis·con·so·late·ness** n., **dis·con·so·la·tion** /-ˌkänsəˈlāSHən/ n.
– ORIGIN late Middle English: from medieval Latin *disconsolatus*, from *dis-* (expressing reversal) + Latin *consolatus* (past participle of *consolari* 'to console').

dis·con·tent /ˌdiskənˈtent/ ▶ **n.** lack of contentment; dissatisfaction with one's circumstances: *popular* **discontent with** *the system had been general for several years | the discontents and anxieties of the working class.* ■ a person who is dissatisfied, typically with the prevailing social or political situation: *the cause attracted a motley crew of discontents and zealots.*
– DERIVATIVES **dis·con·tent·ment** n.

dis·con·tent·ed /ˌdiskənˈtentid/ ▶ **adj.** dissatisfied, esp. with one's circumstances: *I am so* **discontented with** *my work | a discontented housewife* | (as plural noun **the discontented**) *the ranks of the discontented were swelled by returning soldiers.*
– DERIVATIVES **dis·con·tent·ed·ly** adv., **dis·con·tent·ed·ness** n.

dis·con·tin·ue /ˌdiskənˈtinyo͞o/ ▶ **v.** (**discontinues, discontinuing, discontinued**) [with obj.] cease doing or providing (something), typically something provided on a regular basis: *he discontinued his visits | the ferry service was discontinued by the proprietors.* ■ (usu. **be discontinued**) stop making (a particular product): *their current top-of-the-range running shoe is being discontinued.* ■ cease taking (a newspaper or periodical) or paying (a subscription).
– DERIVATIVES **dis·con·tin·u·ance** /-yo͞oəns/ n., **dis·con·tin·u·a·tion** /-ˌtinyo͞oˈāSHən/ n.
– ORIGIN late Middle English (in the sense 'interrupt, disrupt'): via Old French from medieval Latin *discontinuare*, from Latin *dis-* 'not' + *continuare* (see CONTINUE).

dis·con·tin·ued /ˌdiskənˈtinyo͞od/ ▶ **adj.** (of a product) no longer available or produced: *discontinued fabrics.*

dis·con·ti·nu·i·ty /ˌdiskäntnˈ(y)o͞oitē/ ▶ **n.** (pl. **discontinuities**) a distinct break in physical continuity or sequence in time: *there is no significant discontinuity between modern and primitive societies.* ■ a sharp difference of characteristics between parts of something: *changes in government have resulted in discontinuities in policy.* ■ Mathematics a point at which a function is discontinuous or undefined.
– ORIGIN late 16th cent.: from medieval Latin *discontinuitas*, from *discontinuus* (see DISCONTINUOUS).

dis·con·tin·u·ous /ˌdiskənˈtinyo͞oəs/ ▶ **adj.** having intervals or gaps: *a person with a discontinuous employment record.* ■ Mathematics (of a function) having at least one discontinuity, and whose differential coefficient may become infinite.
– DERIVATIVES **dis·con·tin·u·ous·ly** adv.
– ORIGIN mid 17th cent. (in the sense 'producing discontinuity'): from medieval Latin *discontinuus*, from *dis-* 'not' + *continuus* (see CONTINUOUS).

dis·cord /ˈdiskôrd/ ▶ **n. 1** disagreement between people: *a prosperous family who showed no signs of discord.* ■ lack of agreement or harmony between things: *the discord between indigenous and Western cultures.*
2 Music lack of harmony between notes sounding together: *the music faded in discord.* ■ a chord that (in conventional harmonic terms) is regarded as unpleasing or requiring resolution by another. ■ any interval except a unison, an octave, a perfect fifth or fourth, a major or minor third and sixth,

d

or their octaves. ■ a single note dissonant with another.
▶ v. [no obj.] archaic (of people) disagree: *we discorded commonly on two points.* ■ (of things) be different or in disharmony: *the party's views were apt to* ***discord with*** *those of the leading members of the administration.*
– ORIGIN Middle English: from Old French *descord* (noun), *descorder* (verb), from Latin *discordare*, from *discors* 'discordant,' from *dis-* (expressing negation, reversal) + *cor, cord-* 'heart.'

d

dis·cord·ant /dis'kôrdnt/ ▶ adj. **1** disagreeing or incongruous: *the principle of meritocracy is discordant with claims of inherited worth.* ■ characterized by quarreling and conflict: *a study of children in discordant homes.*
2 (of sounds) harsh and jarring because of a lack of harmony: *bombs, guns, and engines mingled in discordant sound.*
– PHRASES **strike a discordant note** appear strange and out of place: *the chair's modernity struck a discordant note in a room full of eighteenth-century furniture.*
– DERIVATIVES **dis·cord·ance** n., **dis·cor·dan·cy** /-dnsē/ n., **dis·cord·ant·ly** adv.
– ORIGIN late Middle English: from Old French *descordant*, present participle of *descorder* (see DISCORD).

dis·co·theque /'diskə,tek/ ▶ n. another term for DISCO (sense 1 of the noun).
– ORIGIN 1950s: from French *discothèque*, originally 'record library,' on the pattern of *bibliothèque* 'library.'

dis·count ▶ n. /'diskount/ a deduction from the usual cost of something, typically given for prompt or advance payment or to a special category of buyers: *many stores will offer a discount on bulk purchases.* ■ Finance a percentage deducted from the face value of a bill of exchange or promissory note when it changes hands before the due date.
▶ v. /'diskount, dis'kount/ [with obj.] **1** deduct an amount from (the usual price of something): (as adj. **discounted**) *current users qualify for a discounted price.* ■ reduce (a product or service) in price: *merchandise that was deeply discounted—up to 50 percent* | (as adj. **discounted**) *discounted books.* ■ buy or sell (a bill of exchange) before its due date at less than its maturity value.
2 regard (a possibility, fact, or person) as being unworthy of consideration because it lacks credibility: *I'd heard rumors, but discounted them.*
▶ adj. /'diskount/ (of a store or business) offering goods for sale at discounted prices: *a discount drugstore chain.* ■ at a price lower than the usual one: *a discount flight.*
– PHRASES **at a discount** below the nominal or usual price: *a plan that allows tenants to buy their homes at a discount.* Compare with AT A PREMIUM (see PREMIUM).
– DERIVATIVES **dis·count·a·ble** /dis'kountəbəl/ adj., **dis·count·er** n.
– ORIGIN early 17th cent. (denoting a reduction in the amount or value of something): from obsolete French *descompte* (noun), *descompter* (verb), or (in commercial contexts) from Italian *(di)scontare*, both from medieval Latin *discomputare*, from Latin *dis-* (expressing reversal) + *computare* (see COMPUTE).

dis·count·ed cash flow ▶ n. Finance a method of assessing investments taking into account the expected accumulation of interest.

dis·coun·te·nance /dis'kountn-əns/ ▶ v. [with obj.] (usu. **be discountenanced**) **1** refuse to approve of (something): *a family in which alcohol consumption is discountenanced.*
2 disturb the composure of: *Amanda was not discountenanced by the accusation.*

dis·count house ▶ n. **1** another term for DISCOUNT STORE.
2 Brit. a company that buys and sells bills of exchange.

dis·count rate ▶ n. Finance **1** the minimum interest rate set by the Federal Reserve for lending to other banks.
2 a rate used for discounting bills of exchange.

dis·count store ▶ n. a store that sells goods at less than the normal retail price.

dis·cour·age /dis'kərij, -'kə-rij/ ▶ v. [with obj.] cause (someone) to lose confidence or enthusiasm: *I don't want to discourage you, but I don't think it's such a good idea.* ■ prevent or seek to prevent (something) by showing disapproval or creating difficulties: *the plan is designed to discourage the use of private cars.* ■ persuade (someone) against an action: *we want to* ***discourage*** *children* ***from*** *smoking.*
– DERIVATIVES **dis·cour·ag·er** n.
– ORIGIN late Middle English: from Old French *descouragier*, from *des-* (expressing reversal) + *corage* 'courage.'

dis·cour·aged /dis'kərijd, -'kə-rijd/ ▶ adj. having lost confidence or enthusiasm; disheartened: *he must be feeling pretty discouraged.*

dis·cour·age·ment /dis'kərijmənt/ ▶ n. **1** a loss of confidence or enthusiasm; dispiritedness: *do not give in to discouragement.*
2 an attempt to prevent something by showing disapproval or creating difficulties; deterrent: *the discouragement of crime.*

dis·cour·ag·ing /dis'kərijiNG/ ▶ adj. causing someone to lose confidence or enthusiasm; depressing: *a discouraging experience.*
– DERIVATIVES **dis·cour·ag·ing·ly** adv.

dis·course ▶ n. /'dis,kôrs/ written or spoken communication or debate: *the language of political discourse* | *an imagined discourse between two people traveling in France.* ■ a formal discussion of a topic in speech or writing: *a discourse on critical theory.* ■ Linguistics a connected series of utterances; a text or conversation.
▶ v. /dis'kôrs/ [no obj.] speak or write authoritatively about a topic: *she could* ***discourse*** *at great length* ***on*** *the history of Europe.* ■ engage in conversation: *he spent an hour* ***discoursing with*** *his supporters in the courtroom.*
– ORIGIN late Middle English (denoting the process of reasoning, also in the phrase *discourse of reason*): from Old French *discours*, from Latin *discursus* 'running to and fro' (in medieval Latin 'argument'), from the verb *discurrere*, from *dis-* 'away' + *currere* 'to run'; the verb influenced by French *discourir*.

dis·course mark·er /'dis,kôrs/ ▶ n. Grammar a word or phrase whose function is to organize discourse into segments, for example *well* or *I mean.*

dis·cour·te·ous /dis'kərtēəs/ ▶ adj. showing rudeness and a lack of consideration for other people: *it would be unkind and discourteous to decline a visit.*
– DERIVATIVES **dis·cour·te·ous·ly** adv., **dis·cour·te·ous·ness** n.

dis·cour·te·sy /dis'kərtəsē/ ▶ n. (pl. **discourtesies**) rude and inconsiderate behavior: *he was able to discourage visitors without obvious discourtesy.* ■ an impolite act or remark: *the fact that senators were not kept informed was an extraordinary discourtesy.*

dis·cov·er /dis'kəvər/ ▶ v. [with obj.] **1** find (something or someone) unexpectedly or in the course of a search: *firemen discovered a body in the debris* | *she discovered her lover in the arms of another woman.* ■ become aware of (a fact or situation): *the courage to discover the truth and possibly be disappointed* | [with clause] *it was a relief to discover that he wasn't in.* ■ be the first to find or observe (a place, substance, or scientific phenomenon): *Fleming discovered penicillin early in the twentieth century.* ■ perceive the attractions of (an activity or subject) for the first time: *a teenager who has recently discovered fashion.* ■ be the first to recognize the potential of (an actor, singer, or musician): *I discovered the band back in the mid 70s.*
2 archaic divulge (a secret): *they contain some secrets which Time will discover.* ■ disclose the identity of (someone): *she at last discovered herself to me.* ■ display (a quality or feeling): *with what agility did these military men discover their skill in feats of war.*
– DERIVATIVES **dis·cov·er·a·bil·i·ty** n., **dis·cov·er·a·ble** adj.
– ORIGIN Middle English (in the sense 'make known'): from Old French *descovrir*, from late Latin *discooperire*, from Latin *dis-* (expressing reversal) + *cooperire* 'cover completely' (see COVER).

dis·cov·ered check ▶ n. Chess a check that results when a player moves a piece or pawn so as to put the opponent's king in check from another piece.

dis·cov·er·er /dis'kəvərər/ ▶ n. the first person to find or explore a place. ■ the first person to find or observe a substance or scientific phenomenon: *many chemical processes are named after their discoverers.*

dis·cov·er·y /dis'kəvərē/ ▶ n. (pl. **discoveries**) **1** the action or process of discovering or being discovered: *the discovery of the body* | *he made some startling discoveries.* ■ a person or thing discovered: *the drug is not a new discovery.*
2 Law the compulsory disclosure, by a party to an action, of relevant documents referred to by the other party.
– ORIGIN mid 16th cent.: from DISCOVER, on the pattern of the pair *recover, recovery.*

dis·cov·er·y well ▶ n. the first successful oil well in a new field.

dis·cred·it /dis'kredit/ ▶ v. (**discredits, discrediting, discredited**) [with obj.] harm the good reputation of (someone or something): *his remarks were taken out of context in an effort to discredit him* | (as adj. **discredited**) *a discredited former governor.* ■ cause (an idea or piece of evidence) to seem false or unreliable: *recent attempts to discredit evolution.*
▶ n. loss or lack of reputation or respect: *they committed crimes that brought discredit upon the administration.* ■ a person or thing that is a source of disgrace: *the ships were* ***a discredit to*** *the country.*
– ORIGIN mid 16th cent.: from DIS- (expressing reversal) + CREDIT, on the pattern of Italian *di) scredito* (noun), *((di)screditare* (verb), and French *discrédit* (noun), *discréditer* (verb).

dis·cred·it·a·ble /dis'kreditəbəl/ ▶ adj. tending to bring harm to a reputation: *allegations of discreditable conduct.*
– DERIVATIVES **dis·cred·it·a·bly** /-blē/ adv.

dis·creet /dis'krēt/ ▶ adj. (**discreeter, discreetest**) careful and circumspect in one's speech or actions, esp. in order to avoid causing offense or to gain an advantage: *we made some discreet inquiries.* ■ intentionally unobtrusive: *a discreet cough.*
– DERIVATIVES **dis·creet·ly** adv., **dis·creet·ness** n.
– ORIGIN Middle English: from Old French *discret*, from Latin *discretus* 'separate,' past participle of *discernere* 'discern,' the sense arising from late Latin *discretio* (see DISCRETION). Compare with DISCRETE.

> **USAGE** The words **discrete** and **discreet** are pronounced in the same way and share the same origin but they do not mean the same thing. **Discrete** means 'separate,' as in *a finite number of discrete categories*, while **discreet** means 'careful and circumspect,' as in *you can rely on him to be discreet.*

dis·crep·an·cy /dis'krepənsē/ ▶ n. (pl. **discrepancies**) a lack of compatibility or similarity between two or more facts: *there's a* ***discrepancy between*** *your account and his.*
– DERIVATIVES **dis·crep·ant** /-pənt/ adj.
– ORIGIN early 17th cent.: from Latin *discrepantia*, from *discrepare* 'be discordant,' from *dis-* 'apart, away' + *crepare* 'to creak.'

dis·crete /dis'krēt/ ▶ adj. individually separate and distinct: *speech sounds are produced as a continuous sound signal rather than discrete units.*
– DERIVATIVES **dis·crete·ly** adv., **dis·crete·ness** n.
– ORIGIN late Middle English: from Latin *discretus* 'separate'; compare with DISCREET.

> **USAGE** On the difference between **discrete** and **discreet**, see usage at DISCREET.

dis·cre·tion /dis'kresHən/ ▶ n. **1** the quality of behaving or speaking in such a way as to avoid causing offense or revealing private information: *she knew she could rely on his discretion.*
2 the freedom to decide what should be done in a particular situation: *it is up to local authorities to use their discretion in setting the charges* | *a pass-fail grading system may be used* ***at the discretion of*** *the department.*
– PHRASES **discretion is the better part of valor** proverb it is better to avoid a dangerous situation than to confront it.
– ORIGIN Middle English (in the sense 'discernment'): via Old French from Latin *discretio(n-)* 'separation' (in late Latin 'discernment'), from *discernere* (see DISCERN).

dis·cre·tion·ar·y /dis'kresHə,nerē/ ▶ adj. available for use at the discretion of the user: *rules are inevitably less flexible than a discretionary policy.* ■ denoting or relating to investment funds placed with a broker or manager who has discretion to invest them on the client's behalf: *discretionary portfolios.*

dis·cre·tion·ar·y in·come ▶ n. income remaining after deduction of taxes, other mandatory charges, and expenditure on necessary items. Compare with DISPOSABLE INCOME.

dis·cret·ize /dis'krē,tīz/ ▶ v. [with obj.] Mathematics represent or approximate (a quantity or series) using a discrete quantity or quantities.
– DERIVATIVES **dis·cret·i·za·tion** /dis,krētə'zāsHən/ n.

dis·crim·i·na·ble /dis'krimənəbəl/ ▶ adj. able to be discriminated; distinguishable: *the target contours will not be discriminable from their background.*
– DERIVATIVES **dis·crim·i·na·bil·i·ty** /dis,krimənə'bilitē/ n., **dis·crim·i·na·bly** /-blē/ adv.
– ORIGIN mid 18th cent.: from DISCRIMINATE, on the pattern of the pair *separate, separable.*

dis·crim·i·nant /dis'krimənənt/ ▶ n. an agent or characteristic that enables things, people, or classes to be distinguished from one another: *anemia is commonly present in patients with both conditions, and is therefore not a helpful discriminant.* ■ Mathematics a function of the coefficients of a polynomial equation whose value gives information about the roots of the polynomial. See also DISCRIMINANT FUNCTION.
– ORIGIN mid 19th cent. (in the sense 'showing discernment'): from Latin *discriminant-* 'distinguishing between,' from the verb *discriminare* (see DISCRIMINATE).

dis·crim·i·nant a·nal·y·sis ▶ **n.** statistical analysis using a discriminant function to assign data to one of two or more groups.

dis·crim·i·nant func·tion ▶ **n.** Statistics a function of several variates used to assign items into one of two or more groups. The function for a particular set of items is obtained from measurements of the variates of items that belong to a known group.

dis·crim·i·nate /dis'krimə,nāt/ ▶ **v.** [no obj.] **1** recognize a distinction; differentiate: *babies can **discriminate between** different facial expressions of emotion.* ■ [with obj.] perceive or constitute the difference in or between: *bats can discriminate a difference in echo delay of between 69 and 98 millionths of a second | features that **discriminate** this species **from** other gastropods.* **2** make an unjust or prejudicial distinction in the treatment of different categories of people or things, esp. on the grounds of race, sex, or age: *existing employment policies **discriminate against** women.*
– DERIVATIVES **dis·crim·i·nate·ly** /-nitlē/ **adv.**, **dis·crim·i·na·tive** /-,nātiv/ **adj.**
– ORIGIN early 17th cent.: from Latin *discriminat-* 'distinguished between,' from the verb *discriminare*, from *discrimen* 'distinction,' from the verb *discernere* (see **DISCERN**).

dis·crim·i·nat·ing /dis'krimə,nātiNG/ ▶ **adj.** (of a person) having or showing refined taste or good judgment: *he became a discriminating collector and patron of the arts.*
– DERIVATIVES **dis·crim·i·nat·ing·ly adv.**

dis·crim·i·na·tion /dis,krimə'nāSHən/ ▶ **n. 1** the unjust or prejudicial treatment of different categories of people or things, esp. on the grounds of race, age, or sex: *victims of racial discrimination | **discrimination against** homosexuals.* **2** recognition and understanding of the difference between one thing and another: *discrimination between right and wrong | young children have difficulties in making fine discriminations.* ■ the ability to discern what is of high quality; good judgment or taste: *those who could afford to buy showed little taste or discrimination.* ■ Psychology the ability to distinguish between different stimuli: [as modifier] *discrimination learning.* **3** Electronics the selection of a signal having a required characteristic, such as frequency or amplitude, by means of a discriminator that rejects all unwanted signals.

dis·crim·i·na·tor /dis'krimə,nātər/ ▶ **n. 1** a characteristic that enables things, people, or classes to be distinguished from one another: *age should not be used as a primary discriminator in recruitment.* **2** Electronics a circuit or device that only produces an output when the input exceeds a fixed value. ■ a circuit that converts a frequency-modulated signal into an amplitude-modulated one.

dis·crim·i·na·to·ry /dis'krimənə,tôrē/ ▶ **adj.** making or showing an unfair or prejudicial distinction between different categories of people or things, esp. on the grounds of race, age, or sex: *discriminatory employment practices.*

dis·cur·sive /dis'kərsiv/ ▶ **adj. 1** digressing from subject to subject: *students often write dull, secondhand, discursive prose.* ■ (of a style of speech or writing) fluent and expansive rather than formulaic or abbreviated: *the short story is concentrated, whereas the novel is discursive.* **2** of or relating to discourse or modes of discourse: *the attempt to transform utterances from one discursive context to another.* **3** Philosophy, archaic proceeding by argument or reasoning rather than by intuition.
– DERIVATIVES **dis·cur·sive·ly adv.**, **dis·cur·sive·ness n.**
– ORIGIN late 16th cent.: from medieval Latin *discursivus*, from Latin *discurs-*, literally 'gone hastily to and fro,' from the verb *discurrere* (see **DISCOURSE**).

dis·cus /'diskəs/ ▶ **n.** (pl. **discuses**) a heavy thick-centered disk thrown by an athlete, in ancient Greek games or in modern field events. ■ the athletic event or sport of throwing the discus: *she had placed first in the discus.*
– ORIGIN via Latin from Greek *diskos*.

discus thrower

dis·cuss /dis'kəs/ ▶ **v.** [with obj.] talk about (something) with another person or group of people: *I **discussed the matter with** my wife* | [with clause] *they were discussing where to go for a drink.* ■ talk or write about (a topic) in detail, taking into account different ideas and opinions: *in Chapter Six I discuss problems that arise in applying Darwin's ideas.*
– DERIVATIVES **dis·cuss·a·ble adj.**, **dis·cuss·er n.**
– ORIGIN late Middle English (in the sense 'dispel, disperse,' also 'examine by argument'): from Latin *discuss-* 'dashed to pieces,' later 'investigated,' from the verb *discutere*, from *dis-* 'apart' + *quatere* 'shake.'

dis·cus·sant /dis'kəsənt/ ▶ **n.** a person who takes part in a discussion, esp. an arranged one.

dis·cus·sion /dis'kəSHən/ ▶ **n.** the action or process of talking about something, typically in order to reach a decision or to exchange ideas: *the proposals are not a blueprint but ideas for discussion | the specific content of the legislation was **under discussion**.* ■ a conversation or debate about a certain topic: *discussions about environmental improvement programs.* ■ a detailed treatment of a particular topic in speech or writing.
– ORIGIN Middle English (denoting judicial examination): via Old French from late Latin *discussio(n-)*, from *discutere* 'investigate' (see **DISCUSS**).

dis·cus·sion board ▶ **n.** another term for **MESSAGE BOARD**.

dis·dain /dis'dān/ ▶ **n.** the feeling that someone or something is unworthy of one's consideration or respect; contempt: *her upper lip curled in disdain | an aristocratic **disdain for** manual labor.*
▶ **v.** [with obj.] consider to be unworthy of one's consideration: *gamblers disdain four-horse races.* ■ refuse or reject (something) out of feelings of pride or superiority: *she remained standing, pointedly disdaining his invitation to sit down* | [with infinitive] *he disdained to discuss the matter further.*
– ORIGIN Middle English: from Old French *desdeign* (noun), *desdeignier* (verb), based on Latin *dedignari*, from *de-* (expressing reversal) + *dignari* 'consider worthy' (from *dignus* 'worthy').

dis·dain·ful /dis'dānfəl/ ▶ **adj.** showing contempt or lack of respect: *with a last disdainful look, she turned toward the door.*
– DERIVATIVES **dis·dain·ful·ly adv.**, **dis·dain·ful·ness n.**

dis·ease /di'zēz/ ▶ **n.** a disorder of structure or function in a human, animal, or plant, esp. one that produces specific signs or symptoms or that affects a specific location and is not simply a direct result of physical injury: *bacterial meningitis is a rare disease | a possible cause of heart disease.* ■ a particular quality, habit, or disposition regarded as adversely affecting a person or group of people: *departmental administration has often led to the dread disease of departmentalitis.*
– ORIGIN Middle English (in the sense 'lack of ease; inconvenience'): from Old French *desaise* 'lack of ease,' from *des-* (expressing reversal) + *aise* 'ease.'

dis·eased /di'zēzd/ ▶ **adj.** suffering from disease: *all the diseased cattle have been removed.* ■ abnormal and corrupt: *I cannot bear your diseased view of mankind.*

di·sease man·age·ment ▶ **n.** a system that seeks to manage the chronic conditions of high-risk, high-cost patients as a group.

dis·e·con·o·my /,disi'känəmē/ ▶ **n.** (pl. **diseconomies**) an economic disadvantage such as an increase in cost arising from an increase in the size of an organization: *in an ideal world, these **diseconomies of scale** would be minimized.*

dis·em·bark /,disem'bärk/ ▶ **v.** [no obj.] leave a ship, aircraft, or other vehicle: *the passengers began to disembark.*
– DERIVATIVES **dis·em·bar·ka·tion** /dis,embär'kāSHən/ **n.**
– ORIGIN late 16th cent.: from French *désembarquer*, Spanish *desembarcar*, or Italian *disimbarcare*, based on Latin *barca* 'ship's boat.'

dis·em·bar·rass /,disem'barəs/ ▶ **v.** (**disembarrass oneself of/from**) free oneself of (a burden or nuisance): *he would do well to disembarrass himself of his too officious advisers.* ■ [with obj.] rare make (someone or something) free from embarrassment.
– DERIVATIVES **dis·em·bar·rass·ment n.**

dis·em·bod·ied /,disem'bädēd/ ▶ **adj.** separated from or existing without the body: *a disembodied ghost.* ■ (of a sound) lacking any obvious physical source: *a disembodied voice at the end of the phone.*

dis·em·bod·y /,disem'bädē/ ▶ **v.** (**disembodies, disembodying, disembodied**) [with obj.] separate or free (something) from its concrete form.
– DERIVATIVES **dis·em·bod·i·ment n.**

dis·em·bogue /,disem'bōg/ ▶ **v.** (**disembogues, disemboguing, disembogued**) [no obj.] literary (of a river or stream) emerge or be discharged in quantity; pour out.
– ORIGIN late 16th cent.: from Spanish *desembocar*, from *des-* (expressing reversal) + *embocar* 'run into a creek or strait' (based on *boca* 'mouth').

dis·em·bow·el /,disem'bouəl/ ▶ **v.** (**disembowels, disemboweling, disemboweled**; Brit. **disembowels, disembowelling, disembowelled**) [with obj.] cut open and remove the internal organs of.
– DERIVATIVES **dis·em·bow·el·ment n.**

dis·em·broil /,disem'broil/ ▶ **v.** [with obj.] archaic free (someone or something) from confusion: *to disembroil a subject that seems to have perplexed even Antiquity.*

dis·em·pow·er /,disem'pouər/ ▶ **v.** [with obj.] make (a person or group) less powerful or confident: *leaving the decision in a government agent's hands disempowers and disrespects women.*
– DERIVATIVES **dis·em·pow·er·ment n.**

dis·en·chant /,disen'CHant/ ▶ **v.** [with obj.] free (someone) from illusion; disappoint: *he may have been disenchanted by the loss of his huge following.*
– DERIVATIVES **dis·en·chant·ing·ly adv.**
– ORIGIN late 16th cent.: from French *désenchanter*, from *dés-* (expressing reversal) + *enchanter* (see **ENCHANT**).

dis·en·chant·ed /,disen'CHantid/ ▶ **adj.** disappointed by someone or something previously respected or admired; disillusioned: *he became **disenchanted with** his erstwhile ally | there are a lot of disenchanted music fans out there.*

dis·en·chant·ment /,disen'CHantmənt/ ▶ **n.** a feeling of disappointment about someone or something you previously respected or admired; disillusionment: *growing **disenchantment with** the leadership.*

dis·en·cum·ber /,disen'kəmbər/ ▶ **v.** [with obj.] free from or relieve of an encumbrance: *it would disencumber the world of a plague.*

dis·en·dow /,disen'dou/ ▶ **v.** [with obj.] deprive (someone or something) of an endowment.
– DERIVATIVES **dis·en·dow·ment n.**

dis·en·fran·chise /,disen'franCHīz/ (also **disfranchise** /dis'franCHīz/) ▶ **v.** [with obj.] deprive (someone) of the right to vote: *the law disenfranchised some 3,000 voters on the basis of a residence qualification.* ■ (as adj. **disenfranchised**) deprived of power; marginalized: *a hard core of kids who are disenfranchised and don't feel connected to the school.* ■ deprive (someone) of a right or privilege: *a measure that would disenfranchise people from access to legal advice.* ■ archaic deprive (someone) of the rights and privileges of a free inhabitant of a borough, city, or country.
– DERIVATIVES **dis·en·fran·chise·ment n.**

dis·en·gage /,disen'gāj/ ▶ **v. 1** [with obj.] separate or release (someone or something) from something to which they are attached or connected: *I **disengaged** his hand **from** mine | they clung together for a moment, then she **disengaged herself**.* ■ [no obj.] become released: *the clutch will not disengage.* ■ remove (troops) from an area of conflict: *the ceasefire gave the commanders a chance to disengage their forces* | [no obj.] *his true intent is to disengage **from** the messy conflict.* **2** [no obj.] Fencing pass the point of one's sword over or under the opponent's sword to change the line of attack.

dis·en·gaged /,disen'gājd/ ▶ **adj.** emotionally detached: *the students were oddly disengaged, as if they didn't believe they could control their lives.*

dis·en·gage·ment /,disen'gājmənt/ ▶ **n. 1** the action or process of withdrawing from involvement in a particular activity, situation, or group: *their steady **disengagement from** politics and politicians.* ■ the withdrawal of military forces or the renunciation of military or political influence in a particular area. ■ the process of separating or releasing something or of becoming separated or released: *the mechanism prevents accidental disengagement.* ■ archaic the breaking off of an engagement to be married. **2** emotional detachment; objectivity: *contemporary criticism can afford neutral disengagement.*

dis·en·tail·ment /,disen'tālmənt/ ▶ **n.** Law the action of freeing property from entail: *the disentailment of the church's landed property.*
– DERIVATIVES **dis·en·tail v.**

dis·en·tan·gle /,disen'taNGgəl/ ▶ **v.** [with obj.] free (something or someone) from an entanglement; extricate: *"I must go," she said, **disentangling** her fingers **from** Gabriel's* | figurative *it was often difficult*

to disentangle fact from fiction. ■ remove knots or tangles from (wool, rope, or hair): *Allen was on his knees disentangling a coil of rope.*
– DERIVATIVES **dis·en·tan·gle·ment** n.

dis·en·thrall /ˌdisenˈTHrôl/ (Brit. **disenthral**) ▶ v. [with obj.] literary set free: *I disenthrall my mind from theories.*
– DERIVATIVES **dis·en·thrall·ment** n.

dis·en·ti·tle /ˌdisenˈtītl/ ▶ v. [with obj.] deprive (someone) of a right: *he was* ***disentitled to*** *gain damages for the injuries.*
– DERIVATIVES **dis·en·ti·tle·ment** n.

dis·en·tomb /ˌdisenˈto͞om/ ▶ v. [with obj.] remove (something) from a tomb: *a mummy that we saw disentombed.*
– DERIVATIVES **dis·en·tomb·ment** n.

dis·e·qui·lib·ri·um /disˌēkwəˈlibrēəm/ ▶ n. a loss or lack of equilibrium or stability, esp. in relation to supply, demand, and prices.

dis·es·tab·lish /ˌdisiˈstablisH/ ▶ v. [with obj.] (usu. **be disestablished**) deprive (an organization, esp. a country's national church) of its official status.
– DERIVATIVES **dis·es·tab·lish·ment** n.

dis·es·teem /ˌdisiˈstēm/ dated ▶ n. low esteem or regard: *language is not insulting unless it is intended to show contempt or disesteem.*
▶ v. [with obj.] have a low opinion of.

di·seuse /dēˈzo͞oz/ ▶ n. a female entertainer who performs monologues.
– ORIGIN late 19th cent.: French, literally 'talker,' feminine of *diseur*, from *dire* 'to say.'

dis·fa·vor /disˈfāvər/ (Brit. **disfavour**) ▶ n. disapproval or dislike: *the headmaster regarded her with disfavor.* ■ the state of being disliked: *raises could be taken away if an employee* ***fell into disfavor.***
▶ v. [with obj.] regard or treat (someone or something) with disfavor: *the hypothesis was favored and disfavored by approximately equal numbers of scientists.*

dis·fel·low·ship /disˈfelōˌsHip/ ▶ n. exclusion from fellowship, esp. as a form of discipline in some Protestant and Mormon churches.
▶ v. (**disfellowships, disfellowshiping, disfellowshiped**; Brit. **disfellowships, disfellowshipping, disfellowshipped**) [with obj.] exclude (someone) from fellowship.

dis·fig·ure /disˈfigyər/ ▶ v. [with obj.] spoil the attractiveness of: *litter disfigures the countryside* | (as adj. **disfiguring**) *a disfiguring birthmark.*
– DERIVATIVES **dis·fig·u·ra·tion** /-ˌfigyəˈrāsHən/ n.
– ORIGIN late Middle English: from Old French *desfigurer*, based on Latin *figura* 'figure.'

dis·fig·ure·ment /disˈfigyərmənt/ ▶ n. the action of spoiling the appearance of something or someone; defacement: *the* ***disfigurement of*** *this very pleasant area.* ■ something that spoils the appearance of someone or something; a blemish: *a severe facial disfigurement.*

dis·fran·chise /disˈfranCHīz/ ▶ v. another term for DISENFRANCHISE.

dis·gorge /disˈgôrj/ ▶ v. [with obj.] **1** cause to pour out: *the combine disgorged a steady stream of grain.* ■ (of a building or vehicle) discharge (the occupants): *an aircraft disgorging paratroopers.* ■ yield or give up (funds, esp. funds that have been dishonestly acquired): *they were made to disgorge all the profits made from the record.* ■ eject (food) from the throat or mouth. ■ [no obj.] (of a river) empty into a sea: *the Nile disgorges into the sea at Rashid.* **2** (usu. **be disgorged**) remove the sediment from (a sparkling wine) after fermentation: *the wine is aged in the bottle before it is disgorged.*
– DERIVATIVES **dis·gorge·ment** n.
– ORIGIN late 15th cent.: from Old French *desgorger*, from *des-* (expressing removal) + *gorge* 'throat.'

dis·gorg·er /disˈgôrjər/ ▶ n. Fishing a device for extracting a hook from a fish's throat.

dis·grace /disˈgrās/ ▶ n. loss of reputation or respect, esp. as the result of a dishonorable action: *he left the army* ***in disgrace*** | *if he'd gone back, it would have brought disgrace on the family.* ■ [in sing.] a person or thing regarded as shameful and unacceptable: *he's* ***a disgrace to*** *the legal profession.*
▶ v. [with obj.] bring shame or discredit on (someone or something): *you have disgraced the family name* | *John stiffened his jaw so he wouldn't disgrace himself by crying.* ■ (**be disgraced**) fall from favor or lose a position of power or honor: *he has been publicly disgraced for offenses of which he was not guilty.*
– ORIGIN mid 16th cent. (as a verb): via French from Italian *disgrazia* (noun), *disgraziare* (verb), from *dis-* (expressing reversal) + Latin *gratia* 'grace.'

dis·graced /disˈgrāst/ ▶ adj. having fallen from favor or a position of power or honor; discredited: *the disgraced Wall Street financier.*

dis·grace·ful /disˈgrāsfəl/ ▶ adj. shockingly unacceptable: *a disgraceful waste of money* | [with clause] *it is disgraceful that they should be denied unemployment benefits.*
– DERIVATIVES **dis·grace·ful·ly** adv.

dis·grun·tled /disˈgrəntld/ ▶ adj. angry or dissatisfied: *judges receive letters from disgruntled members of the public.*
– DERIVATIVES **dis·grun·tle·ment** n.
– ORIGIN mid 17th cent.: from DIS- (as an intensifier) + dialect *gruntle* 'utter little grunts,' from GRUNT.

dis·guise /disˈgīz/ ▶ v. [with obj.] give (someone or oneself) a different appearance in order to conceal one's identity: *he* ***disguised himself as*** *a girl* | *Brian was disguised as a priest.* ■ make (something) unrecognizable by altering its appearance, sound, taste, or smell: *does holding a handkerchief over the mouthpiece really disguise your voice?* ■ conceal the nature or existence of (a feeling or situation): *he made no effort to disguise his contempt.*
▶ n. a means of altering one's appearance or concealing one's identity: *his bizarre disguise drew stares from fellow shoppers.* ■ the state of having altered one's appearance in order to conceal one's identity: *I told them you were a policewoman* ***in disguise.*** ■ the concealing of one's true intentions or feelings: *rows of small children looked at her without disguise.*
– DERIVATIVES **dis·guise·ment** n. (archaic).
– ORIGIN Middle English (meaning 'change one's usual style of dress,' with no implication of concealing one's identity): from Old French *desguisier.*

dis·gust /disˈgəst/ ▶ n. a feeling of revulsion or profound disapproval aroused by something unpleasant or offensive: *the sight filled her with disgust* | *some of the audience walked out* ***in disgust.***
▶ v. [with obj.] cause (someone) to feel revulsion or profound disapproval: *I was disgusted with myself for causing so much misery* | (as adj. **disgusted**) *a disgusted look.*
– DERIVATIVES **dis·gust·ed·ly** adv.
– ORIGIN late 16th cent.: from early modern French *desgoust* or Italian *disgusto*, from Latin *dis-* (expressing reversal) + *gustus* 'taste.'

dis·gust·ful /disˈgəstfəl/ ▶ adj. old-fashioned term for DISGUSTING.

dis·gust·ing /disˈgəstiNG/ ▶ adj. arousing revulsion or strong indignation: *he had the most disgusting rotten teeth* | *I think the decision is disgusting.*
– DERIVATIVES **dis·gust·ing·ly** adv., **dis·gust·ing·ness** n.

dish /disH/ ▶ n. **1** a shallow, typically flat-bottomed container for cooking or serving food: *an ovenproof dish.* ■ the food contained or served in such a container: ***a dish of*** *oysters.* ■ a particular variety or preparation of food served as part of a meal: *fresh fish dishes* | *pasta was served as a* ***main dish.*** ■ (**the dishes**) all the items that have been used in the preparation, serving, and eating of a meal: *it was our turn to wash the dishes.* ■ [usu. with modifier] a shallow, concave receptacle, esp. one intended to hold a particular substance: *a soap dish.* ■ (also **dish aerial**) a bowl-shaped radio antenna. See also SATELLITE DISH.
2 informal a sexually attractive person: *I gather she's quite a dish.* ■ (**one's dish**) dated a thing that one particularly enjoys or does well: *as a public relations man this was my dish and the campaign was right up my street.*
3 (**the dish**) informal information that is not generally known or available: *if he has the real dish I wish he'd tell us.*
4 concavity of a spoked wheel resulting from a difference in spoke tension on each side and consequent sideways displacement of the rim in relation to the hub.
▶ v. [with obj.] **1** (**dish something out/up**) put (food) onto a plate or plates before a meal: *Steve was dishing up vegetables.* ■ (**dish something out**) dispense something in a casual or indiscriminate way: *the banks dished out loans to all and sundry.* ■ (**dish something up**) offer or present something, esp. something regarded as substandard: *is your ISP short-changing you by dishing up outdated and perhaps incorrect information?* ■ (**dish it out**) informal subject others to criticism or punishment: *you can dish it out but you can't take it.* ■ [no obj.] informal gossip or share information, esp. information of an intimate or scandalous nature: *groups gather to brag about babies and dish about romances.*
2 informal, chiefly Brit. utterly destroy, confound, or defeat (someone or something).
3 give concavity to (a wheel) by tensioning the spokes. See sense 4 of the noun.
– PHRASES **dish the dirt** informal reveal or spread scandalous information or gossip.
– PHRASAL VERBS **dish something off** pass the ball to a teammate, esp. in basketball.
– DERIVATIVES **dish·ful** /-ˌfo͝ol/ n. (pl. **dishfuls**).
– ORIGIN Old English *disc* 'plate, bowl' (related to Dutch *dis*, German *Tisch* 'table'), based on Latin *discus* (see DISCUS).

dis·ha·bille /ˌdisəˈbēl/ (also **deshabille**) ▶ n. the state of being only partly or scantily clothed: *the relaxed dishabille of Lely's portraits.*
– ORIGIN late 17th cent.: from French *déshabillé*, 'undressed.'

dish an·ten·na ▶ n. a receiver or transmitter of electromagnetic energy, esp. microwaves or radio waves, that consists of a reflector shaped like a shallow dish.

dis·har·mo·ny /disˈhärmənē/ ▶ n. lack of harmony or agreement.
– DERIVATIVES **dis·har·mo·ni·ous** /-ˌhärˈmōnēəs/ adj., **dis·har·mo·ni·ous·ly** /-ˌhärˈmōnēəslē/ adv.

dish·cloth /ˈdisHˌklôTH/ ▶ n. a cloth for washing or drying dishes.

dish·cloth gourd ▶ n. another term for LOOFAH.

dis·heart·en /disˈhärtn/ ▶ v. [with obj.] cause (someone) to lose determination or confidence: *the farmer was disheartened by the damage to his crops.*
– DERIVATIVES **dis·heart·en·ing·ly** adv., **dis·heart·en·ment** n.

dished /disHt/ ▶ adj. having the shape of a dish; concave: *overloaded timber floors are likely to sag, producing a dished or sloping floor surface.*

di·shev·eled /diˈsHevəld/ (Brit. **dishevelled**) ▶ adj. (of a person's hair, clothes, or appearance) untidy; disordered: *a man with long, disheveled hair.*
– DERIVATIVES **di·shev·el** /-ˈsHevəl/ v., **di·shev·el·ment** n.
– ORIGIN late Middle English: from obsolete *dishevely*, from Old French *deschevele*, past participle of *descheveler* (based on *chevel* 'hair,' from Latin *capillus*). The original sense was 'having the hair uncovered'; later, referring to the hair itself, 'hanging loose,' hence 'disordered, untidy' Compare with UNKEMPT.

dis·hon·est /disˈänist/ ▶ adj. behaving or prone to behave in an untrustworthy or fraudulent way: *he was a dishonest hypocrite prepared to exploit his family.* ■ intended to mislead or cheat: *he gave the editor a dishonest account of events.*
– DERIVATIVES **dis·hon·est·ly** adv.
– ORIGIN late Middle English (in the sense 'dishonorable, unchaste'): from Old French *deshoneste*, Latin *dehonestus.*

dis·hon·es·ty /disˈänəstē/ ▶ n. (pl. **dishonesties**) deceitfulness shown in someone's character or behavior: *the dismissal of thirty civil servants for dishonesty and misconduct.* ■ a fraudulent or deceitful act.
– ORIGIN late Middle English (in the sense 'dishonor, sexual misconduct'): from Old French *deshoneste* 'indecency' (see DISHONEST).

dis·hon·or /disˈänər/ (Brit. **dishonour**) ▶ n. a state of shame or disgrace: *the incident brought dishonor upon the police.*
▶ v. [with obj.] **1** bring shame or disgrace on: *the mayor dishonors his good battle by resorting to sniping.* ■ archaic violate the chastity of (a woman); rape. **2** fail to observe or respect (an agreement or principle): *the community has its own principles it can itself honor or dishonor.* ■ refuse to accept or pay (a check or a promissory note).
– ORIGIN Middle English: from Old French *deshonor* (noun), *deshonorer* (verb), based on Latin *honor* 'honor.'

dis·hon·or·a·ble /disˈänərəbəl/ (Brit. **dishonourable**) ▶ adj. bringing shame or disgrace on someone or something: *his crimes are petty and dishonorable.*
– DERIVATIVES **dis·hon·or·a·ble·ness** n., **dis·hon·or·a·bly** /-blē/ adv.

dis·hon·or·a·ble dis·charge ▶ n. the dismissal of someone from the armed forces as a result of criminal or morally unacceptable actions.

dish·pan /ˈdisHˌpan/ ▶ n. a large basin in which dishes are washed.

dish·pan hands ▶ plural n. red, rough, or chapped hands caused by sensitivity to or excessive use of household detergents or other cleaning agents.

dish·rag /ˈdisHˌrag/ ▶ n. a dishcloth.

dish tow·el ▶ n. a cloth for drying washed dishes, utensils, and glasses.

dish·wash·er /ˈdisHˌwôsHər, -ˌwäsH-/ ▶ n. **1** a machine for washing dishes automatically. **2** a person employed to wash dishes.

dish·wa·ter /ˈdisHˌwôtər, -ˌwätər/ ▶ n. dirty water in which dishes have been washed: *as for the coffee, dishwater would probably have tasted better.*
– PHRASES **dull as dishwater** see DULL.

dish·y /ˈdishē/ ▶ **adj.** (**dishier, dishiest**) informal sexually attractive. ■ scandalous or gossipy: *she's the perfect candidate for a dishy biography.*

dis·il·lu·sion /ˌdisəˈlo͞ozhən/ ▶ **n.** disappointment resulting from the discovery that something is not as good as one believed it to be: *enthusiasm for the government evaporated into a more cynical disillusion.*
▶ **v.** [with obj.] cause (someone) to realize that a belief or an ideal is false: *if they think we have a magic formula to solve the problem, don't disillusion them.*

dis·il·lu·sioned /ˌdisəˈlo͞ozhənd/ ▶ **adj.** disappointed in someone or something that one discovers to be less good than one had believed: *the minority groups were completely* ***disillusioned with*** *the party.*

dis·il·lu·sion·ment /ˌdisəˈlo͞ozhənmənt/ ▶ **n.** a feeling of disappointment resulting from the discovery that something is not as good as one believed it to be: *the high abstention rate at the election reflected the voters' growing* ***disillusionment with*** *politics.*

dis·in·car·nate /ˌdisinˈkärnit, -nāt/ ▶ **adj.** another term for DISCARNATE.

dis·in·cen·tive /ˌdisinˈsentiv/ ▶ **n.** a factor, esp. a financial disadvantage, that tends to discourage people from doing something: *spiraling house prices are beginning to act as a disincentive to development.*

dis·in·cen·tiv·ize /ˌdisinˈsentivīz/ ▶ **v.** [with obj.] discourage (a person or course of action) by removing an incentive: *would such legislation disincentivize marriage?*

dis·in·cli·na·tion /disˌinkləˈnāshən, disˌiNGklə-/ ▶ **n.** [in sing.] a reluctance or lack of enthusiasm: *Lucy felt a strong* ***disinclination to*** *talk about her engagement.*

dis·in·clined /ˌdisinˈklīnd/ ▶ **adj.** [predic., with infinitive] unwilling; reluctant: *the rural community was disinclined to abandon the old ways.*

dis·in·cor·po·rate /ˌdisinˈkôrpəˌrāt/ ▶ **v.** [with obj.] dissolve (a corporate body).

dis·in·fect /ˌdisinˈfekt/ ▶ **v.** [with obj.] clean (something) with a disinfectant in order to destroy bacteria: *he disinfected and dressed the cut on his forehead.*
– DERIVATIVES **dis·in·fec·tion** /-ˈfekshən/ **n.**
– ORIGIN late 16th cent. (in the sense 'rid of infection'): from French *désinfecter*, from *dés-* (expressing reversal) + *infecter* 'to infect.'

dis·in·fect·ant /ˌdisinˈfektənt/ ▶ **n.** a chemical liquid that destroys bacteria.
▶ **adj.** causing the destruction of bacteria: *cleansing and disinfectant products.*

dis·in·fest /ˌdisinˈfest/ ▶ **v.** [with obj.] rid (someone or something) of infesting vermin.
– DERIVATIVES **dis·in·fes·ta·tion** /-ˌinfeˈstāshən/ **n.**

dis·in·fla·tion /ˌdisinˈflāshən/ ▶ **n.** reduction in the rate of inflation.
– DERIVATIVES **dis·in·fla·tion·ar·y** /-ˌnerē/ **adj.**

dis·in·for·ma·tion /disˌinfərˈmāshən/ ▶ **n.** false information that is intended to mislead, esp. propaganda issued by a government organization to a rival power or the media.
– ORIGIN 1950s: formed on the pattern of Russian *dezinformatsiya.*

dis·in·gen·u·ous /ˌdisinˈjenyo͞oəs/ ▶ **adj.** not candid or sincere, typically by pretending that one knows less about something than one really does.
– DERIVATIVES **dis·in·gen·u·ous·ly adv.**, **dis·in·gen·u·ous·ness n.**

dis·in·her·it /ˌdisinˈherit/ ▶ **v.** (**disinherits, disinheriting, disinherited**) [with obj.] change one's will or take other steps to prevent (someone) from inheriting one's property.
– DERIVATIVES **dis·in·her·i·tance** /-ˈheritəns/ **n.**
– ORIGIN late Middle English (superseding earlier *disherit*): from DIS- (expressing removal) + *inherit* in the obsolete sense 'make someone an heir.'

dis·in·hib·it /ˌdisinˈhibit/ ▶ **v.** (**disinhibits, disinhibiting, disinhibited**) [with obj.] make (someone or something) less inhibited: *as well as disinhibiting me, he educated me.*
– DERIVATIVES **dis·in·hi·bi·tion** /disˌinhiˈbishən/ **n.**

dis·in·te·grate /disˈintəˌgrāt/ ▶ **v.** [no obj.] break up into small parts, typically as the result of impact or decay: *when the missile struck, the car disintegrated in a sheet of searing flame.* ■ (of a society, family, or other social group) weaken or break apart: *the marriage disintegrated amid allegations that she was having an affair.* ■ Physics undergo or cause to undergo disintegration at a subatomic level: [no obj.] *a meson can spontaneously disintegrate* | [with obj.] *it has become a relatively easy matter to disintegrate almost any atom.*
– DERIVATIVES **dis·in·te·gra·tive** /-ˌgrātiv/ **adj.**, **dis·in·te·gra·tor** /-ˌgrātər/ **n.**

dis·in·te·gra·tion /disˌintəˈgrāshən/ ▶ **n.** the process of losing cohesion or strength: *the twin problems of economic failure and social disintegration.* ■ the process of coming to pieces: *the disintegration of infected cells.* ■ Physics a process in which a nucleus or other subatomic particle emits a smaller particle or divides into smaller particles.

dis·in·ter /ˌdisinˈtər/ ▶ **v.** (**disinters, disinterring, disinterred**) [with obj.] dig up (something that has been buried, esp. a corpse). ■ discover (something that is well hidden): *he has disinterred and translated an important collection of writings.*
– DERIVATIVES **dis·in·ter·ment n.**
– ORIGIN early 17th cent.: from French *désenterrer*, from *dis-* (expressing reversal) + *enterrer* 'to inter.'

dis·in·ter·est /disˈint(ə)rist/ ▶ **n. 1** the state of not being influenced by personal involvement in something; impartiality: *I do not claim any scholarly disinterest with this book.*
2 lack of interest in something: *he chided Dennis for his* ***disinterest in*** *anything that is not his own idea.*

dis·in·ter·est·ed /disˈintəˌrestid, -tristid/ ▶ **adj.**
1 not influenced by considerations of personal advantage: *a banker is under an obligation to give disinterested advice.*
2 having or feeling no interest in something: *her father was so disinterested in her progress that he only visited the school once.*
– DERIVATIVES **dis·in·ter·est·ed·ly adv.**, **dis·in·ter·est·ed·ness n.**
– ORIGIN early 17th cent.: past participle of the rare verb *disinterest* 'rid of interest or concern,' from DIS- (expressing removal) + the verb INTEREST.

> **USAGE** One of the most contended questions of usage is the difference between **disinterested** and **uninterested**. According to traditional guidelines, **disinterested** should never be used to mean 'not interested' (i.e., it is not a synonym for **uninterested**) but only to mean 'impartial,' as in *the judgments of* ***disinterested*** *outsiders are likely to be more useful.* Ironically, the earliest recorded sense of **disinterested** is for the disputed sense. Today, the 'incorrect' use of **disinterested** is widespread: around a quarter of citations in the Oxford English Corpus for **disinterested** are for this sense.

dis·in·ter·me·di·a·tion /ˌdisintərˌmēdēˈāshən/ ▶ **n.** reduction in the use of intermediaries between producers and consumers, for example by investing directly in the securities market rather than through a bank.

dis·in·vent /ˌdisinˈvent/ ▶ **v.** [with obj.] undo the invention of (something): *you can't disinvent nuclear power.*

dis·in·vest /ˌdisinˈvest/ ▶ **v.** [no obj.] withdraw or reduce an investment: *the oil industry began to disinvest, and oil share prices have fallen* | [with obj.] *they opposed the move to disinvest shares.*
– DERIVATIVES **dis·in·vest·ment n.**

dis·in·vite /ˌdisinˈvīt/ ▶ **v.** [with obj.] withdraw or cancel an invitation to (someone): *the White House called to disinvite him from the president's party.*

dis·in·vol·tu·ra /disˌinvälˈtyo͝orə, -vôl-/ ▶ **n.** self-assurance; lack of constraint.
– ORIGIN mid 19th cent.: from Italian, from *disinvolto* 'unembarrassed,' from *disinvolgere* 'unwind.'

dis·jec·ta mem·bra /disˈjektə ˈmembrə/ ▶ **plural n.** scattered fragments, esp. of written work.
– ORIGIN Latin, alteration of *disjecti membra poetae* (used by Horace) 'limbs of a dismembered poet.'

dis·join /disˈjoin/ ▶ **v.** separate; take or come apart: [no obj.] *the paired chromosomes fail to separate or disjoin during cell division.*
– ORIGIN late Middle English: from Old French *desjoindre*, from Latin *disjungere*, from *dis-* (expressing reversal) + *jungere* 'to join.'

dis·joint /disˈjoint/ ▶ **v.** [with obj.] disturb the cohesion or organization of: *the loss of the area disjointed military plans.* ■ dated take apart at the joints: *disjoint a four-pound chicken, put in a pot, and simmer until tender.*
▶ **adj.** Mathematics (of two or more sets) having no elements in common.
– ORIGIN late Middle English (as an adjective in the sense 'disjointed'): from Old French *desjoint* 'separated,' from the verb *desjoindre* (see DISJOIN).

dis·joint·ed /disˈjointid/ ▶ **adj.** lacking a coherent sequence or connection: *piecing together disjointed fragments of information.*
– DERIVATIVES **dis·joint·ed·ly adv.**, **dis·joint·ed·ness n.**

dis·junct ▶ **adj.** /disˈjəNGkt/ disjoined and distinct from one another: *these items of evidence are just phrases and clauses, often wildly disjunct.* ■ of or relating to the movement of a melody from one note to another by a leap.
▶ **n.** /ˈdisˌjəNGkt/ **1** Logic each of the terms of a disjunctive proposition.
2 Grammar another term for SENTENCE ADVERB.
– ORIGIN late Middle English: from Latin *disjunctus* 'disjoined, separated,' from the verb *disjungere*.

dis·junc·tion /disˈjəNGkshən/ ▶ **n. 1** a lack of correspondence or consistency: *there is a disjunction between the skills taught in education and those demanded in the labor market.*
2 Logic the relationship between two distinct alternatives. ■ a statement expressing this relationship (esp. one using the word "or").
– ORIGIN late Middle English: from Latin *disjunctio(n-)*, from *disjungere* 'disjoin' (see DISJUNCT).

dis·junc·tive /disˈjəNGktiv/ ▶ **adj. 1** lacking connection: *the novel's disjunctive detail.*
2 Grammar (of a conjunction) expressing a choice between two mutually exclusive possibilities, for example *or* in *she asked if he was going or staying.* Compare with COPULATIVE. ■ Logic (of a proposition) expressing alternatives.
▶ **n.** Grammar a disjunctive conjunction or other word. ■ Logic a disjunctive proposition.
– DERIVATIVES **dis·junc·tive·ly adv.**
– ORIGIN late Middle English (sense 2 of the adjective): from Latin *disjunctivus*, from *disjunct-* 'disjoined' (see DISJUNCT).

dis·junc·ture /disˈjəNGkCHər/ ▶ **n.** a separation or disconnection: *the monstrous disjuncture between his private and his public life.*
– ORIGIN late Middle English: from medieval Latin *disjunctura*, from Latin *disjunct-* 'disjoined' (see DISJUNCT).

disk /disk/ (also **disc**) ▶ **n. 1** a flat, thin, round object: *heavy metal disks the size of hockey pucks* | *onion soup ladled over a disk of cheese.* ■ an information storage device for a computer in the shape of a round flat plate that can be rotated to give access to all parts of the surface. The data may be stored either magnetically (in a **magnetic disk**) or optically (in an **optical disk** such as a CD-ROM). ■ (**disc**) a CD or record. ■ (**discs**) one of the suits in some tarot packs, corresponding to coins in others.
2 a shape or surface that is round and flat in appearance: *the smudged yellow disk of the moon.*
3 a roundish, flattened part in an animal or plant, in particular: ■ (**disc** or **intervertebral disc**) a layer of cartilage separating adjacent vertebrae in the spine: *he suffered a prolapsed disc.* ■ Botany (in a composite flower head of the daisy family) a close-packed cluster of disk florets in the center, forming the yellow part of the flower head.
▶ **v.** [with obj.] cultivate (a field) with a disk harrow.
– DERIVATIVES **disk·less adj.**
– ORIGIN mid 17th cent. (originally referring to the seemingly flat round form of the sun or moon): from French *disque* or Latin *discus* (see DISCUS).

> **USAGE** Generally speaking, the US spelling is **disk** and the British spelling is **disc**, although there is much overlap and variation between the two. In particular, the spelling for senses relating to computers is nearly always **disk**, as in **floppy disk**, **disk drive**, etc., but **disc** is the norm for **compact disc, disc brakes,** and **disc camera.**

disk drive ▶ **n.** a device that allows a computer to read from and write to computer disks.

disk·ette /disˈket/ ▶ **n.** another term for FLOPPY DISK.

disk flo·ret ▶ **n.** Botany (in a composite flower head of the daisy family) any of a number of small, tubular and usually fertile florets that form the disk. In rayless plants such as the tansy, the flower head is composed entirely of disk florets. Compare with RAY FLORET.

disk har·row ▶ **n.** a harrow with cutting edges consisting of a row of concave disks set at an oblique angle.

disk jock·ey ▶ **n.** variant spelling of DISC JOCKEY.

Dis·ko /ˈdiskō/ an island with extensive coal deposits on the western coast of Greenland. Its chief settlement is Godhavn.

disk op·er·at·ing sys·tem ▶ **n.** see **DOS.**

disk wheel ▶ **n.** a wheel, esp. a bicycle wheel, with a central disk in place of spokes.

dis·like /disˈlīk/ ▶ **v.** [with obj.] feel distaste for or hostility toward: *he was not distressed by the death of a man he had always disliked.*
▶ **n.** a feeling of distaste or hostility: *despite her dislike of publicity, she was quite a celebrated figure* | *they had* ***taken a dislike to*** *each other.* ■ a thing to which one feels aversion: *I know all his likes and dislikes.*
– DERIVATIVES **dis·like·a·ble** (also **dislikable**) **adj.**

d

dis·lo·cate /dis'lōkāt, 'dislō,kāt/ ▶ **v.** [with obj.] disturb the normal arrangement or position of (something, typically a joint in the body): *he dislocated his shoulder in training.* ■ disturb the organization of; disrupt: *trade was dislocated by a famine.* ■ move from its proper place or position: *the symbol is dislocated from its political context.*
– ORIGIN late 16th cent.: probably a back-formation from DISLOCATION, but perhaps from medieval Latin *dislocatus* 'moved from a former position,' from the verb *dislocare.*

d

dis·lo·ca·tion /,dislō'kāsHən/ ▶ **n.** disturbance from a proper, original, or usual place or state: *he fell prey to loneliness and a wrenching sense of dislocation | the social dislocations caused by government policies.* ■ injury or disability caused when the normal position of a joint or other part of the body is disturbed: *congenital dislocation of the hip | dealing with fractures and dislocations.* ■ Crystallography a displacement of part of a crystal lattice structure.
– ORIGIN late Middle English: from Old French, or from medieval Latin *dislocatio(n-)*, from the verb *dislocare* (see DISLOCATE), based on Latin *locare* 'to place.'

dis·lodge /dis'läj/ ▶ **v.** [with obj.] knock or force out of position: *the hoofs of their horses dislodged loose stones.* ■ remove from a position of power or authority: *government opponents failed to dislodge the prime minister.*
– DERIVATIVES **dis·lodge·a·ble** adj., **dis·lodg·ment** (also **dislodgement**) n.
– ORIGIN late Middle English: from Old French *deslogier*, from *des-* (expressing reversal) + *logier* 'encamp,' from *loge* (see LODGE).

dis·loy·al /dis'loiəl/ ▶ **adj.** failing to be loyal to a person, country, or body to which one has obligations: *she felt that inquiring into her father's past would be* **disloyal to** *her mother.* ■ (of an action, speech, or thought) demonstrating a lack of loyalty: *disloyal mutterings about his leadership.*
– DERIVATIVES **dis·loy·al·ly** adv.
– ORIGIN late 15th cent.: from Old French *desloial*, from *des-* (expressing negation) + *loial* 'loyal.'

dis·loy·al·ty /dis'loiəltē/ ▶ **n.** the quality of not being loyal to a person, country, or organization; unfaithfulness: *an accusation of disloyalty and betrayal.*

dis·mal /'dizməl/ ▶ **adj.** depressing; dreary: *the dismal weather made the late afternoon seem like evening.* ■ (of a person or a mood) gloomy: *his dismal mood was not dispelled by finding the house empty.* ■ informal pitifully or disgracefully bad: *he shuddered as he watched his team's dismal performance.*
– DERIVATIVES **dis·mal·ly** adv., **dis·mal·ness** n.
– ORIGIN late Middle English: from earlier *dismal* (noun), denoting the two days in each month that in medieval times were believed to be unlucky, from Anglo-Norman French *dis mal*, from medieval Latin *dies mali* 'evil days.'

dis·mal sci·ence ▶ **n.** [in sing.] (usu. **the dismal science**) humorous economics.

Dis·mal Swamp another name for GREAT DISMAL SWAMP.

dis·man·tle /dis'mantl/ ▶ **v.** [with obj.] take (a machine or structure) to pieces: *the engines were dismantled and the bits piled into a heap* | figurative *the old regime was dismantled.*
– DERIVATIVES **dis·man·tle·ment** n., **dis·man·tler** /-t(ə)lər/ n.
– ORIGIN late 16th cent. (in the sense 'destroy the defensive capability of (a fortification)'): from Old French *desmanteler*, from *des-* (expressing reversal) + *manteler* 'fortify' (from Latin *mantellum* 'cloak').

dis·mast /dis'mast/ ▶ **v.** [with obj.] break or topple the mast or masts of (a ship): (as adj. **dismasted**) *a dismasted ship wallowing in stormy seas.*

dis·may /dis'mā/ ▶ **v.** [with obj.] cause (someone) to feel consternation and distress: *they were dismayed by the U-turn in policy.*
▶ **n.** consternation and distress, typically that caused by something unexpected: ***to his dismay,*** *she left him.*
– DERIVATIVES **dis·may·ing·ly** adv.
– ORIGIN Middle English: from Old French, based on Latin *dis-* (expressing negation) + the Germanic base of MAY[1].

dis·mem·ber /dis'membər/ ▶ **v.** [with obj.] cut off the limbs of (a person or animal): *I can picture you in a white jacket dismembering rats* | (as adj. **dismembered**) *he buried their dismembered bodies in the back yard.* ■ partition or divide up (a territory or organization): *Russia intended to dismember the Ottoman Empire.*
– DERIVATIVES **dis·mem·ber·ment** n.
– ORIGIN Middle English: from Old French *desmembrer*, based on Latin *dis-* 'apart' + *membrum* 'limb.'

dis·miss /dis'mis/ ▶ **v.** [with obj.] order or allow to leave; send away: *she dismissed the taxi at the corner of the road.* ■ discharge from employment or office: *CBS Records dismissed another 120 people.* ■ treat as unworthy of serious consideration: *it would be easy to* **dismiss** *him* **as** *all brawn and no brain.* ■ deliberately cease to think about: *he suspected a double meaning in her words, but dismissed the thought.* ■ [no obj.] (of a group assembled under someone's authority) disperse: *he told his company to dismiss.* ■ Law refuse further hearing to (a case): *the judge dismissed the case for lack of evidence.*
– DERIVATIVES **dis·miss·i·ble** adj.
– ORIGIN late Middle English: from medieval Latin *dismiss-*, variant of Latin *dimiss-* 'sent away,' from the verb *dimittere.*

dis·miss·al /dis'misəl/ ▶ **n. 1** the act of ordering or allowing someone to leave: *their controversial* **dismissal from** *the competition.* ■ the act of removing someone from employment or office; discharge: *the dismissal of an employee | a claim for unfair dismissal.* ■ Cricket an instance of ending a batsman's innings or of having one's innings ended: *marring his effort was his dismissal in the next over.* **2** the act of treating something as unworthy of serious consideration; rejection: *the government's dismissal of the report.* ■ Law a decision not to continue hearing a case: *the dismissal of the appeal.*

dis·mis·sive /dis'misiv/ ▶ **adj.** feeling or showing that something is unworthy of consideration: *he is too dismissive of the importance of the industrialists.*
– DERIVATIVES **dis·mis·sive·ly** adv., **dis·mis·sive·ness** n.

dis·mount /dis'mount/ ▶ **v. 1** [no obj.] alight from a horse, bicycle, or other thing that one is riding. ■ [with obj.] cause to fall or alight. **2** [with obj.] remove (something) from its support: *we have to dismount the pump.* ■ Computing make (a disk or disk drive) unavailable for use.
▶ **n.** Gymnastics a move in which a gymnast jumps off an apparatus or completes a floor exercise.
– ORIGIN mid 16th cent.: from DIS- + MOUNT[1], probably on the pattern of Old French *desmonter*, medieval Latin *dismontare.*

Dis·ney /'diznē/, Walt (1901–66), US animator and movie and television producer; full name *Walter Elias Disney.* He became known for his cartoon characters that included Mickey Mouse (who first appeared in 1928), Donald Duck, Goofy, and Pluto. *Snow White and the Seven Dwarfs* (1937) was the first full-length cartoon with sound and color. Other notable animated movies: *Pinocchio* (1940), *Dumbo* (1941), *Bambi* (1942), *Cinderella* (1950), and *Peter Pan* (1953).

Dis·ney·land ▶ **n.** a theme park in Anaheim, California, that opened in 1955. [from Walt *Disney.*] ■ a large, bustling place filled with colorful attractions. ■ a place of fantasy or make-believe: *their own think tank, their own Disneyland of future ideas* | [as modifier] *Disneyland conceptions of defense which have no genuine relevance.*

Dis·ney World an amusement park in Lake Buena Vista, southwest of Orlando, Florida, that opened in 1971. Formally ***Walt Disney World.***

dis·o·be·di·ence /,disə'bēdēəns/ ▶ **n.** failure or refusal to obey rules or someone in authority: *he made no allowances for neglect or disobedience of orders.*

dis·o·be·di·ent /,disə'bēdēənt/ ▶ **adj.** refusing to obey rules or someone in authority: *Larry was stern with disobedient employees.*
– DERIVATIVES **dis·o·be·di·ent·ly** adv.
– ORIGIN late Middle English: from Old French *desobedient*, based on Latin *oboedient-* 'obeying' (see OBEDIENT).

dis·o·bey /,disə'bā/ ▶ **v.** [with obj.] fail to obey (rules, a command, or someone in authority): *around 1,000 soldiers had disobeyed orders and surrendered.*
– DERIVATIVES **dis·o·bey·er** n.
– ORIGIN late Middle English: from Old French *desobeir*, based on Latin *oboedire* 'obey' (see OBEY).

dis·o·blige /,disə'blīj/ ▶ **v.** [with obj.] offend (someone) by not acting in accordance with their wishes: *one didn't disoblige them if one could help it.*
– ORIGIN late 16th cent. (in the sense 'release from an obligation'): from French *désobliger*, based on Latin *obligare* 'oblige.'

dis·o·blig·ing /,disə'blījiNG/ ▶ **adj.** deliberately unhelpful; uncooperative.

di·so·my /dī'sōmē/ ▶ **n.** Genetics the condition of having a chromosome represented twice in a chromosomal complement.
– DERIVATIVES **di·so·mic** /-mik/ adj.
– ORIGIN late 20th cent.: from DI-[1] 'two' + -SOME[3] + -Y[3].

dis·or·der /dis'ôrdər/ ▶ **n.** a state of confusion: *tiresome days of mess and disorder.* ■ the disruption of peaceful and law-abiding behavior: *recurrent food crises led to periodic outbreaks of disorder.* ■ Medicine a disruption of normal physical or mental functions; a disease or abnormal condition: *eating disorders | an improved understanding of mental disorder.*
▶ **v.** [with obj.] (usu. as adj. **disordered**) disrupt the systematic functioning or neat arrangement of: *she went to comb her disordered hair | his sleep is disordered.* ■ Medicine disrupt the healthy or normal functioning of: *a patient who is mentally disordered.*
– ORIGIN late 15th cent. (as a verb in the sense 'upset the order of'): alteration, influenced by ORDER, of earlier *disordain*, from Old French *desordener*, ultimately based on Latin *ordinare* 'ordain.'

dis·or·der·ly /dis'ôrdərlē/ ▶ **adj.** lacking organization; untidy: *his life was as disorderly as ever | a disorderly pile of books.* ■ involving or contributing to a breakdown of peaceful and law-abiding behavior: *they had no intention of staging a disorderly protest.*
– DERIVATIVES **dis·or·der·li·ness** n.

dis·or·der·ly con·duct ▶ **n.** Law unruly behavior constituting a minor offense.

dis·or·der·ly house ▶ **n.** Law, archaic a brothel.

dis·or·gan·ize /dis'ôrgə,nīz/ ▶ **v.** [with obj.] disrupt the systematic order or functioning of: *attacks on leading government figures might disorganize the regime.*
– DERIVATIVES **dis·or·gan·i·za·tion** /-,ôrgənə'zāsHən/ n.
– ORIGIN late 18th cent. (dating from the French Revolution): from French *désorganiser.*

dis·or·gan·ized /dis'ôrgə,nīzd/ ▶ **adj.** not properly planned and controlled: *the campaign was hopelessly disorganized.* ■ (of a person) unable to plan one's activities efficiently: *my boss decided that I was unproductive and disorganized.*

dis·o·ri·ent /dis'ôrē,ent/ ▶ **v.** [with obj.] (often as adj. **disoriented**) make (someone) lose their sense of direction: *she was so disoriented that Joe had to walk her to her room.* ■ make (someone) feel confused: *jet lag leaves you irritable, disoriented, and tired.*
– ORIGIN mid 17th cent.: from French *désorienter* 'turn from the east.'

dis·o·ri·en·tate /dis'ôrēən,tāt/ ▶ **v.** another term for DISORIENT.
– DERIVATIVES **dis·o·ri·en·ta·tion** /-,ôrēən'tāsHən/ n.

dis·own /dis'ōn/ ▶ **v.** [with obj.] refuse to acknowledge or maintain any connection with: *Howard's rich family had disowned him because of his marriage.*
– DERIVATIVES **dis·own·er** n., **dis·own·ment** n.

dis·par·age /di'sparij/ ▶ **v.** [with obj.] regard or represent as being of little worth: *he never missed an opportunity to disparage his competitors.*
– DERIVATIVES **dis·par·age·ment** n.
– ORIGIN late Middle English (in the sense 'marry someone of unequal rank,' also 'bring discredit on'): from Old French *desparagier* 'marry someone of unequal rank,' based on Latin *par* 'equal.'

dis·par·ag·ing /di'sparijiNG/ ▶ **adj.** expressing the opinion that something is of little worth; derogatory: *disparaging remarks about public housing.*
– DERIVATIVES **dis·par·ag·ing·ly** adv.

dis·pa·rate /'dispərit, di'sparit/ ▶ **adj.** essentially different in kind; not allowing comparison: *they inhabit disparate worlds of thought.* ■ containing elements very different from one another: *a culturally disparate country.*
▶ **n.** (**disparates**) archaic things so unlike that there is no basis for comparison.
– DERIVATIVES **dis·pa·rate·ly** adv., **dis·pa·rate·ness** n.
– ORIGIN late Middle English: from Latin *disparatus* 'separated,' from the verb *disparare*, from *dis-* 'apart' + *parare* 'to prepare'; influenced in sense by Latin *dispar* 'unequal.'

dis·par·i·ty /di'sparitē/ ▶ **n.** (pl. **disparities**) a great difference: *economic disparities between different regions of the country | the great disparity of weight between the sun and the planets.*
– ORIGIN mid 16th cent.: from French *disparité*, from late Latin *disparitas*, based on Latin *paritas* 'parity.'

dis·pas·sion·ate /dis'pasHənit/ ▶ **adj.** not influenced by strong emotion, and so able to be rational and impartial: *she dealt with life's disasters in a calm, dispassionate way.*
– DERIVATIVES **dis·pas·sion** /-sHən/ n., **dis·pas·sion·ate·ly** adv., **dis·pas·sion·ate·ness** n.

dis·patch /dis'pacH/ (also **despatch**) ▶ **v.** [with obj.] **1** send off to a destination or for a purpose: *he dispatched messages back to base* | [with obj. and infinitive] *the mayor dispatched 150 police officers to restore order.*

2 deal with (a task, problem, or opponent) quickly and efficiently: *they dispatched the opposition.* ■ kill: *he dispatched the animal with one blow.*
▶ **n. 1** the sending of someone or something to a destination or for a purpose: *a resolution authorizing the dispatch of a peacekeeping force.* ■ speed in action: *the situation might change, so he should proceed* ***with dispatch.***
2 an official report on state or military affairs: *in his battle dispatch he described the gunner's bravery.* ■ a report sent in by a newspaper's correspondent from a faraway place.
3 the killing of someone or something: *the legendary dispatch of villains by a hero.*
– DERIVATIVES **dis·patch·er n.**
– ORIGIN early 16th cent.: from Italian *dispacciare* or Spanish *despachar* 'expedite,' from *dis-*, *des-* (expressing reversal) + the base of Italian *impacciare*, Spanish *empachar* 'hinder.'

dis·patch box ▶ **n.** (also **dispatch case**) a container for dispatches, esp. official state or military documents.

dis·patch rid·er ▶ **n.** chiefly Brit. a messenger who delivers urgent business documents or military dispatches by motorcycle or (formerly) on horseback.

dis·pel /dis'pel/ ▶ **v.** (**dispels, dispelling, dispelled**) [with obj.] make (a doubt, feeling, or belief) disappear: *the brightness of the day did nothing to dispel Elaine's dejection.*
– DERIVATIVES **dis·pel·ler n.**
– ORIGIN late Middle English: from Latin *dispellere*, from *dis-* 'apart' + *pellere* 'to drive.'

dis·pen·sa·ble /dis'pensəbəl/ ▶ **adj.** able to be replaced or done without; superfluous: *tiny battlefield robots will be cheap and dispensable.* ■ (of a law or other rule) able to be relaxed in special cases.
– DERIVATIVES **dis·pen·sa·bil·i·ty** /-ˌpensə'bilitē/ **n.**
– ORIGIN early 16th cent. (in the sense 'permissible in special circumstances'): from medieval Latin *dispensabilis*, from Latin *dispensare* (see **DISPENSE**).

dis·pen·sa·ry /dis'pensərē/ ▶ **n.** (pl. **dispensaries**)
1 a room where medicines are prepared and provided.
2 a clinic provided by public or charitable funds.
– ORIGIN late 17th cent.: from medieval Latin *dispensarium*, neuter (used as a noun) of *dispensarius*, from Latin *dispensare* (see **DISPENSE**).

dis·pen·sa·tion /ˌdispən'sāsHən, -pen-/ ▶ **n.**
1 exemption from a rule or usual requirement: *although she was too young, she was given special dispensation to play two matches | they were given a dispensation to take most of the first week off.* ■ permission to be exempted from the laws or observances of a church: *he received papal dispensation to hold a number of benefices.*
2 a system of order, government, or organization of a nation, community, etc., esp. as existing at a particular time: *scholarship is conveyed to a wider audience than under the old dispensation.* ■ (in Christian theology) a divinely ordained order prevailing at a particular period of history: *the Mosaic dispensation.* ■ archaic an act of divine providence: *the laws to which the creator in all his dispensations conforms.*
3 the action of distributing or supplying something: *regulations controlling dispensation of medications.*
– DERIVATIVES **dis·pen·sa·tion·al** /-sHənl/ **adj.**
– ORIGIN late Middle English: from Latin *dispensatio(n-)*, from the verb *dispensare* (see **DISPENSE**).

dis·pen·sa·tion·al·ism /ˌdispən'sāsHənlˌizəm, -pen-/ ▶ **n.** Christian Theology belief in a system of historical progression, as revealed in the Bible, consisting of a series of stages in God's self-revelation and plan of salvation.
– DERIVATIVES **dis·pen·sa·tion·al·ist n.**

dis·pense /dis'pens/ ▶ **v. 1** [with obj.] distribute or provide (a service or information) to a number of people: *he dispensed a gentle pat on Claude's back.* ■ (of a machine) supply (a product or cash): *the machines dispense a range of drinks and snacks.* ■ (of a pharmacist) make up and give out (medicine) according to a doctor's prescription.
2 [no obj.] (**dispense with**) manage without; get rid of: *let's dispense with the formalities, shall we?* ■ give special exemption from (a law or rule): *the secretary of state was empowered to dispense with the nationality requirement in individual cases.* ■ [with obj.] grant (someone) an exemption from a religious obligation: *the pope personally nominated him as bishop,* ***dispensing him from*** *his impediment.*
– PHRASES **dispense with someone's services** dismiss someone from a job.
– ORIGIN late Middle English: via Old French from Latin *dispensare* 'continue to weigh out or disburse,' from the verb *dispendere*, based on *pendere* 'weigh.'

dis·pens·er /dis'pensər/ ▶ **n.** a person or thing that dispenses something: *his role as protector of the weak and dispenser of justice.* ■ [usu. with modifier] an automatic machine or container that is designed to release a specific amount of something: *a paper towel dispenser.*

dis·per·sal /dis'pərsəl/ ▶ **n.** the action or process of distributing things or people over a wide area: *the dispersal of people to increasingly distant suburbs.* ■ the splitting up of a group or gathering of people, causing them to leave in different directions: *the dispersal of the crowd by mounted police.* ■ the splitting up and selling off of a collection of artifacts or books: *the dispersal of the John Willett Collection.*

dis·per·sant /dis'pərsənt/ ▶ **n.** a liquid or gas used to disperse small particles in a medium.

dis·perse /dis'pərs/ ▶ **v.** [with obj.] distribute or spread over a wide area: *storms can disperse seeds via high altitudes | camping sites could be* ***dispersed among*** *trees so as to be out of sight.* ■ go or cause to go in different directions or to different destinations: [no obj.] *the crowd dispersed* | [with obj.] *the police used tear gas to disperse the protesters.* ■ (with reference to gas, smoke, mist, or cloud) thin out or cause to thin out and disappear: [no obj.] *the earlier mist had dispersed* | [with obj.] *winds dispersed the bomb's radioactive cloud high in the atmosphere.* ■ Physics divide (light) into constituents of different wavelengths. ■ Chemistry distribute (small particles) uniformly in a medium.
▶ **adj.** [attrib.] Chemistry denoting a phase dispersed in another phase, as in a colloid: *emulsions should be examined after storage for droplet size of the disperse phase.*
– DERIVATIVES **dis·pers·er n.**, **dis·pers·i·ble adj.**, **dis·per·sive** /-siv/ **adj.**
– ORIGIN late Middle English: from Latin *dispers-* 'scattered,' from the verb *dispergere*, from *dis-* 'widely' + *spargere* 'scatter, strew.'

dis·per·sion /dis'pərZHən, -SHən/ ▶ **n.** the action or process of distributing things or people over a wide area: *some seeds rely on birds for dispersion.* ■ the state of being dispersed over a wide area: *the general dispersion of Hellenistic culture.* ■ Ecology the pattern of distribution of individuals within a habitat. ■ (also **the Dispersion**) another term for **DIASPORA**. ■ a mixture of one substance dispersed in another medium. ■ Physics the separation of white light into colors, or the separation of any radiation according to wavelength. ■ Statistics the extent to which values of a variable differ from a fixed value such as the mean.
– ORIGIN late Middle English: from late Latin *dispersio(n-)*, from Latin *dispergere* (see **DISPERSE**).

dis·pir·it /di'spirit/ ▶ **v.** [with obj.] cause (someone) to lose enthusiasm or hope: *the army was dispirited by the uncomfortable winter conditions.*

dis·pir·it·ed /dis'spiritid/ ▶ **adj.** having lost enthusiasm and hope; disheartened: *she was determined to appear unworried in front of her dispirited family.*
– DERIVATIVES **dis·pir·it·ed·ly adv.**, **dis·pir·it·ed·ness n.**

dis·pir·it·ing /dis'spiritiNG/ ▶ **adj.** causing someone to lose enthusiasm and hope; disheartening: *it was a dispiriting occasion.*
– DERIVATIVES **dis·pir·it·ing·ly adv.**

dis·place /dis'plās/ ▶ **v.** [with obj.] take over the place, position, or role of (someone or something): *in the northern states of India, Hindi has largely displaced English.* ■ cause (something) to move from its proper or usual place: *he seems to have displaced some vertebrae.* ■ (usu. **be displaced**) force (someone) to leave their home, typically because of war, persecution, or natural disaster: *thousands of people have been displaced by the civil war.* ■ remove (someone) from a job or position of authority against their will: *his aides were discredited and displaced.*
– DERIVATIVES **dis·plac·er n.**
– ORIGIN mid 16th cent.: from Old French *desplacer*.

dis·placed per·son ▶ **n.** a person who is forced to leave their home country because of war, persecution, or natural disaster; a refugee.

dis·place·ment /dis'plāsmənt/ ▶ **n. 1** the moving of something from its place or position: *vertical displacement of the shoreline | a displacement of the vertebra at the bottom of the spine.* ■ the removal of someone or something by someone or something else that takes their place: *males may be able to resist displacement by other males.* ■ the enforced departure of people from their homes, typically because of war, persecution, or natural disaster: *the displacement of farmers by guerrilla activity.* ■ the amount by which a thing is moved from its normal position: *a displacement of 6.8 meters along the San Andreas fault.*
2 the occupation by a submerged body or part of a body of a volume that would otherwise be occupied by a fluid. ■ the amount or weight of fluid that would fill such a volume in the case of a floating ship, used as a measure of the ship's size: *the submarine has a surface displacement of 2,185 tons.* ■ technical the volume swept by a reciprocating system, as in a pump or engine.
3 Psychoanalysis the unconscious transfer of an intense emotion from its original object to another one: *this phobia was linked with the displacement of fear of his father.*
4 Physics the component of an electric field due to free separated charges, regardless of any polarizing effects. ■ the vector representing such a component. ■ the flux density of such an electric field.

d

dis·place·ment ac·tiv·i·ty ▶ **n.** Psychology an animal or human activity that seems inappropriate to the context, such as head-scratching when one is confused, considered to arise unconsciously when a conflict between antagonistic urges cannot be resolved.

dis·place·ment pump ▶ **n.** a pump in which liquid is moved out of the pump chamber by a moving surface or by the introduction of compressed air or gas.

dis·place·ment ton ▶ **n.** see **TON**[1] (sense 1).

dis·play /dis'plā/ ▶ **v.** [with obj.] make a prominent exhibition of (something) in a place where it can be easily seen: *the palace used to display a series of Flemish tapestries | a handwritten notice was displayed in the ticket office.* ■ (of a computer or other device) show (information) on a screen. ■ give a conspicuous demonstration of (a quality, emotion, or skill): *the aggressive kind of baseball he displayed as a player.* ■ [no obj.] (of a male bird, reptile, or fish) engage in a specialized pattern of behavior that is intended to attract a mate: *she photographed the peacock, which chose that moment to display.*
▶ **n. 1** a performance, show, or event intended for public entertainment: *a display of fireworks.* ■ a collection of objects arranged for public viewing: *the museum houses an informative display of rocks | work by lesser-known artists is also* ***on display*** | [as modifier] *a display case.* ■ a notable or conspicuous demonstration of a particular type of behavior, emotion, or skill: *a display of great virtuosity.* ■ conspicuous or flashy exhibition; ostentation: *a flagrant display of wealth.* ■ a specialized pattern of behavior by the males of some species of birds, reptiles, and fish that is intended to attract a mate: *the teal were indulging in delightful courtship displays.* ■ Printing the arrangement and choice of type in a style intended to attract attention.
2 an electronic device for the visual presentation of data: *a 17-inch color display* | [as modifier] *a visual display screen.* ■ the process or facility of presenting data on a computer screen or other device: *the processing and display of high volumes of information.* ■ the data shown on a computer screen or other device.
– DERIVATIVES **dis·play·er n.**
– ORIGIN Middle English (in the sense 'unfurl, unfold'): from Old French *despleier*, from Latin *displicare* 'scatter, disperse' (in medieval Latin 'unfold'). Compare with **DEPLOY**.

dis·play ad ▶ **n.** a large advertisement, esp. in a newspaper or magazine, that features eye-catching type or illustrations.

dis·played /dis'plād/ ▶ **adj. 1** (of information) shown on a computer screen or other device: *a utility designed to allow you to cut up pieces of displayed graphics.*
2 Heraldry (of a bird of prey) depicted with the wings extended. ■ (of the wings of a bird of prey) extended.

dis·play type ▶ **n.** large or eye-catching type used for headings or advertisements.

dis·please /dis'plēz/ ▶ **v.** [with obj.] make (someone) feel annoyed or dissatisfied: *the tone of the letter displeased him* | (as adj. **displeasing**) *it was not entirely displeasing to be the center of such a drama.*
– DERIVATIVES **dis·pleas·ing·ly adv.**
– ORIGIN late Middle English: from Old French *desplaisir*, from *des-* (expressing reversal) + *plaisir* 'to please,' from Latin *placere*.

dis·pleas·ure /dis'pleZHər/ ▶ **n.** a feeling of annoyance or disapproval: *his grin turns into thin-lipped displeasure.*
▶ **v.** [with obj.] archaic annoy; displease: *not for worlds would I do aught that might displeasure thee.*
– ORIGIN late Middle English: from Old French *desplaisir* (see **DISPLEASE**), influenced by **PLEASURE**.

d

dis·port /dis'pôrt/ ▶ **v.** [no obj.] archaic or humorous enjoy oneself unrestrainedly; frolic: *a painting of lords and ladies **disporting themselves** by a lake.*
▶ **n.** diversion from work or serious matters; recreation or amusement: *the King and all his Court were met for solace and disport.* ■ archaic a pastime, game, or sport.
– ORIGIN late Middle English: from Old French *desporter*, from *des-* 'away' + *porter* 'carry' (from Latin *portare*).

dis·pos·a·ble /dis'pōzəbəl/ ▶ **adj. 1** (of an article) intended to be used once, or until no longer useful, and then thrown away: *disposable diapers | a disposable razor.* ■ (of a person or idea) able to be dispensed with; easily dismissed: *the poor performer is motivated by the fear that he or she is highly disposable.*
2 (chiefly of financial assets) readily available for the owner's use as required: *he made a mental inventory of his disposable assets.*
▶ **n.** an article designed to be thrown away after use: *don't buy disposables, such as razors, cups, and plates.*
– DERIVATIVES **dis·pos·a·bil·i·ty** /-ˌpōzə'bilitē/ **n.**

dis·pos·a·ble in·come ▶ **n.** income remaining after deduction of taxes and other mandatory charges, available to be spent or saved as one wishes. Compare with DISCRETIONARY INCOME.

dis·pos·al /dis'pōzəl/ ▶ **n. 1** the action or process of throwing away or getting rid of something: *the disposal of radioactive waste.* ■ (also **disposer**) informal an electrically operated device fitted to the waste pipe of a kitchen sink for grinding up food waste: *garbage disposals that never worked.*
2 the sale of shares, property, or other assets: *the disposal of his shares in the company.*
3 the arrangement or positioning of something: *she brushed her hair carefully, as if her success lay in the sleek disposal of each gleaming black thread.*
– PHRASES **at one's disposal** available for one to use whenever or however one wishes: *a helicopter was put at their disposal.*

dis·pose /dis'pōz/ ▶ **v. 1** [no obj.] (**dispose of**) get rid of by throwing away or giving or selling to someone else: *whose responsibility is it to dispose of scrap materials? | people now have substantial assets to dispose of after their death.* ■ informal kill; destroy: *her lover came up with hundreds of schemes for disposing of her husband.* ■ overcome (a rival or threat): *team members were buoyant after they disposed of the champions.* ■ informal consume (food or drink) quickly or enthusiastically: *she watched him dispose of a large slice of cheese.*
2 [with obj.] arrange in a particular position: *the chief disposed his attendants in a circle.* ■ bring (someone) into a particular frame of mind: *prolactin is released, **disposing you toward** sleep | cruelty that brutalizes young minds and disposes them to violence.* ■ [no obj.] literary determine the course of events: *the city proposed, but the unions disposed.* [from the proverb 'Man proposes, (but) God disposes,' translating Latin *Homo proponit, sed Deus disponit* (Thomas à Kempis's *De Imitatione Christi* I. xix).]
– DERIVATIVES **dis·pos·er n.** *a waste disposer | a disposer of grants and subsidies.*
– ORIGIN late Middle English: from Old French *disposer*, from Latin *disponere* 'arrange,' influenced by *dispositus* 'arranged' and Old French *poser* 'to place.'

dis·posed /dis'pōzd/ ▶ **adj.** [predic., usu. with infinitive] inclined or willing: *James didn't seem disposed to take the hint.* ■ [with submodifier] having a specified attitude to or toward: *it is expected that he will be favorably **disposed toward** the proposals.*

dis·po·si·tion /ˌdispə'zisʜən/ ▶ **n. 1** a person's inherent qualities of mind and character: *a sweet-natured girl of a placid disposition.* ■ [often with infinitive] an inclination or tendency: *the cattle showed a decided disposition to run | the judge's **disposition toward** clemency.*
2 the way in which something is placed or arranged, esp. in relation to other things: *the plan need not be accurate so long as it shows the disposition of the rooms.* ■ the action of arranging or ordering people or things in a particular way: *the prerogative gives the state widespread powers regarding the disposition and control of the armed forces.* ■ (**dispositions**) military preparations, in particular the stationing of troops ready for attack or defense: *the new strategic dispositions of our forces.*
3 Law the action of distributing or transferring property or money to someone, in particular by bequest: *this is a tax that affects the disposition of assets on death.*
4 the power to deal with something as one pleases: *if Napoleon had had railroads **at his disposition**, he would have been invincible.* ■ archaic the determination of events, esp. by divine power.
– ORIGIN late Middle English: via Old French from Latin *dispositio(n-)*, from *disponere* 'arrange' (see DISPOSE).

dis·pos·i·tive /dis'päzitiv/ ▶ **adj.** relating to or bringing about the settlement of an issue or the disposition of property: *such litigation will rarely be dispositive of any question.* ■ Law dealing with the disposition of property by deed or will: *the testator had to make his signature after making the dispositive provisions.* ■ dealing with the settling of international conflicts by an agreed disposition of disputed territories: *a peace settlement in the nature of a dispositive treaty.*
– ORIGIN late Middle English (in the sense 'contributory, conducive'): from Old French, or from medieval Latin *dispositivus*, from Latin *disposit-* 'arranged, disposed,' from the verb *disponere* (see DISPOSE).

dis·pos·sess /ˌdispə'zes/ ▶ **v.** [with obj.] deprive (someone) of something that they own, typically land or property: *they were **dispossessed of** lands and properties at the time of the Reformation* | (as plural noun **the dispossessed**) *a champion of the poor and the dispossessed.* ■ oust (a person) from a dwelling or position: *he used to ride out and dispossess his tenants as the spirit moved him.*
– DERIVATIVES **dis·pos·ses·sion** /-'zesʜən/ **n.**
– ORIGIN late 15th cent.: from Old French *despossesser*, from *des-* (expressing reversal) + *possesser* 'possess.'

dis·praise /dis'prāz/ ▶ **n.** rare censure; criticism: *this engraving has on occasion elicited dispraise for Raphael.*
▶ **v.** [with obj.] archaic express censure or criticism of (someone): *men cannot praise Dryden without dispraising Coleridge.*
– ORIGIN Middle English: from Old French *despreisier*, based on late Latin *depreciare* (see DEPRECIATE).

dis·proof /dis'pro͞of/ ▶ **n.** a set of facts that prove that something is untrue: *the theory also provides a disproof of the principle of closure.* ■ the action of proving that something is untrue: *considerations that are subject to scientific verification or disproof.*

dis·pro·por·tion /ˌdisprə'pôrsʜən/ ▶ **n.** an instance of being out of proportion with something else: *there is a disproportion between the scale of expenditure and any benefit that could possibly result.*
– DERIVATIVES **dis·pro·por·tion·al** /-sʜənl/ **adj.**, **dis·pro·por·tion·al·i·ty** /-ˌpôrsʜə'nalitē/ **n.**, **dis·pro·por·tion·al·ly** /-sʜənl-ē/ **adv.**
– ORIGIN mid 16th cent.: from DIS- (expressing absence) + PROPORTION, on the pattern of French *disproportion.*

dis·pro·por·tion·ate[1] /ˌdisprə'pôrsʜənit/ ▶ **adj.** too large or too small in comparison with something else: *people on lower incomes spend a disproportionate amount of their income on fuel | their sentences were disproportionate to the offenses they had committed.*
– DERIVATIVES **dis·pro·por·tion·ate·ly adv.**, **dis·pro·por·tion·ate·ness n.**
– ORIGIN mid 16th cent.: from DIS- (expressing absence) + PROPORTIONATE, on the pattern of French *disproportionné.*

dis·pro·por·tion·ate[2] /ˌdisprə'pôrsʜəˌnāt/ ▶ **v.** [no obj.] Chemistry undergo disproportionation: *water disproportionates to oxygen and hydrogen.*

dis·pro·por·tion·a·tion /ˌdisprəˌpôrsʜə'nāsʜən/ ▶ **n.** Chemistry a reaction in which a substance is simultaneously oxidized and reduced, giving two different products.

dis·prove /dis'pro͞ov/ ▶ **v.** [with obj.] prove that (something) is false: *he has given the Department of Transportation two months to disprove the allegation.*
– DERIVATIVES **dis·prov·a·ble adj.**
– ORIGIN late Middle English: from Old French *desprover.*

dis·put·a·ble /dis'pyo͞otəbəl/ ▶ **adj.** not established as fact, and so open to question or debate: *whether it can be described as art criticism may be disputable.*
– DERIVATIVES **dis·put·a·bly** /-blē/ **adv.**
– ORIGIN late 15th cent.: from Latin *disputabilis*, from the verb *disputare* 'to estimate,' later 'to dispute' (see DISPUTE).

dis·pu·ta·tion /ˌdispyo͝o'tāsʜən/ ▶ **n.** debate or argument: *promoting consensus rather than disputation | a lengthy disputation about the rights and wrongs of a particular request.* ■ formal academic debate: *the founding father of logical disputation | scholastic disputations.*
– DERIVATIVES **dis·put·a·tive** /-'pyo͞otətiv/ **adj.**
– ORIGIN late Middle English: from Latin *disputatio(n-)*, from the verb *disputare* (see DISPUTE).

dis·pu·ta·tious /ˌdispyo͝o'tāsʜəs/ ▶ **adj.** fond of or causing heated arguments: *a congenial hangout for disputatious academics | disputatious council meetings.*
– DERIVATIVES **dis·pu·ta·tious·ly adv.**, **dis·pu·ta·tious·ness n.**

dis·pute /dis'pyo͞ot/ ▶ **n.** a disagreement, argument, or debate: *a territorial dispute between the two countries | the question **in dispute** is altogether insignificant.* ■ a disagreement between management and employees that leads to an action of protest by the employees: *if this dispute cannot be resolved quickly, a formal strike is inevitable.*
▶ **v.** [with obj.] **1** argue about (something); discuss heatedly: *I disputed the charge on the bill* | [no obj.] *he taught and **disputed with** local poets.* ■ question whether (a statement or alleged fact) is true or valid: *the accusations are not disputed* | [with clause] *the estate disputes that it is responsible for the embankment.*
2 compete for; strive to win: *the two drivers crashed while disputing the lead.* ■ archaic resist (a landing or advance): *I formed my line and prepared to dispute the advance of the foe.*
– PHRASES **beyond dispute** certain or certainly; without doubt: *the main part of his argument was beyond dispute.* **open to dispute** not definitely decided: *such estimates are always open to dispute.*
– DERIVATIVES **dis·pu·tant** /-'pyo͞otnt/ **n.**, **dis·put·er n.**
– ORIGIN Middle English: via Old French from Latin *disputare* 'to estimate' (in late Latin 'to dispute'), from *dis-* 'apart' + *putare* 'reckon.'

dis·qual·i·fi·ca·tion /disˌkwäləfi'kāsʜən/ ▶ **n.** the action of disqualifying or the state of being disqualified. ■ a fact or condition that disqualifies someone from a position or activity: *such an offense is no longer a disqualification for office.*

dis·qual·i·fy /dis'kwäləˌfī/ ▶ **v.** (**disqualifies, disqualifying, disqualified**) [with obj.] pronounce (someone) ineligible for an office or activity because of an offense or infringement: *he was **disqualified from** driving for six months.* ■ eliminate (someone) from a competition because of an infringement of the rules: *he was disqualified after failing a drug test.* ■ (of a feature or characteristic) make (someone) unsuitable for an office or activity: *a heart murmur disqualified him for military service.*

dis·qui·et /dis'kwī-it/ ▶ **n.** a feeling of anxiety or worry: *public disquiet about animal testing.*
▶ **v.** [with obj.] (usu. as adj. **disquieted**) make (someone) worried or anxious: *she felt disquieted at the lack of interest the girl had shown.*

dis·qui·et·ing /dis'kwī-itiɴɢ/ ▶ **adj.** inducing feelings of anxiety or worry: *he found Jean's gaze disquieting.*
– DERIVATIVES **dis·qui·et·ing·ly adv.**

dis·qui·e·tude /dis'kwī-iˌt(y)o͞od/ ▶ **n.** a state of uneasiness or anxiety.

dis·qui·si·tion /ˌdiskwə'zisʜən/ ▶ **n.** a long or elaborate essay or discussion on a particular subject: *nothing can kill a radio show quicker than a disquisition on intertextual analysis.*
– DERIVATIVES **dis·qui·si·tion·al** /-sʜənl/ **adj.** (archaic).
– ORIGIN late 15th cent.: via French from Latin *disquisitio(n-)* 'investigation,' based on *quaerere* 'seek.' The original sense was 'topic for investigation,' whence 'discourse in which a subject is investigated' (mid 17th cent).

Dis·rae·li /diz'rālē/, Benjamin, 1st Earl of Beaconsfield (1804–81), British statesman; prime minister 1868 and 1874–80. He was largely responsible for the introduction of the second Reform Act (1867). He also ensured that Britain bought a controlling interest in the Suez Canal (1875) and made Queen Victoria empress of India.

dis·rate /dis'rāt/ ▶ **v.** [with obj.] (usu. **be disrated**) reduce (a sailor) to a lower rank.

dis·re·gard /ˌdisri'gärd/ ▶ **v.** [with obj.] pay no attention to; ignore: *the body of evidence is too substantial to disregard.*
▶ **n.** the action or state of disregarding or ignoring something: *blatant **disregard for** the law.*

dis·rel·ish /dis'relisʜ/ archaic ▶ **n.** a feeling of dislike or distaste: *disrelish for any pursuit is ample reason for abandoning it.*
▶ **v.** [with obj.] regard (something) with dislike or distaste: *I am not surprised that some members should disrelish your report.*

dis·re·mem·ber /ˌdisri'membər/ ▶ **v.** [with obj.] dialect fail to remember: *they had a word for it, but I disremember it now.*

dis·re·pair /ˌdisri'pe(ə)r/ ▶ **n.** poor condition of a building or structure due to neglect: *the station gradually **fell into disrepair**.*

dis·rep·u·ta·ble /dis'repyətəbəl/ ▶ **adj.** not considered to be respectable in character or appearance: *think twice before buying cheap fireworks from disreputable sources | he was heavy, grubby, and vaguely disreputable.*
– DERIVATIVES **dis·rep·u·ta·ble·ness n.**, **dis·rep·u·ta·bly** /-blē/ **adv.**

dis·re·pute /ˌdisrəˈpyo͞ot/ ▶ n. the state of being held in low esteem by the public: *one of the top clubs in the country is close to bringing the game* ***into disrepute***.

dis·re·spect /ˌdisriˈspekt/ ▶ n. lack of respect or courtesy: *growing disrespect for the rule of law.* ▶ v. [with obj.] informal show a lack of respect for; insult: *a young brave who disrespects his elders.*

dis·re·spect·ful /ˌdisriˈspektfəl/ ▶ adj. showing a lack of respect or courtesy; impolite: *a deeply disrespectful attitude toward women.*
– DERIVATIVES **dis·re·spect·ful·ly** /-fəlē/ adv.

dis·robe /disˈrōb/ ▶ v. [no obj.] take off one's clothes: *the girl disrobed slowly and climbed into the high bed.* ■ take off the clothes worn for an official ceremony: *they walked to the vestry to disrobe.* ■ [with obj.] undress (someone): *Kate remembers being disrobed.*
– ORIGIN late Middle English: from DIS- (expressing reversal) + ROBE, perhaps on the pattern of French *desrober*.

dis·rupt /disˈrəpt/ ▶ v. [with obj.] interrupt (an event, activity, or process) by causing a disturbance or problem: *a rail strike that could disrupt both passenger and freight service.* ■ drastically alter or destroy the structure of (something): *alcohol can disrupt the chromosomes of an unfertilized egg.*
– DERIVATIVES **dis·rupt·er** (also **disruptor** /-tər/) n.
– ORIGIN late Middle English: from Latin *disrupt-* 'broken apart,' from the verb *disrumpere*.

dis·rup·tion /disˈrəpSHən/ ▶ n. disturbance or problems that interrupt an event, activity, or process: *the schedule was planned to minimize disruption* | *there had been no delays or* ***disruptions to*** *flights.*

dis·rup·tive /disˈrəptiv/ ▶ adj. causing or tending to cause disruption: *disruptive and delinquent children* | *the hours of work are* ***disruptive to*** *home life.* ■ innovative or groundbreaking: *breaking a disruptive technology into the market is never easy.*
– DERIVATIVES **dis·rup·tive·ly** adv., **dis·rup·tive·ness** n.

> **WORD TRENDS** Is it bad to be **disruptive**? The Oxford English Corpus would suggest it is, with *violent, destructive, dangerous,* and *antisocial* all commonly paired with the word. However, a new form of **disruption** is emerging—one that many people are welcoming and even encouraging. *Disruptive behavior* may be the most common combination in the Corpus, but it is closely followed by *disruptive technology,* a concept first described in 1995. The new sense refers to innovations that improve products or services in an unexpected way, and thus disrupt the established market: *a market ripe for breakout disruptive technologies* | *disruptive innovations often see failure before success.*

diss ▶ v. variant spelling of DIS.

dis·sat·is·fac·tion /disˌsatisˈfakSHən/ ▶ n. lack of satisfaction: *widespread public* ***dissatisfaction with*** *incumbent politicians.*

dis·sat·is·fied /disˈsatisˌfīd/ ▶ adj. not content or happy with something: *small investors* ***dissatisfied with*** *rates on certificates of deposit* | *dissatisfied customers.*
– DERIVATIVES **dis·sat·is·fied·ly** adv.

dis·sat·is·fy /disˈsatisˌfī/ ▶ v. (**dissatisfies, dissatisfying, dissatisfied**) [with obj.] fail to satisfy (someone).

dis·sav·ing /disˈsāviNG/ ▶ n. the action of spending more than one has earned in a given period. ■ (**dissavings**) the excess amount spent.
– DERIVATIVES **dis·sav·er** /-vər/ n.

dis·sect /diˈsekt, dī-/ ▶ v. [with obj.] methodically cut up (a body, part, or plant) in order to study its internal parts. ■ analyze (something) in minute detail: *novels that dissect our obsession with cities and urban angst.*
– DERIVATIVES **dis·sec·tor** /-tər/ n.
– ORIGIN late 16th cent.: from Latin *dissect-* 'cut up,' from the verb *dissecare*, from *dis-* 'apart' + *secare* 'to cut.'

dis·sect·ed /diˈsektid, dī-/ ▶ adj. **1** having been cut up for anatomical study.
2 having a divided form or structure, in particular: ■ Botany (of a leaf) divided into many deep lobes. ■ Geology (of a plateau or upland) divided by a number of deep valleys.

dis·sec·tion /diˈsekSHən, dī-/ ▶ n. the action of dissecting a body or plant to study its internal parts: *the dissection of animals for scientific research.* ■ very detailed analysis of a text or idea: *this dissection of modern relationships.*

dis·sem·ble /diˈsembəl/ ▶ v. [no obj.] conceal one's true motives, feelings, or beliefs: *an honest, sincere person with no need to dissemble.* ■ [with obj.] disguise or conceal (a feeling or intention): *she smiled, dissembling her true emotion.*
– DERIVATIVES **dis·sem·blance** /-bləns/ n., **dis·sem·bler** /-b(ə)lər/ n.
– ORIGIN late Middle English: alteration (suggested by SEMBLANCE) of obsolete *dissimule*, via Old French from Latin *dissimulare* 'disguise, conceal.'

dis·sem·i·nate /diˈseməˌnāt/ ▶ v. [with obj.] spread or disperse (something, esp. information) widely: *health authorities should foster good practice by disseminating information.* ■ (usu. as adj. **disseminated**) spread throughout an organ or the body: *disseminated colonic cancer.*
– DERIVATIVES **dis·sem·i·na·tor** /-ˌnātər/ n.
– ORIGIN late Middle English: from Latin *disseminat-* 'scattered,' from the verb *disseminare*, from *dis-* 'abroad' + *semen, semin-* 'seed.'

dis·sem·i·na·tion /diˌseməˈnāSHən/ ▶ n. the act of spreading something, esp. information, widely; circulation: *dissemination of public information.*

dis·sem·i·nule /diˈseməˌnyo͞ol/ ▶ n. Botany a part of a plant that serves to propagate it, such as a seed or a fruit.
– ORIGIN early 20th cent.: formed irregularly from *dissemination* (see DISSEMINATE) + -ULE.

dis·sen·sion /diˈsenSHən/ ▶ n. disagreement that leads to discord: *this maneuver caused dissension within feminist ranks.*
– ORIGIN Middle English: via Old French from Latin *dissensio(n-)*, from the verb *dissentire* (see DISSENT).

dis·sen·sus /diˈsensəs/ ▶ n. widespread dissent: *analysis reveals notable dissensus in evaluations of occupational roles.*
– ORIGIN 1960s: from DIS- (expressing reversal) + a shortened form of CONSENSUS, or from Latin *dissensus* 'disagreement.'

dis·sent /diˈsent/ ▶ v. [no obj.] hold or express opinions that are at variance with those previously, commonly, or officially expressed: *two members* ***dissented from*** *the majority* | (as adj. **dissenting**) *there were only a couple of dissenting voices.* ■ separate from an established or orthodox church because of doctrinal disagreement.
▶ n. the expression or holding of opinions at variance with those previously, commonly, or officially held: *there was no* ***dissent from*** *this view.* ■ (also **Dissent**) refusal to accept the doctrines of an established or orthodox church; Nonconformity.
– ORIGIN late Middle English: from Latin *dissentire* 'differ in sentiment.'

dis·sent·er /diˈsentər/ ▶ n. a person who dissents. ■ (**Dissenter**) Brit. historical a member of a nonestablished church; a Nonconformist.

dis·sen·tient /diˈsenSHənt/ ▶ adj. in opposition to a majority or official opinion: *dissentient voices were castigated as "hopeless bureaucrats."*
▶ n. a person who opposes a majority or official opinion.
– ORIGIN early 17th cent.: from Latin *dissentient-* 'differing in opinion,' from the verb *dissentire*.

dis·sep·i·ment /diˈsepəmənt/ ▶ n. Botany & Zoology a partition in a part or organ; a septum.
– ORIGIN early 18th cent.: from Latin *dissaepimentum*, from *dissaepire* 'make separate,' from *dis-* (expressing separation) + *saepire* 'divide by a hedge.'

dis·ser·ta·tion /ˌdisərˈtāSHən/ ▶ n. a long essay on a particular subject, esp. one written as a requirement for the Doctor of Philosophy degree: *Joe wrote his doctoral dissertation on Thucydides* | figurative *she went on then into a dissertation on her family's love of Ireland.*
– DERIVATIVES **dis·ser·ta·tion·al** /-SHənl/ adj.
– ORIGIN early 17th cent. (in the sense 'discussion, debate'): from Latin *dissertatio(n-)*, from *dissertare* 'continue to discuss,' from *disserere* 'examine, discuss.'

dis·serv·ice /disˈsərvis/ ▶ n. [usu. in sing.] a harmful action: *you have* ***done a disservice to*** *the African people by ignoring this fact.*

dis·sev·er /diˈsevər/ ▶ v. [with obj.] rare divide or sever (something).
– DERIVATIVES **dis·sev·er·ance** /-ˈsev(ə)rəns/ n., **dis·sev·er·ment** n.
– ORIGIN Middle English (in the sense 'separate'): from Old French *dessevrer*, from late Latin *disseparare*, from *dis-* (expressing intensive force) + Latin *separare* 'to separate.'

dis·si·dence /ˈdisidəns/ ▶ n. protest against official policy; dissent.
– ORIGIN mid 17th cent.: from Latin *dissidentia*, from *dissident-* 'sitting apart' (see DISSIDENT).

dis·si·dent /ˈdisidənt/ ▶ n. a person who opposes official policy, esp. that of an authoritarian state: *a dissident who had been jailed by a military regime.*
▶ adj. in opposition to official policy: *there is only one explicitly dissident voice to be heard.*
– ORIGIN mid 16th cent. (in the sense 'differing in opinion or character'): from Latin *dissident-* 'sitting apart, disagreeing,' from *dis-* 'apart' + *sedere* 'sit.'

dis·sim·i·lar /disˈsimilər/ ▶ adj. not alike; different: *a collection of dissimilar nations lacking overall homogeneity* | *the pleasures of the romance novel are* ***not dissimilar from*** *those of the chocolate bar.*
– DERIVATIVES **dis·sim·i·lar·ly** adv.
– ORIGIN late 16th cent.: from DIS- (expressing reversal) + SIMILAR, on the pattern of Latin *dissimilis*, French *dissimilaire*.

dis·sim·i·lar·i·ty /disˌsiməˈlaritē/ ▶ n. difference; variance: *the similarity or* ***dissimilarity between*** *humans and other animals.*

dis·sim·i·late /diˈsiməˌlāt/ ▶ v. [with obj.] Linguistics change (a sound in a word) in order to be unlike the sounds near it: *in "pilgrim," from Latin "peregrinus," the first "r" is dissimilated to "l."* ■ [no obj.] (of a sound) undergo such a change: *the first "r" dissimilates to "l."*
– DERIVATIVES **dis·sim·i·la·tion** /-ˌsiməˈlāSHən/ n., **dis·sim·i·la·to·ry** /-ləˌtôrē/ adj.
– ORIGIN mid 19th cent.: from DIS- (expressing reversal) + Latin *similis* 'like, similar,' on the pattern of *assimilate*.

dis·si·mil·i·tude /ˌdis-siˈmiliˌt(y)o͞od/ ▶ n. formal dissimilarity or diversity.
– ORIGIN late Middle English: from Latin *dissimilitudo*, from *dissimilis* 'unlike,' from *dis-* (expressing reversal) + *similis* 'like, similar.'

dis·sim·u·late /diˈsimyəˌlāt/ ▶ v. [with obj.] conceal or disguise (one's thoughts, feelings, or character): *a country gentleman who dissimulates his wealth beneath ragged pullovers* | [no obj.] *now that they have power, they no longer need to dissimulate.*
– DERIVATIVES **dis·sim·u·la·tor** /-ˌlātər/ n.
– ORIGIN late Middle English: from Latin *dissimulat-* 'hidden, concealed,' from the verb *dissimulare*.

dis·sim·u·la·tion /diˌsimyəˈlāSHən/ ▶ n. concealment of one's thoughts, feelings, or character; pretense: *an attempt at dissimulation.*

dis·si·pate /ˈdisəˌpāt/ ▶ v. **1** [no obj.] disperse or scatter: *the cloud of smoke dissipated.* ■ (with reference to a feeling or other intangible thing) disappear or cause to disappear: [no obj.] *the concern she'd felt for him had wholly dissipated* | [with obj.] *he wanted to dissipate his anger.*
2 [with obj.] squander or fritter away (money, energy, or resources): *he had dissipated his entire fortune.* ■ (usu. **be dissipated**) Physics cause (energy) to be lost, typically by converting it to heat.
– DERIVATIVES **dis·si·pa·tive** /-ˌpātiv/ adj., **dis·si·pa·tor** /-ˌpātər/ (also **dissipater**) n.
– ORIGIN late Middle English: from Latin *dissipat-* 'scattered,' from the verb *dissipare*, from *dis-* 'apart, widely' + *supare* 'to throw.'

dis·si·pat·ed /ˈdisəˌpātid/ ▶ adj. (of a person or way of life) overindulging in sensual pleasures: *dissipated behavior.*

dis·si·pa·tion /ˌdisəˈpāSHən/ ▶ n. **1** dissipated living: *a descent into drunkenness and sexual dissipation.*
2 squandering of money, energy, or resources: *the dissipation of the country's mineral wealth.* ■ Physics loss of energy, esp. by its conversion into heat.
– ORIGIN late Middle English (in the sense 'complete disintegration'): from Latin *dissipatio(n-)*, from the verb *dissipare* (see DISSIPATE).

dis·so·ci·a·ble /diˈsōSHəbəl/ ▶ adj. able to be dissociated; separable: *language and cognition are not dissociable.*
– ORIGIN mid 19th cent.: from French, from Latin *dissociabilis*, from *dissociare* 'to separate.'

dis·so·ci·ate /diˈsōSHēˌāt, -ˈsōsē-/ ▶ v. [with obj.] **1** disconnect or separate (used esp. in abstract contexts): *voices should not be* ***dissociated from*** *their social context.* ■ (**dissociate oneself from**) declare that one is not connected with or a supporter of (someone or something): *he took pains to dissociate himself from the religious radicals.* ■ (usu. **be dissociated**) Psychiatry split off (a component of mental activity) to act as an independent part of mental life.
2 Chemistry (with reference to a molecule) to split into separate smaller atoms, ions, or molecules, esp. reversibly: [with obj.] *these compounds are dissociated by solar radiation to yield atoms of chlorine.*
– DERIVATIVES **dis·so·ci·a·tive** /-ˌātiv, -SHətiv/ adj.
– ORIGIN mid 16th cent.: from Latin *dissociat-* 'separated,' from the verb *dissociare*, from *dis-* (expressing reversal) + *sociare* 'join together' (from *socius* 'companion').

d

dis·so·ci·at·ed per·son·al·i·ty ▶ **n.** another term for MULTIPLE PERSONALITY.

dis·so·ci·a·tion /diˌsōsēˈāsHən/ ▶ **n.** the disconnection or separation of something from something else or the state of being disconnected: *the dissociation between the executive and the judiciary is the legacy of the Act of Settlement.* ■ Chemistry the splitting of a molecule into smaller molecules, atoms, or ions, esp. by a reversible process. ■ Psychiatry separation of normally related mental processes, resulting in one group functioning independently from the rest, leading in extreme cases to disorders such as multiple personality.

d

dis·so·ci·a·tion con·stant ▶ **n.** Chemistry a quantity expressing the extent to which a particular substance in solution is dissociated into ions, equal to the product of the concentrations of the respective ions divided by the concentration of the undissociated molecule.

dis·sol·u·ble /diˈsälyəbəl/ ▶ **adj.** able to be dissolved, loosened, or disconnected: *permitting divorce would render every marriage dissoluble.*
– DERIVATIVES **dis·sol·u·bil·i·ty** /-ˌsälyəˈbilitē/ **n.**
– ORIGIN mid 16th cent.: from Latin *dissolubilis*, from the verb *dissolvere* (see DISSOLVE).

dis·so·lute /ˈdisəˌlo͞ot/ ▶ **adj.** lax in morals; licentious: *a dissolute, drunken, disreputable rogue.*
– DERIVATIVES **dis·so·lute·ly adv.**, **dis·so·lute·ness n.**
– ORIGIN late Middle English: from Latin *dissolutus* 'disconnected, loose,' from the verb *dissolvere* (see DISSOLVE).

dis·so·lu·tion /ˌdisəˈlo͞osHən/ ▶ **n. 1** the closing down or dismissal of an assembly, partnership, or official body: *the dissolution of their marriage | Henry VIII declared the abbey's dissolution in 1540.* ■ technical the action or process of dissolving or being dissolved: *minerals susceptible to dissolution.* ■ disintegration; decomposition: *the dissolution of the flesh.* ■ formal death.
2 debauched living; dissipation: *an advanced state of dissolution.*
– ORIGIN late Middle English: from Latin *dissolutio(n-)*, from the verb *dissolvere* (see DISSOLVE).

dis·solve /diˈzälv/ ▶ **v. 1** (with reference to a solid) become or cause to become incorporated into a liquid so as to form a solution: [no obj.] *glucose dissolves easily in water* | [with obj.] *dissolve a bouillon cube in a pint of hot water.* ■ [no obj.] (of something abstract, esp. a feeling) disappear: *my courage dissolved.* ■ [no obj.] subside uncontrollably into (an expression of strong feelings): *she suddenly* ***dissolved into*** *floods of tears.* ■ [no obj.] (in a movie) change gradually to (a different scene or picture): ***dissolve to*** *side view, looking down the street.*
2 [with obj.] close down or dismiss (an assembly or official body): *the country's president can dissolve parliament under certain circumstances.* ■ annul or put an end to (a partnership or marriage): *it only takes 28 days to dissolve a domestic partnership.*
▶ **n.** (in a movie) an act or instance of moving gradually from one picture to another.
– DERIVATIVES **dis·solv·a·ble adj.**, **dis·solv·er n.**
– ORIGIN late Middle English (also in the sense 'break down into component parts'): from Latin *dissolvere*, from *dis-* 'apart' + *solvere* 'loosen or solve.'

dis·sol·vent /diˈzälvənt/ ▶ **n.** a substance that dissolves something else.
– ORIGIN mid 17th cent.: from Latin *dissolvent-* 'dissolving,' from the verb *dissolvere* (see DISSOLVE).

dis·so·nance /ˈdisənəns/ ▶ **n.** Music lack of harmony among musical notes: *an unusual degree of dissonance for such choral styles | the harsh dissonances give a sound that is quite untypical of the Renaissance.* ■ a tension or clash resulting from the combination of two disharmonious or unsuitable elements: *dissonance between campaign rhetoric and personal behavior.*
– ORIGIN late Middle English: from Old French, from late Latin *dissonantia*, from Latin *dissonant-* 'not agreeing in sound,' from the verb *dissonare*.

dis·so·nant /ˈdisənənt/ ▶ **adj.** Music lacking harmony: *irregular, dissonant chords.* ■ unsuitable or unusual in combination; clashing: *Jackson employs both harmonious and dissonant color choices.*
– DERIVATIVES **dis·so·nant·ly adv.**
– ORIGIN late Middle English (in the sense 'clashing'): from Old French, or from Latin *dissonant-* 'being discordant or inharmonious,' from the verb *dissonare*, from *dis-* 'apart' + *sonare* 'to sound.'

dis·suade /diˈswād/ ▶ **v.** [with obj.] persuade (someone) not to take a particular course of action: *his friends tried to* ***dissuade*** *him* ***from*** *flying.*
– DERIVATIVES **dis·suad·er n.**, **dis·sua·sion** /-ˈswāzHən/ **n.**, **dis·sua·sive** /-ˈswāsiv/ **adj.**
– ORIGIN late 15th cent. (in the sense 'advise against'): from Latin *dissuadere*, from *dis-* (expressing reversal) + *suadere* 'advise, persuade.'

dis·syl·la·ble /dīˈsiləbəl/ ▶ **n.** variant spelling of DISYLLABLE.
– DERIVATIVES **dis·syl·lab·ic** /ˌdīsiˈlabik/ **adj.**

dis·sym·me·try /disˈsimitrē/ ▶ **n.** (pl. **dissymmetries**) lack of symmetry. ■ technical the symmetrical relation of mirror images, the left and right hands, or crystals with two corresponding forms.
– DERIVATIVES **dis·sym·met·ric** /ˌdis-siˈmetrik/ **adj.**, **dis·sym·met·ri·cal** /ˌdis-siˈmetrikəl/ **adj.**

dis·taff /ˈdistaf/ ▶ **n.** a stick or spindle onto which wool or flax is wound for spinning. ■ [as modifier] of or concerning women.
– ORIGIN Old English *distæf*: the first element is apparently related to Middle Low German *dise*, *disene* 'distaff, bunch of flax'; the second is STAFF[1]. The extended sense arose because spinning was traditionally done by women.

dis·taff side ▶ **n.** the female side of a family: *the family title could be passed down through the distaff side.* The opposite of SPEAR SIDE. ■ the female members of a group: *this fascination was not limited to the distaff side of society.*
– ORIGIN late 19th cent.: because spinning (see DISTAFF) was traditionally done by women while men did the weaving.

dis·tal /ˈdistl/ ▶ **adj.** Anatomy situated away from the center of the body or from the point of attachment: *the distal end of the tibia | axons* ***distal to*** *the injury will degenerate.* The opposite of PROXIMAL. ■ Geology relating to or denoting the outer part of an area affected by geological activity: *the distal zone.* Often contrasted with PROXIMAL.
– DERIVATIVES **dis·tal·ly adv.**
– ORIGIN early 19th cent.: from DISTANT, on the pattern of words such as *dorsal*.

dis·tance /ˈdistəns/ ▶ **n. 1** an amount of space between two things or people: *I bicycled the short distance home | the* ***distance between*** *front and rear wheels.* ■ the condition of being far off; remoteness: *distance makes things look small* | figurative *a significant distance between German and Allied understandings of the war.* ■ a far-off point or place: *watching them* ***from a distance.*** ■ (**the distance**) the more remote part of what is visible or discernible: *I heard police sirens* ***in the distance*** *| they sped off* ***into the distance.*** ■ an interval of time: *a distance of more than twenty years.*
2 the full length of a race: *he claimed the 10,000 meter title in only his second race over the distance.* ■ the distance from the winning post that a horse must have reached when the winner finishes in order to qualify for a subsequent heat. ■ (**the distance**) Boxing the scheduled length of a fight: *he has won his first five fights* ***inside the distance.***
3 the avoidance of familiarity; aloofness or reserve: *a mix of warmth and distance makes a good neighbor.*
▶ **v.** [with obj.] make (someone or something) far off or remote in position or nature: *her mother wished to* ***distance*** *her* ***from*** *the rough village children.* ■ (**distance oneself from**) declare that one is not connected with or a supporter of (someone or something): *he sought to distance himself from the proposals.* ■ Horse Racing beat (a horse) by a distance.
– PHRASES **go the distance** Boxing complete a fight without being knocked out: *he went the distance after being floored in the first round.* ■ (of a boxing match) last the scheduled length: *six of his fights went the distance.* ■ Baseball pitch for the entire length of a game. ■ last for a long time: *this amplifier system should go the distance.* **keep one's distance** stay far away: *keep your distance from birds feeding their young.* ■ maintain one's reserve: *you had to say nothing and keep your distance.* **within —— distance** near enough to reach by the means specified: *the parking lot is within easy walking distance | he wanted to be* ***within driving distance of*** *his grandparents.* **within striking distance** near enough to hit or achieve something: *the aircraft carrier is dispatched to deep waters within striking distance of Moscow.*
– ORIGIN Middle English (in the sense 'discord, debate'): from Old French or from Latin *distantia*, from *distant-* 'standing apart,' from the verb *distare* (see DISTANT).

dis·tance learn·ing ▶ **n.** a method of studying in which lectures are broadcast or classes are conducted by correspondence or over the Internet, without the student's needing to attend a school or college. Also called **distance education**.

dis·tance post ▶ **n.** a post placed at a specified distance before the finishing post on a racecourse, which a horse must have passed when the winner finishes in order to qualify for a subsequent heat.

dis·tance run·ner ▶ **n.** an athlete who competes in long- or middle-distance races.

dis·tant /ˈdistənt/ ▶ **adj. 1** far away in space or time: *distant parts of the world | I remember that distant afternoon.* ■ [predic.] (after a measurement) at a specified distance: *the star is 30,000 light years* ***distant from*** *earth | the town lay half a mile distant.* ■ (of a sound) faint or vague because far away: *the distant bark of some farm dog.* ■ remote or far apart in resemblance or relationship: *a distant acquaintance.* ■ [attrib.] (of a person) not closely related: *a distant cousin.*
2 (of a person) not intimate; cool or reserved: *his children found him strangely distant | she and my father were* ***distant with*** *each other.* ■ remote; abstracted: *a distant look in his eyes.*
– ORIGIN late Middle English: from Latin *distant-* 'standing apart,' from the verb *distare*, from *dis-* 'apart' + *stare* 'stand.'

dis·tant ear·ly warn·ing (abbr.: **DEW**) ▶ **n.** a radar system in North America set up during the Cold War for the early detection of a missile attack.

dis·tant·ly /ˈdistəntlē/ ▶ **adv.** far away: *distantly he heard shouts.* ■ not closely: *they are distantly related to the elephants.* ■ coolly or remotely: *she smiled distantly.*

dis·taste /disˈtāst/ ▶ **n.** [in sing.] mild dislike or aversion: *Harry nurtured* ***a distaste for*** *all things athletic | his mouth twisted with distaste.*
– ORIGIN late 16th cent.: from DIS- (expressing reversal) + TASTE, on the pattern of early modern French *desgout*, Italian *disgusto*. Compare with DISGUST.

dis·taste·ful /disˈtāstˌfəl/ ▶ **adj.** causing dislike or disgust; offensive; unpleasant: *customers complained about the distasteful odor.*
– DERIVATIVES **dis·taste·ful·ly adv.**, **dis·taste·ful·ness n.**
– ORIGIN early 17th cent.

dist. atty. ▶ **abbr.** district attorney.

dis·tem·per[1] /disˈtempər/ ▶ **n. 1** a viral disease of some animals, esp. dogs, causing fever, coughing, and catarrh.
2 archaic political disorder: *an attempt to illuminate the moral roots of the modern world's distemper.*
– ORIGIN mid 16th cent. (originally in the sense 'bad temper,' later 'illness'): from Middle English *distemper* 'upset, derange,' from late Latin *distemperare* 'soak, mix in the wrong proportions,' from *dis-* 'thoroughly' + *temperare* 'mingle.' Compare with TEMPER. Sense 1 dates from the mid 18th cent.

dis·tem·per[2] ▶ **n.** a kind of paint using glue or size instead of an oil base, for use on walls or for scene-painting. ■ a method of mural and poster painting using this.
▶ **v.** [with obj.] (often as adj. **distempered**) paint (something) with distemper: *the distempered roof timbers.*
– ORIGIN late Middle English (originally as a verb in the senses 'dilute' and 'steep'): from Old French *destemprer* or late Latin *distemperare* 'soak.'

dis·tend /disˈtend/ ▶ **v.** swell or cause to swell by pressure from inside: [no obj.] *the abdomen distended rapidly* | [with obj.] *air is introduced into the stomach to distend it.*
– DERIVATIVES **dis·ten·si·bil·i·ty** /-ˌtensəˈbilitē/ **n.**, **dis·ten·si·ble** /-ˈtensəbəl/ **adj.**, **dis·ten·sion** /-ˈtensHən/ **n.**
– ORIGIN late Middle English: from Latin *distendere*, from *dis-* 'apart' + *tendere* 'to stretch.'

dis·tend·ed /disˈtendəd/ ▶ **adj.** swollen due to pressure from inside; bloated: *a distended belly.*

dis·tich /ˈdistik/ ▶ **n.** Prosody a pair of verse lines; a couplet.
– ORIGIN early 16th cent.: via Latin from Greek *distikhon (metron)* '(measure) of two lines,' neuter of *distikhos*, from *di-* 'twice' + *stikhos* 'line.'

dis·ti·chous /ˈdistikəs/ ▶ **adj.** Botany (of parts) arranged alternately in two opposite vertical rows.
– DERIVATIVES **dis·ti·chous·ly adv.**
– ORIGIN mid 18th cent.: via Latin from Greek *distikhos* (see DISTICH) + -OUS.

dis·till /disˈtil/ (Brit. **distil**) ▶ **v.** [with obj.] **1** purify (a liquid) by vaporizing it, then condensing it by cooling the vapor, and collecting the resulting liquid: *they managed to distill a small quantity of water* | (as adj. **distilled**) *dip the slide in distilled water.* ■ make (something, esp. liquor or an essence) in this way: *whiskey is* ***distilled from*** *a mash of grains* | (as noun **distilling**) *the distilling industry.* ■ extract the essence of (something) by heating it with a solvent. ■ remove (a volatile constituent) of a mixture by using heat: *coal tar is made by* ***distilling out*** *the volatile products in coal.* ■ [no obj.] literary emanate as a vapor or in minute drops: *she drew back from the dank breath that distilled out of the earth.*
2 extract the essential meaning or most important aspects of: *my travel notes were* ***distilled into*** *a book |*

(as adj. **distilled**) *the employee report is a distilled version of the main accounts.*
– DERIVATIVES **dis·til·la·to·ry** /-ə,tôrē/ adj.
– ORIGIN late Middle English: from Latin *distillare*, variant of *destillare*, from *de-* 'down, away' + *stillare* (from *stilla* 'a drop').

dis·til·late /'distilit, -,lāt/ ▶ n. something formed by distilling: *petroleum distillates | natural gas mixed with distillate.*
– ORIGIN mid 19th cent.: from Latin *distillatus* 'fallen in drops,' from the verb *distillare* (see DISTILL).

dis·til·la·tion /,distə'lāsHən/ ▶ n. **1** the action of purifying a liquid by a process of heating and cooling: *the petroleum distillation process.*
2 the extraction of the essential meaning or most important aspects of something: *the film is a distillation of personal experiences.*

dis·till·er /dis'tilər/ ▶ n. a person or company that manufactures liquor: *barrels that the master distiller deems to be of superior quality.*

dis·till·er·y /dis'tilərē/ ▶ n. (pl. **distilleries**) a place where liquor is manufactured: *the world's oldest whiskey distillery.*

dis·tinct /dis'tiNGkt/ ▶ adj. **1** recognizably different in nature from something else of a similar type: *the patterns of spoken language are* ***distinct from*** *those of writing | there are two distinct types of sickle cell disease.* ■ physically separate: *the gallery is divided into five distinct spaces.*
2 readily distinguishable by the senses: *a distinct smell of nicotine.* ■ [attrib.] (used for emphasis) so clearly apparent as to be unmistakable; definite: *he got the distinct impression that Melissa wasn't pleased.*
– DERIVATIVES **dis·tinct·ness** n.
– ORIGIN late Middle English (in the sense 'differentiated'): from Latin *distinctus* 'separated, distinguished,' from the verb *distinguere* (see DISTINGUISH).

dis·tinc·tion /dis'tiNGksHən/ ▶ n. **1** a difference or contrast between similar things or people: *there is a sharp* ***distinction between*** *domestic politics and international politics | I was completely unaware of class distinctions.* ■ the separation of things or people into different groups according to their attributes or characteristics: *these procedures were to be applied to all births, without distinction.*
2 excellence that sets someone or something apart from others: *a novelist of distinction.* ■ a decoration or honor awarded to someone in recognition of outstanding achievement: *he gained the highest distinction awarded for excellence in photography.* ■ recognition of outstanding achievement, such as on an examination: *I made a distinction in Greek.* Compare with MERIT.
– PHRASES **distinction without a difference** an artificially created distinction where no real difference exists. **have the distinction of** be different from others of a similar type by virtue of a notable characteristic or achievement: *pinto beans have the distinction of being one of the quickest beans to cook.*
– ORIGIN Middle English (in the sense 'subdivision, category'): via Old French from Latin *distinctio(n-)*, from the verb *distinguere* (see DISTINGUISH).

dis·tinc·tive /dis'tiNGktiv/ ▶ adj. characteristic of one person or thing, and so serving to distinguish it from others: *juniper berries give gin its distinctive flavor.*
– DERIVATIVES **dis·tinc·tive·ly** adv., **dis·tinc·tive·ness** n.
– ORIGIN late Middle English (in the sense 'serving to differentiate'): from late Latin *distinctivus*, from Latin *distinct-* 'distinguished' (see DISTINCT).

dis·tinct·ly /dis'tiNGktlē/ ▶ adv. in a way that is readily distinguishable by the senses; clearly: *reading each word slowly and distinctly.* ■ (used for emphasis) in a way that is very noticeable or apparent; decidedly: *two distinctly different cultures | he looked distinctly uncomfortable.*

dis·tin·gué /,distaNG'gā/ ▶ adj. (fem. **distinguée** pronunc. **same**) having a distinguished manner or appearance: *he was lean and distingué, with a small goatee.*
– ORIGIN early 19th cent.: French, literally 'distinguished.'

dis·tin·guish /dis'tiNGgwisH/ ▶ v. [with obj.] recognize or treat (someone or something) as different: *the child is perfectly capable of* ***distinguishing*** *reality* ***from*** *fantasy.* ■ [no obj.] perceive or point out a difference: *bees are unable to* ***distinguish between*** *red, black, and various grays.* ■ manage to discern (something barely perceptible): *it was too dark to distinguish anything more than their vague shapes.* ■ be an identifying or characteristic mark or property of: *what* ***distinguishes*** *sports* ***from*** *games?* ■ (**distinguish oneself**) make oneself prominent and worthy of respect through one's behavior or achievements: *many distinguished themselves in the fight.*
– ORIGIN late 16th cent.: formed irregularly from French *distinguer* or Latin *distinguere*, from *dis-* 'apart' + *stinguere* 'put out' (from a base meaning 'prick').

dis·tin·guish·a·ble /dis'tiNGgwisHəbəl/ ▶ adj. clear enough to be recognized or identified as different; discernible: *distinguishable features | this particular case is* ***distinguishable from*** *others.* ■ clear enough to be discerned or perceived: *his words were barely distinguishable.*

dis·tin·guished /dis'tiNGgwisHt/ ▶ adj. successful, authoritative, and commanding great respect: *a distinguished American educationist.* ■ showing dignity or authority in one's appearance or manner: *that hairstyle makes you look quite distinguished.*

Dis·tin·guished Fly·ing Cross (abbr.: **DFC**) ▶ n. a US or British military decoration for heroism or distinguished achievement while on aerial duty.

dis·tin·guish·ing /dis'tiNGgwisHiNG/ ▶ adj. characteristic of one thing or person, so serving to identify it; distinctive: *a house with no distinguishing features.*

dis·tort /dis'tôrt/ ▶ v. [with obj.] **1** pull or twist out of shape: *a grimace distorted her fine mouth.* ■ [no obj.] become twisted out of shape: *the pipe will distort as you bend it.*
2 give a misleading or false account or impression of: *many factors can distort the results.*
3 change the form of (an electrical signal or sound wave) during transmission, amplification, or other processing: *you're distorting the sound by overdriving the amp.*
– ORIGIN late 15th cent. (in the sense 'twist to one side'): from Latin *distort-* 'twisted apart,' from the verb *distorquere*, from *dis-* 'apart' + *torquere* 'to twist.'

dis·tort·ed /dis'tôrtid/ ▶ adj. **1** pulled or twisted out of shape; contorted.
2 giving a misleading or false account or impression; misrepresented: *his report gives a distorted view of the meeting.*
3 affected by electrical distortion: *distorted guitars.*
– DERIVATIVES **dis·tort·ed·ly** adv., **dis·tort·ed·ness** n.

dis·tor·tion /dis'tôrsHən/ ▶ n. **1** the action of distorting or the state of being distorted: *the virus causes distortion of the leaves | deliberate distortions of pitch and timbre.* ■ a distorted form or part: *a distortion in the eye's shape or structure.*
2 the action of giving a misleading account or impression: *we're tired of the media's continuing distortion of our issues.*
3 change in the form of an electrical signal or sound wave during processing.
– DERIVATIVES **dis·tor·tion·al** /-'tôrsHənl/ adj., **dis·tor·tion·less** /-'tôrsHənləs/ adj.

distr. ▶ abbr. ■ distribution. ■ distributor. ■ district.

dis·tract /dis'trakt/ ▶ v. [with obj.] prevent (someone) from giving full attention to something: *don't allow noise to* ***distract you from your work*** | (as adj. **distracting**) *she found his nearness distracting.* ■ divert (attention) from something: *it was another attempt to* ***distract attention from the*** *truth.* ■ (**distract oneself**) divert one's attention from something worrying or unpleasant by doing something different or more pleasurable: *I tried to distract myself by concentrating on Jane.* ■ archaic perplex and bewilder: *horror and doubt distract His troubl'd thoughts.*
– ORIGIN late Middle English (also in the sense 'pull in different directions'): from Latin *distract-* 'drawn apart,' from the verb *distrahere*, from *dis-* 'apart' + *trahere* 'to draw, drag.'

dis·tract·ed /dis'traktəd/ ▶ adj. unable to concentrate because one's mind is preoccupied: *Charlotte seemed too distracted to give him much attention | she ran her fingers through her hair in a distracted fashion.*
– DERIVATIVES **dis·tract·ed·ly** adv.

dis·tract·ing /dis'traktiNG/ ▶ adj. preventing concentration or diverting attention; disturbing: *she found his nearness distracting.*
– DERIVATIVES **dis·tract·ing·ly** adv. [as submodifier] *some of my classmates are distractingly pretty.*

dis·trac·tion /dis'traksHən/ ▶ n. **1** a thing that prevents someone from giving full attention to something else: *the company found passenger travel* ***a distraction from*** *the main business of moving freight.* ■ a diversion or recreation: *there are plenty of distractions such as sailing.*
2 extreme agitation of the mind or emotions: *he knew she was nervous by her uncharacteristic air of distraction.*
– PHRASES **to distraction** (in hyperbolic use) intensely: *she loved him to distraction.*
– ORIGIN late Middle English: from Latin *distractio(n-)*, from the verb *distrahere* (see DISTRACT).

dis·trac·tor /dis'traktər/ ▶ n. a person or thing that distracts. ■ an incorrect option in a multiple-choice question: *four pictures, three of which are distractors.*

dis·train /dis'trān/ ▶ v. [with obj.] Law seize (someone's property) to obtain payment of rent or other money owed: *legislation has restricted the right to distrain goods found on the premises.* ■ seize the property of (someone) for this purpose: *the government applied political pressure by distraining debtors.*
– DERIVATIVES **dis·train·er** n., **dis·train·ment** n.
– ORIGIN Middle English: from Old French *destreindre*, from Latin *distringere* 'stretch apart,' from *dis-* 'apart' + *stringere* 'tighten.'

dis·traint /dis'trānt/ ▶ n. Law the seizure of someone's property in order to obtain payment of money owed, esp. rent: *many faced heavy fines and the distraint of goods.*
– ORIGIN mid 18th cent.: from DISTRAIN, on the pattern of *constraint*.

dis·trait /dis'trā/ ▶ adj. (fem. **distraite** /dis'trāt/) [predic.] distracted or absentminded: *he seemed oddly distrait.*
– ORIGIN mid 18th cent.: French, from Old French *destrait*, past participle of *destraire* 'distract,' from Latin *distrahere* 'pull apart' (see DISTRACT).

dis·traught /dis'trôt/ ▶ adj. deeply upset and agitated: *a distraught woman sobbed and screamed for help | he appeared on television, grief-ravaged and distraught.*
– ORIGIN late Middle English: alteration of the obsolete adjective *distract* (from Latin *distractus* 'pulled apart'), influenced by *straught*, archaic past participle of STRETCH.

dis·tress /dis'tres/ ▶ n. **1** extreme anxiety, sorrow, or pain: *to his distress he saw that she was trembling.* ■ the state of a ship or aircraft when in danger or difficulty and needing help: *vessels* ***in distress*** *on or near the coast.* ■ suffering caused by lack of money or the basic necessities of life: *the poor were helped in their distress.* ■ Medicine a state of physical strain, exhaustion, or, in particular, breathing difficulty: *they said the baby was in distress.*
2 Law another term for DISTRAINT.
▶ v. [with obj.] **1** cause (someone) anxiety, sorrow, or pain: *I didn't mean to distress you* | [with obj. and infinitive] *he was distressed to find that Anna would not talk to him.*
2 give (furniture, leather, or clothing) simulated marks of age and wear: *the manner in which leather jackets are industrially distressed.*
– DERIVATIVES **dis·tress·ful** /-fəl/ adj.
– ORIGIN Middle English: from Old French *destresce* (noun), *destrecier* (verb), based on Latin *distringere* 'stretch apart.'

dis·tressed /dis'trest/ ▶ adj. suffering from anxiety, sorrow, or pain: *I was distressed at the news of his death.* ■ dated impoverished: *women in distressed circumstances.* ■ (of furniture, leather, or clothing) having simulated marks of age and wear: *a distressed leather jacket.* ■ (of property) for sale at unusually low prices or at a loss, esp. due to mortgage foreclosure or because it is part of an insolvent estate.

dis·tress·ing /dis'tresiNG/ ▶ adj. causing anxiety, sorrow or pain; upsetting: *some very distressing news.*
– DERIVATIVES **dis·tress·ing·ly** adv. [as submodifier] *the pattern was distressingly familiar.*

dis·tress sale ▶ n. a sale of goods or assets at reduced prices to raise much-needed funds.

dis·tress sig·nal ▶ n. a signal from a ship or aircraft in danger.

dis·trib·u·tar·y /dis'tribyoo͞,terē/ ▶ n. (pl. **distributaries**) a branch of a river that does not return to the main stream after leaving it (as in a delta).

dis·trib·ute /dis'tribyoo͞t/ ▶ v. [with obj.] **1** give shares of (something); deal out: *information leaflets are being distributed to hotels and guest houses.* ■ supply (goods) to stores and other businesses that sell to consumers: *the journal is distributed worldwide.* ■ (**be distributed**) occur throughout an area: *the birds are mainly distributed in marshes and river valleys.* ■ Printing separate (metal type that has been set up) and return the characters to their separate compartments in a type case.
2 Logic use (a term) to include every individual of the class to which it refers: *the middle term must be distributed, at least once, in the premises.*

d

– DERIVATIVES **dis·trib·ut·a·ble** adj.
– ORIGIN late Middle English: from Latin *distribut-* 'divided up,' from the verb *distribuere*, from *dis-* 'apart' + *tribuere* 'assign.'

dis·trib·ut·ed sys·tem ▶ n. a number of independent computers linked by a network.

dis·tri·bu·tion /ˌdistrəˈbyo͞oSHən/ (abbr.: **distr.**) ▶ n. the action of sharing something out among a number of recipients: *she had it printed for distribution among her friends.* ■ the way in which something is shared out among a group or spread over an area: *changes undergone by the area have affected the distribution of its wildlife.* ■ the action or process of supplying goods to stores and other businesses that sell to consumers: *a manager has the choice of four types of distribution* | [as modifier] *an established distribution channel.* ■ Bridge the different number of cards of each suit in a player's hand: *strength has two ingredients, high cards and distribution.*
– DERIVATIVES **dis·tri·bu·tion·al** /-SHənl/ adj.
– ORIGIN late Middle English: from Latin *distributio(n-)*, from the verb *distribuere* (see DISTRIBUTE).

dis·tri·bu·tion func·tion ▶ n. short for CUMULATIVE DISTRIBUTION FUNCTION.

dis·tri·bu·tive /disˈtribyətiv/ ▶ adj. **1** concerned with the supply of goods to stores and other businesses that sell to consumers: *transportation and distributive industries.* ■ concerned with the way in which things are shared between people: *the distributive effects of public expenditure* | *distributive justice.*
2 Grammar (of a determiner or pronoun) referring to each individual of a class, not to the class collectively, e.g., *each, either.*
3 Mathematics (of an operation) fulfilling the condition that, when it is performed on two or more quantities already combined by another operation, the result is the same as when it is performed on each quantity individually and the products then combined.
▶ n. Grammar a distributive word.
– DERIVATIVES **dis·trib·u·tive·ly** adv.
– ORIGIN late Middle English: from Old French *distributif, -ive* or late Latin *distributivus*, from Latin *distribut-* 'divided up,' from the verb *distribuere* (see DISTRIBUTE).

dis·trib·u·tor /disˈtribyətər/ (abbr.: **distr.**) ▶ n. **1** an agent who supplies goods to stores and other businesses that sell to consumers: *a wholesale liquor distributor* | *the movie's distributor booked the film into theaters.*
2 a device in a gasoline engine for passing electric current to each spark plug in turn.

dis·trib·ut·or cap ▶ n. an insulated cap that fits over the distributor in a gasoline engine and that distributes voltage to the spark plugs.

dis·trict /ˈdistrikt/ ▶ n. (abbr.: **distr.**) an area of a country or city, esp. one regarded as a distinct unit because of a particular characteristic: *an elegant shopping district.* ■ a region defined for an administrative purpose: *the city school district.* ■ (**the District**) the District of Columbia; Washington, DC.
▶ v. [with obj.] divide into districts.
– ORIGIN early 17th cent. (denoting the territory under the jurisdiction of a feudal lord): from French, from medieval Latin *districtus* '(territory of) jurisdiction,' from Latin *distringere* 'draw apart.'

dis·trict at·tor·ney (abbr.: **DA**) ▶ n. a public official who acts as prosecutor for the state or the federal government in court in a particular district.

dis·trict court ▶ n. a state of federal trial court.

Dis·trict of Co·lum·bi·a (abbr.: **DC**) a federal district of the US, coextensive with the city of Washington, on the Potomac River with boundaries on the states of Virginia and Maryland.

dis·tro /ˈdistrō/ ▶ n. (pl. **distros**) Computing a distributor or distributed version, esp. of Linux software or of webzines: *I was excited enough about this distro that I forked over the cash to buy it.*
– ORIGIN by shortening and alteration.

dis·trust /disˈtrəst/ ▶ n. the feeling that someone or something cannot be relied on: *his distrust of his mother's new suitor.*
▶ v. [with obj.] doubt the honesty or reliability of; regard with suspicion: *like a skillful gambler, Dave distrusted a sure thing.*
– DERIVATIVES **dis·trust·er** n., **dis·trust·ful** /-fəl/ adj., **dis·trust·ful·ly** /-fəlē/ adv.

dis·turb /disˈtərb/ ▶ v. [with obj.] interfere with the normal arrangement or functioning of: *being sent to jail had apparently not disturbed his cheerfulness* | *the site surface had been disturbed by bulldozer activity.* ■ cause to feel anxious: *I am disturbed by the document I have just read.* ■ interrupt the sleep, relaxation, or privacy of: *I'll see my patient now and we are not to be disturbed.*
– DERIVATIVES **dis·turb·er** n.
– ORIGIN Middle English: from Old French *destourber*, from Latin *disturbare*, from *dis-* 'utterly' + *turbare* 'disturb' (from *turba* 'tumult').

dis·tur·bance /disˈtərbəns/ ▶ n. the interruption of a settled and peaceful condition: *a helicopter landing can cause disturbance to residents.* ■ a breakdown of peaceful and law-abiding behavior; a riot: *the disturbances were precipitated when four men were refused bail.* ■ the disruption of healthy functioning: *her severe mental disturbance was diagnosed as schizophrenia.* ■ Meteorology a local variation from normal or average wind conditions, usually a small tornado or cyclone. ■ Law interference with rights or property; molestation.
– ORIGIN Middle English: from Old French *destourbance*, from *destourber* (see DISTURB).

dis·turbed /disˈtərbd/ ▶ adj. having had its normal pattern or function disrupted: *disturbed sleep.* ■ suffering or resulting from emotional and mental problems: *the treatment of disturbed children* | *disturbed behavior.*

dis·turb·ing /disˈtərbiNG/ ▶ adj. causing anxiety; worrying: *disturbing unemployment figures.*
– DERIVATIVES **dis·turb·ing·ly** adv. [as submodifier] *a woman who looked disturbingly familiar.*

di·sub·sti·tut·ed /dīˈsəbstiˌt(y)o͞otid/ ▶ adj. Chemistry (of a molecule) having two substituent groups.

di·sul·fide /dīˈsəlˌfīd/ (Brit. **disulphide**) ▶ n. Chemistry a sulfide containing two atoms of sulfur in its molecule or empirical formula. ■ an organic compound containing the group –S–S– bonded to other groups.

di·sul·fir·am /dīˈsəlfəˌram/ ▶ n. Medicine a synthetic compound used in the treatment of alcoholics to make drinking alcohol produce unpleasant aftereffects. Also called ANTABUSE (trademark). ● Alternative name: **tetraethylthiuram disulfide**; chem. formula: $(C_2H_5)_2NCSSCN(C_2H_5)_2$.
– ORIGIN 1940s: blend of *disulfide* (see DISULFIDE) and *thiuram* (from THIO- + UREA + AMIDE).

dis·un·ion /disˈyo͞onyən/ ▶ n. the breaking up of something such as a federation: *his rejection of disunion was consistent with his nationalism.*

dis·u·nit·ed /ˌdisyo͞oˈnītid/ ▶ adj. lacking unity: *a disunited nation.*
– DERIVATIVES **dis·u·nite** v.

dis·u·ni·ty /disˈyo͞onitē/ ▶ n. disagreement and conflict within a group: *the disunity among opposition parties.*

dis·use /disˈyo͞os/ ▶ n. the state of not being used: *the machines **fell into disuse** with the advent of computers.*
– PHRASES **fall into disuse** cease to be used: *the old tracks fell into disuse and neglect.*

dis·used /disˈyo͞ozd/ ▶ adj. no longer being used: *they held an exhibition in a disused warehouse.*

dis·u·til·i·ty /ˌdisyo͞oˈtilitē/ ▶ n. Economics the adverse or harmful effects associated with a particular activity or process, esp. when carried out over a long period.

dis·val·ue /disˈvalyo͞o/ ▶ v. (**disvalues, disvaluing, disvalued**) [with obj.] undervalue (something or someone): *I'm not going to disvalue the way they feel.*
▶ n. a negative value or worth.
– DERIVATIVES **dis·val·u·a·tion** /-ˌvalyo͞oˈāSHən/ n.

di·syl·lab·ic /ˌdīsiˈlabik, di-/ (also **dissyllabic**) ▶ adj. (of a word or metrical foot) consisting of two syllables. ■ (of a bird's call) consisting of two distinct sounds, such as the call of the cuckoo.
– ORIGIN mid 17th cent.: from French *dissyllabique*, via Latin from Greek *disullabos* 'of two syllables.'

di·syl·la·ble /dīˈsiləbəl, di-/ (also **dissyllable**) ▶ n. Prosody a word or metrical foot consisting of two syllables.
– ORIGIN late 16th cent.: alteration (influenced by SYLLABLE) of French *disyllabe*, via Latin from Greek *disullabos* 'of two syllables,' from *di-* 'two' + *sullabē* 'syllable.'

dit /dit/ ▶ n. (in Morse code) another term for DOT[1].
– ORIGIN World War II: imitative.

ditch /diCH/ ▶ n. a narrow channel dug in the ground, typically used for drainage alongside a road or the edge of a field.
▶ v. [with obj.] **1** provide with ditches: *he was praised for ditching the coastal areas.* ■ [no obj.] make or repair ditches: (as noun **ditching**) *they would have to pay for hedging and ditching.*
2 informal get rid of; give up: *it crossed her mind to ditch her shoes and run* | *plans for the road were ditched following a public inquiry.* ■ informal end a relationship with (someone) peremptorily; abandon: *she ditched her husband to marry the window cleaner.* ■ informal be truant from (school or another obligation): *maybe she could ditch school and run away.*
3 informal bring (an aircraft) down on water in an emergency: *he was picked up by a frigate after ditching his plane in the Mediterranean.* ■ [no obj.] (of an aircraft) make a forced landing on water: *the aircraft was obliged to ditch in the sea off the North African coast.* ■ derail (a train).
– DERIVATIVES **ditch·er** n.
– ORIGIN Old English *dīc*, of Germanic origin; related to Dutch *dijk* 'ditch, dike' and German *Teich* 'pond, pool,' also to DIKE[1].

ditch·wa·ter /ˈdiCHˌwôtər, -ˌwä-/ ▶ n. stagnant water in a ditch.
– PHRASES **dull as ditchwater** see DULL.

di·the·ism /ˈdīTHēˌizəm, dīˈTHē-/ ▶ n. a belief in two gods, esp. as independent and opposed principles of good and evil.
– DERIVATIVES **di·the·ist** n.

dith·er /ˈdiT͟Hər/ ▶ v. **1** [no obj.] be indecisive: *he was dithering about the election date.*
2 [with obj.] add white noise to (a digital recording) to reduce distortion of low-amplitude signals. ■ display or print (a color image) in such a way that there appears to be more colors in it than are really available: (as adj. **dithered**) *dithered bitmaps.*
▶ n. **1** informal indecisive behavior: *after months of dither they had still not agreed.*
2 [in sing.] a state of agitation: *buses are jammed and dirty and everyone is **in a dither** over taxis.*
– DERIVATIVES **dith·er·er** n., **dith·er·y** adj.
– ORIGIN mid 17th cent. (in the dialect sense 'tremble, quiver'): variant of dialect *didder*; related to DODDER[1].

di·thi·o·nite /dīˈTHīəˌnīt/ ▶ n. Chemistry a salt containing the anion $S_2O_4^{2-}$.
– ORIGIN mid 20th cent.: from DI-[1] 'two' + Greek *theion* 'sulfur' + -ITE[1].

di·thi·zone /dīˈTHīˌzōn/ ▶ n. Chemistry a synthetic compound used as a reagent for the analysis and separation of lead and other metals. ● Alternative name: **diphenylthiocarbazone**; chem. formula: $C_{13}H_{12}N_4S$.
– ORIGIN 1920s: from elements of the systematic name (see above).

dith·y·ramb /ˈdiTHəˌram/ ▶ n. a wild choral hymn of ancient Greece, esp. one dedicated to Dionysus. ■ a passionate or inflated speech, poem, or other writing.
– DERIVATIVES **dith·y·ram·bic** /ˌdiTHəˈrambik/ adj.
– ORIGIN early 17th cent.: via Latin from Greek *dithurambos*, of unknown ultimate origin.

di·tran·si·tive /dīˈtranzətiv/ ▶ adj. Grammar (of a verb) taking two objects, for example *give* as in *I gave her the book.*

dit·sy ▶ adj. variant spelling of DITZY.

dit·ta·ny /ˈditn-ē/ ▶ n. any of a number of aromatic herbaceous or shrubby plants. ● (also **dittany of Crete**) a dwarf shrub with white woolly leaves and pink flowers, native to Crete and Greece (*Origanum dictamnus*, family Labiatae). ● (also **American dittany**) an American herb used in cooking and herbal medicine (genus *Cunila*, family Labiatae). ● another term for GAS PLANT.
– ORIGIN late Middle English: from Old French *ditain* or medieval Latin *ditaneum*, from Latin *dictamnus, dictamnum*, from Greek *diktamnon*, perhaps from *Diktē*, the name of a mountain in Crete.

dit·to /ˈditō/ ▶ n. (pl. **dittos**) **1** used in accounts and lists to indicate that an item is repeated (often indicated by a ditto mark under the word or figure to be repeated). ■ informal used to indicate that something already said is applicable a second time: *if one folds his arms, so does the other; if one crosses his legs, ditto.*
2 a similar thing; a duplicate.
– ORIGIN early 17th cent. (in the sense 'in the aforesaid month'): from Tuscan dialect, variant of Italian *detto* 'said,' from Latin *dictus* 'said.'

dit·tog·ra·phy /diˈtägrəfē/ ▶ n. (pl. **dittographies**) a mistaken repetition of a letter, word, or phrase by a copyist.
– DERIVATIVES **dit·to·graph·ic** /ˌditəˈgrafik/ adj.
– ORIGIN late 19th cent.: from Greek *dittos* 'double' + -GRAPHY.

dit·to mark ▶ n. a symbol (") representing "ditto."

dit·ty /ˈditē/ ▶ n. (pl. **ditties**) a short simple song: *a lovely little music-hall ditty.*
– ORIGIN Middle English: from Old French *dite* 'composition,' from Latin *dictatum* (neuter) 'something dictated,' from *dictare* 'to dictate.'

dit·ty bag (also **ditty box**) ▶ n. a receptacle for odds and ends, esp. one used by sailors or fishermen.
– ORIGIN mid 19th cent.: of unknown origin.

ditz /dits/ ▶ n. informal a scatterbrained person.
– ORIGIN 1970s: back-formation from DITZY.

dit·zy /ˈditsē/ (also **ditsy**) ▶ **adj.** informal silly or scatterbrained: *don't tell me my ditzy secretary didn't send you an invitation!*
– DERIVATIVES **dit·zi·ness** n.
– ORIGIN 1970s: of unknown origin.

di·u·re·sis /ˌdīyəˈrēsis/ ▶ **n.** Medicine increased or excessive production of urine. Compare with POLYURIA.
– ORIGIN late 17th cent.: modern Latin, from DI-³ 'through' + Greek *ourēsis* 'urination.'

di·u·ret·ic /ˌdīyəˈretik/ Medicine ▶ **adj.** (chiefly of drugs) causing increased passing of urine.
▶ **n.** a diuretic drug.
– ORIGIN late Middle English: from Old French *diuretique*, or via late Latin from Greek *diourētikos*, from *diourein* 'urinate,' from *dia* 'through' + *ouron* 'urine.'

di·ur·nal /dīˈərnl/ ▶ **adj.** **1** of or during the day. ■ Zoology (of animals) active in the daytime. ■ Botany (of flowers) open only during the day.
2 daily; of each day: *diurnal rhythms.* ■ Astronomy of or resulting from the daily rotation of the earth.
– DERIVATIVES **di·ur·nal·ly** adv.
– ORIGIN late Middle English (as a term in astronomy): from late Latin *diurnalis*, from Latin *diurnus* 'daily,' from *dies* 'day.'

div ▶ **abbr.** divergence (in mathematical equations).

Div. ▶ **abbr.** ■ Division. ■ divorced.

di·va /ˈdēvə/ ▶ **n.** a famous female opera singer: *your average opera isn't over till the diva trills her high notes.* ■ a famous female singer of popular music: *a pop diva.* ■ a woman regarded as temperamental or haughty: *she's such a diva that she won't enter a restaurant until they change the pictures on the walls to her liking.*
– ORIGIN late 19th cent.: via Italian from Latin, literally 'goddess.'

di·va·gate /ˈdīvəˌgāt/ ▶ **v.** [no obj.] literary stray; digress: *Yeats divagated into Virgil's territory only once.*
– DERIVATIVES **di·va·ga·tion** /ˌdīvəˈgāsHən/ n.
– ORIGIN late 16th cent.: from Latin *divagat-* 'wandered around,' from the verb *divagari*, from *di-* 'widely' + *vagari* 'wander.'

di·va·lent /dīˈvālənt/ ▶ **adj.** Chemistry having a valence of two.

Di·va·li ▶ **n.** variant spelling of DIWALI.

di·van ▶ **n.** **1** /diˈvan, ˈdīˌvan/ a long low sofa without a back or arms, typically placed against a wall.
2 /diˈvan, -ˈvän/ historical a legislative body, council chamber, or court of justice in the Ottoman Empire or elsewhere in the Middle East.
– ORIGIN late 16th cent. (sense 2): via French or Italian from Turkish *dīvān*, from Persian *dīwān* 'anthology, register, court, or bench'; compare with DIWAN. As a piece of furniture, a *divan* was originally (early 18th cent.) a low bench or raised section of floor used as a long seat against the wall of a room, common in Middle Eastern countries; European imitation of this led to the sense 'low flat sofa or bed' (late 19th cent).

di·var·i·cate ▶ **v.** /dīˈvariˌkāt, di-/ [no obj.] technical or literary stretch or spread apart; diverge widely.
▶ **adj.** /-kit, -ˌkāt/ Botany (of a branch) coming off the stem almost at a right angle.
– DERIVATIVES **di·var·i·ca·tion** /-ˌvariˈkāsHən/ n.
– ORIGIN early 17th cent.: from Latin *divaricat-* 'stretched apart,' from the verb *divaricare*, from *di-* (expressing intensive force) + *varicare* 'stretch the legs apart' (from *varicus* 'straddling').

dive /dīv/ ▶ **v.** (past **dived** or **dove** /dōv/; past participle **dived**) [no obj.] **1** [with adverbial of direction] plunge head first into water: *she walked to the deep end, then she dived in | he dived off the bridge for a bet.* ■ (of a fish, a submarine, or a vessel used for underwater exploration) go to a deeper level in water: *the fish dive down to about 1,400 feet and then swim southwest.* ■ swim underwater using breathing equipment: *he had been diving in the area to test equipment.*
2 (of an aircraft or bird) plunge steeply downward through the air: *the aircraft dove for the ground to avoid the attack.* ■ move quickly or suddenly in a specified direction: *a bullet passed close to his head, and he dived for cover* | (as adj. **diving**) *he attempted a diving catch.* ■ (of prices or profits) drop suddenly: *profits before tax dived by 61 percent.* ■ informal put one's hand quickly into something, esp. a pocket or purse, in order to find something: *she dived into her bag and extracted a card.* ■ Soccer & Ice Hockey (of a player) deliberately fall when challenged in order to deceive the referee into awarding a foul.
▶ **n.** **1** a plunge head first into water: *he hit the sea in a shallow dive | a high dive.* ■ an instance of swimming or going deeper under water: *divers should have a good intake of fluid before each dive.*
2 a steep descent by an aircraft or bird: *the jumbo jet went into a dive.* See also NOSEDIVE. ■ a sudden movement in a specified direction: *she made a dive for the fridge to quench her raging thirst.* ■ a sudden and significant fall in prices or profits: *an 11 percent dive in profits.* ■ Soccer & Ice Hockey a deliberate fall by a player, intended to deceive the referee into awarding a foul.
3 informal a disreputable nightclub or bar: *he got into a fight in some dive.*
– PHRASES **take a dive** Boxing pretend to be knocked out. ■ (of prices, hopes, fortunes, etc.) fall suddenly: *profits could take a dive as easily as they could soar | her reputation took a dive from which it has not recovered.*
– PHRASAL VERBS **dive in** help oneself to food. **dive into** occupy oneself suddenly and enthusiastically with (a meal, or an engrossing subject or activity): *dive into a barbecued beef burrito.*
– ORIGIN Old English *dūfan* 'dive, sink' and *dȳfan* 'immerse,' of Germanic origin; related to DEEP and DIP.

dive-bomb ▶ **v.** [with obj.] bomb (a target) while diving steeply downward in an aircraft: *news that they had dive-bombed a US destroyer.* ■ (of a bird or flying insect) attack (something) by swooping down on it: *the crow folded its wings and dive-bombed the vulture.*
– DERIVATIVES **dive-bomb·er** n.

dive·mas·ter /ˈdīvˌmastər/ ▶ **n.** a person who is in charge of an underwater diving expedition.

div·er /ˈdīvər/ ▶ **n.** **1** a person or animal that dives, in particular: ■ a person who dives as a sport: *an Olympic diver.* ■ a person who wears a diving suit to work underwater: *a diver at the oil terminal | a police diver.*
2 British term for LOON¹.

di·verge /diˈvərj, dī-/ ▶ **v.** [no obj.] **1** (of a road, route, or line) separate from another route, esp. a main one, and go in a different direction. ■ develop in a different direction: *howler and spider monkeys* ***diverged from*** *a common ancestor.* ■ (of an opinion, theory, approach, etc.) differ markedly: *the coverage by the columnists* ***diverged from*** *that in the main news stories* | (as adj. **diverging**) *studies from different viewpoints yield diverging conclusions.* ■ deviate from a set course or standard: *suddenly he* ***diverged from*** *his text.*
2 Mathematics (of a series) increase indefinitely as more terms are added.
– ORIGIN mid 17th cent.: from medieval Latin *divergere*, from Latin *dis-* 'in two ways' + *vergere* 'to turn or incline.'

di·ver·gence /diˈvərjəns, dī-/ ▶ **n.** **1** the process or state of diverging: *the divergence between primates and other groups.* ■ a difference or conflict in opinions, interests, wishes, etc.: *a fundamental divergence of attitude.* ■ a place where airflows or ocean currents diverge, typically marked by downwelling (of air) or upwelling (of water).
2 Mathematics the inner product of the operator del and a given vector, which gives a measure of the quantity of flux emanating from any point of the vector field or the rate of loss of mass, heat, etc., from it.

di·ver·gent /diˈvərjənt, dī-/ ▶ **adj.** **1** tending to be different or develop in different directions: *divergent interpretations | varieties of English can remain astonishingly* ***divergent from*** *one another.* ■ Psychology (of thought) using a variety of premises, esp. unfamiliar premises, as bases for inference, and avoiding common limiting assumptions in making deductions.
2 Mathematics (of a series) increasing indefinitely as more of its terms are added.
– DERIVATIVES **di·ver·gen·cy** n., **di·ver·gent·ly** adv.

di·vers /ˈdīvərz/ ▶ **adj.** [attrib.] archaic or literary of varying types; several: *in divers places.*
– ORIGIN Middle English: via Old French from Latin *diversus* 'diverse,' from *divertere* 'turn in separate ways' (see DIVERT).

di·verse /diˈvərs, dī-/ ▶ **adj.** showing a great deal of variety; very different: *a culturally diverse population | subjects as diverse as architecture, language teaching, and the physical sciences.*
– DERIVATIVES **di·verse·ly** adv.
– ORIGIN Middle English: variant of DIVERS.

di·ver·si·fy /diˈvərsiˌfī, dī-/ ▶ **v.** (**diversifies, diversifying, diversified**) make or become more diverse or varied: [no obj.] ***the trilobites diversified into*** *a great number of species* | [with obj.] *they seek to diversify their approach to teaching* | (as adj. **diversified**) *a diversified economy.* ■ [no obj.] (of a company) enlarge or vary its range of products or field of operation: *the company expanded rapidly and* ***diversified into*** *computers.* ■ [with obj.] (often as adj. **diversified**) enlarge or vary the range of products or the field of operation of (a company): *the rise of the diversified corporation.*
– DERIVATIVES **di·ver·si·fi·ca·tion** /-ˌvərsifiˈkāsHən/ n.
– ORIGIN late Middle English (in the sense 'show diversity'): via Old French from medieval Latin *diversificare* 'make dissimilar,' from Latin *diversus*, past participle of *divertere* (see DIVERT).

di·ver·sion /diˈvərZHən, dī-/ ▶ **n.** **1** an instance of turning something aside from its course: *a diversion of resources from defense to civil research.* ■ Brit. an alternative route for use by traffic when the usual road is temporarily closed; a detour: *the road was closed and diversions put into operation.*
2 an activity that diverts the mind from tedious or serious concerns; a recreation or pastime: *our chief diversion was reading.* ■ something intended to distract someone's attention from something more important: *a subsidiary raid was carried out on the airfield to create a diversion.*
– DERIVATIVES **di·ver·sion·ar·y** /-ˌnerē/ adj.
– ORIGIN late Middle English: from late Latin *diversio(n-)*, from Latin *divertere* 'turn aside' (see DIVERT).

di·ver·si·ty /diˈvərsitē, dī-/ ▶ **n.** (pl. **diversities**) the state of being diverse; variety: *there was considerable diversity in the style of the reports.* ■ [usu. in sing.] a range of different things: *newspapers were obliged to allow a diversity of views to be printed.*
– ORIGIN Middle English: from Old French *diversite*, from Latin *diversitas*, from *diversus* 'diverse,' past participle of *divertere* 'turn aside' (see DIVERT).

di·vert /diˈvərt, dī-/ ▶ **v.** [with obj.] **1** cause (someone or something) to change course or turn from one direction to another: *a scheme to* ***divert*** *water* ***from*** *the river to irrigate agricultural land.* ■ [no obj.] (of a vehicle or person) change course: *an aircraft has diverted and will be with you shortly.* ■ reallocate (something, esp. money or resources) to a different purpose: *more of their advertising budget was* ***diverted into*** *promotions.*
2 distract (someone or their attention) from something: *public relations policies are sometimes intended to divert attention away from criticism.* ■ (usu. as adj. **diverting**) draw the attention of (someone) away from tedious or serious concerns; entertain or amuse: *a diverting book | nursery rhymes can calm and divert all but the most fractious child.*
– DERIVATIVES **di·vert·er** n., **di·vert·ing·ly** adv.
– ORIGIN late Middle English: via French from Latin *divertere*, from *di-* 'aside' + *vertere* 'to turn.'

di·ver·tic·u·la /ˌdīvərˈtikyələ/ plural form of DIVERTICULUM.

di·ver·tic·u·lar /ˌdīvərˈtikyələr/ ▶ **adj.** [attrib.] Medicine of or relating to diverticula.

di·ver·tic·u·lar dis·ease ▶ **n.** a condition in which muscle spasm in the colon (lower intestine) in the presence of diverticula causes abdominal pain and disturbance of bowel function without inflammation.

di·ver·tic·u·li·tis /ˌdīvərˌtikyəˈlītis/ ▶ **n.** Medicine inflammation of a diverticulum, esp. in the colon, causing pain and disturbance of bowel function. Compare with DIVERTICULOSIS.

di·ver·tic·u·lo·sis /ˌdīvərˌtikyəˈlōsis/ ▶ **n.** Medicine a condition in which diverticula are present in the intestine without signs of inflammation. Compare with DIVERTICULITIS.

di·ver·tic·u·lum /ˌdīvərˈtikyələm/ ▶ **n.** (pl. **diverticula** /-lə/) Anatomy & Zoology a blind tube leading from a cavity or passage. ■ Medicine an abnormal sac or pouch formed at a weak point in the wall of the alimentary tract.
– ORIGIN early 19th cent.: from medieval Latin, variant of Latin *deverticulum* 'byway,' from *devertere* 'turn down or aside.'

di·ver·ti·men·to /diˌvərtəˈmentō/ ▶ **n.** (pl. **divertimenti** /-ˈmentē/ or **divertimentos**) Music a light and entertaining composition, typically one in the form of a suite for chamber orchestra.
– ORIGIN mid 18th cent. (denoting a diversion or amusement): Italian, literally 'diversion.'

di·ver·tisse·ment /diˈvərtismənt/ ▶ **n.** a minor entertainment or diversion: *as a Sunday divertissement Wittgenstein would play Schubert quartets.* ■ Ballet a short dance within a ballet that displays a dancer's technical skill without advancing the plot or character development.
– ORIGIN early 18th cent. (specifically denoting a short ballet): French, from *divertiss-*, stem of *divertir*, from Latin *divertere* 'turn in separate ways.'

Di·ves /ˈdīˌvēz/ ▶ **n.** literary used to refer to a typical or hypothetical rich man: *there must be rich and poor, Dives says, smacking his claret.*

– ORIGIN late Middle English: from late Latin, used in the Vulgate translation of the Bible (Luke 16).

di·vest /di'vest, dī-/ ▶ v. [with obj.] deprive (someone) of power, rights, or possessions: *men are unlikely to be **divested of** power without a struggle.* ■ deprive (something) of a particular quality: *he has **divested** the original play **of** its charm.* ■ [no obj.] rid oneself of something that one no longer wants or requires, such as a business interest or investment: *it appears easier to carry on in the business than to divest* | *the government's policy of **divesting itself of** state holdings.* ■ dated or humorous relieve (someone) of something being worn or carried: *she divested him of his coat.*
– ORIGIN early 17th cent.: alteration of *devest*, from Old French *desvestir*, from *des-* (expressing removal) + Latin *vestire* (from *vestis* 'garment').

di·vest·i·ture /di'vesti,CHər, -,CHŏŏr, dī-/ (also **divesture** /-'vesCHər, -CHŏŏr/) ▶ n. the action or process of selling off subsidiary business interests or investments: *the divestiture of state-owned assets.*
– ORIGIN early 17th cent.: from medieval Latin *divestit-* 'divested' (from the verb *divestire*) + **-URE**.

di·vest·ment /di'vestmənt, dī-/ ▶ n. another term for **DIVESTITURE**.

div·i ▶ n. (pl. **divis**) Brit. variant spelling of **DIVVY**.

di·vide /di'vīd/ ▶ v. **1** separate or be separated into parts: [with obj.] *consumer magazines can be **divided into** a number of different categories* | [no obj.] *the cell clusters began to divide rapidly.* ■ [with obj.] separate (something) into portions and distribute a share to each of a number of people: *Jack **divided up** the rest of the cash* | *the property was **divided among** his heirs.* ■ [with obj.] allocate (different parts of one's time, attention, or efforts) to different activities or places: *the last years of her life were **divided between** Bermuda and Paris.* ■ [with obj.] form a boundary between (two people or things): *the artificial barrier that has **divided** an academic education **from** a vocational one.* ■ (of a legislative assembly) separate or be separated into two groups for voting: [no obj.] *the House divided: 287 for, 196 against.*
2 disagree or cause to disagree: [with obj.] *the question had divided Frenchmen since the Revolution* | (as adj. **divided**) *a divided party leadership* | [no obj.] *cities where politicians frequently divide along racial lines.*
3 [with obj.] Mathematics find how many times (a number) contains another: *36 **divided by** 2 equals 18* | [no obj.] *the program helps children to multiply and divide quickly and accurately.* ■ [no obj.] (of a number) be susceptible to division without a remainder: *30 does not divide by 8.* ■ find how many times (a number) is contained in another: ***divide** 4 **into** 20.* ■ [no obj.] (of a number) be contained in a number without a remainder: *3 divides into 15.*
▶ n. a wide divergence between two groups, typically producing tension or hostility: *there was still a profound cultural **divide between** the parties.* ■ a boundary between two things: *symbolically, the difference of sex is a divide.* ■ a ridge or line of high ground forming the division between two valleys or river systems.
– PHRASES **divide and conquer** (or **rule**) the policy of maintaining control over one's subordinates or subjects by encouraging dissent between them. **divided against itself** (of a group that should be coherent) split by factional interests: *the regime is profoundly divided against itself.*
– ORIGIN Middle English (as a verb): from Latin *dividere* 'force apart, remove.' The noun dates from the mid 17th cent.

di·vid·ed high·way ▶ n. a road with a median strip between the traffic in opposite directions and typically two or more lanes in each direction.

di·vid·ed skirt ▶ n. dated culottes.

div·i·dend /'divi,dend/ ▶ n. **1** a sum of money paid regularly (typically quarterly) by a company to its shareholders out of its profits (or reserves). ■ a payment divided among a number of people, e.g., members of a cooperative or creditors of an insolvent estate. ■ an individual's share of a dividend. ■ (**dividends**) a benefit from an action or policy: *persistence **pays dividends**.* See also **PEACE DIVIDEND**.
2 Mathematics a number to be divided by another number.
– ORIGIN late 15th cent. (in the general sense 'portion, share'): from Anglo-Norman French *dividende*, from Latin *dividendum* 'something to be divided,' from the verb *dividere* (see **DIVIDE**).

div·i·dend cov·er·age ▶ n. the ratio of a company's dividends to its net income.

div·i·dend yield ▶ n. a dividend expressed as a percentage of a current share price.

di·vid·er /di'vīdər/ ▶ n. **1** a person or thing that divides a whole into parts. ■ an issue on which opinions are divided: *the big divider was still nuclear weapons.* ■ (also **room divider**) a screen or piece of furniture that divides a room into two parts.
2 (**dividers**) a measuring compass, esp. one with a screw for making fine adjustments.

di·vid·ing line ▶ n. the boundary between two areas: ***the dividing line between** eastern and western zones.* ■ a distinction or set of distinctions marking the difference between two related things: ***the dividing line between** drama and reality.*

div·i·div·i /,divē 'divē/ ▶ n. (pl. **divi-divis**) a tropical American tree of the pea family, bearing curled pods. ● *Caesalpinia coriaria*, family Leguminosae. ■ these pods, used as a source of tannin.
– ORIGIN mid 19th cent.: via American Spanish from Carib.

div·i·na·tion /,divə'nāSHən/ ▶ n. the practice of seeking knowledge of the future or the unknown by supernatural means.
– DERIVATIVES **di·vin·a·to·ry** /di'vinə,tôrē/ adj.
– ORIGIN late Middle English: from Latin *divinatio(n-)*, from *divinare* 'predict' (see **DIVINE²**).

di·vine¹ /di'vīn/ ▶ adj. (**diviner, divinest**) **1** of, from, or like God or a god: *heroes with divine powers* | *paintings of shipwrecks being prevented by divine intervention.* ■ devoted to God; sacred: *divine liturgy.*
2 informal, dated excellent; delightful: *that succulent clementine tasted divine* | *he had the most divine smile.*
▶ n. **1** dated a cleric or theologian.
2 (**the Divine**) providence or God.
– DERIVATIVES **di·vine·ly** adv., **di·vine·ness** n.
– ORIGIN late Middle English: via Old French from Latin *divinus*, from *divus* 'godlike' (related to *deus* 'god').

di·vine² ▶ v. [with obj.] discover (something) by guesswork or intuition: *his brother usually divined his ulterior motives* | [with clause] *they had divined that he was a fake.* ■ have supernatural or magical insight into (future events): *frauds who claimed to divine the future in chickens' entrails.* ■ discover (water) by dowsing.
– DERIVATIVES **di·vin·er** n.
– ORIGIN late Middle English: from Old French *deviner* 'predict,' from Latin *divinare*, from *divinus* (see **DIVINE¹**).

Di·vine Of·fice ▶ n. see **OFFICE** (sense 4).

di·vine right of kings ▶ n. the doctrine that kings derive their authority from God, not from their subjects, from which it follows that rebellion is the worst of political crimes. It was claimed in Britain by the earlier Stuarts and is also associated with the absolutism of Louis XIV of France.

di·vine serv·ice ▶ n. public Christian worship.

div·ing /'dīviNG/ ▶ n. **1** the sport or activity of swimming or exploring underwater.
2 the sport or activity of diving into water from a diving board.

div·ing bee·tle ▶ n. a predatory water beetle that has fringed back legs for swimming and stores air under its wing cases while diving. ● Family Dytiscidae: numerous genera and species, including the **great diving beetle** (*Dytiscus marginalis*).

div·ing bell ▶ n. an open-bottomed chamber supplied with compressed air, in which a person can be let down under water.

div·ing board ▶ n. an elevated board projecting over a swimming pool or other body of water, from which people dive or jump in.

div·ing duck ▶ n. a duck of a type that dives under water for food, such as the pochard, scaup, tufted duck, and goldeneye. Compare with **DABBLING DUCK**. ● Tribes Aythyini and Mergini, family Anatidae: several genera, in particular *Aythya* and *Bucephala*.

div·ing pet·rel ▶ n. a stocky auklike seabird of southern oceans, having black upper parts and white underparts. ● Family Pelecanoididae and genus *Pelecanoides*: four species, in particular the **common** (or **northern**) **diving petrel** (*P. urinatrix*).

div·ing suit ▶ n. a watertight suit, typically with a helmet and an air supply, worn for working or exploring deep underwater.

di·vin·ing rod ▶ n. a stick or rod used for dowsing.

di·vin·i·ty /di'vinitē/ ▶ n. **1** (pl. **divinities**) the state or quality of being divine: *Christ's divinity.* ■ the study of religion; theology: *a doctor of divinity.* ■ a divine being; a god or goddess: *busts of various Roman divinities.* ■ (**the Divinity**) God.
2 a fluffy, creamy candy made with stiffly beaten egg whites.
– ORIGIN Middle English: from Old French *divinite*, from Latin *divinitas*, from *divinus* 'belonging to a deity' (see **DIVINE¹**).

div·i·nize /'divə,nīz/ ▶ v. [with obj.] make (someone) divine; deify: *this brush with death seems to have divinized her.*
– ORIGIN mid 17th cent.: from French *diviniser*, from *divin* 'divine.'

di·vi·si /di'vēzē/ ▶ adj. a musical direction indicating that a section of players should be divided into two or more groups, each playing a different part: [postpositive] *violas divisi* | *divisi passages.*
▶ n. (pl. **same**) a passage written or played in this manner.
– ORIGIN Italian, literally 'divided' (plural), from *dividere* 'to divide.'

di·vis·i·ble /di'vizəbəl/ ▶ adj. capable of being divided: *the marine environment is divisible into a number of areas.* ■ Mathematics (of a number) capable of being divided by another number without a remainder: *24 **is divisible by** 4.*
– DERIVATIVES **di·vis·i·bil·i·ty** /-,vizə'bilitē/ n.
– ORIGIN late Middle English: from late Latin *divisibilis*, from *divis-* 'divided,' from the verb *dividere* (see **DIVIDE**).

di·vi·sion /di'viZHən/ ▶ n. **1** the action of separating something into parts, or the process of being separated: *the division of the land into small fields* | *a gene that helps regulate cell division.* ■ the distribution of something separated into parts: *the **division of** his estates **between** the two branches of his family.* ■ an instance of members of a legislative body separating into two groups to vote for or against a bill: *the new clause was agreed without a division.* ■ the action of splitting the roots of a perennial plant into parts to be replanted separately, as a means of propagation: *the plant can also be easily increased by division in autumn.* ■ Logic the action of dividing a wider class into two or more subclasses.
2 disagreement between two or more groups, typically producing tension or hostility: *a growing sense of **division between** north and south* | *a country with ethnic and cultural divisions.*
3 the process or skill of dividing one number by another. See also **LONG DIVISION, SHORT DIVISION**. ■ Mathematics the process of dividing a matrix, vector, or other quantity by another under specific rules to obtain a quotient.
4 each of the parts into which something is divided: *the main divisions of the book.* ■ a major unit or section of an organization, typically one handling a particular kind of work: *a retail division.* ■ a group of army brigades or regiments: *an infantry division.* ■ a number of teams or competitors grouped together in a sport for competitive purposes according to such characteristics as ability, size, or geographic location: *the team will finish in fifth place in Division One.* ■ a part of a county, country, or city defined for administrative or political purposes: *a licensing division of a district.* ■ Brit. a part of a county or borough forming a parliamentary constituency: *he was MP for the Lancaster division of North Lancashire.* ■ Botany a principal taxonomic category that ranks above class and below kingdom, equivalent to the phylum in zoology. ■ Zoology any subsidiary category between major levels of classification.
5 a partition that divides two groups or things: *the villagers lived in a communal building and there were no solid divisions between neighbors.*
– PHRASES **division of labor** the assignment of different parts of a manufacturing process or task to different people in order to improve efficiency.
– ORIGIN late Middle English: from Old French *devisiun*, from Latin *divisio(n-)*, from the verb *dividere* (see **DIVIDE**).

di·vi·sion·al /di'viZHənl/ ▶ adj. of or relating to an organizational or administrative division: *a divisional manager.* ■ forming a partition: *divisional walls.*
– DERIVATIVES **di·vi·sion·al·ly** adv.

di·vi·sion·al·ize /di'viZHənl,īz/ ▶ v. [with obj.] (usu. as adj. **divisionalized**) subdivide (a company or other organization) into a number of separate divisions: *a large divisionalized Western corporation.* ■ [no obj.] undergo this process.
– DERIVATIVES **di·vi·sion·al·i·za·tion** /di,viZHənələ'zāSHən/ n.

di·vi·sion·ism /di'viZHə,nizəm/ ▶ n. another term for **POINTILLISM**.

di·vi·sion sign ▶ n. the sign ÷, placed between two numbers showing that the first is to be divided by the second, as in $6 \div 3 = 2$.

di·vi·sive /di'vīsiv/ ▶ adj. tending to cause disagreement or hostility between people: *the highly divisive issue of abortion.*
– DERIVATIVES **di·vi·sive·ly** adv., **di·vi·sive·ness** n.
– ORIGIN mid 16th cent. (as a noun denoting something that divides or separates): from late Latin *divisivus*, from Latin *dividere* (see **DIVIDE**).

di·vi·sor /di'vīzər/ ▶ n. Mathematics a number by which another number is to be divided. ■ a number that divides into another without a remainder: *the greatest common divisor.*
– ORIGIN late Middle English: from French *diviseur* or Latin *divisor*, from *dividere* (see **DIVIDE**).

di·vorce /di'vôrs/ ▶ **n.** the legal dissolution of a marriage by a court or other competent body: *her divorce from her first husband* | *one in three marriages ends in divorce* | [as modifier] *divorce proceedings*. ■ a legal decree dissolving a marriage. ■ [in sing.] a separation between things that were or ought to be connected: *the bitter divorce between the company and its largest shareholder*.
▶ **v.** [with obj.] legally dissolve one's marriage with (someone): *he divorced his first wife after 10 months* | (as adj. **divorced**) *a divorced couple* | [no obj.] *they divorced eight years later*. ■ separate or dissociate (something) from something else: *we knew how to divorce an issue from an individual*. ■ (**divorce oneself from**) distance or dissociate oneself from (something): *he wanted to divorce himself from all contact with the syndicate*.
– DERIVATIVES **di·vorce·ment n.**
– ORIGIN late Middle English: the noun from Old French *divorce*, from Latin *divortium*, based on *divertere* (see DIVERT); the verb from Old French *divorcer*, from late Latin *divortiare*, from *divortium*.

di·vor·cee /divôr'sē/ (masc. **divorcé**, fem. **divorcée** /-'sā/) ▶ **n.** a divorced person.
– ORIGIN early 19th cent.: from French *divorcé(e)* 'divorced man (or woman).'

div·ot /'divət/ ▶ **n.** a piece of turf cut out of the ground by a golf club in making a stroke. ■ chiefly Scottish a piece of turf, as formerly used for roofing cottages.
– ORIGIN early 16th cent.: of unknown origin.

di·vulge /di'vəlj, dī-/ ▶ **v.** [with obj.] make known (private or sensitive information): *I am too much of a gentleman to divulge her age*.
– DERIVATIVES **div·ul·ga·tion** /,divəl'gāsHən/ **n.**, **di·vul·gence** /-jəns/ **n.**
– ORIGIN late Middle English (in the sense 'announce publicly'): from Latin *divulgare*, from *di-* 'widely' + *vulgare* 'publish' (from *vulgus* 'common people').

div·vy /'divē/ informal ▶ **v.** (**divvies, divvying, divvied**) [with obj.] divide up and share: *they divvied up the proceeds*.
▶ **n.** **1** (also **divi**) (pl. **divies**) Brit. a dividend or share, esp. of profits earned by a cooperative. **2** a distribution. ■ a portion or share.
– ORIGIN late 19th cent.: abbreviation of DIVIDEND.

Di·wa·li /di'wälē/ (also **Divali** /di'välē/) ▶ **n.** a Hindu festival of lights, held in the period October to November. It is particularly associated with Lakshmi, the goddess of prosperity, and marks the beginning of the fiscal year in India.
– ORIGIN from Hindi *dīvālī*, from Sanskrit *dīpāvali* 'row of lights,' from *dīpa* 'lamp' + *vali* 'row.'

di·wan /di'wän/ (also **dewan**) ▶ **n.** **1** (in Islamic societies) a central finance department, chief administrative office, or regional governing body. **2** a chief treasury official, finance minister, or prime minister in some Indian states.
– ORIGIN Urdu, from Persian *dīwān* 'fiscal register'; compare with DIVAN.

Dix /diks/, Dorothea Lynde (1802–87), US social reformer. She was a pioneer in US prison reform, a creator of insane asylums, and superintendent of women army nurses during the Civil War.

Dix·ie 1 an informal name for the southern US states. It was used in the song "Dixie" (1859), a marching song popular with Confederate soldiers in the Civil War. **2** short for DIXIELAND.
– PHRASES **whistle Dixie** engage in unrealistic fantasies; waste one's time: *until you nail down the facts, you're just whistling Dixie*.

Dix·ie·crat /'diksē,krat/ ▶ **n.** informal any of the Southern Democrats who seceded from the party in 1948 in opposition to its policy of extending civil rights.

Dix·ie Cup ▶ **n.** trademark a brand of disposable paper cup.

Dix·ie·land /'diksē,land/ ▶ **n.** a kind of jazz with a strong two-beat rhythm and collective improvisation that originated in New Orleans in the early 20th century.

DIY ▶ **abbr.** do-it-yourself.

Di·yar·ba·kir /di'yär,bəkər/ a city in southeastern Turkey; pop. 592,600 (est. 2007).

di·zy·got·ic /,dīzī'gätik/ (also **dizygous** /dī'zīgəs/) ▶ **adj.** (of twins) derived from two separate ova, and so not identical.

diz·zy /'dizē/ ▶ **adj.** (**dizzier, dizziest**) having or involving a sensation of spinning around and losing one's balance: *Jonathan had begun to suffer dizzy spells* | figurative *he looked around, dizzy with happiness*. ■ causing such a sensation: *a sheer, dizzy drop* | figurative *a dizzy range of hues*. ■ informal (of a woman) silly but attractive: *he only married me because he wanted a dizzy blonde*.
▶ **v.** (**dizzies, dizzying, dizzied**) [with obj.] (usu. as adj. **dizzying**) make (someone) feel unsteady, confused, or amazed: *the dizzying rate of change* | *her nearness dizzied him*.
– DERIVATIVES **diz·zi·ly** /'dizəlē/ **adv.**, **diz·zi·ness n.**
– ORIGIN Old English *dysig* 'foolish'; related to Low German *dusig, dösig* 'giddy' and Old High German *tusic* 'foolish, weak.'

DJ ▶ **n.** (pl. **DJs**) a disc jockey. ■ a person who uses samples of recorded music to make techno, rap, or dance music.

Dja·kar·ta variant spelling of JAKARTA.

djeb·el ▶ **n.** variant spelling of JEBEL.

djel·la·ba /jə'läbə/ (also **djellabah** or **jellaba**) ▶ **n.** a loose hooded cloak, typically woolen, of a kind traditionally worn by Arabs.
– ORIGIN early 19th cent.: from Moroccan Arabic *jellāba, jellābiyya*.

djem·be /'jembə, -bā/, ▶ **n.** Music a kind of goblet-shaped hand drum originating in West Africa.
– ORIGIN French *djembé*, from Mande *jembe*.

DJIA ▶ **abbr.** Dow Jones Industrial Average.

djib·ba /'jibə/ (also **djibbah**) ▶ **n.** variant spelling of JIBBA.

Dji·bou·ti /jə'bōōtē/ (also **Jibuti**) a country on the northeastern coast of Africa; pop. 724,600 (est. 2009); capital, Djibouti; languages, Arabic and French (official), Somali and other Cushitic languages. ■ the capital of Djibouti, a port at the western end of the Gulf of Aden; pop. 583,000 (est. 2007).

> The territory became a French protectorate under the name of French Somaliland in 1897. It was renamed the French Territory of the Afars and Issas in 1946 because the Afars and the Issas are the country's two main ethnic groups. In 1977, the country achieved independence as the Republic of Djibouti.

– DERIVATIVES **Dji·bou·ti·an** /-tēən/ **adj. & n.**

djinn /jin/ ▶ **n.** variant spelling of JINN.

dkl ▶ **abbr.** dekaliter(s).

dkm ▶ **abbr.** dekameter(s).

DL ▶ **abbr.** ■ Football defensive lineman. ■ disabled list.

dl ▶ **abbr.** deciliter(s).

D lay·er ▶ **n.** the lowest layer of the ionosphere, able to reflect low-frequency radio waves.
– ORIGIN 1930s: from an arbitrary use of the letter *D*.

DLitt (also **DLit**) ▶ **abbr.** ■ Doctor of Letters. ■ Doctor of Literature.
– ORIGIN from Latin *Doctor Litterarum*.

DLL ▶ **abbr.** Computing dynamic link library, a collection of subroutines stored on disk, which can be loaded into memory and executed when accessed by a running program.

DM (also **D-mark**) ▶ **abbr.** Deutschmark.

dm ▶ **abbr.** decimeter(s).

DMA ▶ **abbr.** ■ Doctor of Musical Arts. ■ direct memory access, a method allowing a peripheral device to transfer data to or from the memory of a computer system using operations not under the control of the central processor.

DMAE ▶ **abbr.** dimethylaminoethanol, a naturally occurring metabolite with cholinergic properties that is used therapeutically in attention and motion disorders, and topically as an antiwrinkle treatment.

D-mark ▶ **n.** short for DEUTSCHMARK.

DMCA ▶ **abbr.** Digital Millennium Copyright Act.

DMD ▶ **abbr.** ■ Doctor of Dental Medicine. [from Latin *Dentariae Medicinae Doctor* or *Doctor Medicinae Dentalis*.] ■ Duchenne muscular dystrophy.

DMSO ▶ **abbr.** Chemistry dimethyl sulfoxide.

DMus ▶ **abbr.** Doctor of Music.

DMV ▶ **abbr.** Department of Motor Vehicles.

DMZ ▶ **abbr.** demilitarized zone, an area from which warring parties agree to remove their military forces.

DNA ▶ **n.** Biochemistry deoxyribonucleic acid, a self-replicating material present in nearly all living organisms as the main constituent of chromosomes. It is the carrier of genetic information.

> Each molecule of DNA consists of two strands coiled around each other to form a double helix, a structure like a spiral ladder. Each rung of the ladder consists of a pair of chemical groups called bases (of which there are four types), which combine in specific pairs so that the sequence on one strand of the double helix is complementary to that on the other. It is the specific sequence of bases that constitutes the genetic information.

■ the fundamental and distinctive characteristics or qualities of someone or something, esp. when regarded as unchangeable: *diversity is part of the company's DNA* | *men just don't get shopping—it's not in our DNA*.

DNA fin·ger·print·ing (also **DNA profiling**) ▶ **n.** the analysis of DNA from samples of body tissues or fluids in order to identify individuals.

DNase /,dē'en,ās, -,āz/ ▶ **n.** Biochemistry an enzyme that catalyzes the hydrolysis of DNA into oligonucleotides and smaller molecules. Also called DEOXYRIBONUCLEASE.
– ORIGIN 1940s: from **DNA** + **-ASE**.

DNA vi·rus ▶ **n.** a virus in which the genetic information is stored in the form of DNA (as opposed to RNA).

Dnie·per /'nēpər, də'nēpər/ a river in eastern Europe that rises in Russia west of Moscow and flows south for about 1,370 miles (2,200 km) through Ukraine to the Black Sea. Ukrainian name **Dnipro**.

Dnies·ter /'nēstər, də'nēstər/ a river in eastern Europe that rises in the Carpathian Mountains in western Ukraine and flows 876 miles (1,410 km) to the Black Sea near Odessa. Russian name **Dnestr**, Ukrainian name **Dnister**.

Dnipro /'(d)nēprō/ Ukrainian name for DNIEPER.

Dni·pro·dzer·zhinsk /də,nyēprōdzir'zHēnsk/ an industrial city and river port in Ukraine, on the Dnieper River; pop. 245,100 (est. 2009). Former name (until 1936) KAMENSKOYE.

Dni·pro·pe·trovsk /də,nyēprōpə'trôfsk/ an industrial city and river port in Ukraine, on the Dnieper River; pop. 1,017,500 (est. 2009). It was known as Yekaterinoslav (Ekaterinoslav) until 1926.

DNR ▶ **abbr.** do not resuscitate.

DNS ▶ **abbr.** ■ domain name server, the system that automatically translates Internet addresses to the numeric machine addresses that computers use. ■ domain name system, the hierarchical method by which Internet addresses are constructed.

do[1] /dōō/ ▶ **v.** (**does** /dəz/; **doing**; past **did** /did/; past participle **done** /dən/) **1** [with obj.] perform (an action, the precise nature of which is often unspecified): *something must be done about the city's traffic* | *she knew what she was doing* | *what can I do for you?* | *Brian was making eyes at the girl, and had been doing so for most of the hearing*. ■ perform (a particular task): *Dad always did the cooking on Sundays*. ■ work on (something) to bring it to completion or to a required state: *it takes them longer to do their hair than me* | *she's the secretary and does the publicity*. ■ make or have available and provide: *he's doing bistro food* | *many hotels don't do single rooms at all* | [with two objs.] *he decided to do her a favor*. ■ solve; work out: *Joe was doing sums aloud*. ■ cook (food) to completion or to a specified degree: *if a knife inserted into the center comes out clean, then your pie is done*. ■ (often in questions) work at for a living: *what does she do?* ■ produce or give a performance of (a particular play, opera, etc.): *the Royal Shakespeare Company is doing Macbeth next month*. ■ perform (a particular role, song, etc.) or imitate (a particular person) in order to entertain people: *he not only does Schwarzenegger and Groucho, he becomes them*. ■ informal take (a narcotic drug): *he doesn't smoke, drink, or do drugs*. ■ attend to (someone): *the barber said he'd do me next*. ■ vulgar slang have sexual intercourse with. ■ (**do it**) informal have sexual intercourse. ■ (**do it**) informal urinate; defecate.
2 [with obj.] achieve or complete, in particular: ■ travel (a specified distance): *one car I looked at had done 112,000 miles*. ■ travel at (a specified speed): *I was speeding, doing seventy-five*. ■ make (a particular journey): *last time I did New York–Philadelphia round trip by train it was over 80 bucks*. ■ achieve (a specified sales figure): *our best-selling album did about a million worldwide*. ■ informal visit as a tourist, esp. in a superficial or hurried way: *the tourists are allotted only a day to "do" Verona*. ■ spend (a specified period of time), typically in prison or in a particular occupation: *he did five years for manslaughter*. ■ [no obj.] informal finish: *you must sit there and wait till I'm done* | [with present participle] *we're done arguing*. ■ (**be done**) be over: *the special formula continues to beautify your tan when the day is done*. ■ (**be/have done with**) give up concern for: have finished with: *I would sell the place and have done with it* | *Steve was not done with her*.
3 [no obj.] act or behave in a specified way: *they are free to do as they please* | *you did well to bring her back*. ■ make progress or perform in a specified way; get on: *when a team is doing badly, it's not easy*

for a new player to settle in | Mrs. Walters, how're you doing? ■ [with obj. and complement] have a specified effect on: *the walk will do me good.* ■ [with obj.] result in: *the years of stagnation did a lot of harm to the younger generation.*
4 [no obj.] be suitable or acceptable: *if he's anything like you, he'll do* | [with obj.] *a couple of bucks'll do me.*
5 [with obj.] informal beat up; kill: *he was the guy who did Maranzano.* ■ (usu. **be done**) ruin: *once you falter, you're done.* ■ rob (a place): *this would be an easy place to do, and there was plenty of money lying around.* ■ Brit. swindle: *in business you had to do your competitors before they did you.*
6 [with obj.] (usu. **be/get done for**) Brit. informal prosecute; convict: *we got done for conspiracy to commit murder.*
▶ **auxiliary v. 1** used before a verb (except *be, can, may, ought, shall, will*) in questions and negative statements: *do you have any pets?* | *did he see me?* | *I don't smoke* | *it does not matter.* ■ used to make tag questions: *you write poetry, don't you?* | *I never seem to say the right thing, do I?* ■ used in negative commands: *don't be silly* | *do not forget.*
2 used to refer to a verb already mentioned: *he looks better than he did before* | *you wanted to enjoy yourself, and you did* | *as the cops get smarter, so do the crooks.*
3 used to give emphasis to a positive verb: *I do want to act on this* | *he did look tired.* ■ used in positive commands to give polite encouragement: *do tell me!* | *do sit down.*
4 used with inversion of a subject and verb when an adverbial phrase begins a clause for emphasis: *only rarely did they succumb* | *not only did the play close, the theater closed.*
▶ **n.** (pl. **dos** or **do's**) **1** (also **'do**) informal short for HAIRDO.
2 informal, chiefly Brit. a party or other social event: *the soccer club Christmas do.*
3 Brit. archaic or informal a swindle or hoax.
– PHRASES **be to do with** be concerned or connected with: *the problems are usually to do with family tension.* **do a ——** informal behave in a manner characteristic of (a specified person): *he did a Garbo after his flop in the play.* **do battle** enter into a conflict. **do one's head** (or **nut**) **in** (or **do one's head**) Brit. informal be extremely angry, worried, or agitated. **do the honors** see HONOR. **do someone/something justice** see JUSTICE. **don't —— me** informal do not use the word —— to me: *"Don't morning me. Where the hell've you been all night?"* **do or die** persist, even if death is the result. ■ used to describe a critical situation where one's actions may result in victory or defeat: *the 72nd hole was do or die.* **dos and don'ts** rules of behavior: *I have no knowledge of the political dos and don'ts.* **do well for oneself** become successful or wealthy. **have (got) —— to do with** be connected with (someone or something) to the extent specified: *half the country believed rock 'n' roll had something to do with national decline* | *John's got a lot to do with that bribery scandal.* **have nothing to do with** have no contact or dealings with: *Billy and his father have had nothing to do with each other for nearly twenty years.* ■ be no business or concern of: *it's my decision—it has nothing to do with you.* ■ be unconnected with: *he says his departure has nothing to do with the calls for his resignation.* **it isn't done** Brit. used to express the speaker's opinion that something contravenes custom, opinion, or propriety: *in such a society it is not done to admit to taking religion seriously.* **it won't do** used to express the speaker's opinion that someone's behavior is unsatisfactory and cannot be allowed to continue: *Don't talk like that—I've told you before, it won't do.* **no you don't** informal used to indicate that one intends to prevent someone from doing what they were about to do: *Sharon went to get in the taxi. "Oh no you don't," said Steve.* **that does it!** informal used to indicate that one will not tolerate something any longer: *That does it! Let's go!* **that's done it!** Brit. informal used to express dismay or anger when something has gone wrong.
– PHRASAL VERBS **do away with** informal put an end to; remove: *the desire to do away with racism.* ■ kill: *he didn't have the courage to do away with her.* **do by** dated treat or deal with in a specified way: *do as you would be done by* | *she did well by them.* **do someone/something down** Brit. informal get the better of someone, typically in an underhanded way. ■ criticize someone or something: *they're always moaning and doing British industry down.* **do for 1** informal defeat, ruin, or kill: *without that contract we're done for.* **2** Brit. informal do the cleaning for (a person or private household): *Florrie usually did for the Shermans in the mornings.* **3** suffice for: *the old version will do for now.* **do something** (or **nothing**) **for** informal enhance (or detract from) the appearance or quality of: *that scarf does nothing for you.* **do someone in** informal kill someone. ■ (usu. **be done in**) informal tire someone out: *after hiking in the hills all day, I was utterly done in.* **do someone out of** informal deprive someone of (something) in an underhanded or unfair way. **do something out** Brit. informal decorate or furnish a room or building in a particular style, color, or material: *the basement is done out in limed oak.* **do someone over** Brit. informal beat someone up. **do something over 1** informal repeat something: *to absorb the lesson, I had to do it over and over.* **2** informal decorate or furnish a room or building. **do someone up** (usu. **be done up**) dress someone up, esp. in an elaborate or impressive way: *Agnes was all done up in a slinky black number.* **do something up** (usu. **be done up**) arrange one's hair in a particular way, esp. so as to be pulled back from one's face or shoulders: *her dark hair was done up in a pony tail.* ■ wrap something up: *unwieldy packages all done up with twine.* **do with** [with modal] would find useful or would like to have or do: *I could do with a cup of coffee.* ■ (**can't/won't be doing with**) Brit. be unwilling to tolerate or be bothered with: *she couldn't be doing with meals for one.* **do without** (usu. **can do without**) manage without: *she could do without cigarettes for a day.* ■ informal would prefer not to have: *I can do without your complaints first thing in the morning.*
– ORIGIN Old English *dōn*, of Germanic origin; related to Dutch *doen* and German *tun*, from an Indo-European root shared by Greek *tithēmi* 'I place' and Latin *facere* 'make, do.'

do² /dō/ ▶ **n.** Music (in solmization) the first and eighth note of a major scale. ■ the note C in the fixed-do system.
– ORIGIN mid 18th cent.: from Italian *do*, an arbitrarily chosen syllable replacing *ut*, taken from a Latin hymn (see SOLMIZATION).

do. ▶ **abbr.** dated ditto.

DOA ▶ **abbr.** dead on arrival, used to describe a person who is declared dead immediately upon arrival at a hospital.

do·a·ble /'dōōəbəl/ ▶ **adj.** informal within one's powers; feasible: *none of the jobs were fun, but they were doable.*

d.o.b. (also **dob**) ▶ **abbr.** date of birth.

dob·bin /'däbin/ ▶ **n.** dated a pet name for a draft horse or a farm horse.
– ORIGIN late 16th cent.: nickname for the given name *Robert*.

dob·by /'däbē/ ▶ **n.** (pl. **dobbies**) a mechanism attached to a loom for weaving small patterns similar to but simpler than those produced by a Jacquard loom.
– ORIGIN late 19th cent.: perhaps an application of the given name *Dobbie*, from *Dob* (alteration of the given name *Rob*). The usage is probably an extension of the earlier sense 'benevolent elf' (who performed household tasks secretly).

dob·by weave ▶ **n.** a style of patterned weave consisting of small geometric devices repeated frequently.

do·be /'dōbē/ ▶ **n.** informal adobe.
– ORIGIN mid 19th cent.: abbreviation.

Do·ber·man /'dōbərmən/ (also **Doberman pinscher** /'pinCHər/) ▶ **n.** a large dog of a German breed with powerful jaws and a smooth coat, typically black with tan markings.
– ORIGIN early 20th cent.: from the name of Ludwig *Dobermann*, 19th-cent. German dog breeder (+ German *Pinscher* 'terrier').

Doberman

Do·bos To·rte /'dôbəs 'tôrtə, ˌtôrt/ ▶ **n.** a rich cake made of alternate layers of sponge and chocolate or mocha cream, with a crisp caramel topping.
– ORIGIN from German *Dobostorte*, named after József C. *Dobos* (1847–1924), Hungarian pastry cook.

do·bra /'dōbrə/ ▶ **n.** the basic monetary unit of São Tomé and Principe, equal to 100 centavos.
– ORIGIN from Portuguese *dóbra* 'doubloon.'

Do·brich /'dôbrēCH/ a city in northeastern Bulgaria, the center of an agricultural region; pop. 93,163 (2008). It was called Tolbukhin 1949–91 after Soviet marshal **Fyodor Ivanovich Tolbukhin**.

do·bro /'dōbrō/ ▶ **n.** (pl. **dobros**) trademark a type of acoustic guitar with steel resonating disks inside the body under the bridge.
– ORIGIN 1950s: from *Do(pěra) Bro(thers)*, the Czech-American inventors of the instrument.

dobro

Do·bru·ja /'dôbrōōˌjä/ a district in eastern Romania and northeastern Bulgaria on the Black Sea coast, bounded on the north and west by the Danube River.

dob·son·fly /'däbsənˌflī/ ▶ **n.** (pl. **dobsonflies**) a large gray North American winged insect related to the alderflies. Its predatory aquatic larva (the hellgrammite) is often used as fishing bait. ● Family Corydalidae, order Neuroptera: several genera and species, in particular *Corydalus cornutus*.
– ORIGIN early 20th cent.: of unknown origin.

Dob·so·ni·an /däb'sōnēən/ ▶ **adj.** relating to or denoting a low-cost Newtonian reflecting telescope with large aperture and short focal length, or the simple altazimuth mount used for it.
– ORIGIN late 20th cent.: from the name of John *Dobson*, American amateur astronomer, + -IAN.

Dob·son u·nit /'däbsən/ (abbr.: **DU**) ▶ **n.** a unit of measurement for the total amount of ozone in the atmosphere above a point on the earth's surface, one Dobson unit being equivalent to a layer of pure ozone 0.01 mm thick at standard temperature and pressure.
– ORIGIN 1980s: from the name of G. M. B. *Dobson* (1889–1976), British meteorologist.

doc /däk/ informal ▶ **abbr.** ■ doctor. ■ Computing document.

do·cent /'dōsənt/ ▶ **n. 1** a person who acts as a guide, typically on a voluntary basis, in a museum, art gallery, or zoo.
2 (in certain universities and colleges) a member of the teaching staff immediately below professorial rank.
– ORIGIN late 19th cent.: via German from Latin *docent-* 'teaching,' from *docere* 'teach.'

Do·ce·tism /dō'sēˌtizəm, 'dōsi-/ ▶ **n.** the doctrine, important in Gnosticism, that Christ's body was not human but either a phantasm or of real but celestial substance, and that therefore his sufferings were only apparent.
– DERIVATIVES **Do·ce·tist n.**
– ORIGIN mid 19th cent.: from medieval Latin *Docetae* (the name, based on Greek *dokein* 'seem,' given to a group of 2nd-cent. Christian heretics) + -ISM.

doc·ile /'däsəl/ ▶ **adj.** ready to accept control or instruction; submissive: *a cheap and docile workforce.*
– DERIVATIVES **doc·ile·ly adv.**, **do·cil·i·ty** /dä'silitē/ **n.**
– ORIGIN late 15th cent. (in the sense 'apt or willing to learn'): from Latin *docilis*, from *docere* 'teach.'

dock¹ /däk/ ▶ **n.** a structure extending alongshore or out from the shore into a body of water, to which boats may be moored: *the gangplank was lowered to the dock.* ■ an enclosed area of water in a port for the loading, unloading, and repair of ships. ■ (**docks**) a group of such enclosed areas of water along with the wharves and buildings near them. ■ short for DRY DOCK. ■ (also **loading dock**) a platform for loading or unloading trucks or freight trains.
▶ **v.** [no obj.] (of a ship) tie up at a dock, esp. in order to load or unload passengers or cargo: *the ship docked at San Francisco.* ■ [with obj.] bring (a ship or boat) into such a place: *the riverbank where the fur traders docked their boats.* ■ (of a spacecraft) join with a space station or another spacecraft in space. ■ attach (a piece of equipment) to another: *the user wants to dock a portable into a desktop computer.*
– ORIGIN late Middle English: from Middle Dutch, Middle Low German *docke*, of unknown origin.

dock² ▶ **v.** [with obj.] (usu. **be docked**) deduct (something, esp. an amount of money): *their wages are docked for public displays of affection* | [with two objs.] *he will be docked an hour's pay.* ■ cut short (an animal's tail): *fifteen of the dogs had had their tails docked.*
▶ **n.** the solid bony or fleshy part of an animal's tail, excluding the hair. ■ the stump left after a tail has been docked.
– ORIGIN late Middle English: perhaps related to Frisian *dok* 'bunch, ball (of string, etc.)' and German *Docke* 'doll.' The original noun sense was 'the solid part of an animal's tail,' whence the verb sense 'cut

short (an animal's tail),' later generalized to 'reduce, deduct.'

dock[3] ▶ **n.** (usu. **the dock**) the enclosure in a criminal court where a defendant is placed: *the nine others in the dock face a combination of charges.*
– ORIGIN late 16th cent.: probably originally slang and related to Flemish *dok* 'chicken coop, rabbit hutch,' of unknown origin.

dock[4] ▶ **n.** a coarse weed of temperate regions, with inconspicuous greenish or reddish flowers. The leaves are popularly used to relieve nettle stings. ● Genus *Rumex*, family Polygonaceae.
– ORIGIN Old English *docce*, of Germanic origin; related to Dutch dialect *dokke*.

dock·age /ˈdäkij/ ▶ **n.** accommodation or berthing of ships at docks. ■ the charge made for using docks.

dock·er /ˈdäkər/ ▶ **n.** another term for LONGSHOREMAN.

dock·et /ˈdäkit/ ▶ **n. 1** a calendar or list of cases for trial or people having cases pending. ■ an agenda or list of things to be done.
2 a document or label listing the contents of a package or delivery.
▶ **v.** (**dockets, docketing, docketed**) [with obj.] **1** enter (a case or suit) onto a list of those due to be heard: *the case will go to the Supreme Court, and may be docketed for the fall term.*
2 mark (goods or a package) with a document or label listing the contents. ■ annotate (a letter or document) with a brief summary of its contents.
– ORIGIN late 15th cent.: perhaps from DOCK[2]. The word originally denoted a short summary or abstract; hence, in the early 18th cent., 'a document giving particulars of a consignment.'

dock·hand /ˈdäkˌhand/ ▶ **n.** a longshoreman.

dock·ing sta·tion ▶ **n.** a device to which a portable computer is connected so that it can be used like a desktop computer, with an external power supply, monitor, data transfer capability, etc.

dock·land /ˈdäkˌland/ ▶ **n.** chiefly Brit. (also **docklands**) the area containing a city's docks: *plans to redevelop London's docklands.*

dock·o·min·i·um /ˌdäkəˈminēəm/ ▶ **n.** (pl. **dockominiums**) a waterfront condominium with a private mooring. ■ a privately owned dock at a marina.
– ORIGIN 1980s: from DOCK[1], on the pattern of *condominium*.

dock·side /ˈdäkˌsīd/ ▶ **n.** [in sing.] the area immediately adjacent to a dock.

dock·work·er /ˈdäkˌwərkər/ ▶ **n.** a longshoreman.

dock·yard /ˈdäkˌyärd/ ▶ **n.** an area or establishment with docks and equipment for repairing and maintaining ships.

Doc Mar·tens /ˌdäk ˈmärtnz/ (also **Dr. Martens** (trademark in the UK)) ▶ **plural n.** trademark a type of heavy lace-up boot or shoe with an air-cushioned sole.
– ORIGIN 1970s: named after Klaus *Maertens*, German inventor of the sole.

doc·tor /ˈdäktər/ ▶ **n. 1** a qualified practitioner of medicine; a physician. ■ a qualified dentist or veterinary surgeon. ■ [with modifier] informal a person who gives advice or makes improvements: *the script doctor rewrote the original.*
2 (**Doctor**) a person who holds a doctorate: *he was made a Doctor of Divinity.* ■ short for DOCTOR OF THE CHURCH. ■ archaic a teacher or learned person: *the wisest doctor is graveled by the inquisitiveness of a child.*
3 an artificial fishing fly.
▶ **v.** [with obj.] **1** change the content or appearance of (a document or picture) in order to deceive; falsify: *the reports could have been doctored.* ■ alter the content of (a drink, food, or substance) by adding strong or harmful ingredients: *he denied doctoring Stephen's drinks.* ■ Baseball tamper with (a ball) so as to affect its movement when pitched.
2 (usu. as noun **doctoring**) informal treat (someone) medically: *he contemplated giving up doctoring.* ■ Brit. remove the sexual organs of (an animal) so that it cannot reproduce. ■ repair (a machine).
– PHRASES **be (just) what the doctor ordered** informal be very beneficial or desirable under the circumstances: *a 2-0 victory is just what the doctor ordered.*
– DERIVATIVES **doc·tor·ly** adj.
– ORIGIN Middle English (in the senses 'learned person' and 'Doctor of the Church'): via Old French from Latin *doctor* 'teacher' (from *docere* 'teach').

doc·tor·al /ˈdäktərəl/ ▶ **adj.** [attrib.] relating to or designed to achieve a doctorate: *a doctoral dissertation.*

doc·tor·ate /ˈdäktərit/ ▶ **n.** the highest degree awarded by a graduate school or other approved educational organization: *a doctorate in Classics.*
– ORIGIN mid 17th cent.: from medieval Latin *doctoratus* 'made a doctor.'

Doc·tor of Phi·los·o·phy (abbr.: **Ph.D.**) ▶ **n.** a doctorate in any discipline except medicine, or sometimes theology. ■ a person holding such a degree.

Doc·tor of the Church ▶ **n.** one of the early Christian theologians regarded as esp. authoritative in the Western Church (particularly St. Augustine of Hippo, St. Jerome, St. Ambrose, and St. Gregory the Great) or later so designated by the pope (e.g., St. Thomas Aquinas, St. Teresa of Ávila). Compare with DOCUMENTARIAN (sense 1).

Doc·tor·ow /ˈdäktəˌrō/, E. L. (1931–), US writer; full name *Edgar Lawrence Doctorow*. His novels include *Ragtime* (1975), *Billy Bathgate* (1989), *The Waterworks* (1994), and *City of God* (2000).

doc·tri·naire /ˌdäktrəˈner/ ▶ **adj.** seeking to impose a doctrine in all circumstances without regard to practical considerations: *a doctrinaire conservative.*
▶ **n.** a person who seeks to impose a theory in such a way.
– DERIVATIVES **doc·tri·nair·ism** /-ˌizəm/ **n.**
– ORIGIN early 19th cent.: from French, from *doctrine* (see DOCTRINE).

doc·tri·nal /ˈdäktrənl/ ▶ **adj.** concerned with a doctrine or doctrines: *doctrinal disputes.*
– DERIVATIVES **doc·tri·nal·ly** adv.
– ORIGIN late Middle English: from late Latin *doctrinalis*, from *doctrina* 'teaching, learning' (see DOCTRINE).

doc·trine /ˈdäktrin/ ▶ **n.** a belief or set of beliefs held and taught by a church, political party, or other group: *the doctrine of predestination.* ■ a stated principle of government policy, mainly in foreign or military affairs: *the Monroe Doctrine.*
– ORIGIN late Middle English: from Old French, from Latin *doctrina* 'teaching, learning,' from *doctor* 'teacher,' from *docere* 'teach.'

doc·u·dra·ma /ˈdäkyəˌdrämə/ ▶ **n.** a dramatized television movie based on real events.
– ORIGIN 1960s: blend of DOCUMENTARY and DRAMA.

doc·u·ment ▶ **n.** /ˈdäkyəmənt/ a piece of written, printed, or electronic matter that provides information or evidence or that serves as an official record.
▶ **v.** /ˈdäkyəˌment/ [with obj.] record (something) in written, photographic, or other form: *the photographer spent years documenting the lives of miners.* ■ support or accompany with documentation.
– DERIVATIVES **doc·u·ment·a·ble** /ˌdäkyəˈmentəbəl/ adj., **doc·u·ment·al** /ˌdäkyəˈmentl/ adj., **doc·u·ment·er** /-ˌmentər/ n.
– ORIGIN late Middle English: from Old French, from Latin *documentum* 'lesson, proof' (in medieval Latin 'written instruction, official paper'), from *docere* 'teach.'

doc·u·men·tar·i·an /ˌdäkyəmenˈte(ə)rēən/ ▶ **n. 1** a photographer specializing in producing a factual record. ■ a director or producer of documentaries.
2 an expert analyst of historical documents.

doc·u·men·ta·rist /ˌdäkyəˈmentərist/ ▶ **n.** another term for DOCUMENTARIAN (sense 1).

doc·u·men·ta·ry /ˌdäkyəˈmentərē/ ▶ **adj.** consisting of official pieces of written, printed, or other matter: *his book is based on documentary sources.* ■ (of a movie, a television or radio program, or photography) using pictures or interviews with people involved in real events to provide a factual record or report: *he has directed documentary shorts and feature films.*
▶ **n.** (pl. **documentaries**) a movie or a television or radio program that provides a factual record or report.

doc·u·men·ta·tion /ˌdäkyəmenˈtāSHən/ ▶ **n. 1** material that provides official information or evidence or that serves as a record: *you will have to complete the relevant documentation.* ■ the written specification and instructions accompanying a computer program or hardware.
2 the process of classifying and annotating texts, photographs, etc.: *she arranged the collection and documentation of photographs.*

doc·u·ment case ▶ **n.** a lightweight, typically flexible case for carrying papers.

doc·u·ment type def·i·ni·tion (abbr. **DTD**) ▶ **n.** Computing a template that sets out the format and tag structure of an XML- or SGML-compliant document.

doc·u·soap /ˈdäkyəˌsōp/ ▶ **n.** a documentary, usually produced for television and having elements of soap opera, following people in a particular occupation or location over a period of time.
– ORIGIN 1990s: blend of *documentary* and *soap (opera)*.

doc·u·tain·ment /ˌdäkyəˈtānmənt/ ▶ **n.** entertainment provided by movies or other presentations that include documentary materials, intended both to inform and to entertain. ■ a movie or other presentation of this kind.
– ORIGIN 1970s: blend of DOCUMENTARY and ENTERTAINMENT.

DOD ▶ **abbr.** Department of Defense.

dod·der[1] /ˈdädər/ ▶ **v.** [no obj.] tremble or totter, typically because of old age: *spent and nerve-weary, I doddered into the foyer of a third-rate hotel* | (as adj. **doddering**) *that doddering old fool.*
– DERIVATIVES **dod·der·er** n., **dod·der·y** adj.
– ORIGIN early 17th cent.: variant of obsolete dialect *dadder*; related to DITHER.

dod·der[2] ▶ **n.** a widely distributed parasitic climbing plant of the morning glory family, with leafless threadlike stems that are attached to the host plant by means of suckers. ● Genus *Cuscuta*, family Convolvulaceae.
– ORIGIN Middle English: related to Middle Low German *doder, dodder*, Middle High German *toter*.

dod·dle /ˈdädl/ ▶ **n.** [in sing.] Brit. informal a very easy task: *this printer is a doddle to set up and use.*
– ORIGIN 1930s: perhaps from dialect *doddle* 'toddle,' of unknown origin.

dodeca- ▶ **comb. form** (used chiefly in scientific and musical terms) twelve; having twelve: *dodecahedron* | *dodecaphonic.*
– ORIGIN from Greek.

do·dec·a·gon /dōˈdekəˌgän/ ▶ **n.** a plane figure with twelve sides.
– DERIVATIVES **do·de·cag·o·nal** /dōdiˈkagənl/ adj.
– ORIGIN late 17th cent.: from Greek *dōdekagōnon*, neuter (used as a noun) of *dōdekagōnos* 'twelve-angled.'

do·dec·a·he·dron /dōˌdekəˈhēdrən/ ▶ **n.** (pl. **dodecahedrons** or **dodecahedra** /-drə/) a three-dimensional shape having twelve plane faces, in particular a regular solid figure with twelve equal pentagonal faces.
– DERIVATIVES **do·dec·a·he·dral** /-drəl/ adj.
– ORIGIN late 16th cent.: from Greek *dōdekaedron*, neuter (used as a noun) of *dōdekaedros* 'twelve-faced.'

dodecahedron

Do·dec·a·nese /dōˌdekəˈnēz, -ˈnēs, ˌdōdekə-/ a group of twelve islands in the southeastern Aegean Sea, of which the largest is Rhodes.

do·dec·a·phon·ic /dōˌdekəˈfänik/ ▶ **adj.** Music another term for TWELVE-TONE.

dodge /däj/ ▶ **v.** [with obj.] **1** avoid (someone or something) by a sudden quick movement: *we ducked inside our doorway to dodge shrapnel that was raining down.* ■ [no obj.] move quickly to one side or out of the way: *Adam dodged between the cars.* ■ avoid (something) in a cunning or dishonest way: *he went after people who had either dodged the war or invented a record in it.*
2 (often as noun **dodging**) Photography expose (one area of a print) less than the rest during processing or enlarging.
▶ **n.** a sudden quick movement to avoid someone or something. ■ a cunning trick or dishonest act, in particular one intended to avoid something unpleasant: *bartering can be seen as a tax dodge.*
– ORIGIN mid 16th cent. (in the senses 'dither' and 'haggle'): of unknown origin.

dodge·ball /ˈdäjˌbôl/ ▶ **n.** a game in which players in a circle try to hit opponents inside the circle, thus eliminating them, with an inflated ball.

Dodge Cit·y /däj/ a city in southwestern Kansas; pop. 25,689 (est. 2008). Established in 1872 as a shipping station on the Santa Fe Trail, it rapidly gained a reputation as a rowdy frontier town.

dodg·em /ˈdäjəm/ (also **dodgem car**) ▶ **n.** another term for BUMPER CAR.
– ORIGIN 1920s: US proprietary name (as *Dodg'em*), from the phrase *dodge them.*

dodg·er /ˈdäjər/ ▶ **n. 1** [often with modifier] a person who engages in cunning tricks or dishonest practices to avoid something unpleasant: *tax dodgers.*
2 Nautical a canvas screen on a ship giving protection from spray.
3 a small handbill or leaflet.
4 see CORN DODGER.

Dodg·son /ˈdäjsən/, Charles Lutwidge, see CARROLL.

dodg·y /ˈdäjē/ ▶ **adj.** (**dodgier, dodgiest**) Brit. informal dishonest or unreliable: *a dodgy secondhand car* salesman. ■ potentially dangerous: *activities like these could be dodgy for your heart.* ■ of low quality.

do·do /ˈdōdō/ ▶ **n.** (pl. **dodos** or **dodoes**) an extinct flightless bird with a stout body, stumpy wings, a large head, and a heavy hooked bill. It was found on Mauritius until the end of the 17th century. ● *Raphus cucullatus*, family Raphidae. See also SOLITAIRE (sense 3). ■ informal an old-fashioned and ineffective person or thing.
– PHRASES **(as) dead as a** (or **the**) **dodo** informal dead (used for emphasis). ■ no longer effective, valid, or interesting: *the campaign was as dead as a dodo.*
– ORIGIN early 17th cent.: from Portuguese *doudo* 'simpleton' (because the bird had no fear of man and was easily killed). Compare with DOTTEREL.

d

Do·do·ma /ˈdōdəmə, -ˌmä/ the capital of Tanzania, in the center of the country; pop. 183,000 (2007).

DOE ▶ **abbr.** Department of Energy.

doe /dō/ ▶ **n.** a female deer. ■ a female of certain other animal species, such as hare, rabbit, rat, ferret, or kangaroo.
– ORIGIN Old English *dā*, of unknown origin.

doe-eyed ▶ **adj.** having large, gentle, dark eyes: *portraits of doe-eyed young girls.*

do·er /ˈdo͞oər/ ▶ **n.** the person who does something: *the doer of the action.* ■ a person who acts rather than merely talking or thinking: *I'm a doer, not a moaner.*

does /dəz/ third person singular present of DO¹.

doe·skin /ˈdōˌskin/ ▶ **n.** leather made from the skin of a female fallow deer. ■ a fine satin-weave woolen cloth resembling such leather.

does·n't /ˈdəzənt/ ▶ **contraction** does not.

do·est /ˈdo͞oist/ archaic second person singular present of DO¹.

do·eth /ˈdo͞oiTH/ archaic third person singular present of DO¹.

doff /däf, dôf/ ▶ **v.** [with obj.] remove (an item of clothing): *he had doffed tie and jacket and rolled up his shirtsleeves.* ■ take off or raise (one's hat) as a greeting or token of respect: *the manager doffed his hat to her.*
– ORIGIN late Middle English: contraction of *do off.* Compare with DON².

dog /dôg/ ▶ **n. 1** a domesticated carnivorous mammal that typically has a long snout, an acute sense of smell, and a barking, howling, or whining voice. It is widely kept as a pet or for work or field sports. ● *Canis familiaris*, family Canidae (the **dog family**); probably domesticated from the wolf in the Mesolithic period. The dog family also includes the wolves, coyotes, jackals, and foxes. ■ a wild animal of the dog family. ■ the male of an animal of the dog family, or of some other mammals such as the otter: [as modifier] *a dog fox.*
2 informal a person regarded as unpleasant, contemptible, or wicked (used as a term of abuse): *come out, Michael, you dog!* ■ [with adj.] dated used to refer to a person of a specified kind in a tone of playful reproof, commiseration, or congratulation: *you lucky dog!* ■ used in various phrases to refer to someone who is abject or miserable, esp. because they have been treated harshly: *I make him work like a dog | Rob was treated like a dog.* ■ informal, derogatory a woman regarded as unattractive. ■ informal a thing of poor quality; a failure: *a dog of a movie.*
3 short for FIREDOG.
4 a mechanical device for gripping.
5 (**dogs**) informal feet: *if only I could sit down and rest my tired dogs.*
▶ **v.** (**dogs, dogging, dogged**) [with obj.] **1** follow (someone or their movements) closely and persistently: *photographers seemed to dog her every step.* ■ (of a problem) cause continual trouble for: *their finance committee has been dogged by controversy.*
2 (**dog it**) informal act lazily; fail to try one's hardest.
3 grip (something) with a mechanical device: [with obj. and complement] *she has dogged the door shut.*
– PHRASES **dog eat dog** used to refer to a situation of fierce competition in which people are willing to harm each other in order to succeed: *in this business, it's always dog eat dog | popular music is a dog-eat-dog industry.* **a dog's age** informal a very long time: *the best I've seen in a dog's age.* **a dog's life** an unhappy existence, full of problems or unfair treatment. **the dogs of war** literary the havoc accompanying military conflict. [from Shakespeare's *Julius Caesar* (III. 1. 274).] **every dog has its day** proverb everyone will have good luck or success at some point in their lives. **go to the dogs** informal deteriorate shockingly: *the country is going to the dogs.* **hair of the dog** see HAIR. **let sleeping dogs lie** see SLEEP. **not a dog's chance** no chance at all. **put on the dog** informal behave in a pretentious or ostentatious way: *we have to put on the dog for Anne Marie.* **rain cats and dogs** see RAIN. **(as) sick as a dog** see SICK¹. **throw someone to the dogs** discard someone as worthless: *the weak and oppressed must not be thrown to the dogs.* **you can't teach an old dog new tricks** proverb you cannot make people change their established patterns of opinion and behavior.
– DERIVATIVES **dog·like** /-ˌlīk/ **adj.**
– ORIGIN Old English *docga*, of unknown origin.

dog and pon·y show ▶ **n.** an elaborate display or presentation, esp. as part of a promotional campaign.

dog·bane /ˈdôgˌbān/ ▶ **n.** a shrubby North American plant, typically having bell-shaped flowers and reputed to be poisonous to dogs. ● Genus *Apocynum*, family Apocynaceae: several species, including the common **spreading dogbane** (*A. androsaemifolium*).

dog·ber·ry /ˈdôgˌberē/ ▶ **n.** (pl. **dogberries**) informal the fruit of the dogwood. ■ (also **dogberry tree**) the dogwood. ■ a fruit of poor eating quality from any of a number of other shrubs or small trees, e.g., the American rowan.

dog bis·cuit ▶ **n.** a hard thick biscuit for feeding to dogs.

dog·cart /ˈdôgˌkärt/ ▶ **n.** a two-wheeled horse-drawn cart, with cross seats back to back, originally incorporating a box under the seat for sportsmen's dogs.

dog·catch·er /ˈdôgˌkaCHər, -ˌkeCH-/ ▶ **n.** an official or employee who rounds up and impounds stray dogs in a community. Also called DOG WARDEN. ■ informal a low-level political official.

dog clutch ▶ **n.** a device for coupling two shafts in order to transmit motion, one part having teeth that engage with slots in another.

dog cock·le ▶ **n.** a burrowing bivalve mollusk that has a highly convex, almost spherical, shell. ● Family Glycimeridae: many species, including the European *Glycymeris glycymeris.*

dog col·lar ▶ **n.** a collar for a dog. ■ informal term for CLERICAL COLLAR.

dog days ▶ **plural n.** the hottest period of the year (reckoned in antiquity from the heliacal rising of Sirius, the Dog Star). ■ a period of inactivity or sluggishness: *in August the baseball races are in the dog days.*

dog·dom /ˈdôgdəm/ ▶ **n.** the world of dogs and dog enthusiasts.

doge /dōj/ ▶ **n.** historical the chief magistrate of Venice or Genoa.
– ORIGIN mid 16th cent.: from French, from Venetian Italian *doze*, based on Latin *dux, duc-* 'leader.'

dog-ear ▶ **v.** [with obj.] fold down the corner of (a book or magazine), typically to mark a place.
▶ **adj.** (**dog-eared**) (of an object made from paper) with the corners worn or battered with use.

dog-end ▶ **n.** Brit. informal a cigarette butt. ■ the last and least pleasing part of something: *the dog-end of a hard day.*

dog·face /ˈdôgˌfās/ ▶ **n.** informal, dated a US soldier, esp. an infantryman.

dog·fall ▶ **n.** a fall in which wrestlers touch the ground together.

dog·fight /ˈdôgˌfīt/ ▶ **n.** a close combat between military aircraft. ■ a ferocious struggle for supremacy between interested parties: *the meeting deteriorated into a dogfight.* ■ a fight between dogs, esp. one organized illegally for public entertainment.
▶ **v.** engage in a dogfight: [no obj.] *resplendent model airplanes dogfighting in the updrafts.*
– DERIVATIVES **dog·fight·er n.**

dog·fish /ˈdôgˌfiSH/ ▶ **n.** (pl. **same** or **dogfishes**) **1** a small sand-colored bottom-dwelling shark with a long tail, common on European coasts. ● *Scyliorhinus canicula*, family Scyliorhinidae. **2** [with modifier] a small shark that resembles or is related to the dogfish, sometimes caught for food. ● Several genera in the families Scyliorhinidae, Squalidae, and Triakidae.

dog·ged /ˈdôgid/ ▶ **adj.** having or showing tenacity and grim persistence: *success required dogged determination.*
– DERIVATIVES **dog·ged·ly adv., dog·ged·ness n.**

dog·ger¹ /ˈdôgər/ ▶ **n.** historical a two-masted, bluff-bowed Dutch sailboat, used for fishing.
– ORIGIN Middle English: from Middle Dutch.

dog·ger² ▶ **n.** Geology a large spherical concretion occurring in sedimentary rock.
– ORIGIN late 17th cent. (originally a dialect word denoting a kind of ironstone): perhaps from DOG.

dog·ger·el /ˈdôgərəl, ˈdäg-/ ▶ **n.** comic verse composed in irregular rhythm. ■ verse or words that are badly written or expressed: *the last stanza deteriorates into doggerel.*
– ORIGIN late Middle English (as an adjective describing such verse): apparently from DOG (used contemptuously, as in DOG LATIN) + -REL.

dog·gie ▶ **n.** variant spelling of DOGGY.

dog·gie bag ▶ **n.** a bag used by a restaurant customer or party guest to take home leftover food, supposedly for their dog.

dog·gish /ˈdôgiSH/ ▶ **adj.** of or like a dog. ■ archaic (of a person) having the bad qualities of a dog, esp. by being bad-tempered or snappish.

dog·go /ˈdôgō/ ▶ **adv.** (in phrase **lie doggo**) informal remain motionless and quiet to escape detection: *a dozen officers had been lying doggo for hours.*
– ORIGIN late 19th cent.: of obscure origin; apparently from DOG + -O.

dog·gone /ˈdôgˈgôn/ informal ▶ **adj.** [attrib.] used to express feelings of annoyance, surprise, or pleasure: *now just a doggone minute* | [as submodifier] *it's doggone good to be home.*
▶ **v.** [with obj.] used to express surprise, irritation, or anger: *from that moment, doggone it if I didn't see a motivation in Joey! | I'll be doggoned if every fourth kid is affected.*
– ORIGIN early 19th cent.: probably from *dog on it*, euphemism for *God damn it.*

dog·gy /ˈdôgē/ ▶ **adj.** of or like a dog: *his doggy brown eyes.* ■ fond of dogs: *it was a doggy household.*
▶ **n.** (also **doggie**) (pl. **doggies**) a child's word for a dog.
– DERIVATIVES **dog·gi·ness n.**

dog·gy style (also **doggy fashion**) ▶ **n.** vulgar slang (in) a position for human sexual intercourse inspired by that of dogs.

dog·house /ˈdôgˌhous/ ▶ **n.** a dog's kennel. ■ Sailing a raised area at the after end of a yacht's coachroof, providing standing room.
– PHRASES **(be) in the doghouse** informal, often humorous (be) in mild or temporary disfavor.

do·gie /ˈdōgē/ ▶ **n.** (pl. **dogies**) a motherless or neglected calf.
– ORIGIN late 19th cent.: of unknown origin.

dog in the man·ger ▶ **n.** a person who has no need of, or ability to use, a possession that would be of use or value to others, but who prevents others from having it: *what a dog in the manger you must be!* | [as adj.] *she can be so dog in the manger about updating things in the office.*
– ORIGIN alluding to the fable of the dog that lay in a manger to prevent the ox and horse from eating the hay.

dog Lat·in ▶ **n.** a debased form of Latin.

dog·leg /ˈdôgˌleg/ ▶ **n.** a thing that bends sharply, in particular a sharp bend in a road or route. ■ Golf a hole at which the player cannot aim directly at the green from the tee.
▶ **adj.** (also **dog-legged**) bent like a dog's hind leg: *the surf splashes over the dogleg concrete jetty.*
▶ **v.** (**doglegs, doglegging, doglegged**) [no obj.] follow a sharply bending route: *Highway 60 now doglegs northwest toward Frankfort.*

dog·ma /ˈdôgmə/ ▶ **n.** a principle or set of principles laid down by an authority as incontrovertibly true: *the Christian dogma of the Trinity | the rejection of political dogma.*
– ORIGIN mid 16th cent.: via late Latin from Greek *dogma* 'opinion,' from *dokein* 'seem good, think.'

dog·mat·ic /dôgˈmatik/ ▶ **adj.** inclined to lay down principles as incontrovertibly true: *he gives his opinion without trying to be dogmatic.*
– DERIVATIVES **dog·mat·i·cal·ly** /-ik(ə)lē/ **adv.**
– ORIGIN early 17th cent. (as a noun denoting a philosopher or physician of a school based on a priori assumptions): via late Latin from Greek *dogmatikos*, from *dogma, dogmat-* (see DOGMA).

dog·mat·ics /dôgˈmatiks/ ▶ **plural n.** [treated as sing.] a system of principles laid down by an authority, esp. the Roman Catholic Church, as incontrovertibly true: *it is a work of analysis, not of dogmatics.*

dog·ma·tism /ˈdôgməˌtizəm/ ▶ **n.** the tendency to lay down principles as incontrovertibly true, without consideration of evidence or the opinions of others: *a culture of dogmatism and fanaticism.*
– DERIVATIVES **dog·ma·tist n.**
– ORIGIN early 17th cent.: via French from medieval Latin *dogmatismus*, from Latin *dogma* (see DOGMA).

dog·ma·tize /ˈdôgməˌtīz/ ▶ **v.** [with obj.] represent as an incontrovertible truth: *I find views dogmatized to the point of absurdity.*
– ORIGIN early 17th cent.: via French and late Latin from Greek *dogmatizein* 'lay down one's opinion,' from *dogma* (see DOGMA).

dog·nap /ˈdôgˌnap/ ▶ **v.** (**dognaps, dognapping, dognapped** or **dognaps, dognaping, dognaped**) [with obj.] informal steal (a dog), esp. in order to sell it.
– DERIVATIVES **dog·nap·per n.**

do·good·er /ˈdo͞o ˌgo͝odər/ ▶ **n.** a well-meaning but unrealistic or interfering philanthropist or reformer.
– DERIVATIVES **do-good adj. & n., do-good·er·y** /-ərē/ **n., do-good·ing n., do-good·ism** /-go͝od,izəm/ **n.**

dog pad·dle ▶ **n.** an elementary swimming stroke like that of a swimming dog.

dog rac·ing ▶ **n.** another term for GREYHOUND RACING.

Dog·rib /ˈdôg,rib/ ▶ **n. 1** a member of a Dene people of northwestern Canada.
2 the Athabaskan language of this people.
▶ **adj.** of or relating to this people or their language.
– ORIGIN translation of Cree *atimospikay*; from the legend that the people's common ancestor was a dog.

dog rose ▶ **n.** a delicately scented Eurasian wild rose with pink or white flowers. ● Genus *Rosa*, family Rosaceae: several closely related species, in particular *R. canina*.

dogs·bod·y /ˈdôgz,bädē/ ▶ **n.** (pl. **dogsbodies**) informal, chiefly Brit. a person who is given boring, menial tasks to do: *I got myself a job as typist and general dogsbody on a small magazine*.
– DERIVATIVES **dogs·bod·y·ing n.**

dog·skin /ˈdôg,skin/ ▶ **n.** leather made of or imitating dog's skin, esp. as used for gloves.

dog·sled /ˈdôg,sled/ (also **dog sled**) ▶ **n.** a sled designed to be pulled by dogs.
▶ **v.** [no obj.] (usu. as noun **dogsledding**) travel by dogsled: *winter activities include cross-country skiing and dogsledding*.

dog's mer·cu·ry ▶ **n.** a Eurasian plant of the spurge family, with hairy stems and small green flowers, widely found as a dominant plant of old woodland. ● *Mercurialis perennis*, family Euphorbiaceae.
– ORIGIN late 16th cent.: translating modern Latin *Mercurialis canina* (former taxonomic name); the plant is poisonous and is contrasted with *Mercurialis annua* 'annual mercury,' useful in medicine.

dogs·tail /ˈdôgz,tāl/ (also **dog's-tail**) ▶ **n.** an Old World fodder grass with spiky flower heads. ● Genus *Cynosurus*, family Gramineae: several species, in particular **crested dogstail** (*C. cristatus*), a common pasture grass.

Dog Star the star Sirius.
– ORIGIN translating Greek *kuon* or Latin *canicula* 'small dog,' both names of the star; so named as it appears to follow at the heels of Orion (the hunter).

dog tag ▶ **n.** a metal tag attached to a dog's collar, typically giving its name and owner's address. ■ informal a soldier's metal identity tag, worn on a chain around the neck.

dog-tired ▶ **adj.** extremely tired; worn out: *he'd gone to bed dog-tired*.

dog·tooth /ˈdôg,to͞oTH/ ▶ **n.** Architecture a small pointed ornament repeated along a molding consisting of four petals radiating from a raised center, used esp. in the Early English style.

dog·tooth vi·o·let ▶ **n.** a plant of the lily family that has backward-curving pointed petals. ● Genus *Erythronium*, family Liliaceae: several species, in particular the trout lily of North America and the Eurasian *E. dens-canis*, with speckled leaves and pinkish-purple flowers.

dog·trot /ˈdôg,trät/ ▶ **n. 1** [in sing.] a gentle easy trot.
2 a breezeway connecting two cabins.
▶ **v.** [no obj.] move at such a pace.

dog vi·o·let ▶ **n.** a scentless wild violet, typically having purple or lilac flowers. ● Genus *Viola*, family Violaceae: several species, in particular *V. conspersa* of eastern North America.

dog war·den ▶ **n.** another term for DOGCATCHER.

dog·watch /ˈdôg,wäCH/ ▶ **n.** either of two short watches on a ship (4–6 or 6–8 p.m.).

dog-wea·ry ▶ **adj.** another term for DOG-TIRED.

dog whelk ▶ **n.** a predatory marine mollusk that typically occurs on the shore or in shallow waters. ● Family Nassaridae, class Gastropoda: *Nucella* and other genera.

dog·wood /ˈdôg,wo͝od/ ▶ **n.** a shrub or small tree of north temperate regions that yields hard timber and is grown for its decorative foliage, red stems, and colorful berries. ● Genus *Cornus*, family Cornaceae: many species, including the **flowering dogwood** (*C. florida*), common to the eastern US. ■ used in names of trees that resemble the dogwood or yield similar hard timber.

flowering dogwood

– ORIGIN so named because the wood was formerly used to make "dogs" (i.e., skewers).

Do·ha /ˈdōhə/ the capital of Qatar, in the eastern part of the country; pop 385,000 (est. 2007).

DOHC ▶ **abbr.** double overhead camshaft.

DOI ▶ **abbr.** Computing digital object identifier.

doi·ly /ˈdoilē/ ▶ **n.** (pl. **doilies**) a small ornamental mat made of lace or paper with a lace pattern, typically placed on a plate under a cake or other sweet foods.
– ORIGIN late 17th cent.: from *Doiley* or *Doyley*, the name of a 17th-cent. London draper. The word originally denoted a woolen material used for summer wear, said to have been introduced by this draper. The current sense (originally *doily napkin*) dates from the early 18th cent.

do·ing /ˈdo͞oiNG/ ▶ **n. 1** (usu. **doings**) the activities in which a particular person engages: *the latest doings of television stars*.
2 effort; activity: *it would take some doing to calm him down*.
3 informal, chiefly Brit. a beating or scolding: *someone had given her a doing*.
– PHRASES **be someone's doing** be the creation or fault of the person named: *he looked at Lisa as though it was all her doing*.

doit /doit/ ▶ **n.** [in sing.] archaic a very small amount of money.
– ORIGIN late 16th cent.: from Middle Low German *doyt*, Middle Dutch *duit*, of unknown origin.

do-it-your·self (abbr. **DIY**) ▶ **adj.** (of work, esp. building, painting, or decorating) done or to be done by an amateur at home: *easy-to-use materials and do-it-yourself kits for plumbing fittings*.
– DERIVATIVES **do-it-your·self·er n.**

do·jo /ˈdō,jō/ ▶ **n.** (pl. **dojos**) a room or hall in which judo and other martial arts are practiced.
– ORIGIN Japanese, from *dō* 'way, pursuit' + *jō* 'a place.'

dol. ▶ **abbr.** dollar(s).

Dol·by /ˈdōlbē, ˈdôl-/ ▶ **n.** trademark an electronic noise-reduction system used in tape recording to reduce hiss. ■ an electronic system used to provide stereophonic sound for movie theaters and television sets.
– ORIGIN 1960s: named after Ray M. *Dolby* (born 1933), the American engineer who devised it.

dol·ce /ˈdōlCHā/ ▶ **adv. & adj.** Music (esp. as a direction) sweetly and softly.
– ORIGIN Italian, literally 'sweet.'

dol·ce far nien·te /ˈdōlCHā fär nēˈentā/ ▶ **n.** pleasant idleness.
– ORIGIN Italian, 'sweet doing nothing.'

dol·ce vi·ta /ˌdōlCHā ˈvētə/ ▶ **n.** [in sing.] (usu. **la dolce vita**) a life of heedless pleasure and luxury.
– ORIGIN Italian, literally 'sweet life.'

dol·drums /ˈdōldrəmz, ˈdäl-, ˈdôl-/ ▶ **plural n.** (**the doldrums**) a state or period of inactivity, stagnation, or depression: *the mortgage market has been in the doldrums for three years*. ■ an equatorial region of the Atlantic Ocean with calms, sudden storms, and light unpredictable winds.
– ORIGIN late 18th cent. (as *doldrum* 'dull, sluggish person'): perhaps from DULL, on the pattern of *tantrums*.

dole[1] /dōl/ ▶ **n. 1** (usu. **the dole**) Brit. informal benefit paid by the government to the unemployed: *she is drawing on the dole*. ■ dated a charitable gift of food, clothes, or money.
2 literary a person's lot or destiny.
▶ **v.** [with obj.] (**dole something out**) distribute shares of something: *the scanty portions of food* ***doled out*** *to them*.
– PHRASES **on the dole** informal registered as unemployed and receiving benefit from the government.
– ORIGIN Old English *dāl* 'division, portion, or share,' of Germanic origin; related to DEAL[1]. The sense 'distribution of charitable gifts' dates from Middle English; the sense 'unemployment benefit' dates from the early 20th cent.

dole[2] ▶ **n.** archaic or literary sorrow; mourning.
– ORIGIN Middle English: from Old French *doel* 'mourning,' from popular Latin *dolus*, from Latin *dolere* 'grieve.'

dole·ful /ˈdōlfəl/ ▶ **adj.** expressing sorrow; mournful: *a doleful look*. ■ causing grief or misfortune: *doleful consequences*.
– DERIVATIVES **dole·ful·ly adv., dole·ful·ness n.**

dol·er·ite /ˈdälə,rīt/ ▶ **n.** Geology a dark, medium-grained igneous rock, typically with ophitic texture, containing plagioclase, pyroxene, and olivine. It typically occurs in dikes and sills. Also called DIABASE.
– ORIGIN mid 19th cent.: from French *dolérite*, from Greek *doleros* 'deceptive' (because it is difficult to distinguish from diorite).

dol·i·cho·ce·phal·ic /ˌdälikōsəˈfalik/ ▶ **adj.** Anatomy having a relatively long skull (typically with the breadth less than 80 [or 75] percent of the length). Often contrasted with BRACHYCEPHALIC.
– DERIVATIVES **dol·i·cho·ceph·a·ly** /-ˈsefəlē/ **n.**
– ORIGIN mid 19th cent.: from Greek *dolikhos* 'long' + -CEPHALIC.

doll /däl/ ▶ **n.** a small model of a human figure, often one of a baby or girl, used as a child's toy. ■ informal an attractive young woman, often with connotations of unintelligence and frivolity. ■ a generous or considerate person: *would you be a doll and set the table?*
▶ **v.** [with obj.] (**doll someone up**) informal dress someone or oneself smartly and attractively: *I got all* ***dolled up*** *for a party*.
– ORIGIN mid 16th cent. (denoting a mistress): nickname for the given name *Dorothy*. The sense 'small model of a human figure' dates from the late 17th cent.

d

dol·lar /ˈdälər/ ▶ **n.** the basic monetary unit of the US, Canada, Australia, and certain countries in the Pacific, Caribbean, Southeast Asia, Africa, and South America.
– PHRASES **dollars to doughnuts** informal used to emphasize one's certainty: *I'd bet dollars to doughnuts he's a medical student*.
– ORIGIN from early Flemish or Low German *daler*, from German *T(h)aler*, short for *Joachimsthaler*, a coin from the silver mine of *Joachimsthal* ('Joachim's valley'), now *Jáchymov* in the Czech Republic. The term was later applied to a coin used in the Spanish American colonies, which was also widely used in the British North American colonies at the time of the American Revolution, hence adopted as the name of the US monetary unit in the late 18th cent.

dol·lar ar·e·a ▶ **n.** the area of the world in which currency is linked to the US dollar.

dol·lar di·plo·ma·cy ▶ **n.** the use of a country's financial power to extend its international influence.

dol·lar gap ▶ **n.** the amount by which a country's import trade with the dollar area exceeds the corresponding export trade.

dol·lar·i·za·tion /ˌdälәriˈzāSHәn/ (also **dollarisation**) ▶ **n.** the process of aligning a country's currency with the US dollar. ■ the dominating effect of the US on the economy of a country.

dol·lar sign (also **dollar mark**) ▶ **n.** the sign $, representing a dollar.

doll·house /ˈdäl,hous/ (also chiefly Brit. **doll's house**) ▶ **n.** a miniature toy house used for playing with dolls.

dol·lop /ˈdäləp/ ▶ **n.** informal a shapeless mass or blob of something, esp. soft food: *great dollops of cream* | figurative *a dollop of romance here and there*.
▶ **v.** (**dollops, dolloping, dolloped**) [with obj.] add (a shapeless mass or blob of something) casually and without measuring: *Chekov stopped him from dolloping sugar into his coffee*.
– ORIGIN late 16th cent. (denoting a clump of grass or weeds in a field): perhaps of Scandinavian origin and related to Norwegian dialect *dolp* 'lump.'

dol·ly /ˈdälē/ ▶ **n.** (pl. **dollies**) **1** a child's word for a doll. ■ informal, dated an attractive and stylish young woman, usually with connotations of unintelligence.
2 a small platform on wheels used for holding heavy objects, typically film or television cameras.
3 historical a short wooden pole for stirring clothes in a washtub.
▶ **v.** (**dollies, dollying, dollied**) [no obj.] (of a film or television camera) be moved on a mobile platform in a specified direction: *the camera dollies back to reveal hundreds of people*.

dol·ly bird ▶ **n.** Brit. informal an attractive and stylish young woman, considered with reference only to her appearance.

dol·ly tub ▶ **n.** historical a washtub.
– ORIGIN late 19th cent.: from dialect *dolly* (used as a term for various contrivances thought to resemble a doll in some way) and TUB.

Dol·ly Var·den /ˌdälē ˈvärdn/ ▶ **n. 1** (also **Dolly Varden hat**) a large hat with one side drooping and with a floral trimming, formerly worn by women.
2 a brightly spotted edible char (fish) occurring in fresh water on both sides of the North Pacific. ● *Salvelinus malma*, family Salmonidae.
– ORIGIN late 19th cent.: from the name of a character in Dickens's *Barnaby Rudge*, who wore a similar hat.

d

dol·ma /ˈdôlmə/ ▶ n. (pl. **dolmas** or **dolmades** /dôlˈmäT͟Hes, -ˈmädes/) a Greek and Turkish delicacy in which ingredients such as rice, meat, and spices are wrapped in vine or cabbage leaves.
– ORIGIN from modern Greek *ntolmas* or its source, Turkish *dolma*, from *dolmak* 'fill, be filled.'

dol·man /ˈdōlmən/ ▶ n. a long Turkish robe open in front. ■ a woman's loose cloak with capelike sleeves.
– ORIGIN late 16th cent.: based on Turkish *dolama*, *dolaman*.

dol·man sleeve ▶ n. a loose sleeve cut in one piece with the body of a garment.

dol·men /ˈdōlmən, ˈdäl-/ ▶ n. a megalithic tomb with a large flat stone laid on upright ones, found chiefly in Britain and France.
– ORIGIN mid 19th cent.: from French, perhaps via Breton from Cornish *tolmen* 'hole of a stone.'

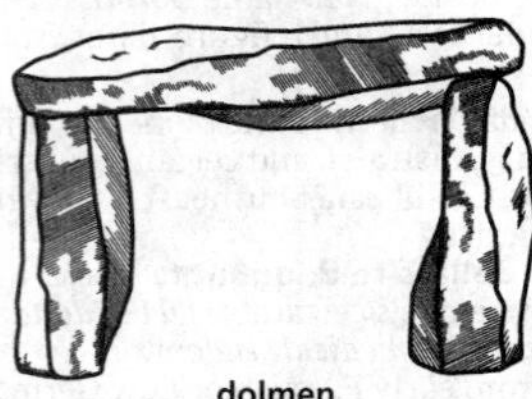
dolmen

do·lo·mite /ˈdäləˌmīt, ˈdō-/ ▶ n. a translucent mineral consisting of a carbonate of calcium and magnesium. ■ a sedimentary rock formed chiefly of this mineral.
– DERIVATIVES **dol·o·mit·ic** /ˌdäləˈmitik/ adj.
– ORIGIN late 18th cent.: from French, from the name of *Dolomieu* (1750–1801), the French geologist who discovered it, + -ITE¹.

Do·lo·mite Moun·tains /ˈdōləˌmīt, ˈdäl-/ (also **the Dolomites**) a mountain range in northern Italy, part of the Alps, so named because the characteristic rock of the region is dolomitic limestone.

do·lor /ˈdōlər/ (Brit. **dolour**) ▶ n. literary a state of great sorrow or distress: *they squatted, hunched in their habitual dolor.*
– ORIGIN Middle English, as *dolor*, (denoting both physical and mental pain or distress), via Old French from Latin *dolor* 'pain, grief.'

do·lo·rim·e·ter /ˌdōləˈrimitər/ ▶ n. an instrument for measuring sensitivity to, or levels of, pain.
– DERIVATIVES **do·lo·rim·e·try** /-itrē/ n.

dol·or·ous /ˈdōlərəs/ ▶ adj. literary feeling or expressing great sorrow or distress.
– DERIVATIVES **dol·or·ous·ly** adv.
– ORIGIN late Middle English: from Old French *doleros*, from late Latin *dolorosus*, from Latin *dolor* 'pain, grief.'

do·lo·stone /ˈdäləˌstōn, ˈdō-/ ▶ n. Geology rock consisting of dolomite.
– ORIGIN mid 20th cent.: from DOLOMITE + STONE.

dol·phin /ˈdälfin, ˈdôl-/ ▶ n. **1** a small gregarious toothed whale that typically has a beaklike snout and a curved fin on the back. Dolphins have become well known for their sociable nature and high intelligence. ● Families Delphinidae (marine) and Platanistidae (the **river dolphins**): several genera and many species.
2 (also **dolphinfish**) another term for MAHIMAHI.
3 a bollard, pile, or buoy for mooring.
4 a structure for protecting the pier of a bridge or other structure from collision with ships.
– ORIGIN late Middle English: from Old French *dauphin*, from Provençal *dalfin*, from Latin *delphinus*, from Greek *delphin*.

dol·phi·nar·i·um /ˌdälfiˈne(ə)rēəm, ˌdôl-/ ▶ n. (pl. **dolphinariums** or **dolphinaria** /-ˈne(ə)rēə/) an aquarium in which dolphins are kept and trained for public entertainment.
– ORIGIN 1960s: from DOLPHIN, on the pattern of *oceanarium*.

dol·phin-safe ▶ adj. (on canned tuna labels) indicating that the tuna has been harvested using fishing methods that are not harmful to dolphins.

dolt /dōlt/ ▶ n. a stupid person.
– ORIGIN mid 16th cent.: perhaps a variant of *dulled*, past participle of DULL.

dolt·ish /ˈdōltisH/ ▶ adj. (of a person) stupid; idiotic: *a doltish character.*
– DERIVATIVES **dolt·ish·ly** adv., **dolt·ish·ness** n.

Dom /däm/ ▶ n. **1** a title prefixed to the names of some Roman Catholic dignitaries and Benedictine and Carthusian monks: *Dom Bede Griffiths.*
2 Portuguese form of DON¹ (sense 2).
– ORIGIN from Latin *dominus* 'master.'

-dom ▶ suffix forming nouns: **1** denoting a state or condition: *freedom.*
2 denoting rank or status: *earldom.*
3 denoting a domain: *fiefdom.*
4 denoting a class of people or the attitudes associated with them, regarded collectively: *officialdom.*
– ORIGIN Old English *-dōm*, originally meaning 'decree, judgment.'

do·main /dōˈmān/ ▶ n. an area of territory owned or controlled by a ruler or government: *the southwestern French domains of the Plantagenets.* ■ a specified sphere of activity or knowledge: *the expanding domain of psychology* | figurative *visual communication is the domain of the graphic designer.* ■ Physics a discrete region of magnetism in ferromagnetic material. ■ Computing a distinct subset of the Internet with addresses sharing a common suffix or under the control of a particular organization or individual. ■ Mathematics the set of possible values of the independent variable or variables of a function.
– DERIVATIVES **do·ma·ni·al** /-nēəl/ adj.
– ORIGIN late Middle English (denoting heritable or landed property): from French *domaine*, alteration (by association with Latin *dominus* 'lord') of Old French *demeine* 'belonging to a lord' (see DEMESNE).

do·maine /dəˈmān/ ▶ n. a vineyard.
– ORIGIN 1960s: from French, literally 'estate' (see DOMAIN).

do·main name ▶ n. Computing the part of a network address that identifies it as belonging to a particular domain.

do·main name sys·tem (abbr.: **DNS**) ▶ n. Computing the system by which Internet domain names and addresses are tracked and regulated.

dome /dōm/ ▶ n. **1** a rounded vault forming the roof of a building or structure, typically with a circular base: *the dome of St. Paul's Cathedral.* ■ the revolving openable hemispherical roof of an observatory. ■ [in names] a sports stadium with a domed roof.
2 a thing shaped like such a roof, in particular: ■ the rounded summit of a hill or mountain: *the great dome of Mont Blanc.* ■ a natural vault or canopy, such as that of the sky or trees: *the dome of the sky.* ■ Geology a rounded uplifted landform or underground structure. ■ informal the top of the head: *a content face topped by a shaved dome.*
3 literary a stately building.
▶ v. [with obj.] (usu. as adj. **domed**) cover with or shape as a dome: *a domed stadium.* ■ [no obj.] (often as noun **doming**) (of stratified rock or a surface) become rounded in formation; swell.
– DERIVATIVES **dome·like** /-ˌlīk/ adj.
– ORIGIN early 16th cent. (sense 3 of the noun): from French *dôme*, from Italian *duomo* 'cathedral, dome,' from Latin *domus* 'house.' Sense 3 of the noun derives directly from Latin *domus*.

Dome of the Rock an Islamic shrine in Jerusalem, for Muslims the third most holy place after Mecca and Medina. It surrounds the sacred rock on which, according to tradition, Abraham prepared to sacrifice his son Isaac and from which the prophet Muhammad made his miraculous night ascent into heaven (the Night Journey).

Dome of the Rock

Domes·day /ˈdo͞omzˌdā/ ▶ n. **1** (also **Domesday Book, Doomsday Book**) a comprehensive record of the extent, value, ownership, and liabilities of land in England, made in 1086 by order of William I.
2 (also **domesday**) archaic spelling of DOOMSDAY.
– ORIGIN Middle English: sense 1 was apparently a popular name applied during the 12th cent. because the book was regarded as a final authority (with allusion to *doomsday* 'the Day of Judgment').

do·mes·tic /dəˈmestik/ ▶ adj. **1** of or relating to the running of a home or to family relations: *domestic chores* | *domestic violence.* ■ chiefly Brit. of or for use in the home rather than in an industrial or office environment: *domestic appliances.* ■ (of a person) fond of family life and running a home: *she was not at all domestic.* ■ (of an animal) tame and kept by humans: *domestic cattle.*
2 existing or occurring inside a particular country; not foreign or international: *the current state of US domestic affairs.*
▶ n. **1** (also **domestic worker** or **domestic help**) a person who is paid to help with menial tasks such as cleaning.
2 a product not made abroad.
– DERIVATIVES **do·mes·ti·cal·ly** /-ik(ə)lē/ adv.
– ORIGIN late Middle English: from French *domestique*, from Latin *domesticus*, from *domus* 'house.'

do·mes·ti·cate /dəˈmestiˌkāt/ ▶ v. [with obj.] (usu. **be domesticated**) tame (an animal) and keep it as a pet or for farm produce: *mammals were first domesticated for their milk.* ■ cultivate (a plant) for food. ■ humorous make (someone) fond of and good at home life and the tasks that it involves: *you've really domesticated him.*
– DERIVATIVES **do·mes·ti·ca·ble** /-kəbəl/ adj., **do·mes·ti·ca·tion** /-ˌmestiˈkāsHən/ n.
– ORIGIN mid 17th cent.: from medieval Latin *domesticat-* 'domesticated,' from the verb *domesticare*, from Latin *domesticus* 'belonging to the house' (see DOMESTIC).

do·mes·ti·cated /dəˈmestiˌkātəd/ ▶ adj. (of an animal) tame and kept as a pet or on a farm: *domesticated dogs.* ■ (of a plant) cultivated for food; naturalized: *domesticated crops.* ■ humorous (of a man) fond of home life and housework: *he is thoroughly domesticated.*

do·mes·tic·i·ty /ˌdōmeˈstisitē/ ▶ n. home or family life: *the atmosphere is one of happy domesticity.*

do·mes·tic part·ner ▶ n. a person who shares a residence with a sexual partner, esp. without a legally recognized union.
– DERIVATIVES **do·mes·tic part·ner·ship** n.

do·mes·tic pi·geon ▶ n. see PIGEON¹ (sense 1).

do·mes·tic sci·ence ▶ n. dated the study of household skills such as cooking or sewing, esp. as taught at school; home economics.

dom·i·cal /ˈdōmikəl, ˈdäm-/ ▶ adj. domed: *an octagonal, domical vault.*

dom·i·cile /ˈdäməˌsīl, ˈdō-, ˈdäməsəl/ ▶ n. formal or Law the country that a person treats as their permanent home, or lives in and has a substantial connection with: *his wife has a domicile of origin in Germany.* ■ a person's residence or home: *the builder I've hired to renovate my new domicile.* ■ the place at which a company or other body is registered, esp. for tax purposes.
▶ v. [with adverbial of place] (**be domiciled**) formal or Law treat a specified country as a permanent home: *the tenant is domiciled in the US.* ■ reside; be based: *he was domiciled in a frame house on the outskirts of town.*
– ORIGIN late Middle English: via Old French from Latin *domicilium* 'dwelling,' from *domus* 'home.'

dom·i·cil·i·ar·y /ˌdäməˈsilēˌerē, ˌdō-/ ▶ adj. concerned with or occurring in someone's home: *a study compared domiciliary care with hospital care.*
– ORIGIN late 19th cent.: from French *domiciliaire*, from medieval Latin *domiciliarius*, from Latin *domicilium* 'dwelling' (see DOMICILE).

dom·i·nance /ˈdämənəns/ ▶ n. power and influence over others: *the worldwide dominance of Hollywood.* ■ Genetics the phenomenon whereby, in an individual containing two allelic forms of a gene, one is expressed to the exclusion of the other. ■ Ecology the predominance of one or more species in a plant (or animal) community.
– DERIVATIVES **dom·i·nan·cy** /-sē/ n.

dom·i·nant /ˈdämənənt/ ▶ adj. most important, powerful, or influential: *they are now in an even more dominant position in the market.* ■ (of a high place or object) overlooking others. ■ Genetics relating to or denoting heritable characteristics that are controlled by genes that are expressed in offspring even when inherited from only one parent. Often contrasted with RECESSIVE. ■ Ecology denoting the predominant species in a plant (or animal) community. ■ in decision theory, (of a choice) at least as good as the alternatives in all circumstances, and better in some: *holding back is here a dominant strategy.*
▶ n. a dominant thing, in particular: ■ Genetics a dominant trait or gene. ■ Ecology a dominant species in a plant (or animal) community. ■ Music the fifth note of the diatonic scale of any key, or the key based on this, considered in relation to the key of the tonic.
– DERIVATIVES **dom·i·nant·ly** adv.
– ORIGIN late Middle English: via Old French from Latin *dominant-* 'ruling, governing,' from the verb *dominari* (see DOMINATE).

dom·i·nant sev·enth ▶ n. Music the common chord of the dominant note in a key, plus the minor seventh from that note (e.g., in the key of C, a chord of G-B-D-F). It is important in conventional harmony, as it naturally resolves to the tonic or subdominant.

dom·i·nate /ˈdäməˌnāt/ ▶ v. [with obj.] have a commanding influence on; exercise control over: *the company dominates the market for operating system software.* ■ be the most important or conspicuous

person or thing in: *the race was dominated by the 1992 champion.* ■ (of something tall or high) have a commanding position over; overlook: *a picturesque city dominated by the cathedral tower.*
– DERIVATIVES **dom·i·na·tor** /-ˌnātər/ **n.**
– ORIGIN early 17th cent.: from Latin *dominat-* 'ruled, governed,' from the verb *dominari*, from *dominus* 'lord, master.'

dom·i·na·tion /ˌdäməˈnāSHən/ ▶ **n. 1** the exercise of control or influence over someone or something, or the state of being so controlled: *evil plans for domination of the universe.*
2 (**dominations**) (in traditional Christian angelology) the fourth highest order of the ninefold celestial hierarchy.
– ORIGIN late Middle English: via Old French from Latin *dominatio(n-)*, from the verb *dominari* (see DOMINATE).

dom·i·na·trix /ˌdäməˈnātriks/ ▶ **n.** (pl. **dominatrices** /-trəˌsēz/ or **dominatrixes**) a dominating woman, esp. one who takes the sadistic role in sadomasochistic sexual activities.
– ORIGIN mid 16th cent. (rare before the late 20th cent.): from Latin, feminine of *dominator*, from *dominat-* 'ruled,' from the verb *dominari* (see DOMINATE).

dom·i·neer /ˌdäməˈni(ə)r/ ▶ **v.** [no obj.] (usu. as adj. **domineering**) assert one's will over another in an arrogant way: *Cathy had been a martyr to her gruff, domineering husband.*
– DERIVATIVES **dom·i·neer·ing·ly adv.**
– ORIGIN late 16th cent.: from Dutch *dominieren*, from French *dominer*, from Latin *dominari* (see DOMINATE).

Do·min·go /dəˈmiNGgō/, Placido (1941–), Spanish opera singer. He moved to Mexico in 1950 and made his debut as an operatic tenor in 1957. His performances in operas by Verdi and Puccini have met with particular acclaim. He was one of the Three Tenors, along with Luciano Pavarotti and José Carreras.

Dom·i·nic, St. /ˈdämənik/ (*c.*1170–1221), Spanish priest and friar; Spanish name *Domingo de Guzmán*. In 1216, he founded the Order of Friars Preachers at Toulouse in France; its members became known as Dominicans or Black Friars. Feast day, August 8.

Dom·i·ni·ca /ˌdäməˈnēkə, dəˈminikə/ a country in the western West Indies, a mountainous island, the most northern of the Windward Islands, in the Caribbean Sea; pop. 72,700 (est. 2009); capital, Roseau; languages, English (official) and Creole.

> The island came into British possession at the end of the 18th century and became an independent republic within the Commonwealth of Nations in 1978.

– ORIGIN named by Columbus, who discovered it on a Sunday (Latin *dies dominica* 'the Lord's day') in 1493.

do·min·i·cal /dəˈminikəl/ ▶ **adj. 1** of Sunday as the Lord's day.
2 of Jesus Christ as the lord.
– ORIGIN Middle English: from late Latin *dominicalis*, from Latin *dominicus*, from *dominus* 'lord, master.'

do·min·i·cal let·ter ▶ **n.** any of the seven letters A–G used in church calendars to indicate the date (January 1–7) on which the first Sunday in the year falls, and hence in dating movable feasts.

Do·min·i·can[1] /dəˈminikən/ ▶ **n.** a member of the Roman Catholic order of preaching friars founded by St. Dominic, or of a religious order for women founded on similar principles.
▶ **adj.** of or relating to St. Dominic or the Dominicans.
– ORIGIN late 16th cent.: from medieval Latin *Dominicanus*, from *Dominicus*, the Latin name of *Domingo de Guzmán* (see DOMINIC, ST.).

Do·min·i·can[2] ▶ **adj.** of or relating to the Dominican Republic or its people.
▶ **n.** a native or inhabitant of the Dominican Republic.
– ORIGIN from Spanish *Dominicana*, influenced by SANTO DOMINGO.

Do·min·i·can[3] ▶ **adj.** of or relating to the island of Dominica or its people.
▶ **n.** a native or inhabitant of the island of Dominica.

Do·min·i·can Re·pub·lic /dəˈminəkən/ a country in the Caribbean Sea that occupies the eastern part of the island of Hispaniola; pop. 9,650,100 (est. 2009); capital, Santo Domingo; official language, Spanish.

> The **Dominican Republic** is the former Spanish colony of Santo Domingo, the part of Hispaniola that Spain retained when it ceded the western portion (now Haiti) to France in 1697. It was proclaimed a republic in 1844.

dom·i·nie /ˈdämənē, ˈdō-/ ▶ **n.** (pl. **dominies**)
1 Scottish a schoolmaster.
2 a pastor or clergyman.
– ORIGIN late 17th cent.: alteration of Latin *domine!* (vocative) 'master!, sir!,' from *dominus* 'lord' (formerly used as a polite form of address to a clergyman or member of one of the professions).

do·min·ion /dəˈminyən/ ▶ **n. 1** sovereignty; control: *man's attempt to establish **dominion** over nature.*
2 (usu. **dominions**) the territory of a sovereign or government: *the Angevin dominions.* ■ (**Dominion**) historical each of the self-governing territories of the British Commonwealth.
3 (**dominions**) another term for DOMINATION (sense 2).
– ORIGIN Middle English: via Old French from medieval Latin *dominio(n-)*, from Latin *dominium*, from *dominus* 'lord, master.'

Do·min·ion Day ▶ **n.** former name for July 1, a national holiday observed in Canada to commemorate the formation of the Dominion in 1867. Since 1982, it has been known as **Canada Day**.

do·min·i·um /dəˈminēəm/ ▶ **n.** Law absolute ownership and control of property.
– ORIGIN mid 18th cent.: from Latin.

Dom·i·no /ˈdäməˌnō/, Fats (1928–), US pianist, singer, and songwriter; born *Antoine Domino*. His music represents part of the transition from rhythm and blues to rock and roll and shows the influence of jazz, boogie-woogie, and gospel music. Notable songs: "Ain't That a Shame" (1955) and "Blueberry Hill" (1956).

dom·i·no /ˈdäməˌnō/ ▶ **n.** (pl. **dominoes** or **dominos**)
1 any of 28 small oblong pieces marked with 0–6 dots (pips) in each half. ■ (**dominoes**) [treated as sing.] the game played with such pieces, in which they are laid down to form a line, each player in turn trying to find and lay down a domino with a value matched by that of a piece at either end of the line already formed.
2 historical a loose cloak, worn with a mask for the upper part of the face at masquerades.
– ORIGIN late 17th cent.: from French, denoting a hood worn by priests in winter, probably based on Latin *dominus* 'lord, master.'

dominoes

dom·i·no ef·fect ▶ **n.** the effect of the domino theory.

dom·i·no the·o·ry ▶ **n.** the theory that a political event in one country will cause similar events in neighboring countries, like a falling domino causing an entire row of upended dominoes to fall.

Do·mi·tian /dəˈmiSHən/ (AD 51–96), son of Vespasian; Roman emperor 81–96; full name *Titus Flavius Domitianus*.

Don /dän/ **1** a river in Russia that rises near Tula, southeast of Moscow, and flows for 1,224 miles (1,958 km) to the Sea of Azov.
2 a river in Scotland that rises in the Grampian Mountains and flows east for 82 miles (131 km) to the North Sea at Aberdeen.
3 a river in northern England that rises in the Pennine Hills and flows east for 70 miles (112 km) to join the Ouse River shortly before it, in turn, joins the Humber River.

don[1] /dän/ ▶ **n. 1** (**Don**) a Spanish title prefixed to a male forename. ■ a Spanish gentleman; a Spaniard. ■ informal a high-ranking member of the Mafia.
2 a university teacher, esp. a senior member of a college at Oxford or Cambridge. [transferred colloquial use of the Spanish title (see above).]
– DERIVATIVES **don·ship** /-ˌSHip/ **n.**
– ORIGIN early 16th cent.: from Spanish, from Latin *dominus* 'lord, master.'

don[2] ▶ **v.** (**dons, donning, donned**) [with obj.] put on (an item of clothing): *in the locker room the players donned their football jerseys.*
– ORIGIN late Middle English: contraction of *do on*. Compare with DOFF.

Don·a·hue /ˈdänəˌhyōō/, Phil (1935–), US talk show host; full name *Phillip John Donahue*. He began his televised "Phil Donahue Show" in 1967 and retired in 1996.

do·nate /ˈdōnāt, dōˈnāt/ ▶ **v.** [with obj.] give (money or goods) for a good cause, for example to a charity: *the proceeds will be donated to an AIDS awareness charity.* ■ allow the removal of (blood or an organ) from one's body for transplantation, transfusion, or other use.
– DERIVATIVES **do·na·tor** /ˈdōnātər/ **n.**
– ORIGIN late 18th cent.: back-formation from DONATION.

Don·a·tel·lo /ˌdänəˈtelō/ (1386–1466), Italian sculptor; born *Donato di Betto Bardi*. He was one of the pioneers of scientific perspective and is known for his lifelike sculptures, including the bronze *David* (*c.*1430–60).

do·na·tion /dōˈnāSHən/ ▶ **n.** something that is given to a charity, esp. a sum of money: *a tax-deductible donation of $200.* ■ the action of donating something.
– ORIGIN late Middle English: via Old French from Latin *donatio(n-)*, from the verb *donare*, based on *donum* 'gift.'

Don·a·tist /ˈdänətist, ˈdō-/ ▶ **n.** a member of a schismatic Christian group in North Africa, formed in 311, who held that only those living a blameless life belonged in the Church. They survived until the 7th century.
– DERIVATIVES **Don·a·tism** /-ˌtizəm/ **n.**
– ORIGIN from *Donatus* (died *c.*355), a Christian prelate in Carthage and the group's leader, + -IST.

don·a·tive /ˈdōnətiv, ˈdän-/ rare ▶ **n.** a donation, esp. one given formally or officially as a largesse.
▶ **adj.** given as a donation. ■ historical (of a benefice) given directly, not presentative.
– ORIGIN late Middle English: from Latin *donativum* 'gift, largesse,' from *donat-* 'given,' from the verb *donare* (see DONATION).

Do·na·tus /dəˈnātəs/, Aelius (4th century), Roman grammarian. The *Ars Grammatica*, which contained his treatises on Latin grammar, was the sole textbook used in schools in the Middle Ages.

Do·nau /ˈdōˌnou/ German name for DANUBE.

Don·bas /dənˈbäs, ˈdänˌbas/ Ukrainian name for DONETS BASIN.

Don·cas·ter /ˈdäNGkəstər/ an industrial town in northern England; pop. 63,800 (est. 2009).

done /dən/ past participle of DO[1].
▶ **v.** informal used as a nonstandard past tense of DO[1]: *I done a lot of rodeoin'.* ■ informal used with a standard past tense verb to indicate absoluteness or completion: *I done told you to zipper your lips.*
▶ **adj. 1** (of food) cooked thoroughly: *the turkey will be done soon.* ■ no longer happening or existing: *her hunting days were done.*
2 informal socially acceptable: *therapy was **not the done thing** then.*
▶ **exclam.** used to indicate that the speaker accepts the terms of an offer: *"I'll give ten to one he misses by a mile!" called Reilly. "Done," said the conductor.*
– PHRASES **a done deal** an agreement that has been finalized. **done for** informal in a situation so bad that it is impossible to get out: *if he gets them, we'll all be done for.* **done in** informal extremely tired: *you look done in.* **over and done with** see OVER.

do·nee /dōˈnē/ ▶ **n.** a person who receives a gift. ■ Law a person who is given a power of appointment.
– ORIGIN early 16th cent.: from DONOR + -EE.

Don·e·gal /ˌdäniˈgôl, ˌdən-/ a county in extreme northwestern Republic of Ireland, part of the old province of Ulster; capital, Lifford.

don·e·gal /ˈdänigəl, -ˌgôl/ (also **Donegal tweed**) ▶ **n.** a tweed characterized by bright flecks randomly distributed on a background usually of light gray, originally woven in County Donegal, northwestern Ireland.

Do·nets /dəˈn(y)ets/ a river in eastern Europe that rises near Belgorod in southern Russia and flows southeast for about 630 miles (1,000 km) through Ukraine before re-entering Russia and joining the Don River near Rostov.

Do·nets Ba·sin a coal-mining and industrial region in southeastern Ukraine that stretches between the valleys of the Donets and lower Dnieper rivers. Ukrainian name DONBAS.

Do·netsk /dəˈn(y)etsk/ a city in the Donets Basin in Ukraine; pop. 974,600 (est. 2009). The city was called Yuzovka 1872–1924, and Stalin or Stalino 1924–61.

dong[1] /dôNG, däNG/ ▶ **v.** [no obj.] (of a bell) make a deep resonant sound.
▶ **n. 1** the deep resonant sound of a large bell.
2 vulgar slang a penis.
– ORIGIN late 16th cent.: imitative.

dong[2] ▶ **n.** the basic monetary unit of Vietnam, equal to 100 xu.
– ORIGIN from Vietnamese *đông* 'coin.'

don·gle /ˈdäNGgəl, ˈdôNG-/ ▶ **n.** a device that is connected to a computer to allow access to wireless broadband or use of protected software.
– ORIGIN 1980s: an arbitrary formation.

Dong-nai Riv·er /ˌdôNG ˈnī/ (also **Donnai** /ˌdôn ˈnī/) a river in Vietnam that flows for 300 miles (483 km) from south central Vietnam to join the Saigon River below Ho Chi Minh City.

dong quai /ˈdŏŏNG ˈkwä, ˈkwī/ ▶ **n.** an aromatic herb of the parsley family, native to China and Japan, the root of which is used to treat premenstrual syndrome, menstrual cramps, menopausal symptoms, and other gynecological complaints. ● *Angelica sinensis*, family Umbelliferae.

Dong·ying /ˈdŏŏNG ˈyiNG/ a city in Hebei province, in eastern China, near the mouth of the Yellow River, in an area rich in oil; pop. 628,400 (est. 2006).

Don·i·zet·ti /ˌdänəˈzetē/, Gaetano (1797–1848), Italian composer. His operas include tragedies such as *Lucia di Lammermoor* (1835) and comedies such as *Don Pasquale* (1843).

d

don·jon /ˈdänjən, ˈdən-/ ▶ **n.** the great tower or innermost keep of a castle.
– ORIGIN Middle English: variant of DUNGEON.

Don Juan /ˌdän ˈ(h)wän/ a legendary Spanish nobleman known for his dissolute life and for seducing women. ■ (as noun **a Don Juan**) a seducer of women; a libertine.

don·key /ˈdôNGkē, ˈdäNG-/ ▶ **n.** (pl. **donkeys**) **1** a domesticated hoofed mammal of the horse family with long ears and a braying call, used as a beast of burden; an ass. ● *Equus asinus*, family Equidae, descended from the wild ass of Africa.
2 informal a stupid or foolish person.
– PHRASES **donkey's years** informal a very long time: *we've been close friends for donkey's years.*
– ORIGIN late 18th cent. (originally pronounced to rhyme with *monkey*): perhaps from DUN¹, or from the given name *Duncan*.

don·key en·gine ▶ **n.** a small or auxiliary engine, esp. on a ship.

don·key·work /ˈdôNGkēˌwərk, ˈdäNG-/ (also **donkey work**) ▶ **n.** informal the boring or laborious part of a job; drudgery: *supervisors who get a research student to do the donkeywork.*

Don·na /ˈdänə, ˈdôn-nä/ ▶ **n.** a title or form of address for an Italian woman.
– ORIGIN early 17th cent.: from Italian, from Latin *domina* 'mistress,' feminine of *dominus* 'lord, master.'

Don·nan e·qui·lib·ri·um /ˈdänən/ ▶ **n.** Chemistry the equilibrium reached between two ionic solutions separated by a semipermeable membrane when one or more of the kinds of ion present cannot pass through the membrane. The result is a difference in osmotic pressure and electrical potential between the solutions.
– ORIGIN early 20th cent.: named after Frederick G. *Donnan* (1870–1956), British physical chemist.

Donne /dən/, John (1572–1631), English poet and clergyman. A metaphysical poet, he is noted for his *Satires* (c.1590–99), *Elegies* (c.1590–99), and love poems, which appeared in the collection *Songs and Sonnets*. As dean of St. Paul's Cathedral, he was one of the most celebrated preachers of his age.

don·née /däˈnā/ (also **donné**) ▶ **n.** **1** a subject or theme of a narrative.
2 a basic fact or assumption.
– ORIGIN late 19th cent.: French, literally 'given.'

Don·ner Pass /ˈdänər/ a site in the Sierra Nevada in northeastern California where some members of an 1844 emigrant party survived a blizzard partly by eating the dead.

don·nish /ˈdänisн/ ▶ **adj.** thought to resemble or suit a college don, particularly because of a pedantic, scholarly manner.
– DERIVATIVES **don·nish·ly** adv., **don·nish·ness** n.

don·ny·brook /ˈdänēˌbrŏŏk/ ▶ **n.** a scene of uproar and disorder; a heated argument: *raucous ideological donnybrooks.*
– ORIGIN mid 19th cent.: from the name of a suburb of Dublin, Ireland, formerly famous for its annual fair.

do·nor /ˈdōnər/ ▶ **n.** a person who donates something, esp. money to a fund or charity: *an anonymous donor has given $25* | [as modifier] *loans from rich donor countries.* ■ a person who provides blood for transfusion, semen for insemination, or an organ or tissue for transplantation. ■ Chemistry an atom or molecule that provides electrons in forming a coordinate bond. ■ Physics an impurity atom in a semiconductor that contributes a conducting electron to the material.
– ORIGIN Middle English: from Old French *doneur*, from Latin *donator*, from *donare* 'give.'

do·nor fa·tigue ▶ **n.** a lessening of public willingness to respond generously to charitable appeals, resulting from the frequency of such appeals.

do-noth·ing ▶ **n.** a person who is idle or lacks ambition.
▶ **adj.** idle or lacking ambition.

Don Quix·o·te /ˌdän kēˈhōtē, -tā/ the hero of a romance (1605–15) by Cervantes, a satirical account of chivalric beliefs and conduct. The character of Don Quixote is typified by a romantic vision and naive, unworldly idealism.

don't /dōnt/ ▶ **contraction** do not. ■ informal does not: *she don't drink tea.*
– PHRASES **dos and don'ts** see DO¹.

do·nut /ˈdōˌnət/ ▶ **n.** variant spelling of DOUGHNUT.

doo·dad /ˈdo͞oˌdad/ ▶ **n.** a trivial ornament or gadget, esp. one whose name the speaker does not know or cannot recall: *the latest electronic doodads.*
– ORIGIN early 20th cent.: of unknown origin.

doo·dle /ˈdo͞odl/ ▶ **v.** [no obj.] scribble absentmindedly: *he was only doodling in the margin.*
▶ **n.** a rough drawing made absentmindedly.
– DERIVATIVES **doo·dler** /-d(ə)lər/ **n.**
– ORIGIN early 17th cent. (originally as a noun denoting a fool, later as a verb in the sense 'make a fool of, cheat'): from Low German *dudeltopf, dudeldopp* 'simpleton.' Current senses date from the 1930s.

doo·dle·bug /ˈdo͞odlˌbəg/ ▶ **n.** informal **1** the larva of an ant lion.
2 an unscientific device for locating oil or minerals; a divining rod.
3 Brit. informal term for V-1.
– ORIGIN mid 19th cent. (sense 1): from 17th-cent. *doodle* 'ninny' + BUG.

doo·dly-squat /ˈdo͞odl-ēˌskwät/ (also **doodly**) ▶ **n.** another term for DIDDLY-SQUAT.

doo-doo /ˈdo͞o ˌdo͞o/ ▶ **n.** a child's word for excrement, used euphemistically in other contexts: *when our fax machine isn't working, we're in deep doo-doo.*

doo·fus /ˈdo͞ofəs/ (also **dufus**) ▶ **n.** (pl. **doofuses**) informal a stupid person.
– ORIGIN 1960s: perhaps an alteration of GOOFUS, or from Scots *doof* 'dolt.'

doo·hick·ey /ˈdo͞oˌhikē/ ▶ **n.** (pl. **doohickeys**) informal a small object or gadget, esp. one whose name the speaker does not know or cannot recall: *a garage filled with electronic parts and other valuable doohickeys.*
– ORIGIN early 20th cent. (originally servicemen's slang): blend of DOODAD and HICKEY.

doo·lal·ly /ˈdo͞oˌlälē/ ▶ **adj.** Brit. informal temporarily deranged or feebleminded: *Uncle Orville's gone doolally again.*
– ORIGIN early 20th cent.: originally *doolally tap*, Indian army slang, from *Deolali* (the name of a town with a military sanatorium and a transit camp) + Urdu *tap* 'fever.'

Doo·ley /ˈdo͞olē/, Thomas Anthony (1927–61), US physician and writer. He established medical missions in Laos in 1956 as well as hospitals in Cambodia, Laos, and Vietnam. In 1957, he established Medico, an international medical aid mission. He wrote about his experiences in *Deliver Us from Evil* (1956), *The Edge of Tomorrow* (1958), and *The Night They Burned the Mountain* (1960).

doo·lie /ˈdo͞olē/ ▶ **n.** (pl. **doolies**) informal a freshman at the US Air Force Academy.
– ORIGIN from Hindi *ḍolī*, diminutive of *ḍolā* 'cradle or litter.'

Doo·lit·tle /ˈdo͞oˌlitl/, Hilda (1886–1961), US poet; pseudonym H.D. From 1911, she lived in London. Her work shows the influence of Ezra Pound and other imagist poets; it also shows the influence of classical mythology.

doom /do͞om/ ▶ **n.** death, destruction, or some other terrible fate: *the aircraft was sent crashing to its doom in the water.* ■ [in sing.] archaic (in Christian belief) the Last Judgment.
▶ **v.** [with obj.] (usu. **be doomed**) condemn to certain destruction or death: *fuel was spilling out of the damaged wing and the aircraft was doomed.* ■ cause to have an unfortunate and inescapable outcome: *her plan was doomed to failure.*
– PHRASES **doom and gloom** (also **gloom and doom**) a general feeling of pessimism or despondency: *the national feeling of doom and gloom.*
– ORIGIN Old English *dōm* 'statute, judgment,' of Germanic origin, from a base meaning 'to put in place'; related to DO¹.

doomed /do͞omd/ ▶ **adj.** likely to have an unfortunate and inescapable outcome; ill-fated: *the moving story of their doomed love affair.*

doom-lad·en ▶ **adj.** conveying a sense of tragedy: *a doom-laden speech.*

doom·say·er /ˈdo͞omˌsāər/ ▶ **n.** a person who predicts disaster, esp. in politics or economics.
– DERIVATIVES **doom·say·ing** /-ˌsāiNG/ **n.**

dooms·day /ˈdo͞omzˌdā/ (also **domesday**) ▶ **n.** [in sing.] the last day of the world's existence. ■ (in Christian belief) the day of the Last Judgment. ■ a time or event of crisis or great danger: [as modifier] *in all the concern over greenhouse warming, one doomsday scenario stands out.*
– PHRASES **till doomsday** informal forever: *we'll be here till doomsday if you don't hurry up.*
– ORIGIN Old English *dōmes dæg* (see DOOM, DAY).

Dooms·day Book ▶ **n.** see DOMESDAY.

doom·y /ˈdo͞omē/ ▶ **adj.** (**doomier, doomiest**) suggesting or predicting disaster; ominous: *doomy forecasts.*
– DERIVATIVES **doom·i·ly** /-məlē/ **adv.**

door /dôr/ ▶ **n.** a hinged, sliding, or revolving barrier at the entrance to a building, room, or vehicle, or in the framework of a cupboard. ■ a doorway: *she walked through the door.* ■ used to refer to the distance from one building in a row to another: *they lived within three doors of each other.*
– PHRASES **at the door** on admission to an event rather than in advance: *tickets will be available at the door.* **close** (or **shut**) **the door on** (or **to**) exclude the opportunity for: *she had closed the door on ever finding out what he was feeling.* (**from**) **door to door 1** from start to finish of a journey: *the trip from door to door could take more than four hours.* **2** visiting all the houses in an area to sell or publicize something: *he went from door to door selling insurance policies* | [as adj.] *a door-to-door salesman.* **lay something at someone's door** regard someone as responsible for something: *the failure is laid at the door of the government.* **leave the door open** ensure that there is still an opportunity for something: *he is leaving the door open for future change.* **open the door to** create an opportunity for: *her research has opened the door to a deeper understanding of the subject.* **out of doors** in or into the open air: *food tastes even better out of doors.* **show someone the door** see SHOW.
– DERIVATIVES **doored adj.** [in combination] *a glass-doored desk.*
– ORIGIN Old English *duru, dor*, of Germanic origin; related to Dutch *deur* 'door' and German *Tür* 'door,' *Tor* 'gate'; from an Indo-European root shared by Latin *foris* 'gate' and Greek *thura* 'door.'

door·bell /ˈdôrˌbel/ ▶ **n.** a bell in a building that can be rung by visitors outside to signal their arrival.

door·bust·er /ˈdôrˌbəstər/ ▶ **n.** informal **1** (in retailing) a special discount price available for a limited period, typically during special early-opening hours.
2 a firearm with special attachments for forcing entry through a door.

do-or-die ▶ **adj.** [attrib.] (of a person's attitude or a situation) showing or requiring a determination not to compromise or be deterred: *the mercenaries fought with a do-or-die resolution.*

door·frame /ˈdôrˌfrām/ (also **door frame**) ▶ **n.** the frame in a doorway into which a door is fitted.

door·jamb /ˈdôrˌjam/ ▶ **n.** each of the two upright parts of a doorframe, on one of which the door is hung.

door·keep·er /ˈdôrˌkēpər/ ▶ **n.** a person on duty at the entrance to a building.

door·knob /ˈdôrˌnäb/ ▶ **n.** a handle on a door that is turned to release the latch.

door knock·er ▶ **n.** a metal or wooden instrument hinged to a door and rapped by visitors to attract attention and gain entry.

door·man /ˈdôrˌman, -mən/ ▶ **n.** (pl. **doormen**) a man such as a porter, bouncer, or janitor who is on duty at the entrance to a large building.

door·mat /ˈdôrˌmat/ ▶ **n.** a mat placed in a doorway, on which people can wipe their shoes on entering a building. ■ a submissive person who allows others to dominate them: *to put up with such treatment you must be either a saint or a doormat.*

door·nail /ˈdôrˌnāl/ ▶ **n.** a stud set in a door for strength or as an ornament.
– PHRASES (**as**) **dead as a doornail** quite dead.

Door Pen·in·su·la a resort region in northeastern Wisconsin that lies between Green Bay and Lake Michigan.

door·plate /ˈdôrˌplāt/ ▶ **n.** a plate on the door of a house or room that gives information about the occupant.

door·post /ˈdôrˌpōst/ ▶ **n.** another term for DOORJAMB.

door prize ▶ **n.** a prize awarded by lottery to the holder of a ticket purchased or distributed at a dance, party, or other function.

door·sill /ˈdôrˌsil/ ▶ **n.** the sill or threshold of a doorway.

door·step /ˈdôrˌstep/ ▶ **n.** a step leading up to the outer door of a house.
– PHRASES **on one's** (or **the**) **doorstep** situated very close by: *the airport is on my doorstep, so flying is easy.*

door·stop /ˈdôrˌstäp/ (also **doorstopper**) ▶ **n.** a fixed or heavy object that keeps a door open or stops it from banging against a wall. ■ a heavy or bulky object (used esp. in reference to a thick book): *his sixth novel is a thumping 400-page doorstop.*

door·way /ˈdôrˌwā/ ▶ **n.** an entrance to a room or building through a door: *Beth stood there in the doorway* | figurative *the doorway to success.*

door·yard /ˈdôrˌyärd/ ▶ **n.** a yard or garden by the door of a house.

doo-wop /ˈdo͞oˌwäp/ ▶ **n.** a style of pop music marked by the use of close harmony vocals using nonsense phrases, originating in the US in the 1950s.
– DERIVATIVES **doo-wop·per n.**
– ORIGIN imitative.

doo·zy /ˈdo͞ozē/ (also **doozie**) ▶ **n.** (pl. **doozies**) informal something outstanding or unique of its kind: *it's gonna be a doozy of a black eye.*
– ORIGIN early 20th cent.: of unknown origin.

do·pa /ˈdōpə/ ▶ **n.** Biochemistry a compound that is present in nervous tissue as a precursor of dopamine, used in the treatment of Parkinson's disease. See also **L-DOPA.** ● An amino acid; alternative name: dihydroxyphenylalanine; chem. formula: $C_9H_{11}NO_4$.
– ORIGIN early 20th cent.: from German, acronym from the systematic name.

do·pa·mine /ˈdōpəˌmēn/ ▶ **n.** Biochemistry a compound present in the body as a neurotransmitter and a precursor of other substances including epinephrine. ● Alternative name: **3,4-dihydroxyphenylethylamine**; chem. formula: $C_8H_{11}NO_2$.
– ORIGIN 1950s: blend of **DOPA** and **AMINE.**

do·pa·min·er·gic /ˌdōpəmiˈnərjik/ ▶ **adj.** Biochemistry releasing or involving dopamine as a neurotransmitter. Drugs with this effect are used in the treatment of Parkinson's disease and some psychiatric disorders; some are subject to abuse.
– ORIGIN 1960s: from *dopamine* + Greek *ergon* 'work' + *-ic.*

dop·ant /ˈdōpənt/ ▶ **n.** Electronics a substance used to produce a desired electrical characteristic in a semiconductor.
– ORIGIN 1960s: from the verb **DOPE** + **-ANT.**

dope /dōp/ ▶ **n. 1** informal a drug taken illegally for recreational purposes, esp. marijuana or heroin. ■ a drug given to a racehorse or greyhound to inhibit or enhance its performance. ■ a drug taken by an athlete to improve performance: [as modifier] *he failed a dope test.*
2 informal a stupid person: *though he wasn't an intellectual giant, he was no dope, either.*
3 informal information about a subject, esp. if not generally known: *our reviewer will give you **the dope on** hot spots around the town.*
4 a varnish applied to the fabric surface of model aircraft to strengthen them and keep them airtight. ■ a thick liquid used as a lubricant.
▶ **v.** [with obj.] **1** administer drugs to (a racehorse, greyhound, or athlete) in order to inhibit or enhance sporting performance: *the horse was doped before the race.* ■ (**be doped up**) informal be heavily under the influence of drugs, typically illegal ones: *he was so doped up that he can't remember a thing.* ■ treat (food or drink) with drugs: *maybe they had doped her Perrier.* ■ [no obj.] informal, dated regularly take illegal drugs.
2 smear or cover with varnish or other thick liquid: *she doped the surface with photographic emulsion.*
3 Electronics add an impurity to (a semiconductor) to produce a desired electrical characteristic.
▶ **adj.** informal very good: *that suit is dope!*
– PHRASAL VERBS **dope something out** informal, dated work out something: *they met to dope out plans for covering the event.*
– DERIVATIVES **dop·er n.**
– ORIGIN early 19th cent. (in the sense 'thick liquid'): from Dutch *doop* 'sauce,' from *doopen* 'to dip, mix.'

dope·ster /ˈdōpstər/ ▶ **n.** informal a person who collects and supplies information, typically on sporting events or elections: *they are inside dopesters with special access to the racing world.*

dope·y /ˈdōpē/ (also **dopy**) ▶ **adj.** (**dopier, dopiest**) informal stupefied by sleep or a drug: *she was under sedation and a bit dopey.* ■ idiotic: *did you ever hear such dopey names?*
– DERIVATIVES **dop·i·ly** /ˈdōpəlē/ **adv.**, **dop·i·ness n.**

dop·pel·gäng·er /ˈdäpəlˌgaNGər/ ▶ **n.** an apparition or double of a living person: *he has a doppelgänger named Donald, his invented twin brother.*
– ORIGIN mid 19th cent.: from German, literally 'double-goer.'

Dop·pler /ˈdäplər/, Christian (1803–53), Austrian physicist. In 1842, he discovered what is now known as the Doppler effect.

Dop·pler broad·en·ing ▶ **n.** Physics the broadening of spectral lines as a result of the different velocities of the emitting atoms giving rise to different Doppler shifts.

Dop·pler ef·fect ▶ **n.** Physics an increase (or decrease) in the frequency of sound, light, or other waves as the source and observer move toward (or away from) each other. The effect causes the sudden change in pitch noticeable in a passing siren, as well as the redshift seen by astronomers.

Dop·pler ra·dar ▶ **n.** Meteorology a radar tracking system using the Doppler effect to determine the location and velocity of a storm, clouds, precipitation, etc.

Dop·pler shift ▶ **n.** Physics a change in frequency due to the Doppler effect.

dop·y /ˈdōpē/ ▶ **adj.** variant spelling of **DOPEY.**

dor /dôr/ (also **dor beetle**) ▶ **n.** a large black dung beetle that makes a droning sound in flight and excavates burrows in which its young develop. ● Family Geotrupidae: several genera and species.
– ORIGIN Old English (denoting a bee or buzzing fly), probably imitative.

Do·ra·do /dəˈrädō/ Astronomy a southern constellation (the Goldfish), containing most of the Large Magellanic Cloud. ■ (as genitive **Doradus** /dəˈrädəs/) used with a preceding letter or numeral to designate a star in this constellation: *the star R Doradus.*
– ORIGIN Spanish (see **DORADO**).

do·ra·do /dəˈrädō/ ▶ **n.** (pl. **dorados**) **1** a South American freshwater fish with a golden body and red fins, popular as a game fish. ● *Salminus maxillosus*, family Characidae.
2 another term for **MAHIMAHI.**
– ORIGIN early 17th cent.: from Spanish, literally 'gilded,' from late Latin *deauratus*, from *deaurare* 'to gild over' (see also **DORY**[1]).

do-rag ▶ **n.** informal a scarf or cloth worn to protect one's hairstyle: *13-year-old kids in big pants, "wife beater" T-shirts, and do-rags dancing to the sound of 50 Cent and calling each other "G."*
– ORIGIN 1990s: from *hairdo* and *rag.*

Do·ra·ti /ˈdôräti, dôˈrätē/, Antal (1906–88), US composer and conductor; born in Hungary. As musical director of symphonies in Dallas 1945–49, Minneapolis 1949–60, Stockholm 1966–70, Washington, DC 1970–77, and Detroit 1977–81, he made over 500 recordings.

Dor·ches·ter /ˈdôrCHəstər, -ˌCHestər/ a residential section of Boston in Massachusetts, south of downtown.

Dor·dogne /dôrˈdōnyə/ a river in western France that rises in the Auvergne region and flows west for 297 miles (472 km) to meet the Garonne River and form the Gironde estuary. ■ a department in southwestern France. It contains caves that have yielded remains of early humans and their artifacts and art, such as at Lascaux.

Dor·drecht /ˈdôrˌdreKHt/ an industrial city and river port in the Netherlands, near the mouth of the Rhine (there called the Waal) River, 12 miles (19 km) southeast of Rotterdam; pop. 118,182 (2008). Also called **DORT.**

Do·ri·an /ˈdôrēən/ ▶ **n.** a member of a Hellenic people speaking the Doric dialect of Greek, thought to have entered Greece from the north *c.*1100 BC. They settled in Peloponnesus and later colonized Sicily and southern Italy.
▶ **adj.** of or relating to this people or to Doris in central Greece.
– ORIGIN via Latin from Greek *Dōrios* 'of Doris' + **-IAN.**

Do·ri·an mode ▶ **n.** Music the mode represented by the natural diatonic scale D–D (containing a minor 3rd and minor 7th).

Dor·ic /ˈdôrik, ˈdär-/ ▶ **adj. 1** relating to or denoting a classical order of architecture characterized by a sturdy fluted column and a thick square abacus resting on a rounded molding.
2 relating to or denoting the ancient Greek dialect of the Dorians. ■ archaic (of a dialect) broad; rustic.
▶ **n. 1** the Doric order of architecture.
2 the ancient Greek dialect of the Dorians. ■ a broad or rustic dialect, esp. the dialect spoken in northeastern Scotland. [by association with the ancient Greek dialect, perceived as rustic.]
– ORIGIN via Latin from Greek *Dōrikos*, from *Dōrios* (see **DORIAN**).

dork /dôrk/ ▶ **n.** informal a dull, slow-witted, or socially inept person. ■ vulgar slang the penis.
– DERIVATIVES **dork·y adj.**
– ORIGIN 1960s (originally US, in the sense 'penis'): perhaps a variant of **DIRK**, influenced by **DICK**[1].

dorm /dôrm/ ▶ **n.** informal a dormitory.
– ORIGIN early 20th cent.: abbreviation.

dor·mant /ˈdôrmənt/ ▶ **adj.** (of an animal) having normal physical functions suspended or slowed down for a period of time; in or as if in a deep sleep: *dormant butterflies* | figurative *the event evoked memories that she would rather had lain dormant.* ■ (of a plant or bud) alive but not actively growing. ■ (of a volcano) temporarily inactive. ■ (of a disease) causing no symptoms but not cured and liable to recur. ■ [usu. postpositive] Heraldry (of an animal) depicted lying with its head on its paws.
– DERIVATIVES **dor·man·cy n.**
– ORIGIN late Middle English (in the senses 'fixed in position' and 'latent'): from Old French, 'sleeping,' present participle of *dormir*, from Latin *dormire* 'to sleep.'

dor·mer /ˈdôrmər/ (also **dormer window**) ▶ **n.** a window that projects vertically from a sloping roof.
– ORIGIN late 16th cent. (denoting the window of a dormitory or bedroom): from Old French *dormeor* 'dormitory,' from *dormir* 'to sleep.'

d

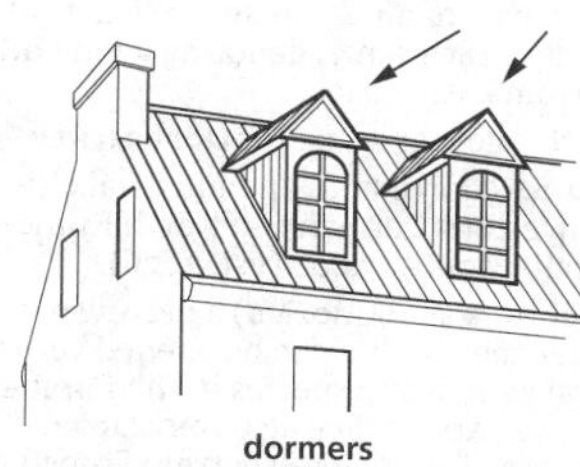
dormers

Dor·mi·tion /dôrˈmiSHən/ ▶ **n.** (in the Orthodox Church) the passing of the Virgin Mary from earthly life. ■ the feast held in honor of this on August 15, corresponding to the Assumption in the Western Church.
– ORIGIN late 15th cent.: from French, from Latin *dormitio(n-)* 'falling asleep,' from *dormire* 'to sleep.'

dor·mi·to·ry /ˈdôrmiˌtôrē/ ▶ **n.** (pl. **dormitories**) a large bedroom for a number of people in a school or institution. ■ a university or college hall of residence or hostel. ■ [as modifier] chiefly Brit. denoting a small town or suburb providing a residential area for those who work in a nearby city.
– ORIGIN late Middle English: from Latin *dormitorium*, neuter (used as a noun) of *dormitorius*, from *dormire* 'to sleep.'

dor·mouse /ˈdôrˌmous/ ▶ **n.** (pl. **dormice** /-ˌmīs/) an agile mouselike rodent with a hairy or bushy tail, found in Africa and Eurasia. Some kinds are noted for spending long periods in hibernation. ● Family Myoxidae: several genera and species, including the **common** (or **hazel**) **dormouse** (*Muscardinus avellanarius*) and the **fat dormouse** (*Myoxus glis*).
– ORIGIN late Middle English: of unknown origin, but associated with French *dormir* or Latin *dormire* 'to sleep' and **MOUSE.**

do·ron·i·cum /dəˈränəkəm/ ▶ **n.** (pl. **doronicums**) a plant of the genus *Doronicum* in the daisy family, esp. (in gardening) leopard's bane.
– ORIGIN modern Latin (Linnaeus), from modern Greek *dōronikon*, from Persian *darūnak.*

dorp /dôrp/ ▶ **n.** chiefly S. African a small rural town or village: *dreary little dorps.*
– ORIGIN late 15th cent.: Dutch, literally 'village' (see **THORP**).

dor·sal /ˈdôrsəl/ ▶ **adj.** Anatomy, Zoology, & Botany of, on, or relating to the upper side or back of an animal, plant, or organ: *a dorsal view of the body* | *the dorsal aorta.* Compare with **VENTRAL.**
– DERIVATIVES **dor·sal·ly adv.**
– ORIGIN late Middle English: from late Latin *dorsalis*, from Latin *dorsum* 'back.'

dor·sal fin ▶ **n.** Zoology an unpaired fin on the back of a fish or whale, e.g., the tall triangular fin of a shark or killer whale.

Dor·set /ˈdôrsit/ a county of southwestern England; county town, Dorchester.

dorsi- ▶ **comb. form 1** of, to, or on the back: *dorsiventral.*
2 another term for **DORSO-.**
– ORIGIN from Latin *dorsum* 'back.'

dor·si·flex /ˈdôrsəˌfleks/ ▶ **v.** [with obj.] Physiology bend (something, typically the hand or foot) dorsally or toward its upper surface: *the subject dorsiflexed his ankle.*
– DERIVATIVES **dor·si·flex·ion** /ˌdôrsəˈflekSHən/ **n.**

dor·si·flex·or /ˈdôrsəˌfleksər/ ▶ **n.** Anatomy a muscle whose contraction dorsiflexes the hand or foot.

dor·si·ven·tral /ˌdôrsəˈventrəl/ ▶ **adj.** chiefly Botany (of a leaf or other part of a plant) having dissimilar dorsal and ventral surfaces. ■ another term for **DORSOVENTRAL.**
– DERIVATIVES **dor·si·ven·tral·i·ty** /-venˈtralitē/ **n.**, **dor·si·ven·tral·ly adv.**

PRONUNCIATION KEY ə *ago, up*; ər *over, fur*; a *hat*; ā *ate*; ä *car*; e *let*; ē *see*; i *fit*; ī *by*; NG *sing*; ō *go*; ô *law, for*; oi *toy*; o͝o *good*; o͞o *goo*; ou *out*; TH *thin*; TH *then*; ZH *vision*

d

dor·so- ▶ comb. form **1** of, to, or on the back and (what is denoted by the second element): *dorsoventral.* **2** another term for DORSI-.
– ORIGIN from Latin *dorsum* 'back.'

dor·so·lat·er·al /ˌdôrsōˈlatərəl/ ▶ adj. Anatomy & Biology of, relating to, or involving the dorsal and lateral surfaces.
– DERIVATIVES **dor·so·lat·er·al·ly** adv.

dor·so·ven·tral /ˌdôrsōˈventrəl/ ▶ adj. Anatomy & Biology extending along or denoting an axis joining the dorsal and ventral surfaces. ■ of, relating to, or involving these surfaces.
– DERIVATIVES **dor·so·ven·tral·ly** adv.

dor·sum /ˈdôrsəm/ ▶ n. (pl. **dorsa**) Anatomy & Zoology the dorsal part of an organism or structure.
– ORIGIN late 18th cent. (denoting a long hill or ridge): from Latin, 'back.'

Dort /dôrt/ another name for DORDRECHT.

Dort·mund /ˈdôrtmənd/ an industrial city in northwestern Germany, in North Rhine–Westphalia; pop. 587,600 (est. 2006).

do·ry[1] /ˈdôrē/ ▶ n. (pl. **dories**) a narrow deep-bodied fish with a mouth that can be opened very wide. ● Several genera and species in the families Zeidae and Oreosomatidae. See also JOHN DORY.
– ORIGIN late Middle English: from French *dorée*, feminine past participle of *dorer* 'gild,' from late Latin *deaurare* 'gild over,' based on Latin *aurum* 'gold.' Compare with DORADO.

do·ry[2] ▶ n. (pl. **dories**) a small flat-bottomed rowboat with a high bow and stern, of a kind originally used for fishing in New England.
– ORIGIN early 18th cent.: perhaps from Miskito *dóri* 'dugout.'

do·ry·phore /ˈdôriˌfôr/ ▶ n. rare a pedantic and annoyingly persistent critic.
– ORIGIN 1950s (introduced by Sir Harold Nicolson): from French, literally 'Colorado beetle,' from Greek *doruphoros* 'spearcarrier.'

DOS /dôs/ ▶ abbr. Computing disk operating system, an operating system originally developed for IBM personal computers.

DoS ▶ abbr. Computing denial of service.

dos-à-dos /ˌdōz ə ˈdō/ ▶ adj. (of two books) bound together with a shared central board and facing in opposite directions.
▶ n. (pl. **same**) **1** a seat or carriage in which the occupants sit back to back.
2 variant spelling of DO-SI-DO.
▶ v. variant spelling of DO-SI-DO.
– ORIGIN mid 19th cent.: French, literally 'back to back.'

dos·age /ˈdōsij/ ▶ n. the size or frequency of a dose of a medicine or drug: *a dosage of 450 milligrams a day | there are recommendations about dosage for elderly patients.* ■ a level of exposure to or absorption of ionizing radiation.

dose /dōs/ ▶ n. a quantity of a medicine or drug taken or recommended to be taken at a particular time: *he took* ***a dose of*** *cough medicine.* ■ an amount of ionizing radiation received or absorbed at one time or over a specified period: ***a dose of*** *radiation exceeding safety limits.* ■ informal a venereal infection. ■ informal a quantity of something regarded as analogous to medicine in being necessary but unpleasant: *I wanted to give you* ***a dose of*** *the hell you put me through.*
▶ v. [with obj.] administer a dose to (a person or animal): *he* ***dosed himself with*** *vitamins.* ■ adulterate or blend (a substance) with another substance: *the champagne was* ***dosed with*** *sugar.*
– PHRASES **in small doses** informal when experienced or engaged in a little at a time: *computer games are great in small doses.*
– ORIGIN late Middle English: from French, via late Latin from Greek *dosis* 'gift,' from *didonai* 'give.'

dose e·quiv·a·lent ▶ n. an estimate of the biological effect of a dose of ionizing radiation, calculated by multiplying the dose received by a factor depending on the type of radiation. It is measured in sieverts.

do·sha /ˈdōsнə/, ▶ n. (in Ayurvedic medicine) each of three energies believed to circulate in the body and govern physiological activity.
– ORIGIN Sanskrit *doṣa*, literally 'fault, disease.'

do-si-do /ˌdō sē ˈdō/ (also **dos-à-dos**) ▶ n. (pl. **do-si-dos**) (in square dancing, and other country dancing) a figure in which two dancers pass around each other back to back and return to their original positions.
▶ v. [no obj.] dance a do-si-do.
– ORIGIN 1920s: alteration of DOS-À-DOS.

do·sim·e·ter /dōˈsimitər/ ▶ n. a device used to measure an absorbed dose of ionizing radiation.
– DERIVATIVES **do·si·met·ric** /ˌdōsəˈmetrik/ adj., **do·sim·e·try** /-ˈsimitrē/ n.

Dos Pas·sos /däs ˈpasəs/, John (Roderigo) (1896–1970), US novelist. He is known for his portrayal of life in the US in such novels as *Manhattan Transfer* (1925) and *U.S.A.* (1938).

doss /däs/ Brit. informal ▶ v. [no obj.] sleep (in rough or inexpensive accommodations): *he* ***dossed down*** *on a friend's floor.*
▶ n. an instance of sleeping in such accommodations. ■ archaic a bed in a cheap lodging house.
– ORIGIN late 18th cent.: perhaps based on Latin *dorsum* 'back.'

dos·sal /ˈdäsəl/ ▶ n. an ornamental cloth hung behind an altar in a church or at the sides of a chancel.
– ORIGIN mid 17th cent. (denoting an ornamental cloth to cover the back of a seat): from medieval Latin *dossale*, from late Latin *dorsalis* 'on the back' (see DORSAL).

doss·house /ˈdäsˌhous/ ▶ n. Brit. informal a cheap lodging house, esp. for homeless people and tramps.

dos·si·er /ˈdôsēˌā, ˈdäs-/ ▶ n. a collection of documents about a particular person, event, or subject: *we have* ***a dossier on*** *him |* ***a dossier of*** *complaints.*
– ORIGIN late 19th cent.: from French, denoting a bundle of papers with a label on the back, from *dos* 'back,' based on Latin *dorsum.*

dost /dəst/ archaic second person singular present of DO[1].

Do·sto·ev·sky /ˌdästəˈyefskē/ (also **Dostoyevsky**), Fyodor (Mikhailovich) (1821–81), Russian novelist. His novels reveal his psychological insight, savage humor, and concern with the religious, political, and moral problems posed by human suffering. Notable works: *Crime and Punishment* (1866), *The Idiot* (1868), and *The Brothers Karamazov* (1880).

DOT ▶ abbr. Department of Transportation.

dot[1] /dät/ ▶ n. a small round mark or spot: *a symbol depicted in colored dots.* ■ such a mark written or printed as part of an *i* or *j*, as a diacritical mark, as one of a series of marks to signify omission, or as a period. ■ Music such a mark used to denote the lengthening of a note or rest by half, or to indicate staccato. ■ the shorter signal of the two used in Morse code. Compare with DASH (sense 3 of the noun). ■ used to refer to an object that appears tiny because it is far away: *the desert shrank figures to mere dots.* ■ used to indicate the punctuation separating parts of an e-mail or website address: *drop me a note at heatvision dot com.*
▶ v. (**dots, dotting, dotted**) [with obj.] mark with a small spot or spots: *wet spots of rain began to dot his shirt.* ■ (of a number of items) be scattered over (an area): *churches dot the countryside.* ■ place a dot over (a letter): *you need to dot the i.* ■ Music mark (a note or rest) to show that the time value is increased by half: (as adj. **dotted**) *a dotted quarter note.*
– PHRASES **dot the i's and cross the t's** informal ensure that all details are correct. **on the dot** informal exactly on time: *he arrived on the dot at nine o'clock.*
– DERIVATIVES **dot·ter** n.
– ORIGIN Old English *dott* 'head of a boil.' The word is recorded only once in Old English, then not until the late 16th cent., when it is found in the sense 'a small lump or clot,' perhaps influenced by Dutch *dot* 'a knot.' The sense 'small mark or spot' dates from the mid 17th cent.

dot[2] ▶ n. archaic a dowry, particularly one from which only the interest or annual income was available to the husband.
– ORIGIN from French, from Latin *dos, dot-* 'dowry' (see DOWER).

dot·age /ˈdōtij/ ▶ n. [in sing.] the period of life in which a person is old and weak: *you could live here and look after me* ***in my dotage.***
– ORIGIN late Middle English: from DOTE + -AGE.

do·tard /ˈdōtərd/ ▶ n. an old person, esp. one who has become weak or senile.
– ORIGIN late Middle English: from DOTE + -ARD.

dot-com (also **dot.com**) ▶ n. a company that relies largely or exclusively on Internet commerce.

dot-com·mer (also **dot.commer**) ▶ n. someone who works for or owns an Internet-based company.

dote /dōt/ ▶ v. [no obj.] **1** (**dote on/upon**) be extremely and uncritically fond of: *she doted on her two young children.*
2 archaic be silly or feebleminded, esp. as a result of old age: *the parson is now old and dotes.*
– DERIVATIVES **dot·er** n.
– ORIGIN Middle English (in the sense 'act or talk foolishly'): of uncertain origin; related to Middle Dutch *doten* 'be silly.'

doth /dəтн/ archaic third person singular present of DO[1].

Do·than /ˈdōтнən/ a city in southeastern Alabama, near the Florida border; pop. 66,505 (est. 2008).

dot·ing /ˈdōtiNG/ ▶ adj. extremely and uncritically fond of someone; adoring: *she was spoiled outrageously by her doting father.*
– DERIVATIVES **dot·ing·ly** adv.

dot ma·trix ▶ n. [usu. as modifier] a grid of dots that are filled selectively to produce an image on a screen or paper: *a dot matrix display board.*

dot ma·trix print·er ▶ n. a printer that forms images of letters, numbers, etc., from a number of tiny dots.

dot-org (also **dot.org**) ▶ n. a nonprofit organization that conducts its business on the Internet.
▶ adj. of or relating to nonprofit business conducted on the Internet.
– ORIGIN from *.org* in an Internet address, indicating a noncommercial site.

dot prod·uct ▶ n. another term for INNER PRODUCT.

dot·ted line ▶ n. a line made up of dots or dashes (often used in reference to the space left for a signature on a contract): *Adam* ***signed on the dotted line.***

dot·ted rhythm ▶ n. Music rhythm in which the beat is unequally subdivided into a long dotted note and a short note.

dot·ter·el /ˈdätərəl/ ▶ n. (pl. **same** or **dotterels**) a small plover with a brown streaked back and a chestnut or buff belly with black below. Dotterels breed in mountainous areas and in the tundra. ● Genus *Eudromias*, family Charadriidae: two species, esp. the Eurasian *E. morinellus*, which is noted for its tameness.
– ORIGIN Middle English: from DOTE (so named because it is easily caught) + -REL. Compare with DODO.

dot·tle /ˈdätl/ ▶ n. a remnant of tobacco left in a pipe after smoking.
– ORIGIN late Middle English (denoting a plug for a barrel or other container): from DOT[1] + -LE[1].

dot·ty /ˈdätē/ ▶ adj. (**dottier, dottiest**) informal (of a person, action, or idea) somewhat mad or eccentric: *he was slightly dotty by the end of his second term.*
– DERIVATIVES **dot·ti·ly** /ˈdätəlē/ adv., **dot·ti·ness** n.
– ORIGIN late 19th cent.: perhaps from obsolete *dote* 'simpleton, fool,' apparently from Dutch *dote* 'folly.'

Dou·a·la /dōōˈälə/ the chief port of and largest city in Cameroon; pop. 1,776,000 (est. 2007).

douane /dwän/ ▶ n. archaic a custom house in France or other Mediterranean countries.
– ORIGIN mid 17th cent.: from French, from Italian *do(g)ana*, from Arabic *dīwān* 'office,' from Persian *dīwān* (see DIVAN). Compare with DIWAN.

Dou·ay Bi·ble /ˈdōō-ā/ (also **Douay version**) ▶ n. an English translation of the Bible formerly used in the Roman Catholic Church, completed at Douai in France early in the 17th century.

dou·ble /ˈdəbəl/ ▶ adj. **1** consisting of two equal, identical, or similar parts or things: *the double doors.* ■ having twice the usual size, quantity, or strength: *she sipped a double brandy.* ■ designed to be used by two people: *a double bed.* ■ having two different roles or interpretations, esp. in order to deceive or confuse: *the* ***double life*** *of a freelance secret agent.*
2 having some essential part or feature twice, in particular: ■ (of a flower variety) having more than one circle of petals: *large double blooms.* ■ (of a domino) having the same number of dots on each half. ■ used to indicate that a letter or number occurs twice in succession: *"otter" is spelled with a double t.*
3 Music lower in pitch by an octave.
▶ predeterminer twice as much or as many: *the jail now houses almost double the number of prisoners it was designed for | I'll pay double what I paid last time.*
▶ adv. at or to twice the amount or extent: *you have to be careful, and this counts double for older people.* ■ as two instead of the more usual one: *she thought she was seeing double.*
▶ n. **1** a thing that is twice as large as usual or is made up of two standard units or things: *join the two sleeping bags together to make a double.* ■ a double measure of liquor. ■ Baseball a hit that allows the batter to reach second base safely: *Sabo came home on a double by O'Neill.* ■ a system of betting in which the winnings and stake from the first bet are transferred to a second. ■ Bridge a call that will increase the points won if the declarer is successful, or increase the penalty points won by the defenders if the declarer fails to make the contract. ■ Darts a hit on the narrow ring enclosed by the two outer circles of a dartboard, scoring double.
2 a person who looks exactly like another: *you could pass yourself off as his double.* ■ a person who stands in for an actor in a film. ■ an apparition of a living person: *she had seen her husband's double.*
3 (**doubles**) (esp. in tennis and badminton) a game or competition involving sides made up of two players: *the semifinals of the doubles.*

▶ **pron.** a number or amount that is twice as large as a contrasting or usual number or amount: *he paid double and had a room all to himself.*
▶ **v. 1** [no obj.] become twice as much or as many: *profits doubled in one year.* ■ [with obj.] make twice as much or as many of (something): *Clare doubled her income overnight.* ■ [with obj.] archaic amount to twice as much as: *thy fifty yet doth double five and twenty.* ■ (**double up**) use the winnings from a bet as stake for another bet. ■ (of a member of the armed forces) move at twice the usual speed; run: *I doubled across the deck to join the others.* ■ (**double up**) share a room: *"Where's Jimmy going to sleep?" "He can double up with Bert."* ■ Baseball (of a batter) get a two-base hit: *Strawberry doubled with two outs.* ■ Bridge make a call increasing the value of the penalty points to be scored on an opponent's bid if it wins the auction and is not fulfilled. ■ informal go out on a double date: *they doubled with his sister and her oafish boyfriend.*
2 [with obj.] fold or bend (paper, cloth, or other material) over on itself: *the muslin is doubled and then laid in a sieve over the bowl.* ■ [no obj.] (**double up**) bend over or curl up, typically because one is overcome with pain or mirth: *Billy started to double up with laughter.* ■ clench (a fist): *he had one arm around her and the other fist doubled.* ■ [no obj.] (usu. **double back**) go back in the direction one has come: *he had to double back to pick them up.* ■ Nautical sail around (a headland): *we struck out seaward to double the headland of the cape.*
3 [no obj.] (of a person or thing) be used in or play another, different role: *a laser printer **doubles as a** photocopier.* ■ [with obj.] (of an actor) play (two parts) in the same piece. ■ Music play two or more musical instruments. ■ [with obj.] Music add the same note in a higher or lower octave to (a note).
– PHRASES **on the double** at running speed; very fast: *he disappeared on the double.* **double or nothing** a gamble to decide whether a loss or debt should be doubled or canceled.
– DERIVATIVES **dou·bler** n.
– ORIGIN Middle English: via Old French from Latin *duplus* (see DUPLE). The verb is from Old French *dobler*, from late Latin *duplare*, from *duplus*.

dou·ble a·cros·tic ▶ **n.** an acrostic in which the first and last letters of each line form a hidden word or words.

dou·ble-act·ing ▶ **adj.** denoting a device or product that combines two different functions: *double-acting hydraulic shock absorbers* | *double-acting baking powder.* ■ (of an engine) having pistons pushed from both sides alternately.

dou·ble-ac·tion ▶ **adj.** another term for DOUBLE-ACTING: *double-action moss killer.* ■ (of a gun) needing to be cocked and fired as two separate actions.

dou·ble a·gent ▶ **n.** an agent who pretends to act as a spy for one country or organization while in fact acting on behalf of an enemy.

dou·ble bar ▶ **n.** a pair of closely spaced bar lines marking the end of a piece or section of music.

dou·ble-bar·reled ▶ **adj.** (of a gun) having two barrels. ■ having two parts or aspects.

dou·ble bass /bās/ ▶ **n.** the largest and lowest-pitched instrument of the violin family, providing the bass line of the orchestral string section and also much used in jazz.

dou·ble bas·soon ▶ **n.** another term for CONTRABASSOON.

dou·ble bill ▶ **n.** a program of entertainment with two main items or personalities: *a double bill of pianist Donegan and alto sax star Woods.*
▶ **v.** [with obj.] (**double-bill**) charge (different accounts) for the same expenses: *her two restaurants were double-billed for the one refrigerator* | [no obj.] *the previous accounting program had a tendency to double-bill.*

dou·ble bind ▶ **n.** a situation in which a person is confronted with two irreconcilable demands or a choice between two undesirable courses of action.

dou·ble-bit·ted ax ▶ **n.** an ax with two blades.

dou·ble-blind ▶ **adj.** denoting a test or trial, esp. of a drug, in which any information that may influence the behavior of the tester or the subject is withheld until after the test. Compare with SINGLE-BLIND.

dou·ble bluff ▶ **n.** an action or statement that is intended to appear as a bluff but is in fact genuine.

dou·ble bo·gey Golf ▶ **n.** a score of two strokes over par for a hole.
▶ **v.** (**double-bogey**) [with obj.] complete (a hole) in two strokes over par.

dou·ble boil·er ▶ **n.** a saucepan with a detachable upper compartment heated by boiling water in the lower one.

dou·ble bond ▶ **n.** a chemical bond in which two pairs of electrons are shared between two atoms.

dou·ble-book ▶ **v.** [with obj.] (usu. **be double-booked**) reserve (something, esp. a seat or a hotel room) for two different customers or parties at the same time: *the hotel was double-booked.* ■ book (someone) into a seat or room that is already reserved for another.

dou·ble-breast·ed ▶ **adj.** (of a jacket or coat) having a substantial overlap of material at the front and showing two rows of buttons when fastened.

dou·ble bri·dle ▶ **n.** a bridle that has both a curb and a snaffle bit, each with its own set of reins.

dou·ble-check ▶ **v.** [with obj.] go over (something) for a second time to ensure that it is accurate or safe: *he double-checked our credentials* | [with clause] *double-check that all windows are firmly locked.*

dou·ble chin ▶ **n.** a roll of fatty flesh below a person's chin.
– DERIVATIVES **dou·ble-chinned** adj.

dou·ble-click ▶ **v.** [no obj.] press a computer mouse button twice in quick succession to select a file, program, or function: *to run a window just double-click on the icon* | [with obj.] *when you double-click this file it should open.*

dou·ble-clutch ▶ **v.** [no obj.] release and reengage the clutch of a vehicle twice when changing gear.

dou·ble con·cer·to ▶ **n.** a concerto for two solo instruments.

dou·ble cream ▶ **n.** British term for HEAVY CREAM.

dou·ble-cross ▶ **v.** [with obj.] deceive or betray (a person with whom one is supposedly cooperating): *he was blackmailed into double-crossing his own government.*
▶ **n.** a betrayal of someone with whom one is supposedly cooperating.
– DERIVATIVES **dou·ble-cross·er** n.

dou·ble-cut ▶ **adj.** (of a file) having two sets of grooves crossing each other diagonally.

dou·ble dag·ger ▶ **n.** a symbol (‡) used in printed text to introduce an annotation.

dou·ble date ▶ **n.** a social outing in which two couples participate.
▶ **v.** [no obj.] (**double-date**) take part in a double date. ■ [with obj.] accompany (someone) on a double date.

Dou·ble·day /ˈdəbəlˌdā/, Abner (1819–93), US army officer. A Union general in the Civil War, he is credited with creating the modern game of baseball, although this claim has been disproved.

dou·ble-deal·ing ▶ **n.** the practice of working to people's disadvantage behind their backs.
▶ **adj.** working deceitfully to injure others: *she is a backstabbing, double-dealing twister.*
– DERIVATIVES **dou·ble-deal·er** n.

dou·ble-deck·er ▶ **n.** something, esp. a bus, that has two floors or levels: [as modifier] *a double-decker bus* | *double-decker sandwiches.*

dou·ble de·com·po·si·tion ▶ **n.** Chemistry another term for METATHESIS (sense 2).

dou·ble-dig·it ▶ **adj.** [attrib.] (of a number, variable, or percentage) between 10 and 99: *double-digit inflation.*
▶ **n.** (**double digits**) another term for DOUBLE FIGURES.

dou·ble-dip ▶ **v.** [no obj.] informal obtain an income from two different sources, typically in an illicit way.
– DERIVATIVES **dou·ble-dip·per** n., **dou·ble-dip·ping** n.

dou·ble dot ▶ **n.** (in musical composition or transcription) two dots placed side by side after a note to indicate that it is to be lengthened by three quarters of its value.
▶ **v.** (**double-dot**) [with obj.] write or perform (music) with a rhythm of alternating long and short notes in a ratio of approximately seven to one, producing a more marked effect than ordinary dotted rhythm.

dou·ble-dou·ble ▶ **n.** chiefly Canadian a cup of coffee with a double serving of both sugar and cream.

dou·ble drib·ble ▶ **n.** Basketball an illegal dribble that occurs when a player dribbles with both hands simultaneously or interrupts a dribble by holding the ball briefly in one or both hands.
▶ **v.** (**double-dribble**) commit or be charged with a double dribble.

dou·ble dum·my ▶ **n.** Bridge a way of playing with two hands exposed, allowing every card to be located, for instructional purposes.

dou·ble Dutch (also **double dutch**) ▶ **n.** a jump-rope game played with two long jump ropes swung in opposite directions so that they cross rhythmically: [as adv.] *three girls jumped double Dutch, the white cords whirring like an electric fan.*

dou·ble-dyed ▶ **adj.** (of an item of clothing) dyed twice in order to give a very deep color. ■ (of a person) thoroughly imbued with a particular quality: *a double-dyed liberal.*

dou·ble ea·gle ▶ **n. 1** a gold coin worth twenty dollars.
2 Golf a score of three strokes under par at a hole.

dou·ble-edged ▶ **adj.** (of a knife or sword) having two cutting edges. ■ having two contradictory aspects or possible outcomes: *the consequences can be double-edged.*
– PHRASES **a double-edged sword** a situation or course of action having both positive and negative effects.

dou·ble ef·fect ▶ **n.** (in ethics) the good and bad effect of an action, compared according to a principle that seeks to justify the action if the bad effect, though foreseen, is outweighed by the good effect.

dou·ble-end·er ▶ **n.** a boat in which stern and bow are similarly tapered.

dou·ble en·ten·dre /ˌdo͞obl ˌänˈtändrə/ ▶ **n.** (pl. **double entendres** pronunc. **same**) a word or phrase open to two interpretations, one of which is usually risqué or indecent. ■ humor using such words or phrases.
– ORIGIN late 17th cent.: from obsolete French (now *double entente*), 'double understanding.'

dou·ble-en·try ▶ **adj.** [attrib.] denoting a system of bookkeeping in which each transaction is entered as a debit in one account and a credit in another.

dou·ble ex·po·sure ▶ **n.** the repeated exposure of a photographic plate or film to light, often producing ghost images.

dou·ble-faced ▶ **adj.** having two faces: *a double-faced clock.* ■ tending to say one thing and do another; deceitful. ■ (of a fabric or material) finished on both sides so that either may be used as the right side.

dou·ble fault ▶ **n.** Tennis an instance of two consecutive faults in serving, counting as a point against the server.
▶ **v.** (**double-fault**) [no obj.] serve a double fault.

dou·ble fea·ture ▶ **n.** a movie program with two full-length films.

dou·ble fig·ures ▶ **plural n.** a number or amount, esp. a percentage, between 10 and 99: *inflation was **in double figures.***

dou·ble flat ▶ **n.** a sign (𝄫) placed before a musical note to indicate that it is to be lowered two semitones. ■ a note so marked or lowered.

dou·ble fugue ▶ **n.** Music a fugue with two subjects, each similarly treated.

dou·ble glaz·ing ▶ **n.** windows that have two layers of glass with a space between them, designed to reduce loss of heat and exclude noise.
– DERIVATIVES **dou·ble-glaze** v.

dou·ble-hand·ed ▶ **adj.** made to be lifted or held with two hands: *a long sword with a double-handed hilt.* ■ using both hands: *a double-handed backhand.*

dou·ble-head·ed ▶ **adj.** having a double head or two heads: *a double-headed monster* | *double-headed nails.* ■ (of a train) pulled by two locomotives. ■ (of a weapon) having two cutting implements, typically one at each end of the shaft: *a double-headed ax.*

dou·ble-head·er /ˌdəbəlˈhedər/ ▶ **n. 1** a sporting event in which two games or contests are played in succession at the same venue, typically between the same teams or players.
2 a train pulled by two locomotives coupled together.

dou·ble he·lix ▶ **n.** a pair of parallel helices intertwined about a common axis, esp. that in the structure of the DNA molecule.

dou·ble-hung ▶ **adj.** (of a window) consisting of two sliding vertical sashes.

dou·ble in·dem·ni·ty ▶ **n.** provision for payment of double the face amount of an insurance policy under certain conditions, e.g., when death occurs as a result of an accident.

dou·ble jeop·ard·y ▶ **n.** Law the prosecution of a person twice for the same offense. ■ risk or disadvantage incurred from two sources simultaneously: *he is **in double jeopardy**, unable to speak either language adequately.*

dou·ble-joint·ed ▶ **adj.** (of a person) having unusually flexible joints, typically those of the fingers, arms, or legs.

dou·ble-knit ▶ **adj.** (of fabric) knit of two joined layers for extra thickness: *a green double-knit suit.*
– ORIGIN mid 19th cent.: *double* with reference to the "doubling" of the yarn to four-ply.

PRONUNCIATION KEY ə *ago, up*; ər *over, fur*; a *hat*; ā *ate*; ä *car*; e *let*; ē *see*; i *fit*; ī *by*; NG *sing*; ō *go*; ô *law, for*; oi *toy*; o͝o *good*; o͞o *goo*; ou *out*; TH *thin*; T͟H *then*; ZH *vision*

d

dou·ble-lock ▶ **v.** [with obj.] lock (a door) with two complete turns of the key so as to engage a second bolt.
▶ **n.** (**double lock**) a type of lock that may be secured in this way.

dou·ble neg·a·tive ▶ **n.** Grammar a negative statement containing two negative elements (for example *didn't say nothing*). ■ a positive statement in which two negative elements are used to produce the positive force, usu. for some particular rhetorical effect (for example *there is not nothing to worry about!*).

USAGE According to standard English grammar, a **double negative** used to express a single negative, such as *I don't know nothing* (rather than *I don't know anything*), is incorrect. The rules dictate that the two negative elements cancel each other out to give an affirmative statement, so that, logically, *I don't know nothing* means *I know something*. In practice, this sort of double negative is widespread in dialect and nonstandard usage and rarely causes confusion about the intended meaning. Double negatives are standard in other languages such as Spanish and Polish, and they have not always been unacceptable in English. They were normal in Old English and Middle English and did not come to be frowned upon until some time after the 16th century. The double negative can be used in speech or in written dialogue for emphasis or other rhetorical effects. Such constructions as 'has not gone unnoticed' or 'not wholly unpersuasive' may be useful for making a point through understatement, but the double negative should be used judiciously because it may cause confusion or annoy the reader.

dou·ble-park ▶ **v.** [with obj.] (usu. **be double-parked**) park (a vehicle) alongside one that is already parked at the side of the road.

dou·ble play ▶ **n.** Baseball a defensive play in which two players are put out.

dou·ble pneu·mo·nia ▶ **n.** pneumonia affecting both lungs.

dou·ble pre·ci·sion ▶ **n.** Computing the use of twice the usual number of bits to represent a number, giving greater arithmetic accuracy.

dou·ble-quick ▶ **adj. & adv.** informal very quick or quickly: [as adj.] *I got changed in **double-quick time*** | [as adv.] *you get upstairs double-quick!*

dou·ble reed ▶ **n.** Music a reed with two slightly separated blades, used for playing a wind instrument such as an oboe or bassoon.

dou·ble re·frac·tion ▶ **n.** Physics division of a single incident light ray or other electromagnetic wave into two separate rays in an anisotropic medium.

dou·ble rhyme ▶ **n.** a feminine rhyme involving one stressed and one unstressed syllable in each rhyming line.

dou·ble salt ▶ **n.** Chemistry a crystalline salt having the composition of a mixture of two simple salts but with a different crystal structure from either.

dou·ble sharp ▶ **n.** a sign (𝄪) placed before a musical note to indicate that it is to be raised two semitones. ■ a note so marked or raised.

dou·ble-sid·ed ▶ **adj.** using or able to be used on both sides: *double-sided adhesive tape.*
– DERIVATIVES **dou·ble-sid·ed·ness n.**

dou·ble-space ▶ **v.** type or format with a full space between lines.

dou·ble·speak /ˈdəbəlˌspēk/ ▶ **n.** deliberately euphemistic, ambiguous, or obscure language: *the art of political doublespeak.*
– ORIGIN 1950s: often attributed incorrectly to George Orwell's novel *Nineteen Eighty-Four.*

dou·ble stand·ard ▶ **n.** a rule or principle that is unfairly applied in different ways to different people or groups: *the smaller pay received by black soldiers demonstrated a double standard.*

dou·ble star ▶ **n.** two stars physically very close together, as a binary star, or apparently so, as an optical double.

dou·ble steal ▶ **n.** Baseball a play in which two base runners each steal a base.

dou·ble stop ▶ **n.** the playing of two notes at once on a violin or similar bowed instrument.
– DERIVATIVES **dou·ble-stop v., dou·ble-stop·ping n.**

dou·blet /ˈdəblət/ ▶ **n. 1** either of a pair of similar things, in particular: ■ either of two words of the same historical source, but with two different stages of entry into the language and different resultant meanings, for example *fashion* and *faction, cloak* and *clock*. ■ (**doublets**) the same number on two dice thrown at once. ■ Physics & Chemistry a pair of associated lines close together in a spectrum or electrophoretic gel. ■ a combination of two simple lenses.
2 a man's short close-fitting padded jacket, commonly worn from the 14th to the 17th century.
– ORIGIN Middle English: from Old French, 'something folded,' also denoting a fur-lined coat, from *double* 'double.'

dou·ble take ▶ **n.** a delayed reaction to something unexpected, immediately after one's first reaction: *Tony glanced at her, then **did a double take**.*

dou·ble-talk ▶ **n.** deliberately unintelligible speech combining nonsense syllables and actual words. ■ another term for DOUBLESPEAK.

dou·ble-team ▶ **v.** [with obj.] (in ball games, esp. basketball) block (an opponent) with two players.
▶ **n.** an act of double-teaming.

dou·ble·think /ˈdəbəlˌTHiNGk/ ▶ **n.** the acceptance of or mental capacity to accept contrary opinions or beliefs at the same time, esp. as a result of political indoctrination.
– ORIGIN 1949: coined by George Orwell in his novel *Nineteen Eighty-Four.*

dou·ble time ▶ **n. 1** a rate of pay equal to double the standard rate, sometimes paid for working on holidays or outside normal working hours.
2 Military a regulation running pace.
3 Music a rhythm that is twice as fast as an earlier one.

dou·ble·ton /ˈdəbəltən/ ▶ **n.** (in card games, esp. bridge) a pair of cards that are the only cards of their suit in a hand. ■ a pair of people or things.
– ORIGIN early 20th cent.: from DOUBLE, on the pattern of *singleton.*

dou·ble tongu·ing ▶ **n.** Music the use of two alternating movements of the tongue (usually as in sounding *t* and *k*) in playing rapid passages on a wind instrument.
– DERIVATIVES **dou·ble-tongue v.**

dou·ble·tree /ˈdəbəlˌtrē/ ▶ **n.** a crossbar in front of a wagon with a swingletree at each end, enabling two horses to be harnessed.
– ORIGIN mid 19th cent.: from DOUBLE, on the pattern of *singletree.*

dou·ble vi·sion ▶ **n.** the simultaneous perception of two images, usually overlapping, of a single scene or object.

dou·ble wham·my ▶ **n.** informal a twofold blow or setback: *a double whammy of taxation and price increases.*
– ORIGIN 1950s: originally with reference to the comic strip *Li'l Abner* (see WHAMMY).

dou·ble-wide ▶ **n.** a semipermanent mobile home consisting of two separate units connected on site: *she left the double-wide empty.*

dou·bloon /dəˈblo͞on/ ▶ **n.** historical a Spanish gold coin.
– ORIGIN from French *doublon* or its source, Spanish *doblón*, from *doble* 'double' (so named because the coin was worth double the value of a pistole).

dou·bly /ˈdəb(ə)lē/ ▶ **adv.** [often as submodifier] to twice the normal extent or degree; especially: *we're going to have to work doubly hard.* ■ two times or in two ways: *doubly mutant cells.*

doubt /dout/ ▶ **n.** a feeling of uncertainty or lack of conviction: ***some doubt has been cast upon** the authenticity of this account* | *they had doubts that they would ever win.*
▶ **v. 1** [with obj.] feel uncertain about: *I doubt my ability to do the job.* ■ question the truth or fact of (something): *who can doubt the value of these services?* | [with clause] *I doubt if anyone slept that night.* ■ disbelieve (a person or their word): *I have no reason to doubt him.* ■ [no obj.] feel uncertain, esp. about one's religious beliefs.
2 [with clause] archaic fear; be afraid of: *I doubt not your contradictions.*
– PHRASES **beyond** (**a** or **a shadow of a**) **doubt** allowing no uncertainty: *you've proved it beyond doubt* | *they knew beyond a shadow of a doubt what made them happy.* **in doubt** open to question: *the outcome is no longer in doubt.* ■ feeling uncertain about something: *by the age of 14 he was in no doubt about his career aims.* **no doubt** used to indicate the speaker's firm belief that something is true even if evidence is not given or available: *those who left were attracted, no doubt, by higher pay.* ■ used to introduce a concession that is subsequently dismissed as unimportant or irrelevant: *they no doubt did what they could to help her, but their best proved insufficient.* **without** (**a**) **doubt** indisputably: *he was without doubt the very worst kind of reporter.*
– DERIVATIVES **doubt·a·ble adj., doubt·ing·ly adv.**
– ORIGIN Middle English: from Old French *doute* (noun), *douter* (verb), from Latin *dubitare* 'hesitate,' from *dubius* 'doubtful' (see DUBIOUS).

doubt·er /doutər/ ▶ **n.** a person who questions or lacks faith in something; a skeptic: *he had proved all his doubters wrong.*

doubt·ful /ˈdoutfəl/ ▶ **adj. 1** feeling uncertain about something: *he looked doubtful, but gave a nod* | *I was **doubtful of** my judgment.*
2 not known with certainty: *the fire was of doubtful origin.* ■ improbable: [with clause] *it is doubtful whether these programs have any lasting effect.* ■ not established as genuine or acceptable: *of doubtful legality.*
– DERIVATIVES **doubt·ful·ly adv., doubt·ful·ness n.**

doubt·ing Thom·as ▶ **n.** a person who is skeptical and refuses to believe something without proof.
– ORIGIN early 17th cent.: with biblical allusion to the apostle Thomas (John 20: 24–29).

doubt·less /ˈdoutlis/ ▶ **adv.** [sentence adverb] used to indicate the speaker's belief that a statement is certain to be true given what is known about the situation: *the company would doubtless find the reduced competition to their liking.* ■ used to refer to a desirable outcome as though it were certain: *doubtless you'll solve the problem.*
– DERIVATIVES **doubt·less·ly adv.**

douce /do͞os/ ▶ **adj.** chiefly Scottish sober, gentle, and sedate: *stories which would have outraged their douce minds.*
– ORIGIN Middle English (in the sense 'pleasant, sweet'): from Old French *dous, douce*, from Latin *dulcis* 'sweet.'

dou·ceur /do͞oˈsər/ ▶ **n.** a financial inducement; a gratuity or bribe: *Pericles gave a handsome douceur to the Spartan commanders to withdraw without fighting.*
– ORIGIN mid 18th cent.: French, literally 'sweetness.'

dou·ceur de vi·vre /do͞oˈsər də ˈvēvrə/ ▶ **n.** a way of living that is pleasant and free from worries.
– ORIGIN mid 20th cent.: French, literally 'sweetness of living (or life).'

douche /do͞osH/ ▶ **n.** a shower of water: *a daily douche.* ■ a jet of liquid applied to part of the body for cleansing or medicinal purposes. ■ a device for washing out the vagina as a contraceptive measure.
▶ **v.** [with obj.] spray or shower with water. ■ [no obj.] use a douche as a method of contraception.
– ORIGIN mid 18th cent. (as a noun): via French from Italian *doccia* 'conduit pipe,' from *docciare* 'pour by drops,' based on Latin *ductus* 'leading' (see DUCT).

douche bag ▶ **n.** a small syringe for douching the vagina, esp. as a contraceptive measure. ■ informal a loathsome or contemptible person (used as a term of abuse).

dough /dō/ ▶ **n. 1** a thick, malleable mixture of flour and liquid, used for baking into bread or pastry.
2 informal money: *lots of dough.*
– DERIVATIVES **dough·i·ness n., dough·y adj.** (**doughier, doughiest**).
– ORIGIN Old English *dāg*, of Germanic origin; related to Dutch *deeg* and German *Teig*, from an Indo-European root meaning 'smear, knead.'

dough·boy /ˈdōˌboi/ ▶ **n. 1** a boiled or deep-fried dumpling.
2 informal a US infantryman, esp. one in World War I. [said to have been a term applied in the Civil War to the large globular brass buttons on the infantry uniform; also said to derive from the use of pipeclay 'dough' to clean the white belts worn by infantrymen.]

dough-faced ▶ **adj.** informal pasty-faced: *his dough-faced niece.*

dough·nut /ˈdōˌnət/ (also **donut**) ▶ **n.** a small fried cake of sweetened dough, typically in the shape of a ball or ring. ■ a ring-shaped object, in particular a vacuum chamber in some types of particle accelerator.

dough·ty /ˈdoutē/ ▶ **adj.** (**doughtier, doughtiest**) archaic, humorous brave and persistent: *his doughty spirit kept him going.*
– DERIVATIVES **dough·ti·ly** /ˈdoutl-ē/ **adv., dough·ti·ness n.**
– ORIGIN late Old English *dohtig*, variant of *dyhtig*, of Germanic origin; related to Dutch *duchtig* and German *tüchtig*.

Doug·las[1] /ˈdəgləs/ the name of a family of US actors. ■ **Kirk** (1916–); born *Issur Danielovitch Demsky*. Notable movies: *Lust for Life* (1957), *Spartacus* (1960), which he also produced, and *Seven Days in May* (1964). ■ **Michael (Kirk)** (1944–); son of Kirk. Notable movies: *The China Syndrome* (1979), which he also produced, *Fatal Attraction* (1987), *Wall Street* (1987), and *Basic Instinct* (1992).

Doug·las[2], Stephen Arnold (1813–61), US lawyer and politician; known as the **Little Giant**. An Illinois Democrat, he was a member of the US House of Representatives 1843–47 and US Senate 1847–61. He is best remembered for the Lincoln-Douglas debates, a series of seven senatorial-campaign debates in 1858 with Republican candidate Abraham Lincoln. He won the Senate seat in 1858, but lost his 1860 bid for the presidency to Lincoln.

Stephen A. Douglas

Doug·las³, William Orville (1898–1980), US Supreme Court associate justice 1939–75. Appointed to the Court by President Franklin D. Roosevelt, he worked to uphold the New Deal programs and was a strong advocate of free speech. He also was noted for defending the environment.

Doug·las fir ▶ **n.** a tall, slender conifer with soft foliage and, in mature trees, deeply fissured bark. It is widely planted as a timber tree. ● Genus *Pseudotsuga*, family Pinaceae: several species, in particular the **common Douglas fir** (*P. menziesii*) of British Columbia and the western US.
– ORIGIN mid 19th cent.: named after David *Douglas* (1798–1834), the Scottish botanist and explorer who introduced it to Europe from North America.

Doug·las-Home /ˌdəgləs ˈhyo͞om/, Sir Alec (1903–95), British Conservative statesman; prime minister 1963–64; born *Alexander Frederick Douglas-Home*.

Doug·lass /ˈdəgləs/, Frederick (1817–95), US abolitionist and writer; born *Frederick Augustus Washington Bailey*. He escaped from slavery in 1838 and became an anti-slavery lecturer. He established an anti-slavery newspaper *North Star* (1847–64) and published his autobiography, *Narrative of the Life of Frederick Douglass* (1845, revised 1892).

Frederick Douglass

dou·la /ˈdo͞olə/ ▶ **n.** a woman who is trained to assist another woman during childbirth and who may provide support to the family after the baby is born.
– ORIGIN 1960s: modern Greek, from Greek *doulē* 'female slave.'

Doul·ton /ˈdōltən, ˈdôltən/ (also **Royal Doulton**) ▶ **n.** trademark fine, decorative pottery or porcelain made at the British factories of John Doulton (1793–1873) or his successors.

doum palm /do͞om/ ▶ **n.** a palm tree with a forked trunk, producing edible fruit and a vegetable ivory substitute. It is native to the Nile region of Upper Egypt. ● *Hyphaene thebaica*, family Palmae.
– ORIGIN early 18th cent.: *doum* from Arabic *dawm*, *dūm*.

dour /do͝or, dou(ə)r/ ▶ **adj.** relentlessly severe, stern, or gloomy in manner or appearance: *a hard, dour, humorless fanatic.*
– DERIVATIVES **dour·ly adv.**, **dour·ness n.**
– ORIGIN late Middle English (originally Scots): probably from Scottish Gaelic *dúr* 'dull, obstinate, stupid,' perhaps from Latin *durus* 'hard.'

Dou·ro /ˈdōˌro͞o/ a river on the Iberian peninsula that rises in central Spain and flows west for 556 miles (900 km) through Portugal to the Atlantic Ocean near Oporto. Spanish name **Duero**.

dou·rou·cou·li /ˌdo͝orəˈko͞olē/ ▶ **n.** (pl. **douroucoulis**) a large-eyed chiefly nocturnal monkey found in South America. Also called **night monkey, owl monkey**. ● Genus *Aotus*, family Cebidae: two or more species.
– ORIGIN mid 19th cent.: probably a South American Indian name.

douse /dous/ (also **dowse**) ▶ **v.** [with obj.] pour a liquid over; drench: *he doused the car with gasoline and set it on fire.* ■ extinguish (a fire or light): *stewards appeared and the fire was doused* | figurative *nothing could douse her sudden euphoria.* ■ Sailing lower (a sail) quickly.
– ORIGIN early 17th cent.: perhaps imitative, influenced by **souse**, or perhaps from dialect *douse* 'strike, beat,' from Middle Dutch and Low German *dossen*.

Dove /dōv/, Rita (1952–), US poet and novelist. The youngest poet and the first African-American woman to hold the post of poet laureate of the US (1993–94), her work includes the Pulitzer Prize–winning poem "Thomas and Beulah" (1987) and the novel *Through the Ivory Gate* (1992).

dove¹ /dəv/ ▶ **n. 1** a stocky seed- or fruit-eating bird with a small head, short legs, and a cooing voice. Doves are generally smaller and more delicate than pigeons, but many kinds have been given both names. ● Family Columbidae: numerous genera and species; white doves are a variety of the domestic pigeon.
2 a person who advocates peaceful or conciliatory policies, esp. in foreign affairs. Compare with **hawk¹** (sense 2 of the noun).
3 (**Dove**) (in Christian art and poetry) the Holy Spirit (as represented in John 1:32).
– DERIVATIVES **dove·like** /-ˌlīk/ **adj.**, **dov·ish adj.** (sense 2).
– ORIGIN Middle English: from Old Norse *dúfa*.

dove² /dōv/ past of **dive**.

dove·cote /ˈdəvˌkōt/ (also **dovecot**) ▶ **n.** a shelter with nest holes for domesticated pigeons.

dove gray /dəv/ ▶ **n.** a light gray.

dove·kie /ˈdəvkē/ ▶ **n.** a small, stubby short-billed auk (seabird) with black plumage and white underparts, breeding in the Arctic. ● *Alle alle*, family Alcidae.
– ORIGIN early 19th cent. (originally denoting the black guillemot, *Cepphus grylle*, also formerly called the *Greenland dove*): from a Scots diminutive of **dove¹**.

Do·ver /ˈdōvər/ **1** a ferry port in Kent, in England, on the coast of the English Channel; pop. 35,200 (est. 2009). It is mainland Britain's nearest point to the Continent, being only 22 miles (35 km) from Calais, France.
2 the capital of Delaware, in the central part of the state; pop. 36,107 (est. 2008).
3 an industrial city in southeastern New Hampshire; pop. 28,609 (est. 2008).
4 a township in southeastern New Jersey, on Barnegat Bay; pop. 89,706 (2000).

Do·ver, Strait of a sea passage between England and France that connects the English Channel with the North Sea.

Do·ver sole ▶ **n.** either of two flatfishes that are highly valued as food. ● a true sole that is common in European waters (*Solea solea*, family Soleidae). ● a relative of the lemon sole found in the eastern Pacific (*Microstomus pacificus*, family Pleuronectidae).

dove·tail /ˈdəvˌtāl/ ▶ **n.** (also **dovetail joint**) a joint formed by one or more tapered projections (tenons) on one piece that interlock with corresponding notches or recesses (mortises) in another. ■ a tenon used in such a joint, typically wider at its extremity.
▶ **v.** [with obj.] join together by means of a dovetail. ■ fit or cause to fit together easily and conveniently: [with obj.] *plan to enable parents to dovetail their career and family commitments* | [no obj.] *flights that dovetail with the working day.*

dovetail

dove tree ▶ **n.** a slender deciduous Chinese tree with flowers that bear large white bracts said to resemble doves' wings, grown as an ornamental. ● *Davidia involucrata*, family Nyssaceae.

Dow /dou/ short for **Dow Jones Industrial Average**: *the Dow fell sharply that summer.*

dow·a·ger /ˈdouəjər/ ▶ **n.** a widow with a title or property derived from her late husband: [as modifier] *the dowager duchess* | [postpositive] *the queen dowager.* ■ informal a dignified elderly woman.
– ORIGIN mid 16th cent.: from Old French *douagiere*, from *douage* 'dower,' from *douer* 'endow,' from Latin *dotare* 'endow' (see **dower**).

dow·a·ger's hump ▶ **n.** forward curvature of the spine resulting in a stoop, typically in women with osteoporosis, caused by collapse of the front edges of the thoracic vertebrae.

dow·dy /ˈdoudē/ ▶ **adj.** (**dowdier, dowdiest**) (of a person, typically a woman, or their clothes) unfashionable and without style in appearance: *she could achieve the kind of casual chic that made every other woman around her look dowdy.*
▶ **n.** (pl. **dowdies**) a woman who is unfashionably and unattractively dressed.
– DERIVATIVES **dow·di·ly** /ˈdoudəlē/ **adv.**, **dow·di·ness n.**
– ORIGIN late 16th cent.: from *dowd* 'person of unfashionable appearance' (of unknown origin) + **-y¹**.

dow·el /ˈdouəl/ ▶ **n.** a peg of wood, metal, or plastic without a distinct head, used for holding together components of a structure.
▶ **v.** (**dowels, doweling, doweled**; Brit. **dowels, dowelling, dowelled**) [with obj.] fasten with a dowel or dowels.
– ORIGIN Middle English: perhaps from Middle Low German *dovel*.

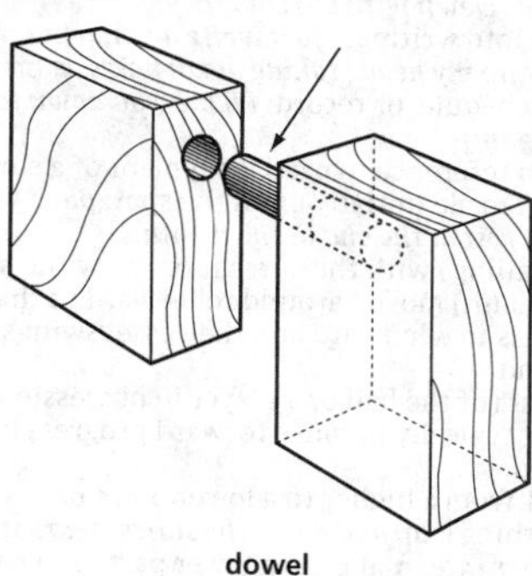

dowel

dow·el·ing /ˈdouəliNG/ (Brit. **dowelling**) ▶ **n.** cylindrical rods for cutting into dowels.

dow·er /ˈdou(-ə)r/ ▶ **n.** a widow's share for life of her husband's estate. ■ archaic a dowry.
▶ **v.** [with obj.] archaic give a dowry to.
– ORIGIN late Middle English: from Old French *douaire*, from medieval Latin *dotarium*, from Latin *dotare* 'endow,' from *dos, dot-* 'dowry'; related to *dare* 'give.'

dow·itch·er /ˈdouiCHər/ ▶ **n.** a wading bird of the sandpiper family, with a long straight bill, breeding in arctic and subarctic North America and eastern Asia. ● Genus *Limnodromus*, family Scolopacidae: three species, in particular the **short-billed dowitcher** (*L. griseus*) and the **long-billed dowitcher** (*L. scolopaceus*).
– ORIGIN mid 19th cent.: from Iroquoian.

Dow Jones In·dus·tri·al Av·er·age /ˈdou ˈjōnz/ (also **Dow Jones Average**) an index of figures indicating the relative price of shares on the New York Stock Exchange, based on the average price of selected stocks.
– ORIGIN from the name of *Dow Jones & Co, Inc.*, a financial news agency founded by Charles H. *Dow* (1851–1902) and Edward D. *Jones* (*c.*1855–1920), American economists whose company compiled the first average of US stock prices in 1884.

Down /doun/ one of the six counties of Northern Ireland, formerly an administrative area; chief town, Downpatrick.

down¹ /doun/ ▶ **adv.** toward or in a lower place or position, esp. to or on the ground or another surface: *she looked down* | *the sun started to go down* | *he put his glass down* | *she flicked the switch up and down* | *he swung the ax to chop down the tree.* ■ at or to a specified distance below: *you can plainly see the bottom 35 feet down.* ■ downstairs: *I went down to put the kettle on.* ■ expressing movement or position away from the north: *they're living down south.* ■ to or at a place perceived as lower (often expressing casualness or lack of hurry): *I'd rather be down at the villa* | *I'm going down to the arcade.* ■ Brit. away from the capital or major city: *there are eight trains a day, four up and four down.* ■ Brit. away from a university, esp. Oxford or Cambridge. ■ (with reference to food or drink swallowed) in or into the stomach: *she couldn't keep anything down.* ■ so as to lie or be fixed flush or flat: *she stuck down a Christmas label.* ■ [as exclamation] used as a command to a person or

PRONUNCIATION KEY ə *ago, up*; ər *over, fur*; a *hat*; ā *ate*; ä *car*; e *let*; ē *see*; i *fit*; ī *by*; NG *sing*; ō *go*; ô *law, for*; oi *toy*; o͝o *good*; o͞o *goo*; ou *out*; TH *thin*; TH *then*; ZH *vision*

d

animal to sit or lie down: *down, boy!* ■ a crossword answer that reads vertically: *how many letters in fifteen down?*
2 to or at a lower level of intensity, volume, or activity: *keep the noise down | the panic was dying down | at night it would cool down.* ■ to or at a lower price, value, or rank: *output was down by 20 percent | soup is down from 59 cents to 49 cents.* ■ to a finer consistency, a smaller amount or size, or a simpler or more basic state: *I must slim down a bit | a formal statement that can't be edited down | thin down an oil-based paint with spirits.* ■ from an earlier to a later point in time or order: *everyone, from the president **down to** the guy selling hot dogs, is outraged.*
3 in or into a weaker or worse position, mood, or condition: *the scandal brought down the government | he was **down with** the flu.* ■ losing or at a disadvantage by a specified amount: *the Braves, down 7–6, rallied for two runs in the sixth inning.* ■ used to express progress through a series of tasks or items: *one down and only six more to go.* ■ (of a computer system) out of action or unavailable for use (esp. temporarily): *the system went down yesterday.* ■ (**down with** ——) shouted to express strong dislike of a specified person or thing: *crowds chanted "Down with bureaucracy!"*
4 in or into writing: *I just **write down** whatever comes into my head | taking down notes.* ■ on or onto a list, schedule, or record: *I'll put you **down for** the evening shift.*
5 (with reference to partial payment of a sum of money) made initially or on the spot: *pay $500 down and the rest at the end of the month.*
6 (of sailing) with the current or the wind. ■ (of a ship's helm) moved around to leeward so that the rudder is to windward and the vessel swings toward the wind.
7 Football (of the ball or a player in possession) not in play, typically because forward progress has been stopped.
▶ **prep. 1** from a higher to a lower point of (something): *up and down the stairs | tears streaming down her face.* ■ at or to a lower part of (a river or stream); nearer the sea: *a dozen miles or so down the Mississippi.* ■ moving or at a point farther along the course of (something): *he lived down the street | I wandered down the road.* ■ informal at or to (a place): *tired of going down to the pub every night.*
2 throughout (a period of time): *astrologers down the ages.*
▶ **adj. 1** [attrib.] directed or moving toward a lower place or position: *the down escalator | click on the down arrow.* ■ Physics denoting a flavor of quark having a charge of $-^1/_3$. Protons and neutrons are thought to be composed of combinations of up and down quarks.
2 [predic.] unhappy; depressed: *he's been so down lately.*
3 [predic.] (of a computer system) temporarily out of action or unavailable: *sorry, but the computer's down.*
4 [predic.] chiefly slang supporting or going along with someone or something: *"You going to the movies?" "Yo, I'm down."* ■ aware of and following the latest fashion: *a seriously down, hip-hop homie.*
▶ **v.** [with obj.] informal **1** knock or bring to the ground: *175 enemy aircraft had been downed | he struck Slater on the face, downing him.*
2 consume (something, typically a drink): *he downed a six-pack.* ■ (of a golfer) sink (a putt).
▶ **n. 1** Football a chance for a team to advance the ball, ending when the ball carrier is tackled or the ball becomes out of play. A team must advance at least ten yards in a series of four downs in order to keep possession.
2 (**downs**) informal unwelcome experiences or events: *there had been more downs than ups during his years at the company.*
3 informal a feeling or period of unhappiness or depression: *everyone gets their downs, their depressive periods.* ■ informal short for DOWNER (sense 1).
– PHRASES **be down on** informal disapprove of; feel hostile or antagonistic toward. **be down to 1** be attributable to (a particular factor or circumstance): *he claimed his problems were down to the media.* ■ be the responsibility of (a particular person): *it's down to you to make sure the boiler receives regular servicing.* **2** be left with only (the specified amount): *I'm down to my last few dollars.* **down in the mouth** informal (of a person or their expression) unhappy; dejected. **down on one's luck** informal experiencing a period of bad luck. **down pat** (or **cold**) memorized or mastered perfectly: *she had the baby's medical routine down pat | a guy who has his art history down cold.* **down to the ground** informal completely. **have** (or **put**) **someone/something down as** judge someone or something to be (a particular type): *I never had Jake down as a ladies' man.*

– ORIGIN Old English *dūn, dūne*, shortened from *adūne* 'downward,' from the phrase *of dūne* 'off the hill' (see DOWN³).

down² ▶ **n.** soft fine fluffy feathers that form the first covering of a young bird or an insulating layer below the contour feathers of an adult bird. ■ such feathers taken from ducks or their nests and used for stuffing cushions, quilts, etc.; eiderdown. ■ fine soft hair on the face or body of a person: *the little girl had a covering of golden down on her head.* ■ short soft hairs on some leaves, fruit, or seeds.
– ORIGIN Middle English: from Old Norse *dúnn*.

down³ ▶ **n.** (usu. **downs**) a gently rolling hill: *the gentle green contours of the downs.* ■ (**the Downs**) ridges of undulating chalk and limestone hills in southern England, with few trees and used mainly for pasture.
– ORIGIN Old English *dūn* 'hill' (related to Dutch *duin* 'dune'), perhaps ultimately of Celtic origin and related to Old Irish *dún* and obsolete Welsh *din* 'fort,' which are from an Indo-European root shared by TOWN.

down-and-dirt·y ▶ **adj.** informal **1** highly competitive or unprincipled: *backstabbing slander and electronic harassment are freely employed in down-and-dirty hacker feuds.*
2 earthy, direct, and explicit: *the down-and-dirty realities about these diseases.* ■ unvarnished; in a raw or prototypical form: *they serve up some down-and-dirty Texas blues.*

down-and-out ▶ **adj.** (of a person) without money, a job, or a place to live; destitute: *a down-and-out homeless vagrant.*
▶ **n.** (also **down-and-outer**) a person without money, a job, or a place to live.

down-at-the-heels (also **down-at-the-heel** or **down-at-heel**) ▶ **adj.** showing signs of neglect and deterioration; shabby: *a down-at-the-heels house.*

down·beat /ˈdounˌbēt/ ▶ **adj.** pessimistic; gloomy: *the assessment of current economic prospects is downbeat.*
▶ **n.** Music an accented beat, usually the first of the bar.

down-bow /ˌbō/ ▶ **n.** Music (on a stringed instrument) a stroke in which the bow, from handle to tip, is slid across the strings in a motion of the hand moving away from the strings.

down·burst /ˈdounˌbərst/ ▶ **n.** a strong downward current of air from a cumulonimbus cloud, usually associated with intense rain or a thunderstorm.

down·cast /ˈdounˌkast/ ▶ **adj. 1** (of a person's eyes) looking downward: *her modestly downcast eyes.*
2 (of a person) feeling despondent.
▶ **n.** a shaft dug in a mine for extra ventilation.

down·code /ˈdounˌkōd/ ▶ **v.** [with obj.] **1** designate (a medical procedure or insurance claim) with a lower value: *an insurer who systematically downcodes professional charge submissions for critical care services* | [no obj.] *we cannot turn to Medicaid to pay if Medicare downcodes.*
2 Computing rewrite or convert (programs or software) into a lower level language: *some of the libraries written into C were downcoded into assembly.*
– DERIVATIVES **down·cod·ing n.**

down·com·er /ˈdounˌkəmər/ ▶ **n.** a pipe for the downward transport of water or gas from the top of a furnace or boiler.

down·con·vert·er /ˈdounkənˌvərtər/ ▶ **n.** Electronics a device that converts a signal to a lower frequency, esp. in television reception.
– DERIVATIVES **down·con·ver·sion** /-ˌvərZHən/ **n.**

down·coun·try /ˈdounˈkəntrē/ ▶ **adj. & adv.** in, into, or relating to the low-lying and generally more densely settled part of a country as opposed to hilly regions: [as adj.] *even the downcountry conservatives support this reform* | [as adv.] *distant summer storms a hundred miles downcountry.*

down·court /ˈdounˈkôrt/ ▶ **adv.** Sports to or into the opposite end of the court, esp. in basketball.

down-curved ▶ **adj.** [attrib.] curved downward: *the slightly down-curved bill of a starling.*

down·cut /ˈdounˌkət/ ▶ **v.** (**downcuts, downcutting**, past and past participle **downcut**) [no obj.] Geology (of a river) erode downward through its bed.

down·draft /ˈdounˌdraft/ (Brit. **downdraught**) ▶ **n.** a downward current or draft of air, esp. one down a chimney into a room.

Down East a name for northeastern New England and for the Maritime Provinces that is derived from an old term for sailing downwind, to the east.

down·er /ˈdounər/ ▶ **n.** informal **1** (usu. **downers**) a depressant or tranquilizing drug, esp. a barbiturate.
2 a dispiriting or depressing experience or factor: *the thought of the danger his son was in put something of a downer on the situation.* ■ a period of consistent failure: *the Red Sox enter the season **on a downer**.*
3 a cow or other animal that is sick or injured and cannot get to its feet unaided.

Dow·ners Grove /ˈdounərz/ a village in northeastern Illinois, west of Chicago; pop. 49,250 (est. 2008).

Dow·ney /ˈdounē/ a city in southwestern California, southeast of Los Angeles; pop. 107,587 (est. 2008).

down·fall /ˈdounˌfôl/ ▶ **n.** a loss of power, prosperity, or status: *the crisis led to the downfall of the government.* ■ the cause of such a loss: *his intractability will prove to be his downfall.*

down·field /ˈdounˈfēld/ ▶ **adv.adj.** Football in or to a position nearer to the opponents' end of a field.

down·force /ˈdounˌfôrs/ ▶ **n.** a force acting on a moving vehicle having the effect of pressing it down toward the ground, giving it increased stability. Downforce is produced by a combination of air resistance and gravity.

down·grade /ˈdounˌgrād/ ▶ **v.** [with obj.] (usu. **be downgraded**) reduce to a lower grade, rank, or level of importance: *some jobs had gradually been downgraded from skilled to semiskilled.*
▶ **n. 1** an instance of reducing someone or something's rank, status, or level of importance.
2 a downward gradient, typically on a railroad track or road.
– PHRASES **on the downgrade** in decline: *profits are on the downgrade.*

down·haul /ˈdounˌhôl/ ▶ **n.** Nautical a rope used for hauling down a sail, spar, etc., esp. in order to control a sail's shape.

down·heart·ed /ˈdounˈhärtid/ ▶ **adj.** discouraged; in low spirits: *fans must not be downhearted even though we lost.*
– DERIVATIVES **down·heart·ed·ly adv.**, **down·heart·ed·ness n.**

down·hill /ˈdounˈhil/ ▶ **adv.** toward the bottom of a slope: *he ran downhill | follow the road downhill.* ■ into a steadily worsening situation: *his marriage continued to slide downhill | the business is **going downhill** fast.*
▶ **adj.** leading down toward the bottom of a slope: *the route is downhill for part of the way.* ■ of or relating to the sport of skiing or cycling downhill: *the world downhill champion.* ■ leading to a steadily worsening situation: *the downhill road to delinquency.* ■ without difficulty or challenge: *we can take the easy road, the downhill road, or we can put America on the path to greatness again.*
▶ **n. 1** a downward slope.
2 Skiing a downhill race. ■ the activity of downhill skiing.
– PHRASES **be downhill all the way 1** be easy in comparison with what came before: *up by six runs in the eighth inning—it should have been downhill all the way.* **2** become worse or less successful: *that had been the start of the present trouble—downhill all the way since then.*

down·hill·er /ˈdounˈhilər/ ▶ **n.** a skier or cyclist who takes part in downhill races.

down-hole (also **downhole**) ▶ **adj. & adv.** (in the oil industry) used, occurring, or performed in a well or borehole.

down-home ▶ **adj.** connected with an unpretentious way of life, esp. that of rural peoples or areas: *some good down-home cooking.*

Down·ing Street /ˈdouniNG/ a street in Westminster, London, between Whitehall and St. James's Park. No. 10 is the official residence of the prime minister; No. 11 is the official home of the chancellor of the exchequer. ■ used allusively for the British government or the prime minister.
– ORIGIN named after the original developer of the site, Sir George *Downing* (*c.*1624–84), a diplomat under both Oliver Cromwell and Charles II.

down·lev·el /ˈdounˌlevəl/ ▶ **adj.** using an earlier version of software, hardware, or an operating system: *there are still 600 million computers, many of them downlevel, that wouldn't have all of these vulnerabilities fixed.*

down·light /ˈdounˌlīt/ (also **downlighter**) ▶ **n.** a light placed or designed so as to throw illumination downward.
– DERIVATIVES **down·light·ing n.**

down·link /ˈdounˌliNGk/ ▶ **n.** a telecommunications link for signals coming to the earth from a satellite, spacecraft, or aircraft.
▶ **v.** [with obj.] relay to the earth (a telecommunications signal or the information it conveys): *any TV station can downlink just about any game.*

down·load /ˈdounˌlōd/ Computing ▶ **v.** [with obj.] copy (data) from one computer system to another or to a disk. Compare with UPLOAD.
▶ **n.** the act or process of copying data in such a way: [as modifier] *a download and upload routine.* ■ a

computer file transferred in such a way: *a popular download from bulletin boards.*
– DERIVATIVES **down·load·a·ble** adj., **down·load·er** n.

down·mar·ket /ˈdoun,märkit/ ▶ adj. & adv. toward or relating to the cheaper or less prestigious sector of the market: [as adj.] *an interview for the downmarket tabloids* | [as adv.] *competition threatens to drive broadcasters further downmarket.*

down pay·ment ▶ n. an initial payment made when something is bought on credit.

down·play /ˈdoun,plā/ ▶ v. [with obj.] make (something) appear less important than it really is: *this report downplays the seriousness of global warming.*

down·pour /ˈdoun,pôr/ ▶ n. a heavy rainfall: *a sudden downpour had filled the gutters and drains.*

down·range /ˈdoun,rānj/ ▶ adv. (of a missile, space launch, etc.) traveling in a specified direction away from the launch site and toward the target: *rounds streaked downrange at more than a mile a second.*

down·rate /ˈdoun,rāt/ ▶ v. [with obj.] make (someone or something) lower in value, standard, or importance.

down·right /ˈdoun,rīt/ ▶ adj. **1** [attrib.] (of something bad or unpleasant) utter; complete (used for emphasis): *it's a downright disgrace.*
2 (of a person's manner or behavior) straightforward; so direct as to be blunt: *her common sense and downright attitude to life surprised him.*
▶ adv. [as submodifier] to an extreme degree; thoroughly: *he was downright rude.*
– DERIVATIVES **down·right·ness** n.

down·riv·er /ˈdounˈrivər/ ▶ adv. & adj. toward or situated at a point nearer the mouth of a river: [as adv.] *the cabin cruiser started to drift downriver* | [as adj.] *the downriver side of the bridge.*

down·scale /ˈdoun,skāl/ ▶ v. [with obj.] reduce in size, scale, or extent: *he was unable to downscale his strongly unionized workforce.*
▶ adj. at the lower end of a scale, esp. a social scale; downmarket: *these brands appeal to downscale shoppers who are looking for a low price.*

down·shift /ˈdoun,sHift/ ▶ v. [no obj.] change to a lower gear in a motor vehicle or bicycle. ■ slow down; slacken off: *well before the country slipped into recession, business was downshifting.* ■ change a financially rewarding but stressful career or lifestyle for a less pressured and less highly paid but more fulfilling one: *they want to downshift from full-time work.*
▶ n. a change to a lower gear in a motor vehicle or bicycle. ■ a change in quality or quantity to a lesser or lower degree: *the downshift of human position from the center of the cosmos.* ■ an instance of changing a financially rewarding but stressful career or lifestyle for a less pressured and less highly paid but more fulfilling one.

down·side /ˈdoun,sīd/ ▶ n. the negative aspect of something, esp. something regarded as in general good or desirable: *a magazine feature on the downside of fashion modeling.*

down·size /ˈdoun,sīz/ ▶ v. [with obj.] make (something) smaller: *I downsized the rear wheel to 26 inches.* ■ make (a company or organization) smaller by eliminating staff positions. ■ [no obj.] (of a company) eliminate staff positions: *recession forced many companies to downsize.*

down·slope /ˈdoun,slōp/ ▶ n. a downward slope.
▶ adv. & adj. at or toward a lower point on a slope.

down·spout /ˈdoun,spout/ ▶ n. a pipe to carry rainwater from a roof to a drain or to ground level.

down·stage /ˈdounˈstāj/ ▶ adj. & adv. at or toward the front of a stage: [as adv.] *all four run for their lives downstage* | [as adj.] *a crowd of dancers occupies the downstage area.*

down·stairs /ˈdounˈste(ə)rz/ ▶ adv. down a flight of stairs: *I tripped over the cat and fell downstairs.* ■ on or to a lower floor: *we were waiting for you downstairs* | *she called him downstairs.*
▶ adj. [attrib.] situated downstairs: *the downstairs bathroom.*
▶ n. the ground floor or lower floors of a building: *the downstairs was hardly damaged at all.*

down·state /ˈdounˈstāt/ ▶ adj. & adv. of, in, or to a part of a state remote from its large cities, esp. the southern part.
▶ n. such an area.
– DERIVATIVES **down·stat·er** n.

down·stream /ˈdounˈstrēm/ ▶ adv. & adj. situated or moving in the direction in which a stream or river flows: [as adv.] *the bridge spanned the river just downstream of the rail line* | [as adj.] *deforestation could have disastrous consequences for downstream regions.* ■ Biology situated in or toward the part of a sequence of genetic material where transcription takes place later than at a given point: *a termination signal was found downstream from the coding region.* ■ at a stage in the process of gas or oil extraction and production after the raw material is ready for refining.

down·stroke /ˈdoun,strōk/ ▶ n. a stroke made downward: *he writes the figure seven with a line through the downstroke* | *the blade angles back on the downstroke.*

down·swing /ˈdoun,swiNG/ ▶ n. **1** another term for DOWNTURN.
2 Golf the downward movement of a club when the player is about to hit the ball.

Down syn·drome /ˈdoun ˈsindrōm/ (also **Down's syndrome**) ▶ n. Medicine a congenital disorder arising from a chromosome defect, causing intellectual impairment and physical abnormalities including short stature and a broad facial profile. It arises from a defect involving chromosome 21, usually an extra copy (trisomy-21).
– ORIGIN 1960s: named after John L. H. *Down* (1828–96), the English physician who first described it.

> **USAGE** Of relatively recent coinage, **Down syndrome** is the accepted term in modern use, and former terms such as **mongol**, **Mongoloid**, and **mongolism**, which are likely to cause offense, should be avoided. See also usage at **MONGOLOID**.

down·tem·po /ˈdoun,tempō/ ▶ adj. (of music) having a relatively slower beat.
▶ n. a genre of electronic dance music with influences from jazz, bossa nova, and dub reggae.

down-the-line ▶ adj. informal thorough and uncompromising: *the party avoids down-the-line support of unions.*

down·throw /ˈdoun,THrō/ Geology ▶ v. (past **downthrew**; past participle **downthrown**) [with obj.] displace (a rock formation) downward.
▶ n. a downward displacement of rock strata.

down tim·ber ▶ n. fallen trees brought down by wind, storm, or other natural agency.

down·time /ˈdoun,tīm/ (also **down time**) ▶ n. time during which a machine, esp. a computer, is out of action or unavailable for use. ■ a time of reduced activity or inactivity: *everyone needs downtime to unwind* | *downtimes for real estate and construction.*

down-to-earth ▶ adj. with no illusions or pretensions; practical and realistic: *a down-to-earth view of marriage.*
– DERIVATIVES **down-to-earth·ness** n.

down·town /ˈdounˈtoun/ ▶ adj. of, in, or characteristic of the central area or main business and commercial area of a town or city: *downtown Chicago* | *a downtown bar.*
▶ adv. in or into such an area: *I drove downtown.*
▶ n. such an area of a town or city: *the heart of Pittsburgh's downtown.*
– DERIVATIVES **down·town·er** n.

down·trend /ˈdoun,trend/ ▶ n. a downward trend, tendency, or movement: *there is not yet a confirmed downtrend in interest rates.*

down·trod·den /ˈdoun,trädn/ ▶ adj. oppressed or treated badly by people in power: *a downtrodden proletarian struggling for social justice.*

down·turn /ˈdoun,tərn/ ▶ n. a decline in economic, business, or other activity: *a downturn in the housing market.*
▶ v. [with obj.] (usu. as adj. **downturned**) turn (something) downward: *his downturned mouth.*

Down Un·der (also **down under**) informal ▶ adv. in or to Australia or New Zealand: *selling wines under the name of the grape variety, just as they do Down Under.*
▶ n. Australia and New Zealand: *thousands of men from Down Under.*
– ORIGIN late 19th cent.: with reference to the position of these countries on a globe.

down·ward /ˈdounwərd/ ▶ adv. (also **downwards**) toward a lower place, point, or level: *he was lying face downward.* ■ used to indicate that something applies to everyone in a certain hierarchy or set: *new rules on sick leave affect employees of all grades, from managers downward.*
▶ adj. moving or leading toward a lower place or level: *the downward curve of the stairs* | *a downward trend in inflation.*
– DERIVATIVES **down·ward·ly** adv.
– ORIGIN Middle English: shortening of Old English *adūnweard.*

down·ward·ly mo·bile ▶ adj. moving to a lower social class; losing wealth and status.
– DERIVATIVES **down·ward mo·bil·i·ty** n.

down·warp /ˈdoun,wôrp/ Geology ▶ n. a broad depression of the earth's surface.
▶ v. [with obj.] displace (a rock formation) downward so as to form such a depression.

down·wash /ˈdoun,wäsH, -,wôsH/ ▶ n. the downward deflection of an airstream by an aircraft wing or helicopter rotor blade.

down·well·ing /ˈdoun,weliNG/ ▶ n. the downward movement of fluid, esp. in the sea, the atmosphere, or deep in the earth.
▶ adj. characterized by or undergoing such movement: *downwelling mantle.*

down·wind /ˈdounˈwind/ ▶ adv. & adj. in the direction in which the wind is blowing: [as adv.] *warnings were issued to people living downwind of the fire* | [as adj.] *downwind landings.*

down·wind·er /ˈdounˈwindər/ ▶ n. a person living downwind of a nuclear test site or reactor, where the risk from fallout or radiation leaks is greatest.

down·y /ˈdounē/ ▶ adj. (**downier**, **downiest**) covered with fine soft hair or feathers: *the baby's downy cheek.* ■ filled with soft feathers: *a downy pillow.* ■ soft and fluffy: *pale downy hair.*
– DERIVATIVES **down·i·ly** /-nəlē/ adv., **down·i·ness** n.

down·y mil·dew ▶ n. mildew on a plant that is marked by a whitish down composed of spore-forming hyphae, penetrating more deeply into the plant than powdery mildew. ● Family Peronosporaceae, subdivision Mastigomycotina.

down·y wood·peck·er ▶ n. a widespread small North American woodpecker with a short bill, black and white plumage, and (on the male) a red patch on the back of the head. ● *Picoides pubescens*, family Picidae.

downy woodpecker

down·zone /ˈdoun,zōn/ ▶ v. [with obj.] assign (land or property) to a zoning grade under which the permitted density of housing and development is reduced.

dow·ry /ˈdou(ə)rē/ ▶ n. (pl. **dowries**) property or money brought by a bride to her husband on their marriage.
– ORIGIN Middle English (denoting a widow's life interest in her husband's estate): from Anglo-Norman French *dowarie*, from medieval Latin *dotarium* (see DOWER).

dowse¹ /douz/ ▶ v. [no obj.] practice dowsing: *water is easy to dowse for.* ■ [with obj.] search for or discover by dowsing: *he dowsed a spiral of energy on the stone.*
– DERIVATIVES **dows·er** n.
– ORIGIN late 17th cent.: of unknown origin.

dowse² ▶ v. variant spelling of DOUSE.

dows·ing /ˈdouziNG/ ▶ n. a technique for searching for underground water, minerals, or anything invisible, by observing the motion of a pointer (traditionally a forked stick, now often paired bent wires) or the changes in direction of a pendulum, supposedly in response to unseen influences: [as modifier] *a dowsing rod.*

dox·ol·o·gy /däkˈsäləjē/ ▶ n. (pl. **doxologies**) a liturgical formula of praise to God.
– DERIVATIVES **dox·o·log·i·cal** /,däksəˈläjikəl/ adj.
– ORIGIN mid 17th cent.: via medieval Latin from Greek *doxologia*, from *doxa* 'appearance, glory' (from *dokein* 'seem') + *-logia* (see -LOGY).

dox·o·ru·bi·cin /,däksəˈro͞obəsin/ ▶ n. Medicine a bacterial antibiotic that is widely used to treat leukemia and various other forms of cancer. ● This is produced by the streptomycete bacterium *Streptomyces peucetius caesius.*
– ORIGIN 1970s: from *deoxy-* (in the sense 'that has lost oxygen') + Latin *rubus* 'red' + -MYCIN.

dox·y /ˈdäksē/ ▶ n. (pl. **doxies**) archaic a lover or mistress. ■ a prostitute.
– ORIGIN mid 16th cent. (originally slang): of unknown origin.

dox·y·cy·cline /,däksēˈsīklēn/ ▶ n. Medicine a broad-spectrum antibiotic of the tetracycline group, which has a long half-life in the body.
– ORIGIN 1960s: from *d(e)oxy-* + TETRACYCLINE.

doy·en /doiˈen, ˈdoi-en/ ▶ n. the most respected or prominent person in a particular field: *the doyen of Canadian poetry.*

– ORIGIN late 17th cent.: via French from Old French *deien* (see DEAN[1]).

doy·enne /doi'en/ ▸ n. a woman who is the most respected or prominent person in a particular field: *she's the doyenne of daytime TV*.
– ORIGIN mid 19th cent.: from French, feminine of *doyen* (see DOYEN).

Doy·enne du Co·mice /doi'en ˌdyo͞o kə'mēs/ ▸ n. see COMICE.

Doyle /doil/, Sir Arthur Conan (1859–1930), Scottish novelist and short-story writer. He is known for his creation of private detective Sherlock Holmes, who first appeared (with his friend Dr. Watson, the narrator of the stories) in *A Study in Scarlet* (1887). Other notable works: *The Adventures of Sherlock Holmes* (1892) and *The Hound of the Baskervilles* (1902).

d

doy·ley ▸ n. dated variant spelling of DOILY.

D'Oy·ly Carte /'doilē 'kärt/, Richard (1844–1901), English impresario and producer. He brought together the librettist Sir W. S. Gilbert and the composer Sir Arthur Sullivan, producing many of their operettas in London's Savoy Theatre, which he had established in 1881.

doz. ▸ abbr. dozen.

doze /dōz/ ▸ v. [no obj.] sleep lightly: *he found his mother dozing by the fire*. ■ (**doze off**) fall lightly asleep: *I dozed off for a few seconds*.
▸ n. [in sing.] a short light sleep.
– ORIGIN mid 17th cent. (in the sense 'stupefy, bewilder, or make drowsy'): perhaps related to Danish *døse* 'make drowsy.'

doz·en /'dəzən/ (abbr.: **dz.**) ▸ n. **1** (pl. **same**) a group or set of twelve: *a dozen bottles of sherry*. ■ (**dozens**) informal a lot: *she has dozens of admirers*.
2 (**the dozens**) an exchange of insults engaged in as a game or ritual among black Americans.
– PHRASES **by the dozen** in large quantities. **talk nineteen to the dozen** Brit. talk incessantly.
– DERIVATIVES **doz·enth** /'dəzənTH/ adj.
– ORIGIN Middle English: from Old French *dozeine*, based on Latin *duodecim* 'twelve.'

doz·er /'dōzər/ ▸ n. informal short for BULLDOZER.

do·zy /'dōzē/ ▸ adj. (**dozier**, **doziest**) drowsy and lazy: *he grew dozy at the end of a long day*.
– DERIVATIVES **do·zi·ly** /-zəlē/ adv., **do·zi·ness** n.

DP ▸ abbr. ■ data processing. ■ dew point. ■ displaced person. ■ Baseball double play.

DPhil ▸ abbr. Doctor of Philosophy.

dpi ▸ abbr. Computing dots per inch, a measure of the resolution of printers, scanners, etc.

DPT (also **DTP**) ▸ abbr. diphtheria, pertussis (whooping cough), and tetanus, a combined vaccine given to small children.

Dr. ▸ abbr. ■ (as a title) Doctor: *Dr. Michael Russell*. ■ (in street names) Drive.

dr. ▸ abbr. ■ debit. [formerly representing *debtor*.] ■ drachma(s). ■ dram(s).

drab[1] /drab/ ▸ adj. (**drabber**, **drabbest**) **1** lacking brightness or interest; drearily dull: *the landscape was drab and gray* | *her drab suburban existence*.
2 of a dull light brown color: *drab camouflage uniforms*.
▸ n. fabric of a dull brownish color.
– DERIVATIVES **drab·ly** adv., **drab·ness** n.
– ORIGIN mid 16th cent. (as a noun denoting undyed cloth): probably from Old French *drap* 'cloth' (see DRAPE).

drab[2] ▸ n. archaic **1** a slovenly woman.
2 a prostitute.
– ORIGIN early 16th cent.: perhaps related to Low German *drabbe* 'mire' and Dutch *drab* 'dregs.'

Drab·ble /'drabəl/, Margaret (1939–), English novelist. Notable works: *The Millstone* (1966), *The Radiant Way* (1987), *The Peppered Moth* (2001), and *The Red Queen* (2004). She is the younger sister of A. S. Byatt.

dra·cae·na /drə'sēnə/ ▸ n. a tropical palmlike shrub or tree with ornamental foliage, popular as a greenhouse or indoor plant. ● Genera *Dracaena* and *Cordyline*, family Agavaceae. See also DRAGON TREE.
– ORIGIN modern Latin, from Greek *drakaina*, feminine of *drakōn* 'serpent, dragon' (the genus *Dracaena* includes *Dracaena draco*, the dragon tree).

drachm /dram/ (abbr.: **dr.**) ▸ n. **1** a unit of weight formerly used by apothecaries, equivalent to 60 grains or one eighth of an ounce. ■ (also **fluid drachm**) a liquid measure formerly used by apothecaries, equivalent to 60 minims or one eighth of a fluid ounce.
2 (in numismatics) an ancient silver coin based on the Attic or Hellenistic drachma. See also DRACHMA.
– ORIGIN late Middle English (denoting the ancient Greek drachma): from Old French *dragme* or late Latin *dragma*, via Latin from Greek *drakhmē* (see DRACHMA).

drach·ma /'dräkmə/ ▸ n. (pl. **drachmas** or **drachmae** /-mē/) the basic monetary unit of Greece (until the introduction of the euro), notionally equal to 100 lepta. ■ a silver coin of ancient Greece.
– ORIGIN via Latin from Greek *drakhmē*, an Attic weight and coin. Compare with DIRHAM and DRACHM.

Dra·co[1] /'drākō/ Astronomy a large northern constellation (the Dragon), stretching around the north celestial pole and said to represent the dragon killed by Hercules. It has no bright stars. ■ (as genitive **Draconis** /drā'kōnis, drə-/) used with a preceding letter or numeral to designate a star in this constellation: *the star Gamma Draconis*.
– ORIGIN Latin.

Dra·co[2] (7th century BC), Athenian legislator. His codification of Athenian law was notorious for its severity; for instance, the death penalty was imposed even for trivial crimes, which gave rise to the adjective *draconian* in English.

dra·co·ni·an /drə'kōnēən, drā-/ ▸ adj. (of laws or their application) excessively harsh and severe.
– DERIVATIVES **dra·con·ic** /-'känik/ adj.
– ORIGIN late 19th cent.: from the Greek name *Drakōn* (see DRACO[2]) + -IAN.

Drac·u·la /'drakyələ/ the Transylvanian vampire in Bram Stoker's novel *Dracula* (1897).
– ORIGIN variant of *Drakula*, *Dragwlya*, names given to Vlad Ţepeş (Vlad the Impaler), a 15th-cent. prince of Wallachia renowned for his cruelty.

draff /draf/ ▸ n. literary dregs or refuse.
– ORIGIN Middle English: perhaps from an unrecorded Old English word related to German *Treber*, *Träber* 'husks, grains,' and perhaps also to DRIVEL.

draft /draft/ ▸ n. **1** a preliminary version of a piece of writing: *the first draft of the party's manifesto* | [as modifier] *a draft document*. ■ a plan, sketch, or rough drawing. ■ (in full **draft mode**) Computing a mode of operation of a printer in which text is produced rapidly but with relatively low definition.
2 (**the draft**) compulsory recruitment for military service: *25 million men were subject to the draft* | [as modifier] *draft cards*. ■ a procedure whereby new or existing sports players are made available for selection or reselection by the teams in a league, usually with the earlier choices being given to the weaker teams. ■ rare a group or individual selected from a larger group for a special duty, e.g., for military service.
3 (Brit. **draught**) a current of cool air in a room or other confined space: *heavy curtains at the windows cut out drafts*.
4 (Brit. **draught**) the action or act of pulling something along, esp. a vehicle or farm implement.
5 a written order to pay a specified sum; a check.
6 (Brit. **draught**) a single act of drinking or inhaling: *she downed the remaining beer in one draft*. ■ the amount swallowed or inhaled in one such act: *he took deep drafts of oxygen into his lungs*.
7 (Brit. **draught**) the depth of water needed to float a ship: *the shallow draft enabled her to get close to shore*.
8 (Brit. **draught**) the drawing in of a fishing net. ■ the fish taken at one drawing; a catch.
▸ v. (Brit. also **draught**) [with obj.] **1** prepare a preliminary version of (a text): *I drafted a letter of resignation*.
2 select (a person or group of people) for a certain purpose: *he was drafted to help with the task force on best safety practices*. ■ conscript (someone) for military service. ■ select (a player) for a sports team through the draft.
3 pull or draw.
4 [no obj.] Auto Racing benefit from reduced wind resistance by driving very closely behind another vehicle.
▸ adj. (Brit. **draught**) [attrib.] **1** denoting beer or other drink that is kept in and served from a barrel or tank rather than from a bottle or can: *draft beer*.
2 denoting an animal used for pulling heavy loads: *draft oxen*.
– PHRASES **on draft** (of beer or other drink) on tap; ready to be drawn from a barrel or tank; not bottled or canned.
– DERIVATIVES **draft·er** n.
– ORIGIN mid 16th cent.: phonetic spelling of DRAUGHT.

draft board ▸ n. a board of civilians that is responsible for registering, classifying, and selecting people for compulsory military service.

draft dodg·er ▸ n. derogatory a person who has avoided compulsory military service.
– DERIVATIVES **draft dodg·ing** n.

draft·ee /draf'tē/ ▸ n. a person conscripted for military service.

draft horse (Brit. **draught horse**) ▸ n. a large horse used for pulling heavy loads, esp. a cart or plow.

draft pick ▸ n. the right of a sports team to select a player during the annual selection process. ■ a player selected during the draft.

drafts·man /'draftsmən/ (Brit. **draughtsman**) ▸ n. (pl. **draftsmen**) **1** a person, esp. a man, who makes detailed technical plans or drawings. ■ an artist skilled in drawing.
2 a person who drafts legal documents.
– DERIVATIVES **drafts·man·ship** /-ˌSHip/ n.

drafts·per·son /'draftsˌpərsən/ ▸ n. (pl. **draftspeople**) a draftsman or draftswoman (used as a neutral alternative).

drafts·wom·an /'draftsˌwo͝omən/ ▸ n. (pl. **draftswomen**) a woman who makes detailed technical plans or drawings.

draft·y /'draftē/ (Brit. **draughty**) ▸ adj. (**draftier**, **draftiest**) (of an enclosed space) cold and uncomfortable because of currents of cool air: *anyone would get pneumonia living in the drafty old house*. ■ (of a door or window) ill-fitting, and so allowing currents of cool air in.
– DERIVATIVES **draft·i·ly** /-təlē/ adv., **draft·i·ness** n.

drag /drag/ ▸ v. (**drags**, **dragging**, **dragged**) **1** [with obj.] pull (someone or something) along forcefully, roughly, or with difficulty: *we dragged the boat up the beach* | figurative *I dragged my eyes away*. ■ take (someone) to or from a place or event, despite their reluctance: *my girlfriend is dragging me off to Atlantic City for a week*. ■ (**drag oneself**) go somewhere wearily, reluctantly, or with difficulty: *I have to drag myself out of bed each day*. ■ move (an icon or other image) across a computer screen using a tool such as a mouse. ■ [no obj.] (of a person's clothes or an animal's tail) trail along the ground: *the nuns walked in meditation, their habits dragging on the grass*. ■ [no obj.] (**drag at**) catch hold of and pull (something): *desperately, Jinny dragged at his arm*. ■ [no obj.] engage in a drag race: *they were caught dragging on Francis Lewis Blvd*. ■ (of a ship) trail (an anchor) along the seabed, causing the ship to drift. ■ [no obj.] (of an anchor) fail to hold, causing a ship or boat to drift. ■ search the bottom of (a river, lake, or the sea) with grapnels or nets: *frogmen had dragged the local river*.
2 [with obj.] (**drag something up**) informal deliberately mention an unwelcome or unpleasant fact: *pieces of evidence about his early life were dragged up*. ■ (**drag someone/something into**) involve someone or something in (a situation or matter), typically when such involvement is inappropriate or unnecessary: *he had no right to drag you into this sort of thing*. ■ (**drag something in/into**) introduce an irrelevant or inappropriate subject: *politics were never dragged into the conversation*. ■ (**drag someone/something down**) bring someone or something to a lower level or standard: *the economy will be dragged down by inefficient firms*.
3 [no obj.] (of time, events, or activities) pass slowly and tediously: *the day dragged—eventually it was time for bed*. ■ (of a process or situation) continue at tedious and unnecessary length: *the dispute between the two families dragged on for years*. ■ [with obj.] (**drag something out**) protract something unnecessarily: *he dragged out the process of serving them*.
4 [no obj.] (**drag on**) informal (of a person) inhale the smoke from (a cigarette).
▸ n. **1** the action of pulling something forcefully or with difficulty: *the drag of the current*. ■ the longitudinal retarding force exerted by air or other fluid surrounding a moving object. ■ [in sing.] a person or thing that impedes progress or development: *Larry was turning out to be a drag on her career*. ■ Fishing unnatural motion of a fishing fly caused by the pull of the line. ■ archaic an iron shoe that can be applied as a brake to the wheel of a cart or wagon.
2 [in sing.] informal a boring or tiresome person or thing: *working nine to five can be a drag*.
3 informal an act of inhaling smoke from a cigarette: *he took a long drag on his cigarette*.
4 clothing more conventionally worn by the opposite sex, esp. women's clothes worn by a man: *a fashion show, complete with men in drag* | [as modifier] *a live drag show*.
5 short for DRAG RACE. ■ informal a street or road: *the main drag*. ■ historical a private vehicle like a stagecoach, drawn by four horses.
6 a thing that is pulled along the ground or through water, in particular: ■ historical a harrow used for breaking up the surface of land. ■ an apparatus for dredging a river or for recovering the bodies of drowned people from a river, a lake, or the sea. ■ another term for DRAGNET.
7 informal influence over other people: *they had the education but they didn't have the drag*.
8 a strong-smelling lure drawn before hounds as a substitute for a fox or other hunted animal. ■ a hunt using such a lure.
9 Music one of the basic patterns (rudiments) of drumming, consisting of a stroke preceded by two grace notes, which are usually played with the other stick. See also RUFF[4].

–PHRASES **drag one's feet** walk slowly and wearily or with difficulty. ■ (also **drag one's heels**) (of a person or organization) be deliberately slow or reluctant to act: *the government has dragged its heels over permanent legislation.* **drag someone/something through the mud** make damaging allegations about someone or something: *he felt enough loyalty to his old school not to drag its name through the mud.* **in drag** wearing the clothing of the opposite sex.
–PHRASAL VERBS **drag something out** extract information from someone against their will: *the truth was being dragged out of us.*
–ORIGIN Middle English: from Old English *dragan* or Old Norse *draga* 'to draw'; the noun partly from Middle Low German *dragge* 'grapnel.'

drag-and-drop Computing ▶ **v.** [with obj.] move (an icon or other image) to another part of the screen using a mouse or similar device, typically in order to perform some operation on a file or document.
▶ **adj.** of, relating to, or permitting the movement of images in this way: *drag-and-drop transfer of messages.*

drag bunt ▶ **n.** Baseball a bunt, usually by a left-handed batter, that is hit down the first baseline.

dra·gée /drä'ZHā/ ▶ **n.** a candy consisting of a center covered with a coating, such as a sugared almond or a chocolate. ■ a small silver ball for decorating cookies or a cake.
–ORIGIN late 17th cent. (also denoting a mixture of spices): French, from Old French *dragie* (see DREDGE[2]).

drag·ger /'dragər/ ▶ **n.** a trawler.

drag·gle /'dragəl/ ▶ **v.** [with obj.] make (something) dirty or wet, typically by trailing it through mud or water: (as adj. **draggled**) *she wore a draggled skirt.* ■ [no obj.] hang untidily: *red hairs draggled from under her cap.* ■ [no obj.] archaic trail behind others; lag behind: *they draggled at the heels of his troop.*
–ORIGIN early 16th cent.: diminutive and frequentative of DRAG.

drag·gle-tailed ▶ **adj.** archaic having untidily trailing skirts: *a draggle-tailed wench.*

drag·gy /'dragē/ ▶ **adj.** (**draggier**, **draggiest**) informal dreary and lacking liveliness: *a long, draggy, boring Friday afternoon.*

drag·line /'drag,līn/ ▶ **n. 1** a large excavator with a bucket pulled in by a wire cable.
2 a rope used for dragging or hauling something. ■ a rope that drags from something, e.g., a mooring line of a hot-air balloon. ■ a line of silk produced by a spider and acting as a safety line or (in newly hatched spiderlings) a parachute.

drag·net /'drag,net/ ▶ **n.** a net drawn through a river or across ground to trap fish or game. ■ a systematic search for someone or something, esp. criminals or criminal activity.

drag·o·man /'dragəmən/ ▶ **n.** (pl. **dragomans** or **dragomen**) an interpreter or guide, esp. in countries speaking Arabic, Turkish, or Persian.
–ORIGIN late Middle English: from obsolete French, from Italian *dragomanno*, from medieval Greek *dragoumanos*, from Arabic *tarjumān* 'interpreter.'

drag·on /'dragən/ ▶ **n. 1** a mythical monster like a giant reptile. In European tradition the dragon is typically fire-breathing and tends to symbolize chaos or evil, whereas in East Asia it is usually a beneficent symbol of fertility, associated with water and the heavens. ■ derogatory a fierce and intimidating person, esp. a woman.
2 another term for FLYING DRAGON. ■ see KOMODO DRAGON.
3 historical (in the 16th and 17th centuries) a short musket carried on the belt of a soldier, esp. a mounted infantryman. ■ a soldier armed with such a musket. Compare with DRAGOON.
–ORIGIN Middle English (also denoting a large serpent): from Old French, via Latin from Greek *drakōn* 'serpent.'

drag·on ar·um ▶ **n.** any of a number of plants of the arum family, in particular the North American green dragon.

drag·on boat ▶ **n.** a boat of a traditional Chinese design, typically decorated to resemble a dragon, propelled with paddles by a large crew and used for racing.

drag·on·et /,dragə'net, 'dragənit/ ▶ **n.** a marine fish that often lies partly buried in the seabed. The male is brightly colored. ● Two genera in the family Callionymidae: several species, in particular the European *Callionymus lyra*.
–ORIGIN Middle English (denoting a small dragon): from Old French, diminutive of *dragon* 'dragon.'

drag·on·fish /'dragən,fish/ ▶ **n.** (pl. **same** or **dragonfishes**) a deep-sea fish with a long slender body. ● a fish with fanglike teeth, a barbel on the chin, and luminous organs on the body (families Stomiatidae and Idiacanthidae). ● (**Antarctic dragonfish**) a fish of southern polar seas with a flattened head (family Bathydraconidae).

drag·on·fly /'dragən,flī/ ▶ **n.** (pl. **dragonflies**) a fast-flying long-bodied predatory insect with two pairs of large transparent wings that are spread out sideways at rest. The voracious aquatic larvae take up to five years to reach adulthood. Compare with DAMSELFLY. ● Suborder Anisoptera, order Odonata: several families. Dragonflies include darners and skimmers.

drag·on·nade /,dragə'nād/ ▶ **n.** one of a series of persecutions directed by Louis XIV against French Protestants, in which troops were quartered upon them.
–ORIGIN early 18th cent.: from French, from *dragon* 'dragon' (see DRAGOON).

drag·on's blood ▶ **n.** a red gum or powder that is derived from the fruit of certain palm trees and from the stem of the dragon tree and related plants.

drag·on's mouth ▶ **n.** another term for ARETHUSA.

drag·on tree ▶ **n.** a slow-growing palmlike tree of the agave family, which is native to the Canary Islands and yields dragon's blood. ● *Dracaena draco*, family Agavaceae.

dra·goon /drə'gōōn/ ▶ **n.** a member of any of several cavalry regiments in the British army. ■ historical a mounted infantryman armed with a short rifle or musket.
▶ **v.** [with obj.] coerce (someone) into doing something: *she had been dragooned into helping with the housework.*
–ORIGIN early 17th cent. (denoting a kind of carbine or musket, thought of as breathing fire): from French *dragon* 'dragon.'

drag queen ▶ **n.** a man who dresses up in women's clothes, typically for the purposes of entertainment.

drag race ▶ **n.** a race between two or more cars over a short distance, usually a quarter of a mile, as a test of acceleration.
–DERIVATIVES **drag rac·er n.**, **drag rac·ing n.**

drag·ster /'dragstər/ ▶ **n.** a car built or modified to take part in drag races.

drag strip ▶ **n.** a straight, paved track or section of road used for drag racing.

drail /'drāl/ ▶ **n.** Fishing a fishhook and line weighted with lead for dragging below the surface of the water.
–ORIGIN late 16th cent. (denoting part of a plow): from the obsolete verb *drail*, an alteration of *trail*.

drain /drān/ ▶ **v.** [with obj.] **1** cause the water or other liquid in (something) to run out, leaving it empty, dry, or drier: *we drained the swimming pool.* ■ cause or allow (liquid) to run off or out of something: *fry the pork and drain off any excess fat.* ■ make (land) drier by providing channels for water to flow away in: *the land was drained and the boggy ground reclaimed.* ■ (of a river) carry off the superfluous water from (a district): *the stream drains a wide moorland above the waterfall.* ■ [no obj.] (of water or another liquid) flow away from, out of, or into something: *the river drains into the Pacific* | figurative *Polly felt the blood drain from her face.* ■ [no obj.] become dry or drier as liquid runs off or away: *dishes left to drain* | *the plant should be watered well and allowed to drain.* ■ (of a person) drink the entire contents of (a glass or other container): *he seized the Scotch set before him and drained it.* ■ [no obj.] (of a feeling or emotion) become progressively less strongly felt: *gradually the tension and stress drained away.*
2 deprive of strength or vitality: *his limbs were drained of all energy* | *Ruth slumped down in her seat, drained by all that had happened.* ■ cause (money, energy, or another valuable resource) to be lost, wasted, or used up: *my mother's hospital bills are draining my income.* ■ [no obj.] (of such a resource) be lost, wasted, or used up: *votes and campaign funds drained away from the Republican candidate.*
3 Golf, informal (of a player) hole (a putt).
▶ **n. 1** a channel or pipe carrying off surplus liquid, esp. rainwater or liquid waste. ■ a tube for drawing off accumulating fluid from a body cavity or an abscess. ■ Electronics the part of a field-effect transistor to which the charge carriers flow after passing the gate.
2 [in sing.] a thing that uses up a particular resource: *nuclear power is a serious drain on the public purse.* ■ the continuous loss or expenditure of a particular resource: *the drain of our heritage.*
–PHRASES **go down the drain** informal be totally wasted: *the government must stop public money from going down the drain.*
–ORIGIN Old English *drēahnian*, *drēhnian* 'strain (liquid),' of Germanic origin; related to DRY.

drain·age /'drānij/ ▶ **n.** the action or process of draining something: *the pot must have holes in the base for good drainage* | *the drainage of wetlands.* ■ the means of removing surplus water or liquid waste; a system of drains.

drain·board /'drān,bôrd/ ▶ **n.** a sloping grooved board or surface, on which washed dishes are left to drain, typically into a sink.

drain·er /'drānər/ ▶ **n.** a device used to drain things, in particular a rack placed on a drainboard to hold washed dishes while they drain. ■ a drainboard. ■ a person or device that drains a flooded area.

drain·pipe /'drān,pīp/ ▶ **n.** a pipe for carrying off rainwater or liquid refuse from a building.

Draize test /drāz/ ▶ **n.** a pharmacological test in which a substance is introduced into the eye or applied to the skin of a laboratory animal in order to ascertain the likely effect of that substance on the corresponding human tissue.
–ORIGIN 1970s: named after John H. *Draize* (1900–92), the American pharmacologist who helped to develop this type of test.

d

Drake /drāk/, Sir Francis (*c.*1540–96), English sailor and explorer. In his ship the *Golden Hind* he was the first Englishman to circumnavigate the globe (1577–80). He also played an important part in the defeat of the Spanish Armada.

drake[1] /drāk/ ▶ **n.** a male duck: *ducks and drakes* | [as modifier] *a drake mallard.*
–ORIGIN Middle English: related to Low German *drake* and German *Enterich*.

drake[2] ▶ **n.** (in fishing) a natural or artificial mayfly, esp. a subadult or gravid female.
–ORIGIN Old English *draca*, from Latin *draco* 'dragon.'

Drake e·qua·tion Astronomy a speculative equation that gives an estimate of the likelihood of discovering intelligent extraterrestrial life in the galaxy, expressed as the product of a series of factors such as the number of stars, the fraction of stars with planets, the fraction of planets on which life evolves, the average lifetime of a civilization, etc. It was formulated by the US astronomer Frank Drake in 1961.

Dra·kens·berg Moun·tains /'dräkənz,bərg/ a mountain range in southern Africa that stretches northeast–southwest for a distance of 700 miles (1,126 km) through Lesotho and parts of South Africa. The highest peak is Thabana Ntlenyana (11,425 feet; 3,482 m).

Drake Pas·sage an area of ocean, noted for its violent storms, that connects the South Atlantic Ocean with the South Pacific Ocean and separates the southern tip of South America (Cape Horn) from the Antarctic Peninsula.
–ORIGIN named after Sir Francis DRAKE.

Drakes Bay /drāks/ an inlet of the Pacific Ocean, northwest of San Francisco in California, visited by Sir Francis Drake in 1579.

DRAM /'dē,ram/ ▶ **n.** Electronics a memory chip that depends upon an applied voltage to keep the stored data.
–ORIGIN acronym from *dynamic random-access memory*.

dram[1] /dram/ ▶ **n. 1** a small drink of whiskey or other spirits (often used in humorous imitation of Scottish speech): *a wee dram to ward off the winter chill.*
2 another term for DRACHM (sense 1).
–ORIGIN late Middle English (sense 2): from Old French *drame* or medieval Latin *drama*, variants of *dragme* and *dragma* (see DRACHM).

dram[2] ▶ **n.** the basic monetary unit of Armenia, equal to 100 luma.

dra·ma /'drämə/ ▶ **n. 1** a play for theater, radio, or television: *a gritty urban drama about growing up in Harlem.* ■ such works as a genre or style of literature: *Renaissance drama.*
2 an exciting, emotional, or unexpected series of events or set of circumstances: *a hostage drama* | *an afternoon of high drama at Fenway Park.*
–ORIGIN early 16th cent.: via late Latin from Greek *drama*, from *dran* 'do, act.'

Dram·a·mine /'dramə,mēn/ ▶ **n.** trademark an antihistamine compound used to counter nausea (esp. travel sickness).
–ORIGIN 1940s: from *dram-* (of unknown origin) + AMINE.

dra·ma queen ▶ **n.** informal a person who habitually responds to situations in a melodramatic way.

dra·mat·ic /drə'matik/ ▶ **adj. 1** [attrib.] of or relating to drama or the performance or study of drama: *the dramatic arts* | *a dramatic society.*

2 (of an event or circumstance) sudden and striking: *a dramatic increase in recorded crime.* ■ exciting or impressive: *he recalled his dramatic escape from the building | dramatic mountain peaks.* ■ (of a person or their behavior) intending or intended to create an effect; theatrical: *with a dramatic gesture, she put a hand to her brow.*
– DERIVATIVES **dra·mat·i·cal·ly** /-ik(ə)lē/ **adv.**
– ORIGIN late 16th cent.: via late Latin from Greek *dramatikos*, from *drama, dramat-* (see DRAMA).

dra·mat·ic i·ro·ny ▶ **n.** see IRONY[1].

dra·mat·ic mon·o·logue ▶ **n.** a poem in the form of a speech or narrative by an imagined person, in which the speaker inadvertently reveals aspects of their character while describing a particular situation or series of events.

d

dra·mat·ics /drəˈmatiks/ ▶ **plural n. 1** [often treated as sing.] the study or practice of acting in and producing plays: *amateur dramatics.*
2 theatrically exaggerated or overemotional behavior: *cut out the dramatics.*

dram·a·tis per·so·nae /ˈdrämətis pərˈsōnē/ ▶ **plural n.** [treated as sing. or pl.] the characters of a play, novel, or narrative.
– ORIGIN mid 18th cent.: Latin, literally 'persons of the drama.'

dram·a·tist /ˈdräməˌtist/ ▶ **n.** a person who writes plays.

dram·a·tize /ˈdräməˌtīz/ ▶ **v.** [with obj.] adapt (a novel) or present (a particular incident) as a play or movie: *the famous play that dramatized the Scopes trial.* ■ exaggerate the seriousness or importance of (an incident or situation): *they have a tendency to dramatize things.*
– DERIVATIVES **dram·a·ti·za·tion** /ˌdrämətiˈzāSHən/ **n.**

dram·a·turge /ˈdräməˌtərj/ (also **dramaturg**) ▶ **n.**
1 a dramatist.
2 a literary editor on the staff of a theater who consults with authors and edits texts.
– ORIGIN mid 19th cent.: via French and German from Greek *dramatourgos*, from *drama, dramat-* 'drama' + *-ergos* 'worker.'

dram·a·tur·gy /ˈdräməˌtərjē/ ▶ **n.** the theory and practice of dramatic composition: *studies of Shakespeare's dramaturgy.*
– DERIVATIVES **dram·a·tur·gic** /-jik/ **adj.**, **dram·a·tur·gi·cal** /ˌdräməˈtərjikəl/ **adj.**, **dram·a·tur·gi·cal·ly** /ˌdräməˈtərjik(ə)lē/ **adv.**

Dram·bu·ie /dramˈbo͞oē/ ▶ **n.** trademark a sweet Scotch whiskey liqueur.
– ORIGIN from Scottish Gaelic *dram buidheach* 'satisfying drink.'

dra·me·dy /ˈdrämədē/ ▶ **n.** (pl. **dramedies**) a movie, play, or broadcast program that combines elements of drama and comedy.

Drang nach O·sten /ˈdräNG näk ˈästən/ ▶ **n.** the former German policy of eastward expansion, esp. that espoused under Nazi rule.
– ORIGIN early 20th cent.: German, literally 'pressure toward the east.'

drank /draNGk/ past of DRINK.

drape /drāp/ ▶ **v.** [with obj.] arrange (cloth or clothing) loosely or casually on or around something: *she draped a shawl around her shoulders.* ■ adorn, cover, or wrap (someone or something) loosely with folds of cloth: *the body was draped in a blanket.* ■ let (oneself or a part of one's body) rest somewhere in a casual or relaxed way: *he draped an arm around her shoulders.* ■ [no obj.] (of fabric) hang or be able to hang in loose, graceful folds: *velvet drapes beautifully.*
▶ **n. 1** (**drapes**) long curtains: *Katherine pulled back the heavy velvet drapes.* ■ Brit. informal a man's suit consisting of a long jacket and narrow trousers, as worn by a Teddy boy: *teds dressed in Edwardian-style drapes and suede shoes.* ■ a cloth for covering parts of a patient's body other than that part on which a surgical operation is being performed.
2 [in sing.] the way in which a garment or fabric hangs: *by fixing the band lower down you obtain a fuller drape in the fabric.*
– DERIVATIVES **drape·y** (also **drapy**) **adj.**
– ORIGIN mid 19th cent.: back-formation from DRAPERY, influenced by French *draper* 'to drape.' The noun senses date from the early 20th cent.

drap·er /ˈdrāpər/ ▶ **n.** Brit. dated a person who sells cloth and dry goods.
– ORIGIN late Middle English (denoting a maker of woolen cloth): from Old French *drapier*, from *drap* 'cloth,' from late Latin *drappus*.

dra·per·y /ˈdrāpərē/ ▶ **n.** (pl. **draperies**) cloth coverings hanging in loose folds: *the hall of the school was hung with green drapery.* ■ (**draperies**) long curtains of heavy fabric. ■ the artistic arrangement of clothing in sculpture or painting: *the effigy is notable for its flowing drapery.*
– ORIGIN Middle English (in the sense 'cloth, fabrics'): from Old French *draperie*, from *drap* 'cloth' (see DRAPER).

dras·tic /ˈdrastik/ ▶ **adj.** likely to have a strong or far-reaching effect; radical and extreme: *a drastic reduction of staffing levels.*
– DERIVATIVES **dras·ti·cal·ly** /-ik(ə)lē/ **adv.**
– ORIGIN late 17th cent. (originally applied to the effect of medicine): from Greek *drastikos*, from *dran* 'do.'

drat /drat/ ▶ **exclam.** (often **drat someone/something**) a mild expression of anger or annoyance: *"Drat!" said Mitchell, kicking the fence | "Drat you!"*
– DERIVATIVES **drat·ted adj.**
– ORIGIN early 19th cent.: shortening of *od rat*, euphemism for *God rot*.

draught ▶ **n.** British spelling of DRAFT (sense 3 of the noun, sense 4 of the noun, sense 6 of the noun, sense 7 of the noun).
▶ **v. & adj.** British spelling of DRAFT.
– ORIGIN Middle English (in the sense 'drawing, pulling'; also 'something drawn, a load'): from Old Norse *dráttr*, of Germanic origin; related to German *Tracht*, also to DRAW. Compare with DRAFT.

draught horse ▶ **n.** British spelling of DRAFT HORSE.

draughts /draf(t)s/ ▶ **n.** Brit. checkers. See CHECKER[2] (sense 2).
– ORIGIN late Middle English: from DRAUGHT; related to obsolete *draught* in the sense 'move' (in chess or any similar game); compare with French *trait*, from Latin *tractus* 'a dragging.'

draughts·man ▶ **n.** British spelling of DRAFTSMAN.

draught·y ▶ **adj.** British spelling of DRAFTY.

Dra·va Riv·er /ˈdrävə/ (also **Drave**) a river that rises in northern Italy and flows for 456 miles (725 km) through southern Austria, Slovenia, and Croatia to join the Danube River near Osijek. It forms part of the border between Hungary and Croatia.

Dra·vid·i·an /drəˈvidēən/ ▶ **adj.** of, relating to, or denoting a family of languages spoken in southern India and Sri Lanka, or the peoples who speak them.
▶ **n. 1** this family of languages.
2 a member of any of the peoples speaking a Dravidian language.

> Dravidian languages were once spoken throughout the Indian subcontinent but were restricted to the south following the arrival of speakers of Indic languages c.1000 BC. Those still used, by over 160 million people, include Tamil, Kannada, Malayalam, and Telugu.

– ORIGIN from Sanskrit *drāviḍa* 'relating to the Tamils' (from *Draviḍa* 'Tamil') + -IAN.

draw /drô/ ▶ **v.** (past **drew** /dro͞o/; past participle **drawn** /drôn/) [with obj.] **1** produce (a picture or diagram) by making lines and marks, esp. with a pen or pencil, on paper: *he drew a map.* ■ produce an image of (someone or something) in such a way: *I asked her to draw me | [no obj.] she draws really well.* ■ trace or produce (a line or mark) on a surface: *she drew a wavering line down the board | figurative where will we draw the outer boundaries of this Europe?*
2 pull or drag (something such as a vehicle) so as to make it follow behind: *a cart drawn by two horses.* ■ pull or move (something) in a specified direction: *I drew back the blanket and uncovered the body.* ■ gently pull or guide (someone) in a specified direction: *"David," she whispered, **drawing him aside.*** ■ [no obj.] move in a slow steady way: *the driver slowed as he drew even with me | the train drew into the station.* ■ [no obj.] come to or arrive at a point in time or a specified point in a process: *the campaign **drew to a close** | the time for the parade itself is **drawing near**.* ■ pull (curtains, blinds, or other such coverings) shut or open: *do you want me to draw the drapes? | she **drew back** the curtains and looked out.* ■ make (wire) by pulling a piece of metal through successively smaller holes.
3 extract (an object or liquid) from a container or receptacle: *he drew his gun and peered into the gloomy apartment | the children went down to the pond to draw water | the syringe **drew off** most of the fluid* | (as adj. **drawn**) *he met them with a drawn sword.* ■ run (a bath): *she drew him a hot bath.* ■ (**draw something from**) obtain something from (a particular source): *an independent panel of judges drawn from members of the public | he draws inspiration from ordinary scenes and simple places.* ■ (**draw on**) use (one's experience, talents, or skills) as a resource: *Sue has a lot of past experience to draw on.* ■ obtain or withdraw (money) from a bank or other source: *this check **draws against** my personal account.* ■ Hunting search (cover) for game. ■ Bridge (of player) force the opponents to play (cards in a particular suit) by leading cards in that suit: *before establishing his diamonds, declarer must draw trumps.* ■ (**draw on**) suck smoke from (a cigarette or pipe). ■ [no obj.] (of a chimney, flue, or fire) allow air to flow in and upward freely, so that a fire can burn: *failure of a fire to draw properly can have a number of causes.* ■ take in (a breath): *Mrs. Feather drew a long breath and let it out.* ■ [no obj.] (of tea) be left standing so that the flavor is extracted from the leaves: *a pot of tea is allowed to draw.* ■ disembowel: *after a mockery of a trial he was **hanged, drawn, and quartered**.*
4 be the cause of (a specified response): *he drew criticism for his lavish spending.* ■ attract (someone) to come to a place or an event: *you really drew the crowds with your playing | customers drawn in by the reductions.* ■ (usu. **be drawn**) induce (someone) to reveal or do something: *I would rather not be **drawn into** your argument.* ■ direct or attract (someone's attention) to something: *it was an outrage and we had to draw people's attention to it.* ■ reach (a conclusion) by deduction or inference from a set of circumstances: *the moral to be drawn is that spending wins votes.* ■ formulate or perceive (a comparison or distinction): *the law drew a clear distinction between innocent and fraudulent misrepresentation.*
5 Golf hit (the ball) so that it travels slightly to the left (for a left-handed player, the right), usually as a result of spin given to the ball: *he had to learn to draw the ball—not least for the tee shots at Augusta.* Compare with FADE (sense 3 of the verb). ■ Billiards impart backspin to (the cue ball), making it move backwards after hitting an object ball.
6 (of a ship) require (a specified depth of water) to float in; have (a certain draft): *boats that **draw only a few inches of water**.*
7 [no obj.] (of a sail) be filled with wind.
8 Brit. finish (a contest or game) with an even score; tie: [with obj. and complement] *Brazil had drawn a stormy match 1–1.*
▶ **n. 1** an act of selecting names randomly, typically by extracting them from a bag or other container, to match competitors in a game or tournament: *the draw has been made for this year's tournament.*
2 a game that ends with the score even; a tie.
3 a person or thing that is very attractive or interesting: *the museum has turned out to be a big draw for schoolchildren in the city.*
4 an act of inhaling smoke from a cigar: *superb cigars offering tons of peppery smoke on each draw.*
5 an act of removing a gun from its holster in order to shoot.
6 Golf a shot causing the ball to deviate to the left (or, for a left-handed golfer, the right). ■ Billiards backspin imparted to a cue ball, causing it to move backwards after hitting an object ball.
– PHRASES **draw a bead on** see BEAD. **draw a blank** see BLANK. **draw blood** cause someone to bleed, esp. in the course of a fight: *the blow drew blood from the corner of his mouth | figurative she knew she'd drawn blood when the smile faded from his face.* **draw fire** attract hostile criticism, usually away from a more important target: *the vaccination campaign continued to draw fire.* **draw the line at** set a limit on what one is willing to do or accept, beyond which one will not go: *she drew the line at prostitution.* **draw lots** see LOT. **draw the short straw** see STRAW. **quick on the draw** very fast in taking one's gun from its holster. ■ very fast in acting or reacting.
– PHRASAL VERBS **draw back** choose not to do something that one was expected to do: *the government has **drawn back from** attempting reform.* **draw on** (of a period of time) pass by and approach its end: *he remembered sitting in silence with his grandmother as evening drew on.* **draw something on** put an item of clothing on: *she drew on her gloves.* **draw someone out** gently or subtly persuade someone to talk or become more expansive: *she drew me out and flattered me.* **draw something out** make something last longer: *the transition was long drawn out.* **draw up** come to a halt: *drivers drew up at the lights.* **draw something up** prepare a plan, proposal, agreement, or other document in detail: *they instructed an attorney to draw up a sales agreement.* **draw oneself up** make oneself stand in a stiffly upright manner: *Sarah drew herself up, full of indignation that he should presume to judge her.*
– ORIGIN Old English *dragan*, of Germanic origin; related to Dutch *dragen* and German *tragen*, also to DRAFT.

draw·back /ˈdrôˌbak/ ▶ **n. 1** a feature that renders something less acceptable; a disadvantage or problem: *the main drawback of fitting catalytic converters is the cost.*
2 an amount of excise or import duty remitted on imported goods that the importer re-exports rather than sells domestically.

draw·bar /ˈdrôˌbär/ ▶ **n. 1** a bar on a vehicle to which something can be attached to pull it or be pulled. ■ a coupler on a railroad car.
2 one of a number of bars that may be pulled out to control harmonics on an electric organ.

draw·bridge /ˈdrôˌbrij/ ▶ **n.** historical a bridge, esp. one over a castle's moat, that is hinged at one end so that it may be raised to prevent people's crossing or to allow vessels to pass under it.

drawbridge

draw·cord /ˈdrôˌkôrd/ ▶ n. Brit. another term for DRAWSTRING.

draw·down /ˈdrôˌdoun/ ▶ n. a reduction in the size or presence of a military force: *the unit is the first to leave Germany as part of the drawdown.* ■ a reduction in the volume of water in a lake or reservoir. ■ a withdrawal of oil or other commodity from stocks.

draw·ee /drôˈē/ ▶ n. the person or organization, typically a bank, who must pay a draft or bill.

draw·er /ˈdrô(ə)r/ ▶ n. **1** a boxlike storage compartment without a lid, made to slide horizontally in and out of a desk, chest, or other piece of furniture.
2 (**drawers**) dated or humorous underpants.
3 a person who draws something, in particular: ■ a person who writes a check. ■ a person who produces a drawing or design. ■ archaic another term for TAPSTER.
– DERIVATIVES **draw·er·ful** /-ˌfo͝ol/ n. (pl. **drawerfuls**).

draw·ing /ˈdrô-iNG/ ▶ n. **1** a picture or diagram made with a pencil, pen, or crayon rather than paint, esp. one drawn in monochrome: *a series of charcoal drawings on white paper.* ■ the art or skill or making such pictures or diagrams: *she took lessons in drawing.*
2 the selection of a winner or winners in a lottery or raffle: *entrants need not be present at the drawing.*

draw·ing board ▶ n. a large flat board on which paper may be spread for artists or designers to work on.
– PHRASES **back to the drawing board** used to indicate that an idea, scheme, or proposal has been unsuccessful and that a new one must be devised: *the government must go back to the drawing board and review the whole issue of youth training.* **on the drawing board** (of an idea, scheme, or proposal) under consideration and not yet ready to put into practice: *there are plans to enlarge the runway, but at present all this remains on the drawing board.*

draw·ing card /ˈdrô-iNG/ (Brit. **drawcard** /ˈdrôˌkärd/) ▶ n. informal a quality or feature that evokes interest or liking; an attraction: *rookie fireball flingers are the prime drawing cards of spring baseball.*

draw·ing pin ▶ n. British term for THUMBTACK.

draw·ing room ▶ n. a room in a large private house in which guests can be received and entertained. ■ a private compartment in a train, typically one that accommodates two or three people.
▶ adj. [attrib.] consciously refined, lighthearted, and elegant: *drawing-room small talk.* ■ (of a song or play) characterized by a polite observance of social proprieties: *a stock figure of Thirties drawing-room comedy.*
– ORIGIN mid 17th cent. (denoting a private room attached to a more public one): abbreviation of 16th-cent. *withdrawing-room* 'a room to withdraw to.'

draw·knife /ˈdrôˌnīf/ ▶ n. (pl. **drawknives** /-ˌnīvz/) a knife consisting of a blade with a handle at each end at right angles to it, which is drawn over a surface, toward the user, with a paring effect.

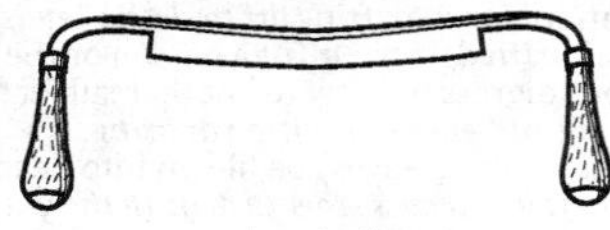
drawknife

drawl /drôl/ ▶ v. [no obj.] speak in a slow, lazy way with prolonged vowel sounds: [with direct speech] *"Suits me fine," he drawled.*
▶ n. [in sing.] a slow, lazy way of speaking or an accent with unusually prolonged vowel sounds: *a Texas drawl.*
– DERIVATIVES **drawl·er** n., **drawl·y** adj.

– ORIGIN late 16th cent.: probably originally slang, from Low German or Dutch *dralen* 'delay, linger.'

drawn /drôn/ past participle of DRAW.
▶ adj. (of a person or a person's face) looking strained from illness, exhaustion, anxiety, or pain: *Cathy was pale and drawn and she looked tired out.*

drawn but·ter ▶ n. melted butter.

drawn-out ▶ adj. (often **long-drawn-out**) lasting or seeming to last longer than is necessary: *a long-drawn-out courtship.*

drawn·work /ˈdrônˌwərk/ (also **drawn threadwork**) ▶ n. ornamental work on linen or other fabric, done by drawing out threads and usually with additional needlework.

draw pok·er ▶ n. a variety of poker in which each player is dealt five cards and, after the first round of betting, may discard some (usually up to three) of these cards and draw replacements from the dealer.

draw reins ▶ n. a pair of reins that are attached to a horse's saddle or girth and pass through the bit rings to the rider's hands.

draw·sheet /ˈdrôˌSHēt/ (also **draw sheet**) ▶ n. a sheet that is placed in such a way that it can be taken from under a patient or invalid without disturbing the bedclothes.

draw·string /ˈdrôˌstriNG/ ▶ n. a string in the seam of the material of a garment or a bag, which can be pulled to tighten or close it.

dray /drā/ ▶ n. a truck or cart for delivering beer barrels or other heavy loads, esp. a low one without sides.
– ORIGIN late Middle English (denoting a sledge): perhaps from Old English *dræge* 'dragnet,' related to *dragan* 'to pull' (see DRAW).

dray horse ▶ n. a large, powerful horse used to pull heavy loads.

dray·man /ˈdrāmən/ ▶ n. (pl. **draymen**) a person who delivers beer for a brewery.

DRC ▶ abbr. Democratic Republic of the Congo.

dread /dred/ ▶ v. [with obj.] anticipate with great apprehension or fear: *Jane was dreading the party* | [with infinitive] *I dread to think what Russell will say.* ■ archaic regard with great awe or reverence.
▶ n. **1** great fear or apprehension: *the thought of returning to New Jersey filled her with dread* | [in sing.] *I used to have a dread of Sunday afternoons.*
2 informal a person with dreadlocks. ■ (**dreads**) dreadlocks.
▶ adj. [attrib.] greatly feared; dreadful: *he was stricken with the dread disease and died.* ■ archaic regarded with awe; greatly revered: *that dread being we dare oppose.*
– ORIGIN Old English *ādrǣdan, ondrǣdan*; related to Old High German *intrātan.*

dread·ed /ˈdredid/ ▶ adj. [attrib.] regarded with great fear or apprehension: *the dreaded news came that Joe had been wounded* | humorous *the dreaded fax machine.*

dread·ful /ˈdredfəl/ ▶ adj. causing or involving great suffering, fear, or unhappiness; extremely bad or serious: *there's been a dreadful accident.* ■ extremely disagreeable: *the weather was dreadful.* ■ [attrib.] used to emphasize the degree to which something is the case, esp. something regarded with sadness or disapproval: *you're a dreadful flirt.* ■ (of a person) unwell or troubled: *she looked dreadful and she was struggling for breath* | *I feel dreadful—I hate myself.*
– DERIVATIVES **dread·ful·ness** n.

dread·ful·ly /ˈdredfəlē/ ▶ adv. **1** [often as submodifier] extremely: *you're dreadfully thin* | *I'm dreadfully sorry!* ■ very much: *I'll miss you dreadfully.*
2 very badly: *the company has performed dreadfully.*

dread·locks /ˈdredˌläks/ ▶ plural n. a hairstyle in which the hair is washed but not combed and twisted while wet into tight braids or ringlets hanging down on all sides.
– DERIVATIVES **dread·locked** adj.

dread·nought /ˈdredˌnôt/ (also **dreadnaught**) ▶ n. **1** historical a type of battleship introduced in the early 20th century, larger and faster than its predecessors and equipped entirely with large-caliber guns. [named after Britain's HMS *Dreadnought*, which was the first to be completed (1906).]
2 archaic a heavy overcoat for stormy weather.

dream /drēm/ ▶ n. a series of thoughts, images, and sensations occurring in a person's mind during sleep: *I had a recurrent dream about falling from great heights.* ■ [in sing.] a state of mind in which someone is or seems to be unaware of their immediate surroundings: *he had been walking around in a dream all day.* ■ a cherished aspiration, ambition, or ideal: *I fulfilled a childhood dream when I became champion* | *the girl of my dreams* | [as modifier] *they'd found their dream home.* ■ an unrealistic or self-deluding fantasy: *maybe he could get a job and earn some money—but he knew this was just a dream.* ■ a person or thing perceived as wonderful or perfect: *her new man's an absolute dream* | *it was a dream of a backhand* | *she's a couturier's dream.*
▶ v. (past and past participle **dreamed** or **dreamt** /dremt/) [no obj.] **1** experience dreams during sleep: *I dreamed about her last night.* ■ [with obj.] see, hear, or feel (something) in a dream: *maybe you dreamed it* | [with clause] *I dreamed that I was going to be executed.* ■ indulge in daydreams or fantasies, typically about something greatly desired: *she had dreamed of a trip to Italy.* ■ [with obj.] (**dream time away**) waste one's time in a lazy, unproductive way.
2 [with negative] contemplate the possibility of doing something or that something might be the case: *I wouldn't dream of foisting myself on you* | [with clause] *I never dreamed anyone would take offense.*
– PHRASES **beyond one's wildest dreams** bigger or better than could be reasonably expected: *stockbrokers command salaries beyond the wildest dreams of most workers.* **in your dreams** used in spoken English to assert that something much desired is not likely ever to happen. **in one's wildest dreams** [with negative] used to emphasize that a situation is beyond the scope of one's imagination: *she could never in her wildest dreams have imagined the summer weather in New York.* **like a dream** informal very well or successfully: *the car is still running like a dream.*
– PHRASAL VERBS **dream on** [in imperative] informal used, esp. in spoken English, as an ironic comment on the unlikely or impractical nature of a plan or aspiration: *Dean thinks he's going to get the job. Dream on, babe.* **dream something up** imagine or invent something: *he's been dreaming up new ways of attracting customers.*
– DERIVATIVES **dream·ful** /-fəl/ adj. (literary), **dream·less** adj.
– ORIGIN Middle English: of Germanic origin, related to Dutch *droom* and German *Traum*, and probably also to Old English *drēam* 'joy, music.'

dream·boat /ˈdrēmˌbōt/ ▶ n. informal a very attractive person, esp. a man.

dream·catch·er /ˈdrēmˌkaCHər, -ˌkeCH-/ ▶ n. a small hoop containing a horsehair mesh, or a similar construction of string or yarn, decorated with feathers and beads, believed to give its owner good dreams. Dreamcatchers were originally made by American Indians.

dreamcatcher

dream·er /ˈdrēmər/ ▶ n. a person who dreams or is dreaming. ■ a person who is unpractical or idealistic: *a rebellious young dreamer.*

dream·land /ˈdrēmˌland/ ▶ n. sleep regarded as a world of dreams: *she tries to lull herself into dreamland.* ■ an imagined and unrealistically ideal world: *there was always in the Cotton Club a certain dreamland aspect.*

dream·like /ˈdrēmˌlīk/ ▶ adj. having the qualities of a dream; unreal: *she snapped out of her dreamlike state.*

dream·scape /ˈdrēmˌskāp/ ▶ n. a landscape or scene with the strangeness or mystery characteristic of dreams: *surrealism's popular manifestations were the dreamscapes of Salvador Dalí.*

dream team ▶ n. a team of people perceived as the perfect combination for a particular purpose: *the two have been linked as the dream team that will revitalize New York Democrats.*

Dream·time /ˈdrēmˌtīm/ ▶ n. (in the mythology of some Australian Aborigines) the "golden age" when the first ancestors were created.

dream·work /ˈdrēmˌwərk/ ▶ n. Psychoanalysis the processes by which the unconscious mind alters the manifest content of dreams in order to conceal their real meaning from the dreamer.

dream·world /ˈdrēmˌwərld/ ▶ n. a fantastic or idealized view of life: *somebody who can live in a romantic dreamworld.*

dream·y /ˈdrēmē/ ▶ adj. (**dreamier, dreamiest**) (of a person) not practical; given to daydreaming: *a dreamy boy who grew up absorbed in poetry.* ■ having a magical or pleasantly unreal quality; dreamlike: *a slow dreamy melody.* ■ informal delightful; gorgeous: *I bet he was really dreamy.*
– DERIVATIVES **dream·i·ly** /-məlē/ adv., **dream·i·ness** n.

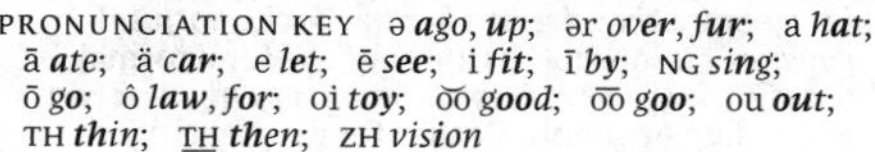
PRONUNCIATION KEY ə ago, up; ər over, fur; a hat; ā ate; ä car; e let; ē see; i fit; ī by; NG sing; ō go; ô law, for; oi toy; o͝o good; o͞o goo; ou out; TH thin; T͟H then; ZH vision

d

drear /dri(ə)r/ ▶ **adj.** literary term for DREARY.
– ORIGIN early 17th cent.: abbreviation.

drear·y /'dri(ə)rē/ ▶ **adj.** (**drearier, dreariest**) dull, bleak, and lifeless; depressing: *the dreary routine of working, eating, and trying to sleep.*
– DERIVATIVES **drear·i·ly** /'dri(ə)rəlē/ **adv.**, **drear·i·ness n.**
– ORIGIN Old English *drēorig* 'gory, cruel,' also 'melancholy,' from *drēor* 'gore,' of Germanic origin; related to German *traurig* 'sorrowful,' also to DROWSY, and probably to DRIZZLE.

dreck /drek/ (also **drek**) ▶ **n.** informal rubbish; trash: *this so-called art is pure dreck.*
– DERIVATIVES **dreck·ish adj.**, **dreck·y adj.**
– ORIGIN early 20th cent.: from Yiddish *drek* 'filth, dregs,' from a Germanic base shared by Old English *threax*; probably related to Greek *skōr* 'dung.'

dredge[1] /drej/ ▶ **v.** [with obj.] clean out the bed of (a harbor, river, or other area of water) by scooping out mud, weeds, and rubbish with a dredge. ■ bring up or clear (something) from a river, harbor, or other area of water with a dredge: *mud was dredged out of the harbor* | [no obj.] *they start to* **dredge for** *oysters in November.* ■ (**dredge something up**) bring to people's attention an unpleasant or embarrassing fact or incident that had been forgotten: *I don't understand why you had to dredge up this story.*
▶ **n.** an apparatus for bringing up objects or mud from a river or seabed by scooping or dragging. ■ a dredger.
– ORIGIN late 15th cent. (as a noun; originally in *dredge-boat*): perhaps related to Middle Dutch *dregghe* 'grappling hook.'

dredge[2] ▶ **v.** [with obj.] sprinkle (food) with a powdered substance, typically flour or sugar: *dredge the bananas with sugar and cinnamon.*
– ORIGIN late 16th cent.: from obsolete *dredge* 'sweetmeat, mixture of spices,' from Old French *dragie*, perhaps via Latin from Greek *tragēmata* 'spices.' Compare with DRAGÉE.

dredg·er /'drejər/ ▶ **n.** a barge or other vessel designed for dredging harbors or other bodies of water.

dree /drē/ ▶ **v.** (**drees, dreeing, dreed**) [with obj.] Scottish or archaic endure (something burdensome or painful): *he dreed pain and dolor.*
– PHRASES **dree one's weird** submit to one's destiny.
– ORIGIN Old English *drēogan*, of Germanic origin; related to Old Norse *drýgja* 'practice, perpetrate.'

dregs /dregz/ ▶ **plural n.** the remnants of a liquid left in a container, together with any sediment or grounds: *coffee dregs.* ■ the most worthless part or parts of something: *the dregs of society.*
– DERIVATIVES **dreg·gy** /'dregē/ **adj.**
– ORIGIN Middle English: probably of Scandinavian origin and related to Swedish *drägg* (plural).

drei·del /'drādl/ ▶ **n.** a small four-sided spinning top with a Hebrew letter on each side, used by the Jews. ■ a gambling game played with such a top, esp. at Hanukkah.
– ORIGIN 1930s: from Yiddish *dreydl*; compare with German *drehen* 'to turn.'

Drei·ser /'drīzər/, Theodore (Herman Albert) (1871–1945), US novelist. His first novel, *Sister Carrie* (1900), caused controversy for its frank treatment of the heroine's sexuality and ambition. Other notable works: *An American Tragedy* (1925) and *America Is Worth Saving* (1941).

drek ▶ **n.** variant spelling of DRECK.

drench /drenCH/ ▶ **v.** [with obj.] **1** wet thoroughly; soak: *I fell in the stream and got drenched* | (as noun **drenching**) *a severe drenching would kill his uncle.* ■ cover (something) liberally or thoroughly: *cool patios drenched in flowers.*
2 forcibly administer a drug in liquid form orally to (an animal).
▶ **n.** a dose of medicine administered to an animal. ■ archaic a draft of a medicinal or poisonous liquid.
– ORIGIN Old English *drencan* 'force to drink,' *drenc* 'a drink or draft,' of Germanic origin; related to German *tränken* (verb), *Trank* (noun), also to DRINK.

Dres·den[1] /'drezdən/ a city in eastern Germany, the capital of Saxony, on the Elbe River; pop. 504,800 (est. 2006). It was almost totally destroyed by Allied bombing in 1945.

Dres·den[2] (also **Dresden china**) ▶ **n.** porcelain ware with elaborate decoration and delicate colorings, made originally at Dresden and (since 1710) at nearby Meissen: [as modifier] *a fine Dresden china cup.*

dress /dres/ ▶ **v. 1** [no obj.] put on one's clothes: *Graham showered and dressed quickly* | *I'll go and get* **dressed.** ■ [with adverbial] wear clothes in a particular way or of a particular type: *she's nice-looking and* **dresses well** | (**be dressed**) *he was dressed in jeans and a thick sweater.* ■ [with obj.] put clothes on (someone): *they dressed her in a white hospital gown.* ■ put on clothes appropriate for a formal occasion: *we* **dressed for dinner** *every night.* ■ [with obj.] design or supply clothes for (a celebrity): *for over four decades he dressed the royal family.* ■ [with obj.] decorate (something) in an artistic or attractive way: *they had dressed the doorframes with sprays of bittersweet.*
2 [with obj.] treat or prepare (something) in a certain way, in particular: ■ clean, treat, or apply a dressing to (a wound). ■ clean and prepare (food, esp. poultry or shellfish) for cooking or eating: (as adj. **dressed**) *dressed crab.* ■ add a dressing to (a salad). ■ apply a fertilizing substance to (a field, garden, or plant). ■ complete the preparation or manufacture of (leather or fabric) by treating its surface in some way. ■ smooth the surface of (stone): (as adj. **dressed**) *a tower built of dressed stone.* ■ arrange or style (one's own or someone else's hair), esp. in an elaborate way.
3 [with obj.] Military draw up (troops) in the proper alignment. ■ [no obj.] (of troops) come into such an alignment.
4 [with obj.] prepare (an artificial fly) for use in fishing: (as adj. **dressed**) *a dressed wet fly.*
▶ **n. 1** a one-piece garment for a woman or girl that covers the body and extends down over the legs.
2 clothing of a specified kind for men or women: *traditional African dress* | figurative *the underlying theme is recognizable even when it appears in feminist dress.* ■ [as modifier] denoting military uniform or other clothing used on formal or ceremonial occasions: *a dress suit.*
– PHRASES **dressed to kill** wearing glamorous clothes intended to create a striking impression. **dressed to the nines** dressed very elaborately.
– PHRASAL VERBS **dress down** dress informally: *Sue dressed down in old jeans and a white blouse.* **dress someone down** informal reprimand someone. **dress ship** decorate a ship with flags, for a special occasion. **dress up** dress in smart or formal clothes. ■ dress in a special costume for fun or as part of an entertainment: *he dressed up as a gorilla.* **dress something up** present something in such a way that it appears better than it really is: *the company dressed up the figures a little.*
– ORIGIN Middle English (in the sense 'put straight'): from Old French *dresser* 'arrange, prepare,' based on Latin *directus* 'direct, straight.'

dres·sage /'dresäZH/ ▶ **n.** the art of riding and training a horse in a manner that develops obedience, flexibility, and balance.
– ORIGIN 1930s: from French, literally 'training.'

dress cir·cle ▶ **n.** the first level of seats above the ground floor in a theater.

dress coat ▶ **n.** another term for TAILCOAT.

dress code ▶ **n.** a set of rules, usually written and posted, specifying the required manner of dress at a school, office, club, restaurant, etc.: *while the dress code doesn't require two-tone shoes, you will get turned away if you wear jeans.* ■ the customary style of dress of a specified group: *jeans or shorts, the standard dress code for producer types.*

dress-down ▶ **adj.** of or relating to dress that is informal or less formal than would be expected: *his genius for casual, dress-down clothes* | *at his company, 'dress-down day' lasts all week.*

dress-down Fri·day ▶ **n.** another term for CASUAL FRIDAY.

dres·ser[1] /'dresər/ ▶ **n.** a chest of drawers. ■ a sideboard with shelves above for storing and displaying plates and kitchen utensils.
– ORIGIN late Middle English (denoting a kitchen sideboard or table on which food was prepared): from Old French *dresseur*, from *dresser* 'prepare' (see DRESS).

dres·ser[2] ▶ **n. 1** [usu. with adj.] a person who dresses in a specified way: *a snappy dresser.* ■ a person who habitually dresses in a smart or elegant way: *she's gorgeous—and she's a dresser.*
2 a person whose job is to look after theatrical costumes and help actors to dress.
3 a person who prepares, treats, or finishes a material or piece of equipment.

dress·ing /'dresiNG/ ▶ **n. 1** (also **salad dressing**) a sauce for salads, typically one consisting of oil and vinegar mixed together with herbs or other flavorings: *vinaigrette dressing.* ■ stuffing: *turkey with apple dressing.*
2 a piece of material placed on a wound to protect it: *an antiseptic dressing.*
3 size or stiffening used in the finishing of fabrics.
4 a fertilizing substance such as compost or manure spread over or plowed into land.

dress·ing-down ▶ **n.** [in sing.] informal a severe reprimand: *the secretary received a public dressing-down.*

dress·ing gown ▶ **n.** a long loose robe, typically worn after getting out of bed or bathing.

dress·ing room ▶ **n.** a room in which actors change clothes before and after their performance. ■ a small room or cubicle in a clothing store, used by customers to try on clothes.

dress·ing ta·ble ▶ **n.** a table with a mirror and drawers for cosmetics, etc., used while dressing or applying makeup.

dress·mak·er /'dres,mākər/ ▶ **n.** a person whose job is making women's clothes.
– DERIVATIVES **dress·mak·ing** /-kiNG/ **n.**

dress pa·rade ▶ **n.** a military parade in full dress uniform.

dress re·hears·al ▶ **n.** the final rehearsal of a live show, in which everything is done as it would be in a real performance.

dress shield ▶ **n.** a piece of waterproof material fastened in the armpit of a dress to protect it from perspiration.

dress shirt ▶ **n.** a man's white shirt worn with a bow tie and a dinner jacket on formal occasions. ■ a man's long-sleeved shirt, suitable for wearing with a tie.

dress·y /'dresē/ ▶ **adj.** (**dressier, dressiest**) (of clothes) suitable for a festive or formal occasion: *wear something dressy, Kate, we're going to a cocktail party.* ■ requiring or given to wearing such clothes: *the sweater can be worn under a blazer for more dressy events.*

drew /dro͞o/ past of DRAW.

Drex·el /'dreksəl/, Anthony Joseph (1826–93), US banker and philanthropist. He joined his father's brokerage firm in 1847 and merged with J. P. Morgan in 1871, making Drexel, Morgan, and Co. the most powerful investment banking house in the US. He was the founder 1892 and benefactor of Drexel Institute of Technology.

drey /drā/ ▶ **n.** (pl. **dreys**) the nest of a squirrel, typically in the form of a mass of twigs in a tree.
– ORIGIN early 17th cent.: of unknown origin.

Drey·fus /'drāfəs, 'drī-/, Alfred (1859–1935), French army officer. In 1894, he was falsely accused of providing military secrets to the Germans; his trial and imprisonment caused a major political crisis in France. He was eventually fully exonerated in 1906.

drib·ble /'dribəl/ ▶ **v. 1** [no obj.] (of a liquid) fall slowly in drops or a thin stream: *rain dribbled down the window.* ■ [with obj.] pour (a liquid) in such a way: *he dribbled cream into his coffee.* ■ allow saliva to run from the mouth: *his mouth was open and he was dribbling.*
2 [with obj.] (chiefly in soccer, field hockey, and basketball) take (the ball) forward past opponents with slight touches of the feet or the stick, or (in basketball) by continuous bouncing: *he attempted to dribble the ball from the goal area* | [no obj.] *he dribbled past a swarm of defenders.*
▶ **n. 1** a thin stream of liquid; a trickle: *a dribble of blood.* ■ saliva running from the mouth.
2 (in soccer, hockey, and basketball) an act or instance of taking the ball forward with repeated slight touches or bounces.
– DERIVATIVES **drib·bler** /-b(ə)lər/ **n.**
– ORIGIN mid 16th cent.: frequentative of obsolete *drib*, variant of DRIP. The original sense was 'shoot an arrow short or wide of its target,' which was also a sense of *drib*.

drib·let /'driblit/ ▶ **n.** a thin stream or small drop of liquid: *driblets of spittle run from her mouth.* ■ a small or insignificant amount: *the prisoners were let out in driblets.*
– ORIGIN late 16th cent. (in the sense 'small sum of money'): from obsolete *drib* (see DRIBBLE) + -LET.

dribs and drabs /'dribz and 'drabz/ ▶ **plural n.** (**in dribs and drabs**) informal in small scattered or sporadic amounts: *doing the work in dribs and drabs.*
– ORIGIN mid 19th cent.: from obsolete *drib* (see DRIBBLE) and *drab* (by reduplication).

dried /drīd/ past and past participle of DRY.

dri·er[1] /'drīər/ ▶ **adj.** comparative of DRY.

dri·er[2] ▶ **n.** variant spelling of DRYER.

drift /drift/ ▶ **v.** [no obj.] **1** be carried slowly by a current of air or water: *the cabin cruiser started to drift downstream* | figurative *excited voices drifted down the hall.* ■ [with adverbial of direction] (of a person) walk slowly, aimlessly, or casually: *people began to drift away.* ■ [with adverbial] move passively, aimlessly, or involuntarily into a certain situation or condition: *I was drifting off to sleep* | *Lewis and his father drifted apart.* ■ (of a person or their attention) digress or stray to another subject: *I noticed my audience's attention drifting.*
2 (esp. of snow or leaves) be blown into heaps by the wind: *fallen leaves start to drift in the gutters* | (as adj. **drifting**) *drifting snow.*
▶ **n. 1** [in sing.] a continuous slow movement from one place to another: *there was a drift to the towns.* ■ the deviation of a vessel, aircraft, or projectile from its intended or expected course as the result of currents or winds: *the pilot had not noticed any appreciable drift.* ■ a steady movement or development from one thing toward another, esp. one that is perceived as unwelcome: *the drift*

toward a more repressive style of policing. ■ a state of inaction or indecision: *after so much drift, any expression of enthusiasm is welcome.*
2 [in sing.] the general intention or meaning of an argument or someone's remarks: *maybe I'm too close to the forest to see the trees, **if you catch my drift**.*
3 a large mass of snow, leaves, or other material piled up or carried along by the wind. ■ Geology glacial and fluvioglacial deposits left by retreating ice sheets. ■ a large mass of flowering plants growing together: *a drift of daffodils.*
4 Mining a horizontal or inclined passage following a mineral vein or coal seam.
– DERIVATIVES **drift·y** adj.
– ORIGIN Middle English (in the sense 'mass of snow, leaves, etc'): originally from Old Norse *drift* 'snowdrift, something driven'; in later use from Middle Dutch *drift* 'course, current'; related to DRIVE.

drift·er /'driftər/ ▶ n. **1** a person who is continually moving from place to place, without any fixed home or job.
2 a fishing boat equipped with a drift net.

drift·fish /'drift,fisн/ ▶ n. (pl. **same** or **driftfishes**) a slender-bodied bottom-dwelling fish found in the deeper waters of warm seas. ● Family Nomeidae (or Stromateidae): several genera, in particular *Ariomma.*

drift ice ▶ n. detached pieces of ice drifting with the wind or ocean currents.

drift net (also **driftnet**) ▶ n. a large net for herring and similar fish, kept upright by weights at the bottom and floats at the top and allowed to drift with the tide.
– DERIVATIVES **drift net·ter** n., **drift net·ting** n.

drift pin ▶ n. a steel pin driven into a hole in a piece of metal to enlarge, shape, or align the hole.

drift·wood /'drift,wo͝od/ ▶ n. pieces of wood that are floating on the sea or have been washed ashore.

drill¹ /dril/ ▶ n. **1** a hand tool, power tool, or machine with a rotating cutting tip or reciprocating hammer or chisel, used for making holes. ■ such a tool used by a dentist for cutting away part of a tooth before filling it.
2 instruction or training in military exercises: *parade-ground drill.* ■ intensive instruction or training in something, typically by means of repeated exercises: *tables can be mastered by drill and practice | language-learning drills.* ■ a rehearsal of the procedure to be followed in an emergency: *air-raid drills.* ■ (**the drill**) informal the correct or recognized procedure or way of doing something: *he didn't know the drill.*
3 a predatory mollusk that bores into the shells of other mollusks in order to feed on the soft tissue. ● Family Muricidae, class Gastropoda: several genera and species, in particular the American **oyster drill** (*Urosalpinx cinerea*), which is a serious pest of oyster beds.

hand drill

▶ v. [with obj.] **1** produce (a hole) in something by or as if by boring with a drill: *drill holes through the tiles for the masonry pins.* ■ make a hole in (something) by boring with a drill: *a power tool for drilling wood.* ■ [no obj.] make a hole in or through something by using a drill: *do not attempt to drill through a joist* | figurative *his eyes drilled into her.* ■ [no obj.] sink a borehole in order to obtain a certain substance, typically oil or water: *they are licensed to **drill for** oil in the area* | (as noun **drilling**) *drilling should begin next year.* ■ (of a dentist) cut away part of (a tooth) before filling it. ■ informal (of a sports player) hit, throw, or kick (a ball or puck) hard and in a straight line: *Rose drilled a ball deep to right center.*
2 subject (someone) to military training exercises: *a sergeant was drilling new recruits.* ■ [no obj.] (of a person) take part in such exercises: *the troops were drilling.* ■ instruct (someone) in something by the means of repeated exercises or practice: *I reacted instinctively because I had been drilled to do just that.* ■ (**drill something into**) cause (someone) to learn something by repeating it regularly: *his mother had drilled into him the need to pay for one's sins.*
– PHRASAL VERBS **drill down** Computing access data that is in a lower level of a hierarchically structured database: *just click on a button and drill down until you find the level of detail you require* | [as modifier] *a drill-down menu of topics.*
– DERIVATIVES **drill·er** n.
– ORIGIN early 17th cent.: from Middle Dutch *drillen* 'bore, turn in a circle.'

drill² ▶ n. a machine that makes small furrows, sows seed in them, and then covers the sown seed. ■ a small furrow, esp. one made by such a machine. ■ a ridge with such a furrow on top. ■ a row of plants sown in such a furrow: *drills of lettuces.*
▶ v. [with obj.] (of a person or machine) sow (seed) with a drill: *crops drilled in autumn.* ■ plant (the ground) in furrows: (as noun **drilling**) *accurate ridging and drilling make hoeing much easier.*
– ORIGIN early 18th cent. (as a noun in the sense 'small furrow'): perhaps from DRILL¹.

drill³ ▶ n. a dark brown baboon with a short tail and a naked blue or purple rump, found in the rain forests of West Africa. Compare with MANDRILL. ● *Mandrillus leucophaeus*, family Cercopithecidae.
– ORIGIN mid 17th cent.: probably a local word. Compare with MANDRILL.

drill⁴ ▶ n. a coarse twilled cotton or linen fabric.
– ORIGIN early 18th cent.: abbreviation of earlier *drilling*, from German *Drillich*, from Latin *trilix* 'triple-twilled,' from *tri-* 'three' + *licium* 'thread.'

drill·ing rig ▶ n. a large structure with equipment for drilling an oil well.

drill·mas·ter /'dril,mastər/ ▶ n. one who instructs or leads others, esp. recruits, in military drills and marching. ■ a rigorous, exacting, or severe instructor; a martinet.

drill press ▶ n. a machine tool for drilling holes, set on a fixed stand.

drill ser·geant ▶ n. a noncommissioned officer who trains soldiers in basic military skills.

drill stem ▶ n. a rotating rod or cylinder used in drilling.

drill·stock /'dril,stäk/ ▶ n. the part of a drilling tool or machine that holds the bit.

dri·ly ▶ adv. variant spelling of DRYLY.

Dri·na Riv·er /'drēnə/ a river that flows for 285 miles (459 km), partly along the border between Bosnia and Herzegovina and Serbia, into the Sava River west of Belgrade in Serbia.

drink /drinɢk/ ▶ v. (past **drank** /drаɴɢk/; past participle **drunk** /drəɴɢk/) [with obj.] **1** take (a liquid) into the mouth and swallow: *we sat by the fire, drinking our coffee* | [no obj.] *he drank thirstily.* ■ [no obj.] consume or be in the habit of consuming alcohol, esp. to excess: *she doesn't drink or smoke | he **drank himself into a stupor*** | (as noun **drinking**) *Les was ordered to cut down his drinking.* ■ [no obj.] (**drink up**) consume the rest of a drink, esp. in a rapid manner. ■ informal (of a plant or a porous substance) absorb (moisture). ■ [no obj.] (of wine) have a specified flavor or character when drunk: *this wine is really drinking beautifully.*
2 (**drink something in**) watch or listen to something with eager pleasure or interest: *she strolled to the window to drink in the view.*
▶ n. a liquid that can be swallowed as refreshment or nourishment: *cans of soda and other drinks | a table covered with food and drink.* ■ a quantity of liquid swallowed: *he had a drink of water.* ■ alcohol, or the habitual or excessive consumption of alcohol: *the effects of too much drink | they both **took to drink**.* ■ a glass of liquid, esp. when alcoholic: *we went for a drink.* ■ (**the drink**) informal the sea or another large area of water.
– PHRASES **drink and drive** drive a vehicle while under the influence of alcohol. **drink deep** take a large draft or drafts of something: figurative *he learned to **drink deep of** the Catholic tradition.* **drink someone's health** express one's good wishes for someone by raising one's glass and drinking a small amount. **drink (a toast) to** celebrate or wish for the good fortune of someone or something by raising one's glass and drinking a small amount. **drink someone under the table** informal consume as much alcohol as one's drinking companion without becoming as drunk. **I'll drink to that** uttered to express one's agreement with or approval of a statement.
– ORIGIN Old English *drincan* (verb), *drinc* (noun), of Germanic origin; related to Dutch *drinken* and German *trinken.*

drink·a·ble /'drinɢkəbl/ ▶ adj. (of a liquid) fit to drink; potable: *a supply of drinkable water.* ■ informal (of a drink) pleasant to taste; palatable: *a very drinkable red wine.*

drink-driv·ing ▶ n. British term for DRUNK DRIVING.
– DERIVATIVES **drink-driv·er** n.

drink·er /'drinɢkər/ ▶ n. a person who drinks a particular drink: *coffee drinkers.* ■ a person who drinks alcohol, esp. to excess: *a heavy drinker.*

drink·ing foun·tain ▶ n. a device producing a small jet of water for drinking.

drink·ing song ▶ n. a hearty song, typically concerning drink and having bawdy lyrics, which is sung while drinking alcohol.

drip /drip/ ▶ v. (**drips, dripping, dripped**) [no obj.] let fall or be so wet as to shed small drops of liquid: *the faucet won't stop dripping | his hands were **dripping with** blood.* ■ [with adverbial] (of liquid) fall in small drops: *water dripped from her clothing.* ■ [with obj.] cause or allow (a liquid) to fall in such a way: *the candle was dripping wax down one side.* ■ display a copious amount or degree of a particular quality or thing: *the women were **dripping with** gold and diamonds* | [with obj.] *her voice dripped sarcasm.*
▶ n. **1** a small drop of a liquid: *she put the bucket on top of the dresser to catch the drips.* ■ [in sing.] the action or sound of liquid falling steadily in small drops: *the drip, drip, drip of the leak in the roof.* ■ short for DRIP FEED.
2 informal a weak and ineffectual person.
3 Architecture a projection or groove on the underside of a cornice, windowsill, or molding that prevents rain from running down the wall below. Compare with DRIPSTONE.
– ORIGIN Old English *dryppan*, *drȳpen*, of Germanic origin; related to Danish *dryppe*, also to DROP.

drip-dry ▶ adj. (of a fabric or garment) capable of drying without creasing when hung up after washing: *drip-dry shirts.*
▶ v. [no obj.] (of fabric or a garment) become dry without forming creases when hung up after washing. ■ [with obj.] dry (fabric or a garment) by hanging it up in this way: *it's easy to wash and simple to drip-dry.*

drip feed ▶ n. a device for introducing fluid drop by drop into a system, e.g., lubricating oil into an engine. ■ Medicine a device that passes fluid, nutrients, or drugs drop by drop into a patient's body on a continuous basis, usually intravenously: *he had been **on a drip feed** for several days.*
▶ v. (**drip-feed**) [with obj.] introduce (fluid) drop by drop: *the oiler drip-feeds oil onto all drive chains.* ■ supply (a patient) with fluid, nutrients, or drugs through a drip feed.

drip·less /'drip,ləs/ ▶ adj. designed to prevent dripping: *dripless valve.*

drip·ping /'dripinɢ/ ▶ n. (**drippings**) fat that has melted and dripped from roasting meat, used in cooking. ■ wax, fat, or other liquid produced from something by the effect of heat.
▶ adj. extremely wet: [as submodifier] ***dripping** wet hair.*

drip·py /'dripē/ ▶ adj. (**drippier, drippiest**) **1** informal weak, ineffectual, or sloppily sentimental: *a drippy love song.*
2 tending to drip: *drippy food.*
– DERIVATIVES **drip·pi·ly** /'dripilē/ adv., **drip·pi·ness** n.

drip·stone /'drip,stōn/ ▶ n. **1** Architecture a molding over a door or window that deflects rain and enhances the opening, typically in medieval architecture.
2 Geology rock deposited by precipitation from dripping water, such as that which forms stalactites and stalagmites.

drive /drīv/ ▶ v. (past **drove** /drōv/; past participle **driven** /'drivən/) **1** [no obj.] operate and control the direction and speed of a motor vehicle: *he got into his car and drove off | they drove back into town.* ■ (of a motor vehicle) travel under the control of a driver: *a car drives up, and a man gets out | a stream of black cars drove by.* ■ [with obj.] own or use (a specified type of motor vehicle): *Sue drives an old Chevy.* ■ be licensed or competent to drive a motor vehicle: *I take it you can drive?* ■ [with obj.] convey (someone) in a vehicle, esp. a private car: *Shelley drove him to the supermarket.*
2 [with obj.] propel or carry along by force in a specified direction: *the wind will drive you onshore.* ■ [no obj.] (of wind, water, or snow) move or fall with great force: *the snow **drove against** him.* ■ (of a source of power) provide the energy to set and keep (an engine or piece of machinery) in motion: *turbines driven by steam.* ■ Electronics (of a device) power or operate (another device): *the interface can be used to drive a printer.* ■ force (a stake or nail) into place by hitting or pushing it: *nails are driven through the boards.* ■ bore (a tunnel). ■ (in ball games) hit or kick (the ball) hard with a free swing of the bat, racket, or foot. ■ Golf strike (a ball) from the tee, typically with a driver.
3 [with obj.] urge or force (animals or people) to move in a specified direction: *they drove a flock of sheep through the center of the city | the French infantry were driven back.* ■ compel to leave: *troops drove out the demonstrators | he wanted to drive me away.*
4 [with obj.] (of a fact or feeling) compel (someone) to act in a particular way, esp. one that is considered undesirable or inappropriate: *he was driven by ambition* | [with obj. and infinitive] *some people are driven to murder their tormentors* | (as adj. **driven**) *my husband is a driven man.* ■ bring (someone) forcibly into a specified negative state: *the thought **drove** him **to despair*** | [with obj. and complement] *my laziness*

d

d

drives my wife crazy. ■ force (someone) to work to an excessive extent: *you're driving yourself too hard.* ■ cause (something abstract) to happen or develop: *the consumer has been driving the economy for a number of years | we need to allow market forces to drive growth in the telecommunications sector.*
▶ n. **1** a trip or journey in a car: *they went for a drive in the country.* ■ [in names] a street or road: *Hammond Drive.* ■ short for DRIVEWAY.
2 Psychology an innate, biologically determined urge to attain a goal or satisfy a need: *her emotional and sexual drives.* ■ the determination and ambition of a person to achieve something: *her drive has sustained her through some shattering personal experiences.*
3 an organized effort by a number of people to achieve a particular purpose, often to raise money: *we're planning a massive membership drive.* ■ Football a series of offensive plays that advance the ball for the purpose of a score: *an 80-yard scoring drive.*
4 the transmission of power to machinery or to the wheels of a motor vehicle. ■ (in a car with automatic transmission) the position of the gear selector in which the car will move forward, changing gears automatically as required: *he threw the car into drive.* ■ Computing short for DISK DRIVE.
5 (in ball games) a forceful stroke made with a free swing of the bat, racket, or foot against the ball. ■ Golf a shot from the tee.
6 an act of driving a group of animals to a particular destination.
– PHRASES **drive something home** see HOME. **what someone is driving at** the point that someone is attempting to make: *I don't understand what you're driving at.*
– DERIVATIVES **driv·a·bil·i·ty** /ˌdrīvəˈbilitē/ (also **driveability**) n., **driv·a·ble** (also **driveable**) adj.
– ORIGIN Old English *drīfan* 'urge (a person or animal) to go forward,' of Germanic origin; related to Dutch *drijven* and German *treiben.*

drive bay ▶ n. Computing a space inside a computer in which a floppy disk, hard disk, or disk drive can be accommodated.

drive belt ▶ n. a belt that transmits drive from a motor, engine, or line shaft to a moving part or machine tool.

drive-by ▶ adj. [attrib.] (of a shooting or other act) carried out from a passing vehicle: *a drive-by shooting.* ■ informal superficial or casual; hurried: *they practice drive-by journalism rather than trying to elevate the level of discussion.*
▶ n. a shooting carried out from a passing vehicle.

drive-by-wire ▶ n. [often as modifier] a semiautomatic and normally computer-regulated system for controlling the engine, handling, suspension, and other functions of a motor vehicle. Also called STEER-BY-WIRE.

drive chain ▶ n. an endless chain with links that engage with toothed wheels in order to transmit power from one shaft to another in an engine or machine tool.

drive-in ▶ adj. [attrib.] denoting a facility such as a restaurant that one can visit without leaving one's car: *it looked like the screen from an old drive-in theater.*
▶ n. a facility of this type.

driv·el /ˈdrivəl/ ▶ n. silly nonsense: *don't talk such drivel!*
▶ v. (**drivels, driveling, driveled**; Brit. **drivels, drivelling, drivelled**) [no obj.] **1** talk nonsense: *he was driveling on about the glory days.*
2 archaic let saliva or mucus flow from the mouth or nose; dribble.
– DERIVATIVES **driv·el·er** (Brit. **driveller**) n.
– ORIGIN Old English *dreflian* (sense 2 of the verb), of uncertain origin; perhaps related to DRAFF.

drive·line /ˈdrīvˌlīn/ ▶ n. another term for DRIVETRAIN.

driv·en /ˈdrivən/ past participle of DRIVE.
▶ adj. **1** [in combination] operated, moved, or controlled by a specified person or source of power: *a chauffeur-driven limousine | wind-driven sand.* ■ motivated or determined by a specified factor or feeling: *a market-driven response to customer needs.*
2 (of snow) piled into drifts or made smooth by the wind: figurative *she was as pure as the driven snow.*

driv·er /ˈdrīvər/ ▶ n. **1** a person who drives a vehicle: *a taxi driver | student drivers.* ■ a person who drives a specified kind of animal: *mule drivers.*
2 a wheel or other part in a mechanism that receives power directly and transmits motion to other parts. ■ Electronics a device or part of a circuit that provides power for output. ■ Computing a program that controls the operation of a device such as a printer or scanner.
3 a factor that causes a particular phenomenon to happen or develop: *the hope of achieving such monopolies becomes the main driver of investment.*
4 a golf club with a flat face and wooden head, used for driving from the tee.
– PHRASES **in the driver's seat** in control of or dominating a situation: *the tax issue is back in the driver's seat of American politics.*
– DERIVATIVES **driv·er·less** adj.

driv·er ant ▶ n. another term for ARMY ANT.

driv·er's li·cense ▶ n. a document permitting a person to drive a motor vehicle.

drive·shaft /ˈdrīvˌSHaft/ ▶ n. a rotating shaft that transmits torque in an engine.

drive sys·tem ▶ n. the part of an engine, computer, or mechanical device that brings about its dynamic movement.

drive-through (also informal **drive-thru**) ▶ adj. [attrib.] denoting a facility through or to which one can drive, esp. to be served without leaving one's car: *a drive-through car wash | drive-through restaurants | the drive-thru window.*
▶ n. a place or facility of this type.

drive time ▶ n. (esp. in broadcasting) the parts of the day when many people commute by car: [as modifier] *drive-time radio.*

drive·train /ˈdrīvˌtrān/ ▶ n. the system in a motor vehicle that connects the transmission to the drive axles.

drive-up ▶ adj. another term for DRIVE-THROUGH.

drive·way /ˈdrīvˌwā/ ▶ n. a short road leading from a public road to a house or garage.

driv·ing /ˈdrīviNG/ ▶ adj. [attrib.] (of rain or snow) falling and being blown by the wind with great force: *driving rain.* ■ having a strong and controlling influence: *Macmillan was the **driving force** behind the plan | a driving ambition.* ■ energetic; dynamic: *driving dance rhythms.*
▶ n. the control and operation of a motor vehicle: *he was convicted of reckless driving* | [as modifier] *a driving course.*

driv·ing li·cence ▶ n. British term for DRIVER'S LICENSE.

driv·ing range ▶ n. an area where golfers can practice drives.

driv·ing wheel ▶ n. **1** any of the large wheels of a locomotive, to which power is applied either directly or via coupling rods.
2 a wheel transmitting motive power in machinery.

driz·zle /ˈdrizəl/ ▶ n. light rain falling in very fine drops: *Boston will be cloudy with patchy drizzle* | [in sing.] *a steady drizzle has been falling since 3 a.m.* ■ [in sing.] Cooking a thin stream of a liquid ingredient trickled over something.
▶ v. [no obj.] (**it drizzles, it is drizzling,** etc.) rain lightly: *it's started to drizzle* | (as adj. **drizzling**) *the drizzling rain.* ■ [with obj.] Cooking cause a thin stream of (a liquid ingredient) to trickle over food: *drizzle the clarified butter over the top.* ■ [with obj.] cause a liquid ingredient to trickle over (food) in this way: *raspberries drizzled with melted chocolate.*
– DERIVATIVES **driz·zly** /-z(ə)lē/ adj.
– ORIGIN mid 16th cent.: probably based on Old English *drēosan* 'to fall,' of Germanic origin; probably related to DREARY.

DRM ▶ abbr. digital rights management.

drogue /drōg/ ▶ n. a device, typically conical or funnel-shaped with open ends, towed behind a boat, aircraft, or other moving object to reduce speed or improve stability. ■ a similar object used as an aerial target for gunnery practice or as a windsock. ■ (in tanker aircraft) a funnel-shaped part on the end of the hose into which a probe is inserted by an aircraft being refueled in flight. ■ short for DROGUE PARACHUTE.
– ORIGIN early 18th cent. (originally a whaling term denoting a piece of stout board attached to a harpoon line, used to slow down or mark the position of a harpooned whale): perhaps related to DRAG.

drogue par·a·chute ▶ n. a small parachute used as a brake or to pull out a larger parachute or other object from an aircraft in flight or a fast-moving vehicle.

droid /droid/ ▶ n. (in science fiction) a robot. ■ a person regarded as lifeless or mechanical: *she will probably leave you for a sales droid.*
– ORIGIN 1970s: shortening of ANDROID.

droit /droit/ ▶ n. Law, historical a right or due.
– ORIGIN late Middle English: from Old French, based on Latin *directus* 'straight, right, direct.'

droit de sei·gneur /ˌdrwä də sānˈyər/ ▶ n. the alleged right of a medieval feudal lord to have sexual intercourse with a vassal's bride on her wedding night.
– ORIGIN French, literally 'lord's right.'

droll /drōl/ ▶ adj. curious or unusual in a way that provokes dry amusement: *his unique brand of droll self-mockery.*
▶ n. archaic a jester or entertainer; a buffoon.
– DERIVATIVES **droll·er·y** /ˈdrōlərē/ n., **droll·ness** n., **drol·ly** adv.
– ORIGIN early 17th cent. (as an adjective): from French *drôle*, perhaps from Middle Dutch *drolle* 'imp, goblin.'

dro·mae·o·sau·rid /ˌdrōmēəˈsôrid/ (also **dromaeosaur** /ˈdrōmēəˌsôr/) ▶ n. a carnivorous bipedal dinosaur of a late Cretaceous family that included deinonychus and the velociraptors. They had a large slashing claw on each hind foot. ● Family Dromaeosauridae, suborder Theropoda, order Saurischia.
– ORIGIN 1970s: from modern Latin *Dromaeosauridae*, based on Greek *dromaios* 'swift-running' + *sauros* 'lizard.'

-drome ▶ comb. form **1** denoting a place for running or racing: *velodrome.*
2 denoting something that runs or proceeds in a certain way: *palindrome.*
– ORIGIN from Greek *dromos* 'course, running.'

drom·e·dar·y /ˈdräməˌderē/ ▶ n. (pl. **dromedaries**) an Arabian one-humped camel, esp. one of a light and swift breed trained for riding or racing.
– ORIGIN Middle English: from Old French *dromedaire* or late Latin *dromedarius* (*camelus*) 'swift camel,' based on Greek *dromas, dromad-* 'runner.'

drone /drōn/ ▶ v. [no obj.] make a continuous low humming sound: *in the far distance a machine droned.* ■ speak tediously in a dull monotonous tone: *he reached for another beer while Jim **droned on**.* ■ [with adverbial of direction] move with a continuous humming sound: *traffic droned up and down the street.*
▶ n. **1** a low continuous humming sound: *he nodded off to the drone of the car engine.* ■ informal a monotonous speech: *only twenty minutes of the hour-long drone had passed.* ■ a continuous musical note, typically of low pitch. ■ a musical instrument, or part of one, sounding such a continuous note, in particular (also **drone pipe**) a pipe in a bagpipe or (also **drone string**) a string in an instrument such as a hurdy-gurdy or a sitar.
2 a male bee in a colony of social bees, which does no work but can fertilize a queen. ■ a person who does no useful work and lives off others.
3 a remote-controlled pilotless aircraft or missile.
– ORIGIN Old English *drān, drǣn* 'male bee,' from a West Germanic verb meaning 'resound, boom'; related to Dutch *dreunen* 'to drone,' German *dröhnen* 'to roar,' and Swedish *dröna* 'to drowse.'

drone fly ▶ n. a hoverfly that resembles a honeybee. Its larva is the rat-tailed maggot. ● *Eristalis tenax*, family Syrphidae.

droog /dro͞og/ ▶ n. informal a young man belonging to a street gang.
– ORIGIN 1962: coined by Anthony Burgess in *Clockwork Orange*; alteration of Russian *drug* 'friend.'

drool /dro͞ol/ ▶ v. [no obj.] drop saliva uncontrollably from the mouth: *the baby begins to drool, then to cough.* ■ informal make an excessive and obvious show of pleasure or desire: *I could imagine him as a teacher being **drooled over** by the girls.*
▶ n. saliva falling from the mouth.
– ORIGIN early 19th cent.: contraction of DRIVEL.

droop /dro͞op/ ▶ v. [no obj.] bend or hang downward limply: *a long black cloak drooped from his shoulders.* ■ sag down from or as if from weariness or dejection: *his eyelids drooped and he became drowsy* | figurative *the scenes are so lengthy that the reader's spirits droop.* ■ [with obj.] cause to bend or hang downward: *James hid his face in his hands and drooped his head.*
▶ n. [in sing.] an act or instance of drooping; a limp or weary attitude: *the exhausted droop of her shoulders.*
– ORIGIN Middle English: from Old Norse *drúpa* 'hang the head'; related to DRIP and DROP.

droop-snoot ▶ n. informal a downward-sloping nose of an aircraft or motor vehicle, esp. one that is of variable pitch, giving an efficient aerodynamic profile.
– DERIVATIVES **droop-snoot·ed** adj.

droop·y /ˈdro͞opē/ ▶ adj. (**droopier, droopiest**) hanging down limply; drooping: *a droopy mustache.* ■ lacking strength or spirit: *the girls looked rather droopy* | figurative *a period of droopy sales.*
– DERIVATIVES **droop·i·ly** /-pəlē/ adv., **droop·i·ness** n.

drop /dräp/ ▶ v. (**drops, dropping, dropped**) [with obj.] **1** let or make (something) fall vertically: *the fire was caused by someone dropping a lighted cigarette | they dropped bombs on London during the raid.* ■ deliver (supplies or troops) by parachute: *the airlift dropped food into the camp.* ■ Rugby score (a goal) by a drop kick. ■ (of an animal, esp. a mare, cow, or ewe) give birth to (young). ■ informal take (a drug, esp. LSD) orally: *he dropped a lot of acid in the Sixties.*
2 [no obj.] fall vertically: *the spoon dropped with a clatter from her hand.* ■ (of a person) allow oneself to fall; let oneself down without jumping: *they escaped by climbing out of the window and dropping to the ground.* ■ (of a person or animal) sink to or

toward the ground: *he dropped to his knees in the mud.* ■ informal collapse or die from exhaustion: *he looked **ready to drop**.* ■ (of ground) slope steeply down: *the cliff drops ninety yards to the valley below.*
3 make or become lower, weaker, or less: *he dropped his voice as she came into the room* | [no obj.] *pretax profits dropped by 37 percent* | *tourism has **dropped off** in the last few years.*
4 abandon or discontinue (a course of action or study): *the charges against him were dropped last year* | *drop everything and get over here!* ■ discard or exclude (someone or something): *they were dropped from the team in the reshuffle.* ■ informal stop associating with: *I was under pressure from family and friends to drop Barbara.* ■ omit (a letter or syllable) in speech: *our English au pair drops her h's.*
5 set down or unload (a passenger or goods), esp. on the way to somewhere else: *he **dropped** the load **off** at a dealer's* | *his mom dropped him outside and drove off to work.* ■ put or leave in a particular place without ceremony or formality: *just drop it in the mail when you've got time.* ■ mention in passing, typically in order to impress: *she dropped a remark about having been included in the selection.*
6 (in sports) fail to win (a point, game, or match). ■ informal lose (money), esp. through gambling: *they drifted into a roulette parlor and dropped about fifteen dollars.*
7 Bridge force or be forced to play (a relatively high card) as a loser under an opponent's higher card, because it is the only card in its suit held in the hand. ■ [no obj.] (of a card) be played in this way: *the queen dropped.*
▶ **n. 1** a small round or pear-shaped portion of liquid that hangs or falls or adheres to a surface: *the first **drops of** rain splashed on the ground.* ■ [often with negative] a very small amount of liquid: *there was not a drop of water in sight.* ■ [usu. with negative] a drink of alcoholic liquor: *he doesn't touch a drop during the week.* ■ (**drops**) liquid medicine to be measured or applied in very small amounts: *eye drops.*
2 [usu. in sing.] an instance of falling or dropping: *they left within five minutes of the drop of the curtain.* ■ an act of dropping supplies or troops by parachute: *the planes finally managed to make the drop.* ■ a fall in amount, quality, or rate: *a significant **drop in** consumer spending.* ■ an abrupt fall or slope: *standing on the lip of a sixty-foot drop.* ■ (**the drop**) Bridge the playing of a high card underneath an opponent's higher card, because it is the only card in its suit held in the hand.
3 something that drops or is dropped, in particular: ■ a section of theatrical scenery lowered from the flies; a drop cloth or drop curtain. ■ a trapdoor on a gallows, the opening of which causes the prisoner to fall and thus be hanged. ■ (**the drop**) execution by hanging.
4 something resembling a drop of liquid in shape, in particular: ■ [usu. with modifier] a piece of candy or a lozenge: *a lemon drop.* ■ a pendant earring.
5 informal a delivery: *I got to the depot and made the drop.* ■ a mailbox. ■ a hiding place for stolen, illicit, or secret things: *the lavatory's toilet tank could be used as a letter drop.*
– PHRASES **at the drop of a hat** informal without delay or good reason: *he used to be very bashful, blushing at the drop of a hat.* **drop the ball** informal make a mistake; mishandle things: *I really dropped the ball on this one.* [with allusion to mishandling in baseball.] **drop dead** die suddenly and unexpectedly: *she had seen her father drop dead of a heart attack.* ■ [in imperative] informal used as an expression of intense scorn or dislike. **drop a** (or **the**) **dime on** informal inform on (someone) to the police. **drop like flies** see FLY[2]. **drop one's guard** abandon one's habitual defensive or protective stance. **drop a hint** (or **drop hints**) let fall a hint or hints, as if casually or unconsciously: *he was dropping hints that in the future he would be taking a back seat in politics.* **a drop in the bucket** (or Brit. **ocean**) a very small amount compared with what is needed or expected: *the $550 million is likely to be a drop in the bucket.* **drop someone a line** send someone a note or letter in a casual manner: *drop me a line at the usual address.* **drop names** see NAME-DROPPING. **drop one's serve** (in tennis) lose a game in which one is serving. **drop a stitch** let a stitch fall off the end of a knitting needle. **drop one's trousers** deliberately let one's trousers fall down, esp. in a public place. **have the drop on** informal have the advantage over: *if your enemy gets the drop on you he can kill you.*
– PHRASAL VERBS **drop back/behind** fall back or get left behind: *the colt was struggling to stay with the pace and started to drop back.* **drop by/in** call informally and briefly as a visitor: *they would unexpectedly drop in on us.* **drop into 1** call casually and informally at (a place): *he'd actually considered dropping into one of the pickup bars.* **2** pass quickly and easily into (a habitual state or manner): *she couldn't help dropping into a Brooklyn accent.* **drop off** fall asleep easily, esp. without intending to: *struggle as she might, she kept dropping off.* **drop out 1** cease to participate in a race or competition. **2** abandon a course of study: *kids who had dropped out of college.* **3** reject conventional society to pursue an alternative lifestyle: *a child of the sixties who had temporarily dropped out.* **4** Rugby restart play with a drop kick. ■ score a drop goal.
– DERIVATIVES **drop·pa·ble** adj.
– ORIGIN Old English *dropa* (noun), *droppian* (verb), of Germanic origin; related to German *Tropfen* 'a drop,' *tropfen* 'to drip,' also to DRIP and DROOP.

drop box ▶ **n. 1** (in weaving) a box situated on either side of the race plate of the loom that is designed to hold shuttles and to bring bobbins of colored thread in line as desired.
2 a secured receptacle into which items such as returned books or videotapes, payments, keys, or donated clothing can be deposited.

drop cloth ▶ **n.** a large sheet for covering furniture or flooring to protect it from dust or while decorating.

drop cur·tain ▶ **n.** a curtain or painted cloth lowered vertically onto a theater stage.

drop-dead ▶ **adj.** informal used to emphasize how attractive someone or something is: *her drop-dead good looks* | [as submodifier] *a **drop-dead gorgeous** Hollywood icon.*

drop-down ▶ **adj.** [attrib.] dropping down or unfolding when required: *an RV with two drop-down beds.* ■ Computing (of a menu) appearing below a menu title when it is selected, and remaining until used or dismissed. Compare with PULL-DOWN.

drop-forged ▶ **adj.** (of a metal object) made by forcing hot metal into or through a die with a drop hammer.
– DERIVATIVES **drop-forg·ing** n.

drop goal ▶ **n.** Rugby a goal scored in open play by drop-kicking the ball over the crossbar, scoring three points (rugby union) or one point (rugby league).

drop ham·mer ▶ **n.** a large heavy weight raised mechanically and allowed to drop, as used in drop-forging and pile-driving.

drop han·dle·bars ▶ **plural n.** bicycle handlebars of which the handles are bent below the rest of the bar, used esp. on racing cycles.

drop-in ▶ **adj. 1** visited on an informal basis without booking or appointments: *a drop-in disco.*
2 (of an object such as a chair seat) designed to drop into position.

drop-in cen·ter ▶ **n.** a place run by a welfare agency or charity where people may call casually for advice or assistance.

drop kick ▶ **n.** (formerly, in football) a kick made by dropping the ball and kicking after it touches the ground. ■ (chiefly in martial arts) a flying kick made against an opponent while dropping to the ground.
▶ **v.** (**drop-kick**) [with obj.] kick using a drop kick.

drop leaf ▶ **n.** a hinged table leaf: *both drop leaves are badly scratched* | [as modifier] *a mahogany drop-leaf table.*

drop·let /ˈdräplit/ ▶ **n.** a very small drop of a liquid: *droplets of water.*

drop·light ▶ **n.** a light that is suspended from a reel so that it can be raised or lowered, typically over a work area.

drop-off ▶ **n. 1** a decline or decrease: *a sudden **drop-off in** tourism.*
2 a sheer downward slope; a cliff: *dizzy drop-offs on either side.*

drop·out /ˈdräpˌout/ ▶ **n. 1** a person who has abandoned a course of study or who has rejected conventional society to pursue an alternative lifestyle: *a college dropout.*
2 a momentary loss of recorded audio signal or an error in reading data on a magnetic tape or disk, usually due to a flaw in the coating.
3 (usu. **dropouts**) a U-shaped slot at the end of a fork on a bicycle, made to receive the axle and enabling the wheel to be changed rapidly.

drop·per /ˈdräpər/ ▶ **n. 1** a short glass tube with a rubber bulb at one end and a tiny hole at the other, for measuring out drops of medicine or other liquids.
2 (in full **dropper line**) Fishing a subsidiary line or loop of filament attached to a main line or leader.
– ORIGIN mid 17th cent. (in the sense 'a person who lets something drop'); sense 1 is first recorded in the late 19th cent.

drop·pings /ˈdräpiNGz/ ▶ **plural n.** the excrement of certain animals, such as rodents, sheep, birds, and insects.

drop scene ▶ **n.** a drop curtain used as part of stage scenery, esp. one in front of which a scene is played while the setting is changed behind. ■ the last scene of a play.

drop scone ▶ **n.** a small thick pancake made by dropping spoonfuls of batter onto a frying pan or other heated surface.

drop·seed /ˈdräpˌsēd/ ▶ **n.** a grass that readily drops its seeds. ● Genus *Sporobolus*, family Gramineae: several species, including the widespread North American **sand dropseed** (*S. cryptandrus*), which has a high yield of edible grain.

drop-ship ▶ **v.** (**drop-ships**, **drop-shipping**, **drop-shipped**) [with obj.] move (goods) from the manufacturer directly to the retailer without going through the usual distribution channels: *the shopping network has begun drop-shipping orders taken by telephone or over the Internet.*
– DERIVATIVES **drop ship·ment** n.

drop shot ▶ **n.** (chiefly in tennis or squash) a softly hit shot, usually with backspin, which drops abruptly to the ground.

drop shoul·der (also **dropped shoulder**) ▶ **n.** a style of shoulder on a garment cut so that the seam is positioned on the upper arm rather than the shoulder.

drop·si·cal /ˈdräpsikəl/ ▶ **adj.** affected with or characteristic of dropsy; edematous.
– ORIGIN late 17th cent.: from DROPSY, replacing earlier *hydropic(al)*, via Latin from Greek *hudrōps* 'dropsy.'

drop·side /ˈdräpˌsīd/ ▶ **adj.** [attrib.] (of a crib or a hospital bed) having a side that drops down to open.
▶ **n.** a side that drops down in this way.

drop-stitch ▶ **adj.** denoting an openwork pattern in knitted garments made by dropping a made stitch at intervals: *a drop-stitch cardigan.*

drop·sy /ˈdräpsē/ ▶ **n.** (pl. **dropsies**) old-fashioned or less technical term for EDEMA. [Middle English: shortening of *idropesie*, earlier form of obsolete *hydropsy*, via Old French and Latin from Greek *hudrōps* 'dropsy,' from *hudōr* 'water.']

drop tank ▶ **n.** an external fuel tank on an aircraft that can be jettisoned when empty.

drop test ▶ **n.** a test of the strength of an object, in which it is dropped under standard conditions or a set weight is dropped on it from a given height.
– DERIVATIVES **drop-test·ing** n.

drop·top /ˈdräpˌtäp/ ▶ **n.** a car having a fabric roof that can be folded down; a convertible.

drop waist (also **dropped waist**) ▶ **n.** a style of waistline on a dress cut so that the seam is positioned at the hips rather than the waist.

drop zone ▶ **n.** a designated area into which troops or supplies are dropped by parachute or in which skydivers land.

dros·er·a /ˈdräsərə/ ▶ **n.** a sundew. ● Genus *Drosera*, family Droseraceae.
– ORIGIN modern Latin, from Greek *droseros* 'dewy' (from the appearance of the glistening hairs on the leaves).

drosh·ky /ˈdräshkē/ ▶ **n.** (pl. **droshkies**) historical a low four-wheeled open carriage of a kind formerly used in Russia.
– ORIGIN early 19th cent.: from Russian *drozhki*, diminutive of *drogi* 'wagon,' from *droga* 'shaft, carriage pole.'

dro·soph·i·la /drəˈsäfələ/ ▶ **n.** a small fruit fly, used extensively in genetic research because of its large chromosomes, numerous varieties, and rapid rate of reproduction. ● Genus *Drosophila*, family Drosophilidae: in particular *D. melanogaster*.
– ORIGIN modern Latin, from Greek *drosos* 'dew, moisture' + *philos* 'loving.'

dross /drôs, dräs/ ▶ **n.** something regarded as worthless; rubbish: *there are bargains if you have the patience to sift through the dross.* ■ foreign matter, dregs, or mineral waste, in particular scum formed on the surface of molten metal.
– DERIVATIVES **dross·y** adj.
– ORIGIN Old English *drōs* (in the sense 'scum on molten metal'); related to Dutch *droesem* and German *Drusen* 'dregs, lees.'

drought /drout/ ▶ **n.** a prolonged period of abnormally low rainfall; a shortage of water resulting from this. ■ [usu. with modifier] a prolonged absence of something specified: *he ended a five-game hitting drought.* ■ archaic thirst.
– DERIVATIVES **drought·i·ness** n., **drought·y** adj.
– ORIGIN late Old English *drūgath* 'dryness,' of Germanic origin; compare with Dutch *droogte*; related to DRY.

drouth /drouTH/ ▶ **n.** dialect or poetic form of DROUGHT.
– DERIVATIVES **drouth·y** adj.

drove[1] /drōv/ past of DRIVE.

drove[2] ▶ **n. 1** a herd or flock of animals being driven in a body: *a drove of cattle.* ■ a large number of people or things doing or undergoing the same

PRONUNCIATION KEY ə *ago, up*; ər *over, fur*; a *hat*; ā *ate*; ä *car*; e *let*; ē *see*; i *fit*; ī *by*; NG *sing*; ō *go*; ô *law, for*; oi *toy*; o͝o *good*; o͞o *goo*; ou *out*; TH *thin*; TH *then*; ZH *vision*

thing: *tourists have stayed away **in droves** this summer.*
2 a broad chisel for use by stonemasons.
– DERIVATIVES **dro·ver n.**
– ORIGIN Old English *drāf*, related to *drīfan* 'to drive.'

drown /droun/ ▶ **v.** [no obj.] die through submersion in and inhalation of water: *she drowned in the pond* | (**be drowned**) *two fishermen were drowned when their motorboat capsized.* ■ [with obj.] deliberately kill (a person or animal) in this way: *he killed his wife then drowned himself in a fit of despair.* ■ [with obj.] submerge or flood (an area): *when the ice melted, the valleys were drowned.* ■ [with obj.] (of a sound) make (another sound) inaudible by being much louder: *his voice was **drowned out** by the approaching engine noise.* ■ [no obj.] (**be drowning in**) be overwhelmed by a large amount of something: *both business and household sectors are drowning in debt* | *art dealers are still **drowning in a sea of** paperwork.* ■ [with obj.] (**drown something in**) cover or immerse food in: *good pizza is not eight inches thick and drowned in tomato sauce.*
– PHRASES **drown one's sorrows** forget one's problems by getting drunk. **like a drowned rat** extremely wet and bedraggled: *she arrived at the church looking like a drowned rat.*
– ORIGIN Middle English (originally northern): related to Old Norse *drukkna* 'to be drowned,' also to **DRINK**.

drowse /drouz/ ▶ **v.** [no obj.] be half asleep; doze intermittently: *he was beginning to drowse in his chair.* ■ [with obj.] archaic make sleepy. ■ archaic be sluggish or inactive: *let not your prudence drowse.*
▶ **n.** [in sing.] a light sleep; a condition of being half asleep.
– ORIGIN late 16th cent.: back-formation from **DROWSY**.

drow·si·ness /ˈdrouzēnis/ ▶ **n.** a feeling of being sleepy and lethargic; sleepiness: *this drug can cause drowsiness.*

drow·sy /ˈdrouzē/ ▶ **adj.** (**drowsier, drowsiest**) sleepy and lethargic; half asleep: *the wine had made her drowsy.* ■ causing sleepiness: *the drowsy heat of the meadows.* ■ (esp. of a place) very peaceful and quiet: *a drowsy suburb.*
– DERIVATIVES **drow·si·ly** /-zəlē/ **adv.**
– ORIGIN late 15th cent.: probably from the stem of Old English *drūsian* 'be languid or slow,' of Germanic origin; related to **DREARY**.

drub /drəb/ ▶ **v.** (**drubs, drubbing, drubbed**) [with obj.] hit or beat (someone) repeatedly. ■ informal defeat thoroughly in a match or contest: *Cleveland drubbed Baltimore 9–0.*
– ORIGIN early 17th cent.: probably from Arabic *ḍaraba* 'to beat, bastinado.' The first recorded uses in English are by travelers in the Near East referring specifically to the punishment of bastinado.

drub·bing /ˈdrəbiNG/ ▶ **n.** a beating; a thrashing: *I'll give the scoundrels a drubbing if I can!* ■ informal a resounding defeat in a match or contest.

drudge /drəj/ ▶ **n.** a person made to do hard, menial, or dull work: *she was little more than a drudge around the house.*
▶ **v.** [no obj.] archaic do such work.
– ORIGIN Middle English (as a noun): of unknown origin; perhaps related to **DRAG**.

drudg·er·y /ˈdrəjərē/ ▶ **n.** hard, menial, or dull work: *domestic drudgery.*

drug /drəg/ ▶ **n.** a medicine or other substance which has a physiological effect when ingested or otherwise introduced into the body: *a new drug aimed at sufferers from Parkinson's disease.* ■ a substance taken for its narcotic or stimulant effects, often illegally: [as modifier] *a drug addict* | figurative *mass adoration is a highly addictive drug.*
▶ **v.** (**drugs, drugging, drugged**) [with obj.] administer a drug to (someone) in order to induce stupor or insensibility: *they were drugged to keep them quiet.* ■ add a drug to (food or drink): *he drugged their coffee.* ■ [no obj.] informal take illegally obtained drugs: *fifteen years of drinking and drugging.*
– PHRASES **do drugs** informal take illegal drugs. **on drugs** taking medically prescribed drugs: *on drugs for high blood pressure.* ■ under the influence of or habitually taking illegal drugs.
– ORIGIN Middle English: from Old French *drogue*, possibly from Middle Dutch *droge vate*, literally 'dry vats,' referring to the contents (i.e., dry goods).

drug a·buse ▶ **n.** the habitual taking of addictive or illegal drugs.

drug ad·dict ▶ **n.** a person who is addicted to an illegal drug.

drug ba·ron ▶ **n.** a person who controls an organization dealing in illegal drugs: *the deportation of a reputed drug baron.*

drugged /drəgd/ ▶ **adj.** (of a person) unconscious or in a stupor as a result of taking or being given a drug: *in his drugged state.* ■ (of food or drink) adulterated with a drug: *he offered them drugged wine.*

drug·get /ˈdrəgit/ ▶ **n.** a floor or table covering made of a coarse woven fabric. ■ the fabric used for such coverings.
– ORIGIN mid 16th cent.: from French *droguet*, from *drogue* in the sense 'poor-quality article.'

drug·gie /ˈdrəgē/ (also **druggy**) ▶ **n.** informal a drug addict.

drug·gist /ˈdrəgist/ ▶ **n.** a pharmacist or retailer of medicinal drugs.
– ORIGIN early 17th cent.: from French *droguiste*, from *drogue* 'drug.'

drug·gy /ˈdrəgē/ informal ▶ **adj.** caused by, involving, or given to taking drugs, esp. illegal ones: *a druggy haze* | *the druggy world of rock and roll.*
▶ **n.** variant spelling of **DRUGGIE**.
– ORIGIN late 16th cent.: from **DRUG** + **-Y¹**.

drug mule ▶ **n.** a person who transports illegal drugs by swallowing them or concealing them in a body cavity.

drug·store /ˈdrəg,stôr/ ▶ **n.** a pharmacy that also sells toiletries and other articles.

drug·store bee·tle ▶ **n.** a small beetle related to the furniture beetle, with larvae that feed on stored foodstuffs such as pasta and seeds. ● *Stegobium paniceum*, family Anobiidae.

Dru·id /ˈdrŏŏid/ ▶ **n.** a priest, magician, or soothsayer in the ancient Celtic religion. ■ a member of a present-day group claiming to represent or be derived from this religion.
– DERIVATIVES **Dru·id·ic** /drŏŏˈidik/ **adj.**, **Dru·id·i·cal** /drŏŏˈidikəl/ **adj.**, **Dru·id·ism** /-,izəm/ **n.**
– ORIGIN from Latin *druidae, druides* (plural), from Gaulish; related to Irish *draoidh* 'magician, sorcerer.'

drum¹ /drəm/ ▶ **n. 1** a percussion instrument sounded by being struck with sticks or the hands, typically cylindrical, barrel-shaped, or bowl-shaped with a taut membrane over one or both ends. ■ (**drums**) a set of drums. ■ (**drums**) the percussion section of a band or orchestra. ■ [in sing.] a sound made by or resembling that of a drum: *the drum of their feet.* ■ historical a military drummer.
2 something resembling or likened to a drum in shape, in particular: ■ a cylindrical container or receptacle. See also **OIL DRUM**. ■ a rotating cylindrical part in a washing machine, in which the laundry is placed. ■ a similar cylindrical part in certain other appliances. ■ Architecture the circular vertical wall supporting a dome. ■ Architecture a stone block forming part of a column.
3 an evening or afternoon tea party of a kind that was popular in the late 18th and early 19th century.
▶ **v.** (**drums, drumming, drummed**) [no obj.] play on a drum. ■ make a continuous rhythmic noise: *she felt the blood drumming in her ears* | (as noun **drumming**) *the drumming of hooves.* ■ [with obj.] beat (the fingers, feet, etc.) repeatedly on a surface, esp. as a sign of impatience or annoyance: *waiting around an empty table, drumming their fingers.* ■ (of a woodpecker) strike the bill rapidly on a dead trunk or branch, esp. as a sound indicating a territorial claim. ■ (of a snipe) vibrate the outer tail feathers in a diving display flight, making a throbbing sound.
– PHRASES **beat** (or **bang**) **the drum for** (or **against**) be ostentatiously in support of (or in opposition to): *he limited campaign contributions in order to beat the drum against political action committees* | *feminists bang the drum for 'quality time.'*
– PHRASAL VERBS **drum something into** drive a lesson into (someone) by constant repetition: *it had been drummed into them to dress correctly.* **drum someone out** expel or dismiss someone with ignominy from a place or institution: *he was drummed out of the air force.* [with allusion to the formal military drumbeat accompanying dismissal from a regiment.] **drum something up** attempt to obtain something by canvassing or soliciting: *the organizers are hoping to drum up support from local businesses.*
– ORIGIN Middle English: from Middle Dutch or Low German *tromme*, of imitative origin.

drum² ▶ **n.** Scottish & Irish a long narrow hill, esp. one separating two parallel valleys.
– ORIGIN early 18th cent.: from Scottish Gaelic and Irish *druim* 'ridge.'

drum³ (also **drumfish**) ▶ **n.** (pl. **same** or **drums**) a fish that makes a drumming sound by vibrating its swim bladder, found mainly in estuarine and shallow coastal waters. Also called **CROAKER**. ● Family Sciaenidae (the **drum family**): many species, including the **black drum** (*Pogonias cromis*) of the western Atlantic. The drum family also includes the mulloway and a number of marine fishes that resemble salmon (e.g., the weakfish).

drum and bass /bās/ ▶ **n.** a type of dance music characterized by bare instrumentation consisting largely of electronic drums and bass, originating in Britain during the early 1990s.

drum·beat /ˈdrəm,bēt/ ▶ **n.** a stroke or pattern of strokes on a drum: *she was aware of a constant, faint drumbeat.*

drum brake ▶ **n.** a type of vehicle brake in which brake shoes press against the inside of a drum on the wheel.

drum·fire /ˈdrəm,fīr/ ▶ **n.** heavy continuous rapid artillery fire.

drum·fish /ˈdrəm,fiSH/ ▶ **n.** (pl. **same** or **drumfishes**) see **DRUM³**.

drum·head /ˈdrəm,hed/ ▶ **n. 1** the membrane or skin of a drum.
2 a winter cabbage of a flat-topped variety.

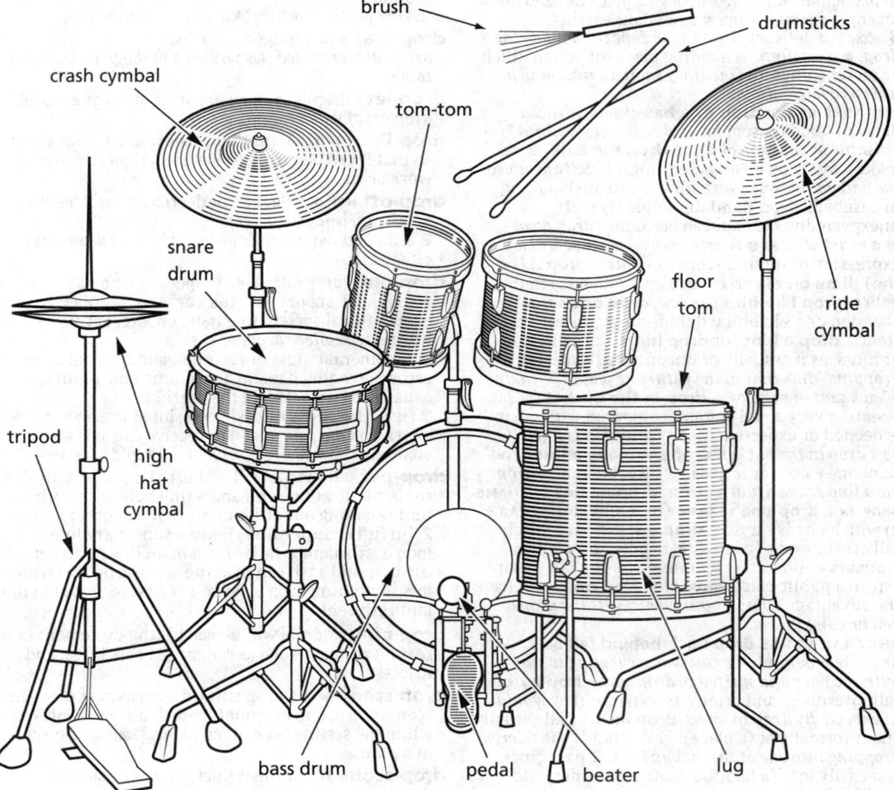

drum kit

3 chiefly historical the circular top of a ship's capstan, with holes into which bars are placed to turn it.
▶ **adj.** [attrib.] carried out by or as if by an army in the field; improvised or summary: *a drumhead court-martial.*

drum kit (also **drum set**) ▶ **n.** a set of drums, cymbals, and other percussion instruments used with drumsticks in jazz and popular music. The most basic components are a foot-operated bass drum, a snare drum, a suspended cymbal, and one or more tom-toms.

drum·lin /ˈdrəmlin/ ▶ **n.** Geology a low oval mound or small hill, typically one of a group, consisting of compacted boulder clay molded by past glacial action.
– ORIGIN mid 19th cent.: probably from DRUM² + *-lin* from -LING.

drum ma·chine ▶ **n.** a programmable electronic device able to imitate the sounds of a drum kit.

drum ma·jor ▶ **n. 1** a noncommissioned officer commanding the drummers of a regimental band. **2** the male leader of a marching band, who often twirls a baton. ■ a male member of a baton-twirling parading group.

drum ma·jor·ette ▶ **n.** the female leader of a marching band. ■ a girl or woman who twirls a baton, typically with a marching band or drum corps.

drum·mer /ˈdrəmər/ ▶ **n. 1** a person who plays a drum or drums.
2 informal a traveling sales representative: *a drummer in electronic software.* [from *drum up* (see DRUM¹).]

drum pad ▶ **n.** an electronic device with one or more flat pads that imitate the sounds of a drum kit when struck.

drum·roll /ˈdrəm,rōl/ (also **drum roll**) ▶ **n.** a rapid succession of beats sounded on a drum, often used to introduce an announcement or event.

drum·stick /ˈdrəm,stik/ ▶ **n.** a stick, typically with a shaped or padded head, used for beating a drum. ■ the lower joint of the leg of a cooked chicken, turkey, or other fowl.

drunk /drəNGk/ past participle of DRINK.
▶ **adj.** affected by alcohol to the extent of losing control of one's faculties or behavior: *he was so drunk he lurched from wall to wall* | *drunk on vodka.* ■ [predic.] (**drunk with**) overcome with (a strong emotion): *the crowd was high on euphoria and drunk with patriotism.*
▶ **n.** a person who is drunk or who habitually drinks to excess. ■ informal a drinking bout; a period of drunkenness: *he used to go on these blind drunks.*
– PHRASES **drunk and disorderly** creating a public disturbance under the influence of alcohol. (**as**) **drunk as a skunk** extremely drunk.

drunk·ard /ˈdrəNGkərd/ ▶ **n.** a person who is habitually drunk.
– ORIGIN Middle English: from Middle Low German *drunkert.*

drunk driv·ing (also **drunken driving**) ▶ **n.** the crime of driving a vehicle with an excess of alcohol in the blood.
– DERIVATIVES **drunk driv·er n.**

drunk·en /ˈdrəNGkən/ ▶ **adj.** [attrib.] drunk or intoxicated: *gangs of drunken youths roamed the streets.* ■ habitually or frequently drunk: *his violent, drunken father.* ■ caused by or showing the effects of drink: *the man's drunken, slurred speech.*
– DERIVATIVES **drunk·en·ly adv.**
– ORIGIN Old English, archaic past participle of DRINK.

drunk·en·ness /ˈdrəNGkən,nəs/ ▶ **n.** the state of being intoxicated; intoxication: *a growing problem of drunkenness.*

drunk tank ▶ **n.** informal a large prison cell for the detention of drunks.

drupe /dro͞op/ ▶ **n.** Botany a fleshy fruit with thin skin and a central stone containing the seed, e.g., a plum, cherry, almond, or olive.
– DERIVATIVES **dru·pa·ceous** /dro͞oˈpāSHəs/ **adj.**
– ORIGIN mid 18th cent.: from Latin *drupa* 'overripe olive,' from Greek *druppa* 'olive.'

drupe·let /ˈdro͞oplit/ ▶ **n.** Botany any of the small individual drupes forming a fleshy aggregate fruit such as a blackberry or raspberry.
– ORIGIN mid 19th cent.: from modern Latin *drupella*, diminutive of *drupa* 'overripe olive' (see DRUPE).

Dru·ry Lane /ˈdro͞orē/ the site in London of the Theatre Royal, one of London's most famous theaters.

druse /dro͞oz/ ▶ **n. 1** Geology a rock cavity lined with a crust of projecting crystals. ■ the crust of crystals lining such a cavity.
2 Botany a rounded cluster of calcium oxalate crystals found in some plant cells.
– DERIVATIVES **drus·y adj.** (Geology).
– ORIGIN early 19th cent.: via French from German *Druse* 'weathered ore.'

druth·er /ˈdrəT͟Hər/ informal ▶ **n.** (usu. **one's druthers**) a person's preference in a matter: *if I had my druthers, I would prefer to be a writer.*
▶ **adv.** rather; by preference.
– ORIGIN late 19th cent.: from a US regional pronunciation of *I'd rather*, contraction of *would rather*. Compare with RUTHER.

Druze /dro͞oz/ (also **Druse**) ▶ **n.** (pl. **same, Druzes** or **Druses** /ˈdro͞oziz/) a member of a political and religious sect of Islamic origin, living chiefly in Lebanon and Syria. The Druze broke away from the Ismaili Muslims in the 11th century; they are regarded as heretical by the Muslim community at large.
– ORIGIN from French, from Arabic *durūz* (plural), from the name of one of their founders, Muhammad ibn Ismail *al-Darazī* (died 1019).

dry /drī/ ▶ **adj.** (**drier, driest**) **1** free from moisture or liquid; not wet or moist: *the jacket kept me warm and dry* | *he wiped it dry with his shirt.* ■ having lost all wetness or moisture over a period of time: *dry paint.* ■ for use without liquid: *the conversion of dry latrines into flush toilets.* ■ with little or no rainfall or humidity: *the West Coast has had two dry winters in a row.* ■ (of a river, lake, or stream) empty of water as a result of evaporation and lack of rainfall: *the river is always dry at this time of year.* ■ (of a source) not yielding a supply of water or oil: *a dry well.* ■ thirsty or thirst-making: *working in the hot sun is making me dry* | *dry work.* ■ (of a cow or other domestic animal) having stopped producing milk. ■ without grease or other moisturizer or lubricator: *cream conditioners for dry hair* | *his throat was dry and sore.* ■ (of bread or toast) without butter or other spreads: *only dry bread and water.*
2 bare or lacking adornment: *the dry facts.* ■ unexciting; dull: *by current tastes the text is dry.* ■ unemotional, undemonstrative, or impassive: *Ralph gave me a dry, silent wave.* ■ (of a joke or sense of humor) subtle, expressed in a matter-of-fact way, and having the appearance of being unconscious or unintentional: *he delighted his friends with a dry, covert sense of humor.*
3 prohibiting the sale or consumption of alcoholic drink: *Indiana stayed dry after the end of prohibition.* ■ (of a person) no longer addicted to or drinking alcohol: *I heard much talk about how sobriety was more than staying straight or dry.*
4 (of an alcoholic drink) not sweet: *a dry, medium-bodied red wine.*
▶ **v.** (**dries, drying, dried**) [no obj.] **1** become dry: *waiting for the paint to dry* | *come in out of the rain and dry off* | *do not let the soil dry out* | *pools are left as the rivers dry up.* ■ [with obj.] cause to become dry: *they had washed and dried their hair.* ■ [with obj.] wipe tears from (the eyes): *she dried her eyes and blew her nose.* ■ wipe dishes dry with a cloth after they have been washed. ■ [with obj.] (usu. as adj. **dried**) preserve by allowing or encouraging evaporation of moisture from: *dried flowers.*
2 theatrical slang forget one's lines: *a colleague of mine once dried in the middle of a scene.*
▶ **n.** (pl. **dries** or **drys**) a person in favor of the prohibition of alcohol.
– PHRASES **come up dry** be unsuccessful: *experiments have so far come up dry.* (**as**) **dry as a bone** extremely dry. (**as**) **dry as dust** extremely dry. ■ extremely dull; lacking emotion, expression, or interest: *what the students learned was as dry as dust.* **there wasn't a dry eye** (**in the house**) (with reference to a play, film, or similar event) everyone in the audience was moved to tears.
– PHRASAL VERBS **dry out** informal (of an alcoholic) abstain from alcoholic drink, esp. as part of a detoxification program: *he intends to dry out and get his life back together again.* **dry up 1** informal cease talking: *then he dried up, and Phil couldn't get another word out of him.* **2** (of something perceived as a continuous flow or source) decrease and stop: *his commissions began to dry up.*
– DERIVATIVES **dry·ish adj.**, **dry·ness n.**
– ORIGIN Old English *drȳge* (adjective), *drȳgan* (verb), of Germanic origin; related to Middle Low German *dröge*, Dutch *droog*, and German *trocken*.

dry·ad /ˈdrī,ad, -əd/ ▶ **n.** (in folklore and Greek mythology) a nymph inhabiting a forest or a tree, esp. an oak tree.
– ORIGIN via Old French and Latin from Greek *druas*, *druad-* 'tree nymph,' from *drus* 'tree.'

dry·ad sad·dle ▶ **n.** a common polypore growing on tree stumps and logs, having a scaly, yellowish-brown upper surface, found in both North America and Eurasia and edible when young.
● *Polyporus squamosus*, family Polyporaceae, class Hymenomycetes.

dry·as /ˈdrīəs/ ▶ **n. 1** a plant of a genus that comprises the mountain avens. ● Genus *Dryas*, family Rosaceae.
2 (**Dryas**) Geology the first and third climatic stages of the late-glacial period in northern Europe, in which cold tundralike conditions prevailed and plants of the genus *Dryas* were abundant. The **Older Dryas** (about 15,000 to 12,000 years ago) followed the last ice retreat, and the **Younger Dryas** (about 10,800 to 10,000 years ago) followed the Allerød stage.
– ORIGIN modern Latin, from Greek *druas* (see DRYAD). The plant (sense 1) has leaves that resemble those of the oak (hence the association with dryads, being originally nymphs of the oak).

dry·as·dust /ˈdrīəz,dəst/ ▶ **n.** a boring, pedantic speaker or writer.
▶ **adj.** (also **dry-as-dust**) dull and boring.
– ORIGIN late 19th cent.: from the name of the character Dr. Jonas *Dryasdust*, featured in prefaces to Sir Walter Scott's novels.

dry bat·ter·y ▶ **n.** an electric battery consisting of one or more dry cells.

dry bulb ▶ **n.** an ordinary exposed thermometer bulb, esp. as used in conjunction with a wet bulb.

dry cell ▶ **n.** an electric cell in which the electrolyte is absorbed in a solid to form a paste, preventing spillage. Compare with WET CELL.

dry-clean ▶ **v.** [with obj.] (usu. **be dry-cleaned**) clean (a garment) with an organic solvent, without using water: *I had my winter coat dry-cleaned recently* | (as noun **dry cleaning**) *premises that offered dry cleaning.*
– DERIVATIVES **dry clean·er n.**

dry cough ▶ **n.** a cough not accompanied by phlegm production.

dry-cure ▶ **v.** another term for DRY-SALT.

Dry·den /ˈdrīdn/, John (1631–1700), English poet, critic, and playwright of the Augustan Age. He is best known for *Marriage à la mode* (1673), *All for Love* (1678), and *Absalom and Achitophel* (1681).

dry dock ▶ **n.** a dock that can be drained of water to allow the inspection and repair of a ship's hull.
▶ **v.** (**dry-dock**) [with obj.] place (a ship) in a dry dock.

dry·er /ˈdrīər/ (also **drier**) ▶ **n. 1** a machine or device for drying something, esp. the hair or laundry.
2 a substance mixed with oil paint or ink to promote drying.
– ORIGIN Middle English (in the sense 'person who dries'): from the verb DRY + -ER¹.

dry·er sheet ▶ **n.** a fabric softener sheet.

dry-eyed ▶ **adj.** (of a person) not crying: *Janet was dry-eyed and stoical under assault.*

dry farm·ing ▶ **n.** another term for DRYLAND FARMING.

dry fly ▶ **n.** an artificial fishing fly that is made to float lightly on the water.
▶ **v.** (**dry-fly**) fish using a dry fly.

dry goods ▶ **plural n.** fabric, thread, clothing, and related merchandise, esp. as distinct from hardware and groceries.

dry hole ▶ **n.** a well drilled for oil or gas but yielding none.

dry hump (also **dry fuck**) ▶ **v.** [with obj.] vulgar slang simulate or unsuccessfully attempt sexual intercourse with (someone or something), usually while fully dressed.

dry ice ▶ **n.** solid carbon dioxide. ■ the cold dense white mist produced by this in air, used for theatrical effects.

dry·ing oil ▶ **n.** an oil that thickens or hardens on exposure to air, esp. one used by artists in mixing paint.

dry land ▶ **n.** land as opposed to the sea or another body of water: *the tide came in and cut off his route to dry land.*

dry·land farm·ing /ˈdrī,land/ (also **dry farming**) ▶ **n.** a method of farming in semiarid areas without the aid of irrigation, using drought-resistant crops and conserving moisture.

dry·lands /ˈdrī,landz/ ▶ **plural n.** an arid area; a region with low rainfall.

dry·ly /ˈdrīlē/ (also **drily**) ▶ **adv. 1** in a matter-of-fact or ironically humorous way: *"How very observant," he said dryly.*
2 in a dry way or condition: *Evans swallowed dryly.*

dry mat·ter ▶ **n.** the part of a foodstuff or other substance that would remain if all its water content was removed.

dry meas·ure ▶ **n.** a measure of volume for loose dry commodities such as grain, tea, and sugar.

dry mop ▶ **n.** another term for DUST MOP.

PRONUNCIATION KEY ə ago, up; ər over, fur; a hat; ā ate; ä car; e let; ē see; i fit; ī by; NG sing; ō go; ô law, for; oi toy; o͝o good; o͞o goo; ou out; TH thin; T͟H then; ZH vision

d

d

dry mount·ing ▶ **n.** Photography a process in which a print is bonded to a mount using a layer of adhesive in a hot press.
– DERIVATIVES **dry-mount v.**, **dry-mount·ed adj.**

dry nurse ▶ **n.** archaic a woman who looks after a baby but does not breastfeed it.
– DERIVATIVES **dry-nurse v.**

Dry·o·pith·e·cus /ˌdrīōˈpiTHikəs/ ▶ **n.** a fossil anthropoid ape of the middle Miocene to early Pliocene epochs, including the supposed common ancestor of gorillas, chimpanzees, and humans.
● Genus *Dryopithecus*, family Pongidae.
– DERIVATIVES **dry·o·pith·e·cine** /-ˈpiTHiˌsēn/ **n. & adj.**
– ORIGIN modern Latin, from Greek *drus* 'tree' + *pithēkos* 'ape.'

dry paint·ing ▶ **n.** another term for **SAND PAINTING**.

dry plate ▶ **n.** Photography a glass plate coated with a light-sensitive gelatin-based emulsion, used formerly as an improvement on the earlier wet plate.

dry point ▶ **n.** a steel needle for engraving on a bare copper plate without acid. ■ an engraving or print so produced. ■ engraving by this means.

dry-roast·ed ▶ **adj.** roasted without fat or oil: *dry-roasted peanuts.*

dry rot ▶ **n. 1** fungal timber decay occurring in poorly ventilated conditions in buildings, resulting in cracking and powdering of the wood.
2 (also **dry rot fungus**) the fungus that causes this.
● *Serpula lacrymans*, family Corticiaceae, class Hymenomycetes.

dry run ▶ **n.** informal a rehearsal of a performance or procedure before the real one: *the president went through a dry run of his speech.*

dry-salt ▶ **v.** [with obj.] cure (meat or fish) with salt rather than in liquid.

dry-salt·er ▶ **n.** Brit. historical a dealer in dyes, gums, and drugs, and sometimes also in pickles and other preserved foodstuffs.

dry sham·poo ▶ **n.** a shampoo in powder form, used without the addition of water.

dry-shod ▶ **adj. & adv.** without wetting one's shoes: [as adj.] *dry-shod evacuation involved getting into a lifeboat at deck level.*

dry sink ▶ **n.** an antique kitchen cabinet with an inset basin, now generally used as an ornament rather than for practical purposes.

dry-ski ▶ **adj.** [attrib.] denoting or relating to skiing on an artificial surface: *a dry-ski slope.*

dry slope ▶ **n.** an artificial ski slope used for practice and training: [as modifier] *dry-slope racers.*

dry·stone /ˈdrīˌstōn/ ▶ **adj.** [attrib.] (of a stone wall) built without using mortar.

dry·suit /ˈdrīˌso͞ot/ ▶ **n.** a waterproof rubber suit worn for water sports and diving, under which warm clothes can be worn.

Dry Tor·tu·gas /tôrˈto͞ogəz/ an island group in southwestern Florida, west of Key West, that is noted for its wildlife. Also called **the Tortugas** or **Tortugas Keys**.

dry val·ley ▶ **n.** a valley cut by water erosion but containing no permanent surface stream, typically one occurring in an area of porous rock such as limestone.

dry·wall /ˈdrīˌwôl/ ▶ **n.** a type of board made from plaster, wood pulp, or other material, used esp. to form the interior walls of houses.

dry wash ▶ **n.** the dry bed of an intermittent stream.

dry well ▶ **n. 1** a shaft or chamber constructed in the ground in order to aid drainage, sometimes containing pumping equipment.
2 another term for **DRY HOLE**.

DS ▶ **abbr.** ■ Music dal segno. ■ document signed.

Ds ▶ **symbol** the chemical element darmstadtium.

DSC ▶ **abbr.** Distinguished Service Cross, (in the US) an Army decoration for heroism in combat or (in the UK) a decoration for distinguished active service at sea.

DSc ▶ **abbr.** Doctor of Science.

DSL ▶ **abbr.** digital subscriber line, a technology for the high-speed transmission of digital information over standard telephone lines. See also **ADSL**.

DSM ▶ **abbr.** Distinguished Service Medal, (in the US) a military decoration for exceptionally meritorious performance of a duty of great responsibility during wartime or (in the UK) a medal for distinguished service at sea.

DSO ▶ **abbr.** Distinguished Service Order, a British military decoration for distinguished service awarded to officers of the army and navy.

DSP ▶ **abbr.** ■ (in genealogy) died without issue. [from Latin *decessit sine prole.*] ■ (in computing and sound reproduction) digital signal processor or processing.

DSS ▶ **abbr.** ■ decision support system.
■ Department of Social Services. ■ digital satellite system; digital satellite services. ■ digital signature standard.

DST ▶ **abbr.** daylight saving time.

DTD ▶ **abbr.** Computing document type definition.

DTP ▶ **abbr.** desktop publishing.

DTs ▶ **plural n.** (usu. **the DTs**) informal delirium tremens.
– ORIGIN mid 19th cent.: abbreviation, originally in the singular form *DT* (now rare).

DTT (also **DTTV**) ▶ **abbr.** digital terrestrial television.

DTV ▶ **abbr.** digital television.

DU ▶ **abbr.** ■ depleted uranium. ■ Dobson unit(s).

du·al /ˈd(y)o͞oəl/ ▶ **adj. 1** [attrib.] consisting of two parts, elements, or aspects: *their dual role at work and home.* ■ Grammar (in some languages) denoting an inflection that refers to exactly two people or things (as distinct from singular and plural): *Old English has dual number for first- and second-person pronouns.* ■ (in an aircraft) using dual controls: *a dual flight.*
2 (often **dual to**) Mathematics (of a theorem, expression, etc.) related to another by the interchange of particular pairs of terms, such as "point" and "line."
▶ **n. 1** Grammar a dual form of a word. ■ the dual number.
2 Mathematics a theorem, expression, etc., that is dual to another.
– DERIVATIVES **du·al·ize** /-ˌlīz/ **v.**, **du·al·ly adv.**
– ORIGIN late Middle English (as a noun denoting either of the two middle incisor teeth in each jaw): from Latin *dualis*, from *duo* 'two.'

du·al car·riage·way ▶ **n.** British term for **DIVIDED HIGHWAY**.

du·al cit·i·zen·ship (also chiefly Brit. **dual nationality**) ▶ **n.** citizenship in two countries concurrently.

du·al con·trol ▶ **adj.** (of an aircraft or a vehicle) having two sets of controls, one of which is used by the instructor: *a dual-control pilot trainer.*
▶ **n.** (usu. **dual controls**) two such sets of controls in an aircraft or vehicle.

du·al her·it·age ▶ **n.** the fact of having parents from different ethnic or cultural backgrounds.

du·al in-line pack·age ▶ **n.** Electronics see **DIP**.

du·al·ism /ˈd(y)o͞oəˌlizəm/ ▶ **n. 1** the division of something conceptually into two opposed or contrasted aspects, or the state of being so divided: *a dualism between man and nature.* ■ Philosophy a theory or system of thought that regards a domain of reality in terms of two independent principles, esp. mind and matter (**Cartesian dualism**). Compare with **IDEALISM**, **MATERIALISM**, and **MONISM**. ■ the religious doctrine that the universe contains opposed powers of good and evil, esp. seen as balanced equals. ■ in Christian theology, the heresy that in the incarnate Christ there were two coexisting persons, human and divine.
2 the quality or condition of being dual; duality.
– DERIVATIVES **du·al·ist n. & adj.**, **du·al·is·tic** /ˌd(y)o͞oəˈlistik/ **adj.**, **du·al·is·ti·cal·ly** /ˌd(y)o͞oəˈlistik(ə)lē/ **adv.**
– ORIGIN late 18th cent.: from **DUAL**, on the pattern of French *dualisme.*

du·al·i·ty /d(y)o͞oˈalitē/ ▶ **n.** (pl. **dualities**) **1** the quality or condition of being dual: *the novel's deep duality about human motive.* ■ Mathematics the property of two theorems, expressions, etc., being dual to each other. ■ Physics the quantum-mechanical property of being regardable as both a wave and a particle.
2 an instance of opposition or contrast between two concepts or two aspects of something; a dualism: *the photographs capitalize on the dualities of light and dark, stillness and movement.*
– ORIGIN late Middle English: from late Latin *dualitas*, from *dualis* (see **DUAL**).

du·al-pur·pose ▶ **adj.** serving two purposes or functions: *a dual-purpose hand and nail cream.*

du·al-use /yo͞os/ ▶ **adj.** (of technology or equipment) designed or suitable for both civilian and military purposes.

dub¹ /dəb/ ▶ **v.** (**dubs, dubbing, dubbed**) **1** [with obj. and complement] give an unofficial name or nickname to (someone or something): *the media dubbed anorexia "the slimming disease."* ■ make (someone) a knight by the ritual touching of the shoulder with a sword: *he should be dubbed Sir Hubert.*
2 [with obj.] dress (an artificial fishing fly) with strands of fur or wool or with other material.
■ incorporate (fur, wool, or other materials) into a fishing fly.
3 [with obj.] smear (leather) with grease. Compare with **DUBBIN**.
4 trim or make smooth (wood) with an adze.
– ORIGIN late Old English (in the sense 'make a knight'): from Old French *adober* 'equip with armor,' of unknown origin. Sense 2 is from the obsolete meaning 'dress or adorn.'

dub² ▶ **v.** (**dubs, dubbing, dubbed**) [with obj.]
1 provide (a film) with a soundtrack in a different language from the original: *the film will be dubbed into French and Flemish.* ■ add (sound effects or music) to a film or a recording: *background sound can be dubbed in at the editing stage.*
2 make a copy of (a sound or video recording).
■ transfer (a recording) from one medium to another. ■ combine (two or more sound recordings) into one composite soundtrack.
▶ **n. 1** an instance of dubbing sound effects or music: *the level of the dub can be controlled manually.*
2 a style of popular music originating from the remixing of recorded music (esp. reggae), typically with the removal of some vocals and instruments and the exaggeration of bass guitar.
– ORIGIN 1920s: abbreviation of **DOUBLE**.

dub³ informal ▶ **n.** an inexperienced or unskillful person.
▶ **v.** (**dubs, dubbing, dubbed**) [with obj.] Golf misplay (a shot).
– ORIGIN late 19th cent.: perhaps from **DUB¹** in the obsolete technical sense 'make blunt.'

Du·bai /do͞oˈbī, də-/ a member state of the United Arab Emirates; pop. 1,775,000 (est. 2009). ■ its capital city, a port on the Persian Gulf; pop. 1,770,500 (est. 2009).

Du Bar·ry /d(y)o͞o ˈbarē/, Marie Jeanne Bécu, Comtesse (1743–93), French courtier and mistress of Louis XV. During the French Revolution she was arrested by the Revolutionary Tribunal and guillotined.

dub·bin /ˈdəbin/ Brit. ▶ **n.** prepared grease used for softening and waterproofing leather.
▶ **v.** (**dubbins, dubbining, dubbined**) [with obj.] apply such a grease to (leather).
– ORIGIN early 19th cent.: alteration of *dubbing*, present participle of **DUB¹** (sense 3).

dub·bing /ˈdəbiNG/ ▶ **n.** material used for the bodies of artificial fishing flies, esp. fur or wool on waxed silk.
– ORIGIN late 17th cent.: from **DUB¹** + **-ING¹**.

Dub·ček /ˈdo͞obCHek/, Alexander (1921–92), Czech statesman, first secretary of the Czechoslovak Communist Party 1968–69. He was the driving force behind the political reforms of 1968, which prompted the Soviet invasion of Czechoslovakia in 1968 and his removal from office. After the collapse of communism in 1989, he was elected speaker of the federal assembly in the new Czechoslovak parliament.

du·bi·e·ty /d(y)o͞oˈbi-itē/ ▶ **n.** formal the state or quality of being doubtful; uncertainty: *his enemies made much of the dubiety of his paternity.*
– ORIGIN mid 18th cent.: from late Latin *dubietas*, from Latin *dubium* 'a doubt.'

Du·bin·sky /do͞oˈbinskē/, David (1892–1982), US labor leader and social reformer; born in Russia. He served as president of the International Ladies' Garment Workers Union 1932–66 and was responsible for reforms such as improved housing and healthcare.

du·bi·ous /ˈd(y)o͞obēəs/ ▶ **adj. 1** hesitating or doubting: *Alex looked dubious, but complied.*
2 not to be relied upon; suspect: *extremely dubious assumptions.* ■ morally suspect: *time-sharing has been brought into disrepute by dubious sales methods.*
■ of questionable value: *she earned the dubious distinction of being the lowest-paid teacher in the nation.*
– DERIVATIVES **du·bi·ous·ly adv.**, **du·bi·ous·ness n.**
– ORIGIN mid 16th cent. (sense 2): from Latin *dubiosus*, from *dubium* 'a doubt,' neuter of *dubius* 'doubtful.'

du·bi·ta·ble /ˈd(y)o͞obitəbəl/ ▶ **adj.** rare (of a belief, conclusion, etc.) open to doubt.
– DERIVATIVES **du·bi·ta·bil·i·ty** /ˌd(y)o͞obitəˈbilitē/ **n.**
– ORIGIN early 17th cent.: from Latin *dubitabilis*, from *dubitare* 'to doubt.'

du·bi·ta·tion /ˌd(y)o͞obiˈtāSHən/ ▶ **n.** formal doubt; hesitation: *a judgment fenced around with proper scholarly dubitation.*
– ORIGIN late Middle English: from Latin *dubitatio(n-)*, from *dubitare* 'to doubt.'

du·bi·ta·tive /ˈd(y)o͞obiˌtātiv/ ▶ **adj.** formal expressing or inclined to doubt or hesitation.
– ORIGIN early 18th cent.: from French *dubitatif, -ive* or late Latin *dubitativus*, from *dubitare* 'to doubt.'

Dub·lin /ˈdəblən/ the capital city of the Republic of Ireland, on the Irish Sea at the mouth of the Liffey River; pop. 506,211 (2006). Irish name **BAILE ÁTHA**

CLIATH. ■ a county in the Republic of Ireland, in the province of Leinster; county town, Dublin.

dub·ni·um /'dəbnēəm/ ▶ **n.** the chemical element of atomic number 105, a very unstable element made by high-energy atomic collisions. (Symbol: **Db**) See also HAHNIUM, JOLIOTIUM.
– ORIGIN 1967: modern Latin, from *Dubna* in Russia, site of the Joint Nuclear Institute.

Du Bois /d(y)ōō 'bois/, W. E. B. (1868–1963), US writer, sociologist, and political activist; full name *William Edward Burghardt Du Bois*. He was an important figure in the movement for equality for black Americans and cofounded the National Association for the Advancement of Colored People (NAACP) in 1909.

Du·bon·net /,d(y)ōōbə'nā/ ▶ **n.** trademark a sweet French red wine.
– ORIGIN from the name of a family of French wine merchants.

dub reg·gae ▶ **n.** a genre of popular dance music made from remixing reggae recordings: *Phase Selector Sound's inventive dub reggae recordings transcend their Music City origins.*

Du·brov·nik /dōō'brôvnik, 'dōō,brôvnik/ a port and resort on the Adriatic coast of Croatia; pop. 26,500 (est. 2009). Italian name (until 1918) **Ragusa**.

dub·step /'dəbstep/ ▶ **n.** a form of dance music, typically instrumental, characterized by a sparse, syncopated rhythm and a strong bassline.

Du·buf·fet /,d(y)ōōbə'fā/, Jean (1901–85), French painter. He rejected traditional techniques and incorporated materials such as sand and plaster in his paintings and produced sculptures made from garbage.

Du·buque /də'byōōk/ an industrial and commercial city in northeastern Iowa, on the Mississippi River; pop. 57,250 (est. 2008).

du·cal /'d(y)ōōkəl/ ▶ **adj.** [attrib.] of, like, or relating to a duke or dukedom: *the ducal palace in Rouen.*
– ORIGIN late 15th cent.: from Old French, from *duc* 'duke.'

duc·at /'dəkət/ ▶ **n. 1** a gold coin formerly current in most European countries. ■ (**ducats**) informal money: *their production of Hamlet has kept the ducats pouring in.*
2 informal a ticket, esp. an admission ticket.
– ORIGIN from Italian *ducato*, originally referring to a silver coin minted by the Duke of Apulia in 1190: from medieval Latin *ducatus* (see DUCHY). Sense 2 dates from the late 19th cent.

Du·ce /'dōōCHā/ (**Il Duce**) the title assumed by Benito Mussolini in 1922.
– ORIGIN Italian, literally 'leader.'

Du·champ /d(y)ōō'SHäN/, Marcel (1887–1968), US artist; born in France. A leading figure of the Dada movement and originator of conceptual art, he invented "ready-mades," mass-produced articles selected at random and displayed as works of art.

Du·chenne mus·cu·lar dys·tro·phy /dōō'SHen/ (abbr.: **DMD**) ▶ **n.** a severe form of muscular dystrophy caused by a genetic defect and usually affecting boys.
– ORIGIN late 19th cent.: named after G. B. A. *Duchenne* (1806–75), the French neurologist who first described it.

duch·ess /'dəCHis/ ▶ **n.** the wife or widow of a duke. ■ a woman holding a rank equivalent to duke in her own right. ■ Brit. informal (esp. among cockneys) an affectionate form of address used by a man to a girl or woman he knows well.
– ORIGIN late Middle English: via Old French from medieval Latin *ducissa*, from Latin *dux*, *duc-* (see DUKE).

duch·esse /d(y)ōō'SHes/ ▶ **n. 1** (also **duchesse satin**) a soft, heavy, glossy kind of satin, usually of silk.
2 a chaise longue resembling two armchairs linked by a stool.
3 (also **duchesse dressing table**) a dressing table with a pivoting mirror.
– ORIGIN late 18th cent. (sense 2): from French, literally 'duchess.'

duch·esse lace ▶ **n.** a kind of Brussels pillow lace characterized by bold floral patterns worked with a fine thread.

duch·esse po·ta·toes ▶ **plural n.** mashed potatoes mixed with egg yolk, formed into small shapes and baked.

duch·y /'dəCHē/ ▶ **n.** (pl. **duchies**) the territory of a duke or duchess; a dukedom.
– ORIGIN Middle English: from Old French *duche*, from medieval Latin *ducatus*, from Latin *dux*, *duc-* (see DUKE).

duck[1] /dək/ ▶ **n.** (pl. **same** or **ducks**) **1** a waterbird with a broad blunt bill, short legs, webbed feet, and a waddling gait. ● Family Anatidae (the **duck family**); domesticated ducks are mainly descended from the mallard. The duck family also includes geese and swans, from which ducks are distinguished by their generally smaller size and shorter necks.
■ such a bird as food: *a duck for tomorrow's dinner.*
2 a pure white thin-shelled bivalve mollusk found off the Atlantic coasts of America. ● Genus *Anatina*, family Mactridae.
3 another term for **DUKW**.
– PHRASES **get** (or **have**) **one's ducks in a row** get (or have) one's facts straight; get (or have) everything organized. **take to something like a duck to water** take to something very readily: *he shows every sign of taking to University politics like a duck to water.* **water off a duck's back** a potentially hurtful or harmful remark or incident that has no apparent effect on the person mentioned: *it was like water off a duck's back to Nick, but I'm sure it upset Paul.*
– ORIGIN Old English *duce*, from the Germanic base of DUCK[2] (expressing the notion of 'diving bird').

duck[2] ▶ **v. 1** [no obj.] lower the head or the body quickly to avoid a blow or so as not to be seen: *spectators ducked for cover | she ducked into the doorway to get out of the line of fire | [with obj.] he ducked his head and entered.* ■ (**duck out**) depart quickly: *I thought I saw you duck out.* ■ [with obj.] avoid (a blow) by moving down quickly: *he ducked a punch from an angry first baseman.* ■ [with obj.] informal evade or avoid (an unwelcome duty or undertaking): *a responsibility that a less courageous man might well have ducked | [no obj.] I was engaged twice and ducked out both times.*
2 [no obj.] plunge one's head or body underwater briefly: *I had to keep ducking down to get my head cool.*
3 Bridge refrain from playing a winning card on a particular trick for tactical reasons.
▶ **n.** [in sing.] a quick lowering of the head.
– DERIVATIVES **duck·er n.**
– ORIGIN Middle English: of Germanic origin; related to Dutch *duiken* and German *tauchen* 'dive, dip, plunge,' also to DUCK[1].

duck[3] (also **ducks**) ▶ **n.** Brit. dear; darling (used as an informal or affectionate form of address, esp. among cockneys).
– ORIGIN late 16th cent.: from DUCK[1].

duck[4] ▶ **n.** a strong linen or cotton fabric, used chiefly for casual or work clothes and sails.
■ (**ducks**) pants made of such a fabric.
– ORIGIN mid 17th cent.: from Middle Dutch *doek* 'linen, linen cloth'; related to German *Tuch* 'cloth.'

duck[5] ▶ **n.** Cricket a batsman's score of zero: *out for a duck.*
– ORIGIN mid 19th cent.: short for *duck's egg*, used for the figure 0 because of its similar outline.

duck·bill /'dək,bil/ ▶ **n.** an animal with jaws resembling a duck's bill, e.g., a platypus or a duck-billed dinosaur.
▶ **adj.** [attrib.] shaped like a duck's bill: *duckbill pliers.*

duck-billed di·no·saur ▶ **n.** another term for HADROSAUR.

duck·bill plat·y·pus (also **duck-billed platypus**) ▶ **n.** see PLATYPUS.

duck·board /'dək,bôrd/ ▶ **n.** (usu. **duckboards**) a board consisting of a number of wooden slats joined together, placed so as to form a path over muddy ground or in a trench.

duck hawk ▶ **n.** dated the peregrine falcon.

duck·ing stool ▶ **n.** historical a chair fastened to the end of a pole, used formerly to plunge offenders into a pond or river as a punishment.

duck·ling /'dəkliNG/ ▶ **n.** a young duck. ■ the flesh of a young duck as food.

duck mus·sel ▶ **n.** a freshwater bivalve mollusk that is smaller and darker than the related swan mussel, found in rivers with sandy or gravelly bottoms. ● *Anodonta anatina*, family Unionidae.

duck·pin /'dək,pin/ ▶ **n.** a short, squat bowling pin. ■ (**duckpins**) [treated as sing.] a game played with such pins.

ducks and drakes ▶ **n.** a game of throwing flat stones so that they skim along the surface of water.
– PHRASES **play ducks and drakes with** trifle with; treat frivolously.
– ORIGIN late 16th cent.: from the movement of the stone over the water.

duck's ass ▶ **n.** another term for DUCKTAIL.

duck soup ▶ **n.** informal an easy task, or someone easy to overcome: *we had some great battles, but against me he was duck soup.*

duck·tail /'dək,tāl/ (also **duck's ass**) (abbr.: **DA**) ▶ **n.** informal a man's hairstyle, associated esp. with the 1950s, in which the hair is slicked back on both sides and tapered at the nape.

duck·walk /'dək,wôk/ ▶ **v.** [no obj.] walk with the body in a squatting posture.
▶ **n.** a walk with the body in this posture.

duck·weed /'dək,wēd/ ▶ **n.** a tiny aquatic flowering plant that floats in large quantities on still water, often forming an apparently continuous green layer on the surface. ● Family Lemnaceae, in particular the genus *Lemna*.

duck·y /'dəkē/ informal ▶ **n.** (pl. **duckies**) Brit. darling; dear (used as a form of address): *come and sit down, ducky.*
▶ **adj.** charming; delightful: *everything here is just ducky.*
– ORIGIN early 19th cent.: from DUCK[3].

duct /dəkt/ ▶ **n.** a channel or tube for conveying something, in particular: ■ (in a building or a machine) a tube or passageway for air, liquid, cables, etc. ■ (in the body) a vessel for conveying lymph or glandular secretions such as tears or bile. ■ (in a plant) a vessel for conveying water, sap, or air.
▶ **v.** [with obj.] (usu. **be ducted**) convey through a duct: *a ventilation system that must be ducted through the wall* | (as adj. **ducted**) *a ducted air system.*
– ORIGIN mid 17th cent. (in the sense 'course' or 'direction'): from Latin *ductus* 'leading, aqueduct,' from *duct-* 'led,' from the verb *ducere.*

duc·tile /'dəktl, -,tīl/ ▶ **adj.** (of a metal) able to be drawn out into a thin wire. ■ able to be deformed without losing toughness; pliable, not brittle. ■ (of a person) docile or gullible.
– DERIVATIVES **duc·til·i·ty** /dək'tilitē/ **n.**
– ORIGIN Middle English (in the sense 'malleable'): from Latin *ductilis*, from *duct-* 'led,' from the verb *ducere.*

duct·ing /'dəktiNG/ ▶ **n.** a system of ducts. ■ tubing or piping forming such a system.

duct·less /'dəktlis/ ▶ **adj.** Anatomy denoting a gland that secretes directly into the bloodstream, such as an endocrine gland or a lymph gland.

duct tape ▶ **n.** strong, cloth-backed, waterproof adhesive tape.
– ORIGIN 1970s: originally used for repairing leaks in ducted ventilation and heating systems.

duc·tule /'dəkt(y)ōōl/ ▶ **n.** Anatomy a minute duct.
– DERIVATIVES **duc·tu·lar** /-tyələr/ **adj.**
– ORIGIN late 19th cent.: Latin, diminutive of *ductus* 'leading.'

duc·tus /'dəktəs/ ▶ **n.** Anatomy a duct.
– ORIGIN mid 17th cent.: from Latin, literally 'leading.'

duct·work /'dəkt,wərk/ ▶ **n.** a system or network of ducts.

dud /dəd/ informal ▶ **n. 1** a thing that fails to work properly or is otherwise unsatisfactory or worthless: *a high-grade collection, not a dud in the lot | all three bombs were duds.* ■ an ineffectual person: *a complete dud, incapable of even hitting the ball.*
2 (**duds**) clothes: *buy yourself some new duds.*
▶ **adj.** not working or meeting standards; faulty: *a dud ignition switch.* ■ counterfeit: *charged with issuing dud checks.*
– ORIGIN Middle English (in the sense 'item of clothing'): of unknown origin.

dude /dōōd/ informal ▶ **n.** a man; a guy: *if some dude smacked me, I'd smack him back.* ■ a stylish, fastidious man: *cool dudes.* [a slang term that came into vogue in New York *c.*1883, in connection with the 'aesthetic' craze of the period.] ■ a city-dweller, esp. one vacationing on a ranch in the western US.
▶ **v.** [no obj.] (**dude up**) dress up elaborately: (as adj. **duded**) *my brother was all duded up in silver and burgundy.*
– DERIVATIVES **dud·ish adj.**
– ORIGIN late 19th cent.: probably from German dialect *Dude* 'fool.'

dude ranch ▶ **n.** (in the western US) a cattle ranch converted to a vacation resort for tourists.

dudg·eon /'dəjən/ ▶ **n.** a feeling of offense or deep resentment: *the manager walked out in high dudgeon.*
– ORIGIN late 16th cent.: of unknown origin.

Dud·ley[1] /'dədlē/ an industrial town in western central England, near Birmingham; pop. 193,200 (est. 2009).

Dud·ley[2], Robert, Earl of Leicester (*c.*1532–88), English nobleman, military commander, and favorite of Elizabeth I.

due /d(y)ōō/ ▶ **adj. 1** [predic.] expected at or planned for at a certain time: *the baby's due in August | he is due back soon* | [with infinitive] *talks are due to adjourn tomorrow.* ■ (of a payment) required at a certain

time: *the May installment was due.* ■ (of a person) having reached a point where the thing mentioned is required or owed: *she was due for a raise | you're more than due a vacation.* ■ (of a thing) required or owed as a legal or moral obligation: *he was only taking back what was* **due to** *him | you must pay any income tax due.*
2 [attrib.] of the proper quality or extent; adequate: *driving without due care and attention.*
▶ **n. 1** (**one's due**) a person's right; what is owed to someone: *he attracts more criticism than is his due.*
2 (**dues**) an obligatory payment; a fee: *he had paid union dues for years.*

d

▶ **adv.** (with reference to a point of the compass) exactly; directly: *we'll head due south again on the same road.*
– PHRASES **due to 1** caused by or ascribable to: *unemployment due to automation will grow steadily.* **2** because of; owing to: *he had to withdraw due to a knee injury.* **give someone their due** be fair to someone: *to give him his due, he was a generous employer.* **in due course** at the appropriate time: *Reynolds will respond in due course to the letter.* **pay one's dues** fulfill one's obligations: *he had paid his dues to society for his previous convictions.* ■ experience difficulties before achieving success: *this drummer has paid his dues with the best.*
– ORIGIN Middle English (in the sense 'payable'): from Old French *deu* 'owed,' based on Latin *debitus* 'owed,' from *debere* 'owe.'

> **USAGE** The use of **due to** as a prepositional phrase meaning 'because of,' as in *he had to retire due to an injury* first appeared in print in 1897, and traditional grammarians have opposed this prepositional usage for more than a century on the grounds that it is a misuse of the adjectival phrase **due to** in the sense of 'attributable to, likely or expected to' (*the train is due to arrive at 11:15*), or 'payable or owed to' (*render unto Caesar what is due to Caesar*). Nevertheless, this prepositional usage is now widespread and common in all types of literature and must be regarded as standard English.The phrase **due to the fact that** is very common in speech, but it is wordy, and, especially in writing, one should use the simple word 'because.'

due date ▶ **n.** the date on which something falls due, esp. the payment of a bill or the expected birth of a baby.
due dil·i·gence ▶ **n.** Law reasonable steps taken by a person in order to satisfy a legal requirement, esp. in buying or selling something. ■ a comprehensive appraisal of a business undertaken by a prospective buyer, esp. to establish its assets and liabilities and evaluate its commercial potential.
du·el /ˈd(y)o͞oəl/ ▶ **n.** chiefly historical a contest with deadly weapons arranged between two people in order to settle a point of honor. ■ (in modern use) a contest or race between two parties: *two eminent critics engaged in a verbal duel.*
▶ **v.** (**duels, dueling, dueled**; Brit. **duels, duelling, duelled**) [no obj.] fight a duel or duels: (as noun **dueling**) *dueling had been forbidden for serving officers.*
– DERIVATIVES **du·el·er** (Brit. **dueller**) **n.**, **du·el·ist** /-ist/ (Brit. **duellist**) **n.**
– ORIGIN late 15th cent.: from Latin *duellum*, archaic form of *bellum* 'war,' used in medieval Latin with the meaning 'combat between two persons,' partly influenced by *dualis* 'of two.' The original sense was 'single combat used to decide a judicial dispute'; the sense 'contest to decide a point of honor' dates from the early 17th cent.
duen·de /do͞oˈendā/ ▶ **n.** a quality of passion and inspiration. ■ a spirit.
– ORIGIN 1920s: from Spanish, contraction of *duen de casa*, from *dueño de casa* 'owner of the house.'
du·en·na /d(y)o͞oˈenə/ ▶ **n.** an older woman acting as a governess and companion in charge of girls, esp. in a Spanish family; a chaperone.
– ORIGIN mid 17th cent.: earlier form of Spanish *dueña*, from Latin *domina* 'lady, mistress.'
due proc·ess (also **due process of law**) ▶ **n.** fair treatment through the normal judicial system, esp. as a citizen's entitlement.
Due·ro /ˈdwerō/ Spanish name for **DOURO**.
du·et /d(y)o͞oˈet/ ▶ **n.** a performance by two people, esp. singers, instrumentalists, or dancers. ■ a musical composition for two performers.
▶ **v.** (**duets, duetting, duetted**) [no obj.] perform a duet.
– DERIVATIVES **du·et·tist n.**
– ORIGIN mid 18th cent.: from Italian *duetto*, diminutive of *duo* 'duet,' from Latin *duo* 'two.'
duff[1] /dəf/ ▶ **n.** [usu. with modifier] a flour pudding boiled or steamed in a cloth bag: *a currant duff.*
– ORIGIN mid 19th cent.: northern English form of **DOUGH**.
duff[2] ▶ **n. 1** decaying vegetable matter covering the ground under trees.
2 Mining coal dust; dross.
▶ **adj.** Brit. informal of very poor quality: *duff lyrics.* ■ incorrect or false: *she played a couple of duff notes.*
– ORIGIN late 18th cent. (denoting something worthless): of unknown origin.
duff[3] ▶ **v.** [with obj.] Brit. informal **1** (**duff someone up**) beat someone up.
2 Golf mishit (a shot).
– ORIGIN early 19th cent.: of uncertain origin; sense 2 is probably a back-formation from **DUFFER**.
duff[4] ▶ **n.** informal a person's buttocks: *I did not get where I am today by sitting on my duff.*
– ORIGIN mid 19th cent.: of unknown origin.
duf·fel /ˈdəfəl/ (also **duffle**) ▶ **n. 1** a coarse woolen cloth with a thick nap. ■ short for **DUFFEL COAT**.
2 sporting or camping equipment. ■ short for **DUFFEL BAG**.
– ORIGIN mid 17th cent.: from *Duffel*, the name of a town in Belgium where the cloth was originally made.
duf·fel bag ▶ **n.** a cylindrical canvas bag closed by a drawstring and carried over the shoulder.
– ORIGIN early 20th cent.: from **DUFFEL** (sense 2), originally denoting a bag for equipment.
duf·fel coat ▶ **n.** a coat made of duffel, typically hooded and fastened with toggles.
duf·fer /ˈdəfər/ ▶ **n.** informal an incompetent or stupid person, esp. an elderly one: *he's the most worthless old duffer.* ■ a person inexperienced at something, esp. at playing golf.
– ORIGIN mid 19th cent.: from Scots *dowfart* 'stupid person,' from *douf* 'spiritless.'
Du Fu /ˈdo͞o ˈfo͞o/ variant of **TU FU**.
du·fus ▶ **n.** variant spelling of **DOOFUS**.
Du·fy /d(y)o͞oˈfē/, Raoul (1877–1953), French painter and textile designer. His characteristic style involved calligraphic outlines sketched on brilliant background washes.
dug[1] /dəg/ past and past participle of **DIG**.
dug[2] ▶ **n.** (usu. **dugs**) the udder, teat, or nipple of a female animal. ■ archaic a woman's breast.
– ORIGIN mid 16th cent.: possibly of Old Norse origin and related to Swedish *dägga*, Danish *dægge* 'suckle.'
du·gong /ˈdo͞ogäNG, -gôNG/ ▶ **n.** (pl. **same** or **dugongs**) an aquatic mammal found on the coasts of the Indian Ocean from eastern Africa to northern Australia. It is distinguished from the manatees by its forked tail. ● *Dugong dugon*, family Dugongidae.
– ORIGIN early 19th cent.: based on Malay *duyong*.

dugong

dug·out /ˈdəgˌout/ ▶ **n. 1** a shelter that is dug in the ground and roofed over, esp. one used by troops in warfare. ■ a low shelter at the side of a baseball field, with seating from which a team's coaches and players not taking part can watch the game.
2 (also **dugout canoe**) a canoe made from a hollowed tree trunk.
duh /də, do͞o/ ▶ **exclam.** informal used to comment on an action perceived as foolish or stupid, or a statement perceived as obvious: *I left the keys in the ignition—duh! | Leopold correctly informs him that the opera is in Italian (duh!).*
DUI ▶ **abbr.** driving under the influence (of drugs or alcohol).
dui·ker /ˈdīkər/ ▶ **n.** (pl. **same** or **duikers**) a small African antelope that typically has a tuft of hair between the horns, found mainly in the rain forest. ● *Cephalophus* and other genera, family Bovidae: several species, including the **common duiker** (*Sylvicapra grimmia*), of southern African savanna and bush, and the very small **blue duiker** (*Philantomba monticola*), prized for its skin.
– ORIGIN late 18th cent.: from South African Dutch, from Dutch, literally 'diver,' from the animal's habit of plunging through bushes when pursued; related to **DUCK**[2].
Duis·burg /ˈd(y)o͞ozˌbərg, ˈd(y)o͞os-, -ˌbo͝ork/ an industrial city in northwestern Germany, in North Rhine–Westphalia; pop. 499,100 (est. 2006).
du jour /də ˈZHo͝or, ˌd(y)o͞o/ ▶ **adj.** [postpositive] (of food in a restaurant) available and being served on this day: *cream of mussel, an occasional soup du jour.* ■ informal used to describe something that is enjoying great but probably short-lived popularity or publicity: *attention deficit disorder is the disease du jour.*
– ORIGIN French, literally 'of the day.'
duke /d(y)o͞ok/ ▶ **n. 1** a male holding the highest hereditary title in the British and certain other peerages. ■ chiefly historical (in some parts of Europe) a male ruler of a small independent state.
2 (**dukes**) informal the fists, esp. when raised in a fighting attitude. [from rhyming slang *Duke of Yorks* 'forks' (= fingers).]
– PHRASES **duke it out** informal fight it out.
– ORIGIN Old English (denoting the ruler of a duchy), from Old French *duc*, from Latin *dux, duc-* 'leader'; related to *ducere* 'to lead.'
duke cher·ry ▶ **n.** a cultivated cherry that is a hybrid between the mazzard and the morello. ● *Prunus* × gondouinii, family Rosaceae.
duke·dom /ˈd(y)o͞okdəm/ ▶ **n.** a territory ruled by a duke. ■ the rank of duke.
DUKW ▶ **n.** an amphibious transport vehicle, esp. as used by the Allies during World War II. Also called **DUCK**[1].
– ORIGIN an official designation, being a combination of factory-applied letters referring to features of the vehicle.
dul·ca·ma·ra /ˌdəlkəˈmerə/ ▶ **n.** an extract of woody nightshade, used in homeopathy esp. for treating skin diseases and chest complaints.
– ORIGIN late 16th cent.: from medieval Latin (used as a specific epithet in *Solanum dulcamara*), from Latin *dulcis* 'sweet' + *amara* 'bitter.'
dul·ce de le·che /ˈdo͞olsā de ˈleCHā/ ▶ **n.** a traditional Argentinian dessert made by caramelizing sugar in milk.
– ORIGIN early 20th cent.: American Spanish, from *dulce* 'sweet' + *de* 'of' + *leche* 'milk.'
dul·cet /ˈdəlsit/ ▶ **adj.** (esp. of sound) sweet and soothing (often used ironically): *record the dulcet tones of your family and friends.*
– ORIGIN late Middle English *doucet*, from Old French *doucet*, diminutive of *doux*, from Latin *dulcis* 'sweet.' The Latin form influenced the modern spelling.
dul·ci·an /ˈdəlsēən/ ▶ **n.** an early type of bassoon made in one piece. ■ any of various organ stops, typically with 8-foot funnel-shaped flue pipes or 8- or 16-foot reed pipes.
– ORIGIN mid 19th cent.: from German *Dulzian*, or a variant of **DULCIANA**.
dul·ci·an·a /ˌdəlsēˈanə, -ˈänə/ ▶ **n.** an organ stop, typically with small conical open metal pipes.
– ORIGIN late 18th cent.: via medieval Latin from Latin *dulcis* 'sweet.'
dul·ci·fy /ˈdəlsəˌfī/ ▶ **v.** (**dulcifies, dulcifying, dulcified**) [with obj.] literary sweeten: *cider pap dulcified with molasses.* ■ calm or soothe: *his voice dulcified the panic.*
– DERIVATIVES **dul·ci·fi·ca·tion** /ˌdəlsəfiˈkāSHən/ **n.**
– ORIGIN late 16th cent. (in the sense 'sweeten'): from Latin *dulcificare* 'sweeten,' from *dulcis* 'sweet.'
dul·ci·mer /ˈdəlsəmər/ ▶ **n.** (also **hammered dulcimer**) a musical instrument with a sounding board or box, typically trapezoidal in shape, over which strings of graduated length are stretched, played by being struck with handheld hammers. ■ (**Appalachian dulcimer**) a musical instrument with a long rounded body and a fretted fingerboard, played by bowing, plucking, and strumming. Also called **MOUNTAIN DULCIMER**.
– ORIGIN late 15th cent.: from Old French *doulcemer*, probably from Latin *dulce melos* 'sweet melody.'

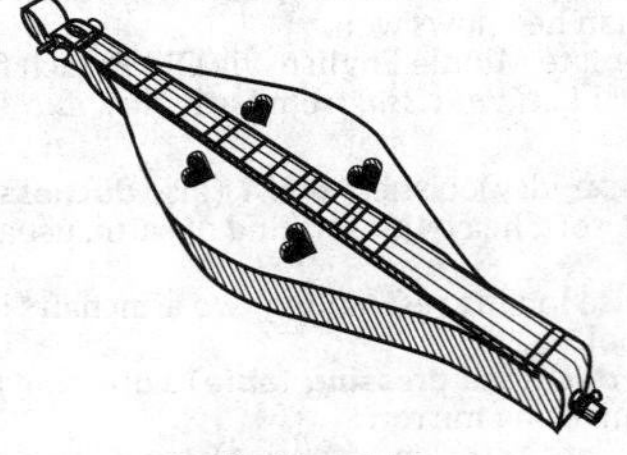

Appalachian dulcimer

dul·ci·tone /ˈdəlsəˌtōn/ ▶ **n.** a musical keyboard instrument in which a series of steel tuning forks is struck by hammers. It was invented in the late 19th century and was superseded by the celesta.
– ORIGIN late 19th cent.: coined by T. Machell, the instrument's inventor, from Latin *dulcis* 'sweet' + *tonus* 'tone.'
du·li·a /d(y)o͞oˈlīə/ ▶ **n.** (in Roman Catholic theology) the reverence accorded to saints and angels. Compare with **LATRIA**.
– ORIGIN late Middle English: via medieval Latin from Greek *douleia* 'servitude,' from *doulos* 'slave.'
dull /dəl/ ▶ **adj. 1** lacking interest or excitement: *your diet doesn't have to be dull and boring.* ■ archaic

(of a person) feeling bored and dispirited: *she said she wouldn't be dull and lonely.*
2 lacking brightness, vividness, or sheen: *his face glowed in the dull lamplight* | *his black hair looked dull.* ■ (of the weather) overcast; gloomy: *next morning dawned dull.* ■ (of sound) not clear; muffled: *a dull thud of hooves.* ■ (of pain) indistinctly felt; not acute: *there was a dull pain in his lower jaw.* ■ (of an edge or blade) blunt: *a lot more people are cut with dull knives than with sharp ones.*
3 (of a person) slow to understand; stupid: *the voice of a teacher talking to a rather dull child.* ■ archaic (of a person's senses) not perceiving things distinctly; insensitive. ■ (of activity) sluggish, slow-moving: *gold closed lower in dull trading.*
▶ **v.** make or become dull or less intense: [with obj.] *time dulls the memory* | [no obj.] *Albert's eyes dulled a little.*
– PHRASES **(as) dull as dishwater** extremely dull. **dull the edge of** cause to be less keenly felt; reduce the intensity or effectiveness of: *she'd have to find something to dull the edges of the pain.*
– DERIVATIVES **dull·ish adj.**, **dull·ness** (also **dulness**) **n.**, **dul·ly adv.**
– ORIGIN Old English *dol* 'stupid,' of Germanic origin; related to Dutch *dol* 'crazy' and German *toll* 'mad, fantastic, wonderful.'

dull·ard /ˈdələrd/ ▶ **n.** a slow or stupid person.
– ORIGIN Middle English: from Middle Dutch *dullaert*, from *dul* 'dull.'

Dul·les /ˈdələs/, John Foster (1888–1959), US statesman and international lawyer. He was the US adviser at the founding of the United Nations in 1945. As secretary of state at the height of the Cold War 1953–59, he urged the stockpiling of nuclear arms to deter Soviet aggression.

dulls·ville /ˈdəlzˌvil/ informal ▶ **n.** a dull or monotonous place or condition.
▶ **adj.** dull or monotonous: *she transforms their dullsville life.*

dull-wit·ted ▶ **adj.** slow to understand; stupid.

du·lo·sis /d(y)o͞oˈlōsis/ ▶ **n.** Entomology the practice by slave-making ants of capturing the pupae of other ant species and rearing them as workers of their own colony.
– DERIVATIVES **du·lot·ic** /-ˈlätik/ **adj.**
– ORIGIN early 20th cent.: from Greek *doulōsis* 'slavery,' from *doulos* 'slave.'

dulse /dəls/ ▶ **n.** a dark red edible seaweed with flattened branching fronds. ● *Rhodymenia palmata*, division Rhodophyta.
– ORIGIN early 17th cent.: from Irish and Scottish Gaelic *duileasg*.

Du·luth /dəˈlo͞oTH/ a port in northeastern Minnesota, at the western end of Lake Superior; pop. 84,284 (est. 2008).

du·ly /ˈd(y)o͞olē/ ▶ **adv.** in accordance with what is required or appropriate; following proper procedure or arrangement: *a document duly signed and authorized by the inspector* | *the ceremony duly began at midnight.* ■ as might be expected or predicted: *I used the tent and was duly impressed.*

dum /dəm/ ▶ **adj.** Indian cooked with steam: *dum aloo.*
– ORIGIN from Hindi *dam*.

Du·ma /ˈdo͞omə/ ▶ **n.** a legislative body in the ruling assembly of Russia and of some other republics of the former Soviet Union.

> **Duma** originally denoted pre-19th-century advisory municipal councils in Russia. It later referred to any of four elected legislative bodies established owing to popular demand in Russia between 1906 and 1917. After the collapse of the Soviet Union in 1991, a new **Duma** was set up as the lower chamber of the Russian parliament.

Du·mas /d(y)o͞oˈmä/ the name of two French novelists and playwrights. ■ **Alexandre** (1802–70); known as **Dumas** *père* (father). He wrote the historical adventure novels *The Three Musketeers* (1844–45) and *The Count of Monte Cristo* (1844–45). ■ **Alexandre** (1824–95), son of Dumas *père*; known as **Dumas** *fils* (son). He wrote the novel (and play) *La Dame aux camélias* (1848), which formed the basis of Verdi's opera *La Traviata* (1853).

Du Mau·ri·er[1] /d(y)o͞o ˈmôrēˌā/, Dame Daphne (1907–89), English novelist; granddaughter of George du Maurier. Notable works: *Jamaica Inn* (1936), *Rebecca* (1938), and *The Birds* (1952).

Du Mau·ri·er[2], George (Louis Palmella Busson) (1834–96), French novelist, cartoonist, and illustrator. He wrote *Trilby* (1894), which included the character Svengali.

dumb /dəm/ ▶ **adj. 1** offensive (of a person) unable to speak, most typically because of congenital deafness: *he was born deaf, dumb, and blind.* ■ (of animals) unable to speak as a natural state and thus regarded as helpless or deserving pity. ■ [predic.] temporarily unable or unwilling to speak: *she stood dumb while he poured out a stream of abuse.* ■ [attrib.] resulting in or expressed by speechlessness: *they stared in dumb amazement.*
2 informal stupid: *a dumb question.* ■ (of a computer terminal) able only to transmit data to or receive data from a computer; having no independent processing capability. Often contrasted with INTELLIGENT.
▶ **v.** [with obj.] **1** (**dumb something down**) informal simplify or reduce the intellectual content of something so as to make it accessible to a larger number of people: *critics have accused publishers of dumbing down books.* ■ [no obj.] (**dumb down**) become less intellectually challenging: *the need to dumb down for mass audiences.*
2 literary make dumb or unheard; silence: *a splendor that dazed the mind and dumbed the tongue.*
– DERIVATIVES **dumb·ly adv.**, **dumb·ness n.**
– ORIGIN Old English, of Germanic origin; related to Old Norse *dumbr* and Gothic *dumbs* 'mute,' also to Dutch *dom* 'stupid' and German *dumm* 'stupid.'

> **USAGE** Although **dumb** meaning 'not able to speak' is the older sense, it has been overwhelmed by the newer sense (meaning 'stupid') to such an extent that the use of the first sense is now almost certain to cause offense. Alternatives such as **speech-impaired** should be used instead. See also usage at DEAF-MUTE.

Dum·bar·ton Oaks /ˈdəmˌbärtn ˈōks/ a historic site in Washington, DC, an estate at which plans for the United Nations were formulated at a 1944 meeting.

dumb-ass ▶ **adj.** [attrib.] informal stupid; brainless: *dumb-ass politicians.*

dumb·bell /ˈdəmˌbel/ ▶ **n. 1** a short bar with a weight at each end, used typically in pairs for exercise or muscle-building. ■ [as modifier] shaped like a dumbbell: *a dumbbell molecule.*
2 informal a stupid person.
– ORIGIN early 18th cent.: originally denoting an apparatus similar to that used to ring a church bell (but without the bell, so noiseless or "dumb"); sense 2 (dating from the 1920s) is an extended use by association with DUMB 'stupid.'

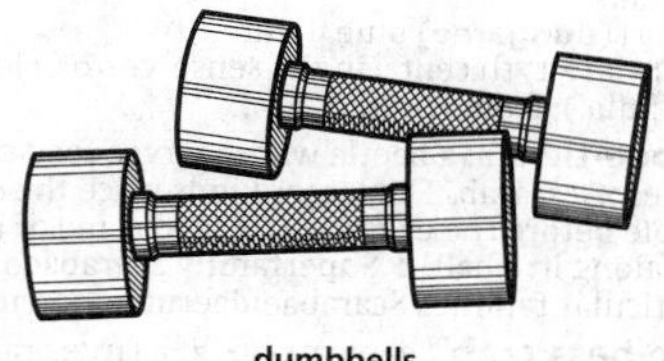
dumbbells

dumb blonde (also **dumb blond**) ▶ **n.** informal a blond-haired woman perceived in a stereotypical way as being attractive but unintelligent.

dumb cane ▶ **n.** a thick-stemmed plant with large variegated leaves, native to tropical America and widely grown as a houseplant. ● Genus *Dieffenbachia*, family Araceae: several species, in particular the Caribbean *D. seguine*, which has a poisonous sap that swells the tongue and temporarily disables the power of speech.

dumb cluck ▶ **n.** informal a stupid person.

dumb·found /ˈdəmˌfound/ (also **dumfound**) ▶ **v.** [with obj.] (usu. **be dumbfounded**) greatly astonish or amaze: *they were dumbfounded at his popularity.*
– ORIGIN mid 17th cent.: blend of DUMB and CONFOUND.

dumb·head /ˈdəmˌhed/ ▶ **n.** informal a stupid person.

dumb i·ron ▶ **n.** historical a curved side piece of a vehicle chassis, to which the front springs are attached.

dum·bo /ˈdəmbō/ ▶ **n.** (pl. **dumbos**) informal a stupid person.
– ORIGIN 1950s: from DUMB + -O, popularized by the 1941 cartoon film *Dumbo*.

dumb·show /ˈdəmˌSHō/ (also **dumb show**) ▶ **n.** gestures used to convey a meaning or message without speech; mime: *they demonstrated in dumbshow how the tea should be made.* ■ a piece of dramatic mime: *there were gags, spoofs, and dumbshows.* ■ (esp. in English drama of the 16th and 17th centuries) a part of a play acted in mime to summarize, supplement, or comment on the main action.

dumb·size /ˈdəmˌsīz/ ▶ **v.** [no obj.] (of a company) reduce staff numbers to levels so low that work can no longer be carried out effectively.
– ORIGIN 1990s: humorously, on the pattern of *downsize*.

dumb·struck /ˈdəmˌstrək/ ▶ **adj.** so shocked or surprised as to be unable to speak: *he was dumbstruck with terror.*

dumb wait·er ▶ **n. 1** a small elevator for carrying things, esp. food and dishes, between the floors of a building.
2 Brit. a movable table, typically with revolving shelves, used in a dining room.

dum·dum /ˈdəmˌdəm/ (also **dumdum bullet**) ▶ **n.** a kind of soft-nosed bullet that expands on impact.
– ORIGIN late 19th cent.: from *Dum Dum*, name of a town and arsenal in eastern India, where such bullets were first produced.

dum-dum ▶ **n.** informal a stupid person.
– ORIGIN 1970s: reduplication of DUMB.

dum·found ▶ **v.** variant spelling of DUMBFOUND.

Dum·fries and Gal·lo·way /dəmˈfrēs and ˈgaləˌwā/ an administrative region in southwestern Scotland, formed in 1975; administrative center, Dumfries.

dum·ka /ˈdo͞omkə/ ▶ **n.** (pl. **dumkas** or **dumky** /-kē/) a piece of Slavic music, originating as a folk ballad or lament, typically melancholy with contrasting lively sections.
– ORIGIN late 19th cent.: via Czech and Polish from Ukrainian.

dumm·kopf /ˈdo͞omˌkôf, -ˌkôpf, ˈdəm-/ ▶ **n.** a stupid person; a blockhead.
– ORIGIN early 19th cent.: from German *dumm* 'dumb' + *Kopf* 'head.'

dum·my /ˈdəmē/ ▶ **n.** (pl. **dummies**) **1** a model or replica of a human being: *a waxwork dummy.* ■ a figure used for displaying or fitting clothes: *a tailor's dummy.* ■ a ventriloquist's doll. ■ Bridge the declarer's partner, whose cards are exposed on the table after the opening lead and played by the declarer. ■ Bridge the exposed hand of the declarer's partner. ■ an imaginary fourth player in whist: [as modifier] *dummy whist.*
2 something designed to resemble and serve as a substitute for the real or usual thing; a counterfeit or sham: *tests using stuffed owls and wooden dummies* | [as modifier] *a dummy torpedo.* ■ a prototype or mock-up, esp. of a book or the layout of a page. ■ a blank round of ammunition. ■ [as modifier] Grammar denoting a word that has no semantic content but is used to maintain grammatical structure.
3 informal a stupid person.
▶ **v.** (**dummies, dummying, dummied**) [with obj.] create a prototype or mock-up of a book or page: *officials dummied up a set of photos.*
– PHRASAL VERBS **dummy up** informal keep quiet; give no information.
– ORIGIN late 16th cent.: from DUMB + -Y[1]. The original sense was 'a person who cannot speak,' then 'an imaginary fourth player in whist' (mid 18th cent.), whence 'a substitute for the real thing' and 'a model of a human being' (mid 19th cent).

dum·my cord ▶ **n.** a cord or strap that secures an object (such as a weapon) to one's person.
▶ **v.** [with obj.] secure an object with such a cord: *he'll show you how to dummy cord your knife.*

dum·my head ▶ **n.** Electronics a model of a human head with a microphone in each ear, used in making binaural and other sound-recording techniques.

du·mor·ti·er·ite /d(y)o͞oˈmôrtēəˌrit/ ▶ **n.** a rare blue or violet mineral occurring typically as needles and fibrous masses in gneiss and schist. It consists of an aluminum and iron borosilicate.
– ORIGIN late 19th cent.: from the name of V.-E. *Dumortier* (1802–76), French geologist, + -ITE[1].

dump /dəmp/ ▶ **n. 1** a site for depositing garbage. ■ [usu. with modifier] a place where a particular kind of waste, esp. dangerous waste, is left: *a nuclear waste dump.* ■ a heap of garbage left at a dump. ■ informal an unpleasant or dreary place: *she says the town has become a dump.* ■ informal an act of defecation.
2 Computing a copying of stored data to a different location, performed typically as a protection against loss. ■ a printout or list of the contents of a computer's memory, occurring typically after a system failure.
▶ **v.** [with obj.] **1** deposit or dispose of (garbage, waste, or unwanted material), typically in a careless or hurried way: *trucks dumped 1,900 tons of refuse here* | [no obj.] *an attempt to prevent people from dumping on vacant lots.* ■ put down or abandon (something) hurriedly in order to make an escape: *the couple dumped the car and fled.* ■ put (something) down firmly or heavily and carelessly: *she dumped her knapsack on the floor.* ■ informal abandon or desert (someone): *his girlfriend dumped him for being fat.* ■ send (goods unsalable in the home market) to a foreign market for sale at a low price: *other countries dump steel in the US at below-*

market prices. ■ informal sell off (assets) rapidly: *investors dumped shares in scores of other consumer-goods firms.*
2 Computing copy (stored data) to a different location, esp. so as to protect against loss. ■ print out or list the contents of (a store), esp. after a system failure.
3 Football tackle (a quarterback) before he can throw a pass.
– PHRASAL VERBS **dump on** informal criticize or abuse (someone); treat badly: *you get dumped on just because of your name.*
– ORIGIN Middle English: perhaps from Old Norse; related to Danish *dumpe* and Norwegian *dumpa* 'fall suddenly' (the original sense in English); in later use partly imitative; compare with THUMP.

d

dump·er /ˈdəmpər/ ▶ **n.** a person or thing that dumps something. ■ (**the dumper**) informal used in reference to a bad or unwanted state: *his career's in the dumper.* ■ (also **dumper truck**) Brit. a dump truck.

dump·ing ground ▶ **n.** a place where garbage or unwanted material is left.

dump·ing syn·drome ▶ **n.** Medicine a group of symptoms, including weakness, abdominal discomfort, and sometimes abnormally rapid bowel evacuation, occurring after meals in some patients who have undergone gastric surgery.

dump·ling /ˈdəmpliNG/ ▶ **n.** a small savory ball of dough (usually made with suet) that may be boiled, fried, or baked in a casserole. ■ a pudding consisting of apples or other fruit enclosed in a sweet dough and baked. ■ humorous a small, fat person: *he was a 250-pound dumpling.*
– ORIGIN early 17th cent.: apparently from the rare adjective *dump* 'of the consistency of dough,' although *dumpling* is recorded much earlier.

dumps /dəmps/ ▶ **plural n.** (in phrase (**down**) **in the dumps**) informal (of a person) depressed or unhappy.
– ORIGIN early 16th cent. (originally singular in the sense 'a dazed or puzzled state'): probably a figurative use of Middle Dutch *domp* 'haze, mist.'

dump·ster /ˈdəmpstər/ (also **Dumpster** trademark) ▶ **n.** a large trash receptacle designed to be hoisted and emptied into a truck.
– ORIGIN 1930s: originally *Dempster Dumpster,* proprietary name (based on DUMP) given by the American manufacturers, Dempster Brothers of Knoxville, Tennessee.

dump·ster div·ing ▶ **n.** the practice of raiding dumpsters to find discarded items that are still useful, can be recycled, and have value.

dump truck ▶ **n.** a truck with a body that tilts or opens at the back for unloading.

dump·y /ˈdəmpē/ ▶ **adj.** (**dumpier, dumpiest**) **1** (of a person) short and stout: *her plain, dumpy sister.*
2 (of a room or building) ugly, dirty, and run-down: *a dumpy little diner with a "closed" sign hanging in the window.*
– DERIVATIVES **dump·i·ly** /-pəlē/ **adv.**, **dump·i·ness n.**
– ORIGIN mid 18th cent.: from DUMPLING + -Y[1].

Dum·yat /do͝omˈyät/ Arabic name for DAMIETTA.

dun[1] /dən/ ▶ **adj.** of a dull grayish-brown color: *a dun cow.* ■ literary dark; dusky: *when the dun evening comes.*
▶ **n. 1** a dull grayish-brown color.
2 a thing that is dun in color, in particular: ■ a horse with a sandy or sandy-gray coat, black mane, tail, and lower legs, and a dark dorsal stripe. ■ a sub-adult mayfly, which has drab coloration and opaque wings. ■ an artificial fishing fly imitating this.
– ORIGIN Old English *dun, dunn,* of Germanic origin; probably related to DUSK.

dun[2] ▶ **v.** (**duns, dunning, dunned**) [with obj.] make persistent demands on (someone), esp. for payment of a debt: *they would very likely start dunning you for payment of your taxes* | (as adj. **dunning**) *she received two dunning letters from the bank.*
▶ **n.** archaic a debt collector or an insistent creditor. ■ a demand for payment.
– ORIGIN early 17th cent. (as a noun): from obsolete *Dunkirk privateer,* from the French port of DUNKIRK.

du·nam /ˈdo͞onəm/ ▶ **n.** a measure of land area used in parts of the former Turkish empire, including Israel (where it is equal to about 900 square meters).
– ORIGIN from modern Hebrew *dûnām* or Arabic *dūnum,* from Turkish *dönüm,* from *dönmek* 'go around.'

Dun·can /ˈdəNGkən/, Isadora (1878–1927), US dancer and teacher. A pioneer of modern dance, she was famous for her "free" barefoot dancing. She died by strangulation when her long scarf became entangled in the wheels of a car.

Dun·can I (*c.*1010–40), king of Scotland 1034–40. He was killed in battle by Macbeth.

dunce /dəns/ ▶ **n.** a person who is slow at learning; a stupid person.
– ORIGIN early 16th cent.: originally an epithet for a follower of John DUNS SCOTUS, whose followers were ridiculed by 16th-cent. humanists and reformers as enemies of learning.

dunce cap (Brit. also **dunce's cap**) ▶ **n.** a paper cone formerly put on the head of a dunce at school as a mark of disgrace.

Dun·dalk /ˈdən,dôk/ a community in north central Maryland, a port just southeast of Baltimore; pop. 62,306 (2000).

Dun·dee /dənˈdē/ a city in eastern Scotland, on the northern side of the Firth of Tay; pop. 141,600 (est. 2009).

Dun·dee cake ▶ **n.** chiefly Brit. a rich fruitcake, typically decorated on top with almonds.

Dun·dee mar·ma·lade ▶ **n.** a type of orange marmalade, originally made in Dundee.

dun·der·head /ˈdəndər,hed/ ▶ **n.** informal a stupid person.
– DERIVATIVES **dun·der·head·ed adj.**
– ORIGIN early 17th cent.: compare with obsolete Scots *dunder, dunner* 'resounding noise'; related to DIN.

dune /d(y)o͞on/ ▶ **n.** a mound or ridge of sand or other loose sediment formed by the wind, esp. on the sea coast or in a desert: *a sand dune.*
– ORIGIN late 18th cent.: from French, from Middle Dutch *dūne*; related to Old English *dūn* 'hill' (see DOWN[3]).

dune bug·gy ▶ **n.** a low, wide-wheeled motor vehicle for recreational driving on sand.

Dun·e·din /dənˈēdn/ a city and port on South Island in New Zealand, founded in 1848 by Scottish settlers; pop. 118,683 (2006).

dung /dəNG/ ▶ **n.** the excrement of animals; manure.
▶ **v.** [with obj.] drop or spread dung on (a piece of ground).
– ORIGIN Old English, of Germanic origin; related to German *Dung,* Swedish *dynga,* Icelandic *dyngja* 'dung, dunghill, heap,' and Danish *dynge* 'heap.'

dun·ga·rees /,dəNGgəˈrēz/ ▶ **plural n. 1** blue jeans or overalls.
2 [in sing.] (**dungaree**) blue denim.
– ORIGIN late 17th cent. (in the sense 'cotton cloth from India'); from Hindi *duṅgrī.*

dung bee·tle ▶ **n.** a beetle whose larvae feed on dung, esp. a scarab. The larger kinds place the dung in a hole before the eggs are laid, and some of them roll it along in a ball. ● Superfamily Scarabaeoidea, in particular families Scarabaeidae and Geotrupidae.

Dun·ge·ness crab /ˈdənjə,nes/ ▶ **n.** a large crab found off the west coast of North America, where it is popular as food. ● *Cancer magister,* family Cancridae.
– ORIGIN mid 20th cent.: from *Dungeness,* the name of a fishing village on the coast of Washington.

dun·geon /ˈdənjən/ ▶ **n.** a strong underground prison cell, esp. in a castle. ■ (in fantasy role-playing games) a labyrinthine subterranean setting. ■ archaic term for DONJON.
▶ **v.** [with obj.] literary imprison (someone) in a dungeon.
– ORIGIN Middle English (also with the sense 'castle keep'): from Old French (perhaps originally with the sense 'lord's tower' or 'mistress tower'), based on Latin *dominus* 'lord, master.' Compare with DONJON.

Dun·geons and Drag·ons ▶ **n.** trademark a fantasy role-playing game set in an imaginary world based loosely on medieval myth.

dung fly ▶ **n.** a hairy fly that lays its eggs in fresh dung. ● Families Scathophagidae and Sphaeroceridae: several species.

dung·hill /ˈdəNG,hil/ (also **dungheap**) ▶ **n.** a heap of dung or refuse, esp. in a farmyard.

du·nite /ˈdənīt/ ▶ **n.** Geology a green to brownish coarse-grained igneous rock consisting largely of olivine.
– ORIGIN mid 19th cent.: from the name of *Dun* Mountain, New Zealand, + -ITE[1].

dunk /dəNGk/ ▶ **v. 1** [with obj.] dip (bread or other food) into a drink or soup before eating it: *she dunked a piece of bread into her coffee.* ■ immerse or dip in water: *the bikers dunked themselves in the ocean* | (as noun **dunking**) *the camera survived a dunking in a stream.*
2 [no obj.] Basketball score by shooting the ball down through the basket with the hands above the rim.
▶ **n.** Basketball a shot downward into the basket with the hands above the rim.
– DERIVATIVES **dunk·er n.**
– ORIGIN early 20th cent.: from Pennsylvania Dutch *dunke* 'dip,' from German *tunken* 'dip or plunge.'

Dunk·ard /ˈdəNGkərd/ ▶ **n.** another term for DUNKER.

Dunk·er /ˈdəNGkər/ ▶ **n.** a member of the German Baptist Brethren, a sect of Baptist Christians founded in 1708 but living in the US since the 1720s.
– ORIGIN early 18th cent.: from Pennsylvania Dutch, from *dunke* (see DUNK).

Dun·kirk /ˈdən,kərk, dənˈkərk/ a port in northern France; pop. 70,654 (2006). It was the scene of the evacuation of 335,000 Allied troops in 1940 by warships, requisitioned civilian ships, and a host of small boats while under constant German attack from the air. French name Dunkerque.

dun·lin /ˈdənlin/ ▶ **n.** (pl. **same** or **dunlins**) a migratory sandpiper with a down-curved bill and (in the breeding season) a reddish-brown back and black belly. It is the most common small wader of the northern hemisphere. ● *Calidris alpina,* family Scolopacidae.
– ORIGIN mid 16th cent.: probably from DUN[1] + -LING, from the grayish-brown winter coloring of its upper parts.

Dun·lop /ˈdənläp/, John Boyd (1840–1921), Scottish inventor. He developed the first successful pneumatic bicycle tire in 1888.

dun·nage /ˈdənij/ ▶ **n.** pieces of wood, matting, or similar material used to keep a cargo in position in a ship's hold. ■ informal a person's belongings, esp. those brought on board ship.
– ORIGIN Middle English: of unknown origin.

dun·no /dəˈnō/ ▶ **contraction** (I) do not know.
– ORIGIN mid 19th cent.: representing an informal pronunciation.

Duns Sco·tus /dənz ˈskōtəs/, John (*c.*1265–1308), Scottish theologian and scholar. He was the first major theologian to defend the theory of the immaculate conception and to oppose St. Thomas Aquinas by arguing that faith is a matter of will rather than something dependent on logical proofs.

Dun·stan, St. /ˈdənstən/ (*c.*909–88), Anglo-Saxon prelate. As archbishop of Canterbury, he introduced the strict Benedictine rule in England and succeeded in restoring monastic life. Feast day, May 19.

dunt /dənt/ chiefly Scottish ▶ **v.** [with obj.] hit or knock firmly with a dull sound: *she dunted my father in the side with her elbow.*
▶ **n.** a firm dull-sounding blow.
– ORIGIN late Middle English: perhaps a variant of DINT.

du·o /ˈd(y)o͞o-ō/ ▶ **n.** (pl. **duos**) **1** a pair of people or things, esp. in music or entertainment: *the comedy duo Laurel and Hardy.*
2 Music a duet: *he wrote two duos for violin and viola.*
– ORIGIN late 16th cent. (sense 2): via Italian from Latin *duo* 'two.'

duo- ▶ **comb. form** two; having two: *duopoly* | *duotone.*
– ORIGIN from Latin.

du·o·dec·i·mal /,d(y)o͞oəˈdesəməl, ,d(y)o͞o-ō-/ ▶ **adj.** relating to or denoting a system of counting or numerical notation that has twelve as a base.
▶ **n.** the system of duodecimal notation.
– DERIVATIVES **du·o·dec·i·mal·ly adv.**
– ORIGIN late 17th cent.: from Latin *duodecimus* 'twelfth' (from *duodecim* 'twelve') + -AL.

du·o·dec·i·mo /,d(y)o͞oəˈdesə,mō, ,d(y)o͞o-ō/ (abbr.: **12mo**) ▶ **n.** (pl. **duodecimos**) a size of book page that results from the folding of each printed sheet into 12 leaves (24 pages). Also called TWELVEMO. ■ a book of this size.
– ORIGIN mid 17th cent.: from Latin (*in*) *duodecimo* 'in a twelfth,' from *duodecimus* 'twelfth.'

du·o·den·a·ry /,d(y)o͞oəˈdenərē, ,d(y)o͞o-ō-/ ▶ **adj.** rare relating to or based on the number twelve.
– ORIGIN mid 19th cent.: from Latin *duodenarius* 'containing twelve,' based on *duodecim* 'twelve.'

du·o·de·ni·tis /,d(y)o͞oədiˈnītis, ,d(y)o͞o-ō-/ ▶ **n.** Medicine inflammation of the duodenum.

duodeno- (also **duoden-** before a vowel) ▶ **comb. form** Anatomy & Medicine relating to the duodenum: *duodenitis.*

du·o·de·num /,d(y)o͞oəˈdēnəm, d(y)o͞oˈädn-əm/ ▶ **n.** (pl. **duodenums** or **duodena** /-nə/) Anatomy the first part of the small intestine immediately beyond the stomach, leading to the jejunum.
– DERIVATIVES **du·o·de·nal** /-ˈdēnl, -ˈädnəl/ **adj.**
– ORIGIN late Middle English: from medieval Latin, from *duodeni* 'in twelves,' its length being equivalent to the breadth of approximately twelve fingers.

du·o·logue /ˈd(y)o͞oə,läg, -,lôg/ ▶ **n.** a play or part of a play with speaking roles for only two actors.
– ORIGIN mid 18th cent.: from DUO-, on the pattern of *monologue.*

duo·mo /ˈdwōmō/ ▶ **n.** (pl. **duomos**) an Italian cathedral.
– ORIGIN Italian, literally 'dome.'

du·op·o·ly /d(y)o͞oˈäpəlē/ ▶ **n.** (pl. **duopolies**) a situation in which two suppliers dominate the market for a commodity or service.

– DERIVATIVES **du·op·o·lis·tic** /-,äpə'listik/ **adj.**
– ORIGIN 1920s: from DUO-, on the pattern of *monopoly.*

du·o·tone /d(y)o͞oə,tōn/ ▶ **n.** a halftone illustration made from a single original with two different colors at different screen angles. ■ the technique or process of making such illustrations: *the best images that duotone can produce.*

du·pat·ta /də'pətə/ ▶ **n.** a length of material worn as a scarf or head covering, typically with a salwar, by women from South Asia.
– ORIGIN from Hindi *dupaṭṭā.*

dupe¹ /d(y)o͞op/ ▶ **v.** [with obj.] deceive; trick: *the newspaper was* **duped into** *publishing an untrue story.*
▶ **n.** a victim of deception: *knowing accomplices or unknowing dupes.*
– DERIVATIVES **dup·a·ble adj.**, **dup·er n.**, **dup·er·y** /-pərē/ **n.**
– ORIGIN late 17th cent.: from dialect French *dupe* 'hoopoe,' from the bird's supposedly stupid appearance.

dupe² ▶ **v. & n.** short for DUPLICATE, esp. in photography.

du·pi·on /'do͞opē,än/ (also **dupioni** /,do͞opē'ōnē/ or **silk dupion**) ▶ **n.** a rough slubbed silk fabric woven from the threads of double cocoons. ■ an imitation of this with other fibers.
– ORIGIN early 19th cent. (in the sense 'double cocoon'): from French *doupion*, from Italian *doppione*, from *doppio* 'double.'

du·ple /'d(y)o͞opəl/ ▶ **adj.** Music (of rhythm) based on two main beats to the measure: *duple time.*
– ORIGIN mid 16th cent.: from Latin *duplus*, from *duo* 'two.'

du·plet /'d(y)o͞oplit/ ▶ **n.** a set of two things. ■ Music a pair of equal notes to be performed in the time of three.
– ORIGIN mid 17th cent. (as a dicing term in the sense of *doublets* (see DOUBLET)): from Latin *duplus* 'duple,' on the pattern of *doublet.* Current senses date from the 1920s.

du·plex /'d(y)o͞opleks/ ▶ **n.** **1** a house divided into two apartments, with a separate entrance for each. ■ an apartment on two floors.
2 Biochemistry a double-stranded polynucleotide molecule.
▶ **adj.** **1** having two parts, in particular: ■ (of a house) consisting of two apartments. ■ (of an apartment) on two floors. ■ (of paper or board) having two differently colored layers or sides. ■ (of a printer or its software) capable of printing on both sides of the paper.
2 (of a communications system, computer circuit, etc.) allowing the transmission of two signals simultaneously in opposite directions. Compare with MULTIPLEX, SIMPLEX.
– ORIGIN mid 16th cent. (as an adjective): from Latin *duplex, duplic-*, from *duo* 'two' + *plicare* 'to fold.' The noun dates from the 1920s.

du·pli·cate ▶ **adj.** /'d(y)o͞opləkit/ [attrib.] **1** exactly like something else, esp. through having been copied: *a duplicate license is issued to replace a valid license which has been lost.*
2 having two corresponding or identical parts: *a duplicate application form.* ■ twice as large or many; doubled: *duplicate taxes on oil and gas.*
▶ **n.** /'d(y)o͞opləkit/ **1** one of two or more identical things: *books may be disposed of if they are duplicates.* ■ a copy of an original: *locksmiths can make duplicates of most keys.*
2 short for DUPLICATE BRIDGE.
3 archaic a pawnbroker's ticket.
▶ **v.** /'d(y)o͞oplə,kāt/ [with obj.] make or be an exact copy of: *a unique scent, impossible to duplicate or forget* | figurative *they have not been able to duplicate his successes.* ■ make or supply copies of (a document): *information sheets had to be typed and duplicated* | (as adj. **duplicating**) *a duplicating machine.* ■ multiply by two; double: *the normal amount of DNA has been duplicated thousands of times.* ■ do (something) again unnecessarily: *most of these proposals duplicated work already done.*
– PHRASES **in duplicate** consisting of two exact copies: *forms to complete in duplicate.*
– DERIVATIVES **du·pli·ca·ble** /-plikəbəl/ **adj.**, **du·pli·ca·tive** /-,kātiv/ **adj.**
– ORIGIN late Middle English (in the sense 'having two corresponding parts'): from Latin *duplicat-* 'doubled,' from the verb *duplicare*, from *duplic-* 'twofold' (see DUPLEX).

du·pli·cate bridge ▶ **n.** a competitive form of bridge in which the same hands are played successively by different partnerships.

du·pli·ca·tion /,d(y)o͞oplə'kāsHən/ ▶ **n.** the action or process of duplicating something. ■ a copy. ■ Genetics a DNA segment in a chromosome that is a copy of another segment.
– ORIGIN late Middle English (used in the mathematical sense 'multiplication by two'): from Old French, or from Latin *duplicatio(n-)*, from *duplicare* 'to double' (see DUPLICATE).

du·pli·ca·tor /'d(y)o͞oplə,kātər/ ▶ **n.** a machine or device for making copies of something, in particular a machine that makes copies of documents by means of fluid ink and a stencil.

du·plic·i·tous /d(y)o͞o'plisitəs/ ▶ **adj.** deceitful: *treacherous, duplicitous behavior.* ■ Law (of a charge or plea) containing more than one allegation.

du·plic·i·ty /d(y)o͞o'plisitē/ ▶ **n.** **1** deceitfulness; double-dealing.
2 archaic doubleness.
– ORIGIN late Middle English: from Old French *duplicite* or late Latin *duplicitas*, from Latin *duplic-* 'twofold' (see DUPLEX).

du Pont /d(y)o͞o 'pänt, 'd(y)o͞o ,pänt/, E. I. (1771–1834), US industrialist; born in France; full name *Éleuthère Irénée du Pont.* His gunpowder manufacturing plant near Wilmington, Delaware, established in 1802, grew into a corporate giant, due largely to the government contracts that ensured its early success, esp. during the War of 1812.

dup·py /'dəpē/ ▶ **n.** (pl. **duppies**) W. Indian a malevolent spirit or ghost.
– ORIGIN late 18th cent.: probably of West African origin.

du Pré /d(y)o͞o 'prā/, Jacqueline (1945–87), English cellist; wife of Daniel Barenboim. She made her solo debut at 16 and was known for her interpretations of cello concertos.

Du·puy·tren's con·trac·ture /də'pwētrənz/ (also **Dupuytren's disease**) ▶ **n.** Medicine a condition in which there is fixed forward curvature of one or more fingers, caused by the development of a fibrous connection between the finger tendons and the skin of the palm.
– ORIGIN late 19th cent.: named after Baron Guillaume *Dupuytren* (1777–1835), the French surgeon who first described the condition.

Du·que de Ca·xi·as /'do͞okē dā kä'sHēəs/ a city in southeastern Brazil, a suburb of Rio de Janeiro; pop. 842,686 (2007).

du·ra¹ /'d(y)o͝orə/ (in full **dura mater**) ▶ **n.** Anatomy the tough outermost membrane enveloping the brain and spinal cord.
– DERIVATIVES **du·ral adj.**
– ORIGIN late 19th cent.: from medieval Latin, literally 'hard mother,' translation of Arabic *al-'umm al-jāfiya* 'coarse mother.'

du·ra² ▶ **n.** variant spelling of DURRA.

du·ra·bil·i·ty /,d(y)o͝orə'bilitē/ ▶ **n.** the ability to withstand wear, pressure, or damage: *the reliability and durability of plastics.*

du·ra·ble /'d(y)o͝orəbəl/ ▶ **adj.** able to withstand wear, pressure, or damage; hard-wearing: *porcelain enamel is strong and durable* | figurative *a durable peace can be achieved.* ■ informal (of a person) having endurance: *the durable Smith lasted the full eight rounds.*
▶ **n.** (**durables**) short for DURABLE GOODS.
– DERIVATIVES **du·ra·ble·ness n.**, **du·ra·bly adv.**
– ORIGIN Middle English (in the sense 'steadfast'): via Old French from Latin *durabilis*, from *durare* 'to last' (see DURATION).

du·ra·ble goods ▶ **plural n.** goods not for immediate consumption and able to be kept for a period of time.

Du·ral·u·min /d(y)o͝or'alyəmin/ ▶ **n.** a hard, light alloy of aluminum with copper and other elements.
– ORIGIN early 20th cent.: perhaps from Latin *durus* 'hard' + ALUMINUM, but probably influenced by *Düren*, the name of the Rhineland town where such alloys were first produced.

du·ra ma·ter /'d(y)o͝orə 'mätər, 'mā-/ ▶ **n.** see DURA¹.

du·ra·men /d(y)o͝or'āmin/ ▶ **n.** Botany the heartwood of a tree.
– ORIGIN mid 19th cent.: from Latin, literally 'hardness,' from *durare* 'harden.'

dur·ance /'d(y)o͝orəns/ ▶ **n.** archaic imprisonment or confinement.
– ORIGIN late Middle English (in the sense 'continuance'): from Old French, from *durer* 'to last,' from Latin *durare.* The sense 'imprisonment' is first recorded in the early 16th cent.

Du·rand /də'rand/, Asher Brown (1796–1886), US artist. He was one of the earliest landscape painters of the Hudson River School.

Du·ran·go /d(y)o͞o'raNGgō/ a state in northern central Mexico. ■ its capital city; pop. 463,830 (2005). Full name VICTORIA DE DURANGO.

Du·ran·te /də'rantē/, Jimmy (1893–1980), US entertainer; born *James Francis Durante.* The gravelly-voiced star of Broadway, movies, radio, and television began his career in vaudeville and became known for his trademark song, "Inka Dinka Doo." His movies include *The Man Who Came to Dinner* (1942).

Du·ras /d(y)o͞o'rä/, Marguerite (1914–96), French novelist, movie director, and playwright; pseudonym of *Marguerite Donnadieu.* Her works include the screenplay for *Hiroshima mon amour* (1959), as well as the semiautobiographical novel *L'Amant* (1984).

du·ra·tion /d(y)o͝or'āsHən/ ▶ **n.** the time during which something continues: *the subway stop has been closed for the duration of the convention* | *a flight of over eight hours' duration.*
– PHRASES **for the duration** until the end of something, esp. a war: *he was in the navy for the duration plus six.* ■ informal for a very long time: *some stains may be there for the duration.*
– DERIVATIVES **du·ra·tion·al adj.**
– ORIGIN late Middle English: via Old French from medieval Latin *duratio(n-)*, from *durare* 'to last,' from *durus* 'hard.'

dur·a·tive /'d(y)o͝orətiv/ ▶ **adj.** Grammar of or denoting continuing action. Contrasted with PUNCTUAL.

Dur·ban /'dərbən/ a seaport and resort in South Africa, on the coast of KwaZulu-Natal; pop. 3,409,100 (est. 2009). Former name (until 1835) PORT NATAL.

dur·bar /'dər,bär/ ▶ **n.** historical the court of an Indian ruler. ■ a public reception held by an Indian prince or by a British governor or viceroy in India.
– ORIGIN Urdu, from Persian *darbār* 'court.'

durch·kom·po·niert /,do͝orKH,kômpō'ni(ə)rt/ ▶ **adj.** another term for THROUGH-COMPOSED.
– ORIGIN from German, from *durch* 'through' + *komponiert* 'composed' (because the music is different throughout).

Dü·rer /'d(y)o͝orər/, Albrecht (1471–1528), German engraver and painter. A leading artist of the Renaissance, he was important for his technically advanced woodcuts and copper engravings and was also noted for his watercolors and drawings.

du·ress /d(y)o͝o'res/ ▶ **n.** threats, violence, constraints, or other action brought to bear on someone to do something against their will or better judgment: *confessions extracted* **under duress.** ■ Law constraint illegally exercised to force someone to perform an act. ■ archaic forcible restraint or imprisonment.
– ORIGIN Middle English (in the sense 'harshness, severity, cruel treatment'): via Old French from Latin *duritia*, from *durus* 'hard.'

Du·rey /d(y)o͝o'rā/, Louis (1888–1979), French composer. A member of the Les Six group until 1921, he later wrote music that had mass appeal, in accordance with communist doctrines on art.

Dur·ga /'do͝orgä/ Hinduism a fierce goddess, wife of Shiva, often identified with Kali. She is usually depicted riding a tiger or lion and slaying the buffalo demon, and with eight or ten arms.

Dur·ga·pur /'do͝orgə,po͝or/ a city in northeastern India, in the state of West Bengal; pop. 543,900 (est. 2009).

Dur·ham¹ /'dərəm, 'do͝or-/ an industrial and academic city in north central North Carolina, noted for its tobacco industry and as the home of Duke University; pop. 223,284 (est. 2008).

Dur·ham² a city in northern England, on the River Wear; pop. 42,100 (est. 2009). It is famous for its 11th-century cathedral, which contains the tomb of the Venerable Bede, and for its university.

Dur·ham quilt /'dərəm/ ▶ **n.** a quilt made by sewing together a piece of fabric, an inner batting, and a lining, the stitches making decorative patterns.

du·ri·an /'do͝orēən, -rē,än/ ▶ **n.** **1** an oval spiny tropical fruit containing a creamy pulp. Despite its fetid smell, it is highly esteemed for its flavor.
2 (also **durian tree**) the large tree that bears this fruit, native to Malaysia. ● *Durio zibethinus*, family Bombacaceae.
– ORIGIN late 16th cent.: from Malay *durian*, from *duri* 'thorn.'

dur·i·crust /'d(y)o͝ori,krəst/ ▶ **n.** Geology a hard mineral crust formed at or near the surface of soil in semiarid regions by the evaporation of groundwater.
– ORIGIN 1920s: from Latin *durus* 'hard' + CRUST.

dur·ing /'d(y)o͝oriNG/ ▶ **prep.** throughout the course or duration of (a period of time): *the restaurant is open during the day* | *the period during which he grew to adulthood.* ■ at a particular point in the course

of: *the stabbing took place during an argument at a party.*
– ORIGIN late Middle English: present participle of the obsolete verb *dure* 'last, endure, extend,' via Old French from Latin *durare* 'to last' (see DURATION).

Durk·heim /ˈdərkˌhīm/, Émile (1858–1917), French sociologist; one of the founders of modern sociology. In 1913, he became the first professor of sociology at the Sorbonne. Notable works: *The Division of Labor in Society* (1893) and *Suicide* (1897).

dur·mast oak /ˈdərˌmast/ ▶ n. a Eurasian oak tree with stalkless, egg-shaped acorns. Also called SESSILE OAK. ● *Quercus petraea*, family Fagaceae.
– ORIGIN late 18th cent.: *durmast* perhaps originally an error for *dunmast*, from DUN[1] + MAST[2].

durn /dərn/ ▶ v., exclam., adj., & adv. dialect form of DARN[2].

durned /dərnd/ ▶ adj. & adv. dialect form of DARNED.

Du·roc /ˈd(y)o͝orāk/ ▶ n. a pig of a reddish breed developed in North America.
– ORIGIN early 19th cent.: from the name of a stallion that is said to have been bought by the breeder Isaac Frink on the same day as the pigs from which he developed the breed.

Du·ro·cher /dəˈrōSHər/, Leo (Ernest) (1905–91), US baseball player and manager. After playing the position of shortstop in the major leagues from 1925 to 1945, he managed the Brooklyn Dodgers 1939–46, 1948, New York Giants 1948–55, Chicago Cubs 1966–72, and Houston Astros 1972–73 and was noted for his cantankerous manner. Baseball Hall of Fame (1994).

dur·ra /ˈdo͝orə/ (also **dura**) ▶ n. grain sorghum of the principal variety grown from northeastern Africa to India. ● *Sorghum bicolor* var. *durra*, family Gramineae; **white durra** is var. cernuum.
– ORIGIN late 18th cent.: from Arabic *ḏura*, *ḏurra*.

Dur·rell /ˈdərəl/, Lawrence (George) (1912–90), English novelist and poet; brother of Gerald Durrell (1925–95). He spent much of his life abroad, particularly in the Mediterranean. Notable works: *Alexandria Quartet* (1957–60) and *Prospero's Cell* (1945).

dur·rie /ˈdərē/ ▶ n. (pl. **durries**) variant spelling of DHURRIE.

durst /dərst/ archaic or regional past of DARE.

du·rum /ˈd(y)o͝orəm/ (also **durum wheat**) ▶ n. a kind of hard wheat grown in arid regions, having bearded ears and yielding flour that is used to make pasta. ● *Triticum durum*, family Gramineae.
– ORIGIN early 20th cent.: from Latin, neuter of *durus* 'hard,' used in the species name since 1798.

Du·shan·be /d(y)o͞oˈSHämbə, -bə/ the capital of Tajikistan; pop. 553,000 (est. 2007). Former name (1929–61) STALINABAD.

dusk /dəsk/ ▶ n. the darker stage of twilight: *dusk was falling rapidly | working the land from dawn to dusk.* ■ semidarkness: *in the dusk of an Istanbul nightclub.*
▶ v. [no obj.] literary grow dark: (as adj. **dusking**) *he saw the lights blaze in the dusking sky.*
▶ adj. literary shadowy, dim, or dark.
– ORIGIN Old English *dox* 'dark, swarthy' and *doxian* 'darken in color,' of Germanic origin; related to Old High German *tusin* 'darkish'; compare with DUN[1]. The noun dates from the early 17th cent. The change in form from *-x* to *-sk* occurred in Middle English.

dusk·y /ˈdəskē/ ▶ adj. (**duskier**, **duskiest**) darkish in color: *dusky red | a dusky complexion.* ■ dated used in euphemistic or poetic reference to black or other dark-skinned people: *a dusky Moorish maiden.* ■ literary dim: *dusky light came from a small window.* ■ [attrib.] used in names of animals with dark coloration, e.g., **dusky dolphin**, **dusky warbler**.
– DERIVATIVES **dusk·i·ly** /-kəlē/ adv., **dusk·i·ness** n.

dusk·y wing ▶ n. a small, dark-winged butterfly of the skipper family, found in North America. ● Genus *Erynnis*, family Hesperiidae; the species are very difficult to tell apart.

Düs·sel·dorf /ˈd(y)o͞osəlˌdôrf/ an industrial city in northwestern Germany, on the Rhine River, capital of North Rhine–Westphalia; pop. 577,500 (est. 2006).

dust /dəst/ ▶ n. **1** fine, dry powder consisting of tiny particles of earth or waste matter lying on the ground or on surfaces or carried in the air: *the car sent up clouds of dust | they rolled and fought in the dust.* ■ [with modifier] any material in the form of tiny particles: *coal dust.* ■ [in sing.] a fine powder: *he ground it into a fine dust.* ■ [in sing.] a cloud of dust. ■ literary a dead person's remains: *scatter my dust and ashes.* ■ literary the mortal human body: *the soul, that dwells within your dust.*
2 [in sing.] an act of dusting: *a quick dust, to get rid of the cobwebs.*
▶ v. [with obj.] **1** remove the dust from the surface of (something) by wiping or brushing it: *I broke the vase I had been dusting | pick yourself up and dust yourself off* | [no obj.] *she washed and dusted and tidied.* ■ (**dust something off**) bring something out for use again after a long period of neglect: *a number of aircraft will be dusted off and returned to flight.* ■ Baseball (**dust someone off**) deliver a pitch very near a batter so they must fall to the dirt to avoid being hit by it.
2 (usu. **be dusted**) cover lightly with a powdered substance: *roll out on a surface dusted with flour.* ■ sprinkle (a powdered substance) onto something: *orange powder was dusted over the upper body.*
3 informal beat up or kill someone: *the officers dusted him up a little bit.*
– PHRASES **dust and ashes** used to convey a feeling of great disappointment or disillusion about something: *the party would be dust and ashes if he couldn't come.* **the dust settles** things quiet down: *she hoped that the dust would settle quickly and the episode be forgotten.* **eat someone's dust** informal fall far behind someone in a competitive situation. **gather** (or **collect**) **dust** remain unused: *some professors let their computers gather dust.* **leave someone/something in the dust** surpass someone or something easily: *today's modems leave their predecessors in the dust.*
– DERIVATIVES **dust·less** adj.
– ORIGIN Old English *dūst*, of Germanic origin; related to Dutch *duist* 'chaff.'

dust·ball /ˈdəstˌbôl/ ▶ n. a ball of dust and fluff.

dust·bath /ˈdəstˌbaTH/ ▶ n. a bird's rolling in dust to clean its feathers.

dust·bin /ˈdəstˌbin/ ▶ n. Brit. a garbage can.

dust bowl ▶ n. an area of land where vegetation has been lost and soil reduced to dust and eroded, esp. as a consequence of drought or unsuitable farming practice. ■ (**the Dust Bowl**) an area of Oklahoma, Kansas, and northern Texas affected by severe soil erosion (caused by windstorms) in the early 1930s, which obliged many people to move.

dust bun·ny ▶ n. informal a ball of dust and fluff.

Dust·bust·er /ˈdəstˌbəstər/ ▶ n. trademark a handheld vacuum cleaner.

dust cov·er ▶ n. a dust jacket.

dust dev·il ▶ n. a small whirlwind or air vortex over land, visible as a column of dust and debris.

dust·er /ˈdəstər/ ▶ n. **1** a cloth or brush for dusting furniture.
2 (also **duster coat**) a woman's loose, lightweight, full-length coat without buttons, of a style originally worn in the 1920s while traveling in an open car. ■ a short, light housecoat.
3 informal a dust storm.

dust·heap /ˈdəstˌhēp/ ▶ n. a heap of household refuse.

dust·ing pow·der ▶ n. powder for dusting over something, in particular talcum powder.

dust jack·et ▶ n. a removable paper cover, generally with a decorative design, used to protect a book from dirt or damage.

dust·man /ˈdəstmən/ ▶ n. (pl. **dustmen**) Brit. a garbage collector.

dust mop ▶ n. a long-handled mop with a soft, fluffy head, used to collect dust from floors and walls.

dust·pan /ˈdəstˌpan/ ▶ n. a flat handheld receptacle into which dust and waste can be swept from the floor.

dust ruf·fle ▶ n. a sheet with a deep pleated or gathered border that is designed to hang down over the mattress and sides of a bed.

dust sheet ▶ n. British term for DROP CLOTH.

dust storm ▶ n. a strong, turbulent wind that carries clouds of fine dust, soil, and sand over a large area.

dust trap ▶ n. something on, in, or under which dust readily gathers.

dust-up ▶ n. informal a fight; a quarrel: *you and Larry had a dust-up over Val?*

dust·y /ˈdəstē/ ▶ adj. (**dustier**, **dustiest**) covered with, full of, or resembling dust: *dusty old records | a hot, dusty road.* ■ (of a color) dull or muted: *patches of pale gold and dusty pink.* ■ staid and uninteresting: *a dusty old bore.*
– DERIVATIVES **dust·i·ly** /ˈdəstəlē/ adv., **dust·i·ness** n.

dust·y mill·er ▶ n. a plant of the daisy family with whitish or grayish foliage. ● Several species in the family Compositae, in particular the cultivated *Artemisia stellerana* of North America and *Senecio cineraria* of the Mediterranean.
– ORIGIN early 19th cent.: named from the fine powder on the flowers and leaves.

Dutch /dəCH/ ▶ adj. **1** of or relating to the Netherlands or its people or their language.
2 of or relating to the people of Germany; German.
▶ n. **1** the West Germanic language of the Netherlands.
2 (as plural noun **the Dutch**) the people of the Netherlands collectively.

> Dutch is most closely related to German and English. It is also the official language of Suriname and the Netherlands Antilles and is spoken in northern Belgium, where it is called Flemish.

– PHRASES **go dutch** share the cost of something, esp. a meal, equally. **in dutch** informal, dated in trouble: *he's been getting in dutch at school.*
– ORIGIN from Middle Dutch *dutsch* 'Dutch, Netherlandish, German': the English word originally denoted speakers of both High and Low German, but became more specific after the United Provinces adopted the Low German of Holland as the national language on independence in 1579.

Dutch auc·tion ▶ n. a method of selling in which the price is reduced until a buyer is found.

Dutch cap ▶ n. a woman's lace cap with triangular flaps on each side, worn as part of Dutch traditional dress.

Dutch cour·age ▶ n. strength or confidence gained from drinking alcohol: *I'll have a couple of drinks to give me Dutch courage.*

Dutch door ▶ n. a door divided into two parts horizontally, allowing one half to be shut and the other left open.

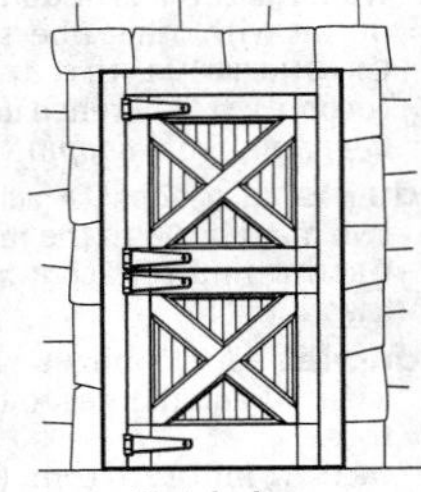
Dutch door

Dutch East In·di·a Com·pa·ny a Dutch trading company founded in 1602 to protect Dutch trading interests in the Indian Ocean. It was dissolved in 1799.

Dutch East In·dies former name (until 1949) of INDONESIA.

Dutch elm dis·ease ▶ n. a fungal disease of elm trees that is spread by elm bark beetles. A virulent strain of the fungus that arose in North America in the early 20th century has destroyed the majority of American elms in many areas. ● The disease is caused by the fungus *Ceratocystis ulmi*, phylum Ascomycota.

Dutch·ess Coun·ty /ˈdəCHis/ a county in southeastern New York, east of the Hudson River, traditionally agricultural but increasingly suburban; pop. 292,878 (est. 2008). Its seat is Poughkeepsie.

Dutch Gui·an·a former name (until 1948) of SURINAME.

Dutch in·te·ri·or ▶ n. a painting of the interior of a Dutch house in a style characteristic of the work of 17th-century genre painters.

Dutch·man /ˈdəCHmən/ ▶ n. (pl. **Dutchmen**) a native or inhabitant of the Netherlands, or a person of Dutch descent. ■ a Dutch ship. ■ a wedge or piece used to conceal a flaw in construction. ■ archaic a German.
– PHRASES **I'm a Dutchman** Brit. used to express one's disbelief or as a way of underlining an emphatic assertion: *if she's seventeen, I'm a Dutchman.*

Dutch·man's breech·es ▶ n. a plant closely related to bleeding heart, but typically having pale yellow or white flowers. ● Genus *Dicentra*, family Fumariaceae: several species, in particular *D. cucullaria*.
– ORIGIN mid 19th cent.: so named because of the shape of the spurred flower.

Dutchman's breeches

Dutch·man's pipe ▶ n. a vigorous climbing vine with hooked tubular flowers, native to eastern North America. ● *Aristolochia durior*, family Aristolochiaceae.

Dutch met·al ▶ n. an alloy of copper and zinc used in imitation of gold leaf.

Dutch New Gui·ea former name (until 1963) of PAPUA (sense 1).

Dutch ov·en ▶ n. a large, heavy cooking pot with a lid. ■ chiefly historical a large metal box serving as a simple oven, heated by being placed under or next to hot coals.

Dutch Re·formed Church a branch of the Protestant Church in the Netherlands, formed during the Reformation. It was disestablished in 1798 and replaced in 1816 by the Netherlands Reformed Church. ■ the dominant branch of the Protestant Church among Afrikaners in South Africa.

Dutch tile ▶ **n.** a kind of glazed white tile painted with traditional Dutch motifs in blue or brown. ▶ **v.** [with obj.] (usu. as adj. **Dutch-tiled**) decorate with such tiles: *Dutch-tiled fireplaces.*

Dutch treat ▶ **n.** an outing, meal, or other special occasion at which each participant pays for their share of the expenses.

Dutch un·cle ▶ **n.** informal a person giving firm but benevolent advice.

Dutch West In·di·a Com·pa·ny a Dutch trading company founded in 1621 to develop Dutch trading interests in competition with Spain and Portugal and their colonies in western India, South America, and West Africa. It was dissolved in 1794.

Dutch·wom·an /ˈdəCH,wo͝omən/ ▶ **n.** (pl. **Dutchwomen**) a female native or inhabitant of the Netherlands, or a woman of Dutch descent.

du·te·ous /ˈd(y)o͞otēəs/ ▶ **adj.** archaic dutiful: *a duteous vassal.*
– DERIVATIVES **du·te·ous·ly** adv., **du·te·ous·ness** n.
– ORIGIN late 16th cent.: from DUTY, on the pattern of words such as *bounteous.*

du·ti·a·ble /ˈd(y)o͞otēəbəl/ ▶ **adj.** liable to customs or other duties: *dutiable goods.*

dut·i·ful /ˈd(y)o͞otəfəl/ ▶ **adj.** conscientiously or obediently fulfilling one's duty: *a dutiful daughter.* ■ motivated by duty rather than desire or enthusiasm: *dutiful applause | a dutiful visit.*
– DERIVATIVES **du·ti·ful·ly** adv., **du·ti·ful·ness** n.

du·ty /ˈd(y)o͞otē/ ▶ **n.** (pl. **duties**) **1** a moral or legal obligation; a responsibility: *it's my duty to uphold the law | she was determined to* **do her duty** *as a citizen | a strong sense of duty.* ■ [as modifier] (of a visit or other undertaking) done from a sense of moral obligation rather than for pleasure: *a fifteen-minute duty visit.*
2 (often **duties**) a task or action that someone is required to perform: *the queen's official duties | your duties will include sweeping the switchboard | Juliet reported for duty.* ■ [as modifier] (of a person) engaged in their regular work: *a duty nurse.* ■ military service: *combat duty in the army.* ■ (also **duties**) performance of prescribed church services by a priest or minister: *he was willing to take Sunday duties.*
3 a payment due and enforced by law or custom, in particular: ■ a payment levied on the import, export, manufacture, or sale of goods: *a 6 percent duty on imports | goods subject to excise duty.*
4 technical the measure of an engine's effectiveness in units of work done per unit of fuel.
– PHRASES **do duty as** (or **for**) serve or act as a substitute for something else: *her mug was doing duty as a wine glass.* **on** (or **off**) **duty** engaged (or not engaged) in one's regular work: *the doorman had gone off duty and the lobby was unattended.*
– ORIGIN late Middle English: from Anglo-Norman French *duete,* from Old French *deu* (see DUE).

du·ty-bound ▶ **adj.** [predic., with infinitive] morally or legally obliged to do something: *legitimate news stories that the press is duty-bound to report.*

du·ty cy·cle ▶ **n.** the cycle of operation of a machine or other device that operates intermittently rather than continuously. ■ the time occupied by this, esp. as a percentage of available time.

du·ty-free ▶ **adj. & adv.** exempt from payment of duty: [as adj.] *the permitted number of duty-free goods* | [as adv.] *most EC goods enter almost duty-free.* ■ [as adj.] (of a shop or area) selling or trading in goods that are exempt from payment of duty.

du·ty of·fi·cer ▶ **n.** an officer, esp. in the police or armed forces, who is on duty at a particular time.

du·um·vir /d(y)o͞oˈəmvər/ ▶ **n.** (in ancient Rome) each of two magistrates or officials holding a joint office.
– ORIGIN Latin, from *duum virum* 'of the two men.'

du·um·vi·rate /d(y)o͞oˈəmvərit/ ▶ **n.** a coalition of two people having joint authority or influence.
– ORIGIN mid 17th cent.: from Latin *duumviratus.*

Du·va·lier /d(y)o͞oˈvälyā/ the name of a family of Haitian statesmen. ■ **François** (1907–71), president 1957–71; known as **Papa Doc.** His regime was noted for its oppressive nature. ■ **Jean-Claude** (1951–), son of François; known as **Baby Doc.** He succeeded to his father's presidency in 1971 but was overthrown by a mass uprising in 1986.

Du·vall, Gabriel (1752–1844), US Supreme Court associate justice 1811–35. Before being appointed to the Court by President Madison, he was a member of the US House of Representatives 1794–96.

du·vet /ˌd(y)o͞oˈvā/ ▶ **n.** a soft quilt filled with down, feathers, or a synthetic fiber, used instead of an upper sheet and blankets.
– ORIGIN mid 18th cent.: from French, literally 'down' (see DOWN[2]).

dux /dəks/ ▶ **n.** (pl. **duces** /ˈd(y)o͞osēz, ˈdo͞okāz/ or **duxes**) a Saxon chief or leader.
– ORIGIN mid 18th cent.: from Latin, 'leader.'

dux·elles /do͞okˈsel/ ▶ **n.** a preparation of mushrooms sautéed with onions, shallots, garlic, and parsley and used to make stuffing or sauce: *chilies stuffed with duxelles.*
– ORIGIN named after the Marquis *d'Uxelles,* a 17th-cent. French nobleman.

DV formal ▶ **abbr.** ■ Deo volente: *this time next week (DV) I shall be among the mountains.* ■ Bible Douay Version.

DVD ▶ **n.** (pl. **DVDs**) a type of compact disc able to store large amounts of data, esp. high-resolution audiovisual material.
– ORIGIN 1990s: abbreviation of *digital versatile disc* (originally of *digital video disc*).

DVD+R ▶ **n.** a blank DVD on which data, including music and movies, can be permanently recorded and read using the DVD+R format. ■ a format for recordable DVDs used by some companies.
– ORIGIN abbreviation of *DVD plus recordable.*

DVD+RW ▶ **n.** a blank DVD that can be recorded, erased, and rerecorded with data many times and read using the DVD+RW format. ■ a format for rewritable DVDs used by some companies. ■ a disc drive that can read and record DVDs.
– ORIGIN abbreviation of *DVD plus rewritable.*

DVD-R ▶ **n.** a blank DVD on which data, including music and movies, can be permanently recorded and read using the DVD-R format. ■ a format for recordable DVDs used by some companies.
– ORIGIN abbreviation of *DVD recordable.*

DVD-RAM ▶ **n.** a blank DVD on which data, including music and movies, can be permanently recorded and read using the DVD-RAM format. A DVD-RAM discs can be recorded over many times, but will only play back in a DVD-RAM drive. ■ a format for recordable DVDs used by some companies.
– ORIGIN abbreviation of *DVD recordable.*

DVD-ROM ▶ **n.** a DVD used as a read-only optical memory device for a computer system.
– ORIGIN abbreviation of *DVD read-only memory.*

DVD-RW ▶ **n.** a blank DVD that can be recorded, erased, and rerecorded with data many times and read using the DVD-RW format. ■ a format for rewritable DVDs used by some companies. ■ a disc drive that can read and record DVDs.
– ORIGIN abbreviation of *DVD rewritable.*

Dvi·na Riv·er /d(ə)vēˈnä/ a river that rises in Russia's Valai Hills and flows west, then north, for 634 miles (1,020 km) across Belarus and Latvia into the Gulf of Riga.

DVM ▶ **abbr.** Doctor of Veterinary Medicine.

Dvo·řák /ˈdvôr,ZHäk/, Antonín (1841–1904), Czech composer. He is best known for his ninth symphony "From the New World" (1892–95).

DVR ▶ **abbr.** digital video recorder.

dwale /dwāl/ ▶ **n.** archaic deadly nightshade or belladonna. ■ a soporific drink formerly made from this.
– ORIGIN Middle English: probably of Scandinavian origin and related to Danish *dvale* 'deep sleep, stupor,' *dvaledrik* 'sleeping draft.'

dwarf /dwôrf/ ▶ **n.** (pl. **dwarfs** or **dwarves** /dwôrvz/) **1** (in folklore or fantasy literature) a member of a mythical race of short, stocky humanlike creatures who are generally skilled in mining and metalworking. ■ often offensive an abnormally small person. ■ [as modifier] denoting something, esp. an animal or plant, that is much smaller than the usual size for its type or species: *a dwarf conifer.*
2 (also **dwarf star**) Astronomy a star of relatively small size and low luminosity, including the majority of main sequence stars.
▶ **v.** [with obj.] cause to seem small or insignificant in comparison: *the buildings surround and dwarf All Saints Church.* ■ stunt the growth or development of: (as adj. **dwarfed**) *the dwarfed but solid branch of a tree.*
– DERIVATIVES **dwarf·ish** adj.
– ORIGIN Old English *dweorg, dweorh,* of Germanic origin; related to Dutch *dwerg* and German *Zwerg.*

> **USAGE** In the sense 'an abnormally small person,' **dwarf** is normally considered offensive. However, there are no accepted alternatives in the general language, since terms such as **person of restricted growth** sound overeuphemistic and have gained little currency.

dwarf·ism /ˈd(w)ôrfizəm/ ▶ **n.** (in medical or technical contexts) unusually or abnormally low stature or small size.

dwarf le·mur ▶ **n.** a small Madagascan primate related to the mouse lemur, feeding primarily on fruit and gums. ● Family Cheirogaleidae: three genera and four species.

dwarf plan·et ▶ **n.** Astronomy a celestial body resembling a small planet but lacking certain technical criteria that are required for it to be classed as such.

dweeb /dwēb/ ▶ **n.** informal a boring, studious, or socially inept person.
– DERIVATIVES **dweeb·ish** adj., **dweeb·y** adj.
– ORIGIN 1980s: perhaps a blend of DWARF and early-20th-cent. *feeb* 'a feebleminded person' (from FEEBLE).

dwell /dwel/ ▶ **v.** (past and past participle **dwelt** /dwelt/ or **dwelled**) [no obj.] **1** [with adverbial of place] formal live in or at a specified place: *groups of gypsies still dwell in these caves.*
2 (**dwell on/upon**) think, speak, or write at length about (a particular subject, esp. one that is a source of unhappiness, anxiety, or dissatisfaction): *I've got better things to do than dwell on the past.* ■ (**dwell on/upon**) (of one's eyes or attention) linger on (a particular object or place): *she let her eyes dwell on them for a moment.*
▶ **n.** technical a slight regular pause in the motion of a machine.
– DERIVATIVES **dwell·er** n. [in combination] *city-dwellers.*
– ORIGIN Old English *dwellan* 'lead astray, hinder, delay' (in Middle English 'tarry, remain in a place'), of Germanic origin; related to Middle Dutch *dwellen* 'stun, perplex' and Old Norse *dvelja* 'delay, tarry, stay.'

dwell·ing /ˈdweliNG/ (also **dwelling place**) ▶ **n.** formal a house, apartment, or other place of residence.

dwell·ing house ▶ **n.** Law a house used as a residence and not for business purposes.

dwell time ▶ **n.** technical time spent in the same position, area, or stage of a process: *dwell time at US airports has reached a new high—almost 70 minutes.*

DWEM ▶ **abbr.** dead white European male.

DWI ▶ **abbr.** driving while intoxicated.

dwin·dle /ˈdwindl/ ▶ **v.** [no obj.] diminish gradually in size, amount, or strength: *traffic has dwindled to a trickle* | (as adj. **dwindling**) *dwindling resources.*
– ORIGIN late 16th cent.: frequentative of Scots and dialect *dwine* 'fade away,' from Old English *dwīnan,* of Germanic origin; related to Middle Dutch *dwīnen* and Old Norse *dvína.*

DWM ▶ **abbr.** ■ (in personal ads) divorced white male. ■ dead white male.

dwt ▶ **abbr.** ■ dead-weight tonnage: *a 40,000 dwt slipway.* ■ pennyweight.

Dy ▶ **symbol** the chemical element dysprosium.

dy·ad /ˈdīad/ ▶ **n.** technical something that consists of two elements or parts: *the mother–child dyad.* ■ Mathematics an operator that is a combination of two vectors. ■ Chemistry a divalent atom or radical.
– DERIVATIVES **dy·ad·ic** /dīˈadik/ adj.
– ORIGIN late 17th cent. (originally denoting the number two or a pair): from late Latin *dyas, dyad-,* from Greek *duas,* from *duo* 'two.' Current senses date from the late 19th cent.

Dy·ak ▶ **n. & adj.** variant spelling of DAYAK.

dy·ar·chy /ˈdī,ärkē/ ▶ **n.** (pl. **dyarchies**) variant spelling of DIARCHY.

dyb·buk /ˈdibək/ ▶ **n.** (pl. **dybbuks** or **dybbukim** /ˌdibo͝oˈkēm/) (in Jewish folklore) a malevolent wandering spirit that enters and possesses the body of a living person until exorcized.
– ORIGIN from Yiddish *dibek,* from Hebrew *dibbūq,* from *dāḇaq* 'cling.'

dye /dī/ ▶ **n.** a natural or synthetic substance used to add a color to or change the color of something.
▶ **v.** (**dyes, dyeing, dyed**) [with obj.] add a color to or change the color of (something) by soaking it in a solution impregnated with a dye: [with complement] *I dyed my hair blonde* | (as adj. **dyed**) *dyed black hair.* ■ [no obj.] take color well or badly during such a process: *it's good material—it should dye well.*
– PHRASES **dyed in the wool** unchanging in a particular belief or opinion; inveterate: *she's a dyed-in-the-wool conservative.* [with allusion to the fact that yarn was dyed in the raw state, producing a more even and permanent color.]
– DERIVATIVES **dye·a·ble** adj.
– ORIGIN Old English *dēag* (noun), *dēagian* (verb). The noun is not recorded from Old English to the

late 16th cent., when it was re-formed from the verb.

dye la·ser ▶ n. a tunable laser using the fluorescence of an organic dye.

dye·line /ˈdīˌlīn/ ▶ n. another term for DIAZO.

dy·er /ˈdīər/ ▶ n. a person whose trade is the dyeing of cloth or other material.

dy·er's green·weed ▶ n. a bushy, yellow-flowered Eurasian plant of the pea family, which has become naturalized in North America. The flowers were formerly used to make a yellow or green dye. ● *Genista tinctoria*, family Leguminosae.

d

dy·er's oak ▶ n. another term for VALONIA.

dy·er's rock·et ▶ n. another term for WELD[2].

dye·stuff /ˈdīˌstəf/ ▶ n. a substance that yields a dye or that can be used as a dye, esp. when in solution.

dy·ing /ˈdī-iNG/ ▶ adj. [attrib.] on the point of death: *he visited his dying mother.* ■ occurring at or connected with the time that someone dies: *he strained to catch her dying words.* ■ gradually ceasing to exist or function; in decline and about to disappear: *stone-cutting is a dying art | the dying embers of the fire.*
– PHRASES **to one's dying day** for the rest of one's life: *I shall remember that to my dying day.*
– ORIGIN late 16th cent.: present participle of DIE[1].

dyke[1] ▶ n. variant spelling of DIKE[1].

dyke[2] /dīk/ ▶ n. offensive a lesbian.
– DERIVATIVES **dyke·y** adj.
– ORIGIN 1940s (earlier as BULLDYKE): of unknown origin.

Dyl·an /ˈdilən/, Bob (1941–), US singer and songwriter; born *Robert Allen Zimmerman*. The leader of an urban folk-music revival in the 1960s, he became known for political and protest songs, such as "The Times They Are A-Changin" (1964). Notable albums: *Highway 61 Revisited* (1965) and *Blood on the Tracks* (1975).

dyn ▶ abbr. dyne.

dy·nam·ic /dīˈnamik/ ▶ adj. **1** (of a process or system) characterized by constant change, activity, or progress: *a dynamic economy.* ■ (of a person) positive in attitude and full of energy and new ideas: *she's dynamic and determined.* ■ Physics of or relating to forces producing motion. Often contrasted with STATIC. ■ Linguistics (of a verb) expressing an action, activity, event, or process. Contrasted with STATIVE. ■ denoting or relating to web pages that update frequently or are generated according to an individual's search terms: *the dynamic content of these sites keeps their audience informed and up to date.* ■ Electronics (of a memory device) needing to be refreshed by the periodic application of a voltage. ■ Electronics of or relating to the volume of sound produced by a voice, instrument, or sound recording equipment.
2 Music relating to the volume of sound produced by an instrument, voice, or recording: *an astounding dynamic range.*
▶ n. **1** a force that stimulates change or progress within a system or process: *evaluation is part of the basic dynamic of the project.*
2 Music another term for DYNAMICS (sense 3).
– DERIVATIVES **dy·nam·i·cal** adj., **dy·nam·i·cal·ly** /-ik(ə)lē/ adv.
– ORIGIN early 19th cent. (as a term in physics): from French *dynamique*, from Greek *dunamikos*, from *dunamis* 'power.'

dy·nam·ic e·qui·lib·ri·um ▶ n. a state of balance between continuing processes.

dy·nam·ic link li·brar·y ▶ n. see DLL.

dy·nam·ic met·a·mor·phism ▶ n. Geology metamorphism produced by mechanical forces.

dy·nam·ic pric·ing ▶ n. the practice of pricing items at a level determined by a particular customer's perceived ability to pay.

dy·nam·ic range ▶ n. the range of acceptable or possible volumes of sound occurring in the course of a piece of music or a performance. ■ the ratio of the largest to the smallest intensity of sound that can be reliably transmitted or reproduced by a particular sound system, measured in decibels.

dy·nam·ics /dīˈnamiks/ ▶ plural n. **1** [treated as sing.] the branch of mechanics concerned with the motion of bodies under the action of forces. Compare with STATICS. ■ [usu. with modifier] the branch of any science in which forces or changes are considered: *chemical dynamics.*
2 the forces or properties that stimulate growth, development, or change within a system or process: *the dynamics of changing social relations.*
3 Music the varying levels of volume of sound in different parts of a musical performance.
– DERIVATIVES **dy·nam·i·cist** /-ˈnaməsist/ n. (sense 1).

dy·nam·ic vis·cos·i·ty ▶ n. a quantity measuring the force needed to overcome internal friction in a fluid.

dy·na·mism /ˈdīnəˌmizəm/ ▶ n. **1** the quality of being characterized by vigorous activity and progress: *the dynamism and strength of the economy.* ■ the quality of being dynamic and positive in attitude: *he was known for his dynamism and strong views.*
2 Philosophy, historical the theory that phenomena of matter or mind are due to the action of forces rather than to motion or matter.
– DERIVATIVES **dy·na·mist** n.
– ORIGIN mid 19th cent.: from Greek *dunamis* 'power' + -ISM.

dy·na·mite /ˈdīnəˌmīt/ ▶ n. a high explosive consisting of nitroglycerine mixed with an absorbent material and typically molded into sticks. ■ something that has the potential to generate extreme reactions or to have devastating repercussions: *that policy is political dynamite.* ■ informal an extremely impressive or exciting person or thing: *both her albums are dynamite | [as modifier] a chick with a dynamite figure.* ■ informal, dated a narcotic, esp. heroin.
▶ v. [with obj.] blow up (something) with dynamite.
– DERIVATIVES **dy·na·mit·er** n.
– ORIGIN mid 19th cent.: from Greek *dunamis* 'power' + -ITE[1].

dy·na·mo /ˈdīnəˌmō/ ▶ n. (pl. **dynamos**) a machine for converting mechanical energy into electrical energy; a generator. ■ informal an extremely energetic person: *she was a dynamo in London politics.*
– ORIGIN late 19th cent.: abbreviation of *dynamo-electric machine*, from Greek *dunamis* 'power.'

dy·na·mom·e·ter /ˌdīnəˈmämitər/ ▶ n. an instrument that measures the power output of an engine.
– ORIGIN early 19th cent.: from French *dynamomètre*, from Greek *dunamis* 'power' + French *-mètre* '(instrument) measuring.'

dy·nast /ˈdīˌnast, -nəst/ ▶ n. a member of a powerful family, esp. a hereditary ruler.
– ORIGIN mid 17th cent.: via Latin from Greek *dunastēs*, from *dunasthai* 'be able.'

dy·nas·ty /ˈdīnəstē/ ▶ n. (pl. **dynasties**) a line of hereditary rulers of a country: *the Tang dynasty.* ■ a succession of people from the same family who play a prominent role in business, politics, or another field: *the Ford dynasty.*
– DERIVATIVES **dy·nas·tic** /dīˈnastik/ adj., **dy·nas·ti·cal·ly** /dīˈnastik(ə)lē/ adv.
– ORIGIN late Middle English: from French *dynastie*, or via late Latin from Greek *dunasteia* 'lordship, power,' from *dunastēs* (see DYNAST).

dyne /dīn/ ▶ n. Physics a unit of force that, acting on a mass of one gram, increases its velocity by one centimeter per second every second along the direction that it acts.
– ORIGIN late 19th cent.: from French, from Greek *dunamis* 'force, power.'

dy·no /ˈdīnō/ ▶ n. (pl. **dynos**) **1** short for DYNAMOMETER.
2 Climbing a rapid move across a rock face in order to reach a hold.
▶ v. (**dynos, dynoing, dyno'd** or **dynoed**) **1** [with obj.] measure (the output of an engine) with a dynamometer.
2 [no obj.] (in mountaineering) climb using dynos.

dys- ▶ comb. form bad; difficult (used esp. in medical terms): *dyspepsia | dysphasia.*
– ORIGIN from Greek *dus-*; related to German *zer-*, also to Old English *to-*.

dys·ar·thri·a /disˈärTHrēə/ ▶ n. Medicine difficult or unclear articulation of speech that is otherwise linguistically normal.
– ORIGIN late 19th cent.: from DYS- 'difficult' + Greek *arthron* 'joint or articulation.'

dys·cal·cu·li·a /ˌdiskalˈkyoolēə/ ▶ n. Psychiatry severe difficulty in making arithmetical calculations, as a result of brain disorder.

dys·cra·sia /disˈkrāZHə/ ▶ n. Medicine an abnormal or disordered state of the body or of a bodily part.
– DERIVATIVES **dys·cras·ic** /-ˈkrazik/ adj.
– ORIGIN late Middle English (denoting an imbalance of physical qualities): via late Latin from Greek *duskrasia* 'bad combination,' from *dus-* 'bad' + *krasis* 'mixture.'

dys·en·ter·y /ˈdisənˌterē/ ▶ n. infection of the intestines resulting in severe diarrhea with the presence of blood and mucus in the feces. ● **bacterial dysentery** is caused by bacteria of the genus *Shigella* and can also spread by contact (see AMEBIC DYSENTERY, SHIGELLA).
– DERIVATIVES **dys·en·ter·ic** /ˌdisənˈterik/ adj.
– ORIGIN late Middle English: from Old French *dissenterie*, or via Latin from Greek *dusenteria*, from *dusenteros* 'afflicted in the bowels,' from *dus-* 'bad' + *entera* 'bowels.'

dys·func·tion /disˈfəNGkSHən/ ▶ n. abnormality or impairment in the function of a specified bodily organ or system: *bowel dysfunction.* ■ deviation from the norms of social behavior in a way regarded as bad: *inner-city dysfunction.*

dys·func·tion·al /disˈfəNGkSHənl/ ▶ adj. not operating normally or properly: *the telephones are dysfunctional.* ■ deviating from the norms of social behavior in a way regarded as bad: *an emotionally dysfunctional businessman | dysfunctional families.*
– DERIVATIVES **dys·func·tion·al·i·ty** n., **dys·func·tion·al·ly** adv.

dys·gen·ic /disˈjenik/ ▶ adj. exerting a detrimental effect on later generations through the inheritance of undesirable characteristics: *dysgenic breeding.*

dys·graph·i·a /disˈgrafēə/ ▶ n. Medicine inability to write coherently, as a symptom of brain disease or damage.
– DERIVATIVES **dys·graph·ic** /-ˈgrafik/ adj.
– ORIGIN 1930s: from DYS- 'difficult' + Greek *-graphia* 'writing.'

dys·ki·ne·sia /ˌdiskiˈnēZHə/ ▶ n. Medicine abnormality or impairment of voluntary movement.
– DERIVATIVES **dys·ki·net·ic** /-ˈnetik/ adj.

dys·la·li·a /disˈlālēə/ ▶ n. Medicine inability to articulate comprehensible speech, esp. when associated with the use of private words or sounds.
– ORIGIN mid 19th cent.: from DYS- 'difficult' + Greek *lalia* 'speech.'

dys·lex·i·a /disˈleksēə/ ▶ n. a general term for disorders that involve difficulty in learning to read or interpret words, letters, and other symbols, but that do not affect general intelligence.
– DERIVATIVES **dys·lec·tic** /-ˈlektik/ adj. & n., **dys·lex·ic** /-ˈleksik/ adj. & n.
– ORIGIN late 19th cent.: coined in German from DYS- 'difficult' + Greek *lexis* 'speech' (apparently by confusion of Greek *legein* 'to speak' and Latin *legere* 'to read').

dys·men·or·rhe·a /ˌdismenəˈrēə/ (Brit. **dysmenorrhoea**) ▶ n. Medicine painful menstruation, typically involving abdominal cramps.

dys·mor·phi·a /disˈmôrfēə/ ▶ n. Medicine deformity or abnormality in the shape or size of a specified part of the body: *muscle dysmorphia.*
– DERIVATIVES **dys·mor·phic** adj.
– ORIGIN late 19th cent.: from Greek *dusmorphia* 'misshapenness, ugliness,' from *dus-* dys- + *morphē* 'form.'

dys·pa·reu·ni·a /ˌdispəˈroonēə/ ▶ n. Medicine difficult or painful sexual intercourse.
– ORIGIN late 19th cent.: from DYS- 'difficult' + Greek *pareunos* 'lying with.'

dys·pep·sia /disˈpepsēə, -ˈpepSHə/ ▶ n. indigestion.
– ORIGIN early 18th cent.: via Latin from Greek *duspepsia*, from *duspeptos* 'difficult to digest.'

dys·pep·tic /disˈpeptik/ ▶ adj. of or having indigestion or consequent irritability or depression.
▶ n. a person who suffers from indigestion or irritability.

dys·pha·gia /disˈfāj(ē)ə/ ▶ n. Medicine difficulty or discomfort in swallowing, as a symptom of disease: *progressive dysphagia.*

dys·pha·sia /disˈfāZHə/ ▶ n. Medicine language disorder marked by deficiency in the generation of speech, and sometimes also in its comprehension, due to brain disease or damage.
– DERIVATIVES **dys·pha·sic** /-ˈfāzik/ adj.
– ORIGIN late 19th cent.: from Greek *dusphatos* 'hard to utter,' from *dus-* 'difficult' + *phatos* 'spoken.'

dys·phe·mism /ˈdisfəˌmizəm/ ▶ n. a derogatory or unpleasant term used instead of a pleasant or neutral one, such as "loony bin" for "mental hospital." The opposite of EUPHEMISM.

dys·pho·ni·a /disˈfōnēə/ ▶ n. Medicine difficulty in speaking due to a physical disorder of the mouth, tongue, throat, or vocal cords.

dys·pho·ri·a /disˈfôrēə/ ▶ n. Psychiatry a state of unease or generalized dissatisfaction with life. The opposite of EUPHORIA.
– DERIVATIVES **dys·phor·ic** /-ˈfôrik/ adj. & n.
– ORIGIN mid 19th cent.: from Greek *dusphoria*, from *dusphoros* 'hard to bear.'

dys·pla·sia /disˈplāZHə/ ▶ n. Medicine the enlargement of an organ or tissue by the proliferation of cells of an abnormal type, as a developmental disorder or an early stage in the development of cancer.
– ORIGIN 1930s: from DYS- 'bad' + Greek *plasis* 'formation.'

dys·plas·tic /disˈplastik/ ▶ adj. exhibiting dysplasia. ■ (of dogs) having malformed joints resulting from a genetic condition. ■ (of moles) generally larger and with irregular and indistinct borders; often symptomatic of melanoma.

dysp·ne·a /disp'nēə/ (Brit. **dyspnoea**) ▸ **n.** Medicine difficult or labored breathing.
– DERIVATIVES **dysp·ne·ic** /disp'nēik/ **adj.**
– ORIGIN mid 17th cent.: via Latin from Greek *duspnoia*, from *dus-* 'difficult' + *pnoē* 'breathing.'

dys·prax·i·a /dis'praksēə/ ▸ **n.** another term for APRAXIA.
– ORIGIN early 20th cent.: from Greek *dus-* 'bad or difficult' + *praxis* 'action.'

dys·pro·si·um /dis'prōzēəm/ ▸ **n.** the chemical element of atomic number 66, a soft silvery-white metal of the lanthanide series. (Symbol: **Dy**)
– ORIGIN late 19th cent.: from Greek *dusprositos* 'hard to get at' + -IUM.

dys·rhyth·mi·a /dis'riTHmēə/ ▸ **n.** Medicine abnormality in a physiological rhythm, esp. in the activity of the brain or heart.
– DERIVATIVES **dys·rhyth·mic** /-mik/ **adj.**, **dys·rhyth·mi·cal** /-mikəl/ **adj.**

dys·thy·mi·a /dis'THīmēə/ ▸ **n.** Psychiatry persistent mild depression.
– DERIVATIVES **dys·thy·mic** /-'THīmik/ **adj.** & **n.**
– ORIGIN mid 19th cent.: from Greek *dusthumia*.

dys·to·ci·a /dis'tōSHə/ ▸ **n.** Medicine & Veterinary Medicine difficult birth, typically caused by a large or awkwardly positioned fetus, by smallness of the maternal pelvis, or by failure of the uterus and cervix to contract and expand normally.
– ORIGIN early 18th cent.: from Greek *dustokia*, from *dus-* 'difficult' + *tokos* 'childbirth.'

dys·to·ni·a /dis'tōnēə/ ▸ **n.** Medicine a state of abnormal muscle tone resulting in muscular spasm and abnormal posture, typically due to neurological disease or a side effect of drug therapy.
– DERIVATIVES **dys·ton·ic** /-'tänik/ **adj.**

dys·to·pi·a /dis'tōpēə/ ▸ **n.** an imagined place or state in which everything is unpleasant or bad, typically a totalitarian or environmentally degraded one. Compare with UTOPIA.
– DERIVATIVES **dys·to·pi·an** (also **dystopic**) **adj.** & **n.**
– ORIGIN late 18th cent.: from DYS- 'bad' + UTOPIA.

dys·troph·ic /dis'träfik/ ▸ **adj. 1** Medicine affected by or relating to dystrophy, esp. muscular dystrophy. **2** Ecology (of a lake) having brown acidic water that is low in oxygen and supports little life, owing to high levels of dissolved humus. Compare with EUTROPHIC and OLIGOTROPHIC.
– ORIGIN late 19th cent.: from Greek *dus-* 'bad' + *-trophia* 'nourishment' + -IC.

dys·tro·phin /dis'trōfin/ ▸ **n.** Biochemistry a protein found in skeletal muscle, which is absent in sufferers from muscular dystrophy.

dys·tro·phy /'distrəfē/ ▸ **n. 1** Medicine & Veterinary Medicine a disorder in which an organ or tissue of the body wastes away. See also MUSCULAR DYSTROPHY. **2** Medicine impaired nourishment of a bodily part.
– ORIGIN late 19th cent.: from modern Latin *dystrophia*, from Greek *dus-* 'bad' + *-trophia* 'nourishment.'

dys·u·ri·a /dis'yo͝orēə/ ▸ **n.** Medicine painful or difficult urination.
– ORIGIN late Middle English: via late Latin from Greek *dusouria*, from *dus-* 'difficult' + *ouron* 'urine.'

DZ ▸ **abbr.** drop zone: *used parachutes were scattered across the DZ.*

dz. ▸ **abbr.** dozen.

Dzau·dzhi·kau /dzou'jēˌkou/ former name (1944–54) of VLADIKAVKAZ.

Dzer·zhinsk /dzir'ZHēnsk/ a city in western central Russia, west of Nizhni Novgorod; pop. 247,500 (est. 2008). Former names CHERNORECHYE (until 1919) and RASTYAPINO (1919–29).

dzo /zō/ ▸ **n.** (pl. **same** or **dzos**) a hybrid of a cow and a yak.
– ORIGIN mid 19th cent.: from Tibetan *mdso*.

Dzong·kha /'zäNGkə/ ▸ **n.** the official language of Bhutan, closely related to Tibetan.

d

Ee

E¹ /ē/ (also **e**) ▶ **n.** (pl. **Es** or **E's**) **1** the fifth letter of the alphabet. ■ denoting the fifth in a set of items, categories, sizes, etc. ■ (**e**) Chess denoting the fifth file from the left, as viewed from White's side of the board. ■ denoting the lowest-earning socioeconomic category for marketing purposes.
2 (**E**) a shape like that of a capital E: [in combination] *an E-shaped stately home.*
3 (usu. **E**) Music the third note of the diatonic scale of C major. ■ a key based on a scale with E as its keynote.

E² ▶ **abbr.** ■ Earth. ■ East or Eastern: *139° E.* ■ Easter. ■ informal the drug Ecstasy or a tablet of Ecstasy. ■ engineer or engineering. ■ English. ■ [in combination] (also **e**) electronic: *E-commerce.* ▶ **symbol** Physics ■ electric field strength. ■ electromotive force. ■ energy: $E = mc^2$.

E³ ▶ **symbol** (€) euro(s).

e¹ ▶ **symbol** ■ (also **e⁻**) Chemistry an electron. ■ (*e*) Mathematics the transcendental number that is the base of Napierian or natural logarithms, approximately equal to 2.71828.

e² /ē/ ▶ **n.** (pl. **e's**) an e-mail system, message, or messages.
▶ **v.** (**e's, e'ing, e'd**) [with obj.] **1** send an e-mail to (someone): *e me to make an offer.*
2 send (a message) by e-mail.
– ORIGIN shortening.

e-¹ ▶ **prefix** variant spelling of **EX-¹** (as in *elect, emit*).

e-² ▶ **prefix** (also **E-**) denoting anything in an electronic state, esp. the use of electronic data transfer in cyberspace for information exchange and financial transactions, esp. through the Internet: *e-business | e-cash | e-world | e-zine.*
– ORIGIN from **ELECTRONIC**, on the pattern of *e-mail.*

ea. ▶ **abbr.** each (used esp. when giving retail prices): *T-shirts for $9.95 ea.*

each /ēCH/ ▶ **determiner & pron.** used to refer to every one of two or more people or things, regarded and identified separately: [as determiner] *each battery is in a separate compartment* | ***each one of** us was asked what went on* | [as pronoun] *Doug had money from **each of** his five uncles | they each have their own personality.*
▶ **adv.** to, for, or by every one of a group (used after a noun or an amount): *they cost $35 each | Paul and Bill have a glass each.*
– PHRASES **each and every** every single (used for emphasis): *taking each and every opportunity.*
– ORIGIN Old English *ǣlc*; related to Dutch *elk* and German *jeglich*, based on a West Germanic phrase meaning 'ever alike' (see **AYE²**, **ALIKE**).

each oth·er ▶ **pron.** used to refer to each member of a group when each does something to or for other members: *they communicate with each other in French.*

Ead·wig /ˈedwig/ variant spelling of **EDWY**.

Ea·gan /ˈēgən/ a city in southeastern Minnesota, just south of St. Paul; pop. 63,985 (est. 2008).

ea·ger /ˈēgər/ ▶ **adj.** (of a person) wanting to do or have something very much: *the man was eager to please | young intellectuals **eager for** knowledge.* ■ (of a person's expression or tone of voice) characterized by keen expectancy or interest: *small eager faces looked up and listened.*
– DERIVATIVES **ea·ger·ly** adv.
– ORIGIN Middle English (also in the sense 'sharp to the senses, pungent, sour'): from Old French *aigre* 'keen,' from Latin *acer, acr-* 'sharp, pungent.'

> **USAGE** See usage at **ANXIOUS**.

ea·ger bea·ver ▶ **n.** informal a keen and enthusiastic person who works very hard.

ea·ger·ness /ˈēgərnəs/ ▶ **n.** enthusiasm to do or to have something; keenness: *the player showed eagerness to play.*

ea·gle /ˈēgəl/ ▶ **n. 1** a large bird of prey with a massive hooked bill and long broad wings, renowned for its keen sight and powerful soaring flight. ● Family Accipitridae: several genera, in particular *Aquila.* ■ a figure of an eagle, esp. as a symbol of the US, or formerly as a Roman or French ensign.
2 Golf a score of two strokes under par at a hole. [suggested by **BIRDIE**.]
3 in the US, a former gold coin worth ten dollars.
▶ **v.** [with obj.] Golf play (a hole) in two strokes under par: *he eagled the last to share fourth place.*
– ORIGIN Middle English: from Old French *aigle*, from Latin *aquila.*

ea·gle eye ▶ **n.** a keen or close watch: *she was keeping an eagle eye on Laura.*
– DERIVATIVES **ea·gle-eyed** /ˌēgəl ˈīd/ **adj.**

ea·gle owl ▶ **n.** a very large Old World owl with ear tufts and a deep hoot. ● Genus *Bubo*, family Strigidae: several species, in particular the Eurasian *B. bubo.*

ea·gle ray ▶ **n.** a large marine ray with long pointed pectoral fins, a long tail, and a distinct head. ● Family Myliobatidae: genera *Myliobatis* and *Aetobatus*, and several species.

ea·glet /ˈēglit/ ▶ **n.** a young eagle.

ea·gre /ˈēgər/ ▶ **n.** dialect term for **BORE³**.
– ORIGIN early 17th cent.: of unknown origin.

Ea·kins /ˈākinz/, Thomas (1844–1916), US painter and photographer. He is known for his portraits and genre pictures of life in Philadelphia. *The Gross Clinic* (1875) aroused controversy because of its explicit depiction of surgery.

-ean ▶ **suffix** forming adjectives and nouns such as *Antipodean, Joycean,* and *Pythagorean.* Compare with **-AN**.
– ORIGIN from Latin *-aeus, -eus* or Greek *-aios, -eios,* + **-AN**.

ear¹ /i(ə)r/ ▶ **n.** the organ of hearing and balance in humans and other vertebrates, esp. the external part of this. ■ an organ sensitive to sound in other animals. ■ [in sing.] an ability to recognize, appreciate, and reproduce sounds, esp. music or language: ***an ear for** melody.* ■ used to refer to a person's willingness to listen and pay attention to something: *she offers a sympathetic ear to worried pet owners.* ■ an ear-shaped thing, esp. the handle of a jug.

> The ear of a mammal is composed of three parts. The outer or external ear consists of a fleshy external flap and a tube leading to the eardrum or tympanum. The middle ear is an air-filled cavity connected to the throat, containing three small linked bones that transmit vibrations from the eardrum to the inner ear. The inner ear is a complex fluid-filled labyrinth including the spiral cochlea (where vibrations are converted to nerve impulses) and the three semicircular canals (forming the organ of balance). The ears of other vertebrates are broadly similar.

– PHRASES **be all ears** informal be listening eagerly and attentively. **bring something (down) about one's ears** bring something, esp. misfortune, on oneself: *she brought her world crashing about her ears.* **one's ears are burning** one is subconsciously aware of being talked about or criticized. **grin** (or **smile**) **from ear to ear** smile broadly. **have something coming out of one's ears** informal have a substantial or excessive amount of something: *that man's got money coming out of his ears.* **have someone's ear** have access to and influence with someone: *he claimed to have the prime minister's ear.* **have** (or **keep**) **an ear to the ground** be well informed about events and trends. **in one ear and out the other** heard but disregarded or quickly forgotten: *whatever he tells me seems to go in one ear and out the other.* **listen with half an ear** not give one's full attention. **be out on one's ear** informal be dismissed or ejected ignominiously. **up to one's ears in** informal very busy with or deeply involved in: *I'm up to my ears in work here.*
– DERIVATIVES **eared** adj. [in combination] *long-eared*, **ear·less** adj.
– ORIGIN Old English *ēare*, of Germanic origin; related to Dutch *oor* and German *Ohr*, from an Indo-European root shared by Latin *auris* and Greek *ous.*

ear² ▶ **n.** the seed-bearing head or spike of a cereal plant. ■ a head of corn.
– ORIGIN Old English *ēar*, of Germanic origin; related to Dutch *aar* and German *Ähre.*

ear·ache /ˈi(ə)rˌāk/ ▶ **n.** pain inside the ear. Also called **OTALGIA**.

ear·bud /ˈi(ə)rˌbəd/ ▶ **n.** a very small headphone, worn inside the ear.

ear can·dy ▶ **n.** light popular music that is pleasant and entertaining but intellectually unchallenging: *the album is mostly ear candy—upbeat melodies and catchy choruses that you can't get out of your head.*

ear drops ▶ **plural n. 1** liquid medication to be applied in small amounts to the ear.
2 (**eardrops**) hanging earrings.

ear·drum /ˈi(ə)rˌdrəm/ ▶ **n.** a membrane of the middle ear that vibrates in response to sound waves; the tympanic membrane.

eared seal ▶ **n.** see **SEAL²**.

ear·flap /ˈi(ə)rˌflap/ ▶ **n.** a flap of material on a hat or cap, covering the ear.

ear·ful /ˈi(ə)rˌfo͝ol/ ▶ **n.** [in sing.] informal a loud blast of a noise: *an earful of static.* ■ a prolonged amount of talking, typically an angry reprimand: *he **gave** his players **an earful** at halftime.*

Ear·hart /ˈe(ə)rˌhärt/, Amelia (Mary) (1897–1937?), US aviator. In 1932, she became the first woman to fly an airplane across the Atlantic Ocean by herself. In 1937, her plane disappeared somewhere over the Pacific Ocean during an around-the-world flight.

Amelia Earhart

ear·hole /ˈi(ə)rˌhōl/ ▶ **n.** the external opening of the ear: *seals can close their earholes under water.* ■ informal a person's ear.

earl /ərl/ ▶ **n.** a British nobleman ranking above a viscount and below a marquess.

–ORIGIN Old English *eorl*, of Germanic origin. The word *earl* originally denoted a man of noble rank, as opposed to a churl; also the word denoted specifically a hereditary nobleman directly above the rank of thane. It was later an equivalent of JARL and, under Canute and his successors, applied to the governor of divisions of England such as Wessex and Mercia. In the late Old English period, as the Saxon court came increasingly under Norman influence, the word was applied to any nobleman bearing the continental title of count (see COUNT[2]).

earl·dom /ˈərldəm/ ▶ n. the rank or title of an earl. ■ historical the territory governed by an earl.

ear·less liz·ard /ˈi(ə)rlis/ ▶ n. a small, long-legged burrowing lizard without visible external ear openings, native to North America. ● *Holbrookia texana*, family Iguanidae.

Earl Grey ▶ n. a kind of China tea flavored with bergamot.
–ORIGIN probably named after the 2nd *Earl Grey* (1764–1845), said to have been given the recipe by a Chinese mandarin.

ear·lobe /ˈi(ə)rˌlōb/ ▶ n. the soft, fleshy lower part of the external ear.

ear·lock /ˈi(ə)rˌläk/ ▶ n. a lock of hair over or above the ear.

earl pal·a·tine ▶ n. (pl. **earls palatine**) historical an earl having royal authority within his country or domain.

Ear·ly /ˈərlē/, Jubal Anderson (1816–94), Confederate army officer. He nearly reached the capital in his 1864 raid on Washington, but was defeated several months later by Sheridan in the Shenandoah Valley and was relieved of his command.

ear·ly /ˈərlē/ ▶ adj. (**earlier, earliest**) **1** happening or done before the usual or expected time: *we ate an early lunch.* ■ (of a plant or crop) flowering or ripening before other varieties: *early potatoes.*
2 happening, belonging to, or done near the beginning of a particular time or period: *an early goal secured victory.* ■ done or occurring near the beginning of the day: *we agreed to meet at 6 a.m. to get an early start.* ■ denoting or belonging to the beginning or opening stages of a historical period, cultural movement, or sphere of activity: *early Impressionism.* ■ occurring at the beginning of a sequence: *the earlier chapters of the book.*
▶ adv. **1** before the usual or expected time: *I was planning to finish work early today.*
2 near the beginning of a particular time or period: *we lost a couple of games early in the season.* ■ near the beginning of the day: *I wrote this piece early one morning.* ■ (**earlier**) before the present time or before the time one is referring to: *you met my husband earlier.*
–PHRASES **at the earliest** not before the time or date specified: *the table won't be delivered until next week at the earliest.* **early bird** humorous a person who rises, arrives, or acts before the usual or expected time. **an early grave** a premature or untimely death: *he worked himself into an early grave.* **the early hours** the time after midnight and before dawn. **an early night** an occasion when someone goes to bed before the usual time. **early** (or **earlier**) **on** at an early (or earlier) stage in a particular time or period: *they discovered early on that the published data were wrong.*
–DERIVATIVES **ear·li·ness** n.
–ORIGIN Old English (as an adverb) *ǣrlīce* (see ERE, -LY[2]), influenced by Old Norse *árliga*. The adjective use dates from Middle English.

ear·ly a·dopt·er ▶ n. a person who starts using a product or technology as soon as it becomes available.

Ear·ly Eng·lish ▶ adj. denoting the earliest stage of English Gothic church architecture, typical of the late 12th and 13th centuries and marked by the use of pointed arches and simple lancet windows without tracery.

ear·ly mu·sic ▶ n. medieval, Renaissance, and early baroque music, esp. as revived and played on period instruments.

ear·ly re·tire·ment ▶ n. the practice of leaving employment before the statutory age, esp. on favorable financial terms.

ear·ly warn·ing sys·tem ▶ n. a network of radar stations established at the boundary of a defended region to provide advanced warning of an aircraft or missile attack. ■ a condition, system, or series of procedures indicating a potential development or impending problem.

ear·mark /ˈi(ə)rˌmärk/ ▶ n. **1** a characteristic or identifying feature: *this car has all the earmarks of a classic.*
2 a congressional directive that funds should be spent on a specific project.
3 a mark on the ear of a domesticated animal indicating ownership or identity.
▶ v. [with obj.] **1** designate (something, typically funds or resources) for a particular purpose: *the new money will be* ***earmarked for*** *cancer research.*
2 mark the ear of (an animal) as a sign of ownership or identity.

ear·muffs /ˈi(ə)rˌməfs/ ▶ plural n. a pair of soft fabric coverings, connected by a band across the top of the head, that are worn over the ears to protect them from cold or noise.

earn /ərn/ ▶ v. [with obj.] (of a person) obtain (money) in return for labor or services: *they earn $35 per hour | he now* ***earns his living*** *as a truck driver.* ■ [with two objs.] (of an activity or action) cause (someone) to obtain (money): *this latest win earned them $50,000 in prize money.* ■ (of capital invested) gain (money) as interest or profit. ■ gain or incur deservedly in return for one's behavior or achievements: *through the years she has earned affection and esteem.*
–PHRASES **earn one's keep** work in return for food and accommodations. ■ be worth the time, money, or effort spent on one.
–PHRASAL VERBS **earn out** (or **earn something out**) (of an author, book, recording artist, etc.) generate sufficient income through sales to equal the amount paid in an advance or royalty: *my experience is that most authors don't earn out | don't confuse earning out the advance with being profitable.*
–ORIGIN Old English *earnian*, from a base shared by Old English *esne* 'laborer.'

earned in·come ▶ n. money derived from paid work. Often contrasted with UNEARNED INCOME.

earned run ▶ n. Baseball a run scored without the aid of errors by the team in the field (i.e., by hits, walks, and outs that advance base runners).

earned run av·er·age ▶ n. Baseball a statistic used to measure a pitcher's effectiveness, obtained by calculating the average number of earned runs scored against the pitcher in every nine innings pitched.

earn·er /ˈərnər/ ▶ n. [with adj. or noun modifier] a person who obtains money in return for labor or services: *higher rates of income tax for high earners | a wage earner.* ■ an activity or product that brings in income of a specified kind or level: *tobacco is a major foreign currency earner.*

ear·nest[1] /ˈərnist/ ▶ adj. resulting from or showing sincere and intense conviction: *an earnest student | two girls were in earnest conversation.*
–PHRASES **in earnest** occurring to a greater extent or more intensely than before: *after Labor Day the campaign begins in earnest.* ■ (of a person) sincere and serious in behavior or convictions.
–DERIVATIVES **ear·nest·ly** adv., **ear·nest·ness** n.
–ORIGIN Old English *eornoste* (adjective), *eornost* (noun), of Germanic origin; related to German *Ernst* (noun).

ear·nest[2] ▶ n. [in sing.] a thing intended or regarded as a sign or promise of what is to come: *the presence of the troops is an earnest of the world's desire not to see the conflict repeated elsewhere.*
–ORIGIN Middle English *ernes*, literally 'installment paid to confirm a contract,' based on Old French *erres*, from Latin *arra*, shortened form of *arrabo* 'a pledge.' The spelling was influenced by words ending in -NESS; the final *-t* is probably by association with EARNEST[1].

ear·nest mon·ey ▶ n. money paid to confirm a contract.

Earn·hardt /ˈərnˌhärt/, Dale (1951–2001), US race car driver; full name *Ralph Dale Earnhardt*. He raced professionally and set many records from 1979 until an accident during the Daytona 500 took his life in February 2001.

earn·ings /ˈərniNGz/ ▶ plural n. money obtained in return for labor or services. ■ income derived from an investment or product: *savers who are attracted by the tax-free earnings.*

earn-out ▶ n. a provision written into some financial transactions whereby the seller of a business will receive additional payments based on the future performance of the business sold.

Earp /ərp/, Wyatt (Berry Stapp) (1848–1929), US marshal and frontiersman. He is best known for the gunfight at the OK Corral (1881), in which he, his brothers, and his friend Doc Holliday fought the Clanton brothers at Tombstone, Arizona.

ear·phone /ˈi(ə)rˌfōn/ ▶ n. (usu. **earphones**) an electrical device worn on the ear to receive radio or telephone communications or to listen to a radio, MP3 player, etc., without other people hearing.

ear·piece /ˈi(ə)rˌpēs/ ▶ n. **1** the part of a telephone, radio receiver, or other aural device that is applied to the ear during use.
2 the part of a pair of glasses that fits around the ear.

ear-pierc·ing ▶ adj. [attrib.] loud and shrill: *the alarm emits an ear-piercing screech.*
▶ n. the practice of making holes in the lobes or edges of the ears to allow the wearing of earrings.

ear·plug /ˈi(ə)rˌpləg/ ▶ n. (usu. **earplugs**) **1** a piece of wax, rubber, or cotton placed in the ear as protection against noise or water.
2 historical an ornament worn in the lobe of the ear.

ear·ring /ˈi(ə)rˌ(r)iNG/ ▶ n. a piece of jewelry worn on the lobe or edge of the ear.

ear shell ▶ n. another term for ABALONE.

ear·shot /ˈi(ə)rˌSHät/ ▶ n. the range or distance over which one can hear or be heard: *she waited until he was* ***out of earshot*** *before continuing.*

ear-split·ting ▶ adj. extremely loud: *an ear-splitting crack of thunder.*

earth /ərTH/ ▶ n. **1** (also **Earth**) the planet on which we live; the world: *the diversity of life* ***on earth***.
■ the surface of the world as distinct from the sky or the sea: *it plummeted back to earth at 60 mph.*
■ the present abode of humankind, as distinct from heaven or hell.

> The earth is the third planet from the sun in the solar system, orbiting between Venus and Mars at an average distance of 90 million miles (149.6 million km) from the sun, and has one natural satellite, the moon. It has an equatorial diameter of 7,654 miles (12,756 km), an average density 5.5 times that of water, and is believed to have formed about 4,600 million years ago. The earth, which is three-quarters covered by oceans and has a dense atmosphere of nitrogen and oxygen, is the only planet known to support life.

2 the substance of the land surface; soil: *a layer of earth.* ■ one of the four elements in ancient and medieval philosophy and in astrology (considered essential to certain signs of the zodiac). ■ a stable, dense, nonvolatile inorganic substance found in the ground. ■ literary the substance of the human body.
3 the underground lair or habitation of a badger or fox.
4 Electrical British term for GROUND[1] (sense 7 of the noun).
▶ v. [with obj.] **1** (**earth something up**) cover the root and lower stem of a plant with heaped-up earth.
2 Hunting drive (a fox) to its underground lair. ■ [no obj.] (of a fox) run to its underground lair.
3 Electrical British term for GROUND[1] (sense 5 of the verb).
–PHRASES **come** (or **bring**) **back** (**down**) **to earth** return or cause to return to reality after a period of daydreaming or excitement. **the earth moved** (or **did the earth move for you?**) humorous one had (or did you have?) an orgasm. **go to earth** (of a hunted animal) hide in an underground burrow. ■ go into hiding: *he'd gone to earth after that meeting.* **like nothing on earth** informal very strange: *they looked like nothing on earth.* **on earth** used for emphasis: *who on earth would venture out in weather like this?*
–ORIGIN Old English *eorthe*, of Germanic origin; related to Dutch *aarde* and German *Erde*.

earth al·mond ▶ n. another term for CHUFA.

earth·bound /ˈərTHˌbound/ ▶ adj. **1** attached or restricted to the earth: *a flightless earthbound bird.*
2 attached or limited to material existence as distinct from a spiritual or heavenly one: *her earthbound view of the sacrament.* ■ lacking in imaginative reach or drive: *an earthbound performance.*
3 (also **earth-bound**) moving toward the earth: *an earthbound spaceship.*

earth clos·et ▶ n. Brit. a basic type of toilet with dry earth used to cover excrement.

earth·en /ˈərTHən/ ▶ adj. [attrib.] (of a floor or structure) made of compressed earth: *the hillside adjacent to the earthen dam.* ■ (of a pot) made of baked or fired clay. ■ literary of, relating to, or characteristic of the earth or material existence.

earth·en·ware /ˈərTHənˌwer/ ▶ n. [often as modifier] pottery made of clay fired to a porous state that can be made impervious to liquids by the use of a glaze: *an earthenware jug.*

earth·light /ˈərTHˌlīt/ ▶ n. another term for EARTHSHINE.

earth·ling /ˈərTHliNG/ ▶ n. an inhabitant of the earth (used esp. in science fiction by members of alien species).

earth loop ▶ n. Electrical British term for GROUND LOOP.

PRONUNCIATION KEY ə ago, up; ər over, fur; a hat; ā ate; ä car; e let; ē see; i fit; ī by; NG sing; ō go; ô law, for; oi toy; o͝o good; o͞o goo; ou out; TH thin; T͟H then; ZH vision

earth·ly /ˈərTHlē/ ▶ **adj. 1** of or relating to the earth or human life on the earth: *water is liquid at normal earthly temperatures.* ■ of or relating to humankind's material existence as distinct from a spiritual or heavenly one: *all earthly happiness is but vanity.*
2 [with negative] informal used for emphasis: *there was no earthly reason why she should not come too.*
– DERIVATIVES **earth·li·ness** n.

earth moth·er ▶ n. (in mythology and primitive religion) a goddess symbolizing fertility and the source of life. ■ a sensual and maternal woman.

earth·mov·er /ˈərthˌmo͞ovər/ ▶ n. a vehicle or machine designed to excavate large quantities of soil.
– DERIVATIVES **earth·mov·ing** n. & adj.

earth·nut /ˈərTHˌnət/ ▶ **n. 1** a Eurasian plant of the parsley family, which has an edible roundish tuber and is typically found in woodland and acid pasture. Also called PIGNUT. ● *Conopodium majus*, family Umbelliferae. ■ the almond-flavored tuber of this plant.
2 chiefly Brit. another term for PEANUT.

earth·quake /ˈərTHˌkwāk/ ▶ n. a sudden and violent shaking of the ground, sometimes causing great destruction, as a result of movements within the earth's crust or volcanic action. ■ a great upheaval: *a political earthquake.*

> Major earthquakes are confined to particular active regions of the earth's crust corresponding to the edges of the crustal plates, and most earthquakes are due to the release of strain energy associated with the relative motions of the plates. The intensity of earthquakes is expressed by the Richter scale, destructive earthquakes generally measuring between about 7 and 9.

earth sci·ence ▶ n. the branch of science dealing with the physical constitution of the earth and its atmosphere. ■ (**earth sciences**) the various branches of this subject, e.g., geology, oceanography, and meteorology.

earth·shak·ing /ˈərTHˌSHākiNG/ ▶ adj. (of music or sound) loud and throbbing: *earthshaking hard-core metal.* ■ another term for EARTH-SHATTERING: *this is not of earthshaking importance.*

earth-shat·ter·ing ▶ adj. (in hyperbolic use) very important, momentous, or traumatic: *tell me this earth-shattering news of yours.*
– DERIVATIVES **earth-shat·ter·ing·ly** adv.

earth·shine /ˈərTHˌSHīn/ (also **earthlight**) ▶ n. Astronomy the glow caused by sunlight reflected off the earth, esp. on the darker portion of a crescent moon.

earth·star /ˈərTHˌstär/ ▶ n. a brownish woodland fungus with a spherical spore-containing fruiting body surrounded by a fleshy star-shaped structure, found in both Eurasia and North America. ● Family Geastraceae, class Gasteromycetes: *Geastrum* and other genera.

earth sta·tion ▶ n. a radio station located on the earth and used for relaying signals from satellites.

earth tone ▶ n. a rich warm color with a brownish hue.

earth trem·or ▶ n. see TREMOR.

earth·ward /ˈərTHwərd/ (also **earthwards**) ▶ **adv. & adj.** toward the earth: [as adv.] *we can watch the parachute as it drifts earthward* | [as adj.] *the bird's earthward plummet.*

earth·work /ˈərTHˌwərk/ ▶ n. a large artificial bank of soil, esp. one made as a defense.

earth·worm /ˈərTHˌwərm/ ▶ n. a burrowing annelid worm that lives in the soil. Earthworms play an important role in aerating and draining the soil and in burying organic matter. ● Family Lumbricidae, class Oligochaeta: *Lumbricus, Allolobophora*, and other genera.

earth·y /ˈərTHē/ ▶ adj. (**earthier, earthiest**) resembling or suggestive of earth or soil: *an earthy smell.* ■ (of a person) direct and uninhibited; hearty: *the storefront is given over to a young, earthy crowd.* ■ (of humor) somewhat coarse or crude: *their good-natured vulgarity and earthy humor.*
– DERIVATIVES **earth·i·ly** adv., **earth·i·ness** n.

ear trum·pet ▶ n. a trumpet-shaped device formerly used as a hearing aid.

ear tuft ▶ n. each of a pair of tufts of longer feathers on the top of the head of some owls. They are unconnected with the true ears.

ear·wax /ˈi(ə)rˌwaks/ ▶ n. the protective yellow waxy substance secreted in the passage of the outer ear. Also called CERUMEN.

ear·wig /ˈi(ə)rˌwig/ ▶ n. a small elongated insect with a pair of terminal appendages that resemble pincers. The females typically care for their eggs and young until they are grown. ● Order Dermaptera: several families.
▶ **v.** (**earwigs, earwigging, earwigged**) [no obj.] informal, chiefly Brit. eavesdrop on a conversation: *he looked behind him to see if anyone was earwigging.* ■ [with obj.] archaic influence (someone) by secret means.
– ORIGIN Old English *ēarwicga*, from *ēare* 'ear' + *wicga* 'earwig' (probably related to *wiggle*). The insect is so named because it was once thought to crawl into the human ear.

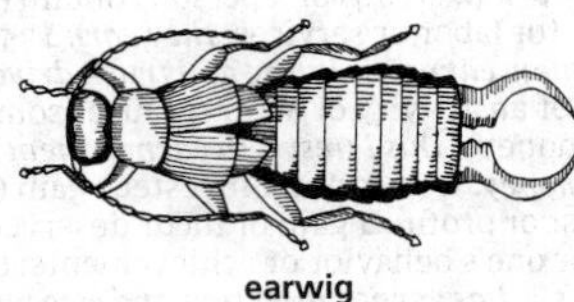
earwig

ear·wit·ness /ˈi(ə)rˌwitnis, ˌi(ə)rˈwit-/ ▶ n. a witness whose testimony is based on what they personally heard.

ear·worm /ˈi(ə)rˌwərm/ ▶ **n. 1** short for CORN EARWORM.
2 informal a catchy song or tune that runs continually through a person's mind.

ease /ēz/ ▶ n. absence of difficulty or effort: *he gave up tobacco and alcohol with ease* | *the guitar's versatility and ease of handling.* ■ absence of rigidity or discomfort; poise: *I was always vexed by her self-contained ease.* ■ freedom from worries or problems, esp. about one's material situation: *a life of wealth and ease.*
▶ **v. 1** [with obj.] make (something unpleasant, painful, or intense) less serious or severe: *a huge road-building program to ease congestion.* ■ [no obj.] become less serious or severe: *the pain doesn't usually ease off for several hours.* ■ [no obj.] (**ease up**) relax one's efforts; do something with more moderation: *I'd ease up on the hard stuff if I were you.* ■ (**ease something away/down/off**) Nautical slacken a rope. ■ (**ease something away/down/off**) Nautical sail slowly or gently. ■ make (something) happen more easily; facilitate: *Tokyo's dominance of government was deemed to ease efficient contact-making.* ■ [no obj.] Finance (of share prices, interest rates, etc.) decrease in value or amount: *these shares should be bought and tucked away for when interest rates ease* | (as noun **easing**) *a slight easing of inflation.*
2 [no obj.] move carefully, gradually, or gently: *I eased down the slope with care* | [with obj.] *the pilot eased the throttle back.* ■ [with obj.] (**ease someone out**) gradually exclude someone from a post or place, esp. by devious or subtle maneuvers: *after the scandal he was eased out of his job.*
– PHRASES **at (one's) ease** free from worry, awkwardness, or problems; relaxed: *she was never quite at ease with Phil.* ■ (**at ease**) Military in a relaxed attitude with the feet apart and the hands behind the back (often as a command): *all right, stand at ease!* **ease someone's mind** alleviate someone's anxiety.
– DERIVATIVES **eas·er** n.
– ORIGIN Middle English: from Old French *aise*, based on Latin *adjacens* 'lying close by,' present participle of *adjacere*. The verb is originally from Old French *aisier*, from the phrase *a aise* 'at ease'; in later use from the noun.

ease·ful /ˈēzfəl/ ▶ adj. literary providing or offering comfort or peace: *life was easeful at that time.*

ea·sel /ˈēzəl/ ▶ n. a self-supporting wooden frame for holding an artist's work while it is being painted or drawn.
– ORIGIN late 16th cent.: from Dutch *ezel* 'ass.' The word "horse" is used in English in a similar way to denote a supporting frame.

artist's easel

ease·ment /ˈēzmənt/ ▶ **n.**
1 Law a right to cross or otherwise use someone else's land for a specified purpose.
2 literary the state or feeling of comfort or peace: *time brings easement.*
– ORIGIN late Middle English: from Old French *aisement*, from *aisier* (see EASE).

ea s·i·ly /ˈēz(ə)lē/ ▶ **adv. 1** without difficulty or effort: *he climbed the mountain easily* | *the area is easily accessible by road.* ■ in a relaxed manner: *he shrugged easily.* ■ more quickly or frequently than is usual: *they get bored easily.*
2 without doubt; by far: *English is easily the reigning language in the financial world.* ■ very probably: *events that could easily become stodgy and predictable.*

east /ēst/ ▶ **n.** (usu. **the east**) **1** the direction toward the point of the horizon where the sun rises at the equinoxes, on the right-hand side of a person facing north, or the point on the horizon itself: *a gale was blowing from the east* | *the Atlantic Ocean is to the east of Florida.* ■ the compass point corresponding to this.
2 the eastern part of the world or of a specified country, region, or town: *a factory in the east of the city.* ■ (usu. **the East**) the regions or countries lying to the east of Europe, esp. China, Japan, and India: *the protection of trade routes to the East.* ■ (usu. **the East**) the eastern part of the US from the Alleghenies on the west and north of the Mason–Dixon line: *Pittsburgh beat up on the bottom three teams in the East.* ■ (usu. **the East**) short for EAST COAST. ■ (usu. **the East**) historical the former communist states of eastern Europe.
3 (**East**) [as name] Bridge the player sitting to the left of North and partnering West.
▶ **adj.** [attrib.] **1** lying toward, near, or facing the east: *the hospital's east wing.* ■ (of a wind) blowing from the east. ■ situated in the part of a church containing the altar or high altar, usually the actual east.
2 (often **East**) of or denoting the eastern part of a specified area, city, or country or its inhabitants: *East Texas* | *East African.*
▶ **adv.** to or toward the east: *traveling east, he met two men* | *the river rises east of the city.*
– ORIGIN Old English *ēast-*, of Germanic origin; related to Dutch *oost* and German *ost*, from an Indo-European root shared by Latin *aurora*, Greek *auōs* 'dawn.'

East Af·ri·ca the eastern part of the African continent, esp. the countries of Kenya, Uganda, and Tanzania.

East An·gli·a /ˈaNGglēə/ a region in eastern England that consists of the counties of Norfolk and Suffolk, as well as parts of Essex and Cambridgeshire counties.

East A·sia the eastern part of the Asian continent, including China and Japan.
– DERIVATIVES **East A·sian** adj.

East Ben·gal the part of the former Indian province of Bengal that was ceded to Pakistan in 1947 and that forms the greater part of the province of East Pakistan. It gained independence as Bangladesh in 1971.

East Ber·lin see BERLIN¹.

east·bound /ˈēs(t)ˌbound/ ▶ adj. leading or traveling toward the east: *the eastbound lane.*

east by north ▶ n. a direction or compass point midway between east and east-northeast.

east by south ▶ n. a direction or compass point midway between east and east-southeast.

East Chi·ca·go an industrial port city in northwestern Indiana, on Lake Michigan, southeast of Chicago, Illinois; pop. 29,978 (est. 2008).

East Chi·na Sea see CHINA SEA.

East Coast ▶ n. the eastern seaboard of the US, esp. the narrow corridor from Boston to Washington, DC.

East End the part of London, England, north of the Thames and east of the City, including the Docklands.
– DERIVATIVES **East End·er** /ˌēst ˈendər/ n.

Eas·ter /ˈēstər/ ▶ n. the most important and oldest festival of the Christian Church, celebrating the resurrection of Jesus Christ and held (in the Western Church) between March 21 and April 25, on the first Sunday after the first full moon following the northern spring equinox. ■ the period in which this occurs, esp. the weekend from Good Friday to Easter Monday.
– ORIGIN Old English *ēastre*; of Germanic origin and related to German *Ostern* and EAST. According to Bede the word is derived from *Ēastre*, the name of a goddess associated with spring.

Eas·ter bun·ny ▶ n. an imaginary rabbit said to bring gifts to children at Easter.

Eas·ter egg ▶ **n. 1** a hard-boiled egg that is dyed and often decorated as part of the Easter celebration. ■ an artificial egg, typically chocolate, given at Easter, esp. to children.
2 an unexpected or undocumented feature in a piece of computer software or on a DVD, included as a joke or a bonus.

Eas·ter Is·land an island in the southeastern Pacific Ocean, west of and administered by Chile; pop. 3,300 (est. 2009). The island, first settled by Polynesians in about AD 400, is famous for its large monolithic statues of human heads that are believed to date from 1000–1600.

statues on Easter Island

Eas·ter lil·y ▸ **n.** a spring-flowering lily. • Genus *Lilium*, family Liliaceae: several species, in particular the tall, white-flowered Japanese lily *L. longiflorum*.

east·er·ly /ˈēstərlē/ ▸ **adj. & adv.** in an eastward position or direction: [as adj.] *the captain ordered an easterly course.* ■ (of a wind) blowing from the east: [as adj.] *the light easterly breeze.*
▸ **n.** (often **easterlies**) a wind blowing from the east.

Eas·ter Mon·day ▸ **n.** the day after Easter Sunday, a public holiday in some places.

east·ern /ˈēstərn/ ▸ **adj.** **1** [attrib.] situated in the east, or directed toward or facing the east: *eastern Long Island | the eastern slopes of the mountain.* ■ (of a wind) blowing from the east.
2 (usu. **Eastern**) living in or originating from the east, in particular the regions or countries lying to the east of Europe: *an Eastern monk.* ■ of, relating to, or characteristic of the East or its inhabitants: *an eastern religion.*
– DERIVATIVES **east·ern·most** /ˈēstərnˌmōst/ **adj.**
– ORIGIN Old English *ēasterne* (as **EAST**, **-ERN**).

East·ern bloc the countries of eastern and central Europe that were under Soviet domination from the end of World War II until the collapse of the Soviet communist system in 1989–91, usually considered to include Poland, East Germany, Czechoslovakia, Hungary, Romania, Bulgaria, and Yugoslavia.

East·ern Church (also **Eastern Orthodox Church**) another name for **ORTHODOX CHURCH**. ■ any of the Christian Churches originating in eastern Europe and the Middle East.

East·ern Des·ert another name of the **ARABIAN DESERT**.

East·ern Em·pire the eastern part of the Roman Empire, after its division in AD 395. See also **BYZANTINE EMPIRE**.

east·ern e·quine en·ceph·a·li·tis ▸ **n.** a rare viral disease that affects horses and humans and is spread by mosquitoes, occurring mainly in eastern US states.

East·ern·er /ˈēstərnər/ (also **easterner**) ▸ **n.** a native or inhabitant of the east, esp. of the eastern US.

East·ern Eu·rope the portion of the European landmass that lies east of Germany and the Alps and west of the Ural Mountains. It includes the former Eastern bloc countries of Poland, the Czech Republic and Slovakia (formerly as Czechoslovakia), Hungary, Romania, and Bulgaria, as well as the Baltic republics of Estonia, Latvia, and Lithuania, and the former Soviet republics of Belarus and Ukraine, along with Russia west of the Urals.

East·ern Ghats see **GHATS**.

east·ern hem·i·sphere the half of the earth that contains Europe, Africa, Asia, and Australia.

East·ern Shore region of eastern Maryland on the Delmarva Peninsula, on the east side of Chesapeake Bay.

East·ern time the standard time in a zone including the eastern states of the US and parts of Canada, specifically. • (**Eastern Standard Time**, abbrev.: **EST**), standard time based on the mean solar time at the meridian 75° W, five hours behind GMT. • (**Eastern Daylight Time**, abbrev.: **EDT**) Eastern time during daylight saving time, four hours behind GMT.

East·ern Zhou see **ZHOU**.

Eas·ter·tide /ˈēstərˌtīd/ ▸ **n.** the Easter period.

East Flan·ders a province in northern Belgium; capital, Ghent. See also **FLANDERS**.

East Fri·sian Is·lands see **FRISIAN ISLANDS**.

East Ger·man·ic ▸ **n.** the extinct eastern group of Germanic languages, including Gothic.
▸ **adj.** of or relating to this group of languages.

East Ger·many (official name *German Democratic Republic*) the former independent nation created in 1949 from the area of Germany occupied by the former Soviet Union after World War II. It was reunited with West Germany after the fall of its communist government in 1990. German name ***Deutsche Demokratische Republik***.

East Hamp·ton a resort town in eastern Long Island in New York, noted for its artists' colony; pop. 22,106 (est. 2008).

East Har·lem a neighborhood of Harlem in northern Manhattan in New York City. Parts of it have been called Italian Harlem and Spanish Harlem, reflecting local ethnic history.

East Hart·ford an industrial town in central Connecticut, across the Connecticut River from Hartford; pop. 48,571 (est. 2008).

East In·di·a another name of **EAST INDIES** (sense 2).

East In·di·a Com·pa·ny a trading company formed in 1600 to develop commerce in the newly colonized areas of Southeast Asia and India. In the 18th century it took administrative control of Bengal and other areas of India, and held it until the British Crown took over in 1858 in the wake of the Indian Mutiny.

East In·di·a·man /ˈindēəmən/ ▸ **n.** historical a trading ship belonging to the East India Company.

East In·dies 1 the islands in Southeast Asia, esp. those of the Malay Archipelago.
2 archaic the whole of Southeast Asia to the east of and including India.
– DERIVATIVES **East In·di·an adj.**

east·ing /ˈēstiNG/ ▸ **n.** distance traveled or measured eastward, esp. at sea. ■ a figure or line representing eastward distance on a map (expressed by convention as the first part of a grid reference, before northing).

East Lan·sing a city in south central Michigan, home to Michigan State University; pop. 45,857 (est. 2008).

East Lon·don a port and resort in South Africa, on the southeastern coast; pop. 452,200 (est. 2009).

East Los An·ge·les a community in southwestern California, a largely Hispanic suburb east of Los Angeles; pop. 124,283 (2000).

East·man[1] /ˈēstmən/, George (1854–1932), US inventor and manufacturer of photographic equipment. He invented flexible roll film that is coated with light-sensitive emulsion and, in 1888, the Kodak camera for use with it.

East·man[2], Linda, see **MCCARTNEY**[2].

east-north·east ▸ **n.** the direction or compass point midway between east and northeast.

East Or·ange a city in northeastern New Jersey, northwest of Newark; pop. 65,390 (est. 2008).

East·port /ˈēstˌpôrt/ a maritime city in eastern Maine, on an island in Passamaquoddy Bay, the easternmost US city; pop. 1,536 (est. 2008).

East Prov·i·dence a city in eastern Rhode Island, across the Seekonk River from Providence; pop. 48,480 (est. 2008).

East Prus·sia the northeastern part of the former kingdom of Prussia, on the Baltic coast, later part of Germany and divided after World War II between the former Soviet Union and Poland.

East Riv·er a tidal inlet in New York City that separates the boroughs of Manhattan and the Bronx from the boroughs of Brooklyn and Queens.

East Si·be·ri·an Sea a part of the Arctic Ocean that lies between the New Siberian Islands and Wrangel Island, to the north of eastern Siberia.

East Side a part of Manhattan in New York City that lies between the East River and Fifth Avenue.

east-south·east ▸ **n.** the direction or compass point midway between east and southeast.

East Ti·mor a country on the eastern part of the island of Timor in the southern part of the Malay Archipelago; pop. 1,131,600 (2009); capital, Dili; languages, Portuguese, Indonesian, English, and indigenous languages. Official name **TIMOR LESTE**.

> Formerly a Portuguese colony, East Timor declared itself independent in 1975. In 1976 it was invaded by Indonesia, which annexed and claimed it as their 27th state. The region was the scene of bitter fighting and of alleged mass killings by the Indonesian government and military forces. In a UN-supervised referendum in 1999, the people voted for independence from Indonesia. Violence continued, but on May 20, 2002, East Timor achieved international recognition as an independent state.

– DERIVATIVES **East Ti·mo·rese n. & adj.**

east·ward /ˈēs(t)wərd/ ▸ **adj.** in an easterly direction: *they followed an eastward course.*
▸ **adv.** (also **eastwards**) toward the east: *the bus rattled its way eastward.*
▸ **n.** (**the eastward**) the direction or region toward the east: *a squall came from the eastward.*
– DERIVATIVES **east·ward·ly adv.**

East·wood /ˈēstˌwo͝od/, Clint (1930–), US movie actor and director. He became known after he starred in *A Fistful of Dollars* (1964), the first cult "spaghetti western." He portrayed detective Harry Callahan in five movies, beginning with *Dirty Harry* (1971). Movies that he directed as well as starred in include *Bird* (1988), *Unforgiven* (1992), *The Bridges of Madison County* (1994), and *Mystic River* (2003).

eas·y /ˈēzē/ ▸ **adj.** (**easier, easiest**) **1** achieved without great effort; presenting few difficulties: *an easy way of retrieving information.* ■ [attrib.] (of an object of attack or criticism) having no defense; vulnerable: *he was vulnerable and an easy target.* ■ informal, derogatory (of a woman) open to sexual advances; sexually available: *her reputation at school for being easy.*
2 (of a period of time or way of life) free from worries or problems: *promises of an easy life in the New World.* ■ (of a person) lacking anxiety or awkwardness; relaxed: *his easy and agreeable manner | they didn't feel easy about what they were doing.*
▸ **adv.** informal without difficulty or effort: *we all scared real easy in those days.*
▸ **exclam.** be careful: *easy, girl—you'll knock me over!*
– PHRASES **be easier said than done** be more easily talked about than put into practice. **(as) easy as pie** see **PIE**[1]. **easy come, easy go** used to indicate that a relationship or possession acquired without effort may be abandoned or lost casually and without regret. **easy does it** used esp. in spoken English to advise someone to approach a task carefully and slowly. **easy on the eye** (or **ear**) informal pleasant to look at (or listen to). **go** (or **be**) **easy on someone** informal refrain from being harsh with or critical of someone. **go easy on something** informal be sparing or cautious in one's use or consumption of something: *go easy on fatty foods.* **have it easy** informal be free from difficulties; be fortunate. **I'm easy** informal said by someone when offered a choice to indicate that they have no particular preference. **of easy virtue** dated (of a woman) sexually promiscuous. **rest** (or **sleep**) **easy** be untroubled by (or go to sleep without) worries: *this insurance policy will let you rest easy.* **take the easy way out** extricate oneself from a difficult situation by choosing the simplest or most expedient course rather than the most honorable or ethical one. **take it easy** proceed calmly and in a relaxed manner. ■ make little effort; rest.
– DERIVATIVES **eas·i·ness n.**
– ORIGIN Middle English (also in the sense 'comfortable, quiet, tranquil'): from Old French *aisie*, past participle of *aisier* 'put at ease, facilitate' (see **EASE**).

eas·y-care ▸ **adj.** [attrib.] (chiefly of man-made fabrics) requiring little effort to wash and dry, and typically no ironing.

eas·y chair ▸ **n.** a large, comfortable chair, typically an armchair.

eas·y·go·ing /ˈēzēˌgōiNG/ ▸ **adj.** relaxed and tolerant in approach or manner: *an outwardly easygoing but fiercely competitive youngster.*

eas·y lis·ten·ing ▸ **n.** popular music that is tuneful and undemanding.

eas·y mark ▸ **n.** informal a person who is easy prey; a weakling or a sucker: *an easy mark for a grifter.*

eas·y mon·ey ▸ **n.** money obtained by dubious means or for little work. ■ money available at relatively low interest.

eas·y street ▸ **n.** informal a state of financial comfort or security: *she keeps complaining about her lot, but I think she's **on easy street**.*

eat /ēt/ ▸ **v.** (past **ate** /āt/; past participle **eaten** /ˈētn/) [with obj.] put (food) into the mouth and chew and swallow it: *he was eating a hot dog | **eat up** all your peas | [no obj.] she watched her son as he ate.* ■ have (a meal): *we ate dinner in a noisy cafe.* ■ [no obj.] (**eat out**) have a meal in a restaurant. ■ [no obj.] (**eat in**) have a meal at home rather than in a restaurant. ■ informal bother; annoy: *she knew what was eating him.* ■ vulgar slang perform fellatio or cunnilingus on (someone). ■ vulgar slang (**eat out**) perform cunnilingus or anilingus on (someone). ■ informal absorb (financial loss or cost).
▸ **n.** (**eats**) informal food or snacks: *people would stop for soft drinks or eats.*
– PHRASES **eat someone alive** informal (of insects) bite someone many times: *we were eaten alive by mosquitoes.* ■ exploit someone's weakness and completely dominate them: *he expects manufacturers to be eaten alive by lawyers in liability suits.* **eat crow** see **CROW**[1]. **eat dirt** see **DIRT**.

eat someone's dust see DUST. **eat one's heart out** suffer from excessive longing, esp. for someone or something unattainable. ■ [in imperative] informal used to encourage feelings of jealousy or regret: *eat your heart out, I'm having a ball!* **eat humble pie** see HUMBLE. **eat like a bird** (or **a horse**) informal eat very little (or a lot). **eat someone out of house and home** informal eat a lot of someone else's food. **eat one's words** retract what one has said, esp. in a humiliated way: *they will eat their words when I win.* **have someone eating out of one's hand** have someone completely under one's control. **I'll eat my hat** informal used to indicate that one thinks the specified thing is extremely unlikely to happen: *if he comes back, I'll eat my hat.*
– PHRASAL VERBS **eat away at** (or **eat something away**) erode or destroy something gradually: *the sun and wind eat away at the ice | prevents bone from being eaten away.* ■ use up (profits, resources, or time), esp. when they are intended for other purposes: *inflation can eat away at the annuity's value over the years.* **eat into** another way of saying EAT AWAY AT. **eat someone up** (usu. as adj. **eaten up**) dominate the thoughts of someone completely: *I'm eaten up with guilt.* **eat something up** use resources or time in very large quantities: *an operating system that eats up 200Mb of disk space.* ■ encroach on something: *this is the countryside that villagers fear will be eaten up by concrete.*
– ORIGIN Old English *etan*, of Germanic origin; related to Dutch *eten* and German *essen*, from an Indo-European root shared by Latin *edere* and Greek *edein*.

eat·a·ble /ˈētəbəl/ ▶ **adj.** fit to be consumed as food: *eatable fruits.*
▶ **n.** (**eatables**) items of food: *parcels of eatables and gifts.*

eat·er /ˈētər/ ▶ **n.** [with adj. or noun modifier] a person or animal that consumes food in a specified way or of a specified kind: *I'm still a big eater | they are meat eaters.*

eat·er·y /ˈētərē/ ▶ **n.** (pl. **eateries**) informal a restaurant or other place where people can be served food.

eat-in ▶ **adj.** [attrib.] (of a kitchen) designed for eating in as well as cooking.

eat·ing ap·ple ▶ **n.** an apple that is suitable for eating raw.

eat·ing dis·or·der ▶ **n.** any of a range of psychological disorders characterized by abnormal or disturbed eating habits (such as anorexia nervosa).

eat·ing house ▶ **n.** a restaurant (usu. used in the names of restaurants): *The Blue Whale Eating House | Mrs. Miller's -- a contemporary pub and fine eating house.*

Eau Claire /ō ˈkler/ a city in west central Wisconsin; pop. 65,426 (est. 2008).

eau de co·logne /ˌō də kəˈlōn/ ▶ **n.** a toilet water with a strong, characteristic scent, originally made in Cologne, Germany.
– ORIGIN early 19th cent.: French, literally 'water of Cologne.'

eau de Nil /ˌō də ˈnē/ ▶ **n.** a pale greenish color.
– ORIGIN late 19th cent.: from French *eau-de-Nil*, literally 'water of the Nile' (from the supposed resemblance in color).

eau de toi·lette /ˌō də twäˈlet/ ▶ **n.** (pl. **eaux de toilette** pronunc. **same**) a dilute form of perfume; toilet water.
– ORIGIN early 20th cent.: French, literally 'toilet water.'

eau-de-vie /ˌō də ˈvē/ ▶ **n.** (pl. **eaux-de-vie** pronunc. **same**) brandy.
– ORIGIN mid 18th cent.: from French *eau-de-vie*, literally 'water of life.'

eaves /ēvz/ ▶ **plural n.** the part of a roof that meets or overhangs the walls of a building.
– ORIGIN Old English *efes* (singular); of Germanic origin; related to German dialect *Obsen*, also probably to OVER.

eaves·drop /ˈēvzˌdräp/ ▶ **v.** (**eavesdrops, eavesdropping, eavesdropped**) [no obj.] secretly listen to a conversation: *she opened the window just enough to eavesdrop on the conversation outside.*
– DERIVATIVES **eaves·drop·per n.**
– ORIGIN early 17th cent.: back-formation from *eavesdropper* (late Middle English) 'a person who listens from under the eaves,' from the obsolete noun *eavesdrop* 'the ground onto which water drips from the eaves,' probably from Old Norse *upsardropi*, from *ups* 'eaves' + *dropi* 'a drop.'

eaves·trough /ˈēvzˌtrôf/ ▶ **n.** Canadian a gutter fixed beneath the edge of a roof.

Eb (also **EB**) ▶ **abbr.** exabyte(s).

e·Bay /ˈēˌbā/ ▶ **v.** [with obj.] buy or sell (goods) through the eBay website.
– DERIVATIVES **e·Bay·er n.**
– ORIGIN 1997: from the proprietary name of the website *eBay* (from Echo Bay Technology Group, the name of a company run by eBay's founder, Pierre Omidyar).

ebb /eb/ ▶ **n.** (usu. **the ebb**) the movement of the tide out to sea: *I knew the tide would be on the ebb | [as modifier] the ebb tide.*
▶ **v.** [no obj.] **1** (of tidewater) move away from the land; recede: *the tide began to ebb.* Compare with FLOW.
2 (of an emotion or quality) gradually lessen or reduce: *my enthusiasm was ebbing away.*
– PHRASES **at a low ebb** in a poor state: *the country was at a low ebb due to the recent war.* **ebb and flow** a recurrent or rhythmical pattern of coming and going or decline and regrowth.
– ORIGIN Old English *ebba* (noun), *ebbian* (verb); related to Dutch *ebbe* (noun), *ebben* (verb), and ultimately to OF, which had the primary sense 'away from.'

EBCDIC /ˈebsēˌdik/ ▶ **abbr.** Extended Binary Coded Decimal Interchange Code, a standard eight-bit character code used in computing and data transmission.

e-bill·ing /ˈēˌbiliNG/ ▶ **n.** the practice by which invoices or bills are electronically delivered or presented to customers, rather than being sent by mail.

EBIT ▶ **abbr.** earnings before interest and tax.

EBITDA ▶ **abbr.** earnings before interest, taxes, depreciation, and amortization.

Eb·la /ˈeblə, ˈēblə/ a city in ancient Syria that was southwest of Aleppo. It became very powerful in the mid-3rd millennium BC, when it dominated a region corresponding to modern Lebanon, northern Syria, and southeastern Turkey.

EbN ▶ **abbr.** east by north.

E-boat /ˈēˌbōt/ ▶ **n.** a German torpedo boat used in World War II.
– ORIGIN from *E-* for *enemy* + BOAT.

Eb·o·la fe·ver /ēˈbōlə/ ▶ **n.** an infectious and generally fatal disease marked by fever and severe internal bleeding, spread through contact with infected body fluids by a filovirus (**Ebola virus**), whose normal host species is unknown.
– ORIGIN 1976: named after a river in the Democratic Republic of the Congo (formerly Zaire), near which the disease was first observed.

eb·on /ˈebən/ ▶ **n.** literary dark brown or black; ebony: [as modifier] *the dark shadows of the mountains gave the river an ebon hue.*

E·bon·ics /ēˈbäniks/ ▶ **plural n.** [treated as sing.] American black English regarded as a language in its own right rather than as a dialect of standard English.
– ORIGIN blend of EBONY and PHONICS.

eb·on·ite /ˈebəˌnīt/ ▶ **n.** another term for VULCANITE.
– ORIGIN mid 19th cent.: from EBONY + -ITE¹.

eb·on·ize /ˈebəˌnīz/ ▶ **v.** [with obj.] (usu. as adj. **ebonized**) make (furniture) look like ebony: *an ebonized casket.*

eb·on·y /ˈebənē/ ▶ **n. 1** heavy blackish or very dark brown timber from a mainly tropical tree. ■ a very dark brown or black color: *his smile flashed against the ebony of his skin | [as modifier] his ebony hair.*
2 a tree of tropical and warm-temperate regions that produces such timber. ● Genera *Diospyros* and *Euclea*, family Ebenaceae: numerous species, in particular *D. ebenum.* ■ used in names of trees of other families that produce similar timber, e.g., **Jamaican** (or **American**) **ebony**.
– ORIGIN late Middle English: from earlier *ebon* (via Old French and Latin from Greek *ebenos* 'ebony tree'), perhaps on the pattern of *ivory*.

e-book /ˈēˌbo͝ok/ ▶ **n.** an electronic version of a printed book that can be read on a computer or handheld device designed specifically for this purpose. ■ a dedicated device for reading electronic versions of printed books.

E·bro /ˈāvrō, ˈābrō/ a river in northeastern Spain that rises in the mountains of the Cantabria region and flows southeast for 570 miles (910 km) into the Mediterranean Sea.

EbS ▶ **abbr.** east by south.

e·bul·lience /iˈbo͝olyəns, iˈbəlyəns/ ▶ **n.** the quality of being cheerful and full of energy; exuberance: *the ebullience of happy children.*

e·bul·lient /iˈbo͝olyənt, iˈbəlyənt/ ▶ **adj. 1** cheerful and full of energy: *she sounded ebullient and happy.*
2 archaic or literary (of liquid or matter) boiling or agitated as if boiling: *misted and ebullient seas.*
– DERIVATIVES **e·bul·lient·ly adv.**
– ORIGIN late 16th cent. (in the sense 'boiling'): from Latin *ebullient-* 'boiling up,' from the verb *ebullire*, from *e-* (variant of *ex-*) 'out' + *bullire* 'to boil.'

eb·ul·li·tion /ˌebəˈliSHən/ ▶ **n.** technical or archaic the action of bubbling or boiling. ■ a sudden outburst of emotion or violence: *in an ebullition of fervor.*
– ORIGIN late Middle English (used to describe a state of agitation of the bodily humors): from late Latin *ebullitio(n-)*, from *ebullire* 'boil up' (see EBULLIENT).

e-busi·ness /ˈēˌbiznis/ another term for E-COMMERCE.

EBV ▶ **abbr.** Epstein-Barr virus.

EC ▶ **abbr.** ■ European Commission. ■ European Community. ■ executive committee.

e·cad /ˈēˌkad, ˈeˌkad/ ▶ **n.** Ecology an organism that is modified by its environment.
– ORIGIN early 20th cent.: from Greek *oikos* 'house' + -AD¹.

é·car·té /ˌākärˈtā/ ▶ **n. 1** a card game for two players, played originally in 19th-century France, in which thirty-two cards are used, and certain cards may be discarded in exchange for others.
2 Ballet a position in which the dancer, facing diagonally toward the audience, extends one leg to the side with the arm of the same side raised above the head and the other arm extended to the side.
– ORIGIN early 19th cent.: French, past participle of *écarter* 'discard, throw out,' from *é* 'out' + *carte* 'card.'

e-cash /ˈēˌkaSH/ ▶ **n.** electronic financial transactions conducted in cyberspace via computer networks.

ec·bol·ic /ekˈbälik/ Medicine ▶ **adj.** inducing contractions of the uterus leading to expulsion of a fetus: *the ecbolic properties of Indian medicinal plants.*
▶ **n.** an agent that induces such contractions.
– ORIGIN mid 18th cent.: from Greek *ekbolē* 'expulsion' + -IC.

Ec·ce Ho·mo /ˈeCHā ˈhōˌmō, ˈeksē, ˈekā/ ▶ **n.** Art a painting of Jesus Christ wearing the crown of thorns.
– ORIGIN early 17th cent.: Latin, literally 'behold the man,' the words of Pontius Pilate to the Jews after Jesus was crowned with thorns (John 19:5).

ec·cen·tric /ikˈsentrik/ ▶ **adj. 1** (of a person or their behavior) unconventional and slightly strange: *my favorite aunt is very eccentric.*
2 technical (of a thing) not placed centrally or not having its axis or other part placed centrally. ■ (of a circle) not centered on the same point as another. ■ (of an orbit) not circular.
▶ **n. 1** a person of unconventional and slightly strange views or behavior: *he enjoys a colorful reputation as an engaging eccentric.*
2 a disc or wheel mounted eccentrically on a revolving shaft in order to transform rotation into backward-and-forward motion, e.g., a cam in an internal combustion engine.
– DERIVATIVES **ec·cen·tri·cal·ly adv.**
– ORIGIN late Middle English (as a noun denoting a circle or orbit not having the earth precisely at its center): via late Latin from Greek *ekkentros*, from *ek* 'out of' + *kentron* 'center.'

ec·cen·tric a·nom·a·ly ▶ **n.** Astronomy the actual anomaly of a planet in an elliptical orbit. Compare with MEAN ANOMALY.

ec·cen·tric·i·ty /ˌeksenˈtrisitē/ ▶ **n.** (pl. **eccentricities**) **1** the quality of being eccentric. ■ (usu. **eccentricities**) an eccentric act, habit, or thing: *her eccentricities were amusing rather than irritating.*
2 technical deviation of a curve or orbit from circularity. ■ a measure of the extent of such deviation: *Halley's Comet has an eccentricity of about 0.9675.*

ec·chy·mo·sis /ˌekəˈmōsis/ ▶ **n.** (pl. **ecchymoses** /ˌekəˈmōˌsēz/) Medicine a discoloration of the skin resulting from bleeding underneath, typically caused by bruising.
– ORIGIN mid 16th cent.: modern Latin, from Greek *ekkhumōsis* 'escape of blood,' from *ekkhumonathai* 'force out blood.'

eccl. ▶ **abbr.** ■ ecclesiastic. ■ ecclesiastical.

Ec·cles /ˈekəlz/, Sir John Carew (1903–97), Australian physiologist, who demonstrated the way in which nerve impulses are conducted by means of chemical neurotransmitters. Nobel Prize for Physiology or Medicine (1963), shared with Alan L. Hodgkin and Andrew F. Huxley.

Eccles. ▶ **abbr.** Bible Ecclesiastes.

ec·cle·si·al /iˈklēzēəl/ ▶ **adj.** formal relating to or constituting a church or denomination: *the modernization of ecclesial buildings.*
– ORIGIN mid 17th cent. (but rare before the 1960s): via Old French from Greek *ekklēsia* 'assembly, church' (see ECCLESIASTIC).

ec·cle·si·arch /iˈklēzēˌärk/ ▶ **n.** archaic a ruler of a church.
– ORIGIN late 18th cent.: from Greek *ekklēsia* 'church' + *arkhos* 'leader.'

Ec·cle·si·as·tes /i,klēzē'astēz/ a book of the Bible traditionally attributed to Solomon, consisting largely of reflections on the vanity of human life.

ec·cle·si·as·tic /i,klēzē'astik/ formal ▶ **n.** a priest or clergyman.
▶ **adj.** another term for ECCLESIASTICAL.
– ORIGIN late Middle English: from French *ecclésiastique*, or via late Latin from Greek *ekklēsiastikos*, from *ekklēsiastēs* 'member of an assembly,' from *ekklēsia* 'assembly, church,' based on *ekkalein* 'summon out.'

ec·cle·si·as·ti·cal /i,klēzē'astikəl/ ▶ **adj.** of or relating to the Christian Church or its clergy: *the ecclesiastical hierarchy.*
– DERIVATIVES **ec·cle·si·as·ti·cal·ly** **adv.**

ec·cle·si·as·ti·cism /i,klēzē'asti,sizəm/ ▶ **n.** excessive attention to details of church practice: *the ecclesiasticism that so often gets in the way of the gospel.*

Ec·cle·si·as·ti·cus /i,klēzē'astikəs/ a book of the Apocrypha containing moral and practical maxims, probably composed or compiled in the early 2nd century BC.

ec·cle·si·ol·o·gy /i,klēzē'äləjē/ ▶ **n.** **1** the study of churches, esp. church building and decoration. **2** theology as applied to the nature and structure of the Christian Church.
– DERIVATIVES **ec·cle·si·o·log·i·cal** /i,klēzēə'läjikəl/ **adj.**, **ec·cle·si·ol·o·gist** /-jist/ **n.**
– ORIGIN mid 19th cent.: from Greek *ekklēsia* 'assembly, church' + -LOGY.

Ec·clus ▶ **abbr.** Bible Ecclesiasticus.

ec·crine /'ekrən, 'ek,rīn, 'ek,rēn/ ▶ **adj.** Medicine relating to or denoting multicellular glands that do not lose cytoplasm in their secretions, esp. the sweat glands found widely distributed on the skin. Compare with APOCRINE.
– ORIGIN 1930s: from Greek *ekkrinein* 'secrete,' from *ek-* 'out' + *krinein* 'sift, separate.'

ECCS ▶ **abbr.** Physics emergency core cooling system.

ec·dys·i·ast /ek'dēzēəst/ ▶ **n.** humorous a striptease performer.
– ORIGIN 1940: coined by H. L. Mencken from Greek *ekdusis* 'shedding,' on the pattern of *enthusiast.*

ec·dy·sis /'ekdəsis/ ▶ **n.** Zoology the process of shedding the old skin (in reptiles) or casting off the outer cuticle (in insects and other arthropods).
– DERIVATIVES **ec·dys·i·al** /ek'dizēəl/ **adj.**
– ORIGIN mid 19th cent.: from Greek *ekdusis*, from *ekduein* 'put off,' from *ek-* 'out, off' + *duein* 'put.'

ec·dy·sone /'ekdi,sōn/ ▶ **n.** Biochemistry a steroid hormone that controls molting in insects and other arthropods.
– ORIGIN 1950s: from Greek *ekdusis* 'shedding' + -ONE.

ECG ▶ **abbr.** ■ electrocardiogram. ■ electrocardiograph.

é·chap·pé /,āsHa'pā/ ▶ **adj.** [postpositive] Ballet (of a movement) progressing from a closed position (first, third, or fifth) to an open position (second or fourth) of the feet.
– ORIGIN French, literally 'escaped.'

ech·e·lon /'esHə,län/ ▶ **n.** **1** a level or rank in an organization, a profession, or society: *the upper echelons of the business world.* ■ [often with modifier] a part of a military force differentiated by position in battle or by function: *the rear echelon.*
2 Military a formation of troops, ships, aircraft, or vehicles in parallel rows with the end of each row projecting farther than the one in front.
▶ **v.** [with obj.] Military arrange in an echelon formation: (as noun **echeloning**) *the echeloning of fire teams.*
– ORIGIN late 18th cent. (sense 2 of the noun): from French *échelon*, from *échelle* 'ladder,' from Latin *scala.*

ech·e·ve·ri·a /,ecHəvə'rēə/ ▶ **n.** a succulent plant with rosettes of fleshy colorful leaves, native to warm regions of America and popular as houseplants. ● Genus *Echeveria*, family Crassulaceae: numerous species and cultivars.
– ORIGIN modern Latin, named after Anastasio *Echeveri* or *Echeverría*, 19th-cent. Mexican botanical illustrator.

e·chid·na /ə'kidnə/ ▶ **n.** a spiny insectivorous egg-laying mammal with a long snout and claws, native to Australia and New Guinea. Also called SPINY ANTEATER. ● Family Tachyglossidae, order Monotremata: two genera and species, in particular *Tachyglossus aculeatus.*
– ORIGIN mid 19th cent.: modern Latin, from Greek *ekhidna* 'viper,' also the name of a mythical creature that gave birth to the many-headed Hydra; compare with *ekhinos* 'sea urchin, hedgehog.'

ech·i·na·cea /,ekə'nāsHə/ ▶ **n.** a North American coneflower. It is used in herbal medicine, largely for its antibiotic and wound-healing properties. ● Genus *Echinacea*, family Compositae: several species, in particular the purple coneflower.
– ORIGIN modern Latin, from Greek *ekhinos* 'hedgehog.'

echi·no·derm /i'kīnə,dərm, 'ekənə,dərm/ ▶ **n.** Zoology a marine invertebrate of the phylum Echinodermata, such as a starfish, sea urchin, or sea cucumber.

Echi·no·der·ma·ta /i,kīnə'dərmətə, ,ekənə-/ Zoology a phylum of marine invertebrates that includes starfishes, sea urchins, brittlestars, crinoids, and sea cucumbers. They have fivefold radial symmetry, a calcareous skeleton, and tube feet operated by fluid pressure.
– ORIGIN modern Latin (plural), from Greek *ekhinos* 'hedgehog, sea urchin' + *derma* 'skin.'

echi·noid /i'kī,noid, 'ekə,noid/ Zoology ▶ **n.** an echinoderm of the class Echinoidea; a sea urchin.
▶ **adj.** relating to or denoting echinoids.

Ech·i·noi·de·a /,ekə'noidēə/ Zoology a class of echinoderms that comprises the sea urchins.
– ORIGIN modern Latin (plural), from ECHINUS.

e·chi·nus /i'kīnəs/ ▶ **n.** (pl. **echini** /-nī/) **1** Zoology a sea urchin. ● Genus *Echinus*, class Echinoidea: several species, including the common European **edible sea urchin** (*E. esculentus*).
2 Architecture a rounded molding below an abacus on a Doric or Ionic capital.
– ORIGIN late Middle English: via Latin from Greek *ekhinos* 'hedgehog, sea urchin.'

Ech·i·u·ra /,ekē'yo͝orə/ Zoology a small phylum of wormlike marine invertebrates that comprises the spoonworms.
– DERIVATIVES **ech·i·u·ran** **n.** & **adj.**, **ech·i·u·roid** /,ekē'yo͝o,roid/ **n.** & **adj.**
– ORIGIN modern Latin (earlier *Echiuroidea*), from Greek *ekhis* 'viper' + *oura* 'tail.'

Ech·o /'ekō/ Greek Mythology a nymph deprived of speech by Hera in order to stop her chatter, and left able only to repeat what others had said.

ech·o /'ekō/ ▶ **n.** (pl. **echoes**) **1** a sound or series of sounds caused by the reflection of sound waves from a surface back to the listener: *the walls threw back the echoes of his footsteps.* ■ a reflected radio or radar beam. ■ the deliberate introduction of reverberation into a sound recording. ■ Linguistics the repetition in structure and content of one speaker's utterance by another.
2 a close parallel or repetition of an idea, feeling, style, or event: *his love for her found an echo in her own feelings.* ■ (often **echoes**) a detail or characteristic that is suggestive of something else: *the cheese has a sharp rich aftertaste with echoes of salty, earthy pastures.*
3 archaic a person who slavishly repeats the words or opinions of another.
4 Bridge a play by a defender of a higher card in a suit followed by a lower one in a subsequent trick, used as a signal to request a further lead of that suit by their partner.
5 a code word representing the letter E, used in radio communication.
▶ **v.** (**echoes**, **echoing**, **echoed**) [no obj.] **1** (of a sound) be repeated or reverberate after the original sound has stopped: *their footsteps echoed on the metal catwalks.* ■ (of a place) resound with or reflect back a sound or sounds: *the house echoed with shouts and thundering feet.* ■ [with obj.] repeat (someone's words or opinions), typically to express agreement: *these criticisms are echoed in a number of other studies* | [with direct speech] *"A trip?" she echoed.*
2 [with obj.] (of an object, movement, or event) be reminiscent of or have shared characteristics with: *a blue suit that echoed the color of her eyes.*
3 [with obj.] Computing send a copy of (an input signal or character) back to its source or to a screen for display: *for security reasons, the password will not be echoed to the screen.*
4 Bridge (of a defender) play a higher card followed by a lower one in the same suit, as a signal to request one's partner to lead that suit.
– DERIVATIVES **ech·o·er** **n.**, **ech·o·ey** /'ekō-ē/ **adj.**, **ech·o·less** **adj.**
– ORIGIN Middle English: from Old French or Latin, from Greek *ēkhō*, related to *ēkhē* 'a sound.'

ech·o·car·di·o·gram /,ekō'kärdēə,gram/ ▶ **n.** Medicine a test of the action of the heart using ultrasound waves to produce a visual display, used for the diagnosis or monitoring of heart disease.

ech·o·car·di·og·ra·phy /,ekō,kärdē'ägrəfē/ ▶ **n.** Medicine the use of ultrasound waves to investigate the action of the heart.
– DERIVATIVES **ech·o·car·di·o·graph** /,ekō'kärdēə,graf/ **n.**, **ech·o·car·di·o·graph·ic** /-,kärdēə'grafik/ **adj.**

ech·o cham·ber ▶ **n.** an enclosed space for producing reverberation of sound.

ech·o·en·ceph·a·lo·gram /,ekōen'sefələ,gram/ ▶ **n.** Medicine a record produced by echoencephalography.

ech·o·en·ceph·a·lo·graph /,ekōen'sefələ,graf/ (abbr.: **EEG**) ▶ **n.** an instrument used to examine the skull and brain by means of reflected ultrasonic waves as part of a painless and noninvasive procedure.
– DERIVATIVES **ech·o·en·ceph·a·lo·graph·ic** /-,sefələ'grafik/ **adj.**

ech·o·en·ceph·a·log·ra·phy /,ekōen,sefə'lägrəfē/ ▶ **n.** Medicine the use of ultrasound waves to investigate structures within the skull.

ech·o·gram /'ekō,gram/ ▶ **n.** a recording of depth or distance under water made by an echo sounder.

ech·o·graph /'ekō,graf/ ▶ **n.** an instrument for recording echograms; an automated echo sounder.

e·cho·ic /e'kō-ik/ ▶ **adj.** of or like an echo. ■ Linguistics representing a sound by imitation; onomatopoeic.
– DERIVATIVES **e·cho·i·cal·ly** **adv.**

ech·o·la·li·a /,ekō'lālēə/ ▶ **n.** Psychiatry meaningless repetition of another person's spoken words as a symptom of psychiatric disorder. ■ repetition of speech by a child learning to talk.
– ORIGIN late 19th cent.: modern Latin, from Greek *ēkhō* 'echo' + *lalia* 'speech.'

ech·o·lo·ca·tion /,ekōlō'kāsHən/ ▶ **n.** the location of objects by reflected sound, in particular that used by animals such as dolphins and bats.

ech·o·prax·i·a /,ekō'praksēə/ ▶ **n.** Psychiatry meaningless repetition or imitation of the movements of others as a symptom of psychiatric disorder.
– ORIGIN early 20th cent.: modern Latin, from Greek *ēkhō* 'echo' + *praxis* 'action.'

ech·o sound·er ▶ **n.** a device for determining the depth of the seabed or detecting objects in water by measuring the time taken for sound echoes to return to the listener.
– DERIVATIVES **ech·o sound·ing** (also **echo-sounding**) **n.**

ech·o·vi·rus /'ekō,vīrəs/ (also **ECHO virus**) ▶ **n.** Medicine any of a group of enteroviruses that can cause a range of diseases, including respiratory infections and a mild form of meningitis.
– ORIGIN 1950s: from *echo* (acronym from *enteric cytopathogenic human orphan*, because the virus was not originally assignable to any known disease) + VIRUS.

echt /ekt/ ▶ **adj.** authentic and typical: *the film's opening was an echt pop snob event.*
▶ **adv.** [as submodifier] authentically and typically: *echt-American writers as Hawthorne and Cooper and Mark Twain.*
– ORIGIN early 20th cent.: German, literally 'genuine, real.'

ECL ▶ **abbr.** Computing emitter-coupled logic.

é·clair /ā'kler, i'kler/ (also **eclair**) ▶ **n.** a small, soft, log-shaped pastry filled with cream and typically topped with chocolate icing.
– ORIGIN mid 19th cent.: from French, literally 'lightning.'

é·clair·cisse·ment /ā,klersēs'mäN/ ▶ **n.** archaic or literary an enlightening explanation of something, typically someone's conduct, that has been hitherto inexplicable.
– ORIGIN French, from *éclaircir* 'clear up,' from *é* (expressing a change of state) + *clair* (see CLEAR).

ec·lamp·si·a /i'klam(p)sēə/ ▶ **n.** Medicine a condition in which one or more convulsions occur in a pregnant woman suffering from high blood pressure, often followed by coma and posing a threat to the health of mother and baby. See also PREECLAMPSIA.
– DERIVATIVES **ec·lamp·tic** /i'klam(p)tik/ **adj.**
– ORIGIN mid 19th cent.: modern Latin, from French *éclampsie*, from Greek *eklampsis* 'sudden development,' from *eklampein* 'shine out.'

é·clat /ā'klä/ ▶ **n.** brilliant display or effect: *she came into prominence briefly but with éclat.* ■ social distinction or conspicuous success: *such action bestows more éclat upon a warrior than success by other means.*
– ORIGIN late 17th cent.: from French, from *éclater* 'burst out.'

ec·lec·tic /i'klektik/ ▶ **adj.** **1** deriving ideas, style, or taste from a broad and diverse range of sources: *her musical tastes are eclectic.*
2 (**Eclectic**) Philosophy of, denoting, or belonging to a class of ancient philosophers who did not belong to or found any recognized school of thought but selected such doctrines as they wished from various schools.
▶ **n.** a person who derives ideas, style, or taste from a broad and diverse range of sources.
– DERIVATIVES **ec·lec·ti·cal·ly** **adv.**, **ec·lec·ti·cism** /i'klekti,sizəm/ **n.**

– ORIGIN late 17th cent. (as a term in philosophy): from Greek *eklektikos*, from *eklegein* 'pick out,' from *ek* 'out' + *legein* 'choose.'

e·clipse /i'klips/ ▶ n. **1** an obscuring of the light from one celestial body by the passage of another between it and the observer or between it and its source of illumination: *an eclipse of the sun.* ■ a loss of significance, power, or prominence in relation to another person or thing: *the election result marked the eclipse of the traditional right and center.*
2 Ornithology a phase during which the distinctive markings of a bird (esp. a male duck) are obscured by molting of the breeding plumage: [as modifier] *eclipse plumage.*
▶ v. [with obj.] (of a celestial body) obscure the light from or to (another celestial body): *as the last piece of the sun was eclipsed by the moon.* ■ literary obscure or block out (light): *a sea of blue sky violently eclipsed by showers.* ■ deprive (someone or something) of significance, power, or prominence: *the state of the economy has eclipsed the environment as the main issue.*
– PHRASES **in eclipse 1** losing or having lost significance, power, or prominence: *his political power was in eclipse.* **2** Ornithology (esp. of a male duck) in its eclipse plumage.
– ORIGIN Middle English: from Old French *e(s)clipse* (noun), *eclipser* (verb), via Latin from Greek *ekleipsis*, from *ekleipein* 'fail to appear, be eclipsed,' from *ek* 'out' + *leipein* 'to leave.'

e·clips·ing bi·na·ry ▶ n. Astronomy a binary star whose brightness varies periodically as the two components pass one in front of the other.

e·clip·tic /i'kliptik/ ▶ n. Astronomy a great circle on the celestial sphere representing the sun's apparent path during the year, so called because lunar and solar eclipses can occur only when the moon crosses it.
▶ adj. of an eclipse or the ecliptic.
– ORIGIN late Middle English: via Latin from Greek *ekleiptikos*, from *ekleipein* 'fail to appear' (see **ECLIPSE**).

ec·lo·gite /'eklə,jīt/ ▶ n. Geology a metamorphic rock containing granular minerals, typically garnet and pyroxene.
– ORIGIN mid 19th cent.: from French, from Greek *eklogē* 'selection' (with reference to the selective content of the rock) + **-ITE**[1].

ec·logue /'ek,lôg, 'ek,läg/ ▶ n. a short poem, esp. a pastoral dialogue.
– ORIGIN late Middle English: via Latin from Greek *eklogē* 'selection,' from *eklegein* 'pick out.'

e·close /i'klōz/ ▶ v. [no obj.] Entomology (of an insect) emerge as an adult from the pupa or as a larva from the egg.
– DERIVATIVES **e·clo·sion** /i'klōZHən/ n.
– ORIGIN late 19th cent. (as *eclosion*): from French *éclore* 'to hatch,' based on Latin *ex-* 'out' + *claudere* 'to close.'

ECM ▶ abbr. electronic countermeasures.

Ec·o /'ekō/, Umberto (1932–), Italian novelist and semiotician. Notable works: *The Name of the Rose* (1981) and *Travels in Hyperreality* (1986).

eco- ▶ comb. form representing **ECOLOGY**.

ec·o·cen·trism /,ekō'sen,trizəm, ,ēkō-/ ▶ n. a point of view that recognizes the ecosphere, rather than the biosphere, as central in importance, and attempts to redress the imbalance created by anthropocentrism.
– DERIVATIVES **ec·o·cen·tric** /-'sentrik/ adj.

ec·o·cide /'ekō,sīd, 'ēkō-/ ▶ n. destruction of the natural environment, esp. when willfully done.

ec·o·cline /'ekō,klīn, 'ēkō-/ ▶ n. Ecology a cline from one ecosystem to another, showing a continuous gradient between the two extremes.

ec·o·con·sum·er /'ekōkən,so͞omər, 'ēkō-/ ▶ n. a consumer who makes purchasing decisions partly or largely on the basis of ecological issues: *sophisticated ecoconsumers are descending upon some destinations that are not capable of delivering the expected services.*

ec·o·fem·i·nism /,ekō'femə,nizəm, ,ēkō-/ ▶ n. a philosophical and political movement that combines ecological concerns with feminist ones, regarding both as resulting from male domination of society.
– DERIVATIVES **ec·o·fem·i·nist** n.

ec·o·freak /'ekō,frēk, 'ēkō-/ ▶ n. informal a person who is unusually enthusiastic about the protection and preservation of the environment.

ec·o-friend·ly ▶ adj. not harmful to the environment: *I use only eco-friendly products.*

ecol. ▶ abbr. ■ ecological. ■ ecology.

ec·o·la·bel·ing ▶ n. the practice of marking products with a distinctive label to show that their manufacture conforms to recognized environmental standards.
– DERIVATIVES **ec·o·la·bel** n.

E. co·li /ē 'kōlī/ ▶ n. a bacterium commonly found in the intestines of humans and other animals, where it usually causes no harm. Some strains can cause severe food poisoning, esp. in old people and children. ● *Escherichia coli*; a motile Gram-negative bacillus.

ec·o·lodge /'ekō,läj, 'ēkō-/ ▶ n. a type of tourist accommodation designed to have the least possible impact on the natural environment in which it is situated.

ec·o·log·i·cal /,ekə'läjikəl, ,ēkə-/ ▶ adj. relating to or concerned with the relation of living organisms to one another and to their physical surroundings: *one of the world's worst ecological disasters | pollution is posing a serious threat to the ecological balance of the oceans.*
– DERIVATIVES **ec·o·log·i·cal·ly** /,ekə'läjik(ə)lē, ,ēkə-/ adv.

ec·o·log·i·cal foot·print ▶ n. the impact of a person or community on the environment, expressed as the amount of land required to sustain their use of natural resources.

e·col·o·gy /i'käləjē/ ▶ n. **1** the branch of biology that deals with the relations of organisms to one another and to their physical surroundings.
2 (also **Ecology**) the political movement that seeks to protect the environment, esp. from pollution.
– DERIVATIVES **e·col·o·gist** /-jist/ n.
– ORIGIN late 19th cent. (originally as *oecology*): from Greek *oikos* 'house' + **-LOGY**.

e-com·merce /'ē,kämərs/ ▶ n. commercial transactions conducted electronically on the Internet.

e·con·o·box /i'känə,bäks/ ▶ n. informal a car that is small and economical rather than luxurious or stylish.
– ORIGIN blend of *economical* and *box*.

e·con·o·met·rics /i,känə'metriks/ ▶ plural n. [treated as sing.] the branch of economics concerned with the use of mathematical methods (esp. statistics) in describing economic systems.
– DERIVATIVES **e·con·o·met·ric** adj., **e·con·o·met·ri·cal** /i,känə'metrikəl, ē,känə-/ adj., **e·con·o·me·tri·cian** /i,känəmə'triSHən/ n., **e·con·o·met·rist** /-'metrist/ n.
– ORIGIN 1930s: from **ECONOMY**, on the pattern of words such as *biometrics* and *psychometrics*.

ec·o·nom·ic /,ekə'nämik, ,ēkə-/ ▶ adj. **1** of or relating to economics or the economy: *the government's economic policy | pest species of great economic importance.* ■ (of a subject) considered in relation to trade, industry, and the creation of wealth: *economic history.*
2 justified in terms of profitability: *many organizations must become larger if they are to remain economic.* ■ requiring fewer resources or costing less money: *solar power may provide a more economic solution.*
– ORIGIN late Middle English: via Old French and Latin from Greek *oikonomikos*, from *oikonomia* (see **ECONOMY**). Originally a noun, the word denoted household management or a person skilled in this, hence the early sense of the adjective (late 16th cent.) 'relating to household management' Modern senses date from the mid 19th cent.

> **USAGE** **Economic** means 'concerning economics': *he's rebuilding a solid* **economic** *base for the country's future.* **Economical** is commonly used to mean 'thrifty, avoiding waste': *small cars should be inexpensive to buy and* **economical** *to run.*

ec·o·nom·i·cal /,ekə'nämikəl, ,ēkə-/ ▶ adj. giving good value or service in relation to the amount of money, time, or effort spent: *a small, economical car.* ■ (of a person or lifestyle) careful not to waste money or resources. ■ using no more of something than is necessary: *this chassis is economical in metal and therefore light in weight.*
– PHRASES **be economical with the truth** (used euphemistically) lie or deliberately withhold information.

> **USAGE** See usage at **ECONOMIC**.

ec·o·nom·i·cal·ly /,ekə'nämik(ə)lē, ,ēkə-/ ▶ adv. in a way that relates to economics or finance: [sentence adverb] *the region is important economically.* ■ in a way that involves careful use of money or resources: *the new building was erected as economically as possible.* ■ in a way that uses no more of something than is necessary: *a précis aims to express a passage more economically.*

ec·o·nom·ic good ▶ n. Economics a product or service that can command a price when sold: *water is an economic good and should be treated as such.*

ec·o·nom·ic in·di·ca·tor ▶ n. a statistic used to gauge future trends in a nation's economy.

ec·o·nom·ic mi·grant ▶ n. a person who travels from one country or area to another in order to improve their standard of living.

ec·o·nom·ic rent ▶ n. Economics the extra amount earned by a resource (e.g., land, capital, or labor) by virtue of its present use.

ec·o·nom·ics /,ekə'nämiks, ,ēkə-/ ▶ plural n. [often treated as sing.] **1** the branch of knowledge concerned with the production, consumption, and transfer of wealth.
2 the condition of a region or group as regards material prosperity: *he is responsible for the island's modest economics.*
– ORIGIN late 16th cent. (denoting the science of household management): from **ECONOMIC** + the plural suffix *-s*, originally on the pattern of Greek *ta oikonomika* (plural), the name of a treatise by Aristotle. Current senses date from the late 18th cent.

e·con·o·mism /i'känə,mizəm/ ▶ n. belief in the primacy of economic causes or factors.
– ORIGIN early 20th cent.: from French *économisme*, based on Greek *oikonomia* 'household management' (see **ECONOMY**).

e·con·o·mist /i'känəmist/ ▶ n. an expert in economics.
– ORIGIN late 16th cent. (originally in the Greek sense): from Greek *oikonomos* 'household manager' (see **ECONOMY**) + **-IST**. The current sense dates from the early 19th cent.

e·con·o·mize /i'känə,mīz/ ▶ v. [no obj.] spend less; reduce one's expenses: *I have to economize where I can | people on low incomes may try to economize on fuel.*
– DERIVATIVES **e·con·o·mi·za·tion** /i,känəmə'zāSHən/ n.

e·con·o·miz·er /i'känə,mīzər/ ▶ n. **1** a device designed to make a machine or system more energy-efficient.
2 a person who reduces expenditure.

e·con·o·my /i'känəmē/ ▶ n. (pl. **economies**) **1** the wealth and resources of a country or region, esp. in terms of the production and consumption of goods and services. ■ a particular system or stage of an economy: *a free-market economy | the less-developed economies.*
2 careful management of available resources: *even heat distribution and fuel economy.* ■ sparing or careful use of something: *economy of words.* ■ (usu. **economies**) a financial saving: *there were many economies to be made by giving up our offices in Manhattan.* ■ (also **economy class**) the cheapest class of air or rail travel: *we flew economy.*
▶ adj. [attrib.] (of a product) offering the best value for the money: [in combination] *an economy pack.* ■ designed to be economical to use: *an economy car.*
– PHRASES **economy of scale** a proportionate saving in costs gained by an increased level of production. **economy of scope** a proportionate saving gained by producing two or more distinct goods, when the cost of doing so is less than that of producing each separately.
– ORIGIN late 15th cent. (in the sense 'management of material resources'): from French *économie*, or via Latin from Greek *oikonomia* 'household management,' based on *oikos* 'house' + *nemein* 'manage.' Current senses date from the 17th cent.

e·con·o·my-class syn·drome ▶ n. deep-vein thrombosis said to be caused by periods of prolonged immobility on long-haul flights.

e·con·o·my-size (also **economy-sized**) ▶ adj. of a size that offers a large quantity for a proportionally lower cost: *an economy-size container.*

e-con·tent /'ē,käntent/ ▶ n. text and images designed for display on web pages: *click on this link to license our e-content* | [as modifier] *e-content solutions.*

ec·o·phys·i·ol·o·gy /,ekō,fizē'äləjē, ,ēkō-/ ▶ n. Biology the study of the interrelationship between the normal physical function of an organism and its environment.

é·cor·ché /,ākôr'SHā/ ▶ n. (pl. **écorchés** pronunc. **same**) a painting or sculpture of a human figure with the skin removed to display the musculature.
– ORIGIN mid 19th cent.: French, literally 'flayed.'

ec·o·re·gion /'ekō,rējən, 'ēkō-/ ▶ n. a major ecosystem defined by distinctive geography and receiving uniform solar radiation and moisture: *the Columbia Basin ecoregion.*

ec·o·sphere /'ekō,sfi(ə)r, 'ēkō-/ ▶ n. the biosphere of the earth or another planet, esp. when the interaction between the living and nonliving components is emphasized. ■ Astronomy the region of space around a sun or star where conditions are such that planets are theoretically capable of sustaining life.

e·cos·saise /,ākō'sāz/ ▶ n. (pl. **ecossaises** pronunc. **same**) an energetic country dance in duple time in which couples form lines facing each other.
– ORIGIN mid 19th cent.: from French, feminine of *écossais* 'Scottish'; the connection with Scotland is unclear.

ec·o·sys·tem /'ekō,sistəm, 'ēkō-/ ▶ n. Ecology a biological community of interacting organisms and their physical environment.

ec·o·tage /ˈekəˌtäzʜ, ēkə-/ ▶ **n.** sabotage carried out for ecological reasons.
– ORIGIN 1970s: blend of *ecological* (see ECOLOGY) and SABOTAGE.

ec·o·ter·ror·ism /ˌekōˈterəˌrizəm, ˈekō-/ ▶ **n.** violence carried out to further environmentalist ends. ■ the action of causing deliberate environmental damage in order to further political ends.
– DERIVATIVES **ec·o·ter·ror·ist** **n.**

ec·o·tone /ˈekəˌtōn, ˈēkəˌtōn/ ▶ **n.** Ecology a region of transition between two biological communities.
– DERIVATIVES **ec·o·ton·al** **adj.**

ec·o·to·pi·a ▶ **n.** an ecologically ideal region or form of society, generally viewed as imaginary.
– DERIVATIVES **ec·o·to·pi·an** **adj.**
– ORIGIN 1975: from the title of a novel by Ernest Callenbach, originally denoting the Pacific coast of the US, from ECO- 'ecological,' on the pattern of *Utopia*.

ec·o·tour·ism /ˌekōˈto͝orizəm, ˌēkō-/ ▶ **n.** tourism directed toward exotic, often threatened, natural environments, esp. to support conservation efforts and observe wildlife.
– DERIVATIVES **ec·o·tour** **n.** & **v.**, **ec·o·tour·ist** **n.**

ec·o·tox·i·col·o·gy /ˌekōˌtäksiˈkäləjē, ˌēkō-/ ▶ **n.** the branch of science that deals with the nature, effects, and interactions of substances that are harmful to the environment.
– DERIVATIVES **ec·o·tox·i·co·log·i·cal** /-kəˈläjikəl/ **adj.**, **ec·o·tox·i·col·o·gist** /-jist/ **n.**

ec·o·type /ˈekōˌtīp, ˈēkō-/ ▶ **n.** Botany & Zoology a distinct form or race of a plant or animal species occupying a particular habitat.

ec·o·vil·lage /ˈēkōˌvilij/ ▶ **n.** a community whose inhabitants seek to live according to ecological principles, causing as little impact on the environment as possible.

ec·o·war·ri·or ▶ **n.** a person actively involved in preventing damage to the environment.

ECOWAS ▶ **abbr.** Economic Community of West African States.

ec·ru /ˈekro͞o/ ▶ **n.** the light beige color of unbleached linen.
– ORIGIN mid 19th cent.: from French *écru* 'unbleached.'

ec·sta·sy /ˈekstəsē/ ▶ **n.** (pl. **ecstasies**) **1** an overwhelming feeling of great happiness or joyful excitement: *there was a look of ecstasy on his face* | *they went into ecstasies over the view.*
2 an emotional or religious frenzy or trancelike state, originally one involving an experience of mystic self-transcendence.
3 (**Ecstasy**) an amphetamine-based synthetic drug with euphoric and hallucinatory effects, originally promoted as an adjunct to psychotherapy. (abbr.: **MDMA**)
– ORIGIN late Middle English (sense 2): from Old French *extasie*, via late Latin from Greek *ekstasis* 'standing outside oneself,' based on *ek-* 'out' + *histanai* 'to place.'

ec·stat·ic /ekˈstatik/ ▶ **adj.** **1** feeling or expressing overwhelming happiness or joyful excitement: *ecstatic fans filled the stadium.*
2 involving an experience of mystic self-transcendence: *an ecstatic vision.*
▶ **n.** a person subject to mystical experiences.
– DERIVATIVES **ec·stat·i·cal·ly** **adv.**

ECT ▶ **abbr.** electroconvulsive therapy.

ecto- ▶ **comb. form** outer; external; on the outside (used commonly in scientific terms): *ectoderm* | *ectoparasite.*
– ORIGIN from Greek *ektos* 'outside.'

ec·to·derm /ˈektəˌdərm/ ▶ **n.** Zoology & Embryology the outermost layer of cells or tissue of an embryo in early development, or the parts derived from this, which include the epidermis and nerve tissue. Compare with ENDODERM and MESODERM.
– DERIVATIVES **ec·to·der·mal** /ˌektōˈdərməl/ **adj.**
– ORIGIN mid 19th cent.: from ECTO- 'outside' + Greek *derma* 'skin.'

ec·to·gen·e·sis /ˌektəˈjenəsis/ ▶ **n.** (chiefly in science fiction) the development of embryos in artificial conditions outside the uterus.
– DERIVATIVES **ec·to·gene** /ˈektəˌjēn/ **n.**, **ec·to·ge·net·ic** /ˌektəˌjəˈnetik/ **adj.**, **ec·to·ge·net·i·cal·ly** /-ˌjəˈnetik(ə)lē/ **adv.**

ec·to·morph /ˈektəˌmôrf/ ▶ **n.** Physiology a person with a lean and delicate body build. Compare with ENDOMORPH and MESOMORPH.
– DERIVATIVES **ec·to·mor·phic** /ˌektəˈmôrfik/ **adj.**, **ec·to·morph·y** **n.**
– ORIGIN 1940s: *ecto-* from *ectodermal* (being the layer of the embryo giving rise to physical characteristics that predominate) + -MORPH.

-ectomy ▶ **comb. form** denoting surgical removal of a specified part of the body: *appendectomy.*
– ORIGIN from Greek *ektomē* 'excision,' from *ek* 'out' + *temnein* 'to cut.'

ec·to·par·a·site /ˌektəˈparəˌsīt/ ▶ **n.** Biology a parasite, such as a flea, that lives on the outside of its host. Compare with ENDOPARASITE.
– DERIVATIVES **ec·to·par·a·sit·ic** /-ˌparəˈsitik/ **adj.**

ec·top·ic /ekˈtäpik/ ▶ **adj.** Medicine in an abnormal place or position.
▶ **n.** an ectopic pregnancy.
– ORIGIN late 19th cent.: from modern Latin *ectopia* 'presence of tissue, cells, etc., in an abnormal place' (from Greek *ektopos* 'out of place') + -IC.

ec·top·ic beat ▶ **n.** another term for EXTRASYSTOLE.

ec·top·ic preg·nan·cy ▶ **n.** a pregnancy in which the fetus develops outside the uterus, typically in a Fallopian tube.

ec·to·plasm /ˈektəˌplazəm/ ▶ **n.** **1** Biology the more viscous, clear outer layer of the cytoplasm in ameboid cells. Compare with ENDOPLASM.
2 a supernatural viscous substance that is supposed to exude from the body of a medium during a spiritualistic trance and form the material for the manifestation of spirits.
– DERIVATIVES **ec·to·plas·mic** /ˌektəˈplazmik/ **adj.**

Ec·to·proc·ta /ˌektəˈpräktə/ Zoology another term for BRYOZOA.
– DERIVATIVES **ec·to·proct** /ˈektəˌpräkt/ **n.**
– ORIGIN modern Latin (plural), from Greek *ektos* 'outside or external' + *prōktos* 'anus.'

ec·to·therm /ˈektəˌᴛʜərm/ ▶ **n.** Zoology an animal that is dependent on external sources of body heat. Often contrasted with ENDOTHERM. Compare with POIKILOTHERM.
– DERIVATIVES **ec·to·ther·mic** **adj.**, **ec·to·ther·my** **n.**

ec·tro·pi·on /ekˈtrōpēən, -pēˌän/ ▶ **n.** Medicine a condition, typically a consequence of advanced age, in which the eyelid is turned outward away from the eyeball.
– ORIGIN late 17th cent.: from Greek, from *ek-* 'out' + *trepein* 'to turn.'

ECU /āˈk(y)o͞o/ (also **ecu**) ▶ **n.** (pl. **same** or **ecus**) the former official monetary unit of the European Union, used to evaluate the exchange rates and reserves of members of the European Monetary System on a common basis and in trading Eurobonds. It was replaced by the euro.
– ORIGIN acronym from *European currency unit.*

Ec·ua·dor /ˈekwəˌdôr/ a republic in northwestern South America, on the Pacific coast; pop. 14,573,100 (est. 2009); capital, Quito; languages, Spanish (official), Quechua.

> Formerly part of the Inca empire, Ecuador was conquered by the Spanish in 1534. It remained part of Spain's American empire until 1822, when independence was gained.

– DERIVATIVES **Ec·ua·dor·i·an** /ˌekwəˈdôrēən/ (also **Ecuadorean**) **adj.** & **n.**

ec·u·men·i·cal /ˌekyəˈmenikəl/ ▶ **adj.** representing a number of different Christian churches. ■ promoting or relating to unity among the world's Christian churches: *ecumenical dialogue.*
– DERIVATIVES **ec·u·men·i·cal·ly** **adv.**
– ORIGIN late 16th cent. (in the sense 'belonging to the universal Church'): via late Latin from Greek *oikoumenikos*, from *oikoumenē* 'the (inhabited) earth.'

Ec·u·men·i·cal Pa·tri·arch ▶ **n.** a title of the Orthodox Patriarch of Constantinople.

ec·u·me·nism /ˈekyəməˌnizəm, eˈkyo͞omə-/ ▶ **n.** the principle or aim of promoting unity among the world's Christian churches.

ec·ze·ma /ˈegzəmə, ˈeksə-, igˈzēmə/ ▶ **n.** a medical condition in which patches of skin become rough and inflamed, with blisters that cause itching and bleeding, sometimes resulting from a reaction to irritation (eczematous dermatitis) but more typically having no obvious external cause.
– DERIVATIVES **ec·zem·a·tous** /igˈzemətəs, ikˈsem-, igˈzē-/ **adj.**
– ORIGIN mid 18th cent.: modern Latin, from Greek *ekzema*, from *ekzein* 'boil over, break out,' from *ek-* 'out' + *zein* 'boil.'

ED ▶ **abbr.** ■ election district. ■ emergency department. ■ erectile dysfunction.

ed. ▶ **abbr.** ■ edited by. ■ edition. ■ editor. ■ education.

-ed[1] ▶ **suffix** forming adjectives: **1** (added to nouns) having; possessing; affected by: *talented* | *diseased.* ■ (added to nouns) characteristic of: *ragged.*
2 used in phrases consisting of adjective and noun: *bad-tempered* | *three-sided.*
– ORIGIN Old English *-ede.*

-ed[2] ▶ **suffix** forming: **1** the past tense and past participle of weak verbs: *landed* | *walked.*
2 participial adjectives: *wounded.*
– ORIGIN Old English *-ed, -ad, -od.*

e·da·cious /iˈdāsʜəs/ ▶ **adj.** rare of, relating to, or given to eating.
– DERIVATIVES **e·dac·i·ty** /iˈdasitē/ **n.**
– ORIGIN early 19th cent.: from Latin *edax, edac-* (from *edere* 'eat') + -IOUS.

E·dam /ˈēdəm/ ▶ **n.** a round Dutch cheese, typically pale yellow with a red wax coating.
– ORIGIN early 19th cent.: named after the town of *Edam* in the Netherlands.

ed·a·ma·me /ˌedəˈmämā/ ▶ **n.** a dish of green soybeans boiled or steamed in their pods.
– ORIGIN Japanese, literally 'beans on a branch.'

e·daph·ic /iˈdafik/ ▶ **adj.** Ecology of, produced by, or influenced by the soil.
– ORIGIN late 19th cent.: coined in German from Greek *edaphos* 'floor' + -IC.

ed·a·pho·saur /ˌedəfōˈsôr/ (also **edaphosaurus** /-ˈsôrəs/) ▶ **n.** a large herbivorous synapsid reptile of the late Carboniferous and early Permian periods, with long knobbly spines on its back supporting a sail-like crest. ● Genus *Edaphosaurus*, order Pelycosauria, subclass Synapsida.
– DERIVATIVES **ed·a·pho·sau·ri·an** **adj.**
– ORIGIN modern Latin, from Greek *edaphos* 'floor' + *sauros* 'lizard.'

Ed·da /ˈedə/ either of two 13th-century Icelandic books, the **Elder** or **Poetic Edda** (a collection of Old Norse poems on Norse legends) and the **Younger** or **Prose Edda** (a handbook to Icelandic poetry by Snorri Sturluson). The Eddas are the chief source of knowledge of Scandinavian mythology.
– ORIGIN either from the name of the great-grandmother in the Old Norse poem *Rigsthul*, or from Old Norse *óthr* 'poetry.'

ed·do /ˈedō/ ▶ **n.** (pl. **eddoes**) a taro corm or plant, esp. of a West Indian variety with many edible cormlets. ● *Colocasia esculenta* var. *antiquorum*, family Araceae.
– ORIGIN late 17th cent.: of West African origin.

Ed·dy /ˈedē/, Mary Baker (1821–1910), US religious leader; founder of the Christian Science movement. Long a victim of various ailments, she believed herself cured by a faith healer, **Phineas Quimby** (1802–1866), and later evolved her own system of spiritual healing.

ed·dy /ˈedē/ ▶ **n.** (pl. **eddies**) a circular movement of water, counter to a main current, causing a small whirlpool. ■ a movement of wind, fog, or smoke resembling this.
▶ **v.** (**eddies, eddying, eddied**) [no obj.] (of water, air, or smoke) move in a circular way: *the mists from the river eddied around the banks.*
– ORIGIN late Middle English: probably from the Germanic base of the Old English prefix *ed-* 'again, back.'

ed·dy cur·rent ▶ **n.** a localized electric current induced in a conductor by a varying magnetic field.

Ed·el·man /ˈādlmən/, Marian Wright (1939–), US human rights activist; president of the Children's Defense Fund, which she founded in 1973. She wrote *A Letter to My Children and Yours* (1992).

e·del·weiss /ˈādlˌwīs, -ˌvīs/ ▶ **n.** a European mountain plant that has woolly white bracts around its small flowers and downy gray-green leaves. ● *Leontopodium alpinum*, family Compositae.
– ORIGIN mid 19th cent.: from German, from *edel* 'noble' + *weiss* 'white.'

e·de·ma /iˈdēmə/ (Brit. also **oedema**) ▶ **n.** a condition characterized by an excess of watery fluid collecting in the cavities or tissues of the body. Also called DROPSY.
– DERIVATIVES **e·dem·a·tous** /iˈdēmətəs/ **adj.**
– ORIGIN late Middle English: modern Latin, from Greek *oidēma*, from *oidein* 'to swell.'

E·den[1] /ˈēdn/, (Robert) Anthony, 1st Earl of Avon (1897–1977), British Conservative statesman; prime minister 1955–57. His premiership was dominated by the Suez crisis of 1956, and widespread opposition to Britain's role in this led to his resignation.

E·den[2] (also **Garden of Eden**) the place where Adam and Eve lived in the biblical account of the Creation, from which they were expelled for disobediently eating the fruit of the tree of the knowledge of good and evil. ■ (as noun **an Eden**) a place or state of great happiness; an unspoiled paradise: *the lost Eden of his childhood.*
– ORIGIN from late Latin (Vulgate), Greek *Ēdēn* (Septuagint), and Hebrew *ʿĒḏen*; perhaps related to Akkadian *edinu*, from Sumerian *eden* 'plain, desert' (but believed to be related to Hebrew *ʿēḏen* 'delight').

E·den Prai·rie a city in southeastern Minnesota, southwest of Minneapolis; pop. 61,191 (est. 2008).

E·den·ta·ta /ˌēdenˈtätə, -ˈtātə/ Zoology another term for **Xenarthra**.

e·den·tate /ēˈdenˌtāt/ ▶ **n.** Zoology a mammal of an order distinguished by the lack of incisor and canine teeth. The edentates, which include anteaters, sloths, and armadillos, are all native to Central and South America. ● Order Xenarthra (or Edentata).
– ORIGIN early 19th cent.: from Latin *edentatus*, past participle of *edentare* 'make toothless,' from *e-* (variant of *ex-*) 'out' + *dens, dent-* 'tooth.'

e·den·tu·lous /ēˈdenCHələs/ ▶ **adj.** Medicine & Zoology lacking teeth.
– ORIGIN early 18th cent.: from Latin *edentulus*, from *e-* (variant of *ex-*) 'out' + *dens, dent-* 'tooth' + **-ulous**.

E·der·le /ˈedərlē/, Gertrude Caroline (1906–2003), US swimmer. The winner of three Olympic medals in 1924, she became the first woman to swim the English Channel 1926, two hours faster than any man had done.

Ed·gar /ˈedgər/ (944–75), king of England 959–975; younger brother of Edwy. He became king of Northumbria and Mercia in 957 when these regions renounced their allegiance to Edwy. He succeeded to the throne of England on Edwy's death.

edge /ej/ ▶ **n. 1** the outside limit of an object, area, or surface; a place or part farthest away from the center of something: *a willow tree at the water's edge* | figurative *these measures are merely tinkering at the edges of a wider issue.* ■ an area next to a steep drop: *the cliff edge.* ■ [in sing.] the point or state immediately before something unpleasant or momentous occurs: *the economy was teetering on the **edge of** recession.*
2 the sharpened side of the blade of a cutting implement or weapon: *a knife with a razor-sharp edge.* ■ the line along which two surfaces of a solid meet. ■ [in sing.] an intense, sharp, or striking quality: *a flamenco singer brings a primitive edge to the music* | *she was still smiling, but there was **an edge to** her voice.* ■ [in sing.] a quality or factor that gives superiority over close rivals or competitors: *the veal had the edge on flavor.*
▶ **v. 1** [with obj.] provide with a border or edge: *the pool is edged with paving.*
2 move gradually, carefully, or furtively in a particular direction: [no obj.] *she tried to edge away from him* | *Nick **edged his way** through the crowd* | [with obj.] *Hazel quietly edged him away from the others.* ■ [with obj.] informal defeat by a small margin: *Connecticut avoided an upset and edged Yale 49–48.*
3 [with obj.] give an intense or sharp quality to: *the bitterness that edged her voice.*
4 [no obj.] ski with one's weight on the edges of one's skis.
– PHRASES **on edge** tense, nervous, or irritable: *never had she felt so on edge before an interview.* **on the edge of one's seat** informal very excited and giving one's full attention to something. **set someone's teeth on edge** (esp. of an unpleasant harsh sound) cause someone to feel intense discomfort or irritation: *a grating that set her teeth on edge.* **take the edge off** reduce the intensity or effect of (something unpleasant or severe): *the tablets will take the edge off the pain.*
– PHRASAL VERBS **edge someone out** remove a person from an organization or role by indirect means: *she was **edged out of** the organization by the director.*
– DERIVATIVES **edged adj.** [in combination] *a black-edged handkerchief*, **edge·less adj.**, **edg·er n.**
– ORIGIN Old English *ecg* 'sharpened side of a blade,' of Germanic origin; related to Dutch *egge* and German *Ecke*, also to Old Norse *eggja* (see **egg**²), from an Indo-European root shared by Latin *acies* 'edge' and Greek *akis* 'point.'

edge cit·y ▶ **n.** a relatively large urban area situated on the outskirts of a city, typically beside a major road.
– ORIGIN 1991: coined by J. Garreau in a book of the same name.

edge con·nec·tor ▶ **n.** an electrical connector with a row of contacts, fitted to the edge of a printed circuit board to facilitate connection to external circuits.

edge tool ▶ **n.** any tool with a sharp cutting edge.

edge·wise /ˈejˌwīz/ (also **edgeways** /-ˌwāz/) ▶ **adv. & adj.** with the edge uppermost or toward the viewer: [as adv.] *could be inserted edgewise between the teeth* | [as adj.] *an edgewise view of our own galaxy.*
– PHRASES **get a word in edgewise** [usu. with negative] contribute to a conversation with difficulty because the other speaker talks almost without pause.

edg·ing /ˈejiNG/ ▶ **n.** a thing forming an edge or border: *the crocheted edging of the cloth.* ■ the process of providing something with an edge or border.

edg·y /ˈejē/ ▶ **adj.** (**edgier, edgiest**) **1** tense, nervous, or irritable: *he became edgy and defensive.* ■ (of a musical performance or a piece of writing) having an intense or sharp quality.
2 informal at the forefront of a trend; experimental or avant-garde: *their songs combine good music and smart, edgy ideas.*
– DERIVATIVES **edg·i·ly** /ˈejəlē/ **adv.**, **edg·i·ness n.**

edh ▶ **n.** variant spelling of **eth**.

EDI ▶ **abbr.** electronic data interchange (a standard for exchanging information between computer systems).

ed·i·ble /ˈedəbəl/ ▶ **adj.** fit to be eaten (often used to contrast with unpalatable or poisonous examples): *nasturtium seeds are edible.*
▶ **n.** (**edibles**) items of food.
– DERIVATIVES **ed·i·bil·i·ty** /ˌedəˈbilitē/ **n.**
– ORIGIN late 16th cent.: from late Latin *edibilis*, from Latin *edere* 'eat.'

e·dict /ˈēdikt/ ▶ **n.** an official order or proclamation issued by a person in authority.
– DERIVATIVES **e·dic·tal** /iˈdiktl/ **adj.**
– ORIGIN Middle English: from Latin *edictum* 'something proclaimed,' neuter past participle of *edicere*, from *e-* (variant of *ex-*) 'out' + *dicere* 'say, tell.'

E·dict of Nantes see **Nantes, Edict of**.

ed·i·fi·ca·tion /ˌedəfiˈkāSHən/ ▶ **n.** formal the instruction or improvement of a person morally or intellectually: *the idea that art's main purpose is to supply moral uplift and edification.*
– ORIGIN late Middle English: from Latin *aedificatio(n-)*, from *aedificare* 'build' (see **edify**).

ed·i·fice /ˈedəfis/ ▶ **n.** formal **1** a building, esp. a large, imposing one.
2 a complex system of beliefs: *the concepts on which the edifice of capitalism was built.*
– ORIGIN late Middle English: via Old French from Latin *aedificium*, from *aedis* 'dwelling' + *facere* 'make.'

ed·i·fy /ˈedəˌfī/ ▶ **v.** (**edifies, edifying, edified**) [with obj.] formal instruct or improve (someone) morally or intellectually.
– ORIGIN Middle English: from Old French *edifier*, from Latin *aedificare* 'build,' from *aedis* 'dwelling' + *facere* 'make' (compare with **edifice**). The word originally meant 'construct a building,' also 'strengthen,' hence to "build up" morally or spiritually.

ed·i·fy·ing /ˈedəˌfī-iNG/ ▶ **adj.** providing moral or intellectual instruction: *edifying literature.*
– DERIVATIVES **ed·i·fy·ing·ly adv.**

E·di·na /ēˈdīnə/ a city in southeastern Minnesota, southwest of Minneapolis; pop. 45,608 (est. 2008).

Ed·in·burg /ˈednˌbərg/ a city in southern Texas, in the Rio Grande valley; pop. 71,520 (est. 2008).

Ed·in·burgh /ˈednˌbərə/ the capital of Scotland, on the southern shore of the Firth of Forth; pop. 449,100 (est. 2009). The city grew up around an 11th-century castle built by Malcolm III on a rocky ridge that dominates the landscape.

Ed·in·burgh, Duke of see **Philip, Prince**.

Ed·in·burgh Fes·ti·val (also **Edinburgh International Festival**) an international festival of the arts held annually in Edinburgh since 1947. In addition to the main program a flourishing fringe festival has developed.

Ed·i·son¹ /ˈedəsən/ a township in eastern New Jersey, northeast of New Brunswick; pop. 99,706 (est. 2008). It is home to Thomas Edison's research laboratory in Menlo Park.

Ed·i·son², Thomas Alva (1847–1931), US inventor. He took out the first of more than 1,000 patents at the age of 21. His inventions include automatic telegraph systems, the carbon microphone for telephones, the phonograph, and the carbon filament lamp.

ed·it /ˈedit/ ▶ **v.** (**edits, editing, edited**) [with obj.] **1** prepare (written material) for publication by correcting, condensing, or otherwise modifying it: *Volume I was edited by J. Johnson.* ■ choose material for (a movie or a radio or television program) and arrange it to form a coherent whole: *the footage wasn't good enough to be edited into broadcast form* | (as adj. **edited**) *an edited version drawn from several prerecorded performances.* ■ change (text) on a computer. ■ (**edit something out**) remove unnecessary or inappropriate words, sounds, or scenes from a text, movie, or radio or television program.
2 be editor of (a newspaper or magazine).
▶ **n.** a change or correction made as a result of editing.
– ORIGIN late 18th cent. (as a verb): partly a back-formation from **editor**, reinforced by French *éditer* 'to edit' (from *édition* 'edition').

edit. ▶ **abbr.** edited. ■ edition. ■ editor.

ed·it·a·ble /ˈeditəbəl/ ▶ **adj.** (of text or software) in a format that can be edited by the user.

e·di·tion /iˈdiSHən/ ▶ **n. 1** a particular form or version of a published text: *a paperback edition.* ■ a particular version of a text that has been revised or created from a substantially new setting of type: *a first edition.* ■ [in sing.] a person or thing that is compared to another as a copy to an original: *the building was a simpler edition of its namesake.*
2 the total number of copies of a book, newspaper, or other published material issued at one time.
3 a particular version or instance of a regular program or broadcast: *the Monday edition will be repeated on Wednesday afternoons.*
– ORIGIN late Middle English: from French *édition*, from Latin *editio(n-)*, from *edere* 'put out,' from *e-* (variant of *ex-*) 'out' + *dare* 'give.'

e·di·ti·o prin·ceps /eˈditēō ˈprinkeps, iˈdiSHēō ˈprinseps/ ▶ **n.** (pl. **editiones principes** /eˌditēˈōnēs ˈpriNGkəˌpez, iˌdiSHēˈōnēz ˈprinsəˌpēz/) the first printed edition of a book.
– ORIGIN Latin, from *editio(n-)* 'edition' and *princeps* 'chief, leader' (from *primus* 'first').

ed·i·tor /ˈeditər/ ▶ **n. 1** a person who is in charge of and determines the final content of a text, particularly a newspaper or magazine: *the editor of The New York Times* | *a sports editor.* ■ a person who works for a publishing company, commissioning or preparing material for publication.
2 a computer program enabling the user to enter or alter text.
– DERIVATIVES **ed·i·tor·ship n.**
– ORIGIN mid 17th cent.: from Latin, 'producer (of games), publisher,' from *edit-* 'produced, put forth,' from the verb *edere*.

ed·i·to·ri·al /ˌediˈtôrēəl/ ▶ **adj.** of or relating to the commissioning or preparing of material for publication: *a pillar of scholarly publishing and editorial excellence.* ■ of or relating to the part of a newspaper or magazine that contains news, information, or comment as opposed to advertising.
▶ **n.** a newspaper article written by or on behalf of an editor that gives an opinion on a topical issue. ■ the parts of a newspaper or magazine that are not advertising.
– DERIVATIVES **ed·i·to·ri·al·ist n.**, **ed·i·to·ri·al·ly adv.**

ed·i·to·ri·al·ize /ˌediˈtôrēəˌlīz/ ▶ **v.** [no obj.] (of a newspaper, editor, or broadcasting organization) make comments or express opinions rather than just report the news.

ed·i·tress /ˈeditris/ ▶ **n.** chiefly Brit. another term for **editrix**.

USAGE See usage at **-ess**¹.

ed·i·trix /ˈeditriks/ ▶ **n.** dated or humorous a female editor.
– ORIGIN early 20th cent.: from **editor** + **-trix**.

ed·it suite ▶ **n.** a room containing equipment for electronically editing video-recorded material.

Ed.M. ▶ **abbr.** master of education.
– ORIGIN from Latin *Educationis Magister*.

Ed·mond /ˈedmənd/ a city in central Oklahoma, an oil center north of Oklahoma City; pop. 79,559 (est. 2008).

Ed·mon·ton /ˈedməntən/ the capital of the province of Alberta, in western Canada, on the North Saskatchewan River; pop. 730,372 (2006).

Ed·mund /ˈedmənd/ the name of two kings of England. ■ **Edmund I** (921–946), reigned 939–946. After succeeding Athelstan, Edmund spent much of his reign trying to win his northern lands back from Norse control. ■ **Edmund II** (*c.*980–1016), son of Ethelred the Unready; reigned 1016; known as **Edmund Ironside**. Edmund led the resistance to Canute's forces in 1015, but was eventually defeated and forced to divide the kingdom with Canute. On Edmund's death, Canute became king of all England.

Ed·mund, St. (*c.*1175–1240), English churchman and teacher; archbishop of Canterbury 1234–40; born *Edmund Rich*. He was the last primate of all of England. Feast day, November 16.

Ed·mund Cam·pi·on, St. see **Campion**.

Ed·mund the Mar·tyr, St. (*c.*841–870), king of East Anglia 855–870. After the defeat of his army by the invading Danes in 870, tradition holds that he was captured and shot with arrows for refusing to reject the Christian faith or to share power with his pagan conqueror. Feast day, November 20.

E·do¹ /ˈedō/ former name of **Tokyo**.

E·do² ▶ **n.** (pl. **same** or **Edos**) **1** a member of a people inhabiting the district of Benin in Nigeria.
2 the Benue-Congo language of this people.
▶ **adj.** of or relating to this people or their language.
– ORIGIN the name of Benin City in Edo.

E·dom·ite /ˈēdəˌmīt/ ▶ **adj.** of or relating to Edom, an ancient region south of the Dead Sea, or its people.

▶ **n.** a member of an ancient people living in Edom in biblical times, traditionally believed to be descended from Esau.

EDP ▶ **abbr.** electronic data processing.

EDT ▶ **abbr.** Eastern Daylight Time (see EASTERN TIME).

EDTA ▶ **abbr.** Chemistry ethylenediamine tetra-acetic acid, a crystalline acid with a strong tendency to form chelates with metal ions. ● Chem. formula: $(CH_2COOH)_2NCH_2CH_2N(CH_2COOH)_2$.

educ. ▶ **abbr.** ■ educated. ■ education. ■ educational.

ed·u·ca·ble /ˈejəkəbəl/ ▶ **adj.** able to be educated: *we must have teachers who believe that every child is educable.*
– DERIVATIVES **ed·u·ca·bil·i·ty** /ˌejəkəˈbilitē/ **n.**

ed·u·cate /ˈejəˌkāt/ ▶ **v.** [with obj.] give intellectual, moral, and social instruction to (someone, esp. a child), typically at a school or university: *she was educated at a boarding school.* ■ provide or pay for instruction for (one's child), esp. at a school. ■ give (someone) training in or information on a particular field: *the need to educate people to conserve water | a plan to* **educate** *the young* **on** *the dangers of drug-taking.*
– ORIGIN late Middle English: from Latin *educat-* 'led out,' from the verb *educare*, related to *educere* 'lead out' (see EDUCE).

ed·u·cat·ed /ˈejəˌkātid/ ▶ **adj.** having been educated: [in combination] *a Harvard-educated lawyer.* ■ resulting from or having had a good education: *educated tastes.*

ed·u·cat·ed guess ▶ **n.** a guess based on knowledge and experience and therefore likely to be correct.

ed·u·ca·tion /ˌejəˈkāsʜən/ ▶ **n.** **1** the process of receiving or giving systematic instruction, esp. at a school or university: *a new system of public education.* ■ the theory and practice of teaching: *colleges of education.* ■ a body of knowledge acquired while being educated: *his education is encyclopedic and eclectic.* ■ information about or training in a particular field or subject: *health education.*
2 (**an education**) an enlightening experience: *a day with those kids was an education in patience and forbearance.*
– DERIVATIVES **ed·u·ca·tion·ist n.**
– ORIGIN mid 16th cent.: from Latin *educatio(n-)*, from the verb *educare* (see EDUCATE).

ed·u·ca·tion·al /ˌejəˈkāsʜənl/ ▶ **adj.** of or relating to the provision of education: *children with special educational needs.* ■ intended or serving to educate or enlighten.
– DERIVATIVES **ed·u·ca·tion·al·ist** /-ist/ **n.**, **ed·u·ca·tion·al·ly adv.**

ed·u·ca·tion·al psy·chol·o·gy ▶ **n.** a branch of psychology that studies children in an educational setting and is concerned with teaching and learning methods, cognitive development, and aptitude assessment.

ed·u·ca·tive /ˈejəˌkātiv/ ▶ **adj.** intended or serving to educate or enlighten; educational: *a useful educative tool.*

ed·u·ca·tor /ˈejəˌkātər/ ▶ **n.** a person who provides instruction or education; a teacher: *the perspective of a professional educator.*

e·duce /iˈd(y)o͞os/ ▶ **v.** [with obj.] formal bring out or develop (something latent or potential): *out of love obedience is to be educed.* ■ infer (something) from data: *more information can be educed from these statistics.*
– DERIVATIVES **e·duc·i·ble** /ēˈd(y)o͞osəbəl, iˈd(y)o͞os-/ **adj.**, **e·duc·tion** /iˈdəksʜən/ **n.**
– ORIGIN late Middle English: from Latin *educere* 'lead out,' from *e-* (variant of *ex-*) 'out' + *ducere* 'to lead.'

ed·u·crat /ˈejəˌkrat/ ▶ **n.** informal, derogatory an education administrator.
– ORIGIN blend of *education* and *bureaucrat.*

e·dul·co·rate /iˈdəlkəˌrāt/ ▶ **v.** [with obj.] rare make (something) more acceptable or palatable.
– DERIVATIVES **e·dul·co·ra·tion** /iˌdəlkəˈrāsʜən/ **n.**
– ORIGIN mid 17th cent.: from medieval Latin *edulcorat-* 'sweetened,' from the verb *edulcorare*, from Latin *e-* (variant of *ex-*) 'out' + *dulcor* 'sweetness.'

ed·u·tain·ment /ˌejəˈtānmənt/ ▶ **n.** entertainment, esp. computer games, with an educational aspect.
– ORIGIN 1980s: blend of EDUCATION and ENTERTAINMENT.

Edw. ▶ **abbr.** Edward.

Ed·ward /ˈedwərd/ the name of six kings of England and also one of Great Britain and Ireland and one of the United Kingdom. ■ **Edward I** (1239–1307), son of Henry III; reigned 1272–1307; known as **the Hammer of the Scots.** His campaign against Prince Llewelyn ended with the annexation of Wales in 1284, but he failed to conquer Scotland. ■ **Edward II** (1284–1327), son of Edward I; reigned 1307–27. In 1314, he was defeated by Robert the Bruce at Bannockburn. In 1326, Edward's wife, Isabella of France, and her lover, Roger de Mortimer, invaded England; Edward was deposed in favor of his son and murdered. ■ **Edward III** (1312–77), son of Edward II; reigned 1327–77. In 1330, he took control of his kingdom, banishing Isabella and executing Mortimer. He supported **Edward de Baliol**, the pretender to the Scottish throne, and started the Hundred Years War. ■ **Edward IV** (1442–83), son of **Richard, Duke of York**; reigned 1461–83. He became king after defeating the Lancastrian Henry VI. Edward was briefly forced into exile 1470–01 by the Earl of Warwick but regained his position with victory at Tewkesbury in 1471. ■ **Edward V** (1470–*c.*1483), son of Edward IV; reigned 1483 but not crowned. Edward and his brother Richard, known as the Princes in the Tower, were probably murdered and the throne was taken by their uncle, Richard III. ■ **Edward VI** (1537–53), son of Henry VIII; reigned 1547–53. His reign saw the establishment of Protestantism as the state religion. ■ **Edward VII** (1841–1910), son of Queen Victoria; reigned 1901–10. Although he played little part in government on coming to the throne, his popularity helped to revitalize the monarchy. ■ **Edward VIII** (1894–1972), son of George V; reigned 1936 but not crowned. Edward abdicated 11 months after coming to the throne in order to marry a US divorcee, Mrs. Wallis Simpson. He was given the title the duke of Windsor by George VI.

Ed·ward, Lake a lake on the border between Uganda and the Democratic Republic of the Congo (formerly Zaire). It is linked to Lake Albert by the Semliki River.

Ed·ward, Prince, Edward Antony Richard Louis, Earl of Wessex (1964–), third son of Elizabeth II. In 1999, he married Sophie Rhys-Jones.

Ed·ward, Prince of Wales see BLACK PRINCE.

Ed·ward·i·an /edˈwôrdēən, -ˈwär-/ ▶ **adj.** of, relating to, or characteristic of the reign of King Edward VII: *the Edwardian era | a fine Edwardian house.*
▶ **n.** a person who lived during this period.

Ed·ward·i·an·a /edˌwôrdēˈanə, -ˌwär-/ ▶ **plural n.** articles, esp. collectors' items, from the reign of Edward VII.

Ed·wards /ˈedwərdz/, Jonathan (1703–58), American cleric and theologian. He was known for the extreme Calvinism of his preaching and writing.

Ed·ward the Con·fes·sor, St. (*c.*1003–66), son of Ethelred the Unready; king of England 1042–66. He founded Westminster Abbey, where he was eventually buried. Feast day, October 13.

Ed·ward the Eld·er (*c.*870–924), son of Alfred the Great; king of Wessex 899–924. His military successes against the Danes made it possible for his son Athelstan to become the first king of all of England in 925.

Ed·ward the Mar·tyr, St. (*c.*963–978), son of Edgar; king of England 975–978. He was faced with a challenge for the throne by supporters of his half-brother, Ethelred, who eventually had him murdered. Feast day, March 18.

Ed·wy /ˈedwē/ (also **Eadwig** /ˈedwig/) (died 959), king of England 955–957. He was about 15 years old when he became king. After Mercia and Northumbria renounced him in favor of his brother Edgar, he ruled over only the lands south of the Thames River.

EE ▶ **abbr.** ■ electrical engineer. ■ electrical engineering.

-ee ▶ **suffix** forming nouns: **1** denoting the person affected directly or indirectly by the action of the formative verb: *employee | lessee.*
2 denoting a person described as or concerned with: *absentee | patentee.*
3 denoting an object of relatively smaller size: *goatee.*
– ORIGIN from Anglo-Norman French *-é*, from Latin *-atus* (past participial ending). Some forms are anglicized modern French nouns (e.g., *refugee* from *réfugié*).

EEA ▶ **abbr.** European Economic Area, a free-trade zone created in 1994, composed of the states of the European Union together with Iceland, Norway, and Liechtenstein.

EEC ▶ **abbr.** ■ European Economic Community. ■ echoencephalograph.

EEG ▶ **abbr.** ■ electroencephalogram. ■ electroencephalograph. ■ electroencephalography.

ee·jit /ˈējit/ ▶ **n.** informal Irish and Scottish form of IDIOT.

eek /ēk/ ▶ **exclam.** informal used as an expression of alarm, horror, or surprise.

eel /ēl/ ▶ **n.** a snakelike fish with a slender elongated body and poorly developed fins, proverbial for its slipperiness: *the man was wanted in a dozen countries but was as slippery as an eel.* ● Order Anguilliformes: many families, in particular Anguillidae, which comprises mainly freshwater eels that breed in the sea, including the common *Anguilla anguilla* of Europe and the **American eel** (*A. rostrata*). ■ used in names of unrelated fishes that resemble the true eels, e.g., **electric eel, moray eel.**
– DERIVATIVES **eel·like** /-ˌlīk/ **adj.**, **eel·y adj.**
– ORIGIN Old English *ǣl*, of Germanic origin; related to Dutch *aal* and German *Aal.*

Ee·lam /ˈēləm, ˈēˌlam/ the proposed homeland of the Tamil people of Sri Lanka, for which the Tamil Tigers separatist group fought until their defeat in 2009.

eel·grass /ˈēlˌgras/ ▶ **n.** **1** a marine plant with long ribbonlike leaves that grows in coastal waters and brackish inlets. ● *Zostera marina*, family Zosteraceae.
2 another term for TAPE GRASS.

eel·pout /ˈēlˌpout/ ▶ **n.** a fish of cool or cold seas, having a broad head with thick lips and an elongated body with the dorsal and anal fins continuous with the tail. ● Family Zoarcidae: numerous genera and species, including the widely distributed northern European viviparous blenny (*Zoarces viviparus*).
– ORIGIN Old English *ǣlepūta* (see EEL, POUT[2]).

eel·worm /ˈēlˌwərm/ ▶ **n.** a nematode, esp. a small soil nematode that can become a serious pest of crops and ornamental plants.

Eem·i·an /ˈēmēən/ (also **Eem** /ēm/) ▶ **adj.** Geology of, relating to, or denoting the most recent interglacial period of the Pleistocene in northern Europe, preceding the Weichsel glaciation. ■ (as noun **the Eemian** or **Eem**) the Eemian interglacial or the system of deposits laid down during it.
– ORIGIN early 20th cent.: from *Eem*, the name of a river in the Netherlands, + -IAN.

e'en /ēn/ literary ▶ **contraction** EVEN[1].

-een ▶ **suffix** Irish forming diminutive nouns such as *colleen.*
– ORIGIN from the Irish diminutive suffix *-ín.*

een·sy /ˈēn(t)sē/ (also **eensy-weensy**) ▶ **adj.** informal extremely small; tiny.

EEO ▶ **abbr.** equal employment opportunity.

EEPROM /ˌē-ēˈpräm, ˈēˌpräm, ˈdəbəl ē ˈpräm/ ▶ **n.** Computing a read-only memory whose contents can be erased and reprogrammed using a pulsed voltage.
– ORIGIN acronym from *electrically erasable programmable ROM.*

e'er /e(ə)r/ literary ▶ **contraction** ever.

-eer ▶ **suffix** **1** (forming nouns) denoting a person concerned with or engaged in an activity: *auctioneer | puppeteer.*
2 (forming verbs) denoting concern or involvement with an activity: *electioneer | profiteer.*
– ORIGIN from French *-ier*, from Latin *-arius*; verbs (sense 2) are often back-formations (e.g., *electioneer* from *electioneering*).

ee·rie /ˈi(ə)rē/ ▶ **adj.** (**eerier, eeriest**) strange and frightening: *an eerie green glow in the sky.*
– DERIVATIVES **ee·ri·ly adv.** [as submodifier] *it was eerily quiet*, **ee·ri·ness n.**
– ORIGIN Middle English (originally northern English and Scots in the sense 'fearful'): probably from Old English *earg* 'cowardly,' of Germanic origin; related to German *arg.*

Ee·yor·ish /ˈēyôrisʜ, ˈēôr-/ (also **Eeyoreish**) ▶ **adj.** Brit. pessimistic or gloomy: *one of the most Eeyorish speeches we have ever heard.*
– ORIGIN 1990s: from *Eeyore*, the name of a donkey in A. A. Milne's *Winnie-the-Pooh* (1926), characterized by his gloomy outlook on life.

ef- ▶ **prefix** variant spelling of EX-[1]. assimilated before *f* (as in *efface, effloresce*).

USAGE See usage at EX-[1].

EFA ▶ **abbr.** essential fatty acid.

eff /ef/ ▶ **n. & v.** chiefly Brit. used as a euphemism for "fuck."
– PHRASES **eff and blind** informal use vulgar expletives; swear: *You can eff and blind all you want; the rules still stand.* [*blind* from its use in vulgar imprecations such as *blind me* (see BLIMEY).]
– DERIVATIVES **eff·ing adj. & adv.**
– ORIGIN 1950s: the letter *F* represented as a word.

eff. ▶ **abbr.** efficiency.

ef·fa·ble /ˈefəbəl/ ▶ **adj.** rare able to be described in words.

– ORIGIN early 17th cent.: from Latin *effabilis*, from *effari* 'utter.'

ef·face /iˈfās/ ▶ **v.** [with obj.] **1** erase (a mark) from a surface: *with time, the words are effaced by the frost and the rain* | figurative *his anger was effaced when he stepped into the open air*.
2 (**efface oneself**) make oneself appear insignificant or inconspicuous.
– DERIVATIVES **ef·face·ment n.**
– ORIGIN late 15th cent. (in the sense 'pardon or be absolved from (an offense)'): from French *effacer*, from *e-* (from Latin *ex-* 'away from') + *face* 'face.'

ef·fect /iˈfekt/ ▶ **n. 1** a change that is a result or consequence of an action or other cause: *the lethal effects of hard drugs* | *politicians really do have some effect on the lives of ordinary people*. ■ the state of being or becoming operative. ■ the extent to which something succeeds or is operative: *wind power can be used to great effect*. ■ [with modifier] Physics a physical phenomenon, typically named after its discoverer: *the Doppler effect*. ■ an impression produced in the mind of a person: *gentle music can have a soothing effect*.
2 (**effects**) the lighting, sound, or scenery used in a play, movie, or broadcast: *the production relied too much on spectacular effects*.
3 (**effects**) personal belongings: *the insurance covers personal effects*.
▶ **v.** [with obj.] cause (something) to happen; bring about: *nature always effected a cure* | *budget cuts that were quietly effected over four years*.
– PHRASES **come into effect** become operative; start to apply: *similar legislation came into effect in Wales on the same date*. **for effect** in order to impress people: *I suspect he's controversial for effect*. **in effect** in operation; in force: *a moratorium in effect since 1985 has been lifted*. ■ used to convey that something is the case in practice even if it is not formally acknowledged to be so: *additional payments that are in effect an entrance tax*. **put** (or **bring** or **carry**) **something into effect** cause something to apply or become operative: *they succeeded in putting their strategies into effect*. **take effect** become operative; start to apply: *the ban is to take effect in six months*. **to the effect that** used to refer to the general sense of something written or spoken: *some comments to the effect that my essay was a little light on analysis*. **to that effect** having that result, purpose, or meaning: *she thought it a foolish rule and put a notice to that effect in a newspaper*.
– ORIGIN late Middle English: from Old French, or from Latin *effectus*, from *efficere* 'accomplish,' from *ex-* 'out, thoroughly' + *facere* 'do, make.' Sense 3 of the noun, 'personal belongings,' arose from the obsolete sense 'something acquired on completion of an action.'

USAGE For the differences in use between **effect** and **affect**, see usage at **AFFECT**[1].

ef·fec·tive /iˈfektiv/ ▶ **adj. 1** successful in producing a desired or intended result: *effective solutions to environmental problems*. ■ (esp. of a law or policy) operative: *the agreements will be* **effective from** *November*.
2 [attrib.] fulfilling a specified function in fact, though not formally acknowledged as such: *the region did not come under effective Dutch control until 1904*. ■ assessed according to actual rather than face value: *an effective price of $176 million*. ■ impressive; striking: *an effective finale*.
▶ **n.** a soldier fit and available for service.
– DERIVATIVES **ef·fec·tiv·i·ty** /ˌefekˈtivitē, ˌēfek-/ **n.**
– ORIGIN late Middle English: from Latin *effectivus*, from *efficere* 'work out, accomplish' (see **EFFECT**).

ef·fec·tive de·mand ▶ **n.** Economics the level of demand that represents a real intention to purchase by people with the means to pay.

ef·fec·tive·ly /iˈfektəvlē/ ▶ **adv.** in such a manner as to achieve a desired result: *make sure that resources are used effectively*. ■ actually but not officially or explicitly: *they were effectively controlled by the people they were supposed to be investigating* | [sentence adverb] *effectively, this means that companies will be able to avoid regulations*.

ef·fec·tive·ness /iˈfektivnis/ ▶ **n.** the degree to which something is successful in producing a desired result; success: *the effectiveness of the treatment*.

ef·fec·tive tem·per·a·ture ▶ **n.** Physics the temperature of an object calculated from the radiation it emits, assuming black-body behavior.

ef·fec·tor /iˈfektər/ ▶ **n.** Biology an organ or cell that acts in response to a stimulus: [as modifier] *effector cells*.

ef·fec·tu·al /iˈfekCHo͞oəl/ ▶ **adj.** (typically of something inanimate or abstract) successful in producing a desired or intended result; effective: *tobacco smoke is the most effectual protection against the mosquito*.
– DERIVATIVES **ef·fec·tu·al·i·ty** /iˌfekCHo͞oˈalitē/ **n.**, **ef·fec·tu·al·ly adv.**, **ef·fec·tu·al·ness n.**
– ORIGIN late Middle English: from medieval Latin *effectualis*, from Latin *effectus* (see **EFFECT**).

ef·fec·tu·ate /iˈfekCHo͞oˌāt/ ▶ **v.** [with obj.] formal put into force or operation: *school choice would effectuate a transfer of power from government to individuals*.
– DERIVATIVES **ef·fec·tu·a·tion** /iˌfekCHo͞oˈāSHən/ **n.**
– ORIGIN late 16th cent.: from medieval Latin *effectuat-* 'caused to happen,' from the verb *effectuare*, from Latin *effectus* (see **EFFECT**).

ef·fem·i·nate /iˈfemənət/ ▶ **adj.** (of a man) having or showing characteristics regarded as typical of a woman; unmanly.
– DERIVATIVES **ef·fem·i·na·cy** /iˈfemənəsē/ **n.**, **ef·fem·i·nate·ly adv.**
– ORIGIN late Middle English: from Latin *effeminatus*, past participle of *effeminare* 'make feminine,' from *ex-* (expressing a change of state) + *femina* 'woman.'

ef·fen·di /iˈfendē/ ▶ **n.** (pl. **effendis** /-dēz/) a man of high education or social standing in an eastern Mediterranean or Arab country. ■ historical a title of respect or courtesy in Turkey.
– ORIGIN early 17th cent.: from Turkish *efendi*, from modern Greek *aphentēs*, from Greek *authentēs* 'lord, master.'

ef·fer·ent /ˈefərənt/ ▶ **adj.** Physiology conducted or conducting outward or away from something (for nerves, the central nervous system; for blood vessels, the organ supplied). The opposite of **AFFERENT**.
– ORIGIN mid 19th cent.: from Latin *efferent-* 'carrying out,' from the verb *efferre*, from *ex-* 'out' + *ferre* 'carry.'

ef·fer·vesce /ˌefərˈves/ ▶ **v.** [no obj.] **1** (of a liquid) give off bubbles.
2 be vivacious and enthusiastic.
– ORIGIN early 18th cent.: from Latin *effervescere*, from *ex-* 'out, up' + *fervescere* 'begin to boil' (from *fervere* 'be hot, boil').

ef·fer·ves·cence /ˌefərˈvesəns/ ▶ **n. 1** bubbles in a liquid; fizz: *the effervescence of sparkling wine*.
2 vivacity and enthusiasm: *he was filled with such effervescence*.

ef·fer·ves·cent /ˌefərˈvesənt/ ▶ **adj. 1** (of a liquid) giving off bubbles; fizzy.
2 vivacious and enthusiastic: *effervescent young people*.
– ORIGIN late 17th cent.: from Latin *effervescent-* 'boiling up,' from the verb *effervescere* (see **EFFERVESCE**).

ef·fete /iˈfēt/ ▶ **adj.** (of a person) affected, overrefined, and ineffectual: *effete trendies from art college*. ■ no longer capable of effective action: *the authority of an effete aristocracy began to dwindle*.
– DERIVATIVES **ef·fete·ness n.**
– ORIGIN early 17th cent. (in the sense 'no longer fertile, past bearing young'): from Latin *effetus* 'worn out by bearing young,' from *ex-* 'out' + *fetus* 'breeding'; related to **FETUS**.

ef·fi·ca·cious /ˌefiˈkāSHəs/ ▶ **adj.** formal (typically of something inanimate or abstract) successful in producing a desired or intended result; effective: *the vaccine has proved both efficacious and safe*.
– DERIVATIVES **ef·fi·ca·cious·ly adv.**, **ef·fi·ca·cious·ness n.**
– ORIGIN early 16th cent.: from Latin *efficax*, *efficac-* (from *efficere* 'accomplish': see **EFFECT**) + **-IOUS**.

ef·fi·ca·cy /ˈefikəsē/ ▶ **n.** the ability to produce a desired or intended result: *there is little information on the efficacy of this treatment*.
– ORIGIN early 16th cent.: from Latin *efficacia*, from *efficax*, *efficac-* (see **EFFICACIOUS**).

ef·fi·cien·cy /iˈfiSHənsē/ ▶ **n.** (pl. **efficiencies**) the state or quality of being efficient: *greater energy efficiency*. ■ an action designed to achieve this: *to increase efficiencies and improve earnings*. ■ technical the ratio of the useful work performed by a machine or in a process to the total energy expended or heat taken in. ■ short for **EFFICIENCY APARTMENT**.
– ORIGIN late 16th cent. (in the sense 'the fact of being an efficient cause'): from Latin *efficientia*, from *efficere* 'accomplish' (see **EFFECT**).

ef·fi·cien·cy a·part·ment (also **efficiency**) ▶ **n.** an apartment in which one room typically contains the kitchen, living, and sleeping quarters, with a separate bathroom.

ef·fi·cient /iˈfiSHənt/ ▶ **adj.** (esp. of a system or machine) achieving maximum productivity with minimum wasted effort or expense: *fluorescent lamps are efficient at converting electricity into light*. ■ (of a person) working in a well-organized and competent way: *an efficient administrator*. ■ [in combination] preventing the wasteful use of a particular resource: *an energy-efficient heating system*.
– DERIVATIVES **ef·fi·cient·ly adv.**
– ORIGIN late Middle English (in the sense 'making, causing,' usually in **EFFICIENT CAUSE**): from Latin *efficient-* 'accomplishing,' from the verb *efficere* (see **EFFECT**). The current sense dates from the late 18th cent.

ef·fi·cient cause ▶ **n.** Philosophy an agent that brings a thing into being or initiates a change.

ef·fi·gy /ˈefijē/ ▶ **n.** (pl. **effigies**) a sculpture or model of a person: *coins bearing the effigy of Maria Theresa of Austria*. ■ a roughly made model of a particular person, made in order to be damaged or destroyed as a protest or expression of anger: *the senator was* **burned in effigy**.
– ORIGIN mid 16th cent.: from Latin *effigies*, from *effingere* 'to fashion (artistically),' from *ex-* 'out' + *fingere* 'to shape.'

ef·fleu·rage /ˌefləˈräZH/ ▶ **n.** a form of massage involving a circular stroking movement made with the palm of the hand.
▶ **v.** [with obj.] massage with such a circular stroking movement: *effleurage the shoulders and press gently*.
– ORIGIN late 19th cent.: from French, from *effleurer* 'skim the surface, stroke lightly,' literally 'remove the flower or "outer beauty" of (something).'

ef·flo·resce /ˌefləˈres/ ▶ **v. 1** [no obj.] (of a substance) lose moisture and turn to a fine powder upon exposure to air. ■ (of salts) come to the surface of brickwork, rock, or other material and crystallize there. ■ (of a surface) become covered with salt particles.
2 reach an optimum stage of development; blossom: *simple concepts that* **effloresce into** *testable conclusions*.
– DERIVATIVES **ef·flo·res·cence** /-ˈresəns/ **n.**, **ef·flo·res·cent adj.**
– ORIGIN late 18th cent.: from Latin *efflorescere*, from *e-* (variant of *ex-*) 'out' + *florescere* 'begin to bloom' (from *florere* 'to bloom,' from *flos*, *flor-* 'flower').

ef·flu·ence /ˈeflo͞oəns/ ▶ **n.** a substance that flows out from something. ■ the action of flowing out.
– ORIGIN late Middle English: from medieval Latin *effluentia*, from Latin *effluere* 'flow out,' from *ex-* 'out' + *fluere* 'to flow.'

ef·flu·ent /ˈeflo͞oənt/ ▶ **n.** liquid waste or sewage discharged into a river or the sea: *the bay was contaminated with the effluent from an industrial plant*.
– ORIGIN late Middle English (in the adjective sense 'flowing out'): from Latin *effluent-* 'flowing out,' from the verb *effluere* (see **EFFLUENCE**). The noun dates from the mid 19th cent.

ef·flu·vi·um /iˈflo͞ovēəm/ ▶ **n.** (pl. **effluvia** /-vēə/) an unpleasant or harmful odor, secretion, or discharge: *the unwholesome effluvia of decaying vegetable matter*.
– ORIGIN mid 17th cent.: from Latin, from *effluere* 'flow out.'

ef·flux /ˈefləks/ ▶ **n.** technical the flowing out of a particular substance or particle. ■ material flowing out. ■ another term for **EFFLUXION** (sense 1).
– ORIGIN mid 16th cent.: from medieval Latin *effluxus*, from *effluere* 'flow out.'

ef·flux·ion /eˈfləkSHən/ ▶ **n. 1** Law (**efflux**) the passing of time, in particular when leading to the expiration of an agreement or contract.
2 archaic the action of flowing out.
– ORIGIN early 17th cent.: from French, or from late Latin *effluxio(n-)*, from *effluere* 'flow out.'

ef·fort /ˈefərt/ ▶ **n.** a vigorous or determined attempt: *hammer birdhouses to country fenceposts* **in an effort to** *bring back the eastern bluebird*. ■ the result of an attempt: *he was a keen gardener, winning many prizes for his efforts*. ■ strenuous physical or mental exertion: *the doctor spared no effort in helping my father*. ■ technical a force exerted by a machine or in a process. ■ [with modifier] the activities of a group of people with a common purpose: *the war effort*.
– DERIVATIVES **ef·fort·ful adj.**, **ef·fort·ful·ly adv.**
– ORIGIN late 15th cent.: from French, from Old French *esforcier*, based on Latin *ex-* 'out' + *fortis* 'strong.'

ef·fort·less /ˈefərtlis/ ▶ **adj.** requiring no physical or mental exertion: *went up the steps in two effortless bounds*. ■ achieved with admirable ease: *her effortless sense of style*.
– DERIVATIVES **ef·fort·less·ly adv.**, **ef·fort·less·ness n.**

ef·fron·ter·y /iˈfrəntərē/ ▶ **n.** insolent or impertinent behavior: *one juror* **had the effrontery to** *challenge the coroner's decision*.
– ORIGIN late 17th cent.: from French *effronterie*, based on late Latin *effrons*, *effront-* 'shameless, barefaced,' from *ex-* 'out' + *frons* 'forehead.'

ef·ful·gent /iˈfo͝oljənt, iˈfəl-/ ▶ **adj.** literary shining brightly; radiant. ■ (of a person or their expression) emanating joy or goodness.

– DERIVATIVES **ef·ful·gence** n., **ef·ful·gent·ly** adv.
– ORIGIN mid 18th cent.: from Latin *effulgent-* 'shining brightly,' from the verb *effulgere*, from *ex-* 'out' + *fulgere* 'to shine.'

ef·fuse /iˈfyo͞oz, iˈfyo͞os/ ▶ v. [with obj.] give off (a liquid, light, smell, or quality). ■ [no obj.] talk in an unrestrained, excited manner: *this was the type of material that they effused about.*
– ORIGIN late Middle English: from Latin *effusus*, past participle of *effundere* 'pour out,' from *ex-* 'out' + *fundere* 'pour.'

ef·fu·sion /iˈfyo͞oZHən/ ▶ n. an instance of giving off something such as a liquid, light, or smell: *a massive effusion of poisonous gas.* ■ Medicine an escape of fluid into a body cavity. ■ an act of talking or writing in an unrestrained or heartfelt way: *literary effusions.*
– ORIGIN late Middle English: from Latin *effusio(n-)*, from *effundere* 'pour out' (see EFFUSE).

ef·fu·sive /iˈfyo͞osiv/ ▶ adj. **1** expressing feelings of gratitude, pleasure, or approval in an unrestrained or heartfelt manner: *an effusive welcome.*
2 Geology (of igneous rock) poured out when molten and later solidified. ■ of or relating to the eruption of large volumes of molten rock.
– DERIVATIVES **ef·fu·sive·ly** adv., **ef·fu·sive·ness** n.

Ef·ik /ˈefik/ ▶ n. (pl. **same**) **1** a member of a people of southern Nigeria.
2 the Benue-Congo language of this people, closely related to Ibibio, and used as a lingua franca.
▶ adj. of or relating to this people or their language.
– ORIGIN the name in Efik.

e-fit /ˈēˌfit/ ▶ n. Brit. an electronic picture of the face of a person being sought by the police, created by a computer program from composite photographs of facial features.
– ORIGIN 1980s: from *e-* 'electronic' and *fit*, on the pattern of PHOTOFIT.

EFL ▶ abbr. English as a foreign language.

EFM ▶ abbr. electronic fetal monitor.

eft /eft/ ▶ n. a newt. ■ Zoology the juvenile stage of a newt.
– ORIGIN Old English *efeta*, of unknown origin. Compare with NEWT.

EFTA /ˈeftə/ ▶ abbr. European Free Trade Association.

EFTPOS ▶ abbr. electronic funds transfer at point of sale.

EFTS ▶ abbr. electronic funds transfer system.

e.g. ▶ abbr. for example.
– ORIGIN from Latin *exempli gratia* 'for the sake of an example.'

e·gad /ēˈgad/ (also **egads**) ▶ exclam. archaic expressing surprise, anger, or affirmation.
– ORIGIN late 17th cent.: representing earlier *A God.*

e·gal·i·tar·i·an /iˌgaləˈterēən/ ▶ adj. of, relating to, or believing in the principle that all people are equal and deserve equal rights and opportunities: *a fairer, more egalitarian society.*
▶ n. a person who advocates or supports such a principle.
– DERIVATIVES **e·gal·i·tar·i·an·ism** n.
– ORIGIN late 19th cent.: from French *égalitaire*, from *égal* 'equal,' from Latin *aequalis* (see EQUAL).

Eg·bert /ˈegbərt/ (died 839), king of Wessex 802–839. In 825, he won a decisive victory that temporarily brought Mercian supremacy to an end.

EGD ▶ n. a technology or system that integrates a computer display with a pair of eyeglasses, using a lens or mirror to reflect images into the eyes: *some EGDs are designed to clip right onto your eyeglasses.*
– ORIGIN abbreviation of 'eyeglass display.'

EGF ▶ abbr. epidermal growth factor.

egg[1] /eg/ ▶ n. **1** an oval or round object laid by a female bird, reptile, fish, or invertebrate, usually containing a developing embryo. The eggs of birds are enclosed in a chalky shell, while those of reptiles are in a leathery membrane. ■ an infertile egg, typically of the domestic hen, used for food. ■ Biology the female reproductive cell in animals and plants; an ovum. ■ a thing resembling a bird's egg in shape: *chocolate eggs.* ■ Architecture a decorative oval molding, used alternately with triangular figures.
2 [with adj.] informal, dated a person possessing a specified quality: *she was a good egg.*
– PHRASES **don't put all your eggs in one basket** proverb don't risk everything on the success of one venture. **go suck an egg** [as imperative] informal used as an expression of anger or scorn. **kill the goose that lays the golden egg** destroy a reliable and valuable source of income. [with allusion to one of Aesop's fables.] **lay an egg** informal be completely unsuccessful; fail badly. **with egg on one's face** informal appearing foolish or ridiculous: *don't underestimate this team, or you'll be left with egg on your face.*
– DERIVATIVES **egg·less** adj.
– ORIGIN Middle English (superseding earlier *ey*, from Old English *ǣg*): from Old Norse.

egg[2] ▶ v. [with obj.] (**egg someone on**) urge or encourage someone to do something, esp. something foolish or risky.
– ORIGIN Middle English: from Old Norse *eggja* 'incite.'

egg and dart ▶ n. Architecture a motif of alternating eggs and darts, used to enrich an ovolo molding.

egg·ar /ˈegər/ ▶ n. a large brownish moth that is often active during the day. The caterpillars typically bear irritant hairs and make an egg-shaped cocoon. ● Many species in the family Lasiocampidae.
– ORIGIN early 18th cent.: probably from EGG[1] + -ER[1].

egg·beat·er /ˈegˌbētər/ ▶ n. a kitchen utensil used for beating ingredients such as eggs or cream. ■ informal a helicopter.

egg-bound ▶ adj. (of a hen) unable through weakness or disease to expel its eggs.

egg·corn /ˈegkôrn/ ▶ n. a word or phrase that results from a mishearing or misinterpretation of another, an element of the original being substituted for one that sounds very similar (e.g. *tow the line* instead of *toe the line*).
– ORIGIN early 21st cent.: with reference to a misinterpretation of ACORN.

egg cream ▶ n. a drink consisting of milk and soda water, flavored with syrup.

egg·cup /ˈegˌkəp/ ▶ n. a small cup for holding a boiled egg upright while it is being eaten.

egg-eat·ing snake (also **egg-eater**) ▶ n. an Old World snake that swallows birds' eggs. It has weak teeth, and breaks shells with sawlike projections inside the gullet. ● Subfamily Dasypeltinae, family Colubridae: genus *Dasypeltis* (of Africa, in particular the widespread *D. scabra*), and *Elachistodon westermanni* (of India).

egg·head /ˈegˌhed/ ▶ n. informal, often derogatory a person who is highly academic or studious; an intellectual.
– DERIVATIVES **egg·head·ed** adj.
– ORIGIN by analogy with a bald head.

egg·nog /ˈegˌnäg, -ˌnôg/ ▶ n. a drink made from a mixture of beaten eggs, cream, and flavorings, often with alcohol.

egg·plant /ˈegˌplant/ ▶ n. **1** the large egg-shaped fruit of an Old World plant, eaten as a vegetable. Its skin is typically dark purple, but the skin of certain cultivated varieties is white or yellow. ■ a dark purple color like the skin of this fruit.
2 the large plant of the nightshade family that bears this fruit. ● *Solanum melongena*, family Solanaceae.

egg roll ▶ n. a Chinese-style snack consisting of diced meat or shrimp and shredded vegetables wrapped in a dough made with egg and deep-fried.

egg sac ▶ n. a protective silken pouch in which a female spider deposits her eggs.

eggs and ba·con (also **egg and bacon**) ▶ n. any of a number of plants that have yellow flowers with orange, red, or brown markings, supposedly suggestive of eggs and bacon, in particular: ● bird's-foot trefoil. ● a shrubby Australian bush plant (*Bossiaea* and other genera, family Leguminosae).

eggs Ben·e·dict ▶ plural n. a dish consisting of poached eggs and sliced ham on toasted English muffins, covered with hollandaise sauce.
– ORIGIN late 19th cent.: of uncertain origin.

egg·shell /ˈegˌSHel/ ▶ n. the thin, hard outer layer of an egg, esp. a hen's egg. ■ (also **eggshell paint**) an oil-based paint that dries with a slight sheen: *the woodwork was painted in eggshell* | [as modifier] *an eggshell finish.* ■ [as modifier] (of china) of extreme thinness and delicacy: *eggshell porcelains.* ■ a pale yellowish-white color.

egg tem·per·a ▶ n. an emulsion of pigment and egg yolk, used in tempera painting.

egg tim·er ▶ n. a device for measuring the time required to cook a boiled egg, traditionally in the form of a miniature hourglass.

egg tooth ▶ n. a hard white protuberance on the beak or jaw of an embryo bird or reptile that is used for breaking out of the shell and is later lost.

egg white ▶ n. the clear, viscous substance around the yolk of an egg that turns white when cooked or beaten. Also called ALBUMEN.

egg·y /ˈegē/ ▶ adj. rich in or covered with egg: *many white wines go passably with eggy dishes.*

eg·lan·tine /ˈeglənˌtēn, -ˌtīn/ ▶ n. another term for SWEETBRIER.
– ORIGIN Middle English: from Old French *eglantine*, from Provençale *aiglentina*, based on Latin *acus* 'needle' or *aculeus* 'prickle.'

e·go /ˈēgō/ ▶ n. (pl. **egos**) a person's sense of self-esteem or self-importance: *a boost to my ego.* ■ Psychoanalysis the part of the mind that mediates between the conscious and the unconscious and is responsible for reality testing and a sense of personal identity. Compare with ID and SUPEREGO. ■ Philosophy (in metaphysics) a conscious thinking subject.
– DERIVATIVES **e·go·less** adj.
– ORIGIN early 19th cent.: from Latin, literally 'I.'

e·go·cen·tric /ˌēgōˈsentrik/ ▶ adj. thinking only of oneself, without regard for the feelings or desires of others; self-centered: *their egocentric tendency to think of themselves as invulnerable.* ■ centered in or arising from a person's own existence or perspective: *egocentric spatial perception.*
▶ n. an egocentric person.
– DERIVATIVES **e·go·cen·tric·al·ly** /-(ə)lē/ adv., **e·go·cen·tric·i·ty** /ˌēgōsenˈtrisitē/ n., **e·go·cen·trism** /ˌēgōˈsentrizəm/ n.
– ORIGIN early 20th cent.: from EGO, on the pattern of words such as *geocentric.*

e·go i·de·al ▶ n. Psychoanalysis (in Freudian theory) the part of the mind that imposes on itself concepts of ideal behavior developed from parental and social standards. ■ (in general use) an idealized conception of oneself.

e·go·ism /ˈēgōˌizəm/ ▶ n. Ethics an ethical theory that treats self-interest as the foundation of morality. ■ another term for EGOTISM.
– DERIVATIVES **e·go·ist** n., **e·go·is·tic** /-ˈistik/ adj., **e·go·is·ti·cal** /-ˈistikəl/ adj., **e·go·is·ti·cal·ly** /-ˈistik(ə)lē/ adv.
– ORIGIN late 18th cent.: from French *égoïsme* and modern Latin *egoismus*, from Latin *ego* 'I.'

> **USAGE** The words **egoism** and **egotism** are frequently confused, as though interchangeable, but there are distinctions worth noting. Both words derive from Latin *ego* ('I'), the first-person singular pronoun. **Egotism**, the more commonly used term, denotes an excessive sense of self-importance, too-frequent use of the word 'I,' and general arrogance and boastfulness. **Egoism**, a more subtle term, is perhaps best left to ethicists, for whom it denotes a view or theory of moral behavior in which self-interest is the root of moral conduct. An **egoist**, then, might devote considerable attention to introspection, but could be modest about it, whereas an **egotist** would have an exaggerated sense of the importance of his or her self-analysis, and would have to tell everyone.

e·go·ma·ni·a /ˌēgōˈmānēə/ ▶ n. obsessive egotism or self-centeredness.
– DERIVATIVES **e·go·ma·ni·ac** /-nēˌak/ n., **e·go·ma·ni·a·cal** /-məˈnīəkəl/ adj.

e·go psy·chol·o·gy ▶ n. Psychology a system of psychoanalytic developmental psychology concerned esp. with personality.
– DERIVATIVES **e·go psy·chol·o·gist** n.

e·go·surf /ˈēgōˌsərf/ ▶ v. [no obj.] informal search the Internet for instances of one's own name or links to one's own website.
– DERIVATIVES **e·go·surf·ing** n.

e·go·tism /ˈēgəˌtizəm/ ▶ n. the practice of talking and thinking about oneself excessively because of an undue sense of self-importance: *in his arrogance and egotism, he underestimated Jill.*
– DERIVATIVES **e·go·tize** /-ˌtīz/ v.
– ORIGIN early 18th cent.: from French *égoïste*, from Latin *ego* 'I.'

> **USAGE** See usage at EGOISM.

e·go·tist /ˈēgətist/ ▶ n. a person who is excessively conceited or self-absorbed; self-seeker: *he is a self-absorbed egotist.*

e·go·tis·ti·cal /ˌēgəˈtistikəl/ ▶ adj. excessively conceited or absorbed in oneself; self-centered: *he's selfish, egotistical, and arrogant.*
– DERIVATIVES **e·go·tis·tic** /ˌēgəˈtistik/ adj., **e·go·tis·ti·cal·ly** /ˌēgəˈtistik(ə)lē/ adv.

e·go trip ▶ n. informal an activity done in order to increase one's sense of self-importance: *driving that car was the biggest ego trip I'd ever had.*

e·gre·gious /iˈgrējəs/ ▶ adj. **1** outstandingly bad; shocking: *egregious abuses of copyright.*
2 archaic remarkably good.
– DERIVATIVES **e·gre·gious·ly** adv., **e·gre·gious·ness** n.

PRONUNCIATION KEY ə *ago, up*; ər *over, fur*; a *hat*; ā *ate*; ä *car*; e *let*; ē *see*; i *fit*; ī *by*; NG *sing*; ō *go*; ô *law, for*; oi *toy*; o͝o *good*; o͞o *goo*; ou *out*; TH *thin*; T͟H *then*; ZH *vision*

e

– ORIGIN mid 16th cent. (sense 2): from Latin *egregius* 'illustrious,' literally 'standing out from the flock,' from *ex-* 'out' + *grex, greg-* 'flock.' The derogatory sense (late 16th cent.) probably arose as an ironical use.

e·gress /ˈēˌgres/ ▶ **n.** the action of going out of or leaving a place: *direct means of access and egress for passengers.* ■ a way out: *a narrow egress.* ■ Law the right or freedom to come out or go out. ■ Astronomy another term for **EMERSION**.
▶ **v.** [with obj.] go out of or leave (a place): *they'd egress the area by heading southwest.*
– ORIGIN mid 16th cent.: from Latin *egressus* 'gone out,' from the verb *egredi*, from *ex-* 'out' + *gradi* 'to step.'

e·gres·sive /iˈgresiv/ ▶ **adj.** Phonetics (of a speech sound) produced using the normal outward-flowing airstream. Compare with **INGRESSIVE**.

e·gret /ˈēgrit, ˈēˌgret, ˈegrit/ ▶ **n.** a heron with mainly white plumage, having long plumes in the breeding season. ● Genus *Egretta* (and *Bubulcus*), family Ardeidae: several species.
– ORIGIN Middle English: from Old French *aigrette*, from Provençal *aigreta*, from the Germanic base of **HERON**.

E·gypt /ˈējəpt/ a country in northeastern Africa, on the Mediterranean Sea; pop. 78,866,600 (est. 2009); capital, Cairo; official language, Arabic.

> The population of Egypt is concentrated chiefly along the fertile valley of the Nile River because the rest of the country is largely desert. Egypt's history spans 5,000 years: the ancient kingdoms of Upper and Lower Egypt were ruled successively by 31 dynasties, which may be divided into the Old Kingdom, the Middle Kingdom, and the New Kingdom. Egypt was a center of Hellenistic culture and then a Roman province before coming under Islamic rule and then becoming part of the Ottoman Empire. Modern Egypt became independent in 1922. From 1958 to 1961 Egypt was united with Syria as the United Arab Republic, a title it retained until 1971. Wars with Israel were fought in 1967 (the Six Day War) and 1973 (the Yom Kippur or October War); the countries signed a peace treaty in 1979.

E·gyp·tian /iˈjipSHən/ ▶ **adj.** of or relating to Egypt or its people. ■ of or relating to Egyptian antiquities: *a large Egyptian collection was sold at Sotheby's.* ■ of or relating to the language of ancient Egypt.
▶ **n. 1** a native of ancient or modern Egypt, or a person of Egyptian descent.
2 the Afro-Asiatic language used in ancient Egypt, attested from *c.*3000 BC. It is represented in its oldest stages by hieroglyphic inscriptions and in its latest form by Coptic; it has been replaced in modern use by Arabic.
– DERIVATIVES **E·gyp·tian·i·za·tion** /iˌjipSHəniˈzāSHən/ **n.**, **E·gyp·tian·ize** /-ˌnīz/ **v.**

E·gyp·tian black ▶ **n.** another term for **BASALT** (stoneware pottery).

E·gyp·tian clo·ver ▶ **n.** another term for **BERSEEM CLOVER**.

E·gyp·tian co·bra ▶ **n.** a large nocturnal African cobra with a thick body and large head. Also called **ASP**. ● *Naja haje*, family Elapidae.

E·gyp·tian goose ▶ **n.** a large African goose that has a dark patch around the eye, pink bill and legs, and either reddish-brown or grayish-brown upper parts. ● *Alopochen aegyptiacus*, family Anatidae.

E·gyp·tian lo·tus ▶ **n.** see **LOTUS** (sense 1).

E·gyp·tian mon·goose ▶ **n.** a mongoose occurring over much of Africa and parts of southwestern Asia and Iberia, noted for its destruction of crocodile eggs. Also called **ICHNEUMON**. ● *Herpestes ichneumon*, family Herpestidae.

E·gyp·tian plov·er ▶ **n.** a ploverlike African bird of the courser family, with a striking pattern of black and white over a mainly bluish back and buff-colored underparts. Also called **CROCODILE BIRD**. ● *Pluvianus aegyptius*, family Glareolidae.

E·gyp·tian vul·ture ▶ **n.** a small white vulture with black wing tips, common in much of southern Eurasia and Africa. ● *Neophron percnopterus*, family Accipitridae.

E·gyp·tol·o·gy /ˌējipˈtäləjē/ ▶ **n.** the study of the language, history, and civilization of ancient Egypt.
– DERIVATIVES **E·gyp·to·log·i·cal** /iˌjiptəˈläjikəl/ **adj.**, **E·gyp·tol·o·gist** /ˌējipˈtäləjist/ **n.**

eh /ā, e/ ▶ **exclam.** used to represent a sound made in speech in a variety of situations, in particular to ask for something to be repeated or explained or to elicit agreement: *"Eh? What's this?" | "Let's hope so, eh?"*
– ORIGIN natural utterance: first recorded in English in the mid 16th cent.

EHF ▶ **abbr.** extremely high frequency.

EHP ▶ **abbr.** ■ effective horsepower. ■ electric horsepower.

EHV ▶ **abbr.** extra-high voltage.

Eich·mann /ˈīkmən/, Adolf (1906–62), German Nazi administrator; full name *Karl Adolf Eichmann*. He administered the concentration camps during World War II. In 1960, he was traced to Argentina by Israeli agents and executed after trial in Israel.

ei·co·sa·pen·ta·e·no·ic ac·id /ˌīkōsəˌpentəˈnō-ik/ ▶ **n.** Chemistry a polyunsaturated fatty acid found esp. in fish oils. In humans it is a metabolic precursor of prostaglandins. ● Chem. formula: $C_{19}H_{29}COOH$.
– ORIGIN 1960s: from Greek *eicosa-* 'twenty' (the number of carbon atoms in the molecule) + **PENTA-** 'five' (the number of unsaturated bonds) + **-ENE** + *-oic* on the pattern of *methanoic*.

Eid /ēd/ (also **Id**) ▶ **n.** a Muslim festival, in particular: ■ (in full **Eid ul-Fitr** /ēd o͝ol ˈfētr/) the feast marking the end of the fast of Ramadan. ■ (in full **Eid ul-Adha** /ēd o͝ol ˈädə/) the festival marking the culmination of the annual pilgrimage to Mecca and commemorating the sacrifice of Abraham.
– ORIGIN from Arabic *ʿīd* 'feast,' from Aramaic.

EIDE ▶ **n.** Computing enhanced integrated drive electronics. See **IDE**.

ei·der /ˈīdər/ ▶ **n.** (also **eider duck**) (pl. **same** or **eiders**) a northern sea duck, of which the male has mainly black and white plumage with a colored head, and the brown female has soft down feathers that are used to line the nest. ● Genus *Somateria* (and *Polysticta*), family Anatidae: four species, in particular the **common eider** (*S. mollissima*). ■ another term for **EIDERDOWN**.
– ORIGIN late 17th cent.: from Icelandic *æthur*, from Old Norse *æthr*.

common eider

ei·der·down /ˈīdərˌdoun/ ▶ **n.** small, soft feathers from the breast of the female eider duck. ■ chiefly Brit. a quilt filled with down (originally from the eider) or some other soft material.

ei·det·ic /īˈdetik/ ▶ **adj.** Psychology relating to or denoting mental images having unusual vividness and detail, as if actually visible.
▶ **n.** a person able to form or recall eidetic images.
– DERIVATIVES **ei·det·i·cal·ly adv.**
– ORIGIN 1920s: coined in German from Greek *eidētikos*, from *eidos* 'form.'

ei·do·lon /īˈdōlən/ ▶ **n.** (pl. **eidolons** or **eidola** /-lə/)
1 an idealized person or thing.
2 a specter or phantom.
– ORIGIN early 19th cent.: from Greek *eidōlon*, from *eidos* 'form.'

ei·dos /ˈīdäs, ˈādäs/ ▶ **n.** (pl. **eide** /ˈīdē, ˈādā/) Anthropology the distinctive expression of the cognitive or intellectual character of a culture or social group.
– ORIGIN 1930s: Greek, literally 'form, type, or idea,' partly in contrast to **ETHOS**.

Eif·fel /ˈīfəl/, Alexandre Gustave (1832–1923), French engineer. He designed and built the Eiffel Tower and was the architect of the inner structure of the Statue of Liberty.

Eif·fel Tow·er a wrought-iron structure erected in Paris for the World Exhibition of 1889. With a height of 984 feet (300 m), it was the tallest man-made structure for many years.

Eiffel Tower

eigen- ▶ **comb. form** Mathematics & Physics proper; characteristic: *eigenfunction*.
– ORIGIN from the German adjective *eigen* 'own.'

ei·gen·fre·quen·cy /ˈīgənˌfrēkwənsē/ ▶ **n.** (pl. **eigenfrequencies**) Mathematics & Physics one of the natural resonant frequencies of a system.

ei·gen·func·tion /ˈīgənˌfəNG(k)SHən/ ▶ **n.** Mathematics & Physics each of a set of independent functions that are the solutions to a given differential equation.

ei·gen·state /ˈīgənˌstāt/ ▶ **n.** Physics a quantum-mechanical state corresponding to an eigenvalue of a wave equation.

ei·gen·val·ue /ˈīgənˌvalyo͞o/ ▶ **n.** Mathematics & Physics
1 each of a set of values of a parameter for which a differential equation has a nonzero solution (an eigenfunction) under given conditions.
2 any number such that a given matrix minus that number times the identity matrix has a zero determinant.

ei·gen·vec·tor /ˈīgənˌvektər/ ▶ **n.** Mathematics & Physics a vector that when operated on by a given operator gives a scalar multiple of itself.

eight /āt/ ▶ **cardinal number** equivalent to the product of two and four; one more than seven, or two less than ten; 8: *a committee of eight members | eight were acquitted | eight of them were unemployed.* (Roman numeral: **viii** or **VIII**) ■ a group or unit of eight people or things: *the win placed Canada closer to the final eight.* ■ eight years old: *children as young as eight.* ■ eight o'clock: *in time for dinner at eight.* ■ short for **FIGURE EIGHT**. ■ a size of garment or other merchandise denoted by eight. ■ a playing card with eight pips. ■ an eight-oared rowboat or its crew.
– ORIGIN Old English *ehta, eahta*, of Germanic origin; related to Dutch and German *acht*, from an Indo-European root shared by Latin *octo* and Greek *oktō*.

eight ball ▶ **n. 1** Billiards the black ball, numbered eight. ■ a game of pool in which one side must pocket all of the striped or solid balls and finally the eight ball to win.
2 (**eightball**) informal a portion of an illegal drug weighing an eighth of an ounce (3.54 g).
– PHRASES **behind the eight ball** informal at a disadvantage.

eight·een /āˈtēn, ˈāˌtēn/ ▶ **cardinal number** equivalent to the product of two and nine; one more than seventeen, or eight more than ten; 18: *she wrote eighteen novels | out of sixty batches checked, eighteen were incorrect | eighteen of the guests were gathered.* (Roman numeral: **xviii** or **XVIII**) ■ a set or team of eighteen individuals. ■ eighteen years old: *he was barely eighteen.* ■ a size of garment or other merchandise denoted by eighteen.
– DERIVATIVES **eight·eenth** /āˈtēnTH, ˈāˌtēnTH/ **ordinal number.**
– ORIGIN Old English *e(a)htatēne* (see **EIGHT**, **-TEEN**).

eight·een·mo /ˌāˈtēnˌmō/ ▶ **n.** (pl. **eighteenmos**) another term for **OCTODECIMO**.

eight·fold /ˈātˌfōld/ ▶ **adj.** eight times as great or as numerous: *an eightfold increase in expenditure.* ■ having eight parts or elements: *an eightfold shape.*
▶ **adv.** by eight times; to eight times the number or amount: *claims have grown eightfold in ten years.*

eight·fold path ▶ **n.** Buddhism the path to nirvana, comprising eight aspects in which an aspirant must become practiced: right views, intention, speech, action, livelihood, effort, mindfulness, and concentration.

eighth /ā(t)TH/ ▶ **ordinal number** constituting number eight in a sequence; 8th: *in the eighth century | the eighth of September | seven men admitted conspiracy, an eighth admitted assisting an offender.* ■ (**an eighth/one eighth**) each of eight equal parts into which something is or may be divided: *an eighth of an inch.* ■ the eighth finisher or position in a race or competition: *she finished eighth of the eleven runners.*
– DERIVATIVES **eighth·ly adv.**

eighth note (Brit. **quaver**) ▶ **n.** Music a note having the time value of an eighth of a whole note or half a quarter note, represented by a large dot with a hooked stem.

eight·pen·ny nail /ˈātˌpenē/ ▶ **n.** a nail that is 2.5 inches (64 mm) long.

eight·y /ˈātē/ ▶ **cardinal number** (pl. **eighties**) equivalent to the product of eight and ten; ten less than ninety; 80: *eighty miles north | a buffet for eighty | eighty of the nurses fled.* (Roman numeral: **lxxx** or **LXXX** eleven) ■ (**eighties**) the numbers from 80 to 89, esp. the years of a century or of a person's life: *his grandmother was in her eighties.* ■ eighty years old: *he was over eighty at the time.*

■ eighty miles an hour: *roaring down the highway doing eighty.*
– DERIVATIVES **eight·i·eth** /ˈātēiTH/ **ordinal number**, **eight·y·fold** /ˈātē,fōld/ **adj. & adv.**
– ORIGIN Old English *hunde(a)htatig*, from *hund* (of uncertain origin) + *e(a)hta* 'eight' + *-tig* (see **-TY²**); the first element was lost early in the Middle English period.

eigh·ty-six /,ātē ˈsiks/ (also **86**) ▶ **v.** [with obj.] informal **1** eject or bar (someone) from a restaurant, bar, etc.: *they were accused of cheating, and eighty-sixed from their favorite casino.*
2 reject, discard, or cancel: *the passwords will be 86ed by next October.*
– ORIGIN 1930s (as a noun, used in restaurants and bars to indicate that a menu item is unavailable or that a customer is not to be served): perhaps rhyming slang for **NIX¹**.

Eijk·man /ˈīkmən/, Christiaan (1858–1930), Dutch physician. His work resulted in a simple cure for beriberi and led to the discovery of the vitamin thiamine. Nobel Prize for Physiology or Medicine (1929), shared with Frederick G. Hopkins.

Ei·lat /āˈlät/ (also **Elat**) the southernmost town in Israel, a port and resort at the head of the Gulf of Aqaba; pop. 46,600 (est. 2008). Founded in 1949 near the ruins of biblical Elath, it is Israel's only outlet to the Red Sea.

Eind·ho·ven /ˈīnt,hōvən, ˈānt-/ a city in the southern Netherlands; pop. 210,333 (2008).

Ein·fühl·ung /ˈīnfo͞o,ləNG/ ▶ **n.** empathy.
– ORIGIN German, from *ein-* 'into' + *Fühlung* 'feeling.'

ein·korn /ˈīn,kôrn/ ▶ **n.** an old kind of Mediterranean wheat with small bearded ears and spikelets that each contain one slender grain, used as fodder in prehistoric times but now rarely grown. Compare with **EMMER**, **SPELT²**. ● *Triticum monococcum*, family Gramineae.
– ORIGIN early 20th cent.: from German, from *ein* 'one' + *Korn* 'seed.'

Ein·stein /ˈīn,stīn/, Albert (1879–1955), US theoretical physicist; born in Germany; founder of the special and general theories of relativity. Often regarded as the greatest scientist of the 20th century, he was influential in the decision to build an atomic bomb. After World War II, however, he spoke out against nuclear weapons. ■ (as noun **an Einstein**) a genius.
– DERIVATIVES **Ein·stein·i·an** /īnˈstīnēən/ **adj.**

Albert Einstein

ein·stein·i·um /īnˈstīnēəm/ ▶ **n.** the chemical element of atomic number 99, a radioactive metal of the actinide series. Einsteinium does not occur naturally and was discovered in 1953 in debris from the first hydrogen bomb explosion. (Symbol: **Es**)
– ORIGIN 1950s: from the name of Albert **EINSTEIN** + **-IUM**.

Eint·ho·ven /ˈīnt,hōvən/, Willem (1860–1927), Dutch physiologist. He devised the first electrocardiograph, a device that records specific muscular contractions in the heart.

Ei·re /ˈerə/ the Gaelic name for Ireland; the official name (1937–49) of the Republic of Ireland.

Ei·rene /īˈrēnē/ Greek Mythology the goddess of peace. Roman equivalent **PAX**.

ei·ren·ic /īˈrenik, -ˈrē-/ ▶ **adj.** variant spelling of **IRENIC**.

Ei·sen·how·er /ˈīzən,hou-ər/, Dwight David (1890–1969), US general and 34th president of the US 1953–61; nicknamed **Ike**. A Kansas Republican, he was one of the most celebrated US military leaders before entering politics. In World War II, he was Supreme Commander of Allied Expeditionary Forces in western Europe 1943–45. As president, he adopted a hard line toward communism in both his domestic and foreign policy.

Dwight D. Eisenhower

Ei·sen·staedt /ˈīzən,SHtat, -,SHtet, -,stat/, Alfred (1898–1995), US photojournalist; born in Dirschau, Germany (now part of Poland). He was one of the original photographers for *Life* magazine 1932–72.

Ei·sen·stein /ˈīzən,SHtīn/, Sergei (Mikhailovich) (1898–1948), Russian movie director, born in Latvia. He is noted for *The Battleship Potemkin* (1925), a commemoration of the Russian Revolution of 1905 that is celebrated for its pioneering use of montage.

eis·tedd·fod /īˈsteT͟H,väd/ ▶ **n.** (pl. **eisteddfods** or **eisteddfodau** /-ˈvädī/) a competitive festival of music and poetry in Wales, in particular the annual National Eisteddfod.
– DERIVATIVES **eis·tedd·fod·ic** /,īsteT͟Hˈvädik/ **adj.**
– ORIGIN Welsh, literally 'session,' from *eistedd* 'sit.'

Eis·wein /ˈīs,vīn/ ▶ **n.** (pl. **Eisweine** /-,vīnə/ or **Eisweins**) wine made from ripe grapes picked while covered with frost.
– ORIGIN from German, from *Eis* 'ice' + *Wein* 'wine.'

ei·ther /ˈēT͟Hər, ˈīT͟Hər/ ▶ **conj. & adv. 1** used before the first of two (or occasionally more) alternatives that are being specified (the other being introduced by "or"): *either I'll accompany you to your room, or I'll wait here* | *available in either black or white.*
2 [adv., with negative] used to indicate a similarity or link with a statement just made: *you don't like him, do you? I don't, either* | *it won't do any harm, but won't really help, either.* ■ for that matter; moreover (used to add information): *I was too tired to go. And I couldn't have paid my way, either.*
▶ **determiner & pron.** one or the other of two people or things: [as determiner] *there were no children of either marriage* | [as pronoun] *they have a mortgage that will be repaid if either of them dies.* ■ [determiner] each of two: *the road was straight with fields of grass on either side.*
– PHRASES **either way** whichever of two given alternatives is the case: *I'm not sure whether he is trying to be clever or controversial, but either way, such writing smacks of racism.*
– ORIGIN Old English *ǣgther*, contracted form of *ǣg(e)hwæther*, of Germanic origin; ultimately related to **AYE¹** and **WHETHER**.

> **USAGE** In good English writing style, it is important that **either** and **or** are correctly placed so that the structures following each word balance and mirror each other. Thus, it is correct to say ***either** I'll accompany you, **or** I'll wait here*. The two expressed choices are parallel, as each includes the subject and its verb phrase: *I'll accompany you; I'll wait here*. It would be incorrect to say ***either** I'll accompany you **or** John* because the first choice includes the subject and its verb phrase, but the second choice is just an object: *I'll accompany you; John*. A corrected version could be *I'll accompany **either** you **or** John* (now the choices are parallel, as each is just the object: *you; John*). See also usage at **NEITHER**.

ei·ther/or /ˈēT͟Hər/ˈôr, ˈīT͟Hər/ˈôr/ (also **either-or**) ▶ **n.** an unavoidable choice between two alternatives: *you can give him an ultimatum—an either/or.*

e·jac·u·late ▶ **v.** /iˈjakyə,lāt/ **1** [no obj.] (of a man or male animal) eject semen from the body at the moment of sexual climax.
2 dated [with direct speech] say something quickly and suddenly: *"Indeed?" ejaculated the stranger.*
▶ **n.** /-,lit/ semen that has been ejected from the body.
– DERIVATIVES **e·jac·u·la·tor n.**, **e·jac·u·la·to·ry** /-lə,tôrē/ **adj.**
– ORIGIN late 16th cent.: from Latin *ejaculat-* 'darted out,' from the verb *ejaculari*, from *e-* (variant of *ex-*) 'out' + *jaculari* 'to dart' (from *jaculum* 'dart, javelin,' from *jacere* 'to throw').

e·jac·u·la·tion /i,jakyəˈlāSHən/ ▶ **n. 1** the action of ejecting semen from the body.
2 dated something said quickly and suddenly.

e·ject /iˈjekt/ ▶ **v.** [with obj.] force or throw (something) out, typically in a violent or sudden way: *many types of rock are ejected from volcanoes as solid, fragmentary material.* ■ cause (something) to drop out or be removed, usually mechanically: *he ejected the spent cartridge.* ■ [no obj.] (of a pilot) escape from an aircraft by being explosively propelled out of it: *he flew to open sea, put the plane in a nosedive, and ejected.* ■ compel (someone) to leave a place: *angry supporters were forcibly **ejected from** the court.* ■ dismiss (someone), esp. from political office: *he was **ejected from** office in July.* ■ emit; give off: *plants utilize carbon dioxide in the atmosphere that animals eject* | (as adj. **ejected**) *ejected electrons.* ■ dispossess (a tenant) by legal process.
– ORIGIN late Middle English: from Latin *eject-* 'thrown out,' from the verb *eicere*, from *e-* (variant of *ex-*) 'out' + *jacere* 'to throw.'

e·jec·ta /iˈjektə/ ▶ **plural n.** [often treated as sing.] material that is forced or thrown out, esp. as a result of volcanic eruption, meteoritic impact, or stellar explosion.
– ORIGIN late 19th cent.: from Latin, 'things thrown out,' neuter plural of *ejectus* 'thrown out,' from *eicere* (see **EJECT**).

e·jec·tion /iˈjekSHən/ ▶ **n. 1** the action of forcing or throwing something out; emission: *an explosive ejection of ash.*
2 the action of forcing someone to leave a place or position; expulsion: *the forcible ejection of a table of rowdy drunks.*

e·jec·tion seat /iˈjekSHən/ ▶ **n.** a device that causes the ejection of a pilot from an aircraft, used in an emergency.

e·jec·tive /iˈjektiv/ Phonetics ▶ **adj.** denoting a type of consonant in some languages, e.g., Hausa, produced by sudden release of pressure from the glottis.
▶ **n.** an ejective consonant.

e·ject·ment /iˈjektmənt/ ▶ **n.** Law the action or process of evicting a tenant from property: *the landlord shall serve a **writ in ejectment**.* ■ the action or process in which a person evicted from property seeks to recover possession and damages.

e·jec·tor /iˈjektər/ ▶ **n.** a device that causes something to be removed or to drop out: *a built-in drill ejector.*

e·ji·do /eˈhēdō/ ▶ **n.** (pl. **ejidos**) (in Mexico) a piece of land farmed communally under a system supported by the state.
– ORIGIN Mexican Spanish, from Spanish, denoting common land on the road leading out of the village.

Eka·te·rin·burg /yi,kətyərinˈbo͝ork, iˈkatərin,bərg/ variant spelling of **YEKATERINBURG**.

E·ka·te·ri·no·dar variant spelling of **YEKATERINODAR**.

E·ka·te·ri·no·slav variant spelling of **YEKATERINOSLAV**.

eke¹ /ēk/ ▶ **v.** [with obj.] (**eke something out**) manage to support oneself or make a living with difficulty: *they eked out their livelihoods from the soil.* ■ make an amount or supply of something last longer by using or consuming it frugally: *the remains of yesterday's stew could be eked out to make another meal.* ■ obtain or create, but just barely: *Tennessee eked out a 74–73 overtime victory.*
– ORIGIN Old English *ēacian*, *ēcan* (in the sense 'increase'), of Germanic origin; related to Old Norse *auka*.

eke² ▶ **adv.** archaic term for **ALSO**.
– ORIGIN Old English, of Germanic origin.

EKG ▶ **abbr.** ■ electrocardiogram. ■ electrocardiograph. ■ electrocardiography.

el /el/ ▶ **n.** (**the El**) an elevated railroad or section of railroad, esp. that in Chicago. ■ a train running on such a railroad.

el. ▶ **abbr.** elevation.

-el ▶ **suffix** variant spelling of **-LE²**.

el-Aa·iún /,elīˈo͞on/ Arabic name of **LAAYOUNE**.

e·lab·o·rate ▶ **adj.** /iˈlab(ə)rit/ involving many carefully arranged parts or details; detailed and complicated in design and planning: *elaborate security precautions* | *elaborate wrought-iron gates.* ■ (of an action) lengthy and exaggerated: *he made an elaborate pretense of yawning.*
▶ **v.** /iˈlabə,rāt/ **1** [with obj.] develop or present (a theory, policy, or system) in detail: *the key idea of the book is expressed in the title and elaborated in*

the text. ■ [no obj.] add more detail concerning what has already been said: *he would not* **elaborate on** *his news.*
2 [with obj.] Biology (of a natural agency) produce (a substance) from its elements or simpler constituents.
– DERIVATIVES **e·lab·o·rate·ly** adv., **e·lab·o·rate·ness** n., **e·lab·o·ra·tion** /iˌlabəˈrāSHən/ n., **e·lab·o·ra·tive** /-ˌrātiv/ adj., **e·lab·o·ra·tor** /-tər/ n.
– ORIGIN late 16th cent. (in the sense 'produced by effort of labor,' also sense 2 of the verb of the verb): from Latin *elaborat-* 'worked out,' from the verb *elaborare*, from *e-* (variant of *ex-*) 'out' + *labor* 'work.'

El·a·gab·a·lus /ˌeləˈgabələs/ variant spelling of **Heliogabalus**.

e

El A·la·mein, Battle of /el ˌäləˈmān, ˌaləˈmān/ a battle of World War II fought in 1942 at El Alamein in Egypt, 60 miles (90 km) west of Alexandria. The German Afrika Korps under Rommel was halted in its advance toward the Nile by the British 8th Army under Montgomery, giving the British a decisive victory.

E·lam /ˈēləm/ an ancient state in southwestern Iran, established in the 4th millennium BC. Susa was one of its chief cities.

E·lam·ite /ˈēləˌmīt/ ▶ n. **1** a native or inhabitant of ancient Elam.
2 the language of ancient Elam, of unknown affinity and spoken from the 3rd millennium to the 4th century BC.
▶ adj. of or relating to the ancient Elamites or their language.

e·lan /āˈlän, āˈlan/ ▶ n. energy, style, and enthusiasm: *a rousing march, played with great elan.*
– ORIGIN mid 19th cent.: from French *élan*, from *élancer* 'to dart,' from *é-* 'out' + *lancer* 'to throw.'

e·land /ˈēlənd/ ▶ n. a spiral-horned African antelope that lives in open woodland and grassland. It is the largest of the antelopes. ● Genus *Taurotragus*, family Bovidae: the **giant eland** (*T. derbianus*) and the **common eland** (*T. oryx*).
– ORIGIN late 18th cent.: via Afrikaans from Dutch,'elk,' from obsolete German *Elend*, from Lithuanian *élnis*.

e·lapse /iˈlaps/ ▶ v. [no obj.] (of time) pass or go by: *weeks elapsed before anyone was charged with the attack* | (as adj. **elapsed**) *a display tells you which track is playing and its elapsed time.*
– ORIGIN late 16th cent. (in the sense 'slip away'): from Latin *elaps-* 'slipped away,' from the verb *elabi*, from *e-* (variant of *ex-*) 'out, away' + *labi* 'to glide, slip.'

e·las·i·pod /əˈlasəˌpäd/ ▶ n. Zoology an aberrant deep-water sea cucumber that lacks a respiratory tree. Most live on the seabed and have leglike appendages, while some swim by means of webbed papillae. ● Order Elasipodida, class Holothuroidea.
– ORIGIN late 19th cent.: from modern Latin *Elasipoda*, from Greek *elasmos* 'beaten metal' + *pous, pod-* 'foot.'

e·las·mo·branch /əˈlazməˌbraNGk/ ▶ n. Zoology a cartilaginous fish of a group that comprises the sharks, rays, and skates. Compare with **selachian**. ● Subclass Elasmobranchii, class Chondrichthyes.
– ORIGIN late 19th cent.: from modern Latin *Elasmobranchii* (plural), from Greek *elasmos* 'beaten metal' + *brankhia* 'gills.'

e·las·mo·saur /əˈlazməˌsôr/ (also **elasmosaurus** /əˌlazməˈsôrəs/) ▶ n. a Cretaceous plesiosaur with a long neck shaped like that of a swan. ● Family Elasmosauridae, infraorder Plesiosauria: several genera, including *Elasmosaurus*.
– DERIVATIVES **e·las·mo·sau·ri·an** adj.
– ORIGIN late 19th cent.: from modern Latin *Elasmosaurus*, from Greek *elasmos* 'beaten metal' + *sauros* 'lizard.'

e·las·tane /əˈlastān/ ▶ n. Brit. an elastic polyurethane material, used esp. for hosiery, underwear, and other close-fitting clothing.
– ORIGIN 1970s: from **elastic** + **-ane**[2].

e·las·tase /iˈlastāz/ ▶ n. Biochemistry a pancreatic enzyme that digests elastin.
– ORIGIN 1940s: from **elastic** + **-ase**.

e·las·tic /iˈlastik/ ▶ adj. (of an object or material) able to resume its normal shape spontaneously after contraction, dilatation, or distortion. ■ able to encompass variety and change; flexible and adaptable: *the definition of nationality is elastic in this cosmopolitan country.* ■ Economics (of demand or supply) sensitive to changes in price or income: *the labor supply is very elastic.* ■ Physics (of a collision) involving no decrease of kinetic energy.
▶ n. cord, tape, or fabric, typically woven with strips of rubber, that returns to its original length or shape after being stretched.
– DERIVATIVES **e·las·ti·cal·ly** /-(ə)lē/ adv., **e·las·ti·cize** /iˈlastəˌsīz/ v.
– ORIGIN mid 17th cent. (originally describing a gas in the sense 'expanding spontaneously to fill the available space'): from modern Latin *elasticus*, from Greek *elastikos* 'propulsive,' from *elaunein* 'to drive.'

e·las·ti·cat·ed /iˈlastəˌkātid/ ▶ adj. chiefly Brit. (of a garment or material) made elastic by the insertion of rubber thread or tape: *ski pants with elasticated waist.*

e·las·tic band ▶ n. a rubber band.

e·las·tic fi·ber ▶ n. Anatomy a yellowish fiber composed chiefly of elastin and occurring in networks or sheets that give elasticity to tissues in the body.

e·las·tic·i·ty /iˌlaˈstisitē, ēˌla-/ ▶ n. **1** the ability of an object or material to resume its normal shape after being stretched or compressed; stretchiness: *aging can decrease the elasticity of your skin.*
2 the ability of something to change and adapt; adaptability.
3 Economics the degree to which a demand or supply is sensitive to changes in price or income.

e·las·tic lim·it ▶ n. Physics the maximum extent to which a solid may be stretched without permanent alteration of size or shape.

e·las·tic mod·u·lus ▶ n. Physics the ratio of the force exerted upon a substance or body to the resultant deformation.

e·las·tin /iˈlastin/ ▶ n. Biochemistry an elastic, fibrous glycoprotein found in connective tissue.
– ORIGIN late 19th cent.: from **elastic** + **-in**[1].

e·las·to·mer /iˈlastəmər/ ▶ n. a natural or synthetic polymer having elastic properties, e.g., rubber.
– DERIVATIVES **e·las·to·mer·ic** /iˌlastəˈmerik/ adj.
– ORIGIN 1930s: from **elastic** + **-mer**.

E·lat variant spelling of **Eilat**.

e·late /iˈlāt/ ▶ v. [with obj.] (usu. as adj. **elated**) make (someone) ecstatically happy: *I felt elated at beating Dennis.*
▶ adj. archaic in high spirits; exultant or proud: *the ladies returned with elate and animated faces.*
– DERIVATIVES **e·lat·ed·ly** adv., **e·lat·ed·ness** n.
– ORIGIN late Middle English (as an adjective): from Latin *elat-* 'raised,' from the verb *efferre*, from *ex-* 'out, from' + *ferre* 'to bear.' The verb dates from the late 16th cent.

e·la·tion /iˈlāSHən/ ▶ n. great happiness and exhilaration: *Richard's* **elation at** *regaining his health was short-lived.*
– ORIGIN late Middle English: from Old French *elacion*, from Latin *elat-* 'raised,' from the verb *efferre* (see **elate**).

E lay·er ▶ n. a layer of the ionosphere able to reflect medium-frequency radio waves.
– ORIGIN 1930s: arbitrary use of the letter *E*, + **layer**.

Ela·zig /ˌeläˈzi/ a commercial city in east central Turkey, east of the upper Euphrates River; pop. 319,400 (est. 2007).

El·ba /ˈelbə/ a small island off the western coast of Italy, known as the place of Napoleon's first exile 1814–15.

El·be /elb(ə)/ a river in central Europe that flows for 720 miles (1,159 km) from the Czech Republic through the German cities of Dresden, Magdeburg, and Hamburg to the North Sea.

El·bert, Mount /ˈelbərt/ a mountain in Colorado, east of Aspen. Rising to 14,431 feet (4,399 m), it is the highest peak in the Rocky Mountains.

el·bow /ˈelˌbō/ ▶ n. the joint between the forearm and the upper arm: *she propped herself up on one elbow.* ■ the part of the sleeve of a garment covering the elbow. ■ a thing resembling an elbow, in particular a piece of piping bent through an angle.
▶ v. [with obj.] **1** strike (someone) with one's elbow: *one player had elbowed another in the face.* ■ [no obj.] move by pushing past people with one's elbows: *people* **elbowed past** *each other to the door* | *furiously, he* **elbowed his way** *through the crowd.*
2 treat (a person or idea) dismissively: *his new TV talk show was elbowed aside in the ratings war.*
– PHRASES **at one's elbow** close at hand; nearby. **elbow-to-elbow** very close together. **up to one's elbows in** informal with one's hands plunged in (something): *I was up to my elbows in the cheese-potato mixture.* ■ deeply involved in (a task or undertaking).
– ORIGIN Old English *elboga, elnboga*, of Germanic origin; related to Dutch *elleboog* and German *Ellenbogen* (see also **ell**[1], **bow**[1]).

el·bow grease ▶ n. informal hard physical work, esp. vigorous polishing or cleaning: *you should be able to get the rust off with a wire brush and elbow grease.*

el·bow room ▶ n. informal adequate space to move or work in: *the car has elbow room for four adults* | figurative *Quebec wants a little more elbow room within the federation.*

El·brus /elˈbro͞os, ˈelˌbro͞os/ a peak in the Caucasus Mountains, on the border between Russia and Georgia. Rising to 18,481 feet (5,642 m), it is the highest mountain in Europe.

El·burz Moun·tains /elˈbo͝orz/ a mountain range in northwestern Iran, close to the southern shore of the Caspian Sea. Damavand is the highest peak, rising to 18,386 feet (5,604 m).

El Ca·jon /ˌel kəˈhōn/ a city in southwestern California, east of San Diego; pop. 92,718 (est. 2008).

El Cap·i·tan /el ˌkapiˈtan/ a peak in Yosemite National Park in California, known for its sheer walls that rise over 3,000 feet (1,000 m) above its base.

El Cen·tro /el ˈsentrō/ a city in southern California, the commercial center of the Imperial Valley; pop. 40,083 (est. 2008).

El·che /ˈelCHā/ a town in southeastern Spain, in the province of Alicante; pop. 228,348 (2008).

el cheap·o /el ˈCHēpō/ ▶ adj. & n. another way of saying **cheapo**.
– ORIGIN 1960s: from **cheap**, on the pattern of Spanish phrases such as *El Dorado* and *El Greco*.

El Cid /el ˈsid/ see **Cid, El**.

eld /eld/ ▶ n. literary old age. ■ former times; the past.
– ORIGIN Old English *ieldu, eldu*, of Germanic origin; related to **elder**[1] and **old**.

eld·er[1] /ˈeldər/ ▶ adj. (of one or more out of a group of related or otherwise associated people) of a greater age: *my elder daughter* | *the elder of the two sons.* ■ (**the Elder**) used to distinguish between related famous people with the same name: *Pliny the Elder.*
▶ n. (usu. **elders**) a person of greater age than someone specified: *schoolchildren were no less fascinated than their elders* | *take a bit of advice from* **your elders and betters**. ■ a person of advanced age. ■ (often **elders**) a leader or senior figure in a tribe or other group: *a council of village elders.* ■ an official in the early Christian Church, or of various Protestant Churches and sects.
– DERIVATIVES **el·der·ship** /-ˌSHip/ n.
– ORIGIN Old English *ieldra, eldra*, of Germanic origin; related to German *älter*, also to **eld** and **old**.

eld·er[2] ▶ n. (also **elderberry**) a small tree or shrub with pithy stems, typically having white flowers and bluish-black or red berries. ● Genus *Sambucus*, family Caprifoliaceae: numerous species, in particular the common North American *S. canadensis* and the Eurasian *S. nigra*.
– ORIGIN Old English *ellærn*; related to Middle Low German *ellern, elderne*.

eld·er·ber·ry /ˈeldərˌberē/ ▶ n. (pl. **elderberries**) the bluish-black or red berry of the elder, used esp. for making jelly or wine. ■ an elder tree or shrub.

el·der·care /ˈeldərˌke(ə)r/ ▶ n. care of people who are elderly or infirm, provided by residential institutions, by paid daily help in the home, or by family members.

el·der·flow·er /ˈeldərˌflou(-ə)r/ ▶ n. the flower of the elder, used to make wines, cordials, and other drinks.

eld·er hand ▶ n. (in card games for two players, e.g., piquet) the player who is the first to receive a complete hand, i.e., the player dealt to.

eld·er·ly /ˈeldərlē/ ▶ adj. (of a person) old or aging: *she was elderly and silver-haired* | (as plural noun **the elderly**) *teams of volunteers to carry out home repairs for the elderly.* ■ (of a machine or similar object) showing signs of age: *a couple of elderly cars.*
– DERIVATIVES **eld·er·li·ness** /-lēnis/ n.

eld·er states·man ▶ n. a person who is experienced and well-respected, esp. a politician.

eld·est /ˈeldəst/ ▶ adj. (of one out of a group of related or otherwise associated people) of the greatest age; oldest: *Swift left the company to his eldest son, Charles* | *he was the eldest of the three.*
– ORIGIN Old English *ieldest, eldest*, of Germanic origin; related to German *ältest*, also to **eld** and **old**.

eld·est hand ▶ n. (in card games for three or more players) the player who is the first to receive a complete hand, usually the player immediately to the left of the dealer.

El Do·ra·do /ˌel dəˈrädō/ the name of a fictitious country or city abounding in gold, formerly believed to exist somewhere in the region of the Orinoco and Amazon rivers. ■ (as noun **an El Dorado** or **eldorado**) (pl. **El Dorados**) a place of great abundance.
– ORIGIN Spanish, literally 'the gilded one.'

el·dritch /ˈeldriCH/ ▶ adj. weird and sinister or ghostly: *an eldritch screech.*
– ORIGIN early 16th cent. (originally Scots): perhaps related to **elf**.

El·ea·nor of Aq·ui·taine /ˈelənər əv ˈakwəˌtān/ (*c.*1122–1204), daughter of the duke of Aquitaine; queen of France 1137–52 and of England 1154–89. She was married to Louis VII of France from 1137; their marriage was annulled in 1152, and she married the future Henry II of England in 1154. She was the mother of Richard I and John I.

El·e·at·ic /ˌelēˈatik/ ▶ **adj.** of or relating to Elea, an ancient Greek city in southwestern Italy, or the school of philosophers that flourished there in about the 5th century BC, including Xenophanes, Parmenides, and Zeno.
▶ **n.** an Eleatic philosopher.
– ORIGIN late 17th cent.: from Latin *Eleaticus*, from *Elea*.

elec. ▶ **abbr.** ■ electric, electrical. ■ electrician. ■ electricity.

el·e·cam·pane /ˌelikamˈpān/ ▶ **n.** a plant that has yellow daisylike flowers with long slender petals and bitter aromatic roots that are used in herbal medicine, native to central Asia. ● *Inula helenium*, family Compositae.
– ORIGIN late Middle English: from medieval Latin *enula* (from Greek *helenion* 'elecampane') + *campana* probably meaning 'of the fields' (from *campus* 'field').

e·lect /iˈlekt/ ▶ **v.** [with obj.] choose (someone) to hold public office or some other position by voting: *the members who were **elected to** the committee* | [with obj. and infinitive] *they elected him leader.* ■ opt for or choose to do something: *freshman year you could elect Industrial Arts* | [no obj.] *more people elected to work at home.* ■ Christian Theology (of God) choose (someone) in preference to others for salvation.
▶ **adj.** (usu. as plural noun **the elect**) (of a person) chosen or singled out: *one of the century's elect.* ■ [postpositive in combination] elected to or chosen for a position but not yet in office: *the president-elect.* ■ Christian Theology chosen by God for salvation.
– DERIVATIVES **e·lect·a·ble** adj., **e·lect·a·bil·i·ty** n.
– ORIGIN late Middle English: from Latin *elect-* 'picked out,' from the verb *eligere*, from *e-* (variant of *ex-*) 'out' + *legere* 'to pick.'

e·lec·tion /iˈleksHən/ ▶ **n.** a formal and organized process of electing or being elected, esp. of members of a political body: *the 1860 presidential election* | [as modifier] *an election year* | *the first of his family to **run for election.*** ■ the act or an instance of electing: *his election to the House of Representatives.*
– ORIGIN Middle English: via Old French from Latin *electio(n-)*, from *eligere* 'pick out' (see **ELECT**).

e·lec·tion·eer /iˌleksHəˈni(ə)r/ ▶ **v.** [no obj.] (usu. as noun **electioneering**) (of a politician or political campaigner) take part actively and energetically in the activities of an election campaign: *the election will not be lost or won as the result of a few weeks of electioneering.*
▶ **n.** a campaigning politician during an election.

e·lec·tive /iˈlektiv/ ▶ **adj. 1** related to or working by means of election: *an elective democracy.* ■ (of a person or office) appointed or filled by election: *he had never held elective office* | *the National Assembly, with 125 elective members.* ■ (of a body or position) possessing or giving the power to elect.
2 (of a course of study) chosen by the student rather than compulsory. ■ (of surgical or medical treatment) chosen by the patient rather than urgently necessary.
▶ **n.** an optional course of study: *up to half the credits in many public high schools are electives.*
– DERIVATIVES **e·lec·tive·ly** adv.
– ORIGIN late Middle English: from Old French *electif, -ive*, from late Latin *electivus*, from *elect-* 'picked out,' from the verb *eligere* (see **ELECT**).

e·lec·tive mut·ism ▶ **n.** see **MUTISM**.

e·lec·tor /iˈlektər, -ˌtôr/ ▶ **n. 1** a person who has the right to vote in an election. ■ (in the US) a member of the electoral college.
2 [usu. as title] historical a German prince entitled to take part in the election of the Holy Roman Emperor: *the Elector of Brandenburg.*
– DERIVATIVES **e·lec·tor·ship** /-ˌSHip/ n.

e·lec·tor·al /iˈlektərəl/ ▶ **adj.** of or relating to elections or electors: *electoral reform.*
– DERIVATIVES **e·lec·tor·al·ly** adv.

e·lec·tor·al col·lege ▶ **n.** (also **Electoral College**) (in the US) a body of people representing the states of the US, who formally cast votes for the election of the president and vice president. ■ a body of electors chosen or appointed by a larger group.

e·lec·tor·ate /iˈlektərət/ ▶ **n. 1** [treated as sing. or pl.] all the people in a country or area who are entitled to vote in an election.
2 historical the office or territories of a German elector.

E·lec·tra /iˈlektrə/ Greek Mythology the daughter of Agamemnon and Clytemnestra. She persuaded her brother Orestes to kill Clytemnestra and Aegisthus (their mother's lover) in revenge for the murder of Agamemnon.

E·lec·tra com·plex ▶ **n.** Psychoanalysis old-fashioned term for the Oedipus complex as manifested in young girls.
– ORIGIN early 20th cent.: named after **ELECTRA**.

e·lec·tress /iˈlektris/ ▶ **n.** [usu. as title] historical the wife of a German elector.

e·lec·tret /iˈlektrit/ ▶ **n.** Physics a permanently polarized piece of dielectric material, analogous to a permanent magnet.
– ORIGIN late 19th cent.: blend of **ELECTRICITY** and **MAGNET**.

e·lec·tric /iˈlektrik/ ▶ **adj. 1** of, worked by, charged with, or producing electricity: *an electric stove* | *an electric current.* ■ (of a musical instrument) amplified through a loudspeaker: *electric bass guitar.* ■ (of a color) brilliant and vivid: *images shot through with jagged streaks of electric blue.*
2 having or producing a sudden sense of thrilling excitement: *the atmosphere was electric.*
▶ **n.** an electric train or other vehicle.
– ORIGIN mid 17th cent.: from modern Latin *electricus*, from Latin *electrum* 'amber,' from Greek *ēlektron* (because rubbing amber causes electrostatic phenomena).

e·lec·tri·cal /iˈlektrikəl/ ▶ **adj.** operating by or producing electricity: *an electrical appliance.* ■ concerned with electricity: *an electrical engineer.*
– DERIVATIVES **e·lec·tri·cal·ly** /-(ə)lē/ **adv.**

e·lec·tri·cal storm ▶ **n.** a thunderstorm or other violent disturbance of the electrical condition of the atmosphere.

e·lec·tric arc ▶ **n.** see **ARC**.

e·lec·tric-arc fur·nace ▶ **n.** another term for **ARC FURNACE**.

e·lec·tric blan·ket ▶ **n.** a blanket that can be heated electrically by an internal element.

e·lec·tric chair ▶ **n.** a chair in which criminals sentenced to death are executed by electrocution.

e·lec·tric eel ▶ **n.** an eellike freshwater fish of South America, using pulses of electricity to kill prey, to assist in navigation, and for defense. ● *Electrophorus electricus*, the only member of the family Electrophoridae.

e·lec·tric eye ▶ **n.** informal a photoelectric cell operating a relay when the beam of light illuminating it is obscured.

e·lec·tric fence ▶ **n.** a fence through which an electric current can be passed, giving an electric shock to any person or animal touching it.

e·lec·tric field ▶ **n.** Physics a region around a charged particle or object within which a force would be exerted on other charged particles or objects.

e·lec·tric gui·tar ▶ **n.** a guitar with a built-in pickup or pickups that convert sound vibrations into electrical signals for amplification.

e·lec·tri·cian /ilekˈtrisHən, ˌēlek-/ ▶ **n.** a person who installs and maintains electrical equipment.

e·lec·tric in·ten·si·ty ▶ **n.** the strength of an electric field at any point, equal to the force per unit charge experienced by a small charge placed at that point.

e·lec·tric·i·ty /ilekˈtrisitē, ˌēlek-/ ▶ **n. 1** a form of energy resulting from the existence of charged particles (such as electrons or protons), either statically as an accumulation of charge or dynamically as a current. ■ the supply of electric current to a house or other building for heating, lighting, or powering appliances: *the electricity was back on.*
2 a state or feeling of thrilling excitement: *the atmosphere was charged with a dangerous sexual electricity.*

e·lec·tric mo·ment ▶ **n.** Physics the product of the distance separating the charges of a dipole and the magnitude of either charge.

e·lec·tric or·gan ▶ **n. 1** an organ (keyboard) in which the sound is produced electrically rather than by pipes.
2 Zoology an organ in certain fishes that is used to produce an electrical discharge for stunning prey, for sensing the surroundings, or as a defense.

e·lec·tric ray ▶ **n.** a sluggish bottom-dwelling marine ray that typically lives in shallow water and can produce an electric shock for the capture of prey and for defense. Also called **TORPEDO RAY** (see **TORPEDO**). ● Family Torpedinidae: several genera, in particular *Torpedo*, and many species.

e·lec·tric ra·zor (also **electric shaver**) ▶ **n.** an electrical device for shaving, with oscillating or rotating blades behind a metal guard.

e·lec·tric shock ▶ **n.** a sudden discharge of electricity through a part of the body.

e·lec·tri·fy /iˈlektrəˌfī/ ▶ **v.** (**electrifies, electrifying, electrified**) [with obj.] **1** charge with electricity; pass an electric current through: (as adj. **electrified**) *an electrified fence.* ■ convert (a machine or system, esp. a railroad line) to the use of electrical power.
2 (often as adj. **electrifying**) impress greatly; thrill: *an electrifying performance.*
– DERIVATIVES **e·lec·tri·fi·ca·tion** /iˌlektrəfiˈkāsHən/ n., **e·lec·tri·fi·er** /-ˌfī(ə)r/ n.
– ORIGIN mid 18th cent.: from **ELECTRIC** + **-FY**.

e·lec·tro /iˈlektrō/ ▶ **n.** (pl. **electros**) **1** short for **ELECTROTYPE** or **ELECTROPLATE**.
2 a style of dance music with a fast beat and synthesized backing track.

electro- ▶ **comb. form 1** relating to or caused by electricity; involving electricity and ...: *electroconvulsive* | *electromagnetism.*
2 relating to music characterized by the use of synthesizers or electronically created sounds: *electropop.*

e·lec·tro·a·cous·tic /iˌlektrōəˈko͞ostik/ ▶ **adj.** involving the direct conversion of electrical into acoustic energy or vice versa. ■ (of a guitar) having both a pickup and a reverberating hollow body.
▶ **n.** an electroacoustic guitar.

e·lec·tro·ac·u·punc·ture (also **electroacupuncture**) ▶ **n.** acupuncture in which the needles used carry a mild electric current.

e·lec·tro·car·di·o·gram /iˌlektrōˈkärdēəˌgram/ (abbr.: **ECG** or **EKG**) ▶ **n.** Medicine a record or display of a person's heartbeat produced by electrocardiography.

e·lec·tro·car·di·o·graph /iˌlektrōˈkärdiəˌgraf/ (abbr.: **ECG** or **EKG**) ▶ **n.** a machine used for electrocardiography.

e·lec·tro·car·di·og·ra·phy /iˌlektrōˌkärdēˈägrəfē/ (abbr.: **ECG** or **EKG**) ▶ **n.** the measurement of electrical activity in the heart and the recording of such activity as a visual trace (on paper or on an oscilloscope screen), using electrodes placed on the skin of the limbs and chest.
– DERIVATIVES **e·lec·tro·car·di·o·graph·ic** /-ˌkärdiəˈgrafik/ **adj.**

e·lec·tro·cau·ter·y /iˌlektrōˈkôtərē/ ▶ **n.** cautery using a needle or other instrument that is electrically heated.

e·lec·tro·chem·is·try /iˌlektrōˈkemistrē/ ▶ **n.** the branch of chemistry that deals with the relations between electrical and chemical phenomena.
– DERIVATIVES **e·lec·tro·chem·i·cal** /-ˈkemikəl/ **adj.**, **e·lec·tro·chem·i·cal·ly** /-ˈkemik(ə)lē/ **adv.**, **e·lec·tro·chem·ist** **n.**

e·lec·tro·chrom·ism /iˌlektrōˈkrōˌmizəm/ ▶ **n.** Chemistry the property of certain dyes of changing color when placed in an electric field.
– DERIVATIVES **e·lec·tro·chro·mic** /-ˈkrōmik/ **adj.**

e·lec·tro·co·ag·u·la·tion /iˈlektrōkōˌagyəˈlāsHən/ ▶ **n.** the coagulation of blood or other tissues by the local application of an electric current to produce concentrated heat.

e·lec·tro·con·vul·sive /iˌlektrōkənˈvəlsiv/ ▶ **adj.** of or relating to the treatment of mental illness by the application of electric shocks to the brain.

e·lec·tro·cor·ti·co·gram /iˌlektrōˈkôrtikōˌgram/ ▶ **n.** Physiology a chart or record of the electrical activity of the brain made using electrodes in direct contact with it.

e·lec·tro·cute /iˈlektrəˌkyo͞ot/ ▶ **v.** [with obj.] injure or kill someone by electric shock: *a man was electrocuted when he switched on the Christmas tree lights.* ■ execute (a convicted criminal) by means of the electric chair.
– DERIVATIVES **e·lec·tro·cu·tion** /iˌlektrəˈkyo͞osHən/ **n.**
– ORIGIN late 19th cent.: from **ELECTRO-**, on the pattern of *execute*.

e·lec·tro·cyte /iˈlektrəˌsīt/ ▶ **n.** Zoology a modified muscle or nerve cell that generates electricity in the electric organ of certain fishes.

e·lec·trode /iˈlektrōd/ ▶ **n.** a conductor through which electricity enters or leaves an object, substance, or region.
– ORIGIN mid 19th cent.: from **ELECTRIC** + Greek *hodos* 'way,' on the pattern of *anode* and *cathode*.

e·lec·tro·der·mal /iˌlektrōˈdərməl/ ▶ **adj.** of or relating to measurement of the electrical conductivity of the skin, esp. as an indicator of someone's emotional responses.

e·lec·tro·di·al·y·sis /iˌlektrōdīˈaləsis/ ▶ **n.** Chemistry dialysis in which the movement of ions is aided by an electric field applied across the semipermeable membrane.

e·lec·tro·dy·nam·ics /iˌlektrōdīˈnamiks/ ▶ **plural n.** [usu. treated as sing.] the branch of mechanics concerned with the interaction of electric currents with magnetic fields or with other electric currents.
– DERIVATIVES **e·lec·tro·dy·nam·ic adj.**

e·lec·tro·dy·na·mom·e·ter /iˌlektrōˌdīnəˈmämitər/ ▶ **n.** an instrument that measures electric current by indicating the strength of repulsion or attraction between the magnetic fields of two sets of coils, one fixed and one movable.

e·lec·tro·en·ceph·a·lo·gram /iˌlektrōənˈsefələˌgram/ (abbr.: **EEG**) ▶ **n.** a test or record of brain activity produced by electroencephalography.

e·lec·tro·en·ceph·a·lo·graph /iˌlektrōənˈsefələˌgraf/ (abbr.: **EEG**) ▶ **n.** a machine used for electroencephalography.

e·lec·tro·en·ceph·a·log·ra·phy /iˌlektrōənˌsefəˈlägrəfē/ ▶ **n.** the measurement of electrical activity in different parts of the brain and the recording of such activity as a visual trace (on paper or on an oscilloscope screen).

e·lec·tro·fish /iˈlektrəˌfisʜ/ ▶ **v.** [with obj.] fish (a stretch of water) using electrocution or a weak electric field.

e·lec·tro·fu·sion /iˌlektrōˈfyo͞ozʜən/ ▶ **n.** fusion (in cells or other materials) that is induced by the application of electric current: *the shell and center are joined by electrofusion, with the reconstructed embryo retaining most of the mother's DNA.*

e·lec·tro·gen·ic /iˌlektrōˈjenik/ ▶ **adj.** Physiology producing a change in the electrical potential of a cell.

e·lec·tro·jet /iˈlektrəˌjet/ ▶ **n.** an intense electric current that occurs in a narrow belt in the lower ionosphere, esp. in the region of strong auroral displays.

e·lec·tro·ki·net·ic /iˌlektrōkəˈnetik/ ▶ **adj.** of or relating to the flow of electricity.

e·lec·tro·less /iˈlektrōlis/ ▶ **adj.** relating to or denoting nickel plating using chemical means, as opposed to electroplating.

e·lec·tro·lier /iˌlektrəˈlir/ ▶ **n.** a chandelier in which the lights are electrical.
– ORIGIN late 19th cent.: from **ELECTRO-**, on the pattern of *chandelier*.

e·lec·trol·o·gist /ilekˈträləjist/ ▶ **n.** a person trained to remove unwanted hair on the body or face or small blemishes on the skin by a method that involves the application of heat using an electric current.

e·lec·tro·lu·mi·nes·cence /iˌlektrōˌlo͞oməˈnesəns/ ▶ **n.** Chemistry luminescence produced electrically, esp. in a phosphor by the application of a voltage.
– DERIVATIVES **e·lec·tro·lu·mi·nes·cent adj.**

e·lec·trol·y·sis /ilekˈträləsis, ˌēlek-/ ▶ **n. 1** Chemistry chemical decomposition produced by passing an electric current through a liquid or solution containing ions.
2 the removal of hair roots or small blemishes on the skin by the application of heat using an electric current.
– DERIVATIVES **e·lec·tro·lyt·ic** /iˌlektrəˈlitik/ **adj.**, **e·lec·tro·lyt·i·cal** /iˌlektrəˈlitikəl/ **adj.**, **e·lec·tro·lyt·i·cal·ly** /iˌlektrəˈlitik(ə)lē/ **adv.**

e·lec·tro·lyte /iˈlektrəˌlīt/ ▶ **n.** a liquid or gel that contains ions and can be decomposed by electrolysis, e.g., that present in a battery. ■ (usu. **electrolytes**) Physiology the ionized or ionizable constituents of a living cell, blood, or other organic matter.
– ORIGIN mid 19th cent.: from **ELECTRO-** + Greek *lutos* 'released' (from *luein* 'loosen').

e·lec·tro·lyt·ic cell /iˌlektəˈlitik/ ▶ **n. 1** a cell in which electrolysis occurs, consisting of an electrolyte through which current from an external source is passed, by a system of electrodes, in order to produce an electrochemical reaction.
2 a cell consisting of an electrolyte, its container, and two electrodes, in which the electrochemical reaction between the electrodes and the electrolyte produces an electric current.

e·lec·tro·lyze /iˈlektrəˌlīz/ ▶ **v.** [with obj.] subject to or treat by electrolysis: *when you electrolyze water, it splits into hydrogen and oxygen.*
– DERIVATIVES **e·lec·tro·lyz·er n.**
– ORIGIN mid 19th cent.: from **ELECTROLYSIS**, on the pattern of *analyze*.

e·lec·tro·mag·net /iˈlektrōˌmagnit/ ▶ **n.** Physics a soft metal core made into a magnet by the passage of electric current through a coil surrounding it.

e·lec·tro·mag·net·ic /iˌlektrōmagˈnetik/ ▶ **adj.** of or relating to the interrelation of electric currents or fields and magnetic fields.
– DERIVATIVES **e·lec·tro·mag·net·i·cal·ly** /-(ə)lē/ **adv.**

e·lec·tro·mag·net·ic field ▶ **n.** Physics a field of force that consists of both electric and magnetic components, resulting from the motion of an electric charge and containing a definite amount of electromagnetic energy.

e·lec·tro·mag·net·ic pulse ▶ **n.** an intense pulse of electromagnetic radiation, esp. one generated by a nuclear explosion and occurring high above the earth's surface.

e·lec·tro·mag·net·ic ra·di·a·tion ▶ **n.** Physics a kind of radiation including visible light, radio waves, gamma rays, and X-rays, in which electric and magnetic fields vary simultaneously.

e·lec·tro·mag·net·ic spec·trum ▶ **n.** Physics the range of wavelengths or frequencies over which electromagnetic radiation extends.

e·lec·tro·mag·net·ic u·nits ▶ **plural n.** Physics a largely obsolete system of electrical units derived primarily from the magnetic properties of electric currents.

e·lec·tro·mag·net·ism /iˌlektrōˈmagnəˌtizəm/ ▶ **n.** the interaction of electric currents or fields and magnetic fields. ■ the branch of physics concerned with this.

e·lec·tro·me·chan·i·cal /iˌlektrōməˈkanikəl/ ▶ **adj.** of, relating to, or denoting a mechanical device that is electrically operated.

e·lec·trom·e·ter /ilekˈträmitər, ˌēlek-/ ▶ **n.** Physics an instrument for measuring electrical potential without drawing any current from the circuit.
– DERIVATIVES **e·lec·tro·met·ric** /iˌlektrəˈmetrik/ **adj.**, **e·lec·trom·e·try** /-ˈträmitrē/ **n.**

e·lec·tro·mo·tive /iˌlektrəˈmōtiv/ ▶ **adj.** Physics producing or tending to produce an electric current.

e·lec·tro·mo·tive force (abbr.: **emf**) ▶ **n.** Physics a difference in potential that tends to give rise to an electric current.

e·lec·tro·my·o·gram /iˌlektrōˈmīəˌgram/ ▶ **n.** Medicine a record or display produced by electromyography.

e·lec·tro·my·og·ra·phy /iˌlektrōmīˈägrəfē/ ▶ **n.** the recording of the electrical activity of muscle tissue, or its representation as a visual display or audible signal, using electrodes attached to the skin or inserted into the muscle.
– DERIVATIVES **e·lec·tro·my·o·graph** /-ˈmīəˌgraf/ **n.**, **e·lec·tro·my·o·graph·ic** /-ˌmīəˈgrafik/ **adj.**, **e·lec·tro·my·o·graph·i·cal·ly** /-ˌmīəˈgrafik(ə)lē/ **adv.**

e·lec·tron /iˈlekˌträn/ ▶ **n.** Physics a stable subatomic particle with a charge of negative electricity, found in all atoms and acting as the primary carrier of electricity in solids.

> The electron's mass is about 9×10^{-28}g, 1,836 times less than that of the proton. Electrons orbit the positively charged nuclei of atoms and are responsible for binding atoms together in molecules and for the electrical, thermal, optical, and magnetic properties of solids. Electric currents in metals and in semiconductors consist of a flow of electrons, and light, radio waves, X-rays, and much heat radiation are all produced by accelerating and decelerating electrons.

– ORIGIN late 19th cent.: from **ELECTRIC** + **-ON**.

e·lec·tron beam ▶ **n.** Physics a stream of electrons in a gas or vacuum.

e·lec·tron-dense ▶ **adj.** (of biological specimens) allowing the passage of few electrons, and so appearing dark in electron micrographs.

e·lec·tron dif·frac·tion ▶ **n.** Physics the diffraction of a beam of electrons by atoms or molecules, used esp. for determining crystal structures.

e·lec·tro·neg·a·tive /iˌlektrəˈnegətiv/ ▶ **adj. 1** Physics electrically negative.
2 Chemistry (of an element) tending to acquire electrons and form negative ions in chemical reactions.
– DERIVATIVES **e·lec·tro·neg·a·tiv·i·ty** /iˌlektrōˌnegəˈtivitē, ēˈˌlektrōˌnegəˈtivədē/ **n.** (sense 2).

e·lec·tron gun ▶ **n.** Physics a device for producing a narrow stream of electrons from a heated cathode.

e·lec·tron·ic /ilekˈtränik, ˌēlek-/ ▶ **adj. 1** (of a device) having or operating with the aid of many small components, esp. microchips and transistors, that control and direct an electric current: *an electronic calculator.* ■ (of music) produced by electronic instruments. ■ of or relating to electronics: *a degree in electronic engineering.*
2 of or relating to electrons.
3 carried out or accessed by means of a computer or other electronic device, esp. over a network: *electronic banking.*
– DERIVATIVES **e·lec·tron·i·cal·ly** /-(ə)lē/ **adv.**
– ORIGIN early 20th cent.: from **ELECTRON** + **-IC**.

e·lec·tron·ic flash ▶ **n.** Photography a flash from a gas-discharge tube, used in high-speed photography.

e·lec·tron·ic mail ▶ **n.** another term for **E-MAIL**.

e·lec·tron·ic mu·sic ▶ **n.** music performed using synthesizers and other electronic instruments.

e·lec·tron·ic or·gan·iz·er ▶ **n.** a pocket-sized computer used for storing and retrieving information such as addresses and appointments.

e·lec·tron·ic pub·lish·ing ▶ **n.** the issuing of books and other material in machine-readable form rather than on paper.

e·lec·tron·ics /ilekˈträniks, ˌēlek-/ ▶ **plural n.** [usu. treated as sing.] the branch of physics and technology concerned with the design of circuits using transistors and microchips, and with the behavior and movement of electrons in a semiconductor, conductor, vacuum, or gas: *electronics is seen as a growth industry* | [as modifier] *electronics engineers.* ■ [treated as pl.] circuits or devices using transistors, microchips, and other components.

e·lec·tron·ic tag·ging ▶ **n.** the attaching of electronic markers to people or goods for monitoring purposes, e.g., to track offenders under house arrest or to deter shoplifters.

e·lec·tron lens ▶ **n.** Physics a device for focusing a stream of electrons by means of electric or magnetic fields.

e·lec·tron mi·cro·scope ▶ **n.** Physics a microscope with high magnification and resolution, employing electron beams in place of light and using electron lenses.

e·lec·tron op·tics ▶ **plural n.** [treated as sing.] the branch of physics that deals with the behavior of electrons and electron beams in magnetic and electric fields.

e·lec·tron pair ▶ **n. 1** Chemistry two electrons occupying the same orbital in an atom or molecule.
2 Physics an electron and a positron produced in a high-energy reaction.

e·lec·tron spin res·o·nance (abbr.: **ESR**) ▶ **n.** Physics a spectroscopic method of locating electrons within the molecules of a paramagnetic substance.

e·lec·tron tube ▶ **n.** Physics an evacuated or gas-filled tube in which a current of electrons flows between electrodes.

e·lec·tron volt (abbr.: **eV**) ▶ **n.** Physics a unit of energy equal to the work done on an electron in accelerating it through a potential difference of one volt.

e·lec·tro·oc·u·lo·gram /iˌlektrōˈäkyələˌgram/ ▶ **n.** a record produced by electrooculography.

e·lec·tro·oc·u·log·ra·phy /iˌlektrōˌäkyəˈlägrəfē/ ▶ **n.** the measurement of the electrical potential between electrodes placed at points close to the eye, used to investigate eye movements esp. in physiological research.
– DERIVATIVES **e·lec·tro·oc·u·lo·graph·ic** /-ləˈgrafik/ **adj.**

e·lec·tro·op·tics /iˌlektrōˈäptiks/ ▶ **plural n.** [treated as sing.] the branch of science that deals with the effect of electric fields on light and on the optical properties of substances.
– DERIVATIVES **e·lec·tro·op·tic adj.**, **e·lec·tro·op·ti·cal** /-ˈäptikəl/ **adj.**

e·lec·tro·os·mo·sis /iˌlektrō-äzˈmōsis, -äs-/ ▶ **n.** osmosis under the influence of an electric field.
– DERIVATIVES **e·lec·tro·os·mot·ic** /-ˈmätik/ **adj.**

e·lec·tro·phil·ic /iˌlektrəˈfilik/ ▶ **adj.** Chemistry (of a molecule or group) having a tendency to attract or acquire electrons. Often contrasted with **NUCLEOPHILIC**.
– DERIVATIVES **e·lec·tro·phile** /iˈlektrəˌfīl/ **n.**

e·lec·tro·pho·re·sis /iˌlektrəfəˈrēsis/ ▶ **n.** Physics & Chemistry the movement of charged particles in a fluid or gel under the influence of an electric field.
– DERIVATIVES **e·lec·tro·pho·rese** /-ˈrēs/ **v.**, **e·lec·tro·pho·ret·ic** /-ˈretik/ **adj.**, **e·lec·tro·pho·ret·i·cal·ly** /-ˈretik(ə)lē/ **adv.**
– ORIGIN early 20th cent.: from **ELECTRO-** + Greek *phorēsis* 'being carried.'

e·lec·troph·o·rus /iˌlekˈträfərəs/ ▶ **n.** Physics a device for repeatedly generating static electricity by induction.
– ORIGIN late 18th cent.: from **ELECTRO-** + Greek *-phoros* 'bearing.'

e·lec·tro·phys·i·ol·o·gy /iˌlektrōˌfizēˈäləjē/ ▶ **n.** the branch of physiology that deals with the electrical phenomena associated with nervous and other bodily activity.
– DERIVATIVES **e·lec·tro·phys·i·o·log·i·cal** /-ˌfizēəˈläjikəl/ **adj.**, **e·lec·tro·phys·i·o·log·i·cal·ly** /-ˌfizēəˈläjik(ə)lē/ **adv.**, **e·lec·tro·phys·i·ol·o·gist** /-jist/ **n.**

e·lec·tro·plate /iˈlektrəˌplāt/ ▶ **v.** [with obj.] (usu. as noun **electroplating**) coat (a metal object) by

electrolytic deposition with chromium, silver, or another metal.
▶ n. electroplated articles.
– DERIVATIVES **e·lec·tro·plat·er** n.

e·lec·tro·plax /i'lektrō,plaks/ (also **electroplaque** /-,plak/) ▶ n. Zoology each of a number of flattened plates of protoplasm that make up the electric organ of certain fishes, e.g., the electric eel.

e·lec·tro·pol·ish /i'lektrō,päliSH/ ▶ v. [with obj.] (often as noun **electropolishing**) give a shiny surface to (metal) using electrolysis.

e·lec·tro·pop /ə'lektrōpôp/ ▶ n. a style of popular music characterized by the use of electronically created sounds, with a synthesizer as the primary instrument.

e·lec·tro·po·ra·tion /i,lektrōpə'rāSHən/ ▶ n. Biology the action or process of introducing DNA or chromosomes into bacteria or other cells using a pulse of electricity to briefly open the pores in the cell membranes.
– DERIVATIVES **e·lec·tro·po·rate** /-'pôr,āt/ v.

e·lec·tro·pos·i·tive /i,lektrə'päzitiv/ ▶ adj. **1** Physics electrically positive.
2 Chemistry (of an element) tending to lose electrons and form positive ions in chemical reactions.

e·lec·tro·re·cep·tion /i,lektrōri'sepSHən/ ▶ n. the detection by an aquatic animal of electric fields or currents.
– DERIVATIVES **e·lec·tro·re·cep·tor** /-'septər/ n.

e·lec·tro·ret·i·no·gram /i,lektrō'retn-ō,gram/ ▶ n. a record of the electrical activity of the retina, used in medical diagnosis and research.

e·lec·tro·scope /i'lektrə,skōp/ ▶ n. Physics an instrument for detecting and measuring electricity, esp. as an indication of the ionization of air by radioactivity.
– DERIVATIVES **e·lec·tro·scop·ic** /i,lektrə'skäpik/ adj.

e·lec·tro·shock /i'lektrə,SHäk/ ▶ adj. [attrib.] of or relating to medical treatment by means of electric shocks: *electroshock therapy*.

e·lec·tro·so·mat·ic /i,lektrōsə'matik/ ▶ adj.
1 pertaining to electronic devices implanted in an organism.
2 pertaining to electrical fields within an organism.

e·lec·tro·stat·ic /i,lektrə'statik/ ▶ adj. Physics of or relating to stationary electric charges or fields as opposed to electric currents.
– ORIGIN mid 19th cent.: from ELECTRO- + STATIC, on the pattern of *hydrostatic*.

e·lec·tro·stat·ic gen·er·a·tor ▶ n. any of various devices used to build up an electric charge to an extreme potential in order to generate electricity, esp. the Van de Graaf generator.

e·lec·tro·stat·ic pre·cip·i·ta·tor ▶ n. a device that removes suspended dust particles from a gas or exhaust by applying a high-voltage electrostatic charge and collecting the particles on charged plates.

e·lec·tro·stat·ics /i,lektrə'statiks/ ▶ plural n. [treated as sing.] Physics the study of stationary electric charges or fields as opposed to electric currents.

e·lec·tro·stat·ic u·nits ▶ plural n. a system of units based primarily on the forces between electric charges.

e·lec·tro·sur·ger·y /i,lektrō'sərjərē/ ▶ n. surgery using a high-frequency electric current to heat and so cut tissue with great precision.
– DERIVATIVES **e·lec·tro·sur·gi·cal** /-'sərjikəl/ adj.

e·lec·tro·tech·nol·o·gy /i,lektrōtek'näləjē/ (also **electrotechnics** /-'tekniks/) ▶ n. the science of the application of electricity in technology.
– DERIVATIVES **e·lec·tro·tech·nic** /-'teknik/ adj., **e·lec·tro·tech·ni·cal** /-'teknikəl/ adj.

e·lec·tro·ther·a·py /i,lektrō'THerəpē/ ▶ n. the use of electric currents passed through the body to stimulate nerves and muscles, chiefly in the treatment of various forms of paralysis.
– DERIVATIVES **e·lec·tro·ther·a·peu·tic** /-,THerə'pyo͞otik/ adj., **e·lec·tro·ther·a·peu·ti·cal** /-,THerə'pyo͞otikəl/ adj., **e·lec·tro·ther·a·pist** /-pist/ n.

e·lec·tro·ther·mal /i,lektrə'THərməl/ ▶ adj. Physics of or relating to heat derived from electricity.

e·lec·tro·type /i'lektrə,tīp/ ▶ v. [with obj.] (often as noun **electrotyping**) make a copy of (something) by the electrolytic deposition of copper on a mold.
▶ n. a copy made in such a way.
– DERIVATIVES **e·lec·tro·typ·er** n.

e·lec·tro·va·lent /i,lektrə'vālənt/ ▶ adj. Chemistry (of bonding) resulting from electrostatic attraction between positive and negative ions; ionic.
– DERIVATIVES **e·lec·tro·va·lence** n., **e·lec·tro·va·len·cy** n.
– ORIGIN 1920s: from ELECTRO- + -*valent*, on the pattern of *trivalent*.

e·lec·tro·weak /i'lektrō,wēk/ ▶ adj. Physics relating to or denoting electromagnetic and weak interactions regarded as manifestations of the same interaction.

e·lec·trum /i'lektrəm/ ▶ n. a natural or artificial alloy of gold with at least 20 percent silver, used for jewelry, esp. in ancient times.
– ORIGIN late Middle English: via Latin from Greek *ēlektron* 'amber, electrum.'

e·lec·tu·ar·y /i'lekCHo͞o,erē/ ▶ n. (pl. **electuaries**) archaic a medicinal substance mixed with honey or another sweet substance.
– ORIGIN late Middle English: from late Latin *electuarium*, probably from Greek *ekleikton*, from *ekleikhein* 'lick up.'

el·ee·mos·y·nar·y /,elə'mäsə,nerē, ,eléə-/ ▶ adj. of, relating to, or dependent on charity; charitable.
– ORIGIN late 16th cent. (as a noun denoting a place where alms were distributed): from medieval Latin *eleemosynarius*, from late Latin *eleemosyna* 'alms,' from Greek *eleēmosunē* 'compassion' (see ALMS).

el·e·gance /'eləgəns/ ▶ n. **1** the quality of being graceful and stylish in appearance or manner; style: *a slender woman with grace and elegance*.
2 the quality of being pleasingly ingenious and simple; neatness: *the simplicity and elegance of the solution*.

el·e·gan·cy /'eligənsē/ ▶ n. **1** graceful and stylish appearance or manner; elegance.
2 something that is elegant: *I do hope you will study a little of the proprieties and elegancies of life*.

el·e·gant /'eləgənt/ ▶ adj. pleasingly graceful and stylish in appearance or manner: *she will look elegant in black | an elegant, comfortable house*.
■ (of a scientific theory or solution to a problem) pleasingly ingenious and simple: *the grand unified theory is compact and elegant in mathematical terms*.
– DERIVATIVES **el·e·gant·ly** adv.
– ORIGIN late 15th cent. (describing a person dressing tastefully): from French, or from Latin *elegans*, *elegant-*, related to *eligere* 'choose, select' (see ELECT).

el·e·gant var·i·a·tion ▶ n. the stylistic fault of studiedly finding different ways to denote the same thing in a piece of writing, merely to avoid repetition.

el·e·gi·ac /,elə'jīək, e'lējē,ak/ ▶ adj. (esp. of a work of art) having a mournful quality: *the movie score is a somber effort, elegiac in its approach*. ■ wistfully mournful.
▶ plural n. (**elegiacs**) verses in an elegiac meter.
– DERIVATIVES **el·e·gi·a·cal·ly** /,elə'jīək(ə)lē/ adv.
– ORIGIN late 16th cent.: from French *élégiaque*, or via late Latin, from Greek *elegeiakos*, from *elegeia* (see ELEGY).

el·e·gi·ac cou·plet ▶ n. a pair of lines consisting of a dactylic hexameter and a pentameter, esp. in Greek and Latin verse.

el·e·gi·ac stan·za ▶ n. a quatrain in iambic pentameter rhymed *abab*. Compare with HEROIC STANZA.

el·e·gize /'elə,jīz/ ▶ v. [no obj.] write in a wistfully mournful way about someone or something.
– DERIVATIVES **el·e·gist** /-jist/ n.

el·e·gy /'eləjē/ ▶ n. (pl. **elegies**) **1** a poem of serious reflection, typically a lament for the dead.
2 (in Greek and Roman poetry) a poem written in elegiac couplets, as notably by Catullus and Propertius.
– ORIGIN early 16th cent.: from French *élégie*, or via Latin, from Greek *elegeia*, from *elegos* 'mournful poem.'

elem. ▶ abbr. elementary.

el·e·ment /'eləmənt/ ▶ n. **1** a part or aspect of something abstract, esp. one that is essential or characteristic: *the death had **all the elements of** a great tabloid story | there are four elements to the proposal*. ■ a small but significant presence of a feeling or abstract quality: *it was the element of danger he loved in flying*. ■ (**elements**) the rudiments of a branch of knowledge: *legal training may include the elements of economics and political science*. ■ [usu. with modifier] (often **elements**) a group of people of a particular kind within a larger group or organization: *extreme right-wing elements in the army*. ■ Mathematics & Logic an entity that is a single member of a set.
2 (also **chemical element**) each of more than one hundred substances that cannot be chemically interconverted or broken down into simpler substances and are primary constituents of matter. Each element is distinguished by its atomic number, i.e., the number of protons in the nuclei of its atoms. ■ any of the four substances (earth, water, air, and fire) regarded as the fundamental constituents of the world in ancient and medieval philosophy. ■ one of these substances considered as a person's or animal's natural environment: *for the islanders, the sea is their kingdom, water their element*. ■ (**the elements**) the weather, esp. strong winds, heavy rain, and other kinds of bad weather: *there was no barrier against the elements*. ■ (**elements**) (in church use) the bread and wine of the Eucharist.
3 a part in an electric teapot, heater, or stove that contains a wire through which an electric current is passed to provide heat. ■ on some electric typewriters, a ball with raised letters that print when the keys are pressed.
– PHRASES **be in** (or **out of**) **one's element** be in (or not in) a situation or environment that one particularly likes and in which one can perform well: *she was in her element with doctors and hospitals*.
– ORIGIN Middle English (denoting fundamental constituents of the world or celestial objects): via Old French from Latin *elementum* 'principle, rudiment,' translating Greek *stoikheion* 'step, component part.'

el·e·men·tal /,elə'mentl/ ▶ adj. **1** primary or basic: *elemental features from which all other structures are compounded*. ■ concerned with chemical elements or other basic components: *elemental analysis*. ■ consisting of a single chemical element.
2 related to or embodying the powers of nature: *a thunderstorm is the inevitable outcome of battling elemental forces*. ■ (of an emotion) having the primitive and inescapable character of a force of nature: *the urge for revenge was too elemental to be ignored*.
▶ n. a supernatural entity or force thought to be physically manifested by occult means.
– DERIVATIVES **el·e·men·tal·ism** /-,izəm/ n., **el·e·men·tal·ly** adv.
– ORIGIN late 15th cent.: from medieval Latin *elementalis*, from *elementum* 'principle, rudiment' (see ELEMENT).

el·e·men·ta·ry /,elə'ment(ə)rē/ ▶ adj. of or relating to the most rudimentary aspects of a subject: *the six stages take students from elementary to advanced level*. ■ easily dealt with; straightforward and uncomplicated: *it's interesting work, although a lot of it is elementary*. ■ not decomposable into elements or other primary constituents.
– DERIVATIVES **el·e·men·tar·i·ly** /-rəlē/ adv., **el·e·men·ta·ri·ness** n.
– ORIGIN late Middle English (in the sense 'composed of the four elements, earth, air, fire, and water'): from Latin *elementarius*, from *elementum* 'principle, rudiment' (see ELEMENT). Current senses dates from the mid 16th cent.

el·e·men·ta·ry par·ti·cle ▶ n. any of various fundamental subatomic particles, including those that are the smallest and most basic constituents of matter (leptons and quarks) or are combinations of these (hadrons, which consist of quarks), and those that transmit one of the four fundamental interactions in nature (gravitational, electromagnetic, strong, and weak). Compare with SUBATOMIC PARTICLE, and see BARYON, BOSON, GLUON, GRAVITON, MESON, PHOTON, W PARTICLE, Z PARTICLE.

el·e·men·ta·ry school ▶ n. a school for the first four to six grades, and usually including kindergarten.

el·e·mi /'eləmē/ ▶ n. an oleoresin obtained from a tropical tree and used in varnishes, ointments, and aromatherapy. ● This resin is obtained from several trees in the family Burseraceae, in particular *Bursera simaruba* (producing **American elemi**) and *Canarium luzanicum* (producing **Manila elemi**).
– ORIGIN mid 16th cent.: perhaps from Arabic *al-lāmī*.

e·len·chus /i'leNGkəs/ ▶ n. (pl. **elenchi** /-kī, -kē/) Logic a logical refutation. See also IGNORATIO ELENCHI. ■ (also **Socratic elenchus**) the Socratic method of eliciting truth by question and answer, esp. as used to refute an argument.
– ORIGIN mid 17th cent. (superseding late Middle English *elench*): via Latin from Greek *elenkhos*.

el·e·phant /'eləfənt/ ▶ n. (pl. **same** or **elephants**)
1 a heavy plant-eating mammal with a prehensile trunk, long curved ivory tusks, and large ears, native to Africa and southern Asia. It is the largest living land animal. ● Family Elephantidae, order Proboscidea: two species. See AFRICAN ELEPHANT, INDIAN ELEPHANT.
2 chiefly Brit. a size of paper, now standardized at 28 × 23 inches (approximately 711 × 584 mm).
– DERIVATIVES **el·e·phan·toid** /,elə'fantoid, 'eləfən,toid/ adj.
– PHRASES **the elephant in the room** a major problem or controversial issue that is obviously

present but avoided as a subject for discussion because it is more comfortable to do so.
– ORIGIN Middle English: from Old French *elefant*, via Latin from Greek *elephas, elephant-* 'ivory, elephant.'

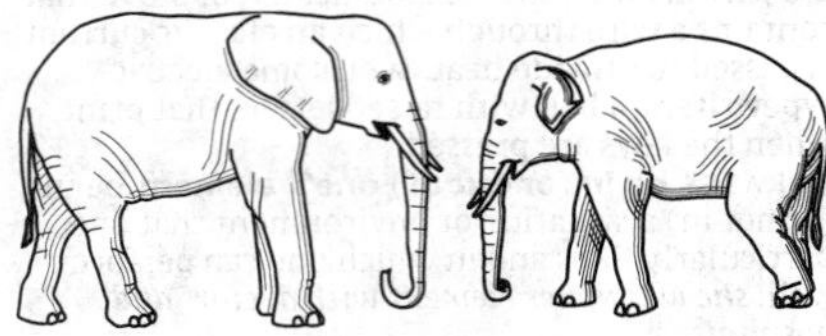

elephants

e

el·e·phant bird ▶ **n.** a heavily built, giant flightless bird, found in Madagascar until it was exterminated in about AD 1000. The eggs, which are still found occasionally, are the largest known. Also called AEPYORNIS. ● Family Aepyornithidae, genera *Aepyornis* and *Mullerornis*: several species, including *A. maximus*.

el·e·phant ear ▶ **n.** any of a number of plants with large heart-shaped leaves.

el·e·phant grass ▶ **n.** a tall robust tropical African grass that is used for fodder and paper. Also called NAPIER GRASS. ● *Pennisetum purpureum*, family Gramineae.

el·e·phan·ti·a·sis /ˌeləfənˈtīəsis/ ▶ **n.** Medicine a condition in which a limb or other part of the body becomes grossly enlarged due to obstruction of the lymphatic vessels, typically by the nematode parasites that cause filariasis.
– ORIGIN mid 16th cent.: via Latin from Greek, from *elephas, elephant-* 'elephant' + -IASIS.

el·e·phan·tine /ˌeləˈfantēn, -ˌtīn, ˈeləfənˌtēn, -ˌtīn/ ▶ **adj.** of, resembling, or characteristic of an elephant or elephants, esp. in being large, clumsy, or awkward: *there was an elephantine thud from the bathroom.*
– ORIGIN early 17th cent.: via Latin from Greek *elephantinos*, from *elephas, elephant-* 'elephant.'

el·e·phant seal ▶ **n.** a large seal that breeds on the west coast of North America and the islands around Antarctica. The male is much larger than the female and has a very thick neck and an inflatable snout. ● Genus *Mirounga*, family Phocidae: two species.

El·eu·sin·i·an mys·ter·ies /ˌelyo͞oˈsinēən/ ▶ **plural n.** the annual rites performed by the ancient Greeks at the village of Eleusis near Athens in honor of Demeter and Persephone.

E·leu·ther·a /iˈlo͞oTHərə/ an island in the central Bahamas, over 100 miles (160 km) long; pop. 8,900 (est. 2009). It was settled by the British in the 1640s.

elev. ▶ **abbr.** elevation.

el·e·vate /ˈeləˌvāt/ ▶ **v.** [with obj.] raise or lift (something) up to a higher position: *the exercise will naturally elevate your chest and head.* ■ raise to a more important or impressive level: *in the 1920s he was* **elevated to** *secretary of state | exotic toppings elevate a pizza from fast food to fine food.* ■ (of a priest) hold up (a consecrated host or chalice) for adoration. ■ increase the level or amount of (something, esp. the level of a component of a person's blood): *high amounts of the drug can elevate blood pressure.* ■ raise the axis of (a piece of artillery) to increase its range.
– DERIVATIVES **el·e·va·to·ry** /-vəˌtôrē/ **adj.**
– ORIGIN late Middle English: from Latin *elevat-* 'raised,' from the verb *elevare*, from *e-* (variant of *ex-*) 'out, away' + *levare* 'lighten' (from *levis* 'light').

el·e·vat·ed /ˈeləˌvātid/ ▶ **adj.** situated or placed higher than the surrounding area: *this hotel has an elevated position above the village | the elevated section of the freeway.* ■ (of a level or amount) higher or greater than what is considered normal: *an elevated temperature.* ■ of a high intellectual or moral standard or level: *the elevated canon of great literary texts.* ■ having a high rank or social standing: *a suitably elevated occupation.*
▶ **n.** an elevated railroad.

el·e·va·tion /ˌeləˈvāSHən/ ▶ **n. 1** the action or fact of elevating or being elevated: *her sudden elevation to the cabinet.* ■ augmentation of or increase in the amount or level of something. ■ (in a Christian Mass) the raising of the consecrated elements for adoration.
2 height above a given level, esp. sea level: *a network of microclimates created by sharp differences in elevation | a total elevation gain of 3,995 feet.* ■ a high place or position: *most early plantation development was at the higher elevations.* ■ the angle of something with the horizontal, esp. of a gun or of the direction of a celestial object. ■ Ballet the ability of a dancer to attain height in jumps.
3 a particular side of a building: *a burglar alarm was prominently displayed on the front elevation.* ■ a drawing or diagram, esp. of a building, made by projection on a vertical plane. Compare with PLAN (sense 3 of the noun).
– DERIVATIVES **el·e·va·tion·al** /-SHənl, -SHnəl/ **adj.**
– ORIGIN late Middle English: from Latin *elevatio(n-)*, from *elevare* 'raise' (see ELEVATE).

el·e·va·tor /ˈeləˌvātər/ ▶ **n. 1** a platform or compartment housed in a shaft for raising and lowering people or things to different floors or levels: *in the elevator she pressed the button for the lobby.* ■ a machine consisting of an endless belt with scoops attached, used typically for raising grain to be stored in an upper story. ■ a tall building used for storing large quantities of grain.
2 a hinged flap on the horizontal stabilizer of an aircraft, typically one of a pair, used to control the motion of the aircraft about its lateral axis.
3 a muscle whose contraction raises a part of the body: *elevators of the upper lip.*
4 North American trademark (also **elevator shoe**) a shoe with a raised insole designed to make the wearer appear taller.
– ORIGIN mid 17th cent. (denoting a levator muscle): modern Latin, from Latin *elevare* 'raise'; in later use directly from ELEVATE.

el·e·va·tor mu·sic ▶ **n.** bland recorded background music played in public places.

el·e·va·tor pitch ▶ **n.** informal a succinct and persuasive sales pitch.
– ORIGIN from the idea of having to impress a senior executive during a brief ride in an elevator.

e·lev·en /iˈlevən/ ▶ **cardinal number** equivalent to the sum of six and five; one more than ten; 11: *the room was about eleven feet wide | eighteen schools were founded, eleven of them in Los Angeles.* (Roman numeral: **xi** or **XI**) ■ eleven years old: *the eldest is only eleven.* ■ eleven o'clock: *she often worked until eleven at night.* ■ a size of garment or other merchandise denoted by eleven. ■ a group or unit of eleven people or things. ■ a sports team of eleven players.
– DERIVATIVES **e·lev·en·fold** /-ˌfōld/ **adj. & adv.**
– ORIGIN Old English *endleofon*, from the base of ONE + a second element (probably expressing the sense 'left over') occurring also in TWELVE; of Germanic origin and related to Dutch and German *elf*.

e·lev·ens·es /iˈlevənziz/ ▶ **plural n.** Brit. informal a short break for light refreshments, usually with tea or coffee, taken about eleven o'clock in the morning.

e·lev·enth /iˈlevənTH/ ▶ **ordinal number** constituting number eleven in a sequence; 11th: *the eleventh century | February the eleventh | the eleventh fairway of a tiny golf course.* ■ (**an eleventh/one eleventh**) each of eleven equal parts into which something is or may be divided. ■ the eleventh grade of a school. ■ Music an interval or chord spanning an octave plus a fourth in the diatonic scale, or a note separated from another by this interval.
– PHRASES **the eleventh hour** the latest possible moment: *he refused to take a public stand until the eleventh hour of the campaign.*

el·e·von /ˈeləˌvän/ ▶ **n.** Aeronautics the movable part of the trailing edge of a delta wing.
– ORIGIN 1940s: blend of ELEVATOR and AILERON (because the elevon combines the functions of both).

ELF ▶ **abbr.** extremely low frequency.

elf /elf/ ▶ **n.** (pl. **elves** /elvz/) a supernatural creature of folk tales, typically represented as a small, elusive figure in human form with pointed ears, magical powers, and a capricious nature.
– DERIVATIVES **elf·ish adj.**, **elv·en** /ˈelvən/ **adj.** (literary), **elv·ish** /ˈelviSH/ **adj.**
– ORIGIN Old English, of Germanic origin; related to German *Alp* 'nightmare.'

elf·in /ˈelfən/ ▶ **adj. 1** (with reference to a person) small and delicate, typically with an attractively mischievous or strange charm: *she looked up at him with an elfin grin.*
2 of or relating to elves: *an enchanted world of fairies in elfin glades.*
▶ **n. 1** archaic an elf.
2 a small North American butterfly that is typically brownish with markings on the wing margins that give the impression of scalloped edges. ● Genus *Incisalia*, family Lycaenidae.
– ORIGIN late 16th cent.: from ELF, probably suggested by Middle English *elvene* 'of elves,' and by *Elphin*, the name of a character in Arthurian romance.

elf·locks /ˈelfˌläks/ ▶ **plural n.** a tangled mass of hair.

elf owl ▶ **n.** a tiny owl that nests in cacti and trees in the arid country of the southern US and Mexico. ● *Micrathene whitneyi*, family Strigidae.

El·gar /ˈelˌgär, -gər/, Sir Edward (William) (1857–1934), English composer. He is known for the five *Pomp and Circumstance* marches (1901–30).

El·gin /ˈeljin/ an industrial city in northeastern Illinois, west of Chicago, formerly noted for its watch manufacturing; pop. 106,330 (est. 2008).

El·gin Mar·bles /ˈelgin ˈmärbəlz, -jin/ a collection of classical Greek marble sculptures and architectural fragments, chiefly from the Parthenon in Athens, brought to England by the diplomat and art connoisseur Thomas Bruce (1766–1841), the 7th Earl of Elgin.

> Executed by Phidias in the 5th century BC, the sculptures were brought from Greece between 1803 and 1812, when the country was under Turkish control. They are currently housed in the British Museum, but are the subject of a repatriation request from the Greek government, which does not accept the legality of the Turkish sale.

el-Gi·za /ˌel ˈgēzə/ another name for GIZA.

El Gre·co /el ˈgrekō/ (1541–1614), Spanish painter; born on Crete; born *Domenikos Theotokopoulos*. His portraits and religious works are characterized by distorted perspective, elongated figures, and strident use of color. In Spanish, his name means "the Greek."

E·li /ˈēlī/ (in the Bible) a priest who acted as a teacher to the prophet Samuel (1 Sam. 1–3).

E·li·a /ˈēlēə/ the pseudonym adopted by Charles Lamb in his *Essays of Elia* (1823) and *Last Essays of Elia* (1833).

e·lic·it /iˈlisit/ ▶ **v.** (**elicits, eliciting, elicited**) [with obj.] evoke or draw out (a response, answer, or fact) from someone in reaction to one's own actions or questions: *they invariably elicit exclamations of approval from guests.* ■ archaic draw forth (something that is latent or potential) into existence: *a corrupt heart elicits in an hour all that is bad in us.*
– DERIVATIVES **e·lic·i·ta·tion** /iˌlisiˈtāSHən/ **n.**, **e·lic·i·tor** /-tər/ **n.**
– ORIGIN mid 17th cent.: from Latin *elicit-* 'drawn out by trickery or magic,' from the verb *elicere*, from *e-* (variant of *ex-*) 'out' + *lacere* 'entice, deceive.'

e·lide /iˈlīd/ ▶ **v.** [with obj.] omit (a sound or syllable) when speaking: (as adj. **elided**) *the indication of elided consonants or vowels.* ■ join together; merge: *whole periods of time are* **elided into** *a few seconds of screen time* | [no obj.] *the two things elided in his mind.*
– ORIGIN mid 16th cent. (in the sense 'annul, do away with,' chiefly as a Scots legal term): from Latin *elidere* 'crush out,' from *e-* (variant of *ex-*) 'out' + *laedere* 'to dash.'

el·i·gi·ble /ˈeləjəbəl/ ▶ **adj.** having the right to do or obtain something; satisfying the appropriate conditions: *customers who are* **eligible for** *discounts* | [with infinitive] *a foreign student is eligible to attend the school.* ■ (of a person) desirable or suitable as a partner in marriage: *the world's most eligible bachelor.*
– DERIVATIVES **el·i·gi·bil·i·ty** /ˌeləjəˈbilitē/ **n.**, **el·i·gi·bly** /-blē/ **adv.**
– ORIGIN late Middle English: via French from late Latin *eligibilis*, from Latin *eligere* 'choose, select' (see ELECT).

E·li·jah /iˈlījə/ (9th century BC), a Hebrew prophet in the time of Jezebel who maintained the worship of Jehovah against that of Baal and other pagan gods.

e·lim·i·nate /iˈliməˌnāt/ ▶ **v.** [with obj.] completely remove or get rid of (something): *a policy that would eliminate inflation.* ■ exclude (someone or something) from consideration: *the police have* **eliminated** *Larry* **from** *their inquiries.* ■ murder (a rival or political opponent). ■ (usu. **be eliminated**) exclude (a person or team) from further participation in a sporting competition following defeat or inadequate results: *the Bears were* **eliminated from** *the playoffs in the first round.* ■ Mathematics remove (a variable) from an equation, typically by substituting another that is shown by a different equation to be equivalent. ■ Chemistry generate or remove (a simple substance) as a product in the course of a reaction involving larger molecules. ■ Physiology expel (waste matter) from the body.
– DERIVATIVES **e·lim·i·na·ble** /-nəbəl/ **adj.**, **e·lim·i·na·tion** /iˌliməˈnāSHən/ **n.**, **e·lim·i·na·tor** /-ˌnātər/ **n.**, **e·lim·i·na·to·ry** /-nəˌtôrē/ **adj.**
– ORIGIN mid 16th cent. (in the sense 'drive out, expel'): from Latin *eliminat-* 'turned out of doors,' from the verb *eliminare*, from *e-* (variant of *ex-*) 'out' + *limen, limin-* 'threshold.'

e·lim·i·na·tion di·et ▶ **n.** a procedure used to identify foods that may be causing an adverse effect in a person, in which all suspected foods are excluded from the diet and then reintroduced one at a time.

ELINT /ˈelint/ ▶ **n.** covert intelligence-gathering by electronic means.
– ORIGIN 1960s: blend of ELECTRONIC and INTELLIGENCE.

El·i·ot[1], Alice, see JEWETT.

El·i·ot² /ˈelēət/, George (1819–80), English novelist; pseudonym of *Mary Ann Evans*. Her novels of provincial life are characterized by their exploration of moral problems and their development of the psychological analysis that marks the modern novel. Notable works: *Adam Bede* (1859), *The Mill on the Floss* (1860), and *Middlemarch* (1871–72).

El·i·ot³, T. S. (1888–1965), British poet, critic, and playwright; born in the US; full name *Thomas Stearns Eliot*. Associated with the rise of literary modernism, he was established as the voice of a disillusioned generation with his long poem *The Waste Land* (1922). *Four Quartets* (1943) revealed his increasing involvement with Christianity. Nobel Prize for Literature (1948).

ELISA /iˈlīzə, iˈlīsə/ ▶ **n.** Biochemistry enzyme-linked immunosorbent assay, an immunological assay technique making use of an enzyme bonded to a particular antibody or antigen.

E·lis·a·beth·ville /əˈlizəbəTH,vil/ former name (until 1966) of LUBUMBASHI.

E·li·sha /iˈlīSHə/ (9th century BC), a Hebrew prophet, disciple, and successor of Elijah.

e·li·sion /iˈliZHən/ ▶ **n.** the omission of a sound or syllable when speaking (as in *I'm, let's, e'en*). ■ an omission of a passage in a book, speech, or film: *the movie's elisions and distortions have been carefully thought out.* ■ the process of joining together or merging things, esp. abstract ideas: *unease at the elision of so many vital questions.*
– ORIGIN late 16th cent.: from late Latin *elision-*, from Latin *elidere* 'crush out' (see ELIDE).

e·lite /əˈlēt, āˈlēt/ ▶ **n. 1** a group of people considered (by others or themselves) to be the best in a particular society or category, esp. because of their power, talent, or wealth: *the wealthy, educated elite* | [as modifier] *an elite combat force.*
2 a size of letter in typewriting, with 12 characters to the inch (about 4.7 to the centimeter).
– ORIGIN late 18th cent.: from French *élite* 'selection, choice,' from *élire* 'to elect,' from a variant of Latin *eligere* (see ELECT). Sense 2 dates from the early 20th cent.

e·lit·ism /əˈlē,tizəm, āˈlē-/ ▶ **n.** the advocacy or existence of an elite as a dominating element in a system or society. ■ the attitude or behavior of a person or group who regard themselves as belonging to an elite: *he accused her of racism and white elitism.*

e·lit·ist /əˈlētist, āˈlētist/ ▶ **n.** a person who believes that a system or society should be ruled or dominated by an elite.
▶ **adj.** favoring, advocating, or restricted to an elite: *the old, elitist image of the string quartet.*

e·lix·ir /iˈliksər/ ▶ **n.** a magical or medicinal potion: *an elixir guaranteed to induce love.* ■ a preparation that was supposedly able to change metals into gold, sought by alchemists. ■ (also **elixir of life**) a preparation supposedly able to prolong life indefinitely. ■ a medicinal solution of a specified type: *a natural herbal cough elixir.*
– ORIGIN late Middle English: via medieval Latin from Arabic *al-ʾiksīr*, from *al* 'the' + *ʾiksīr* from Greek *xērion* 'powder for drying wounds' (from *xēros* 'dry').

E·liz·a·beth /iˈlizəbəTH/ an industrial port city in northeastern New Jersey, on Newark Bay; pop. 124,755 (est. 2008).

E·liz·a·beth I /əˈlizəbəTH/ (1533–1603), daughter of Henry VIII and Anne Boleyn; queen of England and Ireland 1558–1603. Succeeding her Catholic sister Mary I, Elizabeth re-established Protestantism as the state religion. Her reign was dominated by the threat of a Catholic restoration and by war with Spain, culminating in the defeat of the Spanish Armada in 1588. Although frequently courted, she never married.

Elizabeth I

E·liz·a·beth II (1926–), daughter of George VI; queen of the United Kingdom since 1952; born *Princess Elizabeth Alexandra Mary*. She married Prince Philip in 1947; they have four children: Prince Charles, Princess Anne, Prince Andrew, and Prince Edward.

Elizabeth II

E·liz·a·beth, the Queen Mother (1900–2002), wife of George VI; born *Lady Elizabeth Angela Marguerite Bowes-Lyon*. She married George VI in 1923 when he was the Duke of York; they had two daughters, Elizabeth II and Princess Margaret.

E·liz·a·be·than /i,lizəˈbēTHən/ ▶ **adj.** of, relating to, or characteristic of the reign of Queen Elizabeth I: *a lady in Elizabethan dress.*
▶ **n.** a person, esp. a writer, of the time of Queen Elizabeth I.

E·liz·a·be·than son·net ▶ **n.** a type of sonnet much used by Shakespeare, written in iambic pentameter and consisting of three quatrains and a final couplet with the rhyme scheme abab cdcd efef gg.

elk /elk/ ▶ **n. 1** (pl. **same** or **elks**) a red deer of a large race native to North America. Also called WAPITI. ● *Cervus canadensis*, family Cervidae. ■ Brit. another term for MOOSE.
2 (**Elk**) (pl. **Elks**) a member of a charitable fraternal organization, the Benevolent and Protective Order of Elks.
– ORIGIN late 15th cent.: probably from Old English *elh, eolh*, with substitution of *k* for *h*. Other words that have undergone this change are dialect *selk* (Old English *seolh* 'seal') and *fark* (Old English *færh* 'farrow').

elk grass another name for BEARGRASS.

Elk·hart /ˈel,kärt, ˈelk,härt/ an industrial city in northern Indiana, a rail center that is also noted for the manufacture of musical instruments; pop. 52,653 (est. 2008).

Elk Hills a range in south central California, near Bakersfield, the site of an oil reserve that was involved in the 1920s Teapot Dome scandal.

elk·hound /ˈelk,hound/ (in full **Norwegian elkhound**) ▶ **n.** a large hunting dog of a Scandinavian breed with a shaggy gray coat.

ell¹ /el/ ▶ **n.** a former measure of length (equivalent to six hand breadths) used mainly for textiles, locally variable but typically about 45 inches.
– ORIGIN Old English *eln*, of Germanic origin; from an Indo-European root shared by Latin *ulna* (see ULNA). Compare with ELBOW and also with CUBIT (the measure was originally linked to the length of the human arm or forearm).

ell² ▶ **n.** something that is L-shaped or that creates an L shape, in particular: ■ an extension of a building or room that is at right angles to the main part. ■ a bend or joint for connecting two pipes at right angles.

el·lag·ic ac·id /əˈlajik/ ▶ **n.** Chemistry a compound extracted from oak galls and various fruits and nuts. It has some ability to inhibit blood flow and retard the growth of cancer cells. ● A tetracyclic phenol; chem. formula: $C_{14}H_6O_8$.
– ORIGIN early 19th cent.: *ellagic* from French *ellagique* (an anagram of *galle* 'gallnut' + *-ique*), thus avoiding the form *gallique*, already in use.

Elles·mere Is·land /ˈelz,mi(ə)r/ the most northern of the islands in the Canadian Arctic.

El·let /ˈelit/, Charles (1810–62), US engineer. In 1841–42, he built the wire suspension bridge that crosses the Schuylkill River in Philadelphia, the first of its kind in the US.

El·lice Is·lands /ˈeləs/ former name of TUVALU.

El·li·cott Cit·y /ˈelikət/ a historic community in north central Maryland, west of Baltimore; pop. 56,397 (2000).

El·ling·ton /ˈeliNGtən/, Duke (1899–1974), US jazz pianist, composer, and bandleader; born *Edward Kennedy Ellington*. Coming to fame in the early 1930s, he wrote over 900 compositions, including *Mood Indigo* (1930), and was one of the first popular musicians to write extended pieces.

el·lipse /iˈlips/ ▶ **n.** a regular oval shape, traced by a point moving in a plane so that the sum of its distances from two other points (the foci) is constant, or resulting when a cone is cut by an oblique plane that does not intersect the base.
– ORIGIN late 17th cent.: via French from Latin *ellipsis* (see ELLIPSIS).

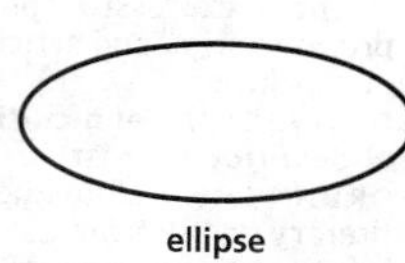
ellipse

el·lip·sis /iˈlipsis/ ▶ **n.** (pl. **ellipses** /-sēz/) the omission from speech or writing of a word or words that are superfluous or able to be understood from contextual clues. ■ a set of dots indicating such an omission.
– ORIGIN mid 16th cent.: via Latin from Greek *elleipsis*, from *elleipein* 'leave out.'

el·lip·soid /iˈlipsoid/ ▶ **n.** a three-dimensional figure whose plane sections are ellipses or circles.
– DERIVATIVES **el·lip·soi·dal** /ilipˈsoidl, ,elip-/ **adj.**

el·lip·tic /iˈliptik/ ▶ **adj.** of, relating to, or having the form of an ellipse.
– ORIGIN early 18th cent.: from Greek *elleiptikos* 'defective,' from *elleipein* 'leave out, fall short.'

el·lip·ti·cal /iˈliptikəl/ ▶ **adj. 1** (of speech or writing) using or involving ellipsis, esp. so as to be difficult to understand: *an elliptical lyrical style.*
2 another term for ELLIPTIC.
– DERIVATIVES **el·lip·ti·cal·ly** /-(ə)lē/ **adv.**

el·lip·tic·i·ty /i,lipˈtisitē, ,elip-/ ▶ **n.** the condition of being elliptic.

El·lis Is·land /ˈeləs/ an island in the bay of New York that served as an entry point for immigrants to the US 1892–1943 and as a detention center for people awaiting deportation until 1954. It is now part of a national monument and houses an immigration museum.

El·li·son /ˈeləsən/, Ralph (Waldo) (1914–94), US writer. He is most noted for his novel *Invisible Man* (1952), but he also published two collections of essays, *Shadow and Act* (1964) and *Going to the Country* (1986), many of which explore blues and African-American folklore.

Ells·berg, Daniel, (1931–) US political analyst, economist, and activist. A former adviser to President Nixon on policy in Southeast Asia, he became an avid opponent of the Vietnam War. Indicted for leaking classified Vietnam-related papers (the "Pentagon Papers") to the press in 1971, he was freed of charges when it was disclosed that Nixon had authorized the theft of Ellsberg's psychiatric records in order to discredit him.

Ells·worth¹ /ˈelzwərTH/, Lincoln (1880–1951), US explorer. He participated in a number of polar expeditions and was the first person to fly over both the North (1926) and South (1935) poles.

Ells·worth², Oliver (1745–1807), US chief justice 1796–1800. As a member of the Continental Congress from 1777 until 1784, he authored the Connecticut Compromise. As a US senator from Connecticut 1789–96, he drafted the Judiciary Act of 1789.

Ells·worth Land a plateau region in Antarctica between the Walgreen Coast and Palmer Land. It rises at the Vinson Massif to 16,863 feet (5,140 m), the highest point in Antarctica.

elm /elm/ (also **elm tree**) ▶ **n.** a tall deciduous tree that typically has rough serrated leaves and propagates from root suckers. ● Genus *Ulmus*, family Ulmaceae: several species, including the **English elm** (*U. procera*) and the **American elm** (*U. americana*), now largely lost to Dutch Elm disease. ■ (also **elmwood**) the wood of this tree.
– ORIGIN Old English, of Germanic origin; related to German dialect *Ilm*, and Swedish and Norwegian *alm*.

El Mon·te /el ˈmäntē/ a city in southwestern California, east of Los Angeles; pop. 121,791 (est. 2008).

El Ni·ño /el ˈnēnyō/ ▶ **n.** (pl. **El Niños**) an irregularly occurring and complex series of climatic changes affecting the equatorial Pacific region and beyond every few years, characterized by the appearance of unusually warm, nutrient-poor water off northern Peru and Ecuador, typically in late December.

– ORIGIN late 19th cent.: Spanish, literally 'the (Christ) child,' because of the occurrence near Christmas.

el·o·cu·tion /ˌeləˈkyo͞osHən/ ▶ **n.** the skill of clear and expressive speech, esp. of distinct pronunciation and articulation. ■ a particular style of speaking.
– DERIVATIVES **el·o·cu·tion·ar·y** /-ˌnerē/ **adj.**, **el·o·cu·tion·ist** /-ist/ **n.**
– ORIGIN late Middle English (denoting oratorical or literary style): from Latin *elocutio(n-)*, from *eloqui* 'speak out' (see ELOQUENCE).

e·lo·de·a /iˈlōdēə/ ▶ **n.** an aquatic plant of a genus that includes the ornamental waterweeds. ● Genus *Elodea*, family Hydrocharitaceae.
– ORIGIN modern Latin, from Greek *helōdēs* 'marshy.'

e

E·lo·him /eˈlōhim, ˌelōˈhēm, ˌelōˈhim/ ▶ **n.** a name for God used frequently in the Hebrew Bible.
– ORIGIN from Hebrew *'ĕlōhīm* (plural).

E·lo·hist /eˈlōhist, ˈelōˌhist/ the postulated author or authors of parts of the Hexateuch in which God is regularly named Elohim. Compare with YAHWIST.
– ORIGIN from Hebrew *'ĕlōhīm* (see ELOHIM) + -IST.

e·lon·gate /iˈlôNGˌgāt, iˈläNG-/ ▶ **v.** [with obj.] make (something) longer, esp. unusually so in relation to its width. ■ [no obj.] chiefly Biology grow longer.
▶ **adj.** chiefly Biology long in relation to width; elongated: *elongate, fishlike creatures.*
– ORIGIN late Middle English (in the sense 'move away, place at a distance'): from late Latin *elongat-* 'placed at a distance,' from the verb *elongare*, from Latin *e-* (variant of *ex-*) 'away' + *longe* 'far off,' *longus* 'long.'

e·lon·gat·ed /iˈlôNGˌgātid, iˈläNG-/ ▶ **adj.** unusually long in relation to its width: *the creature had two sets of arms and an elongated face.*

e·lon·ga·tion /iˌlôNGˈgāsHən, ēˌlôNG-, iˌläNG-, ēˌläNG-/ ▶ **n.** the lengthening of something. ■ a part of a line formed by lengthening; a continuation. ■ the amount of extension of an object under stress, usually expressed as a percentage of the original length. ■ Astronomy the angular separation of a planet from the sun or of a satellite from a planet, as seen by an observer.
– ORIGIN late Middle English: from late Latin *elongatio(n-)*, from *elongare* 'place at a distance' (see ELONGATE).

e·lope /iˈlōp/ ▶ **v.** [no obj.] run away secretly in order to get married, esp. without parental consent: *later he eloped with one of the maids.*
– DERIVATIVES **e·lope·ment** **n.**, **e·lop·er** **n.**
– ORIGIN late 16th cent. (in the general sense 'abscond, run away'): from Anglo-Norman French *aloper*, perhaps related to LEAP.

el·o·quence /ˈeləkwəns/ ▶ **n.** fluent or persuasive speaking or writing: *a preacher of great power and eloquence.*
– ORIGIN late Middle English: via Old French from Latin *eloquentia*, from *eloqui* 'speak out,' from *e-* (variant of *ex-*) 'out' + *loqui* 'speak.'

el·o·quent /ˈeləkwənt/ ▶ **adj.** fluent or persuasive in speaking or writing: *an eloquent speech.* ■ clearly expressing or indicating something: *the touches of fatherliness are eloquent of the real man.*
– DERIVATIVES **el·o·quent·ly** **adv.**
– ORIGIN late Middle English: via Old French from Latin *eloquent-* 'speaking out,' from the verb *eloqui* (see ELOQUENCE).

El Pas·o /el ˈpasō/ a city in western Texas, on the Rio Grande, opposite Ciudad Juárez in Mexico; pop. 613,190 (est. 2008).

el-Qa·hi·ra /ˌel käˈhērə/ variant spelling of AL-QAHIRA.

El Sal·va·dor /el ˈsalvəˌdôr, ˌsälväˈdôr/ a country in western Central America, on the Pacific coast; pop. 7,185,200 (est. 2009); capital, San Salvador; official language, Spanish.

The territory was conquered by the Spanish in 1524 and gained its independence in 1821. Between 1979 and 1992 El Salvador was devastated by a civil war that was marked by the activities of right-wing death squads and resistance by left-wing guerrillas. A UN-brokered peace accord was agreed upon in 1992.

else /els/ ▶ **adv.** **1** [with indefinite pronoun or adv.] in addition; besides: ***anything else** you need to know?* | *I just brought basics—I wasn't sure **what else** you'd want* | *they will offer low prices but **little else**.*
2 [with indefinite pronoun or adv.] different; instead: *isn't there **anyone else** you could ask?* | *it's fate, destiny, or **whatever else** you like to call it.*
3 short for OR ELSE below.
– PHRASES **or else** used to introduce the second of two alternatives: *she felt tempted either to shout at him or else to let his tantrums slide by.* ■ in circumstances different from those mentioned; if it were not the case: *they can't want it, or else they'd request it.* ■ used to warn what will happen if something is not carried out: *you go along with this or else you're going to jail.* ■ used as a warning or a threat: *she'd better shape up, or else.*
– ORIGIN Old English *elles*, of Germanic origin; related to Middle Dutch *els* and Swedish *eljest*.

else·where /ˈelsˌ(h)wer/ ▶ **adv.** in, at, or to some other place or other places: *he is seeking employment elsewhere.*
▶ **pron.** some other place: *all Hawaiian plants originally came from elsewhere.*
– ORIGIN Old English *elles hwǣr* (see ELSE, WHERE).

El·si·nore /ˈelsəˌnôr/ a port on the northeastern coast of the island of Zealand in Denmark; pop. 61,053 (2009). It is the site of the 16th-century Kronborg Castle, which is the setting for Shakespeare's *Hamlet*. Danish name **HELSINGØR**.

ELSS ▶ **abbr.** extravehicular life support system.

El·ster /ˈelstər/ ▶ **n.** [usu. as modifier] Geology a Pleistocene glaciation in northern Europe, corresponding to the Anglian of Britain (and possibly the Mindel of the Alps). ■ the system of deposits laid down at this time.
– DERIVATIVES **El·ster·i·an** /elˈsti(ə)rēən/ **adj.** & **n.**
– ORIGIN 1930s: the name of a tributary of the Elbe River in Germany.

el·u·ant /ˈelyo͞oənt/ ▶ **n.** Chemistry a fluid used to elute a substance.
– ORIGIN 1940s: from Latin *eluent-* 'washing out,' from the verb *eluere* (see ELUTE).

el·u·ate /ˈelyo͞oit, -ˌāt/ ▶ **n.** Chemistry a solution obtained by elution.
– ORIGIN 1930s: from Latin *eluere* 'wash out' + -ATE[1].

e·lu·ci·date /iˈlo͞osiˌdāt/ ▶ **v.** [with obj.] make (something) clear; explain: *work such as theirs will help to elucidate this matter* | [with clause] *in what follows I shall try to elucidate what I believe the problems to be* | [no obj.] *they would not elucidate further.*
– DERIVATIVES **e·lu·ci·da·tive** /-ˌdātiv/ **adj.**, **e·lu·ci·da·tor** /-ˌdātər/ **n.**, **e·lu·ci·da·to·ry** /-dəˌtôrē/ **adj.**
– ORIGIN mid 16th cent.: from late Latin *elucidat-* 'made clear,' from the verb *elucidare*, from *e-* (variant of *ex-*) 'out' + *lucidus* 'lucid.'

e·lu·ci·da·tion /iˌlo͞osiˈdāsHən/ ▶ **n.** explanation that makes something clear; clarification: *work that led to the elucidation of the structure of proteins.*

e·lude /iˈlo͞od/ ▶ **v.** [with obj.] evade or escape from (a danger, enemy, or pursuer), typically in a skillful or cunning way: *he managed to elude his pursuers by escaping into an alley.* ■ (of an idea or fact) fail to be grasped or remembered by (someone): *the logic of this eluded most people.* ■ (of an achievement, or something desired or pursued) fail to be attained by (someone): *sleep still eluded her.* ■ avoid compliance with or subjection to (a law, demand, or penalty).
– DERIVATIVES **e·lu·sion** /iˈlo͞ozHən/ **n.**
– ORIGIN mid 16th cent. (in the sense 'delude, baffle'): from Latin *eludere*, from *e-* (variant of *ex-*) 'out, away from' + *ludere* 'to play.'

el·u·ent /ˈelyo͞oənt/ ▶ **n.** variant spelling of ELUANT.

E·lul /ˈeləl, eˈlo͞ol/ ▶ **n.** (in the Jewish calendar) the twelfth month of the civil and sixth of the religious year, usually coinciding with parts of August and September.
– ORIGIN from Hebrew *'ĕlūl*.

el-Uq·sur /el ˈo͝okˌso͝or/ (also **al-Uqsur** /äl/) Arabic name for LUXOR.

e·lu·sive /iˈlo͞osiv/ ▶ **adj.** difficult to find, catch, or achieve: *success will become ever more elusive.* ■ difficult to remember or recall: *the elusive thought he had had moments before.*
– DERIVATIVES **e·lu·sive·ly** **adv.**, **e·lu·sive·ness** **n.**
– ORIGIN early 18th cent.: from Latin *elus-* 'eluded' (from the verb *eludere*) + -IVE.

e·lute /iˈlo͞ot/ ▶ **v.** [with obj.] Chemistry remove (an adsorbed substance) by washing with a solvent, esp. in chromatography.
– DERIVATIVES **e·lu·tion** /iˈlo͞osHən/ **n.**
– ORIGIN 1920s: from Latin *elut-* 'washed out,' from the verb *eluere*, suggested by German *eluieren*.

e·lu·tri·ate /iˈlo͞otrēˌāt/ ▶ **v.** [with obj.] Chemistry separate (lighter and heavier particles in a mixture) by suspension in an upward flow of liquid or gas. ■ purify by straining.
– DERIVATIVES **e·lu·tri·a·tion** /iˌlo͞otrēˈāsHən/ **n.**
– ORIGIN mid 18th cent.: from Latin *elutriat-* 'washed out,' from the verb *elutriare*, from *e-* (variant of *ex-*) 'out' + *lutriare* 'to wash.'

el·van /ˈelvən/ ▶ **n.** Geology hard intrusive igneous rock found in Cornwall, England, typically quartz porphyry.
– ORIGIN early 18th cent.: perhaps via Cornish from Welsh *elfen* 'element.'

el·ver /ˈelvər/ ▶ **n.** a young eel, esp. when undergoing mass migration upriver from the sea.
– ORIGIN mid 17th cent.: variant of dialect *eel-fare* 'the passage of young eels up a river,' also 'a brood of young eels,' from EEL + FARE in its original sense 'a journey.'

elves /elvz/ plural form of ELF.

E·lyr·ia /iˈli(ə)rēə/ an industrial city in northern Ohio, west of Cleveland; pop. 54,979 (est. 2008).

E·ly·sée Pal·ace /ˌeléˈzā/ a building in Paris that has been the official residence of the French president since 1870. It was built in 1718 and was occupied by Madame de Pompadour, Napoleon I, and Napoleon III.

E·ly·sian /iˈlizHən, iˈlē-/ ▶ **adj.** of, relating to, or characteristic of heaven or paradise: *Elysian visions.*
– PHRASES **the Elysian Fields** another name for ELYSIUM.

E·ly·si·um /iˈlizHēəm, iˈlizēəm, iˈlē-/ Greek Mythology the place at the ends of the earth to which certain favored heroes were conveyed by the gods after death. ■ (as noun **an Elysium**) a place or state of perfect happiness.
– ORIGIN via Latin from Greek *Elusion (pedion)* '(plain) of the blessed.'

el·y·tron /ˈeləˌträn/ ▶ **n.** (pl. **elytra** /-trə/) Entomology each of the two wing cases of a beetle.
– DERIVATIVES **el·y·trous** /-trəs/ **adj.**
– ORIGIN mid 18th cent. (denoting a sheath or covering, specifically that of the spinal cord): from Greek *elutron* 'sheath.'

El·ze·vir /ˈelzəˌvi(ə)r/ a family of Dutch printers. Fifteen members were active 1581–1712; **Bonaventure** (1583–1652) and **Abraham** (1592–1652) managed the firm in its prime.

EM ▶ **abbr.** ■ electromagnetic. ■ Engineer of Mines. ■ enlisted man (men).

em /em/ ▶ **n.** Printing a unit for measuring the width of printed matter, equal to the height of the type size being used. ■ a unit of measurement equal to twelve points.
– ORIGIN late 18th cent.: the letter *M* represented as a word, since it is approximately this width.

'em /əm/ ▶ **pron.** short for THEM, esp. in informal use: *let 'em know who's boss.*
– ORIGIN Middle English: originally a form of *hem*, dative and accusative third person plural pronoun in Middle English; now regarded as an abbreviation of THEM.

em- ▶ **prefix** variant spelling of EN-[1], EN-[2] assimilated before *b*, *p* (as in *emblazon, emplacement*).

e·ma·ci·at·ed /iˈmāsHēˌātid/ ▶ **adj.** abnormally thin or weak, esp. because of illness or a lack of food: *she was so emaciated she could hardly stand.*

e·ma·ci·a·tion /iˌmāsHēˈāsHən/ ▶ **n.** the state of being abnormally thin or weak: *thin to the point of emaciation.*

e-mail /ˈēmāl/ (also **email**) ▶ **n.** messages distributed by electronic means from one computer user to one or more recipients via a network: *reading e-mail has become the first task of the morning* | [as modifier] *e-mail messages.* ■ the system of sending messages by such electronic means: *a contract communicated by e-mail.* ■ a message sent by e-mail: *I got three e-mails from my mother today.*
▶ **v.** [with obj.] send an e-mail to (someone): *you can e-mail me at my normal address.* ■ send (a message) by e-mail: *employees can e-mail the results back.*
– DERIVATIVES **e-mail·er** **n.**
– ORIGIN 1980s: abbreviation of ELECTRONIC MAIL.

em·a·lan·gen·i /ˌeməläNGˈgenē/ plural form of LILANGENI.

em·a·nate /ˈeməˌnāt/ ▶ **v.** [no obj.] (**emanate from**) (of something abstract but perceptible) issue or spread out from (a source): *warmth emanated from the fireplace* | *she felt an undeniable charm emanating from him.* ■ originate from; be produced by: *the proposals emanated from a committee.* ■ [with obj.] give out or emit (something abstract but perceptible): *he emanated a powerful brooding air.*
– DERIVATIVES **em·a·na·tive** /-ˌnātiv/ **adj.**, **em·a·na·tor** /-ˌnātər/ **n.**
– ORIGIN mid 18th cent.: from Latin *emanat-* 'flowed out,' from the verb *emanare*, from *e-* (variant of *ex-*) 'out' + *manare* 'to flow.'

em·a·na·tion /ˌeməˈnāsHən/ ▶ **n.** an abstract but perceptible thing that issues or originates from a source: *she saw the insults as emanations of his own tortured personality.* ■ the action or process of issuing from a source: *the risk of radon gas emanation.* ■ a tenuous substance or form of radiation given off by something: *vaporous emanations surround the mill's foundations.* ■ Chemistry, archaic a radioactive gas formed by radioactive decay of a solid. ■ (in various mystical traditions) a being or force that is a manifestation of God.

e·man·ci·pate /iˈmansəˌpāt/ ▶ **v.** [with obj.] set free, esp. from legal, social, or political restrictions: *the citizen must be **emancipated from** the obsessive secrecy of government.* ■ Law set (a child) free from the authority of its father or parents. ■ free from slavery: *it is estimated that he emancipated 8,000 slaves.*
– DERIVATIVES **e·man·ci·pa·tor** /-ˌpātər/ **n.**, **e·man·ci·pa·to·ry** /-pəˌtôrē/ **adj.**
– ORIGIN early 17th cent.: from Latin *emancipat-* 'transferred as property,' from the verb *emancipare*, from *e-* (variant of *ex-*) 'out' + *mancipium* 'slave.'

e·man·ci·pat·ed /iˈmansəˌpātəd/ ▶ **adj.** free from legal, social, or political restrictions; liberated: *emancipated young women.*

e·man·ci·pa·tion /iˌmansəˈpāSHən/ ▶ **n.** the fact or process of being set free from legal, social, or political restrictions; liberation: *the emancipation of feminist ideas.* ■ the freeing of someone from slavery.

E·man·ci·pa·tion Proc·la·ma·tion /iˌmansəˈpāSHən/ the announcement made by President Lincoln during the Civil War on September 22, 1862, emancipating all black slaves in states still engaged in rebellion against the Union. Although implementation was strictly beyond Lincoln's powers, the declaration turned the war into a crusade against slavery. It went into effect on January 1, 1863.

e·mas·cu·late /iˈmaskyəˌlāt/ ▶ **v.** [with obj.] make (a person, idea, or piece of legislation) weaker or less effective: *our winner-take-all elections emasculate fringe parties.* ■ (usu. as adj. **emasculated**) deprive (a man) of his male role or identity: *he feels emasculated because he cannot control his sons' behavior.* ■ archaic castrate (a man or male animal). ■ Botany remove the anthers from a flower.
– DERIVATIVES **e·mas·cu·la·tion** /iˌmaskyəˈlāSHən/ **n.**, **e·mas·cu·la·tor** /-ˌlātər/ **n.**, **e·mas·cu·la·to·ry** /-ləˌtôrē/ **adj.**
– ORIGIN early 17th cent.: from Latin *emasculat-* 'castrated,' from the verb *emasculare*, from *e-* (variant of *ex-*, expressing a change of state) + *masculus* 'male.'

em·balm /emˈbä(l)m/ ▶ **v.** [with obj.] **1** (often as noun **embalming**) preserve (a corpse) from decay, originally with spices and now usually by arterial injection of a preservative: *the Egyptian method of embalming.* ■ preserve (someone or something) in an unaltered state: *the band was all about revitalizing pop greats and embalming their legacy.*
2 archaic give a pleasant fragrance to: *the sweetness of the linden trees embalmed all the air.*
– DERIVATIVES **em·balm·er n.**, **em·balm·ment n.**
– ORIGIN Middle English: from Old French *embaumer*, from *em-* 'in' + *baume* 'balm,' variant of *basme* (see **BALM**).

em·bank /emˈbaNGk/ ▶ **v.** [with obj.] construct a wall or bank of earth or stone in order to confine (a river) within certain limits. ■ construct a bank of earth or stone to carry (a road or railroad) over an area of low ground.

em·bank·ment /emˈbaNGkmənt/ ▶ **n.** a wall or bank of earth or stone built to prevent a river flooding an area. ■ a bank of earth or stone built to carry a road or railroad over an area of low ground.

em·bar·go /emˈbärgō/ ▶ **n.** (pl. **embargoes**) an official ban on trade or other commercial activity with a particular country: *an **embargo on** grain sales | the oil embargo of 1973.* ■ an official prohibition on any activity. ■ historical an order of a state forbidding foreign ships to enter, or any ships to leave, its ports. ■ archaic a stoppage, prohibition, or impediment.
▶ **v.** (**embargoes, embargoing, embargoed**) [with obj.] **1** (usu. **be embargoed**) impose an official ban on (trade or a country or commodity): *the country has been virtually embargoed by most of the noncommunist world.* ■ officially ban the publication of: *documents of national security importance are routinely embargoed.*
2 archaic seize (a ship or goods) for state service.
– ORIGIN early 17th cent.: from Spanish, from *embargar* 'arrest,' based on Latin *in-* 'in, within' + *barra* 'a bar.'

em·bark /emˈbärk/ ▶ **v.** [no obj.] go on board a ship, aircraft, or other vehicle: *he **embarked for** India in 1817.* ■ [with obj.] put or take on board a ship or aircraft: *its passengers were ready to be embarked.* ■ (**embark on/upon**) begin (a course of action, esp. one that is important or demanding): *he embarked on a new career.*
– DERIVATIVES **em·bar·ka·tion** /ˌembärˈkāSHən/ **n.**, **em·bark·ment n.**
– ORIGIN mid 16th cent.: from French *embarquer*, from *em-* 'in' + *barque* 'bark, ship.'

em·bar·ras de ri·chesses /äNbäˈrä də rēˈSHes/ (also **embarras de choix** /SHwä/) ▶ **n.** more options or resources than one knows what to do with: *he had presented us with an embarras de richesses of history and culture.*
– ORIGIN mid 18th cent.: French, literally 'embarrassment of riches (or choice).'

em·bar·rass /emˈbarəs/ ▶ **v.** [with obj.] cause (someone) to feel awkward, self-conscious, or ashamed: *she wouldn't embarrass either of them by making a scene.* ■ (**be embarrassed**) be caused financial difficulties: *he would be embarrassed by an inheritance tax.* ■ archaic hamper or impede (a person, movement, or action): *the state of the rivers will embarrass the enemy in a considerable degree.* ■ archaic make difficult or intricate; complicate.
– ORIGIN early 17th cent. (in the sense 'hamper, impede'): from French *embarrasser*, from Spanish *embarazar*, probably from Portuguese *embaraçar* (from *baraço* 'halter').

em·bar·rassed /emˈbarəst/ ▶ **adj.** feeling or showing embarrassment: *he became embarrassed at his own effusiveness | an embarrassed silence.* ■ having or showing financial difficulties.
– DERIVATIVES **em·bar·rassed·ly** /-əstlē, -əsidlē/ **adv.**

em·bar·rass·ing /emˈbarəsiNG/ ▶ **adj.** causing embarrassment: *an embarrassing muddle.*
– DERIVATIVES **em·bar·rass·ing·ly adv.**

em·bar·rass·ment /-mənt/ ▶ **n.** a feeling of self-consciousness, shame, or awkwardness: *I turned red with embarrassment.* ■ a person or thing causing such feelings: *he was an embarrassment who was safely left ignored | her extreme views might be an **embarrassment to** the movement.* ■ financial difficulty: *his temporary financial embarrassment.*
– PHRASES **embarrassment of riches** (or **choice**) more options or resources than one knows what to do with: *picking a highlight from such an embarrassment of riches is hard.*

em·bas·sage /ˈembəsij/ ▶ **n.** archaic the business or message of an envoy. ■ a body of people sent as a deputation to or on behalf of a head of state. ■ archaic term for **EMBASSY**.
– ORIGIN late 15th cent. (denoting the action of sending an envoy): from Old French *ambasse* 'message or embassy' + **-AGE**.

em·bas·sy /ˈembəsē/ ▶ **n.** (pl. **embassies**) **1** the official residence or offices of an ambassador: *the Chilean embassy in Moscow.* ■ the staff working in such a building: *the embassy denied any involvement in the murder.* ■ the position or function of an ambassador.
2 chiefly historical a deputation or mission sent by one ruler or state to another.
– ORIGIN late 16th cent. (originally also as *ambassy* denoting the position of ambassador): from Old French *ambasse*, based on Latin *ambactus* 'servant.' Compare with **AMBASSADOR**.

em·bat·tle /emˈbatl/ ▶ **v.** [with obj.] archaic set (an army) in battle array: *it was three o'clock before the king's army was embattled.* ■ fortify (a building or place) against attack.
– ORIGIN Middle English: from Old French *embataillier*.

em·bat·tled /emˈbatld/ ▶ **adj. 1** (of a place or people) involved in or prepared for war, esp. because surrounded by enemy forces: *the embattled Yugoslavian republics.* ■ (of a person) beset by problems or difficulties: *the worst may not be over for the embattled senator.*
2 [postpositive] Heraldry divided or edged by a line of square notches like battlements in outline.

em·bay /emˈbā/ ▶ **v.** [with obj.] (usu. **be embayed**) (chiefly of the wind) confine (a sailing vessel) to a bay: *ships were embayed between two headlands.* ■ (as adj. **embayed**) formed into bays; hollowed out by or as if by the sea: *the embayed island.* ■ chiefly Geology enclose (something) in a recess or hollow.

em·bay·ment /emˈbāmənt/ ▶ **n.** a recess in a coastline forming a bay.

em·bed /emˈbed/ (also **imbed** /im-/) ▶ **v.** (**embeds, embedding, embedded**) [with obj.] **1** fix (an object) firmly and deeply in a surrounding mass: *he had an operation to remove a nail **embedded in** his chest.* ■ implant (an idea or feeling) within something else so it becomes an ingrained or essential characteristic of it: *the Victorian values **embedded in** Tennyson's poetry.* ■ Linguistics place (a phrase or clause) within another clause or sentence. ■ Computing incorporate (a text or code) within the body of a file or document. ■ (often as adj. **embedded**) design and build (a microprocessor) as an integral part of a system or device.
2 attach (a journalist) to a military unit during a conflict.
▶ **n.** /ˈemˌbed/ an embedded journalist: *most of the embeds found themselves covering construction and civil works projects.*

– DERIVATIVES **em·bed·ment n.**

em·bel·lish /emˈbeliSH/ ▶ **v.** [with obj.] make (something) more attractive by the addition of decorative details or features: *blue silk embellished with golden embroidery.* ■ make (a statement or story) more interesting or entertaining by adding extra details, esp. ones that are not true: *she had real difficulty telling the truth because she liked to embellish things.*
– DERIVATIVES **em·bel·lish·er n.**
– ORIGIN late Middle English: from Old French *embelliss-*, lengthened stem of *embellir*, based on *bel* 'handsome,' from Latin *bellus*.

em·bel·lish·ment /emˈbeliSHmənt/ ▶ **n.** a decorative detail or feature added to something to make it more attractive: *architectural embellishments.* ■ a detail, esp. one that is not true, added to a statement or story to make it more interesting or entertaining. ■ the action of adding such details or features.

em·ber /ˈembər/ ▶ **n.** (usu. **embers**) a small piece of burning or glowing coal or wood in a dying fire: *the dying embers in the fireplace* | figurative *the flickering embers of nationalism.*
– ORIGIN Old English *ǣmyrge*, of Germanic origin; related to Old High German *eimuria* 'pyre,' Danish *emmer*, Swedish *mörja* 'embers.' The *b* was added in English for ease of pronunciation when the vowel of the second syllable (*y*) disappeared.

Em·ber day ▶ **n.** any of a number of days reserved for fasting and prayer in the Western Christian Church. Ember days traditionally comprise the Wednesday, Friday, and Saturday following St. Lucy's Day (December 13), the first Sunday in Lent, Pentecost (Whitsun), and Holy Cross Day (September 14), though other days are observed locally.
– ORIGIN Old English *ymbren*, perhaps an alteration of *ymbryne* 'period,' from *ymb* 'around' + *ryne* 'course,' perhaps influenced in part by ecclesiastical Latin *quatuor tempora* 'four periods' (on which the equivalent German *Quatember* is based).

em·bez·zle /emˈbezəl/ ▶ **v.** [with obj.] steal or misappropriate (money placed in one's trust or belonging to the organization for which one works): *she had embezzled $5,600,000 in company funds.*
– DERIVATIVES **em·bez·zler** /emˈbezlər/ **n.**
– ORIGIN late Middle English (in the sense 'steal'): from Anglo-Norman French *embesiler*, from *besiler* in the same sense (compare with Old French *besillier* 'maltreat, ravage'), of unknown ultimate origin. The current sense dates from the late 16th cent.

em·bez·zle·ment /emˈbezəlmənt/ ▶ **n.** theft or misappropriation of funds placed in one's trust or belonging to one's employer: *charges of fraud and embezzlement.*

Em·bi·op·ter·a /ˌembēˈäptərə, ˌembī-/ Entomology a small order of insects that comprises the web-spinners.
– DERIVATIVES **em·bi·op·ter·an n. & adj.**
– ORIGIN modern Latin (plural), from *Embia* (genus name) + Greek *pteron* 'wing.'

em·bit·ter /emˈbitər/ ▶ **v.** [with obj.] (usu. as adj. **embittered**) cause (someone) to feel bitter or resentful: *he died an embittered man.* ■ literary give a sharp or pungent taste or smell to: *the smell of orange zest and smoke embittered the air.*
– DERIVATIVES **em·bit·ter·ment n.**

em·bla·zon /emˈblāzn/ ▶ **v.** [with obj.] conspicuously inscribe or display (a design) on something: *T-shirts **emblazoned with** the names of baseball teams.* ■ depict (a heraldic device): *the cardinal's coat of arms is emblazoned on the door panel.* ■ archaic celebrate or extol publicly: *their success was emblazoned.*
– DERIVATIVES **em·bla·zon·ment n.**

em·blem /ˈembləm/ ▶ **n.** a heraldic device or symbolic object as a distinctive badge of a nation, organization, or family: *America's national emblem, the bald eagle.* ■ (**emblem of**) a thing serving as a symbolic representation of a particular quality or concept: *our child would be a dazzling emblem of our love.*
– ORIGIN late 16th cent. (as a verb): from Latin *emblema* 'inlaid work, raised ornament,' from Greek *emblēma* 'insertion,' from *emballein* 'throw in, insert,' from *em-* 'in' + *ballein* 'to throw.'

em·blem·at·ic /ˌembləˈmatik/ ▶ **adj.** serving as a symbol of a particular quality or concept; symbolic: *this case is emblematic of a larger problem.*

– DERIVATIVES **em·blem·at·i·cal** /ˌembləˈmatikəl/ **adj.**, **em·blem·at·i·cal·ly** /ˌembləˈmatik(ə)lē/ **adv.**

em·blem·a·tist /emˈblemətist/ ▶ **n.** a creator or user of emblems, esp. in allegorical pictures.

em·blem·a·tize /emˈbleməˌtīz/ ▶ **v.** [with obj.] formal serve as a symbolic representation of (a quality or concept).

em·ble·ments /ˈembləmənts/ ▶ **plural n.** Law the profit from growing crops that have been sown, regarded as personal property.
– ORIGIN late 15th cent.: from Old French *emblaement*, from *emblaier* 'sow with corn' (based on *blé* 'corn').

em·bod·i·ment /emˈbädēmənt, im-/ ▶ **n.** a tangible or visible form of an idea, quality, or feeling: *she seemed to be a living embodiment of vitality.* ■ the representation or expression of something in such a form: *it was in Germany alone that his hope seemed capable of embodiment.*

em·bod·y /emˈbädē/ ▶ **v.** (**embodies, embodying, embodied**) [with obj.] **1** be an expression of or give a tangible or visible form to (an idea, quality, or feeling): *a team that embodies competitive spirit and skill.* ■ provide (a spirit) with a physical form.
2 include or contain (something) as a constituent part: *the changes in law* ***embodied in*** *the Freedom of Information Act.*
3 archaic form (people) into a body, esp. for military purposes.
– DERIVATIVES **em·bod·i·er** /-ˈbädēər/ **n.**
– ORIGIN mid 16th cent.: from **EM-** + **BODY**, on the pattern of Latin *incorporare.*

em·bold·en /emˈbōldən/ ▶ **v.** [with obj.] **1** give (someone) the courage or confidence to do something or to behave in a certain way: *emboldened by robust passenger traffic, the airlines put through major fare increases.*
2 cause (a piece of text) to appear in a bold typeface: *center, embolden, and underline the heading.*

em·bo·lec·to·my /ˌembəˈlektəmē/ ▶ **n.** (pl. **embolectomies**) surgical removal of an embolus.

em·bo·lism /ˈembəˌlizəm/ ▶ **n.** **1** Medicine obstruction of an artery, typically by a clot of blood or an air bubble.
2 the periodic intercalation of days or a month to correct the accumulating discrepancy between the calendar year and the solar year, as in a leap year.
– ORIGIN mid 19th cent.: via late Latin from Greek *embolismos*, from *emballein* 'insert.'

em·bo·li·za·tion /ˌembəliˈzāSHən/ ▶ **n.** Medicine the artificial or natural formation or development of an embolus.

em·bo·lus /ˈembələs/ ▶ **n.** (pl. **emboli** /-ˌlī, -ˌlē/) a blood clot, air bubble, piece of fatty deposit, or other object that has been carried in the bloodstream to lodge in a vessel and cause an embolism.
– DERIVATIVES **em·bol·ic** /emˈbälik/ **adj.**
– ORIGIN mid 17th cent. (denoting something inserted or moving within another, specifically the plunger of a syringe): from Latin, literally 'piston,' from Greek *embolos* 'peg, stopper.' The current sense dates from the mid 19th cent.

em·bon·point /ˌänbônˈpwan/ ▶ **n.** the plump or fleshy part of a person's body, in particular a woman's bosom.
– ORIGIN late 17th cent.: from French *en bon point* 'in good condition.'

em·bos·om /emˈbo͝ozəm/ ▶ **v.** [with obj.] (usu. **be embosomed**) literary take or press to one's bosom; embrace. ■ enclose or surround (something) protectively.

em·boss /emˈbôs, -ˈbäs/ ▶ **v.** [with obj.] (usu. as adj. **embossed**) carve or mold a design on (a surface) so that it stands out in relief: *an embossed brass dish.* ■ decorate (a surface) with a raised design.
– DERIVATIVES **em·boss·er n.**, **em·boss·ment n.**
– ORIGIN late Middle English: from the Old French base of obsolete French *embosser*, from *em-* 'into' + *boce* 'protuberance.'

em·bou·chure /ˌämbo͞oˈsHo͝or/ ▶ **n.** **1** Music the way in which a player applies the mouth to the mouthpiece of a brass or wind instrument. ■ the mouthpiece of a flute or a similar instrument.
2 archaic the mouth of a river or valley.
– ORIGIN mid 18th cent.: French, from *s'emboucher* 'discharge itself by the mouth,' from *emboucher* 'put in or to the mouth,' from *em-* 'into' + *bouche* 'mouth.'

em·bour·geoise·ment /emˈbo͝orZHwäzmənt, -ˌmänt/ ▶ **n.** the proliferation in a society of values perceived as characteristic of the middle class, esp. of materialism.
– ORIGIN 1930s: French, from *embourgeoiser* 'become or make bourgeois.'

em·bowed /emˈbōd/ ▶ **adj.** literary bent, arched, or vaulted. ■ [postpositive] Heraldry (of an arm) bent at the elbow; (of a dolphin) with the body curved.

em·bow·el /emˈbouəl/ ▶ **v.** (**embowels, emboweling, emboweled**; Brit. **embowels, embowelling, embowelled**) archaic term for **DISEMBOWEL**.
– ORIGIN early 16th cent.: from Old French *emboweler*, alteration of *esboueler*, from *es-* 'out' + *bouel* 'bowel.'

em·bow·er /emˈbou(-ə)r/ ▶ **v.** [with obj.] (usu. **be embowered**) literary surround or shelter (a place or a person), esp. with trees or climbing plants: *the house stood remote,* ***embowered in*** *trees.*

em·brace /emˈbrās/ ▶ **v.** [with obj.] **1** hold (someone) closely in one's arms, esp. as a sign of affection: *Aunt Sophie embraced her warmly* | [no obj.] *the two embraced, holding each other tightly.*
2 accept or support (a belief, theory, or change) willingly and enthusiastically: *besides traditional methods, artists are embracing new technology.*
3 include or contain (something) as a constituent part: *his career embraces a number of activities—composing, playing, and acting.*
▶ **n.** **1** an act of holding someone closely in one's arms: *they were locked in an embrace.* ■ used to refer to something that is regarded as surrounding, holding, or restricting someone: *the transformations brought about by the embrace of mass media.*
2 [in sing.] an act of accepting or supporting something willingly or enthusiastically: *their eager embrace of foreign influences.*
– DERIVATIVES **em·brace·a·ble adj.**, **em·brace·ment n.**, **em·brac·er n.**
– ORIGIN Middle English (in the sense 'encircle, surround, enclose'; formerly also as *imbrace*): from Old French *embracer*, based on Latin *in-* 'in' + *bracchium* 'arm.'

em·bra·sure /emˈbrāZHər/ ▶ **n.** a small opening in a parapet of a fortified building, splayed on the inside.
– DERIVATIVES **em·bra·sured adj.**
– ORIGIN early 18th cent.: from French, from obsolete *embraser* (earlier form of *ébraser*) 'widen a door or window opening,' of unknown ultimate origin.

em·brit·tle /emˈbritl/ ▶ **v.** make or become brittle.
– DERIVATIVES **em·brit·tle·ment n.**

em·bro·ca·tion /ˌembrəˈkāSHən/ ▶ **n.** a liquid used for rubbing on the body to relieve pain from sprains and strains.
– ORIGIN late Middle English: from medieval Latin *embrocatio(n-)*, from the verb *embrocare*, based on Greek *embrokhē* 'lotion.'

em·broi·der /emˈbroidər/ ▶ **v.** [with obj.] **1** decorate (cloth) by sewing patterns on it with thread: *she had already embroidered a dozen little nighties for the babies* | (as adj. **embroidered**) *an embroidered handkerchief* | [no obj.] *she was teaching one of the girls how to embroider.* ■ produce (a design) on cloth in this way: (as adj. **embroidered**) *a chunky knit sweater with embroidered flowers.*
2 add fictitious or exaggerated details to (an account) to make it more interesting: *she embroidered her stories with colorful detail.*
– DERIVATIVES **em·broi·der·er n.**
– ORIGIN late Middle English: from Anglo-Norman French *enbrouder*, from *en-* 'in, on' + Old French *brouder*, *broisder* 'decorate with embroidery,' of Germanic origin.

em·broi·der·y /emˈbroid(ə)rē/ ▶ **n.** (pl. **embroideries**) **1** the art or pastime of embroidering cloth. ■ cloth decorated in this way.
2 embellishment or exaggeration in the description or reporting of an event: *fanciful embroidery of the facts.*
– ORIGIN late Middle English: from Anglo-Norman French *enbrouderie*, from *enbrouder* 'embroider.'

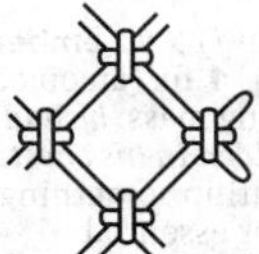

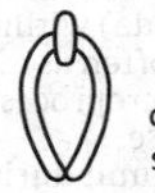

embroidery stitches

em·broil /emˈbroil/ ▶ **v.** [with obj.] (often as adj. **embroiled**) involve (someone) deeply in an argument, conflict, or difficult situation: *she became* ***embroiled in*** *a dispute between two women she hardly knew* | *the movie's about a journalist who becomes* ***embroiled with*** *a nightclub owner.* ■ bring into a state of confusion or disorder.
– DERIVATIVES **em·broil·ment n.**
– ORIGIN early 17th cent.: from French *embrouiller* 'to muddle.'

em·bry·ec·to·my /ˌembrēˈektəmē/ ▶ **n.** (pl. **embryectomies**) the surgical removal of an embryo, esp. one implanted outside the uterus in an ectopic pregnancy.

em·bry·o /ˈembrēˌō/ ▶ **n.** (pl. **embryos**) **1** an unborn or unhatched offspring in the process of development. ■ an unborn human baby, esp. in the first eight weeks from conception, after implantation but before all the organs are developed. Compare with **FETUS**.
2 Botany the part of a seed that develops into a plant, consisting (in the mature embryo of a higher plant) of a plumule, a radicle, and one or two cotyledons.
3 a thing at a rudimentary stage that shows potential for development: *a simple commodity economy is merely the embryo of a capitalist economy.*
– PHRASES **in embryo** at a rudimentary stage with the potential for further development.
– ORIGIN late Middle English: via late Latin from Greek *embruon* 'fetus,' from *em-* 'into' + *bruein* 'swell, grow.'

embryo- ▶ **comb. form** representing **EMBRYO**.

em·bry·o·gen·e·sis /ˌembrē-ōˈjenəsis/ ▶ **n.** Biology the formation and development of an embryo.
– DERIVATIVES **em·bry·o·ge·net·ic** /-jəˈnetik/ **adj.**, **em·bry·o·gen·ic** /-ˈjenik/ **adj.**, **em·bry·og·e·ny** /ˌembrēˈäjənē/ **n.**

em·bry·ol·o·gy /ˌembrēˈäləjē/ ▶ **n.** the branch of biology and medicine concerned with the study of embryos and their development.
– DERIVATIVES **em·bry·o·log·ic** /ˌembrēəˈläjik/ **adj.**, **em·bry·o·log·i·cal** /ˌembrēəˈläjikəl/ **adj.**, **em·bry·o·log·i·cal·ly** /ˌembrēəˈläjik(ə)lē/ **adv.**, **em·bry·ol·o·gist** /-jist/ **n.**

em·bry·o·nate /ˈembrēəˌnāt/ ▶ **adj.** (of an egg) containing an embryo.
▶ **v.** [no obj.] (usu. as adj. **embryonated**) (of an egg) develop into an embryo: *embryonated duck eggs* | *the eggs were allowed two weeks to embryonate.*

em·bry·on·ic /ˌembrēˈänik/ ▶ **adj.** (also **embryonal** /ˈembrēənəl/) **1** of or relating to an embryo.
2 (of a system, idea, or organization) in a rudimentary stage with potential for further development: *the plan is still in its embryonic stages.*
– DERIVATIVES **em·bry·on·i·cal·ly** /-(ə)lē/ **adv.**
– ORIGIN mid 19th cent.: from late Latin *embryo*, *embryon-* 'embryo' + **-IC**.

em·bry·op·a·thy /ˌembrēˈäpəTHē/ ▶ **n.** (pl. **embryopathies**) a developmental defect in an embryo or fetus.

em·bry·o sac ▶ **n.** a cell inside the ovule of a flowering plant where fertilization occurs and which becomes the female gametophyte, containing the endosperm nucleus and the fertilized ovum that develops into the embryo.

em·cee /ˌemˈsē/ informal ▶ **n.** a master of ceremonies.
▶ **v.** (**emcees, emceeing, emceed**) [with obj.] perform the role of a master of ceremonies at (a public entertainment or a large social occasion).
– ORIGIN 1930s: representing the pronunciation of **MC**.

em dash ▶ **n.** a long dash used in punctuation.

-eme ▶ **suffix** Linguistics forming nouns denoting linguistic units that are in systemic contrast with one other: *grapheme* | *phoneme.*
– ORIGIN abstracted from **PHONEME**.

e·mend /iˈmend/ ▶ **v.** [with obj.] make corrections and improvements to (a text). ■ alter (something) in such a way as to correct it: *the year of his death might need to be emended to 652* | [with clause] *he hesitated and quickly emended what he had said.*
– DERIVATIVES **e·mend·a·ble adj.**, **e·mend·er n.**
– ORIGIN late Middle English: from Latin *emendare*, from *e-* (variant of *ex-*) 'out of' + *menda* 'a fault.' Compare with **AMEND**.

e·men·da·tion /ˌēmənˈdāSHən, ˌemən-/ ▶ **n.** the process of making a revision or correction to a text. ■ a correction or revision to a text: *here are some suggested emendations.*

emer. ▶ **abbr.** emerita or emeritus.

em·er·ald /ˈem(ə)rəld/ ▶ **n.** **1** a bright green precious stone consisting of a chromium-rich variety of beryl.
2 a bright green color like that of an emerald: [as modifier] *the leaves are emerald green.*

3 a small hummingbird with bright metallic green plumage and darker wings and tail, found mainly in the area of the Caribbean and Central America. ● Three genera, in particular *Chlorostilbon* and *Amazilia*, family Trochilidae: numerous species. ▶ **adj.** bright green in color: *beyond the airport lay emerald hills.*
– ORIGIN Middle English: from Old French *e(s)meraud*, ultimately via Latin from Greek *(s)maragdos*, via Prakrit from Semitic (compare with Hebrew *bāreqeṯ*, from *bāraq* 'flash, sparkle').

em·er·ald-cut ▶ **adj.** (of a gem) cut in a rectangular shape with stepped facets.

Em·er·ald Isle a name for Ireland.

e·merge /i'mərj/ ▶ **v.** [no obj.] move out of or away from something and come into view: *black ravens emerged from the fog.* ■ become apparent, important, or prominent: *Philadelphia has* ***emerged as the clear favorite*** | (as adj. **emerging**) *a world of emerging economic giants.* ■ (of facts or circumstances) become known: *reports of a deadlock emerged during preliminary discussions* | [with clause] *during the trial it emerged that she had been suffering from a rare personality disorder.* ■ recover from or survive a difficult or demanding situation: *the economy has started to emerge from recession.* ■ (of an insect or other invertebrate) break out from an egg, cocoon, or pupal case.
– ORIGIN late 16th cent. (in the sense 'become known, come to light'): from Latin *emergere*, from *e-* (variant of *ex-*) 'out, forth' + *mergere* 'to dip.'

e·mer·gence /i'mərjəns/ ▶ **n. 1** the process of coming into view or becoming exposed after being concealed: *I misjudged the timing of my emergence.* ■ the escape of an insect or other invertebrate from an egg, cocoon, pupal case, etc. ■ Botany an outgrowth from a stem or leaf composed of epidermal and subepidermal tissue, as the prickles on a thistle plant.
2 the process of coming into being, or of becoming important or prominent: *the emergence of the environmental movement* | *Japan's emergence as a modern state.*
– ORIGIN mid 17th cent. (in the sense 'unforeseen occurrence'): from medieval Latin *emergentia*, from Latin *emergere* 'bring to light' (see **EMERGE**).

e·mer·gen·cy /i'mərjənsē/ ▶ **n.** (pl. **emergencies**) a serious, unexpected, and often dangerous situation requiring immediate action: *your quick response in an emergency could be a lifesaver* | *times of emergency.* ■ [as modifier] arising from or needed or used in an emergency: *an emergency exit.* ■ a person with a medical condition requiring immediate treatment. ■ short for **EMERGENCY ROOM**: *he was rushed into emergency.*
– ORIGIN mid 17th cent.: from medieval Latin *emergentia*, from Latin *emergere* 'arise, bring to light' (see **EMERGE**).

e·mer·gen·cy med·i·cal tech·ni·cian (abbr.: **EMT**) ▶ **n.** a person who is specially trained and certified to administer basic emergency services to victims of trauma or acute illness before and during transportation to a hospital or other healthcare facility.

e·mer·gen·cy room ▶ **n.** the department of a hospital that provides immediate treatment for acute illnesses and trauma.

e·mer·gen·cy serv·ic·es ▶ **plural n.** the public organizations that respond to and deal with emergencies when they occur, esp. those that provide police, ambulance, and firefighting services.

e·mer·gent /i'mərjənt/ ▶ **adj. 1** in the process of coming into being or becoming prominent: *the emergent democracies of eastern Europe.* ■ Philosophy (of a property) arising as an effect of complex causes and not analyzable simply as the sum of their effects.
2 Ecology of or denoting a plant that is taller than the surrounding vegetation, esp. a tall tree in a forest. ■ of or denoting a water plant with leaves and flowers that appear above the water surface.
▶ **n.** Philosophy **1** an emergent property.
2 Botany an emergent tree or other plant.
– ORIGIN late Middle English (in the sense 'occurring unexpectedly'): from Latin *emergent-* 'arising from,' from the verb *emergere* (see **EMERGE**).

e·mer·i·ta /i'meritə/ ▶ **adj.** [postpositive] (of a woman who is the former holder of an office, esp. a female college professor) having retired but allowed to retain her title as an honor: *a professor emerita* | *the librarian emerita of Wellesley College.*

e·mer·i·tus /i'merətəs/ ▶ **adj.** (of the former holder of an office, esp. a college professor) having retired but allowed to retain their title as an honor: *emeritus professor of microbiology* | [postpositive] *the gallery's director emeritus.*
– ORIGIN mid 18th cent.: from Latin, past participle of *emereri* 'earn one's discharge by service,' from *e-* (variant of *ex-*) 'out of, from' + *mereri* 'earn.'

e·mersed /i'mərst/ ▶ **adj.** Botany denoting or characteristic of an aquatic plant reaching above the surface of the water. Contrasted with **SUBMERSED** (see **SUBMERSE**).
– ORIGIN late 17th cent.: from Latin *emersus* 'arisen,' past participle of *emergere* (see **EMERGE**).

e·mer·sion /i'mərZHən/ ▶ **n.** the process or state of emerging from or being out of water after being submerged. ■ Astronomy the reappearance of a celestial body after its eclipse or occultation.
– ORIGIN mid 17th cent.: from late Latin *emersio(n-)*, from Latin *emergere* (see **EMERGE**).

Em·er·son /'emərsən/, Ralph Waldo (1803–82), US philosopher and poet. In 1832, while visiting Britain, he became associated with German idealism. On his return to the US, he evolved the concept of transcendentalism, which found expression in his essay *Nature* (1836).

em·er·y /'em(ə)rē/ ▶ **n.** a grayish-black mixture of corundum and magnetite, used in powdered form as an abrasive. ■ [as modifier] denoting materials coated with emery for polishing, smoothing, or grinding: *emery paper.*
– ORIGIN late 15th cent.: from French *émeri*, from Old French *esmeri*, from Italian *smeriglio*, based on Greek *smuris, smiris* 'polishing powder.'

em·er·y board ▶ **n.** a strip of thin wood or card coated with emery or another abrasive and used as a nail file.

em·e·sis /'eməsis/ ▶ **n.** technical the action or process of vomiting.
– ORIGIN late 19th cent.: from Greek, from *emein* 'to vomit.'

e·met·ic /i'metik/ ▶ **adj.** (of a substance) causing vomiting. ■ informal nauseating or revolting: *that emetic music in department stores.*
▶ **n.** a medicine or other substance that causes vomiting.
– ORIGIN mid 17th cent.: from Greek *emetikos*, from *emein* 'to vomit.'

em·e·tine /'emi,tēn/ ▶ **n.** an alkaloid present in ipecac and formerly used in the treatment of amebic infections and as an emetic in aversion therapy.
– ORIGIN early 19th cent.: from Greek *emetos* 'vomiting' + **-INE**[4].

EMF ▶ **abbr.** ■ electromagnetic field(s). ■ **(emf)** electromotive force. ■ European Monetary Fund.

EMG ▶ **abbr.** ■ electromyogram. ■ electromyography.

-emia (also **-hemia**, Brit. **-aemia** or **-haemia**) ▶ **comb. form** in nouns denoting that a substance is present in the blood, esp. in excess: *septicemia* | *leukemia.*
– ORIGIN from modern Latin *-aemia*, from Greek *-aimia*, from *haima* 'blood.'

e·mic /'ēmik/ Anthropology ▶ **adj.** relating to or denoting an approach to the study or description of a particular language or culture in terms of its internal elements and their functioning rather than in terms of any existing external scheme. Often contrasted with **ETIC**.
▶ **plural n.** (**emics**) [treated as sing.] study adopting this approach.
– ORIGIN 1950s: abstracted from such words as *phonemic* (see **PHONEME**) and **SYSTEMIC**.

em·i·grant /'emigrənt/ ▶ **n.** a person who leaves their own country in order to settle permanently in another: *the first emigrants to America* | [as modifier] *emigrant workers.*
▶ **adj.** used by emigrants: *an emigrant ship.*
– ORIGIN mid 18th cent.: from Latin *emigrant-* 'migrating from,' from the verb *emigrare* (see **EMIGRATE**).

em·i·grate /'emi,grāt/ ▶ **v.** [no obj.] leave one's own country in order to settle permanently in another: *Rosa's parents* ***emigrated from*** *Argentina.*
– DERIVATIVES **em·i·gra·tion** /,emi'grāSHən/ **n.**
– ORIGIN late 18th cent.: from Latin *emigrat-* 'emigrated,' from the verb *emigrare*, from *e-* (variant of *ex-*) 'out of' + *migrare* 'migrate.'

> **USAGE** To **emigrate** is to leave a country, especially one's own, intending to remain away. To **immigrate** is to enter a country, intending to remain there: *my aunt* ***emigrated from*** *Poland and* ***immigrated to*** *Canada.*

é·mi·gré /'emə,grā/ (also **emigre**) ▶ **n.** a person who has left their own country in order to settle in another, usually for political reasons.
– ORIGIN late 18th cent. (originally denoting a person escaping the French Revolution): French, past participle of *émigrer* 'emigrate.'

em·i·nence /'emənəns/ ▶ **n. 1** fame or recognized superiority, esp. within a particular sphere or profession: *her eminence in cinematography.* ■ an important, influential, or distinguished person: *the Lord Chancellor canvassed the views of various legal eminences.* ■ (**His/Your Eminence**) a title given to a Roman Catholic cardinal, or used in addressing him: *His Eminence, Thomas Cardinal Wolsey.*
2 formal or literary a piece of rising ground: *an eminence commanding the River Emme.* ■ Anatomy a slight projection from the surface of a part of the body.
– ORIGIN Middle English: from Latin *eminentia*, from *eminere* 'jut, project.'

é·mi·nence grise /āmēnäns 'grēz/ ▶ **n.** (pl. **éminences grises** pronunc. **same**) a person who exercises power or influence in a certain sphere without holding an official position.
– ORIGIN 1930s: French, literally 'gray eminence.' The term was originally applied to Cardinal Richelieu's gray-cloaked private secretary, Père Joseph (1577–1638).

em·i·nent /'emənənt/ ▶ **adj.** (of a person) famous and respected within a particular sphere or profession: *one of the world's most eminent statisticians.* ■ [attrib.] used to emphasize the presence of a positive quality: *the guitar's eminent suitability for recording studio work.*
– ORIGIN late Middle English: from Latin *eminent-* 'jutting, projecting,' from the verb *eminere*.

em·i·nent do·main ▶ **n.** Law the right of a government or its agent to expropriate private property for public use, with payment of compensation.

em·i·nent·ly /'emənəntlē/ ▶ **adv.** [often as submodifier] to a notable degree; very: *an eminently readable textbook.*

e·mir /ə'mi(ə)r/ (also **amir**) ▶ **n.** a title of various Muslim (mainly Arab) rulers: *the emir of Kuwait.* ■ historical a Muslim (usually Arab) military commander or local chief.
– ORIGIN late 16th cent. (denoting a male descendant of Muhammad): from French *émir*, from Arabic *'amīr* (see **AMIR**).

e·mir·ate /ə'mi(ə)r,āt, ə'mi(ə)rit, 'emərit/ ▶ **n.** the rank, lands, or reign of an emir.

em·is·sar·y /'emə,serē/ ▶ **n.** (pl. **emissaries**) a person sent on a special mission, usually as a diplomatic representative.
– ORIGIN early 17th cent.: from Latin *emissarius* 'scout, spy,' from *emittere* 'send out' (see **EMIT**).

e·mis·sion /i'miSHən/ ▶ **n.** the production and discharge of something, esp. gas or radiation: *the effects of lead emission on health* | *cuts in carbon dioxide emissions.* ■ an ejaculation of semen.
– ORIGIN late Middle English (in the sense 'emanation'): from Latin *emissio(n-)*, from *emiss-* 'sent out,' from the verb *emittere* (see **EMIT**).

e·mis·sion neb·u·la ▶ **n.** Astronomy a nebula that shines with its own light.

e·mis·sion spec·trum ▶ **n.** a spectrum of the electromagnetic radiation emitted by a source. Compare with **ABSORPTION SPECTRUM**.

e·mis·sions trad·ing ▶ **n.** a system by which countries and organizations receive permits to produce a specified amount of carbon dioxide and other greenhouse gases, which they may trade with others.

e·mis·sive /i'misiv/ ▶ **adj.** technical having the power to radiate something, esp. light, heat, or radiation.
– DERIVATIVES **em·is·siv·i·ty** /,emə'sivitē, ,ēmə-/ **n.**
– ORIGIN mid 17th cent. (in the sense 'that is emitted'): from Latin *emiss-* 'emitted, sent out' (from the verb *emittere*) + **-IVE**.

e·mit /i'mit/ ▶ **v.** (**emits, emitting, emitted**) [with obj.] produce and discharge (something, esp. gas or radiation): *coal-fired power stations continue to emit large quantities of sulfur dioxide.* ■ make (a sound): *she emitted a sound like laughter.* ■ issue formally and with authority; put into circulation, esp. currency.
– ORIGIN early 17th cent.: from Latin *emittere*, from *e-* (variant of *ex-*) 'out of' + *mittere* 'send.'

e·mit·ter /i'mitər/ ▶ **n.** a machine, device, etc., that emits something. ■ Electronics a region in a bipolar transistor producing carriers of current.

Em·man·u·el /i'manyōōəl/ (also **Immanuel**) the name given to Christ as the deliverer of Judah prophesied by Isaiah (Isa. 7:14, 8:8; Matt. 1:23).

em·men·a·gogue /ə'menə,gôg, -,gäg, -'mēnə-/ ▶ **n.** Medicine a substance that stimulates or increases menstrual flow.
– ORIGIN early 18th cent.: from Greek *emmēna* 'menses' + *agōgos* 'eliciting.'

Em·men·tal /'emən,täl/ (also **Emmenthal**) ▶ **n.** a kind of hard Swiss cheese with many holes in it, similar to Gruyère.
– ORIGIN from German *Emmentaler*, from *Emmental*, the name of a valley in Switzerland where the cheese was originally made.

em·mer /'emər/ ▶ **n.** an old kind of Eurasian wheat with bearded ears and spikelets that each contain two grains, now grown mainly for fodder and breakfast cereals. Compare with EINKORN, SPELT[2]. ● *Triticum dicoccum*, family Gramineae.
– ORIGIN early 20th cent.: from German, from Old High German *amer* 'spelt.'

em·met /'emit/ ▶ **n.** archaic an ant.
– ORIGIN Old English *ǣmete* (see ANT).

Em·my /'emē/ ▶ **n.** (pl. **Emmys**) a statuette awarded annually to an outstanding television program or performer.
– ORIGIN 1940s: said to be from *Immy*, short for *image orthicon tube* (a kind of television camera tube).

e·mol·lient /i'mälyənt/ ▶ **adj.** having the quality of softening or soothing the skin: *an emollient cream.* ■ attempting to avoid confrontation or anger; soothing or calming: *the president's emollient approach to differences.*
▶ **n.** a preparation that softens the skin: *formulated with rich emollients.*
– DERIVATIVES **e·mol·lience** **n.**
– ORIGIN mid 17th cent.: from Latin *emollient-* 'making soft,' from the verb *emollire*, from *e-* (variant of *ex-*) 'out' + *mollis* 'soft.'

e·mol·u·ment /i'mälyəmənt/ ▶ **n.** (usu. **emoluments**) formal a salary, fee, or profit from employment or office: *the directors' emoluments.*
– ORIGIN late Middle English: from Latin *emolumentum*, originally probably 'payment to a miller for grinding grain,' from *emolere* 'grind up,' from *e-* (variant of *ex-*) 'out, thoroughly' + *molere* 'grind.'

E·mo·na /i'mōnə/ Roman name of LJUBLJANA.

e·mote /i'mōt/ ▶ **v.** [no obj.] (esp. of an actor) portray emotion in a theatrical manner.
– DERIVATIVES **e·mot·er** **n.**
– ORIGIN early 20th cent. (originally US): back-formation from EMOTION.

e·mo·ti·con /i'mōtə,kän/ ▶ **n.** a representation of a facial expression such as:-) (representing a smile), formed by various combinations of keyboard characters and used in electronic communications to convey the writer's feelings or intended tone.
– ORIGIN 1990s: blend of EMOTION and ICON.

e·mo·tion /i'mōSHən/ ▶ **n.** a natural instinctive state of mind deriving from one's circumstances, mood, or relationships with others: *she was attempting to control her emotions | his voice was low and shaky with emotion | fear had become his dominant emotion.* ■ instinctive or intuitive feeling as distinguished from reasoning or knowledge: *responses have to be based on historical insight, not simply on emotion.*
– ORIGIN mid 16th cent. (denoting a public disturbance or commotion): from French *émotion*, from *émouvoir* 'excite,' based on Latin *emovere*, from *e-* (variant of *ex-*) 'out' + *movere* 'move.' The sense 'mental agitation' dates from the mid 17th cent., the current general sense from the early 19th cent.

e·mo·tion·al /i'mōSHənəl/ ▶ **adj.** of or relating to a person's emotions: *children with emotional difficulties.* ■ arousing or characterized by intense feeling: *an emotional speech.* ■ (of a person) having feelings that are easily excited and openly displayed: *he was a strongly emotional young man.*
– DERIVATIVES **e·mo·tion·al·ism** /-,izəm/ **n.**, **e·mo·tion·al·ist** /-ist/ **n. & adj.**, **e·mo·tion·al·i·ty** /i,mōSHə'nalitē/ **n.**, **e·mo·tion·al·ize** /-,līz/ **v.**, **e·mo·tion·al·ly** **adv.**

USAGE See usage at EMOTIVE.

e·mo·tion·less /i'mōSHənləs/ ▶ **adj.** not showing any emotion; unemotional: *her voice was flat and emotionless.*

e·mo·tive /i'mōtiv/ ▶ **adj.** arousing or able to arouse intense feeling: *animal experimentation is an emotive subject | the issue has proved highly emotive.* ■ expressing a person's feelings rather than being neutrally or objectively descriptive: *the comparisons are emotive rather than analytic.*
– DERIVATIVES **e·mo·tive·ly** **adv.**, **e·mo·tive·ness** **n.**, **e·mo·tiv·i·ty** /,ēmō'tivitē/ **n.**
– ORIGIN mid 18th cent.: from Latin *emot-* 'moved,' from the verb *emovere* (see EMOTION).

USAGE The words **emotive** and **emotional** share similarities but are not interchangeable. **Emotive** is used to mean 'arousing intense feeling,' while **emotional** tends to mean 'characterized by intense feeling.' Thus an *emotive issue* is one likely to arouse people's passions, while an *emotional response* is one that is itself full of passion. In sentences such as *we took our* **emotive** *farewells*, **emotive** has been used where **emotional** is appropriate.

e·mo·tiv·ism /i'moti,vizəm/ ▶ **n.** Philosophy an ethical theory that regards ethical and value judgments as expressions of feeling or attitude and prescriptions of action, rather than assertions or reports of anything.
– DERIVATIVES **e·mo·tiv·ist** **n.**

EMP ▶ **abbr.** electromagnetic pulse.

emp. ▶ **abbr.** ■ emperor. ■ empire. ■ empress.

em·pa·na·da /empə'nädə/ ▶ **n.** a Spanish or Latin American pastry turnover filled with a variety of savory ingredients and baked or fried.
– ORIGIN Spanish, feminine past participle (used as a noun) of *empanar* 'roll in pastry,' based on Latin *panis* 'bread.'

em·pan·el /em'panl/ ▶ **v.** variant spelling of IMPANEL.
– DERIVATIVES **em·pan·el·ment** **n.**

em·path /'empaTH/ ▶ **n.** (chiefly in science fiction) a person with the paranormal ability to apprehend the mental or emotional state of another individual.

em·pa·thize /'empə,THīz/ ▶ **v.** [no obj.] understand and share the feelings of another: *counselors need to be able to* **empathize with** *people.*

em·pa·thy /'empəTHē/ ▶ **n.** the ability to understand and share the feelings of another.
– DERIVATIVES **em·pa·thet·ic** /,empə'THetik/ **adj.**, **em·pa·thet·i·cal·ly** /,empə'THetik(ə)lē/ **adv.**, **em·path·ic** /em'paTHik/ **adj.**, **em·path·i·cal·ly** /em'paTHik(ə)lē/ **adv.**
– ORIGIN early 20th cent.: from Greek *empatheia* (from *em-* 'in' + *pathos* 'feeling') translating German *Einfühlung*.

Em·ped·o·cles /em'pedə,klēz/ (*c.*493–*c.*433 BC), Greek philosopher, born in Sicily. He taught that the universe is composed of fire, air, water, and earth, which mingle and separate under the influence of the opposing principles of Love and Strife.

em·pen·nage /,ämpə'näzh, 'empənij/ ▶ **n.** Aeronautics an arrangement of stabilizing surfaces at the tail of an aircraft.
– ORIGIN early 20th cent.: from French, from *empenner* 'to feather an arrow,' from *em-* 'in' + *penne* 'a feather' (from Latin *penna*).

em·per·or /'emp(ə)rər/ ▶ **n. 1** a sovereign ruler of great power and rank, esp. one ruling an empire. **2** (also **emperor butterfly**) an orange and brown North American butterfly with a swift dodging flight, breeding chiefly on hackberries. ● Genus *Asterocampa*, subfamily Apaturinae, family Nymphalidae: several species, in particular the **tawny emperor** (*A. clyton*).
– DERIVATIVES **em·per·or·ship** /-,SHip/ **n.**
– ORIGIN Middle English (esp. representing the title given to the head of the Roman Empire): from Old French *emperere*, from Latin *imperator* 'military commander,' from *imperare* 'to command,' from *in-* 'toward' + *parare* 'prepare, contrive.'

em·per·or moth ▶ **n.** a large moth of the silkworm moth family with eyespots on all four wings. ● *Saturnia* and other genera, family Saturniidae: several species, in particular the common European *S. pavonia*.

em·per·or pen·guin ▶ **n.** the largest species of penguin. It has a yellow patch on each side of the head and rears its young during the Antarctic winter. ● *Aptenodytes forsteri*, family Spheniscidae.

em·pha·sis /'emfəsis/ ▶ **n.** (pl. **emphases** /-,sēz/) special importance, value, or prominence given to something: *they placed great emphasis on the individual's freedom | different emphases and viewpoints.* ■ stress laid on a word or words to indicate special meaning or particular importance. ■ vigor or intensity of expression: *he spoke with emphasis and with complete conviction.*
– ORIGIN late 16th cent.: via Latin from Greek, originally 'appearance, show,' later denoting a figure of speech in which more is implied than is said (the original sense in English), from *emphainein* 'exhibit,' from *em-* 'in, within' + *phainein* 'to show.'

em·pha·size /'emfə,sīz/ ▶ **v.** [with obj.] give special importance or prominence to (something) in speaking or writing: *he jabbed a finger into the tabletop to emphasize his point* | [with clause] *he* **emphasized that** *the drug works in only 30 percent of cases.* ■ lay stress on (a word or phrase) when speaking. ■ make (something) more clearly defined: *a one-piece bathing suit that emphasized her build.*

em·phat·ic /em'fatik/ ▶ **adj.** showing or giving emphasis; expressing something forcibly and clearly: *the children were* **emphatic that** *they would like to repeat the experience | an emphatic movement of his hand.* ■ (of an action or event or its result) definite and clear: *he walked stiffly, with an emphatic limp.* ■ (of word or syllable) bearing the stress. ■ Linguistics denoting certain Arabic consonants that are pronounced with both dental articulation and constriction of the pharynx.
▶ **n.** Linguistics an emphatic consonant.
– ORIGIN early 18th cent.: via late Latin from Greek *emphatikos*, from *emphasis* (see EMPHASIS).

em·phat·i·cal·ly /em'fatik(ə)lē/ ▶ **adv.** in a forceful way. ■ [as submodifier] without doubt; clearly: *Jane, though born in California, feels emphatically Canadian* | [sentence adverb] *Greg is emphatically not a slacker.*

em·phy·se·ma /,emfə'sēmə, -'zēmə/ ▶ **n.** Medicine **1** (also **pulmonary emphysema**) a condition in which the air sacs of the lungs are damaged and enlarged, causing breathlessness. **2** a condition in which air is abnormally present within the body tissues.
– DERIVATIVES **em·phy·sem·a·tous** /,emfə'semətəs, -'sēmə-, -'zemə-, -'zēmə-/ **adj.**, **em·phy·se·mic** **adj.**
– ORIGIN mid 17th cent. (sense 2): via late Latin from Greek *emphusēma*, from *emphusan* 'puff up.'

em·pire /'em,pī(ə)r/ ▶ **n. 1** an extensive group of states or countries under a single supreme authority, formerly esp. an emperor or empress: [in names] *the Roman Empire.* ■ a large commercial organization owned or controlled by one person or group: *her business empire grew.* ■ an extensive operation or sphere of activity controlled by one person or group: *the kitchen had once been the ladies' empire.* ■ supreme political power over several countries when exercised by a single authority: *he encouraged the Greeks in their dream of empire in Asia Minor.* ■ archaic absolute control over a person or group. **2** a variety of apple.
▶ **adj.** also /'äm'pi(ə)r/ (usu. **Empire**) [attrib.] denoting a style of furniture, decoration, or dress fashionable during the First or (less commonly) the Second Empire in France. The decorative style was neoclassical but marked by an interest in Egyptian and other ancient motifs probably inspired by Napoleon's Egyptian campaigns.
– ORIGIN Middle English: via Old French from Latin *imperium*, related to *imperare* 'to command' (see EMPEROR).

empire (adj.)

em·pire build·er ▶ **n.** a person who adds to or strengthens an empire. ■ a person who seeks more power, responsibility, or staff within an organization for the purposes of self-aggrandizement.
– DERIVATIVES **em·pire-build·ing** **n.**

Em·pire State a nickname for the state of NEW YORK.

Em·pire State Build·ing a skyscraper on Fifth Avenue, New York City, which was for several decades the tallest building in the world. When first erected, in 1930–31, it measured 1,250 feet (381 m); the addition of a television mast in 1951 brought its height to 1,472 feet (449 m).

Empire State Building

Em·pire State of the South a nickname for the state of **Georgia**.

em·pir·ic /em'pirik/ ▶ **adj.** another term for **empirical**.
▶ **n.** archaic a person who, in medicine or other branches of science, relies solely on observation and experiment. ■ a quack doctor.
– ORIGIN late Middle English: via Latin from Greek *empeirikos*, from *empeiria* 'experience,' from *empeiros* 'skilled' (based on *peira* 'trial, experiment').

em·pir·i·cal /em'pirikəl/ ▶ **adj.** based on, concerned with, or verifiable by observation or experience rather than theory or pure logic: *they provided considerable empirical evidence to support their argument.*
– DERIVATIVES **em·pir·i·cal·ly** adv.

em·pir·i·cal for·mu·la ▶ **n.** Chemistry a formula giving the proportions of the elements present in a compound but not the actual numbers or arrangement of atoms. Compare with **molecular formula, structural formula**.

em·pir·i·cism /em'pirə,sizəm/ ▶ **n.** Philosophy the theory that all knowledge is derived from sense-experience. Stimulated by the rise of experimental science, it developed in the 17th and 18th centuries, expounded in particular by John Locke, George Berkeley, and David Hume. Compare with **phenomenalism**.
– DERIVATIVES **em·pir·i·cist** n. & adj.

em·place·ment /em'plāsmənt/ ▶ **n. 1** a structure on or in which something is firmly placed. ■ a platform or defended position where a gun is placed for firing.
2 chiefly Geology the process or state of setting something in place or being set in place.
– DERIVATIVES **em·place** v.
– ORIGIN early 19th cent.: from French, from *em-* 'in' + *place* 'a place.'

em·plane /em'plān/ ▶ **v.** variant spelling of **enplane**.

em·ploy /em'ploi/ ▶ **v.** [with obj.] **1** give work to (someone) and pay them for it: *the firm employs 150 people* | [with obj. and infinitive] *temps can be employed to do much of the work.* ■ keep occupied: *most of the newcomers are employed in developing the technology into a product.*
2 make use of: *the methods they have employed to collect the data.*
▶ **n.** [in sing.] the state or fact of being employed for wages or a salary: *I started work in the employ of a grocer and wine merchant.* ■ archaic employment: *her place of employ.*
– DERIVATIVES **em·ploy·a·bil·i·ty** /em,ploi-ə'bilitē/ n., **em·ploy·a·ble** adj., **em·ployed** adj.
– ORIGIN late Middle English (formerly also as *imploy*): from Old French *employer*, based on Latin *implicari* 'be involved in or attached to,' passive form of *implicare* (see **imply**). In the 16th and 17th cent. the word also had the senses 'enfold, entangle' and 'imply,' derived directly from Latin; compare with **implicate**.

em·ploy·ee /em'ploi-ē, ,emploi'ē/ ▶ **n.** a person employed for wages or salary, esp. at nonexecutive level.

em·ploy·er /em'ploi-ər/ ▶ **n.** a person or organization that employs people.

em·ploy·ment /em'ploimənt/ ▶ **n.** the condition of having paid work: *a fall in the numbers in full-time employment.* ■ a person's trade or profession. ■ the action of giving work to someone: *the employment of a full-time tutor.*

em·ploy·ment a·gen·cy ▶ **n.** an agency that finds employers or employees for those seeking them.

Em·po·ria /em'pôrēə/ a commercial city in east central Kansas, associated with William Allen White and his Emporia *Gazette*, which he published from 1895 until 1944; pop. 26,380 (est. 2008).

em·po·ri·um /em'pôrēəm/ ▶ **n.** (pl. **emporiums** or **emporia** /-'pôrēə/) a large retail store selling a wide variety of goods. ■ a business establishment that specializes in products or services on a large scale (often used for humorously formal effect): *the world-famous food emporium* | *you know those half-automated carwash emporia that advertise an "all-cloth wash?"* ■ archaic a principal center of commerce; a market.
– ORIGIN late 16th cent.: from Latin, from Greek *emporion*, from *emporos* 'merchant,' based on a stem meaning 'to journey.'

em·pow·er /em'pou(-ə)r/ ▶ **v.** [with obj. and infinitive] give (someone) the authority or power to do something: *nobody was empowered to sign checks on her behalf.* ■ [with obj.] make (someone) stronger and more confident, esp. in controlling their life and claiming their rights: *movements to empower the poor.*
– DERIVATIVES **em·pow·er·ment** n.

em·press /'empris/ ▶ **n.** a female emperor. ■ the wife or widow of an emperor.
– ORIGIN Middle English: from Old French *emperesse*, feminine of *emperere* (see **emperor**).

em·presse·ment /,änpres'män/ ▶ **n.** archaic animated eagerness or friendliness; effusion.
– ORIGIN from French, from *empresser* 'rush eagerly.'

em·press tree ▶ **n.** a fast-growing paulownia widely grown as an ornamental in the US and now considered an ecological threat, in light of its prolific growth and reproductive capacity.
● *paulownia tomentosa*, family Scrophulariaceae.

emp·ti·ness /'em(p)tēnis/ ▶ **n. 1** the state of containing nothing: *the vast emptiness of space.*
2 the quality of lacking meaning or sincerity; meaninglessness: *he realizes the emptiness of his statement.*
3 the quality of having no value or purpose; futility: *feelings of emptiness and loneliness.*

emp·ty /'em(p)tē/ ▶ **adj.** (**emptier, emptiest**)
1 containing nothing; not filled or occupied: *he took his empty coffee cup back to the counter* | *the room was empty of furniture.* ■ Mathematics (of a set) containing no members or elements.
2 (of words or a gesture) lacking meaning or sincerity: *his answer sounded a little empty* | *empty threats.*
3 having no value or purpose: *her life felt empty and meaningless.*
4 informal hungry.
▶ **v.** (**empties, emptying, emptied**) [with obj.] remove all the contents of (a container): *we empty the cash register each night at closing time* | *pockets were emptied of loose change.* ■ remove (the contents) from a container: *he emptied out the contents of his briefcase.* ■ [no obj.] (of a place) be vacated by people in it: *the bar suddenly seemed to empty.* ■ [no obj.] (**empty into**) (of a river) discharge itself into (the sea or a lake).
▶ **n.** (pl. **empties**) (usu. **empties**) informal a container (esp. a bottle or glass) left empty of its contents.
– PHRASES **running on empty** exhausted of all one's resources or sustenance. **empty vessels make the most noise** (or **sound**) proverb those with least wisdom or knowledge are always the most talkative. **on an empty stomach** see **stomach**.
– DERIVATIVES **emp·ti·ly** /-təlē/ adv.
– ORIGIN Old English *ǣmtig, ǣmetig* 'at leisure, unoccupied, empty,' from *ǣmetta* 'leisure,' perhaps from *ā* 'no, not' + *mōt* 'meeting' (see **moot**).

emp·ty cal·o·ries ▶ **plural n.** calories derived from food containing no nutrients.

emp·ty-hand·ed ▶ **adj.** [predic.] having failed to obtain or achieve what one wanted: *the burglars fled empty-handed.*

emp·ty-head·ed ▶ **adj.** unintelligent and foolish: *why did they promote that empty-headed man?*

emp·ty nest·er ▶ **n.** informal a parent whose children have grown up and left home.

Emp·ty Quar·ter another name for **Rub' al-Khali**.

emp·ty suit ▶ **n.** informal a prominent person regarded as lacking substance, personality, or ability: *they're a bunch of Ivy League empty suits.*

emp·ty word ▶ **n.** Grammar a word that has only a grammatical function, and no meaning in itself (for example, the infinitive marker *to* in English).

em·pur·ple /em'pərpəl/ ▶ **v.** make or become purple: [no obj.] *his face empurpled with fury.*

em·py·e·ma /,empī'ēmə/ ▶ **n.** Medicine the collection of pus in a cavity in the body, esp. in the pleural cavity.
– ORIGIN late Middle English: via late Latin from Greek *empuēma*, from *empuein* 'suppurate,' from *em-* 'in' + *puon* 'pus.'

em·py·re·an /em'pirēən, ,empə'rēən/ (also **empyreal** /-əl/) ▶ **adj.** belonging to or deriving from heaven.
▶ **n.** (**the empyrean**) heaven, in particular the highest part of heaven. ■ literary the visible heavens; the sky.
– ORIGIN late Middle English (as an adjective): via medieval Latin from Greek *empurios*, from *en-* 'in' + *pur* 'fire.' The noun dates from the mid 17th cent.

EMS ▶ **abbr.** ■ emergency medical service. ■ European Monetary System. ■ expanded memory system, a system for increasing the amount of memory available to a computer, now largely superseded by XMS.

EMT ▶ **abbr.** emergency medical technician.

EMU ▶ **abbr.** European Monetary Union.

e·mu /'ēm(y)o͞o/ ▶ **n.** a large flightless fast-running Australian bird resembling the ostrich, with shaggy gray or brown plumage, bare blue skin on the head and neck, and three-toed feet. ● *Dromaius novaehollandiae*, the only member of the family Dromaiidae.
– ORIGIN early 17th cent.: from Portuguese *ema*. The word originally denoted the cassowary, later the greater rhea; current usage dates from the early 19th cent.

em·u·late /'emyə,lāt/ ▶ **v.** [with obj.] match or surpass (a person or achievement), typically by imitation: *lesser men trying to emulate his greatness.* ■ imitate: *hers is not a hairstyle I wish to emulate.* ■ Computing reproduce the function or action of (a different computer, software system, etc.).
– DERIVATIVES **em·u·la·tion** /,emyə'lāsHən/ n., **em·u·la·tive** /-,lātiv/ adj., **em·u·la·tor** /-,lātər/ n.
– ORIGIN late 16th cent.: from Latin *aemulat-* 'rivaled, equaled,' from the verb *aemulari*, from *aemulus* 'rival.'

em·u·lous /'emyələs/ ▶ **adj.** (often **emulous of**) formal seeking to emulate or imitate someone or something. ■ motivated by a spirit of rivalry: *emulous young writers.*
– DERIVATIVES **em·u·lous·ly** adv., **em·u·lous·ness** n.
– ORIGIN late Middle English (in the sense 'resembling, imitating'): from Latin *aemulus* 'rival.' Current senses date from the mid 16th cent.

e·mul·si·fi·er /i'məlsə,fī(ə)r/ ▶ **n.** a substance that stabilizes an emulsion, in particular a food additive used to stabilize processed foods. ■ an apparatus used for making an emulsion by stirring or shaking a substance.

e·mul·si·fy /i'məlsə,fī/ ▶ **v.** (**emulsifies, emulsifying, emulsified**) make into or become an emulsion: [with obj.] *mustard helps to emulsify a vinaigrette.*
– DERIVATIVES **e·mul·si·fi·a·ble** /-,fīəbəl/ adj., **e·mul·si·fi·ca·tion** /i,məlsəfi'kāsHən/ n.

e·mul·sion /i'məlsHən/ ▶ **n. 1** a fine dispersion of minute droplets of one liquid in another in which it is not soluble or miscible. ■ a fine dispersion of one liquid or puréed food substance in another: *ravioli with pea and ginger emulsion.*
2 (also **emulsion paint**) a water-based paint used for walls. ■ a light-sensitive coating for photographic films and plates, containing crystals of a silver compound dispersed in a medium such as gelatin.
– ORIGIN early 17th cent. (denoting a milky liquid made by crushing almonds in water): from modern Latin *emulsio(n-)*, from the verb *emulgere* 'milk out,' from *e-* (variant of *ex-*) 'out' + *mulgere* 'to milk.'

en /en/ ▶ **n.** Printing a unit of measurement equal to half an em and approximately the average width of typeset characters, used esp. for estimating the total amount of space a text will require.
– ORIGIN late 18th cent.: the letter *N* represented as a word, since it is approximately this width.

en-[1] (also **em-**) ▶ **prefix 1** forming verbs (added to nouns) expressing entry into the specified state or location: *engulf* | *embed.*
2 forming verbs (added to nouns and adjectives) expressing conversion into the specified state (as in *encrust, ennoble*). ■ often forming verbs having the suffix *-en* (as in *embolden, enliven*).
3 (added to verbs) in; into; on: *ensnare.* ■ as an intensifier: *entangle.*
– ORIGIN from French, from Latin *in-*. See also **in-**[2], a commonly found by-form.

en-[2] (also **em-**) ▶ **prefix** within; inside: *encyst* | *endemic* | *embolism* | *empyema.*
– ORIGIN from Greek.

-en[1] ▶ **suffix** forming verbs: **1** (from adjectives) denoting the development, creation, or intensification of a state: *widen* | *deepen* | *loosen.*
2 from nouns (such as *strengthen* from *strength*).
– ORIGIN Old English *-nian*, of Germanic origin.

-en[2] ▶ **suffix** (also **-n**) forming adjectives from nouns:
1 made or consisting of: *earthen* | *woolen.*
2 resembling: *golden* | *silvern.*
– ORIGIN Old English, of Germanic origin.

-en[3] (also **-n**) ▶ **suffix** forming past participles of strong verbs: **1** as a regular inflection: *spoken.*
2 as an adjective: *mistaken* | *torn.* ■ often with a restricted adjectival sense: *drunken* | *sunken.*
– ORIGIN Old English, of Germanic origin.

-en[4] ▶ **suffix** forming the plural of a few nouns such as *children, oxen*.
– ORIGIN Middle English reduction of the earlier suffix *-an*.

-en[5] ▶ **suffix** forming diminutives of nouns (such as *chicken, maiden*).
– ORIGIN Old English, of Germanic origin.

-en[6] ▶ **suffix 1** forming feminine nouns such as *vixen*. **2** forming abstract nouns such as *burden*.
– ORIGIN Old English, of Germanic origin.

en·a·ble /en'ābəl/ ▶ **v.** [with obj.] **1** give (someone or something) the authority or means to do something: [with obj. and infinitive] *the evidence would enable us to arrive at firm conclusions*. ■ make possible: *a number of courses are available to enable an understanding of a broad range of issues*.
2 chiefly Computing make (a device or system) operational; activate. ■ (as adj., in combination **-enabled**) adapted for use with the specified application or system: *WAP-enabled mobile phones*.
– DERIVATIVES **en·a·ble·ment** n., **en·a·bler** n.
– ORIGIN late Middle English (formerly also as *inable*): from **EN-**[1], **IN-**[2], + **ABLE**.

en·a·bling act ▶ **n.** a statute empowering a person or body to take certain action, esp. to make regulations, rules, or orders.

en·act /en'akt/ ▶ **v.** [with obj.] **1** make (a bill or other proposal) law: *legislation was enacted in 1987 to attract international companies*. ■ put into practice (a belief, idea, or suggestion).
2 act out (a role or play) on stage.
– DERIVATIVES **en·act·a·ble** adj., **en·ac·tion** /en'aksʜən/ n., **en·ac·tor** /-tər/ n.
– ORIGIN late Middle English (formerly also as *inact*): from **EN-**[1], **IN-**[2], + **ACT**, suggested by medieval Latin *inactare, inactitare*.

en·act·ment /en'aktmənt/ ▶ **n. 1** the process of passing legislation. ■ a law that is passed.
2 a process of acting something out: *the story becomes an enactment of his fantasies*.
– DERIVATIVES **en·ac·tive** /-tiv/ adj.

e·nam·el /i'naməl/ ▶ **n.** an opaque or semitransparent glassy substance applied to metallic or other hard surfaces for ornament or as a protective coating. ■ a work of art executed in such a substance. ■ the hard glossy substance that covers the crown of a tooth. ■ (also **enamel paint**) a paint that dries to give a smooth, hard coat. ■ dated nail polish.
▶ **v.** (**enamels, enameling, enameled**; Brit. **enamels, enamelling, enamelled**) [with obj.] (often as adj. **enameled**) coat or decorate (a metallic or hard object) with enamel: *an enameled roasting pan*. ■ dated apply nail polish to (fingernails or toenails).
– DERIVATIVES **e·nam·el·er** n., **e·nam·el·ist** /-ist/ n.
– ORIGIN late Middle English (originally as a verb; formerly also as *inamel*): from Anglo-Norman French *enamailler*, from *en-* 'in, on' + *amail* 'enamel,' ultimately of Germanic origin.

e·nam·el·ware /i'naməl,wer/ ▶ **n.** enameled kitchenware.

e·nam·el·work /i'naməl,wərk/ ▶ **n.** the craft of inlaying or decorating metal objects with enamel.

en·am·or /i'namər/ (chiefly Brit. **enamour**) ▶ **v.** (**be enamored of/with/by**) be filled with a feeling of love for: *it is not difficult to see why Edward is enamored of her*. ■ have a liking or admiration for: *she was truly enamored of New York*.
– ORIGIN Middle English (formerly also as *inamour*): from Old French *enamourer*, from *en-* 'in' + *amour* 'love.'

en·an·the·ma /,enan'ᴛʜēmə/ ▶ **n.** Medicine an ulcer or eruption occurring on a mucus-secreting surface such as the inside of the mouth.
– ORIGIN mid 19th cent.: from **EN-**[2] 'within' + a shortened form of **EXANTHEMA**.

en·an·ti·o·dro·mi·a /i,nantēə'drōmēə/ ▶ **n.** rare the tendency of things to change into their opposites, esp. as a supposed governing principle of natural cycles and of psychological development.
– ORIGIN early 20th cent.: from Greek, literally 'running in opposite ways.'

en·an·ti·o·mer /i'nantēəmər/ ▶ **n.** Chemistry each of a pair of molecules that are mirror images of each other.
– DERIVATIVES **en·an·ti·o·mer·ic** /i,nantēə'merik/ adj., **en·an·ti·o·mer·i·cal·ly** /-ik(ə)lē/ adv.
– ORIGIN 1930s: from Greek *enantios* 'opposite' + **-MER**.

en·an·ti·o·morph /i'nantēə,môrf/ ▶ **n.** each of two crystalline or other geometric forms that are mirror images of each other.
– DERIVATIVES **en·an·ti·o·mor·phic** /i,nantēə',môrfik/ adj., **en·an·ti·o·mor·phism** /i,nantēə'môrfizəm/ n., **en·an·ti·o·mor·phous** /i,nantēə'môrfəs/ adj.
– ORIGIN late 19th cent.: from Greek *enantios* 'opposite' + **-MORPH**.

en·ar·gite /en'ärjit, 'enər,jit/ ▶ **n.** a dark gray mineral consisting of a sulfide of copper and arsenic.
– ORIGIN mid 19th cent.: from Greek *enargēs* 'clear, distinct' (referring to evident cleavage) + **-ITE**[1].

en·ar·thro·sis /,enär'ᴛʜrōsis/ ▶ **n.** (pl. **enarthroses** /-sēz/) Anatomy a ball-and-socket joint.
– ORIGIN late 16th cent.: from Greek *enarthrōsis*, from *enarthros* 'jointed,' from *en-* 'inside' + *arthron* 'joint.'

e·na·tion /ē'nāsʜən/ ▶ **n.** Botany an outgrowth from the surface of a leaf or other part of a plant.
– ORIGIN mid 19th cent.: from Latin *enatio(n-)*, from *enasci* 'issue forth.'

en bloc /äɴ 'bläk/ ▶ **adv.** all together or all at the same time: *various private museums offered to purchase the trove en bloc*.
– ORIGIN mid 19th cent.: French.

en bro·chette /äɴ brō'sʜet/ ▶ **adj.** Cooking (of a dish) cooked on a skewer.
– ORIGIN French *en brochette* 'on a skewer.'

en brosse /äɴ 'brôs/ ▶ **adj.** [postpositive] (of a person's hair) cut in a short and bristly style.
– ORIGIN early 20th cent.: French, literally 'in the form of a brush.'

enc. ▶ **abbr.** ■ enclosed. ■ enclosure.

en·cage /en'kāj/ ▶ **v.** [with obj.] literary confine in or as in a cage.

en·camp /en'kamp/ ▶ **v.** [no obj.] settle in or establish a camp, esp. a military one: *we encamped for the night by the side of a river*.

en·camp·ment /en'kampmənt/ ▶ **n.** a place with temporary accommodations consisting of huts or tents, typically for troops or nomads. ■ the process of setting up a camp.

en·cap·si·date /en'kapsi,dāt/ ▶ **v.** [with obj.] Biochemistry enclose (a gene or virus particle) in a protein shell.
– DERIVATIVES **en·cap·si·da·tion** /en,kapsi'dāsʜən/ n.

en·cap·su·late /en'kaps(y)ə,lāt/ ▶ **v.** [with obj.] enclose (something) in or as if in a capsule. ■ express the essential features of (someone or something) succinctly: *the conclusion is encapsulated in one sentence*. ■ Computing enclose (a message or signal) in a set of codes that allow use by or transfer through different computer systems or networks. ■ Computing provide an interface for (a piece of software or hardware) to allow or simplify access for the user. ■ (as adj. **encapsulated**) enclosed by a protective coating or membrane.
– DERIVATIVES **en·cap·su·la·tion** /en,kaps(y)ə'lāsʜən/ n.
– ORIGIN late 19th cent. (also as *incapsulate*): from **EN-**[1], **IN-**[2] 'into' + Latin *capsula* (see **CAPSULE**).

en·case /en'kās/ (also dated **incase**) ▶ **v.** [with obj.] enclose or cover in a case or close-fitting surround.
– DERIVATIVES **en·case·ment** n.

en·caus·tic /en'kôstik/ ▶ **adj.** (esp. in painting and ceramics) using pigments mixed with hot wax that are burned in as an inlay.
▶ **n.** the art or process of encaustic painting.
– ORIGIN late 16th cent.: via Latin from Greek *enkaustikos*, from *enkaiein* 'burn in,' from *en-* 'in' + *kaiein* 'to burn.'

-ence /əns, ns/ ▶ **suffix** forming nouns: **1** denoting a quality or an instance of it: *impertinence*.
2 denoting an action or its result: *reference* | *reminiscence*.
– ORIGIN from French *-ence*, from Latin *-entia, -antia* (from present participial stems *-ent-, -ant-*). Since the 16th cent. many inconsistencies have occurred in the use of *-ence* and *-ance*.

en·ceinte[1] /en'sānt, än'sant/ ▶ **n.** archaic an enclosure or the enclosing wall of a fortified place.
– ORIGIN early 18th cent.: from French, from Latin *incincta*, feminine past participle of *incingere* 'gird in,' from *in-* 'in' + *cingere* 'to gird.'

en·ceinte[2] ▶ **adj.** archaic pregnant.
– ORIGIN early 17th cent.: from French.

En·cel·a·dus /en'selədəs/ Astronomy a satellite of Saturn, the eighth closest to the planet, discovered by W. Herschel in 1789. Probably composed mainly of ice, it has a diameter of 311 miles (500 km).
– ORIGIN named after a Greek mythological giant killed by Athene.

en·ce·phal·ic /,ensə'falik/ ▶ **adj.** Anatomy relating to, affecting, or situated in the brain.
– ORIGIN mid 19th cent.: from Greek *enkephalos* 'brain' (from *en-* 'in' + *kephalē* 'head') + **-IC**.

en·ceph·a·li·tis /en,sefə'lītis/ ▶ **n.** inflammation of the brain, caused by infection or an allergic reaction.
– DERIVATIVES **en·ceph·a·lit·ic** /-'litik/ adj.

en·ceph·a·li·tis le·thar·gi·ca /li'ᴛʜärjikə/ ▶ **n.** a form of encephalitis caused by a virus and characterized by headache and drowsiness leading to coma. Also called **SLEEPING SICKNESS**.

en·ceph·a·li·za·tion /en,sefəli'zāsʜən/ ▶ **n.** Zoology an evolutionary increase in the complexity or relative size of the brain, involving a shift of function from noncortical parts of the brain to the cortex.

encephalo- ▶ **comb. form** of or relating to the brain: *encephalopathy*.
– ORIGIN from Greek *enkephalos*.

en·ceph·a·lo·gram /en'sefələ,gram/ ▶ **n.** Medicine an image, trace, or other record of the structure or electrical activity of the brain.

en·ceph·a·log·ra·phy /en,sefə'lägrəfē/ ▶ **n.** Medicine any of various techniques for recording the structure or electrical activity of the brain.
– DERIVATIVES **en·ceph·a·lo·graph** /en'sefələ,graf/ n., **en·ceph·a·lo·graph·ic** /-lə'grafik/ adj.

en·ceph·a·lo·my·e·li·tis /en,sefələ,mīə'lītis/ ▶ **n.** Medicine inflammation of the brain and spinal cord, typically due to acute viral infection.

en·ceph·a·lon /en'sefə,län, -lən/ ▶ **n.** Anatomy the brain.
– ORIGIN mid 18th cent.: from Greek *enkephalon* 'what is inside the head,' from *en-* 'inside' + *kephalē* 'head.'

en·ceph·a·lop·a·thy /en,sefə'läpəᴛʜē/ ▶ **n.** (pl. **encephalopathies**) Medicine a disease in which the functioning of the brain is affected by some agent or condition (such as viral infection or toxins in the blood).

en·chain /en'ᴄʜān/ ▶ **v.** [with obj.] literary bind with or as with chains.
– DERIVATIVES **en·chain·ment** n.
– ORIGIN late Middle English: from Old French *enchainer*, based on Latin *catena* 'chain.'

en·chaîne·ment /,äɴsʜen'mäɴ/ ▶ **n.** (pl. **enchaînements** pronunc. **same**) Ballet a linked sequence of steps or movements constituting a phrase.
– ORIGIN mid 19th cent.: French, 'chaining together.'

en·chant /en'ᴄʜant/ ▶ **v.** [with obj.] fill (someone) with great delight; charm: *Isabel was enchanted with the idea*. ■ put (someone or something) under a spell: (as adj. **enchanted**) *an enchanted garden*.
– DERIVATIVES **en·chant·ed·ly** adv.
– ORIGIN late Middle English (in the senses 'put under a spell' and 'delude'; formerly also as *inchant*): from French *enchanter*, from Latin *incantare*, from *in-* 'in' + *cantare* 'sing.'

en·chant·er /en'ᴄʜantər/ ▶ **n.** a person who uses magic or sorcery, esp. to put someone or something under a spell.

en·chant·er's night·shade ▶ **n.** a woodland plant with small white flowers and fruit with hooked bristles, native to Eurasia and North America.
● Genus *Circaea*, family Onagraceae: several species, including *C. quadrisulcata* and the smaller *C. alpina*.
– ORIGIN late 16th cent.: believed by early botanists to be the herb used by Circe to charm Odysseus' companions.

en·chant·ing /en'ᴄʜantiɴɢ/ ▶ **adj.** delightfully charming or attractive: *Dinah looked enchanting*.
– DERIVATIVES **en·chant·ing·ly** adv.

en·chant·ment /en'ᴄʜantmənt/ ▶ **n. 1** a feeling of great pleasure; delight: *the enchantment of the mountains*.
2 the state of being under a spell; magic: *a world of mystery and enchantment*.

en·chant·ress /en'ᴄʜantris/ ▶ **n.** a woman who uses magic or sorcery, esp. to put someone or something under a spell. ■ a very attractive and beguiling woman.
– ORIGIN late Middle English: from Old French *enchanteresse*, from *enchanter* (see **ENCHANT**).

en·chase /en'ᴄʜās/ ▶ **v.** [with obj.] decorate (a piece of jewelry or work of art) by inlaying, engraving, or carving. ■ place (a jewel) in a setting.
– ORIGIN late Middle English (in the sense 'decorate with figures in relief'): from Old French *enchasser* 'set gems, encase,' from *en-* 'in' + *chasse* 'a case.'

en·chi·la·da /,enᴄʜə'lädə/ ▶ **n.** a rolled tortilla with a filling typically of meat and served with a chili sauce.
– PHRASES **the big enchilada** informal a person or thing of great importance. **the whole enchilada** informal the whole situation; everything.

– ORIGIN Latin American Spanish, feminine past participle of *enchilar* 'season with chili.'

en·chi·rid·i·on /ˌenGkəˈridēən, ˌenkī-/ ▶ **n.** (pl. **enchiridions** or **enchiridia** /-ˈridēə/) formal a book containing essential information on a subject.
– ORIGIN late Middle English: via late Latin from Greek *enkheiridion*, from *en-* 'within' + *kheir* 'hand' + the diminutive suffix *-idion*.

En·ci·ni·tas /ˌensiˈnētəs/ a city in southwestern California, northwest of San Diego; pop. 60,372 (est. 2008).

en·ci·pher /enˈsīfər/ ▶ **v.** [with obj.] convert (a message or piece of text) into a coded form; encrypt.
– DERIVATIVES **en·ci·pher·ment** n.

en·cir·cle /enˈsərkəl/ ▶ **v.** [with obj.] form a circle around; surround: *the town is encircled by fortified walls.*
– DERIVATIVES **en·cir·cle·ment** n.

encl. (also **enc.**) ▶ **abbr.** ■ enclosed. ■ enclosure.

en clair /äN ˈkler/ ▶ **adj. & adv.** (esp. of a telegram or official message) in ordinary language, rather than in code or cipher.
– ORIGIN French, literally 'in clear.'

en·clasp /enˈklasp/ ▶ **v.** [with obj.] formal hold tightly in one's arms.

en·clave /ˈenˌklāv, ˈänG-/ ▶ **n.** a portion of territory within or surrounded by a larger territory whose inhabitants are culturally or ethnically distinct. ■ a place or group that is different in character from those surrounding it: *the engineering department is traditionally a male enclave.*
– ORIGIN mid 19th cent.: from French, from Old French *enclaver* 'enclose, dovetail,' based on Latin *clavis* 'key.'

en·clit·ic /enˈklitik/ Linguistics ▶ **n.** a word pronounced with so little emphasis that it is shortened and forms part of the preceding word, e.g., *n't* in *can't*. Compare with **PROCLITIC**.
▶ **adj.** denoting or relating to such a word.
– DERIVATIVES **en·clit·i·cal·ly** /-(ə)lē/ **adv.**
– ORIGIN mid 17th cent.: via late Latin from Greek *enklitikos*, from *enklinein* 'lean on,' from *en-* 'in, on' + *klinein* 'to lean.'

en·close /enˈklōz/ (also dated **inclose**) ▶ **v.** [with obj.] **1** surround or close off on all sides: *the entire estate was enclosed with walls* | (as adj. **enclosed**) *a dark enclosed space.* ■ historical fence in (common land) so as to make it private property. ■ (usu. as adj. **enclosed**) seclude (a religious order or other community) from the outside world. ■ chiefly Mathematics bound on all sides; contain.
2 place (something) in an envelope together with a letter: *I enclose a copy of the job description.*
– ORIGIN Middle English (in the sense 'shut in, imprison'): from Old French *enclos*, past participle of *enclore*, based on Latin *includere* 'shut in.'

en·clo·sure /enˈklōZHər/ (also dated **inclosure**) ▶ **n.** **1** an area that is sealed off with an artificial or natural barrier. ■ an artificial or natural barrier that seals off an area.
2 the state of being enclosed, esp. in a religious community: *the nuns kept strict enclosure.* ■ historical the process or policy of fencing in waste or common land so as to make it private property, as pursued in much of Britain in the 18th and early 19th centuries: *one of the chief effects of enclosure was to increase the number of landless workers.*
3 a document or object placed in an envelope together with a letter.
– ORIGIN late Middle English: from legal Anglo-Norman French and Old French, from *enclos* 'closed in' (see **ENCLOSE**).

en·code /enˈkōd/ ▶ **v.** [with obj.] convert into a coded form. ■ Computing convert (information or an instruction) into a particular form: *the amount of time required to encode a WAV file to MP3 format.* ■ Biochemistry (of a gene) be responsible for producing (a substance or behavior).
– DERIVATIVES **en·cod·a·ble** adj., **en·cod·er** n., **en·code·ment** n.

en·co·mi·ast /enˈkōmēˌast/ ▶ **n.** formal a person who publicly praises or flatters someone else.
– DERIVATIVES **en·co·mi·as·tic** /enˌkōmēˈastik/ **adj.**, **en·co·mi·as·ti·cal·ly** /enˌkōmēˈastik(ə)lē/ **adv.**
– ORIGIN early 17th cent.: from Greek *enkōmiastēs*, from *enkōmiazein* 'to praise,' from *enkōmion* (see **ENCOMIUM**).

en·co·mi·en·da /enˌkōmēˈendə, -ˌkämē-/ ▶ **n.** historical a grant by the Spanish Crown to a colonist in America conferring the right to demand tribute and forced labor from the Indian inhabitants of an area.
– ORIGIN Spanish, literally 'commission, charge.'

en·co·mi·um /enˈkōmēəm/ ▶ **n.** (pl. **encomiums** or **encomia** /-mēə/) formal a speech or piece of writing that praises someone or something highly.
– ORIGIN mid 16th cent.: Latin, from Greek *enkōmion* 'eulogy,' from *en-* 'within' + *komos* 'revel.'

en·com·pass /enˈkəmpəs/ ▶ **v.** **1** [with obj.] surround and have or hold within: *a vast halo encompassing the Milky Way galaxy.* ■ include comprehensively: *no studies encompass all aspects of medical care.*
2 archaic cause (something) to take place: *an act designed to encompass the death of the king.*
– DERIVATIVES **en·com·pass·ment** n.

en·co·pre·sis /ˌenkəˈprēsis/ ▶ **n.** Medicine involuntary defecation, esp. associated with emotional disturbance or psychiatric disorder.

en·core /ˈänˌkôr/ ▶ **n.** a repeated or additional performance of an item at the end of a concert, as called for by an audience.
▶ **exclam.** called out by an audience at the end of a concert to request such a performance.
▶ **v.** [with obj.] give or call for a repeated or additional performance of (an item) at the end of a concert.
– ORIGIN early 18th cent.: French, literally 'still, again.'

en·coun·ter /enˈkoun(t)ər/ ▶ **v.** [with obj.] unexpectedly experience or be faced with (something difficult or hostile): *we have encountered one small problem.* ■ meet (someone) unexpectedly.
▶ **n.** an unexpected or casual meeting with someone or something. ■ a confrontation or unpleasant struggle: *his close encounter with death.*
– ORIGIN Middle English (in the senses 'meet as an adversary' and 'a meeting of adversaries'; formerly also as *incounter*): from Old French *encontrer* (verb), *encontre* (noun), based on Latin *in-* 'in' + *contra* 'against.'

en·coun·ter group ▶ **n.** a group of people who meet to gain psychological benefit through close contact with one another.

en·cour·age /enˈkərij, -ˈkə-rij/ ▶ **v.** [with obj.] give support, confidence, or hope to (someone): *we were encouraged by the success of this venture* | (as adj. **encouraged**) *I feel much encouraged.* ■ give support and advice to (someone) so that they will do or continue to do something: [with obj. and infinitive] *pupils are encouraged to be creative.* ■ help or stimulate (an activity, state, or view) to develop: *the intention is to encourage new writing talent.*
– DERIVATIVES **en·cour·ag·er** n.
– ORIGIN Middle English (formerly also as *incourage*): from French *encourager*, from *en-* 'in' + *corage* 'courage.'

en·cour·age·ment /enˈkərijmənt/ ▶ **n.** the action of giving someone support, confidence, or hope: *thank you for all your support and encouragement.* ■ persuasion to do or to continue something: *incentives and encouragement to play sports.* ■ the act of trying to stimulate the development of an activity, state, or belief: *the encouragement of foreign investment.*

en·cour·ag·ing /enˈkərijiNG/ ▶ **adj.** giving someone support or confidence; supportive: *she gave me an encouraging smile.* ■ positive and giving hope for future success; promising: *the results are very encouraging.*
– DERIVATIVES **en·cour·ag·ing·ly** adv. [sentence adverb] *encouragingly, there is more research being done today* | [as submodifier] *the level of activity continues to be encouragingly high.*

en·croach /enˈkrōCH/ ▶ **v.** [no obj.] (usu. **encroach on/upon**) intrude on (a person's territory or a thing considered to be a right): *rather than encroach on his privacy, she might have kept to her room.* ■ advance gradually beyond usual or acceptable limits: *the sea has encroached all around the coast.*
– DERIVATIVES **en·croach·er** n.
– ORIGIN late Middle English (in the sense 'obtain unlawfully, seize'; formerly also as *incroach*): from Old French *encrochier* 'seize, fasten upon,' from *en-* 'in, on' + *crochier* (from *croc* 'hook,' from Old Norse *krókr*).

en·croach·ment /enˈkrōCHmənt/ ▶ **n.** **1** intrusion on a person's territory, rights, etc.: *minor encroachments on our individual liberties.* ■ a gradual advance beyond usual or acceptable limits: *urban encroachment of habitat.*
2 Football a penalty in which a defensive player is positioned in the neutral zone at the start of a play.

en croute /äN ˈkro͞ot/ ▶ **adj. & adv.** in a pastry crust: [as postpositive adj.] *salmon en croute* | [as adv.] *goat's cheese is particularly tasty baked en croute.*
– ORIGIN French *en croûte*.

en·crust /enˈkrəst/ (also **incrust**) ▶ **v.** [with obj.] cover (something) with a hard surface layer: *the mussels encrust navigation buoys* | (as adj. **encrusted**) *the dried and encrusted blood.* ■ [no obj.] form a crust.
– ORIGIN early 17th cent. (in the sense 'cause to form a crust'): from French *incruster* or *encroûter*, both from Latin *incrustare*, from *in-* 'into' + *crusta* 'a crust.'

en·crus·ta·tion /ˌenkrəsˈtāSHən/ (also **incrustation**) ▶ **n.** the action of encrusting or state of being encrusted. ■ a crust or hard coating on the surface of something: *the sides are white with encrustations of salt.* ■ Architecture a facing of marble on a building.
– ORIGIN early 17th cent. (originally as *incrustation*): from late Latin *incrustatio(n-)*, from the verb *incrustare* (see **ENCRUST**).

en·crypt /enˈkript/ ▶ **v.** [with obj.] convert (information or data) into a cipher or code, esp. to prevent unauthorized access. ■ (**encrypt something in**) conceal information or data in something by this means.
– DERIVATIVES **en·cryp·tion** /-ˈkripSHən/ **n.**
– ORIGIN 1950s (originally US): from **EN-**[1] 'in' + Greek *kruptos* 'hidden.'

en·cul·tu·ra·tion /enˌkəlCHəˈrāSHən/ (also **inculturation**) ▶ **n.** the gradual acquisition of the characteristics and norms of a culture or group by a person, another culture, etc. ■ the adaptation of Christian liturgy to a non-Christian cultural background.

en·cum·ber /enˈkəmbər/ ▶ **v.** [with obj.] restrict or burden (someone or something) in such a way that free action or movement is difficult: *she was encumbered by her heavy skirts* | *they had arrived encumbered with families.* ■ saddle (a person or estate) with a debt or mortgage: *an estate heavily encumbered with debt.* ■ fill or block up (a place): *we tripped over sticks and stones, which encumber most of the trail.*
– ORIGIN Middle English (in the sense 'cause trouble to, entangle'; formerly also as *incumber*): from Old French *encombrer* 'block up,' from *en-* 'in' + *combre* 'river barrage.'

en·cum·brance /enˈkəmbrəns/ ▶ **n.** a burden or impediment. ■ Law a mortgage or other charge on property or assets. ■ archaic a person, esp. a child, who is dependent on someone else for support.
– ORIGIN Middle English (denoting an encumbered state; formerly also as *incumbrance*): from Old French *encombrance*, from *encombrer* 'block up' (see **ENCUMBER**).

ency. ▶ **abbr.** encyclopedia.

-ency /ənsē, n-sē/ ▶ **suffix** forming nouns: **1** denoting a quality: *efficiency.*
2 denoting a state: *presidency.*
– ORIGIN from Latin *-entia* (compare with **-ENCE**).

encyc. ▶ **abbr.** encyclopedia.

encycl. ▶ **abbr.** encyclopedia.

en·cyc·li·cal /enˈsiklikəl/ ▶ **n.** a papal letter sent to all bishops of the Roman Catholic Church.
▶ **adj.** of or relating to such a letter.
– ORIGIN mid 17th cent. (as an adjective): via late Latin from Greek *enkuklios* 'circular, general,' from *en-* 'in' + *kuklos* 'a circle.'

en·cy·clo·pe·di·a /enˌsīkləˈpēdēə/ (also chiefly Brit. **encyclopaedia**) ▶ **n.** a book or set of books giving information on many subjects or on many aspects of one subject and typically arranged alphabetically.
– ORIGIN mid 16th cent.: modern Latin, from pseudo-Greek *enkuklopaideia* for *enkuklios paideia* 'all-around education.'

en·cy·clo·pe·dic /enˌsīkləˈpēdik/ (also chiefly Brit. **encyclopaedic**) ▶ **adj.** comprehensive in terms of information: *he has an almost encyclopedic knowledge of food.* ■ relating to or containing names of famous people and places and information about words that is not simply linguistic: *a dictionary with encyclopedic material.*
– DERIVATIVES **en·cy·clo·pe·di·cal·ly** /-(ə)lē/ **adv.**

en·cy·clo·pe·dism /enˌsīkləˈpēˌdizəm/ (also chiefly Brit. **encyclopaedism**) ▶ **n.** comprehensive learning or knowledge.

en·cy·clo·pe·dist /enˌsīkləˈpēdist/ (also chiefly Brit. **encyclopaedist**) ▶ **n.** a person who writes, edits, or contributes to an encyclopedia.

en·cyst /enˈsist/ ▶ **v.** Zoology enclose or become enclosed in a cyst.
– DERIVATIVES **en·cys·ta·tion** /ˌensiˈstāSHən/ **n.**, **en·cyst·ment** n.

PRONUNCIATION KEY ə *ago, up*; ər *over, fur*; a *hat*; ā *ate*; ä *car*; e *let*; ē *see*; i *fit*; ī *by*; NG *sing*; ō *go*; ô *law, for*; oi *toy*; o͝o *good*; o͞o *goo*; ou *out*; TH *thin*; T̲H̲ *then*; ZH *vision*

end /end/ ▶ **n. 1** a final part of something, esp. a period of time, an activity, or a story: *the end of the year* | *Mario led the race* ***from beginning to end***. ■ a termination of a state or situation: *the party called for* ***an end to*** *violence* | *one notice will be effective to* ***bring*** *the tenancy* ***to an end***. ■ used to emphasize that something, typically a subject of discussion, is considered finished: *you will go to church and* ***that's the end of it***. ■ death or ruin: *if she's caught stealing again, it will* ***be the end of*** *her career*. ■ archaic (in biblical use) an ultimate state or condition: *the end of that man is peace*.
2 the farthest or most extreme part or point of something: *a length of wire with a hook at the end* | [as modifier] *the end house*. ■ a small piece that is left after something has been used: *a box of candle ends*. ■ a specified extreme point on a scale: *homebuyers at the lower end of the market*. ■ the part or share of an activity with which someone is concerned: *you're going to honor your end of the deal*. ■ a place that is linked to another by a telephone call, letter, or journey: *"Hello," said a voice at the other end*. ■ the part of an athletic field or court defended by one team or player.
3 a goal or result that one seeks to achieve: *each would use the other* ***to further his own ends*** | ***to this end***, *schools were set up for peasant women*.
4 Lawn Bowling & Curling a session of play in one particular direction across the playing area.
5 Football an offensive or defensive lineman positioned nearest to the sideline.
▶ **v.** come or bring to a final point; finish: [no obj.] *when the war ended, policy changed* | *the chapter* ***ends with*** *a case study* | [with obj.] *she wanted to end the relationship*. ■ [no obj.] reach a point and go no further: *the boundary where agnosticism ends and atheism begins*. ■ [no obj.] perform a final act: *the man* ***ended by*** *attacking a police officer*. ■ [no obj.] (**end in**) have as its final part, point, or result: *one in three marriages is now likely to end in divorce*. ■ [no obj.] (**end up**) eventually reach or come to a specified place, state, or course of action: *I ended up in Connecticut* | *you could* ***end up with*** *a higher income*.
– PHRASES **at the end of the day** informal when everything is taken into consideration: *at the end of the day, I'm responsible for what happens in the school*. **be at** (or **have come to**) **an end** be finished or completed. ■ (of a supply of something) become exhausted: *our patience has come to an end*. **be at the end of** be close to having no more of (something): *he was at the end of his ability to cope*. **be the end** informal be the limit of what one can tolerate: *you really are the end!* **come to** (or **meet**) **a bad end** be led by one's own actions to ruin or an unpleasant death. **end one's days** (or **life**) spend the final part of one's existence in a specified place or state: *the last passenger pigeon ended her days in the Cincinnati Zoo*. **an end in itself** a goal that is pursued in its own right to the exclusion of others. **end in tears** have an unhappy or painful outcome (often as a warning): *this treaty will end in tears*. **end it all** commit suicide. **the end of the road** (or **line**) the point beyond which progress or survival cannot continue: *if the lawsuit is not dropped it could be* ***the end of the road*** *for the publisher*. **the end of one's rope** (or **tether**) having no patience or energy left to cope with something: *after enduring four years of mice in the house, we were* ***at the end of our rope*** | *they have* ***reached the end of their tether***. **the end of the world** the termination of life on the earth. ■ informal a complete disaster: *it's not the end of the world if you're not great at sports*. **end on** with the farthest point of an object facing toward one: *seen end on, their sharp, rocky summits point like arrows*. ■ with the farthest point of an object touching that of another: *slim stone tiles had been layered end on with incredible skill*. **end to end** in a row with the farthest point of one object touching that of another object. **in the end** eventually or on reflection: *in the end, I saw that she was right*. **keep** (or **hold**) **one's end up** informal perform well in a difficult or competitive situation. **make an end of** cause (someone or something) to stop existing. **make** (**both**) **ends meet** earn enough money to live without getting into debt. **never** (or **not**) **hear the end of** be continually reminded of (an unpleasant topic or cause of annoyance). **no end** informal to a great extent; very much: *this cheered me up no end*. **no end of** informal a vast number or amount of (something): *we shared no end of good times*. **on end 1** continuing without stopping for a specified period of time: *sometimes they'll be gone for days on end*. **2** in an upright position: *he brushed his hair, leaving a tuft standing on end*. **put an end to** cause someone or something to stop existing: *injury put an end to his career*. **a —— to end all ——s** informal used to emphasize how impressive or successful something is of its kind: *it was a party to end all parties*. **without end** without a limit or boundary: *a war without end*.
– ORIGIN Old English *ende* (noun), *endian* (verb), of Germanic origin; related to Dutch *einde* (noun), *einden* (verb) and German *Ende* (noun), *enden* (verb).

-end ▶ **suffix** denoting a person or thing to be treated in a specified way: *dividend* | *reverend*.
– ORIGIN from Latin *-endus*, gerundive ending.

end-all ▶ **n.** (**the end-all**) the thing that is final or definitive.

en·dan·ger /en'dānjər/ ▶ **v.** [with obj.] put (someone or something) at risk or in danger: *he was driving in a manner likely to endanger life*.
– DERIVATIVES **en·dan·ger·ment n.**

en·dan·gered /en'dānjərd/ ▶ **adj.** (of a species) seriously at risk of extinction.

end-a·round ▶ **n.** Football a play in which an end carries the ball around the opposing side of the line of scrimmage.
▶ **adj.** Computing involving the transfer of a digit from one end of a register to the other.

end·ar·ter·ec·to·my /ˌendärtə'rektəmē/ ▶ **n.** (pl. **endarterectomies**) surgical removal of part of the inner lining of an artery, together with any obstructive deposits, most often carried out on the carotid artery or on vessels supplying the legs.

end·ar·te·ri·tis /ˌendärtə'rītis/ ▶ **n.** Medicine inflammation of the inner lining of an artery.

en dash ▶ **n.** a short dash, the width of an en, used in punctuation.

en·dear /en'di(ə)r/ ▶ **v.** [with obj.] cause to be loved or liked: *Flora's spirit and character* ***endeared her to*** *everyone who met her*.

en·dear·ing /en'di(ə)riNG/ ▶ **adj.** inspiring love or affection: *an endearing little grin*.
– DERIVATIVES **en·dear·ing·ly adv.**

en·dear·ment /en'di(ə)rmənt/ ▶ **n.** a word or phrase expressing love or affection. ■ love or affection: *a term of endearment*.

en·deav·or /en'devər/ (Brit. **endeavour**) ▶ **v.** [no obj.] try hard to do or achieve something: *he is endeavoring to help the Third World*.
▶ **n.** an attempt to achieve a goal: [with infinitive] *an endeavor to reduce serious injury*. ■ earnest and industrious effort, esp. when sustained over a period of time: *enthusiasm is a vital ingredient in all human endeavor*. ■ an enterprise or undertaking: *a political endeavor*.
– ORIGIN late Middle English (in the sense 'exert oneself'): from the phrase *put oneself in devoir* 'do one's utmost' (see **DEVOIR**).

en·dem·ic /en'demik/ ▶ **adj. 1** (of a disease or condition) regularly found among particular people or in a certain area: *areas where malaria is endemic* | *complacency* ***is endemic in*** *industry today*. ■ [attrib.] denoting an area in which a particular disease is regularly found.
2 (of a plant or animal) native or restricted to a certain country or area: *a marsupial* ***endemic to*** *northeastern Australia*.
▶ **n.** an endemic plant or animal.
– DERIVATIVES **en·dem·i·cal·ly** /-(ə)lē/ **adv.**, **en·de·mic·i·ty** /ˌendə'misitē/ **n.**, **en·de·mism** /'endəˌmizəm/ **n.** (sense 2 of the adjective).
– ORIGIN mid 17th cent. (as a noun): from French *endémique* or modern Latin *endemicus*, from Greek *endēmios* 'native' (based on *dēmos* 'people').

> **USAGE** On the difference between **endemic**, **epidemic**, and **pandemic**, see usage at **EPIDEMIC**.

En·der·by Land /'endərbē länd, länt/ a part of Antarctica that is claimed by Australia.

end·er·gon·ic /ˌendər'gänik/ ▶ **adj.** Biochemistry (of a metabolic or chemical process) accompanied by or requiring the absorption of energy, the products being of greater free energy than the reactants. The opposite of **EXERGONIC**.
– ORIGIN mid 20th cent.: from **ENDO-** 'within' + Greek *ergon* 'work' + **-IC**.

En·ders /'endərz/, John Franklin (1897–1985), US virologist. With Frederick C. Robbins (1916–92) and Thomas H. Weller (1915–2008), he devised a method of growing viruses in tissue cultures, which led to the development of vaccines against mumps, polio, and measles. Nobel Prize for Physiology or Medicine (1954), shared with Robbins and Weller.

end·game /'en(d)ˌgām/ (also **end game**) ▶ **n.** the final stage of a game such as chess or bridge, when few pieces or cards remain: *the knight was trapped in the endgame* | figurative *the retaliatory endgame of nuclear warfare*.

end·gate /'en(d)ˌgāt/ ▶ **n.** another term for **TAILGATE**.

end grain ▶ **n.** the grain of wood seen when it is cut across the growth rings.

end·i·an /'endēən/ ▶ **adj.** Computing denoting or relating to a system of ordering data in a computer's memory whereby the most significant (**big-endian**) or least significant (**little-endian**) byte is put first.
– ORIGIN 1980s: a reference to Swift's *Gulliver's Travels*, in which the Lilliputians were divided into two camps, those who ate their eggs by opening the 'big' end and those who ate them by opening the 'little' end.

end·ing /'endiNG/ ▶ **n.** an end or final part of something, esp. a period of time, an activity, or a book or movie: *the ending of the Cold War*. ■ the farthest part or point of something: *a nerve ending*. ■ the final part of a word, constituting a grammatical inflection or formative element.
– ORIGIN Old English *endung* 'termination, completion' (see **END**, **-ING**[1]).

en·dive /'enˌdīv, 'änˌdēv/ ▶ **n. 1** an edible Mediterranean plant whose bitter leaves may be blanched and used in salads. ● *Cichorium endivia*, family Compositae (including both curly-leaved and smooth-leaved varieties).
2 (also **Belgian endive**) a young, typically blanched chicory plant, eaten as a cooked vegetable or in salads.
– ORIGIN late Middle English (also denoting the sow thistle): via Old French from medieval Latin *endivia*, based on Greek *entubon*.

end·less /'en(d)ləs/ ▶ **adj.** having or seeming to have no end or limit: *endless ocean wastes* | *the list is endless*. ■ countless; innumerable: *we smoked endless cigarettes*. ■ (of a belt, chain, or tape) having the ends joined to form a loop allowing continuous action.
– DERIVATIVES **end·less·ly adv.**, **end·less·ness n.**
– ORIGIN Old English *endelēas* (see **END**, **-LESS**).

end·less screw ▶ **n.** the threaded cylinder in a worm gear.

end line ▶ **n.** Football the line that marks the back of the end zone.

end·long /'endˌlôNG, -ˌläNG/ ▶ **adv.** archaic from end to end; lengthwise.

end man ▶ **n. 1** a man at the end of a row, line, or series.
2 historical a man at the end of a line of performers in a minstrel show who engaged in comic repartee with the interlocutor.

end·most /'en(d)ˌmōst/ ▶ **adj.** nearest to the end.

end·note /'en(d)ˌnōt/ ▶ **n.** a note printed at the end of a book or section of a book.

endo- ▶ **comb. form** internal; within: *endoderm* | *endogenous*.
– ORIGIN from Greek *endon* 'within.'

en·do·car·di·al /ˌendō'kärdēəl/ ▶ **adj.** Anatomy & Medicine **1** of or relating to the endocardium.
2 situated inside the heart.

en·do·car·di·tis /ˌendōˌkär'dītis/ ▶ **n.** Medicine inflammation of the endocardium.
– DERIVATIVES **en·do·car·dit·ic** /-'ditik/ **adj.**

en·do·car·di·um /-'kärdēəm/ ▶ **n.** the thin, smooth membrane that lines the inside of the chambers of the heart and forms the surface of the valves.
– ORIGIN late 19th cent.: modern Latin, from **ENDO-** 'within' + Greek *kardia* 'heart.'

en·do·carp /'endəˌkärp/ ▶ **n.** Botany the innermost layer of the pericarp that surrounds a seed in a fruit. It may be membranous (as in apples) or woody (as in the stone of a peach or cherry).
– DERIVATIVES **en·do·car·pic** /ˌendō'kärpik/ **adj.**
– ORIGIN early 19th cent.: from **ENDO-** 'within' + a shortened form of **PERICARP**.

en·do·cen·tric /ˌendō'sentrik/ ▶ **adj.** Linguistics denoting or being a construction in which the whole has the same syntactic function as the head, for example *big black dogs*. Contrasted with **EXOCENTRIC**.

en·do·crine /'endəkrin/ ▶ **adj.** Physiology of, relating to, or denoting glands that secrete hormones or other products directly into the blood: *the endocrine system*.
– ORIGIN early 20th cent.: from **ENDO-** 'within' + Greek *krinein* 'sift.'

en·do·cri·nol·o·gy /ˌendəkrə'näləjē/ ▶ **n.** the branch of physiology and medicine concerned with endocrine glands and hormones.
– DERIVATIVES **en·do·crin·o·log·i·cal** /-ˌkrinə'läjikəl/ **adj.**, **en·do·cri·nol·o·gist** /-jist/ **n.**

en·do·cy·to·sis /ˌendōsī'tōsis/ ▶ **n.** Biology the taking in of matter by a living cell by invagination of its membrane to form a vacuole.
– DERIVATIVES **en·do·cy·tose** /ˌendōsī'tōs, -'tōz/ **v.**, **en·do·cy·tot·ic** /-'tätik/ **adj.**

en·do·derm /ˈendəˌdərm/ (also **entoderm**) ▶ **n.** Zoology & Embryology the innermost layer of cells or tissue of an embryo in early development, or the parts derived from this, which include the lining of the gut and associated structures. Compare with ECTODERM and MESODERM.
– DERIVATIVES **en·do·der·mal** /ˌendəˈdərməl, ˌendō-/ **adj.**, **en·do·der·mic** /ˌendəˈdərmik, ˌendō-/ **adj.**
– ORIGIN mid 19th cent.: from ENDO- 'within' + Greek *derma* 'skin.'

en·do·der·mis /ˌendōˈdərməs/ ▶ **n.** Botany an inner layer of cells in the cortex of a root and of some stems, surrounding a vascular bundle.
– ORIGIN early 20th cent.: from ENDO- 'within' + modern Latin *dermis* 'skin.'

en·dog·a·my /enˈdägəmē/ ▶ **n.** Anthropology the custom of marrying only within the limits of a local community, clan, or tribe. Compare with EXOGAMY. ■ Biology the fusion of reproductive cells from related individuals; inbreeding; self-pollination.
– DERIVATIVES **en·do·gam·ic** /ˌendōˈgamik/ **adj.**, **en·dog·a·mous** /-gəməs/ **adj.**
– ORIGIN mid 19th cent.: from ENDO- 'within' + Greek *gamos* 'marriage,' on the pattern of *polygamy*.

en·do·ge·net·ic /ˌendōjəˈnetik/ ▶ **adj.** another term for ENDOGENIC.

en·do·gen·ic /ˌendōˈjenik/ ▶ **adj.** Geology formed or occurring beneath the surface of the earth. Often contrasted with EXOGENIC.

en·dog·e·nous /enˈdäjənəs/ ▶ **adj.** having an internal cause or origin: *the expected rate of infection is endogenous to the system*. Often contrasted with EXOGENOUS. ■ Biology growing or originating from within an organism: *endogenous gene sequences*. ■ chiefly Psychiatry (of a disease or symptom) not attributable to any external or environmental factor: *endogenous depression*. ■ confined within a group or society.
– DERIVATIVES **en·dog·e·nous·ly** **adv.**

en·do·glos·sic /ˌendōˈglôsik/ ▶ **n.** Linguistics denoting or relating to an indigenous language that is used as the first or official language in a country or community. Compare with EXOGLOSSIC.
– ORIGIN 1980s: from ENDO-, Greek *glōssa* 'language, tongue,' and -IC.

en·do·lith·ic /ˌendōˈliTHik/ ▶ **adj.** Biology living in or penetrating into stone: *endolithic algae*.

en·do·lymph /ˈendəˌlimf/ ▶ **n.** Anatomy the fluid in the membranous labyrinth of the ear.

en·do·me·tri·o·sis /ˌendōˌmētrēˈōsis/ ▶ **n.** Medicine a condition resulting from the appearance of endometrial tissue outside the uterus and causing pelvic pain.

en·do·me·tri·tis /ˌendōmiˈtrītis/ ▶ **n.** Medicine inflammation of the endometrium.

en·do·me·tri·um /ˌendōˈmētrēəm/ ▶ **n.** Anatomy the mucous membrane lining the uterus, which thickens during the menstrual cycle in preparation for possible implantation of an embryo.
– DERIVATIVES **en·do·me·tri·al** /-trēəl/ **adj.**
– ORIGIN late 19th cent.: modern Latin, from ENDO- 'within' + Greek *mētra* 'womb.'

en·do·morph /ˈendəˌmôrf/ ▶ **n.** **1** Physiology a person with a soft round body build and a high proportion of fat tissue. Compare with ECTOMORPH and MESOMORPH.
2 Mineralogy a mineral or crystal enclosed within another.
– DERIVATIVES **en·do·mor·phic** /ˌendəˈmôrfik/ **adj.**, **en·do·mor·phy** /-ˌmôrfē/ **n.**
– ORIGIN 1940s: *endo-* from *endodermal* (being the layer of the embryo giving rise to the physical characteristics that predominate) + -MORPH.

en·do·nu·cle·ase /ˌendōˈn(y)o͞oklēˌās, -ˌāz/ ▶ **n.** Biochemistry an enzyme that cleaves a polynucleotide chain by separating nucleotides other than the two end ones.

en·do·par·a·site /ˌendōˈparəˌsīt/ ▶ **n.** Biology a parasite, such as a tapeworm, that lives inside its host. Compare with ECTOPARASITE.
– DERIVATIVES **en·do·par·a·sit·ic** /-ˌparəˈsitik/ **adj.**

en·do·pep·ti·dase /ˌendōˈpeptiˌdās/ ▶ **n.** Biochemistry an enzyme that breaks peptide bonds other than terminal ones in a peptide chain.

en·doph·o·ra /enˈdäfərə/ ▶ **n.** Linguistics the set of relationships among words having the same reference within a text, contributing to textual cohesion; anaphora and cataphora. Compare with EXOPHORA.
– DERIVATIVES **en·do·phor·ic** /ˌendəˈfôrik, -fär-/ **adj.**
– ORIGIN late 20th cent.: from ENDO- 'within,' on the pattern of *anaphora*.

en·do·phyte /ˈendəˌfīt/ ▶ **n.** Botany a plant, esp. a fungus, that lives inside another plant.
– DERIVATIVES **en·do·phyt·ic** /ˌendəˈfitik/ **adj.**, **en·do·phyt·i·cal·ly** /ˌendəˈfitik(ə)lē/ **adv.**

en·do·plasm /ˈendōˌplazəm/ ▶ **n.** Biology, dated the more fluid, granular inner layer of the cytoplasm in ameboid cells. Compare with ECTOPLASM (sense 1).

en·do·plas·mic re·tic·u·lum /ˌendōˈplazmik riˈtikyələm/ ▶ **n.** Biology a network of membranous tubules within the cytoplasm of a eukaryotic cell, continuous with the nuclear membrane. It usually has ribosomes attached and is involved in protein and lipid synthesis.

en·dop·o·dite /enˈdäpəˌdīt/ (also **endopod** /ˈendəˌpäd/) ▶ **n.** Zoology the inner branch of the biramous limb or appendage of a crustacean. Compare with EXOPODITE, PROTOPODITE.
– ORIGIN late 19th cent.: from ENDO- 'within' + Greek *pous, pod-* 'foot' + -ITE.

end or·gan ▶ **n.** **1** Anatomy a specialized, encapsulated ending of a peripheral sensory nerve, which acts as a receptor for a stimulus.
2 another term for TARGET ORGAN.

en·dor·phin /enˈdôrfin/ ▶ **n.** Biochemistry any of a group of hormones secreted within the brain and nervous system and having a number of physiological functions. They are peptides that activate the body's opiate receptors, causing an analgesic effect.
– ORIGIN 1970s: blend of ENDOGENOUS and MORPHINE.

en·dorse /enˈdôrs/ (also dated **indorse**) ▶ **v.** [with obj.] **1** declare one's public approval or support of: *the report was endorsed by the college*. ■ recommend (a product) in an advertisement.
2 sign (a check or bill of exchange) on the back to make it payable to someone other than the stated payee or to accept responsibility for paying it. ■ (usu. **be endorsed on**) write (a comment) on the front or back of a document.
– DERIVATIVES **en·dors·a·ble** **adj.**, **en·dors·er** **n.**
– ORIGIN late 15th cent. (in the sense 'write on the back of'; formerly also as *indorse*): from medieval Latin *indorsare*, from Latin *in-* 'in, on' + *dorsum* 'back.'

en·dor·see /ˌendôrˈsē/ ▶ **n.** a person to whom a check or bill of exchange is made payable instead of the stated payee.

en·dorse·ment /enˈdôrsmənt/ (also dated **indorsement**) ▶ **n.** **1** an act of giving one's public approval or support to someone or something.
2 a clause in an insurance policy detailing an exemption from or change in coverage.
3 the action of endorsing a check or bill of exchange.

en·do·scope /ˈendəˌskōp/ ▶ **n.** Medicine an instrument that can be introduced into the body to give a view of its internal parts.
– DERIVATIVES **en·do·scop·ic** /ˌendəˈskäpik/ **adj.**, **en·do·scop·i·cal·ly** /ˌendəˈskäpik(ə)lē/ **adv.**, **en·dos·co·pist** /enˈdäskəpist/ **n.**, **en·dos·co·py** /enˈdäskəpē/ **n.**

en·do·skel·e·ton /ˌendōˈskelitn/ ▶ **n.** Zoology an internal skeleton, such as the bony or cartilaginous skeleton of vertebrates. Compare with EXOSKELETON.
– DERIVATIVES **en·do·skel·e·tal** /-ˈskelitl/ **adj.**

en·do·sperm /ˈendəˌspərm/ ▶ **n.** Botany the part of a seed that acts as a food store for the developing plant embryo, usually containing starch with protein and other nutrients.

en·do·spore /ˈendəˌspôr/ ▶ **n.** Biology a resistant asexual spore that develops inside some bacteria cells. ■ the inner layer of the membrane or wall of some spores and pollen grains.
– DERIVATIVES **en·dos·por·ous** /enˈdäspərəs, ˌendəˈspôrəs/ **adj.**

en·do·sym·bi·o·sis /ˌendōˌsimbēˈōsis, -ˌsimbī-/ ▶ **n.** Biology symbiosis in which one of the symbiotic organisms lives inside the other.
– DERIVATIVES **en·do·sym·bi·ont** /-ˈsimbēˌänt, -ˈsimbī-/ **n.**, **en·do·sym·bi·ot·ic** /-ˈätik/ **adj.**

en·do·the·li·um /ˌendəˈTHēlēəm/ ▶ **n.** (pl. **endothelia** /-lēə/) the tissue that forms a single layer of cells lining various organs and cavities of the body, esp. the blood vessels, heart, and lymphatic vessels. It is formed from the embryonic mesoderm. Compare with EPITHELIUM.
– DERIVATIVES **en·do·the·li·al** /-lēəl/ **adj.**
– ORIGIN late 19th cent.: modern Latin, from ENDO- 'within' + Greek *thēlē* 'nipple.'

en·do·therm /ˈendəˌTHərm/ ▶ **n.** Zoology an animal that is dependent on or capable of the internal generation of heat; a warm-blooded animal. Often contrasted with ECTOTHERM. Compare with HOMEOTHERM.
– DERIVATIVES **en·do·ther·my** **n.**
– ORIGIN 1940s: from ENDO- 'within,' on the pattern of *homoiotherm*.

en·do·ther·mic /ˌendəˈTHərmik/ ▶ **adj.** **1** (also **endothermal**) Chemistry (of a reaction or process) accompanied by or requiring the absorption of heat. The opposite of EXOTHERMIC. ■ (of a compound) requiring a net input of heat for its formation from its constituent elements.
2 Zoology (of an animal) dependent on or capable of the internal generation of heat.
– DERIVATIVES **en·do·ther·mi·cal·ly** /-(ə)lē/ **adv.**

en·do·tox·in /ˈendəˌtäksin/ ▶ **n.** Microbiology a toxin that is present inside a bacterial cell and is released when the cell disintegrates. It is sometimes responsible for the characteristic symptoms of a disease, e.g., in botulism. Compare with EXOTOXIN.
– DERIVATIVES **en·do·tox·ic** /ˌendōˈtäksik/ **adj.**

en·do·tra·che·al /ˌendōˈtrākēəl/ ▶ **adj.** situated or occurring within or performed by way of the trachea: *endotracheal tube*.
– DERIVATIVES **en·do·tra·che·al·ly** **adv.**

en·dow /enˈdou/ ▶ **v.** [with obj.] give or bequeath an income or property to (a person or institution): *he endowed the church with lands*. ■ establish (a college post, annual prize, or project) by donating the funds needed to maintain it. ■ (usu. **be endowed with**) provide with a quality, ability, or asset: *he was endowed with tremendous physical strength*.
– DERIVATIVES **en·dow·er** **n.**
– ORIGIN late Middle English (also in the sense 'provide a dower or dowry'; formerly also as *indow*): from legal Anglo-Norman French *endouer*, from *en-* 'in, toward' + Old French *douer* 'give as a gift' (from Latin *dotare*: see DOWER).

en·dow·ment /enˈdoumənt/ ▶ **n.** the action of endowing something or someone: *he tried to promote the endowment of a Chair of Psychiatry*. ■ an income or form of property given or bequeathed to someone. ■ (usu. **endowments**) a quality or ability possessed or inherited by someone. ■ [usu. as modifier] a form of life insurance involving payment of a fixed sum to the insured person on a specified date, or to their estate should they die before this date: *an endowment policy*.

end·pa·per /ˈen(d)ˌpāpər/ (also **end paper**) ▶ **n.** a blank or decorated leaf of paper at the beginning or end of a book, esp. one fixed to the inside of the cover.

end plate ▶ **n.** a flattened piece at or forming the end of something such as a motor or generator. ■ Anatomy each of the discoid expansions of a motor nerve where its branches terminate on a muscle fiber.

end·play /ˈen(d)ˌplā/ Bridge ▶ **n.** a way of playing the last few tricks that forces an opponent to make a disadvantageous lead.
▶ **v.** [with obj.] force (an opponent) to make such a lead.

end·point /ˈen(d)ˌpoint/ (also **end point**) ▶ **n.** the final stage of a period or process. ■ Chemistry the point in a titration at which a reaction is complete, often marked by a color change. ■ Mathematics a point or value that marks the end of a ray or one of the ends of a line segment or interval.

end prod·uct ▶ **n.** that which is produced as the final result of an activity or process, esp. the finished article in a manufacturing process.

end re·sult ▶ **n.** the final result or outcome of an activity or process.

en·drin /ˈendrin/ ▶ **n.** a toxic insecticide that is a stereoisomer of dieldrin.
– ORIGIN mid 20th cent.: from ENDO- 'within' + a shortened form of DIELDRIN.

end run ▶ **n.** Football an attempt by the ballcarrier to run around the end of the defensive line. ■ an evasive tactic or maneuver.
▶ **v.** (**end-run**) [with obj.] evade; circumvent: *an attempt to end-run regulations for fire protection*.

end-stopped ▶ **adj.** (of verse) having a pause at the end of each line.

end times ▶ **plural n.** (in some religious beliefs) the period leading up to Judgment Day: *people in every age have wondered if the end times were going to occur during their lifetimes*.

en·due /enˈd(y)o͞o/ ▶ **v.** (**endues, enduing, endued**) [with obj.] literary endow or provide with a quality or ability: *our sight would be endued with a far greater sharpness*.
– ORIGIN late Middle English (also in the sense 'induct into an ecclesiastical living'): from

e

PRONUNCIATION KEY ə *ago, up*; ər *over, fur*; a *hat*; ā *ate*; ä *car*; e *let*; ē *see*; i *fit*; ī *by*; NG *sing*; ō *go*; ô *law, for*; oi *toy*; o͝o *good*; o͞o *goo*; ou *out*; TH *thin*; T͟H *then*; ZH *vision*

Old French *enduire*, partly from Latin *inducere* 'lead in' (see **INDUCE**), reinforced by the sense of Latin *induere* 'put on clothes.'

en·dur·a·ble /en'd(y)o͝orəbəl/ ▶ **adj.** able to be endured; bearable: *my journey was long but endurable.*

en·dur·ance /en'd(y)o͝orəns/ ▶ **n.** the fact or power of enduring an unpleasant or difficult process or situation without giving way: *she was close to the limit of her endurance.* ■ the capacity of something to last or to withstand wear and tear.
– ORIGIN late 15th cent. (in the sense 'continued existence, ability to last'; formerly also as *indurance*): from Old French, from *endurer* 'make hard' (see **ENDURE**).

e

en·dure /en'd(y)o͝or/ ▶ **v. 1** [with obj.] suffer (something painful or difficult) patiently: *it seemed impossible that anyone could endure such pain.*
2 [no obj.] remain in existence; last: *these cities have endured through time.*
– DERIVATIVES **en·dur·er n.**
– ORIGIN Middle English: from Old French *endurer*, from Latin *indurare* 'harden,' from *in-* 'in' + *durus* 'hard.'

en·dur·ing /en'd(y)o͝oriNG/ ▶ **adj.** continuing or long-lasting: *he formed a number of enduring relationships with women | an enduring problem.*
– DERIVATIVES **en·dur·ing·ly adv.**

en·dur·o /en'd(y)o͝orō/ ▶ **n.** (pl. **enduros**) a long-distance race, esp. for motor vehicles, motorcycles, or bicycles, typically over rough terrain, designed to test endurance.
– ORIGIN 1950s: from **ENDURANCE** + the informal suffix **-o**.

end use ▶ **n.** the application or function for which something is designed or for which it is ultimately used.

end us·er ▶ **n.** the person who actually uses a particular product.

end·ways /'en(d),wāz/ (also **endwise** /-,wīz/) ▶ **adv.** with its end facing upward, forward, or toward the viewer: *a little town looking endways on to the river.* ■ in a row with the end of one object touching that of another: *strips of rubber cemented endways.*

En·dym·i·on /en'dimēən/ Greek Mythology a remarkably beautiful young man, loved by the Moon (Selene). According to one story, he was put in an eternal sleep by Zeus for having fallen in love with Hera, and was then visited every night by Selene.

end zone ▶ **n. 1** Football the rectangular area at each end of the field into which the ball must be carried or passed and caught to score a touchdown.
2 Hockey the area at either end of the rink, extending from the blue line to the boards behind the goal.

ENE ▶ **abbr.** east-northeast.

-ene ▶ **suffix 1** denoting an inhabitant: *Nazarene.*
2 Chemistry forming names of unsaturated hydrocarbons containing a double bond: *benzene | ethylene.*
– ORIGIN from Greek *-ēnos*.

en éch·e·lon /än 'esHə,län/ ▶ **adj. & adv.** chiefly Geology in approximately parallel formation at an oblique angle to a particular direction.
– ORIGIN early 19th cent.: French, literally 'in rung formation.'

en·e·ma /'enəmə/ ▶ **n.** (pl. **enemas** or rare **enemata** /ə'nemətə/) a procedure in which liquid or gas is injected into the rectum, typically to expel its contents, but also to introduce drugs or permit X-ray imaging. ■ a quantity of fluid or a syringe used in such a procedure.
– ORIGIN late Middle English: via late Latin from Greek, from *enienai* 'send or put in,' from *en-* 'in' + *hienai* 'send.'

en·e·my /'enəmē/ ▶ **n.** (pl. **enemies**) a person who is actively opposed or hostile to someone or something. ■ **(the enemy)** [treated as sing. or pl.] a hostile nation or its armed forces or citizens, esp. in time of war: *the enemy shot down four helicopters |* [as modifier] *enemy aircraft.* ■ a thing that harms or weakens something else: *routine is the enemy of art.*
– PHRASES **be one's own worst enemy** act in a way contrary to one's own interests.
– ORIGIN Middle English: from Old French *enemi*, from Latin *inimicus*, from *in-* 'not' + *amicus* 'friend.'

en·er·get·ic /,enər'jetik/ ▶ **adj.** showing or involving great activity or vitality: *energetic exercise.* ■ Physics characterized by a high level of energy (in the technical sense): *energetic X-rays.* ■ of or relating to energy (in the technical sense).
– DERIVATIVES **en·er·get·i·cal·ly** /-(ə)lē/ **adv.**
– ORIGIN mid 17th cent. (in the sense 'powerfully effective'): from Greek *energētikos*, from *energein* 'operate, work in or upon' (based on *ergon* 'work').

en·er·get·ics /,enər'jetiks/ ▶ **plural n. 1** the properties of something in terms of energy.
2 [treated as sing.] the branch of science dealing with the properties of energy and the way in which it is redistributed in physical, chemical, or biological processes.
– DERIVATIVES **en·er·get·i·cist** /-'jetisist/ **n.**

en·er·gize /'enər,jīz/ ▶ **v.** [with obj.] give vitality and enthusiasm to: *people were energized by his ideas.* ■ supply energy, typically kinetic or electrical energy, to (something).
– DERIVATIVES **en·er·giz·er n.**

en·er·gu·men /,enər'gyo͞omən/ ▶ **n.** archaic a person believed to be possessed by the devil or a spirit.
– ORIGIN early 18th cent. (also denoting an enthusiast or fanatic): via late Latin from Greek *energoumenos*, passive participle of *energein* 'work in or upon.'

en·er·gy /'enərjē/ ▶ **n.** (pl. **energies**) **1** the strength and vitality required for sustained physical or mental activity: *changes in the levels of vitamins can affect energy and well-being.* ■ **(energies)** a person's physical and mental powers, typically as applied to a particular task or activity.
2 power derived from the utilization of physical or chemical resources, esp. to provide light and heat or to work machines.
3 Physics the property of matter and radiation that is manifest as a capacity to perform work (such as causing motion or the interaction of molecules): *a collision in which no energy is transferred.* ■ a degree or level of this capacity possessed by something or required by a process.
– ORIGIN mid 16th cent. (denoting force or vigor of expression): from French *énergie*, or via late Latin from Greek *energeia*, from *en-* 'in, within' + *ergon* 'work.'

en·er·gy au·dit ▶ **n.** an assessment of the energy needs and efficiency of a building or buildings.

en·er·gy ef·fi·cien·cy ra·ti·o (abbr.: **EER**) ▶ **n.** the ratio of a heating or cooling system's output, per hour, in British thermal units to the input in watts, used to measure the system's efficiency.

en·er·gy lev·el ▶ **n.** Physics the fixed amount of energy that a system described by quantum mechanics, such as a molecule, atom, electron, or nucleus, can have.

en·er·vate ▶ **v.** /'enər,vāt/ [with obj.] cause (someone) to feel drained of energy or vitality; weaken.
▶ **adj.** /'enərvit/ literary lacking in energy or vitality: *the enervate slightness of his frail form.*
– DERIVATIVES **en·er·va·tor** /-,vātər/ **n.**
– ORIGIN early 17th cent.: from Latin *enervat-* 'weakened (by extraction of the sinews),' from the verb *enervare*, from *e-* (variant of *ex-*) 'out of' + *nervus* 'sinew.'

en·er·vat·ing /'enər,vātiNG/ ▶ **adj.** causing one to feel drained of energy or vitality: *the enervating humidity of the coast.*

en·er·va·tion /,enər'vāsHən/ ▶ **n.** a feeling of being drained of energy or vitality; fatigue: *a sense of enervation.*

En·e·we·tak variant spelling of **ENIWETOK**.

en face /äN 'fäs/ ▶ **adv. & adj.** facing forward.
– ORIGIN mid 18th cent.: French.

en fa·mille /,äN fä'mē/ ▶ **adv.** with one's family: *when they went out en famille, Steven always drove.*
– ORIGIN early 18th cent.: French, literally 'in family.'

en·fant ter·ri·ble /äN,fäN te'rēbl(ə)/ ▶ **n.** (pl. **enfants terribles** pronunc. **same**) a person whose unconventional or controversial behavior or ideas shock, embarrass, or annoy others.
– ORIGIN mid 19th cent.: French, literally 'terrible child.'

en·fee·ble /en'fēbəl/ ▶ **v.** [with obj.] make weak or feeble: (as adj. **enfeebled**) *trade unions are in an enfeebled state.*
– DERIVATIVES **en·fee·ble·ment n., en·fee·bler** /-'fēblər/ **n.**
– ORIGIN Middle English: from Old French *enfeblir*, from *en-* (expressing a change of state) + *feble* 'feeble.'

en·feoff /en'fēf/ ▶ **v.** [with obj.] historical (under the feudal system) give (someone) freehold property or land in exchange for their pledged service. ■ give (property or land) in this way: *the lands were enfeoffed to the baron.*
– DERIVATIVES **en·feoff·ment n.**
– ORIGIN late Middle English: from Anglo-Norman French *enfeoffer*, from Old French *en-* 'in' + *fief* 'fief.' Compare with **FEOFFMENT**.

en·fet·ter /en'fetər/ ▶ **v.** [with obj.] literary restrain (someone) with shackles.

en·fe·vered /en'fēvərd/ ▶ **adj.** literary having or showing the signs of fever.

en·fi·lade /'enfə,lād, -,läd/ ▶ **n. 1** a volley of gunfire directed along a line from end to end.
2 a suite of rooms with doorways in line with each other.
▶ **v.** [with obj.] direct a volley of gunfire along the length of (a target).
– ORIGIN early 18th cent. (denoting the position of a military post commanding the length of a line): from French, from *enfiler* 'thread on a string, pierce from end to end,' from *en-* 'in, on' + *fil* 'thread.'

en·flesh /en'flesH/ ▶ **v.** [with obj.] literary give bodily form to; make real or concrete.
– DERIVATIVES **en·flesh·ment n.**

en·fleu·rage /,äNflə'räzH/ ▶ **n.** the extraction of essential oils and perfumes from flowers using odorless animal or vegetable fats.
– ORIGIN mid 19th cent.: French, from *enfleurer* 'saturate with the perfume from flowers.'

en·flu·rane /en'flo͞o,rān/ ▶ **n.** Medicine a volatile organic liquid used as a general anesthetic.
● A halogenated ether; chem. formula: CHF_2OCF_2CHFCl.
– ORIGIN 1970s: from *en-* (of unknown origin) + **FLUORO-** + **-ANE**[2].

en·fold /en'fōld/ (also dated **infold**) ▶ **v.** [with obj.]
1 surround; envelop: *he shut off the engine and silence enfolded them.* ■ hold or clasp (someone) lovingly in one's arms.
2 fold or shape into folds.
– DERIVATIVES **en·fold·ment n.**
– ORIGIN late Middle English (in the sense 'involve, entail, imply'; formerly also as *infold*): from **EN-**[1], **IN-**[2] 'within' + **FOLD**[1].

en·force /en'fôrs/ ▶ **v.** [with obj.] compel observance of or compliance with (a law, rule, or obligation). ■ cause (something) to happen by necessity or force: *there is no outside agency to enforce cooperation between the players.*
– DERIVATIVES **en·force·a·bil·i·ty** /-,fôrsə'bilitē/ **n., en·force·a·ble** /-əbəl/ **adj., en·forc·er n.**
– ORIGIN Middle English (in the senses 'strive' and 'impel by force'; formerly also as *inforce*): from Old French *enforcir, enforcier*, based on Latin *in-* 'in' + *fortis* 'strong.'

en·forced /en'fôrst/ ▶ **adj.** caused by necessity or force; compulsory: *a period of enforced idleness.*
– DERIVATIVES **en·forc·ed·ly** /-sidlē/ **adv.**

en·force·ment /en'fôrsmənt/ ▶ **n.** the act of compelling observance of or compliance with a law, rule, or obligation: *the strict enforcement of environmental regulations.*

en·fran·chise /en'fran,CHīz/ ▶ **v.** [with obj.] give the right to vote to: *a proposal that foreigners should be enfranchised for local elections.* ■ historical free (a slave).
– DERIVATIVES **en·fran·chise·ment n.**
– ORIGIN late Middle English (formerly also as *infranchise*): from Old French *enfranchiss-*, lengthened stem of *enfranchir*, from *en-* (expressing a change of state) + *franc, franche* 'free.'

ENG ▶ **abbr.** electronic news gathering.

eng. ▶ **abbr.** ■ engine. ■ engineer. ■ engineering. ■ engraved. ■ engraver. ■ engraving.

en·gage /en'gāj/ ▶ **v. 1** [with obj.] occupy, attract, or involve (someone's interest or attention): *he plowed on, trying to outline his plans and engage Sutton's attention.* ■ **(engage someone in)** cause someone to become involved in (a conversation or discussion). ■ arrange to employ or hire (someone): *he was engaged as a trainee copywriter.* ■ [with infinitive] pledge or enter into a contract to do something: *he engaged to pay them $10,000 against a bond.* ■ dated reserve (accommodations, a place, etc.) in advance: *he had engaged a small sailboat.*
2 [no obj.] **(engage in)** participate or become involved in: *organizations engage in a variety of activities |* **(be engaged in)** *some are actively engaged in crime.* ■ **(engage with)** establish a meaningful contact or connection with: *the teams needed to engage with local communities.* ■ (of a part of a machine or engine) move into position so as to come into operation: *the clutch will not engage |* [with obj.] *he engaged the gears and pulled out into the road.* ■ [with obj.] (of fencers or swordsmen) bring (weapons) together preparatory to fighting. ■ [with obj.] enter into conflict or combat with (an adversary).
– ORIGIN late Middle English (formerly also as *ingage*): from French *engager*, ultimately from the base of **GAGE**[1]. The word originally meant 'to pawn or pledge something,' later 'pledge oneself (to do

something),' hence 'enter into a contract' (mid 16th cent.), 'involve oneself in an activity,' 'enter into combat' (mid 17th cent.), giving rise to the notion 'involve someone or something else.'

en·ga·gé /,äNGgä'ZHā/ ▶ **adj.** (of a writer, artist, or their works) morally committed to a particular aim or cause.
– ORIGIN French, past participle of *engager* (see **ENGAGE**).

en·gaged /en'gājd/ ▶ **adj. 1** [predic.] busy; occupied: *I told him I was otherwise engaged.* ■ Brit. (of a telephone line) unavailable because already in use. ■ (of a toilet) already in use.
2 having formally agreed to marry.
3 Architecture (of a column) attached to or partly let into a wall.

en·gage·ment /en'gājmənt/ ▶ **n. 1** a formal agreement to get married. ■ the duration of such an agreement: *a good long engagement to give you time to be sure.*
2 an arrangement to do something or go somewhere at a fixed time: *a dinner engagement.*
3 the action of engaging or being engaged: *Britain's continued* **engagement** *in open trading* | *the engagement of the gears.*
4 a fight or battle between armed forces.
– ORIGIN early 17th cent. (in the general sense 'a legal or moral obligation'): French, from *engager* 'to pledge' (see **ENGAGE**).

en·gage·ment ring ▶ **n.** a ring given by a man to a woman when they agree to marry.

en·gag·ing /en'gājiNG/ ▶ **adj.** charming and attractive: *Sophie had a sunny personality that was very engaging.*
– DERIVATIVES **en·gag·ing·ly adv.**, **en·gag·ing·ness n.**

en garde /än 'gärd, än/ ▶ **exclam.** Fencing a direction to be ready to fence, taking the opening position for action.
– ORIGIN French *en garde* '(be) on guard.'

En·gel·mann spruce /'eNGgəlmən/ (also **Engelmann's spruce**) ▶ **n.** a tall spruce found in the mountains of western North America and Mexico.
● *Picea engelmannii*, family Pinaceae.
– ORIGIN mid 19th cent.: named after George *Engelmann* (1809–84), American botanist.

En·gels /'eNGgəlz/, Friedrich (1820–95), German socialist and political philosopher. He collaborated with Karl Marx in the writing of the *Communist Manifesto* (1848) and translated and edited Marx's later work.

en·gen·der /en'jendər/ ▶ **v.** [with obj.] cause or give rise to (a feeling, situation, or condition): *the issue engendered continuing controversy.* ■ archaic (of a father) beget (offspring).
– ORIGIN Middle English (formerly also as *ingender*): from Old French *engendrer*, from Latin *ingenerare*, from *in-* 'in' + *generare* 'beget' (see **GENERATE**).

en·gine /'enjən/ ▶ **n. 1** a machine with moving parts that converts power into motion. ■ a thing that is the agent or instrument of a particular process: *exports used to be the engine of growth.*
2 a railroad locomotive. ■ short for **FIRE ENGINE**.
■ historical a mechanical device or instrument, esp. one used in warfare: *a siege engine.*
– DERIVATIVES **en·gined adj.** [in combination] *a twin-engined helicopter*, **en·gine·less adj.**
– ORIGIN Middle English (formerly also as *ingine*): from Old French *engin*, from Latin *ingenium* 'talent, device,' from *in-* 'in' + *gignere* 'beget'; compare with **INGENIOUS**. The original sense was 'ingenuity, cunning' (surviving in Scots as *ingine*), hence 'the product of ingenuity, a plot or snare,' also 'tool, weapon,' later specifically denoting a large mechanical weapon; whence a machine (mid 17th cent.), used commonly later in combinations such as *steam engine, internal combustion engine.*

en·gine block ▶ **n.** see **BLOCK** (sense 1 of the noun).

en·gine driv·er ▶ **n.** Brit. a driver of a locomotive; an engineer.

en·gi·neer /,enjə'ni(ə)r/ ▶ **n.** a person who designs, builds, or maintains engines, machines, or public works. ■ a person qualified in a branch of engineering, esp. as a professional: *an aeronautical engineer.* ■ the operator or supervisor of an engine, esp. a railroad locomotive or the engine on an aircraft or ship. ■ a skillful contriver or originator of something: *the prime engineer of the approach.*
▶ **v.** [with obj.] design and build (a machine or structure): *the men who engineered the tunnel.* ■ skillfully or artfully arrange for (an event or situation) to occur: *she engineered another meeting with him.* ■ modify (an organism) by manipulating its genetic material: [as adj., with submodifier] (**engineered**) *genetically engineered plants.*
– ORIGIN Middle English (denoting a designer and constructor of fortifications and weapons; formerly also as *ingineer*): in early use from Old French *engigneor*, from medieval Latin *ingeniator*, from *ingeniare* 'contrive, devise,' from Latin *ingenium* (see **ENGINE**); in later use from French *ingénieur* or Italian *ingegnere*, also based on Latin *ingenium*, with the ending influenced by **-EER**.

en·gi·neer·ing /,enjə'ni(ə)riNG/ ▶ **n.** the branch of science and technology concerned with the design, building, and use of engines, machines, and structures. ■ the work done by, or the occupation of, an engineer. ■ the action of working artfully to bring something about: *if not for Keegan's shrewd engineering, the election would have been lost.*

en·gi·neer·ing sci·ence (also **engineering sciences**) ▶ **n.** the parts of science concerned with the physical and mathematical basis of engineering and machine technology.

en·gine room ▶ **n.** the room containing the engines, esp. in a ship.

en·gine·ry /'enjənrē/ ▶ **n.** archaic engines collectively; machinery.

en·gine turn·ing ▶ **n.** the decoration of metal or ceramic objects with regular engraved patterns using a lathe.
– DERIVATIVES **en·gine-turned adj.**

en·gir·dle /en'gərdl/ (also **engird**) ▶ **v.** [with obj.] literary surround; encircle: *railroads engirdled this tract of country.*

en·gla·cial /en'glāsHəl/ ▶ **adj.** situated, occurring, or formed inside a glacier.
– DERIVATIVES **en·gla·cial·ly adv.**

Eng·land /'iNG(g)lənd/ a European country that forms the largest and most southern part of Great Britain and of the United Kingdom, surrounded on three sides by water (Irish Sea on west, English Channel on south, North Sea on east); pop. 51,446,000 (est. 2008); capital, London; language, English.

> England was conquered by the Romans in the first century AD, when it was inhabited by Celtic peoples. It was a Roman province until the early 5th century. During the 3rd–7th centuries Germanic-speaking tribes, traditionally known as Angles, Saxons, and Jutes, established a number of independent kingdoms there. England emerged as a distinct political entity in the 9th century before being conquered by William, Duke of Normandy, in 1066.

Eng·lish /'iNG(g)lisH/ ▶ **adj.** of or relating to England or its people or language.
▶ **n. 1** the West Germanic language of England, now widely used in many varieties throughout the world.
2 (as plural noun **the English**) the people of England.
3 spin given to a ball, esp. in pool or billiards.

> English is the principal language of Great Britain, the US, Ireland, Canada, Australia, New Zealand, and many other countries. There are some 400 million native speakers, and it is the medium of communication for many millions more; it is the most widely used second language in the world. It belongs to the West Germanic group of Indo-European languages though its vocabulary has been much influenced by Old Norse, Norman French, and Latin.

– DERIVATIVES **Eng·lish·man n.** (pl. **Englishmen**), **Eng·lish·ness n.**, **Eng·lish·wom·an n.** (pl. **Englishwomen**).
– ORIGIN Old English *Englisc* (see **ANGLE**, **-ISH**[1]). The word originally denoted the early Germanic settlers of Britain (Angles, Saxons, and Jutes), or their language (now called **OLD ENGLISH**).

Eng·lish bond ▶ **n.** Building a bond used in brickwork consisting of alternate courses of stretchers and headers.

Eng·lish break·fast (also **full English breakfast**) ▶ **n.** a substantial breakfast including hot cooked food such as bacon and eggs.

Eng·lish Ca·na·di·an ▶ **n.** a Canadian whose principal language is English.
▶ **adj.** of or relating to English-speaking Canadians.

Eng·lish Chan·nel a sea channel that separates southern England from northern France. It is 22 miles (35 km) wide at its narrowest point. A railroad tunnel (the Channel Tunnel) underneath the channel opened in 1994.

Eng·lish Civ·il War the war between Charles I and his Parliamentary opponents, 1642–49.

> Civil war broke out after Charles refused to accede to a series of demands made by Parliament. The king's forces (the Royalists or Cavaliers) were decisively defeated by the Parliamentary forces (or Roundheads) at the Battle of Naseby (1645), and an attempt by Charles to regain power in alliance with the Scots was defeated in 1648. Charles himself was tried and executed by Parliament in 1649.

Eng·lish horn ▶ **n.** Music an alto woodwind instrument of the oboe family, having a bulbous bell and sounding a fifth lower than the oboe.

English horn

Eng·lish i·vy ▶ **n.** see **IVY**.

Eng·lish muf·fin ▶ **n.** a flat circular spongy bread roll made from yeast dough and eaten split, toasted, and buttered.

Eng·lish mus·tard ▶ **n.** a kind of mustard made from mustard seeds milled to a powder, having a very hot taste and typically bright yellow in color.

e

Eng·lish Pale (also **the Pale**) that part of Ireland over which England exercised jurisdiction before the whole country was conquered. Centered in Dublin, it varied in extent at different times from the reign of Henry II until the full conquest under Elizabeth I.
– ORIGIN *Pale* from **PALE**[2].

Eng·lish set·ter ▶ **n.** a setter of a breed of dog with a long white or partly white coat.

Eng·lish son·net ▶ **n.** another term for **ELIZABETHAN SONNET**.

Eng·lish spar·row ▶ **n.** another term for **HOUSE SPARROW**.

Eng·lish spring·er ▶ **n.** (usu. **English springer spaniel**) see **SPRINGER** (sense 1).

en·globe /en'glōb/ ▶ **v.** [with obj.] literary enclose in or shape into a globe.

en·gorge /en'gôrj/ ▶ **v. 1** [with obj.] cause to swell with blood, water, or another fluid: *the river was engorged by a day-long deluge.*
2 (**engorge oneself**) archaic eat to excess.
– DERIVATIVES **en·gorge·ment n.**
– ORIGIN late 15th cent. (in the sense 'gorge; eat or fill to excess'): from Old French *engorgier* 'feed to excess,' from *en-* 'into' + *gorge* 'throat.'

engr. ▶ **abbr.** ■ engineer. ■ engraved. ■ engraver. ■ engraving.

en·graft /en'graft/ (also **ingraft**) ▶ **v.** another term for **GRAFT**[1].
– DERIVATIVES **en·graft·ment n.**

en·grailed /en'grāld/ ▶ **adj.** chiefly Heraldry having semicircular indentations along the edge. Compare with **INVECTED**.

en·grain /en'grān/ ▶ **v.** variant spelling of **INGRAIN**.

en·grained /en'grānd/ ▶ **adj.** variant spelling of **INGRAINED**.

en·gram /'engram/ ▶ **n.** a hypothetical permanent change in the brain accounting for the existence of memory; a memory trace.
– DERIVATIVES **en·gram·mat·ic** /,engrə'matik/ **adj.**
– ORIGIN early 20th cent.: coined in German from Greek *en-* 'within' + *gramma* 'letter of the alphabet.'

en·grave /en'grāv/ ▶ **v.** [with obj.] (usu. **be engraved**) cut or carve (a text or design) on the surface of a hard object: *my name was engraved on the ring.* ■ cut or carve a text or design on (such an object). ■ cut (a design) as lines on a metal plate for printing. ■ (**be engraved on** or **in**) be permanently fixed in (one's memory or mind): *the image would be forever engraved in his memory.*
– PHRASES **be engraved in stone** see **STONE**.
– DERIVATIVES **en·grav·er n.**
– ORIGIN late 15th cent. (formerly also as *ingrave*): from **EN-**[1], **IN-**[2] 'in, on' + **GRAVE**[3], influenced by obsolete French *engraver.*

en·grav·ing /en'grāviNG/ ▶ **n.** a print made from an engraved plate, block, or other surface. ■ the process or art of cutting or carving a design on a hard surface, esp. so as to make a print.

en·gross /en'grōs/ ▶ **v.** [with obj.] **1** absorb all the attention or interest of: *the notes totally engrossed him.* ■ archaic gain or keep exclusive possession of (something): *the country had made the best of its position to engross trade.* [from Old French *en gros*, from medieval Latin *in grosso* 'wholesale.']
2 Law produce (a legal document) in its final or definitive form.
– DERIVATIVES **en·gross·ment n.**
– ORIGIN late Middle English (formerly also as *ingross*): based on **EN-**[1], **IN-**[2] 'in' + late Latin *grossus* 'large.'

en·grossed /en'grōst/ ▶ **adj.** [predic.] having all one's attention or interest absorbed by someone or something: *they seemed to be* **engrossed in** *conversation.*

en·gross·ing /en'grōsiNG/ ▶ **adj.** absorbing all one's attention or interest: *the most engrossing parts of the book.*
– DERIVATIVES **en·gross·ing·ly adv.**

en·gulf /en'gəlf/ ▶ **v.** [with obj.] (of a natural force) sweep over (something) so as to surround or cover it completely: *the cafe was engulfed in flames* | figurative *Europe might be engulfed by war.* ■ eat or swallow (something) whole.
– DERIVATIVES **en·gulf·ment n.**

en·hance /en'hans/ ▶ **v.** [with obj.] intensify, increase, or further improve the quality, value, or extent of: *his refusal does nothing to enhance his reputation* | *computer techniques that enhance images.*
– DERIVATIVES **en·hanc·er n.**
– ORIGIN Middle English (formerly also as *inhance*): from Anglo-Norman French *enhauncer*, based on Latin *in-* (expressing intensive force) + *altus* 'high.' The word originally meant 'elevate' (literally and figuratively), later 'exaggerate, make appear greater,' also 'raise the value or price of something.' Current senses date from the early 16th cent.

en·hance·ment /en'hansmənt/ ▶ **n.** an increase or improvement in quality, value, or extent: *these enhancements will improve the customer experience* | *the enhancement of civic amenities.*

en·har·mon·ic /ˌenhär'mänik/ ▶ **adj.** Music of or relating to notes that are the same in pitch (in modern tuning) though bearing different names (e.g., F sharp and G flat or B and C flat). ■ of or having intervals smaller than a semitone (e.g., between notes such as F sharp and G flat, in systems of tuning that distinguish them).
– DERIVATIVES **en·har·mon·i·cal·ly adv.**
– ORIGIN early 17th cent. (designating ancient Greek music based on a tetrachord divided into two quartertones and a major third): via late Latin from Greek *enarmonikos*, from *en-* 'in' + *harmonia* 'harmony.'

E·nid /'ēnid/ a city in north central Oklahoma; pop. 47,396 (est. 2008).

e·nig·ma /i'nigmə/ ▶ **n.** (pl. **enigmas**) a person or thing that is mysterious, puzzling, or difficult to understand.
– ORIGIN mid 16th cent.: via Latin from Greek *ainigma*, from *ainissesthai* 'speak allusively,' from *ainos* 'fable.'

en·ig·mat·ic /ˌenig'matik/ (also **enigmatical**) ▶ **adj.** difficult to interpret or understand; mysterious: *he took the money with an enigmatic smile.*
– DERIVATIVES **en·ig·mat·i·cal·ly** /-(ə)lē/ **adv.**
– ORIGIN early 17th cent.: from French *énigmatique* or late Latin *aenigmaticus*, based on Greek *ainigma* 'riddle' (see **ENIGMA**).

en·isle /en'īl/ ▶ **v.** [with obj.] literary isolate on or as if on an island: *in the sea of life enisled, we mortal millions live alone.*

En·i·we·tok /ˌenə'wēˌtäk, ə'nēwi-/ (also **Enewetak**) an uninhabited island in the North Pacific Ocean, one of the Marshall Islands. After its population was evacuated, it was used by the US as a testing ground for atom bombs 1948–54.

en·jambed /en'jamd/ ▶ **adj.** (of a line, couplet, or stanza of verse) ending partway through a sentence or clause that continues in the next.
– ORIGIN late 19th cent.: from French *enjamber* 'stride over' + **-ED**[2].

en·jamb·ment /en'jam(b)mənt/ (also **enjambement**) ▶ **n.** (in verse) the continuation of a sentence without a pause beyond the end of a line, couplet, or stanza.
– ORIGIN mid 19th cent.: from French *enjambement*, from *enjamber* 'stride over, go beyond,' from *en-* 'in' + *jambe* 'leg.'

en·join /en'join/ ▶ **v.** [with obj.] instruct or urge (someone) to do something: [with obj. and infinitive] *the code enjoined members to trade fairly.* ■ prescribe (an action or attitude) to be performed or adopted: *the charitable deeds enjoined on him by religion.* ■ (**enjoin someone from**) Law prohibit someone from performing (a particular action) by issuing an injunction.
– DERIVATIVES **en·join·er n.**, **en·join·ment n.**
– ORIGIN Middle English (formerly also as *injoin*): from Old French *enjoindre*, from Latin *injungere* 'join, attach, impose,' from *in-* 'in, toward' + *jungere* 'to join.'

en·join·der /en'joindər/ ▶ **n.** Law a prohibition ordered by an injunction.

en·joy /en'joi/ ▶ **v.** [with obj.] **1** take delight or pleasure in (an activity or occasion): *Joe enjoys reading Icelandic family sagas.* ■ (**enjoy oneself**) have a pleasant time: *I could never enjoy myself, knowing you were in your room alone.* ■ [no obj., in imperative] informal used to urge someone to take pleasure in what is being offered or is about to happen: *Bake until the filling starts to bubble and the crust turns golden brown. Enjoy!*
2 possess and benefit from: *the security forces enjoy legal immunity from prosecution.*
– DERIVATIVES **en·joy·er n.**
– ORIGIN late Middle English: from Old French *enjoier* 'give joy to' or *enjoïr* 'enjoy,' both based on Latin *gaudere* 'rejoice.'

en·joy·a·ble /en'joi-əbəl/ ▶ **adj.** (of an activity or occasion) giving delight or pleasure: *the decision is aimed at making shopping more enjoyable.*
– DERIVATIVES **en·joy·a·bil·i·ty** /enˌjoi-ə'bilitē/ **n.**, **en·joy·a·ble·ness n.**, **en·joy·a·bly** /-əblē/ **adv.**

en·joy·ment /en'joimənt/ ▶ **n. 1** the state or process of taking pleasure in something: *the enjoyment of a good wine.* ■ a thing that gives pleasure: *one of his particular enjoyments was campfire singing.*
2 the action of possessing and benefiting from something.

en·keph·al·in /en'kefəlin/ ▶ **n.** Biochemistry either of two compounds that occur naturally in the brain. They are peptides related to the endorphins, with similar physiological effects.
– ORIGIN 1970s: from Greek *enkephalos* 'brain' (from *en-* 'in' + *kephalē* 'head') + **-IN**[1].

en·kin·dle /en'kindl/ ▶ **v.** [with obj.] literary set on fire. ■ arouse or inspire (an emotion): *fresh remembrance of vexation must still enkindle rage.*

enl. ▶ **abbr.** ■ enlarge. ■ enlarged. ■ enlisted.

en·lace /en'lās/ ▶ **v.** [with obj.] literary entwine or entangle: *a web of green enlaced the thorn trees.*
– ORIGIN Middle English: from Old French *enlacier*, based on Latin *laqueus* 'noose.'

en·large /en'lärj/ ▶ **v.** make or become bigger or more extensive: [with obj.] *recently my son enlarged our garden pond* | [no obj.] *lymph nodes enlarge and become hard* | (as adj. **enlarged**) *an enlarged spleen.* ■ [with obj.] develop a bigger print of (a photograph).
– PHRASAL VERBS **enlarge on/upon** speak or write about (something) in greater detail: *I would like to enlarge on this theme.*
– ORIGIN Middle English (formerly also as *inlarge*): from Old French *enlarger*, from *en-* (expressing a change of state) + *large* 'large.'

en·large·ment /en'lärjmənt/ ▶ **n.** the action or state of enlarging or being enlarged. ■ a photograph that is larger than the negative from which it is produced or than a print that has already been made from it.

en·larg·er /en'lärjər/ ▶ **n.** Photography an apparatus for enlarging or reducing negatives or positives.

en·light·en /en'lītn/ ▶ **v.** [with obj.] give (someone) greater knowledge and understanding about a subject or situation: *Christopher had not enlightened Frances as to their relationship.* ■ give (someone) spiritual knowledge or insight. ■ archaic shed light on (an object).
– DERIVATIVES **en·light·en·er n.**
– ORIGIN Middle English (in the sense 'make luminous'; formerly also as *inlighten*): in early use from Old English *inlīhtan* 'to shine'; later from **EN-**[1], **IN-**[2] (as an intensifier) + **LIGHTEN**[2] or the noun **LIGHT**[1].

en·light·ened /en'lītnd/ ▶ **adj.** having or showing a rational, modern, and well-informed outlook: *the more enlightened employers offer better terms.* ■ spiritually aware.

en·light·en·ment /en'lītnmənt/ ▶ **n. 1** the action of enlightening or the state of being enlightened: *Robbie looked to me for enlightenment.* ■ the action or state of attaining or having attained spiritual knowledge or insight, in particular (in Buddhism) that awareness which frees a person from the cycle of rebirth.
2 (**the Enlightenment**) a European intellectual movement of the late 17th and 18th centuries emphasizing reason and individualism rather than tradition. It was heavily influenced by 17th-century philosophers such as Descartes, Locke, and Newton, and its prominent exponents include Kant, Goethe, Voltaire, Rousseau, and Adam Smith.

en·list /en'list/ ▶ **v.** enroll or be enrolled in the armed services: [no obj.] *he enlisted in the army* | [with obj.] *hundreds of thousands of recruits had been enlisted.* ■ [with obj.] engage (a person or their help or support): *the company enlisted the help of independent consultants.*
– DERIVATIVES **en·list·er n.**, **en·list·ment n.**
– ORIGIN mid 16th cent. (formerly also as *inlist*): from **EN-**[1], **IN-**[2] 'in, on' + **LIST**[1], perhaps suggested by Dutch *inlijsten* 'put on a list.'

en·list·ed man ▶ **n.** a member of the armed forces below the rank of NCO.

en·liv·en /en'līvən/ ▶ **v.** [with obj.] make (something) more entertaining, interesting, or appealing: *the wartime routine was enlivened by a series of concerts.* ■ make (someone) more cheerful or animated: *the visit had clearly enlivened my mother.*
– DERIVATIVES **en·liv·en·er n.**, **en·liv·en·ment n.**
– ORIGIN mid 17th cent. (in the sense 'restore to life, give life to'; formerly also as *inliven*): from 16th-cent. *enlive*, *inlive* (in the same sense), from **EN-**[1], **IN-**[2] (as an intensifier) + **LIFE**.

en masse /än 'mas/ ▶ **adv.** in a group; all together: *the board of directors resigned en masse.*
– ORIGIN late 18th cent.: French, literally 'in a mass.'

en·mesh /en'mesH/ ▶ **v.** [with obj.] (usu. **be enmeshed in**) cause to become entangled in something: *whales enmeshed in drift nets.* ■ involve (someone) in a difficult situation from which it is hard to escape: *he is enmeshed in an adulterous affair.*
– DERIVATIVES **en·mesh·ment n.**

en·mi·ty /'enmitē/ ▶ **n.** (pl. **enmities**) the state or feeling of being actively opposed or hostile to someone or something: *enmity between Protestants and Catholics* | *family feuds and enmities.*
– ORIGIN Middle English: from Old French *enemi(s)tie*, based on Latin *inimicus* (see **ENEMY**).

en·ne·ad /'enēˌad/ ▶ **n.** rare a group or set of nine.
– ORIGIN mid 16th cent.: from Greek *enneas*, *ennead-*, from *ennea* 'nine.'

en·ne·a·gram /'enēəˌgram/ ▶ **n.** a nine-sided figure used in a particular system of analysis to represent the spectrum of possible personality types.
– ORIGIN from Greek *ennea* 'nine' + **-GRAM**[1].

En·ni·us /'enēəs/, Quintus (239–169 BC), Roman epic poet and playwright. He was largely responsible for the creation of a native Roman literature based on Greek models.

en·no·ble /en'nōbəl/ ▶ **v.** [with obj.] give (someone) a noble rank or title. ■ lend greater dignity or nobility of character to: *the theater is a moral instrument to ennoble the mind.*
– DERIVATIVES **en·no·ble·ment n.**
– ORIGIN late 15th cent. (formerly also as *innoble*): from French *ennoblir*, from *en-* (expressing a change of state) + *noble* 'noble.'

en·nui /än'wē/ ▶ **n.** a feeling of listlessness and dissatisfaction arising from a lack of occupation or excitement.
– ORIGIN mid 18th cent.: French, from Latin *mihi in odio est* 'it is hateful to me.' Compare with **ANNOY**.

E·noch /'ēnək, 'ēˌnäk/ **1** (in the Bible) the eldest son of Cain. ■ the first city, built by Cain (Gen. 4:17).
2 a Hebrew patriarch, father of Methuselah.

e·no·ki /i'nōkē/ (also **enoki mushroom**) ▶ **n.** an edible Japanese mushroom, growing in clusters, with slender stems and small caps.
– ORIGIN 1980s: from Japanese *enoki-take*, from *enoki* 'nettle-tree' + *take* 'mushroom.'

e·nol·o·gy /ē'näləjē/ (also **oenology**) ▶ **n.** the study of wines.
– DERIVATIVES **e·no·log·i·cal** /ˌēnə'läjikəl/ **adj.**, **e·nol·o·gist** /-jist/ **n.**
– ORIGIN early 19th cent.: from Greek *oinos* 'wine' + **-LOGY**.

e·no·phile ▶ **n.** variant spelling of **OENOPHILE**.

e·nor·mi·ty /i'nôrmitē/ ▶ **n.** (pl. **enormities**)
1 (**the enormity of**) the great or extreme scale, seriousness, or extent of something perceived as bad or morally wrong: *a thorough search disclosed the full enormity of the crime.* ■ (in neutral use) the large size or scale of something: *I began to get a sense of the enormity of the task.*
2 a grave crime or sin: *the enormities of the regime.*
– ORIGIN late Middle English: via Old French from Latin *enormitas*, from *enormis*, from *e-* (variant of *ex-*) 'out of' + *norma* 'pattern, standard.' The word originally meant 'deviation from legal or moral rectitude' and 'transgression' Current senses have been influenced by **ENORMOUS**.

> **USAGE** **Enormity** traditionally means 'the extreme scale or seriousness of something bad or morally wrong,' as in *they were struggling to deal with the enormity of the crime.* Today, however, a more neutral sense as a synonym for **hugeness** or **immensity**, as in *he soon discovered the enormity of the task*, is common. Some people regard this use as wrong, arguing that **enormity** in its original sense meant 'an extreme wickedness' and should therefore continue to be used only of contexts in which a negative moral judgment is implied. Nevertheless, the sense of 'great size' is now broadly accepted in standard English, although it generally relates to something difficult, such as a task, challenge, or achievement.

e·nor·mous /i'nôrməs/ ▶ **adj.** very large in size, quantity, or extent: *her enormous blue eyes* | *the possibilities are enormous.*
– DERIVATIVES **e·nor·mous·ness n.**

–ORIGIN mid 16th cent.: from Latin *enormis* 'unusual, huge' (see **ENORMITY**) + **-OUS**.

e·nor·mous·ly /iˈnôrməslē/ ▶ **adv.** to a very great degree or extent; considerably: *quality of life varies enormously from one place to another* | [as submodifier] *she has been enormously successful.*

e·no·sis /iˈnōsis, ēˈnō-, ˈenōsēs/ ▶ **n.** the political union of Cyprus and Greece, as an aim or ideal of certain Greeks and Cypriots.
–ORIGIN 1920s: from modern Greek *henōsis*, from *hena* 'one.'

e·nough /iˈnəf/ ▶ **determiner & pron.** as much or as many as required: [as determiner] *too much work and not **enough** people to do it* | *there was just **enough** room for two cars* | [as pronoun] *they ordered **more than enough** for five people* | *getting **enough** of the right things to eat* | [as postpositive adj.] *there will be time **enough** to tell you when we meet.* ■ used to indicate that one is unwilling to tolerate any more of something undesirable: [as determiner] *we've got enough problems without that* | [as pronoun] *I've **had enough** of this arguing* | *that's enough, pack it in.*
▶ **adv. 1** to the required degree or extent (used after an adjective, adverb, or verb); adequately: *before he was old **enough** to shave* | *you're not big **enough** for basketball.*
2 to a moderate degree; fairly: *he can get there easily enough* | *he seems nice enough.*
3 [with sentence adverb] used for emphasis: *curiously enough, there is no mention of him.*
▶ **exclam.** used to express an impatient desire for the cessation of undesirable behavior or speech: *Enough! After six years of your arguing, I've had it!*
–PHRASES **enough is enough** no more will be tolerated. **enough said** there is no need to say more; all is understood.
–ORIGIN Old English *genōg*, of Germanic origin; related to Dutch *genoeg* and German *genug*.

en pa·pil·lote /än ˌpapēˈyōt/ ▶ **adj. & adv.** (of food) cooked and served in a paper wrapper: [as postpositive adj.] *fish en papillote.*

en pas·sant /ˌän päˈsänt, än päˈsän/ ▶ **adv.** by the way; incidentally: *the group's disbandment was announced, almost en passant, by the president.* ■ Chess by the en passant rule.
–PHRASES **en passant rule** (or **law**) Chess the rule that a pawn making a first move of two squares instead of one may nevertheless be immediately captured by an opposing pawn on the fifth rank.
–ORIGIN early 17th cent.: French, literally 'in passing.'

en·plane /enˈplān/ (also **emplane**) ▶ **v.** go or put on board an aircraft.

en pointe /än ˈpwant/ ▶ **adj. & adv.** see **ON POINTE** at **POINTE**.
–ORIGIN French.

en poste /än ˈpôst/ ▶ **adv.** in an official diplomatic position at a particular place.

en pri·meur /än prēˈmœr/ ▶ **adj. & adv.** (of wine) newly produced and made available.
–ORIGIN late 20th cent.: French, literally 'as being new.'

en prise /än ˈprēz/ ▶ **adj.** [predic.] Chess (of a piece or pawn) in a position to be taken.
–ORIGIN early 19th cent.: French.

en·queue /enˈkyo͞o/ ▶ **v.** (**enqueues, enqueuing** or **enqueueing, enqueued**) [with obj.] Computing add (an item of data awaiting processing) to a queue of such items.

en·quire /enˈkwīr/ ▶ **v.** chiefly Brit. another term for **INQUIRE**.
–DERIVATIVES **en·quir·er** **n.**
–ORIGIN Middle English *enquere*, from Old French *enquerre*, based on Latin *inquirere* (based on *quaerere* 'seek').

en·quir·ing /enˈkwī(ə)riNG/ ▶ **adj.** chiefly Brit. another term for **INQUIRING**.

en·quir·y /enˈkwī(ə)rē, ˈenkwərē/ ▶ **n.** (pl. **enquiries**) chiefly Brit. another term for **INQUIRY**.

en·rage /enˈrāj/ ▶ **v.** [with obj.] (usu. **be enraged**) make very angry: *the students were enraged at these new rules.*
–ORIGIN late 15th cent. (formerly also as *inrage*): from French *enrager*, from *en-* 'into' + *rage* 'rage, anger.'

en·raged /enˈrājd/ ▶ **adj.** very angry; furious: *an enraged mob screamed abuse.*

en rap·port /ˌän raˈpôr/ ▶ **adv.** having a close and harmonious relationship: *his improvisation indicates that he is **en rapport** with the rhythm of the band.*
–ORIGIN French (see **RAPPORT**).

en·rapt /enˈrapt/ ▶ **adj.** fascinated; enthralled: *the enrapt audience.*

en·rap·ture /enˈrapCHər/ ▶ **v.** [with obj.] (usu. **be enraptured**) give intense pleasure or joy to: *Ruth was enraptured by the child who was sleeping in her arms so peacefully.*

en·rich /enˈriCH/ ▶ **v.** [with obj.] **1** improve or enhance the quality or value of: *her exposure to museums enriched her life in France.* ■ add to the nutritive value of (food) by adding vitamins or nutrients: *cereal enriched with extra oat bran.* ■ (usu. as adj. **enriched**) increase the proportion of a particular isotope in (an element), esp. that of the fissile isotope U-235 in uranium so as to make it more powerful or explosive. ■ Architecture embellish a molding by carving or otherwise forming a sculpted, ornamental pattern, such as egg and dart: *one may enrich the echinus of a Doric capital with the egg and dart motif.*
2 make (someone) wealthy or wealthier: *top party members had enriched themselves.*
–DERIVATIVES **en·rich·ment** **n.**
–ORIGIN late Middle English (in the sense 'make wealthy'): from Old French *enrichir*, from *en-* 'in' + *riche* 'rich.'

en·robe /enˈrōb/ ▶ **v.** [with obj.] formal dress in a robe or vestment.

en·roll /enˈrōl/ (Brit. **enrol**) ▶ **v.** (**enrolls, enrolling, enrolled**) [no obj.] officially register as a member of an institution or a student on a course: *he enrolled in drama school* | [with obj.] *the school enrolls approximately 1,000 students* | *he enrolled in drama school.* ■ [with obj.] recruit (someone) to perform a service: *a campaign to enroll more foster families.* ■ [with obj.] Law, historical enter (a deed or other document) among the rolls of a court of justice. ■ archaic write the name of (someone) on a list or register.
–DERIVATIVES **en·roll·ee** /ˌenrōˈlē/ **n.**
–ORIGIN late Middle English (formerly also as *inroll*): from Old French *enroller*, from *en-* 'in' + *rolle* 'a roll' (names being originally written on a roll of parchment).

en·roll·ment /enˈrōlmənt/ (Brit. **enrolment**) ▶ **n.** the action of enrolling or being enrolled: *the amount due must be paid on enrollment in October* | *enrollments for teacher training have dropped off sharply.* ■ the number of people enrolled, typically at a school or college.

en route /än ˈro͞ot, en, än/ ▶ **adv.** during the course of a journey; on the way: *he stopped in Turkey en route to Geneva.*
–ORIGIN late 18th cent.: French (see **ROUTE**).

ENS ▶ **abbr.** ensign.

En·sche·de /ˈenskəˌdā/ a city in the eastern Netherlands; pop. 154,753 (2008).

en·sconce /enˈskäns/ ▶ **v.** [with obj.] establish or settle (someone) in a comfortable, safe, or secret place: *Agnes **ensconced herself** in their bedroom* | *spectators who were once comfortably ensconced in the old stadium's box seats.*
–ORIGIN late 16th cent. (in the senses 'fortify' and 'shelter within or behind a fortification'; formerly also as *insconce*): from **EN-**[1], **IN-**[2] 'in' + **SCONCE**[2].

en·sem·ble /änˈsämbəl/ ▶ **n. 1** a group of musicians, actors, or dancers who perform together: *a Bulgarian folk ensemble.* ■ a scene or passage written for performance by a whole cast, choir, or group of instruments. ■ the coordination between performers executing such a passage: *a high level of tuning and ensemble is guaranteed.*
2 a group of items viewed as a whole rather than individually: *the buildings in the square present a charming provincial ensemble.* ■ [usu. in sing.] a set of clothes chosen to harmonize when worn together. ■ chiefly Physics a group of similar systems, or different states of the same system, often considered statistically.
–ORIGIN late Middle English (as an adverb (long rare) meaning 'at the same time'): from French, based on Latin *insimul*, from *in-* 'in' + *simul* 'at the same time.' The noun dates from the mid 18th cent.

En·se·na·da /ˌensəˈnädə/ a city in northwestern Mexico, in Baja California state, on the Pacific Ocean; pop. 248,446 (2005).

en·sheathe /enˈSHēT͟H/ (also **ensheath**) ▶ **v.** [with obj.] chiefly Biology enclose (an organism, tissue, structure, etc.) in or as in a sheath.
–DERIVATIVES **en·sheath·ment** **n.**

en·shrine /enˈSHrīn/ ▶ **v.** [with obj.] (usu. **be enshrined**) place (a revered or precious object) in an appropriate receptacle: *relics are enshrined under altars.* ■ preserve (a right, tradition, or idea) in a form that ensures it will be protected and respected: *the right of all workers to strike was **enshrined in** the new constitution.*
–DERIVATIVES **en·shrine·ment** **n.**

en·shroud /enˈSHroud/ ▶ **v.** [with obj.] literary envelop completely and hide from view: *heavy gray clouds enshrouded the city.*

en·si·form /ˈensəˌfôrm/ ▶ **adj.** chiefly Botany shaped like a sword blade; long and narrow with sharp edges and a pointed tip.
–ORIGIN mid 16th cent.: from Latin *ensis* 'sword' + **-FORM**.

en·si·form car·ti·lage ▶ **n.** another term for **XIPHOID PROCESS**.

en·sign ▶ **n. 1** /ˈensən, ˈenˌsīn/ a flag or standard, esp. a military or naval one indicating nationality. ■ archaic a sign or emblem of a particular thing: *all the ensigns of our greatness.*
2 /ˈensən/ a commissioned officer of the lowest rank in the US Navy and Coast Guard, ranking above chief warrant officer and below lieutenant. ■ historical the lowest rank of commissioned infantry officer in the British army. ■ historical a standard-bearer.
–ORIGIN late Middle English: from Old French *enseigne*, from Latin *insignia* 'signs of office' (see **INSIGNIA**). Compare with **ANCIENT**[2].

en·si·lage /ˈensəlij/ ▶ **n.** another term for **SILAGE**.
▶ **v.** another term for **ENSILE**.
–ORIGIN late 19th cent.: from French, from *ensiler* (see **ENSILE**).

en·sile /enˈsīl/ ▶ **v.** [with obj.] put (grass or another crop) into a silo in order to preserve it as silage.
–ORIGIN late 19th cent.: from French *ensiler*, from Spanish *ensilar*, from *en-* 'in' + *silo* 'silo.'

en·slave /enˈslāv/ ▶ **v.** [with obj.] make (someone) a slave. ■ cause (someone) to lose their freedom of choice or action: *they were enslaved by their need to take drugs.*
–DERIVATIVES **en·slav·er** **n.**
–ORIGIN early 17th cent. (in the sense 'make (a person) subject to a superstition, passion, etc'; formerly also as *inslave*): from **EN-**[1], **IN-**[2] (as an intensifier) + **SLAVE**.

en·slave·ment /enˈslāvmənt/ ▶ **n.** the action of making someone a slave; subjugation: *the enslavement of millions of Africans.*

en·snare /enˈsner/ ▶ **v.** [with obj.] catch in or as in a trap: *they were ensnared in downtown traffic.*
–DERIVATIVES **en·snare·ment** **n.**

en·snarl /enˈsnärl/ ▶ **v.** [with obj.] cause to become caught up in complex difficulties or problems.

En·sor /ˈensôr/, James (Sydney), Baron (1860–1949), Belgian painter and engraver. Noted for macabre subjects, his work is significant both for symbolism and for the development of 20th-century expressionism.

en·sor·cell /enˈsôrsəl/ (also **ensorcel**) ▶ **v.** (**ensorcells, ensorcelling, ensorcelled**; also **ensorcells, ensorceling, ensorceled**) [with obj.] literary enchant; fascinate.
–DERIVATIVES **en·sor·cell·ment** (also **ensorcelment**) **n.**
–ORIGIN mid 16th cent.: from Old French *ensorceler*, alteration of *ensorcerer*, from *sorcier* 'sorcerer.'

en·soul /enˈsōl/ ▶ **v.** [with obj.] endow with a soul.
–DERIVATIVES **en·soul·ment** **n.**

en·sta·tite /ˈenstəˌtīt/ ▶ **n.** a translucent crystalline mineral of varying colors that occurs in some igneous rocks and stony meteorites. It consists of magnesium silicate and is a member of the pyroxene group.
–DERIVATIVES **en·sta·tit·ic** /ˌenstəˈtitik/ **adj.**
–ORIGIN mid 19th cent.: from Greek *enstatēs* 'adversary' (because of its refractory nature) + **-ITE**[1].

en·sue /enˈso͞o/ ▶ **v.** (**ensues, ensuing, ensued**) [no obj.] happen or occur afterward or as a result: *the difficulties that **ensued from** their commitment to Cuba* | (as adj. **ensuing**) *there were repeated clashes in the ensuing days.*
–ORIGIN late Middle English (formerly also as *insue*): from Old French *ensivre*, from Latin *insequi*, based on *sequi* 'follow.'

en suite /än ˈswēt/ ▶ **adj. & adv.** (of a bathroom) immediately adjoining a bedroom and forming part of the same set of rooms. ■ [as adj.] (of a bedroom) having such a bathroom.
–ORIGIN late 18th cent. (in the sense 'in agreement or harmony'): from French, literally 'in sequence.'

en·sure /enˈSHo͝or/ ▶ **v.** [with obj.] make certain that (something) shall occur or be the case: [with clause] *the client must ensure that accurate records be kept.* ■ make certain of obtaining or providing (something): [with two objs.] *she would ensure him a place in society.* ■ [no obj.] (**ensure against**) make sure that (a problem) shall not occur.

PRONUNCIATION KEY ə *ago, up*; ər *over, fur*; a *hat*; ā *ate*; ä *car*; e *let*; ē *see*; i *fit*; ī *by*; NG *sing*; ō *go*; ô *law, for*; oi *toy*; o͝o *good*; o͞o *goo*; ou *out*; TH *thin*; T͟H *then*; ZH *vision*

e

–ORIGIN late Middle English (in the senses 'convince' and 'make safe'): from Anglo-Norman French *enseurer*, alteration of Old French *aseurer*, earlier form of *assurer* (see **ASSURE**). Compare with **INSURE**.

USAGE On the difference between **ensure** and **insure**, see usage at **INSURE**.

en·swathe /en'swäTH, en'swāTH/ ▶ **v.** [with obj.] literary envelop or wrap in a garment or piece of fabric.

ENT ▶ **abbr.** ear, nose, and throat (as a department in a hospital).

-ent /ənt, nt/ ▶ **suffix 1** (forming adjectives) denoting an occurrence of action: *refluent*. ■ denoting a state: *convenient*.
2 (forming nouns) denoting an agent: *coefficient*.
–ORIGIN from French, or from the Latin present participial verb stem *-ent-* (see also **-ANT**).

en·tab·la·ture /en'tablәCHәr, -,CHŏŏr/ ▶ **n.** Architecture a horizontal, continuous lintel on a classical building supported by columns or a wall, comprising the architrave, frieze, and cornice.
–ORIGIN early 17th cent. (formerly also as *intablature*): from Italian *intavolatura* 'boarding' (partly via French *entablement* 'entablement'), from *intavolare* 'board up' (based on *tavola* 'table').

en·ta·ble·ment /en'tābәlmәnt/ ▶ **n.** Architecture a platform supporting a statue, above the dado and base.
–ORIGIN mid 17th cent. (in the sense 'entablature'): from French, based on *table* 'table.'

en·tail ▶ **v.** /en'tāl/ [with obj.] **1** involve (something) as a necessary or inevitable part or consequence: *a situation that entails considerable risks*. ■ Logic have as a logically necessary consequence.
2 Law settle the inheritance of (property) over a number of generations so that ownership remains within a particular group, usually one family: *her father's estate was* ***entailed on*** *a cousin*. ■ archaic cause to experience or possess in a way perceived as permanent or inescapable: *I cannot get rid of the disgrace that you have* ***entailed upon*** *us*.
▶ **n.** /'en,tāl/ Law a settlement of the inheritance of property over a number of generations so that it remains within a family or other group. ■ a property that is bequeathed under such conditions.
–DERIVATIVES **en·tail·ment n.**
–ORIGIN late Middle English (referring to settlement of property; formerly also as *intail*): from **EN-**[1], **IN-**[2] 'into' + Old French *taille* 'notch, tax' (see **TAIL**[2]).

ent·a·me·ba /,entә'mēbә/ (also **entamoeba**) ▶ **n.** (pl. **entamebae** /-'mēbē/ or **entamebas**) an ameba that typically lives harmlessly in the gut, though one kind can cause amebic dysentery. ● Genus *Entamoeba*, phylum Rhizopoda, kingdom Protista.
–ORIGIN modern Latin, from Greek *entos* 'within' + **AMEBA**.

en·tan·gle /en'taNGgәl/ ▶ **v.** [with obj.] (usu. **be entangled**) cause to become twisted together with or caught in: *fish attempt to swim through the mesh and become entangled*. ■ involve (someone) in difficulties or complicated circumstances from which it is difficult to escape: *the case of murder in which she had found herself so painfully entangled*.

en·tan·gle·ment /en'taNGgәlmәnt/ ▶ **n.** the action or fact of entangling or being entangled: *many dolphins die from entanglement in fishing nets*. ■ a complicated or compromising relationship or situation: *romantic entanglements*. ■ an extensive barrier, typically made of interlaced barbed wire and stakes, erected to impede enemy soldiers or vehicles: *the attackers were caught up on wire entanglements*.

en·ta·sis /'entәsis/ ▶ **n.** (pl. **entases** /-sēz/) Architecture a slight convex curve in the shaft of a column, introduced to correct the visual illusion of concavity produced by a straight shaft.
–ORIGIN mid 17th cent.: modern Latin, from Greek, from *enteinein* 'to stretch or strain.'

en·tel·e·chy /en'telәkē/ ▶ **n.** (pl. **entelechies**) Philosophy the realization of potential. ■ the supposed vital principle that guides the development and functioning of an organism or other system or organization. ■ Philosophy the soul.
–ORIGIN late Middle English: via late Latin from Greek *entelekheia* (used by Aristotle), from *en-* 'within' + *telos* 'end, perfection' + *ekhein* 'be in a certain state.'

en·tel·lus /en'telәs/ (also **entellus monkey**) ▶ **n.** another term for **HANUMAN**.
–ORIGIN mid 19th cent.: from the name of an aged Trojan in Virgil's *Aeneid*.

en·tente /än'tänt/ ▶ **n.** (also **entente cordiale** /kôr'dyäl/) a friendly understanding or informal alliance between states or factions: *the growing entente between former opponents*. ■ a group of states in such an alliance. ■ (**the Entente Cordiale**) the understanding between Britain and France reached in 1904, forming the basis of Anglo-French cooperation in World War I.
–ORIGIN mid 19th cent.: French *entente (cordiale)* '(friendly) understanding.'

en·ter /'entәr/ ▶ **v. 1** come or go into (a place): [with obj.] *she entered the kitchen* | [no obj.] *the door opened and Karl entered* | figurative *reading the Bible, we enter into an amazing new world of thoughts*. ■ [no obj.] used as a stage direction to indicate when a character comes on stage: *enter Hamlet*. ■ [with obj.] penetrate (something): *the bullet entered his stomach*. ■ [with obj.] (of a man) insert the penis into the vagina of (a woman). ■ [with obj.] come or be introduced into: *the thought never entered my head*.
2 [with obj.] begin to be involved in: *in 1941 America entered the war*. ■ become a member of or start working in (an institution or profession): *that autumn, he entered college*. ■ register as a competitor or participant in (a tournament, race, or examination). ■ start or reach (a stage or period of time) in an activity or situation: *the election campaign entered its final phase*. ■ [no obj.] (of a particular performer in an ensemble) start or resume playing or singing.
3 write or key (information) in a book, computer, etc., so as to record it: *children can enter the data into the computer*. ■ Law submit (a statement) in an official capacity, usually in a court of law: *an attorney entered a plea of guilty on her behalf*.
▶ **n.** (also **enter key**) a key on a computer keyboard that is used to perform various functions, such as executing a command or selecting options on a menu.
–PHRASAL VERBS **enter into** become involved in (an activity, situation, or matter): *they have entered into a relationship*. ■ undertake to bind oneself by (an agreement or other commitment): *the council entered into an agreement with a private firm*. ■ form part of or be a factor in: *medical ethics also enter into the question*. **enter on/upon 1** formal begin (an activity or job); start to pursue (a particular course in life): *he entered upon a turbulent political career*. **2** Law (as a legal entitlement) go freely into property as or as if the owner.
–ORIGIN Middle English: from Old French *entrer*, from Latin *intrare*, from *intra* 'within.'

en·ter·al /'entәrәl/ ▶ **adj.** Medicine (chiefly of nutrition) involving or passing through the intestine, either naturally via the mouth and esophagus, or through an artificial opening. Often contrasted with **PARENTERAL**.
–DERIVATIVES **en·ter·al·ly adv.**
–ORIGIN early 20th cent.: from Greek *enteron* 'intestine' + **-AL**, partly as a back-formation from **PARENTERAL**.

en·ter·ic /en'terik/ ▶ **adj.** of, relating to, or occurring in the intestines.
–ORIGIN early 19th cent.: from Greek *enterikos*, from *enteron* 'intestine.'

en·ter·ic fe·ver ▶ **n.** another term for **TYPHOID** or **PARATYPHOID**.

en·ter·i·tis /,entә'rītis/ ▶ **n.** Medicine inflammation of the intestine, esp. the small intestine, usually accompanied by diarrhea.

entero- ▶ **comb. form** of or relating to the intestine: *enterovirus*.
–ORIGIN from Greek *enteron*.

en·ter·o·coc·cus /'entәrō,käkәs/ ▶ **n.** (pl. **enterococci** /-,käk(s)ī, -,käk(s)ē/) a streptococcus of a group that occurs naturally in the intestine but causes inflammation and blood infection if introduced elsewhere in the body (e.g., by injury or surgery). ● Genus *Streptococcus* (or *Enterococcus*); Gram-positive cocci.
–DERIVATIVES **en·ter·o·coc·cal** /,entәrō'käkәl/ **adj.**

en·ter·o·coele /'entәrō,sēl/ (also **enterocoel**) ▶ **n.** Zoology a coelom or coelomic cavity developed from the wall of the archenteron in some invertebrates.
–DERIVATIVES **en·ter·o·coe·lic** /,entәrō'sēlik/ **adj.**, **en·ter·o·coe·ly** /-,sēlē/ **n.**

en·ter·o·co·li·tis /,entәrōkә'lītis/ ▶ **n.** Medicine inflammation of both the small intestine and the colon.

en·ter·o·cyte /'entәrō,sīt/ ▶ **n.** Physiology a cell of the intestinal lining.

en·ter·o·hep·a·tic /,entәrōhi'patik/ ▶ **adj.** Physiology relating to or denoting the circulation of bile salts and other secretions from the liver to the intestine, where they are reabsorbed into the blood and returned to the liver.

en·ter·op·a·thy /,entә'räpәTHē/ ▶ **n.** (pl. **enteropathies**) Medicine a disease of the intestine, esp. the small intestine.

en·ter·os·to·my /,entә'rästәmē/ ▶ **n.** (pl. **enterostomies**) an ileostomy or similar surgical operation in which the small intestine is diverted to an artificial opening in the abdominal wall or in another part of the intestine. ■ an opening in the abdominal wall formed in this way.

en·ter·ot·o·my /,entә'rätәmē/ ▶ **n.** the surgical cutting open of the intestine.

en·ter·o·tox·e·mi·a /,entәrō,täk'sēmēә/ (Brit. **enterotoxaemia**) ▶ **n.** chiefly Veterinary Medicine blood poisoning caused by an enterotoxin.

en·ter·o·tox·i·gen·ic /'entәrō,täksi'jenik/ ▶ **adj.** Medicine (of bacteria) producing an enterotoxin.

en·ter·o·tox·in /,entәrō'täksin/ ▶ **n.** Medicine a toxin produced in or affecting the intestines, such as those causing food poisoning or cholera.

en·ter·o·vi·rus /,entәrō'vīrәs/ ▶ **n.** Medicine any of a group of RNA viruses (including those causing polio and hepatitis A) that typically occur in the gastrointestinal tract, sometimes spreading to the central nervous system or other parts of the body.

en·ter·prise /'entәr,prīz/ ▶ **n. 1** a project or undertaking, typically one that is difficult or requires effort: *a joint enterprise between French and Japanese companies*. ■ initiative and resourcefulness: *success came quickly, thanks to a mixture of talent, enterprise, and luck*.
2 a business or company: *a state-owned enterprise*. ■ entrepreneurial economic activity.
–DERIVATIVES **en·ter·pris·er n.**
–ORIGIN late Middle English: from Old French, 'something undertaken,' feminine past participle (used as a noun) of *entreprendre*, based on Latin *prendere, prehendere* 'to take.'

en·ter·prise cul·ture ▶ **n.** a capitalist society in which taking on financial risks in the hope of profit is encouraged.

en·ter·prise zone ▶ **n.** an impoverished area in which incentives such as tax concessions are offered to encourage business investment and provide jobs for the residents.

en·ter·pris·ing /'entәr,prīziNG/ ▶ **adj.** having or showing initiative and resourcefulness: *some enterprising teachers have started their own recycling programs*.
–DERIVATIVES **en·ter·pris·ing·ly adv.**

en·ter·tain /,entәr'tān/ ▶ **v.** [with obj.] **1** provide (someone) with amusement or enjoyment: *a tremendous game that thoroughly entertained the crowd*. ■ receive (someone) as a guest and provide them with food and drink: *a private dining room where members could entertain groups of friends*.
2 give attention or consideration to (an idea, suggestion, or feeling): *Washington entertained little hope of an early improvement in relations*.
–ORIGIN late Middle English: from French *entretenir*, based on Latin *inter* 'among' + *tenere* 'to hold.' The word originally meant 'maintain, continue,' later 'maintain in a certain condition, treat in a certain way,' also 'show hospitality' (late 15th cent).

en·ter·tain·er /,entәr'tānәr/ ▶ **n.** a person, such as a singer, dancer, or comedian, whose job is to entertain others.

en·ter·tain·ing /,entәr'tāniNG/ ▶ **adj.** providing amusement or enjoyment: *the magazine is both entertaining and informative*.
–DERIVATIVES **en·ter·tain·ing·ly adv.**

en·ter·tain·ment /,entәr'tānmәnt/ ▶ **n.** the action of providing or being provided with amusement or enjoyment: *everyone just sits in front of the TV for entertainment*. ■ an event, performance, or activity designed to entertain others: *a theatrical entertainment*. ■ the action of receiving a guest or guests and providing them with food and drink.

en·thal·py /'en,THalpē, en'THalpē/ ▶ **n.** Physics a thermodynamic quantity equivalent to the total heat content of a system. It is equal to the internal energy of the system plus the product of pressure and volume. (Symbol: **H**) ■ the change in this quantity associated with a particular chemical process.
–ORIGIN 1920s: from Greek *enthalpein* 'warm in,' from *en-* 'within' + *thalpein* 'to heat.'

en·the·o·gen /en'thēә,jen, -jәn/ ▶ **n.** a chemical substance, typically of plant origin, that is ingested to produce a nonordinary state of consciousness for religious or spiritual purposes.
–DERIVATIVES **en·the·o·gen·ic** /en,thēә'jenik/ **adj.**
–ORIGIN 1970s: from Greek, literally 'becoming divine within'; coined by an informal committee studying the inebriants of shamans.

en·thrall /en'THrôl/ (also Brit. **enthral**) ▶ **v.** (**enthralls, enthralling, enthralled**) [with obj.] capture the fascinated attention of: *she had been so enthralled by the adventure that she had hardly noticed the cold*. ■ (also **inthrall**) archaic enslave.

– DERIVATIVES **en·thrall·ment** (Brit. also **enthralment**) **n.**
– ORIGIN late Middle English (in the sense 'enslave'; formerly also as *inthrall*): from EN-[1], IN-[2] (as an intensifier) + THRALL.

en·thral·ling /en'THrôliNG/ ▶ **adj.** capturing and holding one's attention; fascinating: *an enthralling bestseller.*

en·throne /en'THrōn/ ▶ **v.** [with obj.] (usu. **be enthroned**) install (a monarch) on a throne, esp. during a ceremony to mark the beginning of their rule. ■ give or ascribe a position of authority to: *he was enthroned as the guru of the avant-garde.*
– DERIVATIVES **en·throne·ment n.**

en·thuse /en'THo͞oz/ ▶ **v.** [reporting verb] say something that expresses one's eager enjoyment, interest, or approval: [no obj.] *they both* **enthused over** *my new look* | [with direct speech] *"This place is superb!" she enthused.* ■ [with obj.] make (someone) interested and eagerly appreciative: *public art is a tonic that can enthuse alienated youth.*

en·thu·si·asm /en'THo͞ozē,azəm/ ▶ **n. 1** intense and eager enjoyment, interest, or approval: *her energy and* **enthusiasm for** *life* | *few expressed enthusiasm about the current leaders.* ■ a thing that arouses such feelings: *the three enthusiasms of his life were politics, religion, and books.*
2 archaic, derogatory religious fervor supposedly resulting directly from divine inspiration, typically involving speaking in tongues and wild, uncoordinated movements of the body.
– ORIGIN early 17th cent. (sense 2): from French *enthousiasme*, or via late Latin from Greek *enthousiasmos*, from *enthous* 'possessed by a god, inspired' (based on *theos* 'god').

en·thu·si·ast /en'THo͞ozē,ast/ ▶ **n.** a person who is highly interested in a particular activity or subject: *a sports car enthusiast.* ■ archaic, derogatory a person of intense and visionary Christian views.
– ORIGIN early 17th cent. (denoting a person believing that he or she is divinely inspired): from French *enthousiaste* or ecclesiastical Latin *enthusiastes* 'member of a heretical sect,' from Greek *enthousiastēs* 'person inspired by a god,' from the adjective *enthous* (see ENTHUSIASM).

en·thu·si·as·tic /en,THo͞ozē'astik/ ▶ **adj.** having or showing intense and eager enjoyment, interest, or approval: *the promoter was enthusiastic about the concert venue.*
– DERIVATIVES **en·thu·si·as·ti·cal·ly adv.**
– ORIGIN early 17th cent.: from Greek *enthousiastikos*, from *enthous* 'possessed by a god' (see ENTHUSIASM).

en·thy·meme /'enTHə,mēm/ ▶ **n.** Logic an argument in which one premise is not explicitly stated.
– ORIGIN mid 16th cent.: via Latin from Greek *enthumēma*, from *enthumeisthai* 'consider,' from *en-* 'within' + *thumos* 'mind.'

en·tice /en'tīs/ ▶ **v.** [with obj.] attract or tempt by offering pleasure or advantage: *a show that should* **entice** *a new audience* **into** *the theater* | [with obj. and infinitive] *the whole purpose of bribes is to entice governments to act against the public interest.*
– DERIVATIVES **en·tic·er n.**
– ORIGIN Middle English (also in the sense 'incite, provoke'; formerly also as *intice*): from Old French *enticier*, probably from a base meaning 'set on fire,' based on an alteration of Latin *titio* 'firebrand.'

en·tice·ment /en'tīsmənt/ ▶ **n.** something used to attract or to tempt someone; a lure: *financial enticements.* ■ the quality of being attractive or tempting: *despite the enticement of low prices, sales fell sharply from 2000's record level.*

en·tic·ing /en'tīsiNG/ ▶ **adj.** attractive or tempting; alluring: *an enticing prospect.*
– DERIVATIVES **en·tic·ing·ly adv.**

en·tire /en'tīr/ ▶ **adj.** [attrib.] with no part left out; whole: *my plans are to travel the entire world.* ■ not broken or decayed. ■ without qualification or reservations; absolute: *an ideological system with which he is in entire agreement.* ■ (of a male horse) not castrated. ■ Botany (of a leaf) without indentations or division into leaflets.
▶ **n.** an uncastrated male horse.
– ORIGIN late Middle English (formerly also as *intire*): from Old French *entier*, based on Latin *integer* 'untouched, whole,' from *in-* 'not' + *tangere* 'to touch.'

en·tire·ly /en'tīrlē/ ▶ **adv.** completely (often used for emphasis): *the juries were made up entirely of men* | [as submodifier] *we have an entirely different outlook.* ■ solely: *eight coaches entirely for passenger transport.*

en·tire·ty /en'tī(ə)rtē, -'tīritē/ ▶ **n.** the whole of something: *she would have to stay in her room over* **the entirety of** *the weekend.*
– PHRASES **in its entirety** as a whole; completely: *the poem is too long to quote in its entirety here.*
– ORIGIN Middle English: from Old French *entierete*, from Latin *integritas*, from *integer* 'untouched, whole' (see ENTIRE). Compare with INTEGRITY.

en·ti·sol /'enti,säl, -sôl/ ▶ **n.** Soil Science a soil of an order comprising mineral soils that have not yet differentiated into distinct horizons.
– ORIGIN mid 20th cent.: from ENTIRE + -SOL.

en·ti·tle /en'tītl/ ▶ **v.** [with obj.] (usu. **be entitled**) **1** give (someone) a legal right or a just claim to receive or do something: *employees are normally* **entitled to** *severance pay* | [with obj. and infinitive] *the landlord is entitled to require references.*
2 give (something, esp. a text or work of art) a particular title: *an article entitled "The Harried Society."* ■ [with obj. and complement] archaic give (someone) a specified title expressing their rank, office, or character: *they entitled him Sultan.*
– ORIGIN late Middle English (formerly also as *intitle*): via Old French from late Latin *intitulare*, from *in-* 'in' + Latin *titulus* 'title.'

en·ti·tle·ment /en'tītlmənt/ ▶ **n.** the fact of having a right to something: ***full* entitlement to** *fees and maintenance should be offered* | *you should be fully aware of your legal entitlements.* ■ the amount to which a person has a right: *annual leave entitlement.*

en·ti·tle·ment pro·gram ▶ **n.** a government program that guarantees certain benefits to a particular group or segment of the population.

en·ti·ty /'entitē/ ▶ **n.** (pl. **entities**) a thing with distinct and independent existence: *church and empire were fused in a single entity.* ■ existence; being: *entity and nonentity.*
– DERIVATIVES **en·ti·ta·tive** /-,tātiv/ **adj.** (chiefly Philosophy).
– ORIGIN late 15th cent. (denoting a thing's existence): from French *entité* or medieval Latin *entitas*, from late Latin *ens, ent-* 'being' (from *esse* 'be').

entom. ▶ **abbr.** entomology.

en·tomb /en'to͞om/ ▶ **v.** [with obj.] (usu. **be entombed**) place (a dead body) in a tomb. ■ bury or trap in or under something: *many people died, most entombed in collapsed buildings.*
– ORIGIN late Middle English (formerly also as *intomb*): from Old French *entomber*, from *en-* 'in' + *tombe* 'tomb.'

en·tomb·ment /en'to͞om,mənt/ ▶ **n.** the placing of a dead body in a tomb; interment: *the entombment of the Unknown Soldier.*

entomo- ▶ **comb. form** of an insect; of or relating to insects: *entomophagous.*
– ORIGIN from Greek *entomon*, neuter (denoting an insect) of *entomos* 'cut up, segmented.'

en·to·mol·o·gy /,entə'mäləjē/ ▶ **n.** the branch of zoology concerned with the study of insects.
– DERIVATIVES **en·to·mo·log·i·cal** /-mə'läjikəl/ **adj., en·to·mol·o·gist** /-jist/ **n.**
– ORIGIN mid 18th cent.: from French *entomologie* or modern Latin *entomologia*, from Greek *entomon* (denoting an insect) + *-logia* (see -LOGY).

en·to·moph·a·gy /,entə'mäfəjē/ ▶ **n.** the practice of eating insects, esp. by people.
– DERIVATIVES **en·to·moph·a·gist** /-jist/ **n., en·to·moph·a·gous** /-'mäfəgəs/ **adj.**

en·to·moph·i·lous /,entə'mäfələs/ ▶ **adj.** Botany (of a plant or flower) pollinated by insects.
– DERIVATIVES **en·to·moph·i·ly** /-'mäfəlē/ **n.**

en·to·par·a·site /,entō'parə,sīt/ ▶ **n.** Biology another term for ENDOPARASITE.
– ORIGIN late 19th cent.: from Greek *entos* 'within' + PARASITE.

En·to·proc·ta /,entə'präktə/ Zoology a small phylum of sedentary aquatic invertebrates that resemble moss animals. They have a rounded body on a long stalk, bearing a ring of tentacles for filtering food from the water.
– DERIVATIVES **en·to·proct** /'entə,präkt/ **n.**
– ORIGIN modern Latin (plural), from Greek *entos* 'within' + *prōktos* 'anus,' the anus being within the ring of tentacles.

ent·op·tic /en'täptik/ ▶ **adj.** (of visual images) occurring or originating inside the eye.
– ORIGIN late 19th cent.: from Greek *entos* 'within' + OPTIC.

en·tou·rage /,änto͞o'räZH/ ▶ **n.** a group of people attending or surrounding an important person: *an entourage of bodyguards.*
– ORIGIN mid 19th cent.: French, from *entourer* 'to surround.'

en·tr'acte /'än,trakt, än'trakt/ ▶ **n.** an interval between two acts of a play or opera. ■ a piece of music or a dance performed during such an interval.
– ORIGIN mid 19th cent.: French (earlier form of *entracte*), from *entre* 'between' + *acte* 'act.'

en·trails /'entrālz, 'entrəlz/ ▶ **plural n.** a person or animal's intestines or internal organs, esp. when removed or exposed. ■ the innermost parts of something: *digging copper out of the entrails of the earth.*
– ORIGIN Middle English: from Old French *entrailles*, from medieval Latin *intralia*, alteration of Latin *interanea* 'internal things,' based on *inter* 'among.'

en·train[1] /en'trān/ ▶ **v.** [no obj.] board a train. ■ [with obj.] put or allow (someone or something) on board a train.

en·train[2] ▶ **v.** [with obj.] **1** (of a current or fluid) incorporate and sweep along in its flow. ■ cause or bring about as a consequence: *the triumph of a revolution was measured in terms of the social revision it entrained.*
2 Biology (of a rhythm or something that varies rhythmically) cause (another) gradually to fall into synchronism with it. ■ [no obj.] (**entrain to**) fall into synchronism with (something) in such a way.
– DERIVATIVES **en·train·ment n.**
– ORIGIN mid 16th cent. (in the sense 'bring on as a consequence'): from French *entraîner*, from *en-* 'in' + *traîner* 'to drag.'

en·trance[1] /'entrəns/ ▶ **n.** an opening, such as a door, passage, or gate, that allows access to a place. ■ [usu. in sing.] an act or instance of going or coming in: *at their abrupt entrance he rose to his feet.* ■ [usu. in sing.] the coming of an actor or performer onto a stage: *her final entrance is as a triumphant princess.* ■ the right, means, or opportunity to enter somewhere or be a member of an institution, society, or other body: *about fifty people attempted to gain entrance* | [as modifier] *an entrance examination.* ■ Music another term for ENTRY.
– PHRASES **make an** (or **one's**) **entrance** (of an actor or performer) come on stage. ■ enter somewhere in a conspicuous or impressive way: *she slowly counted to ten before making her entrance.*
– ORIGIN late 15th cent. (in the sense 'right or opportunity of admission'): from Old French, from *entrer* 'enter.'

en·trance[2] /en'trans/ ▶ **v.** [with obj.] fill (someone) with wonder and delight, holding their entire attention: *I was entranced by a cluster of trees that were lit up by fireflies* | (as adj. **entrancing**) *he had never seen a more entrancing woman.* ■ cast a spell on: *Orpheus entranced the wild beasts.*
– DERIVATIVES **en·trance·ment n., en·tranc·ing·ly adv.**

en·trance·way /'entrəns,wā/ ▶ **n.** a way into a place or thing, esp. a doorway or corridor at the entrance to a building.

en·trant /'entrənt/ ▶ **n.** a person or group that enters, joins, or takes part in something.
– ORIGIN early 17th cent. (denoting a person taking legal possession of land or property): from French, literally 'entering,' present participle of *entrer* (see ENTER).

en·trap /en'trap/ ▶ **v.** (**entraps, entrapping, entrapped**) [with obj.] catch (someone or something) in or as in a trap: *she was entrapped by family expectations.* ■ trick or deceive (someone), esp. by inducing them to commit a crime in order to secure their prosecution.
– DERIVATIVES **en·trap·ment n., en·trap·per n.**
– ORIGIN mid 16th cent.: from Old French *entraper*, from *en-* 'in' + *trappe* 'a trap.'

en tra·ves·ti /än ,trave'stē/ ▶ **adv. & adj.** dressed as a member of the opposite sex, esp. for a theatrical role.
– ORIGIN mid 20th cent.: from French, literally '(dressed) in disguise, cross-dressed.'

en·treat /en'trēt/ ▶ **v. 1** [reporting verb] ask someone earnestly or anxiously to do something: [with obj. and infinitive] *his friends entreated him not to go.* ■ [with obj.] ask earnestly or anxiously for (something): *a message had been sent, entreating aid for the Navajos.*
2 [with obj.] archaic treat (someone) in a specified manner: *the King, I fear, hath ill entreated her.*
– DERIVATIVES **en·treat·ing·ly adv., en·treat·ment n.**
– ORIGIN late Middle English (in the sense 'treat, act toward (someone)'; formerly also as *intreat*): from Old French *entraitier*, based on *traitier* 'to treat,' from Latin *tractare* 'to handle.'

en·treat·y /en'trētē/ ▶ **n.** (pl. **entreaties**) an earnest or humble request: *the king turned a deaf ear to his entreaties.*
– ORIGIN late Middle English (in the sense 'treatment, management'; formerly also as *intreaty*): from ENTREAT, on the pattern of *treaty.*

e

en·tre·chat /ˌäntrəˈSHä/ ▶ **n.** Ballet a vertical jump during which the dancer repeatedly crosses the feet and beats them together.
– ORIGIN French, from Italian (*capriola*) *intrecciata* 'complicated (caper).'

en·tre·côte /ˈäntrəˌkōt/ ▶ **n.** a boned steak cut off the sirloin.
– ORIGIN French, from *entre* 'between' + *côte* 'rib.'

en·trée /ˈänˌtrā, ˌänˈtrā/ (also **entree**) ▶ **n.** the main course of a meal. ■ Brit. a dish served between the fish and meat courses at a formal dinner.
– ORIGIN early 18th cent. (denoting a piece of instrumental music forming the first part of a suite): French, feminine past participle of *entrer* 'enter' (see **ENTRY**).

e

en·tre·mets /ˌäntrəˈmā/ ▶ **n.** a light dish served between two courses of a formal meal.
– ORIGIN French, from *entre* 'between' + *mets* 'dish.'

en·trench /enˈtrenCH/ (also dated **intrench**) ▶ **v.** **1** [with obj.] establish (an attitude, habit, or belief) so firmly that change is very difficult or unlikely: *ageism is entrenched in our society.* ■ establish (a person or their authority) in a position of great strength or security: *by 1947 de Gaulle's political opponents were firmly entrenched in power.* ■ apply extra legal safeguards to (a right, esp. a constitutional right, guaranteed by legislation). ■ establish (a military force, camp, etc.) in trenches or other fortified positions.
2 [no obj.] (**entrench on/upon**) archaic encroach or trespass upon.
– DERIVATIVES **en·trench·ment** n.
– ORIGIN mid 16th cent. (in the sense 'place within a trench'): from **EN-**[1], **IN-**[2] 'into' + **TRENCH**.

en·trenched /enˈtrencHt/ ▶ **adj.** (of an attitude, habit, or belief) firmly established and difficult or unlikely to change; ingrained: *an entrenched resistance to change.*

en·tre nous /ˌäntrə ˈno͞o/ ▶ **adv.** between ourselves; privately: *entre nous, the old man's a bit of a problem.*
– ORIGIN late 17th cent.: French.

en·tre·pôt /ˈäntrəˌpō/ ▶ **n.** (pl. **entrepôts** pronunc. **same** or /-ˌpōz/) a port, city, or other center to which goods are brought for import and export, and for collection and distribution.
– ORIGIN early 18th cent.: French, from *entreposer* 'to store,' from *entre* 'among' + *poser* 'to place.'

en·tre·pre·neur /ˌäntrəprəˈno͝or, -ˈnər/ ▶ **n.** a person who organizes and operates a business or businesses, taking on greater than normal financial risks in order to do so. ■ a promoter in the entertainment industry.
– DERIVATIVES **en·tre·pre·neur·ism** n., **en·tre·pre·neur·ship** n.
– ORIGIN early 19th cent. (denoting the director of a musical institution): from French, from *entreprendre* 'undertake' (see **ENTERPRISE**).

en·tre·pre·neur·i·al /ˌäntrəprəˈno͝orēəl/ ▶ **adj.** characterized by the taking of financial risks in the hope of profit; enterprising: *an entrepreneurial culture | our entrepreneurial spirit thrives on meeting the next challenge.*
– DERIVATIVES **en·tre·pre·neur·i·al·ism** n., **en·tre·pre·neur·i·al·ly** adv.

en·tre·sol /ˈentərˌsäl, ˈäntrəˌsäl, -sôl/ ▶ **n.** a low story between the first floor and the second floor of a building; a mezzanine floor.
– ORIGIN early 18th cent.: French, from Spanish *entresuelo*, from *entre* 'between' + *suelo* 'story.'

en·tro·pi·on /enˈtrōpēˌän, -pēən/ ▶ **n.** Medicine a condition in which the eyelid is rolled inward against the eyeball, typically caused by muscle spasm or by inflammation or scarring of the conjunctiva (as in diseases such as trachoma), and resulting in irritation of the eye by the lashes (trichiasis).
– ORIGIN late 19th cent.: from **EN-**[2] 'inside,' on the pattern of *ectropion*.

en·tro·py /ˈentrəpē/ ▶ **n.** **1** Physics a thermodynamic quantity representing the unavailability of a system's thermal energy for conversion into mechanical work, often interpreted as the degree of disorder or randomness in the system. (Symbol: **S**)
2 lack of order or predictability; gradual decline into disorder: *a marketplace where entropy reigns supreme.*
3 (in information theory) a logarithmic measure of the rate of transfer of information in a particular message or language.
– DERIVATIVES **en·tro·pic** /enˈträpik/ adj., **en·tro·pi·cal·ly** /enˈträpik(ə)lē/ adv.
– ORIGIN mid 19th cent.: from **EN-**[2] 'inside' + Greek *tropē* 'transformation.'

en·trust /enˈtrəst/ ▶ **v.** [with obj.] assign the responsibility for doing something to (someone): *I've been entrusted with the task of getting him safely back.* ■ put (something) into someone's care or protection: *you persuade people to entrust their savings to you.*
– DERIVATIVES **en·trust·ment** n.

en·try /ˈentrē/ ▶ **n.** (pl. **entries**) **1** an act of going or coming in: *the door was locked, but he forced an entry.* ■ a place of entrance, such as a door or lobby. ■ the right, means, or opportunity to enter a place or be a member of something: *undocumented workers seeking entry to the United States.* ■ the action of undertaking something or becoming a member of something: *more young people are postponing their entry into full-time work.* ■ Bridge a card providing an opportunity to transfer the lead to a particular hand. ■ Law the action of taking up the legal right to property. ■ Music the point in a piece of music at which a particular performer in an ensemble starts or resumes playing or singing. ■ dialect a passage between buildings.
2 an item written or printed in a diary, list, ledger, or reference book. ■ the action of recording such an item: *sophisticated features to help ensure accurate data entry.*
3 a person or thing competing in a race or competition: *from the hundreds of entries we received, twelve winners were finally chosen.* ■ [in sing.] the number of competitors in a particular race or competition. ■ the action of participating in a race or competition.
4 the forward part of a ship's hull below the waterline, considered in terms of breadth or narrowness.
– ORIGIN Middle English: from Old French *entree*, based on Latin *intrata*, feminine past participle of *intrare* (see **ENTER**).

en·try form ▶ **n.** an application form for a competition.

en·try in·hib·i·tor ▶ **n.** a class of anti-HIV drugs that work by blocking the entry of the virus into a host cell.

en·try-lev·el ▶ **adj.** at the lowest level in an employment hierarchy: *he was hired as an entry-level research assistant.* ■ (of a product) suitable for a beginner or first-time user; basic: *entry-level computers.*

en·try·way /ˈentrēˌwā/ ▶ **n.** a way in to somewhere or something; an entrance.

en·try word ▶ **n.** a word, phrase, or name that is the subject of and heading for an entry in a dictionary, glossary, or encyclopedia, and is usu. set in boldface or another distinctive type; a headword or lemma.

en·try wound /wo͞ond/ ▶ **n.** a wound made by a bullet or other missile at the point where it entered the body.

en·twine /enˈtwīn/ ▶ **v.** [with obj.] wind or twist together; interweave: *they lay entwined in each other's arms* | figurative *the nations' histories were closely entwined.*
– DERIVATIVES **en·twine·ment** n.

e·nu·cle·ate /iˈn(y)o͞oklēˌāt/ ▶ **v.** [with obj.] **1** Biology remove the nucleus from (a cell).
2 surgically remove (a tumor or gland, or the eyeball) intact from its surrounding capsule.
▶ **adj.** Biology (of a cell) lacking a nucleus.
– DERIVATIVES **e·nu·cle·a·tion** /iˌn(y)o͞oklēˈāSHən/ n.
– ORIGIN mid 16th cent. (in the sense 'clarify, explain'): from Latin *enucleat-* 'extracted, made clear,' from the verb *enucleare*, from *e-* (variant of *ex-*) 'out of' + *nucleus* 'kernel' (see **NUCLEUS**).

e·nu·mer·a·ble /iˈn(y)o͞omərəbəl/ ▶ **adj.** Mathematics able to be counted by one-to-one correspondence with the set of all positive integers.

e·nu·mer·ate /iˈn(y)o͞oməˌrāt/ ▶ **v.** [with obj.] mention (a number of things) one by one: *there is not space to enumerate all his works.* ■ formal establish the number of: *the 2000 census enumerated 10,493 households in the county.*
– DERIVATIVES **e·nu·mer·a·tion** /iˌn(y)o͞oməˈrāSHən/ n., **e·nu·mer·a·tive** /-rətiv, -ˌrātiv/ adj.
– ORIGIN early 17th cent.: from Latin *enumerat-* 'counted out,' from the verb *enumerare*, from *e-* (variant of *ex-*) 'out' + *numerus* 'number.'

e·nu·mer·a·tor /iˈn(y)o͞oməˌrātər/ ▶ **n.** a person employed in taking a census of the population.

e·nun·ci·ate /iˈnənsēˌāt/ ▶ **v.** [with obj.] say or pronounce clearly: *she enunciated each word slowly.* ■ express (a proposition or theory) in clear or definite terms: *a written document enunciating this policy.* ■ proclaim: *a prophet enunciating the Lord's wisdom.*
– DERIVATIVES **e·nun·ci·a·tion** /iˌnənsēˈāSHən/ n., **e·nun·ci·a·tive** /iˈnənsēətiv, -ˌātiv/ adj., **e·nun·ci·a·tor** /-ˌātər/ n.
– ORIGIN mid 16th cent. (as *enunciation*): from Latin *enuntiat-* 'announced clearly,' from the verb *enuntiare*, from *e-* (variant of *ex-*) 'out' + *nuntiare* 'announce' (from *nuntius* 'messenger').

en·ure /iˈn(y)o͝or/ ▶ **v.** variant spelling of **INURE**.

en·u·re·sis /ˌenyəˈrēsis/ ▶ **n.** Medicine involuntary urination, esp. by children at night.
– DERIVATIVES **en·u·ret·ic** /-ˈretik/ adj. & n.
– ORIGIN early 19th cent.: modern Latin, from Greek *enourein* 'urinate in,' from *en-* 'in' + *ouron* 'urine.'

en·urn /inˈərn/ ▶ **v.** variant spelling of **INURN**.
– DERIVATIVES **en·urn·ment** n.

en·vel·op /enˈveləp/ ▶ **v.** (**envelops, enveloping, enveloped**) [with obj.] wrap up, cover, or surround completely: *a figure enveloped in a black cloak* | figurative *a feeling of despair enveloped him.* ■ (of troops) surround (an enemy force).
– DERIVATIVES **en·vel·op·ment** n.
– ORIGIN late Middle English (formerly also as *invelop(e)*): from Old French *envoluper*, from *en-* 'in' + a second element (also found in **DEVELOP**) of unknown origin.

> **USAGE** Envelop is a verb, stressed on the second syllable and meaning 'wrap completely.' The noun meaning 'paper container for a letter' is **envelope**, stressed on the first syllable.

en·vel·ope /ˈenvəˌlōp, ˈänvə-/ ▶ **n.** **1** a flat paper container with a sealable flap, used to enclose a letter or document.
2 a covering or containing structure or layer: *the external envelope of the swimming pool.* ■ the outer metal or glass housing of a vacuum tube, electric light, etc. ■ the structure within a balloon or nonrigid airship containing the gas. ■ Microbiology a membrane forming the outer layer of certain viruses. ■ Electronics a curve joining the successive peaks of a modulated wave. ■ Mathematics a curve or surface tangent to each of a family of curves or surfaces. ■ Astronomy the nebulous covering of the head of a comet; coma.
– PHRASES **push the envelope** informal approach or extend the limits of what is possible: *these are extremely witty and clever stories that consistently push the envelope of TV comedy.* [originally aviation slang, relating to graphs of aerodynamic performance.]
– ORIGIN mid 16th cent. (in the sense 'wrapper, enveloping layer'): from French *enveloppe*, from *envelopper* 'envelop.' The sense 'covering of a letter' dates from the early 18th cent.

en·ven·om /enˈvenəm/ ▶ **v.** [with obj.] archaic put poison on or into; make poisonous.
– ORIGIN Middle English (formerly also as *invenom*): from Old French *envenimer*, from *en-* 'in' + *venim* 'venom.'

en·ven·o·mate /enˈvenəˌmāt/ ▶ **v.** [with obj.] Zoology & Medicine (of a snake, scorpion, spider, or insect) poison by biting or stinging.
– DERIVATIVES **en·ven·o·ma·tion** /enˌvenəˈmāSHən/ n.

En·ver Pa·sha /enˈver pəˈSHä/ (1881–1922), Turkish political and military leader. A leader of the Young Turks in 1908, he was part of a ruling triumvirate that followed a coup d'état in 1913.

en·vi·a·ble /ˈenvēəbəl/ ▶ **adj.** arousing or likely to arouse envy: *an enviable reputation for academic achievement.*
– DERIVATIVES **en·vi·a·bly** /-əblē/ adv.

en·vi·ous /ˈenvēəs/ ▶ **adj.** feeling or showing envy: *I'm envious of their happiness | an envious glance.*
– DERIVATIVES **en·vi·ous·ly** adv.
– ORIGIN Middle English: from Old French *envieus*, from *envie* 'envy,' on the pattern of Latin *invidiosus* 'invidious.'

en·vi·ro /enˈvīrō/ ▶ **n.** (pl. **enviros**) informal an environmentalist: *command-and-control solutions demanded by the more radical enviros.*
▶ **adj.** environmental: *an enviro group that combats the committee's advocates for Western ranching, mining, and energy interests.*
– ORIGIN shortening.

en·vi·ron /enˈvīrən, -ˈvī(ə)rn/ ▶ **v.** [with obj.] formal surround; enclose: *the stone circle was environed by an expanse of peat soil.*
– ORIGIN Middle English (formerly also as *inviron*): from Old French *environer*, from *environ* 'surroundings,' from *en* 'in' + *viron* 'circuit' (from *virer* 'to turn, veer').

en·vi·ron·ment /enˈvīrənmənt, -ˈvī(ə)rn-/ ▶ **n.** **1** the surroundings or conditions in which a person, animal, or plant lives or operates. ■ [usu. with modifier] the setting or conditions in which a particular activity is carried on: *a good learning environment.* ■ [with modifier] Computing the overall structure within which a user, computer, or program operates: *a desktop development environment.*
2 (**the environment**) the natural world, as a whole or in a particular geographical area, esp. as affected by human activity.

en·vi·ron·men·tal /enˌvīrənˈmen(t)l, -ˌvī(ə)rn-/ ▶ **adj.** **1** relating to the natural world and the impact of human activity on its condition: *acid rain may*

have caused major environmental damage. ■ aiming or designed to promote the protection of the natural world: *environmental tourism.*
2 relating to or arising from a person's surroundings: *environmental noise.*
– DERIVATIVES **en·vi·ron·men·tal·ly** adv.

en·vi·ron·men·tal art ▶ n. **1** the production of artistic works intended to enhance or become part of an urban or other outdoor environment. ■ the production of works of art by manipulation of the natural landscape.
2 the production of works of art in the form of large installations or assemblages that surround the observer.

en·vi·ron·men·tal au·dit ▶ n. an assessment of the extent to which an organization is observing practices that seek to minimize harm to the environment.

en·vi·ron·men·tal·ist /en,vīrən'men(t)l-ist, -,vī(ə)rn-/ ▶ n. **1** a person who is concerned with or advocates the protection of the environment.
2 a person who considers that environment, as opposed to heredity, has the primary influence on the development of a person or group.
– DERIVATIVES **en·vi·ron·men·tal·ism** n.

en·vi·ron·men·tal med·i·cine ▶ n. a branch of medicine that studies environmental inputs and the individual's physical, mental, and emotional responses to them.

en·vi·ron·ment-friend·ly ▶ adj. another term for ECO-FRIENDLY.

en·vi·rons /en'vīrənz, -'vī(ə)rnz/ ▶ plural n. the surrounding area or district: *the picturesque environs of the lake.*
– ORIGIN mid 17th cent.: from French, plural of *environ* (see ENVIRON).

en·vis·age /en'vizij/ ▶ v. [with obj.] contemplate or conceive of as a possibility or a desirable future event: *the Rome Treaty envisaged free movement across frontiers.* ■ form a mental picture of (something not yet existing or known): *he knew what he liked but had difficulty envisaging it.*
– ORIGIN early 19th cent.: from French *envisager*, from *en-* 'in' + *visage* 'face.'

en·vi·sion /en'vizHən/ ▶ v. [with obj.] imagine as a future possibility; visualize: *she envisioned the admiring glances of guests seeing her home.*

en·voi /'en,voi, 'än,voi/ (also **envoy**) ▶ n. **1** a short stanza concluding a ballade.
2 literary an author's concluding words.
– ORIGIN late Middle English: from Old French *envoi*, from *envoyer* 'send' (see ENVOY).

en·voy /'en,voi, 'än,voi/ ▶ n. **1** a messenger or representative, esp. one on a diplomatic mission.
2 short for ENVOY EXTRAORDINARY.
– ORIGIN mid 17th cent.: from French *envoyé*, past participle of *envoyer* 'send,' from *en voie* 'on the way,' based on Latin *via* 'way.'

en·voy ex·traor·di·nar·y ▶ n. (pl. **envoys extraordinary**) a minister plenipotentiary, ranking below an ambassador and above a chargé d'affaires.

en·vy /'envē/ ▶ n. (pl. **envies**) a feeling of discontented or resentful longing aroused by someone else's possessions, qualities, or luck: *she felt a twinge of envy for the people on board.* ■ (**the envy of**) a person or thing that inspires such a feeling: *their national health service is the envy of many in Europe.*
▶ v. (**envies, envying, envied**) [with obj.] desire to have a quality, possession, or other desirable attribute belonging to (someone else): *he envied people who did not have to work on weekends* | [with two objs.] *I envy Jane her happiness.* ■ desire for oneself (something possessed or enjoyed by another): *a lifestyle that most of us would envy.*
– DERIVATIVES **en·vi·er** /'envēər/ n.
– ORIGIN Middle English (also in the sense 'hostility, enmity'): from Old French *envie* (noun), *envier* (verb), from Latin *invidia*, from *invidere* 'regard maliciously, grudge,' from *in-* 'into' + *videre* 'to see.'

en·wrap /en'rap/ ▶ v. (**enwraps, enwrapping, enwrapped**) [with obj.] wrap; envelop: *the book jacket enwraps a plain blue paper binding.* ■ engross or absorb (someone): *they were enwrapped in conversation.*

en·wreathe /en'rēTH/ ▶ v. [with obj.] (usu. **be enwreathed**) literary surround or envelop (something): *the lofty battlements, thickly enwreathed with ivy.*

en·zo·ot·ic /,enzō'ätik/ ▶ adj. of, relating to, or denoting a disease that regularly affects animals in a particular district or at a particular season. Compare with EPIZOOTIC, ENDEMIC (sense 1 of the adjective).
– ORIGIN late 19th cent.: from EN-[2] 'within' + Greek *zōion* 'animal' + -IC.

en·zyme /'enzīm/ ▶ n. Biochemistry a substance produced by a living organism that acts as a catalyst to bring about a specific biochemical reaction.

> Most enzymes are proteins with large complex molecules whose action depends on their particular molecular shape. Some enzymes control reactions within cells and some, such as the enzymes involved in digestion, outside them.

– DERIVATIVES **en·zy·mat·ic** /,enzə'matik/ adj., **en·zy·mat·i·cal·ly** /,enzə'matik(ə)lē/ adv., **en·zy·mic** /en'zīmik, -'zimik/ adj., **en·zy·mi·cal·ly** /en'zīmik(ə)lē, -zim-/ adv.
– ORIGIN late 19th cent.: coined in German from modern Greek *enzumos* 'leavened,' from *en-* 'within' + Greek *zumē* 'leaven.'

en·zy·mol·o·gy /,enzə'mäləjē/ ▶ n. the branch of biochemistry concerned with enzymes.
– DERIVATIVES **en·zy·mo·log·i·cal** /-mə'läjikəl/ adj., **en·zy·mol·o·gist** /-jist/ n.

EO ▶ abbr. executive order.

e.o. ▶ abbr. ex officio.

eo- ▶ comb. form early, primeval: *eohippus.*
– ORIGIN from Greek, *ēōs*, 'dawn.'

E·o·cene /'ēə,sēn/ ▶ adj. Geology of, relating to, or denoting the second epoch of the Tertiary period, between the Paleocene and Oligocene epochs. ■ (as noun **the Eocene**) the Eocene epoch or the system of rocks deposited during it.

> The Eocene epoch lasted from 56.5 million to 35.4 million years ago. It was a time of rising temperatures, and there was an abundance of mammals, including the first horses, bats, and whales.

– ORIGIN mid 19th cent.: from Greek *ēōs* 'dawn' + *kainos* 'new.'

e·o·hip·pus /,ē-ō'hipəs/ ▶ n. (pl. **eohippuses**) another term for HYRACOTHERIUM.
– ORIGIN late 19th cent.: from Greek *ēōs* 'dawn' + *hippos* 'horse.'

e·o ip·so /'ē-ō 'ipsō, 'ā-ō/ ▶ adv. formal by that very act or quality; thereby: *such a grand theory would eo ipso give an account of how we communicate using language.*
– ORIGIN Latin, ablative of *id ipsum* 'the thing itself.'

e·o·li·an /ē'ōlēən/ ▶ adj. (also **aeolian**) chiefly Geology relating to or arising from the action of the wind: *fluvial and eolian sediments.*

e·o·lith /'ēə,liTH/ ▶ n. Archaeology a roughly chipped flint found in Tertiary strata, originally thought to be an early artifact but probably of natural origin.
– ORIGIN late 19th cent.: from Greek *ēōs* 'dawn' + *lithos* 'stone.'

E·o·lith·ic /,ēə'liTHik/ ▶ adj. Archaeology, dated of, relating to, or denoting a period at the beginning of the Stone Age, preceding the Paleolithic and characterized by the earliest crude stone tools. ■ (as noun **the Eolithic**) the Eolithic period.
– ORIGIN late 19th cent.: from French *éolithique*, from Greek *ēōs* 'dawn' + *lithikos* (from *lithos* 'stone').

e.o.m. ▶ abbr. end of the month.

e·on /'ēən, 'ē,än/ (chiefly Brit. also **aeon**) ▶ n. (often **eons**) an indefinite and very long period of time, often a period exaggerated for humorous or rhetorical effect: *he reached the crag eons before I arrived* | *his eyes searched her face for what seemed like eons.* ■ Astronomy & Geology a unit of time equal to a billion years. ■ Geology a major division of geological time, subdivided into eras: *the Precambrian eon.* ■ Philosophy (in Neoplatonism, Platonism, and Gnosticism) a power existing from eternity; an emanation or phase of the supreme deity.
– ORIGIN mid 17th cent.: via ecclesiastical Latin from Greek *aiōn* 'age.'

E·os /'ē,äs/ Greek Mythology the Greek goddess of the dawn. Roman equivalent AURORA[2].

e·o·sin /'ēəsin/ ▶ n. a red fluorescent dye that is a bromine derivative of fluorescein, or one of its salts or other derivatives.
– ORIGIN late 19th cent.: from Greek *ēōs* 'dawn' + -IN[1].

e·o·sin·o·phil /,ēə'sinə,fil/ ▶ n. Physiology a white blood cell containing granules that are readily stained by eosin.

e·o·sin·o·phil·i·a /,ēə,sinə'filēə/ ▶ n. Medicine an increase in the number of eosinophils in the blood, occurring in response to some allergens, drugs, and parasites, and in some types of leukemia.

e·o·sin·o·phil·ic /,ēə,sinə'filik/ ▶ adj. **1** Physiology (of a cell or its contents) readily stained by eosin.
2 Medicine relating to or marked by eosinophilia.

EOT ▶ abbr. ■ Computing end of tape. ■ Telecommunications end of transmission.

-eous ▶ suffix (forming adjectives) resembling; displaying the nature of: *aqueous* | *erroneous.*
– ORIGIN from the Latin suffix *-eus* + -OUS.

EP ▶ abbr. ■ electroplate. ■ European Parliament. ■ European plan. ■ extended-play (of a record or compact disc): *an EP of remixes.* ■ extreme pressure (used in grading lubricants).

Ep. ▶ abbr. Epistle.

e.p. ▶ abbr. Chess en passant.

ep- ▶ prefix variant spelling of EPI- before a vowel or *h* (as in *eparch, ephemeral*).

EPA ▶ abbr. Environmental Protection Agency.

e

e·pact /'ē,pakt/ ▶ n. [in sing.] the number of days by which the solar year differs from the lunar year. ■ the number of days into the moon's phase cycle at the beginning of the solar (calendar) year.
– ORIGIN mid 16th cent. (denoting the age of the moon in days at the beginning of the calendar year): from French *épacte*, via late Latin from Greek *epaktai* (*hēmerai*) 'intercalated (days),' from *epagein* 'bring in,' from *epi* 'in addition' + *agein* 'bring.'

ep·arch /'ep,ärk/ ▶ n. the chief bishop of an eparchy.
– ORIGIN mid 17th cent. (denoting the governor of an administrative division of Greece): from Greek *eparkhos*, from *epi* 'above' + *arkhos* 'ruler.'

ep·ar·chy /'ep,ärkē/ ▶ n. (pl. **eparchies**) a province of the Orthodox Church.
– ORIGIN late 18th cent.: from Greek *eparkhia*, from *eparkhos* (see EPARCH).

é·pa·ter /ā'pätā/ ▶ v. (in phrase **épater les bourgeois**) shock people who are conventional or complacent.
– ORIGIN early 20th cent.: French, literally 'startle, shock.'

ep·au·let /'epə,let, ,epə'let/ (also **epaulette**) ▶ n. an ornamental shoulder piece on an item of clothing, typically on the coat or jacket of a military uniform.
– ORIGIN late 18th cent.: from French *épaulette*, diminutive of *épaule* 'shoulder,' from Latin *spatula* in the late Latin sense 'shoulder blade.'

epaulet

ep·ax·i·al /e'paksēəl/ ▶ adj. Anatomy & Zoology situated on the dorsal side of an axis: *epaxial muscles.*

e·pa·zo·te /,epə'zōtā/ ▶ n. a pungent herb used in Latin-American cooking and for tea.

é·pée /,e'pā/ ▶ n. a sharp-pointed dueling sword, designed for thrusting and used, with the end blunted, in fencing. ■ the sport of fencing with an épée.
– DERIVATIVES **épéeist** /-ist/ n.
– ORIGIN late 19th cent.: French, 'sword,' from Old French *espee* (see SPAY).

ep·ei·rog·e·ny /,epī'räjənē/ ▶ n. Geology the regional uplift of an extensive area of the earth's crust.
– DERIVATIVES **e·pei·ro·gen·e·sis** /i,pīrə'jenəsis/ n., **e·pei·ro·gen·ic** /i,pīrō'jenik/ adj.
– ORIGIN late 19th cent.: from Greek *ēpeiros* 'mainland' + -GENY.

ep·en·dy·ma /ə'pendəmə/ ▶ n. Anatomy the thin membrane of glial cells lining the ventricles of the brain and the central canal of the spinal cord.
– DERIVATIVES **ep·en·dy·mal** adj.
– ORIGIN late 19th cent.: from Greek *ependuma*, from *ependuein* 'put on over.'

ep·en·the·sis /i'penTHəsis/ ▶ n. (pl. **epentheses** /-,sēz/) the insertion of a sound or letter within a word, e.g., the *b* in *thimble.*
– DERIVATIVES **ep·en·thet·ic** /,epen'THetik/ adj.
– ORIGIN mid 16th cent.: via late Latin from Greek, from *epentithenai* 'insert,' from *epi* 'in addition' + *en-* 'within' + *tithenai* 'to place.'

e·pergne /i'pərn, ā'pərn/ ▶ n. an ornamental centerpiece for a dining table, typically used for holding fruit or flowers.
– ORIGIN early 18th cent.: perhaps an altered form of French *épargne* 'saving, economy.'

ep·ex·e·ge·sis /e,peksə'jēsis/ ▶ n. (pl. **epexegeses** /-sēz/) the addition of words to clarify meaning. ■ words added for such a purpose.

– DERIVATIVES **ep·ex·e·get·ic** /-'jetik/ **adj.**, **ep·ex·e·get·i·cal** /-'jetikəl/ **adj.**, **ep·ex·e·get·i·cal·ly** /-'jetik(ə)lē/ **adv.**
– ORIGIN late 16th cent.: from Greek *epexēgēsis*, from *epi* 'in addition' + *exēgēsis* 'explanation' (see EXEGESIS).

Eph. ▶ **abbr.** Bible Ephesians.

e·phah /'ēfə, 'ēfä/ ▶ **n.** an ancient Hebrew dry measure equivalent to a bushel (35 l).
– ORIGIN from Hebrew *'ēpāh*, probably from Egyptian.

e·phebe /'efēb, i'fēb/ ▶ **n.** (in ancient Greece) a young man of 18–20 years undergoing military training.
– DERIVATIVES **e·phe·bic** /i'fēbik, e'fēbik/ **adj.**
– ORIGIN via Latin from Greek *ephēbos*, from *epi* 'near to' + *hēbē* 'early manhood.'

e·phed·ra /ə'fedrə, 'efidrə/ ▶ **n.** an evergreen shrub of warm, arid regions that has trailing or climbing stems and tiny, scalelike leaves. Some kinds are a source of ephedrine and are used medicinally. ● Family Ephedraceae and genus *Ephedra*.
– ORIGIN modern Latin, from Latin, 'equisetum,' literally 'horse tail' (which it resembles), from Greek *ephedra*, equivalent to *hippouris*,'horse tail.'

e·phed·rine /ə'fedrin, 'efə,drēn/ ▶ **n.** Medicine a crystalline alkaloid drug obtained from some ephedras. It causes constriction of the blood vessels and widening of the bronchial passages and is used to relieve asthma and hay fever. ● Alternative name: **1-phenyl-2-methylaminopropanol**; chem. formula: $C_{10}H_{15}NO$.
– ORIGIN late 19th cent.: from EPHEDRA + -INE[4].

e·phem·er·a /ə'fem(ə)rə/ ▶ **plural n.** things that exist or are used or enjoyed for only a short time. ■ items of collectible memorabilia, typically written or printed ones, that were originally expected to have only short-term usefulness or popularity: *Mickey Mouse ephemera*.
– ORIGIN late 16th cent.: plural of EPHEMERON. Current use has been influenced by plurals such as *trivia* and *memorabilia*.

e·phem·er·al /ə'fem(ə)rəl/ ▶ **adj.** lasting for a very short time: *fashions are ephemeral*. ■ (chiefly of plants) having a very short life cycle.
▶ **n.** an ephemeral plant.
– DERIVATIVES **e·phem·er·al·i·ty** /ə,femə'ralitē/ **n.**, **e·phem·er·al·ly** **adv.**, **e·phem·er·al·ness** **n.**
– ORIGIN late 16th cent.: from Greek *ephēmeros* (see EPHEMERA) + -AL.

e·phem·er·is /i'fem(ə)ris/ ▶ **n.** (pl. **ephemerides** /-ərədēz/) Astronomy & Astrology a table or data file giving the calculated positions of a celestial object at regular intervals throughout a period. ■ a book or set of such tables or files.
– ORIGIN early 16th cent.: from Latin, from Greek *ephēmeros* 'lasting only a day.'

e·phem·er·is time ▶ **n.** time on a scale defined by the orbital period rather than the axial rotation of the earth.

e·phem·er·on /i'femə,rän/ ▶ **n.** (pl. **ephemerons**) an insect that lives only for a day or a few days.
– ORIGIN from Greek, neuter of *ephēmeros* 'lasting only a day.'

E·phem·er·op·ter·a /ə,femə'räptərə/ Entomology an order of insects that comprises the mayflies. ■ (as plural noun **ephemeroptera**) insects of this order; mayflies.
– DERIVATIVES **e·phem·er·op·ter·an** /-tərən/ **n. & adj.**
– ORIGIN modern Latin (plural), from *Ephemera* (genus name) + *pteron* 'wing.'

E·phe·sians /i'fēzHəns/ a book of the New Testament ascribed to St. Paul, consisting of an epistle to the Church at Ephesus.

Eph·e·sus /'efəsəs/ an ancient Greek city on the western coast of Asia Minor, in modern Turkey, site of the temple of Diana. It is an important center of early Christianity. St. Paul preached here and St. John is said to have lived here.

eph·od /'efäd, 'ēfäd/ ▶ **n.** (in ancient Israel) a sleeveless garment worn by Jewish priests.
– ORIGIN late Middle English: from Hebrew *'ēpōd*.

eph·or /'efôr, 'efər/ ▶ **n.** (in ancient Greece) one of five senior Spartan magistrates.
– DERIVATIVES **eph·or·ate** /'efə,rāt, 'efərit/ **n.**
– ORIGIN from Greek *ephoros* 'overseer,' from *epi* 'above' + the base of *horan* 'see.'

eph·y·ra /'efərə/ ▶ **n.** (pl. **ephyrae** /-,rē/) Zoology a larval jellyfish, after it has separated from the scyphistoma.
– ORIGIN mid 19th cent.: modern Latin, from Greek *Ephura*, denoting a Nereid and an Oceanid.

epi- (also **ep-**) ▶ **prefix 1** on; upon: *epicycle* | *epigraph*. **2** above: *epicotyl* | *epicontinental*. **3** in addition: *epigenesis* | *epiphenomenon*.
– ORIGIN from Greek *epi* 'upon, near to, in addition.'

ep·i·ben·thos /,epə'ben,THäs/ ▶ **n.** Ecology the flora and fauna living on the surface of the bottom of a sea or lake.
– DERIVATIVES **ep·i·ben·thic** /-'benTHik/ **adj.**
– ORIGIN early 20th cent.: from Greek *epi* 'upon' + *benthos* 'depth of the sea.'

ep·i·blast /'epə,blast/ ▶ **n.** Embryology the outermost layer of an embryo before it differentiates into ectoderm and mesoderm.

ep·ic /'epik/ ▶ **n.** a long poem, typically one derived from ancient oral tradition, narrating the deeds and adventures of heroic or legendary figures or the history of a nation. ■ the genre of such poems: *the romances display gentler emotions not found in Greek epic*. ■ a long film, book, or other work portraying heroic deeds and adventures or covering an extended period of time: *a Hollywood biblical epic*.
▶ **adj.** of, relating to, or characteristic of an epic or epics: *England's national epic poem Beowulf*. ■ heroic or grand in scale or character: *his epic journey around the world* | *a tragedy of epic proportions*.
– DERIVATIVES **ep·i·cal** **adj.**, **ep·i·cal·ly** /-(ə)lē/ **adv.**
– ORIGIN late 16th cent. (as an adjective): via Latin from Greek *epikos*, from *epos* 'word, song,' related to *eipein* 'say.'

ep·i·can·thic /,epi'kanTHik/ ▶ **adj.** denoting a fold of skin from the upper eyelid covering the inner angle of the eye, typical in many peoples of eastern Asia and found as a congenital abnormality elsewhere.

ep·i·car·di·um /,epi'kärdēəm/ ▶ **n.** Anatomy a serous membrane that forms the innermost layer of the pericardium and the outer surface of the heart.
– DERIVATIVES **ep·i·car·di·al** /-dēəl/ **adj.**
– ORIGIN mid 19th cent.: from EPI- 'above' + Greek *kardia* 'heart,' on the pattern of *pericardium*.

ep·i·ce·di·um /,epi'sēdēəm/ ▶ **n.** (pl. **epicedia** /-dēə/) formal a funeral ode.
– DERIVATIVES **ep·i·ce·di·an** /-dēən/ **adj.**
– ORIGIN mid 16th cent. (originally in the anglicized form *epicede* and the Greek form *epicedeon*): from Latin, from Greek *epikēdeion*, neuter of *epokēdeios* 'of a funeral' (based on *kēdos* 'care, grief').

ep·i·cene /'epi,sēn/ ▶ **adj.** having characteristics of both sexes or no characteristics of either sex; of indeterminate sex: *the sort of epicene beauty peculiar to boys of a certain age*. ■ effeminate; effete: *the actor infused the role with an epicene languor*.
▶ **n.** an epicene person.
– ORIGIN late Middle English (as a grammatical term): via late Latin from Greek *epikoinos* (based on *koinos* 'common').

ep·i·cen·ter /'epi,sentər/ (Brit. **epicentre**) ▶ **n.** the point on the earth's surface vertically above the focus of an earthquake. ■ the central point of something, typically a difficult or unpleasant situation: *the patient was at the epicenter of concern*.
– DERIVATIVES **ep·i·cen·tral** /,epi'sentrəl/ **adj.**
– ORIGIN late 19th cent.: from Greek *epikentros* 'situated on a center,' from *epi* 'upon' + *kentron* 'center.'

ep·i·con·dyle /,epi'kän,dīl, -'kändl/ ▶ **n.** Anatomy a protuberance above or on the condyle of a long bone, esp. either of the two at the elbow end of the humerus.
– DERIVATIVES **ep·i·con·dyl·ar** /-'kändl-ər/ **adj.**
– ORIGIN mid 19th cent.: from French *épicondyle*, modern Latin *epicondylus* (see EPI-, CONDYLE).

ep·i·con·dy·li·tis /,epi,kändī'lītis, -,kändl'ītis/ ▶ **n.** Medicine a painful inflammation of tendons surrounding an epicondyle.

ep·i·con·ti·nen·tal /,epi,käntə'nen(t)l/ ▶ **adj.** denoting those areas of sea or ocean overlying the continental shelf.

ep·i·cor·mic /,epi'kôrmik/ ▶ **adj.** Botany (of a shoot or branch) growing from a previously dormant bud on the trunk or a limb of a tree.
– ORIGIN early 20th cent.: from EPI- 'upon' + Greek *kormos* 'tree trunk.'

ep·i·cot·yl /,epi'kätl/ ▶ **n.** Botany the region of an embryo or seedling stem above the cotyledon.

ep·i·crit·ic /,epi'kritik/ ▶ **adj.** Physiology relating to or denoting those sensory nerve fibers of the skin that are capable of fine discrimination of touch or temperature stimuli. Often contrasted with PROTOPATHIC.
– ORIGIN early 20th cent.: from Greek *epikritikos* 'giving judgment over,' from *epi* 'upon or over' + *krinein* 'to judge.'

Ep·ic·te·tus /,epik'tētəs/ (*c.*AD 55–*c.*135), Greek philosopher. He preached the common brotherhood of man and advocated a Stoic philosophy.

ep·i·cure /'epi,kyŏŏr/ ▶ **n.** a person who takes particular pleasure in fine food and drink.
– DERIVATIVES **ep·i·cur·ism** /-,rizəm, ,epi'kyŏŏ-/ **n.**
– ORIGIN late Middle English (denoting a disciple of EPICURUS): via medieval Latin from Greek *Epikouros* 'Epicurus.'

Ep·i·cu·re·an /,epikyə'rēən, ,epi'kyŏŏrēən/ ▶ **n.** a disciple or student of the Greek philosopher Epicurus. ■ (**epicurean**) a person devoted to sensual enjoyment, esp. that derived from fine food and drink.
▶ **adj.** of or concerning Epicurus or his ideas: *Epicurean philosophers*. ■ (**epicurean**) relating to or suitable for an epicure: *epicurean feasts*.

Ep·i·cu·re·an·ism /,epəkyə'rēə,nizəm, -'kyŏŏrēə-/ ▶ **n.** an ancient school of philosophy founded in Athens by Epicurus. The school rejected determinism and advocated hedonism (pleasure as the highest good), but of a restrained kind: mental pleasure was regarded more highly than physical, and the ultimate pleasure was held to be freedom from anxiety and mental pain, esp. that arising from needless fear of death and of the gods.

Ep·i·cu·rus /,epə'kyŏŏrəs/ (341–270 BC), Greek philosopher, founder of Epicureanism. His physics is based on Democritus' theory of a materialist universe composed of indestructible atoms moving in a void, unregulated by divine providence.

ep·i·cu·ti·cle /,epi'kyŏŏtikəl/ ▶ **n.** Botany & Zoology the thin, waxy, protective outer layer covering the surfaces of some plants, fungi, insects, and other arthropods.
– DERIVATIVES **ep·i·cu·tic·u·lar** /-kyŏŏ'tikyələr/ **adj.**

ep·i·cy·cle /'epi,sīkəl/ ▶ **n.** Geometry a small circle whose center moves around the circumference of a larger one. ■ historical a circle of this type used to describe planetary orbits in the Ptolemaic system.
– DERIVATIVES **ep·i·cy·clic** /,epi'sīklik, 'epi-/ **adj.**
– ORIGIN late Middle English: from Old French, or via late Latin from Greek *epikuklos*, from *epi* 'upon' + *kuklos* 'circle.'

ep·i·cy·cloid /,epi'sī,kloid/ ▶ **n.** Mathematics a curve traced by a point on the circumference of a circle rolling on the exterior of another circle.
– DERIVATIVES **ep·i·cy·cloi·dal** /-sī'kloidl/ **adj.**

ep·i·deic·tic /,epi'dīktik/ ▶ **adj.** formal characterized by or designed to display rhetorical or oratorical skill.
– ORIGIN late 18th cent.: from Greek *epideiktikos* (based on *deiknunai* 'to show').

ep·i·dem·ic /,epi'demik/ ▶ **n.** a widespread occurrence of an infectious disease in a community at a particular time: *a flu epidemic*. ■ a disease occurring in such a way. ■ a sudden, widespread occurrence of a particular undesirable phenomenon: *an epidemic of violent crime*.
▶ **adj.** of, relating to, or of the nature of an epidemic: *shoplifting has reached epidemic proportions*. Compare with ENDEMIC, PANDEMIC, EPIZOOTIC.
– ORIGIN early 17th cent. (as an adjective): from French *épidémique*, from *épidémie*, via late Latin from Greek *epidēmia* 'prevalence of disease,' from *epidēmios* 'prevalent,' from *epi* 'upon' + *dēmos* 'the people.'

USAGE A disease that quickly and severely affects a large number of people and then subsides is an **epidemic**: *throughout the Middle Ages, successive epidemics of the plague killed millions*. **Epidemic** is also used as an adjective: *she studied the causes of epidemic cholera*. A disease that is continually present in an area and affects a relatively small number of people is **endemic**: *malaria is* **endemic in** (or **to**) *hot, moist climates*. A **pandemic** is a widespread epidemic that may affect entire continents or even the world: *the pandemic of 1918 ushered in a period of frequent epidemics of gradually diminishing severity*. Thus, from an epidemiologist's point of view, the Black Death in Europe and AIDS in sub-Saharan Africa are pandemics rather than epidemics.

ep·i·de·mi·ol·o·gy /,epi,dēmē'äləjē/ ▶ **n.** the branch of medicine that deals with the incidence, distribution, and possible control of diseases and other factors relating to health.
– DERIVATIVES **ep·i·de·mi·o·log·i·cal** /-ə'läjikəl/ **adj.**, **ep·i·de·mi·ol·o·gist** /-jist/ **n.**
– ORIGIN late 19th cent.: from Greek *epidēmia* 'prevalence of disease' + -LOGY.

ep·i·der·mal growth fac·tor (abbr.: **EGF**) ▶ **n.** a mitogenic protein thought to be involved in such physical processes as normal cell growth, wound healing, and the formation of tumors.
– ORIGIN First observed in 1959.

ep·i·der·mis /,epi'dərmis/ ▶ **n.** Biology the outer layer of cells covering an organism, in particular: ■ Zoology & Anatomy the surface epithelium of the skin of an animal, overlying the dermis. ■ Botany the outer layer of tissue in a plant, except where it is replaced by periderm.

– DERIVATIVES **ep·i·der·mal** /ˌ-ˈdərməl/ **adj.**, **ep·i·der·mic** /-ˈdərmik/ **adj.**, **ep·i·der·moid** /-ˈdərˌmoid/ **adj.**
– ORIGIN early 17th cent.: via late Latin from Greek, from *epi* 'upon' + *derma* 'skin.'

ep·i·der·mol·y·sis /ˌepidərˈmäləsis/ (also **epidermolysis bullosa** /bəˈlōsə/) ▶ **n.** Medicine loosening of the epidermis, with extensive blistering of the skin and mucous membranes, occurring either after injury, or as a spontaneous and potentially dangerous condition, particularly in children.

ep·i·di·a·scope /ˌepiˈdīəˌskōp/ ▶ **n.** an optical projector capable of giving images of both opaque and transparent objects.
– ORIGIN early 20th cent.: from EPI- + DIA- + -SCOPE.

ep·i·did·y·mis /ˌepiˈdidəməs/ ▶ **n.** (pl. **epididymides** /-ˈdidəmiˌdēz, -diˈdimiˌdēz/) Anatomy a highly convoluted duct behind the testis, along which sperm passes to the vas deferens.
– DERIVATIVES **ep·i·did·y·mal** /-məl/ **adj.**
– ORIGIN early 17th cent.: from Greek *epididumis*, from *epi* 'upon' + *didumos* 'testicle' (from *duo* 'two').

ep·i·dote /ˈepiˌdōt/ ▶ **n.** a lustrous yellow-green crystalline mineral, common in metamorphic rocks. It consists of a hydroxyl silicate of calcium, aluminum, and iron.
– ORIGIN early 19th cent.: from French *épidote*, from Greek *epididonai* 'give additionally' (because of the length of the crystals).

ep·i·du·ral /ˌepiˈd(y)o͝orəl/ ▶ **adj.** Anatomy & Medicine on or around the dura mater, in particular (of an anesthetic), introduced into the space around the dura mater of the spinal cord.
▶ **n.** an epidural anesthetic, used esp. in childbirth to produce loss of sensation below the waist.
– ORIGIN late 19th cent.: from EPI- 'upon' + DURA[1] + -AL.

ep·i·fau·na /ˌepəˈfônə/ ▶ **n.** Ecology animals living on the surface of the seabed or a riverbed, or attached to submerged objects or aquatic animals or plants. Compare with INFAUNA.
– DERIVATIVES **ep·i·fau·nal** /-ˈfônl/ **adj.**
– ORIGIN early 20th cent.: from EPI- 'upon' + FAUNA.

ep·i·fluo·res·cence /ˌepəflo͝oˈresəns/ ▶ **n.** Optics the fluorescence of an object in an optical microscope when irradiated from the viewing side.

ep·i·gas·tri·um /ˌepiˈgastrēəm/ ▶ **n.** (pl. **epigastria** /-trēə/) Anatomy the part of the upper abdomen immediately over the stomach.
– DERIVATIVES **ep·i·gas·tric** /-trik/ **adj.**
– ORIGIN late 17th cent.: via late Latin from Greek *epigastrion*, neuter of *epigastrios* 'over the belly,' from *epi* 'upon' + *gastēr* 'belly.'

ep·i·ge·al /ˌepiˈjēəl/ ▶ **adj.** Botany growing on or close to the ground. Compare with HYPOGEAL. ■ (of seed germination) with one or more seed leaves appearing above the ground.
– ORIGIN mid 19th cent.: from Greek *epigeios* (from *epi* 'upon' + *gē* 'earth') + -AL.

ep·i·gene /ˈepiˌjēn/ ▶ **adj.** Geology taking place or produced on the surface of the earth.
– ORIGIN early 19th cent.: from French *épigène*, from Greek *epigenēs*, from *epi* 'upon' + *genēs* (see -GEN).

ep·i·gen·e·sis /ˌepiˈjenəsis/ ▶ **n.** Biology the theory, now generally held, that an embryo develops progressively from an undifferentiated egg cell. Often contrasted with PREFORMATION.
– DERIVATIVES **ep·i·gen·e·sist** /-sist/ **n. & adj.**
– ORIGIN mid 17th cent.: from EPI- 'in addition' + GENESIS.

ep·i·ge·net·ic /ˌepijəˈnetik/ ▶ **adj.** Biology resulting from external rather than genetic influences: *epigenetic carcinogens.* ■ Biology of, relating to, or of the nature of epigenesis. ■ Geology formed later than the surrounding or underlying rock formation.
– DERIVATIVES **ep·i·ge·net·i·cal·ly** /-(ə)lē/ **adv.**, **ep·i·ge·net·i·cist** /-ˈnetisist/ **n.**

ep·i·glot·tis /ˌepiˈglätəs/ ▶ **n.** a flap of cartilage at the root of the tongue, which is depressed during swallowing to cover the opening of the windpipe.
– DERIVATIVES **ep·i·glot·tal** /-ˈglätl/ **adj.**, **ep·i·glot·tic** /-ˈglätik/ **adj.**
– ORIGIN late Middle English: from Greek *epiglōttis*, from *epi* 'upon, near to' + *glōtta* 'tongue.'

ep·i·gone /ˈepiˌgōn/ ▶ **n.** (pl. **epigones** /ˈepiˌgōnz/ or **epigoni** /iˈpigəˌnī/) a less distinguished follower or imitator of someone, esp. an artist or philosopher: *the epigone's habit of exaggerating his master's voice.*
– ORIGIN mid 18th cent.: plurals from French *épigones* and Latin *epigoni*, from Greek *epigonoi* 'those born afterward' (based on *gignesthai* 'be born').

ep·i·gram /ˈepiˌgram/ ▶ **n.** a pithy saying or remark expressing an idea in a clever and amusing way. ■ a short poem, esp. a satirical one, having a witty or ingenious ending.
– DERIVATIVES **ep·i·gram·ma·tist** /ˌepiˈgramətist/ **n.**, **ep·i·gram·ma·tize** /ˌepiˈgraməˌtīz/ **v.**
– ORIGIN late Middle English: from French *épigramme*, or Latin *epigramma*, from Greek, from *epi* 'upon, in addition' + *gramma* (see -GRAM[1]).

ep·i·gram·mat·ic /ˌepigrəˈmatik/ ▶ **adj.** of the nature or in the style of an epigram; concise, clever, and amusing: *an epigrammatic style.*
– DERIVATIVES **ep·i·gram·mat·i·cal·ly** /-(ə)lē/ **adv.**
– ORIGIN early 17th cent.: from late Latin *epigrammaticus*, from Latin *epigramma* (see EPIGRAM).

ep·i·graph /ˈepiˌgraf/ ▶ **n.** an inscription on a building, statue, or coin. ■ a short quotation or saying at the beginning of a book or chapter, intended to suggest its theme.
– ORIGIN late 16th cent. (denoting the heading of a document or letter): from Greek *epigraphē*, from *epigraphein* 'write on.'

e·pig·ra·phy /iˈpigrəfē/ ▶ **n.** the study and interpretation of ancient inscriptions. ■ epigraphs collectively.
– DERIVATIVES **e·pig·ra·pher** **n.**, **ep·i·graph·ic** /ˌepiˈgrafik/ **adj.**, **ep·i·graph·i·cal** /ˌepiˈgrafikəl/ **adj.**, **ep·i·graph·i·cal·ly** /ˌepiˈgrafik(ə)lē/ **adv.**, **e·pig·ra·phist** /-fist/ **n.**

e·pig·y·nous /iˈpijənəs/ ▶ **adj.** Botany (of a plant or flower) having the ovary enclosed in the receptacle, with the stamens and other floral parts situated above. Compare with HYPOGYNOUS, PERIGYNOUS.
– DERIVATIVES **e·pig·y·ny** /iˈpijənē/ **n.**
– ORIGIN mid 19th cent.: from modern Latin *epigynus*, from EPI- 'upon, above' + Greek *gunē* 'woman' + -OUS.

ep·i·la·tion /ˌepəˈlāsʜən/ ▶ **n.** the removal of hair by the roots.
– DERIVATIVES **ep·i·late** /ˈepəˌlāt/ **v.**, **ep·i·la·tor** /ˈepəˌlātər/ **n.**
– ORIGIN late 19th cent.: from French *épiler*, from *é-* (expressing removal) + Latin *pilus* 'strand of hair,' on the pattern of *depilation*.

ep·i·lep·sy /ˈepəˌlepsē/ ▶ **n.** a neurological disorder marked by sudden recurrent episodes of sensory disturbance, loss of consciousness, or convulsions, associated with abnormal electrical activity in the brain.
– ORIGIN mid 16th cent.: from French *épilepsie*, or via late Latin from Greek *epilēpsia*, from *epilambanein* 'seize, attack,' from *epi* 'upon' + *lambanein* 'take hold of.'

ep·i·lep·tic /ˌepəˈleptik/ ▶ **adj.** of, relating to, or having epilepsy: *he had an epileptic fit.*
▶ **n.** a person who has epilepsy.
– ORIGIN early 17th cent.: from French *épileptique*, via late Latin from Greek *epilēptikos*, from *epilēpsia* (see EPILEPSY).

ep·i·lep·to·gen·ic /ˌepəˌleptəˈjenik/ ▶ **adj.** Medicine capable of causing an epileptic attack.

ep·i·lim·ni·on /ˌepəˈlimnēˌän, -nēən/ ▶ **n.** (pl. **epilimnionia** /-nēə/) the upper layer of water in a stratified lake.
– ORIGIN early 20th cent.: from EPI- 'above' + Greek *limnion* (diminutive of *limnē* 'lake').

ep·i·lith·ic /ˌepəˈlitʜik/ ▶ **adj.** Botany (of a plant) growing on the surface of rock.
– ORIGIN early 20th cent.: from EPI- 'upon' + Greek *lithos* 'stone' + -IC.

ep·i·logue /ˈepəˌlôg, -ˌläg/ (also **epilog**) ▶ **n.** a section or speech at the end of a book or play that serves as a comment on or a conclusion to what has happened.
– ORIGIN late Middle English: from French *épilogue*, via Latin from Greek *epilogos*, from *epi* 'in addition' + *logos* 'speech.'

ep·i·mer /ˈepəmər/ ▶ **n.** Chemistry each of two isomers with different configurations of atoms around one of several asymmetric carbon atoms present.
– DERIVATIVES **ep·i·mer·ic** /ˌepəˈmerik/ **adj.**, **ep·i·mer·ism** /-ˌrizəm/ **n.**

ep·i·mer·ize /ˈepəməˌrīz/ ▶ **v.** [with obj.] Chemistry convert from one epimeric form into the other.

ep·i·me·ron /ˌepəˈmi(ə)rˌän, iˈpiməˌrän/ ▶ **n.** (pl. **epimerons** or **epimera** /-ˈmi(ə)rə/) Entomology (in insects) the posterior part of the sidewall of a thoracic segment.
– ORIGIN mid 19th cent.: from EPI- 'near' + Greek *mēros* 'thigh.'

ep·i·my·si·um /ˌepəˈmizēəm, -ˈmizʜēəm/ ▶ **n.** Anatomy a sheath of fibrous elastic tissue surrounding a muscle.
– ORIGIN modern Latin, from EPI- 'upon' + Greek *mus* 'muscle.'

ep·i·neph·rine /ˌepiˈnefrin/ ▶ **n.** Biochemistry a hormone secreted by the adrenal glands, esp. in conditions of stress, increasing rates of blood circulation, breathing, and carbohydrate metabolism and preparing muscles for exertion. Also called ADRENALINE.
– ORIGIN late 19th cent.: from EPI- 'above' + Greek *nephros* 'kidney' + -INE[4].

e·piph·a·ny /iˈpifənē/ ▶ **n.** (pl. **epiphanies**) (also **Epiphany**) the manifestation of Christ to the Gentiles as represented by the Magi (Matthew 2:1–12). ■ the festival commemorating this on January 6. ■ a manifestation of a divine or supernatural being. ■ a moment of sudden revelation or insight.
– DERIVATIVES **ep·i·phan·ic** /ˌepəˈfanik/ **adj.**
– ORIGIN Middle English: from Greek *epiphainein* 'reveal.' The sense relating to the Christian festival is via Old French *epiphanie* and ecclesiastical Latin *epiphania*.

ep·i·phe·nom·e·non /ˌepəfəˈnäməˌnän, -ˈnämənən/ ▶ **n.** (pl. **epiphenomena** /-ˈnämənə/) a secondary effect or byproduct that arises from but does not causally influence a process, in particular: ■ Medicine a secondary symptom, occurring simultaneously with a disease or condition but not directly related to it. ■ a mental state regarded as a byproduct of brain activity.
– DERIVATIVES **ep·i·phe·nom·e·nal** /-ˈnämənl/ **adj.**

e·piph·o·ra /əˈpifərə/ ▶ **n. 1** Medicine excessive watering of the eye.
2 Rhetoric another term for EPISTROPHE.
– ORIGIN late 16th cent. (sense 2): via Latin from Greek *epi* 'upon' + *pherein* 'to bear or carry.' Sense 1 dates from the mid 17th cent.

ep·i·phyl·lum /ˌepəˈfiləm/ ▶ **n.** (pl. **epiphyllums**) a cactus with flattened stems and large, fragrant red or yellow flowers. ● Genus *Epiphyllum*, family Cactaceae: several species, in particular the night-flowering cactus (*E. hookeri*).
– ORIGIN modern Latin, from EPI- 'upon' + Greek *phullon* 'leaf.'

e·piph·y·sis /əˈpifəsis/ ▶ **n.** (pl. **epiphyses** /-ˌsēz/) **1** the end part of a long bone, initially growing separately from the shaft. Compare with DIAPHYSIS.
2 another term for PINEAL.
– ORIGIN mid 17th cent.: modern Latin, from Greek *epiphusis*, from *epi* 'upon, in addition' + *phusis* 'growth.'

ep·i·phyte /ˈepəˌfīt/ ▶ **n.** Botany a plant that grows on another plant but is not parasitic, such as the numerous ferns, bromeliads, air plants, and orchids growing on tree trunks in tropical rain forests.
– DERIVATIVES **ep·i·phyt·al** /ˌepəˈfītl/ **adj.**, **ep·i·phyt·ic** /ˌepəˈfitik/ **adj.**
– ORIGIN mid 19th cent.: from EPI- 'in addition' + Greek *phuton* 'plant.'

EPIRB ▶ **abbr.** emergency position-indicating radio beacon.

E·pi·rus /iˈpīrəs/ a coastal region in northwestern Greece; capital, Ioánnina. Greek name **Ipiros**. ■ an ancient country that included the modern region of Epirus and extended north to Illyria and east to Macedonia and Thessaly.

Epis. ▶ **abbr.** ■ Episcopal. ■ Episcopalian. ■ Epistle.

Episc. ▶ **abbr.** ■ Episcopal. ■ Episcopalian.

e·pis·co·pa·cy /iˈpiskəpəsē/ ▶ **n.** (pl. **episcopacies**) government of a church by bishops. ■ (**the episcopacy**) the bishops of a region or church collectively. ■ another term for EPISCOPATE.
– ORIGIN mid 17th cent.: from ecclesiastical Latin *episcopatus* 'episcopate,' on the pattern of *prelacy*.

e·pis·co·pal /iˈpiskəpəl/ ▶ **adj.** of a bishop or bishops: *episcopal power.* ■ (of a church) governed by or having bishops.
– DERIVATIVES **e·pis·co·pal·ism** /-ˌlizəm/ **n.**, **e·pis·co·pal·ly** **adv.**
– ORIGIN late Middle English: from French *épiscopal* or ecclesiastical Latin *episcopalis*, from *episcopus* 'bishop,' from Greek *episkopos* 'overseer' (see BISHOP).

E·pis·co·pal Church the Anglican Church in the US and Scotland.

e·pis·co·pa·lian /iˌpiskəˈpālēən/ ▶ **adj.** of or advocating government of a church by bishops. ■ of or belonging to an episcopal church. ■ (**Episcopalian**) of or belonging to the Episcopal Church.
▶ **n.** an adherent of episcopacy. ■ (**Episcopalian**) a member of the Episcopal Church.
– DERIVATIVES **e·pis·co·pa·lian·ism** /-ˌnizəm/ **n.**

e·pis·co·pate /iˈpiskəpət, -ˌpāt/ ▶ **n.** the office or term of office of a bishop. ■ (**the episcopate**) the bishops of a church or region collectively.

PRONUNCIATION KEY ə *ago, up*; ər *over, fur*; a *hat*; ā *ate*; ä *car*; e *let*; ē *see*; i *fit*; ī *by*; NG *sing*; ō *go*; ô *law, for*; oi *toy*; o͝o *good*; o͞o *goo*; ou *out*; TH *thin*; TH *then*; ZH *vision*

–ORIGIN mid 17th cent.: from ecclesiastical Latin *episcopatus* 'made a bishop,' from *episcopus* 'bishop,' from Greek *episkopos* 'overseer' (see **BISHOP**).

ep·i·scope /'epə,skōp/ ▶ **n.** an optical projector that gives images of opaque objects.

ep·i·se·mat·ic /,epəsə'matik/ ▶ **adj.** Zoology (of coloration or markings) serving to help animals recognize other individuals of the same species.
–ORIGIN late 19th cent.: from **EPI-** 'upon' + Greek *sēma* 'sign' + **-ATIC**.

e·pi·si·ot·o·my /i,pēzē'ätəmē/ ▶ **n.** (pl. **episiotomies**) a surgical cut made at the opening of the vagina during childbirth, to aid a difficult delivery and prevent rupture of tissues.
–ORIGIN late 19th cent.: from Greek *epision* 'pubic region' + **-TOMY**.

ep·i·sode /'epi,sōd/ ▶ **n.** an event or a group of events occurring as part of a larger sequence; an incident or period considered in isolation: *the latest episode in the feud.* ■ each of the separate installments into which a serialized story or radio or television program is divided. ■ a finite period in which someone is affected by a specified illness: *acute psychotic episodes.* ■ Music a passage containing distinct material or introducing a new subject. ■ a section between two choric songs in Greek tragedy.
–ORIGIN late 17th cent. (denoting a section between two choric songs in Greek tragedy): from Greek *epeisodion*, neuter of *epeisodios* 'coming in besides,' from *epi* 'in addition' + *eisodos* 'entry' (from *eis* 'into' + *hodos* 'way').

ep·i·sod·ic /,epə'sädik/ ▶ **adj.** containing or consisting of a series of loosely connected parts or events: *an episodic narrative.* ■ occurring occasionally and at irregular intervals: *volcanic activity is highly episodic in nature.* ■ (of a television or radio program or magazine story) broadcast or published as a series of installments.
–DERIVATIVES **ep·i·sod·i·cal·ly** /-(ə)lē/ **adv.**

ep·i·some /'epi,sōm/ ▶ **n.** Microbiology a genetic element inside some bacterial cells, esp. the DNA of some bacteriophages, that can replicate independently of the host and also in association with a chromosome with which it becomes integrated. Compare with **PLASMID**.

Epist. ▶ **abbr.** Epistle.

e·pis·ta·sis /ə'pistəsis/ ▶ **n.** Genetics the interaction of genes that are not alleles, in particular the suppression of the effect of one such gene by another.
–DERIVATIVES **ep·i·stat·ic** /,epi'statik/ **adj.**
–ORIGIN early 19th cent.: from Greek, literally 'stoppage,' from *ephistanai* 'to stop.'

ep·i·stax·is /,epə'staksis/ ▶ **n.** Medicine bleeding from the nose.
–ORIGIN late 18th cent.: modern Latin, from Greek, from *epistazein* 'bleed from the nose,' from *epi* 'upon, in addition' + *stazein* 'to drip.'

ep·i·ste·mic /,epə'stemik, -'stē-/ ▶ **adj.** of or relating to knowledge or to the degree of its validation.
–DERIVATIVES **ep·i·ste·mi·cal·ly** /-(ə)lē/ **adv.**
–ORIGIN 1920s: from Greek *epistēmē* 'knowledge' (see **EPISTEMOLOGY**) + **-IC**.

e·pis·te·mol·o·gy /i,pistə'mäləjē/ ▶ **n.** Philosophy the theory of knowledge, esp. with regard to its methods, validity, and scope. Epistemology is the investigation of what distinguishes justified belief from opinion.
–DERIVATIVES **e·pis·te·mo·log·i·cal** /-mə'läjikəl/ **adj.**, **e·pis·te·mo·log·i·cal·ly** /-mə'läjik(ə)lē/ **adv.**, **e·pis·te·mol·o·gist** /-jist/ **n.**
–ORIGIN mid 19th cent.: from Greek *epistēmē* 'knowledge,' from *epistasthai* 'know, know how to do.'

ep·i·ster·num /,epi'stərnəm/ ▶ **n.** (pl. **episternums** or **episterna** /-nə/) Zoology a bone between the clavicles, esp. (in mammals) the upper part of the sternum. ■ Entomology (in insects) the anterior part of the sidewall of a thoracic segment.

e·pis·tle /i'pisəl/ ▶ **n.** formal a letter. ■ a poem or other literary work in the form of a letter or series of letters. ■ (also **Epistle**) a book of the New Testament in the form of a letter from an Apostle: *St. Paul's epistle to the Romans.* ■ an extract from an Epistle (or another New Testament book not a Gospel) that is read in a church service.
–ORIGIN Old English, via Latin from Greek *epistolē*, from *epistellein* 'send news,' from *epi* 'upon, in addition' + *stellein* 'send.' The word was reintroduced in Middle English from Old French.

e·pis·to·lar·y /i'pistə,lerē/ ▶ **adj.** relating to or denoting the writing of letters or literary works in the form of letters: *an epistolary novel.*
–ORIGIN mid 17th cent.: from French *épistolaire* or Latin *epistolaris*, from *epistola* (see **EPISTLE**).

e·pis·tro·phe /ə'pistrəfē/ ▶ **n.** Rhetoric the repetition of a word at the end of successive clauses or sentences.
–ORIGIN late 16th cent.: from Greek *epistrophē*, from *epistrephein* 'to turn around,' from *epi* 'in addition' + *strephein* 'to turn.'

ep·i·style /'epi,stīl/ ▶ **n.** Architecture an architrave.
–ORIGIN mid 16th cent. (in the Latin form *epistylium*): from French *épistyle* or via Latin, from Greek *epistulion*, from *epi* 'upon' + *stulos* 'pillar.'

ep·i·taph /'epi,taf/ ▶ **n.** a phrase or statement written in memory of a person who has died, esp. as an inscription on a tombstone.
–ORIGIN late Middle English: from Old French *epitaphe*, via Latin from Greek *epitaphion* 'funeral oration,' neuter of *ephitaphios* 'over or at a tomb,' from *epi* 'upon' + *taphos* 'tomb.'

ep·i·tax·y /'epi,taksē/ ▶ **n.** Crystallography the natural or artificial growth of crystals on a crystalline substrate determining their orientation.
–DERIVATIVES **ep·i·tax·i·al** /,epi'taksēəl/ **adj.**
–ORIGIN 1930s: from French *épitaxie*, from Greek *epi* 'upon' + *taxis* 'arrangement.'

ep·i·tha·la·mi·um /,epəTHə'lāmēəm/ (also **epithalamion** /-mēən/) ▶ **n.** (pl. **epithalamiums** or **epithalamia** /-mēə/ also **epithalamions**) a song or poem celebrating a marriage.
–DERIVATIVES **ep·i·tha·lam·ic** /-'lamik/ **adj.**
–ORIGIN late 16th cent.: via Latin from Greek *epithalamion*, from *epi* 'upon' + *thalamos* 'bridal chamber.'

ep·i·thal·a·mus /,epə'THaləməs/ ▶ **n.** (pl. **epithalami** /-,mī/) Anatomy a part of the dorsal forebrain including the pineal gland and a region in the roof of the third ventricle of the brain.

ep·i·the·li·al·ize /,epə'THēlēə,līz/ ▶ **v.** [with obj. & no obj.] cover or become covered with epithelial tissue, e.g. during the healing of a wound.
–DERIVATIVES **ep·i·the·li·al·i·za·tion** /,epə,THēlēəli'zāSHən/ **n.**

ep·i·the·li·um /,epə'THēlēəm/ ▶ **n.** (pl. **epithelia** /-lēə/) Anatomy the thin tissue forming the outer layer of a body's surface and lining the alimentary canal and other hollow structures. ■ more specifically, the part of this derived from embryonic ectoderm and endoderm, as distinct from endothelium and mesothelium.
–DERIVATIVES **ep·i·the·li·al** /-lēəl/ **adj.**
–ORIGIN mid 18th cent.: modern Latin, from **EPI-** 'above' + Greek *thēlē* 'teat.'

ep·i·thet /'epə,THet/ ▶ **n.** an adjective or descriptive phrase expressing a quality characteristic of the person or thing mentioned: *old men are often unfairly awarded the epithet "dirty."* ■ such a word or phrase as a term of abuse: *the woman begins to hurl racial epithets at them.*
–DERIVATIVES **ep·i·thet·ic** /epə'THetik/ **adj.**, **ep·i·thet·i·cal** /epə'THetikəl/ **adj.**, **ep·i·thet·i·cal·ly** /epə'THetik(ə)lē/ **adv.**
–ORIGIN late 16th cent.: from French *épithète*, or via Latin from Greek *epitheton*, neuter of *epithetos* 'attributed,' from *epitithenai* 'add,' from *epi* 'upon' + *tithenai* 'to place.'

e·pit·o·me /i'pitəmē/ ▶ **n. 1** (**the epitome of**) a person or thing that is a perfect example of a particular quality or type: *she looked the epitome of elegance and good taste.*
2 a summary of a written work; an abstract. ■ archaic a thing representing something else in miniature.
–DERIVATIVES **e·pit·o·mist** /-mist/ **n.**
–ORIGIN early 16th cent.: via Latin from Greek *epitomē*, from *epitemnein* 'abridge,' from *epi* 'in addition' + *temnein* 'to cut.'

e·pit·o·mize /i'pitə,mīz/ ▶ **v.** [with obj.] **1** be a perfect example of: *Hearst's newspapers epitomized bare-knuckle yellow journalism.*
2 archaic give a summary of (a written work).
–DERIVATIVES **e·pit·o·mi·za·tion** /i,pitəmi'zāSHən/ **n.**

ep·i·tope /'epi,tōp/ ▶ **n.** Biochemistry the part of an antigen molecule to which an antibody attaches itself. Also called **ANTIGENIC DETERMINANT**.
–ORIGIN 1960s: from **EPI-** 'upon' + Greek *topos* 'place.'

ep·i·zo·ic /,epi'zō-ik/ ▶ **adj.** Biology (of a plant or animal) growing or living nonparasitically on the exterior of a living animal.
–DERIVATIVES **ep·i·zo·ite** /,epi'zō-īt/ **n.**
–ORIGIN mid 19th cent.: from **EPI-** 'upon' + Greek *zōion* 'animal' + **-IC**.

ep·i·zo·on /,epi'zō,än/ ▶ **n.** (pl. **epizoa** /-'zōə/) Zoology an animal that lives on the body of another animal, esp. as a parasite.
–ORIGIN mid 19th cent.: from **EPI-** 'upon' + Greek *zōion* 'animal.'

ep·i·zo·ot·ic /,epizō'ätik/ ▶ **adj.** of, relating to, or denoting a disease that is temporarily prevalent and widespread in an animal population. Compare with **ENZOOTIC, EPIDEMIC**.
▶ **n.** an outbreak of such a disease.
–ORIGIN late 18th cent. (as an adjective): from French *épizootique*, from *épizootie*, from Greek *epi* 'upon' + *zōion* 'animal.'

e plu·ri·bus u·num /'ē 'plōōrəbəs '(y)ōōnəm/ ▶ **n.** out of many, one (the motto of the US).

EPNS ▶ **abbr.** electroplated nickel silver.

EPO ▶ **abbr.** erythropoietin, esp. when isolated as a drug for medical use or for illegal use by athletes.

ep·och /'epək/ ▶ **n.** a period of time in history or a person's life, typically one marked by notable events or particular characteristics: *the Victorian epoch.* ■ the beginning of a distinctive period in the history of someone or something: *welfare reform was an epoch in the history of U.S. social policy.* ■ Geology a division of time that is a subdivision of a period and is itself subdivided into ages, corresponding to a series in chronostratigraphy: *the Pliocene epoch.* ■ Astronomy an arbitrarily fixed date relative to which planetary or stellar measurements are expressed.
–ORIGIN early 17th cent. (in the Latin form *epocha*; originally in the general sense of a date from which succeeding years are numbered): from modern Latin *epocha*, from Greek *epokhē* 'stoppage, fixed point of time,' from *epekhein* 'stop, take up a position,' from *epi* 'upon, near to' + *ekhein* 'stay, be in a certain state.'

ep·och·al /'epəkəl/ ▶ **adj.** forming or characterizing an epoch; epoch-making.

ep·och-mak·ing ▶ **adj.** of major importance; likely to have a significant effect on a particular period of time.

ep·ode /'epōd/ ▶ **n. 1** a form of lyric poem written in couplets, in which a long line is followed by a shorter one.
2 the third section of an ancient Greek choral ode, or of one division of such an ode. Compare with **STROPHE** and **ANTISTROPHE**.
–ORIGIN early 17th cent.: from French *épode*, or via Latin *epodos*, from Greek *epōidos*, from *epi* 'upon' + *ōidē* (see **ODE**).

ep·o·nym /'epə,nim/ ▶ **n.** a person after whom a discovery, invention, place, etc., is named or thought to be named. ■ a name or noun formed in such a way.
–DERIVATIVES **e·pon·y·my** /ə'pänəmē/ **n.**
–ORIGIN mid 19th cent.: from Greek *epōnumos* 'given as a name, giving one's name to someone or something,' from *epi* 'upon' + *onuma* 'name.'

e·pon·y·mous /ə'pänəməs/ ▶ **adj.** (of a person) giving their name to something: *the eponymous hero of the novel.* ■ (of a thing) named after a particular person: *Roseanne's eponymous hit TV series.*

EPOS ▶ **abbr.** electronic point of sale (used to describe retail outlets that record information electronically).

ep·ox·ide /e'päk,sīd/ ▶ **n.** Chemistry an organic compound whose molecule contains a three-membered ring involving an oxygen atom and two carbon atoms.
–ORIGIN 1930s: from **EPI-** 'in addition' + **OXIDE**.

ep·ox·y /i'päksē/ ▶ **n.** (pl. **epoxies**) (also **epoxy resin**) an adhesive, plastic, paint, or other material made from a class of synthetic thermosetting polymers containing epoxide groups.
▶ **adj.** [attrib.] consisting of or denoting such a material: *epoxy cement.*
▶ **v.** (**epoxies, epoxying, epoxied**) [with obj.] glue (something) using epoxy resin.
–ORIGIN early 20th cent.: from **EPI-** 'in addition' + **OXY-²**.

EPROM /'ē,präm/ ▶ **n.** Electronics a read-only memory whose contents can be erased by ultraviolet light or other means and reprogrammed using a pulsed voltage.
–ORIGIN 1970s: acronym from *erasable programmable ROM.*

eps ▶ **abbr.** earnings per share.

ep·si·lon /'epsi,län/ ▶ **n.** the fifth letter of the Greek alphabet (Ε, ε), transliterated as 'e.' ■ [as modifier] denoting the fifth in a series of items, categories, etc. ■ (**Epsilon**) [followed by Latin genitive] Astronomy the fifth star in a constellation: *Epsilon Carinae.*
▶ **symbol** (ε) permittivity.
–ORIGIN early 18th cent.: Greek, 'plain or simple E,' from *psilos* 'plain,' referring to the need to distinguish epsilon from the diphthong *ai*: in late Greek the two had the same pronunciation.

Ep·som /'epsəm/ a town in Surrey, southeastern England; pop. 35,000 (est. 2009). Its natural mineral waters were used in the production of Epsom salts.

The annual Derby and Oaks horse races are held at its racecourse on Epsom Downs.

Ep·som salts ▶ **plural n.** crystals of hydrated magnesium sulfate used as a purgative or for other medicinal use. ● Chem. formula: $MgSO_4.7H_2O$.
– ORIGIN mid 18th cent.: named after the town of **EPSOM**, where it was first found occurring naturally.

Ep·stein /ˈepˌstīn/, Sir Jacob (1880–1959), British sculptor; born in the US. A founder of the Vorticist group, he later had great success with his modeled portraits of the famous, in particular *Einstein* (1933).

Ep·stein–Barr vi·rus /ˈepstīn ˈbär/ (abbr.: **EBV**) ▶ **n.** Medicine a herpesvirus causing infectious mononucleosis and associated with certain cancers, for example Burkitt's lymphoma.
– ORIGIN 1960s: named after Michael A. *Epstein* (born 1921), British virologist, and Y. M. *Barr* (born 1932), Irish-born virologist.

e·pyl·li·on /əˈpilēən, -ˌän/ ▶ **n.** (pl. **epyllia** /əˈpilēə/) a narrative poem that resembles an epic poem in style but is notably shorter.
– ORIGIN late 19th cent.: from Greek *epullion*, diminutive of *epos* 'word, song,' from *eipein* 'say.'

EQ ▶ **abbr.** ■ educational quotient. ■ emotional quotient. [after IQ, 'intelligence quotient.'] ■ (with reference to sound reproduction) equalizer or equalization.

eq. ▶ **abbr.** ■ equal. ■ equation. ■ equivalent.

eq·ua·ble /ˈekwəbəl/ ▶ **adj.** (of a person) not easily disturbed or angered; calm and even-tempered. ■ not varying or fluctuating greatly: *an equable climate.*
– DERIVATIVES **eq·ua·bil·i·ty** /ˌekwəˈbilitē/ **n.**, **eq·ua·bly** /-blē/ **adv.**
– ORIGIN mid 17th cent. (in the sense 'fair, equitable'): from Latin *aequabilis*, from *aequare* 'make equal' (see **EQUATE**).

e·qual /ˈēkwəl/ ▶ **adj. 1** being the same in quantity, size, degree, or value: *add equal amounts of water and flour* | *1 liter is roughly equal to 1 quart.* ■ (of people) having the same status, rights, or opportunities. ■ uniform in application or effect; without discrimination on any grounds: *a dedicated campaigner for equal rights.* ■ evenly or fairly balanced: *it was hardly an equal contest.*
2 [predic.] **(equal to)** having the ability or resources to meet (a challenge): *the players proved equal to the task.*
▶ **n.** a person or thing considered to be the same as another in status or quality: *we all treat each other as equals* | *it was a day without equal in market history.*
▶ **v.** (**equals, equaling, equaled**; also chiefly Brit. **equals, equalling, equalled**) [with obj.] be the same as in number or amount: *four plus six divided by two equals five* | *the total debits should equal the total credits.* ■ match or rival in performance or extent: *he equaled the world record of 9.93 seconds.* ■ be equivalent to: *his work is concerned with why private property equals exploitation.*
– PHRASES **(the) first among equals** the person or thing having the highest status in a group. **other** (or **all**) **things being equal** provided that other factors or circumstances remain the same: *it follows that, other things being equal, the price level will rise.*
– ORIGIN late Middle English: from Latin *aequalis*, from *aequus* 'even, level, equal.'

> **USAGE** It is widely held that adjectives such as **equal** and **unique** have absolute meanings and therefore can have no degrees of comparison. Hence they should not be modified, and it is incorrect to say **more equal** or **very unique** on the grounds that these are adjectives that refer to a logical or mathematical absolute. For more discussion of this question, see usage at **UNIQUE**.

e·qual·i·tar·i·an /iˌkwäliˈterēən/ ▶ **n.** another term for **EGALITARIAN**.
– DERIVATIVES **e·qual·i·tar·i·an·ism** /-ˌnizəm/ **n.**

e·qual·i·ty /iˈkwälitē/ ▶ **n.** the state of being equal, esp. in status, rights, and opportunities: *an organization aiming to promote racial equality.* ■ Mathematics a symbolic expression of the fact that two quantities are equal; an equation.
– ORIGIN late Middle English: via Old French from Latin *aequalitas*, from *aequalis* (see **EQUAL**).

E·qual·i·ty State a nickname for the state of **WYOMING**.

e·qual·ize /ˈēkwəˌlīz/ ▶ **v.** [with obj.] make the same in quantity, size, or degree throughout a place or group: *incentives to equalize funding for school districts.* ■ [no obj.] become equal to a specified or standard level: *equal volumes tend to equalize in temperature.* ■ [with obj.] make uniform in application or effect: *the act was structured to equalize the status of a defendant.*
– DERIVATIVES **e·qual·i·za·tion** /ˌēkwəliˈzāSHən/ **n.**
– ORIGIN late 16th cent. (in the sense 'be equal to'): from **EQUAL** + **-IZE**, partly suggested by French *égaliser*.

e·qual·iz·er /ˈēkwəˌlīzər/ ▶ **n.** a thing that has an equalizing effect: *education is the great equalizer.* ■ informal a weapon, esp. a gun. ■ Electronics a passive network designed to modify a frequency response, esp. to compensate for distortion.

e·qual·ly /ˈēkwəlē/ ▶ **adv. 1** in the same manner: *all children should be treated equally.* ■ in amounts or parts that are the same in size: *the money can be divided equally between you.*
2 to the same extent or degree: [as submodifier] *follow-up discussion is equally important.* ■ [sentence adverb] in addition and having the same importance (used to introduce a further comment on a topic): *not all who live in inner cities are poor; equally, many poor people live outside inner cities.*

> **USAGE** The construction **equally as**—for example in *follow-up discussion is equally as important*—is relatively common but is sometimes criticized on the grounds of redundancy. **Equally** used alone is adequate: *follow-up discussion is equally important.*

e·qual op·por·tu·ni·ty ▶ **n.** the policy of treating employees and others without discrimination, esp. on the basis of their sex, race, or age: [as modifier] *an equal opportunity employer.*

E·qual Rights A·mend·ment (abbr.: **ERA**) ▶ **n.** a proposed amendment to the US Constitution stating that civil rights may not be denied on the basis of one's sex.

e·quals sign (also **equal sign**) ▶ **n.** the symbol =.

e·qual tem·per·a·ment ▶ **n.** Music see **TEMPERAMENT** (sense 2).

e·qual time ▶ **n.** (in broadcasting) a principle of allowing equal air time to opposing points of view, esp. to political candidates for two or more parties.

e·qua·nim·i·ty /ˌēkwəˈnimitē, ˌekwə-/ ▶ **n.** mental calmness, composure, and evenness of temper, esp. in a difficult situation: *she accepted both the good and the bad with equanimity.*
– DERIVATIVES **e·quan·i·mous** /iˈkwänəməs/ **adj.**
– ORIGIN early 17th cent. (also in the sense 'fairness, impartiality'): from Latin *aequanimitas*, from *aequus* 'equal' + *animus* 'mind.'

e·quant /ˈēkwənt/ ▶ **adj.** Geology (of a crystal or particle) having its different diameters approximately equal, so as to be roughly cubic or spherical in shape.
– ORIGIN mid 16th cent.: from Latin *aequant-* 'making equal,' from the verb *aequare*.

e·quate /iˈkwāt/ ▶ **v.** [with obj.] consider (one thing) to be the same as or equivalent to another: *customers equate their name with quality.* ■ [no obj.] **(equate to/with)** (of one thing) be the same as or equivalent to (another): *that sum equates to half a million pounds today.* ■ cause (two or more things) to be the same in quantity or value: *the level of prices will move to equate supply and demand.*
– DERIVATIVES **e·quat·a·ble** /-təbəl/ **adj.**
– ORIGIN Middle English (in the sense 'make equal, balance'): from Latin *aequat-* 'made level or equal,' from the verb *aequare*, from *aequus* (see **EQUAL**). Current senses date from the mid 19th cent.

e·qua·tion /iˈkwāZHən/ ▶ **n. 1** Mathematics a statement that the values of two mathematical expressions are equal (indicated by the sign =).
2 the process of equating one thing with another: *the equation of science with objectivity.* ■ **(the equation)** a situation or problem in which several factors must be taken into account: *money also came into the equation.*
3 Chemistry a symbolic representation of the changes that occur in a chemical reaction, expressed in terms of the formulae of the molecules or other species involved.
– PHRASES **equation of the first order**, (**second order**, etc.) Mathematics an equation involving only the first derivative, second derivative, etc.
– ORIGIN late Middle English: from Latin *aequatio(n-)*, from *aequare* 'make equal' (see **EQUATE**).

e·qua·tion·al /iˈkwāZHənəl/ ▶ **adj.** another term for **EQUATIVE**.

e·qua·tion of state ▶ **n.** Chemistry an equation showing the relationship between the values of the pressure, volume, and temperature of a quantity of a particular substance.

e·qua·tion of time ▶ **n.** the difference between mean solar time (as shown by clocks) and apparent solar time (indicated by sundials), which varies with the time of year.

eq·ua·tive /iˈkwātiv/ ▶ **adj.** Grammar denoting a sentence or other structure in which one term is identified with another, as in *the winner is Jill.*
– DERIVATIVES **eq·ua·tive·ly adv.**

e·qua·tor /iˈkwātər/ ▶ **n.** an imaginary line drawn around the earth equally distant from both poles, dividing the earth into northern and southern hemispheres and constituting the parallel of latitude 0°. ■ a corresponding line on a planet or other body. ■ Astronomy short for **CELESTIAL EQUATOR**.
– ORIGIN late Middle English: from medieval Latin *aequator*, in the phrase *circulus aequator diei et noctis* 'circle equalizing day and night,' from Latin *aequare* 'make equal' (see **EQUATE**).

e·qua·to·ri·al /ˌekwəˈtôrēəl/ ▶ **adj.** of, at, or near the equator: *equatorial regions.*
– DERIVATIVES **e·qua·to·ri·al·ly** /ˌekwəˈtôrēəlē/ **adv.**

e

E·qua·to·ri·al Guin·ea a small country in West Africa, on the Gulf of Guinea, comprising several offshore islands and a coastal settlement between Cameroon and Gabon; pop. 633,400 (est. 2009); capital, Malabo (on the island of Bioko); languages, Spanish (official), local Niger–Congo languages, pidgin.

> Formerly a Spanish colony, the country became fully independent in 1968. It is the only independent Spanish-speaking state on the continent of Africa. Since 1991 it has been nominally a constitutional democracy.

– DERIVATIVES **E·qua·to·ri·al Guin·e·an adj. & n.**

e·qua·to·ri·al mount (also **equatorial mounting**) ▶ **n.** Astronomy a telescope mounting with one axis aligned to the celestial pole, which allows the movement of celestial objects to be followed by motion about this axis alone. Compare with **ALTAZIMUTH** (sense 1).

e·qua·to·ri·al tel·e·scope ▶ **n.** an astronomical telescope on an equatorial mount.

eq·uer·ry /ˈekwərē, əˈkwerē/ ▶ **n.** (pl. **equerries**) an officer of the British royal household who attends or assists members of the royal family. ■ historical an officer of the household of a prince or noble who had charge over the stables.
– ORIGIN early 16th cent. (formerly also as *esquiry*): from Old French *esquierie* 'company of squires, prince's stables,' from Old French *esquier* 'esquire,' perhaps associated with Latin *equus* 'horse.' The historical sense is apparently based on Old French *esquier d'esquierie* 'squire of stables.'

e·ques /ˈekwes/ singular form of **EQUITES**.

e·ques·tri·an /iˈkwestrēən/ ▶ **adj.** of or relating to horse riding: *his amazing equestrian skills.* ■ depicting or representing a person on horseback: *an equestrian statue.*
▶ **n.** (fem. **equestrienne** /iˌkwestrēˈen/) a rider or performer on horseback.
– ORIGIN mid 17th cent. (as an adjective): from Latin *equester* 'belonging to a horseman' (from *eques* 'horseman, knight,' from *equus* 'horse') + **-IAN**.

e·ques·tri·an·ism /iˈkwestrēəˌnizəm/ ▶ **n.** the skill or sport of horse riding. As an Olympic sport it is divided into three disciplines: show jumping, dressage, and the three-day event (combining show jumping, dressage, and cross-country riding).

equi- ▶ **comb. form** equal; equally: *equiangular* | *equidistant.*
– ORIGIN from Latin *aequi-*, from *aequus* 'equal.'

e·qui·an·gu·lar /ˌēkwēˈaNGgyələr, ˌekwē-/ ▶ **adj.** having equal angles.

e·qui·an·gu·lar spi·ral ▶ **n.** another term for **LOGARITHMIC SPIRAL**.

eq·uid /ˈēkwid, ˈekwid/ ▶ **n.** Zoology a mammal of the horse family (Equidae).
– ORIGIN late 19th cent.: from modern Latin *Equidae* (plural), from Latin *equus* 'horse.'

e·qui·dis·tant /ˌēkwiˈdistənt, ˌekwi-/ ▶ **adj.** at equal distances: *he wants to be equidistant from both political parties.*
– DERIVATIVES **e·qui·dis·tance n.**, **e·qui·dis·tant·ly adv.**

e·qui·fi·nal /ˌēkwəˈfīnəl, ˌekwə-/ ▶ **adj.** technical having the same end or result.
– DERIVATIVES **e·qui·fi·nal·i·ty** /ˌēkwəfīˈnalitē, ˌekwə-/ **n.**, **e·qui·fi·nal·ly adv.**

e·qui·lat·er·al /ˌēkwəˈlatərəl, ˌekwə-/ ▶ **adj.** having all its sides of the same length: *an equilateral triangle.*
– ORIGIN late 16th cent.: from French *équilatéral* or late Latin *aequilateralis*, from *aequilaterus* 'equal-sided' (based on Latin *latus, later-* 'side').

e·quil·i·brate /iˈkwiləˌbrāt/ ▶ **v.** [with obj.] technical bring into or keep in equilibrium. ■ [no obj.] approach or attain a state of equilibrium.
– DERIVATIVES **e·quil·i·bra·tion** /iˌkwiləˈbrāSHən/ **n.**
– ORIGIN mid 17th cent.: from late Latin *aequilibrat-* 'made to balance,' from the verb *aequilibrare*, from *aequi-* 'equally' + *libra* 'balance.'

e·quil·i·brist /iˈkwiləbrist/ ▶ **n.** chiefly archaic an acrobat who performs balancing feats, esp. a tightrope walker.
– ORIGIN mid 18th cent.: from EQUILIBRIUM + -IST.

e·qui·lib·ri·um /ˌēkwəˈlibrēəm, ˌekwə-/ ▶ **n.** (pl. **equilibria** /-ˈlibrēə/) a state in which opposing forces or influences are balanced: *the maintenance of social equilibrium.* ■ a state of physical balance: *I stumbled over a rock and recovered my equilibrium.* ■ a calm state of mind: *his intensity could unsettle his equilibrium.* ■ Chemistry a state in which a process and its reverse are occurring at equal rates so that no overall change is taking place: *ice is in **equilibrium with** water.* ■ Economics a situation in which supply and demand are matched and prices stable.
– DERIVATIVES **e·qui·lib·ri·al** /-ˈlibrēəl/ **adj.**
– ORIGIN early 17th cent. (in the sense 'well-balanced state of mind'): from Latin *aequilibrium*, from *aequi-* 'equal' + *libra* 'balance.'

e·quine /ˈekwīn, ˈēˌkwīn/ ▶ **adj.** of, relating to, or affecting horses or other members of the horse family: *equine infectious anemia.* ■ resembling a horse: *her somewhat equine features.*
▶ **n.** a horse or other member of the horse family.
– ORIGIN late 18th cent.: from Latin *equinus*, from *equus* 'horse.'

e·quine en·ceph·a·li·tis ▶ **n.** a category of viral diseases that affects horses and, in some cases, humans. See also EASTERN EQUINE ENCEPHALITIS.

e·qui·noc·tial /ˌēkwəˈnäkSHəl, ˌekwə-/ ▶ **adj.** happening at or near the time of an equinox. ■ of or relating to equal day and night. ■ at or near the equator.
▶ **n.** (also **equinoctial line** or **equinoctial circle**) another term for CELESTIAL EQUATOR.
– ORIGIN late Middle English (in the sense 'relating to equal periods of day and night'): via Old French from Latin *aequinoctialis*, from *aequinoctium* (see EQUINOX).

e·qui·noc·tial point ▶ **n.** either of two points at which the ecliptic cuts the celestial equator.

e·qui·noc·tial year ▶ **n.** see YEAR (sense 1).

e·qui·nox /ˈekwəˌnäks, ˈēkwə-/ ▶ **n.** the time or date (twice each year) at which the sun crosses the celestial equator, when day and night are of equal length (about September 22 and March 20). ■ another term for EQUINOCTIAL POINT.
– ORIGIN late Middle English: from Old French *equinoxe* or Latin *aequinoctium*, from *aequi-* 'equal' + *nox, noct-* 'night.'

e·quip /iˈkwip/ ▶ **v.** (**equips, equipping, equipped**) [with obj.] supply with the necessary items for a particular purpose: *all bedrooms **are equipped with** a color TV | they **equipped** themselves **for** the campaign.* ■ prepare (someone) mentally for a particular situation or task: *I don't think he's equipped for the modern age.*
– DERIVATIVES **e·quip·per n.**
– ORIGIN early 16th cent.: from French *équiper*, probably from Old Norse *skipa* 'to man (a ship),' from *skip* 'ship.'

equip. ▶ **abbr.** equipment.

eq·ui·page /ˈekwəpij/ ▶ **n. 1** archaic the equipment for a particular purpose.
2 historical a carriage and horses with attendants.
– ORIGIN mid 16th cent. (denoting the crew of a ship): from French *équipage*, from *équiper* 'equip.'

e·qui·par·ti·tion /ˌēkwəpärˈtiSHən, ˌekwə-/ (also **equipartition of energy**) ▶ **n.** Physics the equal distribution of the kinetic energy of a system among its various degrees of freedom. ■ the principle that this exists for a system in thermal equilibrium.
– DERIVATIVES **e·qui·par·ti·tioned adj.**

e·quip·ment /iˈkwipmənt/ ▶ **n.** the necessary items for a particular purpose: *office equipment.* ■ the process of supplying someone or something with such necessary items: *the construction and equipment of new harbor facilities.* ■ mental resources: *they lacked the intellectual equipment to recognize the jokes.* ■ informal used euphemistically to refer to a man's penis and testicles.
– ORIGIN early 18th cent.: from French *équipement*, from *équiper* 'equip.'

e·qui·poise /ˈekwəˌpoiz/ ▶ **n.** balance of forces or interests: *this temporary equipoise of power.* ■ a counterbalance or balancing force: *capital flows act as an **equipoise to** international imbalances in savings.*
▶ **v.** [with obj.] balance or counterbalance (something).
– ORIGIN mid 17th cent.: from EQUI- 'equal' + the noun POISE¹, replacing the phrase *equal poise.*

e·qui·pol·lent /ˌēkwəˈpälənt, ˌekwə-/ archaic ▶ **adj.** equal or equivalent in power, effect, or significance.
▶ **n.** a thing that has equal or equivalent power, effect, or significance.
– DERIVATIVES **e·qui·pol·lence n.**, **e·qui·pol·len·cy n.**
– ORIGIN late Middle English: from Old French *equipolent*, from Latin *aequipollent-* 'of equal value,' from *aequi-* 'equally' + *pollere* 'be strong.'

e·qui·po·tent /ˌēkwəˈpōtnt, ˌekwə-/ ▶ **adj.** technical (chiefly of chemicals and medicines) equally powerful; having equal potencies.

e·qui·po·ten·tial /ˌēkwəpəˈtenCHəl, ˌekwə-/ ▶ **adj.** [attrib.] Physics (of a surface or line) composed of points all at the same potential.
▶ **n.** an equipotential line or surface.

e·qui·prob·a·ble /ˌēkwəˈpräbəbəl, ˌekwə-/ ▶ **adj.** Mathematics & Logic (of two or more things) equally likely to occur; having equal probability.
– DERIVATIVES **e·qui·prob·a·bil·i·ty** /-ˌpräbəˈbilitē/ **n.**

eq·ui·se·tum /ˌekwiˈsētəm/ ▶ **n.** (pl. **equiseta** /-ˈsētə/ or **equisetums**) Botany a plant of a genus that comprises the horsetails. ● Genus *Equisetum*, family Equisetaceae.
– ORIGIN modern Latin, from Latin *equus* 'horse' + *saeta* 'bristle.'

eq·ui·ta·ble /ˈekwitəbəl/ ▶ **adj. 1** fair and impartial: *an equitable balance of power.*
2 Law valid in equity as distinct from law: *the beneficiaries have an equitable interest in the property.*
– DERIVATIVES **eq·ui·ta·bil·i·ty** /ˌekwitəˈbilitē/ **n.**, **eq·ui·ta·ble·ness n.**, **eq·ui·ta·bly** /-əblē/ **adv.**
– ORIGIN mid 16th cent.: from French *équitable*, from *équité* (see EQUITY).

eq·ui·tant /ˈekwitənt/ ▶ **adj.** Botany (of a leaf) having its base folded and partly enclosing the leaf next above it, as in an iris.
– ORIGIN late 18th cent.: from Latin *equitant-* 'riding on horseback,' from the verb *equitare*.

eq·ui·ta·tion /ˌekwiˈtāSHən/ ▶ **n.** formal the art and practice of horsemanship and horse riding.
– ORIGIN mid 16th cent.: from French *équitation* or Latin *equitatio(n-)*, from *equitare* 'ride a horse,' from *eques, equit-* 'horseman' (from *equus* 'horse').

eq·ui·tes /ˈekwəˌtās, -ˌtēz/ ▶ **plural n.** (sing. **eques** /ˈekwes, -wēz/) (in ancient Rome) a class of citizens who originally formed the cavalry of the Roman army and at a later period were a wealthy class of great political importance.
– ORIGIN Latin, plural of *eques* 'horseman.'

eq·ui·ty /ˈekwitē/ ▶ **n.** (pl. **equities**) **1** the quality of being fair and impartial: *equity of treatment.* ■ Law a branch of law that developed alongside common law in order to remedy some of its defects in fairness and justice, formerly administered in special courts. ■ (**Equity**) (in the US, UK, and several other countries) a trade union to which most professional actors belong.
2 the value of the shares issued by a company: *he owns 62% of the group's equity.* ■ (**equities**) stocks and shares that carry no fixed interest.
3 the value of a mortgaged property after deduction of charges against it.
– ORIGIN Middle English: from Old French *equité*, from Latin *aequitas*, from *aequus* 'equal.'

eq·ui·ty of re·demp·tion ▶ **n.** Law the right of a mortgagor over the mortgaged property, esp. the right to redeem the property on payment of the principal, interest, and costs.

eq·ui·ty stock ▶ **n.** capital stock, either common stock or preferred stock.

equiv. ▶ **abbr.** equivalent.

e·quiv·a·lence /iˈkwivələns/ ▶ **n.** the condition of being equal or equivalent in value, worth, function, etc.

e·quiv·a·lence class /iˈkwivələns/ ▶ **n.** Mathematics & Logic the class of all members of a set that are in a given equivalence relation.

e·quiv·a·lence prin·ci·ple ▶ **n.** Physics a basic postulate of general relativity, stating that at any point of space-time the effects of a gravitational field cannot be experimentally distinguished from those due to an accelerated frame of reference.

e·quiv·a·lence re·la·tion ▶ **n.** Mathematics & Logic a relation between elements of a set that is reflexive, symmetric, and transitive. It thus defines exclusive classes whose members bear the relation to each other and not to those in other classes (e.g., "having the same value of a measured property").

e·quiv·a·len·cy /iˈkwivələnsē/ ▶ **n.** (pl. **equivalencies**) another term for EQUIVALENCE. ■ short for GENERAL EQUIVALENCY DEGREE.

e·quiv·a·lent /iˈkwivələnt/ ▶ **adj.** equal in value, amount, function, meaning, etc.: *one unit is **equivalent to** one glass of wine.* ■ [predic.] (**equivalent to**) having the same or a similar effect as: *some regulations are equivalent to censorship.* ■ Mathematics belonging to the same equivalence class.
▶ **n.** a person or thing that is equal to or corresponds with another in value, amount, function, meaning, etc.: *the French equivalent of the FBI.* ■ (also **equivalent weight**) Chemistry the mass of a particular substance that can combine with or displace one gram of hydrogen or eight grams of oxygen, used in expressing combining powers, esp. of elements.
– DERIVATIVES **e·quiv·a·lent·ly adv.**
– ORIGIN late Middle English (describing persons who were equal in power or rank): via Old French from late Latin *aequivalent-* 'being of equal worth,' from the verb *aequivalere*, from *aequi-* 'equally' + *valere* 'be worth.'

e·quiv·o·cal /iˈkwivəkəl/ ▶ **adj.** open to more than one interpretation; ambiguous: *the equivocal nature of her remarks.* ■ uncertain or questionable in nature: *the results of the investigation were equivocal.*
– DERIVATIVES **e·quiv·o·cal·i·ty** /iˌkwivəˈkalitē/ **n.**, **e·quiv·o·cal·ly adv.**, **e·quiv·o·cal·ness n.**
– ORIGIN mid 16th cent.: from late Latin *aequivocus*, from Latin *aequus* 'equally' + *vocare* 'to call.'

e·quiv·o·cate /iˈkwivəˌkāt/ ▶ **v.** [no obj.] use ambiguous language so as to conceal the truth or avoid committing oneself: [with direct speech] *"Not that we are aware of," she equivocated.*
– DERIVATIVES **e·quiv·o·ca·tor** /-ˌkātər/ **n.**, **e·quiv·o·ca·to·ry** /-kəˌtôrē/ **adj.**
– ORIGIN late Middle English (in the sense 'use a word in more than one sense'): from late Latin *aequivocat-* 'called by the same name,' from the verb *aequivocare*, from *aequivocus* (see EQUIVOCAL).

e·quiv·o·ca·tion /iˌkwivəˈkāSHən/ ▶ **n.** the use of ambiguous language to conceal the truth or to avoid committing oneself; prevarication: *I say this without equivocation.*

eq·ui·voque /ˈekwəˌvōk, ˈēkwə-/ (also **equivoke**) ▶ **n.** an expression capable of having more than one meaning; a pun. ■ the fact of having more than one meaning or possible interpretation; ambiguity.
– ORIGIN late Middle English (as an adjective in the sense 'equivocal'): from Old French *equivoque* or late Latin *aequivocus* (see EQUIVOCAL).

E·quu·le·us /ēˈkwōolēəs/ Astronomy a small northern constellation (the Foal or Little Horse), perhaps representing the brother of Pegasus. It has no bright stars. ■ (as genitive **Equulei** /ēˈkwōolēˌī/) used with a preceding letter or numeral to designate a star in this constellation: *the star Delta Equulei.*
– ORIGIN Latin.

ER ▶ **abbr.** ■ emergency room. ■ Queen Elizabeth. [from Latin *Elizabetha Regina.*]

Er ▶ **symbol** the chemical element erbium.

er /ə, ər/ ▶ **exclam.** expressing hesitation: *"Would you like some tea?" "Er ... yes ... thank you."*
– ORIGIN natural utterance: first recorded in English in the mid 19th cent.

-er[1] /ər/ ▶ **suffix 1** denoting a person, animal, or thing that performs a specified action or activity: *farmer | sprinkler.*
2 denoting a person or thing that has a specified attribute or form: *foreigner | two-wheeler.*
3 denoting a person concerned with a specified thing or subject: *milliner | philosopher.*
4 denoting a person belonging to a specified place or group: *city-dweller | New Yorker.*
– ORIGIN Old English *-ere*, of Germanic origin.

-er[2] ▶ **suffix** forming the comparative of adjectives (as in *bigger*) and adverbs (as in *faster*).
– ORIGIN Old English suffix *-ra* (adjectival), *-or* (adverbial), of Germanic origin.

-er[3] ▶ **suffix** forming frequentative verbs such as *glimmer, patter.*
– ORIGIN Old English *-erian, -rian*, of Germanic origin.

-er[4] ▶ **suffix** forming nouns: **1** such as *sampler*. Compare with -AR¹. [ending corresponding to Latin *-aris.*] ■ such as *butler, danger.* [ending corresponding to Latin *-arius, -arium.*] ■ such as *border.* [ending corresponding (via Old French *-eure*) to Latin *-atura.*] ■ such as *laver.* See LAVER². [ending corresponding (via Old French *-eor*) to Latin *-atorium.*]
2 equivalent to -OR¹.
– ORIGIN via Old French or Anglo-Norman French (see above).

-er[5] ▶ **suffix** chiefly Law (forming nouns) denoting verbal action or a document effecting such action: *disclaimer | misnomer.*
– ORIGIN from Anglo-Norman French (infinitive ending).

ERA ▶ abbr. ■ Baseball earned run average. ■ Equal Rights Amendment.

e·ra /'i(ə)rə, 'erə/ ▶ n. a long and distinct period of history with a particular feature or characteristic: *his death marked the end of an era | the era of glasnost.* ■ a system of chronology dating from a particular noteworthy event: *the dawn of the Christian era.* ■ Geology a major division of time that is a subdivision of an eon and is itself subdivided into periods: *the Mesozoic era.* ■ archaic a date or event marking the beginning of a new and distinct period of time.
– ORIGIN mid 17th cent.: from late Latin *aera*, denoting a number used as a basis of reckoning, an epoch from which time is reckoned, plural of *aes, aer-* 'money, counter.'

e·rad·i·cate /i'radi,kāt/ ▶ v. [with obj.] destroy completely; put an end to: *this disease has been eradicated from the world.*
– DERIVATIVES **e·rad·i·ca·ble** /-kəbəl/ adj., **e·rad·i·cant** /-kənt/ n., **e·rad·i·ca·tor** /-,kātər/ n.
– ORIGIN late Middle English (in the sense 'pull up by the roots'): from Latin *eradicat-* 'torn up by the roots,' from the verb *eradicare*, from *e-* (variant of *ex-*) 'out' + *radix, radic-* 'root.'

e·rad·i·cat·ed /i'radə,kātid/ ▶ adj. [postpositive] Heraldry (of a tree or plant) depicted with the roots exposed.

e·rad·i·ca·tion /i,radi'kāSHən/ ▶ n. the complete destruction of something: *the eradication of poverty.*

e·rase /i'rās/ ▶ v. [with obj.] rub out or remove (writing or marks): *graffiti had been erased from the wall.* ■ remove all traces of (a thought, feeling, or memory): *the magic of the landscape erased all else from her mind.* ■ remove recorded material from (a magnetic tape or medium); delete (data) from a computer's memory.
– DERIVATIVES **e·ras·a·ble** /-əbəl/ adj.
– ORIGIN late 16th cent. (originally as a heraldic term meaning 'represent the head or limb of an animal with a jagged edge'): from Latin *eras-* 'scraped away,' from the verb *eradere*, from *e-* (variant of *ex-*) 'out' + *radere* 'scrape.'

e·rased /i'rāst/ ▶ adj. [postpositive] Heraldry (of a head or limb) depicted as cut off in a jagged line.

e·ras·er /i'rāsər/ ▶ n. an object, typically a piece of soft rubber or plastic, used to rub out something written.

E·ras·mus /i'razməs/, Desiderius (*c.*1469–1536), Dutch humanist and scholar; Dutch name *Gerhard Gerhards.* He was the foremost Renaissance scholar of northern Europe, and paved the way for the Reformation with his satires on the Catholic Church.

E·ras·tian·ism /i'rastēə,nizəm, i'rasCHə-/ ▶ n. the doctrine that the state should have supremacy over the Church in ecclesiastical matters (wrongly attributed to Erastus).
– DERIVATIVES **E·ras·tian** /i'rastēən, i'rasCHən/ n. & adj.

E·ras·tus /i'rastəs/ (1524–83), Swiss theologian and physician; Swiss name *Thomas Lieber*, also *Liebler* or *Lüber.* Professor of medicine at Heidelberg from 1558, he opposed the imposition of a Calvinistic system of church government in the city.

e·ra·sure /i'rāSHər/ ▶ n. the removal of writing, recorded material, or data. ■ the removal of all traces of something; obliteration: *the erasure of prior history.*

Er·a·to /'erə,tō/ Greek & Roman Mythology the Muse of lyric poetry and hymns.
– ORIGIN Greek, literally 'lovely.'

Er·a·tos·the·nes /,erə'tästHə,nēz/ (*c.*275–194 BC), Greek scholar, geographer, and astronomer. The first systematic geographer of antiquity, he accurately calculated the circumference of the earth.

er·bi·um /'ərbēəm/ ▶ n. the chemical element of atomic number 68, a soft silvery-white metal of the lanthanide series. (Symbol: **Er**)
– ORIGIN mid 19th cent.: modern Latin, from (*Ytt*)*erb*(*y*), in Sweden, where it was first found. Compare with **YTTERBIUM**.

Er·drich /'ərdrik/, Louise (1954–), US writer; a Native American (Ojibwa). Her novels include *Love Medicine* (1984), *The Bingo Palace* (1994), *Tales of Burning Love* (1996), *The Antelope Wife* (1998), and *The Plague of Doves* (2008).

ere /e(ə)r/ ▶ prep. & conj. literary or archaic before (in time): [as prep.] *we hope you will return ere long* | [as conjunction] *I was driven for some half mile ere we stopped.*
– ORIGIN Old English *ǣr*, of Germanic origin; related to Dutch *eer* and German *eher.*

e-read·er /'ē,rēdər/ ▶ n. a device or application to facilitate or enhance the reading of electronic material.

Er·e·bus /'erəbəs/ Greek Mythology the primeval god of darkness, son of Chaos.

Er·e·bus, Mount a volcanic peak on Ross Island, Antarctica. Rising to 12,452 feet (3,794 m), it is the world's most southern active volcano.
– ORIGIN named after the *Erebus*, the ship of Sir James Ross's expedition to the Antarctic.

E·rech /'er,ek, 'ē,rek/ biblical name for **URUK**.

E·rech·the·um /i'rikTHēəm, ,erik'THēəm/ a marble temple of the Ionic order built on the Acropolis in Athens *c.*421–406 BC, with shrines to Athena, Poseidon, and Erechtheus, a legendary king of Athens. It is most famous for its southern portico, in which the entablature is supported by six caryatids.

e·rect /i'rekt/ ▶ adj. rigidly upright or straight: *she stood erect with her arms by her sides.* ■ (of the penis, clitoris, or nipples) enlarged and rigid, esp. in sexual excitement.
▶ v. [with obj.] construct (a building, wall, or other upright structure): *the guest house was erected in the eighteenth century | the police had erected roadblocks.* ■ create or establish (a theory or system): *the party that erected the welfare state.*
– DERIVATIVES **e·rect·a·ble** adj., **e·rect·ly** adv., **e·rect·ness** n.
– ORIGIN late Middle English: from Latin *erect-* 'set up,' from the verb *erigere*, from *e-* (variant of *ex-*) 'out' + *regere* 'to direct.'

e·rec·tile /i'rektl, -,tīl/ ▶ adj. able to become erect: *erectile spines.* ■ denoting tissues that are capable of becoming of temporarily engorged with blood, particularly those of the penis or other sexual organs. ■ relating to this process: *men with erectile dysfunction.*
– ORIGIN mid 19th cent.: from French *érectile*, from Latin *erigere* 'set up' (see **ERECT**).

e·rec·tile dys·func·tion ▶ n. inability of a man to maintain an erection sufficient for satisfying sexual activity: *a treatment proven safe for erectile dysfunction.*

e·rec·tion /i'rekSHən/ ▶ n. **1** the action of erecting a structure or object: *fees will be levied for the erection of monuments.* ■ a building or other upright structure.
2 an enlarged and rigid state of the penis, typically in sexual excitement.

e·rec·tor /i'rektər/ ▶ n. a person or thing that erects something. ■ a muscle that maintains an erect state of a part of the body or an erect posture of the body.

ere·long /e(ə)r'lôNG, -'läNG/ ▶ adv. archaic before long; soon.

er·e·mite /'erə,mīt/ ▶ n. a Christian hermit or recluse.
– DERIVATIVES **er·e·mit·ic** /,erə'mitik/ adj., **er·e·mit·i·cal** /,erə'mitikəl/ adj.
– ORIGIN Middle English: from Old French *eremite*, from late Latin *eremita* (see **HERMIT**).

er·e·thism /'erə,THizəm/ ▶ n. **1** excessive sensitivity or rapid reaction to stimulation of a part of the body, esp. the sexual organs.
2 a state of abnormal mental excitement or irritation.
– ORIGIN early 19th cent.: from French *éréthisme*, from Greek *erethismos*, from *erethizein* 'irritate.'

E·re·van /,yeri'vän/ another name for **YEREVAN**.

ere·while /er'(h)wīl/ ▶ adv. archaic a while before; some time ago.
– ORIGIN Middle English: from **ERE** + **WHILE**.

Er·furt /'er,fŏŏrt/ an industrial city in central Germany; pop. 202,700 (est. 2006).

erg[1] /ərg/ ▶ n. Physics a unit of work or energy, equal to the work done by a force of one dyne when its point of application moves one centimeter in the direction of action of the force.
– ORIGIN late 19th cent.: from Greek *ergon* 'work.'

erg[2] /erg/ ▶ n. an area of shifting sand dunes in the Sahara.
– ORIGIN late 19th cent.: from French, from Arabic *'irq, 'erg.*

er·ga·tive /'ərgətiv/ Grammar ▶ adj. relating to or denoting a case of nouns (in some languages, e.g., Basque and Eskimo) that identifies the subject of a transitive verb and is different from the case that identifies the subject of an intransitive verb. ■ (of a language) possessing this case. ■ (in English) denoting verbs that can be used both transitively and intransitively to describe the same action, with the object in the former case being the subject in the latter, as in *I boiled the kettle* and *the kettle boiled.* Compare with **INCHOATIVE**.
▶ n. an ergative word. ■ (**the ergative**) the ergative case.
– DERIVATIVES **er·ga·tiv·i·ty** /,ərgə'tivitē/ n.
– ORIGIN 1950s: from Greek *ergatēs* 'worker' (from *ergon* 'work') + **-IVE**.

er·go /'ərgō, 'ergō/ ▶ adv. [sentence adverb] therefore: *she was the sole beneficiary of the will, ergo the prime suspect.*
– ORIGIN late Middle English: Latin.

er·go·cal·cif·er·ol /,ərgəkal'sifəräl, -rôl/ ▶ n. Biochemistry another term for **CALCIFEROL, VITAMIN D2**.
– ORIGIN 1950s: blend of **ERGOT** and **CALCIFEROL**.

er·god·ic /ər'gädik/ ▶ adj. Mathematics relating to or denoting systems or processes with the property that, given sufficient time, they include or impinge on all points in a given space and can be represented statistically by a reasonably large selection of points.
– DERIVATIVES **er·go·dic·i·ty** /,ərgə'disitē/ n.
– ORIGIN early 20th cent.: from German *ergoden*, from Greek *ergon* 'work' + *hodos* 'way' + **-IC**.

er·go·gen·ic /,ərgə'jenik/ ▶ adj. (not in technical use) intended to enhance physical performance, stamina, or recovery: *ergogenic supplements.*

er·go·graph /'ərgə,graf/ ▶ n. an instrument for measuring and recording the work done by a particular muscle group.

er·gom·e·ter /ər'gämitər/ ▶ n. an apparatus that measures work or energy expended during a period of physical exercise.

er·go·met·rine /,ərgə'metrēn/ ▶ n. Chemistry an alkaloid present in ergot. An amide of lysergic acid, it has oxytocic activity and is given to control bleeding after childbirth.
– ORIGIN 1930s: from **ERGOT** + Greek *mētra* 'womb' + **-INE[4]**.

er·go·nom·ic /ərgə'nämik/ ▶ adj. (esp. of workplace design) intended to provide optimum comfort and to avoid stress or injury.

er·go·nom·ics /,ərgə'nämiks/ ▶ plural n. [treated as sing.] the study of people's efficiency in their working environment.
– DERIVATIVES **er·gon·o·mist** /ər'gänəmist/ n.
– ORIGIN 1950s: from Greek *ergon* 'work,' on the pattern of *economics.*

er·go·sphere /'ərgō,sfir/ ▶ n. Astronomy a postulated region around a black hole, from which energy could escape.

er·gos·ter·ol /ər'gästə,rôl, -,räl/ ▶ n. Biochemistry a compound present in ergot and many other fungi. A steroid alcohol, it is converted to vitamin D_2 when irradiated with ultraviolet light.
– ORIGIN early 20th cent.: from **ERGOT**, on the pattern of *cholesterol.*

er·got /'ərgət, -,gät/ ▶ n. **1** a fungal disease of rye and other cereals in which black, elongated, fruiting bodies grow in the ears of the cereal. Eating contaminated food can result in ergotism. ● The fungus is *Claviceps purpurea*, subdivision Ascomycotina. ■ the fruiting bodies of this fungus, used as a source of certain medicinal alkaloids, esp. for inducing uterine contractions or controlling postpartum bleeding.
2 a small, horny protuberance on the back of each of a horse's fetlocks.
– ORIGIN late 17th cent.: from French, from Old French *argot* 'cock's spur' (because of the appearance produced by the disease).

er·got·a·mine /ər'gätə,mēn, -min/ ▶ n. Medicine a compound present in some kinds of ergot. An alkaloid, it causes constriction of blood vessels and is used in the treatment of migraine.

er·got·ism /'ərgə,tizəm/ ▶ n. poisoning produced by eating food affected by ergot, typically resulting in headache, vomiting, diarrhea, and gangrene of the fingers and toes.

er·hu /ər'hŏŏ/ (also **erh hu**) ▶ n. a Chinese two-stringed musical instrument held in the lap and played with a bow.
– ORIGIN early 20th cent.: Chinese, from *èr* 'two' + *hú* 'bowed instrument.'

er·i·ca /'erikə/ ▶ n. a plant of the genus *Erica* (family Ericaceae), esp. (in gardening) heather.
– ORIGIN modern Latin, from Greek *ereikē.*

er·i·ca·ceous /,eri'kāSHəs/ ▶ adj. Botany of, relating to, or denoting plants of the heath family (Ericaceae).
– ORIGIN mid 19th cent.: from modern Latin *Ericaceae* (plural), from the genus name *Erica* (see **ERICA**).

Er·ics·son[1] /'eriksən/, John (1803–89), Swedish engineer whose inventions included the marine screw propeller (1836) and a steam railroad locomotive that rivaled George Stephenson's *Rocket.*

Er·ics·son² (also **Ericson** or **Eriksson**), Leif, Norse explorer; son of Eric the Red. He sailed west from Greenland (*c.*1000) and reputedly discovered land (variously identified as Labrador, Newfoundland, or New England), which he named Vinland because of the vines he claimed to have found growing there.

Er·ic the Red /'erik/ (*c.*940–*c.*1010), Norse explorer. He left Iceland in 982 in search of land to the west and explored Greenland, establishing a Norse settlement there in 986.

E·rid·a·nus /ə'ridn-əs/ Astronomy a long, straggling southern constellation (the River), said to represent the river into which Phaethon fell when struck by Zeus' thunderbolt. ■ (as genitive **Eridani** /ə'ridn,ē, -,ī/) used with a preceding letter or numeral to designate a star in this constellation: *the star Phi Eridani.*
– ORIGIN Latin.

E·rie /'i(ə)rē/ an industrial port city in northwestern Pennsylvania, on Lake Erie; pop. 103,817 (est. 2008).

E·rie, Lake /'i(ə)rē/ one of the five Great Lakes in North America, on the border between Canada and the US. It is linked to Lake Huron by the Detroit River and to Lake Ontario by the Welland Ship Canal and the Niagara River, which is its only natural outlet.

E·rie Ca·nal a historic canal that connects the Hudson River at Albany in eastern New York with the Niagara River and the Great Lakes. Opened in 1825, it spurred the growth of New York City. Today it is chiefly recreational.

e·rig·er·on /ə'rijərən, -,rän/ ▶ **n.** a widely distributed herbaceous plant of the daisy family, which is sometimes cultivated as an ornamental. ● Genus *Erigeron*, family Compositae.
– ORIGIN early 17th cent.: modern Latin, from Latin, 'groundsel' (the original sense in English), from Greek *ērigerōn*, from *ēri* 'early' + *gerōn* 'old man' (because the plant flowers early in the year, and some species bear gray down).

Er·iks·son variant spelling of **ERICSSON²**.

Er·in /'erən/ ▶ **n.** archaic or poetic/literary name for Ireland.

E·rin·ys /i'rinəs/ ▶ **n.** (pl. **Erinyes** /i'rinē-ēz/) (in Greek mythology) a Fury.

er·is·tic /i'ristik/ formal ▶ **adj.** of or characterized by debate or argument. ■ (of an argument or arguer) aiming at winning rather than at reaching the truth.
▶ **n.** a person given to debate or argument. ■ the art or practice or debate or argument.
– DERIVATIVES **er·is·ti·cal·ly** /-(ə)lē/ **adv.**
– ORIGIN mid 17th cent.: from Greek *eristikos*, from *erizein* 'to wrangle,' from *eris* 'strife.'

Er·i·tre·a /,erə'trēə, -'trāə/ an independent state in northeastern Africa, on the Red Sea; pop. 5,647,200 (est. 2009); capital, Asmara; languages, Tigre and Cushitic.

> Eritrea was an Italian colony from 1890 to 1952, when it became part of Ethiopia. After a long guerrilla war, it became internally self-governing in 1991 and fully independent in 1993.

– DERIVATIVES **Er·i·tre·an adj. & n.**
– ORIGIN from Italian, from Latin *Mare Erythraeum* the Red Sea.

Er·lan·gen /'er,läNGən/ an industrial city in southern Germany, on the Regnitz River; pop. 104,700 (est. 2007).

Er·lan·ger /'ər,laNGər/, Joseph (1874–1965), US physiologist. Collaborating with Herbert Gasser, he showed that the velocity of a nerve impulse is proportional to the diameter of the fiber. Nobel Prize for Physiology or Medicine (1944), shared with Gasser.

Er·len·mey·er flask /'ərlən,mīər, 'erlən-/ ▶ **n.** a conical, flat-bottomed laboratory flask with a narrow neck.
– ORIGIN late 19th cent.: named after Emil *Erlenmeyer* (1825–1909), German chemist.

Erl King /'ərl ,kiNG/ ▶ **n.** (in Germanic mythology) a bearded giant or goblin who lures little children to the land of death.
– ORIGIN late 18th cent.: from German *Erlkönig* 'alder king,' a mistranslation of Danish *ellerkonge* 'king of the elves.'

ERM ▶ **abbr.** Exchange Rate Mechanism.

er·mine /'ərmən/ ▶ **n.** (pl. **same** or **ermines**) **1** a stoat, esp. when in its white winter coat. ■ the white fur of the stoat, used for trimming garments, esp. the ceremonial robes of judges or peers. ■ Heraldry fur represented as black spots on a white ground, as a heraldic tincture.
2 (also **ermine moth**) a stout-bodied moth that has cream or white wings with black spots, and a very hairy caterpillar. ● Family Arctiidae: several genera and species.
– DERIVATIVES **er·mined adj.**
– ORIGIN Middle English: from Old French *hermine*, probably from medieval Latin (*mus*) *Armenius* 'Armenian (mouse).'

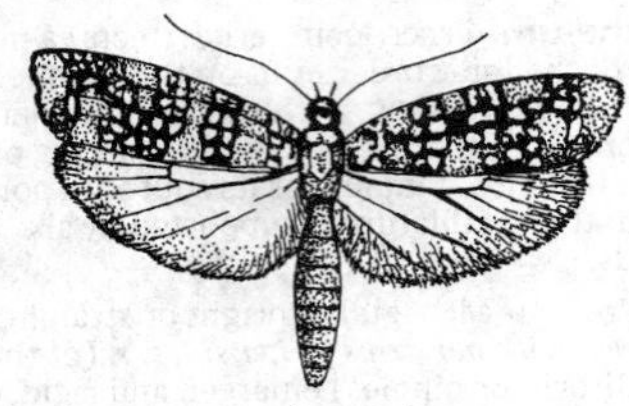
ermine moth

er·mines /'ərmənz/ ▶ **n.** Heraldry fur resembling ermine but with white spots on a black ground.
– ORIGIN mid 16th cent.: perhaps from Old French *hermines*, plural of *herminet*, diminutive of *hermine* 'ermine.'

er·mi·nois /,ərmə'noiz/ ▶ **n.** Heraldry fur resembling ermine but with black spots on a gold ground.
– ORIGIN mid 16th cent.: from Old French, from *hermine* 'ermine.'

-ern ▶ **suffix** forming adjectives such as *northern.*
– ORIGIN Old English *-erne*, of Germanic origin.

erne /ərn/ ▶ **n.** literary the sea eagle.
– ORIGIN Old English *earn* 'eagle,' of Germanic origin; related to Dutch *arend.*

Ernst /ərnst/, Max (1891–1976), German artist. A leader of the Dada movement, he developed the techniques of collage, photomontage, and frottage.

e·rode /i'rōd/ ▶ **v.** [with obj.] (of wind, water, or other natural agents) gradually wear away (soil, rock, or land): *the cliffs have been eroded by the sea.* ■ [no obj.] (of soil, rock, or land) be gradually worn away by such natural agents. ■ gradually destroy or be gradually destroyed: [with obj.] *this humiliation has eroded what confidence Jean has* | [no obj.] *profit margins are eroding.* ■ Medicine (of a disease) gradually destroy (bodily tissue).
– DERIVATIVES **e·rod·i·ble** /i'rōdəbəl/ **adj.**
– ORIGIN early 17th cent.: from French *éroder* or Latin *erodere*, from *e-* (variant of *ex-*) 'out, away' + *rodere* 'gnaw.'

e·rog·e·nous /i'räjənəs/ ▶ **adj.** (of a part of the body) sensitive to sexual stimulation: *erogenous zones.*
– ORIGIN late 19th cent.: from **EROS** + **-GENOUS**.

E·ros /'eräs, 'i(ə)räs/ **1** Greek Mythology the god of love, son of Aphrodite. Roman equivalent **CUPID**. ■ sexual love or desire. ■ (in Freudian theory) the life instinct. Often contrasted with **THANATOS**. ■ (in Jungian psychology) the principle of personal relatedness in human activities, associated with the anima. Often contrasted with **LOGOS**.
2 Astronomy asteroid 433, discovered in 1898, which comes at times nearer to the earth than any celestial body except the moon.
– ORIGIN Latin, from Greek, literally 'sexual love.'

e·ro·sion /i'rōZHən/ ▶ **n.** the process of eroding or being eroded by wind, water, or other natural agents: *the problem of soil erosion.* ■ the gradual destruction or diminution of something: *the erosion of support for the party.* ■ Medicine the gradual destruction of tissue or tooth enamel by physical or chemical action. ■ Medicine a place where surface tissue has been gradually destroyed: *patients with gastric erosions.*
– DERIVATIVES **e·ro·sion·al adj.**, **e·ro·sive** /i'rōsiv/ **adj.**
– ORIGIN mid 16th cent.: via French from Latin *erosio(n-)*, from *erodere* 'wear or gnaw away' (see **ERODE**).

e·rot·ic /i'rätik/ ▶ **adj.** of, relating to, or tending to arouse sexual desire or excitement.
– DERIVATIVES **e·rot·i·cal·ly** /-ik(ə)lē/ **adv.**
– ORIGIN mid 17th cent.: from French *érotique*, from Greek *erōtikos*, from *erōs*, *erōt-* 'sexual love.'

e·rot·i·ca /i'rätikə/ ▶ **n.** literature or art intended to arouse sexual desire.
– ORIGIN mid 19th cent.: from Greek *erōtika*, neuter plural of *erōtikos* (see **EROTIC**).

e·rot·i·cism /i'räti,sizəm/ ▶ **n.** the quality or character of being erotic: *a disturbing blend of violence and eroticism.* ■ sexual desire or excitement.

e·rot·i·cize /i'rätə,sīz/ ▶ **v.** [with obj.] give (something or someone) erotic qualities: *certain symbols and body shapes are eroticized.*
– DERIVATIVES **e·rot·i·ci·za·tion** /i,rätəsə'zāSHən/ **n.**

er·o·tism /'erə,tizəm/ ▶ **n.** sexual desire or excitement; eroticism.
– ORIGIN mid 19th cent.: from Greek *erōs*, *erōt-* 'sexual love' + **-ISM**.

eroto- ▶ **comb. form** relating to eroticism: *erotomania.*
– ORIGIN from Greek *erōs*, *erōt-* 'sexual love.'

e·ro·to·gen·ic /i,rätə'jenik, -rōtə-/ (also **erotogenous** /erə'täjənəs/) ▶ **adj.** another term for **EROGENOUS**.

er·o·tol·o·gy /,erə'täləjē/ ▶ **n.** the study of sexual love and behavior.

e·ro·to·ma·ni·a /i,rätə'mānēə, -,rōtə-/ ▶ **n.** Psychiatry excessive sexual desire. ■ a delusion in which a person (typically a woman) believes that another person (typically of higher social status) is in love with them. Also called **DE CLERAMBAULT'S SYNDROME**.
– DERIVATIVES **e·ro·to·ma·ni·ac** /-'mānē,ak/ **n.**

err /ər, er/ ▶ **v.** [no obj.] formal be mistaken or incorrect; make a mistake: *the judge had erred in ruling that the evidence was inadmissible.* ■ (often as adj. **erring**) sin; do wrong: *the erring brother who had wrecked his life.*
– PHRASES **err on the right side** act so that the least harmful of possible mistakes or errors in is the most likely to occur. **err on the side of** display more rather than less of (a specified quality) in one's actions: *it is better to err on the side of caution.* **to err is human, to forgive divine** proverb it is human nature to make mistakes oneself while finding it hard to forgive others.
– ORIGIN Middle English (in the sense 'wander, go astray'): from Old French *errer*, from Latin *errare* 'to stray.'

er·rand /'erənd/ ▶ **n.** a short journey undertaken in order to deliver or collect something, often on someone else's behalf: *she asked Tim to* ***run an errand*** *for her.* ■ archaic the purpose or object of such a journey: *she knew that if she stated her errand, she would not be able to see him.*
– PHRASES **errand of mercy** a mission carried out to help someone in difficulty.
– ORIGIN Old English *ǣrende* 'message, mission,' of Germanic origin; related to Old High German *ārunti*, and obscurely to Swedish *ärende* and Danish *ærinde.*

er·rand boy ▶ **n.** dated a boy employed in a shop or office to make deliveries and run other errands. ■ informal a man who is in the lowest rank of an organization: *Louis was Harry's errand boy, a gofer.*

er·rant /'erənt/ ▶ **adj. 1** [attrib.] erring or straying from the proper course or standards: *he could never forgive his daughter's errant ways.* ■ Zoology (of a polychaete worm) of a predatory kind that moves about actively and is not confined to a tube or burrow.
2 [often postpositive] archaic or literary traveling in search of adventure: *that same lady errant.* See also **KNIGHT ERRANT**.
– DERIVATIVES **er·ran·cy** /'erənsē/ **n.** (sense 1), **er·rant·ry** /-trē/ **n.** (sense 2).
– ORIGIN Middle English (sense 2): sense 1 from Latin *errant-* 'erring,' from the verb *errare*; sense 2 from Old French *errant* 'traveling,' present participle of *errer*, from late Latin *iterare* 'go on a journey,' from *iter* 'journey.' Compare with **ARRANT**.

er·rat·ic /i'ratik/ ▶ **adj.** not even or regular in pattern or movement; unpredictable: *her breathing was erratic.*
▶ **n.** (also **erratic block** or **boulder**) Geology a rock or boulder that differs from the surrounding rock and is believed to have been brought from a distance by glacial action.
– DERIVATIVES **er·rat·i·cal·ly** /-(ə)lē/ **adv.**, **er·rat·i·cism** /i'rati,sizəm/ **n.**
– ORIGIN late Middle English: from Old French *erratique*, from Latin *erraticus*, from *errare* 'to stray, err.'

er·ra·tum /i'rätəm, -'rā-, -'rat-/ ▶ **n.** (pl. **errata** /-tə/) an error in printing or writing. ■ (**errata**) a list of corrected errors appended to a book or published in a subsequent issue of a journal.
– ORIGIN mid 16th cent.: from Latin, 'error,' neuter past participle of *errare* 'err.'

Er Rif /ər rif/ another name for **RIF MOUNTAINS**.

er·ro·ne·ous /i'rōnēəs/ ▶ **adj.** wrong; incorrect: *employers sometimes make erroneous assumptions.*
– DERIVATIVES **er·ro·ne·ous·ly adv.**, **er·ro·ne·ous·ness n.**
– ORIGIN late Middle English: from Latin *erroneus* (from *erro(n-)* 'vagabond,' from *errare* 'to stray, err') + **-OUS**.

er·ror /'erər/ ▶ **n.** a mistake: *spelling errors* | *an error of judgment.* ■ the state or condition of being wrong in conduct or judgment: *the money had been paid*

in error | *the crash was caused by human error.* ■ Baseball a misplay by a fielder that allows a batter to reach base or a runner to advance. ■ technical a measure of the estimated difference between the observed or calculated value of a quantity and its true value. ■ Law a mistake of fact or of law in a court's opinion, judgment or order.
– PHRASES **see the error of one's ways** realize or acknowledge one's wrongdoing.
– DERIVATIVES **er·ror·less adj.**
– ORIGIN Middle English: via Old French from Latin *error*, from *errare* 'to stray, err.'

er·ror bar ▶ **n.** Mathematics a line through a point on a graph, parallel to one of the axes, which represents the uncertainty or error of the corresponding coordinate of the point.

er·ror cor·rec·tion ▶ **n.** Computing the automatic correction of errors that arise from the incorrect transmission of digital data.

er·ror mes·sage ▶ **n.** Computing a message displayed on a monitor screen or printout, indicating that an incorrect instruction has been given, or that there is an error resulting from faulty software or hardware.

er·satz /'er,säts, -,zäts, er'zäts/ ▶ **adj.** (of a product) made or used as a substitute, typically an inferior one, for something else: *ersatz coffee.* ■ not real or genuine: *ersatz emotion.*
– ORIGIN late 19th cent.: from German, literally 'replacement.'

Erse /ərs/ ▶ **n.** dated the Scottish or Irish Gaelic language.
– ORIGIN early Scots form of **IRISH**.

erst /ərst/ ▶ **adv.** archaic long ago; formerly: *the friends whom erst you knew.*
– ORIGIN Old English *ǣrest*, superlative of *ǣr* (see **ERE**).

erst·while /'ərst,(h)wīl/ ▶ **adj.** [attrib.] former: *his erstwhile rivals.*
▶ **adv.** archaic formerly: *Mary Anderson, erstwhile the queen of America's stage.*

e·ru·cic ac·id /i'rōōsik/ ▶ **n.** Chemistry a solid compound present in mustard and rape seeds. ● An unsaturated fatty acid: chem. formula: $C_{21}H_{41}COOH$.
– ORIGIN mid 19th cent.: *erucic* from Latin *eruca* 'rocket' (denoting the plant) + **-IC**.

e·ruct /i'rəkt/ ▶ **v.** [no obj.] technical emit stomach gas noisily through the mouth; belch.

e·ruc·ta·tion /i,rək'tāsHən/ ▶ **n.** formal a belch.
– ORIGIN late Middle English: from Latin *eructatio(n-)*, from the verb *eructare*, from *e-* (variant of *ex-*) 'out' + *ructare* 'belch.'

er·u·dite /'er(y)ə,dīt/ ▶ **adj.** having or showing great knowledge or learning.
– DERIVATIVES **er·u·dite·ly adv.**
– ORIGIN late Middle English: from Latin *eruditus*, past participle of *erudire* 'instruct, train' (based on *rudis* 'rude, untrained').

er·u·di·tion /'er(y)ōō,disHən/ ▶ **n.** the quality of having or showing great knowledge or learning; scholarship: *he writes with great erudition.*

e·rum·pent /i'rəmpənt/ ▶ **adj.** Biology bursting forth or through a surface: *perithecia separately or collectively erumpent* | figurative *a spectacle of erumpent patriotism.*

e·rupt /i'rəpt/ ▶ **v.** [no obj.] (of a volcano) become active and eject lava, ash, and gases: *Mount Pinatubo began erupting in June.* ■ be ejected from an active volcano: *hot lava erupted from the crust.* ■ (of an object) explode with fire and noise resembling an active volcano: *smoke bombs erupted everywhere.* ■ break out or burst forth suddenly and dramatically: *fierce fighting erupted between the army and guerrillas* | *cheers erupted from the crowd.* ■ give vent to anger, enthusiasm, amusement, or other feelings in a sudden and noisy way: *the soldiers erupted in fits of laughter.* ■ (of a pimple, rash, or other prominent mark) suddenly appear on the skin. ■ (of the skin) suddenly develop such a pimple, rash, or mark. ■ (of a tooth) break through the gums during normal development.
– ORIGIN mid 17th cent.: from Latin *erupt-* 'broken out,' from the verb *erumpere*, from *e-* (variant of *ex-*) 'out' + *rumpere* 'burst out, break.'

e·rup·tion /i'rəpsHən/ ▶ **n.** an act or instance of erupting: *the eruption of Vesuvius* | *magma is stored in crustal reservoirs before eruption.* ■ a sudden outbreak of something, typically something unwelcome or noisy: *a sudden eruption of street violence.* ■ a spot, rash, or other prominent and reddish mark appearing suddenly on the skin.
– ORIGIN late Middle English: from Old French, or from Latin *eruptio(n-)*, from the verb *erumpere* (see **ERUPT**).

e·rup·tive /i'rəptiv/ ▶ **adj.** of, relating to, or formed by volcanic activity: *a history of the eruptive activity in an area.* ■ producing or characterized by eruptions: *an acute eruptive disease.*

er·uv /'erōōv/ ▶ **n.** (pl. usu. **eruvim** /,erōō'vēm/) Judaism an urban area enclosed by a wire boundary that symbolically extends the private domain of Jewish households into public areas, permitting activities within it that are normally forbidden in public on the Sabbath.
– ORIGIN from Hebrew *'ērūb*, from a base meaning 'mixture.'

Er·ving /'ərviNG/, Julius Winfield (1950–), US basketball player; known as **Dr. J.** He played for the Philadelphia 76ers 1977–87. Basketball Hall of Fame (1993).

-ery (also **-ry**) ▶ **suffix** forming nouns: **1** denoting a class or kind: *confectionery* | *greenery.*
2 denoting an occupation, a state, a condition, or behavior: *archery* | *bravery* | *slavery.* ■ with depreciatory reference: *knavery* | *tomfoolery.*
3 denoting a place set aside for an activity or a grouping of things, animals, etc.: *orangery* | *rookery.*
– ORIGIN from French *-erie*, based on Latin *-arius* and *-ator.*

e·ryn·gi·um /i'rinjēəm/ ▶ **n.** (pl. **eryngiums**) a plant of the genus *Eryngium* in the parsley family, esp. (in gardening) sea holly.
– ORIGIN late 16th cent.: modern Latin, from Latin *eryngion*, from a diminutive of Greek *ērungos* 'sea holly.'

e·ryn·go /ə'riNGgō/ ▶ **n.** (pl. **eryngos** or **eryngoes**) another term for **SEA HOLLY** or **ERYNGIUM**.
– ORIGIN late 16th cent.: from Italian and Spanish *eringio*, from Latin *eryngion* (see **ERYNGIUM**).

er·y·sip·e·las /,erə'sipələs/ ▶ **n.** Medicine an acute, sometimes recurrent disease caused by a bacterial infection. It is characterized by large, raised red patches on the skin, esp. that of the face and legs, with fever and severe general illness. ● This is caused by *Streptococcus pyogenes*, a Gram-positive coccus.
– ORIGIN late Middle English: via Latin from Greek *erusipelas*; perhaps related to *eruthros* 'red' and *pella* 'skin.'

er·y·sip·e·loid /,erə'sipə,loid/ ▶ **n.** Medicine dermatitis of the hands due to bacterial infection, occurring mainly among handlers of meat and fish products. ● This is caused by *Erysipelothrix rhusiopathiae*, a Gram-positive bacterium occurring either as slightly curved rods or as filaments.

er·y·the·ma /,erə'THēmə/ ▶ **n.** Medicine superficial reddening of the skin, usually in patches, as a result of injury or irritation causing dilatation of the blood capillaries.
– DERIVATIVES **er·y·the·mal** /-məl/ **adj.**, **er·y·them·a·tous** /-'THemətəs, -'THēmətəs/ **adj.**
– ORIGIN late 18th cent.: from Greek *eruthēma*, from *eruthainein* 'be red,' from *eruthros* 'red.'

e·ryth·rism /'erə,THrizəm, i'riTH-/ ▶ **n.** Zoology a congenital condition of abnormal redness in an animal's fur, plumage, or skin.
– ORIGIN late 19th cent.: from Greek *eruthros* 'red' + **-ISM**.

e·ryth·ri·tol /ə'riTHrə,tôl, -,täl/ ▶ **n.** Chemistry a sweet substance extracted from certain lichens and algae. It is used medicinally as a vasodilator. ● A tetrahydric alcohol; chem. formula: $C_4H_{10}O_4$.
– ORIGIN late 19th cent.: from *erythrite* (earlier name for *erythritol*) + **-OL**.

erythro- ▶ **comb. form** (used commonly in zoological and medical terms) red: *erythrocyte.*
– ORIGIN from Greek *eruthros* 'red.'

e·ryth·ro·blast /i'riTHrō,blast/ ▶ **n.** Physiology an immature erythrocyte containing a nucleus.
– DERIVATIVES **e·ryth·ro·blas·tic** /i,riTHrō'blastik/ **adj.**

e·ryth·ro·blas·to·sis /i,riTHrōbla'stōsis/ ▶ **n.** Medicine the abnormal presence of erythroblasts in the blood. ■ (also **erythroblastosis fetalis**) another term for **HEMOLYTIC DISEASE OF THE NEWBORN**.

e·ryth·ro·cyte /i'riTHrə,sīt/ ▶ **n.** a red blood cell that (in humans) is typically a biconcave disc without a nucleus. Erythrocytes contain the pigment hemoglobin, which imparts the red color to blood, and transport oxygen and carbon dioxide to and from the tissues.
– DERIVATIVES **e·ryth·ro·cyt·ic** /i,riTHrə'sitik/ **adj.**

e·ryth·ro·gen·ic /i,riTHrə'jenik/ ▶ **adj.** Medicine (of a bacterial toxin) causing inflammation and reddening of the skin.

er·y·throid /i'riTH,roid/ ▶ **adj.** Physiology of or relating to erythrocytes.

e·ryth·ro·leu·ke·mi·a /i,riTHrōlōō'kēmēə/ ▶ **n.** Medicine a rare acute form of leukemia in which there is proliferation of immature red and white blood cells.

e·ryth·ro·my·cin /i,riTHrə'mīsin/ ▶ **n.** Medicine an antibiotic used in the treatment of infections caused by Gram-positive bacteria. It is similar in its effects to penicillin. ● This is obtained from the streptomycete bacterium *Streptomyces erythreus.*
– ORIGIN 1950s: from elements of the modern Latin taxonomic name (see above) + **-IN**[1].

er·y·thro·ni·um /,eri'THrōnēəm/ ▶ **n.** (pl. **erythroniums** or **erythronia** /-nēə/) a plant of a genus that includes dogtooth violet. ● Genus *Erythronium*, family Liliaceae.
– ORIGIN modern Latin, from Greek (*saturion*) *eruthronion* 'red-flowered (orchid).'

e·ryth·ro·poi·e·sis /i,riTHrōpoi'ēsis/ ▶ **n.** Physiology the production of red blood cells.
– DERIVATIVES **e·ryth·ro·poi·et·ic** /-'etik/ **adj.**

e·ryth·ro·poi·e·tin /i,riTHrō'poi-itn/ ▶ **n.** Biochemistry a hormone secreted by the kidneys that increases the rate of production of red blood cells in response to falling levels of oxygen in the tissues.

Erz·ge·bir·ge /'ertsgə,birgə/ a mountain range on the border between Germany and the Czech Republic. Also called the **ORE MOUNTAINS**.

Er·zu·rum /,erzōōr'ōōm/ a city in northeastern Turkey, capital of a mountainous province of the same name; pop. 338,100 (est. 2007).

Es ▶ **symbol** the chemical element einsteinium.

-es[1] ▶ **suffix 1** forming plurals of nouns ending in sibilant sounds: *boxes* | *kisses.*
2 forming plurals of certain nouns ending in *-o*: *potatoes* | *heroes.*
– ORIGIN variant of **-S**[1].

-es[2] ▶ **suffix** forming the third person singular of the present tense: **1** in verbs ending in sibilant sounds: *pushes.*
2 in verbs ending in *-o* (but not *-oo*): *goes.*
– ORIGIN variant of **-S**[2].

ESA ▶ **abbr.** European Space Agency.

E·sa·ki /e'säkē/, Leo (1925–), Japanese physicist. He investigated and pioneered the development of quantum-mechanical tunneling of electrons in semiconductor devices. He designed the tunnel diode. He shared the 1973 Nobel Prize for Physics with Ivar Giaever (1929–) and Brian D. Josephson (1940–). See **TUNNEL DIODE**.

E·sau /'ēsô/ (in the Bible) the elder of the twin sons of Isaac and Rebecca, who sold his birthright to his brother Jacob and was tricked out of his father's blessing by his brother (Gen. 25, 27).

es·ca·be·che /,eskə'becHā/ ▶ **n.** a Spanish dish consisting of fried fish that is marinated and served cold.
– ORIGIN Spanish.

es·ca·drille /'eskə,dril, ,eskə'dril/ ▶ **n.** a French squadron of aircraft.
– ORIGIN early 20th cent.: French, literally 'flotilla, flight.'

es·ca·lade /,eskə'lād, 'eskə,lād/ ▶ **n.** historical the scaling of fortified walls using ladders, as a form of military attack.
– ORIGIN late 16th cent.: from French, or from Spanish *escalada, escalado*, from medieval Latin *scalare* 'to scale, climb,' from Latin *scala* 'ladder.'

es·ca·late /'eskə,lāt/ ▶ **v.** [no obj.] increase rapidly: *the price of tickets escalated* | (as adj. **escalating**) *the escalating cost of health care.* ■ become or cause to become more intense or serious: [no obj.] *the disturbance escalated into a full-scale riot* | [with obj.] *we do not want to escalate the war.*
– ORIGIN 1920s (in the sense 'travel on an escalator'): back-formation from **ESCALATOR**.

es·ca·la·tion /,eskə'lāsHən/ ▶ **n.** a rapid increase; a rise: *cost escalations.* ■ an increase in the intensity or seriousness of something; an intensification: *an escalation of violence.*

es·ca·la·tor /'eskə,lātər/ ▶ **n.** a moving staircase consisting of an endlessly circulating belt of steps driven by a motor, conveying people between the floors of a public building.
– ORIGIN early 20th cent. (originally as a trade name): from *escalade* 'climb a wall by ladder' (from the noun **ESCALADE**), on the pattern of *elevator.*

es·ca·la·tor clause ▶ **n.** a clause in a contract that allows for an increase or a decrease in wages or prices under certain conditions.

e

es·cal·lop /iˈskäləp, iˈskal-/ ▶ **n. 1** variant spelling of **ESCALOPE.**
2 another term for **SCALLOP** (sense 2 of the noun).
3 Heraldry a scallop shell as a charge.
▶ **v.** (**escallops, escalloping, escalloped**) another term for **SCALLOP** (sense 3 of the noun).
– ORIGIN late 15th cent. (sense 2 of the noun): from Old French *escalope* 'shell.' Compare with **ESCALOPE** and **SCALLOP.**

es·ca·lope /ˌeskəˈlōp, iˈskäləp, -ˈskal-/ ▶ **n.** a thin slice of meat without any bone, typically a special cut of veal from the leg that is coated, fried, and served in a sauce. Also called **SCALLOP.**
– ORIGIN French; compare with **ESCALLOP** and **SCALLOP.**

es·ca·pade /ˈeskəˌpād/ ▶ **n.** an act or incident involving excitement, daring, or adventure.
– ORIGIN mid 17th cent. (in the sense 'an escape'): from French, from Provençal or Spanish, from *escapar* 'to escape,' based on medieval Latin *ex-* 'out of' + *cappa* 'cloak.' Compare with **ESCAPE.**

es·cape /iˈskāp/ ▶ **v. 1** [no obj.] break free from confinement or control: *two burglars have just escaped from prison* | (as adj. **escaped**) *escaped convicts.* ■ [with obj.] elude or get free from (someone): *he drove along I-84 to escape the police.* ■ succeed in avoiding or eluding something dangerous, unpleasant, or undesirable: *the driver escaped with a broken knee* | [with obj.] *a baby boy narrowly escaped death.* ■ (of a gas, liquid, or heat) leak from a container. ■ [with obj.] (of words or sounds) issue involuntarily or inadvertently from (someone or their lips): *a sob escaped her lips.* [with obj.] fail to be noticed or remembered by (someone): *the name escaped him* | *it may have escaped your notice, but this is not a hotel.*
3 [with obj.] Computing interrupt (an operation) by means of the escape key. ■ cause (a subsequent character or characters) to be interpreted differently.
▶ **n.** an act of breaking free from confinement or control: *the story of his escape from a POW camp* | *he could think of no way of escape, short of rudeness.* ■ an act of successfully avoiding something dangerous, unpleasant, or unwelcome: *the couple had a narrow escape from serious injury.* ■ a means of escaping from somewhere: [as modifier] *he had planned his escape route.* ■ a form of temporary distraction from reality or routine: *romantic novels should present an escape from the dreary realities of life.* ■ a leakage of gas, liquid, or heat from a container. ■ a garden plant or pet animal that has gone wild and (esp. in plants) become naturalized. ■ (also **escape key**) Computing a key on a computer keyboard that either interrupts the current operation or causes subsequent characters to be interpreted differently.
– DERIVATIVES **es·cap·a·ble adj., es·cap·er n.**
– ORIGIN Middle English: from Old French *eschaper*, based on medieval Latin *ex-* 'out' + *cappa* 'cloak.' Compare with **ESCAPADE.**

es·cape clause ▶ **n.** a clause in a contract that specifies the conditions under which one party can be freed from an obligation.

es·cap·ee /iˌskāˈpē, eskāˈpē/ ▶ **n.** a person who has escaped from somewhere, esp. prison.

es·cape hatch ▶ **n.** a hatch for use as an emergency exit, esp. from a submarine, ship, or aircraft.

es·cape mech·an·ism ▶ **n.** Psychology a mental process such as daydreaming that enables a person to avoid acknowledging unpleasant or threatening aspects of reality.

es·cape·ment /iˈskāpmənt/ ▶ **n.** a mechanism in a clock or watch that alternately checks and releases the train by a fixed amount and transmits a periodic impulse from the spring or weight to the balance wheel or pendulum. ■ a mechanism in a typewriter that shifts the carriage a small fixed amount to the left after a key is pressed and released. ■ the part of the mechanism in a piano that enables the hammer to fall back as soon as it has struck the string.
– ORIGIN late 18th cent.: from French *échappement*, from *échapper* 'to escape.'

es·cape ve·loc·i·ty ▶ **n.** the lowest velocity that a body must have in order to escape the gravitational attraction of a particular planet or other object.

es·cape wheel ▶ **n.** a toothed wheel in the escapement of a watch or clock.

es·cap·ism /iˈskāpˌizəm/ ▶ **n.** the tendency to seek distraction and relief from unpleasant realities, esp. by seeking entertainment or engaging in fantasy.
– DERIVATIVES **es·cap·ist n. & adj.**

es·cap·ol·o·gist /iˌskāˈpäləjist, ˌeskā-/ ▶ **n.** an entertainer specializing in escaping from the confinement of such things as ropes, handcuffs, and chains.
– DERIVATIVES **es·cap·ol·o·gy** /-ˈpäləjē/ **n.**

es·car·got /ˌeskärˈgō/ ▶ **n.** a snail, esp. as an item on a menu.
– ORIGIN French, from Old French *escargol*, from Provençal *escaragol.*

es·ca·role /ˈeskəˌrōl/ ▶ **n.** an endive of a variety with broad undivided leaves and a slightly bitter flavor, used in salads.
– ORIGIN early 20th cent.: from French, from Italian *scar(i)ola*, based on Latin *esca* 'food.'

es·carp·ment /iˈskärpmənt/ ▶ **n.** a long, steep slope, esp. one at the edge of a plateau or separating areas of land at different heights.
– ORIGIN early 19th cent.: from French *escarpement*, *escarpe* 'scarp,' from Italian *scarpa* 'slope.' Compare with **SCARP.**

Es·caut /esˈkō/ French name for **SCHELDT.**

-esce ▶ **suffix** forming verbs, often denoting the initiation of action: *coalesce* | *effervesce.*
– ORIGIN from or suggested by Latin verbs ending in *-escere.*

-escence ▶ **suffix** forming nouns corresponding to adjectives ending in *-escent* (such as *fluorescence* corresponding to *fluorescent*).
– ORIGIN see **-ESCENT.**

-escent ▶ **suffix** forming adjectives denoting a developing state or action: *coalescent* | *fluorescent.*
– ORIGIN from French, or from Latin *-escent-* (present participial stem of verbs ending in *-escere*).

es·char /ˈesˌkär/ ▶ **n.** Medicine a dry, dark scab or falling away of dead skin, typically caused by a burn, or by the bite of a mite, or as a result of anthrax infection.
– ORIGIN late Middle English: from French *eschare* or late Latin *eschara* 'scar or scab,' from Greek (see also **SCAR**).

es·cha·tol·o·gy /ˌeskəˈtäləjē/ ▶ **n.** the part of theology concerned with death, judgment, and the final destiny of the soul and of humankind.
– DERIVATIVES **es·cha·to·log·i·cal** /eˌskatlˈäjikəl, ˌeskatl-/ **adj., es·cha·tol·o·gist** /-jist/ **n.**
– ORIGIN mid 19th cent.: from Greek *eskhatos* 'last' + **-LOGY.**

es·cha·ton /ˈeskəˌtän/ ▶ **n.** (**the eschaton**) Theology the final event in the divine plan; the end of the world.
– ORIGIN 1930s: from Greek *eskhaton*, neuter of *eskhatos* 'last.'

es·cheat /esˈCHēt/ chiefly historical ▶ **n.** the reversion of property to the state, or (in feudal law) to a lord, on the owner's dying without legal heirs. ■ an item of property affected by this.
▶ **v.** [no obj.] (of land) revert to a lord or the state by escheat. ■ [with obj.] (usu. as adj. **escheated**) hand over (land) as an escheat.
– ORIGIN Middle English: from Old French *eschete*, based on Latin *excidere* 'fall away,' from *ex-* 'out of, from' + *cadere* 'to fall.'

Esch·er /ˈesHər/, M. C. (1898–1972), Dutch graphic artist; full name *Maurits Corneille Escher.* His prints are characterized by their sophisticated use of visual illusion.

es·chew /esˈCHōō/ ▶ **v.** [with obj.] deliberately avoid using; abstain from: *he appealed to the crowd to eschew violence.*
– DERIVATIVES **es·chew·al n.**
– ORIGIN late Middle English: from Old French *eschiver*, ultimately of Germanic origin and related to German *scheuen* 'shun,' also to **SHY**[1].

Es·cof·fier /ˌeskäfˈyā/, Georges-Auguste (1846–1935), French chef. He gained an international reputation while working in London at the Savoy Hotel 1890–99 and later at the Carlton 1899–1919.

es·co·lar /ˌeskəˈlär/ ▶ **n.** a large, elongated predatory fish occurring in tropical and temperate oceans throughout the world. Also called **SNAKE MACKEREL.** ● Family Gempylidae: several genera and species.
– ORIGIN mid 19th cent.: from Spanish, literally 'scholar,' so named because the ringed markings around the eyes resemble spectacles.

Es·con·di·do /ˌeskənˈdēdō/ a commercial city in southwestern California, north of San Diego; pop. 137,103 (est. 2008).

Es·co·ri·al /eˈskôrēəl, ˌeskôrˈyäl/ a monastery and palace in central Spain, near Madrid, built in the late 16th century by Philip II.

es·cort ▶ **n.** /ˈesˌkôrt/ a person, vehicle, ship, or aircraft, or a group of these, accompanying another for protection, security, or as a mark of rank: *a police escort* | *he was driven away under armed escort.* ■ a man who accompanies a woman to a particular social event. ■ a person, typically a woman, who may be hired to accompany someone socially: [as modifier] *an escort agency.*
▶ **v.** /iˈskôrt/ [with obj.] accompany (someone or something) somewhere, esp. for protection or security, or as a mark of rank: *Shiona escorted Janice to the door* | *the shipment was escorted by armed patrol boats.*
– ORIGIN late 16th cent. (originally denoting a body of armed men escorting travelers): from French *escorte* (noun), *escorter* (verb), from Italian *scorta*, feminine past participle of *scorgere* 'to conduct, guide,' based on Latin *ex-* 'out of' + *corrigere* 'set right' (see **CORRECT**).

es·cri·toire /ˌeskriˈtwär/ ▶ **n.** a small writing desk with drawers and compartments.
– ORIGIN late 16th cent.: from French, from medieval Latin *scriptorium* 'writing room' (see **SCRIPTORIUM**).

es·crow /ˈeskrō/ Law ▶ **n.** a bond, deed, or other document kept in the custody of a third party, taking effect only when a specified condition has been fulfilled. ■ [usu. as modifier] a deposit or fund held in trust or as a security: *an escrow account.* ■ the state of being kept in custody or trust in this way: *the board holds funds in escrow.*
▶ **v.** [with obj.] place in custody or trust in this way.
– ORIGIN late 16th cent.: from Old French *escroe* 'scrap, scroll,' from medieval Latin *scroda*, of Germanic origin; related to **SHRED.**

es·cu·do /iˈskōōdō/ ▶ **n.** (pl. **escudos**) the basic monetary unit of Portugal (until the introduction of the euro) and Cape Verde, equal to 100 centavos.
– ORIGIN Spanish and Portuguese, from Latin *scutum* 'shield.'

es·cu·lent /ˈeskyələnt/ formal ▶ **adj.** fit to be eaten; edible.
▶ **n.** a thing, esp. a vegetable, fit to be eaten.
– ORIGIN early 17th cent.: from Latin *esculentus*, from *esca* 'food,' from *esse* 'eat.'

es·cutch·eon /iˈskəCHən/ ▶ **n. 1** a shield or emblem bearing a coat of arms.
2 (also **escutcheon plate**) a flat piece of metal for protection and often ornamentation, around a keyhole, door handle, or light switch.
– PHRASES **a blot on one's escutcheon** a stain on one's reputation or character. **escutcheon of pretense** a small shield within a coat of arms, bearing another coat or device to which the bearer has a claim, esp. one to which a man's wife is heiress.
– DERIVATIVES **es·cutch·eoned adj.**
– ORIGIN late 15th cent.: from Anglo-Norman French *escuchon*, based on Latin *scutum* 'shield.'

Esd. ▶ **abbr.** Esdras, either in the Apocrypha or the Vulgate (in biblical references).

Es·dras /ˈezdrəs/ **1** either of two books of the Apocrypha. The first is mainly a compilation from Chronicles, Nehemiah, and Ezra; the second is a record of angelic revelation.
2 (in the Vulgate) the books of Ezra and Nehemiah.

ESE ▶ **abbr.** east-southeast.

-ese ▶ **suffix** forming adjectives and nouns: **1** denoting an inhabitant or language of a country or city: *Japanese* | *Viennese.*
2 often derogatory (esp. with reference to language) denoting character or style: *journalese* | *officialese.*
– ORIGIN from Old French *-eis*, based on Latin *-ensis.*

es·em·plas·tic /ˌesemˈplastik/ ▶ **adj.** rare molding into one; unifying.
– DERIVATIVES **es·em·plas·ti·cal·ly** /-(ə)lē/ **adv.**
– ORIGIN early 19th cent.: from Greek *es* 'into' + *hen* (neuter of *heis* 'one') + **PLASTIC**; formed irregularly by Coleridge, probably suggested by German *Ineinsbildung*, in the same sense.

es·er·ine /ˈesəˌrēn, ˈesərin/ ▶ **n.** Chemistry another term for **PHYSOSTIGMINE.**
– ORIGIN mid 19th cent.: from French *ésérine*, from Efik *esere.*

Es·fa·han /ˌesfəˈhän/ variant spelling of **ISFAHAN.**

Esk. ▶ **abbr.** Eskimo.

es·ker /ˈeskər/ ▶ **n.** Geology a long ridge of gravel and other sediment, typically having a winding course, deposited by meltwater from a retreating glacier or ice sheet.
– ORIGIN mid 19th cent.: from Irish *eiscir.*

Es·ki·mo /ˈeskəˌmō/ ▶ **n.** (pl. **same** or **Eskimos**) **1** often (esp. in Canada & Greenland) offensive a member of an indigenous people inhabiting northern Canada, Alaska, Greenland, and eastern Siberia, traditionally living by hunting (esp. of seals) and by fishing.
2 either of the two main languages of this people (Inuit and Yupik), forming a major division of the Eskimo-Aleut family.
▶ **adj.** of or relating to the Eskimos or their languages.
– ORIGIN via French *Esquimaux*, possibly from Spanish *esquimao, esquimal*, from Montagnais *ayas̄kimew* 'person who laces a snowshoe,' probably

applied first to the Micmac and later to the Eskimo (see **husky²**).

> **USAGE** 1 In recent years, **Eskimo** has come to be regarded as offensive because of one of its possible etymologies (Abnaki *askimo* 'eater of raw meat'), but this descriptive name is accurate since Eskimos traditionally derived their vitamins from eating raw meat. This dictionary gives another possible etymology above, but the etymological problem is still unresolved. **2** The peoples inhabiting the regions from northwestern Canada to western Greenland call themselves **Inuit** (see usage at **Inuit**), but in the US, **Eskimo** is the only term that can be properly applied to all of the peoples as a whole, and it is still widely used in anthropological and archaeological contexts. The broader term **Native American** is sometimes used to refer to Eskimo and Aleut peoples. See usage at **Native American**.

Es·ki·mo-Al·eut ▶ **n.** the family of languages comprising Inuit, Yupik, and Aleut.
▶ **adj.** of or relating to this family of languages.

Es·ki·mo cur·lew ▶ **n.** a small New World curlew with a striped head, formerly common in the arctic tundra but now close to extinction. ● *Numenius borealis*, family Scolopacidae.

Es·ki·mo pie ▶ **n.** trademark a bar of chocolate-coated ice cream.

Es·ki·mo roll ▶ **n.** a complete rollover in kayaking, from upright to capsized to upright.

Es·ki·se·hir /ˌeskisʜəˈhi(ə)r/ an industrial and spa city in west central Turkey, the capital of Eskisehir province; pop. 570,900 (est. 2007).

ESL ▶ **abbr.** English as a second language.

ESN ▶ **abbr.** electronic serial number, a unique identifying number programmed into a cellular phone.

ESOL /ˈēˌsäl/ ▶ **abbr.** English for speakers of other languages.

ESOP ▶ **abbr.** employee stock ownership plan; a plan by which a company's capital stock is bought by its employees or workers.

e·soph·a·gi·tis /iˌsäfəˈjītis/ ▶ **n.** Medicine inflammation of the esophagus.

e·soph·a·go·scope /iˈsäfəgəˌskōp/ ▶ **n.** an instrument for the inspection or treatment of the esophagus.

e·soph·a·gus /iˈsäfəgəs/ (Brit. **oesophagus**) ▶ **n.** (pl. **esophagi** /-ˌgī, -ˌjī/ or **esophaguses**) the part of the alimentary canal that connects the throat to the stomach; the gullet. In humans and other vertebrates it is a muscular tube lined with mucous membrane.
– DERIVATIVES **e·soph·a·ge·al** /iˌsäfəˈjēəl/ **adj.**
– ORIGIN late Middle English: modern Latin, from Greek *oisophagos*.

es·o·ter·ic /ˌesəˈterik/ ▶ **adj.** intended for or likely to be understood by only a small number of people with a specialized knowledge or interest: *esoteric philosophical debates*.
– DERIVATIVES **es·o·ter·i·cal·ly** /-(ə)lē/ **adv.**, **es·o·ter·i·cism** /-ˈterəˌsizəm/ **n.**, **es·o·ter·i·cist** /-ˈterəsist/ **n.**
– ORIGIN mid 17th cent.: from Greek *esōterikos*, from *esōterō*, comparative of *esō* 'within,' from *es, eis* 'into.' Compare with **exoteric**.

es·o·ter·i·ca /ˌesəˈterikə/ ▶ **n.** esoteric or highly specialized subjects or publications.
– ORIGIN early 20th cent.: from Greek *esōterika*, neuter plural of *esōterikos* 'esoteric.'

ESP ▶ **abbr.** ■ electrostatic precipitator. ■ extrasensory perception.

esp. ▶ **abbr.** especially.

es·pa·drille /ˈespəˌdril/ ▶ **n.** a light canvas shoe with a plaited fiber sole.
– ORIGIN late 19th cent.: from French, from Provençal *espardi(l)hos*, from *espart* 'esparto,' from Latin *spartum* (see **esparto**).

espadrille

es·pal·ier /iˈspalyər, -yā/ ▶ **n.** a fruit tree or ornamental shrub whose branches are trained to grow flat against a wall, supported on a lattice or a framework of stakes. ■ a lattice or framework of this type.
▶ **v.** [with obj.] train (a tree or shrub) in such a way.
– ORIGIN mid 17th cent.: from French, from Italian *spalliera*, from *spalla* 'shoulder,' from Latin *spatula* (see **spatula**), in late Latin 'shoulder blade.'

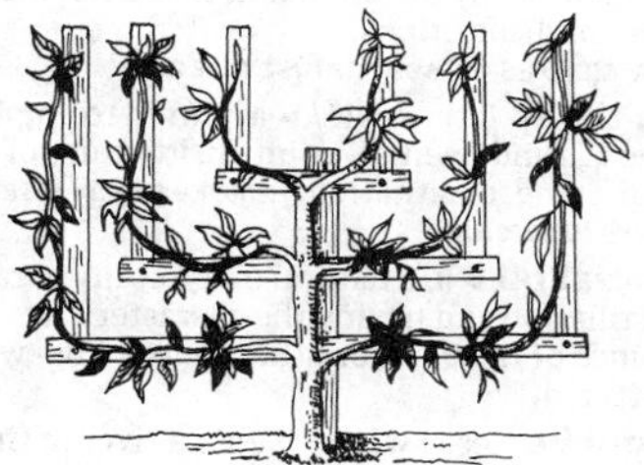
espalier

Es·pa·ña /esˈpänyə/ Spanish name for **Spain**.

es·par·to /iˈspärtō/ (also **esparto grass**) ▶ **n.** (pl. **espartos**) a coarse grass with tough narrow leaves, native to Spain and North Africa. It is used to make ropes, wickerwork, and high-quality paper. ● *Stipa tenacissima*, family Gramineae.
– ORIGIN mid 19th cent.: from Spanish, via Latin from Greek *sparton* 'rope.'

es·pe·cial /iˈspesʜəl/ ▶ **adj.** [attrib.] better or greater than usual; special: *these traditions are of especial interest to feminists*. ■ for or belonging chiefly to one person or thing: *her outburst was for my especial benefit*.
– ORIGIN late Middle English: via Old French from Latin *specialis* 'special,' from *species* (see **species**).

es·pe·cial·ly /iˈspesʜəlē/ ▶ **adv.** **1** used to single out one person, thing, or situation over all others: *he despised them all, especially Sylvester* | *a new song, written especially for Jonathan*.
2 to a great extent; very much: *he didn't especially like dancing* | [as submodifier] *sleep is especially important for growing children*.

> **USAGE** There is some overlap in the uses of **especially** and **specially**. In the broadest terms, both words mean 'particularly,' and the preference for one word over the other is linked with particular conventions of use rather than with any deep difference in meaning. For example, there is little to choose between *written* ***especially*** *for Jonathan* and *written* ***specially*** *for Jonathan*, and neither is more correct than the other. On the other hand, in sentences such as *he despised them all,* ***especially*** *Sylvester*, substitution of **specially** is found in informal uses but should not be used in written English, while in *the car was* ***specially*** *made for the occasion*, substitution of **especially** is somewhat unusual. Overall, **especially** is by far the more common of the two, occurring twenty times as frequently as **specially** in the Oxford English Corpus.

Es·pe·ran·to /ˌespəˈräntō/ ▶ **n.** an artificial language devised in 1887 as an international medium of communication, based on roots from the chief European languages.
– DERIVATIVES **Es·pe·ran·tist** /-tist/ **n.**
– ORIGIN from the name *Dr. Esperanto*, used as a pen name by the inventor of the language, Ludwik L. Zamenhof (1858–1917), Polish physician; the literal sense is 'one who hopes' (based on Latin *sperare* 'to hope').

es·pi·al /iˈspī(ə)l/ ▶ **n.** archaic the action of watching or catching sight of something or someone or the fact of being seen: *he withdrew from his point of espial*.
– ORIGIN late Middle English (in the sense 'spying'): from Old French *espiaille*, from *espier* 'espy.'

es·pi·o·nage /ˈespēəˌnäzʜ, -ˌnäj/ ▶ **n.** the practice of spying or of using spies, typically by governments to obtain political and military information.
– ORIGIN late 18th cent.: from French *espionnage*, from *espionner* 'to spy,' from *espion* 'a spy.'

Es·pi·ri·tu San·to /eˈspiritōō ˈsäntōō/ a volcanic island in northwestern Vanuatu, the largest in the country. Largely agricultural, it was the site of US bases during World War II.

es·pla·nade /ˈespləˌnäd, -ˌnād/ ▶ **n.** a long, open, level area, typically beside the sea, along which people may walk for pleasure. ■ an open, level space separating a fortress from a town.
– ORIGIN late 16th cent. (denoting an area of flat ground on top of a rampart): from French, from Italian *spianata*, from Latin *explanatus* 'flattened, leveled,' from *explanare* (see **explain**).

Es·po·si·to /ˌespəˈzētō/, Phil (1942–), Canadian ice hockey player. He played for the Chicago Blackhawks 1964–67, the Boston Bruins 1967–75, and the New York Rangers 1975–81. Hockey Hall of Fame (1984).

es·pous·al /iˈspouzəl, -səl/ ▶ **n.** **1** [in sing.] an act of adopting or supporting a cause, belief, or way of life: *his espousal of the leftist cause*.
2 archaic a marriage or engagement.
– ORIGIN late Middle English: from Old French *espousaille*, from Latin *sponsalia* 'betrothal,' neuter plural of *sponsalis* (adjective), from *sponsare* 'espouse, betroth.'

es·pouse /iˈspouz/ ▶ **v.** [with obj.] **1** adopt or support (a cause, belief, or way of life): *he turned his back on the modernism he had espoused in his youth*.
2 archaic marry: *Edward had espoused the Lady Grey*. ■ (**be espoused to**) (of a woman) be engaged to (a particular man).
– DERIVATIVES **es·pous·er** **n.**
– ORIGIN late Middle English (in the sense 'take as a spouse'): from Old French *espouser*, from Latin *sponsare*, from *sponsus* 'betrothed,' past participle of *spondere*.

es·pres·si·vo /ˌespreˈsēvō/ ▶ **adv. & adj.** Music (esp. as a direction) with expression of feeling.
– ORIGIN Italian, from Latin *expressus* 'distinctly presented.'

es·pres·so /eˈspresō/ ▶ **n.** (pl. **espressos**) strong black coffee made by forcing steam through ground coffee beans.
– ORIGIN 1940s: from Italian (*caffè*) *espresso*, literally 'pressed out (coffee).'

> **USAGE** The often-occurring variant spelling expresso—and its pronunciation /ikˈspresō/—is incorrect and was probably formed by analogy with express.

es·prit /eˈsprē/ ▶ **n.** the quality of being lively, vivacious, or witty.
– ORIGIN French, from Latin *spiritus* 'spirit.'

es·prit de corps /eˌsprē də ˈkôr/ ▶ **n.** a feeling of pride, fellowship, and common loyalty shared by the members of a particular group.
– ORIGIN late 18th cent.: French, literally 'spirit of the body.'

es·prit de l'es·ca·lier /eˌsprē də ˌleskalˈyā/ ▶ **n.** used to refer to the fact that a witty remark or retort often comes to mind after the opportunity to make it has passed.
– ORIGIN early 20th cent.: French, literally 'wit of the staircase.'

es·py /iˈspī/ ▶ **v.** (**espies, espying, espied**) [with obj.] literary catch sight of: *she espied her daughter rounding the corner*.
– ORIGIN Middle English: from Old French *espier*, ultimately of Germanic origin and related to Dutch *spieden* and German *spähan*. Compare with **spy**.

Esq. ▶ **abbr.** Esquire.

-esque ▶ **suffix** (forming adjectives) in the style of; resembling: *carnivalesque* | *Reaganesque* | *Houdini-esque*.
– ORIGIN from French, via Italian *-esco* from medieval Latin *-iscus*.

es·quire /ˈeskwīr, iˈskwīr/ ▶ **n.** **1** (**Esquire**) (abbr.: **Esq.**) a title appended to a lawyer's surname. ■ Brit. a polite title appended to a man's name when no other title is used, typically in the address of a letter or other documents: *Robert A. Pearson Esquire*.
2 historical a young nobleman who, in training for knighthood, acted as an attendant to a knight. ■ an officer in the service of a king or nobleman. ■ [as title] a landed proprietor or country squire.
– ORIGIN late Middle English: from Old French *esquier*, from Latin *scutarius* 'shield-bearer,' from *scutum* 'shield'; compare with **squire**. Sense 2 was the original denotation, sense 1 being at first a courtesy title given to such a person.

es·qui·va·li·ence /eskwəˈvālēəns/ ▶ **n.** the willful avoidance of one's official responsibilities; the shirking of duties: *after three subordinates attested to his esquivalience, Lieutenant Claiborne was dismissed*. ■ an unwillingness to work, esp. as part of a group effort: *Bovich was chided by teammates for her esquivalience*. ■ lack of interest or motivation: *a teenager's esquivalience is not necessarily symptomatic of depression*.
– DERIVATIVES **es·qui·va·li·ent** **adj.**, **es·qui·va·li·ent·ly** **adv.**
– ORIGIN late 19th cent.: perhaps from French *esquiver* 'dodge, slink away.'

ESR ▶ **abbr.** Physics electron spin resonance.

ess /es/ ▶ **n.** a thing shaped like the letter S.
– ORIGIN mid 16th cent.: the letter *S* represented as a word.

-ess[1] ▶ **suffix** forming nouns denoting female gender: *abbess | adulteress | tigress*.
– ORIGIN from French *-esse*, via late Latin from Greek *-issa*.

> **USAGE** The suffix **-ess** has been used since the Middle Ages to form nouns denoting female persons, using a neutral or a male form as the base (such as **hostess** and **actress** from **host** and **actor**). Despite the apparent equivalence between the male and female pairs of forms, however, they are rarely equivalent in terms of actual use and connotation in modern English (consider the differences in meaning and use between **manager** and **manageress**). In the late 20th century, as the role of women in society changed, some of these feminine forms became problematic and are now regarded as old-fashioned, sexist, and patronizing (e.g., **poetess, authoress, editress**). The 'male' form is increasingly being used as the 'neutral' form, where the gender of the person concerned is simply unspecified.

e

-ess[2] ▶ **suffix** forming abstract nouns from adjectives, such as *largess*.
– ORIGIN Middle English via French *-esse* from Latin *-itia*.

es·say ▶ **n.** /ˈesā/ **1** a short piece of writing on a particular subject.
2 formal an attempt or effort: *a misjudged essay*. ■ a trial design of a postage stamp yet to be accepted.
▶ **v.** /eˈsā/ [with obj.] formal attempt or try: *essay a smile*.
– ORIGIN late 15th cent. (as a verb in the sense 'test the quality of'): alteration of ASSAY, by association with Old French *essayer*, based on late Latin *exagium* 'weighing,' from the base of *exigere* 'ascertain, weigh'; the noun (late 16th cent.) is from Old French *essai* 'trial.'

es·say·ist /ˈesā-ist/ ▶ **n.** a person who writes essays, esp. as a literary genre.

es·say·is·tic /ˌesāˈistik/ ▶ **adj.** characteristic of or used in essays; discursive; informal.

es·se /ˈesē, ˈese/ ▶ **n.** Philosophy essential nature or essence. See also IN ESSE.
– ORIGIN mid 16th cent.: Latin, literally 'to be' (used as a noun).

Es·sen /ˈesən/ an industrial city in the Ruhr valley, in northwestern Germany; pop. 583,200 (est. 2006).

es·sence /ˈesəns/ ▶ **n.** the intrinsic nature or indispensable quality of something, esp. something abstract, that determines its character: *conflict is the essence of drama*. ■ Philosophy a property or group of properties of something without which it would not exist or be what it is. ■ an extract or concentrate obtained from a particular plant or other matter and used for flavoring or scent.
– PHRASES **in essence** basically and without regard for peripheral details; fundamentally: *in detail the class system is complex but in essence it is simple*. **of the essence** critically important: *time will be of the essence*.
– ORIGIN late Middle English: via Old French from Latin *essentia*, from *esse* 'be.'

Es·sene /iˈsēn, ˈesēn/ ▶ **n.** a member of an ancient Jewish ascetic sect of the 2nd century BC–2nd century AD in Palestine, who lived in highly organized groups and held property in common. The Essenes are widely regarded as the authors of the Dead Sea Scrolls.
– ORIGIN from Latin *Esseni* (plural), from Greek *Essēnoi*, perhaps from Aramaic.

es·sen·tial /iˈsenCHəl/ ▶ **adj. 1** absolutely necessary; extremely important: [with infinitive] *it is essential to keep up-to-date records | fiber is an essential ingredient*. ■ [attrib.] fundamental or central to the nature of something or someone: *the essential weakness of the plaintiff's case*. ■ Biochemistry (of an amino acid or fatty acid) required for normal growth but not synthesized in the body and therefore necessary in the diet.
2 Medicine (of a disease) with no known external stimulus or cause; idiopathic: *essential hypertension*.
▶ **n.** (usu. **essentials**) a thing that is absolutely necessary: *we had only the bare essentials in the way of gear*. ■ (**essentials**) the fundamental elements or characteristics of something: *he was quick to grasp the essentials of an opponent's argument*.
– DERIVATIVES **es·sen·ti·al·i·ty** /iˌsenCHēˈalitē/ **n.**, **es·sen·tial·ness n.**
– ORIGIN Middle English (in the sense 'in the highest degree'): from late Latin *essentialis*, from Latin *essentia*.

es·sen·tial·ism /iˈsensHəˌlizəm/ ▶ **n.** Philosophy a belief that things have a set of characteristics that make them what they are, and that the task of science and philosophy is their discovery and expression; the doctrine that essence is prior to existence. Compare with EXISTENTIALISM. ■ the view that all children should be taught on traditional lines the ideas and methods regarded as essential to the prevalent culture. ■ the view that categories of people, such as women and men, or heterosexuals and homosexuals, or members of ethnic groups, have intrinsically different and characteristic natures or dispositions.
– DERIVATIVES **es·sen·tial·ist n. & adj.**

es·sen·tial·ly /iˈsensHəlē/ ▶ **adv.** used to emphasize the basic, fundamental, or intrinsic nature of a person, thing, or situation: [sentence adverb] *essentially, they are amateurs*.

es·sen·tial oil ▶ **n.** a natural oil typically obtained by distillation and having the characteristic fragrance of the plant or other source from which it is extracted.

Es·se·qui·bo /ˌesəˈkwēbō, -ˈkēbō/ a river in Guyana that rises in the Guiana Highlands and flows north for about 600 miles (965 km) to the Atlantic Ocean.

Es·sex /ˈesiks/ **1** a county in eastern England; county town, Chelmsford.
2 a town in northwestern Vermont that includes the village of Essex Junction; pop. 19,649 (est. 2008).

EST ▶ **abbr.** Eastern Standard Time (see EASTERN TIME).

est /est/ ▶ **n.** a system for self-improvement aimed at developing a person's potential through intensive group awareness and training sessions.
– ORIGIN 1970s: acronym from *Erhard Seminars Training*, from the name of Werner *Erhard* (born 1935), the American businessman who devised the technique.

est. ▶ **abbr.** ■ established. ■ estimated.

-est[1] /əst, ist/ ▶ **suffix** forming the superlative of adjectives (such as *shortest, widest*), and of adverbs (such as *soonest*).
– ORIGIN Old English *-ost-, -ust-, -ast-*.

-est[2] /əst, ist/ (also **-st** /st/) ▶ **suffix** archaic forming the second person singular of verbs: *canst | goest*.
– ORIGIN Old English *-est, -ast, -st*.

es·tab·lish /iˈstablisH/ ▶ **v.** [with obj.] **1** set up (an organization, system, or set of rules) on a firm or permanent basis: *the British established a rich trade with Portugal*. ■ initiate or bring about (contact or communication): *the two countries established diplomatic relations*.
2 achieve permanent acceptance or recognition for: *the principle of the supremacy of national parliaments needs to be firmly established | he had established himself as a film star*. ■ introduce (a character, set, or location) into a film or play and allow its identification: *establish the location with a wide shot*.
3 show (something) to be true or certain by determining the facts: [with clause] *the police established that the two passports were forgeries*.
4 Bridge ensure that one's remaining cards in (a suit) will be winners (if not trumped) by playing off the high cards in that suit.
– DERIVATIVES **es·tab·lish·er n.**
– ORIGIN late Middle English (recorded earlier as *stablish*): from Old French *establiss-*, lengthened stem of *establir*, from Latin *stabilire* 'make firm,' from *stabilis* (adjective) 'stable.'

es·tab·lished /iˈstablisHt/ ▶ **adj. 1** having been in existence for a long time and therefore recognized and generally accepted: *the ceremony was an established event in the annual calendar | an established artist*. ■ (of a plant) having taken root; growing well.
2 (of a church or religion) recognized by the government as the national church or religion.
– PHRASES **the Established Church** the Church of England or of Scotland.

es·tab·lish·ment /iˈstablisHmənt/ ▶ **n. 1** the action of establishing something or being established: *the establishment of a scholarship renews that personal interest of donors in students*. ■ archaic a marriage.
2 a business organization, public institution, or household: *hotels or catering establishments*.
3 (usu. **the Establishment**) a group in a society exercising power and influence over matters of policy or taste, and seen as resisting change. ■ [with adj.] an influential group within a specified profession or area of activity: *rumblings of discontent among the medical establishment*.
4 (**the Establishment** or **the Church Establishment**) the ecclesiastical system organized by law. ■ the Church of England or of Scotland.

es·tab·lish·men·tar·i·an /iˌstablisHmənˈterēən/ ▶ **adj.** adhering to, advocating, or relating to the principle of an established church.
▶ **n.** a person adhering to or advocating this.
– DERIVATIVES **es·tab·lish·men·tar·i·an·ism** /-izəm/ **n.**

Es·tab·lish·ment Clause ▶ **n.** Law the clause in the First Amendment of the US Constitution that prohibits the establishment of religion by Congress.

es·ta·mi·net /esˌtaməˈnā/ ▶ **n.** a small cafe in France that sells alcoholic drinks.
– ORIGIN French, from Walloon *staminé* 'cowshed,' from *stamo* 'a pole for tethering a cow,' probably from German *Stamm* 'stem.'

es·tan·cia /eˈstänsēə/ ▶ **n.** a cattle ranch in Latin America or the southwestern US.
– ORIGIN mid 17th cent.: from Spanish, literally 'station,' from medieval Latin *stantia*, based on Latin *stare* 'to stand.'

es·tate /iˈstāt/ ▶ **n. 1** an area or amount of land or property, in particular: ■ an extensive area of land in the country, usually with a large house, owned by one person or organization. ■ all the money and property owned by a particular person, esp. at death: *in his will, he divided his estate between his wife and daughter*. ■ a property where coffee, rubber, grapes, or other crops are cultivated. ■ Brit. a housing or commercial development.
2 (also **estate of the realm**) a class or order regarded as forming part of the body politic, in particular (in Britain), one of the three groups constituting Parliament, now the Lords Spiritual (the heads of the Church), the Lords Temporal (the peerage), and the Commons. They are also known as **the three estates**. ■ dated a particular class or category of people in society: *the spiritual welfare of all estates of men*.
3 archaic or literary a particular state, period, or condition in life: *programs for the improvement of man's estate | the holy estate of matrimony*. ■ grandeur, pomp, or state: *a chamber without a chair of estate*.
– ORIGIN Middle English (in the sense 'state or condition'): from Old French *estat*, from Latin *status* 'state, condition,' from *stare* 'to stand.'

es·tate a·gent ▶ **n.** Brit. a real estate agent.
– DERIVATIVES **es·tate a·gen·cy n.**

es·tate car ▶ **n.** Brit. a station wagon.

es·tate of the realm ▶ **n.** see ESTATE (sense 2).

Es·tates Gen·er·al /iˈstāts/ another term for STATES-GENERAL.

es·tate tax ▶ **n.** a tax levied on the net value of the estate of a deceased person before distribution to the heirs. Also called DEATH TAX.

es·teem /iˈstēm/ ▶ **n.** respect and admiration, typically for a person: *he was held in high esteem by colleagues*.
▶ **v.** [with obj.] (usu. **be esteemed**) respect and admire: *many of these qualities are esteemed by managers* | [as adj., with submodifier] (**esteemed**) *a highly esteemed scholar*. ■ formal consider; deem: [with two objs.] *I should esteem it a favor if you could speak to them*.
– ORIGIN Middle English (as a noun in the sense 'worth, reputation'): from Old French *estime* (noun), *estimer* (verb), from Latin *aestimare* 'to estimate.' The verb was originally in the Latin sense, also 'appraise' (compare with ESTIMATE), used figuratively to mean 'assess the merit of.' Current senses date from the 16th cent.

es·ter /ˈestər/ ▶ **n.** Chemistry an organic compound made by replacing the hydrogen of an acid by an alkyl or other organic group. Many naturally occurring fats and essential oils are esters of fatty acids.
– DERIVATIVES **es·ter·i·fy** /iˈsterəˌfī/ **v.** (**esterifies, esterifying, esterified**).
– ORIGIN mid 19th cent.: from German, probably from a blend of *Essig* 'vinegar' and *Äther* 'ether.'

es·ter·ase /ˈestərās, -rāz/ ▶ **n.** Biochemistry an enzyme that hydrolyzes particular esters into acids and alcohols or phenols.

es·ter·i·fi·ca·tion /esˌterəfiˈkāsHən/ ▶ **n.** Chemistry a reaction of an alcohol with an acid to produce an ester and water.

Esth. ▶ **abbr.** Bible Esther.

Es·ther /ˈestər/ (in the Bible) a woman chosen on account of her beauty by the Persian king Ahasuerus (generally supposed to be Xerxes I) to be his queen. She used her influence with him to save the Israelites in captivity from persecution. ■ a book of the Bible containing an account of these events; a part survives only in Greek and is included in the Apocrypha.

es·thete ▶ **n.** variant spelling of AESTHETE.

es·thet·ic, etc. ▶ **adj.** AESTHETIC, etc.

es·ti·ma·ble /ˈestəməbəl/ ▶ **adj.** worthy of great respect.
– DERIVATIVES **es·ti·ma·bly** /-blē/ **adv.**
– ORIGIN late 15th cent. (in the sense 'able to be estimated or appraised'; earlier in *inestimable*): via Old French from Latin *aestimabilis*, from *aestimare* 'to estimate.'

es·ti·mate ▶ **v.** /ˈestəˌmāt/ [with obj.] roughly calculate or judge the value, number, quantity, or extent of: *the aim is to estimate the effects of macroeconomic policy on the economy* | [with clause] *it is estimated that*

smoking causes 100,000 premature deaths every year | (as adj. **estimated**) *an estimated cost of $140,000,000.* ▶ **n.** /ˈestəmit/ an approximate calculation or judgment of the value, number, quantity, or extent of something: *at a rough estimate, our staff is recycling a quarter of the paper used.* ■ a written statement indicating the likely price that will be charged for specified work or repairs: *compare costs by getting estimates from at least two firms.* ■ a judgment of the worth or character of someone or something: *his high estimate of the poem.*
– DERIVATIVES **es·ti·ma·tive** /ˈestəˌmātiv/ **adj.**
– ORIGIN late Middle English: from Latin *aestimat-* 'determined, appraised,' from the verb *aestimare*. The noun originally meant 'intellectual ability, comprehension' (only in late Middle English), later 'valuing, a valuation' (compare with **ESTIMATION**). The verb originally meant 'to think well or badly of someone or something' (late 15th cent.), later 'regard as being, consider to be' (compare with **ESTEEM**).

es·ti·ma·tion /ˌestəˈmāSHən/ ▶ **n.** a rough calculation of the value, number, quantity, or extent of something: *estimations of protein concentrations.* ■ [usu. in sing.] a judgment of the worth or character of someone or something: *the pop star rose in my estimation.*
– ORIGIN late Middle English (originally in the sense 'comprehension, intuition,' also 'valuing, a valuation'): from Latin *aestimatio(n-)*, from *aestimare* 'determine, appraise' (see **ESTIMATE**).

es·ti·ma·tor /ˈestəˌmātər/ ▶ **n. 1** Statistics a rule, method, or criterion for arriving at an estimate of the value of a parameter. ■ a quantity used or evaluated as such an estimate.
2 a person who estimates the price, value, number, quantity, or extent of something.

es·ti·val /ˈestəvəl, eˈstī-/ (also **aestival**) ▶ **adj.** technical belonging to or appearing in summer.
– ORIGIN late Middle English: from Latin *aestivalis*, from *aestivus*, from *aestus* 'heat.'

es·ti·vate /ˈestəˌvāt/ (also **aestivate**) ▶ **v.** [no obj.] Zoology (of an animal, particularly an insect, fish, or amphibian) spend a hot or dry period in a prolonged state of torpor or dormancy.
– ORIGIN early 17th cent. (in the sense 'pass the summer'): from Latin *aestivat-*, from *aestivare* 'spend the summer,' from *aestus* 'heat.'

es·ti·va·tion /ˌestəˈvāSHən/ (also **aestivation**) ▶ **n.**
1 Zoology prolonged torpor or dormancy of an animal during a hot or dry period.
2 Botany the arrangement of petals and sepals in a flower bud before it opens. Compare with **VERNATION**.

es·toile /eˈstoil/ ▶ **n.** Heraldry a star with (usually six) wavy points or rays.
– ORIGIN late 16th cent.: via Old French from Latin *stella* 'star.'

Es·to·ni·a /eˈstōnēə/ a Baltic country on the southern coast of the Gulf of Finland; pop. 1,299,400 (est. 2009); capital, Tallinn; languages, Estonian (official) and Russian.

> Previously ruled by the Teutonic Knights and then by Sweden, Estonia was ceded to Russia in 1721. It was proclaimed an independent republic in 1918 but was annexed by the Soviet Union in 1940 as a constituent republic, the Estonian SSR. With the breakup of the Soviet Union, Estonia regained its independence in 1991. In 2004 it joined both NATO and the EU.

Es·to·ni·an /eˈstōnēən/ ▶ **adj.** of or relating to Estonia or its people or their language.
▶ **n. 1** a native or inhabitant of Estonia, or a person of Estonian descent.
2 the Finno-Ugric language of Estonia, closely related to Finnish.

es·top /eˈstäp/ ▶ **v.** (**estops, estopping, estopped**) [with obj.] (usu. **be estopped from**) Law bar or preclude by estoppel.
– ORIGIN late Middle English (in the sense 'stop up, dam, plug'): from Old French *estopper* 'stop up, impede,' from late Latin *stuppare*, from Latin *stuppa* 'tow, oakum.' Compare with **STOP** and **STUFF**.

es·top·pel /eˈstäpəl/ ▶ **n.** Law the principle that precludes a person from asserting something contrary to what is implied by a previous action or statement of that person or by a previous pertinent judicial determination.
– ORIGIN mid 16th cent.: from Old French *estoupail* 'bung,' from *estopper* (see **ESTOP**).

es·tra·di·ol /ˌestrəˈdīôl, -ˌäl/ (Brit. **oestradiol**) ▶ **n.** Biochemistry a major estrogen produced in the ovaries.
– ORIGIN 1930s: from **ESTRUS** + **DI-**[1] + **-OL**.

es·trange /iˈstrānj/ ▶ **v.** [with obj.] cause (someone) to be no longer close or affectionate to someone; alienate: *are you deliberately seeking to estrange your readers?*
– ORIGIN late 15th cent.: from Old French *estranger*, from Latin *extraneare* 'treat as a stranger,' from *extraneus* 'not belonging to the family,' used as a noun to mean 'stranger.' Compare with **STRANGE**.

es·tranged /iˈstrānjd/ ▶ **adj.** (of a person) no longer close or affectionate to someone; alienated: *Harriet felt more **estranged from** her daughter than ever* | *her estranged father.* ■ (of a wife or husband) no longer living with their spouse.

es·trange·ment /iˈstrānjmənt/ ▶ **n.** the fact of no longer being on friendly terms or part of a social group: *the growing estrangement of the police from their communities.* ■ the fact of no longer living with one's spouse; separation.

es·treat /iˈstrēt/ Law, chiefly historical ▶ **v.** [with obj.] enforce the forfeit of (a surety for bail or other recognizance).
▶ **n.** a copy of a court record for use in the enforcement of a fine or forfeiture of a recognizance.
– DERIVATIVES **es·treat·ment n.**
– ORIGIN Middle English: from Old French *estraite*, feminine past participle of *estraire*, from Latin *extrahere* 'draw out' (see **EXTRACT**).

es·tri·ol /ˈestrīˌôl, -ˌäl, eˈstrīôl, eˈstrīäl/ (also **oestriol**) ▶ **n.** Biochemistry an estrogen that is one of the metabolic products of estradiol.
– ORIGIN 1930s: from *estrane* (the parent molecule of most estrogens) + **TRI-** + **-OL**.

es·tro·gen /ˈestrəjən/ (Brit. **oestrogen**) ▶ **n.** any of a group of steroid hormones that promote the development and maintenance of female characteristics of the body. Such hormones are also produced artificially for use in oral contraceptives or to treat menopausal and menstrual disorders.
– DERIVATIVES **es·tro·gen·ic** /ˌestrəˈjenik/ **adj.**
– ORIGIN 1920s: from **ESTRUS** + **-GEN**.

es·trone /ˈestrōn/ (Brit. **oestrone**) ▶ **n.** Biochemistry an estrogen similar to but less potent than estradiol.
– ORIGIN 1930s: from *estrane* (parent molecule of most estrogens) + **-ONE**.

es·trous cy·cle /ˈestrəs/ ▶ **n.** the recurring reproductive cycle in many female mammals, including estrus, ovulation, and changes in the uterine lining.

es·trus /ˈestrəs/ (also **estrum** or chiefly Brit. **oestrus**) ▶ **n.** a recurring period of sexual receptivity and fertility in many female mammals; heat: *a mare in estrus.*
– DERIVATIVES **es·trous** /ˈestrəs/ **adj.**
– ORIGIN late 17th cent.: from Greek *oistros* 'gadfly or frenzy.'

es·tu·ar·y /ˈesCHo͞oˌerē/ ▶ **n.** (pl. **estuaries**) the tidal mouth of a large river, where the tide meets the stream.
– DERIVATIVES **es·tu·ar·i·al** /ˌesCHo͞oˈe(ə)rēəl/ **adj.**, **es·tu·a·rine** /ˈesCHo͞oəˌrīn, -əˌrēn/ **adj.**
– ORIGIN mid 16th cent. (denoting a tidal inlet of any size): from Latin *aestuarium* 'tidal part of a shore,' from *aestus* 'tide.'

Es·tu·ar·y Eng·lish ▶ **n.** (in the UK) a type of accent identified as spreading outward from London and containing features of both received pronunciation and London speech.

es·tu·fa /eˈsto͞ofə/ ▶ **n. 1** a heated chamber in which Madeira wine is stored and matured.
2 an underground chamber in which a fire is kept permanently alight, used as a place of assembly by Pueblo Indians.
– ORIGIN mid 19th cent.: from Spanish, probably based on Greek *tuphos* 'steam or smoke.'

esu ▶ **abbr.** electrostatic unit(s).

e·su·ri·ent /iˈso͝orēənt/ ▶ **adj.** archaic hungry or greedy.
– DERIVATIVES **e·su·ri·ent·ly adv.**
– ORIGIN late 17th cent.: from Latin *esurient-* 'being hungry,' from the verb *esurire*, from *esse* 'eat.'

ESV ▶ **abbr.** earth satellite vehicle.

ET ▶ **abbr.** ■ Eastern time. ■ extraterrestrial.

-et[1] ▶ **suffix** forming nouns that were originally diminutives: *baronet* | *hatchet* | *tablet.*
– ORIGIN from Old French *-et, -ete.*

-et[2] (also **-ete**) ▶ **suffix** forming nouns such as *comet*, and often denoting people: *athlete* | *poet.*
– ORIGIN from Greek *-ētēs.*

ETA[1] /ˌētēˈā/ ▶ **abbr.** estimated time of arrival, in particular the time at which an aircraft or ship is expected to arrive at its destination.

ETA[2] /ˈetə/ a Basque separatist movement in Spain, founded in 1959.
– ORIGIN Basque acronym, from *Euzkadi ta Azkatasuna* 'Basque homeland and liberty.'

e·ta /ˈātə, ˈētə/ ▶ **n.** the seventh letter of the Greek alphabet (Η, η), transliterated as 'e' or 'ē.' ■ (**Eta**) [followed by Latin genitive] Astronomy the seventh star in a constellation: *Eta Carinae.*

e·ta·gere /ˌātäˈZHer/ (also **étagère**) ▶ **n.** (pl. **etageres** /ˌātäˈZHer(z)/) a piece of furniture with a number of open shelves for displaying ornaments.
– ORIGIN French *étagère*, from *étage* 'shelf.'

e-tail·er /ˈēˌtālər/ ▶ **n.** trademark a retailer selling goods via electronic transactions on the Internet.
– ORIGIN 1990s: blend of *e-* 'electronic' and *retailer.*

et al. /ˌet ˈal, ˌet ˈäl/ ▶ **abbr.** and others (used esp. in referring to academic books or articles that have more than one author): *the conclusions of Gardner et al.*
– ORIGIN from Latin *et alii.*

> **USAGE** See usage at **ET CETERA**.

e·ta·lon /ˈātlˌän/ ▶ **n.** Physics a device consisting of two reflecting plates for producing interfering light beams.
– ORIGIN early 20th cent.: from French *étalon*, literally 'standard of measurement.'

etc. ▶ **abbr.** et cetera.

et cet·er·a /et ˈsetərə, ˈsetrə/ (also **etcetera**) ▶ **adv.** used at the end of a list to indicate that further, similar items are included: *we're trying to resolve problems of obtaining equipment, drugs, et cetera.* ■ indicating that a list is too tedious or clichéd to give in full: *we've all got to do our duty, pull our weight, et cetera, et cetera.*
– ORIGIN Latin, from *et* 'and' and *cetera* 'the rest' (neuter plural of *ceterus* 'left over').

> **USAGE** Et cetera (a Latin phrase meaning 'and the other things, the rest') is sometimes mispronounced '*ex cetera*,' and its abbreviation, properly etc., is often misspelled 'ect.' The phrase 'and et cetera' is redundant, for *et* means 'and' in Latin. This abbreviation should be used for things, not for people. **Et al.** (an abbreviation of *et alii*, 'and other people, and others') is properly used for others (people) too numerous to mention, as in a list of multiple authors: *Bancroft, Fordwick, et al.* In general, both terms (and their abbreviations) are common enough that it is not necessary to italicize or underline them.

et·cet·er·as /etˈsetərəz, etˈsetrəz/ ▶ **plural n.** unspecified or typical extra items: *she began to pack her compact, comb, and other etceteras.*

etch /eCH/ ▶ **v.** [with obj.] **1** engrave (metal, glass, or stone) by coating it with a protective layer, drawing on it with a needle, and then covering it with acid to attack the parts the needle has exposed, esp. in order to produce prints from it: (as adj. **etched**) *etched glass windows.* ■ use such a process to produce (a print or design). ■ (of an acid or other solvent) corrode or eat away the surface of (something). ■ selectively dissolve the surface of (a semiconductor or printed circuit) with a solvent, laser, or stream of electrons.
2 cut or carve (a text or design) on a surface: *her initials were **etched on** the table* | figurative *his name is etched in baseball history.* ■ mark (a surface) with a carved text or design: *a Pictish stone **etched with** mysterious designs* | figurative *her face was **etched with** tiredness.* ■ cause to stand out or be clearly defined or visible: *Jo watched the outline of the town **etched against** the sky* | (as adj. **etched**) *her finely etched profile.* ■ (**be etched**) (of an experience, image, etc.) be permanently fixed in someone's memory: *the events remain etched in the minds of all who witnessed them.*
▶ **n.** the action or process of etching something.
– DERIVATIVES **etch·er n.**
– ORIGIN mid 17th cent.: from Dutch *etsen*, from German *ätzen*, from a base meaning 'cause to eat'; related to **EAT**.

etch·ant /ˈeCHənt/ ▶ **n.** an acid or corrosive chemical used in etching; a mordant.

etch·ing /ˈeCHiNG/ ▶ **n.** a print produced by the process of etching: *etchings of animals and wildflowers.* ■ the art or process of producing etched plates or objects.

ETD ▶ **abbr.** estimated time of departure.

-ete ▶ **suffix** variant spelling of **-ET**[2] (as in *athlete*).

e·ter·nal /iˈtərnl/ ▶ **adj.** lasting or existing forever; without end or beginning: *the secret of eternal youth* | *fear of eternal damnation.* ■ (of truths, values, or questions) valid for all time; essentially unchanging: *eternal truths of art and life.* ■ informal seeming to last or persist forever, esp. on account of being tedious or annoying: *eternal nagging*

demands | she is an eternal optimist. ■ used to emphasize expressions of admiration, gratitude, or other feelings: *to his eternal credit, he maintained his dignity throughout.* ■ (**the Eternal**) used to refer to an everlasting or universal spirit, as represented by God.
– PHRASES **the Eternal City** a name for the city of Rome. **eternal triangle** a relationship between three people, typically a couple and the lover of one of them, involving sexual rivalry.
– DERIVATIVES **e·ter·nal·i·ty** /ˌētərˈnalitē/ **n.**, **e·ter·nal·ize** /iˈtərnlˌīz/ **v.**, **e·ter·nal·ness n.**
– ORIGIN late Middle English: via Old French from late Latin *aeternalis*, from Latin *aeternus*, from *aevum* 'age.'

e·ter·nal·ly /iˈtərnlē/ ▶ **adv. 1** in a way that continues or lasts forever; permanently: [as submodifier] *his eternally optimistic attitude.* ■ informal in an annoying or tedious way that seems to last forever; constantly: *he was rattling on eternally.*
2 [as submodifier] used to emphasize expressions of admiration, gratitude, etc.: *I'll be eternally grateful.*

e·ter·ni·ty /iˈtərnitē/ ▶ **n.** (pl. **eternities**) infinite or unending time: *their love was sealed for eternity | this state of affairs has lasted for all eternity.* ■ a state to which time has no application; timelessness. ■ Theology endless life after death: *immortal souls destined for eternity.* ■ used euphemistically to refer to death: *he could have crashed the car and taken them both to eternity.* ■ (**an eternity**) informal a period of time that seems very long, esp. on account of being tedious or annoying: *a silence that lasted an eternity.*
– ORIGIN late Middle English: from Old French *eternite*, from Latin *aeternitas*, from *aeternus* 'without beginning or end' (see ETERNAL).

e·ter·nize /iˈtərˌnīz/ ▶ **v.** [with obj.] literary make eternal; cause to live or last forever.

e·te·sian wind /iˈtēZHən wind/ (also **Etesian wind**) ▶ **n.** another term for MELTEMI.
– ORIGIN early 17th cent.: *etesian* from Latin *etesius* 'annual' (from Greek *etēsios*, from *etos* 'year') + -AN.

eth /eTH/ (also **edh**) ▶ **n.** an Old English letter, ð or Ð, representing the dental fricatives /TH/ and /TH/. It was superseded by the digraph *th*, but is now used as a phonetic symbol for the voiced dental fricative /TH/ in the International Phonetic Alphabet (IPA) system. Compare with THORN (sense 3).
– ORIGIN from Danish *edh*, perhaps representing the sound of the letter.

Eth. ▶ **abbr.** Ethiopia.

-eth[1] ▶ **suffix** variant spelling of -TH[1] (as in *fiftieth*).

-eth[2] (also **-th**) ▶ **suffix** archaic forming the third person singular of the present tense of verbs: *doeth | saith.*
– ORIGIN Old English *-eth, -ath, -th.*

eth·a·cryn·ic ac·id /ˌeTHəˈkrinik/ ▶ **n.** Medicine a powerful diuretic drug used in the treatment of fluid retention, esp. that associated with heart, liver, and kidney disorders. ● Alternative name: **2,3-dichloro-4-(2-ethylacryloyl) phenoxyacetic acid**; chem. formula: $C_{13}H_{12}Cl_2O_4$.
– ORIGIN 1960s: *ethacrynic* from elements of the systematic name (see above).

eth·am·bu·tol /eˈTHambyəˌtôl, -ˌtäl/ ▶ **n.** Medicine a synthetic compound with bacteriostatic properties, used in combination with other drugs in the treatment of tuberculosis. ● A derivative of ethylenediamine; chem. formula: $C_{10}H_{24}N_2O_2$.
– ORIGIN 1960s: from *eth(yl)* + *am(ine)* + *but(an)ol.*

eth·a·nal /ˈeTHəˌnäl/ ▶ **n.** systematic chemical name for ACETALDEHYDE.
– ORIGIN late 19th cent.: blend of ETHANE and ALDEHYDE.

eth·an·a·mide /eˈTHanəˌmīd/ ▶ **n.** systematic chemical name for ACETAMIDE.

eth·ane /ˈeTHˌān/ ▶ **n.** Chemistry a colorless, odorless, flammable gas that is a constituent of petroleum and natural gas. It is the second member of the alkane series. ● Chem. formula: C_2H_6.
– ORIGIN late 19th cent.: from ETHER + -ANE[2].

eth·ane·di·ol /ˌeTHˌānˈdīˌôl/ ▶ **n.** systematic chemical name for ETHYLENE GLYCOL.

eth·a·no·ic ac·id /ˌeTHəˈnō-ik/ ▶ **n.** systematic chemical name for ACETIC ACID.

eth·a·nol /ˈeTHəˌnôl, -ˌnäl/ ▶ **n.** systematic chemical name for ETHYL ALCOHOL (see ALCOHOL).
– ORIGIN early 20th cent.: blend of ETHANE and ALCOHOL.

eth·chlor·vy·nol /ˌeTHklôrˈvīnl/ ▶ **n.** another name for PLACIDYL.

Eth·el·red /ˈeTHəlˌred/ the name of two English kings. ■ **Ethelred I** (died 871), king of Wessex and Kent 865–871; elder brother of Alfred. His reign was marked by the continuing struggle against the invading Danes. ■ **Ethelred II** (*c.*969–1016), king of England 978–1016; known as **Ethelred the Unready**. His inability to confront the Danes after he succeeded his murdered half-brother St. Edward the Martyr led to his payment of tribute to prevent their attacks. [*Unready*, later form of obsolete *unredy* 'badly advised.']

eth·ene /ˈeTHēn/ ▶ **n.** systematic chemical name for ETHYLENE.
– ORIGIN mid 19th cent.: from ETHER + -ENE.

e·ther /ˈēTHər/ ▶ **n. 1** Chemistry a pleasant-smelling, colorless, volatile liquid that is highly flammable. It is used as an anesthetic and as a solvent or intermediate in industrial processes. ● Alternative names: **diethyl ether**, ethoxyethane; chem. formula: $C_2H_5OC_2H_5$. ■ any organic compound with a similar structure to this, having an oxygen atom linking two alkyl or other organic groups: *methyl t-butyl ether.*
2 (also **aether**) chiefly literary the clear sky; the upper regions of air beyond the clouds: *nasty gases and smoke disperse into the ether.* ■ (**the ether**) informal air regarded as a medium for radio: *choral evensong still wafts across the ether.*
3 (also **aether**) Physics, archaic a very rarefied and highly elastic substance formerly believed to permeate all space, including the interstices between the particles of matter, and to be the medium whose vibrations constituted light and other electromagnetic radiation.
– DERIVATIVES **e·ther·ic** /iˈTHerik, iˈTHi(ə)rik/ **adj.**
– ORIGIN late Middle English: from Old French, or via Latin from Greek *aithēr* 'upper air,' from the base of *aithein* 'burn, shine.' Originally the word denoted a substance believed to occupy space beyond the sphere of the moon. Sense 3 arose in the mid 17th cent. and sense 1 in the mid 18th cent.

e·the·re·al /iˈTHi(ə)rēəl/ ▶ **adj. 1** extremely delicate and light in a way that seems too perfect for this world: *her ethereal beauty | a singer who has a weirdly ethereal voice.* ■ heavenly or spiritual: *ethereal, otherworldly visions.*
2 Chemistry (of a solution) having diethyl ether as a solvent.
– DERIVATIVES **e·the·re·al·i·ty** /iˌTHi(ə)rēˈalitē/ **n.**, **e·the·re·al·ize** /-ˌlīz/ **v.**, **e·the·re·al·ly adv.**
– ORIGIN early 16th cent.: via Latin from Greek *aitherios* (from *aithēr* 'ether') + -AL.

e·ther·ize /ˈēTHəˌrīz/ ▶ **v.** [with obj.] chiefly historical anesthetize (a person or animal) with ether.
– DERIVATIVES **e·ther·i·za·tion** /ˌēTHəriˈzāSHən/ **n.**

E·ther·net /ˈēTHərˌnet/ ▶ **n.** Computing, trademark a system for connecting a number of computer systems to form a local area network, with protocols to control the passing of information and to avoid simultaneous transmission by two or more systems. ■ a network using this.
– ORIGIN 1970s: blend of ETHER and NETWORK.

eth·ic /ˈeTHik/ ▶ **n.** [in sing.] a set of moral principles, esp. ones relating to or affirming a specified group, field, or form of conduct: *the puritan ethic was being replaced by the hedonist ethic.*
▶ **adj.** rare of or relating to moral principles or the branch of knowledge dealing with these.
– ORIGIN late Middle English (denoting ethics or moral philosophy; also used attributively): from Old French *éthique*, from Latin *ethice*, from Greek (*hē*) *ēthikē* (*tekhnē*) '(the science of) morals,' based on *ēthos* (see ETHOS).

eth·i·cal /ˈeTHikəl/ ▶ **adj. 1** of or relating to moral principles or the branch of knowledge dealing with these: *ethical issues in nursing | ethical churchgoing men.* ■ morally good or correct: *can a profitable business be ethical?* ■ avoiding activities or organizations that do harm to people or the environment: *an expert on ethical investment | switching to more ethical products | ethical holidays.*
2 [attrib.] (of a medicine) legally available only on a doctor's prescription and usually not advertised to the general public.
– DERIVATIVES **eth·i·cal·i·ty** /ˌeTHəˈkalitē/ **n.**, **eth·i·cal·ly** /-ik(ə)lē/ **adv.** *is capitalism ethically justifiable?.*

eth·ics /ˈeTHiks/ ▶ **plural n. 1** [usu. treated as pl.] moral principles that govern a person's or group's behavior: *Judeo-Christian ethics.* ■ the moral correctness of specified conduct: *the ethics of euthanasia.*
2 [usu. treated as sing.] the branch of knowledge that deals with moral principles.

> Schools of ethics in Western philosophy can be divided, very roughly, into three sorts. The first, drawing on the work of Aristotle, holds that the virtues (such as justice, charity, and generosity) are dispositions to act in ways that benefit both the person possessing them and that person's society. The second, defended particularly by Kant, makes the concept of duty central to morality: humans are bound, from a knowledge of their duty as rational beings, to obey the categorical imperative to respect other rational beings. Thirdly, utilitarianism asserts that the guiding principle of conduct should be the greatest happiness or benefit of the greatest number.

– DERIVATIVES **eth·i·cist** /ˈeTHisist/ **n.**

E·thi·o·pi·a /ˌēTHēˈōpēə/ a country in northeastern Africa, on the Red Sea; pop. 85,237,300 (est. 2009); capital, Addis Ababa; languages, Amharic (official) and several other Afro-Asiatic languages. Former name ABYSSINIA.

> Ethiopia is the oldest independent country in Africa, having a recorded civilization that dates from the 2nd millennium BC. Little known to Europeans until the late 19th century, it was invaded and conquered by Italy in 1935. The emperor Haile Selassie was restored by the British in 1941 and ruled until he was overthrown in a Marxist coup in 1974. The subsequent period was marked by civil war, fighting against separatist guerrillas in Eritrea and Tigray, and repeated famines; after the fall of the government in 1991, a multiparty system was adopted, and elections were held in 1995.

– ORIGIN via Latin from Greek *Aethiops*, from *aithein* 'to burn' + *ōps* 'the face.'

E·thi·o·pi·an /ˌēTHēˈōpēən/ ▶ **n.** a native or inhabitant of Ethiopia, or a person of Ethiopian descent. ■ archaic a black person.
▶ **adj. 1** of or relating to Ethiopia or its people.
2 Zoology of, relating to, or denoting a zoogeographical region comprising Africa south of the Sahara, together with the tropical part of the Arabian peninsula and (usually) Madagascar. Distinctive animals include the giraffes, hippopotamuses, aardvark, elephant shrews, tenrecs, and lemurs. Also called AFROTROPICAL.

E·thi·op·ic /ˌēTHēˈäpik, -ˈōpik/ ▶ **n.** another term for GE'EZ.
▶ **adj.** of, in, or relating to Ge'ez.
– ORIGIN mid 17th cent. (as an adjective): via Latin from Greek *aithiopikos*, from *Aethiops* (see ETHIOPIA).

eth·moid /ˈeTHˌmoid/ (also **ethmoid bone**) ▶ **n.** Anatomy a square bone at the root of the nose, forming part of the cranium, and having many perforations through which the olfactory nerves pass to the nose.
– DERIVATIVES **eth·moi·dal** /eTHˈmoidl/ **adj.**
– ORIGIN mid 18th cent.: from Greek *ēthmoeidēs*, from *ēthmos* 'a sieve.'

eth·nic /ˈeTHnik/ ▶ **adj.** of or relating to a population subgroup (within a larger or dominant national or cultural group) with a common national or cultural tradition: *leaders of ethnic communities.* ■ of or relating to national and cultural origins: *two playwrights of different ethnic origins.* ■ denoting origin by birth or descent rather than by present nationality: *ethnic Albanians in Kosovo.* ■ characteristic of or belonging to a non-Western cultural tradition: *ethnic dishes | folk and ethnic music.* ■ archaic neither Christian nor Jewish; pagan or heathen.
▶ **n.** a member of an ethnic minority.
– DERIVATIVES **eth·ni·cal·ly** /-(ə)lē/ **adv.** [sentence adverb] *Denmark is ethnically Scandinavian.*
– ORIGIN late Middle English (denoting a person not of the Christian or Jewish faith): via ecclesiastical Latin from Greek *ethnikos* 'heathen,' from *ethnos* 'nation.' Current senses date from the 19th cent.

eth·nic cleans·ing ▶ **n.** the mass expulsion or killing of members of an unwanted ethnic or religious group in a society.

eth·nic·i·ty /eTHˈnisitē/ ▶ **n.** (pl. **ethnicities**) the fact or state of belonging to a social group that has a common national or cultural tradition: *the interrelationship between gender, ethnicity, and class | the diverse experience of women of different ethnicities.*

eth·nic mi·nor·i·ty ▶ **n.** a group that has different national or cultural traditions from the main population.

ethno- ▶ **comb. form** ethnic; ethnological: *ethnocentric | ethnology.*
– ORIGIN from Greek *ethnos* 'nation.'

eth·no·bot·a·ny /ˌeTHnōˈbätn-ē/ ▶ **n.** the scientific study of the traditional knowledge and customs of a people concerning plants and their medical, religious, and other uses.
– DERIVATIVES **eth·no·bo·tan·ic** /-bəˈtanik/ **adj.**, **eth·no·bo·tan·i·cal** /-bəˈtanikəl/ **adj.**, **eth·no·bot·a·nist** /-ˈbätn-ist/ **n.**

eth·no·cen·tric /ˌeTHnōˈsentrik/ ▶ **adj.** evaluating other peoples and cultures according to the standards of one's own culture.
– DERIVATIVES **eth·no·cen·tri·cal·ly** /-(ə)lē/ **adv.**, **eth·no·cen·tric·i·ty** /-ˌsenˈtrisitē/ **n.**, **eth·no·cen·trism** /-ˌtrizəm/ **n.**

eth·no·cide /ˈeTHnəˌsīd/ ▶ **n.** the deliberate and systematic destruction of the culture of an ethnic group.

eth·no·cul·tur·al /ˌeTHnōˈkəlCHərəl/ ▶ **adj.** relating to or denoting a particular ethnic group.

eth·nog·ra·phy /eTHˈnägrəfē/ ▶ **n.** the scientific description of the customs of individual peoples and cultures.
– DERIVATIVES **eth·nog·ra·pher** /-fər/ **n.**, **eth·no·graph·ic** /ˌeTHnəˈgrafik/ **adj.**, **eth·no·graph·i·cal** /ˌeTHnəˈgrafikəl/ **adj.**, **eth·no·graph·i·cal·ly** /ˌeTHnəˈgrafik(ə)lē/ **adv.**

eth·no·his·to·ry /ˌeTHnōˈhist(ə)rē/ ▶ **n.** the branch of anthropology concerned with the history of peoples and cultures, esp. non-Western ones.
– DERIVATIVES **eth·no·his·to·ri·an** /-hiˈstôrēən/ **n.**, **eth·no·his·tor·ic** /-hiˈstôrik, -ˈstär-/ **adj.**, **eth·no·his·tor·i·cal** **adj.**, **eth·no·his·tor·i·cal·ly** **adv.**

eth·no·lin·guis·tics /ˌeTHnōliNGˈgwistiks/ ▶ **plural n.** [treated as sing.] the branch of linguistics concerned with the relations between linguistic and cultural behavior.
– DERIVATIVES **eth·no·lin·guist** /-ˈliNGgwist/ **n.**, **eth·no·lin·guis·tic** **adj.**

eth·nol·o·gy /eTHˈnäləjē/ ▶ **n.** the study of the characteristics of various peoples and the differences and relationships between them.
– DERIVATIVES **eth·no·log·ic** /ˌeTHnəˈläjik/ **adj.**, **eth·no·log·i·cal** /ˌeTHnəˈläjikəl/ **adj.**, **eth·no·log·i·cal·ly** /ˌeTHnəˈläjik(ə)lē/ **adv.**, **eth·nol·o·gist** /-jist/ **n.**

eth·no·meth·od·ol·o·gy /ˌeTHnōˌmeTHəˈdäləjē/ ▶ **n.** a method of sociological analysis that examines how individuals use everyday conversation and gestures to construct a common-sense view of the world.
– DERIVATIVES **eth·no·meth·od·o·log·i·cal** /-dəˈläjikəl/ **adj.**, **eth·no·meth·od·ol·o·gist** /-jist/ **n.**

eth·no·mu·si·col·o·gy /ˌeTHnōˌmyo͞oziˈkäləjē/ ▶ **n.** the study of the music of different cultures, esp. non-Western ones.
– DERIVATIVES **eth·no·mu·si·co·log·ic** /-kəˈläjik/ **adj.**, **eth·no·mu·si·co·log·i·cal** /-kəˈläjikəl/ **adj.**, **eth·no·mu·si·col·o·gist** /-jist/ **n.**

eth·no·sci·ence /ˌeTHnōˈsīəns/ ▶ **n.** the study of the different ways the world is perceived and categorized in different cultures.

e·tho·gram /ˈēTHəˌgram/ ▶ **n.** Zoology a catalog or table of all the different kinds of behavior or activity observed in an animal.
– ORIGIN 1930s: from Greek *ēthos* 'nature, disposition' + **-GRAM**[1].

e·thol·o·gy /ēˈTHäləjē/ ▶ **n.** the science of animal behavior. ■ the study of human behavior and social organization from a biological perspective.
– DERIVATIVES **e·tho·log·i·cal** /ˌēTHəˈläjikəl/ **adj.**, **e·thol·o·gist** /-jist/ **n.**
– ORIGIN late 19th cent.: via Latin from Greek *ēthologia*, from *ēthos* (see **ETHOS**).

e·thos /ˈēTHäs/ ▶ **n.** the characteristic spirit of a culture, era, or community as manifested in its beliefs and aspirations: *a challenge to the ethos of the 1960s*.
– ORIGIN mid 19th cent.: from modern Latin, from Greek *ēthos* 'nature, disposition,' (plural) 'customs.'

eth·ox·y·eth·ane /əˌTHäksēˈeTHˌān/ ▶ **n.** systematic chemical name for **DIETHYL ETHER** (see **ETHER** (sense 1)).

eth·yl /ˈeTHəl/ ▶ **n.** [usu. as modifier] Chemistry of or denoting the hydrocarbon radical $-C_2H_5$, derived from ethane and present in many organic compounds: *ethyl acetate* | *an ethyl group*.
– ORIGIN mid 19th cent.: from German, from *Äther* 'ether' + **-YL**.

eth·yl ac·e·tate ▶ **n.** Chemistry a colorless, volatile liquid with a fruity smell, used as a plastics solvent and in flavorings and perfumes. ● Chem. formula: $CH_3COOC_2H_5$.

eth·yl al·co·hol ▶ **n.** see **ALCOHOL**.

eth·yl·ben·zene /ˌeTHəlˈbenˌzēn, ˌeTHəlbenˈzēn/ ▶ **n.** Chemistry a colorless, flammable liquid hydrocarbon, used in the manufacture of styrene. ● Chem. formula: $C_6H_5C_2H_5$.

eth·yl·ene /ˈeTHəˌlēn/ ▶ **n.** Chemistry a flammable hydrocarbon gas of the alkene series, occurring in natural gas, coal gas, and crude oil and given off by ripening fruit. It is used in chemical synthesis, esp. in the manufacture of polyethylene. ● Alternative name: **ethene**; chem. formula: C_2H_4.

eth·yl·ene·di·a·mine /ˌeTHəlēnˈdīəˌmēn/ ▶ **n.** Chemistry a viscous liquid used in making detergents and emulsifying agents. ● Chem. formula: $NH_2CH_2CH_2NH_2$.

eth·yl·ene gly·col ▶ **n.** Chemistry a colorless viscous hygroscopic liquid used as an antifreeze, in the manufacture of polyesters, and in the preservation of ancient waterlogged timbers. ● Alternative name: **ethanediol**; chem. formula: $CH_2(OH)CH_2OH$.

eth·yl·ene ox·ide ▶ **n.** Chemistry a flammable toxic gas used as an intermediate and fumigant. ● An epoxide; chem. formula: $(CH_2)_2O$.

eth·yne /ˈeTHīn, eˈTHīn/ ▶ **n.** systematic chemical name for **ACETYLENE**.

et·ic /ˈetik/ Anthropology ▶ **adj.** relating to or denoting an approach to the study or description of a particular language or culture that is general, nonstructural, and objective in its perspective. Often contrasted with **EMIC**.
▶ **plural n.** (**etics**) [treated as sing.] study adopting this approach.
– ORIGIN 1950s: abstracted from **PHONETIC**.

-etic ▶ **suffix** forming adjectives and nouns such as *pathetic, peripatetic*.
– ORIGIN from Greek *-ētikos* or *-ētikos*.

e-tick·et /ˈēˌtikit/ ▶ **n.** trademark a reservation for an airline flight for which the details are recorded electronically without the issuing of a paper ticket.

e·ti·o·lat·ed /ˈētēəˌlātid/ ▶ **adj.** (of a plant) pale and drawn out due to a lack of light: *etiolated mung bean seedlings*. ■ having lost vigor or substance; feeble: *a tone of etiolated nostalgia*.
– DERIVATIVES **e·ti·o·la·tion** /ˌētēəˈlāsHən/ **n.**
– ORIGIN late 18th cent.: from the verb *etiolate* (from French *étioler*, from Norman French *étieuler* 'grow into haulm') + **-ED**[2].

e·ti·ol·o·gy /ˌētēˈäləjē/ (Brit. **aetiology**) ▶ **n.** (pl. **etiologies**) **1** Medicine the cause, set of causes, or manner of causation of a disease or condition: *a disease of unknown etiology* | *a group of distinct diseases with different etiologies*. ■ the causation of diseases and disorders as a subject of investigation.
2 the investigation or attribution of the cause or reason for something, often expressed in terms of historical or mythical explanation.
– DERIVATIVES **e·ti·o·log·ic** /ˌētēəˈläjik/ **adj.**, **e·ti·o·log·i·cal** /ˌētēəˈläjikəl/ **adj.**, **e·ti·o·log·i·cal·ly** /ˌētēəˈläjik(ə)lē/ **adv.**
– ORIGIN mid 16th cent.: via medieval Latin from Greek *aitiologia*, from *aitia* 'a cause' + *-logia* (see **-LOGY**).

et·i·quette /ˈetikit, -ˌket/ ▶ **n.** the customary code of polite behavior in society or among members of a particular profession or group.
– ORIGIN mid 18th cent.: from French *étiquette* 'list of ceremonial observances of a court,' also 'label, etiquette,' from Old French *estiquette* (see **TICKET**).

Et·na, Mount /ˈetnə/ a volcano in eastern Sicily that rises to 10,902 feet (3,323 m). It is the highest and most active volcano in Europe.

ETO ▶ **abbr.** (in World War II) European Theater of Operations.

E·ton col·lar /ˈētn/ ▶ **n.** a broad, stiff white collar worn outside the coat collar, esp. with an Eton jacket.

E·ton Col·lege a boys' secondary school in southern England, on the Thames River opposite Windsor, founded in 1440 by Henry VI to prepare scholars for King's College, Cambridge.

E·to·ni·an /ēˈtōnēən/ ▶ **n.** a past or present member of Eton College: *an Old Etonian*.
▶ **adj.** relating to or typical of Eton College.

E·ton jack·et ▶ **n.** a short jacket reaching only to the waist, typically black and having a point at the back, formerly worn by students at Eton College.

E·to·sha Pan /ēˈtōsHə ˈpan/ a depression in the plateau in northern Namibia that is filled with salt water and has no outlets. It covers an area of 1,854 square miles (4,800 sq km).

é·touf·fée /āˌto͞oˈfā/ ▶ **n.** a spicy Cajun stew made with vegetables and seafood.

e·tri·er /ˈātrēˌā, ˌātrēˈā/ ▶ **n.** Climbing a short rope ladder with a few rungs of wood or metal.
– ORIGIN 1950s: from French *étrier* 'stirrup.'

E·tru·ri·a /iˈtro͝orēə/ an ancient region in western Italy, between the Arno and Tiber rivers, corresponding approximately to modern Tuscany and parts of Umbria. It was the center of the Etruscan civilization.
– DERIVATIVES **E·tru·ri·an** **n. & adj.**

E·trus·can /iˈtrəskən/ ▶ **adj.** of or relating to ancient Etruria, its people, or their language. The Etruscan civilization was at its height *c.*500 BC and was an important influence on the Romans, who subdued the Etruscans by the end of the 3rd century BC.
▶ **n.** **1** a native of ancient Etruria.
2 the language of ancient Etruria, of unknown affinity, written in an alphabet derived from Greek.
– ORIGIN from Latin *Etruscus* + **-AN**.

et seq. (also **et seqq.**) ▶ **adv.** and what follows (used in page references): *see volume 35, p. 329 et seq.*
– ORIGIN from Latin *et sequens* 'and the following,' or from *et sequentes, et sequentia* 'and the following things.'

-ette ▶ **suffix** forming nouns: **1** denoting relatively small size: *kitchenette*.
2 denoting an imitation or substitute: *flannelette*.
3 denoting female gender: *suffragette*.
– ORIGIN from Old French *-ette*, feminine of **-ET**[1].

> **USAGE** The use of **-ette** as a feminine suffix for forming new words is relatively recent: it was first recorded in the word **suffragette** at the beginning of the 20th century and has since been used to form only a handful of well-established words, including **usherette** and **drum majorette**. In the modern context, where the tendency is to use gender-neutral words, the suffix **-ette** is not very productive and new words formed using it tend to be restricted to the deliberately flippant or humorous, as, for example, **bimbette** and **punkette**.

e

é·tude /āˈt(y)o͞od/ ▶ **n.** a short musical composition, typically for one instrument, designed as an exercise to improve the technique or demonstrate the skill of the player.
– ORIGIN mid 19th cent.: from French, literally 'study.'

e·tui /āˈtwē/ ▶ **n.** (pl. **etuis**) dated a small ornamental case for holding needles, cosmetics, and other articles.
– ORIGIN early 17th cent.: from French *étui*, from Old French *estui* 'prison,' from *estuier* 'shut up, keep.' Compare with **TWEEZERS**.

-etum ▶ **suffix** (forming nouns) denoting a collection or plantation of trees or other plants: *arboretum* | *pinetum*.
– ORIGIN from Latin.

ETV ▶ **abbr.** educational television.

etym. ▶ **abbr.** ■ etymological. ■ etymology.

et·y·mol·o·gize /ˌetəˈmäləˌjīz/ ▶ **v.** [with obj.] (usu. **be etymologized**) give or trace the etymology of (a word).
– ORIGIN mid 16th cent.: from medieval Latin *etymologizare*, from Latin *etymologia* (see **ETYMOLOGY**).

et·y·mol·o·gy /ˌetəˈmäləjē/ ▶ **n.** (pl. **etymologies**) the study of the origin of words and the way in which their meanings have changed throughout history. ■ the origin of a word and the historical development of its meaning.
– DERIVATIVES **et·y·mo·log·i·cal** /-məˈläjikəl/ **adj.**, **et·y·mo·log·i·cal·ly** /-məˈläjik(ə)lē/ **adv.**, **et·y·mol·o·gist** /-jist/ **n.**
– ORIGIN late Middle English: from Old French *ethimologie*, via Latin from Greek *etumologia*, from *etumologos* 'student of etymology,' from *etumon*, neuter singular of *etumos* 'true.'

et·y·mon /ˈetəˌmän/ ▶ **n.** (pl. **etymons** or **etyma** /-mə/) a word or morpheme from which a later word is derived.
– ORIGIN late 16th cent. (denoting the original form of a word): via Latin from Greek *etumon* 'true thing' (see **ETYMOLOGY**).

EU ▶ **abbr.** European Union.

Eu ▶ **symbol** the chemical element europium.

eu- ▶ **comb. form** good; well; easily; normal: *eupeptic* | *euphony*.
– ORIGIN from Greek *eu* 'well,' from *eus* 'good.'

eu·bac·te·ri·um /ˌyo͞obakˈti(ə)rēəm/ ▶ **n.** (pl. **eubacteria** /-ˈti(ə)rēə/) **1** a bacterium of a large group typically having simple cells with rigid cell walls and often flagella for movement. The group comprises the "true" bacteria and cyanobacteria, as distinct from archaebacteria. ● Kingdom Eubacteria; this group is sometimes taken to exclude nonrigid forms such as spirochetes and mycoplasmas.
2 a bacterium found mainly in the intestines of vertebrates and in the soil. ● Genus *Eubacterium*; Gram-positive, anaerobic, rod-shaped bacteria.
– DERIVATIVES **eu·bac·te·ri·al** /-ti(ə)rēəl/ **adj.**

Eu·boe·a /yo͞oˈbēə/ an island in Greece in the western Aegean Sea that is separated from the mainland by a narrow channel at Chalcis, which is its capital. Greek name **ÉVVOIA**.

eu·ca·lyp·tus /ˌyo͞okəˈliptəs/ (also **eucalypt** /ˈyo͞okəˌlipt/) ▶ **n.** (pl. **eucalyptuses** or **eucalypti** /-tī/) a fast-growing evergreen Australasian tree that has been widely introduced elsewhere. It is valued for its timber, oil, gum, and resin, and as an ornamental tree. Also called **GUM[1], GUM TREE**. ● Genus *Eucalyptus*, family Myrtaceae: numerous species. ■ (also **eucalyptus oil**) the oil from eucalyptus leaves, chiefly used for its medicinal properties.
– ORIGIN modern Latin, from Greek *eu* 'well' + *kaluptos* 'covered' (from *kaluptein* 'to cover'), because the unopened flower is protected by a cap.

eu·car·y·ote /yo͞oˈkerēˌōt/ ▶ **n.** variant spelling of **EUKARYOTE**.

eu·ca·tas·tro·phe /ˌyo͞okəˈtastrəfē/ ▶ **n.** rare a sudden and favorable resolution of events in a story; a happy ending.
– ORIGIN mid 20th cent.: said to have been coined by J. R. R. Tolkien.

Eu·cha·rist /ˈyo͞okərist/ ▶ **n.** the Christian ceremony commemorating the Last Supper, in which bread and wine are consecrated and consumed. ■ the consecrated elements, esp. the bread.

> The bread and wine are referred to as the body and blood of Christ, though much theological controversy has focused on how substantially or symbolically this is to be interpreted. The service of worship is also called **Holy Communion** or (chiefly in the Protestant tradition) **the Lord's Supper** or (chiefly in the Catholic tradition) **the Mass** or (chiefly in the Eastern Orthodox tradition) **the Divine Liturgy**. See also **CONSUBSTANTIATION, TRANSUBSTANTIATION**.

– DERIVATIVES **Eu·cha·ris·tic** /ˌyo͞okəˈristik/ **adj.**, **Eu·cha·ris·ti·cal** /ˌyo͞okəˈristikəl/ **adj.**
– ORIGIN late Middle English: from Old French *eucariste*, based on ecclesiastical Greek *eukharistia* 'thanksgiving,' from Greek *eukharistos* 'grateful,' from *eu* 'well' + *kharizesthai* 'offer graciously' (from *kharis* 'grace').

eu·chre /ˈyo͞okər/ ▶ **n.** a card game for two to four players, usually played with the thirty-two highest cards, the aim being to win at least three of the five tricks played.
▶ **v.** [with obj.] (in such a card game) gain the advantage over (another player) by preventing them from taking three tricks. ■ informal deceive, outwit, or cheat (someone): *the merchant can be euchred out of his caftan by hard bargaining*.
– ORIGIN early 19th cent.: from German dialect *Jucker(spiel)*.

eu·chro·ma·tin /yo͞oˈkrōmətin/ ▶ **n.** Genetics chromosome material that does not stain strongly except during cell division. It represents the major genes and is involved in transcription. Compare with **HETEROCHROMATIN**.
– DERIVATIVES **eu·chro·mat·ic** /ˌyo͞okrəˈmatik/ **adj.**

Eu·clid[1] /ˈyo͞oklid/ a city in northeastern Ohio, northeast of Cleveland; pop. 47,415 (est. 2008).

Eu·clid[2] (*c*.300 BC), Greek mathematician. His *Elements of Geometry*, which covered plane geometry, the theory of numbers, irrationals, and solid geometry, was the standard work until other kinds of geometry were discovered in the 19th century.

Eu·clid·e·an /yo͞oˈklidēən/ ▶ **adj.** of or relating to Euclid, in particular: ■ of or denoting the system of geometry based on the work of Euclid and corresponding to the geometry of ordinary experience. ■ of such a nature that the postulates of this system of geometry are valid. Compare with **NON-EUCLIDEAN**.

eu·crite /ˈyo͞okrīt/ ▶ **n.** Geology a highly basic form of gabbro containing anorthite or bytownite with augite. ■ a stony meteorite that contains no chondrules and consists mainly of anorthite and augite.
– ORIGIN mid 19th cent.: from Greek *eukritos* 'easily discerned,' from *eu-* 'well' + *kritos* 'separated' (from *krinein* 'to separate').

eu·cryph·i·a /yo͞oˈkrifēə/ ▶ **n.** a shrub or small tree with glossy dark green leaves and large white flowers, native to Australia and South America. ● Genus *Eucryphia*, family Eucryphiaceae.
– ORIGIN modern Latin, from Greek *eu* 'well' + *-kruphos* 'hidden' (with reference to its joined sepals).

eu·dae·mon·ic /ˌyo͞odəˈmänik/ (also **eudemonic**) ▶ **adj.** formal conducive to happiness.
– DERIVATIVES **eu·dae·mo·ni·a** /-ˈmōnēə/ **n.**
– ORIGIN mid 19th cent.: from Greek *eudaimonikos*, from *eudaimōn* 'happy' (see **EUDAEMONISM**).

eu·dae·mon·ism /yo͞oˈdēməˌnizəm/ (also **eudemonism**) ▶ **n.** a system of ethics that bases moral value on the likelihood that good actions will produce happiness.
– DERIVATIVES **eu·dae·mon·ist n.**, **eu·dae·mon·is·tic** /-ˌdēməˈnistik/ **adj.**
– ORIGIN early 19th cent.: from Greek *eudaimonismos* 'system of happiness,' from *eudaimōn* 'happy,' from *eu* 'well' + *daimōn* 'guardian spirit.'

eu·di·om·e·ter /ˌyo͞odēˈämitər/ ▶ **n.** Chemistry a graduated glass tube in which mixtures of gases can be made to react by an electric spark, used to measure changes in volume of gases during chemical reactions.
– DERIVATIVES **eu·di·o·met·ric** /ˌyo͞odēəˈmetrik/ **adj.**, **eu·di·o·met·ri·cal** /ˌyo͞odēəˈmetrikəl/ **adj.**, **eu·di·om·e·try** /-trē/ **n.**
– ORIGIN late 18th cent. (denoting an instrument used to measure amounts of oxygen, thought to be greater in fine weather): from Greek *eudios* 'clear, fine' (weather), from *eu* 'well' + *dios* 'heavenly.'

Eu·gene /yo͞oˈjēn/ a city in west central Oregon, on the Willamette River, home to the University of Oregon; pop. 150,104 (est. 2008).

eu·gen·ics /yo͞oˈjeniks/ ▶ **plural n.** [treated as sing.] the science of improving a human population by controlled breeding to increase the occurrence of desirable heritable characteristics. Developed largely by Francis Galton as a method of improving the human race, it fell into disfavor only after the perversion of its doctrines by the Nazis.
– DERIVATIVES **eu·gen·ic adj.**, **eu·gen·i·cal·ly** /-ik(ə)lē/ **adv.**, **eu·gen·i·cist** /-ˈjenisist/ **n. & adj.**, **eu·gen·ist** /-ˈjenist/ **n. & adj.**

Eu·gé·nie /yo͞ozhāˈnē/ (1826–1920), Spanish empress of France 1853–70 and wife of Napoleon III; born *Eugénia María de Montijo de Guzmán*. She was an important influence on her husband's foreign policy.

eu·ge·nol /ˈyo͞ojəˌnôl, -ˌnäl/ ▶ **n.** Chemistry a colorless or pale yellow liquid compound present in oil of cloves and other essential oils and used in perfumery. ● Alternative name: **4-allyl-2-methoxyphenol**; chem. formula: $C_{10}H_{12}O_2$.
– ORIGIN late 19th cent.: from *Eugenia* (genus name of the tree from which oil of cloves is obtained, named in honor of Prince *Eugene* of Savoy (1663–1736)) + **-OL**.

eu·gle·na /yo͞oˈglēnə/ ▶ **n.** Biology a green, single-celled, freshwater organism with a flagellum, sometimes forming a green scum on stagnant water. ● Genus *Euglena*, division Euglenophyta (or phylum Euglenophyta, kingdom Protista).
– ORIGIN modern Latin, from **EU-** 'well' + Greek *glēnē* 'eyeball, socket of joint.'

eu·gle·noid /yo͞oˈglēnoid/ Biology ▶ **n.** a flagellated single-celled organism of a group that comprises euglena and its relatives. ● Division (or phylum) Euglenophyta.
▶ **adj.** of or relating to organisms of this group. ■ (of cell locomotion) achieved by peristaltic waves that pass along the cell, characteristic of the euglenoids.

eu·he·dral /yo͞oˈhēdrəl/ ▶ **adj.** Geology (of a mineral crystal in a rock) bounded by faces corresponding to its regular crystal form unconstrained by adjacent minerals.

eu·kar·y·ote /yo͞oˈkarēˌōt, -ēət/ (also **eucaryote**) ▶ **n.** Biology an organism consisting of a cell or cells in which the genetic material is DNA in the form of chromosomes contained within a distinct nucleus. Eukaryotes include all living organisms other than the eubacteria and archaebacteria. Compare with **PROKARYOTE**.
– DERIVATIVES **eu·kar·y·ot·ic** /-ˌkarēˈätik/ **adj.**
– ORIGIN 1960s: from **EU-** 'easily (formed)' + **KARYO-** 'kernel' + *-ote* as in *zygote*.

EULA /ˈyo͞olə/ ▶ **abbr.** end user license agreement.

eu·la·chon /ˈyo͞oləˌkän/ ▶ **n.** (pl. **same**) another term for **CANDLEFISH**.
– ORIGIN mid 19th cent.: from Lower Chinook *ulâkân*.

Eu·ler[1] /ˈoilər/, Leonhard (1707–83), Swiss mathematician. He attempted to elucidate the nature of functions, and his study of infinite series led his successors, notably Neils Abel and Augustin Cauchy, to introduce ideas of convergence and rigorous argument into mathematics.

Eu·ler[2], Ulf Svante von (1905–83), Swedish physiologist; son of Hans Euler-Chelpin. He was the first to discover a prostaglandin, which he isolated from semen. Euler also identified norepinephrine as the principal chemical neurotransmitter of the sympathetic nervous system. He shared the 1970 Nobel Prize for Physiology or Medicine with Bernard Katz (1911–2003) and Julius Axelrod (1912–2004).

Eu·ler-Chel·pin /ˌoilər ˈkelpin/, Hans Karl August Simon von (1873–1964), Swedish biochemist; born in Germany. He worked mainly on enzymes and vitamins and explained the role of enzymes in the alcoholic fermentation of sugar. He shared the 1929 Nobel Prize for Chemistry with Arthur Harden (1865–1940).

Eu·ler's con·stant Mathematics a constant used in numerical analysis, approximately equal to 0.577216. It represents the limit of the series $1 + \frac{1}{2} + \frac{1}{3} + \frac{1}{4} + \ldots \frac{1}{n}$ – (natural logarithm of n), as n tends to infinity. It is not known whether this is a rational number or not.
– ORIGIN mid 19th cent.: named after L. *Euler* (see **EULER[1]**).

Eu·ler's for·mu·la the geometric formula $V - E + F = 2$, where V, E, and F are the numbers of vertices, edges, and faces of any simple convex polyhedron or of an equivalent topological graph.

eu·lo·gi·um /yo͞oˈlōjēəm/ ▶ **n.** (pl. **eulogia** /-jēə/ or **eulogiums**) another term for **EULOGY**.
– ORIGIN early 17th cent.: from medieval Latin, 'praise.'

eu·lo·gize /ˈyo͞oləˌjīz/ ▶ **v.** [with obj.] praise highly in speech or writing: *contemporaries eulogized him as a great US senator* | *a plaque that eulogizes the workers*.
– DERIVATIVES **eu·lo·gist** /-jist/ **n.**, **eu·lo·gis·tic** /ˌyo͞oləˈjistik/ **adj.**, **eu·lo·gis·ti·cal·ly** /ˌyo͞oləˈjistik(ə)lē/ **adv.**

eu·lo·gy /ˈyo͞oləjē/ ▶ **n.** (pl. **eulogies**) a speech or piece of writing that praises someone or something highly, typically someone who has just died: *his good friend delivered a brief eulogy*.
– ORIGIN late Middle English (in the sense 'high praise'): from medieval Latin *eulogium*, *eulogia* (from Greek *eulogia* 'praise'), apparently influenced by Latin *elogium* 'inscription on a tomb' (from Greek *elegia* 'elegy'). The current sense dates from the late 16th cent.

Eu·men·i·des /yo͞oˈmeniˌdēz/ Greek Mythology a name given to the Furies. The Eumenides probably originated as well-disposed deities of fertility, whose name was given to the Furies either by confusion or euphemistically.
– ORIGIN via Latin from Greek, from *eumenēs* 'well disposed,' from *eu* 'well' + *menos* 'spirit.'

eu·nuch /ˈyo͞onək/ ▶ **n.** a man who has been castrated, esp. (in the past) one employed to guard the women's living areas at an oriental court. ■ an ineffectual person: *a nation of political eunuchs*.
– ORIGIN Old English, via Latin from Greek *eunoukhos*, literally 'bedroom guard,' from *eunē* 'bed' + a second element related to *ekhein* 'to hold.'

eu·nuch·oid /ˈyo͞onəˌkoid/ ▶ **adj.** chiefly Medicine resembling a eunuch, typically in having reduced or indeterminate sexual characteristics.
– DERIVATIVES **eu·nuch·oid·ism** /-izəm/ **n.**

eu·on·y·mus /yo͞oˈänəməs/ ▶ **n.** a shrub or small tree that is widely cultivated for its autumn colors and bright fruit. ● Genus *Euonymus*, family Celastraceae: numerous species, including the spindle tree.
– ORIGIN modern Latin (named by Linnaeus), from Latin *euonymos*, from Greek *euōnumos* 'having an auspicious or honored name,' from *eus* 'good' + *onoma* 'name.'

eu·pep·tic /yo͞oˈpeptik/ ▶ **adj.** of or having good digestion or a consequent air of healthy good spirits.
– ORIGIN late 17th cent. (in the sense 'helping digestion'): from Greek *eupeptos*, from *eu* 'well, easily' + *peptein* 'to digest.'

eu·phau·si·id /yo͞oˈfôzēid/ ▶ **n.** Zoology a shrimplike, planktonic marine crustacean of an order that includes krill. Many kinds are luminescent. ● Order Euphausiaceae, subclass Malacostraca.
– ORIGIN late 19th cent.: from modern Latin *Euphausia* (genus name from Greek *eu* 'well' + *phainein* 'to show' + *ousia* 'substance') + **-ID[2]**.

eu·phe·mism /ˈyo͞ofəˌmizəm/ ▶ **n.** a mild or indirect word or expression substituted for one considered to be too harsh or blunt when referring to something unpleasant or embarrassing: *"downsizing" as a euphemism for cuts*. The opposite of **DYSPHEMISM**.
– ORIGIN late 16th cent.: from Greek *euphēmismos*, from *euphēmizein* 'use auspicious words,' from *eu* 'well' + *phēmē* 'speaking.'

eu·phe·mis·tic /ˌyo͞ofəˈmistik/ ▶ **adj.** using or of the nature of a euphemism: *the euphemistic terms she uses to describe her relationships*.
– DERIVATIVES **eu·phe·mis·ti·cal·ly** /-(ə)lē/ **adv.**

eu·phe·mize /ˈyo͞ofəˌmīz/ ▶ **v.** [with obj.] refer to (something unpleasant or embarrassing) by means of a euphemism.

– ORIGIN mid 19th cent.: from Greek *euphēmizein* 'use auspicious words' (see EUPHEMISM).

eu·pho·ni·ous /yo͞o'fōnēəs/ ▶ **adj.** (of sound, esp. speech) pleasing to the ear: *this successful candidate delivers a stream of fine, euphonious phrases.*
– DERIVATIVES **eu·pho·ni·ous·ly adv.**

eu·pho·ni·um /yo͞o'fōnēəm/ ▶ **n.** a valved brass musical instrument resembling a small tuba of tenor pitch, played mainly in military and brass bands.
– ORIGIN mid 19th cent.: from Greek *euphōnos* 'having a pleasing sound' + -IUM.

eu·pho·ny /'yo͞ofənē/ ▶ **n.** (pl. **euphonies**) the quality of being pleasing to the ear, esp. through a harmonious combination of words. ■ the tendency to make phonetic change for ease of pronunciation.
– DERIVATIVES **eu·phon·ic** /yo͞o'fänik/ **adj.**, **eu·pho·nize** /-ˌnīz/ **v.**
– ORIGIN late Middle English: from French *euphonie*, via late Latin from Greek *euphōnia*, from *euphōnos* 'well sounding' (based on *phōnē* 'sound').

eu·phor·bi·a /yo͞o'fôrbēə/ ▶ **n.** a plant of a genus that comprises the spurges. ● Genus *Euphorbia*, family Euphorbiaceae.
– ORIGIN late Middle English: from Latin *euphorbea*, named after *Euphorbus*, Greek physician to the reputed discoverer of the plant, Juba II of Mauretania (1st cent. BC).

eu·pho·ri·a /yo͞o'fôrēə/ ▶ **n.** a feeling or state of intense excitement and happiness: *the euphoria of success will fuel your desire to continue training.*
– ORIGIN late 17th cent. (denoting well-being produced in a sick person by the use of drugs): modern Latin, from Greek, from *euphoros* 'borne well, healthy,' from *eu* 'well' + *pherein* 'to bear.'

eu·pho·ri·ant /yo͞o'fôrēənt/ ▶ **adj.** (chiefly of a drug) producing a feeling of euphoria.
▶ **n.** a euphoriant drug.

eu·phor·ic /yo͞o'fôrik, -'fär-/ ▶ **adj.** characterized by or feeling intense excitement and happiness: *a euphoric sense of freedom.*
– DERIVATIVES **eu·phor·i·cal·ly** /yo͞o'fôrik(ə)lē, -'fär-/ **adv.**

eu·phra·sia /yo͞o'frāZHə/ ▶ **n.** a plant of the genus *Euphrasia* in the figwort family, esp. eyebright. ■ a preparation of eyebright used in herbal medicine and homeopathy, esp. for treating eye problems.
– ORIGIN early 18th cent.: via medieval Latin from Greek, literally 'cheerfulness.'

Eu·phra·tes /yo͞o'frātēz/ a river of southwestern Asia that rises in the mountains of eastern Turkey and flows for 1,700 miles (2,736 km) through Syria and Iraq to join the Tigris River to form the Shatt al-Arab waterway.

eu·phu·ism /'yo͞ofyəˌwizəm/ ▶ **n.** formal an artificial, highly elaborate way of writing or speaking.
– DERIVATIVES **eu·phu·ist n.**, **eu·phu·is·tic** /ˌyo͞ofyə'wistik/ **adj.**, **eu·phu·is·ti·cal·ly** /ˌyo͞ofyə'wistik(ə)lē/ **adv.**
– ORIGIN late 16th cent.: from *Euphues*, the name of a character in John Lyly's prose romance of the same name (1578–80), from Greek *euphuēs* 'well endowed by nature,' from *eu* 'well' + the base of *phuē* 'growth.'

eu·ploid /'yo͞oploid/ ▶ **adj.** Biology (of a nucleus, cell, or organism) having an exact multiple of the haploid number of chromosomes.
– ORIGIN from EU- + -PLOID.

Eur·a·sia /yo͝o'rāZHə/ a term used to describe the combined continental landmass of Europe and Asia.

Eur·a·sian /yo͝or'āZHən/ ▶ **adj. 1** of mixed European (or European-American) and Asian parentage. **2** of or relating to Eurasia.
▶ **n.** a person of mixed European (or European-American) and Asian parentage.

> **USAGE** In the 19th century, the word **Eurasian** was normally used to refer to a person of mixed British and Indian parentage. In its modern uses, however, the **-asian** part of the term more often implies Southeast Asian, and **Eurasian** is often used as a synonym for **Amerasian**.

Eu·re·ka /yo͞o'rēkə, yə-/ a port city in northwestern California, on Humboldt Bay off the Pacific Ocean, a noted lumbering center; pop. 25,300 (est. 2008).

eu·re·ka /yo͞o'rēkə, yə-/ ▶ **exclam.** a cry of joy or satisfaction when one finds or discovers something.
– ORIGIN early 17th cent.: from Greek *heurēka* 'I have found it' (from *heuriskein* 'find'), said to have been uttered by Archimedes when he hit upon a method of determining the purity of gold. The noun dates from the early 20th cent.

eu·rhyth·mics ▶ **plural n.** variant spelling of EURYTHMICS.

eu·rhyth·my ▶ **n.** variant spelling of EURYTHMY.

Eu·rip·i·des /yo͞o'ripəˌdēz/ (480–*c.*406 BC), Greek playwright. His 19 surviving plays show important innovations in the handling of traditional myths, such as the introduction of realism, an interest in feminine psychology, and the portrayal of abnormal and irrational states of mind. Notable works: *Medea, Hippolytus, Electra, Trojan Women*, and *Bacchae*.

Eu·ro /'yərō, 'yo͝orō/ ▶ **adj.** informal European, esp. concerned with the European Union: *he voted with the government in the Euro debate.*

eu·ro[1] /'yərō, 'yo͝orō/ ▶ **n.** (pl. **euros** or **euro**) the single European currency, which replaced the national currencies of France, Germany, Spain, Italy, Greece, Portugal, Luxembourg, Austria, Finland, the Republic of Ireland, Belgium, and the Netherlands in 2002. Sixteen member states of the European Union now use the euro.

eu·ro[2] ▶ **n.** (pl. **euros**) the common wallaroo (see WALLAROO).
– ORIGIN mid 19th cent.: from Adnyamadhanha *yuru*.

Euro- ▶ **comb. form** European; European and ...: *Euro-American.* ■ relating to Europe or the European Union: *Eurocommunism | a Euro-MP.*

Eu·ro·bond /'yərəˌbänd, 'yo͝orō-/ ▶ **n.** an international bond issued in Europe or elsewhere outside the country in whose currency its value is stated (usually the US or Japan).

Eu·ro·cen·tric /ˌyərō'sentrik, ˌyo͝orō-/ ▶ **adj.** focusing on European culture or history to the exclusion of a wider view of the world; implicitly regarding European culture as preeminent.
– DERIVATIVES **Eu·ro·cen·tric·i·ty** /-ˌsen'trisitē/ **n.**, **Eu·ro·cen·trism** /-'senˌtrizəm/ **n.**

Eu·ro·com·mu·nism /ˌyərō'kämyəˌnizəm, ˌyo͝orō-/ ▶ **n.** a political system advocated by some communist parties in western European countries, stressing independence from the former Soviet Communist Party and preservation of many elements of Western liberal democracy.
– DERIVATIVES **Eu·ro·com·mu·nist adj. & n.**

Eu·ro·crat /'yərəˌkrat, 'yo͝orə-/ ▶ **n.** informal, chiefly derogatory a bureaucrat in the administration of the European Union.

eu·ro·creep /'yərōˌkrēp, 'yo͝orō-/ (also **Eurocreep**) ▶ **n.** informal the gradual acceptance of the euro in European Union countries that have not yet officially adopted it as their national currency.

Eu·ro·cur·ren·cy /'yərōˌkərənsē, 'yo͝orō-/ ▶ **n. 1** a form of money held or traded outside the country in whose currency its value is stated (originally US dollars held in Europe).
2 [in sing.] a single currency for use by the member states of the European Union.

Eu·ro·dol·lar /'yərōˌdälər, 'yo͝orō-/ ▶ **n.** a US dollar deposit held in Europe or elsewhere outside the US.

eu·ro·land /'yərōˌland, 'yo͝orō-/ another term for EUROZONE.

Eu·ro·mar·ket /'yərōˌmärkit, 'yo͝orō-/ ▶ **n. 1** a financial market that deals with Eurocurrencies.
2 the European Union regarded as a single commercial or financial market.

Eu·ro·pa /yo͞o'rōpə/ **1** Greek Mythology a princess of Tyre who was courted by Zeus in the form of a bull. She was carried off by him to Crete, where she bore him three sons (Minos, Rhadamanthus, and Sarpedon).
2 Astronomy one of the Galilean moons of Jupiter, the sixth closest satellite to the planet, having a network of dark lines on a bright icy surface and a diameter of 1,951 miles (3,140 km).

Eu·rope /'yo͝orəp/ a continent in the northern hemisphere, separated from Africa on the south by the Mediterranean Sea and from Asia on the east roughly by the Bosporus, the Caucasus Mountains, and the Ural Mountains. Europe contains approximately 10 percent of the world's population. It consists of the western part of the landmass of which Asia forms the eastern (and greater) part and includes the British Isles, Iceland, and most of the Mediterranean islands. Its recent history has been dominated by the decline of European states from their former colonial and economic preeminence, the emergence of the European Union among the wealthy democracies of western Europe, and the collapse of the Soviet Union with consequent changes of power in central and eastern Europe.

Eu·rope, Council of an association of European states founded in 1949 to safeguard the political and cultural heritage of Europe and promote economic and social cooperation. One of the Council's principal achievements is the European Convention on Human Rights.

Eu·ro·pe·an /ˌyərə'pēən, ˌyo͝orə-/ ▶ **adj.** of, relating to, or characteristic of Europe or its inhabitants. ■ of or relating to the European Union: *a single European currency.*
▶ **n.** a native or inhabitant of Europe. ■ a national of a state belonging to the European Union. ■ a person who is committed to the European Union: *they claimed to be the party of good Europeans.* ■ a person of European parentage.
– DERIVATIVES **Eu·ro·pe·an·ism** /-ˌnizəm/ **n.**
– ORIGIN from French *européen*, from Latin *europaeus*, based on Greek *Eurōpē* 'Europe.'

Eu·ro·pe·an Com·mis·sion a group, appointed by agreement among the governments of the European Union, which initiates Union action and safeguards its treaties. It meets in Brussels.

Eu·ro·pe·an Com·mis·sion for Hu·man Rights an institution of the Council of Europe, set up to examine complaints of alleged breaches of the Convention. It is based in Strasbourg.

Eu·ro·pe·an Com·mu·ni·ty (abbr.: **EC**) an economic and political association of certain European countries, incorporated since 1993 in the European Union.

> The European Community was formed in 1967 and includes the European Commission, the European Parliament, and the European Court of Justice. Until 1987 it was commonly known as the EEC. The name European Communities is still used in legal contexts where the three distinct organizations are recognized. See also **EUROPEAN UNION**.

Eu·ro·pe·an Court of Jus·tice an institution of the European Union, with thirteen judges appointed by its member governments, meeting in Luxembourg. Established in 1958, it exists to safeguard the law in the interpretation and application of Community treaties.

Eu·ro·pe·an cur·ren·cy u·nit ▶ **n.** see **ECU**.

Eu·ro·pe·an Ec·o·nom·ic Com·mu·ni·ty (abbr.: **EEC**) an institution of the European Union, an economic association of western European countries set up by the Treaty of Rome (1957). The original members were France, West Germany, Italy, Belgium, the Netherlands, and Luxembourg. See also **EUROPEAN COMMUNITY** and **EUROPEAN UNION**.

Eu·ro·pe·an Free Trade As·so·ci·a·tion (abbr.: **EFTA**) a customs union of western European countries, established in 1960 as a trade grouping without the political implications of the European Economic Community. The original members were Austria, Denmark, Norway, Portugal, Sweden, Switzerland, and the UK.

Eu·ro·pe·an In·vest·ment Bank a bank set up in 1958 by the Treaty of Rome to finance capital investment projects promoting the balanced development of members of the European Community. It is based in Luxembourg.

Eu·ro·pe·an·ize /ˌyərə'pēəˌnīz, ˌyo͝orə-/ ▶ **v.** [with obj.] (often as adj. **Europeanized**) give (someone or something) a European character or scope: *a highly Europeanized city.* ■ transfer to the control or responsibility of the European Union.
– DERIVATIVES **Eu·ro·pe·an·i·za·tion** /ˌyərəˌpēəni'zāSHən, ˌyo͝orə-/ **n.**

Eu·ro·pe·an kitch·en ▶ **n.** a compact kitchen with fitted cabinets and appliances, usually white.

Eu·ro·pe·an Mon·e·tar·y Sys·tem (abbr.: **EMS**) a monetary system inaugurated by the European Community in 1979 to coordinate and stabilize the exchange rates of the currencies of member countries, as a prelude to monetary union. It is based on the use of the Exchange Rate Mechanism.

Eu·ro·pe·an Mon·e·tar·y Un·ion (abbr.: **EMU**) a European Union program intended to work toward full economic unity in Europe based on the phased introduction of a common currency (originally, the ECU). The program was announced in 1989; the second stage came into effect on January 1, 1994 under the terms of the Maastricht Treaty, and in 2002 the euro replaced the currencies of twelve European Union countries.

Eu·ro·pe·an Par·lia·ment the Parliament of the European Community, originally established in 1952. From 1958 to 1979 it was composed of representatives drawn from the parliaments of member countries, but since 1979 direct elections have taken place every five years. Through the Single European Act (1987) it assumed a degree of sovereignty over national parliaments. The European Parliament meets in Strasbourg, and its committee is in Brussels.

Eu·ro·pe·an plan ▶ **n.** a system of charging for a hotel room only, without meals. Often contrasted with **AMERICAN PLAN**.

Eu·ro·pe·an Re·cov·er·y Pro·gram official name for the **MARSHALL PLAN**.

Eu·ro·pe·an Space A·gen·cy (abbr.: **ESA**) an organization set up in 1975 to coordinate the national space programs of the collaborating countries. It is based in Paris.

Eu·ro·pe·an Un·ion (abbr.: **EU**) an economic and political association of European countries as a unit with internal free trade and common external tariffs.

> The European Union was created on November 1, 1993. It consists of 27 member states, 16 of which use the common currency unit, the euro. The terms **European Economic Community** (EEC) and **European Community** (EC) continue to be used loosely to refer to what is now the European Union.

e

Eu·ro·phile /ˈyərōˌfīl/ ▶ **n.** a person who admires Europe or favors participation in the European Union.

Eu·ro·phobe /ˈyərōˌfōb/ ▶ **n.** a person who strongly dislikes Europe or opposes participation in the European Union.
– DERIVATIVES **Eu·ro·pho·bic adj.**

eu·ro·pi·um /yəˈrōpēəm/ ▶ **n.** the chemical element of atomic number 63, a soft silvery-white metal of the lanthanide series. Europium oxide is used with yttrium oxide as a red phosphor in color television screens. (Symbol: **Eu**)
– ORIGIN early 20th cent.: modern Latin, based on **EUROPE**.

Eu·ro·poort /ˈyo͝orōˌpôrt/ a major European port in the Netherlands, near Rotterdam.

Eu·ro·skep·tic (also **Eurosceptic**) /ˌyərōˈskeptik, ˈyo͝orō-/ ▶ **n.** a person who is opposed to increasing the powers of the European Union.
– DERIVATIVES **Eu·ro·skep·ti·cism n.**

Eu·ro·trash /ˈyərōˌtrasʜ, ˈyo͝orō-/ ▶ **n.** informal rich European socialites, esp. those living or working in the US.

eur·o·zone /ˈyərəˌzōn, ˈyo͝orə-/ ▶ **n.** the group of European Union nations whose national currency is the euro.

eury- ▶ **comb. form** denoting a wide variety or range of something specified: *eurytopic*.
– ORIGIN from Greek *eurus* 'wide.'

eu·ry·ap·sid /ˌyo͝orēˈapsid/ ▶ **n.** a Mesozoic marine reptile of a group characterized by a single upper temporal opening in the skull, including the nothosaurs, plesiosaurs, and ichthyosaurs. ● Sometimes placed in a subclass Euryapsida, though this taxon is no longer widely recognized.
– ORIGIN from Greek *eurus* 'wide' + *apsis, apsid-* 'arch.'

Eu·ryd·i·ce /yəˈridəsē/ Greek Mythology the wife of Orpheus. After she was killed by a snake, Orpheus secured her release from the underworld on the condition that he not look back at her on their way back to the world of the living. But Orpheus did look back, whereupon Eurydice disappeared.

eu·ry·ha·line /ˌyərəˈhālīn, -ˈhal-/ ▶ **adj.** Ecology (of an aquatic organism) able to tolerate a wide range of salinity. Often contrasted with **STENOHALINE**.
– ORIGIN late 19th cent.: from Greek *eurus* 'wide' + *halinos* 'of salt.'

eu·ryp·ter·id /yəˈriptərid/ ▶ **n.** an extinct marine arthropod of a group occurring in the Paleozoic era. They are related to horseshoe crabs and resemble large scorpions with a terminal pair of paddle-shaped swimming appendages. ● Subclass Eurypterida, class Merostomata, subphylum Chelicerata.
– ORIGIN late 19th cent.: from modern Latin *Eurypterus* (genus name), from **EURY-** + Greek *pteron* 'wing' + **-ID**[2].

eu·ry·ther·mal /ˌyo͝orəˈᴛʜərməl/ (also **eurythermic** /-ˈᴛʜərmik/) ▶ **adj.** Ecology (of an organism) able to tolerate a wide range of temperatures. Often contrasted with **STENOTHERMAL**.

eu·ryth·mic /yəˈriᴛʜmik, yo͞o-/ ▶ **adj.** rare (esp. of architecture or art) in or relating to harmonious proportion.
– ORIGIN mid 19th cent.: based on Greek *eurhuthmia* 'proportion' + **-IC**.

eu·ryth·mics /yəˈriᴛʜmiks, yo͞o-/ ▶ **plural n.** [treated as sing.] a system of rhythmical physical movements to music used to teach musical understanding (esp. in Steiner schools) or for therapeutic purposes, created by Émile Jaques-Dalcroze.
– ORIGIN early 20th cent.: from **EU-** 'well' + **RHYTHM** + **-ICS**.

eu·ryth·my /yo͞oˈriᴛʜmē/ ▶ **n.** another term for **EURYTHMICS**.

– ORIGIN early 17th cent. (also as *eurythmia* in early use): via Latin from Greek *euruthmia*, from *eu-* 'well' + *rhuthmos* 'proportion, rhythm.'

eu·ry·top·ic /ˌyərəˈtäpik, yo͝orə-/ ▶ **adj.** Ecology (of an organism) able to tolerate a wide range of habitats or ecological conditions. Often contrasted with **STENOTOPIC**.

Eu·se·bi·us /yo͞oˈsēbēəs/ (c.AD 264–c.340), bishop and church historian; known as **Eusebius of Caesaria**. His *Ecclesiastical History* is the principal source for the history of Christianity (esp. in the Eastern Church) from the age of the Apostles until 324.

eu·so·cial /yo͞oˈsōsʜəl/ ▶ **adj.** Zoology (of an animal species, esp. an insect) showing an advanced level of social organization, in which a single female or caste produces the offspring and nonreproductive individuals cooperate in caring for the young.
– DERIVATIVES **eu·so·ci·al·i·ty** /-ˌsōsʜēˈalitē/ **n.**

Eu·sta·chian tube /yo͞oˈstāsʜ(ē)ən, -kēən/ ▶ **n.** Anatomy a narrow passage leading from the pharynx to the cavity of the middle ear, permitting the equalization of pressure on each side of the eardrum.
– ORIGIN mid 18th cent.: named after Bartolomeo *Eustachio* (died 1574), the Italian anatomist who identified and described it.

eu·sta·sy /ˈyo͞ostəsē/ ▶ **n.** a change of sea level throughout the world, caused typically by movements of parts of the earth's crust or melting of glaciers.
– DERIVATIVES **eu·sta·tic** /yo͞oˈstatik/ **adj.**
– ORIGIN 1940s: back-formation from *eustatic*, coined in German from Greek *eu* 'well' + *statikos* 'static.'

Eus·ton Road /ˈyo͞ostn/ ▶ **n.** [as modifier] relating to or denoting a group of English post-Impressionist realistic painters of the 1930s.
– ORIGIN from the name of a road in London, England, site of a former School of Drawing and Painting (1938–39).

eu·stress /yo͞oˈstres/ ▶ **n.** moderate or normal psychological stress interpreted as being beneficial for the experiencer.
– ORIGIN late 20th cent.: **EU-** + **STRESS**, on the pattern of *distress*.

eu·tec·tic /yo͞oˈtektik/ Chemistry ▶ **adj.** relating to or denoting a mixture of substances (in fixed proportions) that melts and solidifies at a single temperature that is lower than the melting points of the separate constituents or of any other mixture of them.
▶ **n.** a eutectic mixture. ■ short for **EUTECTIC POINT**.
– ORIGIN late 19th cent.: from Greek *eutēktos* 'easily melting,' from *eu* 'well, easily' + *tēkein* 'melt.'

eu·tec·tic point (also **eutectic temperature**) ▶ **n.** Chemistry the temperature at which a particular eutectic mixture freezes or melts.

eu·tec·toid /yo͞oˈtektoid/ Metallurgy ▶ **adj.** relating to or denoting an alloy that has a minimum transformation temperature between a solid solution and a simple mixture of metals.
▶ **n.** a eutectoid mixture or alloy.

Eu·ter·pe /yo͞oˈtərpē/ Greek & Roman Mythology the Muse of flute playing and lyric poetry.
– ORIGIN Greek, literally 'well-pleasing.'

eu·tha·na·sia /ˌyo͞oᴛʜəˈnāzʜə/ ▶ **n.** the painless killing of a patient suffering from an incurable and painful disease or in an irreversible coma. The practice is illegal in most countries.
– ORIGIN early 17th cent. (in the sense 'easy death'): from Greek, from *eu* 'well' + *thanatos* 'death.'

eu·tha·nize /ˈyo͞oᴛʜəˌnīz/ ▶ **v.** [with obj.] (usu. **be euthanized**) put (a living being, esp. a dog or cat) to death humanely.
– ORIGIN 1970s: formed irregularly from **EUTHANASIA** + **-IZE**.

Eu·the·ri·a /yo͞oˈᴛʜi(ə)rēə/ Zoology a major group of mammals that comprises the placentals. Compare with **METATHERIA**. ● Infraclass Eutheria, subclass Theria.
– ORIGIN modern Latin (plural), from **EU-** 'well, prospering' + Greek *thērion* 'wild beast.'

eu·the·ri·an /yo͞oˈᴛʜi(ə)rēən/ Zoology ▶ **n.** a mammal of the major group Eutheria, which includes all the placentals and excludes the marsupials and monotremes.
▶ **adj.** relating to or denoting eutherians.

eu·thy·roid /yo͞oˈᴛʜīˌroid/ ▶ **adj.** Medicine having a normally functioning thyroid gland.

eu·troph·ic /yo͞oˈträfik, -trō-/ ▶ **adj.** Ecology (of a lake or other body of water) rich in nutrients and so supporting a dense plant population, the decomposition of which kills animal life by depriving it of oxygen. Compare with **DYSTROPHIC** and **OLIGOTROPHIC**.

– ORIGIN early 18th cent. (denoting a medicine promoting good nutrition): from Greek *eutrophia*, from *eu* 'well' + *trephein* 'nourish.' The current sense dates from the 1930s.

eu·troph·i·ca·tion /yo͞oˌträfiˈkāsʜən/ ▶ **n.** excessive richness of nutrients in a lake or other body of water, frequently due to runoff from the land, which causes a dense growth of plant life and death of animal life from lack of oxygen.
– DERIVATIVES **eu·troph·i·cate** /yo͞oˈträfiˌkāt/ **v.**

eV ▶ **abbr.** electron-volt(s).

EVA ▶ **abbr.** ■ ethyl vinyl acetate, a material used as cushioning in running shoes, consisting of a rubbery copolymer of ethylene and vinyl acetate. ■ (in space) extravehicular activity.

e·vac·u·ant /iˈvakyo͞oənt/ ▶ **n.** a medicine that induces some kind of bodily discharge, such as an emetic, a sudorific, or esp. a laxative.
▶ **adj.** (of a medicine or treatment) acting to induce some kind of bodily discharge.
– ORIGIN mid 18th cent.: from Latin *evacuant-* 'emptying (the bowels),' from the verb *evacuare*, later in the more general sense 'remove (contents).'

e·vac·u·ate /iˈvakyəˌwāt/ ▶ **v.** [with obj.] **1** remove (someone) from a place of danger to a safe place: *several families were evacuated from their homes*. ■ leave or cause the occupants to leave (a place of danger): *fire alarms forced staff to evacuate the building* | [no obj.] *residents have to evacuate because of a hurricane*. ■ (of troops) withdraw from (a place): *the last American troops evacuated the Canal Zone*.
2 technical remove air, water, or other contents from (a container): *when it springs a leak, evacuate the pond* | (as adj. **evacuated**) *an evacuated bulb*. ■ empty (the bowels or another bodily organ). ■ discharge (feces or other matter) from the body. ■ deprive (something) of contents, value, or force: *he evacuated time and history of significance*.
– ORIGIN late Middle English (in the sense 'clear the contents of'): from Latin *evacuat-* '(of the bowels) emptied,' from the verb *evacuare*, from *e-* (variant of *ex-*) 'out of' + *vacuus* 'empty.'

e·vac·u·a·tion /iˌvakyo͞oˈāsʜən/ ▶ **n.** **1** the action of evacuating a person or a place: *there were waves of evacuation during the blitz* | *a full-scale evacuation of the city center*.
2 the action of emptying the bowels or another bodily organ. ■ a quantity of matter discharged from the bowels or another bodily organ. ■ technical the action of emptying a container of air, water, or other contents.

e·vac·u·a·tive /iˈvakyəˌwātiv/ ▶ **adj. & n.** another term for **EVACUANT**.

e·vac·u·ee /iˌvakyo͞oˈē/ ▶ **n.** a person evacuated from a place of danger to somewhere safe.
– ORIGIN early 20th cent. (originally in the French form): from French *évacué*, past participle of *évacuer*, from Latin *evacuare* (see **EVACUATE**).

e·vade /iˈvād/ ▶ **v.** escape or avoid, esp. by cleverness or trickery: *friends helped him to evade capture for a time* | *he tried to kiss her, but she evaded him*. ■ (of an abstract thing) elude (someone): *sleep still evaded her*. ■ avoid giving a direct answer to (a question): *he denied evading the question*. ■ avoid dealing with or accepting; contrive not to do (something morally or legally required): *difficulties to be faced and not evaded*. ■ escape paying (tax or duty), esp. by illegitimate presentation of one's finances. ■ defeat the intention of (a law or rule), esp. while complying with its letter.
– DERIVATIVES **e·vad·a·ble adj.**, **e·vad·er n.**
– ORIGIN late 15th cent.: from French *évader*, from Latin *evadere*, from *e-* (variant of *ex-*) 'out of' + *vadere* 'go.'

e·vag·i·nate /iˈvajəˌnāt/ ▶ **v.** Biology & Physiology (with reference to a tubular or pouch-shaped organ or structure) turn or be turned inside out.
– DERIVATIVES **e·vag·i·na·tion** /iˌvajəˈnāsʜən/ **n.**
– ORIGIN mid 17th cent.: from Latin *evaginat-* 'unsheathed,' from the verb *evaginare*, from *e-* (variant of *ex-*) 'out of' + *vagina* 'sheath.'

e·val·u·ate /iˈvalyo͞oˌāt/ ▶ **v.** [with obj.] form an idea of the amount, number, or value of; assess: *when you evaluate any hammer, look for precision machining* | [with clause] *computer simulations evaluated how the aircraft would perform*. ■ Mathematics find a numerical expression or equivalent for (an equation, formula, or function).
– DERIVATIVES **e·val·u·a·tive** /-yo͞oˌātiv, -ətiv/ **adj.**, **e·val·u·a·tor** /-yo͞oˌātər/ **n.**
– ORIGIN mid 19th cent.: back-formation from *evaluation*, from French *évaluer*, from *es-* (from Latin *ex-*) 'out, from' + Old French *value* 'value.'

e·val·u·a·tion /iˌvalyo͞oˈāsʜən/ ▶ **n.** the making of a judgment about the amount, number, or value of something; assessment: *the evaluation of each method | an initial evaluation of the program.*

evan. ▶ **abbr.** ■ evangelical. ■ evangelist.

ev·a·nesce /ˌevəˈnes/ ▶ **v.** [no obj.] literary pass out of sight, memory, or existence.
– ORIGIN mid 19th cent.: from Latin *evanescere,* from *e-* (variant of *ex-*) 'out of' + *vanus* 'empty.'

ev·a·nes·cent /ˌevəˈnesənt/ ▶ **adj.** chiefly literary soon passing out of sight, memory, or existence; quickly fading or disappearing: *a shimmering evanescent bubble.* ■ Physics denoting a field or wave that extends into a region where it cannot propagate and whose amplitude therefore decreases with distance.
– DERIVATIVES **ev·a·nes·cence n., ev·a·nes·cent·ly adv.**
– ORIGIN early 18th cent. (in the sense 'almost imperceptible'): from Latin *evanescent-* 'disappearing,' from the verb *evanescere* (see EVANESCE).

evang. (or **Evang.**) ▶ **abbr.** ■ evangelical. ■ evangelist.

e·van·gel /iˈvanjəl/ ▶ **n. 1** archaic the Christian gospel. ■ any of the four Gospels.
2 another term for EVANGELIST.
– ORIGIN Middle English (in the sense 'gospel'): from Old French *evangile,* via ecclesiastical Latin from Greek *euangelion* 'good news,' from *euangelos* 'bringing good news,' from *eu-* 'well' + *angelein* 'announce.'

e·van·gel·i·cal /ˌivanˈjelikəl/ ▶ **adj.** of or according to the teaching of the gospel or the Christian religion. ■ of or denoting a tradition within Protestant Christianity emphasizing the authority of the Bible, personal conversion, and the doctrine of salvation by faith in the Atonement. ■ zealous in advocating something.
▶ **n.** a member of the evangelical tradition in the Christian Church.
– DERIVATIVES **e·van·gel·ic** /-ˈjelik/ **adj., e·van·gel·i·cal·ism** /-izəm/ **n., e·van·gel·i·cal·ly adv.**
– ORIGIN mid 16th cent.: via ecclesiastical Latin from ecclesiastical Greek *euangelikos,* from *euangelos* (see EVANGEL).

e·van·ge·lism /iˈvanjəˌlizəm/ ▶ **n.** the spreading of the Christian gospel by public preaching or personal witness. ■ zealous advocacy of a cause.

e·van·ge·list /iˈvanjəlist/ ▶ **n. 1** a person who seeks to convert others to the Christian faith, esp. by public preaching. ■ a layperson engaged in Christian missionary work. ■ a zealous advocate of something: *he is an evangelist of junk bonds.*
2 the writer of one of the four Gospels (Matthew, Mark, Luke, or John): *St. John the Evangelist.*
– ORIGIN Middle English (sense 2): from Old French *évangéliste,* via ecclesiastical Latin from ecclesiastical Greek *euangelistēs,* from *euangelizesthai* 'evangelize.'

e·van·ge·lis·tic /iˌvanjəˈlistik/ ▶ **adj.** seeking to convert others to the Christian faith; missionary: *an evangelistic preacher.* ■ zealously advocating a particular cause; campaigning: *an almost evangelistic zeal for the product.*

e·van·ge·lize /iˈvanjəˌlīz/ ▶ **v.** [with obj.] convert or seek to convert (someone) to Christianity. ■ [no obj.] preach the Christian gospel: *the Church's mission to evangelize and declare the faith.*
– DERIVATIVES **e·van·ge·li·za·tion** /iˌvanjəliˈzāsHən/ **n., e·van·ge·liz·er n.**
– ORIGIN late Middle English: from ecclesiastical Latin *evangelizare,* from Greek *euangelizesthai,* from *euangelos* (see EVANGEL).

Ev·ans[1] /ˈevənz/, Sir Arthur (John) (1851–1941), English archaeologist. His excavations at Knossos (1899–1935) resulted in the discovery of the Bronze Age civilization of Crete, which he named Minoan after the legendary Cretan king Minos.

Ev·ans[2], Mary Ann, see ELIOT[2].

Ev·ans·ton /ˈevənstən/ a city in northeastern Illinois, just north of Chicago, home to Northwestern University; pop. 77,693 (est. 2008).

Ev·ans·ville /ˈevənzˌvil/ an industrial port city in southwestern Indiana, on the Ohio River; pop. 116,309 (est. 2008).

evap. ▶ **abbr.** evaporate.

e·vap·o·rate /iˈvapəˌrāt/ ▶ **v.** turn from liquid into vapor: [no obj.] *cook until most of the liquid has evaporated* | [with obj.] *this gets the oil hot enough to evaporate any moisture.* ■ lose or cause to lose moisture or solvent as vapor: [with obj.] *the solution was evaporated to dryness.* ■ [no obj.] (of something abstract) cease to exist: *the militancy of earlier years had evaporated in the wake of defeat.*
– DERIVATIVES **e·vap·o·ra·ble** /-rəbəl/ **adj., e·vap·o·ra·tion** /iˌvapəˈrāsHən/ **n., e·vap·o·ra·tor** /-ˌrātər/ **n.**
– ORIGIN late Middle English: from Latin *evaporat-* 'changed into vapor,' from the verb *evaporare,* from *e-* (variant of *ex-*) 'out of' + *vapor* 'steam, vapor.'

e·vap·o·rat·ed milk ▶ **n.** a processed form of milk that has had some of the liquid removed by evaporation.

e·vap·o·rat·ing dish /iˈvapəˌrātiNG/ ▶ **n.** Chemistry a small ceramic dish in which liquids are heated over a flame so that they evaporate, leaving a solid residue.

e·vap·o·ra·tive /iˈvapəˌrātiv/ ▶ **adj.** relating to or involving evaporation: *evaporative water loss.*
– ORIGIN late Middle English: from late Latin *evaporativus,* from *evaporare* 'change into vapor' (see EVAPORATE).

e·vap·o·ra·tive cool·ing ▶ **n.** reduction in temperature resulting from the evaporation of a liquid, which removes latent heat from the surface from which evaporation takes place. This process is employed in industrial and domestic cooling systems, and is also the physical basis of sweating.
– DERIVATIVES **e·vap·o·ra·tive cool·er n.**

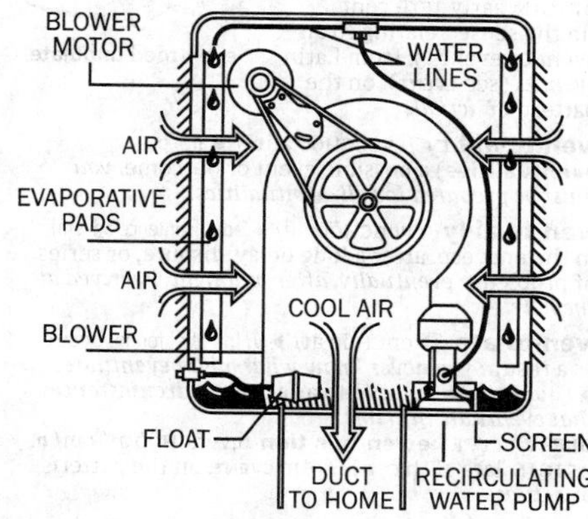

evaporative cooler

e·vap·o·rite /iˈvapəˌrīt/ ▶ **n.** Geology a natural salt or mineral deposit left after the evaporation of a body of water.
– ORIGIN 1920s: alteration of EVAPORATE (see also -ITE[1]).

e·vap·o·tran·spi·ra·tion /iˌvapōˌtranspəˈrāsHən/ ▶ **n.** the process by which water is transferred from the land to the atmosphere by evaporation from the soil and other surfaces and by transpiration from plants.

e·va·sion /iˈvāZHən/ ▶ **n.** the action of evading something: *their adroit evasion of almost all questions.* ■ an indirect answer; a prevaricating excuse: *the protestations and evasions of a witness.*
– ORIGIN late Middle English (in the sense 'prevaricating excuse'): via Old French from Latin *evasio(n-),* from *evadere* (see EVADE).

e·va·sive /iˈvāsiv/ ▶ **adj.** tending to avoid commitment or self-revelation, esp. by responding only indirectly: *she was evasive about her phone number.* ■ directed toward avoidance or escape: *they decided to take evasive action.*
– DERIVATIVES **e·va·sive·ly adv., e·va·sive·ness n.**
– ORIGIN early 18th cent.: from Latin *evas-* 'evaded' (from the verb *evadere*) + -IVE.

Eve /ēv/ (in the Bible) the first woman, wife of Adam and mother of Cain and Abel.

eve /ēv/ ▶ **n.** the day or period of time immediately before an event or occasion: ***on the eve of*** *her departure he gave her a little parcel.* ■ the evening or day before a religious festival: *the service for Passover eve.* ■ chiefly literary evening: *a bitter winter's eve.*
– ORIGIN late Middle English (in the sense 'close of day'): short form of EVEN[2].

e·vec·tion /iˈveksHən/ ▶ **n.** Astronomy regular variation in the eccentricity of the moon's orbit around the earth, caused mainly by the sun's attraction.
– ORIGIN mid 17th cent. (in the sense 'elevation, exaltation'): from Latin *evectio(n-),* from *evehere* 'carry out or up,' from *e-* (variant of *ex-*) 'out' + *vehere* 'carry.'

Eve hy·poth·e·sis ▶ **n.** the hypothesis (based on study of mitochondrial DNA) that modern humans have a common female ancestor who lived in Africa around 200,000 years ago. Also called AFRICAN EVE HYPOTHESIS.

E·ven /ˈāwən, ˈevən/ ▶ **n.** (pl. **same**) **1** a member of an indigenous people of eastern Siberia.
2 the language of this people, a Tungusic language with about 6,000 speakers, closely related to Evenki.
▶ **adj.** of or relating to this people or their language.

e·ven[1] /ˈēvən/ ▶ **adj.** (**evener, evenest**) **1** flat and smooth: *prepare the site, then lay an even bed of mortar.* ■ in the same plane or line; level: *run a file along the saw to make all of the teeth even with each other.*
2 equal in number, amount, or value: *an even gender balance among staff and students.* ■ equally balanced: *it's not an even fight.* ■ having little variation in quality; regular: *they traveled at an even and leisurely pace.* ■ (of a person's temper or disposition) equable; calm: *a man of good humor and even temper.*
3 (of a number, such as 2, 6, or 108) divisible by two without a remainder. ■ bearing such a number: *headers can be placed on odd or even pages or both.* ■ exactly equal to a round number; not having any fractions: *the Dow Jones ended at an even 10,000.*
▶ **v.** make or become even: [with obj.] *she cut the hair again to* ***even up*** *the ends.*
▶ **adv.** used to emphasize something surprising or extreme: *they have never even heard of the US | they wore fur hats, even in summer.* ■ used in comparisons for emphasis: *he knows even less about it than I do.*
– PHRASES **even as** at the very same time as: *even as he spoke, their baggage was being unloaded.* **an even break** informal a fair chance: *suckers never get an even break.* **even if** despite the possibility that; no matter whether: *always try everything even if it turns out to be a dud.* ■ despite the fact that: *he is a great president, even if he has many enemies.* **even now** (or **then**) **1** now (or then) as well as before: *even now, after all these years, it upsets me.* **2** in spite of what has (or had) happened: *even then he never raised his voice to me.* **3** at this (or that) very moment: *very likely you are even now picking up the telephone to call.* **even so** in spite of that; nevertheless: *not the most exciting of places, but even so I was having a good time.* **even though** despite the fact that: *even though he was bigger, he never looked down on me.* **get** (or **be**) **even** informal inflict trouble or harm on someone similar to that which they have inflicted on oneself: *I'll get even with you for this.* **of even date** Law or formal of the same date. **on an even keel** (of a ship or aircraft) having the same draft forward and aft. ■ (of a person or situation) functioning normally after a period of difficulty: *getting her life back on to an even keel after their breakup had been difficult.*
– DERIVATIVES **e·ven·ly adv., e·ven·ness n.**
– ORIGIN Old English *efen* (adjective), *efne* (adverb), of Germanic origin; related to Dutch *even, effen* and German *eben.*

e·ven[2] ▶ **n.** archaic or literary the end of the day; evening: *bring it to my house this even.*
– ORIGIN Old English *ǣfen,* of Germanic origin; related to Dutch *avont* and German *Abend.*

e·ven-aged ▶ **adj.** Forestry (of woodland) composed of trees of approximately the same age. ■ (of trees) of approximately the same age.

e·ven-hand·ed ▶ **adj.** fair and impartial in treatment or judgment: *an even-handed approach.*
– DERIVATIVES **e·ven-hand·ed·ly adv., e·ven-hand·ed·ness n.**

eve·ning /ˈēvniNG/ ▶ **n.** the period of time at the end of the day, usually from about 6 p.m. to bedtime: *it was seven o'clock* ***in the evening*** | [as modifier] *the evening meal.* ■ this time characterized by a specified type of activity or particular weather conditions: *they could have a relaxing evening.* ■ [as modifier] prescribed by fashion as suitable for relatively formal social events held in the evening: *a couple in evening dress.*
▶ **adv.** (**evenings**) informal in the evening; every evening: *Saturday evenings he invariably fell asleep.*
▶ **exclam.** informal short for GOOD EVENING.
– ORIGIN Old English *ǣfnung* 'dusk falling, the time around sunset,' from *ǣfnian* 'approach evening,' from *ǣfen* (see EVEN[2]).

eve·ning gown ▶ **n.** a long, elegant dress suitable for wearing on formal occasions.

eve·ning gros·beak ▶ **n.** a grosbeak native to North America, with yellow coloring.
● *Coccothraustes vespertinus.*

PRONUNCIATION KEY ə *ago, up;* ər *over, fur;* a *hat;* ā *ate;* ä *car;* e *let;* ē *see;* i *fit;* ī *by;* NG *sing;* ō *go;* ô *law, for;* oi *toy;* o͝o *good;* o͞o *goo;* ou *out;* TH *thin;* T͟H *then;* ZH *vision*

e

eve·ning prayer ▶ **n.** (usu. **evening prayers**) a formal act of worship held in the evening. ■ [in sing.] (in the Anglican Church) the service of evensong.

eve·ning prim·rose ▶ **n.** a plant with yellow flowers that open in the evening and yield seeds from which a medicinal oil is extracted. ● Genus *Oenothera*, family Onagraceae: numerous species, in particular the **common evening primrose** (*O. biennis*).

common evening primrose

eve·ning star ▶ **n.** (**the evening star**) the planet Venus, seen shining in the western sky after sunset.

eve·ning wear ▶ **n.** clothing, esp. for women, that is suitable for formal social occasions.

E·ven·ki /i'weNGkē, i'veNGkē/ ▶ **n.** (pl. **same** or **Evenkis**) **1** a member of an indigenous people of northern Siberia. Also called TUNGUS. **2** the Tungusic language of this people. ▶ **adj.** of or relating to this people or their language.

e·ven mon·ey ▶ **n.** (in betting) odds offering an equal chance of winning or losing, with the amount won being the same as the stake: *players bet on each throw for even money* | [as modifier] *Romany King swept past the even-money favorite Paco's Boy.* ■ [as modifier] (of a chance) equally likely to happen or not; fifty-fifty: *above those engines there was an even-money chance of being heard.*

e·ven·song /'ēvən,sôNG, 'evən,säNG/ (also **Evensong**) ▶ **n.** (in the Christian Church) a service of evening prayers, psalms, and canticles, conducted according to a set form, esp. that of the Anglican Church: *choral evensong.*
– ORIGIN Old English *ǣfensang*, originally applied to the pre-Reformation service of vespers (see EVEN[2], SONG).

e·ven-ste·ven /,ēvən 'stēvən/ ▶ **adj. & adv.** informal used in reference to fair and equal competition or distribution of resources: [as adj.] *the race was an even-steven affair* | [as adv.] *I split the money with my wife even-steven.*
– ORIGIN mid 19th cent.: rhyming phrase, used as an intensive.

e·vent /i'vent/ ▶ **n.** a thing that happens, esp. one of importance: *one of the main political events of the late 20th century.* ■ a planned public or social occasion: *events to raise money for charity.* ■ each of several particular contests making up a sports competition: *a star sprinter in the 100- and 200-meter events.* ■ Physics a single occurrence of a process, e.g., the ionization of one atom.
– PHRASES **in any event** (or **at all events**) whatever happens or may have happened: *in any event, there was one promise the trickster did keep.* **in the event** chiefly Brit. as it turns (or turned) out: *he was sent on this important and, in the event, quite fruitless mission.* **in the event of —— if —— happens:** *this will reduce the chance of serious injury in the event of an accident.* **in the event that** if; should it happen that: *in the event that an attack is launched, the defenders will have been significantly weakened by air attacks.* **in that event** if that happens: *in that event, the US would incline toward a lifting of the arms embargo.*
– DERIVATIVES **e·vent·less adj.**, **e·vent·less·ness n.**
– ORIGIN late 16th cent.: from Latin *eventus*, from *evenire* 'result, happen,' from *e-* (variant of *ex-*) 'out of' + *venire* 'come.'

e·ven-tem·pered ▶ **adj.** not easily annoyed or angered: *a gentle and even-tempered man.*

e·vent·er /i'ventər/ ▶ **n.** Brit. a horse or rider that takes part in eventing.
– ORIGIN 1970s: from EVENT, in *three-day event* (see EVENTING).

e·vent·ful /i'ventfəl/ ▶ **adj.** marked by interesting or exciting events: *his long and eventful life.*
– DERIVATIVES **e·vent·ful·ly adv.**, **e·vent·ful·ness n.**

e·vent ho·ri·zon ▶ **n.** Astronomy a theoretical boundary around a black hole beyond which no light or other radiation can escape. ■ a point of no return: *we're nearing the event horizon of the presidential election.*

e·ven·tide /'ēvən,tīd/ ▶ **n.** archaic or literary the end of the day; evening: *the moon flower opens its white, trumpetlike flowers at eventide.*
– ORIGIN Old English *ǣfentīd* (see EVEN[2], TIDE).

e·vent·ing /i'ventiNG/ ▶ **n.** an equestrian sport in which competitors must take part in each of several contests, usually cross-country, dressage, and show jumping.
– ORIGIN 1960s: from EVENT, in *three-day event*, horse trials held on three consecutive days. Compare with EVENTER.

e·vent·ive /i'ventiv/ ▶ **adj.** Linguistics (of the subject or object of a sentence) denoting an event.

e·ven-toed un·gu·late ▶ **n.** a hoofed mammal of an order that includes the ruminants, camels, pigs, and hippopotamuses. Mammals of this group have either two or four toes on each foot. Compare with ODD-TOED UNGULATE. ● Order Artiodactyla: three suborders. See also RUMINANT, TYLOPOD.

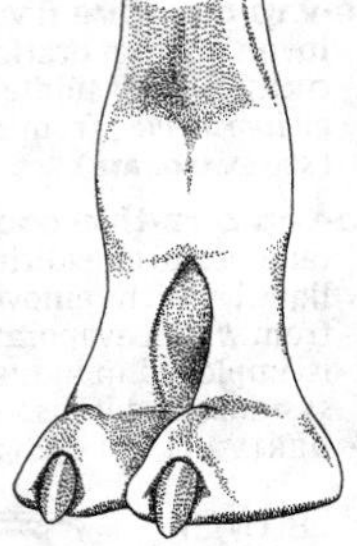
even-toed ungulate

e·ven·tu·al /i'venCHōōəl/ ▶ **adj.** [attrib.] occurring at the end of or as a result of a series of events; final; ultimate: *it's impossible to predict the eventual outcome of the competition.*
– ORIGIN early 17th cent. (in the sense 'relating to an event or events'): from Latin *eventus* (see EVENT), on the pattern of *actual.*

e·ven·tu·al·i·ty /i,venCHōō'alitē/ ▶ **n.** (pl. **eventualities**) a possible event or outcome: *you must be prepared for all eventualities.*

e·ven·tu·al·ly /i'venCHōōəlē/ ▶ **adv.** [sentence adverb] in the end, esp. after a long delay, dispute, or series of problems: *eventually, after midnight, I arrived at the hotel.*

e·ven·tu·ate /i'venCHōō,āt/ ▶ **v.** [no obj.] formal occur as a result: *you never know what might eventuate.* ■ (**eventuate in**) lead to as a result: *circumstances that eventuate in crime.*
– DERIVATIVES **e·ven·tu·a·tion** /i,venCHōō'āSHən/ **n.**
– ORIGIN late 18th cent.: from EVENT, on the pattern of *actuate.*

ev·er /'evər/ ▶ **adv. 1** [usu. with negative or in questions] at any time: *nothing ever seemed to ruffle her* | *don't you ever regret giving up all that money?* ■ used in comparisons for emphasis: *they felt better than ever before* | *our biggest ever range.*
2 at all times; always: *ever the man of action, he was impatient with intellectuals* | *it remains as popular as ever* | *they lived* **happily ever after** | [in combination] *he toyed with his ever-present cigar.*
3 [with comparative] increasingly; constantly: *having to borrow ever larger sums.*
4 used for emphasis in questions and other remarks, expressing astonishment or outrage: *who ever heard of a grown man being frightened of the dark?* | *don't you ever forget it!*
– PHRASES **ever and anon** archaic occasionally: *ever and anon the stillness is rent by the scream of a gibbon.* [from Shakespeare's *Love's Labour's Lost* (v. ii. 101).] **ever since** throughout the period since: *she had lived alone ever since her husband died.* **ever so** very: *I am ever so grateful.* **ever such** Brit. informal very much: *ever such a pretty little cat.* **for ever** see FOREVER. **yours ever** (also **ever yours**) Brit. a formula used to end an informal letter, before the signature.
– ORIGIN Old English *ǣfre*, of unknown origin.

ev·er·bloom·ing /'evər'blōōmiNG/ ▶ **adj.** (of a plant) in bloom throughout most or all of the growing season: *others prefer an everblooming variety like the rugosa roses.*

Ev·er·est, Mount /'ev(ə)rəst/ a mountain in the Himalayas, on the border between Nepal and Tibet. Rising to 29,028 feet (8,848 m), it is the highest mountain in the world; it was first climbed in 1953 by Sir Edmund Hillary and Tenzing Norgay. Tibetan name QOMOLUNGMA.
– ORIGIN named after Sir George *Everest* (1790–1866), a supervisor for the British government in India.

Ev·er·ett /'ev(ə)rit/ an industrial port city in northwestern Washington, north of Seattle, noted for its huge Boeing aircraft-assembly plant; pop. 98,212 (est. 2008).

ev·er·glade /'evər,glād/ ▶ **n.** a marshy tract of land that is mostly under water and covered with tall grass.

Ev·er·glades /'evər,glādz/ a vast area of marshland and coastal mangrove in southern Florida, part of which is protected as a national park.

ev·er·green /'evər,grēn/ ▶ **adj.** of or denoting a plant that retains green leaves throughout the year: *the glossy laurel is hardy and evergreen* | *evergreen shrubs.* Often contrasted with DECIDUOUS.
▶ **n.** a plant that retains green leaves throughout the year: *evergreens planted to cut off the east wind.*

ev·er·green oak ▶ **n.** another term for HOLM OAK.

Ev·er·green State a nickname for the state of WASHINGTON[1].

ev·er·last·ing /,evər'lastiNG/ ▶ **adj.** lasting forever or for a very long time: *the damned would suffer everlasting torment* | *it would be an everlasting reminder of this evening.*
▶ **n. 1** literary eternity.
2 (also **everlasting flower**) a flower of the daisy family with a papery texture, retaining its shape and color after being dried, esp. a helichrysum. Also called IMMORTELLE.
– DERIVATIVES **ev·er·last·ing·ly adv.**, **ev·er·last·ing·ness n.**

ev·er·more /,evər'môr/ ▶ **adv.** (chiefly used for rhetorical effect or in ecclesiastical contexts) always: *we pray that we may evermore dwell in him and he in us.*

Ev·ers /'evərz/, Medgar Wiley (1925–63), US civil rights leader. He was Mississippi field secretary of the NAACP from 1954; his assassination was a factor in President Kennedy's call for new, comprehensive civil rights legislation.

E·vert /'evərt/, Chris (1954–), US tennis player; full name *Christine Marie Evert*. During 1974–86, she won the women's singles title at seven French Open, six US Open, three Wimbledon, and two Australian Open tournaments.

e·vert /i'vərt/ ▶ **v.** [with obj.] Biology & Physiology turn (a structure or organ) outward or inside out: (as adj. **everted**) *the characteristic facial appearance of full, often everted lips.*
– DERIVATIVES **e·ver·si·ble** /i'vərsəbəl/ **adj.**, **e·ver·sion** /i'vərZHən, -SHən/ **n.**
– ORIGIN mid 16th cent. (in the sense 'upset, overthrow'): from Latin *evertere*, from *e-* (variant of *ex-*) 'out' + *vertere* 'to turn.' The current sense dates from the late 18th cent.

ev·er·where /'evər,(h)we(ə)r/ ▶ **adv.** dialect
1 everywhere.
2 wherever.

ev·er·which /'evər,(h)wiCH/ ▶ **adj.** dialect whichever.

eve·ry /'evrē/ ▶ **determiner** (preceding a singular noun) used to refer to all the individual members of a set without exception: *the hotel assures every guest of personal attention* | [with possessive determiner] *the children hung on his every word.* ■ used before an amount to indicate something happening at specified intervals: *tours are every thirty minutes* | *they had every third week off.* ■ (used for emphasis) all possible; the utmost: *you have every reason to be disappointed.*
– PHRASES **every bit as** (in comparisons) equally as: *the planning should be every bit as enjoyable as the event itself.* **every inch** see INCH[1]. **every last** (or **every single**) used to emphasize that every member of a group is included: *unbelievers, every last one of them* | *they insist you weigh every single thing.* **every man has his price** proverb everyone is open to bribery if the inducement offered is large enough. **every now and then** (or **now and again**) from time to time; occasionally: *I used to see him every now and then.* **every other** (or **every second**) each second in a series; each alternate: *I train with weights every other day* | *the auctions are held every second week.* **every so often** from time to time; occasionally: *every so often I need a laugh to stay sane.* **every time** without exception: *it brews a perfect blend of coffee every time.* **every which way** informal in all directions: *you can see cracks moving every which way.* ■ by all available means: *since then he has tried every which way to avoid contact with his ex.*
– ORIGIN Old English *ǣfre ǣlc* (see EVER, EACH).

eve·ry·bod·y /'evrē,bädē, -,bədē/ ▶ **pron.** every person: *everybody agrees with his views* | *it's not everybody's cup of tea.*

USAGE Everybody, along with everyone, traditionally uses a singular pronoun of reference: *everybody must sign* **his** *own name.* Because the use of *his* in this context is now perceived as sexist by some, a second option became popular: *everybody must sign* **his or her** *own name.* But *his or her* is often awkward, and many feel that the plural simply makes more sense: *everybody must sign* **their** *own name.* Although this violates what many consider standard, it is in fact standard in British English and increasingly so in US English. In some sentences, only *they* makes grammatical sense: *everybody agreed to convict the defendant, and* **they** *voted unanimously.*

ev·ery·day /'evrē,dā/ ▶ **adj.** [attrib.] happening or used every day; daily: *everyday chores like shopping and housework.* ■ commonplace: *everyday drugs like aspirin.*
▶ **adv.** (**every day**) each day; daily: *I get up at six every day.*

> **USAGE** The adjective **everyday**, meaning 'happening or used every day' or 'commonplace' (*everyday activities*), is written as one word, whereas the adverb meaning 'each day, daily' (*I get up at six every day*) is written as two.

Eve·ry·man /'evrē,man/ ▶ **n.** [in sing.] an ordinary or typical human being: *it is Everyman's dream car.*
– ORIGIN early 20th cent.: the name of the principal character in a 15th-cent. morality play.

eve·ry·one /'evrē,wən/ ▶ **pron.** every person: *everyone needs time to unwind | he knew everyone in the business.*

eve·ry one ▶ **pron.** each one.

> **USAGE** The pronoun **everyone**, meaning 'every person,' is spelled as one word: *everyone had a great time at the party*. The pronoun **every one**, meaning 'each one,' is spelled as two words: *every one of the employees got a bonus at the end of the year.*

eve·ry·place /'evrē,plās/ ▶ **adv.** informal term for EVERYWHERE.

eve·ry·thing /'evrē,THiNG/ ▶ **pron.** **1** all things; all the things of a group or class: *he taught me everything I know | herbal cures for* ***everything from*** *leprosy* ***to*** *rheumatism.* ■ all things of importance; a great deal: *I lost everything in the crash | he owed everything to his years in Munich.* ■ the most important thing or aspect: *money isn't everything.* **2** the current situation; life in general: *how's everything? | everything is going okay.*
– PHRASES **and everything** informal used to refer vaguely to other things associated with what has been mentioned: *you'll still get paid and everything.* **have everything** informal possess every attraction or advantage: *she was articulate, she was fun—it seemed to me she had everything.*

eve·ry·where /'evrē,(h)wer/ ▶ **adv.** in or to all places: *I've looked everywhere | everywhere she went she was fêted.* ■ in many places; common or widely distributed: *sandwich bars are everywhere.*
▶ **n.** all places or directions: *everywhere was in darkness.*
– PHRASES **everywhere else** in all other places: *they are the same machines used everywhere else in the world.*
– ORIGIN Middle English: formerly also as two words.

Eve·ry·wom·an /'evrē,wŏŏmən/ ▶ **n.** the ordinary or typical woman: *the book is a compilation of memorably silly moments in the life of a hapless Everywoman.*

evg. ▶ **abbr.** evening.

e·vict /i'vikt/ ▶ **v.** [with obj.] expel (someone) from a property, esp. with the support of the law: *he had court orders to evict the trespassers* ***from*** *three camps.*
– DERIVATIVES **e·vic·tor** /-tər/ **n.**
– ORIGIN late Middle English (in the sense 'recover property, or the title to property, by legal process'): from Latin *evict-* 'overcome, defeated,' from the verb *evincere*, from *e-* (variant of *ex-*) 'out' + *vincere* 'conquer.'

e·vic·tion /i'vikSHən/ ▶ **n.** the action of expelling someone, esp. a tenant, from a property; expulsion: *the forced eviction of residents.*

ev·i·dence /'evədəns/ ▶ **n.** the available body of facts or information indicating whether a belief or proposition is true or valid: *the study finds little evidence of overt discrimination.* ■ Law information given personally, drawn from a document, or in the form of material objects, tending or used to establish facts in a legal investigation or admissible as testimony in court: *without evidence, they can't bring a charge.* ■ signs; indications: *there was no obvious evidence of a break-in.*
▶ **v.** [with obj.] (usu. **be evidenced**) be or show evidence of: *that it has been populated from prehistoric times is evidenced by the remains of Neolithic buildings.*
– PHRASES **give evidence** Law give information and answer questions formally and in person in court or at an inquiry. **in evidence** noticeable; conspicuous: *his dramatic flair is still very much in evidence.* **turn state's** (or Brit. **King's** or **Queen's**) **evidence** Law (of a criminal) give information in court against one's partners in order to receive a less severe punishment oneself.
– ORIGIN Middle English: via Old French from Latin *evidentia*, from *evident-* 'obvious to the eye or mind' (see EVIDENT).

ev·i·dence-based ▶ **adj.** Medicine denoting disciplines of health care that proceed empirically with regard to the patient and reject more traditional protocols.

ev·i·dent /'evədənt/ ▶ **adj.** plain or obvious; clearly seen or understood: *she ate the cookies with evident enjoyment.*
– ORIGIN late Middle English: from Old French, or from Latin *evidens*, *evident-* 'obvious to the eye or mind,' from *e-* (variant of *ex-*) 'out' + *videre* 'to see.'

ev·i·den·tial /,evi'denCHəl/ ▶ **adj.** formal of or providing evidence: *the evidential value of the record.*
– DERIVATIVES **ev·i·den·ti·al·i·ty** /,evi,denCHē'alitē/ **n.**, **ev·i·den·tial·ly adv.**
– ORIGIN early 17th cent.: from medieval Latin *evidentialis*, from Latin *evidentia* (see EVIDENCE).

ev·i·den·tia·ry /,evi'densHərē/ ▶ **adj.** chiefly Law another term for EVIDENTIAL.

ev·i·dent·ly /'evidəntlē, 'evi,dentlē, ,evə'dentlē/ ▶ **adv.** **1** plainly or obviously; in a way that is clearly seen or understood: *a work so evidently laden with significance.*
2 [sentence adverb] it is plain that; it would seem that: *evidently Mrs. Smith thought differently.* ■ used as an affirmative response or reply: *"Were they old pals or something?" "Evidently."*

e·vil /'ēvəl/ ▶ **adj.** profoundly immoral and malevolent: *his evil deeds | no man is so evil as to be beyond redemption.* ■ (of a force or spirit) embodying or associated with the forces of the devil: *we have been driven out of the house by this evil spirit.* ■ harmful or tending to harm: *the evil effects of high taxes.* ■ (of something seen or smelled) extremely unpleasant: *a bathroom with an evil smell.*
▶ **n.** profound immorality, wickedness, and depravity, esp. when regarded as a supernatural force: *the world is stalked by relentless evil | good and evil in eternal opposition.* ■ a manifestation of this, esp. in people's actions: *the evil that took place last Thursday.* ■ something that is harmful or undesirable: *sexism, racism, and all other unpleasant social evils.*
– PHRASES **the evil eye** a gaze or stare superstitiously believed to cause material harm: *he gave me the evil eye as I walked down the corridor.* **the Evil One** archaic the Devil. **put off the evil day** (or **hour**) postpone something unpleasant for as long as possible. **speak evil of** slander: *it is a sin to speak evil of the king.*
– DERIVATIVES **e·vil·ly** /'ēvəl(l)ē/ **adv.**, **e·vil·ness n.**
– ORIGIN Old English *yfel*, of Germanic origin; related to Dutch *euvel* and German *Übel*.

e·vil·do·er /'ēvəl,dŏŏər/ ▶ **n.** a person who commits profoundly immoral and malevolent deeds.
– DERIVATIVES **e·vil·do·ing** /'ēvəl,dŏŏiNG/ **n.**

e·vil-mind·ed ▶ **adj.** having wicked thoughts, ideas, or intentions.

e·vince /i'vins/ ▶ **v.** [with obj.] formal reveal the presence of (a quality or feeling): *his letters evince the excitement he felt at undertaking this journey.* ■ be evidence of; indicate: *man's inhumanity to man as evinced in the use of torture.*
– ORIGIN late 16th cent. (in the sense 'prove by argument or evidence'): from Latin *evincere* 'overcome, defeat' (see EVICT).

e·vis·cer·ate /i'visə,rāt/ ▶ **v.** [with obj.] formal disembowel (a person or animal): *the goat had been skinned and neatly eviscerated.* ■ deprive (something) of its essential content: *myriad little concessions that would eviscerate the project.* ■ Surgery remove the contents of (a body organ).
– DERIVATIVES **e·vis·cer·a·tion** /i,visə'rāsHən/ **n.**
– ORIGIN late 16th cent.: from Latin *eviscerat-* 'disemboweled,' from the verb *eviscerare*, from *e-* (variant of *ex-*) 'out' + *viscera* 'internal organs.'

ev·i·ter·ni·ty /,evi'tərnitē/ ▶ **n.** archaic or literary eternal existence; everlasting duration.
– DERIVATIVES **ev·i·ter·nal** /-'tərnl/ **adj.**
– ORIGIN late 16th cent.: from Latin *aeviternus* 'eternal' + -ITY.

e·voc·a·tive /i'väkətiv/ ▶ **adj.** bringing strong images, memories, or feelings to mind: *powerfully evocative lyrics | the building's cramped interiors are highly evocative of past centuries.*
– DERIVATIVES **e·voc·a·tive·ly adv.**, **e·voc·a·tive·ness n.**
– ORIGIN mid 17th cent.: from Latin *evocativus*, from *evocat-* 'called forth,' from the verb *evocare* (see EVOKE).

e·voke /i'vōk/ ▶ **v.** [with obj.] **1** bring or recall to the conscious mind: *the sight of American asters evokes pleasant memories of childhood.* ■ elicit (a response): *the awkward kid who evoked giggles from his sisters.*
2 invoke (a spirit or deity).
– DERIVATIVES **ev·o·ca·tion** /,ēvō'kāsHən, ,evə-/ **n.**, **e·vok·er n.**
– ORIGIN early 17th cent. (sense 2): from Latin *evocare*, from *e-* (variant of *ex-*) 'out of, from' + *vocare* 'to call.'

ev·o·lute /'evə,lōōt/ (also **evolute curve**) ▶ **n.** Mathematics a curve that is the locus of the centers of curvature of another curve (its involute).
– ORIGIN mid 18th cent.: from Latin *evolutus*, past participle of *evolvere* 'roll out' (see EVOLVE).

ev·o·lu·tion /,evə'lōōsHən/ ▶ **n.** **1** the process by which different kinds of living organisms are thought to have developed and diversified from earlier forms during the history of the earth.

> The idea of organic evolution was proposed by some ancient Greek thinkers but was long rejected in Europe as contrary to the literal interpretation of the Bible. Lamarck proposed a theory that organisms became transformed by their efforts to respond to the demands of their environment, but he was unable to explain a mechanism for this. Lyell demonstrated that geological deposits were the cumulative product of slow processes over vast ages. This helped Darwin toward a theory of gradual evolution over a long period by the natural selection of those varieties of an organism slightly better adapted to the environment and hence more likely to produce descendants. Combined with the later discoveries of the cellular and molecular basis of genetics, Darwin's theory of evolution has, with some modification, become the dominant unifying concept of modern biology.

2 the gradual development of something, esp. from a simple to a more complex form: *the forms of written languages undergo constant evolution.*
3 Chemistry the giving off of a gaseous product, or of heat.
4 a pattern of movements or maneuvers: *silk ribbons waving in fanciful evolutions.*
5 Mathematics, dated the extraction of a root from a given quantity.
– DERIVATIVES **ev·o·lu·tion·al** /-sHənl/ **adj.**, **ev·o·lu·tion·al·ly** /-(ə)lē/ **adv.**, **ev·o·lu·tion·ar·i·ly** /,evə,lōōsHə'ne(ə)rəlē/ **adv.**, **ev·o·lu·tion·ar·y** /-,nerē/ **adj.**, **ev·o·lu·tive** /-'lōōtiv/ **adj.**
– ORIGIN early 17th cent.: from Latin *evolutio(n-)* 'unrolling,' from the verb *evolvere* (see EVOLVE). Early senses related to physical movement, first recorded in describing a tactical "wheeling" maneuver in the realignment of troops or ships. Current senses stem from a notion of "opening out" and "unfolding," giving rise to a general sense of 'development.'

ev·o·lu·tion·ist /,evə'lōōsHənist/ ▶ **n.** a person who believes in the theories of evolution and natural selection.
▶ **adj.** of or relating to the theories of evolution and natural selection: *an evolutionist model.*
– DERIVATIVES **ev·o·lu·tion·ism** /-,nizəm/ **n.**

e·volve /i'välv/ ▶ **v.** **1** develop gradually, esp. from a simple to a more complex form: [no obj.] *the company has evolved into a major chemical manufacturer | the Gothic style evolved steadily and naturally* ***from*** *the Romanesque* | [with obj.] *each school must evolve its own way of working.* ■ (with reference to an organism or biological feature) develop over successive generations, esp. as a result of natural selection: [no obj.] *the populations are cut off from each other and evolve independently.*
2 [with obj.] Chemistry give off (gas or heat).
– DERIVATIVES **e·volv·a·ble adj.**, **e·volve·ment n.**
– ORIGIN early 17th cent. (in the general sense 'make more complex, develop'): from Latin *evolvere*, from *e-* (variant of *ex-*) 'out of' + *volvere* 'to roll.'

EVOO ▶ **abbr.** extra virgin olive oil.

Év·ros /'ev,rôs/ Greek name for the MARITSA.

e·vul·sion /i'vəlsHən/ ▶ **n.** the action of plucking something out by force; violent or forcible extraction.

Év·voi·a /'evyä, 'evēä/ Greek name for EUBOEA.

ev·zone /'ev,zōn/ ▶ **n.** a kilted soldier belonging to a select Greek infantry regiment.
– ORIGIN late 19th cent.: from modern Greek *euzōnos*, from Greek, 'dressed for exercise' (from *eu-* 'fine' + *zōnē* 'belt'), because of their distinctive uniform, which includes a fustanella.

EW ▶ **abbr.** enlisted woman (women).

Ewe /'āwā, 'āvā/ ▶ **n.** (pl. **same**) **1** a member of a people of Ghana, Togo, and Benin.
2 the Kwa language of this people.

▶ **adj.** of or relating to this people or their language.
– ORIGIN the name in Ewe.

ewe /yo͞o/ ▶ **n.** a female sheep.
– ORIGIN Old English *eowu*, of Germanic origin; related to Dutch *ooi* and German *Aue*.

ewe neck ▶ **n.** a horse's neck of which the upper outline curves downward instead of upward.
– DERIVATIVES **ewe-necked adj.**

ew·er /ˈyo͞oər/ ▶ **n.** a large jug with a wide mouth, formerly used for carrying water for someone to wash in.
– ORIGIN late Middle English: from Anglo-Norman French *ewer*, variant of Old French *aiguiere*, based on Latin *aquarius* 'of water,' from *aqua* 'water.'

Ew·ing /ˈyo͞o-iNG/, Patrick (1962–), US basketball player. A center for the New York Knicks 1985–2000, he led the US Olympic team to gold medals in 1984 and 1992. He later played for the Seattle SuperSonics 2000–2001 and the Orlando Magic 2001–2002.

eww /ˈēo͞o/ ▶ **exclam.** informal used to express disgust or distaste: *eww, how can you eat that?*
– ORIGIN 1970s: imitative.

ex[1] /eks/ ▶ **prep. 1** (of goods) sold direct from: *carpet tiles offered at a special price, ex stock.*
2 without; excluding: *the discount and market price are ex dividend.*
– ORIGIN mid 19th cent. (sense 2): from Latin, 'out of.'

ex[2] ▶ **n.** informal a former husband, wife, or partner in a relationship: *I don't want my ex to spoil what I have now.*
– ORIGIN early 19th cent.: independent usage of **EX-**[1].

Ex. ▶ **abbr.** Bible Exodus.

ex-[1] (also **e-**) ▶ **prefix 1** out; outside of: *expand | express.*
2 up and away; upward: *excel | extol.*
3 thoroughly: *exacerbate | excruciate.*
4 removal or release: *excommunicate | exculpate | expel.*
5 forming verbs expressing inducement of a state: *exasperate | excite.*
6 forming nouns (from titles of office, status, etc.) expressing a former state: *ex-husband | ex-convict.*
– ORIGIN from Latin *ex* 'out of.'

ex-[2] ▶ **prefix** out: *exodus | exorcism.*
– ORIGIN from Greek *ex* 'out of.'

exa- ▶ **comb. form** (used in units of measurement) denoting a factor of 10^{18}: *exajoule.*
– ORIGIN from *(h)exa-* (see **HEXA-**), based on the supposed analogy of *tera-* and *tetra-*.

ex·a·byte /ˈeksəbīt/ (abbrev.: **Eb** or **EB**) ▶ **n.** Computing a unit of information equal to one quintillion (10^{18}) bytes, or one billion gigabytes.

ex·ac·er·bate /igˈzasərˌbāt/ ▶ **v.** [with obj.] make (a problem, bad situation, or negative feeling) worse: *the forest fire was exacerbated by the lack of rain.*
– DERIVATIVES **ex·ac·er·ba·tion** /igˌzasərˈbāSHən/ **n.**
– ORIGIN mid 17th cent.: from Latin *exacerbat-* 'made harsh,' from the verb *exacerbare*, from *ex-* (expressing inducement of a state) + *acerbus* 'harsh, bitter.' The noun *exacerbation* (late Middle English) originally meant 'provocation to anger.'

> **USAGE** On the difference between **exacerbate** and **exasperate**, see usage at **EXASPERATE**.

ex·act /igˈzakt/ ▶ **adj.** not approximated in any way; precise: *the exact details were still being worked out.* ■ accurate or correct in all details: *an exact replica, two feet tall, was constructed.* ■ (of a person) tending to be accurate and careful about minor details: *she was an exact, clever manager.* ■ (of a subject of study) permitting precise or absolute measurements as a basis for rigorously testable theories: *psychomedicine isn't an exact science yet.*
▶ **v.** [with obj.] demand and obtain (something, esp. a payment) from someone: *tributes exacted from the Slavic peoples | William's advisers exacted an oath of obedience from the clergy.* ■ inflict (revenge) on someone: *a frustrated woman bent on exacting a cruel revenge for his rejection.*
– DERIVATIVES **ex·act·a·ble adj.**, **ex·ac·ti·tude** /-təˌt(y)o͞od/ **n.**, **ex·ac·tor** /-tər/ **n.**
– ORIGIN late Middle English (as a verb): from Latin *exact-* 'completed, ascertained, enforced,' from the verb *exigere*, from *ex-* 'thoroughly' + *agere* 'perform.' The adjective dates from the mid 16th cent. and reflects the Latin *exactus* 'precise.'

ex·act·a /igˈzaktə/ ▶ **n.** a bet in which the first two places in a race must be predicted in the correct order. Compare with **QUINELLA**.
– ORIGIN 1960s: from American Spanish (*quiniela*) *exacta* 'exact (quinella).'

ex·act·ing /igˈzaktiNG/ ▶ **adj.** making great demands on one's skill, attention, or other resources: *living up to such exacting standards.*
– DERIVATIVES **ex·act·ing·ly adv.**, **ex·act·ing·ness n.**

ex·ac·tion /igˈzakSHən/ ▶ **n.** formal the action of demanding and obtaining something from someone, esp. a payment or service: *he supervised the exaction of tolls at various ports.* ■ a sum of money demanded in such a way. ■ an act of demanding unfair and exorbitant payment; an act of extortion.
– ORIGIN late Middle English: from Latin *exactio(n-)*, from *exigere* 'ascertain, perfect, enforce' (see **EXACT**).

ex·act·ly /igˈzak(t)lē/ ▶ **adv. 1** without discrepancy (used to emphasize the accuracy of a figure or description): *they met in 1989 and got married exactly two years later | fold the second strip of paper in exactly the same way.*
2 in exact terms; without vagueness: *what exactly are you looking for?*
3 used as a reply to confirm or agree with what has just been said: *"You mean that you're going to tell me the truth?" "Exactly."*
– PHRASES **not exactly** informal **1** not at all: *that was not exactly convincing.* **2** not quite but close to being: *not exactly agitated, but disturbed.*

ex·act·ness /igˈzak(t)nəs/ ▶ **n.** the quality of being accurate or correct; precision: *it is impossible to calculate with mathematical exactness.*

ex·ag·ger·ate /igˈzajəˌrāt/ ▶ **v.** [with obj.] represent (something) as being larger, greater, better, or worse than it really is: *they were apt to exaggerate any aches and pains | [no obj.] I couldn't sleep for three days—I'm not exaggerating.* ■ (as adj. **exaggerated**) enlarged or altered beyond normal or due proportions: *her plump thighs, exaggerated hips, and minuscule waist.*
– DERIVATIVES **ex·ag·ger·at·ed·ly adv.**, **ex·ag·ger·a·tive** /-ˌrātiv/ **adj.**, **ex·ag·ger·a·tor** /-ˌrātər/ **n.**
– ORIGIN mid 16th cent.: from Latin *exaggerat-* 'heaped up,' from the verb *exaggerare*, from *ex-* 'thoroughly' + *aggerare* 'heap up' (from *agger* 'heap'). The word originally meant 'pile up, accumulate,' later 'intensify praise or blame,' 'dwell on a virtue or fault,' giving rise to current senses.

ex·ag·ger·a·tion /igˌzajəˈrāSHən/ ▶ **n.** a statement that represents something as better or worse than it really is: *it would be an exaggeration to say I had morning sickness, but I did feel queasy.* ■ the action of making such statements: *he was prone to exaggeration.*

ex·alt /igˈzôlt/ ▶ **v.** [with obj.] hold (someone or something) in very high regard; think or speak very highly of: *the party will continue to exalt its hero.* ■ raise to a higher rank or a position of greater power: *this naturally exalts the peasant above his brethren in the same rank of society.* ■ make noble in character; dignify: *romanticism liberated the imagination and exalted the emotions.*
– ORIGIN late Middle English: from Latin *exaltare*, from *ex-* 'out, upward' + *altus* 'high.'

ex·al·ta·tion /ˌegzôlˈtāSHən, ˌeksôl-/ ▶ **n. 1** a feeling or state of extreme happiness: *she beams with exaltation.*
2 the action of elevating someone in rank, power, or character: *the resurrection and exaltation of Christ.* ■ the action of praising someone or something highly: *the exaltation of the army as a place for brotherhood.*
– ORIGIN late Middle English (in the sense 'the action of raising high'): from late Latin *exaltatio(n-)*, from Latin *exaltare* 'raise aloft' (see **EXALT**).

ex·alt·ed /igˈzôltid, eg-/ ▶ **adj. 1** (of a person or their rank or status) placed at a high or powerful level; held in high regard: *it had taken her years of hard infighting to reach her present exalted rank.* ■ (of an idea) noble; lofty: *his exalted hopes of human progress.*
2 in a state of extreme happiness: *I felt exalted and newly alive.*
– DERIVATIVES **ex·alt·ed·ly adv.**, **ex·alt·ed·ness n.**

ex·am /igˈzam/ ▶ **n. 1** short for **EXAMINATION** (sense 2): *he was likely to fail his exams again | [as modifier] exam results.*
2 [with adj. or noun modifier] a medical test of a specified kind: *routine eye exams.*

ex·a·men /igˈzāmən/ ▶ **n.** a formal examination of the soul or conscience, made usually daily by Jesuits and some other Roman Catholics.
– ORIGIN mid 17th cent.: from Latin, in the figurative sense 'examination' (literally 'tongue of a balance'), from *exigere* 'weigh accurately.'

ex·am·i·na·tion /igˌzaməˈnāSHən/ ▶ **n. 1** a detailed inspection or investigation: *an examination of marketing behavior | a medical examination is conducted without delay.* ■ the action or process of conducting such an inspection or investigation: *the treaty is under examination by the Senate Foreign Relations Committee.*
2 a formal test of a person's knowledge or proficiency in a particular subject or skill: *he scraped through the examinations at the end of his first year.*
3 Law the formal questioning of a witness in court.
– ORIGIN late Middle English (also in the sense 'testing (one's conscience) by a standard'): via Old French from Latin *examinatio(n-)*, from *examinare* 'weigh, test' (see **EXAMINE**).

ex·am·i·na·tion-in-chief ▶ **n.** another term for **DIRECT EXAMINATION**.

ex·am·ine /igˈzamən/ ▶ **v.** [with obj.] **1** inspect (someone or something) in detail to determine their nature or condition; investigate thoroughly: *a doctor examined me and said I might need a caesarean | this forced us to examine every facet of our business.*
2 test the knowledge or proficiency of (someone) by requiring them to answer questions or perform tasks: *the colleges set standards by examining candidates.* ■ Law formally question (a witness) in court. Compare with **CROSS-EXAMINE**.
– DERIVATIVES **ex·am·in·a·ble adj.**, **ex·am·i·nee** /igˌzaməˈnē/ **n.**
– ORIGIN Middle English: from Old French *examiner*, from Latin *examinare* 'weigh, test,' from *examen* (see **EXAMEN**).

ex·am·in·er /igˈzamənər/ ▶ **n. 1** a person whose job is to inspect something; an inspector: *a police vehicle examiner.*
2 a person who administers and grades examinations to test people's knowledge or proficiency.

ex·am·ple /igˈzampəl/ ▶ **n. 1** a thing characteristic of its kind or illustrating a general rule: *it's a good example of how European action can produce results | some of these carpets are among the finest examples of the period.* ■ a printed or written problem or exercise designed to illustrate a rule.
2 a person or thing regarded in terms of their fitness to be imitated or the likelihood of their being imitated: *it is vitally important that parents should set an example | she **followed** her brother's **example** and deserted her family.*
▶ **v.** (**be exampled**) be illustrated or exemplified: *the extent of Allied naval support is exampled by the navigational specialists provided.*
– PHRASES **for example** used to introduce something chosen as a typical case: *many, like Helen, for example, come from very poor backgrounds.* **make an example of** punish as a warning to others.
– ORIGIN late Middle English: from Old French, from Latin *exemplum*, from *eximere* 'take out,' from *ex-* 'out' + *emere* 'take.' Compare with **SAMPLE**.

ex an·te /ˈeks ˈantē/ ▶ **adj. & adv.** based on forecasts rather than actual results: [as adj.] *this is an ex ante estimate of the variance.*
– ORIGIN modern Latin, from Latin *ex* 'from, out of' + *ante* 'before.'

ex·an·the·ma /ˌegzanˈTHēmə/ ▶ **n.** (pl. **exanthemata** /-ˈTHemətə/) Medicine a skin rash accompanying a disease or fever.
– DERIVATIVES **ex·an·the·mat·ic** /egˌzanTHəˈmatik/ **adj.**, **ex·an·them·a·tous** /-ˈTHemətəs/ **adj.**
– ORIGIN mid 17th cent.: via late Latin from Greek *exanthēma* 'eruption,' from *ex-* 'out' + *antheein* 'to blossom' (from *anthos* 'flower').

ex·arch /ˈekˌsärk/ ▶ **n. 1** (in the Orthodox Church) a bishop lower in rank than a patriarch and having jurisdiction wider than the metropolitan of a diocese.
2 historical a governor of a distant province under the Byzantine emperors.
– ORIGIN late 16th cent.: via ecclesiastical Latin from Greek *exarkhos*, from *ex-* 'out of' + *arkhos* 'ruler.'

ex·ar·chate /ˈeksärˌkāt/ ▶ **n.** historical a distant province governed by an exarch under the Byzantine emperors.
– ORIGIN mid 16th cent.: from medieval Latin *exarchatus*, from ecclesiastical Latin *exarchus*, from Greek (see **EXARCH**).

ex·as·per·ate /igˈzaspəˌrāt/ ▶ **v.** [with obj.] irritate intensely; infuriate: *this futile process exasperates prison officials* | (as adj. **exasperated**) *she grew exasperated with his inability to notice anything.*
– DERIVATIVES **ex·as·per·at·ed·ly adv.**
– ORIGIN mid 16th cent.: from Latin *exasperat-* 'irritated to anger,' from the verb *exasperare* (based on *asper* 'rough').

> **USAGE** The verbs **exasperate** and **exacerbate** are sometimes confused. **Exasperate**, the more common of the two, means 'irritate or annoy to an extreme degree' (*He calls me three times a day asking for money. It's exasperating!*). **Exacerbate** means 'increase the bitterness or severity of' (*the star shortstop's loud self-congratulations only exacerbated his teammates' resentment*).

ex·as·per·at·ing /igˈzaspəˌrātiNG/ ▶ **adj.** intensely irritating; infuriating: *they suffered a number of exasperating setbacks.*
– DERIVATIVES **ex·as·per·at·ing·ly adv.**

ex·as·per·a·tion /igˌzaspəˈrāsHən/ ▶ **n.** a feeling of intense irritation or annoyance: *she rolled her eyes in exasperation.*

Exc. ▶ **abbr.** Excellency.

exc. ▶ **abbr.** ■ except. ■ exception. ■ excursion.

Ex·cal·i·bur /ekˈskaləbər/ (in Arthurian legend) King Arthur's magic sword.

ex ca·the·dra /ˌeks kəˈTHēdrə/ ▶ **adv. & adj.** with the full authority of office (esp. of the pope's infallibility as defined in Roman Catholic doctrine): [as adv.] *for an encyclical to be infallible the pope must speak ex cathedra.*
– ORIGIN early 19th cent.: Latin, 'from the (teacher's) chair,' from *ex* 'from' and *cathedra* 'seat' (from Greek *kathedra*).

ex·ca·vate /ˈekskəˌvāt/ ▶ **v.** [with obj.] **1** make (a hole or channel) by digging: *the cheapest way of doing this was to excavate a long trench.* ■ dig out material from (the ground): *the ground was largely excavated by hand.* ■ extract (material) from the ground by digging: *a very large amount of gravel would be excavated to form the channel.*
2 remove earth carefully and systematically from (an area) in order to find buried remains. ■ reveal or extract (buried remains) in this way: *clothing and weapons were excavated from the burial site.*
– ORIGIN late 16th cent.: from Latin *excavat-* 'hollowed out,' from the verb *excavare*, from *ex-* 'out' + *cavare* 'make or become hollow' (from *cavus* 'hollow').

ex·ca·va·tion /ˌekskəˈvāsHən/ ▶ **n.** the action of excavating something, esp. an archaeological site: *the methods of excavation have to be extremely rigorous | students often participate in excavations.* ■ a site that is being or has been excavated.

ex·ca·va·tor /ˈekskəˌvātər/ ▶ **n.** a person who removes earth carefully and systematically from an archaeological site in order to find buried remains. ■ a large machine for removing soil from the ground, esp. on a building site.

ex·ceed /ikˈsēd/ ▶ **v.** [with obj.] be greater in number or size than (a quantity, number, or other measurable thing): *production costs have exceeded $60,000.* ■ go beyond what is allowed or stipulated by (a set limit, esp. of one's authority): *the Tribunal's decision clearly exceeds its powers under the statute.* ■ be better than; surpass: *catalog sales have exceeded expectations.*
– DERIVATIVES **ex·ceed·ance n.**
– ORIGIN late Middle English (in the sense 'go over a boundary or specified point'): from Old French *exceder*, from Latin *excedere*, from *ex-* 'out' + *cedere* 'go.'

ex·ceed·ing /ikˈsēdiNG/ archaic or literary ▶ **adj.** very great: *she spoke warmly of his exceeding kindness.*
▶ **adv.** [as submodifier] extremely; exceedingly: *an ale of exceeding poor quality.*

ex·ceed·ing·ly /ikˈsēdiNGlē/ ▶ **adv. 1** [as submodifier] extremely: *the team played exceedingly well.*
2 archaic to a great extent: *the supply multiplied exceedingly.*

ex·cel /ikˈsel/ ▶ **v.** (**excels, excelling, excelled**) [no obj.] be exceptionally good at or proficient in an activity or subject: *a sturdy youth who excelled at football.*
– ORIGIN late Middle English: from Latin *excellere*, from *ex-* 'out, beyond' + *celsus* 'lofty.'

ex·cel·lence /ˈeksələns/ ▶ **n.** the quality of being outstanding or extremely good: *the award for excellence in engineering | a center of academic excellence.* ■ archaic an outstanding feature or quality.
– ORIGIN late Middle English: from Latin *excellentia*, from the verb *excellere* 'surpass' (see **EXCEL**).

ex·cel·len·cy /ˈeksələnsē/ ▶ **n.** (pl. **excellencies**) **1** (**His, Your**, etc., **Excellency**) a title given to certain high officials of state, esp. ambassadors, or of the Roman Catholic Church, or used in addressing them: *His Excellency the Indian Consul General.*
2 archaic an outstanding feature or quality.
– ORIGIN Middle English (in the sense 'excellence'): from Latin *excellentia*, from *excellere* 'surpass' (see **EXCEL**). The use of the word as a title dates from the mid 16th cent.

ex·cel·lent /ˈeksələnt/ ▶ **adj.** extremely good; outstanding: *a 3-bedroom house in excellent condition | their results are excellent.*
▶ **exclam.** used to indicate approval or pleasure: *"What a lovely idea! Excellent!"*
– DERIVATIVES **ex·cel·lent·ly adv.**
– ORIGIN late Middle English (in the general sense 'excelling, outstanding,' referring to either a good or bad quality): from Old French, from Latin *excellent* 'being preeminent,' from *excellere* (see **EXCEL**). The current appreciatory sense dates from the early 17th cent.

ex·cel·si·or /ikˈselsēər/ ▶ **n.** used in the names of hotels, newspapers, and other products to indicate superior quality: *they stayed at the Excelsior.* ■ softwood shavings used for packing fragile goods or stuffing furniture.
– ORIGIN late 18th cent. (as an exclamation): from Latin, comparative of *excelsus*, from *ex-* 'out, beyond' + *celsus* 'lofty.'

Ex·cel·si·or State a nickname for the state of **NEW YORK**.

ex·cen·tric /ikˈsentrik/ ▶ **adj.** chiefly Biology not centrally placed or not having its axis or other part placed centrally: *a distinct excentric nucleus.*
– DERIVATIVES **ex·cen·tri·cal·ly** /-(ə)lē/ **adv.**

ex·cept /ikˈsept/ ▶ **prep.** not including; other than: *naked **except for** my socks | they work every day except Sunday.*
▶ **conj.** used before a statement that forms an exception to one just made: *I didn't tell him anything, **except that** I needed the money | our berets were the same except mine had a leather band inside.* ■ archaic unless: *she never offered advice, except it were asked of her.*
▶ **v.** [with obj.] formal specify as not included in a category or group; exclude: *he excepted from his criticism a handful of distinguished writers.*
– ORIGIN late Middle English: from Latin *except-* 'taken out,' from the verb *excipere*, from *ex-* 'out of' + *capere* 'take.'

> **USAGE** See usage at **ACCEPT**.

ex·cept·ed /ikˈseptid/ ▶ **adj.** [postpositive] not included in the category or group specified: *most museums (the Getty excepted) have small acquisitions budgets.*

ex·cept·ing /ikˈseptiNG/ ▶ **prep.** formal except for; apart from: *excepting some of the dialogue, the book is in every way superior to the movie.*

ex·cep·tion /ikˈsepsHən/ ▶ **n.** a person or thing that is excluded from a general statement or does not follow a rule: *the drives between towns are a delight, and the journey to Graz is **no exception** | while he normally shies away from introducing resolutions, he **made an exception** in this case.*
– PHRASES **the exception proves the rule** proverb the fact that some cases do not follow a rule proves that the rule applies in all other cases. [From Latin *exceptio probat regulam in casibus non exceptis* 'The exception confirms the rule in the cases not excepted.' The exception here is 'the action of excepting,' not 'that being excepted.' By specifically excluding cases where the rule doesn't apply, you make the rule stronger for the cases still governed by it.] **take exception to** object strongly to; be offended by: *they took exception to his bohemian demeanor.* **with the exception of** except; not including. **without exception** with no one or nothing excluded.
– ORIGIN late Middle English: via Old French from Latin *exceptio(n-)*, from *excipere* 'take out' (see **EXCEPT**).

ex·cep·tion·a·ble /ikˈsepsHənəbəl/ ▶ **adj.** formal open to objection; causing disapproval or offense: *his drawings are almost the only exceptionable part of his work.*

> **USAGE** **Exceptionable** means 'open to objection' and is usually found in negative contexts: *there was nothing exceptionable in the evidence.* It is sometimes confused with the much more common **exceptional**, meaning 'unusual, outstanding.' Their opposites, **unexceptionable** ('unobjectionable, beyond criticism') and **unexceptional** ('ordinary'), are also sometimes confused. See also usage at **UNEXCEPTIONABLE**.

ex·cep·tion·al /ikˈsepsHənəl/ ▶ **adj.** unusual; not typical: *crimes of exceptional callousness and cruelty.* ■ unusually good; outstanding: *a pepper offering exceptional flavor and juiciness.* ■ (of a child) mentally or physically disabled so as to require special schooling: *helping parents of exceptional children.*
– DERIVATIVES **ex·cep·tion·al·i·ty** /ikˌsepsHəˈnalitē/ **n.**

> **USAGE** See usage at **EXCEPTIONABLE**.

ex·cep·tion·al·ly /ikˈsepsHənəlē/ ▶ **adv.** to a greater degree than normal; unusually: [as submodifier] *the weather was exceptionally mild for the time of the year.* ■ only in unusual circumstances: *the court allows half an hour in most cases, one hour exceptionally for a very important case.*

ex·cerpt ▶ **n.** /ˈekˌsərpt/ a short extract from a film, broadcast, or piece of music or writing.
▶ **v.** /ikˈsərpt/ [with obj.] take (a short extract) from a text: *the notes are excerpted from his forthcoming biography.* ■ take an excerpt or excerpts from (a text).
– DERIVATIVES **ex·cerpt·i·ble** /ekˈsərptəbəl, ik-/ **adj.**, **ex·cerp·tion** /ekˈsərpsHən, ik-/ **n.**
– ORIGIN mid 16th cent. (as a verb): from Latin *excerpt-* 'plucked out,' from the verb *excerpere*, from *ex-* 'out of' + *carpere* 'to pluck.'

ex·cess /ikˈses, ˈekses/ ▶ **n. 1** an amount of something that is more than necessary, permitted, or desirable: *are you suffering from **an excess of** stress in your life?* ■ the amount by which one quantity or number exceeds another: *the excess of imports over exports rose $1.4 billion.*
2 lack of moderation in an activity, esp. eating or drinking: *bouts of alcoholic excess.* ■ (**excesses**) outrageous or immoderate behavior: *the worst excesses of the French Revolution.*
3 the action of exceeding a permitted limit: *there is no issue as to excess of jurisdiction.*
▶ **adj.** [attrib.] exceeding a prescribed or desirable amount: *trim any excess fat off the meat.*
– PHRASES **in** (or **to**) **excess** exceeding the proper amount or degree: *she insisted that he did not drink to excess.* **in excess of** more than; exceeding: *a top speed in excess of 20 knots.*
– ORIGIN late Middle English: via Old French from Latin *excessus*, from *excedere* 'go out, surpass' (see **EXCEED**).

ex·cess bag·gage ▶ **n.** luggage weighing more than the limit allowed on an aircraft and liable to an extra charge. ■ a thing that is surplus to requirements, and therefore unwanted or inconvenient.

ex·ces·sive /ikˈsesiv/ ▶ **adj.** more than is necessary, normal, or desirable; immoderate: *he was drinking excessive amounts of brandy.*
– DERIVATIVES **ex·ces·sive·ness n.**
– ORIGIN late Middle English: from Old French *excessif, -ive*, from medieval Latin *excessivus*, from Latin *excedere* 'surpass' (see **EXCEED**).

ex·ces·sive·ly /ikˈsesivlē/ ▶ **adv.** to a greater degree or in greater amounts than is necessary, normal, or desirable; inordinately: *they don't drink excessively* | [as submodifier] *excessively high taxes.*

exch. ▶ **abbr.** ■ exchange. ■ exchequer.

ex·change /iksˈCHānj/ ▶ **n.** an act of giving one thing and receiving another (esp. of the same type or value) in return: *negotiations should eventually lead to **an exchange of** land **for** peace | an exchange of prisoners of war | opportunities for the exchange of information.* ■ a visit or visits in which two people or groups from different countries stay with each other or do each other's jobs: [as modifier] *nine colleagues were away on an exchange visit to Germany.* ■ a short conversation; an argument: *there was a heated exchange.* ■ the giving of money for its equivalent in the money of another country. ■ the fee or percentage charged for converting the currency of one country into that of another. ■ a system or market in which commercial transactions involving currency, shares, commodities, etc., can be carried out within or between countries. See also **FOREIGN EXCHANGE**. ■ a central office or station of operations providing telephone service: *private branch exchanges to automate internal telephone networks.* ■ Chess a move or short sequence of moves in which both players capture material of comparable value, or particularly (**the exchange**) in which one captures a rook in return for a knight or bishop (and is said to *win the exchange*). ■ a building or institution used for the trading of a particular commodity or commodities: *the New York Stock Exchange.*
▶ **v.** [with obj.] give something and receive something of the same kind in return: *we exchanged addresses | he **exchanged** a concerned glance **with** Stephen.* ■ give or receive one thing in place of another: *we regret that tickets cannot be exchanged | she **exchanged** her suburban housewife look **for** leathers and tattoos.*
– PHRASES **in exchange** as a thing exchanged: *at 8, he was carrying bags of groceries **in exchange for** a nickel.*
– DERIVATIVES **ex·change·a·bil·i·ty** /iksˌCHānjəˈbilitē/ **n.**, **ex·change·a·ble adj.**, **ex·chang·er n.**
– ORIGIN late Middle English: from Old French *eschange* (noun), *eschangier* (verb), based on *changer* (see **CHANGE**). The spelling was influenced by Latin *ex-* 'out, utterly' (see **EX-**[1]).

ex·change con·trol ▶ **n.** a governmental restriction on the movement of currency between countries.

PRONUNCIATION KEY ə **ago, up**; ər **over, fur**; a **hat**; ā **ate**; ä **car**; e **let**; ē **see**; i **fit**; ī **by**; NG **sing**; ō **go**; ô **law, for**; oi **toy**; o͝o **good**; o͞o **goo**; ou **out**; TH **thin**; T̲H̲ **then**; ZH **vision**

e

ex·change rate ▶ n. (also **rate of exchange**) the value of one currency for the purpose of conversion to another.

ex·change rate mech·an·ism (abbr.: **ERM**) an arrangement within the European Monetary System that allows the value of participating currencies to fluctuate to a defined degree in relation to each other so as to control exchange rates. Each currency is given a rate of exchange with the euro, from which it is allowed to fluctuate by no more than a specified amount; if it moves beyond this the government in question must alter its economic policies or reset the currency's rate with the euro.

ex·change trans·fu·sion ▶ n. Medicine the simultaneous removal of a patient's blood and replacement by donated blood, used in treating serious conditions such as hemolytic disease of the newborn.

e

ex·cheq·uer /eks'cHekər, iks-/ ▶ n. a royal or national treasury. ■ (**Exchequer**) Brit. the bank account into which tax receipts and other public monies are paid; the funds of the British government. ■ (**Exchequer**) Brit. historical the former government office responsible for collecting revenue and making payments on behalf of the sovereign, auditing official accounts, and trying legal cases relating to revenue.
– ORIGIN Middle English: from Old French *eschequier*, from medieval Latin *scaccarium* 'chessboard,' from *scaccus* (see **CHECK**[1]). The original sense was 'chessboard.' Current senses derive from the department of state established by the Norman kings of England to deal with the royal revenues, named *Exchequer* from the checkered tablecloth on which accounts were kept by means of counters. The spelling was influenced by Latin *ex-* 'out' (see **EX**[1]). Compare with **CHEQUER**.

ex·ci·mer /'eksəmər/ ▶ n. Chemistry an unstable molecule that is formed in an excited state by the combination of two smaller molecules or atoms and rapidly dissociates with emission of radiation. Such species are utilized in some kinds of lasers.
– ORIGIN 1960s: blend of **EXCITED** and **DIMER**.

ex·cip·i·ent /ik'sipēənt/ ▶ n. an inactive substance that serves as the vehicle or medium for a drug or other active substance.
– ORIGIN early 18th cent. (as an adjective in the sense 'that takes exception'): from Latin *excipient-* 'taking out,' from the verb *excipere*.

ex·cise[1] ▶ n. /'ek,sīz/ [usu. as modifier] a tax levied on certain goods and commodities produced or sold within a country and on licenses granted for certain activities: *excise taxes on cigarettes*.
▶ v. /ik'sīz, ek-/ [with obj.] (usu. as adj. **excised**) charge excise on (goods): *excised goods*.
– ORIGIN late 15th cent. (in the general sense 'a tax or toll'): from Middle Dutch *excijs, accijs*, perhaps based on Latin *accensare* 'to tax,' from *ad-* 'to' + *census* 'tax' (see **CENSUS**).

ex·cise[2] /ik'sīz/ ▶ v. [with obj.] cut out surgically: *the precision with which surgeons can excise brain tumors* | (as adj. **excised**) *excised tissue*. ■ remove (a section) from a text or piece of music: *the clauses were excised from the treaty*.
– DERIVATIVES **ex·ci·sion** /-'sizHən/ n.
– ORIGIN late 16th cent. (in the sense 'notch or hollow out'): from Latin *excis-* 'cut out,' from the verb *excidere*, from *ex-* 'out of' + *caedere* 'to cut.'

ex·cise·man /'ek,sīzmən, -man/ ▶ n. (pl. **excisemen**) Brit. historical an official responsible for collecting excise tax and preventing infringement of the excise laws (esp. by smuggling).

ex·cit·a·ble /ik'sītəbəl/ ▶ adj. responding rather too readily to something new or stimulating; too easily excited: *Chip could be a bit wayward and excitable*. ■ (of tissue or a cell) responsive to stimulation.
– DERIVATIVES **ex·cit·a·bil·i·ty** /ik,sītə'bilitē/ n., **ex·cit·a·bly** /-əblē/ adv.

ex·cit·ant /ik'sītnt/ ▶ n. Biology a substance that elicits an active physiological or behavioral response.
– ORIGIN early 17th cent.: perhaps suggested by French *excitant*.

ex·ci·ta·tion /ek,sī'tāsHən/ ▶ n. **1** technical the application of energy to a particle, object, or physical system, in particular: ■ Physics the process in which an atom or other particle adopts a higher energy state when energy is supplied: *thermal excitation*. ■ Physiology the state of enhanced activity or potential activity of a cell, organism, or tissue that results from its stimulation. ■ Physics the process of applying current to the winding of an electromagnet to produce a magnetic field. ■ Electronics the process of applying a signal voltage to the control electrode of an electron tube or the base of a transistor.
2 the action or state of exciting or being excited; excitement: *a state of sexual excitation*.
– ORIGIN late Middle English: from Old French, from late Latin *excitatio(n-)*, from *excitare* 'rouse, call forth' (see **EXCITE**).

ex·cit·a·tive /ik'sītətiv/ ▶ adj. rare causing excitation.

ex·cit·a·to·ry /ik'sītə,tôrē/ ▶ adj. chiefly Physiology characterized by, causing, or constituting excitation: *the excitatory action of these impulses*.

ex·cite /ik'sīt/ ▶ v. [with obj.] **1** cause strong feelings of enthusiasm and eagerness in (someone): *flying still excites me* | *Gould was excited by these discoveries*. ■ arouse (someone) sexually: *his kiss thrilled and excited her*.
2 bring out or give rise to (a feeling or reaction): *the ability to excite interest in others*.
3 produce a state of increased energy or activity in (a physical or biological system): *the energy of an electron is sufficient to excite the atom*.
– ORIGIN Middle English (in the sense 'stir someone up, incite someone to do something'): from Old French *exciter* or Latin *excitare*, frequentative of *exciere* 'call out or forth.' Sense 1 dates from the mid 19th cent.

ex·cit·ed /ik'sītid/ ▶ adj. **1** very enthusiastic and eager: *they were excited about the prospect* | *the excited children*. ■ sexually aroused.
2 Physics of or in an energy state higher than the normal or ground state.
– DERIVATIVES **ex·cit·ed·ly** adv.

ex·cite·ment /ik'sītmənt/ ▶ n. a feeling of great enthusiasm and eagerness: *her cheeks were flushed with excitement* | *the excitement of seeing a live leopard*. ■ something that arouses such a feeling; an exciting incident: *the excitements of the previous night*. ■ sexual arousal.

ex·cit·er /ik'sītər/ ▶ n. a thing that produces excitation, in particular a device that provides a magnetizing current for the electromagnets in a motor or generator.

ex·cit·ing /ik'sītiNG/ ▶ adj. causing great enthusiasm and eagerness: *an exciting breakthrough*. ■ sexually arousing.
– DERIVATIVES **ex·cit·ing·ly** adv., **ex·cit·ing·ness** n.

ex·ci·ton /'eksi,tän, ik'sītän/ ▶ n. Physics a mobile concentration of energy in a crystal formed by an excited electron and an associated hole.
– ORIGIN 1930s: from **EXCITATION** + **-ON**.

excl. ▶ abbr. ■ exclamation. ■ excluding. ■ exclusive.

ex·claim /ik'sklām/ ▶ v. [no obj.] cry out suddenly, esp. in surprise, anger, or pain: *she looked in the mirror, exclaiming in dismay at her appearance* | [with direct speech] *"Well, I never," she exclaimed*.
– ORIGIN late 16th cent.: from French *exclamer* or Latin *exclamare*, from *ex-* 'out' + *clamare* 'to shout.'

ex·cla·ma·tion /,eksklə'māsHən/ ▶ n. a sudden cry or remark, esp. expressing surprise, anger, or pain: *Meg gave an involuntary exclamation* | *an exclamation of amazement*.
– ORIGIN late Middle English: from Latin *exclamatio(n-)*, from *exclamare* 'shout out' (see **EXCLAIM**).

ex·cla·ma·tion point (Brit. **exclamation mark**) ▶ n. a punctuation mark (!) indicating an exclamation.

ex·clam·a·to·ry /ik'sklamə,tôrē/ ▶ adj. of or relating to a sudden cry or remark, esp. one expressing surprise, anger, or pain.

ex·clave /'ek,sklāv/ ▶ n. a portion of territory of one state completely surrounded by territory of another or others, as viewed by the home territory. Compare with **ENCLAVE**.
– ORIGIN late 19th cent.: from **EX-**[1] 'out' + a shortened form of **ENCLAVE**.

ex·clo·sure /ik'sklōzHər/ ▶ n. Forestry an area from which unwanted animals are excluded.
– ORIGIN 1920s: from **EX-**[1] 'out' + **CLOSURE**, on the pattern of *enclosure*.

ex·clude /ik'sklo͞od/ ▶ v. [with obj.] deny (someone) access to or bar (someone) from a place, group, or privilege: *women had been excluded from many scientific societies*. ■ keep (something) out of a place: *apply flux to exclude oxygen*. ■ remove from consideration; rule out: *computer software is excluded from the mandatory 15-year write-off*. ■ prevent the occurrence of; preclude: *clauses seeking to exclude liability for loss or damage*.
– PHRASES **law** (or **principle**) **of the excluded middle** Logic the principle that one (and one only) of two contradictory propositions must be true.
– DERIVATIVES **ex·clud·a·ble** adj., **ex·clud·er** n.
– ORIGIN late Middle English: from Latin *excludere*, from *ex-* 'out' + *claudere* 'to shut.'

ex·clud·ing /ik'sklo͞odiNG/ ▶ prep. not taking someone or something into account; apart from; except: *you have eight more days, excluding Sundays*.

ex·clu·sion /ik'sklo͞ozHən/ ▶ n. the process or state of excluding or being excluded: *drug users are subject to exclusion from the military*. ■ an item or risk specifically not covered by an insurance policy or other contract: *exclusions can be added to your policy*.
– PHRASES **to the exclusion of** so as to exclude something specified: *don't revise a few topics to the exclusion of all others*.
– DERIVATIVES **ex·clu·sion·ar·y** /-,nerē/ adj.
– ORIGIN late Middle English: from Latin *exclusio(n-)*, from *excludere* 'shut out' (see **EXCLUDE**).

ex·clu·sion·ar·y rule /ik'sklo͞ozHə,nerē/ ▶ n. a law that prohibits the use of illegally obtained evidence in a criminal trial.

ex·clu·sion clause ▶ n. (in a contract) a clause disclaiming liability for a particular risk.

ex·clu·sion·ist /ik'sklo͞ozHənist/ ▶ adj. acting to shut out or bar someone from a place, group, or privilege: *an exclusionist foreign policy*.
▶ n. a person favoring the exclusion of someone from a place, group, or privilege.

ex·clu·sion prin·ci·ple (in full **Pauli exclusion principle**) ▶ n. see **PAULI**.

ex·clu·sion zone ▶ n. an area into which entry is forbidden, esp. by ships or aircraft of particular nationalities.

ex·clu·sive /ik'sklo͞osiv/ ▶ adj. **1** excluding or not admitting other things: *my exclusive focus is on San Antonio issues*. ■ unable to exist or be true if something else exists or is true: *these approaches are not exclusive; many students will combine them* | ***mutually exclusive** political views*. ■ (of terms) excluding all but what is specified.
2 restricted or limited to the person, group, or area concerned: *the couple had exclusive possession of the condo* | *the jaguar and puma are **exclusive to** the New World*. ■ (of an item or story) not published or broadcast elsewhere: *an exclusive interview*. ■ (of a commodity) not obtainable elsewhere: *exclusive designer jewelry*.
3 catering or available to only a few, select people; high class and expensive: *an exclusive Georgetown neighborhood*.
4 [predic.] (**exclusive of**) not including; excepting: *prices are exclusive of tax and delivery*.
▶ n. an item or story published or broadcast by only one source.
– DERIVATIVES **ex·clu·sive·ness** n., **ex·clu·siv·i·ty** /,eksklo͞o'sivitē/ n.
– ORIGIN late 15th cent. (as a noun denoting something that excludes or causes exclusion): from medieval Latin *exclusivus*, from Latin *excludere* 'shut out' (see **EXCLUDE**).

Ex·clu·sive Breth·ren ▶ plural n. the more rigorous of two principal divisions of the Plymouth Brethren (the other being the Open Brethren). The Exclusive Brethren restrict their contact with outsiders and with modern technology.

ex·clu·sive ec·o·nom·ic zone ▶ n. an area of coastal water and seabed within a certain distance of a country's coastline, to which the country claims exclusive rights for fishing, drilling, and other economic activities.

ex·clu·sive·ly /ik'sklo͞osəvlē/ ▶ adv. to the exclusion of others; only; solely: *paints produced exclusively for independent retailers* | [as submodifier] *exclusively female concerns*.

ex·clu·sive OR ▶ n. Electronics a Boolean operator working on two variables that has the value of one if one but not both of the variables has a value of one. Also called **XOR**. ■ (also **exclusive OR gate**) a circuit that produces an output signal when a signal is received through one and only one of its two inputs.

ex·clu·siv·ism /ik'sklo͞osə,vizəm/ ▶ n. the action or policy of excluding a person or group from a place, group, or privilege.
– DERIVATIVES **ex·clu·siv·ist** adj. & n.

ex·cog·i·tate /ek'skäji,tāt/ ▶ v. [with obj.] formal think out, plan, or devise: *scholars straining to excogitate upon subjects of which they know little*.
– DERIVATIVES **ex·cog·i·ta·tion** /ek,skäji'tāsHən/ n.
– ORIGIN early 16th cent.: from Latin *excogitat-* 'found by process of thought,' from the verb *excogitare*, from *ex-* 'out' + *cogitare* 'think.'

ex·com·mu·ni·cate ▶ v. /,ekskə'myo͞oni,kāt/ [with obj.] officially exclude (someone) from participation in the sacraments and services of the Christian Church.
▶ adj. /,ekskə'myo͞onikit/ excommunicated: *all violators were to be pronounced excommunicate*.
▶ n. /,ekskə'myo͞onikit/ an excommunicated person.
– DERIVATIVES **ex·com·mu·ni·ca·tion** /,ekskə,myo͞oni'kāsHən/ n., **ex·com·mu·ni·ca·tive**

/-ˌkātiv/ **adj.**, **ex·com·mu·ni·ca·tor** /-ˌkātər/ **n.**, **ex·com·mu·ni·ca·to·ry** /-kəˌtôrē/ **adj.**
– ORIGIN late Middle English: from ecclesiastical Latin *excommunicat-* 'excluded from communication with the faithful,' from the verb *excommunicare*, from *ex-* 'out' + Latin *communis* 'common to all,' on the pattern of Latin *communicare* (see **COMMUNICATE**).

ex-con ▶ **n.** informal an ex-convict; a former inmate of a prison.
– ORIGIN early 20th cent.: abbreviation.

ex·co·ri·ate /ikˈskôrēˌāt/ ▶ **v.** [with obj.] **1** formal censure or criticize severely: *the papers that had been excoriating him were now lauding him.*
2 chiefly Medicine damage or remove part of the surface of (the skin).
– DERIVATIVES **ex·co·ri·a·tion** /ikˌskôrēˈāsHən/ **n.**
– ORIGIN late Middle English: from Latin *excoriat-* 'skinned,' from the verb *excoriare*, from *ex-* 'out, from' + *corium* 'skin, hide.'

ex·cre·ment /ˈekskrəmənt/ ▶ **n.** waste matter discharged from the bowels; feces.
– DERIVATIVES **ex·cre·men·tal** /ˌekskrəˈmen(t)l/ **adj.**
– ORIGIN mid 16th cent.: from French *excrément* or Latin *excrementum*, from *excernere* 'to sift out' (see **EXCRETE**).

ex·cres·cence /ikˈskresəns/ ▶ **n.** a distinct outgrowth on a human or animal body or on a plant, esp. one that is the result of disease or abnormality. ■ an unattractive or superfluous addition or feature: *removing the excrescences of later interpretation.*
– ORIGIN late Middle English: from Latin *excrescentia*, from *excrescere* 'grow out,' from *ex-* 'out' + *crescere* 'grow.'

ex·cres·cent /ikˈskresənt/ ▶ **adj. 1** forming or constituting an excrescence.
2 (of a speech sound) added without etymological justification (e.g., the *-t* at the end of the surname *Bryant*).

ex·cre·ta /ikˈskrētə/ ▶ **n.** [treated as sing. or pl.] waste matter discharged from the body, esp. feces and urine.
– ORIGIN mid 19th cent.: from Latin, 'things sifted out,' neuter plural of *excretus*, past participle of *excernere* (see **EXCRETE**).

ex·crete /ikˈskrēt/ ▶ **v.** [with obj.] (of a living organism or cell) separate and expel as waste (a substance, esp. a product of metabolism): *excess bicarbonate is excreted by the kidney* | [no obj.] *the butterfly pupa neither feeds nor excretes.*
– DERIVATIVES **ex·cret·er n.**, **ex·cre·tive** /ˈekskritiv, ikˈskrētiv/ **adj.**
– ORIGIN early 17th cent. (in the sense 'cause to excrete'): from Latin *excret-* 'sifted out,' from the verb *excernere*, from *ex-* 'out' + *cernere* 'sift.'

ex·cre·tion /ikˈskrēsHən/ ▶ **n.** (in living organisms and cells) the process of eliminating or expelling waste matter. ■ a product of this process: *bodily excretions.*
– ORIGIN early 17th cent.: from French *excrétion* or Latin *excretio(n-)*, from *excernere* 'sift out' (see **EXCRETE**).

ex·cre·to·ry /ˈekskriˌtôrē/ ▶ **adj.** of, relating to, or concerned with excretion: *the excretory organs.*

ex·cru·ci·ate /ikˈskrōōsHēˌāt/ ▶ **v.** [with obj.] rare torment (someone) physically or mentally: *I stand back, excruciated by the possibility.*
– DERIVATIVES **ex·cru·ci·a·tion** /ikˌskrōōsHēˌāsHən/ **n.**
– ORIGIN late 16th cent.: from Latin *excruciat-* 'tormented,' from the verb *excruciare* (based on *crux, cruc-* 'a cross').

ex·cru·ci·at·ing /ikˈskrōōsHēˌātiNG/ ▶ **adj.** intensely painful: *excruciating back pain.* ■ mentally agonizing; very embarrassing, awkward, or tedious: *excruciating boredom.*
– DERIVATIVES **ex·cru·ci·at·ing·ly adv.** [as submodifier] *the sting can prove excruciatingly painful.*

ex·cul·pate /ˈekskəlˌpāt/ ▶ **v.** [with obj.] formal show or declare that (someone) is not guilty of wrongdoing: *the article exculpated the mayor.*
– DERIVATIVES **ex·cul·pa·tion** /ˌekskəlˈpāsHən/ **n.**, **ex·cul·pa·to·ry** /eksˈkəlpəˌtôrē/ **adj.**
– ORIGIN mid 17th cent.: from medieval Latin *exculpat-* 'freed from blame,' from the verb *exculpare*, from *ex-* 'out, from' + Latin *culpa* 'blame.'

ex·cur·rent /ekˈskərənt/ ▶ **adj.** chiefly Zoology (of a vessel or opening) conveying fluid outward. The opposite of **INCURRENT**.
– ORIGIN early 17th cent.: from Latin *excurrent-* 'running out,' from the verb *excurrere*.

ex·cur·sion /ikˈskərZHən/ ▶ **n. 1** a short journey or trip, esp. one engaged in as a leisure activity: *an excursion to Mount Etna* | figurative *an excursion into theology.*
2 technical an instance of the movement of something along a path or through an angle. ■ a deviation from a regular pattern, path, or level of operation.
3 archaic a digression.
4 archaic a military sortie (see **ALARUM**).
– DERIVATIVES **ex·cur·sion·ist** /-ist/ **n.**
– ORIGIN late 16th cent. (in the sense 'act of running out,' also meaning 'sortie' in the phrase *alarums and excursions* (see **ALARUM**)): from Latin *excursio(n-)*, from the verb *excurrere* 'run out,' from *ex-* 'out' + *currere* 'to run.'

ex·cur·sive /ikˈskərsiv/ ▶ **adj.** formal of the nature of an excursion; ranging widely; digressive.
– DERIVATIVES **ex·cur·sive·ly adv.**, **ex·cur·sive·ness n.**
– ORIGIN late 17th cent.: from Latin *excurs-* 'digressed, run out' (from the verb *excurrere*) + **-IVE**, perhaps influenced by *discursive*.

ex·cur·sus /ekˈskərsəs/ ▶ **n.** (pl. **same** or **excursuses**) a detailed discussion of a particular point in a book, usually in an appendix. ■ a digression in a written text.
– ORIGIN early 19th cent.: from Latin, 'excursion,' from *excurrere* 'run out.'

ex·cus·a·ble /ikˈskyōōzəbəl/ ▶ **adj.** able to be justified or forgiven; forgivable: *the error is excusable.*
– DERIVATIVES **ex·cus·a·bly** /-zəblē/ **adv.**

ex·cus·al /ikˈskyōōzəl/ ▶ **n.** (typically in legal contexts) the action or fact of excusing or being excused: *he harbored views that would prevent or substantially impair the performance of his duties so as to support his excusal for cause.*
– ORIGIN late 16th cent.: from *excuse* (verb) + *-al*.

ex·cuse ▶ **v.** /ikˈskyōōz/ [with obj.] **1** attempt to lessen the blame attaching to (a fault or offense); seek to defend or justify: *he did nothing to hide or excuse Jacob's cruelty.* ■ forgive (someone) for a fault or offense: *you must excuse my sister* | *he* ***could be excused for*** *feeling that he was born at the wrong time.* ■ overlook or forgive (a fault or offense): *sit down—excuse the mess.* ■ (of a fact or circumstance) serve in mitigation of (a person or act): *his ability excuses most of his faults.*
2 release (someone) from a duty or requirement: *it will not be possible to excuse you from jury duty.* ■ (used in polite formulas) allow (someone) to leave a room or gathering: *now, if you'll excuse us, we have to be getting along.* ■ (**excuse oneself**) say politely that one is leaving. ■ (**be excused**) (used esp. by school pupils) be allowed to leave the room, esp. to go to the bathroom: *please, can I be excused?*
▶ **n.** /ikˈskyōōs/ **1** a reason or explanation put forward to defend or justify a fault or offense: *there can be no possible* ***excuse for*** *any further delay* | *no one will have the* ***excuse that*** *they didn't know.* ■ a reason put forward to conceal the real reason for an action; a pretext: *they use their hunting as an excuse to get away from the womenfolk.*
2 (**an excuse for**) informal a poor or inadequate example of: *that pathetic excuse for a man!*
– PHRASES **excuse me** said politely in various contexts, for example when attempting to get someone's attention, asking someone to move so that one may pass, or interrupting or disagreeing with a speaker. ■ said when asking someone to repeat what they have just said. **make one's excuses** say politely that one is leaving or cannot be present.
– DERIVATIVES **ex·cus·a·to·ry** /-zəˌtôrē/ **adj.**
– ORIGIN Middle English: from Old French *escuser* (verb), from Latin *excusare* 'to free from blame,' from *ex-* 'out' + *causa* 'accusation, cause.'

ex div. ▶ **abbr.** ex dividend.

ex div·i·dend ▶ **adj. & adv.** (of stocks or shares) not including the next dividend.

ex·ec /egˈzek/ ▶ **n.** informal an executive: *top execs.*
– ORIGIN late 19th cent.: abbreviation.

ex·e·cra·ble /ˈeksikrəbəl/ ▶ **adj.** extremely bad or unpleasant: *execrable cheap wine.*
– DERIVATIVES **ex·e·cra·bly** /-blē/ **adv.**
– ORIGIN late Middle English (in the sense 'expressing or involving a curse'): via Old French from Latin *execrabilis*, from *exsecrari* 'to curse' (see **EXECRATE**).

ex·e·crate /ˈeksiˌkrāt/ ▶ **v.** [with obj.] feel or express great loathing for: *they were execrated as dangerous and corrupt.* ■ [no obj.] archaic curse; swear.
– DERIVATIVES **ex·e·cra·tion** /ˌeksiˈkrāsHən/ **n.**, **ex·e·cra·tive** /-ˌkrātiv/ **adj.**, **ex·e·cra·to·ry** /-krəˌtôrē/ **adj.**
– ORIGIN mid 16th cent.: from Latin *exsecrat-* 'cursed,' from the verb *exsecrari*, based on *sacrare* 'dedicate' (from *sacer* 'sacred').

ex·e·cut·a·ble /ˈeksiˌkyōōtəbəl/ Computing ▶ **adj.** (of a file or program) able to be run by a computer.
▶ **n.** an executable file or program.

ex·ec·u·tant /igˈzekyətənt/ formal ▶ **n.** a person who carries something into effect: *executants of the publisher's will.* ■ a person who performs music or makes a work of art or craft.
▶ **adj.** of or relating to the performance of music or the making of works of art or craft: *music is both an art and an executant skill.*
– ORIGIN mid 19th cent.: from French *exécutant* 'carrying out,' present participle of *exécuter* (see **EXECUTE**).

ex·e·cute /ˈeksiˌkyōōt/ ▶ **v.** [with obj.] **1** carry out or put into effect (a plan, order, or course of action): *the corporation executed a series of financial deals.* ■ produce (a work of art): *not only does she execute embroideries, she designs them, too.* ■ perform (an activity or maneuver requiring care or skill): *they had to execute their dance steps with the greatest precision.* ■ Law make (a legal instrument) valid by signing or sealing it. ■ Law carry out (a judicial sentence, the terms of a will, or other order): *police executed a search warrant.* ■ Computing carry out an instruction or program.
2 carry out a sentence of death on (a legally condemned person): *he was convicted of treason and executed.* ■ kill (someone) as a political act.
– ORIGIN late Middle English: from Old French *executer*, from medieval Latin *executare*, from Latin *exsequi* 'follow up, carry out, punish,' from *ex-* 'out' + *sequi* 'follow.'

ex·e·cu·tion /ˌeksiˈkyōōsHən/ ▶ **n. 1** the carrying out or putting into effect of a plan, order, or course of action: *he was fascinated by the entire operation and its execution.* ■ the technique or style with which an artistic work is produced or carried out: *the opera's creative execution.* ■ Law the putting into effect of a legal instrument or order. ■ Law seizure of the property or person of a debtor in default of payment. ■ Law short for **WRIT OF EXECUTION**. ■ Computing the performance of an instruction or program.
2 the carrying out of a sentence of death on a condemned person: *the execution of juveniles is prohibited by international law* | *executions of convicted murderers.* ■ the killing of someone as a political act.

ex·e·cu·tion·er /ˌeksiˈkyōōsH(ə)nər/ ▶ **n.** an official who carries out a sentence of death on a legally condemned person.

ex·ec·u·tive /igˈzekyətiv, eg-/ ▶ **adj.** [attrib.] having the power to put plans, actions, or laws into effect: *an executive chairman* | *executive authority.* ■ relating to managing an organization or political administration and putting into effect plans, policies, or laws: *the executive branch of government* | *the state has various executive functions.* Often contrasted with **LEGISLATIVE**.
▶ **n. 1** a person with senior managerial responsibility in a business organization. ■ [as modifier] suitable or appropriate for a senior business executive: *the executive suite* | *an executive jet.* ■ an executive committee or other body within an organization: *the union executive.*
2 (**the executive**) the person or branch of a government responsible for putting policies or laws into effect.
– DERIVATIVES **ex·ec·u·tive·ly adv.**
– ORIGIN late Middle English (as an adjective): from medieval Latin *executivus*, from *exsequi* 'carry out' (see **EXECUTE**).

ex·ec·u·tive a·gree·ment ▶ **n.** an international agreement, usu. regarding routine administrative matters not warranting a formal treaty, made by the executive branch of the US government without ratification by the Senate.

ex·ec·u·tive of·fi·cer ▶ **n.** an officer with executive power. ■ (in naval vessels and some other military contexts) the officer who is second in command to the captain or commanding officer.

ex·ec·u·tive or·der ▶ **n.** a rule or order issued by the president to an executive branch of the government and having the force of law.

ex·ec·u·tive priv·i·lege ▶ **n.** the privilege, claimed by the president for the executive branch of the US government, of withholding information in the public interest.

ex·ec·u·tive sec·re·tar·y ▶ **n.** a secretary with administrative responsibilities, esp. one managing the business affairs and activities of an executive or an organization.

ex·ec·u·tive ses·sion ▶ **n.** a meeting, esp. a private one, of a legislative body for executive business.

ex·ec·u·tor ▶ **n. 1** /igˈzekyətər/ Law a person or institution appointed by a testator to carry out the terms of their will.
2 /ˈeksəˌkyo͞otər/ a person who produces something or puts something into effect: *the makers and executors of policy.*
– DERIVATIVES **ex·ec·u·to·ri·al** /igˌzekyəˈtôrēəl/ **adj.** (rare), **ex·ec·u·tor·ship** /-ˌship/ **n.**, **ex·ec·u·to·ry** /-ˌtôrē/ **adj.**
– ORIGIN Middle English: via Anglo-Norman French from Latin *execut-* 'carried out,' from *exsequi* (see EXECUTE).

ex·ec·u·trix /igˈzekyəˌtriks/ ▶ **n.** (pl. **executrices** /-ˌtrisēz/ or **executrixes** /-ˌtriksiz/) Law a female executor of a will.
– ORIGIN late Middle English: from late Latin, from Latin *executor* (see EXECUTOR).

e

ex·e·dra /ˈeksidrə, ikˈsēdrə/ ▶ **n.** (pl. **exedrae** /-drē/) Architecture a room, portico, or arcade with a bench or seats where people may converse, esp. in ancient Roman and Greek houses and gymnasia, typically semicircular in plan. ■ an outdoor recess containing a seat.
– ORIGIN Latin, from Greek *ex-* 'out of' + *hedra* 'seat.'

ex·e·ge·sis /ˌeksiˈjēsis/ ▶ **n.** (pl. **exegeses** /-sēz/) critical explanation or interpretation of a text, esp. of scripture: *the task of biblical exegesis | a close exegesis of the plot.*
– DERIVATIVES **ex·e·get·ic** /-ˈjetik/ **adj.**, **ex·e·get·i·cal** /-ˈjetikəl/ **adj.**
– ORIGIN early 17th cent.: from Greek *exēgēsis*, from *exēgeisthai* 'interpret,' from *ex-* 'out of' + *hēgeisthai* 'to guide, lead.'

ex·e·gete /ˈeksəˌjēt/ ▶ **n.** an expounder or textual interpreter, esp. of scripture.
▶ **v.** [with obj.] expound or interpret (a text, esp. scripture): *I am able to exegete the scriptures in ways that make sense.*
– ORIGIN mid 18th cent.: from Greek *exēgētēs*, from *exēgeisthai* 'interpret.'

ex·em·plar /igˈzemplər, -ˌplär/ ▶ **n.** a person or thing serving as a typical example or excellent model: *he became the leading exemplar of conservative philosophy.*
– ORIGIN late Middle English: from Old French *exemplaire*, from late Latin *exemplarium*, from Latin *exemplum* 'sample, imitation' (see EXAMPLE).

ex·em·pla·ry /igˈzemplərē/ ▶ **adj. 1** serving as a desirable model; representing the best of its kind: *an award for exemplary community service.*
2 (of a punishment) serving as a warning or deterrent: *exemplary sentencing may discourage the ultraviolent minority.* ■ Law (of damages) exceeding the amount needed for simple compensation.
– DERIVATIVES **ex·em·pla·ri·ly** /-əlē/ **adv.**, **ex·em·pla·ri·ness n.**, **ex·em·plar·i·ty** /ˌegzemˈplaritē/ **n.**
– ORIGIN late 16th cent.: from late Latin *exemplaris*, from Latin *exemplum* 'sample, imitation' (see EXAMPLE).

ex·em·pli·fy /igˈzempləˌfī/ ▶ **v.** (**exemplifies, exemplifying, exemplified**) [with obj.] be a typical example of: *rock bands that best exemplify the spirit of the age.* ■ give an example of; illustrate by giving an example. ■ Law make an attested copy of (a document) under an official seal.
– DERIVATIVES **ex·em·pli·fi·ca·tion** /igˌzempləfiˈkāshən/ **n.**
– ORIGIN late Middle English (in the sense 'illustrate by examples'): from medieval Latin *exemplificare*, from Latin *exemplum* 'sample' (see EXAMPLE).

ex·em·plum /igˈzempləm/ ▶ **n.** (pl. **exempla** /-plə/) an example or model, esp. a moralizing or illustrative story.
– ORIGIN late 19th cent.: Latin, literally 'example.'

ex·empt /igˈzem(p)t/ ▶ **adj.** free from an obligation or liability imposed on others: *these patients are exempt from all charges | they are not exempt from criticism.*
▶ **v.** [with obj.] free (a person or organization) from an obligation or liability imposed on others: *they were exempted from paying the tax.*
▶ **n.** a person who is exempt from something, esp. the payment of tax.
– ORIGIN late Middle English: from Latin *exemptus* 'taken out, freed,' past participle of *eximere*.

ex·emp·tion /igˈzem(p)shən/ ▶ **n.** the process of freeing or state of being free from an obligation or liability imposed on others: *exemption from prescription charges | regulatory exemptions.* ■ (also **personal exemption**) the process of exempting a person from paying taxes on a specified amount of income for themselves and their dependents. ■ an item or amount exempted in this way: *a series of exemptions from the partnership tax rules.*
– ORIGIN late Middle English: from Old French, or from Latin *exemptio(n-)*, from *eximere* 'take out, free.'

ex·en·ter·a·tion /igˌzentəˈrāshən/ ▶ **n.** complete surgical removal of a body organ, esp. the eyeball and other contents of the eye socket, usually in cases of malignant cancer.
– ORIGIN mid 17th cent. (originally in the sense 'disembowelment'): from Latin *exenterat-* 'removed,' from the verb *exenterare* (suggested by Greek *exenterizein*), from *ex-* 'out of' + *enteron* 'intestine.'

ex·e·qua·tur /ˌeksəˈkwātər/ ▶ **n.** an official recognition by a government of a consul, agent, or other representative of a foreign state, authorizing them to exercise the duties of office.
– ORIGIN early 17th cent.: Latin, literally 'let him or her perform.'

ex·e·quy /ˈeksikwē/ ▶ **n.** (**exequies**) formal funeral rites; obsequies: *he attended the exequies for the dead pope.*
– ORIGIN late Middle English: via Old French from Latin *exequias*, accusative of *exsequiae* 'funeral ceremonies,' from *exsequi* 'follow after.'

ex·er·cise /ˈeksərˌsīz/ ▶ **n. 1** activity requiring physical effort, carried out esp. to sustain or improve health and fitness: *exercise improves your heart and lung power | loosening-up exercises.* ■ a task or activity done to practice or test a skill: *there are exercises at the end of each chapter to check comprehension.* ■ a process or activity carried out for a specific purpose, esp. one concerned with a specified area or skill: *an exercise in public relations.* ■ (often **exercises**) a military drill or training maneuver. ■ (**exercises**) ceremonies: *graduation exercises.*
2 the use or application of a faculty, right, or process: *the free exercise of religion.*
▶ **v.** [with obj.] **1** use or apply (a faculty, right, or process): *control is exercised by the Board | anyone receiving a suspect package should exercise extreme caution.*
2 [no obj.] engage in physical activity to sustain or improve health and fitness; take exercise: *she still exercised every day.* ■ exert (part of the body) to promote or improve muscular strength: *raise your knee to exercise the upper leg and hip muscles.* ■ cause (an animal) to engage in exercise: *she exercised her dogs before breakfast.*
3 occupy the thoughts of; worry or perplex: *the knowledge that a larger margin was possible still exercised him.*
– DERIVATIVES **ex·er·cis·a·ble** /-əbəl/ **adj.**
– ORIGIN Middle English (in the sense 'application of a faculty, right, or process'): via Old French from Latin *exercitium*, from *exercere* 'keep busy, practice,' from *ex-* 'thoroughly' + *arcere* 'keep in or away.'

ex·er·cise ball ▶ **n.** a lightweight, inflated plastic ball with a diameter of 18–36 inches (45–91 cm), used in various fitness and physiotherapeutic exercises. Also called STABILITY BALL.

ex·er·cise bike (also **exercise bicycle**) ▶ **n.** a piece of exercise equipment having handlebars, pedals, and a saddle like a bicycle, on which the user replicates the movements of bicycling.

ex·er·cise book ▶ **n.** a book containing printed exercises for the use of students.

ex·er·cise price ▶ **n.** Stock Market the price per share at which the owner of a traded option is entitled to buy or sell the underlying security.

ex·er·cis·er /ˈeksərˌsīzər/ ▶ **n.** a person who exercises. ■ an apparatus used to exercise.

ex·er·cise yard ▶ **n.** an enclosed outdoor area used for physical exercise in a prison.

Ex·er·cy·cle /ˈeksərˌsīkəl/ ▶ **n.** trademark an exercise bike.
– ORIGIN 1930s: blend of EXERCISE and BICYCLE.

ex·er·gon·ic /ˌeksərˈgänik/ ▶ **adj.** Biochemistry (of a metabolic or chemical process) accompanied by the release of energy. The opposite of ENDERGONIC.
– ORIGIN mid 20th cent.: from EX-[2] 'out of' + Greek *ergon* 'work' + -IC.

ex·ergue /igˈzərg, ˈeksərg, ˈegzərg/ ▶ **n.** a small space or inscription below the principal emblem on a coin or medal, usually on the reverse side.
– ORIGIN late 17th cent.: from French, from medieval Latin *exergum*, from *ex-* 'out' + Greek *ergon* 'work' (probably as a rendering of French *hors d'oeuvre* 'something lying outside the work').

ex·ert /igˈzərt/ ▶ **v.** [with obj.] **1** apply or bring to bear (a force, influence, or quality): *the moon* **exerts** *a force* **on** *the Earth |* **exerting** *influence* **over** *the next generation.*
2 (**exert oneself**) make a physical or mental effort: *he needs to exert himself to try to find an answer.*
– ORIGIN mid 17th cent. (in the sense 'perform, practice'): from Latin *exserere* 'put forth,' from *ex-* 'out' + *serere* 'bind.'

ex·er·tion /igˈzərshən/ ▶ **n. 1** physical or mental effort: *she was panting with the exertion | a well-earned rest after their mental exertions.*
2 the application of a force, influence, or quality: *the exertion of authority.*

Ex·e·ter[1] /ˈeksətər, ˈegzətər/ a city in southwestern England, the county town of Devon, on the Exe River; pop. 109,200 (est. 2009). Exeter was founded by the Romans, who called it Isca.

Ex·e·ter[2] /ˈeksitər, ˈegzitər/ a historic town in southeastern New Hampshire, home to Phillips (Exeter) Academy; pop. 14,762 (est. 2008).

ex·e·unt /ˈeksēənt, ˈeksēˌo͞ont/ ▶ **v.** used as a stage direction in a printed play to indicate that a group of characters leave the stage: *exeunt Hamlet and Polonius.* See also EXIT.
– PHRASES **exeunt omnes** used in this way to indicate that all the actors leave the stage.
– ORIGIN late 15th cent.: Latin, literally 'they go out.'

ex·fil·trate /eksˈfilˌtrāt/ ▶ **v.** [with obj.] withdraw (troops or spies) surreptitiously, esp. from a dangerous position.
– DERIVATIVES **ex·fil·tra·tion** /ˌeksfilˈtrāshən/ **n.**
– ORIGIN late 20th cent.: back-formation from *exfiltration*, perhaps suggested by the pair *infiltration, infiltrate*.

ex·fo·li·ant /eksˈfōlēənt/ ▶ **n.** a cosmetic product designed to remove dead cells from the surface of the skin.
– ORIGIN 1980s: from EXFOLIATE + -ANT.

ex·fo·li·ate /eksˈfōlēˌāt/ ▶ **v.** [no obj.] (of a material) come apart or be shed from a surface in scales or layers: *the bark exfoliates in papery flakes.* ■ [with obj.] cause to do this: *salt solutions exfoliate rocks on evaporating.* ■ [with obj.] wash or rub (a part of the body) with a granular substance to remove dead cells from the surface of the skin: *exfoliate your legs to get rid of dead skin.* ■ [with obj.] shed (material) in scales or layers.
– DERIVATIVES **ex·fo·li·a·tion** /eksˌfōlēˈāshən/ **n.**, **ex·fo·li·a·tive** /-ˌātiv/ **adj.**, **ex·fo·li·a·tor** /-ˌātər/ **n.**
– ORIGIN mid 17th cent.: from late Latin *exfoliat-* 'stripped of leaves,' from the verb *exfoliare*, from *ex-* 'out, from' + *folium* 'leaf.'

ex gra·ti·a /eks ˈgrāshēə/ ▶ **adv. & adj.** (esp. with reference to the paying of money) done from a sense of moral obligation rather than because of any legal requirement: [as adj.] *an ex gratia payment.*
– ORIGIN mid 18th cent.: Latin, literally 'from favor,' from *ex* 'from' and *gratia* (see GRACE).

ex·ha·la·tion /ˌeks(h)əˈlāshən/ ▶ **n.** the process or action of exhaling. ■ an expiration of air from the lungs: *he let his breath out in a long exhalation of relief.* ■ an amount of vapor or fumes given off.

ex·hale /eksˈhāl, ˈeksˌhāl/ ▶ **v.** breathe out in a deliberate manner: [no obj.] *she sat back and exhaled deeply* | [with obj.] *he exhaled the smoke toward the ceiling.* ■ [with obj.] give off (vapor or fumes): *the jungle exhaled mists of early morning.*
– DERIVATIVES **ex·hal·a·ble adj.**
– ORIGIN late Middle English (in the sense 'be given off as vapor'): from Old French *exhaler*, from Latin *exhalare*, from *ex-* 'out' + *halare* 'breathe.'

ex·haust /igˈzôst/ ▶ **v.** [with obj.] **1** drain (someone) of their physical or mental resources; tire out: *her day trip had exhausted her.*
2 use up (resources or reserves) completely: *the country has exhausted its treasury reserves.* ■ expound on, write about, or explore (a subject or options) so fully that there is nothing further to be said or discovered: *she seemed to have exhausted all permissible topics of conversation.*
3 expel (gas or steam) from or into a particular place.
▶ **n.** waste gases or air expelled from an engine, turbine, or other machine in the course of its operation: *buses spewing out black clouds of exhaust* | [as modifier] *exhaust fumes.* ■ the system through which such gases are expelled: [as modifier] *an exhaust pipe.*
– DERIVATIVES **ex·haust·er n.**, **ex·haust·i·bil·i·ty** /igˌzôstəˈbilitē/ **n.**, **ex·haust·i·ble adj.**
– ORIGIN mid 16th cent. (in the general sense 'draw off or out'): from Latin *exhaust-* 'drained out,' from the verb *exhaurire*, from *ex-* 'out' + *haurire* 'draw (water), drain.'

ex·haust·ed /igˈzôstid/ ▶ **adj. 1** drained of one's physical or mental resources; very tired: *I was cold and exhausted | she returned home,* **exhausted from** *her day in the city.*
2 (of resources or reserves) completely used up: *Karl spat, his patience suddenly exhausted.*
– DERIVATIVES **ex·haust·ed·ly adv.**

ex·haust·ing /igˈzôstiNG/ ▶ **adj.** making one feel very tired; very tiring: *a long and exhausting journey.*
– DERIVATIVES **ex·haust·ing·ly adv.**

ex·haus·tion /igˈzôsCHən/ ▶ **n.** **1** a state of extreme physical or mental fatigue: *he was pale with exhaustion.*
2 the action or state of using something up or of being used up completely: *the rapid exhaustion of fossil fuel reserves.* ■ Logic the process of establishing a conclusion by eliminating all the alternatives.
– ORIGIN early 17th cent.: from late Latin *exhaustio(n-)*, from Latin *exhaurire* 'drain out' (see EXHAUST).

ex·haus·tive /igˈzôstiv/ ▶ **adj.** examining, including, or considering all elements or aspects; fully comprehensive: *she has undergone exhaustive tests since becoming ill.*
– DERIVATIVES **ex·haus·tive·ly** adv., **ex·haus·tive·ness** n.

ex·haust trail ▶ **n.** another term for CONTRAIL.

ex·hib·it /igˈzibit/ ▶ **v.** [with obj.] **1** publicly display (a work of art or item of interest) in an art gallery or museum or at a trade fair: *only one sculpture was exhibited in the artist's lifetime.* ■ [no obj.] (of an artist) display one's work to the public in an art gallery or museum: *she was invited to exhibit at several French museums.* ■ (usu. **be exhibited**) publicly display the work of (an artist) in an art gallery or museum: *no foreign painters were exhibited.*
2 manifest or deliberately display (a quality or a type of behavior): *he could exhibit a saintlike submissiveness.* ■ show as a sign or symptom: *patients with alcoholic liver disease exhibit many biochemical abnormalities.*
▶ **n.** an object or collection of objects on public display in an art gallery or museum or at a trade fair: *the museum is rich in exhibits.* ■ an exhibition: *people flocked to the exhibit in record-breaking numbers.* ■ Law a document or other object produced in a court as evidence.
– ORIGIN late Middle English (in the sense 'submit for consideration,' also specifically 'present a document as evidence in court'): from Latin *exhibit-* 'held out,' from the verb *exhibere*, from *ex-* 'out' + *habere* 'hold.'

ex·hi·bi·tion /ˌeksəˈbisHən/ ▶ **n.** **1** a public display of works of art or other items of interest, held in an art gallery or museum or at a trade fair: *an exhibition of French sculpture* | *he never lent his treasures out for exhibition.*
2 a display or demonstration of a particular skill: *fields that have been plowed with a supreme exhibition of the farm worker's skills* | [as modifier] *exhibition games.* ■ [in sing.] an ostentatious or insincere display of a particular quality or emotion: *a false but convincing exhibition of concern for smaller nations.*
3 [usu. as modifier] (in sports) a game whose outcome does not affect a team's standing, typically one played before the start of a regular season: *an exhibition game.*
4 Brit. a scholarship awarded to a student at a school or college, usually after a competitive examination.
– PHRASES **make an exhibition of oneself** behave in a conspicuously foolish way in public.
– ORIGIN late Middle English (in the sense 'maintenance, support'; hence sense 4, mid 17th cent.): via Old French from late Latin *exhibitio(n-)*, from Latin *exhibere* 'hold out' (see EXHIBIT).

ex·hi·bi·tion·er /ˌeksəˈbisHənər/ ▶ **n.** Brit. a student who has been awarded an exhibition (scholarship).

ex·hi·bi·tion·ism /ˌeksəˈbisHəˌnizəm/ ▶ **n.** extravagant behavior that is intended to attract attention to oneself. ■ Psychiatry a mental condition characterized by the compulsion to display one's genitals in public.

ex·hi·bi·tion·ist ▶ **n.** a person who behaves in an extravagant way in order to attract attention: *I am something of an exhibitionist.*
▶ **adj.** behaving extravagantly in order to attract attention.
– DERIVATIVES **ex·hi·bi·tion·is·tic** /-ˌbisHəˈnistik/ adj., **ex·hi·bi·tion·is·ti·cal·ly** /-ˌbisHəˈnistik(ə)lē/ adv.

ex·hib·i·tor /igˈzibitər/ ▶ **n.** a person who displays works of art or other items of interest at an exhibition.

ex·hil·a·rate /igˈziləˌrāt/ ▶ **v.** make (someone) feel very happy, animated, or elated: *the children were exhilarated by a sense of purpose* | (as adj. **exhilarated**) *all this hustle and bustle makes me feel exhilarated.*
– ORIGIN mid 16th cent.: from Latin *exhilarat-* 'made cheerful,' from the verb *exhilarare*, from *ex-* (expressing inducement of a state) + *hilaris* 'cheerful.'

ex·hil·a·rat·ing /igˈziləˌrātiNG/ ▶ **adj.** making one feel very happy, animated, or elated; thrilling: *an exhilarating two-hour rafting experience.*
– DERIVATIVES **ex·hil·a·rat·ing·ly** adv.

ex·hil·a·ra·tion /igˌziləˈrāsHən/ ▶ **n.** a feeling of excitement, happiness, or elation: *they felt the exhilaration of victory.*

ex·hort /igˈzôrt/ ▶ **v.** [with obj. and infinitive] strongly encourage or urge (someone) to do something: *the media have been exhorting people to turn out for the demonstration* | [with direct speech] *"Come on, you guys," exhorted Linda.*
– DERIVATIVES **ex·hort·a·tive** /-tətiv/ adj., **ex·hort·a·to·ry** /-təˌtôrē/ adj., **ex·hort·er** n.
– ORIGIN late Middle English: from Old French *exhorter* or Latin *exhortari*, from *ex-* 'thoroughly' + *hortari* 'encourage.'

ex·hor·ta·tion /ˌegzôrˈtāsHən, ˌeksôr-/ ▶ **n.** an address or communication emphatically urging someone to do something: *exhortations to eat well* | *no amount of exhortation had any effect.*

ex·hume /igˈz(y)o͞om, eksˈ(y)o͞om/ ▶ **v.** [with obj.] dig out (something buried, esp. a corpse) from the ground. ■ (usu. **be exhumed**) Geology expose (a land surface) that was formerly buried.
– DERIVATIVES **ex·hu·ma·tion** /ˌegz(y)o͞oˈmāsHən, ˌeks(h)yo͞o-/ n.
– ORIGIN late Middle English: from medieval Latin *exhumare*, from *ex-* 'out of' + *humus* 'ground.'

ex hy·poth·e·si /ˌeks hīˈpäTHəˌsī/ ▶ **adv.** according to the hypothesis proposed.
– ORIGIN modern Latin, from *ex* 'from' and *hypothesi*, ablative of late Latin *hypothesis* (see HYPOTHESIS).

ex·i·gence /ˈeksijəns/ ▶ **n.** another term for EXIGENCY.

ex·i·gen·cy /ˈeksijənsē, igˈzijənsē/ ▶ **n.** (pl. **exigencies**) an urgent need or demand: *women worked long hours when the exigencies of the family economy demanded it* | *he put financial exigency before personal sentiment.*
– ORIGIN late 16th cent.: from late Latin *exigentia*, from Latin *exigere* 'enforce' (see EXACT).

ex·i·gent /ˈeksijənt/ ▶ **adj.** formal pressing; demanding: *the exigent demands of the music took a toll on her voice.*
– ORIGIN early 17th cent.: from Latin *exigent-* 'completing, ascertaining,' from the verb *exigere* (see EXACT).

ex·i·gi·ble /ˈeksijəbəl/ ▶ **adj.** (of a tax, duty, or other payment) able to be charged or levied.
– ORIGIN early 17th cent.: from French, from *exiger* 'demand, exact,' from Latin *exigere* (see EXACT).

ex·ig·u·ous /igˈzigyo͞oəs, ikˈsig-/ ▶ **adj.** formal very small in size or amount: *my exiguous musical resources.*
– DERIVATIVES **ex·i·gu·i·ty** /ˌeksiˈgyo͞oitē/ n., **ex·ig·u·ous·ly** adv., **ex·ig·u·ous·ness** n.
– ORIGIN mid 17th cent.: from Latin *exiguus* 'scanty' (from *exigere* 'weigh exactly') + -OUS.

ex·ile /ˈegˌzīl, ˈekˌsīl/ ▶ **n.** the state of being barred from one's native country, typically for political or punitive reasons: *he knew now that he would die in exile.* ■ a person who lives away from their native country, either from choice or compulsion: *the return of political exiles.* ■ (**the Exile**) another term for BABYLONIAN CAPTIVITY.
▶ **v.** [with obj.] (usu. **be exiled**) expel and bar (someone) from their native country, typically for political or punitive reasons: *a corrupt dictator who had been exiled from his country* | *he was exiled to Tasmania in 1849* | (as adj. **exiled**) *supporters of the exiled king.*
– ORIGIN Middle English: the noun partly from Old French *exil* 'banishment' and partly from Old French *exile* 'banished person'; the verb from Old French *exiler*; all based on Latin *exilium* 'banishment,' from *exul* 'banished person.'

ex·il·ic /egˈzilik, ekˈsilik/ ▶ **adj.** of or relating to a period of exile, esp. that of the Jews in Babylon in the 6th century BC.

ex·ine /ˈekˌsēn, -ˌsīn/ ▶ **n.** Botany the decay-resistant outer coating of a pollen grain or spore. It typically bears a highly characteristic surface pattern that is used in palynology.
– ORIGIN late 19th cent.: perhaps from EX-[2] 'out' + Greek *is, in-* 'fiber.'

ex·ist /igˈzist/ ▶ **v.** [no obj.] **1** have objective reality or being: *remains of these baths still exist on the south side of the Pantheon* | *there existed no organization to cope with espionage.* ■ be found, esp. in a particular place or situation: *two conflicting stereotypes of housework exist in popular thinking today.*
2 live, esp. under adverse conditions: *how am I going to exist without you?* | *only a minority of people exist on unemployment benefits alone.*
– ORIGIN early 17th cent.: probably a back-formation from EXISTENCE.

ex·ist·ence /igˈzistəns/ ▶ **n.** the fact or state of living or having objective reality: *the plane was the oldest Boeing remaining in existence* | *the need to acknowledge the existence of a problem.* ■ continued survival: *she helped to keep the company alive when its very existence was threatened.* ■ a way of living: *living in a city was more expensive than a rural existence.* ■ any of a person's supposed current, future, or past lives on this earth: *reaping the consequences of evil deeds sown in previous existences.* ■ archaic a being or entity. ■ all that exists.
– ORIGIN late Middle English: from Old French, or from late Latin *existentia*, from Latin *exsistere* 'come into being,' from *ex-* 'out' + *sistere* 'take a stand.'

ex·ist·ent /igˈzistənt/ ▶ **adj.** formal having reality or existence: *the technique has been existent for some years.*
– ORIGIN mid 16th cent.: from Latin *existent-* 'coming into being, emerging,' from the verb *exsistere* (see EXISTENCE).

ex·is·ten·tial /ˌegziˈstenCHəl/ ▶ **adj.** of or relating to existence. ■ Philosophy concerned with existence, esp. human existence as viewed in the theories of existentialism. ■ Logic (of a proposition) affirming or implying the existence of a thing.
– DERIVATIVES **ex·is·ten·tial·ly** adv.
– ORIGIN late 17th cent.: from late Latin *existentialis*, from *existentia* (see EXISTENCE).

ex·is·ten·tial·ism /ˌegziˈstenCHəˌlizəm/ ▶ **n.** a philosophical theory or approach that emphasizes the existence of the individual person as a free and responsible agent determining their own development through acts of the will.

> Generally taken to originate with Kierkegaard and Nietzsche, existentialism tends to be atheistic (although there is a strand of Christian existentialism deriving from the work of Kierkegaard), to disparage scientific knowledge, and to deny the existence of objective values, stressing instead the reality and significance of human freedom and experience. The approach was developed chiefly in 20th-century Europe, notably by Martin Heidegger, Jean-Paul Sartre, Albert Camus, and Simone de Beauvoir.

– DERIVATIVES **ex·is·ten·tial·ist** n. & adj.
– ORIGIN translating Danish *existents-forhold* 'condition of existence' (frequently used by Kierkegaard), from EXISTENTIAL.

ex·is·ten·tial quan·ti·fi·er ▶ **n.** Logic a formal expression used in asserting that something exists of which a stated general proposition can be said to be true.

ex·ist·ing /igˈzistiNG/ ▶ **adj.** [attrib.] in existence or operation at the time under consideration; current: *opponents of the existing political system.*

ex·it /ˈegzit, ˈeksit/ ▶ **n.** **1** a way out, esp. of a public building, room, or passenger vehicle: *she slipped out by the rear exit* | *a fire exit.* ■ a ramp where traffic can leave a highway, major road, or traffic circle: *he pulled off at an exit and stopped his Mercedes-Benz.*
2 an act of going out of or leaving a place: *he made a hasty **exit from** the room.* ■ a departure of an actor from the stage: *the brief soliloquy following Clarence's exit.* ■ a departure from a particular situation: *Australia's early **exit from** the World Cup.*
▶ **v.** (**exits, exiting, exited**) [no obj.] go out of or leave a place: *they **exited from** the aircraft* | *the bullet entered her back and exited through her chest* | [with obj.] *elephants enter and exit the forest on narrow paths.* ■ (of an actor) leave the stage. ■ (**exit**) used as a stage direction in a printed play to indicate that a character leaves the stage: *exit Pamela.* See also EXEUNT. ■ leave a particular situation: *organizations that do not have freedom to exit from unprofitable markets.* ■ Computing terminate a process or program, usually returning to an earlier or more general level of interaction: *this key enables you to temporarily exit from a LIFESPAN option.* ■ Bridge relinquish the lead.
– ORIGIN mid 16th cent. (as a stage direction): from Latin *exit* 'he or she goes out,' third person singular present tense of *exire*, from *ex-* 'out' + *ire* 'go.' The noun use (late 16th cent.) is from Latin *exitus* 'going out,' from the verb *exire*, and the other verb uses (early 17th cent.) are from the noun.

ex·it line ▶ **n.** a line spoken by an actor immediately before leaving the stage. ■ a parting remark.

ex·it poll ▶ **n.** a poll of people leaving a polling place, asking how they voted.

ex·it strat·e·gy ▶ **n.** a preplanned means of extricating oneself from a situation that is likely to become difficult or unpleasant.

ex·it vi·sa (also **exit permit**) ▶ **n.** a document giving authorization to leave a particular country.

ex·it wound /wo͞ond/ ▶ **n.** a wound made by a bullet or other missile passing out of the body.

ex li·bris /eks 'lēbris, 'lībris/ ▶ **adv.** used as an inscription on a bookplate to show the name of the book's owner: *ex libris Edith Wharton.*
▶ **n.** (pl. **same**) a bookplate inscribed in such a way, esp. a decorative one.
– ORIGIN late 19th cent.: Latin, literally 'out of the books or library (of someone).'

ex ni·hi·lo /'eks 'nē(h)əlō, 'nī(h)əlō/ ▶ **adv.** formal out of nothing: *the fashioning of life ex nihilo by God.*
– ORIGIN late 16th cent.: Latin.

exo- ▶ **prefix** external; from outside: *exodermis.*
– ORIGIN from Greek *exō* 'outside.'

ex·o·at·mos·pher·ic /'eksō,atmə'sfi(ə)rik, -'sferik/ ▶ **adj.** operating or taking place outside the atmosphere.

ex·o·bi·ol·o·gy /,eksōbī'äləjē/ ▶ **n.** the branch of science that deals with the possibility and likely nature of life on other planets or in space.
– DERIVATIVES **ex·o·bi·o·log·i·cal** /-,bīə'läjikəl/ **adj.**, **ex·o·bi·ol·o·gist** /-jist/ **n.**

ex·o·carp /'eksō,kärp/ ▶ **n.** Botany the outer layer of the pericarp of a fruit.

ex·o·cen·tric /,eksō'sentrik/ ▶ **adj.** Linguistics denoting or being a construction that has no explicit head, for example *John slept*. Contrasted with **ENDOCENTRIC**.

Ex·o·cet /'eksō,set/ ▶ **n.** trademark a French-made guided anti-ship missile.
– ORIGIN 1970s: from French, literally 'flying fish,' via Latin from Greek *ekōkoitos* 'fish that comes up on the beach' (literally 'out of bed').

ex·o·crine /'eksə,krin, 'eksə,krēn/ ▶ **adj.** Physiology relating to or denoting glands that secrete their products through ducts opening onto an epithelium rather than directly into the bloodstream. Often contrasted with **ENDOCRINE**.
– ORIGIN early 20th cent.: from **EXO-** 'outside' + Greek *krinein* 'sift.'

ex·o·cy·to·sis /'eksōsī'tōsis/ ▶ **n.** Biology a process by which the contents of a cell vacuole are released to the exterior through fusion of the vacuole membrane with the cell membrane.
– DERIVATIVES **ex·o·cy·tot·ic** /-'tätik/ **adj.**

ex·o·der·mis /,eksō'dərməs/ ▶ **n.** Botany a specialized layer in a root beneath the epidermis or velamen.
– ORIGIN early 20th cent.: from **EXO-** 'outside,' on the pattern of *endodermis, epidermis.*

Ex·o·dus /'eksədəs/ the second book of the Bible, which recounts the departure of the Israelites from slavery in Egypt, their journey across the Red Sea and through the wilderness led by Moses, and the giving of the Ten Commandments. The events have been variously dated by scholars between about 1580 and 1200 BC.
– ORIGIN Old English, via ecclesiastical Latin from Greek *exodos*, from *ex-* 'out of' + *hodos* 'way.'

ex·o·dus /'eksədəs/ ▶ **n.** a mass departure of people, esp. emigrants. ■ (**the Exodus**) the departure of the Israelites from Egypt.
– ORIGIN early 17th cent.: from Greek (see **EXODUS**).

ex·o·en·zyme /,eksō'en,zīm/ ▶ **n.** Biochemistry an enzyme that acts outside the cell that produces it.

ex of·fi·ci·o /'eks ə'fisHēō/ ▶ **adv. & adj.** by virtue of one's position or status: [as adj.] *an ex officio member of the committee.*
– ORIGIN Latin, from *ex* 'out of, from' + *officium* 'duty.'

ex·og·a·my /ek'sägəmē/ ▶ **n.** Anthropology the custom of marrying outside a community, clan, or tribe. Compare with **ENDOGAMY**. ■ Biology the fusion of reproductive cells from distantly related or unrelated individuals; outbreeding; cross-pollination.
– DERIVATIVES **ex·og·a·mous** /-məs/ **adj.**

ex·o·gen·ic /,eksə'jenik/ ▶ **adj.** Geology formed or occurring on the surface of the earth. Often contrasted with **ENDOGENIC**.

ex·og·e·nous /ek'säjənəs/ ▶ **adj.** of, relating to, or developing from external factors. Often contrasted with **ENDOGENOUS**. ■ Biology growing or originating from outside an organism: *an exogenous hormone.* ■ chiefly Psychiatry (of a disease, symptom, etc.) caused by an agent or organism outside the body: *exogenous depression.* ■ relating to an external group or society: *exogenous marriage.*
– DERIVATIVES **ex·og·e·nous·ly adv.**
– ORIGIN mid 19th cent.: from modern Latin *exogena* (denoting an exogenous plant, suggested by classical Latin *indigena* 'native') + **-OUS**.

ex·o·glos·sic /,eksō'glôsik/ ▶ **n.** Linguistics denoting or relating to a nonindigenous language that is used as an official or second language in a particular country or community. Compare with **ENDOGLOSSIC**.
– ORIGIN 1980s: from **EXO-**, Greek *glōssa* 'language, tongue,' and **-IC**.

ex·on /'eksän/ ▶ **n.** Biochemistry a segment of a DNA or RNA molecule containing information coding for a protein or peptide sequence. Compare with **INTRON**.
– DERIVATIVES **ex·on·ic adj.**
– ORIGIN late 20th cent.: from *expressed* (see **EXPRESS[1]**) + **-ON**.

ex·on·er·ate /ig'zänə,rāt/ ▶ **v.** [with obj.] **1** (esp. of an official body) absolve (someone) from blame for a fault or wrongdoing, esp. after due consideration of the case: *the court-martial exonerated me | they should exonerate these men from this crime.*
2 (**exonerate someone from**) release someone from (a duty or obligation).
– DERIVATIVES **ex·on·er·a·tive** /-,rātiv/ **adj.**
– ORIGIN late Middle English: from Latin *exonerat-* 'freed from a burden,' from the verb *exonerare*, from *ex-* 'from' + *onus, oner-* 'a burden.'

ex·on·er·a·tion /ig,zänə'rāsHən/ ▶ **n. 1** the action of officially absolving someone from blame; vindication: *the defendants' eventual exoneration.* **2** the release of someone from a duty or obligation.

ex·o·nu·cle·ase /,eksō'n(y)o͞oklē,ās/ ▶ **n.** Biochemistry an enzyme that removes successive nucleotides from the end of a polynucleotide molecule.

ex·o·pep·ti·dase /,eksō'pepti,dās/ ▶ **n.** Biochemistry an enzyme that breaks the terminal peptide bond in a peptide chain.

ex·oph·o·ra /ek'säfərə/ ▶ **n.** Linguistics reference in a text or utterance to something external to it, which is only fully intelligible in terms of information about the extralinguistic situation. Compare with **ENDOPHORA**.
– DERIVATIVES **ex·o·phor·ic** /,eksō'fôrik, -fär-/ **adj.**

ex·oph·thal·mic /,eksäf'THalmik/ ▶ **adj.** Medicine having or characterized by protruding eyes.

ex·oph·thal·mic goi·ter ▶ **n.** another term for **GRAVES' DISEASE**.

ex·oph·thal·mos /,eksäf'THalməs/ (also **exophthalmus** or **exophthalmia** /-mēə/) ▶ **n.** Medicine abnormal protrusion of the eyeball or eyeballs.
– ORIGIN early 17th cent.: from modern Latin *exophthalmus*, from Greek *exophthalmos* 'having prominent eyes,' from *ex-* 'out' + *ophthalmos* 'eye.'

ex·o·plan·et /'eksō,planit/ ▶ **n.** a planet that orbits a star outside the solar system: *most of the 100 known exoplanets are comparable in mass to Jupiter.*

ex·op·o·dite /ek'säpə,dīt/ (also **exopod** /'eksə,päd/) ▶ **n.** Zoology the outer branch of the biramous limb or appendage of a crustacean. Compare with **ENDOPODITE, PROTOPODITE**.
– ORIGIN late 19th cent.: from **EXO-** 'outside' + Greek *pous, pod-* 'foot' + **-ITE[1]**.

exor. ▶ **abbr.** an executor (of a will).

ex·or·bi·tant /ig'zôrbitənt/ ▶ **adj.** (of a price or amount charged) unreasonably high: *the exorbitant price of tickets.*
– DERIVATIVES **ex·or·bi·tance** /eg'zôrbətns/ **n.**, **ex·or·bi·tant·ly adv.**
– ORIGIN late Middle English (originally as a legal term describing a case that is outside the scope of a law): from late Latin *exorbitant-* 'going off the track,' from *exorbitare*, from *ex-* 'out from' + *orbita* 'course, track.'

ex·or·cise /'eksôr,sīz, 'eksər-/ (also **exorcize**) ▶ **v.** [with obj.] drive out or attempt to drive out (an evil spirit) from a person or place: *an attempt to exorcise an unquiet spirit* | figurative *inflation has been exorcised.* ■ rid (a person or place) of an evil spirit: *infants were exorcised prior to baptism.*
– ORIGIN late Middle English: from French *exorciser* or ecclesiastical Latin *exorcizare*, from Greek *exorkizein*, from *ex-* 'out' + *horkos* 'oath.' The word originally meant 'conjure up or command an evil spirit'; the specific sense of driving out an evil spirit dates from the mid 16th cent.

ex·or·cism /'eksôr,sizəm, 'eksər-/ ▶ **n.** the expulsion or attempted expulsion of an evil spirit from a person or place.
– DERIVATIVES **ex·or·cist n.**
– ORIGIN late Middle English: via ecclesiastical Latin from ecclesiastical Greek *exorkismos*, from *exorkizein* 'exorcize.'

ex·or·di·um /ig'zôrdēəm, ik'sôr-/ ▶ **n.** (pl. **exordiums** or **exordia** /-dēə/) formal the beginning or introductory part, esp. of a discourse or treatise.
– DERIVATIVES **ex·or·di·al** /-dēəl/ **adj.**
– ORIGIN late 16th cent.: from Latin, from *exordiri* 'begin,' from *ex-* 'out, from' + *ordiri* 'begin.'

ex·o·skel·e·ton /'eksō,skelitn/ ▶ **n.** Zoology a rigid external covering for the body in some invertebrate animals, esp. arthropods, providing both support and protection. Compare with **ENDOSKELETON**.
– DERIVATIVES **ex·o·skel·e·tal** /,eksō'skelətl/ **adj.**

ex·o·sphere /'eksō,sfi(ə)r/ ▶ **n.** Astronomy the outermost region of a planet's atmosphere.
– DERIVATIVES **ex·o·spher·ic** /,eksō'sfi(ə)rik, -'sferik/ **adj.**

ex·o·spore /'eksō,spôr/ ▶ **n. 1** the outer layer of the membrane in some spores.
2 a spore formed by separation and release from a sporophore, the spore-bearing structure of a fungus.
– DERIVATIVES **ex·o·spor·al** /,eksə'spôrəl/ **adj.**

ex·o·spor·i·um /,eksō'spôrēəm/ ▶ **n.** (pl. **exosporia**) Botany another term for **EXINE**.
– DERIVATIVES **ex·o·spor·ial** /-'spôrēəl/ **adj.**

ex·os·to·sis /,eksä'stōsis/ ▶ **n.** (pl. **exostoses** /-sēz/) Medicine a benign outgrowth of cartilaginous tissue on a bone.
– ORIGIN late 16th cent.: from Greek, from *ex-* 'out' + *osteon* 'bone.'

ex·o·ter·ic /,eksə'terik/ ▶ **adj.** formal (esp. of a doctrine or mode of speech) intended for or likely to be understood by the general public: *an exoteric, literal meaning and an esoteric, inner teaching.* The opposite of **ESOTERIC**.
– ORIGIN mid 17th cent.: via Latin from Greek *exōterikos*, from *exōterō* 'outer,' comparative of *exō* 'outside.'

ex·o·ther·mic /,eksə'THərmik/ ▶ **adj.** Chemistry (of a reaction or process) accompanied by the release of heat. The opposite of **ENDOTHERMIC** (sense 1). ■ (of a compound) formed from its constituent elements with a net release of heat.
– DERIVATIVES **ex·o·ther·mi·cal·ly** /-(ə)lē/ **adv.**
– ORIGIN late 19th cent.: from French *exothermique*.

ex·ot·ic /ig'zätik/ ▶ **adj.** originating in or characteristic of a distant foreign country: *exotic birds | they loved to visit exotic places.* ■ attractive or striking because colorful or out of the ordinary: *an exotic outfit* | (as noun **the exotic**) *there was a touch of the exotic in her appearance.* ■ of a kind not used for ordinary purposes or not ordinarily encountered: *exotic elementary particles as yet unknown to science.*
▶ **n.** an exotic plant or animal: *he planted exotics in the sheltered garden.*
– DERIVATIVES **ex·ot·i·cal·ly** /-(ə)lē/ **adv.**, **ex·ot·i·cism** /ig'zätə,sizəm/ **n.**
– ORIGIN late 16th cent.: via Latin from Greek *exōtikos* 'foreign,' from *exō* 'outside.'

ex·ot·i·ca /ig'zätikə/ ▶ **plural n.** objects considered strange or interesting because they are out of the ordinary, esp. because they originated in a distant foreign country.
– ORIGIN late 19th cent.: from Latin, neuter plural of *exoticus* 'foreign' (see **EXOTIC**).

ex·ot·ic danc·er ▶ **n.** a striptease dancer.

ex·o·tox·in /'eksō,täksin/ ▶ **n.** Microbiology a toxin released by a living bacterial cell into its surroundings. Compare with **ENDOTOXIN**.

exp. ▶ **abbr.** ■ expenses. ■ experience (usually in the context of job advertisements): *previous exp. an advantage.* ■ (**Exp.**) experimental (in titles of periodicals): *J. Exp. Biol.* ■ expiration: *exp. date.* ■ Mathematics the exponential function raising *e* to the power of the given quantity: *it is reduced by exp.* $(-U)$. ■ exposures (in the context of photography): *$4.45 for 24 exp.* ■ express.

ex·pand /ik'spand/ ▶ **v.** become or make larger or more extensive: [no obj.] ***their business expanded into other hotels and properties*** | [with obj.] ***baby birds cannot expand and contract their lungs.*** ■ [no obj.] Physics (of the universe) undergo a continuous change whereby, according to theory based on observed redshifts, all the galaxies recede from one another. ■ [no obj.] (**expand on**) give a fuller version or account of: *Anne expanded on the theory.*
– DERIVATIVES **ex·pand·a·ble adj.**, **ex·pand·er n.**, **ex·pan·si·bil·i·ty** /ik,spansə'bilitē/ **n.**, **ex·pan·si·ble** /-'spansəbəl/ **adj.**
– ORIGIN late Middle English: from Latin *expandere* 'to spread out,' from *ex-* 'out' + *pandere* 'to spread.'

ex·pand·ed /ik'spandid/ ▶ **n.** being or having been enlarged, extended, or broadened, in particular: ■ denoting materials which have a light cellular structure: *expanded polystyrene.* ■ denoting sheet metal slit and stretched into a mesh, used to reinforce concrete and other brittle materials. ■ relatively broad in shape: *the expanded fins of the ray.*

ex·panse /ik'spans/ ▶ **n.** an area of something, typically land or sea, presenting a wide continuous surface: *the green expanse of the forest.* ■ the distance to which something expands or can be

expanded: *the moth has a wing expanse of 20 to 24 mm.*
– ORIGIN mid 17th cent.: from modern Latin *expansum* 'something expanded,' neuter past participle of *expandere* (see EXPAND).

ex·pan·sile /ik'spansəl, -ˌsīl/ ▶ **adj.** Physics of, relating to, or capable of expansion.

ex·pan·sion /ik'spanSHən/ ▶ **n.** the action of becoming larger or more extensive: *the rapid expansion of suburban Washington | a small expansion of industry.* ■ extension of a state's territory by encroaching on that of other nations, pursued as a political strategy: *German expansion in the 1930s.* ■ a thing formed by the enlargement, broadening, or development of something: *the book is an expansion of a lecture given last year.* ■ the increase in the volume of fuel on combustion in the cylinder of an engine, or the piston stroke in which this occurs.
– ORIGIN early 17th cent.: from late Latin *expansion-*, from Latin *expandere* (see EXPAND).

ex·pan·sion·ar·y /ik'spanSHəˌnerē/ ▶ **adj.** (of a policy or action) intended to result in economic or political expansion: *an expansionary budget.*

ex·pan·sion bolt ▶ **n.** a bolt that expands when inserted, no thread being required in the surrounding material.

ex·pan·sion card (also **expansion board**) ▶ **n.** Computing a circuit board that can be inserted in a computer to give extra facilities or memory.

ex·pan·sion·ism /ik'spanSHəˌnizəm/ ▶ **n.** the policy of territorial or economic expansion: *the post-colonial critique of Western expansionism.*
– DERIVATIVES **ex·pan·sion·ist** n. & adj., **ex·pan·sion·is·tic** /ikˌspanSHə'nistik/ adj.

ex·pan·sion joint ▶ **n.** a joint that makes allowance for thermal expansion of the parts joined without distortion.

ex·pan·sion slot ▶ **n.** Computing a place in a computer where an expansion card can be inserted.

ex·pan·sion team ▶ **n.** a new team added to an established professional sport league.

ex·pan·sive /ik'spansiv/ ▶ **adj. 1** covering a wide area in terms of space or scope; extensive or wide-ranging: *deep, expansive canyons.*
2 (of a person or their manner) open, demonstrative, and communicative: *she felt expansive and inclined to talk.*
3 tending toward economic or political expansion: *expansive domestic economic policies.*
– DERIVATIVES **ex·pan·sive·ly** adv., **ex·pan·sive·ness** n.

ex·pan·siv·i·ty /ˌekspan'sivitē/ ▶ **n.** Physics the amount a material expands or contracts per unit length due to a one-degree change in temperature.

ex par·te /eks 'pärtē/ ▶ **adj. & adv.** Law with respect to or in the interests of one side only or of an interested outside party.
– ORIGIN late 17th cent.: Latin, literally 'from a side.'

ex·pat /eks'pat/ ▶ **n. & adj.** informal short for EXPATRIATE.

ex·pa·ti·ate /ik'spāSHēˌāt/ ▶ **v.** [no obj.] speak or write at length or in detail: *she* ***expatiated on*** *working-class novelists.*
– DERIVATIVES **ex·pa·ti·a·tion** /ikˌspāSHē'āSHən/ n.
– ORIGIN mid 16th cent. (in the sense 'roam freely'): from Latin *exspatiari* 'move beyond one's usual bounds,' from *ex-* 'out, from' + *spatiari* 'to walk' (from *spatium* 'space').

ex·pa·tri·ate ▶ **n.** /eks'pātrēit/ a person who lives outside their native country: *American expatriates in London.* ■ archaic a person exiled from their native country.
▶ **adj.** /eks'pātrēit/ [attrib.] (of a person) living outside their native country: *expatriate writers and artists.* ■ archaic expelled from one's native country.
▶ **v.** /eks'pātrēˌāt/ [no obj.] settle oneself abroad: *candidates should be willing to expatriate.*
– DERIVATIVES **ex·pa·tri·a·tion** /eksˌpātrē'āSHən/ n.
– ORIGIN mid 18th cent. (as a verb): from medieval Latin *expatriat-* 'gone out from one's country,' from the verb *expatriare*, from *ex-* 'out' + *patria* 'native country.'

ex·pect /ik'spekt/ ▶ **v.** [with obj.] regard (something) as likely to happen: *we expect the best* | [with obj. and infinitive] *he expects the stock market to sink further* | [with clause] *we expect that farmers will harvest 63 million acres of hay.* ■ regard (someone) as likely to do or be something: [with obj. and infinitive] *they were not expecting him to continue.* ■ believe that (someone or something) will arrive soon: *Celia was expecting a visitor.* ■ look for (something) from someone as rightfully due or requisite in the circumstances: *we expect great things* ***of*** *you.* ■ require (someone) to fulfill an obligation: [with obj. and infinitive] *we expect employers to pay a reasonable salary.* ■ (**I expect**) informal used to indicate that one supposes something to be so, but has no firm evidence or knowledge: *they're just friends of his, I expect* | [with clause] *I expect you know them?*
– PHRASES **be expecting** (**a baby**) informal be pregnant. **to be expected** completely normal: *wild swings in the weather are to be expected.* **what can** (or **do**) **you expect?** used to emphasize that there was nothing unexpected about a person or event, however disappointed one might be.
– DERIVATIVES **ex·pect·a·ble** adj.
– ORIGIN mid 16th cent. (in the sense 'defer action, wait'): from Latin *exspectare* 'look out for,' from *ex-* 'out' + *spectare* 'to look' (frequentative of *specere* 'see').

ex·pect·an·cy /ik'spektənsē/ ▶ **n.** (pl. **expectancies**) the state of thinking or hoping that something, esp. something pleasant, will happen or be the case: *they waited with an air of expectancy.*
– ORIGIN early 17th cent.: from Latin *exspectantia*, from *exspectare* 'look out for' (see EXPECT).

ex·pect·ant /ik'spektənt/ ▶ **adj.** having or showing an excited feeling that something is about to happen, esp. something pleasant and interesting: *an expectant conference crowd.* ■ [attrib.] (of a woman) pregnant: *an expectant mother.*
▶ **n.** archaic a person who anticipates receiving something, esp. high office.
– DERIVATIVES **ex·pect·ant·ly** adv.
– ORIGIN late Middle English: from Latin *exspectant-* 'expecting,' from the verb *exspectare* (see EXPECT).

ex·pec·ta·tion /ˌekspek'tāSHən/ ▶ **n.** a strong belief that something will happen or be the case in the future: *reality had not lived up to expectations* | *an* ***expectation that*** *the government will provide the resources* | *he drilled his men* ***in expectation of*** *a Prussian advance.* ■ a belief that someone will or should achieve something: *students had high expectations for their future.* ■ (**expectations**) archaic one's prospects of inheritance. ■ Mathematics another term for EXPECTED VALUE.

ex·pect·ed u·til·i·ty ▶ **n.** Mathematics & Economics a predicted utility value for one of several options, calculated as the sum of the utility of every possible outcome each multiplied by the probability of its occurrence.

ex·pect·ed val·ue ▶ **n.** Mathematics a predicted value of a variable, calculated as the sum of all possible values each multiplied by the probability of its occurrence.

ex·pec·to·rant /ik'spektərənt/ ▶ **n.** a medicine that promotes the secretion of sputum by the air passages, used esp. to treat coughs.
– ORIGIN mid 18th cent.: from Latin *expectorant-* 'expelling from the chest,' from the verb *expectorare* (see EXPECTORATE).

ex·pec·to·rate /ik'spektəˌrāt/ ▶ **v.** [no obj.] cough or spit out phlegm from the throat or lungs. ■ [with obj.] spit out (phlegm) in this way.
– DERIVATIVES **ex·pec·to·ra·tion** /ikˌspektə'rāSHən/ n.
– ORIGIN early 17th cent. (in the sense 'enable sputum to be coughed up,' referring to medicine): from Latin *expectorat-* 'expelled from the chest,' from the verb *expectorare*, from *ex-* 'out' + *pectus, pector-* 'breast.'

ex·pe·di·en·cy /ik'spēdēənsē/ ▶ **n.** the quality of being convenient and practical despite possibly being improper or immoral; convenience: *an act of political expediency.*

ex·pe·di·ent /ik'spēdēənt/ ▶ **adj.** (of an action) convenient and practical, although possibly improper or immoral: *either side could break the agreement if it were expedient to do so.* ■ (of an action) suitable or appropriate: *holding a public inquiry into the scheme was not expedient.*
▶ **n.** a means of attaining an end, esp. one that is convenient but considered improper or immoral: *the current policy is a political expedient.*
– DERIVATIVES **ex·pe·di·ence** n., **ex·pe·di·ent·ly** adv.
– ORIGIN late Middle English: from Latin *expedient-* 'extricating, putting in order,' from the verb *expedire* (see EXPEDITE). The original sense was neutral; the depreciatory sense, implying disregard of moral considerations, dates from the late 18th cent.

ex·pe·dite /'ekspəˌdīt/ ▶ **v.** [with obj.] make (an action or process) happen sooner or be accomplished more quickly: *he promised to expedite economic reforms.*
– DERIVATIVES **ex·pe·dit·er** (also **expeditor** /-tər/) n.
– ORIGIN late 15th cent. (in the sense 'perform quickly'): from Latin *expedire* 'extricate (originally by freeing the feet), put in order,' from *ex-* 'out' + *pes, ped-* 'foot.'

ex·pe·di·tion /ˌekspə'diSHən/ ▶ **n. 1** a journey or voyage undertaken by a group of people with a particular purpose, esp. that of exploration, scientific research, or war: *an expedition to the jungles of the Orinoco* | informal *a shopping expedition.* ■ the people involved in such a journey or voyage: *many of the expedition have passed rigorous courses.*
2 formal promptness or speed in doing something: *the landlord shall remedy the defects with all possible expedition.*
– ORIGIN late Middle English: via Old French from Latin *expeditio(n-)*, from *expedire* 'extricate' (see EXPEDITE). Early senses included 'prompt supply of something' and 'setting out with aggressive intent' The notions of 'speed' and 'purpose' are retained in current senses. Sense 1 dates from the late 16th cent.

ex·pe·di·tion·ar·y /ˌekspə'diSHəˌnerē/ ▶ **adj.** [attrib.] of or forming an expedition, esp. a military expedition: *an expeditionary force.*

ex·pe·di·tious /ˌekspə'diSHəs/ ▶ **adj.** done with speed and efficiency: *an expeditious investigation.*
– DERIVATIVES **ex·pe·di·tious·ly** adv., **ex·pe·di·tious·ness** n.
– ORIGIN late 15th cent.: from EXPEDITION + -OUS.

ex·pel /ik'spel/ ▶ **v.** (**expels, expelling, expelled**) [with obj.] deprive (someone) of membership of or involvement in a school or other organization: *she was* ***expelled from*** *school.* ■ force (someone) to leave a place, esp. a country. ■ force out or eject (something), esp. from the body: *she expelled a shuddering breath.*
– DERIVATIVES **ex·pel·la·ble** adj., **ex·pel·lee** /ˌekspel'lē/ n., **ex·pel·ler** n.
– ORIGIN late Middle English (in the general sense 'eject, force to leave'): from Latin *expellere*, from *ex-* 'out' + *pellere* 'to drive.'

ex·pend /ik'spend/ ▶ **v.** [with obj.] spend or use up (a resource such as money, time, or energy): *we do not need to expend energy working on our marriage.*
– ORIGIN late Middle English: from Latin *expendere*, from *ex-* 'out' + *pendere* 'weigh, pay.' Compare with SPEND.

ex·pend·a·ble /ik'spendəbəl/ ▶ **adj.** (of an object) designed to be used only once and then abandoned or destroyed: *the need for unmanned and expendable launch vehicles.* ■ of little significance when compared to an overall purpose, and therefore able to be abandoned: *the region is expendable in the wider context of national politics.*
– DERIVATIVES **ex·pend·a·bil·i·ty** /ikˌspendə'bilitē/ n., **ex·pend·a·bly** /-əblē/ adv.

ex·pend·i·ture /ik'spendiCHər/ ▶ **n.** the action of spending funds: *the expenditure of taxpayers' money.* ■ an amount of money spent: *cuts in public expenditure.*
– ORIGIN mid 18th cent.: from EXPEND, suggested by obsolete *expenditor* 'officer in charge of expenditure,' from medieval Latin, from *expenditus*, irregular past participle of Latin *expendere* 'pay out' (see EXPEND).

ex·pense /ik'spens/ ▶ **n.** the cost required for something; the money spent on something: *we had ordered suits* ***at great expense*** | *the committee does not expect members* ***to be put to any expense.*** ■ (**expenses**) the costs incurred in the performance of one's job or a specific task, esp. one undertaken for another person: *his hotel and travel expenses.* ■ a thing on which one is required to spend money: *tolls are a daily expense.*
▶ **v.** [with obj.] (usu. **be expensed**) offset (an item of expenditure) as an expense against taxable income.
– PHRASES **at someone's expense** paid for by someone: *the document was printed at the taxpayer's expense.* ■ with someone as the victim, esp. of a joke: *my friends all had a good laugh at my expense.* **at the expense of** so as to cause harm to or neglect of: *the pursuit of profit at the expense of the environment* | *language courses that emphasize communication skills at the expense of literature.*
– ORIGIN late Middle English: from Anglo-Norman French, alteration of Old French *espense*, from late Latin *expensa* (*pecunia*) '(money) spent,' from Latin *expendere* 'pay out' (see EXPEND).

ex·pense ac·count ▶ **n.** an arrangement under which sums of money spent in the course of business by an employee are later reimbursed by their employer.

ex·pen·sive /ik'spensiv/ ▶ **adj.** costing a lot of money: *keeping a horse is expensive* | *an expensive bottle of wine.*
– DERIVATIVES **ex·pen·sive·ly** adv., **ex·pen·sive·ness** n.

e

– ORIGIN early 17th cent. (in the sense 'lavish, extravagant'): from Latin *expens-* 'paid out,' from the verb *expendere* (see EXPEND), + -IVE.

ex·pe·ri·ence /ik'spi(ə)rēəns/ ▶ n. practical contact with and observation of facts or events: *he had already learned his lesson by painful experience* | *he spoke from experience.* ■ the knowledge or skill acquired by such means over a period of time, esp. that gained in a particular profession by someone at work: *older men whose experience could be called upon* | *candidates with the necessary experience.* ■ an event or occurrence that leaves an impression on someone: *for the younger players it has been a* ***learning experience.***
▶ v. [with obj.] encounter or undergo (an event or occurrence): *the company is experiencing difficulties.* ■ feel (an emotion): *an opportunity to experience the excitement of New York.*
– DERIVATIVES **ex·pe·ri·ence·a·ble** adj., **ex·pe·ri·enc·er** n.
– ORIGIN late Middle English: via Old French from Latin *experientia*, from *experiri* 'try.' Compare with EXPERIMENT and EXPERT.

ex·pe·ri·enced /ik'spi(ə)rēənst/ ▶ adj. having knowledge or skill in a particular field, esp. a profession or job, gained over a period of time: *an experienced social worker* | *she was* ***experienced in*** *marketing.*

ex·pe·ri·en·tial /ek,spi(ə)rē'enCHəl/ ▶ adj. involving or based on experience and observation: *the experiential learning associated with employment.*
– DERIVATIVES **ex·pe·ri·en·tial·ly** adv.
– ORIGIN early 19th cent.: from EXPERIENCE, on the pattern of words such as *inferential.*

ex·per·i·ment ▶ n. /ik'sperəmənt/ a scientific procedure undertaken to make a discovery, test a hypothesis, or demonstrate a known fact: *laboratory* ***experiments on*** *guinea pigs* | *I have tested this by experiment.* ■ a course of action tentatively adopted without being sure of the eventual outcome: *the previous* ***experiment in*** *liberal democracy had ended in disaster.*
▶ v. /ik'sperə,ment/ [no obj.] perform a scientific procedure, esp. in a laboratory, to determine something: *she* ***experimented on*** *chickens as well as mice.* ■ try out new concepts or ways of doing things: *the designers* ***experimented with*** *new ideas in lighting.*
– DERIVATIVES **ex·per·i·men·ta·tion** /ik,sperəmən'tāSHən/ n., **ex·per·i·ment·er** n.
– ORIGIN Middle English: from Old French, or from Latin *experimentum*, from *experiri* 'try.' Compare with EXPERIENCE and EXPERT.

ex·per·i·men·tal /ik,sperə'men(t)l/ ▶ adj. (of a new invention or product) based on untested ideas or techniques and not yet established or finalized: *an experimental drug.* ■ (of a work of art or an artistic technique) involving a radically new and innovative style: *experimental music.* ■ of or relating to scientific experiments: *experimental results.* ■ archaic based on experience as opposed to authority or conjecture: *an experimental knowledge of God.*
– DERIVATIVES **ex·per·i·men·tal·ism** /-izəm/ n., **ex·per·i·men·tal·ist** /-ist/ n., **ex·per·i·men·tal·ly** adv.
– ORIGIN late 15th cent. (in the sense 'having personal experience,' also 'experienced, observed'): from medieval Latin *experimentalis*, from Latin *experimentum* (see EXPERIMENT).

ex·per·i·men·tal psy·chol·o·gy ▶ n. the branch of psychology concerned with the scientific investigation of basic psychological processes such as learning, memory, and cognition in humans and animals.

ex·per·i·ment·er ef·fect /ik'sperə,mentər/ ▶ n. an influence exerted by the experimenter's expectations or other characteristics on the results of an experiment, esp. in psychology.

ex·pert /'ek,spərt/ ▶ n. a person who has a comprehensive and authoritative knowledge of or skill in a particular area: ***experts in*** *child development* | *a financial expert.*
▶ adj. having or involving such knowledge or skill: *he had received expert academic advice* | *he is* ***expert at*** *handling the media.*
– DERIVATIVES **ex·pert·ly** adv., **ex·pert·ness** n.
– ORIGIN Middle English (as an adjective): from French, from Latin *expertus*, past participle of *experiri* 'try.' The noun use dates from the early 19th cent. Compare with EXPERIENCE and EXPERIMENT.

ex·per·tise /,ekspər'tēz, -'tēs/ ▶ n. expert skill or knowledge in a particular field: *technical expertise.*
– ORIGIN mid 19th cent.: from French, from *expert* (see EXPERT).

ex·pert sys·tem ▶ n. Computing a piece of software programmed using artificial intelligence techniques. Such systems use databases of expert knowledge to offer advice or make decisions in such areas as medical diagnosis and trading on the stock exchange.

ex·pert wit·ness ▶ n. a person who is permitted to testify at a trial because of special knowledge or proficiency in a particular field that is relevant to the case.

ex·pi·ate /'ekspē,āt/ ▶ v. [with obj.] atone for (guilt or sin): *their sins must be expiated by sacrifice.*
– DERIVATIVES **ex·pi·a·ble** /'ekspēəbəl/ adj., **ex·pi·a·tor** /-,ātər/ n., **ex·pi·a·to·ry** /'ekspēə,tôrē/ adj.
– ORIGIN late 16th cent. (in the sense 'end (rage, sorrow, etc.) by suffering it to the full'): from Latin *expiat-* 'appeased by sacrifice,' from the verb *expiare*, from *ex-* 'out' + *piare* (from *pius* 'pious').

ex·pi·a·tion /,ekspē'āSHən/ ▶ n. the act of making amends or reparation for guilt or wrongdoing; atonement: *an act of public expiation.*

ex·pi·ra·tion /,ekspə'rāSHən/ ▶ n. **1** the ending of the fixed period for which a contract is valid: *the expiration of the lease.* ■ the end of a period of time: *the expiration of three years.*
2 technical exhalation of breath.
– ORIGIN late Middle English (denoting a vapor or exhalation): from Latin *exspiratio(n-)*, from the verb *exspirare* (see EXPIRE).

ex·pir·a·to·ry /ik'spīrə,tôrē/ ▶ adj. of or relating to the exhalation of air from the lungs.

ex·pire /ik'spīr/ ▶ v. **1** [no obj.] (of a document, authorization, or agreement) cease to be valid, typically after a fixed period of time: *the old contract had expired.* ■ (of a period of time) come to an end: *the three-year period has expired.* ■ (of a person) die.
2 [with obj.] technical exhale (air) from the lung.
– ORIGIN late Middle English: from Old French *expirer*, from Latin *exspirare* 'breathe out,' from *ex-* 'out' + *spirare* 'breathe.'

ex·pi·ry /ik'spī(ə)rē, ek-/ ▶ n. Brit. & Canadian the end of the period for which something is valid: *the expiry of the patent* | [as modifier] *an expiry date.* ■ the end of a fixed period of time: *the expiry of the six-month period.* ■ archaic death.

ex·plain /ik'splān/ ▶ v. [reporting verb] make (an idea, situation, or problem) clear to someone by describing it in more detail or revealing relevant facts or ideas: [with clause] *they explained that their lives centered on the religious rituals* | [with direct speech] *"my daddy has spells," Ben explained* | [with obj.] *he explained the situation.* ■ [with obj.] account for (an action or event) by giving a reason as excuse or justification: *Callie found it necessary to explain her blackened eye* | [with clause] *he makes athletes explain why they made a mistake* | [no obj.] *she had tried to explain about Adam, hadn't she?* ■ (**explain something away**) minimize the significance of an embarrassing fact or action by giving an excuse or justification: *they know stories about me that I can't explain away.*
– PHRASES **explain oneself** expand on what one has said in order to make one's meaning clear. ■ give an account of one's motives or conduct in order to excuse or justify oneself: *he was too panicked to stay and explain himself to the policeman.*
– DERIVATIVES **ex·plain·a·ble** adj., **ex·plain·er** n.
– ORIGIN late Middle English: from Latin *explanare*, based on *planus* 'plain.'

ex·pla·nan·dum /,eksplə'nandəm/ ▶ n. (pl. **explananda** /-də/) Philosophy another term for EXPLICANDUM.
– ORIGIN late 19th cent.: from Latin, '(something) to be explained.'

ex·pla·nans /ek'splā,nans/ ▶ n. (pl. **explanantia** /,eksplə'nanCHēə/) Philosophy another term for EXPLICANS.
– ORIGIN 1940s: Latin, 'explaining.'

ex·pla·na·tion /,eksplə'nāSHən/ ▶ n. a statement or account that makes something clear: *the birth rate is central to any explanation of population trends.* ■ a reason or justification given for an action or belief: *Freud tried to make sex the explanation for everything* | *my application was rejected without explanation.*
– ORIGIN late Middle English: from Latin *explanatio(n-)*, from the verb *explanare* (see EXPLAIN).

ex·plan·a·to·ry /ik'splanə,tôrē/ ▶ adj. serving to explain something: *explanatory notes.*
– DERIVATIVES **ex·plan·a·to·ri·ly** /ik,splanə'tôrəlē/ adv.

ex·plant Biology ▶ v. /ek'splant/ [with obj.] (often as adj. **explanted**) transfer (living cells, tissues, or organs) from animals or plants to a nutrient medium.
▶ n. /'eks,plant/ a cell, organ, or piece of tissue that has been transferred in this way.
– DERIVATIVES **ex·plan·ta·tion** /,eksplan'tāSHən/ n.
– ORIGIN early 20th cent.: from modern Latin *explantare*, from *ex-* 'out' + *plantare* 'to plant.'

ex·ple·tive /'eksplitiv/ ▶ n. an oath or swear word. ■ Grammar a word or phrase used to fill out a sentence or a line of verse without adding to the sense.
▶ adj. Grammar (of a word or phrase) serving to fill out a sentence or line of verse.
– ORIGIN late Middle English (as an adjective): from late Latin *expletivus*, from *explere* 'fill out,' from *ex-* 'out' + *plere* 'fill.' The general noun sense 'word used merely to fill out a sentence' (early 17th cent.) was applied specifically to an oath or swear word in the early 19th cent.

ex·pli·ca·ble /ek'splikəbəl, 'eksplik-/ ▶ adj. able to be accounted for or understood: *the English class system is not entirely explicable in terms of money.*
– ORIGIN mid 16th cent.: from French, or from Latin *explicabilis*, from *explicare* (see EXPLICATE).

ex·pli·can·dum /,ekspli'kandəm/ ▶ n. (pl. **explicanda** /-də/) Philosophy the fact, thing, or expression that is to be explained or explicated. Compare with EXPLICANS.
– ORIGIN mid 19th cent.: Latin, 'something to be explained,' neuter gerundive of *explicare.*

ex·pli·cans /'ekspli,kanz/ ▶ n. (pl. **explicantia** /-,kanSHēə/) Philosophy the explanation or explication given for a fact, thing, or expression. Compare with EXPLICANDUM.
– ORIGIN late 19th cent.: Latin, present participle of *explicare* 'explain.'

ex·pli·cate /'ekspli,kāt/ ▶ v. [with obj.] analyze and develop (an idea or principle) in detail: *attempting to explicate the relationship between crime and economic forces.* ■ analyze (a literary work) in order to reveal its meaning.
– DERIVATIVES **ex·pli·ca·tion** /,ekspli'kāSHən/ n., **ex·pli·ca·tive** /-,kātiv/ adj., **ex·pli·ca·tor** /-,kātər/ n., **ex·pli·ca·to·ry** /ik'splikə,tôrē/ adj.
– ORIGIN mid 16th cent.: from Latin *explicat-* 'unfolded,' from the verb *explicare*, from *ex-* 'out' + *plicare* 'to fold.'

ex·plic·it /ik'splisit/ ▶ adj. stated clearly and in detail, leaving no room for confusion or doubt: *the speaker's intentions were not made explicit.* ■ (of a person) stating something in such a way: *let me be explicit.* ■ describing or representing sexual activity in a graphic fashion: *explicit photos showing poses and acts.*
▶ n. the closing words of a text, manuscript, early printed book, or chanted liturgical text. Compare with INCIPIT. [Middle English: late Latin, 'here ends,' or abbreviation of *explicitus est liber* 'the scroll is unrolled.']
– DERIVATIVES **ex·plic·it·ly** adv., **ex·plic·it·ness** n.
– ORIGIN early 17th cent. (as an adjective): from French *explicite* or Latin *explicitus*, past participle of *explicare* 'unfold' (see EXPLICATE).

ex·plode /ik'splōd/ ▶ v. [no obj.] **1** burst or shatter violently and noisily as a result of rapid combustion, decomposition, excessive internal pressure, or other process, typically scattering fragments widely: *a large bomb exploded in a park.* ■ [with obj.] cause (a bomb) to do this: *the USSR had not yet exploded its first nuclear weapon.* ■ technical undergo a violent expansion in which much energy is released as a shock wave: *lead ensures that gasoline burns rather than explodes.* ■ (of a person) suddenly give expression to violent and uncontainable emotion, esp. anger: *he can* ***explode with*** *anger* | [with direct speech] *"This is ludicrous!" she exploded.* ■ (of a violent emotion or a situation) arise or develop suddenly: *tension that could* ***explode into*** *violence at any time.* ■ (**explode into**) suddenly begin to move or start a new activity: *a bird exploded into flight.* ■ increase suddenly or rapidly in size, number, or extent: *the car population of Warsaw has exploded.* ■ (as adj. **exploded**) (of a diagram or drawing) showing the components of a mechanism as if separated by an explosion but in the normal relative positions: *an exploded diagram of the rifle's parts.*
2 [with obj.] show (a belief or theory) to be false or unfounded: *the myths that link smoking with glamour need to be exploded.*
– DERIVATIVES **ex·plod·er** n.
– ORIGIN mid 16th cent. (in the sense 'reject scornfully, discard'): from Latin *explodere* 'drive out by clapping, hiss off the stage,' from *ex-* 'out' + *plaudere* 'to clap.' Sense 2 is derived from the original sense of the word. Sense 1 (late 18th cent.) evolved via an old sense 'expel with violence and sudden noise,' perhaps influenced by obsolete *displode* 'burst with a noise.'

ex·ploit ▶ v. /ik'sploit/ [with obj.] make full use of and derive benefit from (a resource): *500 companies sprang up to exploit this new technology.* ■ use (a situation or person) in an unfair or selfish way: *the company was exploiting a legal loophole* | *accusations that he exploited a wealthy patient.* ■ benefit unfairly from the work of (someone), typically by overworking or underpaying them: *making money does not always mean exploiting others.*

▶ **n.** /ˈekˌsploit/ a bold or daring feat: *the most heroic and secretive exploits of the war.*
–DERIVATIVES **ex·ploit·a·ble** **adj.**, **ex·ploit·a·tive** /ikˈsploitətiv/ **adj.**, **ex·ploit·er** /ikˈsploitər/ **n.**, **ex·ploit·ive** /ikˈsploitiv/ **adj.**
–ORIGIN Middle English: from Old French *esploit* (noun), based on Latin *explicare* 'unfold' (see EXPLICATE). The early notion of 'success, progress' gave rise to the sense 'attempt to capture,' 'military expedition,' hence the current sense of the noun. Current verb senses (mid 19th cent.) are taken from modern French *exploiter.*

ex·ploi·ta·tion /ˌeksploiˈtāSHən/ ▶ **n.** **1** the action or fact of treating someone unfairly in order to benefit from their work: *the exploitation of migrant workers.*
2 the action of making use of and benefiting from resources: *the Bronze Age saw exploitation of gold deposits.* ■ the fact of making use of a situation to gain unfair advantage for oneself: *this administration's exploitation of the fear of crime.*

ex·plo·ra·tion /ˌekspləˈrāSHən/ ▶ **n.** the action of traveling in or through an unfamiliar area in order to learn about it: *voyages of exploration* | *an exploration of the African interior.* ■ thorough analysis of a subject or theme: *an exploration of the religious dimensions of our lives.*
–DERIVATIVES **ex·plo·ra·tion·al** /-ˈrāSHənl/ **adj.**
–ORIGIN mid 16th cent. (denoting an investigation): from French, or from Latin *exploratio(n-)*, from the verb *explorare* (see EXPLORE). The current sense dates from the early 19th cent.

Ex·plor·a·to·ri·um /ikˌsplôrəˈtôrēəm/ ▶ **n.** [usu. in names] trademark a scientific museum or similar center at which visitors have the opportunity of performing prearranged experiments or demonstrations.
–ORIGIN 1970s: from EXPLORATION + -ORIUM.

ex·plor·a·to·ry /ikˈsplôrəˌtôrē/ ▶ **adj.** relating to or involving exploration or investigation: *surgeons performed an exploratory operation* | *exploratory talks.*
–ORIGIN late Middle English: from Latin *exploratorius*, from *explorare* (see EXPLORE).

ex·plore /ikˈsplôr/ ▶ **v.** [with obj.] travel in or through (an unfamiliar country or area) in order to learn about or familiarize oneself with it: *the best way to explore Iceland's northwest* | figurative *the project encourages children to explore the world of photography.* ■ [no obj.] (**explore for**) search for resources such as mineral deposits: *the company explored for oil.* ■ inquire into or discuss (a subject or issue) in detail: *he sets out to explore fundamental questions.* ■ examine or evaluate (an option or possibility): *you continue to explore new ways to generate income.* ■ examine by touch: *her fingers explored his hair.* ■ Medicine surgically examine (a wound or body cavity) in detail.
–DERIVATIVES **ex·plor·a·tive** /-rətiv/ **adj.**
–ORIGIN mid 16th cent. (in the sense 'investigate (why)'): from French *explorer*, from Latin *explorare* 'search out,' from *ex-* 'out' + *plorare* 'utter a cry.'

ex·plor·er /ikˈsplôrər/ ▶ **n.** a person who explores an unfamiliar area; an adventurer: *a polar explorer.*

ex·plo·sion /ikˈsplōZHən/ ▶ **n.** a violent and destructive shattering or blowing apart of something, as is caused by a bomb. ■ technical a violent expansion in which energy is transmitted outward as a shock wave. ■ a sudden outburst of something such as noise, light, or violent emotion, esp. anger: *an explosion of anger.* ■ a sudden political or social upheaval. ■ a rapid or sudden increase in amount or extent: *an explosion in the adder population.* ■ Phonetics another term for PLOSION.
–ORIGIN early 17th cent.: from Latin *explosio(n-)* 'scornful rejection,' from the verb *explodere* (see EXPLODE).

ex·plo·sive /ikˈsplōsiv/ ▶ **adj.** able or likely to shatter violently or burst apart, as when a bomb explodes: *an explosive device.* ■ likely to cause an eruption of anger or controversy: *Marco's explosive temper* | *the idea was politically explosive.* ■ of or relating to a sudden and dramatic increase in amount or extent: *the explosive growth of personal computers in the 1980s.* ■ (of a vocal sound) produced with a sharp release of air. ■ Phonetics another term for PLOSIVE.
▶ **n.** (often **explosives**) a substance that can be made to explode, esp. any of those used in bombs or shells.
–DERIVATIVES **ex·plo·sive·ly** **adv.**, **ex·plo·sive·ness** **n.**

ex·plo·sive bolt ▶ **n.** a bolt that can be released by being blown out of position by an integral explosive charge.

ex·po /ˈekspō/ ▶ **n.** (pl. **expos**) a large exhibition.
–ORIGIN 1960s (referring to the World Fair held in Montreal in 1967): abbreviation of EXPOSITION.

ex·po·nent /ikˈspōnənt, ˈekspōnənt/ ▶ **n.** **1** a person who believes in and promotes the truth or benefits of an idea or theory: *an early* **exponent** *of the teachings of Thomas Aquinas.* ■ a person who has and demonstrates a particular skill, esp. to a high standard: *he's the world's leading exponent of country rock guitar.*
2 Mathematics a quantity representing the power to which a given number or expression is to be raised, usually expressed as a raised symbol beside the number or expression (e.g., 3 in $2^3 = 2 \times 2 \times 2$).
3 Linguistics a linguistic unit that realizes another, more abstract unit.
–ORIGIN late 16th cent. (as an adjective in the sense 'expounding'): from Latin *exponent-* 'putting out,' from the verb *exponere* (see EXPOUND).

ex·po·nen·tial /ˌekspəˈnenCHəl/ ▶ **adj.** Mathematics of or expressed by a mathematical exponent: *an exponential curve.* ■ (of an increase) becoming more and more rapid: *the social security budget was rising at an exponential rate.*
–DERIVATIVES **ex·po·nen·tial·ly** **adv.**
–ORIGIN early 18th cent.: from French *exponentiel*, from Latin *exponere* 'put out' (see EXPOUND).

ex·po·nen·tial func·tion ▶ **n.** Mathematics a function whose value is a constant raised to the power of the argument, esp. the function where the constant is *e.*

ex·po·nen·tial growth ▶ **n.** growth whose rate becomes ever more rapid in proportion to the growing total number or size.

ex·po·nen·ti·a·tion /ˌekspəˌnenCHēˈāSHən/ ▶ **n.** Mathematics the operation of raising one quantity to the power of another.
–DERIVATIVES **ex·po·nen·ti·ate** /-ˈnenCHēˌāt/ **v.**

ex·port ▶ **v.** /ikˈspôrt, ˈekspôrt/ [with obj.] send (goods or services) to another country for sale: *we exported $16 million worth of mussels to Japan.* ■ spread or introduce (ideas and beliefs) to another country: *the Greeks exported Hellenic culture around the Mediterranean basin.* ■ Computing transfer (data) in a format that can be used by other programs.
▶ **n.** /ˈekˌspôrt/ (usu. **exports**) a commodity, article, or service sold abroad: *wool and mohair were the principal exports.* ■ (**exports**) sales of goods or services to other countries, or the revenue from such sales: *meat exports.* ■ the selling and sending out of goods or services to other countries: *the export of Western technology.* ■ [as modifier] of a high standard suitable for export: *high-grade export coal.*
–DERIVATIVES **ex·port·a·bil·i·ty** /ikˌspôrtəˈbilitē/ **n.**, **ex·port·a·ble** /ikˈspôrtəbəl/ **adj.**, **ex·por·ta·tion** /ˌekspôrˈtāSHən/ **n.**, **ex·port·er** **n.**
–ORIGIN late 15th cent. (in the sense 'take away'): from Latin *exportare*, from *ex-* 'out' + *portare* 'carry.' Current senses date from the 17th cent.

ex·port sur·plus ▶ **n.** the amount by which the value of a country's exports exceeds that of its imports.

ex·pose /ikˈspōz/ ▶ **v.** [with obj.] make (something) visible, typically by uncovering it: *at low tide the sands are exposed.* ■ (often as adj. **exposed**) leave (something) uncovered or unprotected, esp. from the weather: *the coast is very exposed to the southwest.* ■ subject (photographic film) to light, esp. when operating a camera. ■ (**expose oneself**) publicly and indecently display one's genitals. ■ (usu. as adj. **exposed**) leave or put (someone) in an unprotected and vulnerable state: *Miranda felt exposed and lonely.* ■ (**expose someone to**) cause someone to experience or be at risk of: *he exposed himself unnecessarily to gunfire in the war.* ■ make (something embarrassing or damaging) public: *investigations exposed a vast network of illegalities.* ■ reveal the true and typically objectionable nature of (someone or something): *he has been* **exposed as** *a liar and a traitor.* ■ (**expose someone to**) introduce someone to (a subject or area of knowledge): *students were exposed to probability and statistics in high school.* ■ leave (a child) in the open to die.
–DERIVATIVES **ex·pos·er** **n.**
–ORIGIN late Middle English: from Old French *exposer*, from Latin *exponere* (see EXPOUND), but influenced by Latin *expositus* 'put or set out' and Old French *poser* 'to place.'

ex·po·sé /ˌekspōˈzā/ ▶ **n.** a report of the facts about something, esp. a journalistic report that reveals something scandalous: *a shocking exposé of a medical cover-up.*
–ORIGIN early 19th cent.: from French, 'shown, set out,' past participle of *exposer* (see EXPOSE).

ex·po·si·tion /ˌekspəˈziSHən/ ▶ **n.** **1** a comprehensive description and explanation of an idea or theory: *the exposition and defense of his ethics.* ■ Music the part of a movement, esp. in sonata form, in which the principal themes are first presented. ■ the part of a play or work of fiction in which the background to the main conflict is introduced.
2 a large public exhibition of art or trade goods. ■ archaic the action of making public; exposure: *the country squires dreaded the exposition of their rustic conversation.*
–DERIVATIVES **ex·po·si·tion·al** /-ziSHənl/ **adj.**
–ORIGIN Middle English: from Latin *expositio(n-)*, from the verb *exponere* 'put out, exhibit, explain.'

ex·pos·i·tor /ikˈspäzitər/ ▶ **n.** a person or thing that explains complicated ideas or theories: *a lucid expositor of difficult ideas.*
–ORIGIN Middle English: via Old French or late Latin, from Latin *exposit-* 'exposed, explained,' from *exponere* (see EXPOUND).

ex·pos·i·to·ry /ikˈspäziˌtôrē/ ▶ **adj.** intended to explain or describe something: *formal expository prose.*

ex post ▶ **adj. & adv.** based on actual results rather than forecasts: [as adj.] *the ex post trade balance* | [as adv.] *the real-wage rate had fallen ex post.*
–ORIGIN modern Latin, from *ex* 'from' and *post* 'after.'

ex post fac·to /ˌeks pōst ˈfaktō/ ▶ **adj. & adv.** with retroactive effect or force: [as adj.] *ex post facto laws.*
–ORIGIN erroneous division of Latin *ex postfacto* 'in the light of subsequent events.'

ex·pos·tu·late /ikˈspäsCHəˌlāt/ ▶ **v.** [no obj.] express strong disapproval or disagreement: *I* **expostulated** *with him in vain.*
–DERIVATIVES **ex·pos·tu·la·tion** /ikˌspäsCHəˈlāSHən/ **n.**, **ex·pos·tu·la·tor** /-lātər/ **n.**, **ex·pos·tu·la·to·ry** /ikˌspäsCHələˌtôrē/ **adj.**
–ORIGIN mid 16th cent. (in the sense 'demand how or why, state a complaint'): from Latin *expostulat-* 'demanded,' from the verb *expostulare*, from *ex-* 'out' + *postulare* 'demand.'

ex·po·sure /ikˈspōZHər/ ▶ **n.** **1** the state of being exposed to contact with something: *the dangers posed by* **exposure to** *asbestos.* ■ a physical condition resulting from being outside in severe weather conditions without adequate protection: *he died of exposure at 8,000 feet.* ■ experience of something: *his* **exposure to** *the banking system.* ■ the action of exposing a photographic film to light or other radiation: *a camera that would give a picture immediately after exposure* | *trial exposures made with a UV filter.* ■ the quantity of light or other radiation reaching a photographic film, as determined by shutter speed and lens aperture. ■ the action of placing oneself at risk of financial losses, e.g., through making loans, granting credit, or underwriting insurance.
2 the revelation of an identity or fact, esp. one that is concealed or likely to arouse disapproval: *she took her life for fear of exposure as a spy.* ■ the publicizing of information or an event: *scientific findings receive regular exposure in the media.*
3 the direction in which a building faces; an outlook: *the exposure is perfect—a gentle slope to the southwest.*
–ORIGIN early 17th cent.: from EXPOSE, on the pattern of words such as *enclosure.*

ex·po·sure me·ter ▶ **n.** another term for LIGHT METER.

ex·pound /ikˈspound/ ▶ **v.** [with obj.] present and explain (a theory or idea) systematically and in detail: *he was expounding a powerful argument* | [no obj.] *he declined to* **expound on** *his decision.* ■ explain the meaning of (a literary or doctrinal work): *the abbess expounded the scriptures to her nuns.*
–DERIVATIVES **ex·pound·er** **n.**
–ORIGIN Middle English *expoune* (in the sense 'explain (what is difficult)'): from Old French *espon-*, present tense stem of *espondre*, from Latin *exponere* 'expose, publish, explain,' from *ex-* 'out' + *ponere* 'put.' The origin of the final *-d* (recorded from the Middle English period) is uncertain (compare with COMPOUND[1], PROPOUND).

ex·press[1] /ikˈspres/ ▶ **v.** [with obj.] **1** convey (a thought or feeling) in words or by gestures and conduct: *he expressed complete satisfaction.* ■ (**express oneself**) say what one thinks or means: *with a diplomatic smile, she expressed herself more subtly.* ■ chiefly Mathematics represent (a number, relation, or property) by a figure, symbol, or formula: *constants can be* **expressed in terms of** *the Fourier transform.* ■ (usu. **be expressed**) Genetics cause (an inherited characteristic or gene) to appear in a phenotype.
2 squeeze out (liquid or air).
–DERIVATIVES **ex·press·er** **n.**, **ex·press·i·ble** **adj.**
–ORIGIN late Middle English (also in the sense 'press out, obtain by squeezing or wringing,' used

figuratively to mean 'extort'): from Old French *expresser*, based on Latin *ex-* 'out' + *pressare* 'to press.'

ex·press² ▶ adj. operating at high speed, in particular: ■ (of a train or other vehicle of public transportation) making few intermediate stops and reaching its destination quickly: *an express train bound for Innsbruck | express bus service | an express elevator*. ■ denoting a service in which letters or packages are delivered by a special service to ensure speed or security: *an express letter*.
▶ adv. by express train or delivery service: *I got my wife to send my gloves express to the hotel.*
▶ n. **1** an express train or other vehicle of public transportation: *we embarked for the south of France on an overnight express.*
2 an overnight or rapid delivery service: *the books arrived by express.*
3 an express rifle.
▶ v. [with obj.] send by express delivery or messenger: *I expressed my clothes to my destination.*
– ORIGIN early 18th cent. (in the sense of the verb): extension of EXPRESS³; sense 1 of the noun from *express train*, so named because it served a particular destination without intermediate stops, reflecting an earlier sense of *express* 'done or made for a special purpose,' later interpreted in the sense 'rapid.' Senses relating to *express delivery* date from the institution of this postal service in Britain in 1891.

ex·press³ ▶ adj. definitely stated, not merely implied: *it was his express wish that the celebration continue.* ■ precisely and specifically identified to the exclusion of anything else: *the schools were founded for the express purpose of teaching deaf children.* ■ archaic (of a likeness) exact.
– ORIGIN late Middle English: from Old French *expres*, from Latin *expressus* 'distinctly presented,' past participle of *exprimere* 'press out, express,' from *ex-* 'out' + *primere* 'press.'

ex·pres·sion /ik'spresʜən/ ▶ n. **1** the process of making known one's thoughts or feelings: *his views found expression in his moral sermons | she accepted his expressions of sympathy.* ■ the conveying of feeling in the face or voice, in a work of art, or in the performance of a piece of music: *eyes empty of expression | their instruments have a rich variety of expression.*
2 the look on someone's face that conveys a particular emotion: *a sad expression.*
3 a word or phrase, esp. an idiomatic one, used to convey an idea: *nowhere is the expression "garbage in, garbage out" any truer.* ■ Mathematics a collection of symbols that jointly express a quantity: *the expression for the circumference of a circle is* $2\pi r$.
4 the production of something, esp. by pressing or squeezing it out: *essential oils obtained by distillation or expression.*
5 Genetics the appearance in a phenotype of a characteristic or effect attributed to a particular gene. ■ (also **gene expression**) the process by which possession of a gene leads to the appearance in the phenotype of the corresponding character.
– DERIVATIVES **ex·pres·sion·al** /ek'spresʜnəl/ adj.
– ORIGIN late Middle English: from Latin *expressio(n-)*, from *exprimere* 'press out, express.' Compare with EXPRESS¹.

ex·pres·sion·ism /ik'spresʜə,nizəm/ ▶ n. a style of painting, music, or drama in which the artist or writer seeks to express emotional experience rather than impressions of the external world.

> Expressionists characteristically reject traditional ideas of beauty or harmony and use distortion, exaggeration, and other nonnaturalistic devices in order to emphasize and express the inner world of emotion. The paintings of El Greco and Grünewald exemplify expressionism in this broad sense, but the term is also used of a late-19th and 20th-century European and specifically German movement tracing its origins to Van Gogh, Edvard Munch, and James Ensor, which insisted on the primacy of the artist's feelings and mood, often incorporating violence and the grotesque.

– DERIVATIVES **ex·pres·sion·ist** n. & adj., **ex·pres·sion·is·tic** /ik,spresʜə'nistik/ adj., **ex·pres·sion·is·ti·cal·ly** /ik,spresʜə'nistik(ə)lē/ adv.

ex·pres·sion·less /ik'spresʜənləs/ ▶ adj. (of a person's face or voice) not conveying any emotion; unemotional: *her face was expressionless.*
– DERIVATIVES **ex·pres·sion·less·ly** adv., **ex·pres·sion·less·ness** n.

ex·pres·sion mark ▶ n. Music a word or phrase on a musical score that indicates the expression required of a performer.

ex·pres·sive /ik'spresiv/ ▶ adj. effectively conveying thought or feeling. ■ [predic.] (**expressive of**) conveying (the specified quality or idea): *the spires are expressive of religious aspiration.*
– DERIVATIVES **ex·pres·sive·ly** adv., **ex·pres·sive·ness** n., **ex·pres·siv·i·ty** /,ekspre'sivitē/ n.
– ORIGIN late Middle English (in the sense 'tending to press out'): from French *expressif, -ive* or medieval Latin *expressivus*, from *exprimere* 'press out' (see EXPRESS³). Compare with EXPRESS¹.

ex·press lane ▶ n. (on a highway) a lane for through traffic, having fewer exits. ■ (in a grocery store) a checkout aisle for shoppers buying only a few items.

ex·press·ly /ik'spreslі/ ▶ adv. explicitly; clearly: *she was expressly forbidden to use the stove.* ■ for a specific purpose; solely: *the house was expressly built for entertaining.*

ex·pres·so /ik'spresō/ ▶ n. see ESPRESSO.

ex·press ri·fle ▶ n. a rifle that discharges a bullet at high speed and is used in big-game hunting.

ex·press·way /ik'spres,wā/ ▶ n. a highway designed for fast traffic, with controlled entrance and exit, a dividing strip between the traffic in opposite directions, and typically two or more lanes in each direction.

ex·pro·pri·ate /,eks'prōprē,āt/ ▶ v. [with obj.] (esp. of the state) take away (property) from its owner: *government plans to expropriate farmland.* ■ dispossess (someone) of property: *the land reform expropriated the Irish landlords.*
– DERIVATIVES **ex·pro·pri·a·tion** /,eks,prōprē'āsʜən/ n., **ex·pro·pri·a·tor** /-,ātər/ n.
– ORIGIN late 16th cent.: from medieval Latin *expropriat-* 'taken from the owner,' from the verb *expropriare*, from *ex-* 'out, from' + *proprium* 'property,' neuter singular of *proprius* 'own.'

expt. ▶ abbr. experiment.

exptl. ▶ abbr. experimental.

ex·pul·sion /ik'spəlsʜən/ ▶ n. the action of depriving someone of membership in an organization: ***expulsion from school.*** ■ the process of forcing someone to leave a place, esp. a country: *the expulsion of the Jesuits from Spain.* ■ the process of forcing something out of the body.
– DERIVATIVES **ex·pul·sive** /ik'spəlsiv/ adj.
– ORIGIN late Middle English: from Latin *expulsio(n-)*, from *expellere* 'drive out' (see EXPEL).

ex·punge /ik'spənj/ ▶ v. [with obj.] erase or remove completely (something unwanted or unpleasant): *I've kind of expunged that period from my CV.*
– DERIVATIVES **ex·punc·tion** /ik'spəɴɢ(k)sʜən/ n., **ex·punge·ment** n., **ex·pung·er** n.
– ORIGIN early 17th cent.: from Latin *expungere* 'mark for deletion by means of points,' from *ex-* 'out' + *pungere* 'to prick.'

ex·pur·gate /'ekspər,gāt/ ▶ v. [with obj.] (often as adj. **expurgated**) remove matter thought to be objectionable or unsuitable from (a book or account): *the expurgated Arabian Nights.*
– DERIVATIVES **ex·pur·ga·tion** /,ekspər'gāsʜən/ n., **ex·pur·ga·tor** n., **ex·pur·ga·to·ry** /ik'spərgə,tôrē/ adj.
– ORIGIN early 17th cent. (in the sense 'purge of excrement'): from Latin *expurgat-* 'thoroughly cleansed,' from the verb *expurgare*, from *ex-* 'out' + *purgare* 'cleanse.'

ex·quis·ite /ek'skwizit, 'ekskwizit/ ▶ adj. extremely beautiful and, typically, delicate: *exquisite, jewellike portraits.* ■ intensely felt: *the most exquisite kind of agony.* ■ highly sensitive or discriminating: *her exquisite taste in painting.*
▶ n. a man who is affectedly concerned with his clothes and appearance; a dandy.
– DERIVATIVES **ex·quis·ite·ly** adv., **ex·quis·ite·ness** n.
– ORIGIN late Middle English (in the sense 'carefully ascertained, precise'): from Latin *exquisit-* 'sought out,' from the verb *exquirere*, from *ex-* 'out' + *quaerere* 'seek.'

exr. ▶ abbr. executor.

exrx. ▶ abbr. executrix.

ex·san·gui·na·tion /ek,saɴɢgwə'nāsʜən/ ▶ n. Medicine the action of draining a person, animal, or organ of blood. ■ severe loss of blood.
– DERIVATIVES **ex·san·gui·nate** /ek'saɴɢgwə,nāt/ v.
– ORIGIN early 20th cent.: from Latin *exsanguinatus* 'drained of blood' (from *ex-* 'out' + *sanguis, sanguin-* 'blood') + -ION.

ex·san·guine /eks'saɴɢgwin/ ▶ adj. literary bloodless; anemic.
– ORIGIN mid 17th cent.: from EX-¹ 'out' + Latin *sanguis, sanguin-* 'blood.'

ex·sert /ek'sərt/ ▶ v. [with obj.] Biology cause to protrude; push out: (as adj. **exserted**) *an exserted stigma.*
– ORIGIN mid 17th cent.: from Latin *exsert-* 'put forth,' from the verb *exserere* (see EXERT).

ex·serv·ice·man ▶ n. (pl. **ex-servicemen**) chiefly Brit. a man who was formerly a member of the armed forces.

ex si·len·ti·o /,eks sə'lencʜē-ō/ ▶ adj. & adv. by the absence of contrary evidence.
– ORIGIN early 20th cent.: Latin, literally 'from silence.'

ex·solve /eks'sälv/ ▶ v. [no obj.] Geology (of a mineral or other substance) separate out from solution, esp. from solid solution in a rock. ■ [with obj.] (usu. as adj. **exsolved**) form (a mineral or other substance) in this way: *coarsely exsolved ilmenites.*
– DERIVATIVES **ex·so·lu·tion** /,eksə'lo͞osʜən/ n.

ext. ▶ abbr. ■ extension (in a telephone number). ■ exterior. ■ external. ■ extra.

ex·tant /'ekstənt, ek'stant/ ▶ adj. (esp. of a document) still in existence; surviving: *the original manuscript is no longer extant.*
– ORIGIN mid 16th cent. (in the sense 'accessible, able to be publicly seen or reached'): from Latin *exstant-* 'being visible or prominent, existing,' from the verb *exstare*, from *ex-* 'out' + *stare* 'to stand.'

ex·tem·po·ra·ne·ous /ik,stempə'rānēəs/ ▶ adj. spoken or done without preparation: *an extemporaneous speech.*
– DERIVATIVES **ex·tem·po·ra·ne·ous·ly** adv., **ex·tem·po·ra·ne·ous·ness** n.

ex·tem·po·rar·y /ik'stempə,rerē/ ▶ adj. another term for EXTEMPORANEOUS.
– DERIVATIVES **ex·tem·po·rar·i·ly** /ik,stempə'rerəlē/ adv., **ex·tem·po·rar·i·ness** n.
– ORIGIN late 16th cent.: from EXTEMPORE, on the pattern of *temporary.*

ex·tem·po·re /ik'stempərē/ ▶ adj. & adv. spoken or done without preparation: [as adj.] *extempore public speaking* | [as adv.] *he recited the poem extempore.*
– ORIGIN mid 16th cent.: from Latin *ex tempore* 'on the spur of the moment' (literally 'out of the time').

ex·tem·po·rize /ik'stempə,rīz/ ▶ v. [no obj.] compose, perform, or produce something such as music or a speech without preparation; improvise: *he extemporized at the piano* | [with obj.] *she was extemporizing touching melodies.*
– DERIVATIVES **ex·tem·po·ri·za·tion** /ik,stempəri'zāsʜən/ n.

ex·tend /ik'stend/ ▶ v. [with obj.] **1** cause to cover a larger area; make longer or wider: *the Forest Service plans to extend a gravel road nearly a mile.* ■ cause to last longer: *high schools may consider extending the class day to seven periods.* ■ postpone (a starting or ending time) beyond the original limit: *he extended the deadline to 4 p.m. today.* ■ straighten or spread out (the body or a limb) at full length: *she is unable to extend her thumb.* ■ [no obj.] spread from a central point to cover a wider area: *the pipeline currently extends 1,200 miles from Santa Barbara.* ■ [no obj.] occupy a specified area or stretch to a specified point: *the mountains extend over the western end of the island | a fault that may extend to a depth of 12 miles.* ■ [no obj.] (**extend to**) include within one's scope; be applicable to: *her generosity did not extend to all adults.*
2 hold (something) out toward someone: *I nod and extend my hand.* ■ offer or make available: *she extended an invitation to her to stay | I can't extend credit indefinitely.*
3 (**extend oneself**) exert or exercise oneself to the utmost: *you have to extend yourself to change rather than keep on doing the same thing.*
– DERIVATIVES **ex·tend·a·bil·i·ty** /ik,stendə'bilitē/ n., **ex·tend·a·ble** adj., **ex·tend·i·bil·i·ty** /ik,stendə'bilitē/ n., **ex·tend·i·ble** /-əbəl/ adj.
– ORIGIN late Middle English: from Latin *extendere* 'stretch out,' from *ex-* 'out' + *tendere* 'stretch.'

ex·tend·ed /ik'stendid/ ▶ adj. made larger; enlarged: *an extended kitchen and new balcony.* ■ lasting longer than is usual or expected; prolonged: *an extended period of time.*

ex·tend·ed fam·i·ly ▶ n. a family that extends beyond the nuclear family, including grandparents, aunts, uncles, and other relatives, who all live nearby or in one household.

ex·tend·ed-play ▶ adj. denoting a record that plays longer than most singles. ■ denoting an audio- or videotape that is thinner and longer than standard.

ex·tend·er /ik'stendər/ ▶ n. a person or thing that extends something. ■ a substance added to a product such as paint, ink, or glue, to dilute its color or increase its bulk. ■ Photography another term for EXTENSION TUBE.

ex·ten·si·ble /ik'stensəbəl/ ▶ adj. able to be extended; extendable: *an extensible architecture designed to accommodate changes.*
– DERIVATIVES **ex·ten·si·bil·i·ty** /ik,stensə'bilitē/ n.

ex·ten·sile /ik'stensəl, -sīl/ ▶ adj. capable of being stretched out or protruded.

–ORIGIN mid 18th cent.: from Latin *extens-* 'stretched out' (from the verb *extendere*) + **-ILE**.

ex·ten·sion /ik'stenSHən/ ▶ n. **1** a part that is added to something to enlarge or prolong it; a continuation: *the railroad's southern extension.* ■ a room or set of rooms added to an existing building. ■ the action or process of becoming or making something larger: *the extension of the president's powers.* ■ an application of an existing system or activity to a new area: *direct marketing is an extension of telephone selling.* ■ an increase in the length of time given to someone to hold office, complete a project, or fulfill an obligation. ■ Computing an optional suffix to a file name, typically consisting of a period followed by several characters, indicating the file's content or function.
2 (also **extension cord**) a length of electric cord that permits the use of an appliance at some distance from a fixed socket. ■ an extra telephone on the same line as the main one. ■ a subsidiary telephone in a set of offices or similar building, on a line leading from the main switchboard but having its own additional number.
3 [usu. as modifier] instruction by a university or college for students who do not attend full time: *extension courses.*
4 (**extensions**) lengths of real or artificial hair woven into a person's own hair to create a long hairstyle.
5 the action of moving a limb from a bent to a straight position: *seizures with sudden rigid extension of the limbs.* ■ the muscle action controlling this: *triceps extension.* ■ Ballet the ability of a dancer to raise one leg above the waist, or an instance of this: *she has amazing extension | he could perform 180-degree extensions.* ■ Medicine the application of traction to a fractured or dislocated limb or to an injured or diseased spinal column to restore it to its normal position. ■ the lengthening of a horse's stride within a particular gait.
6 Logic the range of a term or concept as measured by the objects that it denotes or contains, as opposed to its internal content. Often contrasted with **INTENSION**. ■ Physics & Philosophy the property of occupying space; spatial magnitude: *nature, for Descartes, was pure extension in space.*
–PHRASES **by extension** taking the same line of argument further: *this raised serious questions about his credibility and, by extension, the credibility of the company.*
–DERIVATIVES **ex·ten·sion·al** /-SHənl/ adj.
–ORIGIN late Middle English: from late Latin *extensio(n-)*, from *extendere* 'stretch out' (see **EXTEND**).

ex·ten·sion lad·der ▶ n. a ladder that can be extended by means of sliding sections.

ex·ten·sion tube ▶ n. Photography a tube fitted to a camera between the body and lens to shorten the distance of closest focus of an object so that close-up pictures can be taken.

ex·ten·sive /ik'stensiv/ ▶ adj. **1** covering or affecting a large area: *an extensive garden.* ■ large in amount or scale: *an extensive collection of silver.*
2 (of agriculture) obtaining a relatively small crop from a large area with a minimum of attention and expense: *extensive farming techniques.* Often contrasted with **INTENSIVE** (sense 1 of the adjective).
–DERIVATIVES **ex·ten·sive·ly** adv., **ex·ten·sive·ness** n.
–ORIGIN late Middle English: from French *extensif, -ive* or late Latin *extensivus*, from *extens-* 'stretched out,' from the verb *extendere* (see **EXTEND**).

ex·ten·som·e·ter /eksten'sämitər/ ▶ n. an instrument for measuring the deformation of a material under stress.
–ORIGIN late 19th cent.: from Latin *extens-* 'extended' (from the verb *extendere*) + **-METER**.

ex·ten·sor /ik'stensər, -sôr/ (also **extensor muscle**) ▶ n. Anatomy a muscle whose contraction extends or straightens a limb or other part of the body. Often contrasted with **FLEXOR**. ■ any of a number of specific muscles in the arm, hand, leg, and foot.
–ORIGIN early 18th cent.: from late Latin, from *extens-* 'stretched out,' from the verb *extendere* (see **EXTEND**).

ex·tent /ik'stent/ ▶ n. [in sing.] the area covered by something: *an enclosure ten acres in extent.* ■ the degree to which something has spread; the size or scale of something: *the extent of AIDS infection.* ■ the amount to which something is or is believed to be the case: *everyone will have to compromise to some extent | they altered the document to such an extent that it contained little in the way of new policy.*
–ORIGIN Middle English (in the sense 'valuation of property, esp. for taxation purposes'): from Anglo-Norman French *extente*, from medieval Latin *extenta*, feminine past participle of Latin *extendere* 'stretch out' (see **EXTEND**).

ex·ten·u·ate /ik'stenyo͞o,āt/ ▶ v. [with obj.] **1** (usu. as adj. **extenuating**) make (guilt or an offense) seem less serious or more forgivable: *there were extenuating circumstances that caused me to say the things I did.*
2 (usu. as adj. **extenuated**) literary make (someone) thin: *drawings of extenuated figures.*
–DERIVATIVES **ex·ten·u·a·tion** /ik,stenyo͞o'āSHən/ n., **ex·ten·u·a·to·ry** /-ə,tôrē/ adj.
–ORIGIN late Middle English (in the sense 'make thin, emaciate'): from Latin *extenuat-* 'made thin,' from the verb *extenuare* (based on *tenuis* 'thin').

ex·te·ri·or /ik'sti(ə)rēər/ ▶ adj. forming, situated on, or relating to the outside of something: *exterior and interior walls.* ■ coming from outside: *exterior noise.* ■ (in filming) outdoor: *exterior locations.*
▶ n. the outer surface or structure of something: *a jar with floral designs on the exterior.* ■ the outer structure of a building: *the museum has a modern exterior.* ■ a person's behavior and appearance, often contrasted with their true character: *beneath that assured exterior, she's vulnerable.* ■ (in filming) an outdoor scene.
–DERIVATIVES **ex·te·ri·or·i·ty** /ik,sti(ə)rē'ôritē, -'ärite/ n., **ex·te·ri·or·ize** /-,rīz/ v., **ex·te·ri·or·ly** adv.
–ORIGIN early 16th cent.: from Latin, comparative of *exter* 'outer.'

ex·te·ri·or an·gle ▶ n. Geometry the angle between a side of a rectilinear figure and an adjacent side extended outward.

ex·ter·mi·nate /ik'stərmə,nāt/ ▶ v. [with obj.] destroy completely: *leftist ideals had not been totally exterminated.* ■ kill (a pest): *they use poison to exterminate moles.*
–DERIVATIVES **ex·ter·mi·na·tor** /-,nātər/ n., **ex·ter·mi·na·to·ry** /-nə,tôrē/ adj.
–ORIGIN late Middle English (in the sense 'drive out, banish'): from Latin *exterminat-* 'driven out, banished,' from the verb *exterminare*, from *ex-* 'out' + *terminus* 'boundary.' The sense 'destroy' (mid 16th cent.) comes from the Latin of the Vulgate.

ex·ter·mi·na·tion /ik,stərmə'nāSHən/ ▶ n. killing, esp. of a whole group of people or animals: *the near extermination of the buffalo herds.* ■ complete destruction.

ex·tern /'ekstərn/ ▶ n. **1** a person working in but not living in an institution, such as nonresident doctor or other worker in a hospital.
2 (in a strictly enclosed order of nuns) a sister who does not live exclusively within the enclosure and goes on outside errands.
–DERIVATIVES **ex·tern·ship** /-SHip/ n.
–ORIGIN mid 16th cent. (as an adjective in the sense 'external'): from French *externe* or Latin *externus*, from *exter* 'outer.' The word was used by Shakespeare to mean 'outward appearance'; current senses date from the early 17th cent.

ex·ter·nal /ik'stərnl/ ▶ adj. **1** belonging to or forming the outer surface or structure of something: *the external walls.* ■ relating to or denoting a medicine or similar substance for use on the outside of the body: *for external application only.*
2 coming or derived from a source outside the subject affected: *for many people the church was a symbol of external authority.* ■ coming from or relating to a foreign country or an outside institution: *responsibility for defense and external affairs.* ■ Computing (of hardware) not contained in the main computer; peripheral. ■ Computing (of storage) using a disk or tape drive rather than the main memory.
▶ n. (**externals**) the outward features of something: *the place has all the appropriate externals, such as chimneys choked with ivy and windows with jasmine.* ■ features that are only superficial; inessentials.
–DERIVATIVES **ex·ter·nal·ly** adv.
–ORIGIN late Middle English: from medieval Latin, from Latin *exter* 'outer.'

ex·ter·nal au·di·to·ry me·a·tus ▶ n. see **MEATUS**.

ex·ter·nal ear ▶ n. the parts of the ear outside the eardrum, esp. the pinna.

ex·ter·nal·ism /ik'stərnə,lizəm/ ▶ n. **1** excessive regard for outward form in religion.
2 Philosophy the view that mental events and acts are essentially dependent on the world external to the mind, in opposition to the Cartesian separation of mental and physical worlds.
–DERIVATIVES **ex·ter·nal·ist** n. & adj.

ex·ter·nal·i·ty /,ekstər'nalitē/ ▶ n. (pl. **externalities**) **1** Economics a side effect or consequence of an industrial or commercial activity that affects other parties without this being reflected in the cost of the goods or services involved, such as the pollination of surrounding crops by bees kept for honey.
2 Philosophy the fact of existing outside the perceiving subject.

ex·ter·nal·ize /ik'stərnə,līz/ ▶ v. [with obj.] (usu. **be externalized**) give external existence or form to: *elements of the internal construction were externalized onto the facade.* ■ express (a thought or feeling) in words or actions: *an urgent need to externalize the experience.* ■ Psychology project (a mental image or process) onto a figure outside oneself: *such neuroses are externalized as interpersonal conflicts.*
–DERIVATIVES **ex·ter·nal·i·za·tion** /ik,stərnəli'zāSHən/ n.

ex·ter·o·cep·tive /,ekstərō'septiv/ ▶ adj. Physiology relating to stimuli that are external to an organism. Compare with **INTEROCEPTIVE**.
–DERIVATIVES **ex·ter·o·cep·tion** /-'sepSHən/ n., **ex·ter·o·cep·tiv·i·ty** /-sep'tivitē/ n.
–ORIGIN early 20th cent.: probably a blend of **EXTERIOR** or **EXTERNAL** and **RECEPTIVE**.

ex·ter·o·cep·tor /,ekstərō'septər/ ▶ n. Physiology a sensory receptor that receives external stimuli. Compare with **INTEROCEPTOR**.

ex·tinct /ik'stiNG(k)t/ ▶ adj. (of a species, family, or other larger group) having no living members: *trilobites and dinosaurs are extinct.* ■ no longer in existence: *an extinct language | the sort of girls' school that is now extinct.* ■ (of a volcano) not having erupted in recorded history. ■ no longer burning: *his now extinct pipe.* ■ (of a title of nobility) having no qualified claimant.
–ORIGIN late Middle English (in the sense 'no longer alight'): from Latin *exstinct-* 'extinguished,' from the verb *exstinguere* (see **EXTINGUISH**).

ex·tinc·tion /ik'stiNG(k)SHən/ ▶ n. **1** the state or process of a species, family, or larger group being or becoming extinct: *the extinction of the great auk | mass extinctions.* ■ the wiping out of a debt.
2 Physics reduction in the intensity of light or other radiation as it passes through a medium or object, due to absorption, reflection, and scattering: *ultraviolet extinction.*
–ORIGIN late Middle English: from Latin *exstinctio(n-)*, from *exstinguere* 'quench' (see **EXTINGUISH**).

ex·tin·guish /ik'stiNGgwiSH/ ▶ v. [with obj.] cause (a fire or light) to cease to burn or shine: *firemen were soaking everything to extinguish the blaze.* ■ put an end to; annihilate: *hope is extinguished little by little.* ■ cancel (a debt) by full payment: *the debt was absolutely extinguished.* ■ Law render (a right or obligation) void: *rights of common pasture were extinguished.*
–DERIVATIVES **ex·tin·guish·a·ble** adj., **ex·tin·guish·ment** n. (Law).
–ORIGIN mid 16th cent.: from Latin *exstinguere*, from *ex-* 'out' + *stinguere* 'quench.' Compare with **DISTINGUISH**.

ex·tin·guish·er /ik'stiNGgwiSHər/ ▶ n. short for **FIRE EXTINGUISHER**.

ex·tir·pate /'ekstər,pāt/ ▶ v. [with obj.] root out and destroy completely: *the use of every legal measure to extirpate this horrible evil from the land.*
–DERIVATIVES **ex·tir·pa·tion** /,ekstər'pāSHən/ n., **ex·tir·pa·tor** /-,pātər/ n.
–ORIGIN late Middle English (as *extirpation*): from Latin *exstirpare*, from *ex-* 'out' + *stirps* 'a stem.'

ex·tol /ik'stōl/ ▶ v. (**extols, extolling, extolled**) [with obj.] praise enthusiastically: *he extolled the virtues of the Russian peoples.*
–DERIVATIVES **ex·tol·ler** n., **ex·tol·ment** n.
–ORIGIN late Middle English: from Latin *extollere*, from *ex-* 'out, upward' + *tollere* 'raise.'

ex·tort /ik'stôrt/ ▶ v. obtain (something) by force, threats, or other unfair means: *he was convicted of trying to extort $1 million from a developer.*
–DERIVATIVES **ex·tort·er** n., **ex·tor·tive** /-tiv/ adj.
–ORIGIN early 16th cent.: from Latin *extort-* 'wrested,' from the verb *extorquere*, from *ex-* 'out' + *torquere* 'to twist.'

ex·tor·tion /ik'stôrSHən/ ▶ n. the practice of obtaining something, esp. money, through force or threats.
–DERIVATIVES **ex·tor·tion·er** n.
–ORIGIN Middle English: from late Latin *extortio(n-)*, from Latin *extorquere* 'wrest' (see **EXTORT**).

ex·tor·tion·ate /ik'stôrSHənit/ ▶ adj. **1** (of a price) much too high; exorbitant: *extortionate ticket prices.*
2 using or given to extortion: *the extortionate power of the unions.*

– DERIVATIVES **ex·tor·tion·ate·ly** adv. [as submodifier] *lobster is extortionately expensive here.*

ex·tor·tion·ist /ik'stôrsHənist/ ▶ n. a person who tries to obtain something through force or violence; a racketeer: *he is a blackmailer and an extortionist.*

ex·tra /'ekstrə/ ▶ adj. added to an existing or usual amount or number: *an extra thirty-five cents an hour.*
▶ adv. 1 [as submodifier] to a greater extent than usual; especially: *he is trying to be extra good.*
2 in addition: *installation will cost about $60 extra.*
▶ n. an item in addition to what is usual or strictly necessary: *I had an education with all the extras.* ■ an item for which an additional charge is made: *the price you pay includes all major charges—there are no hidden extras.* ■ a person engaged temporarily to fill out a scene in a movie or play, esp. as one of a crowd. ■ dated a special issue of a newspaper.
– ORIGIN mid 17th cent. (as an adjective): probably a shortening of EXTRAORDINARY, suggested by similar forms in French and German.

extra- ▶ prefix outside; beyond: *extracellular | extraterritorial.* ■ beyond the scope of: *extracurricular.*
– ORIGIN via medieval Latin from Latin *extra* 'outside.'

ex·tra-base hit ▶ n. Baseball a base hit that allows a batter to safely reach second base, third base, or home without the benefit of a fielding error; a double, triple, or home run.

ex·tra·cel·lu·lar /,ekstrə'selyələr/ ▶ adj. Biology situated or taking place outside a cell or cells: *extracellular space in the cortex.*
– DERIVATIVES **ex·tra·cel·lu·lar·ly** adv.

ex·tra·chro·mo·so·mal /,ekstrə,krōmə'sōməl/ ▶ adj. Biology situated or operating outside the chromosome: *extrachromosomal DNA.*

ex·tra·con·sti·tu·tion·al /,ekstrə,känstə't(y)ōōsHənl/ ▶ adj. not based on or authorized by a political constitution: *the dubious legality of extraconstitutional courts.*

ex·tra·cor·po·re·al /'ekstrəkôr'pôrēəl/ ▶ adj. chiefly Surgery situated or occurring outside the body. ■ denoting a technique of lithotripsy using shock waves generated externally.

ex·tract ▶ v. /ik'strakt/ [with obj.] remove or take out, esp. by effort or force: *the decayed tooth will have to be extracted.* ■ obtain (something such as money or an admission) from someone in the face of initial unwillingness: *I won't let you go without trying to extract a promise from you.* ■ obtain (a substance or resource) from something by a special method: *lead was extracted from the copper.* ■ select (a passage from a piece of writing, music, or film) for quotation, performance, or reproduction: *the table is extracted from the report.* ■ derive (an idea or the evidence for it) from a body of information: *the desire to extract meaningful lessons from a few experiments.* ■ Mathematics calculate (a root of a number).
▶ n. /'ek,strakt/ 1 a short passage taken from a piece of writing, music, or film: *an extract from a historical film.*
2 a preparation containing the active ingredient of a substance in concentrated form: *vanilla extract | extract of chamomile.*
– DERIVATIVES **ex·tract·a·bil·i·ty** /ik,straktə'bilitē/ n., **ex·tract·a·ble** adj.
– ORIGIN late Middle English: from Latin *extract-* 'drawn out,' from the verb *extrahere*, from *ex-* 'out' + *trahere* 'draw.'

ex·trac·tion /ik'straksHən/ ▶ n. 1 the action of taking out something, esp. using effort or force: *mineral extraction | a dental extraction.*
2 [with adj.] the ethnic origin of someone's family: *a worker of Polish extraction.*
– ORIGIN late Middle English: via Old French from late Latin *extractio(n-)*, from Latin *extrahere* 'draw out' (see EXTRACT).

ex·trac·tive /ik'straktiv/ ▶ adj. of or involving extraction, esp. the extensive extraction of natural resources without provision for their renewal: *extractive industry.*

ex·trac·tor /ik'straktər/ ▶ n. [often with modifier] a machine or device used to extract something: *a juice extractor.* ■ [as modifier] denoting a device used to ventilate and remove bad smells from an area: *the engine room's extractor fans.*

ex·tra·cur·ric·u·lar /,ekstrəkə'rikyələr/ ▶ adj. (of an activity at a school or college) pursued in addition to the normal course of study: *extracurricular activities include sports, drama, music, chess.* ■ often humorous outside the normal routine, esp. that provided by a job or marriage: *Harriet's extracurricular sweetheart.*
– DERIVATIVES **ex·tra·cur·ric·u·lar·ly** adv.

ex·tra·dit·a·ble /'ekstrə,dītəbəl, ,ekstrə'dītəbəl/ ▶ adj. (of a crime) making a criminal liable to extradition: *possession of explosives will be an extraditable offense.* ■ (of a criminal) liable to extradition.

ex·tra·dite /'ekstrə,dīt/ ▶ v. [with obj.] hand over (a person accused or convicted of a crime) to the jurisdiction of the foreign state in which the crime was committed: *Greece refused to extradite him to Italy.*
– ORIGIN mid 19th cent.: back-formation from EXTRADITION.

ex·tra·di·tion /,ekstrə'disHən/ ▶ n. the action of extraditing a person accused or convicted of a crime: *they fought to prevent his extradition to the US | extraditions of drug suspects.*
– ORIGIN mid 19th cent.: from French, from *ex-* 'out, from' + *tradition* 'delivery.'

ex·tra·dos /'ekstrə,däs/ ▶ n. (pl. **same** or **extradoses**) Architecture the upper or outer curve of an arch. Often contrasted with INTRADOS.
– ORIGIN late 18th cent.: from French, from Latin *extra* 'outside' + French *dos* 'back' (from Latin *dorsum*).

ex·tra·du·ral /,ekstrə'd(y)ōōrəl/ ▶ adj. Medicine another term for EPIDURAL.

ex·tra·flo·ral /,ekstrə'flôrəl/ ▶ adj. Botany (of a nectary) situated outside a flower, esp. on a leaf or stem.

ex·tra·ga·lac·tic /,ekstrəgə'laktik/ ▶ adj. Astronomy situated, occurring, or originating outside the Milky Way galaxy: *extragalactic radio sources.*

ex·tra in·nings ▶ n. Baseball the continuation of a tie game beyond the usual nine innings. ■ any continuation beyond the expected or scheduled time.

ex·tra·ju·di·cial /,ekstrəjōō'disHəl/ ▶ adj. Law (of a sentence) not legally authorized: *there have been reports of extrajudicial executions.* ■ (of a settlement, statement, or confession) not made in court; out-of-court.
– DERIVATIVES **ex·tra·ju·di·cial·ly** adv.

ex·tra·le·gal /,ekstrə'lēgəl/ ▶ adj. (of an action or situation) beyond the authority of the law; not regulated by the law.

ex·tra·lim·it·al /,ekstrə'limitl/ ▶ adj. chiefly Biology situated, occurring, or derived from outside a particular area.

ex·tra·lin·guis·tic /,ekstrəliNG'gwistik/ ▶ adj. not involving or beyond the bounds of language.

ex·tra·mar·i·tal /,ekstrə'maritl/ ▶ adj. (esp. of sexual relations) occurring outside marriage: *an extramarital affair.*
– DERIVATIVES **ex·tra·mar·i·tal·ly** adv.

ex·tra·mun·dane /,ekstrəmən'dān/ ▶ adj. rare outside or beyond the physical world.

ex·tra·mu·ral /,ekstrə'myōōrəl/ ▶ adj. outside the walls or boundaries of a town, college, or institution: *extramural researchers.* ■ additional to one's work or course of study and typically not connected with it: *extramural activities.*
– DERIVATIVES **ex·tra·mu·ral·ly** adv.
– ORIGIN mid 19th cent.: from Latin *extra muros* 'outside the walls' + -AL.

ex·tra·ne·ous /ik'strānēəs/ ▶ adj. irrelevant or unrelated to the subject being dealt with: *one is obliged to wade through many pages of extraneous material.* ■ of external origin: *when the transmitter pack is turned off, no extraneous noise is heard.* ■ separate from the object to which it is attached: *other insects attach extraneous objects or material to themselves.*
– DERIVATIVES **ex·tra·ne·ous·ly** adv., **ex·tra·ne·ous·ness** n.
– ORIGIN mid 17th cent.: from Latin *extraneus* + -OUS.

ex·tra·net /'ekstrə,net/ ▶ n. an intranet that can be partially accessed by authorized outside users, enabling businesses to exchange information over the Internet securely.
– ORIGIN 1990s: from *extra-* 'outside' + *net*, by analogy with *intranet.*

ex·tra·nu·cle·ar /,ekstrə'n(y)ōōklēər/ ▶ adj.
1 situated in or affecting parts of a cell outside the nucleus.
2 situated or occurring outside the nucleus of an atom.

ex·tra·oc·u·lar mus·cle /,ekstrə'äkyələr/ ▶ n. each of six small voluntary muscles controlling movement of the eyeball within the socket.

ex·tra·or·di·naire /,ekstrə,ôrdn'er/ ▶ adj. [postpositive] informal outstanding or remarkable in a particular capacity: *memories of a gardener extraordinaire.*
– ORIGIN 1940s: French, 'extraordinary.'

ex·traor·di·nar·y /ik'strôrdn,erē, ,ekstrə'ôrdn-/ ▶ adj. very unusual or remarkable: *the extraordinary plumage of the male* | [with clause] *it is extraordinary that no consultation took place.* ■ unusually great: *young children need extraordinary amounts of attention.* ■ [attrib.] (of a meeting) specially convened: *an extraordinary session of the Congress.* ■ [postpositive] (of an official) additional; specially employed: *his appointment as Ambassador Extraordinary in London.*
▶ n. (usu. **extraordinaries**) an item in a company's accounts not arising from its normal activities. Compare with EXCEPTIONAL.
– DERIVATIVES **ex·traor·di·nar·i·ly** /-,erəlē/ adv. [as submodifier] *an extraordinarily beautiful girl,* **ex·traor·di·nar·i·ness** n.
– ORIGIN late Middle English: from Latin *extraordinarius*, from *extra ordinem* 'outside the normal course of events.'

ex·traor·di·nar·y ray ▶ n. Optics (in double refraction) the light ray that does not obey the ordinary laws of refraction. Compare with ORDINARY RAY.

ex·traor·di·nar·y ren·di·tion ▶ n. see RENDITION (sense 2).

ex·tra point ▶ n. Football a point awarded for a successful placekick following a touchdown.

ex·trap·o·late /ik'strapə,lāt/ ▶ v. [with obj.] extend the application of (a method or conclusion, esp. one based on statistics) to an unknown situation by assuming that existing trends will continue or similar methods will be applicable: *the results cannot be extrapolated to other patient groups* | [no obj.] *it is always dangerous to extrapolate from a sample.* ■ estimate or conclude (something) in this way: *attempts to extrapolate likely human cancers from laboratory studies.* ■ Mathematics extend (a graph, curve, or range of values) by inferring unknown values from trends in the known data: (as adj. **extrapolated**) *a set of extrapolated values.*
– DERIVATIVES **ex·trap·o·la·tion** /ik,strapə'lāsHən/ n., **ex·trap·o·la·tive** /-,lātiv/ adj., **ex·trap·o·la·tor** /-,lātər/ n.
– ORIGIN late 19th cent.: from EXTRA- 'outside' + a shortened form of INTERPOLATE.

ex·tra·po·si·tion /,ekstrəpə'zisHən/ ▶ n. Grammar the placing of a word or group of words outside or at the end of a clause, while retaining the sense. The subject is often postponed and replaced by *it* at the start, as in *it's no use crying over spilt milk* rather than *crying over spilt milk is no use.*

ex·tra·py·ram·i·dal /,ekstrəpə'ramidl/ ▶ adj. Anatomy & Medicine relating to or denoting nerves concerned with motor activity that descend from the cortex to the spine and are not part of the pyramidal system: *extrapyramidal symptoms.*

ex·tra·sen·so·ry per·cep·tion /,ekstrə'sensərē/ (abbr.: **ESP**) ▶ n. the faculty of perceiving things by means other than the known senses, e.g., by telepathy or clairvoyance.

ex·tra·so·lar /,ekstrə'sōlər/ ▶ adj. existing or occurring outside the solar system: *extrasolar planets.*

ex·tra·sys·to·le /,ekstrə'sistəlē/ ▶ n. Medicine a heartbeat outside the normal rhythm, as often occurs in normal individuals.

ex·tra·ter·res·tri·al /,ekstrətə'restrēəl/ ▶ adj. of or from outside the earth or its atmosphere: *searches for extraterrestrial intelligence.*
▶ n. a hypothetical or fictional being from outer space, esp. an intelligent one.

ex·tra·ter·ri·to·ri·al /,ekstrə,terə'tôrēəl/ ▶ adj. (of a law or decree) valid outside a country's territory. ■ denoting the freedom of an ambassador or other embassy staff from the jurisdiction of the territory of residence: *foreign embassies have extraterritorial rights.* ■ situated outside a country's territory: *extraterritorial industrial zones.*
– DERIVATIVES **ex·tra·ter·ri·to·ri·al·i·ty** /-,tôrē'alitē/ n.
– ORIGIN mid 19th cent.: from Latin *extra territorium* 'outside the territory' + -AL.

ex·tra·trop·i·cal /,ekstrə'träpikəl/ ▶ adj. chiefly Meteorology situated, existing, or occurring outside the tropics.

ex·tra·u·ter·ine /,ekstrə'yōōtərin, -rin/ ▶ adj. Medicine existing, formed, or occurring outside the uterus: *the first hour of extrauterine life.*

ex·trav·a·gance /ik'stravəgəns/ ▶ n. lack of restraint in spending money or use of resources: *his reckless extravagance with other people's money.* ■ a thing on which too much money has been spent or which has used up too many resources: *salmon trout is an unnecessary extravagance.* ■ excessive elaborateness of style, speech, or action: *the extravagance of the decor.*
– DERIVATIVES **ex·trav·a·gan·cy** /-gənsē/ n.
– ORIGIN mid 17th cent.: from French, from medieval Latin *extravagant-* 'diverging greatly,' from the verb *extravagari* (see EXTRAVAGANT).

ex·trav·a·gant /ik'stravəgənt/ ▶ **adj.** lacking restraint in spending money or using resources: *it was rather extravagant to buy both.* ■ costing too much money: *extravagant gifts like computer games.* ■ exceeding what is reasonable or appropriate; absurd: *extravagant claims for its effectiveness.*
– DERIVATIVES **ex·trav·a·gant·ly** adv.
– ORIGIN late Middle English (in the sense 'unusual, abnormal, unsuitable'): from medieval Latin *extravagant-* 'diverging greatly,' from the verb *extravagari*, from Latin *extra-* 'outside' + *vagari* 'wander.'

ex·trav·a·gan·za /ik,stravə'ganzə/ ▶ **n.** an elaborate and spectacular entertainment or production: *an extravaganza of dance in many forms.*
– ORIGIN mid 18th cent. (in the sense 'extravagance in language or behavior'): from Italian *estravaganza* 'extravagance.' The change was due to association with words beginning with EXTRA-.

ex·trav·a·sate /ik'stravə,sāt/ ▶ **v.** [with obj.] (usu. as adj. **extravasated**) chiefly Medicine let or force out (a fluid, esp. blood) from the vessel that naturally contains it into the surrounding area.
– DERIVATIVES **ex·trav·a·sa·tion** /ik,stravə'sāsHən/ **n.**
– ORIGIN mid 17th cent.: from EXTRA- 'outside' + Latin *vas* 'vessel' + -ATE³.

ex·tra·vas·cu·lar /,ekstrə'vaskyələr/ ▶ **adj.** Medicine situated or occurring outside the vascular system: *extravascular fluid.*

ex·tra·ve·hic·u·lar /,ekstrəvē'hikyələr/ ▶ **adj.** of or relating to an activity performed in space outside a spacecraft.

ex·tra·vert ▶ **n.** variant spelling of EXTROVERT.

ex·tra vir·gin ▶ **adj.** denoting a particularly fine grade of olive oil made from the first pressing of the olives and containing a maximum of one percent oleic acid.

ex·tre·ma /ik'strēmə/ plural form of EXTREMUM.

ex·treme /ik'strēm/ ▶ **adj. 1** reaching a high or the highest degree; very great: *extreme cold.* ■ not usual; exceptional: *in extreme cases the soldier may be discharged.* ■ very severe or serious: *expulsion is an extreme sanction.* ■ (of a person or their opinions) advocating severe or drastic measures; far from moderate, esp. politically: *the party has expelled some of its more extreme members.* ■ denoting or relating to a sport performed in a hazardous environment and involving great physical risk, such as parachuting or whitewater rafting. **2** [attrib.] farthest from the center or a given point; outermost: *the extreme northwest of Scotland.*
▶ **n. 1** either of two abstract things that are as different from each other as possible: *unbridled talk at one extreme and total silence at the other.* ■ the highest or most extreme degree of something: *extremes of temperature.* ■ a very severe or serious act: *he was unwilling to go to the extreme of civil war.* **2** Logic the subject or predicate in a proposition, or the major or minor term in a syllogism (as contrasted with the middle term).
– PHRASES **extremes meet** proverb opposite extremes have much in common. **go** (or **take something**) **to extremes** take an extreme course of action; do something to an extreme degree: *we may go to extremes to find peace and quiet.* **in the extreme** to an extreme degree: *the reasoning was convoluted in the extreme.*
– DERIVATIVES **ex·treme·ness** n.
– ORIGIN late Middle English: via Old French from Latin *extremus* 'outermost, utmost,' superlative of *exterus* 'outer.'

ex·treme·ly /ik'strēmlē/ ▶ **adv.** [as submodifier] to a very great degree; very: *this is an extremely difficult thing to do.*

ex·treme unc·tion ▶ **n.** (in the Roman Catholic Church) a former name for the sacrament of anointing of the sick, esp. when administered to the dying.

ex·trem·ism /ik'strē,mizəm/ ▶ **n.** the holding of extreme political or religious views; fanaticism: *the dangers of religious extremism.*

ex·trem·ist /ik'strēmist/ ▶ **n.** a person who holds extreme or fanatical political or religious views, esp. one who resorts to or advocates extreme action: *political extremists* | [as modifier] *an extremist conspiracy.*

ex·trem·i·ty /ik'stremitē/ ▶ **n.** (pl. **extremities**) **1** the farthest point or limit of something: *the peninsula's western extremity.* ■ (**extremities**) the hands and feet: *tingling and numbness in the extremities.* **2** the extreme degree or nature of something: *the extremity of the violence concerns us.* ■ a condition of extreme adversity or difficulty: *the terror of an animal in extremity.*
– ORIGIN late Middle English: from Old French *extremite* or Latin *extremitas*, from *extremus* 'utmost' (see EXTREME).

ex·trem·o·phile /ek'stremə,fīl/ ▶ **n.** Biology a microorganism, esp. an archaean, that lives in conditions of extreme temperature, acidity, alkalinity, or chemical concentration.

ex·tre·mum /ik'strēməm/ ▶ **n.** (pl. **extremums** or **extrema** /-mə/) [usu. as modifier] Mathematics the maximum or minimum value of a function.
– ORIGIN early 20th cent.: from Latin, neuter of *extremus* 'utmost' (see EXTREME).

ex·tri·cate /'ekstri,kāt/ ▶ **v.** [with obj.] free (someone or something) from a constraint or difficulty: *he was trying to extricate himself from official duties.*
– DERIVATIVES **ex·tri·ca·ble** /'ekstrikəbəl, ik'strik-/ **adj.**, **ex·tri·ca·tion** /,ekstri'kāsHən/ **n.**
– ORIGIN early 17th cent. (in the sense 'unravel, untangle'): from Latin *extricat-* 'unraveled,' from the verb *extricare*, from *ex-* 'out' + *tricae* 'perplexities.'

ex·trin·sic /ik'strinzik, -sik/ ▶ **adj.** not part of the essential nature of someone or something; coming or operating from outside: *extrinsic factors that might affect time budgets* | *the idea that power is extrinsic to production and profits.* ■ (of a muscle, such as any of the eye muscles) having its origin some distance from the part that it moves.
– DERIVATIVES **ex·trin·si·cal·ly** /-(ə)lē/ **adv.**
– ORIGIN mid 16th cent. (in the sense 'outward'): from late Latin *extrinsecus* 'outward,' from Latin *extrinsecus* 'outwardly,' based on *exter* 'outer'; the ending was altered under the influence of -IC.

ex·tro·py /'ekstrəpē/ ▶ **n.** the pseudoscientific principle that life will expand indefinitely and in an orderly, progressive way throughout the entire universe by the means of human intelligence and technology.
– DERIVATIVES **Ex·tro·pi·an** /ek'strōpēən/ **adj. & n.**
– ORIGIN 1980s: from EX-¹ 'out' + a shortened form of ENTROPY.

ex·trorse /'ek,strôrs/ ▶ **adj.** Botany & Zoology turned outward. The opposite of INTRORSE. ■ (of anthers) releasing their pollen on the outside of the flower.
– DERIVATIVES **ex·trorse·ly** adv.
– ORIGIN mid 19th cent.: from late Latin *extrorsus* 'outward' (adverb).

ex·tro·vert /'ekstrə,vərt/ (also **extravert**) ▶ **n.** an outgoing, overtly expressive person. ■ Psychology a person predominantly concerned with external things or objective considerations. Compare with INTROVERT.
▶ **adj.** of, denoting, or typical of an extrovert: *his extrovert personality made him the ideal host.*
– DERIVATIVES **ex·tro·ver·sion** /,ekstrə'vərZHən/ **n.**, **ex·tro·vert·ed** adj.
– ORIGIN early 20th cent.: from *extro-* (variant of EXTRA-, on the pattern of *intro-*) + Latin *vertere* 'to turn.'

> **USAGE** The original spelling extravert is now rare in general use but is found in technical use in psychology.

ex·trude /ik'strōōd/ ▶ **v.** [with obj.] (usu. **be extruded**) thrust or force out: *lava was being extruded from the volcano.* ■ shape (a material such as metal or plastic) by forcing it through a die.
– DERIVATIVES **ex·trud·a·ble** adj., **ex·tru·sile** /ik'strōōsəl, -,sīl/ **adj.**, **ex·tru·sion** /ik'strōōZHən/ **n.**
– ORIGIN mid 16th cent.: from Latin *extrudere*, from *ex-* 'out' + *trudere* 'to thrust.'

ex·tru·sive /ik'strōōsiv/ ▶ **adj.** Geology relating to or denoting rock that has been extruded at the earth's surface as lava or other volcanic deposits.

ex·u·ber·ance /ig'zōōbərəns/ ▶ **n.** the quality of being full of energy, excitement, and cheerfulness; ebullience: *a sense of youthful exuberance.* ■ the quality of growing profusely; luxuriance: *houseplants growing with wild exuberance.*

ex·u·ber·ant /ig'zōōbərənt/ ▶ **adj.** filled with or characterized by a lively energy and excitement: *giddily exuberant crowds* | *flamboyant and exuberant architectural invention.* ■ growing luxuriantly or profusely: *exuberant foliage.*
– DERIVATIVES **ex·u·ber·ant·ly** adv.
– ORIGIN late Middle English (in the sense 'overflowing, abounding'): from French *exubérant*, from Latin *exuberant-* 'being abundantly fruitful,' from the verb *exuberare* (based on *uber* 'fertile').

ex·u·date /'eksyōō,dāt, 'eksə-/ ▶ **n.** an exuded substance, in particular: ■ Medicine a mass of cells and fluid that has seeped out of blood vessels or an organ, esp. in inflammation. ■ Botany & Entomology a substance secreted by a plant or insect.
– ORIGIN late 19th cent.: from Latin *exsudat-* 'exuded,' from the verb *exsudare*.

ex·ude /ig'zōōd/ ▶ **v.** [with obj.] **1** discharge (moisture or a smell) slowly and steadily: *the beetle exudes a caustic liquid.* ■ [no obj.] (of moisture or a smell) be discharged by something in such a way: *slime exudes from the fungus.* **2** (of a person) display (an emotion or quality) strongly and openly: *Mr. Thomas exuded friendship and goodwill.* ■ (of a place) have a strong atmosphere of: *the building exudes an air of tranquility.*
– DERIVATIVES **ex·u·da·tion** /,eksyōō'dāsHən, ,eksə-/ **n.**, **ex·u·da·tive** /ig'zōōdətiv, 'eksə,dātiv, 'eksyōō-/ **adj.**
– ORIGIN late 16th cent.: from Latin *exsudare*, from *ex-* 'out' + *sudare* 'to sweat.'

ex·ult /ig'zəlt/ ▶ **v.** [no obj.] show or feel elation or jubilation, esp. as the result of a success: *exulting in her escape, Annie closed the door behind her.*
– DERIVATIVES **ex·ult·ing·ly** adv.
– ORIGIN late 16th cent.: from Latin *exsultare*, frequentative of *exsilire* 'leap up,' from *ex-* 'out, upward' + *salire* 'to leap.'

ex·ult·ant /ig'zəltnt/ ▶ **adj.** triumphantly happy: *she felt exultant and powerful.*
– DERIVATIVES **ex·ult·an·cy** /-'zəltnsē/ **n.**, **ex·ult·ant·ly** adv.
– ORIGIN mid 17th cent.: from Latin *exsultant-* 'exulting,' from the verb *exsultare*.

ex·ul·ta·tion /,eksəl'tāsHən, ,egzəl-/ ▶ **n.** a feeling of triumphant elation or jubilation; rejoicing: *she laughs in exultation.*

Ex·u·ma Cays /ik'sōōmə 'kēz, ig'zōōmə/ a group of about 350 small islands in the Bahamas.

ex·urb /'eksərb/ ▶ **n.** a district outside a city, esp. a prosperous area beyond the suburbs.
– DERIVATIVES **ex·ur·ban** /ek'sərbən/ **adj.**, **ex·ur·ban·ite** /ek'sərbə,nīt/ **n. & adj.**
– ORIGIN 1955: coined by A. C. Spectorsky (1919–72), American author and editor, either from Latin *ex* 'out of' + *urbs* 'city,' or as a back-formation from the earlier adjective *exurban*.

ex·ur·bi·a /ek'sərbēə/ ▶ **n.** the exurbs collectively; the region beyond the suburbs.
– ORIGIN 1955: from EX-¹ 'out of' + *-urbia*, on the pattern of *suburbia*. See EXURB.

ex·u·vi·ae /ig'zōōvē,ē, -ī/ ▶ **plural n.** [also treated as sing.] Zoology an animal's cast or sloughed skin, esp. that of an insect larva.
– DERIVATIVES **ex·u·vi·al** /-vēəl/ **adj.**
– ORIGIN mid 17th cent.: from Latin, literally 'animal skins, spoils of the enemy,' from *exuere* 'divest oneself of.'

ex·u·vi·ate /ig'zōōvē,āt/ ▶ **v.** [with obj.] technical shed (a skin or shell).
– DERIVATIVES **ex·u·vi·a·tion** /ig,zōōvē'āsHən/ **n.**
– ORIGIN mid 19th cent.: from EXUVIAE + -ATE³.

ex-vo·to /eks 'vōtō/ ▶ **n.** (pl. **ex-votos**) a religious offering given in order to fulfill a vow.
– ORIGIN late 18th cent.: from Latin *ex voto* 'from a vow.'

-ey ▶ **suffix** variant spelling of -Y² (as in *Charley, Limey*).

ey·as /'īəs/ (also **eyass**) ▶ **n.** (pl. **eyasses**) a young hawk, esp. (in falconry) an unfledged nestling taken from the nest for training.
– ORIGIN late 15th cent. (originally *nyas*): from French *niais*, based on Latin *nidus* 'nest.' The initial *n* was lost by wrong division of *a nyas*; compare with ADDER, APRON, and UMPIRE.

eye /ī/ ▶ **n. 1** each of a pair of globular organs in the head through which people and vertebrate animals see, the visible part typically appearing almond-shaped in animals with eyelids: *my cat is blind in one eye* | *closing her eyes, she tried to relax.* ■ the corresponding visual or light-detecting organ of many invertebrate animals. ■ the region of the face surrounding the eyes: *her eyes were swollen with crying.* ■ a person's eye as characterized by the color of the iris: *he had piercing blue eyes.* ■ used to refer to someone's power of vision and in descriptions of the manner or direction of someone's gaze: *his sharp eyes had missed nothing* | *I couldn't take my eyes off him.* ■ used to refer to someone's opinion or attitude toward something: ***in the eyes of** his younger colleagues, Mr. Arnett was an eccentric* | ***to** European **eyes**, it may seem that the city is overcrowded.*

> The basic components of the vertebrate eye are a transparent cornea, an adjustable iris, a lens for focusing, a sensitive retina lining the back of the eye, and a clear fluid- or jelly-filled center. The most primitive animals only have one or two eyespots, while many other invertebrates have several simple eyes or a pair of compound eyes.

2 a thing resembling an eye in appearance, shape, or relative position, in particular: ■ the small hole in a needle through which the thread is passed. ■ a small metal loop into which a hook is fitted as a fastener on a garment. See also **HOOK AND EYE**. ■ Nautical a loop at the end of a rope, esp. one at the top end of a shroud or stay. ■ a rounded eyelike marking on an animal, such as those on the tail of a peacock; an eyespot. ■ a round, dark spot on a potato from which a new shoot can grow. ■ a center cut of meat: *eye of round*. ■ the center of a flower, esp. when distinctively colored. ■ the calm region at the center of a storm or hurricane. See also **THE EYE OF THE STORM** below. ■ **(eyes)** Nautical the extreme forward part of a ship: *it was hanging in the eyes of the ship*.
▶ **v.** **(eyes, eyeing** or **eying, eyed)** [with obj.] look at or watch closely or with interest: *Rose eyed him warily*.
– PHRASES **all eyes** used to convey that a particular person or thing is currently the focus of public interest or attention: ***all eyes are on** the hot spots of eastern Europe*. **be all eyes** be watching eagerly and attentively. **before** (or **under**) **one's** (**very**) **eyes** right in front of one (used for emphasis, esp. in the context of something surprising or unpleasant): *he saw his life's work destroyed before his very eyes*. **close** (or **shut**) **one's eyes to** refuse to notice or acknowledge something unwelcome or unpleasant: *he couldn't close his eyes to the truth—he had cancer*. **an eye for an eye and a tooth for a tooth** used to refer to the belief that punishment in kind is the appropriate way to deal with an offense or crime. [with biblical allusion to Exod. 21: 24.] **the eye of the storm** the calm region at the center of a storm. ■ the most intense part of a tumultuous situation: *he was in the eye of the storm of abstract art*. **the eye of the wind** (also **the wind's eye**) the direction from which the wind is blowing. **eyes front** (or **left** or **right**) a military command to turn the head in the particular direction stated. **a ——'s-eye view** a view from the position or standpoint of a ——: *a satellite's-eye view of global warming*. See also **BIRD'S-EYE VIEW, WORM'S-EYE VIEW**. **give someone the eye** informal look at someone in a way that clearly indicates one's sexual interest in them: *this blonde was giving me the eye*. **half an eye** used in reference to a slight degree of perception or attention: *he kept **half an eye on** the house as he worked*. **have an eye for** be able to recognize, appreciate, and make good judgments about: *applicants should have an eye for detail*. **have** (or **keep**) **one's eye on** keep under careful observation. ■ **(have one's eye on)** hope or plan to acquire: *the county sheriff has his eye on retirement*. **have** (or **with**) **an eye to** have (or having) as one's objective: *with an eye to transatlantic business, he made a deal in New York*. ■ consider (or be considering) prudently; look (or be looking) ahead to: *the charity must have an eye to the future*. **have** (or **with**) **an eye to** (or **for** or **on**) **the main chance** look or be looking for an opportunity to take advantage of a situation for personal gain, typically a financial one: *a developer with an eye on the main chance*. **one's eyes are bigger than one's stomach** one has asked for or taken more food than one can actually eat. (**only**) **have eyes for** be (exclusively) interested in or attracted to: *he has eyes for no one but you*. **have eyes in the back of one's head** know what is going on around one even when one cannot see it. **hit someone between the eyes** (or **in the eye**) informal be very obvious or impressive: *he wouldn't notice talent if it hit him right between the eyes*. **keep an eye** (or **a sharp eye**) **on** keep under careful observation: *dealers are keeping an eye on the currency markets*. **keep an eye out** (or **open**) look out for something with particular attention: ***keep an eye out for** his car*. **keep one's eyes open** (or **peeled** or Brit. **skinned**) be on the alert; watch carefully or vigilantly for something: *visitors should **keep their eyes peeled for** lions*. **lay** (or **set** or **clap**) **eyes on** informal see: *Harry has not laid eyes on Alice for twenty years*. **make eyes at someone** look at someone in a way that indicates one's sexual interest. **my eye** informal, dated used esp. in spoken English to indicate surprise or disbelief. [said to be originally nautical slang.] **open someone's eyes** enlighten someone about certain realities; cause someone to realize or discover something: *the letter finally **opened my eyes to** the truth*. **see eye to eye** have similar views or attitudes to something; be in full agreement: *Mr. Trumble and I do not always see eye to eye*. **a twinkle** (or **gleam**) **in someone's eye** something that is as yet no more than an idea or dream: *not every gleam in a grocer's eye becomes a store*. **what the eye doesn't see, the heart doesn't grieve over** proverb if you're unaware of an unpleasant fact or situation, you can't be troubled by it. **with one's eyes open** fully aware of the possible difficulties or consequences: *I went into this job with my eyes open*. **with one's eyes shut** (or **closed**) **1** without having to make much effort; easily: *I could do it with my eyes shut*. **2** without considering the possible difficulties or consequences: *she didn't go to Hollywood with her eyes closed*. **with one eye on** giving some but not all one's attention to: *I sat with one eye on the clock, waiting for my turn*.
– DERIVATIVES **eyed** /īd/ **adj.** [in combination] *a brown-eyed girl*, **eye·less adj.**
– ORIGIN Old English *ēage*, of Germanic origin; related to Dutch *oog* and German *Auge*.

eye·ball /ˈīˌbôl/ ▶ **n.** the round part of the eye of a vertebrate, within the eyelids and socket. In mammals it is typically a firm, mobile, spherical structure enclosed by the sclera and the cornea.
▶ **v.** [with obj.] informal look or stare at closely: *we eyeballed one another*.
– PHRASES **eyeball to eyeball** face to face with someone, esp. in an aggressive way: *he wheeled around to confront John eyeball to eyeball*. **give someone the hairy eyeball** informal stare at someone disapprovingly or angrily, esp. with one's eyelids partially lowered. **up to one's eyeballs** informal used to emphasize the extreme degree of an undesirable situation or condition: *he's **up to his eyeballs** in debt*.

eye·black /ˈīˌblak/ ▶ **n.** old-fashioned term for **MASCARA**.

eye·bolt /ˈīˌbōlt/ ▶ **n.** a bolt or bar with an eye at the end for attaching a hook or ring to.

eye·bright /ˈīˌbrīt/ ▶ **n.** a small plant of the figwort family with little snapdragonlike flowers. Found in dry fields and along roadsides, it was formerly used as a remedy for eye problems. ● Genus *Euphrasia*, family Scrophulariaceae: several species, in particular the European *E. officinalis* and the North American *E. americana*.

eye·brow /ˈīˌbrou/ ▶ **n.** the strip of hair growing on the ridge above a person's eye socket.
– PHRASES **raise one's eyebrows** (or **an eyebrow**) show surprise, disbelief, or mild disapproval.

eye·brow pen·cil ▶ **n.** a cosmetic pencil for defining or accentuating the eyebrows.

eye can·dy ▶ **n.** informal visual images that are superficially attractive and entertaining but intellectually undemanding: *the film's success rested on a promotional campaign showcasing its relentless eye candy*.

eye-catch·ing ▶ **adj.** immediately appealing or noticeable; striking: *an eye-catching poster*.
– DERIVATIVES **eye-catch·er n.**, **eye-catch·ing·ly adv.**

eye con·tact ▶ **n.** the act of looking directly into one another's eyes: ***make eye contact** with your interviewers*.

eye·cup /īˌkəp/ ▶ **n. 1** a piece of an optical device such as a microscope, camera, or pair of binoculars that is contoured to provide a comfortable rest against the user's eye.
2 a small container used for applying cleansing solutions to the eye.

eye·ful /ˈīˌfo͝ol/ ▶ **n.** [in sing.] informal a long, steady look at something: *they wanted to get an eyeful of Lily*. ■ a visually striking person or thing: *she was quite an eyeful*. ■ a quantity or piece of something thrown or blown into the eye: ***an eyeful of** fluid*.

eye·glass /ˈīˌglas/ ▶ **n.** a single lens for correcting or assisting defective eyesight, esp. a monocle. ■ **(eyeglasses)** another term for **GLASSES**. ■ another term for **EYEPIECE**.

eye·hole /ˈīˌhōl/ ▶ **n.** a hole to look through, esp. in a curtain or mask.

eye·lash /ˈīˌlash/ ▶ **n.** each of the short curved hairs growing on the edges of the eyelids, serving to protect the eyes from dust particles.

eye·let /ˈīlit/ ▶ **n.** a small round hole in leather or cloth for threading a lace, string, or rope through. ■ a metal ring used to reinforce such a hole. ■ a small hole ornamented with stitching around its edge, used as a form of decoration in embroidery. ■ a small hole or slit in a wall for looking through.
▶ **v.** **(eyelets, eyeleting, eyeleted)** [with obj.] make eyelets in (fabric).
– ORIGIN late Middle English *oilet*, from Old French *oillet*, diminutive of *oil* 'eye,' from Latin *oculus*. The change in the first syllable in the 17th cent. was due to association with **EYE**.

eye lev·el ▶ **n.** the level of the eyes looking straight ahead: *pictures hung at eye level*.

eye·lid /ˈīˌlid/ ▶ **n.** each of the upper and lower folds of skin that cover the eye when closed.

eye·lin·er /ˈīˌlīnər/ ▶ **n.** a cosmetic applied as a line around the eyes to make them appear larger or more noticeable.

eye-o·pen·er ▶ **n.** informal **1** [in sing.] an event or situation that proves to be unexpectedly enlightening: *a visit to the docks can be a fascinating eye-opener*.
2 an alcoholic drink taken early in the day.
– DERIVATIVES **eye-o·pen·ing adj.**

eye·patch /ˈīˌpaCH/ ▶ **n.** a patch worn to protect an injured eye.

eye pen·cil ▶ **n.** a pencil for applying makeup around the eyes.

eye·piece /ˈīˌpēs/ ▶ **n.** the lens or group of lenses that is closest to the eye in a microscope, telescope, or other optical instrument. Also called **EYEGLASS** or **OCULAR**.

eye-pop·ping ▶ **adj.** informal astonishingly large, impressive, or blatant: *the company has doubled its assets to an eye-popping $113 billion*.

eye rhyme ▶ **n.** a similarity between words in spelling but not in pronunciation, e.g., *love* and *move*.

eye·shade /ˈīˌSHād/ ▶ **n.** a translucent visor used to protect the eyes from strong light.

eye·shad·ow /ˈīˌSHadō/ ▶ **n.** a colored cosmetic, typically in powder form, applied to the eyelids or to the skin around the eyes to accentuate them.

eye·shot /ˈīˌSHät/ ▶ **n.** the distance for which one can see: *he is **within eyeshot***.

eye·sight /ˈīˌsīt/ ▶ **n.** a person's ability to see: *poor eyesight ended his plans for a naval career*.

eye sock·et ▶ **n.** the cavity in the skull that encloses an eyeball with its surrounding muscles. Also called **ORBIT**.

eyes-on·ly ▶ **adj.** intended to be seen or read only by the person addressed; confidential, secret: *a top-secret, eyes-only telegram for the president*.

eye·sore /ˈīˌsôr/ ▶ **n.** a thing that is very ugly, esp. a building that disfigures a landscape.

eye splice ▶ **n.** a splice made by turning the end of a rope back on itself and interlacing the strands, thereby forming a loop.

eye·spot /ˈīˌspät/ ▶ **n. 1** Zoology a light-sensitive pigmented spot on the bodies of invertebrate animals such as flatworms, starfishes, and microscopic crustaceans, and also in some unicellular organisms.
2 a rounded eyelike marking on an animal, esp. on the wing of a butterfly or moth.
3 a fungal disease of cereals, sugar cane, and other cultivated grasses, characterized by yellowish oval spots on the leaves and stems. ● The fungus is typically *Pseudocercosporella herpotrichoides*, subdivision Deuteromycotina.

eye·stalk /īˌstôk/ ▶ **n.** Zoology a movable stalk that bears an eye near its tip, esp. in crabs, shrimps, and related crustaceans, and in some mollusks.

eye strain ▶ **n.** fatigue of the eyes, such as that caused by reading or looking at a computer screen for too long.

eye·stripe /īˌstrīp/ ▶ **n.** a stripe on a bird's head that encloses or appears to run through the eye.

eye·tooth /ˈīˈˌto͞oTH/ ▶ **n.** a canine tooth, esp. one in the upper jaw.
– PHRASES **give one's eyeteeth for** (or **to be**) do anything in order to have or be something: *I'd give my eyeteeth for a lover*.

eye track·ing ▶ **n.** a technology that monitors eye movements as a means of detecting abnormalities or of studying how people interact with text or online documents: *a company that uses eye tracking to evaluate visual products*.

eye wall ▶ **n.** Meteorology the area immediately outside the eye of a hurricane or cyclone, associated with tall clouds, heavy rainfall, and high winds.

eye·wash /ˈīˌwôSH, -ˌwäSH/ ▶ **n. 1** cleansing solution for a person's eye.
2 informal insincere talk; nonsense: *their rhetoric about reducing intrusive federal rules is so much eyewash*.

eye·wear /īˌwer/ ▶ **n.** things worn on the eyes, such as spectacles and contact lenses.

eye·wit·ness /ˈīˈwitnəs/ ▶ **n.** [often as modifier] a person who has personally seen something happen and so can give a first-hand description of it: ***eyewitness** accounts of the London blitz*.

eye worm ▶ **n.** either of two parasitic nematode worms that affect the eyes of mammals. ● a filarial worm of equatorial Africa, infesting humans and other primates, causing loiasis and sometimes passing across the cornea (*Loa loa*, class Phasmida). ● a nematode that occurs in the region of the eyelid and tear duct, found chiefly in hoofed mammals (genus *Thelazia*, class Phasmida).

ey·ra /ˈe(ə)rə/ ▶ **n.** a reddish-brown form of the jaguarundi.

– ORIGIN early 17th cent.: from Spanish, from Tupi *eirara, irara.*

eyre /e(ə)r/ ▶ **n.** historical a circuit court held in medieval England by a judge (a **justice in eyre**) who rode from county to county for that purpose.
– ORIGIN Middle English: from Old French *eire*, from Latin *iter* 'journey.'

Eyre, Lake /e(ə)r/ a lake in northeastern South Australia, in southern Australia, the country's largest salt lake.
– ORIGIN named after explorer E. J. Eyre (1815–1901).

ey·rie /'e(ə)rē, 'i(ə)rē/ ▶ **n.** variant spelling of AERIE.

ey·rir /'āri(ə)r/ ▶ **n.** (pl. **aurar** /'irär/) a monetary unit of Iceland, equal to one hundredth of a krona.

Ey·senck /'īsəNGk/, Hans (Jürgen) (1916–97), British psychologist; born in Germany. He was noted for his strong criticism of Freudian psychoanalysis and for his ideas concerning the assessment of intelligence and personality.

E·ze·ki·el /i'zēkēəl/ a Hebrew prophet of the 6th century BC who prophesied the forthcoming destruction of Jerusalem and the Jewish nation and inspired hope for the future well-being of a restored state. ■ a book of the Bible containing his prophecies.

e-zine /'ē,zēn/ ▶ **n.** a magazine published only in electronic form on a computer network.

Ez·ra /'ezrə/ a Jewish priest and scribe who played a central part in the reform of Judaism in the 5th or 4th century BC, continuing the work of Nehemiah and forbidding mixed marriages. ■ a book of the Bible telling of Ezra, the return of the Jews from Babylon, and the rebuilding of the Temple.

e

PRONUNCIATION KEY ə ago, up; ər over, fur; a hat; ā ate; ä car; e let; ē see; i fit; ī by; NG sing; ō go; ô law, for; oi toy; o͝o good; o͞o goo; ou out; TH thin; T͟H then; ZH vision

Ff

f

F[1] /ef/ (also **f**) ▶ **n.** (pl. **Fs** or **F's**) **1** the sixth letter of the alphabet. ■ denoting the next after E in a set of items, categories, etc. ■ the sixth highest or lowest class of academic marks (also used to represent "Fail"). ■ (**f**) Chess denoting the sixth file from the left, as viewed from White's side of the board.
2 (usu. **F**) Music the fourth note of the diatonic scale of C major. ■ a key based on a scale with F as its keynote.

F[2] ▶ **abbr.** ■ Fahrenheit: *60°F.* ■ failure. ■ false. ■ farad(s). ■ Chemistry faraday(s). ■ (in racing results) favorite. ■ February. ■ Fellow. ■ female. ■ fighter (in designations of US aircraft types): *the F117 Stealth fighter.* ■ forint. ■ (in auto racing) formula: *an F1 driver.* ■ Franc(s). ■ France. ■ French. ▶ **symbol** ■ the chemical element fluorine. ■ Physics force: $F = ma$.

f ▶ **abbr.** ■ farad. ■ farthing. ■ father. ■ fathom. ■ feet. ■ Grammar feminine. ■ female. ■ [in combination] (in units of measurement) femto- (10^{-15}). ■ filly. ■ fine. ■ (in textual references) folio. ■ following. ■ foot. ■ form. ■ Music forte. ■ (in racing results) furlong(s). ■ franc. ■ from. ■ Chemistry denoting electrons and orbitals possessing three units of angular momentum: *f-orbitals.* [*f* from *fundamental*, originally applied to lines in atomic spectra.] ▶ **symbol** ■ focal length: *apertures of f/5.6 to f/11.* See also **F-NUMBER**. ■ Mathematics a function of a specified variable: *the value of f(x).* ■ Electronics frequency.

f/ ▶ **abbr.** f-number.

F_1 (also **F1**) ▶ **abbr.** Biology the first filial generation, i.e., the generation of hybrids arising from a first cross. The second filial generation is designated **F_2** (or **F2**), and so on.

fa /fä/ ▶ **n.** Music (in solmization) the fourth note of a major scale. ■ the note F in the fixed-do system.
– ORIGIN Middle English: representing (as an arbitrary name for the note) the first syllable of *famuli*, taken from a Latin hymn (see **SOLMIZATION**).

FAA ▶ **abbr.** Federal Aviation Administration.

f.a.a. ▶ **abbr.** free of all average.

fab[1] /fab/ ▶ **adj.** informal fabulous; wonderful.
– ORIGIN 1960s: abbreviation.

fab[2] ▶ **n.** Electronics a microchip fabrication plant. ■ a particular fabrication process in such a plant.
– ORIGIN late 20th cent.: abbreviation of *fabrication* (see **FABRICATE**).

Fa·ber·gé /ˌfabərˈZHā/, Peter Carl (1846–1920), Russian goldsmith and jeweler. He is known for the intricate Easter eggs that he made for Tsar Alexander III and other royalty.

Fa·bi·an /ˈfābēən/ ▶ **n.** a member or supporter of the Fabian Society, an organization of socialists aiming at the gradual rather than revolutionary achievement of socialism.
▶ **adj.** relating to or characteristic of the Fabians: *the Fabian movement.* ■ employing a cautiously persistent and dilatory strategy to wear out an enemy: *Fabian tactics.*
– DERIVATIVES **Fa·bi·an·ism** /-izəm/ **n.**, **Fa·bi·an·ist** /-əst/ **n.**
– ORIGIN late 18th cent.: from the name of *Quintus Fabius Maximus Verrucosus* (see **FABIUS**), after whom the Fabian Society is also named.

Fa·bi·us /ˈfābēəs/ (died 203 BC), Roman general and statesman; full name *Quintus Fabius Maximus Verrucosus*; known as **Fabius Cunctator** (Fabius the Delayer). After Hannibal's defeat of the Roman army at Cannae in 216 BC, Fabius successfully wore down the Carthaginian invaders.

fa·ble /ˈfābəl/ ▶ **n.** a short story, typically with animals as characters, conveying a moral. ■ a story, typically a supernatural one incorporating elements of myth and legend. ■ myth and legend: *the unnatural monsters of fable.* ■ a false statement or belief.
▶ **v.** [no obj.] archaic tell fictitious tales: *I do not dream nor fable.* ■ [with obj.] fabricate or invent (an incident, person, or story).
– DERIVATIVES **fa·bler** /ˈfāb(ə)lər/ **n.**
– ORIGIN Middle English: from Old French *fable* (noun), from Latin *fabula* 'story,' from *fari* 'speak.'

fa·bled /ˈfābəld/ ▶ **adj.** [attrib.] well known for being of great quality or rarity; famous: *a fabled art collection.* ■ mythical; imaginary: *the fabled kingdom.*

fab·less /ˈfablis/ ▶ **adj.** denoting or relating to a company that designs microchips but contracts out their production rather than owning its own factory: *the newcomers' strategy was fabless production.*
– ORIGIN 1980s: from *fab* 'a microchip fabrication plant' + *-less.*

fab·li·au /ˈfablēˌō/ ▶ **n.** (pl. **fabliaux** /-ˌōz/) a metrical tale, typically a bawdily humorous one, of a type found chiefly in early French poetry.
– ORIGIN from Old French (Picard dialect) *fabliaux*, plural of *fablel* 'short fable,' diminutive of *fable.*

Fa·bri·a·no, Gentile da, see **GENTILE DA FABRIANO**.

fab·ric /ˈfabrik/ ▶ **n. 1** cloth, typically produced by weaving or knitting textile fibers: *heavy silk fabric | waterproof fabrics.*
2 the walls, floor, and roof of a building. ■ the body of a car or aircraft. ■ the essential structure of anything, esp. a society or culture: *the fabric of society.*
– ORIGIN late 15th cent.: from French *fabrique*, from Latin *fabrica* 'something skillfully produced,' from *faber* 'worker in metal, stone, etc.' The word originally denoted a building, later a machine or appliance, the general sense being 'something made,' hence sense 1 (mid 18th cent., originally denoting any manufactured material). Sense 2 dates from the mid 17th cent.

fab·ri·cate /ˈfabrəˌkāt/ ▶ **v.** [with obj.] invent or concoct (something), typically with deceitful intent: *officers fabricated evidence.* ■ construct or manufacture (something, esp. an industrial product), esp. from prepared components: *you will have to fabricate an exhaust system.*
– DERIVATIVES **fab·ri·ca·tor** /-ˌkātər/ **n.**
– ORIGIN late Middle English: from Latin *fabricat-* 'manufactured,' from the verb *fabricare*, from *fabrica* 'something skillfully produced' (see **FABRIC**).

fab·ri·ca·tion /ˌfabrəˈkāSHən/ ▶ **n.** the action or process of manufacturing or inventing something: *the assembly and fabrication of electronic products.* ■ an invention; a lie: *the story was a complete fabrication.*

fab·ric soft·en·er ▶ **n.** liquid used to soften clothes when they are being washed, or specially treated squares of cloth used to soften clothes in the dryer.

Fa·bry–Pé·rot in·ter·fe·rom·e·ter /fäˈbrē päˈrō/ ▶ **n.** an interferometer that incorporates an etalon, used chiefly in astronomy.
– ORIGIN early 20th cent.: named after Charles *Fabry* (1867–1945) and Alfred *Pérot* (1863–1925), French physicists.

fab·u·late /ˈfabyəˌlāt/ ▶ **v.** [with obj.] relate (an event or events) as a fable or story. ■ [no obj.] relate untrue or invented stories.
– DERIVATIVES **fab·u·la·tion** /ˌfabyəˈlāSHən/ **n.**, **fab·u·la·tor** /-ˌlātər/ **n.**
– ORIGIN early 17th cent.: from Latin *fabulat-* 'narrated as a fable,' from the verb *fabulari*, from *fabula* (see **FABLE**).

fab·u·list /ˈfabyəlist/ ▶ **n.** a person who composes or relates fables. ■ a liar, esp. a person who invents elaborate, dishonest stories.
– ORIGIN late 16th cent.: from French *fabuliste*, from Latin *fabula* (see **FABLE**).

fab·u·lous /ˈfabyələs/ ▶ **adj.** extraordinary, esp. extraordinarily large: *fabulous riches.* ■ informal amazingly good; wonderful: *a fabulous two-week vacation.* ■ having no basis in reality; mythical: *fabulous creatures.*
– DERIVATIVES **fab·u·los·i·ty** /ˌfabyəˈläsətē/ **n.**, **fab·u·lous·ly adv.**, **fab·u·lous·ness n.**
– ORIGIN late Middle English (in the sense 'known through fable, unhistorical'): from French *fabuleux* or Latin *fabulosus* 'celebrated in fable,' from *fabula* (see **FABLE**).

fac. ▶ **abbr.** ■ facsimile. ■ faculty.

fa·cade /fəˈsäd/ (also **façade**) ▶ **n.** the face of a building, esp. the principal front that looks onto a street or open space. ■ an outward appearance that is maintained to conceal a less pleasant or creditable reality: *her flawless public facade masked private despair.*
– ORIGIN mid 17th cent.: from French *façade*, from *face* 'face,' on the pattern of Italian *facciata.*

face /fās/ ▶ **n. 1** the front part of a person's head from the forehead to the chin, or the corresponding part in an animal. ■ the face as expressing emotion; an expression shown on the face: *the happy faces of these children.* ■ a manifestation or outward aspect of something: *the unacceptable face of social drinking.* ■ [with adj.] a person of a particular type: *this season's squad has a lot of old faces in it.*
2 the surface of a thing, esp. one that is presented to the view or has a particular function, in particular: ■ Geometry each of the surfaces of a solid: *the faces of a cube.* ■ a vertical or sloping side of a mountain or cliff: *the south face of Broad Peak.* ■ the side of a planet or moon facing the observer. ■ the front of a building. ■ the plate of a clock or watch bearing the digits or hands. ■ the distinctive side of a playing card. ■ short for **TYPEFACE**. ■ the side of a coin showing the head or principal design.
▶ **v.** [with obj.] **1** be positioned with the face or front toward (someone or something): *he turned to face her.* ■ [no obj.] have the face or front pointing in a specified direction: *the house faces due east.* ■ [no obj.] (of a soldier) turn in a particular direction: *they immediately faced about.*
2 confront and deal with or accept: *honesty forced her to* ***face facts*** | [no obj.] *the candidates choose not to face up to the pragmatic issues.* ■ (**face someone/something down**) overcome someone or something by a show of determination: *he faced down persistent hecklers at a noontime rally.* ■ have (a difficult event or situation) in prospect: *each defendant faced a maximum sentence of 10 years.* ■ (of a problem or difficult situation) present itself to and require action from (someone): *if you were suddenly faced with an emergency, would you know how to cope?*
3 (usu. **be faced with**) cover the surface of (a thing) with a layer of a different material: *the external basement walls were faced with granite slabs.*
– PHRASES **face down** with the face or surface turned toward the ground: *he lay face down on his bed.* **face the music** be confronted with the unpleasant consequences of one's actions. **the face of the earth** used for emphasis or exaggeration, to refer to the existence or disappearance of someone or something: *he's just disappeared* ***off the face of***

the earth | *the most grueling training* ***on the face of the earth.*** **face up** with the face or surface turned upward to view: *place the panel face up before cutting.* **get out of someone's face** [usu. as imperative] informal stop harassing or annoying someone: *shut up and get out of my face.* **have the face to do something** dated have the effrontery to do something. **in one's face** directly at or against one; as one approaches: *she slammed the door in my face.* **in the face of** when confronted with: *her resolution in the face of the enemy.* ■ in spite of: *reform had been introduced in the face of considerable opposition.* **in your face** see IN-YOUR-FACE. **lose face** suffer a loss of respect; be humiliated: *the code of conduct required that he strike back or lose face.* **loss of face** a loss of respect; humiliation: *he could step aside now without loss of face.* **make a face** (or **faces**) produce an expression on one's face that shows dislike, disgust, or some other negative emotion, or that is intended to be amusing: *she made a face and tossed her purse at him.* **on the face of it** without knowing all of the relevant facts; at first glance: *on the face of it, these improvements look to be insignificant.* **put a good** (or **brave** or **bold**) **face on something** act as if something unpleasant or upsetting is not as bad as it really is: *he tried to put a good face on the financial picture.* **put one's face on** informal apply makeup to one's face. **save face** retain respect; avoid humiliation: *an outcome that allows them all to save face.* **set one's face against** oppose or resist with determination: *he had set his face against the idea.* **throw something back in someone's face** reject something in a brusque or ungracious manner: *she'd given him her trust and he'd thrown it back in her face.* **to one's face** openly in one's presence: *you're telling me to my face I'm a liar.*

– PHRASAL VERBS **face off** take up an attitude of confrontation, esp. at the start of a fight or game: *close to a million soldiers face off in the desert.* ■ Ice Hockey start or restart play with a face-off.

– DERIVATIVES **faced** /fāst/ **adj.** [in combination] *red-faced.*

– ORIGIN Middle English: from Old French, based on Latin *facies* 'form, appearance, face.'

face a·mount ▶ **n.** another term for DEATH BENEFIT.

face card ▶ **n.** a playing card that is a king, queen, or jack of a suit.

face-cen·tered ▶ **adj.** denoting a crystal structure in which there is an atom at each vertex and at the center of each face of the unit cell. Compare with BODY-CENTERED.

face·cloth /ˈfāsˌklôTH/ ▶ **n.** a washcloth.

face·less /ˈfāsləs/ ▶ **adj.** (of a person) remote and impersonal; anonymous: *the faceless bureaucrats who made the rules.* ■ (of a building or place) characterless and dull.

– DERIVATIVES **face·less·ness n.**

facelift /ˈfāslift/ ▶ **n.** a cosmetic surgical operation to remove unwanted wrinkles by tightening the skin of the face. ■ a procedure carried out to improve the appearance of something: *the station has undergone a multimillion-dollar facelift.*

face mask ▶ **n.** a protective mask covering the nose and mouth or nose and eyes.

face-off ▶ **n.** a direct confrontation between two people or groups: *a face-off for the championship title.* ■ Ice Hockey the start or a restart of play, in which the referee drops the puck between two opposing players.

face paint ▶ **n.** bold-colored paint used to decorate the face.

– DERIVATIVES **face paint·er n., face paint·ing n.**

face·plate /ˈfāsˌplāt/ ▶ **n. 1** an enlarged end or attachment on the end of the mandrel on a lathe, with slots and holes on which work can be mounted. ■ a plate protecting a piece of machinery, a light switch, or an electrical outlet. ■ the part of a cathode ray tube that carries the phosphor screen. **2** the transparent window of a diver's or astronaut's helmet.

face pow·der ▶ **n.** flesh-tinted cosmetic powder used to improve the appearance of the face by reducing shine and concealing blemishes.

face·print /ˈfāsˌprint/ ▶ **n.** a digital scan or photograph of a human face, used for identifying individuals from the unique characteristics of facial structure: *hidden cameras and faceprints are used to single out individuals in a crowd.*

– ORIGIN on the pattern of *fingerprint.*

face·print·ing /ˈfāsˌprintiNG/ ▶ **n.** the process of creating a digital faceprint and using software to compare it with a database of photographs, esp. to identify known criminals.

– ORIGIN on the pattern of *fingerprinting.*

fac·er /ˈfāsər/ ▶ **n.** informal, chiefly Brit. a blow to the face. ■ a sudden difficulty or obstacle.

face-sav·ing ▶ **adj.** preserving one's reputation, credibility, or dignity: *a face-saving solution for both sides.*

– DERIVATIVES **face-sav·er n.**

fac·et /ˈfasət/ ▶ **n.** one side of something many-sided, esp. of a cut gem. ■ a particular aspect or feature of something: *participation by the laity in all facets of church life.* ■ Zoology any of the individual units (ommatidia) that make up the compound eye of an insect or crustacean.

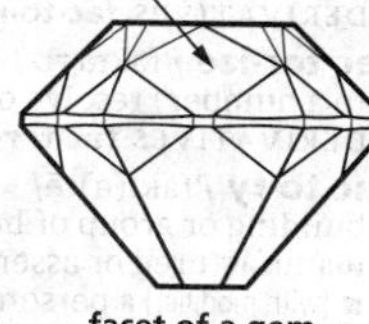
facet of a gem

– DERIVATIVES **fac·et·ed** /ˈfasətid/ **adj.** [in combination] *multifaceted.*

– ORIGIN early 17th cent.: from French *facette*, diminutive of *face* 'face, side' (see FACE).

fa·ce·ti·ae /fəˈsēSHēˌē, -SHēˌī/ ▶ **plural n. 1** dated pornographic literature. **2** archaic humorous or witty sayings.

– ORIGIN early 16th cent.: from Latin, plural of *facetia* 'jest,' from *facetus* 'witty.'

face time ▶ **n.** informal time spent in face-to-face contact with someone. ■ time spent being filmed or photographed by the media.

fa·ce·tious /fəˈsēSHəs/ ▶ **adj.** treating serious issues with deliberately inappropriate humor; flippant.

– DERIVATIVES **fa·ce·tious·ly adv., fa·ce·tious·ness n.**

– ORIGIN late 16th cent. (in the general sense 'witty, amusing'): from French *facétieux*, from *facétie*, from Latin *facetia* 'jest,' from *facetus* 'witty.'

face to face ▶ **adv. & adj.** with the people involved being close together and looking directly at each other: [as adv.] *the two men stood face to face* | [as adj.] *a face-to-face conversation.* ■ [as adv.] in direct confrontation: *he came face to face with a tiger.*

face val·ue ▶ **n.** the value printed or depicted on a coin, banknote, postage stamp, ticket, etc., esp. when less than the actual or intrinsic value. ■ the superficial appearance or implication of something: *she felt the lie was unconvincing, but he seemed to take it at face value.*

fa·cia /ˈfaSH(ē)ə, ˈfā-/ ▶ **n.** chiefly Brit. variant spelling of FASCIA (sense 1).

fa·cial /ˈfāSHəl/ ▶ **adj.** of or affecting the face: *facial expressions.*
▶ **n.** a beauty treatment for the face.

– DERIVATIVES **fa·cial·ly adv.**

– ORIGIN early 17th cent. (as a theological term meaning 'face to face, open'): from medieval Latin *facialis*, from *facies* (see FACE). The current sense of the adjective dates from the early 19th cent.

fa·cial·ist /ˈfāSHəlist/ ▶ **n.** a person who gives facials and other beauty treatments for the face.

fa·cial nerve ▶ **n.** Anatomy each of the seventh pair of cranial nerves, supplying the facial muscles and the tongue.

fa·cial pro·fil·ing ▶ **n.** the recording and analysis of a person's facial characteristics, esp. to assist in identifying an individual: *the police have set up a system of facial profiling at major sporting events.*

fa·cial tis·sue ▶ **n.** tissue that is used to blow one's nose, contain a sneeze, etc.

-facient ▶ **comb. form** producing a specified action or state: *abortifacient.*

– ORIGIN from Latin *facient-* 'doing, making.'

fa·ci·es /ˈfāˌSHēz, ˈfāSHēˌēz/ ▶ **n.** (pl. **same**) **1** Medicine the appearance or facial expression of an individual that is typical of a particular disease or condition. **2** Geology the character of a rock expressed by its formation, composition, and fossil content.

– ORIGIN early 17th cent. (denoting the face): from Latin, 'form, appearance, face.'

fac·ile /ˈfasəl/ ▶ **adj. 1** (esp. of a theory or argument) appearing neat and comprehensive only by ignoring the true complexities of an issue; superficial. ■ (of a person) having a superficial or simplistic knowledge or approach: *a man of facile and shallow intellect.* **2** (of success, esp. in sports) easily achieved; effortless: *a facile victory.* ■ acting or done in a quick, fluent, and easy manner: *he was revealed to be a facile liar.*

– DERIVATIVES **fac·ile·ly** /ˈfasəl(l)ē/ **adv., fac·ile·ness n.**

– ORIGIN late 15th cent. (in the sense 'easily accomplished'): from French, or from Latin *facilis* 'easy,' from *facere* 'do, make.'

fa·cil·i·tate /fəˈsiliˌtāt/ ▶ **v.** [with obj.] make (an action or process) easy or easier: *schools were located on the same campus to facilitate the sharing of resources.*

– DERIVATIVES **fa·cil·i·ta·tive** /-ˌtātiv/ **adj., fa·cil·i·ta·tor** /-ˌtātər/ **n., fa·cil·i·ta·to·ry** /-təˌtôrē/ **adj.**

– ORIGIN early 17th cent.: from French *faciliter*, from Italian *facilitare*, from *facile* 'easy,' from Latin *facilis* (see FACILE).

fa·cil·i·ta·tion /fəˌsiləˈtāSHən/ ▶ **n.** the action of facilitating something. ■ Physiology the enhancement of the response of a neuron to a stimulus following stimulation.

fa·cil·i·ty /fəˈsilətē/ ▶ **n.** (pl. **facilities**) **1** space or equipment necessary for doing something: *cooking facilities* | *facilities for picnicking, camping, and hiking.* ■ an amenity or resource, esp. one connected with leisure or hygiene: *facilities include two swimming pools.* ■ (**the facilities**) a public toilet. ■ an establishment set up to fulfill a particular function or provide a particular service, typically an industrial or medical one: *a manufacturing facility.* ■ an option or service that gives the opportunity to do or benefit from something: *the program includes a help facility and interactive windows.* **2** [usu. in sing.] an ability to do or learn something well and easily; a natural aptitude: *he had a facility for languages.* ■ absence of difficulty or effort: *the pianist played with great facility.*

– ORIGIN early 16th cent. (denoting the means or unimpeded opportunity for doing something): from French *facilité* or Latin *facilitas*, from *facilis* 'easy' (see FACILE).

fac·ing /ˈfāsiNG/ ▶ **n. 1** a layer of material covering part of a garment and providing contrast, decoration, or strength. ■ (**facings**) the cuffs, collar, and lapels of a military jacket, contrasting in color with the rest of the garment. **2** an outer layer covering the surface of a wall.
▶ **adj.** [attrib.] positioned with the front toward a certain direction; opposite: *a book with Italian and English lyrics printed on facing pages* | [in combination] *a south-facing garden.*

FACP ▶ **abbr.** Fellow of the American College of Physicians.

FACS ▶ **abbr.** Fellow of the American College of Surgeons.

fac·sim·i·le /fakˈsiməlē/ ▶ **n.** an exact copy, esp. of written or printed material. ■ another term for FAX.
▶ **v.** (**facsimiles, facsimileing, facsimiled**) [with obj.] make a copy of: *the ride was facsimiled for Disney World.*

– PHRASES **in facsimile** as an exact copy.

– ORIGIN late 16th cent. (originally as *fac simile*, denoting the making of an exact copy, esp. of writing): modern Latin, from Latin *fac!* (imperative of *facere* 'make') and *simile* (neuter of *similis* 'like').

fact /fakt/ ▶ **n.** a thing that is indisputably the case: *she lacks political experience—a fact that becomes clear when she appears in public* | *a body of fact.* ■ (**the fact that**) used in discussing the significance of something that is the case: *the real problem facing them is the fact that their funds are being cut.* ■ (usu. **facts**) a piece of information used as evidence or as part of a report or news article. ■ chiefly Law the truth about events as opposed to interpretation: *there was a question of fact as to whether they had received the letter.*

– PHRASES **before** (or **after**) **the fact** before (or after) the committing of a crime: *an accessory before the fact.* **a fact of life** something that must be accepted as true and unchanging, even if it is unpleasant: *it is a fact of life that young girls write horrible things about people in their diaries.* **facts and figures** precise details. **the facts of life** information about sexual functions and practices, esp. as given to children. **the fact of the matter** the truth. **in** (**point of**) **fact** used to emphasize the truth of an assertion, esp. one contrary to what might be expected or what has been asserted: *Aunt Madeline isn't in fact an aunt but a more distant relative.*

– ORIGIN late 15th cent.: from Latin *factum*, neuter past participle of *facere* 'do.' The original sense was 'an act or feat,' later 'bad deed, a crime,' surviving in the phrase *before* (*or after*) *the fact.* The earliest of the current senses ('truth, reality') dates from the late 16th cent.

fact-find·ing ▶ **adj.** [attrib.] (esp. of a committee or its activity) having the purpose of discovering and establishing the facts of an issue: *a fact-finding mission.*
▶ **n.** the discovery and establishment of the facts of an issue.

– DERIVATIVES **fact-find·er n.**

fac·tic·i·ty /fakˈtisətē/ ▶ **n.** the quality or condition of being fact: *the facticity of death.*

fac·tion[1] /ˈfakSHən/ ▶ **n.** a small, organized, dissenting group within a larger one, esp. in politics:

f

the left-wing faction of the party. ■ a state of conflict within an organization; dissension.
– ORIGIN late 15th cent. (denoting the action of doing or making something): via French from Latin *factio(n-)*, from *facere* 'do, make.'

fac·tion[2] ▶ **n.** a literary and cinematic genre in which real events are used as a basis for a fictional narrative or dramatization.
– ORIGIN 1960s: blend of FACT and FICTION.

-faction ▶ **comb. form** in nouns of action derived from verbs ending in *-fy* (such as *satisfaction* from *satisfy*).
– ORIGIN from Latin *factio(n)-*, from *facere* 'do, make.'

fac·tion·al /'faksHənl/ ▶ **adj.** relating or belonging to a faction: *factional leaders.* ■ characterized by dissent: *factional conflicts.*
– DERIVATIVES **fac·tion·al·ism** /-,izəm/ **n.**, **fac·tion·al·ly adv.**

fac·tion·al·ize /'faksHənl-īz/ ▶ **v.** [no obj.] (esp. of a political party or other organized group) split or divide into factions: *there was a tendency for students to factionalize.*

fac·tious /'faksHəs/ ▶ **adj.** relating or inclined to a state of faction: *a factious country.*
– DERIVATIVES **fac·tious·ly adv.**, **fac·tious·ness n.**
– ORIGIN mid 16th cent.: from French *factieux* or Latin *factiosus*, from *factio* (see FACTION[1]).

fac·ti·tious /fak'tisHəs/ ▶ **adj.** artificially created or developed: *a largely factitious national identity.*
– DERIVATIVES **fac·ti·tious·ly adv.**, **fac·ti·tious·ness n.**
– ORIGIN mid 17th cent. (in the general sense 'made by human skill or effort'): from Latin *facticius* 'made by art,' from *facere* 'do, make.'

fac·ti·tive /'faktətiv/ ▶ **adj.** Linguistics (of a verb) having a sense of causing a result and taking a complement as well as an object, as in *he appointed me captain.*
– ORIGIN mid 19th cent.: from modern Latin *factitivus*, formed irregularly from Latin *factitare*, frequentative of *facere* 'do, make.'

fac·tive /'faktiv/ ▶ **adj.** Linguistics denoting a verb that assigns the status of an established fact to its object (normally a clausal object), e.g., *know, regret, resent.*

fac·toid /'fak,toid/ ▶ **n.** a brief or trivial item of news or information. ■ an assumption or speculation that is reported and repeated so often that it becomes accepted as fact.

fac·tor /'faktər/ ▶ **n. 1** a circumstance, fact, or influence that contributes to a result or outcome: *his legal problems were not a factor in his decision* | *she worked fast, conscious of the time factor.* ■ Biology a gene that determines a hereditary characteristic: *the Rhesus factor.*
2 a number or quantity that when multiplied with another produces a given number or expression. ■ Mathematics a number or algebraic expression by which another is exactly divisible.
3 Physiology any of a number of substances in the blood, mostly identified by numerals, which are involved in coagulation. See FACTOR VIII.
4 a business agent; a merchant buying and selling on commission. ■ a company that buys a manufacturer's invoices at a discount and takes responsibility for collecting the payments due on them. ■ archaic an agent, deputy, or representative.
▶ **v.** [with obj.] **1** Mathematics another term for FACTORIZE.
2 sell (one's receivable debts) to a factor.
– PHRASES **the —— factor** used to indicate that something specified will have a powerful, though unpredictable, influence on a result or outcome: *the feel-good factor.*
– PHRASAL VERBS **factor something in** (or **out**) include (or exclude) something as a relevant element when making a calculation or decision: *when the psychological costs are factored in, a different picture will emerge.*
– DERIVATIVES **fac·tor·a·ble adj.**
– ORIGIN late Middle English (meaning 'doer, perpetrator,' also in the Scots sense 'agent'): from French *facteur* or Latin *factor*, from *fact-* 'done,' from the verb *facere.*

fac·tor VIII (also **factor eight**) ▶ **n.** Physiology a blood protein (a beta globulin) involved in clotting. A deficiency of this causes one of the main forms of hemophilia.

fac·tor·age /'faktərij/ ▶ **n.** the commission or charges payable to a factor.

fac·tor a·nal·y·sis ▶ **n.** Statistics a process in which the values of observed data are expressed as functions of a number of possible causes in order to find which are the most important.

fac·tor cost ▶ **n.** the cost of an item or a service in terms of the various factors that have played a part in its production or availability, and exclusive of tax costs.

fac·to·ri·al /fak'tôrēəl/ ▶ **n.** Mathematics the product of an integer and all the integers below it; e.g., factorial four (*4!*) is equal to 24. (Symbol: !) ■ the product of a series of factors in an arithmetic progression.
▶ **adj.** chiefly Mathematics relating to a factor or such a product: *a factorial design.*
– DERIVATIVES **fac·to·ri·al·ly adv.**

fac·tor·ize /'faktə,rīz/ ▶ **v.** Mathematics (with reference to a number) resolve or be resolvable into factors.
– DERIVATIVES **fac·tor·i·za·tion** /,faktərə'zāsHən/ **n.**

fac·to·ry /'fakt(ə)rē/ ▶ **n.** (pl. **factories**) **1** a building or group of buildings where goods are manufactured or assembled chiefly by machine. ■ [with modifier] a person, group, or institution that continually produces a great quantity of something specified: *a huge factory of lying, slander, and bad English.*
2 historical an establishment for traders carrying on business in a foreign country.
– ORIGIN late 16th cent. (in sense 2): from medieval Latin *factoria* from Latin *factor* (see FACTOR). Sense 1 from late Latin *factoria*, literally 'oil press.'

fac·to·ry farm·ing ▶ **n.** a system of rearing livestock using intensive methods, by which poultry, pigs, or cattle are confined indoors under strictly controlled conditions.
– DERIVATIVES **fac·to·ry farm n.**

fac·to·ry floor ▶ **n.** the workers in a company or industry, rather than the management: *the unions had almost no influence on the factory floor.*

fac·to·ry out·let ▶ **n.** a store in which goods, esp. surplus stock, are sold directly by the manufacturers at a discount.

fac·to·ry ship ▶ **n.** a fishing or whaling ship, or a ship accompanying a fishing or whaling fleet, with facilities for immediate processing of the catch.

fac·to·tum /fak'tōtəm/ ▶ **n.** (pl. **factotums**) an employee who does all kinds of work: *he was employed as the general factotum.*
– ORIGIN mid 16th cent. (originally in the phrases *dominum* (or *magister*) *factotum*, translating roughly as 'master of everything,' and *Johannes factotem* 'John do-it-all' or 'Jack of all trades'): from medieval Latin, from Latin *fac!* 'do!' (imperative of *facere*) + *totum* 'the whole thing' (neuter of *totus*).

fact sheet ▶ **n.** a sheet of paper giving useful information about a particular issue, esp. one distributed for publicity purposes.

fac·tu·al /'fakCHōōəl/ ▶ **adj.** concerned with what is actually the case rather than interpretations of or reactions to it: *a mixture of comment and factual information.* ■ actually occurring: *cases mentioned are factual.*
– DERIVATIVES **fac·tu·al·i·ty** /,fakCHōō'alitē/ **n.**, **fac·tu·al·ly adv.**, **fac·tu·al·ness n.**
– ORIGIN mid 19th cent.: from FACT, on the pattern of *actual.*

fac·tum /'faktəm/ ▶ **n.** (pl. **factums** /-təmz/ or **facta** /-tə/) Law chiefly Canadian a statement of the facts of a case.
– ORIGIN late 18th cent.: from Latin, literally 'something done or made.'

fac·ture /'fakCHər/ ▶ **n.** the quality of the execution of a painting; an artist's characteristic handling of the paint: *Manet's sensuous facture.*
– ORIGIN late Middle English (in the general sense 'construction, workmanship'): via Old French from Latin *factura* 'formation, manufacture,' from *facere* 'do, make.' The current sense dates from the late 19th cent.

fac·u·la /'fakyələ/ ▶ **n.** (pl. **faculae** /-,lē/) Astronomy a bright region on the surface of the sun, linked to the subsequent appearance of sunspots in the same area. ■ a bright spot on the surface of a planet.
– DERIVATIVES **fac·u·lar** /-lər/ **adj.**
– ORIGIN early 18th cent.: from Latin, diminutive of *fax, fac-* 'torch.'

fac·ul·ta·tive /'fakəl,tātiv/ ▶ **adj.** occurring optionally in response to circumstances rather than by nature: *prison-style, facultative homosexuality.* ■ Biology capable of but not restricted to a particular function or mode of life: *a facultative parasite.* Often contrasted with OBLIGATE.
– DERIVATIVES **fac·ul·ta·tive·ly adv.**
– ORIGIN early 19th cent.: from French *facultatif, -ive*, from *faculté* (see FACULTY).

fac·ul·ty /'fakəltē/ ▶ **n.** (pl. **faculties**) **1** an inherent mental or physical power: *her critical faculties.* ■ an aptitude or talent for doing something: *the author's faculty for philosophical analysis.*
2 the teaching staff of a university or college, or of one of its departments or divisions, viewed as a body: *there were then no tenured women on the faculty* | *the English faculty.* ■ a group of university departments concerned with a major division of knowledge: *the Faculty of Arts and Sciences.* ■ dated the members of a particular profession, esp. medicine, considered collectively.
3 a license or authorization, esp. from a church authority.
– ORIGIN late Middle English: from Old French *faculte*, from Latin *facultas*, from *facilis* 'easy,' from *facere* 'make, do.'

FAD ▶ **abbr.** Biochemistry flavin adenine dinucleotide, a coenzyme derived from riboflavin and important in various metabolic reactions.

fad /fad/ ▶ **n.** an intense and widely shared enthusiasm for something, esp. one that is short-lived and without basis in the object's qualities; a craze: *prairie restoration is the latest gardening fad in the Midwest.*
– DERIVATIVES **fad·dish adj.**, **fad·dish·ly adv.**, **fad·dish·ness n.**, **fad·dism** /-,izəm/ **n.**, **fad·dist** /-ist/ **n.**
– ORIGIN mid 19th cent. (originally dialect): probably the second element of *fidfad*, contraction of FIDDLE-FADDLE.

fade /fād/ ▶ **v.** [no obj.] **1** gradually grow faint and disappear: *the noise faded away* | figurative *hopes of peace had faded.* ■ lose or cause to lose color or brightness: [no obj.] *the fair hair had faded to a dusty gray* | [with obj.] (usu. as adj. **faded**) *faded jeans.* ■ (of a flower) lose freshness and wither. ■ gradually become thin and weak, esp. to the point of death. ■ (of a racehorse, runner, etc.) lose strength or drop back, esp. after a promising start: *she faded near the finish.* ■ (of a radio signal) gradually lose intensity: *the signal faded away.* ■ (of a vehicle brake) become temporarily less efficient as a result of frictional heating.
2 [with adverbial] (with reference to film and television images) come or cause to come gradually into or out of view, or to merge into another shot: [no obj.] *fade into scenes of rooms strewn with festive remains* | [with obj.] *some shots have to be faded in.* ■ (with reference to recorded sound) increase or decrease in volume or merge into another recording: [no obj.] *they let you edit the digital data, making it fade in and out* | [with obj.] *fade up natural sound.*
3 Golf (of the ball) deviate to the right (or, for a left-handed golfer, the left), typically as a result of spin given to the ball. ■ [with obj.] cause (the ball) to move in such a way: *he had to fade the ball around a light pole.* Compare with DRAW (sense 5 of the verb).
4 [with obj.] informal (in craps) match the bet of (another player): *Lovejoy faded him for twenty-five cents.*
▶ **n. 1** the process of becoming less bright: *the sun can cause color-fade.* ■ an act of causing a film or television picture to darken and disappear gradually: *a fade to black would bring the sequence to a close.* Compare with FADE-OUT.
2 Golf a shot causing the ball to deviate to the right (or, for a left-handed golfer, the left), usually purposely.
– PHRASES **do a fade** informal run away.
– PHRASAL VERBS **fade back** Football move back from the scrimmage line.
– DERIVATIVES **fade·less adj.**
– ORIGIN Middle English (in the sense 'grow weak, waste away'; compare with *fade away*): from Old French *fader*, from *fade* 'dull, insipid,' probably based on a blend of Latin *fatuus* 'silly, insipid' and *vapidus* 'vapid.'

fade·a·way /'fādə,wā/ ▶ **adj.** Basketball another term for FALLAWAY.

fade-in ▶ **n.** a filmmaking and broadcasting technique whereby an image is made to appear gradually or the volume of sound is gradually increased from zero.

fade-out ▶ **n.** a filmmaking and broadcasting technique whereby an image is made to disappear gradually or the sound volume is gradually decreased to zero. ■ a gradual and temporary loss of a broadcast signal: *radio fade-outs.*

fad·er /'fādər/ ▶ **n.** a device for varying the volume of sound, the intensity of light, or the gain on a video or audio signal.

fade-up ▶ **n.** an instance of increasing the brightness of an image or the volume of a sound.

fa·do /'fäTHōō/ ▶ **n.** (pl. **fados**) a type of popular Portuguese song, usually with a melancholy theme and accompanied by mandolins or guitars. ■ the music for such a song.
– ORIGIN early 20th cent.: Portuguese, literally 'fate.'

fae·ces ▶ **n.** British spelling of FECES.

fa·er·ie /'ferē/ (also **faery**) ▶ **n.** archaic or literary fairyland: *the world of faerie.* ■ a fairy. ■ [as modifier] imaginary; mythical: *faerie dragons.*
– ORIGIN late 16th cent. (introduced by Spenser): pseudoarchaic variant of FAIRY.

Faer·oe Is·lands /'ferō/ variant spelling of FAROE ISLANDS.

Faer·o·ese /ˌfe(ə)rōˈēz, -ˈēs/ ▶ **adj. & n.** variant spelling of **FAROESE**.

FAF ▶ **abbr.** Financial Aid Form.

fag[1] /fag/ ▶ **n.** [in sing.] informal, chiefly Brit. a tiring or unwelcome task: *it's too much of a fag to drive all the way there and back again.* ■ Brit. a junior pupil at a private preparatory school who works and runs errands for a senior pupil.
▶ **v.** (**fags, fagging, fagged**) [no obj.] Brit. informal work hard, esp. at a tedious job or task: *he didn't have to fag away in a lab to get the right answer.* ■ Brit. (of a pupil at a private preparatory school) work and run errands for a senior pupil.
– ORIGIN mid 16th cent. (as a verb in the sense 'grow weary'): of unknown origin. Compare with **FLAG**[1].

fag[2] ▶ **n.** informal, derogatory a male homosexual.
– DERIVATIVES **fag·gy adj.**
– ORIGIN 1920s: short for **FAGGOT**.

fag[3] ▶ **n.** Brit. informal a cigarette.
– ORIGIN late 19th cent.: elliptically from **FAG END**.

fag end ▶ **n.** informal, chiefly Brit. a cigarette butt. ■ an inferior and useless remnant of something: *the fag ends of rope* | figurative *a culture reaching the fag end of its existence.*
– ORIGIN early 17th cent. (in the sense 'remnant'): from 15th-cent. *fag* 'a flap,' of unknown origin. The sense 'a cigarette butt' dates from the early 20th cent.

fagged /fagd/ ▶ **adj.** [predic.] extremely tired; exhausted: *we were all absolutely fagged out.*

fag·got /ˈfagət/ ▶ **n. 1** informal, chiefly offensive a male homosexual. See usage at **QUEER**.
2 British spelling of **FAGOT**.
– DERIVATIVES **fag·got·y adj.**
– ORIGIN early 20th cent.: perhaps from the obsolete sense of *fagot* 'contemptible woman.'

fag hag ▶ **n.** informal a heterosexual woman who spends much of her time with homosexual men.

fag·ot /ˈfagət/ (Brit. **faggot**) ▶ **n.** a bundle of sticks or twigs bound together as fuel. ■ a bundle of iron rods bound together for reheating, welding, and hammering into bars.

fag·ot·ing /ˈfagətiNG/ (Brit. **faggoting**) ▶ **n.** embroidery in which threads are fastened together in bundles: *a black silk dress with tiers of fagoting.*

Fahd /fäd/ (1921–2005), king of Saudi Arabia 1982–2005; full name *Fahd ibn Abdul-Aziz al-Saud.*

fahl·erz /ˈfälərts/ ▶ **n.** a gray copper ore, of which tetrahedrite and tennantite are the typical minerals.
– ORIGIN late 18th cent.: from German, from *fahl* 'ash-colored' + *Erz* 'ore.'

Fahr. ▶ **abbr.** Fahrenheit.

Fahr·en·heit /ˈfarənˌhīt/ (abbr.: **F**) ▶ **adj.** [postpositive when used with a numeral] of or denoting a scale of temperature on which water freezes at 32° and boils at 212° under standard conditions.
▶ **n.** (also **Fahrenheit scale**) this scale of temperature.
– ORIGIN mid 18th cent.: named after Gabriel Daniel *Fahrenheit* (1686–1736), German physicist.

FAIA ▶ **abbr.** Fellow of the American Institute of Architects.

fa·ience /fīˈäns, fā-/ ▶ **n.** glazed ceramic ware, in particular decorated tin-glazed earthenware of the type that includes delftware and maiolica.
– ORIGIN late 17th cent. (originally denoting pottery made at Faenza, Italy): from French *faïence*, from *Faïence*, the French name for *Faenza.*

fail /fāl/ ▶ **v.** [no obj.] **1** be unsuccessful in achieving one's goal: *he failed in his attempt to secure election* | [with infinitive] *they failed to be ranked in the top ten.* ■ [with obj.] be unsuccessful in (an examination, test, or interview): *she failed her finals.* ■ [with obj.] (of a person or a commodity) be unable to meet the standards set by (a test of quality or eligibility): *the player has failed a drug test.* ■ [with obj.] judge (someone, esp. in an examination) not to have passed.
2 neglect to do something: [with infinitive] *the firm failed to give adequate risk warnings.* ■ [with infinitive] behave in a way contrary to hopes or expectations by not doing something: *commuter chaos has again failed to materialize.* ■ (**cannot fail to be/do something**) used to express a strong belief that something must be the case: *you cannot fail to be deeply impressed.* ■ (**never fail to do something**) used to indicate that something invariably happens: *such comments never failed to annoy him.* ■ [with obj.] desert or let down (someone): *at the last moment her nerve failed her.*
3 break down; cease to work well: *a truck whose brakes had failed.* ■ become weaker or of poorer quality; die away: *the light began to fail* | (as adj. **failing**) *his failing health.* ■ (esp. of a rain or a crop or supply) be lacking or insufficient when needed or expected. ■ (of a business or a person) be obliged to cease trading because of lack of funds; become bankrupt.
▶ **n.** a grade that is not high enough to pass an examination or test.
– PHRASES **without fail** absolutely predictably; with no exception: *he writes every week without fail.*
– ORIGIN Middle English: from Old French *faillir* (verb), *faille* (noun), based on Latin *fallere* 'deceive.' An earlier sense of the noun was 'failure to do or perform a duty,' surviving in the phrase *without fail.*

failed /fāld/ ▶ **adj.** [attrib.] **1** (of an undertaking or a relationship) not achieving its end or not lasting; unsuccessful: *a failed coup attempt.* ■ (of a person) unsuccessful in a particular activity, esp. not good enough to make a living by it: *a failed writer.* ■ (of a business) unable to continue due to financial difficulties.
2 (of a mechanism) not functioning properly; broken-down: *an aircraft with a failed engine.*

fail·ing /ˈfāliNG/ ▶ **n.** a weakness, esp. in character; a shortcoming: *pride is a terrible failing.*
▶ **prep.** in default of; in the absence of: *she longed to be with him and, failing that, to be on her own.*

faille /fīl/ ▶ **n.** a soft, light-woven fabric having a ribbed texture and originally made of silk.
– ORIGIN mid 16th cent. (denoting a kind of hood or veil worn by women): from Old French. The current sense dates from the mid 19th cent.

fail·o·ver /ˈfālˌōvər/ ▶ **n.** Computing a method of protecting computer systems from failure, in which standby equipment automatically takes over when the main system fails.

fail-safe ▶ **adj.** causing a piece of machinery or other mechanism to revert to a safe condition in the event of a breakdown or malfunction: *a forklift with a fail-safe device.* ■ unlikely or unable to fail: *the computer that runs the place is supposed to be fail-safe.*
▶ **n.** [usu. in sing.] a system or plan that comes into operation in the event of something going wrong or that is there to prevent such an occurrence: *the secondary safety system is indeed a fail-safe.*

fail·ure /ˈfālyər/ ▶ **n. 1** lack of success: *an economic policy that is doomed to failure* | *the failures of his policies.* ■ an unsuccessful person, enterprise, or thing: *bad weather had resulted in crop failures.*
2 the omission of expected or required action: *their failure to comply with the basic rules.* ■ a lack or deficiency of a desirable quality: *a failure of imagination.*
3 the action or state of not functioning: *symptoms of heart failure* | *an engine failure.* ■ a sudden cessation of power. ■ the collapse of a business.
– ORIGIN mid 17th cent. (originally as *failer*, in the senses 'nonoccurrence' and 'cessation of supply'): from Anglo-Norman French *failer* for Old French *faillir* (see **FAIL**).

fain /fān/ archaic ▶ **adj.** pleased or willing under the circumstances: *the traveler was fain to proceed.* ■ compelled by the circumstances; obliged: *he was fain to acknowledge that the agreement was sacrosanct.*
▶ **adv.** with pleasure; gladly: *I am weary and would fain get a little rest.*
– ORIGIN Old English *fægen* 'happy, well pleased,' of Germanic origin, from a base meaning 'rejoice'; related to **FAWN**[2].

fai·né·ant /ˈfānēənt/ ▶ **adj.** archaic idle or ineffective.
– ORIGIN early 17th cent.: from French, from *fait* 'does' + *néant* 'nothing.'

faint /fānt/ ▶ **adj. 1** (of a sight, smell, or sound) barely perceptible: *the faint murmur of voices.* ■ (of a hope, chance, or possibility) slight; remote: *there is a faint chance that the enemy may flee.* ■ lacking in strength or enthusiasm; feeble :*the faint beat of a butterfly's wing.*
2 [predic.] weak and dizzy; close to losing consciousness: *the heat made him feel faint.*
▶ **v.** [no obj.] lose consciousness for a short time because of a temporarily insufficient supply of oxygen to the brain. ■ archaic grow weak or feeble; decline: *the fires were fainting.*
▶ **n.** [in sing.] a sudden loss of consciousness: *she hit the floor in a dead faint.*
– PHRASES **not have the faintest** informal have no idea: *I haven't the faintest what it means.*
– DERIVATIVES **faint·ness n.**
– ORIGIN Middle English (sense 2 of the adjective; also in the sense 'cowardly,' surviving in **FAINT HEART**): from Old French *faint*, past participle of *faindre* (see **FEIGN**). Compare with **FEINT**[1].

faint heart ▶ **n.** a person who has a timid or reserved nature.
– PHRASES **faint heart never won fair lady** proverb timidity will prevent you from achieving your objective.

faint-heart·ed ▶ **adj.** lacking courage; timid: *they were feeling faint-hearted at the prospect of war* | (as plural noun **the faint-hearted**) *litigation is not for the faint-hearted.*
– DERIVATIVES **faint-heart·ed·ly adv., faint-heart·ed·ness n.**

faint·ly /ˈfāntlē/ ▶ **adv.** in a faint manner; indistinctly: *she smiled faintly.* ■ [as submodifier] slightly: *his faintly ridiculous hair.*

fair[1] /fe(ə)r/ ▶ **adj. 1** in accordance with the rules or standards; legitimate: *the group has achieved fair and equal representation for all its members.* ■ just or appropriate in the circumstances: *to be fair, this subject poses special problems.* ■ archaic (of a means or procedure) gentle; not violent. ■ Baseball (of a batted ball) within the field of play marked by the first and third baselines. ■ Baseball pertaining to this part of the field: *the ball was hit into fair territory.*
2 (of hair or complexion) light; blond. ■ (of a person) having such a complexion or hair.
3 considerable though not outstanding in size or amount: *he did a fair bit of coaching.* ■ moderately good though not outstandingly so: *he believes he has a fair chance of success.*
4 (of weather) fine and dry. ■ (of the wind) favorable: *they set sail with a fair wind.*
5 archaic beautiful: attractive: *the fairest of her daughters.* ■ (of words, a speech, or a promise) false, despite being initially attractive or pleasing; specious.
▶ **adv. 1** without cheating or trying to achieve unjust advantage: *no one could say he played fair.*
2 [as submodifier] dialect to a high degree: *she'll be fair delighted to see you.*
▶ **n.** archaic a beautiful woman.
▶ **v.** [no obj.] dialect (of the weather) become fine: *looks like it's fairing off some.*
– PHRASES **all's fair in love and war** proverb in certain highly charged situations, any method of achieving your objective is justifiable. **by fair means or foul** using whatever means are necessary: *they were determined to ensure victory for themselves, by fair means or foul.* **fair and square** honestly and straightforwardly: *we won the match fair and square.* **a fair deal** equitable treatment. **fair dinkum** see **DINKUM**. **fair enough** informal used to admit that something is reasonable or acceptable: *"I can't come because I'm working late." "Fair enough."* **fair-to-middling** slightly above average: *she manages to capitalize on some fair-to-middling material.* **fair name** dated a good reputation. **the fair sex** (also **the fairer sex**) dated or humorous women. **fair's fair** informal used to request just treatment or assert that an arrangement is just: *Fair's fair—we were here first.* **for fair** informal, dated completely and finally: *then we'd be rid of him for fair.* **in a fair way to do something** dated having nearly done something, and likely to achieve it: *he is in a fair way to get well.* **it's a fair cop** Brit. an admission that the speaker has been caught doing wrong and deserves punishment. **no fair** informal unfair (often used in or as a petulant protestation): *no fair—we're the only kids in the whole school who don't get to watch TV on school nights.*
– DERIVATIVES **fair·ish adj., fair·ness n.**
– ORIGIN Old English *fæger* 'pleasing, attractive,' of Germanic origin, related to Norwegian *vakker*, 'beautiful.'

fair[2] ▶ **n.** a gathering of stalls and amusements for public entertainment. ■ (also **agricultural fair**) a competitive exhibition of livestock, agricultural products, and household skills held annually by a town, county, or state and also featuring entertainment and educational displays. ■ a periodic gathering for the sale of goods. ■ an exhibition to promote particular products: *the Contemporary Art Fair.*
– ORIGIN Middle English (in the sense 'periodic gathering for the sale of goods'): from Old French *feire*, from late Latin *feria*, singular of Latin *feriae* 'holy days' (on which such fairs were often held).

fair[3] ▶ **v.** [with obj.] (usu. as adj. **faired**) streamline (a vehicle, boat, or aircraft) by adding fairings.
– ORIGIN Old English in the senses 'beautify' and 'appear or become clean' The current sense dates from the mid 19th cent.

Fair·banks[1] /ˈfe(ə)rˌbaNGks/ the second-largest city in Alaska, in the central part of the state, near the junction of the Chena and Tanana rivers; pop. 35,132 (est. 2008).

Fair·banks[2] the name of a family of US actors.
■ **Douglas** (1883–1939); born *Douglas Elton Ulman.* He cofounded United Artists in 1919 and became known for his swashbuckling roles in such silent movies as *The Mark of Zorro* (1920), *Robin Hood* (1922), and *The Thief of Baghdad* (1924). ■ **Douglas, Jr.** (1909–2000); born *Douglas Elton Ulman Fairbanks.* The son of Douglas, several of his roles

were also in the swashbuckling tradition. Notable movies: *The Prisoner of Zenda* (1937), *The Corsican Brothers* (1941), and *That Lady in Ermine* (1948).

fair catch ▶ n. Football a catch of a punt in which a player raises a hand and does not advance the ball.

fair cop·y ▶ n. written or printed matter transcribed or reproduced after final correction.

Fair·fax Coun·ty a county in northeastern Virginia that incorporates many suburbs of Washington, DC; pop. 1,015,302 (est. 2008).

Fair·field /ˈfe(ə)rˌfēld/ **1** a city in north central California, an agricultural processing center; pop. 103,683 (est. 2008).
2 a residential town in southwestern Connecticut; pop. 57,345 (est. 2008).
3 a city in southwestern Ohio, north of Cincinnati; pop. 42,384 (est. 2008).

fair game ▶ n. a person or thing that is considered a reasonable target for criticism, exploitation, or attack.

fair·ground /ˈfe(ə)rˌground/ (often **fairgrounds**) ▶ n. an outdoor area where a fair is held.

fair-haired ▶ adj. **1** having light-colored hair.
2 (of a person) favorite; cherished: *the fair-haired boy of American advertising*.

fair·ies' bon·nets ▶ plural n. a small toadstool with a grooved, yellowish-brown, thimble-shaped cap, growing in large clusters on rotten wood or in soil. ● *Coprinus disseminatus*, family Coprinaceae, class Hymenomycetes.

fair·ing /ˈfe(ə)riNG/ ▶ n. an external metal or plastic structure added to increase streamlining and reduce drag, esp. on a high-performance car, motorcycle, boat, or aircraft.

Fair I·saac Cor·po·ra·tion (abbr.: **FICO**) ▶ n. Finance the largest and best known of several companies that provide software for calculating a person's credit score.

Fair Isle one of the Shetland Islands, about halfway between Orkney and the main Shetland group. ■ [usu. as adj.] traditional multicolored geometric designs used in woolen knitwear: *Fair Isle sweaters*.

fair·lead /ˈfe(ə)rˌlēd/ ▶ n. a ring mounted on a boat or ship to guide a rope, keeping it clear of obstructions and preventing it from being cut or chafed.

fair·ly /ˈfe(ə)rlē/ ▶ adv. **1** with justice: *he could not fairly be accused of wasting police time*.
2 [usu. as submodifier] to quite a high degree: *I was fairly certain she had nothing to do with the affair*. ■ actually (used to emphasize something surprising or extreme): *he fairly snarled at her*.
– PHRASES **fairly and squarely** another term for **FAIR AND SQUARE** (see **FAIR[1]**).

fair-mar·ket val·ue ▶ n. a selling price for an item to which a buyer and seller can agree.

fair-mind·ed ▶ adj. impartial in judgment; just: *a fair-minded employer*.
– DERIVATIVES **fair-mind·ed·ly** adv., **fair-mind·ed·ness** n.

fair·ness doc·trine ▶ n. a former federal policy requiring television and radio broadcasters that presented one side of a controversy to provide the opportunity for opposing points of view to be expressed at no charge.

fair play ▶ n. respect for the rules or equal treatment of all concerned.

fair-spo·ken ▶ adj. archaic (of a person) courteous and pleasant.

fair trade ▶ n. trade in which fair prices are paid to producers in developing countries.

fair-trade a·gree·ment ▶ n. an agreement, typically illegal, between a manufacturer of a trademarked item in the US and its retail distributors to sell the item at a price at or above that designated by the manufacturer.

fair use ▶ n. (in US copyright law) the doctrine that brief excerpts of copyright material may, under certain circumstances, be quoted verbatim for purposes such as criticism, news reporting, teaching, and research, without the need for permission from or payment to the copyright holder.

fair·wa·ter /ˈfe(ə)rˌwôtər, -ˌwätər/ ▶ n. a structure that improves the streamlining of a ship to assist its smooth passage through water.

fair·way /ˈfe(ə)rˌwā/ ▶ n. **1** the part of a golf course between a tee and the corresponding green, where the grass is kept short.
2 a navigable channel in a river or harbor. ■ a regular course or track followed by ships.

fair-weath·er friend ▶ n. a person who stops being a friend in times of difficulty.

fair·y /ˈfe(ə)rē/ ▶ n. (pl. **fairies**) **1** a small imaginary being of human form that has magical powers, esp. a female one.
2 informal, offensive a male homosexual.
▶ adj. belonging to, resembling, or associated with fairies: *fairy gold*.
– DERIVATIVES **fair·y·like** /-līk/ adj.
– ORIGIN Middle English (denoting fairyland, or fairies collectively): from Old French *faerie*, from *fae* 'a fairy,' from Latin *fata* 'the Fates,' plural of *fatum* (see **FATE**). Compare with **FAY**.

fair·y ar·ma·dil·lo ▶ n. a very small burrowing armadillo found in southern South America. ● Genus *Clamyphorus*, family Dasypodidae: two species.

fair·y dust ▶ n. another term for **PIXIE DUST**.

fair·y fly ▶ n. a minute parasitic wasp that lays its eggs in the eggs of other insects. ● Family Mymaridae, order Hymenoptera: numerous genera.

fair·y god·moth·er ▶ n. a female character in some fairy tales who has magical powers and brings unexpected good fortune to the hero or heroine.

fair·y·land /ˈfe(ə)rēˌland/ ▶ n. the imaginary home of fairies. ■ a beautiful or seemingly enchanted place: [as modifier] *a fairyland castle*. ■ an imagined ideal place; a utopia.

fair·y ring ▶ n. a circular area of grass that is darker in color than the surrounding grass due to the growth of certain fungi. They were popularly believed to have been caused by fairies dancing.

fair·y shrimp ▶ n. a small, transparent crustacean that typically swims on its back, using its legs to filter food particles from the water. ● Order Anostraca, class Branchiopoda: many species, including brine shrimps.

fair·y tale (also **fairy story**) ▶ n. a children's story about magical and imaginary beings and lands. ■ [as modifier] denoting something regarded as resembling a fairy story in being magical, idealized, or extremely happy: *a fairy-tale romance*. ■ a fabricated story, esp. one intended to deceive.

fair·y tern ▶ n. a small white tropical tern that lays its single egg on a narrow ledge or on the bare branch of a tree. When it flies against a bright sky, the wings appear somewhat translucent, allowing the bone structure to be seen. ● *Gygis alba*, family Sternidae.

fair·y wren ▶ n. a small Australian songbird with a long cocked tail, the male of which has partly or mainly blue plumage. ● Genus *Malurus*, family Maluridae: several species, in particular the common **superb fairy wren** or blue wren (*M. cyaneus*).

Fai·sal /ˈfīsəl/ the name of two kings of Iraq. ■ **Faisal I** (1885–1933); reigned 1921–33. He was supported by the British and by fervent Arab nationalists. Under his rule, Iraq achieved full independence in 1932. ■ **Faisal II** (1935–58), grandson of Faisal I; reigned 1939–58.He was assassinated in a military coup, after which a republic was established.

Fai·sa·la·bad /ˌfīˌsäləˈbäd, -ˈbad/ an industrial city in Punjab, Pakistan; pop. 2,793,700 (est. 2009). Until 1979 it was known as Lyallpur.

fait ac·com·pli /ˈfet əkämˈplē, ˈfāt/ ▶ n. [in sing.] a thing that has already happened or been decided before those affected hear about it, leaving them with no option but to accept: *the results were presented to shareholders as a fait accompli*.
– ORIGIN mid 19th cent.: from French, literally 'accomplished fact.'

faith /fāTH/ ▶ n. **1** complete trust or confidence in someone or something: *this restores one's faith in politicians*.
2 strong belief in God or in the doctrines of a religion, based on spiritual apprehension rather than proof. ■ a system of religious belief: *the Christian faith*. ■ a strongly held belief or theory: *the faith that life will expand until it fills the universe*.
– PHRASES **break** (or **keep**) **faith** be disloyal (or loyal): *an attempt to make us break faith with our customers*.
– ORIGIN Middle English: from Old French *feid*, from Latin *fides*.

faith-based ▶ adj. affiliated with or based on religion or a religious group: *a faith-based plan that bilked investors out of millions*.

faith·ful /ˈfāTHfəl/ ▶ adj. **1** loyal, constant, and steadfast: *he exhorted them to remain faithful to the principles of Reaganism* | *employees who had notched up decades of faithful service* | (as plural noun **the faithful**) *the struggle to please the party faithful*. ■ (of a spouse or partner) never having a sexual relationship with anyone else: *her husband was faithful to her*. ■ (of an object) reliable: *my faithful compass*.
2 (usu. as plural noun **the faithful**) having a strong belief in a particular religion, esp. Islam.
3 true to the facts or the original: *the rugs they make today remain faithful to their ancestors' methods*.

faith·ful·ly /ˈfāTHfəlē/ ▶ adv. **1** in a loyal manner.
2 in a manner that is true to the facts or the original: *she translated the novel as faithfully as possible*.
– PHRASES **yours faithfully** chiefly Brit. a formula for ending a formal letter to someone whose name you do not know.

faith·ful·ness /ˈfāTHfəlnəs/ ▶ n. the quality of being faithful; fidelity: *faithfulness in marriage*.

faith heal·ing ▶ n. healing achieved by religious belief and prayer, rather than by medical treatment.
– DERIVATIVES **faith heal·er** n.

faith·less /ˈfāTHlis/ ▶ adj. **1** disloyal, esp. to a spouse or partner; untrustworthy: *her faithless lover*.
2 without religious faith.
– DERIVATIVES **faith·less·ly** adv., **faith·less·ness** n.

fa·ji·ta /fəˈhētə/ ▶ n. a dish of Mexican origin consisting of strips of spiced beef or chicken, chopped vegetables, and grated cheese, wrapped in a soft tortilla and often served with sour cream.
– ORIGIN late 20th cent.: Mexican Spanish, literally 'little strip or belt.'

fake[1] /fāk/ ▶ n. a thing that is not genuine; a forgery or sham: *the painting was a fake*. ■ a person who appears or claims to be something that they are not. ■ a pretense or trick: *his excuse for coming was a fake*.
▶ adj. not genuine; counterfeit: *fake designer clothing* | *expressing fake emotions*. ■ (of a person) claiming to be something that one is not: *a fake doctor*.
▶ v. [with obj.] forge or counterfeit (something): *the woman faked her spouse's signature*. ■ pretend to feel or suffer from (an emotion or illness): *he had begun to fake a bad stomachache*. ■ make (an event) appear to happen: *he faked his own death*. ■ accomplish (a task) by improvising: *all the experts agree that you can't fake it*. ■ Music improvise: *he fakes the melody line of a standard tune*.
– DERIVATIVES **fak·er** n., **fak·er·y** /ˈfākərē/ n.
– ORIGIN late 18th cent. (as an adjective; originally slang): origin uncertain; perhaps ultimately related to German *fegen* 'sweep, thrash.' Compare with **FIG[2]**.

fake[2] ▶ n. & v. variant spelling of **FLAKE[4]**.
– ORIGIN late Middle English (as a verb): of unknown origin.

fake bake ▶ n. informal the process of getting a sunless tan, as under sunlamps or by applying a sunless-tanning lotion: *they're advertising reasonable prices for fake bakes*.
▶ v. [no obj.] (usu. **fake-bake**) get a sunless tan: *in the winter months, she likes to fake-bake about once a week*.

fake book ▶ n. Music a book of music containing the basic chord sequences of jazz or other tunes.

fak·ie /ˈfākē/ ▶ n. (pl. **fakies**) (in skateboarding or snowboarding) a movement in which the board is ridden backward.
▶ adv. with such a movement: *once you can do it forward, try it fakie*.

fa·kir /fəˈki(ə)r, ˈfākər/ (also **fakeer, faqir, faquir**) ▶ n. a Muslim (or, loosely, a Hindu) religious ascetic who lives solely on alms.
– ORIGIN early 17th cent.: via French from Arabic *fakīr* 'needy man.'

Fa·la·bel·la /ˌfaləˈbelə/ ▶ n. a horse of a miniature breed, the adult of which does not usually exceed 30 inches (75 cm) in height.
– ORIGIN late 20th cent.: named after Julio *Falabella* (died 1981), an Argentinian breeder.

fa·la·fel /fəˈläfəl/ (also **felafel**) ▶ n. a Middle Eastern dish of spiced mashed chickpeas or other pulses formed into balls or fritters and deep-fried, usually eaten with or in pita bread.
– ORIGIN from colloquial Egyptian Arabic *falāfil*, plural of Arabic *fulful, filfil* 'pepper.'

Fa·lange /fəˈlanj, ˈfāˌlanj/ the Spanish Fascist movement that merged with traditional right-wing elements in 1937 to form the ruling party, the Falange Española Tradicionalista, under General Franco. It was formally abolished in 1977.
– DERIVATIVES **Fa·lan·gism** /-izəm/ n., **Fa·lan·gist** /-jist/ n. & adj.
– ORIGIN Spanish, from Latin *phalanx, phalang-* (see **PHALANX**).

Fa·la·sha /fəˈläsHə/ ▶ n. (pl. **same** or **Falashas**) often offensive a member of a group of people in Ethiopia who hold the Jewish faith but use Ge'ez rather than Hebrew as a liturgical language. The Falashas were not formally recognized as Jews until 1975, and many of them were airlifted to Israel in 1984–85 and after.

– ORIGIN early 18th cent.: Amharic, literally 'exile, immigrant.'

fal·cate /ˈfal,kāt, ˈfôl-/ ▶ **adj.** Botany & Zoology curved like a sickle; hooked: *the mandibles are falcate.*
– ORIGIN early 19th cent.: from Latin *falcatus,* from *falx, falc-* 'sickle.'

fal·cat·ed teal ▶ **n.** a small duck that is native to China and northeastern Asia. ● *Anas falcata,* family Anatidae.
– ORIGIN early 18th cent.: named from the long sickle-shaped inner secondary feathers of the male.

fal·chion /ˈfôlCHən, -SHən/ ▶ **n.** historical a broad, slightly curved sword with the cutting edge on the convex side.
– ORIGIN Middle English *fauchon,* from Old French, based on Latin *falx, falc-* 'sickle.' The *-l-* was added in the 16th cent. to conform with the Latin spelling.

fal·ci·form /ˈfalsə,fôrm/ ▶ **adj.** Anatomy & Zoology curved like a sickle; hooked: *the falciform ligament.*
– ORIGIN mid 18th cent.: from Latin *falx, falc-* 'sickle' + **-IFORM**.

fal·cip·a·rum /falˈsipərəm/ (also **falciparum malaria**) ▶ **n.** the most severe form of malaria, caused by infection with *Plasmodium falciparum*: [as modifier] *the falciparum parasite.*
– ORIGIN 1930s: modern Latin, from Latin *falx, falc-* 'sickle' + *-parum* (from *-parus* 'bearing').

fal·con /ˈfalkən, ˈfôl-/ ▶ **n.** a diurnal bird of prey with long pointed wings and a notched beak, typically catching prey by diving on it from above. Compare with **HAWK**[1] (sense 1 of the noun). ● Family Falconidae, in particular the genus *Falco*: many species, including the peregrine, hobby, merlin, and kestrel.
■ Falconry the female of such a bird, esp. a peregrine. Compare with **TERCEL**.
– ORIGIN Middle English *faucon* (originally denoting any diurnal bird of prey used in falconry): from Old French, from late Latin *falco.* The *-l-* was added in the 15th cent. to conform with the Latin spelling.

fal·con·er /ˈfalkənər, ˈfôl-/ ▶ **n.** a person who keeps, trains, or hunts with falcons, hawks, or other birds of prey.
– ORIGIN late Middle English: from Old French *fauconier,* from *faucon* (see **FALCON**).

fal·co·net /,falkəˈnət, ,fôl-/ ▶ **n. 1** historical a light cannon. [mid 16th cent.: from Italian *falconetto,* diminutive of *falcone* 'falcon,' from Latin *falco* (see **FALCON**).]
2 a very small South Asian (or South American) falcon, typically having bold black-and-white plumage. [mid 19th cent.: from **FALCON** + **-ET**[1].]
● Genus *Microhierax* (and *Spiziapteryx*), family Falconidae: six species.

fal·con·ry /ˈfalkənrē, ˈfôl-/ ▶ **n.** the sport of hunting with falcons or other birds of prey; the keeping and training of such birds.
– ORIGIN late 16th cent.: from French *fauconnerie,* from *faucon* (see **FALCON**).

fal·de·ral ▶ **n.** variant spelling of **FOLDEROL**.

Fal·do /ˈfôldō/, Nick (1957–), English golfer; full name *Sir Nicholas Alexander Faldo.* He won the British Open championship in 1987, 1990, and 1992 and the US Masters in 1989, 1990, and 1996.

fald·stool /ˈfôl(d),sto͞ol/ ▶ **n. 1** a folding chair used by a bishop when not occupying the throne or when officiating in a church other than his own.
2 a small movable folding desk or stool for kneeling at prayer.
– ORIGIN late Old English *fældestōl,* of Germanic origin, from the base of **FOLD**[1] and **STOOL**, influenced by medieval Latin *faldistolium,* from Germanic. Compare with **FAUTEUIL**.

Falk·land Is·lands /ˈfôklənd/ (also **the Falklands**) a group of more than 100 islands in the South Atlantic Ocean, an overseas territory of the UK, about 300 miles (500 km) east of the Strait of Magellan; pop. 3,100 (est. 2008); capital, Stanley (on East Falkland). They were occupied and colonized by Britain in 1832–33, following the expulsion of an Argentine garrison. Argentina has contested British sovereignty and continues to refer to the islands by their old Spanish name, the Malvinas. In 1982, an Argentine invasion led to the Falklands War, which ended in a successful British reoccupation.

Falk·land Is·lands De·pen·den·cies a British overseas territory in the South Atlantic Ocean that consists of the South Sandwich Islands and South Georgia (which is administered from the Falkland Islands).

Falk·lands War an armed conflict between Britain and Argentina in 1982.

> On the orders of Argentina's military junta, Argentine forces invaded the Falkland Islands in support of their claim to sovereignty. In response, Britain sent a task force of ships and aircraft, which forced the Argentine forces to surrender.

fall /fôl/ ▶ **v.** (past **fell** /fel/; past participle **fallen** /ˈfôlən/) [no obj.] **1** move downward, typically rapidly and freely without control, from a higher to a lower level: *bombs could be seen **falling from** the planes* | (as adj. **falling**) *the power lines had been brought down by falling trees.* ■ (**fall off**) become detached accidentally and drop to the ground: *my sunglasses fell off and broke on the pavement.* ■ hang down: *hair that was allowed to fall to the shoulders.* ■ (of land) slope downward; drop away: *the land fell away in a steep bank.* ■ (**fall into**) (of a river) flow or discharge itself into. ■ (of someone's eyes or glance) be directed downward. ■ (of someone's face) show dismay or disappointment by appearing to sag or droop: *her face fell as she thought about her life with George.* ■ occur, arrive, or become apparent as if by dropping suddenly: *when night fell we managed to crawl back to our lines* | *the information might **fall into** the wrong hands.*
2 (of a person) lose one's balance and collapse: *she **fell down** at school today.* ■ throw oneself down, typically in order to worship or implore someone: *they fell on their knees, rendering thanks to God.*
■ (of a tree, building, or other structure) collapse to the ground: *the house looked as if it were going to **fall down** at any moment.* ■ (of a building or place) be captured or defeated: *their mountain strongholds **fell to** enemy attack.* ■ die in battle: *an English leader who had fallen at the hands of the Danes.* ■ archaic commit sin; yield to temptation: *it is their husband's fault if wives do fall.* ■ (of a government or leader) lose office. ■ (in sports) lose or be eliminated from play.
3 decrease in number, amount, intensity, or quality: *in 1987 imports into Britain **fell by** 12 percent* | *we're worried that standards are falling.* ■ find a lower level; subside or abate: *the water table in the Rift Valley fell.* ■ (of a measuring instrument) show a lower reading: *the barometer had fallen a further ten points.*
4 pass into a specified state: *many of the buildings **fell into** disrepair* | *she fell pregnant.* ■ (**fall to doing something**) begin to do something: *he fell to musing about how it had happened.* ■ be drawn accidentally into: *you must not **fall into** this common error.*
■ occur at a specified time: *Mother's birthday fell on Flag Day.* ■ be classified or ordered in the way specified: *canals **fall within** the Minister's brief.*
▶ **n. 1** [usu. in sing.] an act of falling or collapsing; a sudden uncontrollable descent: *his mother had a fall, hurting her leg as she alighted from a train.* ■ a controlled act of falling, esp. as a stunt or in martial arts. ■ Wrestling a move which pins the opponent's shoulders on the ground for a count of three. ■ a state of hanging or drooping downward: *the fall of her hair.* ■ a downward difference in height between parts of a surface: *at the corner of the massif this fall is interrupted by other heights of considerable stature.* ■ a sudden onset or arrival as if by dropping: *the fall of darkness.*
2 a thing that falls or has fallen: *in October came the first thin fall of snow* | *a rock fall.* ■ (usu. **falls**) a waterfall or cascade. ■ chiefly literary a downward turn in a melody: *that strain again, it had a dying fall.* ■ (**falls**) the parts or petals of a flower that bend downward, esp. the outer perianth segments of an iris.
3 a decrease in size, number, rate, or level; a decline: *a big **fall in** unemployment.*
4 a loss of office: *the fall of the government.* ■ the loss of a city or fortified place during battle: *the fall of Jerusalem.* ■ a person's moral descent, typically through succumbing to temptation. ■ (**the Fall** or **the Fall of Man**) the lapse of humankind into a state of sin, ascribed in traditional Jewish and Christian theology to the disobedience of Adam and Eve as described in Genesis.
5 (also **Fall**) autumn.
– PHRASES **fall foul** (or **afoul**) **of** come into conflict with and be undermined by: *any commitment of resources is likely to fall foul of government cash limitations.* **fall in** (or **into**) **line** conform with others or with accepted behavior. [with reference to military formation.] **fall into place** (of a series of events or facts) begin to make sense or cohere: *once he knew what to look for, the theory fell quickly into place.* **fall on stony ground** see **STONY**. **fall over oneself to do something** informal be excessively eager to do something: *critics and audiences fell over themselves to compliment him.* **fall prey to** see **PREY**. **fall short** (**of**) (of a missile) fail to reach its target. ■ figurative be deficient or inadequate; fail to reach a required goal: *the total vote fell short of the required two-thirds majority.* **fall to pieces** see **FALL APART** below. **fall victim to** see **VICTIM**. **take the fall** informal receive blame or punishment, typically in the place of another person.
– PHRASAL VERBS **fall apart** (or **to pieces**) break up, come apart, or disintegrate: *their marriage is likely to fall apart.* ■ (of a person) lose one's capacity to cope: *Angie fell to pieces because she had lost everything.* **fall back** move or turn back; retreat. **fall back on** have recourse to when in difficulty: *they normally fell back on one of three arguments.* **fall behind** fail to keep up with one's competitors. ■ fail to meet a commitment to make a regular payment: *borrowers **falling behind with** their mortgage payments.* **fall down** be shown to be inadequate or false; fail: *the deal fell down partly because there were a lot of unanswered questions.* **fall for** informal **1** be captivated by; fall in love with. **2** be deceived by (something): *he should have known better than to expect Duncan to fall for a cheap trick like that.* **fall in 1** take one's place in a military formation: *the soldiers fell in by the side of the road.* **2** (of a structure) collapse inward. **fall in with 1** meet by chance and become involved with: *he fell in with thieves.* **2** act in accordance with (someone's ideas or suggestions); agree to: *falling in with other people's views.* **fall on** (or **upon**) **1** attack fiercely or unexpectedly: *the army fell on the besiegers.* ■ seize enthusiastically: *she fell on the sandwiches as though she had not eaten in weeks.* **2** (of someone's eyes or gaze) be directed toward: *her gaze fell on the mud-stained coverlet.* **3** (of a burden or duty) be borne or incurred by: *the cost of tuition should not fall on the student.* **fall out 1** (of the hair, teeth, etc.) become detached and drop out. **2** have an argument: *he had **fallen out with** his family.* **3** leave one's place in a military formation, or on parade: *the two policemen at the rear fell out of the formation.* **4** happen; turn out: *matters fell out as Stephen arranged.* **fall through** come to nothing; fail: *the project fell through due to lack of money.* **fall to** (of a task) become the duty or responsibility of: *it fell to me to write to Shephard.* ■ (of property) revert to the ownership of.
– ORIGIN Old English*fallan, feallan,* of Germanic origin; the noun is partly from the verb, partly from Old Norse *fall* 'downfall, sin.'

fal·la·cious /fəˈlāSHəs/ ▶ **adj.** based on a mistaken belief: *fallacious arguments.*
– DERIVATIVES **fal·la·cious·ly** /fəˈlāSHəslē/ **adv.**, **fal·la·cious·ness** /fəˈlāSHəsnəs/ **n.**
– ORIGIN early 16th cent.: from Old French *fallacieux,* from Latin *fallaciosus,* from *fallacia* (see **FALLACY**).

fal·la·cy /ˈfaləsē/ ▶ **n.** (pl. **fallacies**) a mistaken belief, esp. one based on unsound argument: *the notion that the camera never lies is a fallacy.* ■ Logic a failure in reasoning that renders an argument invalid. ■ faulty reasoning; misleading or unsound argument: *the potential for fallacy which lies behind the notion of self-esteem.*
– ORIGIN late 15th cent. (in the sense 'deception, guile'; gradually superseding Middle English *fallace*): from Latin *fallacia,* from *fallax, fallac-* 'deceiving,' from *fallere* 'deceive.'

fal·la·cy of com·po·si·tion ▶ **n.** the error of assuming that what is true of a member of a group is true for the group as a whole.

fal·la·way /ˈfôlə,wā/ ▶ **n.** [usu. as modifier] made or done while moving or falling away, esp. (in basketball) from the basket: *he hit a **fallaway jumper** with five minutes left in the half.*

fall·back /ˈfôl,bak/ ▶ **n. 1** an alternative plan that may be used in an emergency: *teaching was a last resort, a fallback.*
2 a reduction or retreat: *the offering will hit the market after a fallback from record highs.*

Fall Clas·sic ▶ **n.** Baseball a nickname for the World Series.

fall·en /ˈfôlən/ past participle of **FALL**.
▶ **adj.** [attrib.] **1** Theology subject to sin or depravity: *fallen human nature.* ■ dated (of a woman) regarded as having lost her honor through engaging in a sexual relationship outside marriage: *a fallen woman with a checkered past.*
2 (of a soldier) killed in battle: *fallen heroes.*
– DERIVATIVES **fall·en·ness n.**

fall·en an·gel ▶ **n.** (in Christian, Jewish, and Muslim tradition) an angel who rebelled against God and was cast out of heaven.

fall·er /ˈfôlər/ ▶ **n.** a person who fells trees for a living.

fall·fish /ˈfôl,fiSH/ ▶ **n.** (pl. **same** or **fallfishes**) a North American freshwater fish resembling the chub. Also called **corporal**. ● *Semotilus corporalis,* family Cyprinidae.

PRONUNCIATION KEY ə *ago, up;* ər *over, fur;* a *hat;* ā *ate;* ä *car;* e *let;* ē *see;* i *fit;* ī *by;* NG *sing;* ō *go;* ô *law, for;* oi *toy;* o͝o *good;* o͞o *goo;* ou *out;* TH *thin;* T͟H *then;* ZH *vision*

fall guy ▶ **n.** informal a scapegoat: *he contends that he is innocent, that he was set up as a fall guy.*

fal·li·bi·lism /ˈfaləbə,lizəm/ ▶ **n.** Philosophy the principle that propositions concerning empirical knowledge can be accepted even though they cannot be proved with certainty.
– DERIVATIVES **fal·li·bi·list n. & adj.**

fal·li·ble /ˈfaləbəl/ ▶ **adj.** capable of making mistakes or being erroneous: *experts can be fallible.*
– DERIVATIVES **fal·li·bil·i·ty** /,faləˈbilətē/ **n.**, **fal·li·bly** /-blē/ **adv.**
– ORIGIN late Middle English: from medieval Latin *fallibilis*, from Latin *fallere* 'deceive.'

fall·ing-out ▶ **n.** [in sing.] a quarrel or disagreement: *the two of them had a falling-out.*

fall·ing sick·ness ▶ **n.** (**the falling sickness**) archaic term for EPILEPSY.

fall·ing star ▶ **n.** a meteor or shooting star.

f

fall line ▶ **n. 1** a narrow zone that marks the geological boundary between an upland region and a plain, distinguished by the occurrence of falls and rapids where rivers and streams cross it. ■ (**the Fall Line**) (in the US) the zone demarcating the Piedmont from the Atlantic coastal plain.
2 (**the fall line**) Skiing the route leading straight down any particular part of a slope.

fall·off /ˈfôl,ôf/ ▶ **n.** [in sing.] a decrease in something: *even top schools have seen a falloff in applications.*

fal·lo·pi·an tube /fəˈlōpēən/ ▶ **n.** (in a female mammal) either of a pair of tubes along which eggs travel from the ovaries to the uterus.
– ORIGIN early 18th cent.: from *Fallopius*, Latinized form of the name of Gabriello *Fallopio* (1523–62), the Italian anatomist who first described them.

fall·out /ˈfôl,out/ ▶ **n. 1** radioactive particles that are carried into the atmosphere after a nuclear explosion or accident and gradually fall back as dust or in precipitation. ■ [usu. with modifier] airborne substances resulting from an industrial process or accident: *acid fallout from power stations.*
2 the adverse side effects or results of a situation: *almost as dramatic as the financial scale of the mess is the growing political fallout.*

fal·low[1] /ˈfalō/ ▶ **adj. 1** (of farmland) plowed and harrowed but left unsown for a period in order to restore its fertility as part of a crop rotation or to avoid surplus production: *incentives for farmers to let the land lie fallow in order to reduce grain surpluses.* ■ inactive: *long fallow periods when nothing seems to happen.*
2 (of a sow) not pregnant.
▶ **n.** a piece of fallow or uncultivated land.
▶ **v.** [with obj.] leave (land) fallow.
– DERIVATIVES **fal·low·ness n.**
– ORIGIN Old English *fealgian* 'to break up land for sowing,' of Germanic origin; related to Low German *falgen*.

fal·low[2] ▶ **n.** a pale brown or reddish yellow color.
– ORIGIN Old English *falu, fealu*.

fal·low deer ▶ **n.** a Eurasian deer with branched palmate antlers, typically having a white-spotted reddish-brown coat in summer. ● *Cervus dama*, family Cervidae.

Fall Riv·er an industrial city in southeastern Massachusetts, a longtime textile center that is also associated with the Lizzie Borden legend; pop. 90,931 (est. 2008).

Fal·mouth /ˈfalməTH/ a commercial town in southeastern Massachusetts, southwest of Cape Cod, home to the Woods Hole ocean science complex; pop. 33,123 (est. 2008).

false /fôls/ ▶ **adj. 1** not according with truth or fact; incorrect: *the test can produce false results* | *the allegations were false.* ■ not according with rules or law: *false imprisonment.*
2 appearing to be the thing denoted; deliberately made or meant to deceive: *check to see if the trunk has a false bottom* | *a false passport.* ■ artificial: *false eyelashes.* ■ feigned: *a horribly false smile.*
3 illusory; not actually so: *sunscreens give users a false sense of security.* ■ [attrib.] used in names of plants, animals, and gems that superficially resemble the thing properly so called, e.g., **false oat, false killer whale**.
4 treacherous; unfaithful: *a false lover.*
– PHRASES **false position** a situation in which one is compelled to act in a manner inconsistent with one's true nature or principles. **play someone false** deceive or cheat someone.
– DERIVATIVES **false·ly adv.**, **false·ness n.**
– ORIGIN Old English *fals* 'fraud, deceit,' from Latin *falsum* 'fraud,' neuter past participle of *fallere* 'deceive'; reinforced or re-formed in Middle English from Old French *fals, faus* 'false.'

false a·ca·cia ▶ **n.** a tree of the same family as the true acacias (Leguminosae), but of a different genus (*Robinia*), in particular the black locust of North America.

false a·larm ▶ **n.** a false report of a fire to a fire department. ■ a warning given about something that fails to happen.

false bed·ding ▶ **n.** Geology another term for CROSS-BEDDING.

false beech·drops ▶ **n.** see PINESAP.

false card Bridge ▶ **n.** a card played in order to give one's opponents a misleading impression of one's strength in the suit led.
▶ **v.** (**false-card**) [with obj.] play (a card) in such a way.

false col·or ▶ **n.** color added during the processing of a photographic or computer image to aid interpretation of the subject.

false con·scious·ness ▶ **n.** (esp. in Marxist theory) a way of thinking that prevents a person from perceiving the true nature of their social or economic situation.

false cor·al snake ▶ **n.** a harmless snake that mimics the bright coloration of the venomous coral snakes. ● Several genera in the family Colubridae, in particular *Simophis* and *Pliocercus* of South America.

false cy·press ▶ **n.** a conifer of a genus that includes Lawson cypress (see PORT ORFORD CEDAR). ● Genus *Chamaecyparis*, family Cupressaceae.

false dawn ▶ **n. 1** a transient light that precedes the rising of the sun by about an hour.
2 a promising situation that comes to nothing: *the latest signs of an economic recovery could be another false dawn.*

false face ▶ **n.** a mask, usually wooden, traditionally worn ceremonially by some North American Indian peoples to cure the sick.

false friend ▶ **n.** a word or expression that has a similar form to one in a person's native language, but a different meaning (for example English *magazine* and French *magasin* 'shop').
– ORIGIN translating French *faux ami*.

false fruit ▶ **n.** a fruit formed from other parts of the plant as well as the ovary, esp. the receptacle, as occurs in the strawberry or fig. Also called PSEUDOCARP.

false gha·ri·al /ˈgerēəl/ ▶ **n.** a rare, narrow-snouted crocodile that resembles the gharial, native to Indonesia and Malaysia. ● *Tomistoma schlegelii*, family Crocodylidae.

false hel·le·bore /ˈhelə,bôr/ ▶ **n.** a herbaceous plant of the lily family, with pleated leaves and a tall spike of densely packed yellow-green flowers, found in damp soils in north temperate regions. Also called INDIAN POKE. ● Genus *Veratrum*, family Liliaceae: several species, in particular *V. viride* of North America.

false·hood /ˈfôls,ho͝od/ ▶ **n.** the state of being untrue: *the truth or falsehood of the many legends that surround her.* ■ a lie. ■ lying: *the right to sue for malicious falsehood.*

false mem·o·ry ▶ **n.** Psychology an apparent recollection of an event that did not actually occur, esp. one of childhood sexual abuse arising from suggestion during psychotherapy: [as modifier] *false memory syndrome.*

false move ▶ **n.** an unwise or careless action that could have dangerous consequences: *one false move would lead to nuclear war.*

false ox·lip ▶ **n.** see OXLIP.

false preg·nan·cy ▶ **n.** Medicine an abnormal condition in which signs of pregnancy such as amenorrhea, nausea, and abdominal swelling are present in a woman who is not pregnant.

false pre·tens·es ▶ **plural n.** behavior intended to deceive others: *he obtained money by false pretenses.*

false rib ▶ **n.** another term for FLOATING RIB.

false scor·pi·on ▶ **n.** another term for PSEUDOSCORPION.

false start ▶ **n.** an invalid or disallowed start to a race, usually due to a competitor beginning before the official signal has been given. ■ an unsuccessful attempt to begin something.

false step ▶ **n.** [usu. in sing.] a slip or stumble: *one false step and we would have fallen in the sea.* ■ a careless or unwise act; a mistake.

false sun·bird ▶ **n.** a small asity of Madagascar that resembles a sunbird. ● Genus *Neodrepanis*, family Philepittidae: two species.

false teeth ▶ **plural n.** another term for DENTURES (see DENTURE).

false to·paz ▶ **n.** another term for CITRINE.

fal·set·to /fôlˈsetō/ ▶ **n.** (pl. **falsettos**) Music a method of voice production used by male singers, esp. tenors, to sing notes higher than their normal range: *he sang in a piercing falsetto* | *he was singing falsetto in this role.* ■ a singer using this method. ■ a voice or sound that is unusually or unnaturally high.
– ORIGIN late 18th cent.: from Italian, diminutive of *falso* 'false,' from Latin *falsus* (see FALSE).

false vam·pire ▶ **n.** a large carnivorous bat that preys on rodents, reptiles, and other small vertebrates. ● an Old World bat (three species in the family Megadermatidae, including the large Australian ghost bat, *Macroderma gigas*). ● a tropical New World bat (*Vampyrum spectrum*, family Phyllostomidae).

false·work /ˈfôls,wərk/ ▶ **n.** temporary framework structures used to support a building during its construction.

fals·ies /ˈfôlsēz/ ▶ **plural n.** informal pads of material in women's clothing used to increase the apparent size of the breasts.

fal·si·fi·ca·tion /,fôlsəfəˈkāSHən/ ▶ **n.** the action of falsifying information or a theory: *an investigation into fraud and the falsification of records.*

fal·si·fy /ˈfôlsə,fī/ ▶ **v.** (**falsifies, falsifying, falsified**) [with obj.] **1** alter (information or evidence) so as to mislead. ■ forge or alter (a document) fraudulently: (as adj. **falsified**) *falsified documents.*
2 prove (a statement or theory) to be false: *the hypothesis is falsified by the evidence.* ■ fail to fulfill (a hope, fear, or expectation); remove the justification for: *changes falsify individual expectations.*
– DERIVATIVES **fal·si·fi·a·bil·i·ty** /,fôlsə,fīəˈbilətē/ **n.**, **fal·si·fi·a·ble** /,fôlsəˈfīəbəl/ **adj.**
– ORIGIN late Middle English (sense 2): from French *falsifier*, from medieval Latin *falsificare*, from Latin *falsificus* 'making false,' from *falsus* 'false.'

fal·si·ty /ˈfôlsətē/ ▶ **n.** the fact of being untrue, incorrect, or insincere: *he exposed the falsity of the claim.*

Fal·staff·i·an /fôlˈstafēən/ ▶ **adj.** of or resembling Shakespeare's character Sir John Falstaff in being fat, jolly, and debauched: *a Falstaffian gusto for life.*

fal·ter /ˈfôltər/ ▶ **v.** [no obj.] start to lose strength or momentum: *her smile faltered and then faded* | (as adj. **faltering**) *his faltering career.* ■ speak in a hesitant or unsteady voice: [with direct speech] *"I c-c-can't," he faltered.* ■ move unsteadily or in a way that shows lack of confidence: *he faltered and finally stopped in midstride.*
– DERIVATIVES **fal·ter·er n.**, **fal·ter·ing·ly adv.**
– ORIGIN late Middle English (in the senses 'stammer' and 'stagger').

Fa·lun Gong /ˈfälo͞on ˈgo͝oNG, ˈgäNG/ (also **Falun Dafa** /ˈfälo͞on ˈdäfä/) **n.** a spiritual exercise and meditation regime with similarities to t'ai chi ch'uan, practiced predominantly in China. ■ a Taoist-Buddhist sect practicing Falun Gong.
– ORIGIN 1990s: Chinese, literally 'wheel of law,' from *fǎ* 'law' + *lún* 'wheel' (+ *gōng* 'skill' or *dà fǎ* 'great method').

Fal·well /ˈfôl,wel/, Jerry Lamon, Sr. (1933–2007), US Baptist clergyman. He was the founder and president of the Moral Majority conservative political action group 1979–89.

FAM ▶ **abbr.** the Family Channel.

fam. ▶ **abbr.** ■ familiar. ■ family.

fame /fām/ ▶ **n.** the condition of being known or talked about by many people, esp. on account of notable achievements: *winning the Olympic title has brought her fame and fortune.*
– PHRASES **fifteen minutes of fame** see FIFTEEN. **of —— fame** having a particular famous association; famous for having or being ——: *the Cariboo country of gold rush fame.*
– ORIGIN Middle English (also in the sense 'reputation,' which survives in the phrase *house of ill fame*): via Old French from Latin *fama*.

famed /fāmd/ ▶ **adj.** known about by many people; renowned: *he is famed for his eccentricities.* ■ archaic widely reported or rumored.
– ORIGIN Middle English: past participle of archaic *fame* (verb), from Old French *famer*, from Latin *fama*.

fa·mil·ia /fəˈmilyə, -ˈmilēə/ ▶ **n.** (pl. **familiae** /-ˈmilē,ē, -ē,ī/) historical a household or religious community under one head, regarded as a unit.
– ORIGIN early 18th cent.: Latin, literally 'family, household.'

fa·mil·ial /fəˈmilēəl, -ˈmilyəl/ ▶ **adj.** of, relating to, or occurring in a family or its members: *the familial Christmas dinner.*
– ORIGIN early 20th cent.: from French, from Latin *familia* 'family.'

fa·mil·iar /fəˈmilyər/ ▶ **adj. 1** well known from long or close association: *their faces will be **familiar to** many of you | a familiar voice.* ■ often encountered or experienced; common: *the situation was all too familiar.* ■ [predic.] (**familiar with**) having a good knowledge of: *ensure that you are familiar with the heating controls.*
2 in close friendship; intimate: *she had not realized they were on such familiar terms.* ■ informal to an inappropriate degree.
▶ **n. 1** (also **familiar spirit**) a demon supposedly attending and obeying a witch, often said to assume the form of an animal.
2 (in the Roman Catholic Church) a person rendering certain services in a pope's or bishop's household.
3 a close friend or associate.
– DERIVATIVES **fa·mil·iar·ly adv.**
– ORIGIN Middle English (in the sense 'intimate,' 'on a family footing'): from Old French *familier*, from Latin *familiaris*, from *familia* 'household servants, household, family,' from *famulus* 'servant.'

fa·mil·iar·i·ty /fəˌmilēˈaritē, -milˈyar-/ ▶ **n.** (pl. **familiarities**) close acquaintance with or knowledge of something: *increase customer **familiarity with** a product.* ■ the quality of being well known; recognizability based on long or close association: *the reassuring familiarity of his parents' home.* ■ relaxed friendliness or intimacy between people: *familiarity allows us to give each other nicknames.* ■ inappropriate and often offensive informality of behavior or language: *the unnecessary familiarity made me dislike him at once.*
– PHRASES **familiarity breeds contempt** proverb extensive knowledge of or close association with someone or something leads to a loss of respect for them or it.
– ORIGIN Middle English (in the senses 'close relationship' and 'sexual intimacy'): via Old French from Latin *familiaritas*, from *familiaris* 'familiar, intimate' (see FAMILIAR).

fa·mil·iar·ize /fəˈmilyəˌrīz/ ▶ **v.** [with obj.] give (someone) knowledge or understanding of something: *to **familiarize** pupils **with** the microscope and its uses.* ■ make (something) better known or more easily grasped: *exercises which will help to familiarize the terms used.*
– DERIVATIVES **fa·mil·iar·i·za·tion** /fəˌmilyərəˈzāSHən/ **n.**

Fam·i·list /ˈfaməlist/ ▶ **n.** a member of the Christian sect of the 16th and 17th centuries called the Family of Love, which asserted the importance of love and the necessity for absolute obedience to any government.

fam·i·list /ˈfaməlist/ ▶ **adj.** of, relating to, or advocating a social framework centered on family relationships rather than on the needs of the individual.
– DERIVATIVES **fam·i·lism** /-izəm/ **n.**, **fam·i·lis·tic** /ˌfaməˈlistik/ **adj.**

fa·mille /fäˈmē(ə)/ ▶ **n.** Chinese enameled porcelain of particular periods in the 17th and 18th centuries with a predominant color, **famille jaune** (yellow), **famille noire** (black), **famille rose** (red), **famille verte** (green).
– ORIGIN late 19th cent.: French, literally 'family.'

fam·i·ly /ˈfam(ə)lē/ ▶ **n.** (pl. **families**) **1** [treated as sing. or pl.] a group consisting of parents and children living together in a household. ■ a group of people related to one another by blood or marriage: *friends and family can provide support.* ■ the children of a person or couple: *she has the sole responsibility for a large family.* ■ a person or people related to one and so to be treated with a special loyalty or intimacy: *I could not turn him away, for he was family.* ■ a group of people united in criminal activity. ■ Biology a principal taxonomic category that ranks above genus and below order, usually ending in *-idae* (in zoology) or *-aceae* (in botany). ■ a group of objects united by a significant shared characteristic. ■ Mathematics a group of curves or surfaces obtained by varying the value of a constant in the equation generating them.
2 all the descendants of a common ancestor: *the house has been owned by the same family for 300 years.* ■ a race or group of peoples from a common stock. ■ all the languages ultimately derived from a particular early language, regarded as a group: *the Austronesian language family.*
▶ **adj.** [attrib.] designed to be suitable for children as well as adults: *a family newspaper.*
– PHRASES **the** (or **one's**) **family jewels** informal a man's genitals. **in the family way** informal pregnant.
– ORIGIN late Middle English (sense 2 of the noun): from Latin *familia* 'household servants, household, family,' from *famulus* 'servant.'

fam·i·ly Bi·ble ▶ **n.** a Bible designed to be used at family prayers, typically one with space on its flyleaves for recording important family events.

fam·i·ly court ▶ **n.** Law a court of law that handles cases involving domestic issues such as divorce, child custody, etc.

fam·i·ly doc·tor (also **family practitioner**) ▶ **n.** another term for GENERAL PRACTITIONER.

fam·i·ly hour ▶ **n.** a period in the evening during which many children and their families watch television, esp. 8 to 9 p.m.: *the rise in the amount of sex and profanity, as well as violence, in the family hour does American families a disservice.*

fam·i·ly leave ▶ **n.** an excused absence from work for the purpose of dealing with family matters, esp. the birth or adoption of a child or to care for a sick parent or spouse.

fam·i·ly man ▶ **n.** a man who lives with his wife and children, esp. one who enjoys home life.

fam·i·ly med·i·cine ▶ **n.** the branch of medicine designed to provide basic health care to all the members of a family.

fam·i·ly name ▶ **n.** a surname. ■ a family's good reputation: *he won't disgrace the family name.*

fam·i·ly plan·ning ▶ **n.** [often as modifier] the practice of controlling the number of children in a family and the intervals between their births, particularly by means of artificial contraception or voluntary sterilization: *family-planning clinics.* ■ artificial contraception.

fam·i·ly style ▶ **adj. 1** designating a style of preparation or serving of food in which diners help themselves from plates of food that have been put on the table: *a family-style Italian restaurant.*
2 suitable for an entire family, including children: *family-style entertainment.*
▶ **adv.** with plates of food from which individual diners can serve themselves: *spaghetti served in a huge bowl, family style.*

fam·i·ly tree ▶ **n.** a diagram showing the relationships between people in several generations of a family; a genealogical tree.

fam·i·ly val·ues ▶ **plural n.** values held to be traditionally learned or reinforced within a family, such as those of high moral standards and discipline.

fam·ine /ˈfamən/ ▶ **n.** extreme scarcity of food: *drought could result in famine throughout the region | the famine of 1921–22.* ■ a shortage: *the cotton famine of the 1860s.* ■ archaic hunger.
– ORIGIN late Middle English: from Old French, from *faim* 'hunger,' from Latin *fames.*

fam·ished /ˈfamiSHt/ ▶ **adj.** informal extremely hungry.
– ORIGIN late Middle English: past participle of the verb *famish*, from Middle English *fame* 'starve,' from Old French *afamer*, based on Latin *fames* 'hunger.'

fa·mous /ˈfāməs/ ▶ **adj.** known about by many people: *the country is **famous for** its natural beauty | a famous star.*
– PHRASES **famous for being famous** having no recognizable or distinct reason for one's fame other than high media exposure. **famous last words** said as an ironic comment on or reply to an overconfident assertion that may well be proved wrong by events: *"I'll be perfectly OK on my own." "Famous last words," she thought to herself.*
– DERIVATIVES **fa·mous·ness n.**
– ORIGIN late Middle English: from Old French *fameus*, from Latin *famosus* 'famed,' from *fama* (see FAME).

fa·mous·ly /ˈfāməslē/ ▶ **adv. 1** informal excellently: *he wasn't difficult at all—we **got on famously**.*
2 indicating that the fact asserted is widely known: *they have famously reclusive lifestyles.*

fam·u·lus /ˈfamyələs/ ▶ **n.** (pl. **famuli** /-ˌlē, -ˌlī/) historical an assistant or servant, esp. one working for a magician or scholar.
– ORIGIN mid 19th cent.: from Latin, 'servant.'

Fan /fan, fän/ ▶ **n. & adj.** variant spelling of FANG.

fan[1] /fan/ ▶ **n. 1** an apparatus with rotating blades that creates a current of air for cooling or ventilation.
2 a device, typically folding and shaped like a segment of a circle when spread out, that is held in the hand and waved so as to cool the person holding it by causing the air to move. ■ a thing or shape resembling such a device when open. ■ an alluvial or talus deposit spread out in such a shape at the foot of a slope. ■ a small sail for keeping the head of a windmill toward the wind.

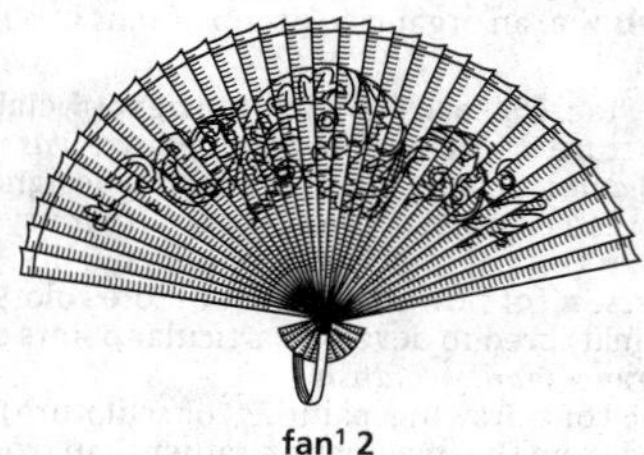
fan[1] 2

3 a device for winnowing grain.
▶ **v.** (**fans, fanning, fanned**) **1** [with obj.] cool (esp. a person or a part of the body) by waving something to create a current of air: *he fanned himself with his hat.* ■ (of breath or a breeze) blow gently on: *his breath fanned her skin as he leaned toward her.* ■ [with obj.] brush or drive away with a waving movement: *a veil of smoke which she **fanned away** with a jeweled hand.* ■ [no obj.] Baseball & Ice Hockey swing at and miss the ball or puck. ■ [no obj.] Baseball (of a batter) strike out. ■ Baseball (of a pitcher) strike out (a batter).
2 [with obj.] increase the strength of (a fire) by blowing on it or stirring up the air near it: *gusty wind fanned fires in Yellowstone Park.* ■ cause (a belief or emotion) to become stronger or more widespread: *long-range weather forecasts fanned fears of drought damage.*
3 [no obj.] disperse or radiate from a central point to cover a wide area: *the arriving passengers began to **fan out** through the town in search of lodgings.* ■ spread out or cause to spread out into a semicircular shape: [no obj.] *a dress made of tiny pleats that **fanned out** as she walked* | [with obj.] *a wind **fanned** her hair **out** behind her.*
– DERIVATIVES **fan·like** /-ˌlīk/ **adj.**, **fan·ner n.**
– ORIGIN Old English *fann* (as a noun denoting a device for winnowing grain), *fannian* (verb), from Latin *vannus* 'winnowing fan.' Compare with VANE.

fan[2] ▶ **n.** a person who has a strong interest in or admiration for a particular sport, art form, or famous person: *football fans | I'm a fan of this author.*
– DERIVATIVES **fan·dom** /ˈfandəm/ **n.**
– ORIGIN late 19th cent. (originally US): abbreviation of FANATIC.

fa·nat·ic /fəˈnatik/ ▶ **n.** a person filled with excessive and single-minded zeal, esp. for an extreme religious or political cause. ■ [often with modifier] informal a person with an obsessive interest in and enthusiasm for something, esp. an activity: *a fitness fanatic.*
▶ **adj.** [attrib.] filled with or expressing excessive zeal: *his fanatic energy.*
– DERIVATIVES **fa·nat·i·cize** /fəˈnatəˌsīz/ **v.**
– ORIGIN mid 16th cent. (as an adjective): from French *fanatique* or Latin *fanaticus* 'of a temple, inspired by a god,' from *fanum* 'temple.' The adjective originally described behavior or speech that might result from possession by a god or demon, hence the earliest sense of the noun 'a religious maniac' (mid 17th cent).

fa·nat·i·cal /fəˈnatikəl/ ▶ **adj.** filled with excessive and single-minded zeal: *fanatical revolutionaries.* ■ obsessively concerned with something: *he was **fanatical about** security at night.*
– DERIVATIVES **fa·nat·i·cal·ly** /-(ə)lē/ **adv.**

fa·nat·i·cism /fəˈnatəˌsizəm/ ▶ **n.** the quality of being fanatical: *the dangers of religious fanaticism.*

fan base ▶ **n.** the fans of a sports team, pop music group, etc., considered as a distinct social grouping.

fan belt ▶ **n.** (in a motor-vehicle engine) a belt that transmits motion from the driveshaft to the radiator fan and the generator or alternator.

fan·boy /ˈfanˌboi/ ▶ **n.** informal, derogatory a male fan, esp. one who is obsessive about movies, comic books, or science fiction.

fan·ci·er /ˈfansēər/ ▶ **n.** [with modifier] a connoisseur or enthusiast of something, esp. someone who has a special interest in or breeds a particular animal: *a pigeon fancier.*

fan·ci·ful /ˈfansəfəl/ ▶ **adj.** (of a person or their thoughts and ideas) overimaginative and unrealistic: *a fanciful story about a pot of gold.* ■ existing only in the imagination or fancy: *the Moon Maiden is one of a number of fanciful lunar inhabitants.* ■ designed to be exotically ornamental rather than practical: *fanciful bonnets.*

f

–DERIVATIVES **fan·ci·ful·ly** /-f(ə)lē/ **adv.**, **fan·ci·ful·ness n.**

fan club ▶ **n.** an organized group of fans of a famous person.

fan·cy /ˈfansē/ ▶ **adj.** (**fancier**, **fanciest**) **1** elaborate in structure or decoration: *the furniture was very fancy* | *a fancy computerized system.* ■ designed to impress: *converted fishing boats with fancy new names.* ■ (esp. of foodstuffs) of high quality: *fancy molasses.* ■ (of flowers) of two or more colors. ■ (of an animal) bred to develop particular points of appearance: *fancy goldfish.*
2 archaic (of a drawing, painting, or sculpture) created from the imagination rather than from life.
▶ **v.** (**fancies**, **fancying**, **fancied**) [with obj.] **1** feel a desire or liking for: *do you fancy a drink?* ■ find sexually attractive: *he saw a woman he fancied.* ■ (**fancy oneself**) informal have an unduly high opinion of oneself, or of one's ability in a particular area: *he fancied himself an amateur psychologist.*
2 [with clause] imagine; think: *he fancied he could smell the perfume of roses.* ■ [in imperative] used to express one's surprise at something: *fancy meeting all those television actors!*
▶ **n.** (pl. **fancies**) **1** a feeling of liking or attraction, typically one that is superficial or transient: *this does not mean that the law should change with every passing fancy.*
2 the faculty of imagination: *my research assistant is prone to flights of fancy.* ■ a thing that one supposes or imagines, typically an unfounded or tentative belief or idea; notion or whim: *scientific fads and fancies.*
3 (in sixteenth and seventeenth cent. music) a composition for keyboard or strings in free or variation form.
–PHRASES **as** (or **when** or **where**) **the fancy takes one** according to one's inclination: *I shall go where the fancy takes me.* **take** (or **catch**) **someone's fancy** appeal to someone: *she'll grab any toy that takes her fancy.* **take a fancy to** become fond of, esp. without an obvious reason.
–DERIVATIVES **fan·ci·ly** /ˈfansəlē/ **adv.**, **fan·ci·ness n.**
–ORIGIN late Middle English: contraction of FANTASY.

fan·cy dress ▶ **n.** an unusual or amusing costume worn to make someone look like a famous person, fictional character, or an animal, esp. as part of a theme at a party.

fan·cy-free ▶ **adj.** free from emotional involvement or commitment to anyone: *her recent divorce meant that she was footloose and fancy-free.*

fan·cy goods ▶ **plural n.** dated items for sale that are purely or chiefly ornamental.

fan·cy man ▶ **n.** dated a woman's lover. ■ archaic a pimp.

fan·cy-pants ▶ **adj.** informal superior or high-class in a pretentious way: *a fancy-pants restaurant.*

fan·cy wom·an ▶ **n.** dated a married man's mistress.

fan·cy·work /ˈfansē,wərk/ ▶ **n.** ornamental needlework, crochet, or knitting, as opposed to plain or purely functional stitches.

fan dance ▶ **n.** a dance in which the female performer is apparently nude and remains partly concealed throughout by large fans.

fan·dan·go /fanˈdaNGgō/ ▶ **n.** (pl. **fandangoes** or **fandangos**) **1** a lively Spanish dance for two people, typically accompanied by castanets or tambourine.
2 a foolish or useless act or thing: *the Washington inaugural fandango.*
–ORIGIN mid 18th cent.: Spanish, of unknown origin.

fane /fān/ ▶ **n.** archaic a temple or shrine.
–ORIGIN late Middle English: from Latin *fanum.*

Fan·euil /ˈfanyəl, ˈfanl/, Peter (1700–43), US merchant. He donated the building known as Faneuil Hall to the city of Boston in 1742.

fan·fare /ˈfan,fer/ ▶ **n.** a short ceremonial tune or flourish played on brass instruments, typically to introduce something or someone important. ■ media attention or elaborate ceremony: *he turned 25 on Saturday with little fanfare.*
–ORIGIN mid 18th cent.: from French, ultimately of imitative origin.

fan·fa·ron·ade /,fan,farəˈnād/ ▶ **n.** arrogant or boastful talk.
–ORIGIN mid 17th cent.: from French *fanfaronnade*, from *fanfaron* 'braggart,' from *fanfare* (see FANFARE).

fan fic·tion (also informal **fanfic**) ▶ **n.** fiction written by a fan of, and featuring characters from, a particular TV series, movie, etc.

Fang /faNG, fäNG/ (also **Fan** /fan, fän/) ▶ **n.** (pl. **same** or **Fangs**) **1** a member of a people inhabiting parts of Cameroon, Equatorial Guinea, and Gabon.
2 the Bantu language of this people.
▶ **adj.** of or relating to this people or their language.
–ORIGIN French, probably from Fang *Pangwe.*

fang /faNG/ ▶ **n.** a large, sharp tooth, esp. a canine tooth of a dog or wolf. ■ the tooth of a venomous snake, by which poison is injected. ■ the biting mouthpart of a spider.
–DERIVATIVES **fanged adj.**, **fang·less adj.**
–ORIGIN late Old English (denoting booty or spoils), from Old Norse *fang* 'capture, grasp'; compare with VANG. A sense 'trap, snare' is recorded from the mid 16th cent.; both this and the original sense survive in Scots. The current sense (also mid 16th cent.) reflects the same notion of 'something that catches and holds.'

fang

fan·girl /ˈfan,gərl/ ▶ **n.** informal, derogatory an obsessive female fan (usually of movies, comic books, or science fiction).
–ORIGIN from FAN[2] + GIRL.

fan·go /ˈfaNGgō/ ▶ **n.** [usu. as modifier] mud from thermal springs in Italy, used in curative treatment at spas and health clubs: *fango therapies.*
–ORIGIN early 20th cent.: Italian, literally 'mud.'

fan-in ▶ **n.** Electronics the number of inputs that can be connected to a circuit.

fan·jet /ˈfan,jet/ ▶ **n.** another term for TURBOFAN.

fan·light /ˈfan,līt/ ▶ **n.** a small semicircular or rectangular window over a door or another window.

fanlight

fan mail ▶ **n.** letters from fans to a famous person they admire.

Fan·nie Mae /ˈfanē ˈmā/ informal name for the Federal National Mortgage Association, a corporation that trades in mortgages.
–ORIGIN 1940s: elaboration of the acronym FNMA, suggested by the given names *Fanny* and *Mae.* Compare with FREDDIE MAC.

fan·ny /ˈfanē/ ▶ **n.** (pl. **fannies**) **1** informal a person's buttocks.
2 Brit. vulgar slang a woman's genitals.
–ORIGIN late 19th cent.: of unknown origin.

fan·ny pack ▶ **n.** a small pouch on a belt, for money and small articles, worn around the waist or hips.

fan-out ▶ **n.** Electronics the number of inputs that can be connected to a specified output.

fan palm ▶ **n.** a palm with large, lobed, fan-shaped leaves. ● *Chamaerops* and other genera, family Palmae: many species, including the **dwarf** (or **European**) **fan palm** (*C. humilis*), which is the only palm native to Europe.

fan·tab·u·lous /fanˈtabyələs/ ▶ **adj.** informal excellent; wonderful: *a fantabulous prize.*
–ORIGIN 1950s: blend of FANTASTIC and FABULOUS.

fan·tail /ˈfan,tāl/ ▶ **n.** a fan-shaped tail or end. ■ the rounded overhanging part of the stern of a vessel, esp. a warship. ■ (also **fantail pigeon**) a domestic pigeon of a broad-tailed variety. ■ the fan of a windmill.
–DERIVATIVES **fan-tailed adj.**

fan-tan ▶ **n. 1** a Chinese gambling game in which players try to guess the remainder after the banker has divided a number of hidden objects into four groups.
2 a card game in which players build on sequences of sevens.
–ORIGIN late 19th cent.: from Chinese *fān tān*, literally 'repeated divisions.'

fan·ta·sia /fanˈtāZHə, fantəˈzēə/ ▶ **n.** a musical composition with a free form and often an improvisatory style. ■ a musical composition that is based on several familiar tunes. ■ a thing that is composed of a mixture of different forms or styles: *the theater is a kind of Moorish and Egyptian fantasia.*
–ORIGIN early 18th cent.: from Italian, 'fantasy,' from Latin *phantasia* (see FANTASY).

fan·ta·size /ˈfantə,sīz/ ▶ **v.** [no obj.] indulge in daydreaming about something desired: *he sometimes fantasized about emigrating.* ■ [with obj.] imagine (something that one wants to happen): *they sometimes fantasize the destruction of the world.*
–DERIVATIVES **fan·ta·sist** /-sist/ **n.**

fan·tast /ˈfan,tast/ (also **phantast**) ▶ **n.** an impractical, impulsive person; a dreamer.
–ORIGIN late 16th cent.: originally via medieval Latin from Greek *phantastēs* 'boaster,' from *phantazein* or *phantazesthai* (see FANTASTIC); in modern use from German *Phantast.*

fan·tas·tic /fanˈtastik/ ▶ **adj. 1** imaginative or fanciful; remote from reality: *novels are capable of mixing fantastic and realistic elements.* ■ of extraordinary size or degree: *the prices were fantastic, far higher than elsewhere.* ■ (of a shape or design) bizarre or exotic; seeming more appropriate to a fairy tale than to reality or practical use: *visions of a fantastic, mazelike building.*
2 informal extraordinarily good or attractive: *your support has been fantastic.*
–DERIVATIVES **fan·tas·ti·cal adj.** (sense 1), **fan·tas·ti·cal·i·ty** /,fan,tastəˈkalitē/ **n.** (sense 1), **fan·tas·ti·cal·ly** /-(ə)lē/ **adv.**
–ORIGIN late Middle English (in the sense 'existing only in the imagination, unreal'): from Old French *fantastique*, via medieval Latin from Greek *phantastikos*, from *phantazein* 'make visible,' *phantazesthai* 'have visions, imagine,' from *phantos* 'visible.' From the 16th to the 19th centuries the Latinized spelling *phantastic* was also used.

fan·tas·ti·cate /fanˈtasti,kāt/ ▶ **v.** [with obj.] rare make (something) seem fanciful or fantastic: *I do not think I have fantasticated these accounts.*
–DERIVATIVES **fan·tas·ti·ca·tion** /,fan,tastiˈkāSHən/ **n.**

fan·ta·sy /ˈfantəsē/ ▶ **n.** (pl. **fantasies**) **1** the faculty or activity of imagining things, esp. things that are impossible or improbable: *his research had moved into the realm of fantasy.* ■ the product of this faculty or activity: *the scene is clearly fantasy.* ■ a fanciful mental image, typically one on which a person dwells at length or repeatedly and which reflects their conscious or unconscious wishes: *the notion of being independent is a child's ultimate fantasy.* ■ an idea with no basis in reality: *it is a misleading fantasy to suggest that the bill can be implemented.* ■ a genre of imaginative fiction involving magic and adventure, esp. in a setting other than the real world.
2 a musical composition, free in form, typically involving variation on an existing work or the imaginative representation of a situation or story; a fantasia.
▶ **v.** (**fantasies**, **fantasying**, **fantasied**) [with obj.] literary imagine the occurrence of; fantasize about.
–ORIGIN late Middle English: from Old French *fantasie*, from Latin *phantasia*, from Greek, 'imagination, appearance,' later 'phantom,' from *phantazein* 'make visible.' From the 16th to the 19th centuries the Latinized spelling *phantasy* was also used.

fan·ta·sy foot·ball ▶ **n.** a competition in which participants select imaginary teams from among the players in a league and score points according to the actual performance of their players.

fan·ta·sy·land /ˈfantəsē,land/ ▶ **n.** a place that is unreal or imaginary or that excites wonder: *living in a fantasyland of endless prosperity and happiness* | [as modifier] *the restaurant is famous for its fantasyland decor of twinkling lights and glitzy mirrors.*

Fan·te /ˈfäntē, ˈfantē/ (also **Fanti**) ▶ **n.** (pl. **same** or **Fantis** /-tēz/) **1** a member of a people of southern Ghana.
2 the dialect of Akan spoken by this people.
▶ **adj.** of or relating to this people or their language.
–ORIGIN the name in Akan.

fan·tod /ˈfan,täd/ ▶ **n.** informal a state or attack of uneasiness or unreasonableness: *the mumbo-jumbo gave me the fantods.*
–ORIGIN mid 19th cent.: of unknown origin.

fan vault ▶ **n.** Architecture a type of vault consisting of a set of concave ribs spreading out from a central point like the ribs of an opened umbrella, used esp. in the English Perpendicular style.
–DERIVATIVES **fan vault·ing n.**

fan worm ▶ **n.** a tube-dwelling marine bristle worm that bears a fanlike crown of filaments that are typically brightly colored and project from the top of the tube, filtering the water for food particles. ● Families Sabellidae and Serpulidae, class Polychaeta: numerous species.

fan·zine /ˈfan,zēn, fanˈzēn/ ▶ **n.** a magazine, usually produced by amateurs, for fans of a particular performer, group, or form of entertainment.
–ORIGIN 1940s (originally US): blend of FAN[2] and MAGAZINE.

FAO ▶ **abbr.** ■ Food and Agriculture Organization. ■ for the attention of.

FAQ ▶ **n.** Computing a list of questions and answers relating to a particular subject, esp. one giving basic information for users of a website.
–ORIGIN 1990s: acronym from *frequently asked questions.*

fa·quir ▶ **n.** variant spelling of FAKIR.

far /fär/ ▶ **adv.** (**farther** /ˈfärT͟Hər/, **farthest** /ˈfärT͟Həst/ or **further** /ˈfərT͟Hər/, **furthest** /ˈfərT͟Həst/) **1** [often with adverbial] at, to, or by a great distance (used to indicate the extent to which one

thing is distant from another): *it was not too far away* | *the mountains far in the distance glowed in the sun.* **2** over a large expanse of space or time: *he had not traveled far* | figurative *that's the reason why we have come so far and done as well as we have.* **3** by a great deal: *he is able to function far better than usual* | *the reality has fallen **far short of** early expectations.*
▶ **adj.** [attrib.] situated at a great distance in space or time: *the far reaches of the universe.* ■ more distant than another object of the same kind: *he was standing in the far corner.* ■ distant from a point seen as central; extreme: *she was brought up in the far north of Scotland* | *the largest electoral success for the far right since the war.*
– PHRASES **as far as** for as great a distance as: *the river stretched away as far as he could see.* ■ for a great enough distance to reach: *I decided to walk as far as the village.* ■ to the extent that: *as far as I am concerned, it is no big deal.* **be a far cry from** be very different from: *the hotel's royal suite is a far cry from the poverty of his home country.* **by far** by a great amount: *this was by far the largest city in the area.* **far and away** by a great amount: *he is far and away the most accomplished player.* **far and near** (also **near and far**) everywhere: *they came from far and near to New York City.* **far and wide** over a large area: *the high plains where bison roamed far and wide.* **far be it from me to** used to express reluctance, esp. to do something that one thinks may be resented: *far be it from me to speculate on his reasons.* **far from** very different from being; tending to the opposite of: *conditions were far from satisfactory.* **far gone** in a bad or worsening state, esp. so as to be beyond recovery: *a few frames from the original film were too far gone to salvage.* ■ advanced in time: *the legislative session is too far gone for the lengthy hearings needed to pass the bill.* **go far 1** achieve a great deal: *he was the bright one, and everyone was sure he would go far.* **2** contribute greatly: *a book that **goes far toward** bridging the gap.* **3** be worth or amount to much: *the money would not go far at this year's prices.* **go so far as to do something** do something regarded as extreme: *surely they wouldn't go so far as to break in?* **go too far** exceed the limits of what is reasonable or acceptable. **how far 1** used to ask how great a distance is: *they wanted to know how far he could travel.* **2** to what extent: *he was not sure how far she was committed.* **so far 1** to a certain limited extent: *the commitment to free trade goes only so far.* **2** (of a trend that seems likely to continue) up to this time: *we've only had one honest man so far.* **(in) so far as** to the extent that: *it was a windless storm so far as blizzards go.* **so far, so good** progress has been satisfactory up to now: *"How's the job going?" "So far, so good."*
– ORIGIN Old English *feorr*; from an Indo-European root shared by Sanskrit *para* and Greek *pera* 'further.'

Far. ▶ **abbr.** faraday.

far·ad /ˈfarəd, -ˌad/ (abbr.: **F**) ▶ **n.** the SI unit of electrical capacitance, equal to the capacitance of a capacitor in which one coulomb of charge causes a potential difference of one volt.
– ORIGIN mid 19th cent.: shortening of FARADAY. The term was originally proposed as a unit of electrical charge.

far·a·da·ic /ˌfarəˈdāik/ ▶ **adj.** another term for FARADIC.
– ORIGIN late 19th cent.: from the name of M. FARADAY + -IC.

Far·a·day /ˈfarəˌdā/, Michael (1791–1867), English physicist and chemist. He contributed significantly to the study of electromagnetism and discovered the laws of electrolysis.

far·a·day /ˈfarəˌdā/ (abbr.: **F**) ▶ **n.** Chemistry a unit of electric charge equal to Faraday's constant.
– ORIGIN early 20th cent.: coined in German from the name of M. FARADAY.

Far·a·day cage ▶ **n.** Physics a grounded metal screen surrounding a piece of equipment to exclude electrostatic and electromagnetic influences.

Far·a·day ef·fect ▶ **n.** Physics the rotation of the plane of polarization of electromagnetic waves in certain substances in a magnetic field.

Far·a·day's con·stant Chemistry the quantity of electric charge carried by one mole of electrons (equal to 96.49 coulombs). Compare with FARADAY.

Far·a·day's law 1 Physics a law stating that when the magnetic flux linking a circuit changes, an electromotive force is induced in the circuit proportional to the rate of change of the flux linkage. **2** Chemistry a law stating that the amount of any substance deposited or liberated during electrolysis is proportional to the quantity of electric charge passed and to the equivalent weight of the substance.

fa·rad·ic /fəˈradik/ (also **faradaic** /ˌfe(ə)rəˈdāik, ˌfar-/) ▶ **adj.** produced by or associated with electrical induction.

Far·al·lon Is·lands /ˈfarəˌlän/ a small, uninhabited island group in the Pacific Ocean, west of San Francisco in California.

far·an·dole /ˌfarənˈdōl, ˈfarənˌdōl/ ▶ **n.** historical a lively Provençal dance in which the dancers join hands and wind in and out in a chain.
– ORIGIN mid 19th cent.: French, from modern Provençal *farandoulo.*

far·a·way /ˈfärəˌwā/ ▶ **adj.** distant in space or time: *exotic and faraway locations.* ■ seeming remote from the immediate surroundings; dreamy: *she had a strange faraway look in her eyes.*

farce /färs/ ▶ **n.** a comic dramatic work using buffoonery and horseplay and typically including crude characterization and ludicrously improbable situations. ■ the genre of such works. ■ an absurd event: *the debate turned into a drunken farce.*
– ORIGIN early 16th cent.: from French, literally 'stuffing,' from *farcir* 'to stuff,' from Latin *farcire.* An earlier sense of 'forcemeat stuffing' became used metaphorically for comic interludes "stuffed" into the texts of religious plays, whence current usage.

far·ceur /färˈsər/ ▶ **n.** a writer of or performer in farces. ■ a joker or comedian.
– ORIGIN late 17th cent.: French, from obsolete *farcer* 'act in farces.'

far·ci·cal /ˈfärsikəl/ ▶ **adj.** of or resembling a farce, esp. because of absurd or ridiculous aspects: *a farcical tangle of events.*
– DERIVATIVES **far·ci·cal·i·ty** /ˌfärsiˈkalitē/ **n.**, **far·ci·cal·ly adv.**

far·cy /ˈfärsē/ ▶ **n.** glanders in horses (or a similar disease in cattle) in which there is inflammation of the lymph vessels, causing nodules (**farcy buds** or **farcy buttons**).
– ORIGIN late Middle English: from Old French *farcin*, from late Latin *farciminum*, from *farcire* 'to stuff' (because of the appearance of the swollen nodules).

far·del /ˈfärdl/ ▶ **n.** archaic a bundle: *a **fardel of** stories, personages, emotions.*
– ORIGIN Middle English: from Old French, diminutive of *fard*, from Arabic *farda* 'piece, pack.'

fare /fer/ ▶ **n. 1** the money a passenger on public transportation has to pay. ■ a passenger paying to travel in a vehicle, esp. a taxicab. **2** a range of food, esp. of a particular type: *delicious Provençal fare.* ■ performance or entertainment of a particular style: *conventional Hollywood fare.*
▶ **v.** [no obj.] **1** [with adverbial] perform in a specified way in a particular situation or over a particular period of time: *the party fared badly in the spring elections.* ■ archaic happen; turn out: *beware that **it fare** not with you as with your predecessor.* **2** archaic travel: *a young knight **fares forth.***
– ORIGIN Old English *fær, faru* 'traveling, a journey or expedition,' *faran* 'to travel,' also 'get on (well or badly),' of Germanic origin; related to Old Norse *ferja* 'ferryboat,' also to FORD. Sense 1 of the noun stems from an earlier meaning 'a journey for which a price is paid'; sense 2 of the noun was originally used with reference to the quality or quantity of food provided, probably from the idea of faring well or badly.

Far East China, Japan, and other countries in eastern Asia.
– DERIVATIVES **Far East·ern adj.**

fare-thee-well (also **fare-you-well**) ▶ **n.** (in phrase **to a fare-thee-well**) to perfection; thoroughly: *the inn is touristy to a fare-thee-well.*

fare·well /ferˈwel/ ▶ **exclam.** used to express good wishes on parting: *farewell, Albert!*
▶ **n.** an act of parting or of marking someone's departure: *the dinner had been arranged as a farewell.* ■ parting good wishes: *he had come on the pretext of **bidding her farewell*** | *I bade him a fond farewell.*
– ORIGIN late Middle English: from the imperative of FARE + the adverb WELL[1].

far·fal·le /färˈfälā, -ˈfalē/ ▶ **n.** small pieces of pasta shaped like bows or butterflies' wings.
– ORIGIN Italian, plural of *farfalla* 'butterfly.'

far·fel /ˈfärfəl/ ▶ **n.** ground noodle dough that when cooked in boiling water forms small pellets, or the pellets so formed, which are used in soups.
– ORIGIN Yiddish *farfl.*

far-fetched ▶ **adj.** unlikely and unconvincing; implausible.

far-flung ▶ **adj.** distant or remote: *the far-flung corners of the world.* ■ widely distributed: *newsletters provided an important link to a far-flung membership.*

Far·go[1] /ˈfärgō/ the largest city in North Dakota, in the southeastern part of the state, across the Red River of the North from Moorhead in Minnesota; pop. 95,531 (est. 2008).

Far·go[2], William, see WELLS, FARGO & CO.

Fa·ri·da·bad /fəˈrēdəˌbäd, -ˌbad/ an industrial city in northern India, south of Delhi, in the state of Haryana; pop. 1,464,100 (est. 2009).

fa·ri·na /fəˈrēnə/ ▶ **n.** flour or meal made of cereal grains, nuts, or starchy roots. ■ archaic a powdery substance, or a substance in powdered form. ■ archaic starch.
– DERIVATIVES **far·i·na·ceous** /ˌfarəˈnāSHəs/ **adj.**
– ORIGIN late Middle English: from Latin, from *far* 'grain.'

far·kle·ber·ry /ˈfärkəlˌberē/ ▶ **n.** (pl. **farkleberries**) a shrub or small tree with thick leathery leaves and inedible black berries, native to the southeastern US. ● *Vaccinium arboreum*, family Ericaceae.
– ORIGIN mid 18th cent.: probably an alteration of WHORTLEBERRY.

farm /färm/ ▶ **n.** an area of land and its buildings used for growing crops and rearing animals, typically under the control of one owner or manager. ■ the main dwelling place on such a site; a farmhouse: *a half-timbered farm.* ■ [with modifier] a place for breeding a particular type of animal or producing a specified crop: *a fish farm.* ■ [with modifier] an establishment at which something is produced or processed: *an energy farm.*
▶ **v. 1** [no obj.] make one's living by growing crops or keeping livestock: *he has farmed organically for five years.* ■ [with obj.] use (land) for growing crops and rearing animals, esp. commercially. ■ [with obj.] breed or grow commercially (a type of livestock or crop, esp. one not normally domesticated or cultivated). **2** [with obj.] (**farm someone/something out**) send out or subcontract work to others: *it saves time and money to farm out some writing work to specialized companies.* ■ arrange for a child or other dependent person to be looked after by someone, usually for payment. ■ send a sports player to a farm team. **3** [with obj.] historical allow someone to collect and keep the revenues from (a tax) on payment of a fee: *the customs had been farmed to the collector for a fixed sum.*
– PHRASES **buy the farm** see BUY.
– DERIVATIVES **farm·a·ble** /ˈfärməbəl/ **adj.**
– ORIGIN Middle English: from Old French *ferme*, from medieval Latin *firma* 'fixed payment,' from Latin *firmare* 'fix, settle' (in medieval Latin 'contract for'), from *firmus* 'constant, firm'; compare with FIRM[2]. The noun originally denoted a fixed annual amount payable as rent or tax; this is reflected in sense 3 of the verb, which later gave rise to 'to subcontract' (sense 2 of the verb). The noun came to denote a lease, and, in the early 16th cent., land leased specifically for farming. The verb sense 'grow crops or keep livestock' dates from the early 19th cent.

Farm Aid an organization whose annual concert of blues, country, and rock music promotes awareness of the need to protect and support family farms in the United States.

Farm Belt the states of the Midwest that are noted particularly for their agricultural production: Iowa, Kansas, Minnesota, Nebraska, North Dakota, and South Dakota.

Far·mer /ˈfärmər/, Fannie Merritt (1857–1915), US educator and author. She opened Miss Farmer's School of Cookery in 1902; her *Boston Cooking School Cook Book* (1896) was known as "the mother of level measurements."

farm·er /ˈfärmər/ ▶ **n. 1** a person who owns or manages a farm. **2** historical a person to whom the collection of taxes was contracted for a fee.
– ORIGIN late Middle English: from Old French *fermier*, from medieval Latin *firmarius*, from *firma* (see FARM). Sense 1 originally denoted a bailiff or steward who farmed land on the owner's behalf, or a tenant farmer.

farm·er cheese (also **farmer's cheese**) ▶ **n.** an unripened cheese that is mild in flavor, firmer than cottage cheese and somewhat crumbly in texture.

far·mer's lung ▶ **n.** informal term for ASPERGILLOSIS.

farm·ers' mar·ket ▶ **n.** a food market, often held in a public place outdoors at regular intervals, at which local farmers sell fruit and vegetables, and often meat, cheese, bakery products, and flowers directly to consumers.

farm·hand /ˈfärmˌhand/ ▶ **n.** a worker on a farm.

farm·house /ˈfärmˌhous/ ▶ **n.** a house attached to a farm, esp. the main house in which the farmer lives.

farm·ing /ˈfärmiNG/ ▶ **n.** the activity or business of growing crops and raising livestock.

Farm·ing·ton /ˈfärmiNGtən/ a city in northwestern New Mexico; pop. 42,637 (est. 2008).

PRONUNCIATION KEY ə *ago, up*; ər *over, fur*; a *hat*; ā *ate*; ä *car*; e *let*; ē *see*; i *fit*; ī *by*; NG *sing*; ō *go*; ô *law, for*; oi *toy*; o͝o *good*; o͞o *goo*; ou *out*; TH *thin*; T͟H *then*; ZH *vision*

Farm·ing·ton Hills a city in southeastern Michigan, west of Detroit; pop. 78,522 (est. 2008).

farm·land /ˈfärm,land/ ▶ **n.** (also **farmlands**) land used for farming.

farm·stead /ˈfärm,sted/ ▶ **n.** a farm and its buildings.

farm team ▶ **n.** Baseball a minor league team that provides players as needed to an affiliated major league team.

farm·work·er /ˈfärm,wərkər/ ▶ **n.** a person employed to work on a farm.

farm·yard /ˈfärm,yärd/ ▶ **n.** a yard or enclosure attached to a farmhouse.

Farne Is·lands /färn/ a group of 17 small islands off the coast of Northumberland, England, noted for their wildlife.

Far·ne·se /färˈnäzā/, Alessandro, see **PAUL III**.

Farn·ham /ˈfärnəm/, Eliza Wood (1815–64), US reformer and writer. As matron of the women's department of Sing Sing prison in Ossining, New York 1844–48, she instituted major reforms.

f

far·o /ˈferō/ ▶ **n.** a gambling card game in which players bet on the order in which the cards will appear.
– ORIGIN early 18th cent. (originally as *pharaoh* or *pharo*): from French *pharaon*(see **PHARAOH**), said to have been the name of the king of hearts.

Far·oe Is·lands /ˈferō/ (also **Faeroe Islands** or **the Faroes**) a group of islands in the North Atlantic Ocean between Iceland and the Shetland Islands that belong to Denmark but are semi-autonomous; pop. 48,900 (est. 2009); capital, Tórshavn.

Far·o·ese /,fe(ə)rōˈēz/ (also **Faeroese**) ▶ **adj.** of or relating to the Faroe Islands or their people or language.
▶ **n.** (pl. **same**) **1** a native or inhabitant of the Faroes, or a person of Faroese descent.
2 the official language of the Faroes, a North Germanic language closely related to Icelandic.

far off ▶ **adj.** remote in time or space: *a far-off country.*

fa·ro·li·to /,faraˈlētō, ,fär-/ ▶ **n.** another term for **LUMINARIA** (sense 1).

fa·rouche /fəˈro͞osн/ ▶ **adj.** sullen or shy in company.
– ORIGIN mid 18th cent.: from French, alteration of Old French *forache*, based on Latin *foras* 'out of doors.'

Fa·rouk /fəˈro͞ok/ (1920–65), king of Egypt; reigned 1936–52. His defeat in the Arab-Israeli conflict of 1948, together with the general corruption of his reign, led to a military coup in 1952. Farouk was forced to abdicate in favor of his infant son, Fuad.

far out ▶ **adj.** unconventional or avant-garde: *far-out politics.* ■ [often as exclamation] informal excellent: *it's really far out!*

Far·quhar /ˈfärkwər/, George (1678–1707), Irish playwright. He was a principal figure in Restoration comedy. Notable works: *The Recruiting Officer* (1706) and *The Beaux' Stratagem* (1707).

far·ra·go /fəˈrägō, -ˈrā-/ ▶ **n.** (pl. **farragoes**) a confused mixture: *a farrago of fact and myth about Abraham Lincoln.*
– DERIVATIVES **far·rag·i·nous** /fəˈrajənəs/ **adj.**
– ORIGIN mid 17th cent.: from Latin, literally 'mixed fodder,' from *far* 'corn.'

Far·ra·gut /ˈfarəgət/, David Glasgow (1801–70), US navy admiral; born *James Glasgow Farragut*. The outstanding naval commander of the Civil War, he captured the city of New Orleans in April 1862 and extended Union control of the Mississippi River north to Vicksburg.

David Farragut

Far·ra·khan /ˈfarə,kan, ˈfärə,kän/, Louis (1933–), US Nation of Islam leader since 1978 and African-American nationalist; born *Louis Eugene Walcott*. He is known for advocating black separatism and black economic power.

far-reach·ing ▶ **adj.** having important and widely applicable effects or implications: *a series of far-reaching political reforms.*

Far·rell[1] /ˈfarəl/, J. T. (1904–79), US novelist; full name *James Thomas Farrell*. He is known for his trilogy about Studs Lonigan: *Young Lonigan* (1932), *The Young Manhood of Studs Lonigan* (1934), and *Judgment Day* (1935).

Far·rell[2], Suzanne (1945–), US dancer; born *Roberta Sue Fricker*. She performed with the New York City Ballet 1961–69, where she became principal dancer 1965–69. She is noted for her performance in the movie version of *A Midsummer Night's Dream* (1966).

far·ri·er /ˈfarēər/ ▶ **n.** a craftsman who trims and shoes horses' hooves.
– DERIVATIVES **far·ri·er·y n.**
– ORIGIN mid 16th cent.: from Old French *ferrier*, from Latin *ferrarius*, from *ferrum* 'iron, horseshoe.'

far·row /ˈfarō/ ▶ **n.** a litter of pigs. ■ an act of giving birth to a litter of pigs.
▶ **v.** [with obj.] (of a sow) give birth to (piglets): *the pig is one of a litter of nine farrowed in July.*
– ORIGIN Old English *fearh, færh* 'young pig,' from an Indo-European root shared by Greek *porkos* and Latin *porcus* 'pig.'

far·ru·ca /fəˈro͞okə/ ▶ **n.** a type of flamenco dance.
– ORIGIN 1930s: Spanish, feminine of *farruco* 'Galician or Asturian,' from *Farruco*, pet form of the given name *Francisco*.

far-see·ing ▶ **adj.** having shrewd judgment and an ability to predict and plan for future eventualities.

Far·si /ˈfärsē/ ▶ **n.** the modern Persian language that is the official language of Iran.
– ORIGIN from Arabic *fārsī*, from *Fārs*, from Persian *Pārs* 'Persia.' Compare with **PARSEE**.

far·sight·ed /ˈfär,sītid, -ˈsītid/ ▶ **adj.** unable to see things clearly, esp. if they are relatively close to the eyes, owing to the focusing of rays of light by the eye at a point behind the retina; hyperopic. ■ seeing or able to see for a great distance. ■ having imagination or foresight: *a farsighted businessman.*
– DERIVATIVES **far·sight·ed·ly adv.**, **far·sight·ed·ness n.**

fart /färt/ informal ▶ **v.** [no obj.] emit gas from the anus. ■ (**fart about/around**) waste time on silly or trivial things.
▶ **n.** an emission of gas from the anus. ■ a boring or contemptible person: *he was such an old fart.*
– ORIGIN Old English (recorded in the verbal noun *feorting* 'farting').

far·ther /ˈfär<u>TH</u>ər/ (also **further** /ˈfər<u>TH</u>ər/) used as comparative of **FAR**.
▶ **adv. 1** at, to, or by a greater distance (used to indicate the extent to which one thing or person is or becomes distant from another): *the farther away you are from your home, the better you should behave* | figurative *his action pushes Haiti even farther away from democratic rule.*
2 over a greater expanse of space or time; for a longer way: *the stream fills the passage, and only a cave diver can explore farther* | figurative *people were trying to get their food dollars to go farther.*
▶ **adj.** more distant in space than another item of the same kind: *the farther side of the mountain.* ■ more remote from a central point: *the farther stretches of the diocese.*

> **USAGE** Traditionally, **farther** and **farthest** were used in referring to physical distance: *the falls were still two or three miles farther up the path.* **Further** and **furthest** were restricted to figurative or abstract senses: *we decided to consider the matter further.* Although **farther** and **farthest** are still restricted to measurable distances, **further** and **furthest** are now common in both senses: *put those plants the furthest from the window.*

far·ther·most /ˈfär<u>TH</u>ər,mōst/ (also **furthermost** /ˈfər-/) ▶ **adj.** (of an edge or extreme) at the greatest distance from a central point or implicit standpoint: *the pitch broke sharply over the farthermost part of the strike zone.*

far·thest /ˈfär<u>TH</u>ist/ (also **furthest** /ˈfər-/) used as superlative of **FAR**.
▶ **adj.** [attrib.] situated at the greatest distance from a specified or understood point: *the farthest door led to a kitchen.* ■ covering the greatest area or distance: *his record for the farthest flight.* ■ extremely remote: *the farthest ends of the earth.*
▶ **adv. 1** at or by the greatest distance (used to indicate how far one thing or person is or becomes distant from another): *the bed farthest from the window.*
2 over the greatest distance or area: *his group probably had farthest to ride.* ■ used to indicate the most distant point reached in a specified direction: *it was the farthest north I had ever traveled.* ■ to the most extreme or advanced point: *countries where industrialization had gone furthest* | *the farthest he'll go is to admit a sort of resentment.*
– PHRASES **at the farthest** at the greatest distance; at most: *the Allied line had been pushed forward, at the farthest, about one mile.*
– ORIGIN late Middle English: formed as a superlative of **FURTHER**.

> **USAGE** On the differences between **farthest** and **furthest**, see **FARTHER**.

far·thing /ˈfär<u>TH</u>iNG/ ▶ **n.** a former monetary unit and coin of the UK, withdrawn in 1961, equal to a quarter of an old penny. ■ [usu. with negative] the least possible amount: *she didn't care a farthing for the woman.*
– ORIGIN Old English *fēorthing*, from *fēortha* 'fourth.'

far·thin·gale /ˈfär<u>TH</u>iNG,gāl/ ▶ **n.** historical a hooped petticoat or circular pad of fabric around the hips, formerly worn under women's skirts to extend and shape them.
– ORIGIN early 16th cent. (formerly also as *vardingale*): from French *verdugale*, alteration of Spanish *verdugado*, from *verdugo* 'rod, stick,' from *verde* 'green.'

fart·lek /ˈfärtlik/ ▶ **n.** Track & Field a system of training for distance runners in which the terrain and pace are continually varied to eliminate boredom and enhance psychological aspects of conditioning.
– ORIGIN 1940s: from Swedish, from *fart* 'speed' + *lek* 'play.'

Far West the region of North America west of the Great Plains.

FAS ▶ **abbr.** ■ fetal alcohol syndrome. ■ Foreign Agricultural Service.

f.a.s. ▶ **abbr.** free alongside ship.

fasc. ▶ **abbr.** fascicle.

fas·ces /ˈfas,ēz/ ▶ **plural n.** historical (in ancient Rome) a bundle of rods with a projecting ax blade, carried by a lictor as a symbol of a magistrate's power. ■ (in Fascist Italy) such items used as emblems of authority.
– ORIGIN Latin, plural of *fascis* 'bundle.'

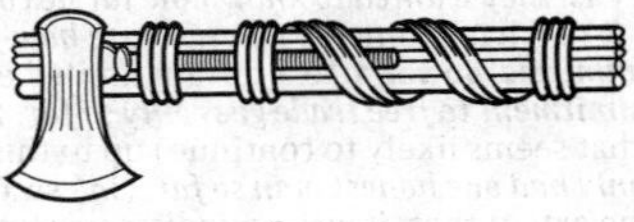

fasces

fas·ci·a /ˈfasн(ē)ə, ˈfā-/ ▶ **n. 1** (chiefly Brit. also **facia**) a wooden board or other flat piece of material such as that covering the ends of rafters. ■ a covering, typically a detachable one, for the front part of a cellular phone. ■ (in classical architecture) a long flat surface between moldings on an architrave. ■ chiefly Brit. the dashboard of a motor vehicle.
2 (pl. **fasciae** /-sнē,ē/) Anatomy a thin sheath of fibrous tissue enclosing a muscle or other organ.
– DERIVATIVES **fas·ci·al** /ˈfasн(ē)əl, fā-/ **adj.** (sense 2).
– ORIGIN mid 16th cent.: from Latin, 'band, doorframe,' related to **FASCES**. Compare with **FESS**'.

fas·ci·at·ed /ˈfasнē,ātəd, ˈfā-/ (also **fasciate**) ▶ **adj. 1** Botany showing abnormal fusion of parts or organs, resulting in a flattened, ribbonlike structure.
2 Zoology striped or banded.
– DERIVATIVES **fas·ci·a·tion** /,fasнēˈāsнən, ,fā-/ **n.**
– ORIGIN mid 18th cent. (in the sense 'striped, banded'): from Latin *fasciatus* (past participle of *fasciare* 'swathe,' from *fascia* 'band') + **-ED**'.

fas·ci·cle /ˈfasikəl/ ▶ **n. 1** (also **fascicule** /-,kyo͞ol/) a separately published installment of a book or other printed work.
2 (also **fasciculus** /fəˈsikyələs/) Anatomy & Biology a bundle of structures, such as nerve or muscle fibers or conducting vessels in plants.
– DERIVATIVES **fas·ci·cled adj.**, **fas·cic·u·lar** /fəˈsikyələr/ **adj.**, **fas·cic·u·late** /fəˈsikyə,lāt, -yəlit/ **adj.**
– ORIGIN late 15th cent. (sense 2): from Latin *fasciculus*, diminutive of *fascis* 'bundle.'

fas·cic·u·la·tion /fə,sikyəˈlāsнən/ ▶ **n. 1** Medicine a brief, spontaneous contraction affecting a small number of muscle fibers, often causing a flicker of movement under the skin. It can be a symptom of disease of the motor neurons.
2 chiefly Biology arrangement in bundles.

fas·ci·i·tis /,fasēˈītəs, ,fasнē-/ ▶ **n.** Medicine inflammation of the fascia of a muscle or organ.

fas·ci·nate /ˈfasə,nāt/ ▶ **v.** [with obj.] (usu. **be fascinated**) draw irresistibly the attention and interest of (someone): *I've always been fascinated by other cultures* | [with obj.] *she was fascinated to learn about this strange land.* ■ archaic (esp. of a snake)

deprive (a person or animal) of the ability to resist or escape by the power of a look or gaze: *the serpent fascinates its prey.*
– DERIVATIVES **fas·ci·na·tor** /-ˌnātər/ **n.**
– ORIGIN late 16th cent. (in the sense 'bewitch, put under a spell'): from Latin *fascinat-* 'bewitched,' from the verb *fascinare,* from *fascinum* 'spell, witchcraft.'

fas·ci·nat·ing /ˈfasəˌnātiNG/ ▶ **adj.** extremely interesting: *fascinating facts.*
– DERIVATIVES **fas·ci·nat·ing·ly adv.**

fas·ci·na·tion /ˌfasəˈnāsHən/ ▶ **n.** the power to fascinate someone; the quality of being fascinating: *television has always held a **fascination for** me.* ■ the state of being fascinated: *he had a lifelong **fascination with** science.*

> **USAGE** The two senses of **fascination** each take a different preposition. A person has a **fascination with** something they are very interested in (*her fascination with the royal family*), whereas something interesting holds a **fascination for** a person (*words have always held a fascination for me*). The Oxford English Corpus shows that the distinction is often blurred today, but it should be maintained in careful writing.

fas·cine /fəˈsēn/ ▶ **n.** a bundle of rods, sticks, or plastic pipes bound together, used in construction or military operations for filling in marshy ground or other obstacles and for strengthening the sides of embankments, ditches, or trenches.
– ORIGIN late 17th cent.: via French from Latin *fascina,* from *fascis* 'bundle.'

fas·ci·o·li·a·sis /fəˌsēəˈlīəsis, fəˌsīə-/ ▶ **n.** Medicine infestation of a human or an animal with the liver fluke.
– ORIGIN late 19th cent.: from modern Latin *Fasciola hepatica,* the name of the liver fluke (from Latin *fasciola* 'small bandage') + **-IASIS.**

fas·cism /ˈfasHˌizəm/ (also **Fascism**) ▶ **n.** an authoritarian and nationalistic right-wing system of government and social organization. ■ (in general use) extreme right-wing, authoritarian, or intolerant views or practice.

> The term Fascism was first used of the totalitarian right-wing nationalist regime of Mussolini in Italy (1922–43), and the regimes of the Nazis in Germany and Franco in Spain were also fascist. Fascism tends to include a belief in the supremacy of one national or ethnic group, a contempt for democracy, an insistence on obedience to a powerful leader, and a strong demagogic approach.

– ORIGIN from Italian *fascismo,* from *fascio* 'bundle, political group,' from Latin *fascis* (see **FASCES**).

fas·cist /ˈfasHist/ ▶ **n.** an advocate or follower of fascism.
▶ **adj.** of or relating to fascism: *a military coup threw out the old fascist regime.*
– DERIVATIVES **fa·scis·tic** /faˈsHistik/ **adj.**

fash·ion /ˈfasHən/ ▶ **n. 1** a popular trend, esp. in styles of dress and ornament or manners of behavior: *his hair is cut in the latest fashion.* ■ the production and marketing of new styles of goods, esp. clothing and cosmetics: [as modifier] *a fashion magazine.*
2 a manner of doing something: *the work is done in a rather casual fashion.*
▶ **v.** [with obj.] (often **be fashioned**) make into a particular or the required form: *the bottles were **fashioned from** green glass.* ■ (**fashion something into**) use materials to make into: *the skins were fashioned into boots and shoes.*
– PHRASES **after a fashion** to a certain extent but imperfectly or unsatisfactorily: *he could read after a fashion.* **after** (or **in**) **the fashion of** in a manner similar to: *she took servants for granted after the fashion of wealthy and pampered girls.* **in** (or **out of**) **fashion** popular (or unpopular) and considered (or not considered) to be attractive at the time in question.
– DERIVATIVES **fash·ion·er n.**
– ORIGIN Middle English (in the sense 'make, shape, appearance,' also 'a particular make or style'): from Old French *façon,* from Latin *factio(n-),* from *facere* 'do, make.'

-fashion ▶ **comb. form** in the manner of something specified: *dog-fashion | castanet-fashion.* ■ in the style associated with a specified place or people: *American-fashion | Bristol-fashion.*

fash·ion·a·ble /ˈfasH(ə)nəbəl/ ▶ **adj.** characteristic of, influenced by, or representing a current popular trend or style: *fashionable clothes.* ■ (of a person) dressing or behaving according to the current trend.
– DERIVATIVES **fash·ion·a·bil·i·ty** /ˌfasH(ə)nəˈbilətē/ **n., fash·ion·a·ble·ness n., fash·ion·a·bly** /-əblē/ **adv.**

fash·ion-for·ward ▶ **adj.** (of a person or style of clothing) very fashionable: *it's become the clothing line of choice for fashion-forward women.*

fash·ion·is·ta /ˌfasHəˈnēstə/ ▶ **n.** informal **1** a designer of haute couture.
2 a devoted follower of fashion: *sleek designs that press all the fashionistas' buttons.*
– ORIGIN 1990s: from *fashion* + Spanish suffix *-ista,* as in *Sandinista, turista.*

fash·ion plate ▶ **n. 1** a person who dresses very fashionably.
2 a picture, typically in a magazine, illustrating a new or current fashion in clothes.

fash·ion vic·tim ▶ **n.** a person who follows popular trends in dress and behavior slavishly.

Fast /fast/, Howard Melvin (1914–2003), US writer. He is best known for his historical novels and as a member of the Communist party 1943–56 who was imprisoned in 1950 for refusing to cooperate with the House Committee on Un-American Activities.

fast[1] /fast/ ▶ **adj. 1** moving or capable of moving at high speed: *a fast and powerful car.* ■ performed or taking place at high speed; taking only a short time: *the journey was fast and enjoyable.* ■ performing or able to perform a particular type of action quickly: *a fast reader.* ■ allowing people or things to move at high speed: *a wide, fast road.* ■ (of a playing field) likely to make the ball bounce or run quickly or to allow competitors to reach a high speed.
2 [predic. or as complement] (of a clock or watch) showing a time ahead of the correct time: *I keep my watch fifteen minutes fast.*
3 firmly fixed or attached: *he **made** a rope **fast** to each corner.* ■ (of friends) close and loyal. ■ (of a dye) not fading in light or when washed.
4 Photography (of a film) needing only a short exposure. ■ (of a lens) having a large aperture and therefore allowing short exposure times.
5 (of a person or lifestyle) engaging in or involving exciting or shocking activities: *the fast life she led in London.*
▶ **adv. 1** at high speed: *he was driving too fast.* ■ within a short time: *they think they're going to get rich fast.*
2 so as to be hard to move; firmly or securely: *the ship was **held fast** by the anchor chain.* ■ (of someone or something sleeping) so as to be hard to wake: *they were too **fast asleep** to reply.*
– PHRASES **pull a fast one** informal try to gain an unfair advantage: *Joey **pulled a fast one on us.***
– ORIGIN Old English *fæst* 'firmly fixed, steadfast' and *fæste* 'firmly, securely' In Middle English the adverb developed the senses 'strongly, vigorously' (compare with *run hard*), and 'close, immediate' (just surviving in the archaic and poetic *fast by;* compare with *hard by*), hence 'closely, immediately' and 'quickly'; the idea of rapid movement was then reflected in adjectival use.

fast[2] ▶ **v.** [no obj.] abstain from all or some kinds of food or drink, esp. as a religious observance.
▶ **n.** an act or period of fasting: *a five-day fast.*
– ORIGIN Old English *fæstan* (verb); related to Old Norse *fasta,* the source of the noun.

fast and fu·ri·ous ▶ **adv. 1** very rapidly: *my heart was beating fast and furious.*
2 eagerly; uproariously.
▶ **adj.** full of rapid action; lively and exciting: *the game was fast and furious.*

fast·back /ˈfas(t)ˌbak/ ▶ **n.** a car with a roofline that slopes continuously down at the back.

fast·ball /ˈfas(t)ˌbôl/ ▶ **n.** a baseball pitch thrown at or near a pitcher's maximum speed. ■ another term for **FAST-PITCH SOFTBALL.**

fast break ▶ **n.** a swift attack from a defensive position in basketball, soccer, and other ball games: *a defense that shut off our fast break altogether* | [as modifier] *there are no fast-break baskets.*
▶ **v.** (**fast-break**) [no obj.] make such an attack: *fast-breaking relentlessly is harder than playing a control game.*

fast breed·er (also **fast breeder reactor**) ▶ **n.** a breeder reactor in which the neutrons causing fission are not slowed by any moderator.

fast buck ▶ **n.** see **BUCK**[2].

fas·ten /ˈfasən/ ▶ **v.** [with obj.] close or join securely: *fasten your seat belts.* ■ [no obj.] be closed or done up in a particular place or part or in a particular way: *a blue nightie that fastens down the back.* ■ fix or hold in place: *she fastened her locket around her neck.* ■ (**fasten something on/upon**) direct one's eyes, thoughts, feelings, etc., intently at: *Maggie fastened her eyes on him* | [no obj.] *speculation fastened on three candidates.* ■ (**fasten something on/upon**) ascribe responsibility to: *blame hadn't been fastened on anyone.* ■ [no obj.] (**fasten on/upon**) single out (someone or something) and concentrate on them or it obsessively: *the critics fastened on two sections of the report.*
– DERIVATIVES **fas·ten·er n.**
– ORIGIN Old English *fæstnian* 'make sure, confirm,' also 'immobilize'; related to **FAST**[1].

fast·en·ing /ˈfasəniNG/ ▶ **n.** a device that closes or secures something: *a front-zip fastening.*

fast food ▶ **n.** food that can be prepared quickly and easily and is sold in restaurants and snack bars as a quick meal or to be taken out: [as modifier] *a fast-food restaurant.*

fast for·ward ▶ **n.** a control on a tape or video player for advancing the tape rapidly: [as modifier] *the fast-forward button.* ■ a facility for cueing audio equipment by allowing the tape to be played at high speed and stopped when the desired place is reached.
▶ **v.** (**fast-forward**) [with obj.] advance (a tape) rapidly, sometimes while simultaneously playing it at high speed. ■ [no obj.] move speedily forward in time when considering or dealing with something over a period: *the text fast-forwards to 1990.*

fast ice ▶ **n.** ice that extends out from the shore and is attached to it.

fas·tid·i·ous /fasˈtidēəs/ ▶ **adj.** very attentive to and concerned about accuracy and detail: *he chooses his words with fastidious care.* ■ very concerned about matters of cleanliness: *the child seemed fastidious about getting her fingers sticky or dirty.*
– DERIVATIVES **fas·tid·i·ous·ly adv., fas·tid·i·ous·ness n.**
– ORIGIN late Middle English: from Latin *fastidiosus,* from *fastidium* 'loathing.' The word originally meant 'disagreeable, distasteful,' later 'disgusted' Current senses date from the 17th cent.

fas·tig·i·ate /fəˈstijēət/ ▶ **adj.** Botany (of a tree or shrub) having the branches sloping upward more or less parallel to the main stem.
– ORIGIN mid 17th cent.: from Latin *fastigium* 'tapering point, gable' + **-ATE**[2].

fast lane ▶ **n.** [usu. in sing.] a lane of a highway for use by traffic that is moving faster than the rest. ■ a hectic or highly pressured lifestyle: *his face showed the strain of a life lived **in the fast lane.***

fast·ness /ˈfas(t)nəs/ ▶ **n. 1** a secure refuge, esp. a place well protected by natural features: *a remote Himalayan mountain fastness.*
2 the ability of a material or dye to maintain its color without fading or washing away: *the dyes differ in their fastness to light.*
– ORIGIN Old English *fæstnes* (see **FAST**[1], **-NESS**).

fast neu·tron ▶ **n.** a neutron with high kinetic energy, esp. one released by nuclear fission and not slowed by any moderator.

fast-pitch soft·ball (also **fast-pitch**) ▶ **n.** a variety of the game of softball featuring fast underhand pitching.

fast re·ac·tor ▶ **n.** a nuclear reactor in which fission is caused mainly by fast neutrons.

fast-talk ▶ **v.** [with obj.] informal pressure (someone) into doing something using rapid or misleading speech: *heroin dealers tried to fast-talk him into a quick sale* | (as adj. **fast-talking**) *a fast-talking confidence trickster.*

fast track ▶ **n.** [in sing.] a route, course, or method that provides for more rapid results than usual: *a career in the fast track of the civil service.*
▶ **v.** (**fast-track**) [with obj.] accelerate the development or progress of (a person or project); compare with **SLOW TRACK**: *the old boys' network fast-tracks men to the top of the corporate ladder.*

fast-twitch ▶ **adj.** [attrib.] Physiology (of a muscle fiber) contracting rapidly, thus providing power rather than endurance.

fat /fat/ ▶ **n.** a natural oily or greasy substance occurring in animal bodies, esp. when deposited as a layer under the skin or around certain organs. ■ a substance of this type, or a similar one made from plant products, used in cooking. ■ the presence of an excessive amount of such a substance in a person or animal, causing them to appear corpulent: *he was a tall man, **running to fat.*** ■ Chemistry any of a group of natural esters of glycerol and various fatty acids, which are solid at room temperature and are the main constituents of animal and vegetable fat. Compare with **OIL.**
▶ **adj.** (**fatter, fattest**) (of a person or animal) having a large amount of excess flesh: *the driver was a fat, wheezing man.* ■ (of an animal bred for food) made plump for slaughter. ■ containing much fat: *fat bacon.* ■ large in bulk or circumference: *a fat cigarette.* ■ informal (of an asset or opportunity) financially substantial or desirable: *a fat profit | fat motion picture deals.* ■ informal used ironically to express the belief that there is none or very little of

something: *fat chance she had of influencing him* | *a fat lot of good that'll do him.* ■ (of coal) containing a high proportion of volatile oils. ■ (of wood) containing a high proportion of resin: *fat pine.*
▶ v. (**fats, fatting, fatted**) archaic make or become fat: [with obj.] *numbers of black cattle are fatted here* | [no obj.] *the hogs have been fatting* | (as adj. **fatted**) *a fatted duck.*
– PHRASES **the fat is in the fire** something has happened that will surely lead to an unpleasant result or angry reaction. **kill the fatted calf** produce one's best food to celebrate, esp. at a prodigal's return. [with biblical allusion to Luke 15.] **live off** (or **on**) **the fat of the land** have the best of everything.
– DERIVATIVES **fat·less** adj., **fat·ly** adv., **fat·ness** n., **fat·tish** adj.
– ORIGIN Old English *fǣtt* 'well fed, plump,' also 'fatty, oily.'

Fa·tah /fəˈtä, ˈfätə/ (also **al-Fatah**) a Palestinian political and military organization founded in 1958 by Yasser Arafat and others to bring about the establishment of a Palestinian state. It dominated the Palestine Liberation Organization from the 1960s, but more recently has been challenged by more extreme groups, and in 2006 was defeated by Hamas in the elections for the Palestinian National Authority.
– ORIGIN Arabic, literally 'victory.'

fa·tal /ˈfātl/ ▶ adj. causing death: *a fatal accident.* ■ leading to failure or disaster: *there were three fatal flaws in the strategy.*
– DERIVATIVES **fa·tal·ly** adv.
– ORIGIN late Middle English (in the senses 'destined by fate' and 'ominous'): from Old French, from Latin *fatalis*, from *fatum* (see **FATE**).

fa·tal·ism /ˈfātl,izəm/ ▶ n. the belief that all events are predetermined and therefore inevitable. ■ a submissive attitude to events, resulting from such a belief.
– DERIVATIVES **fa·tal·ist** n., **fa·tal·is·tic** /,fātlˈistik/ adj., **fa·tal·is·ti·cal·ly** /,fātlˈistik(ə)lē/ adv.

fa·tal·i·ty /fāˈtalətē, fə-/ ▶ n. (pl. **fatalities**) **1** an occurrence of death by accident, in war, or from disease: *shooting was heard and there were fatalities.* ■ a person killed in this way.
2 helplessness in the face of fate: *the plot needs a darker sense of fatality to cover its absurdities.*
– ORIGIN late 15th cent. (denoting the quality of causing death or disaster): from French *fatalité*, from late Latin *fatalitas*, from Latin *fatalis* 'decreed by fate,' from *fatum* (see **FATE**). Sense 1 dates from the mid 19th cent.

Fa·ta Mor·ga·na /ˈfätə môrˈgänə/ ▶ n. a mirage.
– ORIGIN Italian, literally 'fairy Morgan'; originally referring to a mirage seen in the Strait of Messina between Italy and Sicily and attributed to **MORGAN LE FAY**, whose legend and reputation were carried to Sicily by Norman settlers.

fat·back /ˈfat,bak/ ▶ n. **1** fat from the upper part of a side of pork, esp. when dried and salted in strips.
2 informal term for **MENHADEN**.

fat bod·y ▶ n. Zoology each of a number of small white structures in the body of an animal, esp. an insect, that act as a store of fats and glycogen.

fat burn·er ▶ n. an over-the-counter drug that claims to burn calories by increasing the rate of the body's metabolism.

fat camp ▶ n. informal a residential summer program for overweight children, promoting exercise and healthy eating to facilitate weight loss.

fat cat ▶ n. derogatory a wealthy and powerful person, esp. a businessman or politician: [as modifier] *a fat-cat developer.*

fat cit·y ▶ n. informal **1** a condition of great prosperity or good fortune: *when school was out, we were in fat city, man!*
2 the condition of being overweight.

fate /fāt/ ▶ n. **1** the development of events beyond a person's control, regarded as determined by a supernatural power: *fate decided his course for him* | *his injury is a cruel twist of fate.* ■ the course of someone's life, or the outcome of a particular situation for someone or something, seen as beyond their control: *he suffered the same fate as his companion.* ■ [in sing.] the inescapable death of a person: *the guards led her to her fate.*
2 (**the Fates**) Greek & Roman Mythology the three goddesses who preside over the birth and life of humans. Each person's destiny was thought of as a thread spun, measured, and cut by the three Fates, Clotho, Lachesis, and Atropos. Also called the **MOIRAI** and the **PARCAE**. ■ (**Fates**) another term for **NORNS**.
▶ v. (**be fated**) be destined to happen, turn out, or act in a particular way: [with infinitive] *the regime was fated to end badly.*
– PHRASES **a fate worse than death** see **DEATH**. **seal someone's fate** make it inevitable that something unpleasant will happen to someone.
– ORIGIN late Middle English: from Italian *fato* or Old French *fator* (later) from their source, Latin *fatum* 'that which has been spoken,' from *fari* 'speak.'

fate·ful /ˈfātfəl/ ▶ adj. having far-reaching and typically disastrous consequences or implications: *a fateful oversight.*
– DERIVATIVES **fate·ful·ly** adv., **fate·ful·ness** n.

fat farm ▶ n. informal a residential establishment where overweight people seek improved health by dieting, exercise, and treatment.

fat-free ▶ adj. (of a food) not containing animal or vegetable fats: *virtually fat-free yogurt.*

fat·head /ˈfat,hed/ ▶ n. informal a stupid person.
– DERIVATIVES **fat·head·ed** adj., **fat·head·ed·ness** n.

fat hen ▶ n. another name for **LAMB'S-QUARTERS**.

fa·ther /ˈfäT͟Hər/ ▶ n. **1** a man in relation to his natural child or children. ■ a male animal in relation to its offspring. ■ (usu. **fathers**) literary an ancestor. ■ (also **founding father**) an important figure in the origin and early history of something: *Dorsey should be remembered as the father of gospel music.* ■ a man who gives care and protection to someone or something: *the prince is widely regarded as the father of the nation.* ■ the oldest or most respected member of a society or other body. ■ (**the Father**) (in Christian belief) the first person of the Trinity; God. ■ (**Father**) literary used in proper names, esp. when personifying time or a river, to suggest an old and venerable character: *Father Thames.*
2 (also **Father**) (often as a title or form of address) a priest: *pray for me, Father.*
3 (**the Fathers** or **the Church Fathers**) early Christian theologians (in particular of the first five centuries) whose writings are regarded as especially authoritative.
▶ v. [with obj.] be the father of: *he fathered three children.* ■ (usu. as noun **fathering**) treat with the protective care usually associated with a father: *the two males share the fathering of the cubs.* ■ be the source or originator of: *a culture which has fathered half the popular music in the world.* ■ (**father someone on**) make a woman pregnant: *he fathered a child on a one-night stand.* ■ assign the paternity of a child or responsibility for a book, idea, or action to: *a collection of Irish stories was fathered on him.* ■ archaic appear as or admit that one is the father or originator of: *a singular letter from a lady, requesting I would father a novel of hers.*
– PHRASES **like father, like son** proverb a son's character or behavior can be expected to resemble that of his father.
– DERIVATIVES **fa·ther·hood** /-,ho͝od/ n., **fa·ther·less** adj., **fa·ther·less·ness** n., **fa·ther·like** /-,līk/ adj. & adv.
– ORIGIN Old English *fæder*; from an Indo-European root shared by Latin *pater* and Greek *patēr*.

Fa·ther Christ·mas chiefly Brit. another name for **SANTA CLAUS**.

fa·ther con·fes·sor ▶ n. a priest or minister who hears confessions. ■ someone with whom one seeks comfort by trusting with one's confidences: *he was growing tired of acting as the father confessor to every student.*

fa·ther fig·ure ▶ n. an older man who is respected for his paternal qualities and may be an emotional substitute for a father.

fa·ther-in-law ▶ n. (pl. **fathers-in-law**) the father of one's spouse.

fa·ther·land /ˈfäT͟Hər,land/ ▶ n. (often **the Fatherland**) a person's native country, esp. when referred to in patriotic terms. ■ chiefly historical Germany, esp. during the period of Hitler's control.

fa·ther·ly /ˈfäT͟Hərlē/ ▶ adj. of, resembling, or characteristic of a father, esp. in being protective and affectionate: *he gave me such a kind and fatherly look.*
– DERIVATIVES **fa·ther·li·ness** n.

Fa·ther's Day ▶ n. the third Sunday in June, a day on which fathers are particularly honored by their children, esp. with gifts and greeting cards.

Fa·ther Time ▶ n. see **TIME** (sense 1 of the noun).

fath·om /ˈfaT͟Həm/ ▶ n. a unit of length equal to six feet (approximately 1.8 m), chiefly used in reference to the depth of water: *sonar says that we're in eighteen fathoms.*
▶ v. [with obj.] **1** [usu. with negative] understand (a difficult problem or an enigmatic person) after much thought: *he could scarcely fathom the idea that people actually lived in Las Vegas* | [with clause] *he couldn't fathom why she was being so anxious.*
2 measure the depth of (water): *an attempt to fathom the ocean.*
– DERIVATIVES **fath·om·a·ble** adj., **fath·om·less** adj.
– ORIGIN Old English *fæthm*. The original sense was 'something that embraces,' (plural) 'the outstretched arms'; hence, a unit of measurement based on the span of the outstretched arms, later standardized to six feet.

Fa·thom·e·ter /faˈT͟Hämətər, ˈfaT͟Hə(m),mētər/ ▶ n. trademark a type of echo sounder.

fa·tigue /fəˈtēg/ ▶ n. **1** extreme tiredness, typically resulting from mental or physical exertion or illness: *he was nearly dead with fatigue.* ■ a reduction in the efficiency of a muscle or organ after prolonged activity. ■ weakness in materials, esp. metal, caused by repeated variations of stress: *metal fatigue.* ■ [with modifier] a lessening in one's response to or enthusiasm for something, typically as a result of overexposure to it: *museum fatigue.*
2 (also **fatigue detail**) a group of soldiers ordered to perform menial, nonmilitary tasks, sometimes as a punishment. ■ (**fatigues**) loose-fitting clothing, typically khaki, olive drab, or camouflaged, of a sort worn by soldiers when performing such menial tasks or while on active duty: *battle fatigues.*
▶ v. (**fatigues, fatiguing, fatigued**) [with obj.] (often **be fatigued**) cause (someone) to feel tired or exhausted: *they were fatigued by their journey.* ■ reduce the efficiency of (a muscle or organ) by prolonged activity. ■ weaken (a material, esp. metal) by repeated variations of stress.
– DERIVATIVES **fa·tigu·a·bil·i·ty** /fə,tēgəˈbilitē/ n., **fa·tigu·a·ble** adj. (also **fatigable**).
– ORIGIN mid 17th cent. (in the sense 'task or duty that causes weariness'): from French *fatigue* (noun), *fatiguer* (verb), from Latin *fatigare* 'tire out,' from *ad fatim, affatim* 'to satiety or surfeit, to bursting.'

Fa·ti·ha /ˈfätē,hä/ (also **Fatihah**) ▶ n. the short first sura of the Koran, used by Muslims as an essential element of ritual prayer.
– ORIGIN from Arabic *al-Fātiḥah* 'the opening (sura),' from *fātiḥa* 'opening,' from *fataḥa* 'to open.'

Fat·i·ma /ˈfatəmə/ (*c.* AD 606–632), youngest daughter of the prophet Muhammad; wife of the fourth caliph, **Ali**. The descendants of Muhammad trace their lineage through her; she is revered, esp. by Shiite Muslims, as the mother of the imams **Hasan** and **Husayn**.

Fá·ti·ma /ˈfatəmə, ˈfätēmə/ a village in western central Portugal, northeast of Lisbon; pop. 8,500 (est. 2008). It became a center of Roman Catholic pilgrimage after the reported sighting there of the Virgin Mary in 1917.

Fat·i·mid /ˈfatəməd, -,mid/ ▶ n. a member of a dynasty that ruled in parts of northern Africa, Egypt, and Syria from 909 to 1171, and founded Cairo as its capital in 969.
▶ adj. of or relating to the Fatimids.
– DERIVATIVES **Fat·i·mite** /-,mīt/ n. & adj.
– ORIGIN from Arabic *Fāṭima* (see **FATIMA**, from whom the dynasty is said to descend) + **-ID**[3].

fat·ling /ˈfatliNG/ ▶ n. a young animal that has been fattened in readiness for slaughter.

fat·so /ˈfatsō/ ▶ n. (pl. **fatsos**) informal, derogatory a fat person.

fat·ten /ˈfatn/ ▶ v. make or become fat or fatter. [with obj.] *he could do with some good food to fatten him up* | [no obj.] *These cattle fatten up quickly.* | figurative *this may fatten their profits.*

fat·ten·ing /ˈfatn-iNG/ ▶ adj. (of a food) causing an increase in the weight of someone who eats it.

fat·toush /faˈto͞oSH/ (also **fatoush**) ▶ n. a Middle Eastern salad consisting of tomatoes, cucumber, and other vegetables together with croutons made from toasted pita bread.
– ORIGIN Arabic *fattūš*.

fat·ty /ˈfatē/ ▶ adj. (**fattier, fattiest**) containing a large amount of fat: *go easy on fatty foods* | *fatty tissue.* ■ Medicine (of a disease or lesion) marked by abnormal deposition of fat in cells: *fatty degeneration of the liver.*
▶ n. (pl. **fatties**) informal a fat person (esp. as a nickname).
– DERIVATIVES **fat·ti·ness** n.

fat·ty ac·id ▶ n. Chemistry a carboxylic acid consisting of a hydrocarbon chain and a terminal carboxyl group, esp. any of those occurring as esters in fats and oils.

fat·ty oil ▶ n. another term for **FIXED OIL**.

fat·u·ous /ˈfaCHo͞oəs/ ▶ adj. silly and pointless: *a fatuous comment.*
– DERIVATIVES **fa·tu·i·ty** /fəˈt(y)o͞oitē/ n. (pl. **fatuities**), **fat·u·ous·ly** adv., **fat·u·ous·ness** n.
– ORIGIN early 17th cent.: from Latin *fatuus* 'foolish' + **-OUS**.

fat·wa /ˈfätwä/ ▶ n. a ruling on a point of Islamic law given by a recognized authority.
– ORIGIN early 17th cent.: from Arabic *fatwā*, from *aftaʼaā* 'decide a point of law.' Compare with **MUFTI**[1].

fau·bourg /ˈfōˌbŏŏr, -ˌbərg/ ▶ **n.** (usu. in place names) a suburb, esp. one in Paris: *the Faubourg Saint-Germain.*
– ORIGIN French (earlier *faux-bourg* 'false borough'), perhaps an alteration of *forsborc,* literally 'outside the town,' but perhaps based on Middle High German *phâlburgere* 'burgers of the pale,' i.e., people living outside the city wall but still inside the palisade.

fau·ces /ˈfôˌsēz/ ▶ **plural n.** Anatomy the arched opening at the back of the mouth leading to the pharynx.
– DERIVATIVES **fau·cial** /ˈfôSHəl/ **adj.**
– ORIGIN late Middle English: from Latin, 'throat.'

fau·cet /ˈfôsit, ˈfäs-/ ▶ **n.** a device by which a flow of liquid or gas from a pipe or container can be controlled; a tap.
– ORIGIN late Middle English (denoting a bung for the vent-hole of a cask, or a tap for drawing liquor from a container): from Old French *fausset,* from Provençal *falset,* from *falsar* 'to bore.' The current sense dates from the mid 19th cent.

faugh /fô/ ▶ **exclam.** dated expressing disgust: *"Faugh! This place stinks!"*
– ORIGIN natural exclamation: first recorded in English in the mid 16th cent.

Faulk·ner /ˈfôknər/, William (1897–1962), US novelist. His works deal with the history and legends of the US South and have a strong sense of a society in decline. Notable works: *The Sound and the Fury* (1929), *As I Lay Dying* (1930), and *Absalom! Absalom!* (1936). Nobel Prize for Literature (1949).
– DERIVATIVES **Faulk·ner·i·an** /fôkˈni(ə)rēən/ **adj.**

fault /fôlt/ ▶ **n. 1** an unattractive or unsatisfactory feature, esp. in a piece of work or in a person's character: *my worst fault is impatience.* ■ a break or other defect in an electrical circuit or piece of machinery: *a fire caused by an electrical fault.* ■ a misguided or dangerous action or habit: *it has been the great fault of our politicians that they have all wanted to do something.* ■ (in tennis and similar games) a service of the ball not in accordance with the rules. ■ (usu. **faults**) (in show jumping) a penalty point imposed for an error.
2 responsibility for an accident or misfortune: *an ordinary man thrust into peril* ***through no fault of his own*** | *it was his fault she had died.*
3 Geology an extended break in a body of rock, marked by the relative displacement and discontinuity of strata on either side of a particular surface.
▶ **v.** [with obj.] **1** criticize for inadequacy or mistakes: *her colleagues and superiors could not fault her dedication to the job* | *you cannot* ***fault him for*** *the professionalism of his approach.* ■ [no obj.] archaic do wrong: *the people of Caesarea faulted greatly when they called King Herod a god.*
2 (**be faulted**) Geology (of a rock formation) be broken by a fault or faults: *rift valleys where the crust has been stretched and faulted* | (as noun **faulting**) *a complex pattern of faulting.*
– PHRASES **at fault 1** responsible for an undesirable situation or event; in the wrong: *we recover compensation from the person at fault.* **2** mistaken or defective: *he suspected that his calculator was at fault.* **find fault** make an adverse criticism or objection, sometimes unfairly or destructively: *he* ***finds fault with*** *everything I do.* **— to a fault** (of someone who displays a particular commendable quality) to an extent verging on excess: *you're kind, caring and generous to a fault.*
– ORIGIN Middle English *faut(e)* 'lack, failing,' from Old French, based on Latin *fallere* 'deceive.' The *-l-* was added (in French and English) in the 15th cent. to conform with the Latin word, but did not become standard in English until the 17th cent., remaining silent in pronunciation until well into the 18th.

fault-find·ing ▶ **n. 1** continual criticism, typically concerning trivial things.
2 the investigation of the cause of malfunction in machinery, esp. electronic equipment.
– DERIVATIVES **fault-find·er n.**

fault·less /ˈfôltləs/ ▶ **adj.** free from defect or error: *your logic is faultless.*
– DERIVATIVES **fault·less·ly adv.**, **fault·less·ness n.**

fault line ▶ **n.** a line on a rock surface or the ground that traces a geological fault. ■ a divisive issue or difference of opinion that is likely to have serious consequences: *religion is now the great fault line of American politics.*

fault·y /ˈfôltē/ ▶ **adj.** (**faultier, faultiest**) working badly or unreliably because of imperfections: *a car with faulty brakes.* ■ (of reasoning and other mental processes) mistaken or misleading because of flaws: *faulty logic.* ■ having or displaying weaknesses: *her character was faulty.*
– DERIVATIVES **fault·i·ly** /ˈfôltəlē/ **adv.**, **fault·i·ness n.**

faun /fôn/ ▶ **n.** Roman Mythology one of a class of lustful rural gods, represented as a man with a goat's horns, ears, legs, and tail.
– ORIGIN late Middle English: from the name of the pastoral god **FAUNUS**.

fau·na /ˈfônə, ˈfänə/ ▶ **n.** (pl. **faunas** /-nəz/) the animals of a particular region, habitat, or geological period: *the* ***flora and fauna*** *of Siberia* | *islands that support one of the richest of all marine faunas.* Compare with **FLORA**. ■ a book or other work describing or listing the animal life of a region.
– DERIVATIVES **fau·nal** /ˈfônl, ˈfänl/ **adj.**, **fau·nis·tic** /fôˈnistik, fä-/ **adj.**
– ORIGIN late 18th cent.: modern Latin application of *Fauna,* the name of a rural goddess, sister of **FAUNUS**.

fau·nal re·gion /ˈfônl, ˈfänl/ ▶ **n.** another term for **ZOOGEOGRAPHICAL REGION**.

Faun·tle·roy /ˈfôntləˌroi/ (also **Little Lord Fauntleroy**) ▶ **n.** an excessively well-mannered or elaborately dressed young boy.
– ORIGIN from the name of the boy hero of Frances Hodgson Burnett's novel *Little Lord Fauntleroy* (1886).

Fau·nus /ˈfônəs, ˈfänəs/ Roman Mythology an ancient Italian pastoral god, grandson of Saturn, associated with wooded places.

Faust /foust/ (also **Faustus** /ˈfoustəs, ˈfô-/) (died *c.*1540), German astronomer and necromancer. Reputed to have sold his soul to the Devil, he became the subject of dramas by Marlowe and Goethe, an opera by Gounod, and a novel by Thomas Mann.
– DERIVATIVES **Faus·ti·an** /ˈfoustēən/ **adj.**

faute de mieux /ˌfōt də ˈmyœ/ ▶ **adv.** for want of a better alternative: *the show is, faute de mieux, the most eagerly anticipated musical of the season to come.*
– ORIGIN mid 18th cent.: French, literally 'for want of (something) better.'

fau·teuil /ˈfōtil, fōˈtœyə/ ▶ **n.** a wooden seat in the form of an armchair with open sides and upholstered arms.
– ORIGIN French, from Old French *faudestuel,* from medieval Latin *faldistolium* (see **FALDSTOOL**).

Fauve /fōv/ (also **fauve**) ▶ **n.** a member of a group of French painters who favored Fauvism: [as modifier] *a Fauve canvas by Matisse.*

Fauv·ism /ˈfōˌvizəm/ (also **fauvism**) ▶ **n.** a style of painting with vivid expressionistic and nonnaturalistic use of color that flourished in Paris from 1905 and, although short-lived, had an important influence on subsequent artists, esp. the German expressionists. Matisse was regarded as the movement's leading figure.
– DERIVATIVES **Fauv·ist n. & adj.**
– ORIGIN from French *fauvisme,* from *fauve* 'wild beast.' The name originated from a remark of the French art critic Louis Vauxcelles at the Salon of 1905; coming across a quattrocento-style statue in the midst of works by Matisse and his associates, he is reputed to have said, "Donatello au milieu des fauves!" ('Donatello among the wild beasts').

faux /fō/ ▶ **adj.** made in imitation; artificial: *a string of faux pearls.* ■ not genuine; fake or false: *their faux concern for the well-being of the voters didn't fool many.*
– ORIGIN French, literally 'false.'

faux-na·ïf /ˌfō näˈēf/ ▶ **adj.** (of a work of art or a person) artificially or affectedly simple or naive: *faux-naif pastoralism.*
▶ **n.** (**faux naif**) a person who pretends to be ingenuous: *the old device of a faux naif observing his own country as a foreigner.*
– ORIGIN mid 20th cent.: from French *faux* 'false' + *naïf* 'naive.'

faux pas /fō ˈpä, ˈfō ˌpä/ ▶ **n.** (pl. **same**) an embarrassing or tactless act or remark in a social situation.
– ORIGIN late 17th cent.: French, literally 'false step.'

fa·va bean /ˈfävə ˌbēn/ ▶ **n.** another term for **BROAD BEAN**.
– ORIGIN Italian *fava,* from Latin *faba* 'bean.'

fave /fāv/ ▶ **n. & adj.** informal short for **FAVORITE**.

fa·ve·la /fəˈvelə/ ▶ **n.** a Brazilian shack or shanty town; a slum.
– DERIVATIVES **fa·ve·la·do** /ˌfävəˈlädō/ **n.**
– ORIGIN Portuguese.

fa·vi·con /ˈfāvəˌkän/ ▶ **n.** an icon associated with a URL that is variously displayed, as in a browser's address bar or next to the site name in a bookmark list.

fa·vor /ˈfāvər/ (Brit. **favour**) ▶ **n. 1** an attitude of approval or liking: *the legislation is viewed with favor.* ■ support or advancement given as a sign of approval: *a struggle between competing aides for presidential favor.* ■ overgenerous preferential treatment: *they accused you of showing favor to one of the players.* ■ a small gift or souvenir: *good party favors include stickers, hair barrettes, or crayons.* ■ archaic a thing such as a badge or knot of ribbons that is given or worn as a mark of liking or support.
2 an act of kindness beyond what is due or usual: *I've come to ask you a favor.* ■ (**one's favors**) dated used with reference to a woman allowing a man to have sexual intercourse with her: *she had granted her favors to him.*
▶ **v.** [with obj.] **1** feel or show approval or preference for: *slashing public spending is a policy that few politicians favor.* ■ give unfairly preferential treatment to: *critics argued that the policy favored the private sector.* ■ work to the advantage of: *natural selection has favored bats.*
2 (**favor someone with**) (often used in polite requests) give someone (something that they want): *please favor me with an answer.*
3 informal resemble (a parent or relative) in facial features: *she's pretty, and she favors you.*
4 treat (an injured limb) gently, not putting one's full weight on it: *he favors his sore leg.*
– PHRASES **do someone a favor** do something for someone as an act of kindness. **in favor 1** meeting with approval: *they were not in favor with the party.* **2** having or showing approval: *the appeals court ruled 2-1* ***in favor of*** *his extradition.* **in one's favor** to one's advantage: *events were moving in his favor.* **in favor of 1** to be replaced by: *he stepped down as leader in favor of his rival.* **2** to the advantage of: *the final score was 25-16 in favor of Washington.* **out of favor** lacking or having lost approval or popularity: *proper dancing has gone out of favor.*
– DERIVATIVES **fa·vor·er n.**
– ORIGIN Middle English (in the noun sense 'liking, preference'): via Old French from Latin *favor,* from *favere* 'show kindness to' (related to *fovere* 'cherish').

fa·vor·a·ble /ˈfāv(ə)rəbəl/ (Brit. **favourable**) ▶ **adj.**
1 expressing approval: *the book received highly favorable reviews.* ■ giving consent: *their demands rarely received a favorable response.*
2 to the advantage of someone or something: *they made a settlement* ***favorable to*** *the unions.* ■ (of a wind) blowing in the direction of travel. ■ (of weather, or a period of time judged in terms of its weather) fine. ■ suggesting a good outcome: *a favorable prognosis.*
– DERIVATIVES **fa·vor·a·ble·ness n.**
– ORIGIN Middle English: via Old French from Latin *favorabilis,* from *favor* (see **FAVOR**).

fa·vor·a·bly /ˈfāv(ə)r(ə)blē/ (Brit. **favourably**) ▶ **adv. 1** with approval: *the audience responded very favorably.*
2 to the advantage of someone or something: *the deal will work out favorably for the company.*

fa·vored /ˈfāvərd/ ▶ **adj.** preferred or recommended: *she was his favored candidate* | *the most favored destination of visitors to Canada.*

fa·vor·ite /ˈfāv(ə)rət/ (Brit. **favourite**) ▶ **adj.** [attrib.] preferred before all others of the same kind: *their favorite Italian restaurant.*
▶ **n.** a person or thing that is especially popular or particularly well liked by someone: *the song is still a favorite after 20 years.* ■ the competitor thought most likely to win a game or contest, esp. by people betting on the outcome: *he was the early favorite to win the South Carolina caucuses.* ■ a record of the address of a website or other data made to enable quick access; a bookmark.
▶ **v.** [with obj.] record the address of (a website or other data) to enable quick access in future: *you can see who else favorited the same pictures.*
– PHRASES **favorite son** a famous man who is particularly popular and praised for his achievements in his native area: *Green Bay's favorite son is equal parts laid-back and hot-blooded.* ■ a person supported as a presidential candidate by delegates from the candidate's home state.
– ORIGIN late 16th cent. (as a noun): from obsolete French *favorit,* from Italian *favorito,* past participle of *favorire* 'to favor,' from Latin *favor* (see **FAVOR**).

WORD TRENDS As with *friend,* the transformation of **favorite** into a verb is an Internet phenomenon. On the Web, you can record the address of a particular site using an online bookmark, to allow you to find it quickly in the future. On Internet Explorer, the bookmarks are called **favorites**, and the browser's dominance has led to the term being adopted as a synonym for **bookmark** (itself used in computing contexts since the 1980s) as both noun and verb: *voting is open for another 17 days, so favorite the* page and do it daily. The term can also refer to the process of tagging and collecting together your favorite online pictures, videos, or messages: *I spent forever on Flickr searching out, and favoriting, examples of my newest passion.*

fa·vor·it·ism /ˈfāv(ə)rəˌtizəm/ ▶ **n.** the practice of giving unfair preferential treatment to one person or group at the expense of another.

fa·vrile glass /fəvˈrē/ ▶ **n.** a richly colored iridescent glass, developed by L. C. Tiffany.
– ORIGIN late 19th cent.: formed as a trademark from the obsolete adjective *fabrile* 'of a craftsman.'

Fawkes /fôks/, Guy (1570–1606), English conspirator. He was hanged for his part in the Gunpowder Plot of November 5, 1605. The occasion is commemorated annually in Britain on November 5 with fireworks, bonfires, and the burning of an effigy called a *guy*.

f

fawn[1] /fôn, fän/ ▶ **n. 1** a young deer in its first year. **2** a light yellowish-brown color.
▶ **v.** [no obj.] (of a deer) produce young.
– PHRASES **in fawn** (of a deer) pregnant.
– ORIGIN late Middle English: from Old French *faon*, based on Latin *fetus* 'offspring'; compare with FETUS.

fawn[2] ▶ **v.** [no obj.] (of a person) give a servile display of exaggerated flattery or affection, typically in order to gain favor or advantage: *congressmen fawn over the President.* ■ (of an animal, esp. a dog) show slavish devotion, esp. by crawling and rubbing against someone.
– ORIGIN Old English *fagnian* 'make or be glad'; related to FAIN.

fawn·ing /ˈfôniNG, ˈfän-/ ▶ **adj.** displaying exaggerated flattery or affection; obsequious: *fawning adoration | fawning interviews with Hollywood celebs.*
– DERIVATIVES **fawn·ing·ly adv.**

fax /faks/ ▶ **n.** an image of a document made by electronic scanning and transmitted as data by telecommunication links. ■ the production or transmission of documents in this way: *he received the report by fax.* ■ (also **fax machine**) a machine for transmitting and receiving such documents.
▶ **v.** [with obj.] send (a document) by such means. ■ contact (someone) by such means: *to obtain a brochure, fax the agent* | [no obj.] *the best way to order materials was to fax.*
– ORIGIN 1940s.: abbreviation of FACSIMILE.

fay /fā/ ▶ **n.** literary a fairy.
– ORIGIN late Middle English: from Old French *fae, faie*, from Latin *fata* 'the Fates,' plural of *fatum* (see FATE). Compare with FAIRY.

fay·al·ite /fəˈyälˌīt/ ▶ **n.** a black or brown mineral that is an iron-rich form of olivine and occurs in many igneous rocks.
– ORIGIN mid 19th cent.: from *Fayal* (the name of an island in the Azores) + -ITE[1].

Fay·ette·ville /ˈfāətˌvil, -vəl/ **1** a commercial city in northwestern Arkansas, home to the University of Arkansas; pop. 73,372 (est. 2008). **2** a commercial city in south central North Carolina; pop. 174,091 (est. 2008).

fayre /fer/ ▶ **n.** pseudoarchaic spelling of FAIR[2] and FARE (sense 2 of the noun).

faze /fāz/ ▶ **v.** [with obj., usu. with negative] informal disturb or disconcert (someone): *she was not fazed by his show of anger.*
– ORIGIN mid 19th cent.: variant of dialect *feeze* 'drive or frighten off,' from Old English *fēsian*.

USAGE **Faze** has no connection with the word phase and should not be spelled with a *ph-*, although this is a common error: almost a quarter of citations for the word in the Oxford English Corpus are for the incorrect spelling.

fa·zen·da /fəˈzendə/ ▶ **n.** an estate or large farm in Portugal, Brazil, and other Portuguese-speaking countries.
– ORIGIN Portuguese (see HACIENDA).

fa·zen·dei·ro /ˌfazənˈdāˌrō/ ▶ **n.** (pl. **fazendeiros**) a person who owns or occupies a fazenda.
– ORIGIN Portuguese.

FB ▶ **abbr.** ■ foreign body. ■ freight bill.

fb (also **f.b.**) ▶ **abbr.** Sports fullback.

FBI ▶ **abbr.** Federal Bureau of Investigation.

f.c. ▶ **abbr.** ■ fielder's choice. ■ follow copy.

FCA ▶ **abbr.** Farm Credit Association.

fcap. ▶ **abbr.** foolscap.

FCC ▶ **abbr.** Federal Communications Commission.

FCS ▶ **abbr.** Fellow of the Chemical Society.

fcy. ▶ **abbr.** fancy.

FD ▶ **abbr.** ■ Defender of the Faith. [from Latin *Fidei Defensor*.] ■ Fire Department.

FDA ▶ **abbr.** Food and Drug Administration.

FDC ▶ **abbr.** first day cover.

FDDI ▶ **abbr.** fiber-distributed data interface, a communications, cabling, and hardware standard for high-speed optical-fiber networks.

FDI ▶ **abbr.** foreign direct investment.

FDIC ▶ **abbr.** Federal Deposit Insurance Corporation, a body that underwrites most private bank deposits.

FDR the nickname of President Franklin Delano Roosevelt (see ROOSEVELT[2]).

Fe ▶ **symbol** the chemical element iron.
– ORIGIN from Latin *ferrum*.

fe·al·ty /ˈfēltē/ ▶ **n.** historical a feudal tenant's or vassal's sworn loyalty to a lord: *they owed fealty to the Earl rather than the King.* ■ formal acknowledgment of this: *a property for which she did fealty.*
– ORIGIN Middle English: from Old French *feau(l)te, fealte*, from Latin *fidelitas* (see FIDELITY).

fear /fi(ə)r/ ▶ **n.** an unpleasant emotion caused by the belief that someone or something is dangerous, likely to cause pain, or a threat: *drivers are threatening to quit their jobs in fear after a cabby's murder | fear of increasing unemployment | he is prey to irrational fears.* ■ archaic a mixed feeling of dread and reverence: *the love and fear of God.* ■ (**fear for**) a feeling of anxiety concerning the outcome of something or the safety and well-being of someone: *police launched a search for the family amid fears for their safety.* ■ the likelihood of something unwelcome happening: *she could observe the other guests without too much fear of attracting attention.*
▶ **v.** [with obj.] be afraid of (someone or something) as likely to be dangerous, painful, or threatening: *he said he didn't care about life so why should he fear death?* | [with clause] *farmers fear that they will lose business.* ■ [no obj.] (**fear for**) feel anxiety or apprehension on behalf of: *I fear for the city with this madman let loose in it.* ■ [with infinitive] avoid or put off doing something because one is afraid: *they aim to make war so horrific that potential aggressors will fear to resort to it.* ■ used to express regret or apology: *I'll buy her book, though not, I fear, the hardback version.* ■ archaic regard (God) with reverence and awe.
– PHRASES **for fear of** (or **that**) to avoid the risk of (or that): *no one dared refuse the order for fear of losing their job.* **never fear** used to reassure someone: *we shall meet again, never fear.* **put the fear of God in** (or **into**) **someone** cause someone to be very frightened. **without fear or favor** impartially: *make all your decisions without fear or favor.*
– ORIGIN Old English *fǣr* 'calamity, danger,' *fǣran* 'frighten,' also 'revere.'

fear·ful /ˈfi(ə)rfəl/ ▶ **adj. 1** feeling afraid; showing fear or anxiety: *bond traders have remained fearful of inflation* | [with clause] *the mothers were fearful that their daughters would marry and move abroad.* ■ causing or likely to cause people to be afraid; horrifying: *a fearful accident.* **2** informal very great: *he could cause a fearful commotion.*
– DERIVATIVES **fear·ful·ness n.**

fear·ful·ly /ˈfi(ə)rfəlē/ ▶ **adv. 1** in an anxious manner; apprehensively: *he glanced over his shoulder fearfully.* **2** [as submodifier] dreadfully; extremely: *she was fearfully worried for the welfare of her family.*

fear·less /ˈfi(ə)rlis/ ▶ **adj.** lacking fear: *a fearless defender of freedom.*
– DERIVATIVES **fear·less·ly adv.**, **fear·less·ness n.**

fear·mon·ger·ing /ˈfi(ə)rˌməNGgəriNG/ ▶ **n.** the action of deliberately arousing public fear or alarm about a particular issue: *his campaign for re-election was based on fearmongering and deception.*
– DERIVATIVES **fear·mon·ger n.**

fear·some /ˈfi(ə)rsəm/ ▶ **adj.** frightening, esp. in appearance: *the cat mewed, displaying a fearsome set of teeth.*
– DERIVATIVES **fear·some·ly adv.**, **fear·some·ness n.**

fea·si·bil·i·ty /ˌfēzəˈbilətē/ ▶ **n.** the state or degree of being easily or conveniently done: *the feasibility of a manned flight to Mars.*

fea·si·bil·i·ty stud·y ▶ **n.** an assessment of the practicality of a proposed plan or method.

fea·si·ble /ˈfēzəbəl/ ▶ **adj.** possible to do easily or conveniently: *it is not feasible to put most finds from excavations on public display.* ■ informal likely; probable: *the most feasible explanation.*
– DERIVATIVES **fea·si·bly** /-zəblē/ **adv.**
– ORIGIN late Middle English: from Old French *faisible*, from *fais-*, stem of *faire* 'do, make,' from Latin *facere*.

USAGE The primary meaning of **feasible** is 'capable of being done or effected.' There is rarely a need to use **feasible** to mean 'likely' or 'probable' when those words can do the job. There are cases, however, in which a careful writer finds that the sense of likelihood or probability (as with an explanation or theory) is more naturally or idiomatically expressed with **feasible** than with *possible* or *probable*.

feast /fēst/ ▶ **n.** a large meal, typically one in celebration of something: *a wedding feast.* ■ a plentiful supply of something enjoyable, esp. for the mind or senses: *the concert season offers a feast of classical music.* ■ an annual religious celebration. ■ a day dedicated to a particular saint: *the feast of St. Joseph.*
▶ **v.** [no obj.] eat and drink sumptuously: *the men would congregate and feast after hunting.* ■ (**feast on**) eat large quantities of: *we sat feasting on barbecued chicken and beer.* ■ [with obj.] give (someone) a plentiful and delicious meal: *he was feasted and invited to all the parties.*
– PHRASES **skeleton at the feast** a person or thing that brings gloom or sadness to an otherwise pleasant or celebratory occasion. **feast one's eyes on** gaze at with pleasure. **feast or famine** either too much of something or too little.
– DERIVATIVES **feast·er n.**
– ORIGIN Middle English: from Old French *feste* (noun), *fester* (verb), from Latin *festa*, neuter plural of *festus* 'joyous.' Compare with FÊTE and FIESTA.

feast day ▶ **n.** a day on which a celebration, esp. an annual Christian one, is held.

Feast of Ded·i·ca·tion ▶ **n.** another name for HANUKKAH.

Feast of Tab·er·nac·les ▶ **n.** another name for SUCCOTH.

Feast of Weeks ▶ **n.** another name for SHAVUOTH.

feat /fēt/ ▶ **n.** an achievement that requires great courage, skill, or strength: *the new printing presses were considerable feats of engineering.*
– ORIGIN late Middle English (in the general sense 'action or deed'): from Old French *fait*, from Latin *factum* (see FACT).

feath·er /ˈfe<u>TH</u>ər/ ▶ **n.** any of the flat appendages growing from a bird's skin and forming its plumage, consisting of a partly hollow horny shaft fringed with vanes of barbs. ■ (often **feathers**) one of these appendages as decoration. ■ one of the feathers or featherlike vanes fastened to the shaft of an arrow or a dart. ■ (**feathers**) a fringe of long hair on the legs of a dog, horse, or other animal. ■ a small side branch on a tree.
▶ **v. 1** [with obj.] rotate the blades of (a propeller) about their own axes in such a way as to lessen the air or water resistance. ■ vary the angle of attack of (rotor blades). ■ Rowing turn (an oar) so that it passes through the air edgewise: *he turned, feathering one oar slowly.* **2** [no obj.] float, move, or wave like a feather: *the green fronds feathered against a blue sky.* ■ [with obj.] touch (someone or something) very lightly. **3** [with obj.] shorten or taper the hair by cutting or trimming: *my sister had her hair feathered.*
– PHRASES **a feather in one's cap** an achievement to be proud of. **feather one's (own) nest** make money illicitly and at someone else's expense. **(as) light as a feather** extremely light and insubstantial.
– DERIVATIVES **feath·er·less adj.**
– ORIGIN Old English *fether*, from an Indo-European root shared by Latin *penna* 'feather' and Greek *pteron* 'wing.'

feath·er·back /ˈfe<u>TH</u>ərˌbak/ ▶ **n.** a tropical freshwater fish native to southern Asia and Africa, with a strongly humped back, a small, featherlike dorsal fin, and a long anal fin that runs from the belly to the tail. ● Family Notopteridae: four genera and several species, in particular the large edible *Notopterus chitala* of Asia.

feath·er·bed /ˈfe<u>TH</u>ərˌbed/ ▶ **n.** (also **feather bed**) a bed that has a mattress stuffed with feathers.
▶ **v.** (also **feather-bed**) [with obj.] provide (someone) with advantageous economic or working conditions: *apart from the fees he earns, a practicing lawyer is not featherbedded in any way.* ■ (usu. as noun **featherbedding**) deliberately limit production or retain excess staff in (a business) in order to create jobs or prevent unemployment, typically as a result of a union contract.

feath·er·brain /ˈfe<u>TH</u>ərˌbrān/ (also **featherhead**) ▶ **n.** a silly or absentminded person.
– DERIVATIVES **feath·er·brained** (also **feather-brained** or **featherheaded**) **adj.**

feath·er dust·er ▶ **n.** a long-handled brush with a head made of feathers, used for dusting. ■ (also **feather duster worm**) another term for FAN WORM.

feath·ered /ˈfeT͟Hərd/ ▶ **adj.** (of a bird) covered with feathers: [in combination] *black-feathered ostriches.* ■ decorated with feathers: *a feathered hat.*

feath·ered friend ▶ **n.** (usu. **feathered friends**) informal, humorous a bird.

feath·er edge ▶ **n.** a fine edge produced by tapering a board or other object.

feath·er·ing /ˈfeT͟HəriNG/ ▶ **n. 1** the plumage of a bird or part of a bird. ■ featherlike markings or structure: *traditional finishes such as marbling and feathering.* ■ the feathers of an arrow. ■ fringes of hairs on the appendages or body of a dog. ■ Architecture cusping in tracery.
2 the action of varying the angle of propellers, rotor blades, or oars so as to reduce air or water resistance.

feath·er·light /ˈfeT͟Hər,līt/ ▶ **adj.** extremely light: *a featherlight touch.*

feath·er star ▶ **n.** an echinoderm with a small disklike body, long feathery arms for feeding and movement, and short appendages for grasping the surface. ● Order Comatulida, class Crinoidea.

feath·er·stitch /ˈfeT͟Hər,stiCH/ ▶ **n.** ornamental zigzag sewing.
▶ **v.** [with obj., usu. as noun] (**featherstitching**) sew (something) with such a stitch.

feath·er·tail glid·er /ˈfeT͟Hər,tāl/ ▶ **n.** an Australian pygmy possum with a flap of skin between the fore- and hind limbs for gliding, and a feathery tail. ● *Acrobates pygmaeus*, family Burramyidae. Alternative name: **flying mouse**.

feath·er·weight /ˈfeT͟Hər,wāt/ ▶ **n.** a weight in boxing and other sports intermediate between bantamweight and lightweight. It ranges from 118 to 126 pounds (54 to 57 kg). ■ a boxer or other competitor of this weight. ■ a very light person or thing. ■ a person or thing not worth serious consideration: *he is an intellectual featherweight.*

feath·er·y /ˈfeT͟H(ə)rē/ ▶ **adj.** having, covered with, or resembling feathers: *wisps of feathery blonde hair.*
– DERIVATIVES **feath·er·i·ness n.**

fea·ture /ˈfēCHər/ ▶ **n. 1** a distinctive attribute or aspect of something: *safety features like dual air bags.* ■ (usu. **features**) a part of the face, such as the mouth or eyes, making a significant contribution to its overall appearance. ■ Linguistics a distinctive characteristic of a linguistic unit, esp. a speech sound or vocabulary item, that serves to distinguish it from others of the same type.
2 a newspaper or magazine article or a broadcast program devoted to the treatment of a particular topic, typically at length: *a feature on Detroit's downtown fishery.* ■ (also **feature film**) a full-length film intended as the main item in a movie theater program.
▶ **v.** [with obj.] have as a prominent attribute or aspect: *the hotel features a large lounge, a sauna, and a coin-operated solarium.* ■ have as an important actor or participant: *the film featured Glenn Miller and his Orchestra.* ■ [no obj.] (often **be featured**) be a significant characteristic of or take an important part in: *this famous photograph is prominently featured in art collections.* ■ [no obj.] be apparent: *women rarely feature in writing on land settlement.*
– DERIVATIVES **fea·tured adj.** [in combination] *fine-featured women*, **fea·ture·less adj.**
– ORIGIN late Middle English (originally denoting the form or proportions of the body, or a physical feature): from Old French *faiture* 'form,' from Latin *factura* (see FACTURE).

fea·ture-length ▶ **adj.** of the length of a typical feature film or program: *a feature-length documentary.*

Feb. ▶ **abbr.** February.

feb·ri·fuge /ˈfebrə,fyo͞oj/ ▶ **n.** a medicine used to reduce fever.
– DERIVATIVES **fe·brif·u·gal** /,fəbrəˈf(y)o͞ogəl/ **adj.**
– ORIGIN late 17th cent.: from French *fébrifuge*, from Latin *febris* 'fever' + *fugare* 'drive away.' Compare with FEVERFEW.

fe·brile /ˈfeb,rīl, ˈfē,brīl/ ▶ **adj.** having or showing the symptoms of a fever: *a febrile illness.* ■ having or showing a great deal of nervous excitement or energy: *a febrile imagination.*
– DERIVATIVES **fe·bril·i·ty** /fēˈbrilətē/ **n.**
– ORIGIN mid 17th cent.: from French *fébrile* or medieval Latin *febrilis*, from Latin *febris* 'fever.'

Feb·ru·ar·y /ˈfeb(y)o͞o,erē, ˈfebro͞o-/ ▶ **n.** (pl. **Februaries**) the second month of the year, in the northern hemisphere usually considered the last month of winter: *even in February the place is busy* | [as modifier] *a freezing February morning.*
– ORIGIN Middle English *feverer*, from Old French *feverier*, based on Latin *februarius*, from *februa*, the name of a purification feast held in this month. The spelling change in the 15th cent. was due to association with the Latin word.

> **USAGE** Note that **February** is spelled with an **r** following the **Feb-**. Precise speakers insist that the **r** should be pronounced, but this is not easy, and most people replace the **r** following **Feb-** with a **y** sound: **Feb-yoo-** rather than **Feb-roo-**. This is now becoming the accepted standard.

Feb·ru·ar·y Rev·o·lu·tion see RUSSIAN REVOLUTION.

fec. ▶ **abbr.** he or she made it.
– ORIGIN from Latin *fecit.*

fe·ces /ˈfēsēz/ (Brit. **faeces**) ▶ **plural n.** waste matter discharged from the bowels after food has been digested; excrement.
– DERIVATIVES **fe·cal** /ˈfēkəl/ **adj.**
– ORIGIN late Middle English: from Latin, plural of *faex* 'dregs.'

feck·less /ˈfekləs/ ▶ **adj.** lacking initiative or strength of character; irresponsible: *a feckless mama's boy* | *an unfortunate example of feckless filmmaking.*
– DERIVATIVES **feck·less·ly adv.**, **feck·less·ness n.**
– ORIGIN late 16th cent.: from Scots and northern English dialect *feck* (from *effeck*, variant of EFFECT) + -LESS.

fec·u·lent /ˈfekyələnt/ ▶ **adj.** of or containing dirt, sediment, or waste matter: *their feet were forever slipping on feculent bog.*
– DERIVATIVES **fec·u·lence n.**
– ORIGIN late 15th cent.: from French *féculent* or Latin *faeculentus*, from *faex*, *faec-* 'dregs.'

fe·cund /ˈfekənd, ˈfē-/ ▶ **adj.** producing or capable of producing an abundance of offspring or new growth; fertile: *a lush and fecund garden* | figurative *her fecund imagination.* ■ technical (of a woman or women) capable of becoming pregnant and giving birth.
– DERIVATIVES **fe·cun·di·ty** /feˈkəndətē, fiˈkən-/ **n.**
– ORIGIN late Middle English: from French *fécond* or Latin *fecundus* 'fruitful.'

fe·cun·date /ˈfekən,dāt/ ▶ **v.** [with obj.] fertilize: *there were no insects to fecundate flowering plants.* ■ literary make fruitful: *he actuates and fecundates our souls.*
– DERIVATIVES **fe·cun·da·tion** /,fēkənˈdāSHən/ **n.**
– ORIGIN mid 17th cent.: from Latin *fecundat-* 'made fruitful,' from the verb *fecundare*, from *fecundus* 'fruitful.'

Fed /fed/ ▶ **n.** informal **1** a federal agent or official, esp. a member of the FBI: *I don't think he has any friends since he ratted to the Feds.*
2 (usu. **the Fed**) short for FEDERAL RESERVE.
– ORIGIN early 20th cent.: abbreviation of FEDERAL. The abbreviation *fed* had previously been used in the late 18th cent. to denote a member of the Federalist party, who advocated a union of American colonies after the American Revolution.

fed /fed/ past and past participle of FEED.

fed. ▶ **abbr.** ■ federal. ■ federated. ■ federation.

fe·da·yeen /,fedäˈēn, -dīˈēn/ ▶ **plural n.** Arab guerrillas operating esp. in Israel and Palestine against the Israeli government, and in Iraq against the occupying coalition forces during and after the Second Gulf War.
– ORIGIN 1950s: from colloquial Arabic *fidā'iyīn*, plural of classical Arabic *fidā'ī* 'one who gives his life for another or for a cause,' from *fadā* 'to ransom someone.' The singular *fedai* (from Arabic and Persian *fidā'ī*) had previously been used (late 19th cent.) to denote an Ismaili Muslim assassin.

fed·er·al /ˈfed(ə)rəl/ ▶ **adj.** having or relating to a system of government in which several states form a unity but remain independent in internal affairs: *Russia's federation treaty shares powers among Russia's federal and local governments.* ■ of, relating to, or denoting the central government as distinguished from the separate units constituting a federation: *the federal agency that provides legal services to the poor.* ■ of, relating to, or denoting the central government of the US. ■ (**Federal**) historical of the northern states in the Civil War: *a loud Federal cheer was heard, proving Stonewall to be hard pressed.*
– DERIVATIVES **fed·er·al·i·za·tion** /,fed(ə)rəliˈzāSHən/ **n.**, **fed·er·al·ize** /-,līz/ **v.**, **fed·er·al·ly adv.**
– ORIGIN mid 17th cent.: from Latin *foedus*, *foeder-* 'league, covenant' + -AL.

Fed·er·al Bu·reau of In·ves·ti·ga·tion (abbr.: **FBI**) an agency of the US federal government that deals principally with internal security and counterintelligence and that also conducts investigations in federal law enforcement. It was established in 1908 as a branch of the Department of Justice, but was substantially reorganized under the controversial directorship (1924–72) of J. Edgar Hoover.

fed·er·al case ▶ **n.** Law a criminal case that falls under the jurisdiction of a federal court. ■ informal a matter of great concern or with dire consequences: *I'm not trying to make a federal case out of this, Christine, but you've got to do something.*

fed·er·al·ism /ˈfed(ə)rə,lizəm/ ▶ **n.** the federal principle or system of government: *the politics of federalism in Canada.* ■ (**Federalism**) the principles of the Federalist Party. ■ in Canada, support of confederation in opposition to Quebec separatism.

fed·er·al·ist /ˈfed(ə)rəlist/ ▶ **n. 1** an advocate or supporter of federalism: *political struggles between centralists and federalists.*
2 (**Federalist**) a member or supporter of the Federalist Party: *captured both the legislative and the executive branches of the federal government from the Federalists.*
▶ **adj. 1** of, pertaining to, or favoring federalism or federalists: *the Quebec Liberal Party and the federalist cause would be greatly strengthened by his candidacy* | *Britain can achieve what it wants, more power to the federalist European Parliament* | *even the moderates here sounded more Reaganite than Ronald Reagan ever did in his federalist riffs.*
2 (**Federalist**) designating or pertaining to the Federalist Party: *it was not a weapon that could reach John Marshall and the other Federalist judges.*

Fed·er·al·ist Pa·pers (also **The Federalist**) a collection of essays written under the pseudonym "Publius" by Alexander Hamilton, John Jay, and James Madison, addressed to "The People of the State of New York," first published in New York City newspapers between October 1787 and August 1788. The purpose of *The Federalist* was to persuade New Yorkers to ratify the Constitution adopted in Philadelphia in September 1787.

Fed·er·al·ist Par·ty an early political party in the US, joined by George Washington during his presidency (1789–97) and in power until 1801. The party's emphasis on strong central government was extremely important in the early years after independence, but by the 1820s it had been superseded by the Democratic-Republican Party.

Fed·er·al O·pen Mar·ket Com·mit·tee ▶ **n.** a committee of the Federal Reserve Board that meets regularly to set monetary policy, including the interest rates that are charged to banks.

Fed·er·al Reg·is·ter ▶ **n.** a daily publication of the US federal government that issues proposed and final administrative regulations of federal agencies.

Fed·er·al Re·pub·lic of Ger·ma·ny former name of **West Germany** (see GERMANY).

Fed·er·al Re·serve the federal banking authority in the US that performs the functions of a central bank and is used to implement the country's monetary policy, providing a national system of reserve cash available to banks. Created in 1913, the Federal Reserve System consists of twelve Federal Reserve Districts, each having a Federal Reserve Bank. These are controlled from Washington, DC, by the Federal Reserve Board consisting of governors appointed by the US president with Senate approval.

Fed·er·al Trade Com·mis·sion ▶ **n.** Finance a federal agency, established in 1914, that administers antitrust and consumer protection legislation in pursuit of free and fair competition in the marketplace.

Fed·er·al Un·ion see UNION (sense 3).

Fed·er·al Way a city in west central Washington that lies between Seattle and Tacoma; pop. 84,309 (est. 2008).

fed·er·ate ▶ **v.** /ˈfedə,rāt/ [no obj.] (of a number of states or organizations) form a single centralized unit, within which each keeps some internal autonomy. ■ [with obj.] (usu. as adj. **federated**) form (states or organizations) into such a centralized unit: *the establishment of 20 federated states in Mindanao.*
▶ **adj.** /ˈfedərit/ of or relating to such an arrangement: *federate armies.*
– DERIVATIVES **fed·er·a·tive** /-,rātiv, -rətiv/ **adj.**
– ORIGIN early 18th cent. (as an adjective): from late Latin *foederatus*, based on *foedus*, *foeder-* 'league, covenant.'

Fed·er·at·ed States of Mi·cro·ne·sia full name for MICRONESIA (sense 2).

fed·er·a·tion /,fedəˈrāSHən/ ▶ **n.** a group of states with a central government but independence in internal affairs: [in names] *should the world be governed by a Pax Americana or by a democratic UN federation?* ■ an organization or group within which smaller divisions have some degree of internal autonomy: [in names] *the best tag team in the World Wrestling Federation.* ■ the action of forming states

or organizations into a single group with centralized control: *a first step in the federation of Europe.*
– DERIVATIVES **fed·er·a·tion·ist** /-ist/ **n.**
– ORIGIN early 18th cent.: from French *fédération,* from late Latin *foederatio(n-),* from the verb *foederare* 'to ally,' from *foedus* 'league.'

fe·do·ra /fəˈdôrə/ ▶ **n.** a low, soft felt hat with a curled brim and the crown creased lengthwise.
– ORIGIN late 19th cent. (originally US): from *Fédora,* the title of a drama (1882) written by the French dramatist Victorien Sardou (1831–1908).

fedora

fed up ▶ **adj.** [predic.] annoyed or upset at a situation or treatment: *he was* **fed up with** *doing all the work.*

f

fee /fē/ ▶ **n. 1** a payment made to a professional person or to a professional or public body in exchange for advice or services. ■ money paid as part of a special transaction, e.g., for a privilege or for admission to something: *the gallery charges an admission fee.* ■ (usu. **fees**) money regularly paid (esp. to a school or similar institution) for continuing services: *high tuition fees required by the schools.*
2 Law, historical an estate of land, esp. one held on condition of feudal service.
▶ **v.** (**fees, feeing, fee'd** or **feed**) [with obj.] rare make a payment to (someone) in return for services.
– PHRASES **hold something in fee** Law, historical hold an estate in return for feudal service to a superior.
– ORIGIN Middle English: from an Anglo-Norman French variant of Old French *feu, fief,* from medieval Latin *feodum, feudum,* ultimately of Germanic origin. Compare with **FEU** and **FIEF**.

feeb /fēb/ informal ▶ **n. 1** a feebleminded person. **2** an FBI agent.

fee·bate /ˈfēˌbāt/ ▶ **n.** a system of charges and rebates whereby energy-efficient or environmentally friendly practices are rewarded while failure to adhere to such practices is penalized.
– ORIGIN 1990s: blend of *fee* and *rebate.*

fee·ble /ˈfēbəl/ ▶ **adj.** (**feebler, feeblest**) lacking physical strength, esp. as a result of age or illness: *my legs are very feeble after the flu.* ■ (of a sound) faint: *his voice sounded feeble and far away.* ■ lacking strength of character: *she overreacted in such a feeble, juvenile way.* ■ failing to convince or impress: *a feeble excuse.*
– DERIVATIVES **fee·ble·ness n., fee·bly** /ˈfēb(ə)lē/ **adv.**
– ORIGIN Middle English: from Old French *fieble,* earlier *fleible,* from Latin *flebilis* 'lamentable,' from *flere* 'weep.'

fee·ble·mind·ed /ˈfēbəlˌmīndəd/ ▶ **adj.** (of a person) unable to make intelligent decisions or judgments. ■ (of an idea or proposal) lacking in sense or clear direction: *a feebleminded policy.* ■ dated (of a person) having less than average intelligence.
– DERIVATIVES **fee·ble·mind·ed·ly** (also **feeble-mindedly**) **adv., fee·ble·mind·ed·ness** (also **feeble-mindedness**) **n.**

feed /fēd/ ▶ **v.** (past and past participle **fed** /fed/) [with obj.] **1** give food to: *the raiders fed the guard dog to keep it quiet* | [with two objs.] *he fed her brownies he had just baked.* ■ [no obj.] (esp. of an animal or baby) take food; eat something: *morays emerge at night to feed.* ■ provide an adequate supply of food for: *the island's simple agriculture could hardly feed its inhabitants.* ■ [no obj.] (**feed on/off**) derive regular nourishment from (a particular substance): *the bird feeds on cliff-top vegetation* | figurative *his powerful mind fed off political discussion.* ■ encourage the growth of: *I could feed my melancholy by reading Romantic poetry.* ■ give fertilizer to (a plant). ■ put fuel on (a fire).
2 supply (a machine) with material, power, or other things necessary for its operation: *the programs are fed into the computer.* ■ [with two objs.] supply (someone) with (information, ideas, etc.): *I think he is feeding his old employer commercial secrets.* ■ supply water to (a body of water): *the pond is fed by a small stream* | [no obj.] *water feeds into the lower pool.* ■ insert further coins into (a meter) to extend the time for which it operates. ■ [with two objs.] prompt (an actor) with (a line): *you were still in the wings feeding Micky his lines.* ■ (in ball games) pass (the ball) to a player: *he took the ball and fed Salley.* ■ distribute (a broadcast) to local television or radio stations via satellite or network: *programs that the national networks feed to local stations.*
3 cause to move gradually and steadily, typically through a confined space: *make holes through which to feed the cables.*
▶ **n. 1** an act of giving food, esp. to animals or a baby, or of having food given to one: *I've just given the horse her feed.* ■ informal a meal: *how 'bout I fix up a nice hot feed?* ■ food for domestic animals: *the crops are grown for animal feed* | *cow feed.*
2 a device or conduit for supplying material to a machine: *the plotter has a continuous paper feed.* ■ the supply of raw material to a machine or device: [as modifier] *a feed pipe.* ■ a broadcast distributed by satellite or network from a central source to a large number of radio or television stations: *a satellite feed from Washington.* ■ Computing a facility for notifying the user of a blog or other frequently updated website that new content has been added: *most blogs and news sites offer RSS feeds of their latest content.*
3 a line or prompt given to an actor on stage. ■ an actor who provides such a line or prompt.
– PHRASES **off one's feed** informal having no appetite.
– PHRASAL VERBS **feed back 1** (of a response) influence the development of the thing that has given rise to it: *what the audience tells me feeds back into my work.* **2** (of an electrical or other system) produce feedback.
– ORIGIN Old English *fēdan* (verb); related to **FOOD**.

feed·back /ˈfēdˌbak/ ▶ **n. 1** information about reactions to a product, a person's performance of a task, etc., used as a basis for improvement.
2 the modification or control of a process or system by its results or effects, e.g., in a biochemical pathway or behavioral response. See also **NEGATIVE FEEDBACK, POSITIVE FEEDBACK**. ■ the return of a fraction of the output signal from an amplifier, microphone, or other device to the input of the same device; sound distortion produced by this.

feed·bag /ˈfēdbag/ ▶ **n.** a strong canvas or leather bag containing grain, fastened over a horse's muzzle for feeding.

feed dog ▶ **n.** the mechanism in a sewing machine that feeds the material under the needle.

feed·er /ˈfēdər/ ▶ **n. 1** a person or animal that eats a particular food or in a particular manner: *a plankton feeder.*
2 a container filled with food for birds or mammals.
3 a person or thing that supplies something, in particular: ■ a device supplying material to a machine: *the automatic sheet feeder holds up to 10 sheets of paper.* ■ a tributary stream. ■ [usu. as modifier] a branch road or railroad line linking outlying districts with a main communication system. ■ a transmission line carrying electricity to a distribution point. ■ [usu. as modifier] a school, sports team, etc., from which members move on to one more advanced: *a feeder school for Florida State University.*

feed·for·ward /ˈfēdˌfôrwərd/ ▶ **n.** the modification or control of a process using its anticipated results or effects.

feed·ing bot·tle ▶ **n.** Brit. a bottle fitted with a nipple for feeding a baby.

feed·ing fren·zy ▶ **n.** an aggressive and competitive group attack on prey by a number of sharks or piranhas. ■ an episode of frantic competition or rivalry for something: *his casual remark caused a media feeding-frenzy.*

feed·lot /ˈfēdˌlät/ ▶ **n.** an area or building where livestock are fed and fattened up.

feed·stock /ˈfēdˌstäk/ ▶ **n.** raw material to supply or fuel a machine or industrial process.

feed·stuff /ˈfēdˌstəf/ ▶ **n.** (usu. **feedstuffs**) a food provided for cattle and other livestock.

feed·through /ˈfēdˌTHro͞o/ ▶ **n.** an electrical connector used to join two parts of a circuit on opposite sides of something, such as a circuit board or a grounding screen.

feel /fēl/ ▶ **v.** (past and past participle **felt** /felt/) [with obj.] **1** be aware of (a person or object) through touching or being touched: *she felt someone touch her shoulder.* ■ be aware of (something happening) through physical sensation: *she felt the ground give way beneath her.* ■ examine or search by touch: *he touched her head and felt her hair* | [no obj.] *he* **felt around** *for the matches.* ■ [no obj.] be capable of sensation: *the dead cannot feel.* ■ [no obj., with complement] give a sensation of a particular physical quality when touched: *the wool feels soft.* ■ (**feel something out**) informal investigate something cautiously: *they want to feel out the situation.* ■ (**feel someone up**) informal fondle someone for one's own sexual stimulation.
2 experience (an emotion or sensation): *I felt a sense of excitement* | [no obj.] *I felt angry and humiliated* | *we* **feel very strongly about** *freedom of expression.* ■ [no obj., with complement] consider oneself to be in a particular state or exhibiting particular qualities: *he doesn't feel obliged to visit every weekend.* ■ (**feel up to**) have the strength and energy to do or deal with: *after the accident she didn't feel up to driving.* ■ [usu. with negative] (**feel oneself**) be healthy and well: *Ruth was not quite feeling herself.* ■ be emotionally affected by: *he didn't feel the loss of his mother so keenly.* ■ (**feel for**) have compassion for: *poor woman—I feel for her.*
3 [with clause] have a belief or impression, esp. without an identifiable reason: *she felt that the woman positively disliked her.* ■ hold an opinion: *I felt I could make a useful contribution.*
▶ **n.** [usu. in sing.] **1** an act of touching something to examine it. ■ the sense of touch: *he worked by feel rather than using his eyes.*
2 a sensation given by an object or material when touched: *nylon cloth with a cotton feel.* ■ the impression given by something: *the restaurant has a modern bistro feel.*
– PHRASES **feel one's age** become aware that one is growing older and less energetic. **feel free (to do something)** have no hesitation or shyness (often used as an invitation or for reassurance): *feel free to say what you like.* **feel like (doing) something** be inclined to have or do: *I feel like celebrating.* **feel one's oats** see **OAT**. **feel the pinch** see **PINCH**. **feel the pulse of** see **PULSE**[1]. **feel small** see **SMALL**. **feel strange** see **STRANGE**. **feel one's way** find one's way by touch rather than sight: *she plunged into the darkness of the tunnel, feeling her way along the walls.* ■ act cautiously, esp. in an area with which one is unfamiliar: *she was new in the job, still feeling her way.* **get a** (or **the**) **feel for** (or **of**) familiarize oneself with: *you can explore to get a feel of the place.* **have a feel for** have a sensitive appreciation or an intuitive understanding of: *you have to have a feel for animals.* **make oneself** (or **one's presence**) **felt** make people keenly aware of one; have a noticeable effect: *the economic crisis began to make itself felt.*
– ORIGIN Old English *fēlan.*

feel·er /ˈfēlər/ ▶ **n.** an animal organ such as an antenna or palp that is used for testing things by touch or for searching for food. ■ a tentative proposal intended to ascertain someone's attitude or opinion: *he* **put out feelers** *about seeking the party nomination.*

feel·er gauge ▶ **n.** a gauge consisting of a number of thin blades of calibrated thickness used for measuring narrow gaps or clearances.

feel-good ▶ **adj.** [attrib.] causing a feeling of happiness and well-being: *a feel-good movie.*
– DERIVATIVES **feel-good·ism** /-ˌgo͝odˌizəm/ **n.**

feel·ing /ˈfēliNG/ ▶ **n. 1** an emotional state or reaction: *a feeling of joy.* ■ (**feelings**) the emotional side of someone's character; emotional responses or tendencies to respond: *I don't want to hurt her feelings.* ■ strong emotion: *"God bless you!" she said with feeling.*
2 a belief, esp. a vague or irrational one: [with clause] *he had the feeling that he was being watched.* ■ an opinion, typically one shared by several people: *a feeling grew that justice had not been done.*
3 the capacity to experience the sense of touch: *a loss of feeling in the hands.* ■ the sensation of touching or being touched by a particular thing: *the feeling of water against your skin.*
4 (**feeling for**) a sensitivity to or intuitive understanding of: *he seems to have little feeling for art.*
▶ **adj.** showing emotion or sensitivity: *he had a warm and feeling heart.*
– DERIVATIVES **feel·ing·less adj.**

feel·ing·ly /ˈfēliNGlē/ ▶ **adv.** (of the expression of an emotion or opinion) in a heartfelt way: *"Thank goodness," she said feelingly.*

fee sim·ple ▶ **n.** (pl. **fees simple**) Law a permanent and absolute tenure of an estate in land with freedom to dispose of it at will, esp. (in full **fee simple absolute**) a freehold tenure, which is the main type of land ownership.

feet /fēt/ plural form of **FOOT**.

fee tail ▶ **n.** (pl. **fees tail**) Law, historical a former type of tenure of an estate in land with restrictions or entailment regarding the line of heirs to whom it may be willed.
– ORIGIN late Middle English: from Anglo-Norman French *fee tailé* (see **FEE, TAIL**[2]).

feet first ▶ **adv. 1** after death; as a corpse: *everyone told me that they were going to carry me out feet first.* **2** without hesitation or preparation: *the show begins in a way that compels the audience to jump in feet first.*

feh /fe/ ▶ **exclam.** conveying disapproval, displeasure, or disgust: *The greatest writer in the English language? Feh!*
– ORIGIN Yiddish.

Feh·ling's so·lu·tion /ˈfāliNGz/ (also **Fehling's reagent**) ▶ **n.** an alkaline solution of copper(II) sulfate and a tartrate, used in a laboratory test for sugars.

Feif·fer /ˈfīfər/, Jules (1929–), US cartoonist and writer. He is best known for his satirical cartoons, which appeared in *The Village Voice* and *The New Yorker*.

feign /fān/ ▶ **v.** [with obj.] pretend to be affected by (a feeling, state, or injury): *she feigned nervousness.* ■ archaic invent (a story or excuse). ■ [no obj.] archaic indulge in pretense.
– ORIGIN Middle English: from Old French *feign-*, stem of *feindre*, from Latin *fingere* 'mold, contrive.' Senses in Middle English (taken from Latin) included 'make something,' 'invent a story, excuse, or allegation,' hence 'make a pretense of a feeling or response' Compare with FICTION and FIGMENT.

feigned /fānd/ ▶ **adj.** simulated or pretended; insincere: *her eyes widened with feigned shock.*

fei·jo·a /fāˈyōə, -ˈhōə/ ▶ **n.** an evergreen shrub or small tree that bears edible green fruit resembling guavas. It is native to tropical South America and cultivated in New Zealand for its fruit. ● Genus *Feijoa*, family Myrtaceae: two species. ■ the fruit of this plant.
– ORIGIN late 19th cent.: modern Latin, named after J. da Silva *Feijó* (1760–1824), Brazilian naturalist.

fei·jo·a·da /ˌfāZHōōˈädə, fāˈjwädə/ ▶ **n.** a Brazilian or Portuguese stew of black beans with pork or other meat and vegetables, served with rice.
– ORIGIN Portuguese, from *feijão*, from Latin *phaseolus* 'bean.'

feint[1] /fānt/ ▶ **n.** a deceptive or pretended blow, thrust, or other movement, esp. in boxing or fencing: *a brief feint at the opponent's face.* ■ a mock attack or movement in warfare, made in order to distract or deceive an enemy.
▶ **v.** [no obj.] make a deceptive or distracting movement, typically during a fight: *he feinted left, drawing a punch and slipping it.* ■ [with obj.] pretend to throw a (punch or blow) in order to deceive or distract an opponent: *Feinting a left, I bobbed to the right.*
– ORIGIN late 17th cent.: from French *feinte*, past participle (used as a noun) of *feindre* 'feign.'

feint[2] ▶ **adj.** denoting paper printed with faint lines as a guide for handwriting. ■ denoting the lines so printed.
– ORIGIN mid 19th cent.: variant of FAINT.

feist·y /ˈfīstē/ ▶ **adj.** (**feistier, feistiest**) informal (of a person, typically one who is relatively small or weak) lively, determined, and courageous: *a feisty heroine who's more than a pretty face* | *a feisty upstart.* ■ touchy and aggressive: *he got a bit feisty and tried to hit me.*
– DERIVATIVES **feist·i·ly** /ˈfīstəlē/ **adv.**, **feist·i·ness** /ˈfīstēnis/ **n.**
– ORIGIN late 19th cent.: from earlier *feist*, *fist* 'small dog,' from *fisting cur* or *hound*, a derogatory term for a lapdog, from Middle English *fist* 'break wind.' Compare with FIZZLE.

fe·la·fel ▶ **n.** variant spelling of FALAFEL.

Fel·den·krais meth·od /ˈfeldənˌkrīs/ ▶ **n.** a system designed to promote bodily and mental well-being by conscious analysis of neuromuscular activity via exercises that improve flexibility and coordination and increase ease and range of motion.
– ORIGIN 1930s: named after Moshe *Feldenkrais* (1904–84), Russian-born physicist and mechanical engineer.

feld·spar /ˈfel(d)ˌspär/ ▶ **n.** an abundant rock-forming mineral typically occurring as colorless or pale-colored crystals and consisting of aluminosilicates of potassium, sodium, and calcium.
– ORIGIN mid 18th cent.: alteration of German *Feldspat*, *Feldspath*, from *Feld* 'field' + *Spat*, *Spath* 'spar' (see SPAR[3]). The form *felspar* is by mistaken association with German *Fels* 'rock.'

feld·spath·ic /fel(d)ˈspaTHik/ ▶ **adj.** Geology (of a mineral or rock) of the nature of or containing feldspar.

feld·spath·oid /fel(d)ˈspaTHˌoid/ ▶ **n.** Geology any of a group of minerals chemically similar to feldspar but containing less silica, such as nepheline and leucite.
– DERIVATIVES **feld·spath·oid·al** /ˌfel(d)spaTHˈoidl/ **adj.**

fe·li·cif·ic /ˌfēləˈsifik/ ▶ **adj.** Ethics relating to or promoting increased happiness: *the institution of a rule against murder is in general felicific.*
– ORIGIN mid 19th cent.: from Latin *felicificus*, from *felix*, *felic-* 'happy.'

fe·lic·i·tate /fəˈlisəˌtāt/ ▶ **v.** [with obj.] congratulate: *the award winner was felicitated by the cultural association.*
– ORIGIN early 17th cent. (in the sense 'regard as or pronounce happy or fortunate'): from late Latin *felicitat-* 'made happy,' from the verb *felicitare*, from Latin *felix*, *felic-* 'happy.'

fe·lic·i·ta·tions /fəˌlisəˈtāSHənz/ ▶ **plural n.** words expressing praise for an achievement or good wishes on a special occasion.

fe·lic·i·tous /fəˈlisətəs/ ▶ **adj.** well chosen or suited to the circumstances: *a felicitous phrase.* ■ pleasing and fortunate: *the view was the room's only felicitous feature.*
– DERIVATIVES **fe·lic·i·tous·ly adv.**, **fe·lic·i·tous·ness n.**

fe·lic·i·ty /fəˈlisətē/ ▶ **n.** (pl. **felicities**) **1** intense happiness: *domestic felicity.*
2 the ability to find appropriate expression for one's thoughts: *speech that pleased by its accuracy, felicity, and fluency.* ■ a particularly effective feature of a work of literature or art: *the King James version, thanks to its felicities of language, ruled supreme.*
– ORIGIN late Middle English: from Old French *felicite*, from Latin *felicitas*, from *felix*, *felic-* 'happy.'

fe·lid /ˈfēlid/ ▶ **n.** Zoology a mammal of the cat family (Felidae); a wild cat.
– ORIGIN late 19th cent.: from modern Latin *Felidae* (plural), from Latin *feles* 'cat.'

fe·line /ˈfēˌlīn/ ▶ **adj.** of, relating to, or affecting cats or other members of the cat family: *feline leukemia.* ■ catlike, esp. in beauty or slyness: *her face was feline in shape.*
▶ **n.** a cat or other member of the cat family.
– DERIVATIVES **fe·lin·i·ty** /fēˈlinətē/ **n.**
– ORIGIN late 17th cent.: from Latin *felinus*, from *feles* 'cat.'

fe·lix cul·pa /ˈfāliks ˈkŏŏlpə, ˈfēliks/ ▶ **n.** Christian Theology the sin of Adam viewed as fortunate, because it brought about the blessedness of the Redemption. ■ an apparent error or disaster with happy consequences: *he presents the revolt of the Noldor as a felix culpa.*
– ORIGIN mid 20th cent.: Latin, literally 'happy fault.'

fell[1] /fel/ past of FALL.

fell[2] ▶ **v.** [with obj.] **1** (usu. **be felled**) cut down (a tree). ■ knock down: *strong winds felled power lines* | figurative *corruption that felled the financial system in Thailand.*
2 (also **flat-fell**) stitch down (the edge of a seam) to lie flat: (as adj. **flat-felled**) *a flat-felled seam.*
▶ **n.** an amount of timber cut.
– ORIGIN Old English *fellan*, of Germanic origin; related to FALL.

fell[3] ▶ **n.** a hill or stretch of high moorland, esp. in northern England: [in place names] *Cross Fell* | *an area of fell and moor.*
– ORIGIN Middle English: from Old Norse *fjall*, *fell* 'hill.'

fell[4] ▶ **adj.** literary of terrible evil or ferocity; deadly: *sorcerers use spells to achieve their fell ends.*
– PHRASES **in (or at) one fell swoop** all at one time: *nothing can topple the government in one fell swoop.* [from Shakespeare's *Macbeth* (IV. iii. 219).]
– ORIGIN Middle English: from Old French *fel*, nominative of *felon* 'wicked (person)' (see FELON[1]).

fell[5] ▶ **n.** archaic an animal's hide or skin with its hair.
– ORIGIN Old English *fel*, *fell*, of Germanic origin; from an Indo-European root shared by Latin *pellis* and Greek *pella* 'skin.'

fel·la /ˈfelə/ (also **fellah**) ▶ **n.** nonstandard spelling of FELLOW, used in representing speech in various dialects: *goodbye, young fella.*

fel·lah /ˈfelə, felˈä/ ▶ **n.** (pl. **fellahin** /ˌfeləˈhēn, fəˌlä-/) an Egyptian peasant.
– ORIGIN from Arabic *fallāḥ* 'tiller of the soil,' from *falaḥa* 'till the soil.'

fel·late /ˈfelˌāt/ ▶ **v.** [with obj.] perform fellatio on (a man).
– ORIGIN late 19th cent.: from Latin *fellat-* 'sucked,' from the verb *fellare*.

fel·la·ti·o /fəˈlāSH(ē)ˌō/ ▶ **n.** oral stimulation of a man's penis.
– DERIVATIVES **fel·la·tor** /ˈfelˌātər/ **n.**
– ORIGIN late 19th cent.: modern Latin, from Latin *fellare* 'to suck.'

Fel·ler /ˈfelər/, Bob (1918–), US baseball player; full name *Robert William Andrew Feller*. He pitched for the Cleveland Indians 1936–56 (with the exception of 1942–44 when he served in the US Navy) and led American League pitchers in strikeouts seven times. Baseball Hall of Fame (1962).

fell·er[1] /ˈfelər/ ▶ **n.** nonstandard spelling of FELLOW, used in representing speech in various dialects.

fell·er[2] ▶ **n.** a person who cuts down trees.

Fel·li·ni /fəˈlēnē/, Federico (1920–93), Italian movie director. Notable movies: *La Strada* (1954), *La Dolce Vita* (1960) and *8½* (1963).

fel·loes /ˈfelōz/ (also **fellies** /ˈfelēz/) ▶ **plural n.** the outer rim of a wheel, to which the spokes are fixed.
– ORIGIN Old English *felg* (singular).

fel·low /ˈfelō/ ▶ **n. 1** informal a man or boy: *he was an extremely obliging fellow.* ■ a boyfriend or lover: *has she got a fellow?*
2 (usu. **fellows**) a person in the same position, involved in the same activity, or otherwise associated with another: *he was learning with a rapidity unique among his fellows.* ■ a thing of the same kind as or otherwise associated with another: *the page has been torn away from its fellows.*
3 a member of a learned society: *he was elected a fellow of the Geological Society.* ■ (also **research fellow**) a student or graduate receiving a fellowship for a period of research. ■ Brit. an incorporated senior member of a college: *a tutorial fellow.* ■ a member of the governing body in some universities.
▶ **adj.** [attrib.] sharing a particular activity, quality, or condition with someone or something: *they urged the troops not to fire on their fellow citizens.*
– ORIGIN late Old English *fēolaga* 'a partner or colleague' (literally 'one who lays down money in a joint enterprise'), from Old Norse *félagi*, from *félag* 'partnership' from *fé* 'cattle, property, money' + *lag* 'a laying down,' from the Germanic base of LAY[1].

fel·low feel·ing ▶ **n.** sympathy and fellowship existing between people based on shared experiences or feelings.

fel·low·ship /ˈfelōˌSHip/ ▶ **n. 1** friendly association, esp. with people who share one's interests: *they valued fun and good fellowship as the cement of the community.* ■ a group of people meeting to pursue a shared interest or aim. ■ a guild or corporation.
2 the status of a fellow of a college or society: *she held the Faulkner fellowship.*

fel·low trav·el·er ▶ **n.** a person who travels with another. ■ a person who is not a member of a particular group or political party (esp. the Communist Party), but who sympathizes with the group's aims and policies.
– DERIVATIVES **fel·low trav·el·ing adj.**

fe·lo de se /ˌfelō də ˈsā/ ▶ **n.** (pl. **felos de se** /ˌfelōz də ˈsā/) suicide.
– ORIGIN from Anglo-Latin, literally 'felon of himself'; formerly a criminal act in the UK.

fel·on[1] /ˈfelən/ ▶ **n.** a person who has been convicted of a felony.
▶ **adj.** [attrib.] archaic cruel; wicked: *the felon undermining hand of dark corruption.*
– ORIGIN Middle English: from Old French, literally 'wicked, a wicked person' (oblique case of *fel* 'evil'), from medieval Latin *fello*, *fellon-*. Compare with FELON[2].

fel·on[2] ▶ **n.** archaic term for WHITLOW.
– ORIGIN Middle English: perhaps a specific use of FELON[1]; medieval Latin *fello*, *fellon-* had the same sense.

fe·lo·ni·ous /fəˈlōnēəs/ ▶ **adj.** of, relating to, or involved in crime: *they turned their felonious talents to the smuggling trade.* ■ Law relating to or of the nature of felony: *his conduct was felonious.*
– DERIVATIVES **fe·lo·ni·ous·ly adv.**

fel·o·ny /ˈfelənē/ ▶ **n.** (pl. **felonies**) a crime, typically one involving violence, regarded as more serious than a misdemeanor, and usually punishable by imprisonment for more than one year or by death: *he pleaded guilty to six felonies* | *an accusation of felony.*

> The distinction between felonies and misdemeanors usually depends on the penalties or consequences attaching to the crime. In English common law, felony originally comprised those offenses (murder, wounding, arson, rape, and robbery) for which the penalty included forfeiture of land and goods.

– ORIGIN Middle English: from Old French *felonie*, from *felon* (see FELON[1]).

fel·sic /ˈfelsik/ ▶ **adj.** Geology of, relating to, or denoting a group of light-colored minerals including feldspar, feldspathoids, quartz, and muscovite. Often contrasted with MAFIC.
– ORIGIN early 20th cent.: from FELDSPAR + a contraction of SILICA.

fel·spar /ˈfelˌspär/ ▶ **n.** Brit. variant spelling of FELDSPAR.

felt[1] /felt/ ▶ **n.** a kind of cloth made by rolling and pressing wool or another suitable textile accompanied by the application of moisture or heat, which causes the constituent fibers to mat together to create a smooth surface.

▶ **v.** [with obj.] make into felt; mat together: *the wood fibers are shredded and felted together.* ■ cover with felt: (as adj. **felted**) *a felted roof.* ■ [no obj.] become matted: *care must be taken in washing, or the wool will shrink and felt.*
– DERIVATIVES **felt·y** adj.
– ORIGIN Old English; related to FILTER.

felt² past and past participle of FEEL.

felt-tip pen (also **felt-tipped pen** or **felt tip**) ▶ **n.** a pen with a writing point made of felt or other tightly packed fibers, typically containing a brightly colored ink.

fe·luc·ca /fə'lo͞okə, -'ləkə/ ▶ **n.** a small vessel propelled by oars or lateen sails or both, used on the Nile and formerly more widely in the Mediterranean region.
– ORIGIN early 17th cent.: from Italian *feluc(c)a*, probably from obsolete Spanish *faluca*, from Arabic *fulk* 'ship,' probably from Greek *epholkion* '(towed) boat.'

fem /fem/ ▶ **n.** variant spelling of FEMME.

fem. ▶ **abbr.** ■ female. ■ feminine.

FEMA /'fēmə/ ▶ **abbr.** Federal Emergency Management Agency.

fe·male /'fē,māl/ ▶ **adj.** of or denoting the sex that can bear offspring or produce eggs, distinguished biologically by the production of gametes (ova) that can be fertilized by male gametes: *a herd of female deer.* ■ relating to or characteristic of women or female animals: *a female audience | a female name.* ■ (of a plant or flower) having a pistil but no stamens. ■ (of parts of machinery, fittings, etc.) manufactured hollow so that a corresponding male part can be inserted.
▶ **n.** a female person, animal, or plant.
– DERIVATIVES **fe·male·ness** n.
– ORIGIN Middle English: from Old French *femelle*, from Latin *femella*, diminutive of *femina* 'a woman.' The change in the ending was due to association with MALE, but the words *male* and *female* are not otherwise linked etymologically.

fe·male cir·cum·ci·sion ▶ **n.** (among some peoples) the action or traditional practice of cutting off the clitoris and sometimes the labia of girls or young women.

fe·male con·dom ▶ **n.** a contraceptive device made of thin rubber, inserted into a woman's vagina before sexual intercourse.

feme cov·ert /'fem 'kəvərt, 'fēm/ ▶ **n.** Law, historical a married woman.
– ORIGIN early 16th cent.: from Anglo-Norman French, literally 'a woman covered (i.e., protected by marriage).'

feme sole /'fem 'sōl, 'fēm/ ▶ **n.** historical Law a woman without a husband, esp. one who is divorced.
– ORIGIN early 16th cent.: from Anglo-Norman French *feme soule* 'a woman alone.'

fem·i·nal /'femənl/ ▶ **adj.** archaic of or relating to a woman.
– DERIVATIVES **fem·i·nal·i·ty** /,femə'nalətē/ n.
– ORIGIN late Middle English: from medieval Latin *feminalis*, from Latin *femina* 'woman.'

fem·i·na·zi /'femi,nätsē/ ▶ **n.** (pl. **feminazis**) derogatory a radical feminist.
– ORIGIN 1990s: blend of FEMINIST and NAZI.

fem·i·ne·i·ty /,femə'nēətē, -'nāətē/ ▶ **n.** archaic the quality of being feminine.
– ORIGIN early 19th cent.: from Latin *femineus* 'womanish' (from *femina* 'woman') + -ITY.

fem·i·nine /'femənin/ ▶ **adj. 1** having qualities or appearance traditionally associated with women, esp. delicacy and prettiness: *a feminine frilled blouse.* ■ of or relating to women; female: *he enjoys feminine company.*
2 Grammar of or denoting a gender of nouns and adjectives, conventionally regarded as female.
3 Music (of a cadence) occurring on a metrically weak beat.
▶ **n.** (**the feminine**) the female sex or gender: *the association of the arts with the feminine.* ■ Grammar a feminine word or form.
– DERIVATIVES **fem·i·nine·ly** adv., **fem·i·nine·ness** n.
– ORIGIN late Middle English: from Latin *femininus*, from *femina* 'woman.'

fem·i·nine rhyme ▶ **n.** Prosody a rhyme between stressed syllables followed by one or more unstressed syllables (e.g., *stocking/shocking, glamorous/amorous.*). Compare with MASCULINE RHYME.

fem·i·nin·i·ty /,femə'ninətē/ ▶ **n.** the quality of being female; womanliness: *she celebrates her femininity by wearing makeup and high heels.*

fem·i·nism /'femə,nizəm/ ▶ **n.** the advocacy of women's rights on the grounds of political, social, and economic equality to men.

> The issue of rights for women first became prominent during the French and American revolutions in the late 18th century. In Britain it was not until the emergence of the suffragette movement in the late 19th century that there was significant political change. A 'second wave' of feminism arose in the 1960s, with an emphasis on unity and sisterhood.

– ORIGIN late 19th cent.: from French *féminisme*.

fem·i·nist /'femənist/ ▶ **n.** a person who supports feminism.
▶ **adj.** of, relating to, or supporting feminism: *feminist literature.*
– ORIGIN late 19th cent.: from French *féministe*, from Latin *femina* 'woman.'

fem·i·nize /'femə,nīz/ ▶ **v.** [with obj.] make (something) more characteristic of or associated with women: *as office roles changed, clerical work was increasingly feminized.* ■ induce female sexual characteristics in (a male).
– DERIVATIVES **fem·i·ni·za·tion** /,femənə'zāsнən/ n.

femme /fem/ (also **fem**) ▶ **n.** informal a lesbian or an effeminate male homosexual who takes a traditionally feminine sexual role. Often contrasted with BUTCH.
– ORIGIN 1960s: French, 'woman.'

femme fa·tale /,fem fə'tal, fə'täl/ ▶ **n.** (pl. **femmes fatales** pronunc. **same**) an attractive and seductive woman, esp. one who will ultimately bring disaster to a man who becomes involved with her.
– ORIGIN early 20th cent.: French, literally 'disastrous woman.'

femto- ▶ **comb. form** (used in units of measurement) denoting a factor of 10^{-15}: *femtosecond.*
– ORIGIN from Danish or Norwegian *femten* 'fifteen.'

fe·mur /'fēmər/ ▶ **n.** (pl. **femurs** or **femora** /'femərə/) Anatomy the bone of the thigh or upper hind limb, articulating at the hip and the knee. ■ Zoology the third segment of the leg in insects and some other arthropods, typically the longest and thickest segment.
– DERIVATIVES **fem·o·ral** /'femərəl/ adj.
– ORIGIN late 15th cent.: from Latin *femur, femor-* 'thigh.'

fen¹ /fen/ ▶ **n.** a low and marshy or frequently flooded area of land: *a flooded fen | 55 acres of fen.* ■ (**the Fens**) flat low-lying areas of eastern England, formerly marshland but largely drained for agriculture since the 17th century. ■ Ecology wetland with alkaline, neutral, or only slightly acid peaty soil. Compare with BOG.
– DERIVATIVES **fen·ny** adj.
– ORIGIN Old English *fen(n)*.

fen² ▶ **n.** (pl. **same**) a monetary unit of China, equal to one hundredth of a yuan.
– ORIGIN from Chinese *fēn* 'a hundredth part.'

fence /fens/ ▶ **n. 1** a barrier, railing, or other upright structure, typically of wood or wire, enclosing an area of ground to mark a boundary, control access, or prevent escape. ■ a large upright obstacle used in equestrian jumping events.
2 a guard or guide on a plane, saw, or other tool.
3 informal a person who deals in stolen goods.
▶ **v. 1** [with obj.] surround or protect with a fence: *our garden was not fully fenced.* ■ (**fence something in/off**) enclose or separate with a fence for protection or to prevent escape: *everything is fenced in to keep out the wolves.* ■ (**fence someone/something out**) use a barrier to exclude someone or something: *Idaho law requires people to fence out cows.*
2 [with obj.] informal deal in (stolen goods): *after stealing your ring, he didn't even know how to fence it.*
3 [no obj.] fight with swords, esp. as a sport. See also FENCING. ■ conduct a discussion or argument in such a way as to avoid the direct mention of something: *we were fencing, not talking about the subject we'd come to talk about.*
– PHRASES **mend (one's) fences** see MEND. **side of the fence** either of the opposing positions involved in a conflict: *whatever side of the fence you are on, the issue is here to stay.* **sit on the fence** avoid making a decision or choice.
– DERIVATIVES **fence·less** adj., **fenc·er** n.
– ORIGIN Middle English (in the sense 'defending, defence'): shortening of DEFENCE. Compare with FEND.

fence liz·ard ▶ **n.** a small gray-brown North American spiny lizard that typically has bright markings and often basks on rail fences, logs, and tree stumps. ● *Sceloporus undulatus*, family Iguanidae.

fence post ▶ **n.** a wooden or metal post set in the ground as a supporting part of a fence.

fence·row /'fens,rō/ ▶ **n.** an uncultivated strip of land on each side of and below a fence.

fenc·ing /'fensiNG/ ▶ **n. 1** the sport of fighting with swords, esp. foils, épées, or sabers, according to a set of rules, in order to score points against an opponent: [as modifier] *a fencing foil.* ■ the action of conducting a discussion or argument so as to avoid the direct mention of something.
2 a series of fences: *security fencing.* ■ material used for the construction of fences: *chestnut is still in demand for fencing.* ■ the erection of fences.

fend /fend/ ▶ **v. 1** [no obj.] (**fend for oneself**) look after and provide for oneself, without any help from others: *you're old enough to fend for yourself.*
2 [with obj.] (**fend someone/something off**) defend oneself from a blow, attack, or attacker. fig. *he fended off the awkward questions.*
– ORIGIN Middle English (in the sense 'defend'): shortening of DEFEND. Compare with FENCE.

Fend·er /'fendər/, Leo (1907–91), US guitar-maker. He pioneered the design and production of electric guitars and founded the company named after him.

fend·er /'fendər/ ▶ **n. 1** a thing used to keep something off or prevent a collision, in particular: ■ the mudguard or area around the wheel well of a vehicle. ■ a plastic cylinder, tire, etc., hung over a ship's side to protect it against impact. ■ a metal frame at the front of a locomotive or streetcar for pushing aside obstacles on the line; a cowcatcher.
2 a low frame bordering a fireplace to contain burning materials.

fend·er bend·er ▶ **n.** informal a minor collision between motor vehicles.

fe·nes·tra /fə'nestrə/ ▶ **n.** (pl. **fenestrae** /-trē, -trī/) **1** Anatomy & Zoology a small natural hole or opening, esp. in a bone. The mammalian middle ear is linked by the **fenestra ovalis** to the vestibule of the inner ear, and by the **fenestra rotunda** to the cochlea.
2 Medicine an artificial opening. ■ an opening in a bandage or cast. ■ a perforation in a forceps blade. ■ a hole made by surgical fenestration.
– ORIGIN early 19th cent. (as a botanical term denoting a small scar left by the separation of the seed from the ovary): from Latin, literally 'window.'

fe·nes·trate /'fenə,strāt/ ▶ **adj.** Botany & Zoology having small windowlike perforations or transparent areas.
– ORIGIN mid 19th cent.: from Latin *fenestratus* 'provided with openings,' from the verb *fenestrare*.

fe·nes·trat·ed /'fenə,strātid/ ▶ **adj.** provided with a window or windows: *the fenestrated heights of nearby buildings.* ■ chiefly Anatomy having perforations, apertures, or transparent areas: *the capillaries have a fenestrated epithelium.*
– ORIGIN early 19th cent.: from Latin *fenestrare* (see FENESTRATE) + -ED².

fen·es·tra·tion /,fenə'strāsнən/ ▶ **n.** Architecture the arrangement of windows and doors on the elevations of a building. ■ Botany & Zoology the condition of being fenestrate. ■ Medicine a surgical operation in which a new opening is formed, esp. in the bony labyrinth of the inner ear to treat certain types of deafness.

fen·flu·ra·mine /fen'flo͝orə,mēn/ ▶ **n.** Medicine an SSRI appetite-suppressant drug once prescribed for obesity, but withdrawn from the US market in 1997 because of safety concerns. It was one component of FEN-PHEN.

feng shui /'fəNG 'sнwē, -'sнwā/ ▶ **n.** (in Chinese thought) a system of laws considered to govern spatial arrangement and orientation in relation to the flow of energy (qi), and whose favorable or unfavorable effects are taken into account when siting and designing buildings.
– ORIGIN Chinese, from *fēng* 'wind' and *shuǐ* 'water.'

Fe·ni·an /'fēnēən/ ▶ **n.** a member of a 19th-century revolutionary nationalist organization among the Irish in the US and Ireland. The Fenians staged an unsuccessful revolt in Ireland in 1867 and were responsible for isolated revolutionary acts against the British until the early 20th century, when they were gradually eclipsed by the IRA. ■ informal, offensive (chiefly in Northern Ireland) a Protestant name for a Catholic.
– DERIVATIVES **Fe·ni·an·ism** /-izəm/ n.
– ORIGIN from Old Irish *féne*, the name of an ancient Irish people, confused with *fiann, fianna* (see FIANNA FÁIL).

fen·land /'fenlənd/ ▶ **n.** (also **fenlands**) land consisting of fens: *thousands of acres of fenland.* ■ (usu. **the Fenland**) the Fens of eastern England.

fen·nec /'fenik/ (also **fennec fox**) ▶ **n.** a small pale fox with large pointed ears, native to the deserts of North Africa and Arabia. ● *Vulpes zerda*, family Canidae.
– ORIGIN late 18th cent.: via Arabic from Persian *fanak, fanaj.*

fen·nel /'fenl/ ▶ **n.** an aromatic yellow-flowered European plant of the parsley family, with feathery leaves. ● *Foeniculum vulgare*, family Umbelliferae:

two subspecies, a hardy perennial (dulce), the seeds and leaves of which are used as culinary herbs, and the annual **Florence** (or **sweet**) **fennel** (azoricum), with swollen leaf bases that are eaten as a vegetable.
– ORIGIN Old English *finule, fenol*, from Latin *faeniculum*, diminutive of *faenum* 'hay.'

fen·ta·nyl /'fentənil, 'fentn-il/ ▶ **n.** a fast-acting narcotic analgesic and sedative that is sometimes abused for its heroinlike effect.

fen·u·greek /'fenyə,grēk/ ▶ **n.** a white-flowered herbaceous plant of the pea family, with aromatic seeds that are used for flavoring, esp. ground and used in curry powder. ● *Trigonella foenum-graecum*, family Leguminosae.
– ORIGIN Old English *fenogrecum* (superseded in Middle English by forms from Old French *fenugrec*), from Latin *faenugraecum*, from *faenum graecum* 'Greek hay' (the Romans used the dried plant as fodder).

Fen·way /'fen,wā/ (**the Fenway**) a park system that incorporates the wetlands in Boston, Massachusetts. Nearby is Fenway Park, the baseball stadium of the Boston Red Sox.

feoff·ee /fef'ē, fē'fē/ ▶ **n.** a trustee invested with a freehold estate to hold in possession for a purpose. ■ historical (in feudal law) a person to whom a grant of freehold property is made.
– ORIGIN late Middle English: from Anglo-Norman French *feoffe* 'enfeoffed,' past participle of *feoffer*, variant of Old French *fieffer* (see **FEOFFMENT**).

feoff·ment /'fēfmənt/ ▶ **n.** historical (in feudal law) a grant of ownership of freehold property to someone.
– DERIVATIVES **feof·for** /'fēfər/ **n.**
– ORIGIN Middle English: from an Anglo-Norman French variant of Old French *fieffer* 'put in legal possession,' from *fief* (see **FEE** and **FIEF**).

FEP ▶ **abbr.** Computing front-end processor.

FEPC ▶ **abbr.** Fair Employment Practices Commission.

FERA ▶ **abbr.** Federal Emergency Relief Administration.

fe·ral /'fi(ə)rəl, 'ferəl/ ▶ **adj.** (esp. of an animal) in a wild state, esp. after escape from captivity or domestication: *a feral cat.* ■ resembling a wild animal: *a feral snarl.*
– ORIGIN early 17th cent.: from Latin *fera* 'wild animal' (from *ferus* 'wild') + **-AL**.

Fer·ber /'fərbər/, Edna (1887–1968), US writer. She wrote the novels *So Big* (1924) and *Giant* (1952), as well as stage plays that include *Dinner at Eight* (1932, with George S. Kaufman).

fer·ber·ite /'fərbə,rit/ ▶ **n.** a black mineral consisting of ferrous tungstate, typically occurring as elongated prisms.
– ORIGIN early 19th cent.: named after Rudolph *Ferber* (1743–90), Swedish mineralogist, + **-ITE**[1].

fer de lance /,fer dl'ans, -'äns/ ▶ **n.** (pl. **fers de lance** pronunc. **same** or /,ferz-/; or **fer de lances**) a large and dangerous pit viper native to central and South America. ● Genus *Bothrops*, family Viperidae: several species, in particular *B. atrox*.
– ORIGIN late 19th cent.: from French, literally 'iron (head) of a lance.'

Fer·di·nand /'fərdn,and/ of Aragon (1452–1516), king of Castile 1474–1516 and of Aragon 1479–1516; known as **Ferdinand the Catholic**. He and his wife Isabella instituted the Spanish Inquisition in 1478 and supported the expedition of Christopher Columbus in 1492. Their capture of Granada from the Moors in the same year effectively united Spain as one country.

fe·ri·a /'fi(ə)rēə, 'fer-/ ▶ **n.** (in Spanish-speaking regions) a local fair or festival, usually in honor of a patron saint.
– ORIGIN mid 19th cent.: Spanish, from Latin, literally 'holiday.'

fe·ri·al /'fi(ə)rēəl, 'fer-/ ▶ **adj.** Christian Church denoting an ordinary weekday, as opposed to one appointed for a festival or fast.
– ORIGIN late Middle English: from medieval Latin *ferialis*, from Latin *feria* 'holiday.' In late Latin *feria* was used with a prefixed ordinal number to mean 'day of the week' (e.g., *secunda feria* 'second day, Monday'), but Sunday (Dominicus) and Saturday (Sabbatum) were usually referred to by their names; hence *feria* came to mean 'ordinary weekday.'

fe·rin·ghee /fə'riNGgē/ (also **feringhi**) ▶ **n. 1** chiefly derogatory (in India and other parts of Asia) a foreigner, esp. one with white skin.
2 archaic a person of Indian–Portuguese parentage.
– ORIGIN via Urdu from Persian *firangī*, from the base of **FRANK**[2].

Fer·lin·ghet·ti /,fərliNG'getē/, Lawrence (Monsanto) (1919–), US poet and publisher; born *Lawrence Ferling*. Identified with San Francisco's beat movement, he founded a publishing house called City Lights. Notable works: *A Coney Island of the Mind* (1958) and *Her* (1960).

Ferm. ▶ **abbr.** Fermanagh.

Fer·man·agh /fər'manə/ one of the six counties of Northern Ireland, formerly an administrative area; chief town, Enniskillen.

Fer·mat /fer'mä/, Pierre de (1601–65), French mathematician. His work on curves led directly to the general methods of calculus introduced by Isaac Newton and Gottfried Leibniz. He is also recognized as the founder of the modern theory of numbers.

fer·ma·ta /fer'mätə, fər-/ ▶ **n.** Music a pause of unspecified length on a note or rest. ■ a mark (𝄐) over a note or rest that is to be lengthened by an unspecified amount.
– ORIGIN Italian, from *fermare* 'to stop.'

Fer·mat's last the·o·rem /fer'mäz/ Mathematics a conjecture by Fermat that if n is an integer greater than 2, the equation $xn + yn = zn$ has no positive integral solutions. Fermat noted that he had "a truly wonderful proof" of the conjecture, but never wrote it down. In 1995 a general proof was published by the Princeton-based British mathematician Andrew Wiles.

fer·ment ▶ **v.** /fər'ment/ **1** [no obj.] (of a substance) undergo fermentation: *the drink had fermented, turning some of the juice into alcohol.* ■ [with obj.] cause the fermentation of (a substance).
2 [with obj.] incite or stir up (trouble or disorder): *the politicians and warlords who are fermenting this chaos.* ■ [no obj.] (of a negative feeling or memory) fester and develop into something worse: *it had been fermenting in my subconscious for a while.*
▶ **n. 1** agitation and excitement among a group of people, typically concerning major change and leading to trouble or violence: *Germany at this time was in a state of religious ferment.*
2 archaic a fermenting agent or enzyme.
– DERIVATIVES **fer·ment·a·ble adj.**
– ORIGIN late Middle English: from Old French *ferment* (noun), *fermenter* (verb), based on Latin *fermentum* 'yeast,' from *fervere* 'to boil.'

fer·men·ta·tion /,fərmən'tāSHən/ ▶ **n.** the chemical breakdown of a substance by bacteria, yeasts, or other microorganisms, typically involving effervescence and the giving off of heat. ■ the process of this kind involved in the making of beer, wine, and liquor, in which sugars are converted to ethyl alcohol. ■ archaic agitation; excitement: *I had found Paris in high fermentation.*
– DERIVATIVES **fer·ment·a·tive** /fər'men(t)ətiv/ **adj.**
– ORIGIN late Middle English: from late Latin *fermentatio(n-)*, from Latin *fermentare* 'to ferment' (see **FERMENT**).

fer·ment·er /fər'mentər/ ▶ **n.** a container in which fermentation takes place. ■ an organism that causes fermentation.

Fer·mi /'fermē/, Enrico (1901–54), US atomic physicist; born in Italy. He directed the first controlled nuclear chain reaction in 1942 and joined the Manhattan Project to work on the atom bomb. Nobel Prize for Physics (1938).

fer·mi /'fermē, 'fər-/ ▶ **n.** (pl. **same**) a unit of length equal to 10^{-15} meter (one femtometer), used in nuclear physics. It is similar to the diameter of a proton.
– ORIGIN early 20th cent.: named after E. **FERMI**.

Fer·mi–Di·rac sta·tis·tics /'fermē də'rak/ ▶ **plural n.** [treated as sing.] Physics a type of quantum statistics used to describe systems of fermions.
– ORIGIN 1920s: named after E. **FERMI** and P. A. M. **DIRAC**.

fer·mi·on /'fermē,än, 'fər-/ ▶ **n.** Physics a subatomic particle, such as a nucleon, that has half-integral spin and follows the statistical description given by Fermi and Dirac.
– ORIGIN 1940s: from the name of E. **FERMI** + **-ON**.

fer·mi·um /'fermēəm, 'fər-/ ▶ **n.** the chemical element of atomic number 100, a radioactive metal of the actinide series. Fermium does not occur naturally and was discovered in 1953 in the debris of the first hydrogen bomb explosion. (Symbol: **Fm**)
– ORIGIN 1950s: from the name of E. **FERMI** + **-IUM**.

fern /fərn/ ▶ **n.** (pl. **same** or **ferns**) a flowerless plant that has feathery or leafy fronds and reproduces by spores released from the undersides of the fronds. Ferns have a vascular system for the transport of water and nutrients. ● Class Filicopsida, division Pteridophyta.
– DERIVATIVES **fern·er·y** /'fərnərē/ **n.** (pl. **ferneries**), **fern·y adj.**
– ORIGIN Old English *fearn*.

Fer·nan·do Pó·o /fər'nandō 'pō/ former name (until 1973) for **BIOKO**.

fern·brake /'fərn,brāk/ ▶ **n.** a bed or thicket of ferns.
– ORIGIN early 17th cent.: from **FERN** + **BRAKE**[4].

fe·ro·cious /fə'rōSHəs/ ▶ **adj.** savagely fierce, cruel, or violent: *the wolverine is nature's most ferocious and violent animal.* ■ (of a conflict) characterized by or involving aggression, bitterness, and determination: *a ferocious argument.* ■ extreme and unpleasant: *a ferocious headache.*
– DERIVATIVES **fe·ro·cious·ly adv.**, **fe·ro·cious·ness n.**
– ORIGIN mid 17th cent.: from Latin *ferox, feroc-* 'fierce' + **-IOUS**.

fe·roc·i·ty /fə'räsətē/ ▶ **n.** (pl. **ferocities**) the state or quality of being ferocious: *the ferocity of the storm caught them by surprise.*
– ORIGIN mid 16th cent.: from French, or from Latin *ferocitas*, from *ferox, feroc-* 'fierce.'

-ferous (usu. **-iferous**) ▶ **suffix** having, bearing, or containing (a specified thing): *Carboniferous* | *pestiferous.*
– ORIGIN from French *-fère* or Latin *-fer* 'producing,' from *ferre* 'to bear.'

-ferously ▶ **comb. form** in adverbs corresponding to adjectives ending in *-ferous* (such as *pestiferously* corresponding to *pestiferous*).

-ferousness ▶ **comb. form** in nouns corresponding to adjectives ending in *-ferous* (such as *pestiferousness* corresponding to *pestiferous*).

Fer·ra·ra /fə'rärə/ a city in northern Italy, capital of a province of the same name; pop. 130,486 (est. 2009).

Fer·ra·ri /fə'rärē/, Enzo (1898–1988), Italian car designer and manufacturer. In 1929, he founded the company named after him.

fer·rate /'fer,āt/ ▶ **n.** Chemistry a salt in which the anion contains both iron (typically ferric iron) and oxygen.
– ORIGIN mid 19th cent.: from Latin *ferrum* 'iron' + **-ATE**[1].

Fer·rel's law /'ferəlz/ Meteorology a law stating that Coriolis forces deflect winds and freely moving objects to the right in the northern hemisphere and to the left in the southern hemisphere.
– ORIGIN early 20th cent.: named after William *Ferrel* (1817–91), American meteorologist.

fer·ret /'ferət/ ▶ **n.** a domesticated polecat kept as a pet or used, esp. in Europe, for catching rabbits. It is typically albino or brown. ● *Mustela putorius furo*, family Mustelidae; descended mainly from the European polecat.
■ (**black-footed ferret**) a rare weasellike animal (*Mustela nigripes*), found in grassland in the US.

ferret

▶ **v.** (**ferrets, ferreting, ferreted**) [no obj.] (of a person) hunt with ferrets, typically for rabbits. ■ clear (a hole or area of ground) of rabbits with ferrets.
■ [with adverbial of place] look around in a place or container in search of something: *he went to the desk and ferreted around.* ■ [with obj.] (**ferret something out**) search tenaciously for and find something: *she had the ability to ferret out the facts.*
– DERIVATIVES **fer·ret·er n.**, **fer·ret·y adj.**
– ORIGIN late Middle English: from Old French *fuiret*, alteration of *fuiron*, based on late Latin *furo* 'thief, ferret,' from Latin *fur* 'thief.'

ferri- ▶ **comb. form** Chemistry of iron with a valence of three; ferric. Compare with **FERRO-**.
– ORIGIN from Latin *ferrum* 'iron.'

fer·ri·age /'ferē-ij/ ▶ **n.** archaic the action of transporting someone or something by ferry. ■ the fare paid for ferry transportation.

fer·ric /'ferik/ ▶ **adj.** of or relating to iron. ■ Chemistry of iron with a valence of three; of iron(III). Compare with **FERROUS**.
– ORIGIN late 18th cent.: from Latin *ferrum* 'iron' + **-IC**.

fer·ri·cy·a·nide /,feri'sīə,nīd/ ▶ **n.** Chemistry a salt containing the anion $Fe(CN)_6^{3-}$.

fer·ri·mag·net·ic /,feri,mag'netik/ ▶ **adj.** Physics (of a substance) displaying a weak form of ferromagnetism associated with parallel but opposite alignment of neighboring atoms. In

PRONUNCIATION KEY ə *ago, up*; ər *over, fur*; a *hat*; ā *ate*; ä *car*; e *let*; ē *see*; i *fit*; ī *by*; NG *sing*; ō *go*; ô *law, for*; oi *toy*; o͝o *good*; o͞o *goo*; ou *out*; TH *thin*; T̲H̲ *then*; ZH *vision*

contrast with antiferromagnetic materials, these alignments do not cancel out and there is a net magnetic moment.
– DERIVATIVES **fer·ri·mag·ne·tism** /ˌferiˈmagnəˌtizəm/ **n.**

Fer·ris wheel /ˈferis/ ▶ **n.** an amusement-park or fairground ride consisting of a giant vertical revolving wheel with passenger cars suspended on its outer edge.
– ORIGIN late 19th cent.: named after George W. G. *Ferris* (1859–96), the American engineer who invented it.

Ferris wheel

fer·rite /ˈferīt/ ▶ **n. 1** a ceramic compound consisting of a mixed oxide of iron and one or more other metals. Ferrite has ferrimagnetic properties and is used in high-frequency electrical components such as antennas. **2** Metallurgy a form of pure iron with a body-centered cubic crystal structure, occurring in low-carbon steel.
– DERIVATIVES **fer·rit·ic** /fəˈritik/ **adj.** (FERRITE (sense 2)).
– ORIGIN mid 19th cent.: from Latin *ferrum* 'iron' + **-ITE**[1].

fer·ri·tin /ˈferətn/ ▶ **n.** Biochemistry a protein produced in mammalian metabolism that serves to store iron in the tissues.
– ORIGIN 1930s: from **FERRI-** + *-t-* (for ease of pronunciation) + **-IN**[1].

ferro- ▶ **comb. form** containing iron: *ferroconcrete.* ■ Chemistry of iron with a valence of two; ferrous. Compare with **FERRI-**.
– ORIGIN from Latin *ferrum* 'iron.'

fer·ro·al·loy /ˌferōˈaloi, -əˈloi/ ▶ **n.** an alloy of iron with one or more other metals, used in the production of steel.

fer·ro·cene /ˈferəˌsēn/ ▶ **n.** Chemistry an orange crystalline compound whose molecule has a sandwich structure in which two planar cyclopentadiene ligands enclose an iron atom. ● Chem. formula: $Fe(C_5H_5)_2$.
– ORIGIN 1950s: from **FERRO-** 'containing iron' + *-cene* from *c(yclopentadi)ene.*

fer·ro·con·crete /ˌferōˈkänˌkrēt/ ▶ **n.** another term for **REINFORCED CONCRETE**.

fer·ro·cy·a·nide /ˌferōˈsīəˌnīd/ ▶ **n.** Chemistry a salt containing the anion $Fe(CN)_6^{4-}$.

fer·ro·e·lec·tric /ˌferō-iˈlektrik/ Physics ▶ **adj.** (of a substance) exhibiting permanent electric polarization that varies in strength with the applied electric field.
▶ **n.** a ferroelectric substance.
– DERIVATIVES **fer·ro·e·lec·tric·i·ty** /ˌferō-iˌlekˈtrisətē/ **n.**

fer·ro·flu·id /ˈferōˌflo͞oid/ ▶ **n.** [often as modifier] a fluid containing a magnetic suspension: *ferrofluid cooling.*

fer·ro·mag·ne·sian /ˌferōˌmagˈnēzʜən, -zēən/ ▶ **adj.** Geology (of a rock or mineral) containing iron and magnesium as major components.

fer·ro·mag·net·ic /ˌferōˌmagˈnetik/ ▶ **adj.** Physics (of a body or substance) having a high susceptibility to magnetization, the strength of which depends on that of the applied magnetizing field, and that may persist after removal of the applied field. This is the kind of magnetism displayed by iron and is associated with parallel magnetic alignment of neighboring atoms.
– DERIVATIVES **fer·ro·mag·ne·tism** /ˌferōˈmagnəˌtizəm/ **n.**

fer·ro·man·ga·nese /ˌferōˈmaɴɢəˌnēz, -ˌnēs/ ▶ **n.** an alloy of iron and manganese used in the production of steel.

fer·ro·sil·i·con /ˌferōˈsilikən, -ˌkän/ ▶ **n.** an alloy of iron and silicon used in the production of steel and some types of iron.

fer·rous /ˈferəs/ ▶ **adj.** (chiefly of metals) containing or consisting of iron. ■ Chemistry of iron with a valence of two; of iron(II). Compare with **FERRIC**.
– ORIGIN mid 19th cent.: from Latin *ferrum* 'iron' + **-OUS**.

fer·rous ox·ide ▶ **n.** a black powder, FeO, used in making steel and glass.

fer·rous sul·fate ▶ **n.** a pale green iron salt used in inks, tanning, water purification, and treatment of anemia. ● Alternative name: **iron(II) sulfate**; chem. formula (crystals): $FeSO_47H_2O$.

fer·ru·gi·nous /fəˈro͞ojənəs/ ▶ **adj.** containing iron oxides or rust: *a band of ferruginous limestone.* ■ reddish brown; rust-colored: *the ferruginous earth of southern Brazil.*
– ORIGIN mid 17th cent.: from Latin *ferrugo, ferrugin-* 'rust, dark red' (from *ferrum* 'iron') + **-OUS**.

fer·rule /ˈferəl/ ▶ **n.** a ring or cap, typically a metal one, that strengthens the end of a handle, stick, or tube and prevents it from splitting or wearing. ■ a metal band strengthening or forming a joint.
– ORIGIN early 17th cent.: alteration (probably by association with Latin *ferrum* 'iron') of obsolete *verrel*, from Old French *virelle*, from Latin *viriola*, diminutive of *viriae* 'bracelets.'

fer·ry /ˈferē/ ▶ **n.** (pl. **ferries**) (also **ferryboat**) a boat or ship for conveying passengers and goods, esp. over a relatively short distance and as a regular service. ■ a service for conveying passengers or goods in this way. ■ the place from which such a service operates. ■ a similar service using another mode of transportation, esp. aircraft.
▶ **v.** (**ferries, ferrying, ferried**) [with obj.] convey in a boat, esp. across a short stretch of water: *riverboats ferried weekend picnickers to the park.* ■ transport (someone or something) from one place to another: *helicopters ferried 4,000 men into the desert.*
– DERIVATIVES **fer·ry·man n.** /ˈferēmən/ (pl. **ferrymen**).
– ORIGIN Middle English: from Old Norse *ferja* 'ferryboat,' of Germanic origin and related to **FARE**.

fer·tile /ˈfərtl/ ▶ **adj.** (of soil or land) producing or capable of producing abundant vegetation or crops: *fields along the fertile flood plains of the river* | figurative *Germany in the 1920s and 30s was fertile ground for such ideas.* ■ (of a seed or egg) capable of becoming a new individual. ■ (of a person, animal, or plant) able to conceive young or produce seed: *Barbara carefully calculated the period when she was most fertile.* ■ (of a person's mind or imagination) producing many new and inventive ideas with ease. ■ (of a situation or subject) fruitful and productive in generating new ideas: *a series of fertile debates within the social sciences.* ■ Physics (of nuclear material) able to become fissile by the capture of neutrons.
– ORIGIN late Middle English: via French from Latin *fertilis*, from *ferre* 'to bear.'

Fer·tile Cres·cent a crescent-shaped area of fertile land in the Middle East that extends from the eastern Mediterranean coast through the valley of the Tigris and Euphrates rivers to the Persian Gulf. It was the center of the Neolithic development of agriculture (from 7000 BC), and the cradle of the Assyrian, Sumerian, and Babylonian civilizations.

fer·til·i·ty /fərˈtilitē/ ▶ **n.** the quality of being fertile; productiveness: *improve the soil fertility by adding compost.* ■ the ability to conceive children or young: *anxiety and stress affect fertility in both men and women.*

fer·til·i·ty cult /fərˈtilitē/ ▶ **n.** a pagan religious system of some agricultural societies in which seasonal rites are performed with the aim of ensuring good harvests and the future well-being of the community.

fer·til·i·za·tion /ˌfərtl-iˈzāsʜən/ ▶ **n.** Biology the action or process of fertilizing an egg, female animal, or plant, involving the fusion of male and female gametes to form a zygote. ■ the action or process of applying a fertilizer to soil or land.

fer·ti·lize /ˈfərtlˌīz/ ▶ **v.** [with obj.] cause (an egg, female animal, or plant) to develop a new individual by introducing male reproductive material. ■ make (soil or land) more fertile or productive by adding suitable substances to it.
– DERIVATIVES **fer·ti·liz·a·ble adj.**

fer·ti·liz·er /ˈfərtlˌīzər/ ▶ **n.** a chemical or natural substance added to soil or land to increase its fertility: *a nitrogenous fertilizer* | *these varieties need pesticides and more fertilizer.*

fer·u·la /ˈfer(y)ələ/ ▶ **n. 1** a tall large-leaved Eurasian plant of a genus that includes asafetida and its relatives. ● Genus *Ferula*, family Umbelliferae.
2 rare term for **FERULE**.
– ORIGIN late Middle English: from Latin, 'giant fennel, rod.'

fer·ule /ˈferəl/ ▶ **n.** historical a flat ruler with a widened end, formerly used for punishing children.
– ORIGIN late Middle English (denoting the giant fennel): from Latin *ferula* (see **FERULA**).

fer·vent /ˈfərvənt/ ▶ **adj.** having or displaying a passionate intensity: *a fervent disciple of tax reform.* ■ archaic hot, burning, or glowing.
– DERIVATIVES **fer·ven·cy** /-vənsē/ **n.**, **fer·vent·ly adv.**
– ORIGIN Middle English: via Old French from Latin *fervent-* 'boiling,' from the verb *fervere*. Compare with **FERVID** and **FERVOR**.

fer·vid /ˈfərvid/ ▶ **adj.** intensely enthusiastic or passionate, esp. to an excessive degree: *a letter of fervid thanks.* ■ literary burning, hot, or glowing.
– DERIVATIVES **fer·vid·ly adv.**
– ORIGIN late 16th cent. (in the sense 'glowing, hot'): from Latin *fervidus*, from *fervere* 'to boil.' Compare with **FERVENT** and **FERVOR**.

fer·vor /ˈfərvər/ (Brit. **fervour**) ▶ **n.** intense and passionate feeling: *he talked with all the fervor of a new convert.* ■ archaic intense heat.
– ORIGIN Middle English: via Old French from Latin *fervor*, from *fervere* 'to boil.' Compare with **FERVENT** and **FERVID**.

Fès /fes/ variant spelling of **FEZ**.

fes·cue /ˈfeskyo͞o/ ▶ **n.** any of a number of narrow-leaved grasses. ● a perennial grass that is a valuable lawn, pasture, and fodder species (genus *Festuca*, family Gramineae). ● an annual grass that typically occurs on drier soils such as on dunes and wasteland (genus *Vulpia*, family Gramineae).
– ORIGIN Middle English *festu, festue* 'straw, twig,' from Old French *festu*, based on Latin *festuca* 'stalk, straw.' The change of *-t-* to *-c-* occurred in the 16th cent.; the current sense dates from the mid 18th cent.

fess[1] /fes/ (also **fesse**) ▶ **n.** Heraldry an ordinary in the form of a broad horizontal stripe across the middle of the shield.
– PHRASES **in fess** across the middle third of the field.
– ORIGIN late 15th cent.: from Old French *fesse*, alteration of *faisse*, from Latin *fascia* 'band.' Compare with **FASCIA**.

fess[2] ▶ **v.** [no obj.] (**fess up**) informal confess; own up: *"Fess up," she demanded. "What were you doing in Peter's private office?"*
– ORIGIN early 19th cent.: shortening of **CONFESS**.

Fes·sen·den /ˈfesəndən/, Reginald Aubrey (1866–1932), US pioneer of radiotelephony, born in Canada. He invented the heterodyne receiver.

fess point ▶ **n.** Heraldry a point at the center of a shield.

-fest ▶ **comb. form** in nouns denoting a festival or large gathering of a specified kind: *gabfest* | *slugfest.*
– ORIGIN from German *Fest* 'festival.'

fes·ta /ˈfestə/ ▶ **n.** (in Italy and other Mediterranean countries) a religious or other festival.
– ORIGIN early 19th cent.: from Italian, 'festival,' from Latin.

fes·tal /ˈfestəl/ ▶ **adj.** of, like, or relating to a celebration or festival: *he appeared in festal array.*
– DERIVATIVES **fes·tal·ly adv.**
– ORIGIN late 15th cent.: via Old French from late Latin *festalis*, from Latin *festum*, (plural) *festa* 'feast.'

fes·ter /ˈfestər/ ▶ **v.** [no obj.] (of a wound or sore) become septic; suppurate: *I developed a tropical sore that festered badly* | (as adj. **festering**) *a festering abscess.* ■ (of food or garbage) become rotten and offensive to the senses: *a gully full of garbage that festered in the shade.* ■ (of a negative feeling or a problem) become worse or more intense, esp. through long-term neglect or indifference: *anger which festers and grows in his heart.* ■ (of a person) undergo physical and mental deterioration in isolated inactivity: *I might be festering in jail now.*
– ORIGIN late Middle English: from the rare word *fester* 'fistula,' later 'festering sore,' or Old French *festrir* (verb), both from Old French *festre* (noun), from Latin *fistula* 'pipe, reed, fistula.'

fes·ti·val /ˈfestəvəl/ ▶ **n.** a day or period of celebration, typically a religious commemoration: *a tabulation of saints' days and other festivals* | [as modifier] *a festival atmosphere.* ■ an annual celebration or anniversary: *highlights of this year's pumpkin festival.* ■ an organized series of concerts, plays, or movies, typically one held annually in the same place: *numbers that are still heard at traditional jazz festivals.*
– ORIGIN Middle English (as an adjective): via Old French from medieval Latin *festivalis*, from Latin *festivus*, from *festum*, (plural) *festa* 'feast.'

fes·ti·val of lights ▶ **n. 1** another term for **HANUKKAH**.
2 another term for **DIWALI**.

Fes·ti·val of the Dead ▶ **n.** another term for **BON**.

fes·tive /ˈfestiv/ ▶ **adj.** of or relating to a festival: *parties are held and festive food is served.* ■ cheerful and jovially celebratory: *the somber atmosphere has given way to a festive mood.*
– DERIVATIVES **fes·tive·ly adv.**, **fes·tive·ness n.**
– ORIGIN mid 17th cent.: from Latin *festivus*, from *festum*, (plural) *festa* 'feast.'

fes·tiv·i·ty /feˈstivətē/ ▶ **n.** (pl. **festivities**) the celebration of something in a joyful and exuberant way: *the season of festivity and goodwill.* ■ a festive celebration: *she had caught Susan taking a bunch of bouquets at the conclusion of an earlier festivity.* ■ (**festivities**) activities or events celebrating a special occasion: *the Chinese New Year is celebrated with a multitude of festivities.*

– ORIGIN late Middle English: from Old French *festivite* or Latin *festivitas*, from *festivus* 'festive,' from *festum*, (plural) *festa* 'feast.'

fes·toon /fes'to͞on/ ▶ **n.** a chain or garland of flowers, leaves, or ribbons, hung in a curve as a decoration. ■ a carved or molded ornament representing such a garland.
▶ **v.** [with obj.] (often **be festooned with**) adorn (a place) with chains, garlands, or other decorations: *the room was festooned with balloons and streamers.*
– ORIGIN mid 17th cent.: from French *feston*, from Italian *festone* 'festal ornament,' from *festum* 'feast.'

Fest·schrift /'fes(t),sHrift/ (also **festschrift**) ▶ **n.** (pl. **Festschriften** /-,sHriftən/ or **Festschrifts**) a collection of writings published in honor of a scholar.
– ORIGIN late 19th cent.: from German, from *Fest* 'celebration' + *Schrift* 'writing.'

FET ▶ **abbr.** field-effect transistor.

fet·a /'fetə/ (also **feta cheese**) ▶ **n.** a white salty Greek cheese made from the milk of ewes or goats.
– ORIGIN from modern Greek *pheta*.

fe·tal /'fētl/ ▶ **adj.** of or relating to a fetus: *nutrients essential for normal fetal growth.* ■ denoting a posture characteristic of a fetus, with the back curved forward and the limbs folded in front of the body: *he retired to his bed, curled in the fetal position.*

fe·tal al·co·hol syn·drome (abbr.: **FAS**) ▶ **n.** Medicine a congenital syndrome caused by excessive consumption of alcohol by the mother during pregnancy, characterized by retardation of mental development and of physical growth, particularly of the skull and face of the infant.

fetch[1] /fecH/ ▶ **v.** [with obj.] **1** go for and then bring back (someone or something): *he ran to fetch help.* ■ archaic bring forth (blood or tears): *kind offers fetched tears from me.* ■ archaic draw or take a (breath); heave (a sigh).
2 achieve (a particular price) when sold: *handwoven blankets and rugs that can fetch as much as $45,000.*
3 [with two objs.] informal inflict (a blow or slap) on (someone): *he always used to slam the gate and try and fetch her shins a wallop.*
4 informal, dated cause great interest or delight in (someone): *Nadine thought his deductions were good, but she was not as fetched by them as Larry was.*
▶ **n. 1** the distance traveled by wind or waves across open water. ■ the distance a vessel must sail to reach open water.
2 archaic a contrivance, dodge, or trick: *it is no ingenious fetches of argument that we want.*
– PHRASES **fetch and carry** run backward and forward bringing things to someone in a servile fashion: *neither is anyone going to fetch and carry for you when you are in bed with influenza.*
– PHRASAL VERBS **fetch up** informal arrive or come to rest somewhere, typically by accident or unintentionally.
– DERIVATIVES **fetch·er** **n.**
– ORIGIN Old English *fecc(e)an*, variant of *fetian*, probably related to *fatian* 'grasp.'

fetch[2] ▶ **n.** chiefly archaic the apparition or double of a living person, formerly believed to be a warning of that person's impending death.
– ORIGIN late 17th cent.: of unknown origin.

fetch·ing /'fecHiNG/ ▶ **adj.** attractive: *a fetching little garment of pink satin.*
– DERIVATIVES **fetch·ing·ly** **adv.**

fête /fāt, fet/ (also **fete**) ▶ **n.** a celebration or festival.
▶ **v.** [with obj.] (usu. **be fêted**) honor or entertain (someone) lavishly: *she was an instant celebrity, fêted by the media.*
– ORIGIN late Middle English (in the sense 'festival, fair'): from French, from Old French *feste* (see **FEAST**).

fête cham·pê·tre /'fāt sHäN'petr(ə), 'fet/ ▶ **n.** (pl. **fêtes champêtres** pronunc. **same**) an outdoor entertainment; a rural festival.
– ORIGIN late 18th cent.: French, literally 'rural festival.'

fête ga·lante /'fāt gə'länt, 'fet/ ▶ **n.** (pl. **fêtes galantes** pronunc. **same** or /',fāts gə'länts/) an outdoor entertainment or rural festival, esp. as depicted in 18th-century French painting. ■ a painting in this genre.
– ORIGIN early 20th cent.: French, literally 'elegant festival.'

fet·ich ▶ **n.** archaic spelling of **FETISH**.

fe·ti·cide /'fētə,sīd/ ▶ **n.** destruction or abortion of a fetus.

fet·id /'fetid/ (Brit. also **foetid**) ▶ **adj.** smelling extremely unpleasant: *the fetid water of the marsh.*
– DERIVATIVES **fet·id·ly** **adv.**, **fet·id·ness** **n.**
– ORIGIN late Middle English: from Latin *fetidus* (often erroneously spelled *foetidus*), from *fetere* 'to stink.' Compare with **FETOR**.

fet·ish /'fetisH/ ▶ **n.** an inanimate object worshiped for its supposed magical powers or because it is considered to be inhabited by a spirit. ■ a course of action to which one has an excessive and irrational commitment: *he had a fetish for writing more opinions each year than any other justice.* ■ a form of sexual desire in which gratification is linked to an abnormal degree to a particular object, item of clothing, part of the body, etc.: *Victorian men developed fetishes focusing on feet, shoes, and boots.*
– DERIVATIVES **fet·ish·ism** /-,izəm/ **n.**, **fet·ish·ist** /-ist/ **n.**, **fet·ish·is·tic** /,feti'sHistik/ **adj.**
– ORIGIN early 17th cent. (originally denoting an object used by the peoples of West Africa as an amulet or charm): from French *fétiche*, from Portuguese *feitiço* 'charm, sorcery' (originally an adjective meaning 'made by art'), from Latin *factitius*(see **FACTITIOUS**).

fet·ish·ize /'feti,sHīz/ ▶ **v.** [with obj.] have an excessive and irrational commitment to or obsession with (something): *an author who fetishizes privacy.* ■ make (something) the object of a sexual fetish: *women's bodies are so intensely fetishized.*
– DERIVATIVES **fet·ish·i·za·tion** /,fetisHi'zāsHən/ **n.**

fet·lock /'fet,läk/ (also **fetlock joint**) ▶ **n.** the joint of a horse's or other quadruped's leg between the cannon bone and the pastern.
– ORIGIN Middle English: ultimately of Germanic origin; related to **FOOT**.

fetlock

feto- ▶ **comb. form** representing **FETUS**.

fe·tor /'fētər/ (Brit. also **foetor**) ▶ **n.** a strong, foul smell: *the fetor of decay.*
– ORIGIN late 15th cent.: from Latin, from *fetere* 'to stink.' Compare with **FETID**.

fet·ter /'fetər/ ▶ **n.** (usu. **fetters**) a chain or manacle used to restrain a prisoner, typically placed around the ankles: *he lay bound with fetters of iron.* ■ a restraint or check on someone's freedom to do something, typically one considered unfair or overly restrictive: *the fetters of discipline and caution.*
▶ **v.** [with obj.] restrain with chains or manacles, typically around the ankles: (as adj. **fettered**) *a ragged and fettered prisoner.* ■ restrict or restrain (someone) in an unfair or undesirable fashion: *he was not fettered by tradition.*
– ORIGIN Old English *feter*, from an Indo-European root shared by **FOOT**.

fet·ter·lock /'fetər,läk/ ▶ **n.** a D-shaped fetter for tethering a horse by the leg, now only as represented as a heraldic charge.

fet·tle /'fetl/ ▶ **n.** condition: *the aircraft remains in fine fettle.*
▶ **v.** [with obj.] trim or clean the rough edges of (a metal casting or a piece of pottery) before firing. ■ N. English make or repair (something): *the familiar sounds of bikes being prepped and fettled.*
– DERIVATIVES **fet·tler** /'fetl-ər/ **n.**
– ORIGIN late Middle English (as a verb in the general sense 'get ready, prepare,' specifically 'prepare oneself for battle, gird up'): from dialect *fettle* 'strip of material, girdle,' from Old English *fetel*.

fet·tuc·ci·ne /,fetə'cHēnē/ (also **fettucini**) ▶ **n.** pasta made in ribbons.
– ORIGIN from Italian, plural of *fettucina*, diminutive of *fetta* 'slice, ribbon.'

fet·tuc·ci·ne Al·fre·do ▶ **n.** a dish of fettuccine served in a sauce of cream, butter, and grated Parmesan cheese.

fe·tus /'fētəs/ (Brit. (in nontechnical use) also **foetus**) ▶ **n.** (pl. **fetuses**) an unborn offspring of a mammal, in particular an unborn human baby more than eight weeks after conception.
– ORIGIN late Middle English: from Latin, 'pregnancy, childbirth, offspring.'

> **USAGE** The spelling **foetus** has no etymological basis but is recorded from the 16th century and until recently was the standard British spelling in both technical and nontechnical use. In technical usage, **fetus** is now the standard spelling throughout the English-speaking world.

feu /fyo͞o/ Scots Law ▶ **n.** a perpetual lease at a fixed rent. ■ a piece of land held by such a lease.
▶ **v.** (**feus**, **feuing**, **feued**) [with obj.] grant (land) on such a lease.
– ORIGIN late 15th cent. (originally denoting a feudal tenure in which an annual payment was made in lieu of military service): from Old French (see **FEE**).

feud /fyo͞od/ ▶ **n.** a state of prolonged mutual hostility, typically between two families or communities, characterized by violent assaults in revenge for previous injuries: *the long-standing feud between two noble families.* ■ a prolonged and bitter quarrel or dispute: *one of the most volatile feuds that currently rock the scientific community.*
▶ **v.** [no obj.] take part in such a quarrel or violent conflict: *these two families have been feuding since the Civil War* | *Hoover* **feuded with** *the CIA for decades.*
– ORIGIN Middle English *fede* 'hostility, ill will,' from Old French *feide*, from Middle Dutch, Middle Low German *vēde*; related to **FOE**.

feud. ▶ **abbr.** ■ feudal. ■ feudalism.

feu·dal /'fyo͞odl/ ▶ **adj.** according to, resembling, or denoting the system of feudalism: *feudal barons.* ■ absurdly outdated or old-fashioned: *his view of patriotism was more than old-fashioned—it was positively feudal.*
– DERIVATIVES **feu·dal·i·za·tion** /,fyo͞odl-i'zāsHən/ **n.**, **feu·dal·ize** /-,īz/ **v.**, **feu·dal·ly** /'fyo͞odl-ē/ **adv.**
– ORIGIN early 17th cent.: from medieval Latin *feudalis*, from *feudum* (see **FEE**).

feu·dal·ism /'fyo͞odl,izəm/ ▶ **n.** historical the dominant social system in medieval Europe, in which the nobility held lands from the Crown in exchange for military service, and vassals were in turn tenants of the nobles, while the peasants (villeins or serfs) were obliged to live on their lord's land and give him homage, labor, and a share of the produce, notionally in exchange for military protection.
– DERIVATIVES **feu·dal·ist** **n.**, **feu·dal·is·tic** /,fyo͞odl'istik/ **adj.**

feu·dal·i·ty /fyo͞o'dalətē/ ▶ **n.** archaic the principles and practice of the feudal system.
– ORIGIN late 18th cent.: from French *féodalité*, from *féodal*, from medieval Latin *feudalis* 'feudal,' from *feudum* (see **FEE**).

feu·da·to·ry /'fyo͞odə,tôrē/ historical ▶ **adj.** owing feudal allegiance to: *they had for a long period been feudatory to the Norwegian Crown.*
▶ **n.** (pl. **feudatories**) a person who holds land under the conditions of the feudal system.
– ORIGIN late 16th cent.: from medieval Latin *feudatorius*, from *feudare* 'enfeoff,' from *feudum* (see **FEE**).

feu de joie /,fœ də 'zHwä/ ▶ **n.** (pl. **feux de joie** pronunc. **same** or /,fœz/) a rifle salute fired by soldiers on a ceremonial occasion, each soldier firing in succession along the ranks to make a continuous sound.
– ORIGIN early 18th cent.: French, literally 'fire of joy.'

feud·ist /'fyo͞odist/ ▶ **n.** a person taking part in a feud.

feuil·le·ton /'foi-itn, ,fœyə'tôN/ ▶ **n.** a part of a newspaper or magazine devoted to fiction, criticism, or light literature. ■ an article printed in such a part.
– ORIGIN mid 19th cent.: French, from *feuillet*, diminutive of *feuille* 'leaf.'

fe·ver /'fēvər/ ▶ **n.** an abnormally high body temperature, usually accompanied by shivering, headache, and in severe instances, delirium: *I would take aspirin to help me with the pain and reduce the fever* | *African equine fever.* ■ a state of nervous excitement or agitation: *I was mystified, and in a fever of expectation.* ■ [with modifier] the excitement felt by a group of people about a particular public event: *election fever reaches its climax tomorrow.*
▶ **v.** [with obj.] archaic bring about a high body temperature or a state of nervous excitement in (someone): *a heart which sin has fevered.*
– ORIGIN Old English *fēfor*, from Latin *febris*; reinforced in Middle English by Old French *fievre*, also from *febris*.

fe·vered /'fēvərd/ ▶ **adj.** having or showing the symptoms associated with a dangerously high temperature: *her fevered eyes.* ■ feeling or displaying an excessive degree of nervous excitement, agitation, or energy: *my fevered adolescent imagination.*

fe·ver·few /'fēvər,fyo͞o/ ▶ **n.** a bushy aromatic Eurasian plant of the daisy family, with feathery

feverfew

PRONUNCIATION KEY ə *ago, up*; ər *over, fur*; a *hat*; ā *ate*; ä *car*; e *let*; ē *see*; i *fit*; ī *by*; NG *sing*; ō *go*; ô *law, for*; oi *toy*; o͝o *good*; o͞o *goo*; ou *out*; TH *thin*; T͟H *then*; ZH *vision*

f

leaves and daisylike flowers. It is used in herbal medicine to treat headaches. ● *Tanacetum* (or *Chrysanthemum*) *parthenium*, family Compositae.
– ORIGIN Old English *feferfuge*, from Latin *febrifuga*, from *febris* 'fever' + *fugare* 'drive away.' Compare with FEBRIFUGE.

fe·ver grass ▶ n. West Indian term for LEMONGRASS.

fe·ver·ish /ˈfēv(ə)risH/ ▶ adj. having or showing the symptoms of a fever: *he suffered from feverish colds.* ■ displaying a frenetic excitement or energy: *the next couple of weeks were spent in a whirl of feverish activity.*
– DERIVATIVES **fe·ver·ish·ly** adv., **fe·ver·ish·ness** n.

fe·ver·ous /ˈfēv(ə)rəs/ ▶ adj. archaic apt to cause fever. ■ feverish.

fe·ver pitch ▶ n. a state of extreme excitement: *the football crowd was at fever pitch.*

fe·ver tree ▶ n. any of a number of trees that are believed either to cause or to cure fever, in particular: ● a North American tree used in the treatment of malaria during the Civil War (*Pinckneya pubens*, family Rubiaceae). ● a southern African tree that was formerly believed to cause malaria (*Acacia xanthophloea*, family Leguminosae).

few /fyo͞o/ ▶ adj. & pron. **1** (**a few**) a small number of: [as adj.] *may I ask a few questions?* | [as pronoun] *I will recount a few of the stories told me* | *many believe it but only a few are prepared to say.*
2 used to emphasize how small a number of people or things is: [as adj.] *he had few friends* | [as pronoun] *few thought to challenge these assumptions* | *very few of the titles have any literary merit* | *one of the few who survived* | [comparative] *a population of fewer than two million* | [as adj.] *sewing was one of her few pleasures* | [superlative] *ask which products have the fewest complaints.*
▶ n. (as plural noun **the few**) the minority of people; the elect: *a world that increasingly belongs to the few.*
– PHRASES **every few** once in every small group of (typically units of time): *she visits every few weeks.* **few and far between** scarce; infrequent: *my inspired moments are few and far between.* **a good few** Brit. a fairly large number of: *it had been around for a good few years.* **have a few** informal drink enough alcohol to be slightly drunk: *I tend to keep my mouth shut, unless I've had a few.* **no fewer than** used to emphasize a surprisingly large number: *there are no fewer than seventy different brand names.* **not a few** a considerable number: *his fiction has caused not a few readers to see red.* **quite a few** a fairly large number: *quite a few people can do it.* **some few** some but not many: *some few people are born without any sense of time.*
– ORIGIN Old English *fēawe, fēawa*; from an Indo-European root shared by Latin *paucus* and Greek *pauros* 'small.'

> **USAGE** Fewer versus less: strictly speaking, the rule is that **fewer**, the comparative form of **few**, is used with words denoting people or countable things (*fewer members; fewer books; fewer than ten contestants*). **Less**, on the other hand, is used with mass nouns, denoting things that cannot be counted (*less money; less music*). In addition, **less** is normally used with numbers (*less than 10,000*) and with expressions of measurement or time (*less than two weeks; less than four miles away*). But to use **less** with count nouns, as in *less people* or *less words*, is incorrect in standard English.

fey /fā/ ▶ adj. giving an impression of vague unworldliness: *his mother was a strange, fey woman.* ■ having supernatural powers of clairvoyance. ■ chiefly Scottish fated to die or at the point of death: *now he is fey, he sees his own death, and I see it too.*
– DERIVATIVES **fey·ly** adv., **fey·ness** n.
– ORIGIN Old English *fǣge* (in the sense 'fated to die soon').

Feyn·man /ˈfīnmən/, Richard Phillips (1918–88), US theoretical physicist. He is noted for his work on quantum electrodynamics. He shared the 1965 Nobel Prize for Physics with Julian Schwinger (1918–94) and Sin-Itiro Tomonaga (1906–97).

Feyn·man di·a·gram ▶ n. Physics a diagram showing electromagnetic interactions between subatomic particles.

Fez /fez/ (also **Fès** /fes/) a city in northern Morocco, founded in 808; pop. 977,946 (2004).

fez /fez/ ▶ n. (pl. **fezzes**) a flat-topped conical red hat with a black tassel on top, worn by men in some Muslim countries (formerly the Turkish national headdress).

fez

– DERIVATIVES **fezzed** adj.
– ORIGIN early 19th cent.: from Turkish *fes* (perhaps via French *fez*), named after FEZ, once the chief place of manufacture.

ff ▶ abbr. Music fortissimo.

ff. ▶ abbr. ■ folios. ■ following pages.

FFA ▶ abbr. ■ free from alongside. ■ Future Farmers of America.

FFV ▶ abbr. ■ First Family of Virginia. ■ flex-fuel vehicle.

FG ▶ abbr. ■ Football & Basketball field goal. ■ fine grain.

FHA ▶ abbr. ■ Federal Housing Administration. ■ Future Homemakers of America.

FHLBB ▶ abbr. Federal Home Loan Bank Board.

f-hole /ˈef ˌhōl/ ▶ n. either of a pair of sound holes resembling an ʃ and a reversed ʃ in shape, cut in the front of musical instruments of the violin family and some other stringed instruments such as semi-acoustic electric guitars and mandolins.

fhp ▶ abbr. friction horsepower.

FIA the international governing body for motor-racing events.
– ORIGIN acronym from French *Fédération Internationale de l'Automobile.*

fi·a·cre /fēˈäkr(ə)/ ▶ n. (pl. **fiacres** /-krə, -krəz/) historical a small four-wheeled carriage for public hire.
– ORIGIN late 17th cent.: from French, named after the Hôtel de St. *Fiacre* in Paris, where such vehicles were first hired out.

fi·an·cé /ˌfēˌänˈsā, fēˈänsā/ ▶ n. a man who is engaged to be married: *my fiancé and I were childhood sweethearts.*
– ORIGIN mid 19th cent.: from French, past participle of *fiancer* 'betroth,' from Old French *fiance* 'a promise,' based on Latin *fidere* 'to trust.'

fi·an·cée /ˌfēˌänˈsā, fēˈänsā/ ▶ n. a woman who is engaged to be married: *he went back to the valley to marry his fiancée.*

fi·an·chet·to /ˌfēənˈCHetō, -ˈketō/ Chess ▶ n. (pl. **fianchettoes**) the development of a bishop by moving it one square to a long diagonal of the board.
▶ v. (**fianchettoes, fianchettoing, fianchettoed**) [with obj.] develop (a bishop) in such a way.
– ORIGIN mid 19th cent.: from Italian, diminutive of *fianco* 'flank,' ultimately of Germanic origin. Compare with FLANK.

Fi·an·na Fáil /ˈfēənə ˈfoil/ one of the two main political parties of the Republic of Ireland. Larger and traditionally more republican than its rival Fine Gael, it was formed in 1926 in opposition to the Anglo-Irish Treaty of 1921 by Eamon de Valera together with some of the moderate members of Sinn Fein.
– ORIGIN Irish, from *fianna* 'band of warriors'; compare with FENIAN) and *Fáil*, genitive of *Fál*, an ancient name for Ireland. The phrase *Fianna Fáil* was used in 15th-cent. poetry in the neutral sense 'people of Ireland,' but the founders of the political party interpreted it to mean 'soldiers of destiny.'

fi·as·co /fēˈaskō/ ▶ n. (pl. **fiascos**) a thing that is a complete failure, esp. in a ludicrous or humiliating way: *his plans turned into a fiasco.*
– ORIGIN mid 19th cent.: from Italian, literally 'bottle, flask,' in the phrase *far fiasco*, literally 'make a bottle,' figuratively 'fail in a performance': the reason for the figurative sense is unexplained.

fi·at /ˈfēət, ˈfēˌät/ ▶ n. a formal authorization or proposition; a decree: *adopting a legislative review program, rather than trying to regulate by fiat.* ■ an arbitrary order: *the appraisal dropped the value from $75,000 to $15,000, rendering it worthless by bureaucratic fiat.*
– ORIGIN late Middle English: from Latin, 'let it be done,' from *fieri* 'be done or made.'

fi·at mon·ey ▶ n. inconvertible paper money made legal tender by a government decree.

fib /fib/ ▶ n. a lie, typically an unimportant one: *parents told little white fibs about out-of-wedlock births.*
▶ v. (**fibs, fibbing, fibbed**) [no obj.] tell an unimportant lie.
– DERIVATIVES **fib·ber** n.
– ORIGIN mid 16th cent.: perhaps a shortening of obsolete *fible-fable* 'nonsense,' reduplication of FABLE.

fi·ber /ˈfībər/ (Brit. **fibre**) ▶ n. **1** a thread or filament from which a vegetable tissue, mineral substance, or textile is formed: *tropical elements like coconut fibers and branches.* ■ a substance formed of such threads or filaments: *ordinary synthetics don't breathe as well as natural fibers* | *high strength carbon fiber.* ■ a threadlike structure forming part of the muscular, nervous, connective, or other tissue in the human or animal body: *there were degenerative changes in muscle fibers* | figurative *she wanted him with every fiber of her being.* ■ strength of character: *a weak person with no moral fiber.*
2 dietary material containing substances such as cellulose, lignin, and pectin, which are resistant to the action of digestive enzymes: *cereals high in fiber.*
– DERIVATIVES **fi·bered** adj. [in combination] *natural-fibered*, **fi·ber·less** adj.
– ORIGIN late Middle English (in the sense 'lobe of the liver,' (plural) 'entrails'): via French from Latin *fibra* 'fiber, filament, entrails.'

fi·ber·board /ˈfībərˌbôrd/ (Brit. **fibreboard**) ▶ n. a building material made of wood or other plant fibers compressed into boards.

fi·ber·fill /ˈfībərˌfil/ ▶ n. synthetic material used for padding and insulation in garments and soft furnishings such as cushions and duvets.

fi·ber·glass /ˈfībərˌglas/ (Brit. **fibreglass**) (also trademark **Fiberglas**) ▶ n. **1** a reinforced plastic material composed of glass fibers embedded in a resin matrix.
2 a textile fabric made from woven glass filaments.

fi·ber op·tics ▶ plural n. [treated as sing.] the use of thin flexible fibers of glass or other transparent solids to transmit light signals, chiefly for telecommunications or for internal examination of the body. ■ [treated as pl.] the fibers and associated devices so used.
– DERIVATIVES **fi·ber-op·tic** adj.

fi·ber·scope /ˈfībərˌskōp/ (Brit. **fibrescope**) ▶ n. a fiber-optic device for viewing inaccessible internal structures, esp. in the human body.

Fi·bo·nac·ci /ˌfēbəˈnäCHē/, Leonardo (c.1170–c.1250), Italian mathematician; known as **Fibonacci of Pisa**. He made many original contributions in complex calculations, algebra, and geometry and pioneered number theory and indeterminate analysis, discovering the Fibonacci series.

Fi·bo·nac·ci se·ries (also **Fibonacci sequence**) ▶ n. Mathematics a series of numbers in which each number (**Fibonacci number**) is the sum of the two preceding numbers. The simplest is the series 1, 1, 2, 3, 5, 8, etc.

fi·bre ▶ n. British spelling of FIBER.

fi·bre·board ▶ n. British spelling of FIBERBOARD.

fi·bre·glass ▶ n. British spelling of FIBERGLASS.

fi·bre tip ▶ n. British term for FELT-TIP PEN.

fi·bril /ˈfībrəl, ˈfib-/ ▶ n. technical a small or slender fiber: *each muscle fiber is subdivided into smaller fibrils.*
– DERIVATIVES **fi·bril·lar** /-lər/ adj., **fi·bril·lar·y** /-ˌlerē/ adj.
– ORIGIN mid 17th cent.: from modern Latin *fibrilla*, diminutive of Latin *fibra* (see FIBER).

fi·bril·late /ˈfibrəˌlāt/ ▶ v. [no obj.] **1** (of a muscle, esp. in the heart) make a quivering movement due to uncoordinated contraction of the individual fibrils: *the atria ceased to fibrillate when the temperature was reduced.*
2 (of a fiber) split up into fibrils. ■ [with obj.] break (a fiber) into fibrils.
– DERIVATIVES **fi·bril·la·tion** /ˌfibrəˈlāSHən/ n.

fi·brin /ˈfībrən/ ▶ n. Biochemistry an insoluble protein formed from fibrinogen during the clotting of blood. It forms a fibrous mesh that impedes the flow of blood.
– DERIVATIVES **fi·brin·oid** /ˈfībrəˌnoid, ˈfib-/ adj., **fi·brin·ous** /ˈfībrənəs, ˈfib-/ adj.
– ORIGIN early 19th cent.: from FIBER + -IN[1].

fi·brin·o·gen /fīˈbrinəjən/ ▶ n. Biochemistry a soluble protein present in blood plasma, from which fibrin is produced by the action of the enzyme thrombin.

fi·brin·o·gen·ic /ˌfībrənōˈjenik/ ▶ adj. of or relating to fibrinogen or to the formation of fibrin.

fi·bri·nol·y·sis /ˌfībrəˈnäləsis/ ▶ n. Physiology the enzymatic breakdown of the fibrin in blood clots.
– DERIVATIVES **fi·bri·no·lyt·ic** /ˈfībrənəˈlitik/ adj.

fibro- ▶ comb. form of, relating to, or characterized by fibers: *fibroblast* | *fibroma.*
– ORIGIN from Latin *fibra* 'fiber.'

fi·bro·ad·e·no·ma /ˌfībrōˌadnˈōmə/ ▶ n. (pl. **fibroadenomas** or **fibroadenomata** /-adnˈōmətə/) Medicine a tumor formed of mixed fibrous and glandular tissue, typically occurring as a benign growth in the breast.

fi·bro·blast /ˈfībrəˌblast, ˈfib-/ ▶ n. Physiology a cell in connective tissue that produces collagen and other fibers.

fi·bro·car·ti·lage /ˌfībrōˈkärtl-ij/ ▶ n. cartilage that contains fibrous bundles of collagen, such as that of the intervertebral disks in the spinal cord.

fi·bro·cys·tic /ˌfībrəˈsistik, ˌfib-/ ▶ adj. [attrib.] Medicine (of a disease) characterized by the development of fibrous tissue and cystic spaces, typically in the pancreas or the breast.

fi·broid /ˈfīˌbroid/ ▶ adj. of or characterized by fibers or fibrous tissue.
▶ n. Medicine a benign tumor of muscular and fibrous tissues, typically developing in the wall of the uterus.

fi·bro·in /'fībrō-in, 'fib-/ ▶ **n.** a protein that is the chief constituent of silk and spider webs.
– ORIGIN mid 19th cent.: from FIBRO- + -IN¹.

fi·bro·lite /'fībrə,līt/ ▶ **n.** another term for SILLIMANITE.

fi·bro·ma /fī'brōmə/ ▶ **n.** (pl. **fibromas** or **fibromata** /-mətə/) Medicine a benign fibrous tumor of connective tissue.
– DERIVATIVES **fi·bro·ma·tous** adj.
– ORIGIN mid 19th cent.: from Latin *fibra* (see FIBER) + -OMA.

fi·bro·my·al·gia /,fībrōmī'alj(ē)ə/ ▶ **n.** a chronic disorder characterized by widespread musculoskeletal pain, fatigue, and tenderness in localized areas.

fi·bro·sar·co·ma /,fībrō,sär'kōmə/ ▶ **n.** (pl. **fibrosarcomas** or **fibrosarcomata** /-'kōmətə/) Medicine a sarcoma in which the predominant cell type is a malignant fibroblast.
– DERIVATIVES **fi·bro·sar·co·ma·tous** /-'kōmətəs, -'käm-/ adj.

fi·bro·sis /fī'brōsəs/ ▶ **n.** Medicine the thickening and scarring of connective tissue, usually as a result of injury.
– DERIVATIVES **fi·brot·ic** /fī'brätik/ adj.
– ORIGIN late 19th cent.: from Latin *fibra* (see FIBER) + -OSIS.

fi·bro·si·tis /,fībrə'sītis/ ▶ **n.** Medicine inflammation of fibrous connective tissue, typically affecting the back and causing stiffness and pain.
– DERIVATIVES **fi·bro·sit·ic** /-'sitik/ adj.
– ORIGIN early 20th cent.: from Latin *fibrosus* 'fibrous' (from *fibra* 'fiber') + -ITIS.

fi·brous /'fībrəs/ ▶ **adj.** consisting of or characterized by fibers: *lignin is the fibrous material that gives wood its strength.*
– DERIVATIVES **fi·brous·ly** adv., **fi·brous·ness** n.

fib·u·la /'fibyələ/ ▶ **n.** (pl. **fibulae** /-,lē, -,lī/ or **fibulas**) **1** Anatomy the outer and usually smaller of the two bones between the knee and the ankle in humans (or the equivalent joints in other terrestrial vertebrates), parallel with the tibia.
2 Archaeology a brooch or clasp.
– DERIVATIVES **fib·u·lar** /'fibyələr/ adj.
– ORIGIN late 16th cent.: from Latin, 'brooch,' perhaps related to *figere* 'to fix.' The bone is so named because the shape it makes with the tibia resembles a clasp, the fibula being the tongue.

-fic (usu. as **-ific**) ▶ **suffix** (forming adjectives) producing; making: *prolific* | *soporific*.
– ORIGIN from French *-fique* or Latin *-ficus* from *facere* 'do, make.'

FICA ▶ **abbr.** Federal Insurance Contributions Act.

-fically (usu. as **-ifically**) ▶ **suffix** forming adverbs corresponding to adjectives ending in *-fic* (such as *prolifically* corresponding to *prolific*).

-fication (usu. as **-ification**) ▶ **suffix** forming nouns of action from verbs ending in *-fy* (such as *simplification* from *simplify*).
– ORIGIN from French, or from Latin *-fication-* (from verbs ending in *-ficare*).

fi·celle /fē'sel/ ▶ **n.** a small, very thin loaf of French bread.
– ORIGIN French 'twine, string.'

fiche /fēsн/ ▶ **n.** short for MICROFICHE.

Fich·te /'fiktə/, Johann Gottlieb (1762–1814), German philosopher. A student of Kant, he postulated that the ego is the basic reality, and the world is posited by the ego in defining and delimiting itself.

fich·u /'fisнo͞o, 'fē-/ ▶ **n.** a small triangular shawl, worn around a woman's shoulders and neck.
– ORIGIN mid 18th cent.: from French, from *ficher* 'to fix, pin,' from Latin *figere*. Compare with FIX and MICROFICHE.

fick·le /'fikəl/ ▶ **adj.** changing frequently, esp. as regards one's loyalties, interests, or affection: *Web patrons are a notoriously fickle lot, bouncing from one site to another on a whim* | *the weather is forever fickle.*
– DERIVATIVES **fick·ly** /'fik(ə)lē/ adv.
– ORIGIN Old English *ficol* 'deceitful.'

fick·le·ness /'fikəlnəs/ ▶ **n.** changeability, esp. as regards one's loyalties or affections: *the fickleness of youth.*

FICO score /'fīkō/ ▶ **n.** Finance a person's credit score calculated with software from Fair Isaac Corporation (FICO).

> The FICO score is a number between 300 and 850, which indicates a person's capacity to repay a loan. The higher the number, the lower the risk that the borrower will default.

fict. ▶ **abbr.** ■ fiction. ■ fictitious.

fic·tile /'fiktl, -,tīl/ ▶ **adj.** made of earth or clay by a potter. ■ of or relating to pottery or its manufacture. ■ capable of being molded; plastic.
– ORIGIN early 17th cent.: from Latin *fictilis*, from *fict-* 'formed, contrived,' from the verb *fingere*.

fic·tion /'fiksнən/ ▶ **n.** literature in the form of prose, esp. short stories and novels, that describes imaginary events and people. ■ invention or fabrication as opposed to fact: *he dismissed the allegation as absolute fiction.* ■ [in sing.] a belief or statement that is false, but that is often held to be true because it is expedient to do so: *the notion of that country being a democracy is a polite fiction.*
– DERIVATIVES **fic·tion·ist** /-nist/ n.
– ORIGIN late Middle English (in the sense 'invented statement'): via Old French from Latin *fictio(n-)*, from *fingere* 'form, contrive.' Compare with FEIGN and FIGMENT.

fic·tion·al /'fiksнənl/ ▶ **adj.** of or relating to fiction; invented for the purposes of fiction: *fictional texts* | *a fictional character.*
– DERIVATIVES **fic·tion·al·i·ty** /,fiksнə'nalətē/ n., **fic·tion·al·i·za·tion** /,fiksнənl-i'zāsнən/ n., **fic·tion·al·ize** /-nə,līz/ v., **fic·tion·al·ly** adv.

fic·ti·tious /fik'tisнəs/ ▶ **adj.** not real or true, being imaginary or having been fabricated: *she pleaded guilty to stealing thousands in taxpayer dollars by having a fictitious employee on her payroll.* ■ of, relating to, or denoting the imaginary characters and events found in fiction: *the people in this novel are fictitious; the background of public events is not.*
– DERIVATIVES **fic·ti·tious·ly** adv., **fic·ti·tious·ness** n.
– ORIGIN early 17th cent.: from Latin *ficticius* (from *fingere* 'contrive, form') + -OUS (see also -ITIOUS²).

fic·tive /'fiktiv/ ▶ **adj.** creating or created by imagination: *the novel's fictive universe.*
– DERIVATIVES **fic·tive·ness** n.
– ORIGIN early 17th cent. (but rare before the 19th cent.): from French *fictif, -ive* or medieval Latin *fictivus*, from Latin *fingere* 'contrive, form.'

fi·cus /'fīkəs/ ▶ **n.** (pl. **same**) a tree, shrub, or climbing plant of a large genus that includes the figs and the rubber plant. They grow in tropical and warm climates, and several species are of commercial importance. ● Genus *Ficus*, family Moraceae.
– ORIGIN mid 19th cent.: from Latin, 'fig, fig tree.'

fid /fid/ ▶ **n.** Nautical a thick peg, wedge, or supporting pin, in particular: ■ a square wooden or iron bar that takes the weight of a topmast stepped to a lower mast by being passed through holes in both masts. ■ a conical pin or spike used in splicing rope.
– ORIGIN early 17th cent.: of unknown origin.

fid. ▶ **abbr.** fiduciary.

fi·da·yeen /,fidä'yēn/ ▶ **plural n.** variant of FIDDLE.

Fid. Def. ▶ **abbr.** Fidei Defensor. See DEFENDER OF THE FAITH.

fid·dle /'fidl/ ▶ **n. 1** informal a violin, esp. when used to play folk music.
2 informal, chiefly Brit. an act of defrauding, cheating, or falsifying: *a major mortgage fiddle.*
3 Nautical a contrivance, such as a raised rim, that prevents things from rolling or sliding off a table in bad weather.
▶ **v.** informal **1** [no obj.] play the fiddle: *he fiddled with the band from 1949 to 1951* | (**fiddling**) *country music with lots of fiddling and banjo playing.* ■ [with obj.] play (a tune) on the fiddle: *Bill Monroe fiddled his last tune at his annual Beanblossom Bluegrass Festival.*
2 [no obj.] touch or fidget with something in a restless or nervous way: *Laura fiddled with her cup.* ■ tinker with something in an attempt to make minor adjustments or improvements: *never fiddle with an electric machine that's plugged in.* ■ (**fiddle around**) pass time aimlessly, without doing or achieving anything of substance.
3 [with obj.] chiefly Brit. falsify (figures, data, or records), typically in order to gain money: *everyone is fiddling their expenses.*
– PHRASES **fiddle while Rome burns** be concerned with relatively trivial matters while ignoring the serious or disastrous events going on around one. **(as) fit as a fiddle** in good health. **on the fiddle** chiefly Brit. informal engaged in cheating or swindling. **play second fiddle to** take a subordinate role to someone or something in a way often considered demeaning: *she had to play second fiddle to the interests of her husband.*
– ORIGIN Old English *fithele*, denoting a violin or similar instrument (originally not an informal or depreciatory term), based on Latin *vitulari* 'celebrate a festival, be joyful,' perhaps from *Vitula*, the name of a Roman goddess of joy and victory. Compare with VIOL.

fid·dle·back /'fidl,bak/ ▶ **n. 1** [usu. as modifier] a thing shaped like the back of a violin, with the sides deeply curved inward, in particular: ■ the back of a chair.
2 a rippled effect in the grain of fine wood, often exploited when making the backs of violins: [as modifier] *fiddleback mahogany.*
3 (also **fiddleback spider**) another term for BROWN RECLUSE.

fid·dle-de-dee /,fidl dē 'dē/ ▶ **n.** [often as exclamation] dated nonsense.
– ORIGIN late 18th cent.: from FIDDLE + a reduplication.

fid·dle-fad·dle /'fidl ,fadl/ ▶ **n.** trivial matters: nonsense: *he's concerned with petty fiddle-faddle about his personal arrangements.*
▶ **v.** [no obj.] bother with trifles; fuss: *you haven't time to fiddle-faddle about like that.*
– ORIGIN late 16th cent.: reduplication of FIDDLE.

fid·dle-foot·ed ▶ **adj.** (of a horse) skittish. ■ (of a person) restless or apt to wander: *he was what we might consider a fiddle-footed missionary, moving from place to place.*

fid·dle·head /'fidl,hed/ ▶ **n. 1** (also **fiddlehead fern**) the young, curled, edible frond of certain ferns.
2 a scroll-like carving at a ship's bow.
– ORIGIN late 18th cent.: from the resemblance to the head of a violin.

fid·dler /'fidlər, 'fidl-ər/ ▶ **n. 1** informal a person who plays the violin, esp. one who plays folk music.
2 Brit. informal a person who cheats or swindles, esp. one indulging in petty theft.
– ORIGIN Old English *fithelere*, from *fithele* (see FIDDLE).

fid·dler crab ▶ **n.** a small amphibious crab, the males of which have one greatly enlarged claw that they wave in territorial display and courtship. ● Genus *Uca*, family Ocypodidae.

Fid·dler's Green the sailor's Elysium, traditionally a place of wine, women, and song.

fid·dle·stick /'fidl,stik/ ▶ **exclam.** (**fiddlesticks**) nonsense.
▶ **n.** informal a violin bow.

fid·dling /'fidliNG, 'fidl-iNG/ ▶ **adj.** annoyingly trivial or petty: *fiddling little details.*

fid·dly /'fidlē/ ▶ **adj.** (**fiddlier, fiddliest**) Brit. informal complicated or detailed and awkward to do or use: *replacing the battery is fiddly.*

fi·de·ism /'fēdā,izəm/ ▶ **n.** the doctrine that knowledge depends on faith or revelation.
– DERIVATIVES **fi·de·ist** n., **fi·de·is·tic** /,fēdā,istik/ adj.
– ORIGIN late 19th cent.: from Latin *fides* 'faith' + -ISM.

fi·del·i·ty /fə'delətē/ ▶ **n.** faithfulness to a person, cause, or belief, demonstrated by continuing loyalty and support: *he sought only the strictest fidelity to justice.* ■ sexual faithfulness to a spouse or partner. ■ the degree of exactness with which something is copied or reproduced: *the 1949 recording provides reasonable fidelity.*
– ORIGIN late Middle English: from Old French *fidelite* or Latin *fidelitas*, from *fidelis* 'faithful,' from *fides* 'faith.' Compare with FEALTY.

fidg·et /'fijit/ ▶ **v.** (**fidgets, fidgeting, fidgeted**) [no obj.] make small movements, esp. of the hands and feet, through nervousness or impatience: *the audience had begun to fidget on their chairs.* ■ [with obj.] make (someone) uneasy or uncomfortable: *she fidgets me with her never-ending spit and polish.*
▶ **n.** a quick, small movement, typically a repeated one, caused by nervousness or impatience: *he disturbed other people with convulsive fidgets.* ■ a person given to such movements, esp. one whom other people find irritating. ■ (usu. **fidgets**) a state of mental or physical restlessness or uneasiness: *a marketing person full of nervous energy and fidgets.*
– DERIVATIVES **fidg·et·er** n.
– ORIGIN late 17th cent.: from obsolete or dialect *fidge* 'to twitch'; perhaps related to Old Norse *fikja* 'move briskly, be restless or eager.'

fidg·et·y /'fijitē/ ▶ **adj.** inclined to fidget; restless or uneasy: *I get nervous and fidgety at the dentist.*
– DERIVATIVES **fidg·et·i·ness** n.

Fi·do /'fīdō/ historical a system for dispersing fog using gasoline burners on the ground to enable aircraft to land. It was developed by the Allies during World War I.
– ORIGIN acronym from *Fog Intensive Dispersal Operation.*

fi·do /'fīdō/ informal, humorous ▶ **n.** a generic name for a pet dog.
– ORIGIN from Latin *fidō* 'I trust.'

fi·du·cial /fə'do͞osнəl/ ▶ **adj.** technical (esp. of a point or line) assumed as a fixed basis of comparison.
– ORIGIN late 16th cent.: from late Latin *fiducialis*, from *fiducia* 'trust,' from *fidere* 'to trust.'

fi·du·ci·ar·y /fə'do͞osнē,erē, -sнərē/ ▶ **adj.** Law involving trust, esp. with regard to the relationship between a trustee and a beneficiary: *the company*

has a fiduciary duty to shareholders. ■ archaic held or given in trust: *fiduciary estates.* ■ Finance (of a paper currency) depending for its value on securities (as opposed to gold) or the reputation of the issuer.
▸ **n.** (pl. **fiduciaries**) a trustee.
– ORIGIN late 16th cent. (in the sense 'something inspiring trust; credentials'): from Latin *fiduciarius*, from *fiducia* 'trust,' from *fidere* 'to trust.'

fi·dus A·cha·tes /ˈfīdəs əˈkātēz/ ▸ **n.** a faithful friend or devoted follower.
– ORIGIN late 16th cent.: Latin, literally 'faithful Achates' (see ACHATES).

fie /fī/ ▸ **exclam.** archaic or humorous used to express disgust or outrage: *if people don't answer your first letter, fie on them!*
– ORIGIN Middle English: via Old French from Latin *fi*, an exclamation of disgust at a stench.

Fied·ler /ˈfēdlər/, Arthur (1894–1979), US conductor. An accomplished violist, he played for the Boston Pops Orchestra 1915–30 and then became its conductor 1930–74.

f

fief /fēf/ ▸ **n. 1** historical an estate of land, esp. one held on condition of feudal service.
2 a person's sphere of operation or control.
– ORIGIN early 17th cent.: from French (see FEE).

fief·dom /ˈfēfdəm/ ▸ **n.** a fief.

Field[1] /fēld/, Marshall (1834–1906), US merchant and philanthropist. In 1881, he organized Marshall Field & Co., which became the largest retail store in the world. He made major donations to the University of Chicago, the Art Institute of Chicago, and the Field Museum of Natural History.

Field[2], Stephen Johnson (1816–99), US Supreme Court associate justice 1863–97. Appointed to the Court by President Lincoln, he was a conservative. His brother **David Dudley** (1805–94) was noted for his expertise in law codification; another brother **Cyrus West** (1819–92) was known for his part in the laying of the undersea cable between the US and Europe 1857–66.

field /fēld/ ▸ **n. 1** an area of open land, esp. one planted with crops or pasture, typically bounded by hedges or fences: *a wheat field | a field of corn.* ■ a piece of land used for a particular purpose, esp. an area marked out for a game or sport: *a football field.* ■ Baseball defensive play or the defensive positions collectively: *he is fast in the field and on the bases.* ■ a large area of land or water completely covered in a particular substance, esp. snow or ice: *an ice field.* ■ an area rich in a natural product, typically oil or gas: *an oil field.* ■ an area on which a battle is fought: *a field of battle.* ■ archaic a battle: *many a bloody field was to be fought.* ■ a place where a subject of scientific study or artistic representation can be observed in its natural location or context.
2 a particular branch of study or sphere of activity or interest: *we talked to professionals in various fields.* ■ Computing a part of a record, representing an item of data. ■ Linguistics & Psychology a general area of meaning within which individual words make particular distinctions. ■ a space or range within which objects are visible from a particular viewpoint or through a piece of apparatus: *the stars drift through this telescope's field of view.* See also FIELD OF VISION. ■ an area on a flag with a single background color: *fifty white stars on a blue field.* ■ Heraldry the surface of an escutcheon or of one of its divisions.
3 (usu. **the field**) all the participants in a contest or sport: *he destroyed the rest of the field with a devastating injection of speed.*
4 Physics the region in which a particular condition prevails, esp. one in which a force or influence is effective regardless of the presence or absence of a material medium. ■ the force exerted or potentially exerted in such an area: *the variation in the strength of the field.* ■ Mathematics a system subject to two binary operations analogous to those for the multiplication and addition of real numbers, and having similar commutative and distributive laws.
▸ **v. 1** [no obj.] Baseball play as a fielder. ■ [with obj.] catch or stop (the ball): *he fielded the ball cleanly, but threw it down the right-field line.*
2 [with obj.] send out (a team or individual) to play in a game: *a high school that traditionally fielded mediocre teams.* ■ (of a political party) nominate (a candidate) to run in an election: *a radical political party that is beginning to field candidates in local elections.* ■ deploy (an army): *no one had the power to field an army of any consequence.*
3 [with obj.] deal with (a difficult question, telephone call, etc.): *she has fielded five calls from salespeople.*
▸ **adj.** [attrib.] carried out or working in the natural environment, rather than in a laboratory or office: *field observations.* ■ (of military equipment) light and mobile for use on campaign: *field artillery.* ■ used in names of animals or plants found in the open country, rather than among buildings or as cultivated varieties: *field ant.* ■ denoting a game played outdoors on a marked field.
– PHRASES **in the field** on campaign; (while) engaged in combat or maneuvers: *troops in the field.* ■ away from the laboratory or studio; engaged in practical work in a natural environment. ■ (of an employee) away from the home office; working while traveling: *he was a salesman in the field.* **keep the field** archaic continue a military campaign. **lead the field** be the leader in a race. ■ be the best or most popular: *in the executive car group, this model leads the field.* **play the field** informal indulge in a series of sexual relationships without committing oneself to anyone. **take the field** (of a sports team) go onto a field to begin a game. ■ Baseball begin one's turn on defense in an inning. ■ start a military campaign.
– ORIGIN Old English *feld* (also denoting a large tract of open country; compare with VELD), of West Germanic origin; related to Dutch *veld* and German *Feld*.

field book ▸ **n.** a book in which a surveyor or other technician or scientist writes down measurements and other technical notes taken in the field.

field boot ▸ **n.** a close-fitting, knee-length military boot.

field corn ▸ **n.** corn grown to feed livestock.

field·craft /ˈfēld,kraft/ ▸ **n.** the techniques involved in living, traveling, or making military or scientific observations in the field, esp. while remaining undetected.

field crick·et ▸ **n.** a cricket that lives in a burrow in grassland and has a musical birdlike chirp. ● Family Gryllidae, numerous species.

field cricket

field day ▸ **n. 1** Military a review or an exercise, esp. in maneuvering.
2 a day devoted to athletic contests or other sporting events, typically at a school.
3 [in sing.] an opportunity for action, success, or excitement, esp. at the expense of others: *shoplifters are having a field day in the store.*
4 a day set aside for the display of agricultural machinery and crops, esp. corn and soybeans.

field-ef·fect tran·sis·tor (abbr.: **FET**) ▸ **n.** Electronics a transistor in which most current is carried along a channel whose effective resistance can be controlled by a transverse electric field.

field e·mis·sion ▸ **n.** Physics the emission of electrons from the surface of a conductor under the influence of a strong electrostatic field, as a result of the tunnel effect.

field·er /ˈfēldər/ ▸ **n.** Baseball & Cricket a player who occupies a defensive position in the field while the other side is batting (typically one other than the pitcher or catcher, or bowler).

field·er's choice ▸ **n.** Baseball a play in which the fielding team's decision to put out another player allows the batter to reach first base safely.

field e·vents ▸ **plural n.** track-and-field contests other than races, such as throwing and jumping events. Compare with TRACK EVENTS.

field·fare /ˈfēld,fe(ə)r/ ▸ **n.** a large migratory thrush with a gray head, breeding in northern Eurasia. ● *Turdus pilaris*, subfamily Turdinae, family Muscicapidae.
– ORIGIN late Old English *feldefare*, perhaps from *feld* 'field' + the base of *faran* 'to travel' (see FARE).

field glass·es ▸ **plural n.** binoculars for outdoor use.

field goal ▸ **n. 1** Football a goal scored by a placekick, scoring three points.
2 Basketball a basket scored while the clock is running and the ball is in play.

field-grade of·fi·cer ▸ **n.** Military a major, lieutenant colonel, or colonel.

field-grade rank ▸ **n.** the rank attained by a military field officer.

field guide ▸ **n.** a book for the identification of birds, flowers, minerals, or other things in their natural environment.

field hand ▸ **n.** a person employed as a farm laborer.

field hock·ey ▸ **n.** a game played between two teams of eleven players who use hooked sticks to drive a small hard ball toward goals at opposite ends of a field.

field hol·ler ▸ **n.** see HOLLER.

field hos·pi·tal ▸ **n.** a temporary hospital set up near a combat zone to provide emergency care for the wounded.

field house ▸ **n. 1** a large building, often part of a college, that provides space for a variety of athletic facilities, such as basketball and squash courts, a running track, a swimming pool, exercise equipment, and often an indoor arena with spectator seating.
2 a building usually adjacent to an athletic field and equipped with changing rooms, lockers, showers, etc., for those using the athletic facility.

Field·ing /ˈfēldiNG/, Henry (1707–54), English novelist. He provoked the introduction of censorship in theaters with his political satire *The Historical Register for 1736*. He then turned to writing picaresque novels, notably *Joseph Andrews* (1742) and *Tom Jones* (1749).

field lens ▸ **n.** in a multiple lens optical system, the lens farthest from the eye.

field mark ▸ **n.** a visible mark or characteristic that can be used in identifying a bird or other animal in the field.

field mar·shal ▸ **n.** an officer of the highest rank in the British and other armies.

field mouse ▸ **n.** a dark brown mouse with a long tail and large eyes. Also called WOOD MOUSE. ● Genus *Apodemus*, family Muridae: several species, in particular the widespread *A. sylvaticus*.

field mush·room ▸ **n.** another term for CHAMPIGNON.

field of·fi·cer ▸ **n.** another term for FIELD-GRADE OFFICER.

field of hon·or ▸ **n.** the place where a duel or battle is fought.

field of vi·sion ▸ **n.** the entire area that a person or animal is able to see when their eyes are fixed in one position.

field pea ▸ **n.** a pea plant of a variety grown chiefly for fodder or as green manure.
– ORIGIN early 18th cent.: said to be so named because they were once the only agricultural peas cultivated in the UK.

Fields, W. C. (1880–1946), US comedian; born *William Claude Dukenfield*. Having made his name as a comedy juggler, he became a vaudeville star and appeared in the *Ziegfeld Follies* revues between 1915 and 1921. Notable movies: *The Bank Dick* (1940) and *Never Give a Sucker an Even Break* (1941).

field sports ▸ **plural n.** outdoor sports, esp. hunting, shooting, and fishing.

field·stone /ˈfēl(d),stōn/ ▸ **n.** [often as modifier] stone used in its natural form: *a fieldstone fireplace.*

field test ▸ **n.** a test carried out in the environment in which a product or device is to be used.
▸ **v.** (**field-test**) [with obj.] test (something) in the environment in such a way.

field the·o·ry ▸ **n.** Physics a theory that explains physical phenomena in terms of a field and the manner in which it interacts with matter or with other fields.

field tri·al ▸ **n. 1** a field test.
2 a competition for hunting dogs to test their levels of skill and training in retrieving or pointing.

field trip ▸ **n.** a trip made by students or research workers to study something at first hand: *a field trip to the power plant was organized.*

field·work /ˈfēld,wərk/ ▸ **n. 1** practical work conducted by a researcher in the natural environment, rather than in a laboratory or office.
2 rare a temporary fortification.
– DERIVATIVES **field·work·er n.**

fiend /fēnd/ ▸ **n.** an evil spirit or demon. ■ (**the fiend**) archaic the Devil. ■ a wicked or cruel person: *a fiend thirsty for blood and revenge.* ■ a person causing mischief or annoyance: *you little fiend!* ■ informal a person who is excessively fond of or addicted to something: *the restaurant's owner is a wine fiend.*
– DERIVATIVES **fiend·like** /-,līk/ **adj.**
– ORIGIN Old English *fēond* 'an enemy, the devil, a demon,' of Germanic origin; related to Dutch *vijand* and German *Feind* 'enemy.'

fiend·ish /ˈfēndisH/ ▸ **adj.** extremely cruel or unpleasant; devilish: *shrieks of fiendish laughter.* ■ extremely awkward or complex: *a fiendish problem.*
– DERIVATIVES **fiend·ish·ly adv.**, **fiend·ish·ness n.**

Fiennes /fīnz/ the name of a family of British actors. ■ **Ralph** (1962–). His best known roles include Hamlet in a 1995 Broadway production (Tony Award) and Lord Voldemort in the *Harry Potter* movies. Other notable movies: *Schindler's List* (1993), *Quiz Show* (1994), *The English Patient* (1996), and *The End of the Affair* (1999). ■ **Joseph** (1970–), the brother of Ralph. Notable movies: *Shakespeare in Love* (1998), *Luther* (2003), and *Running with Scissors* (2006).

fierce /fi(ə)rs/ ▸ **adj.** (**fiercer**, **fiercest**) having or displaying an intense or ferocious aggressiveness: *as women, we need to accept that we can be fierce, cunning, and predatory | the fierce air battles that*

ensued over the Pacific. ■ (of a feeling, emotion, or action) showing a heartfelt and powerful intensity: *he kissed her with a fierce, demanding passion.* ■ (of the weather or temperature) powerful and destructive in extent or intensity: *fierce storms lashed the country.*
– PHRASES **something fierce** informal to a great and almost overwhelming extent: *he said he missed me something fierce.*
– DERIVATIVES **fierce·ly** adv., **fierce·ness** n.
– ORIGIN Middle English: from Old French *fiers* 'fierce, brave, proud,' from Latin *ferus* 'untamed.' Compare with FERAL.

fi·e·ri fa·ci·as /ˌfīərē ˈfāsH(ē)əs/ ▶ n. Law a writ to a sheriff for executing a judgment.
– ORIGIN late Middle English Latin, 'you shall make happen.'

fier·y /ˈfī(ə)rē/ ▶ adj. (**fierier**, **fieriest**) consisting of fire or burning strongly and brightly: *the sun was a fiery ball low on the hills* | [as submodifier] figurative *a fiery hot chili sauce.* ■ having the bright color of fire: *the car was painted a fiery red.* ■ (of a person) having a passionate, quick-tempered nature: *a fiery, imaginative Aries.* ■ (of behavior or words) passionately angry and deeply felt: *a fiery speech.*
– DERIVATIVES **fier·i·ly** /ˈfī(ə)rəlē/ adv., **fier·i·ness** n.

fier·y cross ▶ n. a burning wooden cross used as a symbol by the Ku Klux Klan. ■ historical a wooden cross, charred and dipped in blood, used among Scottish clans to summon men to battle.

fi·es·ta /fēˈestə/ ▶ n. (in Spanish-speaking regions) a religious festival: *the yearly fiesta of San Juan.* ■ an event marked by festivities or celebration: *a balloon fiesta.*
– ORIGIN Spanish, from Latin *festum*, (plural) *festa* (see FEAST).

FIFA /ˈfēfə/ the international governing body of soccer, formed in 1904 and based in Zurich, Switzerland.
– ORIGIN acronym from French *Fédération internationale de football association.*

fi. fa. ▶ abbr. fieri facias.

fife /fīf/ ▶ n. a kind of small shrill flute used esp. with the drum in military bands.

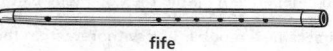

fife

▶ v. [no obj.] archaic play the fife.
– DERIVATIVES **fif·er** n.
– ORIGIN mid 16th cent.: from German *Pfeife* 'pipe,' or from French *fifre* from Swiss German *Pfifre* 'piper.' Compare with PIPE.

fife rail ▶ n. chiefly historical a rail around the mainmast of a sailing ship, holding belaying pins. ■ the rail on top of the bulwark at the edge of a sailing ship's poop or forecastle.
– ORIGIN early 18th cent.: of unknown origin.

FIFO /ˈfīˌfō/ ▶ abbr. first in, first out (chiefly with reference to methods of stock valuation and data storage). Compare with LIFO.

fif·teen /fifˈtēn, ˈfifˌtēn/ ▶ cardinal number equivalent to the product of three and five; one more than fourteen, or five more than ten; 15: *all fifteen species of cranes mate for life* | *fifteen feet high* | *fifteen of the passengers made their appearance.* (Roman numeral: **xv** or **XV**) ■ fifteen years old: *she must be fifteen by now.*
– PHRASES **fifteen minutes of fame** a brief period of fame that a person enjoys before fading back into obscurity. [adapted from Andy Warhol's comment 'in the future everybody will be world famous for fifteen minutes' (1968).]
– ORIGIN Old English *fīftēne, fiftiene* (see FIVE, -TEEN).

fif·teenth /fifˈtēnTH, ˈfifˌtēnTH/ ▶ ordinal number constituting number fifteen in a sequence; 15th: *August the fifteenth* | *the fifteenth century* | *on the fifteenth floor.* ■ (**a fifteenth/one fifteenth**) each of fifteen equal parts into which something is or may be divided. ■ an organ stop sounding a register of pipes two octaves (fifteen notes) above the diapason.

fifth /fi(f)TH/ ▶ ordinal number constituting number five in a sequence; 5th: *the fifth century* BC | *her mother had just given birth to another child, her fifth* | *the world's fifth-largest oil exporter* | *the fifth of November.* ■ (**a fifth/one fifth**) each of five equal parts into which something is or may be divided. ■ the fifth finisher or position in a race or competition: *he finished fifth.* ■ (in some vehicles) the fifth (and typically highest) in a sequence of gears: *in my panic I changed from third to fifth.* ■ fifthly (used to introduce a fifth point or reason): *fourth, it can aid the process of life review, and fifth, it is an enjoyable and stimulating experience.* ■ Music an interval spanning five consecutive notes in a diatonic scale, in particular (also **perfect fifth**) an interval of three whole steps and a half step (e.g., C to G): *strings tuned a fifth apart.* ■ Music the note that is higher by such an interval than the root of a diatonic scale. ■ (**a fifth of**) a fifth of a gallon, as a measure of liquor, or a bottle of this capacity: *a fifth of whiskey.* ■ the fifth grade of a school.
– PHRASES **take** (or **plead**) **the Fifth**(**Amendment**) (in the US) exercise the right guaranteed by the Fifth Amendment to the Constitution of refusing to answer questions in order to avoid incriminating oneself.
– DERIVATIVES **fifth·ly** adv.

fifth col·umn ▶ n. a group within a country at war who are sympathetic to or working for its enemies.
– DERIVATIVES **fifth col·umn·ist** n.
– ORIGIN The term dates from the Spanish Civil War, when General Mola, leading four columns of troops toward Madrid, declared that he had a fifth column inside the city.

fifth-gen·er·a·tion ▶ adj. denoting a proposed new class of computer or programming language employing artificial intelligence.

Fifth-mon·ar·chy-man ▶ n. historical a member of a 17th-century sect expecting the immediate Second Coming of Christ and repudiating all other government.
– ORIGIN from *Fifth Monarchy*, denoting the last of the five great empires prophesied by Daniel (Dan. 2:44).

fifth po·si·tion ▶ n. **1** Ballet a posture in which the feet are turned outward, one immediately in front of but touching the other so that the toe of the back foot just protrudes beyond the heel of the front foot. ■ a position of the arms in which they are held curved in front of the body, at hip level, waist level, or above the head, with the palms facing the body. **2** Music a position of the left hand on the fingerboard of a stringed instrument nearer to the bridge than the fourth position, enabling a higher set of notes to be played.

Fifth Re·pub·lic the republican regime established in France with de Gaulle's introduction of a new constitution in 1958.

fifth wheel ▶ n. **1** an extra wheel for a four-wheeled vehicle. ■ informal a superfluous person or thing. **2** a coupling between a trailer and a vehicle used for towing. ■ (also **fifth-wheel trailer**) a trailer with accommodations for camping out. ■ historical a horizontal turntable over the front axle of a carriage as an extra support to prevent its tipping.

fif·ty /ˈfiftē/ ▶ cardinal number (pl. **fifties**) the number equivalent to the product of five and ten; half of one hundred; 50: *only fifty percent of the aircraft were serviceable* | *about fifty of us filed in* | *a fifty-pound salmon.* (Roman numeral: **l** or **L**) ■ (**fifties**) the numbers from 50 to 59, esp. the years of a century or of a person's life: *Elvis is the icon of the Fifties.* ■ fifty years old: *she looked about fifty.* ■ fifty miles an hour: *doing about fifty.* ■ a fifty-dollar bill.
– DERIVATIVES **fif·ti·eth** /ˈfiftē-iTH/ ordinal number, **fif·ty·fold** /-ˌfōld/ adj. & adv.
– ORIGIN Old English *fīftig* (see FIVE, -TY[2]).

fif·ty-fif·ty ▶ adj. the same in share or proportion; equal: *fifty-fifty partners.* ■ used to refer to one of two possibilities that are equally likely to happen: *he has a fifty-fifty chance of surviving the operation.*
▶ adv. equally; half and half: *they divided the spoils fifty-fifty.*

fig[1] /fig/ ▶ n. **1** a soft pear-shaped fruit with sweet dark flesh and many small seeds, eaten fresh or dried. **2** (also **figtree**) the deciduous Old World tree or shrub that bears this fruit. ● *Ficus carica*, family Moraceae.
■ used in names of other plants of this genus, or in names of nonrelated plants that bear a similar fruit.
– PHRASES **not give** (or **care**) **a fig** not have the slightest concern about: *Karla didn't give a fig for Joe's comfort or his state of mind.*
– ORIGIN Middle English: from Old French *figue*, from Provençal *fig(u)a*, based on Latin *ficus*.

fig[2] informal ▶ n. (in phrase **full fig**) smart clothes, esp. those appropriate to a particular occasion or profession: *a soldier walking up the street in full fig.*
▶ v. (**figs, figging, figged**) [with obj.] archaic dress up (someone) to look smart: *he was figged out in the latest modes.*
– ORIGIN late 17th cent. (as a verb): variant of obsolete *feague* 'liven up' (earlier 'whip'); perhaps related to German *fegen* 'sweep, thrash'; compare with FAKE[1]. An early sense of the verb was 'fill the head with nonsense'; later (early 19th cent.) 'cause (a horse) to be lively and carry its tail well (by applying ginger to its anus)'; hence 'smarten up.'

fig. ▶ abbr. figure: *see fig.34.*

fight /fīt/ ▶ v. (past and past participle **fought** /fôt/) [no obj.] take part in a violent struggle involving the exchange of physical blows or the use of weapons: *the men were fighting* | *they fight with other children.* ■ [with obj.] engage in (a war or battle): *there was another war to fight.* ■ [no obj.] *we fought and died for this country.* ■ quarrel or argue: *she didn't want to fight with her mother all the time* | *they were fighting over who pays the bill.* ■ [with obj.] struggle to put out (a fire, esp. a large one): *two fire trucks raced to the scene to fight the blaze.* ■ [with obj.] endeavor vigorously to win (an election or other contest). ■ campaign determinedly for or against something, esp. to put right what one considers unfair or unjust: *I will fight for more equitable laws.* ■ [with obj.] struggle or campaign against (something): *the best way to fight fascism abroad and racism at home.* ■ [with obj.] attempt to repress (a feeling or an expression of a feeling): *she had to fight back tears of frustration.* ■ [with obj.] take part in a boxing match against (an opponent). ■ (**fight one's way**) move forward with difficulty, esp. by pushing through a crowd or overcoming physical obstacles: *she watched him fight his way across the room.* ■ [with obj.] archaic command, manage, or maneuver (troops, a ship, or military equipment) in battle: *General Hill fights his troops well.*
▶ n. a violent confrontation or struggle: *we'll get into a fight and wind up with bloody noses.* ■ a boxing match. ■ a battle or war: *the country was not eager for a fight with the US.* ■ a vigorous struggle or campaign for or against something: *a long fight against cancer.* ■ an argument or quarrel: *she had a fight with her husband.* ■ the inclination or ability to fight or struggle: *Ginny felt the fight trickle out of her.*
– PHRASES **fight fire with fire** use the weapons or tactics of one's enemy or opponent, even if one finds them distasteful. **fight like cats and dogs** (of two people) be continually arguing with one another. **fight a losing battle** be fated to fail in one's efforts: *he was fighting a losing battle to stem the tears.* **fight shy of** be unwilling to undertake or become involved with: *these musicians fight shy of change.* **make a fight of it** put up a spirited show of resistance in a fight or contest: *the Chargers certainly made a fight of it in the second half.* **fight or flight** the instinctive physiological response to a threatening situation, which readies one either to resist forcibly or to run away. **put up a fight** offer resistance to an attack.
– PHRASAL VERBS **fight back** counterattack or retaliate in a fight, struggle, or contest. **fight it out** settle a dispute by fighting or competing aggressively: *they fought it out with a tug-of-war.* **fight someone/something off** defend oneself against an attack by someone or something: *well-fed people are better able to fight off infectious disease.*
– ORIGIN Old English *feohtan* (verb), *feoht(e), gefeoht* (noun); related to Dutch *vechten, gevecht* and German *fechten, Gefecht.*

fight·er /ˈfītər/ ▶ n. **1** a person or animal that fights, esp. as a soldier or a boxer. ■ a person who does not easily admit defeat in spite of difficulties or opposition: *there'll be months of physiotherapy but medical staff say she's a fighter.* **2** a fast military aircraft designed for attacking other aircraft: *designers employ stealth to render a fighter invisible to radar* | [as modifier] *fighter pilots.*

> **WORD TRENDS** Labels are powerful things, carrying with them a great raft of associations and assumptions, and **terrorist** is one of the most inflammatory. Since the War on Terror was proclaimed in 2001 and wars were initiated in Iraq and Afghanistan, frequency of the word **terrorist** in the Oxford English Corpus peaked sharply but has now declined, whereas evidence for **fighter, insurgent,** and **militant**, more neutral labels for nongovernmental forces opposing Western troops, has steadily increased. However, the neutrality of **fighter** is a matter of debate: in the Corpus it is typically associated with such positive tags as *liberation, heroic,* and *courageous.* Such words are not attached to **terrorist**, which is far more likely to be linked to *fanatical, dangerous,* or *deadly.*

fight·er-bomb·er ▶ n. an aircraft serving as both a fighter and bomber.

fight·ing /ˈfītiNG/ ▶ n. the action of fighting; violence or conflict: *terrible fighting broke out in the streets.*
▶ adj. displaying or engaging in violence, combat, or aggression: *he was a fighting man* | *he put up his fists and took a fighting stance.*

fight·ing chair ▶ n. a fixed chair on a boat used by a person trying to catch large fish.

PRONUNCIATION KEY ə *ago, up*; ər *over, fur*; a *hat*; ā *ate*; ä *car*; e *let*; ē *see*; i *fit*; ī *by*; NG *sing*; ō *go*; ô *law, for*; oi *toy*; o͝o *good*; o͞o *goo*; ou *out*; TH *thin*; T͟H *then*; ZH *vision*

fight·ing chance ▶ n. a possibility of success if great effort is made: *they still have a fighting chance of clinching the title.*

fight·ing fish (also **Siamese fighting fish**) ▶ n. a small labyrinth fish native to Thailand, the males of which fight vigorously. It has been bred in a variety of colors for fighting and for aquariums. ● *Betta splendens*, family Belontiidae.

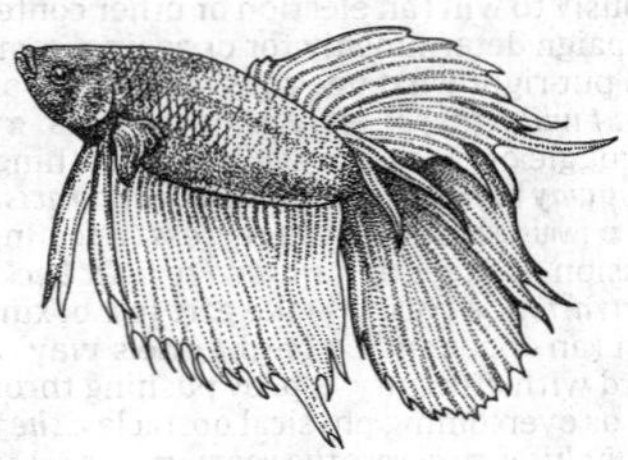

fighting fish

f

fight·ing words ▶ plural n. informal words indicating a willingness to fight or challenge someone. ■ words expressing an insult, esp. of an ethnic, racial, or sexist nature.

fig leaf ▶ n. a leaf of a fig tree, often depicted as concealing the genitals in paintings and sculpture. ■ a thing designed to conceal a difficulty or embarrassment: *the amendment was just a fig leaf designed to cover the cracks in the party.*
– ORIGIN early 16th cent.: with reference to the story of Adam and Eve (Gen. 3:7).

fig·ment /ˈfigmənt/ ▶ n. a thing that someone believes to be real but that exists only in their imagination: *it really was Ross and not **a figment of her overheated imagination**.*
– ORIGIN late Middle English (denoting an invented statement or story): from Latin *figmentum*, related to *fingere* 'form, contrive.' Compare with FEIGN and FICTION. The current sense dates from the early 17th cent.

fi·gu·ra /fiˈgyo͝orə/ ▶ n. (pl. **figurae** /-ˌrē/) (in literary theory) a person or thing representing or symbolizing a fact or ideal.
– ORIGIN mid 20th cent.: Latin, literally 'figure' (representing an early use of *figure* to denote an emblem or type).

fig·ur·al /ˈfigyərəl/ ▶ adj. **1** another term for FIGURATIVE (sense 1)). ■ (in postmodernist writing) relating to or denoting a form of signification that relies on imagery and association rather than on rational and linguistic concepts.
2 Art another term for FIGURATIVE (sense 2)).
– ORIGIN late Middle English: from Old French, or from late Latin *figuralis*, from *figura* 'form, shape' (see FIGURE).

fig·u·rant /ˈfigyərənt, ˌfigyəˈränt/ ▶ n. (fem. **figurante** /ˌfigyəˈräntē, -ˈränt/) a supernumerary actor.
– ORIGIN French, present participle of *figurer* 'to figure.'

fig·u·ra·tion /ˌfigyəˈrāsʜən/ ▶ n. **1** ornamentation by means of figures or designs. ■ Music use of florid counterpoint: *the figuration of the accompaniment comes out too strongly.*
2 allegorical representation: *the figuration of "The Possessed" is much more complex | the opening parable may be read as a figuration of the main idea behind the novel.*
– ORIGIN Middle English (in the senses 'outline' and 'making of arithmetical figures'): from Latin *figuratio(n-)*, from *figurare* 'to form or fashion,' from *figura* (see FIGURE).

fig·ur·a·tive /ˈfigyərətiv/ ▶ adj. **1** departing from a literal use of words; metaphorical: *gold, in the figurative language of the people, was "the tears wept by the sun."*
2 (of an artist or work of art) representing forms that are recognizably derived from life.
– DERIVATIVES **fig·ur·a·tive·ly** adv., **fig·ur·a·tive·ness** n.
– ORIGIN Middle English: from late Latin *figurativus*, from *figurare* 'to form or fashion,' from *figura* (see FIGURE).

fig·ure /ˈfigyər/ ▶ n. **1** a number, esp. one that forms part of official statistics or relates to the financial performance of a company: *official census figures | a figure of 30,000 deaths annually from snakebite.* ■ a numerical symbol, esp. any of the ten in Arabic notation: *the figure 7.* ■ one of a specified number of digits making up a larger number, used to give a rough idea of the order of magnitude: *their market price runs into five figures* | [in combination] *a six-figure salary.* ■ an amount of money: *a figure of two thousand dollars.* ■ (**figures**) arithmetical calculations: *she has no **head for figures**.*
2 a person's bodily shape, esp. that of a woman and when considered to be attractive: *she had always been so proud of her figure.* ■ a person seen indistinctly, esp. at a distance: *a backpacked figure appeared in the distance.* ■ a person of a particular kind, esp. one who is important or distinctive in some way: *Williams became something of a cult figure.* ■ a representation of a human or animal form in drawing or sculpture: *starkly painted figures.*
3 a shape defined by one or more lines in two dimensions (such as a circle or a triangle), or one or more surfaces in three dimensions (such as a sphere or a cuboid), either considered mathematically in geometry or used as a decorative design: *a red ground with white and blue geometric figures.* ■ a diagram or illustrative drawing, esp. in a book or magazine: *figure 1 shows an ignition circuit.* ■ Figure Skating a movement or series of movements following a prescribed pattern and often beginning and ending at the same point. ■ a pattern formed by the movements of a group of people, for example in square dancing or synchronized swimming, as part of a longer dance or display. ■ archaic the external form or shape of a thing.
4 Music a short succession of notes producing a single impression.
5 Logic the form of a syllogism, classified according to the position of the middle term.
▶ v. [no obj.] **1** be a significant and noticeable part of something: *the issue of nuclear policy **figured** prominently in the talks.* ■ (of a person) play a significant role in a situation or event: *he figured largely in opposition to the bill.* ■ (of a fictional character) play a part in a novel, play, or movie: *the four characters who **figure in** Ridley's play.*
2 [with obj.] calculate or work out (an amount or value) arithmetically.
3 [with clause] informal think, consider, or expect to be the case: *I figure that wearing a suit makes you look like a bank clerk* | [with obj.] *for years, teachers had figured him for a dullard.* ■ (of a recent event or newly discovered fact) be logical and unsurprising: *well, she supposed **that figured**.*
4 [with obj.] represent (something) in a diagram or picture: *varieties of this Cape genus are figured from drawings made there.* ■ (usu. as adj. **figured**) embellish (something) with a pattern: *the floors were covered with figured linoleum.*
– PHRASES **figure of fun** a person who is considered ridiculous. **figure of speech** a word or phrase used in a nonliteral sense to add rhetorical force to a spoken or written passage: *calling her a crab is just a figure of speech.* **lose** (or **keep**) **one's figure** lose (or retain) a slim and attractive bodily shape.
– PHRASAL VERBS **figure on** informal count or rely on something happening or being the case in the future: *anyone thinking of salmon fishing should figure on paying $200 a day.* **figure something out** informal solve or discover the cause of a problem: *he was trying to figure out why the camera wasn't working.* **figure someone out** reach an understanding of a person's actions, motives, or personality.
– DERIVATIVES **fig·ure·less** adj.
– ORIGIN Middle English (in the senses 'distinctive shape of a person or thing,' 'representation of something material or immaterial,' and 'numerical symbol,' among others): from Old French *figure* (noun), *figurer* (verb), from Latin *figura* 'shape, figure, form'; related to *fingere* 'form, contrive.'

fig·ured bass ▶ n. Music a bass line with the intended harmonies indicated by figures rather than written out as chords, typical of continuo parts in baroque music.

fig·ure eight (Brit. **figure of eight**) ▶ n. an object or movement having the shape of the number eight.

fig·ure-ground ▶ adj. [attrib.] Psychology & Art relating to or denoting the perception of images by the distinction of objects from a background from which they appear to stand out, esp. in contexts where this distinction is ambiguous.

fig·ure·head /ˈfigyərˌhed/ ▶ n. **1** a nominal leader or head without real power.

figurehead 2

2 a carving, typically a bust or a full-length figure, set at the prow of an old-fashioned sailing ship.

fig·ure-hug·ging ▶ adj. (of a garment) fitting closely to the contours of a woman's body: *a low-cut, figure-hugging dress.*

fig·ure of mer·it ▶ n. a numerical expression representing the performance or efficiency of a given device, material, or procedure.

fig·ure skat·ing ▶ n. the competitive sport of ice skating in prescribed patterns (*figures*) and choreographed free skating.
– DERIVATIVES **fig·ure skat·er** n.

fig·ur·ine /ˌfigyəˈrēn/ ▶ n. a statuette, esp. one of a human form.
– ORIGIN mid 19th cent.: from French, from Italian *figurina*, diminutive of *figura*, from Latin *figura* (see FIGURE).

fig wasp ▶ n. a tiny Old World wasp that lays its eggs inside the flower of the wild fig. It was introduced into the New World to effect cross-fertilization of the cultivated fig. ● *Blastophaga psenes*, family Agaonidae, superfamily Chalcidoidea.

fig·wort /ˈfigˌwərt, -ˌwôrt/ ▶ n. a widely distributed herbaceous plant with purplish-brown two-lobed flowers. It was formerly considered to be effective in the treatment of scrofula. ● Genus *Scrophularia*, family Scrophulariaceae (the **figwort family**): several species. Plants of this family have distinctive two-lobed flowers and include the snapdragons, toadflaxes, foxgloves, mulleins, monkey flowers, and speedwells.
– ORIGIN mid 16th cent.: from obsolete *fig* 'piles' + WORT. The word originally denoted the pilewort, or lesser celandine, which was used as a treatment for piles; the current sense dates from the late 16th cent.

Fi·ji /ˈfējē/ a republic in the South Pacific consisting of a group of more than 800 islands, of which about a hundred are inhabited; pop. 944,700 (est. 2009); capital, Suva; languages, English (official), Fijian, and Hindi.

> First visited by Abel Tasman in 1643, the Fiji Islands became a British Crown Colony in 1874 and independent within the Commonwealth of Nations in 1970. In 1987, following a coup, Fiji became a republic and withdrew from the Commonwealth.

Fi·ji·an /ˌfējēən, fiˈjēən/ ▶ adj. of or relating to Fiji, its people, or language.
▶ n. **1** a native or inhabitant of Fiji, or a person of Fijian descent.
2 the Austronesian language of the indigenous people of Fiji.

fil·a·beg /ˈfiləˌbeg/ ▶ n. variant spelling of FILIBEG.

fil·a·gree /ˈfiləˌgrē/ ▶ n. variant spelling of FILIGREE.

fil·a·ment /ˈfiləmənt/ ▶ n. a slender threadlike object or fiber, esp. one found in animal or plant structures: *a filament of cellulose.* ■ a conducting wire or thread with a high melting point, forming part of an electric bulb or vacuum tube and heated or made incandescent by an electric current. ■ Botany the slender part of a stamen that supports the anther. ■ Astronomy a narrow streamer from the sun's chromosphere or in its corona. ■ Astronomy a narrow streamer of gas in an interstellar cloud or nebula.
– DERIVATIVES **fil·a·men·ta·ry** /ˌfiləˈmentərē/ adj., **fil·a·ment·ed** adj., **fil·a·men·tous** /-ˌmentəs/ adj.
– ORIGIN late 16th cent.: from French, or from modern Latin *filamentum*, from late Latin *filare* 'to spin,' from Latin *filum* 'thread.'

fi·lar·i·a /fəˈle(ə)rēə/ ▶ n. (pl. **filariae** /-ˈle(ə)rēˌē, -ēˌī/) a threadlike parasitic nematode worm transmitted by biting flies and mosquitoes, causing filariasis and related diseases. ● Superfamily Filarioidea, class Phasmida.
– DERIVATIVES **fi·lar·i·al** /-ˈle(ə)rēəl/ adj.
– ORIGIN mid 19th cent.: from modern Latin *Filaria* (former genus name), from Latin *filum* 'thread.'

fil·a·ri·a·sis /ˌfiləˈrīəsəs/ ▶ n. Medicine a tropical disease caused by the presence of filarial worms, esp. in the lymph vessels where heavy infestation can result in elephantiasis.

fil·a·ture /ˈfiləˌcʜər, -ˌcʜo͝or/ ▶ n. the process of obtaining silk thread from silkworm cocoons. ■ an establishment where such activity takes place.
– ORIGIN mid 18th cent.: from French, from Italian *filatura*, from *filare* 'to spin.'

fil·bert /ˈfilbərt/ ▶ n. **1** a cultivated hazel tree that bears edible oval nuts. ● Genus *Corylus*, family Betulaceae: several species, in particular the **giant filbert** (*Corylus maxima*). ■ the nut of this tree.
2 (also **filbert brush**) a brush with bristles forming a flattened oval head, used in oil painting.
– ORIGIN Middle English *fylberd*, from Anglo-Norman French *philbert*, dialect French *noix de*

filbert (so named because it is ripe about August 20, the feast day of *St. Philibert*).

filch /filCH/ ▶ **v.** [with obj.] informal pilfer or steal (something, esp. a thing of small value) in a casual way: *I was promptly accused of filching Mr. Muir's idea.*
– DERIVATIVES **filch·er n.**
– ORIGIN Middle English: of unknown origin.

file[1] /fīl/ ▶ **n.** a folder or box for holding loose papers that are typically arranged in a particular order for easy reference: *a file of correspondence.* ■ the contents of such a folder or box. ■ Computing a collection of data, programs, etc., stored in a computer's memory or on a storage device under a single identifying name: *do you want to save this file?* | [as modifier] *a file name.*
▶ **v.** [with obj.] place (a document) in a cabinet, box, or folder in a particular order for preservation and easy reference: *the contract, when signed, is filed* | figurative *he still had the moment filed away in his memory.* ■ submit (a legal document, application, or charge) to be placed on record by the appropriate authority: *criminal charges were filed against the firm* | [no obj.] *the company had filed for bankruptcy.* ■ (of a reporter) send (a story) to a newspaper or news organization.
– PHRASES **on file** in a file or filing system.
– DERIVATIVES **fil·er n.**
– ORIGIN late Middle English (as a verb meaning 'string documents on a thread or wire to keep them in order'): from French *filer* 'to string,' *fil* 'a thread,' both from Latin *filum* 'a thread.' Compare with **FILE[2]**.

file[2] ▶ **n.** a line of people or things one behind another: *Plains Cree warriors riding in file down the slopes.* ■ Military a small detachment of troops: *a file of English soldiers had ridden out from Perth.* ■ Chess each of the eight rows of eight squares on a chessboard running away from the player toward the opponent. Compare with **RANK[1]** (sense 2 of the noun)).
▶ **v.** [no obj.] (of a group of people) walk one behind the other, typically in an orderly and solemn manner: *the mourners filed into the church.*
– ORIGIN late 16th cent.: from French *file,* from *filer* 'to string.'

file[3] ▶ **n.** a tool with a roughened surface or surfaces, typically of steel, used for smoothing or shaping a hard material: *it is possible to make the necessary notch with a file.*
▶ **v.** [with obj.] smooth or shape (something) with such a tool: *when I have nothing else to do, I file my nails.* ■ (**file something away/off**) remove something by grinding it off with a file: *the engine numbers were filed away.*
– DERIVATIVES **fil·er n.**
– ORIGIN Old English *fīl*; related to Dutch *vijl* and German *Feile.*

fi·lé /fi'lā, 'fēlā/ ▶ **n.** pounded or powdered sassafras leaves used to flavor and thicken soup, esp. gumbo.
– ORIGIN mid 19th cent.: from French, past participle of *filer* 'to twist.'

file cab·i·net ▶ **n.** another term for **FILING CABINET.**

file ex·ten·sion ▶ **n.** Computing a group of letters occurring after a period in a file name, indicating the format of the file.

file·fish /'fīl,fisH/ ▶ **n.** (pl. **same** or **filefishes**) a fish with a dorsal spine and rough scales, related to the triggerfishes and occurring in tropical and sometimes temperate seas. ● Numerous genera and species, family Balistidae (or Monacanthidae).
– ORIGIN late 18th cent.: from **FILE[3]** (because of its rough skin, suggesting the surface of a file).

file·name /'fīl,nām/ ▶ **n.** an identifying name given to a computer file.

Fi·lene /fī'lēn/, Edward Albert (1860–1937), US merchant. As the president of Wm. Filene & Sons, he brought about many innovations, including the bargain basement and charge accounts. In 1921, he helped to establish the Credit Union National Extension Bureau.

file serv·er ▶ **n.** Computing a device that controls access to separately stored files, as part of a multiuser system.

file-shar·ing ▶ **n.** the practice of or ability to transmit files from one computer to another over a network or the Internet: [often as modifier] *file-sharing software.*

fi·let /fi'lā, 'filā/ ▶ **n. 1** French spelling of **FILLET**, used esp. in the names of French or French-sounding dishes: *filet de boeuf.*
2 a kind of net or lace with a square mesh. [late 19th cent.: from French, 'net.']

fi·let mi·gnon /fi,lā mēn'yōN/ ▶ **n.** a small tender piece of beef from the end of the tenderloin.
– ORIGIN mid 20th cent.: French, literally 'dainty fillet.'

File Trans·fer Pro·to·col another term for **FTP**.

fil·i·al /'filēəl, 'filyəl/ ▶ **adj.** of or due from a son or daughter: *a display of filial affection.* ■ Biology denoting the generation or generations after the parental generation. See also **F1**.
– DERIVATIVES **fil·i·al·ly adv.**
– ORIGIN late Middle English: from Old French, or from ecclesiastical Latin *filialis,* from *filius* 'son,' *filia* 'daughter.'

fil·i·a·tion /,filē'āSHən/ ▶ **n.** the fact of being or of being designated the child of a particular parent or parents: *relationships based on ties of filiation as opposed to marriage.* ■ the manner in which a thing is related to another from which it is derived or descended in some respect: *the filiation of Old Norse manuscripts.* ■ a branch of a society or language.
– ORIGIN late Middle English: from French, from ecclesiastical and medieval Latin *filiatio(n-),* from Latin *filius* 'son,' *filia* 'daughter.'

fil·i·beg /'filə,beg/ (also **philibeg, filabeg**) ▶ **n.** Scottish chiefly historical a kilt.
– ORIGIN mid 18th cent.: from Scottish Gaelic *feileadh-beag* 'little kilt,' from *feileadh* 'plaid' and *beag* 'little.'

fil·i·bus·ter /'filə,bəstər/ ▶ **n. 1** an action such as a prolonged speech that obstructs progress in a legislative assembly while not technically contravening the required procedures: *it was defeated by a Senate filibuster in June.*
2 historical a person engaging in unauthorized warfare against a foreign country.
▶ **v.** [no obj.] (often as noun **filibustering**) act in an obstructive manner in a legislature, esp. by speaking at inordinate length: *several measures were killed by Republican filibustering.* ■ [with obj.] obstruct (a measure) in such a way.
– ORIGIN late 18th cent.: from French *flibustier,* first applied to pirates who pillaged the Spanish colonies in the West Indies, ultimately from Dutch *vrijbuiter*; see **FREEBOOTER**. In the mid 19th cent. (via Spanish *filibustero*), the term denoted American adventurers who incited revolution in several Latin American states, whence sense 2 of the noun. The verb was used to describe tactics intended to sabotage congressional proceedings, whence sense 1 of the noun.

fil·i·cide /'filə,sīd/ ▶ **n.** the killing of one's son or daughter: *maternal filicide.* ■ a person who kills their son or daughter.
– ORIGIN mid 17th cent. from Latin *filius* 'son,' *filia* 'daughter' + **-CIDE**.

Fi·li·cop·si·da /,filə'käpsədə/ Botany a class of pteridophyte plants that comprises the ferns.
– ORIGIN modern Latin (plural), from Latin *filix, filic-* 'fern' + *opsis* 'appearance.'

fil·i·form /'filə,fôrm/ ▶ **adj.** Biology threadlike: *the antennae are filiform.*
– ORIGIN mid 18th cent.: from Latin *filum* 'thread' + **-IFORM**.

fil·i·gree /'filə,grē/ (also **filagree**) ▶ **n.** ornamental work of fine (typically gold or silver) wire formed into delicate tracery: [as modifier] *delicate silver filigree earrings.* ■ a thing resembling such fine ornamental work: *a wedding cake of gold and white filigree.*
– ORIGIN late 17th cent. (earlier as *filigreen, filigrane*): from French *filigrane,* from Italian *filigrana* (from Latin *filum* 'thread' + *granum* 'seed').

fil·i·greed /'filə,grēd/ (also **filagreed**) ▶ **adj.** ornamented with or resembling filigree work: *white filigreed stockings.*

fil·ing /'fīliNG/ ▶ **n.** (usu. **filings**) a small particle rubbed off by a file when smoothing or shaping something: *iron filings.*

fil·ing cab·i·net ▶ **n.** a piece of office furniture, typically made of steel, with deep drawers for storing documents.

Fi·li·o·que /,filē'ōkwē, -,kwā/ the word inserted in the Western version of the Nicene Creed to assert the doctrine of the procession of the Holy Ghost from the Son as well as from the Father, which is not admitted by the Eastern Church. It was one of the central issues in the Great Schism of 1054.
– ORIGIN Latin, literally 'and from the Son.'

Fil·i·pi·no /,filə'pēnō/ (also **Pilipino**) ▶ **adj.** of or relating to the Philippines, the Filipinos, or their language.
▶ **n.** (pl. **Filipinos**) **1** (fem. **Filipina** /,filə'pēnə/) a native or national of the Philippines, or a person of Filipino descent.
2 the national language of the Philippines, a standardized form of Tagalog.
– ORIGIN Spanish, from *las Islas Filipinas* 'the Philippine Islands.'

Fí·lip·poi /'fēlē,pē/ Greek name for **PHILIPPI**.

fill /fil/ ▶ **v.** [with obj.] put someone or something into (a space or container) so that it is completely or almost completely full: *I filled up the bottle with water* | *the office was filled with reporters.* ■ [no obj.] (**fill with**) become full of: *Eleanor's eyes filled with tears.* ■ become an overwhelming presence in: *a pungent smell of garlic filled the air.* ■ cause (someone) to have an intense experience of an emotion or feeling: *his presence filled us with foreboding.* ■ appoint a person to hold (a vacant position): *the number of high-tech jobs and the people who can fill them.* ■ hold and perform the expected duties of (a position or role): *she fills the role of the "good" child.* ■ occupy or take up (a period of time): *the next few days were filled with meetings.* ■ be supplied with the items described in (a prescription or order): *she needed to fill a prescription.* ■ block up (a cavity in a tooth) with cement, amalgam, or gold. ■ [no obj.] (of a sail) curve out tautly as the wind blows into it. ■ (of a weather system) increase in barometric pressure. Compare with **DEEPEN**. ■ [with obj.] (of the wind) blow into (a sail), causing it to curve outward. ■ Poker complete (a good hand) by drawing the necessary cards.
▶ **n. 1** (**one's fill**) an amount of something that is as much as one wants or can bear: *we have eaten our fill* | *I've had my fill of surprises for one day.*
2 an amount of something that will occupy all the space in a container. ■ material, loose or compacted, that fills a space, esp. in building or engineering work: *loose polystyrene fill.* ■ the action of filling something, esp. of shading in a region of a computer graphics display. ■ (in popular music) a short interjected phrase on a particular instrument.
– PHRASES **fill the bill** see **BILL[1]**. **fill someone's shoes** informal take over someone's function or duties and fulfill them satisfactorily.
– PHRASAL VERBS **fill in** act as a substitute for someone when they are unable to do their job: *my producer will have to have someone standing by to fill in for me.* **fill someone in 1** inform someone more fully of a matter, giving all the details: *the cab driver filled me in on much important economic and sociological data.* **2** Brit. informal, dated hit or punch someone: *I filled in a chap and took his money.* **fill something in** put material into a hole, trench, or space so that it is completely full: *the canal is now disused and partly filled in.* ■ complete a drawing by adding color or shade to the spaces within an outline: *incised letters, filled in with gold.* ■ chiefly Brit. add information to complete something, typically a form or other official document: *he filled in all the forms.* **fill out** (of a person) put on weight to a noticeable extent. **fill something out** add information to complete an official form or document: *he filled out the requisite forms.* ■ give more details to add to someone's understanding of something: *he filled out the background by going into historical questions.* **fill up** become completely full: *the dining car filled up.* ■ fill the fuel tank of a car.
– ORIGIN Old English *fyllan* (verb), *fyllu* (noun) of Germanic origin; related to Dutch *vullen* and German *füllen* (verbs), *Fülle* (noun), also to **FULL[1]**.

fille de joie /,fē(yə) də 'ZHwä/ ▶ **n.** (pl. **filles de joie**) used euphemistically to refer to a prostitute.
– ORIGIN early 18th cent.: French, literally 'girl of pleasure.'

filled gold ▶ **n.** a relatively inexpensive metal with a layer of gold applied over it.

fill·er[1] /'filər/ ▶ **n. 1** [usu. in combination] a thing put in a space or container to fill it: *these plants are attractive gap-fillers or ground cover.* ■ a substance used for filling cracks or holes in a surface, esp. before painting it: *quick-hardening wood filler.* ■ material used to fill a cavity or increase bulk: *foam filler* | *good quality paints should contain little or no filler.* ■ an item serving only to fill space or time, esp. in a newspaper, broadcast, or recording. ■ a word or sound filling a pause in an utterance or conversation (e.g., *er, well, you know*). ■ a linguistic unit that fills a particular slot in syntactic structure. ■ the tobacco blend used in a cigar.
2 [in combination] a person or thing that fills a space or container: *supermarket shelf-fillers.*

fill·er[2] ▶ **n.** (pl. **same**) a monetary unit of Hungary, equal to one hundredth of a forint.
– ORIGIN from Hungarian *fillér.*

fil·let ▶ **n. 1** /fi'lā, 'filā/ (also **filet**) a fleshy boneless piece of meat from near the loins or the ribs of an animal: *a chicken breast fillet* | *roast fillet of lamb.*

PRONUNCIATION KEY ə *ago, up;* ər *over, fur;* a *hat;* ā *ate;* ä *car;* e *let;* ē *see;* i *fit;* ī *by;* NG *sing;* ō *go;* ô *law, for;* oi *toy;* o͝o *good;* o͞o *goo;* ou *out;* TH *thin;* T͟H *then;* ZH *vision*

■ (also **fillet steak**) a beef steak cut from the lower part of a sirloin. ■ a boned side of a fish.
2 /ˈfilit/ a band or ribbon worn around the head, esp. for binding the hair. ■ Architecture a narrow flat band separating two moldings. ■ Architecture a small band between the flutes of a column. ■ a plain or decorated line impressed on the cover of a book. ■ a roller used to impress such a line.
3 /ˈfilit/ a concave strip of material roughly triangular in cross section that rounds off an interior angle between two surfaces: *a splayed mortar fillet at the junction of the roof with the chimney stack* | [as modifier] *a fillet weld.*
▸ **v.** /fiˈlā, ˈfilā/ (**fillets, filleting, filleted**) [with obj.] remove the bones from (a fish). ■ cut (fish or meat) into boneless strips.
– DERIVATIVES **fil·let·er** n.
– ORIGIN Middle English (denoting a band worn around the head): from Old French *filet* 'thread,' based on Latin *filum* 'thread.'

f

fill·ing /ˈfiliNG/ ▸ **n.** a quantity of material that fills or is used to fill something: *a cushion with polyester filling.* ■ a piece of material used to fill a cavity in a tooth: *a gold filling.* ■ an edible substance placed between the layers of a sandwich, cake, or other foodstuff: *a Swiss roll with a chocolate filling.* ■ another term for **WEFT**.
▸ **adj.** (of food) leaving one with a pleasantly satiated feeling: *a filling spicy bean soup.*

fill·ing sta·tion ▸ **n.** another term for **GAS STATION**.

fil·lip /ˈfiləp/ ▸ **n. 1** something that acts as a stimulus or boost to an activity: *the halving of the automobile tax would provide a fillip to sales.*
2 archaic a movement made by bending the last joint of a finger against the thumb and suddenly releasing it; a flick of the finger: *the Prince, by a fillip, made some of the wine fly in Oglethorpe's face.* ■ a slight smart stroke or tap given in such a way: *she began to give him dainty fillips on the nose with a soft forepaw.*
▸ **v.** (**fillips, filliping, filliped**) [with obj.] archaic propel (a small object) with a flick of the finger: *our aforesaid merchant filliped a nut sharply against his bullying giant.* ■ strike (someone or something) slightly and smartly: *he filliped him over the nose.* ■ stimulate or urge (someone or something): *pour, that the draught may fillip my remembrance.*
– ORIGIN late Middle English (in the sense 'make a fillip with the fingers'): symbolic; compare with **FLICK, FLIP**[1].

fill light ▸ **n.** a supplementary light used in photography or filming that does not change the character of the main light and is used chiefly to lighten shadows.

Fill·more /ˈfilmôr/, Millard (1800–74), 13th president of the US 1850–53. A New York Whig, he served in the US House of Representatives 1833–35, 1837–43 and became US vice president in 1849. Seventeen months later, he succeeded to the presidency upon the death of President Zachary Taylor. Fillmore was an advocate of compromise on the slavery issue, but his unpopular enforcement of the 1850 Fugitive Slave Act hastened the end of the Whig Party.

Millard Fillmore

fill-up ▸ **n.** an instance of making something completely full, esp. the fuel tank of an automobile: *free coffee with fill-up.*

fil·ly /ˈfilē/ ▸ **n.** (pl. **fillies**) a young female horse, esp. one less than four years old. ■ dated a lively girl or young woman.
– ORIGIN late Middle English: from Old Norse *fylja*, of Germanic origin; related to **FOAL**.

film /film/ ▸ **n. 1** a thin flexible strip of plastic or other material coated with light-sensitive emulsion for exposure in a camera, used to produce photographs or motion pictures: *he had already shot a whole roll of film* | *a new range of films and cameras.* ■ material in the form of a thin flexible sheet: *clear plastic film between the layers of glass.* ■ a thin layer covering a surface: *she quickly wiped away the light film of sweat.* ■ archaic a fine thread or filament: *films of silk.*
2 a motion picture; a movie: *a horror film* | [as modifier] *a film director.* ■ movies considered as an art or industry: *a critical overview of feminist writing on film.*
▸ **v. 1** [with obj.] capture on film as part of a series of moving images; make a movie of (a story or event): *she glowered at the television crew who were filming them.* ■ [no obj.] (**film well/badly**) be well or badly suited to portrayal in a film: *an adventure story that would film well.*
2 [no obj.] become or appear to become covered with a thin layer of something: *his eyes had filmed over.*
– DERIVATIVES **film·dom** n. (sense 2 of the noun).
– ORIGIN Old English *filmen* 'membrane'; related to **FELL**[5].

film badge ▸ **n.** a device containing photographic film that registers the wearer's exposure to radiation.

film·go·er /ˈfilm,gōər/ ▸ **n.** a person who goes to the movies, esp. regularly.
– DERIVATIVES **film·go·ing** /-,gōiNG/ n.

film·ic /ˈfilmik/ ▸ **adj.** of or relating to movies or cinematography: *he has reconceived the stage production in filmic terms.*

film·mak·er /ˈfilm,mākər/ ▸ **n.** a person who directs or produces movies for the theater or television.
– DERIVATIVES **film·mak·ing** n.

film noir /,film ˈnwär/ ▸ **n.** a style or genre of cinematographic film marked by a mood of pessimism, fatalism, and menace. The term was originally applied (by a group of French critics) to American thriller or detective films made in the period 1944–54 and to the work of directors such as Orson Welles, Fritz Lang, and Billy Wilder. ■ a film of this genre.
– ORIGIN mid 20th cent.: French, literally 'black film.'

film·og·ra·phy /filˈmägrəfē/ ▸ **n.** (pl. **filmographies**) a list of films by one director or actor, or on one subject.
– ORIGIN 1960s: from **FILM** + **-GRAPHY**, on the pattern of *bibliography.*

film·set·ting /ˈfilm,setiNG/ ▸ **n.** British term for **PHOTOCOMPOSITION**.
– DERIVATIVES **film·set** /-,set/ v., **film·set·ter** n.

film star ▸ **n.** another term for **MOVIE STAR**.

film stock ▸ **n.** see **STOCK** (sense 1 of the noun).

film·strip /ˈfilm,strip/ ▸ **n.** a series of transparencies in a strip for projection, used esp. as a teaching aid.

film·y /ˈfilmē/ ▸ **adj.** (**filmier, filmiest**) (esp. of fabric) thin and translucent: *filmy white voile.* ■ covered with or forming a thin layer of something: *her eyes were dull and filmy.*
– DERIVATIVES **film·i·ly** /ˈfilməlē/ adv., **film·i·ness** /ˈfilmēnis/ n.

film·y fern ▸ **n.** a small fern of damp shady places, with wiry creeping stems and delicate forked fronds that are only one cell thick. They occur chiefly in tropical and subtropical regions. • Family Hymenophyllaceae: *Hymenophyllum* and other genera.

fi·lo /ˈfēlō/ ▸ **n.** variant spelling of **PHYLLO**.

Fi·lo·fax /ˈfīlō,faks, ˈfīlə,-/ ▸ **n.** trademark a loose-leaf notebook for recording appointments, addresses, and notes.
– ORIGIN 1930s: representing a colloquial pronunciation of *file of facts.*

fil·o·po·di·um /,filəˈpōdēəm, ,fī-/ ▸ **n.** (pl. **filopodia** /-ˈpōdēə/) Biology a long, slender, tapering pseudopodium, as found in some protozoans and in embryonic cells.
– DERIVATIVES **fil·o·po·di·al** /-ˈpōdēəl/ adj.
– ORIGIN early 20th cent.: from Latin *filium* 'thread' + **PODIUM**.

fil·o·selle /ˈfilə,sel/ ▸ **n.** floss silk, or silk thread resembling this, used in embroidery.
– ORIGIN mid 16th cent.: from French, from Italian *filosello* 'raw silk from a cocoon,' of uncertain ultimate origin.

fi·lo·vi·rus /ˈfēlō,vīrəs, ˈfī-/ ▸ **n.** a filamentous RNA virus of a genus that causes severe hemorrhagic fevers in humans and primates, and that includes the Ebola and Marburg viruses.

fils[1] /fils/ ▸ **n.** (pl. **same**) a monetary unit of Iraq, Bahrain, Jordan, Kuwait, and Yemen, equal to one hundredth of a riyal in Yemen and one thousandth of a dinar elsewhere.
– ORIGIN from a colloquial pronunciation of Arabic *fals*, denoting a small copper coin, from Latin *follis* 'purse, coin'; compare with **FOLLIS, FOOL**[1].

fils[2] /fēs/ ▸ **n.** used after a surname to distinguish a son from a father of the same name: *Alexandre Dumas fils.* Compare with **PÈRE**.
– ORIGIN late 19th cent.: French, literally 'son.'

fil·ter /ˈfiltər/ ▸ **n.** a porous device for removing impurities or solid particles from a liquid or gas passed through it: *an oil filter.* ■ short for **FILTER TIP**: [as modifier] *a cheap filter cigarette.* ■ a screen, plate, or layer of a substance that absorbs light or other radiation or selectively absorbs some of its components: *filters can be used in photography to reduce haze.* ■ a device for suppressing electrical or sound waves of frequencies not required. ■ Computing a piece of software that processes text, for example to remove unwanted spaces or to format it for use in another application. ■ Brit. an arrangement whereby vehicles may turn left (or right) while other traffic waiting to go straight ahead or turn right (or left) is stopped by a red light: [as modifier] *a filter lane.*
▸ **v.** [with obj.] **1** pass (a liquid, gas, light, or sound) through a device to remove unwanted material: *the patient is hooked up to a dialysis machine twice a week to filter out the cholesterol in the blood* | figurative *you'll be put through to a secretary whose job it is to filter calls.* ■ [no obj., with adverbial of direction] move slowly or in small quantities or numbers through something or in a specified direction: *people filtered out of the concert during the last set.* ■ [no obj., with adverbial] (of information) gradually become known: *the news began to filter in from the hospital.*
2 Computing [with obj.] process or treat with a filter.
– ORIGIN late Middle English (denoting a piece of felt): from French *filtre*, from medieval Latin *filtrum* 'felt used as a filter,' related to **FELT**[1].

fil·ter·a·ble /ˈfiltərəbəl/ (also **filtrable** /-trəbəl/) ▸ **adj. 1** capable of passing through a filter.
2 capable of being separated out by a filter: *filterable virus* | *filterable solids.*

fil·ter bed ▸ **n.** a tank or pond containing a layer of sand or gravel, used for filtering large quantities of liquid.

fil·ter cake ▸ **n.** a deposit of insoluble material left on a filter.

fil·ter feed·ing ▸ **n.** Zoology (of an aquatic animal) feeding by filtering out plankton or nutrients suspended in the water.
– DERIVATIVES **fil·ter-feed** v., **fil·ter feed·er** n.

fil·ter pa·per ▸ **n.** a piece of porous paper for filtering liquids, used esp. in chemical processes and coffee-making.

fil·ter press ▸ **n.** a device consisting of a series of cloth filters fixed to frames, used for the large-scale filtration of liquid under pressure.

fil·ter tip ▸ **n.** a filter attached to a cigarette for removing some components from the inhaled smoke. ■ a cigarette with such a filter.
– DERIVATIVES **fil·ter-tipped** adj.

filth /filTH/ ▸ **n.** disgusting dirt: *stagnant pools of filth.* ■ obscene and offensive language or printed material. ■ corrupt behavior; decadence. ■ used as a term of abuse for a person or people one greatly despises: *I can't believe she married that filth.* ■ (as plural noun **the filth**) Brit. informal, derogatory the police.
– ORIGIN Old English *fȳlth* 'rotting matter, rottenness,' also 'corruption, obscenity,' of Germanic origin; related to Dutch *vuilte*, also to **FOUL**.

filth·y /ˈfilTHē/ ▸ **adj.** (**filthier, filthiest**) disgustingly dirty: *a filthy hospital with no sanitation.* ■ obscene and offensive: *filthy language.* ■ informal used to express one's anger and disgust: *you filthy beast.* ■ (of a mood) bad-tempered and aggressive: *he arrived at the meeting half an hour late in a filthy temper.* ■ Brit. informal (of weather) very unpleasant: *it looked like a filthy night.*
▸ **adv.** [as submodifier] informal to an extreme and often disgusting extent: *he has become filthy rich.*
– DERIVATIVES **filth·i·ly** /ˈfilTHəlē/ adv., **filth·i·ness** /ˈfilTHēnəs/ n.

filth·y lu·cre ▸ **n.** money, esp. when gained in a dishonest or dishonorable way.
– ORIGIN early 16th cent.: with biblical allusion to Tit. 1:11.

fil·tra·ble /ˈfiltrəbəl/ ▸ **adj.** variant spelling of **FILTERABLE**.

fil·trate /ˈfil,trāt/ ▸ **n.** a liquid that has passed through a filter: *filtrates of bacterial cultures* | *drops of clear filtrate.*
▸ **v.** [with obj.] filter: *the remaining alkali is filtrated.*
– ORIGIN early 17th cent.: from modern Latin *filtrat-* 'filtered,' from the verb *filtrare*, from medieval Latin *filtrum* (see **FILTER**).

fil·tra·tion /filˈtrāSHən/ ▸ **n.** the action or process of filtering something: *small particles are difficult to remove without filtration.*

fim·bri·a /ˈfimbrēə/ ▸ **n.** (pl. **fimbriae** /-brē,ē, -brē,ī/) chiefly Anatomy a series of threads or other projections resembling a fringe. ■ [usu. in pl.] an individual thread in such a structure, esp. a fingerlike projection at the end of the Fallopian tube near the ovary.

– DERIVATIVES **fim·bri·al** /-brēəl/ **adj.**
– ORIGIN mid 18th cent.: from late Latin, literally 'border, fringe.'

fim·bri·at·ed /ˈfimbrēˌātid/ (also **fimbriate**) ▶ **adj.** **1** Biology having a fringe or border of hairlike or fingerlike projections.
2 Heraldry having a narrow border, typically of a specified tincture.
– ORIGIN late 15th cent. (sense 2): from Latin *fimbriatus* (from *fimbria* 'fringe') + -ED¹.

fin /fin/ ▶ **n.** a flattened appendage on various parts of the body of many aquatic vertebrates and some invertebrates, including fish and cetaceans, used for propelling, steering, and balancing. ■ an underwater swimmer's flipper. ■ a small flattened projecting surface or attachment on an aircraft, rocket, or automobile, providing aerodynamic stability or serving as a design element. ■ a flattened projection on a device, such as a radiator, used for increasing heat transfer.
▶ **v.** (**fins, finning, finned**) [no obj.] swim underwater by means of flippers: *I finned madly for the surface.*
– DERIVATIVES **fin·less** **adj.**, **finned** **adj.** [in combination] *primitive ray-finned fishes.*
– ORIGIN Old English *finn, fin*, of Germanic origin; related to Dutch *vin* and probably ultimately to Latin *pinna* 'feather, wing.'

fin. ▶ **abbr.** ■ finance. ■ financial. ■ finish.

fi·na·gle /fəˈnāgəl/ ▶ **v.** [with obj.] informal obtain (something) by devious or dishonest means: *Ted attended all the football games he could finagle tickets for.* ■ [no obj.] act in a devious or dishonest manner: *they wrangled and finagled over the fine points.*
– DERIVATIVES **fi·na·gler** /fəˈnāg(ə)lər/ **n.**
– ORIGIN 1920s (originally U.S.): from dialect *fainaigue* 'cheat'; perhaps from Old French *fornier* 'deny.'

fi·nal /ˈfīnl/ ▶ **adj.** coming at the end of a series: *the final version of the report was presented.* ■ reached or designed to be reached as the outcome of a process or a series of events: *the final cost will easily run into six figures.* ■ allowing no further doubt or dispute: *the decision of the judging panel is final.*
▶ **n.** **1** the last game in a sports tournament or other competition, which decides the winner of the tournament. ■ (**finals**) a series of games constituting the final stage of a competition: *the World Cup finals.*
2 (**final**) an examination at the end of a term, academic year, or particular class. ■ (**finals**) Brit. a series of examinations at the end of a degree course: *she was doing her history finals.*
3 Music the principal note in a mode.
4 (**finals**) Brit. the final approach of a landing aircraft to a runway: *the plane piloted by Richards was on finals.*
– PHRASES **the final straw** see STRAW.
– ORIGIN Middle English (in the adjectival sense 'conclusive'): from Old French, or from Latin *finalis*, from *finis* 'end.' Compare with FINISH.

fi·nal cause ▶ **n.** Philosophy the purpose or aim of an action or the end toward which a thing naturally develops.

fi·nal drive ▶ **n.** the last part of the transmission system in a motor vehicle.

fi·na·le /fəˈnalē, -ˈnälē/ ▶ **n.** the last part of a piece of music, a performance, or a public event, esp. when particularly dramatic or exciting: *the festival ends with a grand finale.*
– ORIGIN mid 18th cent.: from Italian, from Latin *finalis* (see FINAL).

Fi·nal Four ▶ **n.** the four teams that qualify for the championship round in the annual NCAA men's or women's college basketball tournament.

fi·nal·ist /ˈfīnl-ist/ ▶ **n.** a competitor or team in the final or finals of a competition.

fi·nal·i·ty /fīˈnalətē, fi-/ ▶ **n.** (pl. **finalities**) the fact or impression of being an irreversible ending: *the abrupt finality of death | there's a dreadful finality about cutting down a tree.* ■ a tone or manner that indicates that no further comment or argument is possible: *"No," she said with finality.* ■ an action or event that ends something irreversibly: *death is the ultimate finality.*
– ORIGIN mid 19th cent.: from French *finalité*, from late Latin *finalitas*, from Latin *finalis* (see FINAL).

fi·nal·ize /ˈfīnlˌīz/ ▶ **v.** [with obj.] produce or agree on a finished and definitive version of: *efforts intensified to finalize plans for postwar reconstruction.*
– DERIVATIVES **fi·nal·i·za·tion** /ˌfīnl-əˈzāsʜən/ **n.**

fi·nal·ly /ˈfīn(ə)lē/ ▶ **adv.** after a long time, typically involving difficulty or delay: *he finally arrived to join us.* ■ as the last in a series of related events or objects: *a referendum followed by local, legislative, and, finally, presidential elections.* ■ [sentence adverb] used to introduce a final point or reason: *finally, it is common knowledge that travel broadens the horizons.* ■ in such a way as to put an end to doubt and dispute: *to dispel finally the belief that auditors were clients of the company.*

fi·nal so·lu·tion ▶ **n.** the Nazi policy of exterminating European Jews. Introduced by Heinrich Himmler and administered by Adolf Eichmann, the policy resulted in the murder of 6 million Jews in concentration camps between 1941 and 1945.
– ORIGIN translation of German *Endlösung*.

fi·nance /ˈfīnans, fəˈnans/ ▶ **n.** the management of large amounts of money, esp. by governments or large companies. ■ monetary support for an enterprise: *housing finance.* ■ (**finances**) the monetary resources and affairs of a country, organization, or person: *the finances of the school were causing serious concern.*
▶ **v.** [with obj.] provide funding for (a person or enterprise): *the city and county originally financed the project.*
– ORIGIN late Middle English: from Old French, from *finer* 'make an end, settle a debt,' from *fin* 'end' (see FINE[2]). The original sense was 'payment of a debt, compensation, or ransom'; later 'taxation, revenue.' Current senses date from the 18th cent., and reflect sense development in French.

fi·nance com·pa·ny (also Brit. **finance house**) ▶ **n.** a company concerned primarily with providing money, as for short-term loans.

fi·nan·cial /fəˈnanCHəl, fī-/ ▶ **adj.** of or relating to finance: *an independent financial adviser.*
– DERIVATIVES **fi·nan·cial·ly** **adv.**

fi·nan·cial·i·za·tion /fəˌnanCHələˈzāsʜən, fī-/ ▶ **n.** the process by which financial institutions, markets, etc., increase in size and influence: *the financialization of the US economy.*

fi·nan·cials /fəˈnansʜəlz/ ▶ **plural n.** shares in financial companies. ■ financial data about a company: *take a look at their financials.*

Fi·nan·cial Times in·dex another term for FTSE INDEX.

fi·nan·cial year ▶ **n.** British term for FISCAL YEAR.

fin·an·cier /ˌfinənˈsi(ə)r, fəˈnanˌsi(ə)r/ ▶ **n.** a person concerned with the management of large amounts of money on behalf of governments or other large organizations.
– ORIGIN early 17th cent.: from French, from *finance* (see FINANCE).

fin·back /ˈfinbak/ (also **finback whale**) ▶ **n.** a large rorqual with a small dorsal fin, a dark gray back, and white underparts. Also called FIN WHALE, COMMON RORQUAL (see RORQUAL). ● *Balaenoptera physalus*, family Balaenopteridae.

fin·ca /ˈfiNGkə/ ▶ **n.** (in Spanish-speaking regions) a country estate; a ranch.

finch /finCH/ ▶ **n.** a seed-eating songbird that typically has a stout bill and colorful plumage.
● The true finches belong to the family Fringillidae (the **finch family**), which includes chaffinches, canaries, linnets, crossbills, etc. Many other finches belong to the bunting, waxbill, or sparrow families.
– ORIGIN Old English *finc*; related to Dutch *vink* and German *Fink*.

find /fīnd/ ▶ **v.** (past and past participle **found** /found/) [with obj.] **1** discover or perceive by chance or unexpectedly: *Lindsey looked up to find Neil watching her | the remains of a headless body had been found.* ■ discover (someone or something) after a deliberate search: *in this climate it could be hard to find a buyer.* ■ (**find oneself**) discover oneself to be in a surprising or unexpected situation: *phobia sufferers often find themselves virtual prisoners in their own home.* ■ succeed in obtaining (something): *she also found the time to raise five children.* ■ summon up (a quality, esp. courage) with an effort: *I found the courage to speak.* ■ [no obj.] (of hunters or hounds) discover game, esp. a fox: *she heard the new halloo—they had found.*
2 recognize or discover (something) to be present: *vitamin B12 is found in dairy products.* ■ become aware of; discover to be the case: *the majority of staff find the magazine to be informative and useful* | [with clause] *she found that none of the local nursery schools had an available slot.* ■ ascertain (something) by study, calculation, or inquiry: *a forum that attempts to find solutions for multimedia publishers.* ■ perceive or experience (something) to be the case: [with obj. and complement] *both men found it difficult to put ideas into words.* ■ (**find oneself**) discover the fundamental truths about one's own character and identity: *I did psychotherapy for years—I wanted to find myself.* ■ Law (of a court) officially declare to be the case: [with obj. and complement] *he was found guilty of speeding* | [with clause] *the court found that a police lab expert had fabricated evidence.*
3 (of a thing) reach or arrive at, either of its own accord or without the human agent being known: *water finds its own level.* ■ (**find one's way**) reach one's destination by one's own efforts, without knowing in advance how to get there: *he found his way to the front door.* ■ (**find one's way**) come to be in a certain situation: *each and every boy found his way into a suitable occupation.* ■ (of a letter) reach (someone). ■ archaic reach the understanding or conscience of (someone): *whatever finds me, bears witness for itself that it has proceeded from a Holy Spirit.*
▶ **n.** a discovery of something valuable, typically something of archaeological interest: *he made his most spectacular finds in the Valley of the Kings | this resort is **a real find**.* ■ a person who is discovered to be useful or interesting in some way: *Paul had been a real find—he could design the whole hotel complex.* ■ Hunting the finding of a fox.
– PHRASES **all found** Brit. dated (of an employee's wages) with board and lodging provided free: *your wages would be five shillings all found.* **find fault** see FAULT. **find favor** be liked or prove acceptable: *the ballets did not find favor with the public.* **find one's feet** stand up and become able to walk. ■ establish oneself in a particular field: *I think he really started to find his feet with this album.* **find God** experience a religious conversion or awakening. **find in favor of** see FIND FOR below. **find it in one's heart to do something** allow or force oneself to do something: *I ask you to find it in your heart to forgive me.*
– PHRASAL VERBS **find against** Law (of a court) make a decision against or judge to be guilty. **find for** (or **find in favor of**) Law (of a court) make a decision in favor of or judge to be innocent: *a jury found for the plaintiff.* **find someone out** detect a person's offensive or immoral actions: *she would always find him out if he tried to lie.* **find something out** (or **find out about something**) discover a fact: *he hadn't time to find out what was bothering her.*
– DERIVATIVES **find·a·ble** /ˈfīndəbəl/ **adj.**
– ORIGIN Old English *findan*, of Germanic origin; related to Dutch *vinden* and German *finden*.

find·er /ˈfīndər/ ▶ **n.** a person who finds someone or something. ■ (in full **finder-scope**) a small telescope attached to a large one to locate an object for observation. ■ the viewfinder of a camera.
– PHRASES **finders keepers** (**losers weepers**) informal used, often humorously, to assert that whoever finds something by chance is entitled to keep it.

find·er's fee ▶ **n.** a fee paid by a business to a person or organization for bringing to its attention financial investors, potential new employees, or buyers or sellers whose relationship with the business will materially benefit it.

fin de siè·cle /ˌfan də sēˈekl(ə)/ ▶ **adj.** relating to or characteristic of the end of a century, esp. the 19th century: *fin-de-siècle art.* ■ decadent: *there was a fin-de-siècle air in the club last night.*
▶ **n.** the end of a century, esp. the 19th century.
– ORIGIN French, 'end of century.'

find·ing /ˈfīndiNG/ ▶ **n.** **1** the action of finding someone or something: *a local doctor reported the finding of numerous dead rats.* ■ (often **findings**) a conclusion reached as a result of an inquiry, investigation, or trial: *experimental findings.*
2 (**findings**) small articles or tools used in making garments, shoes, or jewelry.

fine[1] /fīn/ ▶ **adj.** **1** of high quality: *this was a fine piece of filmmaking | fine wines.* ■ (of a person) worthy of or eliciting admiration: *what a fine human being he is.* ■ good; satisfactory: *relations in the group were fine.* ■ used to express one's agreement with or acquiescence to something: *anything you want is **fine by me**, Linda | he said such a solution would be fine.* ■ in good health and feeling well: *"I'm fine, just fine. And you?"* ■ (of the weather) bright and clear: *it was another fine winter day.* ■ of imposing and dignified appearance or size: *a very fine Elizabethan mansion.* ■ (of speech or writing) sounding impressive and grand but ultimately insincere: *fine words seemed to produce few practical benefits.* ■ denoting or displaying a state of good, though not excellent, preservation in stamps, books, coins, etc. ■ (of gold or silver) containing a specified high proportion of pure metal: *the coin is struck in .986 fine gold.*
2 (of a thread, filament, or person's hair) thin: *I have always had fine and dry hair.* ■ (of a point) sharp: *I sharpened the leads to a fine point.* ■ consisting of small particles: *the soils were all fine silt.* ■ having or requiring an intricate delicacy of touch: *exquisitely fine work.* ■ (of something abstract) subtle and therefore perceived only with

PRONUNCIATION KEY ə ago, up; ər over, fur; a hat; ā ate; ä car; e let; ē see; i fit; ī by; NG sing; ō go; ô law, for; oi toy; o͝o good; o͞o goo; ou out; TH thin; T̲H̲ then; ZH vision

difficulty and care: *the fine distinctions between the new and old definitions of refugee.* ■ (of feelings) refined; elevated: *you might appeal to their finer feelings.*
▶ **n.** (**fines**) very small particles found in mining, milling, etc.
▶ **adv.** informal in a satisfactory or pleasing manner; very well: *"And how's the job-hunting going?" "Oh, fine."*
▶ **v. 1** [with obj.] clarify (beer or wine) by causing the precipitation of sediment during production. ■ [no obj.] (of liquid) become clear: *the ale hadn't had quite time to fine down.*
2 make or become thinner: [with obj.] *it can be fined right down to the finished shape* | [no obj.] *she'd certainly fined down—her face was thinner.*
– PHRASES **cut it** (or **things**) **fine** allow a very small margin of something, esp. time: *boys who have cut it rather fine are scuttling into chapel.* **do fine** be entirely satisfactory: *an omelet will do fine.* ■ be healthy or well: *the baby's doing fine.* ■ do something in a satisfactory manner: *he was doing fine acquiring all the necessary disciplines in finance.* **do someone fine** suit or be enough for someone. **fine feathers make fine birds** proverb beautiful clothes or an eye-catching appearance make a person appear similarly beautiful or impressive. **the finer points of** the more complex or detailed aspects of: *he went on to discuss the finer points of his work.* **——'s finest** informal the police of a particular city: *Moscow's finest.* **one's finest hour** the time of one's greatest success. **fine words butter no parsnips** proverb nothing is achieved by empty promises or flattery. **not to put too fine a point on it** to speak bluntly: *not to put too fine a point on it, your Emily is a liar.* [figuratively, with reference to the sharpening of a weapon, tool, etc.] **one fine day** at some unspecified or unknown time: *you want to be the Chancellor one fine day.*
– DERIVATIVES **fine·ly adv.**, **fine·ness n.**
– ORIGIN Middle English: from Old French *fin*, based on Latin *finire* 'to finish' (see FINISH).

fine² /fīn/ ▶ **n.** a sum of money exacted as a penalty by a court of law or other authority: *a parking fine.*
▶ **v.** [with obj.] (often **be fined**) punish (someone) by making them pay a sum of money, typically as a penalty for breaking the law: *he was fined $600 and sentenced to one day in jail.*
– DERIVATIVES **fine·a·ble** /ˈfīnəbəl/ **adj.**
– ORIGIN Middle English: from Old French *fin* 'end, payment,' from Latin *finis* 'end' (in medieval Latin denoting a sum paid on settling a lawsuit). The original sense was 'conclusion' (surviving in the phrase IN FINE); also used in the medieval Latin sense, the word came to denote a penalty of any kind, later specifically a monetary penalty.

fine³ /fēn/ ▶ **n.** French brandy of high quality made from distilled wine rather than from pomace. ■ short for FINE CHAMPAGNE.

fi·ne⁴ /ˈfēnā/ ▶ **n.** (in musical directions) the place where a piece of music finishes (when this is not at the end of the score but at the end of an earlier section that is repeated at the end of the piece).
– ORIGIN Italian, from Latin *finis* 'end.'

fine art ▶ **n. 1** (also **fine arts**) creative art, esp. visual art, whose products are to be appreciated primarily or solely for their imaginative, aesthetic, or intellectual content: *the convergence of popular culture and fine art.*
2 an activity requiring great skill or accomplishment: *he'll have to learn the fine art of persuasion.*
– PHRASES **have** (or **get**) **something down to a fine art** achieve a high level of skill, facility, or accomplishment in some activity through experience: *Mike had gotten the breakfast routine down to a fine art.*

fine cham·pagne ▶ **n.** brandy from the Champagne district of the Cognac region of which half or more of the content comes from the central Grande Champagne.
– ORIGIN mid 19th cent.: French, literally 'fine (brandy from) Champagne.'

fine chem·i·cals ▶ **plural n.** chemical substances prepared to a very high degree of purity for use in research and industry.

fine-draw ▶ **v.** [with obj.] sew together (two pieces of cloth or edges of a tear) so that the join is imperceptible: *a table cover composed of cloth fine-drawn together.*

Fi·ne Gael /ˌfēnə ˈgāl/ one of the two major political parties of the Republic of Ireland (the other being Fianna Fáil). Founded in 1923 as Cumann na nGaedheal, it changed its name in 1933. It has advocated the concept of a united Ireland achieved by peaceful means.
– ORIGIN Irish, literally 'tribe of Gaels.'

fine-grained ▶ **adj.** (chiefly of wood) having a fine or delicate arrangement of fibers. ■ (chiefly of rock) consisting of small particles. ■ involving great attention to detail: *fine-grained analysis.*

fine nee·dle as·pi·ra·tion ▶ **n.** Medicine a procedure in which a thin needle is used to draw cells or fluid from a lump or mass under the skin.

fine print ▶ **n.** printed matter in small type. ■ inconspicuous details or conditions printed in an agreement or contract, esp. ones that may prove unfavorable: *read the fine print of whatever loan document is shoved under your nose.*

fin·er·y¹ /ˈfīnərē/ ▶ **n.** expensive or ostentatious clothes or decoration: *officers in their blue, gold, and scarlet finery.*
– ORIGIN late 17th cent.: from FINE¹, on the pattern of *bravery.*

fin·er·y² ▶ **n.** (pl. **fineries**) historical a hearth where pig iron was converted into wrought iron.
– ORIGIN late 16th cent.: from French *finerie*, from Old French *finer* 'refine.'

fines herbes /ˌfēn(z)ˈerb/ ▶ **plural n.** mixed herbs used in cooking, esp. fresh herbs chopped as a flavoring for omelets.
– ORIGIN mid 19th cent.: French, literally 'fine herbs.'

fine-spun ▶ **adj.** (esp. of fabric) fine or delicate in texture. ■ subtle; overly refined.

fi·nesse /fəˈnes/ ▶ **n. 1** intricate and refined delicacy: *orchestral playing of great finesse.* ■ artful subtlety, typically that needed for tactful handling of a difficulty: *clients want advice and action that calls for considerable finesse.*
2 (in bridge and whist) an attempt to win a trick with a card that is not a certain winner.
▶ **v.** [with obj.] **1** do (something) in a subtle and delicate manner: *his third shot, which he attempted to finesse, failed by a fraction.* ■ slyly attempt to avoid blame or censure when dealing with (a situation or action): *the administration's attempts to finesse its mishaps.*
2 (in bridge and whist) play (a card that is not a certain winner) in the hope of winning a trick with it: *the declarer finesses ♦J.*
– ORIGIN late Middle English (in the sense 'purity, delicacy'): from French, related to FINE¹.

fine struc·ture ▶ **n.** the composition of an object, substance, or energy phenomenon as viewed on a small scale and in considerable detail. ■ Physics the presence of groups of closely spaced lines in spectra corresponding to slightly different energy levels.

fine-struc·ture con·stant ▶ **n.** Physics a fundamental and dimensionless physical constant, equal to approximately $^1/_{137}$, that occurs in expressions describing the fine structure of atomic spectra.

fine-tooth comb (also **fine-toothed comb**) ▶ **n.** a comb with narrow teeth that are close together. ■ [in sing.] used with reference to a very thorough search or analysis of something: *you should check the small print with a fine-tooth comb.*

fine-tune ▶ **v.** [with obj.] make small adjustments to (something) in order to achieve the best or a desired performance: *the advanced angler seeking to fine-tune his angling skills.*

fin·ger /ˈfiNGgər/ ▶ **n.** each of the four slender jointed parts attached to either hand (or five, if the thumb is included): *she raked her hair back with her fingers.* ■ a part of a glove intended to cover a finger. ■ a measure of liquor in a glass, based on the breadth of a finger: *he poured three fingers of vodka into a juice glass.* ■ an object that has roughly the long, narrow shape of a finger: *a shortbread finger.*
▶ **v.** [with obj.] **1** touch or feel (something) with the fingers: *the thin man fingered his mustache.* ■ play (a musical instrument) with the fingers, esp. in a tentative or casual manner: *a woman fingered a lute.*
2 informal inform on (someone) to the police: *you fingered me for those burglaries.* ■ (**finger someone for**) identify or choose someone for (a particular purpose): *a research biologist with impeccable credentials was fingered for team leader.*
3 Music play (a passage) with a particular sequence of positions of the fingers. See also FINGERING. ■ mark (music) with signs showing which fingers are to be used.
– PHRASES **be all fingers and thumbs** Brit. informal be clumsy or awkward in one's actions. **give someone the finger** informal make an obscene gesture with the middle finger raised as a sign of contempt, meaning 'fuck you.' **have a finger in every pie** be involved in a large and varied number of activities or enterprises. **have** (or **keep**) **one's finger on the pulse** be aware of all the latest news or developments: *he keeps his finger on the pulse of world music.* **keep one's fingers crossed** see CROSS. **lay a finger on someone** touch someone, esp. with the intention of harming them. **lift a finger** see LIFT. **put one's finger on something** identify something exactly: *he cannot put his finger on what has gone wrong.* **twist** (or **wind** or **wrap**) **someone around one's little finger** see LITTLE FINGER. **work one's fingers to the bone** see BONE.
– DERIVATIVES **fin·gered adj.** [in combination] *a two-fingered whistle*, **fin·ger·less adj.**
– ORIGIN Old English, of Germanic origin; related to Dutch *vinger* and German *Finger.*

fin·ger·board /ˈfiNGgərˌbôrd/ ▶ **n.** a flat or roughly flat strip on the neck of a stringed instrument, against which the strings are pressed to shorten the vibrating length and produce notes of higher pitches.

fin·ger bowl ▶ **n.** a small bowl holding water for rinsing the fingers during or after a meal.

fin·ger-dry ▶ **v.** [with obj.] dry and style (hair) by repeatedly running one's fingers through it.

fin·ger food ▶ **n.** food served in such a form and style that it can conveniently be eaten with the fingers.

fin·ger·ing /ˈfiNGgəriNG/ ▶ **n.** a manner or technique of using the fingers, esp. to play a musical instrument: *he once studied keyboard fingering* | *the tuning makes some chord fingerings awkward.* ■ an indication of this in a musical score.

Fin·ger Lakes a region in central New York that is named for its series of narrow glacial lakes that lie parallel in a North-South orientation. Canandaigua, Keuka, Seneca, and Cayuga lakes are among the better known.

fin·ger-lick·ing ▶ **adj.** tasty; delicious: *a finger-licking meal* | [as submodifier] *finger-licking good.*

fin·ger·ling /ˈfiNGgərliNG/ ▶ **n. 1** a small young fish, esp. a salmon parr. [from FINGER (with reference to its transverse dusky bars) + -LING.]
2 a variety of potato having a pink, yellow, blue or light tan skin and flesh.

fin·ger·mark /ˈfiNGgərˌmärk/ ▶ **n.** a mark left on a surface by a dirty or greasy finger.

fin·ger·nail /ˈfiNGgərˌnāl/ ▶ **n.** the flattish horny part on the upper surface of the tip of each finger.

fin·ger of God (also **finger of fate**) ▶ **n.** Astrology an aspect between three planets where one is quincunx to each of the other two, which are sextile to each other.
– ORIGIN so named because of the resemblance of the aspect to a pointed finger.

fin·ger paint ▶ **n.** thick paint designed to be applied with the fingers, used esp. by young children.
▶ **v.** (**finger-paint**) [no obj.] (esp. of children) apply paint with the fingers.
– DERIVATIVES **fin·ger paint·ing n.**

fin·ger·pick /ˈfiNGgərˌpik/ ▶ **v.** [with obj.] play (a guitar or similar instrument) using the fingernails or small plectrums worn on the fingertips to pluck the strings: *black southern guitarists were fingerpicking guitars long before white musicians* | [no obj.] *he fingerpicked with facility.*
▶ **n.** a plectrum worn on a fingertip.
– DERIVATIVES **fin·ger·pick·er n.**

fin·ger-point·ing ▶ **n.** informal actions or words that bring attention to a particular person or issue.

fin·ger·post /ˈfiNGgərˌpōst/ ▶ **n.** a post at a road junction from which signs project in the direction of the place or route indicated.

fin·ger·print /ˈfiNGgərˌprint/ ▶ **n.** an impression or mark made on a surface by a person's fingertip, esp. as used for identifying individuals from the unique pattern of whorls and lines: *the police had his fingerprints on file.* ■ a distinctive identifying characteristic: *the faint chemical fingerprint of plastic explosives.*
▶ **v.** [with obj.] record the fingerprints of (someone): *I was booked, fingerprinted, and locked up for the night.*

fin·ger·spell·ing /ˈfiNGgərˌspeliNG/ ▶ **n.** a form of sign language in which individual letters are formed by the fingers to spell out words.

fin·ger·tip /ˈfiNGgərˌtip/ ▶ **n.** the tip of a finger.
▶ **adj.** [attrib.] using or operated by the fingers: *fingertip electronic controls.* ■ reaching to the fingertips: *the silhouette is close to the waist and flared to fingertip length.*
– PHRASES **at one's fingertips** (esp. of information) readily available; accessible: *until we have more facts at our fingertips, there is no use in speculating.* **by one's fingertips** only with difficulty; precariously: *the general was clinging to power by his fingertips.* **to one's fingertips** completely: *he is a professional to his fingertips.*

fin·ger-wag·ging ▶ **n.** the action of reprimanding or warning someone: [as modifier] *a finger-wagging speech.*

fin·ger wave ▶ **n.** a wave set in wet hair using the fingers.

fin·i·al /ˈfinēəl/ ▶ **n.** a distinctive ornament at the apex of a roof, pinnacle, canopy, or similar structure in a building. ■ an ornament at the top, end, or corner of an object: *ornate curtain poles with decorative finials.*
– ORIGIN late Middle English: from Old French *fin* or Latin *finis* 'end.'

finial

fin·i·cal /ˈfinikəl/ ▶ **adj.** another term for **FINICKY.**
– DERIVATIVES **fin·i·cal·i·ty** /ˌfiniˈkalitē/ **n.**, **fin·i·cal·ly** /-(ə)lē/ **adv.**, **fin·i·cal·ness n.**
– ORIGIN late 16th cent. (probably originally college slang): probably from **FINE**[1] + **-ICAL**, perhaps suggested by Middle Dutch *fijnkens* 'accurately, neatly, prettily.'

fin·ick·ing /ˈfinikiNG/ ▶ **adj.** another term for **FINICKY.**
– ORIGIN mid 17th cent.: from **FINICAL** + **-ING**[2].

fin·ick·y /ˈfinikē/ ▶ **adj.** (of a person) fussy about one's needs or requirements: *a finicky eater.* ■ showing or requiring great attention to detail: *a finicky, almost fetishistic collector.*
– DERIVATIVES **fin·ick·i·ness** /-kēnis/ **n.**

fin·ing /ˈfīniNG/ ▶ **n.** (usu. **finings**) a substance used for clarifying liquid, esp. beer or wine. ■ the process of clarifying wine or beer: [as modifier] *a fining agent.*

fin·is /ˈfinis, fiˈnē/ ▶ **n.** the end (printed at the end of a book or shown at the end of a film).
– ORIGIN late Middle English: from Latin.

fin·ish /ˈfiniSH/ ▶ **v.** [with obj.] **1** bring (a task or activity) to an end; complete: *they were straining to finish the job* | [with present participle] *we finished eating our meal* | [no obj.] *the musician finished to thunderous applause.* ■ consume or get through the final amount or portion of (something, esp. food or drink): *finish your fajita while it's still hot* | *Jerry finished off a margarita.* ■ [no obj.] (of an activity) come to an end: *the war has finished but nothing has changed.* ■ [no obj.] (**finish with**) have no more need for or nothing more to do with: *"I've finished with Tom," Gloria said.* ■ reach the end of a race or other sporting competition, typically in a particular position: [with complement] *she finished third in the 3-meter springboard diving.*
2 (usu. **be finished**) complete the manufacture or decoration of (a material, object, or place) by giving it an attractive surface appearance: *the interior was finished with V-jointed American oak.* ■ complete the fattening of (livestock) before slaughter. ■ dated prepare (a girl) for entry into fashionable society.
▶ **n. 1** [usu. in sing.] an end or final part or stage of something: *a bowl of raspberries was the perfect finish to the meal* | *I really enjoyed the film from start to finish.* ■ a point or place at which a race or competition ends: *he surged into a winning lead 200 meters from the finish.*
2 the manner in which the manufacture of an article is completed in detail: *wide variation in specification and finish.* ■ the surface appearance of a manufactured material or object, or the material used to produce this: *lightweight nylon with a shiny finish.* ■ the final taste impression of a wine or beer: *the wine has a lemony tang on the finish.*
– PHRASES **a fight to the finish** a fight or contest that ends only with the complete defeat of one of the parties involved.
– PHRASAL VERBS **finish someone off** kill, destroy, or comprehensively defeat someone. **finish up** complete an action or process: *he hadn't finished up the paperwork on it.* ■ end a period of time or course of action by doing something or being in a particular position: *Tony started out running the back elevator and finished up as bell captain* | *we finished up with a plate of meats.*
– ORIGIN Middle English: from Old French *feniss-*, lengthened stem of *fenir*, from Latin *finire*, from *finis* 'end.'

fin·ished /ˈfiniSHt/ ▶ **adj.** (of an action, activity, or piece of work) having been completed or ended: *a preparatory drawing for the finished painting.* ■ [predic.] (of a person) having completed or ended an action or activity: *they'll be finished here in an hour.* ■ [predic.] having lost effectiveness, power, or prestige: *he was told he was finished at the club.* ■ (of an object or room) having been given a particular decorative surface as the final stage in its manufacture or decoration: [in combination] *plastic-finished lining paper.* ■ [attrib.] (of livestock) having completed fattening before slaughter: *a reduction in prices for finished cattle.*

fin·ish·er /ˈfiniSHər/ ▶ **n. 1** a person or thing that finishes something, in particular: ■ a person who reaches the end of a race or other sporting competition: *a third-place finisher.* ■ (in soccer) a player who scores a goal: *he is one of the best finishers at the club.* ■ a worker or machine performing the last operation in a manufacturing process.
2 an animal that has been fattened ready for slaughter: [as modifier] *finisher pigs.*

fin·ish·ing school ▶ **n.** a private school where girls are prepared for entry into fashionable society.

fin·ish·ing touch ▶ **n.** (usu. **finishing touches**) a final detail or action completing and enhancing a piece of work: *now they're putting the finishing touches to a new album.*

fin·ish line ▶ **n.** a line marking the end of a race.

fi·nite /ˈfīnīt/ ▶ **adj. 1** having limits or bounds: *every computer has a finite amount of memory.* ■ not infinitely small: *one's chance of winning may be small, but it is finite.*
2 Grammar (of a verb form) having a specific tense, number, and person. Contrasted with **NONFINITE.**
– DERIVATIVES **fi·nite·ly adv.**, **fi·nite·ness n.**
– ORIGIN late Middle English: from Latin *finitus* 'finished,' past participle of *finire*(see **FINISH**).

fi·nit·ism /ˈfīnəˌtizəm/ ▶ **n.** Philosophy & Mathematics rejection of the belief that anything can actually be infinite.
– DERIVATIVES **fi·nit·ist n.**

fi·ni·to /fəˈnētō/ ▶ **adj.** [predic.] informal finished: *it's all done—finito.*
– ORIGIN Italian.

fin·i·tude /ˈfinəˌtōōd, ˈfī-/ ▶ **n.** formal the state of having limits or bounds: *one quickly senses the finitude of his patience.*

Fink /fiNGk/, Mike (c.1770–1823), US frontiersman. His exploits as a marksman, Indian scout, trapper, and keelboat man were legendary.

fink /fiNGk/ informal ▶ **n.** an unpleasant or contemptible person, in particular: ■ a person who informs on people to the authorities: *he was assumed by some to be the management's fink.* ■ dated a strikebreaker.
▶ **v.** [no obj.] **1** (**fink on**) inform on to the authorities: *there was no shortage of people willing to fink on their neighbors.*
2 (**fink out**) fail to do something promised or expected because of a lack of courage or commitment: *administration officials had finked out.* ■ cease to function: *your immune system begins finking out and you get sick.*
– ORIGIN late 19th cent.: of unknown origin; perhaps from German, literally 'finch,' but also a pejorative term. Students started to refer to nonmembers of fraternities as *finks*, probably by association with the freedom of wild birds as opposed to caged ones. The term was later generalized to denote those not belonging to organizations such as trade unions.

fin keel ▶ **n.** a boat's keel shaped like an inverted dorsal fin.

Fin·land /ˈfinlənd/ a country on the Baltic Sea, between Sweden and Russia; pop. 5,250,300 (est. 2009); capital, Helsinki; official languages, Finnish and Swedish. Finnish name **SUOMI.**

> The northern third of the country lies within the Arctic Circle. Long an area of Swedish–Russian rivalry, Finland was ceded to Russia in 1809 but became an independent republic after the Russian Revolution of 1917. Wars with the former Soviet Union were fought in 1939–40. Finland joined the European Union in 1995.

Fin·land, Gulf of an arm of the Baltic Sea between Finland and Estonia that extends east to St. Petersburg in Russia.

Fin·land·i·za·tion /ˌfinləndiˈzāSHən/ ▶ **n.** historical the process or result of being obliged for economic reasons to favor, or at least not oppose, the interests of the former Soviet Union despite not being politically allied to it.
– DERIVATIVES **Fin·land·ize** /ˈfinlənˌdīz/ **v.**
– ORIGIN 1960s: translation of German *Finnlandisierung*, referring to the case of Finland after 1944.

Finn /fin/ ▶ **n.** a native or inhabitant of Finland or a person of Finnish descent.
– ORIGIN Old English *Finnas* (plural), originally applied more widely to denote a people of Scandinavia and northeastern Europe speaking a Finno-Ugric language.

fin·nan /ˈfinən/ (also **finnan haddie** /ˈhadē/) ▶ **n.** haddock cured with the smoke of green wood, turf, or peat.
– ORIGIN early 18th cent.: alteration of *Findon*, the name of a fishing village near Aberdeen in Scotland, but sometimes confused with the Scottish river and village of *Findhorn*.

finnes·ko /ˈfinəˌskō/ ▶ **n.** (pl. **same**) a boot of tanned reindeer skin with the hair on the outside.
– ORIGIN late 19th cent.: from Norwegian *finnsko*, from *Finn* (see **FINN**) + *sko* (see **SHOE**).

Finn·ic /ˈfinik/ ▶ **adj. 1** of, relating to, or denoting the group of Finno-Ugric languages that includes Finnish and Estonian.
2 of, relating to, or denoting the group of peoples that includes the Finns and the Estonians.

Finn·ish /ˈfiniSH/ ▶ **adj.** of or relating to the Finns or their language.
▶ **n.** the Finno-Ugric language of the Finns, spoken in Finland and in parts of Russia and Sweden.

Fin·no-U·gric /ˌfinō ˈ(y)ōōgrik/ (also **Finno-Ugrian** /ˈ(y)ōōgrēən/) ▶ **adj.** of or relating to the major group of Uralic languages, whose main branches are Finnic and Ugric.
▶ **n.** this group of languages.

fin·ny /ˈfinē/ ▶ **adj.** literary of, relating to, or resembling a fish: *it transfixes its finny prey.*

fi·no /ˈfēnō/ ▶ **n.** (pl. **finos**) a light-colored dry sherry.
– ORIGIN mid 19th cent.: Spanish, literally 'fine,' based on Latin *finire* 'to finish' (see **FINISH**).

fi·noc·chi·o /fəˈnōkēˌō/ ▶ **n.** another term for **FLORENCE FENNEL** (see **FENNEL**).
– ORIGIN early 18th cent.: from Italian, from a popular Latin variant of Latin *faeniculum* (see **FENNEL**).

fin ray ▶ **n.** see **RAY**[1] (sense 2 of the noun).

fin whale ▶ **n.** another term for **FINBACK.**

fiord ▶ **n.** variant spelling of **FJORD.**

fio·ri·tu·ra /fēˌôriˈtōōrə/ ▶ **n.** (pl. **fioriture** /-ˈtōōˌrā/) Music an embellishment of a melody, esp. as improvised by an operatic singer.
– ORIGIN Italian, literally 'flowering,' from *fiorire* 'to flower.'

fip·ple /ˈfipəl/ ▶ **n.** the mouthpiece of a recorder or similar wind instrument that is blown endwise, in which a thin channel cut through a block directs a stream of air against a sharp edge. The term has been applied to various parts of this, including the block and the channel.
– ORIGIN early 17th cent.

fip·ple flute ▶ **n.** a flute, such as a recorder, played by blowing endwise.

fir /fər/ ▶ **n.** (also **fir tree**) an evergreen coniferous tree with upright cones and flat needle-shaped leaves, typically arranged in two rows. Firs are an important source of timber and resins. ● Genus *Abies*, family Pinaceae: many species.
– DERIVATIVES **fir·ry adj.**
– ORIGIN late Middle English: probably from Old Norse *fyri-* (recorded in *fyriskógr* 'fir-woods').

fire /fīr/ ▶ **n. 1** combustion or burning, in which substances combine chemically with oxygen from the air and typically give out bright light, heat, and smoke: *his house was destroyed by fire.* ■ one of the four elements in ancient and medieval philosophy and in astrology. ■ a destructive burning of something: *a fire at a hotel.* ■ a collection of fuel, esp. wood or coal, burned in a controlled way to provide heat or a means for cooking: *our small kettle was kept constantly on the fire.* ■ a burning sensation in the body: *the whiskey lit a fire in the back of his throat.* ■ fervent or passionate emotion or enthusiasm: *the fire of their religious conviction.* ■ literary luminosity; glow: *their soft smiles light the air like a star's fire.*
2 the shooting of projectiles from weapons, esp. bullets from guns: *a burst of machine-gun fire.* ■ strong criticism or antagonism: *he directed his fire against policies promoting American capital flight.*
▶ **v.** [with obj.] **1** discharge a gun or other weapon in order to explosively propel (a bullet or projectile): *he fired a shot at the retreating prisoners* | *they fired off a few rounds.* ■ discharge (a gun or other weapon): *another gang fired a pistol* | [no obj.] *troops fired on crowds.* ■ [no obj.] (of a gun) be discharged. ■ direct (questions or statements, esp. unwelcome ones) toward someone in rapid succession: *they fired questions at me for what seemed like ages.* ■ (**fire something off**) send a message aggressively, esp. as one of a series: *he fired off a letter informing her that he regarded the matter with the utmost seriousness.*
2 informal dismiss (an employee) from a job: *having to fire men who've been with me for years* | *you're fired!*
3 supply (a furnace, engine, boiler, or power station) with fuel. ■ [no obj.] (of an internal combustion engine, or a cylinder in one) undergo ignition of its fuel when started: *the engine fired and she pushed her foot down on the accelerator.* ■ archaic set fire to: *I fired the straw.*

4 stimulate or excite (the imagination or an emotion): *India fired my imagination.* ■ fill (someone) with enthusiasm: *in the locker room they were really fired up.* ■ [no obj.] (**fire up**) archaic show sudden anger: *If I were to hear anyone disparage you, I would fire up in a flash.*
5 bake or dry (pottery, bricks, etc.) in a kiln.
6 start (an engine or other device): *with a flick of his wrist he fired up the chainsaw.*
–PHRASES **breathe fire** be extremely angry: *I don't want an indignant boyfriend on my doorstep breathing fire.* **catch fire** begin to burn. ■ become interesting or exciting: *the show never caught fire.* **fire and brimstone** the torments of hell: *his father was preaching fire and brimstone sermons.* **fire away** informal used to give someone permission to begin speaking, typically to ask questions: *"I want to clear up some questions that have been puzzling me." "Fire away."* **fire in the** (or **one's**) **belly** a powerful sense of ambition or determination. **firing on all** (**four**) **cylinders** working or functioning at a peak level. **go through fire** (**and water**) face any peril. **light a fire under someone** stimulate someone to work or act more quickly or enthusiastically. **on fire** in flames; burning. ■ in a state of excitement: *Wright is now on fire with confidence.* **open fire** see OPEN. **play with fire** see PLAY. **set fire to** (or **set something on fire**) cause to burn; ignite. **set the world** (or Brit. **the Thames**) **on fire** do something remarkable or sensational: *the film hasn't exactly set the world on fire.* **take fire** Brit. start to burn. **under fire** being shot at: *observers sent to look for the men came under heavy fire.* ■ being rigorously criticized: *the president was under fire from all sides.* **where's the fire?** informal used to ask someone why they are in such a hurry or state of excitement.
–DERIVATIVES **fire·less** adj., **fir·er** n.
–ORIGIN Old English *fȳr* (noun), *fȳrian* 'supply with material for a fire'; related to Dutch *vuur* and German *Feuer*.

fire a·larm ▶ n. a device making a loud noise that gives warning of a fire.

fire-and-for·get ▶ adj. [attrib.] (of a missile) able to guide itself to its target once fired.

fire ant ▶ n. a tropical American ant that has a painful and sometimes dangerous sting. ● Genus *Solenopsis*, family Formicidae: several species, in particular the South American *S. invicta*, which has become a serious pest in the southeastern US.

fire·arm /ˈfī(ə)rˌärm/ ▶ n. a rifle, pistol, or other portable gun.

fire·back /ˈfīrˌbak/ ▶ n. the back wall of a fireplace. ■ a metal plate covering such a wall.

fire·ball /ˈfīrˌbôl/ ▶ n. a ball of flame or fire: *a crashed tanker exploded in a fireball.* ■ a large bright meteor. ■ historical a ball filled with combustibles or explosives, fired at an enemy or enemy fortifications. ■ a person with a fiery temper or a great deal of energy.

fire·ball·er /ˈfīrˌbôlər/ ▶ n. Baseball a pitcher who throws a good fastball.
–DERIVATIVES **fire·ball·ing** adj.

fire·base /ˈfīrˌbās/ ▶ n. an area in a war zone in which artillery can be massed to provide heavy firepower in support of other military units.

fire-bel·lied toad ▶ n. a warty European aquatic toad, the underside of which is vividly marked in red, orange, yellow, black, and white. ● Genus *Bombina*, family Discoglossidae: in particular *B. bombina*.

fire·blight /ˈfīrˌblīt/ ▶ n. a serious bacterial disease of plants of the rose family, esp. fruit trees, giving the leaves a scorched appearance. ● The bacterium is *Erwinia amylovora*.

fire·bomb /ˈfīrˌbäm/ ▶ n. a bomb designed to cause a fire.
▶ v. [with obj.] attack or destroy (something) with such a bomb: *he suspects that someone firebombed his business.*

fire·box /ˈfīrˌbäks/ ▶ n. the chamber of a boiler in which the fuel is burned.

fire·brand /ˈfīrˌbrand/ ▶ n. **1** a person who is passionate about a particular cause, typically inciting change and taking radical action: *a political firebrand.*
2 a piece of burning wood.

fire·brat /ˈfīrˌbrat/ ▶ n. a fast-moving brownish insect, a type of bristletail, that frequents warm places indoors. ● *Thermobia domestica*, family Lepismatidae, order Thysanura.

fire·break /ˈfīrˌbrāk/ ▶ n. an obstacle to the spread of fire: *a fire-resistant door designed to be a firebreak* | figurative *a firebreak against the spread of revolution from Russia.* ■ a strip of open space in a forest or other area of dense vegetation.

fire·brick /ˈfīrˌbrik/ ▶ n. a brick capable of withstanding intense heat, used esp. to line furnaces and fireplaces.

fire bri·gade ▶ n. chiefly Brit. an organized body of people trained and employed to extinguish fires.

fire·bug /ˈfīrˌbəg/ ▶ n. informal an arsonist.

fire·clay /ˈfīrˌklā/ ▶ n. clay capable of withstanding high temperatures, chiefly used for making firebricks.

fire com·pa·ny ▶ n. another term for FIRE DEPARTMENT.

fire con·trol ▶ n. **1** the process of targeting and firing heavy weapons.
2 the prevention and monitoring of forest fires and grass fires.

fire cor·al ▶ n. a colonial corallike hydrozoan, the heavy external skeleton of which forms reefs. The polyps bear nematocysts that can inflict painful stings. ● Genus *Millepora*, order Hydroida (or Milleporina), class Hydrozoa.

fire·crack·er /ˈfīrˌkrakər/ ▶ n. a loud, explosive firework, typically wrapped in paper and lit with a fuse. ■ an outstanding, exciting, or attractive person or thing: *the book was hardly a literary firecracker.*

fire·crest /ˈfīrˌkrest/ ▶ n. a small warbler having a red and orange crest and occurring mainly in Europe. ● *Regulus ignicapillus*, family Sylviidae.

fire·damp /ˈfīrˌdamp/ ▶ n. methane, esp. as forming an explosive mixture with air in coal mines.

fire de·part·ment ▶ n. the department of a local or municipal authority in charge of preventing and fighting fires.

fire·dog /ˈfīrˌdôg/ ▶ n. another term for ANDIRON.

fire door ▶ n. a fire-resistant door to prevent the spread of fire. ■ a door to the outside of a building used only as an emergency exit.

fire·drake /ˈfīrˌdrāk/ ▶ n. Germanic Mythology a fiery dragon.
–ORIGIN Old English *fȳr-draca*, from *fȳr* (see FIRE) + *draca* 'dragon,' from Latin *draco*.

fire drill ▶ n. **1** a practice of the emergency procedures to be used in case of fire.
2 a primitive device for kindling fire by frictional heating, consisting of a pointed stick that is twirled in a hole in a flat piece of soft wood.

fire-eat·er ▶ n. **1** an entertainer who appears to eat fire.
2 dated a person prone to quarreling or fighting.

fire en·gine ▶ n. a vehicle carrying firefighters and equipment for fighting large fires.

fire es·cape ▶ n. a staircase or other apparatus used for escaping from a building on fire.

fire ex·tin·guish·er ▶ n. a portable device that discharges a jet of water, foam, gas, or other material to extinguish a fire.

fire·fight /ˈfīrˌfīt/ ▶ n. Military a battle using guns rather than bombs or other weapons.

fire·fight·er /ˈfīrˌfītər/ ▶ n. a person whose job is to extinguish fires.

fire·fight·ing /ˈfīrˌfītiNG/ ▶ n. **1** the action or process of extinguishing fires, as a person's job.
2 (in business) the practice of dealing with problems as they arise rather than planning strategically to avoid them.

fire·fly /ˈfīrˌflī/ ▶ n. (pl. **fireflies**) a soft-bodied beetle related to the glowworm, the winged male and flightless female of which both have luminescent organs. The light is chiefly produced as a signal between the sexes, esp. in flashes. ● Family Lampyridae: many species.

firefly

fire·guard /ˈfī(ə)rˌgärd/ ▶ n. **1** a protective screen or grid placed in front of an open fire.
2 a firebreak in a forest.

fire·hall /ˈfīrˌhôl/ ▶ n. a fire station.

fire hose ▶ n. a large-diameter hose used in extinguishing fires.

fire·house /ˈfīrˌhous/ ▶ n. another term for FIRE STATION.

fire i·rons ▶ plural n. implements for tending a domestic fire, typically tongs, a poker, and a shovel.

Fire Is·land a barrier island on the southern shore of Long Island in New York, the site of numerous small resort communities.

fire·less cook·er /ˈfīrləs/ ▶ n. an insulated container capable of maintaining a temperature at which food can be cooked.

fire·light /ˈfīrˌlīt/ ▶ n. light from a fire in a fireplace.
–ORIGIN Old English *fȳr-lēoht* (see FIRE, LIGHT[1]).

fire line ▶ n. a firebreak in a forest.

fire·lock /ˈfīrˌläk/ ▶ n. historical a firearm in which the priming is ignited by sparks.

fire·man /ˈfīrmən/ ▶ n. (pl. **firemen** /-mən/) **1** a firefighter.
2 a person who tends a furnace or the fire of a steam engine or steamship; a stoker. ■ an enlisted person in the US navy who maintains and operates a ship's machinery.

Fi·ren·ze /fēˈrentsā/ Italian name of FLORENCE.

fire o·pal ▶ n. another term for GIRASOL (sense 1).

fire·pit /ˈfī(ə)rpit/ ▶ n. a pit dug into the ground or a freestanding metal vessel, in which a contained outdoor fire is made.

fire·place /ˈfīrˌplās/ ▶ n. a place for a domestic fire, esp. a grate or hearth at the base of a chimney. ■ a structure surrounding such a place.

fire·plug /ˈfīrˌpləg/ ▶ n. a hydrant for a fire hose. ■ informal a short, stocky person, esp. an athlete.

fire·pow·er /ˈfīrˌpou(-ə)r/ ▶ n. the destructive capacity of guns, missiles, or a military force (used with reference to the number and size of weapons available): *the enormous disparity in firepower between the two sides* | figurative *the well-funded legal firepower of the tobacco companies.*

fire·proof /ˈfīrˌpro͞of/ ▶ adj. able to withstand fire or great heat: *a fireproof dish.*
▶ v. [with obj.] make (something) fireproof: *nearby museum buildings will be fireproofed.*

fire-rais·er ▶ n. Brit. an arsonist.
–DERIVATIVES **fire-raising** n.

fire sal·a·man·der ▶ n. a robust short-tailed nocturnal salamander that has black skin with bright red, orange, and yellow markings, native to upland forests of Europe, northwestern Africa, and southwestern Asia. ● *Salamandra salamandra*, family Salamandridae.

fire sale ▶ n. a sale of goods remaining after the destruction of commercial premises by fire. ■ a sale of goods or assets at a very low price, typically when the seller is facing bankruptcy.

fire screen ▶ n. a screen or grid placed in front of an open fire to deflect the direct heat or to protect against sparks.

fire serv·ice ▶ n. Brit. an organization in charge of preventing and fighting fires.

fire·ship /ˈfīrˌSHip/ ▶ n. historical a ship loaded with burning material and explosives and set adrift to ignite and blow up an enemy's ships.

fire·side /ˈfīrˌsīd/ ▶ n. the area around a fireplace (used esp. with reference to a person's home or family life): *he preferred the warmth of his own fireside.* ■ a fireside chat.

fire·side chat ▶ n. an informal conversation. ■ one of a series of radio broadcasts made by President Franklin Delano Roosevelt to the nation, beginning in 1933.

fire start·er ▶ n. a piece of flammable material used to help start a fire.

fire sta·tion ▶ n. a facility where fire engines and other equipment of a fire department are housed.

fire step ▶ n. a step or ledge on which soldiers in a trench stand to fire.

Fire·stone /ˈfīrˌstōn/, Harvey Samuel (1868–1938), US industrialist. He organized the Firestone Tire & Rubber Company in 1900 and was its president 1903–32 and chairman 1932–38.

fire·stone /ˈfīrˌstōn/ ▶ n. stone that can withstand fire and great heat, used esp. for lining furnaces and ovens.

fire·storm /ˈfīrˌstôrm/ ▶ n. an intense and destructive fire (typically one caused by bombing) in which strong currents of air are drawn into the blaze, making it burn more fiercely: *within the firestorm every building was burned to a shell* | figurative *the incident ignited a firestorm of controversy.*

fire·thorn /ˈfīr,THôrn/ ▶ **n.** another term for PYRACANTHA.

fire tow·er ▶ **n.** a tower, often at a high elevation, that esp. in former years was staffed by a lookout for the detection of fires occurring over a wide area.

fire trail ▶ **n.** a track through forest or bush for use in fighting fires.

fire·trap /ˈfīr,trap/ ▶ **n.** a building without proper provision for escape in case of fire.

fire truck ▶ **n.** another term for FIRE ENGINE.

fire-walk·ing ▶ **n.** the practice of walking barefoot over something such as hot stones or wood ashes, often as part of a traditional ceremony.
– DERIVATIVES **fire-walk·er n.**

fire·wall /ˈfīr,wôl/ ▶ **n.** a wall or partition designed to inhibit or prevent the spread of fire. ■ Computing a part of a computer system or network that is designed to block unauthorized access while permitting outward communication. ■ another term for CHINESE WALL.

fire ward·en ▶ **n.** a person employed to prevent or extinguish fires, esp. in a town, camp, or forest.

fire·wa·ter /ˈfīr,wôtər, -,wätər/ ▶ **n.** informal strong liquor.

fire·weed /ˈfīr,wēd/ ▶ **n.** a plant that springs up on burned land, esp. the pink-flowered *Epilobium angustifolium*, a widespread willow herb.

FireWire /ˈfī(ə)r,wī(ə)r/ ▶ **n.** Computing, trademark a technology that allows high-speed communication and data exchange between a computer and a peripheral or between two computers.

fire·wood /ˈfīr,wo͝od/ ▶ **n.** wood burned as fuel.

fire·work /ˈfīr,wərk/ ▶ **n.** a device containing gunpowder and other combustible chemicals that causes a spectacular explosion when ignited, used typically for display or in celebrations: *they were oohing and aahing as if they were watching the fireworks* | [as modifier] *a firework display.* ■ (**fireworks**) an outburst of anger or other emotion, or a display of brilliance or energy: *when you put these men together, you're bound to get fireworks.*

fir·ing /ˈfīriNG/ ▶ **n.** the action of setting fire to something: *the deliberate firing of 600 oil wells.* ■ the discharging of a gun or other weapon: *the prolonged firing caused heavy losses* | *no missile firings were planned.* ■ the dismissal of an employee from a job: *the recent firing of the head of the department.* ■ the baking or drying of pottery or bricks in a kiln.

fir·ing line ▶ **n.** the line of positions from which gunfire is directed at targets. ■ the front line of troops in a battle. ■ a position where one is subject to criticism or blame because of one's responsibilities or position: *the referee in the firing line is an experienced official.*

fir·ing pin ▶ **n.** a movable pin in a firearm that strikes the primer of a cartridge to set off the charge.

fir·ing squad ▶ **n.** a group of soldiers detailed to shoot a condemned person. ■ a group of soldiers detailed to fire the salute at a military funeral.

fir·kin /ˈfərkən/ ▶ **n.** chiefly historical a small cask used chiefly for liquids, butter, or fish. ■ a unit of liquid volume equal to half a kilderkin (about 11 gallons or 41 liters).
– ORIGIN Middle English *ferdekyn*, probably from the Middle Dutch diminutive of *vierde* 'fourth' (a firkin originally contained a quarter of a barrel).

firm[1] /fərm/ ▶ **adj. 1** having a solid, almost unyielding surface or structure: *the bed should be reasonably firm, but not too hard.* ■ solidly in place and stable: *no building can stand without firm foundations* | figurative *he was unable to establish the store on a firm financial footing.* ■ having steady but not excessive power or strength: *you need a firm grip on the steering.* ■ (of a person, action, or attitude) showing resolute determination and strength of character: *he didn't like being firm with Larry, but he had to.*
2 strongly felt and unlikely to change: *he retains a firm belief in the efficacy of prayer.* ■ (of a person) steadfast and constant: *we became firm friends.* ■ decided upon and fixed or definite: *she had no firm plans for the next day.* ■ (of a currency, a commodity, or shares) having a steady value or price that is more likely to rise than fall: *the dollar was firm against the yen.*
▶ **v.** [with obj.] make (something) physically solid or resilient: *an exercise program designed to firm up muscle tone.* ■ fix (a plant) securely in the soil. ■ [no obj.] (of a price) rise slightly to reach a level considered secure: *he believed house prices would firm by the end of the year.* ■ make (an agreement or plan) explicit and definite: *archaeologists have now firmed up this new view.*
▶ **adv.** in a resolute and determined manner: *she will stand firm against the government's proposal.*
– PHRASES **be on firm ground** be sure of one's facts or secure in one's position, esp. in a discussion. **a firm hand** strict discipline or control.
– DERIVATIVES **firm·ly adv.**, **firm·ness n.**
– ORIGIN Middle English: from Old French *ferme*, from Latin *firmus*.

firm[2] ▶ **n.** a business concern, esp. one involving a partnership of two or more people: *a law firm.*
– ORIGIN late 16th cent.: from Italian *firma*, from medieval Latin, from Latin *firmare* 'fix, settle' (in late Latin 'confirm by signature'), from *firmus* 'firm'; compare with FARM. The word originally denoted one's autograph or signature; later (mid 18th cent.) the name under which the business of a firm was transacted, hence the firm itself (late 18th cent).

fir·ma·ment /ˈfərməmənt/ ▶ **n.** literary the heavens or the sky, esp. when regarded as a tangible thing. ■ a sphere or world viewed as a collection of people: *one of the great stars in the American golfing firmament.*
– DERIVATIVES **fir·ma·men·tal** /,fərməˈmentl/ **adj.**
– ORIGIN Middle English: via Old French from Latin *firmamentum*, from *firmare* 'fix, settle.'

fir·man /ˈfərmən, fərˈmän/ ▶ **n.** (pl. **firmans**) **1** a Near Eastern sovereign's edict.
2 a grant or permit.
– ORIGIN early 17th cent.: from Persian *firmān*, Sanskrit *pramāṇa* 'right measure, standard, authority.'

firm·ware /ˈfərm,wer/ ▶ **n.** Computing permanent software programmed into a read-only memory.

firn /fi(ə)rn/ ▶ **n.** granular snow, esp. on the upper part of a glacier, where it has not yet been compressed into ice.
– ORIGIN mid 19th cent.: from German, from Old High German *firni* 'old'; related to Swedish *forn* 'former.'

first /fərst/ ▶ **ordinal number 1** coming before all others in time or order; earliest; 1st: *his first wife* | *the first of five daughters.* ■ never previously done or occurring: *her first day at school.* ■ coming next after a specified or implied time or occurrence: *I didn't take the first bus.* ■ met with or encountered before any others: *the first house I came to.* ■ originally: *many valuable drugs have been recognized first as poisons.* ■ before doing something else specified or implied: *do you mind if I take a shower first?* ■ for the first time: *she first picked up a guitar out of sheer boredom.* ■ firstly; in the first place (used to introduce a first point or reason): *first, it is wrong that the victims should have no remedy.* ■ in preference; rather (used when strongly rejecting a suggestion or possibility): *she longed to go abroad, but not at this man's expense—she'd die first!* ■ with a specified part or person in a leading position: *it plunged nose first into the river.* ■ informal the first occurrence of something notable: *we traveled by air, a first for both of us.* ■ the first in a sequence of a vehicle's gears: *he stuck the car in first and revved.* ■ Baseball first base: *he made it all the way home from first.* ■ the first grade of a school. ■ a first edition of a book.
2 foremost in position, rank, or importance: *the doctor's first duty is to respect this right* | *career women who put work first* | *football must come first.* ■ [often with infinitive] the most likely, pressing, or suitable: *he is the first to admit he was not the best of patients* | *his first problem is where to live.* ■ the first finisher or position in a race or competition. ■ Music performing the highest or chief of two or more parts for the same instrument or voice: *the first violins.* ■ (**firsts**) goods of the best quality: *factory firsts, seconds, and discontinued styles.* ■ Brit. a place in the top grade in an examination, esp. that for a degree: *he took a first in Classics.* ■ Brit. a person having achieved such a degree.
– PHRASES **at first** at the beginning; in the initial stage or stages: *at first Hugh tried to be patient.* **at first glance** see GLANCE[1]. **at first hand** see FIRSTHAND. **at first instance** see INSTANCE. **at first sight** see SIGHT. **(the) first among equals** see EQUAL. **first blood** see BLOOD. **first come, first served** used to indicate that people will be dealt with in the order in which they arrive or apply: *tickets are available on a first come, first served basis.* **first and foremost** most importantly; more than anything else: *I'm first and foremost a writer.* **first and last** fundamentally; on the whole: *museums are first and last about curatorship.* **first of all** before doing anything else; at the beginning: *first of all, let me ask you something.* ■ most importantly: *German unity depends first of all on the German people.* **first off** informal as a first point; first of all: *first off, I owe you a heck of an apology.* **first past the post** (of a contestant, esp. a horse, in a race) winning a race by being the first to reach the finish line. ■ [attrib.] Brit. denoting an electoral system in which a candidate or party is selected by achievement of a simple majority: *our first-past-the-post electoral system.* **first thing** early in the morning; before anything else: *I have to meet Josh first thing tomorrow.* **first things first** used to assert that important matters should be dealt with before other things. **from the (very) first** from the beginning or the early stages: *he should have realized it from the first.* **from first to last** from beginning to end; throughout: *it's a fine performance that commands attention from first to last.* **get to first base** see BASE[1]. **in the first place** as the first consideration or point: *political reality was not quite that simple—in the first place, divisions existed within the parties.* ■ at the beginning; to begin with (esp. in reference to the time when an action was being planned or discussed): *I should have told you in the first place.* **of the first order** (or **magnitude**) used to denote something that is excellent or considerable of its kind: *it is a media event of the first order.* **of the first water** see WATER.
– ORIGIN Old English*fyr(e)st*; of Germanic origin, related to Old Norse *fyrstr* and German *Fürst* 'prince,' from an Indo-European root shared by Sanskrit *prathama*, Latin *primus*, and Greek *prōtos*.

USAGE First, second, third, etc., are adverbs as well as adjectives: *first, dice three potatoes; second, add the bouillon.* Firstly, secondly, etc., are also correct, but make sure not to mix the two groups: *first, second, third*; not *first, secondly, thirdly.* See also usage at FORMER[1].

First A·dar /ˈädär/ see ADAR.

first aid ▶ **n.** help given to a sick or injured person until full medical treatment is available: *an expert in emergency first aid* | [as modifier] *a first-aid kit.*
– DERIVATIVES **first aid·er** /ˈādər/ **n.**

first·born /ˈfərst,bôrn/ ▶ **adj.** (of a person's child) the first to be born; the eldest: *his new album and his firstborn child are due in the same week.*
▶ **n.** a person's first child: *their firstborn arrived.*

First Cause ▶ **n.** Philosophy a supposed ultimate cause of all events, which does not itself have a cause, identified with God.

first class ▶ **n.** a set of people or things grouped together as the best. ■ the best accommodations in a plane, train, or ship: *a seat in first class.* ■ Brit. the highest division in the results of the examinations for a university degree.
▶ **adj. & adv.** of the best quality: [as adj.] *a full-scale grand opera needs a first-class orchestra.* ■ of or relating to the best accommodations in a train, ship, or plane: [as adj.] *first-class air transportation* | [as adv.] *you can travel first class on any train.* ■ of or relating to a class of mail given priority: [as adj.] *first-class mail* | [as adv.] *send it first class.* ■ [as adj.] Brit. of or relating to the highest division in a university examination: *a first-class honors degree.*

First Con·sul the title held by Napoleon Bonaparte from 1799 to 1804, when he became Emperor of France.

first cost ▶ **n.** another term for PRIME COST.

first cous·in ▶ **n.** see COUSIN.

first-day cov·er (also **first day cover**) ▶ **n.** an envelope bearing a stamp or stamps postmarked on their day of issue.

first-de·gree ▶ **adj.** [attrib.] **1** Medicine denoting burns that affect only the surface of the skin and cause reddening.
2 Law denoting the most serious category of a crime, esp. murder.
– PHRASES **first-degree relative** a person's parent, sibling, or child.

first down ▶ **n.** Football a gain of ten yards or more in field position during a series of downs, permitting the offensive team to attempt another series of downs.

First Em·pire the period of the reign of Napoleon I as emperor of the French (1804–15).

first fam·i·ly ▶ **n.** a family considered to rank first in social prestige or pedigree in a particular place. ■ the family of the president of the US or of the governor of a US state, or of the chief executive of another political unit.

first fin·ger ▶ **n.** the finger next to the thumb; the forefinger; the index finger.

first floor ▶ **n.** the ground floor of a building. ■ chiefly Brit. the floor of a building just above the ground floor.

PRONUNCIATION KEY ə *ago, up*; ər *over, fur*; a *hat*; ā *ate*; ä *car*; e *let*; ē *see*; i *fit*; ī *by*; NG *sing*; ō *go*; ô *law, for*; oi *toy*; o͝o *good*; o͞o *goo*; ou *out*; TH *thin*; T͟H *then*; ZH *vision*

first-foot ▶ **v.** [with obj.] be the first person to cross the threshold of the house of (someone) in the New Year, in accordance with a Scottish custom.
▶ **n.** the first person to cross a threshold in the New Year.
– DERIVATIVES **first-foot·er** /ˈfo͝otər/ **n.**

first fruits ▶ **plural n.** the first agricultural produce of a season, esp. when given as an offering to God. ■ the initial results of an enterprise or endeavor: *the first fruits of the companies' collaboration.* ■ historical a payment to a superior by the new holder of an office.

first gear ▶ **n.** the lowest in a set of gears on a vehicle, used when traveling very slowly. ■ used in reference to a failure to make progress: *in a scrappy first half, neither team seemed to* ***get out of first gear.***

first-gen·er·a·tion ▶ **adj. 1** designating the first of a generation to become a citizen in a new country. ■ designating the first of a generation to be born in a country of parents who had immigrated: *a first-generation Canadian whose parents were born on a farm in Vietnam.*
2 designating the first version of a type made available: *first-generation descrambler technology.*

first·hand /ˈfərstˈhand/ ▶ **adj. & adv.** (of information or experience) from the original source or personal experience; direct: [as adj.] *neither of them had any firsthand knowledge of Andean culture* | [as adv.] *this is something you have to hear firsthand.*
– PHRASES **at first hand** directly or from personal experience: *scientists observed the process at first hand.*

first in·ten·tion ▶ **n.** Medicine the healing of a wound by natural contact of the parts involved: *healing* ***by first intention.*** Compare with **SECOND INTENTION.**

First In·ter·na·tion·al see **INTERNATIONAL** (sense 2 of the noun).

First La·dy ▶ **n.** the wife of the president of the US or other head of state. ■ (usu. **first lady**) the leading woman in a particular activity or profession: *the first lady of rock.*

first lan·guage ▶ **n.** a person's native language.

first lieu·ten·ant ▶ **n.** a commissioned officer in the US Army, Air Force, or Marine Corps ranking above second lieutenant and below captain.

first light ▶ **n.** the time when light first appears in the morning; dawn: *you are to set off at first light.*

first-line ▶ **adj.** of first resort: *first-line drugs for HIV exposure.*

first·ling /ˈfərstliNG/ ▶ **n.** (usu. **firstlings**) archaic the first agricultural produce or animal offspring of a season.

first·ly /ˈfərstlē/ ▶ **adv.** used to introduce a first point or reason: *firstly it is wrong and secondly it is extremely difficult to implement.*

> **USAGE** See usage at **FIRST.**

first mate ▶ **n.** the deck officer second in command to the master of a merchant ship.

first min·is·ter ▶ **n.** the leader of the ruling political party in some regions or countries.

first name ▶ **n.** a personal name given to someone at birth or baptism and used before a family name.
– PHRASES **on a first-name basis** having a friendly and informal relationship: *an amateur ecologist who is on a first-name basis with most reptiles.*

First Na·tion ▶ **n.** (in Canada) an indigenous American Indian community officially recognized as an administrative unit by the federal government or functioning as such without official status.

first night ▶ **n.** the first public performance of a play or show: [as modifier] *first-night nerves.*

first-night·er ▶ **n.** a person who attends a first night.

first of·fend·er ▶ **n.** a person who is convicted of a criminal offense for the first time.

first of·fi·cer ▶ **n.** the first mate on a merchant ship. ■ the second in command to the captain on an aircraft.

first-or·der ▶ **adj.** of or relating to the simplest or most fundamental level of organization, experience, or analysis; primary or immediate: *for a teacher, of course, drama must be a first-order experience.* ■ technical having an order of one, esp. denoting mathematical equations involving only the first power of the independent variable or only the first derivative of a function.

first per·son ▶ **n.** see **PERSON** (sense 2).

first po·si·tion ▶ **n. 1** Ballet a posture in which the feet are turned outward with the heels touching. ■ a position of the arms in which both are held curved in front of the body at waist level, with the palms facing the body.
2 Music the lowest position of the hand on the fingerboard of a stringed instrument.

First Pres·i·den·cy ▶ **n.** see **PRESIDENCY.**

first prin·ci·ples ▶ **plural n.** the fundamental concepts or assumptions on which a theory, system, or method is based: *I think we have to start again and go right back to first principles.*

first-rate ▶ **adj.** of the best class or quality; excellent: *first-rate musicians.* ■ in good health or condition; very well: *I think you look first-rate.*

first read·ing ▶ **n.** (in the UK) the first presentation of a bill to Parliament, to permit its introduction.

first re·fus·al ▶ **n.** the privilege of deciding whether to accept or reject something before it is offered to others: *tenants have a* ***right of first refusal*** *if the landlord proposes to sell the property.*

First Reich see **REICH¹.**

First Re·pub·lic the republican regime in France from the abolition of the monarchy in 1792 until Napoleon's accession as emperor in 1804.

first re·spond·er ▶ **n.** someone designated or trained to respond to an emergency.

first ser·geant ▶ **n.** (in the US Army or Marine Corps) the highest-ranking noncommissioned officer in a company or equivalent unit.

First State a nickname for the state of **DELAWARE¹.**

first strike ▶ **n.** an attack with nuclear weapons designed to destroy the enemy's nuclear weapons before their use.

first string ▶ **n.** Sports the best players on a team, the ones that normally play the most. ■ the best or most talented individuals in any endeavor.

First World ▶ **n.** the industrialized capitalist countries of western Europe, North America, Japan, Australia, and New Zealand. Compare with **SECOND WORLD** and **THIRD WORLD.**

First World War another term for **WORLD WAR I.**

Firth /fərTH/, J. R. (1890–1960), English linguist; full name *John Rupert Firth.* Firth was noted for his contributions to linguistic semantics and prosodic phonology.

firth /fərTH/ ▶ **n.** a narrow inlet of the sea; an estuary.
– ORIGIN Middle English (originally Scots), from Old Norse *fjǫrthr* (see **FJORD**).

fir tree ▶ **n.** see **FIR.**

fisc /fisk/ ▶ **n.** Roman History the public treasury of Rome or the emperor's privy purse. ■ a public treasury or exchequer.
– ORIGIN late 16th cent.: from French, or from Latin *fiscus* 'rush basket, purse, treasury.'

fis·cal /ˈfiskəl/ ▶ **adj.** of or relating to government revenue, esp. taxes: *monetary and fiscal policy.* ■ of or relating to financial matters: *the domestic fiscal crisis.* ■ used to denote a fiscal year: *the budget deficit for fiscal 1996.*
▶ **n.** archaic a legal or treasury official in some countries.
– DERIVATIVES **fis·cal·ly adv.**
– ORIGIN mid 16th cent.: from French, or from Latin *fiscalis,* from *fiscus* 'purse, treasury' (see **FISC**).

fis·cal year ▶ **n.** a year as reckoned for taxing or accounting purposes: *the farm is expected to turn a profit for its fiscal year ending April 30.*

Fisch·er¹ /ˈfisHər/, Bobby (1943–2008), US chess player; full name *Robert James Fischer.* He defeated Boris Spassky in 1972 to become the world champion, a title he held until 1975.

Fisch·er², Emil Hermann (1852–1919), German organic chemist. He studied the structure of sugars, other carbohydrates, and purines and synthesized many of them. He also confirmed that peptides and proteins consist of chains of amino acids. Nobel Prize for Chemistry (1902).

Fisch·er³, Hans (1881–1945), German organic chemist. He determined the structure of the porphyrin group of many natural pigments. Nobel Prize for Chemistry (1930).

fish¹ /fisH/ ▶ **n.** (pl. **same** or **fishes**) a limbless cold-blooded vertebrate animal with gills and fins and living wholly in water: *the sea is thick with fish.* ■ the flesh of such animals as food: *hot crab appetizers stuffed with fish.* ■ (**the Fish** or **Fishes**) the zodiacal sign or constellation Pisces. ■ used in names of invertebrate animals living wholly in water, e.g., **cuttlefish, shellfish, jellyfish.** ■ [with adj.] informal a person who is strange in a specified way: *he is generally thought to be a bit of a* ***cold fish.*** ■ informal a torpedo.
▶ **v.** [no obj.] catch or try to catch fish, typically by using a net or hook and line: *he was* ***fishing for*** *bluefish* | *I've told the girls we've* ***gone fishing.*** ■ [with obj.] catch or try to catch fish in (a particular body of water): *they did fish the mountain streams when game grew scarce.* ■ search, typically by groping or feeling for something concealed: *he fished for his registration certificate and held it up to the policeman's flashlight.* ■ try subtly or deviously to elicit a response or some information from someone: *I was not* ***fishing for compliments.*** ■ [with obj.] (**fish something out**) pull or take something out of water or a container: *the body of a woman had been fished out of the river.*
– PHRASES **a big fish** an important or influential person: *he became a big fish in the world of politics.* **a big fish in a small** (or **little**) **pond** a person seen as important and influential only within the limited scope of a small organization or group. **drink like a fish** drink excessive amounts of alcohol. **fish or cut bait** see **BAIT. a fish out of water** a person in a completely unsuitable environment or situation. **fished out** depleted of fish: *the grayling here have hardly been fished out.* **have other** (or **bigger**) **fish to fry** have other (or more important) matters to attend to. **like shooting fish in a barrel** extremely easy: *picking cultivated berries is like shooting fish in a barrel.* **neither fish nor fowl** (**nor good red herring**) of indefinite character and difficult to identify or classify. **there are plenty more fish in the sea** used to console someone whose romantic relationship has ended by pointing out that there are many other people with whom they may have a successful relationship in the future.
– DERIVATIVES **fish·like adj.**
– ORIGIN Old English *fisc* (as a noun denoting any animal living exclusively in water), *fiscian* (verb), of Germanic origin; related to Dutch *vis, vissen* and German *Fisch, fischen.*

> **USAGE** The normal plural of fish is fish (*a shoal of fish; he caught two huge fish*). The older form fishes is still used, but almost exclusively when referring to different kinds of fish (*freshwater fishes of the Great Lakes*).

fish² /fisH/ ▶ **n.** a flat plate of metal, wood, or another material that is fixed on a beam or across a joint in order to give additional strength, esp. on a ship's damaged mast or spar as a temporary repair.
▶ **v.** [with obj.] mend or strengthen (a beam, joint, mast, etc.) with a fish. ■ join (rails in a railroad track) with a fishplate.
– ORIGIN early 16th cent.: probably from French *fiche,* from *ficher* 'to fix,' based on Latin *figere.*

fish and chips ▶ **n.** a dish of fried fish fillets served with French fries.

fish·bowl /ˈfisH,bōl/ ▶ **n.** a round glass bowl for keeping pet fish in. ■ a place open to public view and criticism: *there was no privacy in his office; it was a fishbowl.*

fishcake /ˈfisHkāk/ ▶ **n.** a patty of shredded fish and mashed potato, typically coated in batter or breadcrumbs and fried.

fish ea·gle ▶ **n.** an eagle that catches and feeds on fish. ● Genus *Haliaetus,* family Accipitridae: two or three species, in particular the white-headed **African fish eagle** (*H. vocifer*).

fish·er /ˈfisHər/ ▶ **n. 1** a fisherman.
2 a large brown marten valued for its fur, found in North American woodland where it frequently preys on porcupines. Also called **PEKAN.** ● *Martes pennanti,* family Mustelidae.
– ORIGIN Old English *fiscere* 'fisherman,' of Germanic origin; related to Dutch *visser* and German *Fischer,* also to **FISH¹.**

Fish·er, St. John /ˈfisHər/ (1469–1535), English cleric. In 1504, he became bishop of Rochester and earned the disfavor of Henry VIII by opposing his divorce from Catherine of Aragon. When he refused to accept the king as supreme head of the English church, he was condemned to death. Feast day, June 22.

fish·er·folk /ˈfisHər,fōk/ ▶ **plural n.** people who catch fish for a living.

fish·er·man /ˈfisHərmən/ ▶ **n.** (pl. **fishermen**) a person who catches fish for a living or for sport. ■ a fishing boat.

fish·er·man knit (also **fisherman's knit**) ▶ **n.** a type of thick ribbed knitting.

fish·er·man's bend ▶ **n.** a knot tied by making a full turn around something (typically the ring of an anchor), a half hitch through the turn, and a half hitch around the standing part of the rope.

fish·er·wom·an /ˈfisHər,wo͝omən/ ▶ **n.** (pl. **fisherwomen**) a woman who catches fish, esp. for a living.

fish·er·y /ˈfisHərē/ ▶ **n.** (pl. **fisheries**) a place where fish are reared for commercial purposes. ■ a fishing ground or area where fish are caught. ■ the occupation or industry of catching or rearing fish.

fish·eye /ˈfisH,ī/ ▶ **n. 1** (also **fisheye lens**) a wide-angle lens with a field of vision covering up to 180°, the scale being reduced toward the edges.
2 informal a suspicious or unfriendly look: *Wally gave him the fisheye.*

fish farm ▶ **n.** a place where fish are artificially bred or cultivated, e.g., for food, to restock lakes for angling, or to supply aquariums.
– DERIVATIVES **fish farm·er n., fish farm·ing n.**

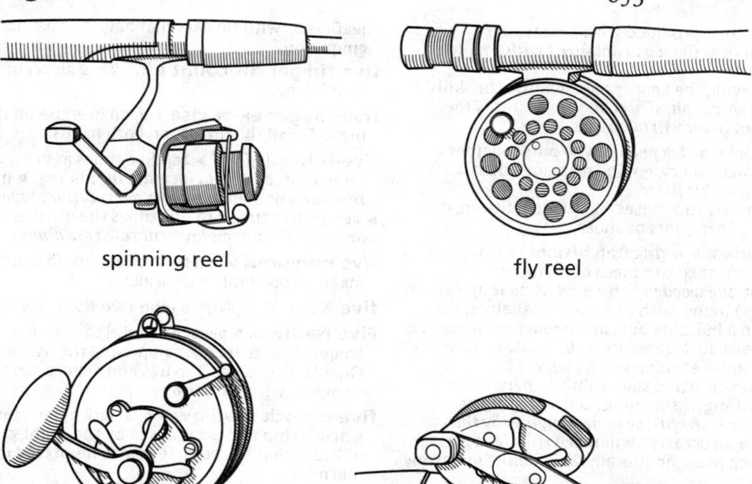

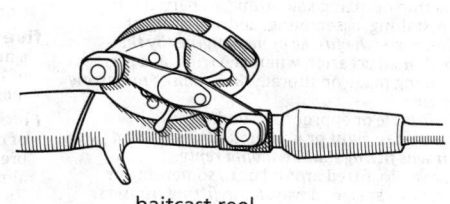

fishing reels

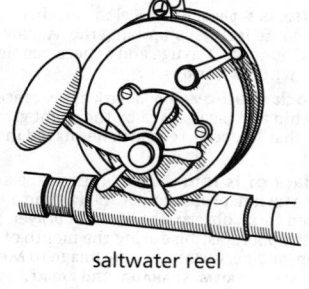

fish fin·ger ▶ **n.** British term for FISH STICK.

fish hawk ▶ **n.** another term for OSPREY.

fish·hook /ˈfisнˌho͝ok/ ▶ **n.** see HOOK (sense 1 of the noun).

fish·ing /ˈfisнiNG/ ▶ **n.** the activity of catching fish, either for food or as a sport.
– PHRASES **fishing expedition** a search or investigation undertaken with the hope, though not the stated purpose, of discovering information: *they worried about an FBI fishing expedition.*

fish·ing cat ▶ **n.** a small wild cat found in wetland habitats in India and Southeast Asia, having a light brown coat with dark spots, a ringed tail, and slightly webbed paws. ● *Felis viverrina*, family Felidae.

fish·ing fly ▶ **n.** a natural or artificial flying insect used as bait in fishing.

fish·ing line ▶ **n.** a long thread of silk or nylon attached to a baited hook, sometimes with a sinker or float, and used for catching fish.

fish·ing pole ▶ **n.** a fishing rod, esp. a simple one with no reel.

fish·ing reel ▶ **n.** a device for winding and unwinding fishing line, designed to be attached to a fishing rod.

fish·ing rod ▶ **n.** a long, tapering rod to which a fishing line is attached, typically on a reel.

fish knife ▶ **n.** a blunt knife with a broad blade for dressing, serving or eating fish.

fish lad·der ▶ **n.** a series of pools built like steps to enable fish to bypass a dam or waterfall.

fish louse ▶ **n.** an aquatic crustacean that is a parasite of fish, typically attached to the skin or gills. ● a free-swimming crustacean with a shieldlike carapace and a pair of suckers (class Branchiura: several genera, in particular *Argulus*). ● an elongated crustacean that becomes permanently attached to the host and typically highly modified (class Copepoda: several orders and numerous species).

fish meal (also **fishmeal**) ▶ **n.** ground dried fish used as fertilizer or animal feed.

fish·mon·ger /ˈfisнˌməNGgər, -ˌmäNGgər/ ▶ **n.** a person or store that sells fish for food.

fish·net /ˈfisнˌnet/ ▶ **n.** a fabric with an open mesh resembling a fishing net: [as modifier] *black fishnet stockings.*

fish·plate /ˈfisнˌplāt/ ▶ **n.** a flat piece of metal used to connect adjacent rails in a railroad track. ■ a flat piece of metal with ends like a fish's tail, used to position masonry.

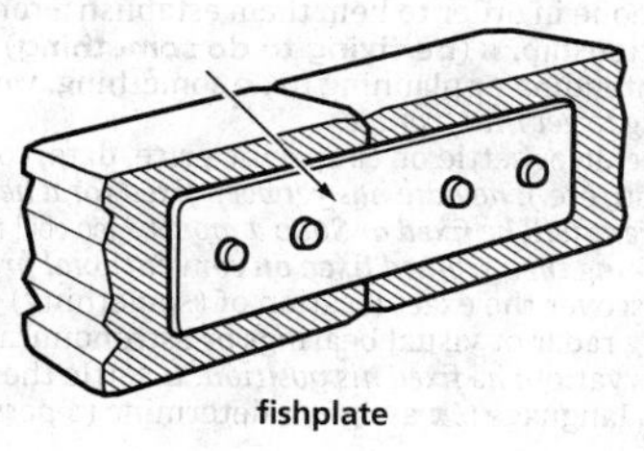
fishplate

fish·pond /ˈfisнˌpänd/ ▶ **n.** a pond in which live fish are kept. ■ an attraction at a fair where contestants use a rod and line to attempt to extract a prize, or a token representing a prize, from a pool or other enclosure.

fish sauce ▶ **n.** a Thai and Vietnamese sauce used as a flavoring or condiment, made from fermented anchovies and salt.

fish stick ▶ **n.** a small, oblong piece of fish fillet, usually breaded and fried.

fish sto·ry ▶ **n.** informal an incredible or far-fetched story.

fish·tail /ˈfisнˌtāl/ ▶ **n.** [usu. as modifier] an object that is forked like a fish's tail: *carved detail including fishtail terminals on the banisters.* ■ an uncontrolled sideways movement of the back of a motor vehicle: *he hit the brakes, sending the car into a fishtail that carried him across the street.*
▶ **v.** [no obj., usu. with adverbial of direction] (of a vehicle) make such a movement: *the vehicle fishtailed from one side of the road to the other.*

fish·way /ˈfisнˌwā/ ▶ **n.** another term for FISH LADDER.

fish·wife /ˈfisнˌwīf/ ▶ **n.** (pl. **fishwives** /-ˌwīvz/) **1** a coarse-mannered woman who is prone to shouting. **2** archaic a woman who sells fish.

fish·y /ˈfisнē/ ▶ **adj.** (**fishier, fishiest**) **1** of, relating to, or resembling fish or a fish: *a fishy smell.* **2** informal arousing feelings of doubt or suspicion: *I'm convinced there is something fishy going on.*
– DERIVATIVES **fish·i·ly** /ˈfisнəlē/ **adv.**, **fish·i·ness n.**

Fisk /fisk/, James (1834–72), US financier. He made his fortune in the stock manipulation that ruined the Erie Railroad, and with Jay Gould he engineered events that involved the US treasury in the Black Friday scandalous attempt to corner the gold market in 1869.

fisk /fisk/ ▶ **n.** Scottish archaic variant spelling of FISC.

fis·sile /ˈfisəl, ˈfisˌīl/ ▶ **adj.** (of an atom or element) able to undergo nuclear fission: *a fissile isotope.* ■ (chiefly of rock) easily split: *flat-bedded and very highly fissile shale.*
– DERIVATIVES **fis·sil·i·ty** /fiˈsilətē/ **n.**
– ORIGIN mid 17th cent. (in the sense 'easily split'): from Latin *fissilis*, from *fiss-* 'split, cracked,' from the verb *findere*.

fis·sion /ˈfisнən, ˈfizнən/ ▶ **n.** the action of dividing or splitting something into two or more parts: *the party dissolved into fission and acrimony.* ■ short for NUCLEAR FISSION. ■ Biology reproduction by means of a cell or organism dividing into two or more new cells or organisms: *bacteria divide by transverse binary fission.*
▶ **v.** [no obj.] (chiefly of atoms) undergo fission: *these heavy nuclei can also fission.*
– ORIGIN early 17th cent.: from Latin *fissio(n-)*, from *findere* 'to split.'

fis·sion·a·ble /ˈfisнənəbəl, ˈfizн-/ ▶ **adj.** another term for FISSILE.

fis·sion bomb ▶ **n.** another term for ATOM BOMB.

fis·sion-track dat·ing ▶ **n.** Geology a technique for establishing the age of a mineral sample from its uranium content. It involves microscopically counting tracks produced by uranium fission fragments and then establishing the existing concentration of uranium by counting again after irradiating the sample with neutrons.

fis·sip·a·rous /fiˈsipərəs/ ▶ **adj.** inclined to cause or undergo division into separate parts or groups: *She was unsuccessful in holding a fissiparous membership together.* ■ Biology (of an organism) reproducing by fission: *small fissiparous worms.*
– DERIVATIVES **fis·sip·a·rous·ness n.**
– ORIGIN mid 19th cent.: from Latin *fissus*, past participle of *findere* 'split,' on the pattern of *viviparous*.

fis·sure /ˈfisнər/ ▶ **n.** a long, narrow opening or line of breakage made by cracking or splitting, esp. in rock or earth. ■ chiefly Anatomy a long narrow opening in the form of a crack or groove, e.g., any of the spaces separating convolutions of the brain. ■ a state of incompatibility or disagreement: *the fissure between private sector business and the newly expanding public sector.*
▶ **v.** [with obj.] (usu. as adj. **fissured**) split or crack (something) to form a long narrow opening: *the skin becomes dry, fissured, and cracked.*
– ORIGIN late Middle English: from Old French, or from Latin *fissura*, from *findere* 'to split.'

fis·sure of Syl·vi·us /ˈsilvēəs/ ▶ **n.** another term for SYLVIAN FISSURE.

fist /fist/ ▶ **n.** a person's hand when the fingers are bent in toward the palm and held there tightly, typically in order to strike a blow or grasp something.
▶ **v. 1** [with obj.] hit with or as with the fists or a fist: *a fastball he fisted into left field.*
2 (also **fist-fuck**) [with obj.] vulgar slang penetrate (a person's anus or vagina) with one's fist.
– PHRASES **make a —— fist of** (or **at**) informal do something to the specified degree of success: *I think he's made a good fist of it.*
– DERIVATIVES **fist·ed adj.** [in combination] *bare-fisted*, **fist·ful** /-ˌfo͝ol/ **n.**
– ORIGIN Old English *fȳst*; related to Dutch *vuist* and German *Faust*.

fist·fight /ˈfistˌfīt/ ▶ **n.** a fight with bare fists.

fist·ic /ˈfistik/ ▶ **adj.** of or relating to boxing; pugilistic.

fist·i·cuffs /ˈfistiˌkəfs/ ▶ **plural n.** fighting with the fists.
– ORIGIN early 17th cent.: probably from obsolete *fisty* 'relating to the fists or to fistfighting' + CUFF².

fis·tu·la /ˈfiscнələ/ ▶ **n.** (pl. **fistulas** or **fistulae** /-lē/) Medicine an abnormal or surgically made passage between a hollow or tubular organ and the body surface, or between two hollow or tubular organs.
– DERIVATIVES **fis·tu·lar** /-lər/ **adj.**, **fis·tu·lous** /-ləs/ **adj.**
– ORIGIN late Middle English: from Latin, 'pipe, flute, fistula.' Compare with FESTER.

fit¹ /fit/ ▶ **adj.** (**fitter, fittest**) **1** [predic.] (of a thing) of a suitable quality, standard, or type to meet the required purpose: *the meat is fit for human consumption* | [with infinitive] *is the water clean and fit to drink?* ■ (of a person) having the requisite qualities or skills to undertake something competently: *he felt himself quite fit for battle* | [with infinitive] *Ted was ghastly pale and fit to do no more than switch channels.* ■ suitable and correct according to accepted social standards: *a fit subject on which to correspond.* ■ [with infinitive] informal (of a person or thing) having reached such an extreme condition as to be on the point of doing the thing specified: *he baited even his close companions until they were fit to kill him.* ■ informal ready: *well, are you fit?*
2 in good health, esp. because of regular physical exercise: *I swim regularly to keep fit* | figurative *the measures would ensure a leaner, fitter company.* ■ Brit. informal sexually attractive; good-looking.
▶ **v.** (**fits, fitting, fitted** or **fit**) [with obj.] **1** be of the right shape and size for: *those jeans still fit me* | [no obj.] *the shoes fit better after being stretched.* ■ (usu. **be fitted for**) try clothing on (someone) in order to make or alter it to the correct size: *she was about to be fitted for her costume.* ■ [no obj.] be of the right size, shape, or number to occupy a particular position or place: *Angela says we can all fit in her car.*
2 fix or put (something) into place: *they fitted smoke alarms to their home.* ■ (often **be fitted with**) provide (something) with a particular component or article: *most tools can be fitted with a new handle.* ■ join or cause to join together to form a whole: [no obj.] *it took a while to figure out how the confounded things fit together* | [with obj.] *many physicists tried to fit together the various pieces of the puzzle.*
3 be in agreement or harmony with; match: *the punishment should fit the crime.* ■ (of an attribute,

qualification, or skill) make (someone) suitable to fulfill a particular role or undertake a particular task: *an MS fits the student for a professional career.* ▶ **n.** the particular way in which something, esp. a garment or component, fits around or into something: *the dress was a perfect fit.* ■ the particular way in which a thing matches something else: *a close fit between teachers' qualifications and their teaching responsibilities.* ■ Statistics the correspondence between observed data and the values expected by theory.

– PHRASES **(as) fit as a fiddle** see FIDDLE. **fit the bill** see BILL[1]. **fit like a glove** see GLOVE. **fit to be tied** informal very angry: *Daddy was fit to be tied when I separated from Hugh.* **fit to bust** informal with great energy: *they laughed fit to bust.* **see** (or **think**) **fit** consider it correct or acceptable to do something: *why did the company see fit to give you the job?*

– PHRASAL VERBS **fit in** (of a person) be socially compatible with other members of a group: *he feels he should become tough to fit in with his friends.* ■ (of a thing) be in harmony with other things within a larger structure: *produce ideas that fit in with an established approach.* ■ (also **fit into**) (of a person or thing) constitute part of a particular situation or larger structure: *where do your sisters fit in?* **fit someone/something in** (or **into**) find room or have sufficient space for someone or something: *can you fit any more books into the box?* ■ succeed in finding time in a busy schedule to see someone or do something: *you're never too busy to fit exercise into your life.* **fit someone/something out** (or **up**) provide with the necessary equipment, supplies, clothes, or other items for a particular situation: *the cabin had been fitted out to a high standard.* **fit someone up** Brit. informal incriminate someone by falsifying evidence against them. **fit something on** Brit. try on (a garment).

– DERIVATIVES **fit·ly** /ˈfitlē/ **adv.**

– ORIGIN late Middle English: of unknown origin.

fit[2] ▶ **n.** a sudden uncontrollable outbreak of intense emotion, laughter, coughing, or other action or activity: *in a fit of temper* | *he got coughing fits.* ■ a sudden attack of convulsions and/or loss of consciousness, typical of epilepsy and some other medical conditions: *he thought she was having a fit.*

– PHRASES **have** (or **throw**) **a fit** informal be very surprised or angry: *my mother would have a fit if she heard that.* **in fits (of laughter)** informal highly amused: *he had us all in fits.* **in** (or **by**) **fits and starts** with irregular bursts of activity: *the machine tends to go forward in fits and starts.*

– ORIGIN Old English *fitt* 'conflict,' in Middle English 'position of danger or excitement,' also 'short period'; the sense 'sudden attack of illness' dates from the mid 16th cent.

fit[3] (also **fytte**) ▶ **n.** archaic a section of a poem.

– ORIGIN Old English *fitt*, perhaps the same word as FIT[2], or related to German *Fitze* 'skein of yarn,' in the obsolete sense 'thread with which weavers mark off a day's work.'

fitch /fiCH/ ▶ **n.** old-fashioned term for POLECAT. ■ (also **fitch fur**) the fur of a polecat.

– ORIGIN late Middle English (denoting the fur of a polecat): from Middle Dutch *visse* 'polecat.'

fitch·é /ˈfiCHˌā/ (also **fitchy** or **fitched**) ▶ **adj.** Heraldry (of a cross) having the foot extended into a point.

– ORIGIN late 16th cent.: from French *fiché*, past participle of *ficher* 'to fix.'

fit·ful /ˈfitfəl/ ▶ **adj.** active or occurring spasmodically or intermittently; not regular or steady: *a few hours' fitful sleep* | *business was fitful.*

– DERIVATIVES **fit·ful·ness n.**

fit·ful·ly /ˈfitfəlē/ ▶ **adv.** not regularly or continuously; intermittently: *he slept fitfully.*

fit·ment /ˈfitmənt/ ▶ **n.** (usu. **fitments**) chiefly Brit. a fixed item of furniture or piece of equipment, esp. in a house.

fit·ness /ˈfitnis/ ▶ **n.** the condition of being physically fit and healthy: *disease and lack of fitness are closely related* | [as modifier] *a fitness test.* ■ the quality of being suitable to fulfill a particular role or task: *he had a year in which to establish his fitness for the office.* ■ Biology an organism's ability to survive and reproduce in a particular environment: *if sharp teeth increase fitness, then genes causing teeth to be sharp will increase in frequency.*

fit-out ▶ **n.** chiefly Brit. an act of providing the necessary equipment for a house or apartment, esp. the final decoration and furniture.

fit·ted /ˈfitid/ ▶ **adj. 1** made or shaped to fill a space or to cover something closely or exactly: *the blouse has a fitted bodice* | *navy blue fitted sheets.* ■ chiefly Brit. (of a room) equipped with matching pieces of furniture built to be fixed into a particular space: *a fitted kitchen.*

2 attached to or provided with a particular component or article: *a pistol fitted with a match-grade barrel.*

3 [predic.] having the appropriate qualities or skills to do something: *physicists may not be fitted for involvement in industrial processes.*

fit·ter /ˈfitər/ ▶ **n. 1** a person who puts together or installs machinery, engine parts, or other equipment: *a pipe fitter.*

2 a person who supervises the cutting, fitting, or alteration of garments or shoes.

fit·ting /ˈfitiNG/ ▶ **n. 1** (often **fittings**) a small part on or attached to a piece of furniture or equipment: *the wooden fittings were made of walnut.* ■ (**fittings**) items, such as a stove or shelves, that are fixed in a building but can be removed when the owner moves: *little remains of the house's Victorian fittings.* Compare with FIXTURE (sense 1).

2 the action of fitting something, in particular: ■ the installing, assembling, and adjusting of machine parts: *the fitting of new engines by the shipyard.* ■ an occasion when one tries on a garment that is being made or altered: *she's coming tomorrow for a fitting.*

▶ **adj. 1** suitable or appropriate under the circumstances; right or proper: *a fitting reward* | [with clause] *it was fitting that he should reply.*

2 [in combination] fitted around or to something or someone in a specified way: *loose-fitting trousers.*

– DERIVATIVES **fit·ting·ly adv.**, **fit·ting·ness n.**

fit·ting room ▶ **n.** a room in a store in which one can try on clothes before deciding whether to purchase them.

Fitz·ger·ald[1], /fitsˈjerəld/ Ella (Jane) (1917–96), US jazz singer. Known for her distinctive style of scat singing, she appeared with Count Basie and Duke Ellington. From the mid 1950s, she made a series of recordings of songs by George Gershwin and Cole Porter.

Ella Fitzgerald

Fitz·ger·ald[2], F. Scott (1896–1940), US novelist; full name *Francis Scott Key Fitzgerald.* His novels, in particular *The Great Gatsby* (1925), provide a vivid portrait of the US during the jazz era of the 1920s. Fitzgerald later became part of an affluent and fashionable set living on the French Riviera; their lifestyle is reflected in *Tender is the Night* (1934), a semiautobiographical novel.

Fitz·Ger·ald con·trac·tion /fitsˈjerəld/ (also **FitzGerald–Lorentz contraction**) ▶ **n.** Physics another term for LORENTZ CONTRACTION.

– ORIGIN named after George. F. *FitzGerald* (1851–1901), Irish physicist, and H. A. LORENTZ, who independently postulated the theory in 1892.

Fiu·me /ˈfyo͞omā/ Italian name of RIJEKA.

five /fīv/ ▶ **cardinal number** equivalent to the sum of two and three; one more than four, or half of ten; 5: *a circlet of five petals* | *five of Sweden's top financial experts.* (Roman numeral: **v** or **V**) ■ a group or unit of five people or things: *the bulbs are planted in threes or fives.* ■ five years old: *he moved with his family to a fish farm when he was five.* ■ five o'clock: *at half past five.* ■ a size of garment or other merchandise denoted by five. ■ a playing card or domino with five spots or pips. ■ a five-dollar bill: *Joe counted his money: six fives and three twenties.*

– ORIGIN Old English *fīf*, of Germanic origin; related to Dutch *vijf* and German *fünf*, from an Indo-European root shared by Latin *quinque* and Greek *pente.*

five-a·larm ▶ **adj.** [attrib.] informal (of a fire) very large or fierce. ■ (of food, such as chilies) extremely pungent; hot.

five-and-dime (also **five-and-dime store** or **five-and-ten**) ▶ **n.** a store selling a wide variety of inexpensive household and personal goods. ■ historical a store where all the articles were priced at five or ten cents.

five-fin·ger (also **fivefinger**) ▶ **n.** any of a number of plants with leaves that are divided into five leaflets or with flowers that have five petals, such as cinquefoil.

five-fin·ger dis·count ▶ **n.** informal an act of shoplifting.

five-fin·ger ex·er·cise ▶ **n.** an exercise on the piano for all the fingers on both hands.

five·fold /ˈfīvˌfōld/ ▶ **adj.** five times as great or as numerous: *a fivefold increase in funding.* ■ having five parts or elements: *fivefold rotational symmetry.* ▶ **adv.** by five times; to five times the number or amount: *the unemployment rate rose almost fivefold.*

five hun·dred ▶ **n.** a form of euchre in which making 500 points wins a game.

five Ks /kāz/ ▶ **plural n.** (**the five Ks**) See KHALSA.

Five Na·tions ▶ **plural n.** historical the original Iroquois confederacy, comprising the Mohawk, Oneida, Onondaga, Cayuga and Seneca peoples. Compare with SIX NATIONS.

five o'clock shad·ow ▶ **n.** a dark appearance on a man's chin and face caused by the slight growth of beard that has occurred since he shaved in the morning.

Five Pil·lars of Is·lam the five duties expected of every Muslim: profession of the faith in a prescribed form, observance of ritual prayer, giving alms to the poor, fasting during the month of Ramadan, and performing a pilgrimage to Mecca. See HAJJ, SALAT, SAWM, SHAHADA, and ZAKAT.

fiv·er /ˈfīvər/ ▶ **n.** informal a five-dollar bill. ■ Brit. a five-pound note.

fives /fīvz/ ▶ **plural n.** [treated as sing.] a game, played esp. in the UK, in which a ball is hit with a gloved hand or a bat against the walls of a court with three walls (**Eton fives**) or four walls (**Rugby fives**).

– ORIGIN mid 17th cent.: plural of FIVE used as a singular noun; the significance is unknown.

five sens·es ▶ **plural n.** (**the five senses**) the faculties of sight, smell, hearing, taste, and touch.

five-spice (also **five-spice powder**) ▶ **n.** a blend of five powdered spices, typically fennel seeds, cinnamon, cloves, star anise, and peppercorns, used in Chinese cuisine.

five-star ▶ **adj.** (esp. of a hotel or restaurant) given five stars in a grading system, typically one in which this denotes the highest class or quality: *a luxury five-star hotel.* ■ (in the US armed forces) having or denoting the highest military rank (awarded only in wartime), distinguished by five stars on the uniform: *a five-star general.*

five-year plan ▶ **n.** (esp. in the former Soviet Union) a government plan for economic development over five years. The first such plan in the Soviet Union was inaugurated in 1928.

fix /fiks/ ▶ **v.** [with obj.] **1** [with obj.] fasten (something) securely in a particular place or position: *fix the clamp on a rail* | *the upper jaw of an amphibian is firmly fixed to the skull.* ■ lodge or implant (an idea, image, or memory) firmly in a person's mind: *he turned back to fix the scene in his mind.*

2 (**fix something on/upon**) direct one's eyes, attention, or mind steadily or unwaveringly toward: *I fixed my attention on the tower.* ■ [no obj.] (**fix on/upon**) (of a person's eyes, attention, or mind) be directed steadily or unwaveringly toward: *her gaze fixed on Jess.* ■ attract and hold (a person's attention or gaze): *their taut relationship fixes your attention.* ■ (**fix someone with**) look at someone unwaveringly: *she fixed her nephew with an unwavering stare.*

3 mend; repair: *you should fix that shelf.* ■ (**fix something up**) do the necessary work to improve or adapt something: *we want to fix up the house before we sell it.* ■ make arrangements for (something); organize: *he's sent her on ahead to fix things up* | *I've fixed it for you to see him on Thursday.* ■ informal restore order or tidiness to (something, esp. one's hair, clothes, or makeup): *Laura was fixing her hair.* ■ informal prepare or arrange for the provision of (food or drink): [with two objs.] *they were fixing him breakfast* | *Ruth fixed herself a cold drink.* ■ (**fix someone up**) informal arrange for someone to have something; provide someone with something: *I'll fix you up with a room.* ■ (**fix someone up**) informal arrange for someone to meet or go out with someone in order to help them establish a romantic relationship. ■ (**be fixing to do something**) informal be intending or planning to do something: *you're fixing to get into trouble.*

4 decide or settle on (a specific price, date, course of action, etc.): *no date has yet been fixed for a hearing* | *the rent will be fixed at $600 a month* | [no obj.] *their thinking then seemed fixed on conventional projects.* ■ discover the exact location of (something) by using radar or visual bearings or astronomical observation: *he fixed his position.* ■ settle the form of (a language). ■ assign or determine (a person's

liability or responsibility) for legal purposes: *there are no facts that fix the defendant with liability.*
5 make (something) permanent or static in nature: *the rate of interest is fixed for the life of the loan.* ■ make (a dye, photographic image, or drawing) permanent. ■ Biology preserve or stabilize (a specimen) with a chemical substance prior to microscopy or other examination: *specimens were fixed in buffered formalin.* ■ (of a plant or microorganism) assimilate (nitrogen or carbon dioxide) by forming a nongaseous compound: *lupines fix gaseous nitrogen in their root nodules.*
6 informal influence the outcome of (something, esp. a race, contest, or election) by illegal or underhanded means: *the foundation denies fixing races.* ■ put (an enemy or rival) out of action, esp. by killing them: *don't you tell nobody, or I'll fix you good!*
7 informal [no obj.] take an injection of a narcotic drug.
8 castrate or spay (an animal); neuter.
▶ **n. 1** [in sing.] informal a difficult or awkward situation from which it is hard to extricate oneself; a predicament: *how on earth did you get into such a fix?*
2 informal a dose of a narcotic drug to which one is addicted: *he hadn't had his fix.* ■ figurative a thing or activity that gives a person a feeling of euphoria or pleasure and that it is difficult to do without: *that rush of adrenaline that is the fix of the professional newsman.*
3 informal a solution to a problem, esp. one that is hastily devised or makeshift: *there is going to be no* **quick fix** *to the recession.*
4 a position determined by visual or radio bearings or astronomical observations.
5 [in sing.] informal a dishonest or underhanded arrangement: *obviously, his appointment was a fix.*
– PHRASES **get a fix on** determine the position of (something) by visual or radio bearings or astronomical observation. ■ informal assess or determine the nature or facts of; obtain a clear understanding of: *it is hard to get a fix on their ages.* **if it ain't broke, don't fix it** proverb don't attempt to improve something that is already working well: *Stick with the plan! If it ain't broke don't fix it.*
– DERIVATIVES **fix·a·ble** /ˈfiksəbəl/ **adj.**
– ORIGIN late Middle English: partly from Old French *fix* 'fixed,' partly from medieval Latin *fixare* 'to fix,' both from Latin *fixus*, past participle of *figere* 'fix, fasten.' The noun dates from the early 19th cent.

fix·ate /ˈfikˌsāt/ ▶ **v.** [with obj.] **1** (usu. **be fixated on/upon**) cause (someone) to acquire an obsessive attachment to someone or something: *she has for some time been fixated on photography.* ■ [no obj.] (**fixate on/upon**) acquire such an obsessive attachment to: *it is important not to fixate on animosity.* ■ (in Freudian theory) arrest (a person or their libidinal energy) at an immature stage, causing an obsessive attachment.
2 technical direct one's eyes toward: *subjects fixated a central point* | [no obj.] *there is tendency to fixate near the beginning of the line of print.*
– ORIGIN late 19th cent.: from Latin *fixus*, past participle of *figere* (see **FIX**) + **-ATE**[3].

fix·a·tion /fikˈsāSHən/ ▶ **n. 1** an obsessive interest in or feeling about someone or something: *his* ***fixation on*** *the details of other people's erotic lives* | *our* ***fixation with*** *diet and fitness.* ■ Psychoanalysis the arresting of part of the libido at an immature stage, causing an obsessive attachment: *fixation at the oral phase might result in dependence on others* | *an oral-maternal fixation.*
2 the action of making something firm or stable: *sand dune fixation.* ■ Biochemistry the process by which some plants and microorganisms incorporate gaseous nitrogen or carbon dioxide to form nongaseous compounds: *his work on nitrogen fixation in plants.* ■ Biology the process of preserving or stabilizing (a specimen) with a chemical substance prior to microscopy or other examination: *biopsy specimens were placed in cassettes before fixation in formalin.*
3 technical the action of concentrating the eyes directly on something: *during the period of total blindness there was a complete absence of visual fixation.*
– ORIGIN late Middle English (originally as an alchemical term denoting the process of reducing a volatile spirit or essence to a permanent bodily form): from medieval Latin *fixatio(n-)*, from *fixare* (see **FIX**).

fix·a·tive /ˈfiksətiv/ ▶ **n. 1** a chemical substance used to preserve or stabilize biological material prior to microscopy or other examination: *an alcoholic fixative* | *ten double drops of fixative.* ■ a substance used to stabilize the volatile components of perfume. ■ a liquid sprayed onto a pastel or charcoal drawing to fix colors or prevent smudging.
2 a substance used to keep things in position or stick them together: *the swift glues these thin twigs to a wall using its own saliva as a fixative.*
▶ **adj.** (of a substance) used to fix or stabilize something.

fixed /fikst/ ▶ **adj. 1** fastened securely in position: *a fixed iron ladder down the port side.* ■ (esp. of a price, rate, or time) predetermined and not subject to or able to be changed: *most trusts locked investors in for a fixed period.* ■ (of a person's expression) held for a long time without changing, esp. to conceal other feelings: *a fixed smile.* ■ (of a view or idea) held inflexibly: *the fixed assumptions of the cold war.*
2 [predic.] (**fixed for**) informal situated with regard to: *how's the club fixed for money now?*
3 (of a sports contest) having the outcome dishonestly predetermined: *the fight's fixed—the ref has your card marked.*
– DERIVATIVES **fix·ed·ly** /ˈfiksidlē/ **adv.**, **fix·ed·ness** /ˈfiksidnis/ **n.**

fixed as·sets ▶ **plural n.** assets that are purchased for long-term use and are not likely to be converted quickly into cash, such as land, buildings, and equipment. Compare with **CURRENT ASSETS**.

fixed cap·i·tal ▶ **n.** capital invested in fixed assets.

fixed charge ▶ **n.** a liability to a creditor that relates to specific assets of a company.

fixed costs ▶ **plural n.** business costs, such as rent, that are constant whatever the quantity of goods or services produced.

fixed-do /dō/ (Brit. **fixed-doh**) ▶ **adj.** [attrib.] Music denoting a system of solmization in which C is called "do," D is called "re," etc., irrespective of the key in which they occur. Compare with **MOVABLE-DO**.

fixed fo·cus ▶ **n.** a camera focus that cannot be adjusted, typically used with a small-aperture lens having a large depth of field.

fixed i·de·a ▶ **n.** another term for **IDÉE FIXE**.

fixed in·come ▶ **n.** an income from a pension or investment that is set at a particular figure and does not vary (as a dividend) or rise with the rate of inflation.

fixed-line ▶ **adj.** denoting or relating to telecommunications systems using cables laid across land, as opposed to cellular radio systems.

fixed oil ▶ **n.** a nonvolatile oil of animal or plant origin.

fixed point ▶ **n.** Physics a well-defined reproducible temperature that can be used as a reference point, e.g., one defined by a change of phase.
▶ **adj.** (**fixed-point**) Computing denoting a mode of representing a number by a single sequence of digits whose values depend on their location relative to a predetermined radix point: *these computers perform arithmetic in fixed-point binary format.* Often contrasted with **FLOATING-POINT**.

fixed star ▶ **n.** see **STAR** (sense 1 of the noun).

fixed-wing ▶ **adj.** [attrib.] denoting aircraft of the conventional type as opposed to those with rotating wings, such as helicopters.

fix·er /ˈfiksər/ ▶ **n. 1** a person who makes arrangements for other people, esp. of an illicit or devious kind.
2 a substance used for fixing a photographic image.

fix·er-up·per ▶ **n.** informal a house in need of repairs (used chiefly in connection with the purchase of such a house).

fix·ing /ˈfiksiNG/ ▶ **n. 1** the action of fixing something: *artificial price fixing.*
2 (**fixings**) apparatus or equipment for a particular purpose: *picnic fixings.* ■ the ingredients necessary to make a dish or meal: *have all the fixings ready before starting.* ■ Brit. screws, bolts, or other items used to fix or assemble building material, furniture, or equipment.

fix·it /ˈfiksit/ ▶ **n.** informal a person known for repairing things or putting things in order: *he pictured himself as a Mr. Fixit.* ■ [usu. as modifier] an act of repairing or putting something right: *a fixit shop.*
– ORIGIN early 20th cent.: from *Little Miss Fixit*, the title of a musical show.

fix·i·ty /ˈfiksitē/ ▶ **n.** the state of being unchanging or permanent: *the fixity of his stare.*
– ORIGIN mid 17th cent. (denoting the property of a substance of not evaporating or losing weight when heated): partly from obsolete *fix* 'fixed,' partly from French *fixité*.

fix·ture /ˈfiksCHər/ ▶ **n. 1** a piece of equipment or furniture that is fixed in position in a building or vehicle: *a light fixture.* ■ (**fixtures**) articles attached to a house or land and considered legally part of it so that they normally remain in place when an owner moves: *the hotel retains many original* ***fixtures and fittings.*** Compare with **FITTING** (sense 1 of the noun)). ■ informal a person or thing that is established in a particular place or situation: *palm readers were a fixture in most '40s nightclubs.*
2 Brit. a sports event that takes place on a particular date.
– ORIGIN late 16th cent. (in the sense 'fixing, becoming fixed'): alteration (first found in Shakespeare) of obsolete *fixure* (from late Latin *fixura*, from Latin *figere* 'to fix'), with *t* inserted on the pattern of *mixture*.

fizz /fiz/ ▶ **v.** [no obj.] (of a liquid) produce bubbles of gas and make a hissing sound: *the mixture fizzed like mad.* ■ make a buzzing or crackling sound: *lightning starts to crackle and fizz.* ■ [with adverbial] move with or display excitement, exuberance, or liveliness: *anticipation began to fizz through his veins.*
▶ **n.** effervescence: *the champagne had lost its fizz.* ■ informal an effervescent drink, esp. sparkling wine: *a bottle of grapefruit fizz.* ■ exuberance; liveliness: *she saw I had lost some of my fizz.*
– ORIGIN mid 17th cent.: imitative.

fiz·zle /ˈfizəl/ ▶ **v.** [no obj.] end or fail in a weak or disappointing way: *their threatened revolt* ***fizzled out*** *at yesterday's meeting.* ■ make a feeble hissing or spluttering sound: *the strobe lights fizzled and flickered.*
▶ **n.** a failure: *in the end the fireworks were a fizzle.* ■ a feeble hissing or spluttering sound: *the electric fizzle of the waves.*
– ORIGIN late Middle English (in the sense 'break wind quietly'): probably imitative (compare with **FIZZ**), but perhaps related to Middle English *fist* (see **FEISTY**). Current senses date from the 19th cent.

fiz·zog /ˈfizˌäg, fizˈäg/ ▶ **n.** another term for **PHIZ**.

fiz·zy /ˈfizē/ ▶ **adj.** (**fizzier**, **fizziest**) (of a beverage) containing bubbles of gas; effervescent: *fizzy mineral water.* ■ full of energy or exuberance; lively: *fizzy new wave pop.*
– DERIVATIVES **fizz·i·ly** /ˈfizəlē/ **adv.**, **fizz·i·ness** /ˈfizēnis/ **n.**

fjord /fēˈôrd, fyôrd/ (also **fiord**) ▶ **n.** a long, narrow, deep inlet of the sea between high cliffs, as in Norway and Iceland, typically formed by submergence of a glaciated valley.
– ORIGIN late 17th cent.: Norwegian, from Old Norse *fjǫrthr*. Compare with **FIRTH**.

FL ▶ **abbr.** Florida (in official postal use).

fL ▶ **abbr.** foot-Lambert.

fl. ▶ **abbr.** ■ floor. ■ floruit. ■ fluid.

Fla. ▶ **abbr.** Florida.

flab /flab/ ▶ **n.** informal soft loose flesh on a person's body; fat.
– ORIGIN 1950s: back-formation from **FLABBY**.

flab·ber·gast /ˈflabərˌgast/ ▶ **v.** [with obj.] (usu. as adj. **flabbergasted**) informal surprise (someone) greatly; astonish: *this news has left me totally flabbergasted.*
– ORIGIN late 18th cent.: of unknown origin.

flab·by /ˈflabē/ ▶ **adj.** (**flabbier**, **flabbiest**) (of a part of a person's body) soft, loose, and fleshy: *this exercise helps to flatten a flabby stomach.* ■ (of a person) having soft loose flesh. ■ not tightly controlled, powerful, or effective: *the quartet playing was uncommitted and flabby.*
– DERIVATIVES **flab·bi·ly** /ˈflabəlē/ **adv.**, **flab·bi·ness** /ˈflabēnis/ **n.**
– ORIGIN late 17th cent.: alteration of earlier *flappy*.

fla·bel·lum /fləˈbeləm/ ▶ **n.** (pl. **flabella** /-ˈbelə/) a fan, esp. an elegant, ornamental one used in Christian ritual. ■ Biology, historical a fan-shaped organ, part, or anatomical structure.

flac·cid /ˈfla(k)səd/ ▶ **adj.** (of part of the body) soft and hanging loosely or limply, esp. so as to look or feel unpleasant: *she took his flaccid hand in hers.* ■ (of plant tissue) drooping or inelastic through lack of water. ■ lacking force or effectiveness: *the flaccid leadership campaign was causing concern.*
– DERIVATIVES **flac·cid·i·ty** /fla(k)ˈsidətē/ **n.**, **flac·cid·ly adv.**
– ORIGIN early 17th cent.: from French *flaccide* or Latin *flaccidus*, from *flaccus* 'flabby.'

flack[1] /flak/ informal ▶ **n.** a publicity agent: *a public relations flack.*
▶ **v.** [with obj.] publicize or promote (something or someone): *a crass ambulance-chaser who flacks* ***himself*** *in TV ads* | [no obj.] *the local news media shamelessly* ***flack for*** *the organizing committee.*
– DERIVATIVES **flack·er·y** /-ərē/ **n.**
– ORIGIN 1940s: of unknown origin.

flack[2] ▶ **n.** variant spelling of **FLAK**.

flac·on /ˈflakən, flaˈkôN/ ▶ **n.** (pl. **flacons** pronunc. same or /-kənz/) a small stoppered bottle, esp. one for perfume.
– ORIGIN early 19th cent.: French, 'flask.'

PRONUNCIATION KEY ə *ago, up*; ər *over, fur*; a *hat*; ā *ate*; ä *car*; e *let*; ē *see*; i *fit*; ī *by*; NG *sing*; ō *go*; ô *law, for*; oi *toy*; o͝o *good*; o͞o *goo*; ou *out*; TH *thin*; T͟H *then*; ZH *vision*

flag[1] /flag/ ▶ **n. 1** a piece of cloth or similar material, typically oblong or square, attachable by one edge to a pole or rope and used as the symbol or emblem of a country or institution or as a decoration during public festivities: *the American flag.* ■ used in reference to the country to which a person has allegiance: *the private's heroism served as an example for every soldier under the flag.* ■ a ship's country of registry. ■ a small piece of cloth, typically attached at one edge to a pole, used as a marker or signal in various sports: *jumped the starter's flag, did he?* ■ the ensign carried by a flagship as an emblem of an admiral's rank.
2 a device, symbol, or drawing typically resembling a flag, used as a marker: *golf courses are indicated by a numbered flag on the map.* ■ Computing a variable used to indicate a particular property of the data in a record.
3 a hook attached to the stem of a musical note, determining the rhythmic value of the note.
▶ **v.** (**flags, flagging, flagged**) [with obj.] **1** mark (an item) for attention or treatment in a specified way: *"greatfully" would be flagged as a misspelling of "gratefully."* ■ draw attention to: *problems often flag the need for organizational change.* ■ Football charge (a player) with a penalty by dropping a penalty flag: *a play in which he was flagged for being offside.*
2 [with obj.] direct (someone) to go in the specified direction by waving a flag or using hand signals: *have him flagged off the course.* ■ (**flag someone/something down**) signal to a vehicle or driver to stop, esp. by waving one's arm: *she flagged down a patrol car.* ■ [no obj.] (of an official in football, soccer, and other sports) raise or throw a flag to indicate a breach of the rules: *the rookie cornerback managed to get flagged for three penalties in one game.*
3 provide or decorate with a flag or flags. ■ register (a vessel) in a specific country, under whose flag it then sails: *the flagging out of much of the fleet to flags of convenience.*
– PHRASES **fly the flag** (of a ship) be registered in a particular country and sail under its flag. ■ (also **show** or **carry** or **wave the flag**) represent or demonstrate support for one's country, political party, or organization, esp. when one is abroad: *he will never consider buying an import, because he likes to fly the flag.* **show the flag** (of a naval vessel) make an official visit to a foreign port, esp. as a show of strength. **wrap oneself in the flag** make an excessive show of one's patriotism, esp. for political ends.
– DERIVATIVES **flag·ger** n.
– ORIGIN mid 16th cent.: perhaps from obsolete *flag* 'drooping,' of unknown ultimate origin.

flag[2] ▶ **n.** a flat stone slab, typically rectangular or square, used for paving.
– DERIVATIVES **flagged** adj. [often in combination] *stone-flagged steps.*
– ORIGIN late Middle English (also in the sense 'turf, sod'): probably of Scandinavian origin and related to Icelandic *flag* 'spot from which a sod has been cut' and Old Norse *flaga* 'slab of stone.'

flag[3] ▶ **n.** a plant with sword-shaped leaves that grow from a rhizome. ● a plant of the iris family (genus *Iris*, family Iridaceae). See **BLUE FLAG** (sense 1); **YELLOW FLAG** (sense 2) ● see **SWEET FLAG.** ■ the long slender leaf of such a plant.
– ORIGIN late Middle English: related to Middle Dutch *flag* and Danish *flæg*; of unknown ultimate origin.

flag[4] ▶ **v.** (**flags, flagging, flagged**) [no obj.] (of a person) become tired, weaker, or less enthusiastic: *if you begin to flag, there is an excellent café to revive you.* ■ (often as adj. **flagging**) (esp. of an activity or quality) become weaker or less dynamic: *she should make another similar film to revive her flagging career.*
– ORIGIN mid 16th cent. (in the sense 'flap about loosely, hang down'): related to obsolete *flag* 'hanging down.'

Flag Day ▶ **n.** June 14, the anniversary of the adoption of the Stars and Stripes as the official US flag in 1777.

flag·el·lant /ˈflajələnt, fləˈjelənt/ ▶ **n.** a person who subjects themselves or others to flogging, either as a religious discipline or for sexual gratification.
– ORIGIN late 16th cent.: from Latin *flagellant-* 'whipping,' from the verb *flagellare*, from *flagellum* 'whip' (see **FLAGELLUM**).

flag·el·late[1] /ˈflajəˌlāt/ ▶ **v.** [with obj.] flog (someone), either as a religious discipline or for sexual gratification: *he flagellated himself with branches.*
– DERIVATIVES **flag·el·la·tor** /-ˌlātər/ n., **flag·el·la·to·ry** /fləˈjeləˌtôrē/ adj.
– ORIGIN early 17th cent.: from Latin *flagellat-* 'whipped,' from *flagellare*.

flag·el·late[2] /ˈflajələt, -ˌlāt/ Zoology ▶ **n.** a protozoan that has one or more flagella used for swimming. ● Several phyla in the kingdom Protista (formerly subphylum Mastigophora, phylum Protozoa), including forms such as euglena that are sometimes regarded as algae.
▶ **adj.** (of a cell or single-celled organism) bearing one or more flagella: *motile flagellate cells.*
– ORIGIN mid 19th cent.: from **FLAGELLUM** + **-ATE**[2].

flag·el·la·tion /ˌflajəˈlāsʜən/ ▶ **n.** flogging or beating, either as a religious discipline or for sexual gratification: *pursuing the path of penance and flagellation.*

fla·gel·lin /fləˈjelən/ ▶ **n.** the structural protein of bacterial flagella.

fla·gel·lum /ˌfləˈjeləm/ ▶ **n.** (pl. **flagella** /-ˈjelə/) Biology a slender threadlike structure, esp. a microscopic whiplike appendage that enables many protozoa, bacteria, spermatozoa, etc., to swim.
– DERIVATIVES **fla·gel·lar** /fləˈjelər, ˈflajələr/ adj.
– ORIGIN early 19th cent. (denoting a whip or scourge): from Latin, diminutive of *flagrum* 'scourge.'

flag·eo·let[1] /ˌflajəˈlet, -ˈlā/ ▶ **n.** a small flutelike instrument resembling a recorder but with four finger holes on top and two thumb holes below. ■ another term for **TIN WHISTLE.**
– ORIGIN mid 17th cent.: from French, diminutive of Old French *flageol*, from Provençal *flaujol*, of unknown origin.

flag·eo·let[2] ▶ **n.** a French kidney bean of a small variety used in cooking.
– ORIGIN late 19th cent.: from French, based on Latin *phaseolus* 'bean.'

flag·fish /ˈflagˌfisʜ/ ▶ **n.** (pl. **same** or **flagfishes**) any of a number of small fish with prominent or boldly marked fins, in particular: ● a colorful freshwater fish with spots and iridescent scales, native to Florida (*Jordanella floridae*, family Cyprinodontidae).

flag-fly·ing ▶ **n.** the action of making a public display to promote the interests of one's country, or of another organization or group.

flag foot·ball ▶ **n.** a modified form of football in which ballcarriers are downed by pulling off a marker, or flag, loosely attached to a belt, rather than by tackling.

Flagg /flag/, James Montgomery (1877–1960), US artist. He created the World War I recruiting poster that features Uncle Sam's pointing finger and the caption "I Want You."

fla·gi·tious /fləˈjisʜəs/ ▶ **adj.** (of a person or their actions) criminal; villainous.
– DERIVATIVES **fla·gi·tious·ly** adv., **fla·gi·tious·ness** n.
– ORIGIN late Middle English: from Latin *flagitiosus*, from *flagitium* 'importunity, shameful crime,' from *flagitare* 'demand earnestly.'

Flag·ler /ˈflaglər/, Henry Morrison (1830–1913), US financier. With John D. Rockefeller, he developed the Standard Oil Company. He organized the Florida East Coast railroad in 1886.

flag·man /ˈflagmən/ ▶ **n.** (pl. **flagmen**) a person who gives signals with a flag, esp. on railroad lines or during road construction.

flag of con·ven·ience ▶ **n.** a flag of a country under which a ship is registered in order to avoid financial charges or restrictive regulations in the owner's country.

flag of·fi·cer ▶ **n.** an admiral, vice admiral, or rear admiral. ■ the commodore of a yacht club.
– ORIGIN mid 17th cent.: *flag*, because the officer had the privilege of carrying a flag that denoted his rank.

flag of truce ▶ **n.** a white flag indicating a desire for a truce.

flag·on /ˈflagən/ ▶ **n.** a large container in which drink is served, typically with a handle and spout: *there was a flagon of beer in his vast fist.* ■ the amount of liquid held in such a container: *he had at least three flagons of wine down him already.* ■ a similar container used to hold the wine for the Eucharist. ■ a large bottle in which wine or cider is sold, typically holding about 2 pints (1.13 liters).
– ORIGIN late Middle English: from Old French *flacon*, based on late Latin *flasco*, *flascon-*, of unknown origin. Compare with **FLASK.**

flag·pole /ˈflagˌpōl/ ▶ **n.** a pole used for flying a flag.
– PHRASES **run something up the flagpole (to see who salutes)** test the popularity of a new idea or proposal: *the idea was first run up the flagpole in 1997.*

flag rank ▶ **n.** the rank attained by flag officers.

fla·grant /ˈflāgrənt/ ▶ **adj.** (of something considered wrong or immoral) conspicuously or obviously offensive: *his flagrant bad taste | a flagrant violation of the law.*
– DERIVATIVES **fla·gran·cy** /-grənsē/ n., **fla·grant·ly** adv.
– ORIGIN late 15th cent. (in the sense 'blazing, resplendent'): from French, or from Latin *flagrant-* 'blazing,' from the verb *flagrare.*

flag·ship /ˈflagˌsʜip/ ▶ **n.** the ship in a fleet that carries the commanding admiral. ■ the best or most important thing owned or produced by a particular organization: ***this bill is the flagship of the administration's legislative program*** | [as modifier] ***their flagship product.***

Flag·staff /ˈflagˌstaf/ a city in north central Arizona, near the San Francisco Peaks, home to Lowell Observatory and the University of Northern Arizona; pop. 60,222 (est. 2008).

flag·staff /ˈflagˌstaf/ ▶ **n.** another term for **FLAGPOLE.**

flag sta·tion (also **flag stop**) ▶ **n.** historical a station at which trains stop only if signaled to do so. ■ a small town or a place of no consequence: *we must go back some years to a little flag station in a pinewood clearing.*

flag·stick /ˈflagˌstik/ ▶ **n.** Golf another term for **PIN** (sense 2 of the noun).

flag·stone /ˈflagˌstōn/ ▶ **n.** a flat stone slab, typically rectangular or square, used for paving.
– DERIVATIVES **flag·stoned** adj.

flag-wav·ing ▶ **n.** the expression of patriotism in a populist and emotional way: *what began as jingoistic flag-waving deteriorated into an international crisis.*
– DERIVATIVES **flag-wav·er** n.

flail /flāl/ ▶ **n.** a threshing tool consisting of a wooden staff with a short heavy stick swinging from it. ■ a similar device used as a weapon or for flogging. ■ a machine for threshing or slashing, with a similar action.
▶ **v. 1** wave or swing or cause to wave or swing wildly: [no obj.] *his arms were flailing helplessly* | [with obj.] *he flailed his arms and drove her away.* ■ [no obj.] flounder; struggle uselessly: *I was flailing about in the water | he flailed around on the snow.*
2 [with obj.] beat; flog: *he escorted them, flailing their shoulders with his cane.*
– ORIGIN Middle English, from Old English *fligel*, based on Latin *flagellum* 'whip' (see **FLAGELLUM**); probably influenced in Middle English by Old French *flaiel* or Dutch *vlegel.*

flair /fler/ ▶ **n. 1** [in sing.] a special or instinctive aptitude or ability for doing something well: *she had a flair for languages | none of us had much artistic flair.*
2 stylishness and originality: *she dressed with flair.*
– ORIGIN late 19th cent.: from French, from *flairer* 'to smell,' based on Latin *fragrare* 'smell sweet.' Compare with **FRAGRANT.**

flak /flak/ (also **flack**) ▶ **n.** antiaircraft fire. ■ strong criticism: *you must be strong enough to take the flak if things go wrong.*
– ORIGIN 1930s: from German, abbreviation of *Fliegerabwehrkanone*, literally 'aircraft-defense gun.'

flake[1] /flāk/ ▶ **n. 1** a small, flat, thin piece of something, typically one that has broken away or been peeled off from a larger piece: *paint peeling off the walls in unsightly flakes | flakes of pastry.* ■ a snowflake. ■ Archaeology a piece of hard stone chipped off for use as a tool by prehistoric humans: [as modifier] *flake tools.* ■ thin pieces of crushed dried food or bait for fish.
2 informal a crazy or eccentric person.
▶ **v. 1** [no obj.] come or fall away from a surface in thin pieces: *the paint had been flaking off for years.* ■ lose small fragments from the surface: *my nails have started to flake at the ends.*
2 [with obj.] break or divide (food) into thin pieces: *flake the fish* | (as adj. **flaked**) *flaked haddock.* ■ [no obj.] (of food, esp. when well cooked) come apart in thin pieces.
– ORIGIN Middle English: the immediate source is unknown, the senses perhaps deriving from different words; probably of Germanic origin and related to **FLAG**[2] and **FLAW**[1].

flake[2] ▶ **n.** a rack or shelf for storing or drying food such as fish.
– ORIGIN Middle English (denoting a wicker framework): perhaps of Scandinavian origin and related to Old Norse *flaki*, *fleki* 'wicker shield' and Danish *flage* 'wicker framework.'

flake[3] ▶ **v.** [no obj.] (**flake out**) informal fall asleep; drop from exhaustion.
– ORIGIN late 15th cent. (in the senses 'become languid' and (of a garment) 'fall in folds'): variant of obsolete *flack* and the verb **FLAG**[4]. The current sense dates from the 1940s.

flake[4] (also **fake** /fāk/) Nautical ▶ **n.** a single turn of a coiled rope or hawser.
▶ **v.** [with obj.] lay (a rope) in loose coils in order to prevent it from tangling: *a cable had to be flaked out.* ■ lay (a sail) down in folds on either side of the boom.
– ORIGIN early 17th cent. (as a noun): of unknown origin; compare with German *Flechte* in the same sense.

flake white ▶ **n.** a pure white pigment made from flakes of white lead.

flak jack·et (also **flak vest**) ▶ **n.** a sleeveless jacket made of heavy fabric reinforced with metal or Kevlar, worn as protection against bullets and shrapnel.

flak·y /ˈflākē/ (also **flakey**) ▶ **adj.** (**flakier**, **flakiest**) **1** breaking or separating easily into small thin pieces: *a tree with flaky bark.* ■ (esp. of skin or paint) tending to crack and come away from a surface in small pieces: *the skin on the shins is often very flaky and dry.*
2 informal crazy or eccentric: *flaky ideas about taxes.* ■ informal (of a device or software) prone to break down; unreliable.
– DERIVATIVES **flak·i·ness** /-kēnis/ **n.**, **flak·i·ly** /-kəlē/ **adv.**

flak·y pas·try ▶ **n.** pastry consisting of thin light layers when baked.

flam /flam/ ▶ **n.** Music one of the basic patterns (rudiments) of drumming, consisting of a stroke preceded by a grace note.
– ORIGIN late 18th cent.: probably imitative.

flam·bé /flämˈbā/ ▶ **adj. 1** [postpositive] (of food) covered with liquor and set alight briefly: *crêpes flambé.*
2 denoting or characterized by a red copper-based porcelain glaze with purple streaks.
▶ **v.** (**flambés, flambéing, flambéed** /-ˈbād/) [with obj.] cover (food) with liquor and set it alight briefly.
– ORIGIN late 19th cent.: French, literally 'singed,' past participle of *flamber*, from *flambe* 'a flame.'

flam·beau /ˈflamˌbō/ ▶ **n.** (pl. **flambeaus** or **flambeaux** /-ˌbōz/) historical a flaming torch, esp. one made of several thick wicks dipped in wax. ■ a large candlestick with several branches.
– ORIGIN mid 17th cent.: from French, from *flambe* 'a flame.'

flam·boy·ant[1] /flamˈboiənt/ ▶ **adj. 1** (of a person or their behavior) tending to attract attention because of their exuberance, confidence, and stylishness: *a flamboyant display of aerobatics | she is outgoing and flamboyant, continuously talking and joking.* ■ (esp. of clothing) noticeable because brightly colored, highly patterned, or unusual in style.
2 Architecture of or denoting a style of French Gothic architecture marked by wavy flamelike tracery and ornate decoration.
– DERIVATIVES **flam·boy·ance n.**, **flam·boy·an·cy** /-ˈboiənsē/ **n.**, **flam·boy·ant·ly adv.**
– ORIGIN mid 19th cent.: from French, literally 'flaming, blazing,' present participle of *flamboyer*, from *flambe* 'a flame.'

flam·boy·ant[2] ▶ **n.** another term for ROYAL POINCIANA. (see POINCIANA).
– ORIGIN late 19th cent.: probably a noun use of the French adjective *flamboyant* 'blazing' (see FLAMBOYANT[1]).

flame /flām/ ▶ **n. 1** a hot glowing body of ignited gas that is generated by something on fire: *the flame of a candle | a sheet of flame blocked my escape.*
2 used in similes and metaphors to refer to something resembling a flame in various respects, in particular: ■ a thing resembling a flame in heat, shape, or brilliance: *red and yellow bunting fluttering like flames in the breeze.* ■ a brilliant orange-red color: [in combination] *a flame-red trench coat.* ■ a thing compared to a flame's ability to burn fiercely or be extinguished: *the flame of hope burns brightly here.* ■ a very intense emotion: *the sound of his laughter fanned the flame of anger to new heights.* ■ a cause that generates passionate feelings: *her father had been keeper of the formalist flame.*
3 a vitriolic or abusive e-mail, typically sent in quick response to another message: *flames about inexperienced users posting stupid messages.*
▶ **v. 1** [no obj.] burn and give off flames: *a great fire flamed in an open fireplace.* ■ [with obj.] set (something) alight: *warm the whiskey slightly, pour over the lobster, and flame it.* ■ shine or glow like a flame: *her thick hair flamed against the light.* ■ (of an intense emotion) appear suddenly and fiercely: *hope flamed in her.* ■ (of a person's face) suddenly become red with intense emotion, esp. anger or embarrassment: *Jess's cheeks flamed.*
2 [with obj.] send (someone) abusive or vitriolic e-mails, typically in a quick exchange.
– PHRASES **burst into flame** (or **flames**) suddenly begin to burn fiercely: *the grass looked ready to burst into flame.* **go up in flames** be destroyed by fire: *last night two factories went up in flames.* **in flames** on fire; burning fiercely: *the plane plunged to the ground in flames.* **old flame** informal a former lover.
– PHRASAL VERBS **flame out** (of a jet engine) lose power through the extinction of the flame in the combustion chamber. ■ informal fail, esp. conspicuously: *journalists had seared him for flaming out in the second round of the Olympics.*
– DERIVATIVES **flame·less adj.**, **flame·like** /-ˌlīk/ **adj.**, **flam·er n.** (Computing)., **flam·y** /ˈflāmē/ **adj.**
– ORIGIN Middle English: from Old French *flame* (noun), *flamer* (verb), from Latin *flamma* 'a flame.'

fla·men /ˈflāmən/ ▶ **n.** (pl. **flamens** or **flamines** /ˈflaməˌnēz/) Roman History a priest serving a particular deity.
– ORIGIN Middle English: Latin, literally 'priest.'

fla·men·co /fləˈmeNGkō/ ▶ **n.** a style of Spanish music, played esp. on the guitar and accompanied by singing and dancing. ■ a style of spirited, rhythmical dance performed to such music, often with castanets.
– ORIGIN late 19th cent.: Spanish, 'like a Gypsy,' literally 'Fleming,' from Middle Dutch *Vlaminc*.

flame·out /ˈflāˌmout/ ▶ **n.** an instance of the flame in the combustion chamber of a jet engine being extinguished, with a resultant loss of power. ■ informal a complete or conspicuous failure: *his first-round flameout at the U.S. Open.*

flame·proof /ˈflāmˌpro͞of/ ▶ **adj.** (esp. of a fabric) treated so as to be nonflammable. ■ (of cookware) able to be used either in an oven or on a stove: *a flameproof casserole.*
▶ **v.** [with obj.] make (something) flameproof.

flame stitch another term for BARGELLO.

flame·throw·er /ˈflāmˌTHrōər/ ▶ **n.** a weapon that sprays out burning fuel.

flame tree ▶ **n.** any of a number of trees with brilliant red flowers, in particular: ● an Australian bottle tree (*Brachychiton acerifolius*, family Sterculiaceae). ● another term for ROYAL POINCIANA (see POINCIANA).

flam·ing /ˈflāmiNG/ ▶ **adj.** [attrib.] **1** burning fiercely and emitting flames: *they dragged her away from the flaming car.* ■ very hot: *flaming June.* ■ glowing with a bright orange or red color: *the flaming autumn maples of the St. Lawrence River valley.* ■ (esp. of an argument) passionate: *Gloria's suddenly flaming jealousy.*
2 informal used for emphasis to express annoyance: *weeds can become a flaming nuisance.*
– DERIVATIVES **flam·ing·ly adv.**

fla·min·go /fləˈmiNGgō/ ▶ **n.** (pl. **flamingos** or **flamingoes**) a tall wading bird with mainly pink or scarlet plumage and long legs and neck. It has a heavy bent bill that is held upside down in the water in order to filter-feed on small organisms. ● Family Phoenicopteridae: three genera and four species, in particular the **greater flamingo** (*Phoenicopterus ruber*).
– ORIGIN mid 16th cent.: from Spanish *flamengo*, earlier form of *flamenco* (see FLAMENCO); associated, because of its color, with Latin *flamma* 'a flame.'

greater flamingo

flam·ma·ble /ˈflaməbəl/ ▶ **adj.** easily set on fire: *the use of highly flammable materials.*
– DERIVATIVES **flam·ma·bil·i·ty** /ˌflaməˈbilətē/ **n.**
– ORIGIN early 19th cent.: from Latin *flammare*, from *flamma* 'a flame.'

USAGE The words **flammable** and **inflammable** mean the same thing, but **flammable** is preferred to avoid confusion: see usage at INFLAMMABLE.

flam·mu·lat·ed owl /ˈflamyəˌlātəd/ ▶ **n.** a small reddish-gray migratory American owl that sometimes occurs in loose colonies. ● *Otus flammeolus*, family Strigidae.

flan /flan/ ▶ **n. 1** a baked dish consisting of an open-topped pastry case with a savory or sweet filling. ■ a sponge base with a sweet topping.
2 a disk of metal such as one from which a coin is made.
– ORIGIN mid 19th cent.: from French (originally denoting a round cake) from Old French *flaon*, from medieval Latin *flado, fladon-*, of West Germanic origin; related to Dutch *vlade* 'custard.'

Flan·ders /ˈflandərz/ a region in the southwestern part of the Low Countries, now divided between Belgium, France, and the Netherlands. It was a powerful medieval principality and the scene of prolonged fighting during World War I.

flâ·ne·rie /ˌflän(ə)ˈrē/ ▶ **n.** aimless idle behavior.
– ORIGIN French, from *flâner* 'saunter, lounge.'

flâ·neur /fläˈnər, -ˈnœr/ (also **flaneur**) ▶ **n.** (pl. **flâneurs** pronunc. **same**) an idler or lounger.
– ORIGIN French, from *flâner* 'saunter, lounge.'

flange /flanj/ ▶ **n.** a projecting flat rim, collar, or rib on an object, serving to strengthen or attach or (on a wheel) to maintain position on a rail: *the flanges that held the tailpipe to the aircraft.*
– DERIVATIVES **flanged adj.**, **flange·less adj.**
– ORIGIN late 17th cent.: perhaps based on Old French *flanchir* 'to bend.'

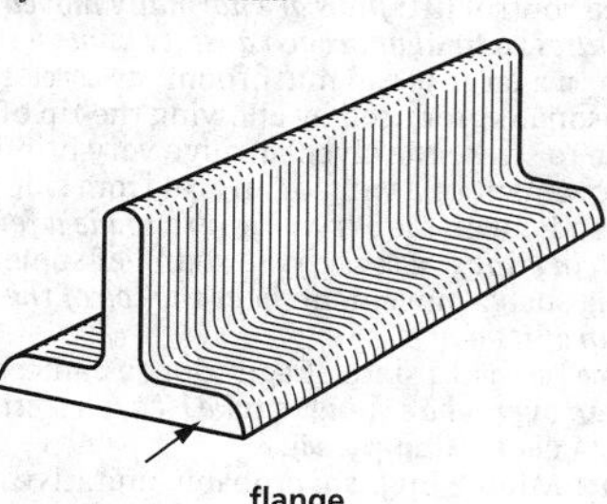
flange

flang·er /ˈflanjər/ ▶ **n.** an electronic device that alters a sound signal by introducing a cyclically varying phase shift into one of two identical copies of the signal and recombining them, used esp. in popular music to alter the sound of an instrument.

flang·ing /ˈflanjiNG/ ▶ **n. 1** the provision of a flange or flanges on an object: *the rim displays the same flanging.*
2 the alteration of sound using a flanger.

flank /flaNGk/ ▶ **n. 1** the side of a person's or animal's body between the ribs and the hip: *leaning against his horse's flanks.* ■ a cut of meat from such a part of an animal: *a thick flank of beef on a spit | two pounds of flank.* ■ the side of something large, such as a mountain, building, or ship: *the northern flank of the volcano.*
2 the right or left side of a body of people such as an army, a naval force, or a soccer team: *the left flank of the Russian Third Army.* ■ the right or left side of a game board such as a chessboard.
▶ **v.** [with obj.] be situated on each side of or on one side of (someone or something): *the fireplace is flanked by built-in bookshelves.* ■ (usu. as adj. **flanking**) guard or strengthen (a military force or position) from the side: *massive walls, defended by four flanking towers.* ■ (usu. as adj. **flanking**) attack down or from the sides, or rake with gunfire from the sides: *a flanking attack from the northeast.*
– ORIGIN late Old English, from Old French *flanc*, of Germanic origin.

flank·er /ˈflaNGkər/ ▶ **n. 1** a person or thing situated on the flank of something, in particular: ■ Football an offensive back who lines up to the outside of an end. ■ Military a fortification guarding or menacing the side of a force or position.
2 Brit. informal, dated a trick; a swindle: *he's certainly pulled a flanker on the army.*

flan·nel /ˈflanl/ ▶ **n. 1** a kind of soft-woven fabric, typically made of wool or cotton and slightly milled and raised: [as modifier] *my longest, thickest flannel nightgown.* ■ (**flannels**) men's trousers made of such material. ■ short for FLANNELETTE.
2 Brit. a washcloth.
3 Brit. informal bland fluent talk indulged in to avoid addressing a difficult subject or situation directly: *a simple admittance of ignorance was much to be preferred to any amount of flannel.*
– ORIGIN Middle English: probably from Welsh *gwlanen* 'woolen article,' from *gwlân* 'wool.'

flan·nel·board /ˈflanlˌbôrd/ ▶ **n.** a board covered with flannel to which paper or cloth cutouts will stick, used as a toy or a teaching aid.

flan·nel cake ▶ **n.** dialect a pancake.

flan·nel·ette /ˌflanlˈet/ ▶ **n.** a napped cotton fabric resembling flannel: [as modifier] *a flannelette nightdress.*

flan·nel·mouth /ˈflanlˌmouTH/ ▶ **n.** informal a person who talks too much, esp. in a boastful or deceitful way.

flap /flap/ ▶ **v.** (**flaps, flapping, flapped**) [with obj.] (of a bird) move (its wings) up and down when flying or preparing to fly: *a pheasant flapped its wings | [no obj.] gulls flapped around uttering their strange*

cries. ■ [no obj.] (of something attached at one point or loosely fastened) flutter or wave around: *the tent bent with the gale, and the corners flapped furiously.* ■ wave (something) around or at something or someone: *she flapped the duster angrily | she began flapping her arms to drive away the permeating cold.* ■ strike or attempt to strike (something) loosely with one's hand, a cloth, or a broad implement, esp. to drive it away.
▶ **n. 1** a piece of something thin, such as cloth, paper, or metal, hinged or attached only on one side, that covers an opening or hangs down from something: *the flap of the envelope | he pushed through the tent flap.* ■ a hinged or sliding section of an aircraft wing used to control lift: *flaps are normally moved by the hydraulics | a final approach at sixty knots with 45° of flap.* ■ a large broad mushroom. ■ Phonetics a type of consonant produced by allowing the tip of the tongue to strike the alveolar ridge very briefly.
2 a movement of a wing or an arm from side to side or up and down: *the surviving bird made a few final despairing flaps.* ■ [in sing.] the sound of something making such a movement: *hear the coo of the dove, the flap of its wings.*
3 [in sing.] informal a state of agitation; a panic: *they're in a flap over who's going to take Henry's lectures.*
– DERIVATIVES **flap·py** adj.
– ORIGIN Middle English: probably imitative.

flap·doo·dle /ˈflapˌdo͞odl/ ▶ **n.** informal nonsense: *people who are prey to dogmatic flapdoodle.* ■ a fool.
– ORIGIN mid 19th cent.: an arbitrary formation.

flap·jack /ˈflapˌjak/ ▶ **n.** a pancake.
– ORIGIN from FLAP (in the dialect sense 'toss a pancake') + JACK¹.

flap·pa·ble /ˈflapəbəl/ ▶ **adj.** excitable and quick to lose one's composure: *he became totally flappable in her presence.*

flap·per /ˈflapər/ ▶ **n.** informal (in the 1920s) a fashionable young woman intent on enjoying herself and flouting conventional standards of behavior. [late 19th cent.: probably from a dialect sense of the noun *flap*, 'a woman of loose character.']

flap valve (also **flapper valve**) ▶ **n.** a valve opened and closed by a plate hinged at one side.

flare /fle(ə)r/ ▶ **n. 1** a sudden brief burst of bright flame or light: *the flare of the match lit up his face.* ■ a device producing a bright flame, used esp. as a signal or marker: *a helicopter spotted a flare set off by the crew | [as modifier] a flare gun.* ■ [in sing.] a sudden burst of intense emotion: *she felt a flare of anger within her.* ■ Astronomy a sudden explosion in the chromosphere and corona of the sun or another star, resulting in an intense burst of radiation. See also SOLAR FLARE. ■ Photography extraneous illumination on film caused by internal reflection in the camera.
2 [in sing.] a gradual widening, esp. of a skirt or pants: *as you knit, add a flare or curve a hem.* ■ an upward and outward curve of a vessel's bow, designed to throw the water outward when under way.
▶ **v.** [no obj.] **1** burn with a sudden intensity: *the blaze across the water flared | the bonfire crackled and flared up.* ■ (of a light or a person's eyes) glow with a sudden intensity: *her eyes flared at the stinging insult.* ■ (of an emotion) suddenly become manifest in a person or their expression: *alarm flared in her eyes | tempers flared.* ■ (**flare up**) (of an illness or chronic medical complaint) recur unexpectedly and cause further discomfort: *Tracy's pain has flared up again, this time almost beyond enduring.* ■ (esp. of an argument, conflict, or trouble) suddenly become more violent or intense: *a recurrent border dispute flared up again.* ■ (**flare up**) (of a person) suddenly become angry: *she flared up, shouting at Jeff.*
2 (often as adj. **flared**) gradually become wider at one end: *a flared skirt | the dress flared out into a huge train.* ■ (of a person's nostrils) dilate: *his head lifted, his nostrils flaring.* ■ [with obj.] (of a person) cause (the nostrils) to dilate.
– ORIGIN mid 16th cent. (in the sense 'spread out (one's hair)'): of unknown origin. Current senses date from the 17th cent.

flare star ▶ **n.** Astronomy a dwarf star that displays spasmodic outbursts of radiation, believed to be due to extremely intense flares.

flare-up ▶ **n.** a sudden outburst of something, esp. violence or a medical condition: *a flare-up between the two countries.*

flash /flasн/ ▶ **v. 1** [no obj.] (of a light or something that reflects light) shine in a bright but brief, sudden, or intermittent way: *the lights started flashing* | (as adj. **flashing**) *a police car with a flashing light.* ■ [with obj.] cause to shine briefly or suddenly: *the oncoming car flashed its lights.* ■ [with obj.] shine or show a light to send (a signal): *red lights started to flash a warning.* ■ [with obj.] give (a swift or sudden look): *Carrie flashed a glance in his direction* | [with two objs.] *she flashed him a withering look.* ■ express a sudden burst of emotion, esp. anger, with such a look: *she glared at him, her eyes flashing.*
2 [with obj.] display (an image, words, or information) suddenly on a television or computer screen or electronic sign, typically briefly or repeatedly: *suddenly the screen flashes a message.* ■ [no obj.] (of an image or message) be displayed in such a way: *the election results flashed on the screen.* ■ informal hold up or show (something, often proof of one's identity) quickly before replacing it: *she opened her purse and flashed her ID card.* ■ informal make a conspicuous display of (something) so as to impress or attract attention: *they all flash their money around.* ■ [no obj.] (often as noun **flashing**) informal (esp. of a man) show one's genitals briefly in public.
3 [no obj.] move or pass very quickly: *a look of terror flashed across Kirov's face | the scenery flashed by | another stray thought flashed through her mind.* ■ [with obj.] send (news or information) swiftly by means of telegraphy or telecommunications: *the story was flashed around the world.*
▶ **n. 1** a sudden brief burst of bright light or a sudden glint from a reflective surface: *the grenade exploded with a yellow flash of light | a lightning flash.*
2 a thing that occurs suddenly and within a brief period of time, in particular: ■ a sudden instance or manifestation of a quality, understanding, or humor: *she had a flash of inspiration.* ■ a news flash.
3 (**Flash**) Computing, trademark a platform for producing and displaying animation and video in Web browsers.
4 a camera attachment that produces a brief very bright light, used for taking photographs in poor light: *an electronic flash | if in any doubt, use flash* | [as modifier] *flash photography.*
5 excess plastic or metal forced between facing surfaces as two halves of a mold close up, forming a thin projection on the finished object.
▶ **adj.** informal, chiefly Brit. **1** (of a thing) ostentatiously expensive, elaborate, or up to date: *a flash new car.* ■ (of a person) superficially attractive because stylish and full of brash charm: *he was carrying this money around and trying to be flash.*
2 archaic of or relating to thieves, prostitutes, or the underworld, esp. their language.
– PHRASES **flash in the pan** a thing or person whose sudden but brief success is not repeated or repeatable: *our start to the season was just a flash in the pan.* [with allusion to the priming of a firearm, the flash arising from an explosion of gunpowder from the pan within the lock.] **in** (or **like**) **a flash** very quickly; immediately: *she was out of the back door in a flash.* (**as**) **quick as a flash** (esp. of a person's response or reaction) very quickly: *quick as a flash, he was at her side.*
– PHRASAL VERBS **flash back** (of a person's thoughts or mind) briefly and suddenly recall a previous time or incident: *her thoughts immediately flashed back to last night.* **flash over** make an electric circuit by sparking across a gap. ■ (of a fire) spread instantly across a gap because of intense heat.
– ORIGIN Middle English (in the sense 'splash water about'): probably imitative; compare with FLUSH¹ and SPLASH.

flash·back /ˈflasнˌbak/ ▶ **n.** a scene in a movie, novel, etc., set in a time earlier than the main story: *in a series of flashbacks, we follow the pair through their teenage years.* ■ a sudden and disturbing vivid memory of an event in the past, typically as the result of psychological trauma or taking LSD.

flash·board /ˈflasнˌbôrd/ ▶ **n.** a board used for increasing the depth of water behind a dam.

flash·bulb /ˈflasнˌbəlb/ ▶ **n.** a light bulb that flashes in order to illuminate a photographic subject, of a type that is used only once: *suddenly flashbulbs were popping and whole rolls of film were squeezed off in seconds.*

flash burn ▶ **n.** a burn caused by sudden intense heat, as from a nuclear explosion.

flash card ▶ **n.** a card containing a small amount of information, held up for students to see, as an aid to learning.

flash drive ▶ **n.** a small electronic device containing flash memory that is used for storing data or transferring it to or from a computer, digital camera, etc.

flash·er /ˈflasнər/ ▶ **n. 1** an automatic device causing a light to flash on and off rapidly. ■ a signal using such a device, for example a car's turn signal.
2 informal a person, esp. a man, who exposes his genitals in public.

flash flood ▶ **n.** a sudden local flood, typically due to heavy rain.

flash-freeze ▶ **v.** [with obj.] freeze (food or other material) rapidly so as to prevent the formation of ice crystals: *the steaks were flash-frozen.*
– DERIVATIVES **flash-freez·er** n.

flash-fry ▶ **v.** [with obj.] (often as adj. **flash-fried**) fry (food) briefly and at a very high temperature.

flash·gun /ˈflasнˌgən/ ▶ **n.** a device that gives a brief flash of intense light, used for taking photographs indoors or in poor light.

flash·ing /ˈflasнiNG/ ▶ **n.** a strip of metal used to stop water from penetrating the junction of a roof with another surface: *flashings around chimneys | the lead flashing on the roof.*
– ORIGIN late 18th cent.: from the earlier synonym *flash* (of unknown origin) + -ING¹.

flash·light /ˈflasнˌlīt/ ▶ **n. 1** a battery-operated portable light.
2 a flashing light used for signals and in lighthouses.
3 a light giving an intense flash, used for photographing at night or indoors.

flash mem·o·ry ▶ **n.** Computing a kind of memory that retains data in the absence of a power supply.

flash mob ▶ **n.** a sudden mass gathering, unanticipated except by participants who communicate electronically: *the flash mob is the idiot child of our instant-communication age.*
▶ **v.** (**flash mobs, flash mobbing, flash mobbed**) [no obj.] hold or subject to a flash mob.

flash·o·ver /ˈflasнˌōvər/ ▶ **n. 1** a high-voltage electric short circuit made through the air between exposed conductors.
2 an instance of a fire spreading very rapidly across a gap because of intense heat.

flash pho·tol·y·sis ▶ **n.** Chemistry the use of an intense flash of light to bring about decomposition or dissociation in a heated gas, usually as a means of generating and studying short-lived molecules.

flash·point /ˈflasнpoint/ (also **flash point**) ▶ **n.**
1 a place, event, or time at which trouble, such as violence or anger, flares up: *the flash point of the conflagration is just blocks away.*
2 Chemistry the temperature at which a particular organic compound gives off sufficient vapor to ignite in air.

flash suit ▶ **n.** a set of heatproof protective clothing.

flash tube ▶ **n.** a gas discharge tube used, esp. in photography, to provide an electronic flash when a current is suddenly passed through it.

flash weld·ing ▶ **n.** a welding process in which the ends of two metal parts are fused by heat generated from their resistance to an electric current and applied pressure.

flash·y /ˈflasнē/ ▶ **adj.** (**flashier, flashiest**) ostentatiously attractive or impressive: *he always had a flashy car.*
– DERIVATIVES **flash·i·ly** /ˈflasнəlē/ **adv.**, **flash·i·ness** /ˈflasнēnis/ **n.**

flask /flask/ ▶ **n.** a container or bottle, in particular: ■ a narrow-necked glass container, typically conical or spherical, used in a laboratory to hold reagents or samples. ■ a metal container for storing a small amount of liquor, typically to be carried in one's pocket: *his silver flask of brandy.* ■ a narrow-necked bulbous glass container, typically with a covering of wickerwork, for storing wine or oil. ■ a vacuum flask. ■ the contents of any of these containers: *a flask of coffee.* ■ historical short for POWDER FLASK.
– ORIGIN Middle English (in the sense 'cask'): from medieval Latin *flasca*. From the mid 16th cent. the word denoted a case of horn, leather, or metal for carrying gunpowder. The sense 'glass container' (late 17th cent.) was influenced by Italian *fiasco*, from medieval Latin *flasco*. Compare with FLAGON.

flat¹ /flat/ ▶ **adj.** (**flatter** /ˈflatə(r)/, **flattest** /ˈflatist/)
1 smooth and even; without marked lumps or indentations: *a flat wall | trim the surface of the cake to make it completely flat.* ■ (of land) without hills: *thirty-five acres of flat countryside.* ■ (of an expanse of water) calm and without waves. ■ not sloping: *the flat roof of a garage.* ■ having a broad level surface but little height or depth; shallow: *a flat rectangular box | a flat cap.* ■ (of the foot) having an arch that is lower than usual. ■ (of shoes) without heels or with very low heels.
2 lacking interest or emotion; dull and lifeless: *"I'm sorry," he said, in a flat voice | her drawings were flat and unimaginative.* ■ (of a person) without energy; dispirited: *his sense of intoxication wore off until he felt flat and weary.* ■ (of a market, prices, etc.) showing little activity; sluggish: *cash flow was flat at $214 million | flat sales in the drinks industry.* ■ (of a sparkling drink) having lost its effervescence: *flat champagne.* ■ (of something kept inflated, esp. a tire) having lost some or all of its air, typically because of a puncture: *you've got a flat tire.* ■ (of a color) uniform: *the dress was a deadly, flat shade of gray.* ■ (of a photographic print or negative) lacking contrast. ■ (of paint) without gloss; matte.

3 [attrib.] (of a fee, wage, or price) the same in all cases, not varying with changed conditions or in particular cases: *a $30 flat fare.* See also FLAT RATE. ■ (of a denial, contradiction, or refusal) completely definite and firm; absolute: *his statement was a flat denial that he had misbehaved.*
4 (of musical sound) below true or normal pitch. ■ [postpositive, in combination] (of a note) a semitone lower than a specified note: *the double basses' opening low E-flat | you never have to change key from B-flat major.* ■ (of a key) having a flat or flats in the signature.
5 (**Flat**) of or relating to flat racing: *the Flat season.*
▶ **adv. 1** in or to a horizontal position: *he was lying flat on his back | she had been knocked flat by the blast.* ■ lying in close juxtaposition, esp. against another surface: *his black curly hair was blown flat across his skull.* ■ so as to become smooth and even: *I hammered the metal flat.*
2 informal completely; absolutely: *I'm turning you down flat* | [as submodifier] *she was going to be flat broke in a couple of days.* ■ after a phrase expressing a period of time to emphasize how quickly something can be done or has been done: *you can prepare a healthy meal **in ten minutes flat**.*
3 below the true or normal pitch of musical sound: *it wasn't a question of singing flat, but of simply singing the wrong notes.*
▶ **n. 1** [in sing.] the flat part of something: *she placed the flat of her hand over her glass.*
2 a flat object, in particular: ■ (often **flats**) an upright section of painted stage scenery mounted on a frame. ■ informal a flat tire. ■ a shallow container in which seedlings are grown and sold. ■ (often **flats**) a shoe with a very low heel or no heel. ■ a railroad car with a flat floor and no sides or roof; a flatcar.
3 (usu. **flats**) an area of low level ground, esp. near water: *the Utah salt flats.* See also MUDFLAT.
4 a musical note lowered a semitone below natural pitch. ■ the sign (♭) indicating this.
▶ **v.** (**flats, flatting, flatted**) [with obj.] **1** (usu. as adj. **flatted**) Music lower (a note) by a semitone: *"blue" harmony emphasizing the flatted third and seventh.*
2 archaic make flat; flatten: *flat the loaves down.*
– PHRASES **fall flat** fail completely to produce the intended or expected effect: *his jokes fell flat.* **fall flat on one's face** fall over forward. ■ fail in an embarrassingly obvious way: *the president could fall flat on his face if the economy doesn't start improving soon.* **(as) flat as a pancake** see PANCAKE. **flat out 1** as fast or as hard as possible: *the whole team is working flat out to satisfy demand* | (as adj. **flat-out**) *the album lacks the flat-out urgency of its predecessor.* **2** informal without hesitation or reservation; unequivocally: *in those early days I'd just flat out vote against foreign aid* | (as adj. **flat-out**) *flat-out perjury.* **3** lying completely stretched out, esp. asleep or exhausted: *she was lying flat out on her pink bath towel.* **that's flat** informal used to indicate that one has reached a decision and will not be persuaded to change one's mind: *he won't go into a home and that's flat.*
– DERIVATIVES **flat·ness** n., **flat·tish** /ˈflatiSH/ adj.
– ORIGIN Middle English: from Old Norse *flatr*; related to PLANT, PLATY-, PLAZA.

flat² ▶ **n.** British term for APARTMENT.
– DERIVATIVES **flat·let** /-lət/ n.
– ORIGIN early 19th cent. (denoting a floor or story): alteration of obsolete *flet* 'floor, dwelling,' of Germanic origin and related to FLAT¹.

flat arch ▶ **n.** Architecture an arch with a flat lower or inner curve. See also JACK ARCH.

flat·bed /ˈflatˌbed/ ▶ **n.** a long flat area or structure: *the flatbed of a truck.* ■ a vehicle with a flat load-carrying area: [as modifier] *a flatbed truck.* ■ [as modifier] denoting a letterpress printing machine in which the form is carried on a horizontal surface: *a flatbed press.* ■ Computing a scanner, plotter, or other device that keeps paper flat during use: [as modifier] *the flatbed technology lets paper enter and exit the printer directly.*

flat-bed press ▶ **n.** a press in which a rotating cylinder equipped with paper makes contact with a horizontal printing surface.

flat·boat /ˈflatˌbōt/ ▶ **n.** a cargo boat with a flat bottom for use in shallow water.

flat·bread /ˈflatˌbred/ ▶ **n.** flat, thin, often unleavened bread.

flat·bug /ˈflatˌbəg/ ▶ **n.** a broad flat bug that typically lives on or under loose bark. ● Family Aradidae, suborder Heteroptera: several species.

Flat·bush /ˈflatˌbo͝oSH/ a residential and commercial section of central Brooklyn in New York City.

flat·car /ˈflatˌkär/ ▶ **n.** a railroad freight car without a roof or sides.

flat-chest·ed ▶ **adj.** (of a woman) having small breasts.

flat-fell ▶ **v.** see FELL² (sense 2 of the verb).

flat file ▶ **n.** Computing a file having no internal hierarchy.

flat·fish /ˈflatˌfiSH/ ▶ **n.** (pl. **same** or **flatfishes**) a flattened marine fish that swims on its side with both eyes on the upper side. They live typically on the seabed and are colored to resemble it. ● Order Pleuronectiformes: several families, in particular Bothidae (left-eye flounders), Pleuronectidae (right-eye flounders), and Soleidae (soles).

flat·foot /ˈflatˌfo͝ot/ ▶ **n. 1** a condition in which the foot has an arch that is lower than usual.
2 (pl. **flatfoots** or **flatfeet** /-ˌfēt/) informal, dated a police officer.

flat-foot·ed ▶ **adj. 1** having flat feet: *a flat-footed, overweight cop.*
2 ■ informal unable to move quickly and smoothly; clumsy: *getting caught in flat-footed ignorance can be uncomfortable.* ■ informal not clever or imaginative; uninspired: *he has little space for anecdote, but the text is no flat-footed catalog.*
– PHRASES **catch someone flat-footed** informal take someone by surprise: *the rise of regional conflicts has caught military planners flat-footed.*
– DERIVATIVES **flat-foot·ed·ly** adv., **flat-foot·ed·ness** n.

flat-four ▶ **adj.** (of an engine) having four horizontal cylinders, two on each side of the crankshaft.
▶ **n.** an engine of this type.

flat·head /ˈflatˌhed/ ▶ **n. 1** (**Flathead**) a member of certain North American Indian peoples such as the Chinook, Choctaw, and Salish, named from their supposed practice of flattening their children's heads artificially. ■ the Salishan language spoken by those people.
2 informal a foolish person.
3 an edible tropical marine fish that has a pointed flattened head with the eyes positioned on the top, typically burrowing in the seabed with just the eyes showing. ● Family Platycephalidae: several genera and species.
4 (of an engine) having the valves and spark plugs in the cylinder block rather than the cylinder head, which is essentially a flat plate. ■ (of a vehicle) having such an engine.
5 [as modifier] (of a screw) countersunk.

Flat·head Range a range of the Rocky Mountains in northwestern Montana. The ***Flathead River*** flows through the area.

flat·i·ron /ˈflatˌīərn/ ▶ **n.** historical an iron that was heated externally and used for pressing clothes.

flat·land /ˈflatˌland/ ▶ **n. 1** (also **flatlands**) land with no hills, valleys, or mountains: *another 100 miles of flatland.*
2 [as place name] an imagined land existing in only two dimensions. [from the title of a book, *Flatland* (1884), by E. A. Abbot.]
3 Brit. an urban area in which the majority of dwellings are flats (apartments): *London flatland.*
– DERIVATIVES **flat·land·er** n. *she's been enthralling flatlanders with her tales of the mountains.*

flat-leafed pars·ley (also **flat-leaf parsley**) ▶ **n.** parsley of a variety with large flat leaves. Also called ITALIAN PARSLEY.

flat·line /ˈflatˌlīn/ ▶ **v.** [no obj.] informal **1** (of a person) die. ■ (of a project or undertaking) fail: *the film has flatlined.*
2 fail to increase; remain static: *their share of the vote has flatlined at about 3%.*
– DERIVATIVES **flat·lin·er** n.
– ORIGIN 1980s: from FLAT¹ + LINE¹ (with reference to the continuous straight line displayed on a heart monitor, indicating death).

flat·ly /ˈflatlē/ ▶ **adv. 1** showing little interest or emotion: *"You'd better go," she said flatly.*
2 in a firm and unequivocal manner; absolutely: *they flatly refused to play* | [as submodifier] *his view seems to me flatly contrary to our evidence.*
3 in a smooth and even way: *I applied the paint flatly.* ■ Photography without marked contrast of light and dark: *the photographs were lit very flatly.*

flat·mate /ˈflatˌmāt/ ▶ **n.** Brit. a person who shares a flat (apartment) with others: *my flatmate moved out a month ago.*

flat·pack ▶ **n.** Electronics a package for an integrated circuit consisting of a rectangular sealed unit with a number of horizontal metal pins protruding from its sides.

flat race ▶ **n.** a horse race over level ground, as opposed to a steeplechase or hurdles.
– DERIVATIVES **flat rac·ing** n.

flat rate ▶ **n.** a charge that is the same in all cases, not varying in proportion with something: *a system of charging a flat rate per household* | [as modifier] *replacing the fee-for-service system with flat-rate payments.* ■ a rate of taxation that is not progressive, but remains at the same proportion on all amounts.

flat screen ▶ **n.** [usu. as modifier] a television or computer screen that is perfectly flat rather than slightly curved and has a slim casing: *a flat-screen TV.*

flat sheet ▶ **n.** an ordinary sheet for a bed as distinct from a fitted one.

flat spin ▶ **n.** Aeronautics a spin in which an aircraft descends in tight circles while remaining almost horizontal.

flat·ten /ˈflatn/ ▶ **v. 1** make or become flat or flatter: [with obj.] *spoon the mixture into the pan, flatten into cakes, and fry until brown* | [no obj.] *the ground **flattened out** and became marshy* | (as adj. **flattened**) *they were dancing on the flattened grass.* ■ [with obj.] press (oneself or one's body) against a surface, typically to get away from something or to let someone pass: *they **flattened themselves** on the pavement as a bomb came whistling down.* ■ [with obj.] Music lower (a note) in pitch by a half step.
2 [with obj.] raze (a building or settlement) to the ground: *the hurricane flattened thousands of homes.* ■ informal knock someone down with power and vigor: *once I'm in the ring, I know I can flatten him.* ■ informal defeat (someone) completely, esp. in a sports contest.
– PHRASAL VERBS **flatten out 1** (of an increasing quantity or rate) show a less marked rise; slow down. **2** make an aircraft fly horizontally after a dive or climb: *he flattened out and made a fine three-point landing.*
– DERIVATIVES **flat·ten·er** n.

flat·ter /ˈflatər/ ▶ **v.** [with obj.] lavish insincere praise and compliments upon (someone), esp. to further one's own interests: *she was flattering him to avoid doing what he wanted.* ■ give an unrealistically favorable impression of: *the portraitist flatters his sitter to the detriment of his art.* ■ (usu. **be flattered**) make (someone) feel honored and pleased: [with obj. and infinitive] *I was very flattered to be given the commission* | [with obj. and clause] *at least I am flattered that you don't find me boring.* ■ (**flatter oneself**) make oneself feel pleased by believing something favorable about oneself, typically something that is unfounded: [with clause] *I flatter myself I'm the best dressed man here.* ■ (of a color or a style of clothing) make (someone) appear more attractive or to the best advantage: *the muted fuchsia shade flattered her pale skin.* ■ archaic please (the ear or eye): *the beauty of the stone flattered the young clergyman's eyes.*
– ORIGIN Middle English: perhaps a back-formation from FLATTERY.

flat·ter·er /ˈflatərər/ ▶ **n.** a person who lavishes praise, often insincerely; a sycophant: *he is not allowing flatterers to deceive him.*

flat·ter·ing /ˈflatəriNG/ ▶ **adj.** (of a person or their remarks) full of praise and compliments: *the article began with some flattering words about us.* ■ pleasing; gratifying: [with infinitive] *it was flattering to have a pretty girl like Frances so obviously fond of him.* ■ enhancing someone's appearance: *I don't think anything sleeveless is very flattering | that's a flattering picture of him.*
– DERIVATIVES **flat·ter·ing·ly** adv.

flat·ter·y /ˈflatərē/ ▶ **n.** (pl. **flatteries**) excessive and insincere praise, esp. that given to further one's own interests: *his healthy distrust of courtiers' flattery.*
– ORIGIN Middle English: from Old French *flaterie*, from *flater* 'stroke, flatter,' probably of Germanic origin and related to FLAT¹.

flat·top /ˈflatˌtäp/ ▶ **n. 1** informal an aircraft carrier.
2 a man's hairstyle in which the hair is cropped short so that it bristles up into a flat surface: *a blond flattop and a faint blond mustache.*

flat·u·lence /ˈflaCHələns/ ▶ **n.** the accumulation of gas in the alimentary canal: *foods that may cause flatulence.* ■ inflated or pretentious speech or writing; pomposity: *the flatulence characterizing his writings.*
– DERIVATIVES **flat·u·len·cy** n.

flat·u·lent /ˈflaCHələnt/ ▶ **adj.** suffering from or marked by an accumulation of gas in the alimentary canal: *treat flatulent cows with caustic soda.* ■ related to or causing this condition: *the flatulent effect of beans.* ■ inflated or pretentious in speech or writing: *the days of flatulent oratory are gone.*
– DERIVATIVES **flat·u·lent·ly** adv.

– ORIGIN late 16th cent.: via French from modern Latin *flatulentus*, from Latin *flatus* 'blowing' (see FLATUS).

fla·tus /ˈflātəs/ ▶ n. formal gas in or from the stomach or intestines, produced by swallowing air or by bacterial fermentation.
– ORIGIN mid 17th cent.: from Latin, literally 'blowing,' from *flare* 'to blow.'

flat·ware /ˈflatˌwe(ə)r/ ▶ n. eating utensils such as knives, forks, and spoons. ■ relatively flat dishes such as plates and saucers. The opposite of HOLLOWWARE.

flat·wa·ter /ˈflatˌwôtər/ ▶ n. slowly moving water in a river, as opposed to rapids: [as modifier] *flatwater kayak and canoe teams.*

flat·worm /ˈflatˌwərm/ ▶ n. a worm of a phylum that includes the planarians together with the parasitic flukes and tapeworms. They are distinguished by having a simple flattened body that lacks blood vessels, and a digestive tract that, if present, has a single opening. ● Phylum Platyhelminthes: several classes.

flat-wo·ven ▶ adj. (of a carpet or rug) woven so as not to form a projecting pile.
– DERIVATIVES **flat-weave** n.

Flau·bert /flōˈber/, Gustave (1821–80), French novelist and short-story writer. A dominant figure in the French realist school, he is noted for *Madame Bovary* (1857), his first published novel.

flaunt /flônt, flänt/ ▶ v. [with obj.] display (something) ostentatiously, esp. in order to provoke envy or admiration or to show defiance: *newly rich consumers eager to flaunt their prosperity.* ■ (**flaunt oneself**) dress or behave in a sexually provocative way.
– PHRASES **if you've got it, flaunt it** informal one should make a conspicuous and confident show of one's wealth or attributes rather than be modest about them.
– DERIVATIVES **flaunt·er** n., **flaunt·y** adj.
– ORIGIN mid 16th cent.: of unknown origin.

> **USAGE** Flaunt and flout may sound similar but they have different meanings. **Flaunt** means 'display ostentatiously,' as in *tourists who liked to* **flaunt** *their wealth,* while **flout** means 'openly disregard (a rule or convention),' as in *new recruits growing their hair and* **flouting** *convention.* It is a common error, recorded since around the 1940s, to use **flaunt** when **flout** is intended, as in *the young woman had been* **flaunting** *the rules and regulations.*

flau·tist /ˈflôtist, ˈflou-/ ▶ n. a flutist.
– ORIGIN mid 19th cent. (superseding 17th-cent. *flutist* in British English use): from Italian *flautista*, from *flauto* 'flute.'

fla·va·none /ˈflāvəˌnōn/ ▶ n. a colorless, crystalline derivative of flavone.

fla·ves·cent /fləˈvesənt/ ▶ adj. yellowish or turning yellow.
– ORIGIN mid 19th cent.: from Latin *flavescent-* 'turning yellow,' from the verb *flavescere*, from *flavus* 'yellow.'

Fla·vi·an /ˈflāvēən/ ▶ adj. of or relating to a dynasty (AD 69–96) of Roman emperors including Vespasian and his sons Titus and Domitian.
▶ n. a member of this dynasty.
– ORIGIN from Latin *Flavianus*, from *Flavius*, a given name used by this dynasty.

fla·vin /ˈflāvin/ ▶ n. Biochemistry any of a group of naturally occurring pigments including riboflavin. They have a tricyclic aromatic molecular structure.
– ORIGIN mid 19th cent.: from Latin *flavus* 'yellow' + -IN[1].

fla·vine /ˈflāˌvēn/ ▶ n. **1** Medicine an antiseptic derived from acridine.
2 Chemistry another term for QUERCETIN.
– ORIGIN early 20th cent.: from Latin *flavus* 'yellow' + -INE[4].

fla·vi·vi·rus /ˈflāvəˌvīrəs/ ▶ n. a virus whose genome consists of positive RNA, that is capable of reproducing in its arthropod vector, and that causes a number of serious human diseases including yellow fever, dengue, Japanese encephalitis, and West Nile virus. ● Family *Flaviviridae*, three genera.

fla·vone /ˈflāˌvōn/ ▶ n. Chemistry a colorless crystalline compound that is the basis of a number of white or yellow plant pigments. ● A tricyclic aromatic compound; chem. formula: $C_{15}H_{10}O_2$. ■ any of these pigments.
– ORIGIN late 19th cent.: from Latin *flavus* 'yellow' + -ONE.

fla·vo·noid /ˈflāvəˌnoid/ ▶ n. Chemistry any of a large class of plant pigments having a structure based on or similar to that of flavone.

fla·vo·pro·tein /ˌflāvəˈprōˌtēn, -ˈprōtēən/ ▶ n. Biochemistry any of a class of conjugated proteins that contain flavins and are involved in oxidation reactions in cells.
– ORIGIN 1930s: blend of FLAVIN and PROTEIN.

fla·vor /ˈflāvər/ (Brit. **flavour**) ▶ n. **1** the distinctive taste of a food or drink: *the yogurt comes in eight fruit flavors | adding sun-dried tomatoes gives the sauce extra flavor.* ■ the general quality of taste in a food: *no other cracker adds so much flavor to the cheese.* ■ a substance used to alter or enhance the taste of food or drink; a flavoring: *we use vanilla and almond flavors.*
2 [in sing.] an indication of the essential character of something: *the extracts give a flavor of the content and tone of the conversation.* ■ [in sing.] a distinctive quality or atmosphere: *whitewashed walls and red pantiles gave the resort a Mediterranean flavor.*
3 a kind, variety, or sort: *various flavors of firewall are evolving.*
4 Physics a quantized property of quarks that differentiates them into at least six varieties (up, down, charmed, strange, top, bottom). Compare with COLOR.
▶ v. [with obj.] alter or enhance the taste of (food or drink) by adding a particular ingredient: *they use a wide range of spices to flavor their foods | chunks of chicken flavored with herbs.* ■ give a distinctive quality to: *the faint exasperation that had flavored her tone.*
– PHRASES **flavor of the month** a person or thing that enjoys a short period of great popularity: *for many law firms, Hong Kong was a flavor of the month.*
– DERIVATIVES **fla·vor·ful** /-fəl/ adj., **fla·vor·less** adj., **fla·vor·some** /-səm/ adj.
– ORIGIN late Middle English (in the sense 'fragrance, aroma'): from Old French *flaor*, perhaps based on a blend of Latin *flatus* 'blowing' and *foetor* 'stench'; the *-v-* appears to have been introduced in Middle English by association with SAVOR. Sense 1 of the noun dates from the late 17th cent.

fla·vored /ˈflāvərd/ (Brit. **flavoured**) ▶ adj. (of food or drink) having a particular type of taste: [in combination] *the peanut oil is light but fairly full-flavored.* ■ (of food or drink) having been given a particular taste by the addition of a flavoring: *a flavored drink* | [in combination] *chicken breasts in lemon-flavored stock.* ■ [in combination] having a particular distinctive quality: *the band knocked out some fine rock 'n' roll-flavored singles.*

fla·vor en·hanc·er ▶ n. a chemical additive, e.g., monosodium glutamate, used to intensify the flavor of food.

fla·vor·ing /ˈflāvəriNG/ (Brit. **flavouring**) ▶ n. a substance used to give a different, stronger, or more agreeable taste to food or drink: *vanilla flavoring | mustard has been used as a flavoring for thousands of years.*

fla·vor·ous /ˈflāvərəs/ ▶ adj. dated having a pleasant or pungent flavor.

flaw[1] /flô/ ▶ n. a mark, fault, or other imperfection that mars a substance or object: *plates with flaws in them were sold at the outlet store.* ■ a fault or weakness in a person's character: *he had his flaws, but he was still a great teacher.* ■ a mistake or shortcoming in a plan, theory, or legal document that causes it to fail or reduces its effectiveness: *there were fundamental flaws in the case for reforming local government.*
▶ v. [with obj.] (usu. **be flawed**) (of an imperfection) mar, weaken, or invalidate (something): *the computer game was flawed by poor programming.*
– ORIGIN Middle English: perhaps from Old Norse *flaga* 'slab'; see FLAG[2]. The original sense was 'a flake of snow,' later, 'a fragment or splinter,' hence 'a defect or imperfection' (late 15th cent).

flaw[2] ▶ n. literary a squall of wind; a short storm.
– ORIGIN early 16th cent.

flawed /flôd/ ▶ adj. blemished, damaged, or imperfect in some way: *flawed crystals.* ■ (of a person) having a weakness in character: *a flawed hero.*

flaw·less /ˈflôləs/ ▶ adj. without any blemishes or imperfections; perfect: *her brown flawless skin.* ■ without any mistakes or shortcomings: *he greeted her in almost flawless English.*
– DERIVATIVES **flaw·less·ly** adv., **flaw·less·ness** n.

flax /flaks/ ▶ n. a blue-flowered herbaceous plant that is cultivated for its seed (linseed) and for textile fiber made from its stalks. ● *Linum usitatissimum*, family Linaceae.
■ textile fiber obtained from this plant: *a mill for the preparation and spinning of flax.*
■ used in names of other plants of the flax family (e.g., **purging flax**) or plants that yield similar fiber (e.g., **false flax**).
– ORIGIN Old English *flæx*; related to Dutch *vlas* and German *Flachs*, from an Indo-European root shared by Latin *plectere* and Greek *plekein* 'to plait, twist.'

flax·en /ˈflaksən/ ▶ adj. of flax. ■ (esp. of hair) of the pale yellow color of dressed flax: *her long flaxen hair.*

flax·seed /ˈflak(s)ˌsēd/ ▶ n. another term for LINSEED. ■ a pupa of the Hessian fly, which resembles a seed of flax.

flay /flā/ ▶ v. [with obj.] peel the skin off (a corpse or carcass): *one shoulder had been flayed to reveal the muscles.* ■ peel (the skin) off a corpse or carcass: *she flayed the white skin from the flesh.* ■ whip or beat (someone) so harshly as to remove their skin: *Matthew flayed them viciously with a branch.* ■ criticize severely and brutally: *he flayed the government for not moving fast enough on economic reform.*
– DERIVATIVES **flay·er** n.
– ORIGIN Old English *flēan*, of Germanic origin; related to Middle Dutch *vlaen*.

F lay·er ▶ n. the highest and most strongly ionized region of the ionosphere.
– ORIGIN 1920s: arbitrary use of *F* + LAYER.

fld. ▶ abbr. ■ field. ■ fluid.

fl dr ▶ abbr. fluid dram.

flea /flē/ ▶ n. a small wingless jumping insect that feeds on the blood of mammals and birds. It sometimes transmits diseases through its bite, including plague and myxomatosis. ● Order Siphonaptera: several families and many species, including the **human flea** (*Pulex irritans*) and the **cat flea** (*Ctenocephalides felis*).
■ short for FLEA BEETLE.
■ a water flea (see DAPHNIA).

cat flea

– PHRASES **a flea in one's ear** a sharp reproof: *she expected to be sent away with a flea in her ear.*
– ORIGIN Old English *flēa*, *flēah*, of Germanic origin; related to Dutch *vlo* and German *Floh*.

flea·bag /ˈflēˌbag/ ▶ n. informal a seedy, run-down hotel or lodging house. ■ a shabby and unpleasant person or thing.

flea·bane /ˈflēˌbān/ ▶ n. a herbaceous plant of the daisy family, reputed to drive away fleas. ● *Erigeron*, *Pulicaria*, and other genera, family Compositae: in particular the pink-flowered **common** (or **Philadelphia**) **fleabane** (*E. philadelphicus*) and the white-flowered **daisy fleabane** (*E. annus*).

flea bee·tle ▶ n. a small jumping leaf beetle that can be a pest of plants such as crucifers. ● *Phyllotreta* and other genera, family Chrysomelidae.

flea·bite /ˈflēˌbīt/ ▶ n. a small red mark caused by the bite of a flea. ■ a trivial injury or cost: *the proposed energy tax amounted to little more than a fleabite.*

flea-bit·ten ▶ adj. bitten by or infested with fleas. ■ sordid, shabby, or disreputable: *this flea-bitten gross-out movie seems to believe that it's about something.*

flea cir·cus ▶ n. a novelty show of performing fleas.

flea col·lar ▶ n. a collar for a cat or dog that is impregnated with insecticide in order to keep the pet free of fleas.

flea-flick·er ▶ n. Football a designed play in which a pass is thrown to a receiver who then laterals to a teammate.

flea mar·ket ▶ n. a market, typically outdoors, selling secondhand goods.

flea·pit /ˈflēˌpit/ ▶ n. chiefly Brit. a dingy, dirty place, esp. a run-down movie theater.

flèche /flāSH, fleSH/ ▶ n. a slender spire, typically over the intersection of the nave and the transept of a Gothic church.
– ORIGIN mid 19th cent.: French, literally 'arrow.'

flé·chette /flāˈSHet, fleSHˈet/ (also **fléchette**) ▶ n. a type of ammunition resembling a small dart, shot from a gun.
– ORIGIN early 20th cent.: from French *fléchette*, diminutive of *flèche* 'arrow.'

fleck /flek/ ▶ n. a very small patch of color or light: *his blue eyes had gray flecks in them | flecks of sunshine.* ■ a small particle or speck of something: *brushing a few flecks of dandruff from his suit.*
▶ v. [with obj.] mark or dot with small patches of color or particles of something: *the minarets are flecked with gold leaf.*
– ORIGIN late Middle English (as a verb): perhaps from Old Norse *flekkr* (noun), *flekka* (verb), or from Middle Low German, Middle Dutch *vlecke*.

flec·tion /ˈflekSHən/ ▶ n. variant spelling of FLEXION.

fled /fled/ past and past participle of FLEE.

fledge /flej/ ▶ **v.** [no obj.] **1** (of a young bird) develop wing feathers that are large enough for flight. ■ [with obj.] bring up (a young bird) until its wing feathers are developed enough for flight.
2 [with obj.] provide (an arrow) with feathers.
– ORIGIN mid 16th cent.: from the obsolete adjective *fledge* 'ready to fly,' from Old English, of Germanic origin; related to Dutch *vlug* 'quick, agile,' also to FLY[1].

fledged /flejd/ ▶ **adj.** (of a young bird) having wing feathers that are large enough for flight; able to fly. See also FULL-FLEDGED. ■ (of a person or thing) having just taken on the role specified: *our discipline is so new fledged that the FBI had to take its cases to the Smithsonian for analysis.* ■ chiefly literary (of an arrow) provided with feathers.

fledg·ling /'flejliNG/ (also **fledgeling**) ▶ **n.** a young bird that has just fledged. ■ [usu. as modifier] a person or organization that is immature, inexperienced, or underdeveloped: *the fledgling democracies of eastern Europe.*
– ORIGIN mid 19th cent.: from the obsolete adjective *fledge* (see FLEDGE), on the pattern of *nestling.*

flee /flē/ ▶ **v.** (**flees, fleeing**; past and past participle **fled** /fled/) [no obj.] run away from a place or situation of danger: *a man was shot twice as he **fled from** five masked youths.* ■ [with obj.] run away from (someone or something): *he was forced to **flee the country** |* figurative *all remaining doubt that he was a guerilla began to flee my mind.*
– ORIGIN Old English *flēon*, of Germanic origin; related to Dutch *vlieden* and German *fliehen.*

fleece /flēs/ ▶ **n. 1** the woolly covering of a sheep or goat: *as the sheep came on board, we grabbed their long shaggy fleeces | he clutched the ram by two handfuls of thick fleece.* ■ the amount of wool shorn from a sheep in a single piece at one time.
2 a thing resembling a sheep's woolly covering, in particular: ■ a soft warm fabric with a texture similar to sheep's wool, used as a lining material. ■ a jacket or other garment made from such a fabric. ■ Heraldry a representation of a fleece suspended from a ring.
▶ **v.** [with obj.] **1** informal obtain a great deal of money from (someone), typically by overcharging or swindling them: *money that authorities say he fleeced from well-to-do acquaintances.*
2 literary cover as if with a fleece: *the sky was half blue, half fleeced with white clouds.*
– DERIVATIVES **fleeced** adj.
– ORIGIN Old English *flēos, flēs*; related to Dutch *vlies* and German *Vlies.*

fleec·y /'flēsē/ ▶ **adj.** (**fleecier, fleeciest**) **1** (esp. of a towel or garment) made of or lined with a soft, warm fabric: *a fleecy sweatshirt.*
2 (esp. of a cloud) white and fluffy.
– DERIVATIVES **fleec·i·ly** /-səlē/ adv., **fleec·i·ness** /-sēnis/ n.

fleer /'fli(ə)r/ ▶ **v.** [no obj.] literary laugh impudently or jeeringly: *he fleered at us.*
▶ **n.** archaic an impudent or jeering look or speech.
– ORIGIN late Middle English: probably of Scandinavian origin and related to Norwegian and Swedish dialect *flira* 'to grin.'

fleet[1] /flēt/ ▶ **n.** the largest group of naval vessels under one commander, organized for specific tactical or other purposes: *an invasion fleet.* ■ (**the fleet**) a country's navy: *the US fleet.* ■ a group of ships sailing together, engaged in the same activity, or under the same ownership: *the small port supports a fishing fleet.* ■ a number of ships, vehicles or aircraft operating together or under the same ownership: ***a fleet of** ambulances took the injured to hospital.*
– ORIGIN Old English *flēot* 'ship, shipping,' from *flēotan* 'float, swim' (see FLEET[4]).

fleet[2] ▶ **adj.** fast and nimble in movement: *a man of advancing years, but **fleet of foot**.*
– DERIVATIVES **fleet·ly** adv., **fleet·ness** n.
– ORIGIN early 16th cent.: probably from Old Norse *fljótr*, of Germanic origin and related to FLEET[4].

fleet[3] ▶ **n.** Brit. a marshland creek, channel, or ditch.
– ORIGIN Old English *flēot*, of Germanic origin; related to Dutch *vliet*, also to FLEET[4].

fleet[4] ▶ **v.** [no obj.] literary move or pass quickly: *a variety of expressions fleeted across his face | time may fleet and youth may fade.* ■ [with obj.] pass (time) rapidly. ■ fade away; be transitory: *the cares of boyhood fleet away.*
– ORIGIN Old English *flēotan* 'float, swim,' of Germanic origin; related to Dutch *vlieten* and German *fliessen*, also to FLIT and FLOAT.

Fleet Ad·mi·ral ▶ **n.** an admiral of the highest rank in the US Navy (awarded only in wartime).

fleet-foot·ed ▶ **adj.** nimble and fast on one's feet: *the fleet-footed sprinter captured his third gold medal.*

fleet·ing /'flētiNG/ ▶ **adj.** lasting for a very short time: *hoping to get a fleeting glimpse of a whale underwater.*
– DERIVATIVES **fleet·ing·ly** adv., **fleet·ing·ness** n.

Fleet Street a street in central London in which the offices of national newspapers were located until the mid-1980s (often used to refer to the British press): *the hottest story in Fleet Street.*

Flem. ▶ **abbr.** Flemish.

Flem·ing[1] /'flemiNG/, Sir Alexander (1881–1955), Scottish bacteriologist. In 1928, Fleming discovered the effect of penicillin on bacteria. Twelve years later, Howard Florey and Ernst Chain established its therapeutic use as an antibiotic. Nobel Prize for Physiology or Medicine (1945), shared with Florey and Chain.

Flem·ing[2], Ian (Lancaster) (1908–64), English novelist. He is known for his spy novels whose hero is the secret agent James Bond. Many of these James Bond stories were made into movies.

Flem·ing[3], Peggy (1948–), US figure skater. She was world champion 1966–68 and won an Olympic gold medal in 1968.

Flem·ing[4], Renée (1959–), US opera singer. She made her debut with the Metropolitan Opera in 1991 and is known for her interpretation of the bel canto repertory and for her enthusiasm for contemporary operas.

Flem·ing[5] ▶ **n. 1** a native of Flanders.
2 a member of the Flemish-speaking people inhabiting northern and western Belgium. Compare with WALLOON.
– ORIGIN late Old English *Flæmingi*, from Old Norse, reinforced by Middle Dutch *Vlāming*, related to *Vlaanderen* 'Flanders.'

Flem·ing's left-hand rule Physics a mnemonic concerning the behavior of a current-carrying conductor in a magnetic field, according to which the directions of the magnetic field, the current, and the force exerted on the conductor are indicated respectively by the first finger, second finger, and thumb of the left hand when these are held out perpendicular to each other.
– ORIGIN 1920s: proposed by English engineer John Ambrose Fleming (1849–1945).

Flem·ing's right-hand rule Physics a mnemonic concerning the behavior of a conductor moving in a magnetic field, according to which the directions of the magnetic field, the induced current, and the motion of the conductor are indicated respectively by the first finger, second finger, and thumb of the right hand when these are held out perpendicular to each other.

Flem·ish /'flemiSH/ ▶ **adj.** of or relating to Flanders, its people, or their language.
▶ **n. 1** the Dutch language as spoken in Flanders, one of the two official languages of Belgium.
2 (**the Flemish**) [as plural noun] the people of Flanders.
– ORIGIN Middle English: from Middle Dutch *Vlāmisch*, related to *Vlaanderen* 'Flanders.'

Flem·ish bond ▶ **n.** Building a pattern of bricks in a wall in which each course consists of alternate headers and stretchers.

flense /flens/ (also **flench** /flenCH/) ▶ **v.** [with obj.] slice the skin or fat from (a carcass, esp. that of a whale). ■ strip (skin or fat) from a carcass: *the skin had been flensed off.*
– DERIVATIVES **flens·er** n.
– ORIGIN early 19th cent.

flesh /fleSH/ ▶ **n.** the soft substance consisting of muscle and fat that is found between the skin and bones of an animal or a human: *she grabbed Anna's arm, her fingers sinking into the flesh.* ■ this substance in an animal or fish, regarded as food: *boned lamb flesh |* [in combination] *a flesh-eater.* ■ the pulpy substance of a fruit or vegetable, esp. the part that is eaten: *halve the avocados and scrape out the flesh.* ■ the skin or surface of the human body with reference to its color, appearance, or sensual properties: *she gasped as the cold water hit her flesh.* ■ (**the flesh**) the human body and its physical needs and desires, esp. as contrasted with the mind or the soul: *I have never been one to deny the **pleasures of the flesh**.* ■ flesh color.
▶ **v. 1** [no obj.] (**flesh out**) put weight on: *he had fleshed out to a solid 220 pounds.* ■ [with obj.] (**flesh something out**) add more details to something that exists only in a draft or outline form: *the theorists have fleshed out a variety of scenarios.*
2 [with obj.] Brit. give (a hound or hawk) a piece of the flesh of game that has been killed in order to incite it. ■ literary initiate (someone) in bloodshed or warfare: *he fleshed his troops by indulging them with enterprises against the enemy's posts.*
3 [with obj.] (often as noun **fleshing**) remove the flesh adhering to (a skin or hide): *after fleshing, the hide is soaked again.*
– PHRASES **all flesh** all human and animal life. **go the way of all flesh** die or come to an end. **in the flesh** in person rather than via a telephone, a movie, the written word, or other means: *they decided that they should meet Alexander in the flesh.* **lose flesh** archaic become thinner. **make someone's flesh creep** (or **crawl**) see MAKE SOMEONE'S SKIN CRAWL at SKIN. **one flesh** used to refer to the spiritual and physical union of two people in a relationship, esp. marriage: *my body is his, his is mine: one flesh.* [with biblical allusion to Gen. 2:24.] **put flesh on (the bones of) something** add more details to something that exists only in a draft or outline form: *he has yet to put flesh on his "big idea."* **put on flesh** put on weight. **sins of the flesh** archaic or humorous sins related to physical indulgence, esp. sexual gratification.
– DERIVATIVES **fleshed** /fleSHt/ adj. [usu. in combination] *a white-fleshed fish*, **flesh·less** adj.
– ORIGIN Old English *flǣsc*, of Germanic origin; related to Dutch *vlees* and German *Fleisch.*

flesh and blood ▶ **n.** used to emphasize that a person is a physical, living being with human emotions or frailties, often in contrast to something abstract, spiritual, or mechanical: *the customer is flesh and blood, not just a sales statistic |* [as modifier] *he seemed more like a creature from a dream than a flesh-and-blood father.*
– PHRASES **one's (own) flesh and blood** a near relative or one's close family: *he felt as much for that girl as if she had been his own flesh and blood.*

flesh col·or ▶ **n.** a light brownish pink.
– DERIVATIVES **flesh-col·ored** adj.

flesh·er /'fleSHər/ ▶ **n. 1** a knife for fleshing hides.
2 a person who fleshes hides.

flesh fly ▶ **n.** a fly that breeds in carrion, typically producing live young that are deposited on a carcass. ● Family Sarcophagidae: *Sarcophaga* and other genera.

flesh·ings /'fleSHiNGz/ ▶ **plural n.** flesh-colored tights worn by actors.

flesh·ly /'fleSHlē/ ▶ **adj.** (**fleshlier, fleshliest**) **1** of or relating to human desire or bodily appetites; sensual: *fleshly pleasures.*
2 having an actual physical presence: *we will shed the lofty metaphysical Cage and incorporate the earlier dynamic and fleshly Cage.*
– ORIGIN Old English *flǣsclic* (see FLESH, -LY[1]).

flesh·pots /'fleSH,päts/ ▶ **plural n.** places providing luxurious or hedonistic living: *he had lived the life of a roué in the fleshpots of London and Paris.*
– ORIGIN early 16th cent.: with biblical allusion to the *fleshpots of Egypt* (Exod. 16:3).

flesh side ▶ **n.** the side of a hide that adjoins the flesh.

flesh wound /wo͞ond/ ▶ **n.** a wound that breaks the skin but does not damage bones or vital organs.

flesh·y /'fleSHē/ ▶ **adj.** (**fleshier, fleshiest**) **1** (of a person or part of the body) having a substantial amount of flesh; plump: *her torso was full, fleshy, and heavy.* ■ (of plant or fruit tissue) soft and thick: *fleshy, greeny-gray leaves.*
2 resembling flesh in appearance or texture.
– DERIVATIVES **flesh·i·ness** n.

fletch /flecH/ ▶ **v.** [with obj.] provide (an arrow) with feathers for flight: *most arrows are fletched with 3- to 5-inch feathers.*
▶ **n.** each of the feathered vanes of an arrow: [in combination] *a four-fletch arrow.*
– ORIGIN mid 17th cent.: alteration of FLEDGE, probably influenced by *fletcher.*

Fletch·er /'flecHər/, John (1579–1625), English playwright. A writer of Jacobean tragicomedies, he wrote about 15 plays with Francis Beaumont and is also believed to have collaborated with William Shakespeare on such plays as *The Two Noble Kinsmen* and *Henry VIII* (both c.1613).

fletch·er /'flecHər/ ▶ **n.** chiefly historical a person who makes and sells arrows.
– ORIGIN Middle English: from Old French *flechier*, from *fleche* 'arrow.'

fletch·ing /'flecHiNG/ ▶ **n.** the feathers of an arrow: *it has good-sized fletching | he repairs damaged fletchings.*

fleur-de-lis /,flər dl'ē, ,flo͝or-/ (also **fleur-de-lys**) ▶ **n.** (pl. **fleurs-de-lis** pronunc. **same** or /-dl'ēz/) **1** Art & Heraldry a stylized lily composed of three petals bound together near their bases. It is especially

fleur-de-lis 1

PRONUNCIATION KEY ə *ago, up*; ər *over, fur*; a *hat*; ā *ate*; ä *car*; e *let*; ē *see*; i *fit*; ī *by*; NG *sing*; ō *go*; ô *law, for*; oi *toy*; o͝o *good*; o͞o *goo*; ou *out*; TH *thin*; T͟H *then*; ZH *vision*

f

known from the former royal arms of France, in which it appears in gold on a blue field.
2 a European iris. ● Genus *Iris*, family Iridaceae, in particular *I.* × germanica 'Florentina' (with bluish-white flowers) or *I. pseudacorus* (the yellow flag).
– ORIGIN Middle English: from Old French *flour de lys* 'flower of the lily.'

fleur de sel /'flər də 'sel, 'flo͝or/ ▶ **n.** French sea salt.

fleu·ron /'flər,än, 'flo͝or-/ ▶ **n.** a flower-shaped ornament, used esp. on buildings, coins, books, and pastry. ■ a small pastry puff used for garnishing.
– ORIGIN late Middle English: from Old French *floron*, from *flour* 'flower.'

fleu·ry /'flərē, 'flo͝orē/ ▶ **adj.** variant spelling of FLORY.

flew /flo͞o/ past of FLY[1].

flews /flo͞oz/ ▶ **plural n.** the thick hanging lips of a bloodhound or similar dog.
– ORIGIN late 16th cent.: of unknown origin.

flex /fleks/ ▶ **v.** [with obj.] bend (a limb or joint): *she saw him flex his ankle and wince.* ■ [no obj.] (of a limb or joint) become bent: *prevent the damaged wrist from flexing.* ■ cause (a muscle) to stand out by contracting or tensing it: *bodybuilders flexing their muscles.* ■ [no obj.] (of a muscle) contract or be tensed: *a muscle flexed in his jaw.* ■ [no obj.] (of a material) be capable of warping or bending and then reverting to shape: *set windows in rubber so they flex during an earthquake.* ■ (usu. as adj. **flexed**) Archaeology place (a corpse) with the legs drawn up under the chin: *a flexed burial.*
▶ **n.** the action or state of flexing: *add rigidity and eliminate brake flex.*
– PHRASES **flex one's muscles** see MUSCLE.
– ORIGIN early 16th cent.: from Latin *flex-* 'bent,' from the verb *flectere.*

flex-fu·el ▶ **adj.** denoting a motor vehicle that will run on gasoline, ethanol, or these two in any combination: *flex-fuel subcompacts have captured 20% of Brazil's new car market.*

flex·i·bil·i·ty /,fleksə'bilətē/ ▶ **n.** the quality of bending easily without breaking: *players gained improved flexibility in their ankles.* ■ the ability to be easily modified: *I enjoyed the flexibility of the schedule.* ■ willingness to change or compromise: *the government has shown flexibility in applying its policy.*

flex·i·ble /'fleksəbəl/ ▶ **adj.** capable of bending easily without breaking: *flexible rubber seals.* ■ able to be easily modified to respond to altered circumstances or conditions: *flexible forms of retirement.* ■ (of a person) ready and able to change so as to adapt to different circumstances: *you can save money if you're flexible about where your room is located.*
– DERIVATIVES **flex·i·bly** /-blē/ **adv.**
– ORIGIN late Middle English: from Old French, or from Latin *flexibilis*, from *flectere* 'to bend.'

flex·ile /'fleksəl, -,sīl/ ▶ **adj.** archaic pliant and flexible: *the serpent's flexile body.*
– DERIVATIVES **flex·il·i·ty** /flek'silətē/ **n.**
– ORIGIN mid 17th cent.: from Latin *flexilis*, from *flectere* 'to bend.'

flex·ion /'flekSHən/ (also **flection**) ▶ **n.** the action of bending or the condition of being bent, esp. the bending of a limb or joint: *flexion of the fingers | these protozoans can move by body flexions.*
– ORIGIN early 17th cent.: from Latin *flexio(n-)*, from *flectere* 'to bend.'

flex·og·ra·phy /flek'sägrəfē/ ▶ **n.** a rotary relief printing method using rubber or plastic plates and fluid inks or dyes for printing on fabrics and impervious materials such as plastics, as well as on paper.
– DERIVATIVES **flex·o·graph·ic** /,fleksə'grafik/ **adj.**
– ORIGIN 1950s: from Latin *flexus* 'a bending' (from the verb *flectere*) + -GRAPHY.

flex·or /'flek,sər, -,sôr/ (also **flexor muscle**) ▶ **n.** Anatomy a muscle whose contraction bends a limb or other part of the body. Often contrasted with EXTENSOR. ■ any of a number of specific muscles in the arm, hand, leg, or foot.

flex·time /'fleks,tīm/ (Brit. **flexitime** /'fleksi-/) ▶ **n.** a system of working a set number of hours with the starting and finishing times chosen within agreed limits by the employee: *no need for day care—the parents can work flextime.*
– ORIGIN 1970s: blend of FLEXIBLE and TIME.

flex·u·ous /'flekSHo͞oəs/ ▶ **adj.** full of bends and curves.
– DERIVATIVES **flex·u·os·i·ty** /,flekSHo͞o'äsitē/ **n.**, **flex·u·ous·ly adv.**
– ORIGIN early 17th cent.: from Latin *flexuosus*, from *flexus* 'a bending,' from the verb *flectere.*

flex·ure /'flekSHər/ ▶ **n.** chiefly Anatomy Geology the action of bending or curving, or the condition of being bent or curved. ■ a bent or curved part: *these lesser hills were flexures of the San Andreas system.*
– DERIVATIVES **flex·ur·al** /-rəl/ **adj.**
– ORIGIN late 16th cent.: from Latin *flexura*, from *flectere* 'to bend.'

flex·wing /'fleks,wiNG/ ▶ **n.** a collapsible fabric delta wing, as used in hang gliders.

flib·ber·ti·gib·bet /'flibərtē,jibit/ ▶ **n.** a frivolous, flighty, or excessively talkative person.
– ORIGIN late Middle English: probably imitative of idle chatter.

flic /flik/ ▶ **n.** informal a French policeman.
– ORIGIN French.

flick /flik/ ▶ **n.** **1** a sudden sharp movement: *the flick of a switch | a flick of the wrist.* ■ the sudden release of a bent finger or thumb, esp. to propel a small object: *he sent his cigarette spinning away with a flick of his fingers.* ■ a light, sharp, quickly retracted blow, esp. with a whip.
2 informal a motion picture: *a Hollywood action flick.* ■ (**the flicks**) chiefly Brit. the movies: *fancy a night at the flicks?*
▶ **v.** [with obj.] propel (something) with a sudden sharp movement, esp. of the fingers: *Emily flicked some ash off her sleeve.* ■ (**flick something on/off**) turn something electrical on or off by means of a switch: *he flicked on the air conditioning.* ■ [no obj.] make a sudden sharp movement: *the finch's tail flicks up and down.* ■ [with obj.] move (a whip) so as to strike.
– PHRASAL VERBS **flick through** another way of saying FLIP THROUGH (see FLIP[1]).
– ORIGIN late Middle English: symbolic, *fl-* frequently beginning words denoting sudden movement.

flick·er[1] /'flikər/ ▶ **v.** [no obj.] **1** (of light or a source of light) shine unsteadily; vary rapidly in brightness: *the interior lights flickered and came on.* ■ (of a flame) burn fitfully, alternately flaring up and dying down: *the candle flickered again* | (as adj. **flickering**) *the flickering flames of the fire.* ■ [with adverbial of place] (of a feeling or emotion) be experienced or show itself briefly and faintly, esp. in someone's eyes: *amusement flickered briefly in his eyes.*
2 make small, quick movements; flutter rapidly: *her eyelids flickered* | [with complement] *the injured killer's eyes flickered open.* ■ [with adverbial of direction] (of someone's eyes) move quickly in a particular direction in order to look at something: *her alert hazel eyes flickered around the room.*
▶ **n.** **1** an unsteady movement of a flame or light that causes rapid variations in brightness: *the flicker of a candle flame caught our eyes.* ■ fluctuations in the brightness of a movie or television image such as occur when the number of frames per second is too small or the refresh rate too low for persistence of vision.
2 a tiny movement: *then a flicker of movement caught his eye.* ■ a brief feeling or indication of emotion: *a flicker of a smile passed across her face | she felt a flicker of alarm.*
– PHRASAL VERBS **flicker out** (of a flame or light) die away and go out after a series of flickers. ■ (of a feeling) die away and finally disappear: *the swift burst of curiosity and eagerness flickered out.*
– ORIGIN Old English *flicorian, flycerian* 'to flutter,' probably of Germanic origin and related to Low German *flickern* and Dutch *flikkeren.*

flick·er[2] ▶ **n.** an American woodpecker that often feeds on ants on the ground. ● Genus *Colaptes*, family Picidae: several species, in particular the **common flicker** (*C. auratus*), occurring in two forms that are distinguished by the underside of the tail and wings, which may be yellow (**yellow-shafted flicker**) or salmon red (**red-shafted flicker**).
– ORIGIN early 19th cent.: imitative of its call.

Flick·er·tail State /'flikər,tāl/ a nickname for the state of NORTH DAKOTA.

flick knife ▶ **n.** British term for SWITCHBLADE.

fli·er /'flīər/ (also **flyer**) ▶ **n.** **1** a person or thing that flies, esp. in a particular way: *a nervous flier.* ■ a person who flies something, esp. an aircraft. ■ informal a fast-moving person or thing.
2 a small handbill advertising an event or product.
3 a speculative investment.
4 a step in a straight flight of stairs.

flight /flīt/ ▶ **n.** **1** the action or process of flying through the air: *an eagle in flight | the history of space flight.* ■ an act of flying; a journey made through the air or in space, esp. a scheduled journey made by an airline: *I got the first flight.* ■ the movement or trajectory of a projectile or ball through the air. ■ [as modifier] relating to or denoting archery in which the main concern is shooting long distances: *short, light flight arrows.* ■ literary swift passage of time: *the never-ending flight of future days.*
2 a group of creatures or objects flying together, in particular: ■ a flock or large body of birds or insects in the air, esp. when migrating: *flights of Canada geese.* ■ a group of aircraft operating together, esp. an air force unit of about six aircraft: *a refueling mission in which his crew topped off three flights of four F-16A jets.*
3 the action of fleeing or attempting to escape: *refugees on the latest stage of their flight from turmoil.*
4 a series of steps between floors or levels: *she has to come up four flights of stairs to her apartment.* ■ a series of hurdles across a racetrack. ■ a closely spaced sequence of locks in a canal.
5 an extravagant or far-fetched idea or account: *ignoring such ridiculous flights of fancy.*
6 the tail of a dart.
▶ **v.** [with obj.] **1** shoot (wildfowl) in flight: (as noun **flighting**) *duck and geese flighting.*
2 Brit. (in soccer, cricket, etc.) deliver (a ball) with well-judged trajectory and pace: *he flighted a free kick into the box.*
– PHRASES **in full flight** escaping as fast as possible. ■ having gained momentum in a run or activity: *when this jazz pianist is in full flight he can be mesmerizing.* **put someone/something to flight** cause someone or something to flee: *a soldier who held off, and eventually put to flight, waves of attackers.* **take flight** **1** (of a bird) take off and fly: *the whole flock took flight* | figurative *my celebrityhood took flight.* **2** flee: *noise that would prompt a spooked horse to take flight.*
– ORIGIN Old English *flyht* 'action or manner of flying,' of Germanic origin; related to Dutch *vlucht* and FLY[1]. This was probably merged in Middle English with an unrecorded Old English word related to German *Flucht* and to FLEE, which is represented by sense 3 of the noun.

flight at·tend·ant ▶ **n.** a steward or stewardess on an aircraft.

flight bag ▶ **n.** a small zippered shoulder bag carried by air travelers.

flight cap·i·tal ▶ **n.** money transferred abroad to avoid taxes or inflation, achieve better investment returns, or to provide for possible emigration.

flight con·trol ▶ **n.** the activity of directing the movement of aircraft: *automatic flight control* | [as modifier] *the flight-control computer.* ■ a control surface on an aircraft.

flight crew ▶ **n.** [treated as sing. or pl.] the personnel responsible for the operation of an aircraft during flight.

flight deck ▶ **n.** **1** the cockpit of a large aircraft, from which the pilot and crew fly it.
2 the deck of an aircraft carrier, used for takeoff and landing.

flight en·gi·neer ▶ **n.** a member of a flight crew responsible for the aircraft's engines and other systems during flight.

flight en·ve·lope ▶ **n.** the range of combinations of speed, altitude, angle of attack, etc., within which a flying object is aerodynamically stable.

flight feath·er ▶ **n.** any of the large primary or secondary feathers in a bird's wing, supporting it in flight. Also called REMEX.

flight·less /'flītlis/ ▶ **adj.** (of a bird or an insect) naturally unable to fly.
– DERIVATIVES **flight·less·ness n.**

flight line ▶ **n.** **1** the part of an airport around the hangars where aircraft can be parked and serviced.
2 a line of flight.

flight path ▶ **n.** the actual or planned course of an aircraft or spacecraft.

flight plan ▶ **n.** Aeronautics a written account of the details of a particular proposed flight.

flight re·cord·er (also **flight data recorder**) ▶ **n.** a device in an aircraft that records technical details during a flight, used in the event of an accident to discover its cause.

flight sim·u·la·tor ▶ **n.** a machine designed to resemble the cockpit of an aircraft, with computer-generated images that mimic the pilot's view, typically with mechanisms that move the entire structure in imitation of an aircraft's motion, used for training pilots.

flight suit ▶ **n.** a one-piece garment worn by the pilot and crew of a military or light aircraft.

flight sur·geon ▶ **n.** a military surgeon specializing in aerospace medicine.

flight test ▶ **n.** a flight of an aircraft, rocket, or equipment to see how well it functions.
▶ **v.** (**flight-test**) [with obj.] test (an aircraft or rocket) by flying it: (as noun **flight-testing**) *it was undergoing cold-weather flight-testing.*

flight·wor·thy /'flīt,wər*TH*ē/ ▶ **adj.** (of an aircraft) capable of being flown safely.

flight·y /ˈflītē/ ▸ adj. (**flightier, flightiest**) fickle and irresponsible: *you may be seen as too flighty and lightweight for real responsibility.*
– DERIVATIVES **flight·i·ly** /ˈflītl-ē/ adv., **flight·i·ness** /ˈflītēnis/ n.
– ORIGIN mid 16th cent.: from FLIGHT + -Y¹.

flim·flam /ˈflim,flam/ informal ▸ n. nonsensical or insincere talk: *I suppose that you suspect me of pseudointellectual flimflam.* ■ a confidence game: *flimflams perpetrated against us by our elected officials.*
▸ v. (**flimflams, flimflamming, flimflammed**) [with obj.] swindle (someone) with a confidence game: *the tribe was flimflammed out of its land.*
– DERIVATIVES **flim·flam·mer** n., **flim·flam·mer·y** /-,flamərē/ n.
– ORIGIN mid 16th cent.: symbolic reduplication.

flim·sy /ˈflimzē/ ▸ adj. (**flimsier, flimsiest**) comparatively light and insubstantial; easily damaged: *voyagers who crossed the sea in flimsy boats.* ■ (of clothing) light and thin: *I wore flimsy clothes and needed warming.* ■ (of a pretext or account) weak and unconvincing: *a pretty flimsy excuse.*
▸ n. (pl. **flimsies**) Brit. a document, esp. a copy, made on very thin paper: *credit-card flimsies.* ■ very thin paper: *sheets of yellow flimsy.*
– DERIVATIVES **flim·si·ly** /ˈflimzəlē/ adv., **flim·si·ness** /-zēnis/ n.
– ORIGIN early 18th cent.: probably from FLIMFLAM.

flinch¹ /flinCH/ ▸ v. [no obj.] make a quick, nervous movement of the face or body as an instinctive reaction to surprise, fear or pain: *she flinched at the acidity in his voice | he had faced death without flinching.* ■ (**flinch from**) avoid doing or becoming involved in (something) through fear or anxiety: *I rarely flinch from a fight when I'm sure of myself.*
▸ n. [in sing.] an act of flinching: *"Don't call me that," he said with a flinch.*
– DERIVATIVES **flinch·er** n., **flinch·ing·ly** adv.
– ORIGIN mid 16th cent. (in the sense 'slink or sneak off'): from Old French *flenchir* 'turn aside,' of West Germanic origin and related to German *lenken* 'to guide, steer.'

flinch² ▸ v. variant spelling of FLENSE.

Flin·ders /ˈflindərz/, Matthew (1774–1814), English explorer. He circumnavigated Australia (1801–03) for the Royal Navy and charted much of its west coast for the first time.

flin·ders /ˈflindərz/ ▸ plural n. small fragments or splinters: *the panel has been smashed to flinders.*
– ORIGIN late Middle English: probably of Scandinavian origin and related to Norwegian *flindra* 'chip, splinter.'

Flin·ders bar ▸ n. a bar of soft iron placed vertically in or near the housing of a ship's compass to correct deviation caused by the local magnetic field of the ship.
– ORIGIN late 19th cent.: name after Captain M. FLINDERS.

fling /fliNG/ ▸ v. (past and past participle **flung** /fləNG/) [with obj.] throw or hurl forcefully: *he picked up the debris and flung it away* | figurative *I was flung into jail.* ■ move or push (something) suddenly or violently: *he flung back the bedclothes* | [with obj.] *Jennifer flung open a door.* ■ (**fling oneself**) throw oneself headlong: *he flung himself down at her feet with a laugh.* ■ (**fling oneself into**) wholeheartedly engage in or begin on (an enterprise): *the producer flung himself into an ugly battle with the studio.* ■ (**fling something on/off**) put on or take off clothes carelessly or rapidly. ■ utter (words) forcefully: *the words were flung at her like an accusation.* ■ [no obj.] go angrily or violently; rush: *he flung away to his study, slamming the door behind him.*
▸ n. **1** a short period of enjoyment or wild behavior: *one final fling before a tranquil retirement.* ■ a short, spontaneous sexual relationship: *I had a fling with someone when I was at college.*
2 short for HIGHLAND FLING.
– DERIVATIVES **fling·er** n.
– ORIGIN Middle English (in the sense 'go violently'): perhaps related to Old Norse *flengja* 'flog.' Sense 1 of the noun is based on an earlier sense 'reckless movement of the body' and dates from the early 19th cent.

Flint /flint/ an industrial city in southeastern Michigan, an auto industry center since the Buick Company was established there in 1903; pop. 112,900 (est. 2008).

flint /flint/ ▸ n. a hard gray rock consisting of nearly pure chert, occurring chiefly as nodules in chalk. ■ a piece of this stone, esp. as flaked or ground in ancient times to form a tool or weapon. ■ a piece of flint used with steel to produce an igniting spark, e.g., in a flintlock gun, or (in modern use) a piece of an alloy used similarly, esp. in a cigarette lighter.
– ORIGIN Old English; related to Middle Dutch *vlint* and Old High German *flins.*

flint corn ▸ n. corn of a variety that has hard, slightly translucent grains.

flint glass ▸ n. a pure lustrous kind of glass originally made with flint.

flint·lock /ˈflint,läk/ ▸ n. **1** an old-fashioned type of gun fired by a spark from a flint.
2 [usu. as modifier] the lock on such a gun: *an antique flintlock pistol.*

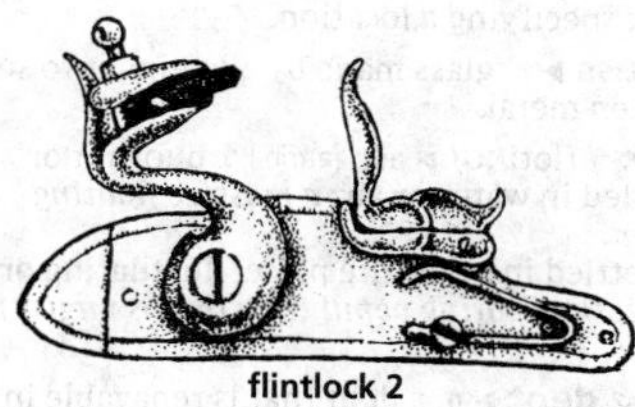
flintlock 2

flint·y /ˈflintē/ ▸ adj. (**flintier, flintiest**) of, containing, or reminiscent of flint: *flinty soil.* ■ (of a person or their expression) very hard and unyielding: *a flinty stare.*
– DERIVATIVES **flint·i·ly** /ˈflintl-ē/ adv., **flint·i·ness** /-tēnis/ n.

flip¹ /flip/ ▸ v. (**flips, flipping, flipped**) **1** turn over or cause to turn over with a sudden sharp movement: [with obj.] *the yacht was flipped by a huge wave* | [no obj.] *the plane flipped over and then exploded.*
2 [with obj.] move, push, or throw (something) with a sudden sharp movement: *she flipped off her dark glasses | she flipped a few coins onto the bar.* ■ turn (an electrical appliance or switch) on or off: *he flipped a switch and the front door opened.* ■ toss (a coin) to decide an issue: *given those odds, one may as well flip a coin* | [no obj.] *you want to flip for it?*
3 [no obj.] informal suddenly lose control or become very angry: *he had clearly flipped under the pressure.* ■ suddenly become very enthusiastic: *I walked into a store, saw the guitar on the wall, and just flipped.*
4 [with obj.] buy and sell (something, esp. real estate or shares) quickly to make a profit: *within one week of starting I flipped a property for a quick $3,000 profit.*
5 [no obj.] informal become an informer: *when he was taken in by the investigators, he flipped immediately.* ■ [with obj.] persuade to become an informer: *the prosecutors won't be able to flip any witnesses to testify against the ex-CEO.*
▸ n. **1** a sudden sharp movement: *the fish made little leaps and flips.* ■ (**a flip through**) a quick look or search through a volume or a collection of papers: *a quick flip through my cookbooks.*
2 Brit. informal a quick tour or pleasure trip: *I did a flip round the post-show party.* [derived from an earlier sense 'short flight in an aircraft.']
▸ adj. glib; flippant: *he couldn't get away with flip, funny conversation.*
▸ exclam. used to express mild annoyance.
– PHRASES **flip one's lid** (or **one's wig**) informal suddenly become deranged or lose one's self-control.
– PHRASAL VERBS **flip through** look or search quickly through (a volume or a collection of papers): *just flip through the phone book and pick a lawyer.*
– ORIGIN mid 16th cent. (as a verb in the sense 'make a flick with the finger and thumb'): probably a contraction of FILLIP.

flip² ▸ n. another term for EGGNOG.
– ORIGIN late 17th cent.: perhaps from FLIP¹ in the sense 'whip up.'

flip chart ▸ n. a large pad of paper bound so that each page can be turned over at the top to reveal the next, used on a stand at presentations.

flip chip ▸ n. a computer chip that is installed on a circuit board face-down, with connections formed by solder bumps rather than wires.
– ORIGIN 1990s: from the fact that the chip is rotated 180 degrees from the traditional mode of attachment.

flip-flop ▸ n. **1** a light sandal, typically of plastic or rubber, with a thong between the big and second toe.
2 a backward handspring.
3 informal an abrupt reversal of policy: *his flip-flop on taxes.*
4 Electronics a switching circuit that works by changing from one stable state to another, or through an unstable state back to its stable state, in response to a triggering pulse.
▸ v. [no obj.] **1** [with adverbial of direction] move with a flapping sound or motion: *she flip-flopped off the porch in battered sneakers.*
2 informal make an abrupt reversal of policy: *the candidate flip-flopped on a number of issues.*
– ORIGIN mid 17th cent. (in the general sense 'something that flaps or flops'): imitative reduplication of FLOP.

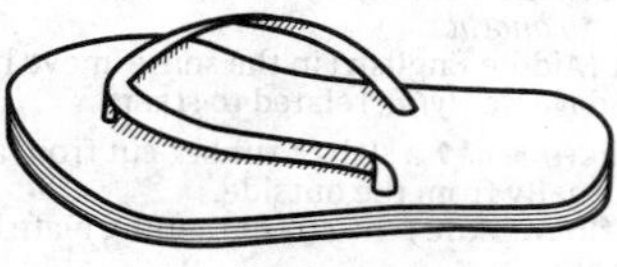
flip-flop 1

flip·pan·cy /ˈflipənsē/ ▸ n. lack of respect or seriousness; frivolousness: *she was infuriated by his careless flippancy.*

flip·pant /ˈflipənt/ ▸ adj. not showing a serious or respectful attitude: *a flippant remark.*
– DERIVATIVES **flip·pant·ly** adv.
– ORIGIN early 17th cent.: from FLIP¹ + -ANT, perhaps on the pattern of heraldic terms such as *couchant* and *rampant.* Early senses included 'nimble' and 'talkative,' hence 'playful,' giving rise to the current use 'lacking seriousness.'

Flip·per /ˈflipər/, Henry Ossian (1856–1940), US soldier and engineer. The first black graduate of West Point 1877, he was court-martialed on false charges in 1882. The charges were not withdrawn until 1970.

flip·per /ˈflipər/ ▸ n. a broad flat limb without fingers, used for swimming by various sea animals such as seals, whales, and turtles. ■ a flat rubber attachment worn on the foot for underwater swimming. ■ a pivoted arm in a pinball machine, controlled by the player and used for sending the ball back up the table. ■ informal a hand.

flip·ping /ˈflipiNG/ ▸ adj. [attrib.] informal, chiefly Brit. used for emphasis or to express mild annoyance: *are you out of your flipping mind?*
– ORIGIN early 20th cent.: from FLIP¹ + -ING².

flip side ▸ n. informal the less important side of a pop single record; the B-side. ■ another aspect or version of something, esp. its reverse or its unwanted concomitant: *virtues are the flip side of vices.*

flip-top ▸ adj. [attrib.] denoting or having a lid or cover that can be easily opened by pulling, pushing, or flicking it with the fingers: *an accessory case with a clear flip-top lid.*
▸ n. a lid or cover of this kind.

flirt /flərt/ ▸ v. **1** [no obj.] behave as though attracted to or trying to attract someone, but for amusement rather than with serious intentions: *it amused him to flirt with her.* ■ (**flirt with**) experiment with or show a superficial interest in (an idea, activity, or movement) without committing oneself to it seriously: *a painter who had flirted briefly with Cubism.* ■ (**flirt with**) deliberately expose oneself to (danger or difficulty): *the need of some individuals to flirt with death.*
2 [with obj.] (of a bird) wave or open and shut (its wings or tail) with a quick flicking motion. ■ [no obj.] move back and forth with a flicking or fluttering motion: *the lark was flirting around the site.*
▸ n. a person who habitually flirts.
– DERIVATIVES **flirt·y** (**flirtier, flirtiest**).
– ORIGIN mid 16th cent.: apparently symbolic, the elements *fl-* and *-irt* both suggesting sudden movement; compare with FLICK and SPURT. The original verb senses were 'give someone a sharp blow' and 'sneer at'; the earliest noun senses were 'joke, gibe' and 'flighty girl' (defined by Dr. Johnson as 'a pert young hussey'), with a notion originally of cheeky behavior, later of playfully amorous behavior.

flir·ta·tion /flərˈtāSHən/ ▸ n. behavior that demonstrates a playful sexual attraction to someone: *Fabia was in no mood for his lighthearted flirtation.* ■ a short or casual relationship: *she had had plenty of flirtations—now she had fallen in love.* ■ a short period of casual experimentation with or interest in a particular idea or activity: *his brief flirtation with the avant-garde in the 1920s.*

flir·ta·tious /flərˈtāSHəs/ ▸ adj. behaving in such a way as to suggest a playful sexual attraction to someone: *she was beautiful and very flirtatious.* ■ expressing a playful sexual attraction: *a flirtatious smile.*
– DERIVATIVES **flir·ta·tious·ly** /-ˈtāSHəslē/ adv., **flir·ta·tious·ness** /-ˈtāSHəsnəs/ n.

flit /flit/ ▸ v. (**flits, flitting, flitted**) [no obj.] move swiftly and lightly: *small birds flitted about in the*

branches | figurative *the idea had flitted through his mind.* ■ Brit. leave one's home or move, typically secretly so as to escape creditors or obligations.
▶ n. Brit. informal an act of leaving one's home or moving, typically secretly so as to escape creditors or obligations: ***moonlight flits** from one insalubrious dwelling to another.*
– ORIGIN Middle English (in the sense 'move house'): from Old Norse *flytja*; related to FLEET[4].

flitch /fliCH/ ▶ n. **1** a slab of timber cut from a tree trunk, usually from the outside.
2 (also **flitch plate**) the strengthening plate in a flitch beam.
3 chiefly dialect a side of bacon.
– ORIGIN Old English *flicce*, originally denoting the salted and cured side of any meat, of Germanic origin; related to Middle Low German *vlicke*.

flitch beam ▶ n. a compound beam made of a steel plate between two slabs of wood.

f

flit·ter /ˈflitər/ ▶ v. [no obj.] move quickly in an apparently random or purposeless manner: *if only you would settle down instead of flittering around the countryside.*
▶ n. a fluttering movement: *the flash and flitter of colored wings.*
– ORIGIN late Middle English: frequentative of FLIT.

flit·ter·mouse /ˈflitərˌmous/ ▶ n. (pl. **flittermice** /-ˌmīs/) old-fashioned term for BAT[2] (sense 1).
– ORIGIN mid 16th cent.: on the pattern of Dutch *vledermuis* or German *Fledermaus*.

fliv·ver /ˈflivər/ ▶ n. informal, dated a cheap car or aircraft, esp. one in bad condition.
– ORIGIN early 20th cent.: of unknown origin.

flix·weed /ˈfliksˌwēd/ ▶ n. a Eurasian plant with small yellow flowers and finely divided leaves, formerly thought to cure dysentery. ● *Descurainia sophia*, family Brassicaceae.
– ORIGIN late 16th cent.: from obsolete *flix* (variant of FLUX) + WEED.

FLN ▶ abbr. Front de Libération Nationale.

float /flōt/ ▶ v. [no obj.] **1** rest or move on or near the surface of a liquid without sinking: *she relaxed, floating gently in the water.* ■ [with obj.] cause (a buoyant object) to rest or move in such a way: *trees were felled and floated downstream.* ■ be suspended freely in a liquid or gas: *fragments of chipped cartilage floated in the joint.*
2 [with adverbial of direction] move or hover slowly and lightly in a liquid or the air; drift: *clouds floated across a brilliant blue sky* | figurative *through the open window floated the sound of traffic.* ■ (**float about/around**) (of a rumor, idea, etc.) circulate: *the notion was floating around Capitol Hill.* ■ (of a sight or idea) come before the eyes or mind: *the advice his father had given him **floated into** his mind.* ■ [with obj.] (in sports) make (the ball) travel lightly and effortlessly through the air: *he floated the kick into the net.*
3 [with obj.] put forward (an idea) as a suggestion or test of reactions. ■ offer the shares of (a company) for sale on the stock market for the first time.
4 (of a currency) fluctuate freely in value in accordance with supply and demand in the financial markets: *a policy of letting the pound float.* ■ [with obj.] allow (a currency) to fluctuate in such a way.
▶ n. **1** a thing that is buoyant in water, in particular: ■ a small object attached to a fishing line to indicate by moving when a fish bites. ■ a cork or buoy supporting the edge of a fishing net. ■ a hollow or inflated organ enabling an organism (such as the Portuguese man-of-war) to float in the water. ■ a hollow structure fixed underneath an aircraft enabling it to take off and land on water. ■ a device floating on the surface of a liquid that forms part of a valve apparatus controlling flow in and out of the enclosing container, e.g., in a toilet tank or a carburetor.
2 a platform mounted on a truck and carrying a display in a parade: *a carnival float.*
3 a hand tool with a rectangular blade used for smoothing plaster or concrete.
4 a soft drink with a scoop of ice cream floating in it: *root-beer floats.*
5 (in critical path analysis) the period of time by which the duration of an activity may be extended without affecting the overall time for the process.
– PHRASES **float someone's boat** informal appeal to or excite someone, esp. sexually: *Kevin doesn't exactly float her boat.*
– ORIGIN Old English *flotian* (verb), of Germanic origin and related to FLEET[4], reinforced in Middle English by Old French *floter*, also from Germanic.

float·a·ble /ˈflōtəbəl/ ▶ adj. capable of floating. ■ (of water) able to support floating objects; deep enough to float in.

float arm ▶ n. the hinged arm attached to the ball float in the ballcock of a toilet tank.

float·a·tion /flōˈtāSHən/ ▶ n. variant spelling of FLOTATION.

float·el /flōˈtel/ (also **flotel**) ▶ n. a floating hotel, esp. a boat used as a hotel. ■ a vessel providing housing for workers on an offshore oil rig.
– ORIGIN 1950s: blend of FLOAT and HOTEL.

float·er /ˈflōtər/ ▶ n. **1** a person or thing that floats, in particular: ■ a worker who is required to do a variety of tasks as the need for each arises. ■ informal a person who frequently changes occupation or residence. ■ a loose particle within the eyeball that is apparent in one's field of vision.
2 an insurance policy covering loss of articles without specifying a location.

float glass ▶ n. glass made by allowing it to solidify on molten metal.

float·ing /ˈflōtiNG/ ▶ adj. [attrib.] **1** buoyant or suspended in water or air: *a massive floating platform.*
2 not settled in a definite place; fluctuating or variable: *the floating population that is migrating to the cities.*

float·ing debt ▶ n. a debt that is repayable in the short term. Compare with FUNDED DEBT.

float·ing dock ▶ n. a submersible floating structure used as a dry dock.

float·ing kid·ney ▶ n. a condition in which the kidneys are abnormally movable. ■ such a kidney.

float·ing-point ▶ adj. Computing denoting a mode of representing numbers as two sequences of bits, one representing the digits in the number and the other an exponent that determines the position of the radix point: *speeds of more than one million **floating-point operations** per second.* Often contrasted with FIXED POINT (adjective).

float·ing rib ▶ n. any of the lower ribs that are not attached directly to the breastbone. Also called FALSE RIB.

float·plane /ˈflōtˌplān/ ▶ n. an aircraft equipped with floats for landing on water; a seaplane.

float valve ▶ n. another term for BALL VALVE.

float·y /ˈflōtē/ ▶ adj. ■ (esp. of a woman's garment or a fabric) light and flimsy: *elegant floaty dresses.*

floc /fläk/ ▶ n. technical a loosely clumped mass of fine particles.
– ORIGIN 1920s: abbreviation of FLOCCULUS.

floc·ci·nau·ci·ni·hil·i·pil·i·fi·ca·tion /ˌfläksəˌnôsəˌnīˌhiləˌpiləfiˈkāSHən/ ▶ n. the action or habit of estimating something as worthless. (The word is used chiefly as a curiosity.).
– ORIGIN mid 18th cent.: from Latin *flocci, nauci, nihili, pili* (words meaning 'at little value') + -FICATION. The Latin elements were listed in a well-known rule of the Latin Grammar used at Eton College, an English public school.

floc·cose /ˈfläkˌōs/ ▶ adj. chiefly Botany covered with or consisting of woolly tufts.
– ORIGIN mid 18th cent.: from late Latin *floccosus*, from Latin *floccus* 'flock.'

floc·cu·lant /ˈfläkyələnt/ ▶ n. a substance that promotes the clumping of particles, esp. one used in treating waste water.

floc·cu·late /ˈfläkyəˌlāt/ ▶ v. technical form or cause to form into small clumps or masses: [no obj.] *it tends to flocculate in high salinities* | [with obj.] *its ability to flocculate suspended silt.*
– DERIVATIVES **floc·cu·la·tion** /ˌfläkyəˈlāSHən/ n.
– ORIGIN late 19th cent.: from modern Latin *flocculus* 'floccule' + -ATE[3].

floc·cule /ˈfläkˌyo͞ol/ ▶ n. a small clump of material that resembles a tuft of wool.
– ORIGIN mid 19th cent.: from modern Latin *flocculus*, diminutive of *floccus* 'flock.'

floc·cu·lent /ˈfläkyələnt/ ▶ adj. having or resembling tufts of wool: *the first snows of winter lay thick and flocculent.* ■ having a loosely clumped texture: *a brown flocculent precipitate.*
– DERIVATIVES **floc·cu·lence** n.
– ORIGIN early 19th cent.: from Latin *floccus* 'tuft of wool' + -ULENT.

floc·cu·lus /ˈfläkyələs/ ▶ n. (pl. **flocculi** /-ˌlī, -ˌlē/) **1** Anatomy a small egg-shaped lobe on the undersurface of the cerebellum.
2 Astronomy a small cloudy wisp on the surface of the sun.
3 a floccule.
– ORIGIN late 18th cent.: modern Latin, diminutive of Latin *floccus* (see FLOCCUS).

floc·cus /ˈfläkəs/ ▶ n. (pl. **flocci** /ˈfläkˌsī, -ˌsē/) a tuft of wool or similar clump of fibers or filaments.
– ORIGIN mid 19th cent.: from Latin, 'lock or tuft of wool.' Compare with FLOCK[2].

flock[1] /fläk/ ▶ n. a number of birds of one kind feeding, resting, or traveling together: ***a flock of** gulls.* ■ a number of domestic animals, esp. sheep, goats, or geese, that are kept together: ***a flock of** sheep.* ■ (**flocks**) large crowds of people: ***flocks of** young people hung around at twilight.* ■ a group of children or students in someone's charge. ■ a Christian congregation or body of believers, esp. one under the charge of a particular minister: *Thomas addressed his flock.* [alluding to the metaphor of Christ or a Christian pastor as a shepherd.]
▶ v. [no obj.] congregate or mass in a flock or large group: *students flocked to spring break sites.*
– ORIGIN Old English *flocc*, of unknown origin. The original sense was 'a band or body of people': this became obsolete, but has been reintroduced as a transferred use of the sense 'a number of animals kept together.'

flock[2] (also **flocking**) ▶ n. [often as modifier] a soft material for stuffing cushions, quilts, and other soft furnishings, made of wool refuse or torn-up cloth: *flock mattresses.* ■ powdered wool or cloth, sprinkled on wallpaper, cloth, or metal to make a raised pattern. ■ a lock or tuft of wool or cotton.
– DERIVATIVES **flock·y** adj.
– ORIGIN Middle English: from Old French *floc*, from Latin *floccus* (see FLOCCUS).

Flod·den, Battle of /ˈflädn/ (also **Flodden Field**) a decisive battle of the Anglo-Scottish war of 1513, at Flodden, a hill near the Northumbrian village of Branxton in northeastern England. A Scottish army under James IV was defeated by a smaller but better-led English force and suffered heavy losses, including the king and most of his nobles.

floe /flō/ (also **ice floe**) ▶ n. a sheet of floating ice.
– ORIGIN early 19th cent. (superseding FLAKE[1] in this sense): probably from Norwegian *flo*, from Old Norse *fló* 'layer.'

flog /fläg/ ▶ v. (**flogs, flogging, flogged**) [with obj.] **1** beat (someone) with a whip or stick as punishment or torture: *the stolen horses will be returned and the thieves flogged* | (as noun **flogging**) *public floggings.* ■ informal promote or talk about (something) repetitively or at excessive length: *rather than **flogging** one idea **to death**, they should be a lighthearted pop group.*
2 Brit. informal sell or offer for sale: *he made a fortune flogging beads to hippies.*
– DERIVATIVES **flog·ger** n.
– ORIGIN late 17th cent. (originally slang): perhaps imitative, or from Latin *flagellare* 'to whip,' from *flagellum* 'whip.'

flo·ka·ti /flōˈkätē/ (also **flokati rug**) ▶ n. (pl. **flokatis**) a Greek woven woolen rug with a thick loose pile.
– ORIGIN mid 20th cent.: from modern Greek *phlokatē* 'peasant's blanket.'

flood /fləd/ ▶ n. **1** an overflowing of a large amount of water beyond its normal confines, esp. over what is normally dry land: *in a thousand miles the flood destroyed every bridge* | *people uprooted by drought or flood* | [as modifier] *a flood barrier.* ■ (**the Flood**) the biblical flood brought by God upon the earth because of the wickedness of the human race (Gen. 6 ff.). ■ the inflow of the tide. ■ literary a river, stream, or sea.
2 an outpouring of tears or emotion: *Rose burst into such **a flood of** tears and sobs as I had never seen.* ■ a very large quantity of people or things that appear or need to be dealt with: *a constant **flood of** callers.*
3 short for FLOODLIGHT.
▶ v. **1** [with obj.] cover or submerge (a place or area) with water: *the dam burst, flooding a small town* | *watching her father flood their backyard skating rink* | (as noun **flooding**) *a serious risk of flooding.* ■ [no obj.] become covered or submerged in this way: *part of the vessel flooded* | figurative *Sarah's eyes **flooded with** tears.* ■ (usu. **be flooded out**) drive someone out of their home or business with a flood: *most of the families who have been flooded out will receive compensation.* ■ (of a river or sea) become swollen and overflow (its banks): *the river flooded its banks* | [no obj.] *the river will flood if it gets much worse.* ■ overfill the carburetor of (an engine) with fuel, causing the engine to fail to start.
2 [no obj.] arrive in overwhelming amounts or quantities: *congratulatory messages flooded in* | *his old fears came flooding back.* ■ [with obj.] overwhelm or swamp with large amounts or quantities: *our switchboard was flooded with calls.* ■ [with obj.] fill or suffuse completely: *she flooded the room with light.*
– PHRASES **be in** (**full**) **flood** (of a river) be swollen and overflowing its banks. ■ (**be in full flood**) (of a person or action) have gained momentum; be at the height of activity: *discussion was already in full flood and refused to be dammed.*
– ORIGIN Old English *flōd*, of Germanic origin; related to Dutch *vloed* and German *Flut*, also to FLOW.

flood·gate /ˈflədˌgāt/ ▶ n. a gate that can be opened or closed to admit or exclude water, esp. the lower gate of a lock. ■ (usu. **the floodgates**) a last restraint holding back an outpouring of something powerful or substantial: *his lawsuit could open the floodgates for thousands of similar claims.*

flood·light /ˈfləd,līt/ ▶ **n.** a large, powerful light, typically one of several used to illuminate a sports field, a stage, or the exterior of a building. ■ the illumination provided by such a light: *a tennis court where you can play by floodlight.*
▶ **v.** (past and past participle **floodlit**) [with obj.] (usu. as adj. **floodlit**) illuminate (a building or outdoor area) with such lights: *floodlit football fields.*

flood·plain /ˈfləd,plān/ ▶ **n.** an area of low-lying ground adjacent to a river, formed mainly of river sediments and subject to flooding.

flood tide ▶ **n.** an incoming tide. ■ a powerful surge or flow of something: *the trickle of tourists has become a flood tide.*

flood·wa·ter /ˈfləd,wôtər, -,wätər/ (also **floodwaters**) ▶ **n.** water overflowing as the result of a flood: *trying to track the rising floodwaters and coordinate relief efforts.*

floor /flôr/ ▶ **n. 1** the lower surface of a room, on which one may walk: *he dropped the cup and it smashed on the floor* | *the kitchen floor.* ■ the bottom of the sea, a cave, or an area of land: *the ocean floor.* ■ informal the ground: *the best way to play is to pass the ball on the floor.* ■ the minimum level of prices or wages: *the dollar's floor against the yen.*
2 all the rooms or areas on the same level of a building; a story: *his office was on the twenty-second floor* | [as modifier, in combination] *a third-floor apartment.*
3 (**the floor**) (in a legislative assembly) the part of the house in which members sit and from which they speak. ■ the right or opportunity to speak next in debate: *other speakers have the floor.* ■ (of the stock exchange) the large central hall where trading takes place.
▶ **v.** [with obj.] **1** provide (a room or area) with a floor: *a hall floored in gleaming white oak* | [as adj., in combination] (**-floored**) *a stone-floored building.*
2 informal knock (someone) to the ground, esp. with a punch. ■ baffle or confound (someone) completely: *that question floored him.*
– PHRASES **cross the floor** see **CROSS**. **from the floor** (of a speech or question) delivered by an individual member at a meeting, not by a representative on the platform: *questions from the floor will be invited.* **take the floor 1** begin to dance on a dance floor. **2** speak in a debate or assembly.
– ORIGIN Old English *flōr*, of Germanic origin; related to Dutch *vloer* and German *Flur*.

floor·board /ˈflôr,bôrd/ ▶ **n.** a long plank making up part of a wooden floor in a building. ■ the floor of a motor vehicle: *the keys had fallen on the floorboard of her car.*

floor·cloth /ˈflôr,klôTH/ ▶ **n.** a thin canvas rug or similar light floor covering.

floor ex·er·cise ▶ **n.** a routine of gymnastic exercises performed without the use any of apparatus.

floor·ing /ˈflôriNG/ ▶ **n.** the boards or other material of which a floor is made.

floor lamp ▶ **n.** a tall lamp designed to stand on the floor.

floor lead·er ▶ **n.** the leader of a party in a legislative assembly.

floor·man /ˈflôrmən/ ▶ **n.** (pl. **floormen**) a person who supervises the gaming tables in a casino.

floor man·ag·er ▶ **n. 1** the stage manager of a television production.
2 an employee in a large store who supervises other salespeople.

floor·pan /ˈflôr,pan/ ▶ **n.** chiefly Brit. the lower part of the body of a motor vehicle, forming the floor of the passenger compartment.

floor plan ▶ **n.** a scale diagram of the arrangement of rooms in one story of a building.

floor sam·ple ▶ **n.** an article of merchandise that has been displayed in a store and that is offered for sale at a reduced price.

floor show ▶ **n.** an entertainment, such as singing or comedy, presented at a nightclub, restaurant, or similar venue.

floor-through a·part·ment ▶ **n.** an apartment that occupies an entire floor of a building.

floor·walk·er /ˈflôr,wôkər/ ▶ **n.** a senior employee of a large store who assists customers and supervises salespeople.

floo·zy /ˈflo͞ozē/ (also **floozie, floosie**) ▶ **n.** (pl. **floozies**) informal a girl or a woman who has a reputation for promiscuity.
– ORIGIN early 20th cent.: perhaps related to **FLOSSY** or to dialect *floosy* 'fluffy.'

flop /fläp/ ▶ **v.** (**flops, flopping, flopped**) **1** [no obj.] fall, move, or hang in a heavy, loose, and ungainly way: *black hair flopped across his forehead.* ■ sit or lie down heavily or suddenly in a specified place, esp. when very tired: *Liz flopped down into the armchair.* ■ informal rest or sleep in a specified place: *I'm going to flop here for the night.*
2 [no obj.] informal (of a performer or show) be completely unsuccessful; fail totally: *prime-time dramas that flopped in the U.S. market.*
▶ **n. 1** a heavy, loose, and ungainly movement, or a sound made by it: *they hit the ground with a flop.* ■ informal a cheap place to sleep.
2 informal a total failure: *the play had been a flop.*
– ORIGIN early 17th cent.: variant of **FLAP**.

-flop ▶ **comb. form** Computing floating-point operations per second (used as a measure of computing power): *a gigaflop computer.*
– ORIGIN acronym; originally spelled *-flops* (*s* = second) but shortened to avoid misinterpretation as plural.

flop·house /ˈfläp,hous/ ▶ **n.** informal a cheap hotel or rooming house.

flop·py /ˈfläpē/ ▶ **adj.** (**floppier, floppiest**) tending to hang or move in a limp, loose, or ungainly way: *the dog had floppy ears* | *floppy hats.*
▶ **n.** (pl. **floppies**) (also **floppy disk**) Computing short for **FLOPPY DISK**.
– DERIVATIVES **flop·pi·ly** /ˈfläpəlē/ **adv.**, **flop·pi·ness n.**

flop·py disk ▶ **n.** Computing a flexible removable magnetic disk, typically encased in hard plastic, used for storing data. Also called **DISKETTE**. Compare with **HARD DISK**.

flop·ti·cal /ˈfläptikəl/ ▶ **adj.** Computing, trademark denoting or relating to a type of floppy-disk drive using a laser to position the read-write head.
▶ **n.** a floppy-disk drive of this type.
– ORIGIN 1980s: blend of **FLOPPY** and **OPTICAL**.

flor /flôr/ ▶ **n.** yeast allowed to develop in a whitish film on the surface of dry (fino) sherries and similar wines during fermentation.
– ORIGIN late 19th cent.: from Spanish, literally 'flower.'

flor. ▶ **abbr.** floruit.

Flo·ra /ˈflôrə/ Roman Mythology the goddess of flowering plants.

flo·ra /ˈflôrə/ ▶ **n.** (pl. **floras** or **florae** /ˈflôrē, ˈflôrī/) the plants of a particular region, habitat, or geological period: *the desert flora give way to oak woodlands* | *the river's **flora and fauna** have been inventoried and protected.* Compare with **FAUNA**. ■ a treatise on or list of such plant life.
– ORIGIN late 18th cent.: from Latin *flos, flor-* 'flower.'

flo·ral /ˈflôrəl/ ▶ **adj.** of flowers: *celebrations of the season's floral abundance.* ■ decorated with or depicting flowers: *a floral pattern.* ■ Botany of flora or floras: *faunal and floral evolution.*
▶ **n.** a fabric with a floral design.
– DERIVATIVES **flo·ral·ly adv.**
– ORIGIN mid 18th cent.: from Latin *flos, flor-* 'flower' + **-AL**.

Flo·ré·al /,flôrāˈäl/ **n.** the eighth month of the French Republican calendar (1793–1805), originally running from April 20 to May 19.
– ORIGIN French, from Latin *floreus* 'flowery,' from *flos, flor-* 'flower.'

Flor·ence /ˈflôrəns, ˈflär-/ **1** a city in western central Italy, the capital of Tuscany, on the Arno River; pop. 365,659 (2008). Florence was a leading center of the Italian Renaissance, esp. under the rule of the Medici family during the 15th century. Italian name **FIRENZE**.
2 an industrial and commercial city in northwestern Alabama, on the Tennessee River, east of Muscle Shoals; pop. 37,877 (est. 2008).

Flor·ence fen·nel ▶ **n.** see **FENNEL**.

Flor·en·tine /ˈflôrən,tēn, -tīn/ ▶ **adj. 1** of or relating to Florence.
2 (**florentine**) [postpositive] (of food) served or prepared on a bed of spinach: *eggs florentine.*
▶ **n. 1** a native or citizen of Florence.
2 (**florentine**) a cookie consisting mainly of nuts and preserved fruit, coated on one side with chocolate.
– ORIGIN Middle English (as a noun): from French *Florentin(e)* or Latin *Florentinus*, from *Florentia* 'Florence.'

Flo·res /ˈflôrəs/ the largest of the Lesser Sunda Islands in Indonesia.

flo·res·cence /flôrˈesəns, fləˈres-/ ▶ **n.** the process of flowering: *the Hieracia are erect throughout the process of florescence* | figurative *a spectacular cultural florescence.*
– ORIGIN late 18th cent.: from modern Latin *florescentia*, from Latin *florescere* 'begin to flower,' based on *flos, flor-* 'flower.'

flo·ret /ˈflôrət/ ▶ **n.** Botany one of the small flowers making up a composite flower head. ■ one of the flowering stems making up a head of cauliflower or broccoli. ■ a small flower.
– ORIGIN late 17th cent.: from Latin *flos, flor-* 'flower' + **-ET**¹.

Flo·rey /ˈflôrē/, Howard Walter, Baron (1898–1968), Australian pathologist. With Ernst Chain, he isolated and purified penicillin. Nobel Prize for Physiology or Medicine (1945), shared with Chain and Alexander Fleming.

Flo·ri·a·nóp·o·lis /,flôrēəˈnôpəlis/ a city in southern Brazil, on the Atlantic coast; pop. 396,723 (2007).

flo·ri·at·ed /ˈflôrē,ātid/ ▶ **adj.** decorated with floral designs.

flo·ri·bun·da /,flôrəˈbəndə/ ▶ **n.** a plant, esp. a rose, that bears dense clusters of flowers.
– ORIGIN late 19th cent.: modern Latin, feminine (used as a noun) of *floribundus* 'freely flowering,' from Latin *flos, flor-* 'flower,' influenced by Latin *abundus* 'copious.'

flo·ri·can /ˈflôrə,kan/ ▶ **n.** a small southern Asian bustard (bird), the male of which has mainly black plumage with white wings. ● Family Otidae: the **Bengal florican** (*Houbaropsis begalensis*) and the **lesser florican** (*Sypheotides indica*).
– ORIGIN late 18th cent.: of unknown origin.

flo·ri·cul·ture /ˈflôri,kəlCHər/ ▶ **n.** the cultivation of flowers.
– DERIVATIVES **flo·ri·cul·tur·al** /,flôriˈkəlCHərəl/ **adj.**, **flo·ri·cul·tur·ist** /,flôriˈkəlCHərist/ **n.**
– ORIGIN early 19th cent.: from Latin *flos, flor-* 'flower' + **CULTURE**, on the pattern of *horticulture*.

flor·id /ˈflôrid, ˈflär-/ ▶ **adj. 1** having a red or flushed complexion: *a stout man with a florid face.*
2 elaborately or excessively intricate or complicated: *florid operatic-style music was out.* ■ (of language) using unusual words or complicated rhetorical constructions: *the florid prose of the nineteenth century.*
3 Medicine (of a disease or its manifestations) occurring in a fully developed form: *florid symptoms of psychiatric disorder.*
– DERIVATIVES **flo·rid·i·ty** /fləˈridətē/ **n.**, **flor·id·ly adv.**, **flor·id·ness n.**
– ORIGIN mid 17th cent.: from Latin *floridus*, from *flos, flor-* 'flower.'

Flor·i·da /ˈflôridə, ˈflär-/ a state in the southeastern US, on a peninsula that extends into the Atlantic Ocean and the Gulf of Mexico; pop. 18,328,340 (est. 2008); capital, Tallahassee; statehood, Mar. 3, 1845 (27). Explored by Ponce de León in 1513, it was purchased from Spain by the US in 1819. It is a popular resort and retirement area.
– DERIVATIVES **Flo·rid·i·an** /fləˈridēən, flô-, flä-/ **adj. & n.**

Flor·i·da Keys a chain of small islands off the tip of the Florida peninsula. Linked to each other and to the mainland by a series of causeways and bridges that form the Overseas Highway, the islands extend southwest over a distance of 100 miles (160 km).

Flor·i·da room ▶ **n.** another term for **SUNROOM**.

Flor·i·da tor·re·ya ▶ **n.** another term for **STINKING CEDAR**.

flo·rif·er·ous /flôˈrifərəs/ ▶ **adj.** (of a plant) producing many flowers.
– ORIGIN mid 17th cent.: from Latin *florifer* (from *flos, flor-* 'flower' + *-fer* 'producing') + **-OUS**.

flo·ri·le·gi·um /,flôrəˈlējēəm/ ▶ **n.** (pl. **florilegia** /-ˈlējēə/ or **florilegiums**) a collection of literary extracts; an anthology.
– ORIGIN early 17th cent.: modern Latin, literally 'bouquet' (from Latin *flos, flor-* 'flower' + *legere* 'gather'), translation of Greek *anthologion* (see **ANTHOLOGY**).

flor·in /ˈflôrən, ˈflär-/ ▶ **n. 1** a former British coin and monetary unit worth two shillings.
2 a foreign coin of gold or silver, esp. a Dutch guilder.
3 the basic monetary unit of Aruba, equal to 100 cents.
– ORIGIN via Old French from Italian *fiorino*, diminutive of *fiore* 'flower,' from Latin *flos, flor-*. The word originally denoted a gold coin issued in Florence, bearing a fleur-de-lis (the city's emblem) on the reverse.

Flor·is·sant /ˈflôrəsənt/ a historic city in east central Missouri, northwest of St. Louis; pop. 50,561 (est. 2008).

flo·rist /ˈflôrist/ ▶ n. a person who sells and arranges plants and cut flowers.
– DERIVATIVES **flo·rist·ry** /-trē/ n.
– ORIGIN early 17th cent.: from Latin *flos, flor-* 'flower,' on the pattern of French *fleuriste* or Italian *florista*.

flo·ris·tic /fləˈristik/ ▶ adj. Botany relating to the study of the distribution of plants.
– DERIVATIVES **flo·ris·ti·cal·ly** /-(ə)lē/ adv.

flo·ris·tics /fləˈristiks/ ▶ plural n. [treated as sing.] Botany the branch of phytogeography concerned with the study of plant species present in an area.

flo·ru·it /ˈflôr(y)o͞oit/ (abbr.: **fl.** or **flor.**) ▶ v. used in conjunction with a specified period or set of dates to indicate when a particular historical figure lived, worked, or was most active.
▶ n. such a period: *they place Nicander's floruit in the middle of the 2nd century bc.*
– ORIGIN mid 19th cent.: Latin, literally 'he or she flourished.'

f

flo·ry /ˈflôrē/ (also **fleury** /ˈflərē, ˈflo͝orē/) ▶ adj. [predic. or postpositive] Heraldry decorated with fleurs-de-lis. ■ (of a cross) having the end of each limb splayed out into three pointed lobes.
– PHRASES **flory counter-flory** decorated with fleurs-de-lis set in alternating directions.
– ORIGIN late Middle English: from Old French *floure*, from *flour* 'flower.'

floss /flôs, fläs/ ▶ n. the rough silk enveloping a silkworm's cocoon. ■ (also **floss silk**) untwisted silk fibers used in embroidery. ■ the silky down in corn and other plants: *milkweed floss.* ■ short for DENTAL FLOSS.
▶ v. [with obj.] clean between (one's teeth) with dental floss: *I flossed my teeth* | [no obj.] *you must floss well.*
– ORIGIN mid 18th cent.: from French (*soie*) *floche* 'floss (silk),' from Old French *flosche* 'down, nap of velvet,' of unknown origin.

floss·y /ˈflôsē, ˈfläsē/ ▶ adj. (**flossier, flossiest**) **1** of or like floss: *short flossy curls.*
2 informal excessively showy: *the flossy gleam of a cheap suit* | *she cultivated flossy friends.*

flo·ta·tion /flōˈtāsHən/ (also **floatation**) ▶ n. the action of floating in a liquid or gas: *the body form is modified to assist in flotation and propulsion.* ■ the process of offering a company's shares for sale on the stock market for the first time. ■ the process of separating small particles of various materials by treatment with chemicals in water in order to make some particles adhere to air bubbles and rise to the surface for removal while others remain in the water. ■ the capacity to float; buoyancy.
– ORIGIN early 19th cent.: alteration of *floatation* (from FLOAT) on the pattern of French *flottaison*. The spelling *flot-* was influenced by FLOTILLA.

flo·ta·tion tank ▶ n. a lightproof, soundproof tank of salt water in which a person floats as a form of deep relaxation.

flo·tel ▶ n. variant spelling of FLOATEL.

flo·til·la /flōˈtilə/ ▶ n. a fleet of ships or boats: *a flotilla of cargo boats.*
– ORIGIN early 18th cent.: from Spanish, diminutive of *flota* 'fleet.'

flot·sam /ˈflätsəm/ ▶ n. the wreckage of a ship or its cargo found floating on or washed up by the sea. Compare with JETSAM. ■ people or things that have been rejected and are regarded as worthless: *the room was cleared of boxes and other flotsam.*
– PHRASES **flotsam and jetsam** useless or discarded objects.
– ORIGIN early 17th cent.: from Anglo-Norman French *floteson*, from *floter* 'to float.'

flounce[1] /flouns/ ▶ v. [no obj.] go or move in an exaggeratedly impatient or angry manner: *he stood up in a fury and flounced out.* ■ move with exaggerated motions: *she flounced around, playing the tart and flirting.*
▶ n. [in sing.] an exaggerated action, typically intended to express one's annoyance or impatience: *she left the room with a flounce.*
– ORIGIN mid 16th cent.: perhaps of Scandinavian origin and related to Norwegian *flunsa* 'hurry,' or perhaps symbolic, like *bounce* or *pounce*.

flounce[2] ▶ n. a wide ornamental strip of material gathered and sewn to a piece of fabric, typically on a skirt or dress; a frill.
▶ v. (as adj. **flounced**) trimmed with a flounce or flounces: *a flounced skirt.*
– DERIVATIVES **flounc·y** /ˈflounsē/ adj.
– ORIGIN early 18th cent.: from an alteration of obsolete *frounce* 'a fold or pleat,' from Old French *fronce*, of Germanic origin; related to RUCK[2].

floun·der[1] /ˈfloundər/ ▶ v. [no obj.] struggle or stagger helplessly or clumsily in water or mud: *he was floundering about in the shallow offshore waters.* ■ struggle mentally; show or feel great confusion: *she floundered, not knowing quite what to say.* ■ be in serious difficulty: *many firms are floundering.*
– DERIVATIVES **floun·der·er** n.
– ORIGIN late 16th cent.: perhaps a blend of FOUNDER[2] and BLUNDER, or perhaps symbolic, *fl-* frequently beginning words connected with swift or sudden movement.

USAGE See usage at FOUNDER[2].

floun·der[2] ▶ n. a small flatfish that typically occurs in shallow coastal water. ● Families Pleuronectidae and Bothidae: several species, in particular the edible *Platichthys flesus* of European waters. ■ (**flounders**) a collective term for flatfishes other than soles. See FLATFISH.
– ORIGIN Middle English: from Old French *flondre*, probably of Scandinavian origin and related to Danish *flynder*.

flour /ˈflou(ə)r/ ▶ n. a powder obtained by grinding grain, typically wheat, and used to make bread, cakes, and pastry. ■ fine soft powder obtained by grinding the seeds or roots of starchy vegetables: *manioc flour.*
▶ v. [with obj.] sprinkle (something, esp. a work surface or cooking utensil) with a thin layer of flour: *grease and flour two round cake pans.* ■ grind (grain) into flour.
– ORIGIN Middle English: a specific use of FLOWER in the sense 'the best part,' used originally to mean 'the finest quality of ground wheat.' The spelling *flower* remained in use alongside *flour* until the early 19th cent.

flour bee·tle ▶ n. a small brown darkling beetle that is a widespread pest of flour and other cereal products. ● Genera *Tribolium, Gnathocerus*, and others, family Tenebrionidae: several species.

flour·ish /ˈflərisH/ ▶ v. **1** [no obj.] (of a person, animal, or other living organism) grow or develop in a healthy or vigorous way, esp. as the result of a particularly favorable environment: *wild plants flourish on the banks of the lake.* ■ develop rapidly and successfully: *the organization has continued to flourish.* ■ [with adverbial] (of a person) be working or at the height of one's career during a specified period: *the caricaturist and wit who flourished in the early years of this century.*
2 [with obj.] (of a person) wave (something) around to attract the attention of others: *"Happy New Year!" he yelled, flourishing a bottle of whiskey.*
▶ n. **1** a bold or extravagant gesture or action, made esp. to attract the attention of others: *with a flourish, she ushered them inside.* ■ an instance of suddenly performing or developing in an impressively successful way: *the Bulldogs produced a late second-half flourish.* ■ an elaborate rhetorical or literary expression. ■ an ornamental flowing curve in handwriting or scrollwork: *spiky gothic letters with an emphatic flourish beneath them.*
2 Music a fanfare played by brass instruments: *a flourish of trumpets.* ■ an ornate musical passage. ■ an improvised addition played esp. at the beginning or end of a composition.
– DERIVATIVES **flour·ish·er** n.
– ORIGIN Middle English: from Old French *floriss-*, lengthened stem of *florir*, based on Latin *florere*, from *flos, flor-* 'a flower.' The noun senses 'ornamental curve' and 'florid expression' come from an obsolete sense of the verb, 'adorn' (originally with flowers).

flour·ish·ing /ˈflərisHiNG/ ▶ adj. developing rapidly and successfully; thriving: *a flourishing career.*

flour moth (in full **Mediterranean flour moth**) ▶ n. a grayish-yellow moth, the caterpillar of which is a pest of flour and cereal products. ● *Ephestia kuehniella*, family Pyralidae.

flour·y /ˈflou(ə)rē/ ▶ adj. covered with flour: *Maggie wiped her floury hands on her apron.* ■ of or resembling flour: *floury white makeup.*
– DERIVATIVES **flour·i·ness** n.

flout /flout/ ▶ v. [with obj.] openly disregard (a rule, law or convention): *these same companies still flout basic ethical practices.* ■ [no obj.] archaic mock; scoff: *the women pointed and flouted at her.*
– ORIGIN mid 16th cent.: perhaps from Dutch *fluiten* 'whistle, play the flute, hiss (in derision)'; German dialect *pfeifen auf*, literally 'pipe at,' has a similar extended meaning.

USAGE **Flout** and **flaunt** do not have the same meaning: see usage at FLAUNT.

flow /flō/ ▶ v. [no obj.] **1** (of a fluid, gas, or electricity) move along or out steadily and continuously in a current or stream: *from here the river flows north* | *a cross-current of electricity seemed to flow between them* | *ventilation channels keep the air flowing.* ■ (of the sea or a tidal river) move toward the land; rise. Compare with EBB.
2 [with adverbial of direction] go from one place to another in a steady stream, typically in large numbers: *the firm is hoping the orders will keep flowing in.* ■ (of clothing or hair) hang loosely in an easy and graceful manner: *her red hair flowed over her shoulders.* ■ proceed or be produced smoothly, continuously, and effortlessly: *talk flowed freely around the table.* ■ be available in copious quantities: *their talk and laughter grew louder as the excellent brandy flowed.* ■ (**flow from**) result from; be caused by: *there are certain advantages that may flow from that decision.*
3 (of a solid) undergo a permanent change of shape under stress, without melting.
▶ n. **1** [in sing.] the action or fact of moving along in a steady, continuous stream: *the flow of water into the pond.* ■ the rate or speed at which such a stream moves: *under the ford the river backs up, giving a deep sluggish flow.* ■ the rise of a tide or a river. Compare with EBB.
2 a steady, continuous stream of something: *she eased the car into the flow of traffic.*
3 the gradual permanent deformation of a solid under stress, without melting.
– PHRASES **go with the flow** informal be relaxed and accept a situation, rather than trying to alter or control it. **in full flow** talking fluently and easily and showing no sign of stopping. ■ performing vigorously and enthusiastically: *Richardson was run out when he was in full flow.*
– ORIGIN Old English *flōwan*, of Germanic origin; related to Dutch *vloeien*, also to FLOOD.

flow chart (also **flowchart** or **flow diagram**) ▶ n. a diagram of the sequence of movements or actions of people or things involved in a complex system or activity. ■ a graphical representation of a computer program in relation to its sequence of functions (as distinct from the data it processes).

flow·er /ˈflou(-ə)r/ ▶ n. **1** the seed-bearing part of a plant, consisting of reproductive organs (stamens and carpels) that are typically surrounded by a brightly colored corolla (petals) and a green calyx (sepals). ■ a brightly colored and conspicuous example of such a part of a plant together with its stalk, typically used with others as a decoration or gift: *I stopped to buy Bridget some flowers.* ■ the state or period in which a plant's flowers have developed and opened: *the roses were just coming into flower.*
2 (**the flower of**) the finest individuals out of a number of people or things: *the flower of college track athletes.* ■ the period of optimum development: *a young policeman in the flower of his life gunned down.*
▶ v. [no obj.] **1** (of a plant) produce flowers; bloom: *these daisies can flower as late as October.* ■ [with obj.] induce (a plant) to produce flowers.
2 be in or reach an optimum stage of development; develop fully and richly: *it is there that the theory of deconstruction has flowered most extravagantly* | (as noun **flowering**) *the flowering of Viennese intellectual life.*
– DERIVATIVES **flow·er·less** adj., **flow·er·like** /-ˌlīk/ adj.
– ORIGIN Middle English *flour*, from Old French *flour, flor*, from Latin *flos, flor-*. The original spelling was no longer in use by the late 17th cent. except in its specialized sense 'ground grain' (see FLOUR).

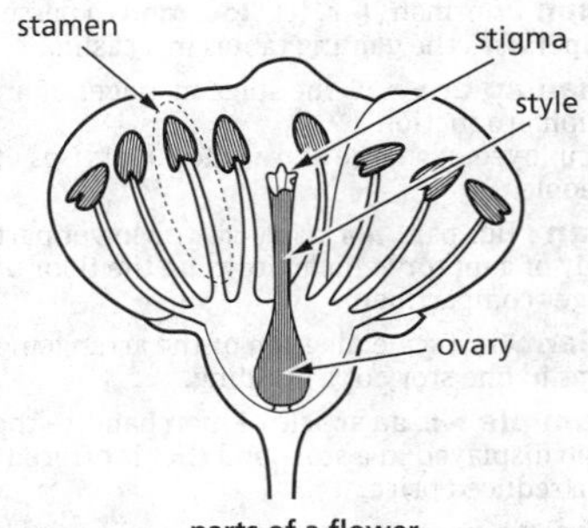

parts of a flower

flow·er·age /ˈflou(-ə)rij/ ▶ n. the process of coming into flower: *the flowerage of Romanticism.*

flow·er bed ▶ n. a garden plot in which flowers are grown.

flow·er bee·tle ▶ n. any of a number of beetles that frequent flowers, in particular: ● an elongated beetle with soft wing cases (chiefly of the family Melyridae). ● a day-flying chafer (family Scarabaeidae).

flow·er child ▶ n. historical a hippie who wore flowers as symbols of peace and love.

flow·ered /'flou(-ə)rd/ ▶ **adj. 1** (esp. of fabric or a garment) having a floral design: *flowered curtains*. **2** [in combination] (of a plant) bearing flowers of a specified kind or number: *yellow-flowered japonica*.

flow·er·er /'flou(-ə)rər/ ▶ **n.** a plant that flowers at a specified time or in a specified manner: *bedding plants and other summer flowerers*.

flow·er es·sence ▶ **n.** a substance prepared from a flowering plant and used therapeutically for its alleged beneficial effects on mood, outlook, etc.

flow·er·et /'flou(-ə)rət/ ▶ **n.** a floret, esp. of cauliflower or broccoli.

flow·er girl ▶ **n. 1** a young girl who carries flowers or scatters them in front of the bride at a wedding; a child bridesmaid.
2 Brit. dated a woman or girl who sells flowers, esp. in the street.

flow·er head (also **flowerhead**) ▶ **n.** a compact mass of flowers at the top of a stem, esp. a capitulum.

flow·er·ing /'flou(-ə)riNG/ ▶ **adj.** (of a plant) in bloom: *a basket of flowering plants*. ■ capable of producing flowers, esp. in contrast to a similar plant with the flowers inconspicuous or absent: *flowering dogwood*. ■ [in combination] producing flowers at a specified time or of a specified type: *winter-flowering heathers*.

flow·er·ing cher·ry ▶ **n.** an ornamental tree grown for its spring blossom, the fruit not being considered edible. ● Genus *Prunus*, family Rosaceae: several species, in particular *P. serrulata* and its hybrids.

flow·er·ing cur·rant ▶ **n.** an ornamental shrub grown for its clusters of small pinkish-red flowers. ● Genus *Ribes*, family Grossulariaceae: several species, in particular the **red-flowering currant** (*R. sanguineum*).

flow·er·ing plant ▶ **n.** a plant that produces flowers; an angiosperm.

flow·er·ing plum ▶ **n.** another term for PURPLE-LEAF PLUM.

flow·er·ing quince ▶ **n.** an Asian shrub of the rose family, with bright red flowers followed by round white, green, or yellow edible fruits. Also called JAPANESE QUINCE, JAPONICA. ● Genus *Chaenomeles*, family Rosaceae: several species, in particular *C. speciosa*, which is grown as an ornamental.

flow·er·ing rush ▶ **n.** a tall rushlike plant with long narrow leaves and pinkish flowers, living in shallow slow-moving water. Native to Eurasia, it has become established in North America. ● *Butomus umbellatus*, the only member of the family Butomaceae.

flow·er·peck·er /'flou(-ə)r,pekər/ ▶ **n.** a small songbird with a short bill and tail, feeding chiefly on insects in flowers and found in Australasia and Southeast Asia. ● Family Dicaeidae (the **flowerpecker family**): two genera, esp. *Dicaeum*. The flowerpecker family also includes the pardalotes and the mistletoe bird.

flow·er·pot /'flou(-ə)r,pät/ ▶ **n.** a small container, typically with sloping sides and made from plastic or earthenware, used for growing a plant in.

flow·er pow·er ▶ **n.** historical the ideas of the flower children, esp. the promotion of peace and love as means of changing the world.

flow·ers of sul·fur ▶ **plural n.** [treated as sing.] Chemistry a fine yellow powdered form of sulfur produced by sublimation.

flow·ers of zinc ▶ **plural n.** [treated as sing.] finely powdered zinc oxide.

flow·er·y /'flou(-ə)rē/ ▶ **adj.** full of, resembling, or smelling of flowers: *a flowery meadow* | *flowery wallpaper*. ■ (of a style of speech or writing) full of elaborate or literary words and phrases: *flowery language*.
– DERIVATIVES **flow·er·i·ness** /-rēnis/ **n.**

flow·ing /'flōiNG/ ▶ **adj.** (esp. of long hair or clothing) hanging or draping loosely and gracefully: *a long flowing gown of lavender silk*. ■ (of a line or contour) smoothly continuous: *the flowing curves of the lawn*. ■ (of language, movement, or style) graceful and fluent: *a flowing prose style*.
– DERIVATIVES **flow·ing·ly adv.**

flow·me·ter /'flō,mētər/ ▶ **n.** an instrument for measuring the rate of flow of a fluid, esp. through a pipe.

flown /flōn/ past participle of FLY[1].

flow·sheet /'flō,SHēt/ ▶ **n.** another term for FLOW CHART.

flow·stone /'flō,stōn/ ▶ **n.** Geology rock deposited as a thin sheet by precipitation from flowing water.

fl. oz. ▶ **abbr.** fluid ounce.

flu /flo͞o/ ▶ **n.** short for INFLUENZA: *I had a bad case of the flu*.
– DERIVATIVES **flu·like adj.**
– ORIGIN mid 19th cent.: abbreviation.

flub /fləb/ informal ▶ **v.** (**flubs, flubbing, flubbed**) [with obj.] botch or bungle (something): *she glanced at her notes and flubbed her lines* | [no obj.] *don't flub again*.
▶ **n.** a thing badly or clumsily done; a blunder: *the textbooks are littered with flubs*.
– ORIGIN 1920s: of unknown origin.

fluc·tu·ant /'flәkCHo͞oәnt/ ▶ **adj.** literary fluctuating; unstable.
– ORIGIN mid 16th cent.: from Old French, 'undulating,' from Latin *fluctuare* 'undulate.'

fluc·tu·ate /'flәkCHo͞o,āt/ ▶ **v.** [no obj.] rise and fall irregularly in number or amount: *trade with other countries tends to fluctuate from year to year* | (as adj. **fluctuating**) *a fluctuating level of demand*.
– ORIGIN mid 17th cent.: from Latin *fluctuat-* 'undulated,' from the verb *fluctuare*, from *fluctus* 'flow, current, wave,' from *fluere* 'to flow.'

fluc·tu·a·tion /,flәkCHo͞o'āSHәn/ ▶ **n.** an irregular rising and falling in number or amount; a variation: *fluctuations in the yearly values could be caused by a variety of factors*.

flue /flo͞o/ ▶ **n.** a duct for smoke and waste gases produced by a fire, a gas heater, a power station, or other fuel-burning installation: *no air rises up the chimney, usually because the flue is blocked* | [as modifier] *flue gases*. ■ a channel for conveying heat.
– ORIGIN late Middle English (denoting the mouthpiece of a hunting horn): of unknown origin. Current senses date from the late 16th cent.

flue-cure ▶ **v.** [with obj.] (often as adj. **flue-cured**) cure (tobacco) using heat from pipes or flues connected to a furnace.

flu·ence /'flo͞oәns/ ▶ **n.** Physics a stream of particles crossing a unit area, usually expressed as the number of particles per second.
– ORIGIN early 17th cent. (in the sense 'a flowing, a stream'): from French, from Latin *fluentia*, from *fluere* 'to flow.'

flu·en·cy /'flo͞oәnsē/ ▶ **n.** the quality or condition of being fluent, in particular: ■ the ability to speak or write a foreign language easily and accurately: *fluency in Spanish is essential*. ■ the ability to express oneself easily and articulately. ■ gracefulness and ease of movement or style: *the horse was jumping with breathtaking fluency*.
– ORIGIN early 17th cent.: from Latin *fluentia*, from *fluere* 'to flow.'

flu·ent /'flo͞oәnt/ ▶ **adj.** (of a person) able to express oneself easily and articulately: *a fluent speaker and writer on technical subjects*. ■ (of a person) able to speak or write a particular foreign language easily and accurately: *she became fluent in French and German*. ■ (of a foreign language) spoken accurately and with facility: *he spoke fluent Spanish*. ■ (of speech, language, movement, or style) smoothly graceful and easy: *his style of play was fast and fluent*. ■ able to flow freely; fluid: *a fluent discharge from the nose*.
– DERIVATIVES **flu·ent·ly adv.**
– ORIGIN late 16th cent. (also in the literal sense 'flowing freely or abundantly'): from Latin *fluent-* 'flowing,' from the verb *fluere*.

flue pipe ▶ **n. 1** a pipe acting as a flue.
2 an organ pipe into which the air enters directly without striking a reed.

flue stop ▶ **n.** an organ stop for a set of flue pipes.

fluff /flәf/ ▶ **n. 1** soft fibers from fabrics such as wool or cotton that accumulate in small light clumps: *he brushed his sleeve to remove the fluff*. ■ any soft downy substance, esp. the fur or feathers of a young mammal or bird.
2 entertainment or writing perceived as trivial or superficial: *the movie is a piece of typical Hollywood fluff*.
3 informal a mistake made in speaking or playing music, or by an actor in delivering lines.
▶ **v.** [with obj.] **1** make (something) appear fuller and softer, typically by shaking or brushing it: *I fluffed up the pillows*.
2 informal fail to perform or accomplish (something) successfully or well (used esp. in a sporting or acting context): *the extra fluffed his only line*.
– ORIGIN late 18th cent.: probably a dialect alteration of 16th-cent. *flue* 'down, nap, fluff,' apparently from Flemish *vluwe*.

fluff·y /'flәfē/ ▶ **adj.** (**fluffier, fluffiest**) **1** of, like, or covered with fluff: *fluffy white clouds* | *a fluffy towel*. ■ (of food) light in texture and containing air: *cream the butter and sugar until pale and fluffy*.
2 informal lacking substance, depth, or seriousness: *the commercial wallows in soft, fluffy, feel-good territory*. ■ (of a person, esp. a woman) frivolous, silly, or vague: *fluffy blondes in leopard-skin pedal pushers*.
– DERIVATIVES **fluff·i·ly** /'flәfәlē/ **adv.**, **fluff·i·ness n.**

flu·gel·horn /'flo͞ogәl,hôrn/ (also **flügelhorn, fluegelhorn**) ▶ **n.** a valved brass musical instrument like a cornet but with a mellower tone.
– ORIGIN mid 19th cent.: from German *Flügelhorn*, from *Flügel* 'wing' + *Horn* 'horn.'

flu·id /'flo͞oid/ ▶ **n.** a substance that has no fixed shape and yields easily to external pressure; a gas or (esp.) a liquid: *we all need several glasses of fluid a day* | *a cleaning fluid*.
▶ **adj.** (of a substance) able to flow easily: *the paint is more fluid than tube watercolors* | *a fluid medium*. ■ not settled or stable; likely or able to change: *our plans are still fluid* | *the fluid political situation of the 1930s*. ■ smoothly elegant or graceful: *her movements were fluid and beautiful to watch*. ■ (of a clutch or coupling) using a liquid to transmit power.
– DERIVATIVES **flu·id·ic** /flo͞o'idik/ **adj.**, **flu·id·i·ty** /flo͞o'idәtē/ **n.**, **flu·id·ly adv.**
– ORIGIN late Middle English (as an adjective): from French *fluide* or Latin *fluidus*, from *fluere* 'to flow.'

flu·id drachm ▶ **n.** see DRACHM.

flu·id·ics /flo͞o'idiks/ ▶ **plural n.** [often treated as sing.] the study and technique of using small interacting flows and fluid jets for functions usually performed by electronic devices.

flu·id·ize /'flo͞oә,dīz/ ▶ **v.** [with obj.] technical cause (a finely divided solid) to acquire the characteristics of a fluid by passing a gas upward through it.
– DERIVATIVES **flu·id·i·za·tion** /,flo͞oәdi'zāSHәn/ **n.**

flu·id·ized bed ▶ **n.** a layer of a fluidized solid, used in chemical processes and in the efficient burning of coal for power generation.

flu·id mech·an·ics ▶ **plural n.** [treated as sing.] the branch of mechanics dealing with the properties of fluids in various states and with their reaction to forces acting upon them.

flu·id ounce (abbr.: **fl. oz.**) ▶ **n. 1** a unit of capacity equal to one sixteenth of a US pint (approximately 0.03 liter).
2 Brit. a unit of capacity equal to one twentieth of a pint (approximately 0.028 liter).

flu·i·dram /,flo͞oi(d)'dram/ ▶ **n.** a fluid drachm. See DRACHM.

fluke[1] /flo͞ok/ ▶ **n.** unlikely chance occurrence, esp. a surprising piece of luck: *their triumph was no fluke*.
– ORIGIN mid 19th cent. (originally a term in games such as billiards denoting a lucky stroke): perhaps a dialect word.

fluke[2] ▶ **n. 1** a parasitic flatworm that typically has suckers and hooks for attachment to the host. Some species are of veterinary or medical importance. ● Classes Trematoda and Monogenea, phylum Platyhelminthes. See DIGENEAN and MONOGENEAN.
2 a flatfish, esp. a flounder.
– ORIGIN Old English *flōc* (sense 2), of Germanic origin; related to German *flach* 'flat.'

fluke[3] ▶ **n.** a broad triangular plate on the arm of an anchor. ■ either of the lobes of a whale's tail.
– ORIGIN mid 16th cent.: perhaps from FLUKE[2] (because of the shape).

fluk·y /'flo͞okē/ (also **flukey**) ▶ **adj.** (**flukier, flukiest**) obtained or achieved more by chance than skill: *a fluky goal*.
– DERIVATIVES **fluk·i·ly** /-kilē/ **adv.**, **fluk·i·ness n.**

flume /flo͞om/ ▶ **n.** a deep narrow channel or ravine with a stream running through it. ■ an artificial channel conveying water, typically used for transporting logs or timber. ■ a water-chute ride at an amusement park.
– ORIGIN Middle English (denoting a river or stream): from Old French *flum*, from Latin *flumen* 'river,' from *fluere* 'to flow.' The sense 'artificial channel' dates from the mid 18th cent.; 'water chute for amusement' is a late 20th-cent. usage.

flum·mer·y /'flәmәrē/ ▶ **n.** (pl. **flummeries**)
1 empty compliments; nonsense: *she hated the flummery of public relations*.
2 a sweet dish, typically made with beaten eggs, sugar, and flavorings.
– ORIGIN early 17th cent. (denoting a dish made with oatmeal or wheatmeal boiled to a jelly): from Welsh *llymru*; perhaps related to *llymrig* 'soft, slippery.'

flum·mox /'flәmәks/ ▶ **v.** [with obj.] (usu. **be flummoxed**) informal perplex (someone) greatly; bewilder: *he was completely flummoxed by the question*.

– ORIGIN mid 19th cent.: probably of dialect origin; compare with dialect *flummock* 'to make untidy, confuse.'

flum·moxed /'fləməkst/ ▶ **adj.** bewildered or perplexed: *he became flummoxed and speechless.*

flump /fləmp/ ▶ **v.** [no obj.] fall or sit down heavily: *he went off to flump into a chair.* ■ [with obj.] set or throw (something) down heavily: *Ellie flumped her hands down on her sewing.*
▶ **n.** [in sing.] the action or sound of such a heavy fall: *the rocks hit the ground with a flump.*
– ORIGIN early 17th cent.: imitative; compare with PLUMP².

flung /fləNG/ past and past participle of FLING.

flunk /fləNGk/ informal ▶ **v.** [with obj.] fail to reach the required standard in (an examination, test, or course of study): *I flunked biology in the tenth grade* | [no obj.] *I didn't flunk but I didn't do too well.* ■ judge (a student or examination candidate) to have failed to reach the required standard: *the teacher flunked thirteen third-graders.* ■ [no obj.] (**flunk out**) (of a student) leave or be dismissed from school or college as a result of failing to reach the required standard: *he had flunked out of college.*
– ORIGIN early 19th cent. (in the general sense 'back down, fail utterly'): perhaps related to FUNK¹ or to *flink* 'be a coward,' perhaps a variant of FLINCH¹.

flun·ky /'fləNGkē/ (also **flunkey**) ▶ **n.** (pl. **flunkies** or **flunkeys**) chiefly derogatory a liveried manservant or footman. ■ a person who performs relatively menial tasks for someone else, esp. obsequiously.
– DERIVATIVES **flun·ky·ism** /-ˌizəm/ **n.**
– ORIGIN mid 18th cent. (originally Scots): perhaps from FLANK in the sense 'a person who stands at one's flank.'

fluo·resce /flo͝o(ə)'res, flôr'es/ ▶ **v.** [no obj.] shine or glow brightly due to fluorescence: *the molecules fluoresce when excited by ultraviolet radiation.*
– ORIGIN late 19th cent.: back-formation from FLUORESCENCE.

fluo·res·ce·in /flo͝o(ə)'resēən, flôr'esēən/ ▶ **n.** Chemistry an orange dye with a yellowish-green fluorescence, used as an indicator and tracer. ● A derivative of resorcinol and phthalic anhydride; chem. formula: $C_{20}H_{12}O_5$.
– ORIGIN late 19th cent.: from FLUORESCENCE + -IN¹.

fluo·res·cence /flo͝o(ə)'resəns, flôr'esəns/ ▶ **n.** the visible or invisible radiation emitted by certain substances as a result of incident radiation of a shorter wavelength such as X-rays or ultraviolet light. ■ the property of absorbing light of short wavelength and emitting light of longer wavelength.
– ORIGIN mid 19th cent.: from FLUORSPAR (which fluoresces), on the pattern of *opalescence.*

fluo·res·cent /ˌflo͝o(ə)'resənt, flôr'esənt/ ▶ **adj.** (of a substance) having or showing fluorescence: *a fluorescent dye.* ■ containing a fluorescent tube: *fluorescent lighting.* ■ vividly colorful: *a fluorescent T-shirt.*
▶ **n.** a fluorescent tube or lamp.

fluo·res·cent screen ▶ **n.** a transparent screen coated with fluorescent material to show images from X-rays.

fluo·res·cent tube (also **fluorescent bulb** or **fluorescent lamp**) ▶ **n.** a glass tube that radiates light when phosphor on its inside surface is made to fluoresce by ultraviolet radiation from mercury vapor.

fluor·i·date /'flo͝orəˌdāt, 'flôr-/ ▶ **v.** [with obj.] add traces of fluorides to (something, esp. a water supply): (as adj. **fluoridated**) *fluoridated toothpaste.*
– DERIVATIVES **fluor·i·da·tion** /ˌflo͝orə'dāSHən, ˌflôr-/ **n.**
– ORIGIN 1940s: back-formation from earlier *fluoridation.*

fluor·ide /'flo͝orˌīd, 'flôr-/ ▶ **n.** Chemistry a compound of fluorine with another element or group, esp. a salt of the anion F⁻ or an organic compound with fluorine bonded to an alkyl group. ■ sodium fluoride or another fluorine-containing salt added to water supplies or toothpaste in order to reduce tooth decay.
– ORIGIN early 19th cent.: from FLUORINE + -IDE.

fluor·i·nate /'flo͝orəˌnāt, 'flôr-/ ▶ **v.** [with obj.] Chemistry introduce fluorine into (a compound). ■ another term for FLUORIDATE.
– DERIVATIVES **fluor·i·na·tion** /ˌflo͝orə'nāSHən, ˌflôr-/ **n.**

fluor·ine /'flo͝orˌēn, flôr-/ ▶ **n.** the chemical element of atomic number 9, a poisonous pale yellow gas of the halogen series. It is the most reactive of all the elements, causing severe burns on contact with skin. (Symbol: **F**)
– ORIGIN early 19th cent.: from *fluor* (see FLUORSPAR) + -INE⁴.

fluo·rite /'flo͝orˌīt, flôr-/ ▶ **n.** a mineral consisting of calcium fluoride that typically occurs as cubic crystals, colorless when pure but often colored by impurities.
– ORIGIN mid 19th cent.: from *fluor* (see FLUORSPAR) + -ITE¹.

fluoro- ▶ **comb. form 1** representing FLUORINE. **2** representing FLUORESCENCE.

fluor·o·car·bon /ˌflo͝orō'kärbən, ˌflôrō-/ ▶ **n.** Chemistry a compound formed by replacing one or more of the hydrogen atoms in a hydrocarbon with fluorine atoms.

fluor·o·chrome /'flo͝orəˌkrōm, 'flôr-/ ▶ **n.** a chemical that fluoresces, esp. one used as a label in biological research.

fluo·rog·ra·phy /flo͝or'ägrəfē, flôr-/ ▶ **n.** photography in which the image is formed by fluorescence, used chiefly in biomedical research.
– DERIVATIVES **fluo·ro·graph** /'flo͝orəˌgraf, 'flôr-/ **n.**

fluo·rom·e·ter /flo͝o'rämitər, flô-/ (also **fluorimeter** /'rimitər/) ▶ **n.** an instrument for measuring the intensity of fluorescence, used chiefly in biochemical analysis.
– DERIVATIVES **fluor·o·met·ric** /ˌflo͝orə'metrik, ˌflôr-/ **adj.**, **fluor·o·met·ri·cal·ly** /ˌflo͝orə'metrik(ə)lē, ˌflôr-/ **adv.**, **fluo·rom·e·try** /flo͝or'ämətrē, flôr-/ **n.**

fluor·o·pol·y·mer /ˌflo͝orō'pälәmər, ˌflôr-/ ▶ **n.** an organic polymer containing fluorine atoms, such as polytetrafluoroethylene.

fluor·o·quin·o·lone /ˌflo͝orō'kwinlˌōn, ˌflôrō-/ ▶ **n.** any of a class of therapeutic antibiotics that are active against a range of bacteria associated with human and animal diseases. Their use in livestock has sparked concerns about the spread of bacteria resistant to them in humans.

fluor·o·scope /'flo͝orəˌskōp, 'flôr-/ ▶ **n.** an instrument with a fluorescent screen used for viewing X-ray images without taking and developing X-ray photographs.
– DERIVATIVES **fluor·o·scop·ic** /ˌflo͝orə'skäpik, ˌflôr-/ **adj.**, **fluor·o·scop·i·cal·ly** /ˌflo͝orə'skäpik(ə)lē, ˌflôr-/ **adv.**, **fluo·ros·co·py** /flo͝or'äskəpē, flôr-/ **n.**

fluo·ro·sis /flo͝or'ōsəs, flôr-/ ▶ **n.** Medicine a chronic condition caused by excessive intake of fluorine compounds, marked by mottling of the teeth and, if severe, calcification of the ligaments.

flu·or·spar /'flo͝orˌspär, 'flôr-/ ▶ **n.** another term for FLUORITE.
– ORIGIN late 18th cent.: from *fluor* 'a flow, a mineral used as a flux, fluorspar' (from Latin *fluor,* from *fluere* 'to flow') + SPAR³.

flu·ox·e·tine /flo͝o'äksəˌtīn/ ▶ **n.** Medicine a synthetic compound that inhibits the uptake of serotonin in the brain and is taken to treat depression. Also called PROZAC (trademark).
– ORIGIN 1970s: from *fluo(rine)* + *ox(y)* + *-etine* (perhaps from *e* + a blend of TOLUENE and AMINE).

flur·ried /'flərēd, 'flə-rēd/ ▶ **adj.** (of a person) agitated, nervous, or anxious: *I sat down, feeling a little flurried and excited.*

flur·ry /'flərē, 'flə-rē/ ▶ **n.** (pl. **flurries**) a small swirling mass of something, esp. snow or leaves, moved by sudden gusts of wind: *a flurry of snow.* ■ a sudden short period of commotion or excitement: *there was a brief flurry of activity in the hall.* ■ a number of things arriving or happening during the same period: *a flurry of editorials hostile to the administration.*
▶ **v.** (**flurries, flurrying, flurried**) [no obj.] (esp. of snow or leaves) be moved in small swirling masses by sudden gusts of wind: *gusts of snow flurried through the door.* ■ (of a person) move quickly in a busy or agitated way: *the waiter flurried between them.*
– ORIGIN late 17th cent.: from obsolete *flurr* 'fly up, flutter, whir' (imitative), probably influenced by HURRY.

flush¹ /fləSH/ ▶ **v. 1** [no obj.] (of a person's skin or face) become red and hot, typically as the result of illness or strong emotion: *Mr. Cunningham flushed angrily.* ■ [with obj.] cause (a person's skin or face) to become red and hot: *the chill air flushed the parson's cheeks.* ■ glow or cause to glow with warm color or light: [no obj.] *the ash in the center of the fire flushed up* | [with obj.] *the sky was flushed with the gold of dawn.*
2 [with obj.] cleanse (something, esp. a toilet) by causing large quantities of water to pass through it: *flush the toilet* | *the nurse flushed out the catheter.* ■ [no obj.] (of a toilet) be cleansed in such a way: *Cally heard the toilet flush.* ■ remove or dispose of (an object or substance) in such a way: *I flushed the pills down the toilet* | *the kidneys require more water to flush out waste products.* ■ cause (a liquid) to flow through something: *0.3 ml of saline is gently flushed through the tube.*
3 [with obj.] drive (a bird, esp. a game bird, or an animal) from its cover: *the grouse were flushed from the woods.* ■ cause to be revealed; force into the open: *they're trying to flush Tilton out of hiding.*
4 [no obj.] (of a plant) send out fresh shoots: *the plant had started to flush by late March.*
▶ **n. 1** a reddening of the face or skin that is typically caused by illness or strong emotion: *a flush of embarrassment rose to her cheeks.* ■ an area of warm color or light: *the bird has a pinkish flush on the breast.*
2 [in sing.] a sudden rush of intense emotion: *I was carried away in a flush of enthusiasm.* ■ a sudden abundance or spate of something: *the frogs feast on the great flush of insects.* ■ a period when something is new or particularly fresh and vigorous: *he is no longer in the first flush of youth.* ■ a fresh growth of leaves, flowers, or fruit.
3 an act of cleansing something, esp. a toilet, with a sudden flow of water: *an old-fashioned toilet uses six or seven gallons per flush* | *leave the hose running to give the system a good flush out.* ■ the device used for producing such a flow of water in a toilet: *he pressed the flush absentmindedly.* ■ [as modifier] denoting a type of toilet that has such a device: *a flush toilet.* ■ a sudden flow: *the melting snow provides a flush of water.*
4 the action of driving a game bird from its cover: *the dogs retrieve the birds after the flush.*
– DERIVATIVES **flush·a·ble** **adj.**, **flush·er** **n.**
– ORIGIN Middle English (in the sense 'move rapidly, spring up,' esp. of a bird 'fly up suddenly'): symbolic, *fl-* frequently beginning words connected with sudden movement; perhaps influenced by FLASH and BLUSH.

flush² ▶ **adj. 1** completely level or even with another surface: *the gates are flush with the adjoining fencing.* ■ (of printed text) not indented or protruding: *each line is flush with the left-hand margin.* ■ (of a door) having a smooth surface, without indented or protruding panels or moldings.
2 [predic.] informal having plenty of something, esp. money: *the banks are flush with funds.* ■ (of money) plentiful: *the years when cash was flush.*
▶ **adv.** so as to be level or even: *the screw must fit flush with the surface.* ■ so as to be directly centered; squarely: *Jumbo reached up and hit Bruno flush on the jaw.*
▶ **v.** [with obj.] fill in (a joint) level with a surface.
– DERIVATIVES **flush·ness** **n.**
– ORIGIN mid 16th cent. (in the sense 'perfect, lacking nothing'): probably related to FLUSH¹.

flush³ ▶ **n.** (in poker) a hand of cards all of the same suit.
– ORIGIN early 16th cent.: from French *flux* (formerly *flus*), from Latin *fluxus* 'a flow' (see FLUX: the use in cards can be compared with English *run*).

flush⁴ ▶ **n.** Ecology a piece of wet ground over which water flows without being confined to a definite channel.
– ORIGIN late Middle English (in the sense 'marshy place').

flushed /fləSHt/ ▶ **adj. 1** (of a person's skin) red and hot, typically as the result of illness or strong emotion: *her flushed cheeks.*
2 (of a person) excited or elated by something: *flushed with success, I was getting into my stride.*

Flush·ing /'fləSHiNG/ a commercial and residential section of northern Queens in New York City, noted for its diverse population.

flust·er /'fləstər/ ▶ **v.** [with obj.] (often as adj. **flustered**) make (someone) agitated or confused: *you need to be able to work under pressure and not get flustered.*
▶ **n.** [in sing.] an agitated or confused state: *the main thing is not to get all in a fluster.*
– ORIGIN early 17th cent. (in the sense 'make slightly drunk'): perhaps of Scandinavian origin and related to Icelandic *flaustra* 'hurry, bustle.'

flute 1

flute /flo͞ot/ ▶ **n. 1** a wind instrument made from a tube with holes along it that are stopped by the fingers or keys, held vertically or horizontally so that the player's breath strikes a narrow edge. ■ a modern orchestral instrument of this type, typically of metal, held horizontally, with the mouthpiece near one end, which is closed. ■ an organ stop with wooden or metal flue pipes producing a similar tone.
2 Architecture an ornamental vertical groove in a column. ■ a trumpet-shaped frill on a dress or other garment. ■ any similar cylindrical groove, as on pastry.
3 a tall, narrow wine glass: *a flute of champagne.*
▶ **v. 1** [with direct speech] speak in a melodious way reminiscent of the sound of a flute: *"What do you do?" she fluted.* ■ [no obj.] literary play, or seem to play, a flute or pipe: *to him who sat upon the rocks, and fluted to the morning sea* | [with obj.] *some swan fluting a wild carol.*

2 [with obj.] (often as adj. **fluted**) make flutes or grooves in: *fluted columns.* ■ make trumpet-shaped frills on (a garment): *a fluted collar.*
– DERIVATIVES **flute·like** /-ˌlīk/ **adj.**
– ORIGIN Middle English: from Old French *flahute*, probably from Provençal *flaüt*, perhaps a blend of *flaujol* 'flageolet' + *laüt* 'lute.'

flut·ed /ˈflo͞otid/ ▶ **adj.** having flutes or grooves; ridged: *fluted pillars.*

flut·ing /ˈflo͞otiNG/ ▶ **n. 1** sound reminiscent of that of a flute: *the silvery fluting of a blackbird.*
2 a groove or set of grooves forming a surface decoration: *a hollow stem with vertical flutings | pieces decorated with fluting.*
▶ **adj.** reminiscent of the sound of a flute: *the golden, fluting voice filled the room.*

flut·ist /ˈflo͞otist/ (also chiefly Brit. **flautist**) ▶ **n.** a flute player.

flut·ter /ˈflətər/ ▶ **v.** [no obj.] (of a bird or other winged creature) fly unsteadily or hover by flapping the wings quickly and lightly: *a couple of butterflies fluttered around the garden.* ■ [with obj.] (of a bird or other winged creature) flap (its wings) quickly and lightly: *the lark fluttered its wings, hovering.* ■ [with adverbial] move or fall with a light irregular or trembling motion: *the remaining petals fluttered to the ground.* ■ [with adverbial of direction] (of a person) move restlessly or uncertainly: *the hostess fluttered forward to greet her guests.* ■ (of a pulse or heartbeat) beat feebly or irregularly.
▶ **n. 1** an act of fluttering: *there was a flutter of wings at the window.* ■ a state or sensation of tremulous excitement: *Sandra felt a flutter in the pit of her stomach | her insides were in a flutter.* ■ Aeronautics undesired oscillation in a part of an aircraft under stress. ■ Medicine disturbance of the rhythm of the heart that is less severe than fibrillation: *atrial flutter | I was diagnosed as having a heart flutter.* ■ Electronics rapid variation in the pitch or amplitude of a signal, esp. of recorded sound. Compare with **WOW**[2].
2 Brit. informal a small bet: *a flutter on the horses.*
– PHRASES **flutter one's eyelashes** open and close one's eyes rapidly in a coyly flirtatious manner.
– DERIVATIVES **flut·ter·er n.**, **flut·ter·ing·ly adv.**, **flut·ter·y adj.**
– ORIGIN Old English *floterian, flotorian*, a frequentative form related to **FLEET**[4].

flut·ter kick ▶ **n.** a brisk, alternating, up-and-down movement of the legs when swimming with certain strokes, such as the crawl.

flut·ter-tongu·ing ▶ **n.** the action of vibrating the tongue (as if rolling an *r*) in playing a wind instrument to produce a whirring effect.

flut·y /ˈflo͞otē/ (also **flutey**) ▶ **adj.** (**flutier**, **flutiest**) reminiscent of the sound of a flute: *a drawn-out fluty whistle.*

flu·vi·al /ˈflo͞ovēəl/ ▶ **adj.** chiefly Geology of or found in a river.
– ORIGIN Middle English: from Latin *fluvialis*, from *fluvius* 'river,' from *fluere* 'to flow.'

flu·vi·a·tile /ˈflo͞ovēəˌtīl/ ▶ **adj.** of, found in, or produced by a river: *fluviatile sediments.*
– ORIGIN late 16th cent.: from French, from Latin *fluviatilis*, from *fluviatus* 'wet,' from *fluvius* 'river.'

fluvio- ▶ **comb. form** river; relating to rivers: *fluvioglacial.*
– ORIGIN from Latin *fluvius* 'river.'

flu·vi·o·gla·cial /ˌflo͞ovēōˈglāSHəl/ ▶ **adj.** Geology relating to or denoting erosion or deposition caused by flowing meltwater from glaciers or ice sheets.

flu·vox·a·mine /flo͞oˈväksəˌmēn, -ˌmin/ ▶ **n.** Medicine a synthetic antidepressant drug that acts by prolonging the effect of the neurotransmitter serotonin on the brain.

flux /fləks/ ▶ **n. 1** the action or process of flowing or flowing out: *the flux of men and women moving back and forth | a localized flux of calcium into the cell.* ■ Medicine an abnormal discharge of blood or other matter from or within the body. ■ (usu. **the flux**) archaic diarrhea or dysentery.
2 continuous change: *the whole political system is in a state of flux.*
3 Physics the rate of flow of a fluid, radiant energy, or particles across a given area. ■ the amount of radiation or number of particles incident on an area in a given time. ■ the total electric or magnetic field passing through a surface.
4 a substance mixed with a solid to lower its melting point, used esp. in soldering and brazing metals or to promote vitrification in glass or ceramics. ■ a substance added to a furnace during metal smelting or glassmaking that combines with impurities to form slag.
▶ **v.** [with obj.] treat (a metal object) with a flux to promote melting.
– ORIGIN late Middle English: from Latin *fluxus*, from *fluere* 'to flow.'

flux den·si·ty ▶ **n.** the magnitude of a magnetic, electric, or other flux passing through a unit area.

flux·gate /ˈfləksˌgāt/ (also **flux gate**) ▶ **n.** a device consisting of one or more soft iron cores each surrounded by primary and secondary windings, used for determining the characteristics of an external magnetic field from the signals produced in the secondary windings.

flux·ion /ˈflәkSHən/ ▶ **n. 1** dated Mathematics a function corresponding to the rate of change of a variable quantity; a derivative.
2 another term for **FLUX** (sense 1 of the noun)).
– DERIVATIVES **flux·ion·al** /-SHənl/ **adj.**
– ORIGIN late 17th cent.: from French, or from Latin *flux-* 'flowed,' from the verb *fluere*.

fly[1] /flī/ ▶ **v.** (**flies** /flīz/, **flying**; past **flew** /flo͞o/; past participle **flown** /flōn/) [no obj.] **1** (of a bird or other winged creature) move through the air under control: *close the door or the moths will fly in | the bird can fly enormous distances.* ■ (of an aircraft or its occupants) travel through the air: *I fly back to New York this evening.* ■ [with obj.] control the flight of (an aircraft); pilot. ■ [with obj.] transport in an aircraft: *helicopters flew the injured to a hospital.* ■ [with obj.] accomplish (a purpose) in an aircraft: *pilots trained to fly combat missions.* ■ [with obj.] release (a bird) to fly, esp. a hawk for hunting or a pigeon for racing.
2 move or be hurled quickly through the air: *balls kept flying over her hedge | he was sent flying by the tackle.* ■ [with adverbial of direction] (past **flied**) Baseball hit a ball high into the air: *Gwynn flied to left.* ■ (past **flied**) (**fly out**) Baseball (of a batter) be put out by hitting a fly ball that is caught. ■ [with adverbial of direction] go or move quickly: *she flew along the path.* ■ informal depart hastily: *I must fly!* ■ (of time) pass swiftly: *how time flies!* ■ (of a report) be circulated among many people: *rumors were flying around Chicago.* ■ (of accusations or insults) be exchanged swiftly and heatedly: *the accusations flew thick and fast.*
3 [with adverbial] (esp. of hair) wave or flutter in the wind: *they were running, hair flying everywhere.* ■ (with reference to a flag) display or be displayed, esp. on a flagpole: *flags were flying at half-mast.*
4 archaic flee; run away: *those that fly may fight again.* ■ [with obj.] flee from; escape from in haste: *you must fly the country for a while.*
5 informal be successful: *that idea didn't fly with most other council members.*
▶ **n.** (pl. **flies**) **1** (Brit. often **flies**) an opening at the crotch of a pair of pants, closed with a zipper or buttons and typically covered with a flap. ■ a flap of material covering the opening or fastening of a garment or of a tent: [as modifier in combination] *a fly-fronted shirt.*
2 (**the flies**) the space over the stage in a theater.
3 Baseball short for **FLY BALL**.
4 (pl. usu. **flys**) Brit. & historical a one-horse hackney carriage.
– PHRASES **fly the coop** informal make one's escape. **fly the flag** see **FLAG**[1]. **fly high** be very successful; prosper: *that young man is the sort to fly high.* **fly in the face of** be openly at variance with (what is usual or expected): *a need to fly in the face of convention.* **fly into a rage** (or **temper**) become suddenly or violently angry. **fly the nest** (of a young bird) leave its nest on becoming able to fly. ■ informal (of a young person) leave their parents' home to set up home elsewhere. **fly off the handle** informal lose one's temper suddenly and unexpectedly. [figuratively, with reference to the loose head of an ax.] **go fly a kite** [in imperative] informal go away. **on the fly** while in motion or progress: *his deep shot was caught on the fly.* ■ Computing during the running of a computer program without interrupting the run.
– PHRASAL VERBS **fly at** attack (someone) verbally or physically: *Robbie flew at him, fists clenched.* ■ (of a hawk) pursue and attack, or habitually pursue (prey). ■ (**fly a hawk at**) send a hawk to pursue and attack (prey).
– DERIVATIVES **fly·a·ble adj.**
– ORIGIN Old English *flēogan*, of Germanic origin; related to Dutch *vliegen* and German *fliegen*, also to **FLY**[2].

fly[2] ▶ **n.** (pl. **flies** /flīz/) a flying insect of a large order characterized by a single pair of transparent wings and sucking (and often also piercing) mouthparts. Flies are noted as vectors of disease. See also **DIPTERA**. ● Order Diptera: numerous families. ■ [usu. in combination] used in names of flying insects of other orders, e.g., **butterfly**, **dragonfly**, **firefly**. ■ an infestation of flying insects on a plant or animal: *cattle to be treated for warble fly.* ■ a natural or artificial flying insect used as bait in fishing, esp. a mayfly.
– PHRASES **die** (or **drop**) **like flies** die or collapse in large numbers: *people in the area seemed to die like flies in the winter.* **a fly in the ointment** a minor irritation that spoils the success or enjoyment of something. **fly on the wall** an unnoticed observer of a particular situation. ■ [as adj.] denoting a filmmaking technique whereby events are observed realistically with minimum interference rather than acted out under direction: *a fly-on-the-wall documentary.* **wouldn't hurt** (or **harm**) **a fly** (of a person or animal) inoffensive and harmless.
– ORIGIN Old English *flȳge, flēoge*, denoting any winged insect; related to Dutch *vlieg* and German *Fliege*, also to **FLY**[1].

fly[3] ▶ **adj.** (**flyer**, **flyest**) informal **1** stylish and fashionable: *they were wearin' fly clothes.*
2 Brit. knowing and clever; worldly-wise: *she's fly enough not to get done out of it.*
– DERIVATIVES **fly·ness n.**
– ORIGIN early 19th cent.: of unknown origin.

fly ag·a·ric ▶ **n.** a poisonous toadstool that has a red cap with fluffy white spots, growing particularly among birch trees. It contains hallucinogenic alkaloids and has long been used by the indigenous peoples of northeastern Siberia. ● *Amanita muscaria*, family Amanitaceae, class Hymenomycetes.

fly ash ▶ **n.** ash produced in small dark flecks, typically from a furnace, and carried into the air.

fly·a·way /ˈflīəˌwā/ ▶ **adj.** (of a person's hair) fine and difficult to control.

fly·back /ˈflīˌbak/ ▶ **n.** the return of the scanning spot in a cathode ray tube to the starting point.

fly ball ▶ **n.** Baseball a ball batted high into the air.

fly·blow /ˈflīˌblō/ ▶ **n.** flies' eggs contaminating food, esp. meat.

fly·blown /ˈflīˌblōn/ ▶ **adj.** dirty or contaminated, esp. through contact with flies and their eggs and larvae: *the room was filthy and flyblown.*

fly·boy /ˈflīˌboi/ ▶ **n.** informal a pilot, esp. one in the air force.

fly·bridge /ˈflīˌbrij/ (also **flying bridge**) ▶ **n.** an open deck above the main bridge of a vessel such as a yacht or cabin cruiser, typically equipped with duplicate controls.

fly·by /ˈflīˌbī/ ▶ **n.** (pl. **flybys**) a flight past a point, esp. the close approach of a spacecraft to a planet or moon for observation.

fly-by-night ▶ **adj.** [attrib.] unreliable or untrustworthy, esp. in business or financial matters: *cheap suits made by fly-by-night operators.*
▶ **n.** (also **fly-by-nighter**) an unreliable or untrustworthy person.

fly-by-wire ▶ **n.** [often as modifier] a semiautomatic and typically computer-regulated system for controlling the flight of an aircraft or spacecraft: *sophisticated fly-by-wire technology.*

fly-cast·ing ▶ **n.** another term for **FLY FISHING**.
– DERIVATIVES **fly-cast v.**

fly·catch·er /ˈflīˌkaCHər, -ˌkeCHər/ ▶ **n.** a bird that catches flying insects, esp. in short flights from a perch. ● Typical Old World flycatchers belong to the family Muscicapidae. Many others belong to the Old World family Monarchidae and the New World family Tyrannidae (**tyrant flycatchers**), while some belong to families Eopsaltridae (Australasia), Platysteiridae (Africa), and Bombycillidae (America).

fly-drive ▶ **adj.** chiefly Brit. denoting a package vacation that includes a flight and car rental at the destination.
▶ **n.** a vacation of this type.

fly·er /ˈflīər/ ▶ **n.** variant spelling of **FLIER**.

fly fish·ing ▶ **n.** the sport of fishing using a rod and an artificial fly as bait.
– DERIVATIVES **fly-fish v.**

fly gal·ler·y ▶ **n.** a raised platform at the side of a stage that contains ropes and equipment for moving props and scenery. Also called **fly floor**.

fly-in ▶ **n.** a meeting for pilots who arrive by air: *they are holding a helicopter fly-in.* ■ an act of transporting people or goods by air: *one or two fly-ins to remote lakes.* ■ [as modifier] denoting a place or activity that is reached using an aircraft: *fly-in canoe trips.*

fly·ing /ˈflī-iNG/ ▶ **adj.** moving or able to move through the air with wings: *a flying ant.* ■ done while hurling oneself through the air: *he took a*

PRONUNCIATION KEY ə *ago, up*; ər *over, fur*; a *hat*; ā *ate*; ä *car*; e *let*; ē *see*; i *fit*; ī *by*; NG *sing*; ō *go*; ô *law, for*; oi *toy*; o͝o *good*; o͞o *goo*; ou *out*; TH *thin*; T͟H *then*; ZH *vision*

f

flying kick at a policeman. ■ moving rapidly, esp. through the air: *one passenger was cut by flying glass.* ■ hasty; brief: *a flying visit.* ■ used in names of animals that can glide by using winglike membranes or other structures, e.g., **flying squirrel**.
▶ n. flight, esp. in an aircraft: *she hates flying.*
– PHRASES **with flying colors** with distinction: *Sylvia had passed her exams with flying colors.*

fly·ing boat ▶ n. a large seaplane that lands with its fuselage in the water.

fly·ing bomb ▶ n. a small pilotless aircraft with an explosive warhead, esp. a V-1.

fly·ing bridge ▶ n. another term for FLYBRIDGE.

fly·ing but·tress ▶ n. Architecture a buttress slanting from a separate pier, typically forming an arch with the wall it supports.

fly·ing change ▶ n. a movement in riding in which the leading leg at the canter is changed without breaking gait while the horse is in the air.

f

fly·ing drag·on ▶ n. an arboreal Southeast Asian lizard that has expanding membranes along the sides of the body, used for gliding between trees. Also called DRAGON. ● Genus *Draco*, family Agamidae: several species.

Fly·ing Dutch·man a legendary spectral ship supposedly seen in the region of the Cape of Good Hope and presaging disaster. ■ the captain of this ship.

fly·ing fish ▶ n. a fish of warm seas that leaps out of the water and uses its winglike pectoral fins to glide over the surface for some distance. ● Family Exocoetidae: several genera and species, in particular *Exocoetus volitans*.

flying fish

fly·ing fox ▶ n. a large fruit bat with a foxlike face, found in Madagascar, Southeast Asia, and northern Australia. ● *Pteropus* and two other genera, family Pteropodidae: numerous species.

fly·ing frog ▶ n. a nocturnal arboreal Asian frog that is able to glide between trees using the large webs between its extended toes. ● *Polypedates leucomystax*, family Rhacophoridae.

fly·ing gur·nard ▶ n. a bottom-dwelling marine fish that has bony armor on the skull, spines behind the head, and large brightly colored pectoral fins. It moves through the water with a gliding or flying motion. ● Family Dactylopteridae: two genera and several species.

fly·ing le·mur ▶ n. a tree-dwelling lemurlike mammal with a membrane between the fore- and hind limbs for gliding from tree to tree. It is nocturnal and native to Southeast Asia. Also called COLUGO. ● Family Cynocephalidae and genus *Cynocephalus*, order Dermoptera: two species.

fly·ing liz·ard ▶ n. another term for FLYING DRAGON.

fly·ing ma·chine ▶ n. an aircraft, esp. an early or unconventional one.

fly·ing mouse ▶ n. **1** Computing a mouse that can be lifted from the desk and used in three dimensions. **2** another term for FEATHERTAIL GLIDER.

fly·ing pha·lan·ger ▶ n. a small Australasian marsupial with a membrane between the fore- and hind limbs for gliding. ● Genera *Petaurus* and *Petauroides*, family Petauridae: five species.

fly·ing sau·cer ▶ n. a disk-shaped flying craft supposedly piloted by aliens; a UFO.

fly·ing snake ▶ n. a greenish semiarboreal Southeast Asian snake that can glide down from a tree in a stiff horizontal position, with the belly hollowed to slow its descent. ● *Chrysopelea ornata*, family Colubridae.

fly·ing squad ▶ n. Brit. a division of a police force or other organization that is capable of reaching an incident quickly.

fly·ing squir·rel ▶ n. a small squirrel that has skin joining the fore and hind limbs for gliding from tree to tree. ● Subfamily Pteromyinae, family Sciuridae (many species in Southeast Asia, northern Eurasia, and North America) and family Anomaluridae (several species in Africa). The two common North American species are the **northern flying squirrel** (*Glaucomys sabrinus*) and the **southern flying squirrel** (*G. volans*).

southern flying squirrel

fly·ing start ▶ n. a start of a race or time trial in which the starting point is passed at speed. ■ a good beginning, esp. one giving an advantage over competitors: *the team got off to a flying start in last year's rally.*

fly·ing tra·peze ▶ n. another term for TRAPEZE (sense 1).

fly·ing wedge ▶ n. a fast-moving group, as of police officers, linked together closely in a V-shaped formation, sometimes used to force a way through a crowd or to protect someone behind them.

fly·ing wing ▶ n. an aircraft with little or no fuselage and no vertical airfoil.

fly-kick ▶ n. a kick, esp. in rugby, made while the ball is still in the air.

fly·leaf /ˈflīˌlēf/ ▶ n. (pl. **flyleaves** /-ˌlēvz/) a blank page at the beginning or end of a book.

Flynn /flin/, Errol (1909–59), US actor; born in Australia; born *Leslie Thomas Flynn.* His usual role was the swashbuckling hero of romantic costume dramas in movies such as *Captain Blood* (1935) and *The Adventures of Robin Hood* (1938).

fly·o·ver /ˈflīˌōvər/ ▶ n. **1** a low flight by one or more aircraft over a specific location: *there were artillery platforms in the hills, making a flyover too risky.* ■ a ceremonial flight of an aircraft past a person or a place.
2 chiefly Brit. an overpass.
3 [as modifier] informal, derogatory denoting central regions of the US regarded as less significant than the East or West coasts: *his appeal extends way beyond the Bible Belt and the flyover states.*

fly·pa·per /ˈflīˌpāpər/ ▶ n. sticky, poison-treated strips of paper that are hung indoors to catch and kill flies.

Fly Riv·er /flī/ a river in Papua New Guinea—the country's longest—that flows for 750 miles (1,200 km) from the border with Indonesia into the Gulf of Papua.

fly rod ▶ n. a lightweight flexible rod used in fly fishing.

flysch /flisH/ ▶ n. Geology a sedimentary deposit consisting of thin beds of shale or marl alternating with coarser strata such as sandstone or conglomerate.
– ORIGIN mid 19th cent.: from Swiss German dialect.

fly·sheet /ˈflīˌsHēt/ ▶ n. **1** a tract or circular of two or four pages.
2 Brit. a fabric cover pitched outside and over a tent to give extra protection against bad weather. See FLY[1] (sense 1 of the noun).

fly·speck /ˈflīˌspek/ ▶ n. a tiny stain made by the excrement of an insect. ■ a thing that is contemptibly small or insignificant: *a sleepy flyspeck of a town.*
– DERIVATIVES **fly·specked** adj.

fly spray ▶ n. a substance sprayed from an aerosol that kills flying insects.

fly strike ▶ n. infestation of an animal with blowfly maggots.

fly swat·ter (also **flyswatter**) ▶ n. an implement used for swatting insects, typically a square of plastic mesh attached to a wire handle.

fly-through ▶ n. a computer-animated simulation of what would be seen by one flying through a particular real or imaginary region.

fly-tip ▶ v. [no obj.] Brit. dump waste illegally.
– DERIVATIVES **fly-tip·per** n.

fly·trap /ˈflīˌtrap/ ▶ n. see VENUS FLYTRAP.

fly-ty·ing ▶ n. the making of the artificial flies used in fly-fishing.

fly·way /ˈflīˌwā/ ▶ n. Ornithology a route regularly used by large numbers of migrating birds.

fly·weight /ˈflīˌwāt/ ▶ n. a weight in boxing and other sports intermediate between light flyweight and bantamweight. In boxing it ranges from 108 to 112 pounds (48 to 51 kg). ■ a boxer or other competitor of this weight.

fly·wheel /ˈflī,(h)wēl/ ▶ n. a heavy revolving wheel in a machine that is used to increase the machine's momentum and thereby provide greater stability or a reserve of available power during interruptions in the delivery of power to the machine.

fly whisk ▶ n. see WHISK (sense 3 of the noun).

FM ▶ abbr. frequency modulation: [as adj.] *an FM radio station.*

Fm ▶ symbol the chemical element fermium.

fm. ▶ abbr. fathom(s).

FMB ▶ abbr. Federal Maritime Board.

FMCG ▶ abbr. fast-moving consumer goods: [as adj.] *the FMCG sector.*

FMCS ▶ abbr. Federal Mediation and Conciliation Service.

FMN ▶ abbr. flavin mononucleotide.

FMV ▶ abbr. full-motion video.

FN ▶ abbr. foreign national.

fn. ▶ abbr. footnote.

FNMA ▶ abbr. Federal National Mortgage Association. Also called FANNIE MAE.

f-num·ber ▶ n. Photography the ratio of the focal length of a camera lens to the diameter of the aperture being used for a particular shot (e.g., *f8*, indicating that the focal length is eight times the diameter).
– ORIGIN early 20th cent.: from *f* (denoting the focal length) and NUMBER.

FO ▶ abbr. ■ field officer. ■ Foreign Office.

Fo /fō/, Dario (1926–), Italian playwright. Notable works: *Accidental Death of an Anarchist* (1970) and *Open Couple* (1983). Nobel Prize for Literature (1997).

fo. ▶ abbr. folio.

FOAF ▶ abbr. ■ friend of a friend: *investigations never do succeed in finding the FOAF who started any of these yarns.* ■ a story or urban legend attributed to one of these.

foal /fōl/ ▶ n. a young horse or related animal.
▶ v. [no obj.] (of a mare) give birth to a foal. ■ (**be foaled**) (of a foal) be born.
– PHRASES **in** (or **with**) **foal** (of a mare) pregnant.
– ORIGIN Old English *fola*, of Germanic origin; related to Dutch *veulen* and German *Fohlen*, also to FILLY.

foam /fōm/ ▶ n. a mass of small bubbles formed on or in liquid, typically by agitation or fermentation: *a beer with a thick head of foam.* ■ a similar mass formed from saliva or sweat. ■ a thick preparation containing many small bubbles: *shaving cream (foam type) does a fine job on my beard.* ■ a lightweight form of rubber or plastic made by solidifying such a liquid. ■ (**the foam**) literary the sea: *Venus rising from the foam.*
▶ v. [no obj.] form or produce a mass of small bubbles; froth: *the sea foamed beneath them.*
– PHRASES **foam at the mouth** informal be very angry.
– DERIVATIVES **foam·less** adj.
– ORIGIN Old English *fām* (noun), *fǣman* (verb); related to Old High German *feim* (noun), *feimen* (verb).

foam·flow·er /ˈfōm,flou(-ə)r/ ▶ n. see TIARELLA.

foam rub·ber ▶ n. a spongy material made of rubber or plastic in the form of foam, used for cushioning and in upholstery.

foam·y /ˈfōmē/ ▶ adj. (**foamier**, **foamiest**) producing or consisting of foam; frothy: *a beach with foamy waves | a mug of foamy beer.*

FOB ▶ abbr. **1** friend of Bill, a friend of Bill Clinton, esp. one of his close circle of advisers and contacts.
2 Forward Operating Base.

fob[1] /fäb/ ▶ n. (also **fob chain**) a chain attached to a watch for carrying in a waistcoat or waistband pocket. ■ a small ornament attached to a watch chain. ■ (also **fob pocket**) a small pocket for carrying a watch. ■ a tab on a key ring.
– ORIGIN mid 17th cent. (denoting a fob pocket in a waistband): origin uncertain; probably related to German dialect *Fuppe* 'pocket.'

fob[2] ▶ v. (**fobs**, **fobbing**, **fobbed**) [with obj.] (**fob someone off**) deceitfully attempt to satisfy someone by making excuses or giving them something inferior: *secretaries fob off most unwanted callers by saying their boss is in a meeting.* ■ (**fob something off on**) give (someone) something inferior to or different from what they want: *he fobbed off the chairmanship on Clifford.*
– ORIGIN late Middle English (in the sense 'cheat out of'): origin uncertain; perhaps related to German *foppen* 'deceive, cheat, banter,' or to FOP.

f.o.b. ▶ abbr. free on board. See FREE.

fo·cac·cia /fō'käCH(ē)ə/ ▶ **n.** a type of flat Italian bread made with yeast and olive oil and flavored with herbs.
– ORIGIN Italian.

fo·cal /'fōkəl/ ▶ **adj.** of or relating to the center or main point of interest: *tapestries in which birds or animals provide the focal interest.* ■ Optics of or relating to the focus of a lens. ■ (of a disease or medical condition) occurring in one particular site in the body.
– DERIVATIVES **fo·cal·ly** adv.
– ORIGIN late 17th cent.: from modern Latin *focalis*, from Latin *focus*, or directly from FOCUS.

fo·cal·ize /'fōkə,līz/ ▶ **v.** [with obj.] technical focus (something), in particular: ■ (in literary theory) provide an internal focus for (a text): *the narrative discourse is focalized around the consciousness of the central protagonist.* ■ Medicine confine (a disease or infection) to a particular site in the body.
– DERIVATIVES **fo·cal·i·za·tion** /,fōkəli'zāSHən/ **n.**

fo·cal length ▶ **n.** the distance between the center of a lens or curved mirror and its focus. ■ the equivalent distance in a compound lens or telescope.

fo·cal plane ▶ **n.** the plane through the focus perpendicular to the axis of a mirror or lens.

fo·cal point ▶ **n.** the point at which rays or waves meet after reflection or refraction, or the point from which diverging rays or waves appear to proceed. ■ the center of interest or activity: *almost every sizable city can have a junior college that can act as a focal point for cultural activity.*

Foch /fôSH/, Ferdinand (1851–1929), French general. He supported the use of offensive warfare, which resulted in many of his 20th Corps being killed at the start of World War I in August 1914.

fo'c'sle /'fōksəl/ (also **fo'c's'le**) ▶ **n.** variant spelling of FORECASTLE.

fo·cus /'fōkəs/ ▶ **n.** (pl. **focuses** or **foci** /'fō,sī, -,kī/)
1 the center of interest or activity: *this generation has made the environment a focus of attention.* ■ an act of concentrating interest or activity on something: *our focus on the customer's requirements.* ■ Geology the point of origin of an earthquake. Compare with EPICENTER. ■ Medicine the principal site of an infection or other disease. ■ Linguistics the part of a sentence given prominence, usually for emphasis or contrast, e.g., *Bob* in *it was Bob who came, not Bill.* Compare with RHEME.
2 the state or quality of having or producing clear visual definition: *his face is rather out of focus.* ■ another term for FOCAL POINT. ■ the point at which an object must be situated with respect to a lens or mirror for an image of it to be well defined. ■ a device on a lens that can be adjusted to produce a clear image.
3 Geometry one of the fixed points from which the distances to any point of a given curve, such as an ellipse or parabola, are connected by a linear relation.
▶ **v.** (**focuses, focusing, focused** or **focusses, focussing, focussed**) [no obj.] **1** (of a person or their eyes) adapt to the prevailing level of light and become able to see clearly: *try to focus on a stationary object.* ■ [with obj.] bring (one's eyes) into such a state: *trying to focus his bleary eyes on Corbett.* ■ [with obj.] adjust the focus of (a telescope, camera, or other instrument): *they were focusing a telescope on a star.* ■ (of rays or waves) meet at a single point. ■ [with obj.] (of a lens) make (rays or waves) meet at a single point. ■ [no obj.] (of light, radio waves, or other energy) become concentrated into a sharp beam of light or energy. ■ [with obj.] (of a lens) concentrate (light, radio waves, or energy) into a sharp beam.
2 (**focus on**) pay particular attention to: *the study will focus on a number of areas in Wales.* ■ [with obj.] concentrate: *the course helps to focus and stimulate your thoughts.* ■ [with obj.] Linguistics place the focus on (a part of a sentence).
– DERIVATIVES **fo·cus·er** **n.**
– ORIGIN mid 17th cent. (as a term in geometry and physics): from Latin, literally 'domestic hearth.'

fo·cus group ▶ **n.** a demographically diverse group of people assembled to participate in a guided discussion about a particular product before it is launched, or to provide ongoing feedback on a political campaign, television series, etc.

fo·cus pull·er ▶ **n.** an assistant to a film or television cameraman who is responsible for keeping the lens focused during filming.

fod·der /'fädər/ ▶ **n.** food, esp. dried hay or feed, for cattle and other livestock. ■ a person or thing regarded only as material for a specific use: *young people ending up as factory fodder.* See also CANNON FODDER.
▶ **v.** [with obj.] give fodder to (cattle or other livestock).
– ORIGIN Old English *fōdor*, of Germanic origin; related to Dutch *voeder* and German *Futter*, also to FOOD.

fo·dy /'fōdē/ ▶ **n.** (pl. **fodies**) a songbird of the weaver family occurring in Madagascar and islands in the Indian Ocean, the male of which typically has mainly red plumage. ● Genus *Foudia*, family Ploceidae: several species.
– ORIGIN a local word.

FoE ▶ **abbr.** Friends of the Earth.

foe /fō/ ▶ **n.** an enemy or opponent: *join forces against the common foe.*
– ORIGIN Old English *fāh* 'hostile' and *gefā* 'enemy'; related to FEUD.

foehn /fān, fœn/ (also **föhn**) ▶ **n.** (often **the foehn**) a hot southerly wind on the northern slopes of the Alps. ■ (also **foehn wind**) Meteorology a warm dry wind of this type developing in the lee of any mountain range.
– ORIGIN mid 19th cent.: from German *Föhn*, based on Latin (*ventus*) *Favonius* 'mild west wind,' *Favonius* being the Roman personification of the west or west wind.

foet·id ▶ **adj.** variant spelling of FETID.

foe·tus ▶ **n.** variant spelling of FETUS (chiefly in British nontechnical use).
– DERIVATIVES **foe·tal** /'fētl/ **adj.**, **foe·ti·cide** /'fētə,sīd/ **n.**

USAGE See usage at FETUS.

fog¹ /fôg, fäg/ ▶ **n. 1** a thick cloud of tiny water droplets suspended in the atmosphere at or near the earth's surface that obscures or restricts visibility (to a greater extent than mist; strictly, reducing visibility to below 1 km): *the collision occurred in thick fog.* ■ [in sing.] an opaque mass of something in the atmosphere: *a whirling fog of dust.* ■ Photography cloudiness that obscures the image on a developed negative or print.
2 [in sing.] something that obscures and confuses a situation or someone's thought processes: *the origins of local government are lost in a fog of detail.*
▶ **v.** (**fogs, fogging, fogged**) **1** (with reference to a glass surface) cover or become covered with steam: [with obj.] *hot steam drifted about her, fogging up the window* | [no obj.] *the windshield was starting to fog up.* ■ Photography make (a film, negative, or print) obscure or cloudy.
2 bewilder or puzzle (someone): *she stared at him, confusion fogging her brain.* ■ make (an idea or situation) difficult to understand: *the government has been fogging the issue.*
3 treat with something, esp. an insecticide, in the form of a spray: *Winnipeg stopped fogging for mosquitoes three years ago.*
– PHRASES **in a fog** in a state of perplexity; unable to think clearly or understand something. **the fog of war** confusion caused by the chaos of war or battle: *he argues that the fog of war clouded everyone's judgment.*
– ORIGIN mid 16th cent.: perhaps a back-formation from FOGGY.

fog² ▶ **n.** the grass that grows in a field after a crop of hay has been taken. ■ long grass left standing in a pasture and used as winter grazing.
– ORIGIN late Middle English: origin uncertain; perhaps related to Norwegian *fogg*.

fog bank ▶ **n.** a dense mass of fog, esp. at sea.

fog·bound /'fôg,bound, 'fäg-/ ▶ **adj.** unable to travel or function normally because of thick fog. ■ enveloped or obscured by fog: *a fogbound forest.*

fog·bow /'fôg,bō, 'fäg-/ ▶ **n.** a phenomenon similar to a rainbow, produced by sunlight shining on fog.

fo·gey /'fōgē/ (also **fogy**) ▶ **n.** (pl. **fogeys** or **fogies**) a person, typically an old one, who is considered to be old-fashioned or conservative in attitude or tastes: *a bunch of old fogeys.*
– DERIVATIVES **fo·gey·dom** /-dəm/ **n.**, **fo·gey·ish** **adj.**, **fo·gey·ism** /,-izəm/ **n.**
– ORIGIN late 18th cent.: related to earlier slang *fogram*, of unknown origin.

Fog·gia /'fôjə, 'fôdjä/ a town in southeastern Italy; pop. 153,239 (2008).

fog·gy /'fôgē, 'fägē/ ▶ **adj.** (**foggier, foggiest**) full of or accompanied by fog: *a dark and foggy night.* ■ unable to think clearly; confused: *she was foggy with sleep.* ■ indistinctly expressed or perceived; obscure: *exactly what the company hopes to achieve is still foggy.*
– PHRASES **not have the foggiest** (**idea** or **notion**) informal have no idea at all.
– DERIVATIVES **fog·gi·ness** **n.**
– ORIGIN late 15th cent.: perhaps from FOG².

Fog·gy Bot·tom informal the US State Department: *Foggy Bottom's strategy for ensuring stability was to leave most of the power structure in place.*
– ORIGIN the name of a riverside area of Washington, DC, where the department is based.

fog·horn /'fôg,hôrn, 'fäg-/ ▶ **n.** a device making a loud, deep sound as a warning to ships in fog.

fog lamp (also **foglight**) ▶ **n.** a bright light on a motor vehicle, used in foggy conditions to improve road visibility or warn other drivers of one's presence.

fo·gy /'fōgē/ ▶ **n.** variant spelling of FOGEY.

föhn ▶ **n.** variant spelling of FOEHN.

foi·ble /'foibəl/ ▶ **n. 1** a minor weakness or eccentricity in someone's character: *they have to tolerate each other's little foibles.*
2 Fencing the weaker part of a sword blade, from the middle to the point. Compare with FORTE¹.
– ORIGIN late 16th cent. (as an adjective in the sense 'feeble'): from obsolete French, in Old French *fieble* (see FEEBLE). Both noun senses also formerly occurred as senses of the word *feeble* and all date from the 17th cent.

foie gras /fwä 'grä/ ▶ **n.** the liver of a specially fattened goose or duck prepared as food. ■ short for PÂTÉ DE FOIE GRAS.
– ORIGIN French, 'fat liver.'

foil¹ /foil/ ▶ **v.** [with obj.] prevent (something considered wrong or undesirable) from succeeding: *a brave policewoman foiled the armed robbery.* ■ frustrate the efforts or plans of: *Errol Flynn was a dashing Mountie foiling Nazi agents in Canada.* ■ Hunting (of a hunted animal) run over or cross (ground or a scent or track) in such a way as to confuse the hounds.
▶ **n. 1** Hunting the track or scent of a hunted animal.
2 archaic a setback in an enterprise; a defeat.
– ORIGIN Middle English (in the sense 'trample down'): perhaps from Old French *fouler* 'to full cloth, trample,' based on Latin *fullo* 'fuller.' Compare with FULL².

foil² ▶ **n. 1** metal hammered or rolled into a thin flexible sheet, used chiefly for covering or wrapping food: *aluminum foil.*
2 a person or thing that contrasts with and so emphasizes and enhances the qualities of another: *the earthy taste of grilled vegetables is a perfect foil for the tart bite of creamy goat cheese.* ■ a thin leaf of metal placed under a precious stone to increase its brilliance.
3 Architecture a leaf-shaped curve formed by the cusping of an arch or circle, typically occurring in groups of three or more in Gothic tracery.
– ORIGIN Middle English: via Old French from Latin *folium* 'leaf.'

foil³ ▶ **n.** a light fencing sword without cutting edges but with a button on its point.
– DERIVATIVES **foil·ist** /-ist/ **n.**
– ORIGIN late 16th cent.: of unknown origin.

foil⁴ ▶ **n.** each of the winglike structures fitted to a hydrofoil's hull to lift it clear of the water at speed.

foist /foist/ ▶ **v.** [with obj.] (**foist someone/something on**) impose an unwelcome or unnecessary person or thing on: *don't let anyone foist inferior goods on you.* ■ (**foist someone/something into**) introduce someone or something surreptitiously or unwarrantably into: *he attempted to foist a new delegate into the conference.*
– ORIGIN mid 16th cent. (in the sense 'palm a false die, so as to produce it at the right moment'): from Dutch dialect *vuisten* 'take in the hand,' from *vuist* (see FIST).

Fo·kine /'fôkyin, fô'kēn/, Michel (1880–1942), US dancer and choreographer; born in Russia; born *Mikhail Mikhailovich Fokin.* He reformed classical ballet. He was Sergi Diaghilev's chief choreographer at the Ballets Russes 1909–14.

Fok·ker /'fäkər/, Anthony Herman Gerard (1890–1939), US aircraft designer and pilot; born in Java. Having built his first aircraft in 1908, he designed fighters used by the Germans in World War I.

fol. ▶ **abbr.** folio. ■ following.

fol·a·cin /'fōləsən, 'fäl-/ ▶ **n.** another term for FOLIC ACID.

fold¹ /fōld/ ▶ **v.** [with obj.] **1** bend (something flexible and relatively flat) over on itself so that one part of it covers another: *she folded all her clothes and packed all her bags.* ■ (**fold something in/into**) mix an ingredient gently with (another ingredient), esp. by lifting a mixture with a spoon so as to enclose it without stirring or beating: *fold the egg whites into the chocolate mixture.* ■ [no obj.] (of a piece of furniture or equipment) be able to be bent or rearranged into a flatter or more compact

shape, typically in order to make it easier to store or carry: [with complement] *the deck chair folds flat* | (as adj. **folding**) *a folding chair.* ■ bend or rearrange (a piece of furniture or equipment) in such a way: *he folded up his tripod.* ■ [no obj.] (**fold out**) be able to be opened out; unfold: *the sofa folds out.* ■ Geology cause (rock strata) to undergo bending or curvature: (as noun **folding**) *a more active period of igneous activity caused intense folding.*
2 [with adverbial] cover or wrap something in (a soft or flexible material): *a plastic bag was folded around the book.* ■ hold or clasp (someone) closely in one's arms with passion or deep affection: *Bob folded her in his arms and kissed her.*
3 [no obj.] informal (of an enterprise or organization) cease operating as a result of financial problems or a lack of support: *the club folded earlier this year.* ■ (esp. of a sports player or team) suddenly stop performing well or effectively: *he folded in the second round.* ■ (of a poker player) drop out of a hand: *an unerring knack for knowing when to fold and when to stay in.*

▶ **n. 1** (usu. **folds**) a form or shape produced by the gentle draping of a loose, full garment or piece of cloth: *the fabric fell in soft folds.* ■ an area of skin that sags or hangs loosely. ■ chiefly Brit. an undulation or gentle curve of the ground; a slight hill or hollow: *the house lay in a fold of the hills.* ■ Geology a bend or curvature of strata.
2 a line or crease produced in paper or cloth as the result of folding it. ■ a piece of paper or cloth that has been folded: *a fold of paper slipped out of the diary.*
– PHRASES **fold one's arms** bring one's arms together and cross them over one's chest. **fold one's hands** bring or hold one's hands together.
– DERIVATIVES **fold·a·ble** adj.
– ORIGIN Old English *falden, fealden,* of Germanic origin; related to Dutch *vouwen* and German *falten.*

fold[2] ▶ **n.** a pen or enclosure in a field where livestock, esp. sheep, can be kept. ■ (**the fold**) a group or community, esp. when perceived as the locus of a particular set of aims and values: *he's performing a ritual to be accepted into the fold.*
▶ **v.** [with obj.] shut (livestock) in a fold.
– ORIGIN Old English *fald,* of Germanic origin; related to Dutch *vaalt.*

-fold ▶ **suffix** forming adjectives and adverbs from cardinal numbers: **1** in an amount multiplied by: *threefold.*
2 consisting of so many parts or facets: *twofold.*
– ORIGIN Old English *-fald, -feald*; related to FOLD[1].

fold·a·way /ˈfōldəˌwā/ ▶ **adj.** [attrib.] adapted or designed to be folded up for ease of storage or transport: *a foldaway table.*

fold·er /ˈfōldər/ ▶ **n.** a folding cover or holder, typically made of stiff paper or cardboard, for storing loose papers. ■ an icon on a computer screen that can be used to access a directory containing related files or documents. ■ a folded leaflet or a booklet made of folded sheets of paper.

fol·de·rol /ˈfäldəˌräl, ˈfôldəˌrôl/ (also **falderal**) ▶ **n.** trivial or nonsensical fuss: *all the folderol of the athletic contests and the cheerleaders.* ■ dated a showy but useless item.

fold·ing door ▶ **n.** a door with vertical jointed sections that can be folded together to one side to allow access to a room or building.

fold·ing mon·ey ▶ **n.** informal paper money; banknotes.

fold·out /ˈfōlˌdout/ ▶ **adj.** [attrib.] (of a page in a book or magazine or a piece of furniture) designed to be opened out for use and then folded away: *a fold-out map.*
▶ **n.** a page or piece of furniture designed in such a way.

fo·ley /ˈfōlē/ ▶ **n.** [as modifier] relating to or concerned with the addition of recorded sound effects after the shooting of a film: *the aural details that foley artists duplicate.*
– ORIGIN named after the inventor of the editing process.

fo·li·a /ˈfōlēə/ plural form of FOLIUM.

fo·li·a·ceous /ˌfōlēˈāsHəs/ ▶ **adj.** of or resembling a leaf or leaves. ■ chiefly Geology consisting of thin sheets or laminae.
– ORIGIN mid 17th cent.: from Latin *foliaceus* 'leafy' (from *folium* 'leaf') + -OUS.

fo·li·age /ˈfōl(ē)ij/ ▶ **n.** plant leaves, collectively: *healthy green foliage.*
– ORIGIN late Middle English *foilage* (in the sense 'design resembling leaves'): from Old French *feuillage,* from *feuille* 'leaf,' from Latin *folium.* The change in the first syllable was due to association with Latin *folium.*

fo·li·age leaf ▶ **n.** Botany a normal leaf, as opposed to petals and other modified leaves.

fo·li·ar /ˈfōlēər/ ▶ **adj.** [attrib.] technical of or relating to leaves: *foliar color and shape.*
– ORIGIN late 19th cent.: from modern Latin *foliaris,* from Latin *folium* 'leaf.'

fo·li·ar feed ▶ **n.** nutrients supplied to the leaves of a plant.
– DERIVATIVES **fo·li·ar feed·ing n.**

fo·li·ate ▶ **adj.** /ˈfōlēət, -ˌāt/ decorated with leaves or leaflike motifs: *foliate scrolls.*
▶ **v.** /ˈfōlēˌāt/ [with obj.] **1** decorate with leaves or leaflike motifs: *the dome is to be foliated.*
2 number the leaves of (a book) rather than the pages.
– ORIGIN mid 17th cent.: from Latin *foliatus* 'leaved,' from *folium* 'leaf.'

fo·li·at·ed /ˈfōlēˌātid/ ▶ **adj.** decorated with leaves or leaflike motifs: *ten columns foliated at the capitals.* ■ Architecture decorated with foils or conventionalized leaves. ■ chiefly Geology consisting of thin sheets or laminae.

fo·li·a·tion /ˌfōlēˈāsHən/ ▶ **n.** chiefly Geology the process of being split into thin sheets or laminae.

fo·lic ac·id /ˈfōlik, ˈfä-/ ▶ **n.** Biochemistry a vitamin of the B complex, found esp. in leafy green vegetables, liver, and kidney. Also called PTEROYLGLUTAMIC ACID, VITAMIN M.
– DERIVATIVES **fo·late** /ˈfōˌlāt/ **n.**
– ORIGIN 1940s: *folic* from Latin *folium* 'leaf' + -IC.

fo·lie à deux /fôˌlē ä ˈdœ/ ▶ **n.** (pl. **folies à deux** /fôˌlēz/) delusion or mental illness shared by two people in close association.
– ORIGIN early 20th cent.: French, literally 'shared madness.'

fo·lie de gran·deur /ˈfôˌlēdəgränˈdər/ ▶ **n.** delusions of grandeur.
– ORIGIN late 19th cent.: French.

Fo·lies-Ber·gère /fôˌlē bərˈzHer, ber-/ a variety theater in Paris, opened in 1869, known for its lavish productions featuring nude and seminude female performers.

fo·li·o /ˈfōlēˌō/ ▶ **n.** (pl. **folios**) an individual leaf of paper or parchment, numbered on the recto or front side only, occurring either loose as one of a series or forming part of a bound volume. ■ Printing the leaf number in a printed book. ■ a sheet of paper folded once to form two leaves (four pages) of a book. ■ a size of book made up of such sheets: *copies in folio.* ■ a book or manuscript made up of sheets of paper folded in such a way; a volume of the largest standard size: *old vellum-bound folios* | [as modifier] *a folio volume.*
– ORIGIN late Middle English: from Latin, ablative of *folium* 'leaf,' in medieval Latin used in references to mean 'on leaf so-and-so.' The original sense of *in folio* (from Italian *in foglio*) was 'in the form of a full-sized sheet or leaf folded once' (designating the largest size of book).

fo·li·ose /ˈfōlēˌōs/ ▶ **adj.** Botany (of a lichen) having a lobed, leaflike shape.
– ORIGIN early 18th cent.: from Latin *foliosus,* from *folium* 'leaf.'

fo·li·um /ˈfōlēəm/ ▶ **n.** (pl. **folia** /-lēə/) technical a thin leaflike structure, e.g., in some rocks or in the cerebellum of the brain.
– ORIGIN mid 18th cent.: from Latin, literally 'leaf.'

fo·li·vore /ˈfōləˌvôr/ ▶ **n.** Zoology an animal that feeds on leaves.
– DERIVATIVES **fo·liv·o·rous** /fōˈlivərəs/ **adj.**

folk /fōk/ ▶ **plural n. 1** (also **folks**) informal people in general: *some folk will do anything for money* | *an old folks' home.* ■ (**folks**) used as a friendly form of address to a group of people: *meanwhile, folks, why not relax and enjoy the show?* ■ (**one's folks**) the members of one's family, esp. one's parents: *I get along all right with your folks.*
2 folk music: *a mixture of folk and reggae.*
▶ **adj.** [attrib.] **1** of or relating to the traditional art or culture of a community or nation: *a revival of interest in folk customs* | *a folk museum.* ■ relating to or originating from the beliefs and opinions of ordinary people: *a folk hero* | *folk wisdom.*
2 of or relating to folk music: *performing at a folk club in Chicago.*
– PHRASES **just (plain) folks** ordinary, down-to-earth, unpretentious people.
– ORIGIN Old English *folc,* of Germanic origin; related to Dutch *volk* and German *Volk.*

folk dance ▶ **n.** a popular dance, considered as part of the tradition or custom of a particular people: *well-known folk dances* | *ballet steps complicated by borrowings from folk dance.*
– DERIVATIVES **folk danc·er n., folk danc·ing n.**

folk et·y·mol·o·gy ▶ **n.** a popular but mistaken account of the origin of a word or phrase. ■ the process by which the form of an unfamiliar or foreign word is adapted to a more familiar form through popular usage.

folk·ie /ˈfōkē/ ▶ **n.** informal a singer, player, or fan of folk music.

folk·ish /ˈfōkisH/ ▶ **adj.** characteristic of ordinary people or traditional culture: *folkish humor.* ■ relating to or like folk music or folk singers: *the most conventionally folkish number on the album.*

folk·life /ˈfōkˌlīf/ ▶ **n.** the way of life of a rural or traditional community.

folk·lore /ˈfōkˌlôr/ ▶ **n.** the traditional beliefs, customs, and stories of a community, passed through the generations by word of mouth. ■ a body of popular myth and beliefs relating to a particular place, activity, or group of people: *Hollywood folklore.*
– DERIVATIVES **folk·lor·ic** /-ˌlôrik/ **adj., folk·lor·ist** /-ist/ **n., folk·lor·is·tic** /ˌfōkləˈristik/ **adj.**

folk mass ▶ **n.** a mass in which folk music is used instead of traditional liturgical music.

folk med·i·cine ▶ **n.** treatment of disease or injury based on tradition, esp. on oral tradition, rather than on modern scientific practice, and often utilizing indigenous plants as remedies.

folk mem·o·ry ▶ **n.** a body of recollections or legends connected with the past that persists among a group of people.

folk mu·sic ▶ **n.** music that originates in traditional popular culture or that is written in such a style. Folk music is typically of unknown authorship and is transmitted orally from generation to generation.

folk rock ▶ **n.** popular music resembling or derived from folk music but incorporating the stronger beat of rock music and using electric instruments.

folk sing·er (also **folksinger**) ▶ **n.** a person who sings folk songs, typically accompanying themselves on a guitar.

folk song ▶ **n.** a song that originates in traditional popular culture or that is written in such a style.

folk·son·o·my /ˌfōkˈsänəmē/ ▶ **n.** (pl. **folksonomies**) a user-generated system of classifying and organizing online content into different categories by the use of metadata such as electronic tags.
– ORIGIN early 21st cent.: blend of *folks* (see FOLK) and TAXONOMY.

folk·sy /ˈfōksē/ ▶ **adj.** (**folksier, folksiest**) having the characteristics of traditional culture and customs, esp. in a contrived or artificial way: *the shop's folksy, small-town image.* ■ (of a person) informal and unpretentious: *his tireless energy and folksy oratory were much in demand at constituency lunches.*
– DERIVATIVES **folk·si·ness** /-sēnis/ **n.**

folk tale ▶ **n.** a story originating in popular culture, typically passed on by word of mouth.

folk·ways /ˈfōkˌwāz/ ▶ **plural n.** the traditional behavior or way of life of a particular community or group of people: *a study of Cherokee folklore and folkways.*

folk·y /ˈfōkē/ ▶ **adj.** (**folkier, folkiest**) another term for FOLKSY or FOLKISH.
– DERIVATIVES **folk·i·ness** /-kēnis/ **n.**

fol·li·cle /ˈfälikəl/ ▶ **n. 1** Anatomy a small secretory cavity, sac, or gland, in particular: ■ (also **hair follicle**) the sheath of cells and connective tissue that surrounds the root of a hair. ■ short for GRAAFIAN FOLLICLE.
2 Botany a dry fruit that is derived from a single carpel and opens on one side only to release its seeds.
– DERIVATIVES **fol·lic·u·lar** /fəˈlikyələr/ **adj., fol·lic·u·late** /fəˈlikyələt, -ˌlāt/ **adj., fol·lic·u·lat·ed** /fəˈlikyəˌlātid/ **adj.**
– ORIGIN late Middle English: from Latin *folliculus* 'little bag,' diminutive of *follis* 'bellows.'

fol·li·cle mite ▶ **n.** a parasitic mite that burrows into the hair follicles, causing demodectic mange.
● Genus *Demodex,* family Demodicidae.

fol·li·cle-stim·u·lat·ing hor·mone (abbr.: **FSH**) ▶ **n.** Biochemistry a hormone secreted by the anterior pituitary gland that promotes the formation of ova or sperm.

fol·lic·u·li·tis /fəˌlikyəˈlītəs/ ▶ **n.** Medicine inflammation of the hair follicles.

fol·lis /ˈfälis/ ▶ **n.** (pl. **folles** /ˈfälēz/) a bronze or copper coin of a type introduced by the Roman emperor Diocletian in AD 296 and also used later in Byzantine currency.
– ORIGIN late 19th cent.: Latin, literally 'bag, purse'; compare with FILS[1], FOOL[1].

fol·low /ˈfälō/ ▶ **v.** [with obj.] **1** go or come after (a person or thing proceeding ahead); move or travel behind: *she went back into the house, and Ben followed her* | [no obj.] *he was following behind in his car.* ■ go after (someone) in order to observe or monitor: *the KGB man followed her everywhere.* ■ archaic strive after; aim at: *I follow fame.* ■ go along (a route or path). ■ (of a route or path) go in the

same direction as or parallel to (another): *the road follows a hidden sweetwater brook.*
2 come after in time or order: *the six years that followed his restoration* | [no obj.] *the rates are as* ***follows.*** ■ happen after (something else) as a consequence: *raucous laughter followed the ribald remark* | [no obj.] *retribution soon followed.* ■ [no obj.] be a logical consequence: *it thus* ***follows from*** *this equation that the value must be negative.* ■ [with obj.] (of a person) do something after (something else): *he follows his surprise hit movie* ***with*** *a paranoid thriller.* ■ (often **be followed by**) have (a dish or course) after another or others in a meal: *turkey was followed by dessert.*
3 act according to (an instruction or precept): *he has difficulty in following written instructions.* ■ conform to: *the film faithfully follows Shakespeare's plot.* ■ act according to the lead or example of (someone): *he follows Aristotle in believing this.* ■ treat as a teacher or guide: *those who seek to follow Jesus Christ.*
4 pay close attention to (something): *I've been following this discussion closely.* ■ keep track of; trace the movement or direction of: *she followed his gaze, peering into the gloom.* ■ maintain awareness of the current state or progress of (events in a particular sphere or account): *young Italians follow football.* ■ (of a person or account) be concerned with the development of (something): *the book follows the life and career of Henry Clay.* ■ understand the meaning or tendency of (a speaker or argument): *I still don't follow you.*
5 practice (a trade or profession). ■ undertake or carry out (a course of action or study): *she followed a strict diet.*
– PHRASES **follow in someone's footsteps** (or **steps**) do as another person did before, esp. in following a particular career. **follow one's nose 1** trust to one's instincts: *you are on the right track so follow your nose.* **2** move along guided by one's sense of smell. **3** go straight ahead. **follow suit** (in bridge, whist, and other card games) play a card of the suit led. ■ conform to another's actions: *Spain cut its rates by half a percent but no other country has followed suit.*
– PHRASAL VERBS **follow through** (in golf, baseball, and other sports) continue one's movement after the ball has been struck or thrown. **follow something through** continue an action or task to its conclusion. **follow something up** pursue or investigate something further: *I decided to follow up the letters with phone calls.*
– ORIGIN Old English *folgian*, of Germanic origin; related to Dutch *volgen* and German *folgen.*

fol·low·er /ˈfälōər/ ▶ **n.** an adherent or devotee of a particular person, cause, or activity: *a freethinker and follower of Voltaire.* ■ a person who moves or travels behind someone or something.

fol·low·ing /ˈfälōiNG/ ▶ **prep.** coming after or as a result of: *police are hunting for two men following a spate of robberies in the area.*
▶ **n. 1** a body of supporters or admirers: *he attracted a worldwide following.*
2 (**the following**) [treated as sing. or pl.] what follows or comes next: *the following are both grammatically correct sentences.*
▶ **adj.** [attrib.] **1** next in time: *the following day there was a ceremony in St. Peter's Square.* ■ about to be mentioned: *you are required to provide us with the following information.*
2 (of a wind or sea) blowing or moving in the same direction as the course of a vehicle or vessel.

fol·low-on ▶ **n.** the action of occurring as a consequence or result of something: [as modifier] *follow-on treatment.* ■ a thing that occurs as a consequence, result, or modification of another: *it will act as the follow-on to the current version of the software.*

fol·low-the-lead·er ▶ **n.** a children's game in which the participants copy the actions and words of a person who has been chosen as leader. ■ the copying of the actions of others, often without consideration of their suitability for oneself: *consumers* ***play follow-the-leader*** *when it comes to buying fashion.*

fol·low-through ▶ **n.** the continuing of an action or task to its conclusion: *the company assures follow-through on all aspects of the contract.* ■ a continuation of the movement of an arm, bat, racket, or club after a ball has been thrown or struck: *he has a characteristic swing and follow-through.*

fol·low-up ▶ **n.** a continuation or repetition of something that has already been started or done, in particular: ■ an activity carried out as part of a study in order to monitor or further develop earlier work: [as modifier] *follow-up interviews.* ■ further observation or treatment of a patient, esp. to monitor earlier treatment: *patients who require proper medical follow-up.* ■ a piece of work that builds on or exploits the success of earlier work: *she is writing* ***a follow-up to*** *Jane Austen's Pride and Prejudice.*

fol·ly /ˈfälē/ ▶ **n.** (pl. **follies**) **1** lack of good sense; foolishness: *an act of sheer folly.* ■ a foolish act, idea, or practice: *the follies of youth.*
2 a costly ornamental building with no practical purpose, esp. a tower or mock-Gothic ruin built in a large garden or park.
3 (**Follies**) a theatrical revue, typically with glamorous female performers: [in names] *the Ziegfeld Follies.*
– ORIGIN Middle English: from Old French *folie* 'madness,' in modern French also 'delight, favorite dwelling' (compare with sense 2), from *fol* 'fool, foolish.'

Fol·som[1] /ˈfōlsəm/ a city in north central California, northeast of Sacramento; pop. 67,788 (est. 2008).

Fol·som[2] ▶ **n.** [usu. as modifier] Archaeology a Paleo-Indian culture of central and North America, dated to about 10,500–8,000 years ago. The culture is distinguished by fluted stone projectile points or spearheads. Compare with CLOVIS[2].
– ORIGIN early 20th cent.: from *Folsom*, northeastern New Mexico, the area where remains were first found.

Fo·mal·haut /ˈfōməl,hôt/ Astronomy the brightest star in the constellation Piscis Austrinus.
– ORIGIN Arabic *fam al-ḥūt* 'mouth of the fish,' from *fam* 'mouth' + *al-* 'the' + *ḥūt* 'fish.'

fo·ment /ˈfō,ment, fōˈment/ ▶ **v.** [with obj.] **1** instigate or stir up (an undesirable or violent sentiment or course of action): *they accused him of fomenting political unrest.*
2 archaic bathe (a part of the body) with warm or medicated lotions.
– DERIVATIVES **fo·ment·er n.**
– ORIGIN late Middle English (sense 2): from French *fomenter*, from late Latin *fomentare*, from Latin *fomentum* 'poultice, lotion,' from *fovere* 'to heat, cherish.'

fo·men·ta·tion /,fōmenˈtāSHən, -mən-/ ▶ **n. 1** the action of instigating or stirring up undesirable sentiment or actions.
2 archaic a poultice.
– ORIGIN late Middle English: from late Latin *fomentatio(n-)*, from the verb *fomentare* (see FOMENT).

fom·i·tes /ˈfōmə,tēz/ ▶ **plural n.** Medicine objects or materials that are likely to carry infection, such as clothes, utensils, and furniture.
– ORIGIN early 19th cent.: from Latin, plural of *fomes*, literally 'kindling wood, tinder.'

Fon /fän/ ▶ **n.** (pl. **same** or **Fons**) **1** a member of a people inhabiting the southern part of Benin.
2 the Kwa language of this people.
▶ **adj.** of or relating to this people or their language.
– ORIGIN the name in Fon.

fond /fänd/ ▶ **adj.** [predic.] (**fond of**) having an affection or liking for: *I'm very fond of Mike* | *he was not too fond of dancing.* ■ [attrib.] affectionate; loving: *waving* ***a fond farewell*** *to her parents* | *reading it brought many fond memories of our childhood.* ■ [attrib.] (of a hope or belief) foolishly optimistic; naive.
– DERIVATIVES **fond·ly adv.**
– ORIGIN late Middle English (in the sense 'infatuated, foolish'): from obsolete *fon* 'a fool, be foolish,' of unknown origin. Compare with FUN.

Fon·da /ˈfändə/ the name of a family of US actors.
■ **Henry (Jaynes)** (1905–82), noted for his roles in such movies as *The Grapes of Wrath* (1939), *Twelve Angry Men* (1957), and *On Golden Pond* (1981).
■ **Jane** (1937–), Henry's daughter. Her movies include *Klute* (1971), *The China Syndrome* (1979), *Nine to Five* (1980), and *On Golden Pond* (1981).
■ **Peter** (1939–), Henry's son. His best known movies are *Easy Rider* (1969) and *Ulee's Gold* (1997). Peter's daughter **Bridget** (1964–) is also an actor.

Henry Fonda

fon·dant /ˈfändənt/ ▶ **n.** a thick paste made of sugar and water and often flavored or colored, used in the making of candy and the icing and decoration of cakes. ■ a candy made of such a paste.
– ORIGIN late 19th cent.: from French, literally 'melting,' present participle of *fondre.*

fon·dant po·ta·toes ▶ **plural n.** potatoes trimmed in the shape of eggs, fried in butter and then baked.

Fond du Lac /ˈfändl,ak, ˈfänjə,lak/ an industrial and commercial city in southeastern Wisconsin, on Lake Winnebago; pop. 42,025 (est. 2008).

fon·dle /ˈfändl/ ▶ **v.** [with obj.] stroke or caress lovingly or erotically: *the dog came over to have his ears fondled* | *charges that he fondled a patient during an examination.*
▶ **n.** an act of fondling.
– DERIVATIVES **fon·dler** /ˈfändlər, ˈfändl-ər/ **n.**
– ORIGIN late 17th cent. (in the sense 'pamper'): back-formation from obsolete *fondling* 'much-loved or petted person,' from FOND + -LING.

fond·ness /ˈfändnis/ ▶ **n.** affection or liking for someone or something: *I remember him with great fondness* | *I have* ***a fondness for*** *spicy food.*

fon·du /fänˈd(y)o͞o/ ▶ **adj.** [postpositive] Ballet (of a position) involving a lowering of the body by bending the knee of the supporting leg: *an arabesque fondu.*
– ORIGIN mid 19th cent.: French, literally 'melted.'

fon·due /fänˈd(y)o͞o/ ▶ **n.** a dish in which small pieces of food are dipped into a hot sauce or a hot cooking medium such as oil or broth: *a Swiss cheese fondue.*
– ORIGIN French, feminine past participle of *fondre* 'to melt.'

Fon·se·ca, Gulf of /fänˈsākə/ an inlet of the Pacific Ocean in western central America. El Salvador lies on its north, Honduras on its east, and Nicaragua on its south.

fons et o·ri·go /ˈfänz et ō ˈrīgō, rē-/ ▶ **n.** the source and origin of something: *they recognized the sixties as the fons et origo of music as they knew it.*
– ORIGIN Latin, originally as *fons et origo mali* 'the source and origin of evil.'

font[1] /fänt/ ▶ **n. 1** a receptacle in a church for the water used in baptism, typically a freestanding stone structure. ■ another term for STOUP. ■ a reservoir for oil in an oil lamp.
2 a fount: *they dip down into the font of wisdom.*
– DERIVATIVES **font·al** /ˈfäntl/ **adj.**
– ORIGIN late Old English: from Latin *fons, font-* 'spring, fountain,' occurring in the ecclesiastical Latin phrase *fons* or *fontes baptismi* 'baptismal water(s).'

font[2] (Brit. also **fount** /fount/) ▶ **n.** Printing a set of type of one particular face and size.
– ORIGIN late 16th cent. (denoting the action or process of casting or founding): from French *fonte*, from *fondre* 'to melt.'

Fon·taine, Joan (de Beauvoir) (1917–), US actress; born in Japan; born *Joan de Havilland*; sister of Olivia de Havilland. Her movies include *Rebecca* (1940), *Suspicion* (1941), and *The Constant Nymph* (1943).

Fon·taine·bleau /,fôNtenˈblō, ˈfäntin,blō/ a town in north central France, southeast of Paris, where King Louis XIV revoked the Edict of Nantes and Napoleon I signed his first abdication; pop. 16,302 (2007).

Fon·tana /fänˈtanə/ a city in southwestern California, east of Los Angeles; pop. 184,984 (est. 2008).

fon·ta·nel /,fäntnˈel/ (also **fontanelle**) ▶ **n.** a space between the bones of the skull in an infant or fetus, where ossification is not complete and the sutures not fully formed. The main one is between the frontal and parietal bones.
– ORIGIN mid 16th cent. (denoting a hollow of the skin between muscles): from French, from modern Latin *fontanella*, from an Old French diminutive of *fontaine* (see FOUNTAIN). The current sense dates from the mid 18th cent.

Fon·tanne /fänˈtan/, Lynn (1887–1983), US actress; born in England. She married actor Alfred Lunt (1892–1977) in 1922, and thereafter they appeared in many plays together, including *The Guardsman* (1924) and *The Visit* (1958).

Fon·teyn /fänˈtān/, Dame Margot (1919–91), English ballet dancer; born *Margaret Hookham.* In 1962, she began a partnership with Rudolf Nureyev, dancing with him in *Giselle* and *Romeo and Juliet.*

SERIF

Bookman
abcdefghijklmnopqrstuvwxyz 1234567890
ABCDEFGHIJKLMNOPQRSTUVWXYZ

Times
abcdefghijklmnopqrstuvwxyz 1234567890
ABCDEFGHIJKLMNOPQRSTUVWXYZ

SANS SERIF

Helvetica
abcdefghijklmnopqrstuvwxyz 1234567890
ABCDEFGHIJKLMNOPQRSTUVWXYZ

Avant Garde
abcdefghijklmnopqrstuvwxyz 1234567890
ABCDEFGHIJKLMNOPQRSTUVWXYZ

SQUARE SERIF

Courier
abcdefghijklmnopqrstuvwxyz 1234567890
ABCDEFGHIJKLMNOPQRSTUVWXYZ

SCRIPT

Boulevard
abcdefghijklmnopqrstuvwxyz 1234567890
ABCDEFGHIJKLMNOPQRSTU
VWXYZ

DISPLAY

ITC Kabel Ultra
abcdefghijklmnopqrstuvwxyz 1234567890
ABCDEFGHIJKLMNOPQRSTUVWXYZ

examples of font families

fon·ti·na /fän'tēnə/ ▶ n. a kind of pale yellow Italian cheese.

Foo·chow /'fōō'jō/ variant of FUZHOU.

food /fōōd/ ▶ n. any nutritious substance that people or animals eat or drink, or that plants absorb, in order to maintain life and growth: *cans of cat food | baby foods.*
– PHRASES **food for thought** something that warrants serious consideration.
– ORIGIN late Old English *fōda*, of Germanic origin; related to FODDER.

Food and Ag·ri·cul·ture Or·gan·i·za·tion (abbr.: **FAO**) an agency of the United Nations established in 1945 to secure improvements in the production and distribution of food and agricultural products and to raise levels of nutrition. Its headquarters are in Rome.

food bank ▶ n. a place supplying food to poor or displaced people.

food bod·y ▶ n. Botany a small nutrient-rich structure developed on the leaves, flowers, or petioles of some tropical plants to attract ants.

food chain ▶ n. a hierarchical series of organisms each dependent on the next as a source of food.

food court ▶ n. an area, typically in a shopping mall, where fast-food outlets, tables, and chairs are located.

food fish ▶ n. a species of fish that is used as food by humans or forms a major part of the diet of a particular predator.

Food Guide Pyr·a·mid ▶ n. a food pyramid developed by the US Department of Agriculture, displaying color-coded food groups arranged according to recommended levels of consumption in a healthy diet.

food·ie /'fōōdē/ ▶ n. informal a person with a particular interest in food; a gourmet.

food mile ▶ n. a mile over which a food item is transported from producer to consumer, as a unit of measurement of the fuel used to do this.

food poi·son·ing ▶ n. illness caused by bacteria or other toxins in food, typically with vomiting and diarrhea.

food proc·es·sor ▶ n. an electric kitchen appliance used for chopping, mixing, or puréeing foods.

food pyr·a·mid ▶ n. **1** a nutritional diagram in the shape of a pyramid, esp. (in the US) the Food Guide Pyramid.
2 Ecology a graphic representation of predatory relationships in the food chain, in which various forms of life are shown on different levels, with each level preying on the one below it.

food stamp ▶ n. a voucher issued by the government to those on low income, exchangeable for food.

food·stuff /'fōōd,stəf/ ▶ n. a substance suitable for consumption as food.

food sup·ple·ment ▶ n. see SUPPLEMENT.

food vac·u·ole ▶ n. Biology a vacuole with a digestive function in the protoplasm of a protozoan.

food val·ue ▶ n. the nutritional value of a foodstuff.

food web ▶ n. Ecology a system of interlocking and interdependent food chains.

foo·fa·raw /'fōōfə,rô/ informal ▶ n. **1** a great deal of fuss or attention given to a minor matter.
2 showy frills added unnecessarily.

foo fight·er /fōō/ ▶ n. an unidentified flying object of a kind reported by US pilots during World War II, usually described as a bright light or ball of fire.
– ORIGIN 1940s: from the comic strip *Smokey Stover* (created in 1935 by Bill Holman (1903–1987)), whose title character used the invented term to mean 'firefighter.'

foo-foo /'fōō ,fōō/ ▶ n. variant spelling of FUFU.

fool[1] /fōōl/ ▶ n. a person who acts unwisely or imprudently; a silly person: *what a fool I was to do this.* ■ historical a jester or clown, esp. one retained in a noble household. ■ informal a person devoted to a particular activity: *he is a running fool.* ■ archaic a person who is duped.
▶ v. [with obj.] trick or deceive (someone); dupe: *he fooled nightclub managers into believing he was a successful businessman | she had been fooling herself in thinking she could remain indifferent.* ■ [no obj.] act in a joking, frivolous, or teasing way: *I shouted at him impatiently to stop fooling around.* ■ [no obj.] (**fool around**) engage in casual or extramarital sexual activity.
▶ adj. [attrib.] informal foolish or silly: *that damn fool waiter.*
– PHRASES **be no** (or **nobody's**) **fool** be a shrewd or prudent person. **a fool and his money are soon parted** proverb a foolish person spends money carelessly and will soon be penniless. **fools rush in where angels fear to tread** proverb people without good sense or judgment will have no hesitation in tackling a situation that even the wisest would avoid. **make a fool of** trick or deceive (someone) so that they look foolish. ■ (**make a fool of oneself**) behave in an incompetent or inappropriate way that makes one appear foolish. **play** (or **act**) **the fool** behave in a playful or silly way. **there's no fool like an old fool** proverb the foolish behavior of an older person seems especially foolish as they are expected to think and act more sensibly than a younger one. **you could have fooled me!** used to express cynicism or doubt about an assertion: *"Fun, was it? Well, you could have fooled me!"*
– PHRASAL VERBS **fool with** toy with; play idly with: *I like fooling with cameras.* ■ tease (a person): *we've just been fooling with you.*
– ORIGIN Middle English: from Old French *fol* 'fool, foolish,' from Latin *follis* 'bellows, bag,' by extension 'empty-headed person'; compare with FILS[1], FOLLIS.

fool[2] ▶ n. [usu. with modifier] chiefly Brit. a cold dessert made of puréed fruit mixed or served with cream or custard: *raspberry fool with cream.*
– ORIGIN late 16th cent.: perhaps from FOOL[1].

fool·er·y /'fōōlərē/ ▶ n. silly or foolish behavior.

fool·har·dy /'fōōl,härdē/ ▶ adj. (**foolhardier, foolhardiest**) recklessly bold or rash: *it would be foolhardy to go into the scheme without support.*
– DERIVATIVES **fool·har·di·ly** /-,härdl-ē/ adv., **fool·har·di·ness** n.
– ORIGIN Middle English: from Old French *folhardi*, from *fol* 'foolish' + *hardi* 'bold' (see HARDY).

fool·ish /'fōōlish/ ▶ adj. (of a person or action) lacking good sense or judgment; unwise: *it was foolish of you to enter into correspondence.*

fool·ish·ly /'fōōlishlē/ ▶ adv. in an unwise manner; stupidly: *they were condemned for acting foolishly | foolishly, I decided to give it a go.*

fool·ish·ness /ˈfo͞olisнnis/ ▶ **n.** lack of good sense or judgment; stupidity: *she was realizing the foolishness of her actions.*

fool·proof /ˈfo͞olˌpro͞of/ ▶ **adj.** incapable of going wrong or being misused: *a foolproof security system.*

fools·cap /ˈfo͞olzˌkap/ ▶ **n.** a size of paper, now standardized at about 13 × 8 (or 13 × 15.75) inches (300 × 200 [or 300 × 400] mm). ■ paper of this size: *several sheets of foolscap.*
– ORIGIN late 17th cent.: said to be named from a former watermark representing a jester's cap.

fool's er·rand ▶ **n.** a task or activity that has no hope of success.

fool's gold ▶ **n.** a brassy yellow mineral, esp. pyrite, that can be mistaken for gold.

fool's par·a·dise ▶ **n.** [in sing.] a state of happiness based on a person's not knowing about or denying the existence of potential trouble: *they were living in a fool's paradise, refusing to accept that they were in debt.*

fool's pars·ley ▶ **n.** a poisonous white-flowered plant of the parsley family, with fernlike leaves and an unpleasant smell, native to Eurasia and North Africa. ● *Aethusa cynapium*, family Umbelliferae.

foos·ball /ˈfo͞osˌbôl/ ▶ **n.** trademark a tabletop version of soccer in which players turn rods fixed on top of a playing box and attached to miniature figures of players, in order to flick the ball and strike it toward the goal.
– ORIGIN mid 20th cent.: from German *Fussball* 'football.'

foot /fo͝ot/ ▶ **n.** (pl. **feet** /fēt/) **1** the lower extremity of the leg below the ankle, on which a person stands or walks. ■ a corresponding part of the leg in vertebrate animals. ■ Zoology a locomotory or adhesive organ of an invertebrate. ■ the part of a sock or stocking that covers the foot. ■ literary a person's manner or speed of walking or running: *fleet of foot.* ■ [treated as pl.] Brit. historical or formal infantry; foot soldiers: *a captain of foot.*
2 the lower or lowest part of something standing or perceived as standing vertically; the base or bottom: *the foot of the stairs.* ■ the end of a table that is furthest from where the host sits. ■ the end of a bed, couch, or grave where the occupant's feet normally rest. ■ a device on a sewing machine for holding the material steady as it is sewn. ■ Botany the part by which a petal is attached. ■ the lower edge of a sail.
3 a unit of linear measure equal to 12 inches (30.48 cm): *shallow water no more than a foot deep.* (Symbol: **′**) ■ [usu. as modifier] Music a unit used in describing sets of organ pipes or harpsichord strings, in terms of the average or approximate length of the vibrating column of air or the string which produces the sound: *a sixteen-foot stop.*
4 Prosody a group of syllables constituting a metrical unit. In English poetry it consists of stressed and unstressed syllables, while in ancient classical poetry it consists of long and short syllables.
▶ **v.** [with obj.] informal **1** pay (the bill) for something, esp. when the bill is considered large or unreasonable.
2 (**foot it**) cover a distance, esp. a long one, on foot: *the rider was left to foot it ten or twelve miles back to camp.* ■ archaic dance: *the dance of fairies, footing it to the cricket's song.*
– PHRASES **at someone's feet** as someone's disciple or subject: *you would like to sit at my feet and thus acquire my wisdom.* **feet of clay** a fundamental flaw or weakness in a person otherwise revered. [with biblical allusion (Dan. 2:33) to the dream of Nebuchadnezzar, in which a magnificent idol has feet "part of iron and part of clay"; Daniel interprets this to signify a future kingdom that will be "partly strong, and partly broken," and will eventually fall.] **get one's feet wet** begin to participate in an activity. **get** (or **start**) **off on the right** (or **wrong**) **foot** make a good (or bad) start at something, esp. a task or relationship. **have something at one's feet** have something in one's power or command: *a perfect couple with the world at their feet.* **have** (or **keep**) **one's** (or **both**) **feet on the ground** be (or remain) practical and sensible. **have a foot in both camps** have an interest or stake concurrently in two parties or sides: *I can have a foot in both the creative and business camps.* **have** (or **get**) **a foot in the door** gain or have a first introduction to a profession or organization. **have one foot in the grave** informal often humorous be near death through old age or illness. **my foot!** informal said to express strong contradiction: *Efficient, my foot!* **off one's feet** so as to be no longer standing: *she was blown off her feet by the shock wave from the explosion.* **on one's feet** standing: *she's in the shop on her feet all day.* ■ well enough after an illness or injury to walk around: *we'll have you back on your feet in no time.* **on** (or **by**) **foot** walking rather than traveling by car or using other transport. **put one's best foot forward** embark on an undertaking with as much effort and determination as possible. **put one's feet up** informal take a rest, esp. when reclining with one's feet raised and supported. **put one's foot down** informal adopt a firm policy when faced with opposition or disobedience. **put one's foot in it** (or **put one's foot in one's mouth**) informal say or do something tactless or embarrassing; commit a blunder or indiscretion. **set foot on** (or **in**) [often with negative] enter; go into: *he hasn't set foot in the place since the war.* **set something on foot** archaic set an action or process in motion: *a plan had lately been set on foot for their relief.* Compare with **AFOOT**. **sweep someone off their feet** charm someone quickly and overpoweringly. **think on one's feet** react to events decisively, effectively, and without prior thought or planning. **to one's feet** to a standing position: *he leaped to his feet.*
– DERIVATIVES **foot·ed** /ˈfo͝otəd/ **adj.** [in combination] *the black-footed ferret*, **foot·less adj.**
– ORIGIN Old English *fōt*, of Germanic origin; related to Dutch *voet* and German *Fuss*, from an Indo-European root shared by Sanskrit *pad, pāda*, Greek *pous, pod-*, and Latin *pes, ped-* 'foot.'

foot·age /ˈfo͝otij/ ▶ **n. 1** a length of film made for movies or television: *film footage of the riot.*
2 size or length measured in feet: *the square footage of the room.*

foot-and-mouth dis·ease ▶ **n.** a contagious viral disease of cattle and sheep, causing ulceration of the hoofs and around the mouth.

foot·ball /ˈfo͝otˌbôl/ ▶ **n. 1** a form of team game played in North America with an oval ball on a field marked out as a gridiron. ■ British term for **SOCCER**. ■ play in such a game, esp. when stylish and entertaining: *his team played some impressive football.*
2 a ball used in football, either oval (as in American football) or round (as in soccer), typically made of leather or plastic and filled with compressed air. ■ a topical issue or problem that is the subject of continued argument or controversy: *the use of education as a political football.*
– DERIVATIVES **foot·ball·er n.**, **foot·ball·ing adj.**

foot·ball pool ▶ **n.** a form of gambling on the results of football games, the winners receiving amounts accumulated from entry money.

foot·bed /ˈfo͝otˌbed/ ▶ **n.** an insole in a boot or shoe, used for cushioning or to provide a better fit.

foot·board /ˈfo͝otˌbôrd/ ▶ **n. 1** an upright panel forming the foot of a bed.
2 a board serving as a step up to a vehicle such as a train.

foot·boy /ˈfo͝otˌboi/ ▶ **n.** historical a boy employed as a servant.

foot·brake /ˈfo͝otˌbrāk/ ▶ **n.** a brake lever in a motor vehicle, which the driver operates by pressing down with the foot.

foot·bridge /ˈfo͝otˌbrij/ ▶ **n.** a bridge designed to be used by pedestrians.

foot-can·dle ▶ **n.** a unit of illumination (now little used) equal to that given by a source of one candela at a distance of one foot (equivalent to one lumen per square foot or 10.764 lux).

foot-drag·ging ▶ **n.** reluctance or deliberate delay concerning a decision or action: *bureaucratic foot-dragging has continued to delay the project.*
– DERIVATIVES **foot-drag·ger n.**

foot·er /ˈfo͝otər/ ▶ **n. 1** [in combination] a person or thing of a specified number of feet in length or height: *a tall, sturdy six-footer.*
2 a line or block of text appearing at the foot of each page of a book or document. Compare with **HEADER**.

foot·fall /ˈfo͝otˌfôl/ ▶ **n. 1** the sound of a footstep or footsteps: *you will recognize his footfall on the stairs.*
2 Brit. the number of people entering a store or shopping area in a given time: *consumer goods shops lost footfall during sunny weekends.*

foot fault ▶ **n.** (in tennis, squash, and similar games) an infringement of the rules made by incorrect placement of the feet when serving.
▶ **v.** (**foot-fault**) [no obj.] (of a player) make a foot fault: *in his anxiety he foot-faulted.* ■ [with obj.] award a foot fault against (a player): *he was foot-faulted by the umpire.*

foot·gear /ˈfo͝otˌgi(ə)r/ ▶ **n.** another term for **FOOTWEAR**.

foot·hill /ˈfo͝otˌhil/ ▶ **n.** (usu. **foothills**) a low hill at the base of a mountain or mountain range: *the camp lies in the foothills of the Andes.*

foot·hold /ˈfo͝otˌhōld/ ▶ **n.** a place where a person's foot can be lodged to support them securely, esp. while climbing. ■ [usu. in sing.] a secure position from which further progress may be made: *the company is attempting to gain a foothold in the Russian market.*

foot·ing /ˈfo͝otiNG/ ▶ **n. 1** (**one's footing**) a secure grip with one's feet: *he suddenly lost his footing.*
2 [in sing.] the basis on which something is established or operates: *attempts to establish the store on a firm financial footing.* ■ the position or status of a person in relation to others: *the suppliers are on an equal footing with the buyers.*
3 (usu. **footings**) the bottommost part of a foundation wall, with a course of concrete wider than the base of the wall.

foo·tle /ˈfo͞otl/ ▶ **v.** [no obj.] chiefly Brit. engage in fruitless activity; mess about: *where's that pesky creature that was footling about outside?*
– ORIGIN late 19th cent.: perhaps from dialect *footer* 'idle, putter about,' from 16th-cent. *foutre* 'worthless thing,' from Old French, literally 'have sexual intercourse with.'

foot·lights /ˈfo͝otˌlīts/ ▶ **plural n.** (usu. **the footlights**) a row of spotlights along the front of a stage at the level of the actors' feet.

foot·ling /ˈfo͞otl-iNG/ ▶ **adj.** trivial and irritating: *year after year you come with the same footling complaint.*

foot·lock·er /ˈfo͝otˌläkər/ ▶ **n.** a small trunk or storage chest, originally stored at the foot of a bed.

foot log ▶ **n.** a log used as a simple footbridge.

foot·long /ˈfo͝otˌlôNG, -ˌläNG/ ▶ **adj.** measuring one foot in length.
▶ **n.** a hot dog one foot long.

foot·loose /ˈfo͝otˌlo͞os/ ▶ **adj.** able to travel freely and do as one pleases due to a lack of responsibilities or commitments: *I am* **footloose** *and fancy-free—I can follow my job wherever it takes me.* ■ chiefly Brit. (of a commercial, industrial, or financial operation) unrestricted in its location or field of operations and able to respond to fluctuations in the market: *modern factories are largely footloose.*

foot·man /ˈfo͝otmən/ ▶ **n.** (pl. **footmen**) **1** a liveried servant whose duties include admitting visitors and waiting at table.
2 historical a soldier in the infantry.
3 archaic a trivet to hang on the bars of a grate.
4 a slender moth that is typically of a subdued color, the caterpillar feeding almost exclusively on lichens. ● Several genera in the family Arctiidae: many species.

foot·mark /ˈfo͝otˌmärk/ ▶ **n.** a footprint.

foot·note /ˈfo͝otˌnōt/ ▶ **n.** an ancillary piece of information printed at the bottom of a page. ■ a thing that is additional or less important: *this incident seemed destined to become a mere footnote in history.*
▶ **v.** [with obj.] add a footnote or footnotes to (a piece of writing).

footpace ▶ **n. 1** walking speed.
2 a raised section of a floor.

foot·pad /ˈfo͝otˌpad/ ▶ **n.** historical a highwayman operating on foot rather than riding a horse.

foot·path /ˈfo͝otˌpaTH/ ▶ **n.** a path for people to walk along, esp. one in the countryside.

foot·plate /ˈfo͝otˌplāt/ ▶ **n.** chiefly Brit. the platform for the crew in the cab of a locomotive. ■ [as modifier] denoting railroad staff responsible for operating trains, as opposed to other employees.

foot-pound ▶ **n. 1** a unit of energy equal to the amount required to raise 1 pound a distance of 1 foot.
2 a unit of torque equal to the force of 1 lb acting perpendicularly to an axis of rotation at a distance of 1 foot.

foot-pound-sec·ond sys·tem ▶ **n.** a system of measurement having the foot, pound, and second as basic units.

foot·print /ˈfo͝otˌprint/ ▶ **n. 1** the impression left by a foot or shoe on the ground or a surface. ■ the impact on the environment of human activity in terms of pollution, damage to ecosystems, and the depletion of natural resources: *these countries are so populous that they can have a very big footprint.* ■ Computing the amount of memory or disk space required by a program.
2 the area covered by something, in particular: ■ the area beneath an aircraft or a land vehicle that is affected by its noise or weight. ■ the area in

which a broadcast signal from a particular source can be received. ■ the space taken up on a surface by a piece of computer hardware.

> **WORD TRENDS** Explorers of the great outdoors have long been urged to 'leave only footprints.' Now we are all being advised to keep an eye on the size of our **footprints**, since the word has become a common metaphor for the impact of human activities on the environment. The first extended use emerged in the 1960s, in reference to the area beneath a vehicle or aircraft that is affected by its noise or pressure, and a few years later the word came to denote the area within which a broadcast signal can be received. **Environmental footprint** is first recorded in the late 1970s, and the word is now very often seen in **carbon footprint**, which refers specifically to the amount of carbon dioxide produced through a person's everyday activities.

foot·rest /ˈfo͝otˌrest/ ▶ **n.** a support for the feet or a foot, used when sitting.

foot rope ▶ **n.** Sailing **1** a rope to which the lower edge of a sail is sewn.
2 a rope below a yard on which a sailor can stand while furling or reefing a sail.

foot rot ▶ **n.** a bacterial disease of the feet in hoofed animals, esp. sheep. ● The bacteria belong to the genera *Bacteroides* and *Fusobacterium*.
■ any of a number of fungal diseases of plants in which the base of the stem rots.

Foot·sie /ˈfo͝otsē/ ▶ **n.** Brit. informal term for **FTSE INDEX**.
– ORIGIN 1980s: fanciful elaboration of *FTSE*, influenced by *footsie*.

foot·sie /ˈfo͝otsē/ ▶ **n.** (also **footsy**) informal the action of touching someone's feet lightly with one's own feet, esp. under a table, as a playful expression of romantic interest: *he was **playing footsie** with Mara under the table.*
– ORIGIN 1940s: humorous diminutive of **FOOT**.

foot·slog /ˈfo͝otˌsläg/ ▶ **v.** (**footslogs, footslogging, footslogged**) [no obj.] (esp. of a soldier) walk or march for a long distance, typically wearily or with effort: *they footslogged around the two villages.*
▶ **n.** a long and exhausting walk or march.
– DERIVATIVES **foot·slog·ger n.**

foot sol·dier ▶ **n.** a soldier who fights on foot; an infantryman. ■ a person who carries out important work but does not have a role of authority in an organization or field: *programmers are the foot soldiers of the computer revolution.*

foot·sore /ˈfo͝otˌsôr/ ▶ **adj.** (of a person or animal) having painful or tender feet from much walking.

foot·stalk /ˈfo͝otˌstôk/ ▶ **n.** the short supporting stalk of a leaf or flower, or various stalklike structures in animals.

foot·step /ˈfo͝otˌstep/ ▶ **n.** a step taken by a person in walking, esp. as heard by another person.

foot·stool /ˈfo͝otˌsto͞ol/ ▶ **n.** a low stool for resting the feet on when sitting.

foot·sure /ˈfo͝otˌsHo͝or/ ▶ **adj.** another term for **SURE-FOOTED**.

foot-tap·ping ▶ **adj.** having or creating a strong rhythmical musical beat: *foot-tapping gospel hymns.*

foot valve ▶ **n.** a one-way valve at the inlet of a pipe or the base of a suction pump.

foot·wall /ˈfo͝otˌwôl/ ▶ **n.** Geology the block of rock that lies on the underside of an inclined fault or of a mineral deposit.

foot·way /ˈfo͝otˌwā/ ▶ **n.** Brit. a path or track for pedestrians.

foot·wear /ˈfo͝otˌwer/ ▶ **n.** outer coverings for the feet, such as shoes, boots, and sandals.

foot·well /ˈfo͝otˌwel/ ▶ **n.** a space for the feet in front of a seat in a vehicle or aircraft.
– ORIGIN 1980s: from **FOOT** + **WELL**[2] (in the sense 'a depression in the floor').

foot·work /ˈfo͝otˌwərk/ ▶ **n.** the manner in which one moves one's feet in various activities such as sports and dancing: *he speaks with other boxers, stopping to comment on punching angles and footwork.* ■ adroit response to sudden danger or new opportunities: *the company had to do a lot of nimble footwork to stay alive.*

foo·ty /ˈfo͝otē/ ▶ **n.** informal **1** Brit. football (soccer).
2 Austral./NZ football (Australian rules).
– ORIGIN by shortening and alteration.

foo yong /ˈfo͞o ˈyəNG/ ▶ **n.** a Chinese dish or sauce made with egg as a main ingredient.
– ORIGIN from Chinese (Cantonese dialect) *foò yung*, literally 'hibiscus.'

foo·zle /ˈfo͞ozəl/ informal ▶ **n.** a clumsy or botched attempt at something, esp. a shot in golf.
▶ **v.** [with obj.] botch; bungle: (as adj. **foozled**) *sliced approach shots and foozled putts.*
– ORIGIN mid 19th cent.: from German dialect *fuseln* 'work badly'; compare with **FUSEL OIL**.

fop /fäp/ ▶ **n.** a man who is concerned with his clothes and appearance in an affected and excessive way; a dandy.
– DERIVATIVES **fop·per·y** /ˈfäpərē/ **n.**
– ORIGIN late Middle English (in the sense 'fool'): perhaps related to **FOB**[2].

fop·pish /ˈfäpisH/ ▶ **adj.** (of a man) concerned with his clothes and appearance in an affected and excessive way: *he is foppish and vain | a foppish dandy.*
– DERIVATIVES **fop·pish·ly adv.**, **fop·pish·ness n.**

for /fôr, fər/ ▶ **prep. 1** in support of or in favor of (a person or policy): *they voted for independence in a referendum.*
2 affecting, with regard to, or in respect of (someone or something): *she is responsible for the efficient running of their department | the demand for money.*
3 on behalf of or to the benefit of (someone or something): *these parents aren't speaking for everyone.* ■ employed by: *it was a good firm to work for.*
4 having (the thing mentioned) as a purpose or function: *she is searching for enlightenment | the necessary tools for making a picture frame.*
5 having (the thing mentioned) as a reason or cause: *Aileen is proud of her family for their support | I could dance and sing for joy.*
6 having (the place mentioned) as a destination: *they are leaving for Swampscott tomorrow.*
7 representing (the thing mentioned): *the "F" is for Fascinating.*
8 in place of or in exchange for (something): *swap these two bottles for that one.* ■ charged as (a price): *copies are available for only a buck.*
9 in relation to the expected norm of (something): *she was tall for her age | warm weather for this time of year.*
10 indicating the length of (a period of time): *he was in prison for 12 years | I haven't seen him for some time.*
11 indicating the extent of (a distance): *he crawled for 300 yards.*
12 indicating an occasion in a series: *the camcorder failed for the third time.*
▶ **conj.** literary because; since: *he felt guilty, for he knew that he bore a share of responsibility for Fanny's death.*
– PHRASES **be for it** Brit. informal be in imminent danger of punishment or other trouble. **for all ——** see **ALL**. **for ever** see **FOREVER**. **for why** informal for what reason: *you're going to and I'll tell you for why.* **oh for ——** I long for ——: *oh for a strong black coffee!* **there's** (or **that's**) **—— for you** used ironically to indicate a particularly poor example of (a quality mentioned): *there's gratitude for you.*
– ORIGIN Old English, probably a reduction of a Germanic preposition meaning 'before' (in place or time); related to German *für*, also to **FORE**.

for. ▶ **abbr.** ■ foreign. ■ forest. ■ forester. ■ forestry.

f.o.r. ▶ **abbr.** free on rail. See **FREE**.

for- ▶ **prefix 1** denoting prohibition: *forbid.*
2 denoting abstention, neglect, or renunciation: *forgive | forget | forgo.*
3 denoting extremity of negative state expressed: *forlorn | forsake.*
– ORIGIN Old English.

fo·ra /ˈfôrə/ plural form of **FORUM** (sense 3).

for·age /ˈfôrij, ˈfär-/ ▶ **v.** [no obj.] (of a person or animal) search widely for food or provisions: *gulls are equipped by nature to forage for food.* ■ [with obj.] obtain (food or provisions): *a girl foraging grass for oxen.* ■ [with obj.] obtain food or provisions from (a place): *a man foraging a dumpster finds some celery.* ■ [with obj.] archaic supply (an animal or person) with food.
▶ **n. 1** bulky food such as grass or hay for horses and cattle; fodder.
2 [in sing.] a wide search over an area in order to obtain something, esp. food or provisions: *the nightly forage produces things that can be sold.*
– DERIVATIVES **for·ag·er n.**
– ORIGIN Middle English: from Old French *fourrage* (noun), *fourrager* (verb), from *fuerre* 'straw,' of Germanic origin and related to **FODDER**.

for·age cap ▶ **n.** a soft cap, usually having a stiff brim, forming part of a soldier's uniform.

for·age fish ▶ **n.** a species of fish of interest to humans chiefly as the prey of more valuable game fish.

for·age har·ves·ter ▶ **n.** a large agricultural machine for harvesting forage crops.

fo·ra·men /fəˈrāmən/ ▶ **n.** (pl. **foramina** /-ˈramənə/) Anatomy an opening, hole, or passage, esp. in a bone.
– ORIGIN late 17th cent.: from Latin, from *forare* 'bore a hole.'

fo·ra·men mag·num ▶ **n.** Anatomy the hole in the base of the skull through which the spinal cord passes.
– ORIGIN late 19th cent.: Latin, 'large opening.'

for·a·min·i·fer /ˌfôrəˈminəfər, ˌfär-/ ▶ **n.** (pl. **foraminifers** or **foraminifera** /fəˌraməˈnifərə/) Zoology a single-celled planktonic animal with a perforated chalky shell through which slender protrusions of protoplasm extend. Most kinds are marine, and when they die, their shells form thick ocean-floor sediments. See also **GLOBIGERINA**. ● Order Foraminiferida, phylum Rhizopoda, kingdom Protista.
– DERIVATIVES **fo·ram·i·nif·er·al** /fəˌraməˈnifərəl/ **adj.**, **fo·ram·i·nif·er·an** /fəˌraməˈnifərən/ **n. & adj.**, **fo·ram·i·nif·er·ous** /fəˌraməˈnifərəs/ **adj.**
– ORIGIN mid 19th cent.: from Latin *foramen*, *foramin-* (see **FORAMEN**) + *-fer* 'bearing' (from *ferre* 'to bear').

for'ard /ˈfôrərd, ˈfär-/ ▶ **adj. & adv.** nonstandard spelling of **FORWARD**, used to represent a nautical pronunciation.

for·as·much as /ˌfôrəzˈməCH əz/ ▶ **conj.** archaic because; since: *forasmuch as the tree returned to life, so too could Arthur be returned to her.*
– ORIGIN Middle English *for as much*, translating Old French *por tant que* 'for so much as.'

for·as·te·ro /ˌfôrəˈsterō/ (also **forastero tree**) ▶ **n.** (pl. **forasteros**) a cacao tree of a widely grown variety that provides the bulk of the world's cocoa beans.
– ORIGIN mid 19th cent.: from Spanish, literally 'foreign,' because the tree was imported into Venezuela from the West Indies, as distinct from the **CRIOLLO** or native variety.

for·ay /ˈfôrˌā, ˈfärˌā/ ▶ **n.** a sudden attack or incursion into enemy territory, esp. to obtain something; a raid: *the garrison made a foray against Richard's camp* | figurative *he made another foray to the bar.* ■ an attempt to become involved in a new activity or sphere: *my first foray into journalism.*
▶ **v.** [no obj.] make or go on a foray: *the place into which they were forbidden to foray.*
– DERIVATIVES **for·ay·er n.**
– ORIGIN Middle English: back-formation from *forayer* 'a person who forays,' from Old French *forrier* 'forager,' from *fuerre* 'straw' (see **FORAGE**).

forb /fôrb/ ▶ **n.** Botany a herbaceous flowering plant other than a grass.
– ORIGIN 1920s: from Greek *phorbē* 'fodder,' from *phorbein* 'to feed.'

for·bade /fərˈbad, fôr-, -ˈbād/ (also **forbad**) past of **FORBID**.

for·bear[1] /fərˈber, fôr-/ ▶ **v.** (past **forbore**; past participle **forborne**) [no obj.] literary or formal politely or patiently restrain an impulse to do something; refrain: *the boy forbore from touching anything* | [with infinitive] *he modestly forbears to include his own work.* ■ [with obj.] refrain from doing or using (something): *Rebecca could not forbear a smile.*
– ORIGIN Old English *forberan* (see **FOR-**, **BEAR**[1]). The original senses were 'endure, bear with,' hence 'endure the absence of something, do without,' also 'bear up against, control oneself,' hence 'refrain from' (Middle English).

for·bear[2] ▶ **n.** variant spelling of **FOREBEAR**.

for·bear·ance /fôrˈberəns, fər-/ ▶ **n.** formal patient self-control; restraint and tolerance: *forbearance from taking action.* ■ Law the action of refraining from exercising a legal right, esp. enforcing the payment of a debt.

for·bear·ing /fôrˈberiNG, fər-/ ▶ **adj.** (of a person) patient and restrained.

for·bid /fərˈbid, fôr-/ ▶ **v.** (**forbids, forbidding**; past **forbade** /-ˈbad, -ˈbād/ or **forbad** /-ˈbad/; past participle **forbidden**) [with obj.] refuse to allow (something): *environmental laws forbid alteration of the coast.* ■ order (someone) not to do something: *I was forbidden from leaving Russia* | [with obj. and infinitive] *my doctor has forbidden me to eat sugar.* ■ refuse (someone or something) entry to a place or area: *all cars are forbidden.* ■ (of a circumstance or quality) make (something) impossible; prevent: *the cliffs forbid any easy turning movement.*
– PHRASES **God** (or **Heaven**) **forbid** used to express a fervent wish that something does not happen: [with clause] *God forbid that this should happen to anyone ever again.*
– ORIGIN Old English *forbēodan* (see **FOR-**, **BID**[2]).

for·bid·den /fər'bidn, fôr-/ ▸ **adj.** not allowed; banned: *a list of forbidden books.* ■ Physics denoting or involving a transition between two quantum-mechanical states that does not conform to some selection rule, esp. for electric dipole radiation.
– PHRASES **the forbidden degrees** the number of steps of descent from the same ancestor that bar two related people from marrying. **forbidden fruit** a thing that is desired all the more because it is not allowed. [with biblical allusion to Gen. 2:17.]

For·bid·den Cit·y 1 an area of Beijing, China, that contains the former imperial palaces, to which entry was forbidden to all except the members of the imperial family and their servants.
2 a name given to Lhasa, Tibet.

Forbidden City

for·bid·ding /fər'bidiNG, fôr-/ ▸ **adj.** unfriendly or threatening in appearance: *a grim and forbidding building.*
– DERIVATIVES **for·bid·ding·ly adv.**

for·bore /fər'bôr, fôr-/ past of FORBEAR[1].

for·borne /fər'bôrn, fôr-/ past participle of FORBEAR[1].

for·bye /fôr'bī/ (also **forby**) ▸ **adv. & prep.** archaic or Scottish in addition; besides: [as adv.] *there's chicken in the fridge, and plenty of soup forbye, if you get hungry again.*

force /fôrs/ ▸ **n. 1** strength or energy as an attribute of physical action or movement: *he was thrown backward by the force of the explosion.* ■ Physics an influence tending to change the motion of a body or produce motion or stress in a stationary body. The magnitude of such an influence is often calculated by multiplying the mass of the body by its acceleration. ■ a person or thing regarded as exerting power or influence: *he might still be a force for peace and unity.* ■ [in combination] used with a number as a measure of wind strength on the Beaufort scale: *a force-nine gale.*
2 coercion or compulsion, esp. with the use or threat of violence: *they ruled by law and not by force.*
3 mental or moral strength or power: *the force of popular opinion.* ■ the state of being in effect or valid: *the law came into force in January.* ■ the powerful effect of something: *the force of her writing is undiminished.*
4 an organized body of military personnel or police: *a soldier in a UN peacekeeping force.* ■ (**forces**) troops and weaponry: *concealment from enemy forces* | figurative *a battle between the forces of good and evil.* ■ a group of people brought together and organized for a particular activity: *a sales force.* ■ (**the force**) informal a police department.
5 Baseball a force out. ■ a situation in which a force out is possible.
▸ **v.** [with obj.] **1** make a way through or into by physical strength; break open by force: *they broke into Fred's house and forced every cupboard door with ax or crowbar.* ■ [with obj.] drive or push into a specified position or state using physical strength or against resistance: *she forced her feet into flat leather sandals* | figurative *Fields was forced out as director.* ■ achieve or bring about (something) by coercion or effort: *Sabine forced a smile* | *she forced her way up the ladder.* ■ push or strain (something) to the utmost: *she knew if she forced it she would rip it.* ■ artificially hasten the development or maturity of (a plant).
2 (often **be forced**) make (someone) do something against their will: *she was forced into early retirement* | [with obj.] *the universities were forced to cut staff.* ■ rape (a woman). ■ Baseball put out (a runner), or cause (a runner) to be put out, at the base to which they are advancing when they are forced to run on a batted ball: *I was forced at second base as the first half of a double play.* ■ (in cards) make a play or bid that compels another player to make (a particular response); make a play or bid that compels (another player) to make such a response: *East could force declarer to ruff another spade.*
– PHRASES **by force of** by means of: *exercising authority by force of arms.* **force the bidding** (at an auction) make bids to raise the price rapidly. **force someone's hand** make someone do something: *the exchange markets may force the Fed's hand.* **force the issue** compel the making of an immediate decision. **force the pace** adopt a fast pace in a race in order to tire out one's opponents quickly. **in force 1** in great strength or numbers: *birdwatchers were out in force.* **2** in effect; valid: *the US has over $8 trillion worth of life insurance in force.*
– PHRASAL VERBS **force something down 1** manage to swallow food or drink when one does not want to: *I forced down a slice of toast.* **2** compel an aircraft to land: *the plane might have been forced down by fighters.* **force oneself on/upon** rape (a woman). **force something on/upon** impose or press something on (a person or organization): *economic cutbacks were forced on the government.*
– DERIVATIVES **force·a·ble adj., forc·er n.**
– ORIGIN Middle English: from Old French *force* (noun), *forcer* (verb), based on Latin *fortis* 'strong.'

forced /fôrst/ ▸ **adj.** obtained or imposed by coercion or physical power: *the brutal regime of forced labor.* ■ (of a gesture or expression) produced or maintained with effort; affected or unnatural: *a forced smile.* ■ (of a plant) having its development or maturity artificially hastened.
– PHRASES **forced march** a fast march by soldiers, typically over a long distance.

forced land·ing ▸ **n.** an act of abruptly bringing an aircraft to the ground or the surface of water in an emergency.
– DERIVATIVES **force-land v.**

force-feed ▸ **v.** [with obj.] force (a person or animal) to eat. ■ [with two objs.] impose or force (information or ideology) upon (someone): *no group has the right to force-feed its beliefs on her.*

force feed·back ▸ **n.** Computing the simulation of physical attributes such as weight in computer gaming and virtual reality, allowing the user to interact directly with virtual objects using touch.

force field ▸ **n.** (chiefly in science fiction) an invisible barrier of exerted strength or impetus: *future land combat vehicles will deflect enemy shells with an electromagnetic force field.*

force·ful /'fôrsfəl/ ▸ **adj.** (esp. of a person or argument) strong and assertive; vigorous and powerful: *she was a forceful personality* | *forceful, imaginative marketing.*
– DERIVATIVES **force·ful·ly adv., force·ful·ness n.**

force ma·jeure /ˌfôrs mä'ZHər/ ▸ **n.**
1 unforeseeable circumstances that prevent someone from fulfilling a contract.
2 irresistible compulsion or greater force.
– ORIGIN late 19th cent.: French, literally 'greater force.'

force·meat /'fôrsˌmēt/ ▸ **n.** a mixture of meat or vegetables chopped and seasoned for use as a stuffing or garnish.
– ORIGIN late 17th cent.: from obsolete *force* 'to stuff,' alteration (influenced by the verb FORCE) of *farce*, from French *farcir* (see FARCE).

force out ▸ **n.** Baseball the putout of a base runner who is forced to go to the next base.

force play ▸ **n.** Baseball a play in which a runner must advance when a ball is hit, thereby allowing a fielder to put the runner out by touching the approached base before the runner gets there.

for·ceps /'fôrsəps, -ˌseps/ (also **a pair of forceps**) ▸ **plural n.** a pair of pincers or tweezers used in surgery or in a laboratory. ■ a large instrument of such a type with broad blades, used to encircle a baby's head and assist in birth: [as modifier] *a forceps delivery.* ■ Zoology an organ or structure resembling forceps, esp. the cerci of an earwig.
– ORIGIN late 16th cent.: from Latin, 'tongs, pincers.'

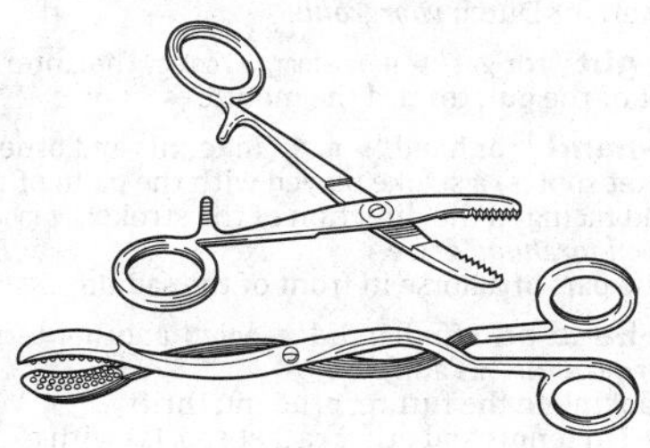
forceps

force pump ▸ **n.** a pump used to move water or other liquid under pressure.

for·ci·ble /'fôrsəbəl/ ▸ **adj.** done by force: *signs of forcible entry.* ■ vigorous and strong; forceful: *they could only be deterred by forcible appeals.*
– ORIGIN late Middle English: from Old French, from *force* (see FORCE).

for·ci·bly /'fôrsəblē/ ▸ **adv.** using force or violence: *no one will be forcibly evicted.* ■ in a forceful way; convincingly: *they argued forcibly against the proposal.*

forc·ing /'fôrsiNG/ ▸ **adj.** Bridge (of a bid) requiring by convention a response from one's partner, no matter how weak their hand may be.

forc·ing house ▸ **n.** a place in which the growth or development of something (esp. plants) is artificially hastened.

Ford[1] /fôrd/, Ford Madox (1873–1939), English novelist and editor; born *Ford Hermann Hueffer*. He is known for his novel *The Good Soldier* (1915).

Ford[2], Gerald Rudolph (1913–2006), 38th president of the US 1974–77; born as *Leslie Lynch King, Jr.* (renamed by his stepfather in 1916). He served in the US House of Representatives 1949–73 and as vice president 1973–74 before succeeding to the presidency upon the resignation of Richard Nixon in the wake of the Watergate affair. Noted for his integrity and candidness, he worked to heal the nation, to curb inflation while stimulating the economy, and to prevent war in the Middle East. He lost the 1976 presidential election to Jimmy Carter.

Gerald Ford

Ford[3], Harrison (1942–), US actor. Best known for his roles in the *Star Wars* trilogy (1977, 1980, 1983) and *Raiders of the Lost Ark* (1981) and its three sequels (1984, 1989, 2008).

Harrison Ford

Ford[4], Henry (1863–1947), US automobile manufacturer. A pioneer of large-scale mass production, he founded the Ford Motor Company, which produced the Model T in 1909. Control of the company passed to his grandson, **Henry Ford II** (1917–1987), in 1945.

Ford[5], John (1895–1973), US movie director; born *Sean Aloysius O'Feeney*. He is chiefly known for his westerns, several of which starred John Wayne, including *Stagecoach* (1939) and *She Wore a Yellow Ribbon* (1949). Other notable movies include *The Grapes of Wrath* (1940).

Ford[6], Whitey (1928–), US baseball player; born *Edward Charles Ford*. His career win percentage (.690) is one of the highest among 20th-century pitchers. Baseball Hall of Fame (1974).

ford /fôrd/ ▸ **n.** a shallow place in a river or stream allowing one to walk or drive across.
▸ **v.** [with obj.] (of a person or vehicle) cross (a river or stream) at a shallow place.

PRONUNCIATION KEY ə *ago, up*; ər *over, fur*; a *hat*; ā *ate*; ä *car*; e *let*; ē *see*; i *fit*; ī *by*; NG *sing*; ō *go*; ô *law, for*; oi *toy*; o͝o *good*; o͞o *goo*; ou *out*; TH *thin*; T͟H *then*; ZH *vision*

– DERIVATIVES **ford·a·ble** adj., **ford·less** adj.
– ORIGIN Old English; related to Dutch *voorde*, also to FARE.

Ford·ham /ˈfôrdəm/ a section of the central Bronx in New York City that takes its name from Fordham University.

fore /fôr/ ▶ **adj.** [attrib.] situated or placed in front: *the fore and hind pairs of wings.*
▶ **n.** the front part of something, esp. a ship.
▶ **exclam.** called out as a warning to people in the path of a golf ball.
▶ **prep.** (also **'fore**) nonstandard form of BEFORE: *we'll be harvesting corn 'fore the end of the month.*
– PHRASES **to the fore** in or to a conspicuous or leading position: *his persistent effort brought this issue to the fore.*
– ORIGIN Old English (as a preposition, also in the sense 'before in time, previously'): of Germanic origin; related to Dutch *voor* and German *vor*. The adjective and noun represent the prefix FORE- used independently (late 15th cent).

fore- ▶ **comb. form 1** (added to verbs) in front: *foreshorten.* ■ beforehand; in advance: *forebode | foreshadow.*
2 (added to nouns) situated in front of: *forecourt.* ■ the front part of: *forebrain.* ■ of or near the bow of a ship: *forecastle.* ■ preceding; going before: *forefather.*
– ORIGIN Old English (see FORE).

fore and aft ▶ **adv.** at the front and rear (often used with reference to a ship or plane): *we're moored fore and aft.* ■ backward and forward: *a sperm whale cannot see directly fore and aft.*
▶ **adj.** [attrib.] backward and forward: *the fore-and-aft motion of the handles.* ■ (of a hat, esp. one worn as part of a uniform) having three corners and a brim at the front and back: *we were in full dress, with fore-and-aft hats and swords.* ■ (of a sail or rigging) set lengthwise, not on transverse yards: *a fore-and-aft-rigged yacht.*
– ORIGIN early 17th cent.: perhaps translating a phrase of Low German origin; compare with Dutch *van voren en van achteren.*

fore·arm[1] /ˈfôrˌärm/ ▶ **n.** the part of a person's arm extending from the elbow to the wrist or the fingertips.

fore·arm[2] /fôrˈärm/ ▶ **v.** [with obj.] prepare (someone) in advance for danger, attack, or another undesirable future event.

fore·bear /ˈfôrˌber/ (also **forbear**) ▶ **n.** (usu. **one's forebears**) an ancestor.
– ORIGIN late 15th cent.: from FORE + *bear*, variant of obsolete *beer* 'someone who exists' (from BE + -ER[1]).

fore·bode /fôrˈbōd/ ▶ **v.** [with obj.] archaic or literary (of a situation or occurrence) act as a warning of (something bad): *this lull foreboded some new assault upon him.* ■ have a presentiment of (something bad): *I foreboded mischief the moment I heard.*

fore·bod·ing /fôrˈbōdiNG/ ▶ **n.** fearful apprehension; a feeling that something bad will happen: *with a sense of foreboding she read the note.*
▶ **adj.** implying or seeming to imply that something bad is going to happen: *when the doctor spoke, his voice was dark and foreboding.*
– DERIVATIVES **fore·bod·ing·ly** adv.

fore·brain /ˈfôrˌbrān/ ▶ **n.** Anatomy the anterior part of the brain, including the cerebral hemispheres, the thalamus, and the hypothalamus. Also called PROSENCEPHALON.

fore·cad·die /ˈfôrˌkadē/ ▶ **n.** (pl. **forecaddies**) a caddie who goes ahead of golfers to see where the balls fall.

fore·cast /ˈfôrˌkast/ ▶ **v.** (past and past participle **forecast** or **forecasted**) [with obj.] predict or estimate (a future event or trend): *rain is forecast for eastern Ohio* | [with obj. and infinitive] *coal consumption is forecast to increase.*
▶ **n.** a prediction or estimate of future events, esp. coming weather or a financial trend.
– DERIVATIVES **fore·cast·er** n.

fore·cas·tle /ˈfōksəl, ˈfôrˌkasəl/ (also **fo'c's'le**) ▶ **n.** the forward part of a ship below the deck, traditionally used as the crew's living quarters. ■ a raised deck at the bow of a ship.

fore·check /ˈfôrˌCHek/ ▶ **v.** [no obj.] Ice Hockey play an aggressive style of defense, checking opponents in their own defensive zone, before they can organize an attack.
– DERIVATIVES **fore·check·er** n.

fore·close /fôrˈklōz/ ▶ **v. 1** [no obj.] take possession of a mortgaged property as a result of the mortgagor's failure to keep up their mortgage payments: *the bank was threatening to foreclose on his mortgage.* ■ [with obj.] take away someone's power of redeeming (a mortgage) and take possession of the mortgaged property.
2 [with obj.] rule out or prevent (a course of action): *the decision effectively foreclosed any possibility of his early rehabilitation.*
– ORIGIN Middle English: from Old French *forclos*, past participle of *forclore*, from *for-* 'out' (from Latin *foras* 'outside') + *clore* 'to close.' The original sense was 'bar from escaping,' in late Middle English 'shut out,' and 'bar from doing something' (sense 2), hence specifically 'bar someone from redeeming a mortgage' (sense 1, early 18th cent).

fore·clo·sure /fôrˈklōZHər/ ▶ **n.** the process of taking possession of a mortgaged property as a result of the mortgagor's failure to keep up mortgage payments.

fore·court /ˈfôrˌkôrt/ ▶ **n. 1** an open area in front of a large building.
2 Tennis the part of the court between the service line and the net.

fore·deck /ˈfôrˌdek/ ▶ **n.** the deck at the forward part of a ship.

fore·doom /fôrˈdo͞om/ ▶ **v.** [with obj.] (usu. **be foredoomed**) condemn beforehand to certain failure or destruction: *the policy is foredoomed to failure.*

fore·dune /ˈfôrˌd(y)o͞on/ ▶ **n.** Ecology a part of a system of sand dunes on the side nearest to the sea.

fore-edge (also **fore edge**) ▶ **n.** technical the outer vertical edge of the pages of a book.

fore·fa·ther /ˈfôrˌfäT͟Hər/ ▶ **n.** (usu. **one's forefathers**) a member of the past generations of one's family or people; an ancestor. ■ a precursor of a particular movement: *the forefathers of rock 'n' roll.*

fore·fend ▶ **v.** variant spelling of FORFEND (sense 2).

fore·fin·ger /ˈfôrˌfiNGgər/ ▶ **n.** the finger next to the thumb; the first or index finger.

fore·foot /ˈfôrˌfo͝ot/ ▶ **n.** (pl. **forefeet**) each of the front feet of a four-footed animal. ■ the forward end of a vessel's keel where it joins the stern.

fore·front /ˈfôrˌfrənt/ ▶ **n.** (**the forefront**) the leading or most important position or place: *we are at the forefront of developments.*

fore·gath·er ▶ **v.** variant spelling of FORGATHER.

fore·go[1] ▶ **v.** variant spelling of FORGO.

fore·go[2] /fôrˈgō/ ▶ **v.** (**foregoes, foregoing, forewent**; past participle **foregone**) [with obj.] archaic precede in place or time.
– DERIVATIVES **fore·go·er** /fôrˈgōər/ n.

fore·go·ing /fôrˈgōiNG/ formal ▶ **adj.** [attrib.] just mentioned or stated; preceding: *the foregoing discussion has juxtaposed management and owner control.*
▶ **n.** (**the foregoing**) [treated as sing. or pl.] the things just mentioned or stated.

fore·gone /ˈfôrˌgôn/ past participle of FOREGO[2].
▶ **adj.** [often postpositive] archaic past: *poets dream of lives foregone in worlds fantastical.*
– PHRASES **a foregone conclusion** a result that can be predicted with certainty.

fore·ground /ˈfôrˌground/ ▶ **n.** (**the foreground**) the part of a view that is nearest to the observer, esp. in a picture or photograph: *the images show vegetation in the foreground.* ■ the most prominent or important position or situation: *whenever books are chosen for children, meaning should always be in the foreground.*
▶ **v.** [with obj.] make (something) the most prominent or important feature: *sexual relationships are foregrounded and idealized.*
– ORIGIN late 17th cent.: from FORE- + GROUND[1], on the pattern of Dutch *voorgrond.*

fore·gut /ˈfôrˌgət/ ▶ **n.** Anatomy & Zoology the anterior part of the gut, toward the mouth.

fore·hand /ˈfôrˌhand/ ▶ **n. 1** (in tennis and other racket sports) a stroke played with the palm of the hand facing in the direction of the stroke: [as modifier] *a good forehand drive.*
2 the part of a horse in front of the saddle.

fore·hand·ed /ˈfôrˈhandid/ ▶ **adj. 1** another term for FOREHAND (as adj.).
2 looking to the future; prudent; thrifty.
▶ **adv.** (in tennis and other racket sports) with a forehand stroke.

fore·head /ˈfôrˌhed, ˈfôrəd/ ▶ **n.** the part of the face above the eyebrows.
– ORIGIN Old English *forhēafod* (see FORE-, HEAD).

for·eign /ˈfôrən, ˈfär-/ ▶ **adj. 1** of, from, in, or characteristic of a country or language other than one's own: *a foreign language.* ■ dealing with or relating to other countries: *foreign policy.* ■ of or belonging to another district or area. ■ coming or introduced from outside: *the quotation is a foreign element imported into the work.* ■ (of a law or restriction) outside the local jurisdiction.
2 strange and unfamiliar: *I suppose this all feels pretty foreign to you.* ■ (**foreign to**) not belonging to or characteristic of: *crime and brutality are foreign to our nature and our country.*
– DERIVATIVES **for·eign·ness** n.
– ORIGIN Middle English *foren, forein*, from Old French *forein, forain*, based on Latin *foras, foris* 'outside,' from *fores* 'door.' The current spelling arose in the 16th cent., by association with SOVEREIGN.

for·eign aid ▶ **n.** money, food, or other resources given or lent by one country to another.

for·eign bill ▶ **n.** a bill of exchange payable in another country.

for·eign bod·y ▶ **n.** an object or piece of extraneous matter that has entered the body by accident or design.

for·eign·er /ˈfôrənər, ˈfär-/ ▶ **n.** a person born in or coming from a country other than one's own. ■ informal a person not belonging to a particular place or group; a stranger or outsider.

for·eign ex·change ▶ **n.** the currency of other countries. ■ an institution or system for dealing in such currency.

For·eign Le·gion a military unit of the French army founded in the 1830s to fight France's colonial wars. Composed, except for the higher ranks, of non-Frenchmen, the Legion was famed for its audacity and endurance. Its most famous campaigns were in French North Africa in the late 19th and early 20th centuries.

for·eign min·is·ter ▶ **n.** (in many countries) a government minister in charge of relations with other countries: *the Tunisian foreign minister will visit Washington.*

for·eign mis·sion ▶ **n. 1** a permanent office established by a nation to represent its interests in a foreign country.
2 a group sent by a church to live in a foreign country for a period of time, esp. to seek converts.

for·eign of·fice in some countries, the department of government in charge of foreign affairs.

for·eign sec·re·tar·y ▶ **n.** (in the UK) a foreign minister.

for·eign serv·ice ▶ **n.** the government department concerned with the representation of a country abroad. ■ (**Foreign Service**) a division of the US State Department staffed by diplomatic and consular personnel.

fore·know /fôrˈnō/ ▶ **v.** (past **foreknew**; past participle **foreknown**) [with obj.] literary be aware of (an event) before it happens: *he foreknows his death like a saint.*

fore·knowl·edge /fôrˈnälij/ ▶ **n.** awareness of something before it happens or exists.

fore·la·dy /ˈfôrˌlādē/ ▶ **n.** (pl. **foreladies**) another term for FOREWOMAN.

fore·land /ˈfôrlənd/ ▶ **n.** an area of land bordering on another or lying in front of a particular feature. ■ a cape or promontory. ■ Geology a stable unyielding block of the earth's crust, against which compression produces a folded mountain range.

fore·leg /ˈfôrˌleg/ ▶ **n.** either of the front legs of a four-footed animal.

fore·limb /ˈfôrˌlim/ ▶ **n.** either of the front limbs of an animal.

fore·lock /ˈfôrˌläk/ ▶ **n.** a lock of hair growing just above the forehead. ■ the part of the mane (of a horse or similar animal) that grows from the poll and hangs down over the forehead.

Fore·man /ˈfôrmən/, George (1949–), US boxer. Having held the world heavyweight championship 1973–74, he regained the title in 1994–95, becoming the oldest man to do so.

fore·man /ˈfôrmən/ ▶ **n.** (pl. **foremen**) a worker, esp. a man, who supervises and directs other workers. ■ (in a court of law) a person, esp. a man, who presides over a jury and speaks on its behalf.
– ORIGIN Middle English: perhaps suggested by Dutch *voorman* (compare with German *Vormann*).

fore·mast /ˈfôrˌmast, -məst/ ▶ **n.** the mast of a ship nearest the bow.

fore·most /ˈfôrˌmōst/ ▶ **adj.** most prominent in rank, importance, or position: *one of the foremost art collectors of his day.*

▶ **adv.** before anything else in rank, importance, or position; in the first place: *O'Keefe's work was, foremost, an expression of the feelings of a woman.*
– PHRASES **first and foremost** see FIRST.
– ORIGIN Old English *formest, fyrmest*, from *forma* 'first' (ultimately a superlative formed from the Germanic base of FORE) + -EST[1]. Compare with FIRST and FORMER[1]. The current spelling arose by association with FORE and MOST.

fore·moth·er /'fôr,məTHər/ ▶ **n.** (usu. **one's foremothers**) a female ancestor or precursor of something.

fore·name /'fôr,nām/ ▶ **n.** another term for FIRST NAME.

fore·noon /'fôr,no͞on/ ▶ **n.** [in sing.] the morning.

fo·ren·sic /fə'renzik, -sik/ ▶ **adj.** of, relating to, or denoting the application of scientific methods and techniques to the investigation of crime: *forensic evidence.* ■ of or relating to courts of law.
▶ **n.** (**forensics**) scientific tests or techniques used in connection with the detection of crime. ■ (also **forensic**) [treated as sing. or pl.] informal a laboratory or department responsible for such tests.
– DERIVATIVES **fo·ren·si·cal·ly** /-(ə)lē/ **adv.**
– ORIGIN mid 17th cent.: from Latin *forensis* 'in open court, public,' from *forum* (see FORUM).

fo·ren·sic ac·count·ing ▶ **n.** the use of accounting skills to investigate fraud or embezzlement and to analyze financial information for use in legal proceedings.

fo·ren·sic med·i·cine ▶ **n.** the application of medical knowledge to the investigation of crime, particularly in establishing the causes of injury or death.

fore·or·dain /,fôrôr'dān/ ▶ **v.** [with obj.] (of God or fate) appoint or decree (something) beforehand: *progress is not foreordained.*
– DERIVATIVES **fore·or·di·na·tion** /fôr,ôrdn'āsHən/ **n.**

fore·part /'fôr,pärt/ ▶ **n.** the part situated at the front of something; the foremost part.

fore·paw /'fôr,pô/ ▶ **n.** either of the front paws of a quadruped.

fore·peak /'fôr,pēk/ ▶ **n.** the forwardmost division of a vessel's hull, often used in ships as a ballast tank.

fore·per·son /'fôr,pərsən/ ▶ **n.** (pl. **forepersons**) a foreman or forewoman (used as a neutral alternative).

fore·play /'fôr,plā/ ▶ **n.** sexual activity that precedes intercourse.

fore·quar·ter /'fôr,kwôrtər/ ▶ **n.** a front quarter of something, esp. of a carcass (of beef, lamb, etc.). ■ (**forequarters**) the front legs and adjoining parts of a quadruped.

fore·run /fôr'rən/ ▶ **v.** (**foreruns, forerunning, foreran**; past participle **forerun**) [with obj.] literary go before or indicate the coming of: *the vast inquietude that foreruns the storm.*

fore·run·ner /'fôr,rənər/ ▶ **n.** a person or thing that precedes the coming or development of someone or something else: *the icebox was a forerunner of today's refrigerator.* ■ a sign or warning of something to come: *overcast mornings are the sure forerunners of steady rain.* ■ archaic an advance messenger.

fore·sail /'fôr,sāl, -səl/ ▶ **n.** the principal sail on a foremast.

fore·see /fôr'sē/ ▶ **v.** (**foresees, foreseeing, foresaw**; past participle **foreseen**) [with obj.] be aware of beforehand; predict: *we did not foresee any difficulties* | [with clause] *it is impossible to foresee how life will work out.*
– DERIVATIVES **fore·se·er** /-'sēər/ **n.**
– ORIGIN Old English *foresēon* (see FORE-, SEE[1]).

fore·see·a·ble /fôr'sēəbəl/ ▶ **adj.** able to be foreseen or predicted: *the situation is unlikely to change in the foreseeable future.*
– DERIVATIVES **fore·see·a·bil·i·ty** /fôr,sēə'bilətē/ **n.**, **fore·see·a·bly** /-'sēəblē/ **adv.**

fore·shad·ow /fôr'sHadō/ ▶ **v.** [with obj.] be a warning or indication of (a future event): *it foreshadowed my preoccupation with jazz.*

fore·sheet /'fôr,sHēt/ ▶ **n. 1** a rope by which the lee corner of a foresail is kept in place.
2 (**foresheets**) the inner part of the bow of a boat.

fore·shock /'fôr,sHäk/ ▶ **n.** a mild tremor preceding the violent shaking movement of an earthquake.

fore·shore /'fôr,sHôr/ ▶ **n.** the part of a shore between high- and low-water marks, or between the water and cultivated or developed land.

fore·short·en /fôr'sHôrtn/ ▶ **v.** [with obj.] portray or show (an object or view) as closer than it is or as having less depth or distance, as an effect of perspective or the angle of vision: *seen from the road, the mountain is greatly foreshortened.* ■ prematurely or dramatically shorten or reduce (something) in time or scale: (as adj. **foreshortened**) *foreshortened reports.*

fore·show /fôr'sHō/ ▶ **v.** (past participle **foreshown**) [with obj.] archaic give warning or promise of (something); foretell.

fore·sight /'fôr,sīt/ ▶ **n.** the ability to predict or the action of predicting what will happen or be needed in the future: *he had the foresight to check that his escape route was clear.*
– ORIGIN Middle English: from FORE- + SIGHT, probably suggested by Old Norse *forsjá, forsjó.*

fore·sight·ed /'fôr,sītid/ ▶ **adj.** having or using foresight.
– DERIVATIVES **fore·sight·ed·ly adv.**, **fore·sight·ed·ness n.**

fore·skin /'fôr,skin/ ▶ **n.** the retractable roll of skin covering the end of the penis. Also called PREPUCE.

for·est /'fôrəst, 'fär-/ ▶ **n.** a large area covered chiefly with trees and undergrowth: *a pine forest* | *much of Europe was covered with forest.* ■ a large number or dense mass of vertical or tangled objects: *a forest of connecting wires.* ■ historical (in England) an area, typically owned by the sovereign and partly wooded, kept for hunting and having its own laws.
▶ **v.** [with obj.] (usu. as adj. **forested**) cover (land) with forest; plant with trees: *a forested area.*
– PHRASES **cannot see the forest for the trees** fail to grasp the main issue because of excessive attention to details.
– DERIVATIVES **for·est·a·tion** /,fôrə'stāsHən, ,fär-/ **n.**
– ORIGIN Middle English (in the sense 'wooded area kept for hunting,' also denoting any uncultivated land): via Old French from late Latin *forestis (silva)*, literally '(wood) outside,' from Latin *foris* 'outside' (see FOREIGN).

fore·stall /fôr'stôl/ ▶ **v.** [with obj.] prevent or obstruct (an anticipated event or action) by taking action ahead of time: ***vitamins may forestall many diseases of aging.*** ■ act in advance of (someone) in order to prevent them from doing something: *she started to rise, but Erica forestalled her and got the telephone.* ■ historical buy up (goods) in order to profit by an enhanced price.
– DERIVATIVES **fore·stall·er n.**, **fore·stall·ment n.**
– ORIGIN Old English *foresteall* 'an ambush' (see FORE- and STALL). As a verb the earliest sense (Middle English) was 'intercept and buy up (goods) before they reach the market, so as to raise the price' (formerly an offense).

fore·stay /'fôr,stā/ ▶ **n.** a stay leading forward and down to support a ship's foremast.

fore·stay·sail /,fôr'stāsəl, -,sāl/ ▶ **n.** a triangular sail set on the forestay.

For·est·er /'fôrəstər/, C. S. (1899–1966), English novelist; pseudonym of *Cecil Lewis Troughton Smith.* He is remembered for his seafaring novels set during the Napoleonic Wars and featuring Captain Horatio Hornblower. He also wrote *The African Queen* (1935).

for·est·er /'fôrəstər, 'fär-/ ▶ **n. 1** a person in charge of a forest or skilled in planting, managing, or caring for trees.
2 chiefly archaic a person or animal living in a forest. ■ Austral. the eastern gray kangaroo. See GRAY KANGAROO.
3 a small black day-flying moth with two white or yellow spots on each wing. ● Family Agaristidae: several genera and species, including the **eight-spotted forester** (*Alypia octomaculata*), common throughout the northeastern US.
– ORIGIN Middle English: from Old French *forestier*, from *forest* (see FOREST).

eight-spotted forester

For·est Hills an affluent residential section of central Queens in New York City that is associated with the US Open in tennis, which was played here until 1978.

for·est·land /'fôrəst,land, 'fär-/ ▶ **n.** an area of land covered by forests.

for·est·ry /'fôrəstrē, 'fär-/ ▶ **n.** the science or practice of planting, managing, and caring for forests.

fore·taste /'fôr,tāst/ ▶ **n.** [in sing.] a sample or suggestion of something that lies ahead: *the freezing rain was a foretaste of winter.*

fore·tell /fôr'tel/ ▶ **v.** (past and past participle **foretold**) [with obj.] predict (the future or a future event): *as he foretold, thousands lost their lives* | [with clause] *a seer had foretold that she would assume the throne.*
– DERIVATIVES **fore·tell·er n.**

fore·thought /'fôr,THôt/ ▶ **n.** careful consideration of what will be necessary or may happen in the future: *Jim had the forethought to book in advance.*

fore·to·ken ▶ **v.** /fôr,tōkən/ [with obj.] literary be a sign of (something to come): *a shiver in the night air foretokening December.*
▶ **n.** /'fôr,tōkən/ a sign of something to come.
– ORIGIN Old English *foretācn* (noun: see FORE-, TOKEN).

fore·told /fôr'tōld/ past and past participle of FORETELL.

fore·top /'fôr,täp/ ▶ **n. 1** a platform around the head of the lower section of a sailing ship's foremast. ■ the front seat on top of a horse-drawn vehicle.
2 another term for FORELOCK.

fore·top·gal·lant mast ▶ **n.** the third section of a sailing ship's foremast, above the fore-topmast.

fore·top·gal·lant sail ▶ **n.** the sail above a sailing ship's fore-topsail.

fore·top·mast ▶ **n.** the second section of a sailing ship's foremast.

fore·top·sail ▶ **n.** the sail above a sailing ship's foresail.

fore·tri·an·gle /'fôr,trī,aNGgəl/ ▶ **n.** the triangular space between the deck, foremast, and forestay of a sailing vessel. ■ the area of sail within this area.

for·ev·er /fə'revər, fô-/ ▶ **adv. 1** for all future time; for always: *she would love him forever.* ■ a very long time (used hyperbolically): *it took forever to get a passport.* ■ used in slogans of support after the name of something or someone: *Elvis Forever!*
2 continually: *she was forever pushing her hair out of her eyes.*

for·ev·er·more /fə,revər'môr/ ▶ **adv.** forever (used for rhetorical effect): *our military will be invincible forevermore.*

fore·warn /fôr'wôrn/ ▶ **v.** [with obj.] inform (someone) of a danger or possible problem: *he had been forewarned of a coup plot.*
– PHRASES **forewarned is forearmed** proverb prior knowledge of possible dangers or problems gives one a tactical advantage.
– DERIVATIVES **fore·warn·er n.**

fore·warn·ing /fôr'wôrniNG/ ▶ **n.** an advance warning: *officials had no forewarning of the attacks.*

fore·went /fôr'went/ past of FOREGO[1], FOREGO[2].

fore·wing /'fôr,wiNG/ ▶ **n.** either of the two front wings of a four-winged insect.

fore·wom·an /'fôr,wo͝omən/ ▶ **n.** (pl. **forewomen**) a female worker who supervises and directs other workers. ■ (in a court of law) a woman who presides over a jury and speaks on its behalf.

fore·word /'fôr,wərd/ ▶ **n.** a short introduction to a book, typically by a person other than the author.
– ORIGIN mid 19th cent.: from FORE- + WORD, on the pattern of German *Vorwort.*

forex /'fô,reks/ ▶ **abbr.** foreign exchange.

fore·yard /'fôr,yärd/ ▶ **n.** the lowest yard on a sailing ship's foremast.

for·feit /'fôrfit/ ▶ **v.** (**forfeits, forfeiting, forfeited**) [with obj.] lose or be deprived of (property or a right or privilege) as a penalty for wrongdoing: *those unable to meet their taxes were liable to forfeit their property.* ■ lose or give up (something) as a necessary consequence of something else: *she didn't mind forfeiting an extra hour in bed to get up and clean the stables.*
▶ **n.** a fine or penalty for wrongdoing or for a breach of the rules in a club or game. ■ Law an item of property or a right or privilege lost as a legal penalty. ■ (**forfeits**) a game in which trivial penalties are exacted. ■ the action of forfeiting something.
▶ **adj.** [predic.] lost or surrendered as a penalty for wrongdoing or neglect: *the lands which he had acquired were automatically forfeit.*

– DERIVATIVES **for·feit·a·ble** adj., **for·feit·er** /ˈfôrfitər/ n.
– ORIGIN Middle English (originally denoting a crime or transgression, hence a fine or penalty for this): from Old French *forfet, forfait*, past participle of *forfaire* 'transgress,' from *for-* 'out' (from Latin *foris* 'outside') + *faire* 'do' (from Latin *facere*).

for·fei·ture /ˈfôrfəCHər/ ▶ n. the loss or giving up of something as a penalty for wrongdoing: *the court ordered the forfeiture of his computer.*

for·fend /fôrˈfend/ ▶ v. [with obj.] **1** archaic avert, keep away, or prevent (something evil or unpleasant). **2** (also **forefend**) protect (something) by precautionary measures.
– PHRASES **Heaven** (or **God**) **forfend** archaic or humorous used to express dismay or horror at the thought of something happening: *Invite him back? Heaven forfend!* | *God forfend that we should allow the media to tell us how to run our business.*

for·gath·er /fôrˈgaT͟Hər/ (also **foregather**) ▶ v. [no obj.] formal assemble or gather together.
– ORIGIN late 15th cent. (originally Scots as *forgadder*): from Dutch *vergaderen*.

for·gave /fərˈgāv/ past of **FORGIVE**.

forge[1] /fôrj/ ▶ v. [with obj.] **1** make or shape (a metal object) by heating it in a fire or furnace and beating or hammering it. ■ create (a relationship or new conditions): *the two women forged a close bond* | *the country is forging a bright new future.*
2 produce a copy or imitation of (a document, signature, banknote, or work or art) for the purpose of deception.
▶ n. a blacksmith's workshop; a smithy. ■ a furnace or hearth for melting or refining metal. ■ a workshop or factory containing such a furnace.
– DERIVATIVES **forge·a·ble** adj.
– ORIGIN Middle English (also in the general sense 'make, construct'): from Old French *forger*, from Latin *fabricare* 'fabricate,' from *fabrica* 'manufactured object, workshop.' The noun is via Old French from Latin *fabrica*.

forge[2] ▶ v. [no obj.] move forward gradually or steadily: *he forged through the crowded side streets.*
– PHRASAL VERBS **forge ahead** move forward or take the lead in a race. ■ continue or make progress with a course or undertaking: *the government is **forging ahead** with reforms.*
– ORIGIN mid 18th cent. (originally of a ship): perhaps an aberrant pronunciation of **FORCE**.

forged /fôrjd/ ▶ adj. copied fraudulently; fake: *they have illegally entered the UK using forged travel documents.*

forg·er /ˈfôrjər/ ▶ n. a person who produces fraudulent copies or imitations: *one of Europe's most notorious art forgers.*

for·ger·y /ˈfôrjərē/ ▶ n. (pl. **forgeries**) the action of forging or producing a copy of a document, signature, banknote, or work of art. ■ a forged or copied document, signature, banknote, or work of art.

for·get /fərˈget/ ▶ v. (**forgets, forgetting**; past **forgot**; past participle **forgotten** or **forgot**) [with obj.] fail to remember: *he had forgotten his lines* | [with clause] *she had completely forgotten how tired and hungry she was.* ■ inadvertently neglect to attend to, do, or mention something: [with infinitive] *she forgot to lock her door* | [no obj.] *I'm sorry, I just forgot.* ■ put out of one's mind; cease to think of or consider: *forget all this romantic stuff* | [no obj.] *for years she had struggled to **forget about** him.* ■ (**forget it**) said when insisting to someone that there is no need for apology or thanks. ■ (**forget it**) said when telling someone that their idea or aspiration is impracticable. ■ (**forget oneself**) stop thinking about one's own problems or feelings: *he must forget himself in his work.* ■ (**forget oneself**) act improperly or unbecomingly.
– PHRASES **not forgetting ——** (at the end of a list) and also ——: *we depend on them for food and shelter and clothing, not forgetting heat in the wintertime.*
– DERIVATIVES **for·get·ter** n.
– ORIGIN Old English *forgietan*; related to Dutch *vergeten* and German *vergessen*, and ultimately to **FOR-** and **GET**.

for·get·ful /fərˈgetfəl/ ▶ adj. apt or likely not to remember: *I'm a bit forgetful these days* | *she was soon **forgetful of** the time.*
– DERIVATIVES **for·get·ful·ly** adv.

for·get·ful·ness /fərˈgetfəlnəs/ ▶ n. lapse of memory: *she teased him for his forgetfulness.*

for·get-me-not ▶ n. a low-growing plant of the borage family that typically has blue flowers and is a popular ornamental. ● *Myosotis* and other genera, family Boraginaceae: several species, in particular the common **water forget-me-not** (*M. scorpioides*), whose bright blue flowers have a yellow, pink, or white center.
– ORIGIN mid 16th cent.: translating the Old French name *ne m'oubliez mye*; said to have the virtue of ensuring that the wearer of the flower would never be forgotten by a lover.

for·get·ta·ble /fərˈgetəbəl/ ▶ adj. easily forgotten, esp. through being uninteresting or mediocre.

for·giv·a·ble ▶ adj. able to be forgiven or tolerated; excusable: *the flaws are forgivable.*
– DERIVATIVES **for·giv·a·bly** /-əblē/ adv.

for·give /fərˈgiv/ ▶ v. (past **forgave**; past participle **forgiven**) [with obj.] stop feeling angry or resentful toward (someone) for an offense, flaw, or mistake: *I don't think I'll ever forgive David for the way he treated her.* ■ (usu. **be forgiven**) stop feeling angry or resentful toward someone for (an offense, flaw, or mistake): *they are not going to pat my head and say **all is forgiven*** | [no obj.] *he was not a man who found it easy to **forgive and forget**.* ■ cancel (a debt): *he proposed that their debts should be forgiven.*
■ used in polite expressions as a request to excuse or regard indulgently one's foibles, ignorance, or impoliteness: *you will have to forgive my suspicious mind.*
– PHRASES **one could** (or **may**) **be forgiven** it would be understandable (if one mistakenly did a particular thing): *the arrangements are so complex that you could be forgiven for feeling confused.*
– DERIVATIVES **for·giv·er** n.
– ORIGIN Old English *forgiefan*, of Germanic origin, related to Dutch *vergeven* and German *vergeben*, and ultimately to **FOR-** and **GIVE**.

for·give·ness /fərˈgivnəs/ ▶ n. the action or process of forgiving or being forgiven: *she is quick to ask forgiveness when she has overstepped the line.*
– ORIGIN Old English *forgiefenes*, from *forgiefen* (past participle of *forgiefan* 'forgive') + the noun suffix *-nes*.

for·giv·ing /fərˈgiviNG/ ▶ adj. ready and willing to forgive: *Taylor was in a forgiving mood* | *he was definitely not inclined to be **forgiving of** anyone spearing his cattle.* ■ (of a thing) easy or safe to deal with: *it's a good, comfortable, forgiving airplane.*
– DERIVATIVES **for·giv·ing·ly** adv.

for·go /fôrˈgō/ (also **forego**) ▶ v. (**forgoes, forgoing, forwent**; past participle **forgone**) [with obj.] omit or decline to take (something pleasant or valuable); go without: *she wanted to forgo the dessert and leave while they could.* ■ refrain from: *we forgo any comparison between the two men.*
– ORIGIN Old English *forgān* (see **FOR-, GO**[1]).

for·got /fərˈgät/ past of **FORGET**.

for·got·ten /fərˈgätn/ past participle of **FORGET**.

for·int /ˈfôrˌint/ ▶ n. the basic monetary unit of Hungary, equal to 100 filler.
– ORIGIN Hungarian, from Italian *fiorino* (see **FLORIN**).

fork /fôrk/ ▶ n. **1** an implement with two or more prongs used for lifting food to the mouth or holding it when cutting. ■ a tool of larger but similar form used for digging or lifting in a garden or farm.
2 a device, component, or part with two or more prongs, in particular: ■ a unit consisting of a pair of supports in which a bicycle or motorcycle wheel revolves. ■ a flash of forked lightning.
3 the point where something, esp. a road or river, divides into two parts. ■ either of two such parts.
4 Chess a simultaneous attack on two or more pieces by one piece.
▶ v. **1** [no obj.] (esp. of a road or other route) divide into two parts: *the place where the road forks.* ■ [no obj.] take or constitute one part or the other at the point where a road or other route divides: *a minor road forked left.*
2 [with obj.] dig, lift, or manipulate (something) with a fork: *fork in some compost.*
3 [with obj.] Chess attack (two pieces) simultaneously with one piece.
– PHRASAL VERBS **fork something over/out/up** (or **fork over/out/up**) informal pay money for something, esp. reluctantly.
– DERIVATIVES **fork·ful** /-ˌfo͝ol/ n. (pl. **forkfuls**).
– ORIGIN Old English *forca, force* (denoting an agricultural implement), based on Latin *furca* 'pitchfork, forked stick'; reinforced in Middle English by Anglo-Norman French *furke* (also from Latin *furca*).

fork·ball /ˈfôrkˌbôl/ ▶ n. Baseball a sinking pitch, released from between the widely spread index finger and middle finger.

Fork·beard /ˈfôrkˌbi(ə)rd/, Sweyn, see **SWEYN I**.

forked /fôrkt/ ▶ adj. having a divided or pronged end or branches; bifurcated: *a deeply forked tail.*
– PHRASES **with forked tongue** humorous untruthfully; deceitfully.

forked light·ning ▶ n. lightning that is visible in the form of a branching line across the sky.

fork·lift /ˈfôrkˌlift/ ▶ n. (also **forklift truck**) a vehicle with a pronged device in front for lifting and carrying heavy loads.
▶ v. [with obj.] lift and carry (a heavy load) with such a vehicle: *blocks of compacted garbage being **forklifted** onto a trailer.*

forklift

for·lorn /fərˈlôrn, fôr-/ ▶ adj. **1** pitifully sad and abandoned or lonely: *forlorn figures at bus stops.*
2 (of an aim or endeavor) unlikely to succeed or be fulfilled; hopeless: *a forlorn attempt to escape.*
– PHRASES **forlorn hope** a persistent or desperate hope that is unlikely to be fulfilled. [mid 16th cent.: from Dutch *verloren hoop* 'lost troop,' from *verloren* (past participle of *verliezen* 'lose') and *hoop* 'company' (related to **HEAP**). The phrase originally denoted a band of soldiers picked to begin an attack, many of whom would not survive; the current sense (mid 17th cent.) derives from a misunderstanding of the etymology.]
– DERIVATIVES **for·lorn·ly** adv., **for·lorn·ness** /fərˈlôrn,nəs/ n.
– ORIGIN Old English *forloren* 'depraved, morally abandoned,' past participle of *forlēosan* 'lose,' of Germanic origin; related to Dutch *verliezen* and German *verlieren*, and ultimately to **FOR-** and **LOSE**. Sense 1 dates from the 16th cent.

form /fôrm/ ▶ n. **1** the visible shape or configuration of something: *the form, color, and texture of the tree.* ■ arrangement of parts; shape: *the entities underlying physical form.* ■ the body or shape of a person or thing: *his eyes scanned her slender form.* ■ arrangement and style in literary or musical composition: *these videos are a triumph of form over content.* ■ Philosophy the essential nature of a species or thing, esp. (in Plato's thought) regarded as an abstract ideal that real things imitate or participate in.
2 a mold, frame, or block in or on which something is shaped. ■ a temporary structure for holding fresh concrete in shape while it sets.
3 a particular way in which a thing exists or appears; a manifestation: *her obsession has taken the form of compulsive exercise.* ■ any of the ways in which a word may be spelled, pronounced, or inflected: *an adjectival rather than adverbial form.* ■ the structure of a word, phrase, sentence, or discourse: *every distinction in meaning is associated with a distinction in form.*
4 a type or variety of something: *sponsorship is a form of advertising.* ■ an artistic or literary genre. ■ Botany a taxonomic category that ranks below variety, which contains organisms differing from the typical kind in some trivial, frequently impermanent, character, e.g., a color variant. Compare with **SUBSPECIES** and **VARIETY**.
5 the customary or correct method or procedure; what is usually done: *an excessive concern for legal form and precedent.* ■ a set order of words; a formula. ■ a formality or item of mere ceremony: *the outward forms of religion.*
6 a printed document with blank spaces for information to be inserted: *an application form.*
7 chiefly Brit. a class or year in a school, usually given a specifying number: *the fifth form.*
8 the state of an athlete or sports team with regard to their current standard of performance: *illness has affected his form* | *they've been **in good form** this season.* ■ details of previous performances by a racehorse or greyhound: *an interested bystander studying the form.*
9 Brit. a long bench without a back.
10 variant spelling of **FORME**.
11 chiefly Brit. a hare's lair.
▶ v. [with obj.] **1** bring together parts or combine to create (something): *the company was formed in 1982.* ■ (**form people/things into**) organize people or things into (a group or body): *peasants and miners were formed into a militia.* ■ go to make up or constitute: *the precepts that form the basis of the book.* ■ [no obj.] gradually appear or develop: *a thick mist was forming all around.* ■ conceive (an idea or plan) in one's mind. ■ enter into or contract (a relationship): *the women would form supportive friendships.* ■ articulate (a word, speech sound, or other linguistic unit). ■ construct (a new word) by derivation or inflection.

2 make or fashion into a certain shape or form: *form the dough into balls.* ■ [no obj.] (**form into**) be made or fashioned into a certain shape or form: *his strong features formed into a smile of pleasure.* ■ (**be formed**) have a specified shape: *her body was slight and flawlessly formed.* ■ shape or develop by training or discipline. ■ influence or shape (something abstract): *the role of the news media in forming public opinion.*
– PHRASES **in form** (of an athlete or sports team) playing or performing well. **off form** (of an athlete or sports team) not playing or performing well.
– DERIVATIVES **form·a·bil·i·ty** /ˌfôrməˈbilətē/ **n.**, **form·a·ble adj.**
– ORIGIN Middle English: from Old French *forme* (noun), *fo(u)rmer* (verb, from Latin *formare* 'to form'), both based on Latin *forma* 'a mold or form.'

-form (usu. as **-iform**) ▶ **comb. form 1** having the form of: *cruciform.*
2 having a particular number of: *multiform.*
– ORIGIN from French *-forme*, from Latin *-formis*, from *forma* 'form.'

for·mal /ˈfôrməl/ ▶ **adj. 1** done in accordance with rules of convention or etiquette; suitable for or constituting an official or important situation or occasion: *a formal dinner party.* ■ (of a person or their manner) prim or stiff. ■ of or denoting a style of writing or public speaking characterized by more elaborate grammatical structures and more conservative and technical vocabulary. ■ (esp. of a house or garden) arranged in a regular, classical, and symmetrical manner.
2 officially sanctioned or recognized: *a formal complaint.* ■ having a conventionally recognized form, structure, or set of rules: *he had little formal education.*
3 of or concerned with outward form or appearance, esp. as distinct from content or matter: *I don't know enough about art to appreciate the purely formal qualities.* ■ having the form or appearance without the spirit: *his sacrifice will be more formal than real.* ■ of or relating to linguistic or logical form as opposed to function or meaning.
▶ **n.** an evening gown. ■ an occasion on which evening dress is worn.
– ORIGIN late Middle English: from Latin *formalis*, from *forma* 'shape, mold' (see FORM).

for·mal cause ▶ **n.** Philosophy (in Aristotelian thought) the pattern that determines the form taken by something.

form·al·de·hyde /fôrˈmaldəˌhīd, fər-/ ▶ **n.** Chemistry a colorless pungent gas in solution made by oxidizing methanol. ● Alternative name: **methanal**; chem. formula: CH_2O.
– ORIGIN late 19th cent.: blend of FORMIC ACID and ALDEHYDE.

for·ma·lin /ˈfôrməlin/ ▶ **n.** a colorless solution of formaldehyde in water, used chiefly as a preservative for biological specimens.
– ORIGIN late 19th cent.: from FORMALDEHYDE + -IN[1].

for·mal·ism /ˈfôrməˌlizəm/ ▶ **n. 1** excessive adherence to prescribed forms: *academic dryness and formalism.* ■ the use of forms of worship without regard to inner significance. ■ the basing of ethics on the form of the moral law without regard to intention or consequences. ■ concern or excessive concern with form and technique rather than content in artistic creation. ■ (in the theater) a symbolic and stylized manner of production. ■ the treatment of mathematics as a manipulation of meaningless symbols.
2 a description of something in formal mathematical or logical terms.
– DERIVATIVES **for·mal·ist n.**, **for·mal·is·tic** /ˌfôrməˈlistik/ **adj.**

for·mal·i·ty /fôrˈmalətē/ ▶ **n.** (pl. **formalities**) the rigid observance of rules of convention or etiquette: *he retained the formality of his social background.* ■ stiffness of behavior or style: *with disconcerting formality, the brothers shook hands.* ■ (usu. **formalities**) a thing that is done simply to comply with requirements of etiquette, regulations, or custom: *legal formalities.* ■ (**a formality**) something that is done as a matter of course and without question; an inevitability: *her saying no was just a formality, and both of them knew it.*
– ORIGIN mid 16th cent. (in the sense 'accordance with legal rules or conventions'): from French *formalité* or medieval Latin *formalitas*, from *formalis* (see FORMAL).

for·mal·ize /ˈfôrməˌlīz/ ▶ **v.** [with obj.] give (something) legal or formal status. ■ give (something) a definite structure or shape: *we became able to formalize our thoughts.*
– DERIVATIVES **for·mal·i·za·tion** /ˌfôrməliˈzāsʜən/ **n.**

for·mal log·ic ▶ **n.** logic based on argument involving deductively necessary relationships and including the use of syllogisms and mathematical symbols.

for·mal·ly /ˈfôrməlē/ ▶ **adv. 1** in accordance with the rules of convention or etiquette: *he was formally attired.*
2 officially: *the mayor will formally open the new railroad station.*
3 [sentence adverb] in outward form or appearance; in theory: *the theorems in question are formally true.* ■ in terms of form or structure: *formally complex types of text.*

for·mal·wear /ˌfôrməlˌwe(ə)r/ ▶ **n.** clothing, such as tuxedos and evening gowns, for formal social occasions.

For·man /ˈfôrmən/, Milos (1932–), US movie director; born in Czechoslovakia. He made *One Flew Over the Cuckoo's Nest* (1975), which won five Academy Awards, and *Amadeus* (1983), which won eight Academy Awards, including that for best director.

for·mant /ˈfôrmənt/ ▶ **n.** Phonetics any of several prominent bands of frequency that determine the phonetic quality of a vowel.
– ORIGIN early 20th cent.: coined in German from Latin *formant-* 'forming,' from the verb *formare*.

for·mat /ˈfôrˌmat/ ▶ **n.** the way in which something is arranged or set out: *the format of the funeral service.* ■ the shape, size, and presentation of a book or periodical. ■ the medium in which a sound recording is made available: *the album is available as a CD as well as on LP and cassette formats.* ■ Computing a defined structure for the processing, storage, or display of data: *a data file in binary format.*
▶ **v.** (**formats, formatting, formatted**) [with obj.] (esp. in computing) arrange or put into a format. ■ prepare (a storage medium) to receive data.
– ORIGIN mid 19th cent.: via French and German from Latin *formatus (liber)* 'shaped (book),' past participle of *formare* 'to form.'

for·mate /ˈfôrˌmāt/ ▶ **n.** a salt or ester of formic acid.

for·ma·tion /fôrˈmāsʜən/ ▶ **n. 1** the action of forming or process of being formed: *the formation of the Great Rift Valley.*
2 a structure or arrangement of something: *a cloud formation.* ■ a formal arrangement of aircraft in flight or troops: *a battle formation | the helicopters hovered overhead in formation.* ■ Geology an assemblage of rocks or series of strata having some common characteristic.
– DERIVATIVES **for·ma·tion·al** /-sʜənl/ **adj.**
– ORIGIN late Middle English: from Latin *formation-*, from *formare* 'to form' (see FORM).

for·ma·tive /ˈfôrmətiv/ ▶ **adj.** serving to form something, esp. having a profound and lasting influence on a person's development: *his formative years.* ■ of or relating to a person's development: *a formative assessment.* ■ Linguistics denoting or relating to any of the smallest meaningful units that are used to form words in a language, typically combining forms and inflections.
▶ **n.** Linguistics a formative element.
– DERIVATIVES **for·ma·tive·ly adv.**
– ORIGIN late 15th cent.: from Old French *formatif, -ive* or medieval Latin *formativus*, from Latin *formare* 'to form' (see FORM).

form class ▶ **n.** Linguistics a class of linguistic forms with grammatical or syntactic features in common; a part of speech or subset of a part of speech.

form crit·i·cism ▶ **n.** analysis of the Bible by tracing the history of its content of parables, psalms, and other literary forms.

form drag ▶ **n.** Aeronautics that part of the drag on an airfoil that arises from its shape. It varies according to the angle of attack and can be decreased by streamlining.

forme /fôrm/ ▶ **n.** Printing a body of type secured in a chase for printing. ■ a quantity of film arranged for making a plate.

form·er[1] /ˈfôrmər/ ▶ **adj.** [attrib.] **1** having previously filled a particular role or been a particular thing: *her former boyfriend.* ■ of or occurring in the past or an earlier period: *in former times.*
2 (**the former**) denoting the first or first mentioned of two people or things: *those who take the former view* | [as noun] *the powers of the former are more comprehensive than those of the latter.*
– ORIGIN Middle English: from Old English *forma* (see FOREMOST) + -ER[2].

> **USAGE** Traditionally, **former** and **latter** are used in relation to pairs of items: either the first of two items (**former**) or the second of two items (**latter**). The reason for this is that **former** and **latter** were formed as comparatives, and comparatives are correctly used with reference to just two things, while a superlative is used where there are more than two things. (So, for example, strictly speaking one should say *the **longest** of the three books* but *the **longer** of the two books.*) In practice, **former** and **latter** are now sometimes used just as synonyms for **first** and **last** and are routinely used to refer to a contrast involving more than two items. Such uses, however, are not acceptable in good English style. Therefore, if you're referring to *winter, spring, and summer*, for example, it would be correct to say *I find the **last** most enjoyable*, not *I find the **latter** most enjoyable.*

form·er[2] ▶ **n. 1** a person or thing that forms something: [in combination] *an opinion-former.* ■ a transverse strengthening part in an aircraft wing or fuselage.
2 [in combination] chiefly Brit. a person in a particular school year: *fifth-formers.*

for·mer·ly /ˈfôrmərlē/ ▶ **adv.** in the past; in earlier times: *Mumbai, formerly Bombay* | [sentence adverb] *the building formerly housed their accounting offices.*

form fac·tor ▶ **n.** a mathematical factor that compensates for irregularity in the shape of an object, usually the ratio between its volume and that of a regular object of the same breadth and height. ■ the physical size and shape of a piece of computer hardware.

form·fit·ting /ˈfôrmˌfitiɴɢ/ ▶ **adj.** (of clothing) fitting the body snugly, so that its shape is clearly visible: said of clothing: *she wore a formfitting dress.*

form ge·nus ▶ **n.** Paleontology a classificatory category used for fossils that are similar in appearance but cannot be reliably assigned to an established animal or plant genus, such as fossil parts of organisms and trace fossils.

For·mi·ca /fôrˈmīkə, fər-/ ▶ **n.** trademark a hard durable plastic laminate used for countertops, cupboard doors, and other surfaces.
– ORIGIN 1920s: of unknown origin.

for·mic ac·id /ˈfôrmik/ ▶ **n.** Chemistry a colorless irritant volatile acid made catalytically from carbon monoxide and steam. It is present in the fluid emitted by some ants. ● Alternative name: **methanoic acid**; chem. formula: HCOOH.
– ORIGIN late 18th cent.: *formic* from Latin *formica* 'ant.'

for·mi·car·y /ˈfôrmiˌkerē/ (also **formicarium** /ˌfôrmiˈke(ə)rēəm/) ▶ **n.** (pl. **formicaries**; **formicaria** /-ˈke(ə)rēə/) an ant's nest, esp. one in an artificial container for purposes of study.
– ORIGIN early 19th cent.: from medieval Latin, from Latin *formica* 'ant.'

for·mi·ca·tion /ˌfôrmiˈkāsʜən/ ▶ **n.** a sensation like insects crawling over the skin.
– ORIGIN early 18th cent.: from Latin *formicatio(n-)*, from *formicare* 'crawl like an ant' (said of the pulse or skin), from *formica* 'ant.'

for·mi·da·ble /ˈfôrmədəbəl, fôrˈmidəbəl, fərˈmid-/ ▶ **adj.** inspiring fear or respect through being impressively large, powerful, intense, or capable: *a formidable opponent.*
– DERIVATIVES **for·mi·da·ble·ness n.**, **for·mi·da·bly** /-əblē/ **adv.**
– ORIGIN late Middle English: from French, or from Latin *formidabilis*, from *formidare* 'to fear.'

> **USAGE** The preferred pronunciation of **formidable** is with the stress on **for-**, although the stress is sometimes heard on the second syllable (in Britain more than in the US).

form·less /ˈfôrmləs/ ▶ **adj.** without a clear or definite shape or structure: *a dark and formless idea.*
– DERIVATIVES **form·less·ly adv.**, **form·less·ness n.**

form let·ter ▶ **n.** a standardized letter to deal with frequently occurring matters.

For·mo·sa /fôrˈmōsə/ former name of TAIWAN.
– ORIGIN Portuguese, literally 'beautiful.'

for·mu·la /ˈfôrmyələ/ ▶ **n. 1** (pl. **formulas** or **formulae** /-ˌlē, -ˌlī/) a mathematical relationship or rule expressed in symbols. ■ (also **chemical formula**) a set of chemical symbols showing the elements present in a compound and their relative proportions, and in some cases the structure of the compound. See EMPIRICAL FORMULA, MOLECULAR FORMULA, STRUCTURAL FORMULA.
2 (pl. **formulas**) a fixed form of words, esp. one used in particular contexts or as a conventional usage: *a legal formula.* ■ a method, statement, or procedure for achieving something, esp. reconciling different aims or positions: *the forlorn hope of finding a peace formula.* ■ a rule or style unintelligently or slavishly followed: [as modifier] *one of those formula*

tunes. ■ a statement that formally enunciates a religious doctrine. ■ a stock epithet, phrase, or line repeated for various effects in literary composition, esp. epic poetry.
3 (pl. **formulas**) a list of ingredients for or constituents of something: *the soft drink company closely guards its secret formula.* ■ a formulation: *an original coal tar formula that helps prevent dandruff.* ■ an infant's liquid food preparation based on cow's milk or soy protein, given as a substitute for breast milk.
4 (usually followed by a number) a classification of race car, esp. by engine capacity.
– ORIGIN early 17th cent. (in the sense 'fixed form of words (for use on ceremonial or social occasions)'): from Latin, diminutive of *forma* 'shape, mold.'

for·mu·la·ic /ˌfôrmyəˈlāik/ ▶ **adj.** constituting or containing a verbal formula or set form of words: *a formulaic greeting.* ■ produced in accordance with a slavishly followed rule or style; predictable: *much romantic fiction is stylized, formulaic, and unrealistic.*
– DERIVATIVES **for·mu·la·i·cal·ly** /-(ə)lē/ **adv.**

For·mu·la One ▶ **n.** trademark an international form of auto racing, whose races are called Grand Prix.

for·mu·lar·ize /ˈfôrmyələˌrīz/ ▶ **v.** [with obj.] make (something) formulaic or predictable: *their stage shows have become a little formularized.*

for·mu·lar·y /ˈfôrmyəˌlerē/ ▶ **n.** (pl. **formularies**) **1** a collection of formulas or set forms, esp. for use in religious ceremonies.
2 an official list giving details of medicines that may be prescribed.
▶ **adj.** relating to or using officially prescribed formulas.
– ORIGIN mid 16th cent.: the noun from French *formulaire* or medieval Latin *formularius* (*liber*) '(book) of formulae,' from Latin *formula* (see FORMULA); the adjective (early 18th cent.) is directly from FORMULA.

for·mu·late /ˈfôrmyəˌlāt/ ▶ **v.** [with obj.] create or devise methodically (a strategy or a proposal): *economists and statisticians were needed to help formulate economic policy.* ■ express (an idea) in a concise or systematic way: *the argument is sufficiently clear that it can be formulated mathematically.*
– DERIVATIVES **for·mu·la·ble** /-ləbəl/ **adj.**, **for·mu·la·tor** /-ˌlātər/ **n.**
– ORIGIN mid 19th cent.: from FORMULA + -ATE[3], on the pattern of French *formuler*, from medieval Latin *formulare.*

for·mu·la·tion /ˌfôrmyəˈlāshən/ ▶ **n. 1** the action of devising or creating something: *the formulation of foreign policy.* ■ a particular expression of an idea, thought, or theory.
2 a material or mixture prepared according to a particular formula.

for·myl /ˈfôrˌmil/ ▶ **n.** [as modifier] Chemistry of or denoting the acyl radical –CHO, derived from formic acid: *N-formyl methionine.*

For·nax /ˈfôrˌnaks/ Astronomy an inconspicuous southern constellation (the Furnace), near Eridanus. ■ (as genitive **Fornacis** /fôrˈnāsis/) used with a preceding letter or numeral to designate a star in this constellation: *the star Beta Fornacis.*
– ORIGIN Latin.

for·ni·cate /ˈfôrniˌkāt/ ▶ **v.** [no obj.] formal or humorous (of two people not married to each other) have sexual intercourse.
– DERIVATIVES **for·ni·ca·tor** /-ˌkātər/ **n.**
– ORIGIN Middle English (as *fornication*): from ecclesiastical Latin *fornicat-* 'arched,' from *fornicari*, from Latin *fornix, fornic-* 'vaulted chamber,' later 'brothel.'

for·ni·ca·tion /ˌfôrniˈkāshən/ ▶ **n.** formal or humorous sexual intercourse between people not married to each other: *laws forbidding adultery and fornication.*

for·nix /ˈfôrniks/ ▶ **n.** (pl. **fornices** /-nəˌsēz/) Anatomy a vaulted or arched structure in the body, in particular: ■ (also **fornix cerebri** /ˈserəˌbrī, ˈkerəˌbrē/) a triangular area of white matter in the mammalian brain between the hippocampus and the hypothalamus.
– ORIGIN late 17th cent.: from Latin, literally 'arch, vaulted chamber.'

for-prof·it ▶ **adj.** [attrib.] denoting an organization that operates to make a profit, esp. one (such as a hospital or school) that would more typically be nonprofit.

For·rest /ˈfôrəst, ˈfär-/, Nathan Bedford (1821–77), Confederate cavalry officer. He led a massacre of 300 black Union soldiers at the surrender of Fort Pillow, Tennessee, April 12, 1864.

for·sake /fərˈsāk, fôr-/ ▶ **v.** (past **forsook** /-ˈso͝ok/; past participle **forsaken** /-ˈsākən/) [with obj.] chiefly literary abandon (someone or something): *he would never forsake Tara.* ■ renounce or give up (something valued or pleasant): *I won't forsake my vegetarian principles.*
– DERIVATIVES **for·sak·er** **n.**
– ORIGIN Old English *forsacan* 'renounce, refuse'; related to Dutch *verzaken*, and ultimately to FOR- and SAKE[1].

for·sak·en /fərˌsākən, fôr-/ ▶ **adj.** abandoned or deserted: *a journey into forgotten and forsaken places.*
– DERIVATIVES **for·sak·en·ness** **n.**

for·sooth /fərˈso͞oth/ ▶ **adv.** [sentence adverb] archaic or humorous indeed (often used ironically or to express surprise or indignation): *forsooth, there is no one I trust more.*
– ORIGIN Old English *forsōth* (see FOR, SOOTH).

For·ster /ˈfôrstər/, E. M. (1879–1970), English novelist and literary critic; full name *Edward Morgan Forster.* His novels include *A Room with a View* (1908) and *A Passage to India* (1924).

for·ster·ite /ˈfôrstəˌrīt/ ▶ **n.** a magnesium-rich variety of olivine, occurring as white, yellow, or green crystals.
– ORIGIN early 19th cent.: from the name of J. R. *Forster* (1729–98), German naturalist, + -ITE[1].

for·swear /fôrˈswe(ə)r/ ▶ **v.** (past **forswore**; past participle **forsworn**) [with obj.] formal agree to give up or do without (something): *he would never forswear the religion of his people.* ■ (**forswear oneself**/**be forsworn**) swear falsely; commit perjury: *I swore that I would lead us safely home and I do not mean to be forsworn.*
– ORIGIN Old English *forswerian*(see FOR-, SWEAR).

For·syth /ˈfôrˌsīth/, Frederick (1938–), English novelist. He is known for political thrillers such as *The Day of the Jackal* (1971), *The Odessa File* (1972), *The Fourth Protocol* (1984), and *The Afghan* (2006).

for·syth·i·a /fərˈsithēə/ ▶ **n.** a widely cultivated ornamental Eurasian shrub whose bright yellow flowers appear in early spring before the leaves.
● Genus *Forsythia*, family Oleaceae: several species.
– ORIGIN modern Latin, named after William *Forsyth* (1737–1804), Scottish botanist and horticulturalist, said to have introduced the shrub into Britain from China.

fort /fôrt/ ▶ **n.** a fortified building or strategic position. ■ a permanent army post. ■ historical a trading post. [so named because such establishments were originally fortified.]
– PHRASES **hold the fort** see HOLD[1].
– ORIGIN late Middle English: from Old French *fort* or Italian *forte*, from Latin *fortis* 'strong.'

fort. ▶ **abbr.** ■ fortification. ■ fortified.

For·ta·le·za /ˌfôrtlˈāzə/ a port in northeastern Brazil, on the Atlantic coast; pop. 2,431,415 (2007).

for·ta·lice /ˈfôrtl-is/ ▶ **n.** a small fort, fortified house, or outwork of fortification.
– ORIGIN late Middle English: from medieval Latin *fortalitia, -itium*, from Latin *fortis* 'strong.'

For·tas /ˈfôrtəs/, Abe (1910–82), US Supreme Court associate justice 1965–69. Criticized for his financial dealings with a known criminal, he was the first justice ever forced to resign by public criticism.

Fort Col·lins /ˈkälinz/ a commercial and industrial city in north central Colorado, home to Colorado State University; pop. 136,509 (est. 2008).

Fort-de-France /ˌfôr də ˈfräns/ the capital of Martinique; pop. 93,000 (est. 2007).

for·te[1] /ˈfôrˌtā, fôrt/ ▶ **n. 1** [in sing.] a thing at which someone excels: *small talk was not his forte.*
2 Fencing the stronger part of a sword blade, from the hilt to the middle. Compare with FOIBLE.
– ORIGIN mid 17th cent. (sense 2; originally as *fort*): from French *fort* (masculine), *forte* (feminine) 'strong,' from Latin *fortis.*

for·te[2] /ˈfôrˌtā/ Music ▶ **adv. & adj.** (esp. as a direction) loud or loudly.
▶ **n.** a passage performed or marked to be performed loudly.
– ORIGIN Italian, literally 'strong, loud,' from Latin *fortis.*

Fort·e·an /ˈfôrtēən/ ▶ **adj.** of, relating to, or denoting paranormal phenomena.
– DERIVATIVES **Fort·e·an·a** /ˌfôrtēˈanə/ **plural n.**
– ORIGIN 1970s: from the name of Charles H. *Fort* (1874–1932), American student of paranormal phenomena.

for·te·pi·an·o /ˌfôrtāpēˈanō, -pēˈänō/ ▶ **n.** (pl. **fortepianos**) Music a piano, esp. of the kind made in the 18th and early 19th centuries.
– ORIGIN mid 18th cent.: from FORTE[2] + PIANO[2].

for·te·pi·an·o /ˌfôrtā pēˈanō, pēˈänō/ ▶ **adv. & adj.** Music (esp. as a direction) loud and then immediately soft.
– ORIGIN Italian.

Forth /fôrth/ a river in central Scotland that rises on Ben Lomond and flows east into the North Sea.

forth /fôrth/ ▶ **adv.** chiefly archaic out from a starting point and forward or into view: *the plants will bush out, putting forth fresh shoots.* ■ onward in time: *from that day forth he gave me endless friendship.*
– PHRASES **and so forth** see SO[1].
– ORIGIN Old English, of Germanic origin; related to Dutch *voort* and German *fort*, from an Indo-European root shared by FORE-.

Forth, Firth of the estuary of the Forth River in Scotland, spanned by a cantilevered railroad bridge and a highway suspension bridge.

forth·com·ing /fôrthˈkəming, ˈfôrthˌkəming/ ▶ **adj. 1** planned for or about to happen in the near future: *the forthcoming baseball season.*
2 [predic. often with negative] (of something required) ready or made available when wanted or needed: *financial support was not forthcoming.* ■ (of a person) willing to divulge information: *their daughter had never been forthcoming about her time in Europe.*
– DERIVATIVES **forth·com·ing·ness** **n.**

forth·right /ˈfôrthˌrīt/ ▶ **adj. 1** (of a person or their manner or speech) direct and outspoken; straightforward and honest: *his most forthright attack yet on the reforms.*
2 archaic proceeding directly forward.
▶ **adv.** archaic directly forward. ■ immediately.
– DERIVATIVES **forth·right·ly** **adv.**, **forth·right·ness** **n.**
– ORIGIN Old English *forthriht* 'straightforward, directly' (see FORTH, RIGHT).

forth·with /fôrthˈwith/ ▶ **adv.** (esp. in official use) immediately; without delay: *we undertake to pay forthwith the money required.*
– ORIGIN Middle English (in the sense 'along with, at the same time'): partly from earlier *forthwithal*, partly representing *forth with* used alone without a following noun.

for·ti·fi·ca·tion /ˌfôrtəfəˈkāshən/ ▶ **n.** (often **fortifications**) a defensive wall or other reinforcement built to strengthen a place against attack. ■ the action of fortifying or process of being fortified: *the fortification of the frontiers.*
– ORIGIN late Middle English: via French from late Latin *fortificatio(n-)*, from *fortificare* (see FORTIFY).

for·ti·fy /ˈfôrtəˌfī/ ▶ **v.** (**fortifies, fortifying, fortified**) [with obj.] strengthen (a place) with defensive works so as to protect it against attack: *the whole town was heavily fortified* | (as adj. **fortified**) *a fortified manor house.* ■ strengthen or invigorate (someone) mentally or physically: *I was fortified by the knowledge that I was in a sympathetic house.* ■ (often as adj. **fortified**) strengthen (a drink) with alcohol: *fortified wine.* ■ increase the nutritive value of (food), esp. with vitamins.
– DERIVATIVES **for·ti·fi·a·ble** **adj.**, **for·ti·fi·er** **n.**
– ORIGIN late Middle English: from French *fortifier*, from late Latin *fortificare*, from Latin *fortis* 'strong.'

for·tis /ˈfôrtis/ ▶ **adj.** Phonetics (of a consonant, in particular a voiceless consonant) strongly articulated, esp. more so than another consonant articulated in the same place. The opposite of LENIS.
– ORIGIN early 20th cent.: from Latin, literally 'strong.'

for·tis·si·mo /fôrˈtisəˌmō/ Music ▶ **adv. & adj.** (esp. as a direction) very loud or loudly.
▶ **n.** (pl. **fortissimos** or **fortissimi** /-ˌmē/) a passage marked to be performed very loudly.
– ORIGIN Italian, from Latin *fortissimus* 'very strong.'

for·ti·tude /ˈfôrtəˌto͞od/ ▶ **n.** courage in pain or adversity: *she endured her illness with great fortitude.*
– ORIGIN Middle English: via French from Latin *fortitudo*, from *fortis* 'strong.'

Fort Knox /näks/ a US military reservation in Kentucky, noted as the site of the depository, which was built in 1936, that holds the bulk of the nation's gold bullion in its vaults.

Fort La·my /ˌfôr ləˈmē/ former name (until 1973) for N'DJAMENA.

Fort Lau·der·dale /ˈlôdərˌdāl/ a resort, commercial, and industrial city in southeastern Florida, north of Miami; pop. 183,126 (est. 2008).

Fort Mc·Hen·ry /məkˈhenrē/ a historic site in the harbor of Baltimore in Maryland, scene of an 1812 British siege that inspired Francis Scott Key to write "The Star Spangled Banner."

Fort My·ers /ˈmī-ərz/ a resort and commercial city in southwestern Florida; pop. 65,394 (est. 2008).

fort·night /ˈfôrtˌnīt/ ▶ **n.** chiefly Brit. a period of two weeks. ■ informal used after the name of a day to indicate that something will take place two weeks after that day.

– ORIGIN Old English *fēowertīene niht* 'fourteen nights.'

fort·night·ly /ˈfôrtˌnītlē/ chiefly Brit. ▶ **adj.** happening or produced every two weeks: *a fortnightly bulletin.* ▶ **adv.** every two weeks: *evening classes will run fortnightly.* ▶ **n.** (pl. **fortnightlies**) a magazine or similar publication issued every two weeks.

Fort Pierce /pi(ə)rs/ a resort and port city in east central Florida; pop. 40,885 (est. 2008).

For·tran /ˈfôrˌtran/ (also **FORTRAN**) ▶ **n.** a high-level computer programming language used esp. for scientific computation.
– ORIGIN 1950s: contraction of *formula translation.*

for·tress /ˈfôrtrəs/ ▶ **n.** a military stronghold, esp. a strongly fortified town fit for a large garrison. ■ a heavily protected and impenetrable building. ■ figurative a person or thing not susceptible to outside influence or disturbance: *he had proved himself to be a fortress of moral rectitude.*
– ORIGIN Middle English: from Old French *forteresse* 'strong place,' based on Latin *fortis* 'strong.'

Fort Smith /smiTH/ an industrial city in western Arkansas, on the Arkansas River; pop. 84,716 (est. 2008).

Fort Sum·ter /ˈsəmtər/ a historic site in the mouth of the harbor of Charleston in South Carolina. Confederate forces fired on US troops here in April 1861, beginning the Civil War.

for·tu·i·tous /fôrˈto͞oətəs/ ▶ **adj.** happening by accident or chance rather than design: *the similarity between the paintings may not be simply fortuitous.* ■ informal happening by a lucky chance; fortunate: *from a cash standpoint, the company's timing is fortuitous.*
– DERIVATIVES **for·tu·i·tous·ly** adv., **for·tu·i·tous·ness** n.
– ORIGIN mid 17th cent.: from Latin *fortuitus,* from *forte* 'by chance,' from *fors* 'chance, luck.'

USAGE The traditional, etymological meaning of **fortuitous** is 'happening by chance': a ***fortuitous meeting*** is a chance meeting, which might turn out to be either a good thing or a bad thing. In modern uses, however, **fortuitous** tends more often to be used to refer to fortunate outcomes, and the word has become more or less a synonym for 'lucky' or 'fortunate.' This use is frowned upon as being not etymologically correct and is best avoided except in informal contexts.

for·tu·i·ty /fôrˈto͞oətē/ ▶ **n.** (pl. **fortuities**) a chance occurrence. ■ the state of being controlled by chance rather than design.

for·tu·nate /ˈfôrCHənət/ ▶ **adj.** favored by or involving good luck or fortune; lucky: [with infinitive] *she'd been fortunate to escape more serious injury* | *it was fortunate that the weather was good.* ■ auspicious or favorable: *a most fortunate match for our daughter.* ■ materially well-off; prosperous: *less fortunate children still converged on the soup kitchens.*
– ORIGIN late Middle English: from Latin *fortunatus,* from *fortuna* (see FORTUNE).

for·tu·nate·ly /ˈfôrCHənətlē/ ▶ **adv.** [sentence adverb] it is fortunate that: *fortunately, no shots were fired and no one was hurt.*

for·tune /ˈfôrCHən/ ▶ **n. 1** chance or luck as an external, arbitrary force affecting human affairs: *some malicious act of fortune keeps them separate.* ■ luck, esp. good luck: *this astounding piece of good fortune that has befallen me.* ■ (**fortunes**) the success or failure of a person or enterprise over a period of time or in the course of a particular activity: *he is credited with turning around the company's fortunes.*
2 a large amount of money or assets: *he eventually inherited a substantial fortune.* ■ (**a fortune**) informal a surprisingly high price or amount of money: *I spent a fortune on drink and drugs.*
– PHRASES **fortune favors the brave** proverb a successful person is often one who is willing to take risks. **the fortunes of war** the unpredictable, haphazard events of war. **make a** (or **one's**) **fortune** acquire great wealth by one's own efforts. **a small fortune** informal a large amount of money. **tell someone's fortune** make predictions about a person's future by palmistry, using a crystal ball, reading tarot cards, or similar divining methods.
– ORIGIN Middle English: via Old French from Latin *Fortuna,* the name of a goddess personifying luck or chance.

For·tune 500 ▶ **n.** trademark an annual list of the five hundred most profitable US industrial corporations.

for·tune cook·ie ▶ **n.** a thin folded cookie containing a slip of paper with a prediction or aphorism written on it, served in Chinese restaurants.

for·tune hunt·er ▶ **n.** a person who seeks to become rich through marrying someone wealthy.

for·tune-tell·er (also **fortune teller**) ▶ **n.** a person who tells people's fortunes.
– DERIVATIVES **for·tune-tell·ing** n.

Fort Wayne /wān/ an industrial and commercial city in northeastern Indiana; pop. 251,591 (est. 2008).

Fort Worth /wərTH/ a city in northern Texas, on the Trinity River, west of Dallas; pop. 703,073 (est. 2008).

for·ty /ˈfôrtē/ ▶ **cardinal number** (pl. **forties**) the number equivalent to the product of four and ten; ten less than fifty; 40: *Troy was only forty miles away* | *forty were arrested* | *there were about thirty or forty of them.* (Roman numeral: **xl** or **XL**) ■ (**forties**) the numbers from forty to forty-nine, esp. the years of a century or of a person's life: *Terry was in his early forties.* ■ forty years old: *a tall woman of about forty.* ■ forty miles an hour: *they were doing about forty.*
– PHRASES **forty winks** informal a short sleep or nap, esp. during the day.
– DERIVATIVES **for·ti·eth** /-tēəTH/ **ordinal number, for·ty·fold** /-ˌfōld/ **adj. & adv.**
– ORIGIN Old English *fēowertig* (see FOUR, -TY²).

for·ty-five ▶ **n. 1** a phonograph record played at 45 rpm; a single.
2 (often **.45**) a 45-caliber revolver.

for·ty-nin·er /ˌfôrtē ˈnīnər/ ▶ **n.** a prospector in the California gold rush of 1849.

for·ty-ninth par·al·lel the parallel of latitude 49° north of the equator, esp. referred to as the boundary between Canada and the US west of Lake of the Woods.

fo·rum /ˈfôrəm/ ▶ **n.** (pl. **forums**) **1** a place, meeting, or medium where ideas and views on a particular issue can be exchanged: *it will be a forum for consumers to exchange their views on medical research.*
2 a court or tribunal.
3 (pl. **fora** /ˈfôrə/) (in an ancient Roman city) a public square or marketplace used for judicial and other business.
– ORIGIN late Middle English (sense 3): from Latin, literally 'what is out of doors,' originally denoting an enclosure surrounding a house; related to *fores* '(outside) door.' Sense 1 dates from the mid 18th cent.

for·ward /ˈfôrwərd/ ▶ **adv.** (also **forwards**) **1** toward the front; in the direction that one is facing or traveling: *he started up the engine and the car moved forward* | *Lori leaned forward over the table.* ■ in, near, or toward the bow or nose of a ship or aircraft. ■ in the normal order or sequence: *the number was the same backward as forward.*
2 onward so as to make progress; toward a successful conclusion: *there's no way forward for the relationship.* ■ into a position of prominence or notice: *he is pushing forward a political ally.*
3 toward the future; ahead in time: *from that day forward, the assembly was at odds with us.* ■ to an earlier time: *the special issue has been moved forward to winter.*
▶ **adj. 1** directed or facing toward the front or the direction that one is facing or traveling: *forward flight* | *the pilot's forward view.* ■ positioned near the enemy lines: *troops moved to the forward areas.* ■ (in sports) moving toward the opponents' goal: *a forward pass.* ■ in, near, or toward the bow or nose of a ship or aircraft. ■ Electronics (of a voltage applied to a semiconductor junction) in the direction that allows significant current to flow.
2 [attrib.] relating to or concerned with the future: *forward planning.*
3 moving or tending onward to a successful conclusion: *the decision is a forward step.* developing or acting earlier than expected or required; advanced or precocious: *an alarmingly forward yet painfully vulnerable child.*
4 (of a person) bold or familiar in manner, esp. in a presumptuous way.
▶ **n. 1** an attacking player in basketball, hockey, or other sports. ■ Football an offensive or defensive lineman.
2 (**forwards**) Finance short for FORWARD CONTRACT.
▶ **v.** [with obj.] **1** send (a letter or e-mail) on to a further destination: (as adj. **forwarding**) *a forwarding address.* ■ hand over or send (an official document): *their final report was forwarded to the Commanding Officer.* ■ dispatch (goods): (as adj. **forwarding**) *a freight forwarding company.*
2 help to advance (something); promote: *the scientists are forwarding the development of biotechnology.*
– DERIVATIVES **for·ward·ly** adv.
– ORIGIN Old English *forweard* (in the sense 'toward the future,' as in *from this day forward*), variant of *forthweard* (see FORTH, -WARD).

for·ward con·tract ▶ **n.** Finance an informal agreement traded through a broker-dealer network to buy and sell specified assets, typically currency, at a specified price at a certain future date. Compare with FUTURES CONTRACT.

for·ward·er¹ /ˈfôrwərdər/ ▶ **n.** a person or organization that supervises the dispatch and delivery of goods, esp. by making banking and insurance arrangements and completing required documents.

for·ward·er² ▶ **adj. & adv.** dated or informal further forward; more advanced: *time was drawing on and we were no forwarder.*

for·ward-look·ing (also **forward-thinking**) ▶ **adj.** favoring innovation and development; progressive.

for·ward·ness /ˈfôrwərdnəs/ ▶ **n.** boldness or overfamiliarity in manner: *he was taken aback by the girl's forwardness.*

for·ward pass ▶ **n.** Football a pass thrown from behind the line of scrimmage in a forward direction, toward the opponent's goal.

for·wards /ˈfôrwərdz/ ▶ **adv.** variant spelling of FORWARD.

for·went /fôrˈwent/ past of FORGO.

FOS ▶ **abbr.** free on steamer.

Fos·bur·y /ˈfäzˌberē/, Dick (1947–), US high jumper; full name *Richard Douglas Fosbury.* He originated the now standard style of jumping known as the "Fosbury flop," in which the jumper clears the bar head first and backward. In 1968, he won the Olympic gold medal using this technique.

fos·sa¹ /ˈfäsə/ ▶ **n.** (pl. **fossae** /ˈfäsē, -sī/) Anatomy a shallow depression or hollow.
– ORIGIN mid 17th cent.: from Latin, literally 'ditch,' feminine past participle of *fodere* 'to dig.'

fos·sa² ▶ **n.** a large nocturnal reddish-brown catlike mammal of the civet family, found in the rain forests of Madagascar. ● *Cryptoprocta ferox,* family Viverridae.
– ORIGIN mid 19th cent.: from Malagasy *fosa.*

Fos·se /ˈfôsē, ˈfäsē/, Bob (1927–87), US jazz dancer, choreographer, and director; full name *Robert Louis Fosse.* He directed and choreographed Broadway musicals such as *Pajama Game* (1954), *Redhead* (1958), and *All That Jazz* (1979) and movies such as *Cabaret* (1972). *Fosse* (1999), a Broadway musical, was dedicated to him.

fosse /fäs/ ▶ **n.** Archaeology a long narrow trench or excavation, esp. in a fortification.
– ORIGIN late Old English, via Old French from Latin *fossa* (see FOSSA¹).

fos·sick /ˈfäsik/ ▶ **v.** [no obj.] Austral./NZ informal rummage; search: *he spent years fossicking through documents.* ■ search for gold in abandoned workings.
– DERIVATIVES **fos·sick·er** /ˈfäsikər/ n.
– ORIGIN mid 19th cent. (referring to mining): probably from the English dialect sense 'obtain by asking' (i.e., 'ferret out').

fos·sil /ˈfäsəl/ ▶ **n.** the remains or impression of a prehistoric organism preserved in petrified form or as a mold or cast in rock. ■ derogatory or humorous an antiquated or stubbornly unchanging person or thing: *he can be a cantankerous old fossil at times.* ■ a word or phrase that has become obsolete except in set phrases or forms, e.g., *hue* in *hue and cry.*
– ORIGIN mid 16th cent. (denoting a fossilized fish found, and believed to have lived, underground): from French *fossile,* from Latin *fossilis* 'dug up,' from *fodere* 'dig.'

fos·sil fu·el ▶ **n.** a natural fuel such as coal or gas, formed in the geological past from the remains of living organisms.

fos·sil i·vo·ry ▶ **n.** ivory from the tusks of a mammoth.

fos·sil·ize /ˈfäsəˌlīz/ ▶ **v.** [with obj.] (usu. **be fossilized**) preserve (an organism) so that it becomes a fossil: *the hard parts of the body are readily fossilized.* ■ [no obj.] become a fossil: *flowers do not readily fossilize.* ■ become or cause to become antiquated, fixed, or incapable of change or development.
– DERIVATIVES **fos·sil·i·za·tion** /ˌfäsəliˈzāSHən/ n.

fos·sil·ized /ˈfäsəˌlīzd/ ▶ **adj.** preserved to become a fossil: *a fossilized bone* | *fossilized human remains.* ■ archaic and incapable of change: *a faltering economy and a fossilized political system.*

PRONUNCIATION KEY ə *ago, up;* ər *over, fur;* a *hat;* ā *ate;* ä *car;* e *let;* ē *see;* i *fit;* ī *by;* NG *sing;* ō *go;* ô *law, for;* oi *toy;* o͝o *good;* o͞o *goo;* ou *out;* TH *thin;* T͟H *then;* ZH *vision*

f

f

fos·so·ri·al /fäˈsôrēəl/ ▶ **adj.** Zoology (of an animal) burrowing. ■ (of limbs) adapted for use in burrowing.
– ORIGIN mid 19th cent.: from medieval Latin *fossorius* (from Latin *fossor* 'digger,' from *fodere* 'to dig') + -AL.

Fos·ter, Stephen (Collins) (1826–64), US composer. He wrote more than 200 songs and, although a Northerner, was best known for songs that purported to capture the Southern plantation spirit, such as "Oh! Susannah" (1848), "Camptown Races" (1850), and "Old Folks at Home" (1851).

fos·ter /ˈfôstər, ˈfäs-/ ▶ **v.** [with obj.] **1** encourage or promote the development of (something, typically something regarded as good): *the teacher's task is to foster learning.* ■ develop (a feeling or idea) in oneself: *appropriate praise helps a child foster a sense of self-worth.*
2 bring up (a child that is not one's own by birth).
▶ **adj.** denoting someone that has a specified family connection through fostering rather than birth: *foster parent | foster child.* ■ involving or concerned with fostering a child: *foster care | foster home.*
– DERIVATIVES **fos·ter·age** /-rij/ **n.**, **fos·ter·er n.**
– ORIGIN Old English *fōstrian* 'feed, nourish,' from *fōster* 'food, nourishment,' of Germanic origin; related to FOOD. The sense 'bring up another's (originally also one's own) child' dates from Middle English.

fos·ter·ling /ˈfôstərlinɢ, ˈfäs-/ ▶ **n.** chiefly archaic a child who is fostered or adopted.
– ORIGIN Old English *fōstorling* (see FOSTER, -LING).

Fou·cault[1] /fo͞oˈkō/, Jean Bernard Léon (1819–68), French physicist. He is chiefly remembered for the huge pendulum that he hung from the roof of the Panthéon in Paris in 1851 to demonstrate the rotation of the earth. He also invented the gyroscope.

Fou·cault[2], Michel (Paul) (1926–84), French philosopher. He was concerned with how society defines categories of abnormality, such as insanity, sexuality, and criminality, and the manipulation of social attitudes toward such things by those in power.

fouet·té /fweˈtā/ ▶ **n.** Ballet a pirouette performed with a circular whipping movement of the raised leg to the side. ■ a quick shift of direction of the upper body, performed with one leg extended.
– ORIGIN French, past participle of *fouetter* 'to whip.'

fought /fôt/ past and past participle of FIGHT.

Fou-hsin variant spelling of FUXIN.

foul /foul/ ▶ **adj.** **1** offensive to the senses, esp. through having a disgusting smell or taste or being unpleasantly soiled: *a foul odor | his foul breath.* ■ informal very disagreeable or unpleasant: *the news had put Michelle in a foul mood.* ■ (of the weather) wet and stormy. ■ Sailing (of wind or tide) opposed to one's desired course.
2 wicked or immoral: *murder most foul.* ■ (of language) obscene or profane. ■ done contrary to the rules of a sport: *a foul tackle.*
3 containing or charged with noxious matter; polluted: *foul, swampy water.* ■ [predic.] (**foul with**) clogged or choked with: *the land was foul with weeds.* ■ Nautical (of a rope or anchor) entangled. ■ (of a ship's bottom) encrusted with algae, barnacles, or other marine growth. ■ Printing (of a first copy or proof) defaced by corrections.
▶ **n.** **1** (in sports) an unfair or invalid stroke or piece of play, esp. one involving interference with an opponent. ■ a collision or entanglement in riding, rowing, or running. ■ short for FOUL BALL.
2 informal, dated a disease in the feet of cattle.
▶ **adv.** unfairly; contrary to the rules. ■ (in sports) in foul territory: *if a batter hits a bunt foul with two strikes, he is out.*
▶ **v.** [with obj.] **1** make foul or dirty; pollute: *factories that fouled the atmosphere.* ■ disgrace or dishonor. ■ (of an animal) make (something) dirty with excrement: *make sure that your pet never fouls the sidewalk.* ■ (**foul oneself**) (of a person) defecate involuntarily.
2 (in sports) commit a foul against (an opponent). ■ Baseball hit a foul ball: *Carter fouled into the glove of Boggs.*
3 (of a ship) collide with or interfere with the passage of (another). ■ cause (a cable, anchor, or other object) to become entangled or jammed: *watch out for driftwood which might foul up the engine.* ■ [no obj.] become entangled in this way.
– PHRASES **fall foul of** see FALL. **foul one's (own) nest** do something damaging or harmful to oneself or one's own interests.
– PHRASAL VERBS **foul out** Basketball be put out of the game for exceeding the permitted number of fouls. ■ Baseball (of a batter) be made out by hitting a foul ball that is caught by an opposing player:: *Wilson has never fouled out against this young pitcher.* **foul something up** (or **foul up**) make a mistake with or spoil something: *leaders should admit when they completely foul things up.*
– DERIVATIVES **foul·ly** /ˈfou(l)lē/ **adv.**, **foul·ness n.**
– ORIGIN Old English *fūl*, of Germanic origin; related to Old Norse *fúll* 'foul,' Dutch *vuil* 'dirty,' and German *faul* 'rotten, lazy,' from an Indo-European root shared by Latin *pus*, Greek *puos* 'pus,' and Latin *putere* 'to stink.'

fou·lard /fo͞oˈlärd/ ▶ **n.** a thin, soft material of silk or silk and cotton, typically having a printed pattern. ■ a tie or handkerchief made of such material.
– ORIGIN mid 19th cent.: from French, of unknown origin.

foul ball ▶ **n.** Baseball a ball struck so that it falls or will fall outside the lines extending from home plate past first and third bases. A foul ball that is not caught counts as a strike against the batter, unless it would be the third strike. The exception is a bunted foul ball, which can be a third strike. Compare with FOUL TIP.

foul brood ▶ **n.** a fatal bacterial disease of larval honeybees. ● This disease is caused by the bacteria *Paenibacillus larvae* or *Melissococcus pluton*.

foul line ▶ **n.** Sports a line marking the boundary of permissible movement or play, in particular: ■ Baseball either of the straight lines extending from home plate past first and third bases into the outfield and marking the limit of the area within which a hit is deemed to be fair. ■ Basketball either of the lines 15 feet in front of each backboard, from which free throws are made. Also called FREE-THROW LINE. ■ (in bowling) a line on the alley, perpendicular to the gutters and 60 feet from the head pin.

foul mouth ▶ **n.** a tendency to use bad language: *he had a foul mouth and an even fouler disposition.*

foul-mouthed /-ˌmouT͟Hd, -ˌmouTHt/ ▶ **adj.** using or characterized by a great deal of bad language: *a foul-mouthed cop.*

foul play ▶ **n.** **1** unfair play in a game or sport.
2 unlawful or dishonest behavior, in particular violent crime resulting in another's death.

foul shot ▶ **n.** Basketball another term for FREE THROW.

foul tip ▶ **n.** Baseball a pitched ball that tips off the bat and travels directly to the catcher's hands. Unlike a foul ball, a foul tip can be a batter's third strike.
– DERIVATIVES **foul-tip v.**

foul-up ▶ **n.** a mistake resulting in confusion.

found[1] /found/ past and past participle of FIND.
▶ **adj.** **1** having been discovered by chance or unexpectedly, in particular: ■ (of an object or sound) collected in its natural state and presented in a new context as part of a work of art or piece of music: *collages of found photos.* ■ (of art) comprising or making use of such objects. ■ (of poetry) formed by reinterpreting metrically the structure of a nonpoetic text.
2 [with submodifier] (of a ship) equipped; supplied: *the ship was two years old, well found and seaworthy.*

found[2] ▶ **v.** [with obj.] **1** establish or originate (an institution or organization), esp. by providing an endowment: *the monastery was founded in 1665* | (as adj. **founding**) *the three founding partners.* ■ plan and begin the building of (a town or colony).
2 (usu. **be founded on/upon**) construct or base (a principle or other abstract thing) according to a particular principle or grounds: *a society founded on the highest principles of religion and education.* ■ (of a thing) serve as a basis for: *the company's fortunes are founded on its minerals business.*
– ORIGIN Middle English: from Old French *fonder*, from Latin *fundare*, from *fundus* 'bottom, base.'

found[3] ▶ **v.** [with obj.] melt and mold (metal). ■ fuse (materials) to make glass. ■ make (an article) by melting and molding metal.
– ORIGIN early 16th cent.: from French *fondre*, from Latin *fundere* 'melt, pour.'

foun·da·tion /founˈdāSHən/ ▶ **n.** **1** (often **foundations**) the lowest load-bearing part of a building, typically below ground level. ■ a body or ground on which other parts rest or are overlaid: *he starts playing melody lines on the bass instead of laying the foundation down.* ■ (also **foundation garment**) a woman's supporting undergarment, such as a girdle. ■ a cream or powder used as a base to even out facial skin tone before applying other cosmetics.
2 an underlying basis or principle for something: *specific learning skills as a foundation for other subjects.* ■ [often with negative] justification or reason: *distorted and misleading accusations with no foundation.*
3 the action of establishing an institution or organization on a permanent basis, esp. with an endowment. ■ an institution established with an endowment, for example a college or a body devoted to financing research or charity.
– DERIVATIVES **foun·da·tion·al** /-SHənl/ **adj.**
– ORIGIN late Middle English: from Old French *fondation*, from Latin *fundatio(n-)*, from *fundare* 'to lay a base for' (see FOUND[2]).

foun·da·tion stone ▶ **n.** a stone laid at a ceremony to celebrate the beginning of construction of a building. ■ a basic or essential element of something.

found·er[1] ▶ **n.** a person who manufactures articles of cast metal; the owner or operator of a foundry: *an iron founder.*
– ORIGIN Middle English: probably from Old French *fondeur*, from *fondre* (see FOUND[3]).

found·er[2] ▶ **v.** [no obj.] (of a ship) fill with water and sink: *six drowned when the yacht foundered off the Florida coast.* ■ (of a plan or undertaking) fail or break down, typically as a result of a particular problem or setback: *the talks **foundered on the issue** of reform.* ■ (of a hoofed animal, esp. a horse or pony) succumb to laminitis.
▶ **n.** laminitis in horses, ponies, or other hoofed animals.
– ORIGIN Middle English (in the sense 'knock to the ground'): from Old French *fondrer*, *esfondrer* 'submerge, collapse,' based on Latin *fundus* 'bottom, base.'

> **USAGE** It is easy to confuse the words **founder** and **flounder**, not only because they sound similar but also because the contexts in which they are used overlap. **Founder** means, in its general and extended use, 'fail or come to nothing, sink out of sight' (*the scheme **foundered** because of lack of organizational backing*). **Flounder**, on the other hand, means 'struggle, move clumsily, be in a state of confusion' (*new recruits **floundering** about in their first week*).

found·er ef·fect ▶ **n.** Biology the reduced genetic diversity that results when a population is descended from a small number of colonizing ancestors.

found·ing fa·ther ▶ **n.** a person who starts or helps to start a movement or institution. ■ (**Founding Father**) a member of the convention that drew up the US Constitution in 1787.

found·ling /ˈfoundlinɢ/ ▶ **n.** an infant that has been abandoned by its parents and is discovered and cared for by others.
– ORIGIN Middle English: from FOUND[1] (past participle) + -LING, perhaps on the pattern of Dutch *vondeling*.

found ob·ject ▶ **n.** objet trouvé.

found·ress /ˈfoundrəs/ ▶ **n.** dated, rare a female founder: *she was the sixth-century foundress of a community of women.*

found·ry /ˈfoundrē/ ▶ **n.** (pl. **foundries**) a workshop or factory for casting metal.
– ORIGIN early 17th cent. (earlier as *foundery*): from FOUND[3] + -RY, perhaps suggested by French *fonderie*.

fount[1] /fänt, fount/ ▶ **n.** a source of a desirable quality or commodity: *our courier was a fount of knowledge.* ■ literary a spring or fountain.
– ORIGIN late 16th cent.: back-formation from FOUNTAIN, on the pattern of the pair *mountain, mount*.

fount[2] ▶ **n.** Brit. variant spelling of FONT[2].

foun·tain /ˈfountn/ ▶ **n.** **1** an ornamental structure in a pool or lake from which one or more jets of water are pumped into the air. ■ short for DRINKING FOUNTAIN. ■ a thing that spurts or cascades into the air: *little fountains of dust.*
2 chiefly literary a natural spring of water. ■ a source of a desirable quality: *the government always quotes this report as the fountain of truth.*
▶ **v.** [no obj.] spurt or cascade like a fountain: *an enormous curtain of lava fountained into the sky.*
– DERIVATIVES **foun·tained** /ˈfountnd/ **adj.** (literary).
– ORIGIN Middle English (sense 2 of the noun): from Old French *fontaine*, from late Latin *fontana*, feminine of Latin *fontanus*, adjective from *fons, font-* 'a spring.'

foun·tain·head /ˈfountnˌhed/ ▶ **n.** an original source of something: *this president was the fountainhead of patronage.*

foun·tain pen ▶ **n.** a pen with a reservoir or cartridge from which ink flows continuously to the nib.

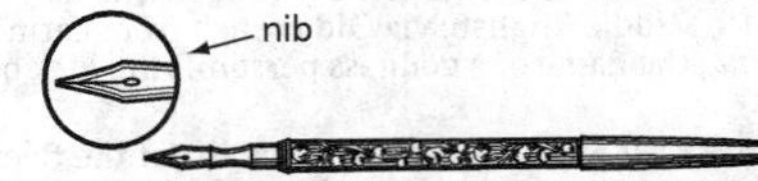

fountain pen

Foun·tain Val·ley a city in southwestern California, southeast of Los Angeles; pop. 55,516 (est. 2008).

four /fôr/ ▸ **cardinal number** equivalent to the product of two and two; one more than three, or six less than ten; 4: *Francesca's got four brothers | it took four of them to lift it | a four-bedroom house.* (Roman numeral: **iv**, **IV**, archaic **iiii** or **IIII**) ■ a group or unit of four people or things: *the girls walked in pairs or fours.* ■ four years old: *I began to teach myself to read at four.* ■ four o'clock: *it's half past four.* ■ a size of garment or other merchandise denoted by four. ■ a playing card or domino with four spots or pips.
– ORIGIN Old English *fēower*, of Germanic origin; related to Dutch and German *vier*, from an Indo-European root shared by Latin *quattuor* and Greek *tessares*.

four-bag·ger ▸ **n.** Baseball a home run.

four-by-four (also **4X4**) ▸ **n.** informal a vehicle with four-wheel drive.

Four Can·tons, Lake of the another name for Lake Lucerne (see LUCERNE, LAKE).

four·chette /fo͝or'sHet/ ▸ **n.** Anatomy a thin fold of skin at the back of the vulva.
– ORIGIN mid 18th cent.: from French, diminutive of *fourche* 'fork.'

four-col·or ▸ **adj.** denoting a color printing process using red, cyan (greenish blue), yellow, and black inks on separate plates that are serially transferred to the same sheet to produce images in full color.

Four Cor·ners the point where Arizona, New Mexico, Colorado, and Utah meet.

four-di·men·sion·al ▸ **adj.** having four dimensions, typically the three dimensions of space (length, breadth, and depth) plus time.

Four·drin·i·er ma·chine /ˌfôrdrə'nir, fôr'drinēər/ ▸ **n.** a machine for making paper as a continuous sheet by drainage on a wire mesh belt.
– ORIGIN mid 19th cent.: named after Henry (died 1854) and Sealy (died 1847) *Fourdrinier*, British papermakers and patentees of such a machine.

four-eyed fish ▸ **n.** a small livebearing freshwater fish of tropical America. Each eye is divided into two, allowing the fish to see both above and below the water while swimming at the surface. ● Family Anablepidae and genus *Anableps*: several species.

four-eyes ▸ **n.** derogatory a person who wears glasses.

four flush ▸ **n.** a poker hand of little value, having four cards of the same suit and one of another. Compare with FLUSH[3].
▸ **v.** (**four-flush**) [no obj.] informal (in poker) bluff when holding a weak hand, particularly a four flush. ■ keep up a pretense; bluff: *your mother will get wise that you're four-flushing.*
– DERIVATIVES **four-flush·er n.**

four·fold /ˈfôrˌfōld/ ▸ **adj.** four times as great or as numerous: *there has been a fourfold increase in break-ins.* ■ having four parts or elements: *fourfold symmetry.*
▸ **adv.** by four times; to four times the number or amount: *the price of electricity rose fourfold.*

four free·doms (usu. **the four freedoms**) the four essential human freedoms as proclaimed in a speech to Congress by President Franklin D. Roosevelt in 1941: freedom of speech and expression, freedom of worship, freedom from want, and freedom from fear.

Four Horse·men of the A·poc·a·lypse four allegorical mounted figures, commonly identified as Pestilence (or Conquest), War, Famine, and Death, whose arrival heralds the end of the world, as described in the biblical book of Revelation. ■ used to refer to people or phenomena seen as agents of imminent catastrophe: *in 2003, the airline industry survived the four horsemen of the apocalypse.*

Four Hun·dred (usu. **the Four Hundred** or **the 400**) ▸ **n.** the social elite of a community: *I would like nothing better than to ask the Four Hundred to meet you.*
– ORIGIN mid 19th cent.: from Ward McAllister's remark "There are only 400 people in New York that one really knows," later popularized in society reports by the New York *Sun*. The notion 'elite' is said to be from the selection of high society guests by the socialite Mrs. William B. Astor Jr., whose ballroom could hold 400.

Fou·rier /'fo͝orēˌā, fo͝or'yā/, Jean Baptiste Joseph (1768–1830), French mathematician. He solved partial differential equations by the method of separation of variables and superposition, which led him to analyze the series and integrals that are now known by his name.

Fou·rier a·nal·y·sis ▸ **n.** Mathematics the analysis of a complex waveform expressed as a series of sinusoidal functions, the frequencies of which form a harmonic series.

Fou·ri·er·ism /'fo͝orēəˌrizəm/ ▸ **n.** a system for the reorganization of society into self-sufficient cooperatives, in accordance with the principles of the French socialist Charles Fourier (died 1837).
– DERIVATIVES **Fou·ri·er·ist n. & adj.**

Fou·rier se·ries ▸ **n.** Mathematics an infinite series of trigonometric functions that represents an expansion or approximation of a periodic function, used in Fourier analysis.

Fou·rier trans·form ▸ **n.** Mathematics a function derived from a given function and representing it by a series of sinusoidal functions.

four-in-hand ▸ **n. 1** a vehicle with four horses driven by one person: [as modifier] *four-in-hand coaches compete this week for the Devon blue ribbon.* ■ a team of four horses.
2 historical a necktie tied in a loose knot with two hanging ends, popular in the late 19th and early 20th centuries. [said to be by association with the sport of driving four-in-hand carriages.]

four-leaf clo·ver (also **four-leafed clover**) ▸ **n.** a clover leaf with four leaflets, rather than the typical three, thought to bring good luck.

four-let·ter word ▸ **n.** any of several short words referring to sexual or excretory functions, regarded as coarse or offensive.

four no·ble truths ▸ **plural n.** the four central beliefs containing the essence of Buddhist teaching. See BUDDHISM.

four-o'clock ▸ **n.** a tropical American herbaceous plant with fragrant trumpet-shaped flowers that open late in the afternoon. Also called MARVEL OF PERU. ● *Mirabilis jalapa*, family Nyctaginaceae.

four-ply ▸ **adj.** (of a material) having four strands or layers: *four-ply yarn.*
▸ **n.** knitting yarn made of four strands.

four-post·er (also **four-poster bed**) ▸ **n.** a bed with a post at each corner, sometimes supporting a canopy.

four·score /'fôr'skôr/ ▸ **cardinal number** archaic eighty.

four·some /'fôrsəm/ ▸ **n.** a group of four people. ■ a golf match between two pairs of players, with partners playing the same ball.

four-square ▸ **adj.** (of a building or structure) having a square shape and solid appearance. ■ (of a person or quality) firm and resolute: *a four-square and formidable hero.*
▸ **adv.** squarely and solidly: *a castle standing four-square and isolated on a peninsula.* ■ firmly or resolutely, esp. in support of someone or something: *they stand four-square behind integration.*

four-star ▸ **adj.** (esp. of a hotel or restaurant) given four stars in a grading system, typically one in which this denotes the highest or next to the highest class or quality. ■ (in the US armed forces) having or denoting the second-highest military rank, distinguished by four stars on the uniform.

four-stroke ▸ **adj.** denoting an internal combustion engine having a cycle of four strokes (intake, compression, combustion, and exhaust). Compare with TWO-STROKE. ■ denoting a vehicle having such an engine.
▸ **n.** an engine or vehicle of this type.

four·teen /ˌfôr'tēn, 'fôrˌtēn/ ▸ **cardinal number** equivalent to the product of seven and two; one more than thirteen, or six less than twenty; 14: *they had spent fourteen days in solitary confinement | all fourteen of us were seated.* (Roman numeral: **xiv** or **XIV**) ■ a size of garment or other merchandise denoted by fourteen. ■ fourteen years old: *he left school at fourteen.*
– DERIVATIVES **four·teenth** /ˌfôr'tēnTH, 'fôrˌtēnTH/ **ordinal number.**
– ORIGIN Old English *fēowertiene* (see FOUR, -TEEN).

fourth /fôrTH/ ▸ **ordinal number** constituting number four in a sequence; 4th: *the fourth and fifth centuries | there were three bedrooms, with potential for a fourth.* ■ (**a fourth/one fourth**) a quarter: *nearly three fourths of that money is now gone.* ■ the fourth finisher or position in a race or competition: *he could do no better than finish fourth.* ■ the fourth (and often highest) in a sequence of a vehicle's gears: *he took the corner at the end of the road in fourth.* ■ fourthly (used to introduce a fourth point or reason): *third, visit popular attractions during lunch; fourth, stay late.* ■ Music an interval spanning four consecutive notes in a diatonic scale, in particular (also **perfect fourth**) an interval of two tones and a semitone (e.g., C to F). ■ Music the note that is higher by this interval than the tonic of a diatonic scale or root of a chord.

fourth-class ▸ **adj.** a class of US mail applying to packages weighing more than sixteen ounces and used esp. for sending general merchandise, books, recordings, and films.

fourth di·men·sion ▸ **n. 1** a postulated spatial dimension additional to those determining length, area, and volume.
2 time regarded as analogous to linear dimensions.

fourth es·tate ▸ **n.** (**the fourth estate**) the press; the profession of journalism: *copy desks are held together by the bad-news contingent of the fourth estate.*
– ORIGIN originally used humorously in various contexts; its first usage with reference to the press has been attributed to Edmund Burke, but this remains unconfirmed.

Fourth In·ter·na·tion·al see INTERNATIONAL (sense 2 of the noun).

fourth·ly /'fôrTHlē/ ▸ **adv.** in the fourth place (used to introduce a fourth point or reason): *fourthly, and last, there are variations in context that influence the process.*

Fourth of Ju·ly ▸ **n.** a national holiday celebrating the anniversary of the adoption of the Declaration of Independence in 1776. Also called INDEPENDENCE DAY.

fourth po·si·tion ▸ **n. 1** Ballet a posture in which the feet are placed turned outward one in front of the other, separated by the distance of one step. ■ a position of the arms in which one is held curved over the head and the other curved in front of the body at waist level.
2 Music a position of the left hand on the fingerboard of a stringed instrument nearer to the bridge than the third position, enabling a higher set of notes to be played.

Fourth Re·pub·lic the republican regime in France between the end of World War II (1945) and the introduction of a new constitution by Charles de Gaulle in 1958.

fourth wall ▸ **n.** (**the fourth wall**) the space that separates a performer or performance from an audience. ■ the conceptual barrier between any fictional work and its viewers or readers: *he breaks **the fourth wall** by having Sam refer to the script and the play he's acting in.*

Fourth World ▸ **n. 1** those countries and communities considered to be the poorest and most underdeveloped of the Third World.
2 those communities that form politically and economically disadvantaged minorities within societies, owing to factors such as urban deprivation or discrimination against tribal peoples.

four-wheel drive ▸ **n.** a transmission system that provides power directly to all four wheels of a vehicle. ■ a vehicle with such a system, typically designed for off-road driving.

fo·ve·a /'fōvēə/ (also **fovea centralis** /sen'trālis/) ▸ **n.** (pl. **foveae** /-vēˌē, -vēˌī/) Anatomy a small depression in the retina of the eye where visual acuity is highest. The center of the field of vision is focused in this region, where retinal cones are particularly concentrated.
– DERIVATIVES **fo·ve·al** /-vēəl/ **adj.**
– ORIGIN late 17th cent.: from Latin, literally 'small pit.'

fowl /foul/ ▸ **n.** (pl. **same** or **fowls**) (also **domestic fowl**) a gallinaceous bird kept chiefly for its eggs and flesh; a domestic cock or hen. ● The domestic fowl is descended from the wild **red junglefowl** of Southeast Asia (see JUNGLE FOWL). ■ any other domesticated bird kept for its eggs or flesh, e.g., the turkey, duck, goose, and guineafowl. ■ the flesh of birds, esp. of the domestic cock or hen, as food; poultry. ■ birds collectively, esp. as the quarry of hunters. ■ archaic a bird.
– ORIGIN Old English *fugol*, originally the general term for a bird, of Germanic origin; related to Dutch *vogel* and German *Vogel*, also to FLY[1].

Fowl·er /'foulər/, H. W. (1858–1933), English lexicographer and grammarian; full name *Henry Watson Fowler*. He compiled the first edition of the *Concise Oxford Dictionary* (1911) with his brother **Francis George Fowler** (1871–1918) and wrote a guide to style and idiom, *Modern English Usage*, which was first published in 1926.

Fowles /foulz/, John (Robert) (1926–2005), English novelist. Notable works: *The Collector* (1963), *The Magus* (1966), and *The French Lieutenant's Woman* (1969).

fowl·ing /'fouliNG/ ▸ **n.** the hunting, shooting, or trapping of wildfowl.
– DERIVATIVES **fowl·er** /'foulər/ **n.**

fowl pest ▸ **n.** either of two similar viral diseases of poultry, Newcastle disease or fowl plague.

f

fowl plague ▸ n. an acute and often fatal infectious viral disease of birds, esp. poultry.

fowl·pox /ˈfoulˌpäks/ ▸ n. a slow-spreading viral disease of birds that produces wartlike nodules on the skin. Infestations sometimes threaten commercial poultry interests. ● *Avipoxvirus*, family Poxviridae.

Fox[1] /fäks/, George (1624–91), English preacher and founder of the Society of Friends (Quakers).

Fox[2], Vicente (1942–), Mexican statesman; president 2000–06; full name *Vicente Fox Quesada*. A member of the conservative National Action Party (PAN), he ended seventy-one years of rule by the Institutional Revolutionary Party (PRI) when elected president.

Vicente Fox Quesada

Fox[3] ▸ n. (pl. **same**) **1** a member of an American Indian people formerly living in southern Wisconsin, and now mainly in Iowa, Nebraska, and Kansas. **2** the Algonquian language of this people.
▸ adj. of or relating to this people or their language.

fox /fäks/ ▸ n. **1** a carnivorous mammal of the dog family with a pointed muzzle and bushy tail, proverbial for its cunning. ● *Vulpes* and three other genera, family Canidae: several species, including the red fox and the arctic fox.
■ the fur of a fox.
2 informal a cunning or sly person: *a wily old fox.* ■ a sexually attractive woman.
▸ v. **1** [with obj.] informal baffle or deceive (someone): *the bad light and dark shadows foxed him.*
2 [with obj.] repair (a boot or shoe) by renewing the upper leather. ■ ornament (the upper of a boot or shoe) with a strip of leather.
– DERIVATIVES **fox·like** /-ˌlīk/ adj.
– ORIGIN Old English, of Germanic origin; related to Dutch *vos* and German *Fuchs*.

foxed /fäkst/ ▸ adj. (of the paper of old books or prints) discolored with brown spots.
– DERIVATIVES **fox·ing** /ˈfäksiNG/ n.

fox·fire /ˈfäksˌfīr/ ▸ n. the phosphorescent light emitted by certain fungi on decaying timber.

fox·glove /ˈfäksˌgləv/ ▸ n. a tall Eurasian plant with erect spikes of flowers, typically pinkish-purple or white, shaped like the fingers of gloves. It is a source of the drug digitalis. ● Genus *Digitalis*, family Scrophulariaceae: many species, in particular *D. purpurea*.

foxglove

fox grape ▸ n. a wild grape-bearing vine native to the eastern US. Also called LABRUSCA, ISABELLA.

fox·hole /ˈfäksˌhōl/ ▸ n. a hole in the ground used by troops as a shelter against enemy fire or as a firing point. ■ a place of refuge or concealment.

fox·hound /ˈfäksˌhound/ ▸ n. a dog of a smooth-haired breed with drooping ears, often trained to hunt foxes in packs over long distances.

fox hunt·ing ▸ n. the sport of hunting a fox across country with a pack of hounds by a group of people on foot and horseback, a traditional sport of the English landed gentry.
– DERIVATIVES **fox hunt·er** n.

fox·tail /ˈfäksˌtāl/ ▸ n. a common meadow grass that has soft brushlike flowering spikes. ● Genus *Alopecurus*, family Gramineae: several species, in particular *A. pratensis*.

fox ter·ri·er ▸ n. a terrier of a short-haired or wire-haired breed originally used for unearthing foxes.

fox·trot /ˈfäksˌträt/ ▸ n. **1** a ballroom dance in 4/4 time, with alternation of two slow and two quick steps. ■ a piece of music written for such a dance. **2** a code word representing the letter F, used in radio communication.
▸ v. (**foxtrots, foxtrotting, foxtrotted**) [no obj.] perform such a ballroom dance.

Fox·woods /ˈfäksˌwo͝odz/ a gambling resort on the Mashantucket Pequot reservation in the town of Ledyard in southeastern Connecticut, north of New London.

fox·y /ˈfäksē/ ▸ adj. (**foxier, foxiest**) resembling or likened to a fox: *a terrier with a foxy expression.* ■ informal cunning or sly in character. ■ informal (chiefly of a woman) sexually attractive. ■ reddish brown in color. ■ (of wine) having a musky flavor. ■ (of paper or other material) marked with spots; foxed.
– DERIVATIVES **fox·i·ly** /ˈfäksəlē/ adv., **fox·i·ness** n.

fo·ya·ite /ˈfoiyəˌīt/ ▸ n. a kind of syenite.

foy·er /ˈfoiər, ˈfoiˌā/ ▸ n. an entrance hall or other open area in a building used by the public, esp. a hotel or theater. ■ an entrance hall in a house or apartment.
– ORIGIN late 18th cent. (denoting the center of attention or activity): from French, 'hearth, home,' based on Latin *focarius* 'kitchen servant,' from *focus* 'domestic hearth.'

Foyt /foit/, A. J. (1935–) US race car driver; full name *Anthony Joseph Foyt, Jr.* He won the Indianapolis 500 four times 1961, 1964, 1967, 1977.

fp ▸ abbr. ■ (**FP**) Fabricated Plate. ■ fireplace. ■ forte-piano. ■ freezing point.

FPC ▸ abbr. ■ Federal Power Commission. ■ fish protein concentrate. ■ Friends Peace Committee.

fpl ▸ abbr. fireplace.

fpm ▸ abbr. feet per minute.

FPO ▸ abbr. ■ Field post office. ■ Fleet post office.

fps (also **f.p.s.**) ▸ abbr. ■ feet per second. ■ foot-pound-second. ■ frames per second.

FPU ▸ abbr. Computing floating-point unit, a processor that performs arithmetic operations.

Fr. ▸ abbr. ■ Father (as a courtesy title of priests): *Fr. Buckley*. [from French *frère*, literally 'brother.'] ■ France. ■ French. ■ Friday. ▸ symbol the chemical element francium.

fr. ▸ abbr. franc(s).

Fra /frä/ ▸ n. a prefixed title given to an Italian monk or friar: *Fra Angelico*.
– ORIGIN Italian, abbreviation of *frate* 'brother,' from Latin *frater*.

frab·jous /ˈfrabjəs/ ▸ adj. humorous delightful; joyous: *"Oh frabjous day!" she giggled.*
– DERIVATIVES **frab·jous·ly** adv.
– ORIGIN 1871: coined by Lewis Carroll in *Through the Looking Glass*, apparently to suggest *fair* and *joyous*.

fra·cas /ˈfrākəs, ˈfrak-/ ▸ n. (pl. **fracases**) a noisy disturbance or quarrel.
– ORIGIN early 18th cent.: French, from *fracasser*, from Italian *fracassare* 'make an uproar.'

frac·tal /ˈfraktəl/ Mathematics ▸ n. a curve or geometric figure, each part of which has the same statistical character as the whole. Fractals are useful in modeling structures (such as eroded coastlines or snowflakes) in which similar patterns recur at progressively smaller scales, and in describing partly random or chaotic phenomena such as crystal growth, fluid turbulence, and galaxy formation.
▸ adj. relating to or of the nature of a fractal or fractals: *fractal geometry*.
– ORIGIN 1970s: from French, from Latin *fract-* 'broken,' from the verb *frangere*.

frac·tion /ˈfrakSHən/ ▸ n. **1** a numerical quantity that is not a whole number (e.g., ½, 0.5). ■ a small or tiny part, amount, or proportion of something: *he hesitated for a fraction of a second | her eyes widened a fraction.* ■ a dissenting group within a larger one. ■ each of the portions into which a mixture may be separated by a process in which the individual components behave differently according to their physical properties.
2 (usu. **the Fraction**) (in the Christian Church) the breaking of the Eucharistic bread.
– ORIGIN late Middle English: via Old French from ecclesiastical Latin *fractio(n-)* 'breaking (bread),' from Latin *frangere* 'to break.'

frac·tion·al /ˈfrakSHənl/ ▸ adj. of, relating to, or expressed as a numerical value that is not a whole number, esp. a fraction less than one. ■ small or tiny in amount: *there was a fractional hesitation before he said yes.* ■ Chemistry relating to or denoting the separation of components of a mixture by making use of their differing physical properties: *fractional crystallization*.
– DERIVATIVES **frac·tion·al·ly** adv.

frac·tion·al dis·til·la·tion ▸ n. Chemistry separation of a liquid mixture into fractions differing in boiling point (and hence chemical composition) by means of distillation, typically using a fractionating column.

frac·tion·al·ize /ˈfrakSHənlˌīz/ ▸ v. [with obj.] (usu. as adj. **fractionalized**) divide (someone or something) into separate groups or parts: *fractionalized consumer markets*.
– DERIVATIVES **frac·tion·al·i·za·tion** /ˌfrakSHənl-iˈzāSHən/ n.

frac·tion·ate /ˈfrakSHəˌnāt/ ▸ v. [with obj.] chiefly technical divide into fractions or components. ■ separate (a mixture) by fractional distillation.
– DERIVATIVES **frac·tion·a·tion** /ˌfrakSHəˈnāSHən/ n.

frac·tion·at·ing col·umn ▸ n. Chemistry a tall, horizontally subdivided or packed container for fractional distillation in which vapor passes upward and condensing liquid flows downward. The vapor becomes progressively enriched in more volatile components as it ascends, and the less volatile components become concentrated in the descending liquid, which can be drawn off.

frac·tious /ˈfrakSHəs/ ▸ adj. (typically of children) irritable and quarrelsome: *they fight and squabble like fractious children.* ■ (of a group or organization) difficult to control; unruly: *the fractious coalition of Social Democrats*.
– DERIVATIVES **frac·tious·ly** adv., **frac·tious·ness** n.
– ORIGIN late 17th cent.: from FRACTION, probably on the pattern of the pair *faction, factious*.

frac·ture /ˈfrakCHər/ ▸ n. **1** the cracking or breaking of a hard object or material: *bone density testing can predict the risk for fracture.* ■ a crack or break in a hard object or material, typically a bone or a body of rock: *a fracture of the left leg.* ■ the physical appearance of a freshly broken rock or mineral, esp. as regards the shape of the surface formed.
2 Phonetics the replacement of a simple vowel by a diphthong owing to the influence of a following sound, typically a consonant. ■ a diphthong substituted in this way.
▸ v. break or cause to break: [no obj.] *the stone has fractured* | [with obj.] *ancient magmas fractured by the forces of wind and ice.* ■ [with obj.] sustain a fracture of (a bone): (as adj. **fractured**) *she suffered a fractured skull.* ■ (with reference to an organization or other abstract thing) split or fragment so as to no longer function or exist: [no obj.] *the movement had fractured without his leadership.* ■ (as adj. **fractured**) (of speech or a language) broken.
– ORIGIN late Middle English: from French, or from Latin *fractura*, from *frangere* 'to break.'

frae /frā/ ▸ prep. Scottish from: *you better collect the tab frae the office.*

frag /frag/ military slang ▸ n. a hand grenade.
▸ v. (**frags, fragging, fragged**) [with obj.] deliberately kill (an unpopular senior officer), typically with a hand grenade.
– ORIGIN 1970s: from *fragmentation grenade*.

frag·ile /ˈfrajəl, -jīl/ ▸ adj. (of an object) easily broken or damaged. ■ flimsy or insubstantial; easily destroyed: *you have a fragile grip on reality.* ■ (of a person) not strong or sturdy; delicate and vulnerable.
– DERIVATIVES **frag·ile·ly** /ˈfrajə(l)lē/ adv.
– ORIGIN late 15th cent. (in the sense 'morally weak'): from Latin *fragilis*, from *frangere* 'to break.' The sense 'liable to break' dates from the mid 16th cent.

frag·ile X syn·drome ▸ n. Medicine an inherited condition characterized by an X chromosome that is abnormally susceptible to damage, esp. by folic acid deficiency. Affected individuals tend to be mentally handicapped.

fra·gil·i·ty /frəˈjilitē/ ▸ n. the quality of being easily broken or damaged: *osteoporosis is characterized by bone fragility.* ■ the quality of being delicate or vulnerable: *a film about the fragility of relationships | his emotional fragility*.

frag·ment ▸ n. /ˈfragmənt/ a small part broken or separated off something: *small fragments of pottery, glass, and tiles.* ■ an isolated or incomplete part of something: *Nathan remembered fragments of that conversation.*
▸ v. /ˈfragˌment/ break or cause to break into fragments: [no obj.] *his followers fragmented into sects.*

– DERIVATIVES **frag·men·tal** /fragˈmentl/ **adj.** (chiefly Geology).
– ORIGIN late Middle English: from French, or from Latin *fragmentum*, from *frangere* 'to break.'

frag·men·tar·y /ˈfragmənˌterē/ ▶ **adj.** consisting of small parts that are disconnected or incomplete: *excavations have revealed fragmentary remains of masonry.*
– DERIVATIVES **frag·men·tar·i·ly** /ˌfragmənˈterəlē/ **adv.**

frag·men·ta·tion /ˌfragmənˈtāSHən/ ▶ **n.** the process or state of breaking or being broken into small or separate parts: *the **fragmentation** of society into a collection of interest groups.* ■ Computing the storing of a file in separate areas of memory scattered throughout a hard disk.

frag·men·ta·tion bomb ▶ **n.** a bomb designed to break into small fragments as it explodes.

Fra·go·nard /ˌfragəˈnär/, Jean-Honoré (1732–1806), French painter in the rococo style. He is known for landscapes and for erotic canvases such as *The Progress of Love* (1771).

fra·grance /ˈfrāgrəns/ ▶ **n.** a pleasant, sweet smell: *the fragrance of fresh-ground coffee | the bushes fill the air with fragrance.* ■ a perfume or aftershave.
– DERIVATIVES **fra·granced** /ˈfrāgrənst/ **adj.**
– ORIGIN mid 17th cent.: from French, or from Latin *fragrantia*, from *fragrare* 'smell sweet.'

fra·gran·cy /ˈfrāgrənsē/ ▶ **n.** (pl. **fragrancies**) dated fragrance.

fra·grant /ˈfrāgrənt/ ▶ **adj.** having a pleasant or sweet smell.
– DERIVATIVES **fra·grant·ly adv.**
– ORIGIN late Middle English: from French, or from Latin *fragrant-* 'smelling sweet,' from the verb *fragrare*.

'fraid /frād/ ▶ **v.** informal nonstandard contraction of "afraid" or "I'm afraid," expressing regret: *'fraid not, doll.*

fraid·y cat /ˈfrādē ˌkat/ ▶ **n.** a child's term for a timid or fearful person, often used as a taunt when addressed to another child.

frail /frāl/ ▶ **adj.** (of a person) weak and delicate: *a frail voice | she looked frail and vulnerable.* ■ easily damaged or broken; fragile or insubstantial: *the balcony is frail | the frail Russian economy.* ■ weak in character or morals.
– DERIVATIVES **frail·ly** /ˈfrā(l)lē/ **adv.**, **frail·ness n.**
– ORIGIN Middle English: from Old French *fraile*, from Latin *fragilis* (see **FRAGILE**).

frail·ty /ˈfrāltē/ ▶ **n.** (pl. **frailties**) the condition of being weak and delicate: *the increasing frailty of old age.* ■ weakness in character or morals: *all drama begins with human frailty | you're too self-righteous to see your own frailties.*
– ORIGIN Middle English (in the sense 'weakness in morals'): from Old French *frailete*, from Latin *fragilitas*, from *fragilis* (see **FRAGILE**).

fraise[1] /frāz/ ▶ **n.** (pl. **same**) (in cooking) a strawberry.
– ORIGIN French, from Latin *fraga* 'wild strawberries.'

fraise[2] ▶ **n. 1** a fortification with sharpened stakes projecting outward.
2 a decorative ruff worn at the neck, esp. in Elizabethan era fashion.

Frak·tur /fräkˈto͝or/ ▶ **n.** a German style of black-letter type.
– ORIGIN late 19th cent.: German, from Latin *fractura* 'fracture' (because of its angularity).

fram·be·sia /framˈbēZH(ē)ə/ ▶ **n.** another term for **YAWS**.
– ORIGIN early 19th cent.: modern Latin, from French *framboise* 'raspberry,' so named because of the red swellings caused by the disease, likened to raspberries.

fram·boise /fränˈbwäz/ ▶ **n.** (in cooking) a raspberry.
– ORIGIN late 16th cent.: French, 'raspberry,' from a conflation of Latin *fraga ambrosia* 'ambrosial strawberry.'

frame /frām/ ▶ **n. 1** a rigid structure that surrounds or encloses something such as a door or window. ■ (**frames**) a metal or plastic structure holding the lenses of a pair of glasses. ■ a case or border enclosing a mirror or picture. ■ the rigid supporting structure of an object such as a vehicle, building, or piece of furniture. ■ a person's body with reference to its size or build: *a shiver shook her slim frame.* ■ a boxlike structure of glass or plastic in which seeds or young plants are grown. ■ [in sing.] archaic or literary the universe, or part of it, regarded as an embracing structure. ■ [in sing.] archaic or literary the structure, constitution, or nature of someone or something: *we have in our inward frame various affections.*
2 [usu. in sing.] a basic structure that underlies or supports a system, concept, or text: *the establishment of conditions provides a frame for interpretation.* ■ technical short for **FRAME OF REFERENCE**: *the Earth's motion relative to the frame of the distant galaxies.* ■ the genre or form of a literary text determining its expected style and content: *my poems look as though they have a classical frame.* ■ [often as modifier] an enclosing section of narrative, esp. one which foregrounds or comments on the primary narrative of a text: *a frame narrator reports the narrative spoken by an inner narrator.*
3 Linguistics a structural environment within which a class of words or other linguistic units can be correctly used. For example *I —— him* is a frame for a large class of transitive verbs.
4 a single complete picture in a series forming a movie, television, or video film. ■ a single picture in a comic strip. ■ Computing a graphic panel in a display window, esp. in an Internet browser, that encloses a self-contained section of data and permits multiple independent document viewing.
5 another term for **RACK**[1] (sense 4 of the noun). ■ a round of play in bowling. ■ informal an inning in a baseball game: *he closed out the game by pitching two hitless frames.*
6 short for **FRAME-UP**.
▶ **v.** [with obj.] **1** place (a picture or photograph) in a frame: *he had the photo framed.* ■ surround so as to create a sharp or attractive image: *a short, strong style cut to frame the face.*
2 erect the framework of a building.
3 create or formulate (a concept, plan, or system): *the staff have proved invaluable in framing the proposals.* ■ form or articulate (words): *he walked out before she could frame a reply.* ■ archaic make or construct (something) by fitting parts together or in accordance with a plan: *what immortal hand or eye could frame thy fearful symmetry?*
4 informal produce false evidence against (an innocent person) so that they appear guilty: *he claims he was framed.*
– PHRASES **frame of mind** a particular mood that influences one's attitude or behavior.
– DERIVATIVES **frame·a·ble** /-məbəl/ **adj.**, **frame·less adj.**, **fram·er n.**
– ORIGIN Old English *framian* 'be useful,' of Germanic origin and related to **FROM**. The general sense in Middle English, 'make ready for use,' probably led to sense 2 of the verb; it also gave rise to the specific meaning 'prepare timber for use in building,' later 'make the wooden parts of a building,' essentially the framework, hence the noun sense 'structure' (late Middle English).

framed /frāmd/ ▶ **adj. 1** (of a picture or similar) held in a frame: *a framed photograph of her father.*
2 [in combination] (of a building) having a frame of a specified material: *a traditional **oak-framed** house.*

frame house ▶ **n.** a house constructed from a wooden skeleton, typically covered with sheathing.

frame of ref·er·ence ▶ **n.** a set of criteria or stated values in relation to which measurements or judgments can be made: *the observer interprets what he sees in terms of his own cultural frame of reference.* ■ (also **reference frame**) a system of geometric axes in relation to which measurements of size, position, or motion can be made.

frame saw ▶ **n.** a saw with a thin blade kept rigid by being stretched in a frame.

frame-up ▶ **n.** [in sing.] informal a conspiracy to falsely incriminate someone.

frame·work /ˈfrāmˌwərk/ ▶ **n.** an essential supporting structure of a building, vehicle, or object: *a conservatory in a delicate framework of iron.* ■ a basic structure underlying a system, concept, or text: *the theoretical framework of political sociology.*

fram·ing /ˈfrāmiNG/ ▶ **n.** the action of framing something. ■ frames collectively.

Fra·ming·ham /ˈfrāmiNGˌham/ an industrial and commercial town in eastern Massachusetts; pop. 64,885 (est. 2008).

franc /franGk/ ▶ **n.** the basic monetary unit of Switzerland and several other countries (including France, Belgium, and Luxembourg until the introduction of the euro), equal to 100 centimes.
– ORIGIN from Old French, from Latin *Francorum Rex* 'king of the Franks,' the legend on gold coins struck in the 14th cent. in the reign of Jean le Bon.

Fran·ca /ˈfränGkə/ an industrial and commercial city in southern Brazil, in São Paulo state; pop. 319,100 (est. 2007).

France[1] /frans, fräNs/ a country in western Europe, on the Atlantic Ocean; pop. 64,420,100 (est. 2009); capital, Paris; official language, French.

France became a major power under the Valois and Bourbon dynasties in the 16th–18th centuries and briefly dominated Europe under Napoleon after the overthrow of the monarchy in the French Revolution 1789. Defeated in the Franco-Prussian War 1870–71, the country also suffered much destruction and loss of life in World War I, and during World War II was occupied by the Germans. France was a founding member of the EEC (now the EU) in 1957.

France[2] /frans/, Anatole (1844–1924), French writer; pseudonym of *Jacques-Anatole-François Thibault*. Works include *Le Crime de Sylvestre Bonnard* (1881), *L'Ile des pingouins* (1908), and *Les Dieux ont soif* (1912). Nobel Prize for Literature (1921).

fran·chise /ˈfranˌCHīz/ ▶ **n. 1** an authorization granted by a government or company to an individual or group enabling them to carry out specified commercial activities, e.g., providing a broadcasting service or acting as an agent for a company's products. ■ a business or service given such authorization to operate. ■ a general title or concept used for creating or marketing a series of products, typically films or television shows: *the Harry Potter franchise.* ■ (chiefly in North America) an ownership structure in professional sports in which a league is limited to a fixed number of teams. ■ an authorization given by a league to own a sports team. ■ informal a professional sports team. ■ (also **franchise player**) informal a star player on a team.
2 (usu. **the franchise**) the right to vote. ■ the rights of citizenship.
▶ **v.** [with obj.] grant a franchise to (an individual or group). ■ grant a franchise for the sale of (goods) or the operation of (a service): *all the catering was franchised out.*
– DERIVATIVES **fran·chi·see** /ˌfranˌCHīˈzē/ **n.**, **fran·chis·er** (also **franchisor** /ˌfranCHəˈzôr/) **n.**
– ORIGIN Middle English (denoting a grant of legal immunity): from Old French, based on *franc*, *franche* 'free' (see **FRANK**[1]). Sense 2 of the noun dates from the late 18th cent. and sense 1 of the noun from the 20th cent.

WORD TRENDS Nowadays a successful movie is rarely just a movie—studios hope their productions will spawn lucrative spin-offs in the form of toys, games, books, DVDs, and, of course, sequels. Such film series are known as **franchises**, borrowing and extending the term used for a proven business model licensed for use by others, such as fast-food restaurants. The Oxford English Corpus shows that **franchise** is increasingly used in the cinematic sense, with common collocates representing familiar Hollywood brands such as *James Bond, Star Trek, Batman*, and *Harry Potter*. A hint of cynicism is creeping in, however, with the sense that franchises are often little more than manufactured moneymaking schemes: *a greedy franchise that doesn't care to develop its characters beyond their punchlines | he managed to milk the franchise on screen for nearly a decade.*

Fran·cis /ˈfransis/, Dick (1920–), English jockey and writer; full name *Richard Stanley Francis*. He was a champion jockey who, after his retirement in 1957, began to write thrillers, mostly set in the world of horse racing.

Fran·cis I (1494–1547), king of France 1515–47. Much of his reign 1521–44 was spent at war with Charles V of Spain. A supporter of the arts, he commissioned the building of the Louvre.

Fran·cis·can /franˈsiskən/ ▶ **n.** a friar, sister, or lay member of a Christian religious order founded in 1209 by St. Francis of Assisi, or of an order based on Franciscan rule. The Franciscan orders are noted for preachers and missionaries.

Divergences of practice led to the separation of the Friars Minor of the Observance (the Observants) and the Friars Minor Conventual (the Conventuals) in 1517, and to the foundation of the stricter Friars Minor Capuchin (the Capuchins) in 1529. The order of Franciscan nuns was founded by St. Clare (*c.*1212) under the direction of St. Francis; they are known as 'Poor Clares.'.

▶ **adj.** of, relating to, or denoting St. Francis or the Franciscans.
– ORIGIN from French *franciscain*, from modern Latin *Franciscanus*, from *Franciscus* 'Francis.'

Fran·cis of As·si·si, St. (*c.*1181–1226), Italian monk; founder of the Franciscan order 1209; born

f

Giovanni di Bernardone. He drew up the original rule, based on complete poverty, of the Franciscan order. He is the patron saint of animals. Feast day, October 4.

Fran·cis of Sales, St. /säl/ (1567–1622), French bishop. A leader of the Counter-Reformation, he was bishop of Geneva 1602–22. The Salesian order (founded in 1859) is named after him. Feast day, January 24.

Fran·cis Xa·vi·er, St., see **XAVIER, ST. FRANCIS**.

fran·ci·um /ˈfransēəm/ ▶ **n.** the chemical element of atomic number 87, a radioactive member of the alkali metal group. Francium occurs naturally as a decay product in uranium and thorium ores. (Symbol: **Fr**)
– ORIGIN 1940s: from **FRANCE**[1] (the discoverer's native country) + **-IUM**.

Franck[1] /frängk/, César (Auguste) (1822–90), French composer and organist; born in Belgium. Notable works: *Symphonic Variations* (1885), the D minor Symphony (1886–88), and the *String Quartet* (1889).

Franck[2], James (1882–1964), US physicist; born in Germany. He worked on the bombardment of atoms by electrons and became involved in the US atom bomb project. He advocated the explosion of the bomb in an uninhabited area to demonstrate its power to Japan.

Fran·co /ˈfrangkō/, Francisco (1892–1975), Spanish general and dictator; head of state 1939–75. Leader of the Nationalists in the Spanish Civil War, he became head of the Falange Party in 1937 and proclaimed himself *Caudillo* ("leader") of Spain. With the defeat of the republic in 1939, he took control of the government and established a dictatorship that ruled Spain until his death.

Francisco Franco

Franco- (also **franco-**) ▶ **comb. form** French; French and ...: *francophone* | *Franco-German*. ■ relating to France.
– ORIGIN from medieval Latin *Francus* 'Frank.'

fran·co·lin /ˈfrangkəlin/ ▶ **n.** a large game bird resembling a partridge, with bare skin on the head or neck, found in Africa and southern Asia. ● Genus *Francolinus*, family Phasianidae: many species.
– ORIGIN mid 17th cent.: from French, from Italian *francolino*, of unknown origin.

Fran·co·ni·a /frangˈkōnēə/ a medieval duchy in southern Germany, inhabited by the Franks.

Fran·co·ni·an /franˈkōnēən/ ▶ **adj.** of or relating to Franconia or its inhabitants.
▶ **n. 1** a native or inhabitant of Franconia.
2 a group of medieval West Germanic dialects, combining features of Low and High German. ■ the group of modern German dialects of Franconia.

Fran·co·nia Notch /frangˈkōnēə/ a valley in the White Mountains of northern New Hampshire, noted for its scenery, including a rock formation called the Old Man of the Mountains.

Fran·co·phile /ˈfrangkəˌfīl/ ▶ **n.** a person who is fond of or greatly admires France or the French.

fran·co·phone /ˈfrangkəˌfōn/ (also **Francophone**) ▶ **adj.** French-speaking: *a summit of francophone countries*.
▶ **n.** a person who speaks French.
– ORIGIN early 20th cent.: from **FRANCO-** 'French' + Greek *phōnē* 'voice.'

Fran·co-Prus·sian War /ˈfrangkō/ the war of 1870–71 between France (under Napoleon III) and Prussia, in which Prussian troops advanced into France and decisively defeated the French at Sedan. The defeat marked the end of the French Second Empire. For Prussia, the proclamation of the new German Empire at Versailles was the climax of Bismarck's ambitions to unite Germany.

fran·gi·ble /ˈfranjəbəl/ ▶ **adj.** formal fragile; brittle.
– ORIGIN late Middle English: from Old French, or from medieval Latin *frangibilis*, from Latin *frangere* 'to break.'

fran·gi·pane /ˈfranjəˌpān, ˌfränjiˈpän/ ▶ **n. 1** an almond-flavored cream or paste. ■ a pastry filled with this.
2 variant spelling of **FRANGIPANI**.
– ORIGIN late 17th cent.: from French, named after the Marquis Muzio *Frangipani* (see **FRANGIPANI**). The term originally denoted the frangipani shrub or tree, the perfume of which is said to have been used to flavor the almond cream.

fran·gi·pan·i /ˌfranjəˈpanē, -ˈpänē/ (also **frangipane**) ▶ **n.** (pl. **same** or **frangipanis**) a tropical American tree or shrub with clusters of fragrant white, pink, or yellow flowers. ● Genus *Plumeria*, family Apocynaceae: several species, in particular *P. rubra*.
■ perfume obtained from this plant.
– ORIGIN mid 19th cent.: named after the Marquis Muzio *Frangipani*, a 16th-cent. Italian nobleman who invented a perfume for scenting gloves.

fran·glais /fränˈglā/ (also **Franglaise** /-ˈglāz/) ▶ **n.** a form of French using many words and idioms borrowed from English.
– ORIGIN 1960s: coined in French, from a blend of *français* 'French' and *anglais* 'English.'

Frank[1] /frangk/, Anne (1929–45), German Jewish girl noted for her diary (*The Diary of a Young Girl*, 1953) that records the experiences of her family, who hid from the Nazis for two years in occupied Amsterdam. They were eventually betrayed and sent to concentration camps; Anne died in the concentration camp at Belsen.

Frank[2] ▶ **n.** a member of a Germanic people that conquered Gaul in the 6th century and controlled much of western Europe for several centuries afterward. ■ (in the eastern Mediterranean region) a person of western European nationality or descent.
– ORIGIN Old English *Franca*, of Germanic origin; perhaps from the name of a weapon and related to Old English *franca* 'javelin' (compare with **SAXON**); reinforced in Middle English by medieval Latin *Francus* and Old French *Franc*, of the same origin and related to **FRENCH**[1].

frank[1] /frangk/ ▶ **adj.** open, honest, and direct in speech or writing, esp. when dealing with unpalatable matters: *a long and frank discussion* | *to be perfectly frank, I don't know*. ■ open, sincere, or undisguised in manner or appearance: *Katherine saw her look at Sam with frank admiration*. ■ Medicine unmistakable; obvious: *frank ulceration*.
– DERIVATIVES **frank·ness** n.
– ORIGIN Middle English (in the sense 'free'): from Old French *franc*, from medieval Latin *francus* 'free,' from *Francus* (see **FRANK**[2]: only Franks had full freedom in Frankish Gaul). Another Middle English sense was 'generous,' which led to the current sense.

frank[2] ▶ **v.** [with obj.] stamp an official mark on (a letter or parcel), esp. to indicate that postage has been paid or does not need to be paid. ■ historical sign (a letter or parcel) to ensure delivery free of charge. ■ archaic facilitate or pay the passage of (someone): *English will frank the traveler through most of North America*.
▶ **n.** an official mark or signature on a letter or parcel, esp. to indicate that postage has been paid or does not need to be paid. [formerly as a superscribed signature of an eminent person entitled to send letters free of charge.]
– DERIVATIVES **frank·er** n.
– ORIGIN early 18th cent.: from **FRANK**[1], an early sense being 'free of obligation.'

frank[3] ▶ **n.** short for **FRANKFURTER**.

Fran·ken·fish /ˈfrangkənˌfish/ ▶ **n.** informal **1** a genetically modified fish.
2 the northern snakehead, so dubbed for its voracious appetite and ability to survive adverse conditions.
– ORIGIN from *Franken(stein)* and *fish*.

Frank·en·food /ˈfrangkənˌfōōd/ ▶ **n.** informal, derogatory genetically modified food: *a cornucopia of pesticide-laden monocrops and lab-engineered Frankenfoods*.
– ORIGIN 1990s: from *Franken(stein)* + *food*.

Frank·en·stein /ˈfrangkənˌstīn/ a character in the novel *Frankenstein, or the Modern Prometheus* (1818) by Mary Shelley. Baron Frankenstein is a scientist who creates and brings to life a manlike monster that eventually turns on him and destroys him. ■ (also **Frankenstein's monster**) [as noun] a thing that becomes terrifying or destructive to its maker.

Frank·fort /ˈfrangkfərt/ the capital of Kentucky, in the northern part of the state; pop. 27,322 (est. 2008).

Frank·furt /ˈfrangkfərt, ˈfrängkˌfōōrt/ a commercial city in western Germany, in the state of Hesse; pop. 652,600 (est. 2006). Full name **Frankfurt am Main**.

Frank·fur·ter /ˈfrangkˌfərtər/, Felix (1882–1965), US Supreme Court associate justice 1939–62; born in Austria. He was a founder of the American Civil Liberties Union in 1920 and was awarded the Presidential Medal of Freedom in 1963.

frank·furt·er /ˈfrangkfərtər, -ˌfərtər/ ▶ **n.** a seasoned smoked sausage typically made of beef and pork.
– ORIGIN from German *Frankfurter Wurst* 'Frankfurt sausage.'

Frank·furt School a school of philosophy of the 1920s whose adherents were involved in a reappraisal of Marxism, particularly in terms of the cultural and aesthetic dimension of modern industrial society. Principal figures include Theodor Adorno, Max Horkheimer, and Herbert Marcuse.

frank·in·cense /ˈfrangkənˌsens/ ▶ **n.** an aromatic gum resin obtained from an African tree and burned as incense. Also called **OLIBANUM, GUM OLIBANUM**.
● This resin is obtained from the tree *Boswellia sacra*, family Burseraceae, native to Somalia.
– ORIGIN late Middle English: from Old French *franc encens*, literally 'high-quality incense,' from *franc* (see **FRANK**[1]) in an obsolete sense 'superior, of high quality' (which also existed in English) + *encens* 'incense.'

frank·ing /ˈfrangking/ ▶ **n.** the action of franking a letter or parcel: [as modifier] *a franking machine*. ■ an official mark or signature on a letter or parcel to indicate that postage has been paid or does not need to be paid.

Frank·ish /ˈfrangkish/ ▶ **adj.** of or relating to the ancient Franks or their language.
▶ **n.** the West Germanic language of the ancient Franks.

Frank·lin[1] /ˈfrangklin/, Aretha (1942–), US soul and gospel singer. She became a hit with the album *I Never Loved a Man (the Way I Love You)* (1967) and went on to record more than 30 albums, including the live gospel set *Amazing Grace* (1972) and *A Rose Is Still a Rose* (1998).

Aretha Franklin

Frank·lin[2], Benjamin (1706–90), American statesman, inventor, and scientist. He was the only individual to sign all three principal documents of the new nation: the Declaration of Independence, the treaty with Great Britain that ended the American Revolution, and the US Constitution. His main scientific achievements were the formulation of a theory of electricity, which introduced positive and negative electricity, and a demonstration of the electrical nature of lightning, which led to the invention of the lightning conductor.

Benjamin Franklin

frank·lin /ˈfrangklən/ ▶ **n.** a landowner of free but not noble birth in the 14th and 15th centuries in England.

–ORIGIN Middle English: from Anglo-Latin *francalanus*, from *francalis* 'held without dues,' from *francus* 'free' (see FRANK¹).

Frank·lin stove ▶ n. a cast-iron stove for heating a room, resembling an open fireplace in shape.
–ORIGIN late 18th cent.: named after Benjamin *Franklin*.

Franklin stove

frank·ly /ˈfraNGklē/ ▶ adv. in an open, honest, and direct manner: *she talks very frankly about herself.* ■ [sentence adverb] used to emphasize the truth of a statement, however unpalatable or shocking this may be: *frankly, I was pleased to leave.*

USAGE See usage at HOPEFULLY.

fran·tic /ˈfrantik/ ▶ adj. wild or distraught with fear, anxiety, or other emotion: *she was frantic with worry.* ■ conducted in a hurried, excited, and chaotic way, typically because of the need to act quickly: *frantic attempts to resuscitate the girl.*
–DERIVATIVES **fran·ti·cal·ly** /-(ə)lē/ adv., **fran·tic·ness** n.
–ORIGIN late Middle English *frentik* 'insane, violently mad,' from Old French *frenetique* (see FRENETIC).

Franz Jo·sef /ˌfränz ˈjōzəf, ˌfränts ˈyōzəf/ (1830–1916), emperor of Austria 1848–1916 and king of Hungary 1867–1916. He gave Hungary equal status with Austria in 1867. His annexation of Bosnia and Herzegovina in 1908 contributed to European political tensions, and the assassination in Sarajevo of his heir apparent, **Archduke Franz Ferdinand**, precipitated World War I.

Franz Jo·sef Land /land, länt/ a group of islands in the Arctic Ocean, discovered in 1873 by an Austrian expedition and annexed by the former Soviet Union in 1928.

frap /frap/ ▶ v. (**fraps, frapping, frapped**) [with obj.] Nautical bind (something) tightly.
–ORIGIN Middle English (in the sense 'strike, beat,' now only dialect): from Old French *fraper* 'to bind, strike,' of unknown origin. The current sense dates from the mid 16th cent.

frap·pé¹ /fraˈpā/ ▶ adj. [postpositive] (of a drink) iced or chilled: *a crème de menthe frappé.*
▶ n. a drink served with ice or frozen to a slushy consistency. ■ (usu. **frappe** /frap/) (chiefly in New England) a milk shake, esp. one made with ice cream.
–ORIGIN mid 19th cent.: French, literally 'iced.'

frap·pé² ▶ adj. [postpositive] Ballet (of a position) involving a beating action of the toe of one foot against the ankle of the supporting leg: *a battement frappé.*
–ORIGIN mid 19th cent.: French, literally 'struck.'

Fras·cat·i /fräsˈkätē/ ▶ n. a wine, typically white, produced in the region of Frascati, Italy.

Fra·ser /ˈfrāzər, ˈfrāZHər/ a river in British Columbia, Canada. It rises in the Rocky Mountains and flows in a wide curve for 850 miles (1,360 km) into the Strait of Georgia, just south of Vancouver.

Fras·er fir ▶ n. a North American fir tree, occurring primarily in the mountains of Virginia, Tennessee, and North Carolina. ● *Abies fraseri*, family Pinaceae.

frass /fras/ ▶ n. fine powdery refuse or fragile perforated wood produced by the activity of boring insects. ■ the excrement of insect larvae.
–ORIGIN mid 19th cent.: from German *Frass*, from *fressen* 'devour.'

frat /frat/ ▶ n. [usu. as modifier] informal a students' fraternity: *a frat party.*
–ORIGIN late 19th cent.: abbreviation.

frat boy ▶ n. informal a young man who behaves in a boisterous or foolish manner considered typical of members of some college fraternities.

fra·ter /ˈfrātər/ ▶ n. historical the dining room or refectory of a monastery.
–ORIGIN Middle English: from Old French *fraitur*, shortening of *refreitor*, from late Latin *refectorium* 'refectory.'

fra·ter·nal /frəˈtərnl/ ▶ adj. **1** of or like a brother or brothers: *his lack of fraternal feeling shocked me.* ■ of or denoting an organization or order for people, esp. men, that have common interests or beliefs.
2 (of twins) developed from separate ova and therefore genetically distinct and not necessarily of the same sex or more similar than other siblings. Compare with IDENTICAL (sense 1).
–DERIVATIVES **fra·ter·nal·ism** /-ˌizəm/ n., **fra·ter·nal·ly** adv.
–ORIGIN late Middle English: from medieval Latin *fraternalis*, from Latin *fraternus*, from *frater* 'brother.'

fra·ter·ni·ty /frəˈtərnətē/ ▶ n. (pl. **fraternities**) **1** [treated as sing. or pl.] a group of people sharing a common profession or interests: *members of the hunting fraternity.* ■ a male students' society in a university or college. ■ a religious or Masonic society or guild.
2 the state or feeling of friendship and mutual support within a group: *the ideals of liberty, equality, and fraternity.*
–ORIGIN Middle English: from Old French *fraternite*, from Latin *fraternitas*, from *fraternus* (see FRATERNAL).

frat·er·nize /ˈfratərˌnīz/ ▶ v. [no obj.] associate or form a friendship with someone, esp. when one is not supposed to: *she ignored Elisabeth's warning glare against* ***fraternizing with the enemy.***
–DERIVATIVES **frat·er·ni·za·tion** /ˌfratərniˈzāSHən/ n.
–ORIGIN early 17th cent.: from French *fraterniser*, from medieval Latin *fraternizare*, from Latin *fraternus* 'brotherly' (see FRATERNAL).

frat·ri·cid·al /ˌfratrəˈsīdl/ ▶ adj. relating to or denoting conflict within a single family or organization: *the fratricidal strife within the party.*

frat·ri·cide /ˈfratrəˌsīd/ ▶ n. the killing of one's brother or sister. ■ a person who kills their brother or sister. ■ the accidental killing of one's own forces in war.
–ORIGIN late 15th cent. (denoting a person who kills their brother or sister, derived from Latin *fratricida*): the primary current sense comes via French from late Latin *fratricidium*, from *frater* 'brother' + *-cidium* (see -CIDE).

Frau /frou/ ▶ n. (pl. **Frauen** /ˈfrou-ən/) a title or form of address for a married or widowed German-speaking woman: *Frau Nordern.*
–ORIGIN early 19th cent.: German, literally 'wife.'

fraud /frôd/ ▶ n. wrongful or criminal deception intended to result in financial or personal gain: *he was convicted of fraud | prosecutions for social security frauds.* ■ a person or thing intended to deceive others, typically by unjustifiably claiming or being credited with accomplishments or qualities: *mediums exposed as tricksters and frauds.*
–DERIVATIVES **fraud·ster** n.
–ORIGIN Middle English: from Old French *fraude*, from Latin *fraus, fraud-* 'deceit, injury.'

fraud·u·lent /ˈfrôjələnt/ ▶ adj. obtained, done by, or involving deception, esp. criminal deception: *the fraudulent copying of American software.* ■ unjustifiably claiming or being credited with particular accomplishments or qualities: *he unmasked fraudulent psychics.*
–DERIVATIVES **fraud·u·lence** n., **fraud·u·lent·ly** adv.
–ORIGIN late Middle English: from Old French, or from Latin *fraudulentus*, from *fraus, fraud-* 'deceit, injury.'

fraught /frôt/ ▶ adj. **1** [predic.] (**fraught with**) (of a situation or course of action) filled with or destined to result in (something undesirable): *marketing any new product is fraught with danger.*
2 causing or affected by great anxiety or stress: *there was a fraught silence | she sounded a bit fraught.*
–ORIGIN late Middle English, 'laden, provided, equipped,' past participle of obsolete *fraught* 'load with cargo,' from Middle Dutch *vrachten*, from *vracht* 'ship's cargo.' Compare with FREIGHT.

Fräu·lein /ˈfroiˌlīn/ ▶ n. a title or form of address for an unmarried German-speaking woman, esp. a young woman: *Fräulein Winkelmann.*
–ORIGIN German, diminutive of FRAU.

Fraun·ho·fer /ˈfrounˌhōfər/, Joseph von (1787–1826), German optician; a pioneer in spectroscopy. He observed and mapped the dark lines in the solar spectrum (**Fraunhofer lines**) that result from the absorption of particular frequencies of light by elements present in the outer layers of the sun.

frax·i·nel·la /ˌfraksəˈnelə/ ▶ n. another term for GAS PLANT.
–ORIGIN mid 17th cent.: modern Latin (former specific epithet), diminutive of Latin *fraxinus* 'ash tree' (because of its leaves, thought to resemble those of the ash).

fray¹ /frā/ ▶ v. [no obj.] (of a fabric, rope, or cord) unravel or become worn at the edge, typically through constant rubbing: *cheap fabric soon frays* | (as adj. **frayed**) *the frayed collar of her old coat.* ■ (of a person's nerves or temper) show the effects of strain. ■ [with obj.] (of a male deer) rub (a bush or small tree) with the head in order to remove the velvet from newly formed antlers, or to mark territory during the rut.
–ORIGIN late Middle English: from Old French *freiier*, from Latin *fricare* 'to rub.'

fray² ▶ n. (**the fray**) a situation of intense activity, typically one incorporating an element of aggression or competition: *nineteen companies intend to bid for the contract, with three more expected to* ***enter the fray.*** ■ a battle or fight.
–ORIGIN late Middle English: from archaic *fray* 'to quarrel,' from *affray* 'startle,' from Anglo-Norman French *afrayer* (see AFFRAY).

frayed /frād/ ▶ adj. (of a fabric, rope, or cord) unraveled or worn at the edge: *the frayed collar of her old coat.* ■ (of a person's nerves or temper) showing the effects of strain: *an effort to soothe frayed nerves.*

Fra·zier /ˈfrāZHər/, Joe (1944–), US heavyweight boxing champion; full name *Joseph Frazier*. He first won the world title in 1968, lost it to George Foreman in 1973, and subsequently lost to Muhammad Ali twice before retiring in 1976.

fra·zil /ˈfrazəl, frəˈzil/ (also **frazil ice**) ▶ n. soft or amorphous ice formed by the accumulation of ice crystals in water that is too turbulent to freeze solid.
–ORIGIN late 19th cent.: from Canadian French *frasil* 'snow floating in the water,' from French *fraisil* 'cinders.'

fraz·zle /ˈfrazəl/ informal ▶ v. [with obj.] (usu. as adj. **frazzled**) cause to feel completely exhausted; wear out: *a frazzled parent.* ■ fray: *change the skirt if it gets frazzled* | figurative *it's enough to frazzle the nerves.*
▶ n. (**a frazzle**) the state of being completely exhausted or worn out: *I'm tired,* ***worn to a frazzle.***
–ORIGIN early 19th cent. (originally dialect): perhaps a blend of FRAY¹ and obsolete *fazle* 'ravel out,' of Germanic origin.

FRB ▶ abbr. ■ Federal Reserve Bank. ■ Federal Reserve Board.

FRCP ▶ abbr. Fellow of the Royal College of Physicians.

FRCS ▶ abbr. Fellow of the Royal College of Surgeons.

freak /frēk/ ▶ n. **1** a very unusual and unexpected event or situation: *the teacher says the accident was a total freak* | [as modifier] *a freak storm.*
2 (also **freak of nature**) a person, animal, or plant with an unusual physical abnormality. ■ informal a person regarded as strange because of their unusual appearance or behavior.
3 [with modifier] informal a person who is obsessed with or unusually enthusiastic about a specified interest: *a fitness freak.* ■ [usu. with modifier] informal a person addicted to a drug of a particular kind: *the twins were cocaine freaks.*
4 archaic a sudden arbitrary change of mind; a whim: *follow this way or that, as the freak takes you.*
▶ v. **1** informal behave or cause to behave in a wild and irrational way, typically because of the effects of extreme emotion, mental illness, or drugs: [no obj.] *I could have* ***freaked out*** *and started smashing the place up* | [with obj.] *he freaks guest stars out on show day.*
2 [with obj.] archaic fleck or streak randomly: *the white pink and the pansy freaked with jet.*

freak·ing /ˈfrēkən, -kiNG/ ▶ adj. informal used as a euphemism for FUCKING: *I'm going out of my freaking mind!*

freak·ish /ˈfrēkiSH/ ▶ adj. bizarre or grotesque; abnormal: *freakish and mischievous elves.* ■ capricious or whimsical; unpredictable: *freakish weather.*
–DERIVATIVES **freak·ish·ly** adv., **freak·ish·ness** n.

freak-out ▶ n. informal a wildly irrational reaction or spell of behavior.

freak show ▶ n. a sideshow at a fair, featuring abnormally developed people or animals. ■ an

f

unusual or grotesque event viewed for pleasure, esp. when in bad taste.

freak·y /ˈfrēkē/ ▶ **adj.** (**freakier, freakiest**) informal very odd, strange, or eccentric.
– DERIVATIVES **freak·i·ly** /-kəlē/ **adv.**, **freak·i·ness n.**

freck·le /ˈfrekəl/ ▶ **n.** a small patch of light brown color on the skin, often becoming more pronounced through exposure to the sun.
▶ **v.** cover or become covered with freckles: [no obj.] *skin that freckles easily* | (as adj. **freckled**) *a freckled face.*
– DERIVATIVES **freck·ly** /ˈfrekl-ē, ˈfreklē/ **adj.**
– ORIGIN late Middle English: alteration of dialect *frecken*, from Old Norse *freknur* (plural).

freck·le-faced ▶ **adj.** having freckles on the face (often used to suggest innocence or wholesomeness): *a freckle-faced schoolboy who never lost the merriment of his youth.*

Fred·die Mac /ˈfredē ˈmak/ informal name for the Federal Home Loan Mortgage Corporation, a corporation that trades in mortgages.
– ORIGIN 1970s: loosely from the initial letters of *Federal Home Loan Mortgage Corporation*, on the model of **FANNIE MAE**.

Fred·er·ick /ˈfred(ə)rik/ a city in northern Maryland; pop. 59,213 (est. 2008).

Fred·er·ick I /ˈfred(ə)rik/ (c.1123–90), king of Germany and Holy Roman Emperor 1152–90; known as **Frederick Barbarossa** ("Redbeard"). He made a sustained effort to subdue Italy and the papacy, but was eventually defeated at the battle of Legnano in 1176.

Fred·er·ick II (1712–86), king of Prussia 1740–86; known as **Frederick the Great**. His campaigns in the War of the Austrian Succession 1740–48 and the Seven Years War 1756–63 succeeded in considerably strengthening Prussia's position; by the end of his reign he had doubled the area of his country.

Fred·er·icks·burg /ˈfred(ə)riks,bərg/ a historic commercial city in northeastern Virginia, on the Rappahannock River; pop. 22,818 (est. 2008).

Fred·er·ick Wil·liam (1620–88), elector of Brandenburg 1640–88; known as **the Great Elector**. His program of reconstruction and reorganization following the Thirty Years War brought stability to his country and laid the foundation for the expansion of Prussian power in the 18th century.

Fred·er·ic·ton /ˈfredriktən/ the capital of New Brunswick, Canada; pop. 50,535 (2006). The city was founded in 1785 by colonists who left the US after the American Revolution out of loyalty to the British crown.
– ORIGIN named after *Frederick* Augustus (1763–1827), second son of the British king George III.

free /frē/ ▶ **adj.** (**freer** /ˈfrēər/, **freest** /ˈfrēəst/)
1 not under the control or in the power of another; able to act or be done as one wishes: *I have no ambitions other than to have a happy life and be free* | *a free choice.* ■ (of a state or its citizens or institutions) subject neither to foreign domination nor to despotic government: *a free press.* ■ [often as complement] not or no longer confined or imprisoned: *the researchers set the birds free.* ■ historical not a slave. ■ [with infinitive] able or permitted to take a specified action: *you are free to leave.* ■ [in names] denoting an ethnic or political group actively opposing an occupying or invading force, in particular the groups that continued resisting the Germans in World War II after the fall of their countries. See also **FREE FRENCH**.
2 [often as complement] not physically restrained, obstructed, or fixed; unimpeded: *she lifted the cat free.* ■ Physics (of power or energy) disengaged or available. See also **FREE ENERGY**. ■ Physics & Chemistry not bound in an atom, a molecule, or a compound: *the atmosphere of that time contained virtually no free oxygen.* See also **FREE RADICAL**. ■ Linguistics (of a morpheme) able to occur in isolation.
3 not subject to or constrained by engagements or obligations: *she spent her free time shopping.* ■ (of a facility or piece of equipment) not occupied or in use: *the bathroom was free.*
4 [predic.] (**free of/from**) not subject to or affected by (a specified thing, typically an undesirable one): *membership is free of charge.*
5 given or available without charge: *free health care.*
6 using or expending something without restraint; lavish: *she was always free with her money.* ■ frank or unrestrained in speech, expression, or action: *he was free in his talk of revolution.* ■ archaic overfamiliar or forward in manner.
7 (of a literary style) not observing the strict laws of form. ■ (of a translation) conveying only the broad sense; not literal.
8 Sailing (of the wind) blowing from a favorable direction to the side or stern of a vessel.
▶ **adv. 1** without cost or payment: *ladies were admitted free.*
2 Sailing with the sheets eased.
▶ **v.** (**frees, freed, freeing**) [with obj.] release from captivity, confinement, or slavery: *they were freed from jail.* ■ release from physical obstruction, restraint, or entanglement: *I had to tug hard and at last freed him.* ■ remove something undesirable or restrictive from: *his inheritance freed him from financial constraints* | *free your mind and body of excess tension.* ■ make available for a particular purpose: *this will free up funds for development elsewhere.*
– PHRASES **for free** informal without cost or payment: *these professionals were giving their time for free.* **free and easy** informal and relaxed. **free, gratis, and for nothing** humorous without charge. **a free hand** freedom to act at one's own discretion. **free on board** (abbr.: **f.o.b.**) including or assuming delivery without charge to the buyer's named destination. **(a) free rein** see **REIN**. **a free ride** a situation in which someone benefits without having to make a fair contribution: *people have been having a free ride, paying so little rent that there is no money for maintenance.* **the free world** the noncommunist countries of the world, as formerly opposed to the Soviet bloc. **it's a free country** said when asserting that a course of action is not illegal or forbidden, often in justification of it. **make free with** treat without ceremony or proper respect: *he'll have something to say about your making free with his belongings.*
– DERIVATIVES **free·ness n.**
– ORIGIN Old English *frēo* (adjective), *frēon* (verb), of Germanic origin; related to Dutch *vrij* and German *frei*, from an Indo-European root meaning 'to love,' shared by **FRIEND**.

> **USAGE** Free means 'without charge,' and a *gift* is 'something given without charge.' The expression "free gift" is therefore a needless repetition.

-free ▶ **comb. form** free of or from: *smoke-free* | *tax-free.*
– ORIGIN from **FREE**.

free a·gent ▶ **n.** a person who does not have any commitments that restrict their actions. ■ a sports player who is not bound by a contract and so is eligible to join any team.

free a·long·side ship (abbr.: **FAS**) ▶ **adv.** without charge for delivery to the boarding area next to a ship, but with the understanding that the buyer is responsible for the item once it is so delivered.

free as·so·ci·a·tion ▶ **n. 1** Psychology the mental process by which one word or image may spontaneously suggest another without any apparent connection. ■ a psychoanalytic technique for investigation of the unconscious mind, in which a relaxed subject reports all passing thoughts without reservation.
2 the forming of a group, political alliance, or other organization without any constraint or external restriction: *it would violate their First Amendment rights of free association and free expression.*
– DERIVATIVES **free-as·so·ci·ate v.** (sense 1).

free·base /ˈfrē,bās/ (also **freebase cocaine**) ▶ **n.** cocaine that has been converted from its salt to its base form by heating with ether or boiling with sodium bicarbonate, taken by inhaling the fumes or smoking the residue.
▶ **v.** [with obj.] prepare or take (cocaine) in such a way.

free·bie /ˈfrēbē/ (also **freebee**) ▶ **n.** informal a thing given free of charge.
– ORIGIN 1940s: an arbitrary formation from **FREE**.

free·board /ˈfrē,bôrd/ ▶ **n.** the height of a ship's side between the waterline and the deck.

free·boot·er /ˈfrē,bo͞otər/ ▶ **n.** a pirate or lawless adventurer.
– DERIVATIVES **free·boot v.**
– ORIGIN late 16th cent.: from Dutch *vrijbuiter*, from *vrij* 'free' + *buit* 'booty,' + the noun suffix *-er*. Compare with **FILIBUSTER**.

free·born /ˈfrē,bôrn/ ▶ **adj.** not born in slavery.

Free Church ▶ **n.** a Christian Church that has dissented or seceded from an established Church.

free climb·ing ▶ **n.** rock climbing without the assistance of devices such as pegs placed in the rock, but occasionally using ropes and belays. Compare with **AID CLIMBING**.
– DERIVATIVES **free climb n. & v.**

freed·man /ˈfrēdmən, -ˌman/ ▶ **n.** (pl. **freedmen**) historical an emancipated slave.

free·dom /ˈfrēdəm/ ▶ **n.** the power or right to act, speak, or think as one wants without hindrance or restraint: *we do have some freedom of choice* | *he talks of revoking some of the freedoms.* ■ absence of subjection to foreign domination or despotic government: *he was a champion of Irish freedom.* ■ the state of not being imprisoned or enslaved: *the shark thrashed its way to freedom.* ■ the state of being physically unrestricted and able to move easily: *the shorts have a side split for freedom of movement.* ■ (**freedom from**) the state of not being subject to or affected by (a particular undesirable thing): *government policies to achieve freedom from want.* ■ the power of self-determination attributed to the will; the quality of being independent of fate or necessity. ■ unrestricted use of something: *the dog is happy having the freedom of the house when we are out.* ■ archaic familiarity or openness in speech or behavior.
– ORIGIN Old English *frēodōm* (see **FREE, -DOM**).

free·dom fight·er ▶ **n.** a person who takes part in a violent struggle to achieve a political goal, esp. in order to overthrow their government.

free·dom march ▶ **n.** a march organized as a demonstration of protest against a political entity for its oppressive policies, which are often directed at a specific group such as a minority.

free·dom of con·science ▶ **n.** the right to follow one's own beliefs in matters of religion and morality.

free·dom of re·li·gion ▶ **n.** the right to practice whatever religion one chooses.

free·dom of speech (also **free speech**) ▶ **n.** the right to express any opinions without censorship or restraint.

free·dom of the seas ▶ **n.** the right of merchant ships to move freely on the seas in peace or war without interference except in territorial zones.

free·dom rid·er ▶ **n.** a person who challenged racial laws in the American South in the 1960s, originally by refusing to abide by the laws designating that seating in buses be segregated by race.

Free·dom Trail a walking tour in Boston, Massachusetts, that takes visitors past historic sites relating to the American Revolution.

free en·er·gy ▶ **n.** Physics a thermodynamic quantity equivalent to the capacity of a system to do work.

free en·ter·prise ▶ **n.** an economic system in which private business operates in competition and largely free of state control.

free fall ▶ **n.** downward movement under the force of gravity only: *the path of a body in free fall.* ■ the part of a parachute-descent before the parachute opens. ■ the movement of a spacecraft in space without thrust from the engines.
▶ **v.** (**free-fall**) [no obj.] move under the force of gravity only; fall rapidly.

free fire zone ▶ **n.** a military combat zone in which there are no restrictions on the use of fire power. ■ an area of activity apparently without rules.

free flight ▶ **n.** the flight of a spacecraft, rocket, or missile when the engine is not producing thrust.

free-float·ing ▶ **adj. 1** not attached to anything and able to move freely: *free-floating aquatic plants.* ■ not assigned to a fixed or particular position, category, or level: *free-floating exchange rates.* ■ (of a person) not committed to a particular cause or political party.
2 Psychiatry (of anxiety) chronic and generalized, without an obvious cause.
– DERIVATIVES **free-float v.**, **free-float·er n.**

free-for-all ▶ **n.** a disorganized or unrestricted situation or event in which everyone may take part, esp. a fight, discussion, or trading market.

free-form ▶ **adj.** not conforming to a regular or formal structure or shape: *a free-form jazz improvisation.*

Free French ▶ **plural n.** an organization of French troops and volunteers in exile formed under General de Gaulle in 1940. Based in London, the movement organized forces that opposed the Axis powers in French Equatorial Africa, Lebanon, and elsewhere, and cooperated with the French Resistance.

free·hand /ˈfrē,hand/ ▶ **adj. & adv.** (esp. with reference to drawing) done manually without the aid of instruments such as rulers: [as adj.] *a freehand sketch* | [as adv.] *the pictures should be drawn freehand.*

free-hand·ed ▶ **adj.** generous, esp. with money.
– DERIVATIVES **free-hand·ed·ly adv.**, **free-hand·ed·ness n.**

free·hold /ˈfrē,hōld/ ▶ **n.** permanent and absolute tenure of land or property with freedom to dispose of it at will. Often contrasted with **LEASEHOLD**. ■ (**the freehold**) the ownership of a piece of land or property by such tenure. ■ a piece of land or property held by such tenure.

▸ **adj.** held by or having the status of freehold.
– DERIVATIVES **free·hold·er** n.

free jazz ▸ **n.** an improvised style of jazz characterized by the absence of set chord patterns or time patterns.

free kick ▸ **n.** (in soccer and rugby) an unimpeded kick of the stationary ball awarded to one side as a penalty for a foul or infringement by the other side.

free·lance /ˈfrēˌlans/ ▸ **adj.** working for different companies at different times rather than being permanently employed by one company: *a freelance journalist.* ■ independent or uncommitted in politics or personal life.
▸ **adv.** earning one's living in such a way: *I work freelance from home.*
▸ **n. 1** a person who earns their living in such a way. **2** historical (often **free lance**) a medieval mercenary.
▸ **v.** [no obj.] earn one's living as a freelance.
– ORIGIN early 19th cent. (denoting a mercenary): originally as two words.

free·lanc·er /ˈfrēˌlansər/ ▸ **n.** a person who works freelance.

free-liv·ing ▸ **adj. 1** freely indulging in pleasures, esp. that of eating; having an unrestricted or independent lifestyle.
2 Biology living freely and independently, not as a parasite or attached to a substrate.

free·load·er /ˈfrēˌlōdər/ ▸ **n.** informal a person who takes advantage of others' generosity without giving anything in return.
– DERIVATIVES **free·load** /ˈfrēˌlōd/ v.

free love ▸ **n.** the idea or practice of having sexual relations according to choice, without being restricted by marriage or other long-term relationships.

free·ly /ˈfrēlē/ ▸ **adv.** not under the control of another; as one wishes: *I roamed freely.* ■ without restriction or interference: *air can freely circulate.* ■ in copious or generous amounts: *she drank freely to keep up her courage.* ■ openly and honestly: *you may speak freely.* ■ willingly and readily; without compulsion: *I freely confess to this failing.*

free·man /ˈfrēmən, -ˌman/ ▸ **n.** (pl. **freemen**) **1** a person who is entitled to full political and civil rights.
2 historical a person who is not a slave or serf.

free mar·ket ▸ **n.** an economic system in which prices are determined by unrestricted competition between privately owned businesses.
– DERIVATIVES **free mar·ket·eer** (also **free-marketeer**) n.

free·mar·tin /ˈfrēˌmärtn/ ▸ **n.** a hermaphrodite or imperfect sterile female calf that is the twin of a male calf whose hormones affected its development.
– ORIGIN late 17th cent.: of unknown origin.

Free·ma·son /ˈfrēˈmāsən/ ▸ **n.** a member of an international order established for mutual help and fellowship, which holds elaborate secret ceremonies.

> The original **freemasons** were itinerant skilled stonemasons of the 14th century, who are said to have recognized fellow craftsmen by secret signs. Modern Freemasonry is usually traced to the formation of the Grand Lodge in London in 1717; members are typically professionals and businessmen.

Free·ma·son·ry /ˈfrēˈmāsənrē/ ▸ **n. 1** the system and institutions of the Freemasons.
2 (**freemasonry**) instinctive sympathy or fellow feeling between people with something in common: *the unshakable freemasonry of actors in a crisis.*

free pass ▸ **n.** an authorization of free admission or travel.

free path see MEAN FREE PATH.

Free·port /ˈfrēˌpôrt/ **1** a port city in the northern Bahamas, on Grand Bahama Island; pop. 44,300 (est. 2009).
2 a commercial village in the town of Hempstead on Long Island in New York; pop. 43,881 (est. 2008).

free port ▸ **n.** a port open to all traders. ■ a port area where goods in transit are exempt from customs duty.

fre·er /ˈfrēər/ ▸ **adj.** comparative of FREE.
▸ **n.** rare a person or agent who frees or sets free someone or something.

free rad·i·cal ▸ **n.** Chemistry an uncharged molecule (typically highly reactive and short-lived) having an unpaired valence electron.

free-range ▸ **adj.** (of livestock, esp. poultry) kept in natural conditions, with freedom of movement. ■ (of eggs) produced by birds reared under such conditions.

free safe·ty ▸ **n.** Football a defensive back who is usually free from an assignment to cover a particular player on the offensive team.

free·sia /ˈfrēZHə/ ▸ **n.** a small southern African plant of the iris family, with fragrant, colorful, tubular flowers, many varieties of which are cultivated for use by florists. ● Genus *Freesia*, family Iridaceae.
– ORIGIN modern Latin, named after Friedrich H. T. *Freese* (died 1876), German physician.

free sil·ver ▸ **adj.** denoting a US political movement for the free coinage of silver, esp. that of the last quarter of the nineteenth century.

free skat·ing ▸ **n.** the sport of performing variable skating figures and jumps to music.
– DERIVATIVES **free skate** n.

free speech ▸ **n.** another term for FREEDOM OF SPEECH.

free spir·it ▸ **n.** an independent or uninhibited person: *they raised their children to be free spirits.*

free-spo·ken ▸ **adj.** archaic speaking candidly and openly.

fre·est /ˈfrēəst/ ▸ **adj.** superlative of FREE.

free·stand·ing /ˈfrēˈstandiNG/ ▸ **adj.** not supported by another structure. ■ not relying on or linked to anything else; independent: *if extracts rather than complete texts are used, they should be freestanding and coherent.*

Free State ▸ **n. 1** historical (before the Civil War) a state of the US in which slavery was illegal. ■ (**the Free State**) a nickname for the state of MARYLAND.
2 a province in central South Africa, situated to the north of the Orange River; capital, Bloemfontein. Formerly called (until 1995) ORANGE FREE STATE.

free·stone /ˈfrēˌstōn/ ▸ **n. 1** rock that can be cut easily in any direction, in particular a fine-grained sandstone or limestone of uniform texture. [from Old French *franche pere* 'excellent rock.']
2 a stone fruit in which the pit is easily separated from the flesh when the fruit is ripe: [as modifier] *freestone peaches.* Contrasted with CLINGSTONE.

free·style /ˈfrēˌstīl/ ▸ **adj.** denoting a contest or version of a sport in which there are few restrictions on the moves or techniques that competitors employ: *freestyle wrestling.*
▸ **n.** a contest of such a kind, in particular a swimming race in which competitors may use any stroke.
– DERIVATIVES **free·styl·er** n.

free-swim·ming ▸ **adj.** Zoology (of an aquatic animal) not attached to an object or substrate and able to swim freely.

free-tailed bat (also **freetail bat**) ▸ **n.** a streamlined fast-flying insectivorous bat with a projecting tail, found in tropical and subtropical countries. ● Family Molossidae: several genera and numerous species, including the mastiff bats and hairless bats.

free·think·er /ˈfrēˈTHiNGkər/ ▸ **n.** a person who rejects accepted opinions, esp. those concerning religious belief.
– DERIVATIVES **free·think·ing** n. & adj.

free throw ▸ **n.** Basketball an unimpeded attempt at a basket (worth one point) awarded to a player following a foul or other infringement.

free-throw line (also **free throw line**) ▸ **n.** Basketball another term for FOUL LINE.

free-to-air ▸ **adj.** denoting or relating to television programs broadcast on standard public or commercial networks, as opposed to subscription satellite or cable.

Free·town /ˈfrēˌtoun/ the capital and chief port of Sierra Leone; pop. 827,000 (est. 2007).

free trade ▸ **n.** international trade left to its natural course without tariffs, quotas, or other restrictions.

free u·ni·ver·si·ty ▸ **n.** a nontraditional educational program of courses often taught by nonprofessionals as an alternative to traditional academic programs, usually offered without prerequisites at low cost or at no cost.

free verse ▸ **n.** poetry that does not rhyme or have a regular meter. Also called VERS LIBRE.

free·ware /ˈfrēˌwe(ə)r/ ▸ **n.** software that is available free of charge.

free·way /ˈfrēˌwā/ ▸ **n.** an express highway, esp. one with controlled access. ■ a toll-free highway.

free weight ▸ **n.** a weight used in weightlifting that is not attached to an apparatus.

free·wheel /ˈfrēˌ(h)wēl/ ▸ **v.** [no obj.] ride a bicycle with the pedals at rest, esp. downhill: *he had come freewheeling down the road.* ■ (usu. as adj. **freewheeling**) act without concern for rules, conventions, or the consequences of one's actions: *the freewheeling drug scene of the sixties.*
▸ **n.** a device that allows a bicycle wheel to revolve forward while the crank is stationary. ■ a device in a motor vehicle transmission allowing the drive shaft to spin faster than the engine.

free will ▸ **n.** the power of acting without the constraint of necessity or fate; the ability to act at one's own discretion.
▸ **adj.** [attrib.] (esp. of a donation) given readily; voluntary: *free-will offerings.*

freeze /frēz/ ▸ **v.** (past **froze** /frōz/; past participle **frozen** /ˈfrōzən/) **1** [no obj.] (of a liquid) be turned into ice or another solid as a result of extreme cold: *in the winter the milk froze.* ■ [with obj.] turn (a liquid) into ice or another solid in such a way. ■ (of something wet or containing liquid) become blocked, covered, or rigid with ice: *the pipes had frozen.* ■ [with obj.] cause (something wet or containing liquid) to become blocked, covered, or rigid with ice: [with complement] *the ground was frozen hard.* ■ be or feel so cold that one is near death (often used hyperbolically): *you'll freeze to death standing there.* ■ [with obj.] (of the weather) cause (someone) to feel so cold that they are near death. ■ (of the weather) be at or below freezing: *at night it froze again.* ■ [with obj.] deprive (a part of the body) of feeling, esp. by the application of a chilled anesthetic substance. ■ [with obj.] treat (someone) with a cold manner; stare coldly at (someone): *she would freeze him with a look when he tried to talk to her.*
2 [with obj.] store (something) at a very low temperature in order to preserve it: *the cake can be frozen.* ■ [no obj.] (of food) be able to be preserved in such a way: *this soup freezes well.*
3 [no obj.] become suddenly motionless or paralyzed with fear or shock: *Mathewson froze on the spot, unable to take the next step.* ■ stop moving when ordered or directed.
4 [with obj.] hold (something) at a fixed level or in a fixed state for a period of time: *new spending on defense was to be frozen.* ■ prevent (assets) from being used for a period of time: *the charity's bank account has been frozen.* ■ stop (a moving image) at a particular frame when filming or viewing: *the camera will set fast shutter speeds to freeze the action.* ■ [no obj.] (of a computer screen) become temporarily locked because of system problems.
▸ **n. 1** an act of holding or being held at a fixed level or in a fixed state: *workers faced a pay freeze.* ■ short for FREEZE-FRAME.
2 a period of frost or very cold weather: *the big freeze surprised the weathermen.*
– PHRASES **freeze one's blood** (or **one's blood freezes**) fill (or be filled) with a sudden feeling of great fear or horror.
– PHRASAL VERBS **freeze someone out** informal behave in a hostile or obstructive way so as to exclude someone from something.
– DERIVATIVES **freez·a·ble** /-zəbəl/ adj.
– ORIGIN Old English *frēosan* (in the phrase *hit frēoseth* 'it is freezing, it is so cold that water turns to ice'), of Germanic origin; related to Dutch *vriezen* and German *frieren*, from an Indo-European root shared by Latin *pruina* 'hoarfrost' and FROST.

freeze-dry ▸ **v.** [with obj.] (usu. as adj. **freeze-dried**) preserve (something) by rapidly freezing it and then subjecting it to a high vacuum that removes ice by sublimation: *freeze-dried beef stew.*

freeze-frame ▸ **n.** the facility of stopping a film or videotape in order to view a motionless image. ■ a motionless image obtained with such a facility.
▸ **v.** [with obj.] use such a facility on (an image or a recording).

freeze-out ▸ **n.** informal an exclusion of a person or organization from something, by boycotting or ignoring them.

freez·er /ˈfrēzər/ ▸ **n.** a refrigerated compartment, cabinet, or room for preserving food at very low temperatures. ■ a device for making frozen desserts such as ice cream or sherbet.

freeze-up ▸ **n.** a period of extreme cold. ■ the freezing over of a body of water such as a lake or river: *until freeze-up, the caribou stay near the lake.*

freez·ing /ˈfrēziNG/ ▸ **adj.** below 32°F (0°C): *strong winds and freezing temperatures.* ■ (used hyperbolically) very cold: *he was freezing and miserable* | [as submodifier] *it was freezing cold outside.* ■ (of fog or rain) consisting of droplets that freeze rapidly on contact with a surface to form ice.
▸ **n.** the freezing point of water: *the temperature was well above freezing.*

freez·ing point ▸ **n.** the temperature at which a liquid turns into a solid when cooled.

f

Fre·ge /ˈfrāgə/, Gottlob (1848–1925), German philosopher and mathematician; founder of modern logic.

Frei·burg /ˈfrībərg, -ˌbo͝ork/ an industrial city in southwestern Germany, in the state of Baden-Württemberg, on the edge of the Black Forest; pop. 220,600 (est. 2009). Full name **Freiburg im Breisgau**.

freight /frāt/ ▶ **n. 1** goods transported by truck, train, ship, or aircraft. ■ the transport of goods by truck, train, ship, or aircraft. ■ a charge for such transport.
2 (in full **freight train**) a train of freight cars: *sugar and molasses moving by freight*.
3 a load or burden.
▶ **v.** [with obj.] transport (goods) in bulk by truck, train, ship, or aircraft: *the metals had been freighted from the city* | [no obj.] *ships freighting to Dublin*.
■ (**be freighted with**) be laden or imbued with (something abstract): *each word was freighted with anger*.
– DERIVATIVES **freight·ing** /ˈfrātiNG/ **n.**
– ORIGIN late Middle English (in the sense 'rental of a ship for transporting goods'): from Middle Dutch, Middle Low German *vrecht*, variant of *vracht* 'ship's cargo.' Compare with FRAUGHT.

freight·age /ˈfrātij/ ▶ **n.** the carrying of goods in bulk. ■ goods carried in bulk; freight.

freight car ▶ **n.** a railroad car for carrying freight.

freight·er /ˈfrātər/ ▶ **n.** a ship or aircraft designed to carry goods in bulk. ■ a person who loads, receives, or forwards goods for transport.

freight ton ▶ **n.** see TON[1] (sense 1).

Fre·li·mo /freˈlēmō/ the nationalist liberation party of Mozambique, founded in 1962. After independence in 1975, Frelimo governed Mozambique as a one-party state until 1990, when a multiparty system was introduced.
– ORIGIN Portuguese, contraction of *Frente de Libertação de Moçambique*, the name of the party.

Fre·man·tle /ˈfrēˌmantl/ a city in southwestern Australia, in the state of Western Australia, the port for Perth; pop. 27,453 (2008).

Fre·mont /ˈfrēˌmänt/ an industrial and commercial city in north central California, south of Oakland, off San Francisco Bay; pop. 202,867 (est. 2008).

Fré·mont /ˈfrēˌmänt/, John Charles (1813–90), US explorer and politician. He explored several viable routes to the Pacific Ocean across the Rocky Mountains in the 1840s. During the Mexican War 1846–48, he fought to win California. In 1856, he unsuccessfully opposed James Buchanan for the presidency.

French[1] /frenCH/ ▶ **adj.** of or relating to France or its people or language.
▶ **n. 1** the Romance language of France, also used in parts of Belgium, Switzerland, and Canada, in several countries of northern and western Africa and the Caribbean, and elsewhere.
2 Brit. short for FRENCH VERMOUTH.
3 (as plural noun **the French**) the people of France collectively.

> French is the first or official language of over 200 million people and is widely used as a second language. It is a Romance language that developed from the Latin spoken in Gaul, the northern dialects becoming dominant after Paris became the capital in the 10th century. French became widely used owing to the cultural influence and colonial expansion of France from the 11th century, and it had a very great influence on English as the language of the Norman ruling class.

– PHRASES (**if you'll**) **excuse** (or **pardon**) **my French** informal used to apologize for swearing.
– DERIVATIVES **French·ness n.**
– ORIGIN Old English *Frencisc*, of Germanic origin, from the base of FRANK[2].

French[2] /frenCH/, Daniel Chester (1850–1931), US sculptor. Among his works are the statue of the Minute Man 1873 at Concord, Massachusetts, and the seated figure of Abraham Lincoln 1922 in the Lincoln Memorial in Washington, DC.

French and In·di·an War North American war (1754–63) between France and Great Britain.

> France's Canadian colonies and American Indian allies were pitted against Britain and its American colonies. The beginning of these hostilities became the prelude to and major cause of the Seven Years War and marked the onset of George Washington's rise to prominence. The conflict ended with the Treaty of Paris; Britain won nearly all of French North America.

French braid ▶ **n.** a hairstyle in which all the hair is gathered into one large braid down the back of the head, starting from the forehead.
▶ **v.** (also **French-braid**) [with obj.] create such a hairstyle.

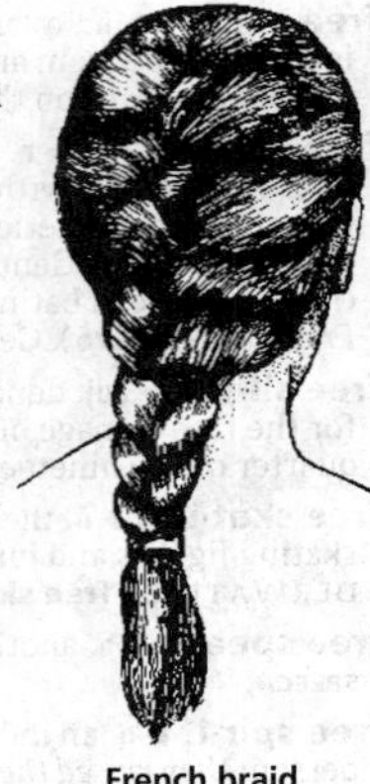
French braid

French bread ▶ **n.** white bread in a long, crisp loaf.

French Ca·na·di·an ▶ **n. 1** a Canadian whose principal language is French.
2 the form of French spoken in Canada.
▶ **adj.** of or relating to French-speaking Canadians or their language.

French chalk ▶ **n.** talc used for marking cloth and removing grease and, in powder form, as a dry lubricant.

French Con·go former name (until 1910) of FRENCH EQUATORIAL AFRICA.

French cuff ▶ **n.** a shirt cuff that is folded back before fastening, creating a double-layered cuff.

French curve ▶ **n.** a template used for drawing curved lines.

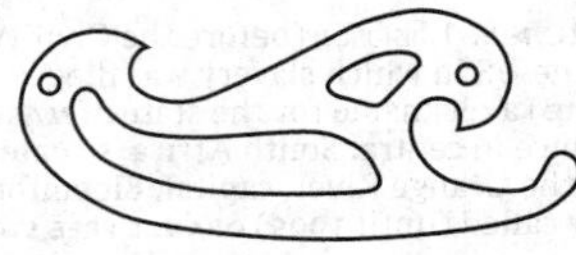
French curve

French-cut ▶ **adj. 1** Cooking sliced obliquely: *French-cut green beans*.
2 (of women's panties) cut so as to reveal much of the upper thigh.

French door ▶ **n.** a door with glass panes throughout its length. ■ a French window.

French doors

French dress·ing ▶ **n.** a salad dressing of vinegar, oil, and seasonings. ■ a sweet, creamy salad dressing commercially prepared from oil, tomato purée, and spices.

French E·qua·to·ri·al Af·ri·ca a former federation of French territories in west central Africa 1910–58. Previously called French Congo, its constituent territories were Chad, Ubanghi Shari (now the central African Republic), Gabon, and Middle Congo (now Congo).

French fries (also **French fried potatoes**) ▶ **plural n.** potatoes cut into strips and deep-fried.

French Gui·an·a /gēˈänə, gīˈanə/ an overseas department of France, in northern South America; pop. 202,000 (est. 2007); capital, Cayenne.

french heel ▶ **n.** a high, curved heel on a woman's shoe.

French horn ▶ **n.** a brass instrument with a coiled tube, valves, and a wide bell, developed from the simple hunting horn in the 17th century. It is played with the right hand in the bell to soften the tone and increase the range of available harmonics.

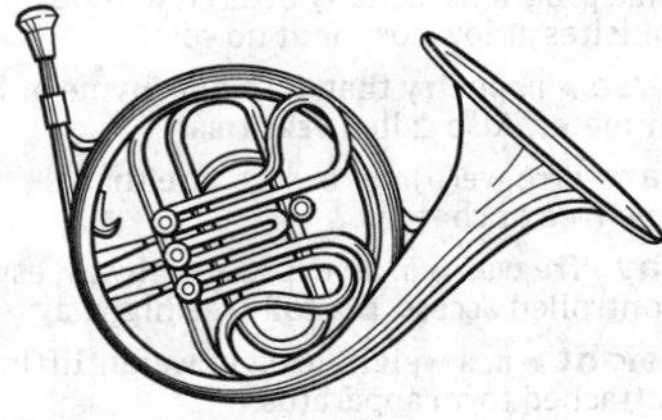
French horn

French·ie /ˈfrenCHē/ ▶ **n.** (pl. **Frenchies**) variant spelling of FRENCHY.

French·i·fy /ˈfrenCHiˌfī/ ▶ **v.** (**Frenchifies, Frenchifying, Frenchified**) [with obj.] (usu. as adj. **Frenchified**) often derogatory make French in form, character, or manners: *she pronounced it without the Frenchified accent*.

French kiss ▶ **n.** a kiss with contact between tongues.
– DERIVATIVES **French kiss·ing n.**

French knot ▶ **n.** (in embroidery) a stitch in which the thread is wound around the needle, which is then passed back through the fabric at almost the same point to form a small dot.

French leave ▶ **n.** informal, dated an unauthorized or unannounced departure; absence without permission: *he seems to have taken French leave*.
– ORIGIN mid 18th cent.: said to derive from the French custom of leaving a dinner or ball without saying goodbye to the host or hostess. The phrase was first recorded shortly after the Seven Years' War (1756–63); the equivalent French expression is *filer à l'Anglaise*, literally 'to escape in the style of the English.'

French let·ter ▶ **n.** Brit. informal a condom.

French·man /ˈfrenCHmən/ ▶ **n.** (pl. **Frenchmen**) a person, esp. a man, who is French by birth or descent.

French man·i·cure ▶ **n.** a style of manicure in which the fingernails are painted pale pink with a white band at the tip.

French pas·try ▶ **n.** a rich pastry, often with a filling of fruit or custard.

French pol·ish ▶ **n.** shellac polish that produces a high gloss on wood.
▶ **v.** [with obj.] treat (wood) with such a polish.

French Pol·y·ne·sia /ˌpäləˈnēZHə/ an overseas territory of France in the South Pacific; pop. 287,000 (est. 2009); capital, Papeete (on the island of Tahiti). French Polynesia includes the Society Islands, the Gambier Islands, the Tuamotu Archipelago, the Tubuai Islands, and the Marquesas. It was granted partial autonomy in 1977.

French Re·pub·li·can cal·en·dar ▶ **n.** a reformed calendar officially introduced by the French Republican government on October 5, 1793.

> The calendar was taken to have started on the equinox of September 22, 1792, the day of the proclamation of the Republic. It had twelve months of thirty days each, with five days of festivals at the year's end (six in leap years). The names of the months were Vendémiaire, Brumaire, Frimaire, Nivose, Pluviose, Ventose, Germinal, Floréal, Plairial, Messidor, Thermidor, and Fructidor. The new calendar was abandoned under the Napoleonic regime, and the Gregorian calendar was formally reinstated on January 1, 1806.

French Rev·o·lu·tion the overthrow of the Bourbon monarchy in France (1789–99).

> The French Revolution began with the meeting of the legislative assembly (the States General) in May 1789 when the French government was already in crisis; the Bastille was stormed in July of the same year. The revolution became steadily more radical and ruthless with power increasingly in the hands of the Jacobins and Robespierre; Louis XVI's execution in January 1793 was followed by Robespierre's Reign of Terror. The revolution failed to produce a stable form of republican government, and after several different forms of administration, the last, the Directory, was overthrown by Napoleon in 1799.

French roll ▶ **n. 1** a crisp roll of French bread.
2 another term for FRENCH TWIST.

French seam ▶ **n.** a seam with the raw edges enclosed.

French So·ma·li·land /səˈmäləˌland/ former name (until 1967) of DJIBOUTI.

French South·ern and Ant·arc·tic Ter·ri·to·ries an overseas territory of France, comprised of Adélie Land in Antarctica, the Kerguelen and Crozet archipelagos, and the islands of Amsterdam and St. Paul in the southern Indian Ocean.

French Su·dan former name of MALI.

French tick·ler ▶ **n.** informal a condom with ribbed protrusions.

French toast ▶ **n.** bread coated in egg and milk and fried.

French twist ▶ **n.** a hairstyle in which the hair is tucked into a vertical roll down the back of the head.

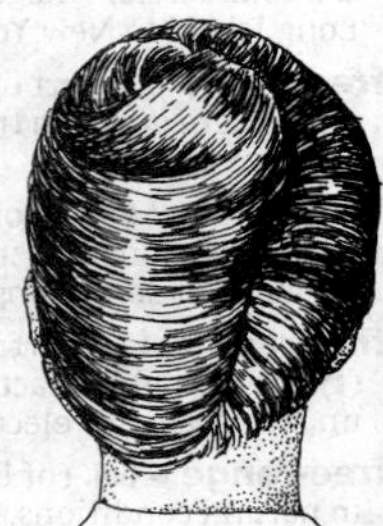
French twist

French ver·mouth ▶ **n.** dry vermouth.

French Wars of Re·li·gion a series of religious and political conflicts in France (1562–98) involving the Protestant Huguenots on one side and Catholic groups on the other. The wars were complicated by interventions from Spain, Rome, England, the Netherlands, and elsewhere, and were not brought to an end until the settlement of the Edict of Nantes.

French West Af·ri·ca a former federation of French territories in northwestern Africa 1895–1959. Its constituent territories were Senegal, Mauritania, French Sudan (now Mali), Upper Volta (now Burkina Faso), Niger, French Guinea (now Guinea), Côte d'Ivoire (Ivory Coast), and Dahomey (now Benin).

French win·dow ▶ n. (usu. **French windows**) each of a pair of casement windows extending to the floor in an outside wall, serving as a window and door.

French·wom·an /'frenCH,wo͝omən/ ▶ n. (pl. **Frenchwomen**) a female who is French by birth or descent.

French·y /'frenCHē/ (also **Frenchie**) ▶ adj. informal, chiefly derogatory perceived as characteristically French: *a perfect example of that kind of progressive Frenchy art.*
▶ n. (pl. **Frenchies**) **1** informal, chiefly derogatory a French person. ■ Canadian a French Canadian.
2 Brit. informal or dated short for FRENCH LETTER.

fren·e·my /'frenəmi/ ▶ n. (pl. **frenemies**) informal a person with whom one is friendly despite a fundamental dislike or rivalry.
– ORIGIN 1950s: blend of FRIEND and ENEMY.

fre·net·ic /frə'netik/ ▶ adj. fast and energetic in a rather wild and uncontrolled way: *a frenetic pace of activity.*
– DERIVATIVES **fre·net·i·cal·ly** /-ik(ə)lē/ adv.
– ORIGIN late Middle English (in the sense 'insane'): from Old French *frenetique*, via Latin from Greek *phrenitikos*, from *phrenitis* 'delirium,' from *phrēn* 'mind.' Compare with FRANTIC.

fren·u·lum /'frenyələm/ ▶ n. Anatomy a small fold or ridge of tissue that supports or checks the motion of the part to which it is attached, in particular a fold of skin beneath the tongue, or between the lip and the gum. ■ Entomology (in some moths and butterflies) a bristle or row of bristles on the edge of the hind wing that keeps it in contact with the forewing.
– ORIGIN early 18th cent.: modern Latin, diminutive of Latin *frenum* 'bridle.'

fre·num /'frēnəm/ ▶ n. another term for FRENULUM.
– ORIGIN mid 18th cent.: from Latin, literally 'bridle.'

fren·zied /'frenzēd/ ▶ adj. wildly excited or uncontrolled: *a frenzied attack.*
– DERIVATIVES **fren·zied·ly** adv.

fren·zy /'frenzē/ ▶ n. (pl. **frenzies**) [usu. in sing.] a state or period of uncontrolled excitement or wild behavior: *Doreen worked herself into a frenzy of rage.*
– ORIGIN Middle English: from Old French *frenesie*, from medieval Latin *phrenesia*, from Latin *phrenesis*, from Greek *phrēn* 'mind.'

Fre·on /'frē,än/ ▶ n. trademark an aerosol propellant, refrigerant, or organic solvent consisting of one or more of a group of chlorofluorocarbons and related compounds.
– ORIGIN 1930s: of unknown origin.

freq. ▶ abbr. ■ frequency. ■ frequent. ■ Grammar frequentative. ■ frequently.

fre·quen·cy /'frēkwənsē/ ▶ n. (pl. **frequencies**) **1** the rate at which something occurs or is repeated over a particular period of time or in a given sample: *shops have closed with increasing frequency during the period.* ■ the fact of being frequent or happening often. ■ Statistics the ratio of the number of actual to possible occurrences of an event. ■ Statistics the (relative) number of times something occurs in a given sample.
2 the rate at which a vibration occurs that constitutes a wave, either in a material (as in sound waves), or in an electromagnetic field (as in radio waves and light), usually measured per second. (Symbol: **f** or ν) ■ the particular waveband at which a radio station or other system broadcasts or transmits signals.
– ORIGIN mid 16th cent. (gradually superseding late Middle English *frequence*; originally denoting a gathering of people): from Latin *frequentia*, from *frequens, frequent-* 'crowded, frequent.'

fre·quen·cy dis·tri·bu·tion ▶ n. Statistics a mathematical function showing the number of instances in which a variable takes each of its possible values.

fre·quen·cy di·vi·sion mul·ti·plex·ing ▶ n. Telecommunications a technique for sending two or more signals over the same telephone line, radio channel, or other medium. Each signal is transmitted as a unique range of frequencies within the bandwidth of the channel as a whole, enabling several signals to be transmitted simultaneously. Compare with TIME DIVISION MULTIPLEXING.

fre·quen·cy mod·u·la·tion (abbr.: **FM**) ▶ n. the modulation of a radio or other wave by variation of its frequency, esp. to carry an audio signal. Often contrasted with AMPLITUDE MODULATION.

fre·quen·cy re·sponse ▶ n. Electronics the dependence on signal frequency of the output–input ratio of an amplifier or other device.

fre·quent ▶ adj. /'frēkwənt/ occurring or done on many occasions, in many cases, or in quick succession: *frequent changes in policy | the showers will become heavier and more frequent.* ■ [attrib.] (of a person) doing something often; habitual: *a frequent visitor to New England.* ■ found at short distances apart: *frequent army roadblocks.* ■ Medicine, dated (of the pulse) rapid.
▶ v. /frē'kwent/ [with obj.] visit (a place) often or habitually: *bars frequented by soldiers* | [as adj., with submodifier] (**frequented**) *one of the most frequented sites.*
– DERIVATIVES **fre·quen·ta·tion** /,frēkwən'tāSHən, ,frēkwen-/ n., **fre·quent·er** /frē'kwentər-/ n.
– ORIGIN late Middle English (in the sense 'profuse, ample'): from French, or from Latin *frequens, frequent-* 'crowded, frequent,' of unknown ultimate origin.

fre·quen·ta·tive /frē'kwentətiv/ Grammar ▶ adj. (of a verb or verbal form) expressing frequent repetition or intensity of action.
▶ n. a verb or verbal form of this type, e.g., *chatter* in English.
– ORIGIN mid 16th cent.: from French *fréquentatif, -ive* or Latin *frequentativus*, from *frequens, frequent-* 'crowded, frequent.'

fre·quent fli·er ▶ n. a person who regularly travels by air on commercial flights, esp. one who is enrolled in a promotional program for such travelers.

fre·quent·ly /'frēkwəntlē/ ▶ adv. regularly or habitually; often: *they go abroad frequently.*

fres·co /'freskō/ ▶ n. (pl. **frescoes** or **frescos**) a painting done rapidly in watercolor on wet plaster on a wall or ceiling, so that the colors penetrate the plaster and become fixed as it dries. ■ this method of painting, used in Roman times and by the great masters of the Italian Renaissance including Giotto, Masaccio, and Michelangelo.
▶ v. [with obj.] paint in fresco: *four scenes had been frescoed on the wall* | [as adj.] *frescoed ceilings.*
– ORIGIN late 16th cent.: Italian, literally 'cool, fresh.' The word was first recorded in the phrase *in fresco*, representing Italian *affresco, al fresco* 'on the fresh (plaster).'

fres·co sec·co /'freskō 'sekō/ ▶ n. see SECCO.

fresh /fresH/ ▶ adj. **1** not previously known or used; new or different: *the court had heard fresh evidence.*
2 recently created or experienced and not faded or impaired: *the memory was still fresh in their minds.* ■ (of food) recently made or obtained; not canned, frozen, or otherwise preserved. ■ [predic.] (of a person) full of energy and vigor: *they are feeling fresh after a good night's sleep.* ■ (of a color or a person's complexion) bright or healthy in appearance. ■ (of a person) attractively youthful and inexperienced. ■ [predic.] (**fresh from/out of**) (of a person) having just had (a particular experience) or come from (a particular place): *we were fresh out of art school.*
3 (of water) not salty. ■ pleasantly clean, pure, and cool: *a bit of fresh air does her good.*
4 (of the wind) cool and fairly strong.
5 informal presumptuous or impudent toward someone, esp. in a sexual way: *some of the men tried to get fresh with the girls.*
6 (of a cow) yielding a renewed or increased supply of milk following the birth of a calf.
▶ adv. [usu. in combination] newly; recently: *fresh-baked bread | fresh-cut grass.*
– PHRASES **be fresh out of** informal have just sold or run out of a supply of (something). (**as**) **fresh as a daisy** see DAISY. **fresh blood** see BLOOD.
– DERIVATIVES **fresh·ness** n.
– ORIGIN Old English *fersc* 'not salt, fit for drinking,' superseded in Middle English by forms from Old French *freis, fresche*; both ultimately of Germanic origin and related to Dutch *vers* and German *frisch*.

fresh breeze ▶ n. a wind of force 5 on the Beaufort scale (17-21 knots or 20–24 mph).

fresh·en /'fresHən/ ▶ v. **1** [with obj.] make (something) newer, cleaner, or more attractive: *it didn't take long to freshen her makeup.* ■ add more liquid to (a drink); top off.
2 [no obj.] (of wind) become stronger and colder.
3 [no obj.] (of a cow) give birth and come into milk.
– PHRASAL VERBS **freshen up** revive oneself by washing oneself or changing into clean clothes: *I freshened up by having a shower.* ■ (**freshen something up**) make something look newer or more attractive.

fresh·er /'fresHər/ ▶ n. Brit. informal term for FRESHMAN.

fresh·et /'fresHət/ ▶ n. the flood of a river from heavy rain or melted snow. ■ a rush of fresh water flowing into the sea.
– ORIGIN late 16th cent.: probably from Old French *freschete*, diminutive of *freis* 'fresh.'

fresh-faced ▶ adj. having a clear and young-looking complexion.

fresh gale ▶ n. a wind of force 8 on the Beaufort scale (34-40 knots or 39-46 mph).

fresh·ly /'fresHlē/ ▶ adv. [usu. as submodifier] newly; recently: *freshly ground black pepper.*

fresh·man /'fresHmən/ ▶ n. (pl. **freshmen**) a first-year student at a university, college, or high school: *we invited the freshmen* | [as modifier] *a freshman second baseman.* ■ a newcomer or novice, esp. someone newly elected to Congress.

fresh·wa·ter /'fresH'wôtər, -'wätər/ ▶ adj. **1** of or found in fresh water; not of the sea: *freshwater and marine fish.*
2 informal (esp. of a school or college) situated in a remote or obscure area; provincial.

fresh·wa·ter flea ▶ n. another term for DAPHNIA.

fresh·wom·an /'fresH,wo͝omən/ ▶ n. (pl. **freshwomen**) a female first-year student at a university, college, or high school.

Fres·nel /frā'nel/, Augustin Jean (1788–1827), French physicist and civil engineer. He correctly postulated that light moves in a wavelike motion transverse to the direction of propagation.

fres·nel /'freznəl, frā'nel/ (also **fresnel lens**) ▶ n. Photography a flat lens made of a number of concentric rings, to reduce spherical aberration.
– ORIGIN mid 19th cent.: named after A. J. FRESNEL.

Fres·no /'freznō/ a city in central California, in the San Joaquin valley; pop. 476,050 (est. 2008).

fret[1] /fret/ ▶ v. (**frets, fretting, fretted**) **1** [no obj.] be constantly or visibly worried or anxious: *she fretted about the cost of groceries* | [with clause] *I fretted that my fingers were so skinny.* ■ [with obj.] cause (someone) worry or distress.
2 [with obj.] gradually wear away (something) by rubbing or gnawing: *the bay's black waves fret the seafront.* ■ form (a channel or passage) by rubbing or wearing away. ■ [no obj.] flow or move in small waves: *soft clay that fretted between his toes.*
▶ n. [in sing.] chiefly Brit. a state of anxiety or worry.
– ORIGIN Old English *fretan* 'devour, consume,' of Germanic origin; related to Dutch *vreten* and German *fressen*, and ultimately to FOR- and EAT.

fret[2] ▶ n. **1** Art & Architecture a repeating ornamental design of interlaced vertical and horizontal lines, such as the Greek key pattern.
2 Heraldry a device of narrow diagonal bands interlaced through a diamond.
▶ v. (**frets, fretting, fretted**) [with obj.] (usu. as adj. **fretted**) decorate with fretwork: *intricately carved and fretted balustrades.*
– ORIGIN late Middle English: from Old French *frete* 'trelliswork' and *freter* (verb), of unknown origin.

fret[3] ▶ n. each of a sequence of bars or ridges on the fingerboard of some stringed musical instruments (such as the guitar), used for fixing the positions of the fingers to produce the desired notes.
▶ v. (**frets, fretting, fretted**) [with obj.] (often as adj. **fretted**) **1** provide (a stringed instrument) with frets.
2 play (a note) while pressing the string down against a fret: *fretted notes.*
– DERIVATIVES **fret·less** adj.
– ORIGIN early 16th cent.: of unknown origin.

fret[3]

fret·board /'fret,bôrd/ ▶ n. a fretted fingerboard on a guitar or other musical instrument.

fret·ful /'fretfəl/ ▶ adj. feeling or expressing distress or irritation: *the baby was crying with a fretful whimper.*
– DERIVATIVES **fret·ful·ly** adv., **fret·ful·ness** n.

fret·saw /ˈfretˌsô/ ▶ **n.** a saw with a narrow blade stretched vertically on a frame, for cutting thin wood in patterns.

fret·work /ˈfretˌwərk/ ▶ **n.** ornamental design in wood, typically openwork, done with a fretsaw.

Freud[1] /froid/, Anna (1895–1982), British psychoanalyst; born in Austria; the youngest child of Sigmund Freud. She introduced important innovations in method and theory to her father's work, notably with regard to disturbed children, and set up a child therapy course and clinic in London.

Freud[2], Lucian (1922–), German-born British painter, grandson of Sigmund Freud. His subjects, typically portraits and nudes, are painted in a powerful naturalistic style based on firm draftsmanship and often using striking angles.

Freud[3], Sigmund (1856–1939), Austrian neurologist and psychotherapist. He was the first to emphasize the significance of unconscious processes in normal and neurotic behavior and was the founder of psychoanalysis as both a theory of personality and a therapeutic practice. He proposed the existence of an unconscious element in the mind that influences consciousness and of conflicts in it between various sets of forces. His theory of the sexual origin of neuroses aroused great controversy.

f

Freud·i·an /ˈfroidēən/ Psychology ▶ **adj.** relating to or influenced by Sigmund Freud and his methods of psychoanalysis, esp. with reference to the importance of sexuality in human behavior. ■ susceptible to analysis in terms of unconscious desires: *he wasn't sure whether his passion for water power had some deep Freudian significance.*
▶ **n.** a follower of Freud or his methods.
– DERIVATIVES **Freud·i·an·ism** /-ˌnizəm/ **n.**

Freud·i·an slip ▶ **n.** an unintentional error regarded as revealing subconscious feelings.

Frey /frā/ (also **Freyr** /frār/) Scandinavian Mythology the god of fertility and dispenser of rain and sunshine.

Frey·a /ˈfrāə/ Scandinavian Mythology the goddess of love and of the night, sister of Frey. She is often identified with Frigga.

Fri. ▶ **abbr.** Friday.

fri·a·ble /ˈfrīəbəl/ ▶ **adj.** easily crumbled: *the soil was friable between her fingers.*
– DERIVATIVES **fri·a·bil·i·ty** /ˌfrīəˈbilətē/ **n.**, **fri·a·ble·ness n.**
– ORIGIN mid 16th cent.: from French, or from Latin *friabilis*, from *friare* 'to crumble.'

fri·ar /ˈfrīər/ ▶ **n.** a member of any of certain religious orders of men, esp. the four mendicant orders (Augustinians, Carmelites, Dominicans, and Franciscans).
– ORIGIN Middle English: from Old French *frere*, from Latin *frater* 'brother.'

fri·ar·bird /ˈfrīərˌbərd/ ▶ **n.** a large Australasian honeyeater with a dark, partly naked head and a long curved bill. ● Genus *Philemon*, family Meliphagidae: many species.

Fri·ar Mi·nor ▶ **n.** a Franciscan friar.
– ORIGIN so named because the Franciscans regarded themselves as of humbler rank than members of other orders.

fri·ar·y /ˈfrīərē/ ▶ **n.** (pl. **friaries**) a building or community occupied by or consisting of friars.

frib·ble /ˈfribəl/ ▶ **n.** informal a frivolous or foolish person. ■ a thing of no great importance.
▶ **v.** (**fribble away**) [with obj.] dated part with lightly and wastefully; fritter: *it is no longer respectable to fribble the days away in idle pleasure.*
– ORIGIN mid 17th cent.: symbolic, from the earlier (now obsolete) verb meaning 'stammer,' also 'act aimlessly or frivolously.'

fric·an·deau /ˈfrikənˌdō/ ▶ **n.** (pl. **fricandeaux** pronunc. **same** or /-ˌdōz/) a slice of meat, esp. veal, cut from the leg. ■ a dish made from such meat, usually fried or stewed and served with a sauce.
– ORIGIN French, probably related to *fricassée* 'stew,' from the verb *fricasser* (see **FRICASSEE**).

fric·as·see /ˈfrikəˌsē, ˌfrikəˈsē/ ▶ **n.** a dish of stewed or fried pieces of meat served in a thick white sauce.
▶ **v.** (**fricassees, fricasseeing, fricasseed**) [with obj.] make a fricassee of (something).
– ORIGIN from French *fricassée*, feminine past participle of *fricasser* 'cut up and cook in sauce' (probably a blend of *frire* 'to fry' and *casser* 'to break').

fric·a·tive /ˈfrikətiv/ Phonetics ▶ **adj.** denoting a type of consonant made by the friction of breath in a narrow opening, producing a turbulent air flow.
▶ **n.** a consonant made in this way, e.g., *f* and *th*.
– ORIGIN mid 19th cent.: from modern Latin *fricativus*, from Latin *fricare* 'to rub.'

Frick /frik/, Henry Clay (1849–1919), US industrialist. He was chairman of the Carnegie Steel Company 1889–1900; his art collection is housed in his former home, now a museum, in New York City.

frick·ing /ˈfrikiNG/ ▶ **adj. & adv.** informal used as a euphemism for **FUCKING**: *they don't have a fricking clue.*

fric·tion /ˈfrikSHən/ ▶ **n.** the resistance that one surface or object encounters when moving over another: *a lubrication system that reduces friction.* ■ the action of one surface or object rubbing against another: *the friction of braking.* ■ conflict or animosity caused by a clash of wills, temperaments, or opinions: *a considerable amount of friction between father and son.*
– DERIVATIVES **fric·tion·less adj.**
– ORIGIN mid 16th cent. (denoting chafing or rubbing of the body or limbs, formerly much used in medical treatment): via French from Latin *frictio(n-)*, from *fricare* 'to rub.'

fric·tion·al /ˈfrikSHənl/ ▶ **adj.** of or produced by the action of one surface or object rubbing against or moving over another: *frictional drag.*

fric·tion·al un·em·ploy·ment ▶ **n.** Economics the unemployment which exists in any economy due to people being in the process of moving from one job to another.

fric·tion clutch ▶ **n.** a clutch in which friction between two moving surfaces is increased until they move in unison.

fric·tion drive ▶ **n.** a transmission system used in motor vehicles that depends upon friction between moving parts in contact to transmit motion.

fric·tion tape ▶ **n.** adhesive tape used chiefly to cover exposed electric wires.

fric·tion weld·ing ▶ **n.** welding in which the heat is produced by rotating one component against the other under compression.

Fri·day /ˈfrīdā, -dē/ ▶ **n.** the day of the week before Saturday and following Thursday: *he was arrested on Friday | the cleaning woman came on Fridays* | [as modifier] *Friday evening.*
▶ **adv.** on Friday: *we'll try again Friday.* ■ (**Fridays**) on Fridays; each Friday: *he goes there Fridays.*
– ORIGIN Old English *Frīgedæg*, named after the Germanic goddess **FRIGGA**; translation of late Latin *Veneris dies* 'day of the planet Venus'; compare with Dutch *vrijdag* and German *Freitag*.

fridge /frij/ ▶ **n.** a refrigerator.
– ORIGIN 1920s: abbreviation, probably influenced by the proprietary name *Frigidaire*.

fried /frīd/ past and past participle of **FRY**[1].
▶ **adj.** **1** (of food) cooked in hot fat or oil: *a breakfast of fried eggs and bacon.*
2 [predic.] informal exhausted or worn out: *I had just come from doing a shoot and I was really fried.* ■ intoxicated with drugs or alcohol.

Frie·dan /friˈdan/, Betty (1921–2006), US feminist and writer. She wrote *The Feminine Mystique* (1963), which presented femininity as an artificial construct and traced the ways in which US women are socialized to become mothers and housewives. In 1966, she founded the National Organization for Women, serving as its president until 1970. Other works: *The Second Stage* (1981) and *The Fountain of Age* (1993).

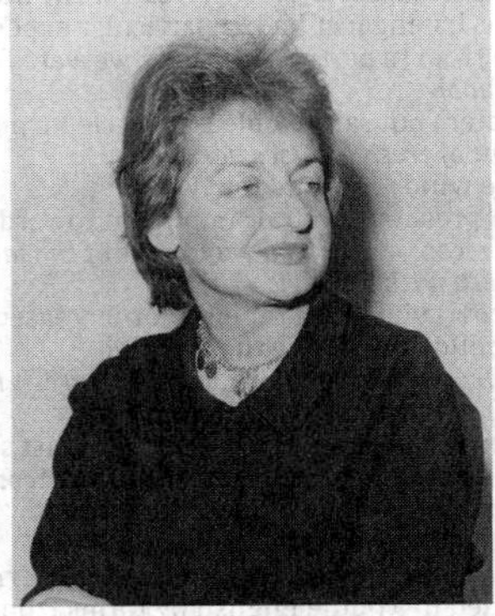
Betty Friedan

Fried·man, Milton (1912–2006), US economist. As a policy adviser to President Ronald Reagan from 1981 to 1989, he advocated free market forces to produce balanced economic growth. Notable works: *Capitalism and Freedom* (1962) and *Free to Choose* (1980, coauthored with his wife). Nobel Prize for Economics (1976).

friend /frend/ ▶ **n.** **1** a person whom one knows and with whom one has a bond of mutual affection, typically exclusive of sexual or family relations. ■ a person who acts as a supporter of a cause, organization, or country by giving financial or other help: *join the Friends of Guilford Free Library.* ■ a person who is not an enemy or who is on the same side: *she was unsure whether he was friend or foe.* ■ a familiar or helpful thing: *he settled for that old friend the compensation grant.* ■ (often as a polite form of address or in ironic reference) an acquaintance or a stranger one comes across: *my friends, let me introduce myself.* ■ a contact associated with a social networking website: *all of a sudden you've got 50 friends online who need to stay connected.*
2 (**Friend**) a member of the Religious Society of Friends; a Quaker.
▶ **v.** [with obj.] **1** add (someone) to a list of contacts associated with a social networking website: *I am friended by 29 people who I have not friended back.*
2 archaic befriend (someone).
– PHRASES **be** (or **make**) **friends with** be (or become) on good or affectionate terms with (someone). **a friend at court** a person in a position to use their influence on one's behalf. **a friend in need is a friend indeed** proverb a person who helps at a difficult time is a truly reliable person. **friends in high places** people in senior positions who are able and willing to use their influence on one's behalf.
– ORIGIN Old English *frēond*, of Germanic origin; related to Dutch *vriend* and German *Freund*, from an Indo-European root meaning 'to love,' shared by **FREE**.

> **WORD TRENDS** Until very recently, the notion of **friending** someone was archaic, confined to dusty tomes or poetic musings. Now, thanks to the growth of social networking sites, the use of **friend** as a verb has been revived, in reference to the process of adding someone to a list of online contacts (*I haven't friended my mother on Facebook and I don't intend to*). This has, of course, opened up whole new realms of social anxiety, from finding those you have **friended** won't **friend** you in return, to discovering that someone has **unfriended** or **defriended** you—removed you from their list of friends (*rather than being an adult about it and telling me how he felt, he unfriended me*).

friend·less /frendləs/ ▶ **adj.** having no friends; alone: *they have been left virtually friendless.*

friend·li·ness /ˈfrendlēnis/ ▶ **n.** the quality of being friendly; affability: *I was overwhelmed by the friendliness of the people here.*

friend·ly /ˈfrendlē/ ▶ **adj.** (**friendlier, friendliest**) kind and pleasant: *they were friendly to me | she gave me a friendly smile.* ■ [predic.] (of a person) on good or affectionate terms: *I was friendly with one of the local farmers.* ■ (of a contest) not seriously or unpleasantly competitive or divisive: *friendly rivalry between the two schools.* ■ Soccer (of a match) not affecting a team's league standings. ■ [in combination] denoting something that is adapted for or is not harmful to a specified thing: *an environment-friendly agronomic practice.* ■ favorable or serviceable: *trees providing a friendly stage on which seedlings begin to grow.* ■ Military (of troops or equipment) of, belonging to, or in alliance with one's own forces.
▶ **adv.** (also **friendlily** /-ləlē/) in a friendly manner.

friend·ly fire ▶ **n.** Military weapon fire coming from one's own side, esp. fire that causes accidental injury or death to one's own forces.

Friend·ly Is·lands another name for **TONGA**.

friend of Dor·o·thy ▶ **n.** (pl. **friends of Dorothy**) informal a gay man.
– ORIGIN from the name of *Dorothy*, a character played by the actress Judy Garland (a gay icon) in the movie *The Wizard of Oz* (1939).

friend·ship /ˈfrendˌSHip/ ▶ **n.** the emotions or conduct of friends; the state of being friends. ■ a relationship between friends: *she formed close friendships with women.* ■ a state of mutual trust and support between allied nations.
– ORIGIN Old English *frēondscipe* (see **FRIEND**, **-SHIP**).

Friends of the Earth (abbr.: **FoE**) an international pressure group established in 1971 to campaign for a better awareness of and response to environmental problems.

fri·er ▶ **n.** variant spelling of **FRYER**.

Fries·land /ˈfrēzlənd/ the western part of the ancient region of Frisia. ■ a northern province in the Netherlands, bounded on the west and north by the IJsselmeer and the North Sea; capital, Leeuwarden.

frieze[1] /frēz/ ▶ **n.** a broad horizontal band of sculpted or painted decoration, esp. on a wall near

the ceiling. ■ a horizontal paper strip mounted on a wall to give a similar effect. ■ Architecture the part of an entablature between the architrave and the cornice.
– ORIGIN mid 16th cent.: from French *frise*, from medieval Latin *frisium*, variant of *frigium*, from Latin *Phrygium* (*opus*) '(work) of Phrygia.'

frieze[2] ▶ **n.** heavy, coarse woolen cloth with a nap, usually on one side only.
– ORIGIN late Middle English: from French *frise*, from medieval Latin *frisia*, 'Frisian wool.'

frig[1] /frig/ vulgar slang ▶ **v.** (**frigs, frigging, frigged**) [with obj.] used as a euphemism for 'fuck.' ■ masturbate.
▶ **exclam.** expressing extreme anger, annoyance, or contempt.
– PHRASAL VERBS **frig around** spend time doing unimportant or trivial things.
– ORIGIN late Middle English: of unknown origin. The original sense was 'move restlessly, wriggle,' later 'rub, chafe,' hence 'masturbate' (late 17th cent).

frig[2] /frij/ (also **'frig**) ▶ **n.** informal short for REFRIGERATOR.

frig·ate /'frigit/ ▶ **n.** a warship with a mixed armament, generally heavier than a destroyer (in the US Navy) and of a kind originally introduced for convoy escort work. ■ historical a sailing warship of a size and armament just below that of a ship of the line.
– ORIGIN late 16th cent. (denoting a light, fast boat that was rowed or sailed): from French *frégate*, from Italian *fregata*, of unknown origin.

frig·ate bird ▶ **n.** a predatory tropical seabird with dark plumage, long narrow wings, a deeply forked tail, and a long hooked bill. Also called MAN-O'-WAR BIRD (see MAN-OF-WAR). ● Family Fregatidae and genus *Fregata*: five species.

Frig·ga /'frigə/ Scandinavian Mythology the wife of Odin and goddess of married love and of the hearth, often identified with Freya. Friday is named after her.

frig·ging /'frigən, -iNG/ (often **friggin'**) ▶ **adj. & adv.** informal used as a euphemism for FUCKING: *that was frigging awesome!*

fright /frīt/ ▶ **n.** a sudden intense feeling of fear: *I jumped up in fright.* ■ an experience that causes one to feel sudden intense fear: *she's had a nasty fright* | *I got **the fright of my life** seeing that woman in the hotel.*
▶ **v.** [with obj.] archaic frighten: *come, be comforted, he shan't fright you.*
– PHRASES **look a fright** informal have a disheveled or grotesque appearance. **take fright** suddenly become frightened or panicked.
– ORIGIN Old English *fryhto*, *fyrhto* (noun), of Germanic origin; related to Dutch *furcht* and German *Furcht*.

fright·en /'frītn/ ▶ **v.** [with obj.] make (someone) afraid or anxious: *the savagery of his thoughts frightened him* | *people were no longer easily frightened into docility.* ■ (**frighten someone/something off**) deter someone or something from involvement or action by making them afraid. ■ [no obj.] (of a person) become afraid or anxious: *at his age, I guess he doesn't frighten any more.*
– DERIVATIVES **fright·en·er** /'frītn-ər/ **n.**

fright·ened /'frītnd/ ▶ **adj.** afraid or anxious: *a frightened child.*

fright·en·ing ▶ **adj.** making someone afraid or anxious; terrifying: *a frightening experience.*
– DERIVATIVES **fright·en·ing·ly** /'frītn-iNGlē/ **adv.**

fright·ful /'frītfəl/ ▶ **adj.** very unpleasant, serious, or shocking: *there's been a frightful accident.* ■ informal used for emphasis, esp. of something bad: *her hair was a frightful mess.*
– DERIVATIVES **fright·ful·ness n.**

fright·ful·ly /'frītfəlē/ ▶ **adv.** [as submodifier] Brit. dated very (used for emphasis): *it was frightfully hot* | *I'm frightfully sorry.*

fright wig ▶ **n.** a wig with the hair arranged standing up or sticking out, as worn by a clown or similar performer.

frig·id /'frijid/ ▶ **adj.** very cold in temperature: *frigid water.* ■ (esp. of a woman) unable or unwilling to be sexually aroused and responsive. ■ showing no friendliness or enthusiasm; stiff or formal in behavior or style: *Henrietta looked back with a frigid calm.*
– DERIVATIVES **fri·gid·i·ty** /frə'jidətē/ **n.**, **frig·id·ly adv.**, **frig·id·ness n.**
– ORIGIN late Middle English: from Latin *frigidus*, from *frigere* 'be cold,' from *frigus* (noun) 'cold.'

frig·id zone ▶ **n.** (also **Frigid Zone**) each of the two areas of the earth respectively north of the Arctic Circle and south of the Antarctic Circle. ■ informal a range of extremely cold temperatures: *winter temperatures can dip into the frigid zone.*

fri·jol /'frēhōl, frē'hōl/ ▶ **n.** (pl. **frijoles** /-hōlz, 'hōlāz, -lēz/) a bean, esp. a red kidney bean or cowpea, used as a staple in Mexican cooking.

fri·jo·les /frē'hōlēz/ ▶ **plural n.** (in Mexican cooking) beans.
– ORIGIN Spanish, plural of *frijol* 'bean.'

fri·jo·les re·fri·tos /rā'frētōs/ ▶ **n.** REFRIED BEANS.

frill /fril/ ▶ **n. 1** a strip of gathered or pleated material sewn by one side onto a garment or larger piece of material as a decorative edging or ornament. ■ a thing resembling such a strip in appearance or function: *a frill of silver hair surrounded a shining bald pate.* ■ a natural fringe of feathers or hair on a bird or other animal. ■ Paleontology an upward-curving bony plate extending behind the skull of many ceratopsian dinosaurs.
2 (usu. **frills**) an unnecessary extra feature or embellishment: *it was just a comfortable apartment with no frills.*
– DERIVATIVES **frilled adj.**, **frill·er·y** /'frilərē/ **n.**
– ORIGIN late 16th cent.: from or related to Flemish *frul.*

frilled liz·ard (also **frill-necked lizard**) ▶ **n.** a large northern Australian lizard with a membrane around the neck that can be erected to form a ruff for defensive display. When disturbed, it runs away on its hind legs. ● *Chlamydosaurus kingii*, family Agamidae.

frilled lizard

frilled shark ▶ **n.** an elongated deep-sea shark of snakelike appearance, with prominent gill covers that give the appearance of a frill around the neck. ● *Chlamydoselachus anguineus*, the only member of the family Clamydoselachidae.

frill·y /'frilē/ ▶ **adj.** (**frillier, frilliest**) decorated with frills or similar ornamentation: *a frilly apron.* ■ overelaborate or showy in character or style: *seafood dishes that avoid being too frilly or rich.*
▶ **plural n.** (**frillies**) informal an item of women's underwear.
– DERIVATIVES **frill·i·ness** /'frilēnis/ **n.**

Fri·maire /frē'mer/ **n.** the third month of the French Republican calendar (1793–1805), originally running from November 21 to December 20.
– ORIGIN French, from *frimas* 'hoarfrost.'

fringe /frinj/ ▶ **n. 1** an ornamental border of threads left loose or formed into tassels or twists, used to edge clothing or material.
2 chiefly British term for BANGS (see BANG[1] (sense 2 of the noun)). ■ a natural border of hair or fibers in an animal or plant.
3 (often **the fringes**) the outer, marginal, or extreme part of an area, group, or sphere of activity: *his uncles were on the fringes of crooked activity.* ■ (**the fringe**) the unconventional, extreme, or marginal wing of a group or sphere of activity: *the lunatic fringe of American political life* | *rap music is no longer something on the fringe.*
4 a band of contrasting brightness or darkness produced by diffraction or interference of light. ■ a strip of false color in an optical image.
5 short for FRINGE BENEFIT.
▶ **adj.** [attrib.] not part of the mainstream; unconventional, peripheral, or extreme: *fringe theater.*
▶ **v.** (**fringes, fringing, fringed**) [with obj.] decorate (clothing or material) with a fringe: *a rich robe of gold, fringed with black velvet.* ■ form a border around (something): *the sea is fringed by palm trees.* ■ (as adj. **fringed**) (of a plant or animal) having a natural border of hair or fiber.
– DERIVATIVES **fringe·less adj.**, **fring·y** /'frinjē/ **adj.**
– ORIGIN Middle English: from Old French *frenge*, based on late Latin *fimbria*, earlier a plural noun meaning 'fibers, shreds.'

fringe ben·e·fit ▶ **n.** an extra benefit supplementing an employee's salary, for example, a company car, subsidized meals, health insurance, etc.

fringed or·chid ▶ **n.** a North American orchid with a flower that has a fringed lip. ● Genus *Habenaria*, family Orchidaceae: many species.

fring·ing reef ▶ **n.** a coral reef that lies close to the shore.

frip·per·y /'fripərē/ ▶ **n.** (pl. **fripperies**) showy or unnecessary ornament in architecture, dress, or language. ■ a tawdry or frivolous thing.
– ORIGIN mid 16th cent. (denoting old or secondhand clothes): from French *friperie*, from Old French *freperie*, from *frepe* 'rag,' of unknown ultimate origin.

Fris. ▶ **abbr.** Frisian.

Fris·bee /'frizbē/ (also **frisbee**) ▶ **n.** trademark a concave plastic disk designed for skimming through the air as an outdoor game or amusement. ■ the game or amusement of skimming such a disk.
– ORIGIN 1950s: said to be named after the *Frisbie* bakery (Bridgeport, Connecticut), whose pie tins could be used similarly.

Frisch[1] /frisH/, Karl von (1886–1982), Austrian zoologist. He worked mainly on honeybees, studying particularly their vision, navigation, and communication. He showed that they perform an elaborate dance in the hive to indicate the direction and distance of food. Nobel Prize in Physiology or Medicine (1973), shared with Konrad Lorenz and Nikolaas Tinbergen.

Frisch[2], Otto Robert (1904–79), British physicist; born in Austria. With his aunt, Lise Meitner, he recognized that Otto Hahn's experiments with uranium had produced a new type of nuclear reaction, which Frisch called nuclear fission. He also indicated the explosive potential of its chain reaction.

Frisch[3], Ragnar (Anton Kittil) (1895–1973), Norwegian economist; a pioneer of econometrics. Nobel Prize for Economics (1969), shared with Jan Tinbergen.

fri·sée /frē'zā/ ▶ **n.** the curly endive (see ENDIVE (sense 1)).
– ORIGIN French, from *chicorée frisée* 'curly endive.'

Fri·sia /'frizHə, 'frēzHə/ an ancient region in northwestern Europe. It included the Frisian Islands and parts of the mainland corresponding to the modern provinces of Friesland and Groningen in the Netherlands and the regions of Ostfriesland and Nordfriesland in northwestern Germany.

Fri·sian /'frizHən, 'frē-/ ▶ **adj.** of or relating to Frisia or Friesland, its people, or language.
▶ **n. 1** a native or inhabitant of Frisia or Friesland.
2 the West Germanic language of Frisia or Friesland, the language most closely related to English.
– ORIGIN late 16th cent.: from Latin *Frisii* 'Frisians' (from Old Frisian *Frīsa*, *Frēsa*) + -IAN.

Fri·sian Is·lands a chain of islands that lie off the coast of northwestern Europe and extend from the IJsselmeer in the Netherlands to Jutland. The **West Frisian Islands** form part of the Netherlands, the **East Frisian Islands** form part of Germany, and the **North Frisian Islands** are divided between Germany and Denmark.

frisk /frisk/ ▶ **v. 1** [with obj.] (of a police officer or other official) pass the hands over (someone) in a search for hidden weapons, drugs, or other items.
2 [no obj.] (of an animal or person) skip or leap playfully; frolic: *this did not deter the foal from **frisking about**.* ■ [with obj.] (of an animal) move or wave (its tail or legs) playfully: *a horse was frisking his back legs like a colt.*
▶ **n. 1** [in sing.] an act of frisking someone.
2 a playful skip or leap.
– DERIVATIVES **frisk·er n.**
– ORIGIN early 16th cent.(sense 2 of the verb): from obsolete *frisk* 'lively, frisky,' from Old French *frisque* 'alert, lively, merry,' perhaps of Germanic origin. Sense 1 of the verb, originally a slang term, dates from the late 18th cent.

fris·ket /'friskit/ ▶ **n.** Printing a thin metal frame keeping the paper in position during printing on a hand press. ■ fluid or adhesive paper used in painting or crafts to cover areas of a surface on which paint is not wanted.
– ORIGIN late 17th cent.: from French *frisquette*, from Provençal *frisqueto*, from Spanish *frasqueta*.

frisk·y /'friskē/ ▶ **adj.** (**friskier, friskiest**) playful and full of energy: *he bounds about like a frisky pup.*
– DERIVATIVES **frisk·i·ly** /'friskəlē/ **adv.**, **frisk·i·ness n.**

fris·son /frē'sôN/ ▶ **n.** a sudden strong feeling of excitement or fear; a thrill: *a frisson of excitement.*
– ORIGIN late 18th cent.: French, literally 'a shiver or thrill.'

PRONUNCIATION KEY ə *ago, up*; ər *over, fur*; a *hat*; ā *ate*; ä *car*; e *let*; ē *see*; i *fit*; ī *by*; NG *sing*; ō *go*; ô *law, for*; oi *toy*; o͝o *good*; o͞o *goo*; ou *out*; TH *thin*; T͟H *then*; ZH *vision*

frit /frit/ ▶ **n.** the mixture of silica and fluxes that is fused at high temperature to make glass. ■ a similar calcined and pulverized mixture used to make soft-paste porcelain or ceramic glazes.
▶ **v.** (**frits, fritting, fritted**) [with obj.] make into frit.
– ORIGIN mid 17th cent.: from Italian *fritta*, feminine past participle of *friggere* 'to fry.'

frites /frēt(s)/ ▶ **plural n.** short for POMMES FRITES.

frit fly ▶ **n.** a very small black fly whose larvae are a serious pest of cereal crops and golf-course turf. ● *Oscinella frit*, family Chloropidae.
– ORIGIN late 19th cent.: from Latin *frit* 'particle on an ear of grain.'

frith /friTH/ ▶ **n.** archaic spelling of FIRTH.

frit·il·lar·y /ˈfritlˌerē/ ▶ **n.** (pl. **fritillaries**) **1** a Eurasian plant of the lily family, with hanging bell-like flowers. ● Genus *Fritillaria*, family Liliaceae: numerous species.
2 a butterfly with orange-brown wings that are checkered with black. ● Subfamilies Argynninae and Melitaeinae, family Nymphalidae: *Argynnis*, *Speyeria*, and other genera, and numerous species, including the North American **great spangled fritillary** (*S. cybele*).
– ORIGIN mid 17th cent.: from modern Latin *fritillaria*, from Latin *fritillus* 'dice box' (probably with reference to the checkered corolla of the snake's-head fritillary).

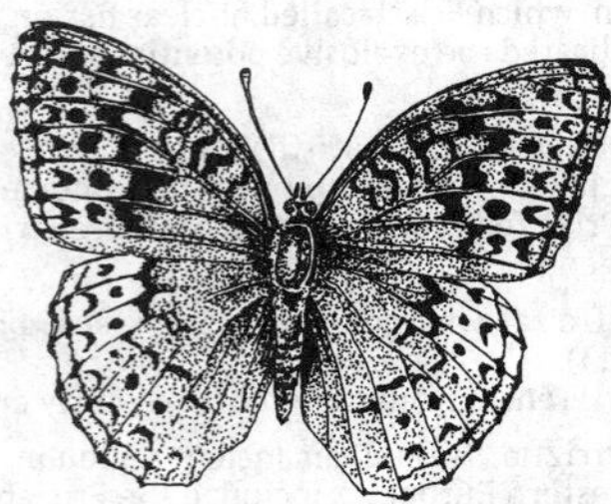
great spangled fritillary

frit·ta·ta /frēˈtätə/ ▶ **n.** an Italian dish made with fried beaten eggs, resembling a Spanish omelet.
– ORIGIN Italian, from *fritto*, past participle of *friggere* 'to fry.' Compare with FRITTER[2].

frit·ter[1] /ˈfritər/ ▶ **v.** [with obj.] **1** (**fritter something away**) waste time, money, or energy on trifling matters: *I wish we hadn't frittered the money away so easily.* ■ [no obj.] dwindle; diminish: *the day fritters.*
2 archaic divide (something) into small pieces: *they become frittered into minute tatters.*
– DERIVATIVES **frit·ter·er n.**
– ORIGIN early 18th cent.: based on obsolete *fitter* 'break into fragments, shred'; perhaps related to German *Fetzen* 'rag, scrap.'

frit·ter[2] ▶ **n.** a piece of fruit, vegetable, or meat that is coated in batter and deep-fried.
– ORIGIN late Middle English: from Old French *friture*, based on Latin *frigere* (see FRY[1]). Compare with FRITTATA.

frit·to mi·sto /ˌfrētō ˈmēstō/ ▶ **n.** a dish of various foods, typically seafood, deep-fried in batter.
– ORIGIN Italian, 'mixed fry.'

fritz /frits/ ▶ **n.** (in phrase **go** or **be on the fritz**) informal (of a machine) stop working properly.
– ORIGIN early 20th cent.: said to be a use of *Fritz*, with allusion to cheap German imports into the US before World War I.

Fri·u·li /frēˈo͝olē/ a historic region in southeastern Europe now divided between Slovenia and the Italian region of Friuli-Venezia Giulia.
– DERIVATIVES **Fri·u·li·an** /-ˈo͝olēən/ **adj. & n.**

Fri·u·li-Ve·ne·zia Giu·lia /frēˌo͝olē väˈnetsēə ˈjo͞olyə/ a region in northeastern Italy, on the border with Slovenia and Austria; capital, Trieste.

friv·ol /ˈfrivəl/ ▶ **v.** (**frivols, frivoling, frivoled**; Brit. **frivols, frivolling, frivolled**) [no obj.] behave in a frivolous way.
– ORIGIN mid 19th cent.: back-formation from FRIVOLOUS.

fri·vol·i·ty /friˈvälətē/ ▶ **n.** lack of seriousness; lightheartedness: *a night of fun and frivolity.*

friv·o·lous /ˈfrivələs/ ▶ **adj.** not having any serious purpose or value: *rules to stop frivolous lawsuits.* ■ (of a person) carefree and not serious.
– DERIVATIVES **friv·o·lous·ly adv., friv·o·lous·ness n.**
– ORIGIN late Middle English: from Latin *frivolus* 'silly, trifling' + -OUS.

frizz /friz/ ▶ **v.** [with obj.] form (hair) into a mass of small, tight curls or tufts: *her hair was frizzed up in a style that seemed matronly.* ■ [no obj.] (of hair) form itself into such a mass: *his hair had frizzed out symmetrically.*
▶ **n.** the state of being formed into such a mass of curls or tufts: *a perm designed to add curl without frizz.*
– ORIGIN late Middle English (in the sense 'dress leather with pumice'): from French *friser*. The sense 'form hair into a mass of curls' dates from the late 16th cent.

friz·zan·te /fritˈsäntā/ ▶ **adj.** (of wine) semi-sparkling.
– ORIGIN Italian.

friz·zle[1] /ˈfrizəl/ ▶ **v.** [no obj.] fry or grill with a sizzling noise: *Elsie had the fat frizzling in the frying pan.* ■ [with obj.] fry until crisp, shriveled, or burned: (as adj. **frizzled**) *add diced frizzled salt pork to taste.*
▶ **n.** [in sing.] the sound or act of frying: *the frizzle of the pan.*
– ORIGIN mid 18th cent.: from FRY[1], probably influenced by SIZZLE.

friz·zle[2] ▶ **v.** [with obj.] form (hair) into tight curls.
▶ **n.** a tight curl in hair.
– DERIVATIVES **friz·zly** /ˈfriz(ə)lē/ **adj.**
– ORIGIN mid 16th cent.: from FRIZZ + -LE[4].

friz·zy /ˈfrizē/ ▶ **adj.** (**frizzier, frizziest**) formed of a mass of small, tight curls or tufts: *frizzy red hair.*
– DERIVATIVES **friz·zi·ness n.**

fro /frō/ ▶ **adv.** see TO AND FRO.
– ORIGIN Middle English: from Old Norse *frá* (see FROM).

Fro·bish·er /ˈfrōbiSHər/, Sir Martin (*c.*1535–94), English explorer. In 1576, he led an unsuccessful expedition in search of the Northwest Passage. Frobisher served in Sir Francis Drake's Caribbean expedition of 1585–86 and took part in the defeat of the Spanish Armada.

frock /fräk/ ▶ **n. 1** a woman's or girl's dress.
2 a loose outer garment, in particular: ■ a long gown with flowing sleeves worn by monks, priests, or clergy. ■ historical a field laborer's smock. ■ short for FROCK COAT.
3 [in sing.] archaic priestly office: *such words as these cost the preacher his frock.*
▶ **v.** [with obj.] provide with or dress in a frock: [as adj., in combination] *a black-frocked Englishman.* ■ archaic invest (someone) with priestly office. Compare with DEFROCK.
– ORIGIN late Middle English: from Old French *froc*, of Germanic origin. The sense 'priest's or monk's gown' is preserved in *defrock*.

frock coat ▶ **n.** a man's double-breasted, long-skirted coat, now worn chiefly on formal occasions.

froe /frō/ ▶ **n.** a cleaving tool with a handle at right angles to the blade.
– ORIGIN late 16th cent.: abbreviation of obsolete *frower*, from FROWARD in the sense 'turned away.'

Froe·bel /ˈfrəbəl/, Friedrich (Wilhelm August) (1782–1852), German educator and founder of the kindergarten system.

frog[1] /frôg, fräg/ ▶ **n. 1** a tailless amphibian with a short squat body, moist smooth skin, and very long hind legs for leaping. ● Frogs are found in most families of the order Anura, but the 'true frogs' are confined to the large family Ranidae.
■ informal a person regarded as repulsive in character or appearance.
2 (**Frog**) informal, offensive a French person.
▶ **v.** [no obj.] hunt for or catch frogs.
– PHRASES **have a frog in one's throat** informal lose one's voice or find it hard to speak because of hoarseness.
– DERIVATIVES **frog·ger n., frog·gy adj.**
– ORIGIN Old English *frogga*, of Germanic origin; related to Dutch *vors* and German *Frosch*. Used as a general term of abuse in Middle English, the term was applied specifically to the Dutch in the 17th cent.; its application to the French (late 18th cent.) is partly alliterative, partly from the reputation of the French for eating frogs' legs.

frog[2] ▶ **n.** a thing used to hold or fasten something, in particular: ■ an ornamental coat fastener or braid consisting of a spindle-shaped button and a loop through which it passes. ■ an attachment to a belt for holding a sword, bayonet, or similar weapon. ■ a perforated or spiked device for holding the stems of flowers in an arrangement. ■ the piece into which the hair is fitted at the lower end of the bow of a stringed instrument. ■ a grooved metal plate for guiding the wheels of a railroad vehicle at an intersection.
– ORIGIN early 18th cent.: perhaps a use of FROG[1], influenced by synonymous Italian *forchetta* or French *fourchette* 'small fork,' because of the shape.

frog[3] ▶ **n.** an elastic horny pad growing in the sole of a horse's hoof, helping to absorb the shock when the hoof hits the ground. ■ a raised or swollen area on a surface.
– ORIGIN early 17th cent.: perhaps from FROG[2].

frog·fish /ˈfrôgˌfiSH/ ▶ **n.** (pl. **same** or **frogfishes**) an anglerfish that typically lives on the seabed, where its warty skin and color provide camouflage. ● Families Antennariidae (numerous species, including *Antennaria hispidus* of the Indo-Pacific), and Brachionichthyidae (four Australian species).

frogged /ˈfrôgd, frägd/ ▶ **adj.** (of a coat) having an ornamental braid or fastening consisting of a spindle-shaped button and a loop.

frog·ging /ˈfrôgiNG, fräg-/ ▶ **n.** ornamental braid or coat fastenings consisting of spindle-shaped buttons and loops.

frog·hop·per /ˈfrôgˌhäpər, fräg-/ ▶ **n.** a jumping, plant-sucking bug, the larva of which produces a frothy mass on plants. Also called SPITTLEBUG. ● Family Cercopidae, suborder Homoptera: several genera.

frog kick ▶ **n.** a movement used in swimming, esp. in the breast stroke, in which the legs are brought toward the body with the knees bent and the feet together and then kicked outward before being brought together again, all in one continuous movement.

frog·let /ˈfrôglət, ˈfräg-/ ▶ **n. 1** a small kind of frog. ● Several genera, including *Crinia* of Australia (family Myobatrachidae), and *Philautus* of Malaysia (family Rhacophoridae).
2 a tiny frog that has recently developed from a tadpole.

frog·man /ˈfrôgˌman, ˈfräg-, -mən/ ▶ **n.** (pl. **frogmen**) a person who swims underwater wearing a rubber suit, flippers, and an oxygen supply.

frog·march /ˈfrôgˌmärCH, ˈfräg-/ ▶ **v.** [with obj.] force (someone) to walk forward by holding and pinning their arms from behind: *the cop frogmarched him down the steep stairs.*

frog·mouth /ˈfrôgˌmouTH, ˈfräg-/ ▶ **n.** a nocturnal bird resembling a nightjar, occurring in Southeast Asia and Australasia. ● Family Podargidae: two genera and several species, in particular the **tawny frogmouth** (*Podargus strigoides*) of Australia.

frog or·chid ▶ **n.** a small orchid with inconspicuous green flowers, growing chiefly on calcareous grassland in north temperate regions. ● *Coeloglossum viride*, family Orchidaceae.

frog's-bit ▶ **n.** a floating freshwater plant with creeping stems that bear clusters of small rounded leaves. ● Two species in the family Hydrocharitaceae: **Eurasian frog's-bit** (*Hydrocharis morsus-ranae*) and **American frog's-bit** (*Limnobium spongia*).

frog·spawn /ˈfrôgˌspôn, ˈfräg-/ ▶ **n.** the eggs of a frog, which are surrounded by transparent jelly.

frog spit ▶ **n.** another term for CUCKOO SPIT.

froi·deur /frwäˈdər/ ▶ **n.** coolness or reserve between people.
– ORIGIN French, from *froid* 'cold.'

frol·ic /ˈfrälik/ ▶ **v.** (**frolics, frolicking, frolicked**) [no obj.] (of an animal or person) play and move about cheerfully, excitedly, or energetically: *Edward frolicked on the sand.* ■ play about with someone in a flirtatious or sexual way: *he denied allegations that he frolicked with a secretary.*
▶ **n.** (often **frolics**) a playful action or movement: *his injuries were inflicted by the frolics of a young filly | the days of fun and frolic were gone for good.* ■ flirtatious or sexual activity or actions: *her poolside frolics.*
▶ **adj.** archaic cheerful, merry, or playful: *a thousand forms of frolic life.*
– DERIVATIVES **frol·ick·er n.**
– ORIGIN early 16th cent. (as an adjective): from Dutch *vrolijk* 'merry, cheerful.'

frol·ic·some /ˈfräliksəm/ ▶ **adj.** lively and playful.
– DERIVATIVES **frol·ic·some·ly adv., frol·ic·some·ness n.**

from /frəm/ ▶ **prep. 1** indicating the point in space at which a journey, motion, or action starts: *she began to walk away from him | I leapt from my bed |* figurative *he was turning the committee away from appeasement.* ■ indicating the distance between a particular place and another place used as a point of reference: *the ambush occurred 50 yards from a checkpoint.*
2 indicating the point in time at which a particular process, event, or activity starts: *the show will run from 10 to 2.*
3 indicating the source or provenance of someone or something: *I'm from Hartford | she phoned him from the hotel | she demanded the keys from her husband.* ■ indicating the date at which something was created: *a document dating from the thirteenth century.*
4 indicating the starting point of a specified range on a scale: *men who ranged in age from seventeen to*

eighty-four. ■ indicating one extreme in a range of conceptual variations: *anything from geography to literature.*
5 indicating the point at which an observer is placed: *you can see the island from here* | figurative *the ability to see things from another's point of view.*
6 indicating the raw material out of which something is manufactured: *a varnish made from copal.*
7 indicating separation or removal: *the party was ousted from power after sixteen years.*
8 indicating prevention: *the story of how he was saved from death.*
9 indicating a cause: *a child suffering from asthma.*
10 indicating a source of knowledge or the basis for one's judgment: *information obtained from papers, books, and presentations.*
11 indicating a distinction: *the courts view him in a different light from that of a manual worker.*
– PHRASES **as from** see AS[1]. **from day to day** (or **hour to hour**, etc.) daily (or hourly, etc.); as the days (or hours, etc.) pass. **from now** (or **then**, etc.) **on** now (or then, etc.) and in the future: *they were friends from that day on.* **from time to time** occasionally.
– ORIGIN Old English *fram, from*, of Germanic origin; related to Old Norse *frá* (see FRO).

fro·mage blanc /frō,mäzʜ 'blänɢk/ ▶ n. a type of soft French cheese made from cow's milk and having a creamy sour taste.
– ORIGIN French, literally 'white cheese.'

Fromm /främ/, Erich (1900–80), US psychoanalyst and social philosopher; born in Germany. His works, which include *Escape from Freedom* (1941), *Man for Himself* (1947), and *The Sane Society* (1955), emphasize the role of culture in neurosis and strongly criticize materialist values.

frond /fränd/ ▶ n. the leaf or leaflike part of a palm, fern, or similar plant: *fronds of bracken* | figurative *her hair escaped in wayward fronds.*
– DERIVATIVES **frond·ed** adj.
– ORIGIN late 18th cent.: from Latin *frons, frond-* 'leaf.'

Fronde /fränd, frôɴd/ a series of civil wars in France 1648–53, in which the nobles rose in rebellion against Mazarin and the court during the minority of Louis XIV. ■ the party which rose in rebellion against Mazarin and the court at this time.
– ORIGIN late 18th cent.: French, from the name for a type of sling used in a children's game played in the streets of Paris at this time.

fron·deur /,frôɴ'dər/ ▶ n. rare a political rebel.
– ORIGIN mid 19th cent.: French, literally 'slinger,' used to denote a member of the FRONDE.

frons /fränz/ ▶ n. (pl. **frontes** /'fräntēz/) Zoology the forehead or equivalent part of an animal, esp. the middle part of an insect's face between the eyes and above the clypeus.
– ORIGIN mid 19th cent.: from Latin, 'front, forehead.'

front /frənt/ ▶ n. **1** the side or part of an object that presents itself to view or that is normally seen or used first; the most forward part of something: *a page at the front of the book had been torn out* | *he sealed the envelope and wrote on the front.* ■ [in sing.] the position directly ahead of someone or something; the most forward position or place: *she quickly turned her head to face the front.* ■ the forward-facing part of a person's body, on the opposite side to their back. ■ the part of a garment covering this: *oatmeal slopped from the tray onto his shirt front.* ■ informal a woman's bust or cleavage. ■ any face of a building, esp. that of the main entrance: *the west front of the cathedral.* ■ chiefly Brit. short for SEAFRONT or WATERFRONT.
2 the foremost line or part of an armed force; the furthest position that an army has reached and where the enemy is or may be engaged: *his regiment was immediately sent to the front.* ■ the direction toward which a line of troops faces when formed. ■ a particular formation of troops for battle. ■ a particular situation or sphere of operation: *there was some good news on the jobs front.* ■ [often in names] an organized political group: *the Palestinian Liberation Front.* ■ Meteorology the forward edge of an advancing mass of air. See COLD FRONT, OCCLUDED FRONT, WARM FRONT.
3 [in sing.] an appearance or form of behavior assumed by a person to conceal their genuine feelings: *she put on a brave front.* ■ a person or organization serving as a cover for subversive or illegal activities: *the CIA identified the company as a front for a terrorist group.* ■ a well-known or prestigious person who acts as a representative, rather than an active member, of an organization. See also FRONTMAN.
4 boldness and confidence of manner: *he's got a bit of talent and a lot of front.*
5 archaic a person's face or forehead.
▶ adj. [attrib.] **1** of or at the front: *the front cover of the magazine* | *she was in the front yard.*
2 Phonetics (of a vowel sound) formed by raising the body of the tongue, excluding the blade and tip, toward the hard palate.
▶ v. [with obj.] **1** (of a building or piece of land) have the front facing or directed toward: *the houses that front Beacon Street* | [no obj.] *we sold the uphill land that fronted on the road.* ■ be or stand in front of: *they reached the hedge fronting the garden.* ■ archaic stand face to face with; confront: *Tom fronted him with unwavering eyes.*
2 (usu. **be fronted**) provide (something) with a front or facing of a particular type or material: *a metal box fronted by an alloy panel* | [as adj., in combination] (**-fronted**) *a glass-fronted bookcase.*
3 lead or be the most prominent member in (an organization, activity, or group of musicians): *the group is fronted by two girl singers.* ■ present or host (a television or radio program). ■ [no obj.] act as a front or cover for someone or something acting illegally or wishing to conceal something: *he fronted for them in illegal property deals.*
4 Phonetics articulate (a vowel sound) with the tongue further forward: (as adj. **fronted**) *all speakers use raised and fronted variants more in spontaneous speech.*
5 Linguistics place (a sentence element) at the beginning of a sentence instead of in its usual position, typically for emphasis or as feature of some dialects, as in *horrible it was.*
▶ exclam. used to summon someone to the front or to command them to assume a forward-facing position, as in calling a bellhop to the front desk or giving orders to troops on parade: *scouts, front and center!*
– PHRASES **in front 1** in a position just ahead of or further forward than someone or something else: *the car in front stopped suddenly.* ■ in the lead in a game or contest: *the Reds were in front until the eighth inning.* **2** on the part or side that normally first presents itself to view: *a house with a wide porch in front.* **in front of 1** in a position just ahead or at the front part of someone or something else: *the lawn in front of the house.* ■ in a position facing someone or something: *she sat in front of the mirror.* **2** in the presence of: *the teacher didn't want his authority challenged in front of the class.* **out front** at or to the front; in front: *two station wagons stopped out front.* ■ in the auditorium of a theater. **up front 1** at or near the front: *the floor plan has an open living area up front.* **2** in advance: *every fee must be paid up front.* **3** open and direct; frank: *I vowed to be up front with her.*
– DERIVATIVES **fron·ting** /'frəntiɴɢ/ n., **front·less** adj., **front·ward** /-wərd/ adj. & adv., **front·wards** /-wərdz/ adv.
– ORIGIN Middle English (denoting the forehead): from Old French *front* (noun), *fronter* (verb), from Latin *frons, front-* 'forehead, front.'

front·age /'frəntij/ ▶ n. the facade of a building. ■ a strip or extent of land abutting on a street or water: *the houses have a narrow frontage to the street* | *our lot has a frontage of 153 feet, with a depth of 170 feet* | *beautiful homes with river frontage.*

front·age road ▶ n. a subsidiary road running parallel to a main road or highway and giving access to houses and businesses. Also called SERVICE ROAD.

fron·tal[1] /'frəntl/ ▶ adj. of or at the front: *the frontal view misses the octagonal tower.* ■ (of an attack) delivered directly on the front, not the side or back: *a frontal assault upon the Iraqi fortifications.* ■ of or relating to the forehead or front part of the skull: *the frontal sinuses.*
– DERIVATIVES **fron·tal·ly** /'frəntl-ē/ adv.
– ORIGIN mid 17th cent. (in the sense 'relating to the forehead'): from modern Latin *frontalis*, from Latin *frons, front-* 'front, forehead.'

fron·tal[2] ▶ n. a decorative cloth for covering the front of an altar.
– ORIGIN Middle English (denoting a band or ornament worn on the forehead): from Old French *frontel*, from Latin *frontale*, from *frons, front-* 'front, forehead.'

fron·tal bone ▶ n. the bone that forms the front part of the skull and the upper part of the eye sockets. ■ either of the pair of bones from which this is formed by fusion in infancy.

fron·tal lobe ▶ n. each of the paired lobes of the brain lying immediately behind the forehead, including areas concerned with behavior, learning, personality, and voluntary movement.

fron·tal lo·bot·o·my ▶ n. lobotomy of the frontal lobe of the cerebrum to sever the white connecting fibers.

front and center ▶ adv. prominently; at the forefront: *standing front and center here today are our bravest heroes.*
▶ adj. prominent; of the greatest importance: *why is this matter suddenly front and center?* | *my front-and-center concerns.*

front bench ▶ n. (in the UK) the foremost seats in the House of Commons, occupied by the members of the cabinet and shadow cabinet.
– DERIVATIVES **front·bench·er** /,frənt'benCHər/ n.

front bot·tom ▶ n. Brit. informal used euphemistically to refer to the female genitalia: *these are women who insist on a "no front bottom" clause.*

front burn·er ▶ n. the focus of attention: *a revamp of the 1872 Mining Law is next up on the front burner.* Compare with BACK BURNER.

front court ▶ n. the part of a basketball court where each team tries to score against its opponent. ■ the players on a team who usually play closest to the other team's basket when trying to score.

Front de Lib·ér·a·tion Na·tion·ale /,frôɴ də ,libə,räs'yôɴ ,näsyə'näl/ (abbr.: **FLN**) a revolutionary political party in Algeria that supported the war of independence against France 1954–62.
– ORIGIN French, 'National Liberation Front.'

front desk ▶ n. the main desk at a hotel or motel, for checking in or out and handling requests from guests.

front door ▶ n. the main entrance to a house.

Fron·te·nac /'frontə,nak, frôɴt(ə)'näk/, Louis de Buade, Comte de (1622–98), French politician. He served as governor of New France 1672–82, 1689–98.

front end ▶ n. **1** the front of a car or other vehicle.
2 the part of a radio or television receiver to which the aerial signal goes first.
3 Computing a part of a computer or program that allows access to other parts.
▶ adj. [attrib.] **1** (of money) paid or charged at the beginning of a transaction: *a front-end fee.*
2 Computing (of a device or program) directly accessed by the user and allowing access to further devices, programs, or databases.

front-end load·er ▶ n. a machine with a scoop or bucket on an articulated arm at the front for digging and loading earth. ■ a hydraulic bucket or scoop that fits onto the front of a tractor.

fron·tes /'fräntēz/ plural form of FRONS.

front-fanged ▶ adj. (of a snake such as a cobra or viper) having the front pair of teeth modified as fangs, with grooves or canals to conduct the venom. Compare with BACK-FANGED.

fron·tier /,frən'ti(ə)r/ ▶ n. a line or border separating two countries. ■ the district near such a line. ■ the extreme limit of settled land beyond which lies wilderness, esp. referring to the western US before Pacific settlement: *his novel of the American frontier.* ■ the extreme limit of understanding or achievement in a particular area: *the success of science in extending the frontiers of knowledge.*
– DERIVATIVES **fron·tier·less** adj.
– ORIGIN late Middle English: from Old French *frontiere*, based on Latin *frons, front-* 'front.'

fron·tiers·man /,frən'ti(ə)rzmən/ ▶ n. (pl. **frontiersmen**) a person, esp. a man, living in the region of a frontier, esp. that between settled and unsettled country.

fron·tiers·wom·an /,frən'ti(ə)rz,wo͝omən/ ▶ n. (pl. **frontierswomen**) a woman living in the region of a frontier, esp. that between settled and unsettled country.

fron·tis·piece /'frəntis,pēs/ ▶ n. **1** an illustration facing the title page of a book.
2 Architecture the principal face of a building. ■ a decorated entrance. ■ a pediment over a door or window.
– ORIGIN late 16th cent. (sense 2): from French *frontispice* or late Latin *frontispicium* 'facade,' from Latin *frons, front-* 'front' + *specere* 'to look.' The change in the ending (early in the word's history) was by association with PIECE.

front·let /'frəntlət/ ▶ n. **1** an ornamental piece of cloth hanging over the upper part of an altar frontal.
2 dated a decorative band or ornament worn on the forehead. ■ another term for PHYLACTERY. ■ a piece of armor or harness for an animal's forehead.
– ORIGIN late 15th cent. (sense 2): from Old French *frontelet*, diminutive of *frontel* (see FRONTAL[2]).

front line (also **frontline**) ▶ n. (usu. **the front line**) the military line or part of an army that is closest

f

to the enemy: [as modifier] *the front-line troops.* ■ the most important or influential position in a debate or movement: *it is doctors who are on the front line of the euthanasia debate.*

front-line state ▶ **plural n.** a country that borders on an area troubled by a war or other crisis: *Germany will no longer be a front-line state with little strategic depth.*

front-load ▶ **v.** [with obj.] distribute or allocate (costs, effort, etc.) unevenly, with the greater proportion at the beginning of an enterprise or process.

front·man /ˈfrənt,man, -mən/ ▶ **n.** (pl. **frontmen**) a person who leads or represents a group or organization, in particular: ■ (also **frontwoman**) the leader of a group of musicians, esp. the lead singer of a pop group. ■ (also **front**) a person who represents an illegal or disreputable organization to give it an air of legitimacy.

front mon·ey ▶ **n.** money received at the beginning of the period of a contract, or money spent in advance of a business operation before income can be obtained: *sought investors willing to put up front money to stage the Broadway musical.*

front of·fice ▶ **n.** the management or administrative officers of a business or other organization.

fron·ton /ˈfrän,tän/ ▶ **n. 1** a building where pelota or jai alai is played.
2 another term for **PEDIMENT**.
– ORIGIN late 17th cent.: from French, from Italian *frontone*, from *fronte* 'forehead,' from Latin *frons, front-* 'front, forehead.'

front-page ▶ **adj.** appearing on the first page of a newspaper or similar publication and containing important or remarkable news: *they ran a front-page story headlined "White-Collar Chic."* ■ worthy of being printed on the first page of a newspaper, etc.: *dishonest research has become front-page news.*
▶ **v.** [with obj.] print (a story) on the first page of a newspaper, etc.: *the paper had front-paged a 1988 discovery at one of his nearby digs.*

Front Range the easternmost range of the Rocky Mountains, chiefly in Colorado, that reaches 14,270 feet (4,349 m) at Grays Peak; also home to Pikes Peak.

front run·ner ▶ **n.** the contestant that is leading in a race or other competition. ■ an athlete or horse that runs best when in the front of the field.

front-run·ning ▶ **adj.** ahead in a race or other competition. ■ (of an athlete or horse) running best when in front of the field.
▶ **n. 1** Stock Market the practice by market makers of dealing on advance information provided by their brokers and investment analysts, before their clients have been given the information.
2 the practice of giving one's support to a competitor because they are in front.

front·side /ˈfrənt,sīd/ ▶ **adj.** [attrib.] denoting a maneuver in surfing and other board sports that is done counterclockwise for a regular rider and clockwise for a goofy rider.

front-wheel drive ▶ **n.** a transmission system that provides power to the front wheels of a motor vehicle.

frore /frôr/ ▶ **adj.** literary frozen; frosty.
– ORIGIN Middle English: archaic past participle of **FREEZE**.

frosh /fräsн/ ▶ **n.** (pl. **same** or **froshes**) informal a college freshman: [as modifier] *frosh week.*
– ORIGIN early 20th cent.: alteration of **FRESHMAN**, perhaps influenced by German *Frosch* 'frog' (in dialect use 'grammar-school student').

Frost /frôst/, Robert (Lee) (1874–1963), US poet, noted for his ironic tone and simple language. Much of his poetry reflects his ties to New England, including the collections *North of Boston* (1914) and *New Hampshire* (1923). He won Pulitzer Prizes in 1924, 1931, and 1937.

frost /frôst/ ▶ **n.** a deposit of small white ice crystals formed on the ground or other surfaces when the temperature falls below freezing. ■ a period of cold weather when such deposits form: *when the hard frosts had set in.* ■ a chilling or dispiriting quality, esp. one conveyed by a cold manner: *there was a light frost of anger in Jack's tone.* ■ [in sing.] informal, chiefly Brit. a failure.
▶ **v.** [with obj.] cover (something) with or as if with small ice crystals; freeze: *each windowpane was frosted along its edges.* ■ [no obj.] become covered with small ice crystals: *a mustache that frosts up when he's ice-climbing.* ■ decorate (a cake, cupcake, or other baked item) with icing. ■ tint hair strands to change the color of isolated strands. ■ injure (a plant) by freezing weather. ■ informal anger or annoy: *such discrimination frosted her no end.*
– DERIVATIVES **frost·less adj.**
– ORIGIN Old English *frost, forst*, of Germanic origin; related to Dutch *vorst* and German *Frost*, also to **FREEZE**.

frost·bite /ˈfrôs(t),bīt/ ▶ **n.** injury to body tissues caused by exposure to extreme cold, typically affecting the nose, fingers, or toes and sometimes resulting in gangrene.

frost·ed /ˈfrôstid/ ▶ **adj.** covered with or as if with frost: *I stood looking out on the frosted garden.* ■ (of glass or a window) having a translucent textured surface so that it is difficult to see through. ■ (of food) decorated or dusted with icing or sugar. ■ (of hair) having isolated strands tinted a light color.

frost flow·er ▶ **n.** any of a group of delicate clusters of ice crystals that form directly from water vapor, typically on the surface of sea ice.

frost-free ▶ **adj.** free of a buildup of ice without defrosting: *a frost-free freezer.*

frost heave ▶ **n.** the uplift of water-saturated soil or other surface deposits due to expansion on freezing. ■ a mound formed in this way, esp. when broken through the pavement of a road.
– DERIVATIVES **frost heav·ing n.**

frost·ing /ˈfrôstiNG/ ▶ **n. 1** icing.
2 a roughened matte finish on otherwise shiny material such as glass or steel.

frost line ▶ **n.** [in sing.] the maximum depth of ground below which the soil does not freeze in winter.

frost·work /ˈfrôst,wərk/ ▶ **n.** attractive patterns made by frost on a window or other surface.

frost·y /ˈfrôstē/ ▶ **adj.** (**frostier, frostiest**) **1** (of the weather) very cold with frost forming on surfaces: *a cold and frosty morning.* ■ covered with or as if with frost: *the dog crouched in the frosty grass.*
2 cold and unfriendly in manner: *Sam gave her a frosty look.*
– DERIVATIVES **frost·i·ly** /ˈfrôstəlē/ **adv.**, **frost·i·ness** /-stēnis/ **n.**

froth /frôᴛʜ/ ▶ **n. 1** a mass of small bubbles in liquid caused by agitation, fermentation, etc.; foam: *leave the yeast until there is a good head of froth.* ■ impure matter that rises to the surface of liquid: *skim off any surface froth.* ■ something that rises or overflows in a soft, light mass: *her skirt swirled in a froth of black lace.*
2 worthless or insubstantial talk, ideas, or activities: *the froth of party politics.*
▶ **v.** [no obj.] form or contain a rising or overflowing mass of small bubbles: *he took a quick sip of beer as it frothed out of the can* | (as adj. **frothing**) *scooping salmon out of the frothing gorge.* ■ [with obj.] agitate (a liquid) so as to produce a mass of small bubbles. ■ rise or overflow in a soft, light mass: *she wore an ivory silk blouse, frothing at neck and cuffs.*
– PHRASES **froth at the mouth** emit a large amount of saliva from the mouth in a bodily seizure. ■ informal display intense anger: *one can barely read a word about them without frothing at the mouth.*
– ORIGIN late Middle English: from Old Norse *frotha, frauth.*

froth·y /ˈfrôᴛʜē, -T͟Hē/ ▶ **adj.** (**frothier, frothiest**) full of or covered with a mass of small bubbles: *steaming mugs of frothy coffee.* ■ light and entertaining but of little substance: *lots of frothy interviews.*
– DERIVATIVES **froth·i·ly** /-ᴛʜəlē, T͟Həlē/ **adv.**, **froth·i·ness** /-ᴛʜēnis, T͟Hēnis/ **n.**

frot·tage /frôˈtäzн/ ▶ **n. 1** Art the technique or process of taking a rubbing from an uneven surface to form the basis of a work of art. ■ a work of art produced in this way.
2 the practice of touching or rubbing against the clothed body of another person in a crowd as a means of obtaining sexual gratification.
– DERIVATIVES **frot·teur** /-ˈtər/ **n.** (pl. **same**) (sense 2), **frot·teur·ism** /-ˈtər,izəm/ **n.** (sense 2).
– ORIGIN 1930s: French, 'rubbing, friction.'

frot·to·la /ˈfrätl-ə/ ▶ **n.** (pl. **frottole** /ˈfrätl-ā/) Music a form of Italian comic or amorous song, esp. from the 15th and 16th centuries.
– ORIGIN Italian, literally 'fib, tall tale.'

Froude num·ber /froud/ ▶ **n.** a dimensionless number used in hydrodynamics to indicate how well a particular model works in relation to a real system.
– ORIGIN mid 19th cent.: named after William *Froude* (1810–79), English civil engineer.

frou·frou /ˈfro͞o,fro͞o/ ▶ **n.** a rustling noise made by someone walking in a dress. ■ frills or other ornamentation, particularly of women's clothes: [as modifier] *a little froufrou skirt.*
– ORIGIN late 19th cent.: from French, imitative.

frounce /frouns/ ▶ **n.** Falconry a form of trichomoniasis affecting hawks, resulting in a sore with a cheesy secretion in the mouth or throat.
– ORIGIN late Middle English: of unknown origin.

fro·ward /ˈfrō(w)ərd/ ▶ **adj.** (of a person) difficult to deal with; contrary.
– DERIVATIVES **fro·ward·ly adv.**, **fro·ward·ness n.**
– ORIGIN late Old English *frāward* 'leading away from, away,' based on Old Norse *frá* (see **FRO, FROM**).

frown /froun/ ▶ **v.** [no obj.] furrow one's brow in an expression of disapproval, displeasure, or concentration: *he frowned as he reread the letter.* ■ (**frown on/upon**) disapprove of: *the old Russian rural system frowned on private enterprise.*
▶ **n.** a facial expression or look characterized by such a furrowing of one's brows: *a frown of disapproval.*
– DERIVATIVES **frown·er n.**, **frown·ing·ly adv.**
– ORIGIN late Middle English: from Old French *froignier*, from *froigne* 'surly look,' of Celtic origin.

frowst /froust/ informal, chiefly Brit. ▶ **n.** [in sing.] a warm, stuffy atmosphere in a room.
▶ **v.** [no obj.] lounge about in such an atmosphere: *don't frowst by the fire all day.*
– DERIVATIVES **frowst·er n.**
– ORIGIN late 19th cent.: back-formation from **FROWSTY**.

frowst·y /ˈfroustē/ ▶ **adj.** (**frowstier, frowstiest**) Brit. having a stale, warm, and stuffy atmosphere: *a small, frowsty office.*
– DERIVATIVES **frowst·i·ness n.**
– ORIGIN mid 19th cent. (originally dialect): variant of **FROWZY**.

frowz·y /ˈfrouzē/ (also **frowsy**) ▶ **adj.** (**frowzier, frowziest**) scruffy and neglected in appearance. ■ dingy and stuffy: *a frowzy nightclub.*
– DERIVATIVES **frowz·i·ness** /-zēnis/ **n.**
– ORIGIN late 17th cent. (originally dialect): of unknown origin.

froze /frōz/ past of **FREEZE**.

fro·zen /ˈfrōzən/ past participle of **FREEZE**.
▶ **adj.** Billiards (of a ball) resting against another ball or a cushion.

fro·zen shoul·der ▶ **n.** the common name for **ADHESIVE CAPSULITIS**.

fro·zen smoke ▶ **n.** another term for **AEROGEL**.

FRS ▶ **abbr.** ■ Federal Reserve System. ■ (in the UK) Fellow of the Royal Society.

frt. ▶ **abbr.** freight.

Fruc·ti·dor /,fro͝oktəˈdôr, frʏk-/ **n.** the twelfth month of the French Republican calendar (1793–1805), originally running from August 18 to September 16.
– ORIGIN French, from Latin *fructus* 'fruit' + Greek *dōron* 'gift.'

fruc·ti·fi·ca·tion /,frəktəfiˈkāsнən/ ▶ **n.** the process of fructifying. ■ Botany a spore-bearing or fruiting structure, esp. in a fungus.
– ORIGIN late 15th cent.: from late Latin *fructificatio(n-)*, from Latin *fructificare* 'fructify,' from *fructus* 'fruit.'

fruc·ti·fy /ˈfrəktə,fī/ ▶ **v.** (**fructifies, fructifying, fructified**) [with obj.] formal make (something) fruitful or productive. ■ [no obj.] bear fruit or become productive.
– ORIGIN Middle English: from Old French *fructifier*, from Latin *fructificare*, from *fructus* 'fruit.'

fruc·tose /ˈfrək,tōs, ˈfro͝ok-, -,tōz/ ▶ **n.** Chemistry a hexose sugar found esp. in honey and fruit.
– ORIGIN mid 19th cent.: from Latin *fructus* 'fruit' + **-OSE**[2].

fruc·tu·ous /ˈfrəkcнo͞oəs, ˈfro͝ok-/ ▶ **adj.** formal full of or producing a great deal of fruit.
– ORIGIN late Middle English: from Latin *fructuosus*, from *fructus* 'fruit.'

frug /fro͞og/ ▶ **n.** a vigorous dance to pop music, popular in the mid-1960s.
▶ **v.** (**frugs, frugging, frugged**) [no obj.] perform such a dance.
– ORIGIN of unknown origin.

fru·gal /ˈfro͞ogəl/ ▶ **adj.** sparing or economical with regard to money or food: *he led a remarkably frugal existence.* ■ simple and plain and costing little: *a frugal meal.*
– DERIVATIVES **fru·gal·ly adv.**
– ORIGIN mid 16th cent.: from Latin *frugalis*, from *frugi* 'economical, thrifty,' from *frux, frug-* 'fruit.'

fru·gal·i·ty /fro͞oˈgalətē/ ▶ **n.** the quality of being economical with money or food; thriftiness: *he scorned the finer things in life and valued frugality and simplicity.*

fru·giv·o·rous /fro͞oˈjivərəs/ ▶ **n.** Zoology (of an animal) feeding on fruit.
– DERIVATIVES **fru·gi·vore** /ˈfro͞oji,vôr/ **n.**

– ORIGIN mid 20th cent.: from Latin *frux, frug-* 'fruit' + *-vore* (see **-VOROUS**).

fruit /froot/ ▶ n. **1** the sweet and fleshy product of a tree or other plant that contains seed and can be eaten as food: *tropical fruits such as mangoes and papaya | eat plenty of fresh fruit and vegetables.* ■ Botany the seed-bearing structure of a plant, e.g., an acorn. ■ the result or reward of work or activity: *the pupils began to appreciate the fruits of their labors | the journal was the first fruit of the creative partnership.* ■ archaic or literary natural produce that can be used for food: *we give thanks for the fruits of the earth.* ■ archaic offspring: *she couldn't bear not to see the fruit of her womb.*
2 informal, offensive a male homosexual.
▶ v. [no obj.] (of a tree or other plant) produce fruit, typically at a specified time: *the trees fruit very early* | (as noun **fruiting**) *cover strawberries with cloches to encourage early fruiting.*
– PHRASES **bear fruit** have good results: *their efforts finally bore fruit in 1993 in a surprise decision by the Supreme Court.* **in fruit** (of a tree or plant) at the stage of producing fruit. **old fruit** Brit. informal, dated a friendly form of address used by one man to another.
– ORIGIN Middle English: from Old French, from Latin *fructus* 'enjoyment of produce, harvest,' from *frui* 'enjoy,' related to *fruges* 'fruits of the earth,' plural (and most common form) of *frux, frug-* 'fruit.'

fruit ac·id ▶ n. another term for **ALPHA-HYDROXY ACID**.

fruit·age /'frootij/ ▶ n. archaic or literary fruit collectively.

fruit·ar·i·an /froo'te(ə)rēən/ ▶ n. a person who eats only fruit.
– DERIVATIVES **fruit·ar·i·an·ism** /-,nizəm/ n.
– ORIGIN late 19th cent.: from **FRUIT**, on the pattern of *vegetarian.*

fruit bat ▶ n. a bat with a long snout and large eyes, feeding chiefly on fruit or nectar and found mainly in the Old World tropics. ● Family Pteropodidae: many genera and numerous species. See also **FLYING FOX**.

fruit bod·y ▶ n. another term for **FRUITING BODY**.

fruit·cake /'froot,kāk/ ▶ n. a cake containing dried fruit and nuts. ■ informal an eccentric or insane person. [compare with *nutty as a fruitcake* (see **NUTTY**).]

fruit cock·tail ▶ n. a finely chopped fruit salad, often commercially produced in cans.

fruit cup ▶ n. a salad made of chopped fruit and served in a glass dish as an appetizer or dessert.

fruit drop ▶ n. the shedding of unripe fruit from a tree.

fruit·ed /'frootid/ ▶ adj. [usu. in combination] (of a tree or plant) producing fruit, esp. of a specified kind: *heavy-fruited plants like tomatoes.*

fruit·er /'frootər/ ▶ n. a tree producing fruit at a specified time or in a specified manner: *the wet-season fruiters.*

fruit·er·er /'frootərər/ ▶ n. a retailer of fruit.
– ORIGIN late Middle English: from **FRUITER** + **-ER**[1]; the reason for the addition of the suffix is unclear.

fruit fly ▶ n. a small fly that feeds on fruit in both its adult and larval stages. ● Families Drosophilidae and Tephritidae: many genera. See also **DROSOPHILA**.

fruit·ful /'frootfəl/ ▶ adj. (of a tree, a plant, or land) producing much fruit; fertile. ■ producing good or helpful results; productive: *years of fruitful collaboration | the two days of talks had been fruitful.* ■ (of a person) producing many offspring.
– DERIVATIVES **fruit·ful·ly** adv., **fruit·ful·ness** n.

fruit·ing bod·y ▶ n. Botany the spore-producing organ of a fungus, often seen as a mushroom or toadstool.

fru·i·tion /froo'isHən/ ▶ n. **1** the point at which a plan or project is realized: *the plans have come to fruition sooner than expected.* ■ [in sing.] the realization of a plan or project: *new methods will come with the fruition of that research.*
2 literary the state or action of producing fruit.
– ORIGIN late Middle English (in the sense 'enjoyment'): via Old French from late Latin *fruitio(n-)*, from *frui* 'enjoy' (see **FRUIT**); the current senses (dating from the late 19th cent.) arose by association with **FRUIT**.

fruit·less /'frootləs/ ▶ adj. **1** failing to achieve the desired results; unproductive or useless: *his fruitless attempts to publish poetry.*
2 (of a tree or plant) not producing fruit.
– DERIVATIVES **fruit·less·ly** adv., **fruit·less·ness** n.

fruit·let /'frootlət/ ▶ n. an immature or small fruit. ■ Botany another term for **DRUPELET**.

fruit loop ▶ n. informal a crazy or foolish person.
– ORIGIN 1970s: from *Froot Loops*, trademark for a breakfast cereal.

fruit ma·chine ▶ n. British term for **SLOT MACHINE**.

fruit pi·geon ▶ n. a fruit-eating pigeon occurring in the Old World tropics. ● a relative of the imperial pigeons occurring in New Guinea (genus *Ducula*, family Columbidae). ● a green pigeon occurring in Africa (genus *Treron*, family Columbidae).

fruit sal·ad ▶ n. a mixture of different types of chopped fruit served in syrup or juice. ■ military slang a display of medals and other decorations.

fruit sug·ar ▶ n. another term for **FRUCTOSE**.

fruit tree ▶ n. a tree grown for its edible fruit.

fruit·wood /'froot,wood/ ▶ n. [usu. as modifier] the wood of a fruit tree, esp. when used in furniture: *a fruitwood dressing table.*

fruit·y /'frootē/ ▶ adj. (**fruitier, fruitiest**) **1** (esp. of food or drink) of, resembling, or containing fruit: *a light and fruity Beaujolais.*
2 (of a voice or sound) mellow, deep, and rich: *Jeff had a wonderfully fruity voice.* ■ Brit. informal sexually suggestive in content or style.
3 informal, offensive relating to or associated with homosexuals.
4 informal eccentric or crazy: *a kind of fruity professor.*
– DERIVATIVES **fruit·i·ly** /'frootl-ē/ adv., **fruit·i·ness** /'frootēnəs/ n.

fru·men·ty /'froomәntē/ (also **furmety**) ▶ n. Brit. an old-fashioned dish consisting of hulled wheat boiled in milk and seasoned with cinnamon and sugar.
– ORIGIN late Middle English: from Old French *frumentee*, from *frument*, from Latin *frumentum* 'corn.'

frump /frəmp/ ▶ n. an unattractive woman who wears dowdy old-fashioned clothes.
– DERIVATIVES **frump·ish** adj., **frump·ish·ly** adv.
– ORIGIN mid 16th cent.: probably a contraction of late Middle English *frumple* 'wrinkle,' from Middle Dutch *verrompelen*. The word originally denoted a mocking speech or action; later (in the plural) ill humor, the sulks; hence a bad-tempered, (later) dowdy woman (early 19th cent).

frump·y ▶ adj. (**frumpier, frumpiest**) (of a woman or her clothes) dowdy and old-fashioned: *a frumpy housewife | her frumpy, shapeless dresses.*
– DERIVATIVES **frump·i·ly** /'frəmpəlē/ adv., **frump·i·ness** /'frəmpēnis/ n.

Frun·ze /'froonzə/ former name (1926–91) of **BISHKEK**.

fru·se·mide /'froosə,mīd, -zə-/ ▶ n. variant spelling of **FUROSEMIDE**.

frus·ta /'frəstə/ plural form of **FRUSTUM**.

frus·trate /'frəs,trāt/ ▶ v. [with obj.] prevent (a plan or attempted action) from progressing, succeeding, or being fulfilled: *his attempt to frustrate the merger.* ■ prevent (someone) from doing or achieving something: *an increasingly popular way to frustrate car thieves.* ■ cause (someone) to feel upset or annoyed, typically as a result of being unable to change or achieve something: (as adj. **frustrating**) *it can be very frustrating to find that the size you want isn't there.*
▶ adj. archaic frustrated.
– DERIVATIVES **frus·trat·er** n., **frus·trat·ing·ly** adv. [as submodifier] *progress turned out to be frustratingly slow.*
– ORIGIN late Middle English: from Latin *frustrat-* 'disappointed,' from the verb *frustrare*, from *frustra* 'in vain.'

frus·trat·ed /'frəs,trātid/ ▶ adj. feeling or expressing distress and annoyance, esp. because of inability to change or achieve something: *young people get frustrated with the system.* ■ [attrib.] (of a person) unable to follow or be successful in a particular career: *a frustrated actor.* ■ [attrib.] prevented from progressing, succeeding, or being fulfilled: *our parents may want us to fulfill their own frustrated dreams.* ■ (of a person or sexual desire) unfulfilled sexually: *jealousies and frustrated passions.*
– DERIVATIVES **frus·trat·ed·ly** adv.

frus·tra·tion /frə'strāsHən/ ▶ n. the feeling of being upset or annoyed, esp. because of inability to change or achieve something: *I sometimes feel like screaming with frustration.* ■ an event or circumstance that causes one to have such a feeling: *the inherent frustrations of assembly line work.* ■ the prevention of the progress, success, or fulfillment of something: *the frustration of their wishes.*
– ORIGIN mid 16th cent.: from Latin *frustratio(n-)*, from *frustrare* 'disappoint' (see **FRUSTRATE**).

frus·tule /'frəs,CHool/ ▶ n. Botany the silicified cell wall of a diatom, consisting of two valves or overlapping halves.

– ORIGIN mid 19th cent.: from Latin *frustulum*, diminutive of *frustum* (see **FRUSTUM**).

frus·tum /'frəstəm/ ▶ n. (pl. **frusta** /-tə/ or **frustums**) Geometry the portion of a cone or pyramid that remains after its upper part has been cut off by a plane parallel to its base, or that is intercepted between two such planes.
– ORIGIN mid 17th cent.: from Latin, 'piece cut off.'

fru·ti·cose /'frooti,kōs, -,kōz/ ▶ adj. Botany (of a lichen) having upright or pendulous branches.
– ORIGIN mid 17th cent.: from Latin *fruticosus*, from *frutex, frutic-* 'bush, shrub.'

Fry /frī/, Christopher (Harris) (1907–2005), English playwright. He is known chiefly for his comic verse dramas, esp. *The Lady's Not for Burning* (1948) and *Venus Observed* (1950).

fry[1] /frī/ ▶ v. (**fries, frying, fried**) [with obj.] **1** cook (food) in hot fat or oil, typically in a shallow pan. ■ [no obj.] (of food) be cooked in such a way: *put half a dozen steaks to fry in a pan.* ■ [no obj.] informal (of a person) burn or overheat: *with the sea and sun and wind you'll fry if you don't take care.*
2 informal destroy: *drugs fry the brain.* ■ execute or be executed by electrocution.
▶ n. (pl. **fries**) [in sing.] a meal of meat or other food cooked in such a way. ■ a social gathering where fried food is served: *you'll explore islands and stop for a fish fry.* ■ (**fries**) another term for **FRENCH FRIES**.
– ORIGIN Middle English: from Old French *frire*, from Latin *frigere.*

fry[2] ▶ plural n. young fish, esp. when newly hatched. ■ the young of other animals produced in large numbers, such as frogs.
– ORIGIN Middle English: from Old Norse *frjó.*

fry·er /'frīər/ (also **frier**) ▶ n. **1** a large, deep container for frying food.
2 a small young chicken suitable for frying.

fry·ing pan (also **frypan**) ▶ n. a shallow pan with a long handle, used for cooking food in hot fat or oil.
– PHRASES **out of the frying pan into the fire** from a bad situation to one that is worse.

fry-up ▶ n. Brit. informal a dish of various types of fried food.

FSBO /'fiz,bō/ ▶ abbr. for sale by owner; designating some aspect of sales of private homes by their owners: *FSBO sellers.*

FSH ▶ abbr. follicle-stimulating hormone.

FSLIC ▶ n. Federal Savings and Loan Insurance Corporation.

f. sp. ▶ abbr. a taxonomic category, esp. of fungi, below that of species and defined by physiological characteristics, esp. as they affect pathogenicity. The abbreviation is used in binomial names, between the species name and a special qualifier.
– ORIGIN abbreviation of Latin *forma specialis*, 'special form.'

FST ▶ abbr. flat-screen television.

f-stop ▶ n. Photography a camera setting corresponding to a particular f-number.

FT ▶ abbr. ■ Basketball free throw. ■ full-time.

Ft. ▶ abbr. Fort: *Ft. Lauderdale.*

ft. ▶ abbr. foot; feet.

FTA ▶ abbr. Free Trade Agreement, used to refer to that signed in 1988 between the US and Canada.

FTC ▶ abbr. Federal Trade Commission.

ft-c ▶ abbr. foot-candle.

fth. ▶ abbr. fathom.

FT in·dex another term for **FTSE INDEX**.

ft-lb ▶ abbr. foot-pound.

FTP Computing ▶ abbr. file transfer protocol, a standard for the exchange of program and data files across a network.
▶ v. (**FTPs, FTP'ing, FTP'd** or **FTP'ed**) [with obj.] informal transfer (a file) from one computer or system to another, esp. on the Internet.

FTSE in·dex a figure (published by the *Financial Times*) indicating the relative prices of shares on the London Stock Exchange, esp. (also **FTSE 100 index**) one calculated on the basis of Britain's one hundred largest public companies.
– ORIGIN *FTSE*, abbreviation of *Financial Times Stock Exchange.*

Fu·ad /foo'äd/ the name of two kings of Egypt. ■ Fuad I (1868–1936), reigned 1922–36. Formerly sultan of Egypt 1917–22, he became Egypt's first

f

king after independence. ■ **Fuad II** (1952–), grandson of Fuad I; reigned 1952–53. Named king as an infant on the forced abdication of his father, Farouk, he was deposed when Egypt became a republic.

fu·bar /ˈfo͞oˌbär/ ▶ **adj.** out of working order; seriously, perhaps irreparably, damaged: *the clock in the hall is fubar*.
– ORIGIN 1940s: acronym from *fucked up beyond all recognition* (or *repair*).

fub·sy /ˈfəbzē/ ▶ **adj.** (**fubsier, fubsiest**) Brit. informal fat and squat.
– ORIGIN late 18th cent.: from dialect *fubs* 'small fat person,' perhaps a blend of FAT and CHUB.

Fuchs[1] /fo͝oks/, Klaus (1911–88), British physicist; born in Germany; full name *Emil Klaus Julius Fuchs*. A communist who fled Nazi persecution, he passed secret information regarding the atom bomb to the former Soviet Union during the 1940s.

Fuchs[2], Sir Vivian (Ernest) (1908–99), English geologist and explorer. He made the first overland crossing of the Antarctic 1955–58. His party met Sir Edmund Hillary's New Zealand contingent, approaching from the opposite direction, at the South Pole.

fuch·sia /ˈfyo͞oSHə/ ▶ **n. 1** a shrub with pendulous tubular flowers that are typically of two contrasting colors. They are native to America and New Zealand and are commonly grown as ornamentals. ● Genus *Fuchsia*, family Onagraceae: many cultivars.
2 a vivid purplish-red color like that of the sepals of a typical fuchsia flower.
– ORIGIN modern Latin, named in honor of Leonhard *Fuchs* (1501–66), German botanist.

fuch·sin /ˈfyo͞oksən, -ˌsēn/ (also **fuchsine**) ▶ **n.** a deep red synthetic dye used as a biological stain and disinfectant. ● A chloride of rosaniline; chem. formula: $C_{20}H_{20}N_3Cl$.
– ORIGIN mid 19th cent.: from German *Fuchs* 'fox,' translating French *Renard* (the name of the chemical company that first produced fuchsin commercially) + -IN[1].

fu·ci /ˈfyo͞osī, -sē/ plural form of FUCUS.

fuck /fək/ vulgar slang ▶ **v.** [with obj.] **1** have sexual intercourse with (someone). ■ [no obj.] (of two people) have sexual intercourse.
2 ruin or damage (something).
▶ **n.** an act of sexual intercourse. ■ [with adj.] a sexual partner.
▶ **exclam.** used alone or as a noun (**the fuck**) or a verb in various phrases to express anger, annoyance, contempt, impatience, or surprise, or simply for emphasis.
– PHRASES **go fuck yourself** an exclamation expressing anger or contempt for, or rejection of, someone. **not give a fuck** (**about**) used to emphasize indifference or contempt.
– PHRASAL VERBS **fuck around** spend time doing unimportant or trivial things. ■ have sexual intercourse with a variety of partners. ■ (**fuck around with**) meddle with. **fuck off** [usu. in imperative] (of a person) go away. **fuck someone over** treat someone in an unfair or humiliating way. **fuck someone up** damage or confuse someone emotionally. **fuck something up** (or **fuck up**) do something badly or ineptly.
– DERIVATIVES **fuck·a·ble** adj.
– ORIGIN early 16th cent.: of Germanic origin (compare Swedish dialect *focka* and Dutch dialect *fokkelen*); possibly from an Indo-European root meaning 'strike,' shared by Latin *pugnus* 'fist.'

> **USAGE** Despite the wideness and proliferation of its use in many sections of society, the word **fuck** remains (and has been for centuries) one of the most taboo words in English. Until relatively recently, it rarely appeared in print; even today, there are a number of euphemistic ways of referring to it in speech and writing, e.g., **the F-word**, **f*****, or **f—k**.

fuck·er /ˈfəkər/ ▶ **n.** vulgar slang a contemptible or stupid person (often used as a general term of abuse).

fuck·head /ˈfəkˌhed/ ▶ **n.** vulgar slang a stupid or contemptible person (often used as a general term of abuse).

fuck·ing /ˈfəkiNG/ ▶ **adj. & adv.** vulgar slang used for emphasis or to express anger, annoyance, contempt, or surprise.

fuck-up ▶ **n.** vulgar slang a mess or muddle. ■ a person who has a tendency to make a mess of things.

fuck·wit /ˈfəkˌwit/ ▶ **n.** chiefly Brit. vulgar slang a stupid or contemptible person (often used as a general term of abuse).

fu·coid /ˈfyo͞oˌkoid/ Botany ▶ **n.** a brown seaweed or fossil plant of a group to which bladderwrack belongs. ● Order Fucales, class Phaeophyceae, including genus *Fucus*.
▶ **adj.** of, relating to, or resembling a brown seaweed, esp. a fucoid.
– ORIGIN mid 19th cent.: from FUCUS + -OID.

fu·co·xan·thin /ˌfyo͞okōˈzanTHin/ ▶ **n.** Chemistry a brown carotenoid pigment occurring in and generally characteristic of the brown algae.
– ORIGIN late 19th cent.: from FUCUS + *xanthin*, variant of XANTHINE.

fu·cus /ˈfyo͞okəs/ ▶ **n.** (pl. **fuci** /ˈfyo͞osī, -sē/) a seaweed of a large genus of brown algae having flat leathery fronds. ● Genus *Fucus*, class Phaeophyceae.
– DERIVATIVES **fu·coid** /-ˌkoid/ adj.
– ORIGIN early 17th cent. (denoting a cosmetic): from Latin, 'rock lichen, red dye, rouge,' from Greek *phukos* 'seaweed,' of Semitic origin.

FUD /fəd/ ▶ **n.** fear, uncertainty and doubt, usually evoked intentionally in order to put a competitor at a disadvantage: [as modifier] *the FUD factor*.
– ORIGIN acronym.

fud·dle /ˈfədl/ ▶ **v.** [with obj.] confuse or stupefy (someone), esp. with alcohol: *my head was aching and my brain seemed fuddled*. ■ [no obj.] archaic go on a drinking bout.
▶ **n.** [in sing.] a state of confusion or intoxication: *through the fuddle of wine he heard some of the conversation*. ■ archaic a drinking bout.
– ORIGIN late 16th cent. (in the sense 'go on a drinking bout'): of unknown origin.

fud·dled /ˈfədld/ ▶ **adj.** confused or stupefied, esp. as a result of drinking alcohol: [in combination] *Benjamin was trying to clear his drink-fuddled brain*.

fud·dy-dud·dy /ˈfədē ˌdədē/ ▶ **n.** (pl. **fuddy-duddies**) informal a person who is old-fashioned and fussy: *he probably thinks I'm an old fuddy-duddy*.
– ORIGIN early 20th cent. (originally dialect): of unknown origin.

fudge /fəj/ ▶ **n. 1** a soft candy made from sugar, butter, and milk or cream. ■ rich chocolate, used esp. as a filling for cakes or a sauce on ice cream: *chocolate cake filled with whipped cream and topped with hot fudge* | [as modifier] *a fudge cake*.
2 an instance of faking or ambiguity: *the new settlement is a fudge rushed out to win cheers at the conference*. ■ archaic nonsense.
3 a piece of late news inserted in a newspaper page.
▶ **v.** [with obj.] present or deal with (something) in a vague, noncommittal, or inadequate way, esp. so as to conceal the truth or mislead: *a temptation to fudge the issue and nudge grades up*. ■ adjust or manipulate (facts or figures) so as to present a desired picture.
▶ **exclam.** dated nonsense (expressing disbelief or annoyance).
– ORIGIN early 17th cent.: probably an alteration of obsolete *fadge* 'to fit' Early usage was as a verb in the sense 'turn out as expected,' also 'merge together': this probably gave rise to its use in confectionery. In the late 17th cent. the verb came to mean 'fit together in a clumsy or underhanded manner,' which included facts or figures being cobbled together in a superficially convincing way: this led to the exclamation 'fudge!' and to sense 3 of the noun.

fudge fac·tor ▶ **n.** informal a figure included in a calculation to account for error or unanticipated circumstances, or to ensure a desired result.

fueh·rer /ˈfyo͝orər/ ▶ **n.** variant spelling of FÜHRER.

fu·el /ˈfyo͞oəl/ ▶ **n.** material such as coal, gas, or oil that is burned to produce heat or power. ■ short for NUCLEAR FUEL. ■ food, drink, or drugs as a source of energy: *any protein intake can also be used as fuel*. ■ a thing that sustains or inflames passion, argument, or other emotion or activity: *the remuneration packages will add fuel to the debate about top-level rewards*.
▶ **v.** (**fuels, fueling, fueled**; Brit. **fuels, fuelling, fuelled**) [with obj.] **1** supply or power (an industrial plant, vehicle, or machine) with fuel: *the plan includes a hydroelectric plant to fuel a paper factory* | figurative *a big novel that is fueled by anger and revenge*. ■ fill up (a vehicle, aircraft, or ship) with oil or gasoline. ■ [no obj.] (**fuel up**) (of a person) eat a meal: *arrive straight from work and fuel up on the complimentary buffet*.
2 cause (a fire) to burn more intensely. ■ sustain or inflame (a feeling or activity): *his rascal heart and private pain fuel his passion as an actor*.
– PHRASES **add fuel to the fire** (or **flames**) cause a situation or conflict to become more intense, esp. by provocative comments.
– ORIGIN Middle English: from Old French *fouaille*, based on Latin *focus* 'hearth' (in late Latin 'fire').

fu·el cell ▶ **n.** a cell producing an electric current directly from a chemical reaction.

fu·el el·e·ment ▶ **n.** an element consisting of nuclear fuel and other materials for use in a reactor.

fu·el in·jec·tion ▶ **n.** the direct introduction of fuel under pressure into the combustion units of an internal combustion engine.
– DERIVATIVES **fu·el-in·ject·ed** adj.

fu·el oil ▶ **n.** oil used as fuel in an engine or furnace.

fu·el rod ▶ **n.** a rod-shaped fuel element in a nuclear reactor.

fu·el·wood /ˈfyo͞oəlˌwo͝od/ ▶ **n.** wood used as fuel.

Fuen·tes /ˈfwentās/, Carlos (1928–), Mexican writer. Notable works: *Where the Air is Clear* (1958), *Terra Nostra* (1975), *The Old Gringo* (1984), and *Happy Families* (2006).

fu·fu /ˈfo͞oˌfo͞o/ (also **foo-foo**) ▶ **n.** dough made from boiled and ground plantain or cassava, used as a staple food in parts of western and central Africa.
– ORIGIN mid 18th cent.: from Twi *fufuu*.

fug /fəg/ ▶ **n.** [in sing.] Brit. informal a warm, stuffy, or smoky atmosphere in a room: *the cozy fug of the music halls*.
– DERIVATIVES **fug·gy** adj.
– ORIGIN late 19th cent. (originally dialect and schoolchildren's slang): of unknown origin.

fu·ga·cious /fyo͞oˈgāSHəs/ ▶ **adj.** literary tending to disappear; fleeting: *she was acutely conscious of her fugacious youth*.
– DERIVATIVES **fu·ga·cious·ly** adv., **fu·ga·cious·ness** n.
– ORIGIN mid 17th cent.: from Latin *fugax, fugac-* (from *fugere* 'flee') + -IOUS.

fu·gac·i·ty /fyo͞oˈgasətē/ ▶ **n. 1** literary the quality of being fleeting or evanescent.
2 Chemistry a thermodynamic property of a real gas that, if substituted for the pressure or partial pressure in the equations for an ideal gas, gives equations applicable to the real gas.

fu·gal /ˈfyo͞ogəl/ ▶ **adj.** of the nature of a fugue: *the virtuosity of the fugal finale*.
– DERIVATIVES **fu·gal·ly** adv.

fu·ga·to /f(y)o͞oˈgätō/ Music ▶ **adj. & adv.** in the style of a fugue, but not in strict or complete fugal form.
▶ **n.** (pl. **fugatos**) a passage in this style.
– ORIGIN Italian.

-fuge ▶ **comb. form** expelling or dispelling either a specified thing or in a specified way: *vermifuge* | *centrifuge*.
– ORIGIN from modern Latin *-fugus*, from Latin *fugare* 'cause to flee.'

fu·gi·tive /ˈfyo͞ojətiv/ ▶ **n.** a person who has escaped from a place or is in hiding, esp. to avoid arrest or persecution: *fugitives from justice* | [as modifier] *fugitive criminals*. ■ [as modifier] quick to disappear; fleeting: *he entertained a fugitive idea that Barbara needed him*.
– ORIGIN late Middle English: from Old French *fugitif, -ive*, from Latin *fugitivus*, from *fugere* 'flee.'

fu·gle·man /ˈfyo͞ogəlmən/ ▶ **n.** (pl. **fuglemen**) historical a soldier placed in front of a regiment or company while drilling to demonstrate the motions and time. ■ a leader, organizer, or spokesman: *fuglemen of the ideological right*.
– ORIGIN early 19th cent.: from German *Flügelmann* 'leader of the file,' from *Flügel* 'wing' + *Mann* 'man.'

fug·ly /ˈfəgli/ ▶ **adj.** (**fuglier, fugliest**) vulgar slang very ugly or unattractive: *I told him we all thought he was fugly*.
– ORIGIN 1970s: blend of FUCKING and UGLY.

fu·gu /ˈf(y)o͞ogo͞o/ ▶ **n.** a puffer fish that is eaten as a Japanese delicacy, after some highly poisonous parts have been removed.
– ORIGIN mid 20th cent.: from Japanese.

fugue /fyo͞og/ ▶ **n. 1** Music a contrapuntal composition in which a short melody or phrase (the subject) is introduced by one part and successively taken up by others and developed by interweaving the parts.
2 Psychiatry a state or period of loss of awareness of one's identity, often coupled with flight from one's usual environment, associated with certain forms of hysteria and epilepsy.
– DERIVATIVES **fugu·ist** /ˈfyo͞ogist/ n.
– ORIGIN late 16th cent.: from French, or from Italian *fuga*, from Latin *fuga* 'flight,' related to *fugere* 'flee.'

füh·rer /ˈfyo͝orər/ (also **fuehrer**) ▶ **n.** a ruthless, tyrannical leader.
– ORIGIN mid 20th cent.: from German *Führer* 'leader,' part of the title *Führer und Reichskanzler* 'Leader and Chancellor of the Empire' assumed in 1934 by Adolf HITLER.

Fu·jai·rah /fo͞oˈjīrə/ (also **al-Fujayrah**) one of the seven member states of the United Arab Emirates; pop. 107,900 (est. 2009).

Fu·ji, Mount /ˈfo͞ojē/ a dormant volcano on the island of Honshu in Japan. Japan's highest mountain, it rises to 12,385 feet (3,776 m). It is regarded as sacred by the Japanese. Also called FUJIYAMA.

Fu·jian /ˈfo͞oˈyän/ (also **Fukien** /ˈfo͞oˈkyen/) a province in southeastern China, on the China Sea; capital, Fuzhou.

Fu·ji·ta scale /fo͞oˈjētə/ (also **Fujita-Pearson scale**) ▶ **n.** Meteorology a scale of tornado severity with numbers from 0 to 6, based on the degree of observed damage.
– ORIGIN mid 20th cent.: named after Dr. Tetsuya Theodore *Fujita* (1920–1988), the meteorologist who chiefly devised it.

Fu·ji·ya·ma /ˌfo͞ojēˈ(y)ämə/ another name for FUJI, MOUNT.

Fu·ku·o·ka /ˌfo͞oko͞oˈōkə/ an industrial city and port in southern Japan, capital of Kyushu island; pop. 1,363,841 (2007).

-ful ▶ **suffix 1** (forming adjectives from nouns) full of: *sorrowful*. ■ having the qualities of: *masterful*.
2 forming adjectives from adjectives or from Latin stems with little change of sense: *grateful*.
3 (forming adjectives from verbs) apt to; able to; accustomed to: *forgetful* | *watchful*.
4 (pl. **-fuls**) forming nouns denoting the amount needed to fill the specified container, holder, etc.: *bucketful* | *handful*.
– ORIGIN from FULL¹.

> **USAGE** The combining form **-ful** is used to form nouns meaning 'the amount needed to fill' (cupful, spoonful, etc.). The plural form of such words is *cupfuls, spoonfuls, etc. Three cups full* would denote the individual cups rather than a quantity measured in cups: *on the sill were three cups full of milk; add three cupfuls of milk to the batter.*

Fu·la /ˈfo͞olə/ ▶ **n.** the Benue-Congo language of the Fulani people, spoken as a first language by about 10 million people and widely used in West Africa as a lingua franca. Also called **Ful, Fulani**.

Fu·la·ni /fo͞oˈlänē/ ▶ **n.** (pl. **same**) **1** a member of a people living in a region of West Africa from Senegal to northern Nigeria and Cameroon. They are traditionally nomadic cattle herders of Muslim faith.
2 another term for FULA.
▶ **adj.** of or relating to this people or their language.
– ORIGIN the name in Hausa.

Ful·bright /ˈfo͝olˌbrīt/, William (1905–95), US senator; full name *James William Fulbright*. An Arkansas Democrat, he sponsored the Fulbright Act of 1946, which authorized funds from the sale of surplus war materials overseas to be used to finance exchange programs of students and teachers between the US and other countries. The program now is supported by federal grants.

ful·crum /ˈfo͝olkrəm, ˈfəl-/ ▶ **n.** (pl. **fulcra** /-krə/ or **fulcrums**) the point on which a lever rests or is supported and on which it pivots. ■ a thing that plays a central or essential role in an activity, event, or situation: *research is the fulcrum of the academic community*.
– ORIGIN late 17th cent. (originally in the general sense 'a prop or support'): from Latin, literally 'post of a couch,' from *fulcire* 'to prop up.'

ful·fill /fo͝olˈfil/ (Brit. **fulfil**) ▶ **v. 1** bring to completion or reality; achieve or realize (something desired, promised, or predicted): *he wouldn't be able to fulfill his ambition to visit Naples*. ■ (**fulfill oneself**) gain happiness or satisfaction by fully developing one's abilities or character. ■ archaic complete (a period of time or piece of work).
2 carry out (a task, duty, or role) as required, pledged, or expected: *some officials were dismissed because they could not fulfill their duties*. ■ satisfy or meet (a requirement or condition): *goods must fulfill three basic conditions*.
– DERIVATIVES **ful·fill·a·ble adj.**, **ful·fill·er n.**
– ORIGIN late Old English *fullfyllan* 'fill up, make full' (see FULL¹, FILL).

ful·filled /fo͝olˈfild/ ▶ **adj.** satisfied or happy because of fully developing one's abilities or character.

ful·fill·ing /fo͝olˈfiliNG/ ▶ **adj.** making someone satisfied or happy because of fully developing their character or abilities: *a fulfilling and rewarding career*.

ful·fill·ment /fo͝olˈfilmənt/ (Brit. **fulfilment**) ▶ **n.**
1 satisfaction or happiness as a result of fully developing one's abilities or character: *she did not believe that marriage was the key to happiness and fulfillment*.
2 the achievement of something desired, promised, or predicted: *winning the championship was the fulfillment of a childhood dream*. ■ the meeting of a requirement or condition: *the fulfillment of statutory requirements*. ■ the performance of a task, duty, or role as required, pledged, or expected.

ful·gent /ˈfəljənt/ ▶ **adj.** literary shining brightly.
– ORIGIN late Middle English: from Latin *fulgent-* 'shining,' from the verb *fulgere*.

ful·gu·ra·tion /ˌfo͝olg(y)əˈrāSHən/ ▶ **n. 1** Medicine the destruction of small growths or areas of tissue using diathermy.
2 literary a flash like that of lightning.
– DERIVATIVES **ful·gu·rant adj.** (FULGURATION (sense 2))., **ful·gu·rate v.** (FULGURATION (sense 2))., **ful·gu·rous adj.** (FULGURATION (sense 2)).
– ORIGIN mid 17th cent. (usually plural in the sense 'flashes of lightning'): from Latin *fulguratio(n-)* 'sheet lightning,' from *fulgur* 'lightning.' Sense 1 dates from the early 20th cent.

ful·gu·rite /ˈfo͝olg(y)əˌrīt/ ▶ **n.** Geology vitreous material formed of sand or other sediment fused by lightning. ■ a piece of such material.
– ORIGIN mid 19th cent.: from Latin *fulgur* 'lightning' + -ITE¹.

fu·lig·i·nous /fyo͞oˈlijənəs/ ▶ **adj.** sooty; dusky.
– ORIGIN late 16th cent. (originally describing a vapor as 'thick and noxious'): from late Latin *fuliginosus*, from *fuligo, fuligin-* 'soot.'

Fu·ling /ˈfo͞oˈliNG/ a city in Sichuan province, in central China, on the Yangtze River at its junction with the Wu River; pop. 168,500 (est. 2009).

full¹ /fo͝ol/ ▶ **adj. 1** containing or holding as much or as many as possible; having no empty space: *wastebaskets full of rubbish* | *she could only nod, for her mouth was full*. ■ having eaten or drunk to one's limits or satisfaction. See also FULL UP below. ■ [predic.] (**full of**) containing or holding much or many; having a large number of: *his diary is full of entries about her*. ■ [predic.] (**full of**) having a lot of (a particular quality): *she was full of confidence*. ■ [predic.] (**full of**) completely engrossed with; unable to stop talking or thinking about: *Anna had been full of her day, saying how Mitch had described England to her*. ■ filled with intense emotion: *she picked at her food, her heart too full to eat*. ■ involving a lot of activities: *he lived a full life*.
2 [attrib.] not lacking or omitting anything; complete: *fill in your full name below* | *full details on request*. ■ (often used for emphasis) reaching the utmost limit; maximum: *he reached for the engine control and turned it up to full power* | *John made full use of all the tuition provided*. ■ having all the privileges and status attached to a particular position: *the country applied for full membership in the European Community*. ■ (of a report or account) containing as much detail or information as possible. ■ used to emphasize an amount or quantity: *he kept his fast pace going for the full 14-mile distance*. ■ [attrib.] (of a covering material in bookbinding) used for the entire cover: *bound in full cloth*.
3 (of a person or part of their body) plump or rounded: *she had full lips* | *the fuller figure*. ■ (of the hair) having body. ■ (of a garment) made using much material arranged in folds or gathers, or generously cut so as to fit loosely: *the dress has a square neck and a full skirt*. ■ (of a sound) strong and resonant. ■ (of a flavor or color) rich or intense.
▶ **adv. 1** straight; directly: *she turned her head and looked full into his face*.
2 very: *he knew full well she was too polite to barge in*. ■ archaic entirely (used to emphasize an amount or quantity): *they talked for full half an hour*.
▶ **n.** (**the full**) archaic the period, point, or state of the greatest fullness or strength; the height of a period of time. ■ the state or time of full moon. ■ archaic or Irish the whole.
▶ **v. 1** [with obj.] black English make (something) full; fill up: *he full up the house with bawling*.
2 [with obj.] gather or pleat (fabric) so as to make a garment full.
3 [no obj.] (of the moon or tide) become full.
– PHRASES **full and by** Sailing close-hauled but with sails filling. **full of beans** see BEAN. **full of oneself** very self-satisfied and with an exaggerated sense of self-worth. **full of years** archaic having lived to a considerable age. **full on 1** running at or providing maximum power or capacity: *he had the heater full on*. **2** so as to make a direct or significant impact: *the recession has hit us full on*. ■ (**full-on**) informal (of an activity or thing) not diluted in nature or effect: *this is full-on ballroom boogie*. **full out 1** as much or as far as possible; with maximum effort or power: *he held his foot to the floor until the car raced full out*. **2** Printing flush with the margin. **full steam** (or **speed**) **ahead** used to indicate that one should proceed with as much speed or energy as possible. **full to the brim** see BRIM. **full up** filled to capacity. ■ having eaten or drunk so much that one is replete. **in full** with nothing omitted: *I shall expect your life story in full*. ■ to the full amount due: *their relocation costs would be paid in full*. ■ to the utmost; completely: *the textbooks have failed to exploit in full the opportunities offered*. **to the full** to the greatest possible extent: *enjoy your free trip to Europe to the full*.
– ORIGIN Old English, of Germanic origin; related to Dutch *vol* and German *voll*.

full² ▶ **v.** [with obj.] (often as noun **fulling**) clean, shrink, and felt (cloth) by heat, pressure, and moisture.
– ORIGIN Middle English: probably a back-formation from FULLER¹, influenced by Old French *fouler* 'press hard upon' or medieval Latin *fullare*, based on Latin *fullo* 'fuller.'

full·back /ˈfo͝olˌbak/ ▶ **n. 1** Football an offensive player in the backfield.
2 (in a game such as soccer or field hockey) a player in a defensive position at the side of the field.

full-blood·ed ▶ **adj. 1** of unmixed race: *a full-blooded Cherokee*.
2 vigorous, enthusiastic, and without compromise: *a full-blooded argument*.
– DERIVATIVES **full blood n.** (sense 1), **full-blood·ed·ly adv.**, **full-blood·ed·ness n.**

full-blown ▶ **adj.** fully developed: *the onset of full-blown AIDS in persons infected with HIV*. ■ (of a flower) in full bloom.

full-bod·ied ▶ **adj.** rich and satisfying in flavor or sound: *a spicy, full-bodied white wine*.

full bore ▶ **adv.** at full speed or maximum capacity: *the boat came full bore toward us*.
▶ **adj.** [attrib.] denoting firearms of relatively large caliber: *full-bore handguns*. ■ complete; thoroughgoing: *a full-bore leftist*.

full-bot·tomed ▶ **adj.** (of a wig) long at the back.

full broth·er ▶ **n.** a brother born of the same mother and father.

full col·or ▶ **n.** the full range of colors: *lively illustrations in full color*.

full-court press ▶ **n.** Basketball a defensive tactic in which members of a team cover their opponents throughout the court and not just near their own basket. ■ an instance of aggressive pressure: *if the president were to mount a full-court press for the space station*.

full dress ▶ **n.** clothes worn on ceremonial or formal occasions.
▶ **adj.** [attrib.] denoting an event, activity, or process that is treated with complete seriousness or that possesses all the characteristics of a genuine example of the type: *shuttle diplomacy might be better than a full-dress conference*.

full dress u·ni·form ▶ **n.** a military uniform worn on ceremonial occasions.

full em·ploy·ment ▶ **n.** the condition in which virtually all who are able and willing to work are employed: *a target of full employment*.

Ful·ler¹ /ˈfo͝olər/, (Sarah) Margaret (1810–50), US literary critic and social reformer. An advocate of cultural education for women, she conducted "Conversations," a popular series of discussion groups in the Boston area before becoming literary critic of the *New York Tribune* 1844–46. Among her books is *Woman in the Nineteenth Century* (1845).

Ful·ler², Melville Weston (1833–1910), US Supreme Court associate justice 1888–1910. He was also a member of the Court of International Arbitration 1900–1910 in The Hague.

Full·er³ /ˈfo͝olər/, R. Buckminster (1895–1983), US designer and architect; full name *Richard Buckminster Fuller*. He is best known for his invention of the geodesic dome and also for his ideals of using the world's resources with maximum purpose and least waste.

full·er¹ /ˈfo͝olər/ ▶ **n.** a person who fulls cloth.
– ORIGIN Old English *fullere*, from Latin *fullo*, of unknown origin.

full·er² ▶ **n.** a grooved or rounded tool on which iron is shaped. ■ a groove made by this, esp. in a horseshoe.
▶ **v.** [with obj.] stamp (iron) with such a tool.
– ORIGIN early 19th cent. (as a verb): of unknown origin.

full·er·ene /ˌfo͝oləˈrēn/ ▶ **n.** Chemistry a form of carbon having a large spheroidal molecule consisting of a hollow cage of atoms, of which buckminsterfullerene was the first known example.
– ORIGIN late 20th cent.: contraction of BUCKMINSTERFULLERENE.

f

ful·ler's earth ▸ n. a type of clay used in fulling cloth and as an adsorbent.

ful·ler's tea·sel ▸ n. a teasel with stiff bracts that curve backward from the prickly flower head. ● *Dipsacus sativus*, family Dipsacaceae.
– ORIGIN so named because it was formerly dried and used for raising the nap on woven cloth.

Ful·ler·ton /'fŏŏlərtən/ a city in southwestern California, southeast of Los Angeles; pop. 131,868 (est. 2008).

full face ▸ adv. with all of the face visible; facing directly at someone or something: *she looked full face at the mirror.*
▸ adj. [attrib.] **1** showing all of the face: *a full-face mug shot.*
2 covering all of the face: *a full-face motorcycle helmet.*

full-fash·ioned ▸ adj. (of women's clothing, esp. hosiery) shaped and seamed to fit the body: *full-fashioned stockings.* ■ (of a knitted garment) shaped by increasing or decreasing the number of loops made along the fabric length without alteration of the stitch.

full-fig·ured ▸ adj. (of women's clothing) designed for large women.

full-fledged ▸ adj. completely developed or established; of full status: *coldlike symptoms that never quite develop into full-fledged colds.*

full flood ▸ n. the tide or a river at its highest. ■ (**in full flood**) speaking enthusiastically and volubly: *she was in full flood about the glories of bicycling.*

full-fron·tal ▸ adj. (of nudity or a nude figure) with full exposure of the front of the body. ■ with nothing concealed or held back: *they put a full-frontal guitar assault to clever lyrics.*

full gain·er ▸ n. Sports (in diving) a dive in which a complete backwards somersault is performed before entering the water feet first.

full-grown ▸ adj. having reached maturity.

full growth ▸ n. the greatest size that a plant or animal naturally attains; maturity.

full-heart·ed ▸ adj. with great enthusiasm and commitment; full of sincere feeling: *full-hearted consent of the electorate.*
– DERIVATIVES **full-heart·ed·ly** adv., **full-heart·ed·ness** n.

full house ▸ n. [in sing.] **1** an audience, or a group of people attending a meeting, that fills the venue for the event to capacity.
2 a poker hand with three of a kind and a pair, beating a flush and losing to four of a kind. ■ a winning card at bingo in which all the numbers have been successfully marked off.

full-length ▸ adj. of the standard length: *a full-length Disney cartoon.* ■ (of a garment or curtain) extending to, or almost to, the ground. ■ (of a mirror or portrait) showing the whole human figure.
▸ adv. (usu. **full length**) (of a person) with the body lying stretched out and flat: *Lucy flung herself full length on the floor.*

full marks ▸ plural n. the maximum award in an examination or assessment. ■ praise for someone's intelligence, hard work, or other quality: *she had to give him full marks for originality.*

full meas·ure ▸ n. the total amount or extent: *the full measure of their worth.*

full moon ▸ n. the phase of the moon in which its whole disk is illuminated. ■ the time when this occurs: *it was several days after full moon.*

full-mo·tion vid·e·o (abbr.: **FMV**) ▸ n. digital video data that is transmitted or stored on video discs for real-time reproduction on a computer (or other multimedia system) at a rate of not less than 25 frames per second.

full-mouthed /'mouTHd, 'mouTHt/ ▸ adj. **1** (of cattle, sheep, etc.) having a full set of adult teeth.
2 spoken loudly or vigorously.

full nel·son ▸ n. see NELSON.

full·ness /'fŏŏlnəs/ (also **fulness**) ▸ n. **1** the state of being filled to capacity: *scores of cans in different states of fullness.* ■ the state of having eaten enough or more than enough and feeling full: *the feeling of fullness you acquire from eating brown rice.* ■ the state of being complete or whole: *the honesty and fullness of the information they provide.* ■ (in or alluding to biblical use) all that is contained in the world: *God's green earth in all its fullness is for the people.*
2 (of a person's body or part of it) the state of being filled out so as to produce a rounded shape: *the childish fullness of his cheeks.* ■ (of a garment or the hair) the condition of having been cut or designed to give a full shape. ■ richness or intensity of flavor, sound, or color: *the coffee is of a luxurious fullness.*
– PHRASES **the fullness of one's** (or **the**) **heart** literary overwhelming emotion. **in the fullness of time** after a due length of time has elapsed; eventually: *he'll tell us in the fullness of time.*

full page ▸ n. [usu. as modifier] an entire page of a newspaper or magazine: *full-page advertisements.*

full pro·fes·sor ▸ n. see PROFESSOR.
– DERIVATIVES **full pro·fes·sor·ship** n.

full-rigged ▸ adj. (of a sailing ship) having three or more masts that all carry square sails.

full-scale ▸ adj. of the same size as the thing represented: *a huge tank containing two full-scale pirate ships.* ■ unrestricted in size, extent, or intensity; complete and thorough: *a full-scale invasion of the mainland.*

full score ▸ n. a score of a musical composition giving the parts for all performers on separate staves.

full sis·ter ▸ n. a sister born of the same mother and father.

full-size ▸ adj. **1** of normal size for its type: *she was still a puppy, not yet full-size.* ■ (of a bed) having the dimensions suitable for two people, specifically 54 inches by 75 inches.
2 enlarged: *click on any item to see a full-size picture.* (Also **full-sized.**)

full stop ▸ n. chiefly Brit. another term for PERIOD (sense 2 of the noun).

full term ▸ n. see TERM (sense 2 of the noun).

full tilt ▸ adv. see TILT.

full-time ▸ adj. occupying or using the whole of someone's available working time, typically 40 hours in a week: *a full-time job.*
▸ adv. on a full-time basis: *both parents were employed full-time.*

full-tim·er ▸ n. a person who does a full-time job.

ful·ly /'fŏŏlē/ ▸ adv. **1** completely or entirely; to the furthest extent: *I fully understand the fears of the workers.* ■ without lacking or omitting anything: *this issue is discussed more fully in chapter seven* | [as submodifier] *a fully equipped gymnasium.*
2 no less or fewer than (used to emphasize an amount): *fully 65 percent of all funerals are by cremation.*
– ORIGIN Old English *fullīce* (see FULL[1], -LY[2]).

-fully ▸ suffix forming adverbs corresponding to adjectives ending in *-ful* (such as *sorrowfully* corresponding to *sorrowful*).

ful·ly fash·ioned ▸ adj. another term for FULL-FASHIONED.

ful·ly fledged ▸ adj. British term for FULL-FLEDGED.

ful·mar /'fŏŏlmər, -,mär/ ▸ n. a gull-sized gray and white seabird of the petrel family, with a stocky body and tubular nostrils. ● Genus *Fulmarus*, family Procellariidae: two species, in particular the **northern fulmar** (*F. glacialis*) of the arctic.
– ORIGIN late 17th cent.: from Hebridean Norn dialect, from Old Norse *fúll* 'stinking, foul' (because of its habit of regurgitating its stomach contents when disturbed) + *már* 'gull.'

ful·mi·nant /'fŏŏlmənənt, 'fəl-/ ▸ adj. Medicine (of a disease or symptom) severe and sudden in onset.
– ORIGIN early 17th cent.: from French, or from Latin *fulminant-* 'striking with lightning,' from the verb *fulminare* (see FULMINATE).

ful·mi·nate /'fŏŏlmə,nāt, 'fəl-/ ▸ v. [no obj.] express vehement protest: *all fulminated against the new curriculum.* ■ literary explode violently or flash like lightning: *thunder fulminated around the house.* ■ [usu. as adj.] Medicine (**fulminating**) (of a disease or symptom) develop suddenly and severely: *fulminating appendicitis.*
▸ n. Chemistry a salt or ester of fulminic acid.
– ORIGIN late Middle English: from Latin *fulminat-* 'struck by lightning,' from *fulmen, fulmin-* 'lightning.' The earliest sense (derived from medieval Latin *fulminare*) was 'denounce formally,' later 'issue formal censures' (originally said of the pope). A sense 'emit thunder and lightning,' based on the original Latin meaning, arose in the early 17th cent., and hence 'explode violently' (late 17th cent).

ful·mi·nate of mer·cu·ry ▸ n. a white or grayish crystalline powder that when dry is extremely volatile when exposed to heat or pressure and is used as an explosive.

ful·mi·na·tion /,fŏŏlmə'nāsHən, -fəl-/ ▸ n. (usu. **fulminations**) an expression of vehement protest: *the fulminations of media moralists.* ■ a violent explosion or a flash like lightning.

ful·min·ic ac·id /fŏŏl'minik, fəl-/ ▸ n. Chemistry a very unstable acid isomeric with cyanic acid. ● Chem. formula: HONC.
– ORIGIN early 19th cent.: *fulminic* from Latin *fulmen, fulmin-* 'lightning' + -IC.

ful·ness /'fŏŏlnəs/ ▸ n. variant spelling of FULLNESS.

ful·some /'fŏŏlsəm/ ▸ adj. **1** complimentary or flattering to an excessive degree: *they are almost embarrassingly fulsome in their appreciation.*
2 of large size or quantity; generous or abundant: *a fulsome harvest.*
– DERIVATIVES **ful·some·ly** adv., **ful·some·ness** n.
– ORIGIN Middle English (in the sense 'abundant'): from FULL[1] + -SOME[1].

> **USAGE** Although the earliest use of **fulsome** (first recorded in the 13th century) was 'generous or abundant,' this meaning is now regarded by some people as wrong. The correct meaning today is held to be 'excessively complimentary or flattering.' However, the word is still often used in its original sense of 'abundant,' especially in sentences such as *she was fulsome in her praise for the people who organized it*, and this use can give rise to ambiguity: for one speaker, **fulsome praise** may be a genuine compliment, while for others it will be interpreted as an insult.

Ful·ton /'fŏŏltn/, Robert (1765–1815), US inventor; pioneer of the steamship. He constructed a steam-propelled "diving-boat" in 1800, which he submerged to a depth of 25 feet (7.6 m). In 1806, he built the first successful paddle steamer, the *Clermont.* Eighteen other steamships were subsequently built, inaugurating the era of commercial steam navigation.

ful·vic ac·id /'fəlvik, 'fŏŏl-/ ▸ n. a highly soluble organic phenol found in humus that chelates elemental mineral nutrients.

ful·vous /'fŏŏlvəs, 'fəl-/ ▸ adj. reddish yellow; tawny.
– ORIGIN mid 17th cent.: from Latin *fulvus* + -OUS.

Fu Man·chu /'fōō man'CHōō/ (in full **Fu Manchu mustache**) ▸ n. a long narrow mustache in which the ends taper and droop down to the chin.
– ORIGIN mid 20th cent.: the kind of mustache worn by *Fu Manchu*, a master criminal in the novels of British writer Sax Rohmer (1883–1959).

Fu Manchu

fu·mar·ic ac·id /fyōō'marik/ ▸ n. Chemistry a crystalline acid, isomeric with maleic acid, present in fumitory and many other plants. ● Alternative name: *trans*-**butenedioic acid**; chem. formula: HOOCCH=CHCOOH.
– DERIVATIVES **fu·ma·rate** /'fyōōmə,rāt/ n.
– ORIGIN mid 19th cent.: *fumaric* from modern Latin *Fumaria* 'fumitory' + -IC.

fu·ma·role /'fyōōmə,rōl/ ▸ n. an opening in or near a volcano, through which hot sulfurous gases emerge.
– DERIVATIVES **fu·ma·rol·ic** /,fyōōmə'rōlik/ adj.
– ORIGIN early 19th cent.: from obsolete Italian *fumaruolo*, from late Latin *fumariolum* 'vent, hole for smoke,' a diminutive based on Latin *fumus* 'smoke.'

fum·ble /'fəmbəl/ ▸ v. [no obj.] use the hands clumsily while doing or handling something: *she fumbled with the lock.* ■ (**fumble around/about**) move clumsily in various directions using the hands to find one's way: *Greg fumbled around in the closet and found his black jacket.* ■ [with obj.] use the hands clumsily to move (something) as specified: *she fumbled a cigarette from her bag.* ■ [with obj.] Football drop or lose control of (the ball), sometimes causing a turnover: *he seldom fumbled a ball.* ■ [with obj.] (in other ball games) fail to catch or field (the ball, a pass, a shot, etc.) cleanly. ■ express oneself or deal with something clumsily or nervously: *asked for explanations, Michael had fumbled for words.*
▸ n. [usu. in sing.] an act of using the hands clumsily while doing or handling something: *just one fumble during a tire change could separate the winners from the losers.* ■ Football an act of dropping or losing control of the ball, sometimes causing a turnover: *his fumble was recovered on the 6-yard line.* ■ (in other ball games) an act of failing to catch or field the ball cleanly. ■ an act of managing or dealing with something clumsily: *we are not talking about subtle errors of judgment, but major fumbles.*
– DERIVATIVES **fum·bler** /'fəmb(ə)lər/ n., **fum·bling·ly** /'fəmb(ə)liNGlē/ adv.
– ORIGIN late Middle English: from Low German *fommeln* or Dutch *fommelen.*

fume /fyōōm/ ▸ n. (usu. **fumes**) gas, smoke, or vapor that smells strongly or is dangerous to inhale: *clouds of exhaust fumes spewed by cars.* ■ a pungent odor of

a particular thing or substance: *he breathed fumes of wine into her face.* ■ literary a watery vapor, steam, or mist rising from the earth or sea.
▶ v. [no obj.] **1** emit gas, smoke, or vapor: *fragments of lava hit the ground, fuming and sizzling.* ■ [with obj.] (usu. as adj. **fumed**) expose (esp. wood) to ammonia fumes in order to produce dark tints: *the fumed oak sideboard.*
2 feel, show, or express great anger: *he is fuming over the interference in his work.*
– DERIVATIVES **fum·ing·ly** /ˈfyo͞omiNGlē/ **adv.**, **fum·y** /ˈfyo͞omē/ **adj.**
– ORIGIN late Middle English: from Old French *fumer* (verb), from Latin *fumare* 'to smoke.'

fume hood ▶ n. a ventilated enclosure in a chemistry laboratory, in which harmful volatile chemicals can be used or kept.

fu·met /fyo͞oˈmā, ˈfyo͞omət/ ▶ n. a concentrated stock, esp. of game or fish, used as flavoring.
– ORIGIN early 18th cent. (in the senses 'smell of game' and 'game flavor'): from French, from *fumer* 'to smoke.' The current sense dates from the early 20th cent.

fu·mi·gate /ˈfyo͞oməˌgāt/ ▶ v. [with obj.] apply the fumes of certain chemicals to (an area) to disinfect it or to rid it of vermin.
– DERIVATIVES **fu·mi·gant** /-gənt/ **n.**, **fu·mi·ga·tion** /ˌfyo͞oməˈgāSHən/ **n.**, **fu·mi·ga·tor** /-ˌgātər/ **n.**
– ORIGIN mid 16th cent. (earlier (late Middle English) as *fumigation*, in the sense 'the action of perfuming'): from Latin *fumigat-* 'fumigated,' from the verb *fumigare*, from *fumus* 'smoke.'

fu·mi·to·ry /ˈfyo͞oməˌtôrē/ ▶ n. an Old World plant with spikes of small tubular pink or white flowers and finely divided grayish leaves, often considered a weed. ● Genus *Fumaria*, family Fumariaceae.
– ORIGIN late Middle English: from Old French *fumeterre*, from medieval Latin *fumus terrae* 'smoke of the earth' (because of its grayish leaves).

fun /fən/ ▶ n. enjoyment, amusement, or lighthearted pleasure: *the children were* ***having fun*** *in the play area | anyone who turns up can join in the fun.* ■ a source of this: *people-watching is great fun.* ■ playful behavior or good humor: *she's full of fun.* ■ behavior or an activity that is intended purely for amusement and should not be interpreted as having serious or malicious purposes: *it was nothing serious; they just enjoyed having some harmless fun.* ■ [attrib.] (of a place or event) providing entertainment or leisure activities for children: *a 33-acre movie-themed fun park.*
▶ adj. (**funner**, **funnest**) informal amusing, entertaining, or enjoyable: *it was a fun evening | what's the funnest part of wakeboarding for you?*
▶ v. (**funs**, **funning**, **funned**) informal joke or tease: [no obj.] *no need to get sore—I was only funning* | [with obj.] *they are just funning you.*
– PHRASES **for fun** (or **for the fun of it**) in order to amuse oneself and not for any more serious purpose. **fun and games** amusing and enjoyable activities: *teaching isn't all fun and games.* **someone's idea of fun** used to emphasize one's dislike for an activity or to mock someone else's liking for it: *being stuck behind a desk all day* ***isn't my idea of fun.*** **in fun** not intended seriously; as a joke: *remember when you meet the press to say that your speech was all in fun.* **like fun** dated an ironic exclamation of contradiction or disbelief in response to a statement. **make fun of** (or **poke fun at**) tease, laugh at, or joke about (someone) in a mocking or unkind way. **not much** (or **a lot of**) **fun** used to indicate that something strikes one as extremely unpleasant and depressing: *it can't be much fun living next door to him.*
– ORIGIN late 17th cent. (denoting a trick or hoax): from obsolete *fun* 'to cheat or hoax,' dialect variant of late Middle English *fon* 'make a fool of, be a fool,' related to *fon* 'a fool,' of unknown origin. Compare with FOND.

> **USAGE** The use of fun as an adjective meaning 'enjoyable,' as in *we had a fun evening*, is now established in informal use, although not accepted in standard English. The adjective now has comparative and superlative forms **funner** and **funnest**, formed as if **fun** were a standard adjective.

Fu·na·ba·shi /ˌfo͞onäˈbäsHē/ a city in central Japan, on eastern Honshu Island, a suburb of Tokyo; pop. 584,152 (2008).

Fu·na·fu·ti /ˌf(y)o͞onəˈf(y)o͞otē/ the capital of Tuvalu, on an island of the same name; pop. 5,000 (est. 2007).

fu·nam·bu·list /fyo͞oˈnambyəlist/ ▶ n. a tightrope walker.
– ORIGIN late 18th cent.: from French *funambule* or Latin *funambulus* (from *funis* 'rope' + *ambulare* 'to walk') + -IST.

Fun·chal /fo͞onˈsHäl, fən-/ the capital and chief port of Madeira, on the south coast of the island; pop. 99,759 (2006).

func·tion /ˈfəNGksHən/ ▶ n. **1** an activity or purpose natural to or intended for a person or thing: *bridges perform the function of providing access across water | Vitamin A is required for good eye function.* ■ practical use or purpose in design: *building designs that prioritize style over function.* ■ a basic task of a computer, esp. one that corresponds to a single instruction from the user.
2 Mathematics a relationship or expression involving one or more variables: *the function (bx + c).* ■ a variable quantity regarded in relation to one or more other variables in terms of which it may be expressed or on which its value depends. ■ Chemistry a functional group.
3 a thing dependent on another factor or factors: *class shame is a function of social power.*
4 a large or formal social event or ceremony: *he was obliged to attend party functions.*
▶ v. [no obj.] work or operate in a proper or particular way: *her liver is functioning normally.* ■ (**function as**) fulfill the purpose or task of (a specified thing): *the museum intends to function as an educational and study center.*
– DERIVATIVES **func·tion·less** **adj.**
– ORIGIN mid 16th cent.: from French *fonction*, from Latin *functio(n-)*, from *fungi* 'perform.'

func·tion·al /ˈfəNGksHənl/ ▶ adj. **1** of or having a special activity, purpose, or task; relating to the way in which something works or operates: *there are important functional differences between left and right brain.* ■ designed to be practical and useful, rather than attractive: *she had assumed the apartment would be functional and simple.* ■ working or operating: *the museum will be fully functional from the opening of the festival.* ■ (of a disease) affecting the operation, rather than the structure, of an organ: *functional diarrhea.* ■ (of a mental illness) having no discernible organic cause: *functional psychosis.*
2 Mathematics of or relating to a variable quantity whose value depends on one or more other variables.
– DERIVATIVES **func·tion·al·ly** **adv.** [sentence adverb] *functionally, the role of the library service is clearly educational.*

func·tion·al food ▶ n. chiefly Brit. another term for NUTRACEUTICAL.

func·tion·al gram·mar ▶ n. a theory of grammar concerned with how the social, cognitive, and pragmatic functions of language relate to structure.

func·tion·al group ▶ n. Chemistry a group of atoms responsible for the characteristic reactions of a particular compound.

func·tion·al il·lit·er·ate ▶ n. a person whose level of ability to read and write is below that needed to do the ordinary tasks required to function normally in society.

func·tion·al·ism /ˈfəNGksHənlˌizəm/ ▶ n. belief in or stress on the practical application of a thing, in particular: ■ (in the arts) the doctrine that the design of an object should be determined solely by its function, rather than by aesthetic considerations, and that anything practically designed will be inherently beautiful. ■ (in the social sciences) the theory that all aspects of a society serve a function and are necessary for the survival of that society. ■ (in the philosophy of mind) the theory that mental states can be sufficiently defined by their cause, their effect on other mental states, and their effect on behavior.
– DERIVATIVES **func·tion·al·ist** **n. & adj.**

func·tion·al·i·ty /ˌfəNGksHəˈnalətē/ ▶ n. **1** the quality of being suited to serve a purpose well; practicality: *I like the feel and functionality of this bakeware.* ■ the purpose that something is designed or expected to fulfill: *manufacturing processes may be affected by the functionality of the product.*
2 the range of operations that can be run on a computer or other electronic system: *new software with additional functionality.*

func·tion·al med·i·cine ▶ n. medical practice or treatments that focus on optimal functioning of the body and its organs, usually involving systems of holistic or alternative medicine: *you don't have to have a disease to benefit from functional medicine.*

func·tion·al shift ▶ n. a shift in the use of a word to a new grammatical function, such as the use of the nouns *contact* and *impact* as verbs.

func·tion·ar·y /ˈfəNGksHəˌnerē/ ▶ n. (pl. **functionaries**) a person who has to perform official functions or duties; an official.

func·tion key ▶ n. Computing a button on a computer keyboard, distinct from the main alphanumeric keys, to which software can assign a particular function.

func·tion word ▶ n. Linguistics a word whose purpose is more to signal grammatical relationship than the lexical meaning of a sentence, e.g., *do* in *do you live here?*

func·tor /ˈfəNGktər/ ▶ n. Logic & Mathematics a function; an operator. ■ Linguistics another term for FUNCTION WORD.
– ORIGIN 1930s: from FUNCTION, on the pattern of words such as *factor*.

fund /fənd/ ▶ n. a sum of money saved or made available for a particular purpose: *he had set up a fund to coordinate economic investment.* ■ (**funds**) financial resources: *the misuse of public funds.* ■ a large stock or supply of something: *a vast* ***fund of*** *information.* ■ (**the funds**) Brit. the stock of the national debt (as a mode of investment). ■ an organization set up for the administration and management of a monetary fund.
▶ v. [with obj.] provide with money for a particular purpose: *the World Bank refused to fund the project* | [in combination] *government-funded research.*
– PHRASES **in funds** Brit. having money to spend.
– ORIGIN mid 17th cent.: from Latin *fundus* 'bottom, piece of landed property.' The earliest sense was 'the bottom or lowest part,' later 'foundation or basis'; the association with money has perhaps arisen from the idea of landed property being a source of wealth.

fun·da /ˈfəndə/ ▶ n. (pl. **fundas**) Indian a basic or fundamental principle underlying something: *her fundas in life are crystal clear.*

fun·dal /ˈfəndəl/ ▶ adj. Medicine of or relating to the fundus of an organ, esp. of the stomach, uterus, or eyeball.

fun·da·ment /ˈfəndəmənt/ ▶ n. **1** the foundation or basis of something.
2 humorous a person's buttocks.
– ORIGIN Middle English (also denoting the base of a building, or the founding of a building or institution): from Old French *fondement*, from Latin *fundamentum*, from *fundare* 'to found.'

fun·da·men·tal /ˌfəndəˈmentl/ ▶ adj. forming a necessary base or core; of central importance: *the protection of fundamental human rights | interpretation of evidence is* ***fundamental to*** *the historian's craft.* ■ affecting or relating to the essential nature of something or the crucial point about an issue: *the fundamental problem remains that of the housing shortage.* ■ so basic as to be hard to alter, resolve, or overcome: *the theories are based on a fundamental error.*
▶ n. (usu. **fundamentals**) a central or primary rule or principle on which something is based: *two courses cover the fundamentals of microbiology.* ■ a fundamental note, tone, or frequency.
– DERIVATIVES **fun·da·men·tal·i·ty** /ˌfəndəmənˈtalətē/ **n.**
– ORIGIN late Middle English: from French *fondamental*, or late Latin *fundamentalis*, from Latin *fundamentum*, from *fundare* 'to found.'

fun·da·men·tal fre·quen·cy ▶ n. Physics the lowest frequency produced by the oscillation of the whole of an object, as distinct from the harmonics of higher frequency.

fun·da·men·tal·ism /ˌfəndəˈmentlˌizəm/ ▶ n. a form of Protestant Christianity that upholds belief in the strict and literal interpretation of the Bible, including its narratives, doctrines, prophecies, and moral laws. ■ strict maintenance of ancient or fundamental doctrines of any religion or ideology, notably Islam.

> Modern Christian fundamentalism arose from American millenarian sects of the 19th century and has become associated with reaction against social and political liberalism, and with the rejection of the theory of evolution. Islamic fundamentalism appeared in the 18th and 19th centuries as a reaction to the disintegration of Islamic political and economic power, asserting that Islam is central to both state and society and advocating strict adherence to the Koran (*Qur'an*) and to Islamic law (*sharia*).

– DERIVATIVES **fun·da·men·tal·ist** **n. & adj.**

fun·da·men·tal·ly /ˌfəndəˈmentl-ē/ ▶ adv. [often as submodifier] in central or primary respects: *two fundamentally different concepts of democracy.*

PRONUNCIATION KEY ə *ago, up*; ər *over, fur*; a *hat*; ā *ate*; ä *car*; e *let*; ē *see*; i *fit*; ī *by*; NG *sing*; ō *go*; ô *law, for*; oi *toy*; o͝o *good*; o͞o *goo*; ou *out*; TH *thin*; T͟H *then*; ZH *vision*

■ [sentence adverb] used to make an emphatic statement about the basic truth of something: *fundamentally, this is a matter for doctors.*

fun·da·men·tal note ▶ n. Music the lowest note of a chord in its original (uninverted) form.

fun·da·men·tal par·ti·cle ▶ n. another term for ELEMENTARY PARTICLE.

fun·da·men·tal tone ▶ n. Music the tone that represents the fundamental frequency of a vibrating object such as a string or bell.

fun·da·men·tal u·nit ▶ n. one of a set of unrelated units of measurement, which are arbitrarily defined and from which other units are derived. For example, in the SI system the fundamental units are the meter, kilogram, and second. ■ a thing that is or is perceived as being the smallest part into which a complex whole can be analyzed: *the house is the fundamental unit of Basque society.*

fund·ed debt ▶ n. debt in the form of securities with long-term or indefinite redemption. Compare with FLOATING DEBT.

fun·di /ˈfənˌdī, -ˌdē/ plural form of FUNDUS.

fund·ie /ˈfəndē/ ▶ n. (pl. **fundies**) informal, chiefly Brit. a fundamentalist, esp. a Christian fundamentalist.
– ORIGIN 1980s: from German, abbreviation of *Fundamentalist* 'fundamentalist.'

fund·ing /ˈfəndiNG/ ▶ n. money provided, esp. by an organization or government, for a particular purpose. ■ the action or practice of providing such money.

fund man·ag·er ▶ n. an employee or department of a large institution (such as a bank, pension fund, or insurance company) that manages the investment of money on its own behalf or on that of an outside client.

fund·rais·er /ˈfəndˌrāzər/ ▶ n. a person whose job or task is to seek financial support for a charity, institution, or other enterprise. ■ an event held to generate financial support for such an enterprise.
– DERIVATIVES **fund·rais·ing** n. & adj.

fun·dus /ˈfəndəs/ ▶ n. (pl. **fundi** /-dī, -dē/) Anatomy the part of a hollow organ (such as the uterus or the gallbladder) that is farthest from the opening. ■ the upper part of the stomach, which forms a bulge higher than the opening of the esophagus (farthest from the pylorus). ■ the part of the eyeball opposite the pupil.
– ORIGIN mid 18th cent.: from Latin, literally 'bottom.'

Fun·dy, Bay of /ˈfəndē/ an arm of the Atlantic Ocean between the Canadian provinces of New Brunswick and Nova Scotia. Its fast-running tides, which are used to generate electricity, are the highest in the world and reach 50–80 feet (12–15 m).

fu·ner·al /ˈfyo͞on(ə)rəl/ ▶ n. the ceremonies honoring a dead person, typically involving burial or cremation. ■ rare a sermon delivered at such a ceremony. ■ archaic or literary a procession of mourners at a burial.
– PHRASES **it's** (or **that's**) **someone's funeral** informal used to warn someone that an unwise act or decision is their responsibility: *"I won't discuss it." "Don't then—it's your funeral."*
– ORIGIN late Middle English: from Old French *funeraille*, from medieval Latin *funeralia*, neuter plural of late Latin *funeralis*, from Latin *funus*, *funer-* 'funeral, death, corpse.'

fu·ner·al di·rec·tor ▶ n. an undertaker.

fu·ner·al home (also **funeral parlor**) ▶ n. an establishment where the dead are prepared for burial or cremation.

fu·ner·al pyre ▶ n. a pile of wood on which a corpse is burned as part of a funeral ceremony in some traditions.

fu·ner·ar·y /ˈfyo͞onəˌrerē/ ▶ adj. relating to a funeral or the commemoration of the dead: *funerary ceremonies.*
– ORIGIN late 17th cent.: from late Latin *funerarius*, from *funus*, *funer-* 'funeral.'

fu·ne·re·al /fyəˈni(ə)rēəl, fyo͞o-/ ▶ adj. having the mournful, somber character appropriate to a funeral: *Lincoln's funereal gloominess was legendary.*
– DERIVATIVES **fu·ne·re·al·ly** adv.
– ORIGIN early 18th cent.: from Latin *funereus* (from *funus*, *funer-* 'funeral') + -AL.

fun·fair /ˈfənˌfer/ ▶ n. chiefly Brit. a fair consisting of rides, sideshows, and other amusements.

fun·gal /ˈfəNGgəl/ ▶ adj. of or caused by a fungus or fungi: *fungal diseases such as mildew.*

fun·gi /ˈfənˌjī, -ˌgī/ plural form of FUNGUS.

fun·gi·ble /ˈfənjəbəl/ ▶ adj. Law (of goods contracted for without an individual specimen being specified) able to replace or be replaced by another identical item; mutually interchangeable: *money is fungible—money that is raised for one purpose can easily be used for another.*
– DERIVATIVES **fun·gi·bil·i·ty** /ˌfənjəˈbilətē/ n.
– ORIGIN late 17th cent.: from medieval Latin *fungibilis*, from *fungi* 'perform, enjoy,' with the same sense as *fungi vice* 'serve in place of.'

fun·gi·cide /ˈfənjəˌsīd, ˈfəNGgə-/ ▶ n. a chemical that destroys fungus.
– DERIVATIVES **fun·gi·cid·al** /ˌfənjəˈsīdl, ˌfəNGgə-/ adj.

fun·gi·form /ˈfənjəˌfôrm, ˈfəNGgəˌ-/ ▶ adj. having the shape of or resembling a fungus or mushroom.

fun·gi·stat·ic /ˌfənjəˈstatik, ˌfəNGgə-/ ▶ adj. inhibiting the growth of fungi.
– DERIVATIVES **fun·gi·stat·i·cal·ly** /-ik(ə)lē/ adv.

fun·giv·or·ous /ˌfənˈjivərəs, -ˈgiv-/ ▶ adj. feeding on fungi or mushrooms.

fun·go /ˈfəNGgō/ ▶ n. (also **fungo fly**) (pl. **fungoes** or **fungos**) Baseball a fly ball hit for fielding practice. ■ (also **fungo bat** or **stick**) a long lightweight bat for hitting practice balls to fielders.
– ORIGIN mid 19th cent.: of unknown origin.

fun·goid /ˈfəNGˌgoid/ ▶ adj. of or caused by a fungus or fungi: *she suffered from a fungoid disease of her feet.* ■ resembling a fungus in shape, texture, or speed of growth: *his skin looked moist and fungoid.*
▶ n. a fungoid plant.

fun·gous /ˈfəNGgəs/ ▶ adj. resembling, caused by, or having the nature of a fungus.
– ORIGIN late Middle English: from Latin *fungosus*, from *fungus* (see FUNGUS).

fun·gus /ˈfəNGgəs/ ▶ n. (pl. **fungi** /-jī, -gī/ or **funguses**) any of a group of unicellular, multicellular, or syncytial spore-producing organisms feeding on organic matter, including molds, yeast, mushrooms, and toadstools. ■ fungal infection (esp. on fish). ■ [in sing.] used to describe something that has appeared or grown rapidly and is considered unpleasant or unattractive: *there was a fungus of outbuildings behind the house.*

> Fungi lack chlorophyll and are therefore incapable of photosynthesis. Many play an ecologically vital role in breaking down dead organic matter; some are an important source of antibiotics or are used in fermentation, and others cause disease. The familiar mushrooms and toadstools are merely the fruiting bodies of organisms that exist mainly as a threadlike mycelium in the soil. Some fungi form associations with other plants, growing with algae to form lichens, or in the roots of higher plants to form mycorrhizas. Fungi are now often classified as a separate kingdom distinct from the green plants.

– ORIGIN late Middle English: from Latin, perhaps related to Greek *spongos*, *sphongos* (see SPONGE).

fun·gus bee·tle ▶ n. a small beetle that feeds chiefly on fungi and is typically black with red or yellow markings. ● Families Mycetophagidae, Erotylidae, and others: several genera.

fun·gus gar·den ▶ n. Entomology a growth of fungus cultivated by certain ants or termites as a source of food.

fun·gus gnat ▶ n. a slender and delicate fly whose larvae feed chiefly on fungi. ● Family Mycetophilidae: numerous species.

fun·house /ˈfənˌhous/ ▶ n. (in an amusement park) a building equipped with trick mirrors, shifting floors, and other devices designed to scare or amuse people as they walk through.

fu·ni·cle /ˈfyo͞onikəl/ ▶ n. Botany a filamentous stalk attaching a seed or ovule to the placenta. Also called FUNICULUS. ■ Entomology a filamentous section of an insect's antenna, supporting the club.
– ORIGIN mid 17th cent.: anglicized form of Latin *funiculus* (see FUNICULUS).

fu·nic·u·lar /fyo͞oˈnikyələr/ ▶ adj. **1** (of a railroad, esp. one on a mountainside) operating by cable with ascending and descending cars counterbalanced. **2** of or relating to a rope or its tension.
▶ n. a railroad operating in such a way.
– ORIGIN mid 17th cent. (in the sense 'of or like a cord or thread'): from Latin *funiculus* (diminutive of *funis* 'rope') + -AR[1].

fu·nic·u·lus /fyo͞oˈnikyələs/ ▶ n. (pl. **funiculi** /-ˌlī, -ˌlē/) Anatomy a bundle of nerve fibers enclosed in a sheath of connective tissue, or forming one of the main tracts of white matter in the spinal cord. ■ another term for FUNICLE.
– ORIGIN mid 17th cent.: from Latin, diminutive of *funis* 'rope.'

Funk /fo͝oNGk, fəNGk/, Casimir (1884–1967), US biochemist; born in Poland. He showed that a number of diseases, including scurvy, rickets, beriberi, and pellagra, were each caused by the deficiency of a particular dietary component. He coined the term *vitamins* for the chemicals concerned.

funk[1] /fəNGk/ informal ▶ n. **1** (also **blue funk**) [in sing.] a state of depression: *I sat absorbed in my own blue funk.* ■ chiefly Brit. a state of great fear or panic: *are you in a blue funk about running out of things to say?* **2** dated, chiefly Brit. a coward.
▶ v. [with obj.] chiefly Brit. avoid (a task or thing) out of fear: *I could have seen him this morning but I funked it.*
– ORIGIN mid 18th cent. (first recorded as slang at Oxford University in Oxford, England): perhaps from FUNK[2] in the slang sense 'tobacco smoke,' or from obsolete Flemish *fonck* 'disturbance, agitation.'

funk[2] ▶ n. **1** a style of popular dance music of US black origin, based on elements of blues and soul and having a strong rhythm that typically accentuates the first beat in the bar. **2** [in sing.] informal, dated a strong musty smell of sweat or tobacco.
– PHRASAL VERBS **funk something up** give music elements of such a style.
– ORIGIN early 17th cent. (in the sense 'musty smell'): perhaps from French dialect *funkier* 'blow smoke on,' based on Latin *fumus* 'smoke.'

funk·a·del·ic /ˌfəNGkəˈdelik/ ▶ adj. denoting a type of dance music that combines funk with elements (such as the use of highly amplified guitars and a heavy drumbeat) derived from rock.
– DERIVATIVES **funkadelia** /-ˈdēlēə/ n.
– ORIGIN 1970s: from the name of a pop group, formed *c.*1970, from FUNK[2] + a shortened form of PSYCHEDELIC.

funk·ster /ˈfəNGkstər/ ▶ n. informal a performer or fan of funky music.

funk·y[1] /ˈfəNGkē/ ▶ adj. (**funkier**, **funkiest**) informal **1** (of music) having or using a strong dance rhythm, in particular that of funk: *some excellent funky beats.* ■ modern and stylish in an unconventional or striking way: *she likes wearing funky clothes.* **2** strongly musty: *cooked greens make the kitchen smell really funky.*
– DERIVATIVES **funk·i·ly** /ˈfuNGkəlē/ adv., **funk·i·ness** n.
– ORIGIN late 18th cent. (in the sense 'smelling strong or bad'): from FUNK[2].

funk·y[2] ▶ adj. (**funkier**, **funkiest**) Brit. archaic or informal frightened, panicky, or cowardly.
– ORIGIN mid 19th cent.: from FUNK[1].

fun·nel /ˈfənl/ ▶ n. a tube or pipe that is wide at the top and narrow at the bottom, used for guiding liquid or powder into a small opening. ■ a thing resembling such a tube or pipe in shape or function: *a funnel of light fell from a circular ceiling.* ■ a metal chimney on a ship or steam engine.
▶ v. (**funnels**, **funneling**, **funneled**; Brit. **funnels**, **funnelling**, **funnelled**) [with obj. and adverbial of direction] guide or channel (something) through or as if through a funnel: *some $12.8 billion was funneled through the Marshall Plan.* ■ [no obj., with adverbial of direction] move or be guided through or as if through a funnel: *the wind funneled down through the valley.* ■ [no obj.] assume the shape of a funnel by widening or narrowing at the end: *the crevice funneled out.*
– DERIVATIVES **fun·nel·like** /-ˌlīk/ adj.
– ORIGIN late Middle English: apparently via Old French from Provençal *fonilh*, from late Latin *fundibulum*, from Latin *infundibulum*, from *infundere*, from *in-* 'into' + *fundere* 'pour.'

fun·nel cake ▶ n. a cake made of batter that is poured through a funnel into hot fat or oil, deep-fried until crisp, and served sprinkled with sugar, of Pennsylvania Dutch origin.

fun·nel cloud ▶ n. a rotating funnel-shaped cloud forming the core of a tornado or waterspout.

fun·nel neck ▶ n. a neck for a knit garment similar to a turtleneck but shorter and without a fold. Compare with MOCK TURTLENECK.

fun·nel-web spi·der ▶ n. any of a number of spiders that build a funnel-shaped web, in particular: ● a large and dangerously venomous Australian spider (genera *Atrax* and *Hadronyche*, family Dipluridae, suborder Mygalomorphae). ● a spider of the family Agelenidae.

fun·ni·ly /ˈfənl-ē/ ▶ adv. in a strange or amusing way: *you do talk funnily.* ■ [sentence adverb] (**funnily enough**) used to admit that a situation or fact is surprising or curious: *funnily enough, I was starting to like the idea.*

fun·ny /ˈfənē/ ▶ adj. (**funnier**, **funniest**) **1** causing laughter or amusement; humorous: *a funny story | the play is hilariously funny.* ■ [predic.] expressing a speaker's objection to another's laughter or mockery: *She started to laugh. "What's so funny?" he asked.* ■ [predic. with negative] informal used to emphasize that something is unpleasant or wrong and should be regarded seriously or avoided: *stealing other people's work isn't funny.*

2 difficult to explain or understand; strange: *I had a funny feeling you'd be around* | *a funny thing, democracy.* ■ unusual or odd; curious: *Bev has a funny little stammer.* ■ unusual in such a way as to arouse suspicion: *there was something funny going on.* ■ used to draw attention to or express surprise at a curious or interesting fact or occurrence: *that's funny!—that vase of flowers has been moved.* ■ informal (of a person or part of the body) not in wholly good health or order; slightly ill: *suddenly my stomach felt funny.*
▶ **plural n.** (**funnies**) informal the comic strips in newspapers: *I read the sports page, funnies, and editorial.*
– PHRASES **see the funny side** (**of something**) appreciate the humorous aspect of a situation or experience.
– DERIVATIVES **fun·ni·ness** /ˈfənēnis/ **n.**

fun·ny bone ▶ **n.** informal the part of the elbow over which the ulnar nerve passes. A knock on the funny bone may cause numbness and pain along the forearm and hand. ■ a person's sense of humor, as located in an imaginary physical organ: *photographs to jostle the mind and the funny bone.*

fun·ny busi·ness ▶ **n.** deceptive, disobedient, or lecherous behavior: *they sent a big strong farmer's lad to make sure there was no funny business.*

fun·ny farm ▶ **n.** informal, offensive a psychiatric hospital: *he should be taken off to the funny farm.*

fun·ny man ▶ **n.** a professional comedian or clown.

fun·ny mon·ey ▶ **n.** informal currency that is forged or otherwise worthless.

fun·ny pa·pers ▶ **plural n.** a section of a newspaper containing comics and humorous matter.

fun run ▶ **n.** informal a noncompetitive run, esp. for sponsored runners in support of a charity.

fun-size (also **fun-sized**) ▶ **adj.** (of a product) smaller than the regular or usual size: *fun-size chocolate bars.*

fun·ster /ˈfənstər/ ▶ **n.** informal a person who makes fun; a joker.

fur /fər/ ▶ **n. 1** the short, fine, soft hair of certain animals: *a long, lean, muscular cat with sleek fur.* ■ the skin of an animal with such hair on it. ■ skins of this type, or fabrics resembling these, used as material for making, trimming, or lining clothes: *jackets made out of yak fur* | [as modifier] *a fur coat.* ■ a garment made of, trimmed, or lined with fur: *she pulled the fur around her.* ■ Heraldry any of several heraldic tinctures representing animal skins in stylized form (e.g., ermine, vair).
2 Brit. a coating formed by hard water on the inside surface of a pipe, kettle, or other container. ■ a coating formed on the tongue as a symptom of sickness.
▶ **v.** (**furs, furring, furred**) [with obj.] **1** [as adj., often in combination] (**furred**) covered with or made from a particular type of fur: *silky-furred lemurs.*
2 Brit. coat or clog with a deposit: *the stuff that furs up coronary arteries.*
3 fix strips of wood to (floor joists, wall studs, etc.) in order to level them or increase their depth.
– PHRASES **fur and feather** game mammals and birds. **make the fur fly** informal cause serious, perhaps violent, trouble.
– DERIVATIVES **fur·less adj.**
– ORIGIN Middle English (as a verb): from Old French *forrer* 'to line, sheathe,' from *forre* 'sheath,' of Germanic origin.

fur. ▶ **abbr.** furlong(s).

fu·ran /ˈfyo͝orˌan, fyo͝oˈran/ ▶ **n.** Chemistry a colorless volatile liquid with a planar unsaturated five-membered ring in its molecule. ● Chem. formula: C_4H_4O.
■ any substituted derivative of this.
– ORIGIN late 19th cent.: from synonymous *furfuran.*

fur·ball /ˈfərˌbôl/ ▶ **n. 1** another term for HAIRBALL.
2 informal a furry pet animal.

fur·bear·er /ˈfərˌbe(ə)rər/ ▶ **n.** an animal whose fur is valued commercially.

fur·be·low /ˈfərbəˌlō/ ▶ **n.** a gathered strip or pleated border of a skirt or petticoat. ■ (**furbelows**) showy ornaments or trimmings: *frills and furbelows just made her look stupid.*
▶ **v.** [with obj.] (usu. as adj. **furbelowed**) literary adorn with trimmings.
– ORIGIN late 17th cent.: from French *falbala* 'trimming, flounce,' of unknown ultimate origin.

fur·bish /ˈfərbisн/ ▶ **v.** [with obj.] (usu. as adj. **furbished**) give a fresh look to (something old or shabby); renovate: *the newly furbished church.* ■ archaic brighten up (a weapon) by polishing it.
– DERIVATIVES **fur·bish·er n.**
– ORIGIN late Middle English: from Old French *forbiss-*, lengthened stem of *forbir*, of Germanic origin.

fur·ca /ˈfərkə/ ▶ **n.** (pl. **furcae** /-kī, -sē/) Zoology a forked appendage or projection in an arthropod, in particular: ■ an ingrowth of the thorax of many insects. ■ the furcula of a springtail.
– DERIVATIVES **fur·cal** /ˈfərkəl/ **adj.**
– ORIGIN early 17th cent.: from Latin, literally 'fork.'

fur·cate technical ▶ **v.** /ˈfərˌkāt, fərˈkāt/ [no obj.] divide into two or more branches; fork: *lines of descent furcating from a common source.*
▶ **adj.** /ˈfərˌkāt, -kit/ divided into two or more branches; forked.
– DERIVATIVES **fur·ca·tion** /fərˈkāsнən/ **n.**
– ORIGIN early 19th cent.: from late Latin *furcatus* 'cloven,' from Latin *furca* 'fork.'

fur·cu·la /ˈfərkyələ/ ▶ **n.** (pl. **furculae** /-ˌlē, -ˌlī/) Zoology a forked organ or structure, in particular: ■ the wishbone of a bird. ■ the forked appendage at the end of the abdomen in a springtail, by which the insect jumps.
– DERIVATIVES **fur·cu·lar adj.**
– ORIGIN mid 19th cent.: from Latin, diminutive of *furca* 'fork.'

fur·fu·ra·ceous /ˌfərf(y)əˈrāsнəs/ ▶ **adj.** Botany & Medicine covered with or characterized by branlike scales.
– ORIGIN mid 17th cent.: from late Latin *furfuraceus* (from Latin *furfur* 'bran') + -OUS.

fur·fur·al /ˈfərf(y)əˌral/ ▶ **n.** Chemistry a colorless liquid used in synthetic resin manufacture, originally obtained by distilling bran. ● An aldehyde derived from furan; chem. formula: C_4H_3OCHO.
– ORIGIN late 19th cent.: from obsolete *furfurol* (in the same sense) + -AL.

fur·fur·al·de·hyde /ˌfərf(y)əˈraldəˌhīd/ ▶ **n.** Chemistry another term for FURFURAL.

fu·ri·o·so /ˌfyo͝orēˈōsō, -zō/ ▶ **adv. & adj.** Music (esp. as a direction) furiously and wildly.
– ORIGIN Italian.

fu·ri·ous /ˈfyo͝orēəs/ ▶ **adj.** extremely angry: *she was furious at this attempt to manipulate her.* ■ full of anger or energy; violent or intense: *he drove at a furious speed.*
– DERIVATIVES **fu·ri·ous·ly adv., fu·ri·ous·ness n.**
– ORIGIN late Middle English: from Old French *furieus*, from Latin *furiosus*, from *furia* 'fury.'

furl /fərl/ ▶ **v.** [with obj.] roll or fold up and secure neatly (a flag, sail, umbrella, or other piece of fabric): *he shouted to the crew to furl sails* | (as adj. **furled**) *a furled umbrella.* ■ [no obj.] literary become rolled up; curl: (as adj. **furled**) *the plant sends up cones of furled leaves.*
– DERIVATIVES **furl·a·ble adj.**
– ORIGIN late 16th cent.: from French *ferler*, from Old French *fer, ferm* 'firm' + *lier* 'bind' (from Latin *ligare*).

fur·long /ˈfərˌlôNG, -ˌläNG/ ▶ **n.** an eighth of a mile, 220 yards.
– ORIGIN Old English *furlang*, from *furh* 'furrow' + *lang* 'long' The word originally denoted the length of a furrow in a common field (formally regarded as a square of ten acres). It was also used as the equivalent of the Roman *stadium*, one eighth of a Roman mile, whence the current sense. Compare with STADIUM.

fur·lough /ˈfərlō/ ▶ **n.** leave of absence, esp. that granted to a member of the armed services: *a civil servant home on furlough* | *a six-week furlough in Australia.* ■ a temporary release of a convict from prison: *a system that allowed murderers to leave prison for weekend furloughs.* ■ a layoff, esp. a temporary one, from a place of employment.
▶ **v.** [with obj.] grant such leave of absence to. ■ lay off (workers), esp. temporarily: *President Reagan furloughed "nonessential" employees* | (as adj. **furloughed**) *factories are apt to recall some furloughed workers.*
– ORIGIN early 17th cent.: from Dutch *verlof*, modeled on German *Verlaub*, of West Germanic origin and related to LEAVE[2].

fur·me·ty /ˈfərmitē/ ▶ **n.** variant of FRUMENTY.

furn. ▶ **abbr.** furnished.

fur·nace /ˈfərnəs/ ▶ **n.** an enclosed structure in which material can be heated to very high temperatures, e.g., for smelting metals. ■ an appliance fired by gas, oil, or wood in which air or water is heated to be circulated throughout a building in a heating system. ■ used to describe a very hot place: *her car was a furnace.*
– ORIGIN Middle English: from Old French *fornais(e)*, from Latin *fornax, fornac-*, from *fornus* 'oven.'

Fur·neaux Is·lands /ˈfərnō/ a group of islands off the coast of northeastern Tasmania, in Australia, in the Bass Strait. The largest island is Flinders Island.

fur·nish /ˈfərnisн/ ▶ **v.** [with obj.] provide (a house or room) with furniture and fittings: *the proprietor has furnished the bedrooms in a variety of styles.*
■ (**furnish someone with**) supply someone with (something); give (something) to someone: *she was able to furnish me with details of the incident.* ■ be a source of; provide: *fish furnish an important source of protein.*
– DERIVATIVES **fur·nish·er n.**
– ORIGIN late Middle English (in the general sense 'provide or equip with what is necessary or desirable'): from Old French *furniss-*, lengthened stem of *furnir*, ultimately of West Germanic origin.

fur·nished /ˈfərnisнt/ ▶ **adj.** (of accommodations) available to be rented with furniture.

fur·nish·ing /ˈfərnisнiNG/ ▶ **n. 1** (usu. **furnishings**) furniture, fittings, and other decorative accessories, such as curtains and carpets, for a house or room.
2 the action of decorating a house or room and providing it with furniture and fittings.
▶ **adj.** denoting fabrics used for curtains, upholstery, or floor coverings: *they create historic furnishing textiles for the finest museums.*

fur·ni·ture /ˈfərnicнər/ ▶ **n. 1** large movable equipment, such as tables and chairs, used to make a house, office, or other space suitable for living or working.
2 [usu. with adj. or noun modifier] small accessories or fittings for a particular use or piece of equipment: *computer hardware, software, and furniture.* ■ the mountings of a rifle. ■ Printing pieces of wood or metal placed around or between metal type to make blank spaces and fasten the matter in the chase.
– PHRASES **part of the furniture** informal a person or thing that has been somewhere so long as to seem a permanent, unquestioned, or invisible feature.
– ORIGIN early 16th cent. (denoting the action of furnishing): from French *fourniture*, from *fournir*, from Old French *furnir* 'to furnish.'

fu·ror /ˈfyo͝orˌôr, -ər/ (also chiefly Brit. **furore**) ▶ **n.** [in sing.] an outbreak of public anger or excitement: *the article raised a furor among mathematicians.* ■ archaic a wave of enthusiastic admiration; a craze.
– ORIGIN late 18th cent.: from Italian *furore*, from Latin *furor*, from *furere* 'be mad, rage.'

fu·ro·se·mide /fyo͝oˈrōsəˌmīd/ (chiefly Brit. also **frusemide**) ▶ **n.** Medicine a synthetic compound with a strong diuretic action, used esp. in the treatment of edema. ● Chem. formula: $C_{12}H_{11}ClN_2O_5S$.
– ORIGIN 1960s: from *fur-* (alteration of *fur(yl)*, denoting a radical derived from furan) + -O- + *sem-* (of unknown origin) + -IDE.

fur·ri·er /ˈfərēər/ ▶ **n.** a person who prepares or deals in furs.
– ORIGIN Middle English: from Old French *forreor*, from *forrer* 'to line, sheathe' (see FUR). The change in the ending in the 16th cent. was due to association with -IER.

fur·ri·er·y /ˈfərēərē/ ▶ **n.** the art or trade of dressing and preparing furs.

fur·ring strip /ˈfəriNG/ ▶ **n.** a length of wood tapering to nothing, used in roofing and other construction work.

fur·row /ˈfərō, ˈfə-rō/ ▶ **n.** a long narrow trench made in the ground by a plow, esp. for planting seeds or for irrigation. ■ a rut, groove, or trail in the ground or another surface: *truck wheels had dug furrows in the sand.* ■ a line or wrinkle on a person's face: *there were deep furrows in his brow.*
▶ **v.** [with obj.] make a rut, groove, or trail in (the ground or the surface of something): *gorges furrowing the deep-sea floor.* ■ (with reference to the forehead or face) mark or be marked with lines or wrinkles caused by frowning, anxiety, or concentration: [with obj.] *a look of concern furrowed his brow* | [no obj.] *her brow furrowed* | (as adj. **furrowed**) *he stroked his furrowed brow.* ■ (with reference to the eyebrows) tighten or be tightened and lowered in anxiety, concentration, or disapproval, so wrinkling the forehead: [no obj.] *his brows furrowed in concentration* | [with obj.] *she furrowed her brows, thinking hard.* ■ (usu. as adj. **furrowed**) use a plow to make a long narrow trench in (land or earth): *furrowed fields.*
– DERIVATIVES **fur·row·y adj.**
– ORIGIN Old English *furh*, of Germanic origin; related to Dutch *voor* and German *Furche*, from an Indo-European root shared by Latin *porca* 'ridge between furrows.'

fur·ry /ˈfərē/ ▶ **adj.** (**furrier, furriest**) covered with fur: *furry creatures in fields.* ■ having a soft surface like fur: *it has soft and furry apple-green leaves.*
– DERIVATIVES **fur·ri·ness** /ˈfərēnis/ **n.**

fur seal ▶ **n.** a gregarious eared seal that frequents the coasts of the Pacific and southern oceans, the male of which is substantially larger than the female. The thick fur on the underside is used commercially as sealskin. ● Two genera in the family Otariidae: the **northern fur seal** (*Callorhinus ursinus*) and the **southern fur seal** (genus *Arctocephalus*).

fur·ther /ˈfərT͟Hər/ used as comparative of FAR.
▶ **adv. 1** (also **farther** /ˈfärT͟Hər/) at, to, or by a greater distance (used to indicate the extent to which one thing or person is or becomes distant from another): *for some time I had wanted to move farther from Lynne* | figurative *the committee seems to have moved further away from its original aims.* ■ [with negative] used to emphasize the difference between a supposed or suggested fact or state of mind and the truth: *as for her being a liar, nothing could be further from the truth* | *nothing could be further from his mind than marrying.*
2 (also **farther** /ˈfär-/) over a greater expanse of space or time; for a longer way: *we had walked further than I realized* | figurative *wages have been driven down even further.* ■ beyond the point already reached or the distance already covered: *Emily decided to drive further up the coast* | *before going any further we need to define our terms.*
3 beyond or in addition to what has already been done: *we are investigating ways to further increase customer satisfaction* | *this theme will be developed further in Chapter 6* | *I shall not trouble you any further.* ■ [sentence adverb] used to introduce a new point relating to or reinforcing a previous statement: *poison hemlock resembles wild carrot, but has a strong, pungent odor; further, young leaves of wild carrot are more finely divided.* ■ at or to a more advanced, successful, or desirable stage: *at the end of three years they were no further on.*
▶ **adj. 1** (also **farther** /ˈfär-/) more distant in space than something else of the same kind: *two men were standing at the further end of the clearing.* ■ more remote from a central point: *the museum is in the further reaches of the town.*
2 additional to what already exists or has already taken place, been done, or been accounted for: *cook for a further ten minutes.*
▶ **v.** [with obj.] help the progress or development of (something); promote: *he had depended on using them to further his own career.*
– PHRASES **not go any further** (of a secret) not be told to anyone else. **until further notice** used to indicate that a situation will not change until another announcement is made: *the museum is closed to the public until further notice.* **until further orders** used to indicate that a situation is only to change when another command is received: *they were to be kept in prison until further orders.*
– DERIVATIVES **fur·ther·er** n.
– ORIGIN Old English *furthor* (adverb), *furthra* (adjective), *fyrthrian* (verb), of Germanic origin; related to FORTH.

USAGE On the differences between **further** and **farther**, see FARTHER.

fur·ther·ance /ˈfərT͟Hərəns/ ▶ **n.** the advancement of a scheme or interest: *acts in furtherance of an industrial dispute.*

fur·ther·more /ˈfərT͟Hərˌmôr/ ▶ **adv.** [sentence adverb] in addition; besides (used to introduce a fresh consideration in an argument): *this species has a quiet charm and, furthermore, is an easy garden plant.*

fur·ther·most /ˈfərT͟Hərˌmōst/ ▶ **adj.** variant form of FARTHERMOST.

fur·thest /ˈfərT͟Hist/ ▶ **adj. & adv.** variant form of FARTHEST.

USAGE On the differences between **furthest** and **farthest**, see FARTHER.

fur·tive /ˈfərtiv/ ▶ **adj.** attempting to avoid notice or attention, typically because of guilt or a belief that discovery would lead to trouble; secretive: *they spent a furtive day together* | *he stole a furtive glance at her.* ■ suggestive of guilty nervousness: *the look in his eyes became furtive.*
– DERIVATIVES **fur·tive·ly** adv., **fur·tive·ness** n.
– ORIGIN early 17th cent.: from French *furtif, -ive* or Latin *furtivus*, from *furtum* 'theft.'

fu·run·cle /ˈfyo͝orˌəNGkəl/ ▶ **n.** technical term for BOIL[2].
– DERIVATIVES **fu·run·cu·lar** /fyo͝oˈrəNGkyələr/ adj., **fu·run·cu·lous** /fyo͝oˈrəNGkyələs/ adj.
– ORIGIN late Middle English: from Latin *furunculus*, literally 'petty thief,' also 'knob on a vine' (regarded as stealing the sap), from *fur* 'thief.'

fu·run·cu·lo·sis /fyo͝oˌrəNGkyəˈlōsəs/ ▶ **n. 1** Medicine the simultaneous or repeated occurrence of boils on the skin.
2 a bacterial disease of salmon and trout.
– ORIGIN late 19th cent.: from FURUNCLE + -OSIS.

fu·ry /ˈfyo͝orē/ ▶ **n.** (pl. **furies**) **1** wild or violent anger: *tears of fury and frustration* | *Rachel shouted, beside herself with fury.* ■ (**a fury**) a surge of violent anger or other feeling: *in a fury, he lashed the horse on.* ■ [in sing.] violence or energy displayed in natural phenomena or in someone's actions: *the fury of a gathering storm* | *she was paddling with a new fury.*
2 (**Fury**) Greek Mythology a spirit of punishment, often represented as one of three goddesses who executed the curses pronounced upon criminals, tortured the guilty with stings of conscience, and inflicted famines and pestilences. The Furies were identified at an early date with the Eumenides. ■ dated used to convey a woman's anger or aggression by comparing her to such a spirit: *she turned on him like a vengeful fury.*
– PHRASES **like fury** informal with great energy or effort: *she fought like fury in his arms.*
– ORIGIN late Middle English: from Old French *furie*, from Latin *furia*, from *furiosus* 'furious,' from *furere* 'be mad, rage.'

furze /fərz/ ▶ **n.** another term for GORSE.
– DERIVATIVES **furz·y** adj.
– ORIGIN Old English *fyrs*, of unknown origin.

fu·sain /ˈfyo͞oˌzān/ ▶ **n.** Geology a crumbly, porous type of coal resembling wood charcoal, used in drawing.
– ORIGIN late 19th cent.: from French, literally 'spindle tree,' also 'fine charcoal' (made from the spindle tree).

fu·sar·i·um /fyo͞oˈzerēəm/ ▶ **n.** a mold of a large genus, many of which cause plant diseases, esp. wilting. ● Genus *Fusarium*, subdivision Deuteromycotina.
■ infestation with any of these or related molds.
– ORIGIN early 20th cent.: modern Latin, from Latin *fusus* 'spindle.'

fus·cous /ˈfəskəs/ ▶ **adj.** technical or literary dark and somber in color.
– ORIGIN mid 17th cent.: from Latin *fuscus* 'dusky' + -OUS.

fuse[1] /fyo͞oz/ ▶ **n.** a safety device consisting of a strip of wire that melts and breaks an electric circuit if the current exceeds a safe level.
▶ **v. 1** [with obj.] join or blend to form a single entity: *intermarriage had fused the families into a large unit.* ■ [no obj.] (of groups of atoms or cellular structures) join or coalesce: *the two nuclei move together and fuse into one nucleus.* ■ melt (a material or object) with intense heat, esp. so as to join it with something else: *powdered glass was fused to a metal base.*
2 [with obj.] provide (a circuit or electrical appliance) with a fuse: (as adj. **fused**) *a fused plug.*
3 [no obj.] Brit. (of an electrical appliance) stop working when a fuse melts: *the crew were left in darkness after the lights fused.* ■ [with obj.] cause (an electrical appliance) to stop working in such a way.
– PHRASES **blow a fuse** use too much power in an electrical circuit, causing a fuse to melt. ■ informal lose one's temper: *it was only a suggestion—there's no need to blow a fuse.*
– ORIGIN late 16th cent.: from Latin *fus-* 'poured, melted,' from the verb *fundere*.

fuse[2] (also **fuze**) ▶ **n.** a length of material along which a small flame moves to explode a bomb or firework, meanwhile allowing time for those who light it to move to a safe distance. ■ a device in a bomb, shell, or mine that makes it explode on impact, after an interval, at set distance from the target, or when subjected to magnetic or vibratory stimulation.
▶ **v.** [with obj.] fit a fuse to (a bomb, shell, or mine): *the bomb was fused to go off during a charity performance.*
– PHRASES **light the** (or **a**) **fuse** set something tense or exciting in motion: *the event lit the fuse for the revolution.* **a short fuse** a tendency to lose one's temper quickly: *watch your tongue—he's got a very short fuse.* ■ (**on a short fuse**) likely to lose one's temper or explode.
– DERIVATIVES **fuse·less** adj.
– ORIGIN mid 17th cent.: from Italian *fuso*, from Latin *fusus* 'spindle.'

fuse box ▶ **n.** a box housing the fuses for circuits in a building.

fused sil·i·ca ▶ **n.** an extremely transparent glass made from fusing silica, commonly used in optical lenses.

fu·see /fyo͞oˈzē/ (also **fuzee**) ▶ **n. 1** a conical pulley or wheel, esp. in a watch or clock.
2 a large-headed match capable of staying lit in strong wind.
3 a railroad signal flare.
– ORIGIN late 16th cent. (denoting a spindle-shaped figure): from French *fusée* 'spindleful,' based on Latin *fusus* 'spindle.'

fu·se·lage /ˈfyo͞osəˌläZH, -zə-/ ▶ **n.** the main body of an aircraft.
– ORIGIN early 20th cent.: from French, from *fuseler* 'shape into a spindle,' from *fuseau* 'spindle.'

fu·sel oil /ˈfyo͞ozəl/ ▶ **n.** a mixture of several alcohols (chiefly amyl alcohol) produced as a byproduct of alcoholic fermentation.
– ORIGIN mid 19th cent.: from German *Fusel* 'bad liquor,' probably related to *fuseln* 'to bungle.'

Fu·shun /ˈfo͞oˈSHo͞on/ a coal-mining city in northeastern China, in the province of Liaoning; pop. 1,264,700 (est. 2006).

fu·si·ble /ˈfyo͞ozəbəl/ ▶ **adj.** able to be fused or melted easily.
– DERIVATIVES **fu·si·bil·i·ty** /ˌfyo͞ozəˈbilətē/ n.
– ORIGIN late Middle English: from Old French, or from medieval Latin *fusibilis*, from *fundere* 'pour, melt.'

fu·si·form /ˈfyo͞ozəˌfôrm/ ▶ **adj.** Botany & Zoology tapering at both ends; spindle-shaped.
– ORIGIN mid 18th cent.: from Latin *fusus* 'spindle' + -IFORM.

fu·sil[1] /ˈfyo͞ozəl/ ▶ **n.** historical a light flintlock musket.
– ORIGIN late 16th cent. (denoting a flint in a tinderbox): from French, ultimately from Latin *focus* 'hearth, fire.'

fu·sil[2] ▶ **n.** Heraldry an elongated lozenge.
– ORIGIN late Middle English: from Old French *fusel*, from a diminutive of Latin *fusus* 'spindle.'

fu·sil·ier /ˌfyo͞ozəˈli(ə)r/ (also **fusileer**) ▶ **n.** (usu. **Fusiliers**) a member of any of several British regiments formerly armed with fusils: *the Royal Scots Fusiliers.* ■ historical a soldier armed with a fusil.
– ORIGIN late 17th cent.: from French, from *fusil* (see FUSIL[1]).

fu·sil·lade /ˈfyo͞osəˌläd, -ˌlād/ ▶ **n.** a series of shots fired or missiles thrown all at the same time or in quick succession: *marchers had to dodge a fusillade of missiles* | figurative *a fusillade of accusations.*
▶ **v.** [with obj.] archaic attack (a place) or shoot down (someone) by a series of shots fired at the same time or in quick succession.
– ORIGIN early 19th cent.: from French, from *fusiller* 'to shoot,' from *fusil* (see FUSIL[1]) + -ADE[1].

fu·sil·li /fyo͞oˈsilē, -ˈsēlē/ ▶ **n.** pasta pieces in the form of short spirals.
– ORIGIN Italian, literally 'little spindles,' diminutive of *fuso*.

fu·si·mo·tor /ˈfyo͞ozəˌmōtər/ ▶ **adj.** Anatomy relating to or denoting the motor neurons with slender fibers that innervate muscle spindles.

fu·sion /ˈfyo͞oZHən/ ▶ **n.** the process or result of joining two or more things together to form a single entity: *a fusion of an idea from anthropology and an idea from psychology* | *malformation or fusion of the three bones in the middle ear.* ■ Physics short for NUCLEAR FUSION. ■ the process of causing a material or object to melt with intense heat, esp. so as to join with another: *the fusion of resin and glass fiber in the molding process.* ■ music that is a mixture of different styles, esp. jazz and rock.
▶ **adj.** referring to food or cooking that incorporates elements of diverse cuisines: *their fusion fare includes a sushi-like roll of gingery rice and eel wrapped in marinated Greek grape leaves.*
– DERIVATIVES **fu·sion·al** /-ZHənl/ adj.
– ORIGIN mid 16th cent.: from Latin *fusio(n-)*, from *fundere* 'pour, melt.'

fu·sion bomb ▶ **n.** a bomb deriving its energy from nuclear fusion, esp. a hydrogen bomb.

fu·sion·ist /ˈfyo͞oZHənist/ ▶ **n. 1** a person who strives for coalition between political parties or factions.
2 a player or fan of music that is mixture of two modern styles.
– DERIVATIVES **fu·sion·ism** /-ˌnizəm/ n.

fuss /fəs/ ▶ **n.** [in sing.] a display of unnecessary or excessive excitement, activity, or interest: *I don't know what all the fuss is about.* ■ a protest or dispute of a specified degree or kind: *he didn't put up too much of a fuss.* ■ elaborate or complex procedures; trouble or difficulty: *they settled in with very little fuss.*
▶ **v.** [no obj.] show unnecessary or excessive concern about something: *she's always fussing about her food.* ■ move around or busy oneself restlessly: *beside him Kelly was fussing with sheets of paper.* ■ [with obj.] Brit. disturb or bother (someone): *when she cries in her sleep, try not to fuss her.*
– PHRASES **make a fuss** become angry and complain. **make a fuss over** (or Brit. **of**) treat (a person or animal) with excessive attention or affection.
– DERIVATIVES **fuss·er** n.
– ORIGIN early 18th cent.: perhaps Anglo-Irish.

fuss·bud·get /ˈfəsˌbəjit/ ▶ **n.** informal a fussy person.

fussed /fəst/ ▶ **adj.** [predic.] Brit. informal (of a person) feeling concern, distress, or annoyance; having strong feelings about something: *it'd be great to be there but I'm not that fussed.*

fuss·pot /ˈfəsˌpät/ ▶ **n.** informal a fussy person.

fuss·y /ˈfəsē/ ▶ **adj.** (**fussier**, **fussiest**) (of a person) fastidious about one's needs or requirements; hard to please: *he is very fussy about what he eats.* ■ showing excessive or anxious concern about detail: *Eleanor patted her hair with quick, fussy movements.* ■ full of unnecessary detail or decoration: *I hate fussy clothes.*
– DERIVATIVES **fuss·i·ly** /ˈfəsəlē/ **adv.**, **fuss·i·ness n.**

fus·ta·nel·la /ˌfəstəˈnelə/ ▶ **n.** a stiff white kilt, worn by men in Albania and Greece.
– ORIGIN mid 19th cent.: from Italian, from modern Greek *phoustani, phoustanela*, probably from Italian *fustagno*, from medieval Latin *fustaneum* (see FUSTIAN).

fus·tian /ˈfəsCHən/ ▶ **n. 1** thick, durable twilled cloth with a short nap, usually dyed in dark colors. **2** pompous or pretentious speech or writing: *a smoke screen of fustian and fantasy.*
– ORIGIN Middle English: from Old French *fustaigne*, from medieval Latin *fustaneum*, from (*pannus*) *fustaneus* 'cloth from *Fostat*,' a suburb of Cairo; sense 2 perhaps from the fact that fustian was sometimes used to cover pillows and cushions, implying that the language was "padded"; compare with BOMBAST.

fus·tic /ˈfəstik/ ▶ **n. 1** archaic a yellow dye obtained from either of two kinds of timber, esp. that of old fustic.
2 (also **old fustic**) a tropical American tree with heartwood that yields dyes and other products. See also YOUNG FUSTIC. ● *Madura* (or *Chlorophora*) *tinctoria*, family Moraceae.
– ORIGIN late Middle English: via French from Spanish *fustoc*, from Arabic *fustuķ*, from Greek *pistakē* 'pistachio tree.'

fus·ty /ˈfəstē/ ▶ **adj.** (**fustier**, **fustiest**) smelling stale, damp, or stuffy: *the fusty odor of decay.* ■ old-fashioned in attitude or style: *grammar in the classroom became a fusty notion.*
– DERIVATIVES **fus·ti·ly** /ˈfəstəlē/ **adv.**, **fus·ti·ness n.**
– ORIGIN late 15th cent.: from Old French *fuste* 'smelling of the cask,' from *fust* 'cask, tree trunk,' from Latin *fustis* 'cudgel.'

fut. ▶ **abbr.** future.

fu·thark /ˈfo͞oˌTHärk/ (also **futhorc** /-ˌTHôrk/, **futhork**) ▶ **n.** the runic alphabet.
– ORIGIN mid 19th cent.: from its first six letters: *f, u, th, a* (or *o*), *r, k.*

fu·tile /ˈfyo͞otl, -ˌtīl/ ▶ **adj.** incapable of producing any useful result; pointless: *a futile attempt to keep fans from mounting the stage.*
– DERIVATIVES **fu·tile·ly adv.**
– ORIGIN mid 16th cent.: from Latin *futilis* 'leaky, futile,' apparently from *fundere* 'pour.'

fu·til·i·tar·i·an /fyo͞oˌtiləˈterēən/ ▶ **adj.** devoted to futile pursuits.
▶ **n.** a person devoted to futile pursuits.

fu·til·i·ty /fyo͞oˈtilətē/ ▶ **n.** pointlessness or uselessness: *the horror and futility of war.*

fu·ton /ˈfo͞oˌtän/ ▶ **n.** a Japanese quilted mattress rolled out on the floor for use as a bed. ■ a type of low wooden sofa bed having such a mattress.
– ORIGIN late 19th cent.: Japanese.

fut·sal /ˈfo͝otsäl/ ▶ **n.** [mass noun] a modified form of soccer played with five players per side on a smaller, typically indoor, field.
– ORIGIN 1980s: partly from Brazilian Portuguese, shortened from *futebol du salão*, and partly from Spanish, shortened from *fútbol sala* or *fútbol de salón.*

fut·tock /ˈfətək/ ▶ **n.** each of the curved timber pieces forming the lower part of a ship's frame.
– ORIGIN Middle English: perhaps from Middle Low German, or from FOOT + HOOK.

fu·ture /ˈfyo͞oCHər/ ▶ **n. 1** (usu. **the future**) the time or a period of time following the moment of speaking or writing; time regarded as still to come: *we plan on getting married in the near future | work on the building will be halted for the foreseeable future.* ■ events that will or are likely to happen in the time to come: *nobody can predict the future.* ■ used to refer to what will happen to someone or something in the time to come: *a blueprint for the future of American fast food.* ■ a prospect of success or happiness: *he'd decided that there was no future in the gang | I began to believe I might have a future as an artist.* ■ Grammar a tense of verbs expressing events that have not yet happened.
2 (**futures**) Finance short for FUTURES CONTRACT.
▶ **adj.** [attrib.] at a later time; going or likely to happen or exist: *the needs of future generations.* ■ (of a person) planned or destined to hold a specified position: *his future wife.* ■ existing after death: *expectation of a future life.* ■ Grammar (of a tense) expressing an event yet to happen.
– PHRASES **for future reference** see REFERENCE. **in future** chiefly Brit. from now on: *she would be more careful in future.*
– DERIVATIVES **fu·ture·less adj.**
– ORIGIN late Middle English: via Old French from Latin *futurus*, future participle of *esse* 'be' (from the stem *fu-*, ultimately from a base meaning 'grow, become').

fu·ture his·to·ry ▶ **n.** (in science fiction) a narration of imagined future events.

fu·ture per·fect ▶ **n.** Grammar a tense of verbs expressing expected completion in the future, in English exemplified by *will have done.*

fu·ture-proof Brit. ▶ **adj.** (of a product) unlikely to become obsolete.
▶ **v.** [with obj.] make (a product or system) future-proof: *this approach allows you to future-proof your applications.*

fu·tures con·tract ▶ **n.** Finance an agreement traded on an organized exchange to buy or sell assets, esp. commodities or shares, at a fixed price but to be delivered and paid for later. Compare with FORWARD CONTRACT.

fu·ture shock ▶ **n.** a state of distress or disorientation due to rapid social or technological change.
– ORIGIN 1970s: popularized by the 1970 book *Future Shock* by Alvin TOFFLER (1928–).

fu·tur·ism /ˈfyo͞oCHəˌrizəm/ ▶ **n.** concern with events and trends of the future or which anticipate the future. ■ (**Futurism**) an artistic movement begun in Italy in 1909 that violently rejected traditional forms so as to celebrate and incorporate into art the energy and dynamism of modern technology. Launched by Filippo Marinetti, it had effectively ended by 1918 but was widely influential, particularly in Russia on figures such as Malevich and Mayakovsky.
– ORIGIN from FUTURE + -ISM, translating Italian *futurismo*, French *futurisme.*

fu·tur·ist /ˈfyo͞oCHərist/ ▶ **n. 1** (**Futurist**) an adherent of futurism.
2 a person who studies the future and makes predictions about it based on current trends.
3 Theology a person who believes that eschatological prophecies are still to be fulfilled.
▶ **adj. 1** (often **Futurist**) of or relating to futurism or the Futurists.
2 relating to a vision of the future, esp. one involving the development of technology: *the grim urban setting of the novel would have been a futurist nightmare.*

fu·tur·is·tic /ˌfyo͞oCHəˈristik/ ▶ **adj. 1** having or involving very modern technology or design: *a swimming pool and futuristic dome.* ■ (of a film or book) set in the future, typically in a world of advanced or menacing technology.
2 (**Futuristic**) dated of or characteristic of Futurism.
– DERIVATIVES **fu·tur·is·ti·cal·ly adv.**

fu·tu·ri·ty /fyo͞oˈto͝orətē, -ˈCHo͝orətē/ ▶ **n.** (pl. **futurities**) the future time: *the tremendous shadows that futurity casts upon the present.* ■ a future event. ■ renewed or continuing existence: *the snowdrops were a promise of futurity.* ■ short for FUTURITY RACE.

fu·tu·ri·ty race (also **futurity stakes**) ▶ **n.** a horse race for young horses for which entries are made long in advance, sometimes before the horses are born.

fu·tur·ol·o·gy /ˌfyo͞oCHəˈräləjē/ ▶ **n.** systematic forecasting of the future, esp. from present trends in society.
– DERIVATIVES **fu·tur·o·log·i·cal** /-rəˈläjikəl/ **adj.**, **fu·tur·ol·o·gist** /-jist/ **n.**

futz /fəts/ ▶ **v.** [no obj.] informal waste time; idle or busy oneself aimlessly: *mother futzed around in the kitchen.* ■ (**futz around with**) deal with (something) in a trifling way; fiddle with: *Mick was futzing around with his camera equipment.*
– ORIGIN 1930s: perhaps an alteration of Yiddish *arumfartzen* 'fart around.'

Fu·xin /ˈfo͞oˈSHin/ (also **Fou-hsin**) an industrial city in northeastern China, in Liaoning province; pop. 691,800 (est. 2006).

fuze /fyo͞oz/ ▶ **n.** variant spelling of FUSE².

fu·zee ▶ **n.** variant spelling of FUSEE.

Fu·zhou /ˈfo͞oˈjō/ (also **Foochow**) a port in southeastern China, capital of Fujian province; pop. 1,457,600 (est. 2006).

fuzz¹ /fəz/ ▶ **n.** a fluffy or frizzy mass of hair or fiber: *a fuzz of black hair | his face was covered with white fuzz.* ■ a blurred image or area: *she saw Jess surrounded by a fuzz of sunlight.* ■ a buzzing or distorted sound, esp. one deliberately produced as an effect on an electric guitar.
▶ **v. 1** make or become blurred or indistinct: [with obj.] *snow fuzzes the outlines of the signs* | [no obj.] *tiny detail can be enlarged to poster size without fuzzing out.*
2 [no obj.] (of hair) become fluffy or frizzy: *her hair fuzzed out uncontrollably in the heat.*
– ORIGIN late 16th cent.: probably of Low German or Dutch origin; compare with Dutch *voos*, Low German *fussig* 'spongy.'

fuzz² ▶ **n.** (**the fuzz**) informal the police.
– ORIGIN 1920s: of unknown origin.

fuzz·ball /ˈfəzˌbôl/ ▶ **n.** a ball of fuzz: *a black and white puppy that looks like a laundered fuzzball.* ■ another term for PUFFBALL (sense 2).

fuzz·box /ˈfəzˌbäks/ ▶ **n.** a device that adds a distorted buzzing quality to the sound of an electric guitar or other instrument.

fuzzed /fəzd/ ▶ **adj.** (of popular music or electric instruments) having or producing a distorted buzzing tone: *fuzzed guitars.*

fuzz·y /ˈfəzē/ ▶ **adj.** (**fuzzier**, **fuzziest**) **1** having a frizzy, fluffy, or frayed texture or appearance: *a girl with fuzzy dark hair.*
2 difficult to perceive clearly or understand and explain precisely; indistinct or vague: *the picture is very fuzzy | that fuzzy line between right and wrong.* ■ (of a person or the mind) unable to think clearly; confused: *my mind felt fuzzy.* ■ another term for FUZZED.
3 Computing & Logic of or relating to a form of set theory and logic in which predicates may have degrees of applicability, rather than simply being true or false. It has important uses in artificial intelligence and the design of control systems.
– PHRASES **warm fuzzy** (or **warm and fuzzy**) informal used to refer to a sentimentally emotional response or something designed to evoke such a response: *babies require a lot of attention, not just momentary warm fuzzies.*
– DERIVATIVES **fuzz·i·ly** /ˈfəzəlē/ **adv.**, **fuzz·i·ness n.**

fuz·zy·head·ed /ˈfəzēˌhedid/ ▶ **adj. 1** muddled in thought or conception: *fuzzyheaded liberals.*
2 slightly dizzy or giddy: *a strange musky scent in the air made her feel fuzzyheaded and distracted.*

FWB ▶ **abbr.** four-wheel brake.

FWD ▶ **abbr.** ■ four-wheel drive. ■ front-wheel drive.

fwd. ▶ **abbr.** forward.

F-word ▶ **n.** informal used instead of or in reference to the word "fuck" because of its taboo nature.

fwy ▶ **abbr.** freeway.

FX ▶ **abbr.** ■ unusual (visual or sound) effects: *computer FX may allow him to redefine cinema.* ■ foreign exchange.
– ORIGIN from the pronunciation of the two letters forming the two syllables of *effects.*

FY ▶ **abbr.** fiscal year.

-fy ▶ **suffix 1** (added to nouns) forming verbs denoting making or producing: *speechify.* ■ denoting transformation or the process of making into: *deify | petrify.*
2 forming verbs denoting the making of a state defined by an adjective: *amplify | falsify.*
3 forming verbs expressing a causative sense: *horrify.*
– ORIGIN from French *-fier*, from Latin *-ficare, -facere*, from *facere* 'do, make.'

FYI ▶ **abbr.** for your information.

fyke /fīk/ (also **fyke net**) ▶ **n.** a bag net for catching fish.
– ORIGIN mid 19th cent.: from Dutch *fuik* 'fish trap.'

fyl·fot /ˈfilˌfät/ ▶ **n.** a swastika.
– ORIGIN late 15th cent.: perhaps from *fill-foot* 'pattern filling the foot of a painted window.'

fyn·bos /ˈfānˌbäs/ ▶ **n.** a distinctive type of vegetation found only on the southern tip of Africa. It includes a wide range of plant species, particularly small heatherlike trees and shrubs.
– ORIGIN Afrikaans, literally 'fine bush.'

fytte ▶ **n.** variant spelling of FIT³.

FZS ▶ **abbr.** Fellow of the Zoological Society.

f

Gg

g

G[1] /jē/ (also **g**) ▶ **n.** (pl. **Gs** or **G's**) **1** the seventh letter of the alphabet. ■ denoting the next after F in a set of items, categories, etc. ■ (**g**) Chess denoting the seventh file from the left, as viewed from White's side of the board.
2 Music the fifth note in the diatonic scale of C major. ■ a key based on a scale with G as its keynote.

G[2] ▶ **abbr.** ■ Physics gauss. ■ German. ■ [in combination] (in units of measurement) giga- (10^9). ■ good. ■ informal grand (a thousand dollars). ■ a unit of gravitational force equal to that exerted by the earth's gravitational field. ▶ **symbol** ■ Chemistry Gibbs free energy. ■ general audiences, a rating in the Voluntary Movie Rating System that all ages may be admitted. ■ Physics the gravitational constant, equal to 6.67×10^{-11}N m² kg⁻². ■ Physics conductance.

g ▶ **abbr.** ■ Chemistry gas. ■ gelding. ■ gram(s). ■ Physics denoting quantum states or wave functions that do not change sign on inversion through the origin. The opposite of **u**. [from German *gerade* 'even.'] ▶ **symbol** Physics the acceleration due to gravity, equal to 9.81 m/s².

G7 ▶ **abbr.** Group of Seven.

G8 ▶ **abbr.** Group of Eight.

G20 ▶ **abbr.** Group of Twenty.

G77 ▶ **abbr.** Group of Seventy-Seven.

GA ▶ **abbr.** ■ Gamblers Anonymous. ■ General Assembly. ■ general aviation. ■ General of the Army. ■ Georgia (in official postal use).

Ga[1] /gä/ ▶ **symbol** the chemical element gallium.

Ga[2] ▶ **abbr.** Bible Galatians.

Ga. ▶ **abbr.** Georgia.

gab /gab/ informal ▶ **v.** (**gabs, gabbing, gabbed**) [no obj.] talk, typically at length, about trivial matters: *Franny walked right past a woman gabbing on the phone.*
▶ **n.** talk; chatter.
– ORIGIN early 18th cent.: variant of **GOB**[1].

GABA ▶ **abbr.** gamma-aminobutyric acid.

gab·ar·dine /ˈgabərˌdēn/ (chiefly Brit. also **gaberdine**) ▶ **n.** a smooth, durable twill-woven cloth, typically of worsted or cotton. ■ Brit. a raincoat made of such cloth. ■ (usu. **gaberdine**) historical a loose long upper garment, worn particularly by Jewish men.
– ORIGIN early 16th cent.: from Old French *gauvardine*, earlier *gallevardine*, perhaps from Middle High German *wallevart* 'pilgrimage' and originally 'a garment worn by a pilgrim.' The textile sense is first recorded in the early 20th cent.

gab·ble /ˈgabəl/ ▶ **v.** [no obj.] talk rapidly and unintelligibly; utter meaningless sounds: *he gabbled on in a panicky way until he was dismissed.*
▶ **n.** rapid, unintelligible talk.
– DERIVATIVES **gab·bler** /ˈgablər/ **n.**
– ORIGIN late 16th cent.: from Dutch *gabbelen*, of imitative origin.

gab·bro /ˈgabrō/ ▶ **n.** (pl. **gabbros**) Geology a dark, coarse-grained plutonic rock of crystalline texture, consisting mainly of pyroxene, plagioclase feldspar, and often olivine.
– DERIVATIVES **gab·bro·ic** /gəˈbrō-ik/ **adj.**, **gab·broid** /-broid/ **adj.**
– ORIGIN mid 19th cent.: from Italian, from Latin *glaber, glabr-* 'smooth.'

gab·by /ˈgabē/ ▶ **adj.** (**gabbier, gabbiest**) informal excessively or annoyingly talkative.

gab·er·dine /ˈgabərˌdēn/ ▶ **n.** chiefly British spelling of **GABARDINE**.

gab·fest /ˈgabˌfest/ ▶ **n.** informal a conference or other gathering with prolonged talking: *these summits are merely empty gabfests.*

ga·bi·on /ˈgābēən/ ▶ **n.** a wirework container filled with rock, broken concrete, or other material, used in the construction of dams, retaining walls, etc.
– DERIVATIVES **ga·bi·on·age** /ˈgābēəˌnäZH/ **n.**
– ORIGIN mid 16th cent.: via French from Italian *gabbione*, from *gabbia* 'cage,' from Latin *cavea*.

Ga·ble /ˈgābəl/, Clark (1901–60), US actor; full name *William Clark Gable*. He was noted for movies such as *It Happened One Night* (1934) and *Gone with the Wind* (1939). His last movie, *The Misfits*, was released posthumously in 1961.

Clark Gable

ga·ble /ˈgābəl/ ▶ **n.** the part of a wall that encloses the end of a pitched roof. ■ (also **gable end**) a wall topped with a gable. ■ a gable-shaped canopy over a window or door.
– DERIVATIVES **ga·bled adj.**
– ORIGIN Middle English: via Old French from Old Norse *gafl*, of Germanic origin; related to Dutch *gaffel* and German *Gabel* 'fork' (the point of the gable originally being the fork of two crossed timbers supporting the end of the rooftree).

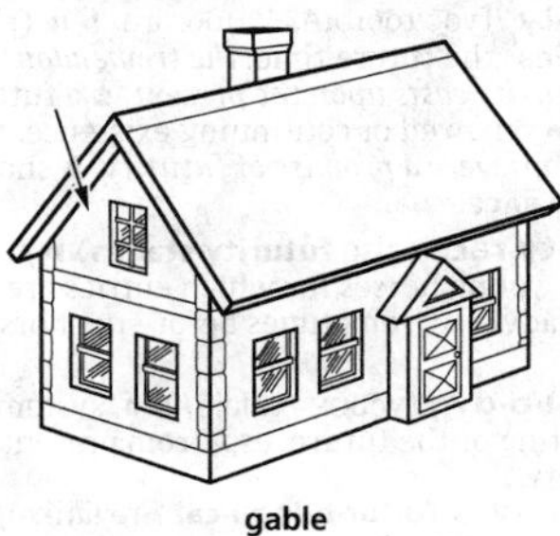
gable

ga·ble roof ▶ **n.** a roof with two sloping sides and a gable at each end.

Ga·bon /gäˈbôN/ a country in West Africa, on the Atlantic coast; pop. 1,515,000 (est. 2009); capital, Libreville; languages, French (official) and West African languages.

> Gabon became a French territory in 1888. Part of French Equatorial Africa from 1910 to 1958, it declared independence in 1960.

– DERIVATIVES **Gab·o·nese** /ˌgabəˈnēz, -ˈnēs/ **adj. & n.**

ga·boon /gəˈbo͞on/ (also **gaboon mahogany**) ▶ **n.** a tropical West African hardwood tree valued for its timber. Also called **OKOUME**. ● *Aucoumea klaineana*, family Burseraceae.
– ORIGIN early 20th cent.: from *Gaboon* (now **GABON**).

Ga·boon vi·per ▶ **n.** a large, thick-bodied venomous African snake with a pair of hornlike scales on the snout, and the scales richly patterned with brown, purple, and cream. ● *Bitis gabonica*, family Viperidae.
– ORIGIN early 20th cent.: named after *Gaboon* (now **GABON**).

Ga·bor /gəˈbôr, ˈgäbôr/, Dennis (1900–79), British electrical engineer; born in Hungary. He conceived the idea of holography. Nobel Prize for Physics (1971).

Ga·bo·ro·ne /ˌgäbəˈrōnā/ the capital of Botswana, in the southern part of the country near the border with South Africa; pop. 223,200 (est. 2009).

Ga·bri·el /ˈgābrēəl/ (in the Bible) the archangel who foretold the birth of Jesus to the Virgin Mary (Luke 1:26–38), and who also appeared to Zacharias, father of John the Baptist, and to Daniel; (in Islam) the archangel who revealed the Koran to the Prophet Muhammad.

Gad[1] /gad/ (in the Bible) a Hebrew patriarch, son of Jacob and Zilpah (Gen. 30:9–11). ■ the tribe of Israel traditionally descended from him.

Gad[2] ▶ **exclam.** used to express dismay or surprise.
– ORIGIN late 15th cent.: euphemistic alteration of **GOD**.

gad /gad/ ▶ **v.** (**gads, gadding, gadded**) [no obj.] informal go around from one place to another, in the pursuit of pleasure or entertainment: *help out around the house and not be gadding about the countryside.*
– ORIGIN late Middle English: back-formation from obsolete *gadling* 'wanderer, vagabond,' (earlier) 'companion,' of Germanic origin.

gad·a·bout /ˈgadəˌbout/ ▶ **n.** a habitual pleasure-seeker.

Gad·a·rene /ˈgadəˌrēn/ ▶ **adj.** involving or engaged in a headlong or potentially disastrous rush to do something.
– ORIGIN early 19th cent. (in the current sense): from New Testament Greek *Gadarēnos* 'inhabitant of *Gadara*' (see Matt. 8:28–32).

Gad·da·fi /gəˈdäfē/ (also **Qaddafi** /kə-/), Mu'ammer Muhammad al- (1942–), Libyan statesman; head of state since 1970. After leading a coup that overthrew **King Idris** in 1969, he established the Libyan Arab Republic and has pursued a policy of Islamic fundamentalism blended with Arab nationalism. He has been accused of supporting international terrorism.

Gad·dis /ˈgadis/, William (1922–98), US writer. He is noted for the novels *JR* (1975), *Carpenter's Gothic* (1985), and *A Frolic of His Own* (1994).

gad·fly /ˈgadˌflī/ ▶ **n.** (pl. **gadflies**) a fly that bites livestock, esp. a horsefly, warble fly, or botfly. ■ an annoying person, esp. one who provokes others into action by criticism.
– ORIGIN late 16th cent.: from **GAD**, or obsolete *gad* 'goad, spike,' from Old Norse *gaddr*, of Germanic origin; related to **YARD**[1].

gadg·et /ˈgajit/ ▶ **n.** a small mechanical device or tool, esp. an ingenious or novel one: *a state-of-the-art kitchen with every conceivable gadget.*
– DERIVATIVES **gadg·e·teer** /ˌgajiˈti(ə)r/ **n.**, **gadg·et·ry** /-trē/ **n.**, **gadg·et·y adj.**
– ORIGIN late 19th cent. (originally in nautical use): probably from French *gâchette* 'lock mechanism' or from the French dialect word *gagée* 'tool.'

ga·did /ˈgādid/ ▶ **n.** Zoology a fish of the cod family (Gadidae).
– ORIGIN late 19th cent.: from modern Latin *Gadidae* (plural), from *gadus* 'cod.'

ga·doid /ˈgādoid/ ▶ **n.** Zoology a bony fish of an order (Gadiformes) that comprises the cods, hakes, and their relatives.

–ORIGIN mid 19th cent.: from modern Latin *gadus* (from Greek *gados* 'cod') + **-OID**.

gad·o·lin·ite /ˈgadl-ə,nīt/ ▶ **n.** a rare dark brown or black mineral, consisting of a silicate of iron, beryllium, and rare earths.
–ORIGIN early 19th cent.: named after Johan *Gadolin* (1760–1852), the Finnish mineralogist who first identified it.

gad·o·lin·i·um /,gadlˈinēəm/ ▶ **n.** the chemical element of atomic number 64, a soft silvery-white metal of the lanthanide series. (Symbol: **Gd**)
–ORIGIN late 19th cent.: from **GADOLINITE**.

ga·droon /gəˈdro͞on/ ▶ **n.** a decorative edging on metal or wood, typically formed by inverted flutings.
–DERIVATIVES **ga·drooned** adj., **ga·droon·ing** n.
–ORIGIN late 17th cent.: from French *godron*, probably related to *goder* 'to pucker,' also to **GODET**.

Gads·den Pur·chase /ˈgadzdən/ an area in New Mexico and Arizona, near the Rio Grande, that covers an area of more than 30,000 square miles (77,700 sq km). It was purchased from Mexico in 1853 by US diplomat **James Gadsden** (1788–1858) with the intention of ensuring a southern railroad route to the Pacific Ocean.

gad·wall /ˈgad,wôl/ ▶ **n.** (pl. **same** or **gadwalls**) a brownish-gray freshwater duck found across Eurasia and North America. ● *Anas strepera*, family Anatidae.
–ORIGIN mid 17th cent.: of unknown origin.

gad·zooks /,gadˈzo͞oks/ ▶ **exclam.** archaic an exclamation of surprise or annoyance.
–ORIGIN late 17th cent.: alteration of *God's hooks*, i.e., the nails by which Jesus Christ was fastened to the cross; see **GAD²**.

Gae·a /ˈjēə/ variant spelling of **GAIA** (sense 1).

Gael /gāl/ ▶ **n.** a Gaelic-speaking person. ■ a person whose ancestors spoke Gaelic.
–DERIVATIVES **Gael·dom** /-dəm/ n.
–ORIGIN from Scottish Gaelic *Gaidheal*.

Gael·ic /ˈgālik/ ▶ **adj.** of or relating to the Goidelic languages, particularly the Celtic language of Scotland, and the culture associated with speakers of these languages and their descendants.
▶ **n.** (also **Scottish Gaelic**) a Goidelic language brought from Ireland in the 5th and 6th centuries AD and spoken in the highlands and islands of western Scotland. ■ (also **Irish Gaelic**) another term for **IRISH** (the language).

Gael·tacht /ˈgāltəKHt/ (**the Gaeltacht**) regions in Ireland, primarily the western coast, where the vernacular language is Irish.
–ORIGIN Irish, earlier *Gaedhealtacht*, from *Gaedheal* 'Gael' + *tacht* 'talk, speech.'

gaff¹ /gaf/ ▶ **n. 1** a stick with a hook, or a barbed spear, for landing large fish.
2 Sailing a spar to which the head of a fore-and-aft sail is bent.
▶ **v.** [with obj.] seize or impale with a gaff.
–ORIGIN Middle English: from Provençal *gaf* 'hook'; related to **GAFFE**.

gaff² ▶ **n.** informal rough treatment; criticism: *if wages increase, perhaps we can stand the gaff.*
–ORIGIN early 19th cent. (in the senses 'outcry; nonsense' and in the phrase *blow the gaff* 'let out a secret'): of unknown origin.

gaff³ ▶ **n.** Brit. informal a house, apartment, or other building, esp. as being a person's home: *John's new gaff is on McDonald Road.*
–ORIGIN 1930s: of unknown origin.

gaffe /gaf/ ▶ **n.** an unintentional act or remark causing embarrassment to its originator; a blunder: *an unforgivable social gaffe.*
–ORIGIN early 20th cent.: from French, literally 'boat hook' (from Provençal *gaf*: see **GAFF¹**), used colloquially to mean 'blunder.'

gaf·fer /ˈgafər/ ▶ **n. 1** the chief electrician in a motion-picture or television production unit.
2 informal an old man.
3 Brit. informal a person in charge of others; a boss.
–ORIGIN late 16th cent.: probably a contraction of **GODFATHER**; compare with **GAMMER**.

gag¹ /gag/ ▶ **n. 1** a piece of cloth put in or over a person's mouth to prevent them from speaking or crying out. ■ a restriction on freedom of speech or dissemination of information: *they lobbied hard for a gag on doctors and nurses.*
2 a device for keeping the patient's mouth open during a dental or surgical operation.
▶ **v.** (**gags, gagging, gagged**) **1** [with obj.] put a gag on (someone): *she was bound and gagged by robbers in her home.* ■ (of a person or body with authority) prevent (someone) from speaking freely or disseminating information: *the administration is trying to gag its critics.*
2 [no obj.] choke or retch: *he gagged on the sourness of the wine.*
–ORIGIN Middle English: perhaps related to Old Norse *gaghāls* 'with the neck thrown back,' or imitative of a person choking.

gag² ▶ **n.** a joke or an amusing story or scene, esp. one forming part of a comedian's act or in a film or play.
▶ **v.** [no obj.] tell jokes.
–ORIGIN mid 19th cent. (originally theatrical slang): of unknown origin.

ga·ga /ˈgä,gä/ ▶ **adj.** informal overexcited or irrational, typically as a result of infatuation or excessive enthusiasm; mentally confused; senile.
–ORIGIN early 20th cent.: from French, 'senile, a senile person,' reduplication based on *gâteux*, variant of *gâteur*, hospital slang in the sense 'bed wetter.'

Ga·ga·rin /gəˈgärin/, Yury (Alekseyevich) (1934–68), Russian cosmonaut. In 1961, he made the first manned space flight, completing a single orbit of the earth in 108 minutes.

gage¹ /gāj/ archaic ▶ **n.** a valued object deposited as a guarantee of good faith. ■ a pledge, esp. a glove, thrown down as a symbol of a challenge to fight.
▶ **v.** [with obj.] offer (a thing or one's life) as a guarantee of good faith.
–ORIGIN Middle English: from Old French *gage* (noun), *gager* (verb), of Germanic origin; related to **WAGE** and **WED**.

gage² ▶ **n. & v.** variant spelling of **GAUGE**.

gage³ ▶ **n.** another term for **GREENGAGE**.

gag·ger /ˈgagər/ ▶ **n.** a person or thing that gags, in particular: ■ a piece of iron used in a foundry mold to keep the core in place.

gag·gle /ˈgagəl/ ▶ **n. 1** a flock of geese.
2 informal a disorderly or noisy group of people: *the gaggle of reporters and photographers that dogged his every step.*
–ORIGIN Middle English (as a verb): imitative of the noise that a goose makes; compare with Dutch *gaggelen* and German *gackern*.

gag·man /ˈgag,man/ (also **gag man**) ▶ **n.** a writer or performer of gags.

gag or·der ▶ **n.** Law a judge's order that a case may not be discussed in public.

gag rule ▶ **n.** a regulation or directive that prohibits public discussion of a particular matter, in particular: ■ a regulation preventing the staff of government-funded family-planning clinics from offering patients information about abortion. ■ a US government policy preventing US aid to foreign family-planning organizations unless they agree not to promote or perform abortions.

gag·ster /ˈgagstər/ ▶ **n.** another term for **GAGMAN**.

gah ▶ **exclam.** used to express exasperation or dismay: *had to go the dentist this morning (arrived late—gah!).*
–ORIGIN natural exclamation: first recorded in English in the early 20th cent.

Gai·a /ˈgīə/ **1** (also **Gaea, Ge**) Greek Mythology the Earth personified as a goddess, daughter of Chaos. She was the mother and wife of Uranus (Heaven); their offspring included the Titans and the Cyclopes. [Greek, 'Earth.']
2 the earth viewed as a vast self-regulating organism. [1970s: coined by James Lovelock, at the suggestion of the writer William Golding, from the name of the goddess *Gaia*.]
–DERIVATIVES **Gai·an** n. & adj.

Gai·a hy·poth·e·sis ▶ **n.** the theory, put forward by James Lovelock, that living matter on the earth collectively defines and regulates the material conditions necessary for the continuance of life. The planet, or rather the biosphere, is thus likened to a vast self-regulating organism.

gai·e·ty /ˈgāitē/ (also **gayety**) ▶ **n.** (pl. **gaieties**) the state or quality of being lighthearted or cheerful: *the sudden gaiety of children's laughter.* ■ merrymaking or festivity: *he seemed to be a part of the gaiety, having a wonderful time.* ■ (**gaieties**) dated entertainments or amusements.
–ORIGIN mid 17th cent.: from French *gaieté*, from *gai* (see **GAY**).

gai·jin /ˈgīˈjin/ ▶ **n.** (pl. **same**) (in Japan) a foreigner.
–ORIGIN Japanese, contraction of *gaikoku-jin*, from *gaikoku* 'foreign country' + *jin* 'person.'

gail·lar·di·a /gəˈlärdēə/ ▶ **n.** an American plant of the daisy family, cultivated for its bright red and yellow flowers. ● Genus *Gaillardia*, family Compositae.
–ORIGIN modern Latin, named in memory of *Gaillard* de Marentonneau, 18th-cent. French amateur botanist.

gai·ly /ˈgālē/ ▶ **adv.** in a cheerful or lighthearted way: *he waved gaily to the crowd.* ■ without thinking of the consequences: *she plunged gaily into speculation on the stock market.* ■ [as submodifier] with a bright or cheerful appearance: *gaily colored sailboats dot the lake.*

gain /gān/ ▶ **v.** [with obj.] **1** obtain or secure (something desired, favorable, or profitable): *a process that has gained the confidence of the industry* | [with two objs.] *their blend of acoustic folk pop gained them several chart hits.* ■ reach or arrive at (a desired destination): *we gained the ridge.* ■ [no obj.] (**gain on**) come closer to (a person or thing pursued): *a huge bear gaining on him with every stride.* ■ archaic bring over to one's interest or views; win over: *to gratify the queen and gain the court.*
2 increase the amount or rate of (something, typically weight or speed): *she had gradually gained weight since her wedding.* ■ [no obj.] increase in value: *stocks also gained for the third day in a row.* ■ [no obj.] (**gain in**) improve or advance in some respect: *canoeing is gaining in popularity.* ■ (of a clock or watch) become fast by (a specific amount of time): *this atomic clock will neither gain nor lose a second in the next 1 million years.*
▶ **n.** an increase in wealth or resources: *the mayor was accused of using municipal funds for personal gain.* ■ a thing that is achieved or acquired: *a balance between water loss and water gain.* ■ the factor by which power or voltage is increased in an amplifier or other electronic device, usually expressed as a logarithm.
–DERIVATIVES **gain·a·ble** adj., **gain·er** n.
–ORIGIN late 15th cent. (as a noun, originally in the sense 'booty'): from Old French *gaigne* (noun), *gaignier* (verb), of Germanic origin.

Gaines·ville /ˈgānz,vil, -vəl/ a city in north central Florida, home to the University of Florida; pop. 114,916 (est. 2008).

gain·ful /ˈgānfəl/ ▶ **adj.** [attrib.] serving to increase wealth or resources: *he soon found gainful employment.*
–DERIVATIVES **gain·ful·ly** adv., **gain·ful·ness** n.

gain·say /,gānˈsā, ˈgān,sā/ ▶ **v.** (past and past participle **gainsaid**) [with obj. with negative] formal deny or contradict (a fact or statement): *the impact of the railroads cannot be gainsaid.* ■ speak against or oppose (someone).
–DERIVATIVES **gain·say·er** n.
–ORIGIN Middle English: from obsolete *gain-* 'against' + **SAY**.

Gains·bor·ough /ˈgānzbərə/, Thomas (1727–88), English painter. He was known for his society portraits, including *Mr. and Mrs. Andrews* (1748) and *The Blue Boy* (c.1770), and for landscapes such as *The Watering Place* (1777).

gain·shar·ing /ˈgān,SHe(ə)riNG/ ▶ **n.** an incentive plan in which employees or customers receive benefits directly as a result of cost-saving measures that they initiate or participate in: [as modifier] *the company's gainsharing program ties bonuses directly to team performance.*

'gainst /genst/ ▶ **prep.** literary short for **AGAINST**.

gait /gāt/ ▶ **n.** a person's manner of walking: *the easy gait of an athlete.* ■ the paces of an animal, esp. a horse or dog.
–ORIGIN late Middle English (originally Scots).

gai·ta /ˈgītə/ ▶ **n.** a kind of bagpipe played in northern Spain and Portugal.
–ORIGIN Spanish and Portuguese.

gait·er /ˈgātər/ ▶ **n.** (usu. **gaiters**) a garment similar to leggings, worn to cover or protect the ankle and lower leg. ■ a shoe or overshoe extending to the ankle or above. ■ a garment of this kind worn as part of the traditional costume of an Anglican bishop.
–DERIVATIVES **gait·ered** adj.
–ORIGIN early 18th cent.: from French *guêtre*, probably of Germanic origin and related to **WRIST**.

Gai·thers·burg /ˈgāTHərz,bərg/ a city in west central Maryland, northwest of Washington, DC; pop. 58,744 (est. 2008).

gal¹ /gal/ ▶ **n.** informal a girl or young woman.
–ORIGIN late 18th cent.: representing a pronunciation.

gal² ▶ **n.** Physics a unit of gravitational acceleration equal to one centimeter per second per second.
–ORIGIN early 20th cent.: named after **GALILEO GALILEI**.

Gal. ▶ **abbr.** Bible Galatians.

gal. ▶ **abbr.** gallon(s).

ga·la /ˈgālə, ˈgalə/ ▶ **n.** a social occasion with special entertainments or performances: [as modifier] *a black-tie gala that begins with a cocktail reception.*

PRONUNCIATION KEY ə *ago, up*; ər *over, fur*; a *hat*; ā *ate*; ä *car*; e *let*; ē *see*; i *fit*; ī *by*; NG *sing*; ō *go*; ô *law, for*; oi *toy*; o͝o *good*; o͞o *goo*; ou *out*; TH *thin*; TH *then*; ZH *vision*

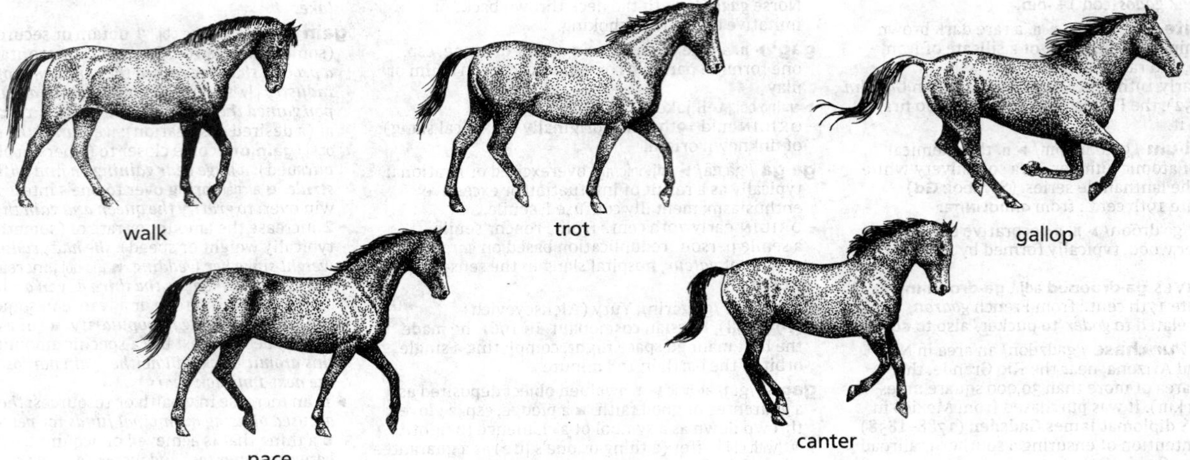

gaits of a horse

g

–ORIGIN early 17th cent. (in the sense 'showy dress'): via Italian and Spanish from Old French *gale* 'rejoicing.'

ga·lac·ta·gogue /gəˈlaktəˌgäg/ ▶ **n.** Medicine a food or drug that promotes or increases the flow of a mother's milk.
–ORIGIN mid 19th cent.: from Greek *gala, galakt-* 'milk' + *agōgos* 'leading.'

ga·lac·tic /gəˈlaktik/ ▶ **adj.** of or relating to a galaxy or galaxies, esp. the Milky Way galaxy. ■ Astronomy measured relative to the galactic equator.
–ORIGIN mid 19th cent.: from Greek *galaktias* (variant of *galaxias* 'galaxy') + **-IC**.

ga·lac·tic e·qua·tor ▶ **n.** Astronomy the great circle passing as closely as possible through the densest parts of the Milky Way.

ga·lac·tic noise ▶ **n.** unidentified radio-frequency radiation coming from beyond the solar system.

ga·lac·tor·rhe·a /gəˌlaktəˈrēə/ ▶ **n.** Medicine excessive or inappropriate production of milk.
–ORIGIN mid 19th cent.: from Greek *gala, galakt-* 'milk' + *rhoia* 'flux, flow.'

ga·lac·tos·a·mine /gəlakˈtäsəˌmēn, -min, -ˈtōsə-/ ▶ **n.** an amino acid derived from the sugar galactose, of which chondroitin is a derivative.
–ORIGIN early 20th cent.: from German *Galaktosamin*.

ga·lac·tose /gəˈlaktōs/ ▶ **n.** Chemistry a sugar of the hexose class that is a constituent of lactose and many polysaccharides.
–ORIGIN mid 19th cent.: from Greek *gala, galakt-* 'milk' + **-OSE²**.

ga·lac·to·si·dase /gəˈlaktōsiˌdās, -ˌdāz, -lakˈtō-/ ▶ **n.** an enzyme, such as lactase, that is involved in the hydrolytic breakdown of a galactoside.

ga·lac·to·side /gəˈlaktəˌsīd/ ▶ **n.** a glycoside yielding galactose on hydrolysis.

ga·la·go /gəˈlāgō, -ˈlägō/ ▶ **n.** (pl. **galagos**) another term for **BUSHBABY**.
–ORIGIN modern Latin (genus name).

ga·lah /gəˈlä/ ▶ **n.** a small Australian cockatoo with a gray back and rosy pink head and underparts, abundant and regarded as a pest. ● *Eulophus roseicapillus*, family Cacatuidae (or Psittacidae).
–ORIGIN mid 19th cent.: from Yuwaalaraay (an Aboriginal language of New South Wales).

Gal·a·had /ˈgaləˌhad/ (also **Sir Galahad**) the noblest of King Arthur's legendary knights; renowned for immaculate purity and destined to find the Holy Grail.

ga·lan·gal /gəˈlaNGgəl/ (also **galingale** /ˈgalinˌgāl/) ▶ **n.** an Asian plant of the ginger family, the aromatic rhizome of which is widely used in cooking and herbal medicine. ● Genera *Alpinia* and *Kaempferia*, family Zingiberaceae.
–ORIGIN Middle English *galingale*, via Old French from Arabic *kalanjān*, perhaps from Chinese *gāoliángjiāng*, from *gāoliáng* (the name of a district in Guangdong Province, China) + *jiāng* 'ginger.'

ga·lant /gəˈlänt/ ▶ **adj.** of, relating to, or denoting a light and elegant style of 18th-century music.
–ORIGIN French and German (see **GALLANT**).

gal·an·tine /ˈgalənˌtēn/ ▶ **n.** a dish of white meat or fish that is boned, cooked, pressed, and served cold in aspic.
–ORIGIN Middle English (in the sense 'sauce for fish'): from Old French, alteration of *galatine*, from medieval Latin *galatina*; the current sense dates from the early 18th cent.

Ga·lá·pa·gos Is·lands /gəˈläpəgəs, -ˈlap-/ a Pacific Ocean archipelago on the equator, about 650 miles (1,045 km) west of Ecuador, to which it belongs; pop. 28,000 (est. 2009). Noted for giant tortoises and many other endemic species, they were the site of Charles Darwin's 1835 observations, which helped him to form his theory of natural selection. Spanish name **ARCHIPIÉLAGO DE COLÓN**.

Gal·a·te·a /ˌgaləˈtēə/ **1** Greek Mythology a sea nymph courted by the Cyclops Polyphemus, who in jealousy killed his rival Acis.
2 the name given to the statue fashioned by Pygmalion and brought to life.

Ga·la·ţi /gäˈläts, -ˈlätsē/ an industrial city in eastern Romania, a port on the lower Danube River; pop. 296,697 (2006).

Ga·la·tia /gəˈlāSH(ē)ə/ an ancient region in central Asia Minor, settled by invading Gauls (the Galatians) in the 3rd century BC. It later became a province of the Roman Empire.
–DERIVATIVES **Ga·la·tian** adj. & n.

Ga·la·tians /gəˈlāSHənz/ a book of the New Testament, an epistle of St. Paul to the Church in Galatia.

gal·ax·y /ˈgaləksē/ ▶ **n.** (pl. **galaxies**) a system of millions or billions of stars, together with gas and dust, held together by gravitational attraction. ■ (**the Galaxy**) the galaxy of which the solar system is a part; the Milky Way. ■ a large group of impressive people or things: *the four musicians have played with a galaxy of stars*.

> The Galaxy in which the earth is located is a disk-shaped spiral galaxy with approximately 100,000 million stars. The sun is located about two thirds of the way out from the center.

–ORIGIN late Middle English (originally referring to the Milky Way): via Old French from medieval Latin *galaxia*, from Greek *galaxias (kuklos)* 'milky (vault),' from *gala, galakt-* 'milk.'

Gal·ba /ˈgalbə/ (*c.*3 BC–AD 69), Roman emperor AD 68–69; full name *Servius Sulpicius Galba*. The successor to Nero, he aroused hostility because of his severity and parsimony and was murdered in a conspiracy organized by Otho.

gal·ba·num /ˈgalbənəm/ ▶ **n.** a bitter aromatic resin produced from kinds of ferula.
–ORIGIN Middle English: via Latin from Greek *khalbanē*, probably of Semitic origin.

Gal·braith /ˈgalˌbrāTH/, John Kenneth (1908–2006), US economist; born in Canada. Well known for his criticism of consumerism and of the power of large multinational corporations, he wrote *The Affluent Society* (1958) and *The New Industrial State* (1967).

gale /gāl/ ▶ **n. 1** a very strong wind: *it was almost blowing a gale* | [as modifier] *gale-force winds*. ■ Meteorology a wind of force 7 to 10 on the Beaufort scale (28-55 knots or 32-63 mph). ■ a storm at sea.
2 (**a gale of/gales of**) a burst of sound, esp. of laughter: *she collapsed into gales of laughter*.
–ORIGIN mid 16th cent.: perhaps related to Old Norse *galinn* 'mad, frantic.'

ga·le·a /ˈgālēə/ ▶ **n.** (pl. **galeae** /-lēˌē/ or **galeas**) Botany & Zoology a structure shaped like a helmet.
–ORIGIN mid 19th cent.: from Latin, literally 'helmet.'

Ga·len /ˈgālən/ (129–199), Greek physician; full name *Claudios Galenos*; Latin name *Claudius Galenus*. While attempting to systematize medicine, he made important discoveries in anatomy and physiology.
–DERIVATIVES **Ga·len·ism** /-ˌnizəm/ n., **Ga·len·ist** /-nist/ adj. & n.

ga·le·na /gəˈlēnə/ ▶ **n.** a bluish, gray, or black mineral of metallic appearance, consisting of lead sulfide. It is the chief ore of lead.
–ORIGIN late 17th cent.: from Latin, 'lead ore' (in a partly purified state).

ga·len·ic /gāˈlenik, gə-/ ▶ **adj.** Medicine (**Galenic**) of or relating to Galen or his methods. ■ (of a medicine) galenical.

ga·len·i·cal /gāˈlenikəl, gə-/ Medicine ▶ **adj.** (of a medicine) made of natural rather than synthetic components. ■ (**Galenical**) of or relating to Galen.
▶ **n.** a medicine of this type.

ga·lère /gaˈler/ ▶ **n.** a group or coterie: *the repulsive galère of Lolita's admirers*.
–ORIGIN mid 18th cent.: French, literally 'galley.' The term was used in Molière's play *Scapin* meaning 'coterie.'

ga·lette /gəˈlet/ ▶ **n.** a flat round cake of pastry or bread. ■ a savory pancake made from potatoes or buckwheat.
–ORIGIN French, from Old French *galet* 'pebble.'

ga·li·a mel·on /ˈgälēə/ ▶ **n.** a small rounded melon of a variety with rough skin and fragrant orange flesh.

Ga·li·bi /gəˈlēbē/ ▶ **n.** another term for **CARIB** (sense 2 of the noun).
–ORIGIN Carib, literally 'strong man.'

Ga·li·cia /gəˈlisHə/ **1** an autonomous region and former kingdom in northwestern Spain; capital, Santiago de Compostela.
2 a region in eastern central Europe, north of the Carpathian Mountains. A former province of Austria, it now forms part of southeastern Poland and western Ukraine.

Ga·li·ci·an /gəˈlisHən/ ▶ **adj. 1** of or relating to Galicia in northwestern Spain, its people, or their language.
2 of or relating to Galicia in east central Europe.
▶ **n. 1** a native or inhabitant of Galicia in northwestern Spain.
2 the Romance language of Galicia in northwestern Spain, closely related to Portuguese.
3 a native or inhabitant of Galicia in east central Europe.

Gal·i·le·an¹ /ˌgaləˈlēən/ ▶ **adj.** of or relating to Galileo or his methods.

Gal·i·le·an² ▶ **adj.** of or relating to Galilee. ■ archaic, derogatory Christian.
▶ **n.** a native of Galilee. ■ archaic, derogatory a Christian.

Gal·i·le·an sat·el·lites Astronomy the four largest moons of Jupiter (Callisto, Europa, Ganymede, and Io), discovered by Galileo in 1610 and independently by the German astronomer Simon Marius (1573–1624).

Gal·i·le·an tel·e·scope ▶ **n.** an astronomical telescope of the earliest type, with a biconvex objective and biconcave eyepiece.

Gal·i·lee /ˈgaləˌlē/ a northern region of ancient Palestine, west of the Jordan River, associated with the ministry of Jesus. It is now part of Israel.

gal·i·lee /ˈgaləˌlē/ ▶ **n.** a chapel or porch at the entrance to some English churches.
–ORIGIN Middle English: from Old French, from medieval Latin *galilea* 'Galilee.' Compare with **GALLERY**.

Gal·i·lee, Sea of a lake in northern Israel. The Jordan River flows through it from north to south. Also called **Tiberias, Lake** or **Kinneret, Lake**.

Gal·i·le·o /ˌgaləˈlāō/ an American space probe to Jupiter launched in 1989. It reached the vicinity of Jupiter in 1995 and released a probe which descended into Jupiter's atmosphere.

Gal·i·le·o Ga·li·lei /ˌgaləˈlāō ˌgaləˈlāē/ (1564–1642), Italian astronomer and physicist. He discovered the constancy of a pendulum's swing, formulated the law of uniform acceleration of falling bodies, and described the parabolic trajectory of projectiles. He applied the telescope to astronomy and observed craters on the moon, sunspots, Jupiter's moons, and the phases of Venus.

gal·in·gale /ˈgalinˌgāl/ ▶ n. **1** a Eurasian sedge with an aromatic rhizome, formerly used in perfumes. [late 16th cent.: variant of **galangal**.] ● *Cyperus longus*, family Cyperaceae.
2 variant spelling of **galangal**.

gal·i·pot /ˈgaləˌpät/ ▶ n. hardened resin deposits formed on the stem of certain species of pine, in particular the maritime pine.
– ORIGIN late 18th cent.: from French, of unknown origin.

gall[1] /gôl/ ▶ n. **1** bold, impudent behavior: *the bank had the gall to demand a fee.*
2 the contents of the gallbladder; bile (proverbial for its bitterness). ■ an animal's gallbladder. ■ used to refer to something bitter or cruel: *accept life's gall without blaming somebody else.*
– ORIGIN Old English *gealla* (denoting bile), of Germanic origin; related to Dutch *gal*, German *Galle* 'gall,' from an Indo-European root shared by Greek *kholē* and Latin *fel* 'bile.'

gall[2] ▶ n. **1** annoyance; irritation: *he imagined Linda's gall as she found herself still married and not rich.*
2 (esp. of a horse) a sore on the skin made by chafing.
▶ v. [with obj.] **1** make (someone) feel annoyed: *he knew he was losing, and it galled him.*
2 make sore by rubbing: *the straps galled their shoulders.*
– ORIGIN Old English *gealle* 'sore on a horse,' perhaps related to **gall[1]**; superseded in Middle English by forms from Middle Low German or Middle Dutch.

gall[3] ▶ n. an abnormal growth formed on plants and trees, esp. oaks, in response to the presence of insect larvae, mites, or fungi. ■ [as modifier] denoting insects or mites that produce such growths: *gall flies.*
– ORIGIN Middle English: via Old French from Latin *galla*.

Gal·la /ˈgalə/ ▶ n. & adj. another term for **Oromo**.
– ORIGIN of unknown origin.

gal·lant ▶ adj. **1** /ˈgalənt/ (of a person or their behavior) brave; heroic: *she had made gallant efforts to pull herself together.* ■ archaic grand; fine: *they made a gallant array as they marched off.*
2 /ˈgalənt/ (of a man or his behavior) giving special attention and respect to women; chivalrous.
▶ n. /gəˈlant, -ˈlänt, ˈgalənt/ dated or literary a man who pays special attention to women. ■ a dashing man of fashion; a fine gentleman.
▶ v. /gəˈlant, -ˈlänt/ [with obj.] archaic (of a man) flirt with (a woman).
– DERIVATIVES **gal·lant·ly** /ˈgaləntlē/ adv.
– ORIGIN Middle English (in the sense 'finely dressed'): from Old French *galant*, from *galer* 'have fun, make a show,' from *gale* 'pleasure, rejoicing.'

gal·lant·ry /ˈgaləntrē/ ▶ n. (pl. **gallantries**)
1 courageous behavior, esp. in battle: *a medal awarded for outstanding gallantry during the raid.*
2 polite attention or respect given by men to women. ■ (**gallantries**) actions or words used when paying such attention.
– ORIGIN late 16th cent. (in the sense 'splendor, ornamentation'): from French *galanterie*, from *galant* (see **gallant**).

Gal·lau·det /ˌgaləˈdet/, Thomas Hopkins (1787–1851), US educator. In 1817, he founded the first free American school for deaf students in Hartford, Connecticut. Gallaudet College in Washington, DC, is named for him.

gall·ber·ry /ˈgôlˌberē/ (also **gallberry holly**) ▶ n. (pl. **gallberries**) a North American holly with shiny leaves and white flowers. ● Genus *Ilex*, family Aquifoliaceae: the **tall gallberry** (*I. coriacea*) of the southeastern US, and the more widespread **low gallberry** (*I. glabra*), with black berries and nearly spineless leaves.

gall·blad·der /ˈgôlˌbladər/ (also **gall bladder**) ▶ n. the small sac-shaped organ beneath the liver, in which bile is stored after secretion by the liver and before release into the intestine.

gal·le·on /ˈgalēən, ˈgalyən/ ▶ n. a sailing ship in use (esp. by Spain) from the 15th through 17th centuries, originally as a warship, later for trade. Galleons were mainly square-rigged and usually had three or more decks and masts.
– ORIGIN early 16th cent.: either via Middle Dutch from French *galion*, from *galie* 'galley,' or from Spanish *galeón*.

galleon

gal·le·ri·a /ˌgaləˈrēə/ ▶ n. a covered or enclosed area, esp. one with commercial establishments for shopping, dining, etc.
– ORIGIN Italian (see **gallery**).

gal·ler·y /ˈgalərē/ ▶ n. (pl. **galleries**) **1** a room or building for the display or sale of works of art. ■ a collection of pictures.
2 a balcony, esp. a platform or upper floor, projecting from the back or sidewall inside a church or hall, providing space for an audience or musicians. ■ (**the gallery**) the highest of such balconies in a theater, containing the cheapest seats. ■ a group of spectators, esp. those at a golf tournament.
3 a long room or passage, esp. one that is partly open at the side to form a portico or colonnade. ■ a horizontal underground passage, esp. in a mine.
– PHRASES **play to the gallery** act in an exaggerated or theatrical manner, esp. to appeal to popular taste.
– DERIVATIVES **gal·ler·ied** adj.
– ORIGIN late Middle English (sense 3): via Old French from Italian *galleria* 'gallery,' formerly also 'church porch,' from medieval Latin *galeria*, perhaps an alteration of *galilea* (see **galilee**).

gal·ley /ˈgalē/ ▶ n. (pl. **galleys**) **1** historical a low, flat ship with one or more sails and up to three banks of oars, chiefly used for warfare, trade, and piracy. ■ a long rowboat used as a ship's boat.
2 the kitchen in a ship or aircraft.
3 (also **galley proof**) a printer's proof in the form of long single-column strips, not in sheets or pages. [*galley* from French *galée* denoting an oblong tray for holding setup type.]
– ORIGIN Middle English: via Old French from medieval Latin *galea*, from medieval Greek *galaia*, of unknown origin.

gal·ley slave ▶ n. historical a person condemned to row in a galley. ■ a person who works very hard, typically performing menial or thankless tasks: *call-center workers are the galley slaves of the twenty-first century.*

Gal·lia·no /galˈyänō/ ▶ n. a golden-yellow Italian liqueur flavored with herbs.
– ORIGIN named after Major Giuseppe Galliáno, noted for halting Ethiopian forces in the war of 1895–96.

gal·liard /ˈgalyərd/ ▶ n. historical a lively dance in triple time for two people, including complicated turns and steps.
– ORIGIN late Middle English (as an adjective meaning 'valiant, sturdy' and 'lively, brisk'): from Old French *gaillard* 'valiant,' of Celtic origin. The current sense dates from the mid 16th cent.

Gal·lic /ˈgalik/ ▶ adj. **1** French or typically French.
2 of or relating to the Gauls.
– DERIVATIVES **Gal·li·cize** /ˈgaləˌsīz/ v.
– ORIGIN late 17th cent.: from Latin *Gallicus*, from *Gallus* 'a Gaul.'

gal·lic ac·id /ˈgalik, ˈgôlik/ ▶ n. Chemistry an acid extracted from oak galls and other vegetable products, formerly used in making ink.
● Alternative name: **3, 4, 5-trihydroxybenzoic acid**; chem. formula: $C_6H_2(OH)_3COOH$.
– DERIVATIVES **gal·late** /ˈgalāt, ˈgôlāt/ n.
– ORIGIN late 18th cent.: *gallic* from Latin *galla* 'oak gall' (see **gall[3]**) + **-ic**.

Gal·li·can /ˈgalikən/ ▶ adj. **1** of or relating to the ancient Church of Gaul or France.
2 of or holding a doctrine (reaching its peak in the 17th century) that asserted the freedom of the Roman Catholic Church in France and elsewhere from the ecclesiastical authority of the papacy. Compare with **ultramontane**.
▶ n. an adherent of the Gallican doctrine.
– DERIVATIVES **Gal·li·can·ism** /-ˌnizəm/ n.
– ORIGIN late Middle English: from Old French *gallican*, or from Latin *Gallicanus*, from *Gallicus* (see **Gallic**).

Gal·li·cism /ˈgaliˌsizəm/ ▶ n. a French expression, esp. one adopted by speakers of another language.
– ORIGIN mid 17th cent.: from French *gallicisme*, from Latin *Gallicus* (see **Gallic**).

Gal·lic Wars Julius Caesar's campaigns 58–51 BC, which established Roman control over Gaul north of the Alps and west of the Rhine River (Transalpine Gaul). During this period Caesar twice invaded Britain (55 and 54 BC).

gal·li·gas·kins /ˌgaliˈgaskinz/ ▶ plural n. Brit. historical loose-fitting breeches, trousers, or gaiters.
– ORIGIN late 16th cent.: perhaps an alteration (influenced by *galley* and *Gascon*) of obsolete French *gargesque*, from Italian *grechesca*, feminine of *grechesco* 'Greek.'

gal·li·mau·fry /ˌgaləˈmôfrē/ ▶ n. (pl. **gallimaufries**) a confused jumble or medley of things. ■ a dish made from diced or minced meat, esp. a hash or ragout.
– ORIGIN mid 16th cent.: from archaic French *galimafrée* 'unappetizing dish,' perhaps from Old French *galer* 'have fun' + Picard *mafrer* 'eat copious quantities.'

gal·li·mi·mus /ˌgaliˈmīməs/ ▶ n. an ostrich dinosaur of the late Cretaceous period. ● Genus *Gallimimus*, infraorder Ornithomimosauria, suborder Theropoda.
– ORIGIN modern Latin, from Latin *galli* 'of a cockerel' (genitive of *gallus*) + *mimus* 'mime, pretense.'

gal·li·na·ceous /ˌgaləˈnāsнəs/ ▶ adj. dated of or relating to birds of an order (Galliformes) which includes domestic poultry and game birds.
– ORIGIN late 18th cent.: from Latin *gallinaceus* (from *gallina* 'hen,' from *gallus* 'cock') + **-ous**.

gall·ing /ˈgôliNG/ ▶ adj. annoying; humiliating: *the loss was particularly galling.*
– DERIVATIVES **gall·ing·ly** adv.

gal·li·nule /ˈgaləˌn(y)o͞ol/ ▶ n. a marsh bird of the rail family, with mainly black, purplish-blue, or dark green plumage, and a red bill. ● Genera *Porphyrio* and *Porphyrula* (or *Gallinula*), family Rallidae: several species, including the **purple gallinule** (*Porphyrula martinica*), found from the southeastern US to Argentina. See also **moorhen**.
– ORIGIN late 18th cent.: from modern Latin *Gallinula* (genus term), diminutive of Latin *gallina* 'hen,' from *gallus* 'cock.'

gal·li·ot /ˈgalēət/ ▶ n. historical a single-masted Dutch cargo boat or fishing vessel. ■ a small fast galley, esp. in the Mediterranean.
– ORIGIN Middle English: from Old French *galiote* or Dutch *galjoot*, from a diminutive of medieval Latin *galea* 'galley.'

Gal·lip·o·li /gəˈlipəlē/ a major campaign of World War I that took place on the Gallipoli peninsula, on the European side of the Dardanelles in 1915–16. The Allies (with heavy involvement of troops from Australia and New Zealand) hoped to gain control of the strait, but the campaign reached stalemate after each side suffered heavy casualties.

gal·li·pot /ˈgaləˌpät/ ▶ n. historical a small pot made from glazed earthenware or metal, used by pharmacists to hold medicines or ointments.
– ORIGIN late Middle English: probably from **galley** + **pot[1]** (because gallipots were brought from the Mediterranean in galleys).

gal·li·um /ˈgalēəm/ ▶ n. the chemical element of atomic number 31, a soft silvery-white metal that melts at about 30°C, just above room temperature. (Symbol: **Ga**)
– ORIGIN late 19th cent.: modern Latin, from Latin *Gallia* 'France' or *gallus* 'cock'; named (either patriotically or as a translation of his own name) by Paul-Émile *Lecoq de Boisbaudran* (1838–1912), the French chemist who discovered it in 1875.

gal·li·um ar·sen·ide ▶ n. a dark-gray crystalline compound containing gallium and arsenic, used in the manufacture of microelectronic components, such as solar cells and semiconductors.

gal·li·vant /ˈgaləˌvant/ ▶ v. [no obj.] informal go around from one place to another in the pursuit of pleasure or entertainment: *she quit her job to go gallivanting around the globe.*
– ORIGIN early 19th cent.: perhaps an alteration of **gallant**.

g

gal·li·wasp /ˈgaləˌwäsp/ ▶ **n.** a marsh lizard found in Central America and the Caribbean. ● Genus *Diploglossus*, family Anguidae: many species, in particular *D. monotropis* of the West Indies.
– ORIGIN late 17th cent.: of unknown origin.

gall midge ▶ **n.** a small, delicate midge that induces gall formation in plants or may cause other damage to crops. ● Family Cecidomyiidae: numerous genera and species.

gall mite ▶ **n.** a minute mite that is parasitic on plants, typically living inside buds and causing them to form hard galls. ● Family Eriophyidae, order Prostigmata: numerous species, in particular *Cecidophyopsis ribis*, which affects black-currant bushes, causing big bud and transmitting the reversion virus.

Gallo- ▶ **comb. form** French; French and ...: *Gallo-German*. ■ relating to France.
– ORIGIN from Latin *Gallus* 'a Gaul.'

gal·lon /ˈgalən/ ▶ **n. 1** a unit of volume for liquid measure equal to four quarts, in particular: ■ US equivalent to 3.79 liters. ■ (also **imperial gallon**) Brit. equivalent to 4.55 liters (also used for dry measure).
2 (**gallons of**) informal a large volume: *gallons of fake blood*.
– DERIVATIVES **gal·lon·age** /-nij/ **n.**
– ORIGIN Middle English: from Anglo-Norman French *galon*, from the base of medieval Latin *galleta*, *galletum* 'pail, liquid measure,' perhaps of Celtic origin.

gal·loon /gəˈlo͞on/ ▶ **n.** a narrow ornamental strip of fabric, typically a silk braid or piece of lace, used to trim clothing or finish upholstery.
– ORIGIN early 17th cent.: from French *galon*, from *galonner* 'to trim with braid,' of unknown ultimate origin.

gal·lop /ˈgaləp/ ▶ **n.** [in sing.] the fastest pace of a horse or other quadruped, with all the feet off the ground together in each stride: *the horse broke into a furious gallop* | *riding at full gallop*. ■ a ride on a horse at this pace: *Will went for a gallop on the beach*. ■ a very fast pace of running or moving.
▶ **v.** (**gallops, galloping, galloped**) [no obj.] **1** (of a horse) go at the pace of a gallop. ■ [with obj.] make (a horse) gallop: *Fred galloped the horse off to the start*. ■ (of a person) run fast and rather boisterously.
2 (of a process or time) progress rapidly in a seemingly uncontrollable manner: *panic about the deadline galloping toward them* | (as adj. **galloping**) *galloping inflation*.
– DERIVATIVES **gal·lop·er n.**
– ORIGIN early 16th cent.: from Old French *galop* (noun), *galoper* (verb), variants of Old Northern French *walop*, *waloper* (see **WALLOP**).

Gal·lo·way /ˈgaləˌwā/ ▶ **n.** an animal of a breed of cattle that originated in Galloway, Scotland. They are hornless and black and are raised for beef.

gal·lows /ˈgalōz/ ▶ **plural n.** [usu. treated as sing.] a structure, typically of two uprights and a crosspiece, for the hanging of criminals. ■ (**the gallows**) execution by hanging: *saved from the gallows by a last-minute reprieve*.
– ORIGIN Old English *galga*, *gealga*, of Germanic origin; related to Dutch *galg* and German *Galgen*; reinforced in Middle English by Old Norse *gálgi*.

gal·lows hu·mor ▶ **n.** grim and ironic humor in a desperate or hopeless situation.

gal·lows tree ▶ **n.** another term for **GALLOWS**.

gall·stone /ˈgôlˌstōn/ ▶ **n.** a small, hard crystalline mass formed abnormally in the gallbladder or bile ducts from bile pigments, cholesterol, and calcium salts. Gallstones can cause severe pain and blockage of the bile duct.

Gal·lup /ˈgaləp/, George Horace (1901–84), US statistician. A pioneer of public opinion polls, he founded the American Institute of Public Opinion in 1935.

Gal·lup poll /ˈgaləp/ ▶ **n.** trademark an assessment of public opinion by the questioning of a statistically representative sample.
– ORIGIN 1940s: named after George H. *Gallup*, US statistician who devised the method.

gal·lus·es /ˈgaləsiz/ ▶ **plural n.** informal suspenders for trousers.
– ORIGIN mid 19th cent.: plural of *gallus*, variant of **GALLOWS**.

gall wasp ▶ **n.** a small winged insect of antlike appearance. The female lays its egg in plant tissue, which swells to form a gall when the larva hatches. ● Superfamily Cynipoidea, order Hymenoptera: several genera.

Ga·lois /gälˈwä/, Évariste (1811–32), French mathematician. His memoir on the conditions for solubility of polynomial equations was posthumously published in 1846.

Ga·lois the·o·ry Mathematics a method of applying group theory to the solution of algebraic equations.

ga·loot /gəˈlo͞ot/ ▶ **n.** informal a clumsy or oafish person (often as a term of abuse).
– ORIGIN early 19th cent. (originally in nautical use meaning 'an inexperienced marine'): of unknown origin.

gal·op /ˈgaləp/ ▶ **n.** a lively ballroom dance in duple time, popular in the late 18th century.
– ORIGIN mid 19th cent.: French, literally 'gallop.'

ga·lore /gəˈlôr/ ▶ **adj.** [postpositive] in abundance: *there were prizes galore for everything*.
– ORIGIN early 17th cent.: from Irish *go leor*, literally 'to sufficiency.'

ga·losh /gəˈläsH/ ▶ **n.** (usu. **galoshes**) a waterproof overshoe, typically made of rubber.
– ORIGIN Middle English (denoting a type of clog): via Old French from late Latin *gallicula*, diminutive of Latin *gallica (solea)* 'Gallic (shoe).' The current sense dates from the mid 19th cent.

gal pal ▶ **n.** informal a female friend.

Gals·wor·thy /ˈgôlzˌwərT͟Hē/, John (1867–1933), British novelist and playwright. He is noted for *The Forsyte Saga* (1906–28), a series of novels. Nobel Prize for Literature (1932).

Gal·ton /ˈgôltn/, Sir Francis (1822–1911), English scientist. He founded eugenics and introduced methods of measuring human mental and physical abilities. He also pioneered the use of fingerprints as a means of identification. He was a cousin of Charles Darwin.

ga·lumph /gəˈləmf/ ▶ **v.** [no obj.] informal move in a clumsy, ponderous, or noisy manner: *she galumphed along beside him* | (as adj. **galumphing**) *a galumphing tortoise*.
– ORIGIN 1871 (in the sense 'prance in triumph'): coined by Lewis Carroll in *Through the Looking Glass*; perhaps a blend of **GALLOP** and **TRIUMPH**.

galv. ▶ **abbr.** galvanic.

Gal·va·ni /gälˈvänē/, Luigi (1737–98), Italian anatomist. He is noted for his discovery of the twitching of frogs' legs in an electric field.

gal·van·ic /galˈvanik/ ▶ **adj. 1** relating to or involving electric currents produced by chemical action.
2 sudden and dramatic: *hurry with awkward galvanic strides*.
– DERIVATIVES **gal·van·i·cal·ly** /-ik(ə)lē/ **adv.**
– ORIGIN late 18th cent.: from French *galvanique*, from **GALVANI**.

gal·van·ic skin re·sponse (also **galvanic skin reflex**) (abbr.: **GSR**) ▶ **n.** a change in the electrical resistance of the skin caused by emotional stress, measurable with a sensitive galvanometer, e.g., in lie-detector tests.

gal·va·nism /ˈgalvəˌnizəm/ ▶ **n.** historical **1** electricity produced by chemical action.
2 the therapeutic use of electric currents.
– ORIGIN late 18th cent.: from French *galvanisme*, from **GALVANI**.

gal·va·nize /ˈgalvəˌnīz/ ▶ **v.** [with obj.] **1** shock or excite (someone), typically into taking action: *the urgency of his voice galvanized them into action*.
2 (often as adj. **galvanized**) coat (iron or steel) with a protective layer of zinc: *an old galvanized bucket*.
– DERIVATIVES **gal·va·ni·za·tion** /ˌgalvəniˈzāsHən/ **n.**, **gal·va·niz·er n.**
– ORIGIN early 19th cent. (in the sense 'stimulate by electricity'): from French *galvaniser* (see **GALVANI**).

gal·va·no·mag·net·ic /ˌgalvənōmagˈnetik, galˈvanō-/ ▶ **adj.** of or relating to the production of an electromagnetic field within a conductor or semiconductor through which a current is flowing.

gal·va·nom·e·ter /ˌgalvəˈnämitər/ ▶ **n.** an instrument for detecting and measuring small electric currents.
– DERIVATIVES **gal·va·no·met·ric** /-nəˈmetrik/ **adj.**

gal·va·no·scope /ˈgalvənəˌskōp/ ▶ **n.** a galvanometer that works by measuring the deflection of a needle in the magnetic field induced by the electric current.
– DERIVATIVES **gal·va·no·scop·ic** /ˌgalvənəˈskäpik/ **adj.**

Gal·ves·ton /ˈgalvəstən/ a port in southeastern Texas, southeast of Houston; pop. 57,086 (est. 2008). It is situated on Galveston Bay, an inlet of the Gulf of Mexico.

Gal·way /ˈgôlˌwā/ a county in the Republic of Ireland, on the western coast of Connacht Province. ■ its county town, a seaport at the head of Galway Bay; pop. 72,414 (2006).

Gal·way Bay an inlet of the Atlantic Ocean on the western coast of Ireland.

gam[1] /gam/ ▶ **n.** informal a leg, esp. in reference to the shapeliness of a woman's leg.
– ORIGIN late 18th cent.: probably a variant of the heraldic term *gamb*, which denotes a charge representing an animal's leg, from Old Northern French *gambe* 'leg.'

gam[2] ▶ **n. 1** a school of whales, porpoises, or dolphins.
2 a social meeting or informal conversation (originally one among whalers at sea).

Ga·ma, Vas·co da see **DA GAMA**.

Ga·may /gaˈmā, ˈgamā/ ▶ **n.** a variety of black wine grape native to the Beaujolais district of France. ■ a fruity red wine made from this grape. ■ (also **Gamay-Beaujolais**) a red wine with a similar flavor.
– ORIGIN from the name of a hamlet in Burgundy, eastern France.

gam·ba /ˈgämbə, ˈgam-/ ▶ **n.** short for **VIOLA DA GAMBA**.

gam·ba·do[1] /gamˈbādō, -ˈbä-/ (also **gambade** /-ˈbād, -ˈbäd/) ▶ **n.** (pl. **gambados** or **gambadoes**) a leap or bound, esp. an exaggerated one.
– ORIGIN early 19th cent.: from Spanish *gambada*, from *gamba* 'leg.'

gam·ba·do[2] ▶ **n.** (pl. **gambados** or **gambadoes**) a gaiter, typically one attached to a saddle to protect a rider's leg from the weather.
– ORIGIN mid 17th cent.: from Italian *gamba* 'leg' + **-ADO**.

Gam·bi·a[1] /ˈgambēə, ˈgäm-/ (also **the Gambia**) a country on the coast of West Africa; pop. 1,778,100 (est. 2009); capital, Banjul; languages, English (official), Malinke and other indigenous languages, and Creole.

> Gambia consists of a narrow strip of territory on either side of the Gambia River that forms an enclave in Senegal. It was created as a British colony in 1843 and became an independent member of the Commonwealth of Nations in 1965 and a republic in 1970.

– DERIVATIVES **Gam·bi·an adj. & n.**

Gam·bi·a[2] /ˈgambēə, ˈgäm-/ a river in West Africa that rises near Labé in Guinea and flows for 500 miles (800 km) through Senegal and Gambia to meet the Atlantic Ocean at Banjul.

gam·bier /ˈgambi(ə)r/ (also **gambir**) ▶ **n.** an astringent extract of a tropical Asiatic plant, used in tanning. ● The chief source of gambier is the climber *Uncaria gambier*, family Rubiaceae.
– ORIGIN early 19th cent.: from Malay *gambir*, the name of the plant.

Gam·bier Is·lands /ˈgamˌbir/ a group of coral islands in the South Pacific Ocean, part of French Polynesia.

gam·bit /ˈgambit/ ▶ **n.** (in chess) an opening in which a player makes a sacrifice, typically of a pawn, for the sake of some compensating advantage. ■ a device, action, or opening remark, typically one entailing a degree of risk, that is calculated to gain an advantage: *his resignation was a tactical gambit*.
– ORIGIN mid 17th cent.: originally *gambett*, from Italian *gambetto*, literally 'tripping up,' from *gamba* 'leg.'

gam·ble /ˈgambəl/ ▶ **v.** [no obj.] **1** play games of chance for money; bet: *she was fond of gambling on cards and horses*. ■ [with obj.] bet (a sum of money) in such a way: *he was gambling every penny he had on the spin of a wheel*.
2 take risky action in the hope of a desired result: [with clause] *the British could only gamble that something would turn up*.
▶ **n.** [usu. in sing.] an act of gambling; an enterprise undertaken or attempted with a risk of loss and a chance of profit or success.
– ORIGIN early 18th cent.: from obsolete *gamel* 'play games,' or from the verb **GAME**.

gam·bler /ˈgamblər/ ▶ **n.** a person who gambles: *a compulsive gambler*.

gam·boge /gamˈbōj, -ˈbo͞ozH/ ▶ **n.** a gum resin produced by various eastern Asian trees, used as a yellow pigment and in medicine as a purgative.
– ORIGIN early 18th cent. (earlier in the Latin form): from modern Latin *gambaugium*, from **CAMBODIA**.

gam·bol /ˈgambəl/ ▶ **v.** (**gambols, gamboling, gamboled**; Brit. **gambols, gambolling, gambolled**) [no obj.] run or jump about playfully: *the mare gamboled toward Connie*.
▶ **n.** [usu. in sing.] an act of running or jumping about playfully.
– ORIGIN early 16th cent.: alteration of obsolete *gambade*, via French from Italian *gambata* 'trip up,' from *gamba* 'leg.'

gam·brel /ˈgambrəl/ (also **gambrel roof**) ▶ **n.** a roof with two sides, each of which has a shallower slope above a steeper one. ■ a hip roof with a small gable forming the upper part of each end.

g

– ORIGIN mid 16th cent. (in the sense 'bent piece of wood or iron used by butchers to hang carcasses on'): from Old Northern French *gamberel*, from *gambier* 'forked stick,' from *gambe* 'leg.' The sense 'hip roof' (mid 19th cent.) is based on an earlier meaning 'joint in the upper part of a horse's hind leg,' the shape of which the roof resembles.

gam·bu·sia /gamˈbyo͞ozHə/ ▶ n. another term for MOSQUITOFISH.
– ORIGIN modern Latin, alteration of American Spanish *gambusino*.

game /gām/ ▶ n. **1** a form of play or sport, esp. a competitive one played according to rules and decided by skill, strength, or luck. ■ a complete episode or period of play, typically ending in a definite result: *a baseball game.* ■ a single portion of play forming a scoring unit in a match, esp. in tennis. ■ Bridge a score of 100 points for tricks bid and made (the best of three games constituting a rubber). ■ a person's performance in a game; a person's standard or method of play: *he will attempt to raise his game to another level.* ■ (**games**) a meeting for sporting contests, esp. track and field: *the Olympic Games.* ■ (**games**) Brit. sports and athletic activities as organized in a school. ■ the equipment for a game, esp. a board game or a computer game.
2 a type of activity or business, esp. when regarded as a game: *this was a game of shuttle diplomacy at which I had become adept.* ■ a secret and clever plan or trick: *I was on to his little game, but I didn't want him to know.*
3 wild mammals or birds hunted for sport or food. ■ the flesh of these mammals or birds, used as food.
▶ adj. eager and willing to do something new or challenging: *they were game for anything after the traumas of Monday.*
▶ v. **1** [no obj.] (often as adj. **gaming**) play games of chance for money. ■ play video or computer games. **2** [with obj.] manipulate (a situation), typically in a way that is unfair or unscrupulous: *it was very easy for a few big companies to game the system | politicians blamed electricity generators for gaming the market.*
– PHRASES **ahead of the game** ahead of one's competitors or peers in the same sphere of activity. **at the top of one's game** see TOP¹. **beat someone at their own game** use someone's own methods to outdo them in their chosen activity. **game over** informal said when a situation is regarded as hopeless or irreversible. **make (a) game of** archaic mock; taunt. **make a game of it** Sports make a contest more closely competitive. **off (or on) one's game** playing badly (or well). **the only game in town** informal the best, the most important, or the only thing worth considering. **play the game** behave in a fair or honorable way; abide by the rules or conventions. **play games** deal with someone or something in a way that lacks due seriousness or respect: *Don't play games with me!*
– DERIVATIVES **game·ly** adv., **game·ness** n., **game·ster** /-stər/ n.
– ORIGIN Old English *gamen* 'amusement, fun,' *gamenian* 'play, amuse oneself,' of Germanic origin.

game bird ▶ n. **1** a bird hunted for sport or food. **2** a bird of a large group that includes pheasants, grouse, quails, guineafowl, guans, etc. ● Order Galliformes: several families.

game·cock /ˈgām,käk/ ▶ n. a rooster bred and trained for cockfighting. Also called **game fowl**.

game en·gine ▶ n. the basic software of a computer game or video game.

game face ▶ n. a sports player's neutral or serious facial expression, displaying determination and concentration.

game fish (also **gamefish** /ˈgām,fisH/) ▶ n. (pl. **same**) a fish caught by anglers for sport, esp. (in fresh water) salmon and trout and (in the sea) billfish, shark, bass, and many members of the mackerel family.

game·keep·er /ˈgām,kēpər/ ▶ n. a person employed to breed and protect game, typically for a large estate.
– DERIVATIVES **game·keep·ing** /-,kēpiNG/ n.

gam·e·lan /ˈgamə,lan/ ▶ n. a traditional instrumental ensemble of Indonesia, typically including many bronze percussion instruments.
– ORIGIN early 19th cent.: from Javanese.

game mis·con·duct ▶ n. Ice Hockey a punitive suspension of a player for the remainder of a game, with a substitution permitted.

game·pad /ˈgām,pad/ ▶ n. a handheld controller for video games.

game plan ▶ n. a strategy worked out in advance, esp. in sports, politics, or business.

game·play /ˈgām,plā/ ▶ n. the tactical aspects of a computer game, such as its plot and the way it is played, as distinct from the graphics and sound effects.

game point ▶ n. (in tennis and other sports) a point that, if won by one contestant, will also win the game.

gam·er /ˈgāmər/ ▶ n. a person who plays a game or games, typically a participant in a computer or role-playing game. ■ (esp. in sports) a person known for consistently making a strong effort.

game room ▶ n. a room for relaxing or socializing in a house or public building, typically furnished with a pool table, Ping-Pong table, dart board, or other recreational amenities.

games con·sole ▶ n. see CONSOLE² (sense 1).

game show ▶ n. a television program in which people compete to win prizes.

games·man·ship /ˈgāmzmən,SHip/ ▶ n. the art of winning games by using various ploys and tactics to gain a psychological advantage.
– DERIVATIVES **games·man** n. (pl. **gamesmen**).

game·some /ˈgāmsəm/ ▶ adj. playful and merry.
– DERIVATIVES **game·some·ly** adv., **game·some·ness** n.

gam·e·tan·gi·um /,gaməˈtanjēəm/ ▶ n. (pl. **gametangia** /-jēə/) Botany a specialized organ or cell in which gametes are formed in algae, ferns, and some other plants.
– ORIGIN late 19th cent.: from modern Latin *gameta* (see GAMETE) + Greek *angeion* 'vessel' + -IUM.

gam·ete /ˈgamēt, gəˈmēt/ ▶ n. Biology a mature haploid male or female germ cell that is able to unite with another of the opposite sex in sexual reproduction to form a zygote.
– DERIVATIVES **ga·met·ic** /gəˈmetik/ adj.
– ORIGIN late 19th cent.: from modern Latin *gameta*, from Greek *gametē* 'wife,' *gametēs* 'husband,' from *gamos* 'marriage.'

game the·o·ry (also **games theory**) ▶ n. the branch of mathematics concerned with the analysis of strategies for dealing with competitive situations where the outcome of a participant's choice of action depends critically on the actions of other participants. Game theory has been applied to contexts in war, business, and biology. Compare with DECISION THEORY.

gameto- ▶ comb. form Biology representing GAMETE.

ga·me·to·cyte /gəˈmētə,sīt/ ▶ n. Biology a cell that divides (by meiosis) to form gametes.

gam·e·to·gen·e·sis /gə,mētəˈjenəsis/ ▶ n. Biology the process in which cells undergo meiosis to form gametes.
– DERIVATIVES **ga·me·to·gen·ic** /-ˈjenik/ adj., **gam·e·tog·e·ny** /,gaməˈtäjənē/ n.

ga·me·to·phyte /gəˈmētə,fīt/ ▶ n. Botany (in the life cycle of plants with alternating generations) the gamete-producing and usually haploid phase, producing the zygote from which the sporophyte arises. It is the dominant form in bryophytes.
– DERIVATIVES **ga·me·to·phyt·ic** /gə,mētəˈfitik/ adj.

game war·den ▶ n. a person who is employed to supervise game and hunting in a particular area.

gam·ey ▶ adj. variant spelling of GAMY.

gam·in /ˈgamin/ ▶ n. dated a street urchin.
– ORIGIN mid 19th cent.: French, originally an eastern dialect word, of unknown origin.

gam·ine /gaˈmēn/ ▶ n. a girl with mischievous or boyish charm. ■ dated a female street urchin.
▶ adj. characteristic of or relating to such a girl.
– ORIGIN late 19th cent.: French, feminine of *gamin* (see GAMIN).

gam·ing house ▶ n. dated a public building where gambling games are played; a casino.

gam·ma /ˈgamə/ ▶ n. the third letter of the Greek alphabet (Γ, γ), transliterated as 'g.' ● The combinations γγ, γκ, and γχ are usually transliterated as 'ng,' 'nc' or 'nk,' and 'nch' or 'nkh.' ■ [as modifier] denoting the third in a series of items, categories, etc. ■ [as modifier] relating to gamma rays: *gamma detector.* ■ (**Gamma**) [followed by Latin genitive] Astronomy the third (usually third-brightest) star in a constellation: *Gamma Orionis.* ■ Physics (pl. **same**) a unit of magnetic field strength equal to 10^{-5} oersted.

gam·ma-a·mi·no·bu·tyr·ic ac·id /ə,mēnōbyo͞oˈtirik/ ▶ n. Biochemistry an amino acid that acts to inhibit the transmission of nerve impulses in the central nervous system. ● Chem. formula: $H_2NCH_2CH_2CH_2COOH$.
– ORIGIN early 20th cent.: *gamma* indicating the relative position of amino on the third carbon away from the acid group.

gam·ma glob·u·lin /ˈgläbyəlin/ ▶ n. see GLOBULIN.

gam·ma-HCH ▶ n. another term for LINDANE.
– ORIGIN *HCH* from *hexachlorocyclohexane.*

gam·ma ra·di·a·tion ▶ n. gamma rays.

gam·ma rays ▶ plural n. penetrating electromagnetic radiation of a kind arising from the radioactive decay of atomic nuclei.

gam·mer /ˈgamər/ ▶ n. archaic an old countrywoman.
– ORIGIN late 16th cent.: probably a contraction of GODMOTHER; see also GAFFER.

gam·mon¹ /ˈgamən/ ▶ n. ham that has been cured or smoked like bacon. ■ the bottom piece of a side of bacon, including a hind leg.
– ORIGIN late 15th cent. (denoting the haunch of a pig): from Old Northern French *gambon*, from *gambe* 'leg.'

gam·mon² ▶ n. a victory in backgammon (carrying a double score) in which the winner removes all their pieces before the loser has removed any.
▶ v. [with obj.] defeat (a backgammon opponent) in such a way.
– ORIGIN mid 18th cent.: apparently from Old English *gamen* or *gamenian* (see GAME), with survival of the *-n* ending.

gam·mon³ informal, dated, chiefly Brit. ▶ n. nonsense; rubbish.
▶ v. [with obj.] hoax or deceive (someone).
– ORIGIN early 18th cent.: origin uncertain; the term was first used as criminals' slang in *give gammon to* 'give cover to (a pickpocket)' and *keep in gammon* 'distract (a victim) for a pickpocket.'

gam·my /ˈgamē/ ▶ adj. Brit. informal (of part of a person's body, esp. the leg) unable to function normally because of injury or chronic pain.
– ORIGIN mid 19th cent. (in the sense 'bad, false'): form of British dialect *game* in the same sense.

Gam·ow /ˈgamôf/, George (1904–68), US physicist; born in Russia. A proponent of the Big Bang theory, he also suggested the triplet code of bases in DNA, which governs the synthesis of amino acids.

gamp /gamp/ ▶ n. Brit. informal, dated an umbrella, esp. a large unwieldy one.
– ORIGIN mid 19th cent.: named after Mrs. *Gamp*, in Charles Dickens's *Martin Chuzzlewit*, who carried such an umbrella.

gam·ut /ˈgamət/ ▶ n. (**the gamut**) **1** the complete range or scope of something: *the whole gamut of human emotion.*
2 Music a complete scale of musical notes; the compass or range of a voice or instrument. ■ historical a scale consisting of seven overlapping hexachords, containing all the recognized notes used in medieval music, covering almost three octaves from bass G to treble E. ■ historical the lowest note in this scale.
– PHRASES **run the gamut** experience, display, or perform the complete range of something: *wines that run the gamut from dry to sweet.*
– ORIGIN late Middle English: from medieval Latin *gamma ut*, originally the name of the lowest note in the medieval scale (bass G an octave and a half below middle C), then applied to the whole range of notes used in medieval music. The Greek letter Γ (gamma) was used for bass G, with *ut* indicating that it was the first note in the lowest of the hexachords or six-note scales (see SOLMIZATION).

gam·y /ˈgāmē/ (also **gamey**) ▶ adj. (**gamier, gamiest**) (of meat) having the strong flavor or smell of game, esp. when it is slightly tainted. ■ racy; disreputable: *gamy language.*
– DERIVATIVES **gam·i·ly** /ˈgāməlē/ adv., **gam·i·ness** n.

ga·nache /gəˈnasH/ ▶ n. a whipped filling of chocolate and cream, used in desserts such as cakes and truffles.
– ORIGIN French.

Ga·na·pa·ti /,gənəˈpətē/ Hinduism another name for GANESH.

Gän·cä /gänˈjä/ an industrial city in Azerbaijan; pop. 307,900 (est. 2008). The city was formerly called Elizavetpol 1804–1918 and Kirovabad 1935–89. Russian name GYANDZHE.

Gand /gäN/ French name of GHENT.

Gan·da /ˈgändə/ ▶ n. & adj. another term for BAGANDA.

Gan·der /ˈgandər/ a town on the island of Newfoundland, on Lake Gander; pop. 9,951 (2006). Its airport served the first regular transatlantic flights during World War II.

gan·der /ˈgandər/ ▶ n. **1** a male goose.
2 [in sing.] informal a look or glance: *take a gander at that luggage.* [from criminals' slang.]
– ORIGIN Old English *gandra*, of Germanic origin; related to Dutch *gander*, also to GANNET.

Gan·dhi¹ /ˈgändē/ the name of a family of Indian political leaders, including: ■ **Indira** (1917–84); prime minister 1966–77 and 1980–84. The daughter

PRONUNCIATION KEY ə *ago, up;* ər *over, fur;* a *hat;* ā *ate;* ä *car;* e *let;* ē *see;* i *fit;* ī *by;* NG *sing;* ō *go;* ô *law, for;* oi *toy;* o͝o *good;* o͞o *goo;* ou *out;* TH *thin;* T͟H *then;* ZH *vision*

of Jawaharlal Nehru, she sought to establish a secular state and to lead India out of poverty. She was assassinated by her own Sikh bodyguards following prolonged religious disturbance. ■ **Rajiv** (1944–91); prime minister 1984–89. The eldest son of Indira, he became prime minister after his mother's assassination. His premiership was marked by continuing unrest, and he was assassinated during an election campaign. His widow, **Sonia** (1946–), born in Italy, entered the political arena in 1998 and was elected head of the Congress Party, leading the party to victory in the 2004 elections.

Gan·dhi², Mahatma (1869–1948), Indian nationalist and spiritual leader; full name *Mohandas Karamchand Gandhi*. Prominent in the opposition to British rule in India, he pursued a policy of nonviolent civil disobedience. Although he never held government office, he was regarded as the country's supreme political and spiritual leader. Gandhi was assassinated by a Hindu following his agreement to the creation of the state of Pakistan.

Gan·dhi·na·gar /ˌgəndiˈnəgər/ a city in western India, capital of the state of Gujarat; pop. 271,300 (est. 2009).

g

G and T (also **G & T**) ▶ **n.** a drink of gin and tonic.

gan·dy danc·er /ˈgandē/ ▶ **n.** informal a track maintenance worker on a railroad.
– ORIGIN early 20th cent.: of unknown origin.

ga·nef /ˈgänəf/ ▶ **n.** a variant spelling of GONIF.

Ga·nesh /gəˈnäsh/ (also **Ganesha** /-ˈnäshə/) Hinduism an elephant-headed deity, son of Shiva and Parvati. Worshiped as the remover of obstacles and patron of learning, he is usually depicted colored red, with a potbelly and one broken tusk, riding a rat. Also called GANAPATI.
– ORIGIN from Sanskrit *Gaṇeśa* 'lord of the ganas' (Shiva's attendants).

gang¹ /gaNG/ ▶ **n. 1** an organized group of criminals. ■ a group of young people involved in petty crime or violence. ■ informal a group of people, esp. young people, who regularly associate together. ■ an organized group of people doing manual work: *ninety days of hard labor on the road gang.*
2 a set of switches, sockets, or other electrical or mechanical devices grouped together.
▶ **v. 1** [no obj.] (**gang together**) (of a number of people) form a group or gang: *the smaller supermarket chains are ganging together to beat the big boys.* ■ (**gang up**) (of a number of people) join together, typically in order to intimidate someone: *he is being unfairly ganged up on.*
2 [with obj.] arrange (electrical devices or machines) together to work in coordination.
– ORIGIN Old English, from Old Norse *gangr, ganga* 'gait, course, going,' of Germanic origin; related to GANG². The original meaning was 'going, a journey,' later in Middle English 'a way, passage,' also 'set of things or people that go together.'

gang² ▶ **v.** [no obj.] Scottish go; proceed: *gang to your bed, lass.*
– PHRASAL VERBS **gang agley** (of a plan) go wrong. [1786: from Robert Burns's 'The best laid schemes o' Mice an' Men, Gang aft agley' (*Poems and Songs*).]
– ORIGIN Old English *gangan*, of Germanic origin; related to GO¹.

Gan·ga /ˈgəNGgə/ Hindi name for GANGES.

gang·bang /ˈgaNG,baNG/ ▶ **n.** informal **1** the successive rape of one person by a group of other people. ■ a sexual orgy involving changes of partner.
2 an instance of violence, esp. a shooting, involving members of a criminal gang.
▶ **v.** [no obj.] participate in a gangbang. ■ [with obj.] victimize (someone) by such participation.
– DERIVATIVES **gang·bang·er n.**

gang·bust·er /ˈgaNG,bəstər/ ▶ **n.** informal a police officer or other person who takes part in breaking up criminal gangs. ■ [as modifier] very successful, esp. commercially: *the restaurant did a gangbuster business.*
– PHRASES **go** (or **like**) **gangbusters** used to refer to great vigor, speed, or success: *the real estate market was going gangbusters | it's growing like gangbusters.*

gang·er /ˈgaNGər/ ▶ **n.** Brit. the foreman of a gang of laborers.

Gan·ges /ˈganˌjēz/ a river in northern India and Bangladesh that rises in the Himalayas and flows southwest for about 1,678 miles (2,700 km) to the Bay of Bengal, where it forms the world's largest delta. The river is regarded by Hindus as sacred. Hindi name GANGA.
– DERIVATIVES **Gan·get·ic** /ganˈjetik/ **adj.**

gang·land /ˈgaNG,land/ ▶ **n.** the world of criminal gangs: [as modifier] *he was the victim of a gangland killing.*

gan·gle /ˈgaNGgəl/ ▶ **v.** [no obj.] move ungracefully.
– ORIGIN mid 20th cent.: back-formation from GANGLING.

gan·gling /ˈgaNGgliNG/ ▶ **adj.** (of a person) tall, thin, and awkward in movements or bearing.
– ORIGIN early 19th cent.: from the verb GANG² + -LE⁴ + -ING².

gan·gli·on /ˈgaNGglēən/ ▶ **n.** (pl. **ganglia** /-glēə/ or **ganglions**) **1** Anatomy a structure containing a number of nerve cell bodies, typically linked by synapses, and often forming a swelling on a nerve fiber. ■ a network of cells forming a nerve center in the nervous system of an invertebrate. ■ a well-defined mass of gray matter within the central nervous system. See also BASAL GANGLIA.
2 Medicine an abnormal benign swelling on a tendon sheath.
– DERIVATIVES **gan·gli·on·ic** /ˌgaNGglēˈänik/ **adj.**
– ORIGIN late 17th cent.: from Greek *ganglion* 'tumor on or near sinews or tendons,' used by Galen to denote the complex nerve centers.

gan·gli·o·side /ˈgaNGglēəˌsīd/ ▶ **n.** Biochemistry any of a group of complex lipids that are present in the gray matter of the human brain.
– ORIGIN 1940s: from GANGLION + *-oside* (see -OSE², -IDE).

gan·gly /ˈgaNGglē/ ▶ **adj.** (**ganglier, gangliest**) another term for GANGLING.

Gang of Four (in China) a group of four associates, including Mao Zedong's wife, involved in implementing the Cultural Revolution. They were among the groups competing for power on Mao's death in 1976, but were arrested and imprisoned.

gang·plank /ˈgaNG,plaNGk/ ▶ **n.** a movable plank used as a ramp to board or disembark from a ship or boat.

gang·plow /ˈgaNG,plou/ ▶ **n.** a type of plow with several blades for turning two or more furrows at one time.

gang rape ▶ **n.** the rape of one person by a group.
– DERIVATIVES **gang-rape v.**

gan·grene /ˈgaNGgrēn, gaNGˈgrēn/ ▶ **n.** Medicine localized death and decomposition of body tissue, resulting from either obstructed circulation or bacterial infection.
▶ **v.** [no obj.] become affected with gangrene.
– DERIVATIVES **gan·gre·nous** /ˈgaNGgrənəs/ **adj.**
– ORIGIN mid 16th cent.: via French from Latin *gangraena*, from Greek *gangraina*.

gang·sta /ˈgaNGstə/ ▶ **n. 1** informal a gang member.
2 (also **gangsta rap**) a type of rap music featuring aggressive lyrics, often with reference to gang violence.
– ORIGIN 1980s: alteration of GANGSTER.

gang·ster /ˈgaNGstər/ ▶ **n.** a member of a gang of violent criminals.
– DERIVATIVES **gang·ster·ism** /-ˌrizəm/ **n.**

Gang·tok /ˈgəNG,tôk/ a city in northern India, in the foothills of the Kanchenjunga Mountains, capital of the state of Sikkim; pop. 32,500 (est. 2009).

gangue /gaNG/ ▶ **n.** the commercially valueless material in which ore is found.
– ORIGIN early 19th cent.: from French, from German *Gang* 'course, lode'; related to GANG¹.

gang·way ▶ **n.** /ˈgaNG,wā/ a raised platform or walkway providing a passage. ■ Brit. a passage between rows of seats, esp. in a theater or aircraft. ■ a movable bridge linking a ship to the shore. ■ an opening in the bulwarks by which a ship is entered or left. ■ a temporary arrangement of planks for crossing muddy or difficult ground on a building site.
▶ **exclam.** /ˈgaNGˈwā/ make way!; get out of the way!

gan·is·ter /ˈganəstər/ ▶ **n.** a close-grained, hard siliceous rock, or a similar synthetic product, used esp. for lining furnaces.
– ORIGIN early 19th cent.: of unknown origin.

gan·ja /ˈgänjə/ ▶ **n.** marijuana.
– ORIGIN early 19th cent.: from Hindi *gāṁjā*.

gan·net /ˈganit/ ▶ **n. 1** a large seabird with mainly white plumage, known for catching fish by plunge-diving. ● Genus *Morus* (or *Sula*), family Sulidae: three species, in particular the **northern gannet** (*M. bassanus*) of the North Atlantic (also called SOLAN GOOSE).
2 Brit. informal a greedy person.
– ORIGIN Old English *ganot*, of Germanic origin; related to Dutch *gent* 'gander,' also to GANDER.

gan·net·ry /ˈganitrē/ ▶ **n.** (pl. **gannetries**) a breeding colony of gannets, usually on an isolated rock.

gan·oid /ˈganoid/ Zoology ▶ **adj.** (of fish scales) hard and bony with a shiny enamellike surface. Compare with CTENOID and PLACOID. ■ (of a fish) having ganoid scales.
▶ **n.** a primitive fish that has ganoid scales, e.g., a bichir, sturgeon, or freshwater garfish.
– ORIGIN mid 19th cent.: from French *ganoïde*, from Greek *ganos* 'brightness.'

Gan·su /ˈgänˈsoo, ˈgan-/ (also **Kansu**) a province in northwestern central China; capital, Lanzhou. This narrow, mountainous province forms a corridor through which the Silk Road passed.

gant·let /ˈgantlit, ˈgônt-/ ▶ **n.** variant spelling of GAUNTLET².

gan·try /ˈgantrē/ ▶ **n.** (pl. **gantries**) a bridgelike overhead structure with a platform supporting equipment such as a crane, railroad signals, lights, or cameras. ■ a movable framework for supporting and servicing a rocket prior to launching.
– ORIGIN late Middle English (denoting a wooden stand for barrels): probably from dialect *gawn* (contraction of GALLON) + TREE.

Gantt chart /gant/ ▶ **n.** a chart in which a series of horizontal lines shows the amount of work done or production completed in certain periods of time in relation to the amount planned for those periods.
– ORIGIN early 20th cent.: named after Henry L. *Gantt* (1861–1919), American management consultant.

Gan·y·mede /ˈganəˌmēd/ **1** Greek Mythology a Trojan youth who was so beautiful that he was carried off by Zeus to be the cupbearer for the Olympic gods.
2 Astronomy one of the Galilean moons of Jupiter, the seventh closest satellite to the planet and the largest satellite in the solar system with a diameter of 3,268 miles (5,260 km).

ganz·feld /ˈgänzˌfeld, ˈgans-/ (also **Ganzfeld**) ▶ **n.** a technique of controlled sensory input used in parapsychology with the aim of improving results in tests of telepathy and other paranormal phenomena.
– ORIGIN late 20th cent.: from German, literally 'whole field.'

GAO ▶ **abbr.** General Accounting Office, a body that undertakes investigations for Congress.

gaol ▶ **n.** Brit. variant spelling of JAIL.
– DERIVATIVES **gaol·er n.**

gap /gap/ ▶ **n. 1** a break or hole in an object or between two objects: *he came through the gap in the hedge.* ■ a pass or way through a range of hills.
2 an unfilled space or interval; a break in continuity: *there are many gaps in our understanding of what happened.* ■ a difference, esp. an undesirable one, between two views or situations: *the media were bridging the gap between government and people.*
– DERIVATIVES **gapped adj.**, **gap·py adj.**
– ORIGIN Middle English: from Old Norse, 'chasm'; related to GAPE.

GAPA ▶ **abbr.** ground-to-air pilotless aircraft.

gape /gāp/ ▶ **v.** [no obj.] stare with one's mouth open wide, typically in amazement or wonder: *they gaped at her as if she were an alien.* ■ be or become wide open: [with complement] *a large duffel bag gaped open by her feet.*
▶ **n.** a wide opening or breach: *a gape of the jaws.* ■ an open-mouthed stare: *she climbed into her sports car to the gapes of passersby.* ■ a widely open mouth or beak: *juvenile birds with yellow gapes.* ■ (**the gapes**) a disease of birds with gaping of the mouth as a symptom, caused by infestation with gapeworm.
– ORIGIN Middle English: from Old Norse *gapa*; related to GAP.

gap·er /ˈgāpər/ ▶ **n. 1** a person who stares, typically in amazement or wonder.
2 a burrowing bivalve mollusk, the shell valves of which have an opening at one or both ends. ● Genus *Mya*, family Myidae.

gape·worm /ˈgāpˌwərm/ ▶ **n.** a parasitic nematode worm that infests the trachea and bronchi of birds, causing the gapes. ● *Syngamus trachea*, class Phasmida.

gap·ing /ˈgāpiNG/ ▶ **adj.** (of a hole, wound, etc.) wide open: *there was a gaping hole in the wall.*
– DERIVATIVES **gap·ing·ly adv.**

gap·ping /ˈgapiNG/ ▶ **n.** Grammar the omission of a verb in the second of two coordinate clauses, as in *I went by bus and Mary by car.*

gap-toothed ▶ **adj.** having or showing gaps between the teeth.

gap year ▶ **n.** chiefly Brit. a period, typically an academic year, taken by a student as a break between secondary school and higher education.

gar /gär/ ▶ **n.** the freshwater garfish of North America.
– ORIGIN mid 18th cent.: abbreviation.

ga·rage /gəˈräzh, -ˈräj/ ▶ **n. 1** a building or shed for housing a motor vehicle or vehicles. ■ an establishment that provides services and repairs for motor vehicles.

2 (also **garage rock**) a style of unpolished energetic rock music associated with suburban amateur bands: [as modifier] *garage band.*
▶ **v.** [with obj.] put or keep (a motor vehicle) in a garage.
– ORIGIN early 20th cent.: from French, from *garer* 'to shelter.'

ga·rage sale ▶ **n.** a sale of miscellaneous household goods, often held in the garage or front yard of someone's house.

ga·ram ma·sa·la /ˌgärəm məˈsälə/ ▶ **n.** a spice mixture used in Indian cooking.
– ORIGIN from Urdu *garam maṣālaḥ*, from *garam* 'hot, pungent' + *maṣālaḥ* 'spice.'

Gar·a·mond /ˈgarəˌmänd/ ▶ **n.** a typeface much used in books.
– ORIGIN mid 19th cent.: named after Claude *Garamond* (1499–1561), French type founder.

garb[1] /gärb/ ▶ **n.** clothing or dress, esp. of a distinctive or special kind: *the black and brown garb of a Franciscan friar.*
▶ **v.** [with obj.] (usu. **be garbed**) dress in distinctive clothes: *she was garbed in Indian shawls.*
– ORIGIN late 16th cent.: via French from Italian *garbo* 'elegance,' of Germanic origin; related to GEAR.

garb[2] ▶ **n.** Heraldry a sheaf of wheat.
– ORIGIN early 16th cent.: from Old Northern French *garbe*; compare with French *gerbe.*

gar·bage /ˈgärbij/ ▶ **n.** wasted or spoiled food and other refuse, as from a kitchen or household. ■ a thing that is considered worthless or meaningless: *a store full of overpriced garbage.* ■ Computing unwanted data in a computer's memory.
– PHRASES **garbage in, garbage out** (abbr.: **GIGO**) used to express the idea that in computing and other spheres, incorrect or poor quality input will always produce faulty output.
– ORIGIN late Middle English (in the sense 'offal'): from Anglo-Norman French, of unknown ultimate origin.

gar·bage can (also **garbage bin**) ▶ **n.** a container, typically plastic or metal, for household refuse.

gar·ban·zo /gärˈbänzō/ (also **garbanzo bean**) ▶ **n.** (pl. **garbanzos**) a chickpea.
– ORIGIN mid 18th cent.: from Spanish.

gar·ble /ˈgärbəl/ ▶ **v.** [with obj.] reproduce (a message, sound, or transmission) in a confused and distorted way: *the connection was awful and kept garbling his voice* | (as adj. **garbled**) *I got a garbled set of directions.*
▶ **n.** a garbled account or transmission.
– DERIVATIVES **gar·bler** /-b(ə)lər/ **n.**
– ORIGIN late Middle English (in the sense 'sift out, cleanse'): from Anglo-Latin and Italian *garbellare*, from Arabic *ġarbala* 'sift,' perhaps from late Latin *cribellare* 'to sieve,' from Latin *cribrum* 'sieve.'

Gar·bo /ˈgärˌbō/, Greta (1905–90), US actress; born in Sweden; born *Greta Gustafsson.* Notable movies: *Anna Christie* (1930), *Mata Hari* (1931), and *Anna Karenina* (1935). After her retirement in 1941, she lived as a recluse.

Greta Garbo

gar·board /ˈgärˌbôrd/ (also **garboard strake**) ▶ **n.** the first range of planks or plates laid on a ship's bottom next to the keel.
– ORIGIN early 17th cent.: from Dutch *gaarboord*, perhaps from *garen* 'gather' + *boord* 'board.'

gar·bol·o·gy /gärˈbäləjē/ ▶ **n.** the study of a community or culture by analyzing its waste.
– DERIVATIVES **gar·bol·o·gist** /-jist/ **n.**
– ORIGIN 1960s: from GARBAGE + -LOGY.

Gar·cí·a Lor·ca /gärˈsēə ˈlôrkə/ see LORCA.

Gar·cí·a Már·quez /gärˈsēə ˈmärkes/, Gabriel (1927–), Colombian novelist. His works include *One Hundred Years of Solitude* (1967), a classic example of magic realism, and *Love in the Time of Cholera* (1985). Nobel Prize for Literature (1982).

gar·çon /gärˈsôN/ ▶ **n.** a waiter in a French restaurant or hotel.
– ORIGIN French, literally 'boy.'

gar·çon·nière /ˌgärsəˈnyer/ ▶ **n.** a bachelor's apartment.
– ORIGIN French, from *garçon* 'boy.'

Gar·da /ˈgärdə/ ▶ **n.** [treated as sing. or pl.] the state police force of the Irish Republic. ■ (pl. **Gardai** /-ˈdē/) a member of the Irish police force.
– ORIGIN from Irish *Garda Síochána* 'Civic Guard.'

Gar·da, Lake /ˈgärdə/ a lake in northeastern Italy that lies between Lombardy and Venetia.

gar·den /ˈgärdn/ ▶ **n. 1** a piece of ground, often near a house, used for growing flowers, fruit, or vegetables. ■ (**gardens**) ornamental grounds laid out for public enjoyment and recreation: *botanical gardens.*
2 [in names] a large public hall: *Madison Square Garden.*
▶ **v.** [no obj.] cultivate or work in a garden.
– ORIGIN Middle English: from Old Northern French *gardin*, variant of Old French *jardin*, of Germanic origin; related to YARD[2].

Gar·de·na /gärˈdēnə/ a city in southwestern California, south of Los Angeles; pop. 58,554 (est. 2008).

gar·den a·part·ment ▶ **n. 1** a low-rise apartment complex with landscaped gardens or lawns.
2 a ground-floor unit of an apartment building, with access to a garden or lawn.

gar·den cress ▶ **n.** a type of cress that is usually grown as a sprouting vegetable, often mixed with sprouting mustard, and used in salads. ● *Lepidium sativum*, family Brassicaceae.

gar·den eel ▶ **n.** an eel of warm seas that lives in a community or "garden." Each individual occupies a burrow from which its head and foreparts protrude, enabling it to catch passing food. ● Several genera and species, family Congridae.

gar·den·er /ˈgärdnər/ ▶ **n.** a person who tends and cultivates a garden as a pastime or for a living: *cultivars grown by amateur gardeners* | *a topiary gardener.*
– ORIGIN Middle English: from Old French *gardinier*, from *gardin* (see GARDEN).

Gar·den Grove a city in southwestern California, southeast of Los Angeles; pop. 165,796 (est. 2008).

gar·de·nia /gärˈdēnyə/ ▶ **n.** a tree or shrub of the bedstraw family, with large fragrant white or yellow flowers. Native to warm climates, it is widely cultivated. ● Genus *Gardenia*, family Rubiaceae: several species, in particular the Cape jasmine.
– ORIGIN modern Latin, named in honor of Dr. Alexander *Garden* (1730–91), Scottish naturalist.

gar·den·ing /ˈgärdniNG, -dn-iNG/ ▶ **n.** the activity of tending and cultivating a garden, esp. as a pastime.

Gar·den of E·den see EDEN[2].

Gar·den of Geth·sem·a·ne see GETHSEMANE, GARDEN OF.

gar·den par·ty ▶ **n.** a social event held outdoors on a lawn or in a garden.

Gar·den State a nickname for the state of NEW JERSEY.

gar·den-va·ri·e·ty ▶ **adj.** [attrib.] of the usual or ordinary type; commonplace: *they are your everyday, garden-variety Americans.*

gar·den war·bler ▶ **n.** a migratory Eurasian songbird with drab plumage, frequenting woodlands. ● *Sylvia borin*, family Sylviidae.

garde·robe /ˈgärdˌrōb/ ▶ **n.** a toilet in a medieval building. ■ a wardrobe or small storeroom, esp. in a medieval building.
– ORIGIN late Middle English: French, from *garder* 'to keep' + *robe* 'robe, dress'; compare with WARDROBE.

Gard·ner[1] /ˈgärdnər/, Ava (Lavinia) (1922–90), US actress. Notable movies: *The Killers* (1946), *Bhowani Junction* (1956), and *The Night of the Iguana* (1964).

Gard·ner[2], Erle Stanley (1899–1970), US novelist and short-story writer. He practiced as a defense lawyer before writing novels that feature lawyer-detective Perry Mason.

Gar·field /ˈgärˌfēld/, James Abram (1831–81), 20th president of the US March–September 1881. He fought for the Union during the Civil War, resigning his command to enter Congress as a Republican. He served in the US House of Representatives 1863–80. Although his presidency was shortened by an assassin, his battle against corruption succeeded in breaking the stronghold of New York senator Roscoe Conkling (1829–88) over the New York Customs House—the US's principal port of entry.

James A. Garfield

g

gar·fish /ˈgärˌfiSH/ ▶ **n.** (pl. **same** or **garfishes**) any of a number of long, slender fish with elongated beaklike jaws containing sharply pointed teeth. ● a marine fish (family Belonidae, in particular the common European *Belone belone*; also called NEEDLEFISH or GARPIKE). ● a freshwater fish (family Lepisosteidae and genus *Lepisosteus*; also called GAR or GARPIKE).
– ORIGIN Middle English: apparently from Old English *gār* 'spear' + FISH[1].

gar·ga·ney /ˈgärgənē/ ▶ **n.** (pl. **same** or **garganeys**) a small Eurasian duck, the male of which has a dark brown head with a white stripe from the eye to the neck. ● *Anas querquedula*, family Anatidae.
– ORIGIN mid 17th cent.: from Italian dialect *garganei*, of imitative origin.

gar·gan·tu·a /gärˈganCHo͞oə/ ▶ **n.** a person of great size; a giant.

gar·gan·tu·an /gärˈganCHo͞oən/ ▶ **adj.** enormous: *a gargantuan appetite.*
– ORIGIN late 16th cent.: from *Gargantua*, the name of a voracious giant in Rabelais' book of the same name (1534), + -AN.

gar·get /ˈgärgit/ ▶ **n.** inflammation of a cow's or ewe's udder.
– ORIGIN early 18th cent.: perhaps a special use of Old French *gargate* 'throat'; related to GARGOYLE. The term was used earlier to denote inflammation of the throat in cattle.

gar·gle /ˈgärgəl/ ▶ **v.** [no obj.] wash one's mouth and throat with a liquid kept in motion by exhaling through it: *instruct patients to gargle with warm water.*
▶ **n.** an act or instance or the sound of gargling: *a swig and gargle of mouthwash.* ■ [usu. in sing.] a liquid used for gargling.
– ORIGIN early 16th cent.: from French *gargouiller* 'gurgle, bubble,' from *gargouille* 'throat' (see GARGOYLE).

gar·goyle /ˈgärˌgoil/ ▶ **n.** a grotesque carved human or animal face or figure projecting from the gutter of a building, typically acting as a spout to carry water clear of a wall.
– DERIVATIVES **gar·goyled** **adj.**
– ORIGIN Middle English: from Old French *gargouille* 'throat,' also 'gargoyle' (because of the water passing through the throat and mouth of the figure); related to Greek *gargarizein* 'to gargle' (imitating the sounds made in the throat).

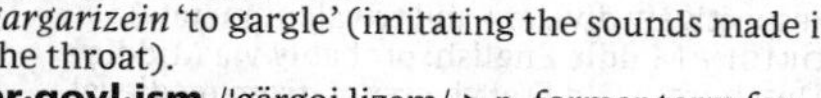

gargoyle

gar·goyl·ism /ˈgärgoiˌlizəm/ ▶ **n.** former term for HURLER'S SYNDROME.
– ORIGIN early 20th cent.: from GARGOYLE (because the deformities that characterize the syndrome were thought to resemble Gothic gargoyles) + -ISM.

Gar·i·bal·di /ˌgarəˈbôldē/, Giuseppe (1807–82), Italian patriot and military leader of the Risorgimento (unification of Italy). With his volunteer force of "Red Shirts," he captured Sicily and southern Italy from the Bourbons in 1860–61, thereby playing a key role in the establishment of a united kingdom of Italy.

gar·i·bal·di /ˌgarəˈbôldē/ ▶ **n.** (pl. **garibaldis**) **1** historical a woman's or children's loose blouse, originally bright red in imitation of the shirts worn by Garibaldi and his followers.

2 a small bright orange marine fish found off California. ● *Hypsypops rubicundus*, family Pomacentridae.
– ORIGIN mid 19th cent.: named after G. GARIBALDI.

gar·ish /ˈgarisʜ/ ▶ **adj.** obtrusively bright and showy; lurid: *garish shirts in all sorts of colors.*
– DERIVATIVES **gar·ish·ly adv., gar·ish·ness n.**
– ORIGIN mid 16th cent.: of unknown origin.

Gar·land[1] /ˈgärlənd/ a city in northeastern Texas, northeast of Dallas; pop. 218,577 (est. 2008).

Gar·land[2], Judy (1922–69), US singer and actress; born *Frances Gumm*. Her best known movie role was as Dorothy in *The Wizard of Oz* (1939). Other notable movies: *Meet Me in St. Louis* (1944) and *A Star is Born* (1954).

gar·land /ˈgärlənd/ ▶ **n.** a wreath of flowers and leaves, worn on the head or hung as a decoration. ■ dated a prize or distinction. ■ archaic a literary anthology or miscellany.
▶ **v.** [with obj.] adorn or crown with a garland: *they were garlanded with flowers.*
– ORIGIN Middle English: from Old French *garlande*, of unknown origin.

gar·lic /ˈgärlik/ ▶ **n. 1** a strong-smelling pungent-tasting bulb, used as a flavoring in cooking and in herbal medicine.
2 the plant, closely related to the onion, that produces this bulb. ● *Allium sativum*, family Liliaceae (or Alliaceae).
– DERIVATIVES **gar·lick·y adj.**
– ORIGIN Old English *gārlēac*, from *gār* 'spear' (because the shape of a clove resembles the head of a spear) + *lēac* 'leek.'

gar·lic chives ▶ **plural n.** another term for CHINESE CHIVES.

gar·lic mus·tard ▶ **n.** a European mustard plant with medicinal and culinary uses that is also an aggressive woodland invader in most of the eastern US. ● *Alliaria petiolata*, family Brassicaceae.

gar·lic press ▶ **n.** a handheld device for crushing cloves of garlic through a sievelike receptacle.

garlic press

gar·ment /ˈgärmənt/ ▶ **n.** an item of clothing.
– ORIGIN Middle English: from Old French *garnement* 'equipment,' from *garnir* 'equip' (see GARNISH).

gar·ment bag ▶ **n.** a large zippered bag incorporating a hanger on which garments may be hung to prevent wrinkling during travel or storage.

Gar·mo, Mount /ˈgärˌmō/ former name (until 1933) of ISMAIL SAMANI PEAK.

Gar·na·cha /ˌgärˈnäCHə/ ▶ **n.** a variety of wine grape grown in Spain. ■ a red or rosé wine made from Garnacha grapes.
– ORIGIN Spanish, from Italian *vernaccia* (see VERNACCIA). The grape is known in France and elsewhere as GRENACHE.

Gar·ner /ˈgärnər/, Errol (Louis) (1923–77), US jazz pianist and composer. He formed his own trio and also recorded with Charlie Parker. He wrote many songs, including "Misty."

gar·ner /ˈgärnər/ ▶ **v.** [with obj.] gather or collect (something, esp. information or approval): *the police struggled to garner sufficient evidence.* ■ archaic store; deposit: *the crop was ready to be reaped and garnered.*
▶ **n.** archaic a storehouse; a granary.
– ORIGIN Middle English (originally as a noun meaning 'granary'): from Old French *gernier*, from Latin *granarium* 'granary,' from *granum* 'grain.'

gar·net /ˈgärnit/ ▶ **n.** a precious stone consisting of a deep red vitreous silicate mineral. ■ Mineralogy any of a class of silicate minerals including this, which belong to the cubic system and have the general chemical formula $A_3B_2(SiO_4)_3$ (A and B being respectively divalent and trivalent metals).
– ORIGIN Middle English: probably via Middle Dutch from Old French *grenat*, from medieval Latin *granatus*, perhaps from *granatum* (see POMEGRANATE), because the garnet is similar in color to the pulp of the fruit.

gar·ni·er·ite /ˈgärnēəˌrīt/ ▶ **n.** a bright green amorphous mineral consisting of a hydrated silicate of nickel and magnesium.
– ORIGIN 1875: named after Jules Garnier (1839–1904), French geologist.

gar·nish /ˈgärnisʜ/ ▶ **v.** [with obj.] **1** decorate or embellish (something, esp. food): *salad garnished with an orange slice.*
2 Law serve with a garnishment. ■ seize (money, esp. part of a person's salary) to settle a debt or claim: *the IRS garnished his earnings.*
▶ **n.** a decoration or embellishment for something, esp. food.
– ORIGIN Middle English (in the sense 'equip, arm'): from Old French *garnir*, probably of Germanic origin and related to WARN. Sense 1 of the verb dates from the late 17th cent.

gar·nish·ee /ˌgärniˈsʜē/ Law ▶ **n.** a third party who is served notice by a court to surrender money in settlement of a debt or claim: [as modifier] *a garnishee order.*
▶ **v.** (**garnishees, garnisheeing, garnisheed**) another term for GARNISH (sense 2 of the verb).

gar·nish·ment /ˈgärnisʜmənt/ ▶ **n. 1** a decoration or embellishment.
2 Law a court order directing that money or property of a third party (usually wages paid by an employer) be seized to satisfy a debt owed by a debtor to a plaintiff creditor.

gar·ni·ture /ˈgärniCHər, -ˌCHo͝or/ ▶ **n.** a set of decorative accessories, in particular vases.
– ORIGIN late 15th cent.: from French, from *garnir* 'to garnish.'

Ga·ronne /gəˈrän, gəˈrôn/ a river in southwestern France that rises in the Pyrenees Mountains and flows northwest for 400 miles (645 km) through Toulouse and Bordeaux to join the Dordogne River at the Gironde estuary.

ga·rotte ▶ **v. & n.** variant spelling of GARROTE.

gar·pike /ˈgärˌpīk/ ▶ **n.** another term for GARFISH.
– ORIGIN late 18th cent.: from GAR + PIKE[1].

gar·ret /ˈgarit/ ▶ **n.** a top-floor or attic room, esp. a small dismal one (traditionally inhabited by an artist).
– ORIGIN Middle English (in the sense 'watchtower'): from Old French *garite*, from *garir* (see GARRISON).

Gar·ri·son /ˈgarəsən/, William Lloyd (1805–79), US social liberal and spearhead for New England abolitionism. He published *The Liberator* 1831–65 and was a founder of the American Anti-Slavery Society in 1833.

gar·ri·son /ˈgarəsən/ ▶ **n.** the troops stationed in a fortress or town to defend it. ■ the building occupied by such troops.
▶ **v.** [with obj.] provide (a place) with a body of troops: *troops are garrisoned in the various territories.* ■ station (troops) in a particular place: *army regiments were garrisoned in Ireland.*
– ORIGIN Middle English (in the sense 'safety, means of protection'): from Old French *garison*, from *garir* 'defend, provide,' of Germanic origin.

gar·ri·son cap ▶ **n.** a cap without a brim, esp. one worn as part of a military uniform.

gar·ri·son town ▶ **n.** a town that has troops permanently stationed in it.

gar·ron /ˈgarən/ ▶ **n.** a small, sturdy workhorse of a breed originating in Ireland and Scotland.
– ORIGIN mid 16th cent.: from Scottish Gaelic *gearran*, Irish *gearrán*.

gar·rote /gəˈrät, -ˈrōt/ (also **garrotte** or **garotte**) ▶ **v.** [with obj.] kill (someone) by strangulation, typically with an iron collar or a length of wire or cord: *he had been garroted with piano wire.*
▶ **n.** a wire, cord, or apparatus used for such a killing.
– ORIGIN early 17th cent.: via French from Spanish, 'a cudgel, a garrote,' perhaps of Celtic origin.

gar·ru·li·ty /gəˈro͞olitē/ ▶ **n.** excessive talkativeness, esp. on trivial matters: *the character's comic garrulity.*

gar·ru·lous /ˈgar(y)ələs/ ▶ **adj.** excessively talkative, esp. on trivial matters: *Polonius is portrayed as a foolish, garrulous old man.*
– DERIVATIVES **gar·ru·lous·ly adv., gar·ru·lous·ness n.**
– ORIGIN early 17th cent.: from Latin *garrulus* (from *garrire* 'to chatter, prattle') + -OUS.

Gar·son /ˈgärsən/, Greer (1908–96), US actress; born in Ireland. She starred in movies such as *Mrs. Miniver* (1942), *Adventure* (1946), and *Sunrise at Campobello* (1960).

gar·ter /ˈgärtər/ ▶ **n. 1** a band worn around the leg to keep up a stocking or sock. ■ a band worn on the arm to keep a shirtsleeve up. ■ a suspender for a sock or stocking.
2 (**the Garter**) short for ORDER OF THE GARTER. ■ the badge or membership of this order.
– DERIVATIVES **gar·tered adj.**
– ORIGIN Middle English: from Old French *gartier*, from *garet* 'bend of the knee, calf of the leg,' probably of Celtic origin.

gar·ter belt ▶ **n.** a belt with attached garters or fasteners, worn as an undergarment to hold up stockings.

gar·ter snake ▶ **n. 1** a common, harmless North American snake that typically has well-defined longitudinal stripes and favors damp habitats. It is occasionally kept as a pet. ● Genus *Thamnophis*, family Colubridae: several species, in particular *T. sirtalis*.
2 a venomous burrowing African snake that is typically dark with lighter bands. ● Genus *Elapsoidea*, family Elapidae: several species.

gar·ter stitch ▶ **n.** knitting in which all of the rows are knitted in knit (plain) stitch, rather than alternating with purl rows.

garth /gärTH/ ▶ **n.** Brit. an open space surrounded by cloisters. ■ archaic a yard or garden.
– ORIGIN Middle English (also, in early use, denoting a hollow): from Old Norse *garthr*; related to YARD[2].

Gar·u·da /gəˈro͞odə/ Hinduism an eaglelike being that Vishnu rides as his mount.
– ORIGIN from Sanskrit *garuḍa*.

Gar·vey /ˈgärvē/, Marcus (Mosiah) (1887–1940), Jamaican political activist and black nationalist leader. He advocated the establishment of an African homeland for black Americans. His thinking was later an important influence on Rastafarianism.

Gar·y /ˈgarē, ˈge(ə)rē/ an industrial city in northwestern Indiana, on Lake Michigan, southeast of Chicago; pop. 95,920 (est. 2008).

gas /gas/ ▶ **n.** (pl. **gases** or **gasses**) **1** an airlike fluid substance which expands freely to fill any space available, irrespective of its quantity: *hot balls of gas that become stars | poisonous gases.* ■ Physics a substance of this type that cannot be liquefied by the application of pressure alone. Compare with VAPOR. ■ a flammable substance of this type used as a fuel. ■ a gaseous anesthetic such as nitrous oxide, used in dentistry. ■ gas or vapor used as a poisonous agent to kill or disable an enemy in warfare. ■ gas generated in the alimentary canal; flatulence. ■ Mining an explosive mixture of firedamp with air.
2 informal short for GASOLINE. ■ used in reference to power or the accelerator of an automobile: *I ordered my friend to step on the gas.*
3 (**a gas**) informal a person or thing that is entertaining or amusing: *the party would be a gas.*
▶ **v.** (**gases, gassed, gassing**) **1** kill or harm by exposure to poisonous gas. ■ [no obj.] (of a storage battery or dry cell) give off gas.
2 fill the tank of (an engine or motor vehicle) with gasoline: *after gassing up the car, he went into the restaurant.*
3 [no obj.] informal talk, esp. excessively, idly, or boastfully: *I thought you'd never stop gassing.*
– PHRASES **run out of gas** informal run out of energy; lose momentum.
– ORIGIN mid 17th cent.: invented by J. B. van Helmont (1577–1644), Belgian chemist, to denote an occult principle that he believed to exist in all matter; suggested by Greek *khaos* 'chaos,' with Dutch *g* representing Greek *kh*.

gas·bag /ˈgasˌbag/ ▶ **n. 1** informal a person who talks too much, typically about unimportant things.
2 the container holding the gas in a balloon or airship.

gas burn·er ▶ **n.** a nozzle or jet through which gas is released to burn, e.g., on a stove.

gas cham·ber ▶ **n.** an airtight room that can be filled with poisonous gas as a means of execution.

gas chro·mat·o·graph ▶ **n.** a device or apparatus used in gas chromatography to separate the constituents of a volatile substance.

gas chro·ma·tog·ra·phy ▶ **n.** chromatography employing a gas as the moving carrier medium. Compare with GAS–LIQUID CHROMATOGRAPHY.

Gas·cogne /gäsˈkôn(yə)/ French name for GASCONY.

Gas·con /ˈgaskən/ ▶ **n. 1** a native or inhabitant of Gascony.
2 (**gascon**) archaic a person who boasts about their achievements or possessions. [with allusion to the perceived character of natives of Gascony.]
▶ **adj.** of or relating to Gascony or its people.
– ORIGIN via Old French from Latin *Vasco, Vascon-*; related to BASQUE.

gas·con·ade /ˌgaskəˈnād/ ▶ **n.** literary extravagant boasting.
– ORIGIN mid 17th cent.: from French *gasconnade*, from *gasconner* 'talk like a Gascon, brag.'

gas con·stant (Symbol: **R**) ▶ **n.** Chemistry the constant of proportionality in the gas equation. It is equal to 8.314 joule kelvin^{-1} mole^{-1}.

Gas·co·ny /ˈgaskənē/ a region and former province in southwestern France, in the northern foothills of the Pyrenees Mountains. French name GASCOGNE.

gas·e·ous /ˈgasēəs, ˈgasʜəs/ ▶ **adj.** of, relating to, or having the characteristics of a gas: *gaseous emissions from motor vehicles | gaseous oxygen.*
– DERIVATIVES **gas·e·ous·ness n.**

gas e·qua·tion ▶ **n.** Chemistry the equation of state of an ideal gas, $PV = nRT$, where P = pressure, V = volume, T = absolute temperature, R = the gas constant, and n = the number of moles of gas.

gas-fired ▶ **adj.** using a combustible gas as its fuel: *gas-fired central heating.*

gas gan·grene ▶ **n.** rapidly spreading gangrene occurring in dirty wounds infected by bacteria that give off a foul-smelling gas. ● This disease is usually caused by anaerobic bacteria of the genus *Clostridium*.

gas gi·ant ▶ **n.** Astronomy a large planet of relatively low density consisting predominantly of hydrogen and helium, such as Jupiter, Saturn, Uranus, or Neptune.

gas guz·zler /ˈgəz(ə)lər/ ▶ **n.** informal an automobile with high fuel consumption.
– DERIVATIVES **gas-guz·zling** **adj.**

gash /gasʜ/ ▶ **n. 1** a long deep slash, cut, or wound: *a bad gash in one leg became infected.* ■ a cleft made as if by a slashing cut: *the blast ripped a 25-foot gash in the hull.*
2 vulgar slang the vulva. ■ offensive women collectively regarded in sexual terms.
▶ **v.** [with obj.] make a gash in; cut deeply: *the jagged edges gashed their fingers.*
– ORIGIN Middle English *garse*, from Old French *garcer* 'to chap, crack,' perhaps based on Greek *kharassein* 'sharpen, scratch, engrave.' The current spelling is recorded from the mid 16th cent.

gas·i·fy /ˈgasəˌfī/ ▶ **v.** (**gasifies, gasifying, gasified**) [with obj.] convert (a solid or liquid, esp. coal) into gas: *5 million tons of coal have been gasified.* ■ [no obj.] become a gas: *if PVC is overheated it will gasify.*
– DERIVATIVES **gas·i·fi·ca·tion** /ˌgasəfiˈkāsʜən/ **n.**

gas jet ▶ **n. 1** another term for GAS BURNER.
2 a flame of illuminated gas from a gas burner.

Gas·kell /ˈgaskəl/, Mrs. Elizabeth (Cleghorn) (1810–65), English novelist. An active humanitarian from a Unitarian background, she wrote *Mary Barton* (1848), *Cranford* (1853), and *North and South* (1855), which display her interest in social concerns. She also wrote a biography (1857) of her friend Charlotte Brontë.

gas·ket /ˈgaskit/ ▶ **n. 1** a shaped piece or ring of rubber or other material sealing the junction between two surfaces in an engine or other device.
2 a cord securing a furled sail to the yard, boom, or gaff of a sailing vessel.

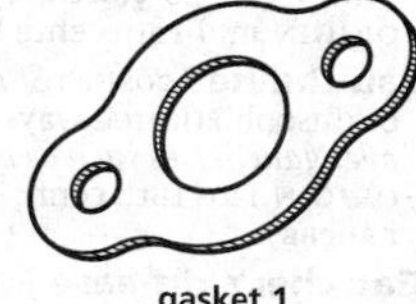
gasket 1

– PHRASES **blow a gasket 1** informal lose one's temper. **2** suffer a leak in a gasket of an engine.
– ORIGIN early 17th cent. (sense 2): perhaps from French *garcette* 'thin rope' (originally 'little girl'), diminutive of *garce*, feminine of *gars* 'boy.'

gas·kin /ˈgaskin/ ▶ **n.** the muscular part of the hind leg of a horse between the stifle and the hock.
– ORIGIN late 16th cent.: perhaps from GALLIGASKINS (the original sense).

gas laws ▶ **plural n.** Chemistry the physical laws that describe the properties of gases, including Boyle's and Charles' laws.

gas·light /ˈgasˌlīt/ ▶ **n.** a type of lamp in which an incandescent mantle is heated by a jet of burning gas. ■ the light produced by such a lamp: *in the gaslight she looked paler than ever.*
– DERIVATIVES **gas·lit** /-ˌlit/ **adj.**

gas–liq·uid chro·ma·tog·ra·phy ▶ **n.** chromatography employing a gas as the moving carrier medium and a liquid as the stationary medium.

gas log ▶ **n.** a gas-burning appliance consisting of a gas burner made to resemble a log, used in a fireplace to simulate the effect of a burning log.

gas·man /ˈgasˌman/ ▶ **n.** (pl. **gasmen**) a person who installs or services gas appliances or reads gas meters.

gas man·tle ▶ **n.** see MANTLE[1] (sense 1 of the noun).

gas mask ▶ **n.** a protective mask used to cover a person's face as a defense against poisonous gas.

gas mask

gas·o·hol /ˈgasəˌhôl, -ˌhäl/ ▶ **n.** a mixture of gasoline and ethyl alcohol used as fuel in internal combustion engines.
– ORIGIN 1970s: blend of GAS and ALCOHOL.

gas oil ▶ **n.** a type of fuel oil distilled from petroleum.

gas·o·line /ˌgasəˈlēn, ˈgasəlēn/ (dated also **gasolene**) ▶ **n.** refined petroleum used as fuel for internal combustion engines.
– ORIGIN mid 19th cent.: from GAS + -OL + -INE[4] (or -ENE).

gas·om·e·ter /gasˈämitər/ ▶ **n.** a tank for storing and measuring gas.
– ORIGIN late 18th cent. (in the sense 'container for holding or measuring a gas'): from French *gazomètre*, from *gaz* 'gas' + *-mètre* '(instrument) measuring.'

gasp /gasp/ ▶ **v.** [no obj.] inhale suddenly with the mouth open, out of pain or astonishment: *a woman gasped in horror at the sight of him.* ■ [with obj.] say (something) while catching one's breath, esp. as a result of strong emotion: *Jeremy gasped out an apology* | [with direct speech] *"It's beautiful!" she gasped, much impressed.* ■ strain to take a deep breath: *she surfaced and gasped for air.*
▶ **n.** a convulsive catching of breath: *his breath was coming in gasps.*
– PHRASES **one's** (or **the**) **last gasp** the point of exhaustion, death, or completion: *the last gasp of the Cold War.*
– ORIGIN late Middle English: from Old Norse *geispa* 'to yawn.'

gas ped·al ▶ **n.** the pedal that controls the speed of a vehicle's engine.

Gas·pé Pen·in·su·la /gasˈpā/ a region in southeastern Quebec in Canada, between the St. Lawrence River and New Brunswick.

gas-per·me·a·ble ▶ **adj.** (of a contact lens) allowing the diffusion of gases into and out of the cornea.

gas plant ▶ **n.** an aromatic Eurasian plant of the rue family, with showy white flowers and fragrant leaves that emit a flammable vapor. This can sometimes be ignited without harming the plant. Also called BURNING BUSH, DITTANY, FRAXINELLA. ● *Dictamnus* (formerly *Fraxinella*) *albus*, family Rutaceae.

Gas·ser /ˈgasər/, Herbert Spencer (1888–1963), US physiologist. In collaboration with Joseph Erlanger, he used an oscilloscope to show that the velocity of a nerve impulse is proportional to the diameter of the fiber. Nobel Prize for Physiology or Medicine (1944), shared with Erlanger.

gas·ser /ˈgasər/ ▶ **n.** informal **1** an idle talker; a chatterer.
2 a very attractive or impressive person or thing: *that story you wrote for me is a gasser!*

gas sta·tion ▶ **n.** an establishment beside a road selling gasoline and oil.

gas·sy /ˈgasē/ ▶ **adj.** (**gassier, gassiest**) **1** of, like, or full of gas: *the carbonated water has a gassy, soda-pop character* | *gassy planets like Jupiter.*
2 informal (of people or language) inclined to be verbose: *a long and gassy book.*
3 (of people) flatulent.
– DERIVATIVES **gas·si·ness** **n.**

Gast·ar·beit·er /ˈgästˌärbītər/ ▶ **n.** (pl. **same** or **Gastarbeiters**) German term for GUEST WORKER.
– ORIGIN German, from *Gast* 'guest' + *Arbeiter* 'worker.'

gast·haus /ˈgästˌhous/ (also **Gasthaus**) ▶ **n.** (pl. **gasthauses** or **gasthäuser** /-ˌhoizər/) a small inn or hotel in a German-speaking country or region.
– ORIGIN from German, from *Gast* 'guest' + *Haus* 'house.'

gas-tight ▶ **adj.** sealed so as to prevent the leakage of gas.

Gas·to·nia /gaˈstōnēə/ an industrial city in southwestern North Carolina; pop. 72,505 (est. 2008).

gastr- ▶ **comb. form** variant spelling of GASTRO- shortened before a vowel (as in *gastrectomy*).

gas·trec·to·my /gaˈstrektəmē/ ▶ **n.** (pl. **gastrectomies**) surgical removal of a part or the whole of the stomach.

gas·tric /ˈgastrik/ ▶ **adj.** of the stomach.
– ORIGIN mid 17th cent.: from modern Latin *gastricus*, from Greek *gastēr, gastr-* 'stomach.'

gas·tric juice ▶ **n.** a thin, clear, virtually colorless acidic fluid secreted by the stomach glands and active in promoting digestion.

gas·trin /ˈgastrin/ ▶ **n.** Biochemistry a hormone that stimulates secretion of gastric juice, and is secreted into the bloodstream by the stomach wall in response to the presence of food.
– ORIGIN early 20th cent.: from GASTRIC + -IN[1].

gas·tri·tis /gaˈstrītis/ ▶ **n.** Medicine inflammation of the lining of the stomach.

gastro- (also **gastr-** before a vowel) ▶ **comb. form** of or relating to the stomach: *gastrectomy* | *gastroenteritis.*
– ORIGIN from Greek *gastēr, gastr-* 'stomach.'

gas·troc·ne·mi·us /ˌgaströ(k)ˈnēmēəs/ (also **gastrocnemius muscle**) ▶ **n.** (pl. **gastrocnemii** /-mēˌī/) Anatomy the chief muscle of the calf of the leg, which flexes the knee and foot. It runs to the Achilles tendon from two heads attached to the femur.
– ORIGIN late 17th cent.: modern Latin, from Greek *gastroknēmia* 'calf of the leg,' from *gastēr, gastr-* 'stomach' + *knēmē* 'leg' (from the bulging shape of the calf).

gas·tro·col·ic /ˌgaströˈkälik/ ▶ **adj.** [attrib.] of or relating to the stomach and the colon.

gas·tro·en·ter·i·tis /ˌgaströˌentəˈrītis/ ▶ **n.** inflammation of the stomach and intestines, typically resulting from bacterial toxins or viral infection and causing vomiting and diarrhea.

gas·tro·en·ter·ol·o·gy /ˌgaströˌentəˈräləjē/ ▶ **n.** the branch of medicine that deals with disorders of the stomach and intestines.
– DERIVATIVES **gas·tro·en·ter·o·log·i·cal** /-tərəˈläjikəl/ **adj.**, **gas·tro·en·te·rol·o·gist** /-jist/ **n.**

gas·tro·in·tes·ti·nal /ˌgaströinˈtestənl/ ▶ **adj.** of or relating to the stomach and the intestines.

gas·tro·lith /ˈgastrəˌlitʜ/ ▶ **n. 1** Medicine a hard concretion in the stomach.
2 Zoology a small stone swallowed by a bird, reptile, or fish, to aid digestion in the gizzard.

gas·tro·nome /ˈgastrəˌnōm/ (also **gastronomer** /gaˈstränəmər/ or **gastronomist** /gaˈstränəˌmist/) ▶ **n.** a gourmet.
– ORIGIN early 19th cent.: from French, from *gastronomie* (see GASTRONOMY).

gas·tron·o·my /gaˈstränəmē/ ▶ **n.** the practice or art of choosing, cooking, and eating good food. ■ the cooking of a particular area: *traditional American gastronomy.*
– DERIVATIVES **gas·tro·nom·ic** /ˌgastrəˈnämik/ **adj.**, **gas·tro·nom·i·cal** /ˌgastrəˈnämikəl/ **adj.**, **gas·tro·nom·i·cal·ly** /ˌgastrəˈnämik(ə)lē/ **adv.**
– ORIGIN early 19th cent.: from French *gastronomie*, from Greek *gastronomia*, alteration of *gastrologia* (see GASTRO-, -LOGY).

gas·tro·pod /ˈgastrəˌpäd/ ▶ **n.** Zoology a mollusk of the large class Gastropoda, such as a snail, slug, or whelk.

Gas·trop·o·da /ˌgastrəˈpōdə/ Zoology a large class of mollusks which includes snails, slugs, whelks, and all terrestrial kinds. They have a large muscular foot for movement and (in many kinds) a single asymmetrical spiral shell.
– ORIGIN modern Latin (plural), from Greek *gastēr, gastr-* 'stomach' + *pous, pod-* 'foot.'

gas·tro·pub /ˈgastrəˌpəb/ ▶ **n.** Brit. a pub that specializes in serving high-quality food.
– ORIGIN 1990s: blend of *gastronomy* and *pub*.

gas·tro·scope /ˈgastrəˌskōp/ ▶ **n.** an optical instrument used for inspecting the interior of the stomach.
– DERIVATIVES **gas·tro·scop·ic** /ˌgastrəˈskäpik/ **adj.**, **gas·tros·co·py** /gaˈsträskəpē/ **n.**

gas·tros·to·my /gaˈsträstəmē/ ▶ **n.** (pl. **gastrostomies**) an opening into the stomach from the abdominal wall, made surgically for the introduction of food. ■ a surgical operation for making such an opening.

Gas·trot·ri·cha /gaˈsträtrikə/ Zoology a small phylum of minute aquatic wormlike animals that bear bristles and cilia. They are thought to be related to the nematode worms and rotifers.
– DERIVATIVES **gas·tro·trich** /ˈgastrəˌtrik/ **n.**
– ORIGIN modern Latin (plural), from Greek *gastēr, gastr-* 'stomach' + *thrix, trikh-* 'hair.'

gas·tru·la /ˈgastrōōlə/ ▶ **n.** (pl. **gastrulae** /-ˌlē/) Embryology an embryo at the stage following the blastula, when it is a hollow cup-shaped structure having three layers of cells.
– DERIVATIVES **gas·tru·la·tion** /ˌgastrəˈlāsʜən/ **n.**
– ORIGIN late 19th cent.: modern Latin, from Greek *gastēr, gastr-* 'stomach' + the Latin diminutive ending *-ula*.

gas tur·bine ▶ **n.** a turbine driven by expanding hot gases produced by burning fuel, as in a jet engine.

gas·works /ˈgasˌwərks/ ▶ **plural n.** [treated as sing.] a place where gas is manufactured and processed.

gat[1] /gat/ ▶ **n.** informal a revolver or pistol.
– ORIGIN early 20th cent.: abbreviation of GATLING GUN.

gat[2] archaic past of GET.

gate /gāt/ ▶ **n. 1** a hinged barrier used to close an opening in a wall, fence, or hedge. ■ a gateway: *she went out through the gate.* ■ an exit from an airport building to an aircraft. ■ [in names] a mountain pass or other natural passage: *the Golden Gate.*
2 the number of people who pay to enter a sports facility, exhibition hall, etc., for any one event: [as modifier] *gate receipts.* ■ the money taken for admission.
3 a device resembling a gate in structure or function, in particular: ■ a hinged or sliding barrier for controlling the flow of water: *a sluice gate.* ■ Skiing an opening through which a skier must pass in a slalom course, typically marked by upright poles. ■ a device for holding each frame of a movie film in position behind the lens of a camera or projector.
4 an electric circuit with an output that depends on the combination of several inputs: *a logic gate.* ■ the part of a field-effect transistor to which a signal is applied to control the resistance of the conductive channel of the device.

▶ v. [with obj.] Brit. (usu. **be gated**) confine (a student) to school or college: *he was gated for the rest of term.*
– PHRASES **get** (or **be given**) **the gate** informal be dismissed from a job.
– ORIGIN Old English *gæt, geat*, plural *gatu*, of Germanic origin; related to Dutch *gat* 'gap, hole, breach.'

-gate ▶ comb. form in nouns denoting an actual or alleged scandal, esp. one involving a cover-up: *Irangate.*
– ORIGIN early 1970s: suggested by the *Watergate* scandal, 1972.

gate ar·ray ▶ n. Computing a regular arrangement of logic gates. ■ an electronic chip consisting of such an arrangement.

ga·teau /gäˈtō, ga-/ ▶ n. (pl. **gateaux** pronunc. **same** or /-ˈtōz/) a rich cake, typically one containing layers of cream or fruit.
– ORIGIN mid 19th cent.: from French *gâteau* 'cake.'

gate-crash·er ▶ n. a person who attends a party or other gathering without an invitation or ticket.
– DERIVATIVES **gate-crash** v.

gat·ed com·mu·ni·ty ▶ n. a residential area with roads that have gates to control the movement of traffic and people into and out of the area.

g

gate·fold /ˈgātˌfōld/ ▶ n. an oversized page in a book or magazine folded to the same size as the other pages but intended to be opened out for reading.

gate·house /ˈgātˌhous/ ▶ n. a house or enclosure near a gateway.

gate·keep·er /ˈgātˌkēpər/ ▶ n. an attendant at a gate who is employed to control who goes through it. ■ a person or thing that controls access to something: *the primary-care doctor serves as the gatekeeper to specialists.*

gate·keep·ing /ˈgātˌkēpiNG/ ▶ n. **1** the activity of controlling, and usually limiting, general access to something: *Wal-Mart's cultural gatekeeping has served to narrow the mainstream for entertainment offerings.*
2 Computing a function or system that controls access or operations to files, computers, networks, or the like: [as modifier] *a gatekeeping mechanism that allows reads under some circumstances and blocks them under others.*

gate·leg ta·ble /ˈgātˌleg/ ▶ n. a table with hinged legs that swing out from the frame to support the drop leaves that make the surface of the table larger.
– DERIVATIVES **gate·legged** /ˈgātˌlegəd/ adj.

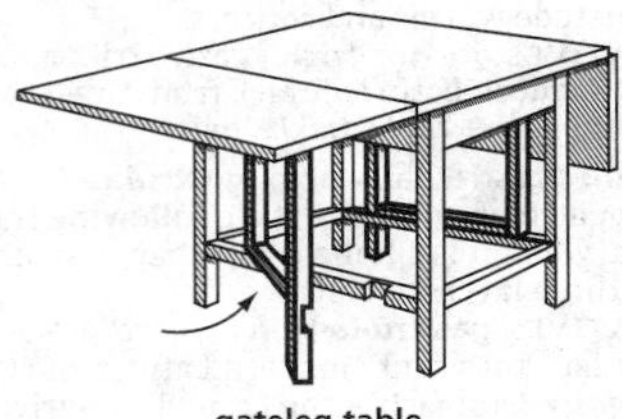
gateleg table

gate·post /ˈgātˌpōst/ ▶ n. a post on which a gate is hinged, or against which it shuts.
– PHRASES **between you and me and the gatepost** see BEDPOST.

Gates[1] /gāts/, Bill (1955–), US computer entrepreneur and philanthropist; full name *William Henry Gates*. In 1975, he cofounded Microsoft, a computer software company, the success of which made him the youngest multibillionaire in US history. With his wife, he established the philanthropic Bill & Melinda Gates Foundation in 2000.

Bill Gates

Gates[2], Horatio (1728–1806), American army officer; born in England. Originally an officer in the British army, he sided with the colonials when the American Revolution broke out. He commanded the Saratoga campaign 1777.

Gates[3], Robert Michael (1943–), US intelligence expert and cabinet member. After 26 years with the CIA, including its directorship 1991–93, he became US secretary of defense in 2006, serving under Presidents George W. Bush and Barack Obama.

Gates·head /ˈgātsˌhed/ an industrial town in northeastern England, on the southern bank of the Tyne River, opposite Newcastle; pop. 73,400 (est. 2009).

gate valve ▶ n. a valve with a sliding part that controls the extent of the aperture.

gate·way /ˈgātˌwā/ ▶ n. an opening that can be closed by a gate: *we turned into a gateway leading to a small cottage.* ■ a frame or arch built around or over a gate: *a big house with a wrought-iron gateway.* ■ a means of access or entry to a place: *Mombasa, the gateway to East Africa.* ■ a means of achieving a state or condition: *curiosity is the gateway to learning.* ■ Computing a device used to connect two different networks, esp. a connection to the Internet.

Gate·way Arch a colossal arch built along the west bank of the Mississippi River in St. Louis, Missouri. The stainless steel arch, 630 feet (192 m) wide and rising 630 feet (192 m) above the banks of the river, was designed by Eero Saarinen and was built 1963–65.

Gateway Arch

gate·way drug ▶ n. a habit-forming drug that, while not itself addictive, may lead to the use of other addictive drugs: *many believe that alcohol and cigarettes are gateway drugs that increase the risk of subsequent involvement with illegal drugs.*

Ga·tha /ˈgätə, -ˌtä/ ▶ n. any of 17 poems attributed to Zoroaster that are the most ancient texts of the Avesta.
– ORIGIN from Avestan *gāthā*.

gath·er /ˈgaTHər/ ▶ v. **1** [no obj.] come together; assemble or accumulate: *a crowd gathered in the square.*
2 [with obj.] bring together and take in from scattered places or sources: *we have gathered the information.* ■ pick up from the ground or a surface: *they gathered up the dirty plates and cups.* ■ collect (grain or other crops) as a harvest. ■ collect (plants, fruits, etc.) for food. ■ draw together or toward oneself: *she gathered the child in her arms.* ■ draw and hold together (fabric or a part of a garment) by running thread through it: *the front is gathered at the waist.*
3 [with obj.] infer; understand: *her clients were, I gathered, a prosperous group.*
4 [with obj.] develop a higher degree of: *the green movement is gathering pace.*
5 [with obj.] summon up (a mental or physical attribute such as one's thoughts or strength) for a purpose: *he lay gathering his thoughts together | he gathered himself for a tremendous leap.*
▶ n. (**gathers**) a part of a garment that is gathered or drawn in.
– PHRASES **gather way** (of a ship) begin to move.
– DERIVATIVES **gath·er·er** n.
– ORIGIN Old English *gaderian*; related to Dutch *gaderen*, also to TOGETHER.

gath·er·ing /ˈgaTHəriNG/ ▶ n. **1** an assembly or meeting, esp. a social or festive one or one held for a specific purpose: *a family gathering.*
2 a set of printed signatures of a book, gathered for binding.

Gat·i·neau /ˌgatnˈō, ga-tēˈnō/ a city in southwestern Quebec in Canada, a largely French-speaking suburb across the Ottawa River from Ottawa in Ontario; pop. 242,124 (2006).

Gat·ling gun /ˈgatliNG/ (also **Gatling**) ▶ n. a rapid-fire, crank-driven gun with a cylindrical cluster of several barrels. The first practical machine gun, it was officially adopted by the US Army in 1866.
– ORIGIN named after Richard J. *Gatling* (1818–1903), its American inventor.

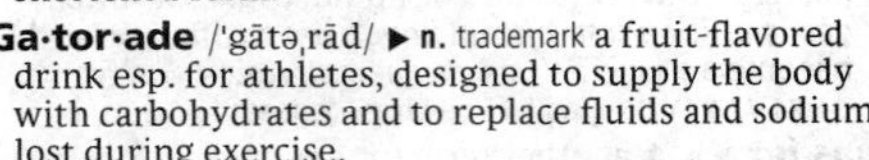
Gatling gun

ga·tor /ˈgātər/ ▶ n. informal an alligator.
– ORIGIN mid 19th cent.: shortened form.

Ga·tor·ade /ˈgātəˌrād/ ▶ n. trademark a fruit-flavored drink esp. for athletes, designed to supply the body with carbohydrates and to replace fluids and sodium lost during exercise.

GATT /gat/ General Agreement on Tariffs and Trade, an international treaty (1948–94) to promote trade and economic development by reducing tariffs and other restrictions. It was superseded by the establishment of the World Trade Organization in 1995.

gauche /gōSH/ ▶ adj. lacking ease or grace; unsophisticated and socially awkward.
– DERIVATIVES **gauche·ly** adv., **gauche·ness** n.
– ORIGIN mid 18th cent.: French, literally 'left.'

gau·che·rie /ˌgōSHəˈrē/ ▶ n. awkward, embarrassing, or unsophisticated ways: *she had long since gotten over gaucheries such as blushing.*
– ORIGIN late 18th cent.: French, from *gauche* (see GAUCHE).

Gau·cher's dis·ease /gōˈSHāz/ ▶ n. a hereditary disease in which the metabolism and storage of fats is abnormal. It results in bone fragility, neurological disturbance, anemia, and enlargement of the liver and spleen.
– ORIGIN mid 20th cent.: named after Phillippe C. E. *Gaucher* (1854–1918), French physician.

gau·cho /ˈgouCHō/ ▶ n. (pl. **gauchos**) a cowboy of the South American pampas.
– ORIGIN Latin American Spanish, probably from Araucanian *kauču* 'friend.'

gaud /gôd/ ▶ n. archaic a showy and purely ornamental thing: *displays of overpriced gauds.*
– ORIGIN Middle English (denoting a trick or pretense): perhaps via Anglo-Norman French from Old French *gaudir* 'rejoice,' from Latin *gaudere*. Current senses may have been influenced by obsolete *gaud* 'a large ornamental bead in a rosary.'

gaud·er·y /ˈgôdərē/ ▶ n. **1** gaudy articles or decoration, esp. clothing or jewelry.
2 tasteless or extravagant display of such articles.

Gau·dí /ˈgoudē/, Antonio (1853–1926), Spanish architect; full name *Antonio Gaudí y Cornet*. He was a leading but idiosyncratic exponent of art nouveau who worked chiefly in Barcelona and is known mainly for his ornate and extravagant church of the Sagrada Familia in Barcelona.

gaud·y[1] /ˈgôdē/ ▶ adj. (**gaudier, gaudiest**) extravagantly bright or showy, typically so as to be tasteless: *silver bows and gaudy ribbons.*
– DERIVATIVES **gaud·i·ly** /-dəlē/ adv., **gaud·i·ness** n.
– ORIGIN late 15th cent.: probably from GAUD + -Y[1].

gaud·y[2] ▶ n. (pl. **gaudies**) Brit. a celebratory reunion dinner or entertainment held by a college.
– ORIGIN mid 16th cent. (in the sense 'rejoicing, a celebration'): from Latin *gaudium* 'joy,' or from *gaude* 'rejoice!,' imperative of *gaudere*.

gauge /gāj/ (chiefly technical also **gage**) ▶ n. **1** an instrument or device for measuring the magnitude, amount, or contents of something, typically with a visual display of such information. ■ a tool for checking whether something conforms to a desired dimension. ■ a means of estimating something; a criterion or test: *emigration is perhaps the best gauge of public unease.*
2 the thickness, size, or capacity of something, esp. as a standard measure, in particular: ■ the diameter of a string, fiber, tube, etc.: [as modifier] *a fine 0.018-inch gauge wire.* ■ [in combination] a measure of the diameter of a gun barrel, or of its ammunition, expressed as the number of spherical pieces of shot of the same diameter as the barrel that can be made from 1 pound (454 g) of lead: [as modifier] *a 12-gauge shotgun.* ■ [in combination] the thickness of sheet metal or plastic: [as modifier] *500-gauge polyethylene.* ■ the distance between the rails of a line of railroad track: *the line was laid to a gauge of 2 ft. 9 in.*
3 (usu. **the gage**) Nautical, historical the position of a sailing vessel to windward (**weather gage**) or leeward (**lee gage**) of another.
▶ v. [with obj.] **1** estimate or determine the magnitude, amount, or volume of: *astronomers can gauge the*

star's intrinsic brightness. ■ form a judgment or estimate of (a situation, mood, etc.): *she is unable to gauge his mood.*
2 measure the dimensions of (an object) with a gauge: *when dry, the assemblies can be gauged exactly and planed to width.* ■ (as adj. **gauged**) made in standard dimensions: *gauged sets of strings.*
– DERIVATIVES **gauge·a·ble** adj., **gaug·er** n.
– ORIGIN Middle English (denoting a standard measure): from Old French *gauge* (noun), *gauger* (verb), variant of Old Northern French *jauge* (noun), *jauger* (verb), of unknown origin.

gauge the·o·ry ▶ n. Physics a quantum theory using mathematical functions to describe subatomic interactions in terms of particles that are not directly detectable.

Gau·guin /gōˈgaN/, (Eugène Henri) Paul (1848–1903), French painter. He lived mainly in Tahiti from 1891, painting in a post-Impressionist style that was influenced by primitive art. Notable works: *The Vision after the Sermon* (1888) and *Faa Iheihe* (1898).

Gau·ha·ti /gouˈhätē/ former name for **GUWAHATI**.

Gaul[1] /gôl/ an ancient region in Europe that corresponds to modern France, Belgium, the southern Netherlands, southwestern Germany, and northern Italy. The area south of the Alps was conquered in 222 BC by the Romans, who called it **Cisalpine Gaul**. The area north of the Alps, known as **Transalpine Gaul**, was taken by Julius Caesar between 58 and 51 BC.

Gaul[2] ▶ n. a native or inhabitant of ancient Gaul.
– ORIGIN from Latin *Gallus*, probably of Celtic origin.

Gau·lei·ter /ˈgouˌlītər/ ▶ n. **1** historical a political official governing a district under Nazi rule.
2 an overbearing official.
– ORIGIN 1930s: German, from *Gau* 'administrative district' + *Leiter* 'leader.'

Gaul·ish /ˈgôlisH/ ▶ adj. of, relating to, or denoting the ancient Gauls.
▶ n. the Celtic language of the ancient Gauls.

Gaulle, Charles de, see **DE GAULLE**.

Gaull·ism /ˈgôˌlizəm/ ▶ n. the principles and policies of Charles de Gaulle, characterized by their conservatism, nationalism, and advocacy of centralized government.
– DERIVATIVES **Gaull·ist** n. & adj.
– ORIGIN 1940s: from French *Gaullisme*.

Gaunt[1] /gônt/ former name of **GHENT**.

Gaunt[2], John of, see **JOHN OF GAUNT**.

gaunt /gônt/ ▶ adj. (of a person) lean and haggard, esp. because of suffering, hunger, or age. ■ (of a building or place) grim or desolate in appearance.
– DERIVATIVES **gaunt·ly** adv., **gaunt·ness** n.
– ORIGIN late Middle English: of unknown origin.

gaunt·let[1] /ˈgôntlit, ˈgänt-/ ▶ n. a stout glove with a long loose wrist. ■ historical an armored glove, as worn by a medieval knight. ■ the part of a glove covering the wrist.
– PHRASES **take up** (or **throw down**) **the gauntlet** accept (or issue) a challenge. [from the medieval custom of issuing a challenge by throwing one's gauntlet to the ground; whoever picked it up was deemed to have accepted the challenge.]
– ORIGIN late Middle English: from Old French *gantelet*, diminutive of *gant* 'glove,' of Germanic origin.

knight's gauntlet

gaunt·let[2] (also **gantlet** /ˈgantlit, ˈgônt-/) ▶ n. (in phrase **run the gauntlet**) **1** go through an intimidating or dangerous crowd, place, or experience in order to reach a goal: *they had to run the gauntlet of television cameras.*
2 historical undergo the military punishment of receiving blows while running between two rows of men with sticks.
– ORIGIN mid 17th cent.: alteration of *gantlope* (from Swedish *gatlopp*, from *gata* 'lane' + *lopp* 'course') by association with **GAUNTLET**[1].

gaur /gou(ə)r/ ▶ n. a large wild ox native to India and Malaysia. Also called **INDIAN BISON, SELADANG**. ● *Bos gaurus*, family Bovidae.
– ORIGIN early 19th cent.: from Sanskrit *gaura*; related to **COW**[1].

Gauss /gous/, Karl Friedrich (1777–1855), German mathematician, astronomer, and physicist. He laid the foundations of number theory.

gauss /gous/ (abbr.: **G**) ▶ n. (pl. **same** or **gausses**) a unit of magnetic induction, equal to one ten-thousandth of a tesla.
– ORIGIN late 19th cent.: named after K. **GAUSS**.

Gauss·i·an dis·tri·bu·tion /ˈgousēən/ ▶ n. Statistics another term for **NORMAL DISTRIBUTION**.
– ORIGIN early 20th cent.: named after K. **GAUSS**, who described it.

Gau·ta·ma /ˈgôtəmə, ˈgou-/, Siddhartha, see **BUDDHA**.

gauze /gôz/ ▶ n. **1** a thin translucent fabric of silk, linen, or cotton. ■ Medicine thin, loosely woven cloth used for dressing and swabs. ■ [in sing.] a transparent haze or film: *they saw the grasslands through a gauze of golden dust.*
2 (also **wire gauze**) a very fine wire mesh.
– ORIGIN mid 16th cent.: from French *gaze*, perhaps from *Gaza*, the name of a town in Palestine.

gauz·y /ˈgôzē/ ▶ adj. (**gauzier**, **gauziest**) resembling gauze; thin and translucent: *a gauzy dress.*
– DERIVATIVES **gauz·i·ly** /-zəlē/ adv., **gauz·i·ness** n.

ga·vage /gəˈväzH/ ▶ n. the administration of food or drugs by force, esp. to an animal, typically through a tube leading down the throat to the stomach.
– ORIGIN late 19th cent.: French, from *gaver* 'force-feed,' from a base meaning 'throat.'

gave /gāv/ past of **GIVE**.

gav·el /ˈgavəl/ ▶ n. a small mallet with which an auctioneer, a judge, or the chair of a meeting hits a surface to call for attention or order.
▶ v. (**gavels**, **gaveling**, **gaveled**; Brit. **gavels**, **gavelling**, **gavelled**) [with obj.] bring (a hearing or person) to order by use of such a mallet: *he gaveled the convention to order.*
– ORIGIN early 19th cent. (originally US in the sense 'stonemason's mallet'): of unknown origin.

gav·el·kind /ˈgavəlˌkīnd/ ▶ n. historical a system of inheritance in which a deceased person's land is divided equally among all male heirs.
– ORIGIN Middle English: from obsolete *gavel* 'payment, rent' + **KIND**[1].

gav·el-to-gav·el ▶ adj. lasting from beginning to end of a formal session or meeting, such as a political convention: *uninterrupted gavel-to-gavel coverage without commentary.*

ga·vi·al /ˈgāvēəl/ ▶ n. variant spelling of **GHARIAL**.
– ORIGIN from French, the *-v-* probably being substituted for *-r-* by scribal error.

ga·votte /gəˈvät/ ▶ n. a medium-paced French dance, popular in the 18th century. ■ a piece of music accompanying or in the rhythm of such a dance, composed in common time beginning on the third beat of the bar.
– ORIGIN French, from Provençal *gavoto* 'dance of the mountain people,' from *Gavot* 'a native of the Alps.'

GAW (or **G.A.W.**) ▶ abbr. guaranteed annual wage.

Ga·wain /gəˈwān, ˈgäˌwān, ˈgäwən/ (in Arthurian legend) one of the knights of the Round Table who quested after the Holy Grail. He is the hero of the medieval poem *Sir Gawain and the Green Knight*.

gawk /gôk/ ▶ v. [no obj.] stare openly and stupidly: *they were gawking at some pinup.*
▶ n. an awkward or shy person.
– DERIVATIVES **gawk·er** n., **gawk·ish** adj.
– ORIGIN late 17th cent. (as a noun): perhaps related to obsolete *gaw* 'to gaze,' from Old Norse *gá* 'heed.'

gawk·y /ˈgôkē/ ▶ adj. (**gawkier**, **gawkiest**) nervously awkward and ungainly: *a gawky teenager.*
– DERIVATIVES **gawk·i·ly** /-kəlē/ adv., **gawk·i·ness** n.

gawp /gôp/ ▶ v. [no obj.] informal stare openly in a stupid or rude manner: *what are you gawping at?*
– DERIVATIVES **gawp·er** n.
– ORIGIN late 17th cent.: perhaps an alteration of **GAPE**.

Gay /gā/, John (1685–1732), English poet and playwright. He is chiefly known for *The Beggar's Opera* (1728).

gay /gā/ ▶ adj. (**gayer**, **gayest**) **1** (of a person, esp. a man) homosexual: *that friend of yours, is he gay?* ■ relating to or used by homosexuals: *feminist, black, and gay perspectives.*
2 lighthearted and carefree: *Nan had a gay disposition and a very pretty face.* ■ brightly colored; showy; brilliant: *a gay profusion of purple and pink sweet peas.*
3 informal foolish; stupid: *making students wait for the light is kind of a gay rule.*
▶ n. a homosexual, esp. a man.
– DERIVATIVES **gay·ness** n.
– ORIGIN Middle English (sense 2 of the adjective): from Old French *gai*, of unknown origin.

USAGE Gay meaning 'homosexual,' dating back to the 1930s (if not earlier), became established in the 1960s as the term preferred by homosexual men to describe themselves. It is now the standard accepted term throughout the English-speaking world. As a result, the centuries-old other senses of **gay** meaning either 'carefree' or 'bright and showy,' once common in speech and literature, are much less frequent. The word **gay** cannot be readily used today in these older senses without sounding old-fashioned or arousing a sense of double entendre, despite concerted attempts by some to keep them alive. **Gay** in its modern sense typically refers to men (**lesbian** being the standard term for homosexual women), but in some contexts it can be used of both men and women.

Ga·ya /gəˈyä/ a city in northeastern India, in the state of Bihar, south of Patna; pop. 470,400 (est. 2009). It is a place of Hindu pilgrimage.

gay·dar /ˈgāˌdär/ ▶ n. informal, humorous the putative ability of homosexuals to recognize one another intuitively or by means of very slight indications. ■ the similar ability of heterosexuals to discern the homosexuality of others.
– ORIGIN 1990s: blend of *gay* and *radar*.

gay·e·ty ▶ n. variant spelling of **GAIETY**.

gay lib·er·a·tion ▶ n. a movement to eliminate social and legal discrimination against homosexuals.

Gay-Lus·sac's law /ˌgā ləˈsak/ Chemistry a law stating that the volumes of gases undergoing a reaction at constant pressure and temperature are in a simple ratio to each other and to that of the product.
– ORIGIN early 19th cent.: named after Joseph L. *Gay-Lussac* (1778–1850), French chemist and physicist.

g

gay pride ▶ n. a sense of dignity and satisfaction in connection with the public acknowledgment of one's own homosexuality.

gay rights ▶ plural n. equal civil and social rights for homosexuals compared with heterosexuals.

gaz. ▶ abbr. ■ gazette. ■ gazetteer.

ga·za·ni·a /gəˈzānēə/ ▶ n. a tropical herbaceous plant of the daisy family, with showy flowers that are typically orange or yellow. ● Genus *Gazania*, family Compositae.
– ORIGIN modern Latin, named after Theodore of *Gaza* (1398–1478), Greek scholar.

Ga·za Strip /ˈgäzə, ˈgazə/ a strip of territory in Palestine, on the southeastern Mediterranean coast, including the town of Gaza; pop. 1,551,900 (est. 2009). Administered by Egypt from 1949 and occupied by Israel from 1967, it became a self-governing enclave under the PLO–Israeli accord of 1994 and elected its own legislative council in 1996.

gaze /gāz/ ▶ v. [no obj.] look steadily and intently, esp. in admiration, surprise, or thought: *he could only gaze at her in astonishment.*
▶ n. a steady intent look: *he turned, following her gaze | offices screened from the public gaze.* ■ [in sing.] (in literary theory) a particular perspective taken to embody certain aspects of the relationship between observer and observed, esp. as reflected in the way in which an author or film director (unconsciously or otherwise) directs attention: *the male gaze.*
– DERIVATIVES **gaz·er** n.
– ORIGIN late Middle English: perhaps related to obsolete *gaw* (see **GAWK**).

ga·ze·bo /gəˈzēbō/ ▶ n. (pl. **gazebos** or **gazeboes**) a roofed structure that offers an open view of the surrounding area, typically used for relaxation or entertainment.
– ORIGIN mid 18th cent.: perhaps humorously from **GAZE**, in imitation of Latin future tenses ending in *-ebo*: compare with **LAVABO**.

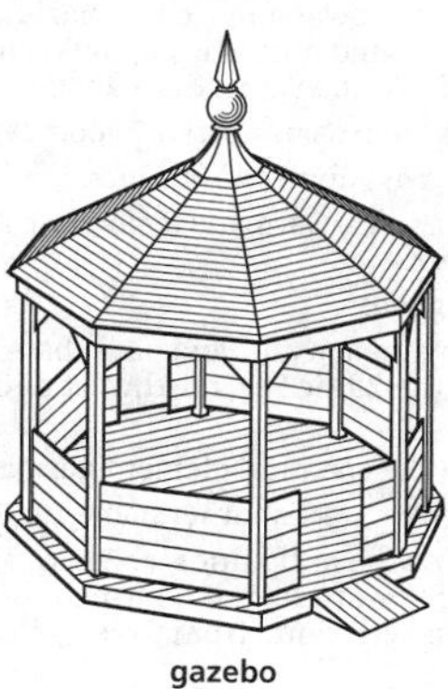

gazebo

ga·zelle /gəˈzel/ ▶ n. (pl. **same** or **gazelles**) a small slender antelope that typically has curved horns and a yellowish-brown coat with white underparts, found in open country in Africa and Asia. ● *Gazella* and other genera, family Bovidae: several species.
– ORIGIN early 17th cent.: from French, probably via Spanish from Arabic *ghazāl*.

PRONUNCIATION KEY ə *ago, up*; ər *over, fur*; a *hat*; ā *ate*; ä *car*; e *let*; ē *see*; i *fit*; ī *by*; NG *sing*; ō *go*; ô *law, for*; oi *toy*; o͝o *good*; o͞o *goo*; ou *out*; TH *thin*; T͟H *then*; ZH *vision*

g

gaze track·ing ▶ n. another term for EYE TRACKING.

ga·zette /gəˈzet/ ▶ n. **1** (used in the names of periodicals) a journal or newspaper.
2 Brit. the official publication of a government organization or institution, listing appointments and other public notices.
▶ v. [with obj.] Brit. announce or publish in an official gazette.
– ORIGIN early 17th cent.: via French from Italian *gazzetta*, originally Venetian *gazeta de la novità* 'a halfpennyworth of news' (because the news-sheet sold for a *gazeta*, a Venetian coin of small value).

gaz·et·teer /ˌgaziˈti(ə)r/ ▶ n. a geographical index or dictionary.
– ORIGIN early 17th cent. (in the sense 'journalist'): via French from Italian *gazzettiere*, from *gazzetta* (see GAZETTE). The current sense comes from a late 17th-cent. gazetteer called *The Gazetteer's: or, Newsman's Interpreter: Being a Geographical Index*.

Ga·zi·an·tep /ˌgäzē-änˈtep/ a city in southern Turkey, near the border with Syria; pop. 1,175,000 (est. 2007). Former name (until 1921): AINTAB.

ga·zil·lion /gəˈzilyən/ (also **kazillion**) ▶ cardinal number informal a very large number or quantity (used jocularly or for emphasis): *I'd like to sell gazillions of books*.
– ORIGIN late 20th cent.: fanciful formation on the pattern of *billion* and *million*.

gaz·pa·cho /gäˈspäCHō/ ▶ n. (pl. **gazpachos**) a Spanish-style soup made from tomatoes and other vegetables and spices, served cold.
– ORIGIN Spanish.

ga·zump /gəˈzəmp/ ▶ v. [with obj.] Brit. **1** (of a seller) raise the contracted price of a property after having informally accepted a lower offer (from an intending buyer).
2 archaic swindle (someone).
– DERIVATIVES **ga·zump·er** n.
– ORIGIN 1920s (sense 2): from Yiddish *gezumph* 'overcharge.' Sense 1 dates from the 1970s.

ga·zund·er /gəˈzəndər/ ▶ v. [with obj.] Brit. (of a buyer) lower the amount of an offer made on a property and accepted by (a seller) at the time of final negotiations.
– ORIGIN late 1980s: humorous blend of GAZUMP and UNDER.

GB ▶ abbr. ■ Computing (also **Gb**) gigabyte(s). ■ Great Britain.

GBH ▶ abbr. grievous bodily harm.

Gbyte ▶ abbr. gigabyte(s).

GCB ▶ abbr. (in the UK) Knight or Dame Grand Cross of the Order of the Bath.

gcd ▶ abbr. Mathematics greatest common divisor.

gcf ▶ abbr. Mathematics greatest common factor.

GCT ▶ abbr. Greenwich Civil Time.

GD ▶ abbr. Grand Duchy.

Gd ▶ symbol the chemical element gadolinium.

gd. ▶ abbr. ■ good. ■ guard.

Gdańsk /gəˈdänsk, -ˈdansk/ an industrial port and shipbuilding center in northern Poland, on an inlet of the Baltic Sea; pop. 456,103 (2007). Disputed between Prussia and Poland during the 19th century, it was a free city under a League of Nations mandate 1919–39, when it was annexed by Nazi Germany, which precipitated hostilities with Poland and the outbreak of World War II. German name DANZIG.

g'day /gəˈdā/ ▶ exclam. Austral./NZ good day.

GDP ▶ abbr. gross domestic product.

GDR ▶ abbr. historical German Democratic Republic. See GERMANY.

gds. ▶ abbr. goods.

Gdy·nia /gəˈdinēə/ a port and naval base in northern Poland, on the Baltic Sea, northwest of Gdańsk; pop. 251,183 (2007).

Ge[1] ▶ symbol the chemical element germanium.

Ge[2] /gā/ Greek Mythology another name for GAIA.

ge·an·ti·cline /jēˈantiˌklīn/ ▶ n. Geology a large-scale anticline or upward fold of stratified rock.
– ORIGIN late 19th cent.: from Greek *gē* 'earth' + ANTICLINE.

gear /gi(ə)r/ ▶ n. **1** (often **gears**) one of a set of toothed wheels that work together to alter the relation between the speed of a driving mechanism (such as the engine of a vehicle or the crank of a bicycle) and the speed of the driven parts (the wheels). ■ a particular function or state of adjustment of engaged gears: *he was tooling along in fifth gear*. ■ used in reference to the level of effort or intensity expended in an activity or undertaking: *from this weekend, the campaign is expected to **step up a gear** | now the champions **moved up a gear***.
2 informal equipment that is used for a particular purpose. ■ a person's personal possessions and clothes. ■ clothing, esp. of a specified kind: *designer gear*. ■ Nautical a ship's rigging.
▶ v. [with obj.] design or adjust the gears in (a machine) to give a specified speed or power output: *it's geared too high for serious off-road use*. ■ (**gear something to**) adjust or adapt something to suit a special purpose or need.
– PHRASES **change** (or **switch** or **shift**) **gears** adopt a different approach to a situation or task: *we have to be prepared to shift gears when things create problems for the government*. **in gear** with a gear engaged: *the captain revved the engines and put them in gear*. ■ proceeding with energy, determination, or speed: *I couldn't get myself into gear early enough on Saturday morning*.
– PHRASAL VERBS **gear down** (or **up**) change to a lower (or higher) gear. **gear for** make ready or prepared: *a nation geared for war*. **gear up** equip or prepare oneself: *the region started to **gear up for** the tourist season*.
– ORIGIN Middle English: of Scandinavian origin; compare with Old Norse *gervi*. Early senses expressed the general meaning 'equipment or apparatus,' later 'mechanism': hence sense 1 of the noun (early 19th cent).

gear·box /ˈgi(ə)rˌbäks/ ▶ n. a set of gears with its casing, esp. in a motor vehicle; the transmission.

gear·ing /ˈgi(ə)riNG/ ▶ n. **1** the set or arrangement of gears in a machine: *the mill's internal waterwheel and gearing survive*.
2 British term for LEVERAGE (sense 2 of the noun).

gear lev·er (also **gearstick**) ▶ n. Brit. another term for GEARSHIFT.

gear ra·ti·o ▶ n. (in a gearbox, transmission, etc.) the ratio between the rates at which the last and first gears rotate.

gear·shift /ˈgi(ə)rˌSHift/ ▶ n. a device used to engage or disengage gears in a transmission or similar mechanism.

gear·wheel /ˈgi(ə)rˌ(h)wēl/ ▶ n. a toothed wheel in a set of gears. ■ (on a bicycle) a cogwheel driven directly by the chain.

geas /gesH/ ▶ n. (pl. **geasa** /ˈgesHə/) (in Irish folklore) an obligation or prohibition magically imposed on a person.
– ORIGIN Irish.

geck·o /ˈgekō/ ▶ n. (pl. **geckos** or **geckoes**) a nocturnal and often highly vocal lizard that has adhesive pads on the feet to assist in climbing on smooth surfaces. It is widespread in warm regions. ● Gekkonidae and related families: numerous genera and species.
– ORIGIN late 18th cent.: from Malay dialect *geko*, *gekok*, imitative of its cry.

GED ▶ abbr. general equivalency degree (or diploma).

gee[1] /jē/ (also **gee-whiz** /ˈjē ˈ(h)wiz/) ▶ exclam. informal a mild expression, typically of surprise, enthusiasm, or sympathy: *Gee, Linda looks great at fifty!*
– ORIGIN mid 19th cent.: perhaps an abbreviation of JESUS.

gee[2] ▶ exclam. (**gee up**) a command to a horse to go faster.
▶ v. (**gees, geeing, geed**) [with obj.] command (a horse) to go faster. ■ encourage (someone) to work more quickly: *I was running around geeing people up*.
– ORIGIN early 17th cent.: of unknown origin.

gee[3] ▶ n. informal a thousand dollars: *we paid five gees*.
– ORIGIN 1930s: representing the initial letter of GRAND.

gee·bung /ˈjēbəNG/ ▶ n. an Australian shrub or small tree that bears creamy-yellow flowers and small green fruit. ● Genus *Persoonia*, family Proteaceae.
– ORIGIN early 19th cent.: from Dharuk.

Gee·chee /ˈgēCHē/ ▶ n. term used of the Gullah dialect, or a speaker of this dialect.
– ORIGIN possibly from the name of the *Ogeechee* River, in Georgia.

geek /gēk/ ▶ n. informal **1** an unfashionable or socially inept person. ■ [usu. with modifier] a knowledgeable and obsessive enthusiast: *a computer geek*.
2 a carnival performer who performs wild or disgusting acts.
– DERIVATIVES **geek·i·ness** n., **geek·y** adj.
– ORIGIN late 19th cent.: from the related English dialect *geck* 'fool,' of Germanic origin; related to Dutch *gek* 'mad, silly.'

WORD TRENDS Is being a geek something to be proud of? A few decades ago, the answer would almost certainly have been no: the word was a cruel and critical label attached to clever, but socially awkward, people: *Trekkies, computer geeks, and unpopular college students*. Then in the 1990s, everything changed. The computer industry helped many **geeks** to achieve great success, and the wider perception of **geeks** began to shift. Being a **geek** was suddenly a positive thing, suggesting an admirable level of knowledge, expertise, and passion: **geeks** could do 'cool stuff,' and they could fix your computer! It's now common for people to be *self-proclaimed* or *self-confessed* **geeks**, with **geekiness** no longer confined to the world of science and technology (*a music geek with an awesome vinyl collection | the kind of film that every true movie geek would give five stars*). **Nerds** have undergone a similar change of image but to a lesser extent, with some negative terms such as *boring* and *pathetic* still commonly attached to the word.

Gee·long /jēˈlôNG/ a port and oil-refining center on the southern coast of Australia, in the state of Victoria; pop. 134,100 (est. 2008).

geese /gēs/ plural form of GOOSE.

gee-string ▶ n. variant spelling of G-STRING.

gee-whiz informal ▶ exclam. another term for GEE[1].
▶ adj. [attrib.] characterized by or causing naive astonishment or wonder, in particular at new technology: *this era of gee-whiz gadgetry*.

geez ▶ exclam. variant spelling of JEEZ.

Ge'ez /gēˈez/ ▶ n. an ancient Semitic language of Ethiopia, which survives as the liturgical language of the Ethiopian Orthodox Church. It is the ancestor of the modern Ethiopian languages such as Amharic. Also called ETHIOPIC.
– ORIGIN of Ethiopic origin.

gee·zer /ˈgēzər/ ▶ n. informal an old man (used as a disparaging term).
– ORIGIN late 19th cent.: representing a dialect pronunciation of earlier *guiser* 'mummer.'

ge·fil·te fish /gəˈfiltə/ ▶ n. a dish of stewed or baked stuffed fish, or of fish cakes boiled in a fish or vegetable broth and usually served chilled.
– ORIGIN late 19th cent.: Yiddish, 'stuffed fish,' from *filn* 'to fill' + FISH[1].

ge·gen·schein /ˈgāgənˌSHīn/ ▶ n. Astronomy a patch of very faint nebulous light sometimes seen in the night sky opposite the position of the sun. It is thought to be the image of the sun reflected from gas and dust outside the atmosphere.
– ORIGIN late 19th cent.: German *Gegenschein*, from *gegen* 'opposite' + *Schein* 'glow, shine.'

Ge·hen·na /gəˈhenə/ (in Judaism and the New Testament) hell.
– ORIGIN via ecclesiastical Latin from Greek *geenna*, from Hebrew *gē' hinnōm* 'hell,' literally 'valley of Hinnom,' a place near Jerusalem where children were sacrificed to Baal (Jer. 19:5,6).

Geh·rig /ˈgerig/, Lou (1903–41), US baseball player; full name *Henry Louis Gehrig*; known as **the Iron Horse**. He played a then-record 2,130 consecutive major league games for the New York Yankees from 1925 to 1939; his stamina earned him his nickname. He died from amyotrophic lateral sclerosis (ALS), often called Lou Gehrig's disease. Baseball Hall of Fame (1939).

Lou Gehrig

Gei·ger /ˈgīgər/, Hans (Johann) Wilhelm (1882–1945), German nuclear physicist. In 1908, he developed a prototype radiation counter for detecting alpha particles.

Gei·ger count·er (also **Geiger-Müller counter** /ˈmələr, ˈmyo͝olər/) ▶ n. a device for measuring radioactivity by detecting and counting ionizing particles.

Gei·sel /ˈgīzəl/, Theodor (Seuss) (1904–91) US writer and illustrator; known as **Dr. Seuss**. His numerous children's books include *And to Think That I Saw It on Mulberry Street* (1937), *Horton Hatches the Egg* (1940), *The Cat in the Hat* (1957), *Green Eggs and Ham* (1960), and *Oh, the Places You'll Go!* (1990). For adults he wrote *You're Only Old Once!* (1986).

gei·sha /ˈgāsHə, ˈgē-/ (also **geisha girl**) ▶ **n.** (pl. **same** or **geishas**) a Japanese hostess trained to entertain men with conversation, dance, and song.
– ORIGIN late 19th cent.: Japanese, 'entertainer,' from *gei* 'performing arts' + *sha* 'person.'

Geiss·ler tube /ˈgīslər/ ▶ **n.** a sealed tube of glass or quartz with a central constriction, filled with vapor for the production of a luminous electrical discharge.
– ORIGIN mid 19th cent.: named after Heinrich *Geissler* (1814–79), the German mechanic and glassblower who invented it.

Geist /gīst/ ▶ **n.** [in sing.] the spirit of an individual or group.
– ORIGIN German; related to **GHOST**.

gei·to·nog·a·my /ˌgītnˈägəmē/ ▶ **n.** Botany the fertilization of a flower by pollen from another flower on the same (or a genetically identical) plant. Compare with **XENOGAMY**.
– DERIVATIVES **gei·to·nog·a·mous** /-məs/ **adj.**
– ORIGIN late 19th cent.: from Greek *geitōn, geitono-* 'neighbor' + *-gamos* 'marrying.'

Ge·jiu /ˈgeˈjo͞o/ (also **Geju**) a city in southern China, near the border with Vietnam; pop. 216,500 (est. 2006).

gel[1] /jel/ ▶ **n.** a jellylike substance containing a cosmetic, medicinal, or other preparation: *try rubbing some teething gel onto sore gums | hair gel.* ■ Chemistry a semisolid colloidal suspension of a solid dispersed in a liquid. ■ Biochemistry a semirigid slab or cylinder of an organic polymer used as a medium for the separation of macromolecules.
▶ **v.** (**gels, gelling, gelled**) [no obj.] Chemistry form into a gel: *the mixture gelled at 7 degrees Celsius.* ■ [with obj.] treat (the hair) with gel.
– ORIGIN late 19th cent.: abbreviation of **GELATIN**.

gel[2] ▶ **v.** (**gels, gelling, gelled**) chiefly Brit. variant spelling of **JELL**.
– ORIGIN late 19th cent.: from **GEL**[1].

gel·a·da /jəˈlädə/ (also **gelada baboon**) ▶ **n.** (pl. **same** or **geladas**) a brownish baboon with a long mane and naked red rump, native to Ethiopia. ● *Theropithecus gelada*, family Cercopithecidae.
– ORIGIN mid 19th cent.: from Amharic *č'äallada.*

ge·la·ti /jəˈlätē/ plural form of **GELATO**.

gel·a·tin /ˈjelətn/ (also chiefly dated **gelatine**) ▶ **n.** a virtually colorless and tasteless water-soluble protein prepared from collagen and used in food preparation as the basis of jellies, in photographic processes, and in glue. ■ (usu. **blasting gelatin**) a high explosive consisting chiefly of a gel of nitroglycerine with added cellulose nitrate.
– ORIGIN early 19th cent.: from French *gélatine*, from Italian *gelatina*, from *gelata*, from Latin (see **JELLY**).

ge·lat·i·nize /jəˈlatn,īz, ˈjelətn,īz/ ▶ **v.** make or become gelatinous or jellylike. ■ [with obj.] (usu. as adj. **gelatinized**) coat with gelatin: *gelatinized glass microscope slides.*
– DERIVATIVES **ge·lat·i·ni·za·tion** /je,latniˈzāsHən/ **n.**

ge·lat·i·nous /jəˈlatn-əs/ ▶ **adj.** having a jellylike consistency: *a sweet, gelatinous drink.* ■ of or like the protein gelatin: *tooth enamel is coated with a gelatinous layer of protein.*
– DERIVATIVES **ge·lat·i·nous·ly adv.**

ge·la·tion[1] /jeˈlāsHən/ ▶ **n.** technical solidification by freezing.
– ORIGIN mid 19th cent.: from Latin *gelatio(n-)*, from *gelare* 'freeze.'

ge·la·tion[2] ▶ **n.** Chemistry the process of forming a gel.

ge·la·to /jəˈlätō/ ▶ **n.** (pl. **gelati** /-tē/) an Italian-style ice cream.
– ORIGIN Italian.

gel·cap ▶ **n.** a gelatin capsule containing liquid medication or other substance to be taken orally.

gel·coat /ˈjel,kōt/ ▶ **n.** the smooth, hard surface layer of polyester resin in a fiberglass structure.

geld /geld/ ▶ **v.** [with obj.] castrate (a male animal). ■ deprive of vitality or vigor: *the English version of the book has been gelded.*
– ORIGIN Middle English: from Old Norse *gelda*, from *geldr* 'barren.'

Gel·der·land /ˈgeldər,länt, ˈKHel-/ a province in the Netherlands, on the border with Germany; capital, Arnhem.

geld·ing /ˈgeldiNG/ ▶ **n.** a castrated animal, esp. a male horse.
– ORIGIN late Middle English: from Old Norse *geldingr*, from *geldr* 'barren.'

gel·id /ˈjelid/ ▶ **adj.** icy; extremely cold: *the gelid pond* | figurative *she gave a gelid reply.*
– ORIGIN early 17th cent.: from Latin *gelidus*, from *gelu* 'frost, intense cold.'

gel·ig·nite /ˈjelig,nīt/ ▶ **n.** a high explosive made from a gel of nitroglycerine and nitrocellulose in a base of wood pulp and sodium or potassium nitrate, used particularly for rock blasting.
– ORIGIN late 19th cent.: probably from **GELATIN** + Latin *(I)ignis* 'wood' + **-ITE**[1].

Gell-Mann /ˌgel ˈmän/, Murray (1929–), US theoretical physicist. He coined the word *quark* and proposed the concept of strangeness in quarks. Nobel Prize for Physics (1969).

gel pen ▶ **n.** a pen that uses a gel-based ink, combining the permanence of oil-based ballpoint ink and the smooth glide of water-based ink.

gel·se·mi·um /jelˈsēmēəm/ ▶ **n. 1** a preparation of the rhizome of yellow jasmine, used in homeopathy to treat flulike symptoms.
2 a plant of a genus that includes the yellow jasmine. ● Genus *Gelsemium*, family Loganiaceae.
– ORIGIN late 19th cent.: modern Latin, from Italian *gelsomino* 'jasmine.'

Gel·sen·kir·chen /ˌgelzənˈki(ə)rKHən/ an industrial city in western Germany, in North Rhine-Westphalia, northeast of Essen; pop. 266,800 (est. 2006).

gelt /gelt/ ▶ **n.** informal money.
– ORIGIN early 16th cent. (originally often used to refer to the pay of a German army): from German *Geld* 'money.'

GEM ▶ **abbr.** ground-effect machine.

gem /jem/ ▶ **n.** a precious or semiprecious stone, esp. when cut and polished or engraved. ■ a person or thing considered to be outstandingly good or special in some respect: *this architectural gem of a palace.* ■ used in names of some brilliantly colored hummingbirds, e.g., **mountain gem**.
▶ **v.** (**gems, gemming, gemmed**) [with obj.] (usu. as adj. **gemmed**) rare decorate with or as with gems.
– DERIVATIVES **gem·like** /-,līk/ **adj.**
– ORIGIN Old English *gim*, from Latin *gemma* 'bud, jewel'; influenced in Middle English by Old French *gemme.*

Ge·ma·ra /gəˈmärə/ ▶ **n.** (**the Gemara**) a rabbinical commentary on the Mishnah, forming the second part of the Talmud.
– ORIGIN from Aramaic *gĕmārā* 'completion.'

ge·ma·tri·a /gəˈmātrēə/ ▶ **n.** a Kabbalistic method of interpreting the Hebrew scriptures by computing the numerical value of words, based on those of their constituent letters.
– ORIGIN mid 17th cent.: from Aramaic *gimaṭrĕyā*, from Greek *geōmetria* (see **GEOMETRY**).

Ge·may·el /jəˈmīəl/, Pierre (1905–84), Lebanese political leader. A Maronite Christian, he founded the right-wing Phalange Party in 1936 and served as a member of parliament 1960–84. His youngest son, **Bashir** (1947–82), was assassinated while president-elect; his eldest son, **Amin** (1942–), served as president 1982–88.

Ge·mein·schaft /gəˈmīn,sHäft, -,sHaft/ ▶ **n.** social relations between individuals, based on close personal and family ties; community. Contrasted with **GESELLSCHAFT**.
– ORIGIN German, from *gemein* 'common' + *-schaft* (see **-SHIP**).

ge·mel·li /jəˈmelē/ ▶ **n.** pasta in the form of two short rods twisted around each other.
– ORIGIN Italian, literally 'twins.'

gem·i·nal /ˈjemənl/ ▶ **adj.** Chemistry denoting substituent atoms or groups, esp. protons, attached to the same atom in a molecule.
– DERIVATIVES **gem·i·nal·ly adv.**
– ORIGIN late 20th cent.: from Latin *geminus* 'twin' + **-AL**.

gem·i·nate Phonetics ▶ **adj.** /ˈjemənit/ consisting of identical adjacent speech sounds, esp. consonants; doubled.
▶ **v.** /ˈjemə,nāt/ [with obj.] double or repeat (a speech sound).
– DERIVATIVES **gem·i·na·tion** /ˌjeməˈnāsHən/ **n.**
– ORIGIN late Middle English: from Latin *geminatus*, past participle of *geminare* 'double, pair with,' from *geminus* 'twin.'

Gem·i·ni /ˈjemə,nī, -,nē/ **1** Astronomy a northern constellation (the Twins), said to represent the mythological twins Castor and Pollux, whose names are given to its two brightest stars. See **DIOSCURI**. ■ (as genitive **Geminorum** /ˌjeməˈnôrəm/) used with a preceding letter or numeral to designate a star in this constellation: *the star Eta Geminorum.*
2 Astrology the third sign of the zodiac, which the sun enters about May 21. ■ (**a Gemini**) (pl. **Geminis**) a person born when the sun is in this sign.
3 a series of twelve manned orbiting space missions, launched by the US in the 1960s in preparation for the Apollo program.
– DERIVATIVES **Gem·i·ni·an** /-,nīən/ **n. & adj.** (sense 2).
– ORIGIN Latin, plural of *geminus* 'twin.'

Gem·i·nids /ˈjemənidz/ Astronomy an annual meteor shower with a radiant in the constellation Gemini, reaching a peak about December 13.

gem·ma /ˈjemə/ ▶ **n.** (pl. **gemmae** /ˈjemē/) Biology a small cellular body or bud that can separate to form a new organism. ■ another term for **CHLAMYDOSPORE**.
– ORIGIN late 18th cent. (denoting a leaf bud, as distinct from a flower bud): from Latin, literally 'bud, jewel.'

gem·ma·tion /jeˈmāsHən/ ▶ **n.** Biology asexual reproduction by the production of gemmae; budding.
– ORIGIN mid 18th cent.: from French, from *gemmer* 'to bud,' from *gemme* 'bud,' from Latin *gemma.*

gem·mip·a·rous /jeˈmipərəs/ ▶ **adj.** Biology (of a plant or animal) reproducing by gemmation.
– ORIGIN late 18th cent.: from modern Latin *gemmiparus*, from Latin *gemma* 'bud, jewel' + *parere* 'produce, give birth to.'

gem·mule /ˈjemyo͞ol/ ▶ **n.** Zoology a tough-coated dormant cluster of embryonic cells produced by a freshwater sponge for development in more favorable conditions.
– DERIVATIVES **gem·mu·la·tion** /ˌjemyəˈlāsHən/ **n.**
– ORIGIN mid 19th cent.: from French, from Latin *gemmula*, diminutive of *gemma* 'bud, jewel.'

gem·ol·o·gy /jeˈmäləjē/ (also **gemmology**) ▶ **n.** the study of precious stones.
– DERIVATIVES **gem·o·log·i·cal** /ˌjeməˈläjikəl/ **adj.**, **gem·ol·o·gist** /-jist/ **n.**
– ORIGIN early 19th cent.: from Latin *gemma* 'bud, jewel' + **-LOGY**.

gems·bok /ˈgemz,bäk/ ▶ **n.** a large antelope that has a gray coat, distinctive black-and-white head markings, and long straight horns, native to southwestern and East Africa. ● *Oryx gazella*, family Bovidae. See also **ORYX**.
– ORIGIN late 18th cent.: via Afrikaans from Dutch, literally 'chamois,' from *gems* 'chamois' + *bok* 'buck.'

Gem State a nickname for **IDAHO**.

gem·stone /ˈjem,stōn/ ▶ **n.** a precious or semiprecious stone, esp. one cut, polished, and used in a piece of jewelry.

ge·müt·lich /gəˈmo͞otlik/ ▶ **adj.** pleasant and cheerful.
– ORIGIN mid 19th cent.: German.

ge·müt·lich·keit /gəˈmo͞otlik,kīt/ (also **Gemütlichkeit**) ▶ **n.** geniality; friendliness.
– ORIGIN mid 19th cent.: German.

Gen. ▶ **abbr.** ■ General: *Gen. Eisenhower.* ■ Bible Genesis.

-gen ▶ **comb. form 1** Chemistry denoting a substance that produces something: *oxygen | allergen.*
2 Botany denoting a substance or plant that is produced: *cultigen.*
– ORIGIN via French *-gène* from Greek *genēs* '-born, of a specified kind,' from *gen-* (root of *gignomai* 'be born, become,' *genos* 'a kind').

ge·na /ˈjēnə/ ▶ **n.** (pl. **genae** /-nē/) Zoology the lateral part of the head of an insect or other arthropod below the level of the eyes.
– DERIVATIVES **ge·nal adj.**
– ORIGIN early 19th cent.: Latin, literally 'cheek.'

gen·darme /ˈZHändärm/ ▶ **n. 1** an armed police officer in France and other French-speaking countries.
2 a rock pinnacle on a mountain, occupying and blocking an arête.
– ORIGIN mid 16th cent. (originally denoting a mounted officer in the French army): French, from *gens d'armes* 'men of arms.' Sense 1 dates from the late 18th cent.

gen·dar·me·rie /ZHänˈdärmərē/ ▶ **n.** a force of gendarmes. ■ the headquarters of such a force.
– ORIGIN mid 16th cent.: French (see **GENDARME**).

gen·der /ˈjendər/ ▶ **n. 1** Grammar (in languages such as Latin, Greek, Russian, and German) each of the classes (typically masculine, feminine, common, neuter) of nouns and pronouns distinguished by the different inflections that they have and require in words syntactically associated with them. Grammatical gender is only very loosely associated with natural distinctions of sex. ■ the property (in nouns and related words) of belonging to such a class: *adjectives usually agree with the noun in gender and number.*
2 the state of being male or female (typically used with reference to social and cultural differences rather than biological ones): *traditional concepts of gender* | [as modifier] *gender roles.* ■ the members of

g

one or other sex: *differences between the genders are encouraged from an early age.*
– DERIVATIVES **gen·der·less** adj.
– ORIGIN late Middle English: from Old French *gendre* (modern *genre*), based on Latin *genus* 'birth, family, nation.' The earliest meanings were 'kind, sort, genus' and 'type or class of noun, etc.' (which was also a sense of Latin *genus*).

USAGE The word **gender** has been used since the 14th century as a grammatical term, referring to classes of noun designated as *masculine, feminine*, or *neuter* in some languages. The sense 'the state of being male or female' has also been used since the 14th century, but this did not become common until the mid 20th century. Although the words **gender** and **sex** both have the sense 'the state of being male or female,' they are typically used in slightly different ways: sex tends to refer to biological differences, while **gender** refers to cultural or social ones.

gen·der bend·er ▶ n. informal **1** a person who dresses and behaves in a way characteristic of the opposite sex.
2 Electronics a device for changing an electrical or electronic connector from male to female, or from female to male.

g

gen·der chang·er ▶ n. an electrical adaptor which allows two male or two female connectors to be connected to each other.

gen·der dys·pho·ri·a ▶ n. Medicine the condition of feeling one's emotional and psychological identity as male or female to be opposite to one's biological sex.
– DERIVATIVES **gen·der dys·phor·ic** adj. & n.

gen·dered /ˈjendərd/ ▶ adj. of, specific to, or biased toward the male or female sex: *gendered occupations.*

gen·der gap ▶ n. the discrepancy in opportunities, status, attitudes, etc., between men and women.

gen·der-neu·tral ▶ adj. **1** denoting a word that cannot be taken to refer to one sex only, e.g., *firefighter* (as opposed to *fireman*).
2 (of language or a piece of writing) using gender-neutral words wherever appropriate.

gene /jēn/ ▶ n. Biology (in informal use) a unit of heredity that is transferred from a parent to offspring and is held to determine some characteristic of the offspring: *proteins coded directly by genes.* ■ (in technical use) a distinct sequence of nucleotides forming part of a chromosome, the order of which determines the order of monomers in a polypeptide or nucleic acid molecule which a cell (or virus) may synthesize.
– ORIGIN early 20th cent.: from German *Gen*, from *Pangen*, a supposed ultimate unit of heredity (from Greek *pan-* 'all' + *genos* 'race, kind, offspring').

ge·ne·a·log·i·cal /ˌjēnēəˈläjikəl/ ▶ adj. of or relating to the study or tracing of lines of family descent: *genealogical research.*
– DERIVATIVES **ge·ne·a·log·i·cal·ly** /-ik(ə)lē/ adv.
– ORIGIN late 16th cent.: from French *généalogique*, via medieval Latin from Greek *genealogikos*, from *genealogia* (see GENEALOGY).

ge·ne·a·log·i·cal tree ▶ n. a diagram showing the lines of descent of a human family or of an animal species, so named because its typical construction is like that of an inverted branching tree.

ge·ne·al·o·gy /ˌjēnēˈäləjē, -ˈal-/ ▶ n. (pl. **genealogies**) a line of descent traced continuously from an ancestor: *combing through the birth records and genealogies.* ■ the study and tracing of lines of descent or development. ■ a plant's or animal's line of evolutionary development from earlier forms.
– DERIVATIVES **ge·ne·al·o·gist** /-jist/ n., **ge·ne·al·o·gize** /-ˌjīz/ v.
– ORIGIN Middle English: via Old French and late Latin from Greek *genealogia*, from *genea* 'race, generation' + *-logia* (see -LOGY).

gene-al·tered ▶ adj. (esp. in journalism) genetically modified: *the much ballyhooed, vine-ripened, gene-altered, rot-resistant tomato.*

gene am·pli·fi·ca·tion /ˌampləfiˈkāsʜən/ ▶ n. the multiple replication of a section of the genome, which occurs during a single cell cycle and results in the production of many copies of a specific sequence of the DNA molecule.

gene dop·ing ▶ n. the nontherapeutic use of gene therapy to enhance athletic performance, such as the supplementation of muscle-building genes.

gene ex·pres·sion ▶ n. see EXPRESSION (sense 1).

gene fre·quen·cy ▶ n. the ratio of a particular allele to the total of all other alleles of the same gene in a given population.

gene map ▶ n. **1** a record of the DNA sequence of a gene: *a cancer gene map.*
2 a genome map.

gene pool ▶ n. the stock of different genes in an interbreeding population.

gen·er·a /ˈjenərə/ plural form of GENUS.

gen·er·al /ˈjenərəl/ ▶ adj. **1** affecting or concerning all or most people, places, or things; widespread: *books of general interest.* ■ not specialized or limited in range of subject, application, activity, etc.: *brush up on your general knowledge.* ■ (of a rule, principle, etc.) true for all or most cases. ■ normal or usual: *it is not general practice to confirm or deny such reports.*
2 considering or including the main features or elements of something, and disregarding exceptions; overall: *they fired in the general direction of the enemy* | *a general introduction to the subject.*
3 [often in titles] chief or principal: *a general manager.*
▶ n. **1** a commander of an army, or an army officer of very high rank. ■ an officer in the US Army, Air Force, or Marine Corps ranking above lieutenant general. ■ the head of a religious order organized on quasi-military lines, e.g., the Jesuits, the Dominicans, or the Salvation Army.
2 (**the general**) archaic the general public.
– PHRASES **as a general rule** in most cases. **in general 1** usually; mainly: *in general, Alexander was a peaceful, loving man.* **2** as a whole: *our understanding of culture in general and of literature in particular.*
– ORIGIN Middle English: via Old French from Latin *generalis*, from *genus, gener-* 'class, race, kind.' The noun primarily denotes a person having overall authority: the sense 'army commander' is an abbreviation of *captain general*, from French *capitaine général* 'commander in chief.'

Gen·er·al A·mer·i·can ▶ n. (in nontechnical use) the variety of English spoken in the greater part of the US, particularly with reference to the lack of regional characteristics.

gen·er·al an·es·the·sia ▶ n. anesthesia that affects the whole body and usually induces a loss of consciousness: *he had the operation under general anesthesia.* Compare with LOCAL ANESTHESIA.

Gen·er·al Bap·tist ▶ n. a member of an Arminian Baptist congregation who rejects the Calvinist doctrine of predestination. Compare with PARTICULAR BAPTIST.

gen·er·al coun·sel ▶ n. the main lawyer who gives legal advice to a company.

gen·er·al court-mar·tial ▶ n. a court-martial for trying serious offenses, consisting of at least five officers with the authority to impose a sentence of dishonorable discharge or death.

gen·er·al·cy /ˈjenərəlsē/ ▶ n. the rank, office, or tenure of a general.

gen·er·al de·liv·er·y ▶ n. mail delivery to a post office for pickup by the addressee.

gen·er·al e·lec·tion ▶ n. a regular election of candidates for office, as opposed to a primary election. ■ a regular election for statewide or national offices.

gen·er·al e·quiv·a·len·cy de·gree (also **general equivalency diploma**) (abbr.: **GED**) ▶ n. a diploma signifying high school graduation, awarded to those who successfully complete a required examination.

gen·er·al head·quar·ters ▶ n. [treated as sing. or pl.] the headquarters of a military commander.

gen·er·al·is·si·mo /ˌjenərəˈlisəˌmō/ ▶ n. (pl. **generalissimos**) the commander of a combined military force consisting of army, navy, and air force units.
– ORIGIN early 17th cent.: Italian, 'having greatest authority,' superlative of *generale* (see GENERAL).

gen·er·al·ist /ˈjenərəlist/ ▶ n. a person competent in several different fields or activities: *with a generalist's education and some specific skills.*

gen·er·al·i·ty /ˌjenəˈralitē/ ▶ n. (pl. **generalities**) **1** a statement or principle having general rather than specific validity or force: *he confined his remarks to generalities.* ■ the quality or state of being general: *policy should be formulated at an appropriate level of generality.*
2 (**the generality**) the majority: *appropriate to the generality of laymen.*
– ORIGIN late Middle English: from Old French *generalite*, from late Latin *generalitas*, from *generalis* (see GENERAL).

gen·er·al·i·za·tion /ˌjenərəliˈzāsʜən/ ▶ n. a general statement or concept obtained by inference from specific cases: *he was making sweeping generalizations.* ■ the action of generalizing: *such anecdotes cannot be a basis for generalization.*

gen·er·al·ize /ˈjenərəˌlīz/ ▶ v. **1** [no obj.] make a general or broad statement by inferring from specific cases: *it is not easy to generalize about the poor* | *it is tempting to generalize from these conclusions.* ■ make or become more widely or generally applicable: [with obj.] *most of what we have observed in this field can be generalized to other fields* | [no obj.] *many of the results generalize to multibody structures.*
2 [with obj.] make (something) more widespread or common: *attempts to generalize an elite education.* ■ (as adj. **generalized**) Medicine (of a disease) affecting much or all of the body; not localized: *a generalized rash and fever.*
– DERIVATIVES **gen·er·al·iz·a·bil·i·ty** /ˌjenərəˌlīzəˈbilitē/ n., **gen·er·al·iz·a·ble** adj., **gen·er·al·iz·er** n.
– ORIGIN Middle English (in the sense 'reduce to a general statement'): from GENERAL + -IZE.

gen·er·al·ly /ˈjenərəlē/ ▶ adv. **1** [sentence adverb] in most cases; usually: *the term of a lease is generally 99 years.*
2 in general terms; without regard to particulars or exceptions: *a decade when France was moving generally to the left.*
3 widely: *the best scheme is generally reckoned to be the Canadian one.*

gen·er·al meet·ing ▶ n. a meeting open to all members of an organization.

gen·er·al of·fi·cer ▶ n. an officer ranking above colonel in the US Army, Air Force, or Marine Corps.

gen·er·al of the air force ▶ n. an officer of the highest rank in the US Air Force, ranking above general (awarded only in wartime).

gen·er·al of the ar·my ▶ n. an officer of the highest rank in the US Army, above general (awarded only in wartime).

gen·er·al prac·ti·tion·er (abbr.: **GP**) ▶ n. a medical doctor who is trained to provide primary health care to patients of either sex and any age.

gen·er·al-pur·pose ▶ adj. having a range of potential uses; not specialized in function or design: *a general-purpose detergent.*

Ge·ne·ral San Mar·tín /ˌkʜānāˈräl ˌsän märˈtēn/ a city in eastern Argentina, northwest of Buenos Aires; pop. 423,200 (est. 2008).

Ge·ne·ral San·tos /ˌkʜānāˈräl ˈsäntōs/ a port city in the Philippines, on southern Mindanao Island, on Saragani Bay; pop. 443,500 (est. 2007).

Ge·ne·ral Sar·mien·to /ˌkʜānāˈräl ˌsärˈmyentō/ (also **Sarmiento** or **San Miguel**) a city in eastern Argentina, west of Buenos Aires; pop. 280,700 (est. 2008).

gen·er·al se·man·tics ▶ plural n. [usu. treated as sing.] a system of linguistic philosophy developed by Alfred Korzybski (1879–1950), which explores the arbitrary nature of words and symbols and attempts to refine ways of using language.

gen·er·al·ship /ˈjenərəlˌsʜip/ ▶ n. the skill or practice of exercising military command.

gen·er·al staff ▶ n. [treated as sing. or pl.] the staff assisting a military commander in planning and executing operations.

gen·er·al store ▶ n. a store, typically in a small town, selling a wide variety of goods.

gen·er·al strike ▶ n. a strike of workers in all or most industries.

Gen·er·al Syn·od ▶ n. the highest governing body of the Church of England, an elected assembly of three houses (bishops, clergy, and laity).

gen·er·al the·o·ry of rel·a·tiv·i·ty ▶ n. see RELATIVITY (sense 2).

gen·er·ate /ˈjenəˌrāt/ ▶ v. [with obj.] cause (something, esp. an emotion or situation) to arise or come about: *changes that are likely to generate controversy* | *generate more jobs in the economy.* ■ produce (energy, esp. electricity). ■ produce (a set or sequence of items) by performing specified mathematical or logical operations on an initial set. ■ Linguistics produce (a sentence or other unit, esp. a well-formed one) by the application of a finite set of rules to lexical or other linguistic input. ■ Mathematics form (a line, surface, or solid) by notionally moving a point, line, or surface.
– DERIVATIVES **gen·er·a·ble** /ˈjenərəbəl/ adj.
– ORIGIN early 16th cent. (in the sense 'beget, procreate'): from Latin *generat-* 'created,' from the verb *generare*, from *genus, gener-* 'stock, race.'

gen·er·a·tion /ˌjenəˈrāsʜən/ ▶ n. **1** all of the people born and living at about the same time, regarded collectively: *one of his generation's finest songwriters.* ■ the average period, generally considered to be about thirty years, during which children are born and grow up, become adults, and begin to have children of their own. ■ a set of members of a family regarded as a single step or stage in descent: [as modifier, in combination] *a third-generation Canadian.* ■ a single stage in the development of a type of product: *a new generation of rear-engined sports cars.*

2 the production of something: *methods of electricity generation | the generation of wealth.* ■ the propagation of living organisms; procreation.
– DERIVATIVES **gen·er·a·tion·al** /-SHənl/ **adj.**, **gen·er·a·tion·al·ly** /-SHənl-ē/ **adv.**
– ORIGIN Middle English: via Old French from Latin *generatio(n-)*, from the verb *generare* (see **GENERATE**).

gen·er·a·tion gap ▶ **n.** (usu. **the generation gap**) differences of outlook or opinion between people of different generations.

gen·er·a·tion-skip·ping tax (abbr. **GST**) ▶ **n.** an estate tax imposed on beneficiaries who are two or more generations removed from the testator.

Gen·er·a·tion X ▶ **n.** the generation born after that of the baby boomers (roughly from the early 1960s to mid 1970s), often perceived to be disaffected and directionless.
– DERIVATIVES **Gen·er·a·tion X·er** /'eksər/ **n.**

Gen·er·a·tion Y ▶ **n.** the generation born in the 1980s and 1990s, comprising primarily the children of the baby boomers and typically perceived as increasingly familiar with digital and electronic technology.
– DERIVATIVES **Gen·er·a·tion Y·er n.**
– ORIGIN 1990s: after **GENERATION X**.

gen·er·a·tive /'jenərətiv, -ˌrātiv/ 'ʤɛnəˌreɪdɪv/ ▶ **adj.** relating to or capable of production or reproduction: *the generative power of the life force.* ■ Linguistics applying principles of generative grammar.
– ORIGIN late Middle English: from late Latin *generativus*, from *generare* 'beget' (see **GENERATE**).

gen·er·a·tive cell ▶ **n.** a reproductive cell, esp. a cell of an angiosperm pollen grain that divides to produce two male gamete nuclei.

gen·er·a·tive gram·mar ▶ **n.** Linguistics a type of grammar that describes a language in terms of a set of logical rules formulated so as to be capable of generating the infinite number of possible sentences of that language and providing them with the correct structural description. ■ a set of rules of this kind.

gen·er·a·tor /'jenəˌrātər/ ▶ **n.** a thing that generates something, in particular: ■ a dynamo or similar machine for converting mechanical energy into electricity. ■ an apparatus for producing gas, steam, or another product. ■ [with modifier] Computing a routine that constructs other routines or subroutines using given parameters, for specific applications: *a report generator.* ■ Mathematics a point, line, or surface regarded as moving and so notionally forming a line, surface, or solid.

gen·er·a·trix /ˌjenə'rātriks/ ▶ **n.** (pl. **generatrices** /-trəˌsēz/) Mathematics another term for **GENERATOR**.
– ORIGIN mid 19th cent.: from Latin (feminine).

ge·ner·ic /jə'nerik/ ▶ **adj. 1** characteristic of or relating to a class or group of things; not specific: *chèvre is a generic term for all goat's milk cheese.* ■ (of goods, esp. medicinal drugs) having no brand name; not protected by a registered trademark: *generic aspirin.*
2 Biology of or relating to a genus.
▶ **n.** a consumer product having no brand name or registered trademark: *substituting generics for brand-name drugs.*
– DERIVATIVES **ge·ner·i·cal·ly** /-ik(ə)lē/ **adv.**
– ORIGIN late 17th cent.: from French *générique*, from Latin *genus, gener-* 'stock, race.'

gen·er·os·i·ty /ˌjenə'räsitē/ ▶ **n.** the quality of being kind and generous: *I was overwhelmed by the generosity of friends and neighbors.* ■ the quality or fact of being plentiful or large: *diners certainly cannot complain about the generosity of portions.*
– ORIGIN late Middle English (denoting nobility of birth): from Latin *generositas*, from *generosus* 'magnanimous' (see **GENEROUS**). Current senses date from the 17th cent.

gen·er·ous /'jenərəs/ ▶ **adj.** (of a person) showing a readiness to give more of something, as money or time, than is strictly necessary or expected: *she was generous with her money.* ■ showing kindness toward others: *it was generous of them to ask her along.* ■ (of a thing) larger or more plentiful than is usual or necessary: *a generous sprinkle of pepper.*
– DERIVATIVES **gen·er·ous·ly adv.**, **gen·er·ous·ness n.**
– ORIGIN late 16th cent.: via Old French from Latin *generosus* 'noble, magnanimous,' from *genus, gener-* 'stock, race.' The original sense was 'of noble birth,' hence 'characteristic of noble birth, courageous, magnanimous, not mean' (a sense already present in Latin).

Gen·e·see Riv·er /ˌjenə'sē, 'jenəˌsē/ a river that flows for 144 miles (232 km) from northwestern Pennsylvania through western New York into Lake Ontario at Rochester.

Gen·e·sis /'jenəsis/ the first book of the Bible, which includes the stories of the creation of the world, Noah's Ark, the Tower of Babel, and the patriarchs Abraham, Isaac, Jacob, and Joseph.
– ORIGIN late Old English, via Latin from Greek, 'generation, creation, nativity, horoscope,' from the base of *gignesthai* 'be born or produced.' The name was given to the first book of the Old Testament in the Greek translation (the Septuagint), hence in the Latin translation (the Vulgate).

gen·e·sis /'jenəsis/ ▶ **n.** [in sing.] the origin or mode of formation of something: *this tale had its genesis in fireside stories.*
– ORIGIN early 17th cent.: from Greek (see **GENESIS**).

Ge·net /jə'nā/, Jean (1910–86), French novelist, poet, and playwright. Much of his work portrayed life in the criminal and homosexual underworlds, of which he was a part. Notable works: *Our Lady of the Flowers* (novel, 1944), *The Maids* (play, 1947), and *The Thief's Journal* (autobiography, 1949).

gen·et[1] /'jenit/ ▶ **n.** a nocturnal, catlike mammal of the civet family with short legs, spotted fur, and a long bushy ringed tail, found in Africa, southwestern Europe, and Arabia. ● Genus *Genetta*, family Viverridae: several species, in particular the **common** (or **small-spotted**) **genet** (*G. genetta*). ■ the fur of the genet.
– ORIGIN Middle English (used in the plural meaning 'genet skins'): from Old French *genete*, probably via Catalan, Portuguese, or Spanish from Arabic *jarnaiṭ*.

gen·et[2] /'jenit/ ▶ **n.** another term for **JENNET** (sense 2).

gene ther·a·py ▶ **n.** the transplantation of normal genes into cells in place of missing or defective ones in order to correct genetic disorders.

ge·net·ic /jə'netik/ ▶ **adj. 1** of or relating to genes or heredity: *all the cells in the body contain the same genetic information.* ■ of or relating to genetics: *an attempt to control mosquitoes by genetic techniques.*
2 of or relating to origin; arising from a common origin: *the genetic relations between languages.*
– DERIVATIVES **ge·net·i·cal adj.**, **ge·net·i·cal·ly** /-ik(ə)lē/ **adv.**
– ORIGIN mid 19th cent. (sense 2): from **GENESIS**, on the pattern of pairs such as *antithesis, antithetic.*

ge·net·i·cal·ly mod·i·fied /jə'netik(ə)lē 'mädəˌfīd/ (abbr.: **GM**) ▶ **adj.** (of an organism or crop) containing genetic material that has been artificially altered so as to produce a desired characteristic: *genetically modified viruses to insert new genes into growing plants.*

ge·net·ic blue·print ▶ **n.** (not in technical use) a gene map, or a genome map.

ge·net·ic code ▶ **n.** the nucleotide triplets of DNA and RNA molecules that carry genetic information in living cells. See **TRIPLET CODE**.

ge·net·ic coun·sel·ing ▶ **n.** the giving of advice to prospective parents concerning the chances of genetic disorders in a future child.

ge·net·ic drift ▶ **n.** Biology variation in the relative frequency of different genotypes in a small population, owing to the chance disappearance of particular genes as individuals die or do not reproduce.

ge·net·ic en·gi·neer·ing ▶ **n.** the deliberate modification of the characteristics of an organism by manipulating its genetic material.

ge·net·ic fin·ger·print·ing (also **genetic profiling**) ▶ **n.** another term for **DNA FINGERPRINTING**.

ge·net·ic load ▶ **n.** Biology the presence of unfavorable genetic material in the genes of a population.

ge·net·ic map ▶ **n.** a graphic representation of a chromosome including the position of its genes.
– DERIVATIVES **ge·net·ic map·ping n.**

ge·net·ic mark·er ▶ **n.** a gene or short sequence of DNA used to identify a chromosome or to locate other genes on a genetic map.

ge·net·ic pol·lu·tion ▶ **n.** the spread of altered genes from genetically engineered organisms to other, nonengineered organisms, esp. by cross-pollination.

ge·net·ics /jə'netiks/ ▶ **plural n.** [treated as sing.] the study of heredity and the variation of inherited characteristics. ■ [treated as sing. or pl.] the genetic properties or features of an organism, characteristic, etc.: *the effects of family genetics on the choice of career.*
– DERIVATIVES **ge·net·i·cist** /-'netəsist/ **n.**

ge·net·ic test·ing (also **genetic screening**) ▶ **n.** the sequencing of human DNA in order to discover genetic differences, anomalies, or mutations that may prove pathological.

Ge·ne·va /jə'nēvə/ a city in southwestern Switzerland, on Lake Geneva; pop. 179,971 (2007). It is headquarters of international bodies such as the Red Cross, various organizations of the United Nations, and the World Health Organization. French name **GENÈVE**.

Ge·ne·va, Lake a lake in southwestern central Europe, between the Jura Mountains and the Alps. Its southern shore forms part of the border between France and Switzerland. French name **LAC LÉMAN**.

Ge·ne·va bands ▶ **plural n.** two white cloth strips attached to the collar of some Protestants' clerical dress.
– ORIGIN late 19th cent.: from the place name **GENEVA**, where they were originally worn by Calvinists.

Ge·ne·va Bi·ble ▶ **n.** an English translation of the Bible published in 1560 by Protestant scholars working in Europe.

Ge·ne·va Con·ven·tion an international agreement first made at Geneva in 1864 and later revised, governing the status and treatment of captured and wounded military personnel and civilians in wartime.

Ge·ne·va cross ▶ **n.** a red cross on a white background, used to identify medical equipment and facilities, esp. in war, and as a sign of neutrality.

Ge·ne·va Pro·to·col any of various protocols drawn up in Geneva, esp. that of 1925 limiting chemical and bacteriological warfare.

Ge·nève /ZHə'nev, -'nāv/ French name for **GENEVA**.

ge·ne·ver /jə'nēvər/ (also literary **geneva** /-'nēvə/) ▶ **n.** Dutch gin.
– ORIGIN early 18th cent.: from Dutch, from Old French *genevre*, from an alteration of Latin *juniperus* (gin being flavored with juniper berries). The variant spelling is due to association with **GENEVA**.

Gen·ghis Khan /ˌgeNGgis 'kän, ˌjeNG-/ (1162–1227), founder of the Mongol empire; born *Temujin*. He took the name Genghis Khan ("ruler of all") in 1206 after uniting the nomadic Mongol tribes. When he died, his empire extended from China to the Black Sea. His grandson Kublai Khan completed the conquest of China.

ge·ni·al[1] /'jēnyəl, -nēəl/ ▶ **adj.** friendly and cheerful: *waved to them in genial greeting.* ■ (esp. of air or climate) pleasantly mild and warm.
– DERIVATIVES **gen·ial·ly adv.**
– ORIGIN mid 16th cent.: from Latin *genialis* 'nuptial, productive,' from *genius* (see **GENIUS**). The Latin sense was adopted into English; hence the senses 'mild and conducive to growth' (mid 17th cent.), later 'cheerful, kindly' (mid 18th cent.).

ge·ni·al[2] ▶ **adj.** Anatomy, rare of or relating to the chin.
– ORIGIN mid 19th cent.: from Greek *geneion* 'chin' (from *genus* 'jaw') + **-AL**.

ge·ni·al·i·ty /ˌjēnē'alitē/ ▶ **n.** the quality of having a friendly and cheerful manner; affability: *he was endowed with geniality and good humor.*

gen·ic /'jenik/ ▶ **adj.** [attrib.] Biology of or relating to genes: *a genic mutation.*

-genic ▶ **comb. form 1** producing: *carcinogenic.* ■ produced by: *iatrogenic.*
2 well suited to: *mediagenic.* [on the pattern of words such as *(photo)genic.*]
– ORIGIN from **-GEN** + **-IC**.

-genically ▶ **suffix** forming adverbs corresponding to adjectives ending in *-genical* (such as *iatrogenically* corresponding to *iatrogenic*).

ge·nic·u·late /jə'nikyəlit, -ˌlāt/ ▶ **adj.** Anatomy bent at a sharp angle.
– ORIGIN mid 17th cent.: from Latin *geniculatus*, from *geniculum* 'small knee, joint (of a plant).'

ge·nic·u·late bod·y (also **geniculate nucleus**) ▶ **n.** Anatomy either of two protuberances on the inferior surface of the thalamus that relay auditory and visual impulses respectively to the cerebral cortex.

ge·nie /'jēnē/ ▶ **n.** (pl. **genies** or **genii** /-nēˌī/) a spirit of Arabian folklore, as traditionally depicted imprisoned within a bottle or oil lamp, and capable of granting wishes when summoned. Compare with **JINN**.
– ORIGIN mid 17th cent. (denoting a guardian or protective spirit): from French *génie*, from Latin *genius* (see **GENIUS**). *Génie* was adopted in the current sense by the 18th-cent. French translators of *The Arabian Nights' Entertainments*, because of its resemblance in form and sense to Arabic *jinnī* 'jinni.'

ge·ni·i /'jēnēˌī/ plural form of **GENIE**, **GENIUS**.

ge·nip /gə'nip/ ▶ **n. 1** the edible fruit of a tropical American tree.

PRONUNCIATION KEY ə *ago, up*; ər *over, fur*; a *hat*; ā *ate*; ä *car*; e *let*; ē *see*; i *fit*; ī *by*; NG *sing*; ō *go*; ô *law, for*; oi *toy*; o͝o *good*; o͞o *goo*; ou *out*; TH *thin*; T͟H *then*; ZH *vision*

g

2 (also **genipap tree** /ˈjenəˌpap/) either of two tropical American trees that yield this fruit. ● (also **guinep** /giˈnep/) a large spreading tree (*Melicoccus bijugatus*, family Sapindaceae). ● another term for GENIPAPO.
– ORIGIN mid 18th cent.: from American Spanish *quenepo* 'guinep tree,' *quenepa*, denoting the fruit.

gen·i·pa·po /ˌjenəˈpapō/ (also **genipap tree** /ˈjenəˌpap/) ▶ n. (pl. **genipapos**) a tropical American tree of the bedstraw family that yields useful timber. Its fruit has a jellylike pulp that is used for flavoring drinks and to make a black dye. Also called GENIP. ● *Genipa americana*, family Rubiaceae. ■ a drink, flavoring, or dye made from this fruit.
– ORIGIN early 17th cent.: from Portuguese *jenipapo*, from Tupi.

genit. ▶ abbr. Grammar genitive.

gen·i·tal /ˈjenitl/ ▶ adj. of or relating to the human or animal reproductive organs: *conditions of the lower genital tract.* ■ Psychoanalysis (in Freudian theory) relating to or denoting the final stage of psychosexual development reached in adulthood.
▶ n. (**genitals**) a person or animal's external organs of reproduction.
– ORIGIN late Middle English: from Old French, or from Latin *genitalis*, from *genitus*, past participle of *gignere* 'beget.'

g

gen·i·tal her·pes ▶ n. a disease characterized by blisters in the genital area, caused by a variety of the herpes simplex virus.

gen·i·ta·li·a /ˌjeniˈtālēə, -ˈtālyə/ ▶ plural n. formal or technical the genitals.
– ORIGIN late 19th cent.: from Latin, neuter plural of *genitalis* (see GENITAL).

gen·i·tal wart ▶ n. a small growth occurring in the anal or genital areas, caused by a virus that is spread esp. by sexual contact.

gen·i·tive /ˈjenitiv/ Grammar ▶ adj. relating to or denoting a case of nouns and pronouns (and words in grammatical agreement with them) indicating possession or close association.
▶ n. a word in the genitive case. ■ (**the genitive**) the genitive case.
– DERIVATIVES **gen·i·ti·val** /ˌjeniˈtīvəl/ adj., **gen·i·ti·val·ly** /ˌjeniˈtīvəlē/ adv.
– ORIGIN late Middle English: from Old French *genitif, -ive* or Latin *genitivus* (*casus*) '(case) of production or origin,' from *gignere* 'beget.'

gen·i·tor /ˈjenitər/ ▶ n. Anthropology a person's biological father. Often contrasted with PATER.
– ORIGIN late Middle English (in the sense 'father'): from Old French *geniteur* or Latin *genitor*, from the root of *gignere* 'beget.' The current sense dates from the mid 20th cent.

gen·i·to·u·ri·nar·y /ˌjenitōˈyo͝orəˌnerē/ ▶ adj. [attrib.] chiefly Medicine of or relating to the genital and urinary organs.

gen·i·ture /ˈjenichər, -ˌcho͝or/ ▶ n. archaic a person's birth or parentage.
– ORIGIN late Middle English: from Old French *geniture* or Latin *genitura*, from the root of *gignere* 'beget.'

gen·ius /ˈjēnyəs/ ▶ n. (pl. **geniuses**) **1** exceptional intellectual or creative power or other natural ability: *she was a teacher of genius* | *Gardner had a real genius for tapping wealth.*
2 a person who is exceptionally intelligent or creative, either generally or in some particular respect: *one of the great musical geniuses of the 20th century.*
3 (pl. **genii** /ˈjēnēˌī/) (in some mythologies) a guardian spirit associated with a person, place, or institution. ■ a person regarded as exerting a powerful influence over another for good or evil: *he sees Adams as the man's evil genius.*
4 (pl. **genii**) the prevalent character or spirit of something such as a nation or age: *Boucher's paintings did not suit the austere genius of neoclassicism.*
– ORIGIN late Middle English: from Latin, 'attendant spirit present from one's birth, innate ability or inclination,' from the root of *gignere* 'beget.' The original sense 'tutelary spirit attendant on a person' gave rise to a sense 'a person's characteristic disposition' (late 16th cent.), which led to a sense 'a person's natural ability,' and finally 'exceptional natural ability' (mid 17th cent.).

ge·ni·us lo·ci /ˈjēnēəs ˈlōsī, -kī/ ▶ n. [in sing.] the prevailing character or atmosphere of a place. ■ the presiding god or spirit of a place.
– ORIGIN early 17th cent.: Latin, literally 'spirit of the place.'

genl. ▶ abbr. general.

gen·lock /ˈjenˌläk/ ▶ n. a device for maintaining synchronization between two different video signals, or between a video signal and a computer or audio signal, enabling video images and computer graphics to be mixed.
▶ v. [no obj.] maintain synchronization between two signals using the genlock technique.
– ORIGIN 1960s: from GENERATOR + the verb LOCK¹.

Gen·o·a /ˈjenōə/ a seaport on the northwestern coast of Italy, capital of Liguria region; pop. 611,171 (2008). It was the birthplace of Christopher Columbus. Italian name GENOVA.
– DERIVATIVES **Gen·o·ese** /ˌjenōˈēz, -ˈēs/ adj. & n.

gen·o·a /ˈjenōə/ ▶ n. (also **genoa jib**) Sailing a large jib or foresail whose foot extends aft of the mast, used esp. on racing yachts.
– ORIGIN late 19th cent.: so named because of association with the city of GENOA.

gen·o·cide /ˈjenəˌsīd/ ▶ n. the deliberate killing of a large group of people, esp. those of a particular ethnic group or nation.
– DERIVATIVES **gen·o·cid·al** /ˌjenəˈsīdl/ adj.
– ORIGIN 1940s: from Greek *genos* 'race' + -CIDE.

ge·noise /zhənˈwäz/ ▶ n. a sponge cake with melted butter incorporated into the batter.

ge·nome /ˈjēˌnōm/ ▶ n. Biology the haploid set of chromosomes in a gamete or microorganism, or in each cell of a multicellular organism. ■ the complete set of genes or genetic material present in a cell or organism.
– DERIVATIVES **ge·no·mic** /jēˈnämik, -ˈnō-, ji-/ adj.
– ORIGIN 1930s: blend of GENE and CHROMOSOME.

ge·nome map ▶ n. a record of the entire genome of an organism, consisting of correctly ordered gene maps.

ge·no·mics /jēˈnōmiks, -ˈnäm-/ ▶ plural n. [treated as sing.] the branch of molecular biology concerned with the structure, function, evolution, and mapping of genomes.
– ORIGIN 1980s: from *genome* 'the complete set of genes present in an organism' + *-ics*.

gen·o·type /ˈjenəˌtīp, ˈjē-/ ▶ n. Biology the genetic constitution of an individual organism. Often contrasted with PHENOTYPE.
▶ v. [with obj.] investigate the genetic constitution of (an individual organism): *the person appointed will be responsible for maintaining and genotyping many different lines of zebra fish.*
– DERIVATIVES **gen·o·typ·ic** /ˌjenəˈtipik, jē-/ adj.
– ORIGIN early 20th cent.: from German *Genotypus*, from Greek *genos* 'race, offspring' + *-tupos* 'type.'

-genous ▶ comb. form **1** producing; inducing: *erogenous.*
2 originating in: *endogenous.*
– ORIGIN from -GEN + -OUS.

Ge·no·va /ˈjenəvə/ Italian name for GENOA.

gen·re /ˈzhänrə/ ▶ n. a category of artistic composition, as in music or literature, characterized by similarities in form, style, or subject matter.
– ORIGIN early 19th cent.: French, literally 'a kind' (see GENDER).

gen·re paint·ing ▶ n. a style of painting depicting scenes from ordinary life, esp. domestic situations. Genre painting is associated particularly with 17th-century Dutch and Flemish artists.
– DERIVATIVES **gen·re paint·er** n.

gens /jenz/ ▶ n. (pl. **gentes** /ˈjentēz/) **1** a group of families in ancient Rome who shared a name and claimed a common origin.
2 Anthropology a group of people who are related through their male ancestors.
– ORIGIN Latin, from the root of *gignere* 'beget.'

Gent /KHent/ Flemish name for GHENT.

gent /jent/ ▶ n. informal a gentleman. ■ (**the Gents**) Brit. a men's public toilet.
– ORIGIN mid 16th cent.: originally a standard written abbreviation; a colloquial usage since the early 19th cent.

gen·ta·mi·cin /ˌjentəˈmīsin/ ▶ n. a broad-spectrum antibiotic used chiefly for severe systemic infections. ● This antibiotic is derived from bacteria of the genus *Micromonospora*.
– ORIGIN mid 20th cent.: from *genta-* (of unknown origin) + *-micin* (alteration of -MYCIN).

gen·teel /jenˈtēl/ ▶ adj. polite, refined, or respectable, often in an affected or ostentatious way.
– DERIVATIVES **gen·teel·ly** adv., **gen·teel·ness** n.
– ORIGIN late 16th cent. (in the sense 'fashionable, stylish'): from French *gentil* 'well-born.' From the 17th cent. to the 19th cent. the word was used in such senses as 'of good social position,' 'having the manners of a well-born person,' 'well-bred.' The ironic or derogatory implication dates from the 19th cent.

gen·teel·ism /jenˈtēlizəm/ ▶ n. a word or expression used because it is thought to be socially more acceptable than the everyday word: *in German usage "sister" was the accepted genteelism for "mistress."*

gen·tes /ˈjentēz/ plural form of GENS.

gen·tian /ˈjenchən/ ▶ n. a plant of temperate and mountainous regions, typically with violet or vivid blue trumpet-shaped flowers. Many kinds are cultivated as ornamentals, esp. as arctic alpines, and some are of medicinal use. ● Genera *Gentiana* and *Gentianella*, family Gentianaceae: numerous species, including the four-petaled **fringed gentian** (*Gentiana crinita*) of North America. ■ a tonic liquor formerly extracted from the root of the gentian.
– ORIGIN late Middle English: from Latin *gentiana*, according to Pliny named after *Gentius*, king of Illyria, who is said to have discovered the medicinal properties of a common species.

fringed gentian

gen·tian vi·o·let ▶ n. a synthetic violet dye derived from rosaniline, used as an antiseptic.

gen·tile /ˈjentīl/ ▶ adj. **1** (**Gentile**) not Jewish: *Christianity spread from Jewish into Gentile cultures.* ■ (of a person) not belonging to one's own religious community. ■ (in the Mormon church) non-Mormon.
2 chiefly Anthropology of, relating to, or indicating a nation or clan, esp. a gens.
▶ n. (**Gentile**) a person who is not Jewish.
– ORIGIN late Middle English: from Latin *gentilis* 'of a family or nation, of the same clan' (used in the Vulgate to refer to non-Jews), from *gens, gent-* 'family, race,' from the root of *gignere* 'beget.'

Gen·ti·le da Fa·bri·a·no /jenˈtēlā də ˌfäbrēˈänō/ (*c.*1370–1427), Italian painter. His major surviving work is *The Adoration of the Magi* (1423), an altarpiece.

gen·til·i·ty /jenˈtilitē/ ▶ n. social superiority as demonstrated by genteel manners, behavior, or appearances: *her grandmother's pretensions to gentility.*
– ORIGIN Middle English (in the sense 'honorable birth'): from Old French *gentilite*, from *gentil* (see GENTLE).

gen·tle /ˈjentl/ ▶ adj. (**gentler, gentlest**) **1** (of a person) mild in temperament or behavior; kind or tender: *he was a gentle, sensitive man.* ■ archaic (of a person) noble or having the qualities attributed to noble birth; courteous; chivalrous.
2 moderate in action, effect, or degree; not harsh or severe: *a little gentle persuasion* | *a gentle breeze.* ■ (of a slope) gradual: *a gentle embankment.*
▶ v. make or become gentle; calm or pacify: [no obj.] *Cobb's tone gentled a little.* ■ [with obj.] make (an animal) docile by gentle handling: *a bird that has been gentled enough to sit on the hand.*
– DERIVATIVES **gen·tle·ness** n., **gen·tly** /-tlē/ adv.
– ORIGIN Middle English: from Old French *gentil* 'highborn, noble,' from Latin *gentilis* 'of the same clan' (see GENTILE). The original sense was 'nobly born,' hence 'courteous, chivalrous,' later 'mild, moderate in action or disposition' (mid 16th cent.).

gen·tle breeze ▶ n. a light wind of force 3 on the Beaufort scale (7–10 knots or 8–12 mph).

gent·le·folk /ˈjentlˌfōk/ ▶ plural n. archaic people of high social position.

gen·tle·la·dy ▶ n. a polite form of a address for a woman, used esp. to a congresswoman during a congressional debate.

gent·le·man /ˈjentlmən/ ▶ n. (pl. **gentlemen**) **1** a chivalrous, courteous, or honorable man: *he behaved like a perfect gentleman.* ■ a man of good social position, esp. one of wealth and leisure. ■ (in the UK) a man of noble birth attached to a royal household.
2 a polite or formal way of referring to a man: *opposite her an old gentleman sat reading.* ■ (**gentlemen**) used as a polite form of address to a group of men: *"Can I help you, gentlemen?"* ■ used as a courteous designation for a male fellow member of the US House of Representatives.
– ORIGIN Middle English (in the sense 'man of noble birth'): from GENTLE + MAN, translating Old French *gentilz hom*. In later use the term denoted a man of

a good family (esp. one entitled to a coat of arms) but not of the nobility.

gen·tle·man-at-arms ▶ **n.** (pl. **gentlemen-at-arms**) one of the bodyguards of the British monarch on ceremonial occasions.

gen·tle·man farm·er ▶ **n.** (pl. **gentlemen farmers**) a well-to-do man who runs a farm for pleasure.

gen·tle·man·ly /ˈjentlmənlē/ ▶ **adj.** (of a man) befitting a gentleman; chivalrous, courteous, or honorable: *a paragon of gentlemanly conduct.*
– DERIVATIVES **gen·tle·man·li·ness** **n.**

gen·tle·man's a·gree·ment (also **gentlemen's agreement**) ▶ **n.** an arrangement or understanding which is based upon the trust of both or all parties, rather than being legally binding.

gen·tle·man's gen·tle·man ▶ **n.** a valet.

gen·tle·peo·ple ▶ **plural n.** a polite or formal way of addressing or referring to a group of people.

gen·tle·wom·an /ˈjentlˌwo͝omən/ ▶ **n.** (pl. **gentlewomen**) archaic a woman of high social standing.

gen·too /ˈjento͞o/ (also **gentoo penguin**) ▶ **n.** a tall penguin with a white triangular patch above the eye, breeding on subantarctic islands. ● *Pygoscelis papua*, family Spheniscidae.
– ORIGIN mid 19th cent.: perhaps from Anglo-Indian *Gentoo* 'a Hindu,' from Portuguese *gentio* 'gentile.'

gen·tri·fy /ˈjentrəˌfī/ ▶ **v.** (**gentrifies**, **gentrifying**, **gentrified**) [with obj.] renovate and improve (esp. a house or district) so that it conforms to middle-class taste. ■ (usu. as adj. **gentrified**) make (someone or their way of life) more refined or dignified.
– DERIVATIVES **gen·tri·fi·ca·tion** /ˌjentrəfiˈkāsHən/ **n.**, **gen·tri·fi·er** **n.**

gen·try /ˈjentrē/ ▶ **n.** (often **the gentry**) people of good social position, specifically (in the UK) the class of people next below the nobility in position and birth: *a member of the landed gentry.* ■ [with adj.] people of a specified class or group: *a New Orleans family of Creole gentry.*
– ORIGIN late Middle English (in the sense 'superiority of birth or rank'): from Anglo-Norman French *genterie*, based on *gentil* (see GENTLE).

ge·nu /ˈjēn(y)o͞o, ˈjen(y)o͞o/ ▶ **n.** (pl. **genua** /ˈjen(y)o͞oə/) Anatomy the knee. ■ Anatomy & Biology a part of certain structures resembling a knee, in particular a bend in the corpus callosum of mammals.
– ORIGIN mid 19th cent.: from Latin.

gen·u·flect /ˈjenyəˌflekt/ ▶ **v.** [no obj.] lower one's body briefly by bending one knee to the ground, typically in worship or as a sign of respect: *she genuflected and crossed herself.* ■ [with adverbial] show deference or servility: *politicians had to genuflect to the far left to advance their careers.*
– DERIVATIVES **gen·u·flec·tion** /ˌjenyəˈfleksHən/ **n.**, **gen·u·flec·tor** /-tər/ **n.**
– ORIGIN mid 17th cent. (in the sense 'bend (the knee)'): from ecclesiastical Latin *genuflectere*, from Latin *genu* 'knee' + *flectere* 'to bend.'

gen·u·ine /ˈjenyo͞oin/ ▶ **adj.** truly what something is said to be; authentic: *each book is bound in genuine leather.* ■ (of a person, emotion, or action) sincere: *she had no doubts as to whether Tom was genuine | a genuine attempt to delegate authority.*
– DERIVATIVES **gen·u·ine·ly** **adv.**, **gen·u·ine·ness** **n.**
– ORIGIN late 16th cent. (in the sense 'natural or proper'): from Latin *genuinus*, from *genu* 'knee' (with reference to the Roman custom of a father acknowledging paternity of a newborn child by placing it on his knee); later associated with *genus* 'birth, race, stock.'

ge·nus /ˈjēnəs/ ▶ **n.** (pl. **genera** /ˈjenərə/ or **genuses**) Biology a principal taxonomic category that ranks above species and below family, and is denoted by a capitalized Latin name, e.g., *Leo.* ■ (in philosophical and general use) a class of things that have common characteristics and that can be divided into subordinate kinds.
– ORIGIN mid 16th cent.: from Latin, 'birth, race, stock.'

Gen-X·er /ˌjen ˈeksər/ ▶ **n.** informal a member of Generation X (born in the 1960s and 1970s). Also called XER.

-geny ▶ **comb. form** denoting the mode by which something develops or is produced: *orogeny | organogeny.*
– ORIGIN related to French *-génie*; both forms derive from Greek *-geneia*, from *gen-* (root of *gignomai* 'be born, become' and *genos* 'a kind').

Gen-Y·er /ˌjen ˈwīər/ ▶ **n.** informal a member of Generation Y (born in the 1980s and 1990s). Also called MILLENNIAL.

Geo. ▶ **abbr.** dated George.

geo- ▶ **comb. form** of or relating to the earth: *geocentric | geochemistry.*
– ORIGIN from Greek *gē* 'earth.'

ge·o·bot·a·ny /ˌjēōˈbätn-ē/ ▶ **n.** another term for PHYTOGEOGRAPHY.
– DERIVATIVES **ge·o·bo·tan·i·cal** /-bəˈtanikəl/ **adj.**, **ge·o·bot·a·nist** /-ˈbätn-ist/ **n.**

ge·o·cach·ing /ˈjēōˌkasHiNG/ ▶ **n.** the recreational activity of hunting for and finding a hidden object by means of GPS coordinates posted on a website.
– DERIVATIVES **ge·o·cach·er** **n.**
– ORIGIN from *geo(graphical)* +*cache* + *-ing.*

ge·o·cen·tric /ˌjēōˈsentrik/ ▶ **adj.** having or representing the earth as the center, as in former astronomical systems. Compare with HELIOCENTRIC. ■ Astronomy measured from or considered in relation to the center of the earth.
– DERIVATIVES **ge·o·cen·tri·cal·ly** /-trik(ə)lē/ **adv.**, **ge·o·cen·trism** /-trizəm/ **n.**

ge·o·chem·is·try /ˌjēōˈkeməstrē/ ▶ **n.** the study of the chemical composition of the earth and its rocks and minerals.
– DERIVATIVES **ge·o·chem·i·cal** /-ˈkemikəl/ **adj.**, **ge·o·chem·ist** /-ˈkemist/ **n.**

ge·o·chro·nol·o·gy /ˌjēōkrəˈnäləjē/ ▶ **n.** the branch of geology concerned with the dating of rock formations and geological events.
– DERIVATIVES **ge·o·chron·o·log·i·cal** /-ˌkränəˈläjikəl/ **adj.**, **ge·o·chro·nol·o·gist** /-jist/ **n.**

ge·o·chron·o·met·ric /ˌjēōˌkränəˈmetrik/ ▶ **adj.** of or relating to geochronological measurement.
– DERIVATIVES **ge·o·chro·nom·e·try** /-krəˈnämətrē/ **n.**

ge·o·code /ˈjēōˌkōd/ ▶ **n.** the characterization of a region, neighborhood, etc., based on population statistics such as the average age or income of its inhabitants, used esp. for marketing purposes.

ge·ode /ˈjēōd/ ▶ **n.** a small cavity in rock lined with crystals or other mineral matter. ■ a rock containing such a cavity.
– DERIVATIVES **ge·od·ic** /jēˈädik/ **adj.**
– ORIGIN late 17th cent.: via Latin from Greek *geōdēs* 'earthy,' from *gē* 'earth.'

ge·o·des·ic /ˌjēəˈdesik, -ˈdē-/ ▶ **adj.** **1** of, relating to, or denoting the shortest possible line between two points on a sphere or other curved surface.
2 another term for GEODETIC.
▶ **n.** a geodesic line or structure.

ge·o·des·ic dome ▶ **n.** a dome constructed of short struts following geodesic lines and forming an open framework of triangles or polygons. The principles of its construction were described by Buckminster Fuller.

geodesic dome

ge·od·e·sy /jēˈädəsē/ ▶ **n.** the branch of mathematics dealing with the shape and area of the earth or large portions of it.
– DERIVATIVES **ge·od·e·sist** /-sist/ **n.**
– ORIGIN late 16th cent.: from modern Latin *geodaesia*, from Greek *geōdaisia*, from *gē* 'earth' + *daiein* 'to divide.'

ge·o·det·ic /ˌjēəˈdetik/ ▶ **adj.** of or relating to geodesy, esp. as applied to land surveying.
– ORIGIN late 17th cent.: from Greek *geōdaitēs* 'land surveyor,' from *geōdaisia* (see GEODESY).

ge·o·det·ic sur·vey ▶ **n.** a land survey with corrections made to account for the curvature of the earth's surface.

ge·o·duck /ˈgo͞oēˌdək/ ▶ **n.** a giant mud-burrowing bivalve mollusk occurring on the west coast of North America, where it is collected for food. Its shell valves are not large enough to enclose its body and very long siphon. ● *Panopea generosa*, family Hyatellidae.
– ORIGIN late 19th cent.: from Puget Sound Salish.

ge·o·ec·o·nom·ics /ˌjēōˌekəˈnämiks, -ēkə-/ ▶ **plural n.** [treated as sing.] **1** the study of the economic trends and conditions of the world's countries and how they are related; economics considered on the broadest global scale.
2 the economic policies or conditions of a country as seen in a global perspective.

ge·o·en·gi·neer·ing /ˌjēōenjəˈni(ə)riNG/ ▶ **n.** the deliberate large-scale manipulation of an environmental process that affects the earth's climate, in an attempt to counteract the effects of global warming.

Geof·frey of Mon·mouth /ˈjefrē əv ˈmänˌməTH/ (*c.*1100–*c.*54), Welsh chronicler. His *Historia Regum Britanniae* (*c.*1139; first printed in 1508), an account of the kings of Britain, was a major source for English literature, esp. for the tales of King Arthur.

geog. ▶ **abbr.** ■ geographer. ■ geographic. ■ geographical. ■ geography.

ge·o·graph·i·cal /ˌjēəˈgrafikəl/ ▶ **adj.** of or relating to geography.
– DERIVATIVES **ge·o·graph·ic** **adj.**, **ge·o·graph·i·cal·ly** /-ik(ə)lē/ **adv.**
– ORIGIN mid 16th cent.: from French *géographique* or late Latin *geographicus*, from Greek *geōgraphikos*, from *geōgraphos* 'geographer,' from *gē* 'earth' + *graphein* 'write, draw.'

ge·o·graph·i·cal mile ▶ **n.** a distance equal to one minute of longitude or latitude at the equator (about 1,850 meters).

ge·og·ra·phy /jēˈägrəfē/ ▶ **n.** the study of the physical features of the earth and its atmosphere, and of human activity as it affects and is affected by these, including the distribution of populations and resources, land use, and industries. ■ [usu. in sing.] the nature and relative arrangement of places and physical features: *knowing the geography and topology of the battlefield.*
– DERIVATIVES **ge·og·ra·pher** /-fər/ **n.**
– ORIGIN late 15th cent.: from French *géographie* or Latin *geographia*, from Greek *geōgraphia*, from *gē* 'earth' + *-graphia* 'writing.'

g

ge·oid /ˈjē-oid/ ▶ **n.** (**the geoid**) the hypothetical shape of the earth, coinciding with mean sea level and its imagined extension under (or over) land areas.
– ORIGIN late 19th cent.: from Greek *geoeidēs*, from *gē* 'earth' + *-oeidēs* (see -OID).

geol. ▶ **abbr.** ■ geologic. ■ geological. ■ geologist. ■ geology.

ge·o·log·i·cal sur·vey ▶ **n.** a detailed and systematic study of the topography, geology, and mineral resources of an area or country.

ge·ol·o·gy /jēˈäləjē/ ▶ **n.** the science that deals with the earth's physical structure and substance, its history, and the processes that act on it. ■ the geological features of an area: *the geology of the Outer Hebrides.* ■ the geological features of a planetary body: *the geology of the surface of Mars.*
– DERIVATIVES **ge·o·log·ic** /ˌjēəˈläjik/ **adj.**, **ge·o·log·i·cal** /ˌjēəˈläjikəl/ **adj.**, **ge·o·log·i·cal·ly** /ˌjēəˈläjik(ə)lē/ **adv.**, **ge·ol·o·gist** /-jist/ **n.**, **ge·ol·o·gize** /-jīz/ **v.**
– ORIGIN late 18th cent.: from modern Latin *geologia*, from Greek *gē* 'earth' + *-logia* (see -LOGY).

geom. ▶ **abbr.** ■ geometric. ■ geometrical. ■ geometry.

ge·o·mag·net·ic e·qua·tor ▶ **n.** a notional circle on the earth's surface, the plane of which is equidistant between the north and south magnetic poles and perpendicular to the magnetic field.

ge·o·mag·net·ism /ˌjēōˈmagniˌtizəm/ ▶ **n.** the branch of geology concerned with the magnetic properties of the earth.
– DERIVATIVES **ge·o·mag·net·ic** /-ˌmagˈnetik/ **adj.**, **ge·o·mag·net·i·cal·ly** /-ˌmagˈnetik(ə)lē/ **adv.**

ge·o·man·cy /ˈjēəˌmansē/ ▶ **n.** **1** the art of placing or arranging buildings or other sites auspiciously.
2 divination from configurations seen in a handful of earth thrown on the ground, or by interpreting lines or textures on the ground.
– DERIVATIVES **ge·o·man·cer** /-sər/ **n.**, **ge·o·man·tic** /ˌjēəˈmantik/ **adj.**

ge·o·mat·ics /ˌjēəˈmatiks/ ▶ **plural n.** [treated as sing.] the application of computerization to information in geography and related fields.
– DERIVATIVES **ge·o·mat·ic** **adj.**
– ORIGIN 1980s: blend of *geography* and *informatics.*

ge·om·e·ter /jēˈämitər/ ▶ **n.** **1** a person skilled in geometry.
2 (also **geometer moth**) Entomology a geometrid moth or its caterpillar.
– ORIGIN late Middle English: from late Latin *geometra*, based on Greek *geōmetrēs*, from *gē* 'earth' + *metrēs* 'measurer.'

ge·o·met·ric /ˌjēəˈmetrik/ ▶ **adj.** **1** of or relating to geometry, or according to its methods.
2 (of a design) characterized by or decorated with regular lines and shapes: *traditional Hopi geometric forms.* ■ (**Geometric**) Archaeology of or denoting a period of Greek culture (around 900–700 BC) characterized by geometrically decorated pottery.
– DERIVATIVES **ge·o·met·ri·cal** **adj.**, **ge·o·met·ri·cal·ly** /-ik(ə)lē/ **adv.**
– ORIGIN mid 17th cent.: via French from Latin *geometricus*, from Greek *geōmetrikos*, from *geōmetrēs* (see GEOMETER).

ge·o·met·ric i·so·mer (also **geometrical isomer**) ▶ n. Chemistry each of two or more compounds that differ from each other in the arrangement of groups with respect to a double bond, ring, or other rigid structure.
– DERIVATIVES **ge·o·met·ric i·som·er·ism** n.

ge·o·met·ric mean ▶ n. the central number in a geometric progression (e.g., *9* in *3, 9, 27*), also calculable as the *n*th root of a product of *n* numbers.

ge·o·met·ric pro·gres·sion ▶ n. a progression of numbers with a constant ratio between each number and the one before (e.g., each subsequent number is increased by a factor of 3 in the progression *1, 3, 9, 27, 81*).

ge·o·met·rics /ˌjēəˈmetriks/ ▶ plural n. straight lines and simple geometric shapes, e.g., circles and squares, used together to form a design or pattern: *their high-quality sheets in florals, classic solids, and bold geometrics can transform the look and feel of a room.*

ge·o·met·ric se·ries ▶ n. a series of numbers or quantities in geometric progression.

ge·om·e·trid /jēˈämətrid/ ▶ n. a moth of a large family (Geometridae), distinguished by having twiglike caterpillars that move by arching and straightening the body. Also called **GEOMETER**.
– ORIGIN late 19th cent.: from modern Latin *Geometridae* (plural), from the genus name *Geometra*, from Latin *geometres* (see **GEOMETER**).

ge·om·e·try /jēˈämətrē/ ▶ n. the branch of mathematics concerned with the properties and relations of points, lines, surfaces, solids, and higher dimensional analogs. ■ (pl. **geometries**) a particular mathematical system describing such properties: *non-Euclidean geometries.* ■ [in sing.] the shape and relative arrangement of the parts of something: *the geometry of spiders' webs.*
– ORIGIN Middle English: via Old French from Latin *geometria*, from Greek *gē* 'earth' + *metria* (see **-METRY**).

ge·o·mor·phic /ˌjēəˈmôrfik/ ▶ adj. of or relating to the form of the landscape and other natural features of the earth's surface.

ge·o·mor·phol·o·gy /ˌjēōˌmôrˈfäləjē/ ▶ n. the study of the physical features of the surface of the earth and their relation to its geological structures.
– DERIVATIVES **ge·o·mor·pho·log·i·cal** /-ˌmôrfəˈläjikəl/ adj., **ge·o·mor·phol·o·gist** /-jist/ n.

ge·o·park /ˈjēōpärk/ ▶ n. a UNESCO-designated area containing one or more sites of particular geological importance, intended to conserve the geological heritage and promote public awareness of it, typically through tourism.

ge·oph·a·gy /jēˈäfəjē/ ▶ n. the practice of eating earth, esp. chalk or clay in famine-stricken regions.
– ORIGIN mid 19th cent.: from **GEO-** 'earth' + Greek *phagia* 'eating, feeding' (from *phagein* 'eat').

ge·o·phys·ics /ˌjēōˈfiziks/ ▶ plural n. [treated as sing.] the physics of the earth.
– DERIVATIVES **ge·o·phys·i·cal** /-ˈfizikəl/ adj., **ge·o·phys·i·cist** /-ˈfizisist/ n.

ge·o·pol·i·tics /ˌjēōˈpäləˌtiks/ ▶ plural n. [treated as sing. or pl.] politics, esp. international relations, as influenced by geographical factors. ■ [treated as sing.] the study of politics of this type.
– DERIVATIVES **ge·o·po·lit·i·cal** /-pəˈlitikəl/ adj., **ge·o·po·lit·i·cal·ly** /-pəˈlitik(ə)lē/ adv., **ge·o·pol·i·ti·cian** /-ˌpäləˈtisHən/ n.

Geor·die /ˈjôrdē/ Brit. informal ▶ n. a person from Tyneside, an area in northeastern England. ■ the English dialect or accent typical of people from Tyneside.
▶ adj. of or relating to Tyneside, its people, or their accent or dialect: *Geordie humor*.
– ORIGIN mid 19th cent.: diminutive of the given name *George*.

George /jôrj/ the name of four kings of Great Britain and Ireland, one of Great Britain and Ireland (from 1920, of the United Kingdom), and one of the United Kingdom. ■ **George I** (1660–1727), great-grandson of James I; reigned 1714–27; elector of Hanover 1698–1727. The first British sovereign of the house of Hanover, he was unpopular in England because of his German manners and his inability to speak English. ■ **George II** (1683–1760), son of George I; reigned 1727–60; elector of Hanover 1727–60. He took an active part in the War of the Austrian Succession 1740–48. ■ **George III** (1738–1820), grandson of George II; reigned 1760–1820; elector of Hanover 1760–1815; king of Hanover 1815–20. He reigned during the time of the American Revolution and the War of 1812. His political influence declined from 1788 after bouts of mental illness. ■ **George IV** (1762–1830), son of George III; reigned 1820–30. Known as a patron of the arts and *bon viveur*, he had a bad reputation that was further damaged by his attempt to divorce his estranged wife **Caroline of Brunswick** just after coming to the throne. ■ **George V** (1865–1936), son of Edward VII; reigned 1910–36. He exercised restrained but important influence over British

Circles

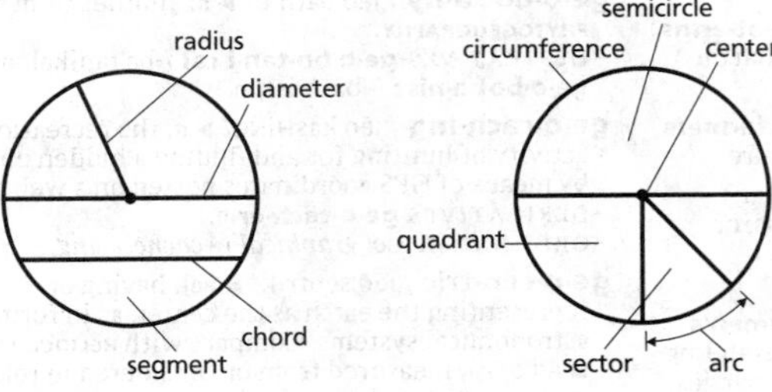

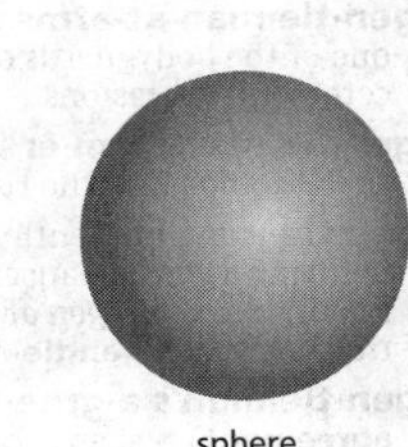

Quadrilaterals

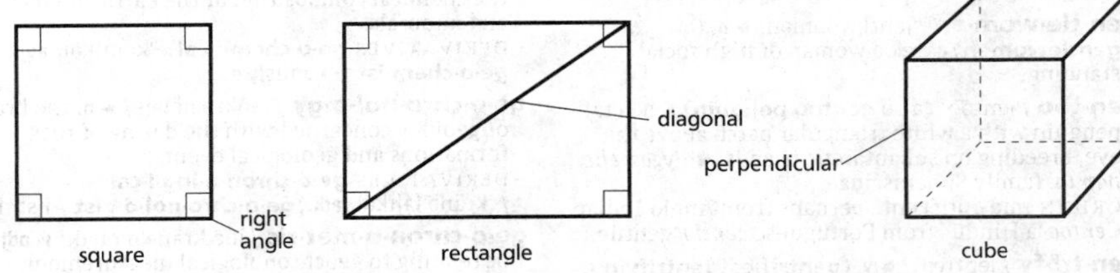

Triangles

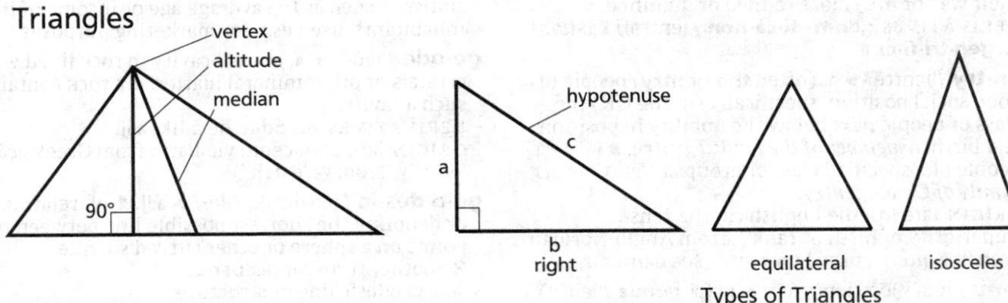

Types of Triangles

Conic Sections

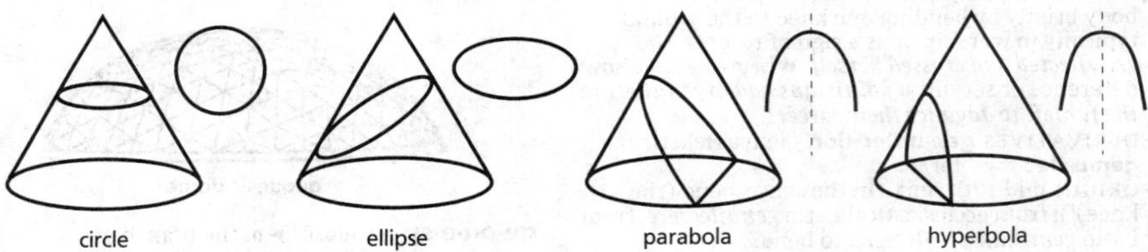

geometric shapes and forms

politics and played a significant role in the formation of the government in 1931. During World War I he changed the name of the royal house to Windsor. ■ **George VI** (1894–1952), son of George V; reigned 1936–52. He came to the throne when his older brother Edward VIII abdicated.

George, Lake /jôrj/ a resort lake in northeastern New York, northeast of Albany, near the Vermont border, scene of many 18th-century military actions.

George, St., patron saint of England. He is reputed in legend to have slain a dragon and may have been martyred near Lydda in Palestine some time before the reign of Constantine. Feast day, April 23.

Geor·ges Bank /ˈjôrjəz/ underwater rise in the Atlantic Ocean, between Massachusetts and Nova Scotia, site of important US and Canadian fishing zones.

George·town /ˈjôrjˌtoun/ **1** the capital of Guyana, a port at the mouth of the Demerara River; pop. 133,000 (est. 2007).
2 an affluent section of northwestern Washington, DC, home to government officials, shopping districts, and Georgetown University.

George Town 1 the capital of the Cayman Islands, on the island of Grand Cayman; pop. 28,000 (est. 2007).
2 the chief port of Malaysia and capital of the state of Penang, on Penang Island; pop. 158,800 (est. 2009). Also called **PENANG**.

geor·gette /jôrˈjet/ ▶ n. a thin silk or crepe dress material.
– ORIGIN early 20th cent.: named after *Georgette* de la Plante (*c.*1900), French dressmaker.

Geor·gia /ˈjôrjə/ **1** a country in southwestern Asia, on the eastern shore of the Black Sea; pop. 4,615,800 (est. 2009); capital, Tbilisi; languages, Georgian (official), Russian, and Armenian.

> An independent kingdom in medieval times, Georgia became part of the Russian empire in the 19th century and then was absorbed into the Soviet Union. When the Soviet Union broke up in 1991, Georgia became an independent republic outside of the Commonwealth of Independent States. Since then, separatist movements among the Abkhazian and South Ossetian minorities have led to outbreaks of ethnic conflict.

2 a state in the southeastern US, on the Atlantic coast; pop. 9,685,744 (est. 2008); capital, Atlanta; statehood, Jan. 2, 1788 (4). Founded as an English colony in 1732 and named after George II, it was one of the original thirteen states. It was the site of General Sherman's "March to the Sea" in 1864 during the Civil War.

Geor·gia, Strait of /ˈjôrjə/ an ocean passage between Vancouver Island and the mainland of British Columbia and Washington.

Geor·gian[1] /ˈjôrjən/ ▶ adj. **1** of or characteristic of the reigns of the British kings George I–IV (1714–1830). ■ of or relating to British architecture of this period that was characterized esp. by restrained elegance and the use of neoclassical styles.
2 of or characteristic of the reigns of the British kings George V and VI (1910–52). ■ of or relating to British literature of 1910–20, in particular pastoral poetry of a type strongly attacked by the early modernists.

Geor·gian[2] ▶ adj. of or relating to the country of Georgia, its people, or their language.

▶ n. 1 a native or inhabitant of Georgia, or a person of Georgian descent.
2 the South Caucasian (or Kartvelian) language, having its own alphabet, that is the official language of Georgia.

Geor·gian[3] ▶ adj. of or relating to the state of Georgia in the US.
▶ n. a native of Georgia.

geor·gic /ˈjôrjik/ ▶ n. a poem or book dealing with agriculture or rural topics. ■ (**Georgics**) the title of a didactic poem on farming by the Roman poet Virgil.
▶ adj. literary rustic; pastoral.
– ORIGIN early 16th cent.: via Latin from Greek *geōrgikos*, from *geōrgos* 'farmer.'

ge·o·sci·ence /ˌjēōˈsīəns, ˈjēōˌsīəns/ ▶ n. (also **geosciences**) earth sciences, esp. geology.
– DERIVATIVES **ge·o·sci·en·tist** /ˌjēōˈsīəntist, ˈjēōˌsīəntist/ n.

ge·o·spa·tial /ˌjēōˈspāsʜəl/ ▶ adj. Geography relating to or denoting data that is associated with a particular location.

ge·o·sphere /ˈjēōˌsfir/ ▶ n. any of the almost spherical concentric regions of matter that make up the earth and its atmosphere, as the lithosphere and hydrosphere.

ge·o·sta·tion·ar·y /ˌjēōˈstāsʜəˌnerē/ ▶ adj. (of an artificial satellite of the earth) moving in a geosynchronous orbit in the plane of the equator, so that it remains stationary in relation to a fixed point on the surface. This orbit is achieved at an altitude of 22,300 miles (35,900 km) above the earth. It is used by communication and meteorological satellites.

ge·o·stroph·ic /ˌjēəˈsträfik/ ▶ adj. Meteorology & Oceanography relating to or denoting the component of a wind or current that arises from a balance between pressure gradients and Coriolis forces.
– ORIGIN early 20th cent.: from **GEO-** 'of the earth' + Greek *strophē* 'a turning' (from *strephein* 'to turn').

ge·o·syn·chro·nous /ˌjēōˈsiɴɢkrənəs/ ▶ adj. (of an earth satellite or its orbit) having a period of rotation synchronous with that of the earth's rotation.

ge·o·syn·cline /ˌjēōˈsinˌklīn/ ▶ n. Geology a large-scale depression in the earth's crust containing very thick deposits.

ge·o·tag·ging /ˈjēōˌtagiɴɢ/ ▶ n. the practice of adding geographical information to digital photographs, typically the latitude and longitude of the location.

ge·o·tax·is /ˌjēōˈtaksis/ ▶ n. Biology the motion of a motile organism or cell in response to the force of gravity.
– DERIVATIVES **ge·o·tac·tic** /-ˈtaktik/ adj.

ge·o·tech·nics /ˌjēōˈtekniks/ ▶ plural n. [treated as sing.] the branch of civil engineering concerned with the study and modification of soil and rocks.
– DERIVATIVES **ge·o·tech·nic** adj., **ge·o·tech·ni·cal** /-nikəl/ adj.

ge·o·tec·ton·ic /ˌjēōtekˈtänik/ ▶ adj. another term for **TECTONIC**.

ge·o·ther·mal /ˌjēōˈᴛʜərməl/ (also **geothermic** /-ˈᴛʜərmik/) ▶ adj. of, relating to, or produced by the internal heat of the earth: *some 70% of Iceland's energy needs are met from geothermal sources.*

ge·o·tro·pism /jēˈätrəˌpizəm/ ▶ n. Botany the growth of the parts of plants with respect to the force of gravity. The upward growth of plant shoots is an instance of **negative geotropism**; the downward growth of roots is **positive geotropism**.
– DERIVATIVES **ge·o·trop·ic** /ˌjēəˈträpik, -ˈtrō-/ adj.
– ORIGIN late 19th cent.: from **GEO-** 'earth' + Greek *tropē* 'turning' + **-ISM**.

ger. ▶ abbr. Grammar ■ gerund. ■ gerundive.

Ge·ra /ˈgärä/ an industrial city in eastern central Germany, in Thuringia; pop. 102,700 (est. 2006).

ge·ra·ni·al /jəˈrānēəl/ ▶ n. Chemistry afragrant oil present in lemongrass oil and used in perfumery. ● an isomer of citral; chem. formula: $C_{10}H_{16}O$.
– ORIGIN late 19th cent.: from German, contraction of *Geraniumaldehyde*.

ge·ra·ni·ol /jəˈrānēˌôl, -ˌäl/ ▶ n. Chemistry a fragrant liquid present in some floral oils and used in perfumery. ● A terpenoid alcohol; chem. formula: $C_{10}H_{18}O$.
– ORIGIN late 19th cent.: from German, from **GERANIUM** + **-OL**.

ge·ra·ni·um /jəˈrānēəm/ ▶ n. a herbaceous plant or small shrub of a genus that comprises the cranesbills and their relatives. Geraniums bear a long narrow fruit that is said to be shaped like the bill of a crane. ● Genus *Geranium*, family Geraniaceae. ■ (in general or informal use) a cultivated pelargonium. ■ the scarlet color of many cultivated pelargoniums.
– ORIGIN modern Latin, from Greek *geranion*, from *geranos* 'crane.'

ger·ber·a /ˈgərbərə/ ▶ n. a plant of the daisy family, native to Asia and Africa, with large brightly colored flowers. ● Genus *Gerbera*, family Compositae: many species, in particular the widely cultivated Transvaal daisy.
– ORIGIN modern Latin, named after Traugott *Gerber* (died 1743), German naturalist.

ger·bil /ˈjərbəl/ ▶ n. 1 a burrowing mouselike rodent that is specially adapted to living in arid conditions, found in Africa and Asia. ● Subfamily Gerbillinae, family Muridae: several genera, in particular *Gerbillus*.
2 another term for **JIRD**.
– ORIGIN mid 19th cent.: from French *gerbille*, from modern Latin *gerbillus*, diminutive of *gerboa* (see **JERBOA**).

ger·e·nuk /ˈgerəˌno͝ok/ ▶ n. a slender East African antelope with a long neck, often browsing on tall bushes by standing on its hind legs. ● *Litocranius walleri*, family Bovidae.
– ORIGIN late 19th cent.: from Somali.

ger·i·at·ric /ˌjerēˈatrik/ ▶ adj. [attrib.] of or relating to old people, esp. with regard to their health care: *a geriatric hospital.*
▶ n. an old person, esp. one receiving special care: *a rest home for geriatrics.*
– ORIGIN 1920s: from Greek *gēras* 'old age' + *iatros* 'doctor,' on the pattern of *pediatric*.

> **USAGE** Geriatric is the normal, semiofficial term used in the US and Britain when referring to the health care of old people (*a geriatric ward; geriatric patients*). When used outside such contexts, however, it typically carries overtones of being worn out and decrepit and can therefore be offensive.

ger·i·at·rics /ˌjerēˈatriks/ ▶ plural n. [treated as sing. or pl.] the branch of medicine or social science dealing with the health and care of old people.
– DERIVATIVES **ger·i·a·tri·cian** /ˌjerēəˈtrisʜən/ n.

Gé·ri·cault /ˌʒʜerēˈkō/, (Jean Louis André) Théodore (1791–1824), French painter. His most noted work, *The Raft of the Medusa* (1819), depicts the survivors of a famous 1816 shipwreck.

germ /jərm/ ▶ n. 1 a microorganism, esp. one that causes disease.
2 a portion of an organism capable of developing into a new one or part of one. Compare with **GERM CELL**. ■ the embryo in a cereal grain or other plant seed. Compare with **WHEAT GERM**. ■ an initial stage from which something may develop: ***the germ of a brilliant idea.***
– DERIVATIVES **germ·y** adj. informal (sense 1).
– ORIGIN late Middle English (sense 2): via Old French from Latin *germen* 'seed, sprout.' Sense 1 dates from the late 19th cent.

Ger·man /ˈjərmən/ ▶ n. 1 a native or inhabitant of Germany. ■ a person of German descent: *Sudeten Germans.*
2 a West Germanic language used in Germany, Austria, and parts of Switzerland, and by communities in the US and elsewhere. See also **HIGH GERMAN, LOW GERMAN**.
3 (in full **German cotillion**) a complex dance in which one couple leads the other couples through a variety of figures and there is a continual change of partners.
▶ adj. of or relating to Germany, its people, or their language.
– ORIGIN from Latin *Germanus*, used to designate related peoples of central and northern Europe, a name perhaps given by Celts to their neighbors; compare with Old Irish *gair* 'neighbor.'

ger·man /ˈjərmən/ ▶ adj. archaic germane.
■ [postpositive] (of a sibling) having the same parents: *my brothers-german.*
– ORIGIN Middle English: from Old French *germain*, from Latin *germanus* 'genuine, of the same parents.'

Ger·man cock·roach ▶ n. a small, brown, common indoor cockroach found worldwide. ● *Blatella germanica*, order Dictyoptera.

Ger·man Dem·o·crat·ic Re·pub·lic (abbr.: **GDR, DDR**) official name for the former state of **East Germany** (see **GERMANY**).

ger·man·der /jərˈmandər/ ▶ n. a widely distributed plant of the mint family. Some kinds are cultivated as ornamentals and some are used in herbal medicine. ● Genus *Teucrium*, family Labiatae: many species, including the **American germander** (*T. canadense*) and the European **wall germander** (*T. chamaedrys*).
– ORIGIN late Middle English: from medieval Latin *germandra*, based on Greek *khamaidrus*, literally 'ground oak,' from *khamai* 'on the ground' + *drus* 'oak' (because the leaves of some species were thought to resemble those of the oak).

ger·man·der speed·well ▶ n. a speedwell with bright blue flowers and leaves resembling those of the germander, native to Eurasia but now common in North America. ● *Veronica chamaedrys*, family Scrophulariaceae.

ger·mane /jərˈmān/ ▶ adj. relevant to a subject under consideration: *that is not germane to our theme.*
– DERIVATIVES **ger·mane·ly** adv., **ger·mane·ness** n.
– ORIGIN early 17th cent.: variant of **GERMAN**, with which it was synonymous from Middle English. The current sense has arisen from a usage in Shakespeare's *Hamlet*.

Ger·man East Af·ri·ca a former German protectorate in East Africa 1891–1918 that corresponds to present-day Tanzania, Rwanda, and Burundi.

Ger·man Em·pire an empire in German-speaking central Europe, created by Bismarck in 1871 after the Franco-Prussian War by the union of twenty-five German states under the Hohenzollern king of Prussia. Also called **SECOND REICH**.

> Forming an alliance with Austria–Hungary, the German Empire became the greatest industrial power in Europe and engaged in colonial expansion in Africa, China, and the Far East. Tensions arising with other colonial powers led to World War I, after which the German Empire collapsed and the Weimar Republic was created.

g

Ger·man·ic /jərˈmanik/ ▶ adj. 1 of, relating to, or denoting the branch of the Indo-European language family that includes English, German, Dutch, Frisian, the Scandinavian languages, and Gothic. ■ of, relating to, or denoting the peoples of ancient northern and western Europe speaking such languages.
2 having characteristics of or attributed to Germans or Germany: *she had an almost Germanic regard for order.*
▶ n. the Germanic languages collectively. See also **EAST GERMANIC, NORTH GERMANIC, WEST GERMANIC**. ■ the unrecorded ancient language from which these developed, thought to have been spoken on the shores of the Baltic Sea in the 3rd millennium BC. Also called **PROTO-GERMANIC**.
– ORIGIN mid 17th cent.: from Latin *Germanicus*, from *Germanus* (see **GERMAN**).

Ger·man·ist /ˈjərmənist/ ▶ n. an expert in or student of the language, literature, and civilization of Germany, or of Germanic languages.

ger·ma·ni·um /jərˈmānēəm/ ▶ n. the chemical element of atomic number 32, a shiny gray semimetal. Germanium was important in the making of transistors and other semiconductor devices, but has been largely replaced by silicon. (Symbol: **Ge**)
– ORIGIN late 19th cent.: modern Latin, from Latin *Germanus* (see **GERMAN**).

Ger·man·ize /ˈjərməˌnīz/ ▶ v. [with obj.] make German; cause to adopt German language and customs: *the Poles had Germanized their family names.*
– DERIVATIVES **Ger·man·i·za·tion** /ˌjərmənīˈzāsʜən/ n.

Ger·man mea·sles ▶ plural n. [usu. treated as sing.] another term for **RUBELLA**.

Germano- ▶ comb. form German; German and ...: *Germanophile*. ■ relating to Germany: *Germanocentric*.

Ger·man·o·phile /jərˈmanəˌfīl/ ▶ n. a person who is fond of or greatly admires Germany or German people or culture.

Ger·man shep·herd (also **German shepherd dog**) ▶ n. a large dog of a breed often used as guard dogs or guide dogs or for police work.

German shepherd

Ger·man sil·ver ▶ n. a white alloy of nickel, zinc, and copper.

Ger·man South West Af·ri·ca a former German protectorate 1884–1918 in southwestern Africa that corresponds to present-day Namibia.

Ger·man·town /ˈjərmənˌtoun/ a historic residential section of northwestern Philadelphia in Pennsylvania, scene of a 1777 battle.

PRONUNCIATION KEY ə *ago, up*; ər *over, fur*; a *hat*; ā *ate*; ä *car*; e *let*; ē *see*; i *fit*; ī *by*; ɴɢ *sing*; ō *go*; ô *law, for*; oi *toy*; o͝o *good*; o͞o *goo*; ou *out*; ᴛʜ *thin*; ᴛʜ *then*; ʒʜ *vision*

Ger·ma·ny /ˈjərmənē/ a country in central Europe, on the Baltic Sea in the north; pop. 82,329,800 (est. 2009); capital, Berlin; official language, German. German name **DEUTSCHLAND**.

The multiplicity of small German states achieved real unity only with the rise of Prussia and the formation of the German Empire in the mid 19th century. After being defeated in World War I, Germany was taken over in the 1930s by the Nazi dictatorship that led to a policy of expansionism and eventually to complete defeat in World War II. Germany was occupied for a time by the victorious Allies and was partitioned. The western part (including West Berlin), which was occupied by the US, Britain, and France, became the Federal Republic of Germany or **West Germany**, with its capital at Bonn. The eastern part, occupied by the former Soviet Union, became the German Democratic Republic or **East Germany**, with its capital in East Berlin. West Germany emerged as a major European industrial power and was a founder member of the EEC, while the East remained under Soviet domination. After the general collapse of communism in eastern Europe, East and West Germany reunited on October 3, 1990.

g

germ cell ▸ **n.** Biology a cell containing half the number of chromosomes of a somatic cell and able to unite with one from the opposite sex to form a new individual; a gamete. ■ an embryonic cell with the potential of developing into a gamete.

ger·mi·cide /ˈjərməˌsīd/ ▸ **n.** a substance or other agent that destroys harmful microorganisms; an antiseptic.
– DERIVATIVES **ger·mi·cid·al** /ˌjərməˈsīdl/ **adj.**

Ger·mi·nal /ˈjərmənl/ ▸ **n.** the seventh month of the French Republican calendar (1793–1805), originally running from March 21 to April 19.

ger·mi·nal /ˈjərmənl/ ▸ **adj.** [attrib.] relating to or of the nature of a germ cell or embryo. ■ in the earliest stage of development. ■ providing material for future development: *the subject was revived in a germinal article by Charles Ferguson.*
– DERIVATIVES **ger·mi·nal·ly adv.**
– ORIGIN early 19th cent.: from Latin *germen, germin-* 'sprout, seed' + **-AL**.

ger·mi·nal disk (also **germinal disc**) ▸ **n.** another term for **BLASTODISK**.

ger·mi·nate /ˈjərməˌnāt/ ▸ **v.** [no obj.] (of a seed or spore) begin to grow and put out shoots after a period of dormancy. ■ [with obj.] cause (a seed or spore) to sprout in such a way. ■ come into existence and develop: *the idea germinated and slowly grew into an obsession.*
– DERIVATIVES **ger·mi·na·ble** /-nəbəl/ **adj.**, **ger·mi·na·tion** /ˌjərməˈnāsHən/ **n.**, **ger·mi·na·tive** /-ˌnātiv/ **adj.**, **ger·mi·na·tor** /-ˌnātər/ **n.**
– ORIGIN late 16th cent.: from Latin *germinat-* 'sprouted forth, budded,' from the verb *germinare*, from *germen, germin-* 'sprout, seed.'

Ger·mis·ton /ˈjərməstən/ a city in South Africa, southeast of Johannesburg; pop. 139,700 (est. 2001). It is the site of a large gold refinery.

germ lay·er ▸ **n.** Embryology each of the three layers of cells (ectoderm, mesoderm, and endoderm) that are formed in the early embryo.

germ line ▸ **n.** Biology a series of germ cells each descended or developed from earlier cells in the series, regarded as continuing through successive generations of an organism.

germ plasm ▸ **n.** Biology germ cells, collectively. ■ the genetic material of such cells.

germ war·fare ▸ **n.** another term for **BIOLOGICAL WARFARE**.

Ge·ron·i·mo[1] /jəˈränəˌmō/ (*c.*1829–1909), Apache chief. He resisted white encroachment on tribal lands in Arizona by leading his people in raids on settlers and US troops before he surrendered in 1886.

Geronimo

Ge·ron·i·mo[2] ▸ **exclam.** used to express exhilaration, esp. when leaping from a great height or moving at a high speed.
– ORIGIN World War II: by association with **GERONIMO**[1], adopted as a slogan by American paratroopers.

ge·ron·tic /jəˈräntik/ ▸ **adj.** of or relating to old age, elderly people, or senescent animals or plants.
– ORIGIN late 19th cent.: from Greek *gerōn, geront-* 'old man' + **-IC**.

ger·on·toc·ra·cy /ˌjerənˈtäkrəsē/ ▸ **n.** a state, society, or group governed by old people. ■ government based on rule by old people.
– DERIVATIVES **ge·ron·to·crat** /jəˈräntəˌkrat/ **n.**, **ge·ron·to·crat·ic** /jəˌräntəˈkratik/ **adj.**
– ORIGIN mid 19th cent.: from Greek *gerōn, geront-* 'old man' + **-CRACY**.

ger·on·tol·o·gy /ˌjerənˈtäləjē/ ▸ **n.** the scientific study of old age, the process of aging, and the particular problems of old people.
– DERIVATIVES **ge·ron·to·log·i·cal** /jəˌräntlˈäjikəl/ **adj.**, **ger·on·tol·o·gist** /-jist/ **n.**
– ORIGIN early 20th cent.: from Greek *gerōn, geront-* 'old man' + **-LOGY**.

-gerous ▸ **comb. form** bearing (a specified thing): *armigerous*.
– ORIGIN from Latin *-ger* 'bearing' (from the root of *gerere* 'to bear, carry') + **-OUS**.

Ger·ry /ˈjerē/, Elbridge (1744–1814), US politician. A signer of the Declaration of Independence in 1776 and vice president of the US 1813–14, his political maneuvering in Massachusetts gave rise to the term "gerrymander."

ger·ry·man·der /ˈjerēˌmandər/ ▸ **v.** [with obj.] (often as noun **gerrymandering**) manipulate the boundaries of (an electoral constituency) so as to favor one party or class. ■ achieve (a result) by such manipulation: *a total freedom to gerrymander the results they want.*
▸ **n.** an instance of such a practice.
– DERIVATIVES **ger·ry·man·der·er n.**
– ORIGIN early 19th cent.: from the name of Governor Elbridge *Gerry* of Massachusetts + **SALAMANDER**, from the supposed similarity between a salamander and the shape of a new voting district on a map drawn when he was in office (1812), the creation of which was felt to favor his party: the map (with claws, wings, and fangs added), was published in the Boston *Weekly Messenger*, with the title *The Gerry-Mander*.

Gersh·win /ˈgərˌsHwin/, George (1898–1937), US composer and pianist; born *Jacob Gershovitz*. He achieved success in 1919 with the song "Swanee" and went on to compose many successful songs and musicals, as well as *Rhapsody in Blue* (1924) and *An American in Paris* (1928) for orchestra and an opera, *Porgy and Bess* (1935). The lyrics for many of these were written by his brother **Ira Gershwin** (1896–1983).

ger·und /ˈjerənd/ ▸ **n.** Grammar a form that is derived from a verb but that functions as a noun, in English ending in *-ing*, e.g., *asking* in *do you mind my asking you?*
– ORIGIN early 16th cent.: from late Latin *gerundium*, from *gerundum*, variant of *gerendum*, the gerund of Latin *gerere* 'do.'

ger·un·dive /jəˈrəndiv/ ▸ **n.** Grammar (in Latin) a form that is derived from a verb but that functions as an adjective, denoting something "that should or must be done."
– ORIGIN Middle English (in the sense 'gerund'): from late Latin *gerundivus* (*modus*) 'gerundive (mood),' from *gerundium* (see **GERUND**).

Ge·sell·schaft /gəˈzelˌsHäft, -ˌsHaft/ ▸ **n.** social relations based on impersonal ties, as duty to a society or organization. Contrasted with **GEMEINSCHAFT**.
– ORIGIN German, from *Gesell(e)* 'companion' + *-schaft* (see **-SHIP**).

ges·ne·ri·ad /gesˈni(ə)rēˌad, jes-/ ▸ **n.** a tropical plant of a family that includes African violets, gloxinias, and their relatives. ● Family Gesneriaceae.
– ORIGIN mid 19th cent.: from modern Latin *Gesneria* (genus name), from the name of Conrad von *Gesner* (1516–65), Swiss naturalist, + **-AD**[1].

ges·so /ˈjesō/ ▸ **n.** (pl. **gessoes**) a hard compound of plaster of Paris or whiting in glue, used in sculpture or as a base for gilding or painting on wood.
– DERIVATIVES **ges·soed adj.**
– ORIGIN late 16th cent.: Italian, from Latin *gypsum* (see **GYPSUM**).

ge·stalt /gəˈsHtält, -ˈsHtôlt/ (also **Gestalt**) ▸ **n.** (pl. **gestalten** /-ˈsHtältn, -ˈsHtôltn/ or **gestalts**) Psychology an organized whole that is perceived as more than the sum of its parts.
– DERIVATIVES **ge·stalt·ism n.**, **ge·stalt·ist n.**
– ORIGIN 1920s: from German *Gestalt*, literally 'form, shape.'

Ge·stalt psy·chol·o·gy ▸ **n.** a movement in psychology founded in Germany in 1912, seeking to explain perceptions in terms of gestalts rather than by analyzing their constituents.

Ge·stalt ther·a·py ▸ **n.** a psychotherapeutic approach developed by Fritz Perls (1893–1970). It focuses on insight into gestalts in patients and their relations to the world, and often uses role-playing to aid the resolution of past conflicts.

Ge·sta·po /gəˈstäpō/ the German secret police under Nazi rule. It ruthlessly suppressed opposition to the Nazis in Germany and occupied Europe and sent Jews and others to concentration camps. From 1936 it was headed by Heinrich Himmler.
– ORIGIN German, from *Geheime Staatspolizei* 'secret state police.'

ges·tate /ˈjeˌstāt/ ▸ **v.** [no obj.] carry a fetus in the womb from conception to birth: ***rabbits gestate for approximately twenty-eight days*** | [with obj.] ***these***

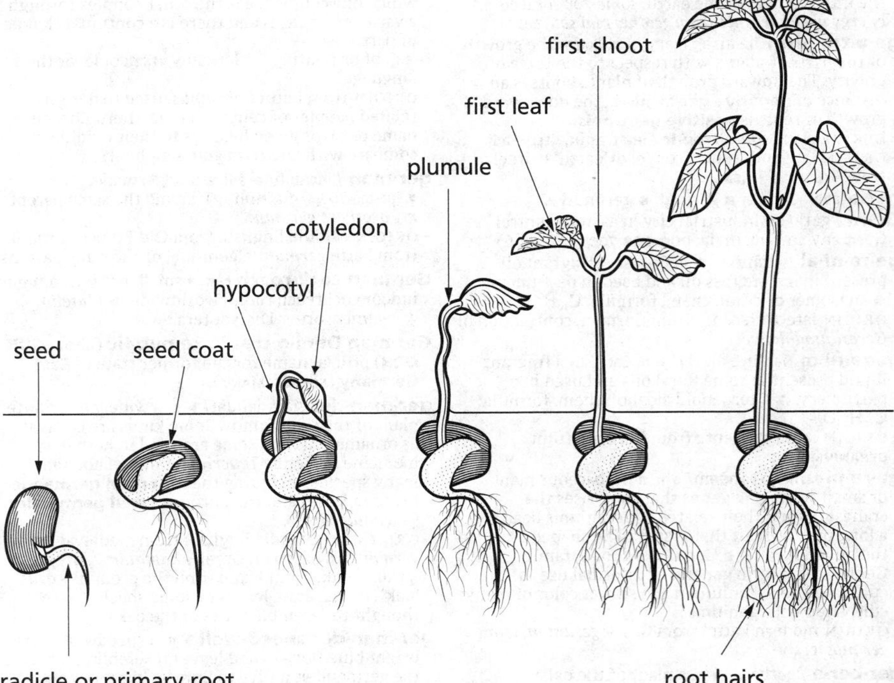

germination of a bean

individuals gestate male-based litters. ■ (of a fetus) undergo gestation. ■ develop over a long period: *a research trip he made while gestating his new book.*
– DERIVATIVES **ges·ta·tive** /je'stātiv, 'jestātiv/ **adj.**
– ORIGIN mid 19th cent.: from Latin *gestat-* 'carried in the womb,' from the verb *gestare.*

ges·ta·tion /je'stāSHən/ ▶ **n.** the process of carrying or being carried in the womb between conception and birth. ■ the development of something over a period of time: *various ideas are in the process of gestation.*
– DERIVATIVES **ges·ta·tion·al** /-SHənl/ **adj.**
– ORIGIN mid 16th cent. (denoting an excursion on horseback, in a carriage, etc., considered as exercise): from Latin *gestatio(n-),* from *gestare* 'carry, carry in the womb,' frequentative of *gerere* 'carry.'

ges·tic·u·late /je'stikyə,lāt/ ▶ **v.** [no obj.] use gestures, esp. dramatic ones, instead of speaking or to emphasize one's words: *they were shouting and gesticulating frantically at drivers who did not slow down.*
– DERIVATIVES **ges·tic·u·la·tive** /-,lātiv/ **adj.**, **ges·tic·u·la·tor** /-,lātər/ **n.**, **ges·tic·u·la·to·ry** /-lə,tôrē/ **adj.**
– ORIGIN early 17th cent.: from Latin *gesticulat-* 'gesticulated,' from the verb *gesticulari,* from *gesticulus,* diminutive of *gestus* 'action.'

ges·tic·u·la·tion /je,stikyə'lāSHən/ ▶ **n.** a gesture, esp. a dramatic one, used instead of speaking or to emphasize one's words: *he punctuated his speech with wild gesticulations | there was a lot of gesticulation.*

ges·ture /'jesCHər/ ▶ **n.** a movement of part of the body, esp. a hand or the head, to express an idea or meaning: *Alex made a gesture of apology | so much is conveyed by gesture.* ■ an action performed to convey one's feelings or intentions: *Maggie was touched by the kind gesture.* ■ an action performed for show in the knowledge that it will have no effect: *I hope the amendment will not be just a gesture.*
▶ **v.** [no obj.] make a gesture: *she gestured meaningfully with the pistol.* ■ [with obj.] express (something) with a gesture or gestures: *he gestured his dissent at this.* ■ [with obj. or infinitive] direct or invite (someone) to move somewhere specified: *he gestured her to a chair.*
– DERIVATIVES **ges·tur·al** **adj.**
– ORIGIN late Middle English: from medieval Latin *gestura,* from Latin *gerere* 'bear, wield, perform.' The original sense was 'bearing, deportment,' hence 'the use of posture and bodily movements for effect in oratory.'

ge·sund·heit /gə'zo͝ontīt/ ▶ **exclam.** used to wish good health to a person who has just sneezed.
– ORIGIN from German *Gesundheit* 'health.'

get /get/ ▶ **v.** (**gets, getting**; past **got** /gät/; past participle **got** or **gotten** /'gätn/) **1** [with obj.] come to have or hold (something); receive: *I got the impression that she wasn't happy.* ■ experience, suffer, or be afflicted with (something bad): *I got a sudden pain in my left eye.* ■ receive as a punishment or penalty: *I'll get the sack if things go wrong.* ■ contract (a disease or ailment): *I might be getting the flu.*
2 [with obj.] succeed in attaining, achieving, or experiencing; obtain: *I need all the sleep I can get.* ■ move in order to pick up or bring (something); fetch: *get another chair* | [with two objs.] *I'll get you a drink.* ■ tend to meet with or find in a specified place or situation: *it was nothing like the winters we get in Florida.* ■ travel by or catch (a bus, train, or other form of transport): *I'll get a taxi and be home in an hour.* ■ obtain (a figure or answer) as a result of calculation. ■ respond to a ring of (a telephone or doorbell) or the knock on (a door): *I'll get it!* ■ [in imperative] informal said as an invitation to notice or look at someone, esp. to criticize or ridicule them: *get her!*
3 [no obj.] enter or reach a specified state or condition; become: *he got very worried | it's getting late* | [with past participle] *you'll get used to it.* ■ [as auxiliary verb] used with a past participle to form the passive mood: *the cat got groomed.* ■ [with obj.] cause to be treated in a specified way: *get the form signed by a doctor.* ■ [with obj.] induce or prevail upon (someone) to do something: *Sophie got Beth to make a fire.* ■ [no obj., with infinitive] have the opportunity to do: *he got to try out a few of these new cars.* ■ [no obj., with present participle or infinitive] begin to be or do something, esp. gradually or by chance: *we got talking one evening.*
4 [no obj.] come, go, or make progress eventually or with some difficulty: *I got to the airport | they weren't going to get anywhere.* ■ move or come into a specified position, situation, or state: *she got into the car.* ■ [with obj.] succeed in making (someone or something) come, go, or make progress: *my honesty often gets me into trouble.* ■ informal reach a specified point or stage: *it's getting so I can't even think.* ■ [usu. in imperative] informal go away.

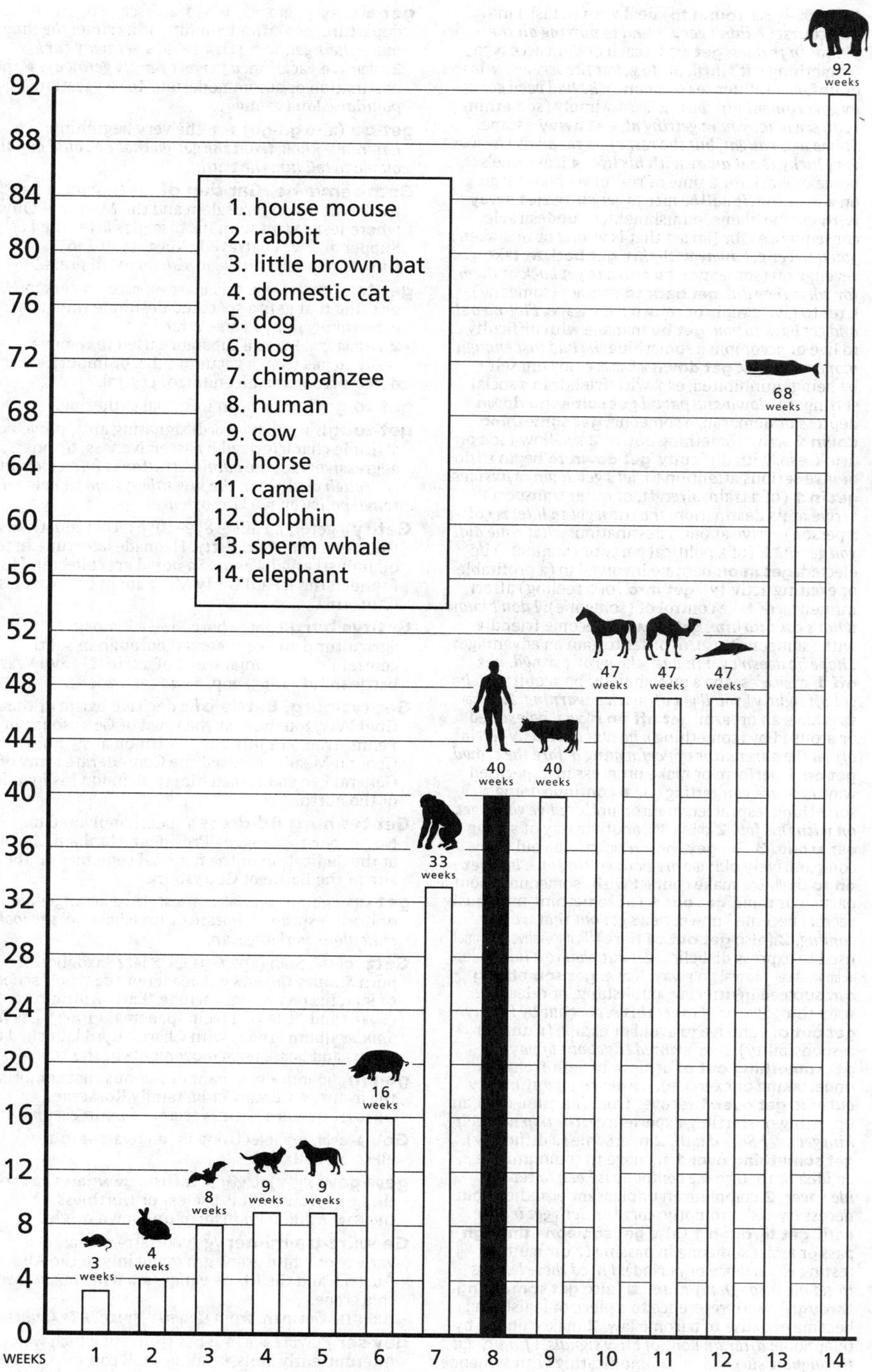

92
88
84
80
76
72
68
64
60
56
52
48
44
40
36
32
28
24
20
16
12
8
4
0

1. house mouse
2. rabbit
3. little brown bat
4. domestic cat
5. dog
6. hog
7. chimpanzee
8. human
9. cow
10. horse
11. camel
12. dolphin
13. sperm whale
14. elephant

3 weeks · 4 weeks · 8 weeks · 9 weeks · 9 weeks · 16 weeks · 33 weeks · 40 weeks · 40 weeks · 47 weeks · 47 weeks · 47 weeks · 68 weeks · 92 weeks

WEEKS 1 2 3 4 5 6 7 8 9 10 11 12 13 14

average gestation periods of selected mammals

5 (**have got**) see **HAVE**.
6 [with obj.] catch or apprehend (someone): *the police have got him.* ■ strike or wound (someone) with a blow or missile: *you got me in the eye!* ■ informal punish, injure, or kill (someone), esp. as retribution: *I'll get you for this!* ■ (**get it**) informal be punished, injured, or killed: *wait until Dad comes home, then you'll get it!* ■ (**get mine, his,** etc.) informal be killed or appropriately punished or rewarded: *I'll get mine, you get yours, we'll all get wealthy.* ■ informal annoy or amuse (someone) greatly: *cleaning the same things all the time, that's what gets me.* ■ informal baffle (someone): *"What's a 'flowery boundary tree'?" "You got me."*
7 [with obj.] informal understand (an argument or the person making it): *What do you mean? I don't get it.*
8 [with obj.] archaic acquire (knowledge) by study; learn: *knowledge which is gotten at school.*
▶ **n. 1** dated an animal's offspring: *he passes this on to his get.*
2 Brit. informal, dialect a person whom the speaker dislikes or despises.
– PHRASES (**as**) —— **as all get out** informal to a great or extreme extent: *he was stubborn as all get out.* **be out to get someone** be determined to punish or harm someone, esp. in retaliation: *he thinks the media are out to get him.* **get in there** informal take positive action to achieve one's aim (often said as an exhortation): *you get in there, son, and you work.* **get it on** informal have sexual intercourse. **get it up** vulgar slang (of a man) achieve an erection. **get-rich-quick** derogatory designed or concerned to make a lot of money fast: *another one of your get-rich-quick schemes.* **get-up-and-go** informal energy, enthusiasm, and initiative.
– PHRASAL VERBS **get something across** manage to communicate an idea clearly. **get ahead** become successful in one's life or career: *how to get ahead in advertising.* **get along 1** have a harmonious or friendly relationship: *they seem to get along pretty well.* **2** manage to live or survive: *don't worry, we'll get along without you.* **get around 1** coax or persuade (someone) to do or allow something that they initially do not want to. **2** deal successfully with (a problem). ■ evade (a regulation or restriction) without contravening it: *the company changed its name to get around the law.* **get around**

to (or chiefly Brit. **round to**) deal with (a task) in due course: *I didn't get around to putting all the photos in frames.* **get at 1** reach or gain access to (something): *it's difficult to get at the screws.* ■ bribe or unfairly influence (someone): *he had been got at by government officials.* **2** informal imply (something): *I can see what you're getting at.* **get away** escape: *Stevie was caught, but the rest of us got away | he was very lucky to get away with his life.* ■ leave one's home or work for a time of rest or recreation; go on a vacation: *it will be nice to get away.* **get away with** escape blame, punishment, or undesirable consequences for (an act that is wrong or mistaken): *you'll never get away with this.* **get back at** take revenge on (someone): *I wanted to get back at them for what they did.* **get back to** contact (someone) later to give a reply or return a message: *I'll find out and get back to you.* **get by** manage with difficulty to live or accomplish something: *he had just enough money to get by.* **get down** informal enjoy oneself by being uninhibited, esp. with friends in a social setting: *get down and party!* **get someone down** depress or demoralize someone. **get something down 1** write something down. **2** swallow food or drink, esp. with difficulty. **get down to** begin to do or give serious attention to: *let's get down to business.* **get in 1** (of a train, aircraft, or other transport) arrive at its destination: *the train got in late.* ■ (of a person) arrive at one's destination: *what time did you get in?* **2** (of a political party or candidate) be elected. **get in on** become involved in (a profitable or exciting activity). **get into** (of a feeling) affect, influence, or take control of (someone): *I don't know what's got into him.* **get in with** become friendly with (someone), esp. in order to gain an advantage: *I hope he doesn't get in with the wrong crowd.* **get off 1** informal escape a punishment; be acquitted: *she got off lightly | you'll get off with a warning.* **2** vulgar slang have an orgasm. **get off on** informal be excited or aroused by (something): *he was obviously getting off on the adrenaline of performing before the crowd.* **get on 1** perform or make progress in a specified way: *how are you getting on?* ■ continue doing something, esp. after an interruption: *I've got to get on with this job.* **2** chiefly Brit. another way of saying GET ALONG. **3** (**be getting on**) informal be old or comparatively old: *we are both getting on a bit.* **get on to** chiefly Brit. make contact with (someone) about a particular topic. **get out 1** (of something previously secret) become known: *news got out that we were coming.* **2** (also **get out of here**) [in imperative] informal used to express disbelief: *get out, you're a liar.* ■ [usu. in imperative] informal go away; leave. **get something out** succeed in uttering, publishing, or releasing something: *we need to get this report out by Friday.* **get out of** contrive to avoid or escape (a duty or responsibility): *they wanted to get out of paying.* **get something out of** achieve benefit from (an undertaking or exercise): *we never got any money out of it.* **get over 1** recover from (an ailment or an upsetting or startling experience): *the trip will help him get over Sal's death.* **2** overcome (a difficulty). **get something over 1** manage to communicate an idea or theory: *the company is keen to get the idea over.* **2** complete an unpleasant or tedious but necessary task promptly: *come on, let's get it over with.* **get through 1** (also **get someone through**) pass or assist someone in passing (a difficult or testing experience or period): *I need these lessons to get me through my exam.* ■ (also **get something through**) (with reference to a piece of legislation) become or cause to become law. **2** make contact by telephone: *after an hour of busy signals, I finally got through.* ■ succeed in communicating with someone in a meaningful way: *I just don't think anyone can get through to these kids.* **get to 1** informal annoy or upset (someone) by persistent action: *he started crying—we were getting to him.* **2** another way of saying GET AROUND TO above. **get together** gather or assemble socially or to cooperate. **get up 1** (also **get someone up**) rise or cause to rise from bed after sleeping. **2** (of wind or the sea) become strong or agitated. **get something up 1** prepare or organize a project or piece of work: *we used to get up little plays.* **2** enhance or refine one's knowledge of a subject.
– DERIVATIVES **get·ta·ble** adj.
– ORIGIN Middle English: from Old Norse *geta* 'obtain, beget, guess'; related to Old English *gietan* (in *begietan* 'beget,' *forgietan* 'forget'), from an Indo-European root shared by Latin *praeda* 'booty, prey,' *praehendere* 'get hold of, seize,' and Greek *khandanein* 'hold, contain, be able.'

ge·ta /ˈgetə, ˈgeˌtä/ ▸ **adj.** (pl. **same** or **getas**) a Japanese wooden shoe with a thong to pass between the first (big) toe and the second toe.

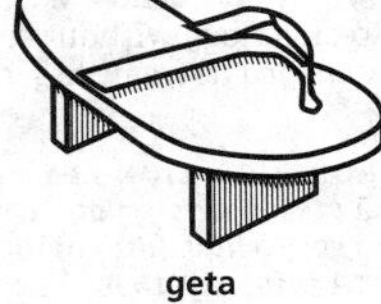
geta

get-at-a·ble /get ˈat əbəl/ (also **getable**) ▸ **adj.** informal accessible.

get·a·way /ˈgetəˌwā/ ▸ **n. 1** an escape or quick departure, esp. after committing a crime: *the thugs made their getaway* | [as modifier] *a getaway car.* **2** informal a vacation: *a perfect family getaway.* ■ the destination or accommodations for a vacation: *a popular island getaway.*

get-go (also **git-go**) ▸ **n.** the very beginning: *Lawrence knew **from the get-go** that he could count on me to tell him the truth.*

Geth·sem·a·ne, Gar·den of /geTHˈsemənē/ a garden between Jerusalem and the Mount of Olives, where Jesus went with his disciples after the Last Supper and was betrayed (Matt. 26:36–46).
– ORIGIN from Hebrew *gath-shemen* 'oil press.'

get·ter /ˈgetər/ ▸ **n. 1** [usu. in combination] a person or thing that gets a specified desirable thing: *an attention-getter | a vote-getter.*
2 Electronics & Physics a substance used to remove residual gas from a vacuum tube, or impurities or defects from a semiconductor crystal.

get-to·geth·er ▸ **n.** an informal gathering.

get-tough ▸ **adj.** informal designating an approach or attitude characterized by assertiveness, firmness, or aggressiveness: *the administration is implementing get-tough changes in the juvenile system | a new get-tough policy on parking offences.*

Get·ty /ˈgetē/, J. Paul (1892–1976), US industrialist; full name *Jean Paul Getty.* He made a fortune in the oil industry and was also a noted art collector. He founded the J. Paul Getty Museum in Los Angeles, California.

Get·tys·burg /ˈgetēzˌbərg, -iz-/ a historic agricultural and commercial borough in south central Pennsylvania, scene of a critical Civil War battle in July 1863; pop. 8,040 (est. 2008).

Get·tys·burg, Battle of a decisive battle of the Civil War, fought near the town of Gettysburg in Pennsylvania in July 1863. A Union army under General Meade repulsed the Confederate army of General Lee and forced him to abandon his invasion of the north.

Get·tys·burg Ad·dress a speech delivered on November 19, 1863, by President Abraham Lincoln at the dedication of the national cemetery on the site of the Battle of Gettysburg.

get·up /ˈgetəp/ ▸ **n.** informal a style or arrangement of dress, esp. an elaborate or unusual one: *she looks ridiculous in that getup.*

Getz /gets/, Stan (1927–91), US jazz saxophonist; born *Stanley Gayetsky.* A leader of the "cool" school of jazz, his recordings include "Early Autumn" (1948) and "The Girl from Ipanema" (1963). His *Jazz Samba* album (1962) with Charlie Byrd launched the samba and bossa nova movements of the 1960s.

ge·um /ˈjēəm/ ▸ **n.** a plant of a genus that comprises the avens. ● Genus *Geum,* family Rosaceae.
– ORIGIN modern Latin, variant of Latin *gaeum.*

GeV ▸ **abbr.** gigaelectronvolt, equivalent to 10^9 electron-volts.

gew·gaw /ˈg(y)o͞oˌgô/ ▸ **n.** (usu. **gewgaws**) a showy thing, esp. one that is useless or worthless.
– ORIGIN Middle English: of unknown origin.

Ge·würz·tra·mi·ner /gəˈvo͝ortstrəˌmēnər/ ▸ **n.** a variety of white grape grown mainly in the Alsace, Austria, and the Rhine valley. ■ a wine made from this grape.
– ORIGIN German, from *Gewürz* 'spice' + TRAMINER.

gey·ser /ˈgīzər/ ▸ **n. 1** a hot spring in which water intermittently boils, sending a tall column of water and steam into the air. ■ a jet or stream of liquid: *the pipe sent up **a geyser of** sewer water into the street.*
2 Brit. a gas-fired water heater through which water flows as it is rapidly heated.
▸ **v.** [no obj.] (esp. of water or steam) gush or burst out with great force: *yellow smoke geysered upward.*
– ORIGIN late 18th cent.: from Icelandic *Geysir,* the name of a particular spring in Iceland; related to *geysa* 'to gush.'

gey·ser·ite /ˈgīzəˌrīt/ ▸ **n.** a hard opaline siliceous deposit occurring around geysers and hot springs.
– ORIGIN early 19th cent.: from GEYSER + -ITE[1].

GF ▸ **n.** (pl. **GFs**) informal a person's girlfriend: *when his GF isn't around, he always flirts with me.*

GFE ▸ **abbr.** government-furnished equipment.

GFWC ▸ **abbr.** General Federation of Women's Clubs.

GGPA ▸ **abbr.** graduate grade-point average.

Gha·ga·ra Ri·ver /gəˈgärə, ˈgägərə/ (also **Gogra**) a river in south central Asia that flows for 570 miles (900 km) from southwestern Tibet through Nepal into India, where it joins the Ganges River.

Gha·na /ˈgänə/ a country in West Africa, with a southern coastline that borders on the Atlantic Ocean; pop. 23,887,800 (est. 2009); capital, Accra; languages, English (official) and West African languages. Former name (until 1957) GOLD COAST.

Formerly a center of the slave trade, the area became the British colony of Gold Coast in 1874. In 1957, it gained independence as a member of the Commonwealth of Nations under the leadership of Kwame Nkrumah. It was the first British colony to become independent.

– DERIVATIVES **Gha·na·ian** /gəˈnāən, gəˈnīən/ **adj.** & **n.**

gha·ri·al /ˈgərēəl/ (also **gavial** /ˈgāvēəl/) ▸ **n.** a large fish-eating crocodile with a long narrow snout that widens at the nostrils, native to the Indian subcontinent. ● *Gavialis gangeticus,* the only member of the family Gavialidae.
– ORIGIN early 19th cent.: from Hindi *ghariyāl.* The spelling *gavial* (from French) is an alteration probably due to scribal error.

ghast·ly /ˈgastlē/ ▸ **adj.** (**ghastlier, ghastliest**)
1 causing great horror or fear; frightful or macabre: *she was overcome with horror at the ghastly spectacle.* ■ informal objectionable; unpleasant: *we had to wear ghastly old-fashioned dresses.*
2 extremely unwell: *he always felt ghastly first thing in the morning.* ■ deathly white or pallid: *a ghastly pallor* | [as submodifier] *he turned ghastly pale and rushed to the bathroom.*
– DERIVATIVES **ghast·li·ness** **n.**
– ORIGIN Middle English: from obsolete *gast* 'terrify,' from Old English *gǣstan,* of Germanic origin; related to GHOST. The *gh* spelling is by association with GHOST. The sense 'objectionable' dates from the mid 19th cent.

ghat /gôt, gät/ (also **ghaut**) ▸ **n. 1** (in South Asia) a flight of steps leading down to a river.
2 (in South Asia) a mountain pass.
– ORIGIN Hindi *ghāṭ.*

Ghats /gôts/ two mountain ranges in central and southern India. Known as **the Eastern Ghats** and **the Western Ghats,** they run parallel to the coast on either side of the Deccan plateau and meet at the southern tip of India.

gha·zal /ˈgəzəl/ ▸ **n.** (in Middle Eastern and Indian literature and music) a lyric poem with a fixed number of verses and a repeated rhyme, typically on the theme of love, and normally set to music.
– ORIGIN via Persian from Arabic *ġazal.*

gha·zi /ˈgäzē/ ▸ **n.** (pl. **ghazis**) (often as an honorific title) a Muslim fighter against non-Muslims.
– ORIGIN from Arabic *al-ġāzī,* participle of *ġazā* 'invade, raid.'

Gha·zi·a·bad /ˈgäzēəˌbäd/ a city in northern India, in Uttar Pradesh, east of Delhi; pop. 1,437,900 (est. 2009).

GHB ▸ **abbr.** (sodium) gamma-hydroxybutyrate, a designer drug with anesthetic properties. ● Chem. formula: $CH_2OH(CH_2)_2COONa$.

ghee /gē/ ▸ **n.** clarified butter made from the milk of a buffalo or cow, used in Indian cooking.
– ORIGIN from Hindi *ghī,* from Sanskrit *ghṛtá* 'sprinkled.'

Ghent /gent/ a city in Belgium, capital of the province of East Flanders, on the Scheldt River; pop. 237,250 (2008). Flemish name GENT, French name GAND.

gher·kin /ˈgərkin/ ▸ **n. 1** a small variety of cucumber, or a young green cucumber used for pickling.
2 a trailing plant with cucumberlike fruits used for pickling. ● *Cucumis anguria,* family Cucurbitaceae. ■ the fresh or pickled fruit of this plant.
– ORIGIN early 17th cent.: from Dutch *augurkje, gurkje,* diminutive of *augurk, gurk,* from Slavic, based on medieval Greek *angourion* 'cucumber.'

ghet·to /ˈgetō/ ▸ **n.** (pl. **ghettos** or **ghettoes**) a part of a city, esp. a slum area, occupied by a minority group or groups. ■ historical the Jewish quarter in a city: *the Warsaw Ghetto.* ■ an isolated or segregated group or area: *the relative security of the gay ghetto.*
▸ **v.** (**ghettoes, ghettoing, ghettoed**) [with obj.] put in or restrict to an isolated or segregated area or group.
– ORIGIN early 17th cent.: perhaps from Italian *getto* 'foundry' (because the first ghetto was established in 1516 on the site of a foundry in Venice), or from Italian *borghetto,* diminutive of *borgo* 'borough.'

ghet·to blast·er ▸ **n.** informal a large portable radio and cassette or CD player.

ghet·to-fab·u·lous ▸ **adj.** informal denoting or exemplifying an ostentatious or flamboyant lifestyle or style of clothing of a type associated with the hip-hop subculture: *ghetto-fabulous rappers.*

ghet·to·ize /ˈgetōˌīz/ ▸ **v.** [with obj.] put in or restrict to an isolated or segregated place, group, or situation: *they called for a policy that seeks to integrate foreign laborers rather than ghettoize them.*
– DERIVATIVES **ghet·to·i·za·tion** /ˌgetō-iˈzāSHən/ **n.**

Ghib·el·line /ˈgibəˌlēn, -ˌlīn, -lin/ ▸ **n.** a member of one of the two great political factions in Italian

medieval politics, traditionally supporting the Holy Roman Emperor against the pope and his supporters, the Guelphs.
– ORIGIN from Italian *Ghibellino*, perhaps from German *Waiblingen*, an estate belonging to Hohenstaufen emperors.

Ghi·ber·ti /gē'bertē/, Lorenzo (1378–1455), Italian sculptor and goldsmith.

ghil·lie ▶ **n.** variant spelling of GILLIE.

Ghir·lan·da·io /,gi(ə)rlən'dīō/ (*c*.1448–94), Italian painter; born *Domenico di Tommaso Bigordi*. He is noted for his religious frescoes, particularly *Christ Calling Peter and Andrew* (1482–84) in the Sistine Chapel in Rome.

ghost /gōst/ ▶ **n.** an apparition of a dead person that is believed to appear or become manifest to the living, typically as a nebulous image: *the building is haunted by the ghost of a monk* | figurative *the ghosts of past deeds*. ■ a faint trace of something: *she gave the ghost of a smile*. ■ a faint secondary image produced by a fault in an optical system or on a cathode ray screen, e.g., by faulty television reception or internal reflection in a mirror or camera.
▶ **v. 1** [with obj.] act as ghostwriter of (a work): *his memoirs were smoothly ghosted by a journalist*.
2 [no obj.] glide smoothly and effortlessly: *they ghosted up the river*.
– PHRASES **the ghost in the machine** Philosophy the mind viewed as distinct from the body (usually used in a derogatory fashion by critics of dualism). [coined by the philosopher Gilbert Ryle (1949).] **give up the ghost** die. ■ (of a machine) stop working. **look as if you have seen a ghost** look very pale and shocked. **not stand a ghost of a chance** have no chance at all.
– DERIVATIVES **ghost·like** /-,līk/ **adj.**
– ORIGIN Old English *gāst* (in the sense 'spirit, soul'), of Germanic origin; related to Dutch *geest* and German *Geist*. The *gh-* spelling occurs first in Caxton, probably influenced by Flemish *gheest*.

ghost·bust·er /'gōst,bəstər/ informal ▶ **n. 1** a person who claims to be able to banish ghosts and poltergeists. ■ a parapsychologist.
2 an investigator of tax fraud.

ghost crab ▶ **n.** a pale yellowish crab that lives in a burrow in the sand above the high-water mark and goes down to the sea at night to feed. ● Genus *Ocypode*, family Ocypodidae.

Ghost Dance an American Indian religious cult of the second half of the 19th century, based on the performance of a ritual dance that, it was believed, would drive away white people and restore the traditional lands and way of life. Advocated by the Sioux chief Sitting Bull, the cult was central to the uprising that was crushed at the Battle of Wounded Knee.

ghost·ing /'gōstiNG/ ▶ **n.** the appearance of a ghost or secondary image on a television or other display screen.

ghost·ly /'gōstlē/ ▶ **adj.** (**ghostlier, ghostliest**) of or like a ghost in appearance or sound; eerie and unnatural: *a ghostly figure with a hood*.
– DERIVATIVES **ghost·li·ness n.**
– ORIGIN Old English *gāstlic*, from *gāst* 'ghost.'

ghost moth (also **ghost swift**) ▶ **n.** a medium to large swift moth, the male of which has white wings. ● Family Hepialidae. See SWIFT (sense 2 of the noun).

ghost sto·ry ▶ **n.** a story involving ghosts or ghostly circumstances, intended to be suspenseful and scary.

ghost town ▶ **n.** a deserted town with few or no remaining inhabitants.

ghost word ▶ **n.** a word that is not actually used but is recorded in a dictionary or other reference work.

ghost·writ·er /'gōst,rītər/ ▶ **n.** a person whose job it is to write material for someone else who is the named author.
– DERIVATIVES **ghost·write v.**

ghoul /gōōl/ ▶ **n.** an evil spirit or phantom, esp. one supposed to rob graves and feed on dead bodies. ■ a person morbidly interested in death or disaster.
– ORIGIN late 18th cent.: from Arabic *ğūl*, 'a desert demon believed to rob graves and devour corpses.'

ghoul·ish /'gōōliSH/ ▶ **adj. 1** resembling or characteristic of a ghoul: *a ghoulish mask*.
2 morbidly interested in death or disaster: *she told the story with ghoulish relish*.
– DERIVATIVES **ghoul·ish·ly adv., ghoul·ish·ness n.**

GHQ ▶ **abbr.** general headquarters.

ghrel·in /'grelin/ ▶ **n.** an enzyme produced by stomach lining cells that stimulates appetite.

Ghul·ghu·leh /gōōl'gōōle/ an ancient city in central Afghanistan. It was destroyed by Genghis Khan *c*.1221.

GHz ▶ **abbr.** gigahertz.

GI[1] ▶ **n.** (pl. **GIs**) a private soldier in the US Army.
– ORIGIN 1930s (originally denoting equipment supplied to US forces): abbreviation of *galvanized iron*; later misinterpreted as an abbreviation of *government* (or *general*) *issue*.

GI[2] ▶ **abbr.** glycemic index.

gi /gē/ ▶ **n.** (pl. **gis**) a lightweight two-piece white garment worn in judo and other martial arts. A gi typically consists of loose-fitting pants and a jacket that is closed with a cloth belt.
– ORIGIN Japanese.

gi

Gia·co·met·ti /,jäkə'metē/, Alberto (1901–66), Swiss sculptor and painter. His most typical works are of emaciated and extremely elongated human forms, such as *Invisible Object* (1934–35) and *Man Pointing* (1947).

gi·ant /'jīənt/ ▶ **n. 1** an imaginary or mythical being of human form but superhuman size. ■ an abnormally tall or large person, animal, or plant. ■ a very large company or organization. ■ a person of exceptional talent or qualities: *a giant among sportsmen*.
2 Astronomy a star of relatively great size and luminosity compared to ordinary stars of the main sequence, and 10–100 times the diameter of the sun.
▶ **adj.** [attrib.] of very great size or force; gigantic: *giant multinational corporations* | *a giant transport plane* | *a giant meteorite*. ■ used in names of very large animals and plants, e.g., **giant hogweed**, **giant tortoise**.
– DERIVATIVES **gi·ant·like** /-,līk/ **adj.**
– ORIGIN Middle English *geant* (with the first syllable later influenced by Latin *gigant-*), from Old French, via Latin from Greek *gigas, gigant-*.

gi·ant ant·eat·er ▶ **n.** a large insectivorous mammal with long coarse fur, large claws, an elongated snout, and a long tongue for catching ants. It is native to Central and South America. ● *Myrmecophaga tridactyla*, family Myrmecophagidae, order Xenartha (or Edentata).

gi·ant clam ▶ **n.** a very large bivalve mollusk that occurs in the tropical Indo-Pacific. ● Family Tridacnidae: several species, including *Tridacna gigas*, which is the largest living shelled mollusk.

gi·ant deer ▶ **n.** another term for IRISH ELK.

gi·ant·ess /'jīəntis/ ▶ **n.** a female giant.

gi·ant gou·ra·mi ▶ **n.** a large edible freshwater fish that is native to Asia. It is widely farmed there and has been introduced elsewhere. ● Family Osphronemidae and genus *Osphronemus*, in particular *O. goramy*.

gi·ant ground·sel ▶ **n.** a large treelike plant of the daisy family, having a thick stem and a few short branches tipped with broad leaves, growing chiefly on high mountains in central and eastern Africa. ● Genus *Senecio* (or *Dendrosenecio*), family Compositae.

gi·ant·ism /'jīən,tizəm/ ▶ **n.** a tendency toward abnormally large size; gigantism.

gi·ant-kill·er ▶ **n.** a person or team that defeats a seemingly much more powerful opponent.
– DERIVATIVES **gi·ant-kill·ing n.**

gi·ant or·der ▶ **n.** Architecture an order whose columns extend through more than one story.

gi·ant pan·da ▶ **n.** see PANDA.

gi·ant pet·rel ▶ **n.** the largest petrel, which is found around southern oceans, has a massive bill, and scavenges from carcasses. ● Genus *Macronectes*, family Procellariidae: two species.

gi·ant puff·ball ▶ **n.** a European fungus that produces a spherical white fruiting body with a diameter of up to 32 inches (80 cm), edible when young. ● *Langermannia gigantea*, family Lycoperdaceae, class Gasteromycetes.

gi·ant reed ▶ **n.** a fast-growing perennial grass native to India that is a principal source for reeds used in musical instruments. In the US it threatens some native plant habitats because of its spreading and dispersal habits. ● *Arundo donax*, family Poaceae.

gi·ant sal·a·man·der ▶ **n.** a very large salamander that is native to North America and eastern Asia, in particular: ● a permanently aquatic salamander (three species in the family Cryptobranchidae), e.g., the American hellbender. ● a terrestrial salamander (three species in the family Dicamptodontidae), of western North America.

gi·ant se·quoi·a ▶ **n.** another term for GIANT REDWOOD (see REDWOOD).

gi·ant silk moth ▶ **n.** see SILKWORM MOTH.

gi·ant sla·lom ▶ **n.** a long-distance slalom with fast, wide turns.

gi·ant squid ▶ **n.** a deep-sea squid that is the largest known invertebrate, reaching a length of 59 feet (18 m) or more. ● Genus *Architeuthis*, order Teuthoidea.

gi·ant toad ▶ **n.** another term for CANE TOAD.

gi·ant tor·toise ▶ **n.** a very large tortoise with a long lifespan, occurring on several tropical oceanic islands. ● Genus *Geochelone*, family Testudinidae: *G. nigra* (Galapagos Islands) and *G. gigantea* (Aldabra and the Seychelles).

giaour /'jou(ə)r/ ▶ **n.** archaic, derogatory a non-Muslim, esp. a Christian.
– ORIGIN from Turkish *gâvur*, from Persian *gaur*, probably from Arabic *kāfir* (see KAFFIR).

Giap /zyäp/, Vo Nguyen (1912–), Vietnamese military and political leader. As North Vietnamese vice-premier and defense minister, he was responsible for the strategy leading to the withdrawal of US forces from South Vietnam in 1973 and the subsequent reunification of the country in 1976.

gi·ar·di·a·sis /,jēär'dīəsis, jär'dī-/ ▶ **n.** infection of the intestine with a flagellate protozoan, which causes diarrhea and other symptoms. ● The protozoan is *Giardia lamblia*, phylum Metamonada, kingdom Protista.
– ORIGIN early 20th cent.: from modern Latin *Giardia* (from the name of Alfred M. *Giard* (1846–1908), French biologist) + -ASIS.

gib /gib/ ▶ **n.** a wood or metal bolt, wedge, or pin for holding part of a machine or structure in place, usually adjusted by a screw or key: [as modifier] *gib screws*.
▶ **v.** [with obj.] fasten (parts) together with a gib.
– ORIGIN late 18th cent.: of unknown origin.

gib·ber /'jibər/ ▶ **v.** [no obj.] speak rapidly and unintelligibly, typically through fear or shock: *they shrieked and gibbered as flames surrounded them* | (as adj. **gibbering**) *a gibbering idiot*.
– ORIGIN early 17th cent.: imitative.

gib·ber·el·lic ac·id /,jibə'relik/ ▶ **n.** a gibberellin that is used commercially, notably in germinating barley for malt.
– ORIGIN 1950s: *gibberellic* from modern Latin *Gibberella* (see GIBBERELLIN) + -IC.

gib·ber·el·lin /,jibə'relin/ ▶ **n.** any of a group of plant hormones that stimulate stem elongation, germination, and flowering.
– ORIGIN 1930s: from modern Latin *Gibberella* (from *Gibberella fujikuroi*, the fungus from which one of the gibberellins was first extracted), diminutive of the genus name *Gibbera*, from Latin *gibber* 'hump,' + -IN[1].

gib·ber·ish /'jibəriSH/ ▶ **n.** unintelligible or meaningless speech or writing; nonsense: *he talks gibberish*.
– ORIGIN early 16th cent.: perhaps from GIBBER (but recorded earlier) + the suffix -ISH[1] (denoting a language as in *Spanish, Swedish*, etc).

gib·bet /'jibit/ historical ▶ **n.** a gallows. ■ an upright post with an arm on which the bodies of executed criminals were left hanging as a warning or deterrent to others. ■ (**the gibbet**) execution by hanging: *the four ringleaders were sentenced to the gibbet*.
▶ **v.** (**gibbets, gibbeting, gibbeted**) [with obj.] hang up (a body) on a gibbet. ■ execute (someone) by hanging. ■ archaic hold up to contempt: *poor Melbourne is gibbeted in the Times*.
– ORIGIN Middle English: from Old French *gibet* 'staff, cudgel, gallows,' diminutive of *gibe* 'club, staff,' probably of Germanic origin.

Gib·bon /'gibən/, Edward (1737–94), English historian. He is best known for his multivolume work, *The History of the Decline and Fall of the Roman Empire* (1776–88).

gib·bon /'gibən/ ▶ **n.** a small, slender tree-dwelling ape with long powerful arms and loud hooting calls, native to the forests of Southeast Asia. See also WHITE-HANDED GIBBON. ● Family Hylobatidae and genus *Hylobates*: several species.
– ORIGIN late 18th cent.: from French, from an Indian dialect word.

gib·bous /'gibəs/ ▶ **adj.** (of the moon) having the observable illuminated part greater than a semicircle and less than a circle. ■ convex or protuberant: *gibbous eyes*.
– DERIVATIVES **gib·bos·i·ty** /gi'bäsitē/ **n.**, **gib·bous·ly adv.**, **gib·bous·ness n.**

g

– ORIGIN late Middle English: from late Latin *gibbosus*, from Latin *gibbus* 'hump.'

Gibbs /gibz/, Josiah Willard (1839–1903), US physical chemist. He was a pioneer in the fields of chemical thermodynamics and statistical mechanics.

Gibbs free en·er·gy ▶ n. Chemistry a thermodynamic quantity equal to the enthalpy (of a system or process) minus the product of the entropy and the absolute temperature. (Symbol: **G**)
– ORIGIN named after J. W. Gibbs (see **GIBBS**).

gibbs·ite /ˈgibzīt/ ▶ n. a colorless mineral consisting of aluminum hydroxide, occurring chiefly as a constituent of bauxite or in encrustations.
– ORIGIN early 19th cent.: named after George *Gibbs* (1776–1833), American mineralogist, + **-ITE**[1].

gibe /jīb/ (also **jibe**) ▶ n. an insulting or mocking remark; a taunt: *a gibe at his old rivals.*
▶ v. [no obj.] make insulting or mocking remarks; jeer: *some cynics in the media might gibe.*
– ORIGIN mid 16th cent. (as a verb): perhaps from Old French *giber* 'handle roughly' (in modern dialect 'kick'); compare with **JIB**[2].

g

gib·lets /ˈjiblits/ ▶ plural n. the liver, heart, gizzard, and neck of a chicken or other fowl, usually removed before the bird is cooked, and often used to make gravy, stuffing, or soup.
– ORIGIN Middle English (in the sense 'an inessential appendage,' later 'garbage, offal'): from Old French *gibelet* 'game bird stew,' probably from *gibier* 'birds or mammals hunted for sport.'

Gi·bral·tar /jəˈbrôltər/ a British overseas territory near the southern tip of the Iberian peninsula, at the eastern end of the Strait of Gibraltar; pop. 28,800 (est. 2009). Occupying a site of great strategic importance, Gibraltar consists of a fortified town and a military base at the foot of a rocky headland called the **Rock of Gibraltar**. Britain captured it during the War of the Spanish Succession in 1704 and is responsible for its defense, external affairs, and internal security.
– DERIVATIVES **Gi·bral·tar·i·an** /jəˌbrôlˈte(ə)rēən, ˌjibˌrôl-/ adj. & n.

Gi·bral·tar, Strait of a channel between the southern tip of the Iberian peninsula and North Africa that forms the only outlet of the Mediterranean Sea to the Atlantic Ocean. It is about 38 miles (60 km) long and varies in width from 15 to 25 miles (24 to 40 km).

Gib·ran /jiˈbrän/ (also **Jubran**), Khalil (1883–1931), US writer and artist; born in Lebanon. His writings in both Arabic and English are deeply romantic, displaying his religious and mystical nature. He is best known for *The Prophet* (1923).

Gib·son[1] /ˈgibsən/, Althea (1927–2003), US tennis player. She was the first black player to succeed at the highest level of tennis, winning all of the major world women's singles titles in the late 1950s.

Gib·son[2], Bob (1935–) US baseball player; full name *Robert Gibson*; born *Pack Gibson*. A pitcher, he played for the St. Louis Cardinals 1959–75. Baseball Hall of Fame (1981).

Gib·son[3], Charles Dana (1867–1944) US artist. A magazine illustrator, he created the "Gibson Girl," typifying a standard of fashion for the times.

Gib·son[4], Mel (1956–), Australian actor and director; born in the US; full name *Mel Columcille Gerard Gibson*. Notable movies: the *Lethal Weapon* trilogy (1987, 1989, and 1992), *Braveheart* (1995), and *The Passion of the Christ* (2004).

Gib·son[5] ▶ n. a dry martini cocktail garnished with a pickled onion.

Gib·son Des·ert /ˈgibsən/ a desert region in western Australia, southeast of the Great Sandy Desert, in eastern central Western Australia. The first European to cross it was Ernest Giles in 1876. He named it after Alfred Gibson, who was lost on an earlier expedition.

Gib·son girl ▶ n. a girl typifying the fashionable ideal of the late 19th and early 20th centuries.
– ORIGIN represented in the work of Charles D. *Gibson* (1867–1944), American artist and illustrator.

gi·bus /ˈjībəs/ (also **gibus hat**) ▶ n. a kind of collapsible top hat.
– ORIGIN mid 19th cent.: named after *Gibus*, the French inventor of this type of hat.

gid·dap /gidˈəp, -ˈap/ ▶ exclam. another term for **GIDDY-UP**.

gid·di·ness /ˈgidēnəs/ ▶ n. **1** a sensation of whirling and a tendency to fall or stagger; dizziness: *symptoms include nausea, vomiting, and giddiness.*
2 a state of excitable frivolity.

gid·dy /ˈgidē/ ▶ adj. (**giddier, giddiest**) having a sensation of whirling and a tendency to fall or stagger; dizzy: *I felt giddy and had to steady myself* | *Luke felt almost giddy with relief.* ■ disorienting and alarming, but exciting: *he has risen to the giddy heights of master.* ■ excitable and frivolous: *her giddy young sister-in-law.*
▶ v. (**giddies, giddying, giddied**) [with obj.] make (someone) feel excited to the point of disorientation: [as adj.] *the giddying speed of the revolving doors.*
– DERIVATIVES **gid·di·ly** /ˈgidəlē/ adv.
– ORIGIN Old English *gidig* 'insane,' literally 'possessed by a god,' from the base of **GOD**. Current senses date from late Middle English.

gid·dy-up /ˌgidē ˈəp/ (also **giddap**) ▶ exclam. used to get a horse to start moving or go faster.
– ORIGIN 1920s (as *giddap*): reproducing a pronunciation of *get up*.

Gide /ZHēd/, André (Paul Guillaume) (1869–1951), French novelist, essayist, and critic; regarded as the father of modern French literature. His notable works include *The Immoralist* (1902), *Strait Is the Gate* (1909), *The Counterfeiters* (1927), and *Journal* (1939–50). Nobel Prize for Literature (1947).

Gid·e·on /ˈgidēən/ **1** (in the Bible) an Israelite leader, described in Judges 6:11.
2 a member of Gideons International.

Gid·e·ons In·ter·na·tion·al an international Christian organization of business and professional people, founded in 1899 in the US with the aim of spreading the Christian faith by placing bibles in hotel rooms and hospital wards.

gie /gē/ ▶ v. (**gies, gieing**; past **gied**; past participle **gied** or **gien** /gēn/) Scottish form of **GIVE**.

Giel·gud /ˈgēlˌgo͝od/, Sir John (1904–2000), English actor and director; full name *Arthur John Gielgud*. A notable Shakespearean actor, particularly remembered for his interpretation of the role of Hamlet, he also appeared in contemporary plays and movies, including the film *Arthur* (1980).

GIF /jif, gif/ ▶ n. Computing a lossless format for compressing image files: [as modifier] *a GIF image.* ■ a file in this format.
– ORIGIN 1980s: acronym from *graphic interchange format*.

GIFT /gift/ ▶ n. Medicine gamete intrafallopian transfer, a technique for assisting conception by introducing mixed ova and sperm into a Fallopian tube.
– ORIGIN 1980s: acronym.

gift /gift/ ▶ n. **1** a thing given willingly to someone without payment; a present: *a Christmas gift* | [as modifier] *a gift shop.* ■ an act of giving something as a present: *his mother's gift of a pen.* ■ informal a very easy task or unmissable opportunity: *that touchdown was an absolute gift.*
2 a natural ability or talent: *he has a gift for comedy.*
▶ v. [with obj.] give (something) as a gift, esp. formally or as a donation or bequest: *the company gifted 2,999 shares to a charity.* ■ present (someone) with a gift or gifts: *the director gifted her with a heart-shaped brooch.* ■ (**gift someone with**) endow someone with (something): *she was gifted with a powerful clairvoyance.*
– PHRASES **the gift of tongues** see **TONGUE**. **look a gift horse in the mouth** find fault with something that has been received as a gift or favor. [earlier as *look a given horse in the mouth*.]
– ORIGIN Middle English: from Old Norse *gipt*; related to **GIVE**.

gift cer·tif·i·cate ▶ n. a voucher given as a present that is exchangeable for a specified cash value of goods or services from a particular place of business.

gift·ed /ˈgiftid/ ▶ adj. having exceptional talent or natural ability: *a gifted amateur musician* | *scholarships for gifted students.*
– DERIVATIVES **gift·ed·ness** n.

gift of gab (chiefly Brit. also **gift of the gab**) ▶ n. the ability to speak with eloquence and fluency.

gift·ware /ˈgiftˌwe(ə)r/ ▶ n. goods sold as being suitable as gifts.

gift wrap (also **gift-wrapping**) ▶ n. decorative paper for wrapping presents.
▶ v. (**gift-wrap**) (**gift wraps, gift wrapping, gift wrapped**) [with obj.] (usu. as adj. **gift-wrapped**) wrap (a present) in decorative paper. ■ hand over (something) as if a gift: *his first on-screen role came gift-wrapped.*

Gi·fu /ˈgēfo͞o/ a city in central Japan, on the island of Honshu; pop. 413,099 (2007).

gig[1] /gig/ ▶ n. **1** chiefly historical a light two-wheeled carriage pulled by one horse.
2 a light, fast, narrow boat adapted for rowing or sailing.
▶ v. [no obj.] travel in a gig.
– ORIGIN late 18th cent.: apparently a transferred sense of obsolete *gig* 'a flighty girl,' which was also applied to various objects or devices that whirled.

gig[2] informal ▶ n. a live performance by or engagement for a musician or group playing popular or jazz music. ■ a job, esp. one that is temporary or that has an uncertain future: *he secured his first gig as an NFL coach.*
▶ v. (**gigs, gigging, gigged**) [no obj.] perform a gig or gigs. ■ [with obj.] use (a piece of musical equipment) at a gig.
– ORIGIN 1920s: of unknown origin.

gig[3] ▶ n. a harpoonlike device used for catching fish or frogs.
▶ v. (**gigs, gigging, gigged**) [no obj.] catch fish or frogs using such a device.
– ORIGIN early 18th cent.: shortening of earlier (rarely used) *fizgig*, probably from Spanish *fisga* 'harpoon.'

gig[4] ▶ n. Computing, informal short for **GIGABYTE**.

giga- ▶ comb. form used in units of measurement.
1 denoting a factor of 10^9: *gigahertz.*
2 Computing denoting a factor of 2^{30}.
– ORIGIN from Greek *gigas* 'giant.'

gig·a·bit /ˈgigəˌbit, ˈjig-/ ▶ n. Computing a unit of information equal to one billion (10^9) or, strictly, 2^{30} bits.

gig·a·byte /ˈgigəˌbīt, ˈjig-/ (abbr.: **GB**) ▶ n. Computing a unit of information equal to one billion (10^9) or, strictly, 2^{30} bytes.

gig·a·flop /ˈgigəˌfläp/ ▶ n. Computing a unit of computing speed equal to one billion floating-point operations per second.
– ORIGIN 1970s: back-formation from *gigaflops* (see **GIGA-**, **-FLOP**).

gi·gan·o·to·sau·rus /jīˌgəˈnōtəsôrəs/ ▶ n. an enormous carnivorous dinosaur of the late Cretaceous period, resembling the tyrannosaurs. ● Genus *Giganotosaurus*, suborder Theropoda, order Saurischia.
– ORIGIN modern Latin, from Greek *gigas* 'giant' + *nōton* 'back' + *sauros* 'lizard.'

gi·gan·tesque /ˌjīgənˈtesk/ ▶ adj. like or appropriate to a giant: *these figures, gigantesque and caricatured, haunted my dreams* | *a gigantesque feat.*
– ORIGIN early 19th cent.: from French, from Italian *gigantesco*, from Greek *gigas, gigant-* (see **GIANT**).

gi·gan·tic /jīˈgantik/ ▶ adj. of very great size or extent; huge or enormous: *a gigantic concrete tower.*
– DERIVATIVES **gi·gan·ti·cal·ly** /-ik(ə)lē/ adv.
– ORIGIN early 17th cent. (in the sense 'like or suited to a giant'): from Latin *gigas, gigant-* (see **GIANT**) + **-IC**.

gi·gan·tism /jīˈgantizəm/ ▶ n. chiefly Biology unusual or abnormal largeness. ■ Medicine excessive growth due to hormonal imbalance. ■ Botany excessive size in plants due to polyploidy.

gi·gan·tom·a·chy /ˌjīgənˈtäməkē/ ▶ n. (in Greek mythology) the struggle between the gods and the giants.
– ORIGIN late 16th cent.: from Greek *gigantomakhia*, from *gigas, gigant-* (see **GIANT**) + *-makhia* 'fighting.'

Gi·gan·to·pi·the·cus /jīˌgantəˈpiTHəkəs/ ▶ n. a very large fossil Asian ape of the late Miocene to early Pleistocene epochs. ● Genus *Gigantopithecus*, family Pongidae.
– ORIGIN modern Latin, from Greek *gigas, gigant-* (see **GIANT**) + *pithēkos* 'ape.'

gig·a·ton /ˈgigəˌtən, ˈjig-/ ▶ n. a unit of explosive force equal to one billion (10^9) tons of trinitrotoluene (TNT).

gig·a·watt /ˈgigəˌwät, ˈjig-/ ▶ n. (abbr. **GW**) a unit of electric power equal to one billion (10^9) watts.

gig·gle /ˈgigəl/ ▶ v. [no obj.] laugh lightly in a nervous, affected, or silly manner: *they giggled at some private joke* | (as adj. **giggling**) *three giggling girls.*
▶ n. a laugh of such a kind. ■ (**the giggles**) continuous uncontrollable giggling: *I got a fit of the giggles.*
– DERIVATIVES **gig·gler** n., **gig·gly** adj. (**gigglier, giggliest**).
– ORIGIN early 16th cent.: imitative.

GIGO /ˈgiˌgō/ ▶ abbr. chiefly Computing garbage in, garbage out. See **GARBAGE**.

gig·o·lo /ˈjigəˌlō, ˈZH-/ ▶ n. (pl. **gigolos**) chiefly derogatory a young man paid or financially supported by an older woman to be her escort or lover.
– ORIGIN 1920s (in the sense 'dancing partner'): from French, formed as the masculine of *gigole* 'dance hall woman,' from colloquial *gigue* 'leg.'

gig·ot /ˈjigət/ ▶ n. a leg of mutton or lamb.
– ORIGIN French, diminutive of colloquial *gigue* 'leg,' from *giguer* 'to hop, jump,' of unknown origin.

gig·ot sleeve ▶ n. a leg-of-mutton sleeve.

gigue /ZHēg/ ▶ n. Music a lively piece of music in the style of a dance, typically of the Renaissance or baroque period, and usually in compound time.
– ORIGIN late 17th cent.: French, literally 'jig.'

Gi·jón /KHēˈKHōn/ a port and industrial city in northern Spain, on the Bay of Biscay; pop. 275,699 (2008).

Gi·la mon·ster /'hēlə/ ▶ **n.** a venomous lizard native to the southwestern US and Mexico. ● *Heloderma suspectum*, family Helodermatidae.
– ORIGIN late 19th cent.: named after *Gila*, a river in New Mexico and Arizona.

Gila monster

Gi·la Riv·er /'hēlə/ a river that flows for 645 miles (1,045 km) from New Mexico across southern Arizona to the Colorado River. Phoenix is in its valley.

Gil·bert[1] /'gilbərt/ a town in southwestern Arizona, part of the Phoenix metropolitan area; pop. 216,449 (est. 2008).

Gil·bert[2], Cass (1859–1934) US architect. He designed the Woolworth building in New York City 1908–13, the annex to the US Treasury building 1918–19, and the US Supreme Court building 1935.

Gil·bert[3], Sir Humphrey (*c.*1539–83), English explorer. He claimed Newfoundland for Elizabeth I in 1583.

Gil·bert[4], William (1544–1603), English physician and physicist. He discovered how to make magnets and coined the term *magnetic pole*.

Gil·bert[5], Sir W. S. (1836–1911), English playwright; full name *William Schwenck Gilbert*. He is best known as a librettist who collaborated on light operas with composer Sir Arthur Sullivan. Notable works: *HMS Pinafore* (1878), *The Pirates of Penzance* (1879), and *The Mikado* (1885).

Gil·bert and El·lice Is·lands /'gilbərt and 'eləs/ a former British colony 1915–75 in the central Pacific Ocean that consisted of two groups of islands: the Gilbert Islands, now a part of Kiribati, and the Ellice Islands, now Tuvalu.

Gil·bert Is·lands a group of islands in the central Pacific Ocean that forms part of Kiribati. The islands straddle the equator and lie immediately west of the International Date Line. They were formerly part of the British colony of the Gilbert and Ellice Islands.

gild[1] /gild/ ▶ **v.** [with obj.] cover thinly with gold.
– PHRASES **gild the lily** try to improve what is already beautiful or excellent. [misquotation, from 'To gild refined gold, to paint the lily; to throw perfume on the violet, ... is wasteful, and ridiculous excess' (Shakespeare's *King John* VI. ii. 11).]
– DERIVATIVES **gild·er n.**
– ORIGIN Old English *gyldan*, of Germanic origin; related to GOLD.

gild[2] ▶ **n.** archaic spelling of GUILD.

gild·ed /'gildid/ ▶ **adj.** covered thinly with gold leaf or gold paint: *an elegant gilded birdcage.* ■ wealthy and privileged: *he saw plain, decent boys transformed to gilded, roistering youths.*

gild·ing /'gildiNG/ ▶ **n.** the process of applying gold leaf or gold paint. ■ the material used in, or the surface produced by, this process.

gi·let /ZHi'lā/ ▶ **n.** (pl. **gilets** pronunc. **same**) a light sleeveless padded jacket.
– ORIGIN late 19th cent.: French, 'waistcoat,' from Spanish *jileco*, from Turkish *yelek*.

Gil·ga·mesh /'gilgə,mesH/ a legendary king of the Sumerian city state of Uruk who is supposed to have ruled sometime during the first half of the 3rd millennium BC. He is the hero of the Babylonian epic of Gilgamesh, which recounts his exploits in an ultimately unsuccessful quest for immortality.

Gill /gil/, Eric (1882–1940), English sculptor, engraver, and typographer; full name *Arthur Eric Rowton Gill*. He did the relief carvings *Stations of the Cross* (1914–18) at Westminster Cathedral and the *Prospero and Ariel* (1931) on Broadcasting House in London. He also designed the first sans serif typeface, Gill Sans.

gill[1] /gil/ ▶ **n.** (often **gills**) **1** the paired respiratory organ of fishes and some amphibians, by which oxygen is extracted from water flowing over surfaces within or attached to the walls of the pharynx. ■ an organ of similar function in an invertebrate animal.
2 the vertical plates arranged radially on the underside of mushrooms and many toadstools.
3 the wattles or dewlap of a fowl. ■ (**gills**) the flesh below a person's jaws and ears: *we stuffed ourselves to the gills with scrambled eggs and toast.*
▶ **v.** [with obj.] **1** gut or clean (a fish).
2 catch (a fish) in a gill net.
– PHRASES **green around** (or **at**) **the gills** (of a person) sickly-looking.
– DERIVATIVES **gilled adj.** [in combination] *a six-gilled shark.*
– ORIGIN Middle English: from Old Norse.

gill[2] /jil/ ▶ **n.** a unit of liquid measure, equal to a quarter of a pint.
– ORIGIN Middle English: from Old French *gille* 'measure or container for wine,' from late Latin *gillo* 'water pot.'

gill[3] /gil/ ▶ **n.** Brit. a deep ravine, esp. a wooded one. ■ a narrow mountain stream.
– ORIGIN Middle English: from Old Norse *gil* 'deep glen.'

gill[4] /jil/ (also **jill**) ▶ **n. 1** archaic a young woman; a sweetheart.
2 a female ferret. Compare with HOB[2] (sense 1).
– ORIGIN late Middle English: abbreviation of the given name *Gillian*.

gill arch ▶ **n.** any of a series of bony or cartilaginous curved bars along the pharynx, supporting the gills of fish and amphibians. ■ any of the corresponding rudimentary structures in the embryos of higher vertebrates.

gill cov·er ▶ **n.** a flap of skin protecting a fish's gills, typically stiffened by bony plates. Also called OPERCULUM.

Gil·les·pie /gə'lespē/, Dizzy (1917–93), US jazz trumpet player and bandleader; born *John Birks Gillespie*. As a virtuoso trumpet player and a leading exponent of bebop style, he formed his own group in 1944 and toured the world.

gil·lie /'gilē/ (also **ghillie**) ▶ **n. 1** (in Scotland) a man or boy who attends someone on a hunting or fishing expedition. ■ historical a Highland chief's attendant.
2 (usu. **ghillie**) a type of shoe with laces along the instep and no tongue, esp. those used for Scottish country dancing.
– ORIGIN late 16th cent.: from Scottish Gaelic *gille* 'lad, servant.' The word was also found in the term *gilliewetfoot*, denoting a servant who carried the chief over a stream, used as a contemptuous name by Lowlanders for the follower of a Highland chief. Sense 2 dates from the 1930s.

gill net ▶ **n.** a fishing net that is hung vertically so that fish get trapped in it by their gills.
– DERIVATIVES **gill-net·ter n.**

gill-o·ver-the-ground ▶ **n.** another term for GROUND IVY.

gill slit /gil/ ▶ **n. 1** any of a series of openings between the gill arches of a fish, through which water passes from the pharynx to the exterior, bathing the gills in the process.
2 any of a similar set of grooves found in embryos of higher vertebrates.

gil·ly·flow·er /'jilē,flou(-ə)r/ (also **gilliflower**) ▶ **n.** any of a number of fragrant flowers, such as the wallflower, clove pink, or white stock.
– ORIGIN Middle English *gilofre* (in the sense 'clove'), from Old French *gilofre, girofle*, via medieval Latin from Greek *karuophullon* (from *karuon* 'nut' + *phullon* 'leaf'). The ending was altered by association with FLOWER, but *gilliver* survived in dialect.

Gil·son·ite /'gilsə,nīt/ ▶ **n.** trademark a very pure, shiny black, brittle form of asphalt, used in making inks, paints, and varnishes.
– ORIGIN late 19th cent.: named after Samuel H. *Gilson*, 19th-cent. American mineralogist, + -ITE.

gilt[1] /gilt/ ▶ **adj.** covered thinly with gold leaf or gold paint.
▶ **n.** gold leaf or gold paint applied in a thin layer to a surface.
– ORIGIN Middle English: archaic past participle of GILD[1].

gilt[2] ▶ **n.** a young sow.
– ORIGIN Middle English: from Old Norse *gyltr*.

gilt-edged ▶ **adj.** (esp. of paper or a book) having a gilded edge or edges. ■ relating to or denoting stocks or other securities that are regarded as extremely reliable investments. ■ of very high quality.

gim·bal /'gimbəl, 'jim-/ ▶ **n.** (often **gimbals**) a mechanism, typically consisting of rings pivoted at right angles, for keeping an instrument such as a compass or chronometer horizontal in a moving vessel or aircraft.
– DERIVATIVES **gim·baled** (or **gimballed**) **adj.**
– ORIGIN late 16th cent. (used in the plural denoting connecting parts in machinery): variant of earlier *gimmal*, itself a variant of late Middle English *gemel* 'twin, hinge, finger ring that can be divided into two rings,' from Old French *gemel* 'twin,' from Latin *gemellus*, diminutive of *geminus*.

gim·crack /'jim,krak/ ▶ **adj.** flimsy or poorly made but deceptively attractive: *plastic gimcrack cookware.*
▶ **n.** a cheap and showy ornament; a knickknack.
– DERIVATIVES **gim·crack·er·y** /-,krakərē/ **n.**
– ORIGIN Middle English *gibecrake*, of unknown origin. Originally a noun, the term denoted some kind of inlaid work in wood, later a fanciful notion or mechanical contrivance, hence a knickknack.

gim·let /'gimlit/ ▶ **n. 1** a small T-shaped tool with a screw-tip for boring holes.
2 a cocktail of gin (or sometimes vodka) and lime juice.
– ORIGIN Middle English: from Old French *guimbelet*, diminutive of *guimble* 'drill,' ultimately of Germanic origin.

gimlet 1

gim·let eye ▶ **n.** an eye with a piercing stare.
– DERIVATIVES **gim·let-eyed adj.**

gim·me /'gimē/ informal ▶ **contraction** give me (not acceptable in standard use): *just gimme the damn thing.*
▶ **n.** a thing that is very easy to perform or obtain, esp. in a game or sport: *the kick would hardly be a gimme in that wind.*

gim·me cap (also **gimme hat**) ▶ **n.** informal a baseball cap that bears a company name or slogan and is given away for publicity purposes.

gim·mick /'gimik/ ▶ **n.** a trick or device intended to attract attention, publicity, or business.
– DERIVATIVES **gim·mick·y adj.**
– ORIGIN 1920s (originally US): of unknown origin but possibly an approximate anagram of *magic*, the original sense being 'a piece of magicians' apparatus.'

gim·mick·ry /'gimikrē/ ▶ **n.** gimmicks collectively; the use of gimmicks: *it does what it says it does, with no design gimmickry.*

gimp[1] /gimp/ ▶ **n. 1** twisted silk, worsted, or cotton with cord or wire running through it, used chiefly as upholstery trimming. ■ (in lacemaking) coarser thread that forms the outline of the design in some techniques.
2 fishing line made of silk bound with wire.
– ORIGIN mid 17th cent.: from Dutch, of unknown ultimate origin.

gimp[2] informal, often offensive ▶ **n.** a physically handicapped or lame person. ■ a limp. ■ a feeble or contemptible person.
▶ **v.** [no obj.] limp; hobble: *she gimped around thereafter on an artificial leg.*
– DERIVATIVES **gimp·y adj.**
– ORIGIN 1920s (originally US): of unknown origin.

gin[1] /jin/ ▶ **n. 1** a clear alcoholic spirit distilled from grain or malt and flavored with juniper berries.
2 (also **gin rummy**) a two-handed form of the card game rummy in which players are dealt ten cards each and attempt to produce a hand in which the point value of unmatched cards adds up to ten or less.
– ORIGIN early 18th cent.: abbreviation of GENEVER.

gin[2] ▶ **n. 1** a machine for separating cotton from its seeds.
2 a machine for raising and moving heavy weights.
3 (also **gin trap**) a snare for catching game.
▶ **v.** (**gins, ginning, ginned**) [with obj.] **1** treat (cotton) in a gin.
2 trap (a person or animal) in a gin.
– DERIVATIVES **gin·ner n.**
– ORIGIN Middle English (in the sense 'a tool or device, a trick'): from Old French *engin* (see ENGINE).

gin·ger /'jinjər/ ▶ **n. 1** a hot fragrant spice made from the rhizome of a plant. It is chopped or powdered for cooking, preserved in syrup, or candied. ■ spirit; mettle: *he had more ginger than her first husband.*
2 a Southeast Asian plant, which resembles bamboo in appearance, from which this rhizome is taken. ● *Zingiber officinale*, family Zingiberaceae.
3 a light reddish-yellow color.
▶ **adj.** (chiefly of hair or fur) of a light reddish-yellow color. ■ (of a person or animal) having ginger hair or fur.
▶ **v.** [with obj.] **1** (usu. as adj. **gingered**) flavor with ginger: *gingered chicken wings.*
2 (**ginger someone/something up**) stimulate; enliven: *she slapped his hand lightly to ginger him up.*

PRONUNCIATION KEY ə *ago, up*; ər *over, fur*; a *hat*; ā *ate*; ä *car*; e *let*; ē *see*; i *fit*; ī *by*; NG *sing*; ō *go*; ô *law, for*; oi *toy*; o͝o *good*; o͞o *goo*; ou *out*; TH *thin*; T͟H *then*; ZH *vision*

g

– DERIVATIVES **gin·ger·y** adj.
– ORIGIN late Old English *gingifer*, conflated in Middle English with Old French *gingimbre*, from medieval Latin *gingiber*, from Greek *zingiberis*, from Pali *siṅgivera*, of Dravidian origin.

gin·ger ale ▶ n. a clear, effervescent nonalcoholic drink flavored with ginger extract.

gin·ger beer ▶ n. a cloudy, effervescent drink made from a mixture of ginger and syrup.

gin·ger·bread /'jinjər,bred/ ▶ n. cake made with molasses and flavored with ginger. ■ fancy decoration, esp. on a building: [as modifier] *a high-gabled gingerbread house.*
– ORIGIN Middle English (originally denoting preserved ginger), from Old French *gingembrat*, from medieval Latin *gingibratum*, from *gingiber* (see GINGER). The change in the ending in the 15th cent. was due to association with BREAD.

gin·ger jar ▶ n. a small ceramic jar with a high rim over which a lid fits.

gin·ger·ly /'jinjərlē/ ▶ adv. in a careful or cautious manner: *Jackson sat down very gingerly.*
▶ adj. showing great care or caution: *with strangers the preliminaries are taken at a gingerly pace.*
– DERIVATIVES **gin·ger·li·ness** n.
– ORIGIN early 16th cent. (in the sense 'daintily, mincingly'): perhaps from Old French *gensor* 'delicate,' comparative of *gent* 'graceful,' from Latin *genitus* 'well-born.'

g

gin·ger snap ▶ n. a thin brittle cookie flavored with ginger.

ging·ham /'giNGəm/ ▶ n. lightweight plain-woven cotton cloth, typically checked in white and a bold color: [as modifier] *gingham curtains.*
– ORIGIN early 17th cent.: from Dutch *gingang*, from Malay *genggang* (originally an adjective meaning 'striped').

gin·gi·va /jin'jīvə, 'jinjəvə/ ▶ n. (pl. **gingivae** /jin'jīvē, 'jinjə,vē/) Medicine the gum.
– DERIVATIVES **gin·gi·val** adj.
– ORIGIN mid 17th cent.: Latin, 'gum.'

gin·gi·vi·tis /,jinjə'vītis/ ▶ n. Medicine inflammation of the gums.

ging·ko ▶ n. variant spelling of GINKGO.

gin·gly·mus /'jiNGgləməs, 'giNG-/ ▶ n. (pl. **ginglymi** /-,mī, -,mē/) Anatomy a hingelike joint, such as the elbow or knee, that allows movement in only one plane.
– ORIGIN late 16th cent.: modern Latin, from Greek *ginglumos* 'hinge.'

gink /giNGk/ ▶ n. informal a foolish or contemptible person.
– ORIGIN early 20th cent. (originally US): of unknown origin.

gink·go /'giNGkō/ (also **gingko**) ▶ n. (pl. **ginkgoes** or **ginkgos**) a deciduous Chinese tree related to the conifers, with fan-shaped leaves and yellow flowers. It has a number of primitive features and is similar to some Jurassic fossils. Also called MAIDENHAIR TREE. ● *Ginkgo biloba*, the only living member of the family Ginkgoaceae and order Ginkgoales, class Coniferopsida.
– ORIGIN late 18th cent.: from Japanese *ginkyō*, from Chinese *yinxing*.

gin mill ▶ n. informal a run-down or seedy nightclub or bar.

gi·nor·mous /ji'nôrməs, jī-/ ▶ adj. informal, humorous extremely large; enormous: *a ginormous five-volume treatment of Greek and Arabic medicine.*
– ORIGIN 1940s (originally military slang): blend of *gigantic* and *enormous*.

gin rum·my ▶ n. see GIN[1].

Gins·berg /'ginzbərg/, Allen (1926–97), US poet. Part of the beat generation and later influential in the hippie movement of the 1960s, he is noted for *Howl and Other Poems* (1956), in which he attacked society for its materialism and complacency.

Gins·burg, Ruth Bader (1933–) US Supreme Court associate justice 1993– . Appointed to the Court by President Clinton, she is one of the more liberal voices on the court.

gin·seng /'jinseNG/ ▶ n. **1** a plant tuber credited with various tonic and medicinal properties, esp. in East Asia.
2 the plant from which this tuber is obtained, native to eastern Asia and North America. ● Genus *Panax*, family Araliaceae: several species, in particular the Asian *P. pseudoginseng* and the North American *P. quinquefolius*.
– ORIGIN mid 17th cent.: from Chinese *rénshēn*, from *rén* 'man' + *shēn*, a kind of herb (because of the supposed resemblance of the forked root to a person).

gin·zo /'ginzō/ informal, offensive ▶ n. (pl. **ginzoes**) an Italian; a person of Italian descent.
▶ adj. Italian.

– ORIGIN mid 20th cent.: perhaps from US slang *Guinea*, denoting an Italian or Spanish immigrant.

Gior·gio·ne /jôr'jōnē/ (*c.*1478–1510), Italian painter; also called **Giorgio Barbarelli** or **Giorgio da Castelfranco**. He introduced the small easel picture in oils that was intended for private collectors. Notable works: *The Tempest* (*c.*1505) and *Sleeping Venus* (*c.*1510).

Giot·to[1] /'jôtō/ (*c.*1267–1337), Italian painter; full name *Giotto di Bondone*. He introduced a naturalistic style showing human expression. His name is associated with the legend of "Giotto's O," in which he is said to have proven his mastery to the pope by drawing a perfect circle freehand. His works include the frescoes in the Arena Chapel in Padua (1305–08) and the church of Santa Croce in Florence (*c.*1320).

Giot·to[2] a European space probe that photographed the nucleus of Halley's comet in March 1986.

Gio·van·ni de' Me·di·ci /jō'vänē də 'medicHē/ the name of the Pope Leo X (see LEO[1]).

gip /jip/ ▶ n. variant spelling of GYP[1].

gip·sy ▶ n. variant spelling of GYPSY.

gi·raffe /jə'raf/ ▶ n. (pl. **same** or **giraffes**) a large African mammal with a very long neck and forelegs, having a coat patterned with brown patches separated by lighter lines. It is the tallest living animal. ● *Giraffa camelopardalis*, family Giraffidae. ■ (**the Giraffe**) the constellation Camelopardalis.
– ORIGIN late 16th cent.: from French *girafe*, Italian *giraffa*, or Spanish and Portuguese *girafa*, based on Arabic *zarāfa*. The animal was known in Europe in the medieval period, and isolated instances of names for it based on the Arabic are recorded in Middle English, when it was commonly called the CAMELOPARD.

giraffe

gir·an·dole /'jirən,dōl/ ▶ n. a branched support for candles or other lights, which either stands on a surface or projects from a wall.
– ORIGIN mid 17th cent. (denoting a revolving cluster of fireworks): from French, from Italian *girandola*, from *girare* 'gyrate, turn,' from Latin *gyrare* (see GYRATE).

gir·a·sol /'jirə,sôl, -,säl/ (also **girasole** /-,sōl/) ▶ n. **1** a kind of opal reflecting a reddish glow.
2 another term for JERUSALEM ARTICHOKE.
– ORIGIN late 16th cent. (in the sense 'sunflower'): from French, or from Italian *girasole*, from *girare* 'to turn' + *sole* 'sun' (because the sunflower turns to follow the path of the sun).

gird[1] /gərd/ ▶ v. (past and past participle **girded** or **girt** /gərt/) [with obj.] literary encircle (a person or part of the body) with a belt or band: *a young man was to be girded with the belt of knighthood.* ■ secure (a garment or sword) on the body with a belt or band: *a white robe girded with a magenta sash.* ■ surround; encircle: *steel rings that gird the elongated, tubular building.*
– PHRASES **gird (up) one's loins** prepare and strengthen oneself for what is to come.
– PHRASAL VERBS **gird oneself for** prepare oneself for (dangerous or difficult future actions).
– ORIGIN Old English *gyrdan*, of Germanic origin; related to Dutch *gorden* and German *gürten*, also to GIRDLE and GIRTH.

gird[2] archaic ▶ v. [no obj.] make cutting or critical remarks: *they girded at the committee.*
▶ n. a cutting or critical remark; a taunt.
– ORIGIN Middle English (in the sense 'strike, stab'): of unknown origin.

gird·er /'gərdər/ ▶ n. a large iron or steel beam or compound structure used for building bridges and the framework of large buildings.
– ORIGIN early 17th cent.: from GIRD[1] in the archaic sense 'brace, strengthen.'

gir·dle /'gərdl/ ▶ n. a belt or cord worn around the waist. ■ a woman's elasticized corset extending from waist to thigh. ■ a thing that surrounds something like a belt or girdle: *a communications girdle around the world.* ■ Anatomy either of two sets of bones encircling the body, to which the limbs are attached. See PECTORAL GIRDLE, PELVIC GIRDLE. ■ the part of a cut gem dividing the crown from the base and embraced by the setting. ■ a ring around a tree made by removing bark.

▶ v. [with obj.] **1** encircle (the body) with or as a girdle or belt: *the Friar loosened the rope that girdled his waist.* ■ surround; encircle: *the chain of volcanoes that girdles the Pacific.*
2 cut through the bark all the way around (a tree or branch), typically in order to kill it or to kill a branch to make the tree more fruitful.
– ORIGIN Old English *gyrdel*, of Germanic origin; related to Dutch *gordel* and German *Gürtel*, also to GIRD[1] and GIRTH.

gir·dler /'gərd(ə)lər/ ▶ n. **1** archaic a maker of girdles.
2 a person or thing that girdles. ■ an insect that removes rings of bark from trees: [in combination] *a twig-girdler.*

girl /gərl/ ▶ n. **1** a female child. ■ a person's daughter, esp. a young one: *he was devoted to his little girl.*
2 a young or relatively young woman. ■ [with modifier] a young woman of a specified kind or having a specified job: *a career girl | a chorus girl.* ■ (**girls**) informal women who mix socially or belong to a particular group, team, or profession: *I look forward to having lunch with the girls.* ■ a person's girlfriend: *his girl eloped with an accountant.* ■ dated a female servant.
– ORIGIN Middle English (denoting a child or young person of either sex): perhaps related to Low German *gör* 'child.'

girl Fri·day ▶ n. a female helper, esp. a junior office worker or a personal assistant to a business executive.
– ORIGIN 1940s: on the pattern of *man Friday*.

girl·friend /'gərl,frend/ ▶ n. a regular female companion with whom a person has a romantic or sexual relationship: *his girlfriend is Australian.* ■ a woman's female friend.

Girl Guide ▶ n. chiefly Brit. a member of the Guide Association.

girl·hood /'gərl,ho͝od/ ▶ n. the state or time of being a girl: *they had been friends since girlhood.*

girl·ie /'gərlē/ ▶ n. (also **girly**) (pl. **girlies**) informal a girl or young woman (often used as a term of address).
▶ adj. **1** (usu. **girly**) often derogatory like, characteristic of, or appropriate to a girl or young woman: *men aren't afraid to be soft, girly, and foppish.*
2 [attrib.] depicting or featuring nude or partially nude young women in erotic poses: *girlie magazines.*

girl·ish /'gərlisH/ ▶ adj. of, like, or characteristic of a girl: *girlish giggles.*
– DERIVATIVES **girl·ish·ly** adv., **girl·ish·ness** n.

Girl Scout ▶ n. a member of an organization of girls, esp. the **Girl Scouts of America**, that promotes character, outdoor activities, good citizenship, and service to others.

gi·ro /'jīrō/ ▶ n. (pl. **giros**) short for AUTOGIRO.

Gi·ronde /ZHē'rôNd/ an estuary in southwestern France, formed at the junction of the Garonne and Dordogne rivers, north of Bordeaux. It flows northwest for 45 miles (72 km) into the Bay of Biscay.

Gi·ron·dist /jə'rändist, ZHə-/ (also **Girondin** /-din/) ▶ n. a member of the French moderate republican party in power 1791–93 during the French Revolution, so called because the party leaders were the deputies from the department of the Gironde.
– ORIGIN from archaic French *Girondiste* (now *Girondin*).

girt[1] /gərt/ past participle of GIRD[1].

girt[2] ▶ n. old-fashioned term for GIRTH.

girth /gərTH/ ▶ n. **1** the measurement around the middle of something, esp. a person's waist. ■ a person's middle or stomach, esp. when large.
2 a band attached to a saddle, used to secure it on a horse by being fastened around its belly.
▶ v. [with obj.] archaic surround; encircle: *the four seas that girth Britain.*
– ORIGIN Middle English (sense 2 of the noun): from Old Norse *gjǫrth*.

GIS ▶ abbr. geographic information system, a system for storing and manipulating geographical information on computer.

Gis·card d'Es·taing /ZHē'skärde'staNG/, Valéry (1926–), French statesman; president 1974–81. As secretary of state for finance 1959–62 and finance minister 1962–66 under President Charles de Gaulle, he was responsible for the policies that formed the basis for France's economic growth. He was a member of the European Parliament 1989–93 and was leader of the center-right Union pour la démocratie française from 1988.

Gish /gisH/, Lillian (1896–1993), US actress. She and her sister **Dorothy** (1898–1968) appeared in a number of D. W. Griffith's movies, including

Hearts of the World (1918) and *Orphans of the Storm* (1922).

Lillian Gish

gis·mo ▶ n. variant spelling of GIZMO.

gist /jist/ ▶ n. [in sing.] **1** the substance or essence of a speech or text: *she noted the gist of each message.* **2** Law the real point of an action: *damage is the gist of the action and without it the plaintiff must fail.*
– ORIGIN early 18th cent.: from Old French, third person singular present tense of *gesir* 'to lie,' from Latin *jacere*. The Anglo-French legal phrase *cest action gist* 'this action lies' denoted that there were sufficient grounds to proceed; *gist* was adopted into English denoting the grounds themselves (sense 2).

git /git/ ▶ n. Brit. informal an unpleasant or contemptible person.
– ORIGIN 1940s: variant of the noun GET (sense 2 of the noun).

Gi·ta /'gētə/ ▶ n. short for BHAGAVADGITA.

gîte /ZHēt/ ▶ n. a small furnished vacation house in France, typically in a rural district.
– ORIGIN French, from Old French *giste*; related to *gésir* 'to lie.'

Git·mo /'git,mō/ informal name for the US naval base or detention facility at Guantánamo Bay, Cuba.
– ORIGIN representing a pronunciation of *GTMO*, an abbreviation of *Guantanamo*.

git·tern /'gitərn/ ▶ n. historical a lutelike medieval stringed instrument, forerunner of the guitar.
– ORIGIN late Middle English: from Old French *guiterne*; perhaps related to CITTERN and GUITAR.

give /giv/ ▶ v. (past **gave** /gāv/; past participle **given** /'givən/) **1** [with two objs.] freely transfer the possession of (something) to (someone); hand over to: *they gave her water to drink* | *the check* ***given to*** *the jeweler proved worthless* | [with obj.] *he gave the papers* ***back***. ■ bestow (love, affection, or other emotional support): *his parents gave him the encouragement he needed to succeed* | (as adj. **giving**) *he was very giving and supportive.* ■ administer (medicine): *she was given antibiotics.* ■ hand over (an amount) in exchange or payment; pay: *how much did you give* ***for*** *that?* ■ (**give something for**) place a specified value on (something): *he never gave anything* ***for*** *French painting or for abstraction.* ■ [with obj.] used hyperbolically to express how greatly one wants to have or do something: *I'd give anything* ***for*** *a cup of tea* | ***I'd give my right arm*** *to be in Othello.* ■ communicate or impart (a message) to (someone): *give my love to all the girls.* ■ [with obj.] commit, consign, or entrust: *a baby* ***given into*** *their care by the accident of her birth.* ■ freely devote, set aside, or sacrifice for a purpose: *all who have* ***given*** *thought* ***to*** *the matter agree* | [no obj.] *committee members who* ***give*** *so generously* ***of*** *their time and effort.* ■ [with obj.] (of a man) sanction the marriage of (his daughter) to someone: *he gave her* ***in marriage*** *to an English noble.* ■ (**give oneself to**) dated consent to have sexual intercourse with (someone). ■ pass on (an illness or infection) to (someone): *I hope I don't give you my cold.* ■ [usu. in imperative] make a connection to allow (someone) to speak to (someone else) on the telephone: *give me the police.* ■ cite or present when making a toast or introducing a speaker or entertainer: *for your entertainment this evening I give you ... Mister Albert DeNiro!*
2 [with two objs.] cause or allow (someone or something) to have (something, esp. something abstract); provide or supply with: *you gave me such a fright* | [with obj.] *this leaflet gives our opening times.* ■ allot or assign (a score) to: *I gave it five out of ten.* ■ sentence (someone) to (a specified penalty): *for the first offense I was given a fine.* ■ concede or yield (something) as valid or deserved in respect of (someone): *give him his due.* ■ allow (someone) to have (a specified amount of time) for an activity or undertaking: *give me a second to bring the car around* | [with obj.] *I'll give you until tomorrow morning.* ■ informal predict that (an activity, undertaking, or relationship) will last no longer than (a specified time): *this is a place that will not improve with time—I give it three weeks.* ■ [with obj.] yield as a product or result: *milk is sometimes added to give a richer cheese.* ■ [with obj.] (**give something off/out/forth**) emit odor, vapor, or similar substances: *it can be burned without giving off toxic fumes.*
3 [with obj.] carry out or perform (a specified action): *I gave a bow* | [with two objs.] *he gave the counter a polish.* ■ utter or produce (a sound): *he gave a gasp.* ■ provide (a party or social meal) as host or hostess: *a dinner given in honor of a Canadian diplomat* | [with two objs.] *Korda gave him a going-away party.*
4 [with obj.] state or put forward (information or argument): *he did not give his name.* ■ pledge or assign as a guarantee: [with two objs.] *I give you my word.* ■ [with two objs., usu. with negative] say to (someone) as an excuse or inappropriate answer: *don't give me any of your back talk.* ■ deliver (a judgment) authoritatively: *I gave my verdict.* ■ present (an appearance or impression): *he gave no sign of life.* ■ [no obj.] informal tell what one knows: *okay, give—what's that all about?*
5 [no obj.] alter in shape under pressure rather than resist or break: *that chair doesn't give.* ■ yield or give way to pressure: *the heavy door didn't give until the fifth push* | figurative *when two people who don't get on are thrust together, something's got to give.* ■ informal concede defeat; surrender: *I give!*
▶ n. capacity to bend or alter in shape under pressure; elasticity: *plastic pots that have enough give to accommodate the vigorous roots.* ■ ability to adapt or comply; flexibility: *there is no give at all in the British position.*
– PHRASES **give oneself airs** act pretentiously or snobbishly. **give and take** mutual concessions and compromises. ■ [as verb] make concessions and compromises. **give as good as one gets** respond with equal force or vehemence when attacked. **give the (whole) game** (or **show**) **away** inadvertently reveal something secret or concealed. **give it to someone** informal scold or punish someone. **give me —** I prefer or admire —: *give me the mainland any day!* **give me a break** informal used to express exasperation, protest, or disbelief. **give or take —** informal to within — (used to express the degree or accuracy of a figure): *three hundred and fifty years ago, give or take a few.* ■ apart from: *give or take a handful of machine tools, there are few new products.* **give rise to** cause or induce to happen: *decisions which give rise to arguments.* **give someone to understand** (or **believe** or **know**) inform someone in a formal and rather indirect way: *I was given to understand that I had been invited.* **give up the ghost** see GHOST. **give someone what for** informal, dated punish or scold someone severely. **not give a damn** (or **hoot**, etc.) informal not care at all: *people who don't give a damn about the environment.* **what gives?** informal what's the news?; what's happening? (frequently used as a friendly greeting).
– PHRASAL VERBS **give someone away 1** reveal the true identity of someone: *his strangely shaped feet gave him away.* ■ reveal information that incriminates someone. **2** hand over a bride ceremonially to her bridegroom as part of a wedding ceremony. **give something away** reveal something secret or concealed. **give in** cease fighting or arguing; yield; surrender: *he reluctantly gave in to the pressure.* **give on to** (or **into**) Brit. (of a window, door, corridor, etc.) overlook or lead into: *a plate glass window gave on to the roof.* **give out** be completely used up: *her energy was on the verge of giving out.* ■ stop functioning; break down: *he curses and swears till his voice gives out.* **give something out** distribute or broadcast something: *I've been giving out leaflets.* **give over** [often in imperative] Brit. informal stop doing something. ■ used to express vehement disagreement or denial: *I suggested her salary might be £100,000. "Give over!"* **give up** cease making an effort; resign oneself to failure. **give it up** [usu. in imperative] informal applaud a performer or entertainer. **give oneself up 1** surrender oneself to law-enforcement agents. **2** dated allow oneself to be taken over by (an emotion or addiction): *he gave himself up to pleasure.* **give someone up 1** deliver a wanted person to authority: *a voice told him to come out and* ***give himself up***. **2** dated stop hoping that someone is still going to arrive: *oh, it's you—we'd almost given you up.* ■ pronounce a sick person incurable. **give something up** part with something that one would prefer to keep: *she would have given up everything for love.* ■ stop the habitual doing or consuming of something: *I've decided to give up drinking.* **give up on** stop having faith or belief in: *they weren't about to give up on their heroes so easily.*
– ORIGIN Old English *giefan, gefan*, of Germanic origin; related to Dutch *geven* and German *geben*.

give·a·way /'givə,wā/ informal ▶ n. **1** a thing that is given free, esp. for promotional purposes: *a preelection tax giveaway.*
2 a thing that makes an inadvertent revelation: *the shape of the parcel was a dead giveaway.*
▶ adj. [attrib.] **1** free of charge: *giveaway goodies.* ■ (of prices) very low.
2 revealing: *small giveaway mannerisms.*

give·back /'giv,bak/ ▶ n. an agreement by workers to surrender benefits and conditions previously agreed upon in return for new concessions or awards.

giv·en /'givən/ past participle of GIVE.
▶ adj. **1** specified or stated: *our level of knowledge on any given subject.*
2 [predic.] (**given to**) inclined or disposed to: *she was not often given to anger.*
3 Law, archaic (of a document) signed and dated: *given under my hand this eleventh day of April.*
▶ prep. taking into account: *given the complexity of the task, they were able to do a good job.*
▶ n. a known or established fact or situation: *at a couture house, attentive service is a given.*

giv·en name ▶ n. another term for FIRST NAME.

giv·er /'givər/ ▶ n. a person who gives something: *a giver of advice* | [in combination] *generous gift-givers.*

Gi·za /'gēzə/ a city southwest of Cairo in northern Egypt, on the western bank of the Nile River, site of the Pyramids and the Sphinx; pop. 2,891,300 (est. 2006). Also called EL-GIZA; Arabic name AL-JIZAH.

giz·mo /'gizmō/ (also **gismo**) ▶ n. (pl. **gizmos**) informal a gadget, esp. one whose name the speaker does not know or cannot recall: *the latest multimedia gizmo.*
– ORIGIN 1940s (originally US): of unknown origin.

giz·zard /'gizərd/ ▶ n. a muscular, thick-walled part of a bird's stomach for grinding food, typically with grit. Also called VENTRICULUS. ■ a muscular stomach of some fish, insects, mollusks, and other invertebrates. ■ informal a person's stomach or throat.
– ORIGIN late Middle English *giser*: from Old French, based on Latin *gigeria* 'cooked entrails of fowl.' The final *-d* was added in the 16th cent.

gjet·ost /'yetôst, 'jet-/ ▶ n. a very sweet, firm, golden-brown Norwegian cheese, traditionally made with goat's milk.
– ORIGIN Norwegian, from *gjet, geit* 'goat' + *ost* 'cheese.'

gl. ▶ abbr. gloss.

GLA ▶ abbr. gamma linolenic acid.

gla·bel·la /glə'belə/ ▶ n. (pl. **glabellae** /-'belē/) Anatomy the smooth part of the forehead above and between the eyebrows.
– DERIVATIVES **gla·bel·lar** /-'belər/ adj.
– ORIGIN early 19th cent.: modern Latin, from Latin *glabellus* (adjective), diminutive of *glaber* 'smooth.'

gla·brous /'glābrəs/ ▶ adj. technical (chiefly of the skin or a leaf) free from hair or down; smooth.
– ORIGIN mid 17th cent.: from Latin *glaber, glabr-* 'hairless, smooth' + -OUS.

gla·cé /gla'sā/ ▶ adj. [attrib.] **1** (of fruit) having a glossy surface due to preservation in sugar: *a glacé cherry.*
2 (of cloth or leather) smooth and highly polished.
▶ v. (**glacés, glacéing, glacéed** /-'sād/ or **glacéd**) [with obj.] glaze with a thin sugar-based coating: [as adj.] *glacéed cape gooseberries.*
– ORIGIN mid 19th cent.: French, literally 'iced,' past participle of *glacer*, from *glace* 'ice.'

gla·cé ic·ing ▶ n. icing made with powdered sugar and water.

gla·cial /'glāSHəl/ ▶ adj. **1** relating to, resulting from, or denoting the presence or agency of ice, esp. in the form of glaciers: *thick glacial deposits* | *a glacial lake.*
2 of ice; icy: *the glacial mountains of New Zealand* | figurative *his glacial blue eyes.* ■ Chemistry denoting pure organic acids (esp. acetic acid) that form icelike crystals on freezing. ■ extremely slow (like the movement of a glacier): *an official described progress in the talks as glacial.*
▶ n. Geology a glacial period.
– DERIVATIVES **gla·cial·ly** adv.
– ORIGIN mid 17th cent.: from French, or from Latin *glacialis* 'icy,' from *glacies* 'ice.'

gla·cial pe·ri·od ▶ n. a period in the earth's history when polar and mountain ice sheets were unusually extensive across the earth's surface.

gla·ci·at·ed /'glāSHē,ātid/ ▶ adj. covered or having been covered by glaciers or ice sheets: *a glaciated valley.*
– ORIGIN mid 19th cent.: past participle of obsolete *glaciate*, from Latin *glaciare* 'freeze,' from *glacies* 'ice.'

gla·ci·a·tion /,glāSHē'āSHən/ ▶ n. Geology the process, condition, or result of being covered by glaciers or ice sheets. ■ a glacial period.

gla·cier /ˈglāsHər/ ▶ **n.** a slowly moving mass or river of ice formed by the accumulation and compaction of snow on mountains or near the poles.
– ORIGIN mid 18th cent.: from French, from *glace* 'ice,' based on Latin *glacies*.

Gla·cier Bay Na·tion·al Park a national park in southeastern Alaska, on the Pacific coast. It covers an area of 4,975 square feet (12,880 sq km).

gla·ci·ol·o·gy /ˌglāsHēˈäləjē/ ▶ **n.** the study of the internal dynamics and effects of glaciers.
– DERIVATIVES **gla·ci·o·log·i·cal** /-SHēəˈläjikəl/ **adj.**, **gla·ci·ol·o·gist** /-jist/ **n.**
– ORIGIN late 19th cent.: from Latin *glacies* 'ice' + **-LOGY**.

gla·cis /ˈglāsis, ˈglas-/ ▶ **n.** (pl. **same** or **glacises**) a gently sloping bank, in particular one that slopes down from a fort, exposing attackers to the defenders' missiles.
– ORIGIN late 17th cent.: from French, from Old French *glacier* 'to slip,' from *glace* 'ice,' based on Latin *glacies*.

glad[1] /glad/ ▶ **adj.** (**gladder, gladdest**) [predic.] pleased; delighted: *she was alive, which was something to be glad about* | [with infinitive] *I'm really glad to hear that.* ■ [attrib.] causing happiness: *glad tidings.* ■ grateful: *he was glad for the excuse to put it off.* ■ [with infinitive] willing and eager (to do something): *he will be glad to carry your bags.*
▶ **v.** (**glads, gladding, gladded**) [with obj.] literary make happy; please: *Albion's lessening shore could grieve or glad mine eye.*
– DERIVATIVES **glad·ness n.**
– ORIGIN Old English *glæd* (originally in the sense 'bright, shining'), of Germanic origin; related to Old Norse *glathr* 'bright, joyous' and German *glatt* 'smooth,' also to Latin *glaber* 'smooth, hairless.'

glad[2] ▶ **n.** informal a gladiolus.
– ORIGIN 1920s: abbreviation.

glad·den /ˈgladn/ ▶ **v.** [with obj.] make glad: *it was a sound that gladdened her heart.*

glade /glād/ ▶ **n.** an open space in a forest.
– ORIGIN late Middle English: of unknown origin; perhaps related to **GLAD**[1] or **GLEAM**, with reference to the comparative brightness of a clearing (obsolete senses of *glade* include 'a gleam of light' and 'a bright space between clouds').

glad-hand ▶ **v.** [with obj.] (esp. of a politician) greet or welcome warmly or with the appearance of warmth: *they had been taking every free minute to glad-hand loyal supporters.*
▶ **n.** (**gladhand**) [in sing.] a warm and hearty, but often insincere, greeting or welcome.
– DERIVATIVES **glad-hand·er n.**

glad·i·a·tor /ˈgladēˌātər/ ▶ **n.** (in ancient Rome) a man trained to fight with weapons against other men or wild animals in an arena.
– DERIVATIVES **glad·i·a·to·ri·al** /ˌgladēəˈtôrēəl/ **adj.**
– ORIGIN late Middle English: from Latin, from *gladius* 'sword.'

glad·i·o·lus /ˌgladēˈōləs/ ▶ **n.** (pl. **gladioli** /-lī/) an Old World plant of the iris family, with sword-shaped leaves and spikes of brightly colored flowers, popular in gardens and as a cut flower. ● Genus *Gladiolus*, family Iridaceae: many species.
– ORIGIN Old English (originally denoting the *gladdon*, a purple-flowered iris), from Latin, diminutive of *gladius* 'sword' (used as a plant name by Pliny).

glad·ly /ˈgladlē/ ▶ **adv.** willingly or eagerly: *I would have gladly paid for it.* ■ with pleasure or gratitude; happily: *she offered me a lift and I gladly accepted.*

glad rags ▶ **plural n.** informal clothes for a special occasion; one's best clothes.

glad·some /ˈgladsəm/ ▶ **adj.** literary (of a person) having a cheerful disposition. ■ filled with, marked by, or causing pleasure.

Glad·stone /ˈgladˌstōn/, William Ewart (1809–98), British statesman; prime minister 1868–74, 1880–85, 1886, and 1892–94. At first a Conservative minister, he later joined the Liberal Party and became its leader in 1867. Elementary education, the Irish Land and the third Reform acts, and the campaign for Irish home rule were introduced during his administrations.

Glad·stone bag ▶ **n.** a bag like a briefcase having two equal compartments joined by a hinge.
– ORIGIN late 19th cent.: named after W. E. **GLADSTONE**, who was noted for the amount of traveling he undertook when electioneering.

Glag·o·lit·ic /ˌglagəˈlitik/ ▶ **adj.** denoting or relating to an alphabet based on Greek minuscules, formerly used in writing some Slavic languages.
▶ **n.** this alphabet.

> The Glagolitic alphabet is of uncertain origin and was introduced in the 9th century at about the same time as the Cyrillic alphabet, which has superseded it except in some Orthodox Church liturgies.

– ORIGIN from modern Latin *glagoliticus*, from *glagòljica*, the name in Croatian of the Glagolitic alphabet, from Old Church Slavic *glagolŭ* 'word.'

glair /gle(ə)r/ ▶ **n.** a preparation made from egg white, used esp. as an adhesive for bookbinding and gilding. ■ dated egg white.
– DERIVATIVES **glair·y adj.**
– ORIGIN Middle English: from Old French *glaire*, based on Latin *clara*, feminine of *clarus* 'clear.'

glaive /glāv/ ▶ **n.** literary a sword.
– ORIGIN Middle English (denoting a lance or halberd): from Old French, apparently from Latin *gladius* 'sword.'

glam /glam/ informal ▶ **adj.** glamorous: *a magician and his glam assistant.* ■ relating to or denoting glam rock.
▶ **n.** glamour: *sass, panache, and a dash of glam.* ■ glam rock.
▶ **v.** (**glams, glamming, glammed**) [no obj.] (**glam up**) make oneself look glamorous.
– ORIGIN 1930s: abbreviation.

glam·a·zon /ˈglaməˌzän, -zən/ ▶ **n.** informal a glamorous, powerfully assertive woman.
– ORIGIN 1960s: from *glam* + *Amazon*.

glam·or·ize /ˈglaməˌrīz/ (also **glamourize**) ▶ **v.** [with obj.] make (something) seem glamorous or desirable, esp. spuriously so: *the lyrics glamorize drugs.*
– DERIVATIVES **glam·or·i·za·tion** /ˌglaməriˈzāsHən/ **n.**

glam·or·ous /ˈglamərəs/ ▶ **adj.** having glamour: *one of the world's most glamorous women.*
– DERIVATIVES **glam·or·ous·ly adv.**

glam·our /ˈglamər/ (also **glamor**) ▶ **n.** the attractive or exciting quality that makes certain people or things seem appealing or special: *the glamour of Monte Carlo* | [as modifier] *the glamour days of Old Hollywood.* ■ beauty or charm that is sexually attractive: *George had none of his brother's glamour.* ■ archaic enchantment; magic: *that maiden, made by glamour out of flowers.*
– ORIGIN early 18th cent. (originally Scots in the sense 'enchantment, magic'): alteration of **GRAMMAR**. Although *grammar* itself was not used in this sense, the Latin word *grammatica* (from which it derives) was often used in the Middle Ages to mean 'scholarship, learning,' including the occult practices popularly associated with learning.

glam·our puss ▶ **n.** dated, informal a glamorous person, esp. a woman.

glam rock ▶ **n.** a style of rock music first popular in the early 1970s, characterized by male performers wearing exaggeratedly flamboyant clothes and makeup.

glance[1] /glans/ ▶ **v.** [no obj.] **1** take a brief or hurried look: *Ginny glanced at her watch.* ■ (**glance at/through**) read quickly or cursorily: *I glanced through your personnel file last night.*
2 hit something at an angle and bounce off obliquely: *he saw a stone glance off a crag and hit Tom on the head.* ■ (esp. of light) reflect off something with a brief flash: *sunlight glanced off the curved body of a dolphin.* ■ [with obj.] (in ball games) deflect (the ball) slightly with a delicate contact: *he glanced the ball into the right corner of the net.*
▶ **n. 1** a brief or hurried look: *Sean and Michael exchanged glances.*
2 literary a flash or gleam of light.
– PHRASES **at a glance** immediately upon looking: *she saw at a glance what had happened.* **at first glance** when seen or considered for the first time, esp. briefly: *good news, at first glance, for frequent travelers.* **glance one's eye** archaic look briefly: *glancing his severe eye around the group.*
– DERIVATIVES **glanc·ing·ly adv.**
– ORIGIN late Middle English (in the sense 'rebound obliquely'): probably a nasalized form of obsolete *glace* in the same sense, from Old French *glacier* 'to slip,' from *glace* 'ice,' based on Latin *glacies*.

glance[2] ▶ **n.** a shiny sulfide ore of lead, copper, or other metal.
– ORIGIN late Middle English: from German *Glanz* 'brightness, luster'; compare with Dutch *glanserts* 'glance ore.'

glanc·ing /ˈglansiNG/ ▶ **adj.** [attrib.] striking someone or something at an angle rather than directly and with full force: *he was struck a glancing blow.*

gland[1] /gland/ ▶ **n.** an organ in the human or animal body that secretes particular chemical substances for use in the body or for discharge into the surroundings. ■ a structure resembling this, esp. a lymph node. ■ Botany a secreting cell or group of cells on or within a plant structure.
– ORIGIN late 17th cent.: from French *glande*, alteration of Old French *glandre*, from Latin *glandulae* 'throat glands.'

gland[2] ▶ **n.** a sleeve used to produce a seal around a piston rod or other shaft.
– ORIGIN early 19th cent.: probably a variant of Scots *glam* 'a vice or clamp'; related to **CLAMP**.

gland·ers /ˈglandərz/ ▶ **plural n.** [usu. treated as sing.] a rare contagious disease that mainly affects horses, characterized by swellings below the jaw and mucous discharge from the nostrils. ● This disease is caused by the bacterium *Pseudomonas mallei*.
– ORIGIN late 15th cent.: from Old French *glandre* (see **GLAND**[1]).

glan·du·lar /ˈglanjələr/ ▶ **adj.** of, relating to, or affecting a gland or glands.
– ORIGIN mid 18th cent.: from French *glandulaire*, from *glandule* 'gland,' from Latin *glandulae* (see **GLAND**[1]).

glan·du·lar fe·ver another term for **INFECTIOUS MONONUCLEOSIS**.

glans /glanz/ ▶ **n.** (pl. **glandes** /ˈglandēz/) Anatomy the rounded part forming the end of the penis (**glans penis**) or clitoris (**glans clitoridis**).
– ORIGIN mid 17th cent.: from Latin, literally 'acorn.'

glare /gle(ə)r/ ▶ **v.** [no obj.] **1** stare in an angry or fierce way: *she glared at him, her cheeks flushing.* ■ [with obj.] express (a feeling, esp. defiance) by staring in such a way: *he glared defiance at the pistols pointing down at him.*
2 [with adverbial] (of the sun or an electric light) shine with a strong or dazzling light: *the sun glared out of a clear blue sky.*
▶ **n. 1** a fierce or angry stare.
2 strong and dazzling light: *Murray narrowed his eyes against the glare of the sun.* ■ oppressive public attention or scrutiny: *he carried on his life in the full glare of publicity.*
3 archaic dazzling or showy appearance; tawdry brilliance: *the pomp and glare of rhetoric.*
– DERIVATIVES **glar·y adj.**
– ORIGIN Middle English (in the sense 'shine brilliantly or dazzlingly'): from Middle Dutch and Middle Low German *glaren* 'to gleam, glare': perhaps related to **GLASS**. The sense 'stare' occurred first in the adjective *glaring* (late Middle English).

glare ice ▶ **n.** smooth, glassy ice.
– ORIGIN mid 19th cent.: probably from obsolete *glare* 'frost'; perhaps related to **GLARE**.

glar·ing /ˈgle(ə)riNG/ ▶ **adj. 1** [attrib.] giving out or reflecting a strong or dazzling light: *the glaring sun.* ■ staring fiercely or fixedly: *their glaring eyes.*
2 highly obvious or conspicuous: *there is a glaring omission in the above data.*
– DERIVATIVES **glar·ing·ly adv.**

Glas·gow /ˈglasgō, ˈglaz-/ a city in Scotland, on the Clyde River; pop. 578,700 (est. 2009). It is the largest city in Scotland.

Glash·ow /ˈglasHō/, Sheldon Lee (1932–), US theoretical physicist. He independently developed a unified theory to explain electromagnetic interactions and the weak nuclear force, and he extended the quark theory of Murray Gell-Mann. Nobel Prize for Physics (1979), shared with Abdus Salam and Steven Weinberg.

glas·nost /ˈglazˌnōst, ˈglas-, ˈgläz-, ˈgläs-/ ▶ **n.** (in the former Soviet Union) the policy or practice of more open consultative government and wider dissemination of information, initiated by leader Mikhail Gorbachev from 1985.
– ORIGIN from Russian *glasnost'*, literally 'the fact of being public,' from *glasnyy* 'public, open' + *-nost'* '-ness.'

glass /glas/ ▶ **n. 1** a hard, brittle substance, typically transparent or translucent, made by fusing sand with soda, lime, and sometimes other ingredients and cooling rapidly. It is used to make windows, drinking containers, and other articles: *a piece of glass* | [as modifier] *a glass door.* ■ any similar substance that has solidified from a molten state without crystallizing.
2 a thing made from, or partly from, glass, in particular: ■ a container to drink from: *a beer glass.* ■ glassware. ■ greenhouses or cold frames considered collectively. ■ chiefly Brit. a mirror. ■ archaic an hourglass.
3 a lens, or an optical instrument containing a lens or lenses, in particular a monocle or a magnifying lens.
4 the liquid or amount of liquid contained in a glass; a glassful: *a glass of lemonade* | *I'll have another glass, please.*
▶ **v.** [with obj.] **1** cover or enclose with glass: *the inn has a long balcony, now glassed in.*
2 (esp. in hunting) scan (one's surroundings) with binoculars: *the first day was spent glassing the rolling hills.*
3 literary reflect in or as if in a mirror: *the opposite slopes glassed themselves in the deep dark water.*
– PHRASES **the glass is half-full** (or **half-empty**) used to refer to an optimistic (or pessimistic) outlook on life: *she remains a person for whom the glass is always half-full* | *I like to think of myself as a glass half-full kind of guy.* **people** (**who live**) **in glass houses shouldn't throw stones** proverb you

shouldn't criticize others when you have similar faults of your own.
– DERIVATIVES **glass·ful** /-ˌfo͝ol/ **n.** (pl. **glassfuls**), **glass·less adj.**, **glass·like** /-ˌlīk/ **adj.**
– ORIGIN Old English *glæs*, of Germanic origin; related to Dutch *glas* and German *Glas*.

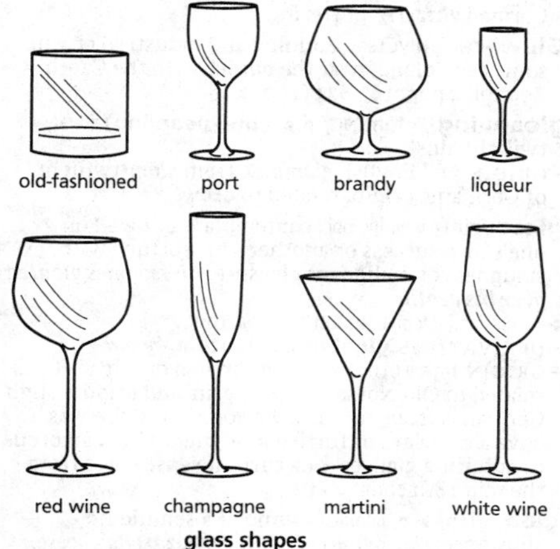

glass shapes

glass·blow·ing /ˈglasˌblō-iNG/ ▶ **n.** the craft of making glassware by blowing air through a tube of semimolten glass.
– DERIVATIVES **glass·blow·er** /-ˌblōər/ **n.**

glass case ▶ **n.** an exhibition display case made mostly from glass.

glass ceil·ing ▶ **n.** [usu. in sing.] an unofficially acknowledged barrier to advancement in a profession, esp. affecting women and members of minorities.

glass cut·ter ▶ **n.** a tool that scores a line on a piece of glass, allowing the glass to be snapped along the line. ■ a person who cuts glass.
– DERIVATIVES **glass cut·ting n.**

glassed-in ▶ **adj.** (of a building or part of a building) covered or enclosed with glass.

glass eel ▶ **n.** an elver at the time that it first enters brackish or fresh water, when it is translucent.

glass·es /ˈglasiz/ ▶ **plural n.** a pair of lenses set in a frame resting on the nose and ears, used to correct or assist defective eyesight or protect the eyes. ■ a pair of binoculars.

glass eye ▶ **n.** an artificial eye made from glass.

glass fi·ber ▶ **n.** a filament of glass. ■ chiefly Brit. a strong plastic, textile, or other material containing embedded glass filaments for reinforcement.

glass har·mon·i·ca ▶ **n.** a musical instrument in which the sound is made by a row of rotating, concentric glass bowls, kept moist and pressed with the fingers or with keys. It was invented in 1761 by Benjamin Franklin and was popular until about 1830.

glass·house /ˈglasˌhous/ ▶ **n.** Brit. a greenhouse.

glass·ine /glaˈsēn/ ▶ **n.** [usu. as modifier] a glossy transparent paper: *glassine envelopes*.
– ORIGIN early 20th cent.: from GLASS + -INE[4].

glass jaw ▶ **n.** Boxing, informal a weak jaw that is easily broken, esp. as an indication of a fighter's vulnerability to an opponent's punches.

glass liz·ard ▶ **n.** a legless burrowing lizard of snakelike appearance, with smooth shiny skin and an easily detached tail, native to Eurasia, Africa, and America. Also called GLASS SNAKE. ● Genus *Ophisaurus*, family Anguidae: several species.

glass·mak·ing /ˈglasˌmākiNG/ ▶ **n.** the manufacture of glass.
– DERIVATIVES **glass·mak·er** /-ˌmākər/ **n.**

glass snake ▶ **n.** another term for GLASS LIZARD.

glass·ware /ˈglasˌwe(ə)r/ ▶ **n.** ornaments and articles made from glass.

glass wool ▶ **n.** glass in the form of fine fibers used for packing and insulation.

glass·work /ˈglasˌwərk/ ▶ **n. 1** the business or technique of cutting and installing glass for windows and doors; glazing.
2 the manufacture of glass and glassware.
3 ornaments and articles made of glass; glassware.

glass·works /ˈglasˌwərks/ ▶ **n.** [treated as sing. or pl.] a factory where glass and glass articles are made.

glass·wort /ˈglasˌwərt, -ˌwôrt/ ▶ **n.** a widely distributed salt-marsh plant with fleshy scalelike leaves. The ashes of the burned plant were formerly used in glassmaking. Also called SAMPHIRE. ● Genus *Salicornia*, family Chenopodiaceae: several species.

glass·y /ˈglasē/ ▶ **adj.** (**glassier**, **glassiest**) **1** of or resembling glass in some way, in particular: ■ having the physical properties of glass; vitreous: *glassy lavas*. ■ (of water) having a smooth surface. ■ (of sound) resembling the sharp or ringing noise made when glass is struck: *a glassy clink*.
2 (of a person's eyes or expression) showing no interest or animation; dull and glazed.
– DERIVATIVES **glass·i·ly** /ˈglasəlē/ **adv.**, **glass·i·ness n.**

Glas·ton·bur·y /ˈglastənb(ə)rē, -ˌberē/ a town in southwestern England; pop. 9,000 (est. 2009). It is the legendary burial place of King Arthur and Queen Guinevere and the site of a ruined abbey held by legend to have been founded by Joseph of Arimathea.

Glas·we·gian /glazˈwējən, -jēən, glas-/ ▶ **adj.** of or relating to Glasgow.
▶ **n.** a native of Glasgow. ■ the dialect or accent of people from Glasgow.
– ORIGIN from GLASGOW, on the pattern of words such as *Norwegian*.

Glat·zer Neisse /ˈglätsər ˌnīsə/ German name for NEISSE (sense 2).

Glau·ber's salt /ˈgloubərz/ ▶ **n.** (also **Glauber's salts**) a crystalline hydrated form of sodium sulfate, used chiefly as a laxative.
– ORIGIN mid 18th cent.: named after Johann R. *Glauber* (1604–1668), the German chemist who first produced the substance artificially.

glau·co·ma /glôˈkōmə/ ▶ **n.** Medicine a condition of increased pressure within the eyeball, causing gradual loss of sight.
– DERIVATIVES **glau·co·ma·tous** /-mətəs/ **adj.**
– ORIGIN mid 17th cent.: via Latin from Greek *glaukōma*, based on *glaukos* 'bluish-green, bluish-gray' (because of the gray-green haze in the pupil).

glau·co·nite /ˈglôkəˌnīt/ ▶ **n.** a greenish clay mineral of the illite group, found chiefly in marine sands.
– DERIVATIVES **glau·co·nit·ic** /ˌglôkəˈnitik/ **adj.**
– ORIGIN mid 19th cent.: from German *Glaukonit*, from Greek *glaukon* (neuter of *glaukos* 'bluish-green') + -ITE[1].

glau·co·phane /ˈglôkəˌfān/ ▶ **n.** a bluish sodium-containing mineral of the amphibole group, found chiefly in schists and other metamorphic rocks.
– ORIGIN mid 19th cent.: from German *Glaukophan*, from Greek *glaukos* 'bluish-green' + *-phanēs* 'shining.'

glau·cous /ˈglôkəs/ ▶ **adj.** technical or literary **1** of a dull grayish-green or blue color.
2 covered with a powdery bloom like that on grapes.
– ORIGIN late 17th cent.: via Latin from Greek *glaukos* 'bluish-green' + -OUS.

glaze /glāz/ ▶ **v.** [with obj.] **1** fit panes of glass into (a window or doorframe or similar structure): *windows can be glazed using laminated glass*. ■ enclose or cover with glass: *the verandas were glazed in*.
2 cover with a glaze or similar finish: *new potatoes that had been glazed in mint-flavored butter*.
3 [no obj.] lose brightness and animation: *the prospect makes my eyes glaze over with boredom* | (as adj. **glazed**) *she had that glazed look in her eyes again*.
▶ **n.** [usu. in sing.] **1** a vitreous substance fused on to the surface of pottery to form a hard, impervious decorative coating. ■ a smooth, shiny surface formed by glazing: *the glaze of the white cups*. ■ chiefly Art a thin topcoat of transparent paint used to modify the tone of an underlying color.
2 a liquid such as milk or beaten egg, used to form a smooth shiny coating on food.
3 a thin, glassy coating of ice on the ground or the surface of water.
– DERIVATIVES **glaz·er n.**
– ORIGIN late Middle English *glase*, from GLASS.

gla·zier /ˈglāZHər/ ▶ **n.** a person whose profession is fitting glass into windows and doors.

glazier's point ▶ **n.** a small triangle of sheet metal, used to hold glass in a window frame until the putty dries.

glaz·ing /ˈglāziNG/ ▶ **n.** the action of installing windows. ■ glass windows: *sealed protective glazing*.

GLBT (also **GLB**) ▶ **abbr.** gay, lesbian, bisexual, or transgendered: [as modifier] *a planned GLBT cable channel*.

GLC ▶ **abbr.** Chemistry gas–liquid chromatography.

gld. ▶ **abbr.** guilder.

gleam /glēm/ ▶ **v.** [no obj.] shine brightly, esp. with reflected light: *light gleamed on the china cats* | *her eyes gleamed with satisfaction*. ■ (of a smooth surface or object) reflect light because well polished: *Victor buffed the glass until it gleamed* | (as adj. **gleaming**) *sleek and gleaming black limousines*. ■ (of an emotion or quality) appear or be expressed through the brightness of someone's eyes or expression: *a hint of mischief gleaming in her eyes*.
▶ **n.** [usu. in sing.] a faint or brief light, esp. one reflected from something: *the gleam of a silver tray*. ■ a brief or faint instance of a quality or emotion, esp. a desirable one: *the gleam of hope vanished*. ■ a brightness in a person's eyes taken as a sign of a particular emotion: *she saw an unmistakable gleam of triumph in his eyes*.
– PHRASES **a gleam in someone's eye** see EYE.
– DERIVATIVES **gleam·ing·ly adv.**, **gleam·y adj.** (archaic).
– ORIGIN Old English *glǣm* 'brilliant light,' of Germanic origin.

glean /glēn/ ▶ **v.** [with obj.] extract (information) from various sources: *the information is gleaned from press clippings*. ■ collect gradually and bit by bit: *objects gleaned from local markets*. ■ historical gather (leftover grain or other produce) after a harvest: (as noun **gleaning**) *the conditions of farm workers in the 1890s made gleaning essential*.
– DERIVATIVES **glean·er n.**, **glean·ing n.**
– ORIGIN late Middle English: from Old French *glener*, from late Latin *glennare*, probably of Celtic origin.

glean·ings /ˈglēniNGz/ ▶ **plural n.** things, esp. facts, that are gathered or collected from various sources rather than acquired as a whole.

Glea·son /ˈglēsən/, Jackie (1916–87), US entertainer; born *Herbert John Gleason*; known as **the Great One**. He is best known for his comedic work on television on *The Jackie Gleason Show* between 1952 and 1970 and as bus driver Ralph Kramden on *The Honeymooners* (1955–56). He also appeared on Broadway in *Take Me Along* (1959) and in movies such as *The Hustler* (1961) and *Nothing in Common* (1986).

glebe /glēb/ ▶ **n.** historical a piece of land serving as part of a clergyman's benefice and providing income. ■ archaic land; fields.
– ORIGIN late Middle English: from Latin *gleba*, *glaeba* 'clod, land, soil.'

glee /glē/ ▶ **n. 1** great delight: *his face lit up with impish glee*.
2 a song for men's voices in three or more parts, usually unaccompanied, of a type popular esp. *c.*1750–1830.
– ORIGIN Old English *glēo* 'entertainment, music, fun,' of Germanic origin. Sense 2 dates from the mid 17th cent.

glee club ▶ **n.** a group organized to sing short choral works, esp. part-songs.

glee·ful /ˈglēfəl/ ▶ **adj.** exuberantly or triumphantly joyful: *she gave a gleeful chuckle*.
– DERIVATIVES **glee·ful·ly adv.**, **glee·ful·ness n.**

glee·man /ˈglēmən/ ▶ **n.** (pl. **gleemen**) historical a professional entertainer, esp. a singer.

glee·some /ˈglēsəm/ ▶ **adj.** archaic gleeful.

gleet /glēt/ ▶ **n.** Medicine a watery discharge from the urethra caused by gonorrheal infection.
– DERIVATIVES **gleet·y adj.**
– ORIGIN Middle English (denoting mucus formed in the stomach): from Old French *glette* 'slime, secretion,' of unknown origin.

Gleich·schal·tung /ˈglikˌSHältoo͝NG/ ▶ **n.** the standardization of political, economic, and social institutions as carried out in authoritarian states.
– ORIGIN German, from *gleich* 'same' + *schalten* 'force or bring into line.'

glen /glen/ ▶ **n.** a narrow valley.
– ORIGIN late Middle English: from Scottish Gaelic and Irish *gleann* (earlier *glenn*).

Glen·dale 1 a city in south central Arizona, northwest of Phoenix; pop. 251,522 (est. 2008).
2 a city in southwestern California, north of Los Angeles; pop. 197,176 (est. 2008).

Glen·do·ra /glenˈdôrə/ a city in southwestern California, northeast of Los Angeles; pop. 49,410 (est. 2008).

glen·gar·ry /glenˈgarē/ ▶ **n.** (pl. **glengarries**) a brimless boat-shaped hat with a cleft down the center, typically having two ribbons hanging at the back, worn as part of Scottish Highland dress.
– ORIGIN mid 19th cent.: from *Glengarry*, the name of a valley in the Highlands of Scotland.

glengarry

Glen More /glen ˈmôr/ another name for GREAT GLEN.

Glenn /glen/, John Herschel, Jr. (1921–), US astronaut and politician. In 1962, he became the first American to orbit the earth. An Ohio Democrat, he served four terms in the US Senate 1975–99. In 1998, in his late 70s, he joined the crew

PRONUNCIATION KEY ə ago, up; ər over, fur; a hat; ā ate; ä car; e let; ē see; i fit; ī by; NG sing; ō go; ô law, for; oi toy; o͝o good; o͞o goo; ou out; TH thin; TH then; ZH vision

g

of the space shuttle *Discovery* in order to help study the effects of space travel on older people.

gle·noid fos·sa /ˈglēnoid ˈfäsə/ (also **glenoid cavity**) ▶ **n.** Anatomy a shallow depression on a bone into which another bone fits to form a joint, esp. that on the scapula into which the head of the humerus fits.
– ORIGIN early 18th cent.: *glenoid* from French *glénoïde*, from Greek *glēnoeidēs*, from *glēnē* 'socket.'

gley /glā/ ▶ **n.** Soil Science a sticky waterlogged soil lacking in oxygen, typically gray to blue in color.
– ORIGIN 1920s: from Ukrainian, literally 'sticky blue clay'; related to CLAY.

gli·a /ˈglēə, ˈglīə/ ▶ **n.** Anatomy the connective tissue of the nervous system, consisting of several different types of cell associated with neurons. Also called NEUROGLIA.
– DERIVATIVES **gli·al** adj.
– ORIGIN late 19th cent.: from Greek, literally 'glue.'

glib /glib/ ▶ **adj.** (**glibber, glibbest**) (of words or the person speaking them) fluent and voluble but insincere and shallow: *she was careful not to let the answer sound too glib.*
– DERIVATIVES **glib·ly** adv., **glib·ness** n.
– ORIGIN late 16th cent. (also in the sense 'smooth, unimpeded'): ultimately of Germanic origin; related to Dutch *glibberig* 'slippery' and German *glibberig* 'slimy.'

g

glide /glīd/ ▶ **v. 1** [no obj.] move with a smooth continuous motion, typically with little noise: *a few gondolas glided past.* ■ [with obj.] cause to move with a smooth continuous motion.
2 [no obj.] make an unpowered flight, either in a glider or in an aircraft with engine failure. ■ (of a bird) fly through the air with very little movement of the wings.
▶ **n.** [in sing.] **1** a smooth continuous movement. ■ a flight in a glider or unpowered aircraft. ■ a smooth continuous step in ballroom dancing.
2 Phonetics a sound produced as the vocal organs move toward or away from articulation of a vowel or consonant, for example /y/ in *mute* /myo͞ot/.
– ORIGIN Old English *glīdan*, of Germanic origin; related to Dutch *glijden* and German *gleiten*.

glide path ▶ **n.** an aircraft's line of descent to land, esp. as indicated by ground radar. ■ a series of events or actions leading smoothly to a particular outcome: *we are on a glide path to success.*

glid·er /ˈglīdər/ ▶ **n. 1** a light aircraft that is designed to fly for long periods without using an engine.
2 a person or thing that glides: *the flying lemur is an efficient glider as well as climber.*
3 a long swinging seat suspended from a frame in a porch.

glide re·flec·tion ▶ **n.** Mathematics a transformation consisting of a translation combined with a reflection about a plane parallel to the direction of the translation.

glid·ing /ˈglīdiNG/ ▶ **n.** the sport of flying in a glider.

glim /glim/ ▶ **n.** archaic, informal a candle or lantern.
– ORIGIN late Middle English (denoting brightness): perhaps an abbreviation of GLIMMER. The current sense dates from the late 17th cent.

glim·mer /ˈglimər/ ▶ **v.** [no obj.] shine faintly with a wavering light: *the moonlight glimmered on the lawn* | (as adj. **glimmering**) *pools of glimmering light.*
▶ **n.** a faint or wavering light. ■ a faint sign of a feeling or quality, esp. a desirable one: *there is one glimmer of hope for Becky.*
– DERIVATIVES **glim·mer·ing·ly** adv.
– ORIGIN late Middle English: probably of Scandinavian origin; related to Swedish *glimra* and Danish *glimre*.

glim·mer·ing /ˈglimәriNG/ ▶ **n.** a glimmer: *the glimmering of an idea.*

glimpse /glimps/ ▶ **n.** a momentary or partial view: *she caught a glimpse of the ocean* | *a glimpse into the world of the wealthy.*
▶ **v.** [with obj.] see or perceive briefly or partially: *he glimpsed a figure standing in the shade.* ■ [no obj.] archaic shine or appear faintly or intermittently: *glowworms glimpsing in the dark.*
– ORIGIN Middle English (in the sense 'shine faintly'): probably of Germanic origin; related to Middle High German *glimsen*, also to GLIMMER.

Glin·ka /ˈgliNGkə/, Mikhail (Ivanovich) (1804–57), Russian composer. He is considered the father of the Russian national school of music. Notable operas: *A Life for the Czar* (1836) and *Russlan and Ludmilla* (1842).

glint /glint/ ▶ **v.** [no obj.] give out or reflect small flashes of light: *her glasses were glinting in the firelight.* ■ (of a person's eyes) shine with a particular emotion: *his eyes glinted angrily.*
▶ **n.** a small flash of light, esp. as reflected from a shiny surface: *the glint of gold in his teeth.* ■ [in sing.] a brightness in someone's eyes seen as a sign of enthusiasm or a particular emotion: *she saw the glint of excitement in his eyes.*
– ORIGIN Middle English (in the sense 'move quickly or obliquely'): variant of dialect *glent*, probably of Scandinavian origin and related to Swedish dialect *glänta, glinta* 'to slip, slide, gleam.'

gli·o·blas·to·ma /ˌglīōblaˈstōmə/ ▶ **n.** (pl. **glioblastomas** or **glioblastomata** /-mətə/) Medicine a highly invasive glioma in the brain.

gli·o·ma /glīˈōmə/ ▶ **n.** (pl. **gliomas** or **gliomata** /-mətə/) Medicine a malignant tumor of the glial tissue of the nervous system.
– ORIGIN late 19th cent.: from Greek *glia* 'glue' + -OMA.

glis·sade /gliˈsäd, -ˈsād/ ▶ **n. 1** a way of sliding down a steep slope of snow or ice, typically on the feet with the support of an ice ax.
2 Ballet a movement, typically used as a joining step, in which one leg is brushed outward from the body, which then takes the weight while the second leg is brushed in to meet it.
▶ **v.** [no obj.] slide down a steep slope of snow or ice with the support of an ice ax.
– ORIGIN mid 19th cent.: French, from *glisser* 'to slip, slide.'

glis·san·do /gliˈsändō/ ▶ **n.** (pl. **glissandi** /-dē/ or **glissandos**) Music a continuous slide upward or downward between two notes.
– ORIGIN Italian, from French *glissant*, present participle of *glisser* 'to slip, slide.'

glis·sé /gləˈsā, glē-/ ▶ **n.** (pl. **same**) Ballet a movement in which weight is transferred from one foot, which is slid outward from the body and briefly extended off the ground, to the other, which is then brought to meet it.
– ORIGIN early 20th cent.: French, literally 'slipped, glided.'

glis·ten /ˈglisən/ ▶ **v.** [no obj.] (of something wet or greasy) shine; glitter: *his cheeks glistened with tears* | (as adj. **glistening**) *the glistening swimming pool.*
▶ **n.** [in sing.] a sparkling light reflected from something wet: *there was a glisten of perspiration across her top lip.*
– DERIVATIVES **glis·ten·ing·ly** adv.
– ORIGIN Old English *glisnian*, of Germanic origin; related to Middle Low German *glisen*. The noun dates from the mid 19th cent.

glis·ter /ˈglistər/ literary ▶ **v.** [no obj.] sparkle; glitter.
▶ **n.** a sparkle.
– ORIGIN late Middle English: probably from Middle Low German *glistern* or Middle Dutch *glisteren*.

glitch /gliCH/ informal ▶ **n.** a sudden, usually temporary malfunction or irregularity of equipment: *a draft version was lost in a computer glitch.* ■ an unexpected setback in a plan: *this has been the first real glitch they've encountered in a three months' tour.* ■ Astronomy a brief irregularity in the rotation of a pulsar.
▶ **v.** [no obj.] suffer a sudden malfunction or irregularity: *her job involves troubleshooting when systems glitch.*
– DERIVATIVES **glitch·y** adj.
– ORIGIN 1960s (originally US): of unknown origin. The original sense was 'a sudden surge of current,' hence 'malfunction, hitch' in astronautical slang.

glit·ter /ˈglitər/ ▶ **v.** [no obj.] shine with a bright, shimmering, reflected light: *trees and grass glittered with dew.* ■ shine as a result of strong feeling: *her eyes were glittering with excitement.*
▶ **n.** [in sing.] **1** bright, shimmering, reflected light: *the blue glitter of the sea.* ■ a glint in a person's eye indicating a particular emotion: *the scathing glitter in his eyes.*
2 tiny pieces of sparkling material used for decoration: *sneakers trimmed with sequins and glitter.*
3 an attractive and exciting but superficial quality: *he avoids the glitter of show business.*
– PHRASES **all that glitters is not gold** proverb the attractive external appearance of something is not a reliable indication of its true nature.
– DERIVATIVES **glit·ter·y** adj.
– ORIGIN late Middle English: from Old Norse *glitra*.

glit·te·ra·ti /ˌglitəˈrätē/ ▶ **plural n.** informal the fashionable set of people engaged in show business or some other glamorous activity.
– ORIGIN 1950s (originally US): blend of GLITTER and LITERATI.

glit·ter·ing /ˈglitəriNG/ ▶ **adj.** [attrib.] shining with a shimmering or sparkling light: *glittering chandeliers.* ■ impressively successful or elaborate: *a glittering military career.*
– DERIVATIVES **glit·ter·ing·ly** adv.

glitz /glits/ informal ▶ **n.** extravagant but superficial display: *the glitz and sophisticated night life of Ibiza.*
▶ **v.** [with obj.] make (something) glamorous or showy: *we need to glitz up the program.*
– ORIGIN 1970s (originally a North American usage): back-formation from GLITZY.

glitz·y /ˈglitsē/ ▶ **adj.** (**glitzier, glitziest**) informal ostentatiously attractive (often used to suggest superficial glamour): *I wanted something glitzy to wear to the launch party.*
– DERIVATIVES **glitz·i·ly** /-səlē/ adv., **glitz·i·ness** n.
– ORIGIN 1960s (originally a North American usage): from GLITTER, suggested by RITZY, and perhaps also by German *glitzerig* 'glittering.'

Gli·wi·ce /gliˈvētsə/ a mining and industrial city in southern Poland, near the border with the Czech Republic; pop. 197,874 (2007).

gloam·ing /ˈglōmiNG/ ▶ **n.** (**the gloaming**) literary twilight; dusk.
– ORIGIN Old English *glōmung*, from *glōm* 'twilight,' of Germanic origin; related to GLOW.

gloat /glōt/ ▶ **v.** [no obj.] contemplate or dwell on one's own success or another's misfortune with smugness or malignant pleasure: *his enemies gloated over his death.*
▶ **n.** [in sing.] informal an act of gloating.
– DERIVATIVES **gloat·er** n., **gloat·ing·ly** adv.
– ORIGIN late 16th cent.: of unknown origin; perhaps related to Old Norse *glotta* 'to grin' and Middle High German *glotzen* 'to stare.' The original sense was 'give a sideways or furtive look,' hence 'cast amorous or admiring glances'; the current sense dates from the mid 18th cent.

glob /gläb/ ▶ **n.** informal a lump of a semiliquid substance: *thick globs of melted mozzarella cheese.*
– ORIGIN early 20th cent.: perhaps a blend of BLOB and GOB[2].

glob·al /ˈglōbəl/ ▶ **adj.** of or relating to the whole world; worldwide: *the downturn in the global economy.* ■ relating to or embracing the whole of something, or of a group of things: *some students may prefer to be given a global picture of what is involved in the task.* ■ Computing operating or applying through the whole of a file, program, etc.: *global searches.*
– DERIVATIVES **glob·al·ly** adv.

glo·bal com·mons ▶ **plural n.** the earth's unowned natural resources, such as the oceans, the atmosphere, and space: *financial speculators and other abusers of our global commons.*

glob·al·ist /ˈglōbəlist/ ▶ **n.** a person who advocates the interpretation or planning of economic and foreign policy in relation to events and developments throughout the world. ■ a person or organization advocating or practicing operations across national divisions.
– DERIVATIVES **glob·al·ism** /-ˌlizəm/ n.

glob·al·ize /ˈglōbəˌlīz/ ▶ **v.** develop or be developed so as to make possible international influence or operation: [with obj.] *communication globalizes capital markets* | [no obj.] *building facilities overseas is part of the strategy of every company that aims to globalize.*
– DERIVATIVES **glob·al·i·za·tion** /ˌglōbəliˈzāSHən/ n.

Glob·al Sur·vey·or (in full **Mars Global Surveyor**) an unmanned American spacecraft that went into orbit around Mars in 1997 to begin detailed photography and mapping of the surface. Contact with the spacecraft was lost in 2006.

glob·al vil·lage ▶ **n.** the world considered as a single community linked by telecommunications.

glob·al warm·ing ▶ **n.** a gradual increase in the overall temperature of the earth's atmosphere generally attributed to the greenhouse effect caused by increased levels of carbon dioxide, chlorofluorocarbons, and other pollutants.

globe /glōb/ ▶ **n. 1** (**the globe**) the earth: *collecting goodies from all over the globe.* ■ a spherical representation of the earth or of the constellations with a map on the surface.
2 a spherical or rounded object: *orange trees clipped into giant globes.* ■ a glass sphere protecting a light. ■ a drinking glass shaped approximately like a sphere: *a brandy globe.* ■ a golden orb as an emblem of sovereignty.
▶ **v.** [with obj.] literary form (something) into a globe.
– DERIVATIVES **globe·like** /-ˌlīk/ adj., **glo·boid** /ˈglōboid/ adj. & n., **glo·bose** /ˈglōbōs/ adj.
– ORIGIN late Middle English (in the sense 'spherical object'): from Old French, or from Latin *globus*.

globe ar·ti·choke ▶ **n.** see ARTICHOKE (sense 1).

globe·fish /ˈglōbˌfiSH/ ▶ **n.** (pl. **same** or **globefishes**)
1 a pufferfish or a porcupine fish.
2 an ocean sunfish. See SUNFISH (sense 1).

globe·flow·er /ˈglōbˌflou(-ə)r/ ▶ **n.** a plant of the buttercup family with globular yellow or orange flowers, native to north temperate regions. ● Genus *Trollius*, family Ranunculaceae.

Globe The·a·tre a theater in Southwark, London, erected in 1599, where many of Shakespeare's plays were first publicly performed. The theater's site was rediscovered in 1989, and a reconstruction of the original theater was opened in 1997.

globe this·tle ▶ **n.** an Old World thistle with globe-shaped heads of metallic blue-gray flowers. ● Genus *Echinops*, family Compositae.

globe·trot·ter /'glōb,trädər/ ▶ **n.** informal a person who travels widely.
– DERIVATIVES **globe-trot v., globe-trot·ting n. & adj.**

glo·big·er·i·na /glō,bijə'rīnə, -'rēnə/ ▶ **n.** (pl. **globigerinas** or **globigerinae** /-nē/) a planktonic marine protozoan with a calcareous shell. The shells collect as a deposit (**globigerina ooze**) over much of the ocean floor. ● Genus *Globigerina*, order Foraminiferida, kingdom Protista.
– ORIGIN modern Latin, from Latin *globus* 'spherical object, globe' (because of the globular chambers in its shell) + *-ger* 'carrying' + **-INA**.

glob·u·lar /'gläbyələr/ ▶ **adj. 1** globe-shaped; spherical.
2 composed of globules.
▶ **n.** Astronomy short for **GLOBULAR CLUSTER**.

glob·u·lar clus·ter ▶ **n.** Astronomy a large compact spherical star cluster, typically of old stars in the outer regions of a galaxy.

glob·ule /'gläbyo͞ol/ ▶ **n.** a small round particle of a substance; a drop: ***globules of fat***. ■ Astronomy a small dark cloud of gas and dust seen against a brighter background such as a luminous nebula.
– DERIVATIVES **glob·u·lous** /-yələs/ **adj.**
– ORIGIN mid 17th cent.: from French, or from Latin *globulus*, diminutive of *globus* 'spherical object, globe.'

glob·u·lin /'gläbyəlin/ ▶ **n.** Biochemistry any of a group of simple proteins soluble in salt solutions and forming a large fraction of blood serum protein. The three principal subsets of globulin are **alpha globulin, beta globulin,** and **gamma globulin,** which are distinguished by their respective degrees of electrophoretic mobility (alpha having the greatest and gamma having the least).
– ORIGIN mid 19th cent.: from **GLOBULE** (in the archaic sense 'blood corpuscle') + **-IN**[1].

glo·bus pal·li·dus /'glōbəs 'palidəs/ ▶ **n.** Anatomy the median part of the lentiform nucleus in the brain.
– ORIGIN late 18th cent.: from Latin, 'pale globus.'

glo·cal·i·za·tion /,glōkələ'zāsнən/ ▶ **n.** the practice of conducting business according to both local and global considerations.
– ORIGIN 1990s: blend of **GLOBAL** + **LOCALIZATION**.

glo·chid /'glōkid/ ▶ **n.** Botany a barbed bristle on the areole of some cacti.
– ORIGIN late 19th cent.: from Greek *glōkhis, glōkhid-* 'arrowhead.'

glo·chid·i·um /glō'kidēəm/ ▶ **n.** (pl. **glochidia** /-'kidēə/) Zoology a parasitic larva of certain freshwater bivalve mollusks, which attaches itself by hooks and suckers to the fins or gills of fish.
– ORIGIN late 19th cent.: modern Latin, based on Greek *glōkhis* 'arrowhead.'

glock·en·spiel /'gläkən,spēl, -,sнpēl/ ▶ **n.** a musical percussion instrument having a set of tuned metal pieces mounted in a frame and struck with small hammers.
– ORIGIN early 19th cent. (denoting an organ stop imitating the sound of bells): from German *Glockenspiel*, literally 'bell-play.'

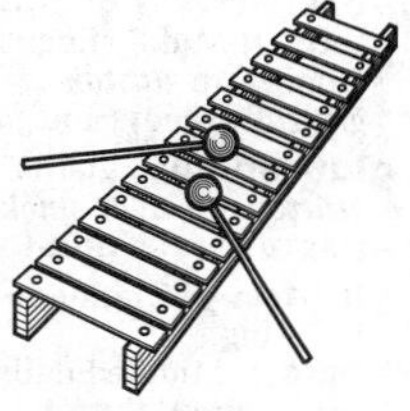
glockenspiel

glom /gläm/ ▶ **v.** (**gloms, glomming, glommed**) [with obj.] informal steal: *I thought he was about to glom my wallet.* ■ [no obj.] (**glom onto**) become stuck or attached to.
– ORIGIN early 20th cent.: variant of Scots *glaum*, of unknown origin.

glo·mer·u·lo·ne·phri·tis /glō,meryəlō,nə'frītis/ ▶ **n.** Medicine acute inflammation of the kidney, typically caused by an immune response.

glo·mer·u·lus /glō'meryələs/ ▶ **n.** (pl. **glomeruli** /-,lī/) Anatomy & Biology a cluster of nerve endings, spores, or small blood vessels, in particular: ■ a cluster of capillaries around the end of a kidney tubule, where waste products are filtered from the blood.
– DERIVATIVES **glo·mer·u·lar** /-lər/ **adj.**
– ORIGIN mid 19th cent.: modern Latin, diminutive of Latin *glomus, glomer-* 'ball of thread.'

gloom /glo͞om/ ▶ **n. 1** partial or total darkness: *he strained his eyes peering into the gloom.* ■ literary a dark or shady place.
2 a state of depression or despondency: *a year of economic gloom for the car industry | his gloom deepened.*
▶ **v.** [no obj.] **1** literary have a dark or somber appearance: *the black gibbet glooms beside the way.* ■ [with obj.] cover with gloom; make dark or dismal: *a black yew gloom'd the stagnant air.*
2 be or look depressed or despondent: *Charles was always glooming about money.*
– PHRASES **gloom and doom** see **DOOM**.
– ORIGIN late Middle English (as a verb): of unknown origin.

gloom·y /'glo͞omē/ ▶ **adj.** (**gloomier, gloomiest**) dark or poorly lit, esp. so as to appear depressing or frightening: *a gloomy corridor.* ■ feeling distressed or pessimistic: *I am by no means gloomy about the prospects for domestic industry.* ■ causing distress or depression: *a gloomy atmosphere.*
– DERIVATIVES **gloom·i·ly** /-məlē/ **adv., gloom·i·ness n.**

gloop /glo͞op/ ▶ **n.** informal another term for **GLOP**.
– DERIVATIVES **gloop·i·ness n., gloop·y adj.** (**gloopier, gloopiest**).
– ORIGIN late 20th cent.: the letters *gl, o,* and *p* are said to be symbolic of semiliquid matter (compare with **GLOP**).

glop /gläp/ ▶ **n.** informal a sticky and amorphous substance, typically something unpleasant: *the snow was sun-softened glop.* ■ a soft, shapeless lump of something: *a glop of creamy dressing.* ■ worthless or overly sentimental writing, music, or other material: *commercialized glop, not worth thinking about.*
– DERIVATIVES **glop·py adj.** (**gloppier, gloppiest**).
– ORIGIN 1940s: symbolic (see **GLOOP**).

Glo·ri·a /'glôrēə/ ▶ **n.** a Christian liturgical hymn or formula beginning (in the Latin text) with *Gloria*, in particular: ■ the hymn beginning *Gloria in excelsis Deo* (Glory be to God in the highest), forming a set part of the Mass. ■ a musical setting of this: *Vivaldi's Gloria.* ■ the doxology beginning *Gloria Patris* (Glory be to the Father), used after psalms and in formal prayer (e.g., in the rosary).
– ORIGIN Middle English: Latin, 'glory.'

Glo·ri·a·na /,glôrē'änə/ the nickname of Queen Elizabeth I.

glo·ri·fied /'glôrə,fīd/ ▶ **adj. 1** [attrib.] (esp. of something or someone ordinary or unexceptional) represented in such a way as to appear more elevated or special: *I did the paperwork and was basically a glorified secretary.*
2 (in religious contexts) made glorious: *the transformed and glorified Jesus.*

glo·ri·fy /'glôrə,fī/ ▶ **v.** (**glorifies, glorifying, glorified**) [with obj.] **1** reveal or make clearer the glory of (God) by one's actions: *God can be glorified through a life of scholarship.* ■ give praise to (God).
2 describe or represent as admirable, esp. unjustifiably or undeservedly: *a football video glorifying violence.*
– DERIVATIVES **glo·ri·fi·ca·tion** /,glôrəfi'kāsнən/ **n., glo·ri·fi·er n.**
– ORIGIN Middle English: from Old French *glorifier*, from ecclesiastical Latin *glorificare*, from late Latin *glorificus*, from Latin *gloria* 'glory.'

glo·ri·ous /'glôrēəs/ ▶ **adj. 1** having, worthy of, or bringing fame or admiration: *the most glorious victory of all time.*
2 having a striking beauty or splendor that evokes feelings of delighted admiration: *a glorious autumn day.*
– DERIVATIVES **glo·ri·ous·ly adv., glo·ri·ous·ness n.**
– ORIGIN Middle English: from Old French *glorieus*, from Latin *gloriosus*, from *gloria* 'glory.'

glo·ry /'glôrē/ ▶ **n.** (pl. **glories**) **1** high renown or honor won by notable achievements: *to fight and die for the glory of one's nation.* ■ praise, worship, and thanksgiving offered to God.
2 magnificence; great beauty: *the train has been restored to all its former glory.* ■ (often **glories**) a thing that is beautiful or distinctive; a special cause for pride, respect, or delight: *the glories of Paris.* ■ the splendor and bliss of heaven: *with the saints in glory.*
3 a luminous ring or halo, esp. as depicted around the head of Jesus Christ or a saint.
▶ **v.** [no obj.] (**glory in**) take great pride or pleasure in: *they were individuals who gloried in their independence.* ■ exult in unpleasantly or boastfully: *readers tended to defend their paper or even to glory in its bias.*
– PHRASES **glory be!** expressing enthusiastic piety. ■ informal used as an exclamation of surprise or delight. ■ (**Glory Be**) [as noun] (esp. in Roman Catholic use) the doxology beginning "Glory be to the Father." **go to glory** die; be destroyed. **in one's glory** informal in a state of extreme joy or exaltation.
– ORIGIN Middle English: from Old French *glorie*, from Latin *gloria*.

glo·ry days ▶ **plural n.** a time in the past regarded as being better than the present: *his glory days as a high school basketball star | the glory days of tourism.*

glo·ry hole ▶ **n. 1** a small furnace used to keep glass malleable so that it can be worked.
2 informal, dated an untidy storage place, esp. a room or cupboard.
3 informal a hole in a wall through which fellatio or masturbation is conducted incognito.
– ORIGIN early 19th cent.: of unknown origin.

gloss[1] /gläs, glôs/ ▶ **n. 1** shine or luster on a smooth surface: *hair with a healthy gloss.* ■ (also **gloss paint**) a type of paint that dries to a bright shiny surface.
2 [in sing.] a superficially attractive appearance or impression: *beneath the gloss of success was a tragic private life.*
▶ **v.** [with obj.] **1** apply a cosmetic gloss to. ■ apply gloss paint to.
2 (**gloss over**) try to conceal or disguise (something embarrassing or unfavorable) by treating it briefly or representing it misleadingly: *the social costs of this growth are glossed over.*
– DERIVATIVES **gloss·er n.**
– ORIGIN mid 16th cent.: of unknown origin.

gloss[2] ▶ **n.** a translation or explanation of a word or phrase. ■ an explanation, interpretation, or paraphrase: *the chapter acts as a helpful gloss on Pynchon's general method.*
▶ **v.** [with obj.] (usu. **be glossed**) provide an explanation, interpretation, or paraphrase for (a text, word, etc.). ■ [no obj.] (**gloss on/upon**) archaic write or make comments, esp. unfavorable ones, about (something): *those laws, which they assumed the liberty of interpreting and glossing upon.*
– ORIGIN mid 16th cent.: alteration of the noun *gloze*, from Old French *glose* (see **GLOZE**), suggested by medieval Latin *glossa* 'explanation of a difficult word,' from Greek *glōssa* 'word needing explanation, language, tongue.'

g

gloss. ▶ **abbr.** glossary.

glos·sa /'gläsə, 'glô-/ ▶ **n.** (pl. **glossae** /-sē/ or **glossas**) a tonguelike structure in the labium of an insect's mouthparts.

glos·sal /'gläsəl, 'glô-/ ▶ **adj.** Anatomy, rare of the tongue; lingual.
– ORIGIN early 19th cent.: from Greek *glōssa* 'tongue' + **-AL**.

glos·sa·ry /'gläsərē, 'glô-/ ▶ **n.** (pl. **glossaries**) an alphabetical list of terms or words found in or relating to a specific subject, text, or dialect, with explanations; a brief dictionary.
– DERIVATIVES **glos·sar·i·al** /glä'se(ə)rēəl, glô-/ **adj., glos·sa·rist** /-rist/ **n.**
– ORIGIN late Middle English: from Latin *glossarium*, from *glossa* (see **GLOSS**[2]).

glos·sa·tor /'glä,sātər, 'glô-, glä'sātər, glô-/ ▶ **n.** chiefly historical a person who writes glosses, esp. a scholarly commentator on the texts of classical, civil, or canon law.
– ORIGIN late Middle English: from medieval Latin, from *glossare*, from Latin *glossa* (see **GLOSS**[2]).

glos·si·tis /glä'sītis, glô-/ ▶ **n.** Medicine inflammation of the tongue.
– ORIGIN early 19th cent.: from Greek *glōssa* 'tongue' + **-ITIS**.

glos·sog·ra·pher /glä'sägrəfər, glô-/ ▶ **n.** a writer of glosses or commentaries.

glos·sog·ra·phy /glä'sägrə,fē/ ▶ **n. 1** the writing of glosses or commentaries.
2 the compiling of glossaries.

glos·so·la·li·a /,gläsə'lālēə, ,glô-/ ▶ **n.** the phenomenon of (apparently) speaking in an unknown language, esp. in religious worship. It is practiced esp. by Pentecostal and charismatic Christians.
– DERIVATIVES **glos·so·la·lic** /-,lālik/ **adj.**
– ORIGIN late 19th cent.: from Greek *glōssa* 'language, tongue' + *lalia* 'speech.'

glos·so·pha·ryn·ge·al nerve /,gläsōfə'rinjēəl, ,glô-/ ▶ **n.** Anatomy each of the ninth pair of cranial nerves, supplying the tongue and pharynx.

gloss·y /'gläsē, 'glô-/ ▶ **adj.** (**glossier, glossiest**) **1** shiny and smooth: *thick, glossy, manageable hair.* ■ (of a magazine or photograph) printed on high-quality smooth shiny paper.
2 superficially attractive and stylish, and suggesting wealth or expense: *glossy TV miniseries and soaps.*
▶ **n.** (pl. **glossies**) informal a magazine printed on glossy paper, expensively produced with many color photographs. ■ a photograph printed on glossy paper.
– DERIVATIVES **gloss·i·ly** /-səlē/ **adv., gloss·i·ness n.**

glot·tal /'glätl/ ▶ **adj.** [attrib.] of or produced by the glottis.

glot·tal stop ▶ **n.** a consonant formed by the audible release of the airstream after complete closure of the glottis. It is widespread in some nonstandard English accents, and in some other languages, such as Arabic, it is a standard consonant.

glot·tis /ˈglätis/ ▶ **n.** the part of the larynx consisting of the vocal cords and the slitlike opening between them. It affects voice modulation through expansion or contraction.
– DERIVATIVES **glot·tic** /ˈglätik/ **adj.**
– ORIGIN late 16th cent.: modern Latin, from Greek *glōttis*, from *glōtta*, variant of *glōssa* 'tongue.'

glot·to·chro·nol·o·gy /ˌglätōkrəˈnäləjē/ ▶ **n.** the use of statistical data to date the divergence of languages from their common sources.
– DERIVATIVES **glot·to·chron·o·log·i·cal** /-ˌkränəˈläjikəl/ **adj.**

Glouces·ter /ˈglôstər, ˈgläs-/ **1** a city in southwestern England, the county town of Gloucestershire; pop. 127,100 (est. 2009).
2 a city in northeastern Massachusetts, on Cape Ann, noted as a fishing and resort center; pop. 30,243 (est. 2008).

Glouces·ter·shire /ˈglôstərSHər, ˈgläs-, -ˌSHi(ə)r/ a county in southwestern England; county town, Gloucester.

glove /gləv/ ▶ **n.** a covering for the hand worn for protection against cold or dirt and typically having separate parts for each finger and the thumb. ■ a padded protective covering for the hand used in boxing, baseball, and other sports.
▶ **v.** [with obj.] informal (of a baseball catcher) catch, deflect, or touch (the ball) with one's glove.
– PHRASES **fit like a glove** (of clothes) fit exactly. **the gloves are off** (or **with the gloves off** or **take the gloves off**) used to express the notion that something will be done in an uncompromising or brutal way, without compunction or hesitation: *for the banks chasing this growing business, the gloves are now definitely off.*
– DERIVATIVES **gloved adj.**, **glove·less adj.**
– ORIGIN Old English *glōf*, of Germanic origin.

glove box (also **glovebox**) ▶ **n. 1** another term for GLOVE COMPARTMENT.
2 a closed chamber into which a pair of gloves projects from openings in the side, used esp. in laboratories and incubators in hospitals to prevent contamination.

glove com·part·ment ▶ **n.** a recess with a hinged door in the dashboard of a motor vehicle, used for storing small items.

glov·er /ˈgləvər/ ▶ **n.** a maker of gloves.

glow /glō/ ▶ **v.** [no obj.] give out steady light without flame: *the tips of their cigarettes glowed in the dark.* ■ have an intense color and a slight shine: [with complement] *faces that glowed red with the cold.* ■ have a heightened color or a bloom on the skin as a result of warmth or health: *he was glowing with health.* ■ feel deep pleasure or satisfaction and convey it through one's expression and bearing: *Katy always glowed when he praised her.*
▶ **n.** [in sing.] a steady radiance of light or heat: *the setting sun cast a deep red glow over the city.* ■ a feeling of warmth in the face or body; the visible effects of this as a redness of the cheeks: *he could feel the brandy filling him with a warm glow.* ■ a strong feeling of pleasure or well-being: *with a glow of pride, Mildred walked away.*
– ORIGIN Old English *glōwan*, of Germanic origin; related to Dutch *gloeien* and German *glühen*.

glow dis·charge ▶ **n.** a luminous sparkless electrical discharge from a pointed conductor in a gas at low pressure.

glow·er /ˈglouər/ ▶ **v.** [no obj.] have an angry or sullen look on one's face; scowl: *she glowered at him suspiciously.*
▶ **n.** [in sing.] an angry or sullen look.
– DERIVATIVES **glow·er·ing adj.**, **glow·er·ing·ly adv.**
– ORIGIN late 15th cent.: perhaps a Scots variant of synonymous dialect *glore*, or from obsolete *glow* 'to stare,' both possibly of Scandinavian origin.

glow·fly /ˈglōˌflī/ another term for FIREFLY.

glow·ing /ˈglōiNG/ ▶ **adj.** [attrib.] expressing great praise: *he received a glowing report from his teachers.*
– DERIVATIVES **glow·ing·ly adv.**

glow stick ▶ **n.** a novelty item consisting of a plastic tube containing two chemicals that combine when the tube is bent, so producing a luminescent glow.

glow·worm /ˈglōˌwərm/ ▶ **n.** a soft-bodied beetle with luminescent organs in the abdomen, esp. the larvalike wingless female, which emits light to attract the flying male. ● Families Lampyridae and Phengodidae: several genera numerous species including the American *Zarhipis integripennis*.

glox·in·i·a /gläkˈsinēə/ ▶ **n.** a tropical American plant with large, velvety, bell-shaped flowers. ● Genera *Gloxinia* and *Sinningia*, family Gesneriaceae: several species, in particular the florists' gloxinia (*S. speciosa*), which is a popular houseplant.
– ORIGIN modern Latin, named after Benjamin P. *Gloxin*, the 18th-cent. German botanist who first described it.

gloze /glōz/ ▶ **v.** [with obj.] rare make excuses for: *the demeanor of Mathews is rather glozed over.* ■ [no obj.] archaic use ingratiating or fawning language. ■ [no obj.] archaic make a comment or comments.
– ORIGIN Middle English: from Old French *gloser*, from *glose* 'a gloss, comment,' based on Latin *glossa* (see GLOSS[2]).

glu·ca·gon /ˈglo͞okəˌgän/ ▶ **n.** Biochemistry a hormone formed in the pancreas that promotes the breakdown of glycogen to glucose in the liver.
– ORIGIN 1920s: from Greek *glukus* 'sweet' + *agōn* 'leading, bringing.'

Gluck /glo͝ok/, Christoph Willibald von (1714–87), German composer. His first operas were in the traditional Italian style, but with *Orfeo ed Euridice* (1762), he initiated a new style in which he united dramatic, musical, and emotional elements, revolutionizing opera. Later works include *Alceste* (1767), *Iphigénie en Aulide* (1774), and *Iphigénie en Tauride* (1779).

glu·co·cor·ti·coid /ˌglo͞okōˈkôrtiˌkoid/ ▶ **n.** Biochemistry any of a group of corticosteroids (e.g., hydrocortisone) that are involved in the metabolism of carbohydrates, proteins, and fats and have anti-inflammatory activity.

glu·co·sa·mine /glo͞oˈkōsəˌmēn, -min/ ▶ **n.** a crystalline compound which occurs widely in connective tissue, esp. as a component of chitin. ■ a synthesized form of this, taken to relieve arthritis pain.

glu·cose /ˈglo͞okōs/ ▶ **n.** Biochemistry a simple sugar that is an important energy source in living organisms and is a component of many carbohydrates. ● A hexose; chem. formula: $C_6H_{12}O_6$. ■ a syrup containing glucose and other sugars, made by hydrolysis of starch and used in the food industry.
– ORIGIN mid 19th cent.: from French, from Greek *gleukos* 'sweet wine,' related to *glukus* 'sweet.'

glu·co·side /ˈglo͞okəˌsīd/ ▶ **n.** Biochemistry a glycoside derived from glucose.
– DERIVATIVES **glu·co·sid·ic** /ˌglo͞okəˈsidik/ **adj.**

glu·cu·ron·ic ac·id /ˌglo͞okyəˈränik/ ▶ **n.** Biochemistry an acid derived from glucose, occurring naturally as a constituent of hyaluronic acid and other glycosaminoglycans. ● A uronic acid; chem. formula: $HOOC(CHOH)_4CHO$.

glue /glo͞o/ ▶ **n.** an adhesive substance used for sticking objects or materials together.
▶ **v.** (**glues, gluing** or **glueing, glued**) [with obj.] fasten or join with or as if with glue: *the wood is cut up into small pieces which are then glued together.* ■ (**be glued to**) informal be paying very close attention to (something, esp. a television or computer screen): *I was glued to the television when the Olympics were on.*
– DERIVATIVES **glue·like** /-ˌlīk/ **adj.**, **glue·y adj.**
– ORIGIN Middle English: from Old French *glu* (noun), *gluer* (verb), from late Latin *glus*, *glut-*, from Latin *gluten*.

glue·pot /ˈglo͞oˌpät/ ▶ **n.** a pot with an outer container holding water, used to heat glue that sets when it cools.

glue sniff·ing ▶ **n.** the practice of inhaling intoxicating fumes from the solvents in adhesives.
– DERIVATIVES **glue sniff·er n.**

glug /gləg/ informal ▶ **v.** (**glugs, glugging, glugged**) [with obj.] drink or pour (liquid) with a hollow gurgling sound: *he glugs down half his beer.*
▶ **n.** a hollow gurgling sound or series of sounds as of liquid being poured from a bottle. ■ an amount of liquid poured from a bottle: *a couple of good glugs of Dubonnet.*
– ORIGIN late 17th cent.: imitative.

glum /gləm/ ▶ **adj.** (**glummer, glummest**) looking or feeling dejected; morose: *they looked glum but later cheered up.*
– DERIVATIVES **glum·ly adv.**, **glum·ness n.**
– ORIGIN mid 16th cent.: related to dialect *glum* 'to frown,' variant of GLOOM.

glume /glo͞om/ ▶ **n.** Botany each of two membranous bracts surrounding the spikelet of a grass (forming the husk of a cereal grain) or one surrounding the florets of a sedge.
– ORIGIN late 18th cent.: from Latin *gluma* 'husk.'

glu·on /ˈglo͞oän/ ▶ **n.** Physics a subatomic particle of a class that is thought to bind quarks together.
– ORIGIN 1970s: from GLUE + -ON.

glut /glət/ ▶ **n.** an excessively abundant supply of something: *there is a glut of cars on the market.*
▶ **v.** (**gluts, glutting, glutted**) [with obj.] (usu. **be glutted**) supply or fill to excess: *the factories for recycling paper are glutted | he was glutting himself on junk food.* ■ archaic satisfy fully: *he planned a treacherous murder to glut his desire for revenge.*
– ORIGIN Middle English: probably via Old French from Latin *gluttire* 'to swallow'; related to GLUTTON.

glu·ta·mate /ˈglo͞otəˌmāt/ ▶ **n.** Biochemistry a salt or ester of glutamic acid. ■ glutamic acid, its salts, or its anion. ■ short for MONOSODIUM GLUTAMATE.

glu·tam·ic ac·id /glo͞oˈtamik/ ▶ **n.** Biochemistry an acidic amino acid that is a constituent of many proteins. ● Chem. formula: $HOOC(CH_2)_2(NH_2)COOH$.
– ORIGIN late 19th cent.: from GLUTEN + AMINE + -IC.

glu·ta·mine /ˈglo͞otəˌmēn/ ▶ **n.** Biochemistry a hydrophilic amino acid that is a constituent of most proteins. ● An amide of glutamic acid; chem. formula: $H_2NCOCH_2CH_2(NH_2)COOH$.
– ORIGIN late 19th cent.: blend of GLUTAMIC ACID and AMINE.

glu·ta·thi·one /ˌglo͞otəˈTHīōn/ ▶ **n.** Biochemistry a compound involved as a coenzyme in oxidation–reduction reactions in cells. It is a tripeptide derived from glutamic acid, cysteine, and glycine.

glute /glo͞ot/ ▶ **n.** (usu. **glutes**) informal short for GLUTEUS.

glu·te·al /ˈglo͞otēəl/ ▶ **adj.** of or relating to the gluteus muscles: *the gluteal region.*
▶ **n.** (usually **gluteals**) a gluteus muscle in the buttocks: *reshaping the gluteals isn't a matter of doing 25 more leg lifts.*
– ORIGIN late 18th cent.: from *gluteus* + *-al*.

glu·ten /ˈglo͞otn/ ▶ **n.** a substance present in cereal grains, esp. wheat, that is responsible for the elastic texture of dough. A mixture of two proteins, it causes illness in people with celiac disease.
– ORIGIN late 16th cent. (originally denoting protein from animal tissue): via French from Latin, literally 'glue.'

glu·te·us /ˈglo͞otēəs/ (also **gluteus muscle**) ▶ **n.** (pl. **glutei** /-tēˌī/) any of three muscles in each buttock that move the thigh, the largest of which is the **gluteus maximus**.
– ORIGIN late 17th cent.: modern Latin, from Greek *gloutos* 'buttock.'

glu·ti·nous /ˈglo͞otn-əs/ ▶ **adj.** like glue in texture; sticky: *glutinous mud.*
– DERIVATIVES **glu·ti·nous·ly adv.**, **glu·ti·nous·ness n.**
– ORIGIN late Middle English: from Old French *glutineux* or Latin *glutinosus*, from *gluten* 'glue.'

glut·ton /ˈglətn/ ▶ **n. 1** an excessively greedy eater. ■ a person who is excessively fond of or always eager for something: ***a glutton for adventure.***
2 another term for WOLVERINE, esp. the European species. [translation of German *Vielfrass* 'glutton,' from Middle Low German *velvratze, velevras* 'wolverine.']
– PHRASES **a glutton for punishment** a person who is always eager to undertake hard or unpleasant tasks.
– DERIVATIVES **glut·ton·ize** /-ˌīz/ **v.**
– ORIGIN Middle English: from Old French *gluton*, from Latin *glutton-*, related to *gluttire* 'to swallow,' *gluttus* 'greedy,' and *gula* 'throat.'

glut·ton·ous /ˈglətnəs/ ▶ **adj.** excessively greedy: ***a gluttonous, cigar-smoking capitalist.***
– DERIVATIVES **glut·ton·ous·ly** /-əslē/ **adv.**

glut·ton·y /ˈglətn-ē/ ▶ **n.** habitual greed or excess in eating.
– ORIGIN Middle English: from Old French *glutonie*, from *gluton* 'glutton.'

gly·ce·mi·a /glīˈsēmēə/ (Brit. **glycaemia**) ▶ **n.** the presence of glucose in the blood.
– DERIVATIVES **gly·ce·mic adj.** /-ˈsēmik/.
– ORIGIN early 20th cent.: from GLYCO- + -EMIA.

gly·ce·mic in·dex /glīˈsēmik/ ▶ **n.** a system that ranks foods on a scale from 1 to 100 based on their effect on blood-sugar levels.

glyc·er·ide /ˈglisəˌrīd/ ▶ **n.** a fatty acid ester of glycerol.

glyc·er·in /ˈglisərin/ (also **glycerine** /-rin, -ˌrēn, ˌglisəˈrēn/) ▶ **n.** another term for GLYCEROL.
– ORIGIN mid 19th cent.: from French *glycérin*, from Greek *glukeros* 'sweet.'

glyc·er·ol /ˈglisəˌrôl, -ˌräl/ ▶ **n.** a colorless, sweet, viscous liquid formed as a byproduct in soap manufacture. It is used as an emollient and laxative, and for making explosives and antifreeze. ● A trihydric alcohol; chem. formula: $CH_2(OH)CH(OH)CH_2(OH)$.
– ORIGIN late 19th cent.: from GLYCERIN + -OL.

glyc·er·yl /ˈglisəˌril/ ▶ **n.** [as modifier] Chemistry of or denoting a radical derived from glycerol by replacement of one or more hydrogen atoms: *glyceryl trinitrate.*
– ORIGIN mid 19th cent.: from GLYCERIN + -YL.

gly·cine /ˈglīsēn/ ▶ **n.** Biochemistry the simplest naturally occurring amino acid. It is a constituent of most proteins. ● Chem. formula: H_2NCH_2COOH.
– ORIGIN mid 19th cent.: from Greek *glukus* 'sweet' + **-INE**[4].

glyco- ▶ **comb. form** of, relating to, or producing sugar: *glycogenesis* | *glycoside*.
– ORIGIN from Greek *glukus* 'sweet.'

gly·co·bi·ol·o·gy /ˌglīkōbīˈäləjē/ ▶ **n.** the scientific study of carbohydrates and their role in biology. ■ this field limited to the study of sugars.

gly·co·gen /ˈglīkəjən/ ▶ **n.** Biochemistry a substance deposited in bodily tissues as a store of carbohydrates. It is a polysaccharide that forms glucose on hydrolysis.
– DERIVATIVES **gly·co·gen·ic** /ˌglīkəˈjenik/ **adj.**

gly·co·gen·e·sis /ˌglīkəˈjenəsis/ ▶ **n.** Biochemistry the formation of glycogen from sugar.

gly·col /ˈglīkôl, -kōl/ ▶ **n.** short for **ETHYLENE GLYCOL**. ■ Chemistry another term for **DIOL**.
– ORIGIN mid 19th cent. (applied to ethylene glycol): from **GLYCERIN** + **-OL** (originally intended to designate a substance intermediate between glycerine and alcohol).

gly·col·ic ac·id /glīˈkälik/ ▶ **n.** a colorless, translucent, crystalline compound, $C_2H_4O_3$, that occurs in cane sugar, unripe grapes, and sugar beets and has numerous industrial uses, esp. in dyeing leather and textiles and in the manufacture of pesticides.

gly·col·y·sis /glīˈkäləsis/ ▶ **n.** Biochemistry the breakdown of glucose by enzymes, releasing energy and pyruvic acid.
– DERIVATIVES **gly·co·lyt·ic** /ˌglīkəˈlitik/ **adj.**

gly·co·pro·tein /ˌglīkōˈprōtēn/ ▶ **n.** Biochemistry any of a class of proteins that have carbohydrate groups attached to the polypeptide chain. Also called **glycopeptide**.

gly·cos·a·mi·no·gly·can /ˌglīkōsəˌmēnōˈglīkan/ ▶ **n.** Biochemistry any of a group of compounds occurring chiefly as components of connective tissue. They are complex polysaccharides containing amino groups. Formerly called **MUCOPOLYSACCHARIDE**.

gly·co·side /ˈglīkəˌsīd/ ▶ **n.** Biochemistry a compound formed from a simple sugar and another compound by replacement of a hydroxyl group in the sugar molecule. Many drugs and poisons derived from plants are glycosides.
– DERIVATIVES **gly·co·sid·ic** /ˌglīkəˈsidik/ **adj.**
– ORIGIN late 19th cent.: from **GLYCO-** 'relating to sugar,' on the pattern of *glucoside*.

gly·cos·u·ri·a /ˌglīkōsyo͝oˈrēə/ ▶ **n.** Medicine a condition characterized by an excess of sugar in the urine, typically associated with diabetes or kidney disease.
– DERIVATIVES **gly·cos·u·ric** /-ˈsyo͝orik/ **adj.**
– ORIGIN mid 19th cent.: from French *glycosurie*, from *glucos* 'glucose.'

glyph /glif/ ▶ **n. 1** a hieroglyphic character or symbol; a pictograph: *flanges painted with esoteric glyphs*. ■ strictly, a sculptured symbol (e.g., as forming the ancient Mayan writing system). ■ Computing a small graphic symbol.
2 Architecture an ornamental carved groove or channel, as on a Greek frieze.
– DERIVATIVES **glyph·ic** /ˈglifik/ **adj.**
– ORIGIN late 18th cent. (sense 2): from French *glyphe*, from Greek *gluphē* 'carving.'

gly·phos·ate /ˈglīfəˌsāt/ ▶ **n.** a synthetic compound that is a nonselective systemic herbicide, particularly effective against perennial weeds. ● Alternative name: *N*-**(phosphonomethyl) glycine**; chem. formula: $C_3H_8NO_5P$.

glyp·tic /ˈgliptik/ ▶ **adj.** of or concerning carving or engraving.
– ORIGIN early 19th cent.: from French *glyptique* or Greek *gluptikos*, from *gluptēs* 'carver,' from *gluphein* 'carve.'

glyp·to·dont /ˈgliptəˌdänt/ ▶ **n.** a fossil South American edentate mammal of the Cenozoic era, related to armadillos but much larger. Glyptodonts had fluted teeth and a body covered in a thick bony carapace. ● Family Glyptodontidae, order Xenarthra (or Edentata): several genera, including *Glyptodon*.
– ORIGIN mid 19th cent.: from Greek *gluptos* 'carved' (from *gluphein* 'carve') + *odous, odont-* 'tooth.'

glyp·tog·ra·phy /glipˈtägrəfē/ ▶ **n.** the art or scientific study of gem engraving.
– ORIGIN late 18th cent.: from Greek *gluptos* 'carved' (from *gluphein* 'carve') + **-GRAPHY**.

GM ▶ **abbr.** ■ general manager. ■ Chess grand master. ■ genetically modified. ■ General Motors.

gm ▶ **abbr.** gram(s).

G-man ▶ **n.** (pl. **G-men**) informal an FBI agent.
– ORIGIN 1930s: probably an abbreviation of *Government man*.

GMAT ▶ **abbr.** ■ Graduate Management Admissions Test. ■ Greenwich Mean Astronomical Time.

GMP ▶ **abbr.** guanosine monophosphate.

GMT ▶ **abbr.** Greenwich Mean Time.

GMW ▶ **abbr.** gram-molecular weight.

gn ▶ **abbr.** guinea(s).

gnarl /närl/ ▶ **n.** a rough, knotty protuberance, esp. on a tree.
– ORIGIN early 19th cent.: back-formation from **GNARLED**.

gnarled /närld/ ▶ **adj.** knobbly, rough, and twisted, esp. with age: *the gnarled old oak tree*.
– ORIGIN early 17th cent.: variant of *knarled*, from **KNAR**.

gnarl·y /ˈnärlē/ ▶ **adj.** (**gnarlier**, **gnarliest**)
1 gnarled.
2 informal difficult, dangerous, or challenging: *she battled through the gnarly first sequence*. [originally surfers' slang, perhaps from the appearance of rough sea.] ■ unpleasant; unattractive: *train stations can be pretty gnarly places*.

gnash /naSH/ ▶ **v.** [with obj.] grind (one's teeth) together, typically as a sign of anger: *no doubt he is gnashing his teeth in rage*. ■ [no obj.] (of teeth) strike together; grind: *the dog's jaws were primed to gnash*.
– ORIGIN late Middle English: perhaps related to Old Norse *gnastan* 'a gnashing.'

gnat /nat/ ▶ **n.** a small two-winged fly that resembles a mosquito. Gnats include both biting and nonbiting forms, and they typically form large swarms. ● Several families, including Simuliidae (black flies) and Ceratopogonidae. ■ a person or thing seen as tiny or insignificant, esp. in comparison with something larger or more important: *I was only a gnat in the affair*.
– ORIGIN Old English *gnæt*, of Germanic origin; related to German *Gnitze*.

gnat·catch·er /ˈnatˌkaCHər, -ˌkeCHər/ ▶ **n.** a tiny gray-backed New World songbird, with a long tail that is often cocked. ● Genus *Polioptila*, family Polioptilidae (or Sylviidae): several species.

gnath·ic /ˈnaTHik/ ▶ **adj.** rare of or relating to the jaws.
– ORIGIN late 19th cent.: from Greek *gnathos* 'jaw' + **-IC**.

Gna·thos·to·mu·li·da /nəˌTHästəˈmyo͞olədə/ Zoology a minor phylum of minute marine worms that appear to be intermediate between coelenterates and flatworms.
– DERIVATIVES **gna·thos·to·mu·lid** /ˌnaTHəˈstômyəlid, ˌnā-/ **n. & adj.**
– ORIGIN modern Latin (plural), from Greek *gnathos* 'jaw' + *stoma* 'mouth.'

gnaw /nô/ ▶ **v.** [no obj.] **1** bite at or nibble something persistently: *watching a dog gnaw at a big bone*. ■ [with obj.] bite at or nibble (something): *she sat gnawing her underlip*.
2 cause persistent and wearing distress or anxiety: *the doubts continued to gnaw at me*.
– ORIGIN Old English *gnagan*, of Germanic origin; related to German *nagen*, ultimately imitative.

gnaw·ing /ˈnô-iNG/ ▶ **adj.** persistently worrying or distressing: *that gnawing pain in her stomach* | *gnawing doubts*.
– DERIVATIVES **gnaw·ing·ly** **adv.**

gnd. ▶ **abbr.** ground.

gneiss /nīs/ ▶ **n.** a metamorphic rock with a banded or foliated structure, typically coarse-grained and consisting mainly of feldspar, quartz, and mica.
– DERIVATIVES **gneiss·ic** /-sik/ **adj.**, **gneiss·oid** /-soid/ **adj.**
– ORIGIN mid 18th cent.: from German, from Old High German *gneisto* 'spark' (because of the rock's sheen).

gnoc·chi /ˈnäkē/ ▶ **plural n.** (in Italian cooking) small dumplings made from potato, semolina, or flour, usually served with a sauce.
– ORIGIN Italian, plural of *gnocco*, alteration of *nocchio* 'knot in wood.'

gnome[1] /nōm/ ▶ **n.** a legendary dwarfish creature supposed to guard the earth's treasures underground. ■ informal a small ugly person. ■ informal a person regarded as having secret or sinister influence, esp. in financial matters: *the gnomes of Zurich*. ■ (also **garden gnome**) a small garden ornament in the form of a bearded man with a pointed hat.
– DERIVATIVES **gnom·ish** **adj.**
– ORIGIN mid 17th cent.: from French, from modern Latin *gnomus*, a word used by Paracelsus as a synonym of *Pygmaeus*, denoting a mythical race of very small people said to inhabit parts of Ethiopia and India (compare with **PYGMY**).

gnome[2] ▶ **n.** a short statement encapsulating a general truth; a maxim.
– ORIGIN late 16th cent.: from Greek *gnōmē* 'thought, opinion' (related to *gignōskein* 'know').

gno·mic /ˈnōmik/ ▶ **adj.** expressed in or of the nature of short, pithy maxims or aphorisms: *that most gnomic form, the aphorism*. ■ enigmatic; ambiguous: *I had to have the gnomic response interpreted for me*.
– DERIVATIVES **gno·mi·cal·ly** /-ik(ə)lē/ **adv.**
– ORIGIN early 19th cent.: from Greek *gnōmikos* (perhaps via French *gnomique*), from *gnōmē* 'thought, judgment,' (plural) *gnōmai* 'sayings, maxims,' related to *gignōskein* 'know.'

gno·mon /ˈnōmän/ ▶ **n. 1** the projecting piece on a sundial that shows the time by the position of its shadow.
2 Geometry the part of a parallelogram left when a similar parallelogram has been taken from its corner.
– DERIVATIVES **gno·mon·ic** /nōˈmänik/ **adj.**
– ORIGIN mid 16th cent.: via Latin from Greek *gnōmōn* 'indicator, carpenter's square' (related to *gignōskein* 'know').

gno·mon·ics /nōˈmäniks/ ▶ **plural n.** [treated as sing.] the art of constructing and using dials and sundials.

g

gno·sis /ˈnōsis/ ▶ **n.** knowledge of spiritual mysteries.
– ORIGIN late 16th cent.: from Greek *gnōsis* 'knowledge' (related to *gignōskein* 'know').

gnos·tic /ˈnästik/ ▶ **adj.** of or relating to knowledge, esp. esoteric mystical knowledge. ■ (**Gnostic**) of or relating to Gnosticism.
▶ **n.** (**Gnostic**) an adherent of Gnosticism.
– ORIGIN late 16th cent. (as a noun): via ecclesiastical Latin from Greek *gnōstikos*, from *gnōstos* 'known' (related to *gignōskein* 'know').

Gnos·ti·cism /ˈnästəˌsizəm/ ▶ **n.** a prominent heretical movement of the 2nd-century Christian Church, partly of pre-Christian origin. Gnostic doctrine taught that the world was created and ruled by a lesser divinity, the demiurge, and that Christ was an emissary of the remote supreme divine being, esoteric knowledge (gnosis) of whom enabled the redemption of the human spirit.

gno·to·bi·ot·ic /ˌnōtōbīˈätik/ ▶ **adj.** Biology of, relating to, or denoting an environment for rearing or culturing organisms in which all the microorganisms are either known or excluded.
– ORIGIN 1940s: from Greek *gnōtos* 'known' + **BIOTIC**.

GNP ▶ **abbr.** gross national product.

GnRH ▶ **abbr.** gonadotropin-releasing hormone.

gns ▶ **abbr.** guineas.

gnu /n(y)o͞o/ ▶ **n.** a large dark antelope with a long head, a beard and mane, and a sloping back. Also called **WILDEBEEST**. ● Genus *Connochaetes*, family Bovidae: two species, in particular the abundant **brindled gnu** or **blue wildebeest** (*C. taurinus*).
– ORIGIN late 18th cent.: from Khoikhoi and San, perhaps imitative of the sound made by the animal when alarmed.

go[1] /gō/ ▶ **v.** (**goes, going**; past **went** /went/; past participle **gone** /gôn, gän/) **1** [no obj.] move from one place or point to another; travel: *he went out to the store* | *she longs to go back home* | *we've got a long way to go*. ■ travel a specified distance: *you just have to go a few miles to get to the road*. ■ travel or move in order to engage in a specified activity or course of action: *let's go and have a beer* | [with infinitive] *we went to see her* | [with present participle] *she used to go hunting*. ■ (**go to**) attend or visit for a particular purpose: *we went to the movies* | *he went to Brown University*. ■ [in imperative] begin motion (used in a starter's order to begin a race): *ready, set, go!* ■ (**go to**) (of a rank or honor) be allotted or awarded: *the top prize went to a twenty-four-year-old sculptor*. ■ (**go into/to/toward**) (of a thing) contribute to or be put into (a whole); be used for or devoted to: *considerable effort went into making the operation successful*. ■ pass a specified amount of time in a particular way or under particular circumstances: *sometimes they **went for** two months without talking*. ■ used to indicate how many people a supply of food, money, or another resource is sufficient for or how much can be achieved using it: *the sale will **go a long way toward** easing the huge debt burden* | *a little luck can **go a long way***. ■ (of a thing) lie or extend in a certain direction: *the scar started just above her ankle and went all the way up inside her leg*. ■ change in level, amount, or rank in a specified direction: *prices **went up** by 15 percent*. ■ informal used to emphasize the speaker's annoyance at a specified action or event: *then he goes and spoils it all* | [with present participle] *don't go poking your nose where you shouldn't*. ■ informal said in various expressions when angrily or contemptuously dismissing someone: *go and get stuffed.*

2 [no obj.] leave; depart: *I really must go.* ■ (of time) pass or elapse: *the hours **went by** | three years **went past**.* ■ come to an end; cease to exist: *a golden age that has now gone for good | 11,500 jobs are due to go by next year.* ■ leave or resign from a post: *I tried to persuade the Chancellor not to go.* ■ be lost or stolen: *when he returned minutes later, his equipment was gone.* ■ die (used euphemistically): *I'd like to see my grandchildren before I go.* ■ (of money) be spent, esp. in a specified way: *the rest of his money **went into** medical expenses.*

3 (**be going to be/do something**) intend or be likely or intended to be or do something; be about to (used to express a future tense): *I'm going to be late for work | she's going to have a baby.*

4 [no obj.] pass into a specified state, esp. an undesirable one: *the food is going bad | her mind immediately went blank | he's gone crazy.* ■ (**go to/into**) enter into a specified state, institution, or course of action: *she turned over and went back to sleep | the car went into a spin | no one went hungry in our house.* ■ make a sound of a specified kind: *the engine went bang.* ■ (of a bell or similar device) make a sound in functioning: *I heard the buzzer go four times.* ■ [with direct speech] informal say: *the kids go, "Yeah, sure."* ■ (**go by/under**) be known or called by (a specified name): *he now goes under the name Charles Perez.*

5 [no obj.] proceed in a specified way or have a specified outcome; turn out: *how did the weekend go? | it all **went off** smoothly.* ■ be successful, esp. in being enjoyable or exciting: *the hosts had to struggle to make things go.* ■ be acceptable or permitted: *underground events where **anything goes**.* ■ (of a song, account, verse, etc.) have a specified content or wording: *if you haven't heard it, the story goes like this.*

6 [no obj.] be harmonious, complementary, or matching: *rosemary **goes with** roast lamb | the earrings and the scarf don't really go.* ■ be found in the same place or situation; be associated: *cooking and eating **go together**.*

7 [no obj.] (of a machine or device) function: *my car won't go.* ■ continue in operation or existence: *the committee was **kept going** even when its existence could no longer be justified.*

8 [no obj.] (of an article) be regularly kept or put in a particular place: *remember which card goes in which slot.* ■ fit or be able to be accommodated in a particular place or space: *you're trying to fit a round peg into a square hole, and it just won't go.*

9 [no obj.] informal use a toilet; urinate or defecate.

▶ **n.** (pl. **goes**) informal **1** an attempt or trial at something: *I thought I'd give it a go.* ■ chiefly Brit. a state of affairs: *this seems a rum sort of go.* ■ chiefly Brit. an attack of illness: *he's had this nasty go of dysentery.* ■ a project or undertaking that has been approved: *tell them the project is a go.* ■ chiefly Brit. used in reference to a single item, action, or spell of activity: *he put it to his lips then knocked it back in one go.*

2 dated spirit, animation, or energy: *there's no go in me at all these days.* ■ vigorous activity: *it's **all go** around here.*

▶ **adj.** [predic.] informal functioning properly: *all systems go.*

– PHRASES **as** (or **so**) **far as it goes** bearing in mind its limitations (said when qualifying praise of something): *the book is a useful catalog as far as it goes.* **as —— go** compared to the average or typical one of the specified kind: *as castles go, it is small and old.* **from the word go** informal from the very beginning. **go figure!** informal said to express the speaker's belief that something is amazing or incredible. **go great guns** see GUN. **go halves** share something equally. **going!(, going!,) gone!** an auctioneer's announcement that bidding is closing or closed. **going on ——** (Brit. also **going on for ——**) approaching a specified time, age, or amount: *I was going on fourteen when I went to my first gig.* **go (to) it** Brit. informal act in a vigorous, energetic, or dissipated way: *Go it, Dad! Give him what for!* **go it alone** see ALONE. **go to show** (or **prove**) (of an occurrence) serve as evidence or proof of something specified. **have a go at 1** make an attempt at; try: *let me have a go at straightening the rim.* **2** chiefly Brit. attack or criticize (someone): *she's always having a go at me.* **have —— going for one** informal used to indicate how much someone has in their favor or to their advantage: *Why did she do it? She had so much going for her.* **make a go of** informal be successful in (something): *he's determined to make a go of his marriage.* **on the go** informal very active or busy: *he's been on the go all evening.* **to go** (of food or drink from a restaurant or cafe) to be eaten or drunk off the premises: *order one large cheese-and-peppers pizza, to go.* **what goes around comes around** proverb the consequences of one's actions will have to be dealt with eventually. **who goes there?** said by a sentry as a challenge.

– PHRASAL VERBS **go about 1** begin or carry on work at (an activity); busy oneself with: *you are going about this in the wrong way.* **2** Sailing change to the opposite tack. **go after** pursue or hunt down (someone). **go against** oppose or resist: *he refused to go against the unions.* ■ be contrary to (a feeling or principle): *these tactics go against many of our instincts.* ■ (of a judgment, decision, or result) be unfavorable for: *the tribunal's decision went against them.* **go ahead** proceed or be carried out without hesitation: *the project will go ahead.* **go along with** give one's consent or agreement to (a person or their views): *the group has decided to go along with the committee's proposal.* **go around 1** (chiefly Brit. **go round**) spin: revolve: *the wheels were going around.* **2** (chiefly Brit. **go round**) (esp. of food) be sufficient to supply everybody present: *there was barely enough food to go around.* ■ (of an aircraft) abort an approach to landing and prepare to make a fresh approach. **go around with** be regularly in the company of: *he goes around with some of the neighborhood kids.* **go at** energetically attack or tackle: *he went at things with a daunting eagerness.* **go back 1** (of a clock) be set to an earlier standard time, esp. at the end of daylight saving time. **2** (of two people) have known each each for a specified, typically long, period of time: *Victor and I go back longer than I care to admit.* **go back on** fail to keep (a promise): *he wouldn't go back on his word.* **go down 1** (of a ship or aircraft) sink or crash: *he saw eleven B-17s go down.* ■ be defeated in a contest: *they went down 2–1.* **2** (of a person, period, or event) be recorded or remembered in a particular way: *his name will now go down in history.* **3** be swallowed: *solids can sometimes go down much easier than liquids.* **4** (of a person, action, or work) elicit a specified reaction: *my slide shows went down reasonably well.* **5** informal happen: *you really don't know what's going down?* **6** Brit. informal leave a university, esp. Oxford or Cambridge, after finishing one's studies: *Dobbins went down last spring.* **7** vulgar slang have sexual intercourse (said by a male of a female). **go down on** vulgar slang perform oral sex on. **go down with** Brit. begin to suffer from (a specified illness): *I went down with an attack of bronchitis.* **go for 1** decide on; choose: *I wished that we had gone for plan B.* ■ tend to find (a particular type of person) attractive: *Dionne went for the outlaw type.* **2** attempt to gain or attain: *he went for a job as a delivery driver.* ■ (**go for it**) strive to the utmost to gain or achieve something (frequently said as an exhortation): *sounds like a good idea—go for it!* **3** launch oneself at (someone); attack: *she went for him with clawed hands.* **4** end up having a specified value or effect: *my good intentions **went for nothing**.* **5** apply to; have relevance for: *the same goes for money-grubbing lawyers.* **go forward** (of a clock) be set to a later standard time, esp. daylight saving time. **go in for** like or habitually take part in (something, esp. an activity): *I don't go in for partying as much as Jesse and Rachel do.* **go into 1** take up in study or as an occupation: *he went into bankruptcy law.* **2** investigate or inquire into (something): *there's no need to go into it now.* **3** (of a whole number) be capable of dividing another, typically without a remainder: *six will go into eighteen, but not into five.* **go off 1** (of a gun, bomb, or similar device) explode or fire. ■ (of an alarm) begin to sound. ■ informal become suddenly angry; lose one's temper: *if you got in an argument with him, he'd just go off.* **2** chiefly Brit. (esp. of food) begin to decompose; become unfit for consumption. **3** informal, chiefly Brit. begin to dislike: *I went off men after my husband left me.* **4** go to sleep: *I went off as soon as my head hit the pillow.* **go on 1** [often with present participle] continue or persevere: *I can't go on protecting you.* ■ talk at great length, esp. tediously or angrily: *she **went on about** how lovely it would be to escape from the city.* ■ continue speaking or doing something after a short pause: [with direct speech] *"I don't understand," she went on.* ■ informal said when encouraging someone or expressing disbelief: *go on, tell him!* **2** happen; take place: *my mom knows what went on.* **3** [often with infinitive] proceed to do: *she went on to do postgraduate work.* **go out 1** (of a fire or light) be extinguished. ■ cease operating or functioning: *the power went out on our block last night.* **2** (of the tide) ebb; recede to low tide. **3** leave one's home to go to an entertainment or social event, typically in the evening: *I'm going out for dinner.* ■ carry on a regular romantic, and sometimes sexual, relationship: *he was **going out with** her best friend.* **4** used to convey someone's deep sympathy or similar feeling: *the boy's heart went out to the pitiful figure.* **5** Golf play the first nine holes in a round of eighteen holes. Compare with COME HOME (see HOME). **6** (in some card games) be the first to dispose of all the cards in one's hand. **go over 1** examine, consider, or check the details of (something): *I want to go over these plans with you again.* **2** change one's allegiance or religion: *he went over to the Democratic Party.* **3** (esp. of an action or performance) be received in a specified way: *his earnestness would go over well in a courtroom.* **go round** chiefly Brit. See GO AROUND. **go through 1** undergo (a difficult or painful period or experience): *the country is going through a period of economic instability.* **2** search through or examine carefully or in sequence: *she started to go through the bundle of letters.* **3** (of a proposal or contract) be officially approved or completed: *the sale of the building is set to go through.* **4** informal use up or spend (available money or other resources). **5** (of a book) be successively published in (a specified number of editions): *within two years it went through thirty-one editions.* **go through with** perform (an action or process) to completion despite difficulty or unwillingness: *he bravely went through with the ceremony.* **go under** (of a business) become bankrupt. ■ (of a person) die or suffer an emotional collapse. **go up 1** (of a building or other structure) be built: *housing developments went up.* **2** explode or suddenly burst into flames: *last night two factories went up in flames.* **3** Brit. informal begin one's studies at a university, esp. Oxford or Cambridge. **go with 1** give one's consent or agreement to (a person or their views). **2** have a romantic or sexual relationship with (someone). **go without** suffer lack or deprivation: *I like to give my children what they want, even if I have to go without.*

– ORIGIN Old English *gān*, of Germanic origin; related to Dutch *gaan* and German *gehen*; the form *went* was originally the past tense of WEND.

> **USAGE** The use of **go** followed by **and**, as in *I must **go and** change* (rather than *I must **go to** change*), is extremely common but is regarded by some grammarians as an oddity. For more details, see usage at **AND**.

go[2] ▶ **n.** a Japanese board game of territorial possession and capture.

– ORIGIN late 19th cent.: Japanese, literally 'small stone,' also the name of the game.

Go·a /ˈgōə/ a state on the western coast of India; capital, Panaji. Formerly a Portuguese territory, it was seized by India in 1961. It formed a Union Territory with Daman and Diu until 1987, when it was made a state.

– DERIVATIVES **Go·an adj. & n., Go·a·nese** /gōəˈnēz, -ˈnēs/ **adj. & n.**

goad /gōd/ ▶ **v.** [with obj.] **1** provoke or annoy (someone) so as to stimulate some action or reaction: *he goaded her on to more daring revelations.*

2 drive or urge (an animal) on with a goad.

▶ **n.** a spiked stick used for driving cattle. ■ a thing that stimulates someone into action: *for him the visit was a goad to renewed effort.*

– ORIGIN Old English *gād*, of Germanic origin.

go-a·head informal ▶ **n.** (usu. **the go-ahead**) permission to proceed: *the government had given the go-ahead for the power station.*

▶ **adj. 1** enthusiastic about new projects; enterprising: *a young and go-ahead managing director.*

2 [attrib.] denoting the run, score, etc., that gives a team the lead in a game.

goal /gōl/ ▶ **n. 1** (in football, soccer, rugby, hockey, and some other games) a pair of posts linked by a crossbar and often with a net attached behind it, forming a space into or over which the ball has to be sent in order to score. ■ an instance of sending the ball into or over this space, esp. as a unit of scoring in a game: *the decisive opening goal | we won by three goals to two.* ■ a cage or basket used similarly in other sports.

2 the object of a person's ambition or effort; an aim or desired result: *going to law school has become the most important goal in his life.* ■ the destination of a journey: *the aircraft bumped toward our goal some 400 miles to the west.* ■ literary a point marking the end of a race.

– PHRASES **in goal** in the position of goalkeeper.

– DERIVATIVES **goal·less adj.**

– ORIGIN Middle English (in the sense 'limit, boundary'): of unknown origin.

goal·hang·er ▶ **n.** Soccer, derogatory a player who spends much of the game near the opposing team's goal in the hope of scoring easy goals.

goal·ie /ˈgōlē/ ▶ **n.** informal term for GOALTENDER or GOALKEEPER.

goal·keep·er /ˈgōlˌkēpər/ ▶ **n.** chiefly Brit. another term for GOALTENDER.

– DERIVATIVES **goal·keep·ing** /-ˌkēpiNG/ **n.**

goal kick ▶ **n.** Soccer a free kick taken by the defending side from within their goal area after attackers send the ball over the end line outside the goal.

goal line ▶ **n.** Sports a line across a football or hockey field at or near its end, on which the goal is placed or which acts as the boundary beyond which a try or touchdown is scored.

goal·mouth /ˈgōlˌmouTH/ ▶ **n.** the area just in front of a goal in soccer, lacrosse, or hockey.

goal·post /ˈgōlˌpōst/ ▶ **n.** either of the two upright posts of a goal.
– PHRASES **move the goalposts** unfairly alter the conditions or rules of a procedure during its course.

goal·tend·er /ˈgōlˌtendər/ ▶ **n.** a player in soccer or hockey whose special role is to stop the ball or puck from entering the goal.

goal·tend·ing /ˈgōlˌtendiNG/ ▶ **n. 1** Soccer & Hockey the action of stopping the ball or puck from entering the goal.
2 Basketball a violation in which a defensive player interferes with a shot when it is on its downward arc or is on or over the rim.

goal to go ▶ **n.** Football the situation in which an offensive team gets a first down within ten yards of the goal line, and thus cannot advance for another first down.

go·an·na /gōˈanə/ ▶ **n.** Australian term for **MONITOR** (sense 4 of the noun).
– ORIGIN mid 19th cent.: alteration of **IGUANA**.

go-a·round (also **go-round**) ▶ **n. 1** a flight path typically taken by an aircraft after an aborted approach to landing.
2 informal a confrontation; an argument: *they had one go-around after another.*

goat /gōt/ ▶ **n. 1** a hardy domesticated ruminant animal that has backward curving horns and (in the male) a beard. It is kept for its milk and meat and is noted for its lively and frisky behavior. ● *Capra hircus*, family Bovidae, descended from the wild bezoar. ■ a wild mammal related to this, such as the ibex, markhor, and tur. See also **MOUNTAIN GOAT**. ■ (**the Goat**) the zodiacal sign Capricorn or the constellation Capricornus.
2 a person likened to a goat, in particular: ■ a lecherous man. ■ a scapegoat.
– PHRASES **get someone's goat** informal irritate someone: *I've tried to get along with her, but sometimes she really gets my goat.*
– DERIVATIVES **goat·ish** adj., **goat·y** adj.
– ORIGIN Old English *gāt* 'nanny goat,' of Germanic origin; related to Dutch *geit* and German *Geiss*, also to Latin *haedus* 'kid.'

goat-an·te·lope ▶ **n.** a ruminant mammal of a group that combines the characteristics of both goats and antelopes. ● Subfamily Caprinae, family Bovidae: tribes Rupicaprini (the chamois, goral, serow, and mountain goat) and Ovibonini (the musk ox and takin).

goat·ee /gōˈtē/ (also **goatee beard**) ▶ **n.** a small, sometimes pointed, beard.
– DERIVATIVES **goat·eed** adj.
– ORIGIN early 19th cent.: so named because of its resemblance to the tuft on a goat's chin.

goat·fish /ˈgōtˌfiSH/ ▶ **n.** (pl. **same** or **goatfishes**) another term for **RED MULLET**.

goat·herd /ˈgōtˌhərd/ ▶ **n.** a person who tends goats.
– ORIGIN Old English, from **GOAT** + obsolete *herd* 'herdsman.'

goat's-beard (also **goatsbeard**) ▶ **n. 1** a plant of the daisy family, with slender grasslike leaves, yellow flowers that typically close at about midday, and downy fruits that resemble those of a dandelion. Native to Eurasia, it has become established in eastern North America. ● *Tragopogon pratensis*, family Compositae.
2 a plant of the rose family, with long plumes of white flowers, found in both Eurasia and North America. ● *Aruncus vulgaris*, family Rosaceae.
– ORIGIN mid 16th cent.: translating Greek *tragopōgon* or Latin *Barba Capri*.

goat·skin /ˈgōtˌskin/ ▶ **n.** the skin of a goat. ■ such a skin, or leather made from it, as a material. ■ a garment or object made out of goatskin.

goat's-rue ▶ **n.** a herbaceous plant of the pea family, which was formerly used in medicine, esp. as a vermifuge. ● Two species in the family Leguminosae: a bushy Eurasian plant that is cultivated as an ornamental (*Galega officinalis*), and a North American plant with pink and yellow flowers and that smells of goats (*Tephrosia virginiana*).

goat·suck·er /ˈgōtˌsəkər/ ▶ **n.** another term for **NIGHTJAR**.
– ORIGIN early 17th cent.: so named because the bird was thought to suck goats' udders.

goat wil·low ▶ **n.** a common European willow with broad leaves and soft fluffy catkins. Also called **GREAT SALLOW** (see **SALLOW**[2]).

gob[1] /gäb/ informal ▶ **n. 1** a lump or clot of a slimy or viscous substance: *a gob of phlegm.* ■ a small lump.
2 (**gobs of**) a lot of: *he wants to make gobs of money selling cassettes.*
– ORIGIN late Middle English: from Old French *gobe* 'mouthful, lump,' from *gober* 'to swallow, gulp,' perhaps of Celtic origin.

gob[2] ▶ **n.** informal, dated an American sailor.
– ORIGIN early 20th cent.: of unknown origin.

gob[3] ▶ **n.** informal, chiefly Brit. a person's mouth: *Jean told him to shut his big gob.*
– ORIGIN mid 16th cent.: perhaps from Scottish Gaelic *gob* 'beak, mouth.'

go-bag ▶ **n.** a bag packed with essential items, kept ready for use in the event of an emergency evacuation of one's home.

gob·bet /ˈgäbit/ ▶ **n.** a piece or lump of flesh, food, or other matter: *they lobbed **gobbets of** fresh bonito off the side of the boat.*
– ORIGIN Middle English: from Old French *gobet*, diminutive of *gobe* (see **GOB**[1]).

gob·ble[1] /ˈgäbəl/ ▶ **v.** [with obj.] eat (something) hurriedly and noisily: *one man **gobbled up** a burger* | [no obj.] *they don't eat, they gobble.* ■ use a large amount of (something) very quickly: *these old houses just **gobble up** money.* ■ (of a large organization or other body) incorporate or take over (a smaller one): *he amassed his packaging empire by **gobbling up** National Can Corporation.*
– ORIGIN early 17th cent.: probably from **GOB**[1].

gob·ble[2] ▶ **v.** [no obj.] (of a male turkey) make a characteristic swallowing sound in the throat. ■ (of a person) make such a sound when speaking, esp. when excited or angry: *she was gobbling to herself faintly in her distress.*
– ORIGIN late 17th cent.: imitative, perhaps influenced by **GOBBLE**[1].

gob·ble·dy·gook /ˈgäbəldēˌgo͝ok, -ˌgo͞ok/ (also **gobbledegook**) ▶ **n.** informal language that is meaningless or is made unintelligible by excessive use of abstruse technical terms; nonsense.
– ORIGIN 1940s (originally US): probably imitating a turkey's gobble.

gob·bler[1] /ˈgäb(ə)lər/ ▶ **n.** a person who eats greedily and noisily.

gob·bler[2] ▶ **n.** informal a turkey cock.

Gob·e·lin /ˈgōbəlin, ˈgäb-/ (also **Gobelin tapestry**) ▶ **n.** a tapestry made at the Gobelins factory in Paris, or in imitation of one.

Gob·e·lins /ˈgōbəlinz, ˈgäb-/ a tapestry and textile factory in Paris, established by the Gobelin family *c.*1440 and taken over by the French Crown in 1662. It was highly successful in the late 17th and 18th centuries, using designs by leading French painters, and tapestry panels became used as alternatives to oil paintings.

go-be·tween ▶ **n.** an intermediary or negotiator.

Go·bi Des·ert /ˈgōbē/ a barren plateau in southern Mongolia and northern China.

Go·bin·eau /ˈgäbəˌnō/, Joseph Arthur, Comte de (1816–82), French writer and anthropologist. His stated view that the races are innately unequal and that the white Aryan race is superior to all others later influenced the ideology and policies of the Nazis.

gob·let /ˈgäblit/ ▶ **n.** a drinking glass with a foot and a stem. ■ archaic a metal or glass bowl-shaped drinking cup, sometimes with a foot and a cover.
– ORIGIN late Middle English: from Old French *gobelet*, diminutive of *gobel* 'cup,' of unknown origin.

gob·let cell ▶ **n.** Anatomy a column-shaped cell found in the respiratory and intestinal tracts, which secretes the main component of mucus.

gob·lin /ˈgäblin/ ▶ **n.** a mischievous, ugly, dwarflike creature of folklore.
– ORIGIN Middle English: from Old French *gobelin*, possibly related to German *Kobold* (see **KOBOLD**) or to Greek *kobalos* 'mischievous goblin.' In medieval Latin *Gobelinus* occurs as the name of a mischievous spirit, said to haunt Évreux in northern France in the 12th cent.

go·bo[1] /ˈgōbō/ ▶ **n.** (pl. **gobos**) a dark plate or screen used to shield a lens from light. ■ Theater a partial screen used in front of a spotlight to project a shape. ■ a shield used to mask a microphone from extraneous noise.
– ORIGIN 1930s: of unknown origin, perhaps from *go between*.

go·bo[2] ▶ **n.** a vegetable root used chiefly in Japanese and Hawaiian cooking.
– ORIGIN Japanese.

go·bo·ny /gəˈbōnē/ ▶ **adj.** Heraldry another term for **COMPONY**.

gob·smacked /ˈgäbˌsmakt/ ▶ **adj.** Brit. informal utterly astonished; astounded.
– DERIVATIVES **gob·smack·ing** /-ˌsmakiNG/ adj.
– ORIGIN 1980s: from **GOB**[1] + **SMACK**[1], with reference to being shocked by a blow to the mouth, or to clapping a hand to one's mouth in astonishment.

gob·stop·per /ˈgäbˌstäpər/ ▶ **n.** chiefly Brit. a jawbreaker.

go·by /ˈgōbē/ ▶ **n.** (pl. **gobies**) a small, usually marine fish that typically has a sucker on the underside. ● Family Gobiidae: numerous genera and species.
– ORIGIN mid 18th cent.: from Latin *gobius*, from Greek *kōbios*, denoting some kind of small fish.

go-by ▶ **n.** (in phrase **give someone the go-by**) informal, dated avoid or snub someone. ■ end a romantic relationship with someone: *her young man's given her the go-by.*

go-cart ▶ **n. 1** variant spelling of **GO-KART**.
2 a handcart. ■ a stroller. ■ archaic a baby walker.
– ORIGIN late 17th cent. (denoting a baby walker): from **GO**[1] (in the obsolete sense 'walk') + **CART**.

God /gäd/ ▶ **n. 1** [without article] (in Christianity and other monotheistic religions) the creator and ruler of the universe and source of all moral authority; the supreme being.
2 (**god**) (in certain other religions) a superhuman being or spirit worshiped as having power over nature or human fortunes; a deity: *a moon god* | *an incarnation of the god Vishnu.* ■ an image, idol, animal, or other object worshiped as divine or symbolizing a god. ■ used as a conventional personification of fate: *he dialed the number and, the gods relenting, got through at once.*
3 (**god**) an adored, admired, or influential person: *he has little time for the fashion victims for whom he is a god.* ■ a thing accorded the supreme importance appropriate to a god: *don't make money your god.*
4 (**the gods**) informal the gallery in a theater. ■ the people sitting in this area.
▶ **exclam.** used for emphasis or to express emotions such as surprise, anger, or distress: *God, what did I do to deserve this?* | *my God! Why didn't you tell us sooner?* | *God, how I hate that woman!*
– PHRASES **for God's sake!** see **SAKE**[1] (sense 3). **God bless** an expression of good wishes on parting. **God damn** (**you, him,** etc) may (you, he, etc.) be damned. **God the Father** (in Christian doctrine) the first person of the Trinity, God as creator and supreme authority. **God forbid** see **FORBID**. **God grant** used to express a wish that something should happen: *God grant he will soon regain his freedom.* **God help** (**you, him,** etc.) used to express the belief that someone is in a difficult, dangerous, or hopeless situation: *God help anyone who tried to cheer me out of my bad mood.* **God the Son** (in Christian doctrine) Christ regarded as the second person of the Trinity; God as incarnate and resurrected savior. **God willing** used to express the wish that one will be able to do as one intends or that something will happen as planned: *one day, God willing, she and John might have a daughter.* **in God's name** used in questions to emphasize anger or surprise: *what in God's name are you doing up there?* **play God** behave as if all-powerful or supremely important. **please God** used to emphasize a strong wish or hope: *please God the money will help us find a cure.* **thank God** see **THANK**. **to God** used after a verb to emphasize a strong wish or hope: *I hope to God you've got something else to put on.* **with God** dead and in heaven.
– DERIVATIVES **god·hood** /-ˌho͝od/ n., **god·ship** /-ˌSHip/ n., **god·ward** /-wərd/ adj. & adv., **god·wards** /-wərdz/ adv.
– ORIGIN Old English, of Germanic origin; related to Dutch *god* and German *Gott*.

God Al·might·y (also **Godalmighty**) ▶ **exclam.** used to express esp. surprise, anger, or exasperation.

Go·dard /gōˈdär(d)/, Jean-Luc (1930–), French movie director, a leading figure of the *nouvelle vague*. His movies include *Breathless* (1960), *Alphaville* (1965), *Wind from the East* (1969), and *Socialisme* (2010).

Go·da·va·ri /gəˈdävərē/ a river in central India that rises in the state of Maharashtra and flows southeast for about 900 miles (1,440 km) across the Deccan plateau to the Bay of Bengal.

god·aw·ful /ˈgädˈôfəl/ (also **God-awful**) ▶ **adj.** informal extremely unpleasant: *it had been the most godawful forty-eight hours.*

god·child /ˈgädˌCHīld/ ▶ **n.** (pl. **godchildren** /-ˌCHildrən/) a person in relation to a godparent.

god·damn /ˈgädˈdam/ (also **goddam** or **goddamned**) ▶ **adj., adv., & n.** informal used for emphasis, esp. to express anger or frustration: [as modifier] *we're sick of this goddamn weather* | [as noun] *I don't give a goddamn what you do!*
– ORIGIN mid 17th cent.: abbreviation of *God damn (me)*.

God·dard /ˈgädərd/, Robert Hutchings (1882–1945), US physicist. He designed and built the first successful liquid-fueled rocket. The National

PRONUNCIATION KEY ə *ago, up*; ər *over, fur*; a *hat*; ā *ate*; ä *car*; e *let*; ē *see*; i *fit*; ī *by*; NG *sing*; ō *go*; ô *law, for*; oi *toy*; o͝o *good*; o͞o *goo*; ou *out*; TH *thin*; TH *then*; ZH *vision*

Aeronautics and Space Administration's (NASA) Goddard Space Flight Center is named for him.

god·daugh·ter /'gäd,dôtər/ ▶ **n.** a female godchild.

god·dess /'gädis/ ▶ **n.** a female deity: *a temple to Athena Nike, goddess of victory.* ■ a woman who is adored, esp. for her beauty: *he had an affair with a screen goddess.*

Gö·del /'gōdl/, Kurt (1906–78), US mathematician; born in Austria. Among his important contributions to mathematical logic is the incompleteness theorem.

Gö·del's in·com·plete·ness the·o·rem see INCOMPLETENESS THEOREM.

go·det /gō'det/ ▶ **n.** a triangular piece of material inserted in a dress, shirt, or glove to make it flared or for ornamentation.
– ORIGIN late 19th cent.: from French.

go·de·tia /gə'dēshə/ ▶ **n.** a North American plant with showy lilac to red flowers. ● Genus *Clarkia* (or *Godetia*), family Onagraceae.
– ORIGIN modern Latin, named after Charles H. *Godet* (1797–1879), Swiss botanist.

g

go·dev·il ▶ **n.** chiefly historical a gadget used in farming, logging, or drilling for oil, in particular: ■ a crude sled, used chiefly for dragging logs. ■ a jointed apparatus for cleaning pipelines.

god·fa·ther /'gäd,fäthər/ ▶ **n.** **1** a male godparent. **2** a man who is influential in a movement or organization, through providing support for it or through playing a leading or innovatory part in it: *the godfather of alternative comedy.* ■ a person directing an illegal organization, esp. a leader of a Mafia family.

God-fear·ing ▶ **adj.** earnestly religious: *an honest, God-fearing woman.*

god·for·sak·en /'gädfər,sākən/ ▶ **adj.** lacking any merit or attraction; dismal: *what are you doing in this godforsaken place?*

God-giv·en ▶ **adj.** received from God: *the God-given power to work miracles.* ■ possessed without question, as if by divine authority: *pedestrians decided it was their God-given right to saunter casually into traffic.*

God·havn /'gōth,houn/ a town in western Greenland, on the south coast of the island of Disko; pop. 1,000 (est. 2009).

god·head /'gäd,hed/ ▶ **n.** (usu. **the Godhead**) God. ■ divine nature. ■ informal an adored, admired, or influential person; an idol.

Go·di·va /gə'dīvə/, Lady (died 1080), English noblewoman; wife of **Leofric, Earl of Mercia**. According to legend, she agreed to her husband's proposition that he would reduce unpopular taxes only if she rode naked on horseback through Coventry's marketplace. According to later versions of the story, nobody watched except peeping Tom, who was struck blind in punishment.

god·less /'gädlis/ ▶ **adj.** not recognizing or obeying God: *a godless country.* ■ without a god: *humanity coming to terms with a godless world.* ■ profane; wicked.
– DERIVATIVES **god·less·ness** n.

god·like /'gäd,līk/ ▶ **adj.** resembling God or a god in qualities such as power, beauty, or benevolence: *our parents are godlike figures to our childish eyes.* ■ befitting or appropriate to a god: *we act as though we have godlike powers to decide our own destiny.*

god·ly /'gädlē/ ▶ **adj.** (**godlier**, **godliest**) devoutly religious; pious: *how to live the godly life.*
– DERIVATIVES **god·li·ness** n.

god·man ▶ **n.** **1** Indian a holy man; a guru. **2** an incarnation of a god in human form. ■ (**God-man**) Jesus Christ.

god·moth·er /'gäd,məthər/ ▶ **n.** a female godparent. ■ a woman who is influential in a movement or organization, through providing support for it or through playing a leading or innovatory part in it: *she has been called the godmother of Quebec business.*

go·down /'gōdoun, gō'doun/ ▶ **n.** (in eastern Asia, esp. India) a warehouse.
– ORIGIN late 16th cent.: from Portuguese *gudão*, from Tamil *kiṭaṅku*, Malayalam *kiṭaṅṅu*, or Kannada *gadaṅgu* 'store, warehouse.'

god·par·ent /'gäd,pe(ə)rənt, -,par-/ ▶ **n.** a person who presents a child at baptism and responds on the child's behalf, promising to take responsibility for the child's religious education.

God's a·cre ▶ **n.** archaic a churchyard.
– ORIGIN early 17th cent.: from German *Gottesacker*, Dutch *Godsakker*.

God Save the Queen (or **King**) ▶ **n.** the British national anthem.
– ORIGIN evidence suggests a 17th-cent. origin for the complete words and tune of the anthem. The ultimate origin is obscure: the phrase "God save the King" occurs in various passages in the Old Testament, while as early as 1545 it was a watchword in the English navy, with "long to reign over us" as a countersign.

God's coun·try ▶ **n.** [in sing.] an area or region, esp. a peaceful, rural one, supposedly favored by God.

god·send /'gäd,send/ ▶ **n.** a very helpful or valuable event, person, or thing: *this highway is **a godsend to** the local community.*
– ORIGIN early 19th cent.: from *God's send* 'what God has sent.'

God's gift ▶ **n.** the ideal or best possible person or thing for someone or something (used chiefly ironically or in negative statements): *he thought he was God's gift to women.*

god·son /'gäd,sən/ ▶ **n.** a male godchild.

God·speed /'gäd'spēd/ ▶ **exclam.** dated an expression of good wishes to a person starting a journey.
– ORIGIN Middle English: from *God speed you* 'may God help you prosper.'

God Squad ▶ **n.** informal used to refer to evangelical Christians, typically suggesting intrusive moralizing and proselytizing.

God's truth ▶ **n.** the absolute truth: *it's done more harm than good, and that's **the God's truth**.*

Godt·håb /'gôt,hôp/ former name (until 1979) of NUUK.

Go·du·nov /'gädn,ôf/, Boris (1550–1605), tsar of Russia 1598–1605. His reign was marked by famine, doubts over his involvement in the earlier death of Ivan the Terrible's **eldest son**, and the appearance of pretender False Dmitri.

God·win /'gädwən/, William (1756–1836), English social philosopher and novelist; the husband of Mary Wollstonecraft and the father of Mary Wollstonecraft Shelley.

God·win-Aus·ten, Mount /,gädwən 'ôstən/ former name for K2.

god·wit /'gädwit/ ▶ **n.** a large, long-legged wader with a long, slightly upturned or straight bill, and typically a reddish-brown head and breast in the breeding male. ● Genus *Limosa*, family Scolopacidae: four species.
– ORIGIN mid 16th cent.: of unknown origin.

God·zil·la /gäd'zilə/ ▶ **n.** informal, humorous **1** a particularly enormous example (of something): *a Godzilla of a condominium tower.* **2** a person or thing likened to a frightful and menacing creature: *Don't let Nurse Godzilla catch you. She'll raise holy hell.*
– ORIGIN from the name of a huge prehistoric monster featured in a series of Japanese films from 1954.

Goeb·bels /'gəbəlz/ (also **Göbbels**), Joseph (1897–1945), German Nazi leader and politician; full name *Paul Joseph Goebbels*. From 1933, he was Adolf Hitler's minister of propaganda. He committed suicide rather than surrender to the Allies.

go·er /'gōər/ ▶ **n.** **1** [in combination] a person who attends a specified place or event, esp. regularly: *a churchgoer | conference-goers.* **2** [with adj.] informal a person or thing that goes in a specified way: *horse no. 7 is a fast goer.* ■ a project likely to be accepted or to succeed: *if the business is a goer, the entrepreneur moves on.*

Goe·ring /'gəriNG/ (also **Göring**), Hermann Wilhelm (1893–1946), German Nazi leader and politician. He was responsible for the German rearmament program, founder of the Gestapo, and director of the German economy. Sentenced to death at the Nuremberg war trials, he committed suicide in his cell.

Goes /gōōs/, Hugo van der (*fl. c.*1467–82), Flemish painter; born in Ghent. His best-known work is the *Portinari Altarpiece* (1475), commissioned for a church in Florence, Italy.

goes /gōz/ third person singular present of GO[1].

go·est /'gō-ist/ archaic second person singular present of GO[1].

go·eth /'gō-ith/ archaic third person singular present of GO[1].

Goe·thals /'gōthəlz/, George Washington (1858–1928), US army officer and engineer. As chief engineer and chairman of the Panama Canal Commission 1907, he oversaw construction of the Panama Canal, which was completed in 1914, and then served as the Canal Zone's governor 1914–17.

Goe·the /'gə(r)tə, 'gœtə/, Johann Wolfgang von (1749–1832), German poet, playwright, novelist, philosopher, and scientist. Involved at first with the *Sturm und Drang* movement, he changed to a more classical style, as in the "Wilhelm Meister" novels 1796–1829. Notable dramas: *Götz von Berlichingen* (1773), *Tasso* (1790), and *Faust* (1808–32).

goe·thite /'gōthīt/ ▶ **n.** a dark reddish-brown or yellowish-brown mineral consisting of oxyhydroxide iron, occurring typically as masses of fibrous crystals.
– ORIGIN early 19th cent.: from the name of J.W. von GOETHE + -ITE[1].

go·fer /'gōfər/ (also **gopher**) ▶ **n.** informal a person who runs errands, esp. on a movie set or in an office.
– ORIGIN 1960s: from *go for* (i.e., go and fetch).

gof·fer /'gäfər/ (also **gauffer** /'gôfər, 'gäf-/) ▶ **v.** [with obj.] (usu. as adj. **goffered**) treat (a lace edge or frill) with heated irons in order to crimp or flute it: *a goffered frill.* ■ (as adj. **goffered**) (of the gilt edges of a book) embossed with a repeating design.
▶ **n.** an iron used to crimp or flute lace.
– ORIGIN late 16th cent.: from French *gaufrer* 'stamp with a patterned tool,' from *gaufre* 'honeycomb,' from Middle Low German *wāfel* (see WAFFLE[2]).

go fish ▶ **n.** a card game in which each player in turn asks an opponent for a particular card and is told to "go fish" from the undealt deck if denied.

Gog and Ma·gog /gôg and mə'gäg/ **1** in the Bible, the names of enemies of God's people. In Ezek. 38–9, Gog is apparently a ruler from the land of Magog, while in Rev. 20:8, Gog and Magog are nations under the dominion of Satan. **2** (in medieval legend) opponents of Alexander the Great, living north of the Caucasus. **3** two giant statues standing in Guildhall, London, representing either the last two survivors of a race of giants supposed to have inhabited Britain before Roman times, or Gogmagog, chief of the giants, and Corineus, a Roman invader.

Go·ge·bic Range /gō'gēbik/ a range of iron-bearing hills in the western Upper Peninsula in Michigan and adjacent areas in Wisconsin.

go-get·ter ▶ **n.** informal an aggressively enterprising person.
– DERIVATIVES **go-get·ting** adj.

gog·gle /'gägəl/ ▶ **v.** [no obj.] look with wide open eyes, typically in amazement or wonder: *"What in the world are you goggling at?"* ■ (of the eyes) protrude or open wide.
▶ **adj.** [attrib.] (of the eyes) protuberant or rolling.
▶ **n.** **1** (**goggles**) close-fitting eyeglasses with side shields, for protecting the eyes from glare, dust, water, etc. ■ informal eyeglasses. **2** [in sing.] a stare with protruding eyes.
– DERIVATIVES **gog·gled** adj.
– ORIGIN Middle English (in the sense 'look to one side, squint'): probably from a base symbolic of oscillating movement.

gog·gle-eye ▶ **n.** any of a number of edible fishes with large eyes that occur widely on reefs in tropical and subtropical seas. ● a nocturnal fish related to the bigeye (*Priacanthus hamrur*, family Priacanthidae). ● (also **goggle-eye jack**) a fish often found in shoals (*Selar crumenophthalmus*, family Carangidae).

gog·gle-eyed ▶ **adj.** having staring or protuberant eyes, esp. through astonishment.

go-go ▶ **adj.** [attrib.] **1** relating to or denoting an unrestrained and erotic style of dancing to popular music: *a go-go bar | go-go dancers.* **2** assertively dynamic: *the go-go bravado of the 1980s.*
– ORIGIN 1960s: reduplication of GO[1], perhaps influenced by A GOGO.

Go·gol /'gōgəl/, Nikolai (Vasilevich) (1809–52), Russian novelist, playwright, and short-story writer; born in Ukraine. His writings are satirical and often explore themes of fantasy and the supernatural. Notable works: *The Government Inspector* (1836), *Notes of a Madman* (1835), and *Dead Souls* (1842).

Goi·â·nia /goi'anēə/ a city in southern central Brazil, capital of the state of Goiás; pop. 1,244,645 (2007). It was founded as a new city in 1933.

Goi·del·ic /goi'delik/ ▶ **adj.** of, relating to, or denoting the northern group of Celtic languages, including Irish, Scottish Gaelic, and Manx. Compare with BRYTHONIC. Also called **Q-CELTIC**.
▶ **n.** these languages collectively.

go·ing /'gōiNG/ ▶ **n.** **1** an act or instance of leaving a place; a departure: *his going left an enormous gap in each of their lives.* **2** [in sing.] the condition of the ground viewed in terms of suitability for walking, riding, or other travel (used esp. in the context of horse racing): *the going was ideal here, with short turf and a level surface.* ■ progress affected by such a condition: *the paths were covered with drifting snow and the going was difficult.* ■ conditions for, or progress in, an endeavor: *when the going gets tough, the tough get going.*
▶ **adj.** **1** [predic.] chiefly Brit. existing or available; to be had: *he asked if there were any other jobs going.* **2** [attrib.] (esp. of a price) generally accepted as fair or correct; current: *people willing to work for the going rate.*

go·ing a·way ▶ **adj.** [attrib.] marking or celebrating a departure: *a going-away party.*
▶ **adv.** informal with victory assured before the end of a race or other sporting contest: *Jordan finished the game with 20 points and Detroit won going away.*

go·ing-o·ver ▶ **n.** [in sing.] informal a thorough treatment, esp. in cleaning or inspection: *give the place a going-over with the vacuum cleaner.* ■ a beating.

go·ings-on ▶ **plural n.** events or behavior, esp. of an unusual or suspect nature.

goi·ter /ˈgoitər/ (Brit. **goitre**) ▶ **n.** a swelling of the neck resulting from enlargement of the thyroid gland: *a woman with a goiter | the belief that amber necklaces were good for curing goiter.*
– DERIVATIVES **goi·tered adj.**, **goi·trous** /ˈgoitrəs/ **adj.**
– ORIGIN early 17th cent.: from French, a back-formation from *goitreux* 'having a goiter,' or from Old French *goitron* 'gullet,' both based on Latin *guttur* 'throat.'

go·ji ber·ry /ˈgōjē/ ▶ **n. 1** a bright red edible berry widely cultivated in China, supposed to contain high levels of certain vitamins. See also **WOLFBERRY**.
2 either of two shrubs (*Lycium barbarum* and *Lycium chinense*) on which goji berries grow.
– ORIGIN from Chinese *gouqi.*

go-kart (also **go-cart**) ▶ **n.** a small racing car with a lightweight or skeleton body.
– DERIVATIVES **go-kart·ing n.**
– ORIGIN 1950s: *kart*, alteration of **CART**.

Go·lan Heights /ˈgōˌlän, -lən/ a range of hills on the border between Syria and Israel, northeast of the Sea of Galilee. Formerly under Syrian control, the area was occupied by Israel in 1967 and annexed in 1981. Negotiations for the withdrawal of Israeli troops from the region began in 1992.

Gol·con·da /gälˈkändə/ ▶ **n.** a source of wealth, advantages, or happiness: *the posters calling emigrants from Europe to the Golconda of the American West.*
– ORIGIN late 19th cent.: from the name of a city near Hyderabad, India, famous for its diamonds.

gold /gōld/ ▶ **n. 1** a yellow precious metal, the chemical element of atomic number 79, valued esp. for use in jewelry and decoration, and to guarantee the value of currencies. (Symbol: **Au**) ■ [with modifier] an alloy of this: *9-carat gold.*

> Gold is quite widely distributed in nature, but economical extraction is only possible from deposits of the native metal or sulfide ores or as a byproduct of copper and lead mining. The use of the metal in coins is now limited, but it is also used in electrical contacts and (in some countries) as a filling for teeth.

2 a deep lustrous yellow or yellow-brown color: *her eyes were light green and flecked with gold.*
3 coins or articles made of gold: *her ankles and wrists were glinting with gold.* ■ money in large sums; wealth: *he proved to be a rabid seeker for gold and power.* ■ a thing that is precious, beautiful, or brilliant: *they scout continents in search of the new green gold.* ■ short for **GOLD MEDAL**.
– PHRASES **go gold** (of a recording) achieve sales meriting a gold disk. **pot** (or **crock**) **of gold** a large but distant or imaginary reward. [with allusion to the story of a crock of gold supposedly to be found by anyone reaching the end of a rainbow.]
– ORIGIN Old English, of Germanic origin; related to Dutch *goud* and German *Gold*, from an Indo-European root shared by **YELLOW**.

gol·darn /ˈgälˈdärn/ ▶ **adj., adv., & n.** informal used as a euphemism for **GODDAMN**.

gold·beat·er /ˈgōldˌbētər/ ▶ **n.** a person who beats gold out into gold leaf.

gold·beat·er's skin ▶ **n.** an animal membrane used to separate leaves of gold during beating.

gold bee·tle (also **goldbug**) ▶ **n.** a leaf beetle with metallic gold coloration. ● Several species in the family Chrysomelidae, in particular *Metriona bicolor*.

Gold·berg[1] /ˈgōldˌbərg/, Arthur Joseph (1908–90), US Supreme Court associate justice 1962–65. He served as US ambassador to the United Nations 1965–68 but resigned because he did not agree with the escalation of the Vietnam War.

Gold·berg[2], Rube (1883–1970), US cartoonist; full name *Reuben Lucius Goldberg*. As creator of the comic strip characters Professor Lucifer Gorgonzola Butts (an inventor of complex mechanical devices to achieve simple tasks), Boob McNutt, and Lala Palooza, he satirized American folkways and modern technology.

gold brick informal ▶ **n.** a thing that looks valuable but is in fact worthless. ■ (also **goldbrick** or **goldbricker**) a con man. ■ a lazy person: [as modifier] *hardworking Amos and goldbrick Andy.*
▶ **v.** (usu. **goldbrick**) [no obj.] invent excuses to avoid a task; shirk: *he wasn't goldbricking; he was really sick.* ■ [with obj.] swindle (someone).

gold·bug /ˈgōldˌbəg/ (also **gold bug**) ▶ **n. 1** informal an advocate of a single gold standard for currency. ■ a person favoring gold as an investment.
2 another term for **GOLD BEETLE**.

gold card ▶ **n.** trademark a charge card or credit card issued to people with a high credit rating and giving benefits not available with the standard card.

Gold Coast former name (until 1957) of **GHANA**. ■ (also **gold coast**) informal any coastal area noted for luxurious living and expensive homes.

gold dig·ger ▶ **n.** informal a person who dates others purely to extract money from them, in particular a woman who strives to marry a wealthy man.

gold dust ▶ **n. 1** fine particles of gold.
2 another term for **BASKET-OF-GOLD**.

gold·en /ˈgōldən/ ▶ **adj. 1** colored or shining like gold: *curls of glossy golden hair | bake until golden.*
2 made or consisting of gold: *a golden crown.*
3 (of a period) very happy and prosperous: *those golden days before World War I.* ■ (of an opportunity) very favorable: *a golden opportunity to boost foreign trade.*
4 (of a singing voice) rich and smooth: *a choir of young golden voices.*
5 denoting the fiftieth year of something: *the American Ballet Theater's golden anniversary extravaganza.*
– DERIVATIVES **gold·en·ly adv.**

gold·en age ▶ **n.** an idyllic, often imaginary past time of peace, prosperity, and happiness. ■ the period when a specified art, skill, or activity is at its peak: *the golden age of cinema.*
– ORIGIN mid 16th cent.: the Greek and Roman poets' name for the first period of history, when the human race lived in an ideal state.

gold·en ag·er ▶ **n.** used euphemistically or humorously to refer to an old person.

gold·en calf ▶ **n.** (in the Bible) an image of gold in the shape of a calf, made by Aaron in response to the Israelites' plea for a god while they awaited Moses' return from Mount Sinai, where he was receiving the Ten Commandments (Exod. 32). ■ a false god, esp. wealth as an object of worship.

gold·en cat ▶ **n.** a small forest-dwelling cat found in Africa and Asia. ● Genus *Felis*, family Felidae: the African *F. aurata*, with a chestnut to silver-gray coat, and the Asiatic *F. temmincki*, with a golden-brown coat and striped head.

Gold·en De·li·cious ▶ **n.** a widely grown dessert apple of a greenish-yellow, soft-fleshed variety.

gold·en ea·gle ▶ **n.** a large Eurasian and North American eagle with yellow-tipped head feathers in the mature adult. ● *Aquila chrysaetos*, family Accipitridae.

gold·en·eye /ˈgōldənˌī/ ▶ **n.** (pl. **same** or **goldeneyes**) a migratory northern diving duck, the male of which has a dark head with a white cheek patch and yellow eyes. ● Genus *Bucephala*, family Anatidae: two species, in particular the **common goldeneye** (*B. clangula*).

Gold·en Fleece Greek Mythology the fleece of a golden ram, guarded by an unsleeping dragon, that was sought and won by Jason with the help of Medea. ■ a goal that is highly desirable but difficult to achieve.

Gold·en Gate a deep channel that connects San Francisco Bay with the Pacific Ocean. It is spanned by the Golden Gate suspension bridge, which was completed in 1937.

Golden Gate Bridge

gold·en glow ▶ **n.** another term for **GREEN-HEADED CONEFLOWER** (see **CONEFLOWER**).

gold·en goose ▶ **n.** a continuing source of wealth or profit that may be exhausted if it is misused: *they were killing the golden goose of tourism.* See also **KILL THE GOOSE THAT LAYS THE GOLDEN EGG** at **EGG**[1].

gold·en ham·ster ▶ **n.** see **HAMSTER**.

gold·en hand·cuffs ▶ **plural n.** informal used to refer to benefits, typically deferred payments, provided by an employer to discourage an employee from taking employment elsewhere.

gold·en hand·shake ▶ **n.** informal a payment given to someone who is laid off or retires early.

Gold·en Hind the ship in which Francis Drake circumnavigated the globe in 1577–80.
– ORIGIN named by Drake in honor of his patron, Sir Christopher Hatton (1540–91), whose crest was a golden hind.

Gold·en Horde the Tartar and Mongol army, led by descendants of Genghis Khan, that overran Asia and parts of eastern Europe in the 13th century and maintained an empire until around 1500 (so called from the richness of the leader's camp).

Gold·en Horn a curved inlet of the Bosporus that forms the harbor of Istanbul. Turkish name **HALIÇ**.

g

gold·en hour ▶ **n.** Medicine the first hour after the occurrence of a traumatic injury, considered the most critical for successful emergency treatment.

gold·en ju·bi·lee ▶ **n.** the fiftieth anniversary of a significant event.

gold·en mean ▶ **n.** [in sing.] **1** the ideal moderate position between two extremes.
2 another term for **GOLDEN SECTION**.

gold·en num·ber ▶ **n.** the number showing a year's place in the Metonic lunar cycle and used to fix the date of Easter for that year.

gold·en old·ie ▶ **n.** informal an old song or movie that is still well known and popular.

gold·en par·a·chute ▶ **n.** informal a large payment or other financial compensation guaranteed to a company executive should the executive be dismissed as a result of a merger or takeover.

gold·en plov·er ▶ **n.** a northern Eurasian and North American plover, with a gold-speckled back and black face and underparts in the breeding season. ● Genus *Pluvialis*, family Charadriidae: three species, in particular *P. apricaria* of Europe and *P. dominica* of Canada.

gold·en rai·sin ▶ **n.** a raisin made from a white grape.

gold·en re·triev·er ▶ **n.** a retriever of a breed with a thick golden-colored coat.

golden retriever

gold·en rice ▶ **n.** a genetically modified variety of rice containing large amounts of the orange or red plant pigment betacarotene, a substance important in the human diet as a precursor of vitamin A.

gold·en·rod /ˈgōldənˌräd/ ▶ **n.** a plant of the daisy family that bears tall spikes of small bright yellow flowers. ● Genus *Solidago*, family Compositae: numerous species, including **tall goldenrod** (*S. altissima*) with plumelike flower clusters, **downy goldenrod** (*S. puberula*) with erect, wandlike flower clusters, and **lance-leaved goldenrod** (*S. graminifolia*) with flat-topped flower clusters.

gold·en rule ▶ **n.** a basic principle that should be followed to ensure success in general or in a particular activity: *one of the golden rules in this class is punctuality.* ■ (often **Golden Rule**) the biblical rule of "do unto others as you would have them do unto you" (Matt. 7:12).

gold·en·seal /ˈgōldənˌsēl/ ▶ **n.** a North American woodland plant of the buttercup family, with a bright yellow root that is used in herbal medicine. ● *Hydrastis canadensis*, family Ranunculaceae.

gold·en sec·tion ▶ **n.** the division of a line so that the whole is to the greater part as that part is to the smaller part (i.e., in a ratio of 1 to $^1/_2$ ($\sqrt{5}+1$)), a proportion that is considered to be particularly pleasing to the eye.

Gold·en State a nickname for the state of **California**.

gold·en syr·up ▶ **n.** Brit. a thick syrup with a buttery aroma, made from cane sugar.

gold·en wat·tle ▶ **n.** an Australian acacia with golden flowers. ● Genus *Acacia*, family Leguminosae: *A. pycnatha*, whose flowers are used as Australia's national emblem, and *A. longifolia*.

gold·en wed·ding (also **golden wedding anniversary**) ▶ **n.** the fiftieth anniversary of a wedding.

gold·field /ˈgōldˌfēld/ ▶ **n.** a district in which gold is found as a mineral.

gold-filled ▶ **adj.** (esp. of jewelry) consisting of a base metal covered in a thin layer of gold.

gold·finch /ˈgōldˌfinCH/ ▶ **n.** a brightly colored finch with yellow feathers in the plumage. ● Genus *Carduelis*, family Fringillidae: four species, esp. the **American goldfinch** (*C. tristis*) and the **Eurasian goldfinch** (*C. carduelis*).
– ORIGIN late Old English *goldfinc* (see **gold, finch**).

g

gold·fish /ˈgōldˌfiSH/ ▶ **n.** (pl. **same** or **goldfishes**) a small reddish-golden Eurasian carp, popular in ponds and aquariums. A long history of breeding in China and Japan has resulted in many varieties of form and color. ● *Carassius auratus*, family Cyprinidae.

gold·fish bowl ▶ **n.** a spherical glass container for goldfish. ■ a place or situation lacking privacy: *a goldfish bowl of publicity*.

gold·i·locks /ˈgōldēˌläks/ ▶ **n.** informal a person with golden hair.

Gold·ing /ˈgōldiNG/, Sir William (Gerald) (1911–93), English novelist. His first novel, *Lord of the Flies* (1954), told of boys stranded on a desert island who revert to savagery. Other notable works: *Rites of Passage* (1980) and *Fire Down Below* (1989). Nobel Prize for Literature (1983).

gold leaf ▶ **n.** gold that has been beaten into a very thin sheet, used in gilding.

Gold·man /ˈgōldmən/, Emma (1869–1940), US political activist; born in Lithuania. She was involved in New York's anarchist movement and was an opponent of US conscription. Notable works: *Anarchism and Other Essays* (1910) and *My Disillusionment in Russia* (1923).

gold med·al ▶ **n.** a medal made of or colored gold, customarily awarded for first place in a race or competition.
– DERIVATIVES **gold med·al·ist n.**

gold mine ▶ **n.** a place where gold is mined. ■ a source of wealth, valuable information, or resources: *this book is a gold mine of information*.
– DERIVATIVES **gold min·er n.**

gold plate ▶ **n.** a thin layer of gold, electroplated or otherwise applied as a coating to another metal. ■ objects coated with gold. ■ plates, dishes, etc., made of gold.
▶ **v.** (**gold-plate**) [with obj.] cover (something) with a thin layer of gold.

gold-plat·ed ▶ **adj.** covered with a thin layer of gold: *a gold-plated tiepin*. ■ likely to prove profitable; secure: *houses are no longer the gold-plated investment they were*.

gold re·serve ▶ **n.** a quantity of gold held by a central bank to support the issue of currency.

gold rush ▶ **n.** a rapid movement of people to a newly discovered goldfield. The first major gold rush, to California in 1848–49, was followed by others in the US, Australia (1851–53), South Africa (1884), and Canada (Klondike, 1897–98).

Golds·bor·o /ˈgōldzˌbərō/ a city in eastern North Carolina, a noted tobacco center; pop. 37,597 (est. 2008).

Gold·smith /ˈgōldˌsmiTH/, Oliver (1728–74), Irish novelist, poet, essayist, and playwright. Notable works: *The Vicar of Wakefield* (1766), *The Deserted Village* (1770), and *She Stoops to Conquer* (1773).

gold·smith /ˈgōldˌsmiTH/ ▶ **n.** a person who makes gold articles.
– ORIGIN late Old English (see **gold, smith**).

gold stand·ard ▶ **n.** historical the system by which the value of a currency was defined in terms of gold, for which the currency could be exchanged. The gold standard was generally abandoned in the Depression of the 1930s. Compare with **silver standard**. ■ the best, most reliable, or most prestigious thing of its type: *you can't rely on lab tests as being the gold standard*.

gold·stone /ˈgōldˌstōn/ ▶ **n.** a variety of aventurine containing sparkling gold-colored particles.

gold·thread /ˈgōldˌTHred/ ▶ **n.** a plant of the buttercup family that yields a yellow dye and is used in herbal medicine as a treatment for mouth ulcers. It grows in North America and northeastern Asia. ● Genus *Coptis*, family Ranunculaceae: several species, in particular *C. groenlandica* and *C. trifolia*.

Gold·wa·ter /ˈgōldˌwôtər, -ˌwä-/, Barry Morris (1909–98), US politician. A conservative, he was a member of the US Senate from Arizona 1953–65, 1969–87 and a Republican presidential candidate in 1964.

Gold·wyn /ˈgōldwən/, Samuel (1882–1974), US movie producer; born in Poland; born *Schmuel Gelbfisz*, changed to *Samuel Goldfish* then *Goldwyn*. He produced his first movie in 1913 and, with Louis B. Mayer, founded Metro-Goldwyn-Mayer (MGM) in 1924.

go·lem /ˈgōləm/ ▶ **n.** (in Jewish legend) a clay figure brought to life by magic. ■ an automaton or robot.
– ORIGIN late 19th cent.: from Yiddish *goylem*, from Hebrew *gōlem* 'shapeless mass.'

golf /gälf, gôlf/ ▶ **n.** 1 a game played on a large open-air course, in which a small hard ball is struck with a club into a series of small holes in the ground, the object being to use the fewest possible strokes to complete the course.

> A golf course usually has 18 holes, each set in a smooth lawn (a green) separated from the others by stretches of smooth grass (fairways), rough ground, sand-filled bunkers, and other hazards. Various clubs are used to hit the ball from a tee toward the green and then putt it into the hole.

2 a code word representing the letter G, used in radio communication.
▶ **v.** [no obj.] play golf: (as noun **golfing**) *a week's golfing*.
– DERIVATIVES **golf·er n.**
– ORIGIN late Middle English (originally Scots): perhaps related to Dutch *kolf* 'club, bat,' used as a term in several Dutch games; *golf*, however, is recorded before these games.

golf bag ▶ **n.** a tall cylindrical bag used for carrying golf clubs and balls.

golf ball ▶ **n.** a small hard ball used in the game of golf.

golf cart ▶ **n.** a small motorized vehicle for golfers and their equipment.

golf club ▶ **n.** 1 a club used to hit the ball in golf, with a heavy wooden or metal head on a slender shaft.
2 an organization of members for playing golf. ■ the premises used by such an organization.

golf course ▶ **n.** a course on which golf is played.

golf links ▶ **plural n.** see **links**.

golf shirt ▶ **n.** a light, short-sleeved shirt with a collar, typically of a knitted fabric and with buttons at the neck only. See also **polo shirt**.

Gol·gi /ˈgôljē/, Camillo (1844–1926), Italian histologist and anatomist. He devised a staining technique to investigate nerve tissue, classified types of nerve cells, and described the structure in the cytoplasm of most cells, now named after him. Nobel Prize for Physiology or Medicine (1906), shared with Santiago Ramón y Cajal.

Gol·gi ap·pa·rat·us (also **Golgi body**) ▶ **n.** Biology a complex of vesicles and folded membranes within the cytoplasm of most eukaryotic cells, involved in secretion and intracellular transport.

Gol·go·tha /ˈgälgəTHə, gôlˈgäTHə/ the site of the crucifixion of Jesus; Calvary.
– ORIGIN from late Latin, via Greek from an Aramaic form of Hebrew *gulgoleth* 'skull' (see Matt. 27:33).

Go·li·ath /gəˈlīəTH/ (in the Bible) a Philistine giant, according to legend slain by David (1 Sam. 17), but according to another tradition slain by Elhanan (2 Sam. 21:19).

go·li·ath bee·tle ▶ **n.** a very large, boldly marked tropical beetle related to the chafers, the male of which has a forked horn on the head. ● Genus *Goliathus*, family Scarabaeidae: several species, in particular *G. giganteus* of Africa, which is the largest known beetle.

gol·li·wog /ˈgäləˌwäg/ ▶ **n.** a soft doll with bright clothes, a black face, and fuzzy hair.
– ORIGIN late 19th cent.: from *Golliwogg*, the name of a doll character in books by Bertha Upton (died 1912), American writer, and Florence K. Upton (died 1922), American illustrator; perhaps suggested by **golly** and **polliwog**.

gol·ly /ˈgälē/ (also **by golly**) ▶ **exclam.** informal, dated used to express surprise or delight: *"Golly! Is that the time?"*
– ORIGIN late 18th cent.: euphemism for **God**.

Go·mel /gôˈm(y)el/ Russian name for **Homel**.

go·mer /ˈgōmər/ ▶ **n.** 1 military slang an inept or stupid colleague, esp. a trainee.
2 informal (used mainly by doctors) a troublesome patient, esp. an elderly or homeless one.
– ORIGIN 1960s: origin uncertain; sense 1 perhaps from the television character *Gomer* Pyle, a bungling Marine Corps enlistee; sense 2 perhaps an acronym from *get out of my emergency room*.

Go·mor·rah /gəˈmôrə/ a town in ancient Palestine, probably south of the Dead Sea. According to Gen. 19:24, it was destroyed by fire from heaven, along with Sodom, for the wickedness of its inhabitants.

Gom·pers /ˈgämpərz/, Samuel (1850–1924), US labor leader; born in England. He helped to found the Federation of Organized Trades and Labor Unions in 1881. When it was reorganized as the American Federation of Labor in 1886, he served as its president until his death and did much to win respect for organized labor.

-gon ▶ **comb. form** in nouns denoting plane figures with a specified number of angles: *hexagon* | *pentagon*.
– ORIGIN from Greek *-gōnos* '-angled.'

go·nad /ˈgōnad/ ▶ **n.** Physiology & Zoology an organ that produces gametes; a testis or ovary.
– DERIVATIVES **go·nad·al** /gōˈnadl/ **adj.**
– ORIGIN late 19th cent.: from modern Latin *gonades*, plural of *gonas*, from Greek *gonē* 'generation, seed.'

go·nad·o·trop·ic hor·mone /gōˌnadəˈträpik, -ˈtrōpik/ (chiefly Brit. also **gonadotrophic hormone** /-ˈträfik, -ˈtrōfik/) ▶ **n.** another term for **gonadotropin**.

go·nad·o·tro·pin /gōˌnadəˈtrōpin/ (chiefly Brit. also **gonadotrophin** /-ˈtrōfin/) ▶ **n.** Biochemistry any of a group of hormones secreted by the pituitary that stimulate the activity of the gonads.

Gon·court /gônˈko͝or/, Edmond de (1822–96) and Jules de (1830–70), French novelists and critics. In his will, Edmond provided for the establishment of the Académie Goncourt, which awards the annual Prix Goncourt.

Gond /gänd/ ▶ **n.** (pl. **same**) 1 a member of an indigenous people living in the hill forests of central India.
2 the Dravidian language of this people.
▶ **adj.** of or relating to the Gonds or their language.
– DERIVATIVES **Gond·i n. & adj.**
– ORIGIN from Sanskrit *goṇḍa*.

gon·do·la /ˈgändələ, gänˈdōlə/ ▶ **n.** a light flat-bottomed boat used on Venetian canals, having a high point at each end and worked by one oar at the stern. ■ a cabin on a suspended ski lift. ■ (also **gondola car**) an open railroad freight car. ■ an enclosed compartment suspended from an airship or balloon.
– ORIGIN mid 16th cent.: from Venetian Italian, from Rhaeto-Romanic *gondolà* 'to rock, roll.'

gondola

gon·do·lier /ˌgändlˈi(ə)r/ ▶ **n.** a person who propels and steers a gondola.
– ORIGIN early 17th cent.: via French from Italian *gondoliere*, from *gondola* (see **gondola**).

Gond·wa·na /gänˈdwänə/ (also **Gondwanaland**) a vast continental area believed to have existed in the southern hemisphere and to have resulted from the breakup of Pangaea in Mesozoic times. It comprised the present Arabia, Africa, South America, Antarctica, Australia, and the peninsula of India.
– ORIGIN late 19th cent. (originally denoting any of a series of rocks in India, esp. fluviatile shales and sandstones): from the name of a region in central northern India, from Sanskrit *goṇḍavana* 'forest of Gond.'

gone /gôn/ past participle of **go**[1].
▶ **adj.** [predic.] 1 no longer present; departed: *while you were gone* | *the bad old days are gone*. ■ no longer in existence; dead or extinct: *an aunt of mine, long since gone*. ■ no longer available: *all 35,000 tickets will be gone by next weekend*. ■ informal in a trance or stupor, esp. through exhaustion, drink, or drugs: *she sat, half-gone, on a folding chair*. ■ [attrib.] lost; hopeless: *spending time and effort on a gone sucker like Galindez*. ■ dated excellent; inspired: *a bunch of real gone cats*.
2 informal having reached a specified time in a pregnancy: *she is now four months gone*.
▶ **prep.** Brit. (of time) past: *it's gone half past eleven*. ■ (of age) older than: *she was gone sixty by then*.
– PHRASES **be gone on** informal be infatuated with: *I always knew he was gone on you*.

gon·er /ˈgônər/ ▶ **n.** informal a person or thing that is doomed or cannot be saved.

gon·fa·lon /ˈgänfələn/ ▶ **n.** a banner or pennant, esp. one with streamers, hung from a crossbar.

–ORIGIN late 16th cent.: from Italian *gonfalone*, from a Germanic compound whose second element is related to VANE.

gon·fa·lon·ier /ˌgänfələˈni(ə)r/ ▶ **n.** the bearer of a gonfalon; a standard-bearer.

gong /gäNG, gôNG/ ▶ **n.** a metal disk with a turned rim, giving a resonant note when struck: *a dinner gong.*
▶ **v.** [no obj.] sound a gong or make a sound like that of a gong being struck.
–ORIGIN early 17th cent.: from Malay *gong, gung*, of imitative origin.

go·ni·a·tite /ˈgōnēəˌtīt/ ▶ **n.** an ammonoid fossil of an early type found chiefly in the Devonian and Carboniferous periods, typically with simple angular suture lines. Compare with AMMONITE and CERATITE. ● Typified by the genus *Goniatites*, order Goniatitida.
–ORIGIN mid 19th cent.: from modern Latin *Goniatites*, from Greek *gōnia* 'angle.'

gon·if /ˈgänəf/ (also **goniff, ganef**) ▶ **n.** informal a disreputable or dishonest person (often used as a general term of abuse).
–ORIGIN mid 19th cent.: from Yiddish *ganev*, from Hebrew *gannāb* 'thief.'

go·ni·om·e·ter /ˌgōnēˈämitər/ ▶ **n.** an instrument for the precise measurement of angles, esp. one used to measure the angles between the faces of crystals.
–DERIVATIVES **go·ni·o·met·ric** /-nēəˈmetrik/ **adj.**, **go·ni·o·met·ri·cal** /-nēəˈmetrikəl/ **adj.**, **go·ni·om·e·try** /-trē/ **n.**
–ORIGIN mid 18th cent.: from French *goniomètre*, from Greek *gōnia* 'angle' + French *-mètre* '(instrument) measuring.'

gon·na /ˈgônə, ˈgənə/ informal ▶ **contraction** going to: *we're gonna win this game.*

gon·o·coc·cus /ˌgänəˈkäkəs/ ▶ **n.** (pl. **gonococci** /-ˈkäkˌsī/) a bacterium that causes gonorrhea. ● *Neisseria gonorrhoeae*, a Gram-negative diplococcus.
–DERIVATIVES **gon·o·coc·cal** /-ˈkäkəl/ **adj.**
–ORIGIN late 19th cent.: from *gono-* (as in GONORRHEA) + COCCUS.

go-no-go ▶ **adj. 1** designating a situation in which one must decide whether or not to continue with a particular course of action, or the moment when such a decision must be made.
2 designating the decision to continue with or abandon a course of action.

gon·or·rhe·a /ˌgänəˈrēə/ (Brit. **gonorrhoea**) ▶ **n.** a venereal disease involving inflammatory discharge from the urethra or vagina.
–DERIVATIVES **gon·or·rhe·al adj.**
–ORIGIN early 16th cent.: via late Latin from Greek *gonorrhoia*, from *gonos* 'semen' + *rhoia* 'flux.'

gon·zo /ˈgänzō/ ▶ **adj.** informal of or associated with journalistic writing of an exaggerated, subjective, and fictionalized style. ■ bizarre or crazy: *the woman was either gonzo or stoned.*
–ORIGIN 1970s: perhaps from Italian *gonzo* 'foolish' or Spanish *ganso* 'goose, fool.'

goo /go͞o/ ▶ **n.** informal **1** a sticky or slimy substance: *he tipped the grayish goo from the test tube.*
2 sickly sentiment.
–ORIGIN early 20th cent. (originally US): perhaps from *burgoo*, a nautical slang term for porridge, based on Persian *bulġūr* 'bruised grain.'

goo·ber /ˈgo͞obər/ ▶ **n.** informal **1** (also **goober pea**) a peanut.
2 often offensive a person from the southeastern US, esp. Georgia or Arkansas. ■ offensive an unsophisticated person; a yokel.

Goo·ber State a nickname for the state of GEORGIA.

good /go͝od/ ▶ **adj.** (**better** /ˈbetər/, **best** /best/) **1** to be desired or approved of: *we live at peace with each other, which is good | a good quality of life.* ■ pleasing and welcome: *she was pleased to hear good news about him.* ■ expressing approval: *the play had good reviews.*
2 having the qualities required for a particular role: *the schools here are good.* ■ appropriate to a particular purpose: *this is a good month for planting seeds.* ■ (of language) with correct grammar and pronunciation: *she speaks good English.* ■ strictly adhering to or fulfilling all the principles of a particular cause, religion, or party: *a good Catholic girl.* ■ (of a ticket) valid: *the ticket is* **good for** *travel from May to September.*
3 possessing or displaying moral virtue: *I've met many good people who made me feel ashamed of my own shortcomings |* (as plural noun **the good**) *the rich and the good shared the same fate as the poor and the bad.* ■ showing kindness: *you are good—thank you.* ■ obedient to rules or conventions: *accustom the child to being rewarded for good behavior.* ■ used to address or refer to people, esp. in a patronizing or humorous way: *the good people of the city were disconcerted.* ■ commanding respect: *he was concerned with establishing and maintaining his good name.* ■ belonging or relating to a high social class: *he comes from a good family.*
4 giving pleasure; enjoyable or satisfying: *the streets fill up with people looking for a good time.* ■ pleasant to look at; attractive: *you're looking pretty good.* ■ (of clothes) smart and suitable for formal wear: *he went upstairs to change out of his good suit.*
5 [attrib.] thorough: *the attic needed a good cleaning | have a good look around.* ■ used to emphasize that a number is at least as great as one claims: *they're a good twenty years younger.* ■ used to emphasize a following adjective: *we had a good long hug.* ■ fairly large: *a good crowd |* figurative *there's a good chance that we may be able to help you.*
6 used in conjunction with the name of God or a related expression as an exclamation of extreme surprise or anger: *good heavens!*
▶ **n. 1** that which is morally right; righteousness: *a mysterious balance of good and evil.*
2 benefit or advantage to someone or something: *he is too clever* **for his own good**.
3 (**goods**) merchandise or possessions: *imports of luxury goods.* ■ Brit. things to be transported, as distinct from passengers: *a means of transporting passengers as well as goods |* [as modifier] *a goods train.* ■ (**the goods**) informal the genuine article.
▶ **adv.** informal well: *my mother could never cook this good.*
–PHRASES **all to the good** to be welcomed without qualification. **as good as ——** very nearly ——: *she's as good as here.* ■ used of a result which will inevitably follow: *if we pass on the information, he's as good as dead.* **be any** (or **no** or **much**) **good** have some (or none or much) merit: *tell me whether that picture is any good.* ■ be of some (or none or much) help in dealing with a situation: *it was no good trying to ward things off.* **be so good as** (or **be good enough**) **to do something** used to make a polite request: *would you be so good as to answer.* **be —— to the good** have a specified net profit or advantage: *I came out $7 to the good.* **come up with** (or **deliver**) **the goods** informal do what is expected or required of one. **do good 1** act virtuously, esp. by helping others. **2** make a helpful contribution to a situation: *could the discussion do any good?* **do someone good** be beneficial to someone, esp. to their health: *the walk will do you good.* **for good** (**and all**) forever; definitively: *the experience almost frightened me away for good.* **get** (or **have**) **the goods on** informal obtain (or possess) information about (someone) that may be used to their detriment. **good and ——** informal used as an intensifier before an adjective or adverb: *it'll be good and dark by then.* (**as**) **good as gold** (esp. of a child) extremely well behaved. (**as**) **good as new** in a very good condition or state, close to the original state again after damage, injury, or illness: *the skirt looked as good as new.* **the Good Book** the Bible. **good for 1** having a beneficial effect on: *smoking is not good for the lungs.* **2** reliably providing: *they found him good for a laugh.* ■ sufficient to pay for: *his money was good for a bottle of whiskey.* **good for you** (or **him**, **her**, etc.)**!** used as an exclamation of approval toward a person, esp. for something that they have achieved: *"I'm taking my driving test next month." "Good for you!"* **the Good Shepherd** a name for Jesus. [with biblical allusion to John 10:1-16.] **good wine needs no bush** see WINE. **a good word** words in recommendation or defense of a person: *I hoped you might* **put in a good word for** *me with your friends.* **have a good mind to do something** see MIND. **in someone's good books** see BOOK. **in good time 1** with no risk of being late: *I arrived in good time.* **2** (also **all in good time**) in due course but without haste: *you shall have a puppy all in good time.* **make good** be successful: *a college friend who made good in Hollywood.* **make something good 1** compensate for loss, damage, or expense: *if I scratched the table, I'd make good the damage.* ■ repair or restore after damage: *make good the wall where you have buried the cable.* **2** fulfill a promise or claim: *I challenged him to make good his boast.* **one good turn deserves another** see TURN. **put a good face on something** see FACE. **take something in good part** not be offended by something: *he took her abruptness in good part.* **up to no good** doing something wrong.
–ORIGIN Old English *gōd*, of Germanic origin; related to Dutch *goed* and German *gut*.

> **USAGE** The adverb corresponding to the adjective **good** is **well**: *she is a good swimmer who performs well in meets.* Confusion sometimes arises because **well** is also an adjective meaning 'in good health, healthy,' for which **good** is widely used informally as a substitute: *I feel well,* meaning 'I feel healthy'—versus the informal *I feel good,* meaning either 'I feel healthy' or 'I am in a good mood.' See also usage at BAD.

good af·ter·noon ▶ **exclam.** expressing good wishes on meeting or parting in the afternoon.

Good·all /ˈgo͝odôl/, Jane (1934–), English zoologist. After working with Louis Leakey in Tanzania from 1957, she made prolonged and intimate studies of chimpanzees at the Gombe Stream Reserve at Lake Tanganyika from 1970.

good·bye /ˌgo͝odˈbī/ (also **goodby** or **good-by**) ▶ **exclam.** used to express good wishes when parting or at the end of a conversation.
▶ **n.** (pl. **goodbyes** or **goodbys**) an instance of saying "goodbye"; a parting: *a final goodbye.*
–ORIGIN late 16th cent.: contraction of *God be with you!*, with *good* substituted on the pattern of phrases such as *good morning*.

good eve·ning ▶ **exclam.** expressing good wishes on meeting or parting during the evening.

good faith ▶ **n.** honesty or sincerity of intention: *the details contained in this brochure have been published* **in good faith**.

good·fel·la /ˈgo͝odˌfelə/ ▶ **n.** informal a gangster, esp. a member of a Mafia family.

good form ▶ **n.** what complies with current social conventions: *it wasn't considered* **in good form** *to show too much enthusiasm.*

good-for-noth·ing ▶ **adj.** (of a person) worthless: *his good-for-nothing son.*
▶ **n.** a worthless person.

Good Fri·day ▶ **n.** the Friday before Easter Sunday, on which the Crucifixion of Jesus Christ is commemorated in the Christian Church. It is traditionally a day of fasting and penance.
–ORIGIN from GOOD, in the sense 'holy, observed as a holy day.'

good-heart·ed ▶ **adj.** kind and well meaning.
–DERIVATIVES **good-heart·ed·ly adv.**, **good-heart·ed·ness n.**

Good Hope, Cape of see CAPE OF GOOD HOPE.

good hu·mor ▶ **n.** a genial disposition or mood: *I admire your dignity and good humor.*

good-hu·mored ▶ **adj.** genial; cheerful.
–DERIVATIVES **good-hu·mored·ly adv.**

good·ie ▶ **n.** variant spelling of GOODY[1].

good·ish /ˈgo͝odiSH/ ▶ **adj.** fairly good: *in goodish working order.* ■ fairly large: *a goodish portion.*

Good-King-Hen·ry (also **Good King Henry**) ▶ **n.** an edible plant of the goosefoot family, with large dark green leaves and insignificant clusters of flowers. Native to Europe, it has become naturalized in North America. ● *Chenopodium bonus-henricus*, family Chenopodiaceae.
–ORIGIN late 16th cent.: of unknown origin.

good-look·ing ▶ **adj.** (chiefly of a person) attractive.
–DERIVATIVES **good-look·er n.**

good·ly /ˈgo͝odlē/ ▶ **adj.** (**goodlier, goodliest**) **1** considerable in size or quantity: *we ran up a goodly bar bill.*
2 archaic attractive, excellent, or admirable.
–DERIVATIVES **good·li·ness n.**
–ORIGIN Old English *gōdlic* (see GOOD, -LY[1]).

Good·man /ˈgo͝odmən/, Benny (1909–86), US jazz clarinetist and bandleader; full name *Benjamin David Goodman*; known as **the King of Swing**. In 1934, he formed his own band, which was the first big band to include both black and white musicians.

good·man /ˈgo͝odmən/ ▶ **n.** (pl. **goodmen**) archaic, chiefly Scottish the male head of a household.

good man·ners ▶ **plural n.** polite or well-bred social behavior: *it's nice to meet a young man with such good manners.*

good mon·ey ▶ **n.** money that might usefully be spent elsewhere; hard-earned money: *I'm not going to pay good money for it.* ■ informal high wages: *I earn good money.*

good morn·ing ▶ **exclam.** expressing good wishes on meeting or parting during the morning.

good na·ture ▶ **n.** a kind and unselfish disposition: *your boy has a good nature.*

good-na·tured ▶ **adj.** kind, friendly, and patient: *everyone was very good-natured about my comments.*
–DERIVATIVES **good-na·tured·ly adv.**

good·ness /ˈgo͝odnis/ ▶ **n.** the quality of being good, in particular: ■ virtue; moral excellence: *a belief in the basic goodness of mankind.* ■ the beneficial or nourishing element of food.
▶ **exclam.** (as a substitution for "God") expressing surprise, anger, etc.: *goodness knows what her rent will be.*
–PHRASES **for goodness' sake** see SAKE[1]. **goodness of fit** Statistics the extent to which observed data match the values expected by theory. **have the**

g

goodness to do something used in exaggeratedly polite requests: *have the goodness to look at me when I'm speaking to you!*
– ORIGIN Old English *gōdnes* (see GOOD, -NESS).

Good News Bi·ble ▶ n. a translation of the Bible in simple everyday English, published 1966–76 by the United Bible Societies.

good night ▶ exclam. expressing good wishes on parting at night or before going to bed.

good old boy ▶ n. a man who embodies some or all of the qualities considered characteristic of many white men of the southern US, including an unpretentious, convivial manner, conservative or intolerant attitudes, and a strong sense of fellowship with and loyalty to other members of his peer group.

goods and chat·tels ▶ plural n. chiefly Law all kinds of personal possessions.

good-sized ▶ adj. of ample size; fairly large: *a good-sized garden.*

good-tem·pered ▶ adj. not easily irritated or made angry.
– DERIVATIVES **good-tem·pered·ly** adv.

good-time ▶ adj. [attrib.] (of a person) recklessly pursuing pleasure: *a good-time party girl | he's just a good-time Charlie.*

good·wife /ˈgŏŏdˌwīf/ ▶ n. (pl. **goodwives**) archaic, chiefly Scottish the female head of a household.

good·will /ˌgŏŏdˈwil/ (also **good will**) ▶ n. **1** friendly, helpful, or cooperative feelings or attitude: *the plan is dependent on goodwill between the two sides* | [as modifier] *a goodwill gesture.*
2 the established reputation of a business regarded as a quantifiable asset, e.g., as represented by the excess of the price paid at a takeover for a company over its fair market value.

Good·win /ˈgŏŏdwin/, Doris Kearns (1943–) US journalist, historian, and writer. Her works include *Lyndon Johnson and the American Dream* (1976), *The Fitzgeralds and the Kennedys* (1989), and *Team of Rivals: The Political Genius of Abraham Lincoln* (2005).

good works ▶ plural n. charitable acts.

good·y[1] /ˈgŏŏdē/ ▶ n. (also **goodie**) (pl. **goodies**) informal (usu. **goodies**) something attractive or desirable, esp. something tasty or pleasant to eat.
▶ exclam. expressing childish delight: *goody, we can have a party.*

good·y[2] ▶ n. (pl. **goodies**) archaic (often as a title prefixed to a surname) an elderly woman of humble station: *the tale of Goody Blake and Harry Gill.*
– ORIGIN mid 16th cent.: pet form of GOODWIFE; compare with HUSSY.

good·y bag ▶ n. a bag containing a selection of desirable products, esp. one given away at a party or as a promotional offer.

Good·year /ˈgŏŏdˌyi(ə)r/, Charles (1800–60), US inventor. He developed the process of the vulcanization of rubber after accidentally dropping some rubber mixed with sulfur and white lead on a hot stove.

good·y-good·y informal ▶ n. a smug or obtrusively virtuous person.
▶ adj. smug or obtrusively virtuous.

good·y two-shoes ▶ n. a smugly or obtrusively virtuous person; a goody-goody.
– ORIGIN from the nickname of the heroine of the *History of Little Goody Two-Shoes* (1766).

goo·ey /ˈgo͞oē/ ▶ adj. (**gooier**, **gooiest**) informal soft and sticky. ■ mawkishly sentimental: *you can love somebody without going all gooey.*
– DERIVATIVES **goo·ey·ness** n.

goof /go͞of/ informal ▶ n. **1** a mistake: *he made one of the most embarrassing goofs of his tenure.*
2 a foolish or stupid person.
▶ v. [no obj.] **1** spend time idly or foolishly; fool around: *I was* **goofing around** *and broke my arm.* ■ (**goof off**) evade a duty; idle or shirk: *he was* **goofing off** *from his math homework.* ■ (**goof on**) make fun of; ridicule: *Lew and I started goofing on Alison's friend.*
2 make a mistake; blunder: *you're scared to say yes in case you* **goof up**.
– ORIGIN early 20th cent.: of unknown origin.

goof·ball /ˈgo͞ofˌbôl/ ▶ n. informal **1** a naive, silly, or stupid person.
2 a narcotic drug in pill form, esp. a barbiturate.

goof-off ▶ n. informal a person who is habitually lazy or does less than their fair share of work.

goof-proof /ˈgo͞ofˌpro͞of/ ▶ adj. (of a product, procedure, etc.) designed to be simple enough for anyone to use or implement: *each comes with complete instructions and detailed illustrations that make the installation nearly goof-proof.*
▶ v. [with obj.] design or adapt (a product, procedure, etc.) so that it is simple for anyone to use: *these simple steps can goof-proof your 1040.*

goof-up ▶ n. informal a stupid mistake.

goof·us /ˈgo͞ofəs/ ▶ n. informal a foolish or stupid person (often used as a general term of abuse).
– ORIGIN 1920s: based on GOOF.

goof·y /ˈgo͞ofē/ ▶ adj. (**goofier**, **goofiest**) informal **1** foolish; harmlessly eccentric.
2 (in surfing and other board sports) with the right leg in front of the left on the board.
– DERIVATIVES **goof·i·ly** /-fəlē/ adv., **goof·i·ness** n.

goo·gle /ˈgo͞ogəl/ ▶ v. [with obj.] informal search for information about (someone or something) on the Internet: *I recently googled my 7th grade teacher and found his current e-mail address* | [no obj.] *she spent the afternoon googling aimlessly.*
– ORIGIN 1990s: from *Google*, a trademark for a popular Internet search engine.

goo·gle bomb·ing ▶ n. the designing of Internet links that will bias search engine results so as to create an inaccurate (often humorous) impression of the search target.

goog·ly /ˈgo͞oglē/ ▶ n. (pl. **googlies**) Cricket a ball bowled with a deceptive bounce.
– ORIGIN early 20th cent.: of unknown origin.

goo·gol /ˈgo͞oˌgôl/ ▶ cardinal number equivalent to ten raised to the power of a hundred (10^{100}).
– ORIGIN 1940s: said to have been coined by the nine-year-old nephew of E. Kasner (1878–1955), American mathematician, at Kasner's request.

goo·gol·plex /ˈgo͞ogôlˌpleks/ ▶ cardinal number equivalent to ten raised to the power of a googol.
– ORIGIN 1940s: from GOOGOL + *-plex* as in *multiplex*.

goo-goo informal ▶ adj. **1** amorously adoring: *making goo-goo eyes at him.*
2 (of speech or vocal sounds) childish or meaningless: *making soothing goo-goo noises.*
– ORIGIN early 20th cent.: possibly related to GOGGLE.

gook[1] /gŏŏk, go͞ok/ ▶ n. informal, offensive a foreigner, esp. a person of Philippine, Korean, or Vietnamese descent.
– ORIGIN 1930s: of unknown origin.

gook[2] ▶ n. informal a sloppy wet or viscous substance: *all that gook she kept putting on her face.*
– ORIGIN 1970s: variant of GUCK.

Goo·la·gong /ˈgo͞oləˌgäNG/, Evonne, see CAWLEY.

goom·bah /ˈgo͞ombä, go͞omˈbä/ ▶ n. informal an associate or accomplice, esp. a senior member of a criminal gang.
– ORIGIN 1960s: probably a dialect alteration of Italian *compàre* 'godfather, friend, accomplice.'

goom·bay /ˈgo͞ombā, ˈgo͞om-/ ▶ n. W. Indian a goatskin drum with a round or squared top, played with the hands. ■ the calypso-style music associated with the playing of such drums. ■ a dance to such drums. ■ (chiefly in the Bahamas) a festival or season of such music and dance.
– ORIGIN perhaps from Kikongo *ngoma*, denoting a type of drum.

goon /go͞on/ ▶ n. informal **1** a silly, foolish, or eccentric person.
2 a bully or thug, esp. one hired to terrorize or do away with opposition: *a squad of goons waving pistols.*
– ORIGIN mid 19th cent.: perhaps from dialect *gooney* 'booby'; influenced by the subhuman cartoon character 'Alice the *Goon*,' created by E. C. Segar (1894–1938), American cartoonist.

goon·ey bird /ˈgo͞onē/ (also **goony bird**) ▶ n. another term for an albatross of the North Pacific. ● Genus *Diomedea*, family Diomedeidae: the Laysan albatross (*D. immutabilis*) and the black-footed albatross (*D. nigripes*).
– ORIGIN mid 19th cent.: of unknown origin.

goop /go͞op/ ▶ n. informal sloppy or sticky semifluid matter, typically something unpleasant. ■ mawkish sentiment.
– DERIVATIVES **goop·i·ness** /-pēnis/ n., **goop·y** adj.
– ORIGIN 1970s: the sounds *g*, *oo*, and *p* are said to be symbolic of semiliquid matter; compare with GLOOP.

goos·an·der /go͞oˈsandər/ ▶ n. (pl. **same** or **goosanders**) British term for COMMON MERGANSER (see MERGANSER).
– ORIGIN early 17th cent.: probably from GOOSE + *-ander* as in dialect *bergander* 'shelduck' (the coloring of the male common merganser resembling that of the shelduck).

goose /go͞os/ ▶ n. (pl. **geese** /gēs/) **1** a large waterbird with a long neck, short legs, webbed feet, and a short broad bill. Generally geese are larger than ducks and have longer necks and shorter bills. ● Several genera in the family Anatidae, esp. *Anser* and *Branta*; most domesticated geese are descended from the greylag. ■ the female of such a bird. ■ the flesh of a goose as food.
2 informal a foolish person: *"Silly goose," he murmured fondly.*
3 (pl. **gooses**) a tailor's smoothing iron.
▶ v. [with obj.] informal **1** poke (someone) between the buttocks.
2 give (something) a boost; invigorate; increase: *the director* **goosed up** *the star's grosses by making him funny.*
– PHRASES **cook someone's goose** see COOK.
– ORIGIN Old English *gōs*, of Germanic origin; related to Dutch *gans* and German *Gans*, from an Indo-European root shared by Latin *anser* and Greek *khēn*.

goose bar·na·cle (also **gooseneck barnacle**) ▶ n. a stalked barnacle that hangs down from driftwood or other slow-moving floating objects, catching passing prey with its feathery legs. ● Genus *Lepas*, class Cirripedia.

goose·ber·ry /ˈgo͞osˌberē/ ▶ n. (pl. **gooseberries**) **1** a round edible yellowish-green or reddish berry with a thin translucent hairy skin.
2 the thorny shrub that bears this fruit. ● *Ribes grossularia*, family Grossulariaceae.
– ORIGIN mid 16th cent.: the first element perhaps from GOOSE, or perhaps based on Old French *groseille*, altered because of an unexplained association with the bird.

goose·bumps /ˈgo͞osˌbəmps/ ▶ plural n. another term for GOOSE PIMPLES.

goose egg informal ▶ n. zero, esp. a zero score in a game: *once again, our team goes home with a big goose egg.*
– ORIGIN late 19th cent.: with reference to the shape of the zero.

goose·fish /ˈgo͞osˌfisH/ ▶ n. (pl. **same** or **goosefishes**) a bottom-dwelling anglerfish. Also called MONKFISH. ● Family Lophiidae: several species, in particular *Lophius americanus* of North American waters.

goose·flesh /ˈgo͞osˌflesH/ ▶ n. a pimply state of the skin with the hairs erect, produced by cold or fright.
– ORIGIN early 19th cent.: so named because the skin resembles that of a plucked goose.

goose·foot /ˈgo͞osˌfŏŏt/ ▶ n. (pl. **goosefoots**) a plant of temperate regions with divided leaves that are said to resemble the foot of a goose. Some kinds are edible and many are common weeds. ● Genus *Chenopodium*, family Chenopodiaceae.

goose·grass /ˈgo͞osˌgras/ ▶ n. another term for CLEAVERS.

goose·neck /ˈgo͞osˌnek/ ▶ n. a support or pipe curved like a goose's neck: [as modifier] *a gooseneck lamp.* ■ Sailing a metal fitting at the end of a boom, connecting it to a pivot or ring near the base of the mast.

goose pim·ples ▶ plural n. the pimples that form gooseflesh.

goose step ▶ n. a military marching step in which the legs are not bent at the knee.
▶ v. (**goose-step**) [no obj.] march with such a step: *soldiers goose-stepped outside.*

goose·y /ˈgo͞osē/ (also **goosy**) ▶ adj. (**goosier**, **goosiest**) having or showing a quality considered to be characteristic of a goose, esp. foolishness or nervousness. ■ informal exhibiting gooseflesh: *I've gone all goosey.*

GOP ▶ abbr. Grand Old Party (Republican Party).

go·pak /ˈgōpak/ (also **hopak**) ▶ n. an energetic Ukrainian dance in duple time, traditionally performed by men.
– ORIGIN 1920s: via Russian, from Ukrainian *hopak*.

go·pher[1] /ˈgōfər/ ▶ n. **1** (also **pocket gopher**) a burrowing rodent with fur-lined pouches on the outside of the cheeks, found in North and Central America. ● Family Geomyidae: several genera and species. ■ informal another term for GROUND SQUIRREL.
2 (also **gopher tortoise**) a tortoise of dry sandy regions that excavates tunnels as shelter from the sun, native to the southern US. ● *Gopherus polyphemus*, family Testudinidae.
3 (also **Gopher**) Computing a menu-based system for Internet searching and document retrieval, largely superseded by the World Wide Web. [1990s: named after the gopher mascot of the University of Minnesota, where the system was invented.]
– ORIGIN late 18th cent.: perhaps from Canadian French *gaufre* 'honeycomb' (because the gopher "honeycombs" the ground with its burrows).

go·pher[2] ▶ n. variant spelling of GOFER.

go·pher ball ▶ n. Baseball a pitch that is hit for a home run.

go·pher snake ▶ n. a large harmless yellowish-cream snake with darker markings, native to western North America. ● *Pituophis catenifer*, family Colubridae. ■ (also **blue gopher snake**) another term for INDIGO SNAKE.

Go·pher State a nickname for the state of MINNESOTA.

go·pher wood ▶ n. **1** (in biblical use) the timber from which Noah's ark was made, from an unidentified tree (Gen. 6:14).

2 (**gopherwood**) either of two North American trees: ● STINKING CEDAR. ● YELLOWWOOD.
– ORIGIN early 17th cent.: *gopher* from Hebrew *gōper*.

go·pik /ˈgōpik/ ▶ **n.** (pl. **same** or **gopiks**) a monetary unit of Azerbaijan, equal to one hundredth of a manat.

Go·rakh·pur /ˈgôrək,po͝or/ an industrial city in northeastern India, in Uttar Pradesh, near the border with Nepal; pop. 719,100 (est. 2009).

go·ral /ˈgôrəl/ ▶ **n.** a long-haired goat-antelope with backward curving horns, found in mountainous regions of eastern Asia. ● Genus *Nemorhaedus*, family Bovidae: two species.
– ORIGIN mid 19th cent.: a local word in the Himalayas.

Gor·ba·chev /ˈgôrbə,CHôf/, Mikhail (Sergeevich) (1931–), Soviet statesman, general secretary of the Communist Party of the former Soviet Union 1985–91 and president 1988–91. Domestically, he introduced major reforms (*glasnost* and *perestroika*), both in the economy and in freedom of information, and his foreign policy helped bring about an end to the Cold War. His resignation following the establishment of the Commonwealth of Independent States effectively dissolved the Soviet Union. Nobel Peace Prize (1990).

gor·bli·mey /gôrˈblīmē/ Brit. informal ▶ **exclam.** an expression of surprise or indignation.
▶ **adj.** [attrib.] common; lower class.
– ORIGIN late 19th cent.: alteration of *God blind me*; also in use as a noun in the early 20th cent. to denote various kinds of unusual clothing.

Gor·di·an knot /ˈgôrdēən/ ▶ **n.** an extremely difficult or involved problem.
– PHRASES **cut the Gordian knot** solve or remove a problem in a direct or forceful way, rejecting gentler or more indirect methods.
– ORIGIN mid 16th cent.: from the legend that *Gordius*, king of Gordium, tied an intricate knot and prophesied that whoever untied it would become the ruler of Asia. It was cut through with a sword by Alexander the Great.

gor·di·an worm ▶ **n.** another term for HORSEHAIR WORM.

Gor·di·mer /ˈgôrdəmər/, Nadine (1923–), South African novelist and short-story writer. Her experience with the effects of apartheid underlies much of her work. Notable novels: *The Conservationist* (Booker Prize, 1974), *Burger's Daughter* (1979), and *Get a Life* (2005). Nobel Prize for Literature (1991).

Nadine Gordimer

Gor·di·um /ˈgôrdēəm/ an ancient city in Asia Minor (now northwestern Turkey), the capital of Phrygia in the 8th and 9th centuries BC.

Gor·don /ˈgôrdn/, Charles George (1833–85), British general and colonial administrator. He is noted for crushing the Taiping Rebellion (1863–64) in China and for fighting Mahdist forces in Sudan in 1884.

Gor·don set·ter ▶ **n.** a setter of a black-and-tan breed, used as a gun dog.
– ORIGIN mid 19th cent.: named after the 4th Duke of *Gordon* (1743–1827), who promoted the breed.

Gor·dy /ˈgôrdē/, Berry, Jr. (1929–), US recording company and popular music producer. He founded Motown Records in 1959 and had huge success in the 1960s and 1970s, popularizing black rhythm-and-blues and soul music.

Gore /gôr/ Al (1948–), US vice president 1993–2001; full name *Albert Arnold Gore, Jr.* A Tennessee Democrat, he served in the US House of Representatives 1977–85 and US Senate 1985–93. He lost the 2000 presidential bid to George W. Bush in one of the closest and most controversial elections in US history. His book *An Inconvenient Truth: The Planetary Emergency of Global Warming and What We Can Do About It* (2006) was the subject of a documentary (2006, Academy Award) and won a 2009 Grammy for Gore's spoken version. Nobel Peace Prize (2007, with the Intergovernmental Panel on Climate Change).

Al Gore

gore[1] /gôr/ ▶ **n.** blood that has been shed, esp. as a result of violence: *the film omitted the **blood and gore** in order to avoid controversy.*
– ORIGIN Old English *gor* 'dung, dirt,' of Germanic origin; related to Dutch *goor*, Swedish *gorr* 'muck, filth.' The current sense dates from the mid 16th cent.

gore[2] ▶ **v.** [with obj.] (of an animal such as a bull) pierce or stab with a horn or tusk.
– ORIGIN late Middle English (in the sense 'stab, pierce'): of unknown origin.

gore[3] ▶ **n.** a triangular or tapering piece of material used in making a garment, sail, or umbrella.
▶ **v.** [with obj.] make with a gore-shaped piece of material: (as adj. **gored**) *a gored skirt.*
– ORIGIN Old English *gāra* 'triangular piece of land,' of Germanic origin; related to Dutch *geer* and German *Gehre*, also probably to Old English *gār* 'spear' (a spearhead being triangular).

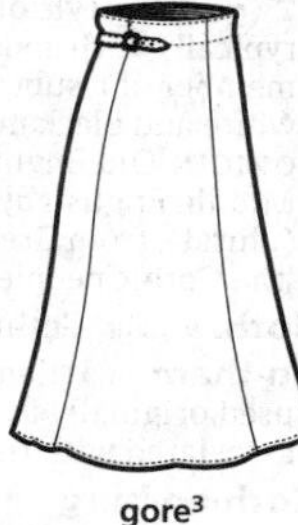
gore[3]

Gó·rec·ki /gəˈretskē/, Henryk (Mikołaj) (1933–), Polish composer. His works include the Third Symphony (1976), known as the *Symphony of Sorrowful Songs.*

Gö·re·me /,gœrāˈmā/ a valley in Cappadocia in central Turkey, noted for its cave dwellings hollowed out of soft tufa rock. In the Byzantine era, these caves contained hermits' cells, monasteries, and more than 400 churches.

Gore-Tex /ˈgôr ,teks/ ▶ **n.** trademark a synthetic waterproof fabric permeable to air and water vapor, used in outdoor and sports clothing.

gorge /gôrj/ ▶ **n. 1** a narrow valley between hills or mountains, typically with steep rocky walls and a stream running through it.
2 archaic the throat. ■ the contents of the stomach.
3 Architecture the neck of a bastion or other outwork; the rear entrance to a fortification.
4 a mass of ice obstructing a narrow passage, esp. a river.
▶ **v.** [no obj.] eat a large amount greedily; fill oneself with food: *the river comes alive during March when fish gorge on caddisworms | we used to go to all the little restaurants there and gorge ourselves.*
– PHRASES **one's gorge rises** one is sickened or disgusted: *looking at it, Wendy felt her gorge rise.*
– DERIVATIVES **gorg·er n.**
– ORIGIN Middle English (as a verb): from Old French *gorger*, from *gorge* 'throat,' based on Latin *gurges* 'whirlpool.' The noun originally meant 'throat' and is from Old French *gorge*; sense 1 of the noun dates from the mid 18th cent.

gorged /gôrjd/ ▶ **adj.** [postpositive] Heraldry having the neck encircled by a coronet or collar, esp. of a specified tincture.
– ORIGIN early 17th cent.: from French *gorge* 'throat' + -ED[2].

gor·geous /ˈgôrjəs/ ▶ **adj.** beautiful; very attractive: *gorgeous colors and exquisite decoration.* ■ informal very pleasant: *a short but gorgeous hot summer.*
– DERIVATIVES **gor·geous·ly adv., gor·geous·ness n.**
– ORIGIN late 15th cent. (describing sumptuous clothing): from Old French *gorgias* 'fine, elegant,' of unknown origin.

gor·get /ˈgôrjit/ ▶ **n. 1** historical an article of clothing that covered the throat. ■ a piece of armor for the throat. ■ a wimple.
2 a patch of color on the throat of a bird or other animal, esp. a hummingbird.
– ORIGIN late Middle English (denoting a piece of armor protecting the throat): from Old French *gorgete*, from *gorge* 'throat' (see GORGE).

gor·gio /ˈgôrjēō/ ▶ **n.** (pl. **gorgios**) the Gypsy name for a non-Gypsy.
– ORIGIN from Romany *gorjo*.

Gor·gon /ˈgôrgən/ (also **gorgon**) ▶ **n.** Greek Mythology each of three sisters, Stheno, Euryale, and Medusa, with snakes for hair, who had the power to turn anyone who looked at them to stone. ■ a fierce, frightening, or repulsive woman.
– ORIGIN via Latin from Greek *Gorgō*, from *gorgos* 'terrible.'

gor·go·nei·on /,gôrgəˈnēän/ ▶ **n.** (pl. **gorgoneia** /-ˈnēə/) a representation of a Gorgon's head.
– ORIGIN Greek, neuter of *gorgoneios* 'of or relating to a Gorgon' (see GORGON).

gor·go·ni·an /gôrˈgōnēən/ Zoology ▶ **n.** a colonial coral of an order distinguished by a horny, treelike skeleton, including the sea fans and precious red coral. Also called HORNY CORAL. ● Order Gorgonacea, class Anthozoa.
▶ **adj.** of or relating to Gorgons or gorgonians.
– ORIGIN mid 19th cent.: from modern Latin *Gorgonia*, from Latin *Gorgo* (see GORGON), with reference to its petrifaction, + -AN.

Gor·gon·zo·la /,gôrgənˈzōlə/ ▶ **n.** a type of rich, strong-flavored Italian cheese with bluish-green veins.
– ORIGIN named after *Gorgonzola*, a village in northern Italy, where it was originally made.

go·ril·la /gəˈrilə/ ▶ **n.** a powerfully built great ape with a large head and short neck, found in the forests of central Africa. It is the largest living primate. ● *Gorilla gorilla*, family Pongidae: three races (two **lowland gorillas** and the **mountain gorilla**). ■ informal a heavily built, aggressive-looking man. ■ [with modifier] a dominant contender within a particular sphere of operation or activity: *the 800-lb gorilla of the home mortgage industry.*
– ORIGIN from an alleged African word for a wild or hairy person, found in the Greek account of the voyage of the Carthaginian explorer Hanno in the 5th or 6th cent. BC; adopted in 1847 as the specific name of the ape.

mountain gorilla

Gor·ky[1] /ˈgôrkē/ former name (1932–91) for NIZHNI NOVGOROD.

Gor·ky[2], Arshile (1904–48), US painter; born in Turkey. An exponent of abstract expressionism, he is best known for his work of the early 1940s, such as *Waterfall* (1943).

Gor·ky[3], Maxim (1868–1936), Russian writer and revolutionary; pseudonym of *Aleksei Maksimovich Peshkov*. After the Russian Revolution, he was proclaimed the founder of the new, officially sanctioned socialist realism. Notable works: *The Lower Depths* (1901) and an autobiographical trilogy (1915–23).

Gor·lov·ka /gôrˈläfkə/ Russian name for HORLIVKA.

gor·mand·ize ▶ **v.** variant spelling of GOURMANDIZE.
– DERIVATIVES **gor·mand·iz·er n.**

Gor·no-Al·tai /,gôrnə älˈtī/ an autonomous republic in south central Russia, on the border with Mongolia; pop. 205,900 (est. 2009); capital, Gorno-Altaisk.

gorp /gôrp/ ▶ **n.** informal another term for TRAIL MIX.

gorse /gôrs/ ▶ **n.** a yellow-flowered shrub of the pea family, the leaves of which are modified to form spines, native to western Europe and North Africa. ● Genus *Ulex*, family Leguminosae: several species, in particular the very spiny *U. europaeus*, which was introduced to North America.
– DERIVATIVES **gors·y adj.**
– ORIGIN Old English *gors, gorst*, from an Indo-European root meaning 'rough, prickly,' shared by German *Gerste* and Latin *hordeum* 'barley.'

gor·y /ˈgôrē/ ▶ **adj.** (**gorier, goriest**) involving or showing violence and bloodshed: *a gory horror film.* ■ covered in blood.
– PHRASES **the gory details** humorous the explicit details of something: *she told him the gory details of her past.*
– DERIVATIVES **gor·i·ly** /-rəlē/ **adv., gor·i·ness n.**

g

gosh /gäsH/ ▶ **exclam.** informal used to express surprise or give emphasis: *gosh, we envy you.* ■ used as a euphemism for "God": *a gosh-awful team.*
– ORIGIN mid 18th cent.: euphemism for **God**.

gos·hawk /ˈgäsˌhôk/ ▶ **n.** a large, short-winged hawk resembling a large sparrow hawk. ● Genus *Accipiter*, family Accipitridae: several species, in particular the **northern goshawk** (*A. gentilis*) of Eurasia and North America.
– ORIGIN Old English *gōshafoc*, from *gōs* 'goose' + *hafoc* 'hawk.'

gosht /gōsHt/ ▶ **n.** Indian red meat (beef, lamb, or mutton): [as modifier] *gosht biryani.*
– ORIGIN from Hindi *gośt*.

gos·ling /ˈgäzliNG/ ▶ **n.** a young goose.
– ORIGIN Middle English (originally *gesling*): from Old Norse *gæslingr*, from *gás* 'goose' + **-LING**, later altered by association with **GOOSE**.

go-slow ▶ **adj.** (of a proposal or course of action) cautious and prudent: *a go-slow policy for the building of nuclear plants.*
▶ **n.** chiefly Brit. a strategy or tactic, esp. a form of protest, in which work or progress is delayed or slowed down: *a reported go-slow by mechanics.*

gos·pel /ˈgäspəl/ ▶ **n. 1** the teaching or revelation of Christ: *it is the Church's mission to preach the gospel.* ■ (also **gospel truth**) a thing that is absolutely true: *they say it's sold out, but don't take that as gospel.* ■ a set of principles or beliefs: *the new economics unit has produced what it reckons to be the approved gospel.*
2 (**Gospel**) the record of Jesus' life and teaching in the first four books of the New Testament. ■ each of these books. ■ a portion from one of these read at a church service.

The four Gospels ascribed to St. Matthew, St. Mark, St. Luke, and St. John all give an account of the ministry, crucifixion, and resurrection of Christ, although the Gospel of John differs greatly from the other three. There are also several later, apocryphal accounts that are recorded as Gospels.

3 (also **gospel music**) a fervent style of black American evangelical religious singing, developed from spirituals sung in Southern Baptist and Pentecostal churches: [as modifier] *gospel singers.*
– ORIGIN Old English *gōdspel*, from *gōd* 'good' + *spel* 'news, a story' (see **SPELL**[2]), translating ecclesiastical Latin *bona annuntiatio* or *bonus nuntius*, used to gloss ecclesiastical Latin *evangelium*, from Greek *euangelion* 'good news' (see **EVANGEL**); after the vowel was shortened in Old English, the first syllable was mistaken for *god* 'God.'

gos·pel·er /ˈgäspələr/ (Brit. **gospeller**) ▶ **n.** a person who zealously teaches or professes faith in the gospel. ■ (in church use) the reader of the Gospel in a Communion service.

gos·pel·ize /ˈgäspəˌlīz/ ▶ **v. 1** [with obj.] rare preach the Gospel to; convert to Christianity.
2 convert (a piece of music) to the style of gospel music: *she gospelizes the hymn "Let There Be Peace."*

Gos·pel side ▶ **n.** (in a church) the north side of the altar, at which the Gospel is read.

gos·sa·mer /ˈgäsəmər/ ▶ **n.** a fine, filmy substance consisting of cobwebs spun by small spiders, which is seen esp. in autumn. ■ used to refer to something very light, thin, and insubstantial or delicate: *in the light from the table lamp, his hair was blond gossamer* | [as modifier] *gossamer wings.*
– DERIVATIVES **gos·sa·mer·y** **adj.**
– ORIGIN Middle English: apparently from **GOOSE** + **SUMMER**[1], perhaps from the time of year around St. Martin's summer, i.e., early November, when geese were eaten (gossamer being common then).

gos·san /ˈgäsən, ˈgäz-/ ▶ **n.** Geology & Mining an iron-containing secondary deposit, largely consisting of oxides and typically yellowish or reddish, occurring above a deposit of a metallic ore.
– ORIGIN late 18th cent.: of unknown origin.

gos·sip /ˈgäsəp/ ▶ **n.** casual or unconstrained conversation or reports about other people, typically involving details that are not confirmed as being true: *he became the subject of much local gossip.* ■ chiefly derogatory a person who likes talking about other people's private lives.
▶ **v.** (**gossips, gossiping, gossiped**) [no obj.] engage in gossip: *they would start **gossiping about** her as soon as she left.*
– DERIVATIVES **gos·sip·er** **n.**, **gos·sip·y** **adj.**
– ORIGIN late Old English *godsibb* 'godfather, godmother, baptismal sponsor,' literally 'a person related to one in God,' from *god* 'God' + *sibb* 'a relative' (see **SIB**). In Middle English the sense was 'a close friend, a person with whom one gossips,' hence 'a person who gossips,' later (early 19th cent.) 'idle talk' (from the verb, which dates from the early 17th cent).

gos·sip col·umn ▶ **n.** a section of a newspaper devoted to gossip about well-known people.
– DERIVATIVES **gos·sip col·um·nist** **n.**

gos·sip·mon·ger /ˈgäsəpˌməNGgər, -ˌmäNG-/ ▶ **n.** derogatory a person who habitually passes on confidential information or spreads rumors.

gos·soon /gäˈso͞on/ ▶ **n.** Irish a lad.
– ORIGIN late 17th cent.: from French *garçon* 'boy.'

gos·sy·pol /ˈgäsəˌpôl, -ˌpäl/ ▶ **n.** Chemistry a toxic crystalline compound present in cottonseed oil. ● A polycyclic phenol; chem. formula: $C_{30}H_{30}O_8$.
– ORIGIN late 19th cent.: from modern Latin *Gossypium* (genus name), from Latin *gossypinum*, *-pion* 'cotton plant' (of unknown origin) + **-OL**.

got /gät/ past and past participle of **GET**.

USAGE See usage at **GOTTEN**.

got·cha /ˈgäCHə/ informal ▶ **exclam.** I have got you (used to express satisfaction at having captured or defeated someone or uncovered their faults).
▶ **n.** an instance of publicly tricking someone or exposing them to ridicule, esp. by means of an elaborate deception.
– ORIGIN 1930s: representing a pronunciation.

go-team ▶ **n.** a group of investigators who can be dispatched immediately to investigate accidents, attacks, and the like: *a go-team from the National Transportation Safety Board is en route to the scene.*

Gö·te·borg /ˈyœtəˌbôr(yə)/ Swedish name of **GOTHENBURG**.

Goth /gäTH/ ▶ **n. 1** a member of a Germanic people that invaded the Roman Empire from the east between the 3rd and 5th centuries. The eastern division, the Ostrogoths, founded a kingdom in Italy, while the Visigoths went on to found one in Spain.
2 (**goth**) a style of rock music derived from punk, typically with apocalyptic or mystical lyrics. ■ a member of a subculture favoring black clothing, white and black makeup, and goth music.
– ORIGIN Old English *Gota*, superseded in Middle English by the adoption of late Latin *Gothi* (plural), from Greek *Gothoi*, from Gothic *Gutthiuda* 'the Gothic people.'

Goth. ▶ **abbr.** Gothic.

Go·tham /ˈgäTHəm/ a nickname for New York City, used originally by Washington Irving and now associated with the Batman stories.

Goth·en·burg /ˈgäTHənˌbərg/ a seaport in southwestern Sweden, on the Kattegat strait; pop. 500,197 (2008). It is the second largest city in Sweden. Swedish name **GÖTEBORG**.

Goth·ic /ˈgäTHik/ ▶ **adj. 1** of or relating to the Goths or their extinct East Germanic language, which provides the earliest manuscript evidence of any Germanic language (4th–6th centuries AD).
2 of or in the style of architecture prevalent in western Europe in the 12th–16th centuries, characterized by pointed arches, rib vaults, and flying buttresses, together with large windows and elaborate tracery.
3 (also pseudoarchaic **Gothick**) belonging to or redolent of the Dark Ages; portentously gloomy or horrifying: *19th-century Gothic horror.*
4 (of lettering) of or derived from the angular style of handwriting with broad vertical downstrokes used in western Europe from the 13th century, including Fraktur and black-letter typefaces.
5 (**gothic**) of or relating to goths or their rock music.
▶ **n. 1** the language of the Goths.
2 the Gothic style of architecture.
3 Gothic type.
– DERIVATIVES **Goth·i·cal·ly** /-ik(ə)lē/ **adv.**, **Goth·i·cism** /ˈgäTHəˌsizəm/ **n.**
– ORIGIN from French *gothique* or late Latin *gothicus*, from *Gothi* (see **GOTH**). It was used in the 17th and 18th centuries to mean 'not classical' (i.e., not Greek or Roman), and hence to refer to medieval architecture that did not follow classical models (sense 2 of the adjective) and a typeface based on medieval handwriting (sense 4 of the adjective).

Goth·ic nov·el ▶ **n.** an English genre of fiction popular in the 18th to early 19th centuries, characterized by an atmosphere of mystery and horror and having a pseudomedieval setting.

Got·land /ˈgätˌland, ˈgôtˌlänt/ an island and province of Sweden, in the Baltic Sea; pop. 57,004 (2008).

go-to guy ▶ **n.** informal a person who can be relied upon for help or support: *a relentlessly hands-on manager who is the go-to guy for any issues related to the 17-day festival.* ■ Sports a member of a sports team who can be relied on to score points if given the opportunity.

got·ta /ˈgätə/ ▶ **contraction** have got to (not acceptable in standard use): *you gotta be careful.*

got·ten /ˈgätn/ past participle of **GET**.

USAGE As past participles of **get**, the words **got** and **gotten** both date back to Middle English. In North American English, **got** and **gotten** are not identical in use. **Gotten** usually implies the process of obtaining something (*he has **gotten** two tickets for the show*), while **got** implies the state of possession or ownership (*he hasn't **got** any money*).

Göt·ter·däm·mer·ung /ˌgätərˈdaməro͞oNG/ (in Germanic mythology) the downfall of the gods.
– ORIGIN German, literally 'twilight of the gods,' popularized by Wagner's use of the word as the title of the last opera of the Ring cycle.

Göt·ting·en /ˈgœtiNGən/ a town in northern central Germany, on the Leine River; pop. 121,600 (est. 2006). It is noted for its university.

gouache /gwäsH, go͞oˈäsH/ ▶ **n.** a method of painting using opaque pigments ground in water and thickened with a gluelike substance. ■ paint of this kind; opaque watercolor. ■ a picture painted in this way.
– ORIGIN late 19th cent.: French, from Italian *guazzo*.

Gou·da /ˈgo͞odə/ ▶ **n.** a flat round cheese with a yellow rind, originally made in the town of Gouda in the Netherlands.

gouge /gouj/ ▶ **n. 1** a chisel with a concave blade, used in carpentry, sculpture, and surgery.
2 an indentation or groove made by gouging.
▶ **v.** [with obj.] **1** make (a groove, hole, or indentation) with or as if with a gouge: *the channel had been **gouged out** by the ebbing water.* ■ make a rough hole or indentation in (a surface), esp. so as to mar or disfigure it: *he had wielded the blade inexpertly, gouging the grass in several places.* ■ (**gouge something out**) cut or force something out roughly or brutally: *one of his eyes had been gouged out.*
2 informal overcharge; swindle: *the airline ends up gouging the very passengers it is supposed to assist.*
– DERIVATIVES **goug·er** **n.**
– ORIGIN late Middle English: from Old French, from late Latin *gubia*, *gulbia*, perhaps of Celtic origin; compare with Old Irish *gulba* 'beak' and Welsh *gylf* 'beak, pointed instrument.'

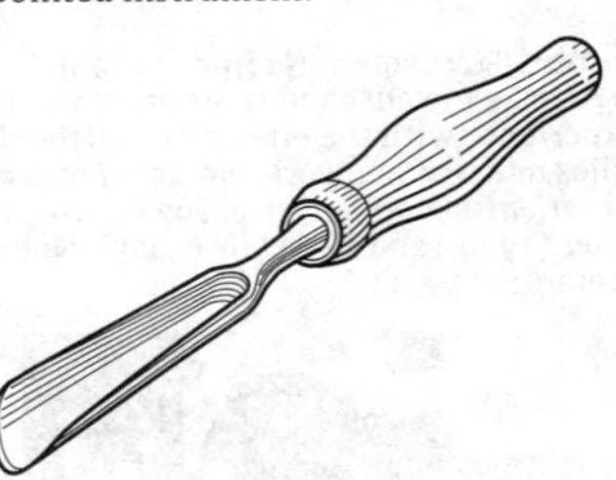
gouge 1

gou·gère /go͞oˈZHe(ə)r/ ▶ **n.** a puff of choux pastry flavored with cheese (usually Gruyère), often stuffed with a savory filling.
– ORIGIN French.

gou·lash /ˈgo͞oˌläsH/ ▶ **n. 1** a highly seasoned Hungarian soup or stew of meat and vegetables, flavored with paprika.
2 (in informal bridge) a redealing of the four hands (unshuffled, with each hand arranged in suits and order of value) after no player has bid. The cards are usually dealt in batches of five, five, and three, and the resulting hands may have very uneven distributions.
– ORIGIN from Hungarian *gulyás-hús*, from *gulyás* 'herdsman' + *hús* 'meat'; sense 2 (dating from the 1920s) is an extended use.

Gould[1] /go͞old/, Glenn (Herbert) (1932–82), Canadian pianist and composer. Best known for his performances of works by Bach, he retired from the concert platform in 1964 to concentrate on recording and broadcasting.

Gould[2], Jay (1836–92), US financier. With James Fisk and Daniel Drew 1797–1879, he gained control of the Erie Railroad in 1868 through stock manipulation. With Fisk, he attempted to corner the gold market, an effort that created the Black Friday panic on September 24, 1869.

Gould[3], Stephen Jay (1941–2002), US paleontologist. A noted popularizer of science, he studied modifications of Darwinian evolutionary theory, proposed the concept of punctuated equilibrium, and wrote on the social context of scientific theory. Notable works: *Ever Since Darwin* (1977), *Bully for Brontosaurus* (1992), *The Lying Stones of Marrakesh: Penultimate Reflections in Natural History* (2000), and *The Structure of Evolutionary Theory* (2002).

Gou·nod /go͞oˈnō/, Charles François (1818–93), French composer, conductor, and organist. He is best known for his opera *Faust* (1859).

gou·ra·mi /go͝oˈrämē/ ▶ n. (pl. **same** or **gouramis**) a small, brightly colored Asian labyrinth fish, popular in aquariums. It builds a nest of bubbles, which is typically guarded by the male. ● Belontiidae and related families: several species.
– ORIGIN late 19th cent.: from Malay *gurami.*

gourd /gôrd, go͝ord/ ▶ n. **1** a fleshy, typically large fruit with a hard skin, some varieties of which are edible. ■ a drinking container, water container, or ornament made from the hard hollowed and dried skin of this fruit.
2 a climbing or trailing plant that bears this fruit. ● Family Cucurbitaceae (the **gourd family**): several genera and species, including the colored **ornamental gourds** (*Cucurbita pepo* var. *ovifera*). The gourd family also includes the marrows, squashes, pumpkins, melons, and cucumbers.
– PHRASES **out of one's gourd** informal out of one's mind; crazy. ■ under the influence or alcohol or drugs: *he was obviously stoned out of his gourd.*
– DERIVATIVES **gourd·ful** /-ˌfo͝ol/ n. (pl. **gourdfuls**).
– ORIGIN Middle English: from Old French *gourde,* based on Latin *cucurbita.*

gourde /go͝ord/ ▶ n. the basic monetary unit of Haiti, equal to 100 centimes.
– ORIGIN the Franco-American name for a dollar.

gour·mand /go͝orˈmänd/ ▶ n. a person who enjoys eating and often eats too much. ■ a connoisseur of good food.
– DERIVATIVES **gour·man·dism** /ˈgo͝ormənˌdizəm/ n.
– ORIGIN late Middle English: from Old French, of unknown origin.

> **USAGE** The words **gourmand** and **gourmet** overlap in meaning but are not identical. Both mean 'a connoisseur of good food,' but **gourmand** more usually means 'a person who enjoys eating and often overeats.'

gour·man·dize /ˈgo͝ormənˌdīz/ ▶ v. [no obj.] indulge in good eating; eat greedily.
▶ n. the action of indulging in or being a connoisseur of good eating.
– ORIGIN late Middle English (as a noun): from French *gourmandise,* from *gourmand;* the verb dates from the mid 16th cent.

gour·met /ˌgôrˈmā, ˌgo͝or-/ ▶ n. a connoisseur of good food; a person with a discerning palate. ■ [as modifier] of a kind or standard suitable for a gourmet: *a gourmet meal.*
– ORIGIN early 19th cent.: French, originally meaning 'wine taster,' influenced by GOURMAND.

> **USAGE** On the distinction between **gourmet** and **gourmand,** see usage at GOURMAND.

gout /gout/ ▶ n. **1** a disease in which defective metabolism of uric acid causes arthritis, esp. in the smaller bones of the feet, deposition of chalkstones, and episodes of acute pain.
2 literary a drop or spot, esp. of blood, smoke, or flame: ***gouts of** flame and phlegm.*
– DERIVATIVES **gout·i·ness** /-tēnis/ n., **gout·y** adj.
– ORIGIN Middle English: from Old French *goute,* from medieval Latin *gutta,* literally 'drop' (because gout was believed to be caused by the dropping of diseased matter from the blood into the joints).

gout·weed /ˈgoutˌwēd/ ▶ n. ground elder, which was formerly used to treat gout.

gov. ▶ abbr. ■ government. ■ governor.

gov·ern /ˈgəvərn/ ▶ v. [with obj.] **1** conduct the policy, actions, and affairs of (a state, organization, or people): *he was incapable of governing the country* | (as adj. **governing**) *the governing coalition.* ■ control, influence, or regulate (a person, action, or course of events): *the future of Jamaica will be governed by geography, not history.* ■ (**govern oneself**) conduct oneself, esp. with regard to controlling one's emotions: *men would give in to passion and become unable to govern themselves.* ■ serve to decide (a legal case).
2 Grammar (of a word) require that (another word or group of words) be in a particular case: *the Latin preposition "cum" governs nouns in the ablative.*
– DERIVATIVES **gov·ern·a·bil·i·ty** /ˌgəvərnəˈbilitē/ n., **gov·ern·a·ble** adj.
– ORIGIN Middle English: from Old French *governer,* from Latin *gubernare* 'to steer, rule,' from Greek *kubernan* 'to steer.'

gov·ern·ance /ˈgəvərnəns/ ▶ n. the action or manner of governing: *a more responsive system of governance will be required.* ■ archaic sway; control: *what, shall King Henry be a pupil still, **under** the surly Gloucester's **governance**?*
– ORIGIN Middle English: from Old French, from *governer* (see GOVERN).

gov·ern·ess /ˈgəvərnis/ ▶ n. a woman employed to teach children in a private household.
– ORIGIN Middle English (originally *governeress,* denoting a female ruler): from Old French *governeresse,* feminine of *governeour* 'governor,' from Latin *gubernator,* from *gubernare* (see GOVERN).

gov·ern·ing bod·y ▶ n. a group of people who formulate the policy and direct the affairs of an institution in partnership with the managers, esp. on a voluntary or part-time basis: *the school's governing body.*

gov·ern·ment /ˈgəvər(n)mənt/ ▶ n. **1** [treated as sing. or pl.] the governing body of a nation, state, or community: *an agency of the federal government* | [as modifier] *government controls.* ■ the system by which a nation, state, or community is governed: *a secular, pluralistic, democratic government.* ■ the action or manner of controlling or regulating a nation, organization, or people: *rules for the government of the infirmary.* ■ the group of people in office at a particular time; administration: *the election of the new government.* ■ another term for POLITICAL SCIENCE.
2 Grammar the relation between a governed and a governing word.
– DERIVATIVES **gov·ern·men·tal** /ˌgəvər(n)ˈmentl/ adj., **gov·ern·men·tal·ly** /ˌgəvər(n)ˈmentl-ē/ adv.
– ORIGIN Middle English: from Old French *governement,* from *governer* (see GOVERN).

Gov·ern·ment House ▶ n. Brit. the official residence of a governor, esp. in a colony or Commonwealth state that regards the British monarch as head of state.

gov·ern·ment-is·sue ▶ adj. (of equipment) provided by the government.

gov·ern·ment se·cu·ri·ties ▶ plural n. bonds or other promissory certificates issued by the government.

gov·ern·ment sur·plus ▶ n. unused equipment sold by the government.

gov·ern·ment·wide /ˈgəvər(n)məntˌwīd/ ▶ adj. & adv. affecting or involving all areas and departments of government: *a governmentwide program to determine if work in the nation's forests could be done better by private contractors.*

gov·er·nor /ˈgəvə(r)nər/ ▶ n. **1** the elected executive head of a state of the US. ■ an official appointed to govern a town or region. ■ the representative of the British Crown in a colony or in a Commonwealth state that regards the monarch as head of state.
2 Brit. the head of a public institution: *the governor of the Bank of England.* ■ a member of a governing body.
3 Brit. informal the person in authority; one's employer.
4 a device automatically regulating the supply of fuel, steam, or water to a machine, ensuring uniform motion or limiting speed.
– DERIVATIVES **gov·er·nor·ate** n., **gov·er·nor·ship** /-ˌSHip/ n.
– ORIGIN Middle English: from Old French *governeour,* from Latin *gubernator,* from *gubernare* (see GOVERN).

gov·er·nor gen·er·al ▶ n. (pl. **governors general**) the chief representative of the Crown in a Commonwealth country of which the British monarch is head of state. ■ chiefly historical an analogous representative of another Crown.

govt. ▶ abbr. government: *local govt.*

gow·an /ˈgouən/ ▶ n. Scottish & N. English a wild white or yellow flower, esp. a daisy.
– ORIGIN mid 16th cent.: probably a variant of dialect *gollan,* denoting various yellow-flowered plants, perhaps related to Old English *golde* 'marigold.'

gowk /gouk/ ▶ n. Brit. dialect **1** an awkward or foolish person (often as a general term of abuse).
2 a cuckoo.
– ORIGIN Middle English (sense 2): from Old Norse *gaukr.*

gown /goun/ ▶ n. a long dress, typically having a close-fitting bodice and a flared or flowing skirt, worn on formal occasions: *a silk ball gown.* ■ a dressing gown. ■ a protective garment worn in a hospital, either by a staff member during surgery or by a patient. ■ a loose cloak indicating one's profession or status, worn by a lawyer, teacher, academic, or college student. ■ the members of a college as distinct from the permanent residents of the college town: *efforts are underway to improve town-gown relations.* Often contrasted with TOWN.
▶ v. (**be gowned**) be dressed in a gown: *she was gowned in luminous silk.*
– ORIGIN Middle English: from Old French *goune,* from late Latin *gunna* 'fur garment'; probably related to Byzantine Greek *gouna* 'fur, fur-lined garment.'

goy /goi/ ▶ n. (pl. **goyim** /ˈgoi-im/ or **goys**) informal, derogatory a Jewish name for a non-Jew.
– DERIVATIVES **goy·ish** adj.
– ORIGIN from Hebrew *gōy* 'people, nation.'

Go·ya /ˈgoiə/ (1746–1828), Spanish painter and etcher; full name *Francisco José de Goya y Lucientes.* He is known for his works concerning the French occupation of Spain 1808–14, including *The Shootings of May 3rd 1808* (1814) and *The Disasters of War* (1810–14), depicting the cruelty and horror of war.

Go·zo /ˈgōzō/ an island in northwest Malta, to the northwest of the main island of Malta.

GP ▶ abbr. general practitioner: *talk over any worries with your GP.*

GPA ▶ abbr. grade point average.

g.p.d. (also **GPD** or **gpd**) ▶ abbr. gallons per day.

gph ▶ abbr. gallons per hour.

gpm ▶ abbr. gallons per minute.

GPO ▶ abbr. ■ general post office. ■ Government Printing Office.

GPRS ▶ abbr. general packet radio services, a technology for radio transmission of small packets of data, esp. between cellular phones and the Internet.

GPS ▶ abbr. Global Positioning System, an accurate worldwide navigational and surveying facility based on the reception of signals from an array of orbiting satellites.

g.p.s. (also **GPS** or **gps**) ▶ abbr. gallons per second.

GPU a Soviet secret police agency 1922–23. See also **OGPU.**
– ORIGIN abbreviation of Russian *Gosudarstvennoe politicheskoe upravlenie* 'State Political Directorate.'

GQ ▶ abbr. general quarters.

gr (also **gr.**) ▶ abbr. ■ grain(s). ■ gram(s). ■ gray. ■ gross.

Graaf·i·an fol·li·cle /ˈgräfēən/ ▶ n. Physiology a fluid-filled structure in the mammalian ovary within which an ovum develops before ovulation.
– ORIGIN mid 19th cent.: named after R. de *Graaf* (1641–73), Dutch anatomist.

grab /grab/ ▶ v. (**grabs, grabbing, grabbed**) [with obj.] **1** grasp or seize suddenly and roughly: *she grabbed him by the shirt collar* | *she grabbed her keys and rushed out.* ■ [no obj.] (**grab at/for**) make a sudden snatch at: *he grabbed at the handle, missed, and nearly fell.* ■ informal obtain or get (something) quickly or opportunistically, sometimes unscrupulously: *I'll grab another drink while there's still time* | *someone's grabbed my seat.* ■ [no obj.] (of a brake on a vehicle) grip the wheel harshly or jerkily: *the brakes grabbed very badly.*
2 [usu. with negative or in questions] informal attract the attention of; make an impression on: *how does that grab you?*
▶ n. **1** [in sing.] a quick, sudden clutch or attempt to seize: *he **made a grab at** the pistol.* ■ an act of obtaining something opportunistically or unscrupulously: *they used the law to effect a land grab.*
2 a mechanical device for clutching, lifting, and moving things, esp. materials in bulk. ■ [as modifier] denoting a bar or strap for people to hold on to for support or in a moving vehicle: *for elderly people, grab rails at strategic places are likely to prevent accidents.*
3 [usu. with modifier] Computing a frame of video or television footage, digitized and stored as a still image in a computer memory for subsequent display, printing, or editing: *a screen grab from Wednesday's program.*
– PHRASES **up for grabs** informal available; obtainable: *great prizes up for grabs.*
– DERIVATIVES **grab·ber** n.
– ORIGIN late 16th cent.: from Middle Low German and Middle Dutch *grabben;* perhaps related to GRIP, GRIPE, and GROPE.

grab bag ▶ n. a container from which a person chooses a wrapped item at random, without knowing the contents. ■ an assortment of miscellaneous items.

grab·ble /ˈgrabəl/ ▶ v. [no obj.] archaic feel or search with the hands; grope about. ■ sprawl or tumble on all fours.
– ORIGIN late 16th cent.: probably from Dutch *grabbelen* 'scramble for a thing,' from Middle Dutch *grabben* (see GRAB).

grab·by /ˈgrabē/ ▶ adj. (**grabbier, grabbiest**) informal having or showing a selfish desire for something; greedy. ■ attracting attention; arousing people's interest: *a grabby angle on a news story.*

gra·ben /ˈgräbən/ ▶ n. (pl. **same** or **grabens**) Geology an elongated block of the earth's crust lying between two faults and displaced downward relative to the blocks on either side, as in a rift valley.
– ORIGIN late 19th cent.: from German *Graben* 'a ditch.'

grace /grās/ ▶ **n. 1** simple elegance or refinement of movement: *she moved through the water with effortless grace.* ■ courteous goodwill: *at least he has the grace to admit his debt to her.* ■ (**graces**) an attractively polite manner of behaving: *she has all the social graces.*
2 (in Christian belief) the free and unmerited favor of God, as manifested in the salvation of sinners and the bestowal of blessings. ■ a divinely given talent or blessing: *the graces of the Holy Spirit.* ■ the condition or fact of being favored by someone: *he fell from grace because of drug use at the Olympics.*
3 (also **grace period**) a period officially allowed for payment of a sum due or for compliance with a law or condition, esp. an extended period granted as a special favor: *another three days' grace.*
4 a short prayer of thanks said before or after a meal: *before dinner the Reverend Newman said grace.*
5 (**His, Her,** or **Your Grace**) used as forms of description or address for a duke, duchess, or archbishop: *His Grace, the Duke of Atholl.*
▶ **v.** [with obj.] do honor or credit to (someone or something) by one's presence: *she bowed out from the sport she has graced for two decades.* ■ (of a person or thing) be an attractive presence in or on; adorn: *Ms. Pasco has graced the front pages of magazines like Elle and Vogue.*
– PHRASES **be in someone's good** (or **bad**) **graces** be regarded by someone with favor (or disfavor). **there but for the grace of God** (**go I**) used to acknowledge one's good fortune in avoiding another's mistake or misfortune. **the** (**Three**) **Graces** Greek Mythology three beautiful goddesses (Aglaia, Thalia, and Euphrosyne), daughters of Zeus. They were believed to personify and bestow charm, grace, and beauty. **with good** (or **bad**) **grace** in a willing and happy (or reluctant and resentful) manner.
– ORIGIN Middle English: via Old French from Latin *gratia*, from *gratus* 'pleasing, thankful'; related to GRATEFUL.

grace-and-fa·vor ▶ **adj.** [attrib.] Brit. denoting accommodations occupied by permission of a sovereign or government.

grace·ful /ˈgrāsfəl/ ▶ **adj.** having or showing grace or elegance: *she was a tall girl, slender and graceful.*
– DERIVATIVES **grace·ful·ly adv.**, **grace·ful·ness n.**

grace·less /ˈgrāslis/ ▶ **adj.** lacking grace, elegance, or charm.
– DERIVATIVES **grace·less·ly adv.**, **grace·less·ness n.**

grace note ▶ **n.** Music an extra note added as an embellishment and not essential to the harmony or melody.

Gra·cias a Di·os, Cape /ˈgräsyäs ä ˈdē-ōs/ a cape that forms the eastern end of the Mosquito Coast in Central America, on the border between Nicaragua and Honduras.

grac·ile /ˈgrasəl, ˈgras,īl/ ▶ **adj.** Anthropology (of a hominid species) of slender build. ■ (of a person) slender or thin, esp. in a charming or attractive way.
– ORIGIN early 17th cent.: from Latin *gracilis* 'slender.'

grac·i·lis /ˈgrasəlis/ (also **gracilis muscle**) ▶ **n.** Anatomy a slender superficial muscle of the inner thigh.
– ORIGIN early 17th cent.: from Latin, literally 'slender.'

gra·cil·i·ty /grəˈsilitē, grə-/ ▶ **n.** formal **1** the state of being gracefully slender.
2 (with reference to a literary style) plain simplicity.

gra·ci·o·so /ˌgrāsHēˈōsō, ˌgräsē-/ ▶ **n.** (pl. **graciosos**) (in Spanish comedy) a buffoon or clown.
– ORIGIN Spanish, literally 'gracious.'

gra·cious /ˈgrāsHəs/ ▶ **adj. 1** courteous, kind, and pleasant: *smiling and gracious in defeat.* ■ elegant and tasteful, esp. as exhibiting wealth or high social status: *the British painter specialized in gracious Victorian interiors | gracious living.*
2 (in Christian belief) showing divine grace: *I am saved by God's gracious intervention on my behalf.*
3 Brit. a polite epithet used of royalty or their acts: *the accession of Her present gracious Majesty.*
▶ **exclam.** expressing polite surprise.
– DERIVATIVES **gra·cious·ly adv.**, **gra·cious·ness n.**
– ORIGIN Middle English: via Old French from Latin *gratiosus*, from *gratia* 'esteem, favor' (see GRACE).

grack·le /ˈgrakəl/ ▶ **n. 1** a songbird of the American blackbird family, the male of which has shiny black plumage with a blue-green sheen. ● Several genera and species, family Icteridae, in particular the **common grackle** (*Quiscalus quiscula*).
2 another term for an Asian mynah or starling, with mainly black plumage. ● *Gracula* and other genera, family Sturnidae; **southern grackle** is another term for GRACKLE (see MYNAH).
– ORIGIN late 18th cent.: from modern Latin *Gracula*, from Latin *graculus* 'jackdaw.'

grad /grad/ ▶ **n.** informal term for GRADUATE.

grad. ▶ **abbr.** ■ gradient. ■ graduate. ■ graduated.

grad·a·ble /ˈgrādəbəl/ ▶ **adj.** Grammar denoting an adjective that can be used in the comparative and superlative and take a submodifier. Contrasted with CLASSIFYING.
– DERIVATIVES **grad·a·bil·i·ty** /ˌgrādəˈbilitē/ **n.**

gra·date /ˈgrādāt/ ▶ **v.** pass or cause to pass by gradations from one shade of color to another: [no obj.] *the black background gradated toward a dark purple.* ■ [with obj.] arrange in steps or grades of size, amount, or quality: (as adj. **gradated**) *the Temple compound became a series of concentric circles of gradated purity.*
– ORIGIN mid 18th cent.: back-formation from GRADATION.

gra·da·tion /grāˈdāsHən/ ▶ **n.** a scale or a series of successive changes, stages, or degrees: *within the woodpecker family, there is a gradation of drilling ability.* ■ a stage or change in such a scale or series: *minute gradations of distance.* ■ a minute change from one shade, tone, or color to another: *amorphous shapes in subtle gradations of green and blue.* ■ (in historical linguistics) another term for ABLAUT.
– DERIVATIVES **gra·da·tion·al** /-sHənl/ **adj.**, **gra·da·tion·al·ly** /-sHənl-ē/ **adv.**
– ORIGIN mid 16th cent.: from Latin *gradatio(n-)*, based on *gradus* 'step.'

grade /grād/ ▶ **n. 1** a particular level of rank, quality, proficiency, intensity, or value: *sea salt is usually available in coarse or fine grades | grade AA butter.* ■ a level in a salary or employment structure. ■ a mark indicating the quality of a student's work: *I got good grades last semester.* ■ Brit. an examination, esp. in music: *I took grade five and got a distinction.* ■ (with specifying ordinal number) those students in a school or school system who are grouped by age or ability for teaching at a particular level for a year: *she teaches first grade.* ■ (in historical linguistics) one in a series of related root forms exhibiting ablaut. ■ Zoology a group of animals at a similar evolutionary level.
2 a gradient or slope: *just over the crest of a long seven percent grade.*
3 [usu. as modifier] a variety of cattle produced by crossing with a superior breed: *grade stock.*
▶ **v.** [with obj.] (usu. **be graded**) **1** arrange in or allocate to grades; class or sort: *they are graded according to thickness* | (as adj. **graded**) *carefully graded exercises.* ■ give a mark to (a student or a piece of work).
2 [no obj.] pass gradually from one level, esp. a shade of color, into another: *the sky graded from blue to white on the horizon.*
3 reduce (a road) to an easy gradient.
4 cross (livestock) with a superior breed.
– PHRASES **at grade** on the same level: *the crossing at grade of two streets.* **make the grade** informal succeed; reach the desired standard.
– ORIGIN early 16th cent.: from French, or from Latin *gradus* 'step.' Originally used as a unit of measurement of angles (a degree of arc), the term later referred to degrees of merit or quality.

grade cross·ing ▶ **n.** a place where a railroad and a road, or two railroad lines, cross at the same level.

grade point ▶ **n.** a numerical value assigned to a letter grade received in a course at a college or university, multiplied by the number of credits awarded for the course.

grade point av·er·age (abbr.: **GPA**) ▶ **n.** an indication of a student's academic achievement at a college or university, calculated as the total number of grade points received over a given period divided by the total number of credits awarded.

grad·er /ˈgrādər/ ▶ **n. 1** a person or thing that grades. ■ a wheeled machine for leveling the ground, esp. in making roads.
2 [in combination] a student of a specified grade in a school: *first-grader.*

grade school ▶ **n.** an elementary school.
– DERIVATIVES **grade school·er n.**

gra·di·ence /ˈgrādēəns/ ▶ **n.** Linguistics the absence of a clear-cut boundary between one category and another, for example between *cup* and *mug* in semantics.

gra·di·ent /ˈgrādēənt/ ▶ **n. 1** an inclined part of a road or railway; a slope: *fail-safe brakes for use on steep gradients.* ■ the degree of such a slope: *the path becomes very rough as the gradient increases.* ■ Mathematics the degree of steepness of a graph at any point.
2 Physics an increase or decrease in the magnitude of a property (e.g., temperature, pressure, or concentration) observed in passing from one point or moment to another. ■ the rate of such a change. ■ Mathematics the vector formed by the operator ∇ acting on a scalar function at a given point in a scalar field.
– ORIGIN mid 19th cent.: from GRADE, on the pattern of *salient*.

gra·dine /grəˈdēn/ (also **gradin** /ˈgrādin/) ▶ **n.** archaic a low step or ledge, esp. one at the back of an altar.
– ORIGIN mid 19th cent.: from Italian *gradino*, diminutive of *grado* 'step.'

gra·di·om·e·ter /ˌgrādēˈämitər/ ▶ **n.** a surveying instrument used for setting out or measuring the gradient of a slope. ■ Physics an instrument for measuring the gradient of an energy field, esp. the horizontal gradient of the earth's gravitational or magnetic field.

grad·u·al /ˈgrajōōəl/ ▶ **adj.** taking place or progressing slowly or by degrees: *the gradual introduction of new methods.* ■ (of a slope) not steep or abrupt.
▶ **n.** (**Gradual**) (in the Western Christian Church) a response sung or recited between the Epistle and Gospel in the Mass. ■ a book of plainsong for the Mass.
– DERIVATIVES **grad·u·al·ness n.**
– ORIGIN late Middle English: from medieval Latin *gradualis*, from Latin *gradus* 'step.' The original sense of the adjective was 'arranged in degrees'; the noun refers to the altar steps in a church, from which the antiphons were sung.

grad·u·al·ism /ˈgrajōōəˌlizəm/ ▶ **n.** a policy of gradual reform rather than sudden change or revolution. ■ Biology the hypothesis that evolution proceeds chiefly by the accumulation of gradual changes (in contrast to the punctuationist model).
– DERIVATIVES **grad·u·al·ist n.**, **grad·u·al·is·tic** /ˌgrajəwəˈlistik/ **adj.**

grad·u·al·ly /ˈgrajōōəlē/ ▶ **adv.** in a gradual way; slowly; by degrees: *the situation gradually improved.*

grad·u·ate ▶ **n.** /ˈgrajōōit/ **1** a person who has successfully completed a course of study or training, esp. a person who has been awarded an undergraduate academic degree. ■ a person who has received a high school diploma: *she is 19, a graduate of Lincoln High.*
2 a graduated cup, tube, flask, or measuring glass, used esp. by chemists and pharmacists.
▶ **v.** /ˈgrajōōˌāt/ **1** [no obj.] successfully complete an academic degree, course of training, or high school: *I graduated from West Point in 1965.* ■ [with obj.] informal receive an academic degree from: *she graduated college in 1970.* ■ [with obj.] confer a degree or other academic qualification on: *the school graduated more than one hundred arts majors in its first year.* ■ (**graduate to**) move up to (a more advanced level or position): *he started with motorbikes but now he's graduated to his first car.*
2 [with obj.] arrange in a series or according to a scale: (as adj. **graduated**) *a graduated tax.* ■ mark out (an instrument or container) in degrees or other proportionate divisions: *the stem was graduated with marks for each hour* | [as adj.] *graduated cylinders.*
3 [with obj.] change (something, typically color or shade) gradually or step by step: *the color is graduated from the middle of the frame to the top.*
▶ **adj.** /ˈgrajōōit/ [attrib.] relating to graduate school education: *the graduate faculty.* ■ having graduated from a school or academic program: *a graduate electrical engineer.*
– ORIGIN late Middle English: from medieval Latin *graduat-* 'graduated,' from *graduare* 'take a degree,' from Latin *gradus* 'degree, step.'

> **USAGE** The traditional use is "be graduated from": *she will be graduated from medical school in June.* However, it is now more common to say "graduate from": *she will graduate from medical school in June.* The use of **graduate** as a transitive verb, as in *he graduated high school last week,* is increasingly common, especially in speech, but is considered incorrect by most traditionalists.

grad·u·ate school ▶ **n.** a division of a university offering advanced programs beyond the bachelor's degree.

grad·u·a·tion /ˌgrajōōˈāsHən/ ▶ **n. 1** the receiving or conferring of an academic degree or diploma. ■ the ceremony at which degrees are conferred.
2 the action of dividing into degrees or other proportionate divisions on a graduated scale. ■ a mark on a container or instrument indicating a degree of quantity.

gra·dus /ˈgrādəs/ ▶ **n.** (pl. **graduses**) historical a manual of classical prosody formerly used in schools to help in writing Greek and Latin verse.
– ORIGIN mid 18th cent.: Latin, from *Gradus ad Parnassum* 'Step(s) to Parnassus,' the title of one such manual.

Grae·cism ▶ **n.** chiefly Brit. variant spelling of GRECISM.

Graeco- ▶ **comb. form** chiefly Brit. variant spelling of GRECO-.
– ORIGIN from Latin *Graecus* (see GREEK).

Grae·co-Ro·man ▶ **adj.** chiefly Brit. variant spelling of **GRECO-ROMAN.**

Graf /graf/, Steffi (1969–), German tennis player; full name *Stefanie Maria Graf.* During 1987–99, she became the only player to win all four Grand Slam singles titles at least four times each. She is also the only player to have won all four singles titles and the Olympic gold medal in the same year (1988).

graf·fi·ti /grəˈfētē/ ▶ **plural n.** (sing. **graffito** /-tō/) [treated as sing. or pl.] writing or drawings scribbled, scratched, or sprayed illicitly on a wall or other surface in a public place: *the walls were covered with graffiti* | [as modifier] *a graffiti artist.*
▶ **v.** [with obj.] write or draw graffiti on (something): *he and another artist graffitied an entire train.* ■ write (words or drawings) as graffiti.
– DERIVATIVES **graf·fi·tist** /-tist/ **n.**
– ORIGIN mid 19th cent.: from Italian (plural), from *graffio* 'a scratch.'

USAGE In Italian, the word **graffiti** is a plural noun, and its singular form is **graffito.** Traditionally, the same distinction has been maintained in English, so that **graffiti**, being plural, would require a plural verb: *the* **graffiti were** *all over the wall.* By the same token, the singular would require a singular verb: *there was a* **graffito** *on the wall.* Today these distinctions survive in some specialist fields such as archaeology, but sound odd to most native speakers. The most common modern use is to treat **graffiti** as if it were a mass noun, similar to a word like **writing**, and not to use **graffito** at all. In this case, **graffiti** takes a singular verb, as in *the* **graffiti was** *all over the wall.* Such uses are now widely accepted as standard and may be regarded as part of the natural development of the language, rather than as mistakes. A similar process is going on with other words such as **agenda, data,** and **media.**

graft[1] /graft/ ▶ **n. 1** a shoot or twig inserted into a slit on the trunk or stem of a living plant, from which it receives sap. ■ an instance of inserting a shoot or twig in this way.
2 Medicine a piece of living tissue that is transplanted surgically. ■ a surgical operation in which tissue is transplanted.
▶ **v.** [with obj.] **1** insert (a shoot or twig) as a graft: *it was common to graft different varieties onto a single tree trunk.* ■ insert a graft on (a stock).
2 Medicine transplant (living tissue) as a graft: *they can graft a new hand onto the arm.*
3 insert or fix (something) permanently to something else, typically in a way considered inappropriate: *western-style government could not easily be* **grafted onto** *a profoundly different country.*
– ORIGIN late Middle English *graff,* from Old French *grafe,* via Latin from Greek *graphion* 'stylus, writing implement' (with reference to the tapered tip of the scion), from *graphein* 'write.' The final *-t* is typical of phonetic confusion between *-f* and *-ft* at the end of words; compare with **TUFT.**

graft[2] ▶ **n.** practices, esp. bribery, used to secure illicit gains in politics or business; corruption: *sweeping measures to curb official graft.* ■ such gains: *government officials grow fat off bribes and graft.*
▶ **v.** [no obj.] make money by shady or dishonest means.
– DERIVATIVES **graft·er n.**
– ORIGIN mid 19th cent.: of unknown origin.

graft[3] Brit. informal ▶ **n.** hard work: *turning those dreams into reality was sheer hard graft.*
▶ **v.** [no obj.] work hard: *I need people prepared to go out and graft.*
– DERIVATIVES **graft·er n.**
– ORIGIN mid 19th cent.: perhaps related to the phrase *spade's graft* 'the amount of earth that one stroke of a spade will move,' based on Old Norse *grǫftr* 'digging.'

graft·age /ˈgraftij/ ▶ **n.** Horticulture the practice, process, or technique of grafting.

graft un·ion ▶ **n.** the point on a plant where the graft is joined to the rootstock.

Gra·ham[1] /gram, ˈgrāəm/, Billy (1918–), US evangelical preacher and author; full name *William Franklin Graham.* A minister of the Southern Baptist Church, he is known for his large evangelistic crusades.

Gra·ham[2], Katherine Meyer (1917–2001), US publisher. In 1940, she married Philip Graham (1915–63), who headed the communications empire started by her father that included *Newsweek* magazine and the *Washington Post.* She became the company's president upon her husband's death and supported the reporting of Carl Bernstein and Bob Woodward that led to the exposure of the Watergate scandal.

Gra·ham[3], Martha (1893–1991), US dancer, teacher, and choreographer. She evolved a new dance language using more flexible movements intended to express psychological complexities and emotional power.

gra·ham /gram, ˈgrāəm/ ▶ **adj.** denoting unbolted wholewheat flour, or cookies or bread made from this: *a box of* **graham crackers.**
– ORIGIN mid 19th cent.: named after Sylvester *Graham* (1794–1851), an American advocate of dietary reform.

Gra·hame /ˈgrāəm, gram/, Kenneth (1859–1932), Scottish writer; known for the children's classic *The Wind in the Willows* (1908).

Gra·ham Land /ˈgrāəm, gram/ the northern part of the Antarctic Peninsula, the only part of Antarctica that lies outside of the Antarctic Circle. Discovered in 1831–32 by English navigator **John Biscoe** (1794–1843), it now forms part of British Antarctic Territory, but is claimed also by Chile and Argentina.

Gra·ham's law Chemistry a law stating that the rates of diffusion and effusion of a gas are inversely proportional to the square root of the density of the gas.
– ORIGIN mid 19th cent.: named after T. *Graham* (1805–1869).

grail /grāl/ ▶ **n. 1** (**the Grail** or **the Holy Grail**) (in medieval legend) the cup or platter used by Jesus at the Last Supper, and in which Joseph of Arimathea received Christ's blood at the Cross. Quests for it undertaken by medieval knights are described in versions of the Arthurian legends written from the early 13th century onward.
2 a thing that is being earnestly pursued or sought after: *profit has become the holy grail.*
– ORIGIN from Old French *graal,* from medieval Latin *gradalis* 'dish.'

grain /grān/ ▶ **n. 1** wheat or any other cultivated cereal crop used as food. ■ the seeds of such cereals: [as modifier] *grain exports.*
2 a single fruit or seed of a cereal: *a few* **grains of** *corn.* ■ a small hard particle of a substance such as salt or sand: *a* **grain of** *salt.* ■ the smallest possible quantity or amount of a quality: *there wasn't* **a grain of truth** *in what he said.* ■ a discrete particle or crystal in a metal, igneous rock, etc., typically visible only when a surface is magnified. ■ a piece of solid propellant for use in a rocket engine.
3 (abbr.: **gr.**) the smallest unit of weight in the troy and avoirdupois systems, equal to $^{1}/_{5760}$ of a pound troy and $^{1}/_{7000}$ of a pound avoirdupois (approximately 0.0648 grams). [because originally the weight was equivalent to that of a grain of wheat.]
4 the longitudinal arrangement or pattern of fibers in wood, paper, etc.: *he scored* **along the grain** *of the table with the knife.* ■ roughness in texture of wood, stone, etc.; the arrangement and size of constituent particles: *the lighter, finer grain of the wood is attractive.* ■ the rough or textured outer surface of leather, or of a similar artificial material. ■ Mining lamination or planes of cleavage in materials such as stone and coal. ■ Photography a granular appearance of a photograph or negative, which is in proportion to the size of the emulsion particles composing it.
5 archaic a person's character or natural tendency.
6 historical kermes or cochineal, or dye made from either of these. [the kermes was thought to consist of grains.]
▶ **v.** [with obj.] **1** (usu. **be grained**) give a rough surface or texture to: *her fingers were* **grained with** *chalk dust.* ■ [no obj.] form into grains: *if the sugar does grain up, add more water.*
2 (usu. as noun **graining**) paint (esp. furniture or interior surfaces) in imitation of the grain of wood or marble: *the art of graining and marbling.*
3 remove hair from (a hide): (as adj. **grained**) *the boots were of best grained leather.*
4 feed (a horse) on grain.
– PHRASES **against the grain** contrary to the natural inclination or feeling of someone or something: *it* **goes against the grain** *to tell outright lies.* [from the fact that wood is easier to cut along the line of the grain.] **in grain** thorough, genuine, by nature, or downright; indelible. [from *dyed in the grain.*]
– DERIVATIVES **grained adj.** [usu. in combination] *coarse-grained sandstone,* **grain·er n., grain·less adj.**
– ORIGIN Middle English (originally in the sense 'seed, grain of wheat'): from Old French *grain,* from Latin *granum.*

grain bee·tle ▶ **n.** a small beetle that infests grain stores and warehouses. ● Cucujidae and other families: several species, in particular the tropical **saw-toothed grain beetle** (*Oryzaephilus surinamensis*), now found worldwide.

grain bor·er ▶ **n.** a beetle that feeds on grain and rice and is a common pest of granaries and flour mills. ● Family Bostrichidae: several species, including the tropical **lesser grain borer** (*Rhizopertha dominica*), now found worldwide.

grain leath·er ▶ **n.** leather dressed with the grain side outward.

grain side ▶ **n.** the side of a hide on which the hair was.

grains of par·a·dise ▶ **plural n.** the seeds of a West African plant of the ginger family, resembling those of cardamom and used as a spice and in herbal medicine. Also called **MALAGUETTA.** ● The plant is *Aframomum melegueta,* family Zingiberaceae.

grain wee·vil ▶ **n.** a weevil that is a common pest of stored grain, which is eaten by the larvae. ● *Sitophilus granarius,* family Curculionidae.

grain whis·key ▶ **n.** whiskey made mainly from corn and barley.

grain·y /ˈgrānē/ ▶ **adj.** (**grainier, grainiest**)
1 granular: *a juicy, grainy texture.* ■ Photography showing visible grains of emulsion, as characteristic of old photographs or modern high-speed film. ■ (of sound, esp. recorded music or a voice) having a rough or gravelly quality: *the grainy sound of bootleg cassettes.*
2 (of wood) having prominent grain.
– DERIVATIVES **grain·i·ness n.**

gral·loch /ˈgraləḵ/ ▶ **n.** the viscera of a dead deer.
▶ **v.** [with obj.] disembowel (a deer that has been shot).
– ORIGIN mid 19th cent.: from Scottish Gaelic *grealach* 'entrails.'

gram[1] /gram/ (Brit. also **gramme**) (abbr.: **g**) ▶ **n.** a metric unit of mass equal to one thousandth of a kilogram.
– ORIGIN late 18th cent.: from French *gramme,* from late Latin *gramma* 'a small weight,' from Greek.

gram[2] ▶ **n.** chickpeas or other legumes used as food.
– ORIGIN early 18th cent.: from Portuguese *grão,* from Latin *granum* 'grain.'

gram[3] ▶ **n.** short for **GRANDMA.**

-gram[1] ▶ **comb. form** in nouns denoting something written or recorded (esp. in a certain way): *cryptogram* | *heliogram.*
– ORIGIN from Greek *gramma* 'thing written, letter of the alphabet,' from *graphein* 'write.'

-gram[2] ▶ **comb. form** in nouns denoting a novelty greeting or message as a humorous or embarrassing surprise for the recipient: *kissogram.*
– ORIGIN on the pattern of *telegram.*

gram·i·ci·din /ˌgraməˈsīdn/ ▶ **n.** Medicine an antibiotic with a wide range of activity, used in many medicinal preparations. ● This antibiotic is obtained from the bacterium *Bacillus brevis.*

gram·i·na·ceous /ˌgraməˈnāsHəs/ ▶ **adj.** Botany of, relating to, or denoting plants of the grass family (Gramineae).
– ORIGIN mid 19th cent.: from Latin *gramen, gramin-* 'grass' + **-ACEOUS.**

gram·i·niv·o·rous /ˌgraməˈnivərəs/ ▶ **adj.** Zoology (of an animal) feeding on grass.
– ORIGIN mid 18th cent.: from Latin *gramen, gramin-* 'grass' + **-VOROUS.**

gram·ma /ˈgramə/ ▶ **n.** informal one's grandmother.

gram·ma·logue /ˈgraməˌlôg, -ˌläg/ ▶ **n.** (in shorthand) a word represented by a single sign or symbol.
– ORIGIN mid 19th cent.: formed irregularly from Greek *gramma* 'letter of the alphabet, thing written' + *logos* 'word,' on the pattern of words such as *catalogue.*

gram·mar /ˈgramər/ ▶ **n.** the whole system and structure of a language or of languages in general, usually taken as consisting of syntax and morphology (including inflections) and sometimes also phonology and semantics. ■ [usu. with modifier] a particular analysis of the system and structure of language or of a specific language. ■ a book on grammar: *my old Latin grammar.* ■ a set of actual or presumed prescriptive notions about correct use of a language: *it was not bad grammar, just dialect.* ■ the basic elements of an area of knowledge or skill: *the grammar of wine.* ■ Computing a set of rules governing what strings are valid or allowable in a language or text.
– ORIGIN late Middle English: from Old French *gramaire,* via Latin from Greek *grammatikē* (*tekhnē*) '(art) of letters,' from *gramma, grammat-* 'letter of the alphabet, thing written.'

gram·mar·i·an /grəˈme(ə)rēən/ ▶ **n.** a person who studies and writes about grammar.
– ORIGIN Middle English: from Old French *gramarien,* from *gramaire* (see **GRAMMAR**).

gram·mar school ▶ n. **1** another term for ELEMENTARY SCHOOL.
2 (in the UK) a state secondary school to which pupils are admitted on the basis of ability. Since 1965 most have been absorbed into the comprehensive school system. ■ a school founded in or before the 16th century for teaching Latin, later becoming a secondary school teaching academic subjects.

-grammatic ▶ comb. form in adjectives corresponding to nouns ending in *-gram* (such as *cryptogrammatic* corresponding to *cryptogram*).

gram·mat·i·cal /grəˈmatikəl/ ▶ adj. of or relating to grammar: *grammatical analysis* | *the grammatical function of a verb.* ■ well formed; in accordance with the productive rules of the grammar of a language: *a grammatical sentence.*
– DERIVATIVES **gram·mat·i·cal·i·ty** /-ˌmatiˈkalitē/ n., **gram·mat·i·cal·ly** /-ik(ə)lē/ adv., **gram·mat·i·cal·ness** n.
– ORIGIN early 16th cent.: from late Latin *grammaticalis*, via Latin from Greek *grammatikos*, from *gramma*, *grammat-* 'letter of the alphabet, thing written.'

g

gram·mat·i·cal·ize /grəˈmatikəˌlīz/ ▶ v. [with obj.] Linguistics change (an element) from one having lexical meaning into one having a largely grammatical function.
– DERIVATIVES **gram·mat·i·cal·i·za·tion** /-ˌmatikəliˈzāSHən/ n.

gramme ▶ n. Brit. variant spelling of GRAM[1].

gram-mo·lec·u·lar weight (abbr.: **GMW**) ▶ n. the quantity of a chemical compound equal to its molecular weight in grams; now usu. replaced by the mole. Also called **gram molecule**. See MOLE[4].

Gram·my /ˈgramē/ ▶ n. (pl. **Grammys** or **Grammies**) each of a number of annual awards given by the American National Academy of Recording Arts and Sciences for achievement in the record industry.
– ORIGIN 1950s: blend of GRAMOPHONE and EMMY.

Gram-neg·a·tive ▶ adj. see GRAM STAIN.

gram·o·phone /ˈgraməˌfōn/ ▶ n. old-fashioned term for RECORD PLAYER.
– ORIGIN late 19th cent.: formed by inversion of elements of *phonogram* 'sound recording.'

gram·o·phone rec·ord ▶ n. old-fashioned term for RECORD (sense 4 of the noun).

gramp /gramp/ (also **gramps**, **grampy** /ˈgramˌpē/) ▶ n. dialect or informal one's grandfather.
– ORIGIN late 19th cent.: contraction of GRANDPAPA.

Gram·pi·an /ˈgrampēən/ a former local government region in northeastern Scotland, dissolved in 1996.

Gram·pi·an Moun·tains (also **the Grampians**) **1** a mountain range in northern central Scotland. Its southern edge forms a natural boundary between the Highlands and the Lowlands.
2 a mountain range in southeastern Australia, in Victoria. It forms a spur of the Great Dividing Range at its western end.

Gram-pos·i·tive ▶ adj. see GRAM STAIN.

gram·pus /ˈgrampəs/ ▶ n. (pl. **grampuses**) a cetacean of the dolphin family, in particular: ■ another term for RISSO'S DOLPHIN. ■ another term for ORCA.
– ORIGIN early 16th cent.: alteration (by association with GRAND 'big') of Old French *grapois*, from medieval Latin *craspiscis*, from Latin *crassus piscis* 'fat fish.'

Gram stain ▶ n. Medicine a staining technique for the preliminary identification of bacteria, in which a violet dye is applied, followed by a decolorizing agent and then a red dye. The cell walls of certain bacteria (denoted **Gram-positive**) retain the first dye and appear violet, while those that lose it (denoted **Gram-negative**) appear red. Also called **Gram's method**.
– ORIGIN late 19th cent.: named after Hans C. J. *Gram* (1853–1938), the Danish physician who devised the method.

gran /gran/ ▶ n. informal, chiefly Brit. one's grandmother.
– ORIGIN mid 19th cent.: abbreviation.

gra·na /ˈgrānə/ ▶ plural n. (sing. **granum** /-nəm/) Botany the stacks of thylakoids embedded in the stroma of a chloroplast.
– ORIGIN late 19th cent.: plural of Latin *granum* 'grain.'

Gra·na·da /grəˈnädə/ **1** a city in southern Spain; pop. 236,988 (2008). Founded in the 8th century, it became the capital of the Moorish kingdom of Granada in 1238.
2 a city in Nicaragua, on the northwestern shore of Lake Nicaragua; pop. 105,171 (2006). Founded by the Spanish in 1523, it is the oldest city in the country.

gran·a·dil·la /ˌgranəˈdilə, -ˈdēyə/ (also **grenadilla**) ▶ n. a passion fruit, or the fruit of a related plant. ● This fruit comes from plants of the genus *Passiflora*, family Passifloraceae, including the **giant granadilla** (*P. quadrangularis*), which has large pale fruits.
– ORIGIN late 16th cent.: Spanish, diminutive of *granada* 'pomegranate.'

gra·na·ry /ˈgrānərē, ˈgran-/ ▶ n. (pl. **granaries**) a storehouse for threshed grain. ■ a region producing large quantities of corn.
– ORIGIN late 16th cent.: from Latin *granarium*, from *granum* 'grain.'

Gran Ca·na·ria /ˌgrän kəˈnäryə/ a volcanic island off the northwestern coast of Africa, one of the Canary Islands. Its chief town, Las Palmas, is the capital of the Canary Islands.

Gran Cha·co /grän ˈCHäkō/ (also **Chaco**) a lowland plain in central South America that extends from southern Bolivia through Paraguay to northern Argentina.

grand /grand/ ▶ adj. **1** magnificent and imposing in appearance, size, or style: *a grand country house* | *the dinner party was very grand.* ■ (of a person) of high rank and with an appearance and manner appropriate to it: *she was such a grand lady.* ■ large or ambitious in scope or scale: *his grand design for the future of Europe* | *collecting on a grand scale.* ■ used in names of places or buildings to suggest size or splendor: *the Grand Canyon* | *the Grand Hotel.*
2 [attrib.] denoting the largest or most important item of its kind: *the grand entrance.* ■ of the highest rank (used esp. in official titles): *the grand duke.* ■ Law (of a crime) serious: *grand theft*. Compare with PETTY (sense 2).
3 informal very good or enjoyable; excellent: *we had a grand day.*
4 [in combination] (in names of family relationships) denoting one generation removed in ascent or descent: *a grand-niece.*
▶ n. **1** (pl. **same**) informal a thousand dollars or pounds: *he gets thirty-five grand a year.*
2 a grand piano.
– PHRASES **a** (or **the**) **grand old man of** a man long and highly respected in (a particular field): *the grand old man of the Republican Party.*
– DERIVATIVES **grand·ly** adv., **grand·ness** n.
– ORIGIN Middle English: from Old French *grant*, *grand*, from Latin *grandis* 'full-grown, big, great.' The original uses were to denote family relationships (sense 4 of the adjective, following Old French usage) and as a title (*the Grand*, translating Old French *le Grand*); hence the senses 'of the highest rank,' 'of great importance.'

gran·dad /ˈgranˌdad/ ▶ n. variant spelling of GRANDDAD.

gran·dam /ˈgranˌdam, -dəm/ (also **granddam**, **grandame**) ▶ n. archaic term for GRANDMOTHER. ■ an old woman. ■ a female ancestor.
– ORIGIN Middle English: from Anglo-Norman French *graund dame* (see GRAND, DAME). Of the English terms of relationship formed with *grand*, this is the oldest.

grand a·part·heid ▶ n. historical (in South Africa) a form of apartheid, prevalent in the 1960s and 1970s, that involved comprehensive racial segregation and measures such as the removal of black people from white areas and the creation of black homelands.

grand·aunt /ˈgrandˌant, -ˌänt/ ▶ n. another term for GREAT-AUNT.

grand·ba·by /ˈgran(d)ˌbābē/ ▶ n. (pl. **grandbabies**) a grandchild who is still a baby.

Grand Banks a submarine plateau of the continental shelf off the southeastern coast of Newfoundland, Canada. It is where the warm Gulf Stream and the cold Labrador Current meet; this promotes the growth of plankton, which makes the waters an important feeding area for fish.

grand batte·ment /ˈgrän bätˈmän/ ▶ n. Ballet a movement in which both legs are kept straight and one leg is kicked outward from the body and in again.

Grand Ca·nal 1 a series of waterways in eastern China that extend south from Beijing to Hangzhou, a distance of 1,060 miles (1,700 km). Built in stages between 486 BC and AD 1327, its original purpose was to transport rice from the river valleys to the cities.
2 the main waterway of Venice, Italy. It is lined on each side by palaces and spanned by the Rialto Bridge.

Grand Can·yon a deep gorge in Arizona, formed by the Colorado River. It is about 277 miles (440 km) long, 5–15 miles (8–24 km) wide, and, in places, 6,000 feet (1,800 m) deep. The area was designated a national park in 1919.

Grand Canyon

Grand Can·yon State a nickname for the state of ARIZONA.

grand·child /ˈgran(d)ˌCHīld/ ▶ n. (pl. **grandchildren** /-ˌCHildrən/) a child of one's son or daughter.

Grand Cou·lee Dam /ˈko͞olē/ a dam on the Columbia River in east central Washington, completed in 1942.

grand cross ▶ n. Astrology an arrangement of four planets in which each is in opposition to one other planet and square to the other two, forming a cross.

grand cru /ˌgrän ˈkrY/ ▶ n. (pl. **grands crus** pronunc. **same**) (chiefly in French official classifications) a wine of the most superior grade, or the vineyard that produces it. Compare with PREMIER CRU.
– ORIGIN early 20th cent.: French, literally 'great growth.'

grand·dad /ˈgranˌdad/ (also **grandad**) ▶ n. informal one's grandfather.

grand·dad·dy /ˈgranˌdadē/ (also **grandaddy**) ▶ n. (pl. **granddaddies**) another term for GRANDDAD. ■ (**the granddaddy of**) used to denote a person or thing that is considered to be the best, largest, or most notable of a particular kind: *that young fellow is going to have the granddaddy of all headaches.*

grand·daugh·ter /ˈgranˌdôtər/ ▶ n. a daughter of one's son or daughter.

grand duch·ess ▶ n. the wife or widow of a grand duke. ■ a princess or noblewoman ruling over a territory in certain European countries. ■ historical a daughter (or son's daughter) of a Russian tsar.

grand duch·y ▶ n. a state or territory ruled by a grand duke or duchess.

grand duke ▶ n. a prince or nobleman ruling over a territory in certain European countries. ■ historical a son (or son's son) of a Russian tsar.

Grande Co·more /ˌgränd kəˈmôr/ the largest of the islands of the Comoros, off the northwestern coast of Madagascar; pop. 316,600 (est. 2006); chief town, Moroni.

grande dame /ˈgran ˈdam, ˈgrän ˈdäm/ ▶ n. a woman of influential position within a particular sphere: *the grande dame of British sculpture.*
– ORIGIN mid 18th cent.: French, literally 'grand lady.'

gran·dee /granˈdē/ ▶ n. a Spanish or Portuguese nobleman of the highest rank. ■ a person of high rank or eminence: *several city grandees and eminent lawyers.*
– ORIGIN late 16th cent.: from Spanish and Portuguese *grande* 'grand,' used as a noun. The change of ending was due to association with -EE.

grande hor·i·zon·tale /ˈgränd ˌôrizänˈtäl/ ▶ n. (pl. **grandes horizontales** pronunc. **same**) humorous a prostitute.
– ORIGIN late 19th cent.: French, literally 'great horizontal.'

gran·deur /ˈgranjər, ˈgranˌdyo͝or/ ▶ n. splendor and impressiveness, esp. of appearance or style: *the austere grandeur of mountain scenery.* ■ high rank or social importance: *for all their grandeur, the chancellors were still officials of the household.*
– ORIGIN late 16th cent. (denoting tall stature): from French, from *grand* 'great, grand' (see GRAND).

grand·fa·ther /ˈgran(d)ˌfäT͟Hər/ ▶ n. the father of one's father or mother. ■ the person who founded or originated something: *Freud is often called the grandfather of psychoanalysis.*
▶ v. [with obj.] informal exempt (someone or something) from a new law or regulation: *smokers who worked here before the ban have been grandfathered.*
– DERIVATIVES **grand·fa·ther·ly** adj.

grand·fa·ther clause ▶ n. informal a clause exempting certain classes of people or things from the requirements of a piece of legislation affecting their previous rights, privileges, or practices.
– ORIGIN early 20th cent.: so called because under constitutional clauses in some southern states, permitting whites to vote and disenfranchising

blacks, the descendants of those voting before 1867 were permitted to vote without having to meet certain stringent conditions.

grand·fa·ther clock ▶ **n.** a clock in a tall freestanding wooden case, driven by weights.

Grand Fleet historical the main British naval fleet, either that based at Spithead in the 18th century or that based at Scapa Flow in World War I.

Grand Forks a city in northeastern North Dakota, on the Red River of the North; pop. 51,313 (est. 2008).

Grand Gui·gnol /grän gēn'yôl/ ▶ **n.** a dramatic entertainment of a sensational or horrific nature, originally a sequence of short pieces as performed at the Grand Guignol theater in Paris.
– ORIGIN French, literally 'Great Punch.'

gran·di·flo·ra /ˌgrandəˈflôrə/ ▶ **adj.** [attrib.] (of a cultivated plant) bearing large flowers.
▶ **n.** a grandiflora plant.
– ORIGIN early 20th cent.: modern Latin (often used in specific names of large-flowered plants), from Latin *grandis* 'great' + *flos, flor-* 'flower.'

gran·dil·o·quent /granˈdiləkwənt/ ▶ **adj.** pompous or extravagant in language, style, or manner, esp. in a way that is intended to impress: *a grandiloquent celebration of Spanish glory.*
– DERIVATIVES **gran·dil·o·quence** n., **gran·dil·o·quent·ly** adv.
– ORIGIN late 16th cent.: from Latin *grandiloquus*, literally 'grand-speaking,' from *grandis* 'grand' + *loqui* 'speak.' The ending was altered in English by association with **ELOQUENT**.

Grand In·quis·i·tor ▶ **n.** historical the director of the court of Inquisition, esp. in Spain and Portugal.

gran·di·ose /ˈgrandēˌōs, ˌgrandēˈōs/ ▶ **adj.** impressive or magnificent in appearance or style, esp. pretentiously so: *the court's grandiose facade.* ■ excessively grand or ambitious: *grandiose plans to reform the world.*
– DERIVATIVES **gran·di·ose·ly** adv., **gran·di·os·i·ty** /ˌgrandēˈäsitē/ n.
– ORIGIN mid 19th cent.: from French, from Italian *grandioso*, from *grande* 'grand.'

Grand Is·land a commercial and industrial city in south central Nebraska; pop. 45,801 (est. 2008).

grand je·té /ˈgrän ZHəˈtā/ ▶ **n.** Ballet a jump in which a dancer springs from one foot to land on the other with one leg forward of their body and the other stretched backward while in the air.

Grand Junc·tion a city in western Colorado, at the junction of the Colorado (formerly the Grand) and Gunnison rivers; pop. 49,688 (est. 2008).

grand ju·ry ▶ **n.** Law a jury, normally of twenty-three jurors, selected to examine the validity of an accusation before trial.

grand·kid /ˈgran(d)ˌkid/ ▶ **n.** informal a grandchild.

grand lar·ce·ny ▶ **n.** Law (in many US states and formerly in Britain) theft of personal property having a value above a legally specified amount.

grand·ma /ˈgran(d)ˌmä, ˈgram-/ ▶ **n.** informal one's grandmother.

grand mal /ˌgran(d) ˈmäl, ˈmal/ ▶ **n.** a serious form of epilepsy with muscle spasms and prolonged loss of consciousness. Compare with **PETIT MAL**. ■ an epileptic fit of this kind.
– ORIGIN late 19th cent.: from French, literally 'great sickness.'

grand·ma·ma /ˈgran(d)ˌmämə, -məˌmä, ˈgram-/ (also **grandmamma**) ▶ **n.** archaic form of **GRANDMA**.

Grand·ma Mo·ses see **MOSES**[2].

grand man·ner ▶ **n.** (**the grand manner**) a style considered appropriate for noble and stately matters: *formal dining in the grand manner.* ■ (**the Grand Manner**) the lofty and rhetorical manner of historical painting exemplified by Raphael and Poussin.

Grand Mar·nier /ˌgrän ˈmärnyā/ ▶ **n.** trademark an orange-flavored cognac-based liqueur.
– ORIGIN French.

grand mas·ter ▶ **n. 1** (usu. **grandmaster**) a chess player of the highest class, esp. one who has won an international tournament.
2 (**Grand Master**) the head of an order of chivalry or of Freemasons.

grand·moth·er /ˈgran(d)ˌməT͟Hər/ ▶ **n.** the mother of one's father or mother.
– PHRASES **teach one's grandmother to suck eggs** presume to advise a more experienced person.
– DERIVATIVES **grand·moth·er·ly** adj.

grand·moth·er clock ▶ **n.** a clock similar to a grandfather clock but about two-thirds the size.

grand·neph·ew /ˈgran(d)ˌnefyo͞o/ ▶ **n.** another term for **GREAT-NEPHEW**.

grand·niece /ˈgran(d)ˌnēs/ ▶ **n.** another term for **GREAT-NIECE**.

grand op·er·a ▶ **n.** an opera on a serious theme in which the entire libretto (including dialogue) is sung. ■ the genre of such opera.

grand·pa /ˈgran(d)ˌpä, ˈgram-/ ▶ **n.** informal one's grandfather.

grand·pa·pa /ˈgran(d)ˌpäpə, -pəˌpä, ˈgram-/ ▶ **n.** old-fashioned term for **GRANDFATHER**.

grand·pap·py /ˈgran(d)ˌpapē, ˈgram-/ ▶ **n.** (pl. **grandpappies**) dialect term for **GRANDFATHER**.

grand·par·ent /ˈgran(d)ˌpe(ə)rənt, -ˌpar-/ ▶ **n.** a parent of one's father or mother; a grandmother or grandfather.
– DERIVATIVES **grand·pa·ren·tal** /ˌgran(d)pəˈrentl/ adj., **grand·par·ent·hood** /-ˌho͝od/ n.

grand pi·an·o ▶ **n.** a large, full-toned piano that has the body, strings, and soundboard arranged horizontally and in line with the keys and is supported by three legs.

grand piano

Grand Prai·rie an industrial city in northeastern Texas, between Dallas and Fort Worth; pop. 160,641 (est. 2008).

Grand Prix /ˌgrän ˈprē, ˌgran/ ▶ **n.** (pl. **Grands Prix** pronunc. **same**) an important sporting event in which participants compete for a major prize. ■ any of a series of auto-racing or motorcycling contests forming part of a world championship series, held in various countries under international rules. ■ (in full **Grand Prix de Paris**) an international horse race for three-year-olds, founded in 1863 and run annually in June at Longchamps, Paris.
– ORIGIN mid 19th cent.: French, literally 'great or chief prize.'

Grand Rap·ids an industrial city in southwestern Michigan, on the Grand River, noted for furniture production; pop. 193,396 (est. 2008).

grand sei·gneur /ˌgrän sänˈyər/ ▶ **n.** a man whose rank or position allows him to command others.
– ORIGIN early 17th cent.: French, literally 'great lord.'

grand siè·cle /ˈgrän sēˈeklə/ ▶ **n.** the reign of Louis XIV, seen as France's period of political and cultural preeminence.
– ORIGIN mid 19th cent.: French, literally 'great century or age.'

grand·sire /ˈgrandˌsī(ə)r/ ▶ **n.** archaic term for **GRANDFATHER**.

grand slam ▶ **n.** the winning of each of a group of major championships or matches in a particular sport in the same year, in particular in tennis or golf. ■ Bridge the bidding and winning of all thirteen tricks. ■ Baseball a home run hit when each of the three bases is occupied by a runner, thus scoring four runs.
– ORIGIN early 19th cent. (as a term in cards, esp. bridge): from **SLAM**[2].

grand·son /ˈgran(d)ˌsən/ ▶ **n.** the son of one's son or daughter.

grand·stand /ˈgran(d)ˌstand/ ▶ **n.** the main seating area, usually roofed, commanding the best view for spectators at racetracks or sports stadiums.
▶ **v.** [no obj.] (usu. as noun **grandstanding**) derogatory seek to attract applause or favorable attention from spectators or the media: *they accused him of political grandstanding.*

Grand Strand a name for the northeastern coast of South Carolina, site of many resorts including Myrtle Beach.

Grand Te·ton Na·tion·al Park /ˈtēˌtän/ a preserve in northwestern Wyoming, just south of Yellowstone National Park, named for the highest of its peaks. Jackson Hole is here.

grand to·tal ▶ **n.** the final amount after everything is added up; the sum of other totals.

grand tour ▶ **n.** a cultural tour of Europe formerly undertaken, esp. in the 18th century, by a young man of the upper classes as a part of his education. ■ informal a guided tour of a building, exhibit, etc.: *he gave me the grand tour of his ranch and studio.*

grand trine /trīn/ ▶ **n.** Astrology an arrangement of three planets in which each planet is in trine with the other two, forming an equilateral triangle.

grand·un·cle /ˈgrandˌəNGkəl/ ▶ **n.** another term for **GREAT-UNCLE**.

grand u·ni·fied the·o·ry ▶ **n.** Physics a theory attempting to give a single explanation of the strong, weak, and electromagnetic interactions between subatomic particles.

Grange /grānj/, Red (1903–91), US football player; born *Harold Edward Grange*; known as the **Galloping Ghost**. He played professionally, mostly with the Chicago Bears, from 1925 until he retired in 1934. Football Hall of Fame (1963).

grange /grānj/ ▶ **n. 1** [usu. in names] Brit. a country house with farm buildings attached: *Biddulph Grange.* ■ historical an outlying farm with tithe barns, belonging to a monastery or feudal lord. ■ archaic a barn.
2 (**the Grange**) (in the US) a farmers' association organized in 1867. The Grange sponsors social activities, community service, and political lobbying. Officially called the **PATRONS OF HUSBANDRY**. ■ a local lodge of this association.
– ORIGIN Middle English (in the sense 'granary, barn'): from Old French, from medieval Latin *granica (villa)* 'grain house or farm,' based on Latin *granum* 'grain.'

grang·er·ize /ˈgrānjəˌrīz/ ▶ **v.** [with obj.] (usu. as adj. **grangerized**) illustrate (a book) by later insertion of material, esp. prints cut from other works.
– DERIVATIVES **grang·er·i·za·tion** /ˌgrānjərəˈzāSHən/ n.
– ORIGIN late 19th cent.: from the name *J. Granger* (1723–76), English biographer.

gran·i·fer·ous /grəˈnifərəs/ ▶ **adj.** Botany (of a plant) producing grain or a grainlike seed.
– ORIGIN mid 17th cent.: from Latin *granum* 'grain' + **-FEROUS**.

gra·ni·ta /grəˈnētə/ ▶ **n.** (pl. **granitas** or **granite** /-tā/) a coarse, Italian-style flavored ice. ■ a drink made with crushed ice.
– ORIGIN Italian.

gran·ite /ˈgranit/ ▶ **n.** a very hard, granular, crystalline, igneous rock consisting mainly of quartz, mica, and feldspar and often used as a building stone.
– DERIVATIVES **gra·nit·ic** /grəˈnitik/ adj., **gran·it·oid** /ˈgraniˌtoid/ adj. & n.
– ORIGIN mid 17th cent.: from Italian *granito*, literally 'grained,' from *grano* 'grain,' from Latin *granum*.

Gran·ite State a nickname for the state of **NEW HAMPSHIRE**.

gran·ite·ware /ˈgranitˌwe(ə)r/ ▶ **n.** a speckled form of earthenware imitating the appearance of granite. ■ a kind of enameled ironware.

gran·it·ize /ˈgraniˌtīz/ ▶ **v.** [with obj.] (usu. as adj. **granitized**) Geology alter (rock) so as to give it a granitic character.
– DERIVATIVES **gran·it·i·za·tion** /ˌgranitiˈzāSHən/ n.

gra·niv·o·rous /grəˈnivərəs/ ▶ **adj.** Zoology (of an animal) feeding on grain.
– DERIVATIVES **gra·ni·vore** /ˈgranəˌvôr/ n.
– ORIGIN mid 17th cent.: from Latin *granum* 'grain' + **-VOROUS**.

gran·ny /ˈgranē/ (also **grannie**) ▶ **n.** (pl. **grannies**) informal one's grandmother.
– ORIGIN mid 17th cent.: from *grannam* (representing a colloquial pronunciation of **GRANDAM**) + **-Y**[2].

gran·ny flat ▶ **n.** informal a part of a house made into self-contained accommodations suitable for an elderly relative.

gran·ny gear ▶ **n.** informal the lowest gear on a bicycle.

gran·ny glass·es ▶ **plural n.** informal round, steel-rimmed or gold-rimmed glasses.

gran·ny knot ▶ **n.** a square knot with the ends crossed the wrong way and therefore liable to slip or jam.

Gran·ny Smith ▶ **n.** a dessert apple of a bright green variety with crisp, sharp-flavored flesh, originating in Australia.
– ORIGIN late 19th cent.: named after Maria Ann *(Granny) Smith* (c.1801–1870), who first produced such apples.

gran·o·di·or·ite /ˌgranəˈdīəˌrīt/ ▶ **n.** Geology a coarse-grained, plutonic rock containing quartz and plagioclase, between granite and diorite in composition.
– ORIGIN late 19th cent.: from **GRANITE** + **DIORITE**.

gra·no·la /grəˈnōlə/ ▶ **n.** a kind of breakfast cereal consisting typically of rolled oats, brown sugar or honey, dried fruit, and nuts. ■ [as modifier] chiefly derogatory denoting those with liberal or environmentalist political views, typified as eating health foods.
– ORIGIN late 19th cent. (as a trademark): from *gran-* (representing **GRANULAR** or **GRAIN**) + *-ola*. The current term dates from the 1970s.

gran·o·lith·ic /ˌgranəˈliTHik/ ▶ **adj.** (of concrete) containing fine granite chippings or crushed granite, used to render floors and surfaces. ■ (of a floor or surface) rendered with such concrete.
▶ **n.** granolithic concrete or rendering.
– ORIGIN late 19th cent.: from *grano-* (irregular combining form from Latin *granum* 'grain') + Greek *lithos* 'stone' + **-IC**.

gran·o·phyre /ˈgranəˌfī(ə)r/ ▶ **n.** Geology a granitic rock consisting of intergrown feldspar and quartz crystals in a medium- to fine-grained groundmass.
– DERIVATIVES **gran·o·phy·ric** /ˌgranəˈfirik/ **adj.**
– ORIGIN late 19th cent.: from German *Granophyr*, from *Granit* 'granite' + *Porphyr* (see PORPHYRY).

Grant[1] /grant/, Cary (1904–86), US actor; born in Britain; born *Alexander Archibald Leach*. He made his mark as a debonair leading man, starring in such movies as *Holiday* (1938), *The Philadelphia Story* (1940), *North by Northwest* (1959), and *Charade* (1963).

Grant[2], Duncan (James Corrow) (1885–1978), Scottish painter and designer; a member of the Bloomsbury Group.

Grant[3], Ulysses Simpson (1822–85), 18th president of the US 1869–77; born *Hiram Ulysses Grant*. As supreme commander of the Union army, he defeated the Confederate army in 1865 with a policy of attrition. As a popular general elected to the presidency, he lacked political experience and was unable to check widespread political corruption and inefficiency. During his first administration, the 15th Amendment was ratified (giving all qualified male citizens the right to vote) and the national park system was established.

Ulysses S. Grant

grant /grant/ ▶ **v.** [with two objs.] **1** agree to give or allow (something requested) to: *a letter granting them permission to smoke.* ■ give (a right, power, property, etc.) formally or legally to: *the amendment that granted women the right to vote.*
2 agree or admit to (someone) that (something) is true: *he hasn't made much progress, I'll grant you that.*
▶ **n. 1** a sum of money given by an organization, esp. a government, for a particular purpose. ■ formal the action of granting something: *we had to recommend the grant or refusal of broadcasting licenses.* ■ Law a legal conveyance or formal conferment: *a grant of land | a grant of probate.*
2 a geographical subdivision in New Hampshire, Vermont, and Maine.
– PHRASES **take someone/something for granted** fail to appreciate someone or something that is very familiar or obvious: *the comforts that people take for granted | she took him for granted.* **take something for granted** ■ assume that something is true without questioning it: *those companies challenged beliefs that everyone else took for granted.*
– DERIVATIVES **grant·a·ble adj., grant·er n.**
– ORIGIN Middle English: from Old French *granter* 'consent to support,' variant of *creanter* 'to guarantee,' based on Latin *credere* 'entrust.'

grant·ed /ˈgrantid/ ▶ **adv.** [sentence adverb] admittedly; it is true (used to introduce a factor that is opposed to the main line of argument but is not regarded as so strong as to invalidate it): *granted, sitting around the house may not be your idea of the perfect retirement, but what's your choice when inflation is eroding the value of your nest egg?*
▶ **conj.** (**granted that**) even assuming that: *granted that officers were used to making decisions, they still couldn't be expected to understand.*

gran·tee /granˈtē/ ▶ **n.** chiefly Law a person to whom a grant or conveyance is made.

Gran·tha /ˈgrəntə/ ▶ **n.** a southern Indian alphabet dating from the 5th century AD, used by Tamil Brahmans when writing Sanskrit transcriptions of their sacred books.
– ORIGIN from Sanskrit *grantha* (see ADI GRANTH).

Granth Sa·hib /ˈgrənt ˈsä(h)ib/ (or **Granth**) short for GURU GRANTH SAHIB.

grant-in-aid ▶ **n.** (pl. **grants-in-aid**) an amount of money given to a local government, an institution, or a particular scholar.

gran·tor /granˈtôr, ˈgrantər/ ▶ **n.** chiefly Law a person or institution that makes a grant or conveyance.

grants·man·ship /ˈgrantsmənˌship/ ▶ **n.** the skill or practice of obtaining grants-in-aid, esp. for research.
– DERIVATIVES **grants·man n.**

gran tu·ris·mo /ˌgran to͝oˈrizmō/ (abbr.: **GT**) ▶ **n.** (pl. **gran turismos**) a high-performance model of automobile.
– ORIGIN mid 20th cent.: Italian, literally 'great touring.'

gran·u·lar /ˈgranyələr/ ▶ **adj. 1** resembling or consisting of small grains or particles. ■ having a roughened surface or structure.
2 technical characterized by a high level of granularity: *a granular database.*
– ORIGIN late 18th cent.: from late Latin *granulum* (see GRANULE) + -AR[1].

gran·u·lar·i·ty /ˌgranyəˈlaritē/ ▶ **n. 1** the quality or condition of being granular.
2 technical the scale or level of detail present in a set of data or other phenomenon: *the granularity of this war is not the sand that covers most of the country, but these details that have proved so elusive.*

gran·u·late /ˈgranyəˌlāt/ ▶ **v. 1** [with obj.] (usu. as adj. **granulated**) form (something) into grains or particles: *granulated sugar.* ■ [no obj.] (of a substance) take the form of grains or particles: *the syrup would not granulate properly.*
2 [no obj.] (often as adj. **granulating**) Medicine (of a wound or lesion) form a grainy surface as part of the healing process. ■ (as adj. **granulated**) chiefly Biology having a roughened surface: *the skin is densely granulated.*
– DERIVATIVES **gran·u·la·tion** /ˌgranyəˈlāshən/ **n., gran·u·la·tor** /-ˌlātər/ **n.**

gran·u·la·tion tis·sue ▶ **n.** new vascular tissue in granular form on an ulcer or the healing surface of a wound.

gran·ule /ˈgranyo͞ol/ ▶ **n.** a small compact particle of a substance: *coffee granules.*
– ORIGIN mid 17th cent.: from late Latin *granulum*, diminutive of Latin *granum* 'grain.'

gran·u·lite /ˈgranyəˌlīt/ ▶ **n.** Geology a fine-grained, granular metamorphic rock in which the main component minerals are typically feldspars and quartz.
– DERIVATIVES **gran·u·lit·ic** /ˌgranyəˈlitik/ **adj.**
– ORIGIN mid 19th cent.: from GRANULE + -ITE[1].

gran·u·lo·cyte /ˈgranyələˌsīt/ ▶ **n.** Physiology a white blood cell with secretory granules in its cytoplasm, e.g., an eosinophil or a basophil.
– DERIVATIVES **gran·u·lo·cyt·ic** /ˌgranyələˈsitik/ **adj.**
– ORIGIN early 20th cent.: from late Latin *granulum* 'granule' + -CYTE.

gran·u·lo·ma /ˌgranyəˈlōmə/ ▶ **n.** (pl. **granulomas** or **granulomata** /-mətə/) Medicine a mass of granulation tissue, typically produced in response to infection, inflammation, or the presence of a foreign substance.
– DERIVATIVES **gran·u·lom·a·tous** /-ˈlämətəs/ **adj.**

gran·u·lo·met·ric /ˌgranyələˈmetrik/ ▶ **adj.** relating to the size, distribution, or measurement of grain sizes in sand, rock, or other deposits.

gran·u·lose /ˈgranyəˌlōs/ ▶ **adj.** consisting of or covered with small grains or granules.

gra·num /ˈgrānəm/ singular form of GRANA.

grape /grāp/ ▶ **n. 1** a berry, typically green (classified as white), purple, red, or black, growing in clusters on a grapevine, eaten as fruit, and used in making wine. ■ (**the grape**) informal wine: *an exploration of the grape.*
2 short for GRAPESHOT.
– DERIVATIVES **grap·ey** (also **grapy**) **adj.** (**grapier, grapiest**).
– ORIGIN Middle English (also in the Old French sense): from Old French, 'bunch of grapes,' probably from *graper* 'gather grapes,' from *grap* 'hook' (denoting an implement used in harvesting grapes), of Germanic origin.

grape·fruit /ˈgrāpˌfro͞ot/ ▶ **n.** (pl. **same**) **1** a large, round, yellow citrus fruit with an acid, juicy pulp.
2 the tree bearing this fruit. ● *Citrus paradisi*, family Rutaceae.
– ORIGIN early 19th cent.: from GRAPE + FRUIT (probably because the fruits grow in clusters).

grape hy·a·cinth ▶ **n.** a small Eurasian plant of the lily family, with clusters of small, globular blue flowers, cultivated as an ornamental or for use in perfume. ● Genus *Muscari*, family Liliaceae.

grape i·vy ▶ **n.** an evergreen climbing plant of the grape family that is grown as a houseplant. ● Genus *Cissus*, family Vitaceae: several species, in particular *C. rhombifolia*.

grape·seed oil /ˈgrāpˌsēd/ ▶ **n.** oil extracted from the residue of grapes that have been juiced.

grape·shot /ˈgrāpˌshät/ ▶ **n.** historical ammunition consisting of a number of small iron balls fired together from a cannon.

grape sug·ar ▶ **n.** dextrose present in or derived from grapes.

grape·vine /ˈgrāpˌvīn/ ▶ **n. 1** a vine native to both Eurasia and North America, esp. one bearing fruit (grapes) used for eating or winemaking. Numerous cultivars and hybrids have been developed for the winemaking industry. ● Genus *Vitis*, family Vitaceae: many species, in particular *V. vinifera* and the American *V. labrusca*.
2 informal used to refer to the circulation of rumors and unofficial information: *I'd heard through the grapevine that the business was nearly settled.*

graph[1] /graf/ ▶ **n.** a diagram showing the relation between variable quantities, typically of two variables, each measured along one of a pair of axes at right angles. ■ Mathematics a collection of points whose coordinates satisfy a given relation.
▶ **v.** [with obj.] plot or trace on a graph.
– ORIGIN late 19th cent.: abbreviation of *graphic formula*.

graph[2] ▶ **n.** Linguistics a visual symbol representing a unit of sound or other feature of speech. Graphs include not only letters of the alphabet but also punctuation marks.
– ORIGIN 1930s: from Greek *graphē* 'writing.'

-graph ▶ **comb. form 1** in nouns denoting something written or drawn in a specified way: *autograph.*
2 in nouns denoting an instrument that records: *seismograph.*
– ORIGIN from French *-graphe*, based on Greek *graphos* 'written, writing.'

graph·eme /ˈgrafēm/ ▶ **n.** Linguistics the smallest meaningful contrastive unit in a writing system. Compare with PHONEME.
– DERIVATIVES **gra·phe·mic** /graˈfēmik/ **adj., gra·phe·mi·cal·ly** /graˈfēmik(ə)lē/ **adv., gra·phe·mics** /graˈfēmiks/ **n.**
– ORIGIN 1930s: from GRAPH[2] + -EME.

graph·ene /ˈgrafēn/ ▶ **n.** a fullerene consisting of bonded carbon atoms in sheet form one atom thick.

-grapher ▶ **comb. form** indicating a person concerned with a subject denoted by a noun ending in *-graphy* (such as *geographer* corresponding to *geography*).
– ORIGIN from Greek *-graphos* 'writer' + -ER[1].

graph·ic /ˈgrafik/ ▶ **adj. 1** of or relating to visual art, esp. involving drawing, engraving, or lettering: *his mature graphic work.* ■ giving a vivid picture with explicit detail: *he gave a graphic description of the torture.* ■ Computing of, relating to, or denoting a visual image: *graphic information such as charts and diagrams.*
2 of or in the form of a graph.
3 [attrib.] Geology of or denoting rocks having a surface texture resembling cuneiform writing.
▶ **n.** Computing a graphical item displayed on a screen or stored as data.
– ORIGIN mid 17th cent.: via Latin from Greek *graphikos*, from *graphē* 'writing, drawing.'

-graphic ▶ **comb. form** in adjectives corresponding to nouns ending in *-graphy* (such as *demographic* corresponding to *demography*).
– ORIGIN from or suggested by Greek *-graphikos*, from *graphē* 'writing, drawing'; partly from -GRAPHY or -GRAPH + -IC.

graph·i·cal /ˈgrafikəl/ ▶ **adj. 1** of, relating to, or in the form of a graph: *flowcharts are graphical presentations.*
2 of or relating to visual art or computer graphics: *a high-resolution graphical display.*
– DERIVATIVES **graph·i·cal·ly** /-ik(ə)lē/ **adv.**

-graphical ▶ **comb. form** equivalent to -GRAPHIC.

-graphically ▶ **comb. form** in adverbs corresponding to nouns ending in *-graphic* (such as *demographically* corresponding to *demographic*).

graph·i·cal us·er in·ter·face (abbr.: **GUI**) ▶ **n.** Computing a visual way of interacting with a computer using items such as windows, icons, and menus, used by most modern operating systems.

graph·ic arts ▶ **plural n.** the visual arts based on the use of line and tone rather than three-dimensional work or the use of color. ■ (**graphic art**) the activity of practicing these arts, esp. as a subject of study.
– DERIVATIVES **graph·ic art·ist n.**

graph·ic de·sign ▶ **n.** the art or skill of combining text and pictures in advertisements, magazines, or books.
– DERIVATIVES **graph·ic de·sign·er n.**

graph·ic e·qual·iz·er ▶ **n.** an electronic device or computer program that allows the separate control of the strength and quality of selected frequency bands.

graph·ic nov·el ▶ **n.** a novel in comic-strip format.

graph·ics /ˈgrafiks/ ▶ **plural n.** [usu. treated as sing.] **1** the products of the graphic arts, esp. commercial design or illustration.
2 the use of diagrams in calculation and design.
3 (also **computer graphics**) [treated as pl.] visual images produced by computer processing. ■ [treated as sing.] the use of computers linked to display screens to generate and manipulate visual images.

graph·ics card ▶ **n.** Computing a printed circuit board that controls the output to a display screen.

graph·ics tab·let ▶ n. Computing an input device consisting of a flat, pressure-sensitive pad that the user draws on or points at with a special stylus, to guide a pointer displayed on the screen.

graph·ite /ˈgraˌfīt/ ▶ n. a gray, crystalline, allotropic form of carbon that occurs as a mineral in some rocks and can be made from coke. It is used as a solid lubricant, in pencils, and as a moderator in nuclear reactors.
– DERIVATIVES **gra·phit·ic** /grəˈfitik/ adj.
– ORIGIN late 18th cent.: coined in German (*Graphit*), from Greek *graphein* 'write' (because of its use as pencil "lead").

graph·i·tize /ˈgrafiˌtīz/ ▶ v. technical convert or be converted into graphite.
– DERIVATIVES **graph·i·ti·za·tion** /ˌgrafitiˈzāsHən/ n.

graph·ol·o·gy /graˈfäləjē/ ▶ n. **1** the study of handwriting, for example, as used to infer a person's character.
2 Linguistics the study of written and printed symbols and of writing systems.
– DERIVATIVES **graph·o·log·i·cal** /ˌgrafəˈläjikəl/ adj., **graph·ol·o·gist** /-jist/ n.
– ORIGIN mid 19th cent.: from Greek *graphē* 'writing' + -LOGY.

graph pa·per ▶ n. paper printed with a network of small squares to assist the drawing of graphs or other diagrams.

graph the·o·ry ▶ n. the mathematical theory of the properties and applications of graphs.

-graphy ▶ comb. form [in nouns denoting:] **1** a descriptive science: *geography*.
2 a technique of producing images: *radiography*.
3 a style or method of writing or drawing: *calligraphy*. ■ writing about (a specified subject): *hagiography*. ■ a written or printed list: *filmography*.
– ORIGIN from or suggested by Greek *-graphia* 'writing.'

grap·nel /ˈgrapnəl/ ▶ n. a grappling hook. ■ a small anchor with several flukes.
– ORIGIN late Middle English: from an Anglo-Norman French diminutive of Old French *grapon*, of Germanic origin.

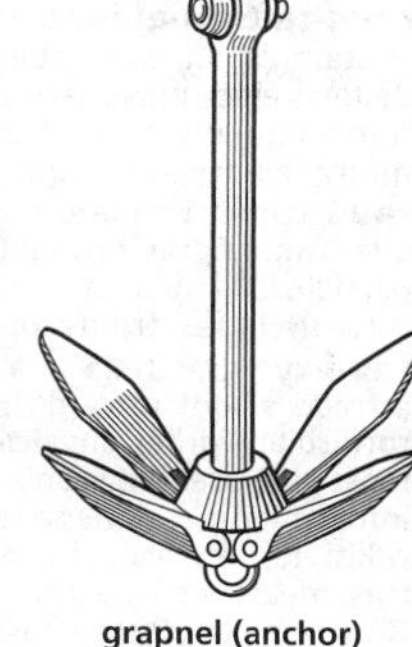
grapnel (anchor)

grap·pa /ˈgräpə/ ▶ n. a brandy distilled from the fermented residue of grapes after they have been pressed in winemaking.
– ORIGIN Italian, literally 'grape stalk,' of Germanic origin.

grap·ple /ˈgrapəl/ ▶ v. **1** [no obj.] engage in a close fight or struggle without weapons; wrestle: *passersby **grappled with** the man after the knife attack*. ■ [with obj.] seize hold of (someone). ■ (**grapple with**) struggle with or work hard to deal with or overcome (a difficulty or challenge): *other towns are still grappling with the problem*.
2 [with obj.] archaic seize or hold with a grapnel.
▶ n. an act of grappling. ■ informal a wrestling match. ■ an instrument for catching hold of or seizing something; a grappling hook.
– DERIVATIVES **grap·pler** /ˈgraplər/ n.
– ORIGIN Middle English (as a noun denoting a grapnel): from Old French *grapil*, from Provençal, diminutive of *grapa* 'hook,' of Germanic origin; related to GRAPE. The verb dates from the mid 16th cent.

grap·pling /ˈgrapliNG/ ▶ n. **1** a grappling hook or grappling iron.
2 a small anchor; a grapnel.

grap·pling hook /ˈgrapliNG/ (also **grappling iron**) ▶ n. a device with iron claws, attached to a rope and used for dragging or grasping.

grap·to·lite /ˈgraptəˌlīt/ ▶ n. an extinct marine invertebrate animal of the Paleozoic era, forming mainly planktonic colonies and believed to be related to the pterobranchs. ● Class Graptolithina, phylum Hemichordata.
– ORIGIN mid 19th cent.: from Greek *graptos* 'marked with letters' + -LITE: so named because of the impressions left on hard shales, resembling markings with a slate pencil.

GRAS ▶ abbr. generally recognized as safe; an FDA label for substances not known to be health hazards.

grasp /grasp/ ▶ v. [with obj.] seize and hold firmly: *she grasped the bottle*. ■ [no obj.] (**grasp at**) try to seize hold of: *they grasped at each other with numbed fingers* | *they had grasped at any means to overthrow him*. ■ get mental hold of; comprehend fully: *the way in which children could grasp complex ideas*. ■ act decisively to the advantage of (something): *we must grasp the opportunities offered*.
▶ n. [in sing.] a firm hold or grip: *the child slipped from her grasp*. ■ a person's power or capacity to attain something: *he knew success was within his grasp*. ■ a person's understanding: *meanings that are beyond my grasp* | *his grasp of detail*.
– PHRASES **grasp at straws** (or **a straw**) see STRAW. **grasp the nettle** Brit. tackle a difficulty boldly. [because a nettle stings when touched lightly, but not when grasped firmly.]
– DERIVATIVES **grasp·a·ble** adj., **grasp·er** n.
– ORIGIN late Middle English: perhaps related to GROPE.

grasp·ing /ˈgraspiNG/ ▶ adj. greedy; avaricious: *grasping, power-hungry individuals*.
– DERIVATIVES **grasp·ing·ly** adv., **grasp·ing·ness** n.

Grass /gräs/, Günter (Wilhelm) (1927–), German novelist, poet, and playwright. His works are intellectual and experimental and often reflect his socialist views. Notable works: *The Tin Drum* (1959), *The Plebeians Rehearse the Uprising* (1966), and *The Flounder* (1977). Nobel Prize for Literature (1999).

grass /gras/ ▶ n. **1** vegetation consisting of typically short plants with long narrow leaves, growing wild or cultivated on lawns and pasture, and as a fodder crop. ■ ground covered with grass: *he sat down on the grass*. ■ pastureland: *the farms were mostly given over to grass*.
2 the mainly herbaceous plant that constitutes such vegetation, which has jointed stems and spikes of small, wind-pollinated flowers.

> Grasses belong to the large family Gramineae (or Poaceae; the **grass family**), and form the dominant vegetation of many areas of the world. The possession of a growing point that is mainly at ground level makes grasses suitable as the food of many grazing animals, and for use in lawns and playing fields.

3 informal marijuana.
4 Brit. informal a police informer. [perhaps related to the 19th-cent. rhyming slang *grasshopper* 'copper.']
▶ v. [with obj.] **1** (usu. **be grassed**) cover (an area of ground) with grass: *hillsides so closely **grassed over**, they seem to be painted green*. ■ feed (livestock) with grass.
2 [no obj.] Brit. informal inform the police of criminal activity or plans: *someone had grassed on the thieves*.
– PHRASES **the grass is always greener on the other side of the fence** proverb other people's lives or situations always seem better than one's own. **not let the grass grow under one's feet** not delay in acting or taking an opportunity.
– DERIVATIVES **grass·less** adj., **grass·like** /-ˌlīk/ adj.
– ORIGIN Old English *græs*, of Germanic origin; related to Dutch *gras*, German *Gras*, also ultimately to GREEN and GROW.

grass carp ▶ n. a large Chinese freshwater fish, farmed for food in Southeast Asia and introduced elsewhere to control the growth of vegetation in waterways. ● *Ctenopharyngodon idella*, family Cyprinidae.

grass·cloth /ˈgrasˌklôTH/ ▶ n. a fine, light cloth resembling linen, woven from the fibers of the inner bark of the ramie plant.

grass·cy·cling /ˈgrasˌsīkliNG/ ▶ n. the leaving of chopped grass clippings on a mowed lawn as a fertilizer.

grass·hop·per /ˈgrasˌhäpər/ ▶ n. a plant-eating insect with long hind legs that are used for jumping and for producing a chirping sound. It frequents grassy places and low vegetation. ● Family Acrididae, order Orthoptera: many genera.

American grasshopper

grass·hop·per mouse ▶ n. a mainly carnivorous North American mouse with a stout body, gray or brownish fur, and a short white-tipped tail. ● Genus *Onychomys*, family Muridae: three species.

grass·land /ˈgrasˌland/ ▶ n. (also **grasslands**) a large open area of country covered with grass, esp. one used for grazing: *rough grassland*.

grass of Par·nas·sus ▶ n. a herbaceous plant of north temperate regions that bears a solitary white flower. ● Genus *Parnassia*, family Saxifragaceae: several species, including *P. glauca* and *P. palustris*.

grass par·rot (also **grass parakeet**) ▶ n. Austral. a small parrot frequenting grassy country. ● Family Psittacidae: several genera, in particular *Psephotus* and *Neophema*.

grass pea ▶ n. a plant of the pea family which is cultivated as food for animals and humans, though excessive consumption can lead to lathyrism. Also called CHICKLING PEA. ● *Lathyrus sativus*, family Leguminosae.

grass·quit /ˈgrasˌkwit/ ▶ n. a small Caribbean and tropical American songbird related to the buntings, the male being partly or mainly black. ● Family Emberizidae (subfamily Emberizinae): three genera, in particular *Tiaris*, and several species.

grass roots (also **grassroots** /ˈgrasˌro͞ots/) ▶ plural n. the most basic level of an activity or organization: *the whole campaign would be conducted **at the grass roots*** | [as modifier] *trying to improve the sport's image at the grass-roots level*. ■ ordinary people regarded as the main body of an organization's membership: *you have lost touch with the grass roots of the party*.

grass ski ▶ n. each of a pair of short skis with rollers on the bottom, for going down grass-covered slopes.
– DERIVATIVES **grass ski·ing** n.

grass skirt ▶ n. a skirt made of long grass and leaves fastened to a waistband, associated esp. with female dancers from some Pacific islands.

grass snake ▶ n. a common harmless Eurasian snake that typically has a yellowish band around the neck and is often found in or near water. ● *Natrix natrix*, family Colubridae. ■ another term for GREEN SNAKE.

g

grass tet·a·ny ▶ n. a disease of livestock caused by magnesium deficiency, occurring esp. when there is a change from indoor feeding to outdoor grazing.

grass wid·ow ▶ n. a woman whose husband is away often or for a prolonged period.
– ORIGIN early 16th cent. (denoting an unmarried woman with a child): from GRASS + WIDOW, perhaps from the idea of the couple having lain on the grass instead of in bed. The current sense dates from the mid 19th cent.; compare with Dutch *grasweduwe* and German *Strohwitwe* 'straw widow.'

grass·y /ˈgrasē/ ▶ adj. (**grassier**, **grassiest**) of or covered with grass: *grassy slopes*. ■ characteristic of grass: *an intense grassy green*.
– DERIVATIVES **grass·i·ness** n.

grate[1] /grāt/ ▶ v. **1** [with obj.] reduce (something, esp. food) to small shreds by rubbing it on a grater: *peel and roughly grate the carrots* | (as adj. **grated**) *grated cheese*.
2 [no obj.] make an unpleasant rasping sound: *the hinges of the door grated*. ■ (**grate against**) rub against something with such a sound: *his helmet grated against the top of the door*. ■ have an irritating effect: *he had a juvenile streak that grated on her nerves*.
– ORIGIN late Middle English: from Old French *grater*, of Germanic origin; related to German *kratzen* 'to scratch.'

grate[2] ▶ n. **1** the recess of a fireplace or furnace. ■ a metal frame confining fuel in a fireplace or furnace.
2 a grating.
– ORIGIN Middle English (meaning 'a grating'): from Old French, based on Latin *cratis* 'hurdle.'

grate·ful /ˈgrātfəl/ ▶ adj. feeling or showing an appreciation of kindness; thankful: *I'm very grateful to you for all your help*. ■ archaic received or experienced with gratitude; welcome: *enjoying the grateful shade*.
– DERIVATIVES **grate·ful·ly** adv., **grate·ful·ness** n.
– ORIGIN mid 16th cent.: from obsolete *grate* 'pleasing, agreeable, thankful' (from Latin *gratus*) + -FUL.

grat·er /ˈgrātər/ ▶ n. a device having a surface covered with holes edged by slightly raised cutting edges, used for grating cheese and other foods.

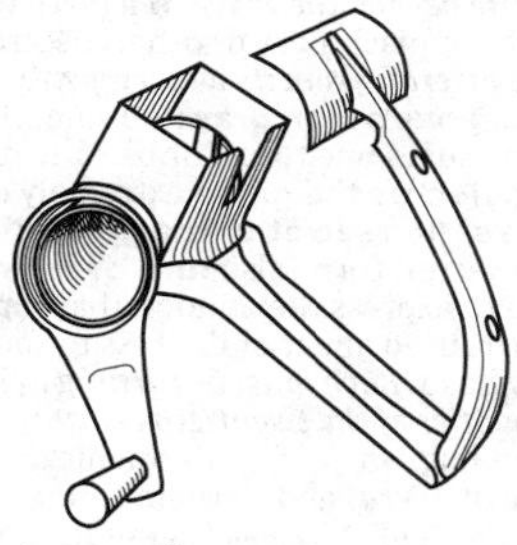
cheese grater

grat·i·cule /ˈgratəˌkyo͞ol/ ▶ n. technical a network of lines representing meridians and parallels, on which a map or plan can be represented.
– ORIGIN late 19th cent.: from French, from medieval Latin *graticula* 'a little grating,' from Latin *craticula* 'gridiron,' diminutive of *cratis* 'hurdle.'

grat·i·fi·ca·tion /ˌgratəfiˈkāSHən/ ▶ **n.** pleasure, esp. when gained from the satisfaction of a desire: *a thirst for sexual gratification.* ■ a source of pleasure.

grat·i·fy /ˈgratəˌfī/ ▶ **v.** (**gratifies, gratifying, gratified**) [with obj.] give (someone) pleasure or satisfaction: *I was gratified to see the coverage in May's issue* | (as adj. **gratifying**) *the results were gratifying.* ■ indulge or satisfy (a desire): *not all the sexual impulses can be gratified.*
– DERIVATIVES **grat·i·fi·er n., gra·ti·fy·ing·ly adv.**
– ORIGIN late Middle English (in the sense 'make pleasing'): from French *gratifier* or Latin *gratificari* 'give or do as a favor,' from *gratus* 'pleasing, thankful.'

grat·in /ˈgrätn, ˈgratn/ ▶ **n.** a dish with a light browned crust of breadcrumbs or melted cheese.
– ORIGIN French, from *gratter*, earlier *grater* 'to grate.'

gra·ti·né /ˌgrätnˈā, ˌgra-/ (also **gratinée**) ▶ **adj.** [postpositive] another term for **AU GRATIN**.
– DERIVATIVES **gra·ti·néed adj.**
– ORIGIN French, past participle of *gratiner* 'cook au gratin.'

grat·ing[1] /ˈgrātiNG/ ▶ **adj.** sounding harsh and unpleasant: *her high, grating voice.* ■ irritating: *a smarty-pants tone that I found grating.*
– DERIVATIVES **grat·ing·ly adv.**

grat·ing[2] ▶ **n.** a framework of parallel or crossed bars, typically preventing access through an opening while permitting communication or ventilation. ■ (also **diffraction grating**) Optics a set of equally spaced parallel wires, or a surface ruled with equally spaced parallel lines, used to produce spectra by diffraction.

grat·is /ˈgratis/ ▶ **adv.** without charge; free: *a monthly program was issued gratis.*
▶ **adj.** given or done for nothing; free: *gratis copies.*
– ORIGIN late Middle English: from Latin, contraction of *gratiis* 'as a kindness,' from *gratia* 'grace, kindness.'

grat·i·tude /ˈgratəˌt(y)o͞od/ ▶ **n.** the quality of being thankful; readiness to show appreciation for and to return kindness: *she expressed her gratitude to the committee for their support.*
– ORIGIN late Middle English: from Old French, or from medieval Latin *gratitudo*, from Latin *gratus* 'pleasing, thankful.'

gra·tu·i·tous /grəˈt(y)o͞oitəs/ ▶ **adj. 1** uncalled for; lacking good reason; unwarranted: *gratuitous violence.*
2 given or done free of charge: *solicitors provide a form of gratuitous legal advice.*
– DERIVATIVES **gra·tu·i·tous·ly adv., gra·tu·i·tous·ness n.**
– ORIGIN mid 17th cent.: from Latin *gratuitus* 'given freely, spontaneous' + **-OUS**.

gra·tu·i·ty /grəˈt(y)o͞oitē/ ▶ **n.** (pl. **gratuities**) formal a tip given to a waiter, taxicab driver, etc.
– ORIGIN late 15th cent. (denoting graciousness or favor): from Old French *gratuité* or medieval Latin *gratuitas* 'gift,' from Latin *gratus* 'pleasing, thankful.'

Grau /grou/, Shirley Ann (1929–), US writer. Her works include *The Keepers of the House* (1964), *The Condor Passes* (1971), and *Roadwalkers* (1994).

gra·va·men /grəˈvāmən/ ▶ **n.** (pl. **gravamina** /-ˈvamənə/) chiefly Law the essence or most serious part of a complaint or accusation. ■ a grievance.
– ORIGIN early 17th cent. (as an ecclesiastical term denoting formal presentation of a grievance): from late Latin, literally 'physical inconvenience,' from Latin *gravare* 'to load,' from *gravis* 'heavy.'

grave[1] /grāv/ ▶ **n.** a place of burial for a dead body, typically a hole dug in the ground and marked by a stone or mound: *the coffin was lowered into the grave.* ■ (**the grave**) used as an allusive term for death: *life beyond the grave.* ■ a place where a broken piece of machinery or other discarded object lies: *lift the aircraft from its watery grave.*
– PHRASES **dig one's own grave** do something foolish that causes one to fail or be ruined. (**as**) **silent** (or **quiet**) **as the grave** extremely quiet. **take the** (or **one's**, etc.) **secret to the grave** die without revealing a secret. **turn** (also **turn over**) **in one's grave** used to express the opinion that something would have caused anger or distress to someone who is now dead: *Bach must be turning in his grave at the vulgarities of the twentieth century.*
– ORIGIN Old English *græf*, of Germanic origin; related to Dutch *graf* and German *Grab*.

grave[2] /grāv/ ▶ **adj.** giving cause for alarm; serious: *a matter of grave concern.* ■ serious or solemn in manner or appearance; somber: *his face was grave.*
▶ **n.** also /gräv/ another term for **GRAVE ACCENT**.
– DERIVATIVES **grave·ly adv., grave·ness n.**
– ORIGIN late 15th cent. (originally of a wound in the sense 'severe, serious'): from Old French *grave* or Latin *gravis* 'heavy, serious.'

grave[3] /grāv/ ▶ **v.** (past participle **graven** /ˈgrāvən/ or **graved**) [with obj.] archaic engrave (an inscription or image) on a surface. ■ literary fix (something) indelibly in the mind: *the times are graven on my memory.*
– ORIGIN Old English *grafan* 'dig,' of Germanic origin; related to German *graben*, Dutch *graven* 'dig' and German *begraben* 'bury,' also to **GRAVE[1]** and **GROOVE**.

grave[4] /grāv/ ▶ **v.** [with obj.] historical clean (a ship's bottom) by burning off the accretions and then tarring it.
– ORIGIN late Middle English: perhaps from French dialect *grave*, variant of Old French *greve* 'shore' (because originally the ship would have been run aground).

gra·ve[5] /ˈgräˌvā/ ▶ **adv. & adj.** Music (as a direction) slowly; with solemnity.
– ORIGIN Italian, 'slow!.'

grave ac·cent /gräv, grāv/ ▶ **n.** a mark (`) placed over certain letters in some languages to indicate an alteration of a sound, as of quality, quantity, or pitch.
– ORIGIN early 17th cent.: French *grave* (see **GRAVE[2]**).

grave·dig·ger /ˈgrāvˌdigər/ ▶ **n.** a person who digs graves.

grav·el /ˈgravəl/ ▶ **n.** a loose aggregation of small water-worn or pounded stones. ■ a mixture of such stones with coarse sand, used for paths and roads and as an aggregate. ■ a stratum or deposit of such stones. ■ Medicine aggregations of crystals formed in the urinary tract.
▶ **v.** (**gravels, graveling, graveled**; Brit. **gravels, gravelling, gravelled**) [with obj.] **1** cover (an area of ground) with gravel.
2 informal make (someone) angry or annoyed: *this was a bad strike, and it graveled him to involve himself in it.* ■ archaic make (someone) feel confused or puzzled.
– ORIGIN Middle English: from Old French, diminutive of *grave* (see **GRAVE[4]**).

grav·el-blind ▶ **adj.** archaic almost completely blind.
– ORIGIN early 17th cent.: originally as *high-gravel-blind*, a humorous usage meaning 'more than sand-blind (= half-blind),' with reference to Shakespeare's *Merchant of Venice*.

grav·el·ly /ˈgravəlē/ ▶ **adj.** resembling, containing, or consisting of gravel: *a dry gravelly soil.* ■ (of a voice) deep and rough-sounding.

grav·en /ˈgrāvən/ past participle of **GRAVE[3]**.

grav·en im·age ▶ **n.** a carved idol or representation of a god used as an object of worship.
– ORIGIN with biblical allusion to Exod. 20:4.

Gra·ven·stein /ˈgrävənˌstīn/ ▶ **n.** a widely grown apple of a large variety having yellow, red-streaked skin, used for cooking and as a dessert apple.
– ORIGIN early 19th cent.: the German form of *Graasten*, a village in Denmark formerly in Schleswig-Holstein, Germany.

grav·er /ˈgrāvər/ ▶ **n.** a burin or other engraving tool. ■ archaic a person who engraves or carves.

Graves[1] /ˈgrāvz/, Robert (Ranke) (1895–1985), English poet, novelist, and critic; professor of poetry at Oxford University 1961–66. Notable prose works: *Goodbye to All That* (1929), *I, Claudius* (1934), and *The White Goddess* (1948).

Graves[2] /ˈgrävz, gräv/ ▶ **n.** a red or white wine from the district of Graves, to the south of Bordeaux in France.

Graves' dis·ease ▶ **n.** a swelling of the neck and protrusion of the eyes resulting from an overactive thyroid gland. Also called **EXOPHTHALMIC GOITER**.
– ORIGIN mid 19th cent.: named after Robert J. *Graves* (1796–1853), the Irish physician who first identified it.

grave·side /ˈgrāvˌsīd/ ▶ **n.** the ground around the edge of a grave.

grave·site /ˈgrāvˌsīt/ ▶ **n.** the location of a person's grave.

grave·stone /ˈgrāvˌstōn/ ▶ **n.** an inscribed headstone marking a grave.

Gra·vett·i·an /grəˈvetēən/ ▶ **adj.** Archaeology of, relating to, or denoting an Upper Paleolithic culture in Europe following the Aurignacian, dated to about 28,000–19,000 years ago. ■ (as noun **the Gravettian**) the Gravettian culture or period.
– ORIGIN 1930s: from *la Gravette*, an archaeological site in southwestern France, where objects from this culture were found.

grave·yard /ˈgrāvˌyärd/ ▶ **n.** a burial ground, esp. one beside a church.

grave·yard shift ▶ **n.** a work shift that runs through the early morning hours, typically covering the period between midnight and 8 a.m.

grav·id /ˈgravid/ ▶ **adj. 1** technical pregnant; carrying eggs or young.
2 full of meaning or a specified quality: *the scene is gravid with unease.*
– ORIGIN late 16th cent.: from Latin *gravidus* 'laden, pregnant,' from *gravis* 'heavy.'

gra·vim·e·ter /grəˈvimitər/ ▶ **n.** an instrument for measuring the difference in the force of gravity from one place to another.
– ORIGIN late 18th cent.: from French *gravimètre*, from *grave* 'heavy' (from Latin *gravis*) + *-mètre* '(instrument) measuring.'

grav·i·met·ric /ˌgravəˈmetrik/ ▶ **adj.** of or relating to the measurement of weight. ■ of or relating to the measurement of gravity.

gra·vim·e·try /grəˈvimətrē/ ▶ **n.** Physics the measurement of weight.

grav·ing dock ▶ **n.** another term for **DRY DOCK**.
– ORIGIN early 19th cent.: *graving* from **GRAVE[4]**.

grav·i·tas /ˈgraviˌtäs/ ▶ **n.** dignity, seriousness, or solemnity of manner: *a post for which he has the expertise and the gravitas.*
– ORIGIN Latin, from *gravis* 'serious.'

grav·i·tate /ˈgraviˌtāt/ ▶ **v.** [no obj.] move toward or be attracted to a place, person, or thing: *they gravitated to the Catholic faith in their hour of need.* ■ Physics move, or tend to move, toward a center of gravity or other attractive force. ■ archaic descend or sink by the force of gravity.
– ORIGIN mid 17th cent.: from modern Latin *gravitat-*, from the verb *gravitare*, from Latin *gravitas* 'weight.'

grav·i·ta·tion /ˌgraviˈtāSHən/ ▶ **n. 1** movement, or a tendency to move, toward a center of attractive force, as in the falling of bodies to the earth. ■ Physics a force of attraction exerted by each particle of matter in the universe on every other particle: *the law of universal gravitation.* Compare with **GRAVITY**.
2 movement toward or attraction to something: *a tentative gravitation toward the prices that we saw before the announcement.*
– DERIVATIVES **grav·i·ta·tion·al** /-SHənl/ **adj., grav·i·ta·tion·al·ly** /-SHənl-ē/ **adv.**
– ORIGIN mid 17th cent.: from modern Latin *gravitatio(n-)*, from the verb *gravitare* (see **GRAVITATE**).

grav·i·ta·tion·al con·stant (abbr.: **G**) ▶ **n.** Physics the constant in Newton's law of gravitation relating gravity to the masses and separation of particles, equal to 6.67×10^{-11}N m^2 kg^{-2}.

grav·i·ta·tion·al field ▶ **n.** Physics the region of space surrounding a body in which another body experiences a force of gravitational attraction.

grav·i·ta·tion·al lens ▶ **n.** Astronomy a region of space containing a massive object whose gravitational field distorts electromagnetic radiation passing through it in a similar way to a lens, sometimes producing a multiple image of a remote object.

grav·i·ton /ˈgraviˌtän/ ▶ **n.** Physics a hypothetical quantum of gravitational energy, regarded as a particle.
– ORIGIN 1940s: from **GRAVITATION** + **-ON**.

grav·i·ty /ˈgravitē/ ▶ **n. 1** Physics the force that attracts a body toward the center of the earth, or toward any other physical body having mass. For most purposes Newton's laws of gravity apply, with minor modifications to take the general theory of relativity into account. ■ the degree of intensity of this, measured by acceleration.
2 extreme or alarming importance; seriousness: *crimes of the utmost gravity.* ■ seriousness or solemnity of manner: *has the poet ever spoken with greater eloquence or gravity?*
– ORIGIN late 15th cent. (sense 2): from Old French, or from Latin *gravitas* 'weight, seriousness,' from *gravis* 'heavy.' Sense 1 dates from the 17th cent.

grav·i·ty feed ▶ **n.** a supply system making use of gravity to maintain the flow of material.
– DERIVATIVES **grav·i·ty-fed adj.**

grav·i·ty wave ▶ **n.** Physics **1** a hypothetical wave carrying gravitational energy, postulated by Einstein to be emitted when a massive body is accelerated.
2 a wave propagated on a liquid surface or in a fluid through the effects of gravity.

grav·lax /ˈgrävˌläks/ ▶ **n.** a Scandinavian dish of dry-cured salmon marinated in herbs.
– ORIGIN Swedish, from *grav* 'trench' + *lax* 'salmon' (from the former practice of burying the salmon in salt in a hole in the ground).

gra·vure /grəˈvyo͝or/ ▶ **n.** an image produced from etching a plate through an intaglio process and producing a print from it. ■ the production of prints in this way.

gra·vy /ˈgrāvē/ ▶ **n.** (pl. **gravies**) **1** the fat and juices exuding from meat during cooking. ■ a sauce made from these juices together with stock and other ingredients.
2 informal unearned or unexpected money.
– ORIGIN Middle English (denoting a spicy sauce): perhaps from a misreading (as *gravé*) of Old French *grané*, probably from *grain* 'spice,' from Latin *granum* 'grain.'

gra·vy boat ▶ **n.** a boat-shaped vessel used for serving gravy or sauce; sauceboat.

gra·vy train ▶ **n.** informal used to refer to a situation in which someone can make a lot of money for very little effort: *come to Hollywood and get on the gravy train.*

Gray[1] /grā/, Asa (1810–88), US botanist. Finding no conflict between evolution and his view of divine design in nature, he supported Darwin's theories at a time when they were unpopular.

Gray[2], Elisha (1835–1901), US inventor. A rival of Alexander Graham Bell for the telephone patent, he founded a small business that eventually became the Western Electric Company.

Gray[3], Horace (1828–1902), US Supreme Court associate justice 1881–1902. Appointed to the Court by President Arthur, he had served as Massachusett's chief justice 1873–81.

Gray[4], Thomas (1716–71), English poet; known for "Elegy Written in a Country Church-Yard" (1751).

gray[1] /grā/ (Brit. **grey**) ▶ **adj. 1** of a color intermediate between black and white, as of ashes or an overcast sky: *gray flannel trousers.* ■ (of a person) having gray hair: *a gray, fatherly gentleman.* ■ informal relating to old people, esp. when seen as an oppressed group: *gray power.* ■ (of the weather) cloudy and dull; without sun: *a cold, gray November day.* ■ (of a person's face) pale, as through tiredness, age, or illness: *a few people, their faces gray and bitter.*
2 dull and nondescript; without interest or character: *gray, faceless men* | *the gray daily routine.*
3 (of financial or trading activity) not accounted for in official statistics: *the gray economy.*
▶ **n. 1** gray color or pigment: *dirty intermediate tones of gray.* ■ gray clothes or material: *the gentleman in gray.* ■ gray hair: *he sighed at the amount of gray at his temple.* ■ (usu. **Gray**) the Confederate army in the Civil War, or a member of that army.
2 a gray thing or animal, in particular a gray or white horse.
▶ **v.** [no obj.] (esp. of hair) become gray with age: *he had put on weight and grayed somewhat* | (as adj. **graying**) *a man of about fifty with graying hair.* ■ (of a person or group) become older; age: (as adj. **graying**) *a graying workforce.*
– PHRASAL VERBS **gray something out** display a menu option in a light font to indicate that it is not available: *all the property fields on the Shortcut tab are either missing or grayed out.*
– DERIVATIVES **gray·ish adj.**, **gray·ly adv.**, **gray·ness n.**
– ORIGIN Old English *grǣg*, of Germanic origin; related to Dutch *grauw* and German *grau.*

gray[2] (abbr.: **Gy**) ▶ **n.** Physics the SI unit of the absorbed dose of ionizing radiation, corresponding to one joule per kilogram.
– ORIGIN 1970s: named after Louis H. *Gray* (1905–65), English radiobiologist.

gray a·re·a ▶ **n.** an ill-defined situation or field not readily conforming to a category or to an existing set of rules: *gray areas in the legislation have still to be clarified.*

gray·beard /ˈgrā,bi(ə)rd/ (Brit. **greybeard**) ▶ **n.**
1 humorous or derogatory an old man.
2 archaic a large stoneware jug used for holding spirits.

Gray code ▶ **n.** a numerical code used in computing in which consecutive integers are represented by binary numbers differing in only one digit.
– ORIGIN mid 20th cent.: named after Frank *Gray* (1887–1969), American physicist.

gray em·i·nence ▶ **n.** another term for **ÉMINENCE GRISE.**

Gray Fri·ar ▶ **n.** a Franciscan friar.
– ORIGIN Middle English: so named because of the color of the order's habit.

gray goods /ˈgrā ,go͝odz/ ▶ **plural n. 1** newly manufactured fabrics that have not been subjected to whitening processes.
2 goods traded in a gray market.

gray goose ▶ **n.** a goose of a group distinguished by having mainly gray plumage. ● Genus *Anser*, family Anatidae: several species, e.g., graylag and white-fronted geese.

gray jay ▶ **n.** a fluffy, long-tailed jay with dark gray upper parts and a whitish face, found in Canada and the northwestern US. ● *Perisoreus canadensis*, family Corvidae.

gray kan·ga·roo ▶ **n.** a large forest-dwelling kangaroo native to Australia. ● Genus *Macropus*, family Macropodidae: the eastern *M. giganteus* (also called **FORESTER**), with silvery-gray fur, and the western *M. fuliginosus*, with brownish fur.

gray·lag /ˈgrā,lag/ (also **graylag goose**) ▶ **n.** a large goose with mainly gray plumage, which is native to Eurasia and is the ancestor of the domestic goose. ● *Anser anser*, family Anatidae.
– ORIGIN early 18th cent.: probably from **GRAY**[1] + dialect *lag* 'goose,' of unknown origin.

gray·ling /ˈgrāliNG/ ▶ **n. 1** an edible freshwater fish of Eurasia and North America that is silvery-gray with horizontal violet stripes and has a long, high dorsal fin. ● Genus *Thymallus*, family Salmonidae: several species.
2 a mainly brown European butterfly that has wings with bright eyespots and grayish undersides. ● *Hipparchia semele*, subfamily Satyrinae, family Nymphalidae.
– ORIGIN Middle English: from **GRAY**[1] + **-LING.**

gray·mail /ˈgrā,māl/ ▶ **n.** a tactic used by the defense in a spy trial, involving the threat to expose government secrets unless charges against the defendant are dropped.

gray mar·ket ▶ **n.** an unofficial market or trade in something, esp. unissued shares or controlled or scarce goods: *the discounting of bonds in the gray market* | [as modifier] *a gray market price.*

gray mat·ter ▶ **n.** the darker tissue of the brain and spinal cord, consisting mainly of nerve cell bodies and branching dendrites. Compare with **WHITE MATTER.** ■ informal intelligence: *I wish I had a little of her gray matter.*

gray mul·let ▶ **n.** a thick-bodied, blunt-headed fish that typically lives in inshore or estuarine waters and is a valued food fish. ● Family Mugilidae: several genera and species.

gray par·rot (also **African gray parrot**) ▶ **n.** a parrot of western equatorial Africa, with gray plumage and a red tail, widely kept as a pet for its mimicking abilities. ● *Psittacus erithacus*, family Psittacidae.

gray·scale /ˈgrā,skāl/ ▶ **n.** Computing a range of gray shades from white to black, as used in a monochrome display or printout: [as modifier] *a grayscale scanner.*

gray seal ▶ **n.** a large seal with a spotted, grayish coat and a convex profile, found commonly in the North Atlantic. Also called **ATLANTIC SEAL.** ● *Halichoerus grypus*, family Phocidae.

gray squir·rel ▶ **n.** an American tree squirrel with mainly gray fur. ● Genus *Sciurus*, family Sciuridae: four species, in particular *Sciurus carolinensis*, native to eastern North America and introduced to Britain and elsewhere.

gray·wacke /ˈgrā,wak, -,wakə/ (Brit. **greywacke**) ▶ **n.** Geology a dark coarse-grained sandstone containing more than 15 percent clay.
– ORIGIN late 18th cent. (as *grauwacke*): from German *Grauwacke*, from *grau* 'gray' + **WACKE.** The anglicized form dates from the early 19th cent.

gray wa·ter ▶ **n.** technical the relatively clean waste water from baths, sinks, washing machines, and other kitchen appliances. Compare with **BLACK WATER.**

gray whale ▶ **n.** a mottled gray baleen whale that typically has heavy encrustations of barnacles on the skin, commonly seen in coastal waters of the northeastern Pacific. ● *Eschrichtius robustus*, the only member of the family Eschrichtiidae.

gray wolf ▶ **n.** another term for **TIMBER WOLF.**

Graz /gräts/ a city in southern Austria, on the Mur River; pop. 247,515 (2006). It is the second largest city in Austria.

graze[1] /grāz/ ▶ **v.** [no obj.] (of cattle, sheep, etc.) eat grass in a field: *cattle **graze on** the open meadows.* ■ [with obj.] (of an animal) feed on (grass or land covered by grass): *llamas graze the tufts of grass.* ■ [with obj.] put (cattle, sheep, etc.) to feed on land covered by grass: *shepherds who grazed animals on common land.* ■ informal (of a person) eat small quantities of food at frequent but irregular intervals: *advertisers should not encourage children **to graze on** snacks or sweets.* ■ informal casually sample something: *we grazed up and down the channels.*
– DERIVATIVES **graz·er n.**
– ORIGIN Old English *grasian*, from *græs* 'grass.'

graze[2] ▶ **v.** [with obj.] scrape the skin of (a part of the body) so as to break the surface but cause little or no bleeding: *she fell down and grazed her knees.* ■ touch or scrape lightly in passing: *his hands just grazed hers.*
▶ **n.** a slight injury where the skin is scraped: *it'll be fine, it's only a graze.*
– ORIGIN late 16th cent.: perhaps a specific use of **GRAZE**[1].

gra·zier /ˈgrāZHər/ ▶ **n.** Brit. a person who rears or fattens cattle or sheep for market.
– ORIGIN Middle English: from **GRASS** + **-IER.**

graz·ing /ˈgrāziNG/ ▶ **n.** grassland suitable for pasturage: *pastures and rough grazing.*

grease ▶ **n.** /grēs/ oily or fatty matter, in particular: ■ a thick oily substance used as a lubricant: *axle grease.* ■ oil or fat used or produced in cooking.
▶ **v.** /grēs, grēz/ [with obj.] smear or lubricate with grease: (as adj. **greased**) *place on a greased baking sheet.*
– PHRASES **grease the palm of** informal bribe (someone). **grease the skids** informal help matters run smoothly: *his mission was to use his budgetary skills to grease the skids for new projects.* **grease the wheels** help something go smoothly: *it is inadequate to grease the wheels of recovery.* **like greased lightning** informal extremely fast: *you come up with plans faster than greased lightning.*
– DERIVATIVES **grease·less adj.**
– ORIGIN Middle English: from Old French *graisse*, based on Latin *crassus* 'thick, fat.'

grease·ball /ˈgrēs,bôl/ ▶ **n.** informal, offensive a foreigner, esp. one of Mediterranean or Latin American origin.

grease gun ▶ **n.** a device for pumping grease under pressure to a particular point.

grease mon·key ▶ **n.** informal a mechanic.

grease·paint /ˈgrēs,pānt/ ▶ **n.** a waxy substance used as makeup by actors.

grease pen·cil ▶ **n.** a pencil made of grease colored with a pigment, used esp. for marking glossy surfaces.

greas·er /ˈgrēsər, -zər/ ▶ **n. 1** an engine mechanic or an unskilled member of a ship's engine-room crew. ■ informal a rough young man, esp. one who greases his hair back and is a member of a motorcycle gang.
2 informal, offensive a Hispanic American, esp. a Mexican.
3 informal a gentle landing of an aircraft.

grease·wood /ˈgrēs,wo͝od/ ▶ **n. 1** a resinous dwarf shrub of the goosefoot family, which yields hard yellow wood used chiefly for fuel. It grows in dry areas of the western US and is toxic to livestock if eaten in large quantities. ● *Sarcobatus vermiculatus*, family Chenopodiaceae.
2 another term for **CHAMISE.**

greas·y /ˈgrēsē, -zē/ ▶ **adj.** (**greasier, greasiest**)
1 covered with or resembling an oily substance: *he wiped his greasy fingers* | *their moisturizers don't feel greasy.* ■ producing more body oils than average: *greasy skin.* ■ containing or cooked with too much oil or fat: *greasy food.* ■ slippery: *the floor was greasy.*
2 (of a person or their manner) effusively polite in a way that is felt to be insincere and repulsive: *the greasy little man from the newspaper.*
– DERIVATIVES **greas·i·ly** /-səlē, -zəlē/ **adv.**, **greas·i·ness n.**

greas·y pole ▶ **n.** informal a pole covered with an oily substance to make it more difficult to climb or walk along, used esp. as a form of entertainment. ■ used to refer to the difficult route to the top of someone's profession: *he steadily climbed the greasy pole toward the job he coveted most.*

greas·y spoon ▶ **n.** informal a cheap, run-down cafe or restaurant serving fried foods.

great /grāt/ ▶ **adj. 1** of an extent, amount, or intensity considerably above the normal or average: *the article was of great interest* | *she showed great potential as an actor.* ■ very large and imposing: *a great ocean between them.* ■ [attrib.] used to reinforce another adjective of size or extent: *a great big grin.* ■ [attrib.] used to express surprise, admiration, or contempt, esp. in exclamations: *you great oaf!* ■ (also **greater**) [attrib.] used in names of animals or plants that are larger than similar kinds, e.g., **great auk, greater flamingo.** ■ (**Greater**) [attrib.] (of a city) including adjacent urban areas: *Greater Cleveland.*
2 of ability, quality, or eminence considerably above the normal or average: *the great Italian conductor* | *we obeyed our great men and leaders* | *great art has the power to change lives.* ■ (**the Great**) a title denoting the most important person of the name: *Alexander the Great.* ■ informal very good or satisfactory; excellent: *this has been another great year* | *what a great guy* | *wouldn't it be great to have him back?* | [as exclamation] *"Great!" said Tom.* ■ [predic.] informal (of a person) very skilled or capable in a particular area: *a brilliant man, great at mathematics.*
3 [attrib.] denoting the element of something that is the most important or the most worthy of consideration: *the great thing is the challenge.* ■ used to indicate that someone or something particularly deserves a specified description: *I was a great fan of Hank's.*
4 [in combination] (in names of family relationships) denoting one degree further removed upward or downward: *great-aunt* | *great-granddaughter* | *great-great-grandfather.*
▶ **n. 1** a great or distinguished person: *the Beatles, Bob Dylan, all the greats.* ■ (as plural noun **the great**) great people collectively: *the lives of the great, including Churchill and Newton.*
2 (**Greats**) Brit. informal another term for **LITERAE HUMANIORES.**
▶ **adv.** informal excellently; very well: *we played awful, they played great.*
– PHRASES **great and small** of all sizes, classes, or types: *all creatures great and small.* **a great deal** see **DEAL**[1]. **a great many** see **MANY.** **a great one for** a

habitual doer of; an enthusiast for: *my father was a great one for buying gadgets.* **Great Scott!** expressing surprise or amazement. [arbitrary euphemism for *Great God!*] **to a great extent** in a substantial way; largely: *we are all to a great extent the product of our culture.*
– ORIGIN Old English *grēat* 'big'; related to Dutch *groot* and German *gross*.

great ape ▶ n. a large ape of a family closely related to humans, including the gorilla, orangutan, and chimpanzees, but excluding the gibbons; an anthropoid ape. ● Family Pongidae, order Primates.

Great At·trac·tor Astronomy a massive grouping of galaxies in the direction of the constellations Hydra and Centaurus, whose gravitational pull is thought to be responsible for deviations in the velocity of other galaxies.

great auk ▶ n. a large, extinct, flightless auk (seabird) of the North Atlantic, resembling a giant razorbill. The great auk was the original "penguin"; many were taken for food, and the last individuals were killed on an islet off Iceland in 1844. ● *Alca* (or *Pinguinus*) *impennis*, family Alcidae.

great-aunt ▶ n. an aunt of one's father or mother.

Great Aus·tra·lian Bight a wide bay on the southern coast of Australia, part of the southern Indian Ocean.

Great Bar·ri·er Reef a coral reef in the western Pacific Ocean, off the coast of Queensland, Australia. It extends for about 1,250 miles (2,000 km), roughly parallel to the coast, and is the largest coral reef in the world.

Great Ba·sin an arid region in the western US between the Sierra Nevada and the Rocky Mountains that includes most of Nevada and parts of the adjacent states.

Great Bear Astronomy the constellation Ursa Major.

Great Bear Lake a large lake in western Northwest Territories, Canada. It drains into the Mackenzie River via the Great Bear River.

Great Bi·ble ▶ n. the edition of the English Bible that Thomas Cromwell ordered in 1538 to be set up in every parish church in England. It was the work of Miles Coverdale and was first issued in 1539.

Great Brit·ain /ˈbritn/ England, Wales, and Scotland considered as a unit. The name is also often used loosely to refer to the United Kingdom.

> **USAGE** Great Britain is the name for the island that comprises England, Scotland, and Wales. The term came into official use in 1603, when King James I (who was also James VI of Scotland) acceded to the throne of England and Wales. Scotland joined this legislative union in 1707. The **United Kingdom** is a political unit that includes these countries and Northern Ireland. The **British Isles** is a geographical term that refers to the United Kingdom, Ireland, and surrounding smaller islands such as the Hebrides and the Channel Islands.

Great Char·ter another name for **MAGNA CARTA**.

great circle ▶ n. a circle on the surface of a sphere that lies in a plane passing through the sphere's center. As it represents the shortest distance between any two points on a sphere, a great circle of the earth is the preferred route taken by a ship or aircraft.

great·coat /ˈgrātˌkōt/ ▶ n. a long heavy overcoat.

great crest·ed grebe ▶ n. a large grebe with a crest and ear ruffs in the breeding season, found from Europe to New Zealand. ● *Podiceps cristatus*, family Podicipedidae.

Great Dane ▶ n. a dog of a very large, powerful, short-haired breed.

Great Dane

Great De·pres·sion see **DEPRESSION**.

Great Dis·mal Swamp (also **Dismal Swamp**) an area of swampland in southeastern Virginia and northeastern North Carolina.

Great Di·vide another name for **CONTINENTAL DIVIDE** or **GREAT DIVIDING RANGE**.

great di·vide ▶ n. a distinction regarded as significant and very difficult to ignore or overcome: *the great divide between workers and management.* ■ the boundary between life and death: *she is still on the human side of the great divide.*

Great Di·vid·ing Range a mountain system in eastern Australia. Curving roughly parallel to the coast, it extends from eastern Victoria to northern Queensland.

great e·gret ▶ n. a large white heron of North and South America. Its yellow bill turns orange when breeding. Also called **AMERICAN EGRET**. ● *Casmerodius albus*, family Ardeidae.

great egret

Great·er An·til·les /anˈtilēz/ see **ANTILLES**.

great·er cel·an·dine /ˈselənˌdīn, -ˌdēn/ ▶ n. a yellow-flowered Eurasian plant of the poppy family. Its toxic orange sap has long been used in herbal medicine, esp. for disorders of the eyes and skin. ● *Chelidonium majus*, family Papaveraceae.

Great·er Sun·da Is·lands /ˈsəndə, ˈso͞ondə/ see **SUNDA ISLANDS**.

Great Ex·hi·bi·tion the first international exhibition of the products of industry, promoted by Prince Albert and held in the Crystal Palace in London in 1851.

Great Falls an industrial city in north central Montana, on the Missouri River; pop. 59,251 (est. 2008).

Great Glen a large fault valley in Scotland that extends southwest for 60 miles (97 km) from the Moray Firth to Loch Linnhe. It contains Loch Ness. Also called **GLEN MORE**.

great-grandchild ▶ n. a son or daughter of one's grandchild.

great-grand·daugh·ter ▶ n. a daughter of one's grandchild.

great-grand·fa·ther ▶ n. the father of one's grandmother or grandfather.

great-grand·moth·er ▶ n. the mother of one's grandmother or grandfather.

great-grand·par·ent ▶ n. the mother or father of one's grandparent.

great-grand·son ▶ n. a son of one's grandchild.

great-heart·ed ▶ adj. dated having a noble, generous, and courageous spirit.
– DERIVATIVES **great-heart·ed·ness** n.

great horned owl ▶ n. a large owl found throughout North and South America, with hornlike ear tufts. ● *Bubo virginianus*, family Strigidae.

great horned owl

Great In·di·an Des·ert another name for **THAR DESERT**.

Great Lakes a group of five large interconnected lakes in central North America that consist of lakes Superior, Michigan, Huron, Erie, and Ontario, and constitute the largest area of fresh water in the world. Lake Michigan is wholly within the US, and the others lie on the Canada–US border. Connected to the Atlantic Ocean by the St. Lawrence Seaway, the Great Lakes form an important commercial waterway.

Great Lake State a nickname for the state of **MICHIGAN**.

Great Land a nickname for the state of **ALASKA**.

Great Leap For·ward an unsuccessful attempt made under Mao Zedong in China 1958–60 to hasten the process of industrialization and improve agricultural production by reorganizing the population into large rural collectives and adopting labor-intensive industrial methods.

great·ly /ˈgrātlē/ ▶ adv. by a considerable amount; very much: *I admire him greatly* | [as submodifier] *they now have greatly increased powers.*

Great Moth·er ▶ n. another name for **MOTHER GODDESS**.

Great Neb·u·la Astronomy **1** (also **Great Nebula in Andromeda**) the Andromeda Galaxy.
2 (also **Great Nebula in Orion**) a bright emission nebula in Orion, visible to the naked eye.

great-neph·ew ▶ n. a son of one's nephew or niece.

great·ness /ˈgrātnəs/ ▶ n. the quality of being great, distinguished, or eminent: *Elgar's greatness as a composer.*

great-niece ▶ n. a daughter of one's nephew or niece.

great north·ern div·er ▶ n. chiefly Brit. another term for **COMMON LOON** (see **LOON**[2]).

great or·gan ▶ n. the chief keyboard in a large organ and its related pipes and mechanism.

Great Ouse /o͞oz/ another name for **OUSE** (sense 1).

Great Plague a serious outbreak of bubonic plague in England in 1665–6, in which about one fifth of the population of London died. It was the last major outbreak in Britain.

Great Plains a vast area of plains east of the Rocky Mountains in North America that extend from the valleys of the Mackenzie River in Canada to southern Texas.

Great Pyrenees ▶ n. a large, heavily built dog of a white breed, with a thick shaggy double coat.

Great Red Spot Astronomy a weather system on the planet Jupiter which measures over 6,200 miles (10,000 km) across and has persisted at least since the beginning of telescopic observations.

Great Rift Val·ley a large system of rift valleys in eastern Africa and the Middle East, the largest in the world, that runs for about 3,000 miles (4,285 km) from the Jordan valley in Syria into Mozambique. It is marked by a chain of lakes and a series of volcanoes, including Mount Kilimanjaro.

great room ▶ n. a large room in a modern house that combines features of a living room with those of a dining room or family room.

Great Rus·sian ▶ adj. & n. former term for **RUSSIAN** (language and people), as distinguished from other peoples and languages of the Russian Empire.

Great St. Ber·nard Pass see **ST. BERNARD PASS**.

Great Salt Lake a salt lake in northern Utah, near Salt Lake City. With an area of about 1,000 square miles (2,590 sq km), it is the largest salt lake in North America.

Great Sand Sea an area of desert in northeastern Africa, on the border between Libya and Egypt.

Great Sand·y Des·ert 1 a large desert in northwestern Australia, in north central Western Australia.
2 another name for **RUB' AL-KHALI**.

Great Schism /ˈs(k)izəm/ **1** the breach between the Eastern and the Western Churches, traditionally dated to 1054 and becoming final in 1472.
2 the period 1378–1417, when the Western Church was divided by the creation of antipopes.

Great Seal ▶ n. a seal used for the authentication of state documents of the highest importance, held by the Secretary of State.

great sku·a /ˈskyo͞oə/ ▶ n. a large North Atlantic skua with mainly brown plumage, feeding by robbing other seabirds. ● *Catharacta skua*, family Stercorariidae.

Great Slave Lake a large lake in southwestern Northwest Territories, Canada. The deepest lake in North America, it reaches a depth of 2,015 feet (615 m). The Mackenzie River flows out of it.

Great Smok·y Moun·tains (also **Smoky Mountains** or **Smokies**) a range of the Appalachian Mountains in southwestern North Carolina and eastern Tennessee. They are named for a frequent haze.

Great So·ci·e·ty ▶ n. a domestic program in the administration of President Lyndon B. Johnson that instituted federally sponsored social welfare programs.

great tit ▶ n. a tit (songbird) with a black head and white cheeks, occurring in many different races from western Europe to eastern Asia. ● *Parus major*, family Paridae.

Great Trek the northward migration 1835–37 of large numbers of Boers, discontented with British rule in the Cape, to the areas where they eventually founded the Transvaal Republic and Orange Free State.

great-un·cle ▶ n. an uncle of one's mother or father.

Great Vic·to·ri·a Des·ert /vikˈtôrēə/ a desert region in Australia that straddles the boundary between Western Australia and South Australia.

Great Wall of Chi·na a fortified wall in northern China, extending some 1,500 miles (2,400 km) from Kansu province to the Yellow Sea north of Beijing. It was first built *c.*210 BC, as a protection against nomad invaders. The present wall dates from the Ming dynasty.

Great Wall of China

Great War another name for **World War I**.

great white shark ▶ **n.** a large, aggressive shark of warm seas, with a brownish or gray back, white underparts, and large triangular teeth. Also called **white pointer**. ● *Carcharodon carcharias*, family Lamnidae.

Great White Way a nickname for **Broadway**.

greave /grēv/ ▶ **n.** historical a piece of armor used to protect the shin.
– ORIGIN Middle English: from Old French *greve* 'shin, greave,' of unknown origin.

grebe /grēb/ ▶ **n.** a diving waterbird with a long neck, lobed toes, and almost no tail, typically having bright breeding plumage used in display. ● Family Podicipedidae: several genera. The several North American species include the **western grebe** (*Aechmorphorus occidentalis*) and the **pied-billed grebe** (*Podilymbus podiceps*).
– ORIGIN mid 18th cent.: from French *grèbe* (term used in the Savoy region), of unknown origin.

pied-billed grebe

Gre·cian /'grēSHən/ ▶ **adj.** of or relating to ancient Greece, esp. its architecture.
– ORIGIN late Middle English: from Old French *grecien*, from Latin *Graecia* 'Greece.'

Gre·cian nose ▶ **n.** a straight nose that continues the line of the forehead without a dip.

Gre·cism /'grēsizəm/ (also chiefly Brit. **Graecism**) ▶ **n.** a Greek idiom or grammatical feature, esp. as imitated in another language. ■ the Greek spirit, style, or mode of expression, esp. as imitated in a work of art.
– ORIGIN late 16th cent.: from French *grécisme* or medieval Latin *Graecismus*, from *Graecus* (see **Greek**).

Gre·co[1] /'grekō/, José (1918–2001), US dancer and choreographer; born in Italy. He had his own dance company from 1931 and also appeared in movies such as *Around the World in 80 Days* (1956).

Gre·co[2] see **El Greco**.

Greco- (also chiefly Brit. **Graeco-**) ▶ **comb. form** Greek; Greek and ...: *Grecophile* | *Greco-Turkish*. ■ relating to Greece.

Gre·co-Ro·man /'grekō/ (also chiefly Brit. **Graeco-Roman**) ▶ **adj.** of or relating to the ancient Greeks and Romans. ■ denoting a style of wrestling in which holds below the waist are prohibited.

Greece /grēs/ a country in southeastern Europe; pop. 10,737,400 (est. 2009); official language, Greek; capital, Athens.

> The age of the classical city states, of which the most prominent were Athens and Sparta, reached its peak in the 5th century BC, after which Greece fell to Macedonia and then became part of the Roman and Byzantine Empires. It was conquered by the Ottoman Turks in 1466 and remained under Turkish rule until the war of independence from 1821 until 1830, after which it became a kingdom. The monarchy was overthrown in a military coup in 1967, and a civilian republic was established in 1974. Greece joined the EC (now the EU) in 1981.

greed /grēd/ ▶ **n.** intense and selfish desire for something, esp. wealth, power, or food.
– ORIGIN late 16th cent.: back-formation from **greedy**.

greed·y /'grēdē/ ▶ **adj.** (**greedier, greediest**) having or showing an intense and selfish desire for something, esp. wealth or power: *greedy thieves who plundered a defense contractor*. ■ having an excessive desire or appetite for food.
– DERIVATIVES **greed·i·ly** /-dəlē/ **adv.**, **greed·i·ness n.**
– ORIGIN Old English *grǣdig*, of Germanic origin.

Greek /grēk/ ▶ **adj.** of or relating to Greece, its people, or their language. Compare with **Hellenic**.
▶ **n. 1** a native or inhabitant of modern Greece, or a person of Greek descent. ■ a Greek-speaking person in the ancient world, typically a native of one of the city states of Greece and the eastern Mediterranean.
2 the ancient or modern language of Greece, the only representative of the Hellenic branch of the Indo-European family.

> The ancient form of Greek was spoken in the southern Balkan peninsula from the 2nd millennium BC. The Greek alphabet, used from the 1st millennium BC onwards, was adapted from the Phoenician alphabet. The dialect of classical Athens formed the basis of the standard dialect (*koine*) from the 3rd century BC onwards, and this remained as a literary language during the periods of the Byzantine Empire and Turkish rule (see **katharevousa**). The colloquial language, however, continued to evolve independently (see **demotic**).

3 a member of a fraternity or sorority having a Greek-letter name.
– PHRASES **beware of Greeks bearing gifts** proverb if a rival or enemy shows one generosity or kindness, one should be suspicious of their motives. [with allusion to Virgil's *Aeneid* (ii. 49).] **it's (all) Greek to me** informal I can't understand it at all.
– DERIVATIVES **Greek·ness n.**
– ORIGIN Old English *Grēcas* 'the Greeks,' from Latin *Graeci*, the name given by the Romans to the people who called themselves the Hellenes, from Greek *Graikoi*, which according to Aristotle was the prehistoric name of the Hellenes.

Greek Cath·o·lic ▶ **n. 1** a member of the Eastern Orthodox Church.
2 a Uniate member of a church observing the Greek rite.

Greek Church another term for **Greek Orthodox Church**.

Greek cof·fee ▶ **n.** very strong black coffee served with the fine grounds in it.

Greek cross ▶ **n.** a cross of which all four arms are of equal length.

Greek fire ▶ **n.** historical a combustible compound emitted by a flame-throwing weapon and used to set light to enemy ships. It was first used by the Greeks besieged in Constantinople (673–78). It ignited on contact with water, and was probably based on naphtha and quicklime.

Greek god ▶ **n.** informal an extremely handsome man.

Greek key ▶ **n.** a pattern of interlocking right-angled spirals.

Greek Or·tho·dox Church (also **Greek Church**) the Eastern Orthodox Church, which uses the Byzantine rite in Greek, in particular the national Church of Greece. See **Orthodox Church**.

Greek re·vi·val ▶ **n.** a neoclassical style of architecture inspired by and incorporating features of Greek temples from the 5th century BC, popular in the US and Europe in the first half of the 19th century.

Greek sal·ad ▶ **n.** a salad consisting of tomatoes, olives, and feta cheese.

Gree·ley[1] /'grēlē/ an agricultural and commercial city in north central Colorado; pop. 91,492 (est. 2008).

Gree·ley[2], Horace (1811–72), US journalist and political leader. He founded the *New York Tribune* in 1841. An abolitionist and supporter of the Free Soil movement, he became known for his advice "Go West, young man."

green /grēn/ ▶ **adj. 1** of the color between blue and yellow in the spectrum; colored like grass or emeralds: *the leaves are bright green*. ■ consisting of fresh vegetables of this color: *a green salad*. ■ denoting a light or flag of this color used as a signal to proceed. ■ (of a ski run) of the lowest level of difficulty, as indicated by colored markers on the run. ■ Physics denoting one of three colors of quark.
2 covered with grass, trees, or other plants: *proposals that would smother green fields with development*. ■ (usu. **Green**) concerned with or supporting protection of the environment as a political principle: *a Green candidate for the European parliament*. ■ (of a product) not harmful to the environment.
3 (of a plant or fruit) young or unripe: *green shoots*. ■ (of wood) unseasoned. ■ (of food or leather) not dried, smoked, or tanned. ■ (of a person) inexperienced, naive, or gullible: *a green recruit fresh from college*. ■ (of a memory) not fading: *clubs devoted to keeping green the memory of Sherlock Holmes*. ■ still strong or vigorous: *first there was green old age, hardly different from middle age*. ■ archaic (of a wound) fresh; not healed.
4 (of the complexion or a person) pale and sickly-looking: *"Are you all right? You look absolutely green."*
▶ **n. 1** green color or pigment: *major roads are marked in green*. ■ green clothes or material: *two girls in red and green*. ■ green foliage or growing plants: *that lovely canopy of green over Puritan Road*. ■ informal, dated money: *you'll save yourself some green*.
2 a green thing, in particular: ■ a green light.
3 a piece of public or common grassy land, esp. in the center of a town: *a house overlooking the green*. ■ an area of smooth, very short grass immediately surrounding a hole on a golf course.
4 (**greens**) green leafy vegetables: *salad greens* | *collard greens*.
5 (usu. **Green**) a member or supporter of an environmentalist group or party.
▶ **v.** make or become green, in particular: ■ [with obj.] make (an urban or desert area) more verdant by planting or encouraging trees or other greenery: *greening the desert*. ■ [with obj.] make less harmful or more sensitive to the environment: *the importance of greening this industry*. ■ [no obj.] become green in color, through age or by becoming covered with plants: *the roof was greening with lichen*.
– DERIVATIVES **green·ish adj.**, **green·ly adv.**, **green·ness n.**
– ORIGIN Old English *grēne* (adjective), *grēnian* (verb), of Germanic origin; related to Dutch *groen*, German *grün*, also to **grass** and **grow**.

green al·gae ▶ **plural n.** photosynthetic algae that contain chlorophyll and store starch in discrete chloroplasts. They are eukaryotic and most live in fresh water, ranging from unicellular flagellates to more complex multicellular forms. ● Treated either as plants (division Chlorophyta) or as protozoans (phylum Chlorophyta, kingdom Protista). The classification of green algae is complex and under review.

green au·dit ▶ **n.** an assessment of a business in terms of its impact on the environment.

Green·a·way /'grēnə,wā/, Kate (1846–1901), English artist; full name *Catherine Greenaway*. She is known esp. for her illustrations of children's books such as *Mother Goose* (1881).

green·back /'grēn,bak/ ▶ **n. 1** informal a dollar bill; a dollar: *the beer she purchased with our last greenback*.
2 informal an animal with a green back, esp. a race of the cutthroat trout found only in Colorado.

Green Bay an industrial port city in northeastern Wisconsin, on Green Bay; pop. 101,025 (est. 2008).

green bean ▶ **n.** the immature pod of any of various bean plants, eaten as a vegetable. See also **string bean**.

green belt ▶ **n. 1** a green belt marking a level of proficiency in judo, karate, or other martial arts below that of a brown belt. ■ a person qualified to wear this.
2 (**greenbelt**) an area of open land around a city, on which building is restricted.

Green Be·ret ▶ **n.** informal a member of the US Army Special Forces.

green·bot·tle /'grēn,bätl/ ▶ **n.** a metallic green fly that sometimes lays eggs in wounds on sheep or other animals. ● Genus *Lucilia*, family Calliphoridae: several species, in particular the common *L. caesar*.

green·bri·er /'grēn,brīər/ (also **greenbriar**) ▶ **n.** a green-stemmed North American vine of the lily family, typically prickly and with blue-black berries. Also called **catbrier**. ● Genus *Smilax*, family Liliaceae: several species, in particular the woody and thorny *S. rotundifolia*.

green·bul /'grēn,bo͝ol/ ▶ **n.** an African bulbul with an olive-green back. ● Family Pycnonotidae: several genera, in particular *Phyllastrephus* and *Pycnonotus*, and numerous species.

green card ▶ **n. 1** (in the US) a permit allowing a foreign national to live and work permanently in the US.
2 (in the UK) an international insurance document for motorists.

green chan·nel ▶ **n.** (at a customs area in an airport or port) the passage that should be taken by arriving passengers who have no goods to declare.

green cheese ▶ **n.** unripened or unmatured cheese.

green·chop /ˈgrēnˌCHäp/ ▶ **v.** [with obj.] cut (grass) in order to bring to cattle or store as silage.

green-col·lar ▶ **adj.** denoting or relating to employment concerned with products and services designed to improve the quality of the environment: *green-collar jobs.*
– ORIGIN on the pattern of WHITE-COLLAR and BLUE-COLLAR.

green corn ▶ **n.** the tender ears of young sweet corn, suitable for cooking and eating.

green crab (also **European green crab**) ▶ **n.** a name for the common shore crab in its capacity as an invasive species in the US.

green drag·on ▶ **n.** a North American arum with a large divided leaf, a greenish-cream spathe, and a very long white spadix. Also called DRAGON ARUM. ● *Arisaema dracontium*, family Araceae.

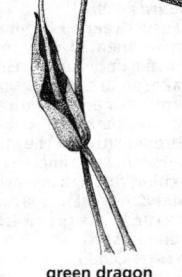

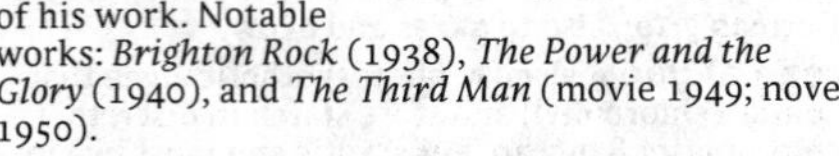
green dragon

Greene[1] /grēn/, (Henry) Graham (1904–91), English novelist. The moral paradoxes he saw in his Roman Catholic faith underlie much of his work. Notable works: *Brighton Rock* (1938), *The Power and the Glory* (1940), and *The Third Man* (movie 1949; novel 1950).

Greene[2], Nathanael (1742–86), American general. Noted as a military strategist, he forced the British out of Georgia and the Carolinas in a series of battles (1781) during the American Revolution.

green earth ▶ **n.** another term for TERRE VERTE.

Green·er /ˈgrēnər/ ▶ **n.** a type of shotgun.
– ORIGIN late 19th cent.: named after William *Greener* (1806–69) or his son William W. *Greener*, gunsmiths and authors.

green·er·y /ˈgrēnərē/ ▶ **n.** green foliage, growing plants, or vegetation.

green·eye /ˈgrēnˌī/ ▶ **n.** a small, slender-bodied fish with iridescent pale green eyes, occurring in deep waters of the western Atlantic. ● Family Chlorophthalmidae: two genera and several species.

green-eyed mon·ster ▶ **n.** (**the green-eyed monster**) informal, humorous jealousy personified.
– ORIGIN from Shakespeare's *Othello* (III. 3. 166).

green fat ▶ **n.** the green, gelatinous part of a turtle, highly regarded by gourmets.

green fee ▶ **n.** another term for GREENS FEE.

green·field /ˈgrēnˌfēld/ ▶ **adj.** [attrib.] relating to or denoting previously undeveloped sites for commercial development or exploitation. Compare with BROWNFIELD.

green·finch /ˈgrēnˌfinCH/ ▶ **n.** a Eurasian finch with green and yellow plumage. ● Genus *Carduelis*, family Fringillidae: three species, in particular the common *C. chloris* of Europe and the Middle East.

green fin·gers ▶ **plural n.** British term for GREEN THUMB.

green·fly /ˈgrēnˌflī/ ▶ **n.** (pl. **same** or **greenflies**) a green aphid that is a common pest of crops and garden plants. ● Several species in the family Aphididae.

green·gage /ˈgrēnˌgāj/ ▶ **n. 1** (also **greengage plum**) a sweet, greenish fruit resembling a small plum. Also called GAGE[3].
2 the tree bearing this fruit. ● *Prunus domestica* subsp. *italica* (or *P. italica*), family Rosaceae.
– ORIGIN early 18th cent.: named after Sir William *Gage* (1657–1727), the English botanist who introduced it to England.

Green God·dess ▶ **n.** a salad dressing made with mayonnaise, garlic, and anchovies, and colored with parsley and green onions.

green goose ▶ **n.** a goose that is killed when under four months old and eaten without stuffing.

green·gro·cer /ˈgrēnˌgrōsər/ ▶ **n.** Brit. a retailer of fruit and vegetables.
– DERIVATIVES **green·gro·cer·y** /-ˌgrōs(ə)rē/ **n.**

green·heart /ˈgrēnˌhärt/ ▶ **n.** a South American evergreen tree of the laurel family, yielding hard greenish timber that is used for marine work because of its resistance to marine borers. ● *Ocotea rodiaei*, family Lauraceae. ■ this timber, or similar timber from various other tropical trees.

green·horn /ˈgrēnˌhôrn/ ▶ **n.** informal a person who is new to or inexperienced at a particular activity.

green·house /ˈgrēnˌhous/ ▶ **n.** a glass building in which plants are grown that need protection from cold weather.

green·house ef·fect ▶ **n.** the trapping of the sun's warmth in a planet's lower atmosphere due to the greater transparency of the atmosphere to visible radiation from the sun than to infrared radiation emitted from the planet's surface.

> It is theorized that on earth the increasing quantity of atmospheric carbon dioxide from the burning of fossil fuels, together with the release of other gases, is causing an increased greenhouse effect and leading to global warming. A greenhouse effect involving CO_2 is also responsible for the very high surface temperature of Venus. See also GLOBAL WARMING.

green·house gas ▶ **n.** a gas that contributes to the greenhouse effect by absorbing infrared radiation, e.g., carbon dioxide and chlorofluorocarbons.

green·ie /ˈgrēnē/ ▶ **n.** informal, often derogatory a person who campaigns for protection of the environment.

Green·ing /ˈgrēniNG/ ▶ **n.** an apple of a variety that is green when ripe.
– ORIGIN early 17th cent. (originally denoting a kind of pear): probably from Middle Dutch *groeninc*, a kind of apple, from *groen* 'green.'

green jer·sey ▶ **n.** (in a cycling race involving stages) a green knit shirt worn each day by the rider accumulating the highest number of points, and presented at the end of the race to the rider with the highest overall points total.

green·keep·er /ˈgrēnˌkēpər/ ▶ **n.** another term for GREENSKEEPER.

Green·land /ˈgrēnlənd/ a large island that lies to the northeast of North America, mostly within the Arctic Circle; pop. 57,600 (est. 2009); capital, Godthåb (Nuuk). Danish name GRØNLAND; called in Inuit KALAALLIT NUNAAT.

> Only 5 percent of Greenland is habitable; the population is largely Inuit. Formerly a Norse and a Danish settlement, Greenland became a dependency of Denmark in 1953 with internal autonomy in 1979. It withdrew from the European Community in 1985.

– DERIVATIVES **Green·land·er n.**

Green·land hal·i·but ▶ **n.** an edible halibut with a black or dark brown upper side that is found in cold, deep waters of the north. ● *Reinhardtius hippoglossoides*, family Pleuronectidae.

Green·land·ic /grēnˈlandik/ ▶ **n.** a dialect of the Inuit language that is the one of the official languages of Greenland, the other being Danish.

> **USAGE** See usage at INUIT.

Green·land right whale (also **Greenland whale**) ▶ **n.** another term for BOWHEAD.

Green·land Sea a sea that lies between the east coast of Greenland and the Svalbard archipelago, part of the Arctic Ocean.

green·let /ˈgrēnlit/ ▶ **n.** a small warblerlike vireo with drab plumage, found in Central and South America. ● Genus *Hylophilus*, family Vireonidae: several species.

green light ▶ **n.** a green traffic light giving permission to proceed. ■ permission to go ahead with a project: *the commission has given the green light for a wind-farm development.*
▶ **v.** (**green-light**) [with obj.] give permission to go ahead with (a project, esp. a movie).

green·ling /ˈgrēnliNG/ ▶ **n.** (pl. **same** or **greenlings**) a spiny-finned, edible fish of the North Pacific. ● Family Hexagrammidae: two genera and several species, including the lingcod.

green liz·ard ▶ **n.** a lizard that is typically green with (esp. in the male) a blue throat, native to Europe and southwestern Asia. ● *Lacerta viridis*, family Lacertidae.

green·mail /ˈgrēnˌmāl/ ▶ **n.** Stock Market the practice of buying enough shares in a company to threaten a takeover, forcing the owners to buy them back at a higher price in order to retain control.
– DERIVATIVES **green·mail·er n.**
– ORIGIN 1980s: blend of GREEN and BLACKMAIL.

green man ▶ **n.** historical a man dressed up in greenery to represent a wild man of the woods or seasonal fertility. ■ a carved image of this, often seen in medieval English churches as a human face with branches and foliage growing out of the mouth.

green ma·nure ▶ **n.** a fertilizer consisting of growing plants that are plowed back into the soil.

green mon·key ▶ **n.** a common African guenon with greenish-brown upper parts and a black face. Compare with GRIVET and VERVET. ● *Cercopithecus aethiops*, family Cercopithecidae, in particular the race *C. a. sabaeus* of West Africa, which is often tamed.

green monkey disease ▶ **n.** another term for MARBURG DISEASE.

Green Moun·tains a range of the Appalachian Mountains that extends north to south through Vermont and reaches 4,393 feet (1,340 m) at Mount Mansfield.

Green Moun·tain State a nickname for the state of VERMONT.

green·ock·ite /ˈgrēnəˌkīt/ ▶ **n.** a mineral consisting of cadmium sulfide and typically occurring as a yellow crust on zinc ores.
– ORIGIN mid 19th cent.: from the name of Lord *Greenock*, who later became Earl Cathcart (1783–1859), + -ITE[1].

green on·ion ▶ **n.** an onion taken from the ground before the bulb has formed, typically eaten raw in salad; a scallion.

Green Par·ty ▶ **n.** an environmentalist political party.

green pep·per ▶ **n.** the unripe fruit of a sweet pepper, which is mild in flavor and widely used in cooking. ■ the plant that yields this fruit. See CAPSICUM.

green pi·geon ▶ **n.** a fruit-eating pigeon with mainly green plumage occurring in the Old World tropics. ● Genus *Treron*, family Columbidae: many species. See also FRUIT PIGEON.

green plov·er ▶ **n.** Brit. the northern lapwing (see LAPWING).

green rev·o·lu·tion ▶ **n.** a large increase in crop production in developing countries achieved by the use of fertilizers, pesticides, and high-yield crop varieties.

Green Riv·er a river that flows for 730 miles (1,130 km) from Wyoming through Colorado and Utah into the Colorado River.

green room ▶ **n.** a room in a theater or studio in which performers can relax when they are not performing.

green·sand /ˈgrēnˌsand/ ▶ **n.** Geology a greenish kind of sandstone, often loosely consolidated.

Greens·boro /ˈgrēnzˌbərə/ a city in north central North Carolina; pop. 250,642 (est. 2008).

green screen ▶ **n.** see BLUE SCREEN.

greens fee (also **green fee**) ▶ **n.** a charge for playing one round or session on a golf course.

green·shank /ˈgrēnˌSHaNGk/ ▶ **n.** a large sandpiper with long, greenish legs and gray plumage, breeding in northern Eurasia and North America. ● Genus *Tringa*, family Scolopacidae: two species, in particular *T. nebularia*.

greens·keep·er /ˈgrēnzˌkēpər/ (also **greenkeeper**) ▶ **n.** a person employed to look after a golf course.

green snake ▶ **n.** a harmless American snake with a green back and white or yellowish underparts. ● Genus *Opheodrys*, family Colubridae: two species.

green space ▶ **n.** an area of grass, trees, or other vegetation set apart for recreational or aesthetic purposes in an otherwise urban environment.

Green·span /ˈgrēnˌspan/, Alan (1926–), US economist. As chairman of the National Commission on Social Security Reform 1981–83, he helped to prevent the bankruptcy of the Social Security system. He served as chairman of the Federal Reserve Board 1987–2006.

green·stick frac·ture /ˈgrēnˌstik/ ▶ **n.** a fracture of the bone, occurring typically in children, in which one side of the bone is broken and the other only bent.

green·stone /ˈgrēnˌstōn/ ▶ **n.** Geology a greenish igneous rock containing feldspar and hornblende. ■ chiefly NZ a variety of nephrite.

green·sward /ˈgrēnˌswôrd/ ▶ **n.** archaic or literary grass-covered ground.

green tea ▶ **n.** tea that is made from unfermented leaves and is pale in color and slightly bitter in flavor, produced mainly in China and Japan. Compare with BLACK TEA.

green thumb ▶ **n.** informal natural talent for growing plants: *you don't need a green thumb to grow them.*

green tur·tle ▶ **n.** a sea turtle with an olive-brown shell, often living close to the coast and extensively hunted for food. ● *Chelonia mydas*, family Cheloniidae.

green turtle

Green·ville /ˈgrēnˌvil, -vəl/ **1** a city in northwestern Mississippi, in the Delta; pop. 35,764 (est. 2008).
2 a city in eastern North Carolina, near the Pamlico River; pop. 79,629 (est. 2008).
3 an industrial city in northwestern South Carolina; pop. 59,988 (est. 2008).

green vit·ri·ol ▶ **n.** archaic crystalline ferrous sulfate.

green·ware /ˈgrēnˌwe(ə)r/ ▶ **n.** unfired pottery.

green·wash /ˈgrēnˌwäsн, -ˌwôsн/ (also **greenwashing**) ▶ **n.** disinformation disseminated by an organization so as to present an environmentally responsible public image: *the recycling bins in the cafeteria are just feeble examples of their corporate greenwash.*
– DERIVATIVES **green·wash·er n.**
– ORIGIN 1980s: from *green* 'not ecologically harmful,' on the pattern of *whitewash*.

green·way /ˈgrēnˌwā/ ▶ **n.** a strip of undeveloped land near an urban area, set aside for recreational use or environmental protection.

green·weed /ˈgrēnˌwēd/ see **DYER'S GREENWEED**.

Green·wich 1 /ˈgrinij, -icн, ˈgren-/ a London borough on the southern bank of the Thames River.
2 /ˈgrenicн/ a town in southwestern Connecticut, on Long Island Sound, an affluent suburb of New York City; pop. 61,937 (est. 2008).

Green·wich Mean Time (abbr.: **GMT**) (also **Greenwich time**) the mean solar time at the Greenwich meridian, adopted as the standard time in a zone that includes the British Isles.

Green·wich me·rid·i·an ▶ **n.** the prime meridian, which passes through the former Royal Observatory at Greenwich, England, adopted internationally as the earth's zero of longitude in 1884.

Green·wich Vil·lage a district of New York City on the lower west side of Manhattan, traditionally associated with writers, artists, and musicians.

green·wood /ˈgrēnˌwo͝od/ ▶ **n.** archaic a wood or forest in leaf (regarded as the typical scene of medieval outlaw life).

green wood·peck·er ▶ **n.** a large green and yellow woodpecker with a red crown and a laughing call, found from Europe to central Asia. ● *Picus viridis*, family Picidae.

green·y /ˈgrēnē/ ▶ **adj.** [often in combination] slightly green: *the greeny-brown surface of the stone.*

Greer /gri(ə)r/, Germaine (1939–), Australian feminist and writer. She first wrote *The Female Eunuch* (1970), an analysis of women's subordination in a male-dominated society. Other books include *The Change* (1991), about social attitudes toward female aging.

greet¹ /grēt/ ▶ **v.** [with obj.] give a polite word or sign of welcome or recognition to (someone) on meeting. ■ receive or acknowledge (something) in a specified way: *everyone present greeted this idea warmly.* ■ (of a sight or sound) become apparent to or be noticed by (someone) on arrival somewhere: *flowers and cheers greeted the shipyard workers.*
– ORIGIN Old English *grētan* 'approach, attack, or salute'; related to Dutch *groeten* and German *grüssen* 'greet.'

greet² ▶ **v.** [no obj.] Scottish weep; cry: *he sat down on the armchair and started to greet.*
– ORIGIN Old English, partly from *grētan* 'cry out, rage,' partly from *grēotan* 'lament,' both of Germanic origin.

greet·er /ˈgrētər/ ▶ **n.** a person who greets people entering a store, church service, or other public place.

greet·ing /ˈgrētiɴɢ/ ▶ **n.** a polite word or sign of welcome or recognition: *Mandy shouted a greeting.* ■ the action of giving such a sign: *she raised her hand in greeting.* ■ (usu. **greetings**) a formal expression of goodwill, said on meeting or in a written message: *warm greetings to you all.*

greet·ing card (Brit. **greetings card**) ▶ **n.** a decorative card sent to convey good wishes on some occasion.

greg·a·rine /ˈgregəˌrin/ Zoology ▶ **adj.** of or relating to a group of microscopic, wormlike protozoans that are internal parasites of insects, annelids, and other invertebrates. ■ (of movement) slow and gliding, as seen in these protozoans.
▶ **n.** a gregarine protozoan. ● Class Gregarina (or subclass Gregarinidia), phylum Sporozoa, kingdom Protista.
– ORIGIN mid 19th cent.: from modern Latin *Gregarina*, from Latin *gregarius* (see **GREGARIOUS**).

gre·gar·i·ous /griˈge(ə)rēəs/ ▶ **adj.** (of a person) fond of company; sociable: *he was a popular and gregarious man.* ■ (of animals) living in flocks or loosely organized communities: *gregarious species forage in flocks from colonies or roosts.* ■ (of plants) growing in open clusters or in pure associations.
– DERIVATIVES **gre·gar·i·ous·ly adv.**, **gre·gar·i·ous·ness n.**
– ORIGIN mid 17th cent.: from Latin *gregarius* (from *grex, greg-* 'a flock') + **-OUS**.

Gre·go·ri·an cal·en·dar /grəˈgôrēən/ ▶ **n.** the calendar introduced in 1582 by Pope Gregory XIII, as a modification of the Julian calendar.

> To bring the calendar back into line with the solar year, 10 days were suppressed, and centenary years were made leap years only if they were divisible by 400. England did not adopt the reformed calendar until 1752, by which time 11 days had to be suppressed. At the same time, New Year's Day was changed from March 25 to January 1, and dates using the new calendar were designated 'New Style.'

Gre·go·ri·an chant ▶ **n.** church music sung as a single vocal line in free rhythm and a restricted scale (plainsong), in a style developed for the medieval Latin liturgy.
– ORIGIN mid 18th cent.: named after St. Gregory the Great (in Latin *Gregorius*), who is said to have standardized it.

Gre·go·ri·an tel·e·scope ▶ **n.** an early reflecting telescope in which light reflected from a concave elliptical secondary mirror passes through a hole in the primary mirror. It was rendered obsolete by the introduction of Newtonian and Cassegrain telescopes.
– ORIGIN mid 18th cent.: named after James *Gregory* (1638–75), the Scottish mathematician who invented it.

Greg·o·ry, St. /ˈgregərē/ (*c.*540–604), pope (as Gregory I) 590–604 and doctor of the Church; known as **St. Gregory the Great**. He sent St. Augustine to England to lead the country's conversion to Christianity. He is also credited with the introduction of Gregorian chant. Feast day, March 12.

Greg·o·ry XIII (1502–85), pope 1572–85; born in Italy. The Gregorian calendar, still in use, was introduced in 1582 as a result of his efforts to correct the errors in the Julian calendar.

Greg·o·ry of Na·zi·an·zus, St. /ˌnāzēˈanzəs/ (329–89), doctor of the Church; bishop of Constantinople. He upheld orthodoxy against the Arian and Apollinarian heresies, and he was influential in restoring adherence to the Nicene Creed. Feast day, (Eastern Church) January 25 and 30; (Western Church) January 2 (formerly May 9).

Greg·o·ry of Nys·sa, St. /ˈnisə/ (*c.*330–*c.*395), doctor of the Eastern Church; bishop of Nyssa in Cappadocia. The brother of St. Basil, he joined with St. Basil and St. Gregory of Nazianzus to oppose Arianism. Feast day, March 9.

Greg·o·ry of Tours, St. /to͝or/ (*c.*540–594), Frankish bishop and historian. He was elected bishop of Tours in 573. Feast day, November 17.

greige /grāzн/ ▶ **n.** a color between beige and gray.
– ORIGIN blend of **GRAY¹** and **BEIGE**, perhaps influenced by French *grège* 'raw (silk).'

grei·sen /ˈgrīzən/ ▶ **n.** Geology a light-colored rock containing quartz, mica, and fluorine-rich minerals, resulting from the alteration of granite by hot vapor from magma.
– ORIGIN late 19th cent.: from German, probably a dialect word, from *greis* 'gray with age.'

grem·lin /ˈgremlin/ ▶ **n.** informal an imaginary mischievous sprite regarded as responsible for an unexplained problem or fault, esp. a mechanical or electronic one: *a gremlin in my computer omitted a line.* ■ such a problem or fault.
– ORIGIN 1940s: perhaps suggested by **GOBLIN**.

Gre·nache /grəˈnäsн/ ▶ **n.** a variety of black wine grape native to the Languedoc-Roussillon region of France. ■ a sweet red dessert wine made from this grape.
– ORIGIN French.

Gre·na·da /grəˈnādə/ a country in the southern Windward Islands, in the Caribbean Sea, that consists of the island of Grenada and the southern Grenadine Islands; pop. 90,700 (est. 2009); capital, St. George's; languages, English (official) and English Creole.

> The island of Grenada was sighted in 1498 by Columbus. Colonized by the French, it was ceded to Britain in 1763, recaptured by the French, and restored to Britain in 1783. It became an independent Commonwealth of Nations state in 1974. Seizure of power by a left-wing military group in 1983 prompted an invasion by the US and some Caribbean countries; they withdrew in 1985.

– DERIVATIVES **Gre·na·di·an** /-ˈdēən/ **adj. & n.**

gre·nade /grəˈnād/ ▶ **n.** a small bomb thrown by hand or launched mechanically. ■ a glass receptacle containing chemicals that are released when the receptacle is thrown and broken, used for testing drains and extinguishing fires.
– ORIGIN mid 16th cent. (in the sense 'pomegranate'): from French, alteration of Old French (*pome*) *grenate* (see **POMEGRANATE**), on the pattern of Spanish *granada*. The bomb was so named because of its shape, supposedly resembling a pomegranate.

gren·a·dier /ˌgrenəˈdi(ə)r/ ▶ **n. 1** a soldier armed with grenades or a grenade launcher. ■ (**Grenadiers** or **Grenadier Guards**) (in the UK) the first regiment of the royal household infantry.
2 a common bottom-dwelling fish with a large head, a long tapering tail, and typically a luminous gland on the belly. Also called **RAT-TAIL**. ● Family Macrouridae: numerous genera and species.
– ORIGIN late 17th cent.: from French, from *grenade* (see **GRENADE**).

gren·a·dil·la /ˌgrenəˈdilə, -ˈdēyə/ ▶ **n.** variant spelling of **GRANADILLA**.

gren·a·dine¹ /ˈgrenəˌdēn, ˌgrenəˈdēn/ ▶ **n.** a sweet syrup made from pomegranates.
– ORIGIN French, from *grenade* 'pomegranate' (see **GRENADE**).

gren·a·dine² ▶ **n.** dress fabric of loosely woven silk or silk and wool.
– ORIGIN mid 19th cent.: from French (earlier *grenade*), 'grained silk,' from *grenu* 'grained,' from *grain* 'grain.'

Gren·a·dine Is·lands /ˌgrenəˈdēn/ (also **the Grenadines**) a chain of small islands in the Caribbean Sea, part of the Windward Islands. They are divided administratively between the islands of St. Vincent and Grenada.

Gren·del /ˈgrendl/ the water monster killed by Beowulf in the Old English epic poem *Beowulf*.

Gre·no·ble /grəˈnōbəl, grəˈnôbl(ə)/ a city in southeastern France; pop. 158,746 (2006).

Gren·ville /ˈgrenvəl/, George (1712–70), British statesman; prime minister 1763–65. The Stamp Act (1765), which aroused great opposition in the North American colonies, was passed during his term of office.

grep /grep/ Computing ▶ **n.** a Unix command used to search files for the occurrence of a string of characters that matches a specified pattern.
▶ **v.** (**greps, grepping, grepped**) [with obj.] search for (a string of characters) using grep.
– ORIGIN from the initial letters of global(ly) search regular expression print.

Gresh·am /ˈgresнəm/ a city in northwestern Oregon, east of Portland; pop. 101,221 (est. 2008).

Gresh·am's law Economics the tendency for money of lower intrinsic value to circulate more freely than money of higher intrinsic and equal nominal value (often expressed as "Bad money drives out good").

Gret·na Green /ˈgretnə/ a village in Scotland just north of the English border, near Carlisle, formerly a popular place for young runaway couples from England to be married without the parental consent required.

Gretz·ky /ˈgretskē/, Wayne (1961–), Canadian hockey player. The all-time leading scorer in the National Hockey League, he was voted most valuable player nine times. Hockey Hall of Fame (1999).

gre·vil·le·a /griˈvilēə/ ▶ **n.** an evergreen tree or shrub bearing conspicuous flowers that lack petals, most kinds of which are native to Australia. ● Genus *Grevillea*, family Proteaceae.
– ORIGIN modern Latin, named after Charles F. *Greville* (1749–1809), Scottish horticulturalist.

grew /gro͞o/ past of **GROW**.

Grey¹ /grā/, Charles, 2nd Earl (1764–1845), British statesman; prime minister 1830–34.

g

Grey[2], Lady Jane (1537–54), niece of Henry VIII; queen of England July 9–19, 1553. In 1553, to ensure a Protestant succession, **John Dudley**, the Duke of Northumberland, forced Jane to marry his son and persuaded the dying Edward VI to name Jane as his successor. She was deposed by forces loyal to Edward's (Catholic) sister Mary and was executed the following year.

Grey[3], Zane (1872–1939), US writer; born *Pearl Grey*. He wrote 54 westerns in a romanticized and formulaic style that sold over 13 million copies during his lifetime.

grey ▶ adj. British spelling of GRAY[1].

grey·beard ▶ n. British spelling of GRAYBEARD.

grey·hen /ˈgrā,hen/ ▶ n. the female of the black grouse.

grey·hound /ˈgrā,hound/ ▶ n. a dog of a tall, slender breed having keen sight and capable of high speed, used since ancient times for hunting small game and now chiefly in racing and coursing.
– ORIGIN Old English *grīghund*; the first element, related to Old Norse *grey* 'bitch,' is of unknown origin.

grey·hound rac·ing ▶ n. a sport in which greyhounds race around a circular or oval track in pursuit of a moving dummy hare and spectators bet on the outcome.

grey·lag ▶ n. British spelling of GRAYLAG.

grey·scale ▶ n. British spelling of GRAYSCALE.

grey·wacke ▶ n. British spelling of GRAYWACKE.

grib·ble /ˈgribəl/ ▶ n. a small marine isopod that bores into submerged wooden structures, often causing damage to pier timbers. ● *Limnoria lignorum*, order Isopoda.
– ORIGIN late 18th cent.: perhaps related to the verb GRUB.

grid /grid/ ▶ n. **1** a framework of spaced bars that are parallel to or cross each other; a grating: *the metal grids had been pulled across the foyer*.
2 a network of lines that cross each other to form a series of squares or rectangles: *a grid of tree-lined streets*. ■ a football field. ■ a network of cables or pipes for distributing power, esp. high-voltage transmission lines for electricity: *the second reactor was not connected to the grid until 1985*. ■ a network of regularly spaced lines on a map that cross one another at right angles and are numbered to enable the precise location of a place. ■ a pattern of lines marking the starting places on a auto-racing track: *first away from the grid*. ■ Electronics an electrode placed between the cathode and anode of a thermionic tube or cathode ray tube, serving to control or modulate the flow of electrons.
3 a number of computers linked together via the Internet so that their combined power may be harnessed to work on difficult problems.
▶ v. [with obj.] (usu. as adj. **gridded**) put into or set out as a grid: *a well-planned core of gridded streets*.
– ORIGIN mid 19th cent.: back-formation from GRIDIRON.

grid bi·as ▶ n. Electronics a fixed voltage applied between the cathode and the control grid of a thermionic tube in order to determine the grid's operating conditions.

grid·der /ˈgridər/ ▶ n. a football player.

grid·dle /ˈgridl/ ▶ n. **1** a heavy, flat iron plate that is heated and used for cooking food.
2 historical a miner's wire-bottomed sieve.
▶ v. [with obj.] **1** cook on a griddle: (as adj. **griddled**) *griddled corn cakes*.
2 historical screen (ore) with a griddle: *black copper ore is generally griddled out*.
– ORIGIN Middle English (denoting a gridiron): from Old French *gredil*, from Latin *craticula*, diminutive of *cratis* 'hurdle'; related to CRATE, GRATE[2], and GRILL[1].

grid·dle cake ▶ n. a flat cake, such as a pancake or a johnny cake, that is cooked on a griddle.

grid·i·ron /ˈgrid,īərn/ ▶ n. **1** a frame of parallel bars or beams, typically in two sets arranged at right angles, in particular: ■ a frame of parallel metal bars used for grilling meat or fish over an open fire. ■ a frame of parallel beams for supporting a ship in dock. ■ (in the theater) a framework over a stage supporting scenery and lighting.
2 a field for football, marked with regularly spaced parallel lines. ■ the game of football: [as modifier] *the national gridiron season*.
3 another term for GRID (sense 2 of the noun).
– ORIGIN Middle English *gredire*, alteration of *gredile* 'griddle' by association with IRON.

grid·lock /ˈgrid,läk/ ▶ n. **1** a traffic jam affecting a whole network of intersecting streets.
2 another term for DEADLOCK (sense 1 of the noun).
– DERIVATIVES **grid·locked** adj.

grid ref·er·ence ▶ n. a map reference indicating a location in terms of a series of vertical and horizontal grid lines identified by numbers or letters.

grief /grēf/ ▶ n. deep sorrow, esp. that caused by someone's death: *she was overcome with grief*. ■ informal trouble or annoyance: *they won't give you any grief in the next few days*.
– PHRASES **come to grief** have an accident; meet with disaster: *many a ship has come to grief along this shore*. **good grief!** an exclamation of irritation, frustration, or surprise.
– ORIGIN Middle English: from Old French *grief*, from *grever* 'to burden' (see GRIEVE).

grief-strick·en ▶ adj. overcome with deep sorrow.

Grieg /grēg/, Edvard (1843–1907), Norwegian composer, conductor, and violinist. Notable works: Piano Concerto in A minor (1869) and the incidental music to Henrik Ibsen's play *Peer Gynt* (1876).

Grier /gri(ə)r/, Robert Cooper (1794–1870), US Supreme Court associate justice 1846–70. Appointed to the Court by President Polk, he was a strong advocate for the Union before, during, and after the Civil War.

griev·ance /ˈgrēvəns/ ▶ n. a real or imagined wrong or other cause for complaint or protest, esp. unfair treatment: *failure to redress genuine grievances*. ■ an official statement of a complaint over something believed to be wrong or unfair: *three pilots have filed grievances against the company*. ■ a feeling of resentment over something believed to be wrong or unfair: *he was nursing a grievance*.
– ORIGIN Middle English (also in the sense 'injury'): from Old French *grevance*, from *grever* 'to burden' (see GRIEVE).

grieve /grēv/ ▶ v. [no obj.] suffer grief: *she grieved for her father*. ■ [with obj.] feel grief for or because of: *she did not have the opportunity to grieve her mother's death*. ■ [with obj.] cause great distress to (someone): *what grieves you, my son?* | [with obj.] *it grieves me to think of you in that house alone*.
– DERIVATIVES **griev·er** n.
– ORIGIN Middle English (also in the sense 'harm, oppress'): from Old French *grever* 'burden, encumber,' based on Latin *gravare*, from *gravis* 'heavy, grave' (see GRAVE[2]).

griev·ous /ˈgrēvəs/ ▶ adj. formal (of something bad) very severe or serious: *his death was a grievous blow* | *the American fleet suffered grievous losses*.
– DERIVATIVES **griev·ous·ly** adv., **griev·ous·ness** n.
– ORIGIN Middle English: from Old French *greveus*, from *grever* (see GRIEVE).

> **USAGE** Grievous ends with -ous and has two syllables: do not pronounce it with three syllables (GREE-vee-us), as if it ended with -ious.

griev·ous bod·i·ly harm (abbr.: **GBH**) ▶ n. Law serious physical injury inflicted on a person by the deliberate action of another.

grif·fin /ˈgrifin/ (also **gryphon**, **griffon** /ˈgrifən/) ▶ n. a mythical creature with the head and wings of an eagle and the body of a lion, typically depicted with pointed ears and with the eagle's legs taking the place of the forelegs.
– ORIGIN Middle English: from Old French *grifoun*, based on late Latin *gryphus*, via Latin from Greek *grups*, *grup-*.

griffin

Grif·fith /ˈgrifiTH/, D. W. (1875–1948), US movie director; full name *David Lewelyn Wark Griffith*. A pioneer in movies, he is responsible for introducing many cinematic techniques, including flashback and fade-out. Notable films: *The Birth of a Nation* (1915), *Intolerance* (1916), and *Broken Blossoms* (1919).

Grif·fith Joy·ner /ˈjoinər/, Florence (1959–98), US track and field athlete; called **Flojo**. She won three gold medals and established world records in the 100- and 200-meter and 4 x 100-meter races at the 1988 Olympic Games.

grif·fon /ˈgrifən/ ▶ n. **1** a dog of any of several terrierlike breeds originating in northwestern Europe. ■ (also **Brussels griffon**) a dog of a toy breed with a flat face and upturned chin.
2 (also **griffon vulture**) a large Old World vulture with predominantly pale brown plumage. ● Genus *Gyps*, family Accipitridae: four species, in particular the Eurasian *G. fulvus* and the African **Ruppell's griffon** (*G. ruepelli*).
3 variant spelling of GRIFFIN.
– ORIGIN Middle English (in sense 2 and sense 3): variant of GRIFFIN; sense 1 was adopted from French in the 18th cent.

grift /grift/ informal ▶ v. [no obj.] engage in petty swindling.
▶ n. a petty swindle.
– DERIVATIVES **grift·er** n.
– ORIGIN early 20th cent.: alteration of GRAFT[2].

grig /grig/ ▶ n. Brit. dialect **1** a small eel.
2 a grasshopper or cricket.
– PHRASES **(as) merry** (or **lively**) **as a grig** full of fun; extravagantly lively.
– ORIGIN Middle English (in the sense 'dwarf'): of unknown origin.

grill[1] /gril/ ▶ n. a metal framework used for cooking food over an open fire; a gridiron. ■ a portable device for cooking outdoors, consisting of such a framework placed over charcoal or gas fuel. ■ a dish of food, esp. meat, cooked using a grill. ■ (also **grill room**) a restaurant serving grilled food.
▶ v. **1** [with obj.] cook (something) using a grill: *grill the trout for about five minutes*.
2 [with obj.] informal subject (someone) to intense questioning or interrogation: *my father grilled us about what we had been doing* | (as noun **grilling**) *they faced a grilling over the latest results*.
– DERIVATIVES **grill·er** n.
– ORIGIN mid 17th cent.: from French *gril* (noun), *griller* (verb), from Old French *graille* 'grille.'

grill[2] ▶ n. variant spelling of GRILLE.

gril·lade /griˈläd, grēˈyäd/ ▶ n. (often **grillades**) a kind of meat stew usually made with beef steak, typical of French regional and Cajun cooking.
– ORIGIN mid 17th cent.: French, literally 'something grilled.'

gril·lage /ˈgrilij/ ▶ n. a heavy framework of cross-timbering or metal beams forming a foundation for building, esp. on soft, wet, or unstable ground.
– ORIGIN late 18th cent.: from French (see GRILLE, -AGE).

grille /gril/ (also **grill**) ▶ n. a grating or screen of metal bars or wires, placed in front of something as protection or to allow ventilation or discreet observation.
– ORIGIN mid 17th cent.: from French, from medieval Latin *craticula*, diminutive of *cratis* 'hurdle'; related to CRATE, GRATE[2], and GRIDDLE.

grill room ▶ n. see GRILL[1].

grill·work /ˈgril,wərk/ ▶ n. metal bars or wires arranged to form a grille.

grilse /grils/ ▶ n. a salmon that has returned to fresh water after a single winter at sea.
– ORIGIN late Middle English: of unknown origin.

grim /grim/ ▶ adj. (**grimmer**, **grimmest**) forbidding or uninviting: *his grim expression* | *long rows of grim, dark housing developments*. ■ (of humor) lacking genuine levity; mirthless; black: *some moments of grim humor*. ■ depressing or worrying to consider: *the grim news of the murder*. ■ unrelentingly harsh; merciless or severe: *few creatures are able to thrive in this grim and hostile land*.
– PHRASES **like grim death** with great determination: *we had to hold on like grim death*.
– DERIVATIVES **grim·ly** adv., **grim·ness** n.
– ORIGIN Old English, of Germanic origin; related to Dutch *grim* and German *grimm*.

grim·ace /ˈgriməs, griˈmās/ ▶ n. an ugly, twisted expression on a person's face, typically expressing disgust, pain, or wry amusement: *she gave a grimace of pain*.
▶ v. [no obj.] make a grimace: *I sipped the coffee and grimaced*.
– ORIGIN mid 17th cent.: from French, from Spanish *grimazo* 'caricature,' from *grima* 'fright.'

Gri·mal·di /grəˈmäldē, -ˈmôl-/, Francesco Maria (1618–63), Italian physicist and astronomer.

gri·mal·kin /griˈmôkin, -ˈmal-/ ▶ n. archaic a cat (used esp. in reference to its characteristically feline qualities). ■ a spiteful old woman.
– ORIGIN late 16th cent.: from GRAY[1] + *Malkin* (nickname for the given name *Matilda*).

grime /grīm/ ▶ n. **1** dirt ingrained on the surface of something, esp. clothing, a building, or the skin.
2 a form of dance music characterized by machinelike sounds and hip-hop vocals.
▶ v. [with obj.] blacken or make dirty with grime: *the beaches are grimed with a foul foam*.
– ORIGIN Middle English: from Middle Low German and Middle Dutch.

Grim·ke /ˈgrimkē/ the name of a family of US reformers, abolitionists, and feminists that included sisters **Sarah Moore** (1792–1872) and **Angelina Emily** (1805–79). They wrote for the American Anti-Slavery Society. Sarah later wrote pamphlets for women's rights, and with Theodore Dwight Weld (1803–95), Angelina's husband, she wrote *American Slavery as It Is: Testimony of a Thousand Witnesses* (1839).

Grimm /grim/, Jacob (Ludwig Carl) (1785–1863) and Wilhelm (Carl) (1786–1859), German philologists and folklorists. In 1852, they inaugurated a dictionary of German on historical principles, which was eventually completed by other scholars in 1960. They also compiled an anthology of German fairy tales, which appeared in three volumes between 1812 and 1822.

Grimm's law Linguistics the observation that certain Indo-European consonants (mainly stops) undergo regular changes in the Germanic languages that are not seen in non-Germanic languages such as Greek or Latin. Examples include *p* becoming *f* so that Latin *pedem* corresponds to English *foot* and German *Fuss*. The principle was set out by Jacob Grimm in his German grammar (2nd edition, 1822).

gri·moire /grim'wär/ ▶ **n.** a book of magic spells and invocations.
– ORIGIN mid 19th cent.: French, alteration of *grammaire* 'grammar.'

Grim Reap·er ▶ **n.** a personification of death in the form of a cloaked skeleton wielding a large scythe.

grim·y /'grīmē/ ▶ **adj.** (**grimier, grimiest**) covered with or characterized by grime: *the grimy industrial city*.
– DERIVATIVES **grim·i·ly** /-məlē/ **adv.**, **grim·i·ness** **n.**

grin /grin/ ▶ **v.** (**grins, grinning, grinned**) [no obj.] smile broadly, esp. in an unrestrained manner and with the mouth open: *Dennis appeared, grinning cheerfully*. ■ [with obj.] express with a broad smile. ■ grimace or appear to grimace grotesquely in a way that reveals the teeth: (as adj. **grinning**) *a grinning skull*.
▶ **n.** a broad smile: *"OK," he said with a grin*.
– PHRASES **grin and bear it** suffer pain or misfortune in a stoical manner.
– DERIVATIVES **grin·ner** **n.**, **grin·ning·ly** **adv.**
– ORIGIN Old English *grennian* 'bare the teeth in pain or anger,' of Germanic origin; probably related to GROAN.

grinch ▶ **n.** informal a person who is mean-spirited and unfriendly.
– ORIGIN mid 20th cent.: from the name of the title character in Dr. Seuss's book *How the Grinch Stole Christmas!* (1957).

grind /grīnd/ ▶ **v.** (past and past participle **ground** /ground/) **1** [with obj.] reduce (something) to small particles or powder by crushing it: *grind some black pepper over the salad* | *they **grind up** fish for fertilizer*. ■ [no obj.] (of a mill or machine) work with a crushing action: *the old mill was grinding again*. ■ sharpen, smooth, or produce (something) by crushing or by friction: *power from a waterwheel was used to grind cutlery*. ■ operate (a mill or machine) by turning the handle: *she was grinding a coffee mill*.
2 rub or cause to rub together gratingly: [no obj.] *tectonic plates that inexorably grind against each other* | [with obj.] *he keeps me awake at night, grinding his teeth*. ■ [no obj.] move noisily and laboriously, esp. against a countering force: *the truck was grinding slowly up the hill*.
3 [no obj.] informal (of a dancer) rotate the hips: *go-go girls grinding to blaring disco*.
▶ **n.** [in sing.] **1** a crushing or grating sound or motion: *the crunch and grind of bulldozers* | figurative *the slow grind of the US legal system*. ■ hard dull work: *relief from the daily grind*. ■ informal an excessively hard-working student. ■ the size of ground particles: *only the right grind gives you all the fine flavor*.
2 informal a dancer's rotary movement of the hips: *a bump and grind*.
– PHRASES **grind to a halt** (or **come to a grinding halt**) move more and more slowly and then stop.
– PHRASAL VERBS **grind away** work or study hard. **grind someone down** wear someone down with continuous harsh or oppressive treatment: *mundane everyday things which just grind people down*. **grind on** continue for a long time in a wearying or tedious way: *the rail talks grind on*. **grind something out** produce something dull or tedious slowly and laboriously: *I must grind out some more fiction*.
– ORIGIN Old English *grindan*, probably of Germanic origin. Although no cognates are known, it may be distantly related to Latin *frendere* 'rub away, gnash.'

grind·er /'grīndər/ ▶ **n.** **1** a machine used for grinding something: *a coffee grinder*. ■ a person employed to grind cutlery, tools, or cereals.
2 a molar tooth. ■ (**grinders**) informal the teeth.
3 informal another term for SUBMARINE SANDWICH.

grind·ing /'grīndiNG/ ▶ **adj.** [attrib.] **1** (of a state) oppressive, tedious, and seemingly without end: *grinding poverty*.
2 (of a sound or motion) harsh and grating: *the group's grinding, ear-splitting guitar*.
– DERIVATIVES **grind·ing·ly** **adv.**

grind·ing wheel ▶ **n.** a wheel used for cutting, grinding, or finishing metal or other objects, and typically made of abrasive particles bonded together.

grind·stone /'grīn(d),stōn/ ▶ **n.** a thick disk of stone or other abrasive material mounted so as to revolve, used for grinding, sharpening, or polishing metal objects. ■ rare another term for MILLSTONE.
– PHRASES **keep one's nose to the grindstone** work hard and continuously.

grin·go /'griNGgō/ ▶ **n.** (pl. **gringos**) informal, often offensive a white person from an English-speaking country (used in Spanish-speaking regions, chiefly Latin America).
– ORIGIN mid 19th cent.: Spanish, literally 'foreign, foreigner, or gibberish,' perhaps an alteration of *griego* 'Greek.'

gri·ot /grē'ō, 'grēō/ ▶ **n.** a member of a class of traveling poets, musicians, and storytellers who maintain a tradition of oral history in parts of West Africa.
– ORIGIN French, earlier *guiriot*, perhaps from Portuguese *criado*.

grip /grip/ ▶ **v.** (**grips, gripping, gripped**) [with obj.] **1** take and keep a firm hold of; grasp tightly: *his knuckles were white as he gripped the steering wheel*. ■ [no obj.] maintain a firm contact, esp. by friction: *a sole that really grips well on wet rock*.
2 (of a feeling or emotion) deeply affect (someone): *she was gripped by a feeling of excitement*. ■ compel the attention or interest of: *she gripped us from the first sentence*.
▶ **n.** **1** [in sing.] a firm hold; a tight grasp or clasp: *his arm was held in a vicelike grip* | figurative *the icy grip of winter*. ■ a manner of grasping or holding something: *I've changed my grip and my backswing*. ■ the ability of something, esp. a wheel or shoe, to maintain a firm contact with a surface: *these shoes have got no grip*. ■ [in sing.] an effective form of control over something: *our firm **grip on** inflation*. ■ [in sing.] an intellectual understanding of something: *you've got a pretty good **grip on** what's going on*.
2 a part or attachment by which something is held in the hand: *handlebar grips*.
3 a traveling bag: *a grip crammed with new clothes*.
4 an assistant in a theater; a stagehand. ■ a member of a camera crew responsible for moving and setting up equipment.
– PHRASES **come** (or **get**) **to grips with** engage in combat with: *they never came to grips with the enemy*. ■ begin to deal with or understand: *a real tough problem to come to grips with*. **get a grip** [usu. in imperative] informal keep or recover one's self-control: *get a grip, guys!* **get a grip on** take control of: *the Fed will have to act to get a grip on inflation*. **in the grip of** dominated or affected by something undesirable or adverse: *people caught in the grip of a drug problem*. **lose one's grip** become unable to understand or control one's situation: *an elderly person who seems to be losing his grip*.
– DERIVATIVES **grip·per** **n.**
– ORIGIN Old English *grippa* (verb), *gripe* 'grasp, clutch' (noun), *gripa* 'handful, sheath'; related to GRIPE.

gripe /grīp/ ▶ **v.** **1** [reporting verb] informal express a complaint or grumble about something, esp. something trivial: [no obj.] *they gripe about the busywork* | [with direct speech] *"Holidays make no difference to Simon," Pat griped*.
2 [with obj.] affect with gastric or intestinal pain: *it gripes my belly like a green apple* | (as adj. **griping**) *then the griping pains started*.
3 [with obj.] archaic grasp tightly; clutch: *Hilyard griped his dagger*.
4 [with obj.] Nautical secure (a boat) with gripes.
5 [no obj.] Sailing (of a ship) turn to face the wind in spite of the helm.
▶ **n.** **1** informal a complaint, esp. a trivial one: *his biggest gripe is that he has lost his sense of privacy*.
2 (usu. **gripes**) gastric or intestinal pain; colic.
3 archaic an act of grasping tightly.
4 (**gripes**) Nautical lashings securing a boat in its place on deck or in davits.
– DERIVATIVES **grip·er** **n.**
– ORIGIN Old English *grīpan* 'grasp, clutch,' of Germanic origin; related to Dutch *grijpen*, German *greifen* 'seize,' also to GRIP and GROPE. Sense 2 of the verb dates from the 17th cent.; sense 1 of the verb, of US origin, dates from the 1930s.

grippe /grip/ ▶ **n.** old-fashioned term for INFLUENZA.
– ORIGIN late 18th cent.: French, from *gripper* 'seize.'

grip·ping /'gripiNG/ ▶ **adj.** firmly holding the attention or interest; exciting: *a gripping TV thriller*.
– DERIVATIVES **grip·ping·ly** **adv.**

grip·py /'gripē/ ▶ **adj.** (of a wheel or shoe) able to grip a surface well: *grippy, quiet tires*.

Gri·qua /'grēkwə/ ▶ **n.** (pl. **same** or **Griquas**) a member of a people of mixed European and Khoikhoi origin, living mainly in the Cape Province of South Africa.
– ORIGIN the name in Nama.

Gris /grēs/, Juan (1887–1927), Spanish painter; born *José Victoriano Gonzales*. A main contributor to the development of the later phase of synthetic cubism, his work features the use of collage and paint in simple fragmented shapes.

gri·saille /gri'zī, -'zāl/ ▶ **n.** Art a method of painting in gray monochrome, typically to imitate sculpture. ■ a painting or stained-glass window in this style.
– ORIGIN mid 19th cent.: French, from *gris* 'gray.'

gris·e·o·ful·vin /,grizēə'fo͝olvin/ ▶ **n.** Medicine an antibiotic used against fungal infections of the hair and skin. ● This antibiotic is obtained from the mold *penicillium griseovulvum*.
– ORIGIN 1930s: from the modern Latin binomial, from medieval Latin *griseus* 'grayish' + Latin *fulvus* 'reddish yellow.'

gri·sette /gri'zet/ ▶ **n.** **1** a common edible woodland mushroom with a brown or gray cap, a slender stem, and white gills. ● *Amanita vaginata* and *A. fulva*, family Amanitaceae, class Hymenomycetes.
2 dated a young working-class Frenchwoman.
– ORIGIN French, from *gris* 'gray' + the diminutive suffix *-ette*; in sense 2 the term derives from the gray dress material typically worn by such women; sense 1 is an extended use.

g

gris-gris /'grē,grē/ ▶ **n.** (pl. **same**) an African or Caribbean charm or amulet. ■ the use of such charms esp. in voodoo: [as modifier] *the New Orleans gris-gris traditions*.
– ORIGIN late 17th cent.: from French *grisgris*, of West African origin.

Grish·am /'grisHəm/, John (Ray) (1955–), US writer and lawyer. His many novels include *A Time to Kill* (1988), *The Firm* (1991), *The Testament* (1999), and *The Brethren* (2000).

gris·kin /'griskin/ ▶ **n.** Brit. the lean part of a loin of pork.
– ORIGIN late 17th cent.: perhaps from archaic *grice* 'pig' + -KIN.

gris·ly /'grizlē/ ▶ **adj.** (**grislier, grisliest**) causing horror or disgust: *the town was shaken by a series of grisly crimes*.
– DERIVATIVES **gris·li·ness** **n.**
– ORIGIN Old English *grislic* 'terrifying,' of Germanic origin; related to Dutch *griezelig*.

gri·son /'grizən/ ▶ **n.** a weasellike mammal with dark fur and a white stripe across the forehead, found in Central and South America. ● Genus *Galictis*, family Mustelidae: two species.
– ORIGIN late 18th cent.: from French, from *gris* 'gray.'

gris·si·ni /gri'sēnē/ ▶ **plural n.** thin, crisp Italian breadsticks.
– ORIGIN Italian.

Gris·som /'grisəm/, Gus (1926–67), US astronaut; full name *Virgil Ivan Grissom*. Part of the original Project Mercury astronaut team in 1959, he was killed in a flash fire in the *Apollo I* capsule along with fellow astronauts **Edward H. White** (1930–67) and **Roger B. Chaffee** (1935–67).

grist /grist/ ▶ **n.** **1** grain that is ground to make flour. ■ malt crushed to make mash for brewing.
2 useful material, esp. to back up an argument: *the research provided the most sensational grist for opponents of tobacco*.
– PHRASES **grist for the mill** useful experience, material, or knowledge.
– ORIGIN Old English, 'grinding,' of Germanic origin; related to GRIND.

gris·tle /'grisəl/ ▶ **n.** cartilage, esp. when found as tough, inedible tissue in meat.
– ORIGIN Old English, of unknown origin.

gris·tly /'gris(ə)lē/ ▶ **adj.** (**gristlier, gristliest**) consisting of or full of gristle: *gristly bits of beef*.

grist·mill /'grist,mil/ ▶ **n.** a mill for grinding grain.

grit /grit/ ▶ **n.** **1** small, loose particles of stone or sand: *she had a bit of grit in her eye*. ■ [as modifier] (with numeral) indicating the grade of fineness of an abrasive: *220-grit paper*. ■ (also **gritstone**) a coarse sandstone: *layers of impervious shales and grits*.
2 courage and resolve; strength of character: *he displayed the true grit of the navy pilot*.
▶ **v.** (**grits, gritting, gritted**) [with obj.] **1** clench (the teeth), esp. in order to keep one's resolve when faced with an unpleasant or painful duty: figurative

Congress must grit its teeth and take action | (as adj. **gritted**) *"Not here," he said through gritted teeth.* **2** [no obj.] move with or make a grating sound: *fine red dust that gritted between the teeth.*
– ORIGIN Old English *grēot* 'sand, gravel,' of Germanic origin; related to German *Griess,* also to GROATS.

grits /grits/ ▶ **plural n.** [also treated as sing.] a dish of coarsely ground corn kernels boiled with water or milk. ■ coarsely ground corn kernels from which this dish is made.
– ORIGIN Old English *grytt, grytte* 'bran, mill dust,' of Germanic origin: related to Dutch *grutten,* German *Grütze,* also to GROATS.

grit·ty /'gritē/ ▶ **adj.** (**grittier, grittiest**) **1** containing or covered with grit.
2 showing courage and resolve: *a gritty pioneer woman.* ■ tough and uncompromising: *a gritty look at urban life.*
– DERIVATIVES **grit·ti·ly** /'gritəlē/ **adv., grit·ti·ness n.**

griv·et /'grivit/ (also **grivet monkey**) ▶ **n.** a common African guenon with greenish-brown upper parts and a black face. Compare with GREEN MONKEY and VERVET. ● *Cercopithecus aethiops,* family Cercopithecidae, in particular the race *C. a. aethiops* of Ethiopia and Sudan, with long white cheek tufts.
– ORIGIN mid 19th cent.: from French, of unknown origin.

griz·zle[1] /'grizəl/ ▶ **adj.** [often in combination] (esp. of hair or fur) having dark and white hairs mixed: *grizzle-haired.*
▶ **n.** a mixture of dark and white hairs.
– ORIGIN Middle English: from Old French *grisel,* from *gris* 'gray.'

griz·zle[2] ▶ **v.** [no obj.] informal, chiefly Brit. (of a child) cry fretfully: (as adj. **grizzling**) *a grizzling baby* | (as noun **grizzling**) *no grizzling, now!* ■ complain; grumble.
– DERIVATIVES **griz·zler** /'griz(ə)lər/ **n.**
– ORIGIN mid 18th cent. (in the sense 'show the teeth, grin'): of unknown origin.

griz·zled /'grizəld/ ▶ **adj.** having or streaked with gray hair: *grizzled hair.*
– ORIGIN late Middle English: from the adjective GRIZZLE[1] + -ED[1].

griz·zly /'grizlē/ ▶ **n.** (pl. **grizzlies**) (also **grizzly bear**) an animal of a large race of the brown bear native to North America. ● *Ursus arctos horribilis,* family Ursidae.
▶ **adj.** (**grizzlier, grizzliest**) gray or gray-haired.
– ORIGIN early 19th cent.: *grizzly* from GRIZZLE[2].

gro. ▶ **abbr.** gross.

groan /grōn/ ▶ **v.** [no obj.] **1** make a deep inarticulate sound in response to pain or despair: *Marty groaned and pulled the blanket over his head.* ■ [with direct speech] say something in a despairing or miserable tone: *"Oh God!" I groaned.* ■ complain; grumble: *they were moaning and groaning about management.*
2 (of a thing) make a low creaking or moaning sound when pressure or weight is applied: *James slumped back into his chair, making it groan and bulge.* ■ (**groan with/under**) be heavily loaded with: *tables groan with joints of venison.* ■ (**groan under/beneath**) be oppressed by: *families groaning under mortgage increases.*
▶ **n. 1** a deep, inarticulate sound made in pain or despair. ■ a complaint: *to listen with sincerity to everyone's moans and groans.*
2 a low creaking or moaning sound made by an object or device under pressure: *the protesting groan of timbers.*
– PHRASES **groan inwardly** feel dismayed by something but remain silent: *everything has a tepid inevitability, and even as you smile you may be groaning inwardly.*
– DERIVATIVES **groan·er n., groan·ing·ly adv.**
– ORIGIN Old English *grānian,* of Germanic origin; related to German *greinen* 'cry, whine,' *grinsen* 'grin,' also probably to GRIN.

groat /grōt/ ▶ **n.** historical any of various medieval European coins, in particular an English silver coin worth four old pence, issued between 1351 and 1662. ■ [in sing. with negative] archaic a small sum: *I do not care a groat.*
– ORIGIN from Middle Dutch *groot* or Middle Low German *grōte* 'great, thick,' hence 'thick penny'; compare with GROSCHEN.

groats /grōts/ ▶ **plural n.** hulled or crushed grain, esp. oats.
– ORIGIN late Old English *grotan* (plural): related to GRIT and GRITS.

gro·cer /'grōsər/ ▶ **n.** a person who sells food and small household goods.
– ORIGIN Middle English (originally 'a person who sold things in the gross' (i.e., in large quantities)): from Old French *grossier,* from medieval Latin *grossarius,* from late Latin *grossus* 'gross.'

gro·cer·y /'grōs(ə)rē/ ▶ **n.** (pl. **groceries**) (also **grocery store**) a grocer's store or business. ■ (**groceries**) items of food sold in such a store.

Grod·no /'grôdnə/ Russian name of HRODNA.

grog /gräg/ ▶ **n.** spirits (originally rum) mixed with water. ■ informal alcoholic drink, esp. beer. ■ crushed unglazed pottery or brick used as an additive in plaster or clay.
– ORIGIN mid 18th cent.: said to be from *Old Grog,* the reputed nickname (because of his grogram cloak) of Admiral Vernon (1684–1757), who in 1740 first ordered diluted (instead of neat) rum to be served out to sailors.

grog·gy /'grägē/ ▶ **adj.** (**groggier, groggiest**) dazed, weak, or unsteady, esp. from illness, intoxication, sleep, or a blow: *the sleeping pills had left her feeling groggy.*
– DERIVATIVES **grog·gi·ly** /'grägəlē/ **adv., grog·gi·ness n.**

grog·ram /'grägrəm/ ▶ **n.** a coarse fabric made of silk, often combined with mohair or wool and stiffened with gum.
– ORIGIN mid 16th cent.: from French *gros grain* 'coarse grain' (see also GROSGRAIN).

groin[1] /groin/ ▶ **n. 1** the area between the abdomen and the thigh on either side of the body. ■ informal the region of the genitals.
2 Architecture a curved edge formed by two intersecting vaults.
– ORIGIN late Middle English *grynde,* perhaps from Old English *grynde* 'depression, abyss.'

groin[2] (also **groyne**) ▶ **n.** a low wall or sturdy timber barrier built out into the sea from a beach to check erosion and drifting.
– ORIGIN late 16th cent.: from dialect *groin* 'snout,' from Old French *groign,* from late Latin *grunium* 'pig's snout,' from Latin *grunnire* 'to grunt.'

groined /groind/ ▶ **adj.** Architecture (of a vault) formed by the intersection of two barrel vaults, usually with plain groins without ribs.

grok /gräk/ ▶ **v.** (**groks, grokking, grokked**) [with obj.] informal understand (something) intuitively or by empathy: *because of all the commercials, children grok things immediately.* ■ [no obj.] empathize or communicate sympathetically; establish a rapport.
– ORIGIN mid 20th cent.: a word coined by Robert Heinlein (1907–88), American science fiction writer, in *Stranger in a Strange Land* (1961).

grom·met /'grämit/ ▶ **n. 1** an eyelet placed in a hole in a sheet or panel to protect or insulate a rope or cable passed through it or to prevent the sheet or panel from being torn.
2 Medicine a tube surgically implanted in the eardrum to drain fluid from the middle ear.
3 informal a young or inexperienced skier, snowboarder, surfer, or skateboarder: *mega moves that make gods out of grommets.*
– ORIGIN early 17th cent. (in nautical use in the sense 'a circle of rope used as a fastening'): from obsolete French *grommette,* from *gourmer* 'to curb,' of unknown ultimate origin. Current senses date from the mid 20th cent.

Gro·my·ko /grə'mēkō/, Andrei (Andreevich) (1909–89), Soviet statesman; foreign minister 1957–85; president of the former Soviet Union 1985–88. His appointment to the presidency, largely a formal position, by Mikhail Gorbachev was widely interpreted as a maneuver to reduce Gromyko's influence and to make an ending of the Cold War possible.

Gro·ning·en /'grōniNGən/ a city in the northern Netherlands, capital of a province with the same name; pop. 182,484 (2008).

groom /groōm, groŏm/ ▶ **v.** [with obj.] **1** look after the coat of (a horse, dog, or other animal) by brushing and cleaning it: *you must be prepared to spend time grooming your dog.* ■ (of an animal) clean the fur or skin of: *their main preoccupation is licking and grooming themselves.* ■ give a neat and tidy appearance to (someone): (as noun **grooming**) *she pays great attention to makeup, grooming, and clothes.* ■ look after (a lawn, ski slope, or other surface).
2 prepare or train (someone) for a particular purpose or activity: *star pupils who are groomed for higher things.* ■ (of a pedophile) prepare (a child) for a meeting, esp. via an Internet chat room, with the intention of committing a sexual offense.
▶ **n. 1** a person employed to take care of horses.
2 a bridegroom.
3 Brit. any of various officials of the royal household.
– ORIGIN Middle English (in the sense 'boy,' later 'man, male servant'): of unknown origin.

grooms·man /'groōmzmən, 'groŏmz-/ ▶ **n.** (pl. **groomsmen**) a male friend officially attending the bridegroom at a wedding.

groove /groōv/ ▶ **n. 1** a long, narrow cut or depression, esp. one made to guide motion or receive a corresponding ridge. ■ a spiral track cut in a phonograph record, into which the stylus fits. ■ Climbing an indentation where two planes of rock meet at an angle of more than 120°.
2 an established routine or habit: *his thoughts were slipping into a familiar groove.*
3 informal a rhythmic pattern in popular or jazz music: *the groove laid down by the drummer and bassist is tough and funky.*
▶ **v. 1** [with obj.] make a groove or grooves in: *deep lines grooved her face.*
2 [no obj.] informal dance or listen to popular or jazz music, esp. that with an insistent rhythm: *they were grooving to Motown.* ■ dated play such music in an accomplished and stylish manner: *the rhythm section grooves in the true Basie manner.* ■ enjoy oneself: *Harley relaxed and began to groove.*
3 [with obj.] Baseball, informal pitch (a ball) in the center of the strike zone. ■ (in the context of other sports) kick or throw (the ball) successfully; score (a goal) with stylish ease: *the San Diego kicker grooved the winning field goal.*
– PHRASES **in** (or **into**) **the groove** informal performing consistently well or confidently: *it might take me a couple of races to get back into the groove.* ■ indulging in relaxed and spontaneous enjoyment, esp. dancing: *get into the groove!*
– ORIGIN Middle English (denoting a mine or shaft): from Dutch *groeve* 'furrow, pit'; related to GRAVE[1].

grooved /groōvd/ ▶ **adj.** provided with or having a groove or grooves.

groov·ing saw ▶ **n.** a circular saw used for cutting grooves.

groov·y /'groōvē/ ▶ **adj.** (**groovier, grooviest**) informal, dated or humorous fashionable and exciting: *sporting a groovy new haircut.* ■ enjoyable and excellent: *he played all the remarkably groovy guitar parts himself.*
– DERIVATIVES **groov·i·ly** /-vəlē/ **adv., groov·i·ness n.**

grope /grōp/ ▶ **v. 1** [no obj.] feel about or search blindly or uncertainly with the hands: *she got up and groped for her spectacles.* ■ (**grope for**) search mentally with hesitation or uncertainty for (a word or answer): *she was groping for the words which would express what she thought* | (as adj. **groping**) *their groping attempts to create a more meaningful existence.* ■ move along with difficulty by feeling objects as one goes: *she blew out the candle and groped her way to the door.*
2 [with obj.] informal feel or fondle (someone) for sexual pleasure, esp. against their will: *he was accused of groping office girls.*
▶ **n.** an act of fondling someone for sexual pleasure: *she and Steve sneaked off for a quick grope.*
– DERIVATIVES **grop·ing·ly adv.**
– ORIGIN Old English *grāpian;* related to GRIPE.

Gro·pi·us /'grōpēəs/, Walter (1883–1969), US architect; born in Germany. He was the first director of the Bauhaus School of Design 1919–28 and a pioneer of the international style. He was one of the designers of the Pan American Building (1962) in New York.

gros·beak /'grōs,bēk/ ▶ **n.** a finch or related songbird with a stout conical bill and typically brightly colored plumage. ● Several genera in the family Fringillidae and subfamily Cardinalinae (family Emberizidae); the **white-fronted grosbeak** or **grosbeak weaver** (*Amblyospiza albifrons*) belongs to the family Ploceidae.
– ORIGIN late 17th cent.: from French *grosbec,* from *gros* 'big, fat' + *bec* 'beak.'

gro·schen /'grōsHən/ ▶ **n.** (pl. **same**) a monetary unit of Austria (until the introduction of the euro), equal to one hundredth of a schilling. ■ historical a small German silver coin. ■ informal a German ten-pfennig piece.
– ORIGIN German, from Middle High German *grosse,* from medieval Latin (*denarius*) *grossus* 'thick (penny)'; compare with GROAT.

gros·grain /'grō,grān/ ▶ **n.** a heavy, ribbed fabric, typically of silk or rayon.
– ORIGIN mid 19th cent.: French, 'coarse grain' (see also GROGRAM).

gros point /grō/ ▶ **n.** a type of needlepoint embroidery consisting of stitches crossing two or more threads of the canvas in each direction.
– ORIGIN mid 19th cent.: French, literally 'large stitch,' from *gros point de Venise,* a type of lace originally from Venice, worked in bold relief. The current sense dates from the 1930s.

gross /grōs/ ▶ **adj. 1** unattractively large or bloated: *I feel fat, gross—even my legs feel flabby.* ■ large-scale; not fine or detailed: *at the gross anatomical level.* ■ complete; blatant: *a gross exaggeration.* ■ vulgar; unrefined: *the duties we felt called upon to perform toward our inferiors were only gross, material ones.* ■ informal very unpleasant; repulsive: *it's disgusting and gross, but it's a fact.*
2 (of income, profit, or interest) without deduction of tax or other contributions; total: *the gross amount of the gift was $1,000* | *the current rate of interest is*

about 6.1 percent gross. Often contrasted with **NET²** (sense 1 of the adjective). ■ (of weight) including all contents, fittings, wrappings, or other variable items; overall: *a projected gross takeoff weight of 500,000 pounds*. ■ (of a score in golf) as actually played, without taking handicap into account.
▶ **adv.** without tax or other contributions having been deducted.
▶ **v.** [with obj.] produce or earn (an amount of money) as gross profit or income: *the film went on to gross $8 million in the U.S.*
▶ **n. 1** (pl. **same**) an amount equal to twelve dozen; 144: *fifty-five gross of tins of processed milk*. [From French *grosse douzaine*, literally 'large dozen.'] **2** (pl. **grosses**) a gross profit or income: *the box-office grosses mounted*.
– PHRASES **by the gross** in large numbers or amounts: *impoverished Mexicans who were arrested here by the gross*.
– PHRASAL VERBS **gross someone out** informal disgust someone, typically with repulsive or obscene behavior or appearance.
– DERIVATIVES **gross·ly adv.** [as submodifier] *Freda was grossly overweight*, **gross·ness n.**
– ORIGIN Middle English (in the sense 'thick, massive, bulky'): from Old French *gros, grosse* 'large,' from late Latin *grossus*.

gross a·nat·o·my ▶ **n.** the branch of anatomy that deals with the structure of organs and tissues that are visible to the naked eye.

gross do·mes·tic prod·uct (abbr.: **GDP**) ▶ **n.** the total value of goods produced and services provided in a country during one year. Compare with **GROSS NATIONAL PRODUCT**.

gross·er /'grōsər/ ▶ **n.** [with adj. or noun modifier] a movie that earns a specified level of gross profit or income: *the 1965 film version was an even bigger grosser | a $50 million-plus grosser*.

gross na·tion·al prod·uct (abbr.: **GNP**) ▶ **n.** the total value of goods produced and services provided by a country during one year, equal to the gross domestic product plus the net income from foreign investments.

gross-out ▶ **n.** informal something disgusting or repellent: [as modifier] *the movie features several gross-out scenes*.

gross ton ▶ **n.** see **TON¹** (sense 1).

gros·su·lar /'gräsyələr/ ▶ **n.** a mineral of the garnet group, consisting essentially of calcium aluminum silicate.
– ORIGIN early 19th cent.: from modern Latin *grossularia* 'gooseberry.' The yellow-green variety is sometimes known as *gooseberry garnet*.

Gros Ventre /'grō ˌvänt/ ▶ **n.** (pl. **Gros Ventres** pronunc. **same**) **1** (also **Gros Ventres of the Missouri**) another term for **HIDATSA**. **2** (also **Gros Ventres of the Prairies**) another term for **ATSINA**.
– ORIGIN French, literally 'big belly.'

grosz /grôsh/ ▶ **n.** (pl. **groszy** /'grôshē/) a monetary unit of Poland, equal to one hundredth of a zloty.
– ORIGIN Polish; compare with **GROSCHEN**.

grot /grät/ ▶ **n.** literary a grotto.
– ORIGIN early 16th cent.: from French *grotte*, from Italian *grotta*, via Latin from Greek *kruptē* 'vault, crypt.'

gro·tesque /grō'tesk/ ▶ **adj.** comically or repulsively ugly or distorted: *grotesque facial distortions*. ■ incongruous or inappropriate to a shocking degree: *a lifestyle of grotesque luxury*.
▶ **n. 1** a very ugly or comically distorted figure, creature, or image: *the rods are carved in the form of a series of gargoyle faces and grotesques*. ■ (**the grotesque**) that which is grotesque: *images of the macabre and the grotesque*. ■ a style of decorative painting or sculpture consisting of the interweaving of human and animal forms with flowers and foliage. **2** Printing a family of 19th-century sans serif typefaces.
– DERIVATIVES **gro·tesque·ly adv.**, **gro·tesque·ness n.**
– ORIGIN mid 16th cent. (as noun): from French *crotesque* (the earliest form in English), from Italian *grottesca*, from *opera* or *pittura grottesca* 'work or painting resembling that found in a grotto'; "grotto" here probably denoted the rooms of ancient buildings in Rome that had been revealed by excavations and contained murals in the grotesque style.

gro·tes·quer·ie /grō'teskərē/ (also **grotesquery**) ▶ **n.** (pl. **grotesqueries**) grotesque quality or grotesque things collectively: *living in a world of grotesquerie and make-believe*. ■ a grotesque figure, object, or action.
– ORIGIN late 17th cent.: French (see **GROTESQUE**).

Gro·ti·us /'grōsh(ē)əs/, Hugo (1583–1645), Dutch jurist and diplomat; Latinized name of *Huig de Groot*. His legal treatise, *De Jure Belli et Pacis* (1625), established the basis of modern international law.

Grot·on /'grätn/ a town in southeastern Connecticut, on the Thames River and Long Island Sound, a submarine manufacturing center; pop. 39,167 (est. 2008).

grot·to /'grätō/ ▶ **n.** (pl. **grottoes** or **grottos**) a small picturesque cave, esp. an artificial one in a park or garden. ■ an indoor structure resembling a cave.
– DERIVATIVES **grot·toed adj.**
– ORIGIN early 17th cent.: from Italian *grotta*, via Latin from Greek *kruptē* (see **CRYPT**).

grot·ty /'grätē/ ▶ **adj.** (**grottier**, **grottiest**) Brit. informal unpleasant and of poor quality: *a grotty little hotel*. ■ [as complement] unwell: *if the person feels very grotty, it is probably true influenza*.
– DERIVATIVES **grot·ti·ness n.**
– ORIGIN 1960s: from **GROTESQUE** + **-Y¹**.

grouch /grouch/ ▶ **n.** a habitually grumpy person: *rock's foremost poet and ill-mannered grouch*. ■ a complaint or grumble: *my only real grouch was that the children's chorus was far less easy on the ear*. ■ a fit of grumbling or sulking: *he's in a thundering grouch*.
▶ **v.** [no obj.] voice one's discontent in an ill-tempered manner; grumble: *there's not a lot to grouch about*.
– ORIGIN late 19th cent.: variant of obsolete *grutch*, from Old French *grouchier* 'to grumble, murmur,' of unknown origin. Compare with **GRUDGE**.

grouch·y /'grouchē/ ▶ **adj.** (**grouchier**, **grouchiest**) irritable and bad-tempered; grumpy; complaining: *the old man grew sulky and grouchy*.
– DERIVATIVES **grouch·i·ly** /-chəlē/ **adv.**, **grouch·i·ness n.**

ground¹ /ground/ ▶ **n. 1** [in sing.] the solid surface of the earth: *he lay on the ground*. ■ a limited or defined extent of the earth's surface; land: *an adjoining area of ground had been purchased*. ■ land of a specified kind: *my feet squelched over marshy ground*. ■ an area of land or sea used for a specified purpose: *shore dumping can pollute fishing grounds and beaches*. ■ (**grounds**) an area of enclosed land surrounding a large house or other building: *the house stands in seven acres of grounds*. ■ [as modifier] (in aviation) of or relating to the ground rather than the air (with particular reference to the maintenance and servicing of an aircraft on the ground): *ground staff | ground crew*. ■ [as modifier] (of an animal) living on or in the ground. ■ [as modifier] (of a fish) bottom-dwelling. ■ [as modifier] (of a plant) low-growing, esp. in relation to similar plants. **2** an area of knowledge or subject of discussion or thought: *third-year courses typically **cover** less **ground** and go into more depth | he shifted the argument onto theoretical grounds of his own choosing*. **3** (**grounds**) factors forming a basis for action or the justification for a belief: *there are some grounds **for** optimism | they called for a retrial **on the grounds** of the new evidence*. **4** chiefly Art a prepared surface to which paint is applied. ■ a substance used to prepare a surface for painting. ■ (in embroidery or ceramics) a plain surface to which decoration is applied. ■ a piece of wood fixed to a wall as a base for boards, plaster, or woodwork. **5** Music short for **GROUND BASS**. **6** (**grounds**) solid particles, esp. of ground coffee, that form a residue; sediment. **7** electrical connection of a circuit or conductor to the earth.
▶ **v.** [with obj.] **1** prohibit or prevent (a pilot or an aircraft) from flying: *a bitter wind blew from the northeast, and the bombers were grounded*. ■ informal (of a parent) refuse to allow (a child) to go out socially as a punishment: *he was grounded for hitting her on the head*. **2** ■ (with reference to a ship) run or go aground: *the larger ships grounded on the riverbed at low tide | rather than be blown up, Muller grounded his ship on a coral reef and surrendered*. **3** (usu. **be grounded in**) give (something abstract) a firm theoretical or practical basis: *the study of history must be grounded in a thorough knowledge of the past*. ■ instruct (someone) thoroughly in a subject: *they were grounded in the classics, in history, and in literature*. **4** place or lay (something) on the ground or hit the ground with it: *he was penalized two strokes for grounding his club in a bunker*. **5** connect (an electrical device) with the ground. **6** [no obj.] Baseball (of a batter) hit a pitched ball so that it bounces on the ground: *he **grounded to** second*. ■ (**ground out**) (of a batter) be put out by hitting a ball on the ground to a fielder who throws it to or touches first base before the batter touches that base: *he **grounded out to** shortstop*.
– PHRASES **be thick** (or **thin**) **on the ground** existing (or not existing) in large numbers or amounts: *new textbooks on particle physics are thin on the ground*. **break ground 1** do preparatory digging or other work prior to building or planting something. **2** another term for **BREAK NEW GROUND** below. **break new** (or **fresh**) **ground** do something innovative that is considered an advance or positive benefit. **cut the ground from under someone's feet** do something that leaves someone without a reason or justification for their actions or opinions. **from the ground up** informal completely or complete: *they needed to learn the business from the ground up*. **gain ground** become more popular or accepted: *new moral attitudes are gaining ground*. **gain ground on** get closer to someone or something one is pursuing or with whom one is competing: *the dollar gained ground on all other major currencies*. **get off the ground** (or **get something off the ground**) start or cause to start happening or functioning successfully: *he doesn't appreciate the steps he must take to get the negotiations off the ground*. **give** (or **lose**) **ground** retreat or lose one's advantage during a conflict or competition: *he refused to give ground on this issue*. **go to ground** (of a fox or other animal) enter its earth or burrow. ■ (of a person) hide or become inaccessible, esp. for a long time: *he had gone to ground following the presidential coup*. **hold** (or **stand**) **one's ground** not retreat or lose one's advantage during a conflict or competition: *you will be able to hold your ground and resist the enemy's attack*. **make up ground** get closer to someone ahead in a race or competition. **on the ground** in a place where real, practical work is done: *the troops on the ground are cynical*. **on one's own ground** in one's own territory or concerning one's own range of knowledge or experience: *I feel reasonably relaxed if I'm interviewed on my own ground*. **prepare the ground** make it easier for something to occur or be developed: *congress approved a series of measures intended to **prepare the ground for** the new economic structure*. **run someone/something to ground** see **RUN**. **work** (or **run**) **oneself into the ground** exhaust oneself by working (or running) very hard.
– ORIGIN Old English *grund*, of Germanic origin; related to Dutch *grond* and German *Grund*.

ground² past and past participle of **GRIND**.
▶ **adj.** [attrib.] reduced to fine particles by crushing or mincing: *ground cumin*. ■ shaped, roughened, or polished by grinding: *the thick opaque ground perimeter of the lenses*.
– PHRASES **ground down** exhausted or worn down.

ground ball ▶ **n.** Baseball a ball hit along the ground.

ground bass /bās/ ▶ **n.** Music a short theme, usually in the bass, that is constantly repeated as the other parts of the music vary.

ground beef ▶ **n.** beef that is cut up into very small pieces in a meat grinder or other machine.

ground bee·tle ▶ **n.** any of a number of beetles that live mainly on or near the ground, in particular a fast-running predatory beetle of the family Carabidae.

ground·break·ing /'groundˌbrākiNG/ ▶ **adj.** breaking new ground; innovative; pioneering.
– DERIVATIVES **ground·break·er** /-ˌbrākər/ **n.**

ground cher·ry ▶ **n.** an American plant of the nightshade family that resembles the cape gooseberry. ● Genus *Physalis*, family Solanaceae: several species, in particular *P. pruinosa*, which yields edible fruit.

ground cloth (also **groundcloth**) ▶ **n.** a waterproof cloth spread under a sleeping bag, directly on the ground or inside a tent. Also called **GROUNDSHEET**.

ground clut·ter ▶ **n.** noise in a radar echo caused by untargeted built or natural landscape features.

ground con·trol ▶ **n.** [treated as sing. or pl.] the ground-based personnel and equipment that monitor and direct the flight and landing of aircraft or spacecraft.
– DERIVATIVES **ground con·trol·ler n.**

ground cov·er ▶ **n.** low-growing, spreading plants that help to stop weeds from growing.

ground crew ▶ **n.** [treated as sing. or pl.] a team of people who maintain and service an aircraft on the ground.

ground dove /dəv/ ▶ **n.** a small dove that spends much of its time on the ground, feeding and frequently nesting there. ● *Columbina, Gallicolumba*, and related genera, family Columbidae: several species, including the **common ground dove** (*C. passerina*) of North and Central America.

g

g

ground·ed /ˈgroundid/ ▶ **adj. 1** well balanced and sensible: *the kids have money and a rock-star dad, but they seem grounded.*
2 (of a pilot or an aircraft) prohibited or prevented from flying: *you don't taunt a grounded flier, especially after he's had a few beers.* ■ informal (of a child being punished) not allowed to participate in social or recreational activities: *the problem is, I've got more grounded friends than available friends.*

ground ef·fect ▶ **n.** the effect of added aerodynamic buoyancy produced by a cushion of air below a vehicle moving close to the ground.

ground el·der ▶ **n.** a common weed of the parsley family, native to Europe, with leaves that resemble those of the elder and spreading, underground stems. ● *Aegopodium podagraria*, family Umbelliferae: a variegated cultivar is sometimes grown as ground cover.

ground·er /ˈgroundər/ ▶ **n.** Baseball a ground ball.

ground floor ▶ **n.** Brit. the floor of a building at ground level.
– PHRASES **get in on the ground floor** informal become part of an enterprise in its early stages.

ground game ▶ **n.** Football play consisting of running from scrimmage to advance the ball.

ground glass ▶ **n. 1** glass with a smooth ground surface that renders it nontransparent while retaining its translucency.
2 glass ground into an abrasive powder.

ground·hog /ˈground,häg, -,hôg/ ▶ **n.** another term for **WOODCHUCK**.

Ground·hog Day ▶ **n.** February 2, when the groundhog is said to come out of its hole at the end of hibernation. If the animal sees its shadow—i.e., if the weather is sunny—it is said to portend six weeks more of winter weather.

ground·hop·per /ˈground,häpər/ ▶ **n.** a small, predominantly brown insect that resembles a grasshopper and has well-developed wings. ● Family Tetrigidae, order Orthoptera: several species.

ground·ing /ˈgroundiNG/ ▶ **n.** [in sing.] basic training or instruction in a subject: *every child needs a good grounding in science and technology.*

ground i·vy ▶ **n.** a creeping plant of the mint family, with bluish-purple flowers. Native to Europe, it has become established in eastern North America. Also called **GILL-OVER-THE-GROUND, CREEPING CHARLIE**. ● *Glechoma hederacea*, family Labiatae.

ground·less /ˈground-lis/ ▶ **adj.** not based on any good reason: *your fears are quite groundless.*
– DERIVATIVES **ground·less·ly adv.**, **ground·less·ness n.**
– ORIGIN Old English *grundlēas* (see **GROUND**[1], **-LESS**).

ground lev·el ▶ **n. 1** the level of the ground: [as modifier] *ground-level ozone pollution.* ■ the ground floor of a building.
2 Physics another term for **GROUND STATE**.

ground·ling /ˈgroundliNG/ ▶ **n. 1** a spectator or reader of inferior taste, such as a member of a theater audience who traditionally stood in the pit below the stage: *Dante is not for groundlings.* [with reference to Shakespeare's *Hamlet* III. ii. 11.]
2 a person on the ground as opposed to one in a spacecraft or aircraft.
3 a fish that lives at the bottom of lakes and streams, esp. a gudgeon or loach.
4 a creeping or dwarf plant.
– ORIGIN early 17th cent. (denoting a fish): from **GROUND**[1] + **-LING**; compare with Dutch *grondeling*, German *Gründling* 'gudgeon.'

ground loop ▶ **n. 1** a violent, uncontrolled horizontal rotation of an aircraft while landing, taking off, or taxiing.
2 an unwanted electric current path in a circuit resulting in stray signals or interference, occurring, e.g., when two earthed points in the same circuit have different potentials.
▶ **v.** (**ground-loop**) [no obj.] (of an aircraft) make a ground loop.

ground·mass /ˈground,mas/ ▶ **n.** [in sing.] Geology the compact, finer-grained material in which the crystals are embedded in a porphyritic rock.

ground·nut /ˈground,nət/ ▶ **n. 1** another term for **PEANUT**.
2 a North American twining vine of the pea family, which bears clusters of fragrant brownish or maroon flowers and which yields a sweet edible tuber. ● Genus *Apios*, family Leguminosae: several species, in particular *A. americana*.

ground·out /ˈground,out/ ▶ **n.** Baseball a play in which a batter is put out by hitting a ball on the ground to a fielder who throws it to or touches first base before the batter touches that base.

ground pine ▶ **n. 1** a small, yellow-flowered Eurasian plant of the mint family that resembles a pine seedling in appearance and smell. ● *Ajuga chamaepitys*, family Labiatae.
2 a North American club moss with small, shiny leaves, resembling a miniature conifer and growing typically in coniferous woodland. ● Genus *Lycopodium*, family Lycopodiaceae: several species, in particular *L. obscurum* and *L. tristachyum*.

ground plan ▶ **n.** the plan of a building at ground level as imagined seen from above. ■ the general outline or basis of a plan.

ground rule ▶ **n.** (usu. **ground rules**) a basic principle: *some ground rules for assessing new machines.* ■ Baseball a rule pertaining to the limits of play on a particular field.

ground run ▶ **n.** the movement of an aircraft along the ground just before takeoff or just after landing.

ground·sel /ˈgroun(d)səl/ ▶ **n. 1** a widely distributed plant of the daisy family, with yellow rayless flowers. ● Genus *Senecio*, family Compositae: several species, in particular the **common groundsel** (*S. vulgaris*), which is a common weed. See also **GIANT GROUNDSEL**.
2 variant spelling of **GROUNDSILL**.
– ORIGIN Old English *gundæswelgiæ* (later *grundeswylige*), probably from *gund* 'pus' + *swelgan* 'to swallow' (with reference to its use in poultices). The later form may be by association with **GROUND**[1], and refer to the plant's rapid growth.

ground·sheet /ˈgroun(d),SHēt/ ▶ **n.** another term for **GROUND CLOTH**.

ground·sill (also **groundsel**) ▶ **n.** the horizontal beam or timber in a building that is secured to the foundation and is the base for the rest of the structure.

grounds·keep·er /ˈgroun(d)z,kēpər/ ▶ **n.** a person who maintains an athletic field, a park, or the grounds of a school or other institution.

ground sloth ▶ **n.** an extinct terrestrial edentate mammal of the Cenozoic era in America, typically of very large size. ● Order Xenarthra (or Edentata). See **MEGATHERIUM, MYLODON**.

grounds·man /ˈgroun(d)zmən/ ▶ **n.** (pl. **groundsmen**) British term for **GROUNDSKEEPER**.

ground·speed /ˈground,spēd/ ▶ **n.** an aircraft's speed relative to the ground. Compare with **AIRSPEED**.

ground squir·rel ▶ **n.** a burrowing squirrel that is typically highly social, found chiefly in North America and northern Eurasia, where it usually hibernates in winter. Also called **GOPHER**[1]. ● *Spermophilus* and other genera, family Sciuridae: many species, including the sousliks and chipmunks.

ground state ▶ **n.** Physics the lowest energy state of an atom or other particle.

ground·stroke /ˈground,strōk/ ▶ **n.** Tennis a stroke played after the ball has bounced, as opposed to a volley.

ground·swell /ˈgroun(d),swel/ ▶ **n.** [in sing.] **1** a buildup of opinion or feeling in a large section of the population: *an unexpected groundswell of opposition developed.*
2 a large or extensive swell in the sea.

ground tack·le ▶ **n.** the equipment used to anchor or moor a boat or ship.

ground·wa·ter /ˈground,wôtər, -,wätər/ ▶ **n.** water held underground in the soil or in pores and crevices in rock.

ground wave ▶ **n.** a radio wave that reaches a receiver from a transmitter directly, without reflection from the ionosphere.

ground·work /ˈground,wərk/ ▶ **n.** preliminary or basic work: *a manned space station is needed to lay the groundwork for a colony on the moon.*

ground ze·ro ▶ **n.** [in sing.] **1** the point on the earth's surface directly above or below an exploding nuclear bomb. ■ the site of the former World Trade Center in New York City in the wake of the terrorist attacks of September 11, 2001.
2 a starting point or base for some activity: *if you're starting at ground zero in terms of knowledge, go to the library.*

group /gro͞op/ ▶ **n.** [treated as sing. or pl.] a number of people or things that are located close together or are considered or classed together: *these bodies fall into four distinct groups.* ■ a number of people who work together or share certain beliefs: *I now belong to my local drama group.* ■ a commercial organization consisting of several companies under common ownership. ■ a number of musicians who play popular music together. ■ Military a unit of the US Air Force, consisting of two or more squadrons. ■ Military a unit of the US Army, consisting of two or more battalions. ■ Art two or more figures or objects forming a design. ■ Chemistry a set of elements occupying a column in the periodic table and having broadly similar properties arising from their similar electronic structure. ■ Chemistry a combination of atoms having a recognizable identity in a number of compounds. ■ Mathematics a set of elements, together with an associative binary operation, that contains an inverse for each element and an identity element. ■ Geology a stratigraphic division consisting of two or more formations.
▶ **v.** [with obj.] put together or place in a group or groups: *three wooden chairs were grouped around a dining table.* ■ put into categories; classify: *we group them into species merely as a convenience.* ■ [no obj.] form a group or groups: *many growers began to group together to form cooperatives.*
– ORIGIN late 17th cent.: from French *groupe*, from Italian *gruppo*, of Germanic origin; related to **CROP**.

group dy·nam·ics ▶ **plural n.** [also treated as sing.] Psychology the processes involved when people in a group interact with each other, or the study of these.

group·er /ˈgro͞opər/ ▶ **n.** a large or very large heavy-bodied fish of the sea bass family, with a big head and wide mouth, found in warm seas. ● Family Serranidae: several genera, in particular *Epinephelus* and *Mycteroperca*. The **Nassau grouper** (*E. striatus*) is the most economically important fish of the Bahamas.
– ORIGIN early 17th cent.: from Portuguese *garoupa*, probably from a local term in South America.

Nassau grouper

group home ▶ **n.** a home where a small number of unrelated people in need of care, support, or supervision can live together, such as those who are elderly or mentally ill.

group·ie /ˈgro͞opē/ ▶ **n.** informal a person, esp. a young woman, who regularly follows a pop music group or other celebrity in the hope of meeting or getting to know them. ■ [with modifier] often derogatory an enthusiastic or uncritical follower: *the contemporary art groupie.*

group·ing /ˈgro͞opiNG/ ▶ **n.** a set of people acting together with a common interest or purpose, esp. within a larger organization: *a grouping of Protestant churches.* ■ the arrangement or formation of people or things in a group or groups: *an alternative form of ability grouping.*

Group of Eight (abbr.: **G8**) the eight leading industrial nations (US, Japan, Germany, France, UK, Italy, Canada, and Russia), whose heads of government meet regularly.

Group of Sev·en 1 (abbr.: **G7**) a group of seven leading industrial nations outside the former communist bloc, consisting of the US, Japan, Germany (originally West Germany), France, the UK, Italy, and Canada.
2 a group of Canadian landscape painters, officially established in 1920, who formed the first major national movement in Canadian art. Their work exhibited a bold and colorful expressionistic style.

Group of Seventy-Seven (abbr.: **G77**) a grouping of the developing countries of the world established after the first United Nations Conference on Trade and Development in 1964 (originally consisting of 77 members but now with 130 member countries).

Group of Twen·ty (abbr.: **G20**) a group of finance ministers and central bank governors from 19 countries and the European Union who meet to discuss global economic issues.

group prac·tice ▶ **n.** a medical practice run by several doctors.

group ther·a·py ▶ **n.** a form of psychotherapy in which a group of patients meet to describe and discuss their problems together under the supervision of a therapist.

group·think /ˈgro͞op,THiNGk/ ▶ **n.** the practice of thinking or making decisions as a group in a way that discourages creativity or individual responsibility: *there's always a danger of groupthink when two leaders are so alike.*
– ORIGIN late 20th cent.: on the pattern of *doublethink*.

grou·pus·cule /gro͞oˈpəs,kyo͞ol/ ▶ **n.** a political or religious splinter group.
– ORIGIN 1960s: from French, diminutive of *groupe* 'group.'

group ve·loc·i·ty ▶ **n.** Physics the speed at which the energy of a wave travels.

group·ware /ˈgro͞opˌwe(ə)r/ ▶ **n.** Computing software designed to facilitate collective working by a number of different users.

group work ▶ **n.** Brit. work done by a group in collaboration.

grouse[1] /grous/ ▶ **n.** (pl. **same**) a medium to large game bird with a plump body and feathered legs, the male being larger and more conspicuously colored than the female. ● Family Tetraonidae (or Phasianidae): several genera, esp. *Lagopus* and *Tetrao*. The family also includes ptarmigans, capercaillies, and prairie chickens. ■ the flesh of this bird as food.
– ORIGIN early 16th cent.: perhaps related to medieval Latin *gruta* or to Old French *grue* 'crane.'

grouse[2] ▶ **v.** [no obj.] complain pettily; grumble: *she heard him grousing about his assistant.*
▶ **n.** a grumble or complaint: *our biggest grouse was about the noise of the construction work.*
– DERIVATIVES **grous·er n.**
– ORIGIN early 19th cent.: of unknown origin; compare with **GROUCH**.

grout[1] /grout/ ▶ **n.** a mortar or paste for filling crevices, esp. the gaps between wall or floor tiles.
▶ **v.** [with obj.] fill in with grout: *the gaps are grouted afterward.*
– ORIGIN mid 17th cent.: perhaps from obsolete *grout* 'sediment,' (plural) 'dregs,' or related to French dialect *grouter* 'grout a wall.'

grout[2] ▶ **n.** (**grouts**) archaic sediment; dregs; grounds: *old women told fortunes in grouts of tea.*
– ORIGIN Old English *grūt*, of Germanic origin; related to Dutch *gruit* 'dregs,' German *Grauss* 'grain, weak beer,' also to **GRITS** and **GROATS**. The original meaning was 'coarse meal, groats,' also denoting the infusion of malt that was fermented to make beer, hence, in Middle English, 'sediment.'

grout·er /ˈgroutər/ ▶ **n.** a tool used for grouting tiles.

grout·ing /ˈgroutiNG/ ▶ **n.** grout, esp. when hardened.

Grove[1] /grōv/, Sir George (1820–1900), English musicologist. He was the founder and first editor of the multivolume *Dictionary of Music and Musicians* (1879–89), which is now named for him in its later editions, and served as the first director of the Royal College of Music 1883–94.

Grove[2], Lefty (1900–1975) US baseball player; full name *Robert Moses Grove*. A pitcher, he played for the Philadelphia Athletics 1925–34 and the Boston Red Sox 1935–41. He led the American League in strikeouts 7 times and had a career total of 2,217. Baseball Hall of Fame (1947).

grove /grōv/ ▶ **n.** a small wood, orchard, or group of trees: *an olive grove* | [in place names] *Ocean Grove.*
– DERIVATIVES **grovy adj.**
– ORIGIN Old English *grāf*, of Germanic origin.

grov·el /ˈgrävəl, ˈgrə-/ ▶ **v.** (**grovels, groveling, groveled**; Brit. **grovels, grovelling, grovelled**) [no obj.] lie or move abjectly on the ground with one's face downward: *she was groveling on the floor in fear.* ■ act in an obsequious manner in order to obtain someone's forgiveness or favor: *everyone expected me to grovel with gratitude* | (as adj. **groveling**) *his groveling references to "great" historians and their "brilliant" works.*
– DERIVATIVES **grov·el·er n.**, **grov·el·ing·ly adv.**
– ORIGIN Middle English: back-formation from the obsolete adverb *grovelling*, from obsolete *groof, grufe* 'the face or front' (in the phrase *on grufe*, from Old Norse *á grúfu* 'face downward') + the suffix *-ling*.

groves of Ac·a·deme ▶ **plural n.** the academic world.
– ORIGIN translating Horace's *silvas Academi*.

grow /grō/ ▶ **v.** (past **grew** /gro͞o/; past participle **grown** /grōn/) [no obj.] **1** (of a living thing) undergo natural development by increasing in size and changing physically; progress to maturity: *he would watch Nick grow to manhood* | (as adj. **growing**) *the linguistic skills acquired by the growing child* | (as adj. **grown**) *the stupidity of grown men hitting a ball with a stick.* ■ (of a plant) germinate and develop: *seaweed grows in the ocean.* ■ [with obj.] produce by cultivation: *more and more land was needed to grow crops for export.* ■ [with obj.] allow or cause (a part of the body) to grow or develop: [with obj.] *she grew her hair long.* ■ (of something abstract) come into existence and develop: *the Vietnamese diaspora grew out of their national tragedy.*
2 become larger or greater over a period of time; increase: *turnover grew to more than $100,000 within three years* | (as adj. **growing**) *a growing number of people are coming to realize this.* ■ [with obj.] cause (something, esp. a business) to expand or increase.
3 [with complement] become gradually or increasingly: *sharing our experiences, we grew braver.* ■ [with infinitive] (of a person) come to feel or know something over time: *she grew to like the friendly, quiet people at the farm.*
– PHRASES **grow on trees** [usu. with negative] informal be plentiful or easily obtained: *money doesn't grow on trees.*
– PHRASAL VERBS **grow apart** (of two or more people) become gradually estranged. **grow into** become as a result of natural development or gradual increase: *Swampscott grew into a fishing village of about three hundred people by the 1850s.* ■ become large enough to wear (a garment) comfortably. **grow on** become gradually more appealing to (someone): *a house has to grow on you.* **grow out** disappear because of normal growth: *Colette's old perm had almost grown out.* **grow out of** become too large to wear (a garment): *blazers that they grew out of.* ■ become too mature to retain (a childish habit): *most children grow out of tantrums by the time they're three.* **grow up** advance to maturity; spend one's childhood and adolescence: *I grew up in a small town in Michigan.* ■ [often in imperative] begin to behave or think sensibly and realistically: *grow up, sister, and come into the real world.* ■ arise; develop: *a school of painting grew up in Cuzco.*
– DERIVATIVES **grow·a·ble adj.**
– ORIGIN Old English *grōwan* (originally referring chiefly to plants), of Germanic origin; related to Dutch *groeien*, also to **GRASS** and **GREEN**.

grow·er /ˈgrōər/ ▶ **n. 1** a person who grows a particular type of crop: *a fruit grower.*
2 [with adj.] a plant that grows in a specified way: *a fast grower.*

grow·ing pains ▶ **plural n.** neuralgic pains that occur in the limbs of some young children. ■ the difficulties experienced in the early stages of an enterprise: *the growing pains of a young republic.*

grow·ing point ▶ **n.** the point at which growth originates. ■ Botany the meristem region at the apex of a plant shoot at which continuous cell division and differentiation occur.

grow·ing sea·son ▶ **n.** the part of the year during which rainfall and temperature allow plants to grow: *a short growing season.*

growl /groul/ ▶ **v.** [no obj.] (of an animal, esp. a dog) make a low guttural sound of hostility in the throat: *the dogs yapped and growled about his heels.* ■ [with direct speech] (of a person) say something in a low grating voice, typically in a threatening manner: *"Keep out of this," he growled.* ■ (of a thing) make a low or harsh rumbling sound, typically one that is felt to be threatening: *thunder growls without warning from a summer sky.*
▶ **n.** a low guttural sound made in the throat, esp. by a dog. ■ a similar sound made by a person, esp. to express hostility or anger. ■ [in sing.] a low throaty sound made by a machine or engine: *the growl of diesel engines.*
– DERIVATIVES **growl·ing·ly adv.**
– ORIGIN mid 17th cent.: probably imitative.

growl·er /ˈgroulər/ ▶ **n. 1** a person or thing that growls.
2 a small iceberg that rises little above the water.
3 informal a pail or other container used for carrying drink, esp. draft beer.
4 an electromagnet with two poles designed to test for short circuits in the windings of an armature.
5 historical a four-wheeled hansom cab.

grown /grōn/ past participle of **GROW**.

grown-up ▶ **adj.** adult: *Joe is married with two grown-up daughters.* ■ suitable for or characteristic of an adult: *it seems a grown-up thing to do.*
▶ **n.** an adult (esp. a child's word): *I don't like it when grown-ups get all serious.*

growth /grōTH/ ▶ **n. 1** the process of increasing in physical size: *the upward growth of plants* | *the growth of the city affects the local climate.* ■ the process of developing or maturing physically, mentally, or spiritually: *keeping a journal can be a vital step in our personal growth.* ■ the increase in number and spread of small or microscopic organisms: *some additives slow down the growth of microorganisms.* ■ the process of increasing in amount, value, or importance: *the rates of population growth are lowest in the north.* ■ increase in economic value or activity: *the government aims to get growth back into the economy.*
2 something that has grown or is growing: *a day's growth of unshaven stubble on his chin.* ■ Medicine & Biology a tumor or other abnormal formation.
3 a vineyard or crop of grapes of a specified classification of quality, or a wine from it.

growth com·pa·ny ▶ **n.** a company that is growing rapidly in comparison to other companies in its field or the economy as a whole.

growth fac·tor ▶ **n.** Biology a substance, such as a vitamin or hormone, that is required for the stimulation of growth in living cells.

growth fund ▶ **n.** a mutual fund that invests primarily in stocks that are expected to increase in capital value rather than yield high income.

growth hor·mone ▶ **n.** a hormone that stimulates growth in animal or plant cells, esp. (in animals) a hormone secreted by the pituitary gland.

growth in·dus·try ▶ **n.** an industry that is developing particularly rapidly.

growth ring ▶ **n.** a concentric layer of wood, shell, or bone developed during an annual or other regular period of growth.

growth stock ▶ **n.** a company stock that tends to increase in capital value rather than yield high income.

groyne ▶ **n.** variant spelling of **GROIN**[2].

groz·ing i·ron /ˈgrōziNG/ ▶ **n.** chiefly historical a pair of pliers for clipping the edges of pieces of glass. ■ historical a tool for smoothing soldered joints in lead pipes.
– ORIGIN Middle English: *grozing* from Middle Dutch, from the stem of *gruizen* 'crush, trim glass,' from *gruis* 'fragments.'

Groz·ny /ˈgrôznē, ˈgräznē/ a city in southwestern Russia, near the border with Georgia, capital of Chechnya; pop. 226,100 (est. 2008).

GRP ▶ **abbr.** glass-reinforced plastic.

grrrl ▶ **n.** see **RIOT GIRL**.

grt ▶ **abbr.** gross registered tonnage, a measure of a ship's size found by dividing the volume of the space enclosed by its hull (measured in cubic feet) by one hundred.

grub /grəb/ ▶ **n. 1** the larva of an insect, esp. a beetle. ■ a maggot or small caterpillar.
2 informal food: *a popular bar serving excellent grub.*
▶ **v.** (**grubs, grubbing, grubbed**) [no obj.] **1** dig or poke superficially at the earth; dig shallowly in soil: *the damage done to pastures by badgers **grubbing for** worms.* ■ [with obj.] remove (something) from the earth by digging it up: *all the vines are **grubbed up** and the land left fallow for a few years.* ■ [with obj.] clear (the ground) of roots and stumps: (as noun **grubbing**) *construction operations including clearing and grubbing.*
2 search for something in a clumsy and unmethodical manner; rummage: *I began grubbing about in the wastepaper basket to find the envelope.* ■ do demeaning or humiliating work in order to achieve something: *she has achieved material independence without having to **grub for** it.* ■ [with obj.] achieve or acquire (something) in such a way: *they were grubbing a living from garbage pails.*
– DERIVATIVES **grub·ber n.**
– ORIGIN Middle English: perhaps related to Dutch *grobbelen*, also to **GRAVE**[1].

grub·by /ˈgrəbē/ ▶ **adj.** (**grubbier, grubbiest**) dirty; grimy: *the grubby face of a young boy.* ■ disreputable; sordid: *grubby little moneylenders.*
– DERIVATIVES **grub·bi·ly** /-bəlē/ **adv.**, **grub·bi·ness n.**

grub·stake /ˈgrəbˌstāk/ informal ▶ **n.** an amount of material, provisions, or money supplied to an enterprise (originally a prospector for ore) in return for a share in the resulting profits.
▶ **v.** [with obj.] provide with a grubstake.

Grub Street /grəb/ ▶ **n.** used in reference to a world or class of impoverished journalists and writers.
– ORIGIN the name of a street (later Milton Street) in Moorgate, London, England, inhabited by such authors in the 17th cent.

grudge /grəj/ ▶ **n.** a persistent feeling of ill will or resentment resulting from a past insult or injury: *she **held a grudge against** her former boss.*
▶ **v.** [with obj.] be resentfully unwilling to give, grant, or allow (something): *he grudged the work and time that the meeting involved.* ■ [with two objs., usu. with negative] feel resentful that (someone) has achieved (something): *I don't grudge him his moment of triumph.*
– PHRASES **bear** (or **owe**) **someone a grudge** maintain a feeling of ill will or resentment toward someone.
– DERIVATIVES **grudg·er n.**
– ORIGIN late Middle English: variant of obsolete *grutch* 'complain, murmur, grumble,' from Old French *grouchier*, of unknown origin. Compare with **GROUCH**.

grudge match ▶ **n.** a contest or other competitive situation based on personal antipathy between the participants.

grudg·ing /ˈgrəjiNG/ ▶ **adj.** given, granted, or allowed only reluctantly or resentfully: *a grudging apology.* ■ (of a person) reluctant or resentfully

unwilling to give, grant, or allow something: *Oliver was grudging about accepting Wickham's innocence.*
– DERIVATIVES **grudg·ing·ly** adv., **grudg·ing·ness** n.

gru·el /'grooəl/ ▶ n. a thin liquid food of oatmeal or other meal boiled in milk or water.
– ORIGIN Middle English: from Old French, of Germanic origin.

gruel·ing /'grooəliNG/ (Brit. **gruelling**) ▶ adj. extremely tiring and demanding: *a grueling schedule.*
– DERIVATIVES **gruel·ing·ly** adv.
– ORIGIN mid 19th cent.: from the verb *gruel* 'exhaust, punish,' from an old phrase *get one's gruel* 'receive one's punishment.'

grue·some /'groosəm/ ▶ adj. causing repulsion or horror; grisly: *a most gruesome murder.* ■ informal extremely unpleasant: *gruesome working hours.*
– DERIVATIVES **grue·some·ly** adv., **grue·some·ness** n.
– ORIGIN late 16th cent.: from Scots *grue* 'to feel horror, shudder' (of Scandinavian origin) + -SOME[1]. Rare before the late 18th cent., the word was popularized by Sir Walter Scott.

gruff /grəf/ ▶ adj. abrupt or taciturn in manner: *penetrate a gruff exterior and you will find him affable.* ■ (of a voice) rough and low in pitch: *she spoke with a gruff, masculine voice.*
– DERIVATIVES **gruff·ly** adv., **gruff·ness** n.
– ORIGIN late 15th cent. (in the sense 'coarse-grained'): from Flemish and Dutch *grof* 'coarse, rude,' of West Germanic origin.

grum·ble /'grəmbəl/ ▶ v. [reporting verb] complain or protest about something in a bad-tempered but typically muted way: [with clause] *his father was grumbling that he hadn't heard a word from him* | [with obj.] *he grumbled something about the decision being unnecessary.* ■ [no obj.] make a low rumbling sound: *thunder was grumbling somewhere in the distance.* ■ [no obj.] (of an internal organ) give intermittent discomfort: *your stomach is grumbling.*
▶ n. a complaint: *the main grumble is that he spends too much time away.* ■ a low rumbling sound.
– DERIVATIVES **grum·bler** /-blər/ n., **grum·bling·ly** /-bliNGlē/ adv., **grum·bly** /-blē/ adj.
– ORIGIN late 16th cent.: from obsolete *grumme* (probably of Germanic origin and related to Dutch *grommen*) + -LE[4].

grump /grəmp/ informal ▶ n. a grumpy person. ■ a fit of sulking: *he walks off in a grump to the other end of the meadow.*
▶ v. [no obj.] act in a sulky, grumbling manner: *he grumped at me when I moved the papers.*
– DERIVATIVES **grump·ish** adj., **grump·ish·ly** adv.
– ORIGIN early 18th cent.: imitating inarticulate sounds expressing displeasure.

grump·y /'grəmpē/ ▶ adj. (**grumpier**, **grumpiest**) bad-tempered and sulky.
– DERIVATIVES **grump·i·ly** /-pəlē/ adv., **grump·i·ness** n.

Grun·dy /'grəndē/ ▶ n. see **MRS. GRUNDY**.

Grü·ne·wald /'groon,väld/, Mathias (*c.*1460–1528), German painter; born *Mathis Nithardt*; also called **Mathis Gothardt** /'gät,härt/. His most noted work is the nine-panel *Isenheim Altar* (completed 1516).

grunge /grənj/ ▶ n. **1** grime; dirt.
2 (also **grunge rock**) a style of rock music characterized by a raucous guitar sound and lazy vocal delivery. ■ the fashion associated with this music, including loose, layered clothing and ripped jeans.
– DERIVATIVES **grun·gi·ness** n., **grun·gy** adj.
– ORIGIN 1970s: back-formation from *grungy*, perhaps suggested by **GRUBBY** and **DINGY**.

grun·ion /'grənyən/ ▶ n. a small, slender Californian fish that swarms onto beaches at night to spawn. The eggs are buried in the sand, and the young fish are swept out to sea on the following spring tide. ● *Leuresthes tenuis*, family Atherinidae.
– ORIGIN early 20th cent.: probably from Spanish *gruñón* 'grunter.'

grunt /grənt/ ▶ v. [no obj.] (of an animal, esp. a pig) make a low, short guttural sound. ■ (of a person) make a low inarticulate sound, typically to express effort or indicate assent: *Graham grunted and heaved as he helped the masons fit a huge slab of stone into place* | [with direct speech] *"What is it?" he grunted irritably.*
▶ n. **1** a low, short guttural sound made by an animal or a person.
2 informal a low-ranking or unskilled soldier or other worker: *he went from grunt to senior executive vice-president in less than five years* | [as modifier] *grunt work.* [alteration of *ground*, from *ground man* (with reference to unskilled railroad work before progressing to lineman).]
3 a dessert made of fruit topped with dough: *blueberry grunt.*
4 an edible shoaling fish of tropical inshore waters and coral reefs, able to make a loud noise by grinding its teeth and amplifying the sound in the swim bladder. ● Family Pomadasyidae: numerous genera and species.
– ORIGIN Old English *grunnettan*, of Germanic origin and related to German *grunzen*; probably originally imitative.

grunt·er /'grəntər/ ▶ n. a fish that makes a grunting noise, esp. when caught, in particular: ● a mainly marine fish of warm waters (family Theraponidae: several genera). ● another term for **GRUNT** (sense 4 of the noun).

grun·tled /'grəntld/ ▶ adj. humorous pleased, satisfied, and contented.
– ORIGIN 1930s: back-formation from **DISGRUNTLED**.

Grus /grəs, groos/ Astronomy a small southern constellation (the Crane), south of Piscis Austrinus. ■ (as genitive **Gruis** /'groois/) used with a preceding letter or numeral to designate a star in this constellation: *the star Delta Gruis.*
– ORIGIN Latin.

Gru·yère /groo'yer, grē-/ ▶ n. a firm, tangy cheese.
– ORIGIN named after *Gruyère*, a district in Switzerland, where it was first made.

gr. wt. ▶ abbr. gross weight.

gryph·on ▶ n. variant spelling of **GRIFFIN**.

grys·bok /'grīs,bäk/ ▶ n. a small mainly nocturnal antelope with small vertical horns and a slightly arched back, found in southwestern Africa. ● Genus *Raphicerus*, family Bovidae: two species.
– ORIGIN late 18th cent.: from Afrikaans, from Dutch *grijs* 'gray' + *bok* 'buck.'

Grøn·land /'grœn,län/ Danish name for **GREENLAND**.

GSA ▶ abbr. ■ General Services Administration. ■ Girl Scouts of America.

GSC ▶ abbr. General Staff Corps.

GSM ▶ abbr. Global System (or Standard) for Mobile, a standardized international system for digital mobile telecommunication.

gsm ▶ abbr. grams per square meter, a measure of weight for paper: *100 gsm paper.*

GSO ▶ abbr. general staff officer.

GSOH ▶ abbr. good sense of humor (used in personal advertisements).

G-spot ▶ n. a sensitive area of the anterior wall of the vagina believed by some to be highly erogenous and capable of ejaculation.
– ORIGIN 1944: *G* from *Gräfenberg*, because first described by Gräfenberg and Dickinson in the *Western Journal of Surgery*.

GSR ▶ abbr. galvanic skin response.

GST ▶ abbr. generation-skipping tax.

Gstaad /gə'SHtät/ a winter-sports resort in western Switzerland.

G-string (also **gee-string**) ▶ n. a garment consisting of a narrow strip of cloth that covers the genitals and is attached to a waistband, worn as underwear or by striptease performers.

G-suit (also **anti-G suit**) ▶ n. a garment with pressurized pouches that are inflatable with air or fluid, worn by fighter pilots and astronauts to enable them to withstand high forces of acceleration.
– ORIGIN 1940s: from *g* (symbol of *gravity*) + **SUIT**.

GT ▶ adj. denoting a high-performance car: *GT cars.*
▶ n. a high-performance car.
– ORIGIN 1960s: abbreviation of Italian **GRAN TURISMO**.

gt. ▶ abbr. ■ gilt. ■ great.

g.t.c. ▶ abbr. ■ good till canceled. ■ good till countermanded.

gtd. ▶ abbr. guaranteed.

GTi ▶ adj. denoting a high-performance car with a fuel-injected engine: *a Peugeot 205 GTi.*
▶ n. a car of this type.
– ORIGIN late 20th cent.: from **GT** + *i* for *injection*.

GTP ▶ abbr. guanosine triphosphate.

GTS ▶ abbr. Nautical gas turbine ship.

GU ▶ abbr. ■ genitourinary. ■ Guam.

gua·ca·mo·le /,gwäkə'mōlē/ ▶ n. a dish of mashed avocado mixed with chopped onion, tomatoes, chili peppers, and seasoning.
– ORIGIN Latin American Spanish, from Nahuatl *ahuacamolli*, from *ahuacatl* 'avocado' + *molli* 'sauce.'

gua·cha·ro /'gwäCHə,rō/ ▶ n. (pl. **guacharos**) a large, nocturnal, fruit-eating bird that resembles a nightjar and lives in caves in Central and South America.
– ORIGIN early 19th cent.: from Spanish *guáchero*, of South American origin.

Gua·da·la·ja·ra /,gwädl-ə'härə/ a city in western central Mexico, capital of the state of Jalisco; pop. 1,600,940 (2005).

Gua·dal·ca·nal /,gwädlkə'nal/ an island in the western Pacific Ocean, the largest of the Solomon Islands; pop. 73,000 (est. 2007). During World War II, it was the scene of the first major US offensive against the Japanese in August 1942.

Gua·dal·quiv·ir /,gwädlki'vir/ a river in southern Spain, in Andalusia. It flows for 410 miles (657 km) through Cordoba and Seville to reach the Atlantic Ocean northwest of Cadiz.

Gua·da·lu·pe Moun·tains /'gwäd,loop, -'oopē/ a range in western Texas and southern New Mexico. Guadalupe Peak at 8,749 feet (2,668 m) is the highest point in Texas. The Carlsbad Caverns are in the New Mexico section.

Gua·de·loupe /,gwädl-'oop/ a group of islands in the Lesser Antilles that form an overseas department of France; pop. 445,000 (est. 2009); capital, Basse-Terre.
– DERIVATIVES **Gua·de·lou·pi·an** /-ēən/ adj. & n.

Gua·dia·na /gwäd'yänə/ a river in Spain and Portugal. Rising in a plateau region southeast of Madrid, it flows southwest for about 350 miles (580 km) before entering the Atlantic Ocean at the Gulf of Cadiz. For the last part of its course, it forms the border between Spain and Portugal.

guai·ac /'gwīak/ ▶ n. brown resin obtained from guaiacum trees, used as a flavoring and in varnishes. It was formerly used medicinally and as a test for traces of blood.

guai·a·col /'gwīə,kôl, -,kōl/ ▶ n. Chemistry an oily yellow liquid with a penetrating odor, obtained by distilling wood tar or guaiac, used as a flavoring and an expectorant. ● Alternative name: *o*-**methoxyphenol**; chem. formula: $HOC_6H_4OCH_3$.
– ORIGIN mid 19th cent.: from **GUAIACUM** + **-OL**.

guai·a·cum /'gwīəkəm/ ▶ n. an evergreen tree of the Caribbean and tropical America, formerly important for its hard, heavy, oily timber but now scarce. Also called **LIGNUM VITAE**. ● *Guaiacum officinale* and *G. sanctum*, family Zygophyllaceae. ■ another term for **GUAIAC**.
– ORIGIN mid 16th cent.: modern Latin, via Spanish from Taino *guayacan*.

guai·fen·e·sin /gwī'fenəsin/ ▶ n. an expectorant used in cough syrups and sometimes for pain relief from fibromyalgia.

Guam /gwäm/ the largest and most southern of the Mariana Islands, administered as an unincorporated territory of the US; pop. 178,400 (est. 2009); capital, Agaña. Guam was ceded to the US by Spain in 1898. It was the site of fighting between the Japanese and the US during World War II.
– DERIVATIVES **Gua·ma·ni·an** /gwä'mānēən/ adj. & n.

guan /gwän/ ▶ n. a large, pheasantlike, tree-dwelling bird of tropical American rain forests. ● Family Cracidae (**the guan family**): several genera, esp. *Penelope*. The guan family also includes curassows and chachalacas.
– ORIGIN late 17th cent.: via American Spanish from Miskito *kwamu*.

gua·na·co /gwə'näkō/ ▶ n. (pl. **guanacos**) a wild Andean mammal similar to the domestic llama, which is probably derived from it. It has a valuable pale brown pelt. ● *Lama guanicoe*, family Camelidae.
– ORIGIN early 17th cent.: via Spanish from Quechua *huanacu*.

Gua·na·jua·to /,gwänə'(h)wätō/ a state in central Mexico. ■ its capital city; pop. 70,798 (2005).

Guan·che /'gwänCHā/ ▶ n. a member of an aboriginal people speaking a Berber language who formerly inhabited the Canary Islands, and were absorbed after the Spanish conquest in the 15th century.
– ORIGIN Spanish.

Guang·dong /'gwäNG'dooNG/ (also **Kwangtung**) a province in southern China, on the South China Sea; capital, Guangzhou (Canton).

Guang·xi Zhuang /'gwäNG'SHē 'jwäNG/ (also **Kwangsi Chuang**) an autonomous region in southern China, on the Gulf of Tonkin; capital, Nanning.

Guang·zhou /'gwäNG'jō/ (also **Kwangchow**) a city in southern China, the capital of Guangdong province; pop. 6,172,800 (est. 2006). It is the leading industrial and commercial center of southern China. Also called **CANTON**[1].

guan·i·dine /'gwänə,dēn/ ▶ n. Chemistry a strongly basic crystalline compound, used in organic synthesis. ● An imide derived from urea; chem. formula: $HNC(NH_2)_2$.
– ORIGIN mid 19th cent.: from **GUANO** + **-IDE** + **-INE**[4].

gua·nine /'gwänēn/ ▶ n. Biochemistry a compound that occurs in guano and fish scales, and is one of the four constituent bases of nucleic acids.

A purine derivative, it is paired with cytosine in double-stranded DNA. ● Alternative name: **6-oxy-2-aminopurine**; chem. formula: $C_5H_5N_5O$.
– ORIGIN mid 19th cent.: from GUANO + -INE[4].

gua·no /ˈgwänō/ ▶ n. (pl. **guanos**) the excrement of seabirds, occurring in thick deposits notably on the islands off Peru and Chile, and used as fertilizer. ■ an artificial fertilizer resembling natural guano, esp. one made from fish.
– ORIGIN early 17th cent.: from Spanish, or from Latin American Spanish *huano*, from Quechua *huanu* 'dung.'

gua·no·sine /ˈgwänəˌsēn/ ▶ n. Biochemistry a compound consisting of guanine combined with ribose, a nucleoside unit in RNA.
– ORIGIN early 20th cent.: from GUANINE, with the insertion of -OSE[2].

gua·no·sine tri·phos·phate /trīˈfäsfāt/ (abbr.: **GTP**) ▶ n. a nucleotide composed of guanine, ribose, and three phosphate groups, which participates in various metabolic reactions, including protein synthesis.

Guan·tá·na·mo Bay /gwänˈtänəmō/ a bay on the southeastern coast of Cuba. It is the site of a US naval base established in 1903, where suspected members of al-Qaeda and the Taliban were held from 2002.

guan·xi /gwanˈCHē/ ▶ n. (in China) the system of social networks and influential relationships that facilitate business and other dealings.
– ORIGIN Mandarin, literally 'connection.'

Guan Yin /ˈgwän ˈyin/ (in Chinese Buddhism) the goddess of compassion.

Gua·po·ré /ˌgwäpəˈrā/ a river that flows northwest for 1,090 miles (1,745 km) from southwestern Brazil, forming much of the Brazil-Bolivia border, to the Mamoré River.

guar /gwär/ ▶ n. a drought-resistant plant of the pea family, which is grown as a vegetable and fodder crop and as a source of guar gum, native to dry regions of Africa and Asia. Also called CLUSTER BEAN. ● *Cyamopsis tetragonoloba*, family Leguminosae. ■ (also **guar gum** or **guar flour**) a fine powder obtained by grinding guar seeds, which has numerous commercial applications, esp. in the food industry, where it is used as a thickener and a binder.
– ORIGIN late 19th cent.: from Hindi *guār*.

guar. ▶ abbr. guaranteed.

gua·ra·che ▶ n. variant spelling of HUARACHE.

gua·ra·na /gwəˈränə/ ▶ n. **1** a substance prepared from the seeds of a Brazilian shrub, used as a tonic or stimulant.
2 the shrub (*Paullinia cupana*) of the soapberry family that yields guarana.
– ORIGIN mid 19th cent.: from Tupi.

Gua·ra·ni /gwärəˈnē/ ▶ n. (pl. **same**) **1** a member of an American Indian people of Paraguay and adjacent regions.
2 the language of this people, one of the main divisions of the Tupi-Guarani language family and a national language of Paraguay.
3 (**guarani**) the basic monetary unit of Paraguay, equal to 100 centimos.
▶ adj. of or relating to the Guarani or their language.
– ORIGIN Spanish.

guar·an·tee /ˌgarənˈtē/ ▶ n. **1** a formal promise or assurance (typically in writing) that certain conditions will be fulfilled, esp. that a product will be repaired or replaced if not of a specified quality and durability: *we offer a 10-year* ***guarantee against*** *rusting*. ■ something that gives a certainty of outcome: *past performance is no* ***guarantee of*** *future results*.
2 (also **guaranty**) Law a formal pledge to pay another person's debt or to perform another person's obligation in the case of default. ■ a thing serving as security for such a pledge. ■ less common term for GUARANTOR.
▶ v. (**guarantees, guaranteeing, guaranteed**) [no obj.] provide a formal assurance or promise, esp. that certain conditions shall be fulfilled relating to a product, service, or transaction: [with clause or infinitive] *the con artist guarantees that the dirt pile will yield at least 20 ounces of gold*. ■ [with obj.] provide such an assurance regarding (something, esp. a product): *the repairs will be guaranteed for three years* | (as adj. **guaranteed**) *the guaranteed bonus is not very high*. ■ [with obj.] provide financial security for; underwrite: *a demand that $100,000 be deposited to guarantee their costs*. ■ [with obj.] promise with certainty: *no one can guarantee a profit on stocks*.
– ORIGIN late 17th cent. (in the sense 'guarantor'): perhaps from Spanish *garante*, corresponding to French *garant* (see WARRANT), later influenced by French *garantie* 'guaranty.'

guar·an·tee fund ▶ n. a sum of money pledged as a contingent indemnity for loss.

guar·an·tor /ˌgarənˈtôr, ˈgarəntər/ ▶ n. a person, organization, or thing that guarantees something: *the role of the police as guarantors of public order*. ■ Law a person or organization who provides a guaranty.

guar·an·ty /ˈgarənˌtē/ ▶ n. (pl. **guaranties**) variant of GUARANTEE (sense 2 of the noun).

guard /gärd/ ▶ v. [with obj.] watch over in order to protect or control: *they were sent to* ***guard*** *villagers* ***from*** *attack by bandits* | *the gates were guarded by uniformed soldiers*. ■ watch over (someone) to prevent them escaping: *his task was to help guard Japanese soldiers*. ■ watch over (someone) to prevent them from escaping: *police officers were guarding inmates who could not be accommodated in prison*. ■ [no obj.] (**guard against**) take precautions against: *farmers must guard against sudden changes in the market*. ■ protect against damage or harm: *the company fiercely guarded its independence*. ■ Basketball stay close to (an opponent) in order to prevent a good shot, pass, or drive.
▶ n. **1** a person who keeps watch, esp. a soldier or other person formally assigned to protect a person or to control access to a place: *a security guard* | [as modifier] *he distracted the soldier on guard duty*. ■ [treated as sing. or pl.] a body of soldiers serving to protect a place or person: *the hound belonged to a member of the castle's guard*. ■ (**Guards**) the household troops of the British army. ■ a prison warder. ■ Brit. an official who rides on and is in general charge of a train. ■ Football each of two offensive players positioned either side of the center. ■ Basketball each of two backcourt players chiefly responsible for running the team's offense.
2 a device worn or fitted to prevent injury or damage: *a retractable blade guard*. ■ a chain attached to a watch or bracelet to prevent loss.
3 a defensive posture adopted in a boxing, fencing, or martial arts contest or in a fight: *this kick can curl around an otherwise effective guard*. ■ a state of caution, vigilance, or preparedness against adverse circumstances: *he let his guard slip enough to make some unwise comments*.
– PHRASES **keep** (or **stand**) **guard** act as a guard. **lower** (or **let down**) **one's guard** relax one's defensive posture, leaving oneself vulnerable to attack: *if you lower your guard or take a step backward, I will throw in the towel*. ■ reduce one's level of vigilance or caution: *she was not ready to let down her guard and confide in him*. **off guard** unprepared for some surprise or difficulty: *the government was caught off guard by the unexpected announcement*. **on guard** on duty to protect or defend something. ■ (also **on one's guard**) prepared for any contingency; vigilant: *we must be* ***on guard against*** *such temptation*. **put up one's guard** adopt a defensive posture. **under guard** being guarded: *he was held in an empty stable under guard*.
– ORIGIN late Middle English (in the sense 'care, custody'): from Old French *garde* (noun), *garder* (verb), of West Germanic origin. Compare with WARD.

guard·ant /ˈgärdnt/ ▶ adj. [usu. postpositive] Heraldry (esp. of an animal) depicted with the body sideways and the face toward the viewer: *three lions passant guardant*.
– ORIGIN late 16th cent.: from French *gardant* 'guarding,' from *garder* 'to guard.'

guard cell ▶ n. Botany each of a pair of curved cells that surround a stoma, becoming larger or smaller according to the pressure within the cells.

guard·ed /ˈgärdid/ ▶ adj. cautious and having possible reservations: *he has given a guarded welcome to the idea*. ■ (of a person's medical condition) serious and of uncertain outcome: *the surviving crewman was in stable but guarded condition*.
– DERIVATIVES **guard·ed·ly** adv., **guard·ed·ness** n.

guard hair ▶ n. long, coarse hair forming an animal's outer fur.

guard·house /ˈgärdˌhous/ ▶ n. a building used to accommodate a military guard or to detain military prisoners. ■ a building accommodating a guard who controls entrance to the grounds of a house, housing development, school, or other facility: *the prestigious islands have opted for guardhouses, where the license plate numbers of visitors are copied down*.

guard·i·an /ˈgärdēən/ ▶ n. a defender, protector, or keeper: *self-appointed guardians of public morality*. ■ a person who looks after and is legally responsible for someone who is unable to manage their own affairs, esp. an incompetent or disabled person or a child whose parents have died. ■ the superior of a Franciscan convent.
– DERIVATIVES **guard·i·an·ship** /-ˌSHip/ n.
– ORIGIN late Middle English: from Old French *garden*, of Germanic origin; compare with WARD and WARDEN. The ending was altered by association with -IAN.

guard·i·an an·gel ▶ n. a spirit that is believed to watch over and protect a person or place.

Guard·mem·ber /ˈgärdˌmembər/ ▶ n. a person who serves in the National Guard.

guard of hon·or ▶ n. a group of soldiers ceremonially welcoming an important visitor or escorting a casket in a funeral. Also called HONOR GUARD.

guard·rail /ˈgärdˌrāl/ ▶ n. a rail that prevents people from falling off or being hit by something. ■ a strong fence at the side of a road or in the middle of an expressway, intended to reduce the risk of serious accidents.

guard ring ▶ n. **1** a ring preventing another ring from slipping off a finger.
2 a ring-shaped electrode used to limit the extent of an electric field, esp. in a capacitor.

guard·room /ˈgärdˌro͞om, -ˌro͝om/ ▶ n. a room in a military base used to accommodate a guard or detain prisoners.

guards·man /ˈgärdzmən/ ▶ n. (pl. **guardsmen**) (in the US) a member of the National Guard. ■ (in the UK) a soldier of a regiment of Guards.

Guar·ne·ri /ˌgwärˈne(ə)rē/, Giuseppe (1687–1744), Italian violin-maker; known as **del Gesù**. He is the most well known of a family of three generations of violin-makers based in Cremona.

Guar·ne·ri·us /gwärˈne(ə)rēəs/ ▶ n. a violin made by a member of the Guarneri family of Cremona, Italy, during the 17th and 18th centuries.

Gua·ru·lhos /gwäˈro͞olyo͞os/ an industrial and commercial city in southeastern Brazil, northeast of São Paulo; pop. 1,236,200 (est. 2007).

Gua·te·ma·la /ˌgwätəˈmälə/ a country in Central America that borders on the Pacific Ocean and has a short coastline on the Caribbean Sea; pop. 13,276,500 (est. 2009); capital, Guatemala City; official language, Spanish.

> A former center of Mayan civilization, Guatemala was conquered by the Spanish in 1523–24. After independence, it formed the core of the short-lived United Provinces of Central America 1828–38 before becoming an independent republic in its own right.

– DERIVATIVES **Gua·te·ma·lan** adj. & n.

Gua·te·ma·la Cit·y the capital of Guatemala; pop. 1,090,000 (est. 2009). At an altitude of 4,920 feet (1,500 m) in the central highlands, it was founded in 1776 to replace the former capital, Antigua Guatemala, which was destroyed by an earthquake in 1773.

gua·va /ˈgwävə/ ▶ n. **1** an edible pale orange tropical fruit with pink, juicy flesh and a strong, sweet aroma.
2 the small tropical American tree that bears this fruit. ● Genus *Psidium*, family Myrtaceae: several species, in particular *P. guajava*.
– ORIGIN mid 16th cent.: from Spanish *guayaba*, probably from Taino.

Gua·via·re Riv·er /gwävˈyärā/ a river that flows east for 650 miles (1,040 km) from the Andes Mountains in Colombia to join the Orinoco River at the Venezuelan border.

guay·a·ber·a /ˌgīəˈberə/ ▶ n. a lightweight open-necked Cuban or Mexican shirt with two breast pockets and two pockets over the hips, typically having short sleeves and worn untucked.
– ORIGIN 1970s: Cuban Spanish, apparently originally from the name of the *Yayabo* river, influenced by Spanish *guayaba* 'guava.'

Gua·ya·quil /ˌgīəˈkēl/ a seaport in western Ecuador, the country's principal port and second largest city; pop. 2,223,200 (est. 2008).

Guay·na·bo /gwīˈnäbō/ a community in northeastern Puerto Rico, south of San Juan; pop. 81,100 (est. 2009).

gua·yu·le /(g)wäˈyo͞olē/ ▶ n. a silver-leaved Mexican shrub of the daisy family that yields large amounts of latex. ● *Parthenium argentatum*, family Compositae. ■ a rubber substitute made from this latex.
– ORIGIN early 20th cent.: via Latin American Spanish from Nahuatl *cuauhuli*.

gu·ber·na·to·ri·al /ˌgo͞obərnəˈtôrēəl/ ▶ **adj.** of or relating to a state governor or the office of state governor: *a gubernatorial election.*
– ORIGIN mid 18th cent.: from Latin *gubernator* 'governor' (from *gubernare* 'steer, govern,' from Greek *kubernan* 'to steer') + -IAL.

guck /gək/ ▶ **n.** informal a slimy, dirty, or otherwise unpleasant substance: *he got mud and cow guck all over his white jersey.*
– ORIGIN possibly a blend of GOO and MUCK.

gudg·eon[1] /ˈgəjən/ ▶ **n. 1** a small, edible, European freshwater fish, often used as bait by anglers. ● *Gobio gobio*, family Cyprinidae.
2 archaic a credulous or easily fooled person.
– ORIGIN late Middle English: from Old French *goujon*, from Latin *gobio(n-)*, from *gobius* 'goby.'

gudg·eon[2] ▶ **n.** a pivot or spindle on which a bell or other object swings or rotates. ■ the tubular part of a hinge into which the pin fits to unite the joint. ■ a socket at the stern of a vessel, into which a rudder is fitted. ■ a pin holding two blocks of stone together.
– ORIGIN Middle English: from Old French *goujon*, diminutive of *gouge* (see GOUGE).

g

gudg·eon pin ▶ **n.** a pin holding a piston rod and a connecting rod together.

Gud·run /ˈgo͝odro͞on/ (in Norse legend) the Norse equivalent of Kriemhild, wife of Sigurd and later of Atli (Attila the Hun).

guel·der rose /ˈgeldər/ ▶ **n.** a deciduous Eurasian shrub of the honeysuckle family with flattened heads of fragrant, creamy-white flowers, followed by clusters of bitter translucent red berries. Similar to the closely related highbush cranberry, it is widely cultivated in North America. ● *Viburnum opulus*, family Caprifoliaceae. See also SNOWBALL BUSH.
– ORIGIN late 16th cent.: from Dutch *geldersche roos* 'rose of *Gelderland*' (see GELDERLAND).

Guelph /gwelf/ ▶ **n. 1** a member of one of two great factions in Italian medieval politics, traditionally supporting the pope against the Holy Roman Emperor. Compare with GHIBELLINE.
2 a member of a princely family of Swabian origin from which the British royal house is descended through George I.
– DERIVATIVES **Guelph·ic** /-fik/ **adj.**
– ORIGIN from Italian *Guelfo*, from Middle High German *Welf*, the name of the founder of one of the two great rival dynasties in the Holy Roman Empire.

gue·non /gəˈnōn/ ▶ **n.** an African monkey found mainly in forests, with a long tail and typically a brightly colored coat. The male is much larger than the female. ● Genus *Cercopithecus*, family Cercopithecidae: several species, including the vervet, mona, and Diana monkeys.
– ORIGIN mid 19th cent.: from French, of unknown origin.

guer·don /ˈgərdn/ chiefly archaic ▶ **n.** a reward or recompense.
▶ **v.** [with obj.] give a reward to (someone): *there might come a time in which he should guerdon them.*
– ORIGIN late Middle English: from Old French, from medieval Latin *widerdonum*, alteration (by association with Latin *donum* 'gift') of a West Germanic compound represented by Old High German *widarlōn* 'repayment.'

Gue·rick·e /ˈgerikə/, Otto von (1602–86), German engineer and physicist. He was the first to investigate the properties of a vacuum, and he devised the Magdeburg hemispheres to demonstrate atmospheric pressure.

Guern·sey[1] /ˈgərnzē/ an island in the English Channel, northwest of Jersey; pop. 65,900 (est. 2009); capital, St. Peter Port.

Guern·sey[2] ▶ **n.** (pl. **Guernseys**) **1** an animal of a breed of dairy cattle from Guernsey, noted for producing rich, creamy milk.
2 (**guernsey**) a thick sweater made with oiled navy blue wool and originally worn by fishermen.

Guern·sey lil·y ▶ **n.** a nerine with large heads of pink lilylike flowers. Native to South Africa, it has long been cultivated and was first described in Guernsey, England. ● *Nerine sarniensis*, family Liliaceae (or Amaryllidaceae).

Guer·re·ro /gəˈre(ə)rō/ a state in southwestern central Mexico, on the Pacific coast; capital, Chilpancingo.

guer·ril·la /gəˈrilə/ (also **guerilla**) ▶ **n.** a member of a small independent group taking part in irregular fighting, typically against larger regular forces: *this small town fell to the guerrillas* | [as modifier] *guerrilla warfare.* ■ [as modifier] referring to actions or activities performed in an impromptu way, often without authorization: *guerrilla theater.*
– ORIGIN early 19th cent. (introduced during the Peninsular War (1808–14)): from Spanish, diminutive of *guerra* 'war.'

> **WORD TRENDS** A new kind of **guerrilla** action is emerging. Like the soldiers of the same name, its proponents are pitted against authority, using ambush and surprise as their primary weapons. Their interests, however, are far from violent: gardening, music, and filmmaking, to be exact. **Guerrilla** is now used to refer to activities performed in an impromptu way, often without permission. **Guerrilla gardening** involves activists planting seeds on abandoned or public land, usually in secret. Then there are the independent filmmakers on low budgets, who shoot their scenes quickly in real locations. Or how about **guerrilla rockers**, who perform unexpectedly in unlikely places: *their live shows have become legendary, including guerrilla gigs on subway trains.*

guess /ges/ ▶ **v.** [with obj.] estimate or suppose (something) without sufficient information to be sure of being correct: *she guessed the child's age to be 14 or 15* | [with clause] *he took her aside, and I guessed that he was offering her a job.* ■ (**guess at**) make a conjecture about: *their motives he could only guess at.* ■ correctly conjecture or perceive: [with clause] *she's guessed where we're going.* ■ (**I guess**) informal used to indicate that although one thinks or supposes something, it is without any great conviction or strength of feeling: [with clause] *I guess I'd better tell you everything.*
▶ **n.** an estimate or conjecture: *my guess is that within a year we will have a referendum.*
– PHRASES **anybody's** (or **anyone's**) **guess** very difficult or impossible to determine: *how well the system will work is anybody's guess.* **keep someone guessing** informal leave someone uncertain or in doubt as to one's intentions or plans.
– DERIVATIVES **guess·a·ble adj.**, **guess·er n.**
– ORIGIN Middle English: origin uncertain; perhaps from Dutch *gissen*, and probably related to GET.

guess·ti·mate (also **guestimate**) informal ▶ **n.** /ˈgestəmit/ an estimate based on a mixture of guesswork and calculation.
▶ **v.** /ˈgestəˌmāt/ [with obj.] form such an estimate of: *the task is to guesstimate the total vote.*
– ORIGIN 1930s: blend of GUESS and ESTIMATE.

guess·work /ˈgesˌwərk/ ▶ **n.** the process or results of guessing.

guest /gest/ ▶ **n.** a person who is invited to visit the home of or take part in a function organized by another: *I have two guests coming to dinner tonight* | [as modifier] *a guest bedroom.* ■ a person invited to participate in an official event: *the bishop went to Cuba as a guest of the Catholic Church* | [as modifier] *a guest speaker.* ■ a person invited to take part in a radio or television program, sports event, or other entertainment: *a regular guest on the morning show* | [as modifier] *a guest appearance.* ■ a person lodging at a hotel or boarding house: *a reduction for guests staying seven nights or more.* ■ a customer at a restaurant. ■ Entomology a small invertebrate that lives unharmed within an ants' nest.
▶ **v.** [no obj.] informal appear as a guest: *he guested on one of her early albums.*
– PHRASES **be my guest** informal please do: *May I choose the restaurant? Be my guest!* **guest of honor** the most important guest at an occasion.
– ORIGIN Middle English: from Old Norse *gestr*, of Germanic origin; related to Dutch *gast* and German *Gast*, from an Indo-European root shared by Latin *hostis* 'enemy' (originally 'stranger').

guestbook ▶ **n.** a book in which visitors to a particular place may write their names, addresses, and remarks. ■ a facility on a website on which visitors to the site may record their comments.

guest house (also **guesthouse**) ▶ **n.** a private house offering accommodations to paying guests. ■ a small, separate house on the grounds of a larger one, used for accommodating guests.

gues·ti·mate ▶ **n.** & **v.** variant spelling of GUESSTIMATE.

guest list ▶ **n.** a list of the people invited to a particular event. ■ a list of people who are to be admitted to a concert or similar event without payment.

guest work·er ▶ **n.** a person with temporary permission to work in another country, esp. in Germany.
– ORIGIN 1960s: translation of the German *Gastarbeiter*.

Gue·va·ra /gəˈvärə/, Che (1928–67), Argentine revolutionary and guerrilla leader; full name *Ernesto Guevara de la Serna*. He played a significant part in the Cuban revolution 1956–59 and became a government minister under Fidel Castro. He was captured and executed by the Bolivian army while training guerrillas for a planned uprising in Bolivia.

guff /gəf/ ▶ **n.** informal trivial, worthless, or insolent talk or ideas.
– ORIGIN early 19th cent. (in the sense 'puff, whiff of a bad smell'): imitative.

guf·faw /gəˈfô/ ▶ **n.** a loud and boisterous laugh.
▶ **v.** [no obj.] laugh in such a way: *both men guffawed at the remark.*
– ORIGIN early 18th cent. (originally Scots): imitative.

Gug·gen·heim /ˈgo͞ogənˌhīm, ˈgo͞o-/, Meyer (1828–1905), US industrialist; born in Switzerland. With his seven sons he established large mining and metal-processing companies. His son **Solomon** (1861–1949) set up several foundations that supported the arts, including the Guggenheim Museum in New York.

gug·gul /ˈgo͞ogəl/ ▶ **n.** an herbal preparation made from the sticky gum of various myrrh trees that has been alleged to aid in lowering serum cholesterol. ● The trees providing the main source are *Commiphora mukul* and *Commiphora wightii*, family Burseraceae.

GUI /ˈgo͞oē/ ▶ **abbr.** Computing graphical user interface.

Gui·a·na /gēˈänə, gīˈanə/ a region in northern South America, bounded by the Orinoco, Negro, and Amazon rivers and the Atlantic Ocean. It now includes Guyana, Suriname, French Guiana, and the Guiana Highlands.

Gui·a·na High·lands a mountainous plateau region in northern South America that lies between the Orinoco and Amazon river basins, largely in southeastern Venezuela and northern Brazil.

guid·ance /ˈgīdns/ ▶ **n. 1** advice or information aimed at resolving a problem or difficulty, esp. as given by someone in authority: *he looked to his father for inspiration and guidance.*
2 the directing of the motion or position of something, esp. a missile: *a surface-to-air missile guidance system.*

guide /gīd/ ▶ **n. 1** a person who advises or shows the way to others: *this lady is going to act as our guide for the rest of the tour.* ■ a professional mountain climber in charge of a group.
2 a thing that helps someone to form an opinion or make a decision or calculation: *here is a guide to the number of curtain hooks you will need.* ■ a book, document, or display providing information on a subject or about a place: *a guide to baby and toddler care.*
3 a structure or marking that directs the motion or positioning of something: *the guides for the bolt needed straightening.*
4 a soldier, vehicle, or ship whose position determines the movements of others.
▶ **v. 1** [with obj.] show or indicate the way to (someone): *he guided her to the front row and sat beside her.* ■ direct the motion or positioning of (something): *the groove in the needle guides the thread.*
2 [with obj.] direct or have an influence on the course of action of (someone or something): *he guided the team to a second successive win in the tournament.*
– DERIVATIVES **guid·a·ble adj.**, **guid·er n.**
– ORIGIN late Middle English: from Old French *guide* (noun), *guider* (verb), of Germanic origin; related to WIT[2].

Guide As·so·ci·a·tion (in the UK) an organization for girls, founded in 1910.

guide·book /ˈgīdˌbo͝ok/ ▶ **n.** a book of information about a place, designed for the use of visitors or tourists.

guid·ed /ˈgīdid/ ▶ **adj.** conducted by a guide: *a guided tour of the castle.* ■ directed by remote control or by internal equipment: *a guided missile.*

guid·ed im·age·ry ▶ **n.** the use of words and music to evoke positive imaginary scenarios in a subject with a view to bringing about some beneficial effect.

guide dog ▶ **n.** a dog trained to lead a blind person.

guide·line /ˈgīdˌlīn/ ▶ **n.** a general rule, principle, or piece of advice.

guide num·ber ▶ **n.** Photography a measure of the power of a flashgun expressed in meters or feet.

guide·post /ˈgīdˌpōst/ ▶ **n.** another term for SIGNPOST.

guide rope ▶ **n.** a rope used to guide the movement of the load of a crane.

guide·way /ˈgīdˌwā/ ▶ **n.** a groove or track along which something moves.

gui·don /'gīdn/ ▶ **n.** a pennant that narrows to a point or fork at the free end, esp. one used as the standard of a light cavalry regiment.
– ORIGIN mid 16th cent.: from French, from Italian *guidone*, from *guida* 'a guide.'

Gui·gnol /gēn'yôl/ the bloodthirsty chief character in a French puppet show of that name that is similar to Punch and Judy. See also **Grand Guignol**.

guild /gild/ (also **gild**) ▶ **n.** a medieval association of craftsmen or merchants, often having considerable power. ■ an association of people for mutual aid or the pursuit of a common goal. ■ Ecology a group of species that have similar requirements and play a similar role within a community.
– ORIGIN late Old English: probably from Middle Low German and Middle Dutch *gilde*, of Germanic origin; related to **yield**.

guild·er /'gildər/ ▶ **n.** (pl. **same** or **guilders**) the basic monetary unit of the Netherlands (until the introduction of the euro), equal to 100 cents. ■ historical a gold or silver coin formerly used in the Netherlands, Germany, and Austria.
– ORIGIN alteration of Dutch *gulden* (see **gulden**).

guild·hall /'gild,hôl/ ▶ **n.** a building used as the meeting place of a guild or corporation. ■ Brit. a town hall. ■ (**Guildhall**) the hall of the Corporation of the City of London, used for ceremonial occasions.

guile /gīl/ ▶ **n.** sly or cunning intelligence: *he used all his guile and guts to free himself from the muddle he was in.*
– DERIVATIVES **guile·ful** /-fəl/ **adj.**, **guile·ful·ly** /-fəlē/ **adv.**
– ORIGIN Middle English: from Old French, probably from Old Norse; compare with **wile**.

guile·less /'gīllis/ ▶ **adj.** devoid of guile; innocent and without deception: *his face, once so open and guileless.*
– DERIVATIVES **guile·less·ly adv.**, **guile·less·ness n.**

Gui·lin /'gwā'lin/ (also **Kweilin**) a city in southern China, on the Li River, in the autonomous region of Guangxi Zhuang; pop. 573,800 (est. 2006).

Guil·lain–Bar·ré syn·drome /gē'yan bə'rā/ ▶ **n.** Medicine an acute form of polyneuritis, often preceded by a respiratory infection, causing weakness and often paralysis of the limbs.
– ORIGIN 1916: named after Georges *Guillain* (1876–1961) and Jean *Barré* (1880–1967), two of those who first described the syndrome.

guil·le·mot /'gilə,mät/ ▶ **n.** a black-breasted auk (seabird) with a narrow pointed bill, typically nesting on cliff ledges. ● Family Alcidae, genus *Cepphus*: several species, in particular the North Atlantic **black guillemot** (*C. grylle*), with a white wing patch in summer and pale plumage in winter.
– ORIGIN late 17th cent.: from French, diminutive of *Guillaume* 'William.'

guil·loche /gi'lōsн/ ▶ **n.** architectural ornamentation resembling braided or interlaced ribbons.
– ORIGIN mid 19th cent.: from French *guillochis*, denoting the ornamentation, or *guilloche*, a carving tool.

guil·lo·tine /'gilə,tēn, 'gēə-/ ▶ **n.** a machine with a heavy blade sliding vertically in grooves, used for beheading people. ■ a device for cutting that incorporates a descending or sliding blade, used typically for cutting paper, card, or sheet metal. ■ a surgical instrument with a sliding blade used typically for the removal of the tonsils. ■ Brit. (in parliament) a procedure used to prevent delay in the discussion of a legislative bill by fixing times at which various parts of it must be voted on: [as modifier] *a guillotine motion.*
▶ **v.** [with obj.] execute (someone) by guillotine. ■ Brit. (in parliament) end discussion by applying a guillotine to (a bill or debate).
– ORIGIN late 18th cent.: from French, named after Joseph-Ignace *Guillotin* (1738–1814), the French physician who recommended its use for executions in 1789.

guillotine

guilt /gilt/ ▶ **n.** the fact of having committed a specified or implied offense or crime: *it is the duty of the prosecution to prove the prisoner's guilt.* ■ a feeling of having done wrong or failed in an obligation: *he remembered with sudden guilt the letter from his mother that he had not yet read.*
▶ **v.** [with obj.] informal make (someone) feel guilty, esp. in order to induce them to do something: *Celeste had been* **guilted into** *going by her parents.*
– PHRASES **guilt by association** guilt ascribed to someone not because of any evidence but because of their association with an offender.
– ORIGIN Old English *gylt*, of unknown origin.

guilt com·plex ▶ **n.** an obsession with the idea of having done wrong.

guilt·less /'giltlis/ ▶ **adj.** having no guilt; innocent: *you don't need a pardon if you're guiltless.*
– DERIVATIVES **guilt·less·ly adv.**, **guilt·less·ness n.**

guilt trip ▶ **n.** an experience of feeling guilty about something, esp. when such guilt is excessive, self-indulgent, or unfounded: *let's skip the guilt trip and talk real, rational reasons.*
▶ **v.** (**guilt-trip**) [with obj.] make (someone) feel guilty, esp. in order to induce them to do something: *a pay increase will not guilt-trip them into improvements.*

guilt·y /'giltē/ ▶ **adj.** (**guiltier**, **guiltiest**) culpable of or responsible for a specified wrongdoing: *the police will soon discover who the guilty party is | he was found* **guilty of** *manslaughter | he found them* **guilty on** *a lesser charge.* See also **find**, **plead**. ■ justly chargeable with a particular fault or error: *she was guilty of a serious error of judgment.* ■ conscious of or affected by a feeling of guilt: *John felt guilty at having deceived the family | she wrestled with a guilty conscience after her adultery.* ■ involving a feeling or a judgment of guilt: *I have no guilty secret to reveal | a guilty verdict.*
– PHRASES **not guilty** innocent, esp. of a formal charge: *he pled not guilty to murder.*
– DERIVATIVES **guilt·i·ly** /-təlē/ **adv.**, **guilt·i·ness n.**
– ORIGIN Old English *gyltig* (see **guilt**, **-y**[1]).

USAGE See usage at **innocent** and **plead**.

guimpe /gimp/ (also **guimp**) ▶ **n.** historical a high-necked blouse or undergarment worn showing beneath a low-necked dress.
– ORIGIN mid 19th cent.: from French; related to German *Wimpel*, Dutch *wimpel* 'pennant, streamer,' also to **wimple** and the rare word *gimp* 'nun's neckerchief.'

Guin·ea /'ginē/ a country on the west coast of Africa; pop. 10,058,000 (est. 2009); capital, Conakry; languages, French (official), Fulani, Malinke, and others.

Part of a feudal Fulani empire from the 16th century, Guinea was colonized by France as part of French West Africa. It became an independent republic in 1958.

– DERIVATIVES **Guin·e·an** /-ēən/ **adj. & n.**

guin·ea /'ginē/ (abbr.: **gn.**) ▶ **n.** Brit. the sum of £1.05 (21 shillings in predecimal currency), now used mainly for determining professional fees and auction prices. ■ historical a former British gold coin that was first minted in 1663 from gold imported from West Africa, with a value that was later fixed at 21 shillings. It was replaced by the sovereign from 1817.
– ORIGIN named after **Guinea** in West Africa.

Guin·ea, Gulf of a large inlet of the Atlantic Ocean that borders on the southern coast of West Africa.

Guin·ea-Bis·sau /'ginē bi'sou/ a country on the western coast of Africa, between Senegal and Guinea; pop. 1,534,000 (est. 2009); capital, Bissau; languages, Portuguese (official), West African languages, Creoles.

The area, a center of the slave trade, was explored by the Portuguese in the 15th century. Formerly called Portuguese Guinea, it became a colony in 1879 and the independent republic of Guinea-Bissau in 1974. A military coup in 1980 brought continuing unrest.

guin·ea fowl ▶ **n.** (pl. **same**) a large African game bird with slate-colored, white-spotted plumage and a loud call. It is sometimes domesticated. ● Family Numididae (or Phasianidae): several genera and species, e.g., the **helmeted guineafowl** (*Numida meleagris*).

guin·ea pig ▶ **n.** a domesticated, tailless South American cavy, originally raised for food. It no longer occurs in the wild and is now typically kept as a pet or for laboratory research. ● *Cavia porcellus*, family Caviidae. ■ a person or thing used as a subject for experiment.

guin·ea worm ▶ **n.** a very long parasitic nematode worm that lives under the skin of infected humans and other mammals in rural Africa and Asia. ● *Dracunculus medinensis*, class Phasmida.

gui·nep /gi'nep/ ▶ **n.** variant spelling of **genip** (sense 2).

Guin·e·vere /'gwinə,vi(ə)r/ (in Arthurian legend) the wife of King Arthur and mistress of Lancelot.

Guin·ness /'ginis/, Sir Alec (1914–2000), English actor. He performed in movies, such as *Bridge on the River Kwai* (1957) and *Star Wars* (1977), and as espionage chief George Smiley in television versions of John Le Carré's novels.

gui·pure /gi'pyŏŏr/ ▶ **n.** a heavy lace consisting of embroidered motifs held together by large connecting stitches.
– ORIGIN mid 19th cent.: from French, from *guiper* 'cover with silk,' of Germanic origin.

gui·ro /'gwi(ə)rō/ ▶ **n.** (pl. **guiros**) a musical instrument with a serrated surface that gives a rasping sound when scraped with a stick, originally made from an elongated gourd and used in Latin American music.
– ORIGIN late 19th cent.: Spanish, literally 'gourd.'

guise /gīz/ ▶ **n.** an external form, appearance, or manner of presentation, typically concealing the true nature of something: *he visited* **in the guise of** *an inspector | telemarketing and selling* **under the guise of** *market research.*
– ORIGIN Middle English: from Old French, of Germanic origin; related to **wise**[2].

gui·tar /gi'tär/ ▶ **n.** a stringed musical instrument with a fretted fingerboard, typically incurved sides, and six or twelve strings, played by plucking or strumming with the fingers or a plectrum. See also **electric guitar**.
– DERIVATIVES **gui·tar·ist** /-rist/ **n.**
– ORIGIN early 17th cent.: from Spanish *guitarra* (partly via French), from Greek *kithara*, denoting an instrument similar to the lyre.

electric guitar acoustic guitar
guitars

gui·tar·fish /gi'tär,fisн/ ▶ **n.** (pl. **same** or **guitarfishes**) a fish of shallow warm seas, related to the rays and having a guitarlike body shape. ● Several species in the family Rhinobatidae, including *Rhinobatus rhinobatus*, common in European waters, and the **Chinese guitarfish** (*Platyrhina sinensis*, family Platyrhinidae).

Gui·yang /'gwā'yäng/ (also **Kweiyang**) an industrial city in southern China, capital of Guizhou province; pop. 1,475,900 (est. 2006).

Gui·zhou /'gwā'jō/ (also **Kweichow**) a province in southern China; capital, Guiyang.

Gu·ja·rat /,gŏŏjə'rät, ,gŏŏj-/ (also **Gujerat**) a state in western India, on the Arabian Sea; capital, Gandhinagar. Formed in 1960 from the northern and western parts of the former state of Bombay, it is one of the most industrialized parts of the country.

Gu·ja·ra·ti /,gŏŏjə'rätē/ (also **Gujerati**) ▶ **n.** (pl. **Gujaratis** /-tēz/) **1** a native or inhabitant of Gujarat.
2 the Indic language of the Gujaratis.
▶ **adj.** of or relating to this people or their language.

Guj·ran·wa·la /,gŏŏjrən'wälə, ,gŏŏj-/ a city in northeastern Pakistan, in Punjab province, northwest of Lahore; pop. 1,526,200 (est. 2009). It was an important center of Sikh influence in the early 19th century.

Guj·rat /'gŏŏj,rät/ a city in northeastern Pakistan, in Punjab province, north of Lahore; pop. 328,500 (est. 2009).

Gu·lag /'gōōläg/ ▶ **n.** [in sing.] a system of labor camps maintained in the former Soviet Union from 1930 to 1955 in which many people died. ■ (**gulag**) a camp in this system, or any political labor camp.
– ORIGIN Russian, from *G(lavnoe) u(pravlenie ispravitel'no-trudovykh) lag(ereĭ)* 'Chief Administration for Corrective Labor Camps.'

gu·lar /'g(y)ōōlər/ Zoology ▶ **adj.** of, relating to, or situated on the throat of an animal, esp. a reptile, fish, or bird.
▶ **n.** a plate or scale on the throat of a reptile or fish.
– ORIGIN early 19th cent.: from Latin *gula* 'throat' + **-ar**[1].

PRONUNCIATION KEY ə *ago, up*; ər *over, fur*; a *hat*; ā *ate*; ä *car*; e *let*; ē *see*; i *fit*; ī *by*; NG *sing*; ō *go*; ô *law, for*; oi *toy*; ŏŏ *good*; ōō *goo*; ou *out*; TH *thin*; TH *then*; ZH *vision*

g

Gul·bar·ga /ˈgo͝olbər,gä/ a city in southern central India, in the state of Karnataka; pop. 532,000 (est. 2009). It was formerly the seat of the Bahmani kings of the Deccan (1347–c.1424).

gulch /gəlCH/ ▶ **n.** a narrow and steep-sided ravine marking the course of a fast stream.
– ORIGIN mid 19th cent.: perhaps from dialect *gulch* 'to swallow.'

gul·den /ˈgo͝oldən/ ▶ **n.** (pl. **same** or **guldens**) another term for GUILDER.
– ORIGIN late 19th cent.: Dutch and German, literally 'golden.'

gules /gyo͞olz/ ▶ **n.** red, as a heraldic tincture: [postpositive] *sword and long cross gules.*
– ORIGIN Middle English: from Old French *goles* (plural of *gole* 'throat,' from Latin *gula*), used to denote pieces of red-dyed fur used as a neck ornament.

gulf /gəlf/ ▶ **n. 1** a deep inlet of the sea almost surrounded by land, with a narrow mouth. ■ **(the Gulf)** informal name for PERSIAN GULF.
2 a deep ravine, chasm, or abyss.
3 a large difference or division between two people or groups, or between viewpoints, concepts, or situations: *a wide gulf between theory and practice.*
– ORIGIN late Middle English: from Old French *golfe*, from Italian *golfo*, based on Greek *kolpos* 'bosom, gulf.'

g

Gulf In·tra·coast·al Wa·ter·way a route that allows sheltered boat passage along the coast of the Gulf of Mexico between Key West in Florida and Brownsville in Texas.

Gulf of A·den, Gulf of Boo·thia, etc. see ADEN, GULF OF; BOOTHIA, GULF OF, etc.

Gulf·port /ˈgəlf,pôrt/ a city in southern Mississippi, on the Gulf of Mexico, west of Biloxi; pop. 70,055 (est. 2008).

Gulf States 1 the countries bordering on the Persian Gulf (Iran, Iraq, Kuwait, Saudi Arabia, Bahrain, Qatar, the United Arab Emirates, and Oman).
2 the US states that border on the Gulf of Mexico (Florida, Alabama, Mississippi, Louisiana, and Texas).

Gulf Stream a warm ocean current that flows from the Gulf of Mexico parallel with the US coast toward Newfoundland, Canada, and then continues across the Atlantic Ocean toward northwestern Europe as the North Atlantic Drift.

Gulf War 1 another name for IRAN–IRAQ WAR.
2 the war of January and February 1991 in which an international coalition of forces under the auspices of the United Nations forced the withdrawal of Saddam Hussein's Iraqi forces from Kuwait, which they had invaded and occupied in August 1990.

Gulf War syn·drome ▶ **n.** a medical condition affecting many veterans of the 1991 Gulf War, causing fatigue, chronic headaches, and skin and respiratory disorders. Its origin is uncertain, though it has been attributed to exposure to a combination of pesticides, vaccines, and other chemicals.

gulf·weed /ˈgəlf,wēd/ ▶ **n.** another term for SARGASSUM.

gull[1] /gəl/ ▶ **n.** a long-winged, web-footed seabird with a raucous call, typically having white plumage with a gray or black mantle. ● Family Laridae: several genera, in particular *Larus*, and numerous species.
– ORIGIN late Middle English: of Celtic origin; related to Welsh *gwylan* and Breton *gwelan*.

gull[2] ▶ **v.** [with obj.] fool or deceive (someone): *workers had been **gulled into** inflicting poverty and deprivation upon themselves.*
▶ **n.** a person who is fooled or deceived.
– ORIGIN late 16th cent.: of unknown origin.

Gul·lah /ˈgələ/ ▶ **n. 1** a member of a black people living on the coast of South Carolina and nearby islands.
2 the Creole language of this people, having an English base with elements from various West African languages. It has about 125,000 speakers.
▶ **adj.** of or relating to this people or their language.
– ORIGIN perhaps a shortening of *Angola*, or from *Gola*, the name of an agricultural people of Liberia and Sierra Leone.

gull·er·y /ˈgələrē/ ▶ **n.** (pl. **gulleries**) a breeding colony, breeding place, or roost of gulls.

gul·let /ˈgəlit/ ▶ **n.** the passage by which food passes from the mouth to the stomach; the esophagus.
– ORIGIN late Middle English: from Old French *goulet*, diminutive of *goule* 'throat,' from Latin *gula*.

gul·ley /ˈgəlē/ ▶ **n.** (pl. **gulleys**) variant spelling of GULLY.

gul·li·ble /ˈgələbəl/ ▶ **adj.** easily persuaded to believe something; credulous: *an attempt to persuade a gullible public to spend their money.*
– DERIVATIVES **gul·li·bil·i·ty** /,gələˈbilitē/ **n.**, **gul·li·bly** /-blē/ **adv.**
– ORIGIN early 19th cent.: from GULL[2] + -IBLE.

gull wing ▶ **n.** [as modifier] (of a door on a car or aircraft) opening upward: *gull-wing doors.*

gul·ly /ˈgəlē/ (also **gulley**) ▶ **n.** (pl. **gullies**) a water-worn ravine. ■ a deep artificial channel serving as a gutter or drain.
▶ **v.** [with obj.] (usu. as adj. **gullied**) erode gullies into (land) by water action: *he began to pick his way over the gullied landscape.*
– ORIGIN mid 16th cent. (in the sense 'gullet'): from French *goulet* (see GULLET).

gulp /gəlp/ ▶ **v.** [with obj.] swallow (drink or food) quickly or in large mouthfuls, often audibly: *he smiled and gulped his milk.* ■ breathe (air) deeply and quickly: *we emerged to gulp great lungfuls of cold night air.* ■ [no obj.] make effortful breathing or swallowing movements, typically in response to strong emotion: *fumes seeped in until she was forced to gulp for air | she **gulped back** the tears.*
▶ **n.** an act of gulping food or drink: *she swallowed the rest of the coffee with a gulp.* ■ a large mouthful of liquid hastily drunk: *Titch took a gulp of beer and wiped his mouth on his sleeve.* ■ a large quantity of air breathed in. ■ a swallowing movement of the throat: *the chairman gave an audible gulp.*
– PHRASES **at a gulp** with one gulp: *having emptied his glass at a gulp, Roger pulled out a cigar.*
– DERIVATIVES **gulp·y adj.**
– ORIGIN Middle English: probably from Middle Dutch *gulpen*, of imitative origin.

gulp·er /ˈgəlpər/ (also **gulper eel**) ▶ **n.** a deep-sea eel with very large jaws that open to give an enormous gape and with eyes near the tip of the snout. ● Order Saccopharyngiformes: several families.

GUM ▶ **abbr.** genitourinary medicine.

gum[1] /gəm/ ▶ **n. 1** a viscous secretion of some trees and shrubs that hardens on drying but is soluble in water, and from which adhesives and other products are made. Compare with RESIN. ■ glue that is used for sticking paper or other light materials together. ■ short for CHEWING GUM or BUBBLEGUM. ■ a gum tree, esp. a eucalyptus. See also SWEET GUM.
2 dated a long rubber boot.
▶ **v.** (**gums, gumming, gummed**) [with obj.] cover with gum or glue: (as adj. **gummed**) *gummed paper.* ■ fasten with gum or glue: *I was gumming small green leaves to a paper tree.* ■ **(gum something up)** clog up a mechanism and prevent it from working properly: *open and close the valves to make sure they don't get gummed up* | figurative *there was no winner and they debated the factors that could have **gummed up the works.***
– ORIGIN Middle English: from Old French *gomme*, based on Latin *gummi*, from Greek *kommi*, from Egyptian *kemai*.

gum[2] ▶ **n.** the firm area of flesh around the roots of the teeth in the upper or lower jaw: *a tooth broken off just above the gum* | [as modifier] *gum disease.*
▶ **v.** (**gums, gumming, gummed**) [with obj.] chew with toothless gums: *some grandmother gumming a meal.*
– ORIGIN Old English *gōma* 'inside of the mouth or throat,' of Germanic origin; related to German *Gaumen* 'roof of the mouth.'

gum[3] ▶ **n.** (in phrase **by gum!**) an exclamation used for emphasis.
– ORIGIN early 19th cent.: euphemistic alteration of *God*.

gum ar·a·bic ▶ **n.** a gum exuded by some kinds of acacia, used in the food industry, in glue, as the binder for watercolor paints, and in incense.

gum·ball /ˈgəm,bôl/ ▶ **n.** a ball of chewing gum, typically with a hard colored sugar coating.

gum ben·ja·min /ˈbenjəmən/ ▶ **n.** another term for BENZOIN (sense 1).

gum ben·zo·in ▶ **n.** see BENZOIN (sense 1).

gum·bo /ˈgəmbō/ ▶ **n.** (pl. **gumbos**) **1** okra, esp. the gelatinous pods used in cooking. ■ (in Cajun cooking) a spicy chicken or seafood soup thickened typically with okra or rice.
2 (**Gumbo**) a French-based patois spoken by some blacks and Creoles in Louisiana.
3 a fine, clayey soil that becomes sticky and impervious when wet.
4 a type of Cajun music consisting of a lively blend of styles and sounds: *New Orleans syncopated gumbo.*
– ORIGIN early 19th cent.: from the Angolan word *kingombo* 'okra.'

gum·boil /ˈgəm,boil/ ▶ **n.** a small swelling formed on the gum over an abscess at the root of a tooth.

gum·boot /ˈgəm,bo͞ot/ ▶ **n.** (usu. **gumboots**) chiefly British term for GUM[1] (sense 2 of the noun).

gum·drop /ˈgəm,dräp/ ▶ **n.** a firm, jellylike, translucent candy made with gelatin or gum arabic.

gum·ma /ˈgəmə/ ▶ **n.** (pl. **gummas** or **gummata** /ˈgəmətə/) Medicine a small, soft swelling that is characteristic of the late stages of syphilis and occurs in the connective tissue of the liver, brain, testes, and heart.
– DERIVATIVES **gum·ma·tous** /ˈgəmətəs/ **adj.**
– ORIGIN early 18th cent.: modern Latin, from Latin *gummi* (see GUM[1]).

gum·mo·sis /gəˈmōsis/ ▶ **n.** the copious production and exudation of gum by a diseased or damaged tree, esp. as a symptom of a disease of fruit trees.

gum·my[1] /ˈgəmē/ ▶ **adj.** (**gummier, gummiest**) viscous; sticky. ■ covered with or exuding a viscous substance: *his eyes are all gummy.*
– DERIVATIVES **gum·mi·ness n.**

gum·my[2] ▶ **adj.** (**gummier, gummiest**) toothless: *a gummy grin.*
▶ **n.** (pl. **gummies**) (also **gummy shark**) a small, edible shark of Australasian coastal waters, with rounded teeth that it uses to crush hard-shelled prey. ● *Mustelus antarcticus*, family Triakidae.
– DERIVATIVES **gum·mi·ly** /ˈgəməlē/ **adv.**

gum o·lib·a·num /ōˈlibənəm/ ▶ **n.** another term for FRANKINCENSE.

gump·tion /ˈgəmpSHən/ ▶ **n.** informal shrewd or spirited initiative and resourcefulness: *she **had the gumption to** put her foot down and head Dan off from those crazy schemes.*
– ORIGIN early 18th cent. (originally Scots): of unknown origin.

gum res·in ▶ **n.** a plant secretion consisting of resin mixed with gum.

gum san·da·rac ▶ **n.** see SANDARAC.

gum·shoe /ˈgəm,SHo͞o/ ▶ **n.** informal a detective.
– ORIGIN early 20th cent.: from *gumshoes* in the sense 'sneakers,' suggesting stealth.

gum trag·a·canth ▶ **n.** see TRAGACANTH.

gum tree ▶ **n.** a tree that exudes gum, esp. a eucalyptus.

gum tur·pen·tine ▶ **n.** see TURPENTINE.

gun /gən/ ▶ **n.** a weapon incorporating a metal tube from which bullets, shells, or other missiles are propelled by explosive force, typically making a characteristic loud, sharp noise. ■ a device for discharging something (e.g., insecticide, grease, or electrons) in a required direction. ■ a gunman: *a hired gun.* ■ **(guns)** dated Nautical slang used as a nickname for a ship's gunnery officer. ■ a starting pistol used in track and field events. ■ the firing of a piece of artillery as a salute or signal: *the boom of the one o'clock gun echoed across the river.*
▶ **v.** (**guns, gunning, gunned**) [with obj.] **1 (gun someone down)** shoot someone with a gun: *they were gunned down by masked snipers.*
2 informal cause (an engine) to race: *as Neil gunned the engine, the boat jumped forward.* ■ accelerate (a vehicle): *he gunned the car away from the curb.*
– PHRASES **big gun** informal an important or powerful person: *the first baseman and the center fielder were the big guns of that team.* **go great guns** informal proceed forcefully, vigorously, or successfully: *the film industry has been going great guns recently.* **jump the gun** informal act before the proper time. **stick to one's guns** informal refuse to compromise or change, despite criticism: *we have stuck to our guns on that issue.* **top gun** a (or the) most important person: *the top guns in contention for the coveted post of chairman.* **under the gun** informal under great pressure: *manufacturers are under the gun to offer alternatives.*
– PHRASAL VERBS **gun for** pursue or act against (someone) with hostility: *the Republican candidate was gunning for his rival over campaign finances.* ■ seek out or strive for (something) determinedly: *he had been gunning for a place in the squad.*
– DERIVATIVES **gun·less adj.**, **gunned adj.** [in combination] *a heavy-gunned ship.*
– ORIGIN Middle English *gunne, gonne*, perhaps from a nickname for the Scandinavian name *Gunnhildr*, from *gunnr* + *hildr*, both meaning 'war.'

gu·na /ˈgo͞onə/ ▶ **n.** (in Vedanta) any of the three interdependent modes or qualities of prakriti: sattva, rajas, or tamas.

gun·boat /ˈgən,bōt/ ▶ **n.** a small, fast ship mounting guns, for use in shallow coastal waters and rivers.

gun·boat di·plo·ma·cy ▶ **n.** foreign policy that is supported by the use or threat of military force.

gun car·riage ▶ **n.** a wheeled support for a piece of artillery.

gun·cot·ton /ˈgən,kätn/ ▶ **n.** a highly nitrated form of nitrocellulose, used as an explosive.

gun deck ▶ **n.** a deck on a vessel on which guns are placed.

gun·di /ˈgəndē/ ▶ **n.** (pl. **gundis**) a small, gregarious rodent living on rocky outcrops in the deserts of North and East Africa. ● Family Ctenodactylidae: four genera and several species.
– ORIGIN late 18th cent.: from North African Arabic.

gun dog ▶ **n.** a dog trained to retrieve game for a hunter.

gun·fight /ˈgən,fīt/ ▶ **n.** a fight involving an exchange of fire with guns.
– DERIVATIVES **gun·fight·er n.**

gun·fire /ˈgən,fī(ə)r/ ▶ **n.** the repeated firing of a gun or guns: *they'd been caught up in gunfire.*

gun·flint /ˈgən,flint/ ▶ **n.** a small piece of flint that is used to ignite the gunpowder in a flintlock gun.

gunge /gənj/ Brit. informal ▶ **n.** a sticky, viscous, and unpleasantly messy material.
▶ **v.** (**gunges, gungeing, gunged**) [with obj.] (**gunge something up**) clog or obstruct something with gunge.
– DERIVATIVES **gun·gy adj.**
– ORIGIN 1960s: perhaps suggested by GOO and GUNK.

gung-ho /,gəNG ˈhō/ ▶ **adj.** unthinkingly enthusiastic and eager, esp. about taking part in fighting or warfare: *the gung-ho soldier who wants all the big military toys.*
– ORIGIN World War II: from Chinese *gōnghé*, taken to mean 'work together' and adopted as a slogan by US Marines.

gun·ite /ˈgənīt/ ▶ **n.** a mixture of cement, sand, and water applied through a pressure hose, producing a dense hard layer of concrete used in building for lining tunnels and structural repairs.
– ORIGIN early 20th cent.: from GUN + -ITE[1].

gunk /gəNGk/ ▶ **n.** informal unpleasantly sticky or messy substance.
– ORIGIN 1930s: the proprietary name of a detergent.

gunk·hole /ˈgəNGk,hōl/ informal ▶ **n.** a shallow inlet or cove that is difficult or dangerous to navigate.
▶ **v.** [no obj.] cruise in and out of such inlets or coves: *they were gunkholing through the coral archipelago.*
– ORIGIN early 20th cent.: of unknown origin.

gun·lock /ˈgən,läk/ ▶ **n.** a mechanism by which the charge of a gun is exploded.

gun·mak·er /ˈgən,mākər/ ▶ **n.** a manufacturer of guns.

gun·man /ˈgənmən/ ▶ **n.** (pl. **gunmen**) a man who uses a gun to commit a crime or terrorist act: *a gang of masked gunmen.* ■ one who has to do with guns or is engaged in their manufacture.

gun·met·al /ˈgən,metl/ ▶ **n.** a gray, corrosion-resistant form of bronze containing zinc, formerly used for making cannon. ■ (also **gunmetal gray**) a dark blue-brown gray color: [as modifier] *the river glinted brass under a gunmetal sky.*

gun mi·cro·phone ▶ **n.** a highly directional microphone with an elongated barrel that can be directed from a distance at a localized sound source.

gun moll ▶ **n.** informal another term for MOLL (sense 1).

gun·nel[1] /ˈgənl/ ▶ **n.** an elongated laterally compressed fish with a dorsal fin that runs along most of the back and reduced or absent pelvic fins. It occurs in cool inshore waters of the northern hemisphere. ● Family Pholidae: two genera and several species.
– ORIGIN late 17th cent.: of unknown origin.

gun·nel[2] ▶ **n.** variant spelling of GUNWALE.

gun·ner /ˈgənər/ ▶ **n. 1** a serviceman who operates or specializes in guns, in particular: ■ historical a naval warrant officer in charge of a ship's guns, gun crews, and ordnance stores. ■ a member of an aircraft crew who operates a gun, esp. (formerly) in a gun turret on a bomber.
2 a person who hunts game with a gun.

gun·ner·a /ˈgənərə/ ▶ **n.** a South American plant that has extremely large leaves resembling rhubarb and that is grown as a waterside ornamental. ● Genus *Gunnera*, family Gunneraceae: several species, in particular *G. manicata* and *G. tinctoria*.
– ORIGIN modern Latin, named after Johann E. *Gunnerus* (1718–73), Norwegian botanist.

gun·ner·y /ˈgənərē/ ▶ **n.** the design, manufacture, or firing of heavy guns: *a pioneer of naval gunnery.*

gun·ner·y ser·geant ▶ **n.** a noncommissioned officer in the US Marine Corps ranking above staff sergeant and below master sergeant.

Gun·ni·son Riv·er /ˈgənəsən/ a river that flows for 180 miles (290 km) through western Colorado to the Colorado River. It is noted for its "Black Canyon."

gun·ny /ˈgənē/ ▶ **n.** coarse fabric, typically made of jute fiber and used esp. for sacks.
– ORIGIN early 18th cent.: from Marathi *gōnī*, from Sanskrit *goṇī* 'sack.'

gun·play /ˈgən,plā/ ▶ **n.** the use of guns: *the struggle started with skirmishes and some scattered gunplay.*

gun·point /ˈgən,point/ ▶ **n.** (in phrase **at gunpoint**) while threatening someone or being threatened with a gun: *two robbers **held a family at gunpoint** while they searched their house.*

gun·port /ˈgən,pôrt/ ▶ **n.** see PORT[4].

gun·pow·der /ˈgən,poudər/ ▶ **n. 1** an explosive consisting of a powdered mixture of saltpeter, sulfur, and charcoal. The earliest known propellant explosive, gunpowder has now largely been superseded by high explosives, although it is still used for quarry blasting and in fuses and fireworks.
2 (also **gunpowder tea**) a fine green China tea of granular appearance.

Gun·pow·der Plot a conspiracy by a small group of Catholic extremists to blow up James I and his Parliament on November 5, 1605.

> The plot is commemorated by the traditional searching of the vaults before the opening of each session of Parliament, and by bonfires and fireworks, with the burning of an effigy of Guy Fawkes, one of the conspirators, annually on November 5.

gun·room /ˈgən,ro͝om, -,ro͞om/ ▶ **n. 1** a room used for storing sporting guns in a house.
2 Brit. dated a set of quarters for midshipmen or other junior officers in a warship.

gun·run·ner /ˈgən,rənər/ ▶ **n.** a person engaged in the illegal sale or importing of firearms.
– DERIVATIVES **gun·run·ning** /-,rəniNG/ **n.**

gun·sel /ˈgənsəl/ ▶ **n.** informal, dated a criminal carrying a gun.
– ORIGIN early 20th cent. (denoting a homosexual youth): from Yiddish *gendzel* 'little goose,' influenced in sense by GUN.

gun·ship /ˈgən,SHip/ ▶ **n.** an airplane or a helicopter heavily armed with machine guns or with machine guns and cannon, providing air support for ground troops in combat.

gun·shot /ˈgən,SHät/ ▶ **n.** a shot fired from a gun. ■ archaic the range of a gun: *we bore down and came nearly within gunshot.*

gun-shy ▶ **adj.** (esp. of a hunting dog) alarmed at the report of a gun. ■ (of a person) nervous and apprehensive.

gun·sight /ˈgən,sīt/ ▶ **n.** a device on a gun that enables it to be aimed accurately.

gun·sling·er /ˈgən,sliNGər/ ▶ **n.** informal a man who carries a gun and shoots well.
– DERIVATIVES **gun·sling·ing** /-,sliNGiNG/ **adj.**

gun·smith /ˈgən,smiTH/ ▶ **n.** a person who makes, sells, and repairs small firearms.

gun·stock /ˈgən,stäk/ ▶ **n.** the stock or support to which the barrel of a gun is attached.

gun·ter /ˈgəntər/ ▶ **n.** Sailing a fore-and-aft sail whose spar is nearly vertical, so that the sail is nearly triangular. ■ (also **gunter rig**) historical a type of rig in which the topmast slides up and down the lower mast on rings.
– DERIVATIVES **gun·ter-rigged adj.**
– ORIGIN late 18th cent.: named after E. *Gunter* (see GUNTER'S CHAIN).

Gun·ter's chain /ˈgəntərz/ ▶ **n.** Surveying a former measuring instrument 66 feet (20.1 m) long, subdivided into 100 links, each of which is a short section of wire connected to the next link by a loop. It has now been superseded by the steel tape and electronic equipment. ■ this length as a unit, equal to $^1/_{10}$ furlong or $^1/_{80}$ mile. Also called CHAIN.
– ORIGIN late 17th cent.: named after Edmund *Gunter* (1581–1626), the English mathematician who devised it.

Gun·ther /ˈgo͝ontər/ (in the Nibelungenlied) the husband of Brunhild and brother of Kriemhild, by whom he was beheaded in revenge for Siegfried's murder.

Gun·tur /go͝onˈto͝or/ a city in eastern India, in Andhra Pradesh; pop. 542,500 (est. 2009).

gun·wale /ˈgənl/ (also **gunnel**) ▶ **n.** (often **gunwales**) the upper edge of the side of a boat or ship.
– PHRASES **to the gunwales** informal so as to be almost overflowing: *the car is stuffed to the gunwales with camera equipment.*
– ORIGIN late Middle English: from GUN + WALE (because it was formerly used to support guns).

Guo·min·dang /ˈgwōˈminˈdäNG/ variant spelling of KUOMINTANG.

gup·pie /ˈgəpē/ ▶ **n.** (pl. **guppies**) informal a homosexual yuppie.
– ORIGIN 1980s: blend of GAY and YUPPIE.

gup·py /ˈgəpē/ ▶ **n.** (pl. **guppies**) a small, livebearing freshwater fish widely kept in aquariums. Native to tropical America, it has been introduced elsewhere to control mosquito larvae. ● *Poecilia reticulata*, family Poeciliidae.
– ORIGIN 1920s: named after R. J. Lechmere *Guppy* (1836–1916), a Trinidadian clergyman who sent the first specimen to the British Museum.

Gup·ta /ˈgo͝optə/ a Hindu dynasty established in AD 320 by **Chandragupta I** in Bihar. At one stage it ruled most of the north of the Indian subcontinent, but it began to disintegrate toward the end of the 5th century.
– DERIVATIVES **Gup·tan adj.**

Gur /go͝or/ ▶ **n.** a branch of the Niger–Congo family of languages, including Senufo, spoken in parts of West Africa. Also called VOLTAIC.
▶ **adj.** of, relating to, or denoting this group of languages.

g

gur·dwa·ra /,gərˈdwärə/ ▶ **n.** a Sikh place of worship.
– ORIGIN from Punjabi *gurduārā*, from Sanskrit *guru* 'teacher' + *dvāra* 'door.'

gur·gle /ˈgərgəl/ ▶ **v.** [no obj.] make a hollow bubbling sound like that made by water running out of a bottle: *my stomach gurgled* | (as adj. **gurgling**) *a faint gurgling noise.* ■ [with adverbial of direction] (of a liquid) run or flow with such a sound: *chemicals gurgle down a drain straight into the sewers.*
▶ **n.** a gurgling sound: *Catherine gave a gurgle of laughter.*
– ORIGIN late Middle English: imitative, or directly from Dutch *gorgelen*, German *gurgeln*, or medieval Latin *gurgulare*, all from Latin *gurgulio* 'gullet.'

Gur·kha /ˈgo͝orkə/ ▶ **n.** a member of any of several peoples of Nepal noted for their military prowess. ■ a member of units of the British army established specifically for Nepalese recruits in the mid 19th century.
– ORIGIN name of a locality, from Sanskrit *gorakṣa* 'cowherd' (from *go* 'cow' + *rakṣ-* 'protect'), used as an epithet of their patron deity.

Gur·mu·khi /ˈgo͝ormə,kē/ ▶ **n.** the script used by Sikhs for writing Punjabi. ■ the Punjabi language as written in this script.
– ORIGIN Punjabi, from Sanskrit *guru* (see GURU) + *mukha* 'mouth.'

gurn /gərn/ ▶ **v.** [no obj.] chiefly Brit. make a grotesque face: (as noun **gurning**) *gurning is one of the fair's most popular competitions.*
– DERIVATIVES **gurn·er n.**
– ORIGIN early 20th cent.: dialect variant of GRIN.

gur·nard /ˈgərnərd/ ▶ **n.** a bottom-dwelling fish of coastal waters, with a heavily boned head and three fingerlike pectoral rays, which it uses for searching for food and for walking on the seabed. ● Family Triglidae: several genera and many species, including the common European *Eutrigla gurnardus*.
– ORIGIN Middle English: from Old French *gornart*, from *grondir* 'to grunt,' from Latin *grundire*, *grunnire*.

gur·ney /ˈgərnē/ ▶ **n.** (pl. **gurneys**) a wheeled stretcher used for transporting hospital patients.
– ORIGIN late 19th cent.: apparently named after J. T. *Gurney* of Boston, Massachusetts, patentee of a new cab design in 1883.

gur·ry /ˈgərē/ ▶ **n.** fish or whale offal.
– ORIGIN late 18th cent.: of unknown origin.

gu·ru /ˈgo͞oro͞o, go͝oˈro͞o/ ▶ **n.** (pl. **gurus**) (in Hinduism and Buddhism) a spiritual teacher, esp. one who imparts initiation. ■ each of the ten first leaders of the Sikh religion. ■ an influential teacher or popular expert: *a management guru.*
– ORIGIN from Hindi and Punjabi, from Sanskrit *guru* 'weighty, grave' (compare with Latin *gravis*), hence 'elder, teacher.'

Gu·ru Granth Sa·hib the principal sacred scripture of Sikhism. Originally compiled under the direction of Arjan Dev (1563–1606), the fifth Sikh guru, it contains hymns and religious poetry as well as the teachings of the first five gurus. Also called ADI GRANTH.

gush /gəsн/ ▶ **v.** [no obj.] **1** [with adverbial of direction] (of a liquid) flow out in a rapid and plentiful stream, often suddenly: *William watched the murky liquid **gushing out*** | figurative *millions of dollars **gushed out** of that office.* ■ [with obj.] send out in a rapid and plentiful stream.
2 speak or write with effusiveness or exaggerated enthusiasm: *a nice old lady reporter who covers the art openings and **gushes about** everything.*
▶ **n. 1** a rapid and plentiful stream or burst.
2 exaggerated effusiveness or enthusiasm.
– ORIGIN late Middle English: probably imitative.

gush·er /ˈgəsнər/ ▶ **n. 1** an oil well from which oil flows profusely without being pumped.
2 an effusive person: *the earnest, ingratiating gusher of numerous television interviews.*

gush·ing /ˈgəsнiNG/ ▶ **adj.** (of speech or writing) effusive or exaggeratedly enthusiastic: *gushing praise.*
– DERIVATIVES **gush·ing·ly** adv.

gush·y /ˈgəsнē/ ▶ **adj.** (**gushier, gushiest**) excessively effusive: *her gushy manner.*
– DERIVATIVES **gush·i·ly** /-sнəlē/ **adv., gush·i·ness n.**

gus·set /ˈgəsit/ ▶ **n.** a piece of material sewn into a garment to strengthen or enlarge a part of it, such as the collar of a shirt or the crotch of an undergarment. ■ a bracket strengthening an angle of a structure.
– DERIVATIVES **gusseted adj.**
– ORIGIN late Middle English: from Old French *gousset*, diminutive of *gousse* 'pod, shell,' of unknown origin.

gus·sy /ˈgəsē/ ▶ **v.** (**gussies, gussying, gussied**) [with obj.] (**gussy someone/something up**) informal make more attractive, esp. in a showy or gimmicky way: *shopkeepers gussied up their window displays.*
– ORIGIN 1940s: perhaps from *Gussie*, nickname for the given name *Augustus*.

gust /gəst/ ▶ **n.** a brief, strong rush of wind. ■ a burst of something such as rain, sound, or emotion: ***gusts of** rain lashed down the narrow alleys.*
▶ **v.** [no obj.] (of the wind) blow in gusts: *the wind was gusting through the branches of the tree.*
– ORIGIN late 16th cent.: from Old Norse *gustr*, related to *gjósa* 'to gush.'

gus·ta·tion /gəˈstāsнən/ ▶ **n.** formal the action or faculty of tasting.
– DERIVATIVES **gus·ta·tive** /ˈgəstətiv/ **adj.**
– ORIGIN late 16th cent.: from Latin *gustatio(n-)*, from *gustare* 'to taste,' from *gustus* 'taste.'

gus·ta·to·ry /ˈgəstəˌtôrē/ ▶ **adj.** formal concerned with tasting or the sense of taste: *gustatory delights.*

Gus·ta·vus Adol·phus /gəˈstävəs əˈdôlfəs/ (1594–1632), king of Sweden 1611–32. His domestic reforms laid the foundation for the modern Swedish state.

gus·to /ˈgəstō/ ▶ **n.** (pl. **gustos** or **gustoes**)
1 enjoyment or vigor in doing something; zest: *she sang it with gusto.* ■ [in sing.] archaic a relish or liking: *he had a particular **gusto for** those sort of performances.*
2 archaic style of artistic execution.
– ORIGIN early 17th cent.: from Italian, from Latin *gustus* 'taste.'

gust·y /ˈgəstē/ ▶ **adj.** (**gustier, gustiest**)
1 characterized by or blowing in gusts: *a gusty morning.*
2 having or showing gusto: *gusty female vocals.*
– DERIVATIVES **gust·i·ly** /ˈgəstəlē/ **adv., gust·i·ness n.**

gut /gət/ ▶ **n. 1** (also **guts**) the stomach or belly: *a painful stabbing feeling in his gut.* ■ Medicine & Biology the lower alimentary canal or a part of this; the intestine: *microbes which naturally live in the human gut.* ■ (**guts**) entrails that have been removed or exposed in violence or by a butcher. ■ (**guts**) the internal parts or essence of something: *the guts of a modern computer.*
2 (**guts**) informal personal courage and determination; toughness of character: *she had both more brains and more guts than her husband* | *you just haven't got the guts to admit it.* ■ [often as modifier] informal used in reference to a feeling or reaction based on an instinctive emotional response rather than considered thought: *a gut feeling* | *I could feel it in my guts—he was out there, watching me.*
3 fiber made from the intestines of animals, used esp. for violin or racket strings or for surgical use: [as modifier] *gut strings.*
4 a narrow passage or strait.
▶ **v.** (**guts, gutting, gutted**) [with obj.] take out the intestines and other internal organs of (a fish or other animal) before cooking it. ■ remove or destroy completely the internal parts of (a building or other structure): *the fire gutted most of the factory.*
– PHRASES **bust a gut** informal **1** make a strenuous effort: *a problem which nobody is going to bust a gut trying to solve.* **2** laugh very heartily: *his facial expressions and ad libs were enough to get audiences to bust a gut.* —— **one's guts out** used to indicate that the specified action is done or performed as hard as possible: *he ran his guts out and finished fourth.* **hate someone's guts** informal feel a strong hatred for someone.
– ORIGIN Old English *guttas* (plural), probably related to *gēotan* 'pour.'

gut·buck·et /ˈgətˌbəkit/ informal ▶ **n.** [as modifier] informal (of jazz or blues) raw and spirited in style: *his gutbucket guitar solos.*
– ORIGIN early 20th cent.: perhaps from the earlier denotation of a one-stringed plucked instrument, with reference to its construction, or referring to the bucket that caught *gutterings* (streams of liquid) from beer barrels in low-class saloons where such music was played.

gut course ▶ **n.** informal a college or university course requiring little work or intellectual ability.

Gu·ten·berg /ˈgo͞otnˌbərg/, Johannes (*c.*1400–68), German printer. He was the first in the West to print by using movable type and to use a press. By *c.*1455, he had produced what later became known as the Gutenberg Bible.

Gu·ten·berg Bi·ble ▶ **n.** the edition of the Bible (Vulgate version) completed by Johannes Gutenberg in about 1455 in Mainz, Germany. It is the first complete book extant in the West and is also the earliest to be printed from movable type.

gut flo·ra ▶ **plural n.** another term for INTESTINAL FLORA.

gut·ful /ˈgətfəl/ informal ▶ **n.** (pl. **gutfuls**) another term for BELLYFUL.

Guth·rie /ˈgəтнrē/, Woody (1912–1967), US folk singer and songwriter; full name *Woodrow Wilson Guthrie.* Social injustice and the hardships of the Depression inspired many of his songs, including "This Land Is Your Land" (1940) and "Deportee" (1948). His son **Arlo** (1947–), also a folk singer and songwriter, is best known for his talking blues song "Alice's Restaurant Massacree" (1967).

Guth·rie test ▶ **n.** Medicine a routine blood test carried out on babies a few days after birth to detect the condition phenylketonuria.
– ORIGIN named after Robert *Guthrie* (born 1916), American microbiologist.

gut·less /ˈgətləs/ ▶ **adj.** informal lacking courage or determination.
– DERIVATIVES **gut·less·ly adv., gut·less·ness n.**

guts·y /ˈgətsē/ ▶ **adj.** (**gutsier, gutsiest**) informal showing courage, determination, and spirit: *she gave a gutsy performance in the tennis tournament.* ■ (of food or drink) strongly flavorsome: *a smooth Bordeaux that is gutsy enough to accompany steak.*
– DERIVATIVES **guts·i·ly** /-sələ/ **adv., guts·i·ness n.**

gut·ta-per·cha /ˌgətə ˈpərcнə/ ▶ **n.** a hard, tough thermoplastic substance that is the coagulated latex of certain Malaysian trees. It consists chiefly of a hydrocarbon isomeric with rubber and is now used chiefly in dentistry and for electrical insulation. ● This substance is obtained from trees of the genus *Palaquium*, family Sapotaceae, in particular *P. gutta.*
– ORIGIN mid 19th cent.: from Malay *getah perca*, from *getah* 'gum' + *perca* 'strips of cloth' (which it resembles), altered by association with obsolete *gutta* 'gum,' from Latin *gutta* 'a drop.'

gut·tate /ˈgətˌāt/ ▶ **adj.** chiefly Biology having drops or droplike markings. ■ in the form of or resembling drops.
– ORIGIN early 19th cent.: from Latin *guttatus* 'speckled,' from *gutta* 'a drop.'

gut·ta·tion /gəˈtāsнən/ ▶ **n.** the secretion of droplets of water from the pores of plants.
– ORIGIN late 19th cent.: from Latin *gutta* 'drop' + -ATION.

gut·ter /ˈgətər/ ▶ **n. 1** a shallow trough fixed beneath the edge of a roof for carrying off rainwater. ■ a channel at the side of a street for carrying off rainwater. ■ (**the gutter**) used to refer to a poor or squalid background or environment: *only moneyed privilege had kept him out of the gutter.* ■ technical a groove or channel for flowing liquid. ■ a channel on either side of a lane in a bowling alley.
2 the blank space between facing pages of a book or between adjacent columns of type or stamps in a sheet.
▶ **v. 1** [no obj.] (of a candle or flame) flicker and burn unsteadily: *the candles had almost guttered out.*
2 [with obj.] archaic channel or furrow with something such as streams or tears: *my cheeks are guttered with tears.* ■ [no obj.] (**gutter down**) stream down: *the raindrops gutter down her visage.*
– ORIGIN Middle English: from Old French *gotiere*, from Latin *gutta* 'a drop'; the verb dates from late Middle English, originally meaning 'cut grooves in' and later (early 18th cent.) used of a candle that melts rapidly because it has become channeled on one side.

gut·ter ball ▶ **n.** (in tenpin bowling) a nonscoring ball that enters the gutter before reaching the pins.

gut·ter·ing /ˈgətəriNG/ ▶ **n.** chiefly Brit. the gutters of a building. ■ material used to make gutters.

gut·ter press ▶ **n.** (**the gutter press**) chiefly Brit. reporters or newspapers engaging in sensational journalism, esp. accounts of the private lives of public figures.

gut·ter·snipe /ˈgətərˌsnīp/ ▶ **n.** derogatory a street urchin.

gut·tur·al /ˈgətərəl/ ▶ **adj.** (of a speech sound) produced in the throat; harsh-sounding. ■ (of a manner of speech) characterized by the use of such sounds: *his parents' guttural central European accent.*
▶ **n.** a guttural consonant (e.g., *k*, *g*) or other speech sound.
– DERIVATIVES **gut·tur·al·ly adv.**
– ORIGIN late 16th cent.: from French, or from medieval Latin *gutturalis*, from Latin *guttur* 'throat.'

gut·tur·al·ize /ˈgətərəˌlīz/ ▶ **v.** [with obj.] **1** say or pronounce in a harsh-sounding guttural manner.
2 articulate (a speech sound) by moving the back of the tongue toward the velum.

gut·ty /ˈgətē/ ▶ **adj.** (**guttier, guttiest**) informal gutsy.

gut-wrench·ing ▶ **adj.** informal extremely unpleasant or upsetting: *the film is a gut-wrenching portrait of domestic violence.*

guv /gəv/ ▶ **n.** Brit. informal (as a form of address) sir: *"Excuse me, guv," he began.*
– ORIGIN late 19th cent.: abbreviation of GUV'NOR.

guv'nor /ˈgəvnər/ ▶ **n.** Brit. informal a man in a position of authority such as one's employer or father (often used as a term of address): *I had a lecture from the guv'nor.*
– ORIGIN mid 19th cent.: representing a nonstandard or colloquial pronunciation.

Guwa·ha·ti /gouˈhätē/ an industrial city in northeastern India, in Assam, a port on the Brahmaputra River; pop. 997,700 (est. 2009). Formerly called GAUHATI.

guy[1] /gī/ ▶ **n. 1** informal a man: *he's a nice guy.* [mid 19th cent.] ■ (**guys**) people of either sex: *you guys want some coffee?*
2 Brit. a figure representing Guy Fawkes, burned on a bonfire on Guy Fawkes' Night, and often displayed by children begging for money for fireworks.
▶ **v.** [with obj.] make fun of; ridicule: *he didn't realize I was guying the whole idea.*
– ORIGIN early 19th cent. (sense 2 of the noun): named after *Guy* Fawkes (see GUNPOWDER PLOT).

guy[2] ▶ **n.** a rope or line fixed to the ground to secure a tent or other structure.
▶ **v.** [with obj.] secure with a line or lines: *it was set on concrete footings and guyed with steel cable.*
– ORIGIN late Middle English: probably of Low German origin; related to Dutch *gei* 'brail' and German *Geitaue* 'brails.'

Guy·a·na /gīˈänə, gīˈanə/ a country on the northeastern coast of South America; pop. 752,900 (est. 2009); capital, Georgetown; languages, English (official), English Creole, and Hindi. Official name COOPERATIVE REPUBLIC OF GUYANA.

> The Spanish explored the area in 1499, and the Dutch settled here in the 17th century. It was occupied by the British from 1796 and established, with adjacent areas, as the colony of British Guiana in 1831. In 1966, it became an independent state of the Commonwealth of Nations.

– DERIVATIVES **Guy·a·nese** /ˌgīəˈnēz, -ˈnēs/ **adj. & n.**
– ORIGIN from an American Indian word meaning 'land of waters.'

guy·ot /gēˈō/ ▶ **n.** Geology a seamount with a flat top.
– ORIGIN 1940s: named after Arnold H. *Guyot* (1807–84), Swiss geographer.

guz·zle /ˈgəzəl/ ▶ **v.** [with obj.] eat or drink (something) greedily: *we guzzle our beer and devour our pizza* | figurative *this car guzzles gas.*
– DERIVATIVES **guz·zler** /-z(ə)lər/ **n.**
– ORIGIN late 16th cent.: perhaps from Old French *gosillier* 'chatter, vomit,' from *gosier* 'throat,' from late Latin *geusiae* 'cheeks.'

Gvozdena Vrata /ˈgvôzdənə ˈvrätə/ Serbian name for IRON GATE.

GVW ▶ **abbr.** gross vehicle weight.

GW ▶ **abbr.** gigawatt.

Gwa·li·or /ˈgwälē,ôr/ a city in central India, in a district of the same name in Madhya Pradesh; pop. 931,800 (est. 2009).

Gy ▶ **abbr.** Physics gray(s).

Gyan·dzhe /gyänˈjə/ Russian name for **GÄNCÄ**.

gybe ▶ **v. & n.** variant spelling of **JIBE²**.

gym /jim/ ▶ **n. 1** a gymnasium. ■ a membership organization that provides a range of facilities designed to improve and maintain physical fitness and health: *we got guest passes to Suzanne's gym.* **2** physical education: *I'm taking just one more semester of gym.*
– ORIGIN late 19th cent.: abbreviation.

gym. ▶ **abbr.** Sports gymnastics.

gym·kha·na /jimˈkänə/ ▶ **n.** a day event comprising races and other competitions between horse riders or car drivers.
– ORIGIN mid 19th cent.: from Urdu *gendḵānah* 'racket court,' from Hindi *geṁd* 'ball' + Persian *ḵānah* 'house,' altered by association with **GYMNASTIC**.

gym·na·si·um /jimˈnāzēəm/ ▶ **n.** (pl. **gymnasiums** or **gymnasia** /-zēə/) **1** a room or building equipped for gymnastics, games, and other physical exercise. **2** /gimˈnäzē,o͝om/ a school in Germany, Scandinavia, or central Europe that prepares pupils for university entrance.
– DERIVATIVES **gym·na·si·al** /-zēəl/ **adj.** (sense 2).
– ORIGIN late 16th cent.: via Latin from Greek *gumnasion*, from *gumnazein* 'exercise naked,' from *gumnos* 'naked.'

gym·nast /ˈjimnist/ ▶ **n.** a person trained in or skilled in gymnastics.
– ORIGIN late 16th cent.: from French *gymnaste* or Greek *gumnastēs* 'trainer of athletes,' from *gumnazein* 'exercise naked' (see **GYMNASIUM**).

gym·nas·tic /jimˈnastik/ ▶ **adj.** of or relating to gymnastics: *a gymnastic display.*
– DERIVATIVES **gym·nas·ti·cal·ly** /-ik(ə)lē/ **adv.**

gym·nas·tics /jimˈnastiks/ ▶ **plural n.** [also treated as sing.] exercises developing or displaying physical agility and coordination. The modern sport of gymnastics typically involves exercises on uneven bars, balance beam, floor, and vaulting horse (for women), and horizontal and parallel bars, rings, floor, and pommel horse (for men). ■ [with adj.] other physical or mental agility of a specified kind: *these vocal gymnastics make the music unforgettable.*

gymno- ▶ **comb. form** bare; naked: *gymnosophist* | *gymnosperm.*
– ORIGIN from Greek *gumnos* 'naked.'

gym·nos·o·phist /jimˈnäsəfist/ ▶ **n.** a member of an ancient Indian sect that wore very little clothing and was given to asceticism and contemplation.
– DERIVATIVES **gym·nos·o·phy** /-fē/ **n.**
– ORIGIN late Middle English: from French *gymnosophiste*, via Latin from Greek *gumnosophistai* (plural), from *gumnos* 'naked' + *sophistēs* 'teacher of philosophy, sophist' (see **SOPHIST**).

gym·no·sperm /ˈjimnə,spərm/ ▶ **n.** Botany a plant that has seeds unprotected by an ovary or fruit. Gymnosperms include the conifers, cycads, and ginkgo. Compare with **ANGIOSPERM**. ● Subdivision Gymnospermae, division Spermatophyta.
– DERIVATIVES **gym·no·sper·mous** /,jimnəˈspərməs/ **adj.**

gym·nure /ˈjim,nyo͝or/ ▶ **n.** another term for **MOONRAT**.
– ORIGIN late 19th cent.: from modern Latin *Gymnura* (former genus name), from Greek *gumnos* 'naked' + *oura* 'tail.'

gyn. ▶ **abbr.** ■ gynecological. ■ gynecologist. ■ gynecology.

gynaeco- chiefly Brit. variant spelling of **GYNECO-**.
– ORIGIN from Greek *gunē, gunaik-* 'woman, female.'

gy·nan·dro·morph /gīˈnandrə,môrf, jinˈan-/ ▶ **n.** Zoology & Medicine an abnormal individual, esp. an insect, having some male and some female characteristics.
– DERIVATIVES **gy·nan·dro·mor·phic** /gī,nandrəˈmôrfik, jin,an-/ **adj.**, **gy·nan·dro·mor·phy** /-fē/ **n.**
– ORIGIN late 19th cent.: from Greek *gunandros* 'of doubtful sex' (see **GYNANDROUS**) + *morphē* 'form.'

gy·nan·drous /gīˈnandrəs, jinˈan-/ ▶ **adj.** Botany (of a flower) having stamens and pistil united in one column, as in orchids. ■ (of a person or animal) hermaphrodite.
– ORIGIN early 19th cent.: from Greek *gunandros* 'of doubtful sex' (from *gunē* 'woman' + *anēr, andr-* 'man, male') + **-OUS**.

gyn·ar·chy /ˈgī,närkē, ˈjin,är-/ ▶ **n.** (pl. **gynarchies**) rule by women or a woman.

gyneco- ▶ **comb. form** relating to women; female: *gynecocracy* | *gynecophobia.*

gyn·e·coc·ra·cy /,gīnəˈkäkrəsē, ,jinə-/ (Brit. **gynaecocracy**) ▶ **n.** another term for **GYNARCHY**.

gy·ne·coid /ˈjini,koid, ˈgīni-, ˈjīni-/ ▶ **adj.** relating to or characteristic of a woman: *people with a pear-shaped figure—also known as the gynecoid pattern because it is more common in women—tend to carry extra weight on their thighs and buttocks.*

gynecol. ▶ **abbr.** ■ gynecological. ■ gynecology.

gy·ne·col·o·gy /,gīnəˈkäləjē, ,jinə-/ (Brit. **gynaecology**) ▶ **n.** the branch of physiology and medicine that deals with the functions and diseases specific to women and girls, esp. those affecting the reproductive system.
– DERIVATIVES **gyn·e·co·log·ic** /-kəˈläjik/ **adj.**, **gyn·e·co·log·i·cal** /-kəˈläjikəl/ **adj.**, **gyn·e·co·log·i·cal·ly** /-kəˈläjik(ə)lē/ **adv.**, **gy·ne·col·o·gist** /-jist/ **n.**

gyn·e·co·mas·ti·a /,gīnəkōˈmastēə/ (Brit. **gynaecomastia**) ▶ **n.** Medicine enlargement of a man's breasts, usually due to hormone imbalance or hormone therapy.

gyn·e·co·pho·bi·a /,gīnəkōˈfōbēə/ (Brit. **gynaecophobia**) ▶ **n.** another term for **GYNOPHOBIA**.

gy·no·cen·tric /,gīnəˈsentrik/ ▶ **adj.** centered on or concerned exclusively with women; taking a female (or specifically a feminist) point of view.

gy·noe·ci·um /jiˈnēsHēəm, gī-, -sēəm/ ▶ **n.** (pl. **gynoecia** /-sHēə, -sēə/) Botany the female part of a flower, consisting of one or more carpels.
– ORIGIN mid 19th cent.: modern Latin, from Greek *gunaikeion* 'women's apartments,' from *gunē, gunaik-* 'woman, female' + *oikos* 'house.'

gy·no·pho·bi·a /,gīnəˈfōbēə, ,jinə-/ ▶ **n.** extreme or irrational fear of women or of the female.
– DERIVATIVES **gy·no·pho·bic** /-bik/ **adj.**

-gynous ▶ **comb. form** Botany having female organs or pistils of a specified kind or number: *epigynous.*
– ORIGIN based on modern Latin *-gynus* (from Greek *-gunos*, from *gunē* 'woman') + **-OUS**.

gyo·za /ˈgyōzə/ ▶ **n.** a Japanese dish consisting of wonton wrappers stuffed with pork and cabbage.
– ORIGIN Japanese, from Chinese *jiaozi.*

gyp¹ /jip/ informal ▶ **v.** (**gyps, gypping, gypped**) [with obj.] cheat or swindle (someone): *that's salesmanship, you have to **gyp** people **into** buying stuff they don't like.*
▶ **n.** (also **gip**) an act of cheating; a swindle.
– ORIGIN late 19th cent.: of unknown origin.

gyp² ▶ **n.** Brit. a college servant at the Universities of Cambridge and Durham.
– ORIGIN mid 18th cent.: perhaps from obsolete *gippo* 'menial kitchen servant,' originally denoting a man's short tunic, from obsolete French *jupeau.*

gyp joint ▶ **n.** informal **1** a business establishment, esp. a store, that has a reputation for cheating customers by charging exorbitant prices for inferior goods or services: *a 42nd Street gyp joint.* **2** a gambling establishment in which the games are run dishonestly.

gyp·po /ˈjipō/ ▶ **n.** (pl. **gyppos**) informal, derogatory a gypsy.

gyp·soph·i·la /jipˈsäfələ/ ▶ **n.** a plant of the genus *Gypsophila* in the pink family, esp. (in gardening) baby's breath.
– ORIGIN modern Latin, from Greek *gupsos* 'chalk, gypsum' + *philos* 'loving.'

gyp·sum /ˈjipsəm/ ▶ **n.** a soft white or gray mineral consisting of hydrated calcium sulfate. It occurs chiefly in sedimentary deposits and is used to make plaster of Paris and fertilizers, and in the building industry.
– DERIVATIVES **gyp·sif·er·ous** /jipˈsifərəs/ **adj.**
– ORIGIN late Middle English: from Latin, from Greek *gupsos.*

gyp·sum board ▶ **n.** another term for **PLASTERBOARD**.

gyp·sy /ˈjipsē/ (also **gipsy**) ▶ **n.** (pl. **gypsies**) **1** (usu. **Gypsy**) a member of a traveling people with dark skin and hair who speak Romany and traditionally live by seasonal work, itinerant trade, and fortune-telling. Gypsies are now found mostly in Europe, parts of North Africa, and North America, but are believed to have originated in South Asia. ■ the language of the gypsies; Romany. **2** a nomadic or free-spirited person.
▶ **adj.** (of a business or business person) nonunion or unlicensed: *gypsy trucking firms.*
– DERIVATIVES **gyp·sy·ish adj.**
– ORIGIN mid 16th cent.: originally *gipcyan*, short for **EGYPTIAN** (because Gypsies were popularly supposed to have come from Egypt).

gyp·sy moth ▶ **n.** a tussock moth having a brown male and larger white female. The caterpillar can be a serious pest of orchards and woodland. ● *Lymantria dispar*, family Lymantriidae.

gy·ral /ˈjīrəl/ ▶ **adj.** chiefly Anatomy of or relating to a gyrus or gyri.

gy·rate /ˈjīrāt/ ▶ **v.** move or cause to move in a circle or spiral, esp. quickly: [no obj.] *their wings gyrate through the water like paddle wheels.* ■ [no obj.] dance in a wild or suggestive manner: *strippers gyrated to rock music on a low stage.*
– DERIVATIVES **gy·ra·tor** /-,rātər/ **n.**
– ORIGIN early 19th cent.: from Latin *gyrat-* 'revolved,' from the verb *gyrare*, from Greek *guros* 'a ring.'

gy·ra·tion /jīˈrāsHən/ ▶ **n.** (usu. **gyrations**) a rapid movement in a circle or spiral; a whirling motion: *the gyrations of the dancers' arms and legs.*

gy·ra·to·ry /ˈjīrə,tôrē/ ▶ **adj.** of or involving circular or spiral motion.

gyre /jīr/ ▶ **v.** [no obj.] literary whirl; gyrate: *a swarm of ghosts gyred around him.*
▶ **n.** a spiral; a vortex. ■ Geography a circular pattern of currents in an ocean basin: *the central North Pacific gyre.*
– ORIGIN late Middle English (in the sense 'whirl (someone or something) around'): from late Latin *gyrare*, from Latin *gyrus* 'a ring,' from Greek *guros*. The noun is from Latin *gyrus.*

gyr·fal·con /ˈjər,falkən, -,fôl-/ ▶ **n.** the largest falcon, found in arctic regions and occurring in several color forms, one of which is mainly white. ● *Falco rusticolus*, family Falconidae.
– ORIGIN Middle English: from Old French *gerfaucon*, of Germanic origin. The first element is probably related to Old High German *gĕr* 'spear'; the spelling *gyr-* arose from a mistaken idea that the bird's name came from Latin *gyrare* 'revolve.'

gy·ri /ˈjīrī/ plural form of **GYRUS**.

gy·ro¹ /ˈjīrō/ ▶ **n.** (pl. **gyros**) short for **GYROSCOPE** or **GYROCOMPASS**.

gy·ro² /ˈyērō, ˈZHirō/ ▶ **n.** (pl. **gyros**) a sandwich made with slices of spiced meat cooked on a spit, served with salad in pita bread.
– ORIGIN 1970s: from modern Greek *guros* 'turning.'

gyro- ▶ **comb. form 1** relating to rotation: *gyromagnetic.* **2** gyroscopic: *gyrostabilizer.*
– ORIGIN from Greek *guros* 'a ring.'

gy·ro·com·pass /ˈjīrō,kəmpəs/ ▶ **n.** a nonmagnetic compass in which the direction of true north is maintained by a continuously driven gyroscope whose axis is parallel to the earth's axis of rotation.

gy·ro·cop·ter /ˈjīrə,käptər/ ▶ **n.** a small, light single-seater autogiro.
– ORIGIN from **GYRO-** 'relating to rotation,' on the pattern of *helicopter.*

gy·ro·mag·net·ic /,jīrōmagˈnetik/ ▶ **adj. 1** Physics of or relating to the magnetic and mechanical properties of a rotating charged particle. **2** (of a compass) combining a gyroscope and a normal magnetic compass.

gy·ron /ˈjīrən/ ▶ **n.** Heraldry a triangular ordinary formed by two lines from the edge of the shield meeting at the fess point at 45 degrees.
– ORIGIN late 16th cent.: from Old French *giron* 'gusset.'

gy·ron·ny /jīˈränē/ ▶ **adj.** Heraldry (of a shield) divided into eight gyrons by straight lines all crossing at the fess point.
– ORIGIN late Middle English: from French *gironné*, from *giron* (see **GYRON**).

gy·ro·pi·lot /ˈjīrə,pīlət/ ▶ **n.** a gyrocompass used to provide automatic steering for a ship or aircraft.

gy·ro·plane /ˈjīrə,plān/ ▶ **n.** an autogiro or similar aircraft.

gy·ro·scope /ˈjīrə,skōp/ ▶ **n.** a device consisting of a wheel or disk mounted so that it can spin rapidly about an axis that is itself free to alter in direction. The orientation of the axis is not affected by tilting of the mounting; so gyroscopes can be used to provide stability or maintain a reference direction in navigation systems, automatic pilots, and stabilizers.
– DERIVATIVES **gy·ro·scop·ic** /,jīrəˈskäpik/ **adj.**, **gy·ro·scop·i·cal·ly** /,jīrəˈskäpik(ə)lē/ **adv.**

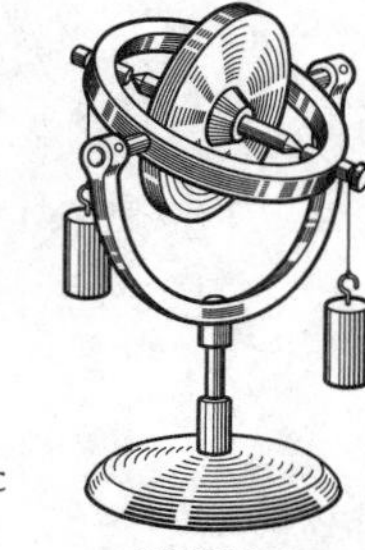
gyroscope

PRONUNCIATION KEY ə ago, up; ər over, fur; a hat; ā ate; ä car; e let; ē see; i fit; ī by; NG sing; ō go; ô law, for; oi toy; o͝o good; o͞o goo; ou out; TH thin; T͟H then; ZH vision

g

– ORIGIN mid 19th cent.: from French, from Greek *guros* 'a ring' + modern Latin *scopium* (see -SCOPE).

gy·ro·sta·bi·lized /ˌjīrō'stābəˌlīzd/ ▶ **adj. 1** (of a vessel) stabilized by a gyrostabilizer.
2 (of cameras, binoculars, and other optical devices) capable of securing a steady view by means of an electronic device that corrects for movement.

gy·ro·sta·bi·liz·er /ˌjīrō'stābəˌlizər/ ▶ **n.** a gyroscopic device for maintaining the equilibrium of something such as a ship, aircraft, or platform.

gy·rus /'jīrəs/ ▶ **n.** (pl. **gyri** /'jīrī/) Anatomy a ridge or fold between two clefts on the cerebral surface in the brain.
– ORIGIN mid 19th cent.: from Latin, from Greek *guros* 'a ring.'

GySgt ▶ **abbr.** gunnery sergeant.

gyt·tja /'yiˌCHä/ ▶ **n.** Geology sediment rich in organic matter deposited at the bottom of a eutrophic lake.
– ORIGIN late 19th cent.: Swedish, literally 'mud, ooze.'

Gyum·ri /'gyo͝omrē/ an industrial city in northwestern Armenia, close to the border with Turkey; pop. 147,000 (est. 2008). The city was destroyed by an earthquake in 1926 and again in 1988. It was formerly called Aleksandropol (1840–1924) and Leninakan (1924–91). Russian name **KUMAYRI**.

gyve /jīv/ ▶ **n.** (usu. **gyves**) archaic a fetter or shackle.
– DERIVATIVES **gyved** adj.
– ORIGIN Middle English: of unknown origin.

Hh

H[1] /āCH/ (also **h**) ▶ **n.** (pl. **Hs** or **H's** /ˈāCHiz/) **1** the eighth letter of the alphabet. ■ denoting the next after G in a set of items, categories, etc. ■ (**h**) Chess denoting the file on the right-hand edge of the board, as viewed from White's side.
2 (**H**) a shape like that of a capital H.
3 (**H**) Music (in the German system) the note B natural.

H[2] ▶ **abbr.** ■ hard (used in describing grades of pencil lead): *a 2H pencil.* ■ height (in giving the dimensions of an object). ■ Physics henry(s). ■ informal heroin. ▶ **symbol** ■ Chemistry enthalpy. ■ the chemical element hydrogen. ■ Physics magnetic field strength.

h /āCH/ ▶ **abbr.** ■ (in measuring the height of horses) hand(s). ■ [in combination] (in units of measurement) hecto-: *wine production reached 624,000 hl last year.* ■ horse. ■ (esp. with reference to water) hot: *nine rooms, all with h & c.* ■ hour(s): *breakfast at 0700 h.* ▶ **symbol** Physics Planck's constant.

ha[1] /hä/ (also **hah**) ▶ **exclam.** used to express surprise, suspicion, triumph, or some other emotion.
– ORIGIN natural utterance: first recorded in Middle English.

ha[2] ▶ **abbr.** hectare(s).

Haar·lem /ˈhärləm/ a city in western Netherlands, near Amsterdam; pop. 147,640 (2008). It is the commercial center of the Dutch bulb industry.

Hab. ▶ **abbr.** Bible Habakkuk.

Ha·bak·kuk /ˈhabəˌko͝ok, həˈbakək/ a Hebrew minor prophet, probably of the 7th century BC. ■ a book of the Bible containing his prophecies.

ha·ba·ne·ra /ˌhäbəˈne(ə)rə, -ˈny(ə)rə/ ▶ **n.** a Cuban dance in slow duple time.
– ORIGIN late 19th cent.: Spanish, short for *danza habanera* 'dance of Havana.'

Ha·ba·ne·ro /ˌhäbəˈne(ə)rō, -ˈnye(ə)rō/ ▶ **n.** (pl. **Habaneros**) a small chili pepper that is the hottest variety available. Also called **Scotch bonnet.**
– ORIGIN Spanish, literally 'of Havana.'

Hab·da·lah /ˌhävdäˈlä, hävˈdôlə/ ▶ **n.** variant spelling of **Havdalah**.

ha·be·as cor·pus /ˈhābēəs ˈkôrpəs/ ▶ **n.** Law a writ requiring a person under arrest to be brought before a judge or into court, esp. to secure the person's release unless lawful grounds are shown for their detention. ■ the legal right to apply for such a writ.
– ORIGIN late Middle English: Latin, literally 'you shall have the body (in court).'

ha·ben·dum /həˈbendəm/ ▶ **n.** Law the part of a deed or conveyance that states the estate or quantity of interest to be granted, e.g., the term of a lease.
– ORIGIN early 17th cent.: Latin, literally '(that is) to be had.'

hab·er·dash·er /ˈhabərˌdasHər/ ▶ **n. 1** a dealer in men's clothing.
2 Brit. a dealer in goods for dressmaking and sewing.
– ORIGIN Middle English: probably based on Anglo-Norman French *hapertas,* perhaps the name of a fabric, of unknown origin. In early use the term denoted a dealer in a variety of household goods, later also specifically a hatter. Current senses date from the early 17th cent.

hab·er·dash·er·y /ˈhabərˌdasHərē/ ▶ **n.** (pl. **haberdasheries**) the goods and wares sold by a haberdasher. ■ the shop of a haberdasher.

hab·er·geon /ˈhabərjən, həˈbərjən/ ▶ **n.** historical a sleeveless coat of mail or scale armor.
– ORIGIN Middle English: from Old French *haubergeon,* from *hauberc* (see **hauberk**), originally denoting a garment protecting the neck; compare with Dutch *halsberg.*

Ha·ber proc·ess /ˈhäbər/ (also **Haber–Bosch process** /ˈhäbər ˈbäsH/) ▶ **n.** an industrial process for producing ammonia from nitrogen and hydrogen, using an iron catalyst at high temperature and pressure.
– ORIGIN named after Fritz *Haber* (1868–1934) and Carl *Bosch* (1874–1940), German chemists.

hab·ile /ˈhabəl/ ▶ **adj.** rare deft; skillful.
– ORIGIN late Middle English: variant of **able**. The spelling change in the 16th and 17th centuries was due to association with French *habile* and Latin *habilis.*

ha·bil·i·ment /həˈbiləmənt/ ▶ **n.** (usu. **habiliments**) archaic clothing.
– ORIGIN late Middle English (in the general sense 'outfit, attire'): from Old French *habillement,* from *habiller* 'fit out,' from Latin *habilis* (see **able**).

ha·bil·i·tate /həˈbiləˌtāt/ ▶ **v. 1** [with obj.] fit out the workings of (a mine).
2 [no obj.] qualify for office, esp. as a teacher in a German university.
– DERIVATIVES **ha·bil·i·ta·tion** /həˌbiləˈtāsHən/ **n.**
– ORIGIN early 17th cent.: from medieval Latin *habilitat-* 'made able,' from the verb *habilitare,* from *habilitas* (see **ability**).

hab·it /ˈhabit/ ▶ **n. 1** a settled or regular tendency or practice, esp. one that is hard to give up: *this can develop into a bad habit | we stayed together out of habit.* ■ informal an addictive practice, esp. one of taking drugs: *a cocaine habit.* ■ Psychology an automatic reaction to a specific situation. ■ general shape or mode of growth, esp. of a plant or a mineral: *a shrub of spreading habit.*
2 a long, loose garment worn by a member of a religious order or congregation. ■ short for **riding habit**. ■ archaic dress; attire.
3 archaic a person's bodily condition or constitution: *a victim to a consumptive habit.*
▶ **v.** [with obj.] (usu. **be habited**) archaic dress; clothe: *a boy habited as a serving lad.*
– PHRASES **break** (or informal **kick**) **the habit** stop engaging in a habitual practice.
– ORIGIN Middle English: from Old French *abit, habit,* from Latin *habitus* 'condition, appearance,' from *habere* 'have, consist of.' The term originally meant 'dress, attire,' later coming to denote physical or mental constitution.

hab·it·a·ble /ˈhabitəbəl/ ▶ **adj.** suitable or good enough to live in.
– DERIVATIVES **hab·it·a·bil·i·ty** /ˌhabətəˈbilətē/ **n.**
– ORIGIN late Middle English: via Old French from Latin *habitabilis,* from *habitare* 'possess, inhabit.'

hab·i·tant /ˈhabitənt, ˈhabətnt/ ▶ **n. 1** [often as modifier] an early French settler in Canada (esp. Quebec) or Louisiana: *the habitant farmhouses of old Quebec.*
2 archaic an inhabitant.
– ORIGIN late Middle English (sense 2): from Old French, from *habiter,* from Latin *habitare* 'inhabit.'

hab·i·tat /ˈhabiˌtat/ ▶ **n.** the natural home or environment of an animal, plant, or other organism: *wild chimps in their natural habitat.* ■ informal a person's usual or preferred surroundings.
– ORIGIN late 18th cent.: from Latin, literally 'it dwells,' from *habitare* (see **habitable**).

hab·i·ta·tion /ˌhabiˈtāsHən/ ▶ **n.** the state or process of living in a particular place: *signs of human habitation.* ■ formal a place in which to live; a house or home.
– DERIVATIVES **hab·i·ta·tive** /ˈhabitəˌtiv/ **adj.**
– ORIGIN late Middle English: via Old French from Latin *habitatio(n-),* from *habitare* 'inhabit.'

hab·it-form·ing ▶ **adj.** (of a drug or activity) addictive.

ha·bit·u·al /həˈbicHo͞oəl/ ▶ **adj.** done or doing constantly or as a habit: *a habitual late sleeper | this pattern of behavior can become habitual.* ■ regular; usual: *his habitual dress.*
– DERIVATIVES **ha·bit·u·al·ly adv.**
– ORIGIN late Middle English (in the sense 'part of one's character'): from medieval Latin *habitualis,* from *habitus* 'condition, appearance' (see **habit**).

ha·bit·u·ate /həˈbicHo͞oˌāt/ ▶ **v.** make or become accustomed or used to something: [with obj.] *she had habituated the chimps to humans.*
– ORIGIN late 15th cent.: from late Latin *habituat-* 'accustomed,' from the verb *habituare,* from *habitus* (see **habit**).

ha·bit·u·a·tion /həˌbicHo͞oˈāsHən/ ▶ **n.** the action of habituating or the condition of being habituated. ■ Psychology the diminishing of a physiological or emotional response to a frequently repeated stimulus.
– ORIGIN late Middle English (in the sense 'formation of habit'): from French or from Latin *habitatio(n)-,* from late Latin *habituare* (see **habituate**).

hab·i·tude /ˈhabiˌt(y)o͞od/ ▶ **n.** rare a habitual tendency or way of behaving.
– ORIGIN late Middle English: via Old French from Latin *habitudo,* from *habere* 'have' (compare with **habit**).

ha·bit·u·é /həˈbicHo͞oˌā/ ▶ **n.** a resident of or frequent visitor to a particular place: *his uncle was a habitué of the French theater.*
– ORIGIN early 19th cent.: French, literally 'accustomed,' past participle of *habituer.*

hab·i·tus /ˈhabitəs/ ▶ **n.** chiefly Medicine & Psychology general constitution, esp. bodily build.
– ORIGIN late 19th cent.: from Latin.

ha·boob /həˈbo͞ob/ ▶ **n.** a violent and oppressive wind blowing in summer, esp. in Sudan, bringing sand from the desert.
– ORIGIN late 19th cent.: from Arabic *habūb* 'blowing furiously.'

Habs·burg /ˈhapsbərg, ˈhäpsˌbo͝ork/ (also **Hapsburg**) one of the principal dynasties of central Europe from medieval to modern times.

> The family established a hereditary monarchy in Austria in 1282 and secured the title of Holy Roman Emperor from 1452. Austrian and Spanish branches were created when Charles divided the territories between his son Philip II and his brother Ferdinand; the Habsburgs ruled Spain 1504–1700, while Habsburg rule in Austria ended with the collapse of Austria–Hungary in 1918.

há·ček /ˈhaˌcHek/ ▶ **n.** a diacritic mark (ˇ) placed over a letter to indicate modification of the sound in Slavic and other languages.
– ORIGIN Czech, diminutive of *hák* 'hook.'

ha·cen·da·do /ˌäsenˈdädō/ (also **haciendado** /ˌäsyen-/) ▶ **n.** (pl. **hacendados**) the owner of a hacienda.
– ORIGIN Spanish.

Ha·chi·o·ji /ˌhäcHēˈōjē/ an industrial city in east central Japan, on east central Honshu Island, west of Tokyo, noted for silk-weaving; pop. 543,737 (2008).

ha·chures /haˈsHo͝orz, ˈhasHərz/ ▶ **plural n.** short parallel lines used in hill-shading on maps, their closeness indicating steepness of gradient.

– DERIVATIVES **ha·chured** /ha'SHŏŏrd, 'hasHərd/ **adj.**
– ORIGIN mid 19th cent.: from French, from *hacher* (see HATCH³).

ha·ci·en·da /ˌhäsē'endə/ ▶ **n.** (in Spanish-speaking regions) a large estate or plantation with a dwelling house.
– ORIGIN Spanish, from Latin *facienda* 'things to be done,' from *facere* 'make, do' (see FAZENDA).

hack¹ /hak/ ▶ **v. 1** [with obj.] cut with rough or heavy blows: *hack off the dead branches* | [no obj.] *a fishmonger* ***hacked at*** *it with a cleaver.*
2 [no obj.] use a computer to gain unauthorized access to data in a system: *they* ***hacked into*** *a bank's computer.* ■ [with obj.] gain unauthorized access to (data in a computer): *hacking private information from computers.*
3 [usu. with negative] (**hack it**) informal manage; cope: *lots of people leave because they* ***can't hack it.***
▶ **n. 1** a rough cut, blow, or stroke: *he was sure one of us was going to take a hack at him.* ■ (in sports) a kick or hit inflicted on another player. ■ a cut or gash. ■ a tool for rough striking or cutting, e.g., a mattock or a miner's pick.
2 informal an act of computer hacking. ■ a piece of computer code that performs some function, esp. an unofficial alternative or addition to a commercial program: *freeware and shareware hacks.*
– PHRASES **hacking cough** a short, dry, frequent cough.
– PHRASAL VERBS **hack around** pass one's time idly or with no definite purpose. **hack someone off** informal annoy or infuriate someone.
– ORIGIN Old English *haccian* 'cut in pieces'; related to Dutch *hakken* and German *hacken.*

hack² ▶ **n. 1** a writer or journalist producing dull, unoriginal work: [as modifier] *a hack scriptwriter.* ■ a person who does dull routine work.
2 a horse for ordinary riding. ■ a good-quality lightweight riding horse, esp. one used in the show ring. ■ a ride on a horse. ■ an inferior or worn-out horse. ■ a horse rented out for riding.
3 a taxicab.
▶ **v.** [no obj.] (usu. as noun **hacking**) ride a horse for pleasure or exercise.
– DERIVATIVES **hack·er·y** /'hakərē/ **n.** (sense 1 of the noun).
– ORIGIN Middle English (sense 2 of the noun): abbreviation of HACKNEY. Sense 1 of the noun dates from the late 17th cent.

hack³ ▶ **n. 1** Falconry a board on which a hawk's meat is laid.
2 a wooden frame for drying bricks, cheeses, etc. ■ a pile of bricks stacked up to dry before firing.
– PHRASES **at hack** (of a young hawk) given partial liberty but not yet allowed to hunt for itself.
– ORIGIN late Middle English (denoting the lower half of a divided door): variant of HATCH¹.

hack·a·more /'hakəˌmôr/ ▶ **n.** a bridle without a bit, operating by exerting pressure on the horse's nose.
– ORIGIN mid 19th cent.: perhaps from Spanish *jaquima*, earlier *xaquima* 'halter.'

hack·ber·ry /'hakˌberē/ ▶ **n.** (pl. **hackberries**) a tree of the elm family that has leaves resembling those of nettles, found in both tropical and temperate regions. See also NETTLE TREE. ● Genus *Celtis*, family Ulmaceae: several species, in particular the **North American hackberry** (*C. occidentalis*), which bears edible purple berries and whose bark becomes ridged and covered with warty knobs.
■ the berry of this tree.
– ORIGIN mid 18th cent.: variant of northern English dialect *hagberry*, of Scandinavian origin.

Hack·en·sack /'hakənˌsak/ a city in northeastern New Jersey, east of Paterson; pop. 42,804 (est. 2008).

hack·er /'hakər/ ▶ **n. 1** a person who uses computers to gain unauthorized access to data. ■ informal an enthusiastic and skillful computer programmer or user.
2 a person or thing that hacks or cuts roughly.

hack·ette /ha'ket/ ▶ **n.** Brit. informal, chiefly derogatory a female journalist.

hack·ing jack·et ▶ **n.** a riding jacket, often tweed, with a tight waist, flared skirt, slits at the side or back, and slanted pockets with flaps.

hack·le /'hakəl/ ▶ **n. 1** (**hackles**) erectile hairs along the back of a dog or other animal that rise when it is angry or alarmed.
2 (often **hackles**) a long, narrow feather on the neck or saddle of a domestic rooster or other bird. ■ Fishing a feather wound around a fishing fly so that its filaments are splayed out. ■ such feathers collectively. ■ a bunch of feathers in a military headdress.
3 a steel comb for separating flax fibers.
▶ **v.** [with obj.] dress or comb with a hackle.
– ORIGIN late Middle English (sense 2 of the noun): variant of HATCHEL.

hack·ma·tack /'hakməˌtak/ ▶ **n.** any of a number of North American coniferous trees, in particular the tamarack.
– ORIGIN late 18th cent.: perhaps from Western Abnaki *akemantak* 'snowshoe-conifer.'

hack·ney /'haknē/ ▶ **n.** (pl. **hackneys**) historical a horse or pony of a light breed with a high-stepping trot, used in harness. ■ [usu. as modifier] a horse-drawn vehicle kept for hire: *a hackney coach.*
– ORIGIN Middle English: probably from *Hackney* in East London, England, where horses were pastured. The term originally denoted an ordinary riding horse (as opposed to a warhorse or draft horse), esp. one available for hire: hence *hackney carriage* or *coach*, and the verb *hackney* meaning 'use (a horse) for general purposes,' later 'make commonplace by overuse' (see HACKNEYED).

hack·ney car·riage ▶ **n.** Brit. a taxicab.

hack·neyed /'haknēd/ ▶ **adj.** (of a phrase or idea) lacking significance through having been overused; unoriginal and trite: *hackneyed old sayings.*

hack·saw /'hakˌsô/ ▶ **n.** a saw with a narrow fine-toothed blade set in a frame, used esp. for cutting metal.
▶ **v.** (past participle **hacksawn** or **hacksawed**) [with obj.] cut (something) using a hacksaw.

hack·tiv·ist /'haktəˌvist/ ▶ **n.** a computer hacker whose activity is aimed at promoting a social or political cause.
– DERIVATIVES **hack·tiv·ism** /-ˌvizəm/ **n.**
– ORIGIN 1990s: blend of *hacker* and *activist.*

had /had/ past and past participle of HAVE.

ha·da·da /'hädəˌdä/ (also **hadada ibis**) ▶ **n.** a large gray-brown African ibis with iridescent patches on the wings and a loud, harsh call. ● *Bostrychia* (or *Hagedashia*) *hagedash*, family Threskiornithidae.
– ORIGIN late 18th cent.: imitative of its call.

ha·dal /'hādl/ ▶ **adj.** of or relating to the zone of the sea greater than approximately 20,000 feet (6,000 m) in depth (chiefly oceanic trenches).
– ORIGIN mid 20th cent.: from HADES + -AL.

had·da /'hadə/ informal ▶ **contraction** had to.

had·dock /'hadək/ ▶ **n.** (pl. **same**) a silvery-gray bottom-dwelling fish of North Atlantic coastal waters, related to the cod. It is popular as a food fish and is of great commercial value. ● *Melanogrammus aeglefinus*, family Gadidae.
– ORIGIN Middle English: from Anglo-Norman French *hadoc*, from Old French *hadot*, of unknown origin.

hade /hād/ Geology ▶ **n.** the inclination of a mineral vein or fault from the vertical.
▶ **v.** [no obj.] (of a shaft, vein, or fault) incline from the vertical: *it was hading eighteen inches for every fathom in depth.*
– ORIGIN late 17th cent.: perhaps a dialect form of the verb HEAD.

Ha·des /'hādēz/ Greek Mythology the underworld; the abode of the spirits of the dead. ■ the god of the underworld, one of the sons of Cronus. Roman equivalent PLUTO.
– DERIVATIVES **Ha·de·an** /'hādēən/ **adj.**
– ORIGIN from Greek *Haidēs*, of unknown origin.

Ha·dith /hə'dēTH/ ▶ **n.** (pl. **same** or **Hadiths**) a collection of traditions containing sayings of the prophet Muhammad that, with accounts of his daily practice (the Sunna), constitute the major source of guidance for Muslims apart from the Koran. ■ one of these sayings.
– ORIGIN from Arabic *ḥadīṯ* 'tradition.'

hadj ▶ **n.** variant spelling of HAJJ.

hadj·i ▶ **n.** variant spelling of HAJI.

Had·ley cell /'hadlē/ ▶ **n.** Meteorology a large-scale atmospheric convection cell in which air rises at the equator and sinks at medium latitudes, typically about 30° north or south.
– ORIGIN 1950s: named after George *Hadley* (1685–1768), English scientific writer.

had·n't /'hadnt/ ▶ **contraction** had not.

Ha·dri·an /'hādrēən/ (AD 76–138), Roman emperor 117–138; full name *Publius Aelius Hadrianus.* The adopted successor of Trajan, he toured the provinces of the empire and secured the frontiers.

Ha·dri·an's Wall /'hādrēənz/ a Roman defensive wall across northern England, stretching from the Solway Firth in the west to the mouth of the Tyne River in the east (about 74 miles; 120 km). It was begun in AD 122, after the emperor Hadrian's visit, to defend the province of Britain against invasions by tribes from the north.

had·ron /'hadˌrän/ ▶ **n.** Physics a subatomic particle of a type including the baryons and mesons that can take part in the strong interaction.
– DERIVATIVES **ha·dron·ic** /had'ränik/ **adj.**
– ORIGIN 1960s: from Greek *hadros* 'bulky' + -ON.

had·ro·saur /'hadrəˌsôr/ (also **hadrosaurus** /ˌhadrə'sôrəs/) ▶ **n.** a large, herbivorous, mainly bipedal dinosaur of the middle to late Cretaceous period, with jaws flattened like the bill of a duck. Also called DUCK-BILLED DINOSAUR. ● Family Hadrosauridae, infraorder Ornithopoda, order Ornithischia.
– DERIVATIVES **had·ro·sau·ri·an adj.**
– ORIGIN late 19th cent.: from modern Latin *Hadrosaurus* (genus name), from Greek *hadros* 'thick, stout' + *sauros* 'lizard.'

hadst /hadst/ archaic second person singular past of HAVE.

haec·ce·i·ty /hak'sēətē/ ▶ **n.** Philosophy that property or quality of a thing by virtue of which it is unique or describable as "this (one)." ■ the property of being a unique and individual thing.
– ORIGIN mid 17th cent.: from medieval Latin *haecceitas*, from Latin *haec*, feminine of *hic* 'this.'

Haeck·el /'hekəl/, Ernst Heinrich (1834–1919), German biologist and philosopher. He popularized Darwin's theories and saw evolution as providing a framework for describing the world, with the German Empire representing the highest evolved form of a civilized nation.

Hae·ju /'hīˌjo͞o/ an industrial port city in southwestern North Korea, on the Yellow Sea; pop. 228,400 (est. 2009).

haem ▶ **n.** British spelling of HEME.

hae·mag·glu·ti·na·tion etc. ▶ **n.** British spelling of HEMAGGLUTINATION etc.

hae·mal ▶ **adj.** British spelling of HEMAL.

haemato- ▶ **comb. form** British spelling of HEMATO-.

-haemia ▶ **comb. form** chiefly Brit. variant spelling of -EMIA.

haemo- ▶ **comb. form** British spelling of HEMO-.

ha·fiz /'häfiz/ ▶ **n.** a Muslim who knows the Koran by heart.
– ORIGIN Persian, from Arabic *ḥāfiẓ* 'guardian,' from *ḥāfiẓa* 'guard, know by heart.'

haf·ni·um /'hafnēəm/ ▶ **n.** the chemical element of atomic number 72, a hard silver-gray metal of the transition series, resembling and often occurring with zirconium. (Symbol: **Hf**)
– ORIGIN 1920s: modern Latin, from *Hafnia*, Latinized form of Danish *Havn*, former name of Copenhagen.

haft /haft/ ▶ **n.** the handle of a knife, ax, or spear.
▶ **v.** [with obj.] (often as adj. **hafted**) provide (a blade, ax head, or spearhead) with a haft.
– ORIGIN Old English *hæft*, of Germanic origin: related to Dutch *heft*, *hecht* and German *Heft*, also to HEAVE.

Haf·to·rah /ˌhäftä'rä, häf'tôrə/ (also **Haphtarah** or **Haphtorah**) ▶ **n.** (pl. **Haftoroth** /-tä'rôt, -'tôrōs/) Judaism a short reading from the Prophets that follows the reading from the Law in a synagogue.
– ORIGIN from Hebrew *hapṭārāh* 'dismissal.'

hag¹ /hag/ ▶ **n. 1** a witch, esp. one in the form of an ugly old woman (often used as a term of disparagement for a woman): *a fat old hag in a dirty apron.*
2 short for HAGFISH.
– DERIVATIVES **hag·gish adj.**
– ORIGIN Middle English: perhaps from Old English *hægtesse*, *hegtes*, related to Dutch *heks* and German *Hexe* 'witch,' of unknown ultimate origin.

hag² ▶ **n.** Scottish & N. English **1** (also **peat hag**) an overhang of peat.
2 a soft place on a moor or a firm place in a bog.
– ORIGIN Middle English (denoting a gap in a cliff): from Old Norse *hogg* 'gap,' from *hoggva* 'hack, hew.'

Hag. ▶ **abbr.** Bible Haggai.

Ha·gar /'hägər/ (in the Bible and in Islamic tradition) the mother of Ishmael (Ismail), son of Abraham.

Ha·gen /'hägən/ an industrial city in northwestern Germany, in North Rhine–Westphalia; pop. 195,700 (est. 2006).

Ha·gers·town /'hāgərzˌtoun/ a city in northwestern Maryland; pop. 39,728 (est. 2008).

hag·fish /'hagˌfisH/ ▶ **n.** (pl. **same** or **hagfishes**) a primitive jawless marine vertebrate distantly related to the lampreys, with a slimy eellike body, a slitlike mouth surrounded by barbels, and a rasping tongue used for feeding on dead or dying fish. ● Class Myxini and family Myxinidae: several genera, in particular *Myxine*, and numerous species.
– ORIGIN early 17th cent.: from HAG¹ + FISH¹.

Hag·ga·dah /hägä'dä, hə'gädə/ (also **Aggadah** /ägä'dä, ə'gädə/) ▶ **n.** (pl. **Haggadoth** or **Haggadot** /-'dôt/) Judaism **1** the text recited at the Seder on the first two nights of the Jewish Passover, including a narrative of the Exodus.

2 a legend, parable, or anecdote used to illustrate a point of the Law in the Talmud. ■ this (nonlegal) element of the Talmud. Compare with **Halacha**.
– DERIVATIVES **Hag·gad·ic** /hə'gädik/ **adj.**, **Hag·ga·dist** /hə'gädist/ **n.**
– ORIGIN mid 18th cent.: from Hebrew *Haggādāh* 'tale, parable,' from *higgīd* 'tell, expound.'

Hag·gai /'hagē,ī, 'hagī/ a Hebrew minor prophet of the 6th century BC. ■ a book of the Bible containing his prophecies of a glorious future in the Messianic age.

hag·gard /'hagərd/ ▶ **adj.** **1** looking exhausted and unwell, esp. from fatigue, worry, or suffering: *I trailed on behind, haggard and disheveled.*
2 (of a hawk) caught for training as a wild adult of more than twelve months. Compare with **passage hawk**.
▶ **n.** a haggard hawk.
– DERIVATIVES **hag·gard·ly** **adv.**, **hag·gard·ness** **n.**
– ORIGIN mid 16th cent. (used in falconry): from French *hagard*; perhaps related to **hedge**; later influenced by **hag**[1].

hag·gis /'hagis/ ▶ **n.** (pl. **same**) a Scottish dish consisting of a sheep's or calf's offal mixed with suet, oatmeal, and seasoning and boiled in a bag, traditionally one made from the animal's stomach.
– ORIGIN late Middle English: probably from earlier *hag* 'hack, hew,' from Old Norse *hǫggva*.

hag·gle /'hagəl/ ▶ **v.** [no obj.] dispute or bargain persistently, esp. over the cost of something: *the two sides are haggling over television rights.*
▶ **n.** a period of such bargaining.
– DERIVATIVES **hag·gler** /'haglər/ **n.**
– ORIGIN late 16th cent. (in the sense 'hack, mangle'): from Old Norse *hǫggva* 'hew.'

hagio- ▶ **comb. form** relating to saints or holiness: *hagiographer*.
– ORIGIN from Greek *hagios* 'holy.'

Hag·i·og·ra·pha /,hagē'ägrəfə, ,hāgē-/ ▶ **plural n.** the books of the Bible comprising the last of the three major divisions of the Hebrew scriptures, other than the Law and the Prophets. The books of the Hagiographa are: Ruth, Psalms, Job, Proverbs, Ecclesiastes, Song of Solomon, Lamentations, Daniel, Esther, Ezra, Nehemiah, and Chronicles. Also called **the Writings** (see **writing**).
– ORIGIN via late Latin from Greek.

hag·i·og·ra·pher /,hagē'ägrəfər, ,hāgē-/ ▶ **n.** **1** a writer of the lives of the saints. ■ derogatory a person who writes in an adulatory way about someone else, esp. in a biography.
2 Theology a writer of any of the Hagiographa.

hag·i·og·ra·phy /,hagē'ägrəfē, ,hāgē-/ ▶ **n.** the writing of the lives of saints. ■ derogatory adulatory writing about another person. ■ biography that idealizes its subject.
– DERIVATIVES **hag·i·o·graph·ic** /,hagēə'grafik, ,hāgēə-/ **adj.**, **hag·i·o·graph·i·cal** /,hagēə'grafəkəl, ,hāgēə-/ **adj.**

hag·i·ol·a·try /,hagē'älətrē, ,hāgē-/ ▶ **n.** the worship of saints. ■ derogatory undue veneration of a famous person.

hag·i·ol·o·gy /,hagē'äləjē, ,hāgē-/ ▶ **n.** literature dealing with the lives and legends of saints.
– DERIVATIVES **hag·i·o·log·i·cal** /,hagēə'läjəkəl, ,hāgēə-/ **adj.**, **hag·i·ol·o·gist** /-jist/ **n.**

hag·i·o·scope /'hagēə,skōp, 'hāgēə-/ ▶ **n.** another term for **squint** (sense 3 of the noun).

hag·rid·den /'hag,ridn/ ▶ **adj.** afflicted by nightmares or anxieties: *it once made parents and doctors hagridden.*

Hague /hāg/ (**The Hague**) the seat of government and administrative center of the Netherlands, on the North Sea coast, capital of the province of South Holland; pop. 475,681 (2008). The International Court of Justice is based here. Dutch name **Den Haag**; also called **'s-Gravenhage**.

hah ▶ **exclam.** variant spelling of **ha**[1].

ha ha ▶ **exclam.** used to represent laughter or amusement.
– ORIGIN natural utterance: first recorded in Old English (compare with **ha**[1]).

ha-ha /'hä ,hä, ,hä 'hä/ ▶ **n.** a ditch with a wall on its inner side below ground level, forming a boundary to a park or garden without interrupting the view.
– ORIGIN early 18th cent.: from French, said to be from the cry of surprise on suddenly encountering such an obstacle.

ha·ham /'hähəm/ ▶ **n.** variant spelling of **chacham**.

Hahn /hän/, Otto (1879–1968), German chemist, pioneer of nuclear fission. Together with Lise Meitner, he discovered the element protactinium in 1917. The pair discovered nuclear fission in 1938 with Fritz Strassmann (1902–80). Nobel Prize for Chemistry (1944), shared with Strassmann.

hahn·i·um /'hänēəm/ ▶ **n.** the name formerly proposed by the American Chemical Society for the chemical element of atomic number 105 (**dubnium**), and by IUPAC for element 108 (**hassium**).
– ORIGIN 1970s: named in honor of O. **Hahn**.

Hai·da /'hīdə/ ▶ **n.** (pl. **same** or **Haidas**) **1** a member of an American Indian people of coastal British Colombia and southeastern Alaska.
2 the language of this people, of unknown affinity.
▶ **adj.** of or relating to this people or their language.
– ORIGIN mid 19th cent.: the name in Haida, literally 'people.'

Hai·fa /'hīfə/ the chief port in Israel, in the northwestern part of the country, on the Mediterranean coast; pop. 264,800 (est. 2008).

Haight-Ash·bury /,hāt 'ash,berē/ a residential and commercial section of central San Francisco in California, associated with youth culture of the 1960s.

haik /hīk/ (also **haick**) ▶ **n.** a large outer wrap, typically white, worn by people from North Africa.
– ORIGIN early 18th cent.: from Arabic *ḥā'ik*.

Hai·kou /'hī'kō/ the capital of Hainan autonomous region in China, a port on the northeastern coast of Hainan island; pop. 864,900 (2006).

hai·ku /'hī,ko͞o, ,hī'ko͞o/ ▶ **n.** (pl. **same** or **haikus**) a Japanese poem of seventeen syllables, in three lines of five, seven, and five, traditionally evoking images of the natural world. ■ an English imitation of this.
– ORIGIN Japanese, contracted form of *haikai no ku* 'light verse.'

hail[1] /hāl/ ▶ **n.** pellets of frozen rain that fall in showers from cumulonimbus clouds. ■ [in sing.] a large number of objects hurled forcefully through the air: *a hail of bullets.*
▶ **v.** [no obj.] **1** (**it hails, it is hailing**, etc.) hail falls: *it hailed so hard we had to stop.*
2 [with adverbial of direction] (of a large number of objects) fall or be hurled forcefully: *missiles and bombs hail down from the sky.*
– ORIGIN Old English *hagol, hægl* (noun), *hagalian* (verb), of Germanic origin; related to Dutch *hagel* and German *Hagel*.

hail[2] ▶ **v.** **1** [with obj.] call out to (someone) to attract attention: *the crew hailed a fishing boat.* ■ signal (an approaching taxicab) to stop: *she raised her hand to hail a cab.*
2 [with obj.] acclaim enthusiastically as being a specified thing: *he has been **hailed as** the new James Dean.*
3 [no obj.] (**hail from**) have one's home or origins in (a place): *he hails from Pittsburgh.*
▶ **exclam.** archaic expressing greeting or acclaim: *hail, Caesar!*
▶ **n.** a shout or call used to attract attention.
– PHRASES **within hail** (or **within hailing distance**) at a distance within which someone may be called to; within earshot.
– DERIVATIVES **hail·er** **n.**
– ORIGIN Middle English: from the obsolete adjective *hail* 'healthy' (occurring in greetings and toasts, such as *wæs hæil*: see **wassail**), from Old Norse *heill*, related to **hale**[1] and **whole**.

Ha'il /'hī(ə)l/ (also **Hail, Hayel**) a city in northwestern Saudi Arabia, on the pilgrimage route from Iraq to Mecca; pop. 267,000 (est. 2004).

Hai·le Se·las·sie /'hīlē sə'lasē/ (1892–1975), emperor of Ethiopia 1930–74; born *Tafari Makonnen*. In exile in Britain during the Italian occupation of Ethiopia 1936–41, he was restored to the throne by the Allies and ruled until he was deposed by a military coup.

hail-fel·low-well-met ▶ **adj.** showing excessive familiarity: *Harold was accustomed to hail-fellow-well-met salesmen.*

Hail Mar·y ▶ **n.** (pl. **Hail Marys**) **1** a prayer to the Virgin Mary used chiefly by Roman Catholics, beginning with part of Luke 1:28. Also called **Ave Maria**. ■ a recitation of such a devotional phrase or prayer: *muttering Hail Marys under her breath.*
2 [usu. as modifier] Football a desperation long pass to try to score late in the game, typically unsuccessful: *they beat the 49ers on a Hail Mary pass in the final seconds.* ■ any attempt with a small chance of success: *a Hail Mary plan.*

hail·stone /'hāl,stōn/ ▶ **n.** a pellet of hail.

hail·storm /'hāl,stôrm/ ▶ **n.** a storm of heavy hail.

Hai·nan /'hī'nän/ an island in the South China Sea that forms an autonomous region of China; pop. 8,450,000 (est. 2007); capital, Haikou.

Hai·naut /(h)ā'nō/ a province in southern Belgium; capital, Mons.

Hai·phong /'hī'fông, -'fäng/ a port in northern Vietnam, on the Gulf of Tonkin, at the delta of the Red River; pop. 485,300 (est. 2009).

hair /he(ə)r/ ▶ **n.** **1** any of the fine threadlike strands growing from the skin of humans, mammals, and some other animals. ■ a similar strand growing from the epidermis of a plant, or forming part of a living cell. ■ (**a hair**) a very small quantity or extent: *his magic takes him a hair above the competition.*
2 such strands collectively, esp. those growing on a person's head: *a woman with shoulder-length fair hair* | [as modifier] *a hair salon.*
– PHRASES **hair of the dog** informal an alcoholic drink taken to cure a hangover. [from *hair of the dog that bit you*, formerly recommended as an efficacious remedy for the bite of a mad dog.] **a hair's breadth** a very small amount or margin: *you escaped death **by a hair's breadth**.* **in** (or **out of**) **someone's hair** informal annoying (or ceasing to annoy) someone: *I'm glad he's out of my hair.* **let one's hair down** informal behave in an uninhibited or relaxed manner: *let your hair down and just have some fun.* **make someone's hair stand on end** alarm or horrify someone. **not a hair out of place** (of a person) extremely neat and tidy in appearance. **not turn a hair** remain apparently unmoved or unaffected: *the old woman didn't turn a hair; she just sat quietly rocking.* **put hair on one's chest** informal (of an alcoholic drink) be very strong. **split hairs** make small and overfine distinctions.
– DERIVATIVES **haired** **adj.** [in combination] *a curly-haired boy*, **hair·like** **adj.**
– ORIGIN Old English *hǣr*, of Germanic origin; related to Dutch *haar* and German *Haar*.

hair·ball /'he(ə)r,bôl/ ▶ **n.** a ball of hair that collects in the stomach of a cat or similar animal as a result of the animal's licking its coat.

hair·band /'he(ə)r,band/ ▶ **n.** a band for securing or tying back one's hair.

hair·breadth /'he(ə)r,bre(d)TH/ ▶ **n.** another term for **a hair's breadth** at **hair**.

hair·brush /'he(ə)r,brəSH/ ▶ **n.** a brush for arranging or smoothing a person's hair.

hair·cloth /'he(ə)r,klôTH/ ▶ **n.** stiff cloth woven with a cotton or linen warp and horsehair weft.

hair·cut /'heər,kət/ ▶ **n.** **1** the style in which a person's hair is cut. ■ an act of cutting a person's hair.
2 informal a reduction in the stated value of an asset: *the banks would probably be willing to take a haircut on the rest.*

hair·do /'he(ə)r,do͞o/ ▶ **n.** (pl. **hairdos**) informal the style of a person's hair. ■ an act of styling a person's hair (used esp. of a woman's hair).

hair·dress·er /'he(ə)r,dresər/ ▶ **n.** a person who cuts and styles hair as an occupation.
– DERIVATIVES **hair·dress·ing** /-,dresiNG/ **n.**

hair dry·er (also **hair drier**) ▶ **n.** an electrical device for drying a person's hair by blowing warm air over it.

hair grass ▶ **n.** a slender-stemmed grass of temperate and cool regions. ● *Deschampsia, Aira*, and other genera, family Gramineae.

hair·less /'he(ə)rlis/ ▶ **adj.** lacking hair; bare or bald: *his hairless chest.*

hair·line /'he(ə)r,līn/ ▶ **n.** **1** the edge of a person's hair, esp. on the forehead.
2 a very thin or fine line: *the boards fitted so tightly together, there was only a hairline between them* | [as modifier] *a hairline fracture.*

hair·net /'he(ə)r,net/ ▶ **n.** a piece of fine mesh fabric for confining the hair.

hair·piece /'he(ə)r,pēs/ ▶ **n.** a quantity or switch of detached hair used to augment a person's natural hair.

hair·pin /'he(ə)r,pin/ ▶ **n.** a U-shaped pin for fastening the hair. ■ a sharp U-shaped curve in a road.
▶ **adj.** shaped like a hairpin; forming a U: *up the steep cliff along a slippery hairpin path* | *a long series of hairpin turns on roads cut into the mountainside.*

hair-rais·ing ▶ **adj.** extremely alarming, astonishing, or frightening: *hair-raising adventures.*
– DERIVATIVES **hair-rais·er** **n.**

hair shirt ▶ **n.** a shirt of haircloth, formerly worn by penitents and ascetics.
▶ **adj.** (**hair-shirt** or **hair-shirted**) austere and self-sacrificing: *a hair-shirted existence advocated by ecofundamentalists.*

hair space ▶ **n.** Printing a very thin space between letters or words.

hair·split·ting /'he(ə)r,splitiNG/ ▶ **adj.** characterized by or fond of small and overfine distinctions: *legal experts have a particularly hairsplitting mentality.*

h

▶ **n.** the action of making small and overfine distinctions; quibbling.
– DERIVATIVES **hair·split·ter** /-ˌsplitər/ **n.**

hair spray (also **hairspray** /ˈhe(ə)rˌsprā/) ▶ **n.** a solution sprayed onto a person's hair to keep it in place.

hair·spring /ˈhe(ə)rˌspriNG/ ▶ **n.** a slender flat coiled spring regulating the movement of the balance wheel in a watch.

hair·streak /ˈhe(ə)rˌstrēk/ ▶ **n.** a butterfly with a narrow streak or row of dots on the underside of the hind wing and a small taillike projection on the hind wing. ● Many genera in the family Lycaenidae.

hair·style /ˈhe(ə)rˌstīl/ ▶ **n.** a particular way in which a person's hair is cut or arranged.

hair·styl·ist /ˈhe(ə)rˌstīlist/ (also **hair stylist**) ▶ **n.** a person who cuts and styles people's hair professionally.
– DERIVATIVES **hair·styl·ing** /-stīliNG/ **n.**

hair trig·ger ▶ **n.** a trigger of a firearm set for release at the slightest pressure. ■ (as modifier **hair-trigger**) liable to change suddenly and violently: *a hair-trigger temper.*

hair·weav·ing /ˈhe(ə)rˌwēviNG/ ▶ **n.** the process of interweaving a hairpiece with one's own hair.

h

hair worm ▶ **n.** another term for **HORSEHAIR WORM.**

hair·y /ˈhe(ə)rē/ ▶ **adj.** (**hairier, hairiest**) **1** covered with hair, esp. thick or long hair: *a hairy chest.* ■ having a rough feel or appearance suggestive of coarse hair: *a hairy tweed coat and skirt.*
2 informal alarming and difficult: *we drove up yet another hairy mountain road.*
– DERIVATIVES **hair·i·ly** /ˈhe(ə)rəlē/ **adv.**, **hair·i·ness n.**

Hai·ti /ˈhātē/ a country in the Caribbean Sea that occupies the western third of the island of Hispaniola; pop. 9,035,500 (est. 2009); capital, Port-au-Prince; official languages, Haitian Creole and French.

> The area was ceded to France by Spain in 1697, and many slaves were imported from West Africa to work on sugar plantations. In 1791, the slaves rose in rebellion under Toussaint L'Ouverture, and the colony was proclaimed an independent state in 1804, under the name of Haiti. It was administered by the US 1915–34 after a succession of corrupt dictatorships. Then, from 1957 until 1986, the country was under the oppressive dictatorship of the Duvalier family. Haiti's first democratically chosen president was elected in 1990 but was overthrown by the military the following year; democracy was restored by US and UN intervention in 1994. Political upheaval occurred again in 2004, resulting in the ouster of the president. Haiti is the poorest country in the Western Hemisphere. In 2010 the area around the capital was devastated by an earthquake.

Hai·tian /ˈhāSHən/ ▶ **adj.** of or relating to Haiti, its inhabitants, or their language.
▶ **n. 1** a native or inhabitant of Haiti.
2 (also **Haitian Creole**) the French-based Creole language spoken in Haiti.

Hai·tink /ˈhīˌtiNGk/, Bernard (Johann Herman) (1929–), Dutch musical director and orchestra conductor.

haj·i /ˈhajē/ (also **hajji** or **hadji**) ▶ **n.** (pl. **hajis**) a Muslim who has been to Mecca as a pilgrim: [as title] *Haji Hadi.*
– ORIGIN from Persian and Turkish *ḥājjī, ḥājī*, from Arabic *ḥajj* (see **HAJJ**).

hajj /haj/ (also **haj** or **hadj**) ▶ **n.** the Muslim pilgrimage to Mecca that takes place in the last month of the year, and that all Muslims are expected to make at least once during their lifetime.
– ORIGIN from Arabic (*al-*) *ḥajj* '(the Great) Pilgrimage.'

ha·ka·ma /ˈhakəmə/ ▶ **n.** [treated as sing. or pl.] loose trousers with many pleats in the front, forming part of Japanese formal dress.
– ORIGIN mid 19th cent.: Japanese.

hake /hāk/ ▶ **n.** (pl. **same** or **hakes**) **1** a large-headed elongated fish with long jaws and strong teeth. It is a valuable commercial food fish. ● Family Merlucciidae and genus *Merluccius*: several species.
2 any of a number of similar fishes related to the true hakes. ● Species in several families, esp. in the northwestern Atlantic genus *Urophycis* (family Phycidae).
– ORIGIN Middle English: perhaps from Old English *haca* 'hook.'

ha·kim /həˈkēm/ ▶ **n. 1** a physician using traditional remedies in India and Muslim countries. [from Arabic *ḥakīm* 'wise man, physician.']
2 a judge, ruler, or governor in India and Muslim countries. [from Arabic *ḥākim* 'ruler.']

Hak·ka /ˈhäkə/ ▶ **n. 1** a member of a people of southeastern China, esp. Canton, Taiwan, and Hong Kong, who migrated from the north during the 12th century.
2 the dialect of Chinese spoken by this people.
▶ **adj.** of or relating to this people or their language.
– ORIGIN from Chinese (Cantonese dialect) *haàk ka* 'stranger.'

Ha·ko·da·te /ˌhäkōˈdätā/ a port in northern Japan, on the southern tip of the island of Hokkaido; pop. 290,873 (2007).

Ha·la·cha /ˌhäläˈKHä, hälôˈKHə/ (also **Halakah**) ▶ **n.** Jewish law and jurisprudence, based on the Talmud.
– DERIVATIVES **Ha·la·chic** /həˈläkHik, həˈlakik/ **adj.**
– ORIGIN from Hebrew *hălāḵāh* 'law.'

ha·lal /həˈläl, həˈlal/ ▶ **adj.** denoting or relating to meat prepared as prescribed by Muslim law: *halal butchers.* ■ religiously acceptable according to Muslim law: *halal banking.*
▶ **n.** halal meat.
– ORIGIN mid 19th cent.: from Arabic *ḥalāl* 'according to religious law.'

ha·la·la /həˈlälə/ ▶ **n.** (pl. **same** or **halalas**) a monetary unit of Saudi Arabia, equal to one hundredth of a riyal.
– ORIGIN Arabic.

Hal·as /ˈhaləs/, George (Stanley) (1895–1983), US football player, coach, and owner; known as **Papa Bear**. He founded the Chicago Bears (originally as the Decatur Staleys) in 1920. As a coach, he set an NFL record with 325 wins. Football Hall of Fame (1963).

ha·la·tion /häˈlāSHən/ ▶ **n.** the spreading of light beyond its proper boundaries to form a fog around the edges of a bright image in a photograph or on a television screen.
– ORIGIN mid 19th cent.: formed irregularly from **HALO** + **-ATION.**

hal·berd /ˈhalbərd, ˈhôl-/ (also **halbert** /-bərt/) ▶ **n.** historical a combined spear and battle-ax.
– ORIGIN late 15th cent.: from French *hallebarde*, from Italian *alabarda*, from Middle High German *helmbarde* (from *helm* 'handle' + *barde* 'hatchet').

hal·berd·ier /ˌhalbərˈdir, ˌhôlbər-/ ▶ **n.** historical a man armed with a halberd.
– ORIGIN early 16th cent.: from French *hallebardier*, from *hallebarde* (see **HALBERD**).

halberd

hal·cy·on /ˈhalsēən/ ▶ **adj.** denoting a period of time in the past that was idyllically happy and peaceful: *the halcyon days of the mid-1980s, when profits were soaring.*
▶ **n. 1** a tropical Asian and African kingfisher with brightly colored plumage. ● Genus *Halcyon*, family Alcedinidae: many species.
2 a mythical bird said by ancient writers to breed in a nest floating at sea at the winter solstice, charming the wind and waves into calm.
– ORIGIN late Middle English (in the mythological sense): via Latin from Greek *alkuōn* 'kingfisher' (also *halkuōn*, by association with *hals* 'sea' and *kuōn* 'conceiving').

Hale[1] /hāl/, Edward Everett (1822–1909), US clergyman, writer, and philanthropist. A Unitarian minister, he wrote the story "A Man Without a Country" (1863).

Hale[2], George Ellery (1868–1938), US astronomer. He discovered that sunspots are associated with strong magnetic fields and invented the spectroheliograph. He also initiated the construction of the 200-inch (5-meter) Hale reflector at Mount Palomar in California.

Hale[3], Nathan (1755–76), American hero. He volunteered in 1776 during the American Revolution to spy behind British lines on Long Island. Disguised as a schoolmaster, he was captured by the British and hanged without trial. His last words are said to have been, "I only regret that I have but one life to lose for my country. "

hale[1] /hāl/ ▶ **adj.** (of a person, esp. an elderly one) strong and healthy: *only just sixty, very hale and hearty.*
– ORIGIN Old English, variant of *hāl* 'whole.'

hale[2] ▶ **v.** [with obj.] archaic drag or draw forcibly: *he haled an old man out of the audience.*
– ORIGIN Middle English: from Old French *haler*, from Old Norse *hala*.

Ha·le·a·ka·la /ˌhäläˌäkəˈlä/ a dormant volcano on eastern Maui in Hawaii.

Hale–Bopp /ˈhālˈbäp/ a periodic comet that passed close to the sun in the spring of 1997 and was one of the brightest of the 20th century.
– ORIGIN named after Alan *Hale* and Thomas *Bopp*, the American astronomers who discovered it (independently of each other).

ha·ler /ˈhälər/ ▶ **n.** (pl. **same** or **haleru** /-ləˌro͞o/) a monetary unit of the Czech Republic, equal to one hundredth of a koruna.
– ORIGIN from Czech *haléř*, from Middle High German *haller*, from *Schwäbisch Hall*, a town in Germany where coins were minted.

Ha·ley[1] /ˈhālē/, Alex (1921–92), US writer; full name *Alexander Murray Palmer Haley*. His best-selling work *Roots: The Saga of an American Family* (1976) chronicled the ancestors of his African-American family. The book and subsequent television miniseries in 1977 each won a Pulitzer Prize. He also wrote *The Autobiography of Malcolm X* (1965) and *Queen* (published posthumously, 1993).

Ha·ley[2], Bill (1925–81), US rock-and-roll singer; full name *William John Clifton Haley*. His song "Rock Around the Clock" (1954) helped to establish the popularity of rock and roll.

half /haf/ ▶ **n.** (pl. **halves** /havz/) either of two equal or corresponding parts into which something is or can be divided: *the northern half of the island | two and a half years | divided in half | reduced by half.* ■ either of two equal periods of time into which a sports game or a performance is divided. ■ Golf a score for an individual hole that is the same as one's opponent's. ■ short for **HALFBACK.**
▶ **predeterminer, pron., & adj.** an amount equal to a half: [as predeterminer] *half an hour | almost half the children turned up* | [as pronoun] *half of the lectures are delivered by him* | [as adj.] *the last half century.* ■ amounting to a part thought of as roughly a half: [as predeterminer] *half the letters were sent first class* | [as pronoun] *half of them are gate-crashers.*
▶ **adv.** to the extent of half: *the glass was half full.* ■ [often in combination] to a certain extent; partly: *the chicken is half-cooked.*
– PHRASES **a —— and a half** informal used to indicate that one considers a particular person or thing to be an impressive example of their kind: *Aunt Edie was a woman and a half.* **at half cock** see **HALF COCK. go halves** share something equally: *she promised to go halves with him.* **half the battle** see **BATTLE. half a chance** informal the slightest opportunity: *given half a chance, he can make anything work.* **half an eye** see **EYE. the half of it** [usu. with negative] informal the most important part or aspect of something: *you don't know the half of it.* **half past one (two,** etc.) thirty minutes after one (two, etc.) o'clock. **half the time** see **TIME. not do things by halves** do things thoroughly or extravagantly. **not half 1** not nearly: *he is not half such a fool as they thought.* **2** informal not at all: *the players are not half bad.* **too —— by half** used to emphasize something bad: *the idea seems too superstitious by half.*
– ORIGIN Old English *half, healf*, of Germanic origin; related to Dutch *half* and German *halb* (adjectives). The earliest meaning of the Germanic base was 'side,' also a noun sense in Old English.

half a doz·en ▶ **n.** another term for **HALF-DOZEN.**

half-and-half ▶ **adv. & adj.** in equal parts: [as adv.] *views were split almost exactly half-and-half* | [as adj.] *a half-and-half mixture.*
▶ **n.** a mixture of milk and cream.

half-assed (also **half-ass**, Brit. **half-arsed**) ▶ **adj.** vulgar slang incompetent; inadequate.

half·back /ˈhafˌbak/ ▶ **n.** Football an offensive back usually positioned behind the quarterback and to the side of the fullback. ■ a usually defensive player in a ball game such as soccer or field hockey whose position is between the line or the forward.

half-baked ▶ **adj.** (of an idea or philosophy) not fully thought through; lacking a sound basis: *half-baked notions of Teutonic superiority.* ■ foolish: *half-baked visionaries without a mission.*

half·beak /ˈhafˌbēk/ ▶ **n.** a slender shoaling fish of coastal areas, with small pectoral fins and the lower jaw lengthened into a beak. It is related to the flying fishes and often skitters along the surface. ● Several genera and species in the family Exocoetidae, including the widely distributed *Euleptorhamphus viridis.*

half bind·ing ▶ **n.** a type of bookbinding in which the spine and corners are bound in one material (typically leather) and the rest of the cover in another.
– DERIVATIVES **half-bound adj.**

half blood ▸ n. **1** dated the relationship between people having one parent in common: *brothers and sisters of the half blood.* ▪ a person related to another in this way.
2 (**half-blood**) offensive another term for HALF-BREED.
– DERIVATIVES **half-blood·ed** adj. (sense 2).

half boot ▸ n. a boot that reaches up to the calf.

half-bot·tle ▸ n. a bottle that is half the standard size.

half-bred ▸ adj. (of an animal) having only one pure-bred parent.
▸ n. an animal of this kind.

half-breed ▸ n. offensive a person whose parents are of different races, esp. the offspring of an American Indian and a person of white European ancestry.

half-broth·er (also **half brother**) ▸ n. a brother with whom one has only one parent in common.

half-caste ▸ n. offensive a person whose parents are of different races, in particular, with a European father and an Indian mother.

half cock ▸ n. the partly raised position of the cock of a gun.

half-cocked ▸ adj. **1** (of a gun) with the cock partly raised.
2 only partly ready; poorly prepared: *half-cocked solutions often change things for the worse | a couple of journalists* ***went off half-cocked*** *and misread a document.*

half crown (also **half a crown**) ▸ n. a former British coin and monetary unit equal to two shillings and sixpence.

half-cut ▸ adj. Brit. informal drunk.

half deck ▸ n. a deck reaching half the length of a ship or boat, fore or aft.
– DERIVATIVES **half-decked** adj.

half dol·lar ▸ n. a US or Canadian coin worth fifty cents. ▪ the sum of fifty cents.

half-door ▸ n. a door of half the usual size, typically covering the bottom half of an opening (e.g., in a stable).

half-doz·en (also **half a dozen**) ▸ n. a set or group of six: *a half-dozen slices of smoked salmon.*

half-du·plex ▸ adj. (of a communications system or computer circuit) allowing the transmission of signals in both directions but not simultaneously.

half gai·ner /ˈgānər/ ▸ n. a dive in which the diver leaves the diving board facing forward, does a half-somersault backward, and enters the water head first facing the board.

half-har·dy ▸ adj. chiefly Brit. (of a plant) able to grow outdoors at all times except in severe frost: *a half-hardy annual.*

half·heart·ed /ˈhafˈhärtid/ ▸ adj. without enthusiasm or energy: *after two years of halfhearted effort, he dropped out of school.*
– DERIVATIVES **half·heart·ed·ly** adv., **half·heart·ed·ness** n.

half hitch ▸ n. a knot formed by passing the end of a rope around its standing part and then through the loop, often used in pairs: *the rope was tied with two half hitches to a long tape.*

half hour ▸ n. (also **half an hour**) a period of thirty minutes: *a slide show presented every half hour.* ▪ a point in time thirty minutes after any full hour of the clock: *the library clock struck the half hour.*
– DERIVATIVES **half-hour·ly** adj. & adv.

half-in·te·ger ▸ n. a number obtained by dividing an odd integer by two ($^1/_2$, $1^1/_2$, $2^1/_2$, etc.).
– DERIVATIVES **half-in·te·gral** adj.

half land·ing ▸ n. Brit. an area of floor approximately halfway up a flight of stairs, typically where it turns a corner.

half-length ▸ adj. of approximately half the normal length. ▪ (of a painting or sculpture) showing a person down to the waist.
▸ n. a painting or sculpture of a person down to the waist.

half-life ▸ n. the time taken for the radioactivity of a specified isotope to fall to half its original value. ▪ the time required for any specified property (e.g., the concentration of a substance in the body) to decrease by half.

half-light ▸ n. dim light such as at dusk: *the trees had a slightly spooky look in the half-light.*

half·ling /ˈhäfliNG/ ▸ n. (in fiction and fantasy) a member of a race of small people.

half-mast ▸ n. the position of a flag that is being flown some way below the top of its staff as a mark of respect for a person who has died. ▪ chiefly humorous a position lower than normal or acceptable, esp. for clothes: *the zipper on his fly always riding at half-mast.*

half meas·ure ▸ n. (usu. **half measures**) an action or policy that is not forceful or decisive enough: *there are* ***no half measures*** *with this company.*

half-moon ▸ n. the moon when only half of its illuminated surface is visible from the earth; the first or last quarter. ▪ the time when this occurs. ▪ a semicircular or crescent-shaped object: [as modifier] *half-moon spectacles.*

half-move ▸ n. Chess a move made by one player (esp. in the context of the analysis of play made by a chess-playing computer program).

half nel·son ▸ n. see NELSON.

half note (Brit. **minim**) ▸ n. Music a note having the time value of two quarter notes or half of a whole note, represented by a ring with a stem.

half pay ▸ n. half of a person's normal or previous salary or wages: *a sabbatical year during which he would receive half pay from Fordham University.*

half·pen·ny /ˈhāp(ə)nē, ˈhafˌpenē/ (also **ha'penny**) ▸ n. (pl. for separate coins **halfpennies**, for a sum of money **halfpence** /-pəns/) a former British coin equal to half an old or new penny. The last halfpenny was withdrawn in 1984.

half·pen·ny·worth /ˈhāpniˌwərTH, ˈhafˌpenē-/ (also **ha'p'orth**) ▸ n. Brit. as much as could be bought for a halfpenny. ▪ [usu. with negative] (**ha'p'orth**) informal a negligible amount: *he's never been a ha'p'orth of bother.*

half pint ▸ n. **1** half of a pint.
2 informal a small or insignificant person or animal.
▸ adj. informal very small; diminutive.

half-pipe ▸ n. a channel made of concrete or cut into the snow with a U-shaped cross section, used by skateboarders, rollerbladers, or snowboarders to perform jumps and other maneuvers.

half-price ▸ adj. & adv. costing half the normal price: [as adj.] *half-price admission.*
▸ n. half the usual price: *many shoes* ***at half price.***

half-round ▸ adj. semicircular in cross section.

half seas o·ver ▸ adj. [predic.] Brit. informal or dated fairly drunk.

half-sis·ter (also **half sister**) ▸ n. a sister with whom one has only one parent in common.

half sov·er·eign ▸ n. a former British gold coin worth ten shillings.

half step ▸ n. Music a semitone.

half-test·er ▸ n. historical a canopy extending over half the length of a bed. ▪ a bed with such a canopy.

half-tim·bered ▸ adj. having walls with a timber frame and a brick or plaster filling.
– DERIVATIVES **half-tim·ber·ing** /ˈtimb(ə)riNG/ n.

half·time /ˈhafˌtīm/ ▸ n. the time at which half of a game or contest is completed, esp. when marked by an intermission: *the most pressure he felt was at halftime when he looked up and saw the score* | [as modifier] *a Super Bowl halftime show.*

half ti·tle ▸ n. the title of a book, printed on the right-hand page before the title page. ▪ the title of a section of a book printed on the right-hand page before the section begins. ▪ a page on which a title of either of these kinds is printed.

half·tone /ˈhafˌtōn/ ▸ n. [usu. as modifier] a reproduction of a photograph or other image in which the various tones of gray or color are produced by variously sized dots of ink: *halftone illustrations.*

half-track ▸ n. a military or other vehicle with wheels at the front and caterpillar tracks at the rear.

half-truth ▸ n. a statement that conveys only part of the truth, esp. one used deliberately in order to deceive someone.

half-vol·ley ▸ n. (in ball games, esp. tennis) a strike of the ball made immediately after it bounces off the ground.

half·way /ˈhafˈwā/ ▸ adv. & adj. at or to a point equidistant between two others: [as adv.] *he stopped halfway down the passage* | [as adj.] *she reached the halfway point.* ▪ in the middle of a period of time: [as adv.] *halfway through the night.* ▪ [as adv.] to some extent: *I'm incapable of doing anything even halfway decent.*
– PHRASES **meet someone halfway** compromise; concede some points in order to gain others: *I'm willing to compromise and meet him halfway.*

half·way house ▸ n. a center for helping former drug addicts, prisoners, psychiatric patients, or others to adjust to life in general society. ▪ the halfway point in a progression: *suspension of the talks was only a halfway house toward complete termination.* ▪ historical an inn midway between two towns.

half·wit /ˈhafˌwit/ ▸ n. informal a foolish or stupid person.

half·wit·ted /ˈhafˌwitid/ ▸ adj. informal foolish or stupid: *a halfwitted proposal.*
– DERIVATIVES **half·wit·ted·ly** adv., **half·wit·ted·ness** n.

half-year·ly ▸ adj. & adv. chiefly Brit. at intervals of six months.

hal·i·but /ˈhaləbət/ ▸ n. (pl. **same**) a northern marine fish that is the largest of the flatfishes and important as a food fish. • Genus *Hippoglossus*, family Pleuronectidae: *H. hippoglossus* of the Atlantic and *H. stenolepis* of the Pacific.
– ORIGIN late Middle English: from *haly* 'holy' + obsolete *butt* 'flatfish' (because it was often eaten on holy days).

Ha·liç /häˈlēCH/ Turkish name of GOLDEN HORN.

Hal·i·car·nas·sus /ˌhaləˈkärnəsəs/ an ancient Greek city on the southwestern coast of Asia Minor, at what is now the Turkish city of Bodrum. It is the site of the Mausoleum of Halicarnassus, one of the Seven Wonders of the World.

hal·ide /ˈhaˌlīd, ˈhā-/ ▸ n. Chemistry a binary compound of a halogen with another element or group.

Hal·i·fax /ˈhaləˌfaks/ the capital of Nova Scotia, Canada; pop. 372,679 (2006). It is Canada's principal ice-free port on the Atlantic coast.

hal·ite /ˈhaˌlīt, ˈhāˌlīt/ ▸ n. sodium chloride as a mineral, typically occurring as colorless cubic crystals; rock salt.
– ORIGIN mid 19th cent.: from Greek *hals* 'salt' + -ITE¹.

hal·i·to·sis /ˌhaliˈtōsəs/ ▸ n. technical term for BAD BREATH.
– ORIGIN late 19th cent.: from Latin *halitus* 'breath' + -OSIS.

Hall¹, Gus (1910–2000), US Communist Party leader; born *Arvo Custa Halberg*. He joined the Communist Party in the US in 1934 and served as national secretary 1950–59 before becoming general secretary. He was the US Communist Party's presidential candidate in four elections from 1972 to 1984.

Hall², Lyman (1724–90), American leader. He was a member of the Continental Congress 1775–78, 1780 and a signer of the Declaration of Independence in 1776.

hall /hôl/ ▸ n. **1** an area in a building onto which rooms open; a corridor. ▪ the room or space just inside the front entrance of a house or apartment: *an entrance hall.*
2 a large room for meetings, concerts, or other events: [in names] *Carnegie Hall.* ▪ a large public room in a mansion or palace used for receptions and banquets. ▪ Brit. the room used for meals in a college, university, or school: *he dined in hall.* ▪ a college or university building containing classrooms, residences, or rooms for other purposes. ▪ the principal living room of a medieval house.
3 [usu. in names] Brit. a large country house, esp. one with a landed estate: *Darlington Hall.*
– ORIGIN Old English *hall, heall* (originally denoting a roofed space, located centrally, for the communal use of a tribal chief and his people); of Germanic origin and related to German *Halle*, Dutch *hall*, also to Norwegian and Swedish *hall.*

Hal·le /ˈhälə/ a city in eastern central Germany, on the Saale River, in Saxony-Anhalt; pop. 235,700 (est. 2006).

Hal·lé /ˈhälə/, Sir Charles (1819–95), German pianist and conductor; born *Karl Halle*. He founded the Hallé Orchestra 1858.

Hall ef·fect ▸ n. Physics the production of a potential difference across an electrical conductor when a magnetic field is applied in a direction perpendicular to that of the flow of current.
– ORIGIN early 20th cent.: named after Edwin H. *Hall* (1855–1938), American physicist.

Hal·lel /häˈlāl, ˈhäˌlāl/ ▸ n. (usu. **the Hallel**) a portion of the service for certain Jewish festivals, consisting of Psalms 113–118: [as modifier] *the Hallel psalms.*
– ORIGIN from Hebrew *hallēl* 'praise.'

hal·le·lu·jah /ˌhaləˈlo͞oyə/ (also **alleluia**) ▸ exclam. God be praised (uttered in worship or as an expression of rejoicing): *He is risen! Alleluia!*
▸ n. an utterance of the word "hallelujah" as an expression of worship or rejoicing. ▪ (usu. **Alleluia**) a piece of music or church liturgy containing this: *the Gospel comes after the Alleluia verse.*
– ORIGIN Old English, via ecclesiastical Latin *alleluia* from Greek *allēlouia* (in the Septuagint), or (from the 16th century) directly from Hebrew *hallĕlūyāh* 'praise ye the Lord.'

Hal·ley /ˈhalē, ˈhā-/, Edmond (1656–1742), English astronomer and mathematician. He is best known for identifying a bright comet (later named after him) and for successfully predicting its return.

Hal·ley's com·et /ˈhalē, ˈhā-/ a periodical comet with an orbital period of about 76 years, its reappearance in 1758–59 having been predicted by Edmond Halley. It was first recorded in 240 BC and last appeared, rather faintly, in 1985–86.

Hal·li·day /ˈhaləˌdā/, Michael Alexander Kirkwood (1925–), English linguist.

hall·mark /ˈhôlˌmärk/ ▶ n. a mark stamped on articles of gold, silver, or platinum in Britain, certifying their standard of purity. ■ a distinctive feature, esp. one of excellence: *the tiny bubbles are the hallmark of fine champagnes.*
▶ v. [with obj.] stamp with a hallmark. ■ designate as distinctive, esp. for excellence.
– ORIGIN early 18th cent. (as a noun): from *Goldsmiths' Hall* in London, England, where articles were tested and stamped with such a mark.

hal·lo /həˈlō/ ▶ exclam., n., & v. variant spelling of HELLO. ■ variant of HALLOO.

hal·loa /həˈlō, ha-/ ▶ exclam., n., & v. variant of HALLOO.

Hall of Fame a national memorial in New York City containing busts and memorials honoring the achievements of famous Americans. ■ [as noun] a similar establishment commemorating the achievements of a particular group of people, esp. athletes in a specified sport: *he was inducted into the Hockey Hall of Fame.*
– DERIVATIVES **Hall of Fam·er** n.

hal·loo /həˈlo͞o/ ▶ exclam. used to attract someone's attention. ■ used to incite dogs to the chase during a hunt.
▶ n. a cry of "halloo."
▶ v. (**halloos, hallooing, hallooed**) [no obj.] cry or shout "halloo" to attract attention or to give encouragement to dogs in hunting. ■ [with obj.] shout to (someone) to attract their attention.
– ORIGIN mid 16th cent.: probably from the rare verb *hallow* 'pursue or urge on with shouts,' from imitative Old French *haloer.*

hal·lou·mi /häˈlo͞omē/ ▶ n. a mild, firm, white Cypriot cheese made from goats' or ewes' milk, used esp. in cooked dishes.
– ORIGIN 1990s: from Egyptian Arabic *ḥalūm,* probably from Arabic *ḥaluma* 'to be mild.'

hal·low /ˈhalō/ ▶ v. [with obj.] honor as holy: *the Ganges is hallowed as a sacred, cleansing river* | (as adj. **hallowed**) *hallowed ground.* ■ make holy; consecrate. ■ (as adj. **hallowed**) greatly revered or respected: *in keeping with a hallowed family tradition.*
▶ n. archaic a saint or holy person.
– ORIGIN Old English *hālgian* (verb), *hālga* (noun), of Germanic origin; related to Dutch and German *heiligen,* also to HOLY.

Hal·low·een /ˌhaləˈwēn, ˌhälə-, -ōˈēn/ (also **Hallowe'en**) ▶ n. the night of October 31, the eve of All Saints' Day, commonly celebrated by children who dress in costume and solicit candy or other treats door-to-door.
– ORIGIN late 18th cent.: contraction of *All Hallow Even* (see HALLOW, EVEN[2]).

Hall·statt /ˈhälˌshtät/ ▶ n. [usu. as modifier] Archaeology a cultural phase of the late Bronze Age and early Iron Age in Europe (*c.*1200–600 BC in temperate continental areas), preceding the La Tène period and associated with the early Celts.
– ORIGIN mid 19th cent.: the name of a village in Austria, site of a burial ground of this period.

hall tree ▶ n. a coatrack in the hall of a house.

hal·lu·ces /ˈhal(y)əˌsēz/ plural form of HALLUX.

hal·lu·ci·nate /həˈlo͞osənˌāt/ ▶ v. [no obj.] experience a seemingly real perception of something not actually present, typically as a result of a mental disorder or of taking drugs: *people sense themselves going mad and hallucinate about spiders.* ■ [with obj.] experience a hallucination of (something): *I don't care if they're hallucinating purple snakes.*
– DERIVATIVES **hal·lu·ci·nant** /-sənənt/ adj. & n., **hal·lu·ci·na·tor** /-ˌātər/ n.
– ORIGIN mid 17th cent. (in the sense 'be deceived, have illusions'): from Latin *hallucinat-* 'gone astray in thought,' from the verb *hallucinari,* from Greek *alussein* 'be uneasy or distraught.'

hal·lu·ci·na·tion /həˌlo͞osənˈāshən/ ▶ n. an experience involving the apparent perception of something not present: *he continued to suffer from horrific hallucinations.*

hal·lu·ci·na·to·ry /həˈlo͞osənəˌtôrē/ ▶ adj. of or resembling a hallucination: *a hallucinatory fantasy.* ■ inducing hallucinations: *a hallucinatory drug.*

hal·lu·ci·no·gen /həˈlo͞osənəˌjən/ ▶ n. a drug that causes hallucinations, such as LSD.
– DERIVATIVES **hal·lu·ci·no·gen·ic** /həˌlo͞osənəˈjenik/ adj.

hal·lux /ˈhaləks/ ▶ n. (pl. **halluces** /ˈhal(y)əˌsēz/) Anatomy a person's big toe. ■ Zoology the innermost digit of the hind foot of vertebrates.
– ORIGIN mid 19th cent.: modern Latin alteration of medieval Latin *allex,* Latin *hallus.*

hall·way /ˈhôlˌwā/ ▶ n. another term for HALL (sense 1).

ha·lo /ˈhālō/ ▶ n. (pl. **haloes** or **halos**) **1** a disk or circle of light shown surrounding or above the head of a saint or holy person to represent their holiness. ■ the glory associated with an idealized person or thing: *he has long since lost his halo for many ordinary Russians.*
2 a circle of white or colored light around the sun, moon, or other luminous body caused by refraction through ice crystals in the atmosphere.
▶ v. (**haloes, haloing, haloed**) [with obj.] surround with or as if with a halo.
– ORIGIN mid 16th cent. (denoting a circle of light around the sun, etc.): from medieval Latin, from Latin *halos,* from Greek *halōs* 'disk of the sun or moon.'

halo- ▶ comb. form **1** relating to salinity: *halophile.* [from Greek *hals, halo-* 'salt.']
2 representing HALOGEN.

hal·o·car·bon /ˈhaləˌkärbən/ ▶ n. Chemistry a chlorofluorocarbon or other compound in which the hydrogen of a hydrocarbon is replaced by halogens.

ha·lo ef·fect ▶ n. the tendency for an impression created in one area to influence opinion in another area: *the convertible furnishes a sporty image and provides a halo effect for other cars in the showrooms.*

hal·o·form /ˈhaləˌfôrm/ ▶ n. Chemistry a compound derived from methane by substituting three hydrogen atoms for halogen atoms, e.g., chloroform.
– ORIGIN 1930s: from HALOGEN, on the pattern of *chloroform.*

hal·o·gen /ˈhaləjən/ ▶ n. Chemistry any of the elements fluorine, chlorine, bromine, iodine, and astatine, occupying group VIIA (17) of the periodic table. They are reactive nonmetallic elements that form strongly acidic compounds with hydrogen, from which simple salts can be made. ■ [as modifier] denoting lamps and radiant heat sources using a filament surrounded by the vapor of iodine or another halogen: *halogen headlights.*
– DERIVATIVES **hal·o·gen·ic** /ˌhaləˈjenik/ adj.
– ORIGIN mid 19th cent.: from Greek *hals, halo-* 'salt' + -GEN.

hal·o·gen·ate /ˈhaləjəˌnāt, haˈläjə-/ ▶ v. [with obj.] (usu. as adj. **halogenated**) Chemistry introduce one or more halogen atoms into (a compound or molecule), usually in place of hydrogen.
– DERIVATIVES **hal·o·gen·a·tion** /ˌhaləjəˈnāshən, həˌläjə-/ n.

hal·on /ˈhāˌlän/ ▶ n. any of a number of unreactive gaseous compounds of carbon with bromine and other halogens, used in fire extinguishers, but now known to damage the ozone layer.
– ORIGIN 1960s: from HALOGEN + -ON.

hal·o·per·i·dol /ˌhaləˈperəˌdôl, -däl/ ▶ n. Medicine a synthetic antidepressant drug used chiefly in the treatment of psychotic conditions.
– ORIGIN 1960s: blend of HALOGEN and PIPERIDINE + -OL.

hal·o·phile /ˈhaləˌfīl/ ▶ n. Ecology an organism, esp. a microorganism, that grows in or can tolerate saline conditions.
– DERIVATIVES **hal·o·phil·ic** /ˌhaləˈfilik/ adj.

hal·o·phyte /ˈhaləˌfīt/ ▶ n. Botany a plant adapted to growing in saline conditions, as in a salt marsh.

hal·o·thane /ˈhaləˌthān/ ▶ n. Medicine a volatile synthetic organic compound used as a general anesthetic. • Chem. formula: $CF_3CHBrCl$.
– ORIGIN 1950s: blend of HALOGEN and ETHANE.

Hals /hälz/, Frans (*c.*1580–1666), Dutch portrait and genre painter. He endowed his portraits with vitality and humor. Notable works: *The Banquet of the Officers of the St. George Militia Company* (1616) and *The Laughing Cavalier* (1624).

Hal·sey /ˈhôlzē/, William Frederick (1882–1959), US naval officer; known as **Bull.** He was commander of Allied naval forces in the South Pacific 1942–44 and of the US Third Fleet 1944–45. He became a fleet admiral in 1945.

Häl·sing·borg /ˈhelsiNGˌbôr(yə)/ Swedish name of HELSINGBORG.

halt[1] /hôlt/ ▶ v. bring or come to an abrupt stop: [with obj.] *there is growing pressure to halt the bloodshed* | [no obj.] *she halted in mid-sentence.* ■ [in imperative] used as a military command to bring marching soldiers to a stop: *company, halt!*
▶ n. a suspension of movement or activity, typically a temporary one: *a halt in production* | *a bus screeched to a halt.*
– PHRASES **call a halt** demand or order a stop: *he decided to call a halt to all further discussion.*
– ORIGIN late 16th cent.: originally in the phrase *make halt,* from German *haltmachen,* from *halten* 'to hold.'

halt[2] archaic ▶ adj. lame.
▶ v. [no obj.] walk with a limp: *he halted slightly in his walk.*
– ORIGIN Old English *healtian* (verb), *halt, healt* (adjective), of Germanic origin.

hal·ter[1] /ˈhôltər/ ▶ n. **1** a rope or strap with a noose or headstall placed around the head of a horse or other animal, used for leading or tethering it. ■ archaic a rope with a noose for hanging a person.
2 [usu. as modifier] a strap by which the bodice of a sleeveless dress or top is fastened or held behind at the neck, leaving the shoulders and back bare: [as modifier] *tourists in halter tops and shorts.*
▶ v. [with obj.] put a halter on (an animal). ■ archaic hang (someone).
– ORIGIN Old English *hælftre,* of Germanic origin, meaning 'something to hold things by'; related to German *Halfter,* also to HELVE.

hal·ter[2] /ˈhal,ti(ə)r/ (also **haltere**) ▶ n. (usu. **halteres**) Entomology the balancing organ of a two-winged fly, seen as either of a pair of knobbed filaments that take the place of the hind wings, vibrating during flight.
– ORIGIN mid 16th cent. (originally plural, denoting a pair of weights like dumbbells held in the hands to give impetus when jumping): from Greek *haltēres* (plural), from *hallesthai* 'to leap.'

halt·er-break ▶ v. [with obj.] accustom (a young horse) to wearing and being handled in a halter.

halt·ing /ˈhôltiNG/ ▶ adj. slow and hesitant, esp. through lack of confidence; faltering: *she speaks halting English with a heavy accent.*
– DERIVATIVES **halt·ing·ly** adv.

hal·vah /ˈhälvä/ (also **halva**) ▶ n. a Middle Eastern confection made of sesame flour and honey.
– ORIGIN Yiddish, or from Turkish *helva,* from Arabic and Persian *ḥalwā* 'sweetmeat.'

halve /hav, häv/ ▶ v. [with obj.] **1** divide into two parts of equal or roughly equal size: *peel and halve the pears.* ■ reduce or be reduced by half: [no obj.] *profits are expected to halve after a tail-off in new customers* | [with obj.] *his pledge to halve the deficit over the next four years.* ■ share (something) equally with another person: *she insisted on halving the bill.* ■ Golf use the same number of strokes as one's opponent and thus tie (a hole or match).
2 (usu. as noun **halving**) fit (crossing timbers) together by cutting out half the thickness of each.
– ORIGIN Middle English: from HALF.

halves /havz, hävz/ plural form of HALF.

hal·wa /ˈhälwä/ (also **halwah**) ▶ n. a sweet Indian dish consisting of carrots or semolina boiled with milk, almonds, sugar, butter, and cardamom.
– ORIGIN from Arabic, literally 'sweetmeat.'

hal·yard /ˈhalyərd/ ▶ n. a rope used for raising and lowering a sail, spar, flag, or yard on a sailing ship.
– ORIGIN late Middle English *halier,* from HALE[2] + -IER. The change in the ending in the 18th cent. was due to association with YARD[1].

Ham /ham/ (in the Bible) a son of Noah (Gen. 10:1), traditional ancestor of the Hamites.

ham[1] /ham/ ▶ n. **1** meat from the upper part of a pig's leg salted and dried or smoked: *thin slices of ham* | *a honey-baked ham.*
2 (**hams**) the backs of the thighs or the thighs and buttocks: *he squatted down on his hams.*
– ORIGIN Old English *ham, hom* (originally denoting the back of the knee), from a Germanic base meaning 'be crooked.' In the late 15th cent. the term came to denote the back of the thigh, hence the thigh or hock of an animal.

ham[2] ▶ n. **1** an excessively theatrical actor: *nobody gets to emote more than a ham on the witness stand.* ■ excessively theatrical acting.
2 informal an amateur radio operator.
▶ v. (**hams, hamming, hammed**) [no obj.] informal overact: *he was hamming it up, doing all the voices and the effects.*
– ORIGIN late 19th cent.: perhaps from the first syllable of AMATEUR; compare with the slang term *hamfatter* 'inexpert performer.' Sense 2 of the noun dates from the early 20th cent.

Ha·ma /ˈhämə/ (also **Hamah**) an industrial city in western Syria, on the Orontes River; pop. 531,000 (est. 2009). Much of the city was destroyed during an unsuccessful uprising against the government in 1982.

ha·ma·chi /həˈmächē/ ▶ n. the Japanese name for Pacific yellowtail, esp. when used in sushi and sashimi.

Ha·ma·da /həˈmädə/, Shoji (1894–1978), Japanese potter. He worked mainly in stoneware to produce utilitarian items of unpretentious simplicity.

Ha·ma·dan /ˌhämäˈdän, ˈhaməˌdan/ a commercial city in western Iran, in the Zagros Mountains between Tehran and Bakhtaran; pop. 479,600 (est. 2006). It is on the site of the ancient city of Ecbatana, which became the capital of the kingdom of Media in the 6th century BC.

ham·a·dry·ad /ˌhaməˈdrīəd/ ▶ **n. 1** (also **Hamadryad**) Greek & Roman Mythology a nymph who lives in a tree and dies when the tree dies. **2** another term for **KING COBRA**.
– ORIGIN via Latin from Greek *hamadruas*, from *hama* 'together' + *drus* 'tree.'

ham·a·dry·as ba·boon /ˌhaməˈdrīəs/ ▶ **n.** a large Arabian and northeastern African baboon, the male of which has a silvery-gray cape of hair and a naked red face and rump. It was held sacred in ancient Egypt. Also called **SACRED BABOON**. ● *Papio hamadryas*, family Cercopithecidae.
– ORIGIN 1930s: modern Latin (see **HAMADRYAD**).

Ha·mah /ˈhämä/ variant spelling of **HAMA**.

Ha·ma·ma·tsu /ˌhäməˈmätso͞o/ an industrial city in Japan, on the southern coast of the island of Honshu; pop. 788,078 (2007).

ham·a·mel·is /ˌhaməˈmēlis/ ▶ **n.** technical name for **WITCH HAZEL**.
– ORIGIN mid 18th cent.: modern Latin (genus name), from Greek *hamamēlis* 'medlar.'

ham-and-egg·er /ˈegər/ ▶ **n.** informal an ordinary person of little consequence.
– ORIGIN originally used in boxing, in the sense 'an average boxer who earns only enough to pay for his meals.'

ha·mar·ti·a /ˌhämärˈtēə/ ▶ **n.** a fatal flaw leading to the downfall of a tragic hero or heroine.
– ORIGIN late 18th cent.: Greek, 'fault, failure, guilt'; the term was used in Aristotle's *Poetics* with reference to ancient Greek tragedy.

Ha·mas /häˈmäs/ a Palestinian Islamic movement founded in 1987 with the aim of establishing a Palestinian state incorporating present-day Israel and the West Bank. In 2006 Hamas defeated the more moderate Fatah in the elections for the Palestinian National Authority.
– ORIGIN Arabic, acronym from the official name of the organization, *Harakat al-Muqāwama al-Islāmiyya* 'Islamic Resistance Movement.'

ha·mate /ˈhāˌmāt/ (also **hamate bone**) ▶ **n.** Anatomy a carpal bone situated on the lower outside edge of the hand. It has a hook-shaped projection on the palmar side to which muscles of the little finger are attached.
– ORIGIN early 18th cent.: from Latin *hamatus* 'hooked,' from *hamus* 'hook.'

ham·bone /ˈhamˌbōn/ ▶ **n.** informal an inferior actor or performer, esp. one who uses a spurious black accent.

Ham·burg /ˈhamˌbərg, ˈhämˌbo͝ork/ **1** a port in northern Germany, on the Elbe River; pop. 1,754,200 (est. 2006). Founded by Charlemagne in the 9th century, it is now the largest port in Germany. **2** a town in western New York, south of Buffalo; pop. 55,868 (est. 2008).

ham·burg /ˈhambərg/ ▶ **n.** (also **Hamburg steak**) another term for **HAMBURGER**.
– ORIGIN from **HAMBURG**.

ham·burg·er /ˈhamˌbərgər/ ▶ **n.** a round patty of ground beef, fried or grilled and typically served on a bun or roll and garnished with various condiments. ■ ground beef.
– ORIGIN late 19th cent. (originally US): from German, from **HAMBURG**.

ham·burg·er bun ▶ **n.** a flattish soft bread roll, often topped with sesame seeds, designed to be filled with a hamburger.

Ham·burg·er Hill a name given to a mountain in central Vietnam, near the border with Laos, where hundreds of US soldiers were killed in a 1969 assault during the Vietnam War.

Ham·den /ˈhamdən/ a town in south central Connecticut, north of New Haven; pop. 57,862 (est. 2008).

Ha·meln /ˈhäməln/ (also **Hamelin** /ˈham(ə)lən/) a town in northwestern Germany, in Lower Saxony, on the Weser River; pop. 58,500 (est. 2006). A medieval market town, it is the setting of the legend of the Pied Piper of Hamelin.

ha·mer·kop ▶ **n.** variant spelling of **HAMMERKOP**.

hames /hāmz/ ▶ **plural n.** two curved pieces of iron or wood forming or attached to the collar of a draft horse, to which the traces are attached.
– ORIGIN Middle English: from Middle Dutch.

ham·fat·ter /ˈhamˌfatər/ (also **hamfat**) ▶ **n.** informal an inexpert or amateurish performer, esp. a mediocre jazz musician: [as modifier] *recordings loaded with that "hamfat" band sound.*
– ORIGIN late 19th cent.: perhaps an alteration of **AMATEUR**.

ham-fist·ed ▶ **adj.** another term for **HAM-HANDED**.
– DERIVATIVES **ham-fist·ed·ly adv.**, **ham-fist·ed·ness n.**

ham-hand·ed ▶ **adj.** informal clumsy; bungling: *a ham-handed attempt.*
– DERIVATIVES **ham-hand·ed·ly adv.**, **ham-hand·ed·ness n.**

Ham·hung /ˈhämˌho͝ong/ an industrial city in eastern North Korea; pop. 773,000 (est. 2007). It was the center of government of northeastern Korea during the Yi dynasty 1392–1910.

Ha·mil·car /həˈmilˌkär/ (*c.*270–229 BC), Carthaginian general, father of Hannibal. He fought Rome in the first Punic War and negotiated the terms of peace after the defeat of the Carthaginians.

Ham·il·ton[1] /ˈhaməltən, -əltn/ **1** a port and industrial city in southern Canada, at the western end of Lake Ontario, in Ontario; pop. 504,559 (2006).
2 a city on North Island in New Zealand; pop. 129,249 (2006).
3 a town in southern Scotland, near Glasgow; pop. 48,000 (est. 2009).
4 the capital of Bermuda; pop. 11,000 (est. 2009).
5 a township in west central New Jersey, southeast of Trenton; pop. 90,402 (est. 2008).
6 an industrial city in southwestern Ohio, north of Cincinnati; pop. 62,477 (est. 2008).

Ham·il·ton[2] /ˈhaməltən/, Alexander (*c.*1757–1804), US politician. He established the US central banking system as secretary of the treasury 1789–95 under President George Washington and advocated a strong central government. He was killed in a duel with Aaron Burr.

Alexander Hamilton

Ham·il·ton[3], Lady Emma (*c.*1765–1815), English mistress of Lord Horatio Nelson; born *Amy Lyon*.

Ham·il·ton[4], Sir William Rowan (1806–65), Irish mathematician and theoretical physicist. Hamilton made influential contributions to optics and to the foundations of algebra and quantum mechanics.

Ham·il·to·ni·an /ˌhaməlˈtōnēən/ ▶ **adj. 1** Physics & Mathematics of, relating to, or invented by the mathematician Sir W. R. Hamilton, esp. denoting concepts employed in the wave-mechanical description of particles.
2 of or relating to the American statesman Alexander Hamilton or his doctrines.
▶ **n. 1** (also **hamiltonian**) Physics & Mathematics a Hamiltonian operator or function.
2 a follower or adherent of Alexander Hamilton or his doctrines.
– DERIVATIVES **Ham·il·to·ni·an·ism** /-izəm/ **n.** (sense 2 of the adjective).

Ham·ite /ˈhaˌmīt/ ▶ **n.** a member of a group of North African peoples, including the ancient Egyptians and Berbers, supposedly descended from Ham, son of Noah.

Ham·it·ic /həˈmitik/ ▶ **adj.** historical of or denoting a hypothetical language family formerly proposed to comprise Berber, ancient Egyptian, the Cushitic languages, and the Chadic languages. These are now recognized as independent branches of the Afro-Asiatic family.
– ORIGIN from *Ham* (the name of a son of Noah) + **-ITE**[1] + **-IC**.

Ham·i·to-Se·mit·ic /ˌhamitō səˈmitik/ ▶ **adj.** former term for **AFRO-ASIATIC**.

Ham·let /ˈhamlit/ a legendary prince of Denmark, hero of a tragedy by Shakespeare.
– PHRASES **Hamlet without the Prince** a performance or event taking place without the principal actor or central figure.

ham·let /ˈhamlit/ ▶ **n.** a small settlement, generally one smaller than a village.
– ORIGIN Middle English: from Old French *hamelet*, diminutive of *hamel* 'little village'; related to **HOME** (*hām* in Old English).

Ham·lisch /ˈhamlisн/, Marvin (Frederick) (1944–), US composer. He composed the music for movies such as *The Way We Were* (1973) and *The Sting* (1973), and for Broadway shows such as *A Chorus Line* (1975) and *Imaginary Friends* (2002).

Hamm /häm/ an industrial city in northwestern Germany, in North Rhine–Westphalia, on the Lippe River; pop. 183,700 (est. 2006).

Ham·mar·skjöld /ˈhamərˌsнōld, ˈhäm-, -ˌsнəld/, Dag (Hjalmar Agne Carl) (1905–61), Swedish diplomat and politician. As secretary general of the United Nations 1953–61, he was influential in the establishment of the UN emergency force in Sinai and Gaza 1956 and also initiated peace moves in the Middle East 1957–58. He was killed in a plane crash while on a peace mission in Congo. Nobel Peace Prize (1961, posthumously).

Dag Hammarskjöld

ham·mer /ˈhamər/ ▶ **n. 1** a tool with a heavy metal head mounted at right angles at the end of a handle, used for jobs such as breaking things and driving in nails. ■ a machine with a metal block for giving a heavy blow to something. ■ an auctioneer's mallet for indicating by a sharp tap that an article is sold. ■ a part of a mechanism that hits another part to make it work, such as one exploding the charge in a gun or one striking the strings of a piano.
2 a metal ball, typically weighing 16 pounds (7.3 kg), attached to a wire for throwing in an athletic contest. ■ (**the hammer**) the sport of throwing such a ball.
3 another term for **MALLEUS**.
▶ **v.** [with obj.] **1** hit or beat (something) with a hammer or similar object: *they are made by heating and hammering pieces of iron.* ■ [no obj.] strike or knock at or on something violently with one's hand or with a hammer or other object: *she **hammered on** his door.* ■ [no obj.] (**hammer away**) work hard and persistently: *for six months I have been **hammering away at** a plot.* ■ [with obj.] drive or secure (something) by striking with or as if with a hammer: *he hammered the tack in | he was hammering leather soles onto a pair of small boots.* ■ (**hammer something in/into**) instill (an attitude, idea, or habit) forcefully or repeatedly: *the "diversity is good" message is hammered into them.*
2 informal attack or criticize forcefully and relentlessly: *he got hammered for an honest mistake.* ■ utterly defeat in a game or contest: *they hammered St. Louis 6–0.*
– PHRASES **come** (or **go**) **under the hammer** be sold at an auction. **hammer and tongs** informal energetically, enthusiastically, or with great vehemence: *all the way to the bottom, Larry could hear them clanging away, hammer and tongs.* **hammer something home** see **HOME**.
– PHRASAL VERBS **hammer something out 1** make something by shaping metal with a hammer. **2** laboriously work out the details of a plan or agreement: *a deal was being hammered out with the Dutch museums.* **3** play a tune loudly or clumsily, esp. on the piano.
– DERIVATIVES **ham·mer·er n.**, **ham·mer·less adj.**

h

– ORIGIN Old English *hamor, hamer*, of Germanic origin: related to Dutch *hamer*, German *Hammer*, and Old Norse *hamarr* 'rock.' The original sense was probably 'stone tool.'

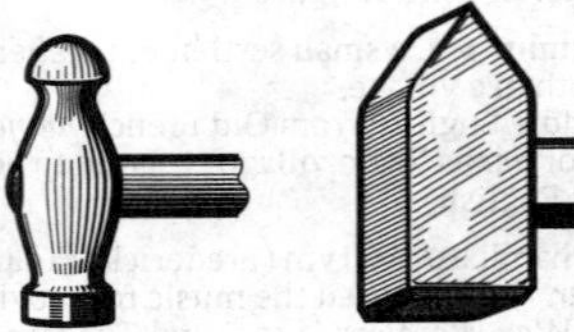
ball-peen hammer sledgehammer

claw hammer

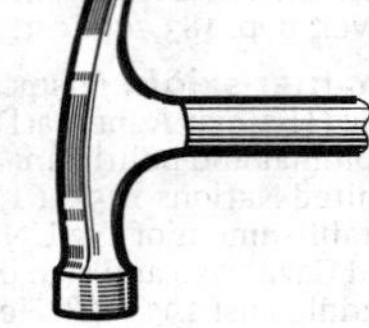
tack hammer

hammer 1

h

ham·mer and sick·le ▶ n. the symbols of the industrial worker and the peasant used as the emblem of the former Soviet Union and of international communism.

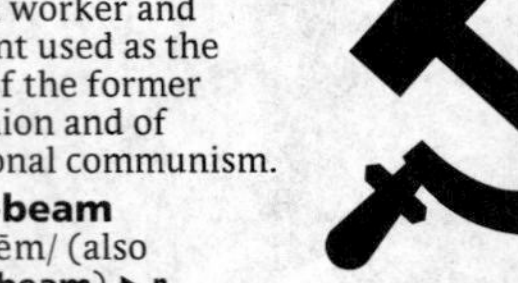
hammer and sickle

ham·mer·beam /ˈhamər,bēm/ (also **hammer beam**) ▶ n. a short wooden beam (typically carved) projecting from a wall to support either a principal rafter or one end of an arch.

ham·mer drill ▶ n. a power drill that works by delivering a rapid succession of blows, used chiefly for drilling in masonry or rock.

Ham·mer·fest /ˈhämər,fest/ a port in northern Norway, on North Kvaløy island; pop. 9,407 (2008). It is the most northern town in Europe.

ham·mer·head /ˈhamər,hed/ ▶ n. **1** (also **hammerhead shark**) a shark of tropical and temperate oceans that has flattened bladelike extensions on either side of the head, with the eyes and nostrils placed at or near the ends. ● Family Sphyrnidae and genus *Sphyrna*: several species. **2** a brown African marsh bird related to the storks, having a crest that looks like a backward projection of the head, and constructing an enormous nest. Also called HAMMERKOP. ● *Scopus umbretta*, the only member of the family Scopidae.

ham·mer·ing /ˈhamәriNG/ ▶ n. **1** the sound or action of hammering something.
2 informal a heavy defeat: *the 7–0 hammering by the Yankees.*
– PHRASES **take a hammering** be subjected to a heavy defeat or harsh treatment.

ham·mer·kop /ˈhamər,käp/ (also **hamerkop**) ▶ n. another term for HAMMERHEAD (sense 2).
– ORIGIN mid 19th cent.: from Afrikaans *hamerkop*, from *hamer* 'hammer' + *kop* 'head.'

ham·mer·lock /ˈhamər,läk/ ▶ n. an armlock in which a person's arm is bent up behind the back.

ham·mer price ▶ n. the price realized by an item sold at auction.

Ham·mer·stein /ˈhamər,stīn/, Oscar (1895–1960), US librettist; full name *Oscar Hammerstein II*. He collaborated with various composers, including Jerome Kern, with whom he wrote *Showboat* (1927), and most notably Richard Rodgers, with whom he wrote *Oklahoma!* (1943), *South Pacific* (1949), and *The Sound of Music* (1959).

ham·mer·toe /ˈhamər,tō/ ▶ n. a toe that is bent permanently downward, typically as a result of pressure from footwear.

Ham·mett /ˈhamət/, (Samuel) Dashiell (1894–1961), US novelist. He developed the hard-boiled style of detective fiction in works such as *The Maltese Falcon* (1930) and *The Thin Man* (1932), both of which were made into successful movies. He lived for many years with playwright Lillian Hellman; they were both persecuted for their left-wing views during the McCarthy era.

ham·mock /ˈhamək/ ▶ n. a bed made of canvas or of rope mesh and suspended by cords at the ends, used as garden furniture or on board a ship.
– ORIGIN mid 16th cent. (in the Spanish form *hamaca*): via Spanish from Taino *hamaka*; the ending was altered in the 16th cent. by association with **-OCK**.

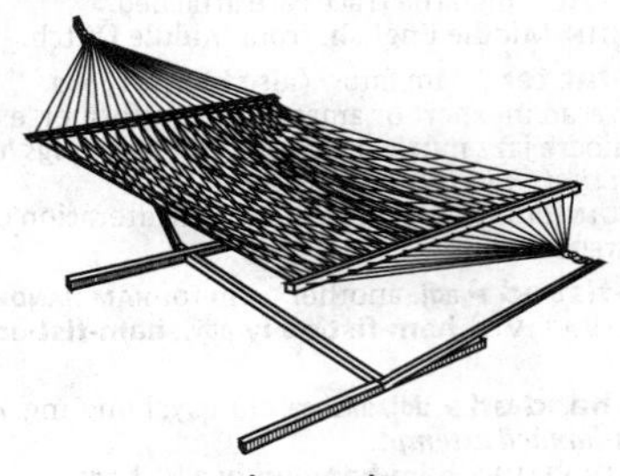
hammock

Ham·mond /ˈhamənd/ an industrial port city in northwestern Indiana, on Lake Michigan, southeast of Chicago in Illinois; pop. 76,732 (est. 2008).

Ham·mond or·gan /ˈhamənd/ ▶ n. trademark a type of electronic organ.
– ORIGIN 1930s: named after Laurens *Hammond* (1895–1973), American mechanical engineer.

Ham·mu·ra·bi /,haməˈräbē, ,hä-/ (died 1750 BC), the sixth king of the first dynasty of Babylonia, reigned 1792–1750 BC. He extended the Babylonian empire and instituted one of the earliest known collections of laws.

ham·my /ˈhamē/ ▶ adj. (**hammier**, **hammiest**) informal (of acting or an actor) exaggerated or overly theatrical: *there is some hammy acting.*
– DERIVATIVES **ham·mi·ly** /ˈhaməlē/ adv., **ham·mi·ness** n.

ham·per¹ /ˈhampər/ ▶ n. a large basket with a lid used for laundry: *a laundry hamper.* ■ a basket with a carrying handle and a hinged lid, used for food, cutlery, and plates on a picnic: *a picnic hamper.*
– ORIGIN Middle English (denoting any large case or casket): from Anglo-Norman French *hanaper* 'case for a goblet,' from Old French *hanap* 'goblet,' of Germanic origin.

ham·per² ▶ v. [with obj.] hinder or impede the movement or progress of: *their work is hampered by lack of funds.*
▶ n. Nautical necessary but cumbersome equipment on a ship.
– ORIGIN late Middle English (in the sense 'shackle, entangle, catch'): perhaps related to German *hemmen* 'restrain.'

Hamp·shire¹ /ˈham(p)SHər/ a county on the coast of southern England; county town, Winchester.

Hamp·shire² /ˈham(p)SHi(ə)r/ ▶ n. a pig of a black breed with a white saddle and prick ears.

Hamp·ton¹ /ˈham(p)tən/ a city in southeastern Virginia, on the harbor of Hampton Roads, on Chesapeake Bay; pop. 145,494 (est. 2008).

Hamp·ton², Lionel Leo (1909–2002), US jazz vibraphonist, drummer, pianist, singer, and bandleader. He played with Benny Goodman in small ensembles before forming his own big band in 1942.

Hamp·ton Roads a deep-water estuary in southeastern Virginia, 4 miles (6 km) long, that is formed by the James River where it joins Chesapeake Bay. It is the site of the battle between the ships *Merrimac* and *Monitor* in 1862 during the Civil War.

Hamp·tons /ˈham(p)tənz/ (**the Hamptons**) a cluster of resort villages in eastern Long Island in New York that include Southampton, East Hampton, and Westhampton Beach.

ham·ster /ˈhamstər/ ▶ n. a solitary burrowing rodent with a short tail and large cheek pouches for carrying food, native to Europe and northern Asia. ● Subfamily Cricetinae, family Muridae: several genera and species, in particular the **golden hamster** (*Mesocricetus auratus*), often kept as a pet or laboratory animal, and the **common hamster** (*Cricetus cricetus*).
– ORIGIN early 17th cent.: from German, from Old High German *hamustro* 'weevil.'

ham·string /ˈham,striNG/ ▶ n. any of five tendons at the back of a person's knee: *he pulled a hamstring.* ■ the great tendon at the back of a quadruped's hock.
▶ v. (past and past participle **hamstrung**) [with obj.] cripple (a person or animal) by cutting their hamstrings. ■ (usu. **be hamstrung**) severely restrict the efficiency or effectiveness of: *we were hamstrung by a total lack of knowledge.*

Ham·sun /ˈhämsən/, Knut (1859–1952), Norwegian novelist; pseudonym of *Knut Pedersen*. Notable works: *Hunger* (1890) and *Growth of the Soil* (1917). Nobel Prize for Literature (1920).

ham·u·lus /ˈhamyələs/ ▶ n. (pl. **hamuli** /-,lī, -,lē/) Anatomy & Zoology a small hook or hooklike projection, esp. one of a number linking the fore- and hind wings of a bee or wasp.
– ORIGIN early 18th cent.: from Latin, diminutive of *hamus* 'hook.'

ham·za /ˈhamzə/ ▶ n. (in Arabic script) a symbol representing a glottal stop. ■ such a sound.
– ORIGIN early 19th cent.: Arabic, literally 'compression.'

Han /han/ **1** the Chinese dynasty that ruled from 206 BC until AD 220 with only a brief interruption. During this period Chinese rule was extended over Mongolia, Confucianism was recognized as the state philosophy, and detailed historical records were kept.
2 the dominant ethnic group in China.

Han·cock¹ /ˈhan,käk/, John (1737–93), American revolutionary and politician. Noted as the first signer of the Declaration of Independence in 1776, he was a member of the Continental Congress 1775–80, 1785, 1786 and its first president 1775–77. He was later governor of Massachusetts 1780–85, 1787–93.

Han·cock², Winfield Scott (1824–86), US army officer. A Union general, he was noted for his defense of Cemetery Ridge at the Battle of Gettysburg 1863. He was the 1880 Democratic presidential candidate, narrowly losing to Garfield.

han·cock /ˈhan,käk/ ▶ v. [with obj.] informal put one's signature to (a document): *Secretary Richardson hancocked a memorandum written to managers across the weapons-complex with the Department's goal spelled out.*
– ORIGIN from *John Hancock*, 'autograph signature.'

Hand /hand/, (Billings) Learned (1872–1961), US jurist and writer. He wrote over 2,000 opinions as judge of the US Court of Appeals, 2nd Circuit 1924–51. He authored *The Spirit of Liberty* (1952) and *The Bill of Rights* (1958).

hand /hand/ ▶ n. **1** the end part of a person's arm beyond the wrist, including the palm, fingers, and thumb: *she placed the money on the palm of her hand | he was leading her by the hand.* ■ a similar prehensile organ forming the end part of a limb of various mammals, such as that on all four limbs of a monkey. ■ [as modifier] operated by or held in the hand: *hand luggage.* ■ [as modifier or in combination] done or made manually rather than by machine: *hand signals | a hand-stitched quilt.* ■ [in sing.] informal a round of applause: *his fans gave him a big hand.* ■ dated a pledge of marriage by a woman: *he wrote to request the hand of her daughter in marriage.*
2 something resembling a hand in form or position, in particular: ■ a pointer on a clock or watch indicating the passing of units of time: *the second hand.* ■ a bunch of bananas.
3 (**hands**) used in reference to the power to direct something: *the day-to-day running of the house was in her hands | taking the law into their own hands.* ■ (usu. **a hand**) an active role in influencing something: *he had a big* ***hand in*** *organizing the event.* ■ (usu. **a hand**) help in doing something: *do you need a hand?* ■ (usu. **hands**) (in sports) skill and dexterity: *he's a receiver with very good hands.* ■ a person's workmanship, esp. in artistic work: *this should be a clue in attributing other work to his hand.* ■ a person's handwriting: *he inscribed the statement in a bold hand.* ■ [with adj.] a person who does something to a specified standard: *I'm a great* ***hand at*** *inventing.*
4 a person who engages in manual labor, esp. in a factory, on a farm, or on board a ship: *a factory hand | the ship was lost with all hands.*
5 the set of cards dealt to a player in a card game. ■ a round or short spell of play in a card game: *his idea of a good time would be a* ***hand of*** *bridge.* ■ Bridge the cards held by declarer as opposed to those in the dummy.
6 a unit of measurement of a horse's height, equal to 4 inches (10.16 cm). [denoting the breadth of a hand, formerly used as a more general lineal measure and taken to equal three inches.]
▶ v. **1** [with two objs.] pick (something) up and give to (someone): *he handed each man a glass | I handed the trowel back to him.* ■ informal make (abusive, untrue, or otherwise objectionable) remarks to (someone): *all the yarns she'd been handing me.* ■ informal make (something) easily obtainable for (someone): *it was a win handed to him on a plate.*
2 [with obj.] hold the hand of (someone) in order to help them move in the specified direction: *he handed him into a carriage.*
3 [with obj.] Sailing take in or furl (a sail): *hand in the main!*
– PHRASES **at hand** nearby: *keep the manual close at hand.* ■ readily accessible when needed. ■ close in time; about to happen: *a breakthrough in combating the disease may be at hand.* **at** (or **by**) **the hands** (or **hand**) **of** through the agency of: *tests he would undergo at the hands of a senior neurologist.* **bind** (or **tie**) **someone hand and foot** tie someone's hands

and feet together. **by hand** by a person and not a machine: *the crop has to be harvested by hand.* **give** (or **lend**) **a hand** assist in an action or enterprise. **hand in glove** in close collusion or association: *they were working **hand in glove** with our enemies.* **hand in hand** (of two people) with hands joined, esp. as a mark of affection. ■ closely associated: *she had the confidence that usually **goes hand in hand** with experience.* (**from**) **hand to mouth** satisfying only one's immediate needs because of lack of money for future plans and investments: *they were flat broke and living hand to mouth* | [as adj.] *a hand-to-mouth existence.* **hands down** easily and decisively; without question: *winning the debate hands down.* **hands off** used as a warning not to touch or interfere with something: *hands off that cake!* ■ (as adj. **hands-off**) not involving or requiring direct control or intervention: *a hands-off management style.* **hands-on** involving or offering active participation rather than theory: *hands-on practice to gain experience.* ■ Computing involving or requiring personal operation at a keyboard. **hands up!** used as an instruction to raise one's hands in surrender or to signify assent or participation: *Hands up! Who saw the program?* **have one's hands full** have as much work as one can do. **have one's hands tied** informal be unable to act freely. **have to hand it to someone** informal used to acknowledge the merit or achievement of someone: *I've got to hand it to you—you've got the magic touch.* **in hand 1** receiving or requiring immediate attention: *he threw himself into the work in hand.* ■ in progress: *negotiations are now well in hand.* **2** ready for use if required; in reserve: *he had $1,000 of borrowed cash in hand.* **3** under one's control: *the police had the situation well in hand.* ■ (of land) farmed directly by its owner and not let to tenants. **in safe hands** protected by someone trustworthy from harm or damage: *the future of the cathedral is in safe hands.* **keep one's hand in** become (or remain) practiced in something. **make** (or **lose** or **spend**) **money hand over fist** informal make (or lose or spend) money very rapidly. **off someone's hands** not having to be dealt with or looked after by the person specified: *they just want the problem off their hands.* **on every hand** all around: *new technologies were springing up on every hand.* **on hand** present, esp. for a specified purpose: *her trainer was on hand to give advice.* ■ readily available. ■ needing to be dealt with: *they had many urgent and pressing matters on hand.* **on someone's hands** used to indicate that someone is responsible for dealing with someone or something: *he has a difficult job on his hands.* ■ used to indicate that someone is to blame for something: *he has my son's blood on his hands.* ■ at someone's disposal: *since I retired I've had more time on my hands.* **on the one** (or **the other**) **hand** used to present factors that are opposed or that support opposing opinions: *a conflict between their rationally held views on the one hand and their emotions and desires on the other.* **out of hand 1** not under control. **2** without taking time to think: *they rejected negotiations out of hand.* **the right hand doesn't know what the left hand is doing** used to convey that there is a state of confusion within a group or organization. **set** (or **put**) **one's hand to** start work on. **stay someone's hand** restrain someone from acting. **take a hand** become influential in determining something; intervene: *fate was about to **take a hand in** the outcome of the championship.* **to hand** within easy reach: *have a pen and paper to hand.* **turn one's hand to** undertake (an activity different from one's usual occupation): *a music teacher who turned his hand to writing books.* **wait on someone hand and foot** attend to all someone's needs or requests, esp. when this is regarded as unreasonable. **with one hand** (**tied**) **behind one's back** with serious limitations or restrictions: *at the moment, the police are tackling record crime rates with one hand tied behind their back.* ■ used to indicate that one could do something without any difficulty: *I could do her job with one hand tied behind my back.*

– PHRASAL VERBS **hand something down 1** pass something on to a younger person or a successor: *songs are handed down from mother to daughter.* **2** announce something, esp. a judgment or sentence, formally or publicly. **hand something in** give something to a person in authority for their attention. **hand something on** pass something to the next person in a series or succession: *he had handed on the family farm to his son.* ■ pass responsibility for something to someone else; delegate. **hand something out 1** give a share of something or one of a set of things to each of a number of people; distribute: *they handed out free drinks to everyone.* **2** impose or inflict a penalty or misfortune on someone. **hand over** pass responsibility to someone else: *he will soon hand over to a new director.* **hand someone/something over** give someone or something, or the responsibility for someone or something, to someone else: *hand the matter over to the police.* **hand something around** offer something to each of a number of people in turn: *a big box of chocolates was handed around.*

– DERIVATIVES **hand·less** adj.

– ORIGIN Old English *hand, hond*, of Germanic origin; related to Dutch *hand* and German *Hand*.

Han·dan /'hän'dän/ industrial city in southern Hebei province in eastern China, a communications and transportation hub on the Fuyang River north of Anyang; pop. 1,221,900 (est. 2006).

hand·bag /'han(d),bag/ ▶ n. a woman's purse.

hand·ball /'han(d),bôl/ ▶ n. **1** a game similar to squash in which a ball is hit with the hand in a walled court. ■ (also **team handball**) a team game similar to soccer in which the ball is thrown or hit with the hands rather than kicked. ■ the ball used in these games.
2 Soccer touching of the ball with the hand or arm, constituting a foul.

hand·bar·row /'hand,barō/ ▶ n. a rectangular frame with poles at each end for being carried by two people.

hand·bell /'han(d),bel/ ▶ n. a small bell with a handle or strap, esp. one of a set tuned to a range of notes and played by a group of people.

hand·bill /'han(d),bil/ ▶ n. a small printed advertisement or other notice distributed by hand.

hand·blown /'hand,blōn/ ▶ adj. (of glassware) made by a glassblower with a handheld blowpipe.

hand·book /'han(d),bo͝ok/ ▶ n. a book giving information such as facts on a particular subject or instructions for operating a machine.

hand·brake /'han(d),brāk/ ▶ n. the emergency or parking brake on a motor vehicle. ■ a brake operated by hand, as on a bicycle.

hand·car /'han(d),kär/ ▶ n. a light railroad vehicle propelled by pushing cranks or levers and used by workers for inspecting the track.

hand·cart /'han(d),kärt/ ▶ n. a small cart pushed or drawn by hand.

hand·clap /'han(d),klap/ ▶ n. a clap of the hands: *the switch is sensitive enough to be activated by a handclap.*

– DERIVATIVES **hand·clap·ping** n.

hand·clasp /'hand,klasp/ ▶ n. the act of clasping someone else's hand; handshake.

hand·craft /'han(d),kraft/ ▶ v. [with obj.] (usu. as adj. **handcrafted**) make skillfully by hand: *a handcrafted rocking chair.*
▶ n. another term for HANDICRAFT.

hand crank ▶ n. a crank that is turned by hand.
▶ v. (**hand-crank**) [with obj.] operate (a device) by turning a crank by hand.

hand cream ▶ n. a moisturizing cream for the hands.

hand·cuff /'han(d),kəf/ ▶ n. (**handcuffs**) a pair of lockable linked metal rings for securing a prisoner's wrists.
▶ v. [with obj.] put handcuffs on (someone): *he was led into court **handcuffed to** a policeman* | figurative *he will not allow his training to handcuff his creativity.*

-handed ▶ comb. form **1** for or involving a specified number of hands: *a two-handed backhand.*
2 chiefly using or designed for use by the hand specified: *a right-handed batter* | *a left-handed guitar.*
3 having hands of a specified kind: *strong-handed.*

-handedly ▶ comb. form in adverbs corresponding to adjectives ending in *-handed* (such as *heavy-handedly* corresponding to *heavy-handed*).

hand·ed·ness /'handid,nis/ ▶ n. the tendency to use either the right or the left hand more naturally than the other: *injury has forced him to change his handedness.*

-handedness ▶ comb. form in nouns corresponding to adjectives ending in *-handed* (such as *left-handedness* corresponding to *left-handed*).

Han·del /'handl/, George Frideric (1685–1759), German composer and organist, resident in Britain from 1712; born *Georg Friedrich Händel*. He is chiefly remembered for his oratorio *Messiah* (1742), his *Water Music* suite (c.1717), and his *Music for the Royal Fireworks* (1749).

hand·ful /'han(d),fo͝ol/ ▶ n. (pl. **handfuls**) **1** a quantity that fills the hand: *a small **handful of** fresh coriander.* ■ a small number or amount: *one of a **handful of** attorneys in the Southwest who specialize in water-rights laws.*
2 informal a person who is very difficult to deal with or control: *the kids could be such a handful.*

hand gal·lop ▶ n. [in sing.] an easily controlled gallop.

hand gre·nade ▶ n. a hand-thrown grenade.

hand·grip /'han(d),grip/ ▶ n. **1** a handle for holding onto something.
2 a grasp with the hand, esp. considered in terms of its strength, as in a handshake.

hand·gun /'han(d),gən/ ▶ n. a gun designed for use by one hand, chiefly either a pistol or a revolver.

hand·held /'hand,held/ ▶ adj. designed to be held in the hand: *a handheld computer.*

hand·hold /'hand,hōld/ ▶ n. something for a hand to grip: *the rock is steep and there are few handholds.*

hand·hold·ing /'hand,hōldiNG/ ▶ n. the provision of careful attention, support, or reassurance to another. ■ the giving of simple, detailed, step-by-step instructions.

hand·i·cap /'handē,kap/ ▶ n. a condition that markedly restricts a person's ability to function physically, mentally, or socially. ■ a circumstance that makes progress or success difficult: *a criminal conviction is a handicap and a label that may stick forever.* ■ a disadvantage imposed on a superior competitor in sports such as golf, horse racing, and competitive sailing in order to make the chances more equal. ■ a race or contest in which such a disadvantage is imposed: [in names] *the trophy for the $75,000 Ak-Sar-Ben Handicap.* ■ the extra weight to be carried in a race by a racehorse on the basis of its previous performance to make its chances of winning the same as those of the other horses. ■ the number of strokes by which a golfer normally exceeds par for a course (used as a method of enabling players of unequal ability to compete with each other): [in combination] *his game struggles along in the 20-handicap range.*
▶ v. (**handicaps, handicapping, handicapped**) [with obj.] act as an impediment to: *lack of funding has handicapped the development of research.* ■ place (someone) at a disadvantage: *without a good set of notes you will handicap yourself when it comes to exams.*

– ORIGIN mid 17th cent.: from the phrase *hand in cap*; originally a pastime in which one person claimed an article belonging to another and offered something in exchange, any difference in value being decided by an umpire. All three deposited forfeit money in a cap; the two opponents showed their agreement or disagreement with the valuation by bringing out their hands either full or empty. If both were the same, the umpire took the forfeit money; if not, it went to the person who accepted the valuation. The term *handicap race* was applied (late 18th cent.) to a horse race in which an umpire decided the weight to be carried by each horse, the owners showing acceptance or dissent in a similar way: hence in the late 19th cent. *handicap* came to mean the extra weight given to the superior horse.

hand·i·capped /'handē,kapt/ ▶ adj. having a condition that markedly restricts one's ability to function physically, mentally, or socially: *a special school for handicapped children* | (as plural noun **the handicapped**) *a home for the handicapped.*

> **USAGE** Handicapped in the sense referring to a person's mental or physical disabilities is first recorded in the early 20th century. For a brief period in the second half of the 20th century, it looked as if **handicapped** would be replaced by **disabled**, but both words are now acceptable and interchangeable in standard American English, and neither word has been overtaken by newer coinages such as *differently abled* or *physically challenged*. See also usage at LEARNING DISABILITY.

hand·i·cap·per /'handē,kapər/ ▶ n. a person appointed to assign or assess a competitor's handicap, esp. in golf or horse racing. ■ [usu. in combination] a person or horse having a specified handicap: *a three-handicapper.*

hand·i·craft /'handē,kraft/ ▶ n. (often **handicrafts**) a particular skill of making decorative objects by hand: *the traditional handicrafts of this region* | *teachers of drawing, design, and handicraft* | [as modifier] *handicraft workshops.* ■ an object made using a skill of this kind: *pottery and handicrafts decorate the rooms and hallways.*

– ORIGIN Middle English: alteration of HANDCRAFT, on the pattern of *handiwork*.

hand·i·work /'handē,wərk/ ▶ n. **1** (**one's handiwork**) something that one has made or done: *the dressmakers stood back to survey their handiwork.*
2 making things by hand, considered as a subject of instruction: *they taught young women reading, writing, and handiwork.*

– ORIGIN Old English *handgeweorc*, from HAND + *geweorc* 'something made,' interpreted in the 16th cent. as *handy* + *work*.

PRONUNCIATION KEY ə *ago, up*; ər *over, fur*; a *hat*; ā *ate*; ä *car*; e *let*; ē *see*; i *fit*; ī *by*; NG *sing*; ō *go*; ô *law, for*; oi *toy*; o͝o *good*; o͞o *goo*; ou *out*; TH *thin*; T͟H *then*; ZH *vision*

h

hand job (also **handjob**) ▶ **n.** vulgar slang an act of male masturbation, esp. as performed on a man by someone else.

hand·ker·chief /ˈhaNGkərCHif, -CHēf/ ▶ **n.** a square of cotton or other finely woven material, typically carried in one's pocket and intended for blowing or wiping one's nose.
– ORIGIN mid 16th cent.: from HAND + KERCHIEF.

han·dle /ˈhandl/ ▶ **v.** [with obj.] **1** feel or manipulate with the hands: *heavy paving slabs can be difficult to handle* | *people who handle food.* ■ drive or control (a vehicle): *where did you learn to handle a boat?* ■ [no obj.] (of a vehicle) respond in a specified manner when being driven or controlled: *a roadworthy bicycle that also handles well off the pavement.*
2 manage (a situation or problem): *a lawyer's ability to handle a case properly.* ■ informal deal with (someone or something): *I don't think I could handle it if they turned me down.* ■ control or manage commercially: *the advertising company that is handling the account.* ■ [with adverbial] (**handle oneself**) conduct oneself in a specified manner: *he handled himself with considerable aplomb.* ■ (**handle oneself**) informal defend oneself physically or verbally: *I can handle myself in a fight.*
▶ **n. 1** the part by which a thing is held, carried, or controlled: *the pan features helpful lifting handles.* ■ (**a handle on**) a means of understanding, controlling, or approaching a person or situation: *it'll give people some kind of handle on these issues* | *get a handle on your life.*
2 informal the name of a person or place: *that's some handle for a baby.*
3 [in sing.] informal the total amount of money bet over a particular time (typically at a casino) or at a particular sporting event: *the monthly handle of a couple of casinos in Las Vegas.*
– DERIVATIVES **han·dle·a·bil·i·ty** /ˌhandl-əˈbilitē/ **n.**, **han·dle·a·ble adj.**, **han·dled adj.** [in combination] *a rope-handled canvas bag,* **han·dle·less adj.**
– ORIGIN Old English *handle* (noun), *handlian* (verb), from HAND.

han·dle·bar /ˈhandlˌbär/ ▶ **n.** (usu. **handlebars**) the steering bar of a bicycle, motorcycle, scooter, or other vehicle, with a handgrip at each end.

han·dle·bar mus·tache ▶ **n.** a wide, thick mustache with the ends curving slightly upward.

handlebar mustache

han·dler /ˈhandlər/ ▶ **n. 1** [usu. with modifier] a person who handles or deals with certain articles or commodities: *a baggage handler* | *a food handler.* ■ a device that handles certain articles or substances.
2 a person who trains or has charge of an animal: *the performance of dog and handler in the ring must be accurate and correct.*
3 a person who trains or manages another person, in particular: ■ a person who trains and acts as second to a boxer. ■ a publicity agent. ■ a person who advises on and directs the activities of a politician or other public figure.

hand·ling /ˈhandl-iNG/ ▶ **n.** the act of taking or holding something in the hands. ■ the packaging and labeling of something to be shipped.

hand·made /ˈhan(d)ˈmād/ ▶ **adj.** made by hand, not by machine, and typically therefore of superior quality: *his expensive handmade leather shoes.*

hand·maid·en /ˈhan(d)ˌmādn/ (also **handmaid**) ▶ **n.** a female servant. ■ a subservient partner or element: *shipping will continue to be the handmaiden of world trade.*

hand-me-down ▶ **n.** (often **hand-me-downs**) a garment or other item that has been passed on from another person.
▶ **adj.** [attrib.] (of a garment or other item) passed on from another person: *he ran in the cold with no mittens and a hand-me-down coat.*

hand·off /ˈhandˌôf, -ˌäf/ ▶ **n.** Football an exchange made by handing the ball to a teammate.

hand·out /ˈhandˌout/ ▶ **n. 1** something given free to a needy person or organization: *hundreds of thousands of refugees subsist on international handouts.*
2 printed information provided free of charge, esp. to accompany a lecture or advertise something: *she was shocked when she saw a one-page handout condemning her campaign.*

hand·o·ver /ˈhandˌōvər/ ▶ **n.** chiefly Brit. an act or instance of handing something over.

hand·phone /ˈhandˌfōn/ ▶ **n.** SE Asian a cordless or cellular phone.

hand·pick /ˈhandˈpik/ ▶ **v.** [with obj.] select carefully with a particular purpose in mind: *the board's executive director handpicked the review panel to ensure the vote* | (as adj. **handpicked**) *a handpicked team.*

hand press ▶ **n.** a printing press that is operated by hand.

hand·print /ˈhandˌprint/ ▶ **n.** the mark left by the impression of a hand.

hand·print·ed /ˈhandˈprintid/ ▶ **adj. 1** written by hand with the letters individually formed.
2 of or bearing a design printed by hand.

hand pup·pet ▶ **n.** a puppet operated by putting one's hand inside it.

hand·rail /ˈhan(d)ˌrāl/ ▶ **n.** a rail fixed to posts or a wall for people to hold on to for support.

hand·roll /ˈhandrōl/ ▶ **n.** a type of sushi consisting of a cone of dried seaweed filled with rice, fish, vegetables, etc.

hand·saw /ˈhan(d)ˌsô/ ▶ **n.** a wood saw worked by one hand.

hand·sel /ˈhansəl/ ▶ **n. & v.** variant spelling of HANSEL.

hand·sel·ling /ˈhandˈseliNG/ ▶ **n.** the practice of promoting books by personal recommendation rather than by publisher-sponsored marketing.
– DERIVATIVES **hand·sell v.** [with obj.].

hand·set /ˈhan(d)ˌset/ ▶ **n.** the part of a telephone that is held up to speak into and listen to. ■ a handheld controller for a piece of electronic equipment, such as a television or video recorder.

hands-free ▶ **adj.** (of a telephone or other electronic device) designed to be operated without using the hands.

hand·shake /ˈhan(d)ˌSHāk/ ▶ **n.** an act of shaking a person's hand with one's own, used as a greeting or to finalize an agreement. ■ a person's particular way of doing this: *her handshake was warm and firm.* ■ Computing an exchange of standardized signals between devices in a computer network regulating the transfer of data.
– DERIVATIVES **hand·shak·ing** /-SHākiNG/ **n.**

hand·some /ˈhansəm/ ▶ **adj.** (**handsomer, handsomest**) **1** (of a man) good-looking. ■ (of a woman) striking and imposing in good looks rather than conventionally pretty. ■ (of a thing) well made, imposing, and of obvious quality: *handsome cookbooks* | *a handsome country town.*
2 (of a number, sum of money, or margin) substantial: *elected by a handsome majority.*
– PHRASES **handsome is as handsome does** proverb character and behavior are more important than appearance.
– DERIVATIVES **hand·some·ly adv.**, **hand·some·ness n.**
– ORIGIN Middle English: from HAND + -SOME[1]. The original sense was 'easy to handle or use,' hence 'suitable' and 'apt, clever' (mid 16th cent.), giving rise to the current appreciatory senses (late 16th cent).

hand·span /ˈhandˌspan/ ▶ **n.** the width of a person's hand, as measured from the tip of the thumb to the tip of the little finger, when the fingers and thumb are spread out.

hand·spike /ˈhandˌspīk/ ▶ **n.** historical a wooden rod with an iron tip, used as a lever on board ship and by artillery soldiers.

hand·spring /ˈhandˌspriNG/ ▶ **n.** an acrobatic jump through the air onto one's hands followed by springing onto one's feet.

hand·stand /ˈhandˌstand/ ▶ **n.** an act of balancing on one's hands with one's feet in the air or against a wall.

hand-to-hand ▶ **adj.** (of fighting) at close quarters: *training in hand-to-hand combat.*

hand tool ▶ **n.** a tool held in the hand and operated without electricity or other power.

hand-wav·ing ▶ **n.** the use of gestures and insubstantial language meant to impress or convince: *their patriotic hand-waving lacked sincerity* | [as modifier] *her path of logic and hand-waving explanations.*

hand·work /ˈhandˌwərk/ ▶ **n.** work done with the hands: *the transition from handwork to machine production.*
– DERIVATIVES **hand·worked adj.**

hand·wo·ven /ˈhandˈwōvən/ ▶ **adj.** made on a hand-operated loom: *handwoven linens.* ■ woven by hand.

hand·wring·ing /ˈhandˌriNGiNG/ ▶ **n.** the clasping together and squeezing of one's hands, esp. when distressed or worried. ■ an excessive display of concern or distress: *his customary handwringing about the need for more local aid.*

hand·writ·ing /ˈhan(d)ˌrītiNG/ ▶ **n.** writing with a pen or pencil. ■ a person's particular style of writing: *her handwriting was small and neat.*
– PHRASES **the handwriting** (or **writing**) **is on the wall** there are clear signs that something unpleasant or unwelcome is going to happen: *the handwriting was on the wall for the old system.* [with biblical allusion to Dan. 5:5, 25–8.]

hand·writ·ten /ˈhan(d)ˌritn/ ▶ **adj.** written with a pen, pencil, or other handheld implement.

Han·dy /ˈhandē/, W. C. (1873–1958), US composer and musician; full name *William Christopher Handy*; known as the **Father of the Blues**. As a cornetist he led the Mahara Minstrels band 1896–1903. Many of his works, including "St. Louis Blues" and "Memphis Blues," were multistrain jazz compositions that utilized elements of the blues.

hand·y /ˈhandē/ ▶ **adj.** (**handier, handiest**)
1 convenient to handle or use; useful: *a handy desktop encyclopedia* | *handy for everyday use.*
2 close at hand: *keep credit cards handy.* ■ placed or occurring conveniently: *a hotel in a handy central location.*
3 skillful: *he's handy with a needle.*
– PHRASES **come in handy** informal turn out to be useful: *the sort of junk that might come in handy one day.*
– DERIVATIVES **hand·i·ly** /ˈhandl-ē, ˈhandəlē/ **adv.**, **hand·i·ness n.**

hand·y·man /ˈhandēˌman/ ▶ **n.** (pl. **handymen**) a person able or employed to do occasional domestic repairs and minor renovations.

Han·ford /ˈhanfərd/ a government reservation in Richland in southeastern Washington, a former US plutonium-production site.

hang /haNG/ ▶ **v.** (past **hung** /həNG/ except in sense 2) **1** suspend or be suspended from above with the lower part dangling free: [with obj.] *that's where people are supposed to hang their wash* | [no obj.] *a chain hanging freely over two pegs.* ■ attach or be attached to a wall: [with obj.] *we could just hang the pictures on the walls* | [no obj.] *the room in which the pictures will hang.* ■ (**be hung with**) be adorned with pictures or other decorations: *the walls of her hall were hung with examples of her work.* ■ attach or be attached so as to allow free movement about the point of attachment: [with obj.] *a long time was spent hanging a couple of doors.* ■ [no obj.] (of fabric or a garment) be arranged in folds so as to droop in a specified way: *this blend of silk and wool hangs well and resists creases.* ■ [with obj.] paste (wallpaper) to a wall. ■ informal way of saying HANG AROUND (sense 2) or HANG OUT (sense 3).
2 (past **hanged**) [with obj.] kill (someone) by tying a rope attached from above around the neck and removing the support from beneath (used as a form of capital punishment): *he was hanged for murder* | *she hanged herself in her cell.* ■ [no obj.] be killed in such a way: *both men were sentenced to hang.* ■ dated used in expressions as a mild oath: [no obj.] *they could all go hang* | [with obj.] *I'm hanged if I know.*
3 [no obj.] remain static in the air: *a haze of smoke hung below the ceiling.* ■ be present or imminent, esp. oppressively or threateningly: *a sense of dread hung over him for days.* ■ [with obj.] Baseball deliver (a breaking pitch) that does not change direction as intended.
4 [with obj.] (of a juror) prevent (a jury) from reaching a verdict by a dissenting vote.
5 Computing come or cause to come unexpectedly to a state in which no further operations can be carried out.
▶ **n.** [in sing.] a downward droop or bend: *the bullish hang of his head.* ■ the way in which something hangs: *the hang of one's clothes.* ■ the way in which pictures are displayed in an exhibition.
– PHRASES **get the hang of** informal learn how to operate or do (something): *it's quite simple when you get the hang of it.* **hang by a thread** see THREAD. **hang fire** delay or be delayed in taking action or progressing. **hang one's hat** informal be resident. **hang heavily** (or **heavy**) (of time) pass slowly. **hang in the air** remain unresolved: *the question that has been hanging in the air.* **hang a left** (or **right**) informal make a left (or right) turn. **hang loose** see LOOSE. **hang someone out to dry** informal leave someone in a difficult or vulnerable situation. **hang ten** Surfing ride a surfboard with all ten toes curled over the board's front edge. **hang tough** informal be or remain inflexible or firmly resolved. **let it all hang out** informal be very relaxed or uninhibited. **not care** (or **give**) **a hang** informal not care at all: *people just don't give a hang about plants.*
– PHRASAL VERBS **hang around 1** loiter; wait around: *undercover officers spent most of their time hanging around bars.* **2** (**hang around with**) associate with (someone): *he never hangs around with that gang.* **hang back** remain behind: *Stephen hung back for fear of being seen.* ■ show reluctance to act or move: *they were hanging back, each unwilling to speak first.* **hang in** informal remain persistent and determined in difficult circumstances: *in the second half, we just had to hang*

in there. **hang on 1** hold tightly: *he hung on to the back of her coat.* ■ informal remain firm or persevere, esp. in difficult circumstances: *we must hang on as best we can.* ■ (**hang on to**) keep; retain: *he is determined to hang on to his job.* **2** informal wait for a short time: *hang on a minute—do you think I might have left anything out?* ■ (on the telephone) remain connected until one is able to talk to a particular person. **3** be contingent or dependent on: *the future of Europe should not hang on a referendum by the French.* **4** listen closely to: *she hung on his every word.* **hang something on** informal attach the blame for something to (someone). **hang out 1** (of laundry) hang from a clothesline to dry. **2** (of a shirttail or other piece of clothing) protrude and hang loosely downward: *with the front tucked in and the tail hanging out.* **3** informal spend time relaxing or enjoying oneself: *musicians hang out with their own kind.* **hang together 1** make sense; be consistent: *it helps the speech to hang together.* **2** (of people) remain associated; help or support each other. **hang up 1** hang from a hook, hanger, etc.: *his good shirt's ironed and hanging up.* **2** end a telephone conversation by cutting the connection. ■ (**hang up on**) end a telephone conversation with (someone) by abruptly cutting the connection. **hang up something** hang something on a hook: *a closet where he could hang up his clothes.* ■ informal cease or retire from the activity associated with the garment or object specified: *he will soon have to hang up his referee's whistle for good.*

– ORIGIN Old English *hangian* (intransitive verb), related to Dutch and German *hangen*, reinforced by the Old Norse transitive verb *hanga*.

> **USAGE** In modern English, **hang** has two past tense and past participle forms: **hanged** and **hung**. **Hung** is the normal form in most general uses (*they* **hung** *out the wash; she* **hung** *around for a few minutes; he had* **hung** *the picture over the fireplace*), but **hanged** is the form normally used in reference to execution by hanging (*she was* **hanged** *as a witch in April 1621*).

hang·ar /ˈhaNGər/ ▶ **n.** a large building with extensive floor area, typically for housing aircraft.
▶ **v.** [with obj.] (usu. **be hangared**) place or store in a hangar: *the army choppers that were hangared out at Springs.*
– DERIVATIVES **hang·ar·age** /-rij/ **n.**
– ORIGIN late 17th cent. (in the sense 'shelter'): from French; probably from Germanic bases meaning 'hamlet' and 'enclosure.'

Hang·chow /ˈhaNGˈCHou, ˈhängˈjō/ variant of **HANGZHOU**.

hang·dog /ˈhaNG,dôg, -,däg/ ▶ **adj.** having a dejected or guilty appearance; shamefaced: *the boys wore hangdog looks as the police marched them down the steps.*

hang·er /ˈhaNGər/ ▶ **n. 1** [in combination] a person who hangs something: *a wallpaper hanger.*
2 (also **coat hanger**) a shaped piece of wood, plastic, or metal with a hook at the top, from which clothes may be hung in order to keep them in shape and free of creases.

hang·er-on ▶ **n.** (pl. **hangers-on**) a person who associates with another person or a group in a sycophantic manner or for the purpose of gaining some personal advantage: *he was a hanger-on who used to come around and drink with Father.*

hang glid·er ▶ **n.** an unpowered flying apparatus for a single person, consisting of a frame with a fabric airfoil stretched over it. The operator is suspended from a harness below and controls flight by body movement. ■ a person flying such an apparatus.
– DERIVATIVES **hang-glide v.**, **hang glid·ing n.**

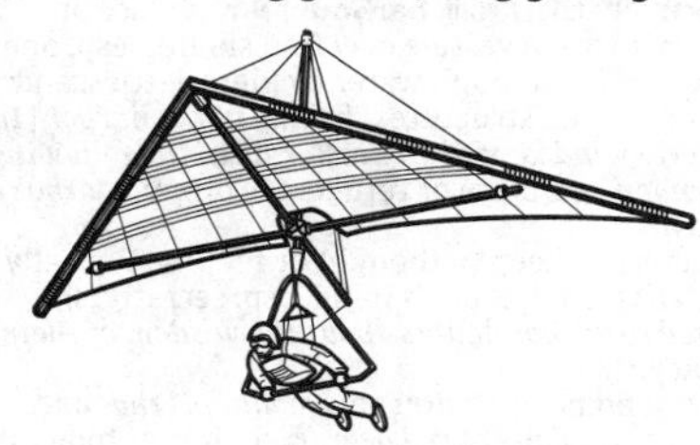
hang glider

hang·ing /ˈhaNGiNG/ ▶ **n. 1** the practice of hanging condemned people as a form of capital punishment.
2 a decorative piece of fabric or curtain hung on the wall of a room or around a bed: *a beautiful wall hanging.*
▶ **adj.** [attrib.] suspended in the air: *hanging palls of smoke.* ■ situated or designed so as to appear to hang down: *hanging gardens.*

hang·ing bas·ket ▶ **n.** a basket or similar container that can be suspended from a building by a small rope or chain and in which decorative flowering plants are grown.

Hang·ing Gar·dens of Bab·y·lon legendary terraced gardens at Babylon, watered by pumps from the Euphrates, whose construction was ascribed to Nebuchadnezzar (*c.*600 BC). They were one of the Seven Wonders of the World.

hang·ing in·dent ▶ **n.** indentation of a paragraph in which all lines except the first are indented.

hang·ing val·ley ▶ **n.** a valley that is cut across by a deeper valley or a cliff.

hang·ing wall ▶ **n.** Geology the block of rock that lies above an inclined fault or an ore body. Compare with **FOOTWALL**.

hang·man /ˈhaNGmən, -,man/ ▶ **n.** (pl. **hangmen**) an executioner who hangs condemned people. ■ a game for two in which one player tries to guess the letters of a word, and failed attempts are recorded by drawing a gallows and someone hanging on it, line by line.

hang·nail /ˈhaNG,nāl/ ▶ **n.** a piece of torn skin at the root of a fingernail.
– ORIGIN late 17th cent.: alteration of *agnail* 'painful swelling around a nail' (from Old English *angnægl*, denoting a corn on the toe), influenced by **HANG**.

hang·out /ˈhaNG,out/ ▶ **n.** informal a place one frequently visits: *I nursed a beer at a favorite college hangout.*

hang·o·ver /ˈhaNG,ōvər/ ▶ **n.** a severe headache or other after effects caused by drinking an excess of alcohol. ■ a thing that has survived from the past: *a hangover from the sixties.*

Hang Seng in·dex /ˈhaNG ˈseNG/ a figure indicating the relative price of shares on the Hong Kong Stock Exchange.
– ORIGIN named after the *Hang Seng Bank* in Hong Kong, where it was devised.

hang time ▶ **n.** Football the number of seconds during which a punted ball is in the air.

hang-up ▶ **n.** informal an emotional problem or inhibition: *people with hang-ups about their age.*

Hang·zhou /ˈhängˈjō/ (also **Hangchow**) a city in eastern China, the capital of Zhejiang province, on an inlet of the Yellow Sea called Hangzhou Bay, at the southern end of the Grand Canal; pop. 2,455,600 (est. 2006).

hank /haNGk/ ▶ **n. 1** a coil or skein of yarn, hair, rope, or other material: *a thick hank of her blonde hair.*
2 a measurement of the length per unit mass of cloth or yarn, which varies according to the type being measured. For example, a hank is equal to 840 yards for cotton yarn and 560 yards for worsted.
3 Sailing a ring for securing a staysail to the stay.
– ORIGIN Middle English: from Old Norse *hǫnk*; compare with Swedish *hank* 'string' and Danish *hank* 'handle.'

hank·er /ˈhaNGkər/ ▶ **v.** [no obj.] (**hanker after/for/to do something**) feel a strong desire for or to do something: *his wife accused him of hankering after adultery | she hankered to go back.*
– DERIVATIVES **hank·er·er n.**
– ORIGIN early 17th cent.: probably related to **HANG**; compare with Dutch *hunkeren*.

hank·er·ing /ˈhaNGk(ə)riNG/ ▶ **n.** a strong desire to have or do something: *a hankering for family life.*

Hanks /haNGks/, Tom (1956–), US actor; full name *Thomas Jeffrey Hanks*. Notable movies: *Splash!* (1984), *Big* (1988), *Sleepless in Seattle* (1993), *Philadelphia* (1993), *Forrest Gump* (1994), *Saving Private Ryan* (1998), and *The Terminal* (2004).

han·ky /ˈhaNGkē/ (also **hankie**) ▶ **n.** (pl. **hankies**) informal a handkerchief.
– ORIGIN late 19th cent.: abbreviation.

han·ky-pan·ky /,haNGkē ˈpaNGkē/ ▶ **n.** informal, humorous behavior, in particular sexual or legally dubious behavior, considered improper but not seriously so: *there's no hanky-panky involved, no dating of customers | suspicions of financial hanky-panky.*
– ORIGIN mid 19th cent.: perhaps an alteration of **HOKEY-POKEY**.

Han·ni·bal[1] /ˈhanəbəl/ a port city in northeastern Missouri, on the Mississippi River, the boyhood home of Mark Twain; pop. 17,432 (est. 2008).

Han·ni·bal[2] /ˈhanəbəl/ (247–182 BC), Carthaginian general. In the second Punic War he attacked Italy by crossing the Alps. He repeatedly defeated the Romans, although he failed to take Rome itself. After being recalled to Africa he was defeated at Zama by Scipio Africanus in 202.

Ha·noi /haˈnoi, hə-/ the capital of Vietnam, on the Red River, in the northern part of the country; pop. 2,632,100 (est. 2009). It was the capital of French Indo-China 1887–1946 and of North Vietnam before the reunification of North and South Vietnam.

Han·o·ver /ˈhan,ōvər, ˈhän-/ **1** an industrial city in northwestern Germany, the capital of Lower Saxony, on the Mittelland Canal; pop. 516,300 (est. 2006). German name **Hannover**. ■ a former state and province in northern Germany. In 1714 the Elector of Hanover succeeded to the British throne as George I, and from then until the accession of Victoria (1837) the same monarch ruled both Britain and Hanover. ■ the British royal house from 1714 to the death of Queen Victoria in 1901.
2 a town in west central New Hampshire, on the Connecticut River, home to Dartmouth College; pop. 11,068 (est. 2008).

Han·o·ve·ri·an /,hanəˈve(ə)rēən/ ▶ **adj.** of or relating to the royal house of Hanover.
▶ **n. 1** (usu. **the Hanoverians**) any of the British sovereigns from George I to Victoria.
2 a medium-built horse of a German breed, developed for use both as a riding horse and in harness.

Han Riv·er /hän/ *1* (Chinese name ***Han Shui***) a river in eastern China that flows southeast for 952 miles (1,532 km) from southwestern Shaanxi province to the Yangtze River in Hubei province. *2* (Chinese name ***Han Jiang***) river in south China that rises in southeastern Fujian province and flows south for 210 miles (338 km) to the South China Sea at Shantou in Guangdong province.

Han·sard /ˈhansərd/ ▶ **n.** the official verbatim record of debates in the British, Canadian, Australian, or New Zealand parliament.
– ORIGIN late 19th cent.: named after Thomas C. *Hansard* (1776–1833), an English printer whose company originally printed it.

Hans·ber·ry /ˈhanz,berē/, Lorraine (1930–65), US playwright and civil rights activist. Her *A Raisin in the Sun* (1959) was the first play by an African-American woman to be produced on Broadway. It was made into a movie in 1961.

Hanse /hans, ˈhänzə/ ▶ **n.** a medieval guild of merchants. ■ (**the Hanse**) the Hanseatic League. ■ a fee payable to a guild of merchants.
– ORIGIN Middle English: from Old French *hanse* 'guild, company,' from Old High German *hansa* 'company, troop.'

Han·se·at·ic League /,hansēˈatik/ a medieval association of northern German cities, formed in 1241 and surviving until the 19th century. In the later Middle Ages it included over 100 towns and functioned as an independent political power.
– ORIGIN *Hanseatic* from medieval Latin *Hanseaticus*, from *hansa* (see **HANSE**).

han·sel /ˈhansəl/ (also **handsel**) ▶ **n.** a gift given for good luck at the beginning of the year or to mark an acquisition or the start of an enterprise. ■ the first installment of a payment.
▶ **v.** (**hansels, hanseling, hanseled**; Brit. **hansels, hanselling, hanselled**) [with obj.] give a hansel to. ■ inaugurate (something), esp. by being the first to try it: *a floodlit fixture to officially hansel the completed stadium.*
– ORIGIN Middle English (denoting luck): apparently related to late Old English *handselen* 'giving into a person's hands,' and Old Norse *handsal* 'giving of the hand to seal a promise,' from **HAND** + an element related to **SELL**; the notion of 'luck,' however, is not present in these words.

Han·sen's dis·ease /ˈhansənz/ ▶ **n.** another name for **LEPROSY**.
– ORIGIN 1930s: named after Gerhard H. A. *Hansen* (1841–1912), the Norwegian physician who discovered the causative agent of the disease.

han·som /ˈhansəm/ (also **hansom cab**) ▶ **n.** historical a two-wheeled horse-drawn carriage accommodating two inside, with the driver seated behind.
– ORIGIN mid 19th cent.: named after Joseph A. *Hansom* (1803–82), English architect, patentee of such a cab in 1834.

hansom

han·ta·vi·rus /ˈhantə,vīrəs/ ▶ **n.** a virus of a genus carried by rodents and causing various febrile

hemorrhagic diseases, often with kidney damage or failure.
– ORIGIN 1980s: from *Hantaan* (the name of a river in Korea where the virus was first isolated) + **VIRUS**.

Ha·nuk·kah /ˈKHänəkə, ˈhänəkə/ (also **Chanukah**) ▶ **n.** a lesser Jewish festival, lasting eight days from the 25th day of Kislev (in December) and commemorating the rededication of the Temple in 165 BC by the Maccabees after its desecration by the Syrians. It is marked by the successive kindling of eight lights.
– ORIGIN from Hebrew *ḥănukkāh* 'consecration.'

han·u·man /ˈhənŏŏ,män/ ▶ **n. 1** (also **hanuman langur**) a pale-colored langur monkey of southern Asia, venerated by Hindus. ● *Presbytis entellus*, family Cercopithecidae.
2 Hinduism (**Hanuman**) a semidivine being of monkeylike form, whose exploits are described in the Ramayana.
– ORIGIN from Sanskrit *hanumant* 'large-jawed.'

Han·zhong /ˈhänˈjŏŏNG/ a city in Shaanxi province, in central China, southwest of Xi'an on the northern bank of the Han River; pop. 420,000.

hao·ma /ˈhoumə/ ▶ **n.** variant of **HOM**.

Hao·ra variant spelling of **HOWRAH**.

hap /hap/ archaic ▶ **n.** luck; fortune. ■ a chance occurrence, esp. an event that is considered unlucky.
▶ **v.** (**haps, happing, happed**) [no obj.] come about by chance: *what can hap to him worthy to be deemed evil?* ■ [with infinitive] have the fortune or luck to do something: *where'er I happ'd to roam.*
– ORIGIN Middle English: from Old Norse *happ*.

hap·ax le·go·me·non /ˈhapaks ləˈgämə,nän/ ▶ **n.** (pl. **hapax legomena** /ləˈgämənə/) a term of which only one instance of use is recorded.
– ORIGIN mid 17th cent.: Greek, 'a thing said once,' from *hapax* 'once' and the passive participle of *legein* 'to say.'

ha'·pen·ny ▶ **n.** variant spelling of **HALFPENNY**.

hap·haz·ard /,hapˈhazərd/ ▶ **adj.** lacking any obvious principle of organization: *the kitchen drawers contained a haphazard collection of silver souvenir spoons.*
– DERIVATIVES **hap·haz·ard·ly adv.**, **hap·haz·ard·ness n.**
– ORIGIN late 16th cent.: from **HAP** + **HAZARD**.

Haph·ta·rah /,häftäˈrä, häfˈtôrə/ (also **Haphtorah**) ▶ **n.** (pl. **Haphtaroth** /-täˈrôt, -ˈtôrōs/) variant spelling of **HAFTORAH**.

hap·ki·do /häpˈkēdō/ ▶ **n.** a Korean martial art characterized by kicking and circular movements.
– ORIGIN Korean: 'way of coordinated strength.'

hap·less /ˈhaplis/ ▶ **adj.** (esp. of a person) unfortunate: *if you're one of the many hapless car buyers who've been shafted.*
– DERIVATIVES **hap·less·ly adv.**, **hap·less·ness n.**
– ORIGIN late Middle English: from **HAP** (in the early sense 'good fortune') + **-LESS**.

haplo- ▶ **comb. form** single; simple: *haplography* | *haploid.*
– ORIGIN from Greek *haploos* 'single.'

hap·lo·chro·mine /,haplōˈkrō,mēn/ Zoology ▶ **adj.** of, relating to, or denoting cichlid fishes of a large and diverse group that are particularly abundant in the large lakes of East Africa.
▶ **n.** a haplochromine fish. ● *Haplochromis* and related genera, family Cichlidae.
– ORIGIN from the modern Latin genus name.

hap·lo·dip·loid /,haplōˈdiploid/ ▶ **adj.** Biology denoting or possessing a genetic system in which females develop from fertilized (diploid) eggs and males from unfertilized (haploid) ones.
– DERIVATIVES **hap·lo·dip·loid·y n.**

hap·log·ra·phy /hapˈlägrəfē/ ▶ **n.** the inadvertent omission of a repeated letter or letters in writing (e.g., writing *philogy* for *philology*).
– ORIGIN late 19th cent.: from Greek *haploos* 'single' + **-GRAPHY**.

hap·loid /ˈhap,loid/ Genetics ▶ **adj.** (of a cell or nucleus) having a single set of unpaired chromosomes. Compare with **DIPLOID**. ■ (of an organism or part) composed of haploid cells.
▶ **n.** a haploid organism or cell.
– DERIVATIVES **hap·loi·dy n.**
– ORIGIN early 20th cent.: from Greek *haploos* 'single' + **-OID**.

hap·lol·o·gy /hapˈläləjē/ ▶ **n.** the omission of an occurrence of a sound or syllable that is repeated within a word, e.g., in *probly* for *probably*.
– ORIGIN late 19th cent.: from Greek *haploos* 'single' + **-LOGY**.

hap·lon·tic /hapˈläntik/ ▶ **adj.** Genetics (chiefly of an alga or other lower plant) having a life cycle in which the main form is haploid, with a diploid zygote being formed only briefly. Compare with **DIPLONTIC** and **DIPLOHAPLONTIC**.
– DERIVATIVES **hap·lont** /ˈhap,länt/ **n.**

hap·lo·sis /hapˈlōsis/ ▶ **n.** Biology the halving of the number of chromosomes in a diploid cell during meiosis, resulting in two haploid cells.

ha'p'orth /ˈhāpərTH/ ▶ **n.** variant spelling of **HALFPENNYWORTH**.

hap·pen /ˈhapən/ ▶ **v.** [no obj.] **1** take place; occur: *the afternoon when the disturbance happened.* ■ ensue as an effect or result of an action or event: *this is what happens when the mechanism goes wrong.* ■ [with infinitive] chance to do something or come about: *we just happened to meet Paul* | *there happens to be a clash of personalities.* ■ [with clause] come about by chance: ***it just so happened*** *that she turned up that afternoon.* ■ (**happen on**) find or come across by chance: *Mike played football as a boy and happened on cycling by accident.* ■ [with infinitive] used as a polite formula in questions: *do you happen to know who her doctor is?*
2 (**happen to**) be experienced by (someone); befall: *the same thing happened to me.* ■ become of: *I don't care what happens to the money.*
– PHRASES **as it happens** actually; as a matter of fact: *we've got a room vacant, as it happens.*
– ORIGIN late Middle English (superseding the verb *hap*): from the noun **HAP** + **-EN**¹.

hap·pen·ing /ˈhap(ə)niNG/ ▶ **n. 1** an event or occurrence: *altogether it was an eerie happening.*
2 a partly improvised or spontaneous piece of theatrical or other artistic performance, typically involving audience participation: *a multimedia happening.*
▶ **adj.** informal fashionable; trendy: *nightclubs for the young are the happening thing.*

hap·pen·stance /ˈhapən,stans/ ▶ **n.** coincidence: *it was just happenstance that I happened to be there* | *an untoward happenstance for Trudy.*
– ORIGIN late 19th cent.: blend of **HAPPEN** and **CIRCUMSTANCE**.

hap·pi /ˈhapē/ (also **happi coat**) ▶ **n.** (pl. **happis**) a loose informal Japanese coat.
– ORIGIN late 19th cent.: Japanese.

hap·pi·ly /ˈhapəlē/ ▶ **adv.** in a happy way: *Eleanor giggled happily.* ■ [sentence adverb] it is fortunate that: *happily, today's situation is very different.*

hap·pi·ness /ˈhapēnis/ ▶ **n.** the state of being happy: *she struggled to find happiness in her life.*

hap·py /ˈhapē/ ▶ **adj.** (**happier, happiest**) **1** feeling or showing pleasure or contentment: *Melissa came in looking happy and excited* | [with clause] *we're just happy that he's still alive* | [with infinitive] *they are happy to see me doing well.* ■ [predic.] (**happy about**) having a sense of confidence in or satisfaction with (a person, arrangement, or situation): *I was never very happy about the explanation* | *I can't say they looked too happy about it, but a deal's a deal.* ■ [predic.] (**happy with**) satisfied with the quality or standard of: *I'm happy with his performance.* ■ [with infinitive] willing to do something: *we will be happy to advise you.* ■ (of an event or situation) characterized by happiness: *we had a very happy, relaxed time.* ■ [attrib.] used in greetings: *happy birthday.*
2 [attrib.] fortunate and convenient: *he had the happy knack of making people like him.*
3 [in combination] informal inclined to use a specified thing excessively or at random: *our litigation-happy society.*
– PHRASES **(as) happy as a clam (at high tide)** extremely happy. **happy hunting ground** a place where success or enjoyment is obtained. [originally referring to the optimistic hope of American Indians for good hunting grounds in the afterlife.]
– ORIGIN Middle English (in the sense 'lucky'): from the noun **HAP** + **-Y**¹.

hap·py-go-luck·y ▶ **adj.** cheerfully unconcerned about the future: *a happy-go-lucky, relaxed attitude.*

hap·py hour ▶ **n.** a period of the day when drinks are sold at reduced prices in a bar or restaurant.

hap·py me·di·um ▶ **n.** a satisfactory compromise: *you have to* ***strike a happy medium between*** *looking like royalty and looking like a housewife.*

Haps·burg /ˈhapsbərg, ˈhäps,bŏŏrk/ variant spelling of **HABSBURG**.

hap·ten /ˈhap,ten/ ▶ **n.** Physiology a small molecule that, when combined with a larger carrier such as a protein, can elicit the production of antibodies that bind specifically to it (in the free or combined state).
– ORIGIN early 20th cent.: from Greek *haptein* 'fasten.'

hap·tic /ˈhaptik/ ▶ **adj.** technical of or relating to the sense of touch, in particular relating to the perception and manipulation of objects using the senses of touch and proprioception.
– ORIGIN late 19th cent.: from Greek *haptikos* 'able to touch or grasp,' from *haptein* 'fasten.'

hap·to·glo·bin /,haptəˈglōbən/ ▶ **n.** Biochemistry a protein present in blood serum that binds to and removes free hemoglobin from the bloodstream.
– ORIGIN 1940s: from Greek *haptein* 'fasten' + *(hemo)globin*.

ha·ra-ki·ri /,härəˈki(ə)rē, ,harə-, ,harē ˈkarē/ ▶ **n.** ritual suicide by disembowelment with a sword, formerly practiced in Japan by samurai as an honorable alternative to disgrace or execution.
– ORIGIN mid 19th cent.: colloquial Japanese, from *hara* 'belly' + *kiri* 'cutting.'

ha·ram /ˈhe(ə)rəm, ˈharəm/ ▶ **adj.** forbidden or proscribed by Islamic law.
– ORIGIN from Arabic *ḥarām* 'forbidden.' Compare with **HAREM**.

ha·rangue /həˈraNG/ ▶ **n.** a lengthy and aggressive speech.
▶ **v.** [with obj.] lecture (someone) at length in an aggressive and critical manner: *the kind of guy who* ***harangued*** *total strangers* ***about*** *PCB levels in whitefish.*
– DERIVATIVES **ha·rangu·er n.**
– ORIGIN late Middle English: from Old French *arenge*, from medieval Latin *harenga*, perhaps of Germanic origin. The spelling was later altered to conform with French *harangue* (noun), *haranguer* (verb).

Ha·rap·pa /həˈrapə/ an ancient city of the Indus valley civilization (*c.*2600–1700 BC), in northern Pakistan. The site of the ruins was discovered in 1920.

Ha·ra·re /həˈrärē, -ˈrärā/ the capital of Zimbabwe; pop. 1,696,000 (est. 2009). Former name (until 1982) **SALISBURY**¹.

ha·rass /həˈras, ˈharəs/ ▶ **v.** [with obj.] subject to aggressive pressure or intimidation: *a warning to men harassing women at work.* ■ make repeated small-scale attacks on (an enemy): *the squadron's task was to harass the retreating enemy forces.*
– DERIVATIVES **ha·rass·er n.**, **ha·rass·ing·ly adv.**
– ORIGIN early 17th cent.: from French *harasser*, from *harer* 'set a dog on,' from Germanic *hare*, a cry urging a dog to attack.

> **USAGE** Traditionally, the word **harass** has been pronounced with stress on the first syllable, as "HAR-us." But the newer pronunciation that puts the stress on the second syllable ("huh-RAS") is increasingly more widespread and is considered standard. This is also true for **harassed** and **harassment**.

ha·rassed /həˈrast, ˈharəst/ ▶ **adj.** feeling or looking strained through having too many demands made on one: *it is a godsend for harassed parents.*

ha·rass·ment /həˈrasm(ə)nt, ˈharəsm(ə)nt/ ▶ **n.** aggressive pressure or intimidation: *they face daily harassment by the police.*

Har·bin /härˈbin, ˈhärbin/ a city in northeastern China, the capital of Heilongjiang province, on the Songhua River; pop. 3,075,300 (est. 2006).

har·bin·ger /ˈhärbənjər/ ▶ **n.** a person or thing that announces or signals the approach of another: *witch hazels are the harbingers of spring.* ■ a forerunner of something: *these works were not yet opera, but they were the most important harbinger of opera.*
– ORIGIN Middle English: from Old French *herbergere*, from *herbergier* 'provide lodging for,' from *herberge* 'lodging,' from Old Saxon *heriberga* 'shelter for an army, lodging' (from *heri* 'army' + a Germanic base meaning 'fortified place'), related to **HARBOR**. The term originally denoted a person who provided lodging, later one who went ahead to find lodgings for an army or for a nobleman and his retinue, hence, a herald (mid 16th cent).

har·bor /ˈhärbər/ (Brit. **harbour**) ▶ **n.** a place on the coast where vessels may find shelter, esp. one protected from rough water by piers, jetties, and other artificial structures: *fishing in the harbor* | *the westerly wind kept us* ***in harbor*** *until the following afternoon.* ■ a place of refuge: *the offered harbor of his arms.*
▶ **v.** [with obj.] **1** keep (a thought or feeling, typically a negative one) in one's mind, esp. secretly: *she started to harbor doubts about the wisdom of their journey.*
2 give a home or shelter to: *woodlands that once harbored a colony of red deer.* ■ shelter or hide (a criminal or wanted person): *he was suspected of harboring an escaped prisoner.* ■ carry the germs of (a disease).
3 [no obj.] archaic (of a ship or its crew) moor in a harbor: *he might have harbored in San Francisco.*
– DERIVATIVES **har·bor·er n.**, **har·bor·less adj.**
– ORIGIN late Old English *herebeorg* 'shelter, refuge,' *herebeorgian* 'occupy shelter,' of Germanic origin; related to Dutch *herberge* and German *Herberge*, also to French *auberge* 'inn'; see also **HARBINGER**.

har·bor·mas·ter /ˈhärbər,mastər/ (also **harbor master**) ▶ **n.** an official in charge of a harbor.

har·bor por·poise ▶ **n.** a porpoise with a dark gray back shading to white underparts, found in the coastal waters of North America and northern Europe. Also called COMMON PORPOISE. ● *Phocoena phocoena*, family Phocoenidae.

har·bor seal ▶ **n.** a seal with a mottled gray-brown coat and a concave profile, found along North Atlantic and North Pacific coasts. ● *Phoca vitulina*, family Phocidae.

har·bor·side /ˈhärbərsīd/ ▶ **n.** the area immediately adjacent to a harbor.

hard /härd/ ▶ **adj. 1** solid, firm, and resistant to pressure; not easily broken, bent, or pierced: *a hard mattress | ground frozen hard as a rock.* ■ (of a person) not showing any signs of weakness; tough: *the hard, tough, honest cop.* ■ (of information) reliable, esp. because based on something true or substantiated: *hard facts about the underclass are maddeningly elusive.* ■ (of a subject of study) dealing with precise and verifiable facts: *efforts to turn psychology into hard science.* ■ (of water) containing mineral salts that make lathering difficult. ■ (of prices of stock, commodities, etc.) stable or firm in value. ■ (of science fiction) scientifically accurate rather than purely fantastic or whimsical: *a hard SF novel.* ■ (of a consonant) pronounced as *c* in *cat* or *g* in *go*.
2 requiring a great deal of endurance or effort: *stooping over all day was hard work.* ■ putting a lot of energy into an activity: *he'd been a hard worker all his life.* ■ difficult to bear; causing suffering: *times were hard at the end of the war | he'd had a hard life.* ■ difficult to understand or solve: *this is a really hard question* | [with infinitive] *she found it hard to believe that he could be involved.* ■ not showing sympathy or affection; strict: *my father is no longer the hard man he once was.* ■ (of a season or the weather) severe: *it's been a long, hard winter.* ■ harsh or unpleasant to the senses: *the hard light of morning.* ■ (of wine) harsh or sharp to the taste, esp. because of tannin.
3 done with a great deal of force or strength: *a hard blow to the head.*
4 potent, powerful, or intense, in particular: ■ (of liquor) strongly alcoholic; denoting distilled spirits rather than beer or wine. ■ (of apple cider) having alcoholic content from fermentation. ■ (of a drug) potent and addictive. ■ denoting an extreme or dogmatic faction within a political party: *the hard left.* ■ (of radiation) highly penetrating. ■ (of pornography) highly obscene and explicit.
▶ **adv. 1** with a great deal of effort: *they work hard at school.* ■ with a great deal of force; violently: *it was raining hard.*
2 so as to be solid or firm: *the mortar has set hard.*
3 to the fullest extent possible: *put the wheel hard over to starboard.*
– PHRASES **be hard on 1** treat or criticize (someone) severely: *you're being too hard on her.* **2** be difficult for or unfair to: *I think the war must have been hard on her.* **3** be likely to hurt or damage: *the monitor flickers, which is hard on the eyes.* **be hard put** [usu. with infinitive] find it very difficult: *you'll be hard put to find a better compromise.* **give someone a hard time** informal deliberately make a situation difficult for someone. **go hard with** dated turn out to (someone's) disadvantage: *it would go hard with the poor.* **hard and fast** (of a rule or a distinction made) fixed and definitive: *it is impossible to lay down any hard and fast rules.* **hard as nails** see NAIL. **hard at it** informal busily working or occupied: *they were hard at it with brooms and mops.* **hard by** close to: *he lived hard by the cathedral.* **hard done by** Brit. harshly or unfairly treated: *she would be justified in feeling hard done by.* **hard feelings** [usu. with negative] feelings of resentment: *there are no hard feelings, and we wish him well.* **hard going** difficult to understand or enjoy: *the studying is at times hard going.* **hard hit** badly affected: *hard hit by falling oil prices.* **a hard nut to crack** informal a person or thing that is difficult to understand or influence. **hard of hearing** not able to hear well. **hard on** (or **upon**) close to; following soon after: *we followed hard on their tracks.* **hard up** informal short of money: *I'm too hard up to buy fancy clothes.* **the hard way** through suffering or learning from the unpleasant consequences of mistakes: *his reputation was earned the hard way.* **play hard to get** informal deliberately adopt an aloof or uninterested attitude, typically in order to make oneself more attractive or interesting.
– DERIVATIVES **hard·ish adj.**
– ORIGIN Old English *hard, heard*, of Germanic origin; related to Dutch *hard* and German *hart*.

hard·back /ˈhärd,bak/ ▶ **adj. & n.** another term for HARDCOVER.

hard·ball /ˈhärd,bôl/ ▶ **n.** baseball, esp. as contrasted with softball. ■ informal uncompromising and ruthless methods or dealings, esp. in politics: *the leadership **played hardball** to win the vote.*

hard-bit·ten (also **hardbitten**) ▶ **adj.** tough and cynical: *joining the hard-bitten reporting veterans at the presidential debate.*

hard·board /ˈhärd,bôrd/ ▶ **n.** stiff board made of compressed and treated wood pulp.

hard·bod·y /ˈhärd,bädē/ ▶ **n.** (pl. **hardbodies**) informal a person with very toned or well-developed muscles: *you're in the cockpit of a ragtop Testarossa with a tanned, blond hardbody at your side.*
– DERIVATIVES **hard·bod·ied adj.**

hard-boiled ▶ **adj. 1** (of an egg) boiled until the white and the yolk are solid.
2 (of a person) tough and cynical. ■ denoting a tough, realistic style of detective fiction set in a world permeated by corruption and deceit: *a hard-boiled thriller.*
– DERIVATIVES **hard-boil v.** (sense 1).

hard case ▶ **n.** informal a tough or intractable person.

hard cash ▶ **n.** negotiable coins and paper money as opposed to other forms of payment.

hard charg·er ▶ **n.** someone with an aggressive, domineering personality. ■ (in car racing) someone who gains a considerably better position during the course of a race.

hard cheese ▶ **n.** see CHEESE[1].

hard clam ▶ **n.** another term for QUAHOG.

hard coal ▶ **n.** another term for ANTHRACITE.

hard-code ▶ **v.** [with obj.] Computing fix (data or parameters) in a program in such a way that they cannot be altered without modifying the program.

hard-cooked ▶ **adj.** another term for HARD-BOILED (sense 1).

hard cop·y ▶ **n.** a printed version on paper of data held in a computer.

hard core ▶ **n.** the most active, committed, or doctrinaire members of a group or movement: *there is always a hard core of trusty stalwarts* | [as modifier] *a hard core following.* ■ popular music that is experimental in nature and typically characterized by high volume and aggressive presentation.
■ pornography of an explicit kind: (as modifier **hard-core**) *hard-core porn.*

hard court ▶ **n.** a tennis court surfaced with asphalt or another hard material: [as adj.] *former national hard court champion.*

hard·cov·er /ˈhärd,kəvər/ ▶ **adj.** (of a book) bound between rigid boards covered in cloth, paper, leather, or film: *hardcover and paperback editions.*
▶ **n.** a hardcover book.
– PHRASES **in hardcover** in a hardcover edition.

hard cur·ren·cy ▶ **n.** currency that is not likely to depreciate suddenly or to fluctuate greatly in value.

hard disk ▶ **n.** Computing a rigid nonremovable magnetic disk with a large data storage capacity.

hard drive ▶ **n.** Computing a high-capacity, self-contained storage device containing a read-write mechanism plus one or more hard disks, inside a sealed unit. Also called **hard disk drive**.

hard-earned ▶ **adj.** having taken a great deal of effort to earn or acquire: *my few hard-earned dollars mean a lot to my family.*

hard-edge ▶ **adj.** of or relating to a style of abstract painting characterized by geometric shapes with sharply defined edges and often in bright colors.

hard-edged ▶ **adj. 1** having sharply defined edges.
2 having an intense, tough, or sharp quality: *hard-edged urban films.*

hard·en /ˈhärdn/ ▶ **v.** make or become hard or harder: [no obj.] *wait for the glue to harden* | [with obj.] *bricks that seem to have been hardened by firing.* ■ make or become more severe and less sympathetic: [with obj.] *she hardened her heart.*
■ make or become tougher and more clearly defined: [no obj.] *suspicion **hardened into** certainty.*
■ [no obj.] (of prices of stocks, commodities, etc.) rise and remain steady at a higher level.
– PHRASES **hardening of the arteries** another term for ARTERIOSCLEROSIS.
– PHRASAL VERBS **harden something off** inure a plant to cold by gradually increasing its exposure to it.
– DERIVATIVES **hard·en·er n.**

hard·ened /ˈhärdnd/ ▶ **adj. 1** having become or been made hard or harder: *hardened steel.* ■ strengthened or made secure against attack, esp. by nuclear weapons: *the silos are **hardened against** air attack.*
2 [attrib.] experienced in a particular job or activity and therefore not easily upset by its more unpleasant aspects: *hardened police officers* | [in combination] *a battle-hardened veteran.* ■ utterly fixed in a habit or way of life seen as bad: *hardened criminals | a hardened liar.*

hard er·ror ▶ **n.** Computing an error or hardware fault causing failure of a program or operating system, esp. one that gives no option of recovery.

hard fern ▶ **n.** a European fern of heathy places, with long, narrow, leathery fronds consisting of a row of thin lobes on each side of the stem.
● *Blechnum spicant*, family Blechnaceae.

hard·gain·er /ˈhärdˈgānər/ ▶ **n.** (in bodybuilding) a person who does not find it easy to gain muscle through exercise.

hard hat ▶ **n.** a rigid protective helmet, as worn by factory and building workers. ■ informal a worker who wears a hard hat. ■ informal a person with reactionary or conservative views.

hard·head /ˈhärd,hed/ ▶ **n.** (also **hardhead catfish**) a marine catfish, the male of which incubates the eggs inside its mouth. It occurs along the Atlantic coast of North America. ● *Arius felis*, family Ariidae.

hard·head·ed /ˈhärd,hedid/ ▶ **adj.** practical and realistic; not sentimental: *as experienced and hardheaded a bunch of legislators as has ever entered Congress.*
– DERIVATIVES **hard·head·ed·ly adv.**, **hard·head·ed·ness n.**

hard·heads /ˈhärd,hedz/ ▶ **plural n.** [treated as sing.] another term for KNAPWEED, esp. the black knapweed.

hard-heart·ed ▶ **adj.** incapable of being moved to pity or tenderness; unfeeling.
– DERIVATIVES **hard-heart·ed·ly adv.**, **hard-heart·ed·ness n.**

hard-hit·ting ▶ **adj. 1** uncompromisingly direct and honest, esp. in revealing unpalatable facts: *some of this season's more hard-hitting episodes deal with urban violence.*
2 (of an athlete or athletes) aggressive and physical: *the game's grunting, hard-hitting defense.*

har·di·hood /ˈhärdē,ho͝od/ ▶ **n.** dated boldness; daring.

har·di·ness /ˈhärdēnis/ ▶ **n.** the ability to endure difficult conditions: *I applaud you on your hardiness.*

Har·ding /ˈhärdiNG/, Warren Gamaliel (1865–1923), 29th president of the US 1921–23. A Republican, he served in the US Senate 1915–21 before becoming president. His administration was marked by corruption and scandal, in particular, the Teapot Dome scandal, in which his secretary of the interior accepted money in return for leasing the Teapot Dome oil reserves in Wyoming to private oil producers. Harding died in office while on a trip to California.

Warren G. Harding

hard la·bor ▶ **n.** heavy manual work as a punishment.

hard land·ing ▶ **n.** a clumsy or rough landing of an aircraft. ■ an uncontrolled landing in which a spacecraft crashes onto the surface of a planet or moon and is destroyed.

hard line ▶ **n.** an uncompromising adherence to a firm policy: *he is known to **take a hard line on** sentencing policy for murder.*
▶ **adj.** (**hard-line**) uncompromising; strict: *a hard-line party activist.*

hard-lin·er ▶ **n.** a member of a group, typically a political group, who adheres uncompromisingly to a set of ideas or policies.

hard-luck sto·ry ▶ **n.** an account of one's problems intended to gain sympathy or help.

hard·ly /ˈhärdlē/ ▶ **adv. 1** scarcely (used to qualify a statement by saying that it is true to an insignificant degree): *the little house in which he lived was hardly bigger than a hut | we hardly know each other.* ■ only a very short time before: *the party had hardly started when the police arrived.* ■ only with great difficulty: *she could **hardly** sit up | I nodded, **hardly***

PRONUNCIATION KEY ə *ago, up*; ər *over, fur*; a *hat*; ā *ate*; ä *car*; e *let*; ē *see*; i *fit*; ī *by*; NG *sing*; ō *go*; ô *law, for*; oi *toy*; o͝o *good*; o͞o *goo*; ou *out*; TH *thin*; T͟H *then*; ZH *vision*

able to breath. ■ no or not (suggesting surprise at or disagreement with a statement): *I hardly think so.* **2** archaic harshly: *the rule worked hardly.*
– PHRASES **hardly any** almost no: *they sold hardly any books.* ■ almost none: *hardly any had previous convictions.* **hardly ever** very rarely: *we hardly ever see them.*

> **USAGE** **1** Words like **hardly**, **scarcely**, and **rarely** should not be used with negative constructions. Thus, it is correct to say *I can hardly wait* but incorrect to say *I can't hardly wait.* This is because adverbs like **hardly** are treated as if they were negatives, and it is a grammatical rule of standard English that double negatives are not acceptable. Words like **hardly** behave as negatives in other respects as well, as for example in combining with terms such as **any** or **at all**, which normally occur only where a negative is present (thus, standard usage is *I've got **hardly any** money*, but not *I've got any money*). See also usage at DOUBLE NEGATIVE. **2 Hardly . . . than** versus **hardly . . . when**: the conjunction *than* is best left to work with comparative adjectives and adverbs (*lovelier than; more quickly than*). Consider a construction such as *Sheila had hardly recovered from the flu when she lost her beloved beagle*: in speech, one might tend to use **than** as the complement to **hardly**, but in careful writing, since time is the point, the word to use is **when**. In a more formal context, however, the idea would be better conveyed: *No sooner had Sheila recovered from the flu than she lost her beloved beagle.* In this sentence, *than* does belong because it is the natural conjunction after the comparative adjective *sooner*. **3** As synonyms, *hardly, barely,* and *scarcely* are almost indistinguishable.

hard·man /ˈhärdman/ ▶ **n.** (pl. **hardmen**) informal a tough, aggressive, or ruthless man.

hard·ness /härdnis/ ▶ **n.** the quality or condition of being hard: *people complained about the hardness of the chairs | a lack of mental hardness.*

hard-nosed ▶ **adj.** informal realistic and determined; tough-minded: *the hard-nosed, tough approach.*

hard nut ▶ **n.** Brit. informal a tough, aggressive, or insensitive person.

hard-on ▶ **n.** vulgar slang an erection of the penis.

hard pal·ate ▶ **n.** the bony front part of the palate.

hard·pan /ˈhärd,pan/ ▶ **n.** a hardened impervious layer, typically of clay, occurring in or below the soil and impairing drainage and plant growth.

hard-paste ▶ **adj.** denoting true porcelain made of fusible and infusible materials (usually kaolin and china stone) fired at a high temperature. Developed in early medieval China, it was not made in Europe until the early 18th century.

hard pow·er ▶ **n.** a coercive approach to international political relations, esp. one that involves the use of military power. Compare with SOFT POWER.

hard-pressed ▶ **adj.** **1** closely pursued: *the hard-pressed French infantry.*
2 burdened with urgent business: *training centers are hard-pressed and insufficient in numbers.* ■ (also **hard pressed**) in difficulties: *creating jobs in the hard-pressed construction industry* | [with infinitive] *many families will **be hard pressed to** support their elderly relations.*

hard rock ▶ **n.** highly amplified rock music with a heavy beat.

hard roe ▶ **n.** see ROE[1].

hard sauce ▶ **n.** a sauce of butter and sugar, typically with brandy, rum, or vanilla added.

hard·scape /ˈhärd,skāp/ ▶ **n.** the nonliving or man-made fixtures of a planned outdoor area: *before you begin to implement your plan, consider the hardscape of your ornamental garden.*

hard·scap·ing /ˈhärd,skāpiNG/ ▶ **n.** the placement of nonplant elements such as fences, walkways, paving, and lighting in a planned outdoor area.

hard·scrab·ble /ˈhärd,skrabəl/ ▶ **adj.** involving hard work and struggle: *her uncle's hardscrabble peanut farm | it was a hardscrabble life in a one-bedroom housing project.*

hard sell ▶ **n.** a policy or technique of aggressive salesmanship or advertising: *they invited 1,000 participants and gave them **the hard sell**.*

hard-shell ▶ **adj.** [attrib.] **1** having a hard shell or outer casing: *hard-shell helmets.*
2 rigid or uncompromising, esp. in fundamentalist religious belief: *I am a hard-shell Baptist.*

hard-shell clam ▶ **n.** another term for QUAHOG.

hard·ship /ˈhärd,SHip/ ▶ **n.** severe suffering or privation: *intolerable levels of hardship | the shared hardships of wartime.*

hard·stand·ing /ˈhärdˈstandiNG/ ▶ **n.** Brit. ground surfaced with a hard material for parking vehicles on.

hard stuff ▶ **n.** (**the hard stuff**) informal strong liquor.

hard·tack /ˈhärd,tak/ ▶ **n.** hard dry bread or biscuit, esp. as rations for sailors.

hard·top /ˈhärd,täp/ ▶ **n.** a motor vehicle with a rigid roof that in some cases is detachable. ■ a roof of this type.

Har·dwar variant spelling of HARIDWAR.

hard·ware /ˈhärd,we(ə)r/ ▶ **n.** tools, machinery, and other durable equipment: *tanks and other military hardware.* ■ the machines, wiring, and other physical components of a computer or other electronic system. Compare with SOFTWARE. ■ tools, implements, and other items used in home life and activities such as gardening.

hard·wear·ing /ˈhärd,we(ə)riNG/ ▶ **adj.** able to stand much wear: *casual loafer shoe with hardwearing sole and heel.*

hard wheat ▶ **n.** wheat of a variety having a hard grain rich in gluten.

hard-wired /härdˈwīrd/ ▶ **adj.** Electronics involving or achieved by permanently connected circuits. ■ informal genetically determined or compelled: *fear is hardwired in our brain.*
– DERIVATIVES **hard-wire** v., **hard-wir·ing** n.

hard·wood /ˈhärd,wo͝od/ ▶ **n.** **1** the wood from a broadleaved tree (such as oak, ash, or beech) as distinguished from that of conifers. ■ a tree producing such wood.
2 (in gardening) mature growth on shrubs and other plants from which cuttings may be taken.

hard-work·ing (also **hardworking**) ▶ **adj.** (of a person) tending to work with energy and commitment; diligent.

Har·dy[1] /ˈhärdē/, Oliver, see LAUREL AND HARDY.

Har·dy[2], Thomas (1840–1928), English novelist and poet. Much of his work deals with the struggle against the indifferent force that inflicts the sufferings and ironies of life. Notable works: *The Mayor of Casterbridge* (1886), *Tess of the D'Urbervilles* (1891), and *Jude the Obscure* (1896).

har·dy /ˈhärdē/ ▶ **adj.** (**hardier**, **hardiest**) robust; capable of enduring difficult conditions. ■ (of a plant) able to survive outside during winter.
– DERIVATIVES **har·di·ly** /-dəlē/ **adv.**
– ORIGIN Middle English (in the sense 'bold, daring'): from Old French *hardi*, past participle of *hardir* 'become bold,' of Germanic origin; related to HARD.

har·dy an·nu·al ▶ **n.** an annual plant that may be sown in the open ground.

har·dy per·en·ni·al ▶ **n.** **1** a perennial plant that can survive outside unprotected over the winter.
2 informal a thing that recurs continually or at regular intervals: *political humor will always be among the hardy perennials of late-night TV.*

hare /he(ə)r/ ▶ **n.** a fast-running, long-eared mammal that resembles a large rabbit, having long hind legs and occurring typically in grassland or open woodland. ● *Lepus* and other genera, family Leporidae: several species.
■ (also **electric hare**) a dummy hare propelled around the track in greyhound racing.
▶ **v.** [no obj.] chiefly Brit. run with great speed: *he hared off between the trees.*
– PHRASES **run with the hare and hunt with the hounds** Brit. try to remain on good terms with both sides in a conflict or dispute.
– ORIGIN Old English *hara*, of Germanic origin: related to Dutch *haas* and German *Hase*.

hare and hounds ▶ **n.** a game in which a group of people (the "hounds") chases across the countryside another person or group (the "hares"), who leave pieces of paper (the "scent") behind them.

hare·bell /ˈhe(ə)r,bel/ ▶ **n.** a widely distributed bellflower with slender stems and pale blue flowers in late summer. Also called BLUEBELL, esp. in Scotland. ● *Campanula rotundifolia*, family Campanulaceae.
– ORIGIN Middle English: probably so named because it is found growing in places frequented by hares.

harebell

hare·brained /ˈhe(ə)r,brānd/ ▶ **adj.** rash; ill-judged: *a harebrained scheme.*

Ha·re·di /KHäreˈdē, häˈrādē/ ▶ **n.** (pl. **Haredim** /-ˈdēm/) a member of any of various Orthodox Jewish sects characterized by strict adherence to the traditional form of Jewish law and rejection of modern secular culture, many of whom do not recognize the modern state of Israel as a spiritual authority.
– ORIGIN Hebrew, literally 'one who trembles (in awe at the word of God).'

Hare·foot /ˈhe(ə)r,fo͝ot/, Harold, see HAROLD.

Ha·re Krish·na /,härē ˈkrishnə, ,harē/ ▶ **n.** a member of the International Society for Krishna Consciousness, a religious sect based mainly in the US and other Western countries. Its devotees typically wear saffron robes, favor celibacy, practice vegetarianism, and chant mantras based on the name of the Hindu god Krishna. ■ this sect.
– ORIGIN 1960s: Sanskrit, literally 'O Vishnu Krishna,' the words of a devotional chant.

hare·lip /ˈhe(ə)r,lip/ ▶ **n.** offensive another term for CLEFT LIP.
– DERIVATIVES **hare·lipped adj.**
– ORIGIN mid 16th cent.: from a perceived resemblance to the mouth of a hare.

> **USAGE** See usage at CLEFT LIP.

har·em /ˈhe(ə)rəm, ˈhar-/ ▶ **n.** **1** (in former times) the separate part of a Muslim household reserved for wives, concubines, and female servants.
2 the women occupying a harem; the wives (or concubines) of a polygamous man. ■ a group of female animals sharing a single mate. ■ chiefly derogatory a group of women perceived as centering around a particular man: *rich men with their expensive harems of buxom blondes.*
– ORIGIN mid 17th cent.: from Arabic *ḥaram, ḥarīm*, literally 'prohibited, prohibited place' (hence 'sanctuary, women's quarters, women'), from *ḥarama* 'be prohibited.' Compare with HARAM.

hare's-tail (also **hare's-tail grass**) ▶ **n.** a Mediterranean grass with white silky flowering heads and woolly gray-green leaves, widely grown as an ornamental, used esp. when dried. ● *Lagurus ovatus*, family Gramineae.

hare wal·la·by ▶ **n.** a small, agile, fast-moving Australian wallaby with orange rings of fur around the eyes. ● Genera *Lagorchestes* and *Lagostrophus*, family Macropodidae: several species.

Har·gei·sa /härˈgāsə/ (also **Hargeysa**) a city in northwestern Somalia; pop. 407,200 (est. 2004).

Har·greaves /ˈhär,grēvz/, James (1720–78), English inventor who invented the spinning jenny around 1764.

har·i·cot /ˈhari,kō/ (also **haricot bean**) ▶ **n.** **1** a bean of a variety with small white seeds, esp. the kidney bean.
2 the dried seed of this bean used as a vegetable.
– ORIGIN mid 17th cent.: French, perhaps from Aztec *ayacotli.*

har·i·cot vert /ˈve(ə)r(t)/ ▶ **n.** (pl. **haricots verts**) a green bean with a very narrow edible pod and very small seeds.
– ORIGIN French, 'green bean.'

Har·idwar /ˈhär,dwär/ (also **Hardwar**) a city in northern India, in Uttar Pradesh, on the Ganges River; pop. 197,300 (est. 2009). It is a place of Hindu pilgrimage.

Har·i·jan /ˈharə,jan/ ▶ **n.** a member of a hereditary Hindu group of the lowest social and ritual status. See UNTOUCHABLE.
– ORIGIN from Sanskrit *harijana*, literally 'a person dedicated to Vishnu,' from *Hari* 'Vishnu' + *jana* 'person.' The term was adopted and popularized by Gandhi.

ha·ris·sa /həˈrēsə/ ▶ **n.** a hot sauce or paste used in North African cuisine, made from chili peppers, paprika, and olive oil.
– ORIGIN from Arabic.

hark /härk/ ▶ **v.** [no obj.] literary listen: *Hark! He knocks.*
– PHRASAL VERBS **hark back** mention or remember something from the past: *if it was such a rotten vacation, why hark back to it?* [originally a hunting term, used of hounds retracing their steps to find a lost scent.] **hark back to** evoke (an older style or genre): *paintings that hark back to Constable and Turner.*
– ORIGIN Middle English: of Germanic origin; related to German *horchen*, also to HEARKEN.

hark·en ▶ **v.** variant spelling of HEARKEN.

Har·lan /ˈhärlən/ US jurists. **John Marshall Harlan** (1833–1911), US Supreme Court associate justice 1877–1911. A strong defender of civil rights, he declared in *Plessy v. Ferguson* (1896) in a dissenting opinion that the Constitution is "color-blind." His grandson and namesake, **John Marshall Harlan** (1899–1971), generally conservative, was a US Supreme Court associate justice 1955–71.

Har·lem /ˈhärləm/ a district in New York City, north of 96th Street in northeastern Manhattan. It has a large black population and in the 1920s and 1930s was noted for its nightclubs and jazz bands.

Har·lem Ren·ais·sance a literary movement in the 1920s that centered on Harlem and was an early manifestation of black consciousness in the US

The movement included writers such as Langston Hughes and Zora Neale Hurston.

har·le·quin /ˈhärlik(w)ən/ ▶ **n.** **1** (**Harlequin**) a mute character in traditional pantomime, typically masked and dressed in a diamond-patterned costume. ■ historical a stock comic character in Italian *commedia dell'arte*.
2 (also **harlequin duck**) a small duck of fast-flowing streams around the Arctic and North Pacific, the male having mainly gray-blue plumage with bold white markings. ● *Histrionicus histrionicus*, family Anatidae.
▶ **adj.** in varied colors; variegated.
– ORIGIN late 16th cent.: from obsolete French, from earlier *Herlequin* (or *Hellequin*), the name of the leader of a legendary troop of demon horsemen; perhaps ultimately related to Old English *Herla cyning* 'King Herla,' a mythical figure sometimes identified with Woden.

har·le·quin·ade /ˌhärlik(w)əˈnād/ ▶ **n.** historical the section of a traditional pantomime in which Harlequin played a leading role. ■ dated a piece of buffoonery.
– ORIGIN late 18th cent.: from French *arlequinade*, from *(h)arlequin* (see HARLEQUIN).

Har·lin·gen /ˈhärlinjən/ a city in southern Texas, northwest of Brownsville; pop. 64,843 (est. 2008).

har·lot /ˈhärlət/ ▶ **n.** archaic a prostitute or promiscuous woman.
– DERIVATIVES **har·lot·ry** /-trē/ **n.**
– ORIGIN Middle English (denoting a vagabond or beggar, later a lecherous man or woman): from Old French *harlot*, *herlot* 'young man, knave, vagabond.'

Har·low /ˈhärlō/, Jean (1911–37), US movie actress; born *Harlean Carpenter*. Noted for her platinum blonde hair and sex appeal, she had her first big success in the movie *Hell's Angels* (1930). Her six movies with Clark Gable included *Red Dust* (1932) and *Saratoga* (1937).

Jean Harlow

harm /härm/ ▶ **n.** physical injury, esp. that which is deliberately inflicted: *it's fine as long as no one is inflicting harm on anyone else*. ■ material damage: *it's unlikely to do much harm to the engine*. ■ actual or potential ill effect or danger: *I can't see any harm in it*.
▶ **v.** [with obj.] physically injure: *the villains didn't harm him*. ■ damage the health of: *smoking when pregnant can harm your baby*. ■ have an adverse effect on: *this could harm his Olympic prospects*.
– PHRASES **come to no harm** be unhurt or undamaged. **do more harm than good** inadvertently make a situation worse rather than better. **do (someone) no harm** used to indicate that a situation or action will not hurt someone, whether or not it will provide any benefit: *the diet of milk and zwieback certainly did him no harm*. **mean no harm** not intend to cause damage or insult: *this was cruel, but they meant no harm by it*. **no harm done** used to reassure someone that what they have done has caused no real damage. **out of harm's way** in a safe place.
– ORIGIN Old English *hearm* (noun), *hearmian* (verb), of Germanic origin; related to German *Harm* and Old Norse *harmr* 'grief, sorrow.'

har·mat·tan /ˌhärməˈtän/ ▶ **n.** a dry, dusty easterly or northeasterly wind on the West African coast, occurring from December to February.
– ORIGIN late 17th cent.: from Twi *haramata*.

harm·ful /ˈhärmfəl/ ▶ **adj.** causing or likely to cause harm: *shield the planet from harmful cosmic rays* | *sugars that can be harmful to the teeth*.
– DERIVATIVES **harm·ful·ly** **adv.**, **harm·ful·ness** **n.**

harm·less /ˈhärmlis/ ▶ **adj.** not able or likely to cause harm: *the venom of most spiders is harmless to humans*. ■ inoffensive: *as an entertainer, he's pretty harmless*.
– DERIVATIVES **harm·less·ly** **adv.**, **harm·less·ness** **n.**

har·mo·lod·ics /ˌhärməˈlädiks/ ▶ **plural n.** [treated as sing.] a form of free jazz in which musicians improvise simultaneously on a melodic line at various pitches.
– DERIVATIVES **harmolodic** **adj.**
– ORIGIN 1970s: coined by the American saxophonist Ornette Coleman (b. 1930) and said to be a blend of *harmony*, *movement*, and *melodic*.

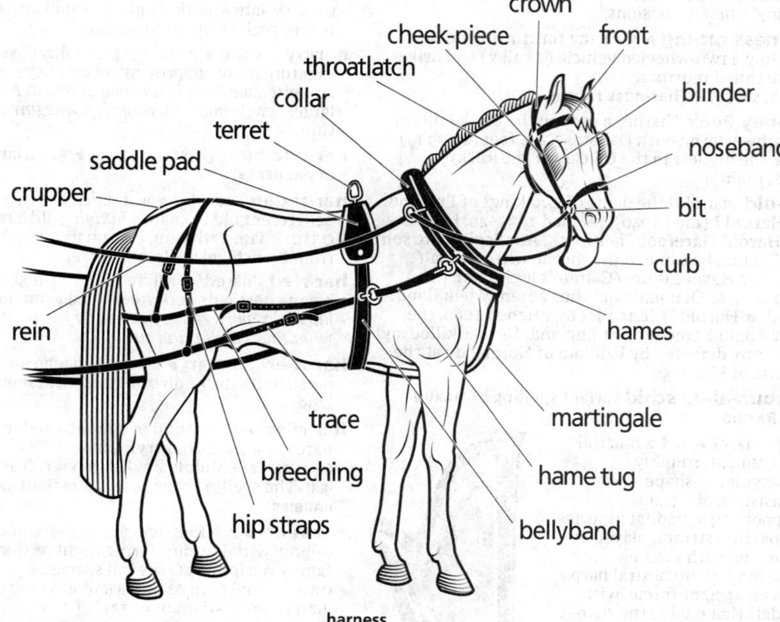

harness

har·mon·ic /härˈmänik/ ▶ **adj.** **1** of, relating to, or characterized by musical harmony: *a basic four-chord harmonic sequence*. ■ Music relating to or denoting a harmonic or harmonics.
2 Mathematics of or relating to a harmonic progression. ■ Physics of or relating to component frequencies of a complex oscillation or wave.
■ Astrology using or produced by the application of a harmonic: *harmonic charts*.
▶ **n.** **1** Music an overtone accompanying a fundamental tone at a fixed interval, produced by vibration of a string, column of air, etc., in an exact fraction of its length. ■ a note produced on a musical instrument as an overtone, e.g., by lightly touching a string while sounding it.
2 Physics a component frequency of an oscillation or wave. ■ Astrology a division of the zodiacal circle by a specified number, used in the interpretation of a birth chart.
– DERIVATIVES **har·mon·i·cal·ly** /-ik(ə)lē/ **adv.**
– ORIGIN late 16th cent. (in the sense 'relating to music, musical'): via Latin from Greek *harmonikos*, from *harmonia* (see HARMONY).

har·mon·i·ca /härˈmänikə/ ▶ **n.** a small rectangular wind instrument with a row of metal reeds along its length, held against the lips and moved from side to side to produce different notes by blowing or sucking. Also called MOUTH ORGAN.
– ORIGIN mid 18th cent.: from Latin, feminine singular or neuter plural of *harmonicus* 'musical' (see HARMONIC).

har·mon·ic mi·nor (also **harmonic minor scale**) ▶ **n.** Music a scale containing a minor third, minor sixth, and major seventh, forming the basis of conventional harmony in minor keys.

har·mon·ic mo·tion ▶ **n.** another term for SIMPLE HARMONIC MOTION.

har·mon·ic pro·gres·sion ▶ **n.** **1** Music a series of chord changes forming the underlying harmony of a piece of music.
2 Mathematics a sequence of quantities whose reciprocals are in arithmetic progression (e.g., 1, $^1/_3$, $^1/_5$, $^1/_7$, etc.).

har·mon·ic se·ries ▶ **n.** **1** Music a set of frequencies consisting of a fundamental and the harmonics related to it by an exact fraction.
2 Mathematics a series of values in harmonic progression.

har·mo·ni·ous /härˈmōnēəs/ ▶ **adj.** tuneful; not discordant: *harmonious music*. ■ forming a pleasing or consistent whole: *the decor is a harmonious blend of traditional and modern*. ■ free from disagreement or dissent: *harmonious relationships*.
– DERIVATIVES **har·mo·ni·ous·ly** **adv.**, **har·mo·ni·ous·ness** **n.**

har·mo·nist /ˈhärmənist/ ▶ **n.** a person skilled in musical harmony.

har·mo·ni·um /härˈmōnēəm/ ▶ **n.** a keyboard instrument in which the notes are produced by air driven through metal reeds by foot-operated bellows.
– ORIGIN mid 19th cent.: from French, from Latin *harmonia* (see HARMONY) or Greek *harmonios* 'harmonious.'

har·mo·nize /ˈhärməˌnīz/ ▶ **v.** [with obj.] add notes to (a melody) to produce harmony. ■ [no obj.] sing in harmony: *she scats and harmonizes simultaneously*. ■ [no obj.] produce a pleasing visual combination: *the containers harmonize in color, texture, and shape with the flowers they display*. ■ make consistent: *the economic group founded to harmonize national development plans*.
– DERIVATIVES **har·mo·ni·za·tion** /ˌhärmənəˈzāsHən/ **n.**
– ORIGIN late 15th cent. (in the sense 'sing or play in harmony'): from French *harmoniser*, from *harmonie* (see HARMONY).

har·mo·ny /ˈhärmənē/ ▶ **n.** (pl. **harmonies**) **1** the combination of simultaneously sounded musical notes to produce chords and chord progressions having a pleasing effect: *four-part harmony in the barbershop style* | *the note played on the fourth beat anticipates the harmony of the following bar*. ■ the quality of forming a pleasing and consistent whole: *delightful cities where old and new blend in harmony*. ■ an arrangement of the four Gospels, or of any parallel narratives, that presents a single continuous narrative text.
2 agreement or concord: *man and machine in perfect harmony*.
– PHRASES **harmony of the spheres** see SPHERE.
– ORIGIN late Middle English: via Old French from Latin *harmonia* 'joining, concord,' from Greek, from *harmos* 'joint.'

har·ness /ˈhärnis/ ▶ **n.** a set of straps and fittings by which a horse or other draft animal is fastened to a cart, plow, etc., and is controlled by its driver. ■ an arrangement of straps for fastening something to a person's body, such as a parachute, or for restraining a young child.
▶ **v.** [with obj.] **1** put a harness on (a horse or other draft animal). ■ (**harness something to**) attach a draft animal to (something) by a harness: *the horse was harnessed to two long shafts*.
2 control and make use of (natural resources), esp. to produce energy: *attempts to harness solar energy* | figurative *projects that harness the creativity of those living in the ghetto*.
– PHRASES **in harness** (of a horse or other animal) used for driving or draft work. ■ in the routine of daily work: *a man who died in harness far beyond the normal age of retirement*. ■ working closely with someone to achieve something: *local and central government should work in harness*.
– DERIVATIVES **har·ness·er** **n.**

h

– ORIGIN Middle English: from Old French *harneis* 'military equipment,' from Old Norse, from *herr* 'army' + *nest* 'provisions.'

har·ness rac·ing ▶ n. racing for trotting horses pulling a two-wheeled vehicle (a sulky) and driver. Also called TROTTING.
– DERIVATIVES **har·ness race** n.

Har·ney Peak /'härnē/ a peak in the Black Hills of southwestern South Dakota, 7,242 feet (2,209 m) tall, the highest in the US east of the Rocky Mountains.

Har·old /'harəld/ the name of two kings of England. ■ **Harold I** (died 1040), reigned 1035–40; known as **Harold Harefoot** /'her,fo͝ot/ . An illegitimate son of Canute, he came to the throne when his half-brother **Hardecanute** (Canute's legitimate heir) was king of Denmark and thus absent when Canute died. ■ **Harold II** (*c.*1019–66), reigned 1066, the last Anglo-Saxon king of England. He was killed and his army defeated by William of Normandy at the Battle of Hastings.

Ha·roun-al-Ra·schid variant spelling of HARUN AR-RASHID.

harp /härp/ ▶ n. **1** a musical instrument, roughly triangular in shape, consisting of a frame supporting a graduated series of parallel strings, played by plucking with the fingers. The modern orchestral harp has an upright frame, with pedals that enable the strings to be retuned to different keys.
2 another term for HARMONICA: *Papa had been teaching him to play the blues harp.* [short for *mouth harp.*]
3 (also **harp shell** or **harp snail**) a marine mollusk that has a large vertically ribbed shell with a wide aperture, found chiefly in the Indo-Pacific. ● Family Harpidae, class Gastropoda.

harp 1

▶ v. [no obj.] **1** talk or write persistently and tediously on a particular topic: *guys who are constantly **harping on about** the war.*
2 archaic play on a harp.
– ORIGIN Old English *hearpe*, of Germanic origin; related to Dutch *harp* and German *Harfe*.

Harp·er /'härpər/, Stephen Joseph (1959–), Canadian Conservative statesman; prime minister since 2006.

harp·er /'härpər/ ▶ n. a musician, esp. a folk musician, who plays a harp.

Har·pers Fer·ry /'härpərz/ a small town in far northeastern West Virginia, at the junction of the Potomac and Shenandoah rivers. It is noted for a raid in October 1859 in which John Brown and a group of abolitionists captured a Federal arsenal located here.

harp·ist /'härpist/ ▶ n. a musician who plays a harp.

Har·poc·ra·tes /här'päkrə,tēz/ Greek name for HORUS.

har·poon /,här'po͞on/ ▶ n. a barbed spearlike missile attached to a long rope and thrown by hand or fired from a gun, used for catching whales and other large sea creatures.
▶ v. [with obj.] spear (something) with a harpoon.
– DERIVATIVES **har·poon·er** n.
– ORIGIN early 17th cent. (denoting a barbed dart or spear): from French *harpon*, from *harpe* 'dog's claw, clamp,' via Latin from Greek *harpē* 'sickle.'

har·poon gun ▶ n. a type of gun used for firing harpoons.

harp seal ▶ n. a slender North Atlantic seal that typically has a dark harp-shaped mark on its gray back. ● *Pagophilus groenlandicus*, family Phocidae.

harp shell ▶ n. see HARP (sense 3 of the noun).

harp·si·chord /'härpsi,kôrd/ ▶ n. a keyboard instrument with horizontal strings that run perpendicular to the keyboard in a long tapering case and are plucked by points of quill, leather, or plastic operated by depressing the keys. It is used chiefly in European classical music of the 16th to 18th centuries.
– DERIVATIVES **harp·si·chord·ist** /-ist/ n.
– ORIGIN early 17th cent.: from obsolete French *harpechorde*, from late Latin *harpa* 'harp' + *chorda* 'string' (the insertion of the letter *s* being unexplained).

harp snail ▶ n. see HARP (sense 3 of the noun).

har·py /'härpē/ ▶ n. (pl. **harpies**) Greek & Roman Mythology a rapacious monster described as having a woman's head and body and a bird's wings and claws or depicted as a bird of prey with a woman's face. ■ a grasping, unpleasant woman.
– ORIGIN late Middle English: from Latin *harpyia*, from Greek *harpuiai* 'snatchers.'

har·py ea·gle ▶ n. a large crested eagle of tropical rain forests, often preying on monkeys. ● Family Accipitridae: *Harpia harpyja* of South America, the largest eagle, and *Harpyopsis novaeguineae* of New Guinea.

har·que·bus /'(h)ärk(w)əbəs/ ▶ n. variant spelling of ARQUEBUS.

har·ri·dan /'haridn/ ▶ n. a strict, bossy, or belligerent old woman: *a bullying old harridan.*
– ORIGIN late 17th cent. (originally slang): perhaps from French *haridelle* 'old horse.'

har·ried /'harēd/ ▶ adj. feeling strained as a result of having demands persistently made on one; harassed: *harried reporters are frequently forced to invent what they cannot find out.*

har·ri·er[1] /'harēər/ ▶ n. a person who engages in persistent attacks on others or incursions into their land.

har·ri·er[2] ▶ n. a hound of a breed used for hunting hares. ■ a cross-country runner.
– ORIGIN late Middle English *hayrer*, from HARE + -ER[1]. The spelling change was due to association with HARRIER[1].

har·ri·er[3] ▶ n. a long-winged, slender-bodied bird of prey with low quartering flight. ● Genus *Circus*, family Accipitridae: several species.
– ORIGIN mid 16th cent. (as *harrower*): from *harrow* 'harry, rob' (variant of HARRY). The spelling change in the 17th cent. was due to association with HARRIER[1].

har·ri·er hawk ▶ n. an African bird of prey with a bare yellow face, resembling a goshawk but flying like a harrier. ● Genus *Polyboroides*, family Accipitridae: two species, in particular *P. typus*.

Har·ri·man /'harəmən/, Averell (1891–1986), US diplomat and financier; full name *William Averell Harriman*. The chairman of the board of the Union Pacific Railroad 1932–46, he was US secretary of commerce 1946–48 and governor of New York 1955–59. He also served as ambassador to the former Soviet Union 1943–46, to Britain 1946, and as ambassador-at-large 1968–69.

Har·ris /'harəs/, Joel Chandler (1848–1908), US writer. He is best known for his Brer Rabbit and Brer Fox stories as told by the fictional Uncle Remus.

Har·ris·burg /'harəs,bərg/ the capital of Pennsylvania, in the southeastern central part of the state, on the Susquehanna River; pop. 47,148 (est. 2008). The nearby nuclear power station at Three Mile Island suffered a serious accident in 1979.

Har·ri·son[1] /'harəsən/, Benjamin (1833–1901), 23rd president of the US 1889–93; the grandson of William Henry Harrison. An Indiana Republican, he served as a US senator 1881–87. During his administration, Oklahoma was settled and the way was paved for the annexation of Hawaii. Due to deterioration of the economy and labor unrest, he was not re-elected.

Benjamin Harrison

Har·ri·son[2], George (1943–2001), English musician and songwriter. He was the lead guitarist of the Beatles, for which he occasionally wrote songs, including "Something" (1969). His interest in India was reflected in his solo career after the group's breakup in 1970.

Har·ri·son[3], William Henry (1773–1841), 9th president of the US, 1841; the grandfather of Benjamin Harrison. As a Whig from Ohio, he became a member of the US House of Representatives 1817–19 and of the US Senate 1825–28. Already a military hero, having led the defeat of the Indians at the Battle of Tippecanoe in 1811 and of Indian chief Tecumseh in 1813, he was a popular candidate for the presidency but served only 32 days before he died of pneumonia.

William Henry Harrison

Har·ri·son·burg /'harəsən,bərg/ a commercial and academic city in northern Virginia, in the Shenandoah Valley; pop. 44,015 (est. 2008).

Har·ris's hawk (also **Harris hawk**) ▶ n. a large chocolate-brown buteo with chestnut shoulder patches and a conspicuous white rump and tail band. Popular with falconers, it occurs in arid country from the southwestern US to South America and frequently nests in tall cacti. ● *Parabuteo unicinctus*, family Accipitridae.

Har·ris tweed ▶ n. trademark handwoven tweed made in the Outer Hebrides in Scotland, esp. on the island of Lewis and Harris.

Har·rods·burg /'harədz,bərg/ a historic city in central Kentucky, the first English settlement (1774) west of the Allegheny Mountains; pop. 8,192 (est. 2008).

Har·ro·vi·an /hə'rōvēən/ ▶ n. a past or present member of Harrow School.
– ORIGIN early 19th cent.: from modern Latin *Harrovia* 'Harrow' + -AN.

har·row /'harō/ ▶ n. an implement consisting of a heavy frame set with teeth or tines that is dragged over plowed land to break up clods, remove weeds, and cover seed.
▶ v. [with obj.] **1** draw a harrow over (land).
2 cause distress to: *Todd could take it, whereas I'm harrowed by it.*
– DERIVATIVES **har·row·er** n.
– ORIGIN Middle English: from Old Norse *herfi*; obscurely related to Dutch *hark* 'rake.'

har·row·ing /'harōiNG/ ▶ adj. acutely distressing: *a harrowing film about racism and violence.*
– DERIVATIVES **har·row·ing·ly** adv.

Har·row·ing of Hell (in medieval Christian theology) the defeat of the powers of evil and the release of its victims by the descent of Christ into hell after his death.
– ORIGIN Middle English: *harrowing* from *harrow*, by-form of the verb HARRY.

Har·row School /'harō/ a boys' preparatory school in northwest London, founded under Queen Elizabeth I in 1571.

har·rumph /hə'rəmf/ ▶ v. [no obj.] clear the throat noisily. ■ grumpily express dissatisfaction or disapproval: *skeptics tend to harrumph at case histories like this.*
▶ n. a noisy clearing of the throat. ■ a grumpy expression of dissatisfaction or disapproval.
– ORIGIN 1930s: imitative.

har·ry /'harē/ ▶ v. (**harries, harrying, harried**) [with obj.] persistently carry out attacks on (an enemy or an enemy's territory). ■ persistently harass: *he bought the house for Jenny, whom he harries into marriage.*
– ORIGIN Old English *herian, hergian*, of Germanic origin, probably influenced by Old French *harier*, in the same sense.

harsh /härsH/ ▶ adj. **1** unpleasantly rough or jarring to the senses: *drenched in a harsh white neon light* | *harsh guttural shouts.*
2 cruel or severe: *a time of harsh military discipline.* ■ (of a climate or conditions) difficult to survive in; hostile: *the harsh environment of the desert.* ■ (of reality or a fact) grim and unpalatable: *the harsh realities of the world news.* ■ having an undesirably strong effect: *she finds soap too harsh and drying.*
– DERIVATIVES **harsh·en** /-SHən/ v., **harsh·ly** adv., **harsh·ness** n.
– ORIGIN Middle English: from Middle Low German *harsch* 'rough,' literally 'hairy,' from *haer* 'hair.'

hars·let /'härslit/ ▶ n. variant spelling of HASLET.

Hart[1] /härt/, Frederick E. (1943–99), US sculptor. He sculpted and cast in bronze the *Three Soldiers* (or *Three Fighting Men*) statue (1984) that stands at the Vietnam Veterans Memorial in Washington, DC. His work also includes the front entrance to the National Cathedral that was completed and dedicated in 1990.

Hart[2], Lorenz (Milton) (1895–1943), US lyricist. His collaborations with composer Richard Rodgers include the scores for the Broadway shows *Babes in Arms* (1937), *The Boys from Syracuse* (1938), and *Pal Joey* (1940). His songs include "Blue Moon" (1934) and "My Funny Valentine" (1937).

Hart[3], Moss (1904–61), US playwright and director. His collaborations with George S. Kaufman include the plays *You Can't Take It with You* (1936) and *The Man Who Came to Dinner* (1939). He also wrote the movie script for *Gentlemen's Agreement* (1947).

hart /härt/ ▶ **n.** an adult male deer, esp. a red deer over five years old.
– ORIGIN Old English *heorot*, *heort*, of Germanic origin; related to Dutch *hert* and German *Hirsch*.

Harte /härt/, Bret (1836–1902), US short-story writer and poet; full name *Francis Bret Harte*. He is chiefly remembered for his stories about life in a California gold-mining town. Notable works: *The Luck of Roaring Camp and Other Sketches* (1870) and *Tales of the Argonauts* (1875).

har·te·beest /'härt(ə),bēst/ ▶ **n.** a large African antelope with a long head and sloping back, related to the gnus. ● Genera *Alcelaphus*, *Damaliscus*, and *Sigmoceros*, family Bovidae: three or four species, in particular the **red hartebeest** (*A. buselaphus*), which typically has a reddish-brown coat.
– ORIGIN late 18th cent.: from South African Dutch, from Dutch *hert* 'hart' + *beest* 'beast.'

Hart·ford /'härtfərd/ the capital of Connecticut, in the center of the state, on the Connecticut River; pop. 124,062 (est. 2008).

harts·horn /'härts,hôrn/ (also **spirit of hartshorn**) ▶ **n.** archaic aqueous ammonia solution used as smelling salts, formerly prepared from the horns of deer.
– ORIGIN Old English *heortes horn* (see **HART**, **HORN**).

hart's tongue (also **hart's tongue fern**) ▶ **n.** a common European fern whose long, narrow undivided fronds are said to resemble the tongues of deer. ● *Phyllitis* (or *Asplenium*) *scolopendrium*, family Aspleniaceae.

har·um-scar·um /,he(ə)rəm 'ske(ə)rəm/ ▶ **adj.** reckless; impetuous: *she shall be frightened out of her wits by your harum-scarum ways.*
▶ **n.** a reckless or impetuous person.
– ORIGIN late 17th cent. (as an adverb): reduplication based on **HARE** and **SCARE**.

Ha·run ar-Ra·shid /hä'ro͞on är rä'sнēd/ (also **Haroun-al-Raschid** /äl/) (763–809), fifth Abbasid caliph of Baghdad 786–809.

ha·rus·pex /hə'rəs,peks, 'harə,speks/ ▶ **n.** (pl. **haruspices** /hə'rəspə,sēz/) (in ancient Rome) a religious official who interpreted omens by inspecting the entrails of sacrificial animals.
– DERIVATIVES **ha·rus·pi·cy** /hə'rəspəsē/ **n.**
– ORIGIN Latin, from an unrecorded element meaning 'entrails' (related to Sanskrit *hirā* 'artery') + *-spex* (from *specere* 'look at').

Har·vard clas·si·fi·ca·tion /'härvərd/ ▶ **n.** Astronomy a system of classification of stars based on their spectral types, the chief classes (O, B, A, F, G, K, M) forming a series from hot bluish-white stars to cool dull red stars.
– ORIGIN 1960s: named after the observatory at **HARVARD UNIVERSITY**, where it was devised.

Har·vard com·ma ▶ **n.** another term for **SERIAL COMMA**.
– ORIGIN a characteristic of the house style of *Harvard* University Press.

Har·vard U·ni·ver·si·ty an Ivy League university in Cambridge, Massachusetts, founded in 1636. It is the oldest American university.
– ORIGIN named after John *Harvard* (1607–38), an English settler who bequeathed his library and half his estate to the university.

har·vest /'härvist/ ▶ **n.** the process or period of gathering in crops: *helping with the harvest.* ■ the season's yield or crop: *a poor harvest.* ■ a quantity of animals caught or killed for human use: *a limited harvest of wild mink.* ■ the product or result of an action: *in terms of science, Apollo yielded a meager harvest.*
▶ **v.** [with obj.] gather (a crop) as a harvest: (as noun **harvesting**) *after harvesting, most of the crop is stored in large buildings.* ■ catch or kill (animals) for human consumption or use. ■ remove (cells, tissue, or an organ) from a person or animal for transplantation or experimental purposes.
– DERIVATIVES **har·vest·a·ble** **adj.**, **har·vest·er** **n.**
– ORIGIN Old English *hærfest* 'autumn,' of Germanic origin; related to Dutch *herfst* and German *Herbst*, from an Indo-European root shared by Latin *carpere* 'pluck' and Greek *karpos* 'fruit.'

har·ves·ter ant ▶ **n.** an ant that gathers and stores seeds and grain as a communal food source for the colony. ● *Messor* and other genera, family Formicidae.

har·vest home ▶ **n.** the gathering in of the final part of the year's harvest. ■ a festival marking the end of the harvest period.

har·vest·man /'härvəstmən/ ▶ **n.** (pl. **harvestmen**) another term for **DADDY LONGLEGS** (sense 1).

har·vest mite ▶ **n.** another term for **CHIGGER** (sense 1).

har·vest moon ▶ **n.** the full moon that is seen nearest to the time of the autumnal equinox.

har·vest mouse ▶ **n.** **1** a nocturnal mouse found in North and Central America. ● Genus *Reithrodontomys*, family Muridae: several species. **2** a small northern Eurasian mouse with a prehensile tail, nesting among the stalks of growing grains and other vegetation. ● *Micromys minutus*, family Muridae.

Har·vey, William (1578–1657), English physician, who first described how blood circulates.

Har·vey Wall·bang·er /'härvē 'wôl,baNGər/ ▶ **n.** a cocktail made from vodka or gin, orange juice, and Galliano.

Ha·ry·a·na /,härē'änə/ a state in northern India; capital, Chandigarh. It was formed in 1966, largely from Hindi-speaking parts of the former state of Punjab.

harz·burg·ite /'härtsbər,gīt/ ▶ **n.** Geology a plutonic rock of the peridotite group consisting largely of orthopyroxene and olivine.
– ORIGIN late 19th cent.: from *Harzburg*, the name of a town in Germany, + **-ITE[1]**.

Harz Moun·tains /härts/ a range of mountains in central Germany, the highest of which is the Brocken.

has /haz/ third person singular present of **HAVE**.

has-been ▶ **n.** informal, derogatory a person or thing considered to be outmoded or no longer of any significance: *a political has-been* | [as modifier] *a has-been film star.*

hash[1] /hasн/ ▶ **n.** a dish of cooked meat cut into small pieces and cooked again, usually with potatoes. ■ a finely chopped mixture: *a hash of raw tomatoes, chilies, and coriander.* ■ a mixture of jumbled incongruous things; a mess.
▶ **v.** [with obj.] **1** make (meat or other food) into a hash. ■ chop (meat or vegetables).
2 (**hash something out**) come to agreement on something after lengthy and vigorous discussion: *they went to the diner to hash out ideas.*
– PHRASES **make a hash of** informal make a mess of; bungle: *listening to other board members make a hash of things.* **settle someone's hash** informal deal with and subdue someone in no uncertain manner. **sling hash** see **SLING[1]**.
– ORIGIN late 16th cent. (as a verb): from French *hacher*, from *hache* (see **HATCHET**).

hash[2] ▶ **n.** informal short for **HASHISH**.

hash[3] (also **hash sign**) ▶ **n.** chiefly Brit. the sign *#*.
– ORIGIN 1980s: probably from **HATCH[3]**, altered by folk etymology.

> **USAGE** The symbol #, called **hash** in British English, has different names, some of them potentially confusing. In the US, it is referred to as either the **number sign** (when used in contexts such as *question #2*) or the **pound sign** (when used as a symbol for pounds of weight: *2# of sugar*). The technical name for it is the **octothorp**.

hash browns (also **hashed browns**) ▶ **plural n.** a dish of cooked potatoes, typically with onions added, that have been chopped into small pieces and fried until brown.

Hash·e·mite /'hasнə,mīt/ ▶ **n.** a member of an Arab princely family claiming descent from Hashim, great-grandfather of Muhammad.
▶ **adj.** of or relating to this family.

Hash·e·mite King·dom of Jor·dan official name for **JORDAN[1]** (sense 1).

hash house ▶ **n.** informal a cheap restaurant.

Ha·shi·mo·to's dis·ease /,hasнi'mōtōz/ ▶ **n.** an autoimmune disease causing chronic inflammation and consequential failure of the thyroid gland.
– ORIGIN 1930s: named after Hakaru *Hashimoto* (1881–1934), Japanese surgeon.

hash·ish /'ha,sнēsн/ ▶ **n.** an extract of the cannabis plant, containing concentrations of the psychoactive resins.
– ORIGIN late 16th cent.: from Arabic *ḥašīš* 'dry herb, powdered hemp leaves.'

hash mark ▶ **n.** **1** a service stripe worn on the left sleeve of an enlisted person's uniform to indicate three years of service in the army or four years in the navy. ■ a similar stripe on any uniform.
2 Football one of a series of marks made along parallel lines that delineate the middle of the field, used to spot the ball after a play ends outside these lines.
3 the symbol #.

hash·tag /'hasнtag/ ▶ **n.** (on social networking websites such as Twitter) a word or phrase preceded by a hash or pound sign (#) and used to identify messages on a specific topic.

Ha·sid /кнä'sēd, 'кнäsid, 'häsid/ (also **Chasid**, **Chassid**, or **Hassid**) ▶ **n.** (pl. **Hasidim** /,кнäsē'dēm, hä'sēdim/) **1** a member of a strictly orthodox Jewish sect in Palestine in the 3rd and 2nd centuries BC that opposed Hellenizing influences on their faith and supported the Maccabean revolt.
2 an adherent of Hasidism.
– DERIVATIVES **Ha·sid·ic** /кнä'sedik, häsēdik/ **adj.**
– ORIGIN from Hebrew *ḥāsīd* 'pious.'

Has·i·dism /'hasi,dizəm/ (also **Chasidism**, **Chassidism**, or **Hassidism**) ▶ **n.** an influential mystical Jewish movement founded in Poland in the 18th century in reaction to the rigid academicism of rabbinical Judaism. The movement declined sharply in the 19th century, but fundamentalist communities developed from it, and Hasidism is still a force in Jewish life, particularly in Israel and New York.

has·let /'haslət, 'hāz-/ (also **harslet**) ▶ **n.** a cold meat preparation consisting of chopped or minced pork offal compressed into a loaf before being cooked.
– ORIGIN late Middle English (originally denoting meat for roasting): from Old French *hastelet*, diminutive of *haste* 'roast meat, spit,' probably of Germanic origin and related to Dutch *harst* 'sirloin.'

h

Has·mo·ne·an /,hazmə'nēən/ ▶ **adj.** of or relating to the Jewish dynasty established by the Maccabees.
▶ **n.** a member of this dynasty.
– ORIGIN from modern Latin *Asmonaeus* (from Greek *Asamonaios*, the grandfather of Mattathias, head of the Maccabees in the 2nd cent. BC) + **-AN**.

has·n't /'haznt/ ▶ **contraction** has not.

hasp /hasp/ ▶ **n.** a slotted hinged metal plate that forms part of a fastening for a door or lid and is fitted over a metal loop and secured by a pin or padlock. ■ a similar metal plate on a trunk or suitcase with a projecting piece that is secured by the lock.

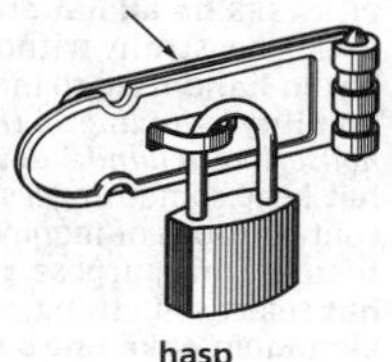
hasp

▶ **v.** [with obj.] archaic lock (a door, window, or lid) by securing the hasp over the loop of the fastening.
– ORIGIN Old English *hæpse*, *hæsp*, of Germanic origin; related to Dutch *haspel* and German *Haspe*.

Has·sid ▶ **n.** variant spelling of **HASID**.

Has·sid·ism ▶ **n.** variant spelling of **HASIDISM**.

has·si·um /'hasēəm/ ▶ **n.** the chemical element of atomic number 108, a very unstable element made by high-energy atomic collisions. (Symbol: **Hs**) See also **HAHNIUM**.
– ORIGIN modern Latin, from Latin *Hassias* 'Hesse' (the German state); it was discovered in Darmstadt in 1984.

has·sle /'hasəl/ informal ▶ **n.** irritating inconvenience: *the hassle of losing a high security key* | *traveling can be a hassle.* ■ deliberate harassment: *if they give you any hassle, just tell them it's for me.* ■ a disagreement; a quarrel: *an election-year hassle with farmers.*
▶ **v.** [with obj.] harass; pester: *squeegee men who hassle drivers for change at stoplights.*
– ORIGIN late 19th cent. (originally dialect in the sense 'hack or saw at'): of unknown origin, perhaps a blend of **HAGGLE** and **TUSSLE**.

has·sock /'hasək/ ▶ **n.** **1** a thick, firmly padded cushion, in particular: ■ a footstool. ■ chiefly Brit. a cushion for kneeling on in church.
2 a firm clump of grass or matted vegetation in marshy or boggy ground.
– ORIGIN Old English *hassuc* (sense 2), of unknown origin.

hast /hast/ archaic second person singular present of **HAVE**.

has·tate /'ha,stāt/ ▶ **adj.** Botany (of a leaf) having a narrow triangular shape like that of a spearhead.
– ORIGIN late 18th cent.: from Latin *hastatus*, from *hasta* 'spear.'

haste /hāst/ ▶ **n.** excessive speed or urgency of movement or action; hurry: *working with feverish haste* | *I write in haste.*

▶ **v.** archaic term for HASTEN.
– PHRASES **make haste** dated hurry; hasten: *I make haste to seal this.* **more haste, less speed** proverb you make better progress with a task if you don't try to do it too quickly.
– ORIGIN Middle English: from Old French *haste* (noun), *haster* (verb), of Germanic origin.

has·ten /ˈhāsən/ ▶ **v.** [no obj., with infinitive] be quick to do something: *he hastened to refute the assertion.* ■ [with adverbial of direction] move or travel hurriedly: *we hastened back to Paris.* ■ [with obj.] cause (something) to happen sooner than it otherwise would: *a move that could hasten peace talks.*
– ORIGIN mid 16th cent.: extended form of HASTE, on the pattern of verbs in -EN[1].

hast·i·ly /ˈhāstəlē/ ▶ **adv.** with excessive speed or urgency; hurriedly: *he hastily changed the subject | maybe I acted too hastily.*

Has·tings, Bat·tle of a decisive battle that took place in 1066 just north of the town of Hastings, East Sussex. William the Conqueror defeated the forces of the Anglo-Saxon king Harold II; Harold died in the battle, leaving the way open for the Norman Conquest of England.

hast·y /ˈhāstē/ ▶ **adj.** (**hastier, hastiest**) done or acting with excessive speed or urgency; hurried: *a hasty attempt to defuse the situation | hasty decisions.* ■ acting with with excessive speed or insufficient consideration: *don't be too* **hasty** *in criticizing a colleague.* ■ archaic quick-tempered.
– DERIVATIVES **hast·i·ness** **n.**
– ORIGIN Middle English: from Old French *hasti, hastif,* from *haste* (see HASTE).

hast·y pud·ding ▶ **n.** a mush containing cornmeal or (in Britain) wheat flour stirred to a thick batter in boiling milk or water.

hat /hat/ ▶ **n.** a shaped covering for the head worn for warmth, as a fashion item, or as part of a uniform. ■ used to refer to a particular role or occupation of someone who has more than one: *wearing her scientific hat, she is director of a pharmacology research group.*
– PHRASES **be all hat and no cattle** informal tend to talk boastfully without acting on one's words. **hat in hand** used to indicate an attitude of humility: *standing on the stoop of his ex-wife's house, hat in hand.* **keep something under one's hat** keep something a secret. **pass the hat** collect contributions of money from a number of people for a specific purpose. **pick something out of a hat** select something, esp. the winner of a contest, at random. **take one's hat off to** (or **hats off to**) used to state one's admiration for (someone who has done something praiseworthy): *I take my hat off to anyone who makes it work | hats off to emergency services for prompt work in the wake of the storms.* **talk through one's hat** see TALK. **throw one's hat in** (or **into**) **the ring** express willingness to take up a challenge, esp. to enter a political race.
– DERIVATIVES **hat·ful** /-ˌfo͝ol/ **n.** (pl. **hatfuls**), **hat·less adj.**, **hat·ted adj.** [in combination] *a white-hatted cowboy.*
– ORIGIN Old English *hætt,* of Germanic origin; related to Old Norse *hǫttr* 'hood,' also to HOOD[1].

hat·band /ˈhatˌband/ ▶ **n.** a decorative ribbon encircling a hat, held in position above the brim.

hat·box /ˈhatˌbäks/ ▶ **n.** a large cylindrical box used to protect a hat when being transported or stored.

hatch[1] /hacн/ ▶ **n.** an opening of restricted size allowing for passage from one area to another, in particular: ■ a door in an aircraft, spacecraft, or submarine. ■ an opening in the deck of a boat or ship leading to the cabin or a lower level, esp. a hold: *a cargo hatch.* ■ an opening in a ceiling leading to a loft. ■ an opening in a kitchen wall for serving or selling food through: *a service hatch.* ■ the rear door of a hatchback car. ■ short for HATCHBACK.
– PHRASES **down the hatch** informal used in a toast; drink up.
– ORIGIN Old English *hæcc* (denoting the lower half of a divided door), of Germanic origin; related to Dutch *hek* 'paling, screen.'

hatch[2] ▶ **v. 1** [no obj.] (of a young bird, fish, or reptile) emerge from its egg: *ten little chicks* **hatched out**. ■ (of an egg) open and produce a young animal: *eggs need to be put in a warm place to hatch.* ■ [with obj.] incubate (an egg): *the eggs are best hatched under broody hens or in incubators.* ■ [with obj.] cause (a young animal) to emerge from its egg: *our penguins were hatched and hand-reared here.*
2 [with obj.] conspire to devise (a plot or plan): *the little plot that you and Sylvia* **hatched up** *last night.*
▶ **n.** a newly hatched brood: *a hatch of mayflies.*
– ORIGIN Middle English *hacche;* related to Swedish *häcka* and Danish *hække.*

hatch[3] ▶ **v.** [with obj.] (in fine art and technical drawing) shade (an area) with closely drawn parallel lines: (as noun **hatching**) *the miniaturist's use of hatching and stippling.*
– ORIGIN late 15th cent. (in the sense 'inlay with strips of metal'): from Old French *hacher,* from *hache* (see HATCHET).

hatch·back /ˈhacнˌbak/ ▶ **n.** a car with a door across the full width at the back end that opens upward to provide easy access for loading.

hat·check /ˈhatˌcнek/ ▶ **adj.** of or employed in a checkroom for hats, coats, and other personal items.

hatch·el /ˈhacнəl/ ▶ **n.** another term for HACKLE (sense 3 of the noun).
▶ **v.** another term for HACKLE.
– ORIGIN Middle English *hechele,* related to HOOK.

hatch·er·y /ˈhacнərē/ ▶ **n.** (pl. **hatcheries**) a place where the hatching of fish or poultry eggs is artificially controlled for commercial purposes.

hatch·et /ˈhacнit/ ▶ **n.** a small ax with a short handle for use in one hand.
– ORIGIN Middle English: from Old French *hachette,* diminutive of *hache* 'ax,' from medieval Latin *hapia,* of Germanic origin.

hatch·et-faced ▶ **adj.** informal with a narrow face and sharp features.

hatch·et·fish /ˈhacнitˌfisн/ ▶ **n.** (pl. **same** or **hatchetfishes**) a deep-bodied laterally compressed tropical freshwater fish of the New World. It is able to fly short distances above the surface of the water by beating its broad pectoral fins. ● Family Gasteropelecidae: three genera, in particular *Gasteropelecus,* and several species.

hatch·et job ▶ **n.** informal a fierce attack on someone or their work, esp. in print: *the author's attempted hatchet job on the judge was totally unjustified and irresponsible.*

hatch·et man ▶ **n.** informal a person employed to carry out controversial or disagreeable tasks, such as the dismissal of a number of people from employment. ■ a person who writes fierce attacks on others or their work.
– ORIGIN late 19th cent.: figuratively, from an early use denoting a hired Chinese assassin.

hatch·ling /ˈhacнliNG/ ▶ **n.** a young animal that has recently emerged from its egg.

hatch·ment /ˈhacнmənt/ ▶ **n.** a large tablet, typically diamond-shaped, bearing the coat of arms of someone who has died, displayed in their honor.
– ORIGIN early 16th cent.: probably from obsolete French *hachement,* from Old French *acesmement* 'adornment.'

hatch·way /ˈhacнˌwā/ ▶ **n.** an opening or hatch, esp. in a ship's deck.

hate /hāt/ ▶ **v.** [with obj.] feel intense or passionate dislike for (someone): *the boys hate each other | he was particularly hated by the extreme right.* ■ have a strong aversion to (something): *he hates flying |* [with infinitive] *I'd hate to live there.* ■ [with infinitive] used politely to express one's regret or embarrassment at doing something: *I hate to bother you.* ■ [no obj.] (**hate on**) informal express strong dislike for; criticize or abuse: *I can't hate on them for trying something new.*
▶ **n.** intense or passionate dislike: *feelings of hate and revenge.* ■ [as modifier] denoting hostile actions motivated by intense dislike or prejudice: *a hate campaign.*
– DERIVATIVES **hat·a·ble** /ˈhātəbəl/ (also **hateable**) **adj.**
– ORIGIN Old English *hatian* (verb), *hete* (noun), of Germanic origin; related to Dutch *haten* (verb) and German *hassen* (verb), *Hass* 'hatred.'

hate crime ▶ **n.** a crime motivated by racial, sexual, or other prejudice, typically one involving violence.

hate·ful /ˈhātfəl/ ▶ **adj.** arousing, deserving of, or filled with hatred: *hateful letters of abuse that had come unsigned.* ■ informal very unpleasant: *I don't have to stay in this hateful place.*
– DERIVATIVES **hate·ful·ly adv.**, **hate·ful·ness n.**

hate mail ▶ **n.** hostile and sometimes threatening letters sent, usually anonymously, to an individual or group.

hat·er /ˈhātər/ ▶ **n.** a person who greatly dislikes a specified person or thing: *a man hater | he's not a hater of modern music.* ■ informal a negative or critical person: *she found it difficult to cope with the haters.*

hath /hatн/ archaic third person singular present of HAVE.

Hath·a·way /ˈhatнəˌwā/, Anne (*c.*1557–1623), the wife of Shakespeare, whom she married in 1582.

hath·a yo·ga /ˈhätнə/ ▶ **n.** a yoga system of physical exercises and breathing control.
– ORIGIN from Sanskrit *haṭha* 'force' and YOGA.

Hath·or /ˈhatнôr/ Egyptian Mythology a sky goddess, the patron of love and joy, represented variously as a cow, with a cow's head or ears, or with a solar disk between a cow's horns.

hat·pin /ˈhatˌpin/ ▶ **n.** a long pin, typically with an ornamental head, that holds a woman's hat in position by securing it to her hair.

hat·rack /ˈhatˌrak/ ▶ **n.** a tall freestanding post fitted with large hooks for hanging hats on.

ha·tred /ˈhātrid/ ▶ **n.** intense dislike or ill will: *racial hatred | his murderous hatred of his brother.*
– ORIGIN Middle English: from HATE + *-red* (from Old English *rǣden* 'condition').

Hat·shep·sut /hatˈsнepˌso͞ot/ (died 1482 BC), Egyptian queen of the 18th dynasty, reigned *c.*1503–1482 BC. On the death of her husband, Tuthmosis II, she became regent for her nephew, Tuthmosis III. She then named herself pharaoh and was often portrayed as male.

hat·stand /ˈhatˌstand/ ▶ **n.** British term for HATRACK.

hat·ter /ˈhatər/ ▶ **n.** a person who makes and sells hats.

Hat·ter·as, Cape /ˈhatərəs/ a peninsula in eastern North Carolina, often called "the Graveyard of the Atlantic" because of the treacherous waters around.

Hat·ties·burg /ˈhatēzˌbərg/ an industrial, commercial, and academic city in southeastern Mississippi; pop. 51,993 (est. 2008).

hat trick ▶ **n.** three successes of the same kind, esp. consecutive ones within a limited period: *the band completes the trilogy, making for a dubious musical hat trick.* ■ (chiefly in ice hockey or soccer) the scoring of three goals in a game by one player. ■ (in cricket) the taking of three wickets by the same bowler with successive balls.
– ORIGIN late 19th cent.: originally referring to the club presentation of a new hat (or some equivalent) to a bowler taking three wickets successively.

hau·berk /ˈhôbərk/ ▶ **n.** historical a piece of armor originally covering only the neck and shoulders but later consisting of a full-length coat of mail or military tunic.
– ORIGIN Middle English: from Old French *hauberc, hausberc,* originally denoting protection for the neck, of Germanic origin.

haugh·ti·ness /ˈhôtēnis/ ▶ **n.** the appearance or quality of being arrogantly superior and disdainful: *her air of haughtiness.*

haugh·ty /ˈhôtē/ ▶ **adj.** (**haughtier, haughtiest**) arrogantly superior and disdainful: *a look of haughty disdain | a haughty aristocrat.*
– DERIVATIVES **haugh·ti·ly** /-təlē/ **adv.**
– ORIGIN mid 16th cent.: extended form of obsolete *haught,* earlier *haut,* from Old French, from Latin *altus* 'high.'

haul /hôl/ ▶ **v. 1** [with obj.] (of a person) pull or drag with effort or force: *he hauled his bike out of the shed |* [no obj., with adverbial] *she* **hauled on** *the reins.* ■ (**haul oneself**) propel or pull oneself with difficulty: *he hauled himself along the cliff face.* ■ informal force (someone) to appear for reprimand or trial: *they will be hauled into court next week.*
2 [with obj.] (of a vehicle) pull (an attached trailer or load) behind it: *the train was hauling a cargo of liquid chemicals.* ■ transport in a truck or cart: *Bennie hauls trash in North Philadelphia.*
3 [no obj.] (esp. of a sailing ship) make an abrupt change of course.
▶ **n. 1** a quantity of something that was stolen or is possessed illegally: *they escaped with a haul of antiques.* ■ the number of points, medals, or titles won by a person or team in a sporting event or over a period. ■ a number of fish caught.
2 a distance to be traversed: *the thirty-mile haul to Tallahassee.* See also LONG HAUL, SHORT HAUL.
– PHRASES **haul ass** informal move or leave fast. **haul off** informal leave; depart. ■ withdraw a little in preparation for some action: *he hauled off and smacked the kid.*
– ORIGIN mid 16th cent. (originally in the nautical sense 'trim sails for sailing closer to the wind'): variant of HALE[2].

haul·age /ˈhôlij/ ▶ **n.** the commercial transport of goods: *road haulage.* ■ a charge for such transport.

haul·er /ˈhôlər/ ▶ **n.** a person or company employed in the transport of goods or materials by road: *private haulers collect the bagged or bundled waste.* ■ a truck used for the transport of goods or materials.

haul·ier /ˈhôlēər/ ▶ **n.** British term for HAULER.

haulm /hôm/ chiefly Brit. ▶ **n.** a stalk or stem. ■ the stalks or stems collectively of peas, beans, or potatoes without the pods or tubers, as used for bedding: *potato haulm.*
– ORIGIN Old English *healm, halm,* of Germanic origin; related to Dutch *halm* and German *Halm,* from an Indo-European root shared by Latin *culmus* 'stalk' and Greek *kalamos* 'reed.'

haunch /hôncн, häncн/ ▶ **n. 1** a buttock and thigh considered together, in a human or animal. ■ the

leg and loin of an animal, such as a deer, as food: *haunch of caribou meat.*
2 Architecture the side of an arch, between the crown and the pier.
– PHRASES **sit on one's haunches** squat with the haunches resting on the backs of the heels.
– ORIGIN Middle English: from Old French *hanche*, of Germanic origin.

haunt /hônt, hänt/ ▶ **v.** [with obj.] (of a ghost) manifest itself at (a place) regularly: *a gray lady who haunts the chapel.* ■ (of a person) frequent (a place): *he haunts used book stores.* ■ be persistently and disturbingly present in (something): *cities haunted by the shadow of cholera.* ■ be persistently in the mind of (someone): *the sight haunted me for years.*
▶ **n.** a place frequented by a specified person or group of people: *I revisited my old haunts | Greenwich Village has been home to a number of literary haunts.*
– DERIVATIVES **haunt·er n.**
– ORIGIN Middle English (in the sense 'frequent (a place)'): from Old French *hanter*, of Germanic origin; distantly related to HOME.

haunt·ed /ˈhôntid, ˈhän-/ ▶ **adj.** (of a place) frequented by a ghost: *it looked like a classic haunted mansion.* ■ having or showing signs of mental anguish or torment: *the hollow cheeks, the haunted eyes.*

haunt·ing /ˈhônting, ˈhän-/ ▶ **adj.** poignant and evocative; difficult to ignore or forget: *the melodies were elaborate and of haunting beauty.*
– DERIVATIVES **haunt·ing·ly adv.**

Haupt·mann /ˈhoupt,män/, Gerhart (1862–1946), German playwright. An early pioneer of naturalism, he is known for *Before Sunrise* (1889) and *The Ascension of Joan* (1893). Nobel Prize for Literature (1912).

hau·ri·ent /ˈhôrēənt/ ▶ **adj.** [postpositive] Heraldry (of a fish or marine creature) depicted swimming vertically, typically with the head upward.
– ORIGIN late 16th cent.: from Latin *haurient-* 'drawing in (air, water, etc.),' from the verb *haurire*.

Hau·sa /ˈhousə, ˈhouzə/ ▶ **n.** (pl. **same** or **Hausas**)
1 a member of a people of northern Nigeria and adjacent regions.
2 the Chadic language of this people, spoken mainly in Nigeria and Niger, and widely used as a lingua franca in parts of West Africa.
▶ **adj.** of or relating to this people or their language.
– ORIGIN the name in Hausa.

haus·frau /ˈhous,frou/ ▶ **n.** a German housewife. ■ informal a woman regarded as overly domesticated or efficient.
– ORIGIN late 18th cent.: from German, from *Haus* 'house' + *Frau* 'woman, wife.'

haus·tel·lum /hôˈsteləm/ ▶ **n.** (pl. **haustella** /hôˈstelə/) Zoology the sucking organ or proboscis of an insect or crustacean.
– DERIVATIVES **haus·tel·late** /hôˈstelit, ˈhôstə,lāt/ **adj.**
– ORIGIN early 19th cent.: modern Latin diminutive of *haustrum* 'scoop,' from *haust-* 'drawn in,' from the verb *haurire*.

haus·to·ri·um /hôˈstôrēəm/ ▶ **n.** (pl. **haustoria** /hôˈstôrēə/) Botany a slender projection from the root of a parasitic plant, such as a dodder, or from the hyphae of a parasitic fungus, enabling the parasite to penetrate the tissues of its host and absorb nutrients from it.
– DERIVATIVES **haus·to·ri·al** /hôstôrēəl/ **adj.**
– ORIGIN late 19th cent.: modern Latin, from Latin *haustor* 'thing that draws in,' from the verb *haurire*.

haut·boy /ˈ(h)ō,boi/ (also **hautbois** /-,boi/) ▶ **n.** archaic form of OBOE.
– ORIGIN mid 16th cent.: from French *hautbois*, from *haut* 'high' + *bois* 'wood.'

haute /ōt/ (or **haut**) ▶ **adj.** fashionably elegant or high-class.

haute bour·geoi·sie /,ōt bōōzhwäˈzē/ ▶ **n.** (**the haute bourgeoisie**) [treated as sing. or pl.] the upper middle class.
– ORIGIN late 19th cent.: French, literally 'high bourgeoisie.'

haute cou·ture /,ōt ,kōōˈtŏŏr/ ▶ **n.** the designing and making of high-quality fashionable clothes by leading fashion houses, esp. to order. ■ clothes of this kind.
– ORIGIN early 20th cent.: French, literally 'high dressmaking.'

haute cui·sine /,ōt ,kwəˈzēn/ ▶ **n.** the preparation and cooking of high-quality food following the style of traditional French cuisine. ■ food produced in such a way.
– ORIGIN early 20th cent.: French, literally 'high cooking.'

haute é·cole /,ōt eˈkôl/ ▶ **n.** the art or practice of advanced classical dressage.
– ORIGIN mid 19th cent.: French, literally 'high school.'

Haute-Nor·man·die /,ōt ,nôrmänˈdē/ a region in northern France, on the coast of the English Channel.

hau·teur /hōˈtər/ ▶ **n.** haughtiness of manner; disdainful pride.
– ORIGIN French, from *haut* 'high.'

haut monde /ō ˈmônd, ˈmänd/ ▶ **n.** (**the haut monde**) fashionable society.
– ORIGIN mid 19th cent.: French, literally 'high world.'

Ha·va·na[1] /həˈvanə/ the capital of Cuba, on the northern coast; pop. 2,148,132 (2008). It was founded in 1515 by Diego Velázquez de Cuéllar. Spanish name LA HABANA.

Ha·van·a[2] /həˈvanə, həˈvänə/ ▶ **n.** a cigar made in Cuba or from Cuban tobacco.

Ha·va·su, Lake /ˈhavə,sōō/ a reservoir and recreational site on the Colorado River between Arizona and southeastern California.

Hav·da·lah /,hävdäˈlä, hävˈdôlə/ (also **Habdalah**) ▶ **n.** a Jewish religious ceremony or formal prayer marking the end of the Sabbath.
– ORIGIN from Hebrew *habdālāh* 'separation, division.'

have /hav/ ▶ **v.** (**has** /haz, (h)əz/, **having, had** /had, (h)əd/) [with obj.] **1** (also **have got**) possess, own, or hold: *he had a new car and a boat | have you got a job yet? | I don't have that much money on me | he's got the equipment with him.* ■ possess or be provided with (a quality, characteristic, or feature): *the ham had a sweet, smoky flavor | she's got blue eyes | the house has gas heat.* ■ (**have oneself**) informal provide or indulge oneself with (something): *he had himself two highballs.* ■ be made up of; comprise: *in 1989 the party had 10,000 members.* ■ used to indicate a particular relationship: *he's got three children | do you have a client named Pedersen?* ■ be able to make use of (something available or at one's disposal): *how much time have I got for the presentation?* ■ have gained (a qualification): *he's got a BA in English.* ■ possess as an intellectual attainment; know (a language or subject): *he knew Latin and Greek; I had only a little French.*
2 experience; undergo: *I went to a few parties and had a good time | I was having difficulty in keeping awake.* ■ (also **have got**) suffer from (an illness, ailment, or disability): *I've got a headache.* ■ (also **have got**) let (a feeling or thought) come into one's mind; hold in the mind: *he had the strong impression that someone was watching him | we've got a few ideas we're kicking around | I've no doubt he's as busy as I am.* ■ [with past participle] experience or suffer the specified action happening or being done to (something): *she had her bag stolen.* ■ cause (someone or something) to be in a particular state or condition: *I want to have everything ready in good time | I had the TV on with the sound turned down.* ■ (also **have got**) informal have put (someone) at a disadvantage in an argument (said either to acknowledge that one has no answer to a point or to show that one knows one's opponent has no answer): *you've got me there; I've never given the matter much thought.* ■ [with past participle] cause (something) to be done for one by someone else: *it is advisable to have your carpet laid by a professional.* ■ tell or arrange for something to be done: *she had her long hair cut | always having the builders in to do something.* ■ (usu. **be had**) informal cheat or deceive (someone): *I realized I'd been had.* ■ vulgar slang engage in sexual intercourse with (someone).
3 (**have to do something** or **have got to do something**) be obliged or find it necessary to do the specified thing: *you don't have to accept this situation | we've got to plan for the future.* ■ need or be obliged to do (something): *he's got a lot to do.* ■ be strongly recommended to do something: *if you think that place is great, you have to try our summer house.* ■ be certain or inevitable to happen or be the case: *there has to be a catch.*
4 perform the action indicated by the noun specified (used esp. in spoken English as an alternative to a more specific verb): *he had a look around | the color green has a restful effect.* ■ organize and bring about: *are you going to have a party?* ■ eat or drink: *I'll have the vegetable plate.* ■ give birth to or be due to give birth to: *she's going to have a baby.*
5 (also **have got**) show (a personal attribute or quality) by one's actions or attitude: *he had little patience with technological gadgetry | if you've got the drive to finish your degree.* ■ [often in imperative] exercise or show (mercy, pity, etc.) toward another person: *God have mercy on me!* ■ [with negative] not accept; refuse to tolerate: *I can't have you insulting Tom like that.*
6 (also **have got**) place or keep (something) in a particular position: *Mary had her back to me | I soon had the trout in a net.* ■ hold or grasp (someone or something) in a particular way: *he had me by the throat.*
7 be the recipient of (something sent, given, or done): *she had a letter from Mark.* ■ take or invite into one's home so as to provide care or entertainment, esp. for a limited period: *we're having the children for the weekend.*
▶ **auxiliary v.** used with a past participle to form the perfect, pluperfect, and future perfect tenses, and the conditional mood: *I have finished | he had asked her | she will have left by now | I could have helped, had I known | "Have you seen him?" "Yes, I have."*
▶ **n.** (**the haves**) informal people with plenty of money and possessions: *an increasing gap between the haves and have-nots.*
– PHRASES **have a care** (or **an eye**, etc.) see CARE, EYE, etc. **have got it bad** informal be very powerfully affected emotionally, esp. by love. ■ be in a situation where one is treated badly or exploited: *if you think you've got it bad now, how would you like to be paid to collect pebbles?* **have had it** informal **1** be in a very poor condition; be beyond repair or past its best: *the car had had it.* ■ be extremely tired: *tomorrow she would drive on through Germany, but for today, she'd had it.* ■ have lost all chance of survival: *looks like your plant's had it.* **2** be unable to tolerate someone or something any longer: *I've had it with him—he's humiliated me once too often!* **have it 1** [with clause] express the view that (used to indicate that the speaker is reporting something that they do not necessarily believe to be fact): *rumor had it that although he lived in a derelict house, he was really very wealthy.* **2** win a decision, esp. after a vote: *the ayes have it.* **3** have found the answer to something: *"I have it!" Rosa exclaimed.* **have it away** (or **off**) Brit. vulgar slang have sexual intercourse. **have it both ways** see BOTH. **have it coming** deserve punishment or downfall. **have (got) it in for** informal feel a particular dislike of (someone) and behave in a hostile manner toward them. **have (got) it in one (to do something)** informal have the capacity or potential (to do something): *everyone thinks he has it in him to produce a literary classic.* **have it out** informal attempt to resolve a contentious matter by confronting someone and engaging in a frank discussion or argument: *give her the chance of a night's rest before you have it out with her.* **have a nice day** used to express good wishes when parting. **have (got) nothing on** informal **1** be not nearly as good as (someone or something), esp. in a particular respect: *bright though his three sons were, they had nothing on Sally.* **2 have nothing** (or **something**) **on someone** know nothing (or something) discreditable or incriminating about someone: *I am not worried—they've got nothing on me.* **have nothing to do with** see DO[1]. **have one too many** see MANY. **have (got) something to oneself** be able to use, occupy, or enjoy something without having to share it with anyone else. **have —— to do with** see DO[1].
– PHRASAL VERBS **have at** attempt or attack forcefully or aggressively. **have someone on** Brit. informal try to make someone believe something that is untrue, esp. as a joke: *that's just too neat—you're having me on.* **have (got) something on 1** be wearing something: *she had a blue dress on.* **2** Brit. be committed to an arrangement: *I've got a lot on at the moment.* **have something out** undergo an operation to extract the part of the body specified: *she had her wisdom teeth out.*
– ORIGIN Old English *habban*, of Germanic origin; related to Dutch *hebben* and German *haben*, also probably to HEAVE.

USAGE 1 Have and have got: there is a great deal of debate on the difference between these two forms. A traditional view is that **have got** is chiefly British, but not correct in formal writing, while **have** is chiefly American. Actual usage is more complicated: **have got** is in fact also widely used in US English. In both US and British usage, **have** is more formal than **have got**, and it is more appropriate in writing to use constructions such as **don't have** (or **do not have**) rather than **haven't got**. See also usage at GOTTEN. **2** A common mistake is to write the word **of** instead of **have** or **'ve**: *I could of told you that* instead of *I could've told you that.* The reason for the mistake is that the pronunciation of **have** in unstressed contexts is the same as that of **of**, and the two words are confused when it comes to writing them down. The error was recorded as early as 1837 and, although common, is unacceptable in standard English. **3** Another controversial issue is the insertion of **have** where it is superfluous, as, for example, *I might have missed it if you **hadn't have** pointed it out* (rather than the standard ... *if you **hadn't** pointed it out*). This construction has been around since at least the 15th century, but only where a hypothetical situation is presented (e.g., statements starting with **if**). More recently, there has been speculation among grammarians and linguists that this insertion of **have** may represent a kind of subjunctive and is actually making a useful distinction in the language. However, it is still regarded as an error in standard English.

Ha·vel /ˈhävəl/, Václav (1936–), Czech playwright and statesman; president of Czechoslovakia 1989–92 and of the Czech Republic 1993–2003. His plays, such as *The Garden Party* (1963), were critical of totalitarianism, and he was twice imprisoned as a dissident.

ha·ve·li /ˌhəvəˈlē/ ▶ **n.** (pl. **havelis**) Indian a mansion.
– ORIGIN via Hindi from Arabic *havelī*.

have·lock /ˈhavˌläk/ ▶ **n.** a cloth covering for a military cap that extends downward to protect the neck from sun and weather.
– ORIGIN mid 19th cent.: named after Sir Henry *Havelock* (1795–1857), an English general who served in India.

havelock

ha·ven /ˈhāvən/ ▶ **n.** a place of safety or refuge: *a haven for wildlife.* ■ an inlet providing shelter for ships or boats; a harbor or small port.
– ORIGIN late Old English *hæfen*, from Old Norse *hǫfn*; related to Dutch *haven*, German *Hafen* 'harbor.'

have-nots ▶ **plural n.** (usu. **the have-nots**) informal economically disadvantaged people: *lack of access to information will perpetuate the division between the haves and have-nots.*

have·n't /ˈhavənt/ ▶ **contraction** have not.

ha·ver /ˈhāvər/ ▶ **v.** [no obj.] Scottish talk foolishly; babble: *Tom havered on.* ■ Brit. act in a vacillating or indecisive manner: (as noun **havering**) *most people giggle at their havering and indecision.*
▶ **n.** (also **havers**) Scottish foolish talk; nonsense.
– ORIGIN early 18th cent.: of unknown origin.

Ha·ver·hill /ˈhāv(ə)rəl/ an industrial city in northeastern Massachusetts, on the Merrimack River; pop. 61,275 (est. 2008).

hav·er·sack /ˈhavərˌsak/ ▶ **n.** a small, sturdy bag carried on the back or over the shoulder, used esp. by soldiers and hikers.
– ORIGIN mid 18th cent.: from French *havresac*, from obsolete German *Habersack*, denoting a bag used by soldiers to carry oats as horse feed, from dialect *Haber* 'oats' + *Sack* 'sack, bag.'

Ha·ver·sian ca·nal /həˈvərZHən/ ▶ **n.** Anatomy any of the minute tubes that form a network in bone and contain blood vessels.
– ORIGIN mid 19th cent.: named after Clopton *Havers* (1650–1702), English anatomist.

Hav·li·cek /ˈhavləˌCHek/, John (1940–), US basketball player; nickname **Hondo**. He played for the Boston Celtics 1962–78, during which time they won eight NBA titles 1963–66, 1968–69, 1974, 1976. Basketball Hall of Fame (1983).

hav·oc /ˈhavək/ ▶ **n.** widespread destruction: *the hurricane ripped through Florida, causing havoc.* ■ great confusion or disorder: *schoolchildren wreaking havoc in the classroom.*
▶ **v.** (**havocs, havocking, havocked**) [with obj.] archaic lay waste to; devastate.
– PHRASES **play havoc with** completely disrupt; cause serious damage to: *shift work plays havoc with the body clock.*
– ORIGIN late Middle English: from Anglo-Norman French *havok*, alteration of Old French *havot*, of unknown origin. The word was originally used in the phrase *cry havoc* (Old French *crier havot*) 'to give an army the order *havoc*,' which was the signal for plundering.

haw¹ /hô/ ▶ **n.** the red fruit of the hawthorn.
– ORIGIN Old English *haga*, of Germanic origin; probably related to HEDGE (compare with Dutch *haag* 'hedge').

haw² ▶ **n.** the third eyelid or nictitating membrane in certain mammals, esp. dogs and cats.
– ORIGIN late Middle English (denoting a discharge from the eye): of unknown origin.

haw³ ▶ **v.** see HEM AND HAW at HEM².

Ha·wai·i /həˈwī(y)ē, -ˈwä(y)ē, -ˈwô(y)ē/ a state in the US that is comprised of a group of islands in the North Pacific Ocean, about 3,000 miles (4,830 km) west of mainland US; pop. 1,288,198 (est. 2008); capital, Honolulu (on Oahu); statehood, Aug. 21, 1959 (50). First settled by Polynesians, Hawaii was discovered by Captain James Cook in 1778. It was annexed by the US in 1898 and is a popular vacation destination. Former name SANDWICH ISLANDS. ■ the largest island in the state of Hawaii.

Ha·wai·i-A·leu·tian Stand·ard Time (abbr.: **HST**) ▶ **n.** the standard time in a zone including the Hawaiian Islands and the western Aleutian Islands, specifically. ■ standard time based on the mean solar time at longitude 150° W., ten hours behind GMT. Also called **Hawaiian Standard Time**.

Ha·wai·ian /həˈwīən, -ˈwoi-ən/ ▶ **n. 1** a native or inhabitant of Hawaii.
2 the Austronesian language of Hawaii.
▶ **adj.** of or relating to Hawaii, its people, or their language. ■ Geology relating to or denoting a type of volcanic eruption in which fluid basaltic lava is produced, as is typical of volcanoes in Hawaii.

Ha·wai·ian goose ▶ **n.** another term for NENE.

Ha·wai·ian gui·tar ▶ **n.** a steel-stringed guitar in which a characteristic glissando effect is produced by sliding a metal bar along the strings as they are plucked.

Ha·wai·ian hon·ey·creep·er ▶ **n.** see HONEYCREEPER (sense 2).

ha·wa·la /həˈwälə, -ˈvälə/ ▶ **n.** a system or agency for transferring money traditionally used in the Muslim world, whereby the money is paid to an agent who then instructs a remote associate to pay the final recipient.
– ORIGIN from Arabic, literally 'change, transform.'

haw·finch /ˈhôˌfinCH/ ▶ **n.** a large Old World finch with a massive bill for cracking open cherry stones and other hard seeds. ● Genus *Coccothraustes*, family Fringillidae: three species, in particular the widespread *C. coccothraustes*.
– ORIGIN late 17th cent.: from HAW¹ + FINCH.

hawk¹ /hôk/ ▶ **n. 1** a diurnal bird of prey with broad rounded wings and a long tail, typically taking prey by surprise with a short chase. Compare with FALCON. ● Family Accipitridae: several genera, esp. *Accipiter*, which includes the Cooper's hawk and goshawk.
■ a bird of prey related to the buteos.
■ Falconry any diurnal bird of prey used in falconry.
2 a person who advocates an aggressive or warlike policy, esp. in foreign affairs. Compare with DOVE¹ (sense 2).
▶ **v.** [no obj.] **1** (of a person) hunt game with a trained hawk: *he spent the afternoon hawking.*
2 (of a bird or dragonfly) hunt on the wing for food: *swifts hawked low over the water* | [with obj.] *dragonflies hawk and feed on flies.*
– PHRASES **have eyes like a hawk** miss nothing of what is going on around one. **watch someone like a hawk** keep a vigilant eye on someone, esp. to check that they do nothing wrong.
– DERIVATIVES **hawk·ish adj.**, **hawk·ish·ly adv.**, **hawk·ish·ness n.**, **hawk·like** /-ˌlīk/ **adj.**
– ORIGIN Old English *hafoc*, *heafoc*, of Germanic origin; related to Dutch *havik* and German *Habicht*.

hawk² ▶ **v.** [with obj.] carry around and offer (goods) for sale, typically advertising them by shouting: *street traders were hawking costume jewelry.*
– ORIGIN late 15th cent.: back-formation from HAWKER¹.

hawk³ ▶ **v.** [no obj.] clear the throat noisily: *he hawked and spat into the flames.* ■ [with obj.] (**hawk something up**) bring phlegm up from the throat.
– ORIGIN late 16th cent.: probably imitative.

hawk⁴ ▶ **n.** a plasterer's square board with a handle underneath for carrying plaster or mortar.
– ORIGIN late Middle English: of unknown origin.

hawk ea·gle ▶ **n.** a small tropical eagle with broad wings and a long tail, and typically a crest. ● Genera *Spizaetus* and *Spizastur*, family Accipitridae: several species.

Hawke Bay a bay on the eastern coast of North Island, in New Zealand.

hawk·er¹ /ˈhôkər/ ▶ **n.** a person who travels around selling goods, typically advertising them by shouting.
– ORIGIN early 16th cent.: probably from Low German or Dutch and related to HUCKSTER.

hawk·er² ▶ **n.** a falconer.
– ORIGIN Old English *hafocere*, from *hafoc* 'hawk.'

hawk-eyed ▶ **adj.** having very good eyesight.
■ watching carefully; vigilant: *a hawk-eyed policeman saved the lives of dozens of shoppers.*

Hawk·eye State /ˈhôˌkī/ a nickname for the state of IOWA.

hawk·fish /ˈhôkˌfiSH/ ▶ **n.** (pl. **same** or **hawkfishes**) a small tropical marine fish found chiefly in the Indo-Pacific region. It typically lives in shallow water and adopts a distinctive perching or "hovering" position just above coral. ● Family Cirrhitidae: three genera and several species.

Hawk·ing /ˈhôkiNG/, Stephen (William) (1942–), English theoretical physicist. His main work has been with space-time, quantum mechanics, and black holes. His book *A Brief History of Time* (1988) was a bestseller.

Hawk·ing ra·di·a·tion ▶ **n.** Physics electromagnetic radiation that, according to theory, should be emitted by a black hole. The radiation is due to the black hole capturing one of a particle-antiparticle pair created spontaneously near to the event horizon.

hawk moth (also **hawkmoth**) ▶ **n.** a large swift-flying moth with a stout body and narrow forewings, typically feeding on nectar while hovering. Also called SPHINX. See also HORNWORM.
● Family Sphingidae: several genera and many species.

hawk moth

hawk-nosed ▶ **adj.** (of a person) having a nose that is curved like a hawk's beak.

hawk owl ▶ **n.** a hawklike owl with a small head and long tail, and typically an obscure facial disk.
● Family Strigidae: three genera, including *Ninox* (several species in Asia and Australasia) and *Surnia*, in particular the diurnal *S. ulula* of northern coniferous forests.

Hawks /hôks/, Howard (Winchester) (1896–1977), US movie director, producer, and screenwriter. He wrote and directed the screenplay for his first movie in 1926 and also directed such movies as *The Big Sleep* (1946), *Gentlemen Prefer Blondes* (1953), and *Rio Bravo* (1959).

hawks·beard /ˈhôksˌbērd/ (also **hawk's beard**) ▶ **n.** a plant of the daisy family that resembles a dandelion but has a branched stem with several flowers. ● Genus *Crepis*, family Compositae: several species, including the **western hawksbeard** (*C. occidentalis*), found in the rocky areas of the western and southwestern US, and the **slender hawksbeard** (*C. atribarba*), found in the open areas of western North America.

hawks·bill /ˈhôksˌbil/ (also **hawksbill turtle**) ▶ **n.** a small tropical sea turtle with hooked jaws and overlapping horny plates on the shell, extensively hunted as the traditional source of tortoiseshell.
● *Eretmochelys imbricata*, family Cheloniidae.

hawksbill

hawk·shaw /ˈhôkˌSHô/ ▶ **n.** informal, dated a detective.
– ORIGIN early 20th cent.: from the name of a detective in the play *The Ticket-of-Leave Man* by Tom Taylor (1817–80), English dramatist; also portrayed in the comic strip *Hawkshaw the Detective* by Augustus Charles ("Gus") Mager (1878–1956), American cartoonist.

hawk·weed /ˈhôkˌwēd/ ▶ **n.** a widely distributed plant of the daisy family, typically having small yellow dandelionlike flower heads and often growing as a weed. ● Genus *Hieracium*, family Compositae.
– ORIGIN late Old English, rendering Latin *hieracium*, based on Greek *hierax* 'hawk.'

Ha·worth /ˈhouˌwərTH/, Sir Walter Norman (1883–1950), English organic chemist. A pioneer in carbohydrate chemistry, he was the first person to make a vitamin artificially when he synthesized vitamin C. He shared the 1937 Nobel Prize for Chemistry with Paul Karrer (1889–1971).

hawse /hôz/ ▶ **n.** the part of a ship's bows through which the anchor cables pass. ■ the space between the head of an anchored vessel and the anchors.
– ORIGIN late Middle English *halse*, probably from Old Norse *háls* 'neck, ship's bow.'

haw·se·hole /ˈhôz,hōl/ ▶ **n.** a hole in the deck of a ship through which an anchor cable passes.

hawse·pipe /ˈhôz,pīp/ ▶ **n.** an inclined pipe leading from a hawsehole to the side of a ship, containing the shank of the anchor when the anchor is raised.

haw·ser /ˈhôzər/ ▶ **n.** a thick rope or cable for mooring or towing a ship.
– ORIGIN Middle English: from Anglo-Norman French *haucer*, from Old French *haucier* 'to hoist,' based on Latin *altus* 'high.'

haw·ser-laid ▶ **adj. 1** another term for **CABLE-LAID**.
2 chiefly historical denoting the ordinary type of rope commonly used in ships' rigging, typically made of three left-handed strands twisted together right-handed.

haw·thorn /ˈhô,THôrn/ ▶ **n.** a thorny shrub or tree of the rose family, with white, pink, or red blossoms and small dark red fruits (haws). Native to north temperate regions, it is commonly used for hedges. Also called **MAY²**, **QUICKTHORN**, or **WHITETHORN**. ● Genus *Crataegus*, family Rosaceae: many species, in particular the European **common hawthorn** (*C. monogyna*).
– ORIGIN Old English *hagathorn*, probably meaning literally 'hedge thorn' (see **HAW¹**, **THORN**); related to Dutch *haagdoorn*, German *Hagedorn*.

Haw·thorne¹ /ˈhô,THôrn/ a city in southwestern California, south of Los Angeles; pop. 84,305 (est. 2008).

Haw·thorne² /ˈhô,THôrn/, Nathaniel (1804–64), US novelist and short-story writer. Much of his fiction explores guilt, sin, and morality. Notable works: *The Scarlet Letter* (1850), *The House of Seven Gables* (1851), and *The Marble Faun* (1860).

Haw·thorne ef·fect ▶ **n.** the alteration of behavior by the subjects of a study due to their awareness of being observed.
– ORIGIN 1960s: from *Hawthorne*, the name of one of the Western Electric Company's plants in Chicago, where the phenomenon was first observed in the 1920s.

Hay /hā/, John Milton (1838–1905), US diplomat and writer. He was US ambassador to Great Britain 1897–98, and then, as US secretary of state 1898–1905, he negotiated the Hay–Pauncefote Treaty 1901 that made possible the construction of the Panama Canal.

hay¹ /hā/ ▶ **n.** grass that has been mown and dried for use as fodder.
– PHRASES **hit the hay** informal go to bed. **make hay (while the sun shines)** proverb make good use of an opportunity while it lasts.
– ORIGIN Old English *hēg*, *hīeg*, *hīg*, of Germanic origin; related to Dutch *hooi* and German *Heu*, also to **HEW**.

hay² ▶ **n.** a country dance with interweaving steps similar to a reel. ■ a winding figure in such a dance.
– ORIGIN early 16th cent.: from an obsolete sense 'a kind of dance' of French *haie* 'hedge,' figuratively 'row of people lining the route of a procession.'

hay·box /ˈhā,bäks/ ▶ **n.** historical a box stuffed with hay in which heated food was left to continue cooking.

hay·cock /ˈhā,käk/ ▶ **n.** a conical heap of hay in a field.

Hay·dn /ˈhīdn/, Franz Joseph (1732–1809), Austrian composer. A major exponent of the classical style, he was musical director to the household of Hungary's Prince Esterházy 1761–90. His work includes 104 symphonies, chamber and keyboard music, and the oratorio *The Creation* (1796–98).

Ha·yek /ˈhīək/, Friedrich August von (1899–1992), British economist; born in Austria. Strongly opposed to Keynesian economics, he was a leading advocate of the free market. Nobel Prize for Economics (1974), shared with Gunnar Myrdal.

Hay·el /ˈhī(ə)l/ variant spelling of **HA'IL**.

Hayes¹ /hāz/, Helen (1900–1993), US actress; born Helen Hayes Brown; known as the **First Lady of the American Theater**. Her Broadway career spanned seven decades and included Tony-winning roles in *Happy Birthday* (1946) and *Time Remembered* (1957). She also appeared in movies such as *The Sin of Madelon Claudet* (1932) and *Airport* (1970).

Hayes², Rutherford B(irchard) (1822–93), 19th president of the US 1877–81. A Republican, he served in the US House of Representatives 1865–68 and as governor of Ohio 1868–72 and 1876–77 before succeeding Ulysses S. Grant to the presidency. During his administration, Reconstruction in the South came to an end. His use of federal troops during the railroad strikes of 1877 cost him the popular support of the people.

Rutherford B. Hayes

hay fe·ver ▶ **n.** an allergy caused by pollen or dust in which the mucous membranes of the eyes and nose are itchy and inflamed, causing a runny nose and watery eyes.

hay·field /ˈhā,fēld/ ▶ **n.** a field where hay is being or is to be made.

hay·fork /ˈhā,fôrk/ ▶ **n.** a hand tool for lifting hay; pitchfork. ■ a machine for lifting hay.

hay·ing /ˈhāiNG/ ▶ **n.** the activity of mowing and drying grass to make hay.

hay·lage /ˈhālij/ ▶ **n.** silage made from grass that has been partially dried.
– ORIGIN 1960s: blend of **HAY¹** and **SILAGE**.

hay·loft /ˈhā,lôft/ ▶ **n.** a loft over a stable or barn used for storing hay or straw.

hay·mak·er /ˈhā,mākər/ ▶ **n. 1** a person who is involved in making hay, esp. one who tosses and spreads it to dry after mowing. ■ an apparatus for shaking and drying hay.
2 informal a forceful blow: *he caught him on the side of the head with a stinging haymaker*.
– DERIVATIVES **hay·mak·ing n.**

Hay·mar·ket Square /ˈhā,märkit/ a historic site in Chicago, in Illinois, site of an 1886 bombing during a labor demonstration.

hay·mow /ˈhā,mō/ ▶ **n.** a stack of hay. ■ a part of a barn in which hay is stored.

hay·rick /ˈhā,rik/ ▶ **n.** another term for **HAYSTACK**.

hay·ride /ˈhā,rīd/ ▶ **n.** a ride taken for pleasure in a wagon carrying hay.

hay·seed /ˈhā,sēd/ ▶ **n. 1** grass seed obtained from hay.
2 informal a person from the country, esp. a simple, unsophisticated one.

hay·stack /ˈhā,stak/ ▶ **n.** a packed pile of hay, typically with a pointed or ridged top.

Hay·ward /ˈhāwərd/ a city in north central California, south of Oakland, on San Francisco Bay; pop. 142,061 (est. 2008).

hay·wire /ˈhā,wīr/ ▶ **adj.** informal erratic; out of control: *her imagination had gone haywire*.
– ORIGIN 1920s (originally US): from **HAY¹** + **WIRE**, from the use of hay-baling wire in makeshift repairs.

Hay·worth /ˈhā,wərTH/, Rita (1918–87), US actress and dancer; born *Margarita Carmen Cansino*. She achieved stardom in movie musicals such as *Cover Girl* (1944) before going on to play roles in film noir, notably in *Gilda* (1946) and *The Lady from Shanghai* (1948).

haz·ard /ˈhazərd/ ▶ **n. 1** a danger or risk: *the hazards of smoking*. ■ a potential source of danger: *a fire hazard | a health hazard*. ■ a permanent feature of a golf course that presents an obstruction to playing a shot, such as a bunker or stream.
2 literary chance; probability.
3 a gambling game using two dice, in which the chances are complicated by arbitrary rules.
▶ **v.** [with obj.] **1** venture to say (something): *he hazarded a guess*.
2 put (something) at risk of being lost: *the cargo business is too risky to hazard money on*.
– ORIGIN Middle English (sense 3 of the noun): from Old French *hasard*, from Spanish *azar*, from Arabic *az-zahr* 'chance, luck,' from Persian *zār* or Turkish *zar* 'dice.'

haz·ard light ▶ **n.** each of a pair of flashing lights on a vehicle, warning that it is stationary or unexpectedly slowing down or reversing.

haz·ard·ous /ˈhazərdəs/ ▶ **adj.** risky; dangerous: *we work in hazardous conditions | it is* **hazardous to** *personal safety*.
– DERIVATIVES **haz·ard·ous·ly adv.**, **haz·ard·ous·ness n.**
– ORIGIN mid 16th cent.: from French *hasardeux*, from *hasard* 'chance' (see **HAZARD**).

haze¹ /hāz/ ▶ **n. 1** a slight obscuration of the lower atmosphere, typically caused by fine suspended particles. ■ a tenuous cloud of something such as vapor or smoke in the air: *a faint haze of steam*.
2 [in sing.] a state of mental obscurity or confusion: *through an alcoholic haze*.
– ORIGIN early 18th cent. (originally denoting fog or hoarfrost): probably a back-formation from **HAZY**.

haze² ▶ **v. 1** [with obj.] force (a new or potential recruit to the military, a college fraternity, etc.) to perform strenuous, humiliating, or dangerous tasks: *rookies were mercilessly hazed*.
2 [with obj.] drive (cattle) in a specified direction while on horseback.
– ORIGIN late 17th cent. (originally Scots and dialect in the sense 'frighten, scold, or beat'): perhaps related to obsolete French *haser* 'tease or insult.'

ha·zel /ˈhāzəl/ ▶ **n. 1** a temperate shrub or small tree with broad leaves, bearing prominent male catkins in spring and round hard-shelled edible nuts in autumn. ● Genus *Corylus*, family Betulaceae: several species, in particular the common **Eurasian hazel** (*C. avellana*), formerly widely managed as coppice.
2 a reddish-brown or greenish-brown color, esp. of someone's eyes.
– ORIGIN Old English *hæsel*, of Germanic origin; related to Dutch *hazelaar* 'hazel tree,' *hazelnoot* 'hazelnut,' and German *Hasel*, from an Indo-European root shared by Latin *corylus*.

ha·zel grouse ▶ **n.** a small Eurasian woodland grouse with mainly grayish plumage. ● *Bonasa bonasia*, family Tetraonidae (or Phasianidae).

ha·zel·nut /ˈhāzəl,nət/ ▶ **n.** a round brown hard-shelled nut that is the edible fruit of the hazel.

haz·ing /ˈhāziNG/ ▶ **n.** the imposition of strenuous, often humiliating, tasks as part of a program of rigorous physical training and initiation: *army cadets were hospitalized for injuries caused by hazing*. ■ humiliating and sometimes dangerous initiation rituals, esp. as imposed on college students seeking membership to a fraternity or sorority.

Haz·litt /ˈhazlət/, William (1778–1830), English essayist and critic. Notable works: *Table Talk* (1821) and *The Spirit of the Age* (1825).

ha·zy /ˈhāzē/ ▶ **adj.** (**hazier**, **haziest**) covered by a haze: *the sky was hazy from irrigation evaporation*. ■ vague, indistinct, or ill-defined: *hazy memories | the picture we have of him as a man is extremely hazy*.
– DERIVATIVES **ha·zi·ly** /-zilē/ **adv.**, **ha·zi·ness n.**
– ORIGIN early 17th cent. (in nautical use in the sense 'foggy'): of unknown origin.

haz·zan /KHäˈzän, ˈKHäzən/ ▶ **n.** (pl. **hazzanim** /,KHäzäˈnēm, KHäˈzônim/) another term for **CANTOR** (sense 1).
– ORIGIN mid 17th cent.: from Hebrew *ḥazzān* 'cantor,' possibly from Assyrian *ḥazannu* 'mayor, village headman.'

HB ▶ **abbr.** ■ half board. ■ (also **hb**) hardback. ■ hard black (used in describing a medium grade of pencil lead). ■ the political wing of the Basque separatist organization ETA. [abbreviation of Basque *Herri Batasuna* 'United People.']

Hb ▶ **symbol** hemoglobin.

HBM ▶ **abbr.** Brit. Her or His Britannic Majesty (or Majesty's).

H-bomb ▶ **n.** another term for **HYDROGEN BOMB**.
– ORIGIN 1950s: from **H²** (denoting hydrogen) + **BOMB**.

HBP ▶ **abbr.** Baseball (in box scores, of a batter) hit by a pitch.

HC ▶ **abbr.** ■ Holy Communion. ■ (in the UK) House of Commons. ■ hydrocarbon: *increasing fuel efficiency decreases the levels of HC*.

h.c. ▶ **abbr.** honoris causa.

HCF ▶ **abbr.** Mathematics highest common factor.

HCFC ▶ **abbr.** hydrochlorofluorocarbon.

HCG ▶ **abbr.** human chorionic gonadotropin.

hd. ▶ **abbr.** ■ hand. ■ head.

hdbk. ▶ **abbr.** handbook.

HDD ▶ **abbr.** Computing hard disk drive.

hdkf. ▶ **abbr.** handkerchief.

HDL ▶ **abbr.** high-density lipoprotein.

hdqrs. ▶ **abbr.** headquarters.

HDTV ▶ **abbr.** high-definition television, using more lines per frame to give a sharper image than a conventional television.

hdwe. ▶ **abbr.** hardware.

HE ▶ **abbr.** ■ high explosive. ■ His Eminence. ■ His or Her Excellency.

He ▶ **symbol** the chemical element helium.

he /hē/ ▶ **pron.** [third person singular] used to refer to a man, boy, or male animal previously mentioned or easily identified: *everyone liked my father—he was the perfect gentleman.* ■ used to refer to a person or animal of unspecified sex (in modern use, now chiefly replaced by "he or she" or "they"): *every child needs to know that he is loved.* ■ any person (in modern use, now chiefly replaced by "anyone" or "the person"): *he who is silent consents.*
▶ **n.** [in sing.] a male; a man: *is that a he or a she?* ■ [in combination] male: *a he-goat.*
– ORIGIN Old English *he, hē*, of Germanic origin; related to Dutch *hij*.

> **USAGE** **1** For a discussion of *I am older than* **he** versus *I am older than* **him**, see usage at **PERSONAL PRONOUN** and **THAN**. **2** Until recently, **he** was used to refer to a person of unspecified sex, as in *every child needs to know that* **he** *is loved*, but this is now generally regarded as old-fashioned or sexist. Since the 18th century, **they** has been an alternative to **he** in this sense, where it occurs after an indefinite pronoun such as **everyone** or **someone** (*everyone needs to feel that* **they** *matter*). It is becoming more and more accepted both in speech and in writing, and is used as the norm in this dictionary. Another alternative is **he or she**, though this can become tiresomely long-winded when used frequently. See also usage at **SHE, THEY,** and **EVERYBODY**.

Head /hed/, Edith (1907–81), US costume designer; born *Edith Claire Posener*. She designed wardrobe for more than 400 movies and won eight Academy Awards. Notable movies: *All About Eve* (1950), *Sabrina* (1954), and *The Sting* (1973).

head /hed/ ▶ **n.** **1** the upper part of the human body, or the front or upper part of the body of an animal, typically separated from the rest of the body by a neck, and containing the brain, mouth, and sense organs. ■ the head regarded as the location of intellect, imagination, and memory: *whatever comes into my head.* ■ (**head for**) an aptitude for or tolerance of: *she had a good head for business.* ■ informal a headache, esp. one resulting from intoxication. ■ the height or length of a head as a measure: *a dazzling woman half a head taller than he was.* ■ (**heads**) the obverse side of a coin (used when tossing a coin): *heads or tails?* ■ the antlers of a deer.
2 a thing having the appearance of a head either in form or in relation to a whole, in particular: ■ the cutting, striking, or operational end of a tool, weapon, or mechanism. ■ the flattened or knobbed end of a nail, pin, screw, or match. ■ the ornamented top of a pillar or column. ■ a compact mass of leaves or flowers at the top of a stem, esp. a capitulum: *huge heads of fluffy cream flowers.* ■ the edible leafy part at the top of the stem of such green vegetables as cabbage and lettuce.
3 the front, forward, or upper part or end of something, in particular: ■ the upper end of a table or bed: *he sat down at the head of the cot.* ■ the flat end of a cask or drum. ■ the front of a line or procession. ■ the top of a page. ■ short for **HEADLINE**. ■ the top of a flight of stairs or steps. ■ the source of a river or stream. ■ the end of a lake or inlet at which a river enters. ■ [usu. in place names] a promontory: *Beachy Head.* ■ the top of a ship's mast. ■ the bows of a ship. ■ the foam on top of a glass of beer, or the cream on the top of milk. ■ short for **CYLINDER HEAD**.
4 a person in charge of something; a director or leader: *the head of the Dutch Catholic Church.* ■ Brit. short for **HEADMASTER** or **HEADMISTRESS**.
5 Grammar the word that governs all the other words in a phrase in which it is used, having the same grammatical function as the whole phrase.
6 a person considered as a numerical unit: *they paid fifty dollars a head.* ■ [treated as pl.] a number of cattle or game as specified: *seventy head of dairy cattle.*
7 a component in an audio, video, or information system by which information is transferred from an electrical signal to the recording medium, or vice versa. ■ short for **PRINTHEAD**.
8 a body of water kept at a particular height in order to provide a supply at sufficient pressure: *an 8 m head of water in the shafts.* ■ the pressure exerted by such water or by a confined body of steam: *a good head of steam on the gauge.*
9 Nautical slang a toilet, esp. on a boat or ship.
10 Geology a superficial deposit of rock fragments, formed at the edge of an ice sheet by repeated freezing and thawing and then moved downhill.
▶ **adj.** [attrib.] chief; principal: *the head waiter.*
▶ **v.** [with obj.] **1** be in the leading position on: *the Palm Sunday procession was headed by the crucifer.* ■ be in charge of: *an organizational unit headed by a line manager | she headed up the Centennial program.*
2 give a title or caption to: *an article headed "The Protection of Human Life."* ■ (as adj. **headed**) having a printed heading, typically the name and address of a person or organization: *headed notepaper.*
3 [no obj.] (also **be headed**) move in a specified direction: *he was heading for the exit | we were headed in the wrong direction.* ■ (**head for**) appear to be moving inevitably toward (something, esp. something undesirable): *the economy is heading for recession.* ■ [with obj.] direct or steer in a specified direction: *she headed the car toward them.*
4 Soccer shoot or pass (the ball) with the head: *a corner kick that he headed into the net.*
5 lop off the upper part or branches of (a plant or tree).
6 [no obj.] (of a lettuce or cabbage) form a head.
– PHRASES **be banging** (or **knocking**) **one's head against a brick wall** be doggedly attempting the impossible and suffering in the process. **bang** (or **knock**) **people's heads together** reprimand people severely, esp. in an attempt to stop their arguing. **be hanging over someone's head** (of something unpleasant) threaten to affect someone at any moment. **be heading for a fall** see **FALL**. **be on someone's** (**own**) **head** be someone's sole responsibility. **bite** (or **snap**) **someone's head off** reply sharply and brusquely to someone. (**down**) **by the head** Nautical (of a boat or ship) deeper in the water forward than astern: *the Boy Andrew went down by the head.* **come to a head** reach a crisis: *the violence came to a head with the deaths of six youths.* ■ suppurate; fester: *abscesses should be allowed to come to a head.* **enter someone's head** [usu. with negative] occur to someone: *such an idea never entered my head.* **from head to toe** (or **foot**) all over one's body: *I was shaking from head to toe.* **get one's head around** (or **round**) [usu. with negative] informal understand or come to terms with something: *I just can't get my head around this idea.* **give someone his** (or **her**) **head** allow someone complete freedom of action. **give someone head** vulgar slang perform oral sex on someone. **go to someone's head** (of alcohol) make someone dizzy or slightly drunk. ■ (of success) make someone conceited. **get something into one's** (or **someone's**) **head** come or cause (someone) to realize or understand: *when will you get it into your head that it's the project that counts, not me?* **head of hair** the hair on a person's head, regarded in terms of its appearance or quantity: *he had a fine head of hair.* —— **one's head off** talk, laugh, etc., unrestrainedly: *he was drunk as a skunk and singing his head off.* **head over heels** **1** turning over completely in forward motion, as in a somersault. **2** (also **head over heels in love**) madly in love: *I immediately fell head over heels for Don.* **a head start** an advantage granted or gained at the beginning of something: *our fine traditions give us a head start on the competition.* **heads will roll** people will be dismissed or forced to resign. **head to head** in open, direct conflict or competition: *the governor and the senator went head to head in a spontaneous debate.* **in one's head** by mental process without use of physical aids: *the piece he'd already written in his head.* **keep one's head** remain calm. **keep one's head above water** avoid succumbing to difficulties, typically debt. **keep one's head down** remain inconspicuous in difficult or dangerous times. **lose one's head** lose self-control; panic. **make head or tail** (or **heads or tails**) **of** [usu. with negative] understand at all: *we couldn't make head or tail of his answer.* **off** (or **out of**) **one's head** informal crazy: *my old man's going off his head, you know.* ■ extremely drunk or severely under the influence of drugs. **off the top of one's head** without careful thought or investigation. **over someone's head** **1** (also **above someone's head**) beyond someone's ability to understand: *the discussion was over my head, I'm afraid.* **2** without someone's knowledge or involvement, esp. when they have a right to it: *the deal was struck over the heads of the regions concerned.* ■ with disregard for someone else's (stronger) claim: *his promotion over the heads of more senior colleagues.* **put their** (or **our** or **your**) **heads together** consult and work together: *they forced the major banks to put their heads together to sort it out.* **put something into someone's head** suggest something to someone: *who's being putting ideas into your head?* **take it into one's head to do something** impetuously decide to do something. **turn someone's head** make someone conceited. **turn heads** attract a great deal of attention or interest: *she recently turned heads with a nude scene.*
– PHRASAL VERBS **head someone/something off** intercept and turn aside: *he ran up the road to head off approaching cars.* ■ forestall: *they headed off a fight by ordering further study of both plans.* **head up** Sailing steer toward the wind.
– DERIVATIVES **head·ed adj.** [in combination] *bald-headed men | woolly-headed New Age thinking,* **head·less adj.**
– ORIGIN Old English *hēafod*, of Germanic origin; related to Dutch *hoofd* and German *Haupt*.

-head[1] ▶ **suffix** equivalent to **-HOOD**.
– ORIGIN Middle English *-hed, -hede*.

-head[2] ▶ **comb. form** **1** denoting the front, forward, or upper part or end of a specified thing: *spearhead | masthead.*
2 in nouns used informally to express disparagement of a person: *airhead | dumbhead.*
3 in nouns used informally to denote an addict or habitual user of a specified drug: *crackhead.* ■ in nouns used informally to denote an enthusiast of a particular thing: *a small community of bloggers and webheads.*

head·ache /ˈhed,āk/ ▶ **n.** a continuous pain in the head. ■ informal a thing or person that causes worry or trouble; a problem: *an administrative headache.*
– DERIVATIVES **head·ach·y** /-,ākē/ **adj.**

head·band /ˈhed,band/ ▶ **n.** **1** a band of fabric worn around the head as a decoration or to keep the hair or perspiration off the face.
2 an ornamental strip of colored silk fastened to the top of the spine of a book.

head·bang·er /ˈhed,baNGər/ ▶ **n.** informal a fan or performer of heavy metal music. Also called **METALHEAD**.

head·board /ˈhed,bôrd/ ▶ **n.** an upright panel forming or placed behind the head of a bed.

head·butt ▶ **n.** an aggressive and forceful thrust with the top of the head, esp. into the face or body of another person.
▶ **v.** [with obj.] attack (someone) with such a thrust of the head.

head case ▶ **n.** informal a mentally ill or unstable person.

head·cheese /ˈhed,CHēz/ ▶ **n.** meat from a pig's or calf's head that is cooked and pressed into a loaf with aspic.

head cold ▶ **n.** a common cold characterized by congested nasal passages, sneezing, and headache.

head count ▶ **n.** an instance of counting the number of people present: *a U.S. Marine turns up missing at a head count.* ■ a total number of people, esp. the number of people employed in a particular organization: *you may decide that by reducing your head count you can reach this quarter's goals.*

head·dress /ˈhed,dres/ ▶ **n.** an ornamental covering or band for the head, esp. one worn on ceremonial occasions.

American Indian headdress

head·end /ˈhed,end/ ▶ **n.** a control center in a cable television system where various signals are brought together and monitored before being introduced into the cable network.

head·er /ˈhedər/ ▶ **n.**
1 Soccer a shot or pass made with the head.
2 informal a headlong fall or dive.
3 a brick or stone laid at right angles to the face of a wall. Compare with **STRETCHER** (sense 4).
4 a line or block of text appearing at the top of each page of a book or document. Compare with **FOOTER** (sense 2).
5 (also **header tank**) a raised tank of water maintaining pressure in a plumbing system.

head first ▶ **adj. & adv.** with the head in front of the rest of the body: [as adv.] *she dived head first into the water* | [as attrib. adj.] *a head-first slide.* ■ without sufficient forethought.

head·ful /ˈhed,fo͝ol/ ▶ **n.** **1** a quantity sufficient to cover the head: *a headful of tight curls.*
2 a great amount (of knowledge or information): *a headful of things to worry about.*

head gas·ket ▶ **n.** the gasket that fits between the cylinder head and the cylinders or cylinder block in an internal combustion engine.

head·gear /ˈhed,gi(ə)r/ ▶ **n.** hats, helmets, and other items worn on the head: *protective headgear.* ■ the parts of a harness around a horse's head.

head·hunt·er /ˈhed,həntər/ ▶ **n.** a person who identifies and approaches suitable candidates employed elsewhere to fill business positions: *a headhunter offering you a wonderful new position at a higher salary.* ■ a member of a society that collects the heads of dead enemies as trophies.
– DERIVATIVES **head·hunt v.**, **head·hunt·ing** /-həntiNG/ **n.**

head·ing /ˈhediNG/ ▶ **n.** **1** a title at the head of a page or section of a book: *chapter headings.* ■ a division or section of a subject; a class or category: *this topic falls under four main headings.*

2 a direction or bearing: *he crawled on a heading of 90 degrees until he came to the track.*
3 a horizontal passage made in preparation for building a tunnel. ■ Mining another term for DRIFT (sense 4 of the noun).
4 a strip of cloth at the top of a curtain above the hooks or wire that suspend the curtain.

head·land /ˈhedlənd, ˈhedˌland/ ▶ **n. 1** a narrow piece of land that projects from a coastline into the sea.
2 a strip of land left unplowed at the end of a field.

head·light /ˈhedˌlīt/ (also **headlamp**) ▶ **n.** a powerful light at the front of a motor vehicle or railroad engine.
– PHRASES **like a deer** (or **rabbit**) **in the headlights** used to refer to a state of fear, panic, or confusion so extreme that it is impossible to act or think normally: *faced with too many choices and not enough real information, we are like deer caught in the headlights | his deer-in-the-headlights expression.*

head·line /ˈhedˌlīn/ ▶ **n.** a heading at the top of an article or page in a newspaper or magazine: *a front-page headline.* ■ (**the headlines**) the most important items of news in a newspaper or in a broadcast news bulletin: *issues that are never long out of the headlines.*
▶ **v. 1** [with obj. and complement] provide with a headline: *a feature that was headlined "Invest in Your Future."*
2 [with obj.] appear as the star performer at (a concert): *an acoustic jam headlined by rappers LL Cool J and De La Soul.*

head·lin·er /ˈhedˌlīnər/ ▶ **n.** a performer or act that is the star attraction on a program and typically performs last.

head·lock /ˈhedˌläk/ ▶ **n.** a method of restraining someone by holding an arm firmly around their head, esp. as a hold in wrestling.

head·long /ˈhedˌlôNG, -ˌläNG/ ▶ **adv. & adj. 1** [as adv.] with the head foremost: *he fell headlong into the tent.*
2 in a rush; with reckless haste: [as attrib. adj.] *a headlong dash through the house* | [as adv.] *those who rush headlong to join in the latest craze.*
– ORIGIN Middle English *headling* (from HEAD + the adverbial suffix *-ling*), altered in late Middle English by association with -LONG.

head louse ▶ **n.** a louse that infests the scalp and hair of the human head and is esp. common among schoolchildren. ● *Pediculus humanus capitis*, family Pediculidae, order Anoplura. See also BODY LOUSE.

head·man /ˈhedmən/ ▶ **n.** (pl. **headmen**) the chief or leader of a community or tribe.

head·mas·ter /ˈhedˌmastər/ ▶ **n.** (esp. in private schools) the man in charge of a school; the principal.
– DERIVATIVES **head·mas·ter·ly adj.**

head·mis·tress /ˈhedˌmistris/ ▶ **n.** (esp. in private schools) the woman in charge of a school; the principal.

head·note /ˈhedˌnōt/ ▶ **n.** a note inserted at the head of an article, reported law case, or other document, summarizing or commenting on the content. ■ Law a summary of a decided case prefixed to the case report, setting out the principles behind the decision and an outline of the facts.

head of state ▶ **n.** the chief public representative of a country, such as a president or monarch, who may also be the head of government.

head-on ▶ **adj. & adv. 1** with or involving the front of a vehicle: [as attrib. adj.] *a head-on collision* | [as adv.] *they hit a bus head-on.*
2 with or involving direct confrontation: [as attrib. adj.] *trying to avoid a head-on clash.*

head·phones /ˈhedˌfōnz/ ▶ **plural n.** a pair of earphones typically joined by a band placed over the head, for listening to audio signals such as music or speech.

headphones

head·piece /ˈhedˌpēs/ ▶ **n. 1** a device worn on the head as an ornament or to serve a function: *her headpiece was a wreath of silk flowers | headpieces for carrying water.*
2 an illustration or ornamental motif printed at the head of a chapter in a book.
3 the part of a halter or bridle that fits over the top of a horse's head behind the ears.

head·quar·ter /ˈhedˌkwôrtər/ ▶ **v.** [with obj.] (usu. **be headquartered**) provide (an organization) with headquarters at a specified location: *UNESCO is headquartered in Paris.*

head·quar·ters /ˈhedˌkwôrtərz/ ▶ **n.** [treated as sing. or pl.] the premises occupied by a military commander and the commander's staff. ■ the place or building serving as the managerial and administrative center of an organization.

head·rail /ˈhedˌrāl/ ▶ **n.** a horizontal rail at the top of something.

head·rest /ˈhedˌrest/ ▶ **n.** a padded part extending from or fixed to the back of a seat or chair, designed to support the head.

head·room /ˈhedˌro͞om, -ˌro͝om/ ▶ **n.** the space above a driver's or passenger's head in a vehicle. ■ the space or clearance between the top of a vehicle and the underside of a bridge or other structure above it.

head·sail /ˈhedˌsāl/ ▶ **n.** a sail on a ship's foremast or bowsprit.

head·scarf /ˈhedˌskärf/ ▶ **n.** (pl. **headscarves**) a square of fabric worn as a covering for the head, often folded into a triangle and knotted under the chin.

head·set /ˈhedˌset/ ▶ **n. 1** a set of headphones, typically with a microphone attached, used esp. in telephone and radio communication.
2 the bearing assembly that links the front fork of a bicycle to its frame.

head·ship /ˈhedˌSHip/ ▶ **n.** the position of leader or chief. ■ chiefly Brit. the position of head teacher in a school.

head shop ▶ **n.** a store that sells drug-related paraphernalia.

head·shot /ˈhedˌSHät/ ▶ **n. 1** a photograph of a person's head. ■ a frame, or a sequence of frames, of videotape or motion-picture film that captures a close-up of a person's head.
2 a bullet or gunshot aimed at the head.

head·shrink·er /ˈhedˌSHriNGkər/ ▶ **n.** historical a headhunter who preserved and shrank the heads of his dead enemies. ■ informal a clinical psychiatrist, psychologist, or psychotherapist. Compare with SHRINK.

heads·man /ˈhedzmən/ ▶ **n.** (pl. **headsmen**) historical a man who was responsible for beheading condemned prisoners.

head·space /ˈhedˌspās/ ▶ **n.** the unfilled space above the contents of a closed container.

head·spring /ˈhedˌspriNG/ ▶ **n. 1** a spring that is the main source of a stream.
2 a somersault similar to a handspring, except that the performer lands on the head as well as the hands.

head·stall /ˈhedˌstôl/ ▶ **n. 1** the part of a bridle or halter that fits around a horse's head.
2 another term for HEADPIECE (sense 3).

head·stand /ˈhedˌstand/ ▶ **n.** the act of balancing on one's head and hands with the feet in the air.

head·stand·er /ˈhedˌstandər/ ▶ **n.** a small deep-bodied freshwater fish of the Amazon region, popular in aquariums. It swims and feeds at an oblique angle with the head down. ● Genus *Abramites*, family Anostomidae: two species.

head·stay /ˈhedˌstā/ ▶ **n.** a forestay, esp. in a small vessel.

head·stock /ˈhedˌstäk/ ▶ **n. 1** a set of bearings in a machine, supporting a revolving part.
2 the widened piece at the end of the neck of a guitar, to which the tuning pegs are fixed.
3 the horizontal end member of the underframe of a railroad vehicle.

head·stone /ˈhedˌstōn/ ▶ **n.** a slab of stone set up at the head of a grave, typically inscribed with the name of the dead person.

head·stream /ˈhedˌstrēm/ ▶ **n.** a headwater stream.

head·strong /ˈhedˌstrôNG/ ▶ **adj.** self-willed and obstinate: *I am headstrong and like getting my own way.*

heads-up informal ▶ **n.** an advance warning of something: *the heads-up came just in time to stop the tanks from launching the final assault.*
▶ **adj.** [attrib.] showing alertness or perceptiveness: *they played a very heads-up game.*

head tax ▶ **n.** a uniform tax imposed on each person: *a 50 cent head tax imposed on departing ferry passengers.*

head-to-head ▶ **adj. & adv.** involving two parties confronting each other: [as adj.] *a head-to-head battle with discounters.*
▶ **n.** a conversation, confrontation, or contest between two parties.

head-trip ▶ **n. 1** an intellectually stimulating experience.
2 an act performed primarily for self-gratification.

head-turn·ing ▶ **adj.** extremely noticeable or attractive: *her skimpy, head-turning costumes.*

head-up dis·play (also **heads-up display**) ▶ **n.** a display of instrument readings in an aircraft or vehicle that can be seen without lowering the eyes, typically through being projected onto the windshield or visor.

head voice ▶ **n.** [in sing.] one of the high registers of the voice in speaking or singing, above chest voice.

head·ward /ˈhedwərd/ ▶ **adj.** in the region or direction of the head. ■ Geology denoting erosion by a stream or river occurring progressively upstream from the original source.
▶ **adv.** (also **headwards**) toward the head.

head·wa·ter /ˈhedˌwôtər, -ˌwätər/ ▶ **n.** (usu. **headwaters**) a tributary stream of a river close to or forming part of its source: *these paths follow rivers right up into their headwaters.*

head·way /ˈhedˌwā/ ▶ **n. 1** (usu. in phrase **make headway**) move forward or make progress, esp. when circumstances make this slow or difficult: *the ship was making very little headway against heavy seas | they appear to be* ***making headway*** *in bringing the rebels under control.*
2 the average interval of time between vehicles moving in the same direction on the same route.

head·wear /ˈhedˌwe(ə)r/ ▶ **n.** coverings for the head, such as hats, caps, and scarves.

head·wind /ˈhedˌwind/ ▶ **n.** a wind blowing from directly in front, opposing forward motion.

head·word /ˈhedˌwərd/ ▶ **n.** a word that begins a separate entry in a reference work such as a dictionary.

head·work /ˈhedˌwərk/ ▶ **n. 1** activities taxing the mind; mental work.
2 (**headworks**) apparatus for controlling the flow of water in a river or canal.

head·y /ˈhedē/ ▶ **adj.** (**headier, headiest**) (of liquor) potent; intoxicating: *several bottles of heady local wine.* ■ having a strong or exhilarating effect: *the heady days of the birth of the women's movement | a heady, exotic perfume.*
– DERIVATIVES **head·i·ly** /ˈhedl-ē/ **adv.**, **head·i·ness n.**

heal /hēl/ ▶ **v.** [with obj.] (of a person or treatment) cause (a wound, injury, or person) to become sound or healthy again: *his concern is to heal sick people.* ■ [no obj.] become sound or healthy again: *he would have to wait until his knee had healed.* ■ alleviate (a person's distress or anguish): *time can heal the pain of grief.* ■ correct or put right (an undesirable situation): *the rift between them was never really healed.*
– DERIVATIVES **heal·a·ble adj.**, **heal·er n.**
– ORIGIN Old English *hǣlan* (in the sense 'restore to sound health'), of Germanic origin; related to Dutch *heelen* and German *heilen*, also to WHOLE.

heal-all ▶ **n.** a universal remedy; a panacea. ■ informal any of a number of medicinal plants, esp. self-heal.

heal·ing /ˈhēliŋ/ ▶ **n.** the process of making or becoming sound or healthy again: *the gift of healing.*
▶ **adj.** tending to heal; therapeutic: *a healing experience | the healing process.*

health /helTH/ ▶ **n.** the state of being free from illness or injury: *he was restored to health* | [as modifier] *a health risk.* ■ a person's mental or physical condition: *bad health forced him to retire* | figurative *a standard for measuring the financial health of a company.* ■ used to express friendly feelings toward one's companions before drinking.
– ORIGIN Old English *hǣlth*, of Germanic origin; related to WHOLE.

health·care /ˈhelTHˌke(ə)r/ (also **health care**) ▶ **n.** the maintenance and improvement of physical and mental health, esp. through the provision of medical services: [as modifier] *healthcare workers.*

health cen·ter ▶ **n.** a building or establishment housing local medical services or the practice of a group of doctors.

health farm ▶ **n.** chiefly Brit. a residential establishment where people seek improved health by a regimen of dieting, exercise, and treatment.

health food ▶ **n.** natural food that is thought to have health-giving qualities.

health·ful /ˈhelTHfəl/ ▶ **adj.** having or conducive to good health: *healthful methods of cooking vegetables.*
– DERIVATIVES **health·ful·ly adv.**, **health·ful·ness n.**

health main·te·nance or·ga·ni·za·tion (abbr.: **HMO**) ▶ **n.** a health insurance organization to which subscribers pay a predetermined fee in return for a range of medical services from physicians and healthcare workers registered with the organization.

health phys·ics ▶ **plural n.** [treated as sing.] the branch of radiology that deals with the health of people working with radioactive materials.

health sav·ings ac·count ▶ n. a savings account used in conjunction with a high-deductible health insurance policy that allows users to save money tax-free against medical expenses (abbr. **HSA**).

health serv·ice ▶ n. a public service providing medical care.

health tour·ism ▶ n. the practice of traveling to a tourist destination with the main purpose of receiving some therapeutic treatment.
– DERIVATIVES **health tour·ist** n.

health·y /ˈhelTHē/ ▶ adj. (**healthier**, **healthiest**) in good health: *I feel fit and healthy* | figurative *the family is the basis of any healthy society*. ■ (of a part of the body) not diseased: *healthy cells*. ■ indicative of, conducive to, or promoting good health: *a healthy appetite* | *a healthy balanced diet*. ■ normal, natural, and desirable: *a healthy contempt for authority* | *healthy competition*. ■ of a satisfactory size or amount: *making a healthy profit*.
– DERIVATIVES **health·i·ly** /ˈhelTHəlē/ adv., **health·i·ness** n.

Hea·ney /ˈhēnē/, Seamus (Justin) (1939–), Irish poet; born in Northern Ireland. He became an Irish citizen in 1972. Notable works: *North* (1975) and *The Haw Lantern* (1987). In 1999 he published an acclaimed new translation of *Beowulf*. Nobel Prize for Literature (1995).

heap /hēp/ ▶ n. an untidy collection of things piled up haphazardly: *she rushed out, leaving her clothes in a heap on the floor*. ■ a mound or pile of a particular substance: ***a heap of** gravel*. ■ informal an untidy or dilapidated place or vehicle: *they climbed back in the heap and headed home*. ■ (**a heap of/heaps of**) informal a large amount or number of something: *we have heaps of room*.
▶ adv. (**heaps**) informal a great deal: *"How do you like Maggie?" "I like you heaps better!"*
▶ v. [with obj.] put in a pile or mound: *she heaped logs on the fire* | ***heaped up** in one corner was a pile of junk*. ■ (**heap something with**) load something copiously with: *he heaped his plate with rice*. ■ (**heap something on/upon**) bestow praise, abuse, or criticism liberally on: *they had once heaped praise on her*. ■ [no obj.] form a heap: *clouds heaped higher in the west*.
– PHRASES **at the top** (or **bottom**) **of the heap** (of a person) at the highest (or lowest) point of a society or organization: *she had come up the hard way from the very bottom of the heap*. **be struck all of a heap** informal be extremely disconcerted. **heap coals of fire on someone's head** go out of one's way to cause someone remorse. [with biblical allusion to Rom. 12:20.] **in a heap** (of a person) with the body completely limp: *he landed in a heap at the bottom of the stairs*.
– ORIGIN Old English *hēap* (noun), *hēapian* (verb), of Germanic origin; related to Dutch *hoop* and German *Haufen*.

hear /hi(ə)r/ ▶ v. (past and past participle **heard** /hərd/) [with obj.] perceive with the ear the sound made by (someone or something): *behind her she could hear men's voices* | [with obj. and infinitive] *she had never been heard to complain* | [no obj.] *he did not hear very well*. ■ be told or informed of: *have you heard the news?* | [with clause] *they heard that I had moved* | [no obj.] *I was shocked to **hear of** her death*. ■ [no obj.] (**have heard of**) be aware of; know of the existence of: *nobody had ever heard of my college*. ■ [no obj.] (**hear from**) be contacted by (someone), esp. by letter or telephone: *if you would like to join the committee, we would love to hear from you*. ■ listen or pay attention to: [with clause] *she just doesn't hear what I'm telling her*. ■ (**hear someone out**) listen to all that someone has to say: *Joseph gravely heard them out but never offered advice*. ■ [no obj.] (**will/would not hear of**) will or would not allow or agree to: *I won't hear of such idiocy*. ■ Law listen to and judge (a case or plaintiff): *an all-woman jury heard the case*. ■ listen to and grant (a prayer): *our Heavenly Father has heard our prayers*.
– PHRASES **be hearing things** see **THING**. **be unable to hear oneself think** informal used to complain about very loud noise or music: *I hate bars where you can't hear yourself think*. **hear! hear!** used to express one's wholehearted agreement, esp. with something said in a speech. **hear tell of** (or **that**) be informed of (or that): *I heard tell that he went out west*.
– DERIVATIVES **hear·a·ble** adj., **hear·er** n.
– ORIGIN Old English *hīeran*, *hēran*, of Germanic origin; related to Dutch *hooren* and German *hören*.

Heard and Mc·Don·ald Is·lands /hərd and məkˈdänəld/ a group of uninhabited islands in the southern Indian Ocean, administered by Australia since 1947 as an external territory.

hear·ing /ˈhi(ə)riNG/ ▶ n. **1** the faculty of perceiving sounds: *people who have very acute hearing*. ■ the range within which sounds may be heard; earshot: *she had moved out of hearing*.
2 an opportunity to state one's case: *I think I had a fair hearing*. ■ Law an act of listening to evidence in a court of law or before an official, esp. a trial before a judge without a jury.

hear·ing aid ▶ n. a small device that fits in or on the ear, worn by a partially deaf person to amplify sound.

hear·ing dog ▶ n. a dog trained to alert people who are deaf or hard of hearing to such sounds as the ringing of an alarm, doorbell, or telephone.

heark·en /ˈhärkən/ (also **harken**) ▶ v. [no obj.] archaic listen: *he refused to hearken to Thomas's words of wisdom*.
– PHRASAL VERBS **hearken back to** another way of saying **HARK BACK TO** (see **HARK**).
– ORIGIN Old English *heorcnian*; probably related to **HARK**. The spelling with *ea* (dating from the 16th cent.) is due to association with **HEAR**.

hear·say /ˈhi(ə)r,sā/ ▶ n. information received from other people that one cannot adequately substantiate; rumor: *according to hearsay, Bob had managed to break his arm*. ■ Law the report of another person's words by a witness, usually disallowed as evidence in a court of law: *everything they had told him would have been ruled out as hearsay* | [as modifier] *hearsay evidence*.

hearse /hərs/ ▶ n. a vehicle for conveying the coffin at a funeral.
– ORIGIN Middle English: from Anglo-Norman French *herce* 'harrow, frame,' from Latin *hirpex* 'a kind of large rake,' from Oscan *hirpus* 'wolf' (with reference to the teeth). The earliest recorded sense in English is 'latticework canopy placed over the coffin (while in church) of a distinguished person,' but this probably arose from the late Middle English sense 'triangular frame (shaped like the ancient harrow) for carrying candles at certain services.' The current sense dates from the mid 17th cent.

Hearst, William Randolph (1863–1951), US newspaper publisher and tycoon. His introduction of features such as large headlines and sensational crime reporting revolutionized US journalism. He was the model for the central character of Orson Welles's movie *Citizen Kane* (1941).

heart /härt/ ▶ n. **1** a hollow muscular organ that pumps the blood through the circulatory system by rhythmic contraction and dilation. In vertebrates there may be up to four chambers (as in humans), with two atria and two ventricles. ■ the region of the chest above the heart: *holding hand on heart for the Pledge of Allegiance*. ■ the heart regarded as the center of a person's thoughts and emotions, esp. love or compassion: *hardening his heart, he ignored her entreaties* | *he poured out his heart to me* | *he has no heart*. ■ one's mood or feeling: *they had a change of heart*. ■ courage or enthusiasm: *they may **lose heart** as the work mounts up* | *Mary **took heart** from the encouragement handed out* | *I **put my heart and soul into** it and then got fired*.
2 the central or innermost part of something: *right in the heart of the city*. ■ the vital part or essence: *the heart of the matter*. ■ the close compact center of a head of a cabbage or lettuce.
3 a conventional representation of a heart with two equal curves meeting at a point at the bottom and a cusp at the top. ■ (**hearts**) one of the four suits in a conventional pack of playing cards, denoted by a red figure of such a shape. ■ a card of this suit. ■ (**hearts**) a card game similar to whist, in which players attempt to avoid taking tricks containing a card of this suit.
4 [usu. with modifier] the condition of agricultural land as regards fertility.
▶ v. [with obj.] informal like very much; love: *I totally heart this song*. [from use of the symbol ♥, first popularized by the 'I ♥ NY' advertising campaign of the late 1970s.]
– PHRASES **after one's own heart** of the type that one likes or understands best; sharing one's tastes: *this is a man after my own heart*. **at heart** in one's real nature, in contrast to how one may appear: *he's a good guy at heart*. **break someone's heart** overwhelm someone with sadness. **by heart** from memory. **close** (or **dear**) **to** (or **near**) **one's heart** of deep interest and concern to one. **from the** (**bottom of one's**) **heart** with sincere feeling: *their warmth and hospitality is right from the heart*. **give** (or **lose**) **one's heart to** fall in love with. **have a heart** [often in imperative] be merciful; show pity. **have a heart of gold** have a generous nature. **have the heart to do something** [usu. with negative] be insensitive or hard-hearted enough to do something: *I don't have the heart to tell her*. **have** (or **put**) **one's heart in** be (or become) keenly involved in or committed to (an enterprise). **have one's heart in one's mouth** be greatly alarmed or apprehensive. **have one's heart in the right place** be sincere or well intentioned. **heart of stone** a stern or cruel nature. **hearts and flowers** used in allusion to extreme sentimentality. **hearts and minds** used in reference to emotional and intellectual support or commitment: *a campaign to win the hearts and minds of America's college students*. **one's heart's desire** a person or thing that one greatly wishes for. **one's heartstrings** used in reference to one's deepest feelings of love or compassion: *the kitten's pitiful little squeak **tugged at her heartstrings***. **in one's heart of hearts** in one's inmost feelings. **take something to heart** take criticism seriously and be affected or upset by it. **wear one's heart on one's sleeve** make one's feelings apparent. **with all one's heart** (or **one's whole heart**) sincerely; completely. **with one's heart in one's boots** in a state of great depression or trepidation: *I had to follow her with my heart in my boots*.
– DERIVATIVES **heart·ed** adj. [in combination] *a generous-hearted woman*.
– ORIGIN Old English *heorte*, of Germanic origin; related to Dutch *hart* and German *Herz*, from an Indo-European root shared by Latin *cor*, *cord-* and Greek *kēr*, *kardia*.

heart·ache /ˈhärt,āk/ ▶ n. emotional anguish or grief, typically caused by the loss or absence of someone loved.

heart at·tack ▶ n. a sudden and sometimes fatal occurrence of coronary thrombosis, typically resulting in the death of part of a heart muscle.

heart·beat /ˈhärt,bēt/ ▶ n. the pulsation of the heart. ■ (usu. **heartbeats**) a single pulsation of the heart: *her heartbeats steadied*. ■ an animating or vital unifying force: *conflict is the essential heartbeat of fiction*.
– PHRASES **a heartbeat away from** very close to; on the verge of: *the man who is just a heartbeat away from the presidency*. **in a heartbeat** instantly; immediately: *I'd do it again in a heartbeat*.

heart·break /ˈhärt,brāk/ ▶ n. overwhelming distress: *an unforgettable tale of joy and heartbreak*.

heart·break·er /ˈhärt,brākər/ ▶ n. **1** a person who is very attractive but who is irresponsible in emotional relationships.
2 a story or event that causes overwhelming distress.

heart·break·ing /ˈhärt,brākiNG/ ▶ adj. causing overwhelming distress; very upsetting.
– DERIVATIVES **heart·break·ing·ly** adv. [as submodifier] *a heartbreakingly lonely place*.

heart·bro·ken /ˈhärt,brōkən/ ▶ adj. (of a person) suffering from overwhelming distress; very upset: *he was **heartbroken at** the thought of leaving the house*.

heart·burn /ˈhärt,bərn/ ▶ n. a form of indigestion felt as a burning sensation in the chest, caused by acid regurgitation into the esophagus.

heart·en /ˈhärtn/ ▶ v. [with obj.] (usu. **be heartened**) make more cheerful or confident: [with obj. and infinitive] *she was heartened to observe that the effect was faintly comic* | (as adj. **heartening**) *this is the most heartening news of all*.
– DERIVATIVES **heart·en·ing·ly** adv.

heart fail·ure ▶ n. severe failure of the heart to function properly, esp. as a cause of death: *her mother had died of heart failure*.

heart·felt /ˈhärt,felt/ ▶ adj. (of a feeling or its expression) sincere; deeply and strongly felt: *our heartfelt thanks*.

hearth /härTH/ ▶ n. the floor of a fireplace: *the crackling blaze on the hearth*. ■ the area in front of a fireplace: *they were sitting around the hearth*. ■ used as a symbol of one's home: *he left **hearth and home** to train in Denmark*. ■ the base or lower part of a furnace, where molten metal collects.
– ORIGIN Old English *heorth*; related to Dutch *haard* and German *Herd*.

hearth·rug /ˈhärTH,rəg/ ▶ n. a rug laid in front of a fireplace to protect the carpet or floor.

hearth·side /ˈhärTH,sīd/ ▶ n. the area around a hearth or fireplace; fireside.

hearth·stone /ˈhärTH,stōn/ ▶ n. a flat stone forming a hearth or part of a hearth.

heart·i·ly /ˈhärtl-ē/ ▶ adv. **1** in a hearty manner: *she laughed heartily* | *they dined heartily*.
2 [as submodifier] very; to a great degree (esp. with reference to personal feelings): *they were heartily sick of the whole subject*.

heart·land /ˈhärt,land/ ▶ n. the central or most important part of a country, area, or field of activity. ■ the center of support for a belief or movement: *the heartland of the rebel cause*. ■ (**the heartland**) the central part of the US; the Midwest: *a recession that battered the coasts while sparing the heartland*.

heart·less /ˈhärtlis/ ▶ adj. displaying a complete lack of feeling or consideration: *heartless thieves stole the stroller of a two-year-old boy*.
– DERIVATIVES **heart·less·ly** adv., **heart·less·ness** n.

heart line ▶ n. (in palmistry) the upper of the two horizontal lines that cross the palm of the hand, linked to a person's physical health and ability to form emotional relationships.

heart-lung ma·chine ▶ n. a machine that temporarily takes over the functions of the heart and lungs, esp. during heart surgery.

heart mas·sage ▶ n. another term for cardiac massage.

heart of palm ▶ n. the edible bud of a palm tree.

heart-rend·ing ▶ adj. (of a story or event) causing great sadness or distress.
– DERIVATIVES **heart-rend·ing·ly** adv.

heart's-blood ▶ n. archaic the blood, as being necessary for life.

heart-search·ing ▶ n. thorough, typically painful examination of one's feelings and motives: *I began to write, but not without much heart-searching.*

hearts·ease /ˈhärts,ēz/ (also **heart's-ease**) ▶ n. a wild European pansy that typically has purple and yellow flowers. It has given rise to the hybrids from which most garden pansies were developed. ● *Viola tricolor*, family Violaceae.
– ORIGIN late Middle English: origin uncertain, the term being applied by herbalists to both the pansy and the wallflower in the 16th cent.

heart·sick /ˈhärt,sik/ ▶ adj. despondent, typically from grief or loss of love.
– DERIVATIVES **heart·sick·ness** n.

heart·sore /ˈhärt,sôr/ ▶ adj. literary grieving; heartsick.

heart-stop·ping ▶ adj. thrilling; full of suspense.
– DERIVATIVES **heart-stop·per** n., **heart-stop·ping·ly** adv.

heart·throb /ˈhärt,THräb/ ▶ n. informal a man, typically a celebrity, whose good looks excite immature romantic feelings in women.

heart-to-heart ▶ adj. (of a conversation) candid, intimate, and personal: *a heart-to-heart chat.*
▶ n. such a conversation: *they had seemed engrossed in a heart-to-heart.*

heart ur·chin ▶ n. a heart-shaped burrowing sea urchin that has a thick covering of fine spines on the shell, giving it a furry appearance. ● Class Echinoidea, order Spatangoida.

heart·warm·ing /ˈhärt,wôrmiNG/ ▶ adj. emotionally rewarding or uplifting.

heart·wood /ˈhärt,wo͝od/ ▶ n. the dense inner part of a tree trunk, yielding the hardest timber.

heart·y /ˈhärtē/ ▶ adj. (**heartier**, **heartiest**) **1** (of a person or their behavior) loudly vigorous and cheerful: *a hearty and boisterous character | he sang in a hearty baritone.* ■ (of a feeling or an opinion) heartfelt: *hearty congratulations.* ■ (of a person) strong and healthy: *a white-bearded but hearty man.*
2 (of food) wholesome and substantial: *a hearty meal cooked over open flames.* ■ (of a person's appetite) robust and healthy: *Jim goes for a long walk to work up a hearty appetite for dinner.*
▶ n. Brit. informal **1** a vigorously cheerful and sporty person.
2 (usu. **me hearties**) a form of address ascribed to sailors.
– DERIVATIVES **heart·i·ness** n.

heat /hēt/ ▶ n. **1** the quality of being hot; high temperature: *it is sensitive to both heat and cold.* ■ hot weather conditions: *the oppressive heat was making both men sweat.* ■ a source or level of heat for cooking: *remove from the heat and beat in the butter.* ■ a spicy quality in food that produces a burning sensation in the mouth: *chili peppers add taste and heat to food.* ■ Physics heat seen as a form of energy arising from the random motion of the molecules of bodies, which may be transferred by conduction, convection, or radiation. ■ technical the amount of heat that is needed to cause a specific process or is evolved in such a process: *the heat of formation.* ■ technical a single operation of heating something, esp. metal in a furnace.
2 intensity of feeling, esp. of anger or excitement: *words few men would dare use to another, even in the heat of anger.* ■ (**the heat**) informal intensive and unwelcome pressure or criticism, esp. from the authorities: *a flurry of legal proceedings **turned up the heat** in the dispute.*
3 a preliminary round in a race or contest: *the 200-meter heats.*
▶ v. make or become hot or warm: [with obj.] *the room faces north and is difficult to heat* | [no obj.] *the pipes expand as they **heat up**.* ■ [no obj.] (**heat up**) (of a person) become excited or impassioned. ■ [no obj.] (**heat up**) become more intense and exciting: *the action really begins to heat up.* ■ [with obj.] archaic inflame; excite: *this discourse had heated them.*
– PHRASES **if you can't stand the heat, get out of the kitchen** proverb if you can't deal with the pressures and difficulties of a situation or task, you should leave others to deal with it rather than complaining. **in the heat of the moment** while temporarily angry, excited, or engrossed, and without stopping for thought. **in heat** (of a female mammal) in the receptive period of the sexual cycle; in estrus.
– ORIGIN Old English *hǣtu* (noun), *hǣtan* (verb), of Germanic origin; related to Dutch *hitte* (noun) and German *heizen* (verb), also to HOT.

heat bar·ri·er ▶ n. the limitation of the speed of an aircraft or other flying object by heat resulting from air friction.

heat ca·pac·i·ty ▶ n. the number of heat units needed to raise the temperature of a body by one degree.

heat death ▶ n. Physics a state of uniform distribution of energy, esp. viewed as a possible fate of the universe. It is a corollary of the second law of thermodynamics.

heat·ed /ˈhētid/ ▶ adj. **1** made warm or hot: *a heated swimming pool.*
2 inflamed with passion or conviction: *she had a heated argument with an official.*
– DERIVATIVES **heat·ed·ly** adv.

heat en·gine ▶ n. a device for producing motive power from heat, such as a gasoline engine or steam engine.

heat·er /ˈhētər/ ▶ n. **1** a person or thing that heats, in particular a device for warming the air or water: *a wall-mounted electric heater | a gas water heater.* ■ Electronics a conductor used for indirect heating of the cathode of a thermionic tube.
2 Baseball a fastball.
3 informal, dated a gun.

heat ex·chang·er ▶ n. a device for transferring heat from one medium to another.

Heath /hēTH/, Sir Edward (Richard George) (1916–2005), British Conservative statesman; prime minister 1970–74. He negotiated Britain's entry into the European Economic Community.

heath /hēTH/ ▶ n. **1** an area of open uncultivated land, esp. in Britain, with characteristic vegetation of heather, gorse, and coarse grasses. ■ Ecology vegetation dominated by dwarf shrubs of the heath family: [as modifier] *heath vegetation.*
2 a dwarf shrub with small leathery leaves and small pink or purple bell-shaped flowers, characteristic of heathland and moorland. ● *Erica* and related genera, family Ericaceae (the **heath family**): many species, including the common European **cross-leaved heath** (*E. tetralix*).
– DERIVATIVES **heath·y** adj.
– ORIGIN Old English *hǣth*, of Germanic origin; related to Dutch *heide* and German *Heide*.

heat haze ▶ n. an obscuration of the atmosphere in hot weather, esp. a shimmering in the air near the ground that distorts distant views.

heath·en /ˈhēT͟Hən/ ▶ n. chiefly derogatory a person who does not belong to a widely held religion (esp. one who is not a Christian, Jew, or Muslim) as regarded by those who do. ■ a follower of a polytheistic religion; a pagan. ■ (**the heathen**) heathen people collectively, esp. (in biblical use) those who did not worship the God of Israel. ■ informal an unenlightened person; a person regarded as lacking culture or moral principles.
▶ adj. of or relating to heathens: *heathen gods.*
– DERIVATIVES **heath·en·dom** /-dəm/ n., **heath·en·ish** adj., **heath·en·ism** /-,nizəm/ n.
– ORIGIN Old English *hǣthen*, of Germanic origin; related to Dutch *heiden* and German *Heide*; generally regarded as a specifically Christian use of a Germanic adjective meaning 'inhabiting open country,' from the base of HEATH.

heath·er /ˈheT͟Hər/ ▶ n. a purple-flowered Eurasian heath that grows abundantly on moorland and heathland. Many ornamental varieties have been developed. Also called LING². ● *Calluna vulgaris*, family Ericaceae. This family includes the rhododendrons and azaleas as well as the blueberries and many other berry-bearing dwarf shrubs.
■ informal any similar plant of this family; a heath.
– DERIVATIVES **heath·er·y** adj.
– ORIGIN Old English *hadre, hedre* (recorded in place names), of unknown origin. The word was chiefly Scots until the 16th cent.; the change in the first syllable in the 18th cent. was due to association with HEATH.

heath·land /ˈhēTH,land/ ▶ n. (also **heathlands**) an extensive area of heath: *1,000 acres of heathland.*

heat in·dex ▶ n. a quantity expressing the discomfort felt as a result of the combined effects of the temperature and humidity of the air.

heat·ing /ˈhētiNG/ ▶ n. equipment or devices used to provide heat, esp. to a building: *baseboard heating.*

heat lamp ▶ n. an electrical device with a bulb that emits mainly heat rather than light, used as a heat source.

heat light·ning ▶ n. a flash or flashes of light seen near the horizon, esp. on warm evenings, believed to be the reflection of distant lightning on high clouds.

Heat-Moon, William Least (1939–), US writer, of Osage ancestry; also known as **William Trogdon**. Notable works: *Blue Highways* (1982), *PrairyErth* (1991), *River-Horse* (1999), and *Roads to Quoz* (2008).

heat·proof /ˈhēt,pro͞of/ ▶ adj. able to resist great heat.

heat pump ▶ n. a device that transfers heat from a colder area to a hotter area by using mechanical energy, as in a refrigerator.

heat rash ▶ n. another term for PRICKLY HEAT.

heat-re·sist·ant ▶ adj. another term for HEATPROOF. ■ not easily becoming hot: *fondue forks with heat-resistant handles.*

heat-seek·ing /ˈhēt,sēkiNG/ ▶ adj. (of a missile) able to detect and home in on infrared radiation emitted by a target, such as the exhaust vent of a jet aircraft.

heat shield ▶ n. a device or coating for protection from excessive heat. ■ an outer covering on a spacecraft, esp. on the nose cone and leading edges, to protect it from the heat generated during re-entry into the earth's atmosphere.

heat sink ▶ n. a device or substance for absorbing excessive or unwanted heat.

heat·stroke /ˈhēt,strōk/ ▶ n. a condition marked by fever and often by unconsciousness, caused by failure of the body's temperature-regulating mechanism when exposed to excessively high temperatures.

heat treat·ment ▶ n. the use of heat for therapeutic purposes in medicine.
– DERIVATIVES **heat-treat** v.

heat wave ▶ n. a prolonged period of abnormally hot weather.

heave /hēv/ ▶ v. (past and past participle **heaved** or chiefly Nautical **hove** /hōv/) **1** [with obj.] lift or haul (a heavy thing) with great effort: *she heaved the sofa back into place | he **heaved himself** out of bed.* ■ Nautical pull, raise, or move (a boat or ship) by hauling on a rope or ropes. ■ informal throw (something heavy): *she heaved half a brick at him.*
2 [with obj.] produce (a sigh): *he heaved a euphoric sigh of relief.*
3 [no obj.] rise and fall rhythmically or spasmodically: *his shoulders heaved as he panted.* ■ make an effort to vomit; retch: *my stomach heaved.*
▶ n. **1** an act of heaving, esp. a strong pull. ■ Geology a sideways displacement in a fault.
2 (**the heaves**) informal a case of retching or vomiting: *waiting for the heaves to subside.*
3 (**heaves**) a disease of horses, with labored breathing.
– PHRASES **heave in sight** (or **into view**) chiefly Nautical come into view: *the three canoes hove into view.*
– PHRASAL VERBS **heave to** Nautical (of a boat or ship) come to a stop, esp. by turning across the wind leaving the headsail backed: *he hove to and dropped anchor.*
– DERIVATIVES **heav·er** n.
– ORIGIN Old English *hebban*, of Germanic origin; related to Dutch *heffen* and German *heben* 'lift up.'

heave-ho /ˈhēv ˈhō/ ▶ exclam. a cry emitted when doing in unison actions that take physical effort.
▶ n. such an exclamation. ■ (**the heave-ho**) expulsion or elimination from an institution, association, or contest: *conjecture over who'll get the heave-ho.*
– ORIGIN late Middle English: from *heave!* (imperative) + HO², originally in nautical use when hauling a rope.

heav·en /ˈhevən/ ▶ n. **1** a place regarded in various religions as the abode of God (or the gods) and the angels, and of the good after death, often traditionally depicted as being above the sky. ■ God (or the gods): *Constantine was persuaded that disunity in the Church was displeasing to heaven.* ■ Theology a state of being eternally in the presence of God after death. ■ informal a place, state, or experience of supreme bliss: *lying by the pool with a good book is my idea of heaven.* ■ used in various exclamations as a substitute for "God": *Heaven knows! | good heavens!*
2 (often **heavens**) literary the sky, esp. perceived as a vault in which the sun, moon, stars, and planets are situated: *Galileo used a telescope to observe the heavens.*
– PHRASES **the heavens open** it suddenly starts to rain heavily. **in seventh heaven** in a state of ecstasy. **move heaven and earth to do something**

make extraordinary efforts to do a specified thing: *if he had truly loved her he would have moved heaven and earth to get her back.* **stink** (or **smell**) **to high heaven** have a very strong and unpleasant odor.
– DERIVATIVES **heav·en·ward** /-wərd/ adj. & adv., **heav·en·wards** /-wərdz/ adv.
– ORIGIN Old English *heofon*, of Germanic origin; related to Dutch *hemel* and German *Himmel*.

heav·en·ly /ˈhevənlē/ ▶ adj. **1** of heaven; divine: *heavenly Father.*
2 of the heavens or sky: *heavenly constellations.*
3 informal very pleasing; wonderful: *their shampoos smell heavenly | it was a heavenly morning for a ride.*
– DERIVATIVES **heav·en·li·ness** n.
– ORIGIN Old English *heofonlic* (see HEAVEN, -LY[1]).

heav·en·ly bod·y ▶ n. a planet, star, or other celestial body.

heav·en·ly host ▶ n. a literary or biblical term for the angels.

heav·en-sent ▶ adj. (of an event or opportunity) occurring at a favorable time; opportune.

heav·i·er-than-air ▶ adj. (of an aircraft) weighing more than the air it displaces.

heav·i·ly /ˈhevəlē/ ▶ adv. **1** to a great degree; in large amounts: *it was raining heavily | he had been drinking heavily for six months.* ■ to a large extent; very or very much: *the country is heavily dependent on banana exports.*
2 with a lot of force or effort; with weight: *she fell heavily to the ground | he sat down heavily in the chair.* ■ in a way that is mentally oppressive or hard to endure: *it is a burden that weighs heavily on his shoulders | tension hung heavily in the air.* ■ slowly and loudly: *she was breathing heavily.* ■ in a slow way that expresses sadness: *he sighed heavily.*

heav·i·ly built ▶ adj. (of a person) having a large, broad, and strong body: *he was tall and heavily built.*

heav·ing /ˈhēviNG/ ▶ adj. Brit. informal (of a place) extremely crowded: *the foyer was absolutely heaving with people.*

heav·ing line ▶ n. a lightweight line with a weight at the end, made to be thrown between a ship and the shore, or from one ship to another, and used to pull a heavier line across.

Heav·i·side /ˈhevēˌsīd/, Oliver (1850–1925), English physicist and electrical engineer. In 1902, he suggested the existence of a layer in the atmosphere responsible for reflecting radio waves back to earth.

Heav·i·side lay·er (also **Heaviside–Kennelly layer** /ˈkenl-ē/) ▶ n. another name for E LAYER.
– ORIGIN early 20th cent.: named after O. HEAVISIDE and A. E. KENNELLY.

heav·y /ˈhevē/ ▶ adj. (**heavier**, **heaviest**) **1** of great weight; difficult to lift or move: *the pan was too heavy for me to carry.* ■ used in questions about weight: *how heavy is it?* ■ [attrib.] (of a class of thing) above the average weight; large of its kind: *heavy artillery.* ■ [predic.] weighed down; full of something: *branches heavy with blossoms.* ■ (of a person's head or eyes) feeling weighed down by weariness: *a heavy head.* ■ Physics of or containing atoms of an isotope of greater than the usual mass. See also HEAVY WATER.
2 of great density; thick or substantial: *heavy gray clouds | a heavy blanket.* ■ (of food or a meal) hard to digest; too filling. ■ (of ground or soil) hard to travel over or work with because muddy or full of clay. ■ not delicate or graceful; coarse: *he had a big mustache and heavy features.* ■ moving slowly or with difficulty: *steering that is heavy when parking.* ■ (of a smell) overpowering: *the air was heavy with the sweet odor of apples.* ■ (of the sky) full of dark clouds; oppressive: *a heavy thundery sky.*
3 of more than the usual size, amount, or force: *rush hour traffic was heavy and I was delayed.* ■ doing something to excess: *a heavy smoker.* ■ (**heavy on**) using a lot of: *stories heavy on melodrama.*
4 striking or falling with force: *a heavy blow to the head | we had heavy overnight rain.* ■ (of music, esp. rock) having a strong bass component and a forceful rhythm.
5 needing much physical effort: *long hours and heavy work.* ■ mentally oppressive; hard to endure: *a heavy burden of responsibility.* ■ important or serious: *a heavy discussion.* ■ (of a literary work) hard to read or understand because overly serious or difficult. ■ feeling or expressing grief: *I left him with a heavy heart.* ■ informal (of a situation) serious and hard to deal with: *things were getting pretty heavy.* ■ informal (of a person) strict or harsh: *the police were really getting heavy.*
▶ n. (pl. **heavies**) **1** a thing, such as a vehicle, that is large or heavy of its kind. ■ informal a large, strong man, esp. one hired for protection: *I needed money to pay off the heavies.* ■ an important person: *music business heavies.* ■ (**heavies**) Brit. informal serious newspapers: *reporters from the Sunday heavies.*
2 chiefly Scottish strong beer, esp. bitter: *a pint of heavy.*
▶ adv. heavily: *his words hung heavy in the air* | [in combination] *heavy-laden.*
– PHRASES **heavy with child** pregnant. **make heavy weather of** see WEATHER.
– DERIVATIVES **heav·i·ness** n., **heav·y·ish** adj.
– ORIGIN Old English *hefig*, of Germanic origin; related to Dutch *hevig*, also to HEAVE.

heav·y breath·ing ▶ n. breathing that is audible through being deep or labored, esp. in sleep or as a result of exertion.

heav·y chain ▶ n. Biochemistry the protein subunit that, as one of a pair, makes up the major part of an immunoglobulin molecule.

heav·y chem·i·cals ▶ plural n. bulk chemicals used in industry and agriculture.

heav·y cream ▶ n. thick cream that contains a lot of butterfat.

heav·y-du·ty ▶ adj. (of material or an article) designed to withstand the stresses of demanding use: *heavy-duty rubber gloves.* ■ informal intense, important, or abundant: *she did some heavy-duty cleaning.*

heav·y-foot·ed ▶ adj. slow and laborious in movement: *the whole occasion could resemble a heavy-footed hippo dance in mud.*

heav·y go·ing ▶ n. a person or situation that is difficult or boring: *she found the technical manuals heavy going.*

heav·y-hand·ed ▶ adj. clumsy or insensitive: *this heavy-handed prose is merely tiresome.* ■ overly forceful or oppressive: *the government's most heavy-handed efforts to muzzle social protest.*
– DERIVATIVES **heav·y-hand·ed·ly** adv., **heav·y-hand·ed·ness** n.

heav·y-heart·ed ▶ adj. feeling depressed or melancholy.

heav·y hit·ter ▶ n. informal **1** an important or powerful person: *a high-profile national issue pitting heavy hitters in the Senate against the Department of Agriculture.*
2 a high-scoring athlete.

heav·y horse ▶ n. a large, strong, heavily built horse of a type or breed used for draft work.

heav·y hy·dro·gen ▶ n. another term for DEUTERIUM.

heav·y in·dus·try ▶ n. the manufacture of large, heavy articles and materials in bulk.

heav·y-lift ▶ adj. [attrib.] (of a vehicle) capable of lifting or transporting extremely heavy loads: *a heavy-lift helicopter.*

heav·y lift·ing ▶ n. the lifting of heavy objects. ■ hard or difficult work: *the heavy lifting in this business is in designing external distribution systems.*

heav·y met·al ▶ n. **1** a type of highly amplified harsh-sounding rock music with a strong beat, characteristically using violent or fantastic imagery.
2 a metal of relatively high density, or of high relative atomic weight.

heav·y oil ▶ n. any of the relatively dense hydrocarbons (denser than water) derived from petroleum, coal tar, and similar materials.

heav·y pet·ting ▶ n. erotic contact between two people involving stimulation of the genitals but stopping short of intercourse.

heav·y·set /ˈhevēˌset/ ▶ adj. having a stocky or stout build.

heav·y sleep·er ▶ n. a person who sleeps deeply and is difficult to wake up.

heav·y wa·ter ▶ n. water in which the hydrogen in the molecules is partly or wholly replaced by the isotope deuterium, used esp. as a moderator in nuclear reactors.

heav·y·weight /ˈhevēˌwāt/ ▶ n. **1** a weight in boxing and other sports, typically the heaviest category. In the amateur boxing scale it ranges from 178 to 200 pounds (81 to 91 kg). ■ a boxer or other competitor of this weight.
2 a person or thing of above-average weight. ■ a person of influence or importance, esp. in a particular sphere: *a political heavyweight with national recognition.*
▶ adj. of above-average weight. ■ serious, important, or influential: *heavyweight news coverage.*

Heb. ▶ abbr. ■ Bible Hebrews. ■ Hebrew.

heb·dom·a·dal /hebˈdämədl/ ▶ adj. formal weekly (used esp. of organizations that meet weekly): *he was forced to eke out a meager living scribbling hebdomadal feuilletons.*
– ORIGIN early 17th cent. (in the sense 'lasting seven days'): from late Latin *hebdomadalis*, from Greek *hebdomas, hebdomad-* 'the number seven, seven days,' from *hepta* 'seven.'

He·be[1] /ˈhēbē/ Greek Mythology the daughter of Hera and Zeus, and cupbearer of the gods.
– ORIGIN from Greek *hēbē* 'youthful beauty.'

Hebe[2] /hēb/ ▶ n. informal, offensive a Jewish person.
– ORIGIN early 20th cent.: abbreviation of HEBREW.

He·bei /ˈhəˈbā/ (also **Hopeh** /ˈhəˈbā, ˈhō-/) a province in northeastern central China; capital, Shijiazhuang.

he·be·phre·ni·a /ˌhēbəˈfrēnēə/ ▶ n. a form of chronic schizophrenia involving disordered thought, inappropriate emotions, hallucinations, and bizarre behavior.
– DERIVATIVES **he·be·phren·ic** /-ˈfrenik/ adj. & n.
– ORIGIN late 19th cent. (originally associated with behavior in puberty): from HEBE[1] + Greek *phrēn* 'mind' + -IA[1].

heb·e·tude /ˈhebəˌt(y)o͞od/ ▶ n. literary the state of being dull or lethargic.
– ORIGIN early 17th cent.: from late Latin *hebetudo*, from *hebes, hebet-* 'blunt.'

Hebr. ▶ abbr. Hebrew or Hebrews.

He·bra·ic /hēˈbrāik/ ▶ adj. of Hebrew or the Hebrews: *a student of Hebraic religious literature.*
– DERIVATIVES **He·bra·i·cal·ly** /-ik(ə)lē/ adv.
– ORIGIN via Christian Latin from late Greek *Hebraikos*, from *Hebraios* (see HEBREW).

He·bra·ism /ˈhēbrāˌizəm/ ▶ n. **1** a Hebrew idiom or expression.
2 the Jewish religion, culture, or character.
– DERIVATIVES **He·bra·is·tic** /ˌhēbrāˈistik/ adj., **He·bra·ize** /-ˌīz/ v.
– ORIGIN late 16th cent.: from French *hébraïsme* or modern Latin *Hebraismus*, from late Greek *Hebraïsmos*, from *Hebraios* (see HEBREW).

He·bra·ist /ˈhēbrāist/ ▶ n. a scholar of the Hebrew language. ■ a student or adherent of the Jewish religion, culture, or character.

He·brew /ˈhēbro͞o/ ▶ n. **1** a member of an ancient people living in what is now Israel and Palestine and, according to biblical tradition, descended from the patriarch Jacob, grandson of Abraham. After the Exodus (*c.*1300 BC) they established the kingdoms of Israel and Judah, and their scriptures and traditions form the basis of the Jewish religion. ■ old-fashioned and sometimes offensive term for JEW.
2 the Semitic language of this people, in its ancient or modern form.
▶ adj. **1** of the Hebrews or the Jews.
2 of or in Hebrew.

> Hebrew is written from right to left in a characteristic alphabet of twenty-two consonants, the vowels sometimes being marked by additional signs. From about AD 500 it was almost entirely restricted to Jewish religious use, but it was revived as a spoken language in the 19th century and, with a vocabulary extended by borrowing from contemporary languages, is now the official language of the state of Israel.

– ORIGIN from Old French *Ebreu*, via Latin from late Greek *Hebraios*, from Aramaic *ʿibray*, based on Hebrew *ʿibrî* understood to mean 'one from the other side (of the river).'

He·brew Bi·ble the sacred writings of Judaism, called by Christians the Old Testament, and comprising the Law (Torah), the Prophets, and the Hagiographa or Writings.

He·brews /ˈhēbro͞oz/ a book of the New Testament, traditionally included among the letters of St. Paul but now generally held to be non-Pauline.

Heb·ri·des /ˈhebrəˌdēz/ a group of about 500 islands off the northwestern coast of Scotland. The **Inner Hebrides** are separated from the **Outer Hebrides** by the Little Minch. Also called WESTERN ISLES.
– DERIVATIVES **Heb·ri·de·an** /ˌhebrəˈdēən/ n. & adj.

He·bron /ˈhēbrən/ a Palestinian city on the West Bank of the Jordan River; pop. 240,200 (est. 2009). As the home of Abraham, it is a holy city of both Judaism and Islam. Israeli forces withdrew from all but a small part of the city in 1997.

Heb·ros /ˈhēbrəs/ (also **Hebrus**) ancient Greek name for MARITSA.

Hec·a·te /ˈhekətē/ Greek Mythology a goddess of dark places, often associated with ghosts and sorcery. She is frequently identified with Artemis and Selene.

hec·a·tomb /ˈhekəˌtōm/ ▶ n. (in ancient Greece or Rome) a great public sacrifice, originally of a hundred oxen. ■ an extensive loss of life for some cause.
– ORIGIN late 16th cent.: via Latin from Greek *hekatombē* (from *hekaton* 'hundred' + *bous* 'ox').

Hecht /hekt/, Ben (1894–1964), US writer and playwright. He wrote the screenplays for *Underworld* (1927) and *The Scoundrel* (1935) and cowrote *The Front Page* (1928).

heck /hek/ ▶ exclam. expressing surprise, frustration, or dismay: *oh heck, I can't for the life of me remember.* ■ (**the heck**) used for emphasis in questions and exclamations: *what the heck's the matter?*

– PHRASES **a heck of a ——** used for emphasis in various statements or exclamations: *it was a heck of a lot of money.*
– ORIGIN late 19th cent. (originally dialect): euphemistic alteration of HELL.

heck·el·phone /ˈhekəlˌfōn/ ▶ n. a woodwind instrument resembling a large oboe, with a range about an octave lower.
– ORIGIN early 20th cent.: from German *Heckelphon*, named after Wilhelm *Heckel* (1856–1909), German instrument maker, on the pattern of *saxophone*.

heck·le /ˈhekəl/ ▶ v. [with obj.] **1** interrupt (a public speaker) with derisive or aggressive comments or abuse: *he was booed and heckled when he tried to address the demonstrators* | [no obj.] *he is merely heckling from the sidelines.*
2 dress (flax or hemp) to split and straighten the fibers for spinning.
▶ n. a heckling comment: *the meeting regularly dissolved into heckles.*
– DERIVATIVES **heck·ler** /ˈhek(ə)lər/ n.
– ORIGIN Middle English (sense 2 of the verb): from *heckle* 'flax comb,' a northern and eastern form of HACKLE. The sense 'interrupt (a public speaker) with aggressive questions' arose in the mid 17th cent.; for the development in sense, compare with TEASE.

heck·uv·a /ˈhekəvə/ nonstandard spelling of A HECK OF A —— (see HECK): *a heckuva lot of people.*

hec·tare /ˈhekˌte(ə)r/ (abbr.: **ha**) ▶ n. a metric unit of square measure, equal to 100 ares (2.471 acres or 10,000 square meters).
– DERIVATIVES **hec·tar·age** /ˈhektərij/ n.
– ORIGIN early 19th cent.: from French, formed irregularly from Greek *hekaton* 'hundred' + ARE[2].

hec·tic /ˈhektik/ ▶ adj. **1** full of incessant or frantic activity: *a hectic business schedule.*
2 Medicine, archaic relating to, affected by, or denoting a regularly recurrent fever typically accompanying tuberculosis, with flushed cheeks and hot, dry skin.
▶ n. Medicine, archaic a hectic fever or flush. ■ a patient suffering from such a fever.
– DERIVATIVES **hec·ti·cal·ly** /-tik(ə)lē/ adv.
– ORIGIN late Middle English *etik*, via Old French from late Latin *hecticus*, from Greek *hektikos* 'habitual,' from *hexis* 'habit, state of mind or body.' The original specific association with the symptoms of tuberculosis (*hectic fever*) gave rise to the early 20th-cent. sense 'characterized by feverish activity.'

hecto- ▶ comb. form (used commonly in units of measurement) a hundred: *hectometer.*
– ORIGIN from French, formed irregularly by contraction of Greek *hekaton* 'hundred.'

hec·to·cot·y·lus /ˌhektōˈkätl-əs/ ▶ n. (pl. **hectocotyli** /-ˈkätlˌī/) Zoology a modified arm used by male octopuses and some other cephalopods to transfer sperm to the female.
– ORIGIN mid 19th cent.: modern Latin, from HECTO- 'hundred' + Greek *kotulē* 'hollow thing,' a name given by Cuvier to what he mistakenly took to be a genus of parasitic worms.

hec·to·gram /ˈhektəˌgram/ (Brit. also **hectogramme**) (abbr.: **hg**) ▶ n. a metric unit of mass equal to one hundred grams.

hec·to·graph /ˈhektəˌgraf/ ▶ n. an apparatus for copying documents by the use of a gelatin plate that receives an impression of the master copy.

hec·to·li·ter /ˈhektəˌlētər/ (Brit. **hectolitre**) (abbr.: **hl**) ▶ n. a metric unit of capacity equal to one hundred liters, used esp. for wine, beer, grain, and other agricultural produce.

hec·to·me·ter /ˈhektəˌmētər/ (Brit. **hectometre**) (abbr.: **hm**) ▶ n. a metric unit of length equal to one hundred meters.

Hec·tor /ˈhektər/ Greek Mythology a Trojan warrior, son of Priam and Hecuba and husband of Andromache. He was killed by Achilles, who dragged his body behind his chariot three times around the walls of Troy.

hec·tor /ˈhektər/ ▶ v. [with obj.] talk to (someone) in a bullying way: *she doesn't hector us about giving up things* | (as adj. **hectoring**) *a brusque, hectoring manner.*
– DERIVATIVES **hec·tor·ing·ly** /ˈhekt(ə)riNGlē/ adv.
– ORIGIN late Middle English: from the Greek name HECTOR. Originally denoting a hero, the sense later became 'braggart or bully' (applied in the late 17th cent. to a member of a gang of youths in London, England), hence 'talk to in a bullying way.'

Hec·u·ba /ˈhekyəbə/ Greek Mythology the queen of Troy, wife of Priam and mother of children including Hector, Paris, Cassandra, and Troilus.

he'd /hēd/ ▶ contraction he had: *he'd seen all he wanted.* ■ he would: *he'd like to see you.*

hed·dle /ˈhedl/ ▶ n. one of a set of looped wires or cords in a loom, with an eye in the center through which a warp yarn is passed before going through the reed to control its movement and divide the threads.
– ORIGIN early 16th cent.: apparently from an alteration of Old English *hefeld.*

he·der /ˈKHādər, ˈhādər/ ▶ n. (pl. **hedarim** /KHəˈdärim/ or **heders**) variant spelling of CHEDER.

hedge /hej/ ▶ n. a fence or boundary formed by closely growing bushes or shrubs: *she was standing barefoot in a corner of the lawn, trimming the hedge.* ■ a contract entered into or asset held as a protection against possible financial loss: *inflation hedges such as real estate and gold.* ■ a word or phrase used to allow for additional possibilities or to avoid commitment, for example, *etc., often, usually,* or *sometimes.*
▶ v. [with obj.] **1** surround or bound with a hedge: *a garden hedged with yews.* ■ (**hedge something in**) enclose.
2 limit or qualify (something) by conditions or exceptions: *experts usually hedge their predictions, just in case.* ■ [no obj.] avoid making a definite decision, statement, or commitment: *she hedged around the one question she wanted to ask.*
3 protect (one's investment or an investor) against loss by making balancing or compensating contracts or transactions: *the company hedged its investment position on the futures market.*
– PHRASES **hedge one's bets** avoid committing oneself when faced with a difficult choice.
– DERIVATIVES **hedg·er** n.
– ORIGIN Old English *hegg*, of Germanic origin; related to Dutch *heg* and German *Hecke.*

hedge fund ▶ n. a limited partnership of investors that uses high risk methods, such as investing with borrowed money, in hopes of realizing large capital gains.

hedge·hog /ˈhejˌhôg, -ˌhäg/ ▶ n. a nocturnal Old World mammal with a spiny coat and short legs, able to roll itself into a ball for defense. ● Family Erinaceidae: four genera and several species, including the **common hedgehog** (*Erinaceus europaeus*) of western and northern Europe, which is predominantly insectivorous.
■ any other animal covered with spines, esp. a porcupine.
– ORIGIN late Middle English: from HEDGE (from its habitat) + HOG (from its piglike snout).

common hedgehog

hedge·hop /ˈhejˌhäp/ ▶ v. [no obj.] fly an aircraft at a very low altitude.
– DERIVATIVES **hedge·hop·per** n.

hedge·row /ˈhejˌrō/ ▶ n. a hedge of wild shrubs and trees, typically bordering a road or field.
– ORIGIN Old English: from HEDGE + obsolete *rew* 'hedgerow,' assimilated to ROW[1].

hedge trim·mer ▶ n. an electric tool resembling a chainsaw used for cutting back bushes, shrubs, and hedges.

he·don·ic /hēˈdänik/ ▶ adj. technical relating to or considered in terms of pleasant (or unpleasant) sensations.
– ORIGIN mid 17th cent.: from Greek *hēdonikos*, from *hēdonē* 'pleasure.'

he·don·ism /ˈhēdnˌizəm/ ▶ n. the pursuit of pleasure; sensual self-indulgence. ■ the ethical theory that pleasure (in the sense of the satisfaction of desires) is the highest good and proper aim of human life.
– ORIGIN mid 19th cent.: from Greek *hēdonē* 'pleasure' + -ISM.

he·don·ist /ˈhēdnist/ ▶ n. a person who believes that the pursuit of pleasure is the most important thing in life; a pleasure-seeker: *she was living the life of a committed hedonist.*

he·don·is·tic /ˌhēdnˈistik/ ▶ adj. engaged in the pursuit of pleasure; sensually self-indulgent: *a hedonistic existence of drink, drugs, and parties.*
– DERIVATIVES **he·don·is·ti·cal·ly** /ˌhēdnˈistik(ə)lē/ adv.

-hedral ▶ comb. form in adjectives corresponding to nouns ending in *-hedron* (such as *dodecahedral* corresponding to *dodecahedron*).

-hedron ▶ comb. form (pl. **-hedra** or **-hedrons**) in nouns denoting geometric solids having a specified number of plane faces: *decahedron.* ■ denoting geometric solids having faces of a specified shape: *rhombohedron.*
– ORIGIN from Greek *hedra* 'seat, base.'

hee·bie-jee·bies /ˌhēbēˈjēbēz/ ▶ plural n. (**the heebie-jeebies**) informal a state of nervous fear or anxiety: *it takes a lot more than a measly poltergeist to give me the heebie-jeebies.*
– ORIGIN 1920s: coined by W. B. DeBeck (1890–1942), American cartoonist, in his comic strip *Barney Google.*

heed /hēd/ ▶ v. [with obj.] pay attention to; take notice of: *he should have heeded the warnings.*
▶ n. careful attention: *if he heard, he paid no heed* | *we must take heed of the suggestions.*
– ORIGIN Old English *hēdan* (originally intransitive); related to Dutch *hoeden* and German *hüten.*

heed·ful /ˈhēdfəl/ ▶ adj. aware of and attentive to: *he is heedful of his own intuitions.*
– DERIVATIVES **heed·ful·ly** adv., **heed·ful·ness** n.

heed·less /ˈhēdlis/ ▶ adj. showing a reckless lack of care or attention: *"Elaine!" she shouted, heedless of attracting unwanted attention* | *his heedless impetuosity.*
– DERIVATIVES **heed·less·ly** adv., **heed·less·ness** n.

hee-haw /ˈhē ˌhô/ ▶ n. the loud, harsh cry of a donkey or mule. ■ [as modifier] informal relating to or denoting unsophisticated rural humor and attitudes: *hee-haw manners.*
▶ v. [no obj.] make the loud, harsh cry of a donkey or mule.
– ORIGIN early 19th cent.: imitative.

h

heel[1] /hēl/ ▶ n. **1** the back part of the foot below the ankle. ■ a corresponding part of the foot in vertebrate animals. ■ the part of the palm of the hand next to the wrist: *he rubbed the heel of his hand against the window.* ■ the part of a shoe or boot supporting the heel: *shoes with low heels.* ■ the part of a sock covering the heel. ■ (**heels**) high-heeled shoes.
2 a thing resembling a heel in form or position, in particular: ■ the end of a violin bow at which it is held. ■ the part of the head of a golf club nearest the shaft. ■ a crusty end of a loaf of bread, or the rind of a cheese. ■ a piece of the main stem of a plant left attached to the base of a cutting.
3 informal an inconsiderate or untrustworthy person: *what kind of a heel do you think I am?*
4 [as exclamation] a command to a dog to walk close behind its owner.
▶ v. [with obj.] **1** fit or renew a heel on (a shoe or boot).
2 (of a dog) follow closely behind its owner: *these dogs are born with the instinctive urge to heel.*
3 [no obj.] touch the ground with the heel when dancing.
4 Golf strike (the ball) with the heel of the club.
– PHRASES **at** (or **to**) **heel** (of a dog) close to and slightly behind its owner. **at the heels of** (or **at someone's heels**) following closely behind: *he headed off with Sammy at his heels.* **bring someone to heel** bring someone under control. **down at heel** (of a shoe) with the heel worn down. ■ having a poor, shabby appearance. **kick up one's heels** have a lively, enjoyable time. **on the heels of** following closely after: *September frosts would be on the heels of the dog days of August.* **set someone back on their heels** astonish or discomfit someone. **turn on one's heel** turn sharply around. **under the heel of** dominated or controlled by: *the Greeks spent several centuries under the heel of the Ottoman Empire.*
– DERIVATIVES **heeled** /hēld/ adj. [in combination] *high-heeled shoes*, **heel·less** adj.
– ORIGIN Old English *hēla, hǣla*, of Germanic origin; related to Dutch *hiel.*

heel[2] ▶ v. [no obj.] (of a boat or ship) be tilted temporarily by the pressure of wind or by an uneven distribution of weight on board. Compare with LIST[2].
■ [with obj.] cause (a boat or ship) to lean over in such a way.
▶ n. an instance of a ship leaning over in such a way.
■ the degree of incline of a ship's leaning measured from the vertical.
– ORIGIN late 16th cent.: from obsolete *heeld, hield* 'incline,' of Germanic origin; related to Dutch *hellen.*

heel[3] ▶ v. [with obj.] (**heel something in**) set a plant in the ground and cover its roots.
– ORIGIN Old English *helian* 'cover, hide,' of Germanic origin, from an Indo-European root shared by Latin *celare* 'hide.'

heel·ball /ˈhēlˌbôl/ ▶ n. a mixture of hard wax and lampblack used by shoemakers for polishing and in brass rubbing.

heel bone ▶ n. the calcaneus.

heel·flip /ˈhēlflip/ ▶ n. (in skateboarding) a maneuver in which the front heel is used to manipulate the board during a jump in such a way that it completes a sideways rotation before landing.

heel·tap /ˈhēlˌtap/ ▶ **n. 1** one of the layers of leather or other material of which a shoe heel is made. **2** dated an amount of liquor left at the bottom of a glass after drinking.

He·fei /ˈhəˈfā/ (also **Hofei**) an industrial city in eastern China, capital of Anhui province; pop. 1,502,800 (est. 2006).

Hef·ner /ˈhefnər/, Hugh (Marston) (1926–), US publisher. He founded *Playboy* magazine in 1953 and Playboy Clubs International, Inc., in 1959.

heft /heft/ ▶ **v.** [with obj.] lift or carry (something heavy): *Donald hefted another pair of sandbags from the stack.* ■ lift or hold (something) in order to test its weight: *Eileen hefted the gun in her hand.* ▶ **n.** the weight of someone or something. ■ ability or influence: *his colleagues wonder if he has the intellectual heft for his new job.*
– ORIGIN late Middle English (as a noun): probably from **HEAVE**, on the pattern of words such as *cleft* and *weft*.

heft·y /ˈheftē/ ▶ **adj.** (**heftier, heftiest**) large, heavy, and powerful: *a hefty young chap.* ■ (of a number or amount) impressively large: *a hefty 10 million* | *hefty Christmas bonuses.*
– DERIVATIVES **heft·i·ly** /-təlē/ **adv.**, **heft·i·ness n.**

He·gang /ˈhəˈgäNG/ a city in Heilongjiang province, in northeastern China, northeast of Harbin; pop. 611,900 (est. 2006).

h

He·gel /ˈhāgəl/, Georg Wilhelm Friedrich (1770–1831), German philosopher. In *Science of Logic* (1812–16) he described the three-stage process of dialectical reasoning, on which Marx based his theory of dialectical materialism.
– DERIVATIVES **He·ge·li·an** /həˈgālēən/ **adj. & n.**, **He·ge·li·an·ism** /həˈgālēəˌnizəm/ **n.**

heg·e·mon·ic /ˌhegəˈmänik/ ▶ **adj.** ruling or dominant in a political or social context: *the bourgeoisie constituted the hegemonic class.*
– ORIGIN mid 17th cent.: from Greek *hēgemonikos* 'capable of commanding,' from *hēgemōn* (see **HEGEMONY**).

he·gem·o·ny /həˈjemənē, ˈhejəˌmōnē/ ▶ **n.** leadership or dominance, esp. by one country or social group over others: *Germany was united under Prussian hegemony after 1871.*
– ORIGIN mid 16th cent.: from Greek *hēgemonia*, from *hēgemōn* 'leader,' from *hēgeisthai* 'to lead.'

He·gi·ra /hiˈjīrə, ˈhejərə/ (also **Hejira** or **Hijra** /ˈhijrə/) ▶ **n.** Muhammad's departure from Mecca to Medina in AD 622, prompted by the opposition of the merchants of Mecca and marking the consolidation of the first Muslim community. ■ the Muslim era reckoned from this date: *the second century of the Hegira.* See also **AH**. ■ (**hegira**) an exodus or migration.
– ORIGIN via medieval Latin from Arabic *hijra* 'departure,' from *hajara* 'emigrate.'

hei·au /ˈhe-ēˌou/ ▶ **n.** (pl. **same** or **heiaus**) an ancient Hawaiian temple or sacred site.
– ORIGIN Hawaiian.

Hei·deg·ger /ˈhīdəgər/, Martin (1889–1976), German philosopher. In *Being and Time* (1927), he examined the ontology of "Being," in particular, human existence as involvement with a world of objects (*Dasein*).

Hei·del·berg /ˈhīdlˌbərg/ a city in southwestern Germany, on the Neckar River, in Baden-Württemberg; pop. 144,600 (est. 2006). Its university is the oldest in Germany.

Hei·del·berg man ▶ **n.** a fossil hominid of the early middle Pleistocene period, identified by only a jawbone found near Heidelberg in 1907. ● an early form of *Homo erectus* (formerly *H. heidelbergensis*), family Hominidae.

Hei·den /ˈhīdn/, Eric (1958–), US speed skater. He was the world champion in speed skating in 1977, 1978, and 1979 before he won five gold medals at the 1980 Olympic games.

heif·er /ˈhefər/ ▶ **n.** a young female cow that has not borne a calf.
– ORIGIN Old English *heahfore*, of unknown origin.

Hei·fetz /ˈhīfits/, Jascha (1901–87), US violinist; born in Lithuania. Recognized as a musical prodigy at age three, he made his US debut at Carnegie Hall in 1917 and went on to become one of the most celebrated violinists of the century.

heigh /hī, hā/ ▶ **exclam.** archaic expressing encouragement or inquiry.
– ORIGIN natural utterance: first recorded in Middle English.

heigh-ho ▶ **exclam.** informal expressing boredom, resignation, or jollity: *it was like talking to a brick wall. Heigh-ho!* | *how pleasant it is to have money, heigh-ho!*

height /hīt/ ▶ **n. 1** the measurement from base to top or (of a standing person) from head to foot: *columns rising to 65 feet in height* | *both men were of average height.* ■ elevation above ground or a recognized level (typically sea level): *the glider is gaining height.* ■ the quality of being tall or high: *his height seems to work to his advantage.* **2** a high place or area: *he's terrified of heights.* **3** the most intense part or period of something: *the height of the tourist season* | *at the height of his career* | *they took consumerism to new heights.* ■ an extreme instance or example of something: *it would be the height of bad manners not to attend the wedding.*
– ORIGIN Old English *hēhthu* (in the sense 'top of something'), of Germanic origin; related to Dutch *hoogte*, also to **HIGH**.

height·en /ˈhītn/ ▶ **v.** [with obj.] make (something) higher. ■ make or become more intense: [with obj.] *the pleasure was heightened by the sense of guilt that accompanied it* | [no obj.] *concern over CFCs has heightened* | (as adj. **heightened**) *the heightened color of her face.*

height·ism /ˈhītizəm/ ▶ **n.** prejudice or discrimination against someone on the basis of their height.
– DERIVATIVES **height·ist adj. & n.**

height of land ▶ **n.** a watershed.

Heil·bronn /ˈhīlˌbrän, -ˌbrôn/ a city in southwestern Germany, on the Neckar River, in Baden-Württemberg; pop. 121,400 (est. 2006).

Hei·long /ˈhāˈlôNG/ Chinese name of **AMUR**.

Hei·long·jiang /ˈhāˈlôNGjēˈäNG/ (also **Heilungkiang** /-ˈlo͝oNG-/) a province in northeastern China, on the Russian frontier; capital, Harbin.

Heim·lich ma·neu·ver /ˈhīmlik, ˈhīmliKH/ ▶ **n.** a first-aid procedure for dislodging an obstruction from a person's windpipe in which a sudden strong pressure is applied on the abdomen, between the navel and the rib cage.
– ORIGIN 1970s: named after Henry J. *Heimlich* (born 1920), the American doctor who developed the procedure.

hei·nie /ˈhīnē/ ▶ **n.** informal a person's buttocks.
– ORIGIN 1960s: alteration of **HINDER²**, variant of **HIND¹**.

hei·nous /ˈhānəs/ ▶ **adj.** (of a person or wrongful act, esp. a crime) utterly odious or wicked: *a battery of heinous crimes.*
– DERIVATIVES **hei·nous·ly adv.**, **hei·nous·ness n.**
– ORIGIN late Middle English: from Old French *haineus*, from *hair* 'to hate,' of Germanic origin.

Heinz /hīnz/, Henry John (1844–1919), US food manufacturer. In 1869 he established a family firm for the manufacture and sale of processed foods.

heir /e(ə)r/ ▶ **n.** a person legally entitled to the property or rank of another on that person's death: *his eldest son and heir* | *she aspired to marry the heir to the throne.* ■ a person inheriting and continuing the legacy of a predecessor: *they saw themselves as the true heirs of the Enlightenment.*
– DERIVATIVES **heir·dom** /-dəm/ **n.**, **heir·less adj.**, **heir·ship** /-ˌSHip/ **n.**
– ORIGIN Middle English: via Old French from Latin *heres*.

heir ap·par·ent ▶ **n.** (pl. **heirs apparent**) an heir whose claim cannot be set aside by the birth of another heir. Compare with **HEIR PRESUMPTIVE**. ■ a person who is most likely to succeed to the place of another: *he was once considered heir apparent to the chairman.*

heir-at-law ▶ **n.** (pl. **heirs-at-law**) an heir by right of blood, esp. to the real property of a person who dies intestate.

heir·ess /ˈe(ə)ris/ ▶ **n.** a female heir, esp. to vast wealth: *an oil heiress.*

heir·loom /ˈe(ə)rˌlo͞om/ ▶ **n.** a valuable object that has belonged to a family for several generations.
– ORIGIN late Middle English: from **HEIR** + **LOOM¹** (which formerly had the senses 'tool, heirloom').

heir pre·sump·tive ▶ **n.** (pl. **heirs presumptive**) an heir whose claim could be set aside by the birth of another heir. Compare with **HEIR APPARENT**.

Hei·sen·berg /ˈhīzənˌbərg/, Werner Karl (1901–76), German mathematical physicist and philosopher. He developed a system of quantum mechanics based on matrix algebra in which he states his well-known uncertainty principle (1927). Nobel Prize for Physics (1932).

Heis·man Tro·phy /ˈhīsmən/ ▶ **n.** an annual award given to the outstanding college football player in the US by the Downtown Athletic Club of New York City.
– ORIGIN named in honor of football pioneer John W. Heisman (1869–1936).

heist /hīst/ informal ▶ **n.** a robbery: *a diamond heist.* ▶ **v.** [with obj.] steal: *he heisted a Pontiac.*
– ORIGIN mid 19th cent.: representing a local pronunciation of **HOIST**.

He·jaz /ˈhēˈjaz, -ˈZHäz/ (also **Hijaz**) a coastal region in western Saudi Arabia that borders the Red Sea.

He·ji·ra ▶ **n.** variant spelling of **HEGIRA**.

He·La cells /ˈhelə/ ▶ **plural n.** human epithelial cells of a strain maintained in tissue culture since 1951 and used in research, esp. in virology.
– ORIGIN 1950s: from the name of *He*nrietta *La*cks, whose cervical carcinoma provided the original cells.

held /held/ past and past participle of **HOLD¹**.

hel·den·ten·or /ˈheldəntəˌnôr, ˈheldnˌtenər/ ▶ **n.** a powerful tenor voice suitable for heroic roles in opera. ■ a singer with such a voice.
– ORIGIN 1920s: German, literally 'hero tenor.'

Hel·en /ˈhelən/ Greek Mythology the daughter of Zeus and Leda, born from an egg. In the Homeric poems she was the outstandingly beautiful wife of Menelaus, and her abduction by Paris (to whom she had been promised, as a bribe, by Aphrodite) led to the Trojan War.

Hel·e·na /ˈhelənə/ the capital of Montana, in the western central part of the state; pop. 29,351 (est. 2008).

Hel·e·na, St. /ˈhelənə/ (*c.*255–*c.*330), Roman empress and mother of Constantine the Great. In 326 she founded basilicas on the Mount of Olives and at Bethlehem and is credited with finding the cross on which Jesus Christ was crucified. Feast day (in the Eastern Church) May 21; (in the Western Church) August 18.

he·len·i·um /həˈlēnēəm/ ▶ **n.** an American plant of the daisy family that bears many red to yellow flowers, each having a prominent central disk. ● Genus *Helenium*, family Compositae: many species, esp. the sneezeweeds.
– ORIGIN modern Latin, from Greek *helenion*. The term originally denoted the herb *elecampane*, possibly in commemoration of Helen of Troy (said to have planted elecampane on the island of Pharos); the current designation was adopted by Linnaeus in the 18th cent.

heli- ▶ **comb. form** relating to helicopters: *heli-skiing* | *helipad.*

he·li·a·cal /həˈlīəkəl/ ▶ **adj.** Astronomy relating to or near the sun.
– ORIGIN mid 16th cent.: via late Latin from Greek *hēliakos* (from *hēlios* 'sun') + **-AL**.

he·li·a·cal ris·ing ▶ **n.** the rising of a celestial object at the same time or just before the sun, or its first visible rising after a period of invisibility due to conjunction with the sun. The last setting before such a period is the **heliacal setting**.
– ORIGIN early 17th cent.: *heliacal*, via late Latin from Greek *hēliakos* (from *hēlios* 'sun') + **-AL**.

he·li·an·the·mum /ˌhēlēˈanTHəməm/ ▶ **n.** a rockrose of the genus *Helianthemum.*
– ORIGIN modern Latin, from Greek *hēlios* 'sun' + *anthemon* 'flower' (because the flowers open in sunlight).

he·li·an·thus /ˌhēlēˈanTHəs/ ▶ **n.** a plant of the genus *Helianthus* in the daisy family, esp. (in gardening) a sunflower.
– ORIGIN modern Latin, from Greek *hēlios* 'sun' + *anthos* 'flower.'

hel·i·cal /ˈhelikəl, ˈhē-/ ▶ **adj.** having the shape or form of a helix; spiral: *helical molecules.*
– DERIVATIVES **hel·i·cal·ly** /-ik(ə)lē/ **adv.**

hel·i·ces /ˈhēləˌsēz/ plural form of **HELIX**.

hel·i·chry·sum /ˌheləˈkrisəm/ ▶ **n.** an Old World plant of the daisy family. Some kinds are grown as everlastings, retaining their shape and color when dried. Compare with **STRAWFLOWER**. ● Genus *Helichrysum*, family Compositae.
– ORIGIN Latin, from Greek *helikhrusos*, from *helix* 'spiral' + *khrusos* 'gold.' It originally denoted a yellow-flowered plant, possibly *Helichrysum stoechas.*

he·lic·i·ty /həˈlisitē/ ▶ **n. 1** chiefly Biochemistry helical character, esp. of DNA. **2** Physics a combination of the spin and the linear motion of a subatomic particle.
– ORIGIN 1950s (sense 2): from Latin *helix, helic-* 'spiral' + **-ITY**.

hel·i·coid /ˈheliˌkoid/ ▶ **n.** an object of spiral or helical shape. ■ Geometry a surface formed by simultaneously moving a straight line along an axis and rotating it around it (like a screw thread). ▶ **adj.** of the form of a helix or helicoid.
– DERIVATIVES **hel·i·coi·dal** /ˌheliˈkoidəl/ **adj.**
– ORIGIN late 17th cent.: from Greek *helikoeidēs* 'of spiral form,' from *helix, helik-* (see **HELIX**).

hel·i·con /ˈheliˌkän, -kən/ ▶ **n.** a large spiral bass tuba played encircling the player's head and resting on the shoulder.
– ORIGIN late 19th cent.: from Latin, associated with **HELIX**.

hel·i·co·nia /ˌheliˈkōnēə/ ▶ **n.** a large-leaved tropical American plant that bears spectacular flowers with brightly colored bracts. ● Genus *Heliconia*, family Heliconiaceae (formerly Musaceae): many species, including the lobster claw.

Hel·i·con, Mount /ˈheləˌkän, -ikən/ a mountain in Boeotia, in central Greece, north of the Gulf of Corinth, that rises to 5,741 feet (1,750 m). It was believed by the ancient Greeks to be the home of the Muses.

hel·i·cop·ter /ˈheliˌkäptər/ ▶ **n.** a type of aircraft that derives both lift and propulsion from one or two sets of horizontally revolving overhead rotors. It is capable of moving vertically and horizontally, the direction of motion being controlled by the pitch of the rotor blades. Compare with **AUTOGIRO**.
▶ **v.** [with obj.] transport by helicopter: *the Coast Guard helicoptered a compressor to one ship.* ■ [no obj.] fly somewhere in a helicopter: *the inspection team helicoptered ashore.*
– ORIGIN late 19th cent.: from French *hélicoptère*, from Greek *helix* 'spiral' + *pteron* 'wing.'

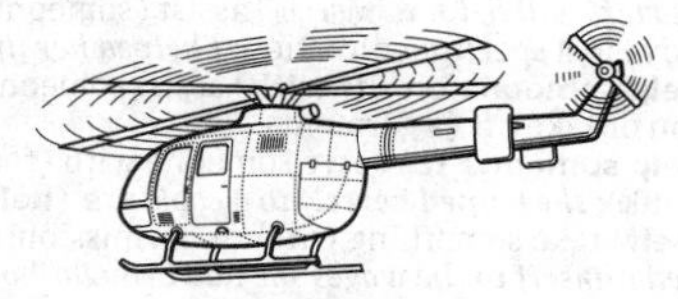
helicopter

he·lic·tite /həˈliktīt, ˈhelikˌtīt/ ▶ **n.** Geology a distorted form of stalactite, typically resembling a twig.
– ORIGIN late 19th cent.: from Greek *heliktos* 'twisted,' on the pattern of *stalactite*.

helio- ▶ **comb. form** of or relating to the sun: *heliogravure* | *heliostat*.
– ORIGIN from Greek *hēlios* 'sun.'

he·li·o·cen·tric /ˌhēlēəˈsentrik/ ▶ **adj.** having or representing the sun as the center, as in the accepted astronomical model of the solar system. Compare with **GEOCENTRIC**. ■ Astronomy measured from or considered in relation to the center of the sun: *heliocentric distance*.
– DERIVATIVES **he·li·o·cen·tri·cal·ly** /-trik(ə)lē/ **adv.**

He·lio·gab·a·lus /ˌhēlēōˈgabələs/ (also **Elagabalus** /ˌeləˈgabələs/) (AD 204–222), Roman emperor 218–222; born *Varius Avitus Bassianus*. He was notorious for his dissipated lifestyle and neglect of state affairs.

he·li·o·gram /ˈhēlēəˌgram/ ▶ **n.** a message sent by reflecting sunlight in flashes from a movable mirror.

he·li·o·graph /ˈhēlēəˌgraf/ ▶ **n.** **1** a signaling device by which sunlight is reflected in flashes from a movable mirror. ■ a message sent in such a way; a heliogram.
2 a telescopic apparatus for photographing the sun.
3 historical a type of early photographic engraving made using a sensitized silver plate and an asphalt or bitumen varnish.
▶ **v.** [with obj.] **1** dated send (a message) by heliograph.
2 historical take a heliographic photograph of.
– DERIVATIVES **he·li·o·graph·ic** /ˌhēlēəˈgrafik/ **adj.**, **he·li·og·ra·phy** /ˌhēlēˈägrəfē/ **n.**

he·li·o·gra·vure /ˌhēlēōgrəˈvyo͝or/ ▶ **n.** another term for **PHOTOGRAVURE**.

he·li·om·e·ter /ˌhēlēˈämitər/ ▶ **n.** Astronomy, historical a refracting telescope with a split objective lens, used for finding the angular distance between two stars.
– ORIGIN mid 18th cent.: from **HELIO-** 'of the sun' + **-METER** (because it was originally used for measuring the diameter of the sun).

he·li·o·pause /ˈhēlēəˌpôz/ ▶ **n.** Astronomy the boundary of the heliosphere.

He·li·op·o·lis /ˌhēlēˈäpələs/ **1** an ancient Egyptian city located near the apex of the Nile delta at what is now Cairo. It was the original site of the obelisks known as Cleopatra's Needles.
2 ancient Greek name for **BAALBEK**.
– ORIGIN from Greek *hēlios* 'sun' + *polis* 'city.'

He·li·os /ˈhēlēˌäs/ Greek Mythology the sun personified as a god, father of Phaethon. He is generally represented as a charioteer driving daily from east to west across the sky.
– ORIGIN Greek *hēlios* 'sun.'

he·li·o·sphere /ˈhēlēəˌsfi(ə)r/ ▶ **n.** Astronomy the region of space, encompassing the solar system, in which the solar wind has a significant influence.
– DERIVATIVES **he·li·o·spher·ic** /ˌhēlēəˈsferik, -ˈsfi(ə)rik/ **adj.**

he·li·o·stat /ˈhēlēəˌstat/ ▶ **n.** an apparatus containing a movable or driven mirror, used to reflect sunlight in a fixed direction. See also **COELOSTAT**.

he·li·o·ther·a·py /ˌhēlēəˈTHerəpē/ ▶ **n.** the therapeutic use of sunlight.

he·li·o·trope /ˈhēlēəˌtrōp/ ▶ **n.** a plant of the borage family, cultivated for its fragrant purple or blue flowers, which are used in perfume. ● Genus *Heliotropium*, family Boraginaceae.
■ a light purple color, similar to that typical of heliotrope flowers.
– ORIGIN Old English *eliotropus* (originally applied to various plants whose flowers turn toward the sun), via Latin from Greek *hēliotropion* 'plant turning its flowers to the sun,' from *hēlios* 'sun' + *trepein* 'to turn.' The spelling was influenced by French *héliotrope*.

he·li·ot·ro·pism /ˌhēlēˈätrəˌpizəm, ˌhēlēəˈtrōpizəm/ ▶ **n.** Botany the directional growth of a plant in response to sunlight. Compare with **PHOTOTROPISM**. ■ Zoology the tendency of an animal to move toward light.
– DERIVATIVES **he·li·o·trop·ic** /ˌhēlēəˈträpik, -ˈtrōpik/ **adj.**

He·li·o·zo·a /ˌhēlēəˈzōə/ Zoology a class of single-celled aquatic animals that are related to the radiolarians. They have a spherical shell with fine radiating needlelike projections. ● Class Heliozoa, phylum Actinopoda, kingdom Protista.
– ORIGIN modern Latin (plural), from Greek *hēlios* 'sun' + *zōion* 'animal.'

he·li·o·zo·an /ˌhēlēəˈzōən/ Zoology ▶ **n.** a single-celled aquatic animal of the phylum Heliozoa. ▶ **adj.** relating to or denoting heliozoans.

hel·i·pad /ˈheləˌpad/ ▶ **n.** a landing and takeoff area for helicopters.

hel·i·port /ˈheləˌpôrt/ ▶ **n.** an airport or landing place for helicopters.
– ORIGIN 1940s: from **HELI-** + **PORT**[1], on the pattern of *airport*.

hel·i·ski·ing /ˈheliˌskē-iNG/ ▶ **n.** skiing in which the skier is taken up the mountain by helicopter.
– DERIVATIVES **hel·i·ski v.**, **hel·i·ski·er n.**

he·li·um /ˈhēlēəm/ ▶ **n.** the chemical element of atomic number 2, an inert gas that is the lightest member of the noble gas series. (Symbol: **He**)

> **Helium** occurs in traces in air and more abundantly in natural gas deposits. It is used as a lifting gas for balloons and airships, and liquid **helium** (boiling point: 4.2 kelvins, −268.9°C) is used as a coolant. **Helium** is produced in stars as the main product of the thermonuclear fusion of hydrogen and is the second most abundant element in the universe after hydrogen.

– ORIGIN late 19th cent.: modern Latin, from Greek *hēlios* 'sun,' because its existence was inferred from an emission line in the sun's spectrum.

he·lix /ˈhēliks/ ▶ **n.** (pl. **helices** /-ləˌsēz/) an object having a three-dimensional shape like that of a wire wound uniformly in a single layer around a cylinder or cone, as in a corkscrew or spiral staircase.
■ Geometry a curve on a conical or cylindrical surface that would become a straight line if the surface were unrolled into a plane. ■ Biochemistry an extended spiral chain of atoms in a protein, nucleic acid, or other polymeric molecule. ■ Architecture a spiral ornament. ■ Anatomy the rim of the external ear.
– ORIGIN mid 16th cent. (in the architectural sense 'spiral ornament'): via Latin from Greek.

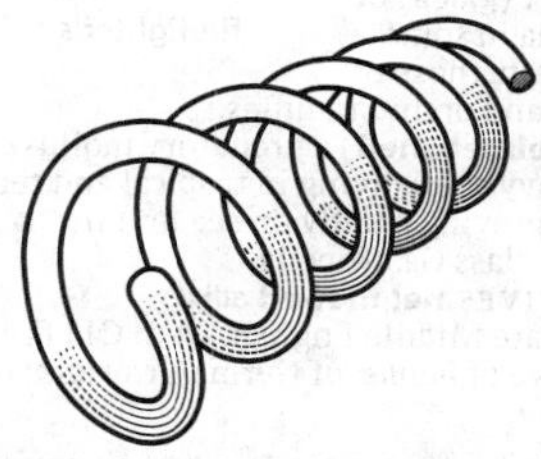
helix

hell /hel/ ▶ **n.** a place regarded in various religions as a spiritual realm of evil and suffering, often traditionally depicted as a place of perpetual fire beneath the earth where the wicked are punished after death. ■ a state or place of great suffering; an unbearable experience: *I've been through hell* | *he made her life hell.*
▶ **exclam.** used to express annoyance or surprise or for emphasis: *oh, hell—where will this all end?* | *hell, no, we were all married.* ■ (**the hell**) informal expressing anger, contempt, or disbelief: *who the hell are you?* | *the hell you are!*
– PHRASES **all hell broke loose** informal suddenly there was pandemonium. **(as) —— as hell** informal used for emphasis: *he's as guilty as hell.* **be hell on** informal be very unpleasant or harmful to: *summer can be hell on a man's skin.* **catch** (or **get**) **hell** informal be severely reprimanded: *Paul kept his mouth shut and looked apologetic—we got hell.* **come hell or high water** whatever difficulties may occur. **for the hell of it** informal just for fun: *she walked on window ledges for the hell of it.* **—— from hell** informal an extremely unpleasant or troublesome instance or example of something: *I've got a hangover from hell.* **get the hell out (of)** informal escape quickly from (a place or situation): *let's all get the hell out of here.* **give someone hell** informal severely reprimand or make things very unpleasant for someone. **go to hell** informal used to express angry rejection of someone or something. **go to** (or **through**) **hell and back** endure an extremely unpleasant or difficult experience. **go to hell in a handbasket** informal undergo a rapid process of deterioration. **hell for leather** as fast as possible. **hell's bells** informal an exclamation of annoyance or anger. **hell hath no fury like a woman scorned** proverb a woman who has been rejected by a man can be ferociously angry and vindictive. **a** (or **one**) **hell of a ——** informal used to emphasize something very bad or great: *it cost us a hell of a lot of money.* **hell's half acre** a great distance. **hell on wheels** a disastrous situation. **like hell** informal **1** very fast, much, hard, etc. (used for emphasis): *it hurts like hell.* **2** used in ironic expressions of scorn or disagreement: *like hell, he thought.* **not a hope in hell** informal no chance at all. **play hell** informal make a fuss; create havoc. ■ cause damage: *the rough road played hell with the tires.* **the road to hell is paved with good intentions** proverb promises and plans must be put into action, or else they are useless. **there will be hell to pay** informal serious trouble will occur as a result of a previous action. **to hell** used for emphasis: *damn it to hell.* **to hell with** informal expressing one's scorn or lack of concern for (someone or something): *to hell with the consequences.* **until** (or **till**) **hell freezes over** for an extremely long time or forever. **what the hell** informal it doesn't matter.
– DERIVATIVES **hell·ward** /-wərd/ **adv. & adj.**
– ORIGIN Old English *hel*, *hell*, of Germanic origin; related to Dutch *hel* and German *Hölle*, from an Indo-European root meaning 'to cover or hide.'

he'll /hēl/ ▶ **contraction** he shall; he will.

hel·la·cious /heˈlāSHəs/ ▶ **adj.** informal very great, bad, or overwhelming: *there was this hellacious hailstorm.*
– DERIVATIVES **hel·la·cious·ly adv.**
– ORIGIN 1930s: from **HELL** + **-ACIOUS**, perhaps suggested by *bodacious*.

Hel·lad·ic /heˈladik/ ▶ **adj.** Archaeology of, relating to, or denoting the Bronze Age cultures of mainland Greece (*c.*3000–1050 BC), of which the latest period is equivalent to the Mycenaean age.
– ORIGIN early 19th cent.: from Greek *Helladikos*, from *Hellas*, *Hellad-* 'Greece.'

Hel·las /ˈheləs/ Greek name for **GREECE**.

hell·bend·er /ˈhelˌbendər/ ▶ **n.** an aquatic giant salamander with grayish skin and a flattened head, native to North America. ● *Cryptobranchus alleganiensis*, family Cryptobranchidae.

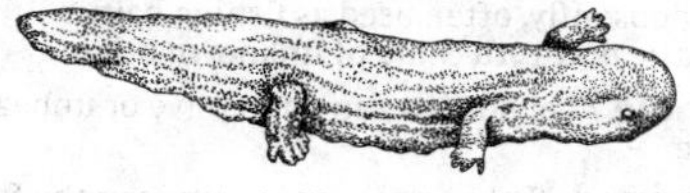
hellbender

hell-bent ▶ **adj.** [predic.] determined to achieve something at all costs: *why are you hell-bent on leaving?*

hell·cat /ˈhelˌkat/ ▶ **n.** a spiteful, violent woman.

hel·le·bore /ˈheləˌbôr/ ▶ **n.** a poisonous winter-flowering Eurasian plant of the buttercup family, typically having coarse divided leaves and large white, green, or purplish flowers. ● Genus *Helleborus*, family Ranunculaceae.
■ another term for **FALSE HELLEBORE**.
– ORIGIN Old English (denoting any of various plants supposed to cure madness), from Old French *ellebre*, *elebore* or medieval Latin *eleborus*, via Latin from Greek *helleboros*.

h

hel·leb·o·rine /ˈheləbəˌrīn, həˈlebərən/ ▶ **n.** a mainly woodland orchid occurring chiefly in north temperate regions. ● Two genera in the family Orchidaceae: *Epipactis* (with greenish or reddish flowers that are sometimes self-fertilized) and *Cephalanthera* (with larger white or pink flowers).
– ORIGIN late 16th cent.: French or Latin, from Greek *helleborinē*, a plant like hellebore, from *helleboros* 'hellebore.'

Hel·len /ˈhelən/ Greek Mythology the son or brother of Deucalion and ancestor of all the Hellenes or Greeks.

Hel·lene /ˈhelēn/ ▶ **n.** an ancient Greek. ■ a native of modern Greece (chiefly in the title of the now exiled royal family): *the King of the Hellenes*.
– ORIGIN from Greek *Hellēn* 'a Greek.' Compare with HELLEN.

Hel·len·ic /heˈlenik/ ▶ **adj.** Greek. ■ Archaeology relating to or denoting Iron Age and Classical Greek culture (between Helladic and Hellenistic).
▶ **n.** the branch of the Indo-European language family comprising classical and modern Greek. ■ the Greek language.
– ORIGIN from Greek *Hellēnikos*, from *Hellēn* (see HELLENE).

Hel·len·ism /ˈheləˌnizəm/ ▶ **n.** the national character or culture of Greece, esp. ancient Greece. ■ the study or imitation of ancient Greek culture.
– DERIVATIVES **Hel·len·ist n.**, **Hel·len·i·za·tion** /ˌheləniˈzāSHən/ **n.**, **Hel·len·ize** /-ˌnīz/ **v.**, **Hel·len·iz·er** /-ˌnīzər/ **n.**
– ORIGIN early 17th cent. (denoting a Greek phrase or idiom): from Greek *Hellēnismos*, from *Hellēnizein* 'speak Greek, make Greek,' from *Hellēn* 'a Greek.'

Hel·len·is·tic /ˌheləˈnistik/ ▶ **adj.** of or relating to Greek history, language, and culture from the death of Alexander the Great to the defeat of Cleopatra and Mark Antony by Octavian in 31 BC. During this period Greek culture flourished, spreading through the Mediterranean and into the Near East and Asia and centering on Alexandria in Egypt and Pergamum in Turkey.

Hel·ler /ˈhelər/, Joseph (1923–99), US novelist. His experiences in the US Army Air Force during World War II inspired his best-known novel *Catch-22* (1961), an absurd black comedy that satirized war and was the source of the expression "catch-22." He also wrote *Something Happened* (1974), *God Knows* (1984), *Picture This* (1988), and *Closing Time* (1994).

hel·ler /ˈhelər/ ▶ **n.** (pl. **same** or **hellers**) a former German or Austrian coin of low value. ■ another term for HALER.
– ORIGIN from German *Heller*, earlier *haller* (see HALER).

Hel·ler·work /ˈhelərˌwərk/ ▶ **n.** trademark a system involving deep tissue massage and exercise, designed to help correct posture, improve mobility, relieve pain, etc.
– ORIGIN 1980s: after Joseph *Heller* (1940–), its inventor.

Hel·les·pont /ˈheləˌspänt/ the ancient name for the Dardanelles, named after the legendary Helle, who fell into the strait and was drowned while escaping with her brother Phrixus from their stepmother, Ino, on a golden-fleeced ram.

hell·fire /ˈhelˌfīr/ ▶ **n.** the fire or fires regarded as existing in hell: *threats of hellfire and damnation*.

hell·gram·mite /ˈhelgrəˌmīt/ ▶ **n.** the aquatic larva of a dobsonfly, often used as fishing bait.
– ORIGIN mid 19th cent.: of unknown origin.

hell·hole /ˈhelˌhōl/ ▶ **n.** an oppressive or unbearable place.

hell·hound /ˈhelˌhound/ ▶ **n.** a demon in the form of a dog.
– ORIGIN Old English: originally referring esp. to Cerberus, the watchdog of Hades in Greek mythology.

hel·lion /ˈhelyən/ ▶ **n.** informal a rowdy, mischievous, or troublemaking person, esp. a child.
– ORIGIN mid 19th cent.: perhaps from dialect *hallion* 'a worthless fellow,' changed by association with HELL.

hell·ish /ˈheliSH/ ▶ **adj.** of or like hell: *an unearthly, hellish landscape*. ■ informal extremely difficult or unpleasant: *it had been a hellish week*.
▶ **adv.** [as submodifier] Brit. informal extremely (used for emphasis): *it was hellish expensive*.
– DERIVATIVES **hell·ish·ly adv.** [as submodifier] *a hellishly dull holiday*, **hell·ish·ness n.**

Hell·man /ˈhelmən/, Lillian (Florence) (1907–84), US playwright. Her plays, such as *The Children's Hour* (1934), *The Little Foxes* (1939), and *Watch on the Rhine* (1941), often reflected her socialist and feminist concerns. She lived with writer Dashiell Hammett, and both were blacklisted during the McCarthy era.

hel·lo /həˈlō, heˈlō/ (also **hallo** or chiefly Brit. **hullo**) ▶ **exclam.** used as a greeting or to begin a telephone conversation: *hello there, Katie!* ■ Brit. used to express surprise: *hello, what's all this then?* ■ used as a cry to attract someone's attention: *"Hello below!" he cried.* ■ /həˈlō, heˈlō/ expressing sarcasm or anger: *hello! did you even get what the play was about?*
▶ **n.** (pl. **hellos**) an utterance of "hello"; a greeting: *she was getting polite nods and hellos from people.*
▶ **v.** (**helloes, helloing, helloed**) [no obj.] say or shout "hello"; greet someone.
– ORIGIN late 19th cent.: variant of earlier *hollo*; related to HOLLA.

hell-rais·er ▶ **n.** a person who causes trouble by drinking, being violent, or otherwise behaving outrageously.
– DERIVATIVES **hell-rais·ing adj. & n.**

Hell's An·gel ▶ **n.** a member of any of a number of gangs ("chapters") of male motorcycle enthusiasts, first formed in California in the 1950s and originally notorious for lawless behavior.

Hell's Can·yon a chasm in Idaho, cut by the Snake River, that forms the deepest gorge in the US. Flanked by the Seven Devils Mountains, the canyon drops to a depth of 7,900 feet (2,433 m).

hell·uv·a /ˈheləvə/ nonstandard spelling of A HELL OF A —— (see HELL): *I'm in a helluva mess.*

helm[1] /helm/ ▶ **n.** (**the helm**) a tiller or wheel and any associated equipment for steering a ship or boat: *she stayed at the helm, alert for tankers.* ■ a position of leadership: *they are family-run empires whose founders remain at the helm.* ■ Nautical a helmsman.
▶ **v.** [with obj.] steer (a boat or ship). ■ manage the running of: *the magazine he helmed in the late eighties.* ■ direct (a movie).
– ORIGIN Old English *helma*; probably related to HELVE.

> **WORD TRENDS** Most of us still think of **helm** as primarily a nautical word, but according to the Oxford English Corpus, the verb is presently more at home in Hollywood than on the deep blue sea. The sense 'direct a movie,' which dates from 1930, is now dominant, with the most common objects of **helm** being *film* and *movie*. *Ship* comes in at number three, but is then followed by a long sequence of film-industry words such as *comedy, remake, adaptation*, and *thriller*.

helm[2] ▶ **n.** archaic a helmet.
– DERIVATIVES **helmed adj.**
– ORIGIN Old English, of Germanic origin; related to Dutch *helm* and German *Helm*, also to HELMET, from an Indo-European root meaning 'to cover or hide.'

Hel·mand /ˈhelmənd/ the longest river in Afghanistan. Rising in the Hindu Kush, it flows southwest for 700 miles (1,125 km) before emptying into marshland near the Iran–Afghanistan frontier. ■ a province in SW Afghanistan.

helm·er /ˈhelmər/ ▶ **n.** informal a film director.

hel·met /ˈhelmit/ ▶ **n. 1** a hard or padded protective hat, various types of which are worn by soldiers, police officers, firefighters, motorcyclists, athletes, and others. **2** Botany the arched upper part (galea) of the corolla in some flowers, esp. those of the mint and orchid families. **3** (also **helmet shell**) a predatory mollusk with a squat heavy shell, living in tropical and temperate seas and preying chiefly on sea urchins. ● Family Cassidae, class Gastropoda.
– DERIVATIVES **hel·met·ed adj.**
– ORIGIN late Middle English: from Old French, diminutive of *helme*, of Germanic origin; related to HELM[2].

firefighter's helmet

hel·minth /ˈhelmənTH/ ▶ **n.** a parasitic worm; a fluke, tapeworm, or nematode.
– DERIVATIVES **hel·min·thic** /helˈminTHik/ **adj.**
– ORIGIN mid 19th cent.: from Greek *helmins, helminth-* 'intestinal worm.'

hel·min·thi·a·sis /ˌhelmənˈTHīəsis/ ▶ **n.** Medicine infestation with parasitic worms.

hel·min·thol·o·gy /ˌhelmənˈTHäləjē/ ▶ **n.** the study of parasitic worms.
– DERIVATIVES **hel·min·tho·log·i·cal** /helˌminTHəˈläjikəl/ **adj.**, **hel·min·thol·o·gist** /-jist/ **n.**

Hel·mont /ˈhelmänt/, Jan Baptista van (1577–1644), Belgian chemist and physician. He made early studies on the conservation of matter, was the first to distinguish gases, and coined the word *gas*.

helms·man /ˈhelmzmən/ ▶ **n.** (pl. **helmsmen**) a person who steers a ship or boat.

Hé·lo·ïse /ˈ(h)eləˌwēz/ (1098–1164), French abbess. She is known for her tragic love affair with the theologian Abelard. She later became abbess of the community of Paraclete.

hel·ot /ˈhelət/ ▶ **n.** a member of a class of serfs in ancient Sparta, intermediate in status between slaves and citizens. ■ a serf or slave.
– DERIVATIVES **hel·ot·age** /-ˌtij/ **n.**, **hel·ot·ism** /-ˌtizəm/ **n.**, **hel·ot·ry** /-trē/ **n.**
– ORIGIN via Latin from Greek *Heilōtes* (plural), traditionally taken as referring to *Helos*, a Laconian town whose inhabitants were enslaved.

help /help/ ▶ **v.** [with obj.] **1** make it easier for (someone) to do something by offering one's services or resources: *Roger's companion helped him with the rent* | [with obj. and infinitive] *she helped him find a buyer* | [no obj.] *the teenager helped out in the corner store.* ■ improve (a situation or problem); be of benefit to: *upbeat comments about prospects helped confidence* | *sore throats can be helped by gargling* | [no obj.] *legislation to fit all new cars with catalytic converters will help.* ■ [with obj.] assist (someone) to move in a specified direction: *I helped her up.* ■ (**help someone on/off with**) assist someone to put on or take off (a garment).
2 (**help someone to**) serve someone with (food or drink): *she helped herself to a cookie.* ■ (**help oneself**) take something without permission: *he helped himself to the wages she had brought home.*
3 (**can/could not help**) cannot or could not avoid: *he could not help laughing* | *you can't help but agree.* ■ (**can/could not help oneself**) cannot or could not stop oneself from acting in a certain way: *she couldn't help herself; she burst into tears.*
▶ **n.** the action of helping someone to do something; assistance: *I asked for help from my neighbors* | *thank you for your help.* ■ [in sing.] a person or thing that helps: *he was a great help.* ■ a domestic servant or employee. ■ (as plural noun **the help**) a group of such employees working for one employer. ■ [as modifier] giving assistance to a computer user in the form of displayed instructions: *a help menu.*
▶ **exclam.** used as an appeal for urgent assistance: *Help! I'm drowning!*
– PHRASES **so help me** (**God**) used to emphasize that one means what one is saying. **there is no help for it** there is no way of avoiding or remedying a situation.
– ORIGIN Old English *helpan* (verb), *help* (noun), of Germanic origin; related to Dutch *helpen* and German *helfen*.

help desk ▶ **n.** a service providing information and support to computer users, esp. within a company.

help·er /ˈhelpər/ ▶ **n.** a person who helps someone else: *there was no shortage of willing helpers.*

help·er cell /ˈhelpər/ (also **helper T cell**) ▶ **n.** Physiology a T cell that influences or controls the differentiation or activity of other cells of the immune system.

help·ful /ˈhelpfəl/ ▶ **adj.** giving or ready to give help: *people are friendly and helpful* | *helpful staff.* ■ useful: *we find it very helpful to receive comments.*
– DERIVATIVES **help·ful·ly adv.**, **help·ful·ness n.**

help·ing /ˈhelpiNG/ ▶ **n.** a portion of food served to one person: *there will be enough for six to eight helpings* | *she asked for a second helping of spinach.*

help·ing hand ▶ **n.** (**a helping hand**) assistance: *she was always ready to lend a helping hand.*

help·less /ˈhelplis/ ▶ **adj.** unable to defend oneself or to act without help: *the cubs are born blind and helpless.* ■ uncontrollable: *they burst into helpless laughter.*
– DERIVATIVES **help·less·ly adv.**, **help·less·ness n.**

help·line /ˈhelpˌlīn/ ▶ **n.** a telephone service providing help with problems.

Help·mann /ˈhelpmən/, Sir Robert (Murray) (1909–86), Australian ballet dancer, choreographer, director, and actor. He began a long partnership with Margot Fonteyn in 1935.

help·mate /ˈhelpˌmāt/ (also **helpmeet** /-ˌmēt/) ▶ **n.** a helpful companion or partner, esp. one's husband or wife.
– ORIGIN late 17th cent. (as *helpmeet*): from an erroneous reading of Gen. 2:18, 20, where Adam's future wife is described as "an help meet for him" (i.e., a suitable helper for him). The variant *helpmate* came into use in the early 18th cent.

Hel·prin /ˈhelprən/, Mark (1947–), US journalist and writer. His works of fiction include *Winter's Tale* (1983), *A Soldier of the Great War* (1991), and *Memoir from Antproof Case* (1995).

Hel·sing·borg /ˈhelsiNG,bôrg(yə)/ a port in southern Sweden, on the Øresund opposite Elsinore in Denmark; pop. 126,754 (2008). Swedish name **Hälsingborg**.

Hel·sing·ør /,helseNGˈœr/ Danish name of **Elsinore**.

Hel·sin·ki /helˈsiNGkē, ˈhelsiNGkē/ the capital of Finland, a port in the southern part of the country, on the Gulf of Finland; pop. 579,504 (2009). Swedish name **Helsingfors** /ˈhelsiNG,fôrz/.

hel·ter-skel·ter /,heltər ˈskeltər/ ▶ **adj. & adv.** in disorderly haste or confusion: [as adj.] *she had blamed her grogginess on a helter-skelter lifestyle* | [as adv.] *hurtling helter-skelter down the pavement.*
▶ **n. 1** [in sing.] disorder; confusion: *the helter-skelter of a school day.*
2 Brit. a tall spiral slide winding around a tower at a fair.
– ORIGIN late 16th cent. (as an adverb): a rhyming jingle of unknown origin, perhaps symbolic of running feet or from Middle English *skelte* 'hasten.'

helve /helv/ ▶ **n.** the handle of a weapon or tool.
– ORIGIN Old English *helfe*, of Germanic origin; related to **halter**[1].

Hel·ve·tia /helˈvēSHə/ Latin name of **Switzerland**.

Hel·ve·tian /helˈvēSHən/ chiefly historical ▶ **adj.** Swiss.
▶ **n.** a native of Switzerland.

Hel·vet·ic /helˈvetik/ ▶ **adj. & n.** another term for **Helvetian**.

Hel·ve·ti·i /helˈvēSHē,ī/ ▶ **plural n.** an ancient Celtic people living in what is now western Switzerland.

hem[1] /hem/ ▶ **n.** the edge of a piece of cloth or clothing that has been turned under and sewn.
▶ **v. (hems, hemming, hemmed)** [with obj.] **1** turn under and sew the edge of (a piece of cloth or clothing).
2 (hem someone/something in) (usu. **be hemmed in**) surround and restrict the space or movement of: *he was hemmed in by the tables.*
– ORIGIN Old English, 'the border of a piece of cloth.' The verb senses date from the mid 16th cent.

hem[2] ▶ **exclam.** used in writing to indicate a sound made when coughing or clearing the throat to attract someone's attention or express hesitation.
▶ **n.** an utterance of such a sound.
▶ **v. (hems, hemming, hemmed)** [no obj.] archaic make such a sound when hesitating or as a signal.
– PHRASES **hem and haw** hesitate; be indecisive: *I waste a lot of time hemming and hawing before going into action.*
– ORIGIN late 15th cent.: imitative.

he·mag·glu·ti·na·tion /,hēmə,glo͞otnˈāSHən/ (Brit. **haemagglutination**) ▶ **n.** Medicine & Biology the clumping together of red blood cells.
– DERIVATIVES **he·mag·glu·ti·nate** /-ˈglo͞otn,āt/ **v.**

he·mag·glu·ti·nin /,hēməˈglo͞otn-in/ (Brit. **haemagglutinin**) ▶ **n.** Medicine & Biology a substance, such as a viral protein, that causes hemagglutination.

he·mal /ˈhēməl/ (Brit. **haemal**) ▶ **adj.** Physiology of or concerning the blood. ■ Zoology situated on the same side of the body as the heart and major blood vessels (i.e., in chordates, ventral).
– ORIGIN mid 19th cent.: from Greek *haima* 'blood' + **-al**.

he-man ▶ **n.** informal a well-built, muscular man, esp. one who is ostentatiously so.

he·man·gi·o·ma /hi,manjēˈōmə/ (Brit. **haemangioma**) ▶ **n.** (pl. **hemangiomas** or **hemangiomata** /-ˈōmətə/) Medicine a benign tumor of blood vessels, often forming a red birthmark.

he·ma·te·in /,hēməˈtē-in, ˈhēmə,tēn/ ▶ **n.** a reddish-brown crystalline dye obtained from logwood and used as a stain and indicator. ● Chem. formula $C_{16}H_{12}O_6$.

he·ma·tem·e·sis /,hēməˈteməsis/ (Brit. **haematemesis**) ▶ **n.** Medicine the vomiting of blood.
– ORIGIN early 19th cent.: from **hemato-** 'of blood' + Greek *emesis* 'vomiting.'

he·mat·ic /hēˈmatik/ (Brit. **haematic**) ▶ **adj.** Medicine, dated, of, relating to, or affecting the blood.
– ORIGIN mid 19th cent.: from Greek *haimatikos*, from *haima, haimat-* 'blood.'

he·ma·tin /ˈhēmə,tin/ (Brit. **haematin**) ▶ **n.** Biochemistry a bluish-black compound derived from hemoglobin by removal of the protein part and oxidation of the iron atom.
– ORIGIN mid 19th cent.: from Greek *haima, haimat-* 'blood' + **-in**[1].

he·ma·tin·ic /,hēməˈtinik/ ▶ **n.** any substance that tends to increase the amount of hemoglobin in the blood.
▶ **adj.** tending to increase the amount of hemoglobin in the blood.

he·ma·tite /ˈhēmə,tīt/ (Brit. **haematite**) ▶ **n.** a reddish-black mineral consisting of ferric oxide. It is an important ore of iron.
– ORIGIN late Middle English: via Latin from Greek *haimatitēs (lithos)* 'bloodlike (stone),' from *haima, haimat-* 'blood.'

hemato- (chiefly Brit. **haemato-**) ▶ **comb. form** of or relating to the blood: *hematoma.*
– ORIGIN from Greek *haima, haimat-* 'blood.'

he·mat·o·blast /hiˈmatə,blast/ ▶ **n.** an immature blood cell.

he·mat·o·cele /hiˈmatə,sēl/ (Brit. **haematocele**) ▶ **n.** Medicine a swelling caused by blood collecting in a body cavity.

he·mat·o·crit /hiˈmatə,krit/ (Brit. **haematocrit**) ▶ **n.** Physiology the ratio of the volume of red blood cells to the total volume of blood. ■ an instrument for measuring this, typically by centrifugation.
– ORIGIN late 19th cent.: from **hemato-** 'of blood' + Greek *kritēs* 'judge.'

he·mat·o·gen·e·sis /,hēmətəˈjenəsis, hi,matə-/ ▶ **n.** another term for **hemopoiesis**.

he·ma·tog·e·nous /,hēməˈtäjənəs/ (Brit. **haematogenous**) ▶ **adj.** Medicine originating in or carried by the blood.

he·ma·tol·o·gy /,hēməˈtäləjē/ (Brit. **haematology**) ▶ **n.** the study of the physiology of the blood.
– DERIVATIVES **he·ma·to·log·ic** /-təˈläjik/ **adj.**, **he·ma·to·log·i·cal** /-təˈläjikəl/ **adj.**, **he·ma·tol·o·gist** /-jist/ **n.**

he·ma·tol·y·sis /hēməˈtäləsis/ ▶ **n.** another term for **hemolysis**.

he·ma·to·ma /,hēməˈtōmə/ (Brit. **haematoma**) ▶ **n.** (pl. **hematomas** or **hematomata** /-ˈtōmətə/) Medicine a solid swelling of clotted blood within the tissues.

he·ma·toph·a·gous /,hēməˈtäfəgəs/ (Brit. **haematophagous**) ▶ **adj.** (of an animal, esp. an insect or tick) feeding on blood.

he·mat·o·poi·e·sis /,hēmətōpoiˈēsis, hi,matə-/ (Brit. **haematopoiesis**) ▶ **n.** another term for **hemopoiesis**.
– DERIVATIVES **he·ma·to·poi·et·ic** /-poiˈetik/ **adj.**

he·ma·tox·y·lin /,hēməˈtäksəlin/ (Brit. **haematoxylin**) ▶ **n.** Chemistry a colorless compound present in logwood that is easily converted into blue, red, or purple dyes and is used as a biological stain. ● A phenol; chem. formula: $C_{16}H_{14}O_6$.
– ORIGIN mid 19th cent.: from modern Latin *Haematoxylum* (genus name), from *haemato-*, variant of **hemato-** 'of blood,' + Greek *xulon* 'wood.'

he·mat·o·zo·on /hi,matəˈzōən, ,hēmətə-/ ▶ **n.** (pl. **hematozoa** /-ˈzōə/) any parasitic organism that lives in the blood.

he·ma·tu·ri·a /,hēməˈt(y)o͝orēə/ (Brit. **haematuria**) ▶ **n.** Medicine the presence of blood in urine.

heme /hēm/ (Brit. **haem**) ▶ **n.** Biochemistry an iron-containing compound of the porphyrin class that forms the nonprotein part of hemoglobin and some other biological molecules.
– ORIGIN 1920s: back-formation from **hemoglobin**.

hem·er·o·cal·lis /,hemərōˈkaləs/ ▶ **n.** (pl. **same**) a plant of a genus that comprises the daylilies. ● Genus *Hemerocallis*, family Liliaceae.
– ORIGIN modern Latin, from Greek *hēmerokallis* 'a lily that flowers for a day,' from *hēmera* 'day' + *kallos* 'beauty.'

hemi- ▶ **prefix** half: *hemicylindrical* | *hemiplegia.*
– ORIGIN from Greek *hēmi-*; related to Latin *semi-*.

-hemia ▶ **comb. form** variant spelling of **-emia**.

hem·i·al·gi·a /,hemēˈalj(ē)ə/ ▶ **n.** pain affecting one half of the body.

hem·i·a·nop·si·a /,hemēəˈnäpsēə/ (also **hemianopia** /-ˈnōpēə/) ▶ **n.** blindness over half the field of vision.

he·mic /hēmik/ ▶ **adj.** of or relating to the blood or the circulatory system.

hem·i·cel·lu·lose /,hemiˈselyəlōs, -lōz/ ▶ **n.** Biochemistry any of a class of substances that occur as constituents of the cell walls of plants and are polysaccharides of simpler structure than cellulose.
– ORIGIN late 19th cent.: coined in German from **hemi-** + **cellulose**.

Hem·i·chor·da·ta /,hemikôrˈdātə/ Zoology a small phylum of marine invertebrates that comprises the acorn worms.
– ORIGIN modern Latin (see **hemi-**, **Chordata**).

hem·i·chor·date /,hemiˈkôrdāt/ Zoology ▶ **n.** a marine invertebrate of the phylum Hemichordata; an acorn worm.
▶ **adj.** relating to or denoting hemichordates.

hem·i·cy·cle /ˈhemi,sīkəl/ ▶ **n.** a semicircular shape or structure.

hem·i·cy·lin·dri·cal /,hemisəˈlindrikəl/ ▶ **adj.** having the shape of half a cylinder (divided lengthways).

hem·i·dem·i·sem·i·qua·ver /,hemē,demēˈsemē,kwāvər/ ▶ **n.** Music chiefly Brit. a note with the time value of half a demisemiquaver; a sixty-fourth note.

hem·i·he·dral /,hemēˈhēdrəl/ ▶ **adj.** Crystallography having half the number of planes required for symmetry of the holohedral form.

hem·i·hy·drate /,hemiˈhīdrāt/ ▶ **n.** Chemistry a crystalline hydrate containing one molecule of water for every two molecules of the compound in question.

hem·i·me·tab·o·lous /,hemәməˈtabələs/ ▶ **adj.** Entomology (of an insect) having no pupal stage in the transition from larva to adult.
– DERIVATIVES **hem·i·met·a·bol·ic** /,hemə,metəˈbälik/ **adj.**

hem·i·mor·phite /,heməˈmôrfīt/ ▶ **n.** a mineral consisting of hydrated zinc silicate, typically occurring as flat white prisms.

Hem·ings /ˈhemiNGz/, Sally (1773–1835), US slave. A slave at Thomas Jefferson's estate, Monticello, she was reported to be his mistress in the *Richmond Recorder* 1802. More recent evidence has shown that they probably had children together.

Hem·ing·way /ˈhemiNGg,wā/, Ernest (Miller) (1899–1961), US novelist, short-story writer, and journalist. He achieved success with *The Sun Also Rises* (1926), which reflected the disillusionment of the postwar "lost generation." In World War II, he joined in the D-Day landings as a war correspondent. Other notable works: *A Farewell to Arms* (1929), *For Whom the Bell Tolls* (1940), and *The Old Man and the Sea* (1952, Pulitzer Prize 1953). Nobel Prize for Literature (1954).

Ernest Hemingway

hem·i·o·la /,hemēˈōlə/ ▶ **n.** Music a musical figure in which, typically, two groups of three beats are replaced by three groups of two beats, giving the effect of a shift between triple and duple meter.
– ORIGIN late Middle English: via medieval Latin from Greek *hēmiolia* 'in the ratio of one and a half to one' (from *hēmi-* 'half' + *holos* 'whole').

hem·i·par·a·site /,heməˈparə,sīt/ ▶ **n.** Botany a plant that obtains or may obtain part of its food by parasitism, e.g., mistletoe, which also photosynthesizes.

hem·i·pa·re·sis /,hemәpəˈrēsis/ ▶ **n.** another term for **hemiplegia**.

hem·i·pe·nis /ˈhemi,pēnis/ ▶ **n.** (pl. **hemipenes** /-,pēnēz/) Zoology each of the paired male reproductive organs in snakes and lizards.

hem·i·ple·gi·a /,heməˈplēj(ē)ə/ ▶ **n.** Medicine paralysis of one side of the body.
– DERIVATIVES **hem·i·ple·gic** /-ˈplējik/ **n. & adj.**
– ORIGIN early 17th cent.: modern Latin, from Greek *hēmiplēgia*, from *hemi-* 'half' + *plēgē* 'stroke.'

He·mip·ter·a /həˈmiptərə/ Entomology a large order of insects that comprises the true bugs, which include aphids, cicadas, leafhoppers, and many others. They have piercing and sucking mouthparts and incomplete metamorphosis. See also **Heteroptera**, **Homoptera**. ■ (as plural noun **hemiptera**) insects of this order; true bugs.
– ORIGIN modern Latin (plural), from Greek *hēmi-* 'half' + *pteron* 'wing' (because of the forewing

structure, partly hardened at the base and partly membranous).

he·mip·ter·an /hə'miptərən/ Entomology ▶ **n.** an insect of the order Hemiptera, such as an aphid, cicada, or leafhopper.
▶ **adj.** relating to or denoting hemipterans.
– DERIVATIVES **he·mip·ter·ous** /-tərəs/ **adj.**

hem·i·sphere /'hemə,sfi(ə)r/ ▶ **n.** a half of a sphere. ■ a half of the earth, usually as divided into northern and southern halves by the equator, or into western and eastern halves by an imaginary line passing through the poles. ■ a half of the celestial sphere. ■ (also **cerebral hemisphere**) each of the two parts of the cerebrum (left and right) in the brain of a vertebrate.
– DERIVATIVES **hem·i·spher·ic** /,hemə'sfi(ə)rik, -'sferik/ **adj.**, **hem·i·spher·i·cal** **adj.**, **hem·i·spher·i·cal·ly** **adv.**
– ORIGIN late Middle English (in the sense 'half the celestial sphere, the sky'): from Old French *emisphere*, via Latin from Greek *hēmisphairion*, from *hēmi-* 'half' + *sphaira* 'sphere.'

hem·i·stich /'hemə,stik/ ▶ **n.** (chiefly in Old English verse) a half of a line of verse.
– ORIGIN late 16th cent.: via late Latin from Greek *hēmistikhion*, from *hēmi-* 'half' + *stikhos* 'row, line of verse.'

h

Hem·kund, Lake /hem'ko͝ond/ a lake in northern India, in the Himalayan foothills, in Uttar Pradesh. It is regarded as holy by the Sikhs.

hem·line /'hem,līn/ ▶ **n.** the level of the lower edge of a garment such as a skirt, dress, or coat: *a long jacket with a lowered hemline at the back.*

hem·lock /'hem,läk/ ▶ **n.** **1** a highly poisonous European plant of the parsley family, with a purple-spotted stem, fernlike leaves, small white flowers, and an unpleasant smell. ● *Conium maculatum*, family Umbelliferae.
■ a sedative or poisonous potion obtained from this plant. Such a potion was said to have been used to poison Socrates.
2 (also **hemlock fir** or **spruce**) a coniferous North American tree with dark green foliage that is said to smell like hemlock when crushed, grown chiefly for timber and pulp production, and also grown in Europe as an ornamental. ● Genus *Tsuga*, family Pinaceae: several species, in particular **eastern hemlock** (*T. canadensis*) and **Carolina hemlock** (*T. caroliniana*).
– ORIGIN Old English *hymlice, hemlic*, of unknown origin.

hemo- (chiefly Brit. **haemo-**) ▶ **comb. form** equivalent to **HEMATO-**.
– ORIGIN from Greek *haima* 'blood.'

he·mo·chro·ma·to·sis /,hēmə,krōmə'tōsis/ (Brit. **haemochromatosis**) ▶ **n.** Medicine a hereditary disorder in which iron salts are deposited in the tissues, leading to liver damage, diabetes mellitus, and bronze discoloration of the skin.

he·mo·coel /'hēmə,sēl/ (Brit. **haemocoel**) ▶ **n.** Zoology the primary body cavity of most invertebrates, containing circulatory fluid.
– ORIGIN late 19th cent.: from **HEMO-** 'of blood' + Greek *koilos* 'hollow, cavity.'

he·mo·cy·a·nin /,hēmə'sīənən/ (Brit. **haemocyanin**) ▶ **n.** Biochemistry a protein containing copper, responsible for transporting oxygen in the blood plasma of arthropods and mollusks.
– ORIGIN mid 19th cent.: from **HEMO-** 'of blood' + **CYAN** + **-IN**[1].

he·mo·cyte /'hēmə,sīt/ ▶ **n.** a blood cell, esp. in an invertebrate.

he·mo·cy·tom·e·ter /,hēməsī'tämitər/ (also **hemacytometer**) (Brit. **haemocytometer**) ▶ **n.** an instrument for visual counting of the number of cells in a blood sample or other fluid under a microscope.

he·mo·di·al·y·sis /,hēmə,dī'aləsis/ (Brit. **haemodialysis**) ▶ **n.** (pl. **hemodialyses** /-,sēz/) Medicine kidney dialysis.

he·mo·dy·nam·ic /,hēmōdī'namik/ (Brit. **haemodynamic**) ▶ **adj.** Physiology of or relating to the flow of blood within the organs and tissues of the body.
– DERIVATIVES **he·mo·dy·nam·i·cal·ly** /-ik(ə)lē/ **adv.**, **he·mo·dy·nam·ics** **n.**

he·mo·flag·el·late /,hēmə'flajə,lāt, -lit/ ▶ **n.** any parasitic flagellate protozoan that lives in the bloodstream.

he·mo·glo·bin /'hēmə,glōbin/ (Brit. **haemoglobin**) ▶ **n.** Biochemistry a red protein responsible for transporting oxygen in the blood of vertebrates. Its molecule comprises four subunits, each containing an iron atom bound to a heme group.
– ORIGIN mid 19th cent.: a contracted form of *hematoglobulin*, in the same sense.

he·mo·glo·bin·op·a·thy /,hēmə,glōbə'näpəTHē/ (Brit. **haemoglobinopathy**) ▶ **n.** (pl. **hemoglobinopathies**) Medicine a hereditary condition involving an abnormality in the structure of hemoglobin.

he·mo·glo·bi·nu·ri·a /,hēmə,glōbə'n(y)o͝orēə/ (Brit. **haemoglobinuria**) ▶ **n.** Medicine excretion of free hemoglobin in the urine.

he·mo·lymph /'hēmə,lim(p)f/ (Brit. **haemolymph**) ▶ **n.** a fluid equivalent to blood in most invertebrates, occupying the hemocoel.

he·mol·y·sin /hi'mälisin, ,hēmə'lī-/ ▶ **n.** a substance in the blood that destroys red blood cells and liberates hemoglobin.

he·mol·y·sis /hē'mäləsis/ (Brit. **haemolysis**) ▶ **n.** the rupture or destruction of red blood cells. Also called **HEMATOLYSIS**.

he·mo·lyt·ic /,hēmə'litik/ (Brit. **haemolytic**) ▶ **adj.** Medicine relating to or involving the rupture or destruction of red blood cells: *hemolytic anemia.*

he·mo·lyt·ic dis·ease of the new·born ▶ **n.** Medicine a severe form of anemia caused in a fetus or newborn infant by incompatibility with the mother's blood type, typically when the mother is Rhesus negative and produces antibodies that attack Rhesus positive fetal blood through the placenta. Also called **ERYTHROBLASTOSIS**.

he·mo·phil·i·a /,hēmə'filēə/ (Brit. **haemophilia**) ▶ **n.** a medical condition in which the ability of the blood to clot is severely reduced, causing the sufferer to bleed severely from even a slight injury. The condition is typically caused by a hereditary lack of a coagulation factor, most often factor VIII.
– DERIVATIVES **he·mo·phil·i·ac** /-'filē,ak/ **n.**, **he·mo·phil·ic** /-'filik/ **adj.**

he·mo·poi·e·sis /,hēməpoi'ēsis/ (Brit. **haemopoiesis**) ▶ **n.** the production of blood cells and platelets, which occurs in the bone marrow. Also called **HEMATOGENESIS**.
– DERIVATIVES **he·mo·poi·et·ic** /-poi'etik/ **adj.**
– ORIGIN early 20th cent.: from **HEMO-** 'of blood' + Greek *poiēsis* 'making.'

he·mop·ty·sis /hē'mäptəsis/ (Brit. **haemoptysis**) ▶ **n.** the coughing up of blood.
– ORIGIN mid 17th cent.: modern Latin, from **HEMO-** 'of blood' + Greek *ptusis* 'spitting.'

hem·or·rhage /'hem(ə)rij/ (Brit. **haemorrhage**) ▶ **n.** an escape of blood from a ruptured blood vessel, esp. when profuse. ■ a damaging loss of valuable people or resources suffered by an organization, group, or country: *a hemorrhage of highly qualified teachers.*
▶ **v.** [no obj.] (of a person) suffer a hemorrhage: *he had begun hemorrhaging in the night.* ■ [with obj.] expend (money) in large amounts in a seemingly uncontrollable manner: *the business was hemorrhaging cash.*
– ORIGIN late 17th cent. (as a noun): alteration of obsolete *hemorrhagy*, via Latin *haemorrhagia* from Greek *haimorrhagia*, from *haima* 'blood' + the stem of *rhēgnunai* 'burst.'

hem·or·rhag·ic /,hemə'rajik/ (Brit. **haemorrhagic**) ▶ **adj.** accompanied by or produced by hemorrhage: *a viral hemorrhagic fever | hemorrhagic colitis.*

hem·or·rhoid /'hem(ə),roid/ (Brit. **haemorrhoid**) ▶ **n.** (usu. **hemorrhoids**) a swollen vein or group of veins in the region of the anus. Also (collectively) called **PILES**.
– DERIVATIVES **hem·or·rhoi·dal** /,hem(ə)'roidl/ **adj.**
– ORIGIN late Middle English: via Old French and Latin from Greek *haimorrhoides (phlebes)* 'bleeding (veins),' from *haima* 'blood' + an element related to *rhein* 'to flow.'

he·mo·sta·sis /,hēmə'stāsəs, heme-/ (Brit. **haemostasis**) ▶ **n.** Medicine the stopping of a flow of blood.
– DERIVATIVES **he·mo·stat·ic** /-'statik/ **adj.**

he·mo·stat /'hēmə,stat/ (Brit. **haemostat**) ▶ **n.** Medicine an instrument for preventing the flow of blood from an open blood vessel by compression of the vessel.

hemp /hemp/ ▶ **n.** (also **Indian hemp**) the cannabis plant, esp. when grown for fiber. ■ the fiber of this plant, extracted from the stem and used to make rope, stout fabrics, fiberboard, and paper. ■ used in names of other plants that yield fiber, e.g., **Manila hemp**. ■ marijuana.
– ORIGIN Old English *henep, hænep*, of Germanic origin; related to Dutch *hennep* and German *Hanf*, also to Greek *kannabis*.

hemp ag·ri·mo·ny ▶ **n.** an erect Eurasian plant of the daisy family, resembling a valerian, with clusters of pale purple flowers and hairy stems. ● *Eupatorium cannabinum*, family Compositae.

hemp·en /'hempən/ ▶ **adj.** [attrib.] made from hemp fiber: *hempen rope.*

hemp net·tle ▶ **n.** a nettlelike plant of the mint family, native to Eurasia but introduced elsewhere. ● Genus *Galeopsis*, family Labiatae: several species, including *G. tetrahit*, found in waste areas of southern Canada and the northern US.

hemp·seed /'hemp,sēd/ ▶ **n.** the seed of hemp, particularly as used for fishing bait.

Hemp·stead /'hem(p),sted/ **1** a town on western Long Island in southeastern New York state, on the eastern boundary of Queens in New York City, that includes the villages of Hempstead, Rockville Centre, Levittown, and many others; pop. 761,101 (est. 2008).
2 a village on western Long Island in the town of Hempstead; pop. 53,915 (est. 2008).

hem·stitch /'hem,stiCH/ ▶ **n.** a decoration used on woven fabric, esp. alongside a hem, in which several adjacent threads are pulled out and the crossing threads are tied into bunches, making a row of small openings.
▶ **v.** [with obj.] incorporate such a decoration in the hem of (a piece of cloth or clothing).

hen /hen/ ▶ **n.** a female bird, esp. of a domestic fowl. ■ (**hens**) domestic fowls of either sex. ■ used in names of birds, esp. waterbirds of the rail family, e.g., **moorhen**. ■ a female lobster, crab, or salmon.
– PHRASES **as rare** (or **scarce**) **as hen's teeth** extremely rare.
– ORIGIN Old English *henn*, of Germanic origin; related to Dutch *hen* and German *Henne*.

He·nan /'hə'nän/ (also **Honan** /'hō'nän/) a province in northeastern central China; capital, Zhengzhou.

hen and chick·ens ▶ **n.** any of a number of plants producing additional small flower heads or offshoots. ● Several species, esp. the houseleeks (family Crassulaceae).

hen·bane /'hen,bān/ ▶ **n.** a coarse and poisonous Eurasian plant of the nightshade family, with sticky hairy leaves and an unpleasant smell. ● *Hyoscyamus niger*, family Solanaceae.
■ a psychoactive drink prepared from this plant.

hen·bit /'hen,bit/ ▶ **n.** a dead-nettle with purple flowers and partly prostrate stems, native to Eurasia, several kinds of which have become widely naturalized in North America. ● Genus *Lamium*, family Labiatae: several species, in particular *L. amplexicaule*.
– ORIGIN late 16th cent.: apparently a translation of Low German or Dutch *hoenderbeet*.

hence /hens/ ▶ **adv.** **1** as a consequence; for this reason: *a stiff breeze and hence a high windchill.*
2 in the future (used after a period of time): *two years hence they might say something quite different.*
3 (also **from hence**) archaic from here: *hence, be gone.*
– ORIGIN Middle English *hennes* (sense 3): from earlier *henne* (from Old English *heonan*, of Germanic origin, related to **HE**) + **-S**[3] (later respelled *-ce* to denote the unvoiced sound).

hence·forth /'hens,fôrTH/ (also **henceforward** /hens'fôrwərd/) ▶ **adv.** from this time on or from that time on: *the company announced that it would henceforth charge royalties.*

hench·man /'henCHmən/ ▶ **n.** (pl. **henchmen**) chiefly derogatory a faithful follower or political supporter, esp. one prepared to engage in crime or dishonest practices by way of service. ■ historical a squire or page of honor to a person of rank.
– ORIGIN Middle English, from Old English *hengest* 'male horse' + **MAN**, the original sense being probably 'groom.'

hen·coop /'hen,ko͞op/ ▶ **n.** a cage or pen for keeping poultry in.

hendeca- ▶ **comb. form** eleven; having eleven: *hendecasyllable.*
– ORIGIN from Greek *hendeka* 'eleven.'

hen·dec·a·gon /hen'dekə,gän/ ▶ **n.** a plane figure with eleven straight sides and angles.
– DERIVATIVES **hen·de·cag·o·nal** /,hendə'kagənl/ **adj.**
– ORIGIN early 18th cent.: from **HENDECA-** 'eleven' + **-GON**, on the pattern of words such as *polygon*.

hen·dec·a·syl·la·ble /hen'dekə,siləbəl, -,dekə'siləbəl/ ▶ **n.** Prosody a line of verse containing eleven syllables.
– DERIVATIVES **hen·dec·a·syl·lab·ic** /hen,dekəsə'labik/ **adj.**

Hen·der·son /'hendərsən/ a city in southeastern Nevada, southeast of Las Vegas; pop. 252,064 (est. 2008).

Hen·der·son·ville /ˈhendərsən,vil/ a city in north central Tennessee, a northeastern suburb of Nashville; pop. 47,725 (est. 2008).

hen·di·a·dys /henˈdīədəs/ ▶ **n.** Rhetoric the expression of a single idea by two words connected with "and," e.g., *nice and warm*, when one could be used to modify the other, as in *nicely warm*.
– ORIGIN late 16th cent.: via medieval Latin from Greek *hen dia duoin* 'one thing by two.'

Hen·drix /ˈhendriks/, Jimi (1942–70), US rock musician; full name *James Marshall Hendrix*. Remembered for the flamboyance and originality of his improvisations, he greatly widened the scope of the electric guitar. Notable songs: "Purple Haze" (1967) and "All Along the Watchtower" (1968).

Jimi Hendrix

hen·e·quen /ˈhenək(w)ən/ ▶ **n.** **1** a fiber resembling sisal, chiefly used for twine and paper pulp.
2 a Central American agave from which such fiber is obtained. ● *Agave fourcroydes*, family Agavaceae.
– ORIGIN early 17th cent.: from Spanish *jeniquen*, from a local word.

henge /henj/ ▶ **n.** a prehistoric monument consisting of a circle of stone or wooden uprights.
– ORIGIN mid 18th cent.: back-formation from STONEHENGE.

hen·house /ˈhen,hous/ ▶ **n.** a small shed for keeping poultry in.

Hen·ie /ˈhenē/, Sonja (1912–69), US figure skater; born in Norway. She won ten consecutive world championships 1927–36 and three Olympic gold medals 1928, 1932, 1936. She starred in movies such as *One in a Million* (1936) and *Sun Valley Serenade* (1941) and toured professionally with her own ice show until 1952.

Hen·le's loop /ˈhenlēz/ ▶ **n.** another term for LOOP OF HENLE.

Hen·ley /ˈhenlē/ (in full **Henley Royal Regatta**) the oldest rowing regatta in Europe, inaugurated in 1839 at Henley-on-Thames, England, and held annually in the first week in July.

hen·ley /ˈhenli/ (also **Henley**) ▶ **n.** a style of casual top with a scoop neck and a short row of buttons in the center of the neckline.
– ORIGIN late 19th cent.: originally a style associated with the Henley Royal Regatta.

hen·na /ˈhenə/ ▶ **n.** **1** the powdered leaves of a tropical shrub, used as a dye to color the hair and decorate the body.
2 the Old World shrub that produces these leaves, with small pink, red, or white flowers. ● *Lawsonia inermis*, family Lythraceae.
▶ **v.** (**hennas, hennaing, hennaed** /ˈhenəd/) [with obj.] dye (hair) with henna.
– ORIGIN early 17th cent.: from Arabic *ḥinnā'*.

Hen·ne·pin /ˈhenəpən/, Louis (1640–c.1701), French missionary, explorer, and writer. He accompanied La Salle as his chaplain through the Great Lakes in 1679, explored the surrounding territory that included the Mississippi River, and described his discoveries in writing.

hen·o·the·ism /ˈhenōᴛʜē,izəm, ,henōˈᴛʜē-/ ▶ **n.** adherence to one particular god out of several, esp. by a family, tribe, or other group.
– ORIGIN mid 19th cent.: from Greek *heis, heno-* 'one' + *theos* 'god' + -ISM.

hen par·ty ▶ **n.** informal a social gathering of women.

hen·peck /ˈhen,pek/ ▶ **v.** [with obj.] (usu. as adj. **henpecked**) (of a woman) continually criticize and give orders to (her husband or other male partner): *henpecked husbands*.

Hen·ri /ˈhenrē/, Robert (1865–1929), US painter. An advocate of realism, he believed that an artist must be a social force. The Ashcan School of painters was formed largely as a result of his influence.

Hen·ri·cian /henˈrisʜēən/ ▶ **adj.** of or relating to the reign and policies of Henry VIII of England.

Hen·ry[1] /ˈhenrē/ the name of eight kings of England. ■ **Henry I** (1068–1135), youngest son of William I; reigned 1100–35. He conquered Normandy in 1105. ■ **Henry II** (1133–89), son of Matilda; reigned 1154–89. The first Plantagenet king, he restored order and extended his kingdom. ■ **Henry III** (1207–72), son of John; reigned 1216–72. ■ **Henry IV** (1367–1413), son of John of Gaunt; reigned 1399–1413; known as **Henry Bolingbroke**. He overthrew Richard II, establishing the Lancastrian dynasty. ■ **Henry V** (1387–1422), son of Henry IV; reigned 1413–22. He renewed the Hundred Years War soon after coming to the throne and defeated the French at Agincourt in 1415. ■ **Henry VI** (1421–71), son of Henry V; reigned 1422–61 and 1470–71. ■ **Henry VII** (1457–1509), the first Tudor king; son of Edmund Tudor, Earl of Richmond; reigned 1485–1509; known as **Henry Tudor**. He defeated Richard III at Bosworth Field and eventually established an unchallenged Tudor dynasty. ■ **Henry VIII** (1491–1547), son of Henry VII; reigned 1509–47. Henry had six wives (Catherine of Aragon, Anne Boleyn, Jane Seymour, Anne of Cleves, Catherine Howard, Katherine Parr) and three children (Mary I, with Catherine of Aragon; Elizabeth I, with Anne Boleyn; and Edward VI, with Jane Seymour). His first divorce, from Catherine of Aragon, was opposed by the pope, leading to England's break with the Roman Catholic Church.

Henry VIII

Hen·ry[2] (1394–1460), Portuguese prince; known as **Henry the Navigator**. The third son of John I of Portugal, he organized many voyages of exploration, most notably south along the African coast, thus laying the foundation for Portuguese imperial expansion around Africa to East Asia.

Hen·ry[3] the name of seven kings of the Germans, six of whom were also Holy Roman Emperors. ■ **Henry I** (c.876–936), reigned 919–936; known as **Henry the Fowler**. He waged war successfully against the Slavs in Brandenburg, the Magyars, and the Danes. ■ **Henry II** (973–1024), reigned 1002–24; Holy Roman Emperor 1014–24; also known as **Saint Henry**. ■ **Henry III** (1017–56), reigned 1039–56; Holy Roman Emperor 1046–56. He brought stability and prosperity to the empire, defeating the Czechs and fixing the frontier between Austria and Hungary. ■ **Henry IV** (1050–1106), son of Henry III; reigned 1056–1105; Holy Roman Emperor 1084–1105. Increasing conflict with **Pope Gregory VII** led Henry to call a council in 1076 to depose the pope, who excommunicated Henry. ■ **Henry V** (1086–1125), reigned 1099–1125; Holy Roman Emperor 1111–25. ■ **Henry VI** (1165–97), reigned 1169–97; Holy Roman Emperor 1191–97. ■ **Henry VII** (c.1269/74–1313), reigned 1308–13; Holy Roman Emperor 1312–13.

Hen·ry[4] John, American folk legend, the "steel-driving man" who tried to save railroad laborers' jobs by competing against a steam-powered hammer. He won by driving in more spikes than the machine, but then collapsed and died.

Hen·ry[5], O (1862–1910), US short-story writer; pseudonym of *William Sydney Porter*. Jailed for embezzlement in 1898, he started writing in prison. His humorous, ironic stories of everyday life depend on coincidence and twists. Collections of his works include *Cabbages and Kings* (1904), *The Voice of the City* (1908), and *Waifs and Strays* (published posthumously in 1917).

Hen·ry[6], Patrick (1736–99), American revolutionary. As a member of the Continental Congress 1774–76, he was noted as an orator. He is best remembered for an impassioned speech in which he urged the colonies into readiness with the statement "Give me liberty, or give me death."

Patrick Henry

hen·ry /ˈhenrē/ (abbr.: **H**) ▶ **n.** (pl. **henries** or **henrys**) Physics the SI unit of inductance, equal to an electromotive force of one volt in a closed circuit with a uniform rate of change of current of one ampere per second.
– ORIGIN late 19th cent.: named after Joseph *Henry* (1797–1878), the American physicist who discovered the phenomenon.

Hen·ry Bo·ling·broke /ˈbôliɴɢ,bro͝ok, ˈbōliɴɢ,bro͝ok/, Henry IV of England (see HENRY[1]).

Hen·ry IV (1553–1610), king of France 1589–1610; known as **Henry of Navarre**. Although leader of Huguenot forces in the latter stages of the French Wars of Religion, on succeeding the Catholic **Henry III**, he became Catholic himself in order to guarantee peace. He established religious freedom with the Edict of Nantes (1598) and restored order after the prolonged civil war.

Hen·ry's law Chemistry a law stating that the mass of a dissolved gas in a given volume of solvent at equilibrium is proportional to the partial pressure of the gas.
– ORIGIN late 19th cent.: named after William *Henry* (1774–1836), English chemist.

Hen·ry the Fow·ler /ˈfoulər/, Henry I, king of the Germans (see HENRY[3]).

Hen·ry Tu·dor /ˈto͞odər/, Henry VII of England (see HENRY[1]).

Hen·son[1] /ˈhensən/, Jim (1936–90), US puppeteer; full name *James Maury Henson*. He created the Muppets, the most commercially successful puppets in history, who became well known as the principal characters on television's *Sesame Street* (1969–) and *The Muppet Show* (1976–81).

Hen·son[2], Matthew (Alexander) (1866–1955), US explorer. He accompanied Peary as his valet when their party became the first to reach the North Pole in 1909. He wrote *A Black Explorer at the North Pole* (1912).

hep /hep/ ▶ **adj.** old-fashioned term for HIP[3].

hep·a·rin /ˈhepərin/ ▶ **n.** Biochemistry a compound occurring in the liver and other tissues that inhibits blood coagulation. A sulfur-containing polysaccharide, it is used as an anticoagulant in the treatment of thrombosis.
– ORIGIN early 20th cent.: via late Latin from Greek *hēpar* 'liver' + -IN[1].

hep·a·rin·ize /ˈhepərə,nīz/ ▶ **v.** [with obj.] add heparin to (blood or a container about to be filled with blood) to prevent it from coagulating.
– DERIVATIVES **hep·a·rin·i·za·tion** /,hepərənəˈzāsʜən/ **n.**

he·pat·ic /həˈpatik/ ▶ **adj.** of or relating to the liver: *right and left hepatic ducts.*
▶ **n.** Botany less common term for LIVERWORT.
– ORIGIN late Middle English: via Latin from Greek *hēpatikos*, from *hēpar, hēpat-* 'liver.'

he·pat·i·ca /həˈpatikə/ ▶ **n.** a plant of the buttercup family, with anemonelike flowers, native to north temperate regions. ● Genus *Hepatica*, family Ranunculaceae.
– ORIGIN from medieval Latin *hepatica (herba)* 'plant having liver-shaped parts, or one used to treat liver diseases,' feminine of *hepaticus* (see HEPATIC).

he·pat·ic por·tal vein ▶ **n.** see PORTAL VEIN.

PRONUNCIATION KEY ə *ago, up*; ər *over, fur*; a *hat*; ā *ate*; ä *car*; e *let*; ē *see*; i *fit*; ī *by*; NG *sing*; ō *go*; ô *law, for*; oi *toy*; o͝o *good*; o͞o *goo*; ou *out*; TH *thin*; T͟H *then*; ZH *vision*

h

hep·a·ti·tis /ˌhepəˈtītis/ ▶ **n.** a disease characterized by inflammation of the liver.
– ORIGIN early 18th cent.: modern Latin, from Greek *hēpar, hēpat-* 'liver' + **-ITIS**.

hep·a·ti·tis A ▶ **n.** a form of viral hepatitis transmitted in food, causing fever and jaundice.

hep·a·ti·tis B ▶ **n.** a severe form of viral hepatitis transmitted in infected blood, causing fever, debility, and jaundice.

hep·a·ti·tis C ▶ **n.** a form of viral hepatitis transmitted in infected blood, causing chronic liver disease. It was formerly called non-A, non-B hepatitis.

hepato- ▶ **comb. form** of or relating to the liver.
– ORIGIN from Greek *hēpar, hēpat-* 'liver.'

hep·a·to·cyte /ˈhepətəˌsīt, həˈpatə-/ ▶ **n.** Physiology a liver cell.

hep·a·to·ma /ˌhepəˈtōmə/ ▶ **n.** (pl. **hepatomas** or **hepatomata** /-ˈtōmətə/) Medicine a cancer of the cells of the liver.

hep·a·to·meg·a·ly /ˌhepətōˈmegəlē/ ▶ **n.** Medicine abnormal enlargement of the liver.

hep·a·to·pan·cre·as /ˌhepətōˈpaNGkrēəs, -ˈpankrēəs/ ▶ **n.** Zoology technical term for **DIGESTIVE GLAND**.

h

hep·a·to·tox·ic /ˌhepətōˈtäksik/ ▶ **adj.** damaging or destructive to liver cells.
– DERIVATIVES **hep·a·to·tox·ic·i·ty** /-täkˈsisətē/ **n.**, **hep·a·to·tox·in** /-ˈtäksən/ **n.**

Hep·burn[1] /ˈhepˌbərn/, Audrey (1929–93), US actress; born in Belgium; born *Edda Kathleen van Heemstra Hepburn-Ruston*. After pursuing a career as a stage and movie actress in Britain, she moved to Hollywood. Notable movies: *Roman Holiday* (1953), *Sabrina* (1954), *Breakfast at Tiffany's* (1961), and *My Fair Lady* (1964).

Hep·burn[2], Katharine (1909–2003), US actress; full name *Katharine Houghton Hepburn*. Making her screen debut in 1932, she starred in a wide range of movies, often opposite Spencer Tracy. She won Academy Awards for her lead roles in *Morning Glory* (1933), *Guess Who's Coming to Dinner* (1967), *The Lion in Winter* (1968), and *On Golden Pond* (1981).

Katharine Hepburn

hep·cat /ˈhepˌkat/ ▶ **n.** informal, dated a stylish or fashionable person, esp. in the sphere of jazz or popular music.
– ORIGIN 1930s: from **HEP** + **CAT**[1].

He·phaes·tus /hiˈfestəs/ Greek Mythology the god of fire and of craftsmen, son of Zeus and Hera; husband of Aphrodite. He was a divine metalworker who was lame as the result of having interfered in a quarrel between his parents. Roman equivalent **VULCAN**.

Hep·ple·white /ˈhepəlˌ(h)wīt/, George (died 1786), English cabinetmaker and furniture designer. The posthumously published book of his designs, *The Cabinetmaker and Upholsterer's Guide* (1788), contains almost 300 designs.

hepta- ▶ **comb. form** seven; having seven: *heptagon* | *heptathlon*.
– ORIGIN from Greek *hepta* 'seven.'

hep·ta·chlor /ˈheptəˌklôr/ ▶ **n.** a chlorinated hydrocarbon used as an insecticide. ● Chem. formula: $C_{10}H_5Cl_7$.

hep·tad /ˈhepˌtad/ ▶ **n.** technical a group or set of seven.
– ORIGIN mid 17th cent.: from Greek *heptas, heptad-*, from *hepta* 'seven.'

hep·ta·gon /ˈheptəˌgän/ ▶ **n.** a plane figure with seven straight sides and angles.
– DERIVATIVES **hep·tag·o·nal** /hepˈtagənl/ **adj.**
– ORIGIN late 16th cent.: from Greek *heptagonon*, neuter (used as a noun) of *heptagonos* 'seven-angled.'

hep·ta·he·dron /heptəˈhēdrən/ ▶ **n.** (pl. **heptahedrons** or **heptahedra** /-ˈhēdrə/) a solid figure with seven plane faces.
– DERIVATIVES **hep·ta·he·dral** /-ˈhēdrəl/ **adj.**
– ORIGIN late 17th cent.: from **HEPTA-** 'seven' + **-HEDRON**, on the pattern of words such as *polyhedron*.

hep·tam·er·ous /hepˈtamərəs/ ▶ **adj.** Botany & Zoology having parts arranged in groups of seven. ■ consisting of seven joints or parts.

hep·tam·e·ter /hepˈtamitər/ ▶ **n.** Prosody a line of verse consisting of seven metrical feet.
– ORIGIN late 19th cent.: via late Latin from Greek *heptametron*, from *hepta-* 'seven' + *metron* 'measure.'

hep·tane /ˈhepˌtān/ ▶ **n.** Chemistry a colorless liquid hydrocarbon of the alkane series, obtained from petroleum. ● Chem. formula: C_7H_{16}; several isomers, esp. the straight-chain isomer (*n*-**heptane**).
– ORIGIN late 19th cent.: from **HEPTA-** 'seven' (denoting seven carbon atoms) + **-ANE**[2].

hep·tar·chy /ˈhepˌtärkē/ ▶ **n.** (pl. **heptarchies**) a country or region consisting of seven smaller, autonomous regions. ■ government by seven rulers.
– DERIVATIVES **hep·tar·chic** /hepˈtärkik/ **adj.**, **hep·tar·chi·cal** /hepˈtärkikəl/ **adj.**
– ORIGIN late 16th cent.: from **HEPTA-** 'seven' + Greek *arkhia* 'rule,' on the pattern of *tetrarchy*.

Hep·ta·teuch /ˈheptəˌt(y)o͞ok/ ▶ **n.** the first seven books of the Bible (Genesis to Judges) collectively.
– ORIGIN late 17th cent.: via late Latin from Greek *heptateukhos*, from *hepta* 'seven' + *teukhos* 'book, volume.'

hep·tath·lon /hepˈtaTHˌlän/ ▶ **n.** a track and field event, in particular one for women, in which each competitor takes part in the same prescribed seven events (100-meter hurdles, high jump, shot put, 200-meter dash, long jump, javelin, and 800-meter run).
– DERIVATIVES **hep·tath·lete** /-ˈtaTHlēt/ **n.**
– ORIGIN 1970s: from **HEPTA-** 'seven' + Greek *athlon* 'contest,' on the pattern of words such as *decathlon*.

hep·ta·va·lent /ˈheptəˌvālənt/ ▶ **adj.** Chemistry having a valence of seven.

hep·tyl /ˈheptəl/ ▶ **n.** [as modifier] Chemistry of or denoting an alkyl radical $-Co_7H_{15}$, derived from heptane.

Hep·worth /ˈhepwərTH/, Barbara (1903–75), English sculptor; full name *Dame Jocelyn Barbara Hepworth*. She worked in wood, stone, and bronze and is noted for her simple monumental works in landscape and architectural settings, including the nine-piece group *The Family of Man* (1972).

her /hər/ ▶ **pron.** [third person singular] **1** used as the object of a verb or preposition to refer to a female person or animal previously mentioned or easily identified: *she knew I hated her* | *I told Hannah I would wait for her*. Compare with **SHE**. ■ referring to a ship, country, or other inanimate thing regarded as female: *the crew tried to sail her through a narrow gap*. ■ often used in place of "she" after the verb "to be" and after "than" or "as" to refer to a female person or animal: *it must be her* | *he was younger than her*.
2 archaic or dialect herself: *peevishly she flung her on her face*.
▶ **possessive determiner 1** belonging to or associated with a female person or animal previously mentioned or easily identified: *Patricia loved her job* | *how the mother crane treats her babies*. ■ belonging to or associated with a ship, country, or other inanimate thing regarded as female.
2 (**Her**) used in titles: *Her Royal Highness*.
– ORIGIN Old English *hire*, genitive and dative of *hīo, hēo* 'she.'

> **USAGE** On whether her or she is the correct pronoun in a comparative construction ("younger than her" or "younger than she"?), see usage at **PERSONAL PRONOUN** and **THAN**.

He·ra /ˈherə/ Greek Mythology a powerful goddess, the wife and sister of Zeus and the daughter of Cronus and Rhea. She was worshiped as the queen of heaven and as a marriage goddess. Roman equivalent **JUNO**.
– ORIGIN from Greek *Hēra* 'lady,' feminine of *hērōs* 'hero,' perhaps used as a title.

Her·a·cles /ˈherəklēz/ (also **Herakles**) Greek equivalent of **HERCULES**.

Her·a·cli·tus /ˌherəˈklītəs/ (*c.*500 BC), Greek philosopher. He believed that fire is the origin of all things and that permanence is an illusion, everything being in a process of constant change.

He·rak·li·on /heˈraklēən/ the capital of Crete, a port on the northern coast of the island; pop. 138,100 (est. 2009). Greek name **IRÁKLION**.

her·ald /ˈherəld/ ▶ **n. 1** an official messenger bringing news.
2 a person or thing viewed as a sign that something is about to happen: *they considered the first primroses as the herald of spring*.
3 historical an official employed to oversee state ceremony, precedence, and the use of armorial bearings, and to make proclamations, carry ceremonial messages, and oversee tournaments.
▶ **v.** [with obj.] be a sign that (something) is about to happen: *the speech heralded a change in policy*. ■ (usu. **be heralded**) acclaim: *the band has been heralded as the industrial supergroup of the '90s*.
– ORIGIN Middle English: from Old French *herault* (noun), *herauder* (verb), of Germanic origin.

he·ral·dic /həˈraldik/ ▶ **adj.** of or relating to heraldry.
– DERIVATIVES **he·ral·di·cal·ly** /-ik(ə)lē/ **adv.**

her·ald·ry /ˈherəldrē/ ▶ **n.** the system by which coats of arms and other armorial bearings are devised, described, and regulated. ■ armorial bearings or other heraldic symbols. ■ colorful ceremony: *all the pomp and heraldry provided a splendid pageant*.
– DERIVATIVES **her·ald·ist** /ˈherəldist/ **n.**

Her·alds' Col·lege /ˈherəldz/ informal name for **COLLEGE OF ARMS**.

He·rat /həˈrät, he-/ a city in western Afghanistan; pop. 349,000 (est. 2006).

herb /(h)ərb/ ▶ **n. 1** any plant with leaves, seeds, or flowers used for flavoring, food, medicine, or perfume: *bundles of dried herbs* | [as modifier] *a formal herb garden*.
2 Botany any seed-bearing plant that does not have a woody stem and dies down to the ground after flowering.
– ORIGIN Middle English: via Old French from Latin *herba* 'grass, green crops, herb.' Although *herb* has always been spelled with an *h*, pronunciation without it was usual in British English until the 19th cent. and is still standard in the US.

her·ba·ceous /(h)ərˈbāsHəs/ ▶ **adj.** of, denoting, or relating to herbs (in the botanical sense).
– ORIGIN mid 17th cent.: from Latin *herbaceus* 'grassy' (from *herba* 'grass, herb') + **-OUS**.

her·ba·ceous bor·der ▶ **n.** a garden border containing herbaceous, typically perennial, flowering plants.

her·ba·ceous per·en·ni·al ▶ **n.** a plant whose growth dies down annually but whose roots or other underground parts survive.

herb·age /ˈ(h)ərbij/ ▶ **n.** herbaceous vegetation. ■ the succulent part of this vegetation, used as pasture. ■ historical the right of pasture on another person's land.
– ORIGIN late Middle English: from Old French *erbage*, based on Latin *herba* 'herb, grass, crops.'

herb·al /ˈ(h)ərbəl/ ▶ **adj.** relating to or made from herbs, esp. those used in cooking and medicine: *herbal remedies*.
▶ **n.** a book that describes herbs and their culinary and medicinal properties.
– ORIGIN early 16th cent. (as a noun): from medieval Latin *herbalis* (adjective), from Latin *herba* 'grass, herb.'

herb·al·ism /ˈ(h)ərbəˌlizəm/ ▶ **n.** the study or practice of the medicinal and therapeutic use of plants, now esp. as a form of alternative medicine.

herb·al·ist /ˈ(h)ərbəlist/ ▶ **n.** a practitioner of herbalism. ■ a dealer in medicinal herbs. ■ an early botanical writer.

her·bar·i·um /(h)ərˈbe(ə)rēəm/ ▶ **n.** (pl. **herbariums** or **herbaria** /-ˈbe(ə)rēə/) a systematically arranged collection of dried plants. ■ a room or building housing such a collection. ■ a box, cabinet, or other receptacle in which dried plants are kept.
– ORIGIN late 18th cent.: from late Latin, from Latin *herba* 'grass, herb.'

herb·a·ry /ˈ(h)ərbərē/ ▶ **n.** (pl. **herbaries**) archaic an herb garden.

herbed /(h)ərbd/ ▶ **adj.** (of food) cooked, flavored, or seasoned with herbs.

Her·bert[1] /ˈhərbərt/, George (1593–1633), English metaphysical poet and clergyman. His poems, collected in *The Temple*, express a sweet and trusting friendliness with God.

Her·bert[2] /ˈhərbərt/, Victor (1859–1924), US composer, conductor, and cellist; born in Ireland. Among his light operas, or operettas, are included *Babes in Toyland* (1903) and *Naughty Marietta* (1910). He conducted the Pittsburgh Symphony 1889–1904.

herb·i·cide /ˈ(h)ərbəˌsīd/ ▶ **n.** a substance that is toxic to plants and is used to destroy unwanted vegetation.

her·biv·ore /ˈ(h)ərbəˌvôr/ ▶ **n.** an animal that feeds on plants.
– DERIVATIVES **her·biv·o·rous** /(h)ərˈbiv(ə)rəs/ **adj.**
– ORIGIN mid 19th cent.: from Latin *herba* 'herb' + *-vore* (see **-VOROUS**).

her·biv·o·ry /(h)ə'bivərē/ ▶ **n.** the eating of plants, esp. ones that are still living: *in response to herbivory, plants defend themselves with arrays of structural and chemical weapons.*
– ORIGIN mid 20th cent.: from *herbivor(ous)* + *-y*.

herb Par·is ▶ **n.** a European woodland plant of the lily family, with a single unbranched stem bearing a green and purple flower above four leaves. ● *Paris quadrifolia*, family Liliaceae (or Trilliaceae).
– ORIGIN translating medieval Latin *herba paris*, probably literally 'herb of a pair,' referring to the resemblance of the four leaves to a true-love knot.

herb Rob·ert ▶ **n.** a common cranesbill with pungent-smelling red-stemmed leaves and pink flowers, native to north temperate regions. ● *Geranium robertianum*, family Geraniaceae.
– ORIGIN translating medieval Latin *herba Roberti*, variously supposed to refer to *Robert* Duke of Normandy, St. *Robert*, or St. Rupert.

herb·y /'(h)ərbē/ ▶ **adj.** (**herbier**, **herbiest**) (of food or drink) containing or tasting or smelling of herbs.

Her·ce·go·vi·na variant spelling of HERZEGOVINA.

Her·cu·la·ne·um /ˌhərkyə'lānēəm/ an ancient Roman town, near Naples, on the lower slopes of Mount Vesuvius. The volcano's eruption in AD 79 buried it, along with Pompeii, deeply under volcanic ash and thus largely preserved it until its accidental rediscovery by a well-digger in 1709.

Her·cu·le·an /ˌhərkyə'lēən, hər'kyo͞olēən/ ▶ **adj.** requiring great strength or effort: *a Herculean task.* ■ (of a person) muscular and strong.
– ORIGIN late 16th cent. (in the sense 'relating to Hercules'): from Latin *Herculeus* 'Hercules' + -AN.

Her·cu·les /'hərkyəˌlēz/ **1** Greek & Roman Mythology a hero of superhuman strength and courage who performed twelve immense tasks or "labors" imposed on him and who after death was ranked among the gods. Greek name HERACLES. ■ (as noun **a Hercules**) a man of exceptional strength or size.
2 Astronomy a large northern constellation, said to represent the kneeling figure of Hercules. It contains the brightest globular cluster in the northern hemisphere, but no bright stars. ■ (as genitive **Herculis** /'hərkyəlis/) used with a preceding letter or numeral to designate a star in this constellation: *the star Delta Herculis.*
– ORIGIN Latin, from Greek *Hēraklēs*.

Her·cu·les bee·tle ▶ **n.** a large tropical American rhinoceros beetle, the male of which has two long curved horns extending from the head and one from the thorax. ● Genus *Dynastes*, family Scarabaeidae: several species, including the **eastern Hercules beetle** (*D. tityus*) of the southeastern US.

Her·cu·les-club ▶ **n.** either of two tall prickly shrubs or small trees of the US. ● the **southern prickly-ash** (*Zanthoxylum clava-herculis*, family Rutaceae), a tree of the rue family with knobby, corky protrusions on its trunk. ● the **devil's walking stick** (*Aralia spinosa*, family Araliaceae), a tree of the ginseng family, with large leaves and black berries. Also called ANGELICA TREE.

Her·cy·ni·an /hər'sinēən/ ▶ **adj.** Geology of, relating to, or denoting a prolonged mountain-forming period (orogeny) in western Europe, eastern North America, and the Andes in the Upper Paleozoic era, esp. the Carboniferous and Permian periods. ■ (as noun **the Hercynian**) the Hercynian orogeny.
– ORIGIN late 16th cent.: from Latin *Hercynia silva*; originally used by the ancient writers to designate an area of forested mountains in central Germany; later (from the late 19th cent.) applied in geology to the Harz Mountains formed in the Hercynian period.

herd /hərd/ ▶ **n.** a large group of animals, esp. hoofed mammals, that live, feed, or migrate together or are kept together as livestock: *a herd of elephants | large farms with big dairy herds.* ■ derogatory a large group of people, typically with a shared characteristic: *I dodged herds of joggers and cyclists | he is not of the common herd.*
▶ **v. 1** [with adverbial of direction] (with reference to a group of people or animals) move in a particular direction: [with obj.] *Nick herded me through the baggage claim and into his Jaguar* | [no obj.] *we all herded into a storage room.*
2 [with obj.] keep or look after (livestock): *Hunter and Tripp herded sheep.*
– ORIGIN Old English *heord*, of Germanic origin; related to German *Herde*.

herd·boy /'hərdˌboi/ ▶ **n.** a boy who looks after a herd of livestock.

herd·er /'hərdər/ ▶ **n.** a person who looks after a herd of livestock or makes a living from keeping livestock, esp. in open country.

herd im·mu·ni·ty ▶ **n.** general immunity to a pathogen in a population based on the acquired immunity to it by a high proportion of members over time.

herd in·stinct ▶ **n.** an inclination in people or animals to behave or think like the majority.

herds·man /'hərdzmən/ ▶ **n.** (pl. **herdsmen**) the owner or keeper of a herd of domesticated animals. ■ (**the Herdsman**) the constellation Boötes.

here /hi(ə)r/ ▶ **adv. 1** in, at, or to this place or position: *they have lived here most of their lives | come here and let me look at them* | [after prep.] *I'm getting out of here | it's too hot in here.* ■ used when pointing or gesturing to indicate the place in mind: *sign here | I have here a letter from the chief of police.* ■ used to draw attention to someone or something that has just arrived: ***here's** my brother* | ***here comes** the bus.* ■ [with infinitive] used to indicate one's role in a particular situation: *I'm here to help you | we're not here to mess around.* ■ used to refer to existence in the world in general: *what are we all doing here?*
2 (usu. **here is/are**) used when introducing something or someone: *here's a dish that is simple and quick to make | here's what you have to do.* ■ used when giving something to someone: *here's the money I promised you | here is my address.*
3 used when indicating a time, point, or situation that has arrived or is happening: *here is your opportunity | here comes summer | here we encounter the main problem.*
▶ **exclam. 1** used to attract someone's attention: *here, let me hold it.*
2 indicating one's presence in a roll call.
– PHRASES **here and now** at this very moment; at the present time: *we're going to settle this here and now* | [as noun] *our obsession with the here and now.* **here and there** in various places: *small bushes scattered here and there.* **here goes** an expression indicating that one is about to start something difficult or exciting. **here's to someone/something** used to wish health or success before drinking: *here's to us! | here's to your safe arrival.* **here today, gone tomorrow** soon over or forgotten; short-lived. **here we are** said on arrival at one's destination. **here we go again** said to indicate that the same events, typically undesirable ones, are recurring. **neither here nor there** of no importance or relevance.
– ORIGIN Old English *hēr*, of Germanic origin; related to Dutch and German *hier*, also to HE.

here·a·bouts /'hirəˌbouts/ (also **hereabout**) ▶ **adv.** near this place: *there is little natural water hereabouts.*

here·af·ter /hi(ə)r'aftər/ ▶ **adv.** formal from now on: *nothing I say hereafter is intended to relate to the second decision.* ■ at some time in the future: *this court is in no way prejudging any such defense which may hereafter be raised.* ■ after death: *a sermon about hope of life hereafter.*
▶ **n.** (**the hereafter**) life after death: *suffering is part of our preparation for the hereafter.*

here·at /ˌhi(ə)r'at/ ▶ **adv.** archaic as a result of this: *greatly distressed hereat, they declared themselves to deserve a fine.*

here·by /ˌhi(ə)r'bī, 'hi(ə)rˌbī/ ▶ **adv.** formal as a result of this document or utterance: *the Port Authority hereby solicits proposals from developers.*

he·red·i·ta·ble /hə'reditəbəl/ ▶ **adj.** less common term for HERITABLE.
– ORIGIN late Middle English: from Old French, or from medieval Latin *hereditabilis*, from ecclesiastical Latin *hereditare* 'inherit,' from Latin *heres, hered-* 'heir.'

her·e·dit·a·ment /ˌherə'ditəmənt/ ▶ **n.** Law, dated any item of property, either a **corporeal hereditament** (such as land or a building) or an **incorporeal hereditament** (such as a rent or a right of way). ■ an item of inheritance.
– ORIGIN late Middle English: from medieval Latin *hereditamentum*, from ecclesiastical Latin *hereditare* 'inherit,' from Latin *heres, hered-* 'heir.'

he·red·i·tar·i·an /həˌredi'te(ə)rēən/ ▶ **adj.** of or relating to the theory that heredity is the primary influence on human behavior, intelligence, or other characteristics.
▶ **n.** an advocate of such a view.
– DERIVATIVES **he·red·i·tar·i·an·ism** /-əˌnizəm/ **n.**

he·red·i·tar·y /hə'rediˌterē/ ▶ **adj.** (of a title, office, or right) conferred by or based on inheritance: *members of the ancient Polish aristocracy who had hereditary right to elect the king.* ■ [attrib.] (of a person) holding a position by inheritance: *I am the hereditary chief of the Piscataway people.* ■ (of a characteristic or disease) determined by genetic factors and therefore able to be passed on from parents to their offspring or descendants: *cystic fibrosis is our most common fatal hereditary disease.* ■ of or relating to inheritance: *a form of hereditary succession and dynastic rule became standard practice.* ■ Mathematics (of a set) defined such that every element that has a given relation to a member of the set is also a member of the set.
– DERIVATIVES **he·red·i·tar·i·ly** /həˌredi'te(ə)rəlē/ **adv.**, **he·red·i·tar·i·ness** /həˌredi'te(ə)rēnis/ **n.**
– ORIGIN late Middle English: from Latin *hereditarius*, from *hereditas* (see HEREDITY).

he·red·i·ty /hə'reditē/ ▶ **n. 1** the passing on of physical or mental characteristics genetically from one generation to another: *few scientists dispute that heredity can create a susceptibility to alcoholism.* ■ a person's ancestry: *he wears a Cossack tunic to emphasize his Russian heredity.*
2 inheritance of title, office, or right: *membership is largely based on heredity.*
– ORIGIN late 18th cent.: from French *hérédité*, from Latin *hereditas* 'heirship,' from *heres, hered-* 'heir.'

Her·e·ford /'hərfərd, 'herə-/ ▶ **n.** an animal of a breed of red and white beef cattle.
– ORIGIN early 19th cent.: named after *Hereford*, England, where it originated.

here·in /ˌhi(ə)r'in/ ▶ **adv.** formal in this document or book: *the author herein recounts his travel adventures.* ■ in this matter; arising from this: *the statues are sensual to the point of erotic and herein lies their interest.*

here·in·af·ter /ˌhi(ə)rin'aftər/ ▶ **adv.** formal further on in this document: *grievous bodily harm (hereinafter GBH).*

here·in·be·fore /ˌhi(ə)rinbi'fôr/ ▶ **adv.** formal before this point in this document.

here·of /ˌhi(ə)r'əv/ ▶ **adv.** formal of this document: *in accordance with section 17 hereof.*

He·re·ro /hə're(ə)rō/ ▶ **n.** (pl. **same** or **Hereros**) **1** a member of a people living in Namibia, Angola, and Botswana.
2 the Bantu language of this people.
▶ **adj.** of or relating to the Herero or their language.
– ORIGIN a local name, from *Otshi-Herero*, the Herero word for the language.

he·re·si·arch /hə'rēzēˌärk, 'herəsē-/ ▶ **n.** the founder of a heresy or the leader of a heretical sect.
– ORIGIN mid 16th cent.: via ecclesiastical Latin from ecclesiastical Greek *hairesiarkhēs* 'leader of a sect,' from *hairesis* 'heretical sect, heresy' + *arkhēs* 'ruler.'

her·e·sy /'herəsē/ ▶ **n.** (pl. **heresies**) belief or opinion contrary to orthodox religious (esp. Christian) doctrine: *Huss was burned for heresy | the doctrine was denounced as a heresy by the pope.* ■ opinion profoundly at odds with what is generally accepted: *cutting capital gains taxes is heresy | the politician's heresies became the conventional wisdom of the day.*
– ORIGIN Middle English: from Old French *heresie*, based on Latin *haeresis*, from Greek *hairesis* 'choice' (in ecclesiastical Greek 'heretical sect'), from *haireisthai* 'choose.'

her·e·tic /'herətik/ ▶ **n.** a person believing in or practicing religious heresy. ■ a person holding an opinion at odds with what is generally accepted.
– ORIGIN Middle English: from Old French *heretique*, via ecclesiastical Latin from Greek *hairetikos* 'able to choose' (in ecclesiastical Greek, 'heretical'), from *haireisthai* 'choose.'

he·ret·i·cal /hə'retikəl/ ▶ **adj.** believing in or practicing religious heresy: *heretical beliefs.* ■ holding an opinion at odds with what is generally accepted: *I feel a bit heretical saying this, but I think the film has too much action.*
– DERIVATIVES **he·ret·i·cal·ly** **adv.**

here·to /ˌhi(ə)r'to͞o/ ▶ **adv.** formal to this matter or document: *the written consent of each of the parties hereto | hereto is appended an estimate of the cost.*

here·to·fore /'hi(ə)rtəˌfôr/ ▶ **adv.** formal before now: *diseases that heretofore were usually confined to rural areas.*

here·un·der /ˌhi(ə)r'əndər/ ▶ **adv.** formal as provided for under the terms of this document: *all expenses incurred hereunder by the bank shall be recoverable.* ■ further on in a document.

here·un·to /hi(ə)r'ənˌto͞o, 'hi(ə)rˌən'to͞o/ ▶ **adv.** archaic or formal to this document: *signed in the presence of us both who have hereunto subscribed our names as witnesses.*

here·up·on /ˌhi(ə)rə'pän/ ▶ **adv.** after or as a result of this.

here·with /ˌhir'wiTH, -'wiT͟H/ ▶ **adv.** formal with this letter: *I send you herewith fifteen dollars.*

her·i·ot /'herēət/ ▶ **n.** Brit. historical a tribute paid to a lord out of the belongings of a tenant who died, often consisting of a live animal or, originally, military equipment that he had been lent during his lifetime.
– ORIGIN Old English *heregeatwa*, from *here* 'army' + *geatwa* 'trappings.'

her·it·a·ble /'heritəbəl/ ▶ **adj.** able to be inherited, in particular: ■ Biology (of a characteristic)

transmissible from parent to offspring. ■ Law (of property) capable of being inherited by heirs-at-law. Compare with **MOVABLE** (sense 2 of the adjective).
– DERIVATIVES **her·it·a·bil·i·ty** /ˌheritəˈbilitē/ **n.**, **her·it·a·bly** /-blē/ **adv.**
– ORIGIN late Middle English: from Old French *heriter* 'inherit,' from ecclesiastical Latin *hereditare*, from Latin *heres*, *hered-* 'heir.'

her·it·age /ˈheritij/ ▶ **n.** [in sing.] **1** property that is or may be inherited; an inheritance. ■ valued objects and qualities such as cultural traditions, unspoiled countryside, and historic buildings that have been passed down from previous generations: *the richness of our diverse cultural heritage | a sense of history and heritage.* ■ [as modifier] (of a plant variety) not hybridized with another; old-fashioned: *heritage roses.*
2 archaic a special or individual possession; an allotted portion. ■ God's chosen people (the people of Israel, or the Christian Church).
– ORIGIN Middle English: from Old French *heritage*, from *heriter* 'inherit' (see **HERITABLE**).

her·i·tor /ˈheritər/ ▶ **n.** a person who inherits.
– ORIGIN late Middle English: from Anglo-Norman French *heriter*, based on Latin *hereditarius* (see **HEREDITARY**). The spelling change in the 16th cent. was by association with words ending in **-OR**[1].

herk·y-jerk·y /ˈhərkē ˌjərkē/ ▶ **adj.** informal characterized by or moving in sudden stops and starts: *there were no windup toys, no herky-jerky contraptions.*
– ORIGIN late 20th cent.: reduplication of **JERKY**[1].

herl /hərl/ ▶ **n.** a barb or filament of a feather used in dressing a fishing fly.
– ORIGIN late Middle English: apparently of Germanic origin and related to Middle Low German *harle*.

Her·len /ˈhərˈlən/ another name for **KERULEN RIVER**.

herm /hərm/ ▶ **n.** a squared stone pillar with a carved head on top (typically of Hermes), used in ancient Greece as a boundary marker or a signpost.
– ORIGIN from the Greek name **HERMES**.

Her·man /ˈhərmən/, Woody (1913–87), US jazz clarinetist, saxophonist, and bandleader; full name *Woodrow Charles Herman*. He led several big bands that were all called Thundering Herds and became known for the song "Woodchoppers' Ball" (1939). "Ebony Concerto" was written for him by Stravinsky and first performed at Carnegie Hall in 1946.

her·maph·ro·dite /hərˈmafrəˌdīt/ ▶ **n.** a person or animal having both male and female sex organs or other sexual characteristics, either abnormally or (in the case of some organisms) as the natural condition. ■ Botany a plant having stamens and pistils in the same flower. ■ archaic a person or thing combining opposite qualities or characteristics.
▶ **adj.** of or denoting a person, animal, or plant of this kind: *hermaphrodite creatures in classical sculpture.*
– DERIVATIVES **her·maph·ro·dit·ic** /-ˌmafrəˈditik/ **adj.**, **her·maph·ro·dit·i·cal** /-ˌmafrəˈditikəl/ **adj.**, **her·maph·ro·dit·ism** /hərˈmafrədiˌtizəm/ (or **hermaphrodism** /-ˌdizəm/) **n.**
– ORIGIN late Middle English: via Latin from Greek *hermaphroditos* (see **HERMAPHRODITUS**).

her·maph·ro·dite brig ▶ **n.** a two-masted sailing ship with a square-rigged foremast and, on the mainmast, a square topsail above a fore-and-aft gaff mainsail.

Her·maph·ro·dit·us /hərˌmafrəˈdītəs/ Greek Mythology a son of Hermes and Aphrodite, with whom the nymph Salmacis fell in love and prayed to be forever united. As a result Hermaphroditus and Salmacis became joined in a single body that retained characteristics of both sexes.

her·me·neu·tic /ˌhərməˈn(y)o͞otik/ ▶ **adj.** concerning interpretation, esp. of the Bible or literary texts.
▶ **n.** a method or theory of interpretation.
– DERIVATIVES **her·me·neu·ti·cal adj.**, **her·me·neu·ti·cal·ly** /-(ə)lē/ **adv.**
– ORIGIN late 17th cent.: from Greek *hermēneutikos*, from *hermēneuein* 'interpret.'

her·me·neu·tics /ˌhərməˈn(y)o͞otiks/ ▶ **plural n.** [usu. treated as sing.] the branch of knowledge that deals with interpretation, esp. of the Bible or literary texts.

Her·mes /ˈhərmēz/ Greek Mythology the son of Zeus and Maia, the messenger of the gods, and god of merchants, thieves, and oratory. He was portrayed as a herald equipped for traveling, with broad-brimmed hat, winged shoes, and a winged rod. Roman equivalent **MERCURY**.
– ORIGIN probably from Greek *herma* 'heap of stones': from early times he was represented by a carved stock or stone and was identified with **THOTH**.

Her·mes Tris·me·gis·tus /ˌtrisməˈjistəs/ a legendary figure regarded by Neoplatonists and others as the author of certain works on astrology, magic, and alchemy.
– ORIGIN Latin, 'thrice-greatest Hermes,' in reference to **THOTH**, identified with **HERMES**.

her·met·ic /hərˈmetik/ ▶ **adj. 1** (of a seal or closure) complete and airtight: *a hermetic seal that ensures perfect waterproofing.* ■ insulated or protected from outside influences: *a hermetic society.*
2 (also **Hermetic**) of or relating to an ancient occult tradition encompassing alchemy, astrology, and theosophy. ■ esoteric; cryptic: *obscure and hermetic poems.*
– DERIVATIVES **her·met·i·cal·ly** /hərˈmetiklē, -ik(ə)lē/ **adv.**, **her·met·i·cism** /hərˈmetiˌsizəm/ **n.**
– ORIGIN mid 17th cent. (sense 2): from modern Latin *hermeticus*, from **HERMES**, identified with **THOTH**, regarded as the founder of alchemy and astrology.

her·mit /ˈhərmit/ ▶ **n. 1** a person living in solitude as a religious discipline. ■ any person living in solitude or seeking to do so.
2 a hummingbird found in the shady lower layers of tropical forests, foraging along a regular route. ● *Phaethornis* and other genera, family Trochilidae: several species.
– DERIVATIVES **her·mit·ic** /hərˈmitik/ **adj.**
– ORIGIN Middle English: from Old French *hermite*, from late Latin *eremita*, from Greek *erēmitēs*, from *erēmos* 'solitary.'

her·mit·age /ˈhərmitij/ ▶ **n. 1** the dwelling of a hermit, esp. when small and remote.
2 (**the Hermitage** /ˌermiˈtäzʜ/) a major art museum in St. Petersburg, Russia, containing among its collections those begun by Catherine the Great. [named with reference to the "retreat" in which the empress displayed her treasures to her friends.]
3 (**the Hermitage** /ˈhərmitij/) an estate, the home of Andrew Jackson, in central Tennessee, northeast of Nashville.
– ORIGIN Middle English: from Old French, from *hermite* (see **HERMIT**).

her·mit crab ▶ **n.** a crab with a soft asymmetrical abdomen that lives in a castoff mollusk shell for protection. In several kinds, the shell becomes covered with sponges, sea anemones, or bryozoans. ● Superfamily Paguroidea.

Her·mi·tian /hərˈmisʜən/ ▶ **adj.** Mathematics denoting or relating to a matrix in which those pairs of elements that are symmetrically placed with respect to the principal diagonal are complex conjugates.
– ORIGIN early 20th cent.: from the name of Charles *Hermite* (1822–1905), French mathematician, + **-IAN**.

her·mit thrush ▶ **n.** a small migratory North American thrush, noted for its melodious song. ● *Catharus guttatus*, subfamily Turdinae, family Muscicapidae.

hermit thrush

Her·mo·sil·lo /ˌermōˈsē(y)ō/ a city in northwestern Mexico, capital of the state of Sonora; pop. 641,791 (2005).

her·ni·a /ˈhərnēə/ ▶ **n.** (pl. **hernias** or **herniae** /-nēˌē/) a condition in which part of an organ is displaced and protrudes through the wall of the cavity containing it (often involving the intestine at a weak point in the abdominal wall).
– DERIVATIVES **her·ni·al adj.**
– ORIGIN late Middle English: from Latin.

her·ni·ate /ˈhərnēˌāt/ ▶ **v.** [no obj.] (usu. as adj. **herniated**) (of an organ) suffer a hernia: *a herniated bowel.*
– DERIVATIVES **her·ni·a·tion** /hərnēˈāsʜən/ **n.**

He·ro[1] /ˈhi(ə)rō/ Greek Mythology a priestess of Aphrodite at Sestos on the European shore of the Hellespont, whose lover Leander, a youth of Abydos on the opposite shore, swam the strait nightly to visit her. One stormy night he was drowned, and Hero in grief threw herself into the sea.

He·ro[2] /ˈhi(ə)rō, ˈhērō/ (1st century), Greek mathematician and inventor; known as **Hero of Alexandria**. He described a number of hydraulic, pneumatic, and other mechanical devices, including elementary applications of the power of steam.

he·ro /ˈhi(ə)rō/ ▶ **n.** (pl. **heroes**) a person, typically a man, who is admired or idealized for courage, outstanding achievements, or noble qualities: *a war hero.* ■ the chief male character in a book, play, or movie, who is typically identified with good qualities, and with whom the reader is expected to sympathize. ■ (in mythology and folklore) a person of superhuman qualities and often semidivine origin, in particular one of those whose exploits and dealings with the gods were the subject of ancient Greek myths and legends. ■ (also **hero sandwich**) another term for **SUBMARINE SANDWICH**.
– ORIGIN Middle English (with mythological reference): via Latin from Greek *hērōs*.

Her·od /ˈherəd/ the name of four rulers of ancient Palestine. ■ **Herod the Great** (*c.*74–4 BC), ruled 37–4 BC. According to the New Testament, Jesus was born during his reign, and he ordered the massacre of the innocents (Matt. 2:16). ■ **Herod Antipas** (22 BC–*c.*AD 40), son of Herod the Great, tetrarch of Galilee and Peraea 4 BC–AD 40. He married Herodias and was responsible for the beheading of John the Baptist. According to the New Testament (Luke 23:7), Pilate sent Jesus to be questioned by him before the Crucifixion. ■ **Herod Agrippa I** (10 BC–AD 44), grandson of Herod the Great; king of Judaea AD 41–44. He imprisoned St. Peter and put St. James the Great to death. ■ **Herod Agrippa II** (AD 27–*c.*93), son of Herod Agrippa I; king of various territories in northern Palestine 50–*c.*93. He presided over the trial of St. Paul (Acts 25:13 ff.).
– DERIVATIVES **He·ro·di·an** /həˈrōdēən/ **adj. & n.**

He·rod·o·tus /heˈrädətəs/ (5th century BC), Greek historian. Known as "the Father of History," he was the first historian to collect his materials systematically, test their accuracy to a certain extent, and arrange them in a well-constructed and vivid narrative.

he·ro·ic /həˈrōik/ ▶ **adj.** having the characteristics of a hero or heroine; very brave: *heroic deeds | a few heroic individuals.* ■ of or representing heroes or heroines: *early medieval heroic poetry.* ■ (of language or a work of art) grand or grandiose in scale or intention: *one passes under pyramids and obelisks, all on a heroic scale.* ■ Sculpture (of a statue) larger than life-size but less than colossal.
▶ **n.** (**heroics**) **1** behavior or talk that is bold or dramatic, esp. excessively or unexpectedly so: *the makeshift team performed heroics.*
2 short for **HEROIC VERSE**.
– DERIVATIVES **he·ro·i·cal·ly** /-ik(ə)lē/ **adv.**
– ORIGIN late Middle English: from Old French *heroique* or Latin *heroicus*, from Greek *hērōikos* 'relating to heroes,' from *hērōs* 'hero.'

he·ro·ic cou·plet ▶ **n.** (in verse) a pair of rhyming iambic pentameters, much used by Chaucer and the poets of the 17th and 18th centuries such as Alexander Pope.

he·ro·ic stan·za ▶ **n.** a rhyming quatrain in heroic verse. Also called **heroic quatrain**. ■ (in English poetry) a quatrain in iambic pentameter rhyming *abab* or *abba*. Compare with **ELEGIAC STANZA**.

he·ro·ic verse ▶ **n.** a type of verse used for epic or heroic subjects, such as the dactylic hexameter, iambic pentameter, or alexandrine. Also called **heroic meter**.

her·o·in /ˈherō-in/ ▶ **n.** a highly addictive analgesic drug derived from morphine, often used illicitly as a narcotic producing euphoria. ● Alternative name: **diacetylmorphine**; chem. formula: $C_{17}H_{17}NO(C_2H_3O_2)_2$.
– ORIGIN late 19th cent.: from German *Heroin*, from Latin *heros* 'hero' (because of its effects on the user's self-esteem).

her·o·ine /ˈherō-in/ ▶ **n.** a woman admired or idealized for her courage, outstanding achievements, or noble qualities: *she was the heroine of a materialist generation.* ■ the chief female character in a book, play, or movie, who is typically identified with good qualities, and with whom the reader is expected to sympathize. ■ (in mythology and folklore) a woman of superhuman qualities and often semidivine origin, in particular one whose dealings with the gods were the subject of ancient Greek myths and legends.
– ORIGIN mid 17th cent. (in the sense 'demigoddess, venerated woman'): from French *héroïne* or Latin *heroina*, from Greek *hērōinē*, feminine of *hērōs* 'hero.'

her·o·ism /ˈherōˌizəm/ ▶ **n.** great bravery.
– ORIGIN early 18th cent.: from French *héroïsme*, from *héros*, from Latin *heros* (see **HERO**).

her·o·ize /ˈhi(ə)rōˌīz/ ▶ **v.** [with obj.] treat or represent as a hero: *the father is heroized for long forbearance.*

her·on /ˈherən/ ▶ **n.** a large fish-eating wading bird with long legs, a long S-shaped neck, and a long pointed bill. ● Family Ardeidae (the **heron family**): several genera and numerous species, including the **great blue heron** (*Ardea herodias*).
– ORIGIN Middle English: from Old French, of Germanic origin.

great blue heron

her·on·ry /ˈherənrē/ ▶ **n.** (pl. **heronries**) a breeding colony of herons, typically in a group of trees.

He·roph·i·lus /həˈräfələs/ (4th–3rd centuries BC), Greek anatomist. He is considered the father of human anatomy for his fundamental discoveries concerning the anatomy of the brain, eye, and reproductive organs.

he·ro's wel·come ▶ **n.** an enthusiastic welcome for someone who has done something brave or praiseworthy.

he·ro wor·ship ▶ **n.** excessive admiration for someone. ■ (in ancient Greece) the worship of superhuman heroes.
▶ **v.** (**hero-worship**) [with obj.] admire (someone) excessively.
– DERIVATIVES **he·ro-wor·ship·er** **n.**

herp /hərp/ ▶ **n.** short for **HERPTILE**.

her·pes /ˈhərpēz/ ▶ **n.** any of a group of viral diseases caused by herpes viruses, affecting the skin (often with blisters) or the nervous system.
– DERIVATIVES **her·pet·ic** /hərˈpetik/ **adj.**
– ORIGIN late Middle English (originally used also of other skin conditions): via Latin from Greek *herpēs* 'shingles,' literally 'creeping,' from *herpein* 'to creep.'

her·pes sim·plex ▶ **n.** a viral infection, caused by a group of herpes viruses, that may produce cold sores, genital inflammation, or conjunctivitis.

her·pes·vi·rus /ˈhərpēzˌvīrəs/ ▶ **n.** Medicine any of a group of DNA viruses causing herpes and other diseases.

her·pes zos·ter /ˈzästər/ ▶ **n.** medical name for **SHINGLES**. ■ a herpesvirus that causes shingles and chickenpox.
– ORIGIN late Middle English: from **HERPES** and Latin *zoster*, from Greek *zōstēr* 'girdle, shingles.'

her·pe·to·fau·na /ˈhərpitōˌfônə/ ▶ **n.** Zoology the reptiles and amphibians of a particular region, habitat, or geological period.
– DERIVATIVES **her·pe·to·fau·nal** /-fônəl/ **adj.**
– ORIGIN modern Latin, from Greek *herpeton* 'creeping thing, reptile' + **FAUNA**.

her·pe·tol·o·gy /ˌhərpəˈtäləjē/ ▶ **n.** the branch of zoology concerned with reptiles and amphibians.
– DERIVATIVES **her·pe·to·log·i·cal** /-təˈläjəkəl/ **adj.**, **her·pe·tol·o·gist** /-jist/ **n.**
– ORIGIN early 19th cent.: from Greek *herpeton* 'reptile' (from *herpein* 'to creep') + **-LOGY**.

herp·tile /ˌhərpˈtīl/ ▶ **n.** a reptile or amphibian.
– ORIGIN blend of **HERPETOLOGY** and **REPTILE**.

Herr /he(ə)r/ ▶ **n.** (pl. **Herren** /ˈhe(ə)rən/) a title or form of address used of or to a German-speaking man, corresponding to *Mr.* and also used before a rank or occupation: *good morning, Herr Weber | my trip with the Herr Doktor was postponed.* ■ a German man.
– ORIGIN German, from Old High German *hērro*, comparative of *hēr* 'exalted.'

Her·ren·volk /ˈherənˌfōk, -ˌfôlk/ ▶ **n.** the German nation as considered by the Nazis to be innately superior to others.
– ORIGIN mid 20th cent.: German, 'master race,' from *Herr* 'master' + *Volk* 'people, folk.'

her·ring /ˈheriNG/ ▶ **n.** a silvery fish that is most abundant in coastal waters and is of great commercial importance as a food fish in many parts of the world. ● *Clupea* and other genera, family Clupeidae (the **herring family**): several species, in particular (*C. harengus*), of the North Atlantic. The herring family also includes the sprats, shads, and pilchards.
– ORIGIN Old English *hǣring, hēring*; related to Dutch *haring* and German *Hering*.

her·ring·bone /ˈheriNGˌbōn/ ▶ **n.** [usu. as modifier] **1** an arrangement or design consisting of columns of short parallel lines, with all the lines in one column sloping one way and all the lines in the next column sloping the other way so as to resemble the bones in a fish, used esp. in the weave of cloth or the placing of bricks: *a brown wool herringbone jacket.* ■ (also **herringbone stitch**) a cross-stitch with a pattern resembling such an arrangement, used in embroidery or for securing an edge.

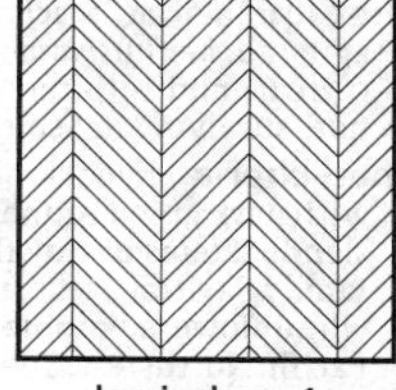
herringbone 1

2 Skiing a method of ascending a slope by walking forward in alternate steps with each ski angled outward.
▶ **v. 1** [with obj.] mark with a herringbone pattern. ■ work with a herringbone stitch.
2 [no obj.] Skiing ascend a slope using the herringbone technique: *we learned how to herringbone up the hills and swoosh down them.*

her·ring gull ▶ **n.** a gull with gray black-tipped wings, abundant and widespread in both Eurasia and North America. ● *Larus argentatus*, family Laridae.

Her·ri·ot /ˈherēət/, James (1916–1995), English short-story writer and veterinary surgeon; pseudonym of *James Alfred Wight*. His experiences as a veterinarian inspired a series of stories including *All Creatures Great and Small* (1972).

Herrn·hut·er /ˈhe(ə)rnˌhōōtər/ ▶ **n.** a member of a Moravian Church.
– ORIGIN mid 18th cent.: German, from *Herrnhut* (literally 'the Lord's keeping'), the name of the first German settlement of the Moravian Church.

hers /hərz/ ▶ **possessive pron.** used to refer to a thing or things belonging to or associated with a female person or animal previously mentioned: *his eyes met hers | the choice was hers | friends of hers warned her.*

Her·schel /ˈhərSHəl/, Sir (Frederick) William (1738–1822), English astronomer; born in Germany. His cataloguing of the skies resulted in the discovery of the planet Uranus.

her·self /hərˈself/ ▶ **pron.** [third person singular] **1** [reflexive] used as the object of a verb or preposition to refer to a female person or animal previously mentioned as the subject of the clause: *she had to defend herself | Jo made herself a cup of tea.*
2 [emphatic] she or her personally (used to emphasize a particular female person or animal mentioned): *she told me herself.*
– PHRASES **(not) be herself** see **NOT BE ONESELF** at **BE**. **by herself** see **BY ONESELF** at **BY**.
– ORIGIN Old English (see **HER, SELF**).

Her·sey /ˈhərsē/, John Richard (1914–93), US writer; born in China of US missionary parents. Among his works are *A Bell for Adano* (1944) and *Hiroshima* (1946).

Her·shey /ˈhərSHē/ a village in southeastern Pennsylvania, created by chocolate manufacturer Milton Hershey (1857–1945); pop. 12,771 (2000).

her·sto·ry /ˈhərstərē/ ▶ **n.** (pl. **herstories**) history viewed from a female or specifically feminist perspective.
– ORIGIN 1970s: from **HER** + **STORY**[1], analogous formation based on the form *history*.

Hertz /hərts/, Heinrich Rudolf (1857–94), German physicist and pioneer in radio communication. He continued the work of Maxwell on electromagnetic waves and was the first to broadcast and receive radio waves.

hertz /hərts/ (abbr.: **Hz**) ▶ **n.** (pl. **same**) the SI unit of frequency, equal to one cycle per second.
– ORIGIN late 19th cent.: named after H. R. **HERTZ**.

Hertz·ian wave /ˈhərtsēən/ ▶ **n.** former term for **RADIO WAVE**.

Hertz·sprung–Rus·sell di·a·gram /ˈhertsˌsprōōNG ˈrəsəl/ ▶ **n.** Astronomy a two-dimensional graph, devised independently by Ejnar Hertzsprung (1873–1967) and Henry Norris Russell (1877–1957), in which the absolute magnitudes of stars are plotted against their spectral types. Stars are found to occupy only certain regions of such a diagram.

He·rut /KHeˈrōōt, he-/ a right-wing Israeli political party founded by Menachem Begin in 1948 from the remains of the Irgun group and one of the parties that combined to form the Likud coalition in 1973.
– ORIGIN Hebrew, 'freedom.'

Her·ze·go·vi·na /ˌhərtsəˈgōvənə, ˌhert-, -gōˈvēnə/ (also **Hercegovina**) a region in the Balkans that forms the southern part of Bosnia and Herzegovina and is separated from the Adriatic Sea by part of Croatia. Its chief town is Mostar.
– DERIVATIVES **Her·ze·go·vi·ni·an** /-gōˈvinēən, -gōˈvēnēən/ **adj. & n.**

Her·zl /ˈhərtsəl/, Theodor (1860–1904), Hungarian journalist, playwright, and Zionist leader. The founder of the Zionist movement in 1897, he worked for most of his life as a writer and journalist in Vienna.

he's /hēz/ ▶ **contraction** he is: *he's going to speak.* ■ he has: *he's given up his job.*

Hesh·van /ˈKHeSHvän, ˈheSHvən/ ▶ **n.** variant spelling of **HESVAN**.

He·si·od /ˈhesēəd/ (*c.*700 BC), Greek poet. One of the earliest known Greek poets, he wrote the *Theogony*, an epic poem on the genealogies of the gods.

hes·i·tan·cy /ˈhezitənsē/ ▶ **n.** the quality or state of being hesitant.
– DERIVATIVES **hes·i·tance** **n.**

hes·i·tant /ˈhezitənt/ ▶ **adj.** tentative, unsure, or slow in acting or speaking: *clients are hesitant about buying | her slow, hesitant way of speaking.*
– DERIVATIVES **hes·i·tant·ly** **adv.**
– ORIGIN late Middle English: from Latin *haesitant-* 'being undecided,' from the verb *haesitare* (see **HESITATE**).

hes·i·tate /ˈheziˌtāt/ ▶ **v.** [no obj.] pause before saying or doing something, esp. through uncertainty: *she hesitated, unsure of what to say.* ■ [with infinitive] be reluctant to do something: *he hesitated to spoil the mood by being inquisitive.*
– PHRASES **he who hesitates is lost** proverb delay or vacillation may have unfortunate or disastrous consequences.
– DERIVATIVES **hes·i·tat·er** /-ˌtātər/ **n.**, **hes·i·tat·ing·ly** /-ˌtātiNGlē/ **adv.**
– ORIGIN early 17th cent.: from Latin *haesitat-* 'stuck fast, left undecided,' from the verb *haesitare*, from *haerere* 'stick, stay.'

hes·i·ta·tion /ˌheziˈtāSHən/ ▶ **n.** the action of pausing or hesitating before saying or doing something: *she answered without hesitation.*

Hes·pe·ri·a /heˈspi(ə)rēə/ a city in southern California, north of San Bernardino; pop. 85,883 (est. 2008).

Hes·pe·ri·an /heˈspi(ə)rēən/ ▶ **adj.** Greek Mythology of or concerning the Hesperides. ■ literary western.
– ORIGIN late 15th cent.: from Latin *hesperius* (from Greek *hesperios*, from *Hesperia* 'land of the west,' from *hesperos* 'western' (see **HESPERUS**)) + **-AN**.

Hes·per·i·des /heˈsperəˌdēz/ Greek Mythology a group of nymphs who were guardians, with the aid of a watchful dragon, of a tree of golden apples in a garden located beyond the Atlas Mountains at the western border of Oceanus, the river encircling the world. One of the labors of Hercules was to fetch the golden apples.

hes·per·id·i·um /ˌhespəˈridēəm/ ▶ **n.** (pl. **hesperidia** /-ˌhespəˈridēə/) Botany a fruit with sectioned pulp inside a separable rind, e.g., an orange or grapefruit.
– ORIGIN mid 19th cent.: based on *Hesperideae*, former name of an order of plants containing citrus fruits, named after the golden apples of the Hesperides (see **HESPERIDES**) + **-IUM**.

Hes·per·us /ˈhespərəs/ ▶ **n.** literary the planet Venus.
– ORIGIN Latin, from Greek *hesperos* 'western,' (as a noun) 'the evening star,' related to Latin *vesper* 'evening (star)' (see **VESPER**).

Hess[1] /hes/, Dame Myra (1890–1965), English pianist. She was noted for her performances of the music of Schumann, Beethoven, Mozart, and Bach.

Hess[2], Rudolf (1894–1987), German politician, deputy leader of the Nazi Party 1934–41; full name *Walther Richard Rudolf Hess*. In 1941, secretly and on his own initiative, he parachuted into Scotland to negotiate peace with Britain. He was imprisoned for the duration of the war and, at the Nuremberg war trials, sentenced to life imprisonment in Spandau prison, Berlin, where he died.

Hess[3], Victor Francis (1883–1964), US physicist; born in Austria; born *Victor Franz Hess*. He showed that some ionizing radiation (later termed cosmic rays) was extraterrestrial in origin but did not come from the sun. Nobel Prize for Physics (1936), shared with Carl D. Anderson.

Hes·se[1] /hes, ˈhesə/ a state in western Germany; capital, Wiesbaden. German name **Hessen**.
– DERIVATIVES **Hes·sian** /ˈheSHən/ **adj. & n.**

Hes·se[2] /ˈhesə/, Hermann (1877–1962), Swiss novelist and poet, born in Germany. His work reflects his interest in spiritual values as expressed in Eastern religion and his involvement in Jungian analysis. Notable works: *Siddhartha* (1922), *Steppenwolf* (1927), and *The Glass Bead Game* (1943). Nobel Prize for Literature (1946).

hes·sian /ˈheSHən/ ▶ **n.** a strong, coarse fabric made from hemp or jute, used for sacks.
– ORIGIN late 19th cent.: from *Hesse* (see **HESSE**[1]) + **-IAN**.

Hes·sian boot ▶ **n.** a high tasseled leather boot, originally worn by Hessian troops.

Hes·sian fly ▶ **n.** a gall midge whose larvae are a pest of cereal crops, occurring in wheat-growing areas. ● *Mayetiola destructor*, family Cecidomyiidae.
– ORIGIN late 18th cent.: so named because it was supposed (erroneously) to have been carried to America by Hessian troops during the American Revolution.

hest /hest/ ▶ **n.** archaic form of **BEHEST**.
– ORIGIN Old English *hǣs*, of Germanic origin; related to **HIGHT**. The spelling change in Middle English was by association with abstract nouns ending in *-t*.

Hes·ton /ˈhestən/, Charlton (1924–2008), US actor and social activist. His movies include *The Ten Commandments* (1956), *Ben-Hur* (1959), and *Planet of the Apes* (1968). He headed the National Rifle Association (NRA) 1998–2003.

h

Hes·van /ˈKHESHvän, ˈhesvən/ (also **Chesvan, Heshvan**) ▶ **n.** (in the Jewish calendar) the second month of the civil and eighth of the religious year, usually coinciding with parts of October and November.
– ORIGIN from Hebrew *ḥešwān*.

Hes·y·chast /ˈhesiˌkast/ ▶ **n.** historical a member of a movement dedicated to contemplation, originating among the Orthodox monks of Mount Athos in the 14th century.
– ORIGIN mid 19th cent.: from late Greek *hēsukhastēs* 'hermit,' from *hēsukhazein* 'be still,' from *hēsukhos* 'still.'

het /het/ ▶ **adj. & n.** informal short for HETEROSEXUAL.

he·tae·ra /hiˈti(ə)rə/ (also **hetaira** /-ˈtīrə/) ▶ **n.** (pl. **hetaeras** or **hetaerae** /-ˈti(ə)rē/) a courtesan or mistress, esp. one in ancient Greece akin to the modern geisha.
– ORIGIN from Greek *hetaira*, feminine of *hetairos* 'companion.'

het·er·o /ˈhetərō/ ▶ **adj. & n.** (pl. **heteros**) informal short for HETEROSEXUAL.

hetero- ▶ **comb. form** other; different: *heteropolar* | *heterosexual*. Often contrasted with HOMO-.
– ORIGIN from Greek *heteros* 'other.'

het·er·o·ar·o·mat·ic /ˌhetərōˌarəˈmatik/ ▶ **adj.** Chemistry denoting an organic compound with a ring structure that is both heterocyclic and aromatic.

het·er·o·at·om /ˌhetərōˈatəm/ ▶ **n.** an atom in the ring of a cyclic compound other than a carbon atom.
– DERIVATIVES **het·e·ro·a·tom·ic** /-əˈtämik/ **adj.**

het·er·o·cer·cal /ˌhetərōˈsərkəl/ ▶ **adj.** Zoology (of a fish's tail) having unequal upper and lower lobes, usually with the vertebral column passing into the upper. Contrasted with DIPHYCERCAL, HOMOCERCAL.
– ORIGIN mid 19th cent.: from HETERO- 'other' + Greek *kerkos* 'tail.'

het·er·o·chro·mat·ic /ˌhetərōkrəˈmatik/ ▶ **adj. 1** of several different colors or (in physics) wavelengths. **2** Biochemistry of or relating to heterochromatin.

het·er·o·chro·ma·tin /ˌhetərōˈkrōmətin/ ▶ **n.** Biology chromosome material of different density from normal (usually greater), in which the activity of the genes is modified or suppressed. Compare with EUCHROMATIN.

het·er·o·chro·mo·some /ˌhetərōˈkrōməˌsōm/ ▶ **n.** another term for SEX CHROMOSOME.

het·er·o·clite /ˈhetərəˌklīt/ formal ▶ **adj.** abnormal or irregular.
▶ **n.** an abnormal thing or person. ■ an irregularly declined word, esp. a Greek or Latin noun.
– DERIVATIVES **het·er·o·clit·ic** /ˌhetərəˈklitik/ **adj.**
– ORIGIN late 15th cent.: via late Latin from Greek *heteroklitos*, from *heteros* 'other' + *-klitos* 'inflected' (from *klinein* 'to lean, inflect').

het·er·o·cy·clic /ˌhetərōˈsīklik, -ˈsiklik/ ▶ **adj.** Chemistry denoting a compound whose molecule contains a ring of atoms of at least two elements (one of which is generally carbon).

het·er·o·cyst /ˈhetərəˌsist/ ▶ **n.** a large, transparent, thick-walled cell found in the filaments of certain blue-green algae and in certain fungi.

het·er·o·dox /ˈhetərəˌdäks/ ▶ **adj.** not conforming with accepted or orthodox standards or beliefs: *heterodox views*.
– DERIVATIVES **het·er·o·dox·y n.**
– ORIGIN early 17th cent. (originally as a noun denoting an unorthodox opinion): via late Latin from Greek *heterodoxos*, from *heteros* 'other' + *doxa* 'opinion.'

het·er·o·dyne /ˈhetərəˌdīn/ Electronics ▶ **adj.** of or relating to the production of a lower frequency from the combination of two almost equal high frequencies, as used in radio transmission.
▶ **v.** [with obj.] combine (a high-frequency signal) with another to produce a lower frequency in this way.
– ORIGIN early 20th cent.: from HETERO- 'other' + *-dyne*, suffix formed irregularly from Greek *dunamis* 'power.'

het·er·oe·cious /ˌhetəˈrēsHəs/ ▶ **adj.** Biology parasitic on different and often unrelated species of host at different stages of life. Compare with HOMOECIOUS.

het·er·o·ga·met·ic /ˌhetərōgəˈmetik/ ▶ **adj.** Biology denoting the sex that has sex chromosomes that differ in morphology, resulting in two different kinds of gamete, e.g., (in mammals) the male and (in birds) the female. The opposite of HOMOGAMETIC.

het·er·og·a·my /ˌhetəˈrägəmē/ ▶ **n. 1** chiefly Zoology the alternation of generations, esp. between sexual and parthenogenetic generations.
2 Botany a state in which the flowers of a plant are of two or more types. Compare with HOMOGAMY (sense 2). ■ another term for ANISOGAMY.
3 marriage between people from different sociological or educational backgrounds. Compare with HOMOGAMY (sense 1).
– DERIVATIVES **het·er·og·a·mous** /-ˈrägəməs/ **adj.**

het·er·o·ge·ne·ous /ˌhetərəˈjēnēəs/ ▶ **adj.** diverse in character or content: *a large and heterogeneous collection*. ■ Chemistry of or denoting a process involving substances in different phases (solid, liquid, or gaseous). ■ Mathematics incommensurable through being of different kinds, degrees, or dimensions.
– DERIVATIVES **het·er·o·ge·ne·i·ty** /-jəˈnēətē/ **n.**, **het·er·o·ge·ne·ous·ly adv.**, **het·er·o·ge·ne·ous·ness n.**
– ORIGIN early 17th cent.: from medieval Latin *heterogeneus*, from Greek *heterogenēs*, from *heteros* 'other' + *genos* 'a kind.'

> **USAGE** The correct spelling for the word meaning 'diverse in character or content' is **heterogeneous**, but a fairly common misspelling is **heterogenous**. The reason for the error probably relates to the pronunciation, which, in rapid speech, often skims over the fifth syllable as if to skip the **e**. Take care to note that **heterogenous** is a different word, which is used in specialized medical and biological senses and means 'originating outside the organism.'

het·er·og·e·nous /ˌhetəˈräjənəs/ ▶ **adj.** Medicine originating outside the organism: *present in the urine are heterogenous proteins*.

> **USAGE** See usage at HETEROGENEOUS.

het·er·o·glos·si·a /ˌhetərōˈgläsēə/ ▶ **n.** the presence of two or more voices or expressed viewpoints in a text or other artistic work.

het·er·o·graft /ˈhetərōˌgraft/ ▶ **n.** another term for XENOGRAFT.

het·er·og·y·nous /ˌhetəˈräjənəs/ ▶ **adj.** having females of two kinds, fertile and neuter, as in bees and ants.

het·er·ol·o·gous /ˌhetəˈrälәgəs/ ▶ **adj.** chiefly Medicine & Biology not homologous.
– DERIVATIVES **het·er·ol·o·gy** /-ˈräləjē/ **n.**

het·er·ol·y·sis /ˌhetəˈräləsis, -rōˈlīsis/ ▶ **n. 1** Biology the dissolution of cells by lysins or enzymes from different species.
2 Chemistry the breakdown of a compound into oppositely charged ions.
– DERIVATIVES **het·er·o·lyt·ic adj.**

het·er·om·er·ous /ˌhetəˈrämərəs/ ▶ **adj.** Biology having or composed of parts that differ in number or position.

het·er·o·mor·phic /ˌhetərəˈmôrfik/ ▶ **adj.** Biology occurring in two or more different forms, esp. at different stages in the life cycle.
– DERIVATIVES **het·er·o·morph** /ˈhetərəˌmôrf/ **n.**, **het·er·o·mor·phy n.** /ˈhetərəˌmôrfē/.

het·er·o·mor·phism /ˌhetərəˈmôrfizəm/ ▶ **n.** Biology the quality or condition of existing in various forms: *chromosomal heteromorphism*.

het·er·on·o·mous /ˌhetəˈränəməs/ ▶ **adj.** subject to a law or standard external to itself. ■ (in Kantian moral philosophy) acting in accordance with one's desires rather than reason or moral duty. Compare with AUTONOMOUS. ■ subject to different laws.
– DERIVATIVES **het·er·on·o·my** /-ˈränəmē/ **n.**

het·er·o·nor·ma·tive /ˌhetərōˈnôrmətiv/ ▶ **adj.** denoting or relating to a world view that promotes heterosexuality as the normal or preferred sexual orientation: *the heteronormative codes of twentieth-century mainstream Western cinema*.
– DERIVATIVES **het·er·o·nor·ma·tiv·i·ty n.**

het·er·o·nym /ˈhetərəˌnim/ ▶ **n.** Linguistics **1** each of two or more words that are spelled identically but have different sounds and meanings, such as *tear* meaning "rip" and *tear* meaning "liquid from the eye."
2 each of two or more words that are used to refer to the identical thing in different geographical areas of a speech community, such as *submarine sandwich*, *hoagie*, and *grinder*.
3 each of two words having the same meaning but derived from unrelated sources, for example *preface* and *foreword*. Contrasted with PARONYM.
– DERIVATIVES **het·er·o·nym·ic** /ˌhetərəˈnimik/ **adj.**, **het·er·on·y·mous** /ˌhetəˈränəməs/ **adj.**

het·er·o·phyte /ˈheərəˌfīt/ ▶ **n.** Botany a plant that derives its nourishment from other organisms.
– DERIVATIVES **het·er·o·phyt·ic** /-rōˈfitik/ **adj.**

het·er·o·plas·ty /ˈhetərəˌplastē/ ▶ **n.** the operation of grafting tissue between two individuals of the same or different species.
– DERIVATIVES **het·er·o·plas·tic** /ˈhetərəˈplastik/ **adj.**

het·er·o·po·lar /ˌhetərōˈpōlər/ ▶ **adj.** chiefly Physics characterized by opposite or alternating polarity. ■ (esp. of an electric motor) with an armature passing north and south magnetic poles alternately.

Het·er·op·ter·a /ˌhetəˈräptərə/ Entomology a group of true bugs in which the forewings are nonuniform, having a thickened base and membranous tip. The predatory and water bugs belong to this group, as well as many plant bugs. Compare with HOMOPTERA. ● Suborder Heteroptera, order Hemiptera. ■ (as plural noun **heteroptera**) bugs of this group.
– ORIGIN modern Latin (plural), from Greek *heteros* 'other' + *pteron* 'wing.'

het·er·op·ter·an /ˌhetəˈräptərən/ Entomology ▶ **n.** a bug of the group Heteroptera. ▶ **adj.** relating to or denoting heteropterans.
– DERIVATIVES **het·er·op·ter·ous** /-ˈräptərəs/ **adj.**

het·er·o·sex·ism /ˌhetərōˈsekˌsizəm/ ▶ **n.** discrimination or prejudice against homosexuals on the assumption that heterosexuality is the normal sexual orientation.
– DERIVATIVES **het·er·o·sex·ist adj.**

het·er·o·sex·u·al /ˌhetərōˈsekSHōōəl/ ▶ **adj.** (of a person) sexually attracted to people of the opposite sex. ■ involving or characterized by sexual attraction between people of the opposite sex: *heterosexual relationships*.
▶ **n.** a heterosexual person.
– DERIVATIVES **het·er·o·sex·u·al·i·ty** /-ˌsekSHōōˈalitē/ **n.**, **het·er·o·sex·u·al·ly adv.**

het·er·o·sis /ˌhetəˈrōsəs/ ▶ **n.** Genetics the tendency of a crossbred individual to show qualities superior to those of both parents. Also called HYBRID VIGOR.
– ORIGIN early 20th cent.: from Greek *heterōsis* 'alteration,' from *heteros* 'other.'

het·er·os·po·rous /ˌhetəˈräspərəs, -ərəˈspôrəs/ ▶ **adj.** Biology producing two different kinds of spores.
– DERIVATIVES **het·er·os·po·ry n.**

het·er·o·sty·ly /ˈhetərəˌstīlē/ ▶ **n.** Botany the condition (e.g., in primroses) of having styles of different lengths relative to the stamens in the flowers of different individual plants, to reduce self-fertilization.
– DERIVATIVES **het·er·o·sty·lous** /ˌhetərəˈstīləs/ **adj.**
– ORIGIN late 19th cent.: from HETERO- 'different' + Greek *stulos* 'column' + -Y³.

het·er·ot·ic /ˌhetəˈrätik/ ▶ **adj. 1** Biology of or relating to heterosis (hybrid vigor).
2 Physics of or relating to a theory of cosmic strings that combines elements of two earlier models.

het·er·o·trans·plant /ˌhetərōˈtransˌplant/ ▶ **n.** another term for XENOGRAFT.

het·er·o·troph /ˈhetərəˌträf, -trōf/ ▶ **n.** Biology an organism deriving its nutritional requirements from complex organic substances. Compare with AUTOTROPH.
– DERIVATIVES **het·er·o·troph·ic** /ˌhetərəˈträfik, -ˈtrō-/ **adj.**, **het·er·ot·ro·phy** /ˌhetəˈrätrəfē/ **n.**
– ORIGIN early 20th cent.: from HETERO- 'other' + Greek *trophos* 'feeder.'

het·er·o·typ·ic /ˌhetərōˈtipik/ ▶ **adj.** different in form, arrangement, or type. ■ Biology of or relating to the first of the two nuclear divisions of meiosis.

het·er·o·zy·go·sis /ˌhetərōzīˈgōsis/ ▶ **n.** Genetics the state of being a heterozygote. ■ Biology the formation of a zygote through the fusion of genetically different gametes.

het·er·o·zy·gote /ˌhetərōˈzīgәt, -ˈzīgōt/ ▶ **n.** Genetics an individual having two different alleles of a particular gene or genes, and so giving rise to varying offspring. Compare with HOMOZYGOTE.
– DERIVATIVES **het·er·o·zy·gos·i·ty** /-zīˈgäsitē/ **n.**, **het·er·o·zy·gous** /-ˈzīgəs/ **adj.**

het·man /ˈhetmən/ ▶ **n.** (pl. **hetmen**) a Polish or Cossack military commander.
– ORIGIN Polish, probably from German *Hauptmann* 'captain.'

het up /ˌhet ˈəp/ ▶ **adj.** [predic.] informal angry and agitated: *her husband is all het up about something*.
– ORIGIN mid 19th cent.: from dialect *het* 'heated, hot,' surviving in Scots.

heu·cher·a /ˈhyōōkərə/ ▶ **n.** a North American plant with dark green round or heart-shaped leaves and slender stems of tiny flowers. ● Genus *Heuchera*, family Saxifragaceae: many species, including the white-flowered **alpine heuchera** (*H. glabra*) of the Pacific Northwest. See also ALUMROOT, CORAL BELLS.
– ORIGIN modern Latin, named after Johann H. von *Heucher* (1677–1747), German botanist.

heu·rig·er /ˈhoirigər/ (also **heurige** /-rigə/) ▶ **n.** (pl. **heurigen** /-rigən/) (esp. in Austria) wine from the latest harvest. ■ an establishment where this is served.
– ORIGIN mid 20th cent.: Austrian German, literally 'this year's (wine).'

heu·ris·tic /hyōōˈristik/ ▶ **adj.** enabling a person to discover or learn something for themselves: *a "hands-on" or interactive heuristic approach to learning*. ■ Computing proceeding to a solution by trial and error or by rules that are only loosely defined.
▶ **n.** a heuristic process or method. ■ (**heuristics**) [usu. treated as sing.] the study and use of heuristic techniques.

– DERIVATIVES **heu·ris·ti·cal·ly** adv.
– ORIGIN early 19th cent.: formed irregularly from Greek *heuriskein* 'find.'

he·ve·a /ˈhēvēə/ ▶ n. a South American tree of a genus that comprises the rubber trees. ● Genus *Hevea*, family Euphorbiaceae.
– ORIGIN modern Latin, from Quechua *hyeve*.

He·ve·sy /ˈhevəSHē/, George Charles de (1885–1966), Hungarian radiochemist. He studied radioisotopes and invented the technique of labeling with isotopic tracers. Hevesy was also codiscoverer of the element hafnium in 1923. Nobel Prize for Chemistry (1943).

HEW ▶ abbr. (Department of) Health, Education, and Welfare.

hew /hyo͞o/ ▶ v. (past participle **hewn** /hyo͞on/ or **hewed**) **1** [with obj.] chop or cut (something, esp. wood) with an ax, pick, or other tool: *we have finished hauling and hewing timber*. ■ (usu. **be hewn**) make or shape (something) by cutting or chopping a material such as wood or stone: *a seat hewn out of a fallen tree trunk*.
2 [no obj.] (**hew to**) conform or adhere to: *some artists took photographs that hewed to more traditional ideas of art*.
– ORIGIN Old English *hēawan*, of Germanic origin; related to Dutch *houwen* and German *hauen*.

hew·er /ˈhyo͞oər/ ▶ n. dated a person who cuts wood, stone, or other materials. ■ a miner who cuts coal from a seam.
– PHRASES **hewers of wood and drawers of water** menial drudges; laborers. [with biblical allusion to Josh. 9:21.]

Hew·lett /ˈhyo͞olit/, William R. (1913–2001), US electrical engineer, inventor, and businessman. He invented an audio oscillator and with David Packard (1912–96) cofounded the Hewlett-Packard Company in 1939.

hex[1] /heks/ ▶ v. [with obj.] cast a spell on; bewitch: *he hexed her with his fingers*.
▶ n. a magic spell; a curse: *a death hex*. ■ a witch.
– ORIGIN mid 19th cent. (as a verb): from Pennsylvania Dutch *hexe* (verb), *Hex* (noun), from German *hexen* (verb), *Hexe* (noun).

hex[2] ▶ adj. & n. **1** short for HEXADECIMAL. **2** short for HEXAGONAL (see HEXAGON).

hexa- (also **hex-** before a vowel) ▶ comb. form six; having six.
– ORIGIN from Greek *hex* 'six.'

hex·a·chlor·o·phene /ˌheksəˈklôrəˌfēn/ ▶ n. a white, odorless compound used as an antibacterial agent. Chem. formula: $(C_6HCl_3OH)_2CH_2$.

hex·a·chord /ˈheksəˌkôrd/ ▶ n. a musical scale of six notes with a half step between the third and fourth. An overlapping series of seven such scales starting on G, C, and F formed the basis of medieval music theory.

hex·ad /ˈhekˌsad/ ▶ n. technical a group or set of six.
– ORIGIN mid 17th cent. (denoting a series of six numbers): from Greek *hexas, hexad-*, from *hex* 'six.'

hex·a·dec·i·mal /ˌheksəˈdes(ə)məl/ ▶ adj. Computing relating to or using a system of numerical notation that has 16 rather than 10 as its base.
– DERIVATIVES **hex·a·dec·i·mal·ly** adv.

hex·a·gon /ˈheksəˌgän/ ▶ n. a plane figure with six straight sides and angles.
– ORIGIN late 16th cent.: via late Latin from Greek *hexagōnon*, neuter (used as a noun) of *hexagōnos* 'six-angled.'

hex·ag·o·nal /hekˈsagənl/ ▶ adj. of or pertaining to a hexagon. ■ (of a solid) having a section that is a hexagon; constructed on a base that is a hexagon. ■ designating or pertaining to a crystal system in which three coplanar axes of equal length are separated by 60° and a fourth axis of a different length is at right angles to these. ■ (of a mineral) crystallizing in this system.
– DERIVATIVES **hex·ag·o·nal·ly** adv.

hex·a·gram /ˈheksəˌgram/ ▶ n. a figure formed of six straight lines, in particular: ■ a star-shaped figure formed by two intersecting equilateral triangles. ■ any of a set of sixty-four figures made up of six parallel whole or broken lines, occurring in the ancient Chinese *I Ching*.
– ORIGIN mid 19th cent.: from HEXA- 'six' + Greek *gramma* 'line.'

hex·a·he·dron /ˌheksəˈhēdrən/ ▶ n. (pl. **hexahedrons** or **hexahedra** /-drə/) a solid figure with six plane faces.
– DERIVATIVES **hex·a·he·dral** /-drəl/ adj.
– ORIGIN late 16th cent.: from Greek *hexaedron*, neuter (used as a noun) of *hexaedros* 'six-faced.'

hex·am·er·ous /hekˈsamərəs/ ▶ n. Botany & Zoology having parts arranged in groups of six. ■ consisting of six joints or parts.

hex·am·e·ter /hekˈsamitər/ ▶ n. Prosody a line of verse consisting of six metrical feet, esp. of six dactyls.
– DERIVATIVES **hex·a·met·ric** /ˌheksəˈmetrik/ adj.
– ORIGIN late Middle English: from Latin, from Greek *hexametros* 'of six measures' (from *hex* 'six' + *metron* 'measure').

hex·ane /ˈhekˌsān/ ▶ n. Chemistry a colorless liquid hydrocarbon of the alkane series. ● Chem. formula: C_6H_{14}; five isomers, esp. the straight-chain isomer (***n*-hexane**).
– ORIGIN late 19th cent.: from HEXA- 'six' (denoting six carbon atoms) + -ANE[2].

hex·a·pla /ˈheksəplə/ ▶ n. a sixfold text in parallel columns, esp. of the Old Testament.
– ORIGIN early 17th cent. (originally referring to Origen's edition of the Old Testament): from Greek, neuter plural of *hexaploos* 'sixfold,' from *hex* 'six' + *ploos* '-fold.'

hex·a·ploid /ˈheksəˌploid/ Genetics ▶ adj. (of a cell or nucleus) containing six homologous sets of chromosomes. ■ (of an organism or species) composed of hexaploid cells.
▶ n. a hexaploid organism, variety, or species.
– DERIVATIVES **hex·a·ploi·dy** n.

Hex·ap·o·da /ˌheksəˈpōdə/ Entomology a class of six-legged arthropods that comprises the insects. The name is used as another term for *Insecta*, esp. when the primitive apterygotes are not considered to be true insects.
– DERIVATIVES **hex·a·pod** /ˈheksəˌpäd/ n.
– ORIGIN modern Latin (plural), from Greek *hexapous, hexapod-*, from *hex* 'six' + *pous* 'foot.'

hex·a·style /ˈheksəˌstīl/ Architecture ▶ n. a six-columned portico.
▶ adj. (of a portico) having six columns.
– ORIGIN early 18th cent.: from Greek *hexastulos*, from *hex* 'six' + *stulos* 'column.'

Hex·a·teuch /ˈheksəˌt(y)o͞ok/ ▶ n. the first six books of the Bible (Genesis to Joshua) collectively.
– ORIGIN late 19th cent.: from HEXA- 'six' + Greek *teukhos* 'book.'

hex·a·va·lent /ˌheksəˈvālənt/ ▶ adj. Chemistry having a valence of six.

hex·ose /ˈhekˌsōs/ ▶ n. Chemistry any of the class of simple sugars whose molecules contain six carbon atoms, such as glucose and fructose. They generally have the chemical formula $C_6H_{12}O_6$.
– ORIGIN late 19th cent.: from HEXA- 'six' + -OSE[2].

hex sign ▶ n. a design usually in the shape of a star, wheel, or rosette on a circular field. Formerly, hex signs were painted on barns, esp. by the Pennsylvania Dutch, and were thought to ward off evil.

hex·yl /ˈheksəl/ ▶ n. [as modifier] Chemistry of or denoting an alkyl radical $-C_6H_{13}$, derived from hexane.

hey /hā/ ▶ exclam. used to attract attention, to express surprise, interest, or annoyance, or to elicit agreement: *hey, what's going on here?* | *hey, don't I know it!* ■ used as a friendly greeting: *I just called to say hey*.
– PHRASES **what the hey** informal used as a euphemism for "what the hell."
– ORIGIN natural exclamation: first recorded in Middle English.

hey·day /ˈhāˌdā/ ▶ n. (usu. **one's heyday**) the period of a person's or thing's greatest success, popularity, or vigor: *the paper has lost millions of readers since its heyday in 1964*.
– ORIGIN late 16th cent. (denoting good spirits or passion): from archaic *heyday!*, an exclamation of joy, surprise, etc.

Hey·er·dahl /ˈhāərˌdäl/, Thor (1914–2002), Norwegian anthropologist. He is noted for his ocean voyages in primitive craft to demonstrate his theories of cultural diffusion, the best known of which was that of the balsa raft *Kon-Tiki* from Peru to the islands east of Tahiti in 1947. In 1969, he successfully crossed from Morocco to Central America in a papyrus boat (*Ra II*).

hey pres·to ▶ exclam. chiefly Brit. & Canadian another way of saying PRESTO.

Hez·bol·lah /ˌhezbəˈlä, hezˈbälə/ (also **Hizbullah**) an extremist Shiite Muslim group that has close links with Iran, created after the Iranian revolution of 1979 and active esp. in Lebanon.
– ORIGIN from Arabic *ḥizbullāh* 'Party of God,' from *ḥezb* 'party' + *'allāh* (see ALLAH).

HF ▶ abbr. Physics high frequency.

Hf ▶ symbol the chemical element hafnium.

hf ▶ abbr. half.

HFC ▶ abbr. hydrofluorocarbon.

hfs ▶ abbr. hyperfine structure.

HG ▶ abbr. Brit. Her or His Grace.

Hg ▶ symbol the chemical element mercury.
– ORIGIN abbreviation of modern Latin *hydrargyrum*.

hg ▶ abbr. hectogram(s).

hgb. ▶ abbr. hemoglobin.

HGH ▶ abbr. human growth hormone.

hgt. ▶ abbr. height.

hgwy. ▶ abbr. highway.

HH ▶ abbr. ■ Brit. Her or His Highness. ■ His Holiness. ■ (used in describing grades of pencil lead) extra hard.

hh. ▶ abbr. hands (as a unit of measurement of a horse's height).

hhd ▶ abbr. hogshead(s).

HHFA ▶ abbr. Housing and Home Finance Agency.

H-hour ▶ n. the time of day at which an attack, landing, or other military operation is scheduled to begin.
– ORIGIN World War I: from *H* (for *hour*) + HOUR.

HHS ▶ abbr. Department of Health and Human Services.

HI ▶ abbr. Hawaii (in official postal use).

hi /hī/ ▶ exclam. informal used as a friendly greeting or to attract attention: *"Hi there. How was the flight?"*
– ORIGIN natural exclamation: first recorded in late Middle English.

Hi·a·le·ah /ˌhīəˈlēə/ a city in southeastern Florida, northwest of Miami; pop. 210,542 (est. 2008).

hi·a·tus /hīˈātəs/ ▶ n. (pl. **hiatuses**) [usu. in sing.] a pause or gap in a sequence, series, or process: *there was a brief hiatus in the war with France*. ■ Prosody & Grammar a break between two vowels coming together but not in the same syllable, as in *the ear* and *cooperate*.
– DERIVATIVES **hi·a·tal** /-ˈātəl/ adj.
– ORIGIN mid 16th cent. (originally denoting a physical gap or opening): from Latin, literally 'gaping,' from *hiare* 'gape.'

hi·a·tus her·ni·a (also **hiatal hernia**) ▶ n. Medicine the protrusion of an organ, typically the stomach, through the esophageal opening in the diaphragm.

Hi·a·wath·a[1] /ˌhīəˈwäTHə/ (*fl. c.*1570), legendary American Indian chief; meaning of name "He Makes Rivers." A member of the Mohawk tribe, he is credited with establishing an Iroquois confederacy—comprised of Onondaga, Mohawk, Oneida, Cayuga, and Seneca tribes—the Five Nations League. His name was used for the hero of Longfellow's poem, "The Song of Hiawatha."

Hi·a·wath·a[2] a fictional Chippewa hero who lived on Lake Superior and who was the hero of a narrative poem by Henry Wadsworth Longfellow called *The Song of Hiawatha* (1855).

hi·ba /ˈhēbə/ ▶ n. a Japanese conifer with evergreen scalelike leaves that form flattened sprays of foliage, widely planted as an ornamental and yielding durable timber. ● *Thujopsis dolabrata*, family Cupressaceae.
– ORIGIN Japanese.

hi·ba·chi /həˈbäCHē/ ▶ n. (pl. **hibachis**) a portable cooking apparatus consisting of a small grill over a brazier. ■ (in Japan) a large earthenware pan or brazier in which charcoal is burned to provide indoor heating.
– ORIGIN mid 19th cent.: Japanese *hibachi, hi-hachi*, from *hi* 'fire' + *hachi* 'bowl, pot.'

hi·ba·ku·sha /ˌhēbəˈko͞oSHə, hēˈbäko͞oˌSHä/ ▶ n. (pl. **same**) (in Japan) a survivor of either of the atomic explosions at Hiroshima or Nagasaki in 1945.
– ORIGIN mid 20th cent.: Japanese, from *hi* 'suffer' + *baku* 'explosion' + *sha* 'person.'

Hib·bing /ˈhibiNG/ a city in northeastern Minnesota, a mining center in the Mesabi Range; pop. 16,209 (est. 2008).

hi·ber·nate /ˈhībərˌnāt/ ▶ v. [no obj.] (of an animal or plant) spend the winter in a dormant state. ■ (of a person) remain inactive or indoors for an extended period: *the pilots who have been hibernating during the winter months get their gliders out again*.
– DERIVATIVES **hi·ber·na·tion** /ˌhībərˈnāSHən/ n., **hi·ber·na·tor** /-ˌnātər/ n.
– ORIGIN early 19th cent.: from Latin *hibernare*, from *hiberna* 'winter quarters,' from *hibernus* 'wintry.'

Hi·ber·ni·an /hīˈbərnēən/ ▶ adj. of or concerning Ireland (now chiefly used in names): *the Royal Hibernian Academy*.
▶ n. a native of Ireland (now chiefly used in names): *the Ancient Order of Hibernians*.
– ORIGIN from Latin *Hibernia* (alteration of *Iverna*, from Greek *I(w)ernē*, of Celtic origin; related to Irish *Éire, Éirinn* 'Ireland': see EIRE, ERIN) + -AN.

PRONUNCIATION KEY ə *ago, up*; ər *over, fur*; a *hat*; ā *ate*; ä *car*; e *let*; ē *see*; i *fit*; ī *by*; NG *sing*; ō *go*; ô *law, for*; oi *toy*; o͝o *good*; o͞o *goo*; ou *out*; TH *thin*; T͟H *then*; ZH *vision*

Hi·ber·ni·an·ism /hīˈbərnēə,nizəm/ (also **Hibernicism** /-ni,sizəm/) ▶ n. an Irish idiom or expression.

Hiberno- ▶ comb. form Irish; Irish and ...: *Hiberno-English.* ■ relating to Ireland.
– ORIGIN from medieval Latin *Hibernus* 'Irish'; see also HIBERNIAN.

hi·bis·cus /hīˈbiskəs/ ▶ n. a plant of the mallow family, grown in warm climates for its large brightly colored flowers or for products such as fiber or timber. ● Genus *Hibiscus,* family Malvaceae: many species, including the rose mallow.
– ORIGIN Latin, from Greek *hibiskos,* which Dioscorides identified with the marsh mallow.

hic /hik/ ▶ exclam. used in writing to express the sound of a hiccup, esp. a drunken one.
– ORIGIN late 19th cent.: imitative.

hic·cup /ˈhikəp/ (also **hiccough** pronounced same) ▶ n. an involuntary spasm of the diaphragm and respiratory organs, with a sudden closure of the glottis and a characteristic sound like that of a cough. ■ (**hiccups**) an attack of such spasms occurring repeatedly for some time: *he got the hiccups.* ■ a temporary or minor difficulty or setback: *just a little hiccup in our usual wonderful service.*
▶ v. (**hiccups, hiccuping, hiccuped**) [no obj.] suffer from or make the sound of a hiccup or series of hiccups.
– DERIVATIVES **hic·cup·y** adj.
– ORIGIN late 16th cent.: imitative; the form *hiccough* arose by association with COUGH.

h

hic ja·cet /ˈhik ˈjāsət/ ▶ n. literary an epitaph.
– ORIGIN early 17th cent.: Latin, 'here lies,' the first two words of a Latin epitaph.

hick /hik/ ▶ n. informal a person who lives in the country, regarded as being unintelligent or provincial: *wondering what a hick from the sticks was doing there* | [as modifier] *a hick town.*
– ORIGIN mid 16th cent.: nickname for the given name *Richard.*

hick·ey /ˈhikē/ ▶ n. (pl. **hickeys**) **1** informal a gadget. **2** informal a skin blemish, esp. a mark caused by a lover biting or sucking the skin. ■ a blemish in printing, esp. an uninked area in a solid, caused by a piece of dirt.
– ORIGIN early 20th cent.: of unknown origin.

Hick·ok /ˈhikäk/, James Butler (1837–76), US frontiersman and marshal; known as **Wild Bill Hickok**. The legend of his invincibility became something of a challenge to gunmen, and he was eventually murdered at Deadwood, South Dakota.

Hick·o·ry /ˈhik(ə)rē/ a city in west central North Carolina, noted for its furniture industry; pop. 41,305 (est. 2008).

hick·o·ry /ˈhik(ə)rē/ ▶ n. a chiefly North American tree of the walnut family that yields useful timber and typically bears edible nuts. ● Genus *Carya,* family Juglandaceae: several species, including the **shagbark hickory** (*C. ovata*), with shaggy peeling bark. See also PECAN, PIGNUT.
■ a stick made of hickory wood.
– ORIGIN late 17th cent.: abbreviation of *pohickery,* the local Virginian name, from Algonquian *pawcohiccora.*

Hicks /hiks/, Sir John Richard (1904–89), English economist. He did pioneering work on general economic equilibrium, the theory that economic forces tend to balance one another rather than simply reflect cyclical trends. Nobel Prize in Economics (1972), shared with Kenneth J. Arrow.

Hicks·ville /ˈhiks,vil/ a village in central Long Island in New York; pop. 41,260 (2000).

hid /hid/ past of HIDE¹.

Hi·dal·go /ēˈdälgō/ a state in southern Mexico; capital, Pachuca de Soto.

hi·dal·go /hiˈdälgō/ ▶ n. (pl. **hidalgos**) (in Spanish-speaking regions) a gentleman.
– ORIGIN late 16th cent.: Spanish, from *hijo de algo,* literally 'son of something' (i.e., of an important person).

Hi·dat·sa /hēˈdätsä/ ▶ n. (pl. **same** or **Hidatsas**) **1** a member of an American Indian people living on the upper Missouri River in North Dakota. **2** the Siouan language of this people.
▶ adj. of or relating to this people or their language.
– ORIGIN a Hidatsa village name.

hid·den /ˈhidn/ past participle of HIDE¹.
▶ adj. kept out of sight; concealed: *hidden dangers* | *her hidden feelings.*
– DERIVATIVES **hid·den·ness** n.

hid·den a·gen·da ▶ n. a secret or ulterior motive for something.

hid·den·ite /ˈhidn,īt/ ▶ n. a rare green gem variety of spodumene.
– ORIGIN late 19th cent.: named after William E. *Hidden* (1832–1918), US mineralogist.

hid·den re·serves ▶ plural n. a company's funds that are not declared on its balance sheet. ■ mental or physical capabilities beyond those normally available to someone: *hidden reserves of power.*

hide¹ /hīd/ ▶ v. (past **hid** /hid/; past participle **hidden** /ˈhidn/) [with obj.] put or keep out of sight; conceal from the view or notice of others: *he hid the money in the house* | *the sacred relic had been* **hidden away** *in a sealed cavern.* ■ (of a thing) prevent (someone or something) from being seen: *clouds hid the moon.* ■ keep secret or unknown: *Hal could hardly hide his dislike.* ■ [no obj.] conceal oneself: *Juliet's first instinct was to hide under the blankets* | *he had a little money and could* **hide out** *until the end of the month.* ■ [no obj.] (**hide behind**) use (someone or something) to protect oneself from criticism or punishment, esp. in a way considered cowardly or unethical: *companies and manufacturers with poor security can hide behind the law.*
▶ n. Brit. a camouflaged shelter used to get a close view of wildlife.
– PHRASES **hide one's head** cover up one's face or keep out of sight, esp. from shame. **hide one's light under a bushel** keep quiet about one's talents or accomplishments. [with biblical allusion to Matt. 5:15.]
– DERIVATIVES **hid·er** n.
– ORIGIN Old English *hȳdan.*

hide² ▶ n. the skin of an animal, esp. when tanned or dressed. ■ used to refer to a person's ability to withstand criticisms or insults: *"I'm sorry I called you a pig." "My hide's thick enough; it didn't bother me."*
– PHRASES **hide or hair of someone** [with negative] the slightest sight or trace of someone: *I could find neither hide nor hair of him.* **save someone's hide** see SAVE¹. **tan** (or **whip**) **someone's hide** beat or flog someone. ■ punish someone severely.
– DERIVATIVES **hid·ed** adj.
– ORIGIN Old English *hȳd,* of Germanic origin; related to Dutch *huid* and German *Haut.*

hide³ ▶ n. a former measure of land used in England, typically equal to between 60 and 120 acres, being the amount that would support a family and its dependents.
– ORIGIN Old English *hīd, hīgid,* from the base of *hīgan, hīwan* 'household members,' of Germanic origin.

hide-and-seek ▶ n. a children's game in which one player tries to find other players who have hidden themselves.

hide·a·way /ˈhīdə,wā/ ▶ n. a place used as a retreat or a hiding place: *an intimate hideaway overlooking the bay.*
▶ adj. designed to be concealed when not in use: *a hideaway bed.*

hide·bound /ˈhīd,bound/ ▶ adj. unwilling or unable to change because of tradition or convention: *you are hidebound by your petty laws.*
– ORIGIN mid 16th cent. (as a noun denoting a condition of cattle): from HIDE² + BOUND⁴. The earliest sense of the adjective (of cattle) was extended to emaciated human beings, and then applied figuratively in the sense 'narrow, cramped, or bigoted in outlook.'

hid·e·ous /ˈhidēəs/ ▶ adj. ugly or disgusting to look at: *his smile made him look more hideous than ever.* ■ extremely unpleasant: *the whole hideous story.*
– DERIVATIVES **hid·e·ous·ly** adv. [as submodifier] *a hideously expensive camera,* **hid·e·ous·ness** n.
– ORIGIN Middle English: from Old French *hidos, hideus,* from *hide, hisde* 'fear,' of unknown origin.

hide·out /ˈhīd,out/ ▶ n. a hiding place, esp. one used by someone who has broken the law.

hid·ey-hole /ˈhīdē ,hōl/ ▶ n. informal a place for hiding something or oneself in, esp. as a retreat from other people.

hid·ing¹ /ˈhīdiNG/ ▶ n. informal a physical beating: *they took off after him, caught him, and gave him a hiding.* ■ a severe defeat: *if they'd played badly, they would have expected a hiding.*
– ORIGIN early 19th cent.: from HIDE² + -ING¹.

hid·ing² ▶ n. the action of concealing someone or something. ■ the state of being hidden: *the shipowner had gone* **into hiding**.
– ORIGIN Middle English: from HIDE¹ + -ING¹.

hid·ing place ▶ n. a place for concealing someone or something.

hi·dro·sis /hiˈdrōsəs, hī-/ ▶ n. Medicine sweating.
– DERIVATIVES **hi·drot·ic** /hiˈdrätik, hī-/ adj.
– ORIGIN mid 19th cent.: from Greek *hidrōsis,* from *hidrōs* 'sweat.'

hie /hī/ ▶ v. (**hies, hieing** or **hying, hied**) [no obj.] go quickly: *I hied down to New Orleans* | *I* **hied myself** *to a screenwriters' conference.*
– ORIGIN Middle English: from Old English *hīgian* 'strive, pant,' of unknown origin.

hi·er·arch /ˈhī(ə),rärk/ ▶ n. a chief priest, archbishop, or other leader.
– ORIGIN late Middle English: via medieval Latin from Greek *hierarkhēs,* from *hieros* 'sacred' + *arkhēs* 'ruler.'

hi·er·ar·chi·cal /,hī(ə)ˈrärkikəl/ ▶ adj. of the nature of a hierarchy; arranged in order of rank: *the hierarchical bureaucracy of a local authority.*
– DERIVATIVES **hi·er·ar·chi·cal·ly** adv.

hi·er·ar·chy /ˈhī(ə),rärkē/ ▶ n. (pl. **hierarchies**) a system or organization in which people or groups are ranked one above the other according to status or authority. ■ (**the hierarchy**) the upper echelons of a hierarchical system; those in authority: *the magazine was read quite widely even by some of the hierarchy.* ■ an arrangement or classification of things according to relative importance or inclusiveness: *a taxonomic hierarchy of phyla, classes, orders, families, genera, and species.* ■ (**the hierarchy**) the clergy of the Catholic or Episcopal Church; the religious authorities. ■ Theology the traditional system of orders of angels and other heavenly beings.
– DERIVATIVES **hi·er·ar·chic** /,hī(ə)ˈrärkik/ adj., **hi·er·ar·chi·za·tion** /,hī(ə),rärkəˈzāSHən/ n., **hi·er·ar·chize** /-,kīz/ v.
– ORIGIN late Middle English: via Old French and medieval Latin from Greek *hierarkhia,* from *hierarkhēs* 'sacred ruler' (see HIERARCH). The earliest sense was 'system of orders of angels and heavenly beings'; the other senses date from the 17th cent.

hi·er·at·ic /,hī(ə)ˈratik/ ▶ adj. of or concerning priests: *he raised both his arms in an outlandish hieratic gesture.* ■ of or in the ancient Egyptian writing of abridged hieroglyphics used by priests. Compare with DEMOTIC. ■ of or concerning Egyptian or Greek styles of art adhering to early methods as laid down by religious tradition.
– DERIVATIVES **hi·er·at·i·cal·ly** /-ik(ə)lē/ adv.
– ORIGIN mid 17th cent. (earlier as *hieratical*): via Latin from Greek *hieratikos,* from *hierasthai* 'be a priest,' from *hiereus* 'priest,' *hieros* 'sacred.'

hiero- ▶ comb. form sacred; holy.
– ORIGIN from Greek *hieros* 'sacred.'

hi·er·oc·ra·cy /,hī(ə)ˈräkrəsē/ ▶ n. (pl. **hierocracies**) rule by priests. ■ a ruling body composed of priests.
– DERIVATIVES **hi·er·o·crat·ic** /,hī(ə)rəˈkratik/ adj.

hi·er·o·glyph /ˈhī(ə)rə,glif/ ▶ n. a stylized picture of an object representing a word, syllable, or sound, as found in ancient Egyptian and other writing systems.
– ORIGIN late 16th cent.: back-formation from HIEROGLYPHIC.

hi·er·o·glyph·ic /,hī(ə)rəˈglifik/ ▶ n. (**hieroglyphics**) writing consisting of hieroglyphs. ■ enigmatic or incomprehensible symbols or writing: *tattered notebooks filled with illegible hieroglyphics.*
▶ adj. of or written in hieroglyphs. ■ (esp. in art) stylized, symbolic, or enigmatic in effect.
– DERIVATIVES **hi·er·o·glyph·i·cal** adj., **hi·er·o·glyph·i·cal·ly** adv.
– ORIGIN late 16th cent.: from French *hiéroglyphique,* from Greek *hierogluphikos,* from *hieros* 'sacred' + *gluphē* 'carving.'

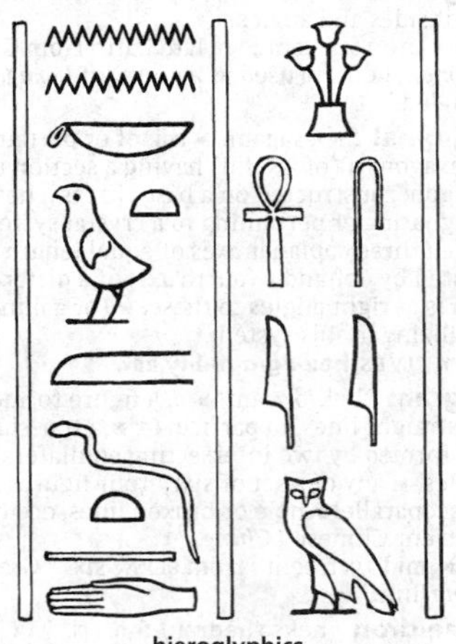

hieroglyphics

hi·er·o·gram /ˈhī(ə)rə,gram/ ▶ n. a sacred inscription or symbol.

hi·er·ol·a·try /,hī(ə)ˈrälətrē/ ▶ n. the worship of saints or sacred things.

hi·er·ol·o·gy /,hī(ə)ˈräləjē/ ▶ n. sacred literature or lore.

hi·er·o·phant /ˈhī(ə)rəˌfant/ ▸ **n.** a person, esp. a priest in ancient Greece, who interprets sacred mysteries or esoteric principles.
– DERIVATIVES **hi·er·o·phan·tic** /ˌhī(ə)rəˈfantik/ **adj.**
– ORIGIN late 17th cent.: via late Latin from Greek *hierophantēs*, from *hieros* 'sacred' + *phainein* 'show, reveal.'

hi-fi /ˈhīˌfī/ ▸ **adj.** of, used for, or relating to the reproduction of music or other sound with high fidelity.
▸ **n.** (pl. **hi-fis**) a set of equipment for high-fidelity sound reproduction, esp. a radio or phonograph.
– ORIGIN 1950s: abbreviation of HIGH FIDELITY.

hig·gle /ˈhigəl/ ▸ **v.** archaic spelling of HAGGLE.

hig·gle·dy-pig·gle·dy /ˌhigəldē ˈpigəldē/ ▸ **adv. & adj.** in confusion or disorder: [as adv.] *bits of paper hanging higgledy-piggledy on the furniture and walls* | [as adj.] *a higgledy-piggledy mountain of newspapers.*
– ORIGIN late 16th cent.: rhyming jingle, probably with reference to the irregular herding together of pigs.

hig·gler /ˈhiglər/ ▸ **n.** W. Indian a person who travels around selling small items; a peddler.

Higgs /higz/ (also **Higgs boson** or **Higgs particle**) ▸ **n.** Physics a subatomic particle whose existence is predicted by the theory that unified the weak and electromagnetic interactions.
– ORIGIN 1970s: named after Peter W. *Higgs* (1929–), English physicist.

high /hī/ ▸ **adj. 1** of great vertical extent: *the top of a high mountain* | *the mast was higher than the tallest building in the city.* ■ (after a measurement and in questions) measuring a specified distance from top to bottom: *a tree forty feet high* | *how high is the fence?* ■ far above ground, sea level, or another point of reference: *a fortress high up on a hill.* ■ extending above the normal or average level: *a round face with a high forehead.* ■ [attrib.] (of territory or landscape) inland and well above sea level: *high prairies.* ■ near to the top of a real or notional list in order of rank or importance: *financial security is* **high on** *your list of priorities.* ■ [attrib.] performed at, to, or from a considerable height: *high diving.* ■ Baseball (of a pitched ball) above a certain level, such as the batter's armpits, as it crosses home plate, and thus outside the strike zone.
2 great, or greater than normal, in quantity, size, or intensity: *a high temperature* | *fudge is* **high in** *calories.* ■ of large numerical or monetary value: *they had been playing for high stakes.* ■ very favorable: *nature had provided him with an admirably high opinion of himself.* ■ extreme in religious or political views: *the high Christology of the Christian creeds.* ■ (of a period or movement) at its peak: *high summer.* ■ (of latitude) close to 90°; near the North or South Pole: *high southern latitudes.*
3 great in rank or status: *he held high office in professional organizations.* ■ ranking above others of the same kind: *they announced the High Commissioner's retirement.* ■ morally or culturally superior: *they believed that nature was driven by something higher than mere selfishness.*
4 (of a sound or note) having a frequency at the upper end of the auditory range: *a high, squeaky voice.* ■ (of a singer or instrument) producing notes of relatively high pitch: *a high soprano voice.*
5 [predic.] informal excited; euphoric: *he was* **high on** *an idea.* ■ intoxicated with drugs: *some of them were already* **high on** *alcohol and Ecstasy.*
6 [predic.] unpleasantly strong-smelling, in particular (of food) beginning to go bad. ■ (of game) slightly decomposed and so ready to cook.
7 Phonetics (of a vowel) produced with the tongue relatively near the palate.
▸ **n. 1** a high point, level, or figure: *commodity prices were at a rare high.* ■ a notably happy or successful moment: *the highs and lows of life.* ■ a high-frequency sound or musical note. ■ an area of high atmospheric pressure; an anticyclone.
2 [usu. in sing.] informal a state of high spirits or euphoria: *the highs I got from cocaine always ended in despair* | *the team is still* **on a high** *from Saturday's victory.*
3 informal high school (chiefly used in names): *I enjoyed my years at McKinley High.*
4 a high power setting: *the vent blower was* **on high.** ■ top gear in a motor vehicle.
▸ **adv. 1** at or to a considerable or specified height: *the sculpture stood about five feet high.*
2 highly: *he ranked high among the pioneers of twentieth-century chemical technology.* ■ at a high price: *buying shares low and selling them high.*
3 (of a sound) at or to a high pitch.
– PHRASES **ace** (or **king** or **queen**, etc.) **high** (in card games) having the ace (or another specified card) as the highest-ranking. **from on high** from a very high place. ■ from remote high authority or heaven: *government programs coming down from on high.* **high and dry** out of the water, esp. the sea as it retreats: *when the tide goes out, a lot of boats are* **left high and dry.** ■ in a difficult position, esp. without resources: *when the plant shut down, hundreds of workers found themselves high and dry.* **high and low** in many different places: *we searched high and low for a new teacher.* **high and mighty** ■ informal thinking or acting as though one is more important than others. **a high old time** informal a most enjoyable time: *they had a high old time at the clambake.* **high, wide, and handsome** informal expansive and impressive. [from *Arizona Nights* by Stewart E. White (1873–1946), US author.] **it is high time that ——** it is past the time when something should have happened or been done: *it was high time that she faced the facts.* **on high** in or to heaven or a high place: *a spotter plane circling on high.* **on one's high horse** informal used to refer to someone's behaving in an arrogant or pompous manner: *get down off your high horse.* **run high** (of a river) be full and close to overflowing, with a strong current. ■ (of feelings) be intense: *passions run high when marriages break up.*
– ORIGIN Old English *hēah*, of Germanic origin; related to Dutch *hoog* and German *hoch.*

high·ball /ˈhīˌbôl/ ▸ **n. 1** a drink consisting of whiskey and a mixer such as soda or ginger ale, served with ice in a tall glass.
2 informal a railroad signal to proceed.
▸ **v.** [no obj.] informal travel fast: *they highballed north.*

high-band ▸ **adj.** relating to or denoting a video system using a relatively high carrier frequency, which allows more bandwidth for the signal.

high beam ▸ **n.** the brightest setting of a vehicle's headlights.

high·bind·er /ˈhīˌbīndər/ ▸ **n.** informal an unscrupulous person, esp. a corrupt politician. ■ an assassin, esp. one belonging to a Chinese-American criminal organization.
– ORIGIN early 19th cent.: first recorded as *Highbinders*, the name of a New York gang.

high-born ▸ **adj.** having noble parents: *the high-born man who inherited wealth and dutifully flaunted it.*

high·boy /ˈhīˌboi/ ▸ **n.** a tall chest of drawers on legs.

high·bred /ˈhīˌbred/ ▸ **adj. 1** bred from superior stock.
2 having or showing good breeding or manners; well-bred.

high·brow /ˈhīˌbrou/ ▸ **adj.** often derogatory scholarly or rarefied in taste: *innovatory art had a small, mostly highbrow following.*
▸ **n.** a person of this type.

high·bush cran·ber·ry /ˈhīˌboosh/ ▸ **n.** a shrub of the honeysuckle family, with round clusters of white flowers followed by red berries. Compare with GUELDER ROSE. ● *Viburnum trilobum*, family Caprifoliaceae.

high chair ▸ **n.** a small chair with long legs for a baby or small child, fitted with a tray that is used as a table at mealtimes.

High Church ▸ **adj.** of or adhering to a tradition within the Anglican Church emphasizing ritual, priestly authority, sacraments, and historical continuity with Catholic Christianity. Compare with LOW CHURCH, BROAD CHURCH.
▸ **n.** [treated as sing. or pl.] the principles or adherents of this tradition.
– DERIVATIVES **High Church·man n.**

high-class ▸ **adj.** of a high standard, quality, or social class: *a high-class boarding school.*

high col·or (also **high coloring**) ▸ **n.** a flushed complexion: *he had a high color to his cheeks.*

high com·e·dy ▸ **n.** comedy employing sophisticated wit and often satirizing the upper classes. Compare with LOW COMEDY.

high com·mand ▸ **n.** the commander in chief and associated senior staff of an army, navy, or air force.

high com·mis·sion ▸ **n.** an embassy of one British Commonwealth country in another.
– DERIVATIVES **high com·mis·sion·er n.**

high con·cept ▸ **n.** (esp. in a movie or television plot) emphasis on a striking and easily communicable idea: *for mainstream media companies, the focus has shifted from high concept to hard cash* | [as modifier] *a series of high-concept videos.*

high-coun·try ▸ **adj.** of or relating to land above the piedmont and below the timberline: *the high-country snowpack often exceeds 10 feet.*

high court ▸ **n.** a supreme court of justice. ■ the US Supreme Court. ■ (in the US) the supreme court in a state. ■ (in some US states) a superior court. ■ (in full **High Court of Justice**) (in England and Wales) the court of unlimited civil jurisdiction comprising three divisions: Queen's Bench, Chancery, and the Family Division.

high day ▸ **n.** Brit. the day of a religious festival.
– PHRASES **high days and holidays** informal special occasions: *the drawing room is used only on high days and holidays.*

high-den·si·ty li·po·pro·tein (abbr.: **HDL**) ▸ **n.** a lipoprotein that removes cholesterol from the blood and is associated with a reduced risk of atherosclerosis and heart disease. Compare with LOW-DENSITY LIPOPROTEIN.

high-end ▸ **adj.** denoting the most expensive of a range of products.

high·er an·i·mals ▸ **plural n.** animals of relatively advanced or developed characteristics, such as mammals and other vertebrates.

high·er court ▸ **n.** Law a court that can overrule the decision of another.

high·er crit·i·cism ▸ **n.** the study of the literary methods and sources discernible in a text, esp. as applied to biblical writings.

high·er ed·u·ca·tion ▸ **n.** education beyond high school, esp. at a college or university.

high·er law ▸ **n.** a moral or religious principle that is believed to overrule secular constitutions and laws.

high·er learn·ing ▸ **n.** education and learning at the college or university level.

high·er math·e·mat·ics ▸ **plural n.** [usu. treated as sing.] advanced mathematics, such as number theory and topology.

h

high·er plants ▸ **plural n.** plants of relatively complex or advanced characteristics, esp. vascular plants (including flowering plants).

high·er-up ▸ **n.** informal a senior person in an organization: *he was looking for a way to impress the higher-ups.*

high·est com·mon fac·tor (abbr.: **HCF**) ▸ **n.** the highest number that can be divided exactly into each of two or more numbers.

high ex·plo·sive ▸ **n.** a chemical explosive that is rapid and destructive, used in shells and bombs.

high·fa·lu·tin /ˌhīfəˈlootn/ (also **highfaluting** /-ˈlootiNG/) ▸ **adj.** informal (esp. of speech, writing, or ideas) pompous or pretentious: *you don't want any highfalutin jargon.*
– ORIGIN mid 19th cent.: perhaps from HIGH + *fluting* (present participle of FLUTE).

high fash·ion ▸ **n.** another term for HAUTE COUTURE.

high fi·del·i·ty ▸ **n.** the reproduction of sound with little distortion, giving a result very similar to the original.

high fi·nance ▸ **n.** financial transactions involving large amounts of money.

high five informal ▸ **n.** a gesture of celebration or greeting in which two people slap each other's palms with their arms raised: *they gave each other an exuberant high five in the middle of the press center.*
▸ **v.** (**high-five**) [with obj.] greet with such a gesture.

high·fli·er /ˈhīflīər/ (also **highflyer**, **high-flyer**) ▸ **n.** a person who is or has the potential to be very successful, esp. academically or in business: *the company cannot expect to recruit many highfliers.*
– DERIVATIVES **high·fly·ing** /-ˈflī-iNG/ **adj.**

high-flown ▸ **adj.** (esp. of language or ideas) extravagant and lofty.

high fre·quen·cy ▸ **n.** (in radio) a frequency of 3–30 megahertz.

high gear ▸ **n.** a gear that causes a wheeled vehicle to move fast, owing to a high ratio between the speed of the wheels and that of the mechanism driving them: *pull away* **in high gear** | figurative *the war against the Mafia has gone into high gear.*

High Ger·man ▸ **n.** the standard literary and spoken form of German, originally used in the highlands in the south of Germany. The establishment of this form as a standard language owes much to the biblical translations of Martin Luther in the 16th century. See also MIDDLE HIGH GERMAN, OLD HIGH GERMAN.

high-grade ▸ **adj.** of very good quality: *high-grade printing papers.* ■ (of ore) rich in metal value and commercially profitable.

high ground ▸ **n. 1** land that is higher than the surrounding area, esp. that which stays dry: *they decided to climb to high ground and serve as lookouts.*
2 (**the high ground**) a position of superiority in a debate: *if he turns it down, he will have lost the moral high ground to the president.*

high-hand·ed ▸ **adj.** using power or authority without considering the feelings of others: *they oppose this cruel and high-handed takeover.*

– DERIVATIVES **high·hand·ed·ly** adv., **high·hand·ed·ness** n.

high hat ▶ n. **1** a tall hat, esp. a top hat. ■ informal a snobbish or supercilious person.
2 (**high-hat**) variant spelling of HI-HAT.
▶ adj. (**high-hat**) informal snobbish.
▶ v. (**high-hat**) (**high-hats, high-hatting, high-hatted**) [with obj.] informal act in a snobbish or supercilious manner toward (someone).

high heels ▶ plural n. women's shoes with tall, thin heels.
– DERIVATIVES **high-heeled** /'hī ˌhēld/ adj.

High Hol·i·days (also **High Holy Days**) ▶ plural n. the Jewish holy days of Yom Kippur and Rosh Hashanah. Also called DAYS OF AWE.

high hur·dles ▶ plural n. [treated as sing.] a race in which runners jump over hurdles 42 inches (107 cm) high.
– DERIVATIVES **high hur·dler** n.

high-im·pact ▶ adj. [attrib.] **1** (of plastic or a similar substance) able to withstand great impact without breaking.
2 denoting exercises, typically aerobics, that place a great deal of harmful stress on the body.

high·jack ▶ v. variant spelling of HIJACK.

high jinks /jiNGks/ (also **hijinks**) ▶ plural n. boisterous fun: *high jinks behind the wheel of a car.*
– ORIGIN late 17th cent.: see JINK.

high jump ▶ n. (**the high jump**) an athletic event in which competitors jump over a bar that is raised until only one competitor can jump over it without dislodging it.
– PHRASES **be for the high jump** Brit. informal be about to be severely reprimanded or punished.
– DERIVATIVES **high jump·er** n.

high-key (also **high-keyed**) ▶ adj. Art & Photography having a predominance of light or bright tones.

high kick ▶ n. a kick with the foot high in the air, for example in dancing or martial arts.
▶ v. [no obj.] (**high-kick**) make such a kick.
– DERIVATIVES **high-kick·ing** adj.

high·land /'hīlənd/ ▶ n. **1** (also **highlands**) an area of high or mountainous land: *the highlands of Madagascar* | [as modifier] *a highland region of Vietnam.*
2 (**the Highlands**) the mountainous part of Scotland, north of Glasgow, often associated with Gaelic culture: [as modifier] *a Highland regiment.*
– DERIVATIVES **high·land·er** n., **high·land·man** n. (pl. **highlandmen**).
– ORIGIN Old English *hēahlond* 'a high promontory' (see HIGH, LAND).

High·land cat·tle ▶ plural n. animals of a shaggy-haired breed of cattle with long, curved, widely spaced horns.

High·land dress ▶ n. clothing in the traditional style of the Scottish Highlands, including the kilt, now chiefly worn on formal occasions.

High·land fling ▶ n. a vigorous Scottish dance consisting of a series of complex steps performed solo, originally to celebrate victory.

High·land Games ▶ plural n. a meeting for athletic events, playing of the bagpipes, and dancing, held in the Scottish Highlands or by Scots elsewhere.

high·land moc·ca·sin ▶ n. the North American copperhead.

high-lev·el ▶ adj. at or of a level above that which is normal or average: *a high-level cistern* | *high-level crop production.* ■ relating to or involving people of high administrative rank or great authority: *high-level negotiations.* ■ Computing denoting a programming language that is relatively accessible to the user, having instructions that resemble a natural language such as English. ■ (of nuclear waste) highly radioactive and requiring long-term storage in isolation.

high life ▶ n. **1** (also **high living**) an extravagant social life as enjoyed by the wealthy.
2 (usu. **highlife**) a style of dance music of West African origin, influenced by rock and jazz.

high·light /'hīˌlīt/ ▶ n. **1** an outstanding part of an event or period of time: *he views that season as the highlight of his career.* ■ (**highlights**) the best parts of a sporting or other event edited for broadcasting or recording: *he never watches TV highlights of games he has umpired.*
2 a bright or reflective area in a painting, picture, or design. ■ (usu. **highlights**) a bright tint in the hair, esp. one produced by bleaching or dyeing.
▶ v. [with obj.] **1** pick out and emphasize: *the issues highlighted by the report* | *speakers at the conference highlighted additional problems faced by women with AIDS.* ■ make visually prominent: *a vast backdrop with the colorful logo highlighted with lasers.* ■ mark with a highlighter: *a photocopy with sections highlighted in green.*
2 create highlights in (hair).

high·light·er /'hīˌlītər/ ▶ n. **1** a broad felt-tipped pen used to overlay transparent fluorescent color on text or a part of an illustration, leaving it legible and emphasized.
2 a cosmetic that is lighter than the wearer's foundation or skin, used to emphasize features such as the eyes or cheekbones.

high-low ▶ n. **1** historical a lace-up boot with a low heel, reaching to the ankle, worn by military personnel in the 18th and early 19th centuries.
2 a poker game in which the high and low hands split the pot.
3 Bridge a signal given to one's partner to lead a suit by playing a high card and then a lower card of the same suit.

high-low-jack ▶ n. a card game in which points are won for the high trump, low trump, jack of trumps, and either the ten of trumps or the most points.

high·ly /'hīlē/ ▶ adv. to a high degree or level: [as submodifier] *a highly dangerous substance* | *highly paid people* | *a highly placed official.* ■ favorably: *he was highly regarded by his colleagues.*
– ORIGIN Old English *hēalīce* (see HIGH, -LY¹).

high-main·te·nance ▶ adj. needing a lot of work to keep in good condition. ■ informal (of a person or relationship) demanding a lot of attention: *Caitlin is our only child and she's very high-maintenance.*

High Mass ▶ n. (in the Roman Catholic Church) formerly, a mass with full ceremonial, including music and incense and typically having the assistance of a deacon and subdeacon.

high-mind·ed ▶ adj. having strong moral principles: *high-minded notions of what good persons want to be.*
– DERIVATIVES **high-mind·ed·ly** adv., **high-mind·ed·ness** n.

high muck-a-muck /'hī 'mək ə ˌmək/ (also **high muckety-muck**) ▶ n. informal a person in a position of authority, esp. one who is overbearing or conceited: *he was once a high muckety-muck at the CIA.*
– ORIGIN mid 19th cent.: perhaps from Chinook *hiyu* 'plenty' + *muckamuck* 'food,' from Nootka *hayo* 'ten' + *ma'ho·maq-* 'choice wheatmeal,' with *high* substituted for *hiyu.*

high·ness /'hīnis/ ▶ n. **1** the state of being high: *the highness of her cheekbones.*
2 (**His/Your**, etc., **Highness**) a title given to a person of royal rank, or used in addressing them: *I am most grateful, Your Highness.*
– ORIGIN Old English *hēanes* (see HIGH, -NESS).

high noon ▶ n. **1** midday.
2 an event or confrontation that is likely to decide the final outcome of a situation: *the high noon of his quest for the presidential nomination.* [popularized by the film *High Noon* (1952).]

high note ▶ n. a successful point in an event or period of time: *he wants to end his managerial career on a high note.*

high-oc·tane ▶ adj. denoting gasoline having a high octane number and thus good anti-knock properties. ■ powerful or dynamic: *a high-octane forty-year-old.*

high-pass ▶ adj. Electronics (of a filter) transmitting all frequencies above a certain value.

high-pitched ▶ adj. **1** (of a sound) high in pitch.
2 (of a roof) steep.

high plac·es ▶ plural n. positions of power or authority: *people in high places were taking note.*

High Point an industrial city in north central North Carolina, noted for furniture manufacturing; pop. 101,835 (est. 2008).

high point ▶ n. the most enjoyable or significant part of an experience or period of time: *the high point of her life had been a trip she took to Vancouver.*

high pol·y·mer ▶ n. a polymer having a high molecular weight, such as those used in plastics and resins.

high-pow·ered (also **high-power**) ▶ adj. (of a machine or device) having greater than normal strength or capabilities: *a high-powered rifle.* ■ dynamic and capable: *a high-powered delegation.*

high-pres·sure ▶ n. a condition of the atmosphere in which the pressure is above average (e.g., in an anticyclone).
▶ adj. **1** involving or using much physical force: *high-pressure jets of freezing water.*
2 involving a high degree of anxiety or stress: *he worked in a high-pressure advertising job.* ■ (of a salesperson or sales pitch) employing a high degree of coercion; insistent: *high-pressure marketing tactics.*

high priest ▶ n. a chief priest of a non-Christian religion, in particular: ■ the chief priest of the historic Jewish religion. ■ the head of a religious cult or similar group. ■ a chief advocate of a belief or practice: *the high priest of the drug culture.*

high priest·ess ▶ n. a female high priest.

high pro·file ▶ n. [in sing.] a position of attracting much attention or publicity: *people who have a high profile in the community.*
▶ adj. (**high-profile**) attracting much attention or publicity: *a high-profile military presence.*

high-rank·ing ▶ adj. having a senior or important position in a particular hierarchy: *a high-ranking government official.*

high re·lief ▶ n. see RELIEF (sense 4).

High Ren·ais·sance see RENAISSANCE.

high-res ▶ adj. variant spelling of HI-RES.

high-rise ▶ adj. (of a building) having many stories: *office towers and high-rise apartments.* ■ taller or set higher than normal: *high-rise handlebars.*
▶ n. a building with many stories.

high-risk ▶ adj. involving or exposed to a high level of danger: *high-risk activities, such as skydiving and downhill skiing.*

high road ▶ n. **1** a main road: *Chris avoided the high road and took a roundabout way through the woods.* ■ a direct or certain route or course.
2 a morally superior approach toward something: *he is winning support for taking the high road in refusing to be drawn into negative campaigning.*

high roll·er ▶ n. informal a person who gambles or spends large amounts of money.
– DERIVATIVES **high-roll·ing** adj.
– ORIGIN with reference to rolling dice.

high school ▶ n. a school that typically comprises grades 9 through 12, attended after primary school or middle school.
– DERIVATIVES **high school·er** n.

high seas ▶ plural n. (**the high seas**) the open ocean, esp. that not within any country's jurisdiction.

high sea·son ▶ n. chiefly Brit. the most popular time of year at a resort, hotel, or tourist attraction, when prices are highest.

high sign ▶ n. informal a surreptitious gesture, often prearranged, giving warning or indicating that all is well: *I'm getting the high sign from my secretary—gotta go.*

High·smith /'hīˌsmiTH/, Patricia (1921–95), US writer of detective fiction; born *Patricia Plangman.* Her novels are noted for their black humor, particularly those featuring Tom Ripley, an amoral antihero living in France. Notable works: *Strangers on a Train* (1949), *The Talented Mr. Ripley* (1956), and *Ripley Under Water* (1991).

high so·ci·e·ty ▶ n. see SOCIETY (sense 1).

high-sound·ing ▶ adj. (of language or ideas) extravagant and lofty.

high-speed ▶ adj. moving, operating, or happening very quickly: *high-speed travel.* ■ (of photographic film) needing little light or only short exposure. ■ (of steel) suitable for drill bits and other tools that cut fast enough to become red-hot.

high spir·its ▶ plural n. lively and cheerful behavior or mood: *the team returned in high spirits.*
– DERIVATIVES **high-spir·it·ed** adj., **high-spir·it·ed·ness** n.

high spot ▶ n. the most enjoyable or significant part of an experience or period of time: *perhaps that summer will mark the high spot of my life.*
– PHRASES **hit the high spots** informal visit the most exciting places in town.

high-stick ▶ v. [no obj.] (usu. as noun **high-sticking**) Ice Hockey strike an opponent on or above the shoulders with one's stick, for which a penalty may be assessed.

high street ▶ n. Brit. the main street of a town, esp. as the traditional site for most stores, banks, and other businesses. ■ [as modifier] (of retail goods) catering to the needs of the ordinary public: *high-street fashion.*

high-strung ▶ adj. nervous and easily upset: *a high-strung racing thoroughbred.*

hight /hīt/ ▶ adj. [predic.] archaic or literary named: *a little pest, hight Tommy Moore.*
– ORIGIN Middle English, from Old English *heht*, past tense of *hātan* 'command, call, or name,' of Germanic origin; related to Dutch *heten* and German *heissen.*

high ta·ble ▶ n. Brit. a table in a dining hall, typically on a platform, for the most important people, such as the fellows of a college: *I sat at high table.*

high·tail /'hīˌtāl/ ▶ v. [no obj.] informal move or travel fast: *I cut my trip short and hightailed it home.*

high tea ▶ n. Brit. a meal eaten in the late afternoon or early evening, typically consisting of a cooked dish, bread and butter, and tea.

high-tech (also **hi-tech**) ▶ adj. employing, requiring, or involved in high technology: *a high-tech security system.* ■ (chiefly in architecture and interior

design) using styles and materials, such as steel, glass, and plastic, that are more usual in industry.
▶ n. (**high tech**) short for HIGH TECHNOLOGY.

high tech·nol·o·gy ▶ n. advanced technological development, esp. in electronics: [as modifier] *high-technology weapons*.

high-ten·sile ▶ adj. (of metal) very strong under tension: *high-tensile steel*.

high ten·sion ▶ n. another term for HIGH VOLTAGE.

high-test ▶ adj. (of gasoline) high-octane. ■ meeting very high standards: *a high-test office*.

high-tick·et ▶ adj. another term for BIG-TICKET.

high tide ▶ n. the state of the tide when at its highest level: *at high tide you have to go inland*. ■ the highest point of something: *the high tide of nationalism*.

high-toned ▶ adj. stylish or superior: *she's getting high-toned and putting on airs*.

high-top (also **hightop**) ▶ adj. denoting a sneaker with a laced upper that extends some distance above the wearer's ankle.
▶ n. (**high-tops**) a pair of such sneakers.

high trea·son ▶ n. see TREASON.

high-up ▶ n. informal a senior person in an organization.

high volt·age ▶ n. an electrical potential large enough to cause injury or damage.

high wa·ter ▶ n. another term for HIGH TIDE.

high-wa·ter mark ▶ n. the level reached by the sea at high tide, or by a lake or river at its highest stand. ■ a maximum recorded level or value: *unemployment and crime both stand at a high-water mark*.

high·way /ˈhīˌwā/ ▶ n. a main road, esp. one connecting major towns or cities: *a six-lane highway* | figurative *the highway to success*. ■ another term for EXPRESSWAY. ■ (chiefly in official use) a public road. ■ Computing a pathway connecting parts of one computer system or between different systems.

high·way·man /ˈhīwāmən/ ▶ n. (pl. **highwaymen**) historical a man, typically on horseback, who held up travelers at gunpoint in order to rob them.

high wine ▶ n. a type of liquor containing a high percentage of alcohol.

high wire ▶ n. a high tightrope. ■ [as modifier] requiring great skill or judgment: *it will take a financial high-wire balancing act to fund the requirements*.

high words ▶ plural n. archaic angry words: *high words passed between them*.

high yel·low ▶ adj. offensive denoting a mulatto or a light-skinned black person.
▶ n. person of this kind.

HIH ▶ abbr. Brit. Her or His Imperial Highness.

hi-hat /ˈhīˌhat/ (also **high-hat**) ▶ n. a pair of foot-operated cymbals forming part of a drum kit.

hi·jab /hiˈjäb/ ▶ n. a head covering worn in public by some Muslim women. ■ the religious code that governs the wearing of such clothing.
– ORIGIN Persian, from Arabic *ḥajaba* 'to veil.'

hi·jack /ˈhīˌjak/ (also **highjack**) ▶ v. [with obj.] illegally seize (an aircraft, ship, or vehicle) in transit and force it to go to a different destination or use it for one's own purposes: *three armed men hijacked a white van* | (as noun **hijacking**) *an eight-hour hijacking*. ■ steal (goods) by seizing them in transit. ■ take over (something) and use it for a different purpose: *the organization had been hijacked by extremists*.
▶ n. an incident or act of hijacking.
– DERIVATIVES **hi·jack·er** n.
– ORIGIN 1920s (originally US): of unknown origin.

Hi·jaz variant spelling of HEJAZ.

hi·ji·ki /hēˈjēkē/ ▶ n. edible Japanese seaweed sold in dried black strips.
– ORIGIN Japanese.

Hij·ra /ˈhijrə/ ▶ n. variant spelling of HEGIRA.

hike /hīk/ ▶ n. **1** a long walk, esp. in the country or wilderness. ■ informal a long distance.
2 a sharp increase, esp. in price: *fears of **a hike in** interest rates*.
3 Football a snap: *he takes the hike, drops back, and fakes to his right*.
▶ v. **1** [no obj.] walk for a long distance, esp. across country or in the woods: *we planned to hike another mile up a steep trail* | (as noun **hiking**) *she enjoys hiking and climbing in her spare time*.
2 [with obj.] pull or lift up (something, esp. clothing): *he **hiked up** his sweatpants and marched to the door*. ■ increase (something, esp. a price) sharply: *some of the local merchants hiked the price of goods*.
3 Football snap (a football).
– PHRASES **take a hike** [usu. in imperative] informal go away (used as an expression of irritation or annoyance).
– DERIVATIVES **hik·er** n.
– ORIGIN early 19th cent. (originally dialect, as a verb): of unknown origin.

hi·ki·ko·mo·ri /hiˌkēkəˈmôri/ ▶ n. (pl. **same**) (in Japan) the abnormal avoidance of social contact, typically by adolescent males. ■ a person who avoids social contact.
– ORIGIN Japanese, literally 'staying indoors, (social) withdrawal.'

hi·la /ˈhīlə/ plural form of HILUM.

hi·lar /ˈhīlər/ ▶ adj. Anatomy & Botany of or relating to a hilus or hilum.

hi·lar·i·ous /həˈle(ə)rēəs/ ▶ adj. extremely amusing: *a hilarious dialogue from characters we never meet again*. ■ boisterously merry: *an old man was in hilarious conversation with three young men*.
– DERIVATIVES **hi·lar·i·ous·ly** adv.
– ORIGIN early 19th cent.: from Latin *hilaris* (from Greek *hilaros* 'cheerful') + **-ous**. The sense 'exceedingly amusing' dates from the 1920s.

hi·lar·i·ty /həˈle(ə)ritē/ ▶ n. extreme amusement, esp. when expressed by laughter: *his incredulous expression was the cause of much hilarity*. ■ boisterous merriment: *the noisy hilarity of the streets*.
– ORIGIN late Middle English (in the sense 'cheerfulness'): from French *hilarité*, from Latin *hilaritas* 'cheerfulness, merriment,' from *hilaris* (see HILARIOUS).

Hil·a·ry, St. /ˈhilərē/ (*c.*315–*c.*367), French bishop. As bishop of Poitiers, he opposed Arianism. Feast day, January 13.

Hil·bert space /ˈhilbərt/ ▶ n. Mathematics an infinite-dimensional analog of Euclidean space.
– ORIGIN early 20th cent.: named after David *Hilbert* (1862–1943), German mathematician.

Hil·da, St. /ˈhildə/ (614–680), English abbess. Related to the Anglo-Saxon kings of Northumbria, she founded a monastery for both men and women at Whitby around 658. Feast day, November 17.

Hil·de·gard of Bin·gen, St. (1098–1179), German abbess, scholar, composer, and mystic. A nun of the Benedictine order, she wrote scientific works, poetry, and music, and described her mystical experiences in *Scivias*.

Hil·des·heim /ˈhildəsˌhīm/ an industrial city in northwestern Germany, in Lower Saxony; pop. 103,200 (est. 2006).

Hil·i·gay·non /ˌhiliˈgīnən/ ▶ n. (pl. **same** or **Hiligaynons**) **1** a member of a people inhabiting Panay, Negros, and other islands in the central Philippines.
2 the Austronesian language of this people.
▶ adj. of or relating to this people or their language.

hill /hil/ ▶ n. **1** a naturally raised area of land, not as high or craggy as a mountain. ■ a sloping piece of road or trail: *they were climbing a steep hill in low gear*. ■ a heap or mound of something: ***a hill of** sliding shingle*.
2 (**the Hill**) informal short for CAPITOL HILL.
▶ v. [with obj.] form (something) into a heap. ■ bank up (a plant) with soil: *if frost threatens our new plants, we hill them up*.
– PHRASES **a hill of beans** [with negative] informal a thing of little value: *the problems of one old actor don't amount to a hill of beans*. **as old as the hills** see OLD. **over the hill** informal old and past one's prime. **up hill and down dale** see UP.
– ORIGIN Old English *hyll*, of Germanic origin; from an Indo-European root shared by Latin *collis* and Greek *kolōnos* 'hill.'

Hil·la·ry /ˈhilərē/, Sir Edmund (Percival) (1919–2008), New Zealand mountaineer and explorer. In 1953, Hillary and Tenzing Norgay, as members of a British expedition, were the first people to reach the summit of Mount Everest.

hill·bil·ly /ˈhilˌbilē/ ▶ n. (pl. **hillbillies**) **1** informal, chiefly derogatory an unsophisticated country person, associated originally with the remote regions of the Appalachians.
2 old-fashioned term for COUNTRY MUSIC.
– ORIGIN early 20th cent.: from HILL + *Billy* (nickname for the given name *William*).

hill climb ▶ n. a race for vehicles up a steep, often winding, hill.
– DERIVATIVES **hill-climb·er** n., **hill-climb·ing** n.

hill·ock /ˈhilək/ ▶ n. a small hill or mound.
– DERIVATIVES **hill·ock·y** adj.

Hills·bo·ro /ˈhilzˌbərō/ a commercial and industrial city in northwestern Oregon; pop. 93,638 (est. 2008).

hill·side /ˈhilˌsīd/ ▶ n. the sloping side of a hill.

hill sta·tion ▶ n. a town in the low mountains of the Indian subcontinent, popular as a holiday resort during the hot season.

hill·top /ˈhilˌtäp/ ▶ n. the summit of a hill.

hill·walk·ing /ˈhilˌwôkiNG/ ▶ n. the pastime of walking in hilly country.
– DERIVATIVES **hill·walk·er** /-ˌwôkər/ n.

hill·y /ˈhilē/ ▶ adj. (**hillier, hilliest**) having many hills.
– DERIVATIVES **hill·i·ness** n.

Hi·lo /ˈhēlō/ a port community in Hawaii, on the northern coast of the island of Hawaii; pop. 40,759 (2000).

hilt /hilt/ ▶ n. the handle of a weapon or tool, esp. a sword, dagger, or knife.
– PHRASES (**up**) **to the hilt** completely: *we're mortgaged to the hilt*.
– DERIVATIVES **hilt·ed** adj.
– ORIGIN Old English *hilt, hilte*, of Germanic origin.

Hil·ton /ˈhiltn/, Conrad (Nicholson) (1887–1979), US businessman. After buying up different hotels during the 1920s, 1930s, and 1940s, he formed the Hilton Hotels Corporation in 1946 and Hilton International in 1948.

Hil·ton Head Is·land a resort town in southeastern South Carolina, on one of the Sea Islands in the Atlantic Ocean, northeast of Savannah in Georgia; pop. 33,913 (est. 2008).

hi·lum /ˈhīləm/ ▶ n. (pl. **hila** /ˈhīlə/) Botany the scar on a seed marking the point of attachment to its seed vessel. ■ a point in a starch granule around which the layers of starch are deposited. ■ Anatomy another term for HILUS.
– ORIGIN mid 17th cent. (in the Latin sense): from Latin, literally 'little thing, trifle,' once thought to mean 'that which sticks to a bean,' hence the current sense (mid 18th cent).

hi·lus /ˈhīləs/ ▶ n. (pl. **hili** /ˈhīlī, -lē/) Anatomy an indentation in the surface of a kidney, spleen, or other organ, where blood vessels, ducts, nerve fibers, etc., enter or leave it.
– ORIGIN mid 19th cent.: modern Latin, alteration of HILUM.

HIM ▶ abbr. Brit. Her or His Imperial Majesty.

him /him/ ▶ pron. [third person singular] **1** used as the object of a verb or preposition to refer to a male person or animal previously mentioned or easily identified: *his wife survived him* | *he took the children with him*. Compare with HE. ■ referring to a person or animal of unspecified sex (in modern use chiefly replaced by "him or her" or "them"): *withdrawing your child from school to educate him at home may seem drastic*. ■ often used in place of "he" after the verb "to be" and after "than" or "as" to refer to a male person or animal: *that's him all right* | *I could never be as good as him*.
2 archaic or dialect himself: *in the depths of him, he too didn't want to go*.
– ORIGIN Old English, dative singular form of *he, hē* 'he' and *hit* 'it.'

USAGE On whether **him** or **he** is the correct pronoun in a comparative construction (*smarter than him* or *smarter than he*?), see usage at PERSONAL PRONOUN and THAN. See also usage at HE.

Hi·ma·chal Pra·desh /həˈmäCHəl prəˈdāSH, -ˈdeSH/ a mountainous state in northern India; capital, Shimla.

Him·a·la·yan /ˌhiməˈlāən/ ▶ adj. of or relating to the Himalayas: *the Himalayan foothills*.
▶ n. a cat of a long-haired breed having blue eyes and a pale coat with dark points, developed by crossing Persian and Siamese cats.

Him·a·la·yas /ˌhiməˈlāəz, həˈmäl(ə)yəz/ a vast mountain system in southern Asia that extends for 1,500 miles (2,400 km) from Kashmir east to Assam. The Himalayas consist of a series of parallel ranges that rise up from the Ganges River basin to the Tibetan plateau. The backbone is the Great Himalayan Range, the highest mountain range in the world, with several peaks rising to over 25,000 feet (7,700 m), the highest being Mount Everest.
– ORIGIN from Sanskrit *Himālaya*, from *hima* 'snow' + *ālaya* 'abode.'

hi·mat·i·on /həˈmatēˌän/ ▶ n. an outer garment worn by the ancient Greeks over the left shoulder and under the right.
– ORIGIN Greek.

him·bo /ˈhimbō/ ▶ n. (pl. **himbos**) informal, humorous an attractive but unintelligent man.
– ORIGIN 1980s: analogous form of *bimbo*.

Himm·ler /ˈhimlər/, Heinrich (1900–45), German leader; chief of the SS (Nazi special police force) 1929–45 and of the Gestapo 1936–45. He established and oversaw the systematic genocide of over 6,000,000 Jews and other disfavored groups between 1941 and 1945. Captured by British forces in 1945, he committed suicide.

Hims /himz, hims/ variant form of **HOMS**.

him·self /himˈself/ ▶ **pron.** [third person singular]
1 [reflexive] used as the object of a verb or preposition to refer to a male person or animal previously mentioned as the subject of the clause: *the steward introduced himself as Pete | he ought to be ashamed of himself.*
2 [emphatic] he or him personally (used to emphasize a particular male person or animal mentioned): *Thomas himself laid down what we should do | he said so himself.* ■ chiefly Irish a third party of some importance, esp. the master of the house: *I'll mention it to himself.*
– PHRASES **(not) be himself** see **NOT BE ONESELF** at **BE**. **by himself** see **BY ONESELF** at **BY**.
– ORIGIN Old English (see **HIM**, **SELF**).

Him·yar·ite /ˈhimyəˌrīt/ ▶ **n.** a member of an ancient people of the southwestern part of the Arabian peninsula, who ruled much of southern Arabia before the 6th century AD.
▶ **adj.** of or relating to this people.
– ORIGIN from the name *Himyar* (the name of a traditional king of Yemen) + **-ITE**[1].

hin /hin/ ▶ **n.** a Hebrew unit of liquid capacity equal to approximately 5.5 quarts (5 l).
– ORIGIN late Middle English: from biblical Hebrew *hīn*.

Hi·na·ya·na /ˌhēnəˈyänə/ (also **Hinayana Buddhism**) ▶ **n.** a pejorative name given by the followers of Mahayana Buddhism to the more conservative schools of early Buddhism. The tradition died out in India, but it survived in Sri Lanka (Ceylon) as the Theravada school and was taken from there to other regions of Southeast Asia. See **THERAVADA**.
– ORIGIN from Sanskrit *hīna* 'lesser' + *yāna* 'vehicle.'

hind[1] /hīnd/ ▶ **adj.** [attrib.] (esp. of a bodily part) situated at the back; posterior: *he snagged a calf by the hind leg.*
– PHRASES **on one's hind legs** see **LEG**.
– ORIGIN Middle English: perhaps shortened from Old English *behindan* (see **BEHIND**).

hind[2] ▶ **n.** **1** a female deer, esp. a red deer or sika in and after its third year.
2 any of several large edible groupers with spotted markings.
– ORIGIN Old English, of Germanic origin; related to Dutch *hinde* and German *Hinde*, from an Indo-European root meaning 'hornless,' shared by Greek *kemas* 'young deer.'

hind[3] ▶ **n.** archaic, chiefly Scottish a skilled farm worker. ■ a peasant or rustic.
– ORIGIN late Old English *hīne* 'household servants,' apparently from *hīgna, hīna*, genitive plural of *hīgan, hīwan* 'family members.'

Hind. ▶ **abbr.** ■ Hindi. ■ Hindu. ■ Hindustan. ■ Hindustani.

hind- ▶ **comb. form** (added to nouns) at the back; posterior: *hindquarters | hindbrain.*

hind·brain /ˈhīn(d)ˌbrān/ ▶ **n.** the lower part of the brainstem, comprising the cerebellum, pons, and medulla oblongata. Also called **RHOMBENCEPHALON**.

Hin·den·burg[1] /ˈhindənˌbərg, -ˌbo͝ork/ former German name (1915–45) of **ZABRZE**.

Hin·den·burg[2] /ˈhindənbərg/, Paul Ludwig von Beneckendorff und von (1847–1934), German field marshal and statesman; president of the Weimar Republic 1925–34.

Hin·den·burg Line /ˈhindənbərg/ (in World War I) a German fortified line of defense on the Western Front to which Paul von Hindenburg directed retreat and which was not breached until near the end of the war. Also called **SIEGFRIED LINE**.

hind·er[1] /ˈhindər/ ▶ **v.** [with obj.] create difficulties for (someone or something), resulting in delay or obstruction: *various family stalemates were hindering communication.*
– ORIGIN Old English *hindrian* 'injure or damage,' of Germanic origin; related to German *hindern*, also to **BEHIND**.

hind·er[2] /ˈhīndər/ ▶ **adj.** [attrib.] (esp. of a bodily part) rear; hind: *the hinder end of its body.*
– ORIGIN Middle English: perhaps from Old English *hinderweard* 'backward,' related to **BEHIND**.

Hin·di /ˈhindē/ ▶ **n.** a form of Hindustani written in Devanagari and with many loanwords from Sanskrit, an official language of India, and the most widely spoken language of northern India.
▶ **adj.** of or relating to Hindi.
– ORIGIN from Urdu *hindī*, from *Hind* 'India.' See **INDUS**[1], **SINDHI**.

hind limb (also **hindlimb**) ▶ **n.** either of the back limbs of an animal.

hind·most /ˈhīn(d)ˌmōst/ ▶ **adj.** furthest back: *the hindmost part of the frog's food canal.*

Hin·doo /ˈhindo͞o/ ▶ **n. & adj.** archaic spelling of **HINDU**.

hind·quar·ters /ˈhīn(d)ˌkwôrtərz/ ▶ **plural n.** the hind legs and adjoining parts of a quadruped.

hin·drance /ˈhindrəns/ ▶ **n.** a thing that provides resistance, delay, or obstruction to something or someone: *a hindrance to the development process | the visitor can wander around without hindrance.*

hind·sight /ˈhīn(d)ˌsīt/ ▶ **n.** understanding of a situation or event only after it has happened or developed: ***with hindsight**, I should never have gone.*

Hin·du /ˈhindo͞o/ ▶ **n.** (pl. **Hindus**) a follower of Hinduism.
▶ **adj.** of or relating to Hindus or Hinduism.
– ORIGIN Urdu, from Persian *hindū*, from *Hind* 'India.'

Hin·du·ism /ˈhindo͞oˌizəm/ ▶ **n.** a major religious and cultural tradition of South Asia, developed from Vedic religion.

> Hinduism is practiced primarily in India, Bangladesh, Sri Lanka, and Nepal. It is a diverse family of devotional and ascetic cults and philosophical schools, all sharing a belief in reincarnation and involving the worship of one or more of a large pantheon of gods and goddesses, including Shiva and Vishnu (incarnate as Rama and Krishna), Kali, Durga, Parvati, and Ganesh. Hindu society was traditionally based on a caste system.

– DERIVATIVES **Hin·du·ize** /-ˌīz/ **v.**

Hin·du Kush /ˈhindo͞o ˈko͞osh/ a mountain range in northern Pakistan and Afghanistan that forms a western continuation of the Himalayas. Several peaks exceed 20,000 feet (6,150 m), the highest being Tirich Mir.

Hin·du·stan /ˌhindo͞oˈstan, -ˈstän/ historical the Indian subcontinent in general, more specifically that part of India north of the Deccan, esp. the plains of the Ganges and Jumna rivers.

Hin·du·sta·ni /ˌhindo͞oˈstänē/ ▶ **n.** a group of Indic dialects spoken in northwestern India, principally Hindi and Urdu. ■ the Delhi dialect of Hindi, widely used throughout India as a lingua franca.
▶ **adj.** of or relating to the culture of northwestern India: *Hindustani classical music.*

> **USAGE** **Hindustani** was the usual term in the 18th and 19th centuries for the native language of northwestern India. The usual modern term is **Hindi** (or **Urdu** in Muslim contexts), although **Hindustani** is still used to refer to the dialect of Hindi spoken around Delhi.

Hin·dut·va /hinˈdətvə/ ▶ **n.** Indian a strong or aggressive sense of Hindu identity, seeking the creation of a Hindu state.
– ORIGIN Hindi.

hind wing (also **hindwing**) ▶ **n.** either of the two back wings of a four-winged insect.

Hines /hīnz/, Earl (Kenneth) (1905–83), US jazz pianist and bandleader; known as **Fatha Hines**. He originated the "trumpet style" of piano playing.

hinge /hinj/ ▶ **n.** a movable joint or mechanism on which a door, gate, or lid swings as it opens and closes, or that connects linked objects. ■ Biology a natural joint that performs a similar function, for example that of a bivalve shell. ■ a central point or principle on which everything depends: *this period can be called the hinge of history.*
▶ **v.** (**hinges**, **hingeing** or **hinging**, **hinged**) [with obj.] attach or join with or as if with a hinge: *the ironing board was set into the wall and hinged at the bottom |* (as adj. **hinged**) *a pocket watch with a hinged lid.* ■ [no obj.] (of a door or part of a structure) hang and turn on a hinge: *the skull's jaw hinged down.* ■ [no obj.] (**hinge on**) depend entirely on: *the future of the industry could hinge on the outcome of next month's election.*
– DERIVATIVES **hinge·less adj.**
– ORIGIN Middle English *henge*; related to **HANG**.

hinge

Hin·gis /ˈhiNGgəs/, Martina (1981–), Swiss tennis player. During 1997–99, she won the women's singles title at one Wimbledon, one US Open, and three Australian Open tournaments.

hink·y /ˈhiNGkē/ ▶ **adj.** (**hinkier**, **hinkiest**) informal (of a person) dishonest or suspect: *he knew the guy was hinky.* ■ (of an object) unreliable: *my brakes are a little hinky.*
– ORIGIN 1950s: of obscure origin.

hin·ny /ˈhinē/ ▶ **n.** (pl. **hinnies**) the offspring of a female donkey and a male horse.
– ORIGIN early 17th cent.: via Latin from Greek *hinnos*.

hi·no·ki /hiˈnōkē/ ▶ **n.** (also **hinoki cypress**) a tall slow-growing tree native to Japan that has bright green leaves and yields a valuable timber.
● *Chamaecyparis obtusa*, family Cupressaceae.
– ORIGIN early 18th cent.: from Japanese.

hint /hint/ ▶ **n.** a slight or indirect indication or suggestion: *he has given no **hint of** his views.* ■ a small piece of practical information or advice: *handy hints about what to buy.* ■ a very small trace of something: *Randy smiled with **a hint of** mockery.*
▶ **v.** [no obj.] suggest or indicate something indirectly or covertly: *there were those who **hinted at** doctored evidence |* [with clause] *Edwards has hinted that he will dispose of his majority shareholding.* ■ (**hint at**) (of a thing) be a slight or possible indication of: *the restrained fronts of the terraced houses only hinted at the wealth within.*
– PHRASES **drop a hint** see **DROP**. **take a** (or **the**) **hint** understand and act on a hint: *she tried to put him off but he didn't take the hint.*
– ORIGIN early 17th cent. (in the sense 'occasion, opportunity'): apparently from obsolete *hent* 'grasp, get hold of,' from Old English *hentan*, of Germanic origin; related to **HUNT**. The basic notion is 'something that may be taken advantage of.'

hin·ter·land /ˈhintərˌland/ (also **hinterlands**) ▶ **n.** **1** the often uncharted areas beyond a coastal district or a river's banks: *early settlers were driven from the coastal areas into the hinterland.* ■ an area surrounding a town or port and served by it: *the city had grown prosperous by exploiting its local western hinterland.*
2 an area lying beyond what is visible or known: *in the hinterland of his mind these things rose, dark and ominous.*
– ORIGIN late 19th cent.: from German, from *hinter* 'behind' + *Land* 'land.'

hip[1] /hip/ ▶ **n.** **1** a projection of the pelvis and upper thigh bone on each side of the body in human beings and quadrupeds. ■ (**hips**) the circumference of the body at the buttocks: *a sweater tied around the hips.* ■ a person's hip joint: *she ran into a fence and dislocated her hip.*
2 the sharp edge of a roof from the ridge to the eaves where two sides meet.
– PHRASES **be joined at the hip** informal (of two people) be inseparable. **on the hip** archaic at a disadvantage.
– ORIGIN Old English *hype*, of Germanic origin; related to Dutch *heup* and German *Hüfte*, also to **HOP**[1].

hip[2] (also **rose hip**) ▶ **n.** the fruit of a rose, esp. a wild kind.
– ORIGIN Old English *hēope, hīope*; related to Dutch *joop* and German *Hiefe*.

hip[3] ▶ **adj.** (**hipper**, **hippest**) informal following the latest fashion, esp. in popular music and clothes: *it's becoming hip to be environmentally conscious.* ■ understanding; aware: *he's trying to show how hip he is to Americana.*
– DERIVATIVES **hip·ly adv.**, **hip·ness n.**
– ORIGIN early 20th cent.: of unknown origin.

hip[4] ▶ **exclam.** introducing a communal cheer: *hip, hip, hooray!*
– ORIGIN mid 18th cent.: of unknown origin.

HIPAA /ˈhipˌô/ ▶ **abbr.** Health Insurance Portability and Accountability Act, a 1996 Federal law that restricts access to individuals' private medical information: [as adj.] *HIPAA regulations.*

hip·bone /ˈhipˌbōn/ ▶ **n.** a large bone forming the main part of the pelvis on each side of the body and consisting of the fused ilium, ischium, and pubis. Also called **INNOMINATE BONE**.

hip boot ▶ **n.** a waterproof boot that reaches the hip.

hip flask ▶ **n.** a small flask for liquor, of a kind intended to be carried in a hip pocket.

hip-hop ▶ **n.** a style of popular music of US black and Hispanic origin, featuring rap with an electronic backing.
– ORIGIN 1980s: reduplication probably based on **HIP**[3].

hip-hug·gers (also **hiphuggers**) ▶ **plural n.** pants hanging from the hips rather than from the waist.

hip joint ▶ **n.** the ball-and-socket joint connecting a leg to the trunk of the body, in which the head of the thigh bone fits into the socket of the ilium.

Hip·par·chus /hiˈpärkəs/ (*c.*170–after 126 BC), Greek astronomer and geographer. He is best known for his discovery of the precession of the equinoxes and is credited with the invention of trigonometry.

hipped¹ /hipt/ ▶ **adj.** [in combination] (of a person or animal) having hips of a specified kind: *a thin-hipped girl.*

hipped² ▶ **adj.** [predic.] (**hipped on**) informal obsessed or infatuated with: *why are you suddenly hipped on discipline?*
– ORIGIN 1920s.: from HIP³, or as the past participle of *hip* 'make someone hip (i.e., aware).'

hipped roof ▶ **n.** another term for HIP ROOF.

hip·pie /ˈhipē/ (also **hippy**) ▶ **n.** (esp. in the 1960s) a person of unconventional appearance, typically having long hair and wearing beads, associated with a subculture involving a rejection of conventional values and the taking of hallucinogenic drugs.
▶ **adj.** of or relating to hippies or the subculture associated with them: *he epitomized the hippie biker.*
– DERIVATIVES **hip·pie·dom** /-dəm/ **n.**, **hip·pi·ness n.**, **hip·py·ish** /ˈhipē-isн/ **adj.**
– ORIGIN 1950s: from HIP³ + -IE (sense 1).

hip·po /ˈhipō/ ▶ **n.** (pl. **same** or **hippos**) informal term for HIPPOPOTAMUS.

hip·po·cam·pus /ˌhipəˈkampəs/ ▶ **n.** (pl. **hippocampi** /-ˈkampī, -ˈkampē/) Anatomy the elongated ridges on the floor of each lateral ventricle of the brain, thought to be the center of emotion, memory, and the autonomic nervous system.
– ORIGIN late 16th cent.: via Latin from Greek *hippokampos*, from *hippos* 'horse' + *kampos* 'sea monster.'

hip pock·et ▶ **n.** a pocket in the back of a pair of pants.
– PHRASES **in someone's hip pocket** completely under someone's control.

hip·po·cras /ˈhipəˌkras/ ▶ **n.** historical wine flavored with spices.
– ORIGIN late Middle English: from Old French *ipocras* 'Hippocrates' (see HIPPOCRATES), translating medieval Latin *vinum Hippocraticum* 'Hippocratic wine' (because it was strained through a filter called a *Hippocrates' sleeve*).

Hip·poc·ra·tes /hiˈpäkrətēz/ (*c.*460–377 BC), Greek physician, traditionally regarded as the father of medicine. His name is associated with the medical profession's Hippocratic oath because of his attachment to a body of ancient Greek medical writings, probably none of which was written by him.

Hip·po·crat·ic oath /ˈhipəˈkratik/ ▶ **n.** an oath stating the obligations and proper conduct of doctors, formerly taken by those beginning medical practice. Parts of the oath are still used in most medical schools.
– ORIGIN mid 18th cent.: *Hippocratic* from medieval Latin *Hippocraticus* 'relating to Hippocrates' (see HIPPOCRATES).

Hip·po·crene /ˈhipəˌkrēn, ˌhipəˈkrēnē/ ▶ **n.** literary used to refer to poetic or literary inspiration.
– ORIGIN early 17th cent.: via Latin from Greek *Hippokrēnē, Hippou krēnē*, literally 'fountain of the horse' (from *hippos* 'horse' + *krēnē* 'fountain'), the name of a fountain on Mount Helicon sacred to the Muses, which according to legend was produced by a stroke of Pegasus' hoof.

hip·po·drome /ˈhipəˌdrōm/ ▶ **n.** **1** [as name] a theater or other performance venue: *"Tuna Does Vegas" is ending this week at the Waco Hippodrome.*
2 (in ancient Greece or Rome) a course for chariot or horse races.
– ORIGIN late 16th cent. (sense 2): from French, via Latin from Greek *hippodromos*, from *hippos* 'horse' + *dromos* 'race, course.' The early sense led to the term's use as a grandiose name for a modern circus, later applied to other places of popular entertainment (late 19th cent).

hip·po·griff /ˈhipəˌgrif/ (also **hippogryph**) ▶ **n.** a mythical creature with the body of a horse and the wings and head of an eagle, born of the union of a male griffin and a filly.
– ORIGIN mid 17th cent.: from French *hippogriffe*, from Italian *ippogrifo*, from Greek *hippos* 'horse' + Italian *grifo* 'griffin.'

hip point·er ▶ **n.** a sports injury in which the point of the hip is deeply bruised and painful.

Hip·pol·y·tus /hiˈpälətəs/ Greek Mythology the son of Theseus, banished and cursed by his father after being falsely accused by Phaedra, his father's wife, of rape. He was killed when a sea monster, sent by Poseidon in response to the curse, frightened his horses as he drove his chariot along a seashore.

hip·po·pot·a·mus /ˌhipəˈpätəməs/ ▶ **n.** (pl. **hippopotamuses** or **hippopotami** /-ˌmī, -ˌmē/) a large thick-skinned semiaquatic African mammal, with massive jaws and large tusks. ● Family Hippopotamidae: the very large *Hippopotamus amphibius*, frequenting rivers and lakes, and the smaller **pygmy hippopotamus** (*Choeropsis liberiensis*), frequenting forests near fresh water in West Africa.
– ORIGIN Middle English: via Latin from Greek *hippopotamos*, earlier *hippos ho potamios* 'river horse' (from *hippos* 'horse,' *potamos* 'river').

Hip·po Re·gi·us /ˈhipō ˈrējēəs/ see ANNABA.

hip·pus /ˈhipəs/ ▶ **n.** Medicine spasmodic or rhythmic contraction of the pupil of the eye, a symptom of some neurological conditions.
– ORIGIN late 17th cent.: modern Latin, from Greek *hippos* 'tremor of the eyes.'

hip·py¹ ▶ **n. & adj.** variant spelling of HIPPIE.

hip·py² ▶ **adj.** having large hips.

hip·py-dip·py /ˌhipē ˈdipē/ ▶ **adj.** informal rejecting conventional practices or behavior in a way perceived to be vague and unconsidered or foolishly idealistic: *despite her hippy-dippy reputation, discipline seems to be the key to her success.*

hip roof (also **hipped roof**) ▶ **n.** a roof with the ends inclined, as well as the sides.

hip·shot /ˈhipˌsнät/ ▶ **adj. & adv.** having a dislocated hip. ■ [as adv.] having a posture with one hip lower than the other.

hip·ster¹ /ˈhipstər/ ▶ **n.** informal a person who follows the latest trends and fashions.
– DERIVATIVES **hip·ster·ism** /-ˌrizəm/ **n.**
– ORIGIN 1940s (used originally as an equivalent term to HEPCAT): from HIP³ + -STER.

hip·ster² ▶ **adj.** (of a garment) having the waistline at the hips rather than the waist.
▶ **n.** (**hipsters**) pants having such a waistline; hip-huggers.

hi·ra·ga·na /ˌhi(ə)rəˈgänə/ ▶ **n.** the more cursive and more widely used form of kana (syllabic writing) used in Japanese, esp. used for function words and inflections. Compare with KATAKANA.
– ORIGIN Japanese, 'plain kana.'

hir·cine /ˈhərˌsīn, -sən/ ▶ **adj.** archaic of or resembling a goat.
– ORIGIN mid 17th cent.: from Latin *hircinus*, from *hircus* 'he-goat.'

hire /hīr/ ▶ **v.** [with obj.] **1** employ (someone) for wages: *management hired and fired labor in line with demand.* ■ employ for a short time to do a particular job: *don't hire a babysitter who's under 16* | (as adj. **hired**) *a hired assassin.* ■ (**hire oneself out**) make oneself available for temporary employment: *he hired himself out as a laborer.*
2 chiefly Brit. obtain the temporary use of (something) for an agreed payment; rent: *she had to hire a dress for the wedding.* ■ (**hire something out**) grant the temporary use of something for an agreed payment.
▶ **n. 1** the action of hiring someone or something.
2 a person who is hired; an employee: *new hires go through six months of training.*
– PHRASES **for** (or **on**) **hire** available to be hired.
– DERIVATIVES **hire·a·ble** (also **hirable**) **adj.**, **hir·er n.**
– ORIGIN Old English *hȳrian* 'employ (someone) for wages,' *hȳr* 'payment under contract for the use of something'; related to Dutch *huren* (verb), *huur* (noun).

hire car ▶ **n.** Brit. a rental car.

hired girl ▶ **n.** a female domestic servant.

hired gun ▶ **n.** informal **1** an expert brought in to resolve complex problems or to lobby for a cause: *it is a chance for an insurance company's hired gun to find some excuse to deny your benefits.*
2 a hired bodyguard, mercenary, or assassin.

hired hand ▶ **n.** a person hired to do short-term manual work.

hired man ▶ **n.** a male domestic servant. ■ another term for HIRED HAND.

hire·ling /ˈhīrlinɢ/ ▶ **n.** chiefly derogatory a person employed to undertake menial work. ■ a person who works purely for material reward: *the government's paid hirelings assure us that we're on our way out of recession.*
– ORIGIN mid 16th cent.: from HIRE + -LING, on the pattern of Dutch *huurling.*

hire pur·chase ▶ **n.** British term for INSTALLMENT PLAN.

hi-res /ˌhīˈrez/ (also **high-res**) ▶ **adj.** informal (of a display or a photographic or video image) showing a large amount of detail.
– ORIGIN late 20th cent.: from *high-resolution.*

Hi·ro·hi·to /ˌhi(ə)rəˈhētō/ (1901–89), emperor of Japan 1926–89; full name *Michinomiya Hirohito.* Regarded as the 124th direct descendant of Jimmu, he refrained from involvement in politics, although he was instrumental in obtaining Japan's agreement to the unconditional surrender that ended World War II. In 1946, the new constitution imposed by the US obliged him to renounce his divinity and become a constitutional monarch.

Hirohito

Hi·ro·shi·ma /ˌhi(ə)rəˈsнēmə, hiˈrōsнəmə/ a city in southwestern Japan, on the southern coast of the island of Honshu; pop. 1,144,572 (2007). It was the target of the first atom bomb, which was dropped by the US on August 6, 1945, and resulted in the deaths of about one third of the city's population of 300,000. This, with a second attack on Nagasaki three days later, led to Japan's surrender and to the end of World War II.

Hirsch·sprung's dis·ease /ˈhirsн,prŏŏnɢz/ ▶ **n.** a congenital condition in which the rectum and part of the colon fail to develop a normal system of nerves, and consequently feces accumulate in the colon following birth.
– ORIGIN early 20th cent.: named after Harald *Hirschprung* (1830–1916), Danish pediatrician.

hir·sute /ˈhərˌsōōt, hərˈsōōt, ˈhi(ə)rˌsōōt/ ▶ **adj.** hairy: *their hirsute chests.*
– DERIVATIVES **hir·sute·ness n.**
– ORIGIN early 17th cent.: from Latin *hirsutus.*

hir·sut·ism /ˈhərsōōˌtizəm, hərˈsōō-, ˈhi(ə)rˌsōō-/ ▶ **n.** Medicine abnormal growth of hair on a person's face and body, esp. on a woman.

hir·un·dine /hiˈrəndin, -ˌdīn/ ▶ **n.** Ornithology a songbird of the swallow family (Hirundinidae).
– ORIGIN mid 19th cent.: from Latin *hirundo* 'swallow' + -INE¹.

his /hiz/ ▶ **possessive determiner 1** belonging to or associated with a male person or animal previously mentioned or easily identified: *James sold his business.* ■ belonging to or associated with a person or animal of unspecified sex (in modern use chiefly replaced by "his or her" or "their"): *any child with delayed speech should have his hearing checked.*
2 (**His**) used in titles: *His Honor* | *His Lordship.*
▶ **possessive pron.** used to refer to a thing or things belonging to or associated with a male person or animal previously mentioned: *he took my hand in his* | *some friends of his.*
– PHRASES **his and hers** (of matching items) for husband and wife, or men and women: *his and hers towels.*
– ORIGIN Old English, genitive singular form of *he, hē* 'he' and *hit* 'it.'

USAGE See usage at HE.

His·pan·ic /hiˈspanik/ ▶ **adj.** of or relating to Spain or to Spanish-speaking countries, esp. those of Latin America. ■ of or relating to Spanish-speaking people or their culture, esp. in the US.
▶ **n.** a Spanish-speaking person living in the US, esp. one of Latin American descent.
– DERIVATIVES **His·pan·i·cize** /hiˈspaniˌsīz/ **v.**
– ORIGIN from Latin *Hispanicus*, from *Hispania* 'Spain.'

USAGE In the US, **Hispanic** is the standard accepted term when referring to Spanish-speaking people living in the US. Other, more specific, terms such as **Latino** and **Chicano** are also used where occasion demands. See also usage at CHICANO.

His·pan·ic A·mer·i·can ▶ **n.** a US citizen or resident of Hispanic descent.
▶ **adj.** of or relating to Hispanic Americans.

His·pan·io·la /ˌhispənˈyōlə/ an island in the Greater Antilles in the Caribbean Sea, divided into the countries of Haiti and the Dominican Republic. After its European discovery by Columbus in 1492, Hispaniola was colonized by the Spaniards, who ceded the western part (now Haiti) to France in 1697.

His·pan·ist /'hispanist/ (also **Hispanicist** /-əsist/) ▶ **n.** an expert in or student of the language, literature, and civilization of Spain and the Spanish-speaking countries of Latin America.

His·pan·o /hi'spanō, -'spänō/ ▶ **n.** (pl. **Hispanos**) a person descended from Spanish settlers in the Southwest before it was annexed to the US. ■ a Hispanic.

Hispano- ▶ **comb. form** Spanish; Spanish and ...: *Hispano-Argentine*. ■ relating to Spain.
– ORIGIN from Latin *Hispanus* 'Spanish.'

His·pan·o·phobe /hi'spanə,fōb/ ▶ **n.** a person who dislikes or fears Spanish-speaking peoples or countries.

his·pid /'hispid/ ▶ **adj.** Botany & Zoology covered with stiff hair or bristles.
– ORIGIN mid 17th cent.: from Latin *hispidus*.

Hiss /his/, Alger (1904–96), US public official. In 1948 he was accused by journalist Whittaker Chambers of passing State Department documents to a Soviet agent.

hiss /his/ ▶ **v.** [no obj.] make a sharp sibilant sound as of the letter *s*: *the escaping gas was now hissing*. ■ (of a person) make such a sound as a sign of disapproval or derision: *the audience hissed loudly at the mention of his name*. ■ [with obj.] express disapproval of (someone) by making such a sound: *he was hissed off the stage*. ■ [reporting verb] whisper something in an urgent or angry way: *he hissed at them to be quiet* | [with direct speech] *"Get back!" he hissed.*
▶ **n.** a sharp sibilant sound: *the spit and hiss of a cornered cat*. ■ a sound such as this used as an expression of disapproval or derision: *a hiss of annoyance*. ■ electrical interference at audio frequencies: *tape hiss*.
– ORIGIN late Middle English (as a verb): imitative.

his·self /hi'self, hiz-/ ▶ **pron.** nonstandard spelling of **HIMSELF**, used in representing informal or dialect speech.

his·sy /'hisē/ (also **hissy fit**) ▶ **n.** an angry outburst or tantrum.

hist /hist/ ▶ **exclam.** archaic used to attract attention or call for silence.
– ORIGIN natural exclamation: first recorded in English in the late 16th cent.

hist. ▶ **abbr.** ■ histology. ■ historian. ■ historical. ■ history.

hist- ▶ **comb. form** variant spelling of **HISTO-** shortened before a vowel (as in *histidine*).

his·ta·mine /'histə,mēn, -,min/ ▶ **n.** Biochemistry a compound that is released by cells in response to injury and in allergic and inflammatory reactions, causing contraction of smooth muscle and dilation of capillaries. ● A heterocyclic amine; chem. formula: $C_5H_9N_3$.
– DERIVATIVES **his·ta·min·ic** /,histə'minik/ **adj.**
– ORIGIN early 20th cent.: blend of **HISTIDINE** and **AMINE**.

his·ti·dine /'histə,dēn/ ▶ **n.** Biochemistry a basic amino acid that is a constituent of most proteins. It is an essential nutrient in the diet of vertebrates, and is the source from which histamine is derived in the body. ● Chem. formula: $C_6H_9N_3O_2$.
– ORIGIN late 19th cent.: from Greek *histos* 'web, tissue' + **-IDE** + **-INE**[4].

his·ti·o·cyte /'histēə,sīt/ ▶ **n.** Physiology a stationary phagocytic cell present in connective tissue.
– ORIGIN early 20th cent.: from Greek *histion* (diminutive of *histos* 'tissue, web') + **-CYTE**.

histo- (also **hist-** before a vowel) ▶ **comb. form** Biology relating to organic tissue: *histochemistry* | *histocompatibility*.
– ORIGIN from Greek *histos* 'web, tissue.'

his·to·chem·is·try /,histə'keməstrē/ ▶ **n.** the branch of science concerned with the identification and distribution of the chemical constituents of tissues by means of stains, indicators, and microscopy.
– DERIVATIVES **his·to·chem·i·cal** /-'kemikəl/ **adj.**, **his·to·chem·i·cal·ly** /-'kəmik(ə)lē/ **adv.**

his·to·com·pat·i·bil·i·ty /,histōkəm,patə'bilitē/ ▶ **n.** Medicine compatibility between the tissues of different individuals, so that one accepts a graft from the other without having an immune reaction.

his·to·gen·e·sis /,histə'jenəsis/ ▶ **n.** Biology the differentiation of cells into specialized tissues and organs during growth.
– DERIVATIVES **his·to·ge·net·ic** /,histəjə'netik/ **adj.**

his·to·gram /'histə,gram/ ▶ **n.** Statistics a diagram consisting of rectangles whose area is proportional to the frequency of a variable and whose width is equal to the class interval.
– ORIGIN late 19th cent.: from Greek *histos* 'mast, web' + **-GRAM**[1].

his·tol·o·gy /hi'stäləjē/ ▶ **n.** Biology the study of the microscopic structure of tissues.
– DERIVATIVES **his·to·log·ic** /,histə'läjik/ **adj.**, **his·to·log·i·cal** /,histə'läjikəl/ **adj.**, **his·tol·o·gist** /-jist/ **n.**

his·tol·y·sis /hi'stäləsis/ ▶ **n.** Biology the breaking down of tissues (e.g., during animal metamorphosis).
– DERIVATIVES **his·to·lyt·ic** /,histə'litik/ **adj.**

his·tone /'hi,stōn/ ▶ **n.** Biochemistry any of a group of basic proteins found in chromatin.
– ORIGIN late 19th cent.: coined in German, perhaps from Greek *histanai* 'arrest' or from *histos* 'web, tissue.'

his·to·pa·thol·o·gy /,histōpə'THäləjē/ ▶ **n.** the study of changes in tissues caused by disease.
– DERIVATIVES **his·to·path·o·log·i·cal** /,histō,paTHə'läjikəl/ **adj.**, **his·to·pa·thol·o·gist** /-jist/ **n.**

his·to·plas·mo·sis /,histōplaz'mōsis/ ▶ **n.** Medicine infection by a fungus found in the droppings of birds and bats in humid areas. It is not serious if confined to the lungs but can be fatal if spread throughout the body. ● The fungus is *Histoplasma capsulatum*.

his·to·ri·an /hi'stôrēən/ ▶ **n.** an expert in or student of history, esp. that of a particular period, geographical region, or social phenomenon: *a military historian*.
– ORIGIN late Middle English: from Old French *historien*, from Latin *historia* (see **HISTORY**).

his·to·ri·at·ed /hi'stôrē,ātid/ ▶ **adj.** (of an initial letter in an illuminated manuscript) decorated with designs representing scenes from the text.
– ORIGIN late 19th cent.: from French *historié*, past participle of *historier* in an obsolete sense 'illustrate,' from medieval Latin *historiare*, from *historia* (see **HISTORY**).

his·tor·ic /hi'stôrik, -'stär-/ ▶ **adj.** **1** famous or important in history, or potentially so: *we are standing on a historic site* | *a time of historic change*. ■ archaic of or concerning history; of the past: *eruptions in historic times*.
2 Grammar (of a tense) used in the narration of past events, esp. Latin and Greek imperfect and pluperfect.
– ORIGIN early 17th cent. (in the sense 'relating to or in accordance with history'): via Latin from Greek *historikos*, from *historia* 'narrative, knowing by inquiry' (see **HISTORY**).

> **USAGE** 1 On the use of *an historic moment* or *a historic moment*, see **AN**. 2 In general, **historic** means 'notable in history, significant in history,' as in a Supreme Court decision, a battlefield, or a great discovery. **Historical** means 'relating to history or past events': (*historical society; historical documents*). To write **historic** instead of **historical** may imply a greater significance than is warranted: a **historical** lecture may simply tell about something that happened, whereas a **historic** lecture would in some way change the course of human events. It would be correct to say, *Professor Suarez's historical lecture on the Old Southwest was given at the historic mission church.*

his·tor·i·cal /hi'stôrikəl, -'stär-/ ▶ **adj.** of or concerning history; concerning past events: *the historical background to such studies*. ■ belonging to the past, not the present: *famous historical figures*. ■ (esp. of a novel or movie) set in the past. ■ (of the study of a subject) based on an analysis of its development over a period: *for the Darwinians, biogeography became a historical science*.
– ORIGIN late Middle English: via Latin from Greek *historikos* (see **HISTORIC**).

> **USAGE** 1 On the difference between **historical** and **historic**, see usage at **HISTORIC**. 2 On the use of *an historical event* or *a historical event*, see **AN**.

his·tor·i·cal lin·guis·tics ▶ **plural n.** [treated as sing.] the study of the history and development of languages.

his·tor·i·cal·ly /hi'stôrik(ə)lē, -'stär-/ ▶ **adv.** with reference to past events: *a historically accurate picture of the time*. ■ [sentence adverb] in the past: *historically, government policy has favored urban dwellers*.

his·tor·i·cal ma·te·ri·al·ism ▶ **n.** another term for **DIALECTICAL MATERIALISM**.

his·tor·i·cism /hi'stôrə,sizəm, -'stär-/ ▶ **n.** **1** the theory that social and cultural phenomena are determined by history. ■ the belief that historical events are governed by laws.
2 the tendency to regard historical development as the most basic aspect of human existence.
3 chiefly derogatory (in artistic and architectural contexts) excessive regard for past styles.
– DERIVATIVES **his·tor·i·cist** **n.**
– ORIGIN late 19th cent.: from **HISTORIC**, translating German *Historismus*.

his·to·ric·i·ty /,histə'risitē/ ▶ **n.** historical authenticity: *an effort to assert the historicity of poetry and the political power of poets*.

his·tor·i·cize /his'stôrə,sīz, -'stär-/ ▶ **v.** [with obj.] treat or represent as historical.
– DERIVATIVES **his·tor·i·ci·za·tion** /hi,stôrəsə'zāSHən, -,stär-/ **n.**

his·tor·ic pres·ent /'prezənt/ ▶ **n.** Grammar the present tense used instead of the past in vivid narrative, esp. in titles, such as *The Empire Strikes Back*, and informally in speech, e.g., "so I say to him."

his·to·ri·og·ra·phy /hi,stôrē'ägrəfē, -,stär-/ ▶ **n.** the study of historical writing. ■ the writing of history.
– DERIVATIVES **his·to·ri·og·ra·pher** /-'ägrəfər/ **n.**, **his·to·ri·o·graph·ic** /-ə'grafik/ **adj.**, **his·to·ri·o·graph·i·cal** /-ə'grafikəl/ **adj.**
– ORIGIN mid 16th cent.: via medieval Latin from Greek *historiographia*, from *historia* 'narrative, history' + *graphia* 'writing.'

his·to·ry /'hist(ə)rē/ ▶ **n.** (pl. **histories**) **1** the study of past events, particularly in human affairs: *medieval European history*. ■ the past considered as a whole: *letters that have changed the course of history*.
2 the whole series of past events connected with someone or something: *the history of Aegean painting*. ■ an eventful past: *the group has quite a history*. ■ a past characterized by a particular thing: *his family had a history of insanity*.
3 a continuous, typically chronological, record of important or public events or of a particular trend or institution: *a history of the labor movement*. ■ a historical play: *Shakespeare's comedies, histories, and tragedies*.
– PHRASES **be history** be perceived as no longer relevant to the present: *the mainframe will soon be history* | *I was making a laughingstock of myself, but that's history now*. ■ informal used to indicate imminent departure, dismissal, or death: *an inch either way and you'd be history*. **go down in history** be remembered or recorded in history. **make history** do something that is remembered in or influences the course of history. **the rest is history** used to indicate that the events succeeding those already related are so well known that they need not be recounted again: *they teamed up, discovered that they could make music, and the rest is history*.
– ORIGIN late Middle English (also as a verb): via Latin from Greek *historia* 'finding out, narrative, history,' from *histōr* 'learned, wise man,' from an Indo-European root shared by **WIT**[2].

his·to·sol /'histə,sôl, -,säl/ ▶ **n.** Soil Science a soil of an order comprising peaty soils, with a deep surface layer of purely organic material.

his·tri·on·ic /,histrē'änik/ ▶ **adj.** overly theatrical or melodramatic in character or style: *a histrionic outburst*. ■ formal of or concerning actors or acting: *histrionic talents*. ■ Psychiatry denoting a personality disorder marked by shallow, volatile emotions, and attention-seeking behavior.
▶ **n.** **1** (**histrionics**) exaggerated dramatic behavior designed to attract attention: *discussions around the issue have been based as much in histrionics as in history*. ■ dramatic performance; theater.
2 archaic an actor.
– DERIVATIVES **his·tri·on·i·cal·ly** /-ik(ə)lē/ **adv.**
– ORIGIN mid 17th cent. (in the sense 'dramatically exaggerated, hypocritical'): from late Latin *histrionicus*, from Latin *histrio(n-)* 'actor.'

hit /hit/ ▶ **v.** (**hits, hitting, hit**) [with obj.] **1** bring one's hand or a tool or weapon into contact with (someone or something) quickly and forcefully: *the woman hit the mugger with her umbrella* | [no obj.] *use your words, but do not hit* | *the police* **hit out** *with billy clubs*. ■ accidentally strike (part of one's body) against something, often causing injury: *she fainted and hit her head on the metal bedstead*. ■ (of a moving object or body) come into contact with (someone or something stationary) quickly and forcefully: *a car hit the barrier*. ■ informal touch or press (part of a machine or other device) in order to work it: *he picked up the phone and hit several buttons*.
2 cause harm or distress to: *the area has been badly hit by business closures*. ■ [no obj.] (**hit out**) make a strongly worded criticism or attack: *he hit out at suppliers for hyping their products*. ■ (of a disaster) occur in and cause damage to (an area) suddenly: *the country was hit by a major earthquake*. ■ informal attack and rob or kill: *if they're cops, maybe it's not a good idea to have them hit*. ■ informal be affected by (an unfortunate and unexpected circumstance or event): *the opening of the town center hit a snag*.
3 (of a missile or a person aiming one) strike (a target): *the sniper fired and hit a third man*. ■ informal

reach (a particular level, point, or figure): *his career hit rock bottom.* ■ informal arrive at or go to (a place): *we hit a diner for coffee and doughnuts | it was still night when we hit the outskirts of Chicago.* ■ be suddenly and vividly realized by: [with obj. and clause] *it hit her that I wanted to settle down here.* ■ [no obj.] informal (of a piece of music, film, or play) be successful: *actors are promised a pay increase if a show hits.* ■ [no obj.] take effect: *we sat waiting for the caffeine to hit.* ■ informal give (someone) a dose of a drug or an alcoholic drink. ■ informal (of a product) become available and make an impact on: *the latest board game to hit the market.* ■ informal used to express the idea that someone is taking up a pursuit or taking it seriously: *more and more teenagers are hitting the books.* ■ (**hit someone for/up for**) informal ask someone for: *she was waiting for the right moment to hit her mother for some cash.*
4 propel (a ball) with a bat, racket, stick, etc., to score or attempt to score runs or points in a game. ■ score (runs or points) in this way: *he had hit 25 home runs.* ■ [no obj.] Baseball (of a batter) make a base hit.
▶ **n. 1** an instance of striking or being struck: *few structures can withstand a hit from a speeding car.* ■ a verbal attack: *he could not resist a* **hit at** *his friend's religiosity.* ■ informal a murder, typically one planned and carried out by a criminal organization. ■ Baseball short for BASE HIT.
2 an instance of striking the target aimed at: *one of the bombers had scored a direct hit.* ■ a successful venture, esp. in entertainment: *he was the director of many big hits* | [as modifier] *a hit comedy.* ■ a successful film, pop record, or song: *he was the director of many big hits.* ■ informal a successful and popular person or thing: *handsome, smiling, and smart, he was an immediate hit.* ■ Computing an instance of identifying an item of data that matches the requirements of a search. ■ an instance of a particular website being accessed by a user: *the site gets an average 350,000 hits per day.*
3 informal a dose of a psychoactive drug.
– PHRASES **hit-and-miss** done or occurring at random: *picking a remedy can be a bit hit-and-miss.* **hit someone below the belt** Boxing give one's opponent an illegal low blow. ■ behave unfairly, esp. so as to gain an unfair advantage. **hit someone for six** see SIX. **hit the bottle** see BOTTLE. **hit the ground running** informal start something and proceed at a fast pace with enthusiasm. **hit the hay** see HAY[1]. **hit home** see HOME. **hit it off** informal be naturally friendly or well suited. **hit the jackpot** see JACKPOT. **hit the mark** be successful in an attempt or accurate in a guess. **hit the nail on the head** find exactly the right answer. **hit-or-miss** /ˈˌhid ôr ˈmis/ as likely to be unsuccessful as successful: *her work can be hit-or-miss.* **hit the right note** see NOTE. **hit the road** (or **trail**) informal set out on a journey. **hit the roof** see ROOF. **hit the sack** see SACK[1]. **hit the spot** see SPOT. **make a hit** be successful or popular: *you made a big hit with her.*
– PHRASAL VERBS **hit on** (or **upon**) **1** discover or think of, esp. by chance: *she hit on a novel idea for fund-raising.* **2** informal make sexual advances toward. **hit someone up** attempt to get something, typically money, from someone: *he hit up some family members.*
– DERIVATIVES **hit·ter** n.
– ORIGIN late Old English *hittan* (in the sense 'come upon, find'), from Old Norse *hitta* 'come upon, meet with,' of unknown origin.

hit-and-run ▶ **adj.** denoting or relating to a motor accident in which the vehicle involved does not stop: *a man on a bicycle had been struck and killed by a hit-and-run driver.* ■ denoting or relating to a swift attack followed by immediate withdrawal: *a hit-and-run guerrilla war in the streets.* ■ done or intended for quickness of effect rather than for permanency: *hit-and-run agents who sign rookies to huge bonuses and buy themselves getaway cars.* ■ Baseball designating an offensive play in which a base runner, not attempting to steal a base, runs before the pitch is thrown, in an attempt to advance further in case of a hit.

hitch /hiCH/ ▶ **v. 1** [with obj.] move (something) into a different position with a jerk: *she hitched the blanket around him | he* **hitched** *his pants* **up**.
2 [no obj.] informal travel by hitchhiking. ■ [with obj.] obtain (a ride) by hitchhiking.
3 [with obj.] fasten or tether with a rope: *he returned to where he had hitched his horse.* ■ harness (a draft animal or team): *Thomas* **hitched** *the pony* **to** *his cart.*
▶ **n. 1** a temporary interruption or problem: *everything went without a hitch.*
2 a knot used for fastening a rope to another rope or something else. ■ a device for attaching one thing to another, esp. the tow bar of a motor vehicle: *a trailer hitch.*
3 informal an act of hitchhiking.
4 informal a period of service: *his 12-year hitch in the navy.*
– PHRASES **get hitched** informal marry. **hitch one's wagon to a star** try to succeed by forming a relationship with someone who is already successful.
– ORIGIN Middle English (in the sense 'lift up with a jerk'): of unknown origin.

Hitch·cock /ˈhiCH,käk/, Sir Alfred (Joseph) (1899–1980), English movie director. Acclaimed in Britain for movies such as *The Thirty-Nine Steps* (1935), he moved to Hollywood in 1939. Among his later works, notable for their suspense and their technical ingenuity, are the thrillers *Strangers on a Train* (1951), *Psycho* (1960), and *The Birds* (1963).

Alfred Hitchcock

hitch·er /ˈhiCHər/ ▶ **n.** a hitchhiker.

hitch·hike /ˈhiCH,hīk/ ▶ **v.** [no obj.] travel by getting free rides in passing vehicles: *he dropped out in 1976 and hitchhiked west.*
▶ **n.** a journey made by hitchhiking.
– DERIVATIVES **hitch·hik·er** n.

hi-tech /ˌhīˈtek/ ▶ **adj.** variant spelling of HIGH-TECH.

hith·er /ˈhiT͟Hər/ ▶ **adv.** archaic or literary to or toward this place: *I little knew then that such calamity would summon me hither!*
▶ **adj.** archaic situated on this side: *on the hither side of the service road.*
– ORIGIN Old English *hider*, of Germanic origin; related to HE and HERE.

hith·er and thith·er (also **hither and yon**) ▶ **adv.** in various directions, esp. in a disorganized way: *the entire household ran hither and thither.*

hith·er·to /ˈhiT͟Hər,to͞o, ˌhiT͟Hərˈto͞o/ ▶ **adv.** until now or until the point in time under discussion: *there is a need to replace what has hitherto been a haphazard method of payment.*

hith·er·ward /ˈhiT͟Hərwərd/ ▶ **adv.** archaic to or toward this place.

Hit·ler /ˈhitlər/, Adolf (1889–1945), German leader, born in Austria; chancellor of Germany 1933–45. He cofounded the National Socialist German Workers' (Nazi) Party in 1919 and came to prominence through his powers of oratory. He wrote *Mein Kampf* (1925), an exposition of his political ideas, while in prison. He established the totalitarian Third Reich in 1933. His expansionist foreign policy precipitated World War II, while his fanatical anti-Semitism led to the Holocaust. ■ (as noun **a Hitler**) a person with authoritarian or tyrannical characteristics: *little Hitlers in the classroom.*
– DERIVATIVES **Hit·ler·i·an** /hitˈle(ə)rēən/ **adj.**, **Hit·ler·ite** /-ˌrīt/ **n. & adj.**

Hit·ler·ism /ˈhitləˌrizəm/ ▶ **n.** the political principles or policy of the Nazi Party in Germany 1933–45.
– ORIGIN named after Adolf HITLER.

Hit·ler mus·tache ▶ **n.** a small square mustache like that worn by Adolf Hitler.

Hit·ler sa·lute ▶ **n.** another term for NAZI SALUTE.

hit list ▶ **n.** a list of people to be killed for criminal or political reasons: *her lover may be on the killer's hit list.* fig. *one of a dozen "corporate welfare" schemes on a Washington hit list.*

hit·mak·er /ˈhitmākər/ ▶ **n.** informal a successful singer or producer of popular music.

hit·man /ˈhitˌman/ ▶ **n.** informal a person who is paid to kill someone, esp. for a criminal or political organization.

hit pa·rade ▶ **n.** dated a weekly listing of the current bestselling pop records.

hit squad ▶ **n.** a team of assassins.

Hitt. ▶ **abbr.** Hittite.

Hit·tite /ˈhitīt/ ▶ **n. 1** a member of an ancient people who established an empire in Asia Minor and Syria that flourished from *c.*1700 to *c.*1200 BC. ■ a subject of this empire or one of their descendants, including the members of a Canaanite or Syrian people mentioned in the Bible (11th to 8th century BC).
2 the Anatolian language of the Hittites, the earliest attested Indo-European language. Written in both hieroglyphic and cuneiform scripts, it was deciphered in the early 20th century.
▶ **adj.** of or relating to the Hittites, their empire, or their language.
– ORIGIN from Hebrew *Ḥittīm*, ultimately from Hittite *Ḫatti*.

HIV ▶ **abbr.** human immunodeficiency virus, a retrovirus that causes AIDS.

hive /hīv/ ▶ **n. 1** a beehive. ■ the bees in a hive. ■ a thing that has the domed shape of a beehive.
2 a place in which people are busily occupied: *the kitchen became* **a hive of activity**.
▶ **v.** [with obj.] place (bees) in a hive. ■ [no obj.] (of bees) enter a hive.
– PHRASAL VERBS **hive something off** chiefly Brit. (esp. in business) separate something from a larger group or organization, esp. from public to private ownership: *the weekly magazine hived off by the BBC.*
– ORIGIN Old English *hȳf*, of Germanic origin.

hive bee ▶ **n.** another term for HONEYBEE.

hives /hīvz/ ▶ **plural n.** [treated as sing. or pl.] another term for URTICARIA.
– ORIGIN early 16th cent. (originally Scots, denoting various conditions causing a rash, esp. in children): of unknown origin.

HIV-pos·i·tive ▶ **adj.** having had a positive result in a blood test for the AIDS virus HIV.

hiya /ˈhīə/ ▶ **exclam.** an informal greeting.
– ORIGIN 1940s: alteration of *how are you?*

Hiz·bul·lah variant spelling of HEZBOLLAH.

HK ▶ **abbr.** Hong Kong.

HL ▶ **abbr.** (in the UK) House of Lords.

hl ▶ **abbr.** hectoliter(s).

hld. ▶ **abbr.** hold.

hlqn ▶ **abbr.** harlequin.

HM ▶ **abbr.** ■ headmaster or headmistress. ■ (in the UK) Her (or His) Majesty('s): *HM Forces.*

hm ▶ **abbr.** hectometer(s).

hmm /(h)m/ (also **h'm**) ▶ **exclam. & n.** variant spelling of HEM[2], HUM[2].

HMO ▶ **abbr.** health maintenance organization.

Hmong /hmôNG/ ▶ **n.** (pl. **same**) **1** a member of a people living traditionally in isolated mountain villages throughout Southeast Asia. Large numbers have emigrated to the US. Also called MIAO.
2 the language of this people, occurring in a large number of highly distinct dialects.
▶ **adj.** relating to or denoting this people or their language.

HMS ▶ **abbr.** Her or His Majesty's Ship, used in the names of ships in the British navy: *HMS Ark Royal.*

HN ▶ **abbr.** head nurse.

hny ▶ **abbr.** honey.

Ho ▶ **symbol** the chemical element holmium.

ho[1] /hō/ (also **hoe**) ▶ **n.** (pl. **hos** or **hoes**) informal a prostitute. ■ derogatory a woman.
– ORIGIN 1960s: representing a dialect pronunciation of WHORE.

ho[2] /hō/ ▶ **exclam. 1** an expression of surprise, admiration, triumph, or derision: *Ho! I'll show you.* ■ [in combination] used as the second element of various exclamations: *what ho! | heave ho.*
2 used to call for attention: *ho there!* ■ [in combination] dated, chiefly Nautical used to draw attention to something seen: *land ho!*
– ORIGIN natural exclamation: first recorded in Middle English.

ho. ▶ **abbr.** house.

hoa·gie /ˈhōgē/ ▶ **n.** (also **hoagy**) (pl. **hoagies**) another term for SUBMARINE SANDWICH.
– ORIGIN of unknown origin.

Hoag·land /ˈhōglənd/, Edward (Morley) (1932–), US writer. His novels include *Seven Rivers West* (1986). He also wrote short stories such as those collected in *The Final Fate of Alligators* (1992) and travel books, which include *African Calliope* (1979).

hoar /hôr/ archaic literary ▶ **adj.** grayish white; gray or gray-haired with age.
▶ **n.** hoarfrost.
– ORIGIN Old English *hār*, of Germanic origin; related to German *hehr* 'majestic, noble.'

hoard /hôrd/ ▶ **n.** a stock or store of money or valued objects, typically one that is secret or carefully guarded: *he came back to rescue* **his little hoard of gold.** ■ an ancient store of coins or other valuable artifacts: *a hoard of Romano-British*

h

bronzes. ■ an amassed store of useful information or facts, retained for future use: *a **hoard** of secret information about his work.*
▶ **v.** [with obj.] amass (money or valued objects) and hide or store away: *thousands of antiques hoarded by a compulsive collector | many of the boat people had hoarded rations.* ■ reserve in the mind for future use: (as adj. **hoarded**) *a year's worth of hoarded resentments and grudges.*
– ORIGIN Old English *hord* (noun), *hordian* (verb), of Germanic origin; related to German *Hort* (noun), *horten* (verb).

USAGE The words **hoard** and **horde** have some similarities in meaning and are pronounced the same, so it is unsurprising that they are sometimes confused. A **hoard** is 'a secret stock or store of something,' as in *a **hoard** of treasure*, while a **horde** is a disparaging word for 'a large group of people,' as in *hordes of fans descended on the stage*. Instances of **hoard** being used instead of **horde** are not uncommon: around a quarter of citations for **hoard** in the Oxford English Corpus are for the incorrect use.

hoard·er /hôrdər/ ▶ **n.** a person who hoards things: *I'm a bit of a hoarder.*

hoard·ing /'hôrdiNG/ ▶ **n.** Brit. a large board in a public place, used to display advertisements; a billboard. ■ a temporary board fence erected around a building site.
– ORIGIN early 19th cent.: from obsolete *hoard* in the same sense (probably based on Old French *hourd*; related to HURDLE) + -ING[1].

hoar·frost /'hôr,frôst, -,fräst/ ▶ **n.** a grayish-white crystalline deposit of frozen water vapor formed in clear still weather on vegetation, fences, etc.

hoar·hound /'hôr',hound/ ▶ **n.** variant spelling of HOREHOUND.

hoarse /hôrs/ ▶ **adj.** (of a person's voice) sounding rough and harsh, typically as the result of a sore throat or of shouting: *a hoarse whisper* | [as complement] *he shouted himself hoarse.*
– DERIVATIVES **hoarse·ly** adv., **hoars·en** /'hôrsən/ v., **hoarse·ness** n.
– ORIGIN Old English *hās*, of Germanic origin; related to Dutch *hees*. The spelling with *r* was influenced in Middle English by an Old Norse cognate.

hoar·y /'hôrē/ ▶ **adj.** (**hoarier, hoariest**) **1** grayish white: *hoary cobwebs.* ■ (of a person) having gray or white hair; aged: *a hoary old fellow with a face of white stubble.* ■ [attrib.] used in names of animals and plants covered with whitish fur or short hairs, e.g., **hoary bat, hoary cress**.
2 old and trite: *that hoary American notion that bigger is better.*
– DERIVATIVES **hoar·i·ly** /'hôrəlē/ adv., **hoar·i·ness** n.

hoar·y mar·mot /'hôrē 'märmət/ ▶ **n.** a large stocky grayish-brown marmot with a whistling call, found in the mountains of northwestern North America. ● *Marmota caligata*, family Sciuridae.

ho·at·zin /wät'sēn/ ▶ **n.** a large tree-dwelling tropical American bird with weak flight. Young hoatzins have hooked claws on their wings, enabling them to climb around among the branches. ● *Opisthocomus hoazin*, the only member of the family Opisthocomidae (order Galliformes or Cuculiformes).
– ORIGIN mid 17th cent.: from American Spanish, from Nahuatl *uatzin*, probably imitative of its call.

hoax /hōks/ ▶ **n.** a humorous or malicious deception: *they recognized the plan as a hoax* | [as modifier] *he was accused of making hoax calls.*
▶ **v.** [with obj.] deceive with a hoax.
– ORIGIN late 18th cent. (as a verb): probably a contraction of HOCUS.

hoax·er /hōksər/ ▶ **n.** a person who tricks or deceives someone by means of a hoax: *improving the tracing of calls has deterred many hoaxers.*

hob[1] /häb/ ▶ **n. 1** a flat metal shelf at the side or back of a fireplace, having its surface level with the top of the grate and used esp. for heating pans.
2 a machine tool used for cutting gears or screw threads.
– ORIGIN late 16th cent.: alteration of HUB. Sense 1, 'metal shelf by a fireplace,' dates from the late 17th cent.

hob[2] ▶ **n. 1** a male ferret. Compare with GILL[4] (sense 2).
2 archaic or dialect a sprite or hobgoblin.
– PHRASES **play** (or **raise**) **hob** cause mischief.
– ORIGIN late Middle English (in the sense 'country fellow'): nickname for *Rob*, short for *Robin* or *Robert*, often referring specifically to ROBIN GOODFELLOW.

Ho·ban /'hōbən/, James (1762–1831), US architect; born in Ireland. He designed the White House in Washington, DC 1793–1801 and, after it was burned in the War of 1812, supervised its restoration and redesign 1815–29.

Ho·bart /'hō,bärt/ the capital and chief port of Tasmania, on the southeastern part of the island; pop. 209,287 (2008).

Hobbes /häbz/, Thomas (1588–1679), English philosopher. He believed that human action was motivated entirely by selfish concerns, notably fear of death. He is best known for his treatise *Leviathan, or the Matter, Form, and Power of a Commonwealth, Ecclesiastical and Civil* (1651).
– DERIVATIVES **Hobbes·i·an** /'häbzēən/ adj.

hob·bit /'häbit/ ▶ **n.** a member of an imaginary race similar to humans, of small size and with hairy feet, in stories by J. R. R. Tolkien.
– ORIGIN 1937: invented by Tolkien in his book *The Hobbit*, and said by him to mean 'hole-dweller.'

hob·ble /'häbəl/ ▶ **v. 1** [no obj.] walk in an awkward way, typically because of pain from an injury: *he was hobbling around on crutches.*
2 [with obj.] tie or strap together (the legs of a horse or other animal) to prevent it from straying. [variant of HOPPLE.] ■ cause (a person or animal) to limp: *Johnson was still hobbled slightly by an ankle injury.* ■ restrict the activity or development of: *cotton farmers hobbled by low prices.*
▶ **n. 1** [in sing.] an awkward way of walking, typically due to pain from an injury: *he finished the game almost reduced to a hobble.*
2 a rope or strap used for hobbling a horse or other animal.
– DERIVATIVES **hob·bler** /'häb(ə)lər/ n.
– ORIGIN Middle English: probably of Dutch or Low German origin and related to Dutch *hobbelen* 'rock from side to side.'

hob·ble·bush /'häbəl,bo͝osH/ ▶ **n.** a North American viburnum that bears clusters of white or pink flowers and purple-black berries. ● *Viburnum alnifolium*, family Caprifoliaceae.

hob·ble·de·hoy /'häbəldē,hoi/ informal, dated ▶ **n.** a clumsy or awkward youth.
▶ **adj.** awkward or clumsy: *his hobbledehoy hands.*
– ORIGIN mid 16th cent.: of unknown origin.

hob·ble skirt ▶ **n.** a style of skirt so narrow at the hem as to impede walking, popular in the 1910s.

hob·by[1] /'häbē/ ▶ **n.** (pl. **hobbies**) **1** an activity done regularly in one's leisure time for pleasure: *her hobbies are reading and gardening.*
2 archaic a small horse or pony. ■ historical an early type of velocipede.
– ORIGIN late Middle English *hobyn, hoby*, from nicknames for the given name *Robin*. Originally sense 2 (compare with DOBBIN), it later came to denote a toy horse or hobbyhorse, hence 'a pastime, something done for pleasure.'

hob·by[2] ▶ **n.** (pl. **hobbies**) a migratory Old World falcon with long narrow wings, catching dragonflies and birds on the wing. ● Genus *Falco*, family Falconidae: four species, e.g., the (**northern**) **hobby** (*F. subbuteo*) of Eurasia.
– ORIGIN late Middle English: from Old French *hobet*, diminutive of *hobe* 'falcon.'

hob·by farm ▶ **n.** a small farm operated for pleasure or supplemental income rather than for primary income.
– DERIVATIVES **hob·by farm·er** n.

hob·by·horse /'häbē,hôrs/ ▶ **n. 1** a child's toy consisting of a stick with a model of a horse's head at one end. ■ a rocking horse. ■ a model of a horse or a horse's head, typically of wicker, used in morris dancing or pantomime.
2 a preoccupation; a favorite topic: *one of her favorite hobbyhorses was about how people had to care for "the child inside."*

hob·by·ist /'häbēist/ ▶ **n.** a person who pursues a particular hobby: *a computer hobbyist.*

hob·gob·lin /'häb,gäblən/ ▶ **n.** (in mythology and fairy tales) a mischievous imp or sprite. ■ a fearsome mythical creature.
– ORIGIN mid 16th cent.: from HOB[2] + GOBLIN.

hob·nail /'häb,nāl/ ▶ **n.** a short heavy-headed nail used to reinforce the soles of boots. ■ a blunt projection, esp. in cut or molded glassware. ■ glass decorated with such projections.
– DERIVATIVES **hob·nailed** adj.
– ORIGIN late 16th cent.: from HOB[1] + NAIL.

hob·nail liv·er (also **hobnailed liver**) ▶ **n.** a liver having many small knobby projections due to cirrhosis.

hob·nob /'häb,näb/ ▶ **v.** (**hobnobs, hobnobbing, hobnobbed**) [no obj.] informal mix socially, esp. with those of higher social status: *a select few who **hobnob** with the biggest celebrities the country has to offer.*
– ORIGIN early 19th cent. (in the sense 'drink together'): from archaic *hob or nob, hob and nob*, probably meaning 'give and take,' used by two people drinking to each other's health, from dialect *hab nab* 'have or not have.'

ho·bo /'hō,bō/ ▶ **n.** (pl. **hoboes** or **hobos**) a homeless person; a tramp or vagrant. ■ a migrant worker.
– ORIGIN late 19th cent.: of unknown origin.

Ho·bo·ken /'hō,bōkən/ an industrial city in northeastern New Jersey, on the Hudson River, opposite New York City; pop. 40,577 (est. 2008).

Hob·son's choice /'häbsənz/ ▶ **n.** a choice of taking what is available or nothing at all.
– ORIGIN mid 17th cent.: named after Thomas *Hobson* (1554–1631), a livery stable owner in Cambridge, England, who gave the customer the "choice" of the horse nearest the door or none at all.

Ho Chi Minh /'hō 'CHē 'min/ (1890–1969), Vietnamese communist statesman; president of North Vietnam 1954–69; born *Nguyen That Thanh*. He led the Vietminh against the Japanese during World War II, fought the French until they were defeated in 1954 and Vietnam was divided into North and South Vietnam, and deployed his forces in the guerrilla struggle that became the Vietnam War.

Ho Chi Minh

Ho Chi Minh Cit·y a city and port on the southern coast of Vietnam; pop. 5,929,500 (est. 2009). As Saigon, it was the capital of the French colony established in Vietnam in the 19th century and became the capital of South Vietnam in the partition of 1954. The name was changed to Ho Chi Minh City in 1975.

Ho Chi Minh Trail a covert system of trails along Vietnam's western frontier, a major supply route for North Vietnamese forces during the Vietnam War.

hock[1] /häk/ ▶ **n. 1** the joint in a quadruped's hind leg between the knee and the fetlock, the angle of which points backward.
2 a knuckle of meat, esp. of pork or ham.
– ORIGIN late Middle English.

hock[2] ▶ **v.** [with obj.] informal term for PAWN[2].
– PHRASES **in hock** having been pawned. ■ in debt: *the company is in hock to the banks.*
– ORIGIN mid 19th cent. (in the phrase *in hock*): from Dutch *hok* 'hutch, prison, debt.'

hock[3] ▶ **n.** Brit. a dry white wine from the German Rhineland.
– ORIGIN abbreviation of obsolete *hockamore*, alteration of German *Hochheimer* (*Wein*) '(wine) from Hochheim.'

hock·et /'häkit/ ▶ **n.** Music a spasmodic or interrupted effect in medieval and contemporary music, produced by dividing a melody between two parts, notes in one part coinciding with rests in the other.
– DERIVATIVES **hock·et·ing** n.
– ORIGIN late 18th cent.: from French *hoquet* 'hiccup'; in Old French the sense was 'hitch, sudden interruption,' which also existed in Middle English.

hock·ey /'häkē/ ▶ **n. 1** short for ICE HOCKEY.
2 short for FIELD HOCKEY.
– ORIGIN early 16th cent.: of unknown origin.

hock·ey mom ▶ **n.** informal a mother who devotes a great deal of time and effort to supporting her children's participation in ice hockey.

Hock·ney /'häknē/, David (1937–), English painter. He is best known for his California work of the mid 1960s, which depicts flat, almost shadowless architecture, lawns, and swimming pools.

ho·cus /'hōkəs/ ▶ **v.** (**hocuses, hocusing, hocused** or Brit. **hocusses, hocussing, hocussed**) [with obj.] archaic deceive (someone): *these people have been hocussed and cheated by the government.*
– ORIGIN late 17th cent.: from an obsolete noun *hocus* 'trickery,' from HOCUS-POCUS.

ho·cus-po·cus /,hōkəs 'pōkəs/ ▶ **n.** meaningless talk or activity, often designed to draw attention

away from and disguise what is actually happening: *some people still view psychology as a lot of hocus-pocus.* ■ a form of words often used by a person performing magic tricks. ■ deception; trickery.
– ORIGIN early 17th cent.: from *hax pax max Deus adimax*, a pseudo-Latin phrase used as a magic formula by conjurors.

hod /häd/ ▶ **n.** a builder's V-shaped open trough on a pole, used for carrying bricks and other building materials. ■ a coal scuttle.
– ORIGIN late 16th cent.: variant of northern English dialect *hot* 'a basket for carrying earth,' from Old French *hotte* 'pannier,' probably of Germanic origin.

hod·den /'hädn/ ▶ **n.** chiefly Scottish & N. English a coarse woolen cloth.
– ORIGIN late 16th cent.: of unknown origin.

Ho·dei·da /hō'dādə/ the chief port of Yemen, on the Red Sea; pop. 410,000 (est. 2004). Arabic name **AL-HUDAYDA**.

hodge·podge /'häj,päj/ (Brit. **hotchpotch**) ▶ **n.** [in sing.] a confused mixture: *Rob's living room was a hodgepodge of modern furniture and antiques.*
– ORIGIN late Middle English: alteration of **HOTCHPOTCH** by association with *Hodge* (a nickname for the given name *Roger*), an archaic British term used as a name for a typical agricultural worker.

Hodg·kin[1] /'häjkin/, Sir Alan Lloyd (1914–1998), English physiologist. With Andrew F. Huxley, he demonstrated the role of sodium and potassium ions in the transmission of nerve impulses between cells. Nobel Prize for Physiology or Medicine (1963), shared with John C. Eccles and Huxley.

Hodg·kin[2], Dorothy (Crowfoot) (1910–94), British chemist. She developed Sir Lawrence Bragg's X-ray diffraction technique for investigating the structure of crystals and applied it to complex organic compounds. She determined the structures of penicillin, vitamin B_{12}, and insulin. Nobel Prize for Chemistry (1964).

Hodg·kin's dis·ease /'häjkinz/ ▶ **n.** a malignant but often curable disease of lymphatic tissues typically causing painless enlargement of the lymph nodes, liver, and spleen.
– ORIGIN mid 19th cent.: named after Thomas *Hodgkin* (1798–1866), the English physician who first described it.

ho·di·er·nal /,hōdē'ərnl, ,hädē-/ ▶ **adj.** rare of or relating to the present day.
– ORIGIN mid 17th cent.: from Latin *hodiernus* (from *hodie* 'today') + **-AL**.

hod·o·graph /'hädə,graf/ ▶ **n.** Mathematics a curve, the radius vector of which represents in magnitude and direction the velocity of a moving object.
– ORIGIN mid 19th cent.: from Greek *hodos* 'way' + **-GRAPH**.

ho·do·scope /'hädə,skōp/ ▶ **n.** Physics an instrument for observing the paths of subatomic particles, esp. those arising from cosmic rays.
– ORIGIN early 20th cent. (denoting a microscope for examination of light paths in crystals): from Greek *hodos* 'way' + **-SCOPE**. The current sense dates from the 1950s.

Hoe /hō/, Richard March (1812–86), US inventor and industrialist. In 1846, he developed a successful rotary press, which greatly increased the speed of printing.

hoe[1] /hō/ ▶ **n.** a long-handled gardening tool with a thin metal blade, used mainly for weeding and breaking up soil.
▶ **v.** (**hoes, hoeing, hoed**) [with obj.] use a hoe to dig (earth) or thin out or dig up (plants).
– DERIVATIVES **ho·er n.**
– ORIGIN Middle English: from Old French *houe*, of Germanic origin; related to German *Haue*, also to **HEW**.

hoe[2] ▶ **n.** variant spelling of **HO**[1].

hoe·cake /'hō,kāk/ ▶ **n.** a coarse cake made of cornmeal, originally baked on the blade of a hoe.

hoe·down /'hō,doun/ ▶ **n.** a social gathering at which lively folk dancing takes place. ■ a lively folk dance.

Ho·fei variant of **HEFEI**.

Hof·fa /'häfə/, Jimmy (1913–*c.*1975), US labor union leader; full name *James Riddle Hoffa*. President of the Teamsters from 1957, he was imprisoned 1967–71 for attempted bribery of a federal court judge, fraud, and looting pension funds. His sentence was commuted by President Nixon and he was given parole in 1971 on condition that he resign as president of the union. He disappeared in 1975 and is thought to have been murdered.

Hoff·mann /'häfmən/, E. T. A. (1776–1822), German novelist, short-story writer, and music critic; full name *Ernst Theodor Amadeus Hoffmann*. His extravagantly fantastic stories provided the inspiration for Offenbach's opera *Tales of Hoffmann* (1881).

Hof·mann /'hôfmän/, Hans (1880–1966), US artist; born in Germany. He was a leader in the style of abstract expressionism.

Hof·manns·thal /'hôfmən,stäl/, Hugo von (1874–1929), Austrian poet and playwright. He wrote the libretti for many of Richard Strauss's operas, including *Elektra* (1909) and *Der Rosenkavalier* (1911). With Strauss and Max Reinhardt, he helped found the Salzburg Festival.

hog /hôg, häg/ ▶ **n. 1** a domesticated pig, esp. one over 120 pounds (54 kg) and reared for slaughter. ■ a feral pig. ■ a wild animal of the pig family, for example, a warthog. ■ informal a greedy person.
2 informal a large, heavy motorcycle.
3 (also **hogg**) Brit. a young sheep before the first shearing.
▶ **v.** (**hogs, hogging, hogged**) **1** [with obj.] informal keep or use all of (something) for oneself in an unfair or selfish way: *he never hogged the limelight.*
2 (with reference to a ship) bend or become bent convex upward along its length as a result either of the hull being supported in the middle and not at the ends (as in a heavy sea) or the vessel's being loaded more heavily at the ends. Compare with **SAG**.
– PHRASES **go (the) whole hog** informal do something completely or thoroughly. [of several origins suggested, one interprets *hog* as a slang term for a ten-cent piece; another refers the idiom to one of Cowper's poems (1779), which discusses Muslim uncertainty about which parts of the pig are acceptable as food, leading to the 'whole hog' being eaten, because of confusion over Muhammad's teaching.] **live high on** (or **off**) **the hog** informal have a luxurious lifestyle.
– DERIVATIVES **hog·ger n., hog·ger·y** /'hôgərē, 'häg-/ **n., hog·gish adj., hog·gish·ly adv., hog·like** /-,lik/ **adj.**
– ORIGIN late Old English *hogg, hocg*, perhaps of Celtic origin and related to Welsh *hwch* and Cornish *hoch* 'pig, sow.'

Ho·gan /'hōgən/, Ben (1912–97), US golfer; full name *William Benjamin Hogan*. His numerous championship titles include the Masters (1951, 1953), the PGA (1946, 1948), the US Open (1948, 1950, 1951, 1953), and the British Open (1953).

ho·gan /'hō,gän, -gən/ ▶ **n.** a traditional Navajo hut of logs and earth.
– ORIGIN Navajo.

hogan

Ho·garth /'hō,gärTH/, William (1697–1764), English painter and engraver. Notable works include his series of engravings on "modern moral subjects," such as *A Rake's Progress* (1735).
– DERIVATIVES **Ho·garth·i·an** /hō'gärTHēən/ **adj.**

hog·back /'hôg,bak, 'häg-/ ▶ **n.** a long hill or mountain ridge with steep sides.

hog deer ▶ **n.** a short-legged heavily built deer having a yellow-brown coat with darker underparts, found in grasslands and paddy fields in Southeast Asia. ● *Cervus porcinus*, family Cervidae.

hog·fish /'hôg,fisн, 'häg-/ ▶ **n.** (pl. **same** or **hogfishes**) a colorful wrasse (fish) that occurs chiefly in the warm waters of the western Atlantic, often acting as a cleaner fish for other species. ● Several genera and species in the family Labridae, in particular the large edible *Lachnolaimus maximus*.

hogg /hôg, häg/ ▶ **n.** variant spelling of **HOG** (sense 3 of the noun).

Hog·gar Moun·tains /'hägər, ,hə'gär/ a mountain range in the Saharan desert in southern Algeria that rises to a height of 9,573 feet (2,918 m) at Tahat. Also called **AHAGGAR MOUNTAINS**.

hog heav·en ▶ **n.** a state of complete happiness: *Bryan stood on the pitcher's mound, knowing he was in hog heaven.*

hog line ▶ **n.** Curling a line marked across either end of a curling rink. No sweeping is allowed until a stone has crossed the first line.

Hog·ma·nay /'hägmə,nā/ ▶ **n.** (in Scotland) New Year's Eve, and the celebrations that take place at this time.
– ORIGIN early 17th cent.: perhaps from *hoguinané*, Norman French form of Old French *aguillanneuf* 'last day of the year, new year's gift.'

hog-nosed bat ▶ **n.** a tiny insectivorous bat with a piglike nose and no tail, native to Thailand. It is the smallest known bat. ● *Craseonycteris thonglongyai*, the only member of the family Craseonycteridae.

hog-nosed skunk ▶ **n.** an American skunk with a bare elongated snout and a black face, found in rugged terrain. ● Genus *Conepatus*, family Mustelidae: several species.

hog·nose snake /'hôg,nōz, 'häg-/ (also **hog-nosed snake**) ▶ **n.** a harmless burrowing American snake with an upturned snout. When threatened it inflates itself with air and hisses, and may feign death. Also called **PUFF ADDER** in North America. ● Genus *Heterodon*, family Colubridae: several species.

hog plum ▶ **n.** a tropical tree that bears edible plumlike fruit, in particular: ● a Caribbean tree (also called **YELLOW MOMBIN**) with yellow fruit (*Spondias mombin*, family Anacardiaceae). ● a tropical American tree (also called **TALLOWWOOD**) with bitter fruit and timber that is used as a sandalwood substitute (*Ximenia americana*, family Olacaceae).
– ORIGIN late 17th cent.: so named because the fruit is common food for hogs in the West Indies and Brazil.

hogs·head /'hôgz,hed, 'hägz-/ (abbr.: **hhd**) ▶ **n.** a large cask. ■ a measure of capacity for wine, equal to 63 gallons (238.7 liters). ■ a measure of capacity for beer, equal to 64 gallons (245.5 liters).
– ORIGIN Middle English: from **HOG** + **HEAD**; the reason for the term is unknown.

hog-tie (also **hogtie**) ▶ **v.** [with obj.] secure by fastening together the hands and feet (of a person) or all four feet (of an animal): *they gagged him and hog-tied him to the front pew.* ■ impede or hinder greatly: *you may be hog-tied by stringent local ordinances or agencies.*

hog·wash /'hôg,wôsн, 'häg,wäsн/ ▶ **n.** informal nonsense.
– ORIGIN mid 15th cent.: from **HOG** + **WASH**; the original sense was 'kitchen swill for pigs.'

hog·weed /'hôg,wēd, 'häg-/ ▶ **n.** a large, coarse, white-flowered weed of the parsley family, native to north temperate regions and formerly used as forage for pigs. ● Genus *Heracleum*, family Umbelliferae: several species, in particular the common European *H. sphondylium* and the introduced **giant hogweed** (*H. mantegazzianum*).

hog-wild ▶ **adj.** informal extremely enthusiastic; out of control: *I'm not hog-wild about this job.*
– PHRASES **go hog-wild** act in an unrestrained manner: *Congress will go hog-wild in its spending.*

Ho·hen·stau·fen /,hōən'stoufən, -'sнtou-/ a German dynastic family, some of whom ruled as Holy Roman Emperors between 1138 and 1254, among them Frederick I (Barbarossa).

Ho·hen·zol·lern /'hōən,zälərn/ a German dynastic family from which came the kings of Prussia from 1701 to 1918 and German emperors from 1871 to 1918.

Hoh·hot /'hə'hôt/ (also **Huhehot** /'hōō'hä'hôt/) the capital of Inner Mongolia autonomous region, in northeastern China; pop. 825,900 (est. 2006). Former name (until 1954) **KWEISUI**.

ho ho /'hō 'hō/ ▶ **exclam.** representing deep, exuberant laughter. ■ used to express triumph, esp. at discovery: *Ho ho! A stranger in our midst!*
– ORIGIN mid 16th cent.: reduplication of **HO**[2].

ho-hum /,hō'həm/ ▶ **exclam.** used to express boredom or resignation.
▶ **adj.** boring: *a ho-hum script.*
– ORIGIN 1920s: imitative of a yawn.

hoick /hoik/ informal ▶ **v.** [with obj.] lift or pull abruptly or with effort: *she hoicked her bag on to the desk.*
▶ **n.** an abrupt pull.
– ORIGIN late 19th cent.: perhaps a variant of **HIKE**.

hoicks /hoiks/ ▶ **exclam.** variant of **YOICKS**.

hoi pol·loi /'hoi pə,loi/ ▶ **plural n.** (usu. **the hoi polloi**) derogatory the masses; the common people: *avoid mixing with the hoi polloi.*
– ORIGIN mid 17th cent.: Greek, literally 'the many.'

USAGE 1 Hoi is the Greek word for **the**, and the phrase **hoi polloi** means 'the many.' This has led some traditionalists to insist that **hoi polloi** should not be used in English with **the**, since that would be to state the word **the** twice. But, once

h

established in English, expressions such as **hoi polloi** are typically treated as fixed units and are subject to the rules and conventions of English. Evidence shows that use with **the** has now become an accepted part of standard English usage: *they kept to themselves, away from the hoi polloi* (rather than . . . *away from hoi polloi*). **2 Hoi polloi** is sometimes used incorrectly to mean 'upper class'—that is, the exact opposite of its normal meaning. It seems likely that the confusion arose by association with the similar-sounding but otherwise unrelated word **hoity-toity**.

hoi·sin /'hoisin, hoi'sin/ (also **hoisin sauce**) ▶ **n.** a sweet, spicy, dark red sauce made from soybeans, vinegar, sugar, garlic, and various spices, widely used in southern Chinese cooking.

hoist /hoist/ ▶ **v.** [with obj.] raise (something) by means of ropes and pulleys: *high overhead great cranes hoisted girders.* ■ raise or haul up: *she hoisted her backpack onto her shoulder.*
▶ **n. 1** an act of raising or lifting something. ■ an act of increasing something: *the government's interest rate hoist.* ■ an apparatus for lifting or raising something.
2 the part of a flag nearest the staff; the vertical dimension of a flag.
3 a group of flags raised as a signal.
– PHRASES **hoist one's flag** (of an admiral) take up command. **hoist the flag** stake one's claim to discovered territory by displaying a flag. **hoist by one's own petard** see PETARD.
– DERIVATIVES **hoist·er n.**
– ORIGIN late 15th cent.: alteration of dialect *hoise*, probably from Dutch *hijsen* or Low German *hiesen*, but recorded earlier.

hoi·ty-toi·ty /ˌhoitē 'toitē/ ▶ **adj. 1** haughty; snobbish: *the moneyed, hoity-toity inhabitants of the island.*
2 archaic frolicsome.
– ORIGIN mid 17th cent. (in the sense 'boisterous or silly behavior'): from obsolete *hoit* 'indulge in riotous mirth,' of unknown origin.

Ho·kan /'hōkən/ ▶ **adj.** relating to or denoting a group of American Indian languages of California and western Mexico, considered as a possible language family and including Yuman, Mojave, and several other languages now extinct or nearly so.
▶ **n.** this hypothetical language family.
– ORIGIN from Hokan *hok* 'about two' + -AN.

hoke /hōk/ ▶ **v.** [with obj.] informal (of an actor) act (a part) in an insincere, sentimental, or melodramatic manner: *just try it straight—don't hoke it up.*
– ORIGIN early 20th cent.: back-formation from HOKUM.

hok·ey /'hōkē/ ▶ **adj.** (**hokier, hokiest**) informal mawkishly sentimental: *a good-hearted, slightly hokey song.* ■ noticeably contrived: *a hokey country-western accent.*
– DERIVATIVES **hok·ey·ness** (also **hokiness**) **n.**
– ORIGIN 1940s: from HOKUM + -Y[1].

ho·key-po·key ▶ **n.** informal **1** (**the hokey-pokey**) a circle dance with a synchronized shaking of the limbs in turn, accompanied by a simple song.
2 hocus-pocus; trickery.
3 dated ice cream sold on the street, esp. by Italian street vendors.
– ORIGIN late 19th cent.: of unknown origin.

Hok·kai·do /hä'kīdō/ the most northern of the four main islands of Japan; pop. 5,570,000 (2007); capital, Sapporo.

hok·ku /'hôˌko͞o, 'hä-/ ▶ **n.** (pl. **same**) another term for HAIKU.
– ORIGIN late 19th cent.: Japanese, literally 'opening verse' (of a linked sequence of comic verses).

ho·kum /'hōkəm/ ▶ **n.** informal nonsense: *they dismissed such corporate homilies as boardroom hokum.* ■ trite, sentimental, or unrealistic situations and dialogue in a movie, play, or piece of writing: *classic B-movie hokum.*
– ORIGIN early 20th cent.: of unknown origin.

Ho·ku·sai /'hōkəˌsī/, Katsushika (1760–1849), Japanese painter and wood engraver. He represented aspects of everyday Japanese life in his woodcuts.

Hol·arc·tic /häl'ärktik, hō'lärk-, -'ärtik/ ▶ **adj.** Zoology of, relating to, or denoting a zoogeographical region comprising the Nearctic and Palearctic regions combined. The two continents have been linked intermittently by the Bering land bridge, and the faunas are closely related. ■ (as noun **the Holarctic**) the Holarctic region.
– ORIGIN late 19th cent.: from HOLO- 'whole' + ARCTIC.

Hol·bein /'hōlˌbīn/, Hans (1497–1543), German painter and engraver; known as **Holbein the Younger**. He was commissioned by Henry VIII to supply portraits of the king's prospective brides.

hold[1] /hōld/ ▶ **v.** (past and past participle **held** /held/)
1 [with obj.] grasp, carry, or support with one's arms or hands: *she was holding a brown leather suitcase* | [no obj.] *he* **held onto** *the back of a chair.* ■ keep or sustain in a specified position: *I held the door open for him.* ■ embrace (someone): *Mark pulled her into his arms and held her close.* ■ be able to bear (the weight of a person or thing): *I reached up to the nearest branch that seemed likely to hold my weight.* ■ (of a vehicle) maintain close contact with (the road), esp. when driven at speed: *the car holds the corners very well.* ■ (of a ship or an aircraft) continue to follow (a particular course): *the ship is holding a southeasterly course.* ■ [no obj.] archaic keep going in a particular direction: *he* **held on his way**, *close behind his friend.*
2 [with obj.] keep or detain (someone): *the police were holding him on a murder charge* | [with obj. and complement] *she was held prisoner for two days.* ■ keep possession of (something), typically in the face of a challenge or attack: *the rebels held the town for many weeks* | [no obj.] *White managed to* **hold onto** *his lead.* ■ keep (someone's interest or attention). ■ (of a singer or musician) sustain (a note). ■ stay or cause to stay at a certain value or level: [no obj.] *the savings rate held at 5%* | [with obj.] *he is determined to hold down inflation.*
3 [no obj.] remain secure, intact, or in position without breaking or giving way: *the boat's anchor would not hold.* ■ (of a favorable condition or situation) continue without changing: *let's hope her luck holds.* ■ be or remain valid or available: *I'll have that coffee now, if the offer still holds.* ■ (of an argument or theory) be logical, consistent, or convincing: *their views still seem to* **hold up** *extremely well.* ■ (**hold to**) refuse to abandon or change (a principle or opinion). ■ [with obj.] (**hold someone to**) cause someone to adhere to (a commitment).
4 [with obj.] contain or be capable of containing (a specified amount): *the tank held twenty-four gallons.* ■ be able to drink (a reasonable amount of alcohol) without becoming drunk or suffering any ill effects: *I can hold my liquor as well as anyone.* ■ have or be characterized by: *I don't know what the future holds.*
5 [with obj.] have in one's possession: *the managing director still holds fifty shares in the company.* ■ [no obj.] informal be in possession of illegal drugs: *he was holding, and the police hauled him off to jail.* ■ have or occupy (a job or position). ■ have or adhere to (a belief or opinion): *I feel nothing but pity for someone who holds such chauvinistic views* | [with clause] *they hold that all literature is empty of meaning.* ■ [with obj. and complement] consider (someone) to be responsible or liable for a particular situation: *you can't hold yourself responsible for what happened.* ■ (**hold someone/something in**) regard someone or something with (a specified feeling): *the speed limit is held in contempt by many drivers.* ■ [with clause] (of a judge or court) rule; decide: *the Court of Appeals held that there was no evidence to support the judge's assessment.*
6 [with obj.] keep or reserve for someone: *a reservation can be held for twenty-four hours.* ■ prevent from going ahead or occurring: *hold your fire!* ■ maintain (a telephone connection) until the person one has telephoned is free to speak: *please hold, and I'll see if he's available* | [no obj.] *will you hold?* ■ informal refrain from adding or using (something, typically an item of food or drink): *a strawberry margarita, but hold the tequila.* ■ (**hold it**) informal used as a way of exhorting someone to wait or to stop doing something: *hold it right there, pal!* ■ [no obj.] archaic restrain oneself.
7 [with obj.] arrange and take part in (a meeting or conversation): *a meeting was held at the church.*
▶ **n. 1** an act or manner of grasping something; a grip: *he* **caught hold of** *her arm* | *he lost his hold and fell.* ■ a particular way of grasping or restraining someone, esp. an opponent in wrestling or judo. ■ a place where one can grip with one's hands or feet while climbing: *he felt carefully with his feet for a hold and swung himself up.* ■ a way of influencing someone: *he discovered that Tom had some kind of* **hold over** *his father.* ■ a degree of power or control: *military forces tightened their* **hold on** *the capital.*
2 archaic a fortress.
– PHRASES **be left holding the bag** (or **baby**) informal be left with an unwelcome responsibility, typically without warning. **don't hold your breath** see BREATH. **get hold of** grasp (someone or something) physically. ■ grasp (something) intellectually; understand. ■ informal obtain: *if you can't get hold of ripe tomatoes, add some tomato purée.* ■ informal find or manage to contact (someone): *I'll try and get hold of Mark.* **hold someone/something at bay** see BAY[5]. **hold one's breath** see BREATH. **hold someone/something cheap** archaic have a low opinion of someone or something. **hold court** be the center of attention amid a crowd of one's admirers. **hold someone/something dear** care for or value someone or something greatly: *fidelity is something most of us hold dear.* **hold fast** remain tightly secured: *the door held fast, obviously locked.* ■ continue to believe in or adhere to an idea or principle: *it is important that we* **hold fast to** *the policies.* **hold the fort** take responsibility for a situation while another person is temporarily absent. **hold one's ground** see GROUND[1]. **hold someone's hand** give a person comfort, guidance, or moral support in a difficult situation. **hold hands** (of two or more people) clasp each other by the hand, typically as a sign of affection. **hold someone/something harmless** Law indemnify someone or something. **hold one's horses** [usu. as imperative] informal wait a moment. **hold the line** not yield to the pressure of a difficult situation: *France's central bank would hold the line.* **hold one's nose** squeeze one's nostrils with one's fingers in order to avoid inhaling an unpleasant smell. **hold one's own** see OWN. **hold one's peace** see PEACE. **hold (one's) serve** (or **service**) (in tennis and other racket sports) win a game in which one is serving. **hold the stage** see STAGE. **hold sway** see SWAY. **hold someone to bail** Law bind by bail. **hold one's tongue** [often in imperative] informal remain silent. **hold someone/something to ransom** see RANSOM. **hold true** (or **good**) remain true or valid: *his views still hold true today.* **hold up one's head** (or **hold one's head high**) see HEAD. **hold water** [often with negative] (of a statement, theory, or line of reasoning) appear to be valid, sound, or reasonable: *this argument just does not hold water.* **no holds barred** (in wrestling) with no restrictions on the kinds of holds that are used. ■ used to convey that no rules or restrictions apply in a conflict or dispute: *no-holds-barred military action.* **on hold** waiting to be connected while making a telephone call. ■ temporarily not being dealt with or pursued: *he* **put** *his career* **on hold**. **take hold** start to have an effect: *the reforms of the late nineteenth century had taken hold.* **there is no holding someone back** used to convey that someone is particularly determined or cannot be prevented from doing something: *there's no holding you back these days.*
– PHRASAL VERBS **hold something against** allow past actions or circumstances to have a negative influence on one's present attitude toward (someone): *he knew that if he failed her, she would hold it against him forever.* **hold back** hesitate to act or speak: *he held back, remembering the mistake he had made before.* **hold someone/something back** prevent or restrict the advance, progress, or development of someone or something: *Jane struggled to hold back her laughter.* ■ (**hold something back**) refuse or be unwilling to make something known: *you're not holding anything back from me, are you?* **hold someone down** keep someone under strict control or severely restrict their freedom: *the people are held down by a repressive military regime.* **hold something down** informal succeed in keeping a job or position for a period of time. **hold forth** talk lengthily, assertively, or tediously about a subject: *he was* **holding forth on** *the merits of the band's debut album.* **hold off** (of bad weather) fail to occur. ■ delay or postpone an action or decision. **hold someone/something off** resist an attacker or challenge: *he held off a late challenge by Vose to win by thirteen seconds.* **hold on 1** [often in imperative] wait; stop: *hold on a minute, I'll be right back!* **2** endure or keep going in difficult circumstances: *if only they could hold on a little longer.* **hold on to** keep: *the industry is trying to hold on to experienced staff.* **hold out** resist or survive in dangerous or difficult circumstances: *Russian troops* **held out against** *constant attacks.* ■ continue to be sufficient: *we can stay here for as long as our supplies hold out.* **hold out for** continue to demand (a particular thing), refusing to accept what has been offered: *he is holding out for a guaranteed 7 percent raise.* **hold out on** informal refuse to give something, typically information, to (someone). **hold something out** offer a chance or hope: *a new drug may hold out hope for patients with lung cancer.* **hold something over 1** postpone something. **2** use a fact or piece of information to threaten or intimidate (someone). **hold together** (or **hold something together**) remain or cause to remain united: *if your party holds together, you will probably win.* **hold up** remain strong or vigorous: *the dollar held up well against the yen.* **hold someone/something up 1** support and prevent something from falling: *concrete pillars hold up the elevated section of the railroad.* **2** display something by holding it above one's waist or head: *he held up the book so she could see the cover.* ■ present or expose someone or something as an example or for particular treatment: *they were* **held up to** *public ridicule.* **3** delay or block the movement or progress of someone or something: *our return flight was held up for seven hours.* **4** rob someone or something using the threat of force or violence: *a masked gunman held up the post office.* **5** Bridge refrain from playing a winning card for tactical reasons. **hold**

with [with negative] informal approve of: *I don't hold with fighting or violence.*
– DERIVATIVES **hold·a·ble** adj.
– ORIGIN Old English *haldan, healdan*, of Germanic origin; related to Dutch *houden* and German *halten*; the noun is partly from Old Norse *hald* 'hold, support, custody.'

hold[2] ▶ n. a large space in the lower part of a ship or aircraft in which cargo is stowed.
– ORIGIN late 16th cent.: from obsolete *holl*, from Old English *hol* (see HOLE). The addition of *-d* was due to association with HOLD[1].

hold·all /'hōld,ôl/ ▶ n. Brit. a large rectangular bag with handles and a shoulder strap, used for carrying clothes and other personal belongings.

hold·back /'hōl(d),bak/ ▶ n. a thing serving to hold something else in place: *a curtain holdback.* ■ a sum of money withheld under certain conditions.

hold but·ton ▶ n. a button on a telephone that temporarily interrupts a call so that another call may be taken.

hold·er /'hōldər/ ▶ n. **1** a device or implement for holding something: *a cigarette holder.*
2 a person who holds something: *US passport holders | holders of two American hostages.* ■ the possessor of a trophy, championship, or record: *the record holder in the 100-meter dash.*
3 Brit. a smallholder.

hold·fast /'hōl(d),fast/ ▶ n. a firm grip. ■ a staple or clamp securing an object to a wall or other surface. ■ Biology a stalked organ by which an alga or other simple aquatic plant or animal is attached to a substrate.

hold·ing /'hōldiNG/ ▶ n. **1** an area of land held by lease. ■ the tenure of such land.
2 (**holdings**) stocks, property, and other financial assets in someone's possession: *commercial property holdings.* ■ books, periodicals, magazines, and other material in a library.

hold·ing com·pa·ny ▶ n. a company created to buy and possess the shares of other companies, which it then controls.

hold·ing ground ▶ n. Nautical an area of seabed where an anchor will hold.

hold·ing pat·tern ▶ n. the flight path maintained by an aircraft awaiting permission to land.

hold·ing tank ▶ n. a large container in which liquids are temporarily held.

hold·out /'hōld,out/ ▶ n. an act of resisting something or refusing to accept what is offered: *a defiant holdout against a commercial culture.* ■ a person or organization acting in such a way.

hold·o·ver /'hōld,ōvər/ ▶ n. a person or thing surviving from an earlier time, esp. someone surviving in office or remaining on a sports team: *the conservative holdover from the Eisenhower years.*

hold·up /'hōld,əp/ ▶ n. **1** a situation that causes delay, esp. to a journey.
2 a robbery conducted with the use of threats or violence: *three dead in armored car holdup.*

hole /hōl/ ▶ n. **1** a hollow place in a solid body or surface: *he dug out a small hole in the snow.* ■ an animal's burrow. ■ an aperture passing through something: *he had a hole in his sock.* ■ a cavity or receptacle on a golf course, typically one of eighteen or nine, into which the ball must be hit. ■ a cavity of this type as representing a division of a golf course or of play in golf: *Stephen lost the first three holes to Eric.* ■ Physics a position from which an electron is absent, esp. one regarded as a mobile carrier of positive charge in a semiconductor. ■ [in place names] a valley: *Jackson Hole.*
2 informal a small or unpleasant place: *she had wasted a whole lifetime in this hole of a town.* ■ informal an awkward situation: *get yourself out of a hole.*
▶ v. [with obj.] **1** make a hole or holes in: *a fuel tank was holed by the attack and a fire started.*
2 Golf hit (the ball) so that it falls into a hole: *alternate shots from each partner until the ball is holed | [no obj.] he holed in one at the third.*
– PHRASES **blow a hole in** ruin the effectiveness of (something): *the amendment could blow a hole in the legislation.* **in the hole** informal in debt: *we're still three thousand dollars in the hole.* **in holes** worn so much that holes have formed: *my clothes are in holes.* **make a hole in** use a large amount of: *holidays can make a big hole in your savings.* **need something like a hole in the head** informal used to emphasize that someone has absolutely no need or desire for something. **a square peg in a round hole** see PEG.
– PHRASAL VERBS **hole out** Golf send the ball into a hole. **hole up** informal hide oneself: *I holed up for two days in a tiny cottage in Pennsylvania.*
– DERIVATIVES **hol·ey** /'hōlē/ adj.
– ORIGIN Old English *hol* (noun), *holian* (verb), of Germanic origin; related to Dutch *hol* (noun) 'cave,' (adjective) 'hollow,' and German *hohl* 'hollow,' from an Indo-European root meaning 'cover, conceal.'

hole-and-cor·ner ▶ adj. attempting to avoid public notice; secret: *a hole-and-corner wedding.*

hole card ▶ n. (in stud or other forms of poker) a card that has been dealt face down. ■ a thing that is kept secret until it can be used to one's own advantage.

hole in one ▶ n. (pl. **holes in one**) Golf a shot that enters the hole from the tee with no intervening shots.

hole in the heart ▶ n. Medicine a congenital defect in the heart septum, resulting in inadequate circulation of oxygenated blood (a cause of blue baby syndrome).

hole in the wall ▶ n. informal **1** a small dingy place, esp. a bar or restaurant: *even though the gallery was only a hole in the wall, I couldn't have afforded it* | [as modifier] *hole-in-the wall bars.*
2 Brit. an automatic cash dispenser installed in the outside wall of a bank.

hole punch ▶ n. a device or tool for punching holes in paper or other thin materials.

hole saw ▶ n. a tool for making circular holes, consisting of a metal cylinder with a toothed edge.

Ho·li /'hōlē/ ▶ n. a Hindu spring festival celebrated in February or March in honor of Krishna.
– ORIGIN via Hindi from Sanskrit *holī*.

Hol·i·day /'hälə,dā/, Billie (1915–59), US jazz singer; born *Eleanora Fagan*. She began her recording career with Benny Goodman's band in 1933 and then went on to perform with many small jazz groups. Her autobiography, *Lady Sings the Blues* (1956), was made into a movie in 1972.

hol·i·day /'häli,dā/ ▶ n. a day of festivity or recreation when no work is done: *December 25 is an official public holiday.* ■ [as modifier] characteristic of a holiday; festive: *a holiday atmosphere.* ■ chiefly Brit. (often **holidays**) a vacation: *I spent my summer holidays on a farm | Fred was **on holiday** in Spain.*
▶ v. [no obj.] chiefly Brit. spend a holiday in a specified place: *he is holidaying in Italy.*
– ORIGIN Old English *hāligdæg* 'holy day.'

hol·i·day camp ▶ n. Brit. a site for vacationers with accommodations, entertainment, and leisure facilities.

hol·i·day·mak·er /'hälidā,mākər/ ▶ n. Brit. a person on vacation away from home.

hol·i·day sea·son ▶ n. the period of time from Thanksgiving until New Year, including such festivals as Christmas, Hanukkah, and Kwanzaa.

ho·li·er-than-thou ▶ adj. characterized by an attitude of moral superiority: *they had quite a critical, holier-than-thou approach.*

ho·li·ness /'hōlēnis/ ▶ n. the state of being holy: *a life of holiness and total devotion to God.* ■ (**His/Your Holiness**) a title given to the pope, Orthodox patriarchs, and the Dalai Lama, or used in addressing them. ■ [as modifier] denoting a Christian renewal movement originating in the mid 19th century among Methodists in the US, emphasizing the Wesleyan doctrine of the sanctification of believers.
– ORIGIN Old English *hālignes* (see HOLY, -NESS).

ho·lism /'hōl,izəm/ ▶ n. chiefly Philosophy the theory that parts of a whole are in intimate interconnection, such that they cannot exist independently of the whole, or cannot be understood without reference to the whole, which is thus regarded as greater than the sum of its parts. Holism is often applied to mental states, language, and ecology. The opposite of ATOMISM. ■ Medicine the treating of the whole person, taking into account mental and social factors, rather than just the physical symptoms of a disease.
– DERIVATIVES **ho·list** adj. & n.
– ORIGIN 1920s: from HOLO- 'whole' + -ISM; coined by J. C. Smuts to designate the tendency in nature to produce organized "wholes" (bodies or organisms) from the ordered grouping of units.

ho·lis·tic /hō'listik/ ▶ adj. chiefly Philosophy characterized by comprehension of the parts of something as intimately interconnected and explicable only by reference to the whole. ■ Medicine characterized by the treatment of the whole person, taking into account mental and social factors, rather than just the physical symptoms of a disease.
– DERIVATIVES **ho·lis·ti·cal·ly** /-ik(ə)lē/ adv.

hol·la /'hälə/ ▶ exclam. archaic used to call attention to something: *"Holla! what storm is this?"*
– ORIGIN early 16th cent. (as an order to stop or cease): from French *holà*, from *ho* 'ho!' + *là* 'there.'

Hol·land /'hälənd/ **1** another name for the NETHERLANDS.
2 a city in southwestern Michigan, noted for its Dutch heritage; pop. 34,076 (est. 2008).

hol·land /'hälənd/ ▶ n. a kind of smooth, durable linen fabric, used chiefly for window shades and furniture covering.
– ORIGIN Middle English: from HOLLAND, the name of a former province of the Netherlands where the cloth was made, from Dutch, earlier *Holtlant* (from *holt* 'wood' + *-lant* 'land').

hol·lan·daise sauce /'hälən,dāz/ ▶ n. a creamy sauce of melted butter, egg yolks, and lemon juice or vinegar, served esp. with fish.
– ORIGIN French *hollandaise*, feminine of *hollandais* 'Dutch,' from *Hollande* 'Holland.'

Hol·land·er /'häləndər/ ▶ n. dated a native of the Netherlands.

Hol·lands /'häləndz/ ▶ n. archaic Dutch gin.
– ORIGIN from archaic Dutch *hollandsch genever* (earlier form of *hollands jenever*) 'Dutch gin.'

hol·ler /'hälər/ informal ▶ v. [no obj.] (of a person) give a loud shout or cry: *he hollers when he wants feeding* | [with direct speech] *"I can't get down," she hollered.*
▶ n. a loud cry or shout. ■ (also **field holler**) a melodic cry with abrupt or swooping changes of pitch, used originally by black slaves at work in the fields and later contributing to the development of the blues.
– ORIGIN late 17th cent. (as a verb): variant of the rare verb *hollo*; related to HALLOO.

Hol·ler·ith /'hälə,riTH/, Herman (1860–1929), US engineer. He invented a tabulating machine using punched cards for computation, an important precursor of the electronic computer, and he founded a company that later expanded to become the IBM Corporation.

hol·low /'hälō/ ▶ adj. **1** having a hole or empty space inside: *each fiber has a hollow core.* ■ (of a thing) having a depression in its surface; concave: *hollow cheeks.* ■ (of a sound) echoing, as though made in or on an empty container: *a hollow cough.*
2 without significance: *the result was a hollow victory.* ■ insincere: *a hollow promise.*
▶ n. a hole or depression in something: *a hollow at the base of a large tree.* ■ a small valley: *the house fell behind as they climbed out of the hollow.*
▶ v. [with obj.] form by making a hole: *a tunnel was **hollowed out** in a mountain range.* ■ make a depression in.
– PHRASES **beat someone hollow** defeat or surpass someone completely or thoroughly. **in the hollow of one's hand** entirely in one's power: *great events lay in the hollow of his hand.*
– DERIVATIVES **hol·low·ly** adv., **hol·low·ness** n.
– ORIGIN Old English *holh* 'cave'; obscurely related to HOLE.

hol·low at·om ▶ n. an atom in which inner-shell electrons are missing, usually as a result of electrical excitation.

hol·low-eyed ▶ adj. (of a person) having deeply sunken eyes, typically as a result of illness or tiredness.

hol·low-heart·ed ▶ adj. archaic insincere; false.

hol·low square ▶ n. historical a body of infantry drawn up in a square with a space in the middle.

hol·low·ware /'hälō,we(ə)r/ ▶ n. serving dishes and accessories, esp. of silver, that are hollow or concave. Contrast with FLATWARE.

Hol·ly /'hälē/, Buddy (1936–59), US rock-and-roll singer, guitarist, and songwriter; born *Charles Hardin Holley*. He recorded such hits as "That'll be the Day" with his band, The Crickets, before going solo in 1958. He was killed in an airplane crash.

hol·ly /'hälē/ ▶ n. a widely distributed shrub, typically having prickly dark green leaves, small white flowers, and red berries. There are several deciduous species of holly but the evergreen hollies are more typical and familiar. ● Genus *Ilex*, family Aquifoliaceae: many species, in particular the **American holly** (*I. opaca*), known as the Christmas holly. See also GALLBERRY, WINTERBERRY, YAUPON. ■ the branches, foliage, and berries of this plant used as Christmas decorations.
– ORIGIN Middle English *holi*, shortened form of Old English *holegn, holen*, of Germanic origin; related to German *Hulst*.

hol·ly fern ▶ n. a small shield fern that has narrow glossy fronds with a double row of stiff bristle-edged lobes, found chiefly in mountainous areas of both Eurasia and North America. ● Several species in the genus *Polystichum*, family Dryopteridaceae, in particular the widespread *P. lonchitis*.

hol·ly·hock /ˈhälēˌhäk/ ▶ **n.** a tall Eurasian plant of the mallow family, widely cultivated for its large showy flowers. ● *Alcea rosea*, family Malvaceae.
– ORIGIN Middle English: from **HOLY** + obsolete *hock* 'mallow,' of unknown origin. It originally denoted the marsh mallow, which has medicinal uses (hence, perhaps, the use of 'holy'); the current sense dates from the mid 16th cent.

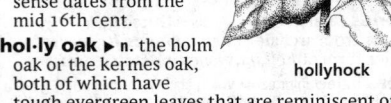

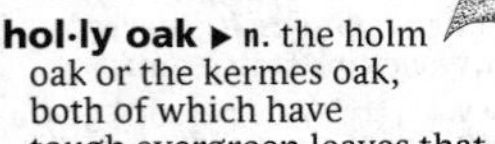
hollyhock

hol·ly oak ▶ **n.** the holm oak or the kermes oak, both of which have tough evergreen leaves that are reminiscent of holly leaves.

Hol·ly·wood /ˈhälēˌwo͝od/ **1** a district in Los Angeles, the principal center of the US movie industry. ■ the US movie industry and the lifestyles of the people associated with it: *he was never seduced by the glitz and money of Hollywood*.
2 a resort city in southeastern Florida, north of Miami, on the Atlantic Ocean; pop. 141,740 (est. 2008).

Hol·ly·wood bed ▶ **n.** a bed consisting of a mattress on a box spring supported on short legs, often with an upholstered headboard.

Hol·ly·wood end·ing ▶ **n.** a conventional ending in a movie, typically regarded as sentimental or simplistic and often featuring an improbably positive outcome.

holm /hōm/ (also **holme**) ▶ **n.** Brit. an islet, esp. in a river or near a mainland. ■ a piece of flat ground by a river that is submerged in time of flood.
– ORIGIN Old English, from Old Norse *holmr*.

Holmes[1] /hōmz/, Oliver Wendell (1809–94), US physician, poet, and essayist; father of US Supreme Court justice Oliver Wendell Holmes. His main contribution to medicine was an essay, written in 1843, on contagion as one cause of puerperal fever. His best-known literary works are the humorous essays known as "table talks," which began with *The Autocrat of the Breakfast Table* (1857–58).

Holmes[2], Oliver Wendell (1841–1935), US Supreme Court associate justice 1902–32; the son of physician and essayist Oliver Wendell Holmes. He became well known for his strong, articulate, and often dissenting opinions.

Holmes[3], Sherlock, an extremely perceptive private detective in stories by Sir Arthur Conan Doyle.
– DERIVATIVES **Holmes·i·an** /-zēən/ **adj.**

hol·mi·um /ˈhōlmēəm/ ▶ **n.** the chemical element of atomic number 67, a soft silvery-white metal of the lanthanide series. (Symbol: **Ho**)
– ORIGIN late 19th cent.: modern Latin, from *Holmia*, Latinized form of *Stockholm*, the capital of Sweden (because many minerals of the yttrium group, to which holmium belongs, are found in that area); discovered by P.T. Cleve, Swedish chemist.

holm oak /hōm/ ▶ **n.** an evergreen southern European oak, with dark green glossy leaves. Also called **EVERGREEN OAK** or **ILEX**. ● *Quercus ilex*, family Fagaceae.
– ORIGIN late Middle English: *holm*, alteration of dialect *hollin*, from Old English *holen* 'holly.'

hol·o /ˈhälō/ ▶ **n.** (pl. **holos**) informal a hologram.

holo- ▶ **comb. form** whole; complete: *holocaust* | *holophytic*.
– ORIGIN from Greek *holos* 'whole.'

ho·lo·blas·tic /ˌhäləˈblastik, ˌhōlə-/ ▶ **adj.** (of an ovum) having cleavage planes that divide the egg into separate blastomeres.

hol·o·caust /ˈhäləˌkôst, ˈhōlə-/ ▶ **n.** **1** destruction or slaughter on a mass scale, esp. caused by fire or nuclear war: *a nuclear holocaust* | *the threat of imminent holocaust*. ■ (**the Holocaust**) the mass murder of Jews under the German Nazi regime during the period 1941–45. More than 6 million European Jews, as well as members of other persecuted groups, such as gypsies and homosexuals, were murdered at concentration camps such as Auschwitz.
2 historical a Jewish sacrificial offering that is burned completely on an altar.
– ORIGIN Middle English: from Old French *holocauste*, via late Latin from Greek *holokauston*, from *holos* 'whole' + *kaustos* 'burned' (from *kaiein* 'burn').

Hol·o·caust de·ni·al ▶ **n.** the belief or assertion that the Holocaust did not happen or was greatly exaggerated.
– DERIVATIVES **Hol·o·caust de·ni·er** **n.**

Hol·o·cene /ˈhäləˌsēn, ˈhōlə-/ ▶ **adj.** Geology of, relating to, or denoting the present epoch, which is the second epoch in the Quaternary period and followed the Pleistocene. Also called **RECENT**. ■ (as noun **the Holocene**) the Holocene epoch or the system of deposits laid down during this time.

> The Holocene epoch has lasted from about 10,000 years ago to the present day. It covers the period since the ice retreated after the last glaciation and is sometimes regarded as just another interglacial period.

– ORIGIN late 19th cent.: coined in French from **HOLO-** 'whole' + Greek *kainos* 'new.'

hol·o·en·zyme /ˌhälōˈenˌzīm, ˌhōlō-/ ▶ **n.** Biochemistry a biochemically active compound formed by the combination of an enzyme with a coenzyme.

Hol·o·fer·nes /ˌhäləˈfərnēz/ (in the Apocrypha) the Assyrian general of Nebuchadnezzar's forces, who was killed by Judith.

hol·o·gram /ˈhäləˌgram, ˈhōlə-/ ▶ **n.** a three-dimensional image formed by the interference of light beams from a laser or other coherent light source. ■ a photograph of an interference pattern that, when suitably illuminated, produces a three-dimensional image.

hol·o·graph /ˈhäləˌgraf, ˈhōlə-/ ▶ **n.** a manuscript handwritten by the person named as its author: [as modifier] *a holograph letter by Abraham Lincoln*.
– ORIGIN early 17th cent.: from French *holographe*, or via late Latin from Greek *holographos*, from *holos* 'whole' + *-graphos* 'written, writing.'

hol·og·ra·phy /hōˈlägrəfē/ ▶ **n.** the study or production of holograms.
– DERIVATIVES **hol·o·graph·ic** /ˌhäləˈgrafik, ˌhōlə-/ **adj.**, **hol·o·graph·i·cal·ly** /ˌhäləˈgrafik(ə)lē, ˌhōlə-/ **adv.**

hol·o·he·dral /ˌhäləˈhēdrəl, ˌhōlə-/ ▶ **adj.** Crystallography having the full number of planes required by the symmetry of a crystal system.

Ho·lon /ˈhōˌlän, KHôˈlôn/ a manufacturing town in west central Israel, part of the Tel Aviv-Jaffa metropolitan area; pop. 170,600 (est. 2008).

ho·loph·ra·sis /həˈläfrəsis/ ▶ **n.** the expression of a whole phrase in a single word, for example *howdy* for *how do you do*. ■ the learning of linguistic elements as whole chunks by very young children acquiring their first language, for example *it's all gone* learned as *allgone*.
– DERIVATIVES **hol·o·phrase** /ˈhäləˌfrāz, ˈhōlə-/ **n.**, **hol·o·phras·tic** /ˌhäləˈfrastik, hōlə-/ **adj.**

hol·o·phyt·ic /ˌhäləˈfitik, ˌhōlə-/ ▶ **adj.** Biology (of a plant or protozoan) able to synthesize complex organic compounds by photosynthesis.

hol·o·thu·ri·an /ˌhäləˈTHo͝orēən, ˌhōlə-/ ▶ **n.** Zoology a sea cucumber.
– ORIGIN mid 19th cent.: from the modern Latin genus name *Holothuria* (from Greek *holothourion*, denoting a kind of zoophyte) + **-AN**.

Hol·o·thu·roi·de·a /ˌhälōTHo͝orˈoidēə, ˌhōlō-/ Zoology a class of echinoderms that comprises the sea cucumbers.
– DERIVATIVES **hol·o·thu·roid** /-ˈTHo͝orˌoid/ **n. & adj.**
– ORIGIN modern Latin (plural), based on Greek *holothourion* (see **HOLOTHURIAN**).

hol·o·type /ˈhäləˌtīp, ˈhōlə-/ ▶ **n.** Botany & Zoology a single type specimen upon which the description and name of a new species is based. Compare with **SYNTYPE**.

hols /hälz/ ▶ **plural n.** Brit. informal holidays.
– ORIGIN early 20th cent.: abbreviation.

Hol·stein /ˈhōlˌstān, -ˌstēn/ ▶ **n.** an animal of a typically black-and-white breed of large dairy cattle.

hol·ster /ˈhōlstər/ ▶ **n.** a holder for carrying a handgun or other firearm, typically made of leather and worn on a belt or under the arm: *the Luger slid easily from the holster*.
▶ **v.** [with obj.] put (a gun) into its holster.
– ORIGIN mid 17th cent.: corresponding to and contemporary with Dutch *holster*, of unknown origin.

holster

holt[1] /hōlt/ ▶ **n.** **1** the den of an animal, esp. that of an otter.
2 dialect a grip or hold.
– ORIGIN late Middle English (in sense 2): variant of **HOLD[1]**.

holt[2] ▶ **n.** archaic or dialect a wood or wooded hill.
– ORIGIN Old English, of Germanic origin; related to Middle Dutch *hout* and German *Holz*, from an Indo-European root shared by Greek *klados* 'twig.'

Holt·er mon·i·tor /ˈhōltər/ ▶ **n.** a portable device that records the rhythm of the heart continuously, typically for 24–48 hours, by means of electrodes attached to the chest.
– ORIGIN 1950s: named after Norman J. *Holter* (1914–83), the American biophysicist who invented it.

> **USAGE** When a patient is fitted with a **Holter monitor**, the recording device may be on a strap that goes around the neck or over the shoulder. This procedure is so suggestive of wearing a **halter** that it is not surprising that many people, including some healthcare professionals, believe they are correct in calling the device a **halter monitor**. In fact, the true name has nothing to do with the way the device is worn, but refers only to the man who invented it: Norman J. **Holter**. Even though the pronunciations of **Holter** and **halter** differ, the mistaken identity is persistent.

ho·lus-bo·lus /ˌhōləs ˈbōləs/ ▶ **adv.** all at once: *swallowing every proposal that is made holus-bolus*.
– ORIGIN mid 19th cent. (originally dialect): perhaps pseudo-Latin for 'whole bolus, whole lump.'

ho·ly /ˈhōlē/ ▶ **adj.** (**holier, holiest**) **1** dedicated or consecrated to God or a religious purpose; sacred: *the Holy Bible* | *the holy month of Ramadan*. ■ (of a person) devoted to the service of God: *saints and holy men*. ■ morally and spiritually excellent: *I do not lead a holy life*.
2 dated or humorous used in exclamations of surprise or dismay: *holy smoke!*
– DERIVATIVES **ho·li·ly** /ˈhōləlē/ **adv.**
– ORIGIN Old English *hālig*, of Germanic origin; related to Dutch and German *heilig*, also to **WHOLE**.

Ho·ly Al·li·ance a loose alliance of European powers pledged to uphold the principles of the Christian religion. It was proclaimed at the Congress of Vienna (1814–15) by the emperors of Austria and Russia and the king of Prussia and was joined by most other European monarchs.

Ho·ly Ark ▶ **n.** see **ARK** (sense 2).

ho·ly bas·il ▶ **n.** a kind of basil that is venerated by Hindus as a sacred plant. Also called **TULSI**. ● *Ocimum sanctum*, family Labiatae.

ho·ly cit·y ▶ **n.** a city held sacred by the adherents of a religion. ■ (**the Holy City**) Jerusalem. ■ (**the Holy City**) (in Christian tradition) Heaven.

Ho·ly Com·mun·ion ▶ **n.** see **COMMUNION** (sense 2).

ho·ly day ▶ **n.** a day on which a religious observance is held.

holy day of obligation ▶ **n.** (in the Roman Catholic Church) a day on which Roman Catholics are required to attend Mass.

Ho·ly Fam·i·ly Jesus as a child with Mary and Joseph (and often also others such as John the Baptist or St. Anne), esp. as a subject for a painting.

Ho·ly Fa·ther ▶ **n.** a title of the pope.

Ho·ly·field /ˈhōlēˌfēld/, Evander (1962–), US boxer. He was a four-time world heavyweight champion 1990–92, 1993–94, 1996–99, and 2000–2001.

ho·ly fool ▶ **n.** a person who appears unintelligent and unsophisticated but who has other redeeming qualities.

Ho·ly Ghost ▶ **n.** another term for **HOLY SPIRIT**.

Ho·ly Grail ▶ **n.** see **GRAIL**.

Ho·ly In·no·cents' Day ▶ **n.** see **INNOCENTS' DAY**.

Ho·ly Joe ▶ **n.** informal a sanctimonious or pious man. ■ a clergyman.
– ORIGIN late 19th cent.: originally nautical slang.

Ho·ly Land a region on the eastern shore of the Mediterranean Sea, in what is now Israel and Palestine, revered by Christians as the place in which Jesus Christ lived and taught, by Jews as the land given to the people of Israel, and by Muslims. ■ a region similarly revered, for example, Arabia in Islam.

Ho·ly League any of various European alliances sponsored by the papacy during the 15th, 16th, and 17th centuries. They include the League of 1511–13, formed by Pope Julius II to expel Louis XII of France from Italy, and the French Holy League (also called the **CATHOLIC LEAGUE**) of 1576 and 1584, a Catholic extremist league formed during the French Wars of Religion.

Ho·ly Name ▶ **n.** (esp. in the Catholic Church) the name of Jesus as an object of formal devotion.

Ho·ly Of·fice the ecclesiastical court of the Roman Catholic Church established as the final court of appeal in trials of heresy. Formed in 1542 as part of the Inquisition, it was renamed the Sacred Congregation for the Doctrine of the Faith in 1965.

ho·ly of ho·lies /'hōlē əv 'hōlēz/ ▶ n. the inner chamber of the sanctuary in the Jewish Temple in Jerusalem, separated by a veil from the outer chamber. It was reserved for the presence of God and could be entered only by the High Priest on the Day of Atonement. ■ a place regarded as most sacred or special: *she had done the wrong thing, venturing into this holy of holies.*

ho·ly or·ders ▶ plural n. the sacrament or rite of ordination as a member of the Christian clergy, esp. in the grades of bishop, priest, or deacon.
– PHRASES **in holy orders** having the status of an ordained member of the clergy. **take holy orders** become an ordained member of the clergy.

ho·ly place ▶ n. a place revered as holy, typically one to which religious pilgrimage is made. ■ historical the outer chamber of the sanctuary in the Jewish Temple in Jerusalem.

Ho·ly Roll·er ▶ n. informal, derogatory a member of an evangelical Christian group that expresses religious fervor by frenzied excitement or trances.

Ho·ly Ro·man Em·pire the empire set up in western Europe following the coronation of Charlemagne as emperor in the year 800. It was created by the medieval papacy in an attempt to unite Christendom under one rule. At times the territory of the empire was extensive and included Germany, Austria, Switzerland, and parts of Italy and the Netherlands.

Ho·ly Sat·ur·day ▶ n. the Saturday preceding Easter Sunday.

Ho·ly Scrip·ture ▶ n. the sacred writings of Christianity contained in the Bible.

Ho·ly See the papacy or the papal court; those associated with the pope in the government of the Roman Catholic Church at the Vatican. Also called **See of Rome**.

Ho·ly Sep·ul·cher the place in which the body of Jesus was laid after being taken down from the Cross. ■ the church in Jerusalem erected over the traditional site of this tomb.

Ho·ly Spir·it ▶ n. (in Christianity) the third person of the Trinity; God as spiritually active in the world.

Ho·ly Spir·it As·so·ci·a·tion for the U·ni·fi·ca·tion of World Chris·ti·an·i·ty another name for **Unification Church**.

ho·ly·stone /'hōlē,stōn/ chiefly historical ▶ n. a piece of soft sandstone used for scouring the decks of ships. ▶ v. [with obj.] scour (a deck) with a holystone.
– ORIGIN early 19th cent.: probably from **holy** + **stone**. Sailors called the stones "bibles" or "prayer books," perhaps because they scrubbed the decks on their knees.

ho·ly ter·ror ▶ n. see **terror** (sense 2).

Ho·ly Thurs·day ▶ n. **1** (chiefly in the Roman Catholic Church) Maundy Thursday. **2** dated (in the Anglican Church) Ascension Day.

Ho·ly Trin·i·ty ▶ n. see **trinity**.

ho·ly war ▶ n. a war declared or waged in support of a religious cause.

ho·ly wa·ter ▶ n. water blessed by a priest and used in religious ceremonies.

Ho·ly Week ▶ n. the week before Easter, starting on Palm Sunday.

Ho·ly Writ ▶ n. the Bible. ■ writings or sayings of unchallenged authority.

Ho·ly Year ▶ n. (in the Roman Catholic Church) a period of remission from the penal consequences of sin, granted under certain conditions for a year usually at intervals of twenty-five years.

hom /hōm/ (also **homa** /'hōmə/, **haoma** /'houmə/) ▶ n. the soma plant, a leafless vine of eastern India. ● *Sarcostemma acidum*, family Asclepiadaceae. ■ the sour, milky juice of this plant, consumed as a sacred drink of the Parsees. See also **soma**[2].
– ORIGIN mid 19th cent.: from Persian *hūm* or Avestan *haoma*.

hom·age /'(h)ämij/ ▶ n. special honor or respect shown publicly: *they **paid homage to** the local boy who became president | a masterly work written **in homage to** Beethoven.* ■ historical formal public acknowledgment of feudal allegiance: *a man doing **homage to** his personal lord.*
– ORIGIN Middle English: Old French, from medieval Latin *hominaticum*, from Latin *homo, homin-* 'man' (the original use of the word denoted the ceremony by which a vassal declared himself to be his lord's "man").

hom·bre /'ämbrā, -brē/ ▶ n. informal a man, esp. one of a particular type: *the Raiders quarterback is one tough hombre.*
– ORIGIN mid 19th cent. (originally denoting a man of Spanish descent): Spanish, 'man,' from Latin *homo, homin-*.

hom·burg /'hämbərg/ ▶ n. a man's felt hat having a narrow curled brim and a tapered crown with a lengthwise indentation.
– ORIGIN late 19th cent.: named after *Homburg*, a town in western Germany, where such hats were first worn.

homburg

home /hōm/ ▶ n. **1** the place where one lives permanently, esp. as a member of a family or household: *I was nineteen when I left home and went to college | they have made Provence their home.* ■ the family or social unit occupying such a place: *he came from a good home and was well educated.* ■ a house or an apartment considered as a commercial property: *low-cost homes for first-time buyers.* ■ a place where something flourishes, is most typically found, or from which it originates: *Piedmont is the home of Italy's finest red wines.* ■ informal a place where an object is kept. **2** an institution for people needing professional care or supervision: *an old people's home.* **3** Sports the goal or end point. ■ the place where a player is free from attack. ■ (in lacrosse) each of the three players stationed nearest their opponents's goal. ■ Baseball short for **home plate**. ■ a game played or won by a team on their own ground.
▶ adj. [attrib.] **1** of or relating to the place where one lives: *I don't have your home address.* ■ made, done, or intended for use in the place where one lives: *traditional home cooking.* ■ relating to one's own country and its domestic affairs: *Japanese competitors are selling cars for lower prices in the US than in their home market.* **2** (of a sports team or player) belonging to the country or locality in which a sporting event takes place: *the home team.* ■ played on or connected with a team's own ground: *their first home game of the season.* **3** denoting the administrative center of an organization: *the company has moved its home office.*
▶ adv. to or at the place where one lives: *what time did he get home last night? | I stayed home with the kids.* ■ to the end or conclusion of a race or something difficult: *the favorite romped home six lengths clear.* ■ Baseball to or toward home plate. ■ to the intended or correct position: *he drove the bolt home noisily.*
▶ v. [no obj.] **1** (of an animal) return by instinct to its territory after leaving it: *a dozen geese homing to their summer nesting grounds.* ■ (of a pigeon bred for long-distance racing) fly back to or arrive at its loft after being released at a distant point. **2** (**home in on**) move or be aimed toward (a target or destination) with great accuracy: *more than 100 missiles were launched, homing in on radar emissions.* ■ focus attention on: *a teaching style that homes in on what is of central importance for each student.*
– PHRASES **at home** in one's own house. ■ in one's own neighborhood, town, or country: *he has been consistently successful both at home and abroad.* ■ comfortable and at ease in a place or situation: *sit down and **make yourself at home**.* ■ confident or relaxed about doing or using something: *he was quite at home talking about Eisenstein or Brecht.* ■ ready to receive and welcome visitors: *she took to her room and was not **at home to** friends.* ■ (with reference to sports fixtures) at a team's own ground: *Houston lost at home to Phoenix.* **bring something home to someone** make someone realize the full significance of something: *her first-hand account brought home to me the pain of the experience.* **close** (or **near**) **to home** (of a remark or topic of discussion) relevant or accurate to the point that one feels uncomfortable or embarrassed. **come home** Golf play the second nine holes in a round of eighteen holes. Compare with **home** (see **go**[1]). **come home to someone** (of the significance of something) become fully realized by someone: *the full enormity of what was happening came home to Sara.* **drive** (or **hammer** or **press** or **ram**) **something home** make something clearly and fully understood by the use of repeated or forcefully direct arguments. **hit** (or **strike**) **home** (of a blow or a missile) reach an intended target. ■ (of words) have the intended, esp. unsettling or painful, effect on their audience: *she could see that her remark had hit home.* ■ (of the significance or true nature of a situation) become fully realized by someone: *the full impact of life as a celebrity began to hit home.* **home free** having successfully achieved or being within sight of achieving one's objective: *at 7–0 they should have been home free.* **a home away from home** a place where one is as happy, relaxed, or comfortable as in one's own home. **home is where the heart is** proverb your home will always be the place for which you feel the deepest affection, no matter where you are. **home sweet home** used as an expression of one's pleasure or relief at being in or returning to one's own home.
– DERIVATIVES **home·like** /'hōm,līk/ adj.
– ORIGIN Old English *hām*, of Germanic origin; related to Dutch *heem* and German *Heim*.

> **USAGE** Note that the phrasal verb meaning 'move accurately toward a target' is **home in on**, not hone in on. More than a third of citations for this expression in the Oxford English Corpus are for the incorrect form.

home bank·ing ▶ n. a system of banking whereby transactions are performed directly by telephone or via a computer and modem.

home base ▶ n. a place from which operations or activities are carried out; headquarters. ■ the objective toward which players progress in certain games.

home·bod·y /'hōm,bädē/ ▶ n. (pl. **homebodies**) informal a person who likes to stay at home, esp. one who is perceived as unadventurous.

home·boy /'hōm,boi/ ▶ n. informal a young acquaintance from one's own town or neighborhood, or from the same social background. ■ (esp. among urban black people) a member of a peer group or gang.

home-bred ▶ adj. bred or raised at home. ■ lacking in worldly experience; unsophisticated.

home brew ▶ n. beer or other alcoholic drink brewed at home: *I observed the town's bootlegger deliver three bottles of home brew.* ■ [as modifier] informal made at home, rather than in a store or factory: *home-brew software.*
– DERIVATIVES **home-brewed** adj.

home·build·er /'hōmbildər/ ▶ n. a company whose business is the construction of private houses.
– DERIVATIVES **home·build·ing** n.

home·buy·er /'hōm,bīər/ ▶ n. a person who buys a house or condominium.

home·com·ing /'hōm,kəmiNG/ ▶ n. an instance of returning home. ■ a high school, college, or university game, dance, or other event to which alumni are invited.

home ec /'hōm 'ek/ ▶ n. informal short for **home economics**.

home ec·o·nom·ics ▶ plural n. [often treated as sing.] cooking and other aspects of household management, esp. as taught at school.

home farm ▶ n. chiefly Brit. & S. African a farm on an estate that is set aside to provide produce for the owner of the estate.

home fries (also **home-fried potatoes**) ▶ plural n. fried sliced potatoes.

home front ▶ n. the civilian population and activities of a nation whose armed forces are engaged in war abroad.

home·girl /'hōm,gərl/ ▶ n. informal a female equivalent of a homeboy.

home·grown /'hōm'grōn/ ▶ adj. grown or produced in one's own garden or country: *a basket of homegrown fruit.* ■ belonging to one's own particular locality or country: *a jazz concert featuring homegrown artists.*

home key ▶ n. **1** Music the basic key in which a work is written; the tonic key. **2** a key on a computer or typewriter keyboard that acts as the base position for one's fingers in touch-typing.

Ho·mel /hô'm(y)el/ an industrial city in southeastern Belarus; pop. 488,100 (est. 2009). Russian name **Gomel**.

home·land /'hōm,land/ ▶ n. a person's or a people's native land: *I could finally go back to my homeland.* ■ an autonomous or semiautonomous state occupied by a particular people: *the group is fighting for a separate homeland.* ■ historical any of ten partially self-governing areas in South Africa designated for particular indigenous African peoples under the former policy of apartheid.

home·less /'hōmlis/ ▶ adj. (of a person) without a home, and therefore typically living on the streets: *the plight of young homeless people* | (as noun **the homeless**) *charities for the homeless.*
– DERIVATIVES **home·less·ness** n.

home loan ▶ n. a loan advanced to a person to assist in buying a house or condominium.

home·ly /'hōmlē/ ▶ adj. (**homelier, homeliest**) **1** (of a person) unattractive in appearance.

PRONUNCIATION KEY ə *ago, up*; ər *over, fur*; a *hat*; ā *ate*; ä *car*; e *let*; ē *see*; i *fit*; ī *by*; NG *sing*; ō *go*; ô *law, for*; oi *toy*; o͝o *good*; o͞o *goo*; ou *out*; TH *thin*; <u>TH</u> *then*; ZH *vision*

2 Brit. (of a place or surroundings) simple but cozy and comfortable, as in one's own home: *a modern hotel with a homely atmosphere.* ■ unsophisticated and unpretentious: *homely pleasures.*
– DERIVATIVES **home·li·ness** n.

home·made /'hō(m)'mād/ ▶ adj. made at home, rather than in a store or factory: *homemade apple pies | it sounds like the homemade album that it is.*

home·mak·er /'hōm,mākər/ ▶ n. a person, esp. a housewife, who manages a home.

home·mak·ing /'hōm,mākiNG/ ▶ n. the creation and management of a home, esp. as a pleasant place in which to live.

home mov·ie ▶ n. a film made at home or without professional equipment or expertise, esp. a movie featuring one's own activities.

ho·me·o·box /'hōmēō,bäks/ ▶ n. Genetics any of a class of closely similar sequences that occur in various genes and are involved in regulating embryonic development in a wide range of species.
– ORIGIN 1980s: from *homeotic* (see **HOMEOSIS**) + the noun **BOX**[1]; first discovered in homeotic genes of *Drosophila* fruit flies.

Home Of·fice the British government department dealing with domestic affairs, including law and order, immigration, and broadcasting, in England and Wales.

h

ho·me·o·mor·phism /,hōmēə'môr,fizəm/ ▶ n. Mathematics an instance of topological equivalence to another space or figure.
– DERIVATIVES **ho·me·o·mor·phic** /-'môrfik/ adj.

ho·me·o·path /'hōmēə,paTH/ (also **homeopathist** /,hōmē'äpəTHist/, Brit. **homoeopath**) ▶ n. a person who practices homeopathy.
– ORIGIN mid 19th cent.: from German *Homöopath* (see **HOMEOPATHY**).

ho·me·op·a·thy /,hōmē'äpəTHē/ (Brit. **homoeopathy**) ▶ n. the treatment of disease by minute doses of natural substances that in a healthy person would produce symptoms of disease. Often contrasted with **ALLOPATHY**.
– DERIVATIVES **ho·me·o·path·ic** /,hōmēə'paTHik/ adj., **ho·me·o·path·i·cal·ly** /,hōmēə'paTHik(ə)lē/ adv.
– ORIGIN early 19th cent.: coined in German from Greek *homoios* 'like' + *patheia* (see **-PATHY**).

ho·me·o·sis /,hōmē'ōsis/ ▶ n. (pl. **homeoses** /-,sēz/) Biology the replacement of part of one segment of an insect or other segmented animal by a structure characteristic of a different segment, esp. through mutation.
– DERIVATIVES **ho·me·ot·ic** /-'ätik/ adj.
– ORIGIN late 19th cent.: from Greek *homoiōsis* 'becoming like,' from *homoios* 'like.'

ho·me·o·sta·sis /,hōmēə'stāsis/ ▶ n. (pl. **homeostases** /-sēz/) the tendency toward a relatively stable equilibrium between interdependent elements, esp. as maintained by physiological processes.
– DERIVATIVES **ho·me·o·stat·ic** /-'statik/ adj.
– ORIGIN 1920s: modern Latin, from Greek *homoios* 'like' + **-STASIS**.

ho·me·o·therm /'hōmēə,THərm/ (also **homoiotherm**) ▶ n. Zoology an organism that maintains its body temperature at a constant level, usually above that of the environment, by its metabolic activity. Often contrasted with **POIKILOTHERM**; compare with **WARM-BLOODED**.
– DERIVATIVES **ho·me·o·ther·mal** /,hōmēə'THərməl/ adj., **ho·me·o·ther·mic** /,hōmēə'THərmik/ adj., **ho·me·o·ther·my** n.
– ORIGIN late 19th cent.: modern Latin, from Greek *homoios* 'like' + *thermē* 'heat.'

home·own·er /'hōm,ōnər/ ▶ n. a person who owns their own home.
– DERIVATIVES **home·own·er·ship** /-SHip/ n.

home page (also **homepage**) ▶ n. the introductory page of a website, typically serving as a table of contents for the site.

home plate ▶ n. Baseball the five-sided flat white rubber base next to which the batter stands and over which the pitcher must throw the ball for a strike. A runner must touch home plate after having reached all the other bases to score a run.

home·port /'hōm,pôrt/ ▶ v. [with obj.] assign (a vessel) to a particular port as its home: *Guam's strategic location makes it the logical place to homeport an aircraft carrier.*

home port ▶ n. the port from which a ship originates or in which it is registered.

Ho·mer[1] /'hōmər/ (8th century BC), Greek epic poet. He is traditionally held to be the author of the *Iliad* and the *Odyssey*, although modern scholarship has revealed the place of the Homeric poems in a preliterate oral tradition. In later antiquity, Homer was regarded as the greatest poet, and his poems were constantly used as a model and source by others.
– PHRASES **Homer sometimes nods** proverb even the most gifted person occasionally makes mistakes.

Ho·mer[2], Winslow (1836–1910), US painter. He is noted for his seascapes, such as *Cannon Rock* (1895), painted in a vigorous naturalistic style that combines imagination and strength and is considered an expression of the American pioneering spirit.

ho·mer /'hōmər/ ▶ n. 1 Baseball a home run.
2 a homing pigeon.
3 informal a referee or official who is thought to favor the team playing at home.
▶ v. [no obj.] Baseball hit a home run: *he homered for the sixth time in seven games.*

home range ▶ n. Zoology an area over which an animal or group of animals regularly travels in search of food or mates, and that may overlap with those of neighboring animals or groups of the same species.

Ho·mer·ic /hō'merik/ ▶ adj. of or in the style of Homer or the epic poems ascribed to him. ■ of Bronze Age Greece as described in these poems: *the mists of the Homeric age.* ■ epic and large-scale: *some of us exert a Homeric effort.*
– ORIGIN via Latin from Greek *Homērikos*, from *Homēros* (see **HOMER**[1]).

home rule ▶ n. the government of a colony, dependent country, or region by its own citizens.

home run ▶ n. Baseball a fair hit that allows the batter to make a complete circuit of the bases without stopping and score a run.

home·school·ing /'hōm'skōōliNG/ ▶ n. the education of children at home by their parents.
– DERIVATIVES **home·school** v., **home·school·er** /'skōōlər/ n.

Home Sec·re·tar·y ▶ n. (in the UK) the Secretary of State in charge of the Home Office.

home shop·ping ▶ n. shopping carried out from one's own home by ordering goods advertised on the Internet, in a catalog, or on a television channel.
– DERIVATIVES **home shop·per** n.

home·shor·ing /'hōmSHôriNG/ ▶ n. the practice of transferring employment that was previously carried out in a company's office or factory to employees' homes.
– ORIGIN early 21st cent.: on the pattern of **OFFSHORING**.

home·sick /'hōm,sik/ ▶ adj. experiencing a longing for one's home during a period of absence from it: *he was homesick for America after five weeks in Europe.*
– DERIVATIVES **home·sick·ness** n.

home·site /'hōm,sīt/ ▶ n. a building plot for a house.

home·sourc·ing /'hōmsôrsiNG/ ▶ n. . another term for **HOMESHORING**.
– ORIGIN early 21st cent.: on the pattern of *outsourcing* (see **OUTSOURCE**).

home·spun /'hōm,spən/ ▶ adj. 1 simple and unsophisticated: *homespun philosophy.*
2 (of cloth or yarn) made or spun at home.
■ denoting a coarse handwoven fabric similar to tweed.
▶ n. cloth of this type: *clad in homespun.*

home stand ▶ n. a series of consecutive games played at a team's home stadium, field, or court.

Home·stead /'hōm,sted/ an agricultural and suburban city in southeastern Florida, southwest of Miami; pop. 57,936 (est. 2008).

home·stead /'hōm,sted/ ▶ n. 1 a house, esp. a farmhouse, and outbuildings.
2 Law a person's or family's residence, which comprises the land, house, and outbuildings, and in most states is exempt from forced sale for collection of debt.
3 historical (as provided by the federal Homestead Act of 1862) an area of public land in the West (usually 160 acres) granted to any US citizen willing to settle on and farm the land for at least five years.
4 (in southern Africa) a hut or cluster of huts occupied by one family or clan, standing alone or as part of a traditional African village.
– DERIVATIVES **home·stead·er** n.
– ORIGIN Old English *hāmstede* 'a settlement' (see **HOME, STEAD**).

Home·stead Act ▶ n. see **HOMESTEAD**.

home·stead·ing /'hōm,stediNG/ ▶ n. life as a settler on a homestead. ■ the granting of homesteads to settlers.

home·stretch /'hōm'streCH/ (also **home stretch**) ▶ n. the concluding straight part of a racecourse: *he drifted in back of the pack halfway down the homestretch.* ■ the last part of an activity or campaign: *this was his last term, the home stretch.*

home stud·y ▶ n. 1 a course of study carried out at home, rather than in a traditional classroom setting.
2 an assessment of prospective adoptive parents to see if they are suitable for adopting a child.

home·style /'hōm,stīl/ ▶ adj. [attrib.] such as would be made or provided at home; simple and unpretentious.

home the·a·ter ▶ n. television and video equipment designed to reproduce at home the experience of being in a movie theater, typically including stereo speakers and a big-screen television set.

home·town /'hōm'toun/ ▶ n. the town where one was born or grew up, or the town of one's present fixed residence.

home truth ▶ n. (usu. **home truths**) an unpleasant fact about oneself, esp. as pointed out by another person: *what he needed was someone to tell him a few home truths.*

home vid·e·o ▶ n. a film on videotape for viewing at home.

home·ward /'hōmwərd/ ▶ adv. (also **homewards** /-wərdz/) toward home: *setting off homeward.*
▶ adj. going or leading toward home: *their homeward journey.*
– ORIGIN Old English *hāmweard* (see **HOME, -WARD**).

home·work /'hōm,wərk/ ▶ n. schoolwork that a student is required to do at home. ■ work or study done in preparation for a certain event or situation: *he had evidently done his homework and read his predecessor's reports.* ■ paid work carried out in one's own home, esp. low-paid piecework.

USAGE See usage at **SCHOOLWORK**.

home·work·er /'hōm,wərkər/ ▶ n. a person who works from home, esp. doing low-paid piecework.

home·wreck·er /'hōm,rekər/ ▶ n. informal one who is blamed for the breakup of a marriage or family, such as an adulterous partner.

hom·ey[1] /'hōmē/ (also **homy**) ▶ adj. (**homier**, **homiest**) (of a place or surroundings) pleasantly comfortable and cozy. ■ unsophisticated; unpretentious: *an idealized vision of traditional peasant life as simple and homey.*
– DERIVATIVES **hom·ey·ness** (also **hominess**) n.

hom·ey[2] ▶ n. (pl. **homeys**) variant spelling of **HOMIE**.

hom·i·cid·al /,hämə'sīdl, ,hōmə-/ ▶ adj. of, relating to, or tending toward murder: *he had homicidal tendencies.*

hom·i·cide /'hämə,sīd, 'hōmə-/ ▶ n. the deliberate and unlawful killing of one person by another; murder: *he was charged with homicide | two thirds of homicides in the county were drug-related.* ■ (**Homicide**) the police department that deals with such crimes: *a detective from Homicide.* ■ dated a murderer.
– ORIGIN Middle English: from Old French, from Latin *homicidium*, from *homo, homin-* 'man.'

hom·ie /'hōmē/ (also **homey**) ▶ n. (pl. **homies**) informal a homeboy or homegirl.

hom·i·let·ic /,hämə'letik/ ▶ adj. of the nature of or characteristic of a homily: *homiletic literature.*
▶ n. (**homiletics**) the art of preaching or writing sermons: *the teaching of homiletics.*
– ORIGIN mid 17th cent.: via late Latin from Greek *homilētikos*, from *homilein* 'converse with, consort,' from *homilia* (see **HOMILY**).

ho·mil·i·ar·y /hä'milē,erē/ ▶ n. (pl. **homiliaries**) historical a book of homilies.
– ORIGIN mid 19th cent.: from medieval Latin *homiliarius*, from ecclesiastical Latin *homilia* (see **HOMILY**).

hom·i·ly /'häməlē/ ▶ n. (pl. **homilies**) a religious discourse that is intended primarily for spiritual edification rather than doctrinal instruction; a sermon. ■ a tedious moralizing discourse: *she delivered her homily about the need for patience.*
– DERIVATIVES **hom·i·list** /-list/ n.
– ORIGIN late Middle English: via Old French from ecclesiastical Latin *homilia*, from Greek, 'discourse, conversation' (in ecclesiastical use, 'sermon'), from *homilos* 'crowd.'

hom·ing /'hōmiNG/ ▶ adj. relating to an animal's ability to return to a place or territory after traveling a distance away from it: *a strong homing instinct.* ■ (of a pigeon) trained to fly home from a great distance and bred for long-distance racing. ■ (of a weapon or piece of equipment) fitted with an electronic device that enables it to find and hit a target.

hom·i·nid /'hämə,nid/ ▶ n. Zoology a primate of a family (Hominidae) that includes humans and their fossil ancestors.
– ORIGIN late 19th cent.: from modern Latin *Hominidae* (plural), from Latin *homo, homin-* 'man.'

hom·i·noid /'hämə,noid/ Zoology ▶ n. a primate of a group that includes humans, their fossil ancestors,

and the great apes. ● Superfamily Hominoidea: families Hominidae and Pongidae.
▶ **adj.** of or relating to primates of this group; hominid or pongid.
– ORIGIN early 20th cent.: from Latin *homo, homin-* 'human being' + **-OID**.

hom·i·ny /ˈhämənē/ ▶ **n.** coarsely ground corn used to make grits: [as modifier] *hominy grits.*
– ORIGIN early 17th cent.: shortened from Virginia Algonquian *uskatahomen.*

Ho·mo /ˈhōmō/ the genus of primates of which modern humans (*Homo sapiens*) are the present-day representatives. ■ [with Latin or pseudo-Latin adj.] denoting kinds of modern human, often humorously: *a textbook example of Homo neuroticus.*

> The genus *Homo* is believed to have existed for at least two million years, and modern humans (*H. sapiens sapiens*) first appeared in the Upper Paleolithic. Among several extinct species are *H. habilis, H. erectus,* and *H. neanderthalensis.*

– ORIGIN Latin, 'man.'

ho·mo /ˈhō,mō/ offensive ▶ **n.** (pl. **homos**) a homosexual man.
▶ **adj.** homosexual.
– ORIGIN 1920s: abbreviation.

homo- ▶ **comb. form 1** same: *homogametic.*
2 relating to homosexual love: *homoerotic.* Often contrasted with **HETERO-**.
– ORIGIN from Greek *homos* 'same.'

ho·mo·cen·tric[1] /,hōmōˈsentrik/ ▶ **adj.** having the same center.
– ORIGIN early 17th cent.: from Greek **HOMO-** 'same' + **-CENTRIC**.

ho·mo·cen·tric[2] ▶ **adj.** another term for **ANTHROPOCENTRIC**.
– ORIGIN early 20th cent.: from Latin *homo* 'human being, man' + **-CENTRIC**.

ho·mo·cer·cal /,hōməˈsərkəl/ ▶ **adj.** Zoology (of a fish's tail) appearing outwardly symmetrical but with the backbone passing into the upper lobe, as in all higher fish. Contrasted with **DIPHYCERCAL, HETEROCERCAL**.
– ORIGIN mid 19th cent.: from **HOMO-** 'same' + Greek *kerkos* 'tail' + **-AL**.

ho·mo·cys·teine /,hōməˈsistēn/ ▶ **n.** Biochemistry an amino acid that occurs in the body as an intermediate in the metabolism of methionine and cysteine. ● Chem. formula: $HSCH_2CH_2CH(NH_2)COOH$.

ho·moe·cious /hōˈmēsHəs, hä-/ ▶ **adj.** Biology parasitic on a single host throughout life. Compare with **HETEROECIOUS**.

ho·moe·o·path ▶ **n.** Brit. variant spelling of **HOMEOPATH**.

ho·moe·op·a·thy ▶ **n.** Brit. variant spelling of **HOMEOPATHY**.

ho·mo·e·rot·ic /,hōmō-iˈrätik/ ▶ **adj.** concerning or arousing sexual desire centered on a person of the same sex: *homoerotic images.*
– DERIVATIVES **ho·mo·e·rot·i·cism** /-,sizəm/ **n.**

ho·mo·ga·met·ic /,hōmōgəˈmetik/ ▶ **adj.** Biology denoting the sex that has sex chromosomes that do not differ in morphology, resulting in only one kind of gamete, e.g., (in mammals) the female and (in birds) the male. The opposite of **HETEROGAMETIC**.

ho·mog·a·my /hōˈmägəmē, hä-/ ▶ **n. 1** Biology inbreeding, esp. as a result of isolation. ■ marriage between people from similar sociological or educational backgrounds. Compare with **HETEROGAMY** (sense 3).
2 Botany a state in which the flowers of a plant are all of one type (either hermaphrodite or of the same sex). Compare with **HETEROGAMY** (sense 2).
3 Botany the simultaneous ripening of the stamens and pistils of a flower, ensuring self-pollination. Compare with **DICHOGAMY**.
– DERIVATIVES **ho·mog·a·mous** /-ˈmägəməs/ **adj.**
– ORIGIN late 19th cent.: from **HOMO-** 'same' + Greek *gamos* 'marriage.'

ho·mog·e·nate /həˈmäjə,nāt, -nət/ ▶ **n.** Biology a suspension of cell fragments and cell constituents obtained when tissue is homogenized.

ho·mo·ge·ne·i·ty /,hōməjəˈnēitē, ,hämə-/ ▶ **n.** the quality or state of being homogeneous: *the cultural homogeneity of our society.*

ho·mo·ge·ne·ous /,hōməˈjēnēəs/ (also **homogenous** /həˈmäjənəs/) ▶ **adj.** of the same kind; alike: *timbermen prefer to deal with homogeneous woods.* ■ consisting of parts all of the same kind: *culturally speaking the farmers constitute an extremely homogeneous group.* ■ Mathematics containing terms all of the same degree.
– DERIVATIVES **ho·mo·ge·ne·ous·ly adv., ho·mo·ge·ne·ous·ness n.**
– ORIGIN early 17th cent. (as **HOMOGENEITY**): from medieval Latin *homogeneus,* from Greek *homogenēs,* from *homos* 'same' + *genos* 'race, kind.'

> **USAGE** The usual spelling is **homogeneous**, and the spelling **homogenous** is traditionally regarded as an error. **Homogenous** is a different word, a specialized biological term meaning 'having a common descent,' which has been largely replaced by **homologous**. From the evidence of the Oxford English Corpus, the spelling **homogeneous** has become significantly less common since 2000, and around a third of citations for the word now use the form **homogenous**. This can now be regarded as an established variant.

ho·mog·e·nize /həˈmäjə,nīz/ ▶ **v.** [with obj.] **1** subject (milk) to a process in which the fat droplets are emulsified and the cream does not separate: (as adj. **homogenized**) *homogenized milk.* ■ Biology prepare a suspension of cell constituents from (tissue) by physical treatment in a liquid.
2 make uniform or similar.
– DERIVATIVES **ho·mog·e·ni·za·tion** /hə,mäjənīˈzāsHən/ **n., ho·mog·e·niz·er n.**

ho·mog·e·nous /həˈmäjənəs/ ▶ **adj. 1** Biology old-fashioned term for **HOMOLOGOUS**.
2 see **HOMOGENEOUS**.
– DERIVATIVES **ho·mog·e·nous·ly adv.**
– ORIGIN late 19th cent.: from **HOMO-** 'same' + Greek *genos* 'race, kind' + **-OUS**.

> **USAGE** See usage at **HOMOGENEOUS**.

ho·mog·e·ny /həˈmäjənē/ ▶ **n.** Biology variant of **HOMOGENEITY**.

ho·mo·graft /ˈhōmə,graft, ˈhämə-/ ▶ **n.** a tissue graft from a donor of the same species as the recipient. Compare with **ALLOGRAFT**.

hom·o·graph /ˈhämə,graf, ˈhōmə-/ ▶ **n.** each of two or more words spelled the same but not necessarily pronounced the same and having different meanings and origins (e.g., **BOW**[1] and **BOW**[2]).
– DERIVATIVES **hom·o·graph·ic** /,häməˈgrafik, ,hōmə-/ **adj.**

ho·moi·o·therm /hōˈmoiə,THərm/ ▶ **n.** variant spelling of **HOMEOTHERM**.

ho·moi·ou·si·an /,hōmoiˈo͞osēən/ ▶ **n.** historical in the fourth-century Arian controversy, a person who held that God the Father and God the Son are of like but not identical substance. Compare with **HOMOOUSIAN**.
– ORIGIN late 17th cent. (as an adjective in the sense 'of similar but not identical substance'): via ecclesiastical Latin from Greek *homoiousios,* from *homoios* 'like' + *ousia* 'essence, substance.' The noun dates from the mid 18th cent.

ho·mo·log ▶ **n.** variant spelling of **HOMOLOGUE**.

ho·mol·o·gate /hōˈmälə,gāt, hə-/ ▶ **v.** [with obj.] formal express agreement with or approval of: *one body of patrons elected the teacher, the others afterward homologating the appointment.* ■ approve (a car, boat, or engine) for sale in a particular market or use in a particular class of racing.
– DERIVATIVES **ho·mol·o·ga·tion** /hō,mäləˈgāsHən, hə-/ **n.**
– ORIGIN late 16th cent.: from medieval Latin *homologat-* 'agreed,' from the verb *homologare,* from Greek *homologein* 'confess.'

ho·mol·o·gize /hōˈmälə,jīz, hə-/ ▶ **v.** [with obj.] formal make or show to have the same relation, relative position, or structure.

ho·mol·o·gous /hōˈmäləgəs, hə-/ ▶ **adj.** having the same relation, relative position, or structure, in particular: ■ Biology (of organs) similar in position, structure, and evolutionary origin but not necessarily in function: *a seal's flipper is homologous with the human arm.* Often contrasted with **ANALOGOUS**. ■ Biology (of chromosomes) pairing at meiosis and having the same structural features and pattern of genes. ■ Chemistry (of a series of chemical compounds) having the same functional group but differing in composition by a fixed group of atoms.
– ORIGIN mid 17th cent.: via medieval Latin from Greek *homologos* 'agreeing, consistent,' from *homos* 'same' + *logos* 'ratio, proportion.'

ho·mo·logue /ˈhōmə,lôg, -,läg/ (also **homolog**) ▶ **n.** technical a homologous thing.
– ORIGIN mid 19th cent.: from French, from Greek *homologos* (see **HOMOLOGOUS**).

ho·mol·o·gy /hōˈmäləjē, hə-/ ▶ **n.** the quality or condition of being homologous. ■ Biology similarity in sequence of a protein or nucleic acid between organisms of the same or different species.

ho·mo·mor·phic /,hōməˈmôrfik/ ▶ **adj.** technical of the same or similar form. ■ Mathematics of, relating to, or of the nature of a homomorphism.
– DERIVATIVES **ho·mo·mor·phi·cal·ly** /,hōməˈmôrfik(ə)lē/ **adv.**

ho·mo·mor·phism /,hōməˈmôr,fizəm/ ▶ **n.** Mathematics a transformation of one set into another that preserves in the second set the relations between elements of the first.

hom·o·nym /ˈhämə,nim, ˈhōmə-/ ▶ **n.** each of two or more words having the same spelling but different meanings and origins (e.g., **POLE**[1] and **POLE**[2]); a homograph. ■ each of two words having the same pronunciation but different meanings, origins, or spelling (e.g., **TO, TOO,** and **TWO**); a homophone. ■ Biology a Latin name that is identical to that of a different organism, the newer of the two names being invalid.
– DERIVATIVES **hom·o·nym·ic** /,häməˈnimik, ,hōmə-/ **adj., ho·mon·y·mous** /hōˈmänəməs/ **adj., ho·mon·y·my** /hōˈmänəmē/ **n.**
– ORIGIN late 17th cent.: via Latin from Greek *homōnumon,* neuter of *homōnumos* 'having the same name,' from *homos* 'same' + *onuma* 'name.'

ho·mo·ou·si·an /,hōmōˈo͞osēən/ (also **homousian**) ▶ **n.** historical in the fourth-century Arian controversy, a person who held that God the Father and God the Son are of the same substance. Compare with **HOMOIOUSIAN**.
– ORIGIN mid 16th cent.: from ecclesiastical Latin *homousianus,* from *homousius,* from Greek *homoousios,* from *homos* 'same' + *ousia* 'essence, substance.'

ho·mo·phile /ˈhōmə,fīl/ ▶ **n.** a homosexual man or woman. ■ a person active in supporting the rights of homosexuals.
▶ **adj.** of or relating to homosexuals. ■ active in supporting the rights of homosexuals.

ho·mo·pho·bi·a /,hōməˈfōbēə/ ▶ **n.** an extreme and irrational aversion to homosexuality and homosexual people.
– DERIVATIVES **ho·mo·phobe** /ˈhōmə,fōb/ **n., ho·mo·pho·bic** /-ˈfōbik/ **adj.**
– ORIGIN 1960s: from **HOMOSEXUAL** + **-PHOBIA**.

ho·mo·phone /ˈhämə,fōn, ˈhōmə-/ ▶ **n.** each of two or more words having the same pronunciation but different meanings, origins, or spelling, e.g., *new* and *knew.* ■ each of a set of symbols denoting the same sound or group of sounds.

ho·mo·phon·ic /,häməˈfänik, ,hōmə-/ ▶ **adj. 1** Music characterized by the movement of accompanying parts in the same rhythm as the melody. Often contrasted with **POLYPHONIC**.
2 another term for **HOMOPHONOUS**.
– DERIVATIVES **ho·mo·phon·i·cal·ly** /-ik(ə)lē/ **adv.**

ho·moph·o·nous /hōˈmäfənəs, hə-/ ▶ **adj.** (of a word or words) having the same pronunciation as another or others but different meaning, origin, or spelling.
– DERIVATIVES **ho·moph·o·ny** /-ˈmäfənē/ **n.**

ho·mo·po·lar /,häməˈpōlər, ,hōmə-/ ▶ **adj.** having equal or constant electrical polarity. ■ (of an electric generator) producing direct current without the use of commutators.

Ho·mop·ter·a /hōˈmäptərə/ Entomology a group of true bugs comprising those in which the forewings are uniform in texture. Plant bugs such as aphids, whitefly, scale insects, and cicadas belong to this group. Compare with **HETEROPTERA**. ● Suborder Homoptera, order Hemiptera.
■ (as plural noun **homoptera**) bugs of this group.
– ORIGIN modern Latin (plural), from **HOMO-** 'equal' + Greek *pteron* 'wing.'

ho·mop·ter·an /hōˈmäptərən/ Entomology ▶ **n.** a bug of the group Homoptera.
▶ **adj.** relating to or denoting homopterans.
– DERIVATIVES **ho·mop·ter·ous** /-tərəs/ **adj.**

ho·mor·gan·ic /,hōmôrˈganik/ ▶ **adj.** denoting sets of speech sounds that are produced using the same vocal organs, e.g., *p, b,* and *m.*

Ho·mo sa·pi·ens /ˈhōmō ˈsāpēənz/ the primate species to which modern humans belong; humans regarded as a species. See also **HOMO**. ■ a member of this species.
– ORIGIN Latin, literally 'wise man.'

ho·mo·sex·u·al /,hōməˈseksHo͞oəl/ ▶ **adj.** (of a person) sexually attracted to people of one's own sex. ■ involving or characterized by sexual attraction between people of the same sex: *homosexual desire.*
▶ **n.** a person who is sexually attracted to people of their own sex.
– DERIVATIVES **ho·mo·sex·u·al·i·ty** /-,seksHo͞oˈalitē/ **n., ho·mo·sex·u·al·ly adv.**
– ORIGIN late 19th cent.: from **HOMO-** 'same' + **SEXUAL**.

ho·mo·so·cial /,hōməˈsōsHəl/ ▶ **adj.** of or relating to social interaction between members of the same sex, typically men.

ho·mo·trans·plant /ˌhōmō'transˌplant/ ▶ **n.** another term for **ALLOGRAFT**.

ho·mo·u·si·an /ˌhōmō'o͞osēən/ ▶ **n.** variant spelling of **HOMOOUSIAN**.

ho·mo·zy·gote /ˌhōmō'zīgōt/ ▶ **n.** Genetics an individual having two identical alleles of a particular gene or genes and so breeding true for the corresponding characteristic. Compare with **HETEROZYGOTE**.
– DERIVATIVES **ho·mo·zy·gos·i·ty** /-zī'gäsitē/ **n.**, **ho·mo·zy·gous** /-'zīgəs/ **adj.**

Homs /hôms/ (also **Hims** /hims/) an industrial city in western Syria, on the Orontes River; pop. 869,700 (est. 2009). It was named in 636 by the Muslims and occupies the site of the ancient city of Emesa.

ho·mun·cu·lus /hə'məngkyələs, hō-/ ▶ **n.** (pl. **homunculi** /-ˌlī/ or **homuncules** /-ˌlēz/) a very small human or humanoid creature. ■ historical a supposed microscopic but fully formed human being from which a fetus was formerly believed to develop.
– ORIGIN mid 17th cent.: from Latin, diminutive of *homo, homin-* 'man.'

hom·y ▶ **adj.** variant spelling of **HOMEY**[1].

hon /hən/ ▶ **n.** informal short for **HONEY** (as a form of address): *It wouldn't interest you, hon.*

Hon. ▶ **abbr.** ■ (in official job titles) Honorary: *the Hon. Secretary.* ■ (in titles of some government officials and judges) Honorable: *the Hon. Charles Rothschild.*

h

Ho·nan /'hō'nan, 'hōˌnän/ **1** variant of **HENAN**. **2** former name for **LUOYANG**.

hon·cho /'hänchō/ informal ▶ **n.** (pl. **honchos**) a leader or manager; the person in charge: *the company's head honcho in the US.*
▶ **v.** (**honchoes**, **honchoed**) [with obj.] be in charge of (a project or situation): *the task at hand was to honcho an eighteen-wheeler to St. Louis.*
– ORIGIN 1940s: from Japanese *hanchō* 'group leader,' a term brought back to the US by servicemen stationed in Japan during the occupation following World War II.

Hon·da /'händə/, Soichiro (1906–92), Japanese motor manufacturer. Opening his first factory in 1934, he began motorcycle manufacture in 1948 and expanded into automobile production during the 1960s.

Hon·du·ras /hän'd(y)o͝orəs/ a country in Central America that borders on the Caribbean Sea and also has a short coastline on the Pacific Ocean; pop. 7,833,700 (est. 2009); capital, Tegucigalpa; official language, Spanish.

> At the southern limit of the Mayan empire, Honduras was visited by Columbus in 1502 and became a Spanish colony. In 1821, it became an independent republic.

– DERIVATIVES **Hon·du·ran** /-rən/ **adj. & n.**

hone /hōn/ ▶ **v.** [with obj.] sharpen with a whetstone. ■ (usu. **be honed**) make sharper or more focused or efficient: *their appetites were honed by fresh air and exercise.*
▶ **n.** a whetstone, esp. one used to sharpen razors.
– ORIGIN Middle English: from Old English *hān* 'stone,' of Germanic origin; related to Old Norse *hein.*

> **USAGE** See usage at **HOME**.

Ho·neck·er /'hōnəkər/, Erich (1912–94), East German statesman; head of state 1976–89. His repressive regime was marked by a close allegiance to the former Soviet Union. He was ousted in 1989 as communism began to collapse throughout Eastern Europe.

hon·est /'änist/ ▶ **adj.** free of deceit and untruthfulness; sincere: *I haven't been totally honest with you.* ■ morally correct or virtuous: *I did the only right and honest thing.* ■ [attrib.] fairly earned, esp. through hard work: *struggling to make an honest living.* ■ (of an action) blameless or well intentioned even if unsuccessful or misguided: *he'd made an honest mistake.* ■ [attrib.] simple, unpretentious, and unsophisticated: *good honest food with no gimmicks.*
▶ **adv.** [sentence adverb] informal used to persuade someone of the truth of something: *you'll like it when you get there, honest.*
– PHRASES **make an honest woman of** dated or humorous marry a woman, esp. to avoid scandal if she is pregnant. [*honest* here originally meant 'respectable,' but was probably associated with the archaic sense 'chaste, virtuous.'] **to be honest** speaking frankly: *I've never been much of a movie buff, to be honest.*
– ORIGIN Middle English (originally in the sense 'held in or deserving of honor'): via Old French from Latin *honestus*, from *honos* (see **HONOR**).

hon·est bro·ker ▶ **n.** an impartial mediator in international, industrial, or other disputes.
– ORIGIN late 19th cent.: translating German *ehrlicher Makler* with reference to **BISMARCK**[2], under whom Germany was united.

hon·est·ly /'änistlē/ ▶ **adv. 1** in a truthful, fair, or honorable way: *he'd come by the money honestly.* **2** used to emphasize the sincerity of an opinion, belief, or feeling: *she honestly believed that she was making life easier for Jack.* ■ [sentence adverb] used to emphasize the sincerity or truthfulness of a statement: *honestly, darling, I'm not upset.* ■ [sentence adverb] used to indicate the speaker's disapproval, annoyance, or impatience: *honestly, that man is the absolute limit!*

hon·est-to-God informal ▶ **adj.** [attrib.] genuine; real: *an honest-to-God celebrity.*
▶ **adv.** genuinely; really: [as exclamation] *"You mean you didn't know?" "Honest to God!"*

hon·est-to-good·ness ▶ **adj.** [attrib.] genuine and straightforward: *an honest-to-goodness family vacation in the sun.*

hon·es·ty /'änistē/ ▶ **n. 1** the quality of being honest: *they spoke with convincing honesty about their fears | it was not, in all honesty, an auspicious debut.* **2** a European plant with purple or white flowers and round, flat, translucent seedpods that are used for indoor flower arrangements. Also called **MONEY PLANT**. ● Genus *Lunaria*, family Brassicaceae.
– ORIGIN Middle English: from Old French *honeste*, from Latin *honestas*, from *honestus* (see **HONEST**). The original sense was 'honor, respectability,' later 'decorum, virtue, chastity.' The plant is so named from its seedpods, translucency symbolizing lack of deceit.

hone·wort /'hōnˌwərt, -ˌwôrt/ ▶ **n.** a wild plant of the parsley family. ● Two species in the family Umbelliferae: *Cryptotaenia canadensis*, a native of North America and eastern Asia that is cultivated for food in Japan, and *Trinia glauca*, a small European plant.
– ORIGIN mid 17th cent.: from obsolete *hone* 'swelling' (for which the plant was believed to be a remedy) + **WORT**.

hon·ey /'hənē/ ▶ **n.** (pl. **honeys**) **1** a sweet, sticky, yellowish-brown fluid made by bees and other insects from nectar collected from flowers. ■ a yellowish-brown or golden color: [as modifier] *her honey skin.* ■ any sweet substance similar to bees' honey. **2** informal an excellent example of something: *it's one honey of an adaptation.* ■ darling; sweetheart (usually as a form of address): *hi, honey!*
– ORIGIN Old English *hunig*, of Germanic origin; related to Dutch *honig* and German *Honig.*

hon·ey ant ▶ **n.** an ant that stores large amounts of honeydew and nectar in its elastic abdomen, which becomes greatly distended. This is then fed to nest mates by regurgitation. ● *Myrmecocystus* and other genera, family Formicidae.

hon·ey badg·er ▶ **n.** another term for **RATEL**.

hon·ey·bee /'hənēˌbē/ ▶ **n.** (also **hive bee**) a stinging winged insect that collects nectar and pollen, produces wax and honey, and lives in large communities. It was domesticated for its honey around the end of the Neolithic period and is usually kept in hives. ● Four species in the genus *Apis*, family Apidae, in particular the widespread *A. mellifera.*

honeybees

hon·ey buck·et ▶ **n.** informal a toilet that does not use water and has to be emptied manually.

hon·ey·bunch /'hənēˌbənch/ (also **honeybun** /-ˌbən/) ▶ **n.** informal darling (used as a form of address).

hon·ey·comb /'hənēˌkōm/ ▶ **n. 1** a structure of hexagonal cells of wax, made by bees to store honey and eggs. **2** a structure of adjoining cavities or cells: *a honeycomb of caves.* ■ a mass of cavities produced by corrosion or dissolution: [as modifier] *honeycomb weathering.* ■ a raised hexagonal or cellular pattern on the face of a fabric. **3** tripe from the second stomach of a ruminant.
▶ **v.** [with obj.] fill with cavities or tunnels: *whole hillsides were honeycombed with mines.* ■ infiltrate and undermine: *their men honeycombed the army.*
– ORIGIN Old English *hunigcamb* (see **HONEY**, **COMB**).

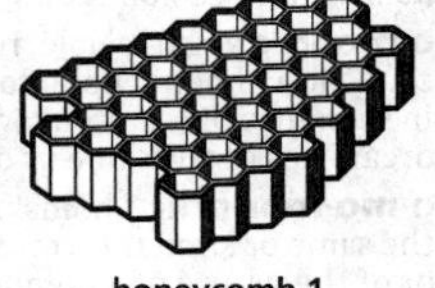
honeycomb 1

hon·ey·creep·er /'hənēˌkrēpər/ ▶ **n. 1** a tropical American tanager with a long curved bill, feeding on nectar and insects. ● Genera *Cyanerpes* and *Chlorophanes*, family Emberizidae (subfamily Thraupinae): five species. **2** (also **Hawaiian honeycreeper**) a Hawaiian songbird of variable appearance and with a specialized bill, several kinds of which are now endangered. ● Family Drepanididae (or Fringillidae): several genera and species, often with Hawaiian names such as the iiwi and ou.

hon·ey·dew /'hənēˌd(y)o͞o/ ▶ **n. 1** a sweet, sticky substance excreted by aphids and often deposited on leaves and stems. ■ literary an ideally sweet substance. **2** (also **honeydew melon**) a melon of a variety with smooth pale skin and sweet green flesh.

hon·ey·eat·er /'hənēˌētər/ ▶ **n.** an Australasian songbird with a long brushlike tongue for feeding on nectar. ● Family Meliphagidae: numerous species and genera.

hon·eyed /'hənēd/ (also **honied**) ▶ **adj. 1** (of food) containing or coated with honey. ■ having a rich sweetness of taste or smell: *as the wine matures, it becomes more honeyed.* ■ having a golden or warm yellow color. **2** (of a person's words or tone of voice) soothing, soft, and intended to please or flatter: *he wooed her with honeyed words.*

hon·ey fun·gus ▶ **n.** another term for **HONEY MUSHROOM**.

hon·ey·guide /'hənēˌgīd/ ▶ **n.** a small bird of the Old World tropics, typically having drab plumage and feeding chiefly on beeswax and bee grubs. Two African kinds attract humans and other mammals, esp. ratels, to bee nests. ● Family Indicatoridae: four genera, esp. *Indicator.*

hon·ey lo·cust ▶ **n.** a tree of the pea family with long branched thorns, although a thornless variety has been cultivated and is typically grown as an ornamental for its fernlike foliage. ● Genus *Gleditsia*, family Leguminosae: several species, in particular the North American *G. triacanthos*, the pods of which contain a sweet pulp.

hon·ey·moon /'hənēˌmo͞on/ ▶ **n.** a vacation spent together by a newly married couple: *romantic hand-holding breakfasts together on their honeymoon.* ■ [often as modifier] an initial period of enthusiasm or goodwill, typically at the start of a new job: *the new president's honeymoon period.*
▶ **v.** [no obj.] spend a honeymoon: *they are honeymooning in the south of France.*
– DERIVATIVES **hon·ey·moon·er** **n.**
– ORIGIN mid 16th cent. (originally denoting the period of time following a wedding): from **HONEY** + **MOON**. The original reference was to affection waning like the moon, but later the sense became 'the first month after marriage.'

hon·ey mush·room ▶ **n.** a widespread parasitic fungus that produces clumps of honey-colored toadstools at the base of trees. The black stringlike hyphae invade a tree, causing decay or death and spreading out to other trees. Also called **HONEY FUNGUS**. ● *Armillaria mellea*, family Tricholomataceae, class Hymenomycetes.

hon·ey pos·sum ▶ **n.** a tiny shrewlike marsupial with a long pointed snout and a prehensile tail, found only in southwestern Australia, where it feeds exclusively upon nectar and pollen. ● *Tarsipes rostratus*, the only member of the family Tarsipedidae.

hon·ey·pot /'hənēˌpät/ ▶ **n. 1** a container in which honey is kept. ■ a place to which many people are attracted: *its elegant shops make Florence a global honeypot.* **2** vulgar slang a woman's genitals.

hon·ey·pot ant ▶ **n.** another term for **HONEY ANT**.

hon·ey·suck·er /'hənēˌsəkər/ ▶ **n.** any of a number of long-billed birds that feed on nectar, esp. (in South Africa) a sunbird.

hon·ey·suck·le /'hənēˌsəkəl/ ▶ **n.** a widely distributed climbing shrub with tubular flowers that are typically fragrant and of two colors or shades, opening in the evening for pollination by moths. ● Genera *Lonicera* and *Diervilla*, family Caprifoliaceae (the **honeysuckle family**): many species, including the common Japanese **honeysuckle** (*L. japonica*), the **trumpet honeysuckle** (*L. sempervirens*), and the **northern bush honeysuckle** (*D. lonicera*). The honeysuckle

family also includes such berry-bearing shrubs as guelder rose, elder, and snowberry.
– ORIGIN Middle English *honysoukil*, extension of *honysouke*, from Old English *hunigsūce* (see HONEY, SUCK). It originally denoted tubular flowers, such as the red clover, which are sucked for their nectar.

hon·ey·trap /ˈhənē,trap/ (also **honey trap**) ▶ **n.** a stratagem in which irresistible bait is used to lure a victim.

hon·ey·wort /ˈhən,wərt, -wôrt/ ▶ **n.** a Mediterranean plant of the borage family with grayish-green leaves and tubular yellow or purple flowers that are a favored source of nectar for bees. ● Genus *Cerinthe*, family Boraginaceae: several species, in particular the yellow-flowered *C. major*.

hong·i /ˈhängē/ ▶ **n.** NZ (usu. **the hongi**) a traditional Maori greeting in which people press their noses together.
– ORIGIN Maori.

Hong Kong /ˈhäng ˈkäng, ˈhông ˈkông/ a special administrative region on the southeastern coast of China, a former British dependency; pop. 7,346,600 (est. 2009). The area comprises Hong Kong Island, ceded by China in 1841; the Kowloon peninsula, ceded in 1860; and the New Territories, additional areas of the mainland that were leased for 99 years in 1898. All were returned to China in 1997. Hong Kong has become one of the world's major financial and manufacturing centers.

Ho·ni·a·ra /,hōnēˈärə/ the capital of the Solomon Islands, a port on the northwestern coast of the island of Guadalcanal; pop. 66,000 (est. 2007).

hon·ied /ˈhənēd/ ▶ **adj.** variant spelling of HONEYED.

ho·ni soit qui mal y pense /,ônē ˈswä kē ,mäl ē ˈpäns/ ▶ **exclam.** shame on him who thinks evil of it (the motto of the Order of the Garter).
– ORIGIN French.

honk /häNGk, hôNGk/ ▶ **n.** the cry of a wild goose. ■ the harsh sound of a car horn.
▶ **v. 1** ■ make or cause to make a honk: [with obj.] *taxi drivers honking their horns* | [no obj.] *geese circled around and honked.*
2 Brit. informal vomit.
– ORIGIN mid 19th cent.: imitative.

honk·er /ˈhäNGkər, ˈhôNG-/ ▶ **n.** a person or thing that honks. ■ informal a wild goose.

hon·ky /ˈhäNGkē, ˈhôNG-/ ▶ **n.** (pl. **honkies**) informal a derogatory term used by black people for a white person or for white people collectively.
– ORIGIN 1960s: of unknown origin.

hon·ky-tonk /ˈhäNGkē ,täNGk, ˈhôNGkē ,tôNGk/ ▶ **n.** informal **1** a cheap or disreputable bar, club, or dance hall, typically where country music is played: *country bands at highway honky-tonks.* ■ [as modifier] squalid and disreputable: *a honky-tonk beach resort.*
2 a style of country and western music of the 1950s associated with honky-tonks: *good-time urban cowboy fare with a hint of honky-tonk and a healthy measure of rock.*
3 [often as modifier] ragtime piano music.
– ORIGIN late 19th cent.: of unknown origin.

hon·nête homme /ôˈnet ˈôm/ ▶ **n.** a decent, cultivated man of the world; a gentleman.
– ORIGIN mid 17th cent.: French, literally 'honest man.'

Hon·o·lu·lu /,hänlˈoolōō, ,hōn-/ the capital of Hawaii, a principal port on the southeastern coast of the island of Oahu; pop. 374,676 (est. 2008).

hon·or /ˈänər/ (Brit. **honour**) ▶ **n. 1** high respect; esteem: *his portrait hangs in the place of honor.* ■ [in sing.] a person or thing that brings credit: *you are an honor to our profession.* ■ adherence to what is right or to a conventional standard of conduct: *I must as a matter of honor avoid any taint of dishonesty.*
2 a privilege: *the great poet of whom it is my honor to speak tonight.* ■ a thing conferred as a distinction, esp. an official award for bravery or achievement: *the highest military honors.* ■ (**honors**) a special distinction for proficiency in an examination: *she passed with honors.* ■ (**honors**) a class or course of degree studies more specialized than that of the ordinary level: [as modifier] *an honors degree in mathematics.* ■ (**His, Your,** etc., **Honor**) a title of respect given to or used in addressing a judge or a mayor. ■ Golf the right of teeing off first, having won the previous hole.
3 dated a woman's chastity or her reputation for this: *she died defending her honor.*
4 Bridge an ace, king, queen, or jack. ■ (**honors**) possession in one's hand of at least four of the ace, king, queen, and jack of trumps, or of all four aces in no trumps, for which a bonus is scored. ■ (in whist) an ace, king, queen, or jack of trumps.
▶ **v.** [with obj.] **1** regard with great respect: *Joyce has now learned to honor her father's memory* | (as adj. **honored**) *an honored guest.* ■ pay public respect to: *talented writers were honored at a special ceremony.*
2 fulfill (an obligation) or keep (an agreement): *make sure the franchisees honor the terms of the contract.* ■ accept (a bill) or pay (a check) when due: *the bank informed him that the check would not be honored.*
– PHRASES **do the honors** informal perform a social duty or small ceremony for others (often used to describe the serving of food or drink to a guest). **honor bright** dated "on my honor": *I'll never do it again, honor bright, I won't.* [from Thomas Moore's *Tom Cribb's Memorial to Congress* (1819).] **in honor bound** another way of saying HONOR. **in honor of** as a celebration of or expression of respect for. **on one's honor** under a moral obligation: *they are on their honor as gentlemen not to cheat.* **on** (or **upon**) **my honor** used as an expression of sincerity: *I promise on my honor.* **there's honor among thieves** proverb dishonest people may have certain standards of behavior that they will respect.
– ORIGIN Middle English: from Old French *onor* (noun), *onorer* (verb), from Latin *honor.*

hon·or·a·ble /ˈänərəbəl/ (Brit. **honourable**) ▶ **adj. 1** bringing or worthy of honor: *this is the only honorable course* | *a decent and honorable man.* ■ formal or humorous (of the intentions of a man courting a woman) directed toward marriage: *the young man's intentions had been honorable.*
2 (**Honorable**) used as a title indicating eminence or distinction, given esp. to judges and certain high officials: *the Honorable Richard Morris Esquire, chief justice of the supreme court of our state.*
– DERIVATIVES **hon·or·a·ble·ness n., hon·or·a·bly adv.**
– ORIGIN Middle English: via Old French from Latin *honorabilis*, from *honor* 'honor.'

hon·or·a·ble dis·charge ▶ **n.** discharge from military service with a favorable record.

hon·or·a·ble men·tion ▶ **n.** a commendation given to a candidate in an examination or competition who is not awarded a prize.

hon·or·and /ˈänərənd, -,rand/ ▶ **n.** a person to be publicly honored, esp. with an honorary degree.
– ORIGIN 1950s: from Latin *honorandus* 'to be honored,' gerundive of *honorare* 'to honor,' from *honor* 'honor.'

hon·o·rar·i·um /,änəˈre(ə)rēəm/ ▶ **n.** (pl. **honorariums** or **honoraria** /-ˈre(ə)rēə/) a payment given for professional services that are rendered nominally without charge.
– ORIGIN mid 17th cent.: from Latin, denoting a gift made on being admitted to public office, from *honorarius* (see HONORARY).

hon·or·ar·y /ˈänə,rerē/ ▶ **adj. 1** conferred as an honor, without the usual requirements or functions: *an honorary doctorate.* ■ (of a person) holding such a title or position: *an honorary member of the club.*
2 Brit. (of an office or its holder) unpaid: *Honorary Secretary of the Association.*
– ORIGIN early 17th cent.: from Latin *honorarius*, from *honor* 'honor.'

hon·o·ree /,änəˈrē/ ▶ **n.** a person who receives an honor.

hon·or guard another term for GUARD OF HONOR.

hon·or·if·ic /,änəˈrifik/ ▶ **adj.** (of an office or position) given as a mark of respect, but having few or no duties. ■ denoting a form of address showing high status, politeness, or respect: *an honorific title for addressing women.*
▶ **n.** a title or word implying or expressing high status, politeness, or respect: *he will be able to put the honorific after his name: licenciado, "college graduate."*
– DERIVATIVES **hon·or·if·i·cal·ly** /ik(ə)lē/ **adv.**
– ORIGIN mid 17th cent.: from Latin *honorificus*, from *honor* 'honor.'

ho·no·ris cau·sa /äˈnôris ˈkôzə, ˈkousə/ ▶ **adv.** (esp. of a degree awarded without examination) as a mark of esteem: *the artist has been awarded the degree honoris causa.*
– ORIGIN early 17th cent.: Latin, literally 'for honor's sake.'

hon·or kill·ing ▶ **n.** in certain cultures, the killing of a relative, esp. a girl or woman, who is perceived to have brought dishonor on the family.

hon·or point ▶ **n.** Heraldry the point halfway between the top of a shield and the fess point.

hon·ors list ▶ **n.** a publicly issued list of people and the distinctions they are to be awarded.

hon·or so·ci·e·ty ▶ **n.** an organization for high-school or college students of high academic achievement.

hon·ors of war ▶ **plural n.** privileges granted to a capitulating force, for example, that of marching out with colors flying.

hon·or sys·tem ▶ **n.** [in sing.] a system of payment or examination that relies solely on the honesty of those concerned.

hon·our ▶ **n. & v.** British spelling of HONOR.

hon·our·a·ble ▶ **adj.** British spelling of HONORABLE.

Hon·shu /ˈhänSHoo/ the largest of the four main islands of Japan; pop 103,000,000 (est. 2005).

Hooch, Pieter de, see DE HOOCH.

hooch¹ /hooCH/ (also **hootch**) ▶ **n.** informal alcoholic liquor, esp. inferior or illicit whiskey.
– ORIGIN late 19th cent.: abbreviation of *Hoochinoo*, the name of an Alaskan Indian people who made liquor.

hooch² /hooCH/ ▶ **n.** informal a shelter or improvised dwelling.
– ORIGIN 1950s (originally military slang): perhaps from Japanese *uchi* 'dwelling.'

hood¹ /hood/ ▶ **n. 1** a covering for the head and neck with an opening for the face, typically forming part of a coat or sweatshirt. ■ a separate garment similar to this worn over a college gown or a surplice to indicate the wearer's degree. ■ Falconry a leather covering for a hawk's head.
2 a thing resembling a hood in shape or use, in particular: ■ a metal part covering the engine of an automobile. ■ a canopy to protect users of machinery or to remove fumes from it. ■ a hoodlike structure or marking on the head or neck of an animal. ■ the upper part of the flower of a plant such as a dead-nettle. ■ Brit. a folding waterproof cover of an automobile, baby carriage, etc.
▶ **v.** [with obj.] put a hood on or over.
– DERIVATIVES **hood·less adj., hood·like** /-,līk/ **adj.**
– ORIGIN Old English *hōd*; related to Dutch *hoed*, German *Hut* 'hat,' also to HAT.

hood² ▶ **n.** informal a gangster or similar violent criminal.
– ORIGIN 1930s: abbreviation of HOODLUM.

hood³ (also **'hood**) ▶ **n.** informal a neighborhood, esp. one's own neighborhood: *I've lived in the hood for 15 years.*
– ORIGIN 1970s: shortening of NEIGHBORHOOD.

-hood ▶ **suffix** forming nouns: **1** denoting a condition or quality: *falsehood* | *womanhood.*
2 denoting a collection or group: *brotherhood.*
– ORIGIN Old English *-hād*, originally an independent noun meaning 'person, condition, quality.'

Hood, Mount /hood/ a peak in the Cascade Range in northwest Oregon, east of Portland, 11,239 feet (3,426 m), the highest point in the state.

hood·ed /ˈhoodid/ ▶ **adj.** (of an article of clothing) having a hood: *a hooded cape in violet silk.* ■ (of a person) wearing a hood: *a hooded figure.* ■ (of eyes) having thick, drooping upper eyelids resembling hoods: *a dark man with hooded eyes.*

hood·ed crow ▶ **n.** a bird of the northern and eastern European race of the carrion crow, having a gray body with a black head, wings, and tail. ● *Corvus corone cornix*, family Corvidae.

hood·ed seal ▶ **n.** a seal with a gray and white blotched coat, found in the Arctic waters of the North Atlantic. The male has a nasal sac that is inflated into a hood during display. ● *Cystophora cristata*, family Phocidae.

hood·i·a /ˈhoodēə/ ▶ **n.** a southern African cactus from which a compound that acts as an appetite suppressant is derived. ● Genus *Hoodia*, family Asclepiadaceae; about 20 species.
– ORIGIN from modern Latin *Hoodia*, from *Hood*, the name of an English plant grower.

hood·ie /ˈhoodē/ (also **hoody**) ▶ **n.** (pl. **hoodies**) a hooded sweatshirt or jacket: *outerwear is either a denim jacket or a hoodie.*
– ORIGIN from *hood* + *-ie* or *-y.*

hood·lum /ˈhoodləm, ˈhood-/ ▶ **n.** a person who engages in crime and violence; a hooligan or gangster.
– ORIGIN late 19th cent. (originally US): of unknown origin.

hood mold (also **hood molding**) ▶ **n.** Architecture another term for DRIPSTONE (sense 1).

hoo·doo /ˈhoo,doo/ ▶ **n. 1** voodoo; witchcraft. ■ a run of bad luck associated with a person or activity: *when is this hoodoo going to end?* ■ a person or thing that brings or causes bad luck.
2 a column or pinnacle of weathered rock: *a towering sandstone hoodoo.*
▶ **v.** (**hoodoos, hoodooing, hoodooed**) [with obj.] bewitch: *she's hoodooed you.* ■ bring bad luck to: *a fine player, but repeatedly hoodooed.*
– ORIGIN late 19th cent. (originally US): apparently an alteration of VOODOO. It originally denoted a person who practiced voodoo, hence a hidden cause of bad luck (sense 1 of the noun). Sense 2 of the

h

noun is apparently due to the resemblance of the rock column to a strange human form, often topped by an overhanging "hat" of harder rock.

hood·wink /ˈho͝odˌwiNGk/ ▶ **v.** [with obj.] deceive or trick (someone): *an attempt to hoodwink the public.*
– ORIGIN mid 16th cent. (originally in the sense 'to blindfold'): from the noun **HOOD**[1] + an obsolete sense of **WINK** 'close the eyes.'

hood·y /ˈho͝odē/ ▶ **n.** variant spelling of **HOODIE**.

hoo·ey /ˈho͞oē/ ▶ **n.** informal nonsense: *your interest is just a lot of hooey and I know it.*
– ORIGIN 1920s (originally US): of unknown origin.

hoof /ho͝of, ho͞of/ ▶ **n.** (pl. **hoofs** or **hooves** /ho͝ovz, ho͞ovz/) the horny part of the foot of an ungulate animal, esp. a horse: *there was a clatter of hoofs as a rider came up to them.*
▶ **v.** [with obj.] informal (**hoof it**) go on foot: *it was awfully hot, but we hoofed it all the way back.* ■ dance: *we hoof it reasonably fancily, and no one guffaws.*
– PHRASES **on the hoof 1** (of livestock) not yet slaughtered. **2** informal without great thought or preparation: *policy was made on the hoof.*
– DERIVATIVES **hoofed** adj.
– ORIGIN Old English *hōf*, of Germanic origin; related to Dutch *hoef* and German *Huf*.

hoof-and-mouth dis·ease ▶ **n.** another term for **FOOT-AND-MOUTH DISEASE**.

hoof·er /ˈho͝ofər, ˈho͞ofər/ ▶ **n.** informal a professional dancer.

Hoo·ghly /ˈho͞oglē/ (also **Hugli**) the most western of the rivers in the Ganges delta, in West Bengal, India. It flows for 120 miles (192 km) into the Bay of Bengal and is navigable to Kolkata (Calcutta).

hoo-ha /ˈho͞oˌhä/ ▶ **n.** [in sing.] informal a commotion; a fuss: *the book was causing such a hoo-ha.*
– ORIGIN 1930s: of unknown origin.

hook /ho͝ok/ ▶ **n. 1** a piece of metal or other material, curved or bent back at an angle, for catching hold of or hanging things on: *a picture hook.* ■ (also **fishhook**) a bent piece of metal, typically barbed and baited, for catching fish.
2 a thing designed to catch people's attention: *companies are looking for a sales hook.* ■ a chorus or repeated instrumental passage in a piece of popular music that gives it immediate appeal and makes it easy to remember.
3 a curved cutting instrument, esp. as used for reaping or shearing.
4 a short swinging punch made with the elbow bent, esp. in boxing: *a perfectly timed right hook to the chin.* ■ Golf a stroke that makes the ball deviate in flight in the direction of the follow-through (from right to left for a right-handed player), typically inadvertently. Compare with **SLICE**.
5 a curved stroke in handwriting, esp. as made in learning to write. ■ Music an added stroke transverse to the stem in the symbol for an eighth note or other note.
6 [usu. in place names] a curved promontory or sand spit.
▶ **v. 1** [with obj.] attach or fasten with a hook or hooks: *the truck had a red lamp hooked to its tailgate | she tried to* **hook up** *her bra* | [no obj.] *a ladder that hooks over the roof ridge.* ■ bend or be bent into the shape of a hook so as to fasten around or to an object: [with obj.] *he hooked his thumbs in his belt* | [no obj.] *her legs hooked around mine.*
2 [with obj.] catch with a hook: *he hooked a 24-lb pike.* ■ informal captivate: *I was hooked by John's radical zeal.* ■ archaic, informal steal.
3 [with obj.] Golf strike (the ball) or play (a stroke) so that the ball deviates in the direction of the follow-through, typically inadvertently. ■ [no obj.] Boxing punch one's opponent with the elbow bent.
4 [with obj.] Rugby push (the ball) backward with the foot from the front line in a scrum.
5 [no obj.] (usu. as noun **hooking**) informal (of a woman) work as a prostitute.
– PHRASES **by hook or by crook** by any possible means: *the government intends, by hook or by crook, to hold on to the land.* **get one's hooks into** informal get hold of: *they were going to move out rather than let Mel get his hooks into them.* **get** (or **give someone**) **the hook** informal be dismissed (or dismiss someone) from a job. **hook, line, and sinker** used to emphasize that someone has been completely deceived or tricked: *he fell hook, line, and sinker for this year's April Fool joke.* [with allusion to the taking of bait by a fish.] **off the hook 1** informal no longer in difficulty or trouble: *I lied to get him off the hook.* **2** (of a telephone receiver) not on its rest, and so preventing incoming calls. **on the hook for** informal (in a financial context) responsible for: *he's on the hook for about $9.5 million.* **on one's own hook** informal, dated on one's own account; by oneself.
– PHRASAL VERBS **hook up 1** (also **hook someone/something up**) link or be linked to electronic equipment: *he was hooked up to an electrocardiograph.* **2** informal (of two people) meet or form a relationship: *she decides to hook up with Jake, a kid from the nearby boys' school.* ■ engage in a casual sexual relationship: *hooking up with total strangers can be very dangerous.*
– DERIVATIVES **hook·less** adj., **hook·let** /-lit/ n., **hook·like** /-ˌlīk/ adj.
– ORIGIN Old English *hōc*, of Germanic origin; related to Dutch *hoek* 'corner, angle, projecting piece of land,' also to German *Haken* 'hook.'

hookah

hook·ah /ˈho͝okə, ˈho͞okə/ ▶ **n.** an oriental tobacco pipe with a long, flexible tube that draws the smoke through water contained in a bowl.
– ORIGIN mid 18th cent.: from Urdu, from Arabic *ḥuḳḳa* 'casket, jar.'

hook and eye ▶ **n.** a small metal hook and loop used together as a fastener on a garment.

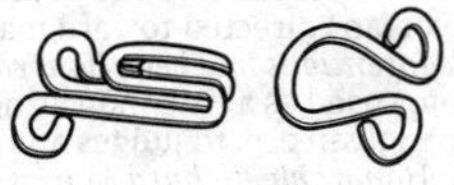

hook and eye

hook-and-lad·der truck ▶ **n.** a fire engine that carries extension ladders and other firefighting and rescue equipment.

Hooke /ho͝ok/, Robert (1635–1703), English scientist. He formulated the law of elasticity (Hooke's law), proposed an undulating theory of light, introduced the term *cell* to biology, postulated elliptical orbits for the earth and moon, and proposed the inverse square law of gravitational attraction.

hooked /ho͝okt/ ▶ **adj. 1** having a hook or hooks: *a hooked gold earring.* ■ curved like a hook: *a golden eagle with hooked beak.*
2 informal captivated; absorbed: *he was* **hooked on** *a video game.* ■ addicted: *a girl who got* **hooked on** *cocaine.*
3 (of a rug or mat) made by pulling yarn through canvas with a hook.

Hook·er[1] /ˈho͝okər/, Sir Joseph Dalton (1817–1911), English botanist and pioneer in phytogeography. He applied Darwin's theories to plants and, with **George Bentham** (1800–84), he produced a work on classification, *Genera Plantarum* (1862–83).

Hook·er[2], Thomas (*c.*1586–1647), American clergyman; born in England. A founding settler of Hartford, Connecticut, in 1636, he helped to write the *Fundamental Orders* (1639), which was Connecticut's original constitution.

hook·er[1] /ˈho͝okər/ ▶ **n. 1** informal a prostitute.
2 Rugby the player in the middle of the front row of the scrum, who tries to hook the ball.

hook·er[2] ▶ **n.** a one-masted sailboat of a kind used esp. in Ireland for fishing. ■ Nautical, informal an old boat.
– ORIGIN mid 17th cent.: from Dutch *hoeker*, from *hoek* 'hook' (used earlier in *hoekboot*, denoting a two-masted Dutch fishing vessel).

hook·er[3] ▶ **n.** informal a glass or drink of undiluted brandy, whiskey, or other liquor.
– ORIGIN mid 19th cent.: of unknown origin.

Hooke's law /ho͝oks/ Physics a law stating that the strain in a solid is proportional to the applied stress within the elastic limit of that solid.

hook·ey ▶ **n.** variant spelling of **HOOKY**[1].

hook-nosed ▶ **adj.** having a prominent aquiline nose.

hook shot ▶ **n.** Basketball a one-handed shot in which a player extends one arm out to the side and over the head toward the basket.

hook·tip /ˈho͝okˌtip/ ▶ **n.** a slender moth that has hooked tips to the forewings. The caterpillar tapers to a point at the rear and rests with both ends raised. ● Family Drepanidae: *Drepana* and other genera.

hook·up /ˈho͝okˌəp/ ▶ **n.** a connection to a public electric, water, or sewer line, or to a similar service: *the campground has 70 sites with water and sewer hookups.* ■ an interconnection of broadcasting equipment for special transmissions: *he reached a global audience on the satellite hookup.*

hook·worm /ˈho͝okˌwərm/ ▶ **n.** a parasitic nematode worm that inhabits the intestines of humans and other animals. It has hooklike mouthparts with which it attaches itself to the wall of the gut, puncturing the blood vessels and feeding on the

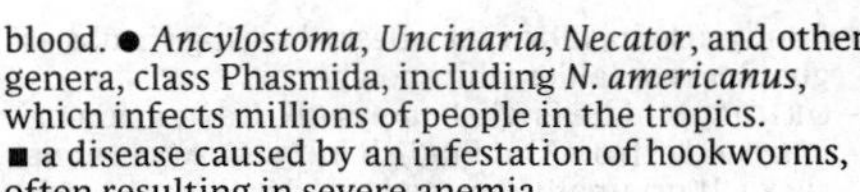

blood. ● *Ancylostoma, Uncinaria, Necator*, and other genera, class Phasmida, including *N. americanus*, which infects millions of people in the tropics. ■ a disease caused by an infestation of hookworms, often resulting in severe anemia.

hook·y[1] /ˈho͝okē/ (also **hookey**) ▶ **n.** (in phrase **play hooky**) informal stay away from school or work without permission or explanation.
– ORIGIN mid 19th cent. (originally US): of unknown origin.

hook·y[2] ▶ **adj.** (of a tune or a component of a tune) having immediate appeal and easy to remember: *a hooky bass line.*

hoo·li·gan /ˈho͞oləgin/ ▶ **n.** a violent young troublemaker, typically one of a gang.
– DERIVATIVES **hoo·li·gan·ism** /-ˌnizəm/ n.
– ORIGIN late 19th cent.: perhaps from *Hooligan*, the surname of a fictional rowdy Irish family in a music-hall song of the 1890s, also of a character in a cartoon.

hoo·lock /ˈho͞oˌläk/ (also **hoolock gibbon**) ▶ **n.** a gibbon with white eyebrows, the male of which has black fur and the female golden, found from northeastern India to Burma (Myanmar). ● *Hylobates hoolock*, family Hylobatidae.
– ORIGIN early 19th cent.: perhaps from Bengali and imitative of the animal's cry.

hoop /ho͞op/ ▶ **n.** a circular band of metal, wood, or similar material, esp. one used for binding the staves of barrels or forming part of a framework. ■ the round metal rim from which a basketball net is suspended. ■ (**hoops**) informal the game of basketball. ■ a large ring used as a toy by being bowled along. ■ a large ring, typically with paper stretched over it, for circus performers to jump through. ■ historical a circle of flexible material used for expanding a woman's petticoat or skirt. ■ short for **HOOP PETTICOAT**. ■ chiefly Brit. a croquet wicket.
▶ **v.** [with obj.] bind or encircle with or as with hoops.
– PHRASES **jump through hoops** perform a difficult and grueling series of tests at someone else's request or command: *we had to jump through all sorts of hoops to win accreditation.* **shoot hoops** play basketball.
– DERIVATIVES **hooped** adj.
– ORIGIN late Old English *hōp*; related to Dutch *hoep*.

hoop·er /ˈho͞opər/ ▶ **n.** old-fashioned term for **COOPER**.
– ORIGIN Middle English: from **HOOP**.

hoop·head ▶ **n.** informal a basketball player or devoted fan.

hoop i·ron ▶ **n.** flattened iron in long thin strips used for binding together the staves of casks or tubs.

hoop·la /ˈho͞oˌplä, ˈho͝opˌlä/ ▶ **n. 1** informal excitement surrounding an event or situation, esp. when considered to be unnecessary fuss: *the hoopla and ceremony of international competition.*
2 Brit. a game in which rings are thrown from behind a line in an attempt to encircle one of several prizes.

hoo·poe /ˈho͞oˌpō, -ˌpo͞o/ ▶ **n.** a salmon-pink Eurasian bird with a long down-curved bill, a large erectile crest, and black and white wings and tail. ● *Upupa epops*, the only member of the family Upupidae.
– ORIGIN mid 17th cent.: alteration of obsolete *hoop*, from Old French *huppe*, from Latin *upupa*, imitative of the bird's call.

hoop pet·ti·coat ▶ **n.** historical a petticoat expanded with hoops of flexible material.

hoop skirt ▶ **n.** historical a skirt worn over a series of hoops that make it spread out.

hoop·ster /ˈho͞opstər/ ▶ **n.** informal a basketball player.

hoo·ray /həˈrā, ho͞o-/ ▶ **exclam.** another term for **HURRAH**.

hoose·gow /ˈho͞osˌgou/ ▶ **n.** informal a prison.
– ORIGIN early 20th cent.: via Latin American Spanish from Spanish *juzgado* 'tribunal,' from Latin *judicatum* 'something judged,' neuter past participle of *judicare*.

Hoo·sier /ˈho͞oZHər/ ▶ **n.** a native or inhabitant of Indiana.
– ORIGIN early 19th cent.: of unknown origin.

Hoo·sier State a nickname for the state of **INDIANA**.

hoot /ho͞ot/ ▶ **n.** a deep or medium-pitched musical sound, often wavering or interrupted, that is the typical call of many kinds of owl. ■ a similar but typically more raucous sound made by a horn, siren, or steam whistle. ■ a shout expressing scorn or disapproval: *there were hoots of derision.* ■ a short outburst of laughter: *the audience broke into hoots of laughter.* ■ (**a hoot**) informal an amusing situation or person: *your mom's a real hoot.*
▶ **v.** [no obj.] (of an owl) utter a hoot. ■ (of a person) make loud sounds of scorn, disapproval, or merriment: *she began to hoot with laughter.* ■ [with obj.] (**hoot something down**) express loud scornful

disapproval of something: *his questions were hooted down or answered obscenely.* ■ (with reference to a horn, siren, etc.) make or cause to make a hoot.
– PHRASES **not care** (or **give**) **a hoot** (or **two hoots**) informal not care at all.
– ORIGIN Middle English (in the sense 'make sounds of derision'): perhaps imitative.

hootch /ho͞oCH/ ▶ n. variant spelling of HOOCH[1].

hoot·en·an·ny /ˈho͞otnˌanē/ ▶ n. (pl. **hootenannies**) informal an informal gathering with folk music and sometimes dancing.
– ORIGIN 1920s (originally US, denoting a gadget or 'thingamajig'): of unknown origin.

hoot·er /ˈho͞otər/ ▶ n. **1** informal a person's nose.
2 (**hooters**) vulgar slang a woman's breasts.
3 Brit. a siren or steam whistle, esp. one used as a signal for work to begin or cease. ■ the horn of a motor vehicle.

Hoo·ver[1] /ˈho͞ovər/ a city in north central Alabama, south of Birmingham; pop. 71,020 (est. 2008).

Hoo·ver[2], Herbert (Clark) (1874–1964), 31st president of the US 1929–33. After serving as secretary of commerce 1921–29 under Presidents Harding and Coolidge, he was elected to the presidency on the Republican ballot. As president, he was faced with the long-term problems of the Depression. Unable to keep his campaign promise of prosperity and to improve his poor record in international affairs, he was defeated by Democrat Franklin D. Roosevelt in 1932.

Herbert Clark Hoover

Hoo·ver[3], J. Edgar (1895–1972), US government official; director of the FBI 1924–72; full name *John Edgar Hoover*. He reorganized the FBI into an efficient, scientific law-enforcement agency, but came under criticism for the organization's role during the McCarthy era and for its reactionary political stance in the 1960s.

Hoo·ver[4], William (Henry) (1849–1932), US industrialist; manufacturer of vacuum cleaners.

Hoo·ver·ville /ˈho͞ovərˌvil/ ▶ n. a shantytown built by unemployed and destitute people during the Depression of the early 1930s.
– ORIGIN named after H.C. HOOVER[1], during whose presidency such accommodations were built (see also -VILLE).

hooves /ho͝ovz, ho͞ovz/ plural form of HOOF.

hop[1] /häp/ ▶ v. (**hops, hopping, hopped**) [no obj.] (of a person) move by jumping on one foot. ■ (of a bird or other animal) move by jumping with two or all feet at once: *a blackbird was hopping around in the sun.* ■ spring or leap a short distance with one jump: *he hopped down from the rock.* ■ [with obj.] jump over (something): *the cow hopped the fence.* ■ informal pass quickly from one place to another: *let's hop over to the bar.* ■ make a quick change of position, location, or activity: *over the years he hopped from one department to another.* ■ [with obj.] informal board (a bus, airplane, or other mode of transportation): *she hopped a train in Winnipeg.* ■ [with obj.] informal jump onto (a moving vehicle): *ex-soldiers looking for work hopped freight trains heading west.* ■ [usu. as noun in combination] (**-hopping**) (of an aircraft or ferry) pass quickly from one place to another: *two-week island-hopping packages.* ■ (**hop it**) Brit. informal go away quickly.
▶ n. **1** a hopping movement. ■ a short journey or distance: *a short hop by cab from Soho.*
2 an informal dance.
– PHRASES **hop, skip, and (a) jump 1** old-fashioned term for TRIPLE JUMP. **2** informal a short distance: *it's just a hop, skip, and a jump from my hometown.* **hop the twig** (or **stick**) Brit. informal depart suddenly or die. **hop to it** begin a task quickly; get busy: *I shall have the experience of snapping my fingers and having people hop to it.* **on the hop** Brit. informal **1** unprepared: *he was caught on the hop.* **2** bustling around; busy: *we were always kept on the hop.*
– PHRASAL VERBS **hop in** (or **out**) informal get into (or out of) a car: *hop in then and we'll be off.*
– ORIGIN Old English *hoppian*, of Germanic origin; related to German dialect *hopfen* and German *hopsen*.

hop[2] ▶ n. a twining climbing plant native to north temperate regions, cultivated for the conelike flowers borne by the female plant, which are used in brewing beer. ● *Humulus lupulus*, family Cannabaceae (or Cannabidaceae).
■ (**hops**) the dried conelike flowers of this plant, used in brewing to give a bitter flavor and as a mild sterilant.
▶ v. (**hops, hopping, hopped**) **1** [with obj.] flavor with hops: *a strong dark beer, heavily hopped.*
2 (**be hopped up**) informal be stimulated or intoxicated by or as if by a psychoactive drug.
– DERIVATIVES **hop·py** adj.
– ORIGIN late Middle English *hoppe* (in the sense 'ripened hop cones for flavoring malt liquor'), from Middle Low German or Middle Dutch.

ho·pak /ˈhōpak/ ▶ n. variant spelling of GOPAK.

Hope /hōp/, Bob (1903–2003), US comedian; born in Britain; born *Leslie Townes Hope*. He often portrayed a cowardly incompetent, cheerfully failing to become a romantic hero, as in the series of *Road* movies (1940–62), in which he starred with Bing Crosby and Dorothy Lamour (1914–96). He is also noted for his annual Christmas television specials 1953–94, many of which telecast the USO shows that he brought to US troops stationed around the world.

hope /hōp/ ▶ n. **1** a feeling of expectation and desire for a certain thing to happen: *he looked through her belongings in the hope of coming across some information* | *I had high hopes of making the Olympic team.* ■ a person or thing that may help or save someone: *their only hope is surgery.* ■ grounds for believing that something good may happen: *he does see some hope for the future.*
2 archaic a feeling of trust.
▶ v. [no obj.] want something to happen or be the case: *he's* ***hoping for*** *an offer of compensation* | [with clause] *I hope that the kids are OK.* ■ [with infinitive] intend if possible to do something: *we're hoping to address all these issues.*
– PHRASES **hope against hope** cling to a mere possibility: *they were hoping against hope that he would find a way out.* **hope for the best** hope for a favorable outcome. **hope springs eternal (in the human breast)** proverb it is human nature to always find fresh cause for optimism. **in hopes of** with the aim of: *I lay on a towel in the park in hopes of getting a tan.* **in hopes that** hoping that: *they are screaming in hopes that a police launch will pick us up.* **not a hope** informal no chance at all.
– DERIVATIVES **hop·er** n.
– ORIGIN late Old English *hopa* (noun), *hopian* (verb), of Germanic origin; related to Dutch *hoop* (noun), *hopen* (verb), and German *hoffen* (verb).

hope chest ▶ n. a chest containing household linen and clothing stored by a woman in preparation for her marriage.

hope·ful /ˈhōpfəl/ ▶ adj. feeling or inspiring optimism about a future event: *a hopeful sign* | [with clause] *he remained hopeful that something could be worked out.*
▶ n. a person likely or hoping to succeed: *a leading gubernatorial hopeful.*
– DERIVATIVES **hope·ful·ness** n.

hope·ful·ly /ˈhōpfəlē/ ▶ adv. **1** in a hopeful manner: *he rode on hopefully.*
2 [sentence adverb] it is to be hoped that: *hopefully, it should be finished by next year.*

USAGE The traditional sense of **hopefully**, 'in a hopeful manner' (*he stared hopefully at the trophy*), has been used since 1593. The first recorded use of **hopefully** as a sentence adverb, meaning 'it is to be hoped that' (*hopefully, we'll see you tomorrow*), appears in 1702 in the *Magnalia Christi Americana*, written by Massachusetts theologian and writer Cotton Mather. This use of **hopefully** is now the most common one. Sentence adverbs in general (*frankly, honestly, regrettably, seriously*) are found in English since at least the 1600s, and their use has become common in recent decades. However, most traditionalists take the view that all sentence adverbs are inherently suspect. Although they concede that the battle over **hopefully** is lost on the popular front, they continue to withhold approval of its use as a sentence adverb. Attentive ears are particularly bothered when the sentence that follows does not match the promise of the introductory adverb, as when *frankly* is followed not by an expression of honesty but by a self-serving proclamation (*frankly, I don't care if you go or not*). See also usage at SENTENCE ADVERB and THANKFULLY.

Ho·peh /ˈhōˈpā/ variant of HEBEI.

hope·less /ˈhōplis/ ▶ adj. **1** feeling or causing despair about something: *his situation was obviously hopeless* | *Jessica looked at him in mute hopeless appeal.*
2 inadequate; incompetent: *I'm* ***hopeless at*** *names.*
– DERIVATIVES **hope·less·ness** n.

hope·less·ly /ˈhōplislē/ ▶ adv. **1** in a way that shows or causes despair: *she sighed hopelessly.*
2 [as submodifier] used to emphasize that a situation is beyond hope of improvement; irredeemably: *before long, he was hopelessly lost.*

hop·head /ˈhäpˌhed/ ▶ n. informal a drug addict.
– ORIGIN early 20th cent.: from HOP[2] + HEAD.

hop horn·beam ▶ n. see HORNBEAM.

Ho·pi /ˈhōpē/ ▶ n. (pl. **same** or **Hopis**) **1** a member of a Pueblo Indian people living chiefly in northeastern Arizona.
2 the Uto-Aztecan language of this people.
▶ adj. of or relating to this people or their language.
– ORIGIN the name in Hopi.

Hop·kins[1] /ˈhäpkənz/, Sir Anthony (1937–), Welsh actor; full name *Philip Anthony Hopkins*. Notable movies: *The Elephant Man* (1980), *The Silence of the Lambs* (1991), *The Remains of the Day* (1993), and *Hannibal* (2001).

Hop·kins[2], Sir Frederick Gowland (1861–1947), English biochemist. He carried out pioneering work on "accessory food factors" essential to the diet, later called vitamins. Nobel Prize for Physiology or Medicine (1929), shared with Christiaan Eijkman.

Hop·kins[3], Gerard Manley (1844–89), English poet. A shipwreck inspired him to write "The Wreck of the Deutschland," which makes use of his "sprung rhythm" technique.

Hop·kins[4], Mark (1802–87), US philosopher and educator. He taught moral philosophy 1830–87 at Williams College and was that institution's president 1836–72. He also served as president of the American Board of Commissioners for Foreign Missions 1857–87.

Hop·kin·son /ˈhäpkənsən/, Francis (1737–91), US public official, musician, and writer. He was a signer of the Declaration of Independence in 1776 and helped to design the first US flag in 1777. A harpsichordist, he is considered the first native-born American composer of classical music.

Hop·kins·ville /ˈhäpkinzˌvil/ a city in southwestern Kentucky, southwest of Bowling Green; pop. 32,076 (est. 2008).

hop·lite /ˈhäpˌlīt/ ▶ n. a heavily armed foot soldier of ancient Greece.
– ORIGIN from Greek *hoplitēs*, from *hoplon* 'weapon.'

Hop·per[1] /ˈhäpər/, Edward (1882–1967), US realist painter. He is best known for his mature works, such as *Early Sunday Morning* (1930) and *Nighthawks* (1942), often depicting isolated figures in bleak scenes from everyday urban life.

Hop·per[2], Grace Murray (1906–92), US admiral, mathematician, and computer scientist. She taught mathematics at Vassar College 1931–44 before serving in the US Navy 1943–86, where she became the highest ranked female officer. From 1959 until 1971, she worked as a computer programmer for the Sperry Rand Corporation.

hop·per /ˈhäpər/ ▶ n. **1** a container for a bulk material such as grain, rock, or trash, typically one that tapers downward and is able to discharge its contents at the bottom. ■ chiefly historical a tapering container, working with a hopping motion, through which grain passed into a mill. ■ (in full **hopper car**) a railroad car able to discharge coal or other bulk material through its floor. ■ a barge for carrying away mud or sediment from a dredging machine and discharging it. ■ (also **hopper head**) a container at the top of a vertical pipe that receives water from a gutter or waste pipe. ■ a box in which bills are put for consideration by a legislature.
2 a person or thing that hops. ■ a hopping insect, esp. a grasshopper.

hop·ping /ˈhäpiNG/ ▶ adj. informal very active or lively: *the delis do a hopping lunch business.*
– PHRASES **hopping mad** informal extremely angry.

hop·ping john ▶ n. (in the southern US and Caribbean) a stew of rice with black-eyed peas, often also containing bacon and red peppers.

hop·ple /ˈhäpəl/ ▶ v. & n. Riding another term for HOBBLE (sense 2 of the verb).
– ORIGIN late 16th cent.: probably of Low German origin and related to early Flemish *hoppelen* and Middle Dutch *hobelen* 'jump, dance'; compare with HOBBLE.

PRONUNCIATION KEY ə *ago, up*; ər *over, fur*; a *hat*; ā *ate*; ä *car*; e *let*; ē *see*; i *fit*; ī *by*; NG *sing*; ō *go*; ô *law, for*; oi *toy*; o͝o *good*; o͞o *goo*; ou *out*; TH *thin*; T͟H *then*; ZH *vision*

h

hop·sack /ˈhäpˌsak/ ▶ **n.** a coarse fabric of a loose plain weave, used for clothing. ▪ a coarse hemp sack used for hops.

hop·scotch /ˈhäpˌskäCH/ ▶ **n.** a children's game in which each child by turn hops into and over squares marked on the ground to retrieve a marker thrown into one of these squares.
▶ **v.** [no obj.] skip from place to place; move erratically: *the blackouts hopscotched around eight Western states | he hopscotched from Indonesia to Hong Kong to Australia to Japan.*
– ORIGIN early 19th cent.: from HOP¹ + SCOTCH¹.

hop·tree /ˈhäpˌtrē/ (also **hop tree**) ▶ **n.** a North American shrub or small tree of the rue family, with bitter fruit that was formerly used in brewing as a substitute for hops. ● *Ptelea trifoliata*, family Rutaceae.

hor. ▶ **abbr.** ▪ horizon. ▪ horizontal. ▪ horology.

ho·ra /ˈhôrə, ˈhōrə/ (also **horah**) ▶ **n.** a Romanian or Israeli dance in which the performers form a ring.
– ORIGIN late 19th cent.: from Romanian *horă*, Hebrew *hōrāh*.

Hor·ace /ˈhôrəs/ (65–68 BC), Roman poet of the Augustan period; full name *Quintus Horatius Flaccus*. A well-known satirist and literary critic, he is noted for his *Odes*. Other works include *Satires* and *Ars Poetica*.

h

ho·ral /ˈhôrəl/ ▶ **adj.** of or relating to an hour or hours; hourly.
– ORIGIN early 18th cent.: from late Latin *horalis*, from Latin *hora* 'hour.'

ho·ra·ry /ˈhôrərē/ ▶ **adj.** archaic of or relating to hours as measurements of time. ▪ occurring every hour: *I took horary observations of the barometer.* ▪ Astrology relating to or denoting a branch of astrology in which answers are given to questions using a chart drawn up for the time a question is posed.
– ORIGIN early 17th cent.: from medieval Latin *horarius*, from Latin *hora* 'hour.'

Ho·ra·tian /həˈrāSHən/ ▶ **adj.** of or relating to the Roman poet Horace or his work. ▪ (of an ode) of several stanzas, each of the same metrical pattern.

hor·cha·ta /ôrˈCHätə/ ▶ **n.** (in Spain and Latin American countries) a milky drink made from ground almonds, tiger nuts, or rice.
– ORIGIN Spanish.

horde /hôrd/ ▶ **n. 1** chiefly derogatory a large group of people: *he was surrounded by a horde of tormenting relatives.* ▪ an army or tribe of nomadic warriors: *Tartar hordes.*
2 Anthropology a loosely knit small social group typically consisting of about five families.
– ORIGIN mid 16th cent. (originally denoting a tribe or troop of Tartar or other nomads): from Polish *horda*, from Turkish *ordu* '(royal) camp.'

USAGE The words **hoard** and **horde** are quite distinct; see usage at HOARD.

hore·hound /ˈhôrˌhound/ (also **hoarhound**) ▶ **n.** a strong-smelling hairy plant of the mint family, with a tradition of use in medicine. ● Two species in the family Labiatae: **white horehound** (*Marrubium vulgare*), a widely distributed plant traditionally used as a medicinal herb, and **black horehound** (*Ballota nigra*), a Eurasian plant that has become naturalized in North America and was formerly reputed to cure the bite of a mad dog.
▪ the bitter aromatic juice of white horehound, used esp. in the treatment of coughs and colds.
– ORIGIN Old English *hāre hūne*, from *hār* (see HOAR) + *hūne*, the name of the white horehound, also applied to related plants.

Hor·gan /ˈhôrgən/, Paul (1903–95), US writer; full name *Paul George Vincent O'Shaughnessy Horgan*. His works, mostly about the southwestern US, include *Great River* (1954) and *Lamy of Santa Fe* (1975).

ho·ri·zon /həˈrīzən/ ▶ **n. 1** [usu. in sing.] the line at which the earth's surface and the sky appear to meet: *the sun rose above the horizon.* ▪ (also **apparent** or **visible horizon**) the circular boundary of the part of the earth's surface visible from a particular point, ignoring irregularities and obstructions. ▪ (also **celestial horizon**) Astronomy a great circle of the celestial sphere, the plane of which passes through the center of the earth and is parallel to that of the apparent horizon of a place.
2 (often **horizons**) the limit of a person's mental perception, experience, or interest: *she wanted to leave home and broaden her horizons.*
3 Geology a layer of soil or rock, or a set of strata, with particular characteristics. ▪ Archaeology a level of an excavated site representing a particular period.
– PHRASES **on the horizon** just imminent or becoming apparent: *trouble could be on the horizon.*
– ORIGIN late Middle English: via Old French from late Latin *horizon*, from Greek *horizōn* (*kuklos*) 'limiting (circle).'

hor·i·zon·tal /ˌhôrəˈzän(t)l/ ▶ **adj. 1** parallel to the plane of the horizon; at right angles to the vertical: *a horizontal line.* ▪ (of machinery) having its parts working in a horizontal direction: *a horizontal steam engine.*
2 combining companies engaged in the same stage or type of production: *a horizontal merger.* ▪ involving social groups of equal status: *horizontal class loyalties.*
3 of or at the horizon: *the horizontal moon.*
▶ **n.** a horizontal line, plane, etc.
– DERIVATIVES **hor·i·zon·tal·i·ty** /-ˌzänˈtalitē/ **n.**, **hor·i·zon·tal·ly adv.**
– ORIGIN mid 16th cent. (sense 3 of the adjective): from French, or from modern Latin *horizontalis*, from late Latin *horizon*, *horizont-* (see HORIZON).

hor·i·zon·tal sta·bi·liz·er ▶ **n.** a horizontal airfoil at the tail of an aircraft.

Hork·heim·er /ˈhôrkˌhīmər/, Max (1895–1973), German philosopher and sociologist; a leading figure of the Frankfurt School.

Hor·liv·ka /ˈhôrləfkə/ an industrial city in southeastern Ukraine, in the Donets Basin; pop. 266,300 (est. 2009). Russian name GORLOVKA.

hor·mone /ˈhôrˌmōn/ ▶ **n.** Physiology a regulatory substance produced in an organism and transported in tissue fluids such as blood or sap to stimulate specific cells or tissues into action. ▪ a synthetic substance with a similar effect. ▪ (**hormones**) a person's sex hormones as held to influence behavior or mood.
– DERIVATIVES **hor·mo·nal** /hôrˈmōnl/ **adj.**
– ORIGIN early 20th cent.: from Greek *hormōn*, present participle of *horman* 'impel, set in motion.'

hor·mone re·place·ment ther·a·py (abbr.: **HRT**) ▶ **n.** treatment with estrogens with the aim of alleviating menopausal symptoms or osteoporosis.

Hor·muz /hôrˈmo͞oz, ˈhôrˌməz/ (also **Ormuz** /ôrˈmo͞oz, ˈôrˌməz/) an Iranian island at the mouth of the Persian Gulf, in the Strait of Hormuz. It is the site of an ancient city that was an important center of commerce in the Middle Ages.

Hor·muz, Strait of a strait that links the Persian Gulf with the Gulf of Oman and that leads to the Arabian Sea and separates Iran from the Arabian peninsula. It is of strategic and economic importance as a waterway through which sea traffic to and from the oil-rich countries of the gulf must pass.

horn /hôrn/ ▶ **n. 1** a hard permanent outgrowth, often curved and pointed, found in pairs on the heads of cattle, sheep, goats, giraffes, etc., and consisting of a core of bone encased in keratinized skin. ▪ a woolly keratinized outgrowth, occurring singly or one behind another, on the snout of a rhinoceros. ▪ a deer's antler. ▪ a hornlike projection on the head of another animal, e.g., a snail's tentacle or the tuft of a horned owl. ▪ (**horns**) archaic a pair of horns as an emblem of a cuckold.
2 the substance of which horns are composed: *powdered rhino horn.* ▪ a receptacle or instrument made of horn, such as a drinking container or powder flask.
3 a horn-shaped projection. ▪ a sharp promontory or mountain peak. ▪ a raised projection on the pommel of a Western saddle: *slung from the horn of his saddle was a leather bag.* ▪ (**the Horn**) Cape Horn. ▪ an arm or branch of a river or bay. ▪ the extremity of the moon or other crescent. ▪ Brit. vulgar slang an erect penis.
4 a wind instrument, conical in shape or wound into a spiral, originally made from an animal horn (now typically brass) and played by lip vibration. ▪ short for FRENCH HORN.
5 an instrument sounding a warning or other signal: *a car horn.*
▶ **v.** [with obj.] (of an animal) butt or gore with the horns.
– PHRASES **blow** (or **toot**) **one's own horn** informal talk boastfully about oneself or one's achievements. **draw** (or **pull**) **in one's horns** become less assertive or ambitious. **on the horn** informal on the telephone: *she got on the horn to complain.* **on the horns of a dilemma** faced with a decision involving equally unfavorable alternatives.
– PHRASAL VERBS **horn in** informal intrude; interfere.
– DERIVATIVES **horn·ist** /-ist/ **n.** (sense 4 of the noun), **horn·less adj.**, **horn·like** /-ˌlik/ **adj.**
– ORIGIN Old English, of Germanic origin; related to Dutch *hoorn* and German *Horn*, from an Indo-European root shared by Latin *cornu* and Greek *keras*.

Horn, Cape the most southern point of South America, on a Chilean island south of Tierra del Fuego. The region is notorious for its storms and, until the opening of the Panama Canal in 1914, constituted the only sea route between the Atlantic and Pacific oceans. Also called **the Horn**.
– ORIGIN named after *Hoorn*, the birthplace of the Dutch navigator William C. Schouten (*c.*1580–1625), who sailed around it in 1616.

horn·beam /ˈhôrnˌbēm/ ▶ **n.** a deciduous tree of north temperate regions, with oval serrated leaves, inconspicuous drooping flowers, and tough winged nuts. It yields hard pale timber. ● Genera *Carpinus* and *Ostrya*, family Betulaceae: several species, including the **American hornbeam** (*C. caroliniana*), the **eastern** (or **hop**) **hornbeam** (*O. virginiana*), and the **European hornbeam** (*C. betulus*).
– ORIGIN late Middle English: so named because of the tree's hard, close-grained wood.

horn·bill /ˈhôrnˌbil/ ▶ **n.** a medium to large tropical Old World bird, having a very large curved bill that typically has a large horny or bony casque. The male often seals up the female inside the nest hole. ● Family Bucerotidae: several genera and numerous species, e.g., the **great Indian hornbill** (*Buceros bicornis*).

horn·blende /ˈhôrnˌblend/ ▶ **n.** a dark brown, black, or green mineral of the amphibole group consisting of a hydroxyl alumino-silicate of calcium, magnesium, and iron, occurring in many igneous and metamorphic rocks.
– ORIGIN late 18th cent.: from German, from *Horn* 'horn' + *blende* (see BLENDE).

horn·book /ˈhôrnˌbo͝ok/ ▶ **n.** historical a teaching aid consisting of a leaf of paper showing the alphabet, and often the ten digits and the Lord's Prayer, mounted on a wooden tablet and protected by a thin plate of horn. ▪ Law a one-volume treatise summarizing the law in a specific field.

horn·dog /ˈhôrndäg/ ▶ **n.** informal a man with strong sexual desires.

Horne /hôrn/, Lena (Calhoun) (1917–2010), US singer and actress. In the early 1940s, she became the first African American to have a long-term contract with a Hollywood studio. Her movies include *Stormy Weather* (1943) and *Till the Clouds Roll By* (1946). In 1981, she opened on Broadway in *Lena Horne: The Lady and Her Music.*

horned /hôrnd/ ▶ **adj. 1** having a horn or horns: *horned cattle* | [in combination] *a long-horned bison.*
2 [attrib.] literary crescent-shaped: *the horned moon.*

horned grebe ▶ **n.** a North American and northern Eurasian grebe with reddish underparts and a black and gold crest. ● *Podiceps auritus*, family Podicipedidae.

horned lark ▶ **n.** a widespread lark of open country, esp. the Arctic and mountains, the male having a black and white head pattern and two small black hornlike crests. ● Genus *Eremophila*, family Alaudidae: two species, in particular *E. alpestris*. British name: **shorelark**.

horned liz·ard ▶ **n.** an American lizard that somewhat resembles a toad, with spiny skin and large spines on the head, typically occurring in dry open country. Also called HORNED TOAD. ● Genus *Phrynosoma*, family Iguanidae: several species, in particular the **Texas horned lizard** (*P. cornutum*) and the **regal horned lizard** (*P. solare*).

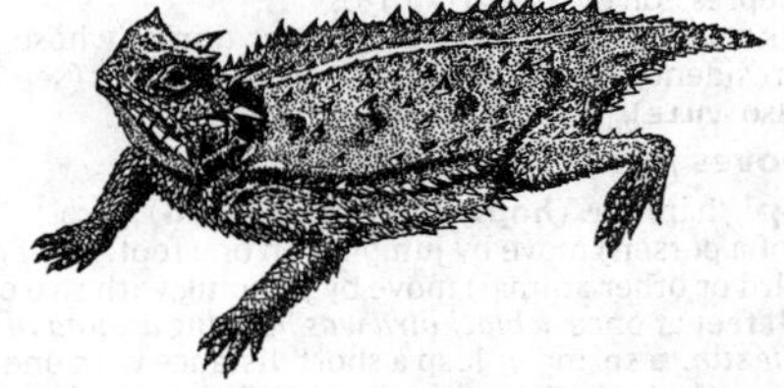

regal horned lizard

horned pop·py (also **horn poppy**) ▶ **n.** a Eurasian poppy with grayish-green lobed leaves, large flowers, and a long curved seed capsule. ● Genus *Glaucium*, family Papaveraceae: several species, in particular the **yellow horned poppy** (*G. flavum*), which has become naturalized in the US, esp. along the coast from Massachusetts to Virginia.

horned toad ▶ **n. 1** another term for HORNED LIZARD.
2 a large toad with horn-shaped projections of skin over the eyes, in particular: ● a Southeast Asian toad (*Megophrys* and other genera, family Peltobatidae). ● a South American toad (*Ceratophrys* and other genera, family Leptodactylidae).

horned vi·per ▶ **n.** a venomous nocturnal snake with an upright projection over each eye, native to the sandy deserts of North Africa and Arabia. It moves in the same way as the sidewinder. ● *Cerastes cerastes*, family Viperidae.

hor·ne·ro /hôrˈne(ə)rō/ ▶ **n.** (pl. **horneros**) a tropical American bird of the ovenbird family, often building its ovenlike mud nest on the top of a fence

post. Also called **ovenbird**. ● Genus *Furnarius*, family Furnariidae: several species, in particular the **rufous hornero** (*F. rufus*).
– ORIGIN late 19th cent.: from Spanish, literally 'baker.'

Hor·ner's syn·drome /ˈhôrnərz/ ▶ **n.** Medicine a condition marked by a contracted pupil, drooping upper eyelid, and local inability to sweat on one side of the face, caused by damage to sympathetic nerves on that side of the neck.
– ORIGIN early 20th cent.: named after Johann F. *Horner* (1831–86), Swiss ophthalmologist.

hor·net /ˈhôrnit/ ▶ **n.** a large stinging wasp that typically nests in hollow trees. ● *Vespa* and other genera, family Vespidae: several species, including the **giant hornet** (*V. crabro*) and the **bald-faced** (or **white-faced**) **hornet** (*V. maculata*).

bald-faced hornet

– PHRASES **a hornets' nest** a situation fraught with difficulties or complications: *the move has stirred up a hornets' nest of academic fear and loathing.*
– ORIGIN Old English *hyrnet*, of Germanic origin; related to German *Hornisse*. The form of the word was probably influenced by Middle Dutch and Middle Low German *hornte*.

hor·net moth ▶ **n.** a clearwing moth that resembles a hornet, with larvae that burrow under tree bark. ● Several species in the family Sesiidae, including *Sesia apiformis*, which can be a pest of poplars.

Hor·ney /ˈhôrˌnī/, Karen (Danielsen) (1885–1952), US psychoanalyst; born in Germany. Expelled from the New York Psychoanalytic Institute for her critique of Freudian practices 1941, she was the founder of the Association for Advancement of Psychoanalysis and the American Institute for Psychoanalysis that same year.

horn·fels /ˈhôrnˌfelz/ ▶ **n.** a dark, fine-grained metamorphic rock consisting largely of quartz, mica, and particular feldspars.
– ORIGIN mid 19th cent.: from German, literally 'horn rock.'

Horn of Af·ri·ca a peninsula in northeastern Africa that includes Somalia and parts of Ethiopia. It lies between the Gulf of Aden and the Indian Ocean. Also called **Somali Peninsula**.

horn of plen·ty ▶ **n. 1** a cornucopia.
2 an edible woodland mushroom with a funnel-shaped cap that bears spores on its grayish outer surface, found in both Eurasia and North America. ● *Craterellus cornucopiodes*, family Cantharellaceae, class Hymenomycetes.

horn·pipe /ˈhôrnˌpīp/ ▶ **n.** a lively dance associated with sailors, typically performed by one person. ■ a piece of music for such a dance.
– ORIGIN late Middle English (denoting a wind instrument made of horn, played to accompany dancing): from **horn** + **pipe**.

horn-rimmed ▶ **adj.** (of glasses) having rims made of horn or a similar substance.

Horns·by /ˈhôrnzbē/, Rogers (1896–1963), US baseball player and manager; known as **Rajah**. A second baseman, he was known for his batting prowess and played mainly for the St. Louis Cardinals 1915–26, 1932. Baseball Hall of Fame (1942).

horn shell ▶ **n.** a mollusk with a long tapering shell, occurring in brackish and marine waters. ● Families Potamididae and Cerithidae, class Gastropoda.

horn·swog·gle /ˈhôrnˌswägəl/ ▶ **v.** [with obj.] (usu. **be hornswoggled**) informal get the better of (someone) by cheating or deception: *you mean to say you were hornswoggled?*
– ORIGIN early 19th cent. (originally US): of unknown origin.

horn·tail /ˈhôrnˌtāl/ ▶ **n.** a large wasplike sawfly that deposits its eggs inside trees and timber. It has a long egg-laying tube but no sting. Also called **woodwasp**. ● Family Siricidae, suborder Symphyta, order Hymenoptera: several species.

horn·worm /ˈhôrnˌwərm/ ▶ **n.** the caterpillar of a hawk moth, having a spike or "horn" on its tail. ● Family Sphingidae: several genera and many species, in particular pests like the **tobacco hornworm** (*Manduca sexta*) and the **tomato hornworm** (*M. quinquemaculata*).

horn·wort /ˈhôrnˌwərt, -ˌwôrt/ ▶ **n.** a submerged aquatic plant with narrow forked leaves that become translucent and horny as they age, occurring worldwide. ● Genus *Ceratophyllum*, family Ceratophyllaceae: two or more species, in particular *C. demersum*.

horn·y /ˈhôrnē/ ▶ **adj.** (**hornier**, **horniest**) **1** of or resembling horn: *a horny beak* | *horny nails.* ■ hard and rough: *horny, dry skin.*
2 informal feeling or arousing sexual excitement.
– DERIVATIVES **horn·i·ness** n.

horn·y cor·al ▶ **n.** see **coral** (sense 2).

horol. ▶ **abbr.** horology.

hor·o·loge /ˈhôrəˌläj/ ▶ **n.** archaic a timepiece.
– ORIGIN late Middle English: from Old French, via Latin from Greek *hōrologion*, from *hōra* 'time' + *-logos* '-telling.'

Hor·o·lo·gi·um /ˌhôrəˈlōjēəm/ Astronomy a faint southern constellation (the Clock), between Hydrus and Eridanus. ■ (as genitive **Horologii** /ˌhôrəˈlōjēˌī, -ˌē/) used with a preceding letter or numeral to designate a star in this constellation: *the star R Horologii.*
– ORIGIN Latin.

ho·rol·o·gy /həˈräləjē/ ▶ **n.** the study and measurement of time. ■ the art of making clocks and watches.
– DERIVATIVES **ho·rol·o·ger** /-jər/ **n.**, **hor·o·log·ic** /ˌhôrəˈläjik/ **adj.**, **hor·o·log·i·cal** /ˌhôrəˈläjikəl/ **adj.**, **ho·rol·o·gist** /-jist/ **n.**
– ORIGIN early 19th cent.: from Greek *hōra* 'time' + **-logy**.

ho·rop·ter /ˈhôˌräptər, həˈräptər/ ▶ **n.** Optics a line or surface containing all those points in space whose images fall on corresponding points of the retinas of the two eyes.
– ORIGIN early 18th cent.: from Greek *horos* 'limit' + *optēr* 'person who looks.'

hor·o·scope /ˈhôrəˌskōp, ˈhärə-/ ▶ **n.** Astrology a forecast of a person's future, typically including a delineation of character and circumstances, based on the relative positions of the stars and planets at the time of that person's birth. ■ a short forecast for people born under a particular sign, esp. as published in a newspaper or magazine. ■ a birth chart. See **chart**.
– DERIVATIVES **hor·o·scop·ic** /ˌhôrəˈskäpik, ˌhärə-/ **adj.**, **ho·ros·co·py** /həˈräskəpē/ **n.**
– ORIGIN Old English: via Latin from Greek *hōroskopos*, from *hōra* 'time' + *skopos* 'observer.'

Hor·o·witz /ˈhôrəˌwits/, Vladimir (1904–89), US pianist, born in Russia. He first toured the US in 1928 and settled there soon afterward. A leading international virtuoso, he was best known for his performances of Scarlatti, Liszt, Scriabin, and Prokofiev.

hor·ren·dous /həˈrendəs, hô-/ ▶ **adj.** extremely unpleasant, horrifying, or terrible: *she suffered horrendous injuries.*
– DERIVATIVES **hor·ren·dous·ly** adv.
– ORIGIN mid 17th cent.: from Latin *horrendus* (gerundive of *horrere* '(of hair) stand on end') + **-ous**.

hor·rent /ˈhôrənt/ ▶ **adj.** literary **1** (of a person's hair) standing on end.
2 feeling or expressing horror: *a horrent cry.*
– ORIGIN mid 17th cent.: from Latin *horrent-* '(of hair) standing on end,' from the verb *horrere*.

hor·ri·ble /ˈhôrəbəl, ˈhär-/ ▶ **adj.** causing or likely to cause horror; shocking: *a horrible massacre.* ■ informal very unpleasant: *the tea tasted horrible.*
– DERIVATIVES **hor·ri·ble·ness** n., **hor·ri·bly** /-blē/ **adv.** [as submodifier] *the plan had gone horribly wrong.*
– ORIGIN Middle English: via Old French from Latin *horribilis*, from *horrere* 'tremble, shudder' (see **horrid**).

hor·rid /ˈhôrid, ˈhär-/ ▶ **adj. 1** causing horror: *a horrid nightmare.* ■ informal very unpleasant or disagreeable: *the teachers at school were horrid* | *a horrid brown color.*
2 literary rough; bristling.
– DERIVATIVES **hor·rid·ly** adv., **hor·rid·ness** n.
– ORIGIN late 16th cent. (in the sense 'rough, bristling'): from Latin *horridus*, from *horrere* 'tremble, shudder, (of hair) stand on end.'

hor·ri·fic /hôˈrifik, hə-/ ▶ **adj.** causing horror: *horrific injuries.*
– DERIVATIVES **hor·rif·i·cal·ly** /ik(ə)lē/ **adv.**
– ORIGIN mid 17th cent.: from Latin *horrificus*, from *horrere* 'tremble, shudder' (see **horrid**).

hor·ri·fy /ˈhôrəˌfī, ˈhär-/ ▶ **v.** (**horrifies**, **horrifying**, **horrified**) [with obj.] (usu. **be horrified**) fill with horror; shock greatly: *they were horrified by the very idea* | (as adj. **horrified**) *the horrified spectators* | (as adj. **horrifying**) *a horrifying incident.*
– DERIVATIVES **hor·ri·fi·ca·tion** /ˌhôrifiˈkāsHən, hə-/ **n.**, **hor·ri·fied·ly** /-ˌfī(ə)dlē/ **adv.**, **hor·ri·fy·ing·ly** **adv.** [as submodifier] *horrifyingly flimsy boats.*
– ORIGIN late 18th cent.: from Latin *horrificare*, from *horrificus* (see **horrific**).

hor·rip·i·la·tion /hôˌripəˈlāsHən, hə-/ ▶ **n.** literary the erection of hairs on the skin due to cold, fear, or excitement.
– DERIVATIVES **hor·rip·i·late** /hôˈripəˌlāt, hə-/ **v.**
– ORIGIN mid 17th cent.: from late Latin *horripilatio(n-)*, from Latin *horrere* 'stand on end' (see **horrid**) + *pilus* 'hair.'

hor·ror /ˈhôrər, ˈhär-/ ▶ **n. 1** an intense feeling of fear, shock, or disgust: *children screamed in horror.* ■ a thing causing such a feeling: *photographs showed the horror of the tragedy* | *the horrors of civil war.* ■ a literary or film genre concerned with arousing such feelings: [as modifier] *a horror movie.* ■ intense dismay: *to her horror she found that a thief had stolen the machine.* ■ [as exclamation] (**horrors**) chiefly humorous used to express dismay: *horrors, two buttons were missing!* ■ [in sing.] intense dislike: *many have a horror of consulting a dictionary.* ■ (**the horrors**) an attack of extreme nervousness or anxiety: *the mere thought of it gives me the horrors.*
2 informal a bad or mischievous person, esp. a child: *that little horror Zach was around.*
– ORIGIN Middle English: via Old French from Latin *horror*, from *horrere* 'tremble, shudder' (see **horrid**).

hor·ror-struck (also **horror-stricken**) ▶ **adj.** (of a person) briefly paralyzed with horror or shock.

hor·ror va·cui /ˈvakyəˌwī/ ▶ **n.** [in sing.] a fear or dislike of leaving empty spaces, esp. in an artistic composition.
– ORIGIN mid 19th cent.: modern Latin, literally 'horror of a vacuum.'

hors con·cours /ˌôr kôNˈko͝or/ ▶ **adj. 1** unrivaled; unequaled: *most husbands are fools, but that one was hors concours.*
2 formal (of an exhibit or exhibitor) not competing for a prize.
– ORIGIN late 19th cent.: French, literally 'out of the competition.'

hors de com·bat /ˌôr də kämˈbä/ ▶ **adj.** out of action due to injury or damage: *their pilots had been rendered temporarily hors de combat.*
– ORIGIN mid 18th cent.: French, literally 'out of the fight.'

hors d'oeuvre /ôr ˈdərv, ˈdœvrə/ ▶ **n.** (pl. **same** or **hors d'oeuvres** pronunc. **same** or /ˈdərvz/) a small savory dish, typically one served as an appetizer at the beginning of a meal.
– ORIGIN mid 18th cent.: French, literally 'outside the work.'

horse /hôrs/ ▶ **n. 1** a solid-hoofed plant-eating domesticated mammal with a flowing mane and tail, used for riding, racing, and to carry and pull loads. ● *Equus caballus*, family Equidae (the **horse family**), descended from the wild Przewalski's horse. The horse family also includes the asses and zebras.
■ an adult male horse; a stallion or gelding.
■ a wild mammal of the horse family.
■ [treated as sing. or pl.] cavalry: *forty horse and sixty foot.*
2 a frame or structure on which something is mounted or supported, esp. a sawhorse. ■ Nautical a horizontal bar, rail, or rope in the rigging of a sailing ship for supporting something. ■ short for **pommel horse** or **vaulting horse**.
3 informal heroin.
4 informal a unit of horsepower: *the huge 63-horse 701-cc engine.*
5 Mining an obstruction in a vein.
▶ **v.** [with obj.] (usu. **be horsed**) provide (a person or vehicle) with a horse or horses.
– PHRASES **don't change horses in midstream** proverb choose a sensible moment to change your mind. **frighten the horses** [usu. with negative] do something likely to cause public outrage or offense: *David's views would not have frightened the horses.* **from the horse's mouth** (of information) from the person directly concerned or another authoritative source. **horses for courses** Brit. proverb different people are suited to different things or situations. **to horse** (as a command) mount your horses! **you can lead** (or **take**) **a horse to water but you can't make him drink** proverb you can give someone an opportunity, but you can't force them to take it.
– PHRASAL VERBS **horse around** informal fool around: *schoolkids laughing and horsing around.*
– DERIVATIVES **horse·like** /-ˌlīk/ **adj.**
– ORIGIN Old English *hors*, of Germanic origin; related to Dutch *ros* and German *Ross*.

horse-and-bug·gy ▶ **adj.** [attrib.] old-fashioned: *horse-and-buggy technology.*

horse·back /ˈhôrsˌbak/ ▶ **adj. & adv.** mounted on a horse: [as adj.] *a horseback rider* | [as adv.] *they rode horseback along the trail.*

– PHRASES **on** (or **by**) **horseback** mounted on a horse.

horse·bean /ˈhôrsˌbēn/ (also **horse bean**) ▶ **n.** another term for BROAD BEAN.

horse chest·nut ▶ **n.** a deciduous tree with large leaves of five leaflets, conspicuous sticky winter buds, and upright conical clusters of white, pink, or red flowers. Unrelated to true chestnuts, the horse chestnut bears unpalatable nuts enclosed in fleshy, thorny husks. ● Genus *Aesculus*, family Hippocastanaceae: several species, in particular *A. hippocastanum*, native east of the Balkans and widely planted over much of Europe and North America.
■ the fruit or seed of this tree.
– ORIGIN late 16th cent.: translating (now obsolete) botanical Latin *Castanea equina*; its fruit is said to have been an Eastern remedy for chest diseases in horses.

horse cloth ▶ **n.** a cloth used to cover a horse, or as part of its trappings.

horse-drawn ▶ **adj.** (of a vehicle) pulled by a horse or horses: *a horse-drawn carriage.*

horse·feath·ers /ˈhôrsˌfeT͟Hərz/ ▶ **exclam.** used to express disagreement, disbelief, or frustration.

h

horse·flesh /ˈhôrsˌflesH/ ▶ **n.** horses considered collectively. ■ the flesh of a horse, esp. when used as food.

horse·fly /ˈhôrsˌflī/ ▶ **n.** (pl. **horseflies**) a stoutly built fly, the female of which is a bloodsucker and inflicts painful bites on horses and other mammals, including humans. ● Genus *Tabanus*, family Tabanidae: numerous species.

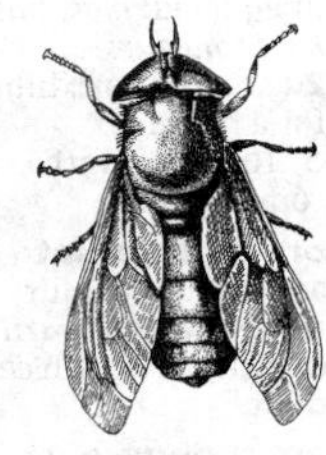
horsefly

Horse Guards ▶ **plural n.** a mounted brigade from the household troops of the British monarch, used for ceremonial occasions.

horse·hair /ˈhôrsˌhe(ə)r/ ▶ **n.** hair from the mane or tail of a horse, typically used in furniture for padding.

horse·hair worm ▶ **n.** a long slender worm related to the nematodes, the larvae being parasites of arthropods and the adults living in water or damp soil. ● Phylum Nematomorpha: two classes.

Horse·head Neb·u·la /ˈhôrsˌhed/ Astronomy a dust nebula in the shape of a horse's head, forming a dark silhouette against a bright emission nebula in Orion.

horse·hide /ˈhôrsˌhīd/ ▶ **n.** **1** the skin of a horse. ■ leather made from the skin of a horse.
2 informal a baseball. [so named because, until replaced by cowhide in late 20th century, the traditional covering of a baseball was horsehide.]

horse lat·i·tudes ▶ **plural n.** a belt of calm air and sea occurring in both the northern and southern hemispheres between the trade winds and the westerlies.
– ORIGIN late 18th cent.: of uncertain origin.

horse·laugh /ˈhôrsˌlaf/ ▶ **n.** a loud, coarse laugh.

horse·leech /ˈhôrsˌlēcH/ ▶ **n.** a large predatory leech of freshwater and terrestrial habitats that feeds on carrion and small invertebrates. ● Genus *Haemopis*, family Hirudidae.

horse·less /ˈhôrslis/ ▶ **adj.** [attrib.] (of a vehicle) not drawn by a horse or horses: *a horseless cabriolet.*

horse·less car·riage ▶ **n.** archaic, humorous an automobile.

horse mack·er·el ▶ **n.** a shoaling edible fish of the eastern Atlantic, commercially fished in southern African waters. Also called SCAD. ● *Trachurus trachurus*, family Carangidae.

horse·man /ˈhôrsmən/ ▶ **n.** (pl. **horsemen**) a rider on horseback, esp. a skilled one.

horse·man·ship /ˈhôrsmənˌsHip/ ▶ **n.** the art or practice of riding on horseback.

horse·meat /ˈhôrsmēt/ ▶ **n.** the flesh of a horse as food.

horse·mint /ˈhôrsˌmint/ ▶ **n.** a tall coarse kind of mint. ● Genera *Mentha* and *Monarda*, family Labiatae: several species and hybrids, including the European *Mentha longifolia* and the North American *Monarda punctata*.
– ORIGIN Middle English: from HORSE (often used in the names of plants to denote a coarse variety) + MINT[1].

horse mush·room ▶ **n.** a large edible mushroom with a creamy-white cap and pinkish-gray gills, found in grassland in both Eurasia and North America. ● *Agaricus arvensis*, family Agaricaceae, class Hymenomycetes.

horse op·er·a ▶ **n.** informal a western movie.

horse pis·tol ▶ **n.** historical a large pistol carried at the pommel of the saddle by a rider.

horse·play /ˈhôrsˌplā/ ▶ **n.** rough, boisterous play.

horse·play·er /ˈhôrsˌplāər/ ▶ **n.** a person who regularly bets on horse races.

horse·pow·er /ˈhôrsˌpou(-ə)r/ (abbr.: **hp**) ▶ **n.** (pl. **same**) a unit of power equal to 550 foot-pounds per second (745.7 watts). ■ the power of an engine measured in terms of this: *a strong 140-horsepower engine.* See also BRAKE HORSEPOWER.

horse race ▶ **n.** **1** a race between two or more horses ridden by jockeys.
2 a very close contest: *eight hours after the polls closed, the election was still a horse race.*

horse rac·ing ▶ **n.** the sport in which horses and their riders take part in races, typically with substantial betting on the outcome.

horse·rad·ish /ˈhôrsˌradisH/ ▶ **n.** a European plant of the cabbage family, with long docklike leaves, grown for its pungent root. ● *Armoracia rusticana*, family Brassicaceae.
■ this root, which is scraped or grated as a condiment and often made into a sauce.

horse sense ▶ **n.** informal common sense.

horse·shit /ˈhôr(s)ˌsHit/ ▶ **n.** vulgar slang nonsense.

horse·shoe /ˈhôr(s)ˌsHo͞o/ ▶ **n.** a shoe for a horse formed of a narrow band of iron in the form of an extended circular arc and secured to the hoof with nails. ■ a shoe of this kind or a representation of one, regarded as bringing good luck. ■ something resembling this in shape: [as modifier] *a horseshoe bend.* ■ (**horseshoes**) [treated as sing.] a game in which horseshoes are thrown at a stake in the ground.

horse·shoe bat ▶ **n.** an insectivorous Old World bat with a horseshoe-shaped ridge on the nose. ● Family Rhinolophidae and genus *Rhinolophus*: numerous species.

horse·shoe crab ▶ **n.** a large marine arthropod with a domed horseshoe-shaped shell, a long tail-spine, and ten legs, little changed since the Devonian. ● Class Merostomata, subphylum Chelicerata: four species, in particular the North American *Limulus polyphemus*.

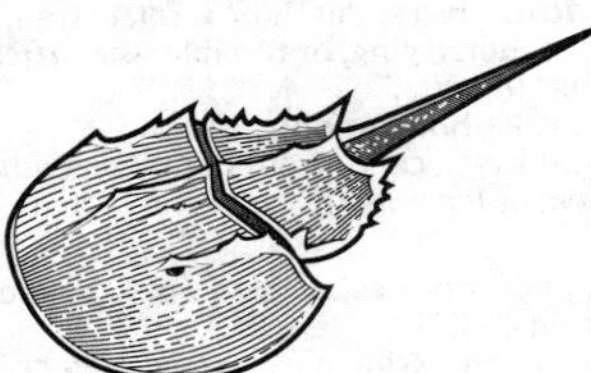
horseshoe crab

Horse·shoe Falls see NIAGARA FALLS.

horse's neck ▶ **n.** informal a drink consisting of ginger ale, a twist of lemon peel, and liquor, typically brandy.

horse·tail /ˈhôrsˌtāl/ ▶ **n.** a nonflowering plant with a hollow jointed stem that bears whorls of narrow leaves, producing spores in cones at the tips of the shoots. ● Genus *Equisetum*, the only surviving genus of the family Equisetaceae and class Sphenopsida, division Pteridophyta.

horse·trad·ing (also **horse trading**) ▶ **n.** the buying and selling of horses. ■ hard and shrewd bargaining, typically in politics.
– DERIVATIVES **horse-trade** v., **horse-trad·er** n.

horse·whip /ˈhôrsˌ(h)wip/ ▶ **n.** a long whip used for driving and controlling horses.
▶ **v.** (**horsewhips, horsewhipping, horsewhipped**) [with obj.] beat with such a whip: *she would horsewhip them mercilessly.*

horse·wom·an /ˈhôrsˌwo͝omən/ ▶ **n.** (pl. **horsewomen**) a woman who rides on horseback, esp. a skilled one.

hors·ey /ˈhôrsē/ (also **horsy**) ▶ **adj.** (**horsier, horsiest**) **1** of or resembling a horse: *wide eyes and big, horsey teeth.*
2 concerned with or devoted to horses or horse racing: *the horsey fraternity.*
– DERIVATIVES **hors·i·ly** /ˈhôrsəlē/ **adv.**, **hors·i·ness** **n.**

horst /hôrst/ ▶ **n.** Geology a raised elongated block of the earth's crust lying between two faults.
– ORIGIN late 19th cent.: from German *Horst* 'heap.'

hort. ▶ **abbr.** horticulture or horticultural.

Hor·ta /ˈhôrtə/, Victor (1861–1947), Belgian architect. His work is notable for its innovative use of iron and glass, and he is considered the originator of Art Nouveau.

hor·ta·to·ry /ˈhôrtəˌtôrē/ ▶ **adj.** tending or aiming to exhort: *the central bank relied on hortatory messages and voluntary compliance.*
– DERIVATIVES **hor·ta·tion** /ˌhôrˈtāsHən/ **n.**, **hor·ta·tive** /ˈhôrtətiv/ **adj.**
– ORIGIN late 16th cent.: from Latin *hortatorius*, from *hortari* 'exhort.'

hor·ti·cul·ture /ˈhôrtiˌkəlcHər/ ▶ **n.** the art or practice of garden cultivation and management.
– DERIVATIVES **hor·ti·cul·tur·al** /ˌhôrtiˈkəlcHərəl/ **adj.**, **hor·ti·cul·tur·al·ist** /ˌhôrtiˈkəlcHərəlist/ **n.**, **hor·ti·cul·tur·ist** /ˌhôrtəˈkəlcHərist/ **n.**
– ORIGIN late 17th cent.: from Latin *hortus* 'garden,' on the pattern of *agriculture*.

hor·tus sic·cus /ˈhôrtəs ˈsikəs/ ▶ **n.** (pl. **horti sicci** /ˈhôrtī ˈsikī, ˈsikē/) an arranged collection of dried plants; a herbarium.
– ORIGIN late 17th cent.: Latin, literally 'dry garden.'

Ho·rus /ˈhôrəs/ Egyptian Mythology a god regarded as the protector of the monarchy, typically represented as a falcon-headed man. He assumed various aspects: in the myth of Isis and Osiris he was the posthumous son of the latter, whose murder he avenged.

Hos. ▶ **abbr.** Bible Hosea.

ho·san·na /hōˈzanə, -ˈzä-/ (also **hosannah**) ▶ **exclam.** (esp. in biblical, Judaic, and Christian use) used to express adoration, praise, or joy.
▶ **n.** an expression of adoration, praise, or joy.
– ORIGIN Old English, via late Latin from Greek *hōsanna*, from Rabbinical Hebrew *hōšaʿnā*, abbreviation of biblical *hōšīʿā-nnā* 'save, we pray' (Ps. 118:25).

hose /hōz/ ▶ **n.** **1** a flexible tube conveying water, used esp. for watering plants and in firefighting.
2 [treated as pl.] stockings, socks, and tights (esp. in commercial use): *a chorus girl's fishnet hose.*
■ historical breeches: *Elizabethan doublet and hose.*
▶ **v.** [with obj.] water, spray, or drench with a hose: *he was hosing down the driveway.*
– ORIGIN Old English *hosa*, of Germanic origin; related to Dutch *hoos* 'stocking' and German *Hosen* 'trousers.' Originally singular, the term denoted a covering for the leg, sometimes including the foot but sometimes reaching only as far as the ankle.

Ho·se·a /hōˈzāə, -ˈzēə/ a Hebrew minor prophet of the 8th century BC. ■ a book of the Bible containing his prophecies.

ho·sel /ˈhōzəl/ ▶ **n.** the socket of a golf club head into which the shaft fits.
– ORIGIN late 16th cent.: diminutive of HOSE, in the dialect sense 'sheathing.'

hose·pipe /ˈhōzˌpīp/ ▶ **n.** British term for HOSE (sense 1 of the noun).

hos·er /ˈhōzər/ ▶ **n.** chiefly Canadian informal a foolish or uncultivated person.
– ORIGIN 1980s: of uncertain origin; popularized by characters on the Canadian television show *SCTV* (1980–2).

ho·sier /ˈhōzHər/ ▶ **n.** a manufacturer or seller of hosiery.

ho·sier·y /ˈhōzHərē/ ▶ **n.** stockings, socks, and tights collectively.

hosp. ▶ **abbr.** hospital.

hos·pice /ˈhäspis/ ▶ **n.** a home providing care for the sick, esp. the terminally ill. ■ archaic a lodging for travelers, esp. one run by a religious order.
– ORIGIN early 19th cent.: from French, from Latin *hospitium*, from *hospes, hospit-* (see HOST[1]).

hos·pi·ta·ble /häˈspitəbəl, ˈhäspitəbəl/ ▶ **adj.** friendly and welcoming to strangers or guests: *two friendly, hospitable brothers run the hotel.* ■ (of an environment) pleasant and favorable for living in: *the Sonoran desert is one of the least hospitable places on earth.*
– DERIVATIVES **hos·pi·ta·bly** /-blē/ **adv.**
– ORIGIN late 16th cent.: from French, from obsolete *hospiter* 'receive a guest,' from medieval Latin *hospitare* 'entertain,' from *hospes, hospit-* (see HOST[1]).

hos·pi·tal /ˈhäˌspitl/ ▶ **n.** **1** an institution providing medical and surgical treatment and nursing care for sick or injured people.
2 historical a hospice, esp. one run by the Knights Hospitaller.
3 [usu. in names] Brit. Law a charitable institution for the education of the young.
– ORIGIN Middle English (sense 2): via Old French from medieval Latin *hospitale*, neuter of Latin *hospitalis* 'hospitable,' from *hospes, hospit-* (see HOST[1]).

hos·pi·tal cor·ners ▶ **plural n.** overlapping folds used to tuck sheets neatly and securely under the mattress at the corners, in a manner typically used by nurses.

hos·pi·tal·er /ˈhäˌspitl-ər/ (also **hospitaller**) ▶ **n.** a member of a charitable religious order, originally the Knights Hospitaler.
– ORIGIN Middle English: from Old French *hospitalier*, from medieval Latin *hospitalarius*, from *hospitale* (see HOSPITAL).

Hos·pi·ta·let /ˌäspitlˈet, ˌōspētäˈlet/ (also **Hospitalet de Llobregat** /dä ˌ(l)yōbriˈgät/) a city and southern suburb of Barcelona in northeastern Spain; pop. 253,800 (est. 2008).

hos·pi·tal fe·ver ▶ **n.** historical louse-borne typhus acquired in overcrowded, insanitary conditions in an old-fashioned hospital.

hos·pi·tal·ism /ˈhäˌspitlˌizəm/ ▶ **n.** the adverse effects of a prolonged stay in the hospital, such as developmental retardation in children.

hos·pi·tal·ist /ˈhäspitl-ist/ ▶ **n.** a dedicated in-patient physician who works exclusively in a hospital.

hos·pi·tal·i·ty /ˌhäspiˈtalitē/ ▶ **n.** the friendly and generous reception and entertainment of guests, visitors, or strangers.
▶ **adj.** relating to or denoting the business of housing or entertaining visitors: *the hospitality industry.*
– ORIGIN late Middle English: from Old French *hospitalite*, from Latin *hospitalitas*, from *hospitalis* 'hospitable' (see HOSPITAL).

hos·pi·tal·ize /ˈhäspitlˌīz/ ▶ **v.** [with obj.] (usu. **be hospitalized**) admit or cause (someone) to be admitted to a hospital for treatment: *Casey was hospitalized for chest pains.*
– DERIVATIVES **hos·pi·tal·i·za·tion** /ˌhäspitl-iˈzāshən/ **n.**

hos·pi·tal·ler ▶ **n.** British spelling of HOSPITALER.

hos·pi·tal ship ▶ **n.** a ship that functions as a hospital, esp. to receive or take home sick or wounded military personnel.

hos·po·dar /ˈhäspəˌdär/ ▶ **n.** historical a governor of Wallachia and Moldavia under the Ottoman Porte.
– ORIGIN from Romanian, from Ukrainian *hospodar*; related to Russian *gospodar'*, from *gospod'* 'lord.'

hoss /hôs/ ▶ **n.** nonstandard spelling of HORSE, used in representing dialect or informal speech.

host[1] /hōst/ ▶ **n. 1** a person who receives or entertains other people as guests: *a dinner-party host.* ■ a person, place, or organization that holds and organizes an event to which others are invited: *Innsbruck once* **played host to** *the Winter Olympics.* ■ an area in which particular living things are found: *Australia* **is host to** *some of the world's most dangerous animals.* ■ often humorous the landlord or landlady of a pub: ***mine host*** *raised his glass of whiskey.* ■ the moderator or emcee of a television or radio program.
2 Biology an animal or plant on or in which a parasite or commensal organism lives. ■ (also **host cell**) a living cell in which a virus multiplies. ■ a person or animal that has received transplanted tissue or a transplanted organ.
3 (also **host computer**) a computer that mediates multiple access to databases mounted on it or provides other services to a computer network.
▶ **v.** [with obj.] act as host at (an event) or for (a television or radio program).
– ORIGIN Middle English: from Old French *hoste*, from Latin *hospes, hospit-* 'host, guest.'

host[2] ▶ **n.** (**a host of** or **hosts of**) a large number of people or things: *a host of memories rushed into her mind.* ■ archaic an army. ■ literary (in biblical use) the sun, moon, and stars: *the starry host of heaven.* ■ another term for HEAVENLY HOST. See also LORD OF HOSTS at LORD.
– ORIGIN Middle English: from Old French *ost, hoost*, from Latin *hostis* 'stranger, enemy' (in medieval Latin 'army').

host[3] ▶ **n.** (usu. **the Host**) the bread consecrated in the Eucharist: *the elevation of the Host.*
– ORIGIN Middle English: from Old French *hoiste*, from Latin *hostia* 'victim.'

hos·ta /ˈhōstə, ˈhästə/ ▶ **n.** an eastern Asian plant cultivated in the West for its shade-tolerant foliage and loose clusters of tubular mauve or white flowers. Also called PLANTAIN LILY. ● Genus *Hosta* (formerly *Funkia*), family Liliaceae.
– ORIGIN modern Latin, named after Nicolaus T. *Host* (1761–1834), Austrian physician.

hos·tage /ˈhästij/ ▶ **n.** a person seized or held as security for the fulfillment of a condition: *the kidnapper had instructed the hostage's family to drop the ransom at noon.*
– PHRASES **hold** (or **take**) **someone hostage** seize and keep someone as a hostage: *they were held hostage by armed rebels | taken hostage at gunpoint.* **a hostage to fortune** an act, commitment, or remark that is regarded as unwise because it invites trouble or could prove difficult to live up to: *making objectives explicit is to give a hostage to fortune.*
– ORIGIN Middle English: from Old French, based on late Latin *obsidatus* 'the state of being a hostage' (the earliest sense in English), from Latin *obses, obsid-* 'hostage.'

hos·tel /ˈhästl/ ▶ **n.** an establishment that provides inexpensive food and lodging for a specific group of people, such as students, workers, or travelers. ■ short for YOUTH HOSTEL. ■ archaic an inn providing accommodations.
– ORIGIN Middle English (in the general sense 'lodging, place to stay'): from Old French, from medieval Latin *hospitale* (see HOSPITAL).

hos·tel·ing /ˈhästl-iNG/ (Brit. **hostelling**) ▶ **n.** the practice of staying in youth hostels when traveling.
– DERIVATIVES **hos·tel·er** /ˈhästl-ər/ **n.**

hos·tel·ry /ˈhästl-rē/ ▶ **n.** (pl. **hostelries**) archaic or humorous an inn.
– ORIGIN late Middle English: from Old French *hostelerie*, from *hostelier* 'innkeeper,' from *hostel* (see HOSTEL).

host·ess /ˈhōstis/ ▶ **n.** a woman who receives or entertains guests: *the perfect dinner-party hostess.* ■ a woman employed at a restaurant to welcome and seat customers. ■ a woman employed to entertain customers at a nightclub, bar, or dance hall. ■ a stewardess on an aircraft, train, etc. ■ a woman who introduces a television or radio program: *a game-show hostess.*
– ORIGIN Middle English: from Old French (*h*)*ostesse*, feminine of (*h*)*oste* (see HOST[1]).

hos·tile /ˈhästl, ˈhäˌstīl/ ▶ **adj.** unfriendly; antagonistic: *a hostile audience | he wrote a ferociously hostile attack.* ■ of or belonging to a military enemy: *hostile aircraft.* ■ [predic.] opposed: *people are very* **hostile to the idea.** ■ (of a takeover bid) opposed by the company to be bought.
– DERIVATIVES **hos·tile·ly adv.**
– ORIGIN late 16th cent.: from French, or from Latin *hostilis*, from *hostis* 'stranger, enemy.'

hos·tile wit·ness ▶ **n.** Law a witness who is antagonistic to the party calling them and, being unwilling to tell the truth, may have to be cross-examined by the party.

hos·til·i·ty /häˈstilitē/ ▶ **n.** (pl. **hostilities**) hostile behavior; unfriendliness or opposition: *their* **hostility to all outsiders.** ■ (**hostilities**) acts of warfare: *he called for an immediate cessation of hostilities.*
– ORIGIN late Middle English: from French *hostilité* or late Latin *hostilitas*, from Latin *hostilis* (see HOSTILE).

hos·tler /ˈ(h)äslər/ (also **ostler**) ▶ **n.** historical a man employed to look after the horses of people staying at an inn.
– ORIGIN late Middle English: from Old French *hostelier* 'innkeeper,' from *hostel* (see HOSTEL).

hot /hät/ ▶ **adj.** (**hotter, hottest**) **1** having a high degree of heat or a high temperature: *it was hot inside the hall | basking under a hot sun.* ■ feeling or producing an uncomfortable sensation of heat: *she felt hot and her throat was parched.* ■ (of food or drink) prepared by heating and served without cooling. ■ informal (of an electric circuit) at a high voltage; live. ■ informal radioactive.
2 (of food) containing or consisting of pungent spices or peppers that produce a burning sensation when tasted: *a very hot dish cooked with green chili.*
3 passionately enthusiastic, eager, or excited: *the idea had been nurtured in his hot imagination.* ■ lustful, amorous, or erotic: *steamy bed scenes that may be too hot for young fans.* ■ (of music, esp. jazz) strongly rhythmical and excitingly played: *hot salsa and lambada dancing.*
4 involving much activity, debate, or intense feeling: *the environment has become a very hot issue.* ■ (esp. of news) fresh or recent and therefore of great interest: *have I got some hot gossip for you!* ■ currently popular, fashionable, or in demand: *they know the hottest dance moves.* ■ difficult to deal with; awkward or dangerous: *he found my story* **simply too hot to handle.** ■ Hunting (of the scent) fresh and strong, indicating that the quarry has passed recently. ■ informal (of goods) stolen and difficult to dispose of because easily identifiable. ■ informal (of a person) wanted by the police. ■ [predic.] (in children's games) very close to finding or guessing something.
5 informal knowledgeable or skillful: *Tony is very* **hot on** *local history.* ■ [predic., usu. with negative] good; promising: *this is* **not so hot** *for business.* ■ [predic.] (**hot on**) informal considering as very important; strict about: *local customs officers are hot on confiscations.*
– PHRASES **get hot** (of an athlete or team) suddenly become effective: *he got hot at the right time and found himself in the title match.* **have the hots for** informal be sexually attracted to. **hot and bothered** see BOTHER. **hot and heavy** informal intense; with intensity: *the competition became very hot and heavy.* **hot on the heels of** following closely: *the two new species come hot on the heels of the discovery of the Vu Quang ox.* **hot to trot** informal ready and eager to engage in an activity. **hot under the collar** informal angry, resentful, or embarrassed. **in hot pursuit** following closely and eagerly. **in hot water** informal in a situation of difficulty, trouble, or disgrace: *he is in hot water for insensitive remarks he made.* **make it** (or **things**) **hot for someone** informal make things unpleasant for someone; persecute.
– PHRASAL VERBS **hot up** (or **hot something up**) Brit. informal become or make hot: *he hotted up the flask in Daisy's hand.* ■ become or make more active, lively, or exciting: *the championship contest hotted up.*
– DERIVATIVES **hot·ness n.**, **hot·tish adj.**
– ORIGIN Old English *hāt*, of Germanic origin; related to Dutch *heet* and German *heiss*.

hot air ▶ **n.** informal empty talk that is intended to impress: *they dismissed the theory as a load of hot air.*

hot-air bal·loon ▶ **n.** see BALLOON (sense 2 of the noun).

hot·bed /ˈhätˌbed/ ▶ **n.** a bed of earth heated by fermenting manure, for raising or forcing plants. ■ an environment promoting the growth of something, esp. something unwelcome: *the country was* **a hotbed of** *revolt and dissension.*

hot-blood·ed ▶ **adj.** lustful; passionate: *hot-blooded, pulse-pounding passion.*

hot box ▶ **n. 1** Railroad an overheated axle box or journal box.
2 another term for SWEATBOX (sense 1).

hot but·ton ▶ **n.** (often as modifier **hot-button**) informal a topic or issue that is highly charged emotionally or politically: *the hot-button issue of nuclear waste disposal.*

hot·cake /ˈhätˌkāk/ (also **hot cake**) ▶ **n.** a pancake.
– PHRASES **sell like hotcakes** informal be sold quickly and in large quantities.

hot cath·ode ▶ **n.** a cathode designed to be heated in order to emit electrons.

hotch·pot /ˈhächˌpät/ ▶ **n.** Law the reunion and blending together of properties for the purpose of securing equal division, esp. of the property of an intestate parent.
– ORIGIN late Middle English (in the sense 'hodgepodge'): from Anglo-Norman French and Old French *hochepot*, from *hocher* 'to shake' (probably of Low German origin) + *pot* 'pot.'

hotch·potch /ˈhächˌpäch/ ▶ **n.** Brit. variant of HODGEPODGE. ■ a mutton stew with mixed vegetables.
– ORIGIN late Middle English: variant of HOTCHPOT.

hot cross bun ▶ **n.** a bun marked with a cross and containing dried fruit, traditionally eaten during Lent.

hot dark mat·ter ▶ **n.** see DARK MATTER.

hot-desk·ing ▶ **n.** the practice in an office of allocating desks to workers when they are required or on a rotating system, rather than giving each worker their own desk.

hot dog ▶ **n. 1** a hot sausage served in a long, soft roll and typically topped with various condiments.
2 informal a person who shows off, esp. a skier or surfer who performs stunts or tricks.
▶ **exclam.** informal used to express delight or enthusiastic approval: *hot dog! I've finally found something I can do that you can't.*
▶ **v.** (**hotdog**) (**hot dogs, hot dogging, hot dogged**) [no obj.] informal perform stunts or tricks; show off: *he chastised the dancers who'd been hotdogging.*
– DERIVATIVES **hot·dog·ger n.**

ho·tel /hōˈtel/ ▶ **n. 1** an establishment providing accommodations, meals, and other services for travelers and tourists.
2 a code word representing the letter H, used in radio communication.
– ORIGIN mid 18th cent.: from French *hôtel*, from Old French *hostel* (see HOSTEL).

hô·tel de ville /ōˈtel də ˈvēl/ ▶ **n.** (pl. **hôtels de ville** pronunc. **same**) (in France) a city hall or town hall.

ho·te·lier /ˌōtelˈyā, hōtlˈi(ə)r/ ▶ **n.** a person who owns or manages a hotel.
– ORIGIN early 20th cent.: from French *hôtelier*, from Old French *hostelier* 'innkeeper' (see HOSTELRY).

ho·tel·ing /hōˈteliNG/ ▶ **n.** the short-term provision of office space to a temporary worker. ■ the short-term letting of surplus office space to employees from other companies.
– ORIGIN from *hotel* + *-ing*.

hot flash ▶ **n.** a sudden feeling of feverish heat, typically as a symptom of menopause.

PRONUNCIATION KEY ə *ago, up;* ər *over, fur;* a *hat;* ā *ate;* ä *car;* e *let;* ē *see;* i *fit;* ī *by;* NG *sing;* ō *go;* ô *law, for;* oi *toy;* o͝o *good;* o͞o *goo;* ou *out;* TH *thin;* T͟H *then;* ZH *vision*

hot flush ▶ n. British term for HOT FLASH.

hot·foot /ˈhät,fo͝ot/ ▶ v. [with obj.] (**hotfoot it**) [with adverbial of direction] walk or run quickly and eagerly: *we hotfooted it after him.*
▶ adv. in eager haste: *he rushed hotfoot to the planning office to object.*

hot·head /ˈhät,hed/ ▶ n. a person who is impetuous or who easily becomes angry and violent.

hot·head·ed /ˈhät,hedid/ ▶ adj. having an impetuous or quick-tempered nature: *a hot-headed youth.*
– DERIVATIVES **hot·head·ed·ly** adv., **hot·head·ed·ness** n.

hot·house /ˈhät,hous/ ▶ n. a heated building, typically made largely of glass, for rearing plants out of season or in a climate colder than is natural for them. ■ an environment that encourages the rapid growth or development of someone or something, esp. in a stifling or intense way: [as modifier] *the hothouse atmosphere of the college.*
▶ v. [with obj.] educate (a child) to a high level at an earlier age than is usual.

hot key ▶ n. Computing a key or a combination of keys providing quick access to a particular function within a program.

hot·line /ˈhät,līn/ (also **hot line**) ▶ n. a direct telephone line set up for a specific purpose, esp. for use in emergencies or for communication between heads of government: *a domestic violence hotline.*

hot·link /ˈhät,liNGk/ Computing ▶ n. a connection between documents or applications that enables material from one source to be incorporated into another, in particular a facility that automatically updates material in a document when an alteration is made to the document from which it originated. ■ a hypertext link.
▶ v. [with obj.] connect (two documents) by means of a hotlink.

hot·list /ˈhät,list/ ▶ n. Computing a personal list of favorite or most frequently accessed websites compiled by an Internet user.

hot·ly /ˈhätlē/ ▶ adv. in a passionate, excited, or angry way: *the rumors were hotly denied | hotly debated issues.*

hot met·al ▶ n. a typesetting technique in which type is newly made each time from molten metal, cast by a composing machine.

hot mon·ey ▶ n. capital that is frequently transferred between financial institutions in an attempt to maximize interest or capital gain.

hot pants ▶ plural n. tight, brief women's shorts, worn as a fashion garment.

hot pep·per ▶ n. any of several varieties of pungent pepper used dried or chopped as a condiment.

hot plate ▶ n. a flat heated surface (or a set of these), typically portable, used for cooking food or keeping it hot.

hot pot (also **hotpot**) ▶ n. Brit. a casserole of meat and vegetables, typically with a covering layer of sliced potato.

hot po·ta·to ▶ n. informal a controversial issue or situation that is awkward or unpleasant to deal with: *dog registration has become a political hot potato.*

hot press ▶ n. a device in which paper or cloth is pressed between glazed boards and hot metal plates in order to produce a smooth or glossy surface. ■ a similar apparatus used in making plywood.
▶ v. (**hot-press**) [with obj.] press with such a device.

hot rod ▶ n. a motor vehicle that has been specially modified to give it extra power and speed.
▶ v. (**hot-rod**) (**hot rods, hot rodding, hot rodded**)
1 [no obj.] drive a hot rod.
2 [with obj.] modify (a vehicle or other device) to make it faster or more powerful.
– DERIVATIVES **hot rod·der** (also **hot-rodder**) n.

hot seat ▶ n. (**the hot seat**) informal **1** the position of a person who carries full responsibility for something, including facing criticism or being answerable for decisions or actions: *it's been a bad week for the men in the hot seat.*
2 the electric chair.

hot shoe ▶ n. Photography a socket on a camera with direct electrical contacts for an attached flashgun or other accessory.

hot·shot /ˈhät,SHät/ ▶ n. informal an important or exceptionally able person: *these three hotshots decide what's what at the firm.*

hot spot ▶ n. **1** a small area or region with a relatively hot temperature in comparison to its surroundings. ■ Geology an area of volcanic activity, esp. where this is isolated. ■ a place of significant activity or danger: *a hot spot of commerce.*
2 (also **hotspot**) an area on a computer screen that can be clicked to activate a function. ■ a public place with an available wireless signal for Internet access.

hot spring ▶ n. a spring of naturally hot water, typically heated by subterranean volcanic activity.

Hot Springs a spa city in central Arkansas; pop. 39,467 (est. 2008).

Hot·spur /ˈhät,spər/ the nickname of Sir Henry Percy (see PERCY[1]).

hot·spur /ˈhät,spər/ ▶ n. archaic a rash, impetuous person.
– ORIGIN late Middle English: literally 'a person whose spur is hot from rash or constant riding.'

hot-stove ▶ adj. [attrib.] denoting a discussion about a favorite sport carried on during the off-season: *hot-stove speculation | these postseason fans—known as the hot-stove league—will be in here all winter arguing about the strike zone.*
– ORIGIN 1950s: by association with discussions conducted around a heater in the winter.

hot-stove league ▶ n. informal sports fans, esp. baseball fans in the off season, who discuss players, teams, and the upcoming season.

hot stuff ▶ n. informal used to refer to a person or thing of outstanding quality, interest, or talent: *he's hot stuff at arithmetic.* ■ used to refer to a sexually exciting person, movie, book, etc.: *Jill was reputed to be hot stuff.*

hot-swap ▶ v. [with obj.] informal fit or replace (a computer part) with the power still connected.
– DERIVATIVES **hot-swap·pa·ble** adj.

hot·sy-tot·sy /,hätsē ˈtätsē/ ▶ adj. **1** informal, dated used as a term of approval: *hotsy-totsy rhythms thrill the air.*
2 another term for HOITY-TOITY.
– ORIGIN early 20th cent.: reduplication of HOT, a fanciful formation by Billie de Beck (died 1942), US cartoonist.

hot-tem·pered ▶ adj. easily angered; quick-tempered.

Hot·ten·tot /ˈhätn,tät/ ▶ n. & adj. used to refer to Khoikhoi peoples.
– ORIGIN Dutch, perhaps from a Nama dancing song, transferred by Dutch sailors to the people themselves, or from German *hotteren-totteren* 'stutter' (with reference to their language, in which clicking sounds are used).

> **USAGE** The word **Hottentot** is first recorded in the late 17th century and was a name applied by white Europeans to the Khoikhoi. It is now regarded as offensive with reference to people and should always be avoided in favor of **Khoikhoi** or the names of the particular peoples. The only standard use for **Hottentot** in modern use is in the names of animals and plants.

hot tick·et ▶ n. informal a person or thing that is much in demand: *he's the current hot ticket on the hard-core hip-hop block* | [as modifier] *a hot-ticket invitation.*

hot·tie /ˈhätē/ (also **hotty**) ▶ n. (pl. **hotties**) informal a sexually attractive person: *a former high school hottie who married a prom queen.*
– ORIGIN from *hot* + *-ie* or *-y*.

hot tip ▶ n. a very reliable prediction or piece of inside information: *I had a hot tip on a horse in the third race.*

hot tub ▶ n. a large tub filled with hot aerated water used for recreation or physical therapy.

hot war ▶ n. a war with active military hostilities.

hot-wa·ter bot·tle (also **hot-water bag**) ▶ n. a flat, oblong container, typically made of rubber, that is filled with hot water and used for warmth.

hot-wire ▶ v. [with obj.] informal start the engine of (a vehicle) by bypassing the ignition system, typically in order to steal it.
▶ adj. [attrib.] (of an electrical instrument) depending on the expansion of a wire when heated or on a change in the electrical resistance of a wire when heated or cooled: *a hot-wire detector.*

hou·ba·ra /ho͞oˈbärə/ (also **houbara bustard**) ▶ n. a bustard of arid open country and semidesert, found from the Canary Islands to central Asia and threatened by hunting. ● *Chlamydotis undulata*, family Otidae.
– ORIGIN early 19th cent.: modern Latin, from Arabic *ḥubārā*.

Hou·di·ni /ho͞oˈdēnē/, Harry (1874–1926), US magician and escape artist; born in Hungary; born *Erik Weisz*. In the early 1900s, he became known for his ability to escape from all kinds of bonds and containers, from prison cells to aerially suspended straitjackets. ■ [as noun] a person skilled at escaping: *you're a regular Houdini.* ■ an ingenious escape: *he will have to do a Houdini to escape from me.*

Harry Houdini

Hou·ma a city in southeastern Louisiana, in the Cajun Country, southwest of New Orleans; pop. 32,512 (est. 2008).

hou·mous ▶ n. variant spelling of HUMMUS.

hound /hound/ ▶ n. a dog of a breed used for hunting, esp. one able to track by scent. ■ [with modifier] a person who avidly pursues something: *he has a reputation as a publicity hound.* ■ informal, dated a despicable or contemptible man. ■ used in names of dogfishes, e.g., **nurse hound, smooth hound.**
▶ v. [with obj.] harass, persecute, or pursue relentlessly: *a tenacious attorney general who had hounded Jimmy Hoffa and other labor bosses | his opponents used the allegations to **hound** him **out of** office.*
– PHRASES **ride to hounds** see RIDE.
– ORIGIN Old English *hund* (in the general sense 'dog'), of Germanic origin; related to Dutch *hond* and German *Hund*, from an Indo-European root shared by Greek *kuōn, kun-* 'dog.'

hound's-tongue ▶ n. a tall plant of the borage family that has a mousy smell and bears long silky hairs, small purplish flowers, and tongue-shaped leaves. ● *Cynoglossum officinale*, family Boraginaceae.

hounds·tooth /ˈhoun(d)z,to͞oTH/ ▶ n. a large checked pattern with notched corners suggestive of a canine tooth, typically used in cloth for jackets and suits.

houndstooth

houn·gan /ˈho͞oNGgən/ ▶ n. a voodoo priest.
– ORIGIN early 20th cent.: from Fon, from *hun*, a deity represented by a fetish, + *ga* 'chief.'

hour /ou(ə)r/ ▶ n. **1** a period of time equal to a twenty-fourth part of a day and night and divided into 60 minutes: *an extra hour of daylight | rates have ranged from $9 to $32 an hour* | [as modifier, usu. with preceding numeral] *a two-hour operation.* ■ a less definite period of time: *during the early hours of the morning.* ■ the distance traveled in one hour: *Ocean City is less than an hour away.*
2 a point in time: *I wondered if my last hour had come.* ■ a time of day specified as an exact number of hours from midnight or midday: *the clock in the sitting room **struck the hour**.* ■ (**hours**) [with preceding numeral] a time so specified on the 24-hour clock: *the first bomb fell at 0051 hours.* ■ the time as formerly reckoned from sunrise: *it was about the ninth hour.*
3 a fixed period of time for an activity, such as work, use of a building, etc.: *shortened working hours | the dinner hour.*
4 (usu. **hours**) (in the Western Church) a short service of psalms and prayers to be said at a particular time of day, esp. in religious communities.
5 Astronomy 15° of longitude or right ascension (one twenty-fourth part of a circle).
– PHRASES **all hours** any time, esp. outside the time considered usual for something: *intruders had access at all hours | teenagers expect to be allowed to stay out to **all hours**.* **keep late hours** get up and go to bed late. **keep regular hours** do the same thing at the same time every day. **on the hour** at an exact hour, or on each hour, of the day or night: *news bulletins on the hour.* **within the hour** after less than an hour.
– ORIGIN Middle English: from Anglo-Norman French *ure*, via Latin from Greek *hōra* 'season, hour.'

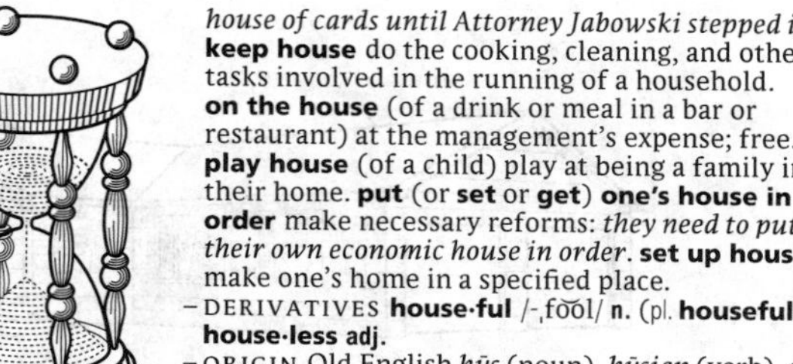
hourglass

hour·glass /ˈou(ə)rˌglas/ ▶ **n.** an invertible device with two connected glass bulbs containing sand that takes an hour to pass from the upper to the lower bulb. ■ [as modifier] shaped like such a device: *her hourglass figure.*

hour hand ▶ **n.** the hand on a clock or watch that indicates the hour.

hou·ri /ˈho͝orē/ ▶ **n.** (pl. **houris**) a beautiful young woman, esp. one of the virgin companions of the faithful in the Muslim Paradise.
– ORIGIN mid 18th cent.: from French, from Persian *ḥūrī*, from Arabic *ḥūr*, plural of *ʼaḥwar* 'having eyes with a marked contrast of black and white.'

hour-long (also **hourlong**) ▶ **adj.** [attrib.] lasting for one hour.

hour·ly /ˈou(ə)rlē/ ▶ **adj. 1** done or occurring every hour: *there is an hourly bus service.* ■ (with numeral or fraction) occurring at intervals measured in hours: *diamorphine was prescribed at four-hourly doses | trains run at half-hourly intervals.*
2 reckoned hour by hour: *to introduce standard fees instead of hourly rates.*
▶ **adv. 1** every hour: *sunscreens should be applied hourly | a train runs hourly from 7 a.m. to 8 p.m.* ■ (with numeral or fraction) at intervals measured in hours: *temperature should be recorded four-hourly.*
2 by the hour: *hourly paid workers.*
3 frequently; continually: *her curiosity was mounting hourly.*

Hou·sa·ton·ic River /ˌho͞osəˈtänik/ a river that flows for 130 miles (210 km) from the Berkshire Hills in western Massachusetts through Connecticut to Long Island Sound.

house ▶ **n.** /hous/ (pl. **houses** /ˈhouziz/) **1** a building for human habitation, esp. one that is lived in by a family or small group of people. ■ the people living in such a building; a household: *do you want the whole house woken up?* ■ (often **House**) a family or family lineage, esp. a noble or royal one; a dynasty: *the power and prestige of **the house of** Stewart.* ■ [with modifier] a building in which animals live or in which things are kept: *a reptile house.*
2 a building in which people meet for a particular activity: *a house of prayer.* ■ a business or institution: *he had purchased a publishing house.* ■ a restaurant or inn: [as modifier] *I ordered a bottle of their house wine.* ■ a residential hall at a school or college, or its residents. ■ a theater: *a hundred musicians performed in front of a full house.* ■ an audience in a theater or concert venue: *the house burst into applause.* ■ a religious community that occupies a particular building: *the Cistercian house at Clairvaux.* ■ dated a brothel. ■ Brit. formal a college of a university.
3 a legislative or deliberative assembly: *the sixty-member National Council, the country's upper house.* ■ (**the House**) the House of Representatives or (in the UK or Canada) the House of Commons or Lords.
4 (also **house music**) a style of popular dance music typically using synthesized drum and bass lines, sparse repetitive vocals, and a fast beat.
5 Astrology any of the twelve divisions of the celestial sphere, based on the positions of the ascendant and midheaven at a given time and place, and determined by any of a number of methods. ■ such a division represented as a sector on an astrological chart, used in allocating elements of character and circumstance to different spheres of human life.
▶ **adj.** /hous/ [attrib.] **1** (of an animal or plant) kept in, frequenting, or infesting buildings.
2 of or relating to a business, institution, or society: *a house journal.* ■ (of a band or group) resident or regularly performing in a club or other venue.
▶ **v.** /houz/ [with obj.] **1** provide (a person or animal) with shelter or living quarters: *attempts by the government to house the poor.*
2 provide space for; accommodate: *the museum houses a collection of Roman sculpture.* ■ insert or fix (something) in a socket or mortise.
– PHRASES **like a house on fire** (or **afire**) informal vigorously; furiously. ■ excellently: *Ben and my aunt got along like a house on fire.* **house and home** a person's home (used for emphasis): *some people sell house and home to sit in a boat writing books.* **a house divided cannot stand** proverb a group or organization weakened by internal dissensions will be unable to withstand external pressures. **house of cards** a structure built out of playing cards precariously balanced together. ■ an insubstantial or insecure situation or scheme: *his case was a house of cards until Attorney Jabowski stepped in.* **keep house** do the cooking, cleaning, and other tasks involved in the running of a household. **on the house** (of a drink or meal in a bar or restaurant) at the management's expense; free. **play house** (of a child) play at being a family in their home. **put** (or **set** or **get**) **one's house in order** make necessary reforms: *they need to put their own economic house in order.* **set up house** make one's home in a specified place.
– DERIVATIVES **house·ful** /-ˌfo͝ol/ **n.** (pl. **housefuls**), **house·less adj.**
– ORIGIN Old English *hūs* (noun), *hūsian* (verb), of Germanic origin; related to Dutch *huis*, German *Haus* (nouns), and Dutch *huizen*, German *hausen* (verbs).

house a·gent ▶ **n.** British term for **REAL ESTATE AGENT.**

house ar·rest ▶ **n.** the state of being kept as a prisoner in one's own house, rather than in a prison: *she was placed **under house arrest**.*

house·boat /ˈhousˌbōt/ ▶ **n.** a boat that is or can be moored for use as a dwelling.

house·bound /ˈhousˌbound/ ▶ **adj.** unable to leave one's house, typically due to illness or old age.

house·boy /ˈhousˌboi/ ▶ **n.** a boy or man employed to undertake domestic duties.

house brand ▶ **n.** a brand name used exclusively by a retailer (or a selected group of retailers) for a product or line of products that are typically sold for prices lower than that of comparable items with manufacturer brand names. ■ a product bearing such a name: *don't get the expensive coffee, get the house brand.*

house·break /ˈhousˌbrāk/ ▶ **v.** (past. **housebroke**; past participle **housebroken**) [with obj.] train (a pet) to urinate and defecate outside the house or only in a special place: *an elephant is exceedingly difficult to housebreak* | (as adj. **housebroken**) *wolves are almost never housebroken.*

house·break·ing /ˈhousˌbrākiNG/ ▶ **n.** the action of breaking into a building, esp. in daytime, to commit a crime.
– DERIVATIVES **house·break·er** /-ˌbrākər/ **n.**

house·build·ing /ˈhousˌbildiNG/ ▶ **n.** the trade or activity of building houses.
– DERIVATIVES **house·build·er n.**

house·carl /ˈhousˌkärl/ (also **housecarle**) ▶ **n.** historical a member of the bodyguard of a Danish or English king or noble.
– ORIGIN late Old English *hūscarl*, from Old Norse *húskarl* 'manservant,' (plural) 'retinue, bodyguard,' from *hús* 'house' + *karl* 'man.'

house church ▶ **n.** a charismatic church independent of traditional denominations, esp. one meeting in a private house.

house·clean·ing /ˈhousˌklēniNG/ ▶ **n. 1** the cleaning of the interior of a dwelling.
2 the removal of unwanted or superfluous items, practices, conditions, or personnel: *the new owner's housecleaning cost a lot of people their jobs.*
– DERIVATIVES **house·clean v.**, **house·clean·er n.**

house·coat /ˈhousˌkōt/ ▶ **n.** a woman's long, loose, lightweight robe for informal wear around the house.

house crick·et ▶ **n.** a chiefly nocturnal cricket with a birdlike warble, native to North Africa and southwestern Asia. It has become established in heated buildings. ● *Acheta domesticus*, family Gryllidae.

house·dress /ˈhousˌdres/ ▶ **n.** a simple, usually washable, dress suitable for wearing while doing housework.

house·fa·ther /ˈhousˌfäT͟Hər/ ▶ **n.** a man in charge of and living in a boarding school dormitory or other group residence.

house finch ▶ **n.** a red-breasted brown finch, now common from Canada to Mexico and sometimes regarded as a pest. ● *Carpodacus mexicanus*, family Fringillidae.

house flag ▶ **n.** a flag indicating the company that a ship belongs to.

house·fly /ˈhousˌflī/ (also **house fly**) ▶ **n.** (pl. **houseflies**) a common small fly occurring worldwide in and around human habitation. Its eggs are laid in decaying material, and the fly can be a health hazard due to its contamination of food. ● *Musca domestica*, family Muscidae.

house geck·o ▶ **n.** a large-eyed nocturnal gecko of the Old World tropics, occupying a range of habitats including houses. ● *Hemidactylus*, *Gehyra*, and other genera, family Gekkonidae: several species, including *H. mabouia* of Africa and tropical America, and *G. mutilata* of Asia.

house guest (also **houseguest**) ▶ **n.** a guest staying for some days in a private house.

house·hold /ˈhousˌ(h)ōld/ ▶ **n.** a house and its occupants regarded as a unit: *the whole household was asleep | ten percent of households had a television* | [as modifier] *household appliances.*

house·hold·er /ˈhousˌ(h)ōldər/ ▶ **n.** a person who owns or rents a house; the head of a household.

house·hold gods ▶ **plural n.** gods presiding over a household, esp. (in Roman History) the lares and penates. ■ possessions held in esteem: *the Fairley household gods—portraits and an assortment of silver.*

house·hold name (also **household word**) ▶ **n.** a person or thing that is well known by the public: *I'd like to sell gazillions of books and become a household name.*

house·hold troops ▶ **plural n.** troops employed to guard a sovereign.

house-hunt ▶ **v.** [no obj.] seek a house to buy or rent and live in.
– DERIVATIVES **house-hunt·er n.**, **house-hunt·ing n.**

house·hus·band /ˈhousˌhəzbənd/ ▶ **n.** a man who lives with a partner and carries out household duties traditionally done by a housewife rather than working outside the home.

house·keep·er /ˈhousˌkēpər/ ▶ **n.** a person, typically a woman, employed to manage a household.
– DERIVATIVES **house·keep v.** (dated).

house·keep·ing /ˈhousˌkēpiNG/ ▶ **n. 1** the management of household affairs. ■ money set aside or given for such a purpose: *writing barely pays my part of the housekeeping.* ■ a department within a hotel or other residential facility that oversees the cleaning of rooms and the provision of necessities such as towels and glassware: *you'll never have to nag housekeeping for a set of dry towels.*
2 operations such as record-keeping or maintenance in an organization or a computer that make work possible but do not directly constitute its performance. ■ Biology the regulation of metabolic functions that are common to all cells: [as modifier] *housekeeping genes.*

house·leek /ˈhousˌlēk/ ▶ **n.** a succulent plant with rosettes of fleshy leaves and small pink flowers. Houseleeks grow on walls and roofs, and are popular cultivated plants. ● *Sempervivum* and related genera, family Crassulaceae: several species, in particular *S. tectorum.*

house lights (also **houselights**) ▶ **plural n.** the lights in the area of a theater where the audience sits: *the show ended and the house lights came up.*

house·maid /ˈhousˌmād/ ▶ **n.** a female domestic employee, esp. one who cleans reception rooms and bedrooms.

house·maid's knee ▶ **n.** inflammation of the fluid-filled cavity covering the kneecap, often due to excessive kneeling; bursitis.

house·man /ˈhousmən/ ▶ **n.** (pl. **housemen**)
1 another term for **HOUSEBOY.**
2 Brit. a hospital intern.

house·mas·ter /ˈhousˌmastər/ ▶ **n.** a teacher, typically male, in charge of a dormitory at a boarding school.

house·mis·tress /ˈhousˌmistris/ ▶ **n.** a female teacher in charge of a dormitory at a boarding school.

house·moth·er /ˈhousˌməT͟Hər/ ▶ **n.** a woman in charge of and living in a boarding school dormitory or children's home.

house mouse ▶ **n.** a grayish-brown mouse found abundantly as a scavenger in human dwellings. It is widely kept as a pet or experimental animal and has been bred in many varieties. ● *Mus musculus*, family Muridae.

house mu·sic ▶ **n.** see **HOUSE** (sense 4 of the noun).

House of Bur·gess·es ▶ **n.** the lower house of the colonial Virginia legislature.

House of Com·mons (in the UK and Canada) the elected chamber of Parliament.

house of cor·rec·tion ▶ **n.** an institution for the short-term confinement of minor offenders.

house of·fi·cer ▶ **n.** Brit. a medical intern.

house of God ▶ **n.** a place of religious worship, esp. a church.

house of ill fame (also **house of ill repute**) ▶ **n.** archaic or humorous a brothel.

House of Lords (in the UK) the higher chamber of Parliament, composed of peers and bishops. ■ a committee of specially qualified members of this,

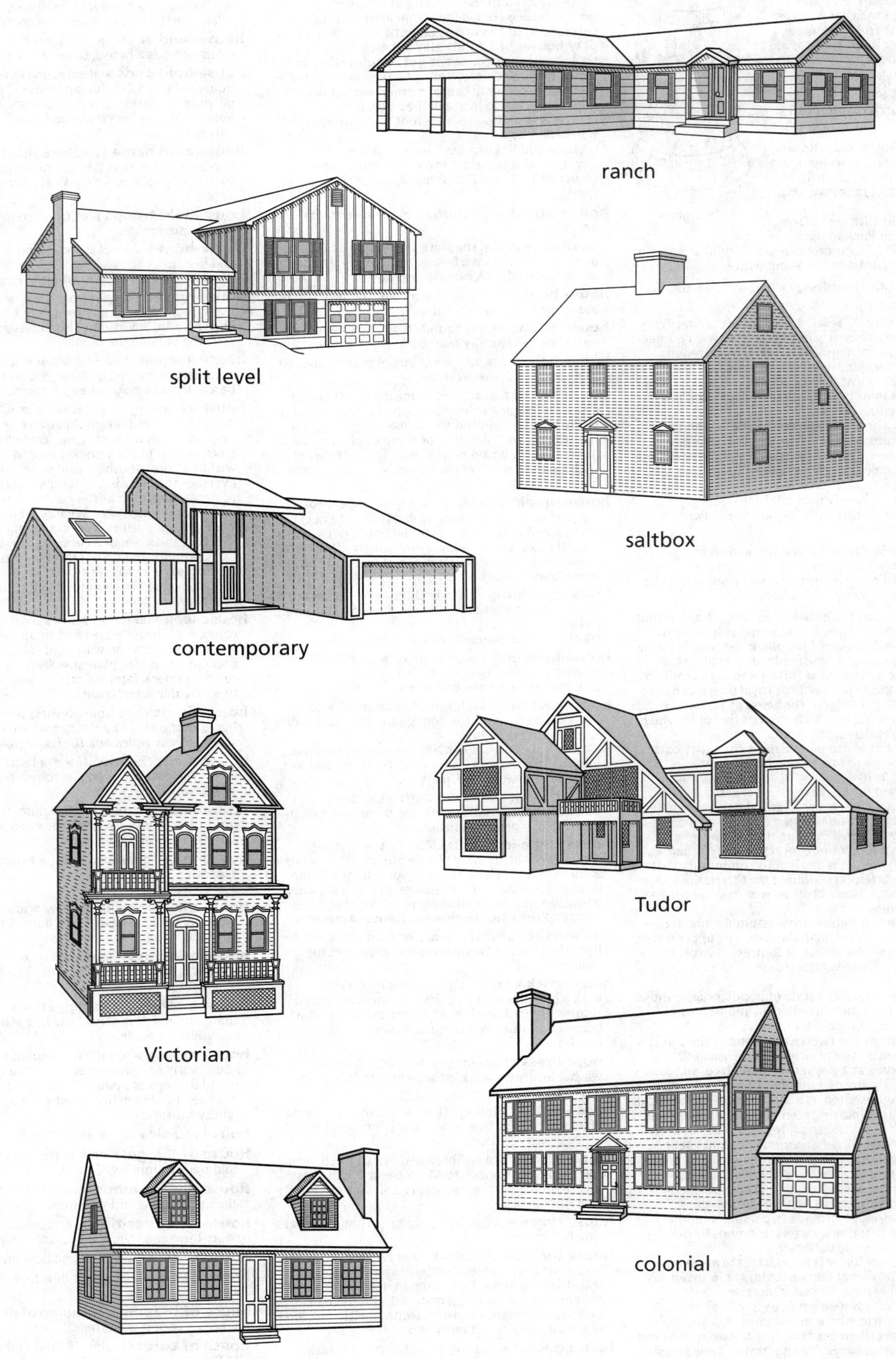

house styles

h

appointed as the ultimate judicial appeal court of England and Wales.

House of Rep·re·sent·a·tives the lower house of the US Congress and other legislatures, including most US state governments.

house or·gan ▶ **n.** a periodical published by a company to be read by its employees and other interested parties and dealing mainly with its own activities.

house·par·ent /ˈhous,pe(ə)rənt, -,parənt/ ▶ **n.** a housemother or housefather.

house par·ty ▶ **n.** a party at which the guests stay at a house overnight or for a few days.

house·plant /ˈhous,plant/ (also **house plant**) ▶ **n.** a plant grown indoors.

house-proud ▶ **adj.** attentive to, or preoccupied with, the care and appearance of one's home.

house rat ▶ **n.** another term for BLACK RAT.

house·room /ˈhous,ro͞om, -,ro͝om/ ▶ **n.** space or accommodations in one's house: *she refused to give houseroom to the canvas her brother had bought.*

house-sit (also **housesit**) ▶ **v.** [no obj.] live in and look after a house while its owner is away.
– DERIVATIVES **house-sit·ter n.**, **house-sit·ting n.**

Hous·es of Par·lia·ment (in the UK) the Houses of Lords and Commons regarded together, or the building where they meet (the Palace of Westminster).

Houses of Parliament

house spar·row ▶ **n.** a brown and gray sparrow that nests in the eaves and roofs of houses, common from Europe to southern Asia and introduced elsewhere. Also called ENGLISH SPARROW. ● *Passer domesticus*, family Passeridae (or Ploceidae).

house style ▶ **n.** a company's preferred manner of presentation and layout of written material: *the document will automatically be set out according to the house style.*

house-to-house ▶ **adj. & adv.** performed at or taken to each house in turn: [as adj.] *a veteran salesman took a rookie on house-to-house canvassing* | [as adv.] *troops searched house to house for agitators.*

house·top /ˈhous,täp/ ▶ **n.** the outer surface of the roof of a house.
– PHRASES **shout something from the housetops** old-fashioned way of saying SHOUT SOMETHING FROM THE ROOFTOPS (see SHOUT).

house-train ▶ **v.** chiefly Brit. another term for HOUSEBREAK.

House Un-A·mer·i·can Ac·tiv·i·ties Com·mit·tee (abbr.: **HUAC**) a committee of the US House of Representatives established in 1938 to investigate subversives. It became notorious for its zealous investigations of alleged communists, particularly in the late 1940s, although it was originally intended to pursue Fascists also.

house·warm·ing /ˈhous,wôrmiNG/ ▶ **n.** [usu. as modifier] a party celebrating a move to a new home: *a housewarming gift.*

house·wife /ˈhous,wīf/ ▶ **n.** (pl. **housewives**) **1** a married woman whose main occupation is caring for her family, managing household affairs, and doing housework.
2 a small case for needles, thread, and other small sewing items.
– DERIVATIVES **house·wife·ly adj.**, **house·wif·er·y** /-,wīfərē/ **n.**
– ORIGIN Middle English *husewif* (see HOUSE, WIFE).

house·work /ˈhous,wərk/ ▶ **n.** regular work done in housekeeping, such as cleaning, shopping, and cooking.

house·y /ˈhousē/ ▶ **adj.** Brit. informal in the style of house music.

hous·ing¹ /ˈhouziNG/ ▶ **n. 1** houses and apartments considered collectively: *affordable housing* | [as modifier] *a housing development.* ■ the provision of accommodations: *the sector that offers housing to the poorest.*
2 a rigid casing that encloses and protects a piece of moving or delicate equipment.
3 a recess or groove cut in one piece of wood to allow another piece to be attached to it.

hous·ing² ▶ **n.** archaic a cloth covering put on a horse for protection or ornament.
– ORIGIN late Middle English (in the general sense 'covering'): from Old French *houce*, from medieval Latin *hultia*, of Germanic origin.

hous·ing de·vel·op·ment (Brit. **housing estate**) ▶ **n.** a residential area in which the houses have all been planned and built at the same time.

hous·ing start ▶ **n.** the beginning of construction of a new house. ■ (**housing starts**) the number of new houses begun during a particular period, used as an indicator of economic conditions.

Hous·man /ˈhousmən/, A. E. (1859–1936), English poet and classical scholar; full name *Alfred Edward Housman*. He is chiefly remembered for his poems collected in *A Shropshire Lad* (1896).

Hous·ton¹ /ˈ(h)yo͞ostən/ an inland port in Texas, linked to the Gulf of Mexico by the Houston Ship Canal; pop. 2,242,193 (est. 2008). Since 1961, it has been a center for space research and manned space flight; it is the site of the NASA Space Center.
– ORIGIN named after Samuel *Houston*.

Hous·ton², Samuel (1793–1863), US soldier and politician. He led the struggle to win control of Texas and to make it part of the US. He was the first president of the republic of Texas 1836–38, 1841–44 and the first US senator from the state of Texas 1846–59. The governor of Texas 1859–61, he was ousted for refusing to swear allegiance to the Confederacy during the Civil War.

Samuel Houston

hove /hōv/ chiefly Nautical past of HEAVE.

hov·el /ˈhəvəl, ˈhävəl/ ▶ **n. 1** a small, squalid, unpleasant, or simply constructed dwelling. ■ archaic an open shed or outbuilding, used for sheltering cattle or storing grain or tools.
2 historical a conical building enclosing a kiln.
– ORIGIN late Middle English: of unknown origin.

hov·er /ˈhəvər/ ▶ **v.** [no obj.] remain in one place in the air: *army helicopters hovered overhead.* ■ remain poised uncertainly in one place or between two states: *her hand **hovered over** the console* | *his expression **hovered between** cynicism and puzzlement.* ■ (of a person) wait or linger close at hand in a tentative or uncertain manner: *she hovered anxiously in the background.* ■ remain at or near a particular level: *inflation will hover around the 4 percent mark.*
▶ **n.** [in sing.] an act of remaining in the air in one place.
– DERIVATIVES **hov·er·er n.**
– ORIGIN late Middle English: from archaic *hove* 'hover, linger,' of unknown origin.

hov·er·craft /ˈhəvər,kraft/ ▶ **n.** (pl. **same**) a vehicle or craft that travels over land or water on a cushion of air provided by a downward blast. A design was first patented by Christopher Cockerell (1910–99) in 1955.

hov·er·port /ˈhəvər,pôrt/ ▶ **n.** a terminal for hovercraft.

hov·er·train /ˈhəvər,trān/ ▶ **n.** a train that travels on a cushion of air.

how¹ /hou/ ▶ **adv.** [usu. interrogative adverb] **1** in what way or manner; by what means: *how does it work?* | *he did not know how he ought to behave* | [with infinitive] *he showed me how to adjust the focus.*
2 used to ask about the condition or quality of something: *how was your vacation?* | *how did they play?* ■ used to ask about someone's physical or mental state: *how are the children?* | *I asked how he was doing.*
3 [with adj. or adv.] used to ask about the extent or degree of something: *how old are you?* | *how long will it take?* | *I wasn't sure how fast to go.* ■ used to express a strong feeling such as surprise about the extent of something: *how kind it was of him* | *how I wish I had been there!*
4 [relative adverb] the way in which; that: *she told us how she had lived out of a suitcase for a week.* ■ in any way in which; however: *I'll do business how I like.*
– PHRASES **and how!** informal very much so (used to express strong agreement): *"Did you miss me?" "And how!"* **here's how!** dated said when drinking to someone's health. **how about 1** used to make a suggestion or offer: *how about a drink?* **2** used when asking for information or an opinion on something: *how about your company?* **the how and why** the methods and reasons for doing something: *tonight's edition demystifies the how and why of television ratings.* **how come?** see COME. **how do?** an informal greeting. **how do you do?** a formal greeting. **how many** what number: *how many books did you sell?* **how much** what amount or price: *just how much did it cost?* **how now?** archaic what is the meaning of this? **how so?** how can you show that that is so? **how's that for ——?** isn't that a remarkable instance of ——?: *how's that for stereotypical thinking?*
– ORIGIN Old English *hū*; related to Dutch *hoe*, also to WHO and WHAT.

how² ▶ **exclam.** a greeting attributed to North American Indians (used in humorous imitation).
– ORIGIN early 19th cent.: perhaps from Sioux *háo* or Omaha *hou*.

How·ard¹ /ˈhou-ərd/, Catherine (*c.*1521–42), fifth wife of Henry VIII. Accused of infidelity, she confessed and was beheaded.

How·ard² see THREE STOOGES.

How·ard³, John (Winston) (1939–), Australian Liberal statesman; prime minister 1996–2007.

How·ard⁴, Leslie (1893–1943), English actor; born *Leslie Howard Stainer*. He was best known for his roles as the archetypal British gentleman in movies such as *The Scarlet Pimpernel* (1935) and *Pygmalion* (1938). Other notable movies include *Gone with the Wind* (1939).

how·be·it /houˈbēit/ ▶ **adv.** archaic nevertheless; however: *howbeit, I've no proof of the thing.*

how·dah /ˈhoudə/ ▶ **n.** (in South Asia) a seat for riding on the back of an elephant or camel, typically with a canopy and accommodating two or more people.
– ORIGIN from Urdu *haudah*, from Arabic *hawdaj* 'litter.'

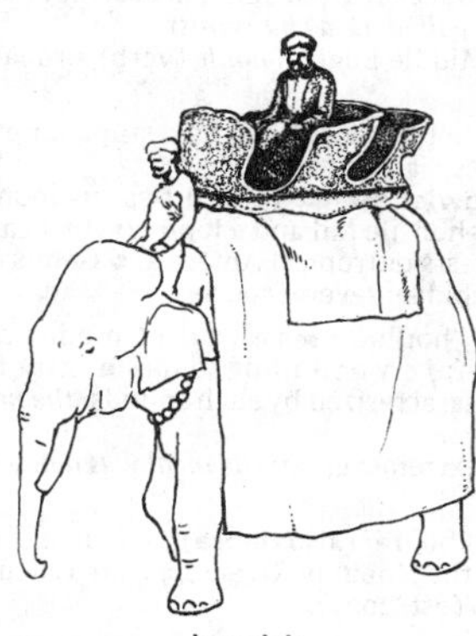
howdah

how-do-you-do (also **how-de-do** or **how-d'ye-do**) ▶ **n.** [in sing.] informal an awkward, messy, or annoying situation: *a fine how-do-you-do that would be!*

how·dy /ˈhoudē/ ▶ **exclam.** an informal friendly greeting, particularly associated with the western states: *howdy, stranger.*
– ORIGIN early 19th cent.: alteration of *how d'ye*.

Howe¹ /hou/, Elias (1819–67), US inventor. In 1846, he patented the first sewing machine. Its principles were adapted by Isaac Merrit Singer and others in violation of Howe's patent rights, and it took a seven-year litigation battle to secure the royalties.

Howe², Gordie (1928–), Canadian hockey player; full name *Gordon Howe*. A prolific scorer, he played for the Omaha Knights 1945–46, the Detroit Red Wings 1946–71, the Houston Aeros 1973–77, and the New England Whalers 1977–80. Hockey Hall of Fame (1972).

how·e'er /houˈe(ə)r/ literary ▶ **contraction** however.

How·ells /ˈhou-əlz/, William Dean (1837–1920), US writer and critic. He was editor-in-chief of *Atlantic Monthly* magazine 1871–81. His novels include *The Rise of Silas Lapham* (1885) and *A Hazard of New Fortunes* (1890).

how·ev·er /hou'evər/ ▶ **adv. 1** used to introduce a statement that contrasts with or seems to contradict something that has been said previously: *People tend to put on weight in middle age. However, gaining weight is not inevitable.*
2 [relative adverb] in whatever way; regardless of how: *however you look at it, you can't criticize that.* ■ [with adj. or adv.] to whatever extent: *he was hesitant to take the risk, however small.*

USAGE When **ever** is used as an intensifier after *how, what, when, where,* or *why,* it should be separated by a space. Thus, *how ever did you find her?* could be rephrased, with no change of meaning, *how did you ever find her?* This rule tends to be more often followed—or more widely understood—in Britain than in the US. **However** in the sense of 'no matter how' (*however gently you correct him, Peter always takes offense*) should be spelled as one word. See also usage at **WHATEVER**.

how·itz·er /'houətsər/ ▶ **n.** a short gun for firing shells on high trajectories at low velocities.
– ORIGIN late 17th cent.: from Dutch *houwitser*, from German *Haubitze*, from Czech *houfnice* 'catapult.'

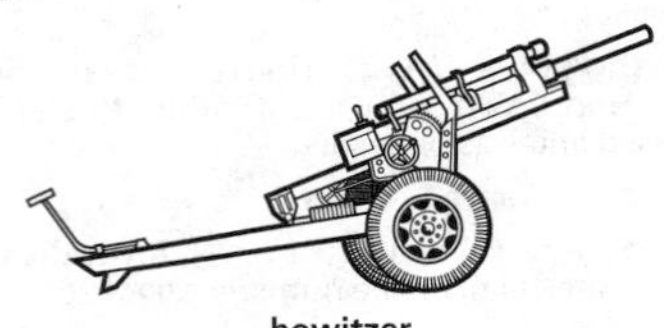

howitzer

howl /houl/ ▶ **n.** a long, loud, doleful cry uttered by an animal such as a dog or wolf. ■ a loud cry of pain, fear, anger, amusement, or derision: *he let out a howl of anguish* | figurative *I got howls of protest from readers.* ■ [in sing.] a prolonged wailing noise such as that made by a strong wind: *they listened to the howl of the gale.* ■ Electronics a wailing noise in a loudspeaker due to electrical or acoustic feedback.
▶ **v.** [no obj.] make a howling sound: *he howled in agony* | *the wind howled around the house.* ■ weep and cry out loudly: *a baby started to howl.* ■ [with obj.] (**howl someone down**) shout in disapproval in order to prevent a speaker from being heard: *they howled me down and called me a chauvinist.*
– ORIGIN Middle English *houle* (verb), probably imitative.

howl·er /'houlər/ ▶ **n. 1** informal a stupid or glaring mistake, esp. an amusing one.
2 (also **howler monkey**) a fruit-eating monkey with a prehensile tail and a loud howling call, native to the forests of tropical America. ● Genus *Alouatta*, family Cebidae: several species.

howl·ing /'houliNG/ ▶ **adj.** [attrib.] **1** producing a long, loud, doleful cry or wailing sound. ■ archaic filled with or characterized by such sounds: *the howling wilderness.*
2 informal extreme; great: *the meal was a howling success.*

How·rah /'hourə/ (also **Haora**) a city in eastern India, on the Hooghly River, opposite Calcutta; pop. 1,034,400 (est. 2009).

how·so·e'er /ˌhousō'e(ə)r/ literary ▶ **contraction** howsoever.

how·so·ev·er /ˌhousō'evər/ formal or archaic ▶ **adv.** [with adj. or adv.] to whatever extent: *any quantity howsoever small.*
▶ **conj.** in whatever way; regardless of how: *howsoever it came into being, it is good to look at.*

how-to informal ▶ **adj.** [attrib.] providing detailed and practical advice: *read a how-to book.*
▶ **n.** (pl. **how-tos**) a book, video, or training session that provides such advice. ■ (**how-tos**) the correct procedures for a particular activity: *you will discover the how-tos of freehand drawing.*

Hox·ha /'hôjə/, Enver (1908–85), Albanian statesman; founder of the Albanian Communist Party in 1941; prime minister 1944–54, and first secretary of the Albanian Communist Party 1954–85. He rigorously isolated Albania from Western influences and implemented a Stalinist program of nationalization and collectivization.

hoy[1] /hoi/ ▶ **exclam.** used to attract someone's attention: *"Hoy! Look!"*
– ORIGIN natural exclamation: first recorded in late Middle English.

hoy[2] ▶ **n.** historical a small coastal sailing vessel, typically carrying one mast rigged fore-and-aft.
– ORIGIN Middle English: from Middle Dutch *hoei*, of unknown origin.

hoy·a /'hoiə/ ▶ **n.** a climbing or sprawling evergreen shrub with ornamental foliage and waxy flowers, native to Southeast Asia and the Pacific and grown as a greenhouse or indoor plant. ● Genus *Hoya*, family Asclepiadaceae.
– ORIGIN modern Latin, named after Thomas *Hoy* (*c.*1750–*c.*1821), English gardener.

hoy·den /'hoidn/ ▶ **n.** dated a boisterous girl.
– DERIVATIVES **hoy·den·ish adj.**
– ORIGIN late 16th cent. (denoting a rude or ignorant man): probably from Middle Dutch *heiden* (see **HEATHEN**).

Hoyle[1] /hoil/, Sir Fred (1915–2001), English astrophysicist and writer. He was one of the proponents of the steady state theory of cosmology, and, mainly with US physicist **William A. Fowler** (1911–95), described the processes of nucleosynthesis inside stars.

Hoyle[2] /hoil/ ▶ **n.** (in phrase **according to Hoyle**) according to plan or the rules.
– ORIGIN early 20th cent.: from the name of Edmond *Hoyle* (1672–1769), English writer on card games.

h.p. (also **HP**) ▶ **abbr.** ■ high pressure. ■ Brit. hire purchase. ■ horsepower.

HPF ▶ **abbr.** highest possible frequency.

HPV ▶ **abbr.** human papilloma virus.

HQ ▶ **abbr.** headquarters.

HR ▶ **abbr.** ■ House of Representatives. ■ human resources.

hr ▶ **abbr.** hour.

Hr. ▶ **abbr.** Herr.

Hra·dec Krá·lo·vé /'(h)rädˌets 'krälôˌve/ a town in the northern Czech Republic, on the Elbe River; pop. 94,134 (2007). German name **KÖNIGGRÄTZ**.

HRE ▶ **abbr.** Holy Roman Empire or Emperor.

H. Rept. ▶ **abbr.** House Report.

H. Res. ▶ **abbr.** House Resolution.

HRH ▶ **abbr.** Brit. Her or His Royal Highness (as a title): *HRH Prince Philip.*

Hrod·na /'KHrôdnə/ a city in western Belarus, on the Neman River, near the borders with Poland and Lithuania; pop. 338,200 (est. 2009). Russian name **GRODNO**.

hrs ▶ **abbr.** hours.

HRT ▶ **abbr.** hormone replacement therapy.

Hr·vat·ska /'KH(ə)rvatskä, 'hərvätskä/ Croatian name for **CROATIA**.

hryv·na /'(h)rivnyə, -nē, hə'riv-/ (also **hryvnia**) ▶ **n.** the basic monetary unit of Ukraine, equal to 100 kopiykas.
– ORIGIN from Ukrainian *gryvnya* '3-kopek coin of pre-independent Ukraine,' from Old Russian *grivina* 'necklace, ring, coin.'

Hs ▶ **symbol** the chemical element hassium.

HSA ▶ **abbr. HEALTH SAVINGS ACCOUNT**.

HSGT ▶ **abbr.** high speed ground transit.

HSH ▶ **abbr.** Her or His Serene Highness (as a title): *HSH Prince Rainer.*

Hsia-men variant spelling of **XIAMEN**.

Hsian variant spelling of **XIAN**.

Hsiang variant spelling of **XIANG**.

Hsi·ning variant spelling of **XINING**.

HST ▶ **abbr.** ■ hypersonic transport. ■ Hubble Space Telescope.

Hsu-chou variant spelling of **XUZHOU**.

HT ▶ **abbr.** ■ halftime. ■ (electrical) high tension.

HTLV ▶ **abbr.** human T cell lymphotropic virus.

HTLV-I ▶ **abbr.** ■ T-cell lymphotrophic virus type I. ■ human lymphotropic virus, type 1.

HTLV-III ▶ **abbr.** human T-cell lymphotropic virus, type III.

HTML ▶ **n.** Computing Hypertext Markup Language, a standardized system for tagging text files to achieve font, color, graphic, and hyperlink effects on World Wide Web pages.

Hts. ▶ **abbr.** Heights.

HTTP ▶ **abbr.** Computing Hypertext Transfer (or Transport) Protocol, the data transfer protocol used on the World Wide Web.

HUAC /'hyo͞o-ak/ ▶ **abbr.** House Un-American Activities Committee.

Huai·bei /'hwī'bā/ an industrial city in northern Anhui province, in eastern China, southwest of Xuzhou; pop. 674,200 (est. 2006).

Huai·nan /'hwī'nän/ a city in east central China, in the province of Anhui; pop. 932,200 (est. 2006).

Hual·la·ga /wä'yägä/ a river in central Peru, one of the headwaters of the Amazon River. Rising in the central Andes, it flows northeast for 700 miles (1,100 km) to the Amazon Basin at Lagunas.

Huam·bo /'wämbō/ a city in the mountains in western Angola; pop. 294,100 (est. 2004). Founded in 1912, it was known by its Portuguese name of Nova Lisboa until 1978.

Huang Hai /'hwäNG 'hī/ Chinese name for **YELLOW SEA**.

Huang Ho /'hō/ (also **Huang He** /'hə/) Chinese name for **YELLOW RIVER**.

Huang·shi /'hwäNG'SHē/ (formerly ***Hwangshih***) an industrial city in Hubei province, in east central China, on the Yangtze River, south of Wuhan; pop. 628,000 (est. 2006).

hua·ra·che /wə'räCHē/ (also **guarache**) ▶ **n.** a leather-thonged sandal, originally worn by Mexican Indians.
– ORIGIN late 19th cent.: Mexican Spanish.

huarache

Huas·ca·rán /ˌwäskə'rän/ an extinct volcano in the Peruvian Andes, in western central Peru, that rises to 22,205 feet (6,768 m). It is the highest peak in Peru.

hub /həb/ ▶ **n.** the central part of a wheel, rotating on or with the axle, and from which the spokes radiate. ■ a place or thing that forms the effective center of an activity, region, or network: *the kitchen was the hub of family life.*
– PHRASES **hub-and-spoke** denoting a system of air transportation in which local airports offer flights to a central airport where international or long-distance flights are available.
– ORIGIN early 16th cent. (denoting a shelf at the side of a fireplace used for heating pans): of unknown origin (compare with **HOB**[1]).

hub·ba hub·ba /'həbə 'həbə/ ▶ **exclam.** informal used to express approval, excitement, or enthusiasm, esp. with regard to a person's appearance: *In walks the willowy Juanita. Hubba hubba!* | [as adj.] *they parodied her hubba-hubba image.*
– ORIGIN 1940s: of unknown origin.

Hub·bard squash /'həbərd/ ▶ **n.** a winter squash of a variety with a green or yellow rind and yellow flesh.

Hub·ble /'həbəl/, Edwin Powell (1889–1953), US astronomer. He studied galaxies and devised a classification scheme for them. In 1929, he proposed what is now known as Hubble's law with its constant of proportionality (Hubble's constant). The Hubble Space Telescope, deployed in space in 1990, is named for him.

hub·ble-bub·ble /'həbəl ˌbəbəl/ ▶ **n.** a hookah.
– ORIGIN mid 17th cent.: imitative repetition of **BUBBLE**.

Hub·ble clas·si·fi·ca·tion Astronomy a simple method of describing the shapes of galaxies, using subdivisions of each of four basic types (elliptical, spiral, barred spiral, and irregular). Hubble's suggestion that they form an evolutionary sequence is no longer accepted.

Hub·ble's con·stant Astronomy the ratio of the speed of recession of a galaxy (due to the expansion of the universe) to its distance from the observer. The reciprocal of the constant is called **Hubble time** and represents the length of time for which the universe has been expanding, and hence the age of the universe.

Hub·ble's law Astronomy a law stating that the redshifts in the spectra of distant galaxies (and hence their speeds of recession) are proportional to their distance.

Hub·ble Space Tel·e·scope an orbiting astronomical observatory launched in 1990. The telescope's high-resolution images are far better than can be obtained from the earth's surface.

hub·bub /'həbəb/ ▶ **n.** [in sing.] a chaotic din caused by a crowd of people: *a hubbub of laughter and shouting.* ■ a busy, noisy situation: *she fought through the hubbub.*
– ORIGIN mid 16th cent.: perhaps of Irish origin; compare with the Irish exclamations *abábú, abú,* used in battle cries.

hub·by /'həbē/ ▶ **n.** (pl. **hubbies**) informal a husband.
– ORIGIN late 17th cent.: familiar abbreviation.

hub·cap /'həbˌkap/ ▶ **n.** a metal or plastic cover for the hub of a motor vehicle's wheel.

Hu·bei /'ho͞o'bā/ (also **Hupeh**) a province in eastern China; capital, Wuhan.

Hub·li /'ho͝oblē/ (also **Hubli-Dharwad** /där'wäd/, **Hubli-Dharwar** /där'wär/) a city in southwestern India; pop. 892,300 (est. 2009). It was united with the adjacent city of Dharwad in 1961.

hu·bris /ˈ(h)yo͞obris/ ▶ **n.** excessive pride or self-confidence. ■ (in Greek tragedy) excessive pride toward or defiance of the gods, leading to nemesis.
– DERIVATIVES **hu·bris·tic** /(h)yo͞oˈbristik/ **adj.**
– ORIGIN Greek.

hu·chen /ˈho͝okən/ ▶ **n.** (pl. **same**) a large, slender, nonmigratory fish of the salmon family that lives only in the Danube River system. ● *Hucho hucho*, family Salmonidae.
– ORIGIN early 20th cent.: from German.

huck·a·back /ˈhəkəˌbak/ ▶ **n.** a strong linen or cotton fabric with a rough surface, used for toweling.
– ORIGIN late 17th cent.: of unknown origin.

huck·le·ber·ry /ˈhəkəlˌberē/ ▶ **n.** (pl. **huckleberries**) **1** a small, round, edible blue-black berry related to the blueberry.
2 the low-growing North American shrub of the heath family that bears this fruit. ● Genus *Gaylussacia*, family Ericaceae: several species, including the common **black huckleberry** (*G. baccata*).
– ORIGIN late 16th cent.: probably originally a dialect name for the blueberry (though early evidence is lacking), from dialect *huckle* 'hip, haunch' (because of the plant's jointed stems).

huck·ster /ˈhəkstər/ ▶ **n.** a person who sells small items, either door-to-door or from a stall or small store. ■ a mercenary person eager to make a profit out of anything. ■ a publicity agent or advertising copywriter, esp. for radio or television.
▶ **v.** [with obj.] promote or sell (something, typically a product of questionable value). ■ [no obj.] bargain; haggle.
– DERIVATIVES **huck·ster·ism** /-izəm/ **n.**
– ORIGIN Middle English (in the sense 'retailer at a stall, hawker'): probably of Low German origin.

HUD /həd/ ▶ **abbr.** ■ (Department of) Housing and Urban Development. ■ head-up display.

Hud·ders·field /ˈhədərzˌfēld/ a town in West Yorkshire, northern England; pop. 136,500 (est. 2009).

hud·dle /ˈhədl/ ▶ **v.** [no obj.] crowd together; nestle closely: *they **huddled together** for warmth.* ■ curl one's body into a small space: *the watchman remained, huddled under his canvas shelter.* ■ draw together for an informal, private conversation: *selection committee members huddled with attorneys.* ■ [with obj.] Brit. heap together in a disorderly manner: *a man with his clothes all huddled on anyhow.*
▶ **n.** a crowded or confused mass of people or things: *a **huddle of** barns and outbuildings.* ■ a brief gathering of players during a game to receive instructions, esp. in football. ■ a small group of people holding an informal, private conversation. ■ archaic confusion; bustle.
– ORIGIN late 16th cent. (in the sense 'conceal'): perhaps of Low German origin.

Hud·son, Henry (*c.*1565–1611), English explorer. He discovered the North American bay, river, and strait that bear his name. In 1610, he attempted to winter in Hudson Bay, but his crew mutinied and set Hudson and a few companions adrift, never to be seen again.

Hud·son Bay an inland sea—the largest in the world—in northeastern Canada. It is connected to the North Atlantic Ocean via Hudson Strait.
– ORIGIN named after the explorer Henry *Hudson*, who discovered it in 1610.

Hud·so·ni·an /hədˈsōnēən/ ▶ **adj.** of or relating to Hudson Bay and the surrounding land. ■ Biology denoting a biogeographical zone represented by the territory around the bay (north of the tree line from Labrador to Alaska).

Hud·son Riv·er a river in eastern New York, that rises in the Adirondack Mountains and flows south for 350 miles (560 km) into the Atlantic Ocean at New York City.
– ORIGIN named after Henry *Hudson*, who in 1609 sailed 150 miles (240 km) up the river as far as Albany.

Hud·son's Bay blan·ket (also **Hudson Bay blanket**) ▶ **n.** Canadian a durable woolen blanket, typically with wide colored stripes.
– ORIGIN late 19th cent.: originally sold by the *Hudson's Bay* Company and frequently used as material for coats.

Hud·son's Bay Com·pa·ny a British colonial trading company set up in 1670 and granted all lands draining into Hudson Bay for purposes of commercial exploitation, principally trade in fur.

hue /(h)yo͞o/ ▶ **n.** a color or shade: *her face lost its golden hue* | *verdigris is greenish-yellow in hue.* ■ the attribute of a color by virtue of which it is discernible as red, green, etc., and which is dependent on its dominant wavelength, and independent of intensity or lightness. ■ character; aspect: *men of all political hues submerged their feuds.*
– DERIVATIVES **hued adj.** [in combination] *rainbow-hued*, **hue·less adj.**
– ORIGIN Old English *hīw, hēow* (also 'form, appearance,' obsolete except in Scots), of Germanic origin; related to Swedish *hy* 'skin, complexion.' The sense 'color, shade' dates from the mid 19th cent.

Hué /(h)wā/ a city in central Vietnam; pop. 233,800 (est. 2009).

hue and cry ▶ **n.** a loud clamor or public outcry. ■ historical a loud cry calling for the pursuit and capture of a criminal. In former English law the cry had to be raised by the inhabitants of a hundred in which a robbery had been committed if they were not to become liable for the damages suffered by the victim.
– ORIGIN late Middle English: from the Anglo-Norman French legal phrase *hu e cri*, literally 'outcry and cry,' from Old French *hu* 'outcry' (from *huer* 'to shout').

Hue·co Moun·tains /ˈwākō/ a range in southern New Mexico and western Texas, near El Paso, that rises to 6,717 feet (2,049 m).

hue·vos ran·che·ros /ˈwāvōs ranˈCHerōs, rän-/ ▶ **n.** a dish of fried or poached eggs served on a tortilla with a spicy tomato sauce.

huff /həf/ ▶ **v.** [no obj.] **1** blow out loudly; puff: *he was huffing under a heavy load.* ■ [with obj.] express (one's annoyance or offense): *he huffed out his sudden irritation.*
2 [with obj.] sniff fumes from (gasoline or solvents) for a euphoric effect: *kids that are huffing spray paint like crazy.*
▶ **n.** [usu. in sing.] a fit of petty annoyance: *she walked off **in a huff**.*
– PHRASES **huff and puff** breathe heavily with exhaustion. ■ express one's annoyance in an obvious or threatening way.
– DERIVATIVES **huff·ish adj.**
– ORIGIN late 16th cent.: imitative of the sound of blowing.

huff·y /ˈhəfē/ ▶ **adj.** (**huffier, huffiest**) annoyed or irritated and quick to take offense at petty things: *ask writers for more than a second draft and they get huffy.*
– DERIVATIVES **huff·i·ly** /ˈhəfəlē/ **adv.**, **huff·i·ness n.**

hug /həg/ ▶ **v.** (**hugs, hugging, hugged**) [with obj.] squeeze (someone) tightly in one's arms, typically to express affection: *he hugged her close to him* | *people kissed and hugged each other* | [no obj.] *we hugged and kissed.* ■ hold (something) closely or tightly around or against part of one's body: *he hugged his knees to his chest.* ■ fit tightly around: *a pair of jeans that hugged the contours of his body.* ■ keep close to: *I headed north, hugging the coastline all the way.* ■ (**hug oneself**) congratulate or be pleased with oneself: *she hugged herself with secret joy.* ■ cherish or cling to (something such as a belief): *a boy hugging a secret.*
▶ **n.** an act of holding someone tightly in one's arms, typically to express affection: *there were hugs and tears as they were reunited.* ■ a squeezing grip in wrestling.
– DERIVATIVES **hug·ga·ble adj.**
– ORIGIN mid 16th cent.: probably of Scandinavian origin and related to Norwegian *hugga* 'comfort, console.'

huge /(h)yo͞oj/ ▶ **adj.** (**huger, hugest**) extremely large; enormous: *a huge area* | *he made a huge difference to the team.*
– DERIVATIVES **huge·ness n.**
– ORIGIN Middle English: shortening of Old French *ahuge*, of unknown origin.

huge·ly /ˈ(h)yo͞ojlē/ ▶ **adv.** [often as submodifier] very much; to a great extent: *a hugely expensive house.*

hug·ger-mug·ger /ˈhəgər ˌməgər/ ▶ **adj.**
1 confused; disorderly: *a spirit of careless frivolity where all was hugger-mugger.*
2 secret; clandestine.
▶ **n. 1** confusion; muddle.
2 secrecy.
– ORIGIN early 16th cent. (sense 2 of the noun): probably related to HUDDLE and to dialect *mucker* 'hoard money, conceal.' This is one of a number of similar formations from late Middle English to the 16th cent., including *hucker-mucker* and *hudder-mudder*, with the basic sense 'secrecy, concealment.'

Hughes[1] /hyo͞oz/, Charles Evans (1862–1948), US chief justice 1930–41 and politician. He was a US Supreme Court associate justice 1910–16 and unsuccessfully ran against Democrat Woodrow Wilson for the presidency in 1916 before becoming chief justice.

Hughes[2], Howard (Robard) (1905–76), US industrialist, movie producer, and aviator. Having acquired a fortune through his father's tool company, he began producing movies in the 1920s and broke many world aviation records during the 1930s. He lived as a recluse for the last 25 years of his life. Notable movies: *Hell's Angels* (1930) and *The Outlaw* (1941).

Hughes[3], Langston (1902–67), US writer; full name *James Mercer Langston Hughes*. A leading voice of the Harlem Renaissance, he began a prolific literary career with *The Weary Blues* (1926), a series of poems on black themes, using blues and jazz rhythms. Other poetry collections include *The Negro Mother* (1931) and *Shakespeare in Harlem* (1941).

Hughes[4], Ted (1930–98), English poet; full name *Edward James Hughes*. His vision of the natural world as a place of violence, terror, and beauty pervades his work. He served as Britain's poet laureate 1984–98. Hughes was married to Sylvia Plath, a marriage he recounted in *Birthday Letters* (1998). Other notable works: *The Hawk in the Rain* (1957) and *Crow* (1970).

Hug·li variant spelling of HOOGHLY.

Hu·go /ˈ(h)yo͞ogō/, Victor (1802–85), French poet, novelist, and playwright; full name *Victor-Marie Hugo*. His belief that theater should express both the grotesque and the sublime of human existence overturned existing conventions. Notable works: *Hernani* (drama, 1830), *Les Feuilles d'automne* (poems, 1831), *Notre-Dame de Paris* (novel, 1831), and *Les Misérables* (novel, 1862).

Hu·gue·not /ˈhyo͞ogəˌnät/ ▶ **n.** a French Protestant of the 16th–17th centuries. Largely Calvinist, the Huguenots suffered severe persecution at the hands of the Catholic majority, and many thousands emigrated from France.
– ORIGIN French, alteration (by association with the name of a Geneva burgomaster, Besançon *Hugues*) of *eiguenot*, from Dutch *eedgenot*, from Swiss German *Eidgenoss* 'confederate,' from *Eid* 'oath' + *Genoss* 'associate.'

huh /hə/ ▶ **exclam.** used to express scorn, anger, disbelief, surprise, or amusement: *"Huh," she snorted, "Over my dead body!"* ■ used in questions to invite agreement or further comment or to express a lack of understanding: *pretty devastating, huh?*
– ORIGIN natural utterance: first recorded in English in the early 17th cent.

Hu·he·hot /ˈho͞ohāˌhōt/ variant of HOHHOT.

hui /ˈho͞o-ē/ ▶ **n.** (pl. **huis** or **huies**) (in Hawaii) a club or association.
– ORIGIN Maori and Hawaiian.

hu·ia /ˈho͞oyə/ ▶ **n.** an extinct New Zealand wattlebird with glossy black plumage, the female having a much longer and more curved bill than the male. The tail feathers were formerly prized by Maoris, and the last huia was seen in 1907. ● *Heteralocha acutirostris*, family Callaeidae.
– ORIGIN mid 19th cent.: from Maori, imitative of its cry.

hui·sa·che /wēˈsäCHē/ ▶ **n.** an acacia tree with violet-scented flowers that yield an essential oil used in perfumery, native to warm regions of America and cultivated elsewhere. Also called SWEET ACACIA, SPONGE TREE. ● *Acacia farnesiana*, family Leguminosae.

huit·la·co·che /ˌwētləˈkōCHā/ ▶ **n.** a fungus that grows on corn, considered a delicacy in Mexico where cooks use it to flavor food.

hu·la /ˈho͞olə/ (also **hula-hula**) ▶ **n.** a dance performed by Hawaiian women, characterized by six basic steps, undulating hips, and gestures symbolizing or imitating natural phenomena or historical or mythological subjects.
– ORIGIN early 19th cent.: Hawaiian.

hu·la hoop (also trademark **Hula-Hoop**) ▶ **n.** a large hoop spun around the body by gyrating the hips, for play or exercise.
▶ **v.** (**hula-hoop**) [no obj.] (usu. as noun **hula-hooping**) spin a hula hoop around the body by gyrating the hips.

hu·la skirt ▶ **n.** a long grass skirt as worn by a hula dancer.

hulk /həlk/ ▶ **n. 1** an old ship stripped of fittings and permanently moored, esp. for use as storage or (formerly) as a prison. ■ any large disused structure: *hulks of abandoned machinery.*
2 a large or unwieldy boat or other object. ■ a large, clumsy-looking person: *a six-foot **hulk of** a man.*
– ORIGIN Old English *hulc* 'fast ship,' probably reinforced in Middle English by Middle Low German and Middle Dutch *hulk*; probably of Mediterranean origin and related to Greek *holkas* 'cargo ship.'

hulk·ing /ˈhəlkiNG/ ▶ **adj.** informal (of a person or object) large, heavy, or clumsy: *a hulking young man.*

PRONUNCIATION KEY ə *ago, up*; ər *over, fur*; a *hat*; ā *ate*; ä *car*; e *let*; ē *see*; i *fit*; ī *by*; NG *sing*; ō *go*; ô *law, for*; oi *toy*; o͝o *good*; o͞o *goo*; ou *out*; TH *thin*; TH *then*; ZH *vision*

Hull[1] /həl/ a city and port in northeastern England, situated at the junction of the Hull and Humber rivers; pop. 263,200 (est. 2009). Official name KINGSTON UPON HULL.

Hull[2], Bobby (1939–), Canadian hockey player; full name *Robert Marvin Hull, Jr.* He played for the Chicago Blackhawks 1957–72, the Winnipeg Jets 1972–79, and the Hartford Whalers 1980–81. Hockey Hall of Fame (1983).

Hull[3], Cordell (1871–1955), US statesman. His tenure as US secretary of state 1933–44 is the longest in US history. A Tennessee Democrat, he had earlier served in the US House of Representatives 1907–21, 1923–31, and the US Senate 1931–33. Nobel Peace Prize (1945).

hull[1] /həl/ ▶ n. the main body of a ship or other vessel, including the bottom, sides, and deck but not the masts, superstructure, rigging, engines, and other fittings.
▶ v. [with obj.] (usu. **be hulled**) hit and pierce the hull of (a ship) with a shell or other missile.
– DERIVATIVES **hulled** adj. [in combination] *a wooden-hulled narrowboat.*
– ORIGIN Middle English: perhaps the same word as HULL[2], or related to HOLD[2].

hull[2] ▶ n. the outer covering of a fruit or seed, esp. the pod of peas and beans, or the husk of grain. ■ the green calyx of a strawberry or raspberry.
▶ v. [with obj.] (usu. as adj. **hulled**) remove the hulls from (fruit, seeds, or grain).
– ORIGIN Old English *hulu*, of Germanic origin; related to Dutch *huls*, German *Hülse* 'husk, pod,' and German *Hülle* 'covering,' also to HEEL[3].

h

hul·la·ba·loo /'hələbə,lo͞o, ,hələbə'lo͞o/ ▶ n. [in sing.] informal a commotion; a fuss: *remember all the hullabaloo over the golf ball?*
– ORIGIN mid 18th cent.: reduplication of *hallo, hullo*, etc.

hul·lo /hə'lō/ ▶ exclam. variant spelling of HELLO.
– ORIGIN first recorded, in this form, in T. Hughes' *Tom Brown's Schooldays* (1857).

hum[1] /həm/ ▶ v. (**hums, humming, hummed**) [no obj.] **1** make a low, steady continuous sound like that of a bee: *the computers hummed.* ■ sing with closed lips: *he hummed softly to himself* | [with obj.] *she was humming a cheerful tune.* ■ (of a place) be filled with a low, steady continuous sound: *the room* ***hummed with*** *an expectant murmur.* ■ informal be in a state of great activity: *the repair shops are humming as the tradesmen set about their various tasks.*
2 Brit. informal smell unpleasant: *when the wind drops this stuff really hums.*
▶ n. [in sing.] a low, steady, continuous sound: *the hum of insects* | *a low hum of conversation.* ■ an unwanted low-frequency noise in an amplifier caused by variation of electric current, esp. the alternating frequency of the power lines.
– DERIVATIVES **hum·ma·ble** adj., **hum·mer** n.
– ORIGIN late Middle English: imitative.

hum[2] ▶ exclam. used to express hesitation or dissent: *"Ah, hum, Elaine, isn't it?"*
– ORIGIN mid 16th cent.: imitative; related to the verb HUM[1].

hu·man /'(h)yo͞omən/ ▶ adj. of, relating to, or characteristic of people or human beings: *the human body.* ■ of or characteristic of people as opposed to God or animals or machines, esp. in being susceptible to weaknesses: *they are only human, and therefore mistakes do occur* | *the risk of human error.* ■ of or characteristic of people's better qualities, such as kindness or sensitivity: *the human side of politics is getting stronger.* ■ Zoology of or belonging to the genus *Homo*.
▶ n. a human being, esp. a person as distinguished from an animal or (in science fiction) an alien.
– DERIVATIVES **hu·man·ness** n.
– ORIGIN late Middle English *humaine*, from Old French *humain(e)*, from Latin *humanus*, from *homo* 'man, human being.' The present spelling became usual in the 18th cent.; compare with HUMANE.

> **USAGE** See usage at HUMANITARIAN.

hu·man be·ing ▶ n. a man, woman, or child of the species *Homo sapiens*, distinguished from other animals by superior mental development, power of articulate speech, and upright stance.

hu·man cap·i·tal ▶ n. the skills, knowledge, and experience possessed by an individual or population, viewed in terms of their value or cost to an organization or country.

hu·man chain ▶ n. a line of people formed for passing things quickly from one site to another. ■ a line or circle of people linking hands in a protest or demonstration.

hu·man cho·ri·on·ic go·nad·o·tro·pin /,kôrē'änik ,gō,nadə'trōpin/ (abbr.: **HCG**) ▶ n. a hormone produced in the human placenta that maintains the corpus luteum during pregnancy.

hu·mane /(h)yo͞o'mān/ ▶ adj. **1** having or showing compassion or benevolence: *regulations ensuring the humane treatment of animals.* ■ inflicting the minimum of pain: *humane methods of killing.*
2 formal (of a branch of learning) intended to have a civilizing or refining effect on people: *the center emphasizes economics as a humane discipline.*
– DERIVATIVES **hu·mane·ly** adv., **hu·mane·ness** n.
– ORIGIN late Middle English: the earlier form of HUMAN, restricted to the senses above in the 18th cent.

hu·man e·col·o·gy ▶ n. see ECOLOGY.

hu·man en·gi·neer·ing ▶ n. the management of industrial labor, esp. with regard to relationships between people and machines; ergonomics.

Hu·man Ge·nome Pro·ject an international project to study the entire genetic material of a human being.

hu·man ge·og·ra·phy ▶ n. the branch of geography dealing with how human activity affects or is influenced by the earth's surface.

hu·man in·ter·est ▶ n. the aspect of a story in the media that interests people because it describes the experiences or emotions of individuals: *the conflict was not lacking in human interest* | [as modifier] *dry and distant matters are often treated from a human-interest angle.*

hu·man·ism /'(h)yo͞omə,nizəm/ ▶ n. an outlook or system of thought attaching prime importance to human rather than divine or supernatural matters. Humanist beliefs stress the potential value and goodness of human beings, emphasize common human needs, and seek solely rational ways of solving human problems. ■ (often **Humanism**) a Renaissance cultural movement that turned away from medieval scholasticism and revived interest in ancient Greek and Roman thought. ■ (among some contemporary writers) a system of thought criticized as being centered on the notion of the rational, autonomous self and ignoring the unintegrated and conditioned nature of the individual.
– DERIVATIVES **hu·man·ist** n. & adj., **hu·man·is·tic** /,(h)yo͞omə'nistik/ adj., **hu·man·is·ti·cal·ly** /,(h)yo͞omə'nistik(ə)lē/ adv.

hu·man·i·tar·i·an /(h)yo͞o,mani'te(ə)rēən/ ▶ adj. concerned with or seeking to promote human welfare: *groups sending humanitarian aid* | *a humanitarian organization.* ■ denoting an event or situation that causes or involves widespread human suffering, esp. one that requires the large-scale provision of aid: *human rights groups have warned of a worsening humanitarian crisis.*
▶ n. a person who seeks to promote human welfare; a philanthropist.
– DERIVATIVES **hu·man·i·tar·i·an·ism** /-,nizəm/ n.

> **USAGE** The primary sense of **humanitarian** is 'concerned with or seeking to promote human welfare.' Since the 1930s, a new sense, exemplified by phrases such as *the worst* ***humanitarian*** *disaster this country has seen*, has been gaining currency, and is now broadly established, especially in journalism, although it is not considered good style by all. In the Oxford English Corpus, the second most common collocation of **humanitarian** is *humanitarian crisis*.

hu·man·i·ty /(h)yo͞o'manitē/ ▶ n. (pl. **humanities**) **1** the human race; human beings collectively: *appalling crimes against humanity.* ■ the fact or condition of being human; human nature: *music is the universal language with which we can express our common humanity.*
2 humaneness; benevolence: *he praised them for their standards of humanity, care, and dignity.*
3 (**humanities**) learning or literature concerned with human culture, esp. literature, history, art, music, and philosophy.
– ORIGIN Middle English: from Old French *humanite*, from Latin *humanitas*, from *humanus* (see HUMAN).

hu·man·ize /'(h)yo͞omə,nīz/ ▶ v. [with obj.] **1** make (something) more humane or civilized: *his purpose was to humanize prison conditions.*
2 give (something) a human character.
– DERIVATIVES **hu·man·i·za·tion** /,hyo͞oməni'zāsHən/ n.
– ORIGIN early 17th cent.: from French *humaniser*, from Latin *humanus* (see HUMAN).

hu·man·kind /'(h)yo͞omən,kīnd/ ▶ n. human beings considered collectively (used as a neutral alternative to "mankind"): *the origin of humankind.*

> **USAGE** See usage at MAN.

hu·man·ly /'(h)yo͞omənlē/ ▶ adv. **1** from a human point of view; in a human manner: *they can grow both humanly and spiritually.* ■ by human means; within human ability: *we did all that was humanly possible.*
2 chiefly archaic with human feeling or kindness.

hu·man na·ture ▶ n. the general psychological characteristics, feelings, and behavioral traits of humankind, regarded as shared by all humans: *he had a poor opinion of human nature.*

hu·man·oid /'(h)yo͞omə,noid/ ▶ adj. having an appearance or character resembling that of a human.
▶ n. (esp. in science fiction) a being resembling a human in its shape.

hu·man pap·il·lo·ma·vi·rus /,papə'lōmə,vīrəs/ ▶ n. a virus with subtypes that cause diseases in humans ranging from common warts to cervical cancer.

hu·man race ▶ n. (**the human race**) human beings in general; humankind: *trees are vital to the survival of the human race.*

hu·man re·la·tions ▶ plural n. relations with or between people, particularly the treatment of people in a professional context.

hu·man re·sourc·es ▶ plural n. the personnel of a business or organization, esp. when regarded as a significant asset. ■ the department of a business or organization that deals with the hiring, administration, and training of personnel: *director of human resources at the company.*

hu·man right ▶ n. (usu. **human rights**) a right that is believed to belong justifiably to every person: *a flagrant disregard for basic human rights* | *communication is a fundamental human right.*

hu·man shield ▶ n. a person or group of people held near a potential target to deter attack.

hu·man T cell lym·pho·trop·ic vi·rus /,limfō'träpik, -'trōpik/ (abbr.: **HTLV**) ▶ n. any of a group of retroviruses that cause disease by attacking T cells.

Hum·ber /'həmbər/ an estuary in northeastern England that is formed at the junction of the Ouse and Trent rivers near Goole and that flows east for 38 miles (60 km) to enter the North Sea at Spurn Head. It has the major port of Hull on its northern bank and is spanned by the world's largest suspension bridge, which opened in 1981 and has a span of 4,626 feet (1,410 m).

hum·ble /'həmbəl/ ▶ adj. (**humbler, humblest**) **1** having or showing a modest or low estimate of one's own importance: *he was humble about his stature as one of rock history's most influential guitarists.* ■ (of an action or thought) offered with or affected by such an estimate of one's own importance: *my humble apologies.*
2 of low social, administrative, or political rank: *she came from a humble, unprivileged background.* ■ (of a thing) of modest pretensions or dimensions: *he built the business empire from humble beginnings.*
▶ v. [with obj.] lower (someone) in dignity or importance: *I knew he had* ***humbled himself*** *to ask for my help.* ■ decisively defeat (another team or competitor, typically one that was previously thought to be superior): *he was humbled by his political opponents.*
– PHRASES **eat humble pie** make a humble apology and accept humiliation. [*humble pie* is from a pun based on UMBLES 'offal,' considered inferior food.] **my humble abode** used to refer to one's home with an ironic or humorous show of modesty or humility. **your humble servant** archaic or humorous used at the end of a letter or as a form of ironic courtesy: *your most humble servant, George Porter.*
– DERIVATIVES **hum·ble·ness** n., **hum·bly** /-blē/ adv.
– ORIGIN Middle English: from Old French, from Latin *humilis* 'low, lowly,' from *humus* 'ground.'

hum·ble-bee ▶ n. another term for BUMBLEBEE.
– ORIGIN late Middle English: probably from Middle Low German *hummelbē*, from *hummel* 'to buzz' + *bē* 'bee.'

Hum·boldt Cur·rent /'həm,bōlt/ another name for PERUVIAN CURRENT.

hum·bug /'həm,bəg/ ▶ n. **1** deceptive or false talk or behavior: *his comments are sheer humbug.* ■ a hypocrite: *you see what a humbug I am.*
2 Brit. a hard candy, esp. one flavored with peppermint.
▶ v. (**humbugs, humbugging, humbugged**) [with obj.] deceive; trick: *to humbug his humble neighbors was not difficult.* ■ [no obj.] dated act like a fraud or sham.
– DERIVATIVES **hum·bug·ger·y** /-,bəg(ə)rē/ n.
– ORIGIN mid 18th cent. (in the senses 'hoax, trick' and 'deceiver'): of unknown origin.

hum·ding·er /'həm'diNGər/ ▶ n. informal a remarkable or outstanding person or thing of its kind: *a humdinger of a funny story.*
– ORIGIN early 20th cent. (originally US): of unknown origin.

hum·drum /'həm,drəm/ ▶ adj. lacking excitement or variety; dull; monotonous: *humdrum routine work.*

▶ **n.** dullness; monotony: *an escape from the humdrum of his life.*
– ORIGIN mid 16th cent.: probably a reduplication of HUM[1].

Hume /hyo͞om/, David (1711–76), Scottish philosopher, economist, and historian. He rejected the possibility of certainty in knowledge. Notable works: *A Treatise of Human Nature* (1739–40) and *History of England* (1754–62).
– DERIVATIVES **Hum·e·an** /'hyo͞omēən/ **adj. & n.**

hu·mec·tant /(h)yo͞o'mektənt/ ▶ **adj.** retaining or preserving moisture.
▶ **n.** a substance, esp. a skin lotion or a food additive, used to reduce the loss of moisture.
– ORIGIN early 19th cent. (denoting a moistening agent): from Latin *humectant-* 'moistening,' from the verb *humectare*, from *humectus* 'moist, wet,' from *humere* 'be moist.'

hu·mer·al /'(h)yo͞omərəl/ ▶ **adj.** [attrib.] **1** of or relating to the humerus of a human or other vertebrate: *a humeral fracture.* ■ Entomology of, relating to, or in the region of the humerus on the wing of an insect: *a humeral lobe.*
2 (in Catholic use) denoting a plain vestment worn around the shoulders when administering the sacrament.
– ORIGIN late 16th cent.: from French, or from late Latin *humeralis*, from Latin *humerus* (see HUMERUS).

hu·mer·us /'(h)yo͞omərəs/ ▶ **n.** (pl. **humeri** /-mə,rī/) Anatomy the bone of the upper arm or forelimb, forming joints at the shoulder and the elbow.
■ Entomology a structure in an insect involving, or in the region of, the front basal corners of the wings or wing cases.
– ORIGIN late Middle English: from Latin, 'shoulder.'

hu·mic /'(h)yo͞omik/ ▶ **adj.** [attrib.] relating to or consisting of humus: *humic acids.*

hu·mid /'(h)yo͞omid/ ▶ **adj.** marked by a relatively high level of water vapor in the atmosphere: *a hot and humid day.*
– DERIVATIVES **hu·mid·ly adv.**
– ORIGIN late Middle English: from French *humide* or Latin *humidus*, from *humere* 'be moist.'

hu·mid·i·fi·er /(h)yo͞o'midə,fī(ə)r/ ▶ **n.** a device for keeping the atmosphere moist in a room.

hu·mid·i·fy /(h)yo͞o'midə,fī/ ▶ **v.** (**humidifies, humidifying, humidified**) [with obj.] (often as adj. **humidified**) increase the level of moisture in (air): *a regulated flow of humidified air.*
– DERIVATIVES **hu·mid·i·fi·ca·tion** /-,midəfi'kāsHən/ **n.**

hu·mid·i·stat /(h)yo͞o'midi,stat/ ▶ **n.** a machine or device that automatically regulates the humidity of the air in a room or building.

hu·mid·i·ty /(h)yo͞o'miditē/ ▶ **n.** (pl. **humidities**) the state or quality of being humid. ■ a quantity representing the amount of water vapor in the atmosphere or a gas: *the temperature is seventy-seven, the humidity in the low thirties.* ■ atmospheric moisture.
– ORIGIN late Middle English: from Old French *humidite* or Latin *humiditas*, from *humidus* (see HUMID).

hu·mi·dor /'(h)yo͞omi,dôr/ ▶ **n.** an airtight container for keeping cigars or tobacco moist.
– ORIGIN early 20th cent.: from HUMID, on the pattern of *cuspidor*.

hu·mi·fy /'(h)yo͞omə,fī/ ▶ **v.** (**humifies, humifying, humified**) [with obj.] convert (plant remains) into humus.
– DERIVATIVES **hu·mi·fi·ca·tion** /,(h)yo͞omifi'kāsHən/ **n.**

hu·mil·i·ate /(h)yo͞o'milē,āt/ ▶ **v.** [with obj.] make (someone) feel ashamed and foolish by injuring their dignity and self-respect, esp. publicly: *you'll humiliate me in front of the whole school!*
– DERIVATIVES **hu·mil·i·a·tor** /-,ātər/ **n.**
– ORIGIN mid 16th cent. (in the sense 'bring low'): from late Latin *humiliat-* 'made humble,' from the verb *humiliare*, from *humilis* (see HUMBLE). The current sense dates from the mid 18th cent.

hu·mil·i·at·ing /(h)yo͞o'milē,ātiNG/ ▶ **adj.** causing someone to feel ashamed and foolish by injuring their dignity and self-respect: *a humiliating defeat.*
– DERIVATIVES **hu·mil·i·at·ing·ly** /-,ātiNGlē/ **adv.**

hu·mil·i·a·tion /(h)yo͞o,milē'āsHən/ ▶ **n.** the action of humiliating someone or the state of being humiliated: *they suffered the humiliation of losing in the opening round.*

hu·mil·i·ty /(h)yo͞o'militē/ ▶ **n.** a modest or low view of one's own importance; humbleness.
– ORIGIN Middle English: from Old French *humilite*, from Latin *humilitas*, from *humilis* (see HUMBLE).

HU·MINT /'(h)yo͞omint/ ▶ **n.** covert intelligence-gathering by agents or others.
– ORIGIN late 20th cent.: from *human intelligence*.

Hum·mel /'həməl/, Berta (1909–46), German artist and nun; also known as **Sister Maria Innocentia**. She created the sketches upon which M. I. Hummel figurines, made by the Franz Goebel Company, are based.

Hum·mer /'həmər/ ▶ **n.** trademark a type of four-wheel-drive all-terrain military vehicle, or a similar vehicle intended for civilian use.

hum·ming·bird /'həmiNG,bərd/ ▶ **n.** a small nectar-feeding tropical American bird that is able to hover and fly backward, typically having colorful iridescent plumage. ● Family Trochilidae: many genera and numerous species, including the **ruby-throated hummingbird** (*Archilochus colubris*) of the eastern US, and the red-crowned **Anna's hummingbird** (*Calypte anna*), found chiefly along the Pacific coast of the US.
– ORIGIN mid 17th cent.: so named because of the humming sound produced by the rapid vibration of the bird's wings.

ruby-throated hummingbird

hum·ming·bird hawk moth (also **hummingbird moth**) ▶ **n.** a migratory day-flying hawk moth that makes an audible hum while hovering in front of flowers to feed on nectar. ● Family Sphingidae.

hum·mock /'həmək/ ▶ **n.** a hillock, knoll, or mound. ■ a hump or ridge in an ice field. ■ a piece of forested ground rising above a marsh.
– DERIVATIVES **hum·mock·y adj.**
– ORIGIN mid 16th cent. (originally in nautical use denoting a small hillock on the coast): of unknown origin.

hum·mus /'ho͝oməs, 'həm-/ (also **houmous**) ▶ **n.** a thick paste or spread made from ground chickpeas and sesame seeds, olive oil, lemon, and garlic, made originally in the Middle East.
– ORIGIN from Arabic *ḥummuṣ*.

hu·mon·gous /(h)yo͞o'mäNGgəs, -'məNG-/ (also **humungous**) ▶ **adj.** informal huge; enormous: *a humongous steak.*
– ORIGIN 1970s (originally US): possibly based on HUGE and MONSTROUS, influenced by the stress pattern of *stupendous*.

hu·mor /'(h)yo͞omər/ (Brit. **humour**) ▶ **n. 1** the quality of being amusing or comic, esp. as expressed in literature or speech: *his tales are full of humor.* ■ the ability to express humor or make other people laugh: *their inimitable brand of humor.*
2 a mood or state of mind: *her good humor vanished | the clash hadn't improved his humor.* ■ archaic an inclination or whim.
3 (also **cardinal humor**) historical each of the four chief fluids of the body (blood, phlegm, yellow bile [choler], and black bile [melancholy]) that were thought to determine a person's physical and mental qualities by the relative proportions in which they were present.
▶ **v.** [with obj.] comply with the wishes of (someone) in order to keep them content, however unreasonable such wishes might be: *she was always humoring him to prevent trouble.* ■ archaic adapt or accommodate oneself to (something).
– PHRASES **out of humor** in a bad mood. **sense of humor** the ability to perceive humor or appreciate a joke.
– ORIGIN Middle English (as *humour*): via Old French from Latin *humor* 'moisture,' from *humere* (see HUMID). The original sense was 'bodily fluid' (surviving in *aqueous humor* and *vitreous humor*, fluids in the eyeball); it was used specifically for any of the cardinal humors (sense 3 of the noun), whence 'mental disposition' (thought to be caused by the relative proportions of the humors). This led, in the 16th cent., to the senses 'state of mind, mood' (sense 2 of the noun) and 'whim, fancy,' hence *to humor someone* 'to indulge a person's whim' sense 1 of the noun dates from the late 16th cent.

hu·mor·al /'(h)yo͞omərəl/ ▶ **adj.** Medicine of or relating to the body fluids, esp. with regard to immune responses involving antibodies in body fluids as distinct from cells (see CELL-MEDIATED). ■ historical of or relating to the four bodily humors. ■ historical (of diseases) caused by or attributed to a disordered state of body fluids or (formerly) the bodily humors.
– ORIGIN late Middle English (in the general sense 'relating to bodily fluids'): from Old French, or from medieval Latin *humoralis*, from Latin *humor* 'moisture' (see HUMOR).

hu·mor·esque /,(h)yo͞omə'resk/ ▶ **n.** a short, lively piece of music.
– ORIGIN late 19th cent.: from German *Humoreske*, from *Humor* 'humor.'

hu·mor·ist /'(h)yo͞omərist/ ▶ **n.** a humorous writer, performer, or artist.

hu·mor·less /'(h)yo͞omərlis/ ▶ **adj.** lacking humor; not able to appreciate or express humor: *they are such a humorless bunch.*
– DERIVATIVES **hu·mor·less·ly adv., hu·mor·less·ness n.**

hu·mor·ous /'(h)yo͞omərəs/ ▶ **adj.** causing lighthearted laughter and amusement; comic: *a humorous and entertaining talk.* ■ having or showing a sense of humor: *his humorous gray eyes.*
– DERIVATIVES **hu·mor·ous·ly adv., hu·mor·ous·ness n.**

hu·mour ▶ **n.** British spelling of HUMOR.

hump /həmp/ ▶ **n. 1** a rounded protuberance found on the back of a camel or other animal or as an abnormality on a person's back.
2 a rounded raised mass of earth or land. ■ a mound over which railroad vehicles are pushed so as to run by gravity to the required place in a switchyard.
▶ **v. 1** [with obj.] informal lift or carry (a heavy object) with difficulty: *he continued to hump cases up and down the hotel corridor.* ■ [no obj.] move heavily and awkwardly: *it was late morning by the time I finally humped into camp.*
2 [with obj.] make hump-shaped: *the cat humped himself into a different shape and purred.*
3 [with obj.] vulgar slang have sexual intercourse with.
– PHRASES **over the hump** over the worst or most difficult part of something.
– DERIVATIVES **hump·less adj., hump·y adj.** (**humpier, humpiest**).
– ORIGIN early 18th cent.: probably related to Low German *humpe* 'hump,' also to Dutch *homp*, Low German *humpe* 'lump, hunk (of bread).'

hump·back /'həmp,bak/ ▶ **n. 1** (also **humpback whale**) a baleen whale that has a hump (instead of a dorsal fin) and long white flippers. It is noted for its lengthy vocalizations or "songs." ● *Megaptera novaeangliae*, family Balaenopteridae.
2 (also **humpback salmon**) another term for PINK SALMON.
3 another term for HUNCHBACK.
– DERIVATIVES **hump·backed adj.**

humped /həm(p)t/ ▶ **adj.** having a hump or humps; hump-shaped: *a breed of humped cattle | a humped bridge.*

Hum·per·dinck /'həmpər,diNGk/, Engelbert (1854–1921), German composer who wrote the opera *Hänsel und Gretel* (1893).

humph /həmf/ ▶ **exclam.** used to express slightly scornful doubt or dissatisfaction.
– ORIGIN natural utterance: first recorded in English in the mid 16th cent.

Hum·phrey /'həmfrē/, Hubert Horatio (1911–78), US politician. He was a US senator from Minnesota 1949–64 before becoming US vice president 1965–69. A Democratic presidential candidate in 1968, he again served in the Senate 1971–78.

Hubert H. Humphrey

Hump·ty Dump·ty /'həm(p)tē 'dəm(p)tē/ (also **humpty dumpty**) ▶ **n.** (pl. **Humpty Dumpties**)

informal **1** a fat, rotund person: [as modifier] *he was a Humpty Dumpty figure of a man.*
2 a person or thing that once overthrown cannot be restored.
– ORIGIN late 18th cent.: from the egglike nursery-rhyme character *Humpty Dumpty*, who fell off a wall and could not be put together again.

hu·mun·gous ▶ **adj.** variant spelling of **HUMONGOUS**.

hu·mus /ˈ(h)yo͞oməs/ ▶ **n.** the organic component of soil, formed by the decomposition of leaves and other plant material by soil microorganisms.
– ORIGIN late 18th cent.: from Latin, literally 'soil.'

Hum·vee /ˈhəmˈvē/ ▶ **n.** trademark a type of modern military vehicle.
– ORIGIN late 20th cent.: alteration, from the initials of *high-mobility multipurpose vehicle*.

Hun /hən/ ▶ **n. 1** a member of a warlike Asiatic nomadic people who ravaged Europe in the 4th–5th centuries. ■ a reckless or uncivilized destroyer of something.
2 informal, derogatory a German (esp. in military contexts during World War I and World War II). ■ (**the Hun**) Germans collectively.
– DERIVATIVES **Hun·nish adj.**
– ORIGIN Old English *Hūne*, *Hūnas* (plural), from late Latin *Hunni*, from Greek *Hounnoi*, of Middle Iranian origin.

h

Hu·nan /ˈho͞oˈnän/ a province in eastern central China; capital, Changsha.

hunch /hənCH/ ▶ **v.** [with obj.] raise (one's shoulders) and bend the top of one's body forward: *he thrust his hands in his pockets, hunching his shoulders* | [no obj.] *he* ***hunched over*** *his glass.* ■ [no obj.] bend one's body into a huddled position: *I* ***hunched up*** *as small as I could.* ■ shove or push; nudge: *she hunched me and winked.*
▶ **n. 1** a feeling or guess based on intuition rather than known facts: *she was* ***acting on a hunch****.*
2 a humped position or thing: *the hunch of his back.*
3 chiefly dialect a thick piece; a hunk: ***a hunch of bread****.*
– ORIGIN late 15th cent.: of unknown origin. The original meaning was 'push, shove' (noun and verb), a sense retained now in Scots as a noun, and in US dialect as a verb. Sense 1 of the noun probably derives from the sense 'nudge someone in order to draw attention to something.'

hunch·back /ˈhənCHˌbak/ ▶ **n.** a back deformed by a sharp forward angle, forming a hump, typically caused by collapse of a vertebra. ■ often offensive a person with such a deformity.
– DERIVATIVES **hunch·backed adj.**

hun·dred /ˈhəndrid/ ▶ **cardinal number** (pl. **hundreds** or (with numeral or quantifying word) **hundred**) (**a/one hundred**) the number equivalent to the product of ten and ten; ten more than ninety; 100: *a hundred yards away* | *there are just a hundred of us here.* (Roman numeral: **c** or **C**) ■ (**hundreds**) the numbers from 100 to 999: *an unknown number, probably in the hundreds, had already been lost.* ■ (**hundreds**) several hundred things or people: *it cost hundreds of dollars.* ■ (usu. **hundreds**) informal an unspecified large number: *hundreds of letters poured in.* ■ (**the —— hundreds**) the years of a specified century: *the early nineteen hundreds.* ■ one hundred years old: *you must be over a hundred!* ■ one hundred miles per hour. ■ a hundred-dollar bill. ■ (chiefly in spoken English) used to express whole hours in the twenty-four-hour system: *thirteen hundred hours.*
▶ **n.** Brit. historical a subdivision of a county or shire, having its own court.
– PHRASES **a** (or **one**) **hundred percent** entirely; completely: *I'm one hundred percent sure.* ■ [usu. with negative] informal completely fit and healthy: *I wasn't exactly one hundred percent.* ■ informal maximum effort and commitment: *he always gave one hundred percent for the team.*
– DERIVATIVES **hun·dred·fold** /-ˌfōld/ **adj. & adv.**, **hun·dredth** /ˈhəndridTH, ˈhəndritTH/ **ordinal number.**
– ORIGIN late Old English, from *hund* 'hundred' (from an Indo-European root shared with Latin *centum* and Greek *hekaton*) + a second element meaning 'number'; of Germanic origin and related to Dutch *honderd* and German *hundert*. The noun sense 'subdivision of a county' is of uncertain origin: it may originally have been equivalent to a hundred hides of land (see **HIDE**[3]).

Hun·dred Flow·ers a period of debate in China 1956–57, when, under the slogan "Let a hundred flowers bloom and a hundred schools of thought contend," citizens were invited to voice their opinions of the communist regime. It was forcibly ended after social unrest and fierce criticism of the government, with those who had voiced their opinions being prosecuted.

hun·dred·weight /ˈhəndridˌwāt/ (abbr.: **cwt**) ▶ **n.** (pl. **same** or **hundredweights**) a unit of weight equal to one twentieth of a ton, in particular: ■ (also **short hundredweight**) (in the US) equal to 100 lb avoirdupois (about 45.4 kg). ■ (also **metric hundredweight**) (in the metric system) equal to 50 kg. ■ (also **long hundredweight**) (in the UK) equal to 112 lb avoirdupois (about 50.8 kg).

Hun·dred Years War a war between France and England, conventionally dated 1337–1453.

> The war consisted of a series of conflicts in which successive English kings attempted to dominate France and included an early string of English military successes, most notably Crécy and Poitiers. In 1415 England, under Henry V, delivered a crushing victory at Agincourt and occupied much of northern France, but, with the exception of Calais, all English conquests had been lost by 1453.

hung /həNG/ past and past participle of **HANG**.
▶ **adj. 1** (of a jury) unable to agree on a verdict. ■ (in the UK and Canada) (of an elected body) having no political party with an overall majority: *a hung parliament.*
2 [predic.] (**hung up**) informal emotionally confused or disturbed: *people are hung up in all sorts of ways.* ■ (**hung up about/on**) have a psychological or emotional obsession or problem about: *guys are so hung up about the way they look.* ■ delayed or detained: *my mother was probably hung up in traffic.*
3 [predic.] vulgar slang used esp. in similes to refer to the size of a man's penis: *he's hung like a horse.*

Hun·gar·i·an /həNGˈge(ə)rēən/ ▶ **adj.** of or relating to Hungary, its people, or their language.
▶ **n. 1** a native or inhabitant of Hungary. ■ a person of Hungarian descent.
2 an Ugric language, the official language of Hungary, spoken also in Romania. Also called **MAGYAR**.
– ORIGIN from medieval Latin *Hungarī* + **-AN**.

Hun·ga·ry /ˈhəNGgərē/ a country in central Europe; pop. 9,905,600 (est. 2009); capital, Budapest; official language, Hungarian. Hungarian name **MAGYARORSZÁG**.

> Hungary was conquered by the Habsburgs in the 17th century and became an equal partner in the Austro-Hungarian Empire in 1867. Following the collapse of the empire in 1918, it became an independent kingdom. After participation in World War II on the Axis side, Hungary was occupied by the former Soviet Union and became a communist state. Although a liberal reform movement was crushed by Soviet troops in 1956, the communist system was abandoned in 1989, and the first multiparty elections were held in 1990. Hungary joined NATO in 1999 and the EU in 2004.

– ORIGIN from medieval Latin *Hungaria* (see also **HUNGARIAN**).

hun·ger /ˈhəNGgər/ ▶ **n.** a feeling of discomfort or weakness caused by lack of food, coupled with the desire to eat: *she was faint with hunger.* ■ a severe lack of food: *they died from cold and hunger.* ■ a strong desire or craving: *her* ***hunger for*** *knowledge.*
▶ **v.** [no obj.] **1** (**hunger after/for**) have a strong desire or craving for: *all actors hunger for such a role.*
2 archaic feel or suffer hunger through lack of food.
– ORIGIN Old English *hungor* (noun), *hyngran* (verb), of Germanic origin; related to Dutch *honger* and German *Hunger*.

hun·ger strike ▶ **n.** a prolonged refusal to eat, carried out as a protest, typically by a prisoner.
– DERIVATIVES **hun·ger strik·er n.**

hung·o·ver /ˈhəNGˌōvər/ (also **hung over**) ▶ **adj.** suffering from a hangover after drinking alcohol.

hun·gry /ˈhəNGgrē/ ▶ **adj.** (**hungrier**, **hungriest**) feeling or displaying the need for food: *I was feeling ravenously hungry* | *children with hungry looks on their faces.* ■ [attrib.] causing hunger: *I always find art galleries hungry work.* ■ having a strong desire or craving: *he was* ***hungry for*** *any kind of excitement* | [in combination] *grasping, power-hungry individuals.*
– DERIVATIVES **hun·gri·ly** /-grəlē/ **adv.**, **hun·gri·ness n.**
– ORIGIN Old English *hungrig*; related to Dutch *hongerig*, German *hungrig*, also to **HUNGER**.

Hun·jiang /ˈho͝oNGˈjyäNG/ an industrial city in Jilin province, in northeastern China, near the border with North Korea; pop. 269,500 (est. 2006).

hunk /həNGk/ ▶ **n. 1** a large piece of something, esp. one of food cut or broken off a larger piece: ***a hunk of bread****.*
2 informal a sexually attractive man, esp. a large, strong one.
– ORIGIN early 19th cent.: probably of Dutch or Low German origin.

hunk·er /ˈhəNGkər/ ▶ **v.** [no obj.] **1** squat or crouch down low: *he* ***hunkered down*** *beside her.* ■ hunch; bend: *burly workers* ***hunkered over*** *the menu of the day.* ■ take shelter in a defensive position: *the best way to deal with your father is to* ***hunker down*** *and let it blow over.*
2 (**hunker down**) apply oneself seriously to a task: *students hunkered down to prepare for the examinations.*
– ORIGIN early 18th cent.: probably related to Dutch *huiken* and German *hocken*.

hun·kers /ˈhəNGkərz/ ▶ **plural n.** informal haunches: *sitting on his hunkers.*
– ORIGIN mid 18th cent. (originally Scots): from **HUNKER**.

hunk·y /ˈhəNGki/ ▶ **adj.** (**hunkier**, **hunkiest**) informal (of a man) large, strong, and sexually attractive: *a hunky guy with rippling stomach muscles.*

hunk·y-do·ry /ˌhəNGkē ˈdôrē/ ▶ **adj.** informal fine; going well: *everything is hunky-dory.*
– ORIGIN mid 19th cent. (originally US): *hunky* from Dutch *honk* 'home, base' (in games); the origin of *dory* is unknown.

Hunt[1] /hənt/, (William) Holman (1827–1910), English painter, cofounder of the Pre-Raphaelite Brotherhood. Notable works: *The Light of the World* (1854) and *The Scapegoat* (1855).

Hunt[2], Ward (1810–86), US Supreme Court associate justice 1873–82. Appointed to the Court by President Grant, he previously served as a judge and then chief judge of the New York state court of appeals 1865–73.

hunt /hənt/ ▶ **v. 1** [with obj.] pursue and kill (a wild animal) for sport or food: *in the autumn they hunted deer* | [no obj.] *they hunted and fished.* ■ (of an animal) chase and kill (its prey): *mice are hunted by weasels and foxes* | [no obj.] *lionesses hunt in groups.* ■ [no obj.] try to find someone or something by searching carefully: *he desperately* ***hunted for*** *a new job.* ■ (**hunt something out/up**) search for something until it is found. ■ [with obj.] (of the police) search for (a criminal): *the gang is being hunted by police* | [no obj.] *police are* ***hunting for*** *her attacker.* ■ (**hunt someone down**) pursue and capture someone.
2 [no obj.] (of a machine, instrument needle, or system) oscillate around a desired speed, position, or state. ■ (of an aircraft or rocket) oscillate around a mean flight path. ■ (of an automatic transmission in a motor vehicle) keep shifting between gears because of improperly designed shift logic.
3 [no obj.] (**hunt down/up**) (in change-ringing) move the place of a bell in a simple progression.
▶ **n. 1** an act of hunting wild animals or game. ■ an association of people who meet regularly to hunt, esp. with hounds. ■ an area where hunting takes place. ■ a search: *police launched a* ***hunt for*** *the killer.*
2 an oscillating motion around a desired speed, position, or state.
– ORIGIN Old English *huntian*, of Germanic origin. The sense in change-ringing dates from the late 17th cent., and is probably based on the idea of the bells pursuing one another; it gave rise to the sense 'oscillate around a desired speed' (late 19th cent).

hunt-and-peck ▶ **adj.** denoting or using an inexpert form of typing in which only one or two fingers are used: *hunt-and-peck computer users.*

hunt·ed /ˈhəntid/ ▶ **adj.** being pursued or searched for: *they ran like hunted hares.* ■ appearing worn or harassed as if one is being pursued: *his eyes had a hunted look.*

hunt·er /ˈhən(t)ər/ ▶ **n. 1** a person or animal that hunts: *a deer hunter.* ■ a person searching for something: *a bargain hunter.* ■ a horse of a breed developed for stamina in fox hunting and ability to jump obstacles. ■ (**the Hunter**) the constellation Orion.
2 a watch with a hinged cover protecting the glass.

hunt·er-gath·er·er ▶ **n.** a member of a nomadic people who live chiefly by hunting, fishing, and harvesting wild food.

hunt·er-kill·er ▶ **adj.** (of a naval vessel, esp. a submarine) equipped to locate and destroy enemy vessels, esp. other submarines.

hunt·er's moon ▶ **n.** the first full moon after a harvest moon.

hunt·ing /ˈhəntiNG/ ▶ **n. 1** the activity of hunting wild animals or game, esp. for food or sport.
2 (also **plain hunting**) Bell-ringing a simple system of changes in which bells move through the order in a regular progression.

hunt·ing dog ▶ **n. 1** a dog of a breed developed for hunting.
2 (also **Cape hunting dog**) an African wild dog that has a dark coat with pale markings and a white-tipped tail, living and hunting in packs. ● *Lycaon pictus*, family Canidae.

hunt·ing ground ▶ **n.** a place used or suitable for hunting. ■ a place where people can observe or acquire what they want: *the circuit is a favorite hunting ground for talent scouts.*

hunt·ing horn ▶ **n.** a horn blown to give signals during hunting.

Hun·ting·ton /ˈhəntiNGtən/ **1** a town in northern Long Island in New York that includes Huntington, Cold Spring Harbor, and other villages; pop. 201,594 (est. 2008).
2 a city in southwestern West Virginia, on the Ohio River; pop. 49,185 (est. 2008).

Hun·ting·ton Beach a city in southern California, on the Pacific coast, south of Long Beach; pop. 192,620 (est. 2008).

Hun·ting·ton's cho·re·a /ˈhəntiNGtənz kəˈrēə/ ▶ **n.** a hereditary disease marked by degeneration of the brain cells and causing chorea and progressive dementia.
– ORIGIN late 19th cent.: named after George *Huntington* (1851–1916), the US neurologist who first described it.

hunt·ress /ˈhəntris/ ▶ **n.** a woman who hunts.

hunts·man /ˈhəntsmən/ ▶ **n.** (pl. **huntsmen**) a person who hunts. ■ a hunt official in charge of hounds.

Hunts·ville /ˈhənts,vil/ a city in northern Alabama; pop. 176,645 (est. 2008). It is a center for space exploration and solar energy research.

hun·yak /ˈhənyak/ ▶ **n.** informal, offensive a person of Hungarian or central European origin, esp. an immigrant.
– ORIGIN early 20th cent.: alteration of **HUNGARIAN**, on the pattern of *Polack*.

Hu·on pine /ˈ(h)yo͞o-än/ ▶ **n.** a tall Tasmanian conifer that has yewlike berries and fragrant red timber. ● *Dacrydium franklinii*, family Podocarpaceae.
– ORIGIN early 19th cent.: from *Huon*, the name of a river in the south of Tasmania.

hup /həp/ ▶ **exclam.** used as a way of encouraging a marching rhythm: *hup, two, three!*

Hu·peh /ˈho͞oˈpā/ variant of **HUBEI**.

hur·dle /ˈhərdl/ ▶ **n. 1** an upright frame, typically one of a series, that athletes in a race must jump over. ■ (**hurdles**) a hurdle race: *the women's 100-meter hurdles.*
2 an obstacle or difficulty: *there are many hurdles to overcome.*
3 chiefly Brit. a portable rectangular frame strengthened with willow branches or wooden bars, used as a temporary fence. ■ a horse race over a series of such frames: *a handicap hurdle.* ■ historical a frame on which traitors were dragged to execution.
▶ **v. 1** [no obj.] (often as noun **hurdling**) take part in a race that involves jumping hurdles. ■ [with obj.] jump over (a hurdle or other obstacle) while running.
2 [with obj.] enclose or fence off with hurdles.
– PHRASES **fall at the first hurdle** meet with failure at a very early stage of an undertaking: *the campaign could fall at the first hurdle if they fail to secure planning permission.*
– ORIGIN Old English *hyrdel* 'temporary fence,' of Germanic origin; related to Dutch *horde* and German *Hürde*.

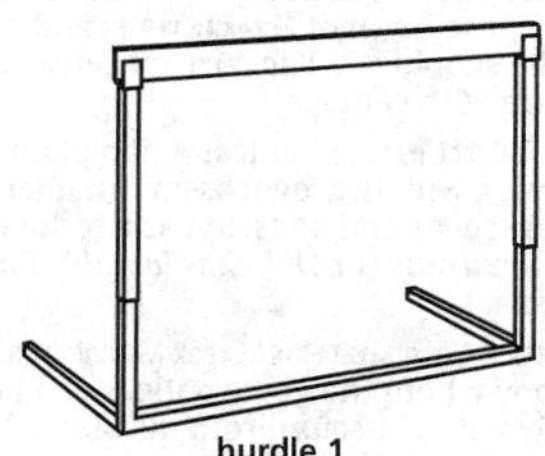
hurdle 1

hur·dler /ˈhərdlər/ ▶ **n.** an athlete, dog, or horse that runs in hurdle races.

hur·dy-gur·dy /ˈhərdē ˌgərdē/ ▶ **n.** (pl. **hurdy-gurdies**) a musical instrument with a droning sound played by turning a handle, which is typically attached to a rosined wheel sounding a series of drone strings, with keys worked by the left hand. ■ informal a barrel organ.
– ORIGIN mid 18th cent.: probably imitative of the sound of the instrument.

hurl /hərl/ ▶ **v.** [with obj.] throw (an object) with great force: *rioters hurled a brick through the windshield of a car.* ■ push or impel (someone) violently: *I seized Nathan and hurled him into the lobby* | figurative *he hurled himself into the job with enthusiasm.* ■ utter (abuse) vehemently: *they were hurling insults over a back fence.* ■ [no obj.] informal vomit: *it made me want to hurl.*
– ORIGIN Middle English: probably imitative, but corresponding in form and partly in sense with Low German *hurreln*.

hurl·er /ˈhərlər/ ▶ **n. 1** informal a baseball pitcher.
2 a player of hurling.

Hurl·er's syn·drome /ˈhərlərz/ ▶ **n.** Medicine a defect in metabolism arising from congenital absence of an enzyme, causing accumulation of lipids and glycosaminoglycans, and resulting in mental retardation, a protruding abdomen, and bone deformities including an abnormally large head.
– ORIGIN 1930s: named after Gertrud *Hurler* (1889–1965), the Austrian pediatrician who first described it.

hurl·ey /ˈhərlē/ ▶ **n.** a stick used in the game of hurling. ■ another term for **HURLING**.
– ORIGIN early 19th cent.: from the verb **HURL**.

hurl·ing /ˈhərliNG/ ▶ **n.** an Irish game resembling field hockey, played with a shorter stick with a broader oval blade. It is the national game of Ireland and may date back to the 2nd millennium BC.

hurl·y-burl·y /ˈhərlē ˌbərlē/ ▶ **n.** busy, boisterous activity: *the hurly-burly of school life.*
– ORIGIN Middle English: reduplication based on **HURL**.

Hu·ron /ˈhyo͝oˌrän/ ▶ **n.** (pl. **same** or **Hurons**)
1 a member of a confederation of native North American peoples formerly living in the region east of Lake Huron and now settled mainly in Oklahoma and Quebec.
2 the extinct Iroquoian language of any of these peoples.
▶ **adj.** of or relating to these peoples or their language.
– ORIGIN French, literally 'having hair standing in bristles on the head,' from Old French *hure* 'head of a wild boar,' of unknown ultimate origin.

Hu·ron, Lake /ˈ(h)yo͝orən, ˈ(h)yo͝orˌän/ the second largest of the five Great Lakes of North America, on the border between Canada and the US.

hur·rah /ho͝oˈrä, hə-/ (also **hooray**, **hurray** /-ˈrā/) ▶ **exclam.** used to express joy or approval: *Hurrah! She's here at last!*
▶ **n.** an utterance of the word "hurrah."
▶ **v.** [no obj.] shout "hurrah."
– ORIGIN late 17th cent.: alteration of archaic *huzza*; perhaps originally a sailors' cry when hauling.

Hur·ri /ˈho͝orē/ ▶ **plural n.** the Hurrian people collectively.
– ORIGIN the name in Hittite and Akkadian.

Hur·ri·an /ˈho͝orēən/ ▶ **adj.** of, relating to, or denoting an ancient people, originally from Armenia, who settled in Syria and northern Mesopotamia during the 3rd–2nd millennia BC and were later absorbed by the Hittites and Assyrians.
▶ **n. 1** a member of this people.
2 the language of the Hurrians, written in cuneiform and of unknown affinity.

hur·ri·cane /ˈhəriˌkān, ˈhə-ri-/ ▶ **n.** a storm with a violent wind, in particular a tropical cyclone in the Caribbean. ■ a wind of force 12 on the Beaufort scale (equal to or exceeding 64 knots or 74 mph).
– ORIGIN mid 16th cent.: from Spanish *huracán*, probably from Taino *hurakán* 'god of the storm.'

Hur·ri·cane Alley a popular term for areas of the US and the Caribbean, such as Florida and the Gulf Coast, that are prone to hurricanes.

hur·ri·cane deck ▶ **n.** a covered deck at or near the top of a ship's superstructure.

hur·ri·cane lamp ▶ **n.** an oil lamp with a glass chimney, designed to protect the flame even in high winds.

hur·ri·cane tape ▶ **n.** a strong type of adhesive tape used on windows to keep the glass in place if it is broken by strong winds.

hur·ried /ˈhərēd/ ▶ **adj.** done in a hurry; rushed: *I ate a hurried breakfast.*
– DERIVATIVES **hur·ried·ly** **adv.**, **hur·ried·ness** **n.**

hur·ry /ˈhərē, ˈhə-rē/ ▶ **v.** (**hurries**, **hurrying**, **hurried**) [no obj.] move or act with haste; rush: *we'd better hurry* | *servants hurried around.* ■ [often in imperative] (**hurry up**) do something more quickly: *hurry up and finish your meal.* ■ [with obj.] cause to move or proceed with haste: *she hurried him across the landing.* ■ [with obj.] do or finish (something) quickly, typically too quickly: *formalities were hurried over.*
▶ **n.** great haste: *in my hurry to leave, I knocked over a pile of books.* ■ [with negative and in questions] a need for haste; urgency: *there's no hurry to get back* | *relax, what's the hurry?*
– PHRASES **in a hurry** rushed; in a rushed manner: *the city offers fast food if you're in a hurry.* ■ eager to get a thing done quickly: *no one seemed in a hurry for the results.* ■ [usu. with negative] informal easily; readily: *an experience you won't forget in a hurry.*
– ORIGIN late 16th cent. (as a verb): imitative.

hur·ry-scur·ry archaic ▶ **n.** disorderly haste; confused hurrying.
▶ **adj. & adv.** with hurry and confusion.
– ORIGIN mid 18th cent.: reduplication of **HURRY**.

hur·ry-up ▶ **adj.** [attrib.] informal showing, involving, or requiring haste or urgency: *the hurry-up atmosphere of the court contributed to the mistake.*

hurst /hərst/ ▶ **n.** a hillock. ■ a sandbank in the sea or a river. ■ [usu. in place names] a wood or wooded rise.
– ORIGIN Old English *hyrst*, of Germanic origin; related to German *Horst*.

Hurs·ton /ˈhərstən/, Zora Neale (1901–60), US novelist. Her novels reflect her interest in folklore, esp. that of the Deep South. Notable works: *Jonah's Gourd Vine* (1934), *Dust Tracks on a Road* (autobiography, 1942), and *Seraph on the Suwanee* (1948).

hurt /hərt/ ▶ **v.** (past and past participle **hurt**) [with obj.] cause physical pain or injury to: *Ow! You're hurting me!* | [no obj.] *does acupuncture hurt?* ■ [no obj.] (of a part of the body) suffer pain: *my back hurts.* ■ cause mental pain or distress to (a person or their feelings): *she didn't want to hurt his feelings.* ■ [no obj.] (of a person) feel mental pain or distress: *he was hurting badly, but he smiled through his tears.* ■ be detrimental to: *high interest rates are hurting the local economy.* ■ [no obj.] (**hurt for**) informal have a pressing need for: *Frank wasn't hurting for money.*
▶ **n.** physical injury; harm. ■ mental pain or distress: *the hurt of being constantly ignored* | *wariness that masked a hurt.*
– ORIGIN Middle English (originally in the senses 'to strike' and 'a blow'): from Old French *hurter* (verb), *hurt* (noun), perhaps ultimately of Germanic origin.

hurt·ful /ˈhərtfəl/ ▶ **adj.** causing distress to someone's feelings: *his hurtful remarks.*
– DERIVATIVES **hurt·ful·ly** **adv.**, **hurt·ful·ness** **n.**

hur·tle /ˈhərtl/ ▶ **v.** move or cause to move at a great speed, typically in a wildly uncontrolled manner: [no obj., with adverbial of direction] *a runaway car hurtled toward them* | [with obj. and adverbial of direction] *the branch flew off and hurtled us into a ditch.*
– ORIGIN Middle English (in the sense 'strike against, collide with'): frequentative of **HURT**.

Hu·sain variant spelling of **HUSSEIN**[1], **HUSSEIN**[2].

hus·band /ˈhəzbənd/ ▶ **n.** a married man considered in relation to his wife: *she and her husband are both retired.*
▶ **v.** [with obj.] use (resources) economically; conserve: *the need to husband his remaining strength.*
– DERIVATIVES **hus·band·er** **n.** (rare), **hus·band·hood** /-ˌho͝od/ **n.**, **hus·band·less** **adj.**, **hus·band·ly** **adj.**
– ORIGIN late Old English (in the senses 'male head of a household' and 'manager, steward'), from Old Norse *húsbóndi* 'master of a house,' from *hús* 'house' + *bóndi* 'occupier and tiller of the soil.' The original sense of the verb was 'till, cultivate.'

hus·band·man /ˈhəzbəndmən/ ▶ **n.** (pl. **husbandmen**) archaic a person who cultivates the land; a farmer.
– ORIGIN Middle English (originally in northern English use denoting the holder of a *husbandland*, i.e., manorial tenancy): from **HUSBAND** in the obsolete sense 'farmer' + **MAN**.

hus·band·ry /ˈhəzbəndrē/ ▶ **n. 1** the care, cultivation, and breeding of crops and animals: *crop husbandry.*
2 management and conservation of resources.
– ORIGIN Middle English: from **HUSBAND** in the obsolete sense 'farmer' + **-RY**; compare with **HUSBANDMAN**.

hush /həsH/ ▶ **v.** [with obj.] make (someone) be quiet or stop talking: *he placed a finger before pursed lips to hush her.* ■ [no obj.] be quiet: *Hush! Someone will hear you.* ■ (**hush something up**) suppress public mention of something: *management took steps to hush up the dangers.*
▶ **n.** [in sing.] a silence: *a hush descended over the crowd.*
– ORIGIN mid 16th cent.: back-formation from obsolete *husht* 'silent, hushed' (taken to be a past participle), from an interjection *husht* 'quiet!'

hush·a·by /ˈhəsHəˌbī/ (also **hushabye**) ▶ **exclam.** archaic used to calm a child.

hushed /həsHt/ ▶ **adj.** having a calm and still silence: *he addressed the hushed courtroom.* ■ (of a voice or conversation) quiet and serious: *the nurses were talking in hushed voices.*

PRONUNCIATION KEY ə *ago, up*; ər *over, fur*; a *hat*; ā *ate*; ä *car*; e *let*; ē *see*; i *fit*; ī *by*; NG *sing*; ō *go*; ô *law, for*; oi *toy*; o͝o *good*; o͞o *goo*; ou *out*; TH *thin*; T͟H *then*; ZH *vision*

hush-hush ▶ **adj.** informal (esp. of an official plan or project) highly secret or confidential: *a hush-hush research unit.*

hush mon·ey ▶ **n.** informal money paid to someone to prevent them from disclosing embarrassing or discreditable information.

hush pup·pies ▶ **plural n.** small cakes of cornmeal dough that are quickly deep-fried.

husk /həsk/ ▶ **n.** the dry outer covering of some fruits or seeds. ■ a dry or rough outer layer or coating, esp. when empty of its contents: *the husks of dead bugs* | figurative *I expect whatever husk of a person emerges from the car to be sheet-white.*
▶ **v. 1** [with obj.] remove the husk or husks from.
2 [with direct speech] say something in a husky voice: *"Help me," husked Miles.*
– ORIGIN late Middle English: probably from Low German *hūske* 'sheath,' literally 'little house.'

husk·ing bee ▶ **n.** another term for CORNHUSKING.

husk·y[1] /ˈhəskē/ ▶ **adj.** (**huskier, huskiest**) **1** (of a voice or utterance) sounding low-pitched and slightly hoarse.
2 strong; hefty: *Patrick looked a husky, strong guy.*
3 like or consisting of a husk or husks.
– DERIVATIVES **husk·i·ly** /ˈhəskəlē/ **adv.**, **husk·i·ness n.**

h

husk·y[2] (also **huskie**) ▶ **n.** (pl. **huskies**) a powerful dog of a breed with a thick double coat that is typically gray, used in the Arctic for pulling sleds.
– ORIGIN mid 19th cent. (originally denoting the Eskimo language or an Eskimo): abbreviation of obsolete *Ehuskemay* or Newfoundland dialect *Huskemaw* 'Eskimo,' probably from Montagnais (see ESKIMO). The term replaced the 18th-cent. term *Eskimo dog.*

Huss /həs, hōōs/, John (*c.*1372–1415), Bohemian religious reformer; Czech name *Jan Hus.*
He supported the views of Wyclif, attacked ecclesiastical abuses, and was excommunicated in 1411. He was later tried and burned at the stake. See also HUSSITE.

hus·sar /həˈzär/ ▶ **n.** historical (in the 15th century) a Hungarian light horseman. ■ a soldier in a light cavalry regiment that had adopted a dress uniform modeled on that of the Hungarian hussars.
– ORIGIN from Hungarian *huszár*, from Old Serbian *husar*, from Italian *corsaro* (see CORSAIR).

Hus·sein[1], Abdullah ibn, see ABDULLAH IBN HUSSEIN.

Hus·sein[2] /hōōˈsān/ (also **Husain**), ibn Talal (1935–99), king of Jordan 1953–99. Hussein sought to maintain good relations both with the West and with other Arab nations, but his moderate policies created problems with Palestinian refugees from Israel within Jordan. During the Gulf War, he supported Iraq, but in 1994 he signed a treaty that normalized relations with Israel. He was succeeded by his son **Abdullah**.

Hus·sein[3] (also **Husain**), Saddam (1937–2006), Iraqi president; prime minister and head of the armed forces 1979–2003; full name *Saddam bin Hussein at-Takriti.* During his presidency, Iraq fought a war with Iran 1980–88 and invaded Kuwait 1990, from which Iraqi forces were expelled in the Gulf War of 1991. His regime was known for its brutality, and the United Nations imposed economic sanctions against the country in 1990. Believing that Hussein was developing weapons of mass destruction, the US, with coalition forces, invaded Iraq in 2003. He was overthrown and later tried for crimes against humanity and executed.

Huss·ite /ˈhəˌsīt/ ▶ **n.** a member or follower of the religious movement begun by John Huss. After Huss's execution the Hussites took up arms against the Holy Roman Empire and demanded a set of reforms that anticipated the Reformation. Most of the demands were granted 1436, and a church was established that remained independent of the Roman Catholic Church until 1620.
▶ **adj.** of or relating to the Hussites.
– DERIVATIVES **Huss·it·ism** /ˈhəˌsīˌtizəm/ **n.**

hus·sy /ˈhəsē, ˈhəzē/ ▶ **n.** (pl. **hussies**) an impudent or immoral girl or woman: *that brazen little hussy!*
– ORIGIN late Middle English: contraction of HOUSEWIFE (the original sense); the current sense dates from the mid 17th cent.

hust·ings /ˈhəstiNGz/ ▶ **n.** (pl. **same**) a meeting at which candidates in an election address potential voters. ■ the campaigning associated with an election: *a formidable political operator at his best* **on the hustings**.
– ORIGIN late Old English *husting* 'deliberative assembly, council,' from Old Norse *hústhing* 'household assembly held by a leader,' from *hús* 'house' + *thing* 'assembly, parliament'; *hustings* was applied in Middle English to the highest court of the City of London, England. Subsequently it denoted the platform where the Lord Mayor and aldermen presided and (early 18th cent.) a temporary platform on which parliamentary candidates were nominated; hence the sense 'electoral proceedings.'

hus·tle /ˈhəsəl/ ▶ **v. 1** [with obj.] force (someone) to move hurriedly or unceremoniously in a specified direction: *they hustled him into the back of a horse-drawn wagon.* ■ push roughly; jostle: *they were hissed and hustled as they went in.* ■ [no obj.] hurry; bustle: *he had to retag second base and hustle back to first.*
2 [with obj.] informal obtain by forceful action or persuasion: *the brothers headed to New York to try and hustle a record deal.* ■ (**hustle someone into**) coerce or pressure someone into doing or choosing something: *don't be hustled into anything.* ■ sell aggressively: *he hustled his company's oil around the country.* ■ obtain by illicit action; swindle; cheat: *Linda hustled money from men she met.*
3 [no obj.] informal engage in prostitution.
▶ **n. 1** busy movement and activity: *the* **hustle and bustle** *of the big cities.*
2 informal a fraud or swindle.
– PHRASES **hustle one's butt** (or vulgar slang **ass**) informal move or act quickly.
– ORIGIN late 17th cent. (originally in the sense 'shake, toss'): from Middle Dutch *hutselen.* Sense 3 of the verb dates from the early 20th cent.

hus·tler /ˈhəslər/ ▶ **n.** informal an aggressively enterprising person; a go-getter. ■ a prostitute.

Hus·ton /ˈhyōōstən/, John (1906–87), US movie director; an Irish citizen from 1964. After a varied background as a boxer, cavalryman, journalist, and actor, he made his debut as a movie director in 1941 with *The Maltese Falcon.* Other notable movies include *The African Queen* (1951) and *Prizzi's Honor* (1985). His father, **Walter** (1884–1950), was an actor noted for his performance in *Treasure of the Sierra Madre* (1948), and his daughter, **Anjelica** (1951–), had leading roles in such movies as *Prizzi's Honor* (1985), *The Addams Family* (1991), and *The Royal Tenenbaums* (2001).

hut /hət/ ▶ **n.** a small single-story building of simple or crude construction, serving as a poor, rough, or temporary house or shelter.
▶ **v.** (**huts, hutting, hutted**) [with obj.] provide with huts: (as adj. **hutted**) *a hutted encampment.*
– DERIVATIVES **hut·like** /-ˌlīk/ **adj.**
– ORIGIN mid 16th cent. (in the sense 'temporary wooden shelter for troops'): from French *hutte*, from Middle High German *hütte.*

hutch /həCH/ ▶ **n. 1** a box or cage, typically with a wire mesh front, for keeping rabbits, ferrets, or other small domesticated animals: *a rabbit hutch.*
2 a storage chest. ■ a cupboard or dresser typically with open shelves above.
– ORIGIN Middle English: from Old French *huche*, from medieval Latin *hutica*, of unknown origin. The original sense was 'storage chest' (sense 2).

Hutch·in·son[1] /ˈhəCHənsən/ a city in south central Kansas; pop. 40,889 (est. 2008).

Hutch·in·son[2], Anne Marbury (1591–1643), American religious leader; born in England. She was banished from Massachusetts Bay Colony in 1637 for her liberal views on grace and salvation. First moving to Rhode Island and then settling in New York in 1642, she and most of her family were killed by Indians.

hut·ment /ˈhətmənt/ ▶ **n.** Military an encampment of huts.

hu·tong /ˈhōōtôNG/ ▶ **n.** (pl. **same** or **hutongs**) a narrow lane or alleyway in a traditional residential area of a Chinese city, esp. Beijing.
– ORIGIN Chinese *hútòng*, probably from Mongolian *gudum.*

Hut·ter·ite /ˈhətəˌrīt/ ▶ **n.** a member of either an Anabaptist Christian sect established in Moravia in the early 16th century, or a North American community holding similar beliefs and practicing an old-fashioned communal way of life.
▶ **adj.** of or relating to Hutterites or their beliefs and practices.
– ORIGIN from the name of Jacob Hutter (died 1536), a Moravian Anabaptist, + -ITE[1].

Hut·ton /ˈhətn/, James (1726–97), Scottish geologist. Although controversial at the time, his description of the processes that have shaped the surface of the earth is now accepted as showing that it is very much older than had previously been believed.

Hu·tu /ˈhōōtōō/ ▶ **n.** (pl. **same** or **Hutus** or **Bahutu** /bəˈhōōtōō/) a member of a Bantu-speaking people forming the majority population in Rwanda and Burundi. They are traditionally a farming people and were historically dominated by the Tutsi people; the antagonism between the peoples led in 1994 to large-scale ethnic violence, esp. in Rwanda.
▶ **adj.** of or relating to this people.
– ORIGIN a local name.

Hux·ley[1] /ˈhəkslē/, Aldous (Leonard) (1894–1963), English novelist and essayist. After writing *Antic Hay* (1923) and *Brave New World* (1932), he moved to California in 1937, where he experimented with psychedelic drugs in 1953 and wrote of his experiences in *The Doors of Perception* (1954).

Hux·ley[2], Sir Andrew Fielding (1917–), British physiologist, the grandson of Thomas Henry Huxley. He worked with Alan L. Hodgkin on the physiology of nerve transmission. Nobel Prize for Physiology or Medicine (1963), shared with John C. Eccles and Hodgkin.

Hux·ley[3], Thomas Henry (1825–95), English biologist. A surgeon and leading supporter of Darwinism, he coined the word *agnostic* to describe his own beliefs.

Huy·gens /ˈhoigənz/, Christiaan (1629–95), Dutch physicist, mathematician, and astronomer. His wave theory of light enabled him to explain reflection and refraction.

huz·zah /həˈzä/ (also **huzza**) archaic ▶ **exclam.** used to express approval or delight; hurrah.
▶ **v.** [no obj.] cry "huzzah."
– ORIGIN late 16th cent.: perhaps used originally as a sailor's cry when hauling.

HV (also **h.v.**) ▶ **abbr.** ■ high velocity. ■ high voltage.

hvy. ▶ **abbr.** heavy.

HW ▶ **abbr.** ■ hardwood. ■ high water. ■ hot water (heat).

HWM ▶ **abbr.** high-water mark.

hwy ▶ **abbr.** highway.

hy·a·cinth /ˈhīəˌsinTH/ ▶ **n. 1** a bulbous plant of the lily family, with straplike leaves and a compact spike of bell-shaped fragrant flowers. Native to western Asia, hyacinths are cultivated outdoors and as houseplants.
● Genus *Hyacinthus*, family Liliaceae: several species, in particular *H. orientalis*, from which the common large-flowered cultivars are derived.
■ a light purplish-blue color typical of some hyacinth flowers.
2 another term for JACINTH.
– DERIVATIVES **hy·a·cin·thine** /ˌhīəˈsinTHin, -ˌTHīn/ **adj.**

hyacinth

– ORIGIN mid 16th cent. (denoting a gem): from French *hyacinthe*, via Latin from Greek *huakinthos*, denoting any of various plants identified with the flower in the myth of HYACINTHUS, and a gem (perhaps the sapphire). The current sense dates from the late 16th cent.

hy·a·cinth bean ▶ **n.** a tropical Asian plant of the pea family, widely grown as an ornamental or for its edible seeds and pods and as a fodder crop.
● *Lablab purpureus* (or *Dolichos lablab*), family Leguminosae.

Hy·a·cin·thus /ˌhīəˈsinTHəs/ Greek Mythology a beautiful boy whom the god Apollo loved but killed accidentally with a discus. From his blood Apollo caused the hyacinth to spring up.

Hy·a·des /ˈhīˌdēz/ Astronomy an open star cluster in the constellation Taurus, appearing to surround the bright star Aldebaran.
– ORIGIN from Greek *Huades*, by folk etymology from *huein* 'to rain,' but perhaps from *hus* 'pig,' the Latin name of the constellation being *Suculae* 'little pigs.'

hy·ae·na ▶ **n.** variant spelling of HYENA.

hy·a·lin /ˈhīəlin/ ▶ **n.** Physiology a clear substance produced esp. by the degeneration of epithelial or connective tissues.
– ORIGIN mid 19th cent.: via Latin from Greek *hualinos*, from *hualos* 'glass.'

hy·a·line /ˈhīəlin, -ˌlīn/ ▶ **adj.** Anatomy & Zoology having a glassy, translucent appearance. ■ relating to, consisting of, or characterized by hyaline material.
▶ **n. 1** (**the hyaline**) literary a thing that is clear and translucent like glass, esp. a smooth sea or a clear sky.
2 another term for HYALIN.
– ORIGIN mid 17th cent.: from Latin *hyalinus* (see HYALIN).

hy·a·line car·ti·lage ▶ **n.** a translucent bluish-white type of cartilage present in the joints, the respiratory tract, and the immature skeleton.

hy·a·line mem·brane dis·ease ▶ **n.** a condition in newborn babies in which the lungs are deficient in surfactant, preventing their proper expansion and causing the formation of hyaline material in the lung spaces. Also called RESPIRATORY DISTRESS SYNDROME.

hy·a·lite /ˈhīəˌlīt/ ▶ **n.** a translucent, colorless variety of opal.
– ORIGIN late 18th cent.: from Greek *hualos* 'glass' + -ITE[1].

hy·a·loid /ˈhīəˌloid/ ▶ **adj.** Anatomy glassy; transparent.
– ORIGIN mid 19th cent.: from French *hyaloïde*, or via late Latin from Greek *hualoeidēs* 'like glass,' from *hualos* 'glass.'

hy·a·loid mem·brane ▶ **n.** a thin transparent membrane enveloping the vitreous humor of the eye.

hy·a·lu·ron·ic ac·id /ˌhīəlo͞oˈränik/ ▶ **n.** Biochemistry a viscous fluid carbohydrate present in connective tissue, synovial fluid, and the humors of the eye.
– DERIVATIVES **hy·a·lu·ro·nate** /hīəˈlo͝orəˌnāt/ **n.**
– ORIGIN 1930s: *hyaluronic* from a blend of HYALOID and URONIC ACID.

Hy·an·nis /hīˈanis/ a commercial village in southeastern Massachusetts, on Cape Cod; pop. 16,000 (est. 2008).

hy·brid /ˈhīˌbrid/ ▶ **n.** **1** Biology the offspring of two plants or animals of different species or varieties, such as a mule (a hybrid of a donkey and a horse): *a **hybrid of** wheat and rye.*
2 a thing made by combining two different elements; a mixture: *the final text is a **hybrid of** the stage play and the film.* ■ a word formed from elements taken from different languages, for example *television* (*tele-* from Greek, *vision* from Latin). ■ (also **hybrid car**) a car with a gasoline engine and an electric motor, each of which can propel it.
▶ **adj.** of mixed character; composed of mixed parts: *Mexico's hybrid postconquest culture.* ■ bred as a hybrid from different species or varieties: *a hybrid variety | hybrid offspring.*
– DERIVATIVES **hy·brid·ism** /ˈhībrəˌdizəm/ **n.**, **hy·brid·i·ty** /hīˈbriditē/ **n.**
– ORIGIN early 17th cent. (as a noun): from Latin *hybrida* 'offspring of a tame sow and wild boar, child of a freeman and slave, etc.'

hy·brid·ize /ˈhībriˌdīz/ ▶ **v.** [with obj.] crossbreed (individuals of two different species or varieties). ■ [no obj.] (of an animal or plant) breed with an individual of another species or variety.
– DERIVATIVES **hy·brid·iz·a·ble adj.**, **hy·brid·i·za·tion** /ˌhībrədiˈzāsʜən/ **n.**

hy·brid vig·or ▶ **n.** another term for HETEROSIS.

hyd. ▶ **abbr.** ■ hydraulics. ■ hydrostatics.

hy·dan·to·in /hīˈdantō-ən/ ▶ **n.** Chemistry a crystalline compound present in sugar beet and used in the manufacture of some anticonvulsant drugs. ● A cyclic derivative of urea; chem. formula: $C_3H_4N_2O_2$.
– ORIGIN mid 19th cent.: from Greek *hudōr* 'water' + *allantoic* (see ALLANTOIS) + -IN[1].

hy·da·thode /ˈhīdəˌᴛʜōd/ ▶ **n.** Botany a modified pore, esp. on a leaf, that exudes drops of water.
– ORIGIN late 19th cent.: from Greek *hudōr, hudat-* 'water' + *hodos* 'way.'

hy·da·tid /ˈhīdətid/ ▶ **n.** Medicine a cyst containing watery fluid. ■ such a cyst formed by and containing a tapeworm larva. ■ a tapeworm larva.
– ORIGIN late 17th cent.: from modern Latin *hydatis*, from Greek *hudatis, hudatid-* 'watery vesicle,' from *hudōr, hudat-* 'water.'

hy·da·tid·i·form mole /ˌhīdəˈtitəˌfôrm/ ▶ **n.** Medicine a cluster of fluid-filled sacs formed in the uterus by the degeneration of chorionic tissue around an aborting embryo.

Hyde[1] /hīd/, Edward, see CLARENDON.

Hyde[2], Mr., see JEKYLL.

Hyde Park /hīd/ **1** a town in southeastern New York, on the Hudson River, north of Poughkeepsie, associated with the family of Franklin D. Roosevelt; pop. 20,270 (est. 2008).
2 a park in western central London, England.

Hy·der·a·bad /ˈhīd(ə)rəˌbad, -ˌbäd/ **1** a city in central India, capital of the state of Andhra Pradesh; pop. 4,025,300 (est. 2009).
2 a former large princely state in southern central India, divided in 1956 between Maharashtra, Mysore, and Andhra Pradesh.
3 a city in southeastern Pakistan, in the province of Sind, on the Indus River; pop. 1,536,400 (est. 2009).

hydr- ▶ **comb. form** variant spelling of HYDRO- shortened before a vowel (as in *hydraulic*).

Hy·dra /ˈhīdrə/ **1** Greek Mythology a many-headed snake whose heads grew again as they were cut off, killed by Hercules. ■ (as noun **hydra**) a thing that is hard to overcome or resist because of its pervasive or enduring quality or its many aspects.
2 Astronomy the largest constellation (the Water Snake or Sea Monster), said to represent the beast slain by Hercules. Its few bright stars are close to the celestial equator. Compare with HYDRUS. ■ (as genitive **Hydrae** /ˈhīdrē/) used with a preceding letter or numeral to designate a star in this constellation: *the star Beta Hydrae.*
– ORIGIN via Latin from Greek *hudra.*

hy·dra /ˈhīdrə/ ▶ **n.** a minute freshwater coelenterate with a stalklike tubular body and a ring of tentacles around the mouth. ● Genus *Hydra*, class Hydrozoa.
– ORIGIN via Latin from Greek *hudra* 'water snake' (see HYDRA), named by Linnaeus because, if cut into pieces, each section can grow into a whole animal.

hy·dram·ni·os /hīˈdramnēˌäs/ ▶ **n.** Medicine a condition in which excess amniotic fluid accumulates during pregnancy.

hy·dran·gea /hīˈdrānjə/ ▶ **n.** a shrub or climbing plant with rounded or flattened flowering heads of small florets, the outer ones of which are typically infertile. Hydrangeas are native to Asia and America. ● Genus *Hydrangea*, family Hydrangeaceae: many species, in particular **late** (or **panicled**) **hydrangea** (*H. paniculata*), an ornamental shrub that blooms in late summer, and **bigleaf hydrangea** (*H. macrophylla*), commonly grown for florists and as a houseplant.
– ORIGIN modern Latin, from Greek *hudro-* 'water' + *angeion* 'vessel' (from the cup shape of its seed capsule).

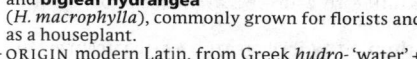

late hydrangea

hy·drant /ˈhīdrənt/ ▶ **n.** an upright water pipe, esp. one in a street, with a nozzle to which a fire hose can be attached.
– ORIGIN early 19th cent. (originally US): formed irregularly from HYDRO- 'relating to water' + -ANT.

hy·drate /ˈhīˌdrāt/ ▶ **n.** Chemistry a compound, typically a crystalline one, in which water molecules are chemically bound to another compound or an element.
▶ **v.** [with obj.] cause to absorb water. ■ Chemistry combine chemically with water molecules: (as adj. **hydrated**) *hydrated silicate crystals.*
– DERIVATIVES **hy·drat·a·ble adj.**, **hy·dra·tion** /hīˈdrāsʜən/ **n.**, **hy·dra·tor** /-tər/ **n.**
– ORIGIN early 19th cent.: coined in French from Greek *hudōr* 'water.'

hy·drau·lic /hīˈdrôlik/ ▶ **adj.** **1** denoting, relating to, or operated by a liquid moving in a confined space under pressure: *hydraulic fluid | hydraulic lifting gear.*
2 of or relating to the science of hydraulics.
3 (of cement) hardening under water.
– DERIVATIVES **hy·drau·li·cal·ly** /-(ə)lē/ **adv.**
– ORIGIN early 17th cent.: via Latin from Greek *hudraulikos*, from *hudro-* 'water' + *aulos* 'pipe.'

hy·drau·lic frac·tur·ing ▶ **n.** the forcing open of fissures in subterranean rocks by introducing liquid at high pressure, esp. to extract oil or gas.

hy·drau·lic ram ▶ **n.** an automatic pump in which a large volume of water flows through a valve that it periodically forces shut, the sudden pressure change being used to raise a smaller volume of water to a higher level.

hy·drau·lics /hīˈdrôliks/ ▶ **plural n.** **1** [usu. treated as sing.] the branch of science and technology concerned with the conveyance of liquids through pipes and channels, esp. as a source of mechanical force or control.
2 hydraulic systems, mechanisms, or forces.

hy·dra·zine /ˈhīdrəˌzēn/ ▶ **n.** Chemistry a colorless volatile alkaline liquid with powerful reducing properties, used in chemical synthesis and in some kinds of rocket fuels. ● Chem. formula: N_2H_4.
– ORIGIN late 19th cent.: from HYDROGEN + AZO- + -INE[4].

hy·dric /ˈhīdrik/ ▶ **adj.** Ecology (of an environment or habitat) containing plenty of moisture; very wet. Compare with MESIC[1] and XERIC.
– ORIGIN early 20th cent.: from HYDRO- + -IC.

hy·dride /ˈhīˌdrīd/ ▶ **n.** Chemistry a binary compound of hydrogen with a metal.

hy·dri·od·ic ac·id /ˌhīdrēˈädik/ ▶ **n.** Chemistry a strongly acidic solution of the gas hydrogen iodide in water. ● Chem. formula: HI.
– ORIGIN early 19th cent.: *hydriodic* from a blend of HYDROGEN and IODINE.

hy·dro /ˈhīdrō/ ▶ **n.** (pl. **hydros**) **1** a hydroelectric power plant. ■ hydroelectricity. ■ Canadian electricity.
2 Brit. a hotel or clinic originally providing hydropathic treatment.
– ORIGIN late 19th cent.: abbreviation.

hydro- (also **hydr-**) ▶ **comb. form** **1** water; relating to water: *hydraulic | hydrocolloid.* ■ Medicine affected with an accumulation of serous fluid: *hydrocephalus.*
2 Chemistry combined with hydrogen: *hydrocarbon.*
– ORIGIN from Greek *hudōr* 'water.'

hy·dro·bro·mic ac·id /ˌhīdrəˈbrōmik/ ▶ **n.** Chemistry a strongly acidic solution of the gas hydrogen bromide in water. ● Chem. formula: HBr.

hy·dro·car·bon /ˈhīdrəˌkärbən/ ▶ **n.** Chemistry a compound of hydrogen and carbon, such as any of those that are the chief components of petroleum and natural gas.

hy·dro·cele /ˈhīdrəˌsēl/ ▶ **n.** Medicine the accumulation of serous fluid in a body sac.

hy·dro·ceph·a·lus /ˌhīdrōˈsefələs/ ▶ **n.** Medicine a condition in which fluid accumulates in the brain, typically in young children, enlarging the head and sometimes causing brain damage.
– DERIVATIVES **hy·dro·ce·phal·ic** /ˌhīdrōsəˈfalik/ **adj.**, **hy·dro·ceph·a·ly** /-ˈsefəlē/ **n.**
– ORIGIN late 17th cent.: modern Latin, from Greek *hudrokephalon*, from *hudro-* 'water' + *kephalē* 'head.'

hy·dro·chlo·ric ac·id /ˌhīdrəˈklôrik/ ▶ **n.** Chemistry a strongly acidic solution of the gas hydrogen chloride in water. ● Chem. formula: HCl.

hy·dro·chlo·ride /ˌhīdrəˈklôˌrīd/ ▶ **n.** Chemistry a compound of a particular organic base with hydrochloric acid: [with adj.] *cocaine hydrochloride.*

hy·dro·chlo·ro·fluor·o·car·bon /ˌhīdrōˌklôrōˈflo͝orōˌkärbən/ (abbr.: **HCFC**) ▶ **n.** Chemistry any of a class of inert compounds of carbon, hydrogen, hydrocarbons, chlorine, and fluorine, used in place of chlorofluorocarbons as being somewhat less destructive to the ozone layer.

hy·dro·col·loid /ˌhīdrōˈkäˌloid/ ▶ **n.** a substance that forms a gel in the presence of water, examples of which are used in surgical dressings and in various industrial applications.

hy·dro·cor·ti·sone /ˌhīdrəˈkôrtiˌzōn/ ▶ **n.** Biochemistry a steroid hormone produced by the adrenal cortex and used medicinally to treat inflammation resulting from eczema and rheumatism.

hy·dro·cy·an·ic ac·id /ˌhīdrōsīˈanik/ ▶ **n.** Chemistry a highly poisonous acidic solution of hydrogen cyanide in water.

hy·dro·dy·nam·ics /ˌhīdrōdīˈnamiks/ ▶ **plural n.** [treated as sing.] the branch of science concerned with forces acting on or exerted by fluids (esp. liquids).
– DERIVATIVES **hy·dro·dy·nam·ic adj.**, **hy·dro·dy·nam·i·cal** /-ˈnamikəl/ **adj.**, **hy·dro·dy·nam·i·cal·ly adv.**, **hy·dro·dy·nam·i·cist** /-ˈnamisist/ **n.**
– ORIGIN late 18th cent.: from modern Latin *hydrodynamica*, from Greek *hudro-* 'water' + *dunamikos* (see DYNAMIC).

hy·dro·e·lec·tric /ˌhīdrōəˈlektrik/ ▶ **adj.** relating to or denoting the generation of electricity using flowing water (typically from a reservoir held behind a dam or other barrier) to drive a turbine that powers a generator.
– DERIVATIVES **hy·dro·e·lec·tric·i·ty** /-əlekˈtrisitē/ **n.**

hy·dro·fluor·ic ac·id /ˌhīdrəˌflo͝orik/ ▶ **n.** Chemistry an acidic and extremely corrosive solution of the liquid hydrogen fluoride in water. ● Chem. formula: HF.

hy·dro·fluor·o·car·bon /ˌhīdrōˈflo͝orəˌkärbən/ (abbr.: **HFC**) ▶ **n.** Chemistry any of a class of partly chlorinated and fluorinated hydrocarbons, used as an alternative to chlorofluorocarbons in foam production, refrigeration, and other processes.

hy·dro·foil /ˈhīdrəˌfoil/ ▶ **n.** a boat whose hull is fitted underneath with shaped vanes (foils) that

lift the hull clear of the water to increase the boat's speed. ■ another term for FOIL[4].
– ORIGIN 1920s: from HYDRO- 'relating to water' + FOIL[4].

hydrofoil

hy·dro·frac·tur·ing /ˈhīdrəˌfrakCHəriNG/ ▶ n. another term for HYDRAULIC FRACTURING.

hy·dro·gel /ˈhīdrəˌjel/ ▶ n. a gel in which the liquid component is water.

hy·dro·gen /ˈhīdrəjən/ ▶ n. a colorless, odorless, highly flammable gas, the chemical element of atomic number 1. (Symbol: **H**)

> Hydrogen is the lightest of the chemical elements and has the simplest atomic structure, a single electron orbiting a nucleus consisting of a single proton. It is by far the commonest element in the universe, although not on the earth, where it occurs chiefly combined with oxygen as water.

– DERIVATIVES **hy·drog·e·nous** /hīˈdräjənəs/ adj.
– ORIGIN late 18th cent.: coined in French from Greek *hudro-* 'water' + *-genēs* (see -GEN).

hy·drog·e·nase /ˈhīdrəjəˌnās, hīˈdräjə-/ ▶ n. [usu. with modifier] Biochemistry an enzyme that catalyzes the reduction of a particular substance by hydrogen.

hy·dro·gen·ate /ˈhīdrəjəˌnāt, hīˈdräjənāt/ ▶ v. [with obj.] (often as adj. **hydrogenated**) charge with or cause to combine with hydrogen.
– DERIVATIVES **hy·dro·gen·a·tion** /ˌhīdrəjəˈnāSHən, hīˌdräjə-/ n.

hy·dro·gen bomb ▶ n. an immensely powerful bomb whose destructive power comes from the rapid release of energy during the nuclear fusion of isotopes of hydrogen (deuterium and tritium), using an atom bomb as a trigger. Compare with ATOM BOMB.

hy·dro·gen bond ▶ n. Chemistry a weak bond between two molecules resulting from an electrostatic attraction between a proton in one molecule and an electronegative atom in the other.

hy·dro·gen cy·a·nide ▶ n. Chemistry a highly poisonous gas or volatile liquid with an odor of bitter almonds, made by the action of acids on cyanides. ● Chem. formula: HCN.

hy·dro·gen per·ox·ide ▶ n. Chemistry a colorless, viscous, unstable liquid with strong oxidizing properties, commonly used in diluted form in disinfectants and bleaches. ● Chem. formula: H_2O_2.

hy·dro·gen sul·fide ▶ n. Chemistry a colorless poisonous gas with a smell of rotten eggs, made by the action of acids on sulfides. ● Chem. formula: H_2S.

hy·dro·ge·ol·o·gy /ˌhīdrəjēˈäləjē/ ▶ n. the branch of geology concerned with water occurring underground or on the surface of the earth.
– DERIVATIVES **hy·dro·ge·o·log·i·cal** /-jēəˈläjikəl/ adj., **hy·dro·ge·ol·o·gist** /-jist/ n.

hy·drog·ra·phy /hīˈdrägrəfē/ ▶ n. the science of surveying and charting bodies of water, such as seas, lakes, and rivers.
– DERIVATIVES **hy·drog·ra·pher** /-fər/ n., **hy·dro·graph·ic** /ˌhīdrəˈgrafik/ adj., **hy·dro·graph·i·cal** /ˌhīdrəˈgrafikəl/ adj., **hy·dro·graph·i·cal·ly** /ˌhīdrəˈgrafik(ə)lē/ adv.

hy·droid /ˈhīˌdroid/ Zoology ▶ n. a coelenterate of an order that includes the hydras. They are distinguished by the dominance of the polyp phase. ● Order Hydroida, class Hydrozoa.
▶ adj. of or relating to coelenterates of this group. ■ another term for POLYPOID (sense 1).
– ORIGIN mid 19th cent.: from HYDRA + -OID.

hy·dro·lase /ˈhīdrəˌlās, -ˌlāz/ ▶ n. [usu. with modifier] Biochemistry an enzyme that catalyzes the hydrolysis of a particular substrate.

hy·drol·o·gy /hīˈdräləjē/ ▶ n. the branch of science concerned with the properties of the earth's water, esp. its movement in relation to land.
– DERIVATIVES **hy·dro·log·ic** /ˌhīdrəˈläjik/ adj., **hy·dro·log·i·cal** /ˌhīdrəˈläjikəl/ adj., **hy·dro·log·i·cal·ly** /ˌhīdrəˈläjik(ə)lē/ adv., **hy·drol·o·gist** /-jist/ n.

hy·drol·y·sate /hīˈdräləˌsāt/ ▶ n. Chemistry a substance produced by hydrolysis.

hy·drol·y·sis /hīˈdräləsis/ ▶ n. Chemistry the chemical breakdown of a compound due to reaction with water.
– DERIVATIVES **hy·dro·lyt·ic** /ˌhīdrəˈlitik/ adj.

hy·dro·lyze /ˈhīdrəˌlīz/ (Brit. **hydrolyse**) ▶ v. [with obj.] Chemistry break down (a compound) by chemical reaction with water. ■ [no obj.] undergo this process.

hy·dro·mag·net·ics /ˌhīdrōmagˈnetiks/ ▶ plural n. another term for MAGNETOHYDRODYNAMICS.
– DERIVATIVES **hy·dro·mag·net·ic** adj.

hy·dro·man·cy /ˈhīdrəˌmansē/ ▶ n. divination by means of signs derived from the appearance of water and its movements.

hy·dro·mas·sage /ˌhīdrōməˈsäzH, -ˈsäj/ ▶ n. massage using jets of water, as a health or beauty treatment.

hy·dro·me·chan·ics /ˌhīdrōməˈkaniks/ ▶ plural n. [treated as sing.] the mechanics of liquids; hydrodynamics, esp. in relation to mechanical applications.
– DERIVATIVES **hy·dro·me·chan·i·cal** /-ˈkanikəl/ adj.

hy·dro·me·du·sa /ˌhīdrōməˈd(y)o͞osə, -zə/ ▶ n. (pl. **hydromedusae** /-ˌsē, -ˌzē/) Zoology the medusoid phase of a hydroid coelenterate.

hy·dro·mel /ˈhīdrəˌmel/ ▶ n. historical a drink similar to mead, made with fermented honey and water.
– ORIGIN late Middle English: from Latin, from Greek *hudromeli*, from *hudro-* 'water' + *meli* 'honey.'

hy·dro·me·te·or /ˌhīdrōˈmētēər/ ▶ n. Meteorology an atmospheric phenomenon or entity involving water or water vapor, such as rain or a cloud.

hy·drom·e·ter /hīˈdrämitər/ ▶ n. an instrument for measuring the density of liquids.
– DERIVATIVES **hy·dro·met·ric** /ˌhīdrəˈmetrik/ adj., **hy·drom·e·try** /-itrē/ n.

hy·dron·ic /hīˈdränik/ ▶ adj. denoting a cooling or heating system in which heat is transported using circulating water.

hy·dro·ni·um i·on /hīˈdrōnēəm/ ▶ n. Chemistry the ion H_3O^+, consisting of a protonated water molecule and present in all aqueous acids.
– ORIGIN early 20th cent.: *hydronium*, from German (a contraction).

hy·drop·a·thy /hīˈdräpəTHē/ ▶ n. the treatment of illness through the use of water, either internally or through external means such as steam baths (not now a part of orthodox medicine). Compare with HYDROTHERAPY.
– DERIVATIVES **hy·dro·path·ic** /ˌhīdrəˈpaTHik/ adj., **hy·drop·a·thist** /-THist/ n.
– ORIGIN mid 19th cent.: from HYDRO- 'of water,' on the pattern of *allopathy* and *homeopathy*.

hy·dro·phil·ic /ˌhīdrəˈfilik/ ▶ adj. having a tendency to mix with, dissolve in, or be wetted by water. The opposite of HYDROPHOBIC.
– DERIVATIVES **hy·dro·phi·lic·i·ty** /-fəˈlisitē/ n.

hy·droph·i·lous /hīˈdräfələs/ ▶ adj. Botany (of a plant) water-pollinated.
– DERIVATIVES **hy·droph·i·ly** /-ˈdräfəlē/ n.

hy·dro·pho·bi·a /ˌhīdrəˈfōbēə/ ▶ n. extreme or irrational fear of water, esp. as a symptom of rabies in humans. ■ rabies, esp. in humans.
– ORIGIN late Middle English: via late Latin from Greek *hudrophobia*, from *hudro-* 'water' + *phobos* 'fear.'

hy·dro·pho·bic /ˌhīdrəˈfōbik/ ▶ adj. **1** tending to repel or fail to mix with water. The opposite of HYDROPHILIC.
2 of or suffering from hydrophobia.
– DERIVATIVES **hy·dro·pho·bic·i·ty** /-fōˈbisitē/ n.

hy·dro·phone /ˈhīdrəˌfōn/ ▶ n. a microphone that detects sound waves under water.

hy·dro·phyte /ˈhīdrəˌfīt/ ▶ n. Botany a plant that grows only in or on water.
– DERIVATIVES **hy·dro·phyt·ic** /ˌhīdrəˈfitik/ adj.

hy·dro·plane /ˈhīdrəˌplān/ ▶ n. **1** a light fast motorboat designed to skim over the surface of water.
2 a finlike attachment that enables a moving submarine to rise or fall in the water.
3 a seaplane.
▶ v. [no obj.] (of a vehicle) slide uncontrollably on the wet surface of a road: *a motorist whose car hydroplaned and crashed into a tree.*

hy·dro·pon·ics /ˌhīdrəˈpäniks/ ▶ plural n. [treated as sing.] the process of growing plants in sand, gravel, or liquid, with added nutrients but without soil.
– DERIVATIVES **hy·dro·pon·ic** adj., **hy·dro·pon·i·cal·ly** /-ˈpänik(ə)lē/ adv.
– ORIGIN 1930s: from HYDRO- 'of water' + Greek *ponos* 'labor' + -ICS.

hy·dro·pow·er /ˈhīdrəˌpouər/ ▶ n. hydroelectric power.

hy·dro·qui·none /ˌhīdrōkwiˈnōn, -ˈkwinˌōn/ ▶ n. Chemistry a crystalline compound made by the reduction of benzoquinone. ● Alternative name: **benzene-1,4-diol**; chem. formula: $C_6H_4(OH)_2$.

hy·dro·sphere /ˈhīdrəˌsfir/ ▶ n. (usu. **the hydrosphere**) all the waters on the earth's surface, such as lakes and seas, and sometimes including water over the earth's surface, such as clouds.

hy·dro·stat·ic /ˌhīdrəˈstatik/ ▶ adj. relating to or denoting the equilibrium of liquids and the pressure exerted by liquid at rest.
– DERIVATIVES **hy·dro·stat·i·cal** adj., **hy·dro·stat·i·cal·ly** /ik(ə)lē/ adv.
– ORIGIN late 17th cent.: probably from Greek *hudrostatēs* 'hydrostatic balance,' from *hudro-* 'water' + *statikos* (see STATIC).

hy·dro·stat·ics /ˌhīdrəˈstatiks/ ▶ plural n. [treated as sing.] the branch of mechanics concerned with the hydrostatic properties of liquids.

hy·dro·sul·fite /ˌhīdrōˈsəlˌfīt/ ▶ n. another term for DITHIONITE.

hy·dro·ther·a·py /ˌhīdrəˈTHerəpē/ ▶ n. another term for HYDROPATHY. ■ the use of exercises in a pool as part of treatment for conditions such as arthritis or partial paralysis.
– DERIVATIVES **hy·dro·ther·a·pist** /-pist/ n.

hy·dro·ther·mal /ˌhīdrəˈTHərməl/ ▶ adj. of, relating to, or denoting the action of heated water in the earth's crust.
– DERIVATIVES **hy·dro·ther·mal·ly** adv.

hy·dro·ther·mal vent ▶ n. an opening in the sea floor out of which heated mineral-rich water flows.

hy·dro·tho·rax /ˌhīdrəˈTHôˌraks/ ▶ n. the condition of having fluid in the pleural cavity.

hy·drot·ro·pism /hīˈdrätrəˌpizəm/ ▶ n. Botany the growth or turning of plant roots toward or away from moisture.

hy·drous /ˈhīdrəs/ ▶ adj. chiefly Chemistry & Geology containing water as a constituent: *a hydrous lava flow.*
– ORIGIN early 19th cent.: from Greek *hudro-* 'water' + -OUS.

hy·drox·ide /hīˈdräkˌsīd/ ▶ n. Chemistry a compound of a metal with the hydroxide ion OH^- (as in many alkalis) or the group –OH.

hy·drox·o·ni·um i·on /ˌhīdräkˈsōnēəm/ ▶ n. Chemistry another term for HYDRONIUM ION.
– ORIGIN 1920s: *hydroxonium* from HYDRO- (relating to hydrogen) + OXY-[2] + the suffix *-onium* (from AMMONIUM).

hydroxy- ▶ comb. form Chemistry representing HYDROXYL or HYDROXIDE: *hydroxyapatite.*

hy·drox·y·a·pa·tite /hīˌdräksēˈapəˌtīt/ ▶ n. a mineral of the apatite group that is the main inorganic constituent of tooth enamel and bone, although it is rare in rocks.

hy·drox·yl /hīˈdräksəl/ ▶ n. [as modifier] Chemistry of or denoting the radical –OH, present in alcohols and many other organic compounds: *a hydroxyl group.*
– ORIGIN mid 19th cent.: from a blend of HYDROGEN and OXYGEN, + -YL.

hy·drox·yl·ate /hīdräksəˌlāt/ ▶ v. [with obj.] (often as adj. **hydroxylated**) Chemistry introduce a hydroxyl group into (a molecule or compound).
– DERIVATIVES **hy·drox·y·la·tion** /hīˌdräksəˈlāSHən/ n.

Hy·dro·zo·a /ˌhīdrəˈzōə/ Zoology a class of coelenterates that includes hydras and Portuguese men-of-war. Many of them are colonial, and some kinds have both polypoid and medusoid phases.
– ORIGIN modern Latin (plural), from HYDRO- 'water' + Greek *zōion* 'animal.'

hy·dro·zo·an /ˌhīdrəˈzōən/ Zoology ▶ n. a coelenterate of the class Hydrozoa, such as a hydra or Portuguese man-of-war. ▶ adj. relating to or denoting hydrozoans.

Hy·drus /ˈhīdrəs/ Astronomy an inconspicuous southern constellation (the Water Snake), between the star Achernar and the south celestial pole. Compare with HYDRA (sense 2). ■ (as genitive **Hydri** /-drī/) used with a preceding letter or numeral to designate a star in this constellation: *the star Delta Hydri.*
– ORIGIN Latin, from Greek *hudros.*

hy·e·na /hīˈēnə/ ▶ n. a doglike African mammal with forelimbs that are longer than the hind limbs and an erect mane. Hyenas are noted as scavengers but most are also effective hunters. ● Family

Hyaenidae: two genera, in particular *Hyaena*, and three species.
– ORIGIN Middle English: via Latin from Greek *huaina*, feminine of *hus* 'pig' (the transference of the term probably being because the animal's mane was thought to resemble a hog's bristles).

hy·giene /ˈhīˌjēn/ ▶ **n.** conditions or practices conducive to maintaining health and preventing disease, esp. through cleanliness: *poor standards of food hygiene | personal hygiene.*
– ORIGIN late 16th cent.: via French from modern Latin *hygieina*, from Greek *hugieinē* (*tekhnē*) '(art) of health,' from *hugiēs* 'healthy.'

hy·gi·en·ic /hīˈjenik, -ˈjē-/ ▶ **adj.** conducive to maintaining health and preventing disease, esp. by being clean; sanitary: *hygienic conditions.*
– DERIVATIVES **hy·gi·en·i·cal·ly** /-(ə)lē/ **adv.**

hy·gien·ist /hīˈjenəst, -jē-/ ▶ **n.** **1** a specialist in the promotion of clean conditions for the preservation of health: *an industrial hygienist.*
2 short for DENTAL HYGIENIST.

hygro- ▶ **comb. form** relating to moisture: *hygrometer.*
– ORIGIN from Greek *hugros* 'wet.'

hy·grom·e·ter /hīˈgrämitər/ ▶ **n.** an instrument for measuring the humidity of the air or a gas.
– DERIVATIVES **hy·gro·met·ric** /ˌhīgrəˈmetrik/ **adj.**, **hy·grom·e·try** /-trē/ **n.**

hy·groph·il·ous /hīˈgräfələs/ ▶ **adj.** Botany (of a plant) growing in damp conditions.

hy·gro·phyte /ˈhīgrəˌfīt/ ▶ **n.** Botany a plant that grows in wet conditions.

hy·gro·scope /ˈhīgrəˌskōp/ ▶ **n.** an instrument that gives an indication of the humidity of the air.

hy·gro·scop·ic /ˌhīgrəˈskäpik/ ▶ **adj.** (of a substance) tending to absorb moisture from the air. ■ relating to humidity or its measurement.
– DERIVATIVES **hy·gro·scop·i·cal·ly** /-(ə)lē/ **adv.**

hy·ing /ˈhī-iNG/ present participle of HIE.

Hyk·sos /ˈhikˌsäs, -ˌsōs/ ▶ **plural n.** a people of mixed Semitic and Asian descent who invaded Egypt and settled in the Nile delta *c.*1640 BC. They formed the 15th and 16th dynasties of Egypt and ruled a large part of the country until driven out *c.*1532 BC.
– ORIGIN from Greek *Huksōs* (interpreted by Manetho as 'shepherd kings' or 'captive shepherds'), from Egyptian *heqa khoswe* 'foreign rulers.'

hy·la /ˈhīlə/ ▶ **n.** a tree frog of a widespread genus, typically bright green in color. ● Genus *Hyla*, family Hylidae: many species.
– ORIGIN modern Latin, from Greek *hulē* 'timber.'

hy·lic /ˈhīlik/ ▶ **adj.** rare of matter; material. The opposite of PSYCHIC (sense 2 of the adjective).
– ORIGIN mid 19th cent.: via late Latin from Greek *hulikos*, from *hulē* 'matter.'

hylo- ▶ **comb. form** of or relating to matter: *hylozoism.*
– ORIGIN from Greek *hulē* 'matter.'

hy·lo·mor·phism /ˌhīləˈmôrˌfizəm/ ▶ **n.** Philosophy the doctrine that physical objects result from the combination of matter and form.
– DERIVATIVES **hy·lo·mor·phic** /-fik/ **adj.**
– ORIGIN late 19th cent.: from HYLO- 'matter' + Greek *morphē* 'form.'

hy·lo·zo·ism /ˌhīləˈzōˌizəm/ ▶ **n.** Philosophy the doctrine that all matter has life.
– ORIGIN late 17th cent.: from HYLO- 'matter' + Greek *zōē* 'life.'

hy·men /ˈhīmən/ ▶ **n.** a membrane that partially closes the opening of the vagina and whose presence is traditionally taken to be a mark of virginity.
– DERIVATIVES **hy·men·al** /ˈhīmənl/ **adj.**
– ORIGIN mid 16th cent.: via late Latin from Greek *humēn* 'membrane.'

hy·me·ne·al /ˌhīməˈnēəl/ ▶ **adj.** literary of or concerning marriage.
– ORIGIN early 17th cent.: from Latin *hymenaeus*, from *Hymen* (from Greek *Humēn*), the name of the god of marriage, + -AL.

hy·me·ni·um /hīˈmēnēəm/ ▶ **n.** (pl. **hymenia** /-nēə/) Botany (in higher fungi) a surface consisting mainly of spore-bearing structures (asci or basidia).
– DERIVATIVES **hy·me·ni·al** /-nēəl/ **adj.**
– ORIGIN early 19th cent.: from Greek *humenion*, diminutive of *humēn* 'membrane.'

Hy·me·nop·ter·a /ˌhīməˈnäptərə/ Entomology a large order of insects that includes the bees, wasps, ants, and sawflies. These insects have four transparent wings and the females often have a sting. ■ (as plural noun **hymenoptera**) insects of this order.
– ORIGIN modern Latin (plural), from Greek *humenopteros* 'membrane-winged,' from *humēn* 'membrane' + *pteron* 'wing.'

hy·me·nop·ter·an /ˌhīməˈnäptərən/ Entomology ▶ **n.** an insect of the order Hymenoptera, such as a bee, wasp, or ant.
▶ **adj.** relating to or denoting hymenopterans.
– DERIVATIVES **hy·me·nop·ter·ous** /-tərəs/ **adj.**

Hy·mie /ˈhīmē/ ▶ **n.** informal, offensive a Jewish person.
– ORIGIN 1980s: colloquial abbreviation of the Jewish male given name *Hyman*.

hymn /him/ ▶ **n.** a religious song or poem, typically of praise to God or a god: *a Hellenistic hymn to Apollo.* ■ a formal song sung during Christian worship, typically by the whole congregation. ■ a song, text, or other composition praising or celebrating someone or something: *a most unusual passage like a hymn to the great outdoors.*
▶ **v. 1** [with obj.] praise or celebrate (something): *Johnson's reply hymns education.*
2 [no obj.] rare sing hymns.
– DERIVATIVES **hym·nic** /ˈhimnik/ **adj.**
– ORIGIN Old English, via Latin from Greek *humnos* 'ode or song in praise of a god or hero,' used in the Septuagint to translate various Hebrew words, and hence in the New Testament and other Christian writings.

hym·nal /ˈhimnəl/ ▶ **n.** a book of hymns.
▶ **adj.** of hymns: *hymnal music.*
– ORIGIN late 15th cent.: from medieval Latin *hymnale*, from Latin *hymnus* (see HYMN).

hym·na·ry /ˈhimnərē/ ▶ **n.** (pl. **hymnaries**) another term for HYMNAL.

hym·no·dy /ˈhimnədē/ ▶ **n.** the singing or composition of hymns.
– DERIVATIVES **hym·no·dist** /-dist/ **n.**
– ORIGIN early 18th cent.: via medieval Latin from Greek *humnōidia*, from *humnos* 'hymn.'

hym·nog·ra·pher /himˈnägrəfər/ ▶ **n.** a writer of hymns.
– DERIVATIVES **hym·nog·ra·phy** /-ˈnägrəfē/ **n.**
– ORIGIN early 17th cent.: from Greek *humnographos*, from *humnos* 'hymn' + *graphos* 'writer.'

hym·nol·o·gy /himˈnäləjē/ ▶ **n.** the study or composition of hymns.
– DERIVATIVES **hym·no·log·i·cal** /ˌhimnəˈläjikəl/ **adj.**, **hym·nol·o·gist** /-jist/ **n.**
– ORIGIN mid 17th cent.: originally from Greek *humnologia* 'hymn-singing,' the early sense until the mid 19th cent.

hy·oid /ˈhīˌoid/ Anatomy & Zoology ▶ **n.** (also **hyoid bone**) a U-shaped bone in the neck that supports the tongue.
▶ **adj.** of or relating to this bone or structures associated with it.
– ORIGIN early 19th cent.: via French from modern Latin *hyoïdes*, from Greek *huoeidēs* 'shaped like the letter upsilon (υ).'

hy·os·cine /ˈhīəˌsēn/ ▶ **n.** another term for SCOPOLAMINE.
– ORIGIN late 19th cent.: from modern Latin *hyoscyamus* (see HYOSCYAMINE) + -INE[4].

hy·os·cy·a·mine /ˌhīəˈsīəmin, -ˌmēn/ ▶ **n.** Chemistry a poisonous compound present in henbane, with similar properties to hyoscine. ● Chem. formula: $C_{17}H_{23}NO_3$.
– ORIGIN mid 19th cent.: from modern Latin *hyoscyamus* (from Greek *huoskuamos* 'henbane,' from *hus, huos* 'pig' + *kuamos* 'bean') + -INE[4].

hyp. ▶ **abbr.** ■ hypotenuse. ■ hypothesis or hypothetical.

hyp- ▶ **comb. form** variant spelling of HYPO- shortened before a vowel or *h* (as in *hypesthesia*).

hyp·aes·the·sia ▶ **n.** British spelling of HYPESTHESIA.

hy·pae·thral ▶ **adj.** variant spelling of HYPETHRAL.

hy·pal·la·ge /hīˈpaləjē, hi-/ ▶ **n.** Rhetoric a transposition of the natural relations of two elements in a proposition, for example in the sentence "Melissa shook her doubtful curls."
– ORIGIN late 16th cent.: via late Latin from Greek *hupallagē*, from *hupo* 'under' + *allassein* 'to exchange.'

hy·pa·lon /ˈhīpəˌlän/ (also trademark **Hypalon**) ▶ **n.** a kind of synthetic rubber made of chlorinated and sulfonated polyethylene.
– ORIGIN mid 20th cent.: of unknown origin.

hy·pan·thi·um /hīˈpanTHēəm, hi-/ ▶ **n.** (pl. **hypanthia** /-THēə/) Botany a cuplike or tubular enlargement of the receptacle of a flower, loosely surrounding the gynoecium or united with it.

Hy·pa·tia /hīˈpāSHə, -patēə/ (*c.*370–415), Greek philosopher, astronomer, and mathematician. She was the head of the Neoplatonist school in Alexandria and was famous for her eloquence and learning. She was murdered by a mob of Christians incited by Cyril, the bishop of Alexandria.

hype[1] /hīp/ informal ▶ **n.** extravagant or intensive publicity or promotion: *she relied on hype and headlines to stoke up interest in her music.* ■ a deception carried out for the sake of publicity.
▶ **v.** [with obj.] promote or publicize (a product or idea) intensively, often exaggerating its importance or benefits: *an industry quick to hype its products.*
– ORIGIN 1920s (originally in the sense 'shortchange, cheat,' or 'person who cheats, etc'): of unknown origin.

hype[2] informal ▶ **n.** a hypodermic needle or injection. ■ a drug addict.
▶ **v.** [with obj.] (usu. **be hyped up**) stimulate or excite (someone): *I was hyped up because I wanted to do well.*
– ORIGIN 1920s (originally US): abbreviation of HYPODERMIC.

hy·per /ˈhīpər/ ▶ **adj.** informal hyperactive or unusually energetic: *eating sugar makes you hyper.*
– ORIGIN 1940s: abbreviation of HYPERACTIVE.

hyper- ▶ **prefix 1** over; beyond; above: *hypernym.* ■ exceeding: *hypersonic.* ■ excessively; above normal: *hyperthyroidism.*
2 relating to hypertext: *hyperlink.*
– ORIGIN from Greek *huper* 'over, beyond.'

hy·per·ac·tive /ˌhīpərˈaktiv/ ▶ **adj.** abnormally or extremely active: *a hyperactive pituitary gland.* ■ (of a child) showing constantly active and sometimes disruptive behavior.
– DERIVATIVES **hy·per·ac·tiv·i·ty** /-ˌakˈtivitē/ **n.**

hy·per·ae·mi·a ▶ **n.** British spelling of HYPEREMIA.

hy·per·aes·the·sia ▶ **n.** British spelling of HYPERESTHESIA.

hy·per·al·ge·si·a /ˌhīpəralˈjēzēə, -ˈjēsēə/ ▶ **n.** Medicine abnormally heightened sensitivity to pain.
– DERIVATIVES **hy·per·al·ge·sic** /-ˈjēzik, -ˈjēsik/ **adj.**

hy·per·al·i·men·ta·tion /ˌhīpərˌaləmənˈtāSHən/ ▶ **n.** Medicine artificial supply of nutrients, typically intravenously.

hy·per·bar·ic /ˌhīpərˈbarik/ ▶ **adj.** of or involving a gas at a pressure greater than normal.
– ORIGIN 1960s: from HYPER- 'above normal' + Greek *baros* 'heavy.'

hy·per·ba·ton /hīˈpərbəˌtän/ ▶ **n.** Rhetoric an inversion of the normal order of words, esp. for the sake of emphasis, as in the sentence "*this I must see.*"
– ORIGIN mid 16th cent.: via Latin from Greek *huperbaton* 'overstepping' (from *huper* 'over, above' + *bainein* 'go, walk').

hy·per·bo·la /hīˈpərbələ/ ▶ **n.** (pl. **hyperbolas** or **hyperbolae** /-bəlē/) a symmetrical open curve formed by the intersection of a circular cone with a plane at a smaller angle with its axis than the side of the cone. ■ Mathematics the pair of such curves formed by the intersection of a plane with two equal cones on opposites of the same vertex.
– ORIGIN mid 17th cent.: modern Latin, from Greek *huperbolē* 'excess' (from *huper* 'above' + *ballein* 'to throw').

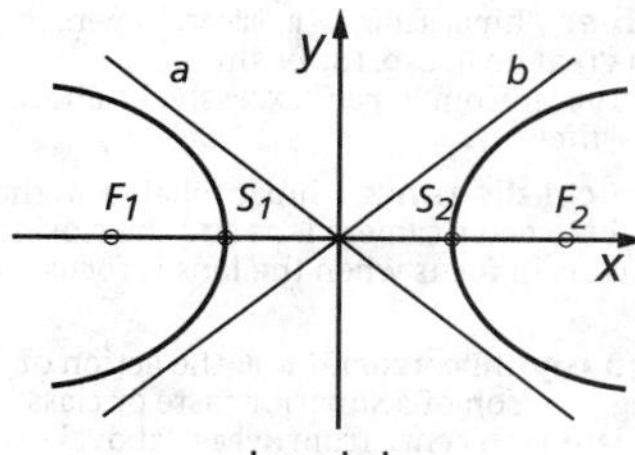

hyperbola

hy·per·bo·le /hīˈpərbəlē/ ▶ **n.** exaggerated statements or claims not meant to be taken literally.
– DERIVATIVES **hy·per·bol·i·cal** /ˌhīpərˈbälikəl/ **adj.**, **hy·per·bol·i·cal·ly** /ˌhīpərˈbälik(ə)lē/ **adv.**, **hy·per·bo·lism** /-ˌlizəm/ **n.**
– ORIGIN late Middle English: via Latin from Greek *huperbolē* (see HYPERBOLA).

hy·per·bol·ic /ˌhīpərˈbälik/ ▶ **adj. 1** of or relating to a hyperbola. ■ Mathematics (of a function, e.g., a cosine) having the same relation to a rectangular hyperbola as the unqualified function does to a circle.
2 (of language) exaggerated; hyperbolical.

hy·per·bol·ic pa·rab·o·loid ▶ **n.** Mathematics a surface whose section parallel to one properly oriented coordinate plane is a hyperbola and whose

PRONUNCIATION KEY ə *ago, up*; ər *over, fur*; a *hat*; ā *ate*; ä *car*; e *let*; ē *see*; i *fit*; ī *by*; NG *sing*; ō *go*; ô *law, for*; oi *toy*; o͝o *good*; o͞o *goo*; ou *out*; TH *thin*; T͟H *then*; ZH *vision*

sections parallel to the other two coordinate planes are parabolas.

hy·per·bo·loid /hī'pərbə,loid/ ▶ **n.** a solid or surface having plane sections that are hyperbolas, ellipses, or circles.
– DERIVATIVES **hy·per·bo·loi·dal** /hī,pərbə'loidl/ **adj.**

hy·per·bo·re·an /,hīpər'bôrēən, -bə'rēən/ literary ▶ **n.** an inhabitant of the extreme north. ■ (**Hyperborean**) Greek Mythology a member of a race worshiping Apollo and living in a land of sunshine and plenty beyond the north wind.
▶ **adj.** of or relating to the extreme north.
– ORIGIN late Middle English: from late Latin *hyperboreanus*, from Greek *huperboreos*, from *huper* 'beyond' + *boreas* 'north wind.'

hy·per·cap·ni·a /,hīpər'kapnēə/ ▶ **n.** Pathology excessive carbon dioxide in the bloodstream, typically caused by inadequate respiration.

hy·per·cho·les·ter·ol·e·mi·a /,hīpərkə,lestərə'lēmēə/ (Brit. **hypercholesterolaemia**) ▶ **n.** Medicine an excess of cholesterol in the bloodstream.
– ORIGIN late 19th cent.: from **HYPER-** 'above normal' + **CHOLESTEROL** + **-EMIA**.

hy·per·con·scious /,hīpər'känsHəs/ ▶ **adj.** acutely or excessively aware: *placing so much emphasis on willpower as to become hyperconscious, if not sometimes even inhibited.*

hy·per·cor·rec·tion /,hīpərkə'reksHən/ ▶ **n.** the erroneous use of a word form or pronunciation based on a false analogy with a correct or prestigious form, such as *between you and I* for the standard *between you and me*.
– DERIVATIVES **hy·per·cor·rect** /-'rekt/ **adj.**

hy·per·crit·i·cal /,hīpər'kritikəl/ ▶ **adj.** excessively and unreasonably critical, esp. of small faults.
– DERIVATIVES **hy·per·crit·i·cal·ly** /-ik(ə)lē/ **adv.**

hy·per·cube /'hīpər,kyo͞ob/ ▶ **n.** a geometric figure in four or more dimensions that is analogous to a cube in three dimensions.

hy·per·drive /'hīpər,drīv/ ▶ **n.** (in science fiction) a propulsion system for travel in hyperspace.

hy·per·e·mi·a /,hīpə'rēmēə/ (Brit. **hyperaemia**) ▶ **n.** Medicine an excess of blood in the vessels supplying an organ or other part of the body.
– DERIVATIVES **hy·per·e·mic** /-'rēmik/ **adj.**
– ORIGIN mid 19th cent.: from **HYPER-** 'above normal' + **-EMIA**.

hy·per·es·the·sia /,hīpərəs'THēZHə/ (Brit. **hyperaesthesia**) ▶ **n.** Medicine excessive physical sensitivity, esp. of the skin.
– DERIVATIVES **hy·per·es·thet·ic** /-'THetik/ **adj.**
– ORIGIN mid 19th cent.: from **HYPER-** 'above normal' + Greek *aisthēsis* 'sensation.'

hy·per·ex·tend /,hīpərik'stend/ ▶ **v.** [with obj.] forcefully extend (a limb or joint) beyond its normal limits, either in exercise or therapy or so as to cause injury.
– DERIVATIVES **hy·per·ex·ten·sion** /-'stensHən/ **n.**

hy·per·fli·er /'hīpər,flīər/ ▶ **n.** informal a person who travels a great deal, esp. for business.
– ORIGIN 1990s: from *hyper-* 'excessively, above normal' + *flier*.

hy·per·fo·cal dis·tance /,hīpər'fōkəl/ ▶ **n.** the distance between a camera lens and the closest object that is in focus when the lens is focused at infinity.

hy·per·ga·my /hī'pərgəmē/ ▶ **n.** the action of marrying a person of a superior caste or class.
– ORIGIN late 19th cent.: from **HYPER-** 'above' + Greek *gamos* 'marriage.'

hy·per·gly·ce·mi·a /,hīpərglī'sēmēə/ (Brit. **hyperglycaemia**) ▶ **n.** Medicine an excess of glucose in the bloodstream, often associated with diabetes mellitus.
– DERIVATIVES **hy·per·gly·ce·mic** /-'sēmik/ **adj.**
– ORIGIN late 19th cent.: from **HYPER-** 'above normal' + **GLYCO-** + **-EMIA**.

hy·per·gol·ic /,hīpər'gälik/ ▶ **adj.** (of a rocket propellant) igniting spontaneously on mixing with another substance.
– ORIGIN 1940s: from German *Hypergol*, probably from **HYPER-** 'beyond' + Greek *ergon* 'work' + **-OL**.

hy·per·i·cin /hī'perəsin/ ▶ **n.** a substance found in St. John's wort, credited with chemical and pharmacological properties similar to those of antidepressants. ● A polycyclic quinone; chem. formula: $C_{30}H_{14}O_8$.
– ORIGIN early 20th cent.: from *hypericum* 'a yellow-flowered plant' + *-in*, chemical suffix.

hy·per·i·cum /hī'perikəm/ ▶ **n.** a yellow-flowered plant of a genus that includes the St. John's worts and rose of Sharon. ● Genus *Hypericum*, family Guttiferae.
– ORIGIN Latin, from Greek *hupereikon*, from *huper* 'over, above' + *ereikē* 'heath.'

hy·per·im·mune /,hīpəri'myo͞on/ ▶ **adj.** Medicine having a high concentration of antibodies produced in reaction to repeated injections of an antigen.
– DERIVATIVES **hy·per·im·mu·nized** /-'imyə,nīzd/ **adj.**

hy·per·in·fla·tion /hīpərin'flāsHən/ ▶ **n.** monetary inflation occurring at a very high rate.

hy·per·in·stru·ment /'hīpər,instrəmənt/ ▶ **n.** a musical instrument designed or adapted to be used with electronic sensors whose output controls the computerized generation or transformation of the sound.

Hy·pe·ri·on /hī'pi(ə)rēən/ Astronomy a satellite of Saturn, the sixteenth closest to the planet, discovered in 1848. It has an irregular shape, with a diameter of 159 miles (255 km).
– ORIGIN named after a Titan of Greek mythology.

hy·per·ker·a·to·sis /,hīpər,kerə'tōsis/ ▶ **n.** Medicine abnormal thickening of the outer layer of the skin.

hy·per·ki·ne·sis /,hīpərki'nēsis/ (also **hyperkinesia** /-'nēZHə/) ▶ **n. 1** Medicine muscle spasm.
2 Psychiatry a disorder of children marked by hyperactivity and inability to concentrate.
– ORIGIN mid 19th cent.: from **HYPER-** 'above normal' + Greek *kinēsis* 'motion.'

hy·per·ki·net·ic /,hīpərkə'netik/ ▶ **adj.** frenetic; hyperactive. ■ of or affected with hyperkinesis.

hy·per·link /'hīpər,liNGk/ Computing ▶ **n.** a link from a hypertext file or document to another location or file, typically activated by clicking on a highlighted word or image on the screen.
▶ **v.** [with obj.] link (a file) in this way: *thumbnail images that are hyperlinked to a larger image.*

hy·per·li·pe·mi·a /,hīpərlə'pēmēə/ (Brit. **hyperlipaemia**) ▶ **n.** another term for **HYPERLIPIDEMIA**.
– DERIVATIVES **hy·per·li·pe·mic** /-'pēmik/ **adj.**

hy·per·lip·i·de·mi·a /,hīpər,lipi'dēmēə/ (Brit. **hyperlipidaemia**) ▶ **n.** Medicine an abnormally high concentration of fats or lipids in the blood.
– DERIVATIVES **hy·per·lip·i·de·mic** /-'dēmik/ **adj.**

hy·per·mar·ket /'hīpər,märkit/ ▶ **n.** chiefly Brit. a very large store with a wide range of goods and a large parking lot, typically situated outside a town.
– ORIGIN 1970s: translation of French *hypermarché*, from **HYPER-** 'beyond, exceeding' + *marché* 'market.'

hy·per·me·di·a /,hīpər'mēdēə/ ▶ **n.** Computing an extension to hypertext providing multimedia facilities, such as those handling sound and video.
– ORIGIN 1960s: from **HYPER-** 'above, beyond' + **MEDIA**[1].

hy·per·me·tro·pi·a /,hīpərmə'trōpēə/ ▶ **n.** another term for **HYPEROPIA**.
– DERIVATIVES **hy·per·me·tro·pic** /-'träpik, -'trō-/ **adj.**
– ORIGIN mid 19th cent.: from Greek *hupermetros* 'beyond measure' (from *huper* 'over, above' + *metron* 'measure') + *ōps* 'eye.'

hy·per·mil·ing /'hīpər,mīliNG/ ▶ **n.** the practice of making adjustments to a vehicle or using driving techniques that will maximize the vehicle's fuel economy.
– DERIVATIVES **hy·per·mil·er n.**

hy·perm·ne·sia /,hīpərm'nēZHə/ ▶ **n.** unusual power or enhancement of memory, typically under abnormal conditions such as trauma, hypnosis, or narcosis.

hy·per·mu·ta·ble /,hīpər'myo͞otəbəl/ ▶ **adj.** Genetics of or in a state in which mutation is abnormally frequent.
– DERIVATIVES **hy·per·mu·ta·tion** /-myo͞o'tāsHən/ **n.**

hy·per·nym /'hīpər,nim/ ▶ **n.** a word with a broad meaning that more specific words fall under; a superordinate. For example, *color* is a hypernym of *red*. Contrasted with **HYPONYM**.
– ORIGIN 1970s: from **HYPER-** 'beyond,' on the pattern of *hyponym*.

hy·per·on /'hīpə,rän/ ▶ **n.** Physics an unstable subatomic particle classified as a baryon, heavier than the neutron and proton.
– ORIGIN 1950s: from **HYPER-** 'beyond, over' + **-ON**.

hy·per·o·pi·a /,hīpə'rōpēə/ ▶ **n.** farsightedness.
– DERIVATIVES **hy·per·op·ic** /-'räpik/ **adj.**
– ORIGIN late 19th cent.: from **HYPER-** 'beyond' + Greek *ōps* 'eye.'

hy·per·par·a·site /,hīpər'parə,sīt/ ▶ **n.** Biology a parasite whose host is itself a parasite.
– DERIVATIVES **hy·per·par·a·sit·ic** /-,parə'sitik/ **adj.**, **hy·per·par·a·sit·ism** /-sī,tizəm, -si-/ **n.**

hy·per·par·a·thy·roid·ism /,hīpər,parə'THīroi,dizəm/ ▶ **n.** Medicine an abnormally high concentration of parathyroid hormone in the blood, resulting in weakening of the bones through loss of calcium.
– DERIVATIVES **hy·per·par·a·thy·roid adj.**

hy·per·phys·i·cal /,hīpər'fizikəl/ ▶ **adj.** supernatural.
– DERIVATIVES **hy·per·phys·i·cal·ly** /-ik(ə)lē/ **adv.**

hy·per·pla·sia /,hīpər'plāZHə/ ▶ **n.** Medicine & Biology the enlargement of an organ or tissue caused by an increase in the reproduction rate of its cells, often as an initial stage in the development of cancer.
– ORIGIN mid 19th cent.: from **HYPER-** 'beyond' + Greek *plasis* 'formation.'

hy·per·re·al /,hīpə(r)'rēəl/ ▶ **adj. 1** exaggerated in comparison to reality.
2 (of artistic representation) extremely realistic in detail.
– DERIVATIVES **hy·per·re·al·ism** /-,lizəm/ **n.**, **hy·per·re·al·ist** /-ist/ **adj.**, **hy·per·re·al·is·tic** /,hīpə(r),rēə'listik/ **adj.**, **hy·per·re·al·i·ty** /,hīpə(r),rē'alitē/ **n.**

hy·per·sen·si·tive /,hīpər'sensitiv/ ▶ **adj.** abnormally or excessively sensitive, either psychologically or in physical response.
– DERIVATIVES **hy·per·sen·si·tive·ness n.**, **hy·per·sen·si·tiv·i·ty** /-,sensi'tivitē/ **n.**

hy·per·son·ic /,hīpər'sänik/ ▶ **adj. 1** relating to speeds of more than five times the speed of sound (Mach 5).
2 relating to sound frequencies above about a thousand million hertz.
– DERIVATIVES **hy·per·son·i·cal·ly** /-ik(ə)lē/ **adv.**
– ORIGIN 1930s (sense 2): from **HYPER-** 'beyond, exceeding,' on the pattern of *supersonic* and *ultrasonic*.

hy·per·space /'hīpər,spās/ ▶ **n.** space of more than three dimensions. ■ (in science fiction) a notional space-time continuum in which it is possible to travel faster than light.
– DERIVATIVES **hy·per·spa·tial** /,hīpər'spāsHəl/ **adj.**

hy·per·sphere /'hīpər,sfi(ə)r/ ▶ **n.** a sphere that exhibits more than three dimensions.

hy·per·sthene /'hīpər,sTHēn/ ▶ **n.** a greenish rock-forming mineral of the orthopyroxene class, consisting of a magnesium iron silicate.
– ORIGIN early 19th cent.: coined in French, from **HYPER-** 'exceeding' + Greek *sthenos* 'strength' (because it is harder than hornblende).

hy·per·ten·sion /,hīpər'tensHən/ ▶ **n.** Medicine abnormally high blood pressure. ■ a state of great psychological stress.

hy·per·ten·sive /,hīpər'tensiv/ ▶ **adj.** exhibiting hypertension.
▶ **n.** Medicine a person with high blood pressure.

hy·per·text /'hīpər,tekst/ ▶ **n.** Computing a software system that links topics on the screen to related information and graphics, which are typically accessed by a point-and-click method. ■ a document presented on a computer in this way.

hy·per·ther·mi·a /,hīpər'THərmēə/ ▶ **n.** Medicine the condition of having a body temperature greatly above normal.
– DERIVATIVES **hy·per·ther·mic** /-'THərmik/ **adj.**
– ORIGIN late 19th cent.: from **HYPER-** 'beyond' + Greek *thermē* 'heat.'

hy·per·thy·roid·ism /,hīpər'THīroi,dizəm/ ▶ **n.** Medicine overactivity of the thyroid gland, resulting in a rapid heartbeat and an increased rate of metabolism. Also called **THYROTOXICOSIS**.
– DERIVATIVES **hy·per·thy·roid adj.**, **hy·per·thy·roid·ic** /-THī'roidik/ **adj.**

hy·per·ton·ic /,hīpər'tänik/ ▶ **adj.** having increased pressure or tone, in particular: ■ Biology having a higher osmotic pressure than a particular fluid, typically a body fluid or intracellular fluid. ■ Physiology of or in a state of abnormally high muscle tone.
– DERIVATIVES **hy·per·to·ni·a** /-'tōnēə/ **n.**, **hy·per·to·nic·i·ty** /,hīpərtə'nisitē/ **n.**

hy·per·tro·phy /hī'pərtrəfē/ ▶ **n.** Physiology the enlargement of an organ or tissue from the increase in size of its cells.
– DERIVATIVES **hy·per·troph·ic** /,hīpər'träfik, -'trō-/ **adj.**, **hy·per·troph·ied** /-trəfēd/ **adj.**
– ORIGIN mid 19th cent.: from **HYPER-** 'beyond, exceeding' + Greek *-trophia* 'nourishment.'

hy·per·ven·ti·late /,hīpər'ventl,āt/ ▶ **v.** [no obj.] **1** breathe or cause to breathe at an abnormally rapid rate, so increasing the rate of loss of carbon dioxide.
2 [with obj.] be or become overexcited: *it was one less thing to hyperventilate about.* ■ (as adj. **hyperventilated**) inflated or pretentious in style; overblown: *hyperventilated prose.*

– DERIVATIVES **hy·per·ven·ti·la·tion** /-ˌventl'āsʜən/ **n.**

hyp·es·the·sia /ˌhipəs'ᴛʜēzʜə, ˌhīpəs-/ (Brit. **hypaesthesia**) ▶ **n.** a diminished capacity for physical sensation, esp. of the skin.
– DERIVATIVES **hyp·es·thet·ic** /-'ᴛʜetik/ **adj.**
– ORIGIN late 19th cent.: from **HYPO-** 'below' + Greek *aisthēsis* 'sensation.'

hy·pe·thral /hi'pēᴛʜrəl, hī-/ (also **hypaethral**) ▶ **adj.** (of a classical building) having no roof; open to the sky: *the hypethral temple.*
– ORIGIN late 18th cent.: via Latin from Greek *hupaithros* (from *hupo* 'under' + *aithēr* 'air') + **-AL**.

hy·pha /'hīfə/ ▶ **n.** (pl. **hyphae** /-fē/) Botany each of the branching filaments that make up the mycelium of a fungus.
– DERIVATIVES **hy·phal adj.**
– ORIGIN mid 19th cent.: modern Latin, from Greek *huphē* 'web.'

Hyph·a·sis /'hifəsis/ ancient Greek name for **BEAS**.

hy·phen /'hīfən/ ▶ **n.** the sign (-) used to join words to indicate that they have a combined meaning or that they are linked in the grammar of a sentence (as in *pick-me-up, rock-forming*), to indicate the division of a word at the end of a line, or to indicate a missing or implied element (as in *short- and long-term*).
▶ **v.** another term for **HYPHENATE**.
– ORIGIN early 17th cent.: via late Latin from Greek *huphen* 'together,' from *hupo* 'under' + *hen* 'one.'

hy·phen·ate ▶ **v.** /'hīfəˌnāt/ [with obj.] write with a hyphen: (as adj. **hyphenated**) *a hyphenated surname.*
▶ **n.** /'hīfənit/ a person who is active in more than one occupation or sphere: *as a supreme hyphenate, she was prepared to carry a heavy load as the director-producer-star of her new film.*
– DERIVATIVES **hy·phen·a·tion** /ˌhīfə'nāsʜən/ **n.**

hy·phen·at·ed A·mer·i·can ▶ **n.** informal an American citizen who can trace their ancestry to another, specified part of the world, such as an African American or an Irish American (so called because terms like *African American* are often written with a hyphen).

hyp·na·gog·ic /ˌhipnə'gäjik, -'gō-/ (also **hypnogogic**) ▶ **adj.** Psychology of or relating to the state immediately before falling asleep.
– DERIVATIVES **hyp·na·gog·i·a n.**
– ORIGIN late 19th cent.: from French *hypnagogique*, from Greek *hupnos* 'sleep' + *agōgos* 'leading' (from *agein* 'to lead').

hypno- ▶ **comb. form** relating to sleep: *hypnopedia.* ■ relating to hypnosis: *hypnotherapy.*
– ORIGIN from Greek *hupnos* 'sleep.'

hyp·no·gog·ic a variant spelling of **HYPNAGOGIC**.
– DERIVATIVES **hyp·no·gog·i·a n.**

hyp·no·pe·di·a /ˌhipnō'pēdēə/ (Brit. **hypnopaedia**) ▶ **n.** learning by hearing while asleep or under hypnosis.

hyp·no·pho·bi·a /ˌhipnə'fōbēə/ ▶ **n.** an abnormal fear of falling asleep.
– DERIVATIVES **hyp·no·pho·bic adj.**

hyp·no·pom·pic /ˌhipnə'pämpik/ ▶ **adj.** Psychology of or relating to the state immediately preceding waking up.
– ORIGIN early 20th cent.: from Greek *hupnos* 'sleep' + *pompē* 'sending away' + **-IC**.

Hyp·nos /'hipˌnäs/ Greek Mythology the god of sleep, son of Nyx (Night).
– ORIGIN from Greek *hupnos* 'sleep.'

hyp·no·sis /hip'nōsis/ ▶ **n.** the induction of a state of consciousness in which a person apparently loses the power of voluntary action and is highly responsive to suggestion or direction. Its use in therapy, typically to recover suppressed memories or to allow modification of behavior by suggestion, has been revived but is still controversial. ■ this state of consciousness.
– ORIGIN late 19th cent.: from Greek *hupnos* 'sleep' + **-OSIS**.

hyp·no·ther·a·py /ˌhipnō'ᴛʜerəpē/ ▶ **n.** the use of hypnosis as a therapeutic technique.
– DERIVATIVES **hyp·no·ther·a·pist** /-pist/ **n.**

hyp·not·ic /hip'nätik/ ▶ **adj. 1** of, producing, or relating to hypnosis: *a hypnotic state.* ■ exerting a compelling, fascinating, or soporific effect: *her voice had a hypnotic quality.*
2 Medicine (of a drug) sleep-inducing.
▶ **n. 1** Medicine a sleep-inducing drug.
2 a person under or open to the influence of hypnotism.
– DERIVATIVES **hyp·not·i·cal·ly** /-(ə)lē/ **adv.**
– ORIGIN early 17th cent.: from French *hypnotique*, via late Latin from Greek *hupnōtikos* 'narcotic, causing sleep,' from *hupnoun* 'put to sleep,' from *hupnos* 'sleep.'

hyp·no·tism /'hipnəˌtizəm/ ▶ **n.** the study or practice of hypnosis.
– DERIVATIVES **hyp·no·tist n.**

hyp·no·tize /'hipnəˌtīz/ ▶ **v.** [with obj.] produce a state of hypnosis in (someone): *a witness had been hypnotized to enhance his memory.* ■ capture the whole attention of (someone); fascinate: *hypnotized by the rain, Eric stared across the street.*
– DERIVATIVES **hyp·no·tiz·a·ble** /-ˌtīzəbəl, ˌhipnə'tīzəbəl/ **adj.**

hy·po¹ /'hīpō/ ▶ **n.** Photography the chemical sodium thiosulphate (formerly called hyposulphite) used as a photographic fixer.
– ORIGIN mid 19th cent.: abbreviation of *hyposulphite.*

hy·po² ▶ **n.** (pl. **hypos**) informal term for **HYPODERMIC**.
– ORIGIN early 20th cent.: abbreviation.

hypo- (also **hyp-**) ▶ **prefix** under: *hypodermic.* ■ below normal: *hypoglycemia.* ■ slightly: *hypomanic.* ■ Chemistry containing an element with an unusually low valence: *hypochlorous.*
– ORIGIN from Greek *hupo* 'under.'

hy·po·al·ler·gen·ic /ˌhīpōˌalər'jenik/ ▶ **adj.** (esp. of cosmetics and textiles) relatively unlikely to cause an allergic reaction.

hy·po·blast /'hīpəˌblast/ ▶ **n.** Biology former term for **ENDODERM**.

hy·po·cal·ce·mi·a /ˌhīpōkal'sēmēə/ (Brit. **hypocalcaemia**) ▶ **n.** Medicine deficiency of calcium in the bloodstream.

hy·po·caust /'hīpəˌkôst/ ▶ **n.** a hollow space under the floor of an ancient Roman building, into which hot air was sent for heating a room or bath.
– ORIGIN from Latin *hypocaustum*, from Greek *hupokauston* 'place heated from below,' from *hupo* 'under' + *kau-* (base of *kaiein* 'to burn').

hy·po·cen·ter /'hīpəˌsentər/ ▶ **n. 1** the underground focus point of an earthquake. Compare with **EPICENTER**.
2 another term for **GROUND ZERO**.

hy·po·chlo·rous ac·id /ˌhīpə'klôrəs/ ▶ **n.** Chemistry a weak acid with oxidizing properties formed when chlorine dissolves in cold water, used in bleaching and water treatment. ● Chem. formula: HOCl.
– DERIVATIVES **hy·po·chlo·rite** /-ˌrīt/ **n.**
– ORIGIN mid 19th cent.: *hypochlorous* from **HYPO-** (denoting an element in a low valency) + **CHLORINE** + **-OUS**.

hy·po·chon·dri·a /ˌhīpə'kändrēə/ ▶ **n.** abnormal anxiety about one's health, esp. with an unwarranted fear that one has a serious disease.
– ORIGIN late Middle English (in the Greek sense): via late Latin from Greek *hupokhondria*, denoting the soft body area below the ribs, from *hupo* 'under' + *khondros* 'sternal cartilage.' Melancholy was originally thought to arise from the liver, gallbladder, spleen, etc.

hy·po·chon·dri·ac /ˌhīpə'kändrēˌak/ ▶ **n.** a person who is abnormally anxious about their health.
▶ **adj.** another term for **HYPOCHONDRIACAL**.
– ORIGIN late 16th cent.: coined in French from Greek *hupokhondriakos*, from *hupokhondria* (see **HYPOCHONDRIA**).

hy·po·chon·dri·a·cal /ˌhīpōkən'drīəkəl/ ▶ **adj.** of or affected by hypochondria.

hy·po·chon·dri·a·sis /ˌhīpōkən'drīəsis/ ▶ **n.** technical term for **HYPOCHONDRIA**.

hy·po·co·ris·tic /ˌhīpəkə'ristik/ ▶ **adj.** denoting, or of the nature of, a pet name or diminutive form of a name.
▶ **n.** a hypocoristic name or form.
– DERIVATIVES **hy·poc·o·rism** /hī'päkəˌrizəm, hi-/ **n.**
– ORIGIN mid 19th cent.: from Greek *hupokorisma*, from *hupokorizesthai* 'play the child,' from *hupo* 'under' + *korē* 'child.'

hy·po·cot·yl /'hīpəˌkätl, ˌhīpə'kätl/ ▶ **n.** Botany the part of the stem of an embryo plant beneath the stalks of the seed leaves, or cotyledons, and directly above the root.

hy·po·cre·tin /hīpə'krētn/ ▶ **n.** another name for **OREXIN**.

hy·poc·ri·sy /hi'päkrisē/ ▶ **n.** (pl. **hypocrisies**) the practice of claiming to have moral standards or beliefs to which one's own behavior does not conform; pretense.
– ORIGIN Middle English: from Old French *ypocrisie*, via ecclesiastical Latin, from Greek *hupokrisis* 'acting of a theatrical part,' from *hupokrinesthai* 'play a part, pretend,' from *hupo* 'under' + *krinein* 'decide, judge.'

hyp·o·crite /'hipəˌkrit/ ▶ **n.** a person who indulges in hypocrisy.
– ORIGIN Middle English: from Old French *ypocrite*, via ecclesiastical Latin from Greek *hupokritēs* 'actor,' from *hupokrinesthai* (see **HYPOCRISY**).

hyp·o·crit·i·cal /ˌhipə'kritikəl/ ▶ **adj.** behaving in a way that suggests one has higher standards or more noble beliefs than is the case: *we don't go to church and we thought it would be hypocritical to have him christened.*
– DERIVATIVES **hyp·o·crit·i·cal·ly** /ˌhipə'kritik(ə)lē/ **adv.**

hy·po·cy·cloid /ˌhīpə'sīˌkloid/ ▶ **n.** Mathematics the curve traced by a point on the circumference of a circle that is rolling on the interior of another circle.
– DERIVATIVES **hy·po·cy·cloi·dal** /ˌhīpə'sīˌkloidl/ **adj.**

hy·po·der·mic /ˌhīpə'dərmik/ ▶ **adj.** [attrib.] Medicine of or relating to the region immediately beneath the skin. ■ (of a needle or syringe) used to inject a drug or other substance beneath the skin. ■ (of a drug or other substance or its application) injected beneath the skin.
▶ **n.** a hypodermic syringe or injection.
– DERIVATIVES **hy·po·der·mi·cal·ly** /-(ə)lē/ **adv.**

hy·po·gas·tri·um /ˌhīpə'gastrēəm/ ▶ **n.** (pl. **hypogastria** /-trēə/) Anatomy the part of the central abdomen that is situated below the region of the stomach.
– DERIVATIVES **hy·po·gas·tric** /-trik/ **adj.**
– ORIGIN late 17th cent.: modern Latin, from Greek *hupogastrion*, from *hupo* 'under' + *gastēr* 'belly.'

hy·po·ge·al /ˌhīpə'jēəl/ (also **hypogean**) ▶ **adj.** Botany underground; subterranean. Compare with **EPIGEAL**. ■ (of seed germination) with the seed leaves remaining below the ground.
– ORIGIN late 17th cent.: via late Latin from Greek *hupogeios* (from *hupo* 'under' + *gē* 'earth') + **-AL**.

hy·po·gene /'hīpəˌjēn/ ▶ **adj.** Geology producing or occurring under the surface of the earth.
– DERIVATIVES **hy·po·gen·ic** /ˌhīpə'jenik/ **adj.**
– ORIGIN mid 19th cent.: from **HYPO-** 'under' + Greek *genēs* '-born, of a certain kind.'

hy·po·ge·um /ˌhīpə'jēəm/ ▶ **n.** (pl. **hypogea** /-'jēə/) an underground chamber.
– ORIGIN mid 17th cent.: from Latin, from Greek *hupogeion*, neuter of *hupogeios* 'underground.'

hy·po·glos·sal nerve /ˌhīpə'gläsəl/ ▶ **n.** Anatomy each of the twelfth pair of cranial nerves, supplying the muscles of the tongue.
– ORIGIN mid 19th cent.: *hypoglossal* from **HYPO-** 'under' + Greek *glōssa* 'tongue' + **-AL**.

hy·po·gly·ce·mi·a /ˌhīpōglī'sēmēə/ (Brit. **hypoglycaemia**) ▶ **n.** Medicine deficiency of glucose in the bloodstream.
– DERIVATIVES **hy·po·gly·ce·mic** /-'sēmik/ **adj.**
– ORIGIN late 19th cent.: from **HYPO-** 'below' + **GLYCO-** + **-EMIA**.

hy·po·gon·ad·ism /ˌhīpō'gōnaˌdizəm/ ▶ **n.** Medicine reduction or absence of hormone secretion or other physiological activity of the gonads (testes or ovaries).
– DERIVATIVES **hy·po·go·nad·al** /ˌhīpəˌgō'nadl/ **adj.**, **hy·po·go·nad·ic** /ˌhīpəgō'nadik/ **n. & adj.**

hy·pog·y·nous /hī'päjənəs/ ▶ **adj.** Botany (of a plant or flower) having the stamens and other floral parts situated below the carpels (or gynoecium). Compare with **EPIGYNOUS**, **PERIGYNOUS**.
– DERIVATIVES **hy·pog·y·ny** /-'päjənē/ **n.**
– ORIGIN early 19th cent.: from modern Latin *hypogynus*, from **HYPO-** 'below' + *gunē* 'woman' (used to represent 'pistil') + **-OUS**.

hy·poid /'hīˌpoid/ (also **hypoid gear**) ▶ **n.** a bevel wheel with teeth engaging with a spiral pinion mounted at right angles to the wheel's axis, used to connect nonintersecting shafts in vehicle transmissions and other mechanisms.
– ORIGIN 1920s: perhaps a contraction of **HYPERBOLOID**.

hy·po·ka·le·mi·a /ˌhīpōkā'lēmēə/ (Brit. **hypokalaemia**) ▶ **n.** Medicine deficiency of potassium in the bloodstream.
– DERIVATIVES **hy·po·ka·le·mic** /-'lēmik/ **adj.**
– ORIGIN 1940s: from **HYPO-** 'below' + modern Latin *kalium* 'potassium.'

hy·po·lim·ni·on /ˌhīpə'limnēˌän, -nēən/ ▶ **n.** (pl. **hypolimnionia** /-nēə/) the lower layer of water in a stratified lake, typically cooler than the water above and relatively stagnant.

h

– ORIGIN early 20th cent.: from **HYPO-** 'below' + Greek *limnion* (diminutive of *limnē* 'lake').

hy·po·mag·ne·se·mi·a /ˌhīpəˌmagnəˈsēmēə/ (Brit. **hypomagnesaemia**) ▶ **n.** Medicine & Veterinary Medicine deficiency of magnesium in the blood, significant in cattle as the cause of grass tetany.
– DERIVATIVES **hy·po·mag·ne·se·mic** /-ˈsēmik/ **adj.**

hy·po·ma·ni·a /ˌhīpəˈmānēə/ ▶ **n.** Psychiatry a mild form of mania, marked by elation and hyperactivity.
– DERIVATIVES **hy·po·man·ic** /-ˈmanik/ **adj.**

hy·po·nym /ˈhīpəˌnim/ ▶ **n.** a word of more specific meaning than a general or superordinate term applicable to it. For example, *spoon* is a hyponym of *cutlery*. Contrasted with **HYPERNYM**.
– DERIVATIVES **hy·pon·y·my** /hīˈpänəmē/ **n.**

hy·po·par·a·thy·roid·ism /ˌhīpōˌparəˈTHīroiˌdizəm/ ▶ **n.** Medicine diminished concentration of parathyroid hormone in the blood, which causes deficiencies of calcium and phosphorus compounds in the blood and results in muscular spasms.
– DERIVATIVES **hy·po·par·a·thy·roid adj.**

hy·poph·y·sis /hīˈpäfəsis/ ▶ **n.** (pl. **hypophyses** /-ˌsēz/) Anatomy technical term for **PITUITARY**.
– DERIVATIVES **hy·po·phys·e·al** /ˌhīpəˈfizēəl, hīˌpäfəˈsēəl/ (also **hypophysial**) **adj.**
– ORIGIN late 17th cent.: modern Latin, from Greek *hupophusis* 'offshoot,' from *hupo* 'under' + *phusis* 'growth.'

hy·po·pi·tu·i·ta·rism /ˌhīpōpiˈt(y)o͞o-itəˌrizəm/ ▶ **n.** Medicine diminished hormone secretion by the pituitary gland, causing dwarfism in children and premature aging in adults.
– DERIVATIVES **hy·po·pi·tu·i·tar·y** /ˌhīpōpə-ˈt(y)o͞oiˌterē/ **adj.**

hy·po·pne·a /hīˈpäpnēə, hi-/ ▶ **n.** abnormally slow or shallow breathing.

hy·po·rhe·ic ▶ **adj.** denoting an area or ecosystem beneath the bed of a river or stream that is saturated with water and that supports invertebrate fauna which play a role in the larger ecosystem: *the hyporheic zone.*

hy·po·sen·si·tiv·i·ty /ˈhīpōˌsensiˈtivitē/ ▶ **n.** a lower than normal sensitivity to stimuli.

hy·po·sen·si·tize /ˌhīpōˈsensiˌtīz/ ▶ **v.** [with obj.] reduce the sensitivity of (a hypersensitive person) to an allergen by frequently injecting small amounts of the allergen; desensitize.
– DERIVATIVES **hy·po·sen·si·ti·za·tion** /ˈhīpōˌsensitiˈzāSHən/ **n.**

hy·po·spa·di·as /ˌhīpəˈspādēəs, ˌhipə-/ ▶ **n.** Medicine a congenital condition in males in which the opening of the urethra is on the underside of the penis.
– ORIGIN early 19th cent.: from Greek *hupospadias* 'person having hypospadias.'

hy·po·spray /ˈhīpōˌsprā/ ▶ **n.** trademark (chiefly in science fiction) a device used to introduce a drug or other substance into the body through the skin without puncturing it.

hy·pos·ta·sis /hīˈpästəsis/ ▶ **n.** (pl. **hypostases** /-ˌsēz/) **1** Medicine the accumulation of fluid or blood in the lower parts of the body or organs under the influence of gravity, as occurs in cases of poor circulation or after death.
2 Philosophy an underlying reality or substance, as opposed to attributes or that which lacks substance. ■ Theology (in Trinitarian doctrine) each of the three persons of the Trinity, as contrasted with the unity of the Godhead. ■ [in sing.] Theology the single person of Christ, as contrasted with his dual human and divine nature.
– ORIGIN early 16th cent. (in theological use): via ecclesiastical Latin from Greek *hupostasis* 'sediment,' later 'essence, substance,' from *hupo* 'under' + *stasis* 'standing.'

hy·pos·ta·size /hīˈpästəˌsīz/ ▶ **v.** another term for **HYPOSTATIZE**.

hy·po·stat·ic /ˌhīpəˈstatik/ ▶ **adj.** Theology relating to the persons of the Trinity.
– DERIVATIVES **hy·po·stat·i·cal adj.**

hy·po·stat·ic un·ion ▶ **n.** Theology the combination of divine and human natures in the single person of Christ.

hy·pos·ta·tize /hīˈpästəˌtīz/ ▶ **v.** [with obj.] formal treat or represent (something abstract) as a concrete reality.

hy·po·sthe·ni·a /ˌhīpäsˈTHēnēə/ ▶ **n.** an abnormal lack of strength.

hy·po·style /ˈhīpəˌstīl/ ▶ **adj.** Architecture (of a building) having a roof supported by pillars, typically in several rows.
▶ **n.** a building having such a roof.
– ORIGIN mid 19th cent.: from Greek *hupostulos*, from *hupo* 'under' + *stulos* 'column.'

hy·po·tax·is /ˌhīpəˈtaksis/ ▶ **n.** Grammar the subordination of one clause to another. Contrasted with **PARATAXIS**.
– DERIVATIVES **hy·po·tac·tic** /ˌhīpəˈtaktik/ **adj.**
– ORIGIN late 19th cent.: from Greek *hupotaxis*, from *hupo* 'under' + *taxis* 'arrangement.'

hy·po·ten·sion /ˌhīpəˈtenSHən/ ▶ **n.** abnormally low blood pressure.

hy·po·ten·sive /ˌhīpōˈtensiv/ ▶ **adj.** lowering the blood pressure: *hypotensive drugs.* ■ relating to or suffering from abnormally low blood pressure.

hy·pot·e·nuse /hīˈpätn̩ˌ(y)o͞os/ ▶ **n.** the longest side of a right triangle, opposite the right angle.
– ORIGIN late 16th cent.: via Latin *hypotenusa* from Greek *hupoteinousa (grammē)* 'subtending (line),' from the verb *hupoteinein* (from *hupo* 'under' + *teinein* 'stretch').

hypoth. ▶ **abbr.** hypothesis or hypothetical.

hy·po·thal·a·mus /ˌhīpəˈTHaləməs/ ▶ **n.** (pl. **hypothalami** /-ˌmī/) Anatomy a region of the forebrain below the thalamus that coordinates both the autonomic nervous system and the activity of the pituitary, controlling body temperature, thirst, hunger, and other homeostatic systems, and involved in sleep and emotional activity.
– DERIVATIVES **hy·po·tha·lam·ic** /ˌhīpōˌTHəˈlamik/ **adj.**

hy·poth·e·cate /həˈpäTHiˌkāt, hī-/ ▶ **v.** [with obj.] pledge (money) by law to a specific purpose.
– DERIVATIVES **hy·poth·e·ca·tion** /həˌpäTHiˈkāSHən, hī-/ **n.**
– ORIGIN early 17th cent.: from medieval Latin *hypothecat-* 'given as a pledge,' from the verb *hypothecare*, based on Greek *hupothēkē*.

hy·po·ther·mal /ˌhīpəˈTHərməl/ ▶ **adj.** not very hot; tepid. ■ relating to or suffering from hypothermia. ■ Geology of or relating to mineral deposits formed at relatively high temperature and pressure.
– DERIVATIVES **hy·po·ther·mic** /-ˈTHərmik/ **adj.**

hy·po·ther·mi·a /ˌhīpəˈTHərmēə/ ▶ **n.** the condition of having an abnormally low body temperature, typically one that is dangerously low.
– DERIVATIVES **hy·po·ther·mic adj.**
– ORIGIN late 19th cent.: from **HYPO-** 'below' + Greek *thermē* 'heat.'

hy·poth·e·sis /hīˈpäTHəsis/ ▶ **n.** (pl. **hypotheses** /-ˌsēz/) a supposition or proposed explanation made on the basis of limited evidence as a starting point for further investigation: *professional astronomers attacked him for popularizing an unconfirmed hypothesis.* ■ Philosophy a proposition made as a basis for reasoning, without any assumption of its truth.
– ORIGIN late 16th cent.: via late Latin from Greek *hupothesis* 'foundation,' from *hupo* 'under' + *thesis* 'placing.'

hy·poth·e·sis test·ing ▶ **n.** Statistics the theory, methods, and practice of testing a hypothesis by comparing it with the null hypothesis. The null hypothesis is only rejected if its probability falls below a predetermined significance level, in which case the hypothesis being tested is said to have that level of significance.

hy·poth·e·size /hīˈpäTHəˌsīz/ ▶ **v.** [with obj.] put (something) forward as a hypothesis: *it was reasonable to hypothesize a viral causality* | [with clause] *they hypothesize that the naturally high insulin levels result from a "thrifty gene."*
– DERIVATIVES **hy·poth·e·siz·er n.**

hy·po·thet·i·cal /ˌhīpəˈTHetikəl/ ▶ **adj.** of, based on, or serving as a hypothesis: *that option is merely hypothetical at this juncture.* ■ supposed but not necessarily real or true: *the hypothetical tenth planet.* ■ Logic denoting or containing a proposition of the logical form *if p then q*.
▶ **n.** (usu. **hypotheticals**) a hypothetical proposition or statement: *Finn talked in hypotheticals, tossing what-if scenarios to Rosen.*
– DERIVATIVES **hy·po·thet·i·cal·ly** /-ik(ə)lē/ **adv.** [sentence adverb] *hypothetically, varying interpretations of the term are possible.*

hy·po·thet·i·co-de·duc·tive /ˌhīpəˌTHetikō diˈdəktiv/ ▶ **adj.** Philosophy of or relating to the testing of the consequences of hypotheses, to determine whether the hypotheses themselves are false or acceptable.

hy·po·thy·roid·ism /ˌhīpōˈTHīroiˌdizəm/ ▶ **n.** Medicine abnormally low activity of the thyroid gland, resulting in retardation of growth and mental development in children and adults.
– DERIVATIVES **hy·po·thy·roid n. & adj.**

hy·po·ton·ic /ˌhīpəˈtänik/ ▶ **adj.** having reduced pressure or tone, in particular: ■ Biology having a lower osmotic pressure than a particular fluid, typically a body fluid or intracellular fluid. ■ Physiology of or in a state of abnormally low muscle tone.
– DERIVATIVES **hy·po·to·ni·a** /-ˈtōnēə/ **n.**, **hy·po·to·nic·i·ty** /ˌhīpōtōˈnisitē/ **n.**

hy·pot·ro·phy /hīˈpätrəfē/ ▶ **n.** (pl. **hypotrophies**) a degeneration of an organ or tissue caused by a loss of cells.

hy·po·ven·ti·la·tion /ˌhīpōˌventlˈāSHən/ ▶ **n.** Medicine breathing at an abnormally slow rate, resulting in an increased amount of carbon dioxide in the blood.

hy·po·vo·le·mi·a /ˌhīpōvəˈlēmēə/ (Brit. **hypovolaemia**) ▶ **n.** Medicine a decreased volume of circulating blood in the body.
– DERIVATIVES **hy·po·vo·le·mic** /-ˈlēmik/ **adj.**
– ORIGIN early 20th cent.: from **HYPO-** 'under' + **VOLUME** + Greek *haima* 'blood.'

hy·po·xan·thine /ˌhīpōˈzanˌTHēn/ ▶ **n.** Biochemistry a compound that is an intermediate in the metabolism of purines in animals and occurs in plant tissues. ● Alternative name: **6-hydroxypurine**; chem. formula: $C_5H_4N_4O$.

hy·pox·e·mi·a /ˌhīpäkˈsēmēə/ (Brit. **hypoxaemia**) ▶ **n.** Medicine an abnormally low concentration of oxygen in the blood. ■ Ecology oxygen deficiency in a biotic environment.
– ORIGIN late 19th cent.: from **HYPO-** (denoting an element in a low valency) + **OXYGEN** + **-EMIA**.

hy·pox·i·a /hīˈpäksēə/ ▶ **n.** Medicine deficiency in the amount of oxygen reaching the tissues. ■ oxygen deficiency in a biotic environment: *aquatic hypoxia.*
– DERIVATIVES **hy·pox·ic** /-sik/ **adj.**
– ORIGIN 1940s: from **HYPO-** (denoting an element in a low valency) + **OXYGEN** + **-IA**¹.

hyp·si·loph·o·dont /ˌhipsəˈläfəˌdänt/ (also **hypsilophodontid** /-ˌläfəˈdäntid/) ▶ **n.** a small bipedal herbivorous dinosaur of the middle Jurassic to late Cretaceous periods, adapted for swift running. ● Family Hypsilophodontidae, infraorder Ornithopoda, order Ornithischia.
– ORIGIN late 19th cent.: from modern Latin *Hypsilophodontidae*, from Greek *hupsilophos* 'high-crested' + *odous, odont-* 'tooth.'

hypso- ▶ **comb. form** relating to height or elevation: *hypsometer*.
– ORIGIN from Greek *hupsos* 'height.'

hyp·sog·ra·phy /hipˈsägrəfē/ ▶ **n.** the branch of geography concerned with the determination and mapping of the relative elevation of areas of land.
– DERIVATIVES **hyp·so·graph·ic** /ˌhipsōˈgrafik/ **adj.**, **hyp·so·graph·i·cal** /ˌhipsōˈgrafikəl/ **adj.**

hyp·som·e·ter /hipˈsämitər/ ▶ **n.** a device for calibrating thermometers at the boiling point of water at a known height above sea level or for estimating height above sea level by finding the temperature at which water boils.

hyp·so·met·ric /ˌhipsōˈmetrik/ ▶ **adj.** of or relating to the use of the hypsometer; hypsographic.

Hy·ra·coi·de·a /ˌhīrəˈkoidēə/ Zoology a small order of mammals that comprises the hyraxes.
– DERIVATIVES **hy·ra·coid** /ˈhīrəˌkoid/ **n. & adj.**
– ORIGIN modern Latin (plural), based on Greek *hurax, hurak-* (see **HYRAX**).

hy·ra·co·the·ri·um /ˌhīrəkōˈTHi(ə)rēəm/ ▶ **n.** the earliest fossil ancestor of the horse. It was a small forest animal of the Eocene epoch, with four toes on the front feet and three on the back. Also called **EOHIPPUS**. ● Genus *Hyracotherium*, family Equidae.
– ORIGIN modern Latin: from *hyraco-* (combining form from **HYRAX**) + Greek *thērion* 'wild animal.'

hy·rax /ˈhīˌraks/ ▶ **n.** a small herbivorous mammal with a compact body and a very short tail, found in arid country in Africa and Arabia. The nearest relatives to hyraxes are the elephants and other subungulates. ● Family Procaviidae and order Hyracoidea: three genera and several species.
– ORIGIN mid 19th cent.: modern Latin, from Greek *hurax* 'shrewmouse.'

hy·son /ˈhīsən/ ▶ **n.** a type of green China tea.
– ORIGIN mid 18th cent.: from Chinese *xīchūn*, literally 'bright spring.'

hys·sop /ˈhisəp/ ▶ **n. 1** a small bushy aromatic plant of the mint family, the bitter minty leaves of which are used in cooking and herbal medicine. ● *Hyssopus officinalis*, family Labiatae.
2 (in biblical use) a wild shrub of uncertain identity whose twigs were used for sprinkling in ancient Jewish rites of purification.
– ORIGIN Old English *hysope* (reinforced in Middle English by Old French *ysope*), via Latin from Greek *hyssōpos*, of Semitic origin.

hys·ter·ec·to·mize /ˌhistəˈrektəˌmīz/ ▶ **v.** [with obj.] perform a hysterectomy on (a woman or a female animal).

hys·ter·ec·to·my /ˌhistəˈrektəmē/ ▶ **n.** (pl. **hysterectomies**) a surgical operation to remove all or part of the uterus.
– ORIGIN late 19th cent.: from Greek *hustera* 'womb' + **-ECTOMY**.

hys·ter·e·sis /ˌhistəˈrēsis/ ▶ **n.** Physics the phenomenon in which the value of a physical property lags behind changes in the effect causing it, as for instance when magnetic induction lags behind the magnetizing force.
– ORIGIN late 19th cent.: from Greek *husterēsis* 'shortcoming, deficiency,' from *husterein* 'be behind,' from *husteros* 'late.'

hys·te·ri·a /hiˈsterēə, -ˈsti(ə)rēə/ ▶ **n.** exaggerated or uncontrollable emotion or excitement, esp. among a group of people: *the mass hysteria that characterizes the week before Christmas.* ■ Psychiatry a psychological disorder (not now regarded as a single definite condition) whose symptoms include conversion of psychological stress into physical symptoms (somatization), selective amnesia, shallow volatile emotions, and overdramatic or attention-seeking behavior. The term has a controversial history as it was formerly regarded as a disease specific to women.
– ORIGIN early 19th cent.: from Latin *hystericus* (see HYSTERIC).

hys·ter·ic /hiˈsterik/ ▶ **n. 1** (**hysterics**) informal a wildly emotional and exaggerated reaction: *the child has been seized with regular fits of hysterics at bedtime.* ■ uncontrollable laughter: *this started them both giggling and they fled upstairs in hysterics.* **2** a person suffering from hysteria.
▶ **adj.** another term for HYSTERICAL (sense 2).
– ORIGIN mid 17th cent. (as an adjective): via Latin from Greek *husterikos* 'of the womb,' from *hustera* 'womb' (hysteria being thought to be specific to women and associated with the womb), related to UTERUS.

hys·ter·i·cal /hiˈsterikəl/ ▶ **adj. 1** deriving from or affected by uncontrolled extreme emotion: *hysterical laughter | the band was mobbed by hysterical fans.* ■ informal extremely funny: *her attempts to teach them to dance were hysterical.* **2** Psychiatry relating to, associated with, or suffering from hysteria: *the doctor thinks the condition is partly hysterical.* ■ another term for HISTRIONIC (denoting personality disorder).
– DERIVATIVES **hys·ter·i·cal·ly adv.** [as submodifier] *isn't it hysterically funny?*

hys·ter·on prot·er·on /ˈhistəˌrän ˈprätəˌrän/ ▶ **n.** Rhetoric a figure of speech in which what should come last is put first, i.e., an inversion of the natural order, for example "*I die! I faint! I fail!*"
– ORIGIN mid 16th cent.: late Latin, from Greek *husteron proteron* 'the latter (put in place of) the former.'

Hys·tri·co·mor·pha /ˌhistrikōˈmôrfə/ Zoology a major division of the rodents that includes the guinea pigs, porcupines, coypu, and their relatives. They occur chiefly in South America. ● Suborder Hystricomorpha, order Rodentia.
– DERIVATIVES **hys·tri·co·morph** /ˈhistrikōˌmôrf/ **n. & adj.**
– ORIGIN modern Latin (plural), from Latin *hystrix, hystric-* 'porcupine' (from Greek *hustrix*) + *morphē* 'form.'

Hy·trel /ˈhīˌtrel/ ▶ **n.** trademark a strong, flexible synthetic resin used in shoes, sports equipment, and other manufactured articles.

Hz ▶ **abbr.** hertz.

h

I i

I[1] /ī/ (also **i**) ▶ **n.** (pl. **Is** or **I's**) **1** the ninth letter of the alphabet. ■ denoting the next after H in a set of items, categories, etc.
2 the Roman numeral for one.
– PHRASES **dot the i's and cross the t's** see DOT[1].

I[2] ▶ **pron.** [first person singular] used by a speaker to refer to himself or herself: *accept me for what I am.*
▶ **n.** (**the I**) Philosophy (in metaphysics) the subject or object of self-consciousness; the ego.
– ORIGIN Old English, of Germanic origin; related to Dutch *ik* and German *ich*, from an Indo-European root shared by Latin *ego* and Greek *egō*.

> **USAGE** On whether it is correct to say *between you and I* or *between you and me*, see usage at BETWEEN and PERSONAL PRONOUN. On whether it is correct to say *Rachel and I went to Paris* or *Rachel and me went to Paris*, see usage at PERSONAL PRONOUN.

I[3] ▶ **abbr.** ■ Independent. ■ (preceding a highway number) Interstate. ■ (**I.**) Island(s) or Isle(s) (chiefly on maps). ▶ **symbol** ■ electric current: $V = I/R$. ■ the chemical element iodine.

i ▶ **symbol** (i) Mathematics the imaginary quantity equal to the square root of minus one. Compare with J.

-i[1] ▶ **suffix** forming the plural: **1** of nouns adopted from Latin ending in *-us*: *foci* | *timpani.*
2 of nouns adopted from Italian ending in *-e* or *-o*: *dilettanti.*

> **USAGE** The suffix **-i** is one of several suffixes in the English language that form foreign plurals (*-a* and *-ae* are two others). Many nouns derived from a foreign language retain their foreign plural, at least when they first enter English, and particularly if they belong to a specialist field. Over time, though, it is quite normal for a word in general use to acquire a regular English plural. This may coexist with the foreign plural (e.g., **cactus**, plural **cacti** or **cactuses**), or it may actually oust a foreign plural. Note that not all Latin words ending in *-us* have a plural that ends in *-i*: for example, the Latin word *apparatus* is unchanged in the plural.

-i[2] ▶ **suffix** forming adjectives from names of countries or regions in the Near or Middle East: *Azerbaijani* | *Pakistani.*
– ORIGIN from Semitic and Indo-Iranian adjectival endings.

-i- ▶ **suffix** a connecting vowel chiefly forming words ending in *-ana, -ferous, -fic, -form, -fy, -gerous, -vorous.* Compare with -O-.

IA ▶ **abbr.** Iowa (in official postal use).

Ia. ▶ **abbr.** Iowa.

i.a. ▶ **abbr.** in absentia.

-ia[1] ▶ **suffix 1** forming nouns adopted unchanged from Latin or Greek (such as *mania, militia*), and modern Latin or Greek terms (such as *utopia*).
2 forming names of. ■ Medicine states and disorders: *anemia* | *diphtheria.* ■ Botany & Zoology genera and higher groups: *dahlia* | *Latimeria.*
3 forming names of countries: *India.*
– ORIGIN representing Latin or Greek endings.

-ia[2] ▶ **suffix** forming noun plurals: **1** from Greek neuter nouns ending in *-ion* or from those in Latin ending in *-ium* or *-e*: *paraphernalia* | *regalia.*
2 Zoology in the names of classes: *Reptilia.*

IAA ▶ **abbr.** Biochemistry indoleacetic acid.

IAAF ▶ **abbr.** International Association of Athletics Federations.

IABA ▶ **abbr.** International Amateur Boxing Association.

Ia·coc·ca /ˌīəˈkōkə/, Lee (1924–) US industrialist; full name *Lido Anthony Iacocca.* He was president of Ford Motor Company 1970–78 before leading the Chrysler Corporation 1978–92. He told his success story in *Iacocca* (1984).

IADB ▶ **abbr.** ■ Inter-American Defense Board. ■ Inter-American Development Bank.

IAEA ▶ **abbr.** International Atomic Energy Agency.

-ial ▶ **suffix** forming adjectives such as *celestial, primordial.*
– ORIGIN from French *-iel* or Latin *-ialis.*

IALC ▶ **abbr.** instrument approach and landing chart.

IAMAW ▶ **abbr.** International Association of Machinists and Aerospace Workers.

i·amb /ˈīˌam(b)/ ▶ **n.** Prosody a metrical foot consisting of one short (or unstressed) syllable followed by one long (or stressed) syllable.

i·am·bic /īˈambik/ ▶ **adj.** Prosody of or using iambs: *iambic pentameters.*
▶ **n.** a verse using iambs. ■ (**iambics**) verse of this kind.
– ORIGIN mid 16th cent.: from French *iambique,* via late Latin from Greek *iambikos,* from *iambos* (see IAMBUS).

i·am·bus /īˈambəs/ ▶ **n.** (pl. **iambuses** or **iambi** /-bī/) Prosody another term for IAMB.
– ORIGIN late 16th cent.: Latin, from Greek *iambos* 'iambus, lampoon,' from *iaptein* 'attack verbally' (because the iambic trimeter was first used by Greek satirists).

-ian /ēən, ən/ ▶ **suffix** forming adjectives and nouns such as *antediluvian* and *Christian.* Compare with -AN.
– ORIGIN from French *-ien* or Latin *-ianus.*

IAP ▶ **abbr.** international airport.

I·ap·e·tus /īˈapetəs, ēˈap-/ Astronomy a satellite of Saturn, the seventeenth closest to the planet, discovered by Cassini in 1671. It has one bright icy side and one very dark side and a diameter of 907 miles (1,460 km).
– ORIGIN named after a Titan of Greek mythology, son of Uranus (Heaven) and Gaia (Earth).

IAQ ▶ **abbr.** indoor air quality.

IARU ▶ **abbr.** International Amateur Radio Union.

IAS ▶ **abbr.** ■ indicated air speed. ■ Institute for Advanced Studies.

Ia·şi /yäsн/ a city in eastern Romania; pop. 316,716 (2006). From 1565 to 1859 it was the capital of the principality of Moldavia. German name JASSY.

-iasis ▶ **suffix** a common form of -ASIS.

IATA /īˈätə/ ▶ **abbr.** International Air Transport Association.

iatro- ▶ **comb. form** relating to a physician or to medical treatment: *iatrogenic.*
– ORIGIN from Greek *iatros* 'physician,' from *iasthai* 'heal.'

i·at·ro·chem·is·try /īˌatrəˈkemistrē/ ▶ **n.** historical a school of thought of the 16th and 17th centuries that sought to understand medicine and physiology in terms of chemistry.
– DERIVATIVES **i·at·ro·chem·i·cal adj.**, **i·at·ro·chem·ist n.**

i·at·ro·gen·ic /īˌatrəˈjenik/ ▶ **adj.** of or relating to illness caused by medical examination or treatment.
– DERIVATIVES **i·at·ro·gen·e·sis** /-ˈjenisis/ **n.**

IAU ▶ **abbr.** ■ International Association of Universities. ■ International Astronomical Union.

ib. ▶ **adv.** short for IBID.

I·ba·dan /ēˈbädn/ the second largest city in Nigeria, 100 miles (160 km) northeast of Lagos; pop. 2,628,000 (est. 2007).

I·ba·gué /ˌēbəˈgā/ a city in west central Colombia, capital of Tolima department; pop. 501,000 (est. 2009).

IBAN /ˈīban/ ▶ **abbr.** International Bank Account Number.

I·bá·rru·ri Gó·mez /iˈbärərē ˈgōmez/, Dolores (1895–1989), Spanish politician and leader of the Republicans during the Spanish Civil War; known as **La Pasionaria.**

I-beam ▶ **n.** a girder that has the shape of an I when viewed in section.

I·be·ri·a /īˈbi(ə)rēə/ the ancient name of the Iberian peninsula.
– ORIGIN Latin, literally 'the country of the *Iberi* or *Iberes,*' from Greek *Ibēres* 'Spaniards.'

I·be·ri·an /īˈbi(ə)rēən/ ▶ **adj.** relating to or denoting Iberia, or the countries of Spain and Portugal.
▶ **n. 1** a native of Iberia, esp. in ancient times.
2 the extinct Romance language spoken in the Iberian peninsula in late classical times. It forms an intermediate stage between Latin and modern Spanish, Catalan, and Portuguese. Also called IBERO-ROMANCE.
3 the extinct Celtic language spoken in the Iberian peninsula in ancient times, known only from a few inscriptions, place names, and references by Latin authors. Also called CELTIBERIAN.

I·be·ri·an pen·in·su·la the extreme southwestern peninsula of Europe that contains Spain and Portugal.

Ibero- ▶ **comb. form** Iberian; Iberian and ...: *Ibero-Roman.* ■ relating to Iberia.

I·be·ro-Ro·mance /īˌbi(ə)rō rōˈmans/ ▶ **n.** another term for IBERIAN (sense 2 of the noun).

i·bex /ˈīˌbeks/ ▶ **n.** (pl. **ibexes**) a wild goat with long, thick ridged horns and a beard, found in the mountains of the Alps, Pyrenees, central Asia, and Ethiopia. ● Genus *Capra,* family Bovidae: the widespread *C. ibex,* and the **Spanish ibex** (*C. pyrenaica*) of the Pyrenees.
– ORIGIN early 17th cent.: from Latin.

IBF ▶ **abbr.** International Boxing Federation.

I·bi·bi·o /iˈbibēō, ibəˈbēō/ ▶ **n.** (pl. **same** or **Ibibios**)
1 a member of a people of southern Nigeria.
2 the Benue-Congo language of this people, closely related to Efik.
▶ **adj.** of or relating to this people or their language.
– ORIGIN the name in Ibibio.

ibid. /ˈibid/ (also **ib.**) ▶ **adv.** in the same source (used to save space in textual references to a quoted work that has been mentioned in a previous reference).
– ORIGIN abbreviation of Latin *ibidem* 'in the same place.'

-ibility ▶ **suffix** forming nouns corresponding to adjectives ending in *-ible* (such as *accessibility* corresponding to *accessible*).
– ORIGIN from French *-ibilité* or Latin *-ibilitas.*

i·bis /ˈībis/ ▶ **n.** (pl. **ibises**) a large wading bird with a long down-curved bill, long neck, and long legs. ● Family Threskiornithidae: several genera and species, including the **sacred ibis** and **white ibis.**
– ORIGIN late Middle English: via Latin from Greek.

i·bis·bill /ˈībisˌbil/ ▶ **n.** an upland wading bird of central Asia, with a long, down-curved bill and black, white, and blue-gray plumage on the head and breast. ● *Ibidorhyncha struthersii,* the only member of the family Ibidorhynchidae.

I·bi·za /iˈbēTHə, iˈvēTHə/ the most western of the Balearic Islands, a popular resort. ■ its capital city and port; pop. 46,835 (2008).
– DERIVATIVES **I·bi·zan** adj. & n.

I·bi·zan hound /iˈbēzən, iˈbēTHən/ ▶ n. a dog of a breed of hound from Ibiza, characterized by large, pointed, pricked ears and white, yellowish-brown, or reddish-brown coloring.

-ible /əbəl, ibəl/ ▶ suffix forming adjectives: **1** able to be: *audible* | *defensible*.
2 suitable for being: *reversible* | *edible*.
3 causing: *terrible* | *horrible*.
4 having the quality to: *descendible* | *passible*.
– ORIGIN from French *-ible* or Latin *-ibilis*.

-ibly ▶ suffix forming adverbs corresponding to adjectives ending in *-ible* (such as *audibly* corresponding to *audible*).

IBM ▶ abbr. International Business Machines, a leading US computer manufacturer.

Ibn Ba·tu·ta /ˌibən bəˈtōōtə/ (*c.*1304–68), Arab explorer. From 1325 to 1354, he traveled through northern and western Africa, India, and China and wrote a vivid account of his journey in the *Rihlah*.

ibn Hus·sein, Abdullah, see **ABDULLAH IBN HUSSEIN**.

Ibn Sa·ud /ˌibən säˈōōd/ (*c.*1880–1953) king of Saudi Arabia 1932–53. He founded Saudi Arabia 1932 after having unified the various domains over which he had assumed sovereignty.

I·bo /ˈēbō/ (also **Igbo** /ˈigˌbō/) ▶ n. (pl. **same** or **Ibos**)
1 a member of a people of southeastern Nigeria.
2 the Kwa language of this people.
▶ adj. of or relating to this people or their language.
– ORIGIN a local name.

i·bo·ga·ine /iˈbōgəˌēn/ ▶ n. a hallucinogenic compound derived from the roots of a West African shrub, sometimes used as a treatment for heroin or cocaine addiction. ● The shrub is *Tabernanthe iboga*, family Apocynaceae.
– ORIGIN from a blend of *iboga* (local name for the compound) and **COCAINE**.

IBRD ▶ abbr. International Bank for Reconstruction and Development.

IBS ▶ abbr. irritable bowel syndrome.

Ib·sen /ˈibsən/, Henrik (1828–1906), Norwegian playwright. He was the first major playwright to write tragedy about ordinary people in prose. Notable works: *Peer Gynt* (1867), *A Doll's House* (1879), *Ghosts* (1881), and *The Master Builder* (1892).

i·bu·pro·fen /ˌībyōōˈprōfən/ ▶ n. a synthetic compound used widely as an analgesic and anti-inflammatory drug. ● Alternative name: **2-(4-isobutylphenyl) propionic acid**; chem. formula: $C_{13}H_{18}O_2$.
– ORIGIN 1960s: from elements of the chemical name.

IC ▶ abbr. ■ integrated circuit. ■ intensive care. ■ internal combustion: *the IC engine*.

i/c ▶ abbr. ■ (esp. in military contexts) in charge of: *the quartermaster general is i/c rations*. ■ in command: *2 i/c = second in command*.

-ic ▶ suffix **1** forming adjectives such as *Islamic*, *terrific*.
2 forming nouns such as *lyric*, *mechanic*.
3 denoting a particular form or instance of a noun ending in *-ics*: *aesthetic* | *dietetic* | *tactic*.
4 Chemistry denoting an element in a higher valence: *ferric* | *sulfuric*. Compare with **-OUS**.
– ORIGIN from French *-ique*, Latin *-icus*, or Greek *-ikos*.

-ical /ikəl/ ▶ suffix forming adjectives: **1** corresponding to nouns or adjectives usually ending in *-ic* (such as *comical* corresponding to *comic*).
2 corresponding to nouns ending in *-y* (such as *pathological* corresponding to *pathology*).

-ically ▶ suffix forming adverbs corresponding to adjectives ending in *-ic* or *-ical* (such as *tactically* corresponding to *tactical*).

ICANN ▶ abbr. Internet Committee for Assigned Names and Numbers, the nonprofit organization that oversees the use of Internet domains.

ICAO ▶ abbr. International Civil Aviation Organization.

Ic·a·rus /ˈikərəs/ Greek Mythology the son of Daedalus, who escaped from Crete using wings made by his father but was killed when he flew too near the sun and the wax attaching his wings melted.
– DERIVATIVES **I·car·i·an** /iˈke(ə)rēən, īˈke(ə)r-/ adj.

ICBM ▶ abbr. intercontinental ballistic missile.

ICC ▶ abbr. ■ Interstate Commerce Commission. ■ International Chamber of Commerce. ■ International Criminal Court.

ICE[1] ▶ abbr. internal combustion engine.

ICE[2] /īs/ ▶ n. an entry stored in one's cellular phone that provides emergency contact information.
▶ v. [with obj.] program (a cellular phone) with such information.
– ORIGIN early 21st cent.: acronym from *in case of emergency*.

ice /īs/ ▶ n. **1** frozen water, a brittle, transparent crystalline solid: *the pipes were blocked with ice*. ■ complete absence of friendliness or affection in manner or expression: *the ice in his voice*.
2 a frozen mixture of fruit juice or flavored water and sugar.
3 informal diamonds.
4 informal an illegal profit made from reselling tickets. ■ money paid in graft or bribery.
5 informal methamphetamine.
▶ v. [with obj.] **1** decorate (a cake) with icing.
2 informal clinch (something such as a victory or deal).
3 informal kill: *a man had been iced by the police*.
4 Ice Hockey shoot (the puck) so as to commit icing.
– PHRASES **break the ice** do or say something to relieve tension or get conversation going at the start of a party or when people meet for the first time. **on ice 1** (of wine or food) kept chilled by being surrounded by ice. ■ (esp. of a plan or proposal) held in reserve for future consideration: *the recommendation was put on ice*. **2** (of an entertainment) performed by skaters: *Cinderella on Ice*. **on thin ice** in a precarious or risky situation: *you're skating on thin ice*.
– PHRASAL VERBS **ice over** (or **up**) become completely covered or blocked with ice: *the wings iced over, forcing the pilot to dive*.
– ORIGIN Old English *īs*, of Germanic origin; related to Dutch *ijs* and German *Eis*.

-ice ▶ suffix forming nouns such as *service*, *police*, and abstract nouns such as *avarice*, *justice*.
– ORIGIN from Old French *-ice*, from Latin *-itia*, *-itius*, *-itium*, or from other sources by assimilation.

ice age ▶ n. a glacial episode during a past geological period. See **GLACIAL PERIOD**. ■ (**the Ice Age**) the series of glacial episodes during the Pleistocene period.

ice ax (also **ice axe**) ▶ n. an ax used by climbers for cutting footholds in ice, having a head with one pointed and one flattened end, and a spike at the foot.

ice bag ▶ n. another term for **ICE PACK** (sense 1).

ice beer ▶ n. a type of strong lager brewed at subzero temperatures so that ice crystals form. These are then strained off to remove impurities and excess water.

ice·berg /ˈīsˌbərg/ ▶ n. a large floating mass of ice detached from a glacier or ice sheet and carried out to sea.
– PHRASES **the tip of the iceberg** the small, perceptible part of a much larger situation or problem that remains hidden.
– ORIGIN late 18th cent.: from Dutch *ijsberg*, from *ijs* 'ice' + *berg* 'hill.'

ice·berg let·tuce ▶ n. a lettuce of a variety having a dense, round head of crisp, pale leaves.

ice·blink /ˈīsˌbliNGk/ ▶ n. a bright appearance of the sky caused by reflection from a distant ice sheet.

ice blue ▶ n. a very pale blue color.

ice·boat /ˈīsˌbōt/ ▶ n. **1** a light, wind-driven vehicle with sails and runners, used for traveling on ice.
2 a boat used for breaking ice on a waterway; an icebreaker.

ice·bound /ˈīsˌbound/ ▶ adj. completely surrounded or covered by ice: *the lake was icebound*.

ice·box /ˈīsˌbäks/ ▶ n. dated a refrigerator. ■ a chilled box or cupboard for keeping something cold, esp. food.

ice·break·er /ˈīsˌbrākər/ ▶ n. a ship designed for breaking a channel through ice. ■ a thing that serves to relieve inhibitions or tension between people, or start a conversation. ■ a thing that breaks up moving ice so as to lessen its impact, esp. a structure protecting the upstream end of a bridge pier.

ice buck·et ▶ n. a cylindrical container holding chunks of ice, either ready to serve in drinks or for chilling a bottle of wine in.

ice cap (also **icecap**) ▶ n. a covering of ice over a large area, esp. on the polar region of a planet.

ice chest ▶ n. a chilled box for keeping something cold, esp. food and beverages.

ice climb·ing ▶ n. the sport or activity of climbing glaciers.
– DERIVATIVES **ice climb·er** n.

ice-cold ▶ adj. **1** (esp. of a liquid) very cold; as cold as ice: *there is plenty of ice-cold beer*.
2 unemotional or dispassionate; unfeeling: *he is the epitome of ice-cold judgment*.

ice cream ▶ n. a soft frozen food made with sweetened and flavored milk fat. ■ a serving of this, typically in a bowl or a wafer cone or on a stick.
– ORIGIN mid 18th cent.: alteration of *iced cream*.

ice cube ▶ n. a small block of ice made in a freezer, esp. for adding to drinks.

iced /īst/ ▶ adj. [attrib.] **1** (of a drink or other liquid) cooled in or mixed with pieces of ice: *iced coffee*. ■ (of a surface or object) covered or coated with ice: *we played hockey on the iced schoolyard*.
2 (of a cake or cookie) decorated with icing.

ice danc·ing ▶ n. a form of ice skating incorporating choreographed dance moves, typically performed by skaters in pairs.
– DERIVATIVES **ice dance** n., **ice danc·er** n.

iced tea (also **ice tea**) ▶ n. a chilled drink of sweetened tea, typically flavored with lemon.

ice·fall /ˈīsˌfôl/ ▶ n. **1** a steep part of a glacier that looks like a frozen waterfall.
2 a fall of loose ice; an avalanche of ice.

ice field ▶ n. a wide flat expanse of floating ice, esp. in polar regions.

ice·fish /ˈīsˌfisH/ ▶ n. (pl. **same** or **icefishes**)
1 another name for **CAPELIN**.
2 a scaleless Antarctic fish of pallid appearance with spiny gill covers and a snout shaped like a duck's bill. ● *Chaenocephalus aceratus*, family Chaenichthyidae.

ice-fish ▶ v. [no obj.] fish through holes in the ice on a lake or river: *ice-fish for perch*.
– DERIVATIVES **ice fish·ing** n.

ice floe ▶ n. see **FLOE**.

ice fog ▶ n. fog formed of minute ice crystals.

ice front ▶ n. the lower edge of a glacier.

ice hock·ey ▶ n. a fast contact sport played on an ice rink between two teams of six skaters, who attempt to drive a small rubber disk (the puck) into the opposing goal with hooked or angled sticks. It developed in Canada in the 19th century.

ice·house /ˈīsˌhous/ ▶ n. a building for storing ice, typically one situated partly or wholly underground.

Ice·land /ˈīslənd/ an island country in the North Atlantic Ocean, just south of the Arctic Circle, at the northern end of the Mid-Atlantic Ridge, volcanically active, only about 20 percent habitable; pop. 306,700 (est. 2009); capital, Reykjavik; official language, Icelandic. Icelandic name **ÍSLAND**.

> First settled by Norse colonists in the 9th century, Iceland was under Norwegian rule from 1262 to 1380, when it passed to Denmark. Granted internal self-government in 1874, it became a fully fledged independent republic in 1944. In 2010, volcanic eruptions in Eyjafjallajökull, an ice cap in southern Iceland, caused major disruptions of air travel across much of Europe.

Ice·land·er /ˈīsləndər/ ▶ n. a native or inhabitant of Iceland. ■ a person of Icelandic descent.

Ice·lan·dic /īsˈlandik/ ▶ adj. of or relating to Iceland or its language.
▶ n. the North Germanic language of Iceland, which is very similar to Old Norse.

Ice·land moss (also **Iceland lichen**) ▶ n. a brown, branching lichen with stiff spines along the margins of the fronds, growing in mountain and moorland habitats. It can be boiled to produce an edible jelly. ● *Cetraria islandica*, order Parmeliales.

Ice·land pop·py (also **Icelandic poppy**) ▶ n. a tall poppy that is widely cultivated for its colorful flowers and suitability for cutting, native to arctic and north temperate regions. ● *Papaver nudicaule*, family Papaveraceae.

Ice·land spar ▶ n. a transparent variety of calcite, showing strong double refraction.

ice·man /ˈīsmən/ ▶ n. (pl. **icemen**) a man who sells or delivers ice.

ice milk ▶ n. a sweet frozen food similar to ice cream but containing less butterfat.

ice pack ▶ n. **1** a bag filled with ice and applied to the body to reduce swelling or lower temperature.
2 another term for **PACK ICE**.

ice pick ▶ n. a sharp, straight, pointed implement with a handle, used to break ice into small pieces for chilling food and drinks.

ice plant ▶ n. either of two succulent plants that are widely cultivated for their flowers. ● a South African plant that has leaves covered with glistening fluid-filled hairs that resemble ice crystals (genera *Mesembryanthemum* and *Dorotheanthus*, family Aizoaceae, in particular *M. crystallinum*). ● an

Asian stonecrop that bears domed heads of tiny pink flowers (*Sedum spectabile*, family Crassulaceae).

ice rink ▶ **n.** see RINK.

ice sheet ▶ **n.** a permanent layer of ice covering an extensive tract of land, esp. a polar region.

ice shelf ▶ **n.** a floating sheet of ice permanently attached to a landmass.

ice show ▶ **n.** an entertainment performed by ice skaters.

ice skate ▶ **n.** a boot with a blade attached to the bottom, used for skating on ice.
▶ **v.** [no obj.] skate on ice as a sport or pastime.
– DERIVATIVES **ice skat·er n.**

figure skate

hockey skate

ice skates

ice skat·ing ▶ **n.** skating on ice as a sport or pastime. Ice skating became a recognized sport in 1876. Skaters are marked for technical and artistic excellence in performing a series of prescribed patterns and free skating (**figure skating**) or a choreographed series of dance moves (**ice dancing**).

ice storm ▶ **n.** a storm of freezing rain that leaves a coating of ice.

ice tea ▶ **n.** another term for ICED TEA.

ice wa·ter ▶ **n.** water melted from ice or with ice added to cool it.

ice wine ▶ **n.** a sweet, concentrated wine made from grapes that froze on the vine.

I Ching /'ē 'CHiNG, 'jiNG/ ▶ **n.** an ancient Chinese manual of divination based on eight symbolic trigrams and sixty-four hexagrams, interpreted in terms of the principles of yin and yang. It was included as one of the "five classics" of Confucianism. English name BOOK OF CHANGES.
– ORIGIN from Chinese *yijing* 'book of changes.'

ich·neu·mon /ik'n(y)ōōmən/ ▶ **n. 1** (also **ichneumon wasp** or **ichneumon fly**) a slender parasitic wasp with long antennae that deposits its eggs in, on, or near the larvae of other insects. ● Family Ichneumonidae, order Hymenoptera: numerous genera and species.
2 another term for EGYPTIAN MONGOOSE.
– ORIGIN late 15th cent. (sense 2): via Latin from Greek *ikhneumōn* 'tracker,' from *ikhneuein* 'to track,' from *ikhnos* 'track, footstep.'

ich·nog·ra·phy /ik'nägrəfē/ ▶ **n.** (pl. **ichnographies**) a ground plan of a building or map of a region.
– ORIGIN late 16th cent.: from French *ichnographie*, or via Latin from Greek *ikhnographia*, from *ikhnos* 'track' + *-graphia* (see -GRAPHY).

i·chor /'ī,kôr/ ▶ **n.** Greek Mythology the fluid that flows like blood in the veins of the gods. ■ literary any bloodlike fluid: *tomatoes drooled ichor from their broken skins.* ■ archaic a watery, fetid discharge from a wound.
– DERIVATIVES **i·chor·ous** /'īkərəs/ **adj.**
– ORIGIN mid 17th cent.: from Greek *ikhōr*.

ichth. ▶ **abbr.** ichthyology.

ich·thus /'ikTHəs/ ▶ **n.** an image of a fish used as a symbol of Christianity.
– ORIGIN from Greek *ikhthus* 'fish': the initial letters of the word are sometimes taken as short for *Iesous Christos, Theou Uios, Soter* (Jesus Christ, Son of God, Savior).

ich·thy·ic /'ikTHē-ik/ ▶ **adj.** archaic fishlike.
– ORIGIN mid 19th cent.: from Greek *ikhthuïkos* 'fishy,' from *ikhthus* 'fish.'

ichthyo- ▶ **comb. form** relating to fish; fishlike: *ichthyosaur.*
– ORIGIN from Greek *ikhthus* 'fish.'

ich·thy·ol·o·gy /,ikTHē'äləjē/ ▶ **n.** the branch of zoology that deals with fishes.
– DERIVATIVES **ich·thy·o·log·i·cal** /-ə'läjikəl/ **adj.**, **ich·thy·ol·o·gist** /-jist/ **n.**

ich·thy·oph·a·gous /,ikTHē'äfəgəs/ ▶ **adj.** formal fish-eating: *Americans are more ichthyophagous than ever.*
– DERIVATIVES **ich·thy·oph·a·gy** /-'äfəjē/ **n.**

ich·thy·orn·is /,ikTHē'ôrnis/ ▶ **n.** an extinct, gull-like, fish-eating bird of the late Cretaceous period, with large toothed jaws. ● Genus *Ichthyornis*, order Ichthyornithiformes.
– ORIGIN modern Latin, from ICHTHYO- + Greek *ornis* 'bird.'

ich·thy·o·saur /'ikTHēə,sôr/ (also **ichthyosaurus** /,ikTHēə'sôrəs/) ▶ **n.** an extinct marine reptile of the Mesozoic era resembling a dolphin, with a long pointed head, four flippers, and a vertical tail. ● Order Ichthyosauria, subclass Diapsida: numerous genera, including *Ichthyosaurus*.
– DERIVATIVES **ich·thy·o·sau·ri·an** /,ikTHēə'sôrēən/ **adj.**
– ORIGIN mid 19th cent.: from ICHTHYO- 'fish' + Greek *sauros* 'lizard.'

ich·thy·o·sis /,ikTHē'ōsis/ ▶ **n.** Medicine a congenital skin condition that causes the epidermis to become dry and rough like fish scales.
– DERIVATIVES **ich·thy·ot·ic** /-'ätik/ **adj.**

I-chun variant of YICHUN.

-ician ▶ **suffix** (forming nouns) denoting a person skilled in or concerned with a field or subject (often corresponding to a noun ending in *-ic* or *-ics*): *politician* | *statistician.*
– ORIGIN from French *-icien.*

i·ci·cle /'īsikəl/ ▶ **n.** a hanging, tapering piece of ice formed by the freezing of dripping water. ■ a thin, shiny strip of plastic or foil hung on a Christmas tree for decoration.
– ORIGIN Middle English: from ICE + dialect *ickle* 'icicle' (from Old English *gicel*).

ic·ing /'īsiNG/ ▶ **n. 1** a mixture of sugar with liquid or butter, typically flavored and colored, and used as a coating for cakes or cookies.
2 the formation of ice on an aircraft, ship, or other vehicle, or in an engine.
3 Ice Hockey the action of shooting the puck from one's own end of the rink to the other but not into the goal, for which the referee calls a face-off in one's own end.
– PHRASES **the icing** (or **frosting**) **on the cake** an attractive but inessential addition or enhancement: *being a scientist is enjoyable, and winning a Nobel is icing on the cake.*

ic·ing sug·ar ▶ **n.** British term for CONFECTIONERS' SUGAR.

-icist ▶ **suffix** equivalent to -ICIAN.
– ORIGIN based on forms ending in -IC, + -IST.

-icity ▶ **suffix** forming abstract nouns esp. from adjectives ending in *-ic* (such as *authenticity* from *authentic*).
– ORIGIN based on forms ending in -IC, + -ITY.

ICJ ▶ **abbr.** International Court of Justice.

ick /ik/ ▶ **exclam.** used to express disgust: *oatmeal—ick!*
▶ **n.** informal a sticky or congealed substance, typically regarded with disgust: *she scrubbed the ick off the back of the stove.*
– ORIGIN 1940s: probably imitative.

-ick ▶ **suffix** archaic variant spelling of -IC.

Ick·es /'ikəs/, Harold LeClair (1874–1952) US lawyer and public official. He served as head of the federal Public Works Administration 1933–39 and as US secretary of the interior 1933–46.

ick·y /'ikē/ ▶ **adj.** (**ickier, ickiest**) informal sticky, esp. unpleasantly so. ■ distastefully sentimental: *a romantic subplot that is just plain icky.* ■ nasty or repulsive (used as a general term of disapproval): *icky boys with all their macho strutting.*
– DERIVATIVES **ick·i·ness n.**
– ORIGIN 1930s: perhaps related to SICK[1] or to the child's word *ickle* 'little.'

i·con /'ī,kän/ ▶ **n. 1** (also **ikon**) a painting of Jesus Christ or another holy figure, typically in a traditional style on wood, venerated and used as an aid to devotion in the Byzantine and other Eastern Churches.
2 a person or thing regarded as a representative symbol of something: *this iron-jawed icon of American manhood.*
3 Computing a symbol or graphic representation on a screen of a program, option, or window, esp. one of several for selection.
4 Linguistics a sign whose form directly reflects the thing it signifies, for example, the word *snarl* pronounced in a snarling way.
– ORIGIN mid 16th cent. (in the sense 'simile'): via Latin from Greek *eikōn* 'likeness, image.' Current senses date from the mid 19th cent. onward.

i·con·ic /ī'känik/ ▶ **adj.** of, relating to, or of the nature of an icon: *language is not in general an iconic sign system.* ■ (of a classical Greek statue) depicting a victorious athlete in a conventional style.
– DERIVATIVES **i·con·i·cal·ly** /-ik(ə)lē/ **adv.**, **i·co·nic·i·ty** /,īkə'nisitē/ **n.**
– ORIGIN mid 17th cent.: from Latin *iconicus*, from Greek *eikonikos*, from *eikōn* 'likeness, image.'

i·con·i·fy /ī'känə,fī/ ▶ **v.** (**iconifies, iconifying, iconified**) [with obj.] Computing reduce (a window on a screen) to a small symbol or graphic representation of itself so as to make room for other windows.

i·con·ize /'īkə,nīz/ ▶ **v.** [with obj.] **1** Computing reduce (a window on a screen) to a small symbol or graphic.
2 treat as an icon: *they iconized him as an iron-jawed symbol of American manhood.*

icono- ▶ **comb. form 1** of an image or likeness: *iconology.*
2 relating to icons: *iconoclast.*
– ORIGIN from Greek *eikōn* 'likeness.'

i·con·o·clasm /ī'känə,klazəm/ ▶ **n. 1** the action of attacking or assertively rejecting cherished beliefs and institutions or established values and practices.
2 the rejection or destruction of religious images as heretical; the doctrine of iconoclasts.
– ORIGIN late 18th cent.: from ICONOCLAST, on the pattern of pairs such as *enthusiast, enthusiasm.*

i·con·o·clast /ī'känə,klast/ ▶ **n. 1** a person who attacks cherished beliefs or institutions.
2 a destroyer of images used in religious worship, in particular: ■ historical a supporter of the 8th- and 9th-century movement in the Byzantine Church that sought to abolish the veneration of icons and other religious images. ■ historical a Puritan of the 16th or 17th century.
– ORIGIN mid 17th cent. (sense 2): via medieval Latin from ecclesiastical Greek *eikonoklastēs*, from *eikōn* 'likeness' + *klan* 'to break.'

i·con·o·clas·tic /ī,känə'klastik/ ▶ **adj.** characterized by attack on cherished beliefs or institutions: *a fresh, even an iconoclastic, influence could work wonders.*
– DERIVATIVES **i·con·o·clas·ti·cal·ly** /ī,känə'klastik(ə)lē/ **adv.**

i·co·nog·ra·phy /,īkə'nägrəfē/ ▶ **n. 1** (pl. **iconographies**) the visual images and symbols used in a work of art or the study or interpretation of these. ■ the visual images, symbols, or modes of representation collectively associated with a person, cult, or movement: *the iconography of pop culture.*
2 a collection of illustrations or portraits.
– DERIVATIVES **i·co·nog·ra·pher** /-fər/ **n.**, **i·con·o·graph·ic** /ī,känə'grafik/ **adj.**, **i·con·o·graph·i·cal** /ī,känə'grafikəl/ **adj.**, **i·con·o·graph·i·cal·ly** /ī,känə'grafik(ə)lē/ **adv.**
– ORIGIN early 17th cent. (denoting a drawing or plan): from Greek *eikonographia* 'sketch, description,' from *eikōn* 'likeness' + *-graphia* 'writing.'

i·co·nol·a·try /,īkə'nälətrē/ ▶ **n.** chiefly derogatory the worship of icons.
– ORIGIN early 17th cent.: from ecclesiastical Greek *eikonolatreia*, from *eikōn* 'likeness' + *-latria* 'worship.'

i·co·nol·o·gy /,īkə'näləjē/ ▶ **n.** the study of visual imagery and its symbolism and interpretation, esp. in social or political terms. ■ symbolism: *the iconology of a work of art.*
– DERIVATIVES **i·con·o·log·i·cal** /ī,känə'läjikəl/ **adj.**

i·co·nos·ta·sis /,īkə'nästəsis/ ▶ **n.** (pl. **iconostases** /-,sēz/) a screen bearing icons, separating the sanctuary of many Eastern churches from the nave.
– ORIGIN mid 19th cent.: from modern Greek *eikonostasis*, from *eikōn* 'likeness' + *stasis* 'standing, stopping.'

i·co·sa·he·dron /ī,kōsə'hēdrən, ī,käsə-/ ▶ **n.** (pl. **icosahedrons** or **icosahedra** /-drə/) a solid figure with twenty plane faces, esp. equilateral triangular ones.
– DERIVATIVES **i·co·sa·he·dral** /-drəl/ **adj.**
– ORIGIN late 16th cent.: via late Latin from Greek *eikosaedron*, neuter (used as a noun) of *eikosaedros* 'twenty-faced.'

ICRC ▶ **abbr.** International Committee of the Red Cross.

-ics ▶ **suffix** (forming nouns) denoting arts or sciences, branches of study, or profession: *classics* | *politics.*
– ORIGIN from French *-iques*, Latin *-ica*, or Greek *-ika*, plural forms.

> **USAGE** A noun ending in **-ics** meaning 'a subject of study or branch of knowledge' will usually take a singular rather than a plural verb: ***politics is*** *a blood sport* | ***classics is*** *hardly studied at all these days.* However, the same word may take a plural verb in cases where the sense is plural: *many of* ***the classics were*** *once regarded with disdain.*

ICSI ▶ **abbr.** intracytoplasmic sperm injection, a technique for in vitro fertilization in which an individual sperm cell is introduced into an egg cell.

ICT ▶ **abbr.** information and communications technology.

ic·tal /'iktl/ ▶ **adj.** Medicine of or relating to a seizure.
– ORIGIN 1950s: from ICTUS + -AL.

ic·ter·us /'iktərəs/ ▶ **n.** Medicine technical term for JAUNDICE.
– DERIVATIVES **ic·ter·ic** /ik'terik/ **adj.**

–ORIGIN early 18th cent.: via Latin from Greek *ikteros*. The Latin term denoted jaundice, also a yellowish-green bird (the sight of which was thought to cure jaundice).

Ic·ti·nus /ik'tīnəs/ (5th century BC), Greek architect. He is said to have designed the Parthenon in Athens with architect Callicrates and sculptor Phidias between 448 and 437 BC.

ic·tus /'iktəs/ ▶ **n.** (pl. **same** or **ictuses**) **1** Prosody a rhythmical or metrical stress.
2 Medicine a stroke or seizure; a fit.
–ORIGIN early 18th cent. (denoting the beat of the pulse): from Latin, literally 'blow.'

ICU ▶ **abbr.** intensive care unit.

i·cy /'īsē/ ▶ **adj.** (**icier, iciest**) covered with or consisting of ice: *there were icy patches on the roads.* ■ very cold: *an icy wind.* ■ (of a person's tone or manner) very unfriendly; hostile: *her voice was icy.*
–DERIVATIVES **i·ci·ly** /'īsilē/ **adv.**, **i·ci·ness n.**

ID ▶ **abbr.** ■ Idaho (in official postal use). ■ identification or identity: *they weren't carrying any ID* | [as adj.] *an ID card.*

Id ▶ **n.** variant spelling of EID.

id /id/ ▶ **n.** Psychoanalysis the part of the mind in which innate instinctive impulses and primary processes are manifest. Compare with EGO and SUPEREGO.
–ORIGIN 1920s: from Latin, literally 'that,' translating German *es*. The term was first used in this sense by Freud, following use in a similar sense by his contemporary, Georg Groddeck.

id. ▶ **abbr.** idem.

I'd /īd/ ▶ **contraction** I would or I should: *I'd like a bath.* ■ I had: *I'd agreed to go.*

-id[1] ▶ **suffix** forming adjectives such as *putrid, torrid.*
–ORIGIN from French *-ide*, from Latin *-idus*.

-id[2] ▶ **suffix 1** forming nouns such as *chrysalid, pyramid.*
2 Biology forming names of structural constituents: *plastid.*
3 Botany forming names of plants belonging to a family with a name ending in *-idaceae*: *orchid.*
–ORIGIN from or suggested by French *-ide*, via Latin *-idis* from Greek *-is, -id-*.

-id[3] ▶ **suffix** forming nouns: **1** Zoology denoting an animal belonging to a family with a name ending in *-idae* or to a class with a name ending in *-ida*: *carabid* | *arachnid.*
2 denoting a member of a specified dynasty or family: *Achaemenid* | *Sassanid.*
3 Astronomy denoting a meteor in a shower radiating from a specified constellation: *Geminids.* ■ denoting a star of a class like one in a specified constellation: *cepheid.*
–ORIGIN from or suggested by Latin *-ides* (plural *-idae, -ida*), from Greek.

IDA ▶ **abbr.** International Development Association.

I·da /'īdə/ **1** a mountain in central Crete, associated in classical times with the god Zeus. Rising to 8,058 ft. (2,456 m.), it is the highest peak on the island.
2 Astronomy asteroid 243, which is 52 km. long and has a tiny moon (Dactyl), which is about 1.5 km. across.

I·da·ho /'īdə,hō/ a state in the northwestern US that borders on the Canadian province of British Columbia on the north and that includes part of the Rocky Mountains; pop. 1,523,816 (est. 2008); capital, Boise; statehood, July 3, 1890 (43). It was explored by Lewis and Clark in 1805 and was crossed by the Oregon Trail that ended at Fort Vancouver in Washington.
–DERIVATIVES **I·da·ho·an** /-,hōən/ **n. & adj.**

I·da·ho Falls a city in southeastern Idaho, on the Snake River; pop. 54,334 (est. 2008).

IDDD ▶ **abbr.** international direct distance dialing.

id·dings·ite /'idiNG,zīt/ ▶ **n.** a brownish mineral deposit consisting of a mixture of silicates, formed by alteration of olivine.
–ORIGIN late 19th cent.: from the name of Joseph P. *Iddings* (1857–1920), American geologist, + -ITE[1].

IDE ▶ **abbr.** Computing Integrated Drive Electronics, a standard for interfacing computers and their peripherals.

-ide ▶ **suffix** Chemistry forming nouns: ■ denoting binary compounds of a nonmetallic or more electronegative element or group: *cyanide* | *sodium chloride.* ■ denoting various other compounds: *peptide* | *saccharide.* ■ denoting elements of a series in the periodic table: *lanthanide.*
–ORIGIN originally used in *oxide*.

i·de·a /ī'dēə/ ▶ **n. 1** a thought or suggestion as to a possible course of action: *they don't think it's a very good idea.* ■ a concept or mental impression: *our menu list will give you some idea of how interesting a low-fat diet can be.* ■ an opinion or belief: *nineteenth-century ideas about drinking.*
2 (**the idea**) the aim or purpose: *I took a job with the idea of getting some money together.*
3 Philosophy (in Platonic thought) an eternally existing pattern of which individual things in any class are imperfect copies. ■ (in Kantian thought) a concept of pure reason, not empirically based in experience.
–PHRASES **get** (or **give someone**) **ideas** informal become (or make someone) ambitious, bigheaded, or tempted to do something against someone else's will, esp. make a sexual advance: *Mac began to get ideas about turning pro.* **have** (**got**) **no idea** informal not know at all: *she had no idea where she was going.* **not someone's idea of** informal not what someone regards as: *it's not my idea of a happy ending.* **put ideas into someone's head** suggest ambitions or thoughts that a person would not otherwise have had. **that's an idea** informal that suggestion or proposal is worth considering. **that's the idea** informal used to confirm to someone that they have understood something or they are doing something correctly: *"A sort of bodyguard?" "That's the idea."* **the very idea!** informal an exclamation of disapproval or disagreement.
–ORIGIN late Middle English (sense 3): via Latin from Greek *idea* 'form, pattern,' from the base of *idein* 'to see.'

i·de·al /ī'dē(ə)l/ ▶ **adj. 1** satisfying one's conception of what is perfect; most suitable: *the swimming pool is ideal for a quick dip* | *this is an ideal opportunity to save money.*
2 [attrib.] existing only in the imagination; desirable or perfect but not likely to become a reality: *in an ideal world, we might have made a different decision.* ■ representing an abstract or hypothetical optimum: *mathematical modeling can determine theoretically ideal conditions.*
▶ **n.** a person or thing regarded as perfect: *you're my ideal of how a man should be.* ■ a standard of perfection; a principle to be aimed at: *tolerance and freedom, the liberal ideals.*
–ORIGIN late Middle English (as a term in Platonic philosophy, in the sense 'existing as an archetype'): from late Latin *idealis*, from Latin *idea* (see IDEA).

i·de·al gas ▶ **n.** Chemistry a hypothetical gas whose molecules occupy negligible space and have no interactions, and that consequently obeys the gas laws exactly.

i·de·al·ism /ī'dē(ə),lizəm/ ▶ **n. 1** the practice of forming or pursuing ideals, esp. unrealistically: *the idealism of youth.* Compare with REALISM. ■ (in art or literature) the representation of things in ideal or idealized form. Often contrasted with REALISM (sense 2).
2 Philosophy any of various systems of thought in which the objects of knowledge are held to be in some way dependent on the activity of mind. Often contrasted with REALISM (sense 3).
–ORIGIN late 18th cent. (sense 2): from French *idéalisme* or German *Idealismus*, from late Latin *idealis* (see IDEAL).

i·de·al·ist /ī'dē(ə),list/ ▶ **n. 1** a person who is guided more by ideals than by practical considerations: *he came to power with the reputation of a left-wing idealist.*
2 Philosophy a person who believes in the theory of idealism.

i·de·al·is·tic /ī,dē(ə)'listik/ ▶ **adj.** characterized by idealism; unrealistically aiming for perfection: *idealistic young doctors who went to work for the rebels.*
–DERIVATIVES **i·de·al·is·ti·cal·ly adv.**

i·de·al·i·ty /,īdē'alitē/ ▶ **n.** (pl. **idealities**) formal the state or quality of being ideal: *the ideality of the island of Aran.* ■ the quality of expressing or being characterized by ideals: *the loftiness and ideality of the Gettysburg Address.* ■ archaic an ideal or idealized thing: *they commenced their married life with idealities about love.*

i·de·al·ize /ī'dē(ə),līz/ ▶ **v.** [with obj.] (often as adj. **idealized**) regard or represent as perfect or better than in reality: *Helen's idealized accounts of their life together.*
–DERIVATIVES **i·de·al·i·za·tion** /ī,dē(ə)li'zāSHən/ **n.**, **i·de·al·iz·er n.**

i·de·al·ly /ī'dē(ə)lē/ ▶ **adv. 1** [as sentence adverb] preferably; in an ideal world: *ideally, you should exercise for 30 minutes every day.*
2 [as submodifier] in the best possible way; perfectly: *her experience makes her ideally suited to the job.*

i·de·ate /'īdē,āt/ ▶ **v.** [with obj.] (often as adj. **ideated**) form an idea of; imagine or conceive: *the arc whose ideated center is a nodal point in the composition.* ■ [no obj.] form ideas; think.
–ORIGIN late 17th cent.: from medieval Latin *ideat-* 'formed as an idea,' from the verb *ideare*, from Latin *idea* (see IDEA).

i·de·a·tion /,īdē'āSHən/ ▶ **n.** Psychology the formation of ideas or concepts: *paranoid ideation.*
–DERIVATIVES **i·de·a·tion·al** /-SHənl/ **adj.**, **i·de·a·tion·al·ly** /-SHənl-ē/ **adv.**

i·deb·e·none /ī'debə,nōn/ ▶ **n.** a benzoquinone compound with strong antioxidant properties. It has therapeutic uses in age-related cognitive dysfunction and skin rejuvenation, owing to its ability to stimulate nerve growth.

i·dée fixe /ēdā 'fēks/ ▶ **n.** (pl. **idées fixes** pronunc. **same**) an idea or desire that dominates the mind; an obsession.
–ORIGIN mid 19th cent.: French, literally 'fixed idea.'

i·dée re·çue /ēdā rə'so͞o/ ▶ **n.** (pl. **idées reçues** /ēdā rə'so͞oz/) a generally accepted concept or idea.
–ORIGIN mid 20th cent.: French, literally 'received idea.'

i·dem /'ī,dem, 'idem/ ▶ **adv.** used in citations to indicate an author or work that has just been mentioned: *Marianne Elliott, Partners in Revolution, 1982; idem, Wolfe Tone, 1989.*
–ORIGIN late Middle English: Latin, literally 'the same.'

i·dem·po·tent /'īdem,pōtənt/ Mathematics ▶ **adj.** denoting an element of a set that is unchanged in value when multiplied or otherwise operated on by itself.
▶ **n.** an element of this type.
–ORIGIN late 19th cent.: from Latin *idem* 'same' + POTENT[1].

ident /ī'dent/ ▶ **n.** short for IDENTIFICATION, esp. in informal or technical use.

i·den·ti·cal /ī'dentikəl/ ▶ **adj. 1** similar in every detail; exactly alike: *four girls in identical green outfits* | *the passage on the second floor was identical to the one below.* ■ (of twins) developed from a single fertilized ovum, and therefore of the same sex and usually very similar in appearance. Compare with FRATERNAL (sense 2). ■ [attrib.] (of something encountered on separate occasions) the same: *she stole a suitcase from the identical station at which she had been arrested before.*
2 Logic & Mathematics expressing an identity: *an identical proposition.*
–DERIVATIVES **i·den·ti·cal·ly** /-ik(ə)lē/ **adv.**
–ORIGIN late 16th cent. (sense 2): from medieval Latin *identicus*, from late Latin *identitas* (see IDENTITY).

i·den·ti·fi·a·ble /ī'denti,fīəbəl/ ▶ **adj.** able to be recognized; distinguishable: *there are no easily identifiable features on the shoreline.*
–DERIVATIVES **i·den·ti·fi·a·bly** /-,fīəblē/ **adv.**

i·den·ti·fi·ca·tion /ī,dentəfi'kāSHən/ ▶ **n.** the action or process of identifying someone or something or the fact of being identified: *each child was tagged with a number for identification* | *it may be impossible for relatives to make positive identifications.* ■ a means of proving a person's identity, esp. in the form of official papers: *I asked to see his identification.* ■ a person's sense of identity with someone or something: *children's identification with storybook characters.* ■ the association or linking of one thing with another: *the traditional Russian identification of democracy with anarchy.*
–ORIGIN mid 17th cent.: originally from medieval Latin *identificat-* 'identified,' from the verb *identificare*; later from IDENTIFY.

i·den·ti·fi·er /ī'dentə,fīər/ ▶ **n.** a person or thing that identifies something: *the new number is to be known as the "unique patient identifier."* ■ Computing a sequence of characters used to identify or refer to a program or an element, such as a variable or a set of data, within it.

i·den·ti·fy /ī'dentə,fī/ ▶ **v.** (**identifies, identifying, identified**) [with obj.] **1** establish or indicate who or what (someone or something) is: *the judge ordered that the girl not be identified* | *the contact would identify himself simply as Cobra.* ■ recognize or distinguish (esp. something considered worthy of attention): *a system that ensures that the student's real needs are identified.*
2 (**identify someone/something with**) associate (someone) closely with; regard (someone) as having strong links with: *he was equivocal about being identified too closely with the peace movement.* ■ equate (someone or something) with: *because of my upstate accent, people identified me with a homely farmer's wife.* ■ [no obj.] (**identify with**) regard oneself as sharing the same characteristics or thinking as someone else: *I liked Fromm and identified with him.*
–ORIGIN mid 17th cent. (in the sense 'treat as being identical with'): from medieval Latin *identificare*,

PRONUNCIATION KEY ə *ago, up;* ər *over, fur;* a *hat;* ā *ate;* ä *car;* e *let;* ē *see;* i *fit;* ī *by;* NG *sing;* ō *go;* ô *law, for;* oi *toy;* o͝o *good;* o͞o *goo;* ou *out;* TH *thin;* T͟H *then;* ZH *vision*

from late Latin *identitas* (see **IDENTITY**) + Latin *-ficare* (from *facere* 'make').

i·den·ti·kit /ī'dentiˌkit/ ▶ **n.** trademark a picture of a person, esp. one sought by the police, reconstructed from typical facial features according to witnesses' descriptions: [as modifier] *an identikit photograph.*
– ORIGIN 1960s: blend of **IDENTITY** and **KIT**[1].

i·den·ti·ty /ī'dentitē/ ▶ **n.** (pl. **identities**) **1** the fact of being who or what a person or thing is: *he knows the identity of the bombers | she believes she is the victim of mistaken identity.* ■ the characteristics determining this: *attempts to define a distinct Canadian identity.* ■ [as modifier] chiefly Brit. (of an object) serving to establish who the holder, owner, or wearer is by bearing their name and often other details such as a signature or photograph: *an identity card.*
2 a close similarity or affinity: *the initiative created an identity between the city and the suburbs.*
3 Mathematics (also **identity operation**) a transformation that leaves an object unchanged. ■ (also **identity element**) an element of a set that, if combined with another element by a specified binary operation, leaves that element unchanged.
4 Mathematics the equality of two expressions for all values of the quantities expressed by letters, or an equation expressing this, e.g., $(x + 1)^2 = x^2 + 2x + 1$.
– ORIGIN late 16th cent. (in the sense 'quality of being identical'): from late Latin *identitas*, from Latin *idem* 'same.'

i·den·ti·ty cri·sis ▶ **n.** Psychiatry a period of uncertainty and confusion in which a person's sense of identity becomes insecure, typically due to a change in their expected aims or role in society.

i·den·ti·ty ma·trix ▶ **n.** Mathematics a square matrix in which all the elements of the principal diagonal are ones and all other elements are zeros. The effect of multiplying a given matrix by an identity matrix is to leave the given matrix unchanged.

i·den·ti·ty pa·rade (also **identification parade**) ▶ **n.** Brit. a police lineup.

i·den·ti·ty pol·i·tics ▶ **plural n.** [treated as sing.] a tendency for people of a particular religion, race, social background, etc., to form exclusive political alliances, moving away from traditional broad-based party politics.

i·den·ti·ty theft ▶ **n.** the fraudulent acquisition and use of a person's private identifying information, usually for financial gain.

id·e·o·gram /'idēəˌgram, 'īdē-/ ▶ **n.** a written character symbolizing the idea of a thing without indicating the sounds used to say it, e.g., numerals and Chinese characters.
– ORIGIN mid 19th cent.: from Greek *idea* 'form' + **-GRAM**[1].

Chinese character for Earth

Roman numeral three

Wheelchair access sign

Biohazard sign

ideograms

id·e·o·graph /'idēəˌgraf, 'īdē-/ ▶ **n.** another term for **IDEOGRAM.**
– DERIVATIVES **id·e·o·graph·ic** /ˌidēə'grafik, ˌīdē-/ **adj.**, **id·e·og·ra·phy** /ˌidē'ägrəfē, ˌīdē-/ **n.**
– ORIGIN mid 19th cent.: from Greek *idea* 'form' + **-GRAPH.**

i·de·o·logue /'īdēəˌlôg, -ˌläg, 'idēə-/ ▶ **n.** an adherent of an ideology, esp. one who is uncompromising and dogmatic: *a conservative ideologue.*
– ORIGIN early 19th cent.: from French *idéologue*; see also **IDEOLOGY.**

i·de·ol·o·gy /ˌīdē'äləjē, ˌidē-/ ▶ **n. 1** (pl. **ideologies**) a system of ideas and ideals, esp. one that forms the basis of economic or political theory and policy: *the ideology of republicanism.* ■ the ideas and manner of thinking characteristic of a group, social class, or individual: *a critique of bourgeois ideology.* ■ archaic visionary speculation, esp. of an unrealistic or idealistic nature.
2 archaic the science of ideas; the study of their origin and nature.
– DERIVATIVES **i·de·o·log·i·cal** /-ə'läjikəl/ **adj.**, **i·de·o·log·i·cal·ly** /-ə'läjik(ə)lē/ **adv.**, **i·de·ol·o·gist** /-jist/ **n.**
– ORIGIN late 18th cent. (sense 2): from French *idéologie*, from Greek *idea* 'form, pattern' + *-logos* (denoting discourse or compilation).

ides /īdz/ ▶ **plural n.** (in the ancient Roman calendar) a day falling roughly in the middle of each month (the 15th day of March, May, July, and October, and the 13th of other months), from which other dates were calculated. Compare with **NONES, CALENDS.**
– ORIGIN late Old English: from Old French, from Latin *idus* (plural), of unknown origin.

i·dig·bo /i'digbō/ ▶ **n.** (pl. **idigbos**) a West African tree that has a distinctive pagodalike shape and yields weather-resistant timber. ● *Terminalia ivorensis*, family Combretaceae.
– ORIGIN a local name.

idio- ▶ **comb. form** distinct; private; personal; own: *idiotype.*
– ORIGIN from Greek *idios* 'own, distinct.'

id·i·o·cy /'idēəsē/ ▶ **n.** (pl. **idiocies**) extremely stupid behavior: *the idiocy of decimating rain forests | every aspect of public administration throws up its own idiocies.*
– ORIGIN early 16th cent. (originally denoting low intelligence): from **IDIOT**, probably on the pattern of pairs such as *lunatic, lunacy.*

id·i·o·graph·ic /ˌidēə'grafik/ ▶ **adj.** of or relating to the study or discovery of particular scientific facts and processes, as distinct from general laws. Often contrasted with **NOMOTHETIC.**

id·i·o·lect /'idēəˌlekt/ ▶ **n.** the speech habits peculiar to a particular person.
– ORIGIN 1940s: from **IDIO-** 'own, personal' + *-lect* as in *dialect.*

id·i·om /'idēəm/ ▶ **n. 1** a group of words established by usage as having a meaning not deducible from those of the individual words (e.g., *rain cats and dogs, see the light*). ■ a form of expression natural to a language, person, or group of people: *he had a feeling for phrase and idiom.* ■ the dialect of a people or part of a country.
2 a characteristic mode of expression in music or art: *they were both working in a neo-Impressionist idiom.*
– ORIGIN late 16th cent.: from French *idiome*, or via late Latin from Greek *idiōma* 'private property, peculiar phraseology,' from *idiousthai* 'make one's own,' from *idios* 'own, private.'

id·i·o·mat·ic /ˌidēə'matik/ ▶ **adj. 1** using, containing, or denoting expressions that are natural to a native speaker: *distinctive idiomatic dialogue.*
2 appropriate to the style of art or music associated with a particular period, individual, or group: *a short Bach piece containing lots of idiomatic motifs.*
– DERIVATIVES **id·i·o·mat·i·cal·ly** /-ik(ə)lē/ **adv.**
– ORIGIN early 18th cent.: from Greek *idiōmatikos* 'peculiar, characteristic,' from *idiōma* (see **IDIOM**).

id·i·o·path·ic /ˌidēə'paTHik/ ▶ **adj.** Medicine relating to or denoting any disease or condition that arises spontaneously or for which the cause is unknown.

id·i·op·a·thy /ˌidē'äpəTHē/ ▶ **n.** (pl. **idiopathies**) Medicine a disease or condition that arises spontaneously or for which the cause is unknown.
– ORIGIN late 17th cent.: from modern Latin *idiopathia*, from Greek *idiopatheia*, from *idios* 'own, private' + *-patheia* 'suffering.'

id·i·o·phone /'idēəˌfōn/ ▶ **n.** Music, technical an instrument the whole of which vibrates to produce a sound when struck, shaken, or scraped, such as a bell, gong, or rattle.

id·i·o·syn·cra·sy /ˌidēə'siNGkrəsē/ ▶ **n.** (pl. **idiosyncrasies**) (usu. **idiosyncrasies**) a mode of behavior or way of thought peculiar to an individual: *one of his little idiosyncrasies was always preferring to be in the car first.* ■ a distinctive or peculiar feature or characteristic of a place or thing: *the idiosyncrasies of the prison system.* ■ Medicine an abnormal physical reaction by an individual to a food or drug.
– ORIGIN early 17th cent. (originally in the sense 'physical constitution peculiar to an individual'): from Greek *idiosunkrasia*, from *idios* 'own, private' + *sun* 'with' + *krasis* 'mixture.'

id·i·o·syn·crat·ic /ˌidēəsiNG'kratik, ˌidē-ō-/ ▶ **adj.** of or relating to idiosyncrasy; peculiar or individual: *she emerged as one of the great idiosyncratic talents of the Nineties.*
– DERIVATIVES **id·i·o·syn·crat·i·cal·ly** /-ik(ə)lē/ **adv.**
– ORIGIN late 18th cent.: from **IDIOSYNCRASY**, on the pattern of Greek *sunkratikos* 'mixed together.'

id·i·ot /'idēət/ ▶ **n.** informal a stupid person. ■ Medicine, archaic a mentally handicapped person.
– ORIGIN Middle English (denoting a person of low intelligence): via Old French from Latin *idiota* 'ignorant person,' from Greek *idiōtēs* 'private person, layman, ignorant person,' from *idios* 'own, private.'

id·i·ot board (also **idiot card**) ▶ **n.** informal a board displaying a television script to a speaker as an aid to memory.

id·i·ot box ▶ **n.** informal a television set.

id·i·ot·ic /ˌidē'ätik/ ▶ **adj.** informal very stupid: *I was able to hum its idiotic theme tune.*
– DERIVATIVES **id·i·ot·i·cal·ly** /ˌidē'ätik(ə)lē/ **adv.**

id·i·ot light ▶ **n.** informal a warning light that goes on when a fault occurs in a device, esp. a light on the instrument panel of a motor vehicle.

id·i·ot sa·vant ▶ **n.** (pl. **idiot savants** or **idiots savants** pronunc. **same**) a person who is considered to be mentally handicapped but displays brilliance in a specific area, esp. one involving memory.
– ORIGIN French, literally 'learned idiot.'

id·i·o·type /'idēəˌtīp/ ▶ **n.** Biology the set of genetic determinants of an individual. ■ Immunology a set of antigen-binding sites that characterizes the antibodies produced by a particular clone of antibody-producing cells.

I·di·ta·rod Riv·er /ī'ditəˌräd/ a river in western Alaska, scene of a 1908 gold rush, route of the Iditarod dogsled race that goes from Anchorage to Nome.

i·dle /'īdl/ ▶ **adj.** (**idler, idlest**) **1** (esp. of a machine or factory) not active or in use: *assembly lines standing idle for lack of spare parts.* ■ (of a person) not working; unemployed. ■ (of a person) avoiding work; lazy. ■ [attrib.] (of time) characterized by inaction or absence of significant activity: *at no time in the day must there be an idle moment.* ■ (of money) held in cash or in accounts paying no interest.
2 without purpose or effect; pointless: *he did not want to waste valuable time in idle chatter.* ■ (esp. of a threat or boast) without foundation: *I knew Ellen did not make idle threats.*
▶ **v.** [no obj.] (of a person) spend time doing nothing; be idle: *four men were idling outside the shop.* ■ move aimlessly or lazily: *Cal idled past MetroHealth at a stately pace.* ■ (of an engine) run slowly while disconnected from a load or out of gear: *the car is noisily idling in the street.* ■ [with obj.] cause (an engine) to idle. ■ [with obj.] take out of use or employment: *he will close the newspaper, idling 2,200 workers.*
– PHRASAL VERBS **idle something away** spend one's time doing nothing or very little.
– DERIVATIVES **i·dle·ness n.**
– ORIGIN Old English *īdel* 'empty, useless'; related to Dutch *ijdel* 'vain, frivolous, useless' and German *eitel* 'bare, worthless.'

i·dler /'īdlər/ ▶ **n. 1** a habitually lazy person. ■ a person who is doing nothing in particular, typically while waiting for something.
2 a pulley that transmits no power but guides or tensions a belt or rope. ■ an idle wheel.

i·dle wheel ▶ **n.** an intermediate wheel between two geared wheels, esp. when its purpose is to allow them to rotate in the same direction.

i·dly /'īdlē/ ▶ **adv.** with no particular purpose, reason, or foundation: *"How was the game?" Katie asked idly.* ■ in an inactive or lazy way: *I can no longer stand idly by and let him take the blame.*

I·do /'ēdō/ ▶ **n.** an artificial universal language developed from Esperanto.
– ORIGIN early 19th cent.: Ido, literally 'offspring.'

i·do·crase /'īdəˌkrās, -ˌkrāz, 'idə-/ ▶ **n.** a mineral consisting of a silicate of calcium, magnesium, and aluminum, occurring typically as dark green to brown prisms in metamorphosed limestone.
– ORIGIN early 19th cent.: from Greek *eidos* 'form' + *krasis* 'mixture.'

i·dol /'īdl/ ▶ **n.** an image or representation of a god used as an object of worship. ■ a person or thing that is greatly admired, loved, or revered: *movie idol Robert Redford.*
– ORIGIN Middle English: from Old French *idole*, from Latin *idolum* 'image, form' (used in ecclesiastical Latin in the sense 'idol'), from Greek *eidōlon*, from *eidos* 'form, shape.'

i·dol·a·ter /ī'dälətər/ ▶ **n.** a person who worships an idol or idols.
– ORIGIN late Middle English: from Old French *idolatre*, based on Greek *eidōlolatrēs*, from *eidōlon* (see **IDOL**) + *-latrēs* 'worshiper.'

i·dol·a·trous /ī'dälətrəs/ ▶ **adj.** worshiping idols: *the idolatrous peasantry.* ■ treating someone or something as an idol: *America's idolatrous worship of the auto.*

i·dol·a·try /ī'dälətrē/ ▶ **n.** worship of idols. ■ extreme admiration, love, or reverence for something or someone: *we must not allow our idolatry of art to obscure issues of political significance.*
– ORIGIN Middle English: from Old French *idolatrie*, based on Greek *eidōlolatreia*, from *eidōlon* (see IDOL) + *-latreia* 'worship.'

i·dol·ize /'īdl,īz/ ▶ **v.** [with obj.] admire, revere, or love greatly or excessively: *he idolized his mother.*
– DERIVATIVES **i·dol·i·za·tion** /,īdl-i'zāshən/ **n.**, **i·dol·iz·er n.**

I·dom·e·neus /ī'dämən(y)o͞os, ī,dämə'nēəs/ Greek Mythology king of Crete, son of Deucalion and descendant of Minos. He was forced to kill his son after vowing to sacrifice the first living thing that he met on his return from the Trojan War.

IDP ▶ **abbr.** ■ integrated data processing. ■ International Driving Permit. ■ internally displaced person.

Id ul-A·dha /'id äl 'äT͟Hä/ see EID.

Id ul-Fi·tr /'id äl 'fētər/ see EID.

i·dyll /'īdl/ ▶ **n.** an extremely happy, peaceful, or picturesque episode or scene, typically an idealized or unsustainable one: *the rural idyll remains strongly evocative in most industrialized societies.* ■ a short description in verse or prose of a picturesque scene or incident, esp. in rustic life.
– ORIGIN late 16th cent. (in the Latin form): from Latin *idyllium*, from Greek *eidullion*, diminutive of *eidos* 'form, picture.'

i·dyl·lic /ī'dilik/ ▶ **adj.** (esp. of a time or place) like an idyll; extremely happy, peaceful, or picturesque: *an attractive hotel in an idyllic setting.*
– DERIVATIVES **i·dyl·li·cal·ly** /-ik(ə)lē/ **adv.**

IE ▶ **abbr.** Indo-European.

i.e. ▶ **abbr.** that is to say (used to add explanatory information or to state something in different words): *a walking boot that is synthetic, i.e., not leather or suede.*
– ORIGIN from Latin *id est* 'that is.'

-ie ▶ **suffix 1** variant spelling of -Y² (as in *auntie*). **2** archaic variant spelling of -Y¹, -Y³.
– ORIGIN earlier form of *-y*.

IEA ▶ **abbr.** International Energy Agency.

IED ▶ **abbr.** improvised explosive device, such as a car bomb.

IEEE ▶ **abbr.** Institute of Electrical and Electronics Engineers.

Ie·per /'yāpər/ Flemish name of YPRES.

-ier ▶ **suffix** forming personal nouns denoting an occupation or interest: **1** pronounced with stress on the preceding element: *glazier.* [Middle English: variant of -ER¹.]
2 pronounced with stress on the final element: *brigadier* | *cashier.* [from French *-ier*, from Latin *-arius*.]

IF ▶ **abbr.** intermediate frequency.

if /if/ ▶ **conj. 1** introducing a conditional clause. ■ on the condition or supposition that; in the event that: *if you have a complaint, write to the director* | *if you like, I'll put in a word for you.* ■ (with past tense) introducing a hypothetical situation: *if you had stayed, this would never have happened.* ■ whenever; every time: *if I go out, she gets nasty.*
2 despite the possibility that; no matter whether: *if it takes me seven years, I shall do it.*
3 (often used in indirect questions) whether: *he asked if we would like some coffee* | *see if you can track it down.*
4 [with modal] expressing a polite request: *if I could trouble you for your names?* | *if you wouldn't mind giving him a message?*
5 expressing an opinion: *that's an awfully long walk, if you don't mind my saying so* | *if you ask me, he's in love.*
6 expressing surprise or regret: *well, if it isn't Frank!* | *if I could just be left alone.*
7 with implied reservation. ■ and perhaps not: *the new leaders have little if any control.* ■ used to admit something as being possible but regarded as relatively insignificant: *if there was any weakness, it was naiveté* | *so what if he did?* ■ despite being (used before an adjective or adverb to introduce a contrast): *she was honest, if a little brutal.*
▶ **n.** a condition or supposition: *there are so many ifs and buts in the policy.*
– PHRASES **if and only if** used to introduce a condition that is necessary as well as sufficient: *witches are real if and only if there are criteria for identifying witches.* **if and when** at a future time (should it arise): *if and when the film gets the green light, be sure you've read the book first.* **if anything** used to suggest tentatively that something may be the case (often the opposite of something previously implied): *I haven't made much of this—if anything, I've played it down.* **if I were you** used to accompany a piece of advice: *I would go to see him if I were you.* **if not** perhaps even (used to introduce a more extreme term than one first mentioned): *hundreds if not thousands of germs.* **if only 1** even if for no other reason than: *Willy would have to tell George more, if only to keep him from pestering.* **2** used to express a wish, esp. regretfully: *if only I had listened to you.* **if so** if that is the case.
– ORIGIN Old English *gif*, of Germanic origin; related to Dutch *of* and German *ob*.

> **USAGE** **If** and **whether** are more or less interchangeable in sentences like *I'll see* **if** *he left an address* and *I'll see* **whether** *he left an address*, although **whether** is generally regarded as more formal and suitable for written use. But, although **if** and **whether** are often interchangeable, a distinction worth noting is that **if** is also used in conditional constructions and **whether** in expressing an alternative or possibility. Thus, *tell me if you're going to be in town next week* could be strictly interpreted as 'you need not reply if you are *not* going to be in town,' whereas *tell me whether you're going to be in town next week* clearly means 'a reply is desired one way or the other.'

IFAD ▶ **abbr.** International Fund for Agricultural Development.

IFC ▶ **abbr.** International Finance Corporation.

Ife /'ēfā/ an industrial city in southwestern Nigeria; pop. 258,300 (est. 2005).

-iferous ▶ **comb. form** common form of -FEROUS.

iff /if/ ▶ **conj.** Logic & Mathematics if and only if.
– ORIGIN 1950s: arbitrary extension of *if*.

if·fy /'ifē/ ▶ **adj.** (**iffier, iffiest**) informal full of uncertainty; doubtful: *the prospect for classes resuming next Wednesday seems iffy.* ■ of doubtful quality or legality: *a good wine merchant will change the iffy bottles for sound ones.*

-ific ▶ **suffix** common form of -FIC.

-ification ▶ **suffix** common form of -FICATION.

IFO ▶ **abbr.** identified flying object.

-iform ▶ **comb. form** common form of -FORM.

IFR ▶ **abbr.** instrument flight rules, used to regulate the flying and navigating of an aircraft using instruments alone.

if·tar /'if,tär/ ▶ **n.** the meal eaten by Muslims after sunset during Ramadan.

IFV ▶ **abbr.** infantry fighting vehicle.

IG ▶ **abbr.** ■ Indo-Germanic. ■ Inspector General.

Ig ▶ **abbr.** immunoglobulin.

Ig·bo /'igbō/ ▶ **n. & adj.** see IBO.

ig·loo /'iglo͞o/ ▶ **n.** a dome-shaped Eskimo house, typically built from blocks of solid snow.
– ORIGIN mid 19th cent.: from Inuit *iglu* 'house.'

igloo

ign. ▶ **abbr.** ignition.

Ig·na·tius Loy·o·la, St. /ig'nāsH(ē)əs loi'ōlə/ (1491–1556), Spanish theologian and founder of the Society of Jesus (the Jesuit order). His *Spiritual Exercises* (1548), an ordered scheme of meditations, is still used in Jesuit training programs. Feast day, July 31.

ig·ne·ous /'ignēəs/ ▶ **adj.** Geology (of rock) having solidified from lava or magma. ■ relating to or involving volcanic processes: *igneous activity.* ■ rare of fire; fiery.
– ORIGIN mid 17th cent.: from Latin *igneus* (from *ignis* 'fire') + -OUS.

ig·nim·brite /'ignim,brīt/ ▶ **n.** Geology a volcanic rock consisting essentially of pumice fragments, formed by the consolidation of material deposited by pyroclastic flows.
– ORIGIN 1930s: from Latin *ignis* 'fire' + *imber, imbr-* 'shower of rain, storm cloud' + -ITE¹.

ig·nis fat·u·us /'ignəs 'facHo͞oəs/ ▶ **n.** (pl. **ignes fatui** /'ignēz 'facHo͞o,ī/) a will-o'-the-wisp. ■ something deceptive or deluding.
– ORIGIN mid 16th cent.: modern Latin, literally 'foolish fire' (because of its erratic movement).

ig·nite /ig'nīt/ ▶ **v.** catch fire or cause to catch fire: [no obj.] *furniture can give off lethal fumes when it ignites* | [with obj.] *sparks flew out and ignited the dry scrub.* ■ [with obj.] arouse or inflame (an emotion or situation): *the words ignited new fury in him.*
– DERIVATIVES **ig·nit·a·bil·i·ty** /ig,nītə'bilitē/ **n.**, **ig·nit·a·ble adj.**
– ORIGIN mid 17th cent. (in the sense 'make intensely hot'): from Latin *ignire* 'set on fire,' from *ignis* 'fire.'

ig·ni·ter /ig'nītər/ ▶ **n. 1** a device for igniting a fuel mixture in an engine.
2 a device for causing an electric arc.

ig·ni·tion /ig'nisHən/ ▶ **n.** the action of setting something on fire or starting to burn: *three minutes after ignition, the flames were still growing.* ■ the process of starting the combustion of fuel in the cylinders of an internal combustion engine. ■ (usu. **the ignition**) the mechanism for bringing this about, typically activated by a key or switch: *he put the key in the ignition.*
– ORIGIN early 17th cent. (denoting the heating of a substance to the point of combustion or chemical change): from medieval Latin *ignitio(n-)*, from the verb *ignire* 'set on fire' (see IGNITE).

ig·ni·tron /'igni,trän/ ▶ **n.** a kind of rectifier with a mercury cathode, able to carry large electric currents.
– ORIGIN 1930s: from IGNITE or IGNITION + -TRON.

ig·no·ble /ig'nōbəl/ ▶ **adj.** (**ignobler, ignoblest**) **1** not honorable in character or purpose: *ignoble feelings of intense jealousy.*
2 of humble origin or social status: *ignoble savages.*
– DERIVATIVES **ig·no·bil·i·ty** /,ignō'bilitē/ **n.**, **ig·no·bly** /-blē/ **adv.**
– ORIGIN late Middle English (sense 2): from French, or from Latin *ignobilis*, from *in-* 'not' + *gnobilis*, older form of *nobilis* 'noble.'

ig·no·min·i·ous /,ignə'minēəs/ ▶ **adj.** deserving or causing public disgrace or shame: *no other party risked ignominious defeat.*
– DERIVATIVES **ig·no·min·i·ous·ly adv.**, **ig·no·min·i·ous·ness n.**
– ORIGIN late Middle English: from French *ignominieux*, or Latin *ignominiosus*, from *ignominia* (see IGNOMINY).

ig·no·min·y /'ignə,minē, ig'näminē/ ▶ **n.** public shame or disgrace: *the ignominy of being imprisoned.*
– ORIGIN mid 16th cent.: from French *ignominie* or Latin *ignominia*, from *in-* 'not' + a variant of *nomen* 'name.'

ig·no·ra·mus /,ignə'rāməs, -'raməs/ ▶ **n.** (pl. **ignoramuses**) an ignorant or stupid person.
– ORIGIN late 16th cent.: Latin, literally 'we do not know' (in legal use 'we take no notice of it'), from *ignorare* (see IGNORE). The modern sense may derive from the name of a character in George Ruggle's *Ignoramus* (1615), a satirical comedy exposing lawyers' ignorance.

ig·no·rance /'ignərəns/ ▶ **n.** lack of knowledge or information: *he acted in ignorance of basic procedures.*
– PHRASES **ignorance is bliss** proverb if you do not know about something, you do not worry about it.
– ORIGIN Middle English: via Old French from Latin *ignorantia*, from *ignorant-* 'not knowing' (see IGNORANT).

ig·no·rant /'ignərənt/ ▶ **adj.** lacking knowledge or awareness in general; uneducated or unsophisticated: *he was told constantly that he was ignorant and stupid.* ■ [predic.] lacking knowledge, information, or awareness about something in particular: *they were ignorant of astronomy.* ■ informal discourteous or rude: *this ignorant, pin-brained receptionist.* ■ black English easily angered: *I is an ignorant man—even police don't meddle with me.*
– DERIVATIVES **ig·no·rant·ly adv.**
– ORIGIN late Middle English: via Old French from Latin *ignorant-* 'not knowing,' from the verb *ignorare* (see IGNORE).

ig·no·ra·ti·o e·len·chi /,ignə'rāsHēō i'lenGkī, -kē/ ▶ **n.** (pl. **ignorationes elenchi** /,ignə,rāsHē'ōnēz/) Philosophy a logical fallacy that consists in apparently refuting an opponent while actually disproving something not asserted.
– ORIGIN late 16th cent.: Latin, literally 'ignorance of the elenchus.'

ig·nore /ig'nôr/ ▶ **v.** [with obj.] refuse to take notice of or acknowledge; disregard intentionally: *he ignored her outraged question.* ■ fail to consider (something significant): *direct satellite broadcasting ignores national boundaries.* ■ Law (of a grand jury) reject (an indictment) as groundless.
– DERIVATIVES **ig·nor·a·ble adj.**, **ig·nor·er n.**
– ORIGIN late 15th cent. (in the sense 'be ignorant of'): from French *ignorer* or Latin *ignorare* 'not know, ignore,' from *in-* 'not' + *gno-*, a base meaning 'know.' Current senses date from the early 19th cent.

ig·no·tum per ig·no·tius /ig'nōtəm pər ig'nōsHəs/ ▶ **n.** the action of offering an explanation that is harder to understand than the thing it is meant to explain.
– ORIGIN late Latin, literally 'the unknown through the more unknown.'

i

I·gua·çu /ˌēgwəˈsoo/ a river in southern Brazil. It rises in the Serra do Mar in southeastern Brazil and flows west for 800 miles (1,300 km) to the Paraná River, which it joins just below Iguaçu Falls, a spectacular series of waterfalls. Spanish name **Iguazú**.

i·gua·na /iˈgwänə/ ▶ **n.** a large, arboreal, tropical American lizard with a spiny crest along the back and greenish coloration, occasionally kept as a pet. ● Genus *Iguana*, family Iguanidae: two species, in particular the common **green iguana** (*I. iguana*). ■ any iguanid lizard.
– ORIGIN mid 16th cent.: from Spanish, from Arawak *iwana*.

i·gua·nid /iˈgwänid/ ▶ **n.** Zoology a lizard of the iguana family (Iguanidae). Iguanids are found mainly in the New World but also occur in Madagascar and on some Pacific islands.
– ORIGIN late 19th cent.: from modern Latin *Iguanidae* (plural), from the genus name *Iguana* (see IGUANA).

i·guan·o·don /iˈgwänəˌdän/ ▶ **n.** a large, partly bipedal, herbivorous dinosaur of the early to mid Cretaceous period, with a broad, stiff tail and the thumb developed into a spike. ● Genus *Iguanodon*, infraorder Ornithopoda, order Ornithischia.
– DERIVATIVES **i·guan·o·dont** /-ˌdänt/ **adj.**
– ORIGIN modern Latin, from IGUANA + Greek *odous, odont-* 'tooth' (because its teeth resemble those of the iguana).

IGY ▶ **abbr.** International Geophysical Year.

i.h.p. ▶ **abbr.** indicated horsepower.

IHS ▶ **abbr.** Jesus.
– ORIGIN Middle English: from late Latin, representing Greek ΙΗΣ as an abbreviation of *Iēsous* 'Jesus' used in manuscripts and also as a symbolic or ornamental monogram, but later often taken as an abbreviation of various Latin phrases, notably *Iesus Hominum Salvator* 'Jesus Savior of Men,' *In Hoc Signo* (*vinces*) 'in this sign (thou shalt conquer),' and *In Hac Salus* 'in this (cross) is salvation.'

i·i·wi /ēˈēˌwē/ ▶ **n.** (pl. **same** or **iiwis**) a Hawaiian honeycreeper with a long, down-curved bill and mainly bright red plumage. ● *Vestiaria coccinea*, family Drepanididae (or Fringillidae).
– ORIGIN late 18th cent.: from Hawaiian.

IJs·sel /ˈīsəl/ a river in the Netherlands. In part, it is a distributary of the Rhine River, which it leaves at Arnhem to join the Oude IJssel ("Old IJssel") a few miles downstream and then flows north for 72 miles (115 km) through the eastern Netherlands to the IJsselmeer.

IJs·sel·meer /ˈīsəlˌmer/ a shallow lake in the northwestern Netherlands that was created in 1932 when a dam was built across the entrance to the old Zuider Zee. Large areas have since been reclaimed as polders.

i·kat /ˈēkät/ ▶ **n.** fabric made using an Indonesian decorative technique in which warp or weft threads, or both, are tie-dyed before weaving.
– ORIGIN 1930s: Malay, literally 'fasten, tie.'

i·ke·ba·na /ˌikəˈbänə, ˌēke-/ ▶ **n.** the art of Japanese flower arrangement, with formal display according to strict rules.
– ORIGIN early 20th cent.: Japanese, literally 'living flowers,' from *ikeru* 'keep alive' + *hana* 'flower.'

Ikh·na·ton /ikˈnätn/ variant form of AKHENATEN.

i·kon ▶ **n.** variant spelling of ICON (sense 1).

Ik·san /ˈēkˌsän/ a commercial city in southwestern South Korea; pop. 312,800 (est. 2008).

IL ▶ **abbr.** Illinois (in official postal use).

il- ▶ **prefix 1** variant spelling of IN-¹, IN-². **2** assimilated before *l* (as in *illustrate, illogical*).

-il ▶ **suffix** forming adjectives and nouns such as *civil* and *fossil*.
– ORIGIN from Old French, from Latin *-ilis*.

ILA ▶ **abbr.** ■ International Law Association. ■ International Longshoremen's Association.

i·lang-i·lang ▶ **n.** variant spelling of YLANG-YLANG.

-ile ▶ **suffix** forming adjectives and nouns such as *agile* and *juvenile*. ■ Statistics forming nouns denoting a value of a variate that divides a population into the indicated number of equal-sized groups, or one of the groups itself: *decile* | *percentile*.
– ORIGIN variant of -IL esp. in adoptions from French.

il·e·a /ˈilēə/ plural form of ILEUM.

Île-de-France /ˌēl də ˈfräns/ a region of north central France, incorporating the city of Paris.

il·e·i·tis /ˌilēˈītis/ ▶ **n.** Medicine inflammation of the ileum.

il·e·os·to·my /ˌilēˈästəmē/ ▶ **n.** (pl. **ileostomies**) a surgical operation in which a piece of the ileum is diverted to an artificial opening in the abdominal wall. ■ an opening so formed.
– ORIGIN late 19th cent.: from ILEUM + Greek *stoma* 'mouth.'

Iles du Vent /ˌēl dy ˈvän/ French name for WINDWARD ISLANDS (sense 2).

I·le·sha /ēˈläshə/ a city in southwestern Nigeria; pop. 192,700 (est. 2005).

il·e·um /ˈilēəm/ ▶ **n.** (pl. **ilea** /ˈilēə/) Anatomy the third portion of the small intestine, between the jejunum and the cecum.
– DERIVATIVES **il·e·ac** /-ˌak/ **adj.**, **il·e·al** /-əl/ **adj.**
– ORIGIN late 17th cent.: from medieval Latin, variant of ILIUM.

il·e·us /ˈilēəs/ ▶ **n.** Medicine a painful obstruction of the ileum or other part of the intestine.
– ORIGIN late 17th cent.: from Latin, from Greek *eileos, ilios* 'colic,' apparently from *eilein* 'to roll.'

i·lex /ˈīˌleks/ ▶ **n. 1** another term for HOLM OAK. **2** a tree or shrub of a genus that includes holly and its relatives. ● Genus *Ilex*, family Aquifoliaceae.
– ORIGIN late Middle English: from Latin, 'holm oak.'

ILGWU ▶ **abbr.** International Ladies' Garment Workers' Union.

il·i·a /ˈilēə/ plural form of ILIUM.

il·i·ac /ˈilēˌak/ ▶ **adj.** of or relating to the ilium or the nearby regions of the lower body: *the iliac artery*.
– ORIGIN early 16th cent.: from late Latin *iliacus*, from *ilia* 'entrails.'

i·li·a·cus /iˈlīəkəs/ (also **iliacus muscle**) ▶ **n.** Anatomy a triangular muscle that passes from the pelvis through the groin on either side and, together with the psoas, flexes the hip.
– ORIGIN early 17th cent.: from late Latin.

Il·i·ad /ˈilēəd, -ˌad/ a Greek hexameter epic poem in twenty-four books, traditionally ascribed to Homer, telling how Achilles killed Hector at the climax of the Trojan War.

Il·i·um /ˈilēəm/ alternative name for TROY, esp. the 7th-century BC Greek city.

il·i·um /ˈilēəm/ ▶ **n.** (pl. **ilia** /ˈilēə/) the large broad bone forming the upper part of each half of the pelvis.
– ORIGIN late 16th cent.: from Latin, singular of *ilia* 'flanks, entrails.'

ilk /ilk/ ▶ **n.** [in sing.] a type of people or things similar to those already referred to: *the veiled suggestions that reporters of his ilk seem to be so good at* | *fascists, racists, and others of that ilk*. ■ **(of that ilk)** Scottish chiefly archaic of the place or estate of the same name: *Sir Iain Moncreiffe of that Ilk*.
– ORIGIN Old English *ilca* 'same,' of Germanic origin; related to ALIKE.

> **USAGE** In modern usage, ilk is used in phrases such as ***of his ilk*** and ***of that ilk*** to mean 'type' or 'sort.' This sense arose out of a misunderstanding of the earlier, Scottish use in the phrase **of that ilk**, where it means 'of the same name or place.' For this reason, some traditionalists regard the modern use as incorrect. It is, however, the only common current use and is now part of standard English.

ill /il/ ▶ **adj. 1** not in full health; sick: *her daughter is seriously ill* | [with submodifier] *a terminally ill patient*. **2** [attrib.] poor in quality: *ill judgment dogs the unsuccessful*. ■ harmful: *she had a cup of the same wine and suffered no ill effects*. ■ (esp. of fortune) not favorable: *no one less deserved such ill fortune than McStay*.
▶ **adv. 1** [usu. in combination] badly, wrongly, or imperfectly: *some of his premises seem ill-chosen* | *it ill becomes one so beautiful to be gloomy*. ■ unfavorably or unpropitiously: *something which boded ill for unwary golfers*. **2** only with difficulty; hardly: *she could ill afford the cost of new curtains*.
▶ **n. 1** (as plural noun **the ill**) people who are ill: *a day center for the mentally ill*. **2** (usu. **ills**) a problem or misfortune: *a lengthy work on the ills of society*. ■ evil; harm: *how could I wish him ill?*
– PHRASES **ill at ease** uncomfortable or embarrassed. **speak** (or **think**) **ill of** say (or think) something critical about.
– ORIGIN Middle English (in the senses 'wicked,' 'malevolent,' 'harmful,' and 'difficult'): from Old Norse *illr* 'evil, difficult,' of unknown origin.

> **USAGE** On the punctuation of ill in compound adjectives, see usage at WELL¹, as the same rules apply.

Ill. ▶ **abbr.** Illinois.

I'll /īl/ ▶ **contraction** I shall; I will: *I'll arrange it*.

ill-ad·vised ▶ **adj.** unwise or imprudent: *you would be ill-advised to go on your own*.
– DERIVATIVES **ill-ad·vis·ed·ly adv.**

ill-af·fect·ed ▶ **adj.** archaic not inclined to be friendly or sympathetic.

ill-as·sort·ed ▶ **adj.** not well matched: *ill-assorted furniture*.

il·la·tion /əˈlāshən/ ▶ **n.** archaic the action of inferring or drawing a conclusion. ■ an inference.
– ORIGIN mid 16th cent.: from Latin *illatio(n-)*, from *illat-* 'brought in,' from the verb *inferre* (see INFER).

il·la·tive /ˈilətiv, iˈlātiv/ ▶ **adj. 1** of the nature of or stating an inference. ■ proceeding by inference. **2** Grammar relating to or denoting a case of nouns in some languages used to express motion into something.
▶ **n.** the illative case, or a word in this case.
– DERIVATIVES **il·la·tive·ly adv.**
– ORIGIN late 16th cent.: from Latin *illativus*, from *illat-* 'brought in' (see ILLATION).

Il·la·war·ra /ˌiləˈwärə, -ˈwôrə/ ▶ **n.** (also **Illawarra shorthorn**) an animal of an Australian breed of red or roan dairy cattle.
– ORIGIN early 20th cent.: from the name of a coastal district south of Sydney, where the breed was developed.

ill-be·haved ▶ **adj.** behaving badly: *the most ill-behaved lot of kids and pets you've ever seen*.

ill-bred ▶ **adj.** badly brought up or rude.
– DERIVATIVES **ill breed·ing n.**

ill-con·ceived ▶ **adj.** not carefully planned or considered: *ill-conceived schemes*.

ill-con·sid·ered ▶ **adj.** badly thought out: *an ill-considered remark*.

ill-de·fined ▶ **adj.** not having a clear description or limits; vague: *ill-defined concepts*.

ill-dis·posed ▶ **adj.** unfriendly or unsympathetic: *this fact was ignored by ill-disposed critics*.

il·le·gal /i(l)ˈlēgəl/ ▶ **adj.** contrary to or forbidden by law, esp. criminal law: *illegal drugs*.
▶ **n.** an illegal immigrant.
– DERIVATIVES **il·le·gal·i·ty** /ˌi(l)liˈgalitē/ **n.** (pl. **illegalities**), **il·le·gal·ly adv.**
– ORIGIN early 17th cent.: from French *illégal* or medieval Latin *illegalis*, from Latin *in-* 'not' + *legalis* 'according to the law.'

il·leg·i·ble /i(l)ˈlejəbəl/ ▶ **adj.** not clear enough to be read: *his handwriting is totally illegible*.
– DERIVATIVES **il·leg·i·bil·i·ty** /i(l)ˌlejəˈbilitē/ **n.**, **il·leg·i·bly** /-blē/ **adv.**

il·le·git·i·mate /ˌi(l)ləˈjitəmit/ ▶ **adj.** not authorized by the law; not in accordance with accepted standards or rules: *an illegitimate exercise of power by the military*. ■ (of a child) born of parents not lawfully married to each other.
▶ **n.** a person who is illegitimate by birth.
– DERIVATIVES **il·le·git·i·ma·cy** /-məsē/ **n.**, **il·le·git·i·mate·ly adv.**
– ORIGIN mid 16th cent.: from late Latin *illegitimus* (from *in-* 'not' + *legitimus* 'lawful'), suggested by LEGITIMATE.

ill-fat·ed ▶ **adj.** destined to fail or have bad luck: *an ill-fated expedition*.

ill-fa·vored (Brit. **ill-favoured**) ▶ **adj.** unattractive or offensive: *he was by anyone's reckoning ill-favored and homely*.

ill feel·ing ▶ **n.** animosity or resentment.

ill-fit·ting ▶ **adj.** (of a garment) of the wrong size or shape for the person wearing it: *an ill-fitting suit*.

ill-found·ed ▶ **adj.** (esp. of an idea or belief) not based on fact or reliable evidence: *ill-founded criticism* | *her fear may be ill-founded*.

ill-got·ten ▶ **adj.** acquired by illegal or unfair means: *the Mafiosi launder their ill-gotten gains*.

ill hu·mor ▶ **n.** irritability or bad temper.

ill-hu·mored ▶ **adj.** bad-tempered; irritable: *a querulous and ill-humored little man*.

il·lib·er·al /i(l)ˈlib(ə)rəl/ ▶ **adj. 1** opposed to liberal principles; restricting freedom of thought or behavior: *illiberal and anti-democratic policies*. **2** rare uncultured or unrefined. **3** rare not generous; mean.
– DERIVATIVES **il·lib·er·al·ism n.**, **il·lib·er·al·i·ty** /-ˌlibəˈralitē/ **n.**, **il·lib·er·al·ly adv.**
– ORIGIN mid 16th cent. (in the sense 'vulgar, ill-bred'): from French *illibéral*, from Latin *illiberalis* 'mean, sordid,' from *in-* 'not' + *liberalis* (see LIBERAL).

Il·lich /ˈilich/, Ivan (1926–2002), US educator and writer; born in Austria. He advocated the deinstitutionalization of education, religion, and medicine. Notable works: *Deschooling Society* (1971) and *Limits to Medicine* (1978).

il·lic·it /i(l)ˈlisit/ ▶ **adj.** forbidden by law, rules, or custom: *illicit drugs* | *illicit sex*.
– DERIVATIVES **il·lic·it·ly adv.**, **il·lic·it·ness n.**
– ORIGIN early 16th cent.: from French, or from Latin *illicitus*, from *in-* 'not' + *licitus* (see LICIT).

il·lim·it·a·ble /i(l)ˈlimitəbəl/ ▶ **adj.** without limits or an end: *the illimitable human capacity for evil.*
– DERIVATIVES **il·lim·it·a·bil·i·ty** /-ˌlimitəˈbilitē/ **n.**, **il·lim·it·a·bly** /-blē/ **adv.**

Il·li·noi·an /ˌiliˈnoi-ən/ ▶ **adj.** Geology of, relating to, or denoting a Pleistocene glaciation in North America, preceding the Wisconsin and approximating to the Saale of northern Europe. ■ (as noun **the Illinoian**) the Illinoian glaciation or the system of deposits laid down during it.
– ORIGIN mid 19th cent.: from **ILLINOIS** + **-AN**.

Il·li·nois /ˌiləˈnoi, -ˈnoiz/ a state in the eastern central US; pop. 12,901,563 (est. 2008); capital, Springfield; statehood, Dec. 3, 1818 (21). Colonized by the French in the 1600s and ceded to Britain in 1763, it was acquired by the US in 1783.
– DERIVATIVES **Il·li·nois·an** /-ˈnoiən, -ˈnoizən/ **n. & adj.**

Il·li·nois Riv·er a river that flows southwest for 273 miles (440 km) through Illinois to the Mississippi River.

il·liq·uid /i(l)ˈlikwid/ ▶ **adj.** (of assets) not easily converted into cash: *illiquid assets.* ■ (of a market) with few participants and a low volume of activity.
– DERIVATIVES **il·li·quid·i·ty** /ˌi(l)liˈkwiditē/ **n.**

il·lite /ˈilīt/ ▶ **n.** a clay mineral of the muscovite mica group, with a lattice structure that does not expand on absorption of water.
– ORIGIN 1930s: from **ILLINOIS** + **-ITE**[1].

il·lit·er·a·cy /i(l)ˈlitərəsē/ ▶ **n.** the inability to read or write: *the ineffective educational system meant that illiteracy was widespread.* ■ lack of knowledge in a particular subject; ignorance: *his economic illiteracy.*

il·lit·er·ate /i(l)ˈlitərit/ ▶ **adj.** unable to read or write: *his parents were illiterate.* ■ [with submodifier] ignorant in a particular subject or activity: *the extent to which voters are politically illiterate.* ■ uncultured or poorly educated: *the ignorant, illiterate town council.* ■ (esp. of a piece of writing) showing a lack of education, esp. an inability to read or write well.
▶ **n.** a person who is unable to read or write.
– PHRASES **functionally illiterate** lacking the literacy necessary for coping with most jobs and many everyday situations.
– DERIVATIVES **il·lit·er·ate·ly adv.**, **il·lit·er·ate·ness n.**
– ORIGIN late Middle English: from Latin *illitteratus*, from *in-* ‘not’ + *litteratus* (see **LITERATE**).

ill-judged ▶ **adj.** lacking careful consideration; unwise: *an ill-judged decision.*

ill-man·nered ▶ **adj.** having bad manners; not behaving well in social situations: *ill-mannered and unruly children.*

ill-matched ▶ **adj.** (of two or more people or items) not well suited to or appropriate for each other: *an ill-matched couple.*

ill na·ture ▶ **n.** the quality of being bad-tempered or mean-spirited.

ill-na·tured ▶ **adj.** bad-tempered or mean-spirited.
– DERIVATIVES **ill-na·tured·ly adv.**

ill·ness /ˈilnis/ ▶ **n.** a disease or period of sickness affecting the body or mind: *he died after a long illness | I've never missed a day's work through illness.*

il·lo·cu·tion /ˌiləˈkyo͞oSHən/ ▶ **n.** Philosophy & Linguistics an act of speaking or writing which in itself effects or constitutes the intended action, e.g. ordering, warning, or promising. Compare with **PERLOCUTION**.
– DERIVATIVES **il·lo·cu·tion·ar·y** /-ˌnerē/ **adj.**

il·log·ic /i(l)ˈläjik/ ▶ **n.** reasoning or thought that is not logical.

il·log·i·cal /i(l)ˈläjikəl/ ▶ **adj.** lacking sense or clear, sound reasoning: *an illogical fear of the supernatural.*
– DERIVATIVES **il·log·i·cal·i·ty** /i(l)ˌläjiˈkalitē/ **n.** (pl. **illogicalities**), **il·log·i·cal·ly** /-ik(ə)lē/ **adv.**

ill-o·mened ▶ **adj.** attended by bad omens: *ill-omened birds of prey.*

ill-pre·pared ▶ **adj.** not ready or prepared for something: *his light clothing left him ill-prepared for the rain.*

ill-starred ▶ **adj.** destined to fail or have many difficulties; unlucky: *an ill-starred expedition.*

ill-suit·ed ▶ **adj.** unsuitable or inappropriate: *the soil is ill-suited to wheat farming.*

ill tem·per ▶ **n.** irritability; anger.

ill-tem·pered ▶ **adj.** irritable or grumpy.
– DERIVATIVES **ill-temperedly adv.**

ill-timed ▶ **adj.** done or occurring at an inappropriate time: *an extremely ill-timed announcement.*

ill-treat ▶ **v.** [with obj.] act cruelly toward (a person or animal).

ill-treat·ment ▶ **n.** cruel or inhumane treatment: *he died from medical neglect and ill-treatment.*

il·lude /iˈlo͞od/ ▶ **v.** [with obj.] literary trick; delude: *he had allowed his imagination to illude him.*
– ORIGIN late Middle English: from Latin *illudere* ‘to mock.’

il·lume /iˈlo͞om/ ▶ **v.** [with obj.] literary light up; illuminate: *sparks from candles illume our faces.*
– ORIGIN late Middle English: abbreviation of **ILLUMINE**.

il·lu·mi·nance /iˈlo͞omənəns/ ▶ **n.** Physics the amount of luminous flux per unit area.

il·lu·mi·nant /iˈlo͞omənənt/ ▶ **n.** technical a means of lighting or source of light: *until 1880, oil was the only illuminant in use.*
▶ **adj.** giving off light.
– ORIGIN mid 17th cent.: from Latin *illuminant-* ‘illuminating,’ from the verb *illuminare* (see **ILLUMINATE**).

il·lu·mi·nate /iˈlo͞oməˌnāt/ ▶ **v. 1** [with obj.] light up: *a flash of lightning illuminated the house* | figurative *his face was illuminated by a smile.* ■ decorate (a building or structure) with lights for a special occasion.
2 (often as adj. **illuminated**) decorate (a page or initial letter in a manuscript) with gold, silver, or colored designs.
3 (usu. as adj. **illuminating**) help to clarify or explain (a subject or matter): *a most illuminating discussion.*
– DERIVATIVES **il·lu·mi·nat·ing·ly adv.**, **il·lu·mi·na·tive** /-ˌnātiv, -nətiv/ **adj.**, **il·lu·mi·na·tor** /-ˌnātər/ **n.**
– ORIGIN late Middle English: from Latin *illuminat-* ‘illuminated,’ from the verb *illuminare*, from *in-* ‘upon’ + *lumen, lumin-* ‘light.’

il·lu·mi·na·ti /iˌlo͞oməˈnätē/ ▶ **plural n.** people claiming to possess special enlightenment or knowledge of something: *some mysterious standard known only to the illuminati of the organization.* ■ (**Illuminati**) a sect of 16th-century Spanish heretics who claimed special religious enlightenment. ■ (**Illuminati**) a Bavarian secret society founded in 1776, organized like the Freemasons.
– DERIVATIVES **il·lu·mi·nism** /iˈlo͞oməˌnizəm/ **n.**, **il·lu·mi·nist** /iˈlo͞omənist/ **n.**
– ORIGIN late 16th cent.: plural of Italian *illuminato* or Latin *illuminatus* ‘enlightened,’ past participle of *illuminare* (see **ILLUMINATE**).

il·lu·mi·na·tion /iˌlo͞oməˈnāSHən/ ▶ **n. 1** lighting or light: *higher levels of illumination are needed for reading.* ■ (often **illuminations**) a display of lights on a building or other structure.
2 Physics another term for **ILLUMINANCE**.
3 the art of illuminating a manuscript. ■ an illuminated design in a manuscript.
4 clarification: *these books form the most sustained analysis and illumination of the subject.* ■ spiritual or intellectual enlightenment.
– ORIGIN Middle English: via Old French from late Latin *illuminatio(n-)*, from the verb *illuminare* (see **ILLUMINATE**).

il·lu·mine /iˈlo͞omən/ ▶ **v.** [with obj.] literary light up; brighten: *the lamplight illumined her pale features.* ■ enlighten (someone) spiritually or intellectually: *he assures himself that he is illumined and not deluded.*
– ORIGIN Middle English: from Old French *illuminer*, from Latin *illuminare* (see **ILLUMINATE**).

illus. ▶ **abbr.** illustrated or illustration.

ill-use /ˌil ˈyo͞oz/ ▶ **v.** [with obj.] ill-treat (someone).
▶ **n.** (**ill use** /ˌil ˈyo͞os/) ill-treatment.

il·lu·sion /iˈlo͞oZHən/ ▶ **n.** a thing that is or is likely to be wrongly perceived or interpreted by the senses: *the illusion makes parallel lines seem to diverge by placing them on a zigzag-striped background.* ■ a deceptive appearance or impression: *the illusion of family togetherness | the tension between illusion and reality.* ■ a false idea or belief: *he had no illusions about the trouble she was in.*
– PHRASES **be under the illusion that** believe mistakenly that: *the world is under the illusion that the original painting still hangs in the Winter Palace.* **be under no illusion** (or **illusions**) be fully aware of the true state of affairs.
– DERIVATIVES **il·lu·sion·al** /-ZHənl/ **adj.**
– ORIGIN Middle English (in the sense ‘deceiving, deception’): via Old French from Latin *illusio(n-)*, from *illudere* ‘to mock,’ from *in-* ‘against’ + *ludere* ‘play.’

il·lu·sion·ism /iˈlo͞oZHəˌnizəm/ ▶ **n.** the principle or technique by which artistic representations are made to resemble real objects or to give an appearance of space by the use of perspective.
– DERIVATIVES **il·lu·sion·is·tic** /iˌlo͞oZHəˈnistik/ **adj.**

il·lu·sion·ist /iˈlo͞oZHənist/ ▶ **n.** a person who performs tricks that deceive the eye; a magician.

il·lu·sive /iˈlo͞osiv/ ▶ **adj.** chiefly literary deceptive; illusory: *that illusive haven.*
– ORIGIN early 17th cent.: from medieval Latin *illusivus*, from Latin *illus-* ‘mocked,’ from the verb *illudere* (see **ILLUSION**).

il·lu·so·ry /iˈlo͞osərē, -zərē/ ▶ **adj.** based on illusion; not real: *she knew the safety of her room was illusory.*
– DERIVATIVES **il·lu·so·ri·ly** /-rəlē/ **adv.**, **il·lu·so·ri·ness n.**

il·lus·trate /ˈiləˌstrāt/ ▶ **v.** [with obj.] provide (a book, newspaper, etc.) with pictures: *the guide is illustrated with full-color photographs.* ■ explain or make (something) clear by using examples, charts, pictures, etc.: *the results are illustrated in Figure 7.* ■ serve as an example of: *a collection of pieces that illustrate Bach's techniques.*
– ORIGIN early 16th cent. (in the sense ‘illuminate, shed light on’): from Latin *illustrat-* ‘lit up,’ from the verb *illustrare*, from *in-* ‘upon’ + *lustrare* ‘illuminate.’

il·lus·trat·ed /ˈiləˌstrātid/ ▶ **adj.** (of a book, newspaper, etc.) containing pictures or other graphical material: *an illustrated collection of poems.*

il·lus·tra·tion /ˌiləˈstrāSHən/ ▶ **n.** a picture illustrating a book, newspaper, etc.: *an illustration of a yacht.* ■ an example serving to clarify or prove something: *this accident is a graphic illustration of the disaster that's waiting to happen.* ■ the action or fact of illustrating something, either pictorially or by exemplification: *by way of illustration, I refer to the following case.*
– DERIVATIVES **il·lus·tra·tion·al** /-SHənl/ **adj.**
– ORIGIN late Middle English (in the sense ‘illumination; spiritual or intellectual enlightenment’): via Old French from Latin *illustratio(n-)*, from the verb *illustrare* (see **ILLUSTRATE**).

il·lus·tra·tive /iˈləstrətiv, ˈiləˌstrātiv/ ▶ **adj.** serving as an example or explanation: *this timetable is provided for illustrative purposes only.*
– DERIVATIVES **il·lus·tra·tive·ly adv.**

il·lus·tra·tor /ˈiləˌstrātər/ ▶ **n.** a person who draws or creates pictures for magazines, books, advertising, etc.

il·lus·tri·ous /iˈləstrēəs/ ▶ **adj.** well known, respected, and admired for past achievements: *his illustrious predecessor | an illustrious career.*
– DERIVATIVES **il·lus·tri·ous·ly adv.**, **il·lus·tri·ous·ness n.**
– ORIGIN mid 16th cent.: from Latin *illustris* ‘clear, bright’ + **-OUS**.

il·lu·vi·a·tion /iˌlo͞ovēˈāSHən/ ▶ **n.** Soil Science the introduction of salts or colloids into one soil horizon from another by percolating water.
– DERIVATIVES **il·lu·vi·al** /iˈlo͞ovēəl, -vyəl/ **adj.**, **il·lu·vi·at·ed** /iˈlo͞ovēˌātid/ **adj.**
– ORIGIN early 20th cent.: from **IL-** ‘in’ + *-luvial* (on the pattern of *alluvial*) + **-ATION**.

ill will ▶ **n.** animosity or bitterness: *he didn't bear his estranged wife any ill will.*

Il·lyr·i·a /iˈli(ə)rēə/ an ancient region along the eastern coast of the Adriatic Sea that included Dalmatia and what is now Montenegro and northern Albania.

Il·lyr·i·an /iˈli(ə)rēən/ ▶ **n.** a native or inhabitant of ancient Illyria. ■ the branch of the Indo-European family of languages possibly represented by modern Albanian.
▶ **adj.** of or relating to the ancient region of Illyria or its language.

il·men·ite /ˈilməˌnīt/ ▶ **n.** a black mineral consisting of iron titanium oxide, of which it is the main ore.
– ORIGIN early 19th cent.: named after the *Ilmen* mountains in the Urals + **-ITE**[1].

ILO ▶ **abbr.** International Labor Organization.

I·lo·ca·no /ˌēlōˈkänō/ ▶ **n.** (pl. **same** or **Ilocanos**) **1** a member of a people inhabiting northwestern Luzon in the Philippines.
2 the Austronesian language of this people.
▶ **adj.** of or relating to this people or their language.
– ORIGIN Philippine Spanish, from *Ilocos*, the name of two provinces in the Philippines.

I·lo·i·lo /ˌēlōˈēlō/ a port on the southern coast of Panay in the Philippines; pop. 418,700 (est. 2007).

I·lo·rin /iˈlôrin/ a city in western Nigeria; pop. 771,000 (est. 2007).

ILS ▶ **abbr.** instrument landing system, a system in which an aircraft's instruments interact with

PRONUNCIATION KEY ə *ago, up*; ər *over, fur*; a *hat*; ā *ate*; ä *car*; e *let*; ē *see*; i *fit*; ī *by*; NG *sing*; ō *go*; ô *law, for*; oi *toy*; o͝o *good*; o͞o *goo*; ou *out*; TH *thin*; T͟H *then*; ZH *vision*

ground-based electronics to enable the pilot to land the aircraft safely in poor visibility.

il·va·ite /ˈilvəˌīt/ ▶ **n.** a mineral consisting of a basic silicate of calcium and iron, typically occurring as black prisms.
– ORIGIN early 19th cent.: from Latin *Ilva* 'Elba' (an Italian island in the Mediterranean) + -ITE[1].

-ily ▶ **suffix** forming adverbs corresponding to adjectives ending in *-y* (such as *happily* corresponding to *happy*).
– ORIGIN see -Y[1], -LY[2].

IM ▶ **abbr.** Computing ■ instant message. ■ instant messaging.

I'm /īm/ ▶ **contraction** I am: *I'm a busy woman.*

im- ▶ **prefix** variant spelling of IN-[1], IN-[2] assimilated before *b, m, p* (as in *imbibe, immure, impart*).

im·age /ˈimij/ ▶ **n. 1** a representation of the external form of a person or thing in art. ■ a visible impression obtained by a camera, telescope, microscope, or other device, or displayed on a computer or video screen. ■ an optical appearance or counterpart produced by light or other radiation from an object reflected in a mirror or refracted through a lens. ■ Mathematics a point or set formed by mapping from another point or set. ■ Computing an exact copy of a computer's hard disk, made for backing up data or setting up new machines. ■ a mental representation or idea: *he had an image of Uncle Walter throwing his crutches away.* ■ [in sing.] a person or thing that closely resembles another: *he's the image of his father.*
2 a simile or metaphor: *he uses the image of a hole to describe emotional emptiness.*
3 the general impression that a person, organization, or product presents to the public: *she strives to project an image of youth.* ■ [in sing.] semblance or likeness: *we are made in the image of God.* ■ (in biblical use) an idol.
▶ **v.** [with obj.] make a representation of the external form of: *artworks that imaged women's bodies.* ■ make a visual representation of (something) by scanning it with a detector or electromagnetic beam: *every point on the Earth's surface was imaged by the satellite* | (as noun **imaging**) *medical imaging.* ■ form a mental picture or idea of: *it is possible for us to image a society in which no one committed crime.*
– DERIVATIVES **im·age·less** adj.
– ORIGIN Middle English: from Old French, from Latin *imago*; related to IMITATE.

im·age in·ten·si·fi·er ▶ **n.** a device used to make a brighter version of an image on a photoelectric screen.

im·age mac·ro ▶ **n.** (on the Internet) a photographic image on which a humorous caption or catchphrase has been digitally superimposed.

im·age·mak·er ▶ **n.** a person employed to identify and create a favorable public image for a person, organization, or product.

im·age proc·ess·ing ▶ **n.** the analysis and manipulation of a digitized image, esp. in order to improve its quality.

im·ag·er /ˈimijər/ ▶ **n.** an electronic or other device that records images of something: *a thermal imager.*

im·age·ry /ˈimij(ə)rē/ ▶ **n.** visually descriptive or figurative language, esp. in a literary work: *Tennyson uses imagery to create a lyrical emotion.* ■ visual images collectively: *the impact of computer-generated imagery on contemporary art.* ■ visual symbolism: *the film's religious imagery.*
– ORIGIN Middle English (in the senses 'statuary, carved images collectively'): from Old French *imagerie*, from *imager* 'make an image,' from *image* (see IMAGE).

im·age·set·ter /ˈimijˌsetər/ ▶ **n.** Computing a very high-quality type of color printer used to print glossy magazines, newsletters, or other documents.

im·ag·i·na·ble /iˈmaj(ə)nəbəl/ ▶ **adj.** possible to be thought of or believed: *the most spectacular views imaginable.*
– DERIVATIVES **i·mag·i·na·bly** /-blē/ adv.
– ORIGIN late Middle English: from late Latin *imaginabilis*, from Latin *imaginare* 'form an image of, represent,' from *imago, imagin-* 'image.'

i·ma·gi·nal ▶ **adj. 1** /iˈmaj(ə)nəl/ of or relating to an image: *imaginal education methods.*
2 /iˈmāgənəl, iˈmä-/ Entomology of or relating to an adult insect or imago.
– ORIGIN late 19th cent.: from Latin *imago, imagin-* 'image' + -AL.

im·ag·i·nar·y /iˈmajəˌnerē/ ▶ **adj. 1** existing only in the imagination: *Chris had imaginary conversations with her.*
2 Mathematics (of a number or quantity) expressed in terms of the square root of a negative number (usually the square root of −1, represented by *i* or *j*). See also COMPLEX.
– DERIVATIVES **im·ag·i·nar·i·ly** /iˌmajəˈne(ə)rəlē/ adv.
– ORIGIN late Middle English: from Latin *imaginarius*, from *imago, imagin-* 'image.'

> **USAGE** Imaginary means 'product of the imagination, unreal.' **Imaginative** means 'showing imagination, original.' Science fiction, for example, deals with **imaginary** people, places, and events; how **imaginative** it is depends on the writer's ability.

im·ag·i·na·tion /iˌmajəˈnāSHən/ ▶ **n.** the faculty or action of forming new ideas, or images or concepts of external objects not present to the senses: *she'd never been blessed with a vivid imagination.* ■ the ability of the mind to be creative or resourceful: *technology gives workers the chance to use their imagination.* ■ the part of the mind that imagines things: *a girl who existed only in my imagination.*
– ORIGIN Middle English: via Old French from Latin *imaginatio(n-)*, from the verb *imaginari* 'picture to oneself,' from *imago, imagin-* 'image.'

im·ag·i·na·tive /iˈmaj(ə)nətiv/ ▶ **adj.** having or showing creativity or inventiveness: *making imaginative use of computer software* | *he was imaginative beyond all other architects.*
– DERIVATIVES **i·mag·i·na·tive·ly** adv., **i·mag·i·na·tive·ness** n.

> **USAGE** See usage at IMAGINARY.

im·ag·ine /iˈmajən/ ▶ **v.** [with obj.] **1** form a mental image or concept of: *imagine a road trip from Philadelphia to Chicago* | [with clause] *I couldn't imagine what she expected to tell them.* ■ (often as adj. **imagined**) believe (something unreal or untrue) to exist or be so: *they suffered from ill health, real or imagined, throughout their lives.*
2 [with clause] suppose or assume: *after Ned died, everyone imagined that Mabel would move away.* ■ [as exclamation] just suppose: *imagine! to outwit Heydrich!*
– DERIVATIVES **i·mag·in·er** n.
– ORIGIN Middle English: from Old French *imaginer*, from Latin *imaginare* 'form an image of, represent' and *imaginari* 'picture to oneself,' both from *imago, imagin-* 'image.'

im·ag·i·neer /iˌmajəˈni(ə)r/ ▶ **n.** a person who devises and implements a new or highly imaginative concept or technology, in particular one who devises the attractions in Walt Disney theme parks.
▶ **v.** [with obj.] (often as noun **imagineering**) devise and implement (such a concept or technology): *theme parks are benefiting from a new era of imagineering.*
– ORIGIN 1940s: from IMAGINE, on the pattern of *engineer.*

im·ag·ines /iˈmāgəˌnēz, iˈmä-/ plural form of IMAGO.

im·ag·in·ings /iˈmajəniNGz/ ▶ **plural n.** thoughts or fantasies: *this was quite beyond his worst imaginings.*

im·ag·ism /ˈiməˌjizəm/ ▶ **n.** a movement in early 20th-century English and American poetry that sought clarity of expression through the use of precise images. The movement derived in part from the aesthetic philosophy of T. E. Hulme and involved Ezra Pound, James Joyce, Amy Lowell, and others.
– DERIVATIVES **im·ag·ist** n., **im·ag·is·tic** /ˌiməˈjistik/ adj.

i·ma·go /iˈmāgō, iˈmä-/ ▶ **n.** (pl. **imagos, imagoes** or **imagines** /iˈmāgəˌnēz/) **1** Entomology the final and fully developed adult stage of an insect, typically winged.
2 Psychoanalysis an unconscious, idealized mental image of someone, esp. a parent, that influences a person's behavior.
– ORIGIN late 18th cent. (sense 1): modern Latin use of Latin *imago* 'image.' Sense 2 dates from the early 20th cent.

i·mam /iˈmäm/ ▶ **n.** the person who leads prayers in a mosque. ■ (**Imam**) a title of various Muslim leaders, esp. of one succeeding Muhammad as leader of Shiite Islam: *Imam Khomeini.*
– DERIVATIVES **i·mam·ate** /-ˌmāt/ n.
– ORIGIN from Arabic *'imām* 'leader,' from *'amma* 'lead the way.'

IMAP /ˈīˌmap/ ▶ **abbr.** Computing Internet Mail Access Protocol.

I·ma·ri /iˈmärē/ ▶ **n.** [usu. as modifier] a type of richly decorated Japanese porcelain: *an Imari vase.*
– ORIGIN late 19th cent.: from the name of a port in northwestern Kyushu, Japan, from which it was shipped.

IMAX /ˈīˌmaks/ ▶ **n.** trademark a technique of widescreen cinematography that produces an image approximately ten times larger than that from standard 35 mm film: [as modifier] *IMAX theaters.*
– ORIGIN 1960s: from *i-* (probably representing a pronunciation of EYE) + *max* (short for MAXIMUM).

im·bal·ance /imˈbaləns/ ▶ **n.** lack of proportion or relation between corresponding things: *tension is generated by the imbalance of power* | *the condition is caused by a hormonal imbalance.*

im·be·cile /ˈimbəsəl, -ˌsil/ ▶ **n.** informal a stupid person.
▶ **adj.** [attrib.] stupid; idiotic: *try not to make imbecile remarks.*
– DERIVATIVES **im·be·cil·ic** /ˌimbəˈsilik/ adj., **im·be·cil·i·ty** /ˌimbəˈsilitē/ n. (pl. **imbecilities**).
– ORIGIN mid 16th cent. (as an adjective in the sense 'physically weak'): via French from Latin *imbecillus*, literally 'without a supporting staff,' from *in-* (expressing negation) + *baculum* 'stick, staff.' The current sense dates from the early 19th cent.

im·bed ▶ **v.** variant spelling of EMBED.

im·bibe /imˈbīb/ ▶ **v.** [with obj.] formal or humorous drink (alcohol): *they were imbibing far too many pitchers of beer* | [no obj.] *having imbibed too freely, he fell over.* ■ absorb or assimilate (ideas or knowledge): *she had imbibed the gospel of modernism from Kandinsky.* ■ chiefly Botany (esp. of seeds) absorb (water) into ultramicroscopic spaces or pores. ■ Botany place (seeds) in water in order to absorb it.
– DERIVATIVES **im·bib·er** n., **im·bi·bi·tion** /ˌimbəˈbiSHən/ n. (chiefly Botany).
– ORIGIN late Middle English (in the senses 'absorb or cause to absorb moisture' and 'take into solution'): from Latin *imbibere*, from *in-* 'in' + *bibere* 'to drink.'

im·bri·cate /ˈimbriˌkāt/ chiefly Zoology & Botany ▶ **v.** (usu. as adj. **imbricated**) arrange (scales, sepals, plates, etc.) so that they overlap like roof tiles: *these molds have spherical bodies composed of imbricated triangular plates.* ■ [no obj.] (usu. as adj. **imbricating**) overlap: *a coating of imbricating scales.*
▶ **adj.** (of scales, sepals, plates, etc.) having adjacent edges overlapping. Compare with VALVATE.
– DERIVATIVES **im·bri·ca·tion** /ˌimbriˈkāSHən/ n.
– ORIGIN early 17th cent. (in the sense 'shaped like a pantile'): from Latin *imbricat-* 'covered with roof tiles,' from the verb *imbricare*, from *imbrex, imbric-* 'roof tile' (from *imber* 'shower of rain').

im·bro·glio /imˈbrōlyō/ ▶ **n.** (pl. **imbroglios**) an extremely confused, complicated, or embarrassing situation: *the Watergate imbroglio.* ■ archaic a confused heap.
– ORIGIN mid 18th cent.: Italian, from *imbrogliare* 'confuse'; related to EMBROIL.

Im·bros /ˈēmˌbrôs/ a Turkish island in the Aegean Sea, near the entrance to the Dardanelles. Turkish name **Imroz.**

im·brue /imˈbro͞o/ (also **embrue** /em-/) ▶ **v.** (**imbrues, imbruing, imbrued**) [with obj.] archaic or literary stain (something, esp. one's hands or sword): *they were unwilling to imbrue their hands in his blood.*
– ORIGIN late Middle English: from Old French *embruer* 'bedaub, bedabble,' ultimately of Germanic origin and related to BROTH.

im·bue /imˈbyo͞o/ ▶ **v.** (**imbues, imbuing, imbued**) [with obj.] (often **be imbued with**) inspire or permeate with a feeling or quality: *the entire performance was imbued with sparkle and elan.*
– ORIGIN late Middle English (in the sense 'saturate'): from French *imbu* 'moistened,' from Latin *imbutus*, past participle of *imbuere* 'moisten.'

IMD ▶ **abbr.** intermodulation distortion.

IMEI ▶ **abbr.** international mobile equipment identity.

IMF ▶ **abbr.** International Monetary Fund.

IMHO ▶ **abbr.** in my humble opinion.

Im·ho·tep /imˈhōˌtep/ (*fl.* 27th century BC), Egyptian architect and scholar, who was later deified. It is thought that he designed the step pyramid built at Saqqara for third-dynasty pharaoh Djoser.

im·id·az·ole /ˌimiˈdazōl/ ▶ **n.** Chemistry a colorless crystalline compound with mildly basic properties, present as a substituent in the amino acid histidine. ● a heterocyclic compound; chem. formula: $C_3H_4N_2$.
– ORIGIN late 19th cent.: from IMIDE + AZO- + -OLE.

im·ide /ˈimīd/ ▶ **n.** Chemistry an organic compound containing the group −CONHCO−, related to ammonia by replacement of two hydrogen atoms by acyl groups.
– ORIGIN mid 19th cent.: from French, arbitrary alteration of AMIDE.

i·mine /iˈmēn, ˈimin/ ▶ **n.** Chemistry an organic compound containing the group −C=NH or −C=NR where R is an alkyl or other group.
– ORIGIN late 19th cent.: from AMINE, on the pattern of the pair *amide, imide.*

im·ip·ra·mine /iˈmiprəˌmēn/ ▶ **n.** a synthetic compound used to treat depression. ● A tricyclic amine; chem. formula: $C_{19}H_{24}N_2$.
– ORIGIN 1950s: from *imi(ne)* + *pr(opyl)* + AMINE.

imit. ▶ **abbr.** imitation or imitative.

im·i·tate /ˈimiˌtāt/ ▶ **v.** take or follow as a model: *his style was imitated by many other writers.* ■ copy (a person's speech or mannerisms), esp. for comic effect: *she imitated my Scottish accent.* ■ copy or simulate: *synthetic fabrics can now imitate everything from silk to rubber.*
– DERIVATIVES **im·i·ta·ble** /ˈimitəbəl/ **adj.**
– ORIGIN mid 16th cent.: from Latin *imitat-* 'copied,' from the verb *imitari*; related to *imago* 'image.'

im·i·ta·tion /ˌimiˈtāsʜən/ ▶ **n.** a thing intended to simulate or copy something else: [as modifier] *an imitation diamond.* ■ the action of using someone or something as a model: *a child learns to speak by imitation.* ■ an act of imitating a person's speech or mannerisms, esp. for comic effect: *he attempted an atrocious imitation of my English accent.* ■ Music the repetition of a phrase or melody in another part or voice, usually at a different pitch.
– PHRASES **imitation is the sincerest form of flattery** proverb copying someone or something is an implicit way of paying them a compliment.
– ORIGIN late Middle English: from Latin *imitatio(n-)*, from the verb *imitari* (see IMITATE).

im·i·ta·tive /ˈimiˌtātiv/ ▶ **adj. 1** copying or following a model or example: *the derring-do of our film heroes inspired us to imitative feats.* ■ following a model or example without any attempt at originality: *an ill-conceived and imitative addition to the museum.*
2 (of a word) reproducing a natural sound (e.g., *fizz*) or pronounced in a way that is thought to correspond to the appearance or character of the object or action described (e.g., *blob*).
– DERIVATIVES **im·i·ta·tive·ly adv.**, **im·i·ta·tive·ness n.**

im·i·ta·tor /ˈimiˌtātər/ ▶ **n.** a person who copies the behavior or actions of another: *the show's success has sparked off many imitators.*

im·mac·u·late /iˈmakyəlit/ ▶ **adj.** (esp. of a person or their clothes) perfectly clean, neat, or tidy: *an immaculate white suit.* ■ free from flaws or mistakes; perfect: *an immaculate safety record.* ■ Theology (in the Roman Catholic Church) free from sin. ■ Botany & Zoology uniformly colored without spots or other marks.
– DERIVATIVES **im·mac·u·la·cy** /-ləsē/ **n.**, **im·mac·u·late·ly adv.**, **im·mac·u·late·ness n.**
– ORIGIN late Middle English (in the sense 'free from moral stain'): from Latin *immaculatus*, from *in-* 'not' + *maculatus* 'stained' (from *macula* 'spot').

Im·mac·u·late Con·cep·tion ▶ **n.** the doctrine that God preserved the Virgin Mary from the taint of original sin from the moment she was conceived; it was defined as a dogma of the Roman Catholic Church in 1854. ■ the feast commemorating the Immaculate Conception on December 8.

im·ma·nent /ˈimənənt/ ▶ **adj.** existing or operating within; inherent: *the protection of liberties is immanent in constitutional arrangements.* ■ (of God) permanently pervading and sustaining the universe. Often contrasted with TRANSCENDENT.
– DERIVATIVES **im·ma·nence n.**, **im·ma·nen·cy n.**, **im·ma·nent·ism** /-ˌtizəm/ **n.**, **im·ma·nent·ist** /-tist/ **n.**
– ORIGIN mid 16th cent.: from late Latin *immanent-* 'remaining within,' from *in-* 'in' + *manere* 'remain.'

Im·man·u·el variant spelling of EMMANUEL.

im·ma·te·ri·al /ˌi(m)məˈti(ə)rēəl/ ▶ **adj.**
1 unimportant under the circumstances; irrelevant: *so long as the band kept the beat, what they played was immaterial.*
2 Philosophy spiritual, rather than physical: *we have immaterial souls.*
– DERIVATIVES **im·ma·te·ri·al·i·ty** /-ˌti(ə)rēˈalitē/ **n.**, **im·ma·te·ri·al·ly adv.**
– ORIGIN late Middle English (sense 2): from late Latin *immaterialis*, from *in-* 'not' + *materialis* 'relating to matter.'

im·ma·te·ri·al·ism /ˌi(m)məˈti(ə)rēəˌlizəm/ ▶ **n.** the belief that material things have no objective existence.
– DERIVATIVES **im·ma·te·ri·al·ist n.**

im·ma·ture /ˌiməˈcʜo͝or, -ˈt(y)o͝or/ ▶ **adj.** not fully developed: *many of the fish caught are immature | immature fruit.* ■ having or showing emotional or intellectual development appropriate to someone younger: *his immature sense of humor.*
– DERIVATIVES **im·ma·ture·ly adv.**
– ORIGIN mid 16th cent. (in the sense 'premature,' referring to death): from Latin *immaturus* 'untimely, unripe,' from *in-* 'not' + *maturus* 'ripe' (see MATURE).

im·ma·tu·ri·ty /ˌiməˈcʜo͝oritē/ ▶ **n.** the state of being immature or not fully grown. ■ behavior that is appropriate to someone younger: *they were shocked by such immaturity in a grown man.*

im·meas·ur·a·ble /iˈmezʜərəbəl/ ▶ **adj.** too large, extensive, or extreme to measure: *immeasurable suffering.*
– DERIVATIVES **im·meas·ur·a·bil·i·ty** /-ˌmezʜərəˈbilitē/ **n.**, **im·meas·ur·a·bly adv.**

im·me·di·a·cy /iˈmēdēəsē/ ▶ **n.** the quality of bringing one into direct and instant involvement with something, giving rise to a sense of urgency or excitement: *electronic mail works because it has the immediacy of a scribbled memo.*

im·me·di·ate /iˈmēdē-it/ ▶ **adj. 1** occurring or done at once; instant: *the authorities took no immediate action | the book's success was immediate.* ■ relating to or existing at the present time: *the immediate concern was how to avoid taxes.*
2 nearest in time, relationship, or rank: *a funeral with only the immediate family in attendance.* ■ nearest or next to in space: *roads in the immediate vicinity of the port.* ■ (of a relation or action) without an intervening medium or agency; direct: *coronary thrombosis was the immediate cause of death.*
3 Philosophy (of knowledge or reaction) gained or shown without reasoning; intuitive.
– DERIVATIVES **im·me·di·ate·ness n.**
– ORIGIN late Middle English (in the sense 'nearest in space or order'): from Old French *immediat*, or from late Latin *immediatus*, from *in-* 'not' + *mediatus* 'intervening,' past participle of *mediare* (see MEDIATE).

im·me·di·ate con·stit·u·ent ▶ **n.** Linguistics each of the constituents of a syntactic unit at the next level down in the hierarchy.

im·me·di·ate·ly /iˈmēdē-itlē/ ▶ **adv. 1** at once; instantly: *I called immediately for an ambulance.*
2 without any intervening time or space: *she was sitting immediately behind me.* ■ in direct or very close relation: *they would be the states most immediately affected by any such action.*
▶ **conj.** chiefly Brit. as soon as: *let me know immediately she arrives.*

im·med·i·ca·ble /iˈmedikəbəl/ ▶ **adj.** archaic unable to be healed or treated; incurable.
– ORIGIN mid 16th cent.: from Latin *immedicabilis*, from *in-* 'not' + *medicabilis* (see MEDICABLE).

Im·mel·mann /ˈiməlmən, -ˌmän/ (also **Immelmann turn**) ▶ **n.** an aerobatic maneuver in which an airplane performs a half loop followed by a half roll, resulting in reversal of direction and increased height.
– ORIGIN early 20th cent.: named after Max *Immelmann* (1890–1916), German fighter pilot.

im·me·mo·ri·al /ˌi(m)məˈmôrēəl/ ▶ **adj.** originating in the distant past; very old: *an immemorial custom.*
– DERIVATIVES **im·me·mo·ri·al·ly adv.**
– ORIGIN early 17th cent.: from medieval Latin *immemorialis*, from *in-* 'not' + *memorialis* 'relating to the memory.'

im·mense /iˈmens/ ▶ **adj.** extremely large or great, esp. in scale or degree: *the cost of restoration has been immense | an immense apartment building.*
– DERIVATIVES **im·men·si·ty** /-sitē/ **n.**
– ORIGIN late Middle English: via French from Latin *immensus* 'immeasurable,' from *in-* 'not' + *mensus* 'measured' (past participle of *metiri*).

im·mense·ly /iˈmenslē/ ▶ **adv.** to a great extent; extremely: [as submodifier] *the president was immensely popular.*

im·merse /iˈmərs/ ▶ **v. 1** dip or submerge in a liquid: *immerse the paper in water for twenty minutes.* ■ baptize (someone) by immersion in water.
2 (**immerse oneself** or **be immersed**) involve oneself deeply in a particular activity or interest: *she immersed herself in her work | she was still immersed in her thoughts.*
– ORIGIN early 17th cent.: from Latin *immers-* 'dipped into,' from the verb *immergere*, from *in-* 'in' + *mergere* 'to dip.'

im·mer·sion /iˈmərzʜən, -sʜən/ ▶ **n.** the action of immersing someone or something in a liquid: *his back was still raw from immersion in the icy Atlantic Ocean.* ■ deep mental involvement: *she seeks total immersion in her own inner world.* ■ a method of teaching a foreign language by the exclusive use of that language, usually at a special school. ■ baptism by immersing a person bodily (but not necessarily completely) in water. ■ Astronomy, rare the disappearance of a celestial body in the shadow of or behind another. See also EMERSION.
– ORIGIN late 15th cent.: from late Latin *immersio(n-)*, from *immergere* 'dip into' (see IMMERSE).

im·mer·sion heat·er ▶ **n.** an electric heating element that is positioned in the liquid to be heated.

im·mer·sive /iˈmərsiv/ ▶ **adj.** (of a computer display or system) generating a three-dimensional image that appears to surround the user.

im·mi·grant /ˈimigrənt/ ▶ **n.** a person who comes to live permanently in a foreign country. ■ Biology an animal or plant living or growing in a region to which it has migrated.
– ORIGIN late 18th cent.: from Latin *immigrant-* 'immigrating,' from the verb *immigrare*, on the pattern of *emigrant*.

im·mi·grate /ˈimiˌgrāt/ ▶ **v.** [no obj.] come to live permanently in a foreign country: *the Mennonites immigrated to western Canada in the 1870s.*
– ORIGIN early 17th cent.: from Latin *immigrat-* 'immigrated,' from the verb *immigrare*, from *in-* 'into' + *migrare* 'migrate.'

USAGE See usage at EMIGRATE.

im·mi·gra·tion /ˌimiˈgrāsʜən/ ▶ **n.** the action of coming to live permanently in a foreign country: *patterns of immigration from the Indian subcontinent to Britain.* ■ the place at an airport or country's border where government officials check the documents of people entering that country.

im·mi·nent /ˈimənənt/ ▶ **adj. 1** about to happen: *they were in imminent danger of being swept away.*
2 archaic overhanging.
– DERIVATIVES **im·mi·nence n.**, **im·mi·nent·ly adv.**
– ORIGIN late Middle English: from Latin *imminent-* 'overhanging, impending,' from the verb *imminere*, from *in-* 'upon, toward' + *minere* 'to project.'

im·mis·ci·ble /i(m)ˈmisəbəl/ ▶ **adj.** (of liquids) not forming a homogeneous mixture when added together: *water is immiscible with suntan oil.*
– DERIVATIVES **im·mis·ci·bil·i·ty** /-ˌmisəˈbilitē/ **n.**, **im·mis·ci·bly** /-blē/ **adv.**
– ORIGIN late 17th cent.: from late Latin *immiscibilis*, from *in-* 'not' + *miscibilis* (see MISCIBLE).

i

im·mis·er·a·tion /i(m)ˌmizəˈrāsʜən/ ▶ **n.** economic impoverishment.
– DERIVATIVES **im·mis·er·ate** /-ˈmizəˌrāt/ **v.**
– ORIGIN 1940s: translating German *Verelendung*.

im·mis·er·i·za·tion /i(m)ˌmizərəˈzāsʜən/ ▶ **n.** another term for IMMISERATION.
– DERIVATIVES **im·mis·er·ize** /-ˈmizəˌrīz/ **v.**

im·mit·i·ga·ble /i(m)ˈmitigəbəl/ ▶ **adj.** archaic unable to be made less severe or serious: *the pain was immitigable.*
– DERIVATIVES **im·mit·i·ga·bly** /-blē/ **adv.**
– ORIGIN late 16th cent.: from late Latin *immitigabilis*, from *in-* 'not' + *mitigabilis* 'able to be mitigated.'

im·mit·tance /i(m)ˈmitns/ ▶ **n.** Physics admittance and impedance (as a combined concept).
– ORIGIN 1950s: blend of IMPEDANCE and ADMITTANCE.

im·mix·ture /iˈmiksCHər/ ▶ **n.** archaic the process of mixing or being involved with something.

im·mo·bile /i(m)ˈmōbəl, -bēl, -bīl/ ▶ **adj.** not moving; motionless: *she sat immobile for a long time.* ■ incapable of moving or being moved: *an immobile workforce.*
– DERIVATIVES **im·mo·bil·i·ty** /ˌi(m)mōˈbilitē/ **n.**
– ORIGIN Middle English: from Old French, from Latin *immobilis*, from *in-* 'not' + *mobilis* (see MOBILE).

im·mo·bil·ism /i(m)ˈmōbəˌlizəm/ ▶ **n.** deep-seated resistance to political change.

im·mo·bi·lize /i(m)ˈmōbəˌlīz/ ▶ **v.** [with obj.] prevent (something or someone) from moving or operating as normal: *I want you to immobilize their vehicle | fear had immobilized her.* ■ restrict the movements of (a limb or patient) to allow healing: *other children in the ward were immobilized in traction.*
– DERIVATIVES **im·mo·bi·li·za·tion** /-ˌmōbəliˈzāsʜən/ **n.**
– ORIGIN late 19th cent.: from French *immobiliser*, from *immobile* (see IMMOBILE).

im·mod·er·ate /i(m)ˈmädərit/ ▶ **adj.** not sensible or restrained; excessive: *immoderate drinking.*
– DERIVATIVES **im·mod·er·ate·ly adv.**
– ORIGIN late Middle English: from Latin *immoderatus*, from *in-* 'not' + *moderatus* 'reduced, controlled' (past participle of *moderare*).

im·mod·er·a·tion /iˌmädəˈrāsʜən/ ▶ **n.** the quality of being excessive and lacking in restraint; overindulgence: *he paid a high price for his immoderation.*

im·mod·est /i(m)ˈmädist/ ▶ **adj.** lacking humility or decency: *she thought Western clothes were ugly and immodest.*
– DERIVATIVES **im·mod·est·ly adv.**, **im·mod·es·ty n.**
– ORIGIN late 16th cent.: from French *immodeste* or Latin *immodestus*, from *in-* 'not' + *modestus* (see MODEST).

im·mo·late /ˈiməˌlāt/ ▶ **v.** [with obj.] kill or offer as a sacrifice, esp. by burning.
– DERIVATIVES **im·mo·la·tion** /ˌiməˈlāsʜən/ **n.**, **im·mo·la·tor** /-ˌlātər/ **n.**

– ORIGIN mid 16th cent.: from Latin *immolat-* 'sprinkled with sacrificial meal,' from the verb *immolare*, from *in-* 'upon' + *mola* 'meal.'

im·mor·al /i(m)ˈmôrəl, -ˈmärəl/ ▶ **adj.** not conforming to accepted standards of morality: *an immoral and unwinnable war*.
– DERIVATIVES **im·mor·al·ly adv.**

> **USAGE** Immoral means 'failing to adhere to moral standards.' **Amoral** is a more neutral, impartial word meaning 'without, or not concerned with, moral standards.' An **immoral** person commits acts that violate society's moral norms. An **amoral** person has no understanding of these norms, or no sense of right and wrong. **Amoral** may also mean 'not concerned with, or outside the scope of morality' (following the pattern of *apolitical, asexual*). **Amoral**, then, may refer to a judicial ruling that is concerned only with narrow legal or financial issues. Whereas **amoral** may be simply descriptive, **immoral** is judgmental.

im·mor·al·ism /iˈmôrəˌlizəm, -ˈmär-/ ▶ **n.** a system of thought or behavior that does not accept moral principles.
– DERIVATIVES **im·mor·al·ist n.**
– ORIGIN early 20th cent.: suggested by German *Immoralismus*.

im·mo·ral·i·ty /ˌiməˈralitē, ˌimô-/ ▶ **n.** (pl. **im·moralities**) the state or quality of being immoral; wickedness: *he believed his father had been punished by God for his immorality*.

i

im·mor·tal /i(m)ˈmôrtl/ ▶ **adj.** living forever; never dying or decaying: *our mortal bodies are inhabited by immortal souls*. ■ deserving to be remembered forever: *the immortal children's classic, "The Adventures of Tom Sawyer."*
▶ **n.** an immortal being, esp. a god of ancient Greece or Rome. ■ a person of enduring fame: *he will always be one of the immortals of hockey*. ■ (**Immortals**) historical the royal bodyguard of ancient Persia. ■ (**Immortal**) a member of the French Academy.
– DERIVATIVES **im·mor·tal·ly adv.**
– ORIGIN late Middle English: from Latin *immortalis*, from *in-* 'not' + *mortalis* (see **MORTAL**).

im·mor·tal·i·ty /ˌi(m)ˌmôrˈtalitē/ ▶ **n.** the ability to live forever; eternal life: *eating the fruit gave the gods immortality*.

im·mor·tal·ize /i(m)ˈmôrtlˌīz/ ▶ **v.** [with obj.] (usu. **be immortalized in**) confer enduring fame upon: *he will be forever immortalized in the history books*.
– DERIVATIVES **im·mor·tal·i·za·tion** /-ˌmôrtl-iˈzāSHən/ **n.**

im·mor·telle /ˌiˌmôrˈtel/ ▶ **n. 1** another term for **EVERLASTING** (sense 2 of the noun).
2 W. Indian a Caribbean tree of the pea family, with a spiny trunk and clusters of red, orange, or pinkish flowers. ● Genus *Erythrina*, family Leguminosae: two species.
– ORIGIN mid 19th cent.: French, literally 'everlasting.'

im·mo·tile /i(m)ˈmōtl/ ▶ **adj.** Biology not motile.

im·mov·a·ble /i(m)ˈmo͞ovəbəl/ ▶ **adj.** not able to be moved: *lock your bike to something immovable like a lamp post*. ■ (of a person) not yielding to argument or pressure. ■ (esp. of a principle) fixed or unchangeable: *an immovable article of faith*. ■ Law (of property) consisting of land, buildings, or other permanent items.
▶ **n.** (**immovables**) Law immovable property.
– DERIVATIVES **im·mov·a·bil·i·ty** /-ˌmo͞ovəˈbilitē/ **n.**, **im·mov·a·bly** /-blē/ **adv.**

immun. ▶ **abbr.** immunity or immunization.

im·mune /iˈmyo͞on/ ▶ **adj.** resistant to a particular infection or toxin owing to the presence of specific antibodies or sensitized white blood cells: *they were naturally immune to hepatitis B*. ■ protected or exempt, esp. from an obligation or the effects of something: *they are immune from legal action*. ■ [predic.] not affected or influenced by something: *no one is immune to his immense charm*. ■ [attrib.] Biology of or relating to immunity: *the body's immune system*.
– ORIGIN late Middle English (in the sense 'free from (a liability)'): from Latin *immunis* 'exempt from public service or charge,' from *in-* 'not' + *munis* 'ready for service.' Senses relating to physiological resistance date from the late 19th cent.

im·mune de·fi·cien·cy ▶ **n.** another term for **IMMUNODEFICIENCY**.

im·mune re·sponse ▶ **n.** the reaction of the cells and fluids of the body to the presence of a substance that is not recognized as a constituent of the body itself.

im·mu·ni·ty /iˈmyo͞onitē/ ▶ **n.** (pl. **immunities**) the ability of an organism to resist a particular infection or toxin by the action of specific antibodies or sensitized white blood cells: *immunity to typhoid seems to have increased spontaneously*. ■ protection or exemption from something, esp. an obligation or penalty: *the rebels were given immunity from prosecution*. ■ Law officially granted exemption from legal proceedings. ■ (**immunity to**) lack of susceptibility, esp. to something unwelcome or harmful: *products must have an adequate level of immunity to interference | exercises designed to build an immunity to fatigue*.
– ORIGIN late Middle English (in the sense 'exemption (from a liability)'): from Latin *immunitas*, from *immunis* (see **IMMUNE**).

im·mu·nize /ˈimyəˌnīz/ ▶ **v.** [with obj.] make (a person or animal) immune to infection, typically by inoculation: *the vaccine is used to immunize children against measles*.
– DERIVATIVES **im·mu·ni·za·tion** /ˌimyəniˈzāSHən/ **n.**, **im·mu·niz·er n.**

immuno- ▶ **comb. form** Medicine representing **IMMUNE**, **IMMUNITY**, or **IMMUNOLOGY**.

im·mu·no·as·say /ˌimyənōˈasā, iˌmyo͞o-/ ▶ **n.** Biochemistry a procedure for detecting or measuring specific proteins or other substances through their properties as antigens or antibodies: *these general principles can be applied to all immunoassays | the uses of immunoassay in industry*.

im·mu·no·blot·ting /ˌimyənōˈblätiNG, iˌmyo͞o-/, ▶ **n.** a technique for analyzing or identifying proteins in a mixture, involving separation by electrophoresis followed by staining with antibodies.

im·mu·no·chem·is·try /ˌimyənōˈkemistrē, iˌmyo͞o-/ ▶ **n.** the branch of biochemistry concerned with immune responses and systems.

im·mu·no·com·pe·tent /ˌimyənōˈkämpitənt, iˌmyo͞o-/ ▶ **adj.** Medicine having a normal immune response.
– DERIVATIVES **im·mu·no·com·pe·tence n.**

im·mu·no·com·pro·mised /ˌimyənōˈkämprəˌmīzd, iˌmyo͞o-/ ▶ **adj.** Medicine having an impaired immune system.

im·mu·no·cy·to·chem·is·try /ˌimyənōˌsītō-ˈkemistrē, iˌmyo͞o-/ ▶ **n.** the range of microscopic techniques used in the study of the immune system.
– DERIVATIVES **im·mu·no·cy·to·chem·i·cal** /-ˈkeməkəl/ **adj.**

im·mu·no·de·fi·cien·cy /ˌimyənōdəˈfiSHənsē, iˌmyo͞o-/ ▶ **n.** failure of the immune system to protect the body adequately from infection, due to the absence or insufficiency of some component process or substance.

im·mu·no·dif·fu·sion /ˌimyənōdiˈfyo͞oZHən, iˌmyo͞o-/ ▶ **n.** Biochemistry a technique for detecting or measuring antibodies and antigens by their precipitation when diffused together through a gel or other medium.

im·mu·no·e·lec·tro·pho·re·sis /ˌimyənō-iˌlektrōfəˈrēsis, iˈmyo͞o-/ ▶ **n.** Biochemistry a technique for the identification of proteins in serum or other fluid by electrophoresis and subsequent immunodiffusion.

im·mu·no·fluo·res·cence /ˌimyənōˌflo͝oˈresəns, -flô-, iˌmyo͞o-/ ▶ **n.** Biochemistry a technique for determining the location of an antigen (or antibody) in tissues by reaction with an antibody (or antigen) labeled with a fluorescent dye.
– DERIVATIVES **im·mu·no·fluo·res·cent adj.**

im·mu·no·gen·ic /ˌimyənōˈjenik, iˌmyo͞o-/ ▶ **adj.** relating to or denoting substances able to produce an immune response.
– DERIVATIVES **im·mu·no·ge·nic·i·ty** /-jəˈnisitē/ **n.**

im·mu·no·glob·u·lin /ˌimyənōˈgläbyələn, iˌmyo͞o-/ ▶ **n.** Biochemistry any of a class of proteins present in the serum and cells of the immune system, that function as antibodies.

im·mu·nol·o·gy /ˌimyəˈnäləjē/ ▶ **n.** the branch of medicine and biology concerned with immunity.
– DERIVATIVES **im·mu·no·log·ic** /ˌimyənəˈläjik, iˌmyo͞o-/ **adj.**, **im·mu·no·log·i·cal** /ˌimyənəˈläjikəl, iˌmyo͞o-/ **adj.**, **im·mu·no·log·i·cal·ly** /ˌimyənəˈläjik(ə)lē, iˌmyo͞o-/ **adv.**, **im·mu·nol·o·gist** /-jist/ **n.**

im·mu·no·sorb·ent /ˌimyənōˈsôrbənt, -ˈzôr-, iˌmyo͞o-/ ▶ **adj.** Biochemistry relating to or denoting techniques making use of the absorption of antibodies by insoluble preparations of antigens.

im·mu·no·sup·pres·sion /ˌimyənōsəˈpreSHən, iˌmyo͞o-/ ▶ **n.** Medicine the partial or complete suppression of the immune response of an individual. It is induced to help the survival of an organ after a transplant operation.
– DERIVATIVES **im·mu·no·sup·pres·sant** /-səˈpresənt/ **n.**, **im·mu·no·sup·pressed** /-səˈprest/ **adj.**

im·mu·no·sup·pres·sive /ˌimyənōsəˈpresiv, iˌmyo͞o-/ ▶ **adj.** Medicine (chiefly of drugs) partially or completely suppressing the immune response of an individual.
▶ **n.** a drug of this kind.

im·mu·no·ther·a·py /ˌimyənōˈTHerəpē, iˌmyo͞o-/ ▶ **n.** Medicine the prevention or treatment of disease with substances that stimulate the immune response.

im·mure /iˈmyo͝or/ ▶ **v.** [with obj.] (usu. **be immured**) enclose or confine (someone) against their will: *her brother was immured in a lunatic asylum*.
– DERIVATIVES **im·mure·ment n.**
– ORIGIN late 16th cent.: from French *emmurer* or medieval Latin *immurare*, from *in-* 'in' + *murus* 'wall.'

im·mu·ta·ble /iˈmyo͞otəbəl/ ▶ **adj.** unchanging over time or unable to be changed: *an immutable fact*.
– DERIVATIVES **im·mu·ta·bil·i·ty** /iˌmyo͞otəˈbilitē/ **n.**, **im·mu·ta·bly** /-blē/ **adv.**
– ORIGIN late Middle English: from Latin *immutabilis*, from *in-* 'not' + *mutabilis* (see **MUTABLE**).

IMO ▶ **abbr.** ■ in my opinion. ■ International Maritime Organization.

i-mode ▶ **n.** trademark a proprietary technology that allows data to be transferred to and from Internet sites via cellular phones.
– ORIGIN early 21st cent.: from *I* (referring to the user's ability to interact directly with the Internet) + *mode*.

IMP /imp/ ▶ **abbr.** Bridge International Match Point.

imp /imp/ ▶ **n.** a mischievous child: *a cheeky young imp*. ■ a small, mischievous devil or sprite.
▶ **v.** [with obj.] repair a damaged feather in (the wing or tail of a trained hawk) by attaching part of a new feather.
– ORIGIN Old English *impa, impe* 'young shoot, scion,' *impian* 'to graft,' based on Greek *emphuein* 'to implant.' In late Middle English, the noun denoted a descendant, esp. of a noble family, and later a child of the devil or a person regarded as such; hence a 'little devil' or mischievous child (early 17th cent).

imp. ▶ **abbr.** ■ imperative. ■ imperfect. ■ imperial. ■ impersonal. ■ implement. ■ import or imported or importer. ■ important. ■ imprimatur. ■ in the first place. [from Latin *imprimīis*.] ■ imprint. ■ improper. ■ improved or improvement.

im·pact ▶ **n.** /ˈimˌpakt/ the action of one object coming forcibly into contact with another: *there was the sound of a third impact | bullets that expand and cause devastating injury on impact*. ■ the effect or influence of one person, thing, or action, on another: *our regional measures have had a significant impact on unemployment*.
▶ **v.** /imˈpakt/ [no obj.] **1** come into forcible contact with another object: *the shell impacted twenty yards away*. ■ [with obj.] come into forcible contact with: *an asteroid impacted the earth some 60 million years ago*. ■ [with obj.] press firmly: *the animals' feet do not impact and damage the soil as cows' hooves do*.
2 (**impact on**) have a strong effect on someone or something: *high interest rates have impacted on retail spending* | [with obj.] *the move is not expected to impact the company's employees*.
– ORIGIN early 17th cent. (as a verb in the sense 'press closely, fix firmly'): from Latin *impact-* 'driven in,' from the verb *impingere* (see **IMPINGE**).

im·pact cra·ter ▶ **n.** a crater on a planet or moon caused by the impact of a meteorite or other object, typically circular with a raised rim.

im·pact·ed /imˈpaktid/ ▶ **adj. 1** chiefly Medicine pressed firmly together, in particular: ■ (of a tooth) wedged between another tooth and the jaw. ■ (of a fractured bone) having the parts crushed together. ■ (of feces) lodged in the intestine.
2 strongly affected by something: *grandiose planning projects have had deleterious effects on impacted social groups*.

im·pact·ful /imˈpaktfəl/ ▶ **adj.** having a major impact or effect: *an eye-catching and impactful design*.

im·pac·tion /imˈpakSHən/ ▶ **n.** Medicine the condition of being or process of becoming impacted, esp. of feces in the intestine.

im·pac·tive /imˈpaktiv/ ▶ **adj.** having a strong effect or influence; making an impression: *impactive color radiates from the sculptures*.

im·pac·tor /imˈpaktər/ ▶ **n.** chiefly Astronomy an object (such as a meteorite) that collides with another body.

im·pair /imˈpe(ə)r/ ▶ **v.** [with obj.] weaken or damage something (esp. a human faculty or function): *drug use that impairs job performance*.
– ORIGIN Middle English *enpeire*, from Old French *empeirier*, based on late Latin *pejorare* (from Latin *pejor* 'worse'). The current spelling is due to association with words derived from Latin beginning with *im-*.

im·paired /im'pe(ə)rd/ ▶ **adj.** having a disability of a specified kind: [in combination] *hearing-impaired children.*

im·pair·ment /im'pe(ə)rmənt/ ▶ **n.** the state or fact of being impaired, esp. in a specified faculty: *a degree of physical or mental impairment | memory impairment.*

im·pal·a /im'palə, -'pälə/ ▶ **n.** (pl. **same**) a graceful antelope often seen in large herds in open woodland in southern and East Africa. ● *Aepyceros melampus*, family Bovidae.
– ORIGIN late 19th cent.: from Zulu *i-mpala.*

impala

im·pale /im'pāl/ ▶ **v.** [with obj.] **1** pierce or transfix with a sharp instrument: *his head was* **impaled on** *a pike and exhibited for all to see.*
2 Heraldry display (a coat of arms) side by side with another on the same shield, separated by a vertical line: (as adj. **impaled**) *the impaled arms of her husband and her father.* ■ (of a coat of arms) adjoin (another coat of arms) in this way.
– DERIVATIVES **im·pale·ment** n., **im·pal·er** n.
– ORIGIN mid 16th cent. (in the sense 'enclose with stakes or pales'): from French *empaler* or medieval Latin *impalare*, from Latin *in-* 'in' + *palus* 'a stake.'

im·pal·pa·ble /im'palpəbəl/ ▶ **adj.** unable to be felt by touch: *an impalpable ghost.* ■ not easily comprehended: *something so impalpable as personhood.*
– DERIVATIVES **im·pal·pa·bil·i·ty** /-,palpə'bilitē/ n., **im·pal·pa·bly** /-blē/ adv.
– ORIGIN early 16th cent.: from French, or from late Latin *impalpabilis*, from *in-* 'not' + *palpabilis* (see PALPABLE).

im·pa·na·tion /,impə'nāsHən/ ▶ **n.** Theology the medieval and Reformation doctrine that the body of Christ is present within the Eucharistic bread and does not replace it. Compare with CONSUBSTANTIATION.
– DERIVATIVES **im·pa·nate** /'impə,nāt, im'panit/ adj.
– ORIGIN mid 16th cent.: from medieval Latin *impanatio(n-)*, from *impanare* 'embody in bread,' from *in-* 'in' + *panis* 'bread.'

im·pan·el /im'panl/ (also **empanel**) ▶ **v.** (**impanels, impaneling, impaneled**; Brit. **impanelling, impanelled**) [with obj.] enlist or enroll (a jury). ■ enroll (someone) onto a jury: *several of her friends have been impaneled.*
– DERIVATIVES **im·pan·el·ment** n.
– ORIGIN late Middle English (originally as *empanel*): from Anglo-Norman French *empaneller*, from *em-* 'in' + Old French *panel* 'panel.'

im·park /im'pärk/ ▶ **v.** [with obj.] historical enclose (animals) in a park. ■ enclose (land) to make it into a park.
– ORIGIN late Middle English: from Old French *emparquer*, from *em-* 'within' + *parc* 'park.'

im·part /im'pärt/ ▶ **v.** [with obj.] make (information) known; communicate: *teachers had a duty to* **impart** *strong morals* **to** *their students.* ■ bestow (a quality): *its main use has been to* **impart** *a high surface gloss* **to** *finished articles.*
– DERIVATIVES **im·par·ta·tion** /,impär'tāsHən/ n.
– ORIGIN late Middle English (in the sense 'give a share of'): from Old French *impartir*, from Latin *impartire*, from *in-* 'in' + *pars, part-* 'part.'

im·par·tial /im'pärsHəl/ ▶ **adj.** treating all rivals or disputants equally; fair and just: *independent and impartial advice.*
– DERIVATIVES **im·par·ti·al·i·ty** /-,pärsHē'alitē/ n., **im·par·tial·ly** adv.

im·pass·a·ble /im'pasəbəl/ ▶ **adj.** impossible to travel along or over: *the narrow channels are impassable to oceangoing ships.*
– DERIVATIVES **im·pass·a·bil·i·ty** /-,pasə'bilitē/ n., **im·pass·a·ble·ness** n., **im·pass·a·bly** /-blē/ adv.

im·passe /'im,pas, im'pas/ ▶ **n.** a situation in which no progress is possible, esp. because of disagreement; a deadlock: *the current political impasse.*
– ORIGIN mid 19th cent.: from French, from *im-* (expressing negation) + the stem of *passer* 'to pass.'

im·pas·si·ble /im'pasəbəl/ ▶ **adj.** chiefly Theology incapable of suffering or feeling pain: *belief in an impassible God.*
– DERIVATIVES **im·pas·si·bil·i·ty** /-,pasə'bilitē/ n., **im·pas·si·bly** /-blē/ adv.
– ORIGIN Middle English: via Old French from ecclesiastical Latin *impassibilis*, from Latin *in-* 'not' + *passibilis* (see PASSIBLE).

im·pas·sion /im'pasHən/ ▶ **v.** [with obj.] make passionate: *her body had once pleased and impassioned him.*
– ORIGIN late 16th cent.: from Italian *impassionare*, from *im-* (expressing intensive force) + *passione* 'passion,' from Christian Latin *passio* (see PASSION).

im·pas·sioned /im'pasHənd/ ▶ **adj.** filled with or showing great emotion: *she made an impassioned plea for help.*

im·pas·sive /im'pasiv/ ▶ **adj.** not feeling or showing emotion: *impassive passersby ignore the performers.*
– DERIVATIVES **im·pas·sive·ly** adv., **im·pas·sive·ness** n., **im·pas·siv·i·ty** /,impə'sivitē/ n.

im·pas·to /im'pastō, -'pästō/ ▶ **n.** Art the process or technique of laying on paint or pigment thickly so that it stands out from a surface. ■ paint applied thickly.
– ORIGIN late 18th cent.: from Italian, from *impastare*, from *im-* 'upon' + *pasta* 'a paste,' from late Latin.

im·pa·tience ▶ **n.** the tendency to be impatient; irritability or restlessness: *she crumpled up the pages in a burst of impatience.*

im·pa·tiens /im'pāsHənz/ ▶ **n.** an East African plant with abundant red, pink, or white flowers. It is often grown as a houseplant, and its many hybrids are grown as bedding plants. ● Genus *Impatiens*, family Balsaminaceae.
– ORIGIN late 18th cent.: modern Latin, from Latin, literally 'impatient' (because the capsules of the plant readily burst open when touched).

im·pa·tient /im'pāsHənt/ ▶ **adj. 1** having or showing a tendency to be quickly irritated or provoked: *an impatient motorist blaring his horn | she was impatient with any restriction.* ■ [predic.] (**impatient of**) intolerant of: *a man impatient of bureaucracy.*
2 restlessly eager: *they are impatient for change |* [with infinitive] *he was impatient to be on his way.*
– DERIVATIVES **im·pa·tient·ly** adv.
– ORIGIN late Middle English (in the senses 'lacking patience' and 'unbearable'): via Old French from Latin *impatient-* 'not bearing, impatient,' from *in-* 'not' + *pati* 'suffer, bear.'

im·peach /im'pēcH/ ▶ **v.** [with obj.] call into question the integrity or validity of (a practice): *there is no basis to Searle's motion to impeach the verdict.* ■ charge (the holder of a public office) with misconduct: *the governor served only one year before being impeached and convicted for fiscal fraud.* ■ Brit. charge with treason or another crime against the state.
– DERIVATIVES **im·peach·a·ble** adj., **im·peach·ment** n.
– ORIGIN late Middle English (also in the sense 'hinder, prevent'; earlier as *empeche*): from Old French *empecher* 'impede,' from late Latin *impedicare* 'catch, entangle' (based on *pedica* 'a fetter,' from *pes, ped-* 'foot'). Compare with IMPEDE.

im·pec·ca·ble /im'pekəbəl/ ▶ **adj.** (of behavior, performance, or appearance) in accordance with the highest standards of propriety; faultless: *a man of impeccable character.* ■ Theology, rare not liable to sin.
– DERIVATIVES **im·pec·ca·bil·i·ty** /-,pekə'bilitē/ n., **im·pec·ca·bly** /-blē/ adv.
– ORIGIN mid 16th cent. (in the theological sense): from Latin *impeccabilis*, from *in-* 'not' + *peccare* 'to sin.'

im·pe·cu·ni·ous /,impə'kyōōnēəs/ ▶ **adj.** having little or no money: *a titled but impecunious family.*
– DERIVATIVES **im·pe·cu·ni·os·i·ty** /-,kyōōnē'äsitē/ n., **im·pe·cu·ni·ous·ness** n.
– ORIGIN late 16th cent.: from IN-[1] 'not' + obsolete *pecunious* 'having money, wealthy' (from Latin *pecuniosus*, from *pecunia* 'money').

im·ped·ance /im'pēdns/ ▶ **n.** the effective resistance of an electric circuit or component to alternating current, arising from the combined effects of ohmic resistance and reactance. See also ACOUSTIC IMPEDANCE. ● Impedance is usually expressed as a complex quantity $Z = R + jX$, where R is resistance, X is reactance, and j is the imaginary square root of -1.

im·pede /im'pēd/ ▶ **v.** [with obj.] delay or prevent (someone or something) by obstructing them; hinder: *the sap causes swelling that can impede breathing.*
– ORIGIN late 16th cent.: from Latin *impedire* 'shackle the feet of,' based on *pes, ped-* 'foot.' Compare with IMPEACH.

im·ped·i·ment /im'pedəmənt/ ▶ **n.** a hindrance or obstruction in doing something: *a serious impediment to scientific progress.* ■ (also **speech impediment**) a defect in a person's speech, such as a lisp or stammer.
– DERIVATIVES **im·ped·i·men·tal** /-,pedə'mentl/ adj.
– ORIGIN late Middle English: from Latin *impedimentum*, from *impedire* (see IMPEDE).

im·ped·i·men·ta /im,pedə'mentə/ ▶ **plural n.** equipment for an activity or expedition, esp. when considered as bulky or an encumbrance.
– ORIGIN early 17th cent.: from Latin, plural of *impedimentum* 'impediment,' from *impedire* (see IMPEDE).

im·pel /im'pel/ ▶ **v.** (**impels, impelling, impelled**) [with obj.] drive, force, or urge (someone) to do something: *financial difficulties impelled him to desperate measures |* [with obj. and infinitive] *a lack of equality impelled the oppressed to fight.* ■ drive forward; propel: *vital energies impel him in unforeseen directions.*
– ORIGIN late Middle English (in the sense 'propel'): from Latin *impellere*, from *in-* 'toward' + *pellere* 'to drive.'

im·pel·ler /im'pelər/ ▶ **n.** the rotating part of a centrifugal pump, compressor, or other machine designed to move a fluid by rotation. ■ a similar device turned by the flow of water past a ship's hull, used to measure speed or distance traveled.

im·pend /im'pend/ ▶ **v.** [no obj.] (usu. as adj. **impending**) be about to happen: *my impending departure.* ■ (of something bad) loom: *danger of collision impends.*
– ORIGIN late 16th cent.: from Latin *impendere*, from *in-* 'toward, upon' + *pendere* 'hang.'

im·pen·e·tra·ble /im'penətrəbəl/ ▶ **adj.**
1 impossible to pass through or enter: *a dark, impenetrable forest.* ■ Physics (of matter) incapable of occupying the same space as other matter at the same time.
2 impossible to understand: *impenetrable interviews with French intellectuals.*
– DERIVATIVES **im·pen·e·tra·bil·i·ty** /-,penətrə'bilitē/ n., **im·pen·e·tra·bly** /-blē/ adv.
– ORIGIN late Middle English: via French from Latin *impenetrabilis*, from *in-* 'not' + *penetrabilis* 'able to be pierced,' from the verb *penetrare* (see PENETRATE).

im·pen·i·tent /im'penitnt/ ▶ **adj.** not feeling shame or regret about one's actions or attitudes.
– DERIVATIVES **im·pen·i·tence** n., **im·pen·i·ten·cy** n., **im·pen·i·tent·ly** adv.
– ORIGIN late Middle English: from ecclesiastical Latin *impaenitent-* 'not repenting,' from Latin *in-* 'not' + *paenitere* 'repent.'

im·per·a·tive /im'perətiv/ ▶ **adj. 1** of vital importance; crucial: *immediate action was imperative |* [with clause] *it is imperative that standards be maintained.*
2 giving an authoritative command; peremptory: *the bell pealed again, a final imperative call.* ■ Grammar denoting the mood of a verb that expresses a command or exhortation, as in *come here!*
▶ **n. 1** an essential or urgent thing: *free movement of labor was an economic imperative.* ■ a factor or influence making something necessary: *the change came about through a financial imperative.*
2 Grammar a verb or phrase in the imperative mood. ■ (**the imperative**) the imperative mood.
– DERIVATIVES **im·per·a·ti·val** /-,perə'tīvəl/ adj., **im·per·a·tive·ly** adv., **im·per·a·tive·ness** n.
– ORIGIN late Middle English (as a grammatical term): from late Latin *imperativus* (literally 'specially ordered,' translating Greek *prostatikē enklisis* 'imperative mood'), from *imperare* 'to command,' from *in-* 'toward' + *parare* 'make ready.'

im·pe·ra·tor /,impə'rätər, -,tôr/ ▶ **n.** Roman History commander (a title conferred under the Republic on a victorious general and under the Empire on the emperor).
– DERIVATIVES **im·per·a·to·ri·al** /im,perə'tôrēəl/ adj.
– ORIGIN Latin, from *imperare* 'to order, command.'

im·per·cep·ti·ble /,impər'septəbəl/ ▶ **adj.** impossible to perceive: *his head moved in an almost imperceptible nod.*
– DERIVATIVES **im·per·cep·ti·bil·i·ty** /-,septə'bilitē/ n., **im·per·cep·ti·bly** /-blē/ adv.
– ORIGIN late Middle English: from French, or from medieval Latin *imperceptibilis*, from *in-* 'not' + *perceptibilis*, from the verb *percipere* (see PERCEIVE).

im·per·cep·tive /,impər'septiv/ ▶ **adj.** lacking in perception or insight: *she dismissed the statement as juvenile or at least imperceptive.*

im·per·cip·i·ent /,impər'sipēənt/ ▶ **adj.** failing to perceive something.
– DERIVATIVES **im·per·cip·i·ence** n.

im·per·fect /im'pərfikt/ ▶ **adj. 1** not perfect; faulty or incomplete: *an imperfect grasp of English.*
2 Grammar (of a tense) denoting a past action in progress but not completed at the time in question.
3 Music (of a cadence) ending on the dominant chord.

PRONUNCIATION KEY ə *ago, up*; ər *over, fur*; a *hat*; ā *ate*; ä *car*; e *let*; ē *see*; i *fit*; ī *by*; NG *sing*; ō *go*; ô *law, for*; oi *toy*; ŏŏ *good*; ōō *goo*; ou *out*; TH *thin*; TH *then*; ZH *vision*

4 Law (of a gift, title, etc.) transferred without all the necessary conditions or requirements being met.
▶ **n.** (**the imperfect**) Grammar the imperfect tense.
– DERIVATIVES **im·per·fect·ly** **adv.**
– ORIGIN Middle English *imparfit, imperfet*, from Old French *imparfait*, from Latin *imperfectus*, from *in-* 'not' + *perfectus* (see PERFECT). The spelling change in the 16th cent. was due to association with the Latin form.

im·per·fect com·pe·ti·tion ▶ **n.** the situation prevailing in a market in which elements of monopoly allow individual producers or consumers to exercise some control over market prices.

im·per·fec·tion /ˌimpərˈfekSHən/ ▶ **n.** a fault, blemish, or undesirable feature: *the imperfections and injustices in our political system.* ■ the state of being faulty or incomplete: *he accepted me without question, in all my imperfection.*
– ORIGIN late Middle English: via Old French from late Latin *imperfectio(n-)*, from *imperfectus* (see IMPERFECT).

im·per·fec·tive /ˌimpərˈfektiv/ Grammar ▶ **adj.** relating to or denoting an aspect of verbs, esp. in Slavic languages, that expresses action without reference to its completion. The opposite of PERFECTIVE.
▶ **n.** the imperfective aspect, or an imperfective form of a verb.

im·per·fect rhyme ▶ **n.** a rhyme in which there is only a partial matching of sounds (e.g., *love* and *move*). See also PARARHYME.

i

im·per·fo·rate /imˈpərfərit/ ▶ **adj.** not perforated, in particular: ■ Anatomy & Zoology lacking the normal opening: *unicellular spores of these parasites have an imperforate wall.* ■ (of a postage stamp or a block or sheet of stamps) lacking perforations, esp. as an error.

im·pe·ri·al /imˈpi(ə)rēəl/ ▶ **adj.** **1** of or relating to an empire: *Britain's imperial era.* ■ of or relating to an emperor: *the imperial family.* ■ majestic; magnificent: *the bedroom is huge and imperial.* ■ imperious or domineering: *the party and its autocratic—many would say imperial—ways.*
2 of, relating to, or denoting the system of nonmetric weights and measures (the ounce, pound, stone, inch, foot, yard, mile, acre, pint, gallon, etc.) formerly used for all measures in the UK, and still used for some.
3 chiefly historical (of a size of paper) measuring roughly 762 × 559 mm (30 × 22 inches).
▶ **n.** a small pointed beard growing below the lower lip (associated with Napoleon III of France).
– DERIVATIVES **im·pe·ri·al·ly** **adv.**
– ORIGIN late Middle English: via Old French from Latin *imperialis*, from *imperium* 'command, authority, empire'; related to *imperare* 'to command.' Compare with EMPEROR, EMPIRE, also with IMPERIOUS.

im·pe·ri·al gal·lon ▶ **n.** see GALLON (sense 1).

im·pe·ri·al·ism /imˈpi(ə)rēəˌlizəm/ ▶ **n.** a policy of extending a country's power and influence through diplomacy or military force: *the struggle against imperialism* | figurative *French ministers protested at US cultural imperialism.* ■ chiefly historical rule by an emperor.
– DERIVATIVES **im·pe·ri·al·is·tic** /-ˌpi(ə)rēəˈlistik/ **adj.**, **im·pe·ri·al·is·ti·cal·ly** **adv.**

im·pe·ri·al·ist /imˈpi(ə)rēəlist/ ▶ **adj.** of, relating to, supporting, or practicing imperialism: *an imperialist regime.*
▶ **n.** chiefly derogatory a person who supports or practices imperialism.

im·pe·ri·al·ize /imˈpi(ə)rēəˌlīz/ ▶ **v.** [with obj.] (usu. as adj. **imperialized**) subject to imperial rule or influence: *people of an imperialized culture.*

im·pe·ri·al pi·geon ▶ **n.** a tropical, fruit-eating pigeon that typically has a pale grayish head and breast and a dark back, occurring in Australasia, Indonesia, and southern Asia. ● Genus *Ducula*, family Columbidae.

Im·pe·ri·al Val·ley an irrigated section of the Colorado Desert, in southeastern California.

im·per·il /imˈperəl/ ▶ **v.** (**imperils, imperiling, imperiled**; Brit. **imperils, imperilling, imperilled**) [with obj.] put at risk of being harmed, injured, or destroyed: *white-band disease imperils coral reefs.*
– DERIVATIVES **im·per·il·ment** **n.**
– ORIGIN late Middle English: from PERIL, probably on the pattern of *endanger*.

im·pe·ri·ous /imˈpi(ə)rēəs/ ▶ **adj.** assuming power or authority without justification; arrogant and domineering: *his imperious demands.*
– DERIVATIVES **im·pe·ri·ous·ly** **adv.**, **im·pe·ri·ous·ness** **n.**
– ORIGIN mid 16th cent.: from Latin *imperiosus*, from *imperium* 'command, authority, empire'; related to *imperare* 'to command.' Compare with IMPERIAL.

im·per·ish·a·ble /imˈperisHəbəl/ ▶ **adj.** enduring forever: *imperishable truths.*
– DERIVATIVES **im·per·ish·a·bil·i·ty** /-ˌperisHəˈbilitē/ **n.**, **im·per·ish·a·ble·ness** **n.**, **im·per·ish·a·bly** **adv.**

im·pe·ri·um /imˈpi(ə)rēəm/ ▶ **n.** absolute power: *it was the high noon of the imperium, an age when there was something empowering about being an American.*
– ORIGIN mid 17th cent.: from Latin, 'command, authority, empire'; related to *imperare* 'to command.'

im·per·ma·nent /imˈpərmənənt/ ▶ **adj.** not permanent.
– DERIVATIVES **im·per·ma·nence** **n.**, **im·per·ma·nen·cy** **n.**, **im·per·ma·nent·ly** **adv.**

im·per·me·a·ble /imˈpərmēəbəl/ ▶ **adj.** not allowing fluid to pass through: *an impermeable membrane.* ■ not liable to be affected by pain or distress; insusceptible or imperturbable: *women who appear* ***impermeable to*** *pain.*
– DERIVATIVES **im·per·me·a·bil·i·ty** /-ˌpərmēəˈbilitē/ **n.**
– ORIGIN late 17th cent.: from French *imperméable*, or from late Latin *impermeabilis*, from *in-* 'not' + *permeabilis* (see PERMEABLE).

im·per·mis·si·ble /ˌimpərˈmisəbəl/ ▶ **adj.** too bad to be allowed: *the prosecution made impermissible use of the testimony.*
– DERIVATIVES **im·per·mis·si·bil·i·ty** /-ˌmisəˈbilitē/ **n.**

im·per·son·al /imˈpərsənl/ ▶ **adj.** **1** not influenced by, showing, or involving personal feelings: *the impersonal march of progress.* ■ (of a place or organization) large, featureless, and anonymous: *large, impersonal institutions.*
2 not existing as a person; having no personality: *he gradually came to believe in an impersonal God.*
3 Grammar (of a verb) used only with a formal subject (in English usually *it*) and expressing an action not attributable to a definite subject (as in *it is snowing*).
– DERIVATIVES **im·per·son·al·i·ty** /-ˌpərsəˈnalitē/ **n.**, **im·per·son·al·ly** **adv.**
– ORIGIN late Middle English (sense 3): from late Latin *impersonalis*, from Latin *in-* 'not' + *personalis* (see PERSONAL).

im·per·son·al pro·noun ▶ **n.** the pronoun *it* when used without definite reference or antecedent, as in *it was snowing* and *it seems hard to believe.*

im·per·son·ate /imˈpərsəˌnāt/ ▶ **v.** [with obj.] pretend to be (another person) as entertainment or in order to deceive someone: *it's a very serious offense to impersonate a police officer.*
– DERIVATIVES **im·per·son·a·tor** /-ˌnātər/ **n.**
– ORIGIN early 17th cent. (in the sense 'personify'): from IN-[2] 'into' + Latin *persona* 'person,' on the pattern of *incorporate*.

im·per·son·a·tion /imˌpərsəˈnāSHən/ ▶ **n.** an act of pretending to be another person for the purpose of entertainment or fraud: *he did an impersonation of Fred Astaire.*

im·per·ti·nence /imˈpərtnəns/ ▶ **n.** lack of respect; rudeness: *they gasped at the impertinence of the suggestion.*

im·per·ti·nent /imˈpərtnənt/ ▶ **adj.** **1** not showing proper respect; rude: *an impertinent question.*
2 formal not pertinent to a particular matter; irrelevant: *talk of "rhetoric" and "strategy" is* ***impertinent to*** *this process.*
– DERIVATIVES **im·per·ti·nent·ly** **adv.**
– ORIGIN late Middle English (sense 2): from Old French, or from late Latin *impertinent-* 'not having reference to,' from Latin *in-* 'not' + *pertinere* 'pertain.'

im·per·turb·a·ble /ˌimpərˈtərbəbəl/ ▶ **adj.** unable to be upset or excited; calm: *an imperturbable tranquility.*
– DERIVATIVES **im·per·turb·a·bil·i·ty** /-tərbəˈbilitē/ **n.**, **im·per·turb·a·bly** **adv.**
– ORIGIN late Middle English: from late Latin *imperturbabilis*, from *in-* 'not' + *perturbare* (see PERTURB).

im·per·vi·ous /imˈpərvēəs/ ▶ **adj.** not allowing fluid to pass through: *an impervious layer of basaltic clay.* ■ [predic.] (**impervious to**) unable to be affected by: *he worked, apparently impervious to the heat.*
– DERIVATIVES **im·per·vi·ous·ly** **adv.**, **im·per·vi·ous·ness** **n.**
– ORIGIN mid 17th cent.: from Latin *impervius* (from *in-* 'not' + *pervius* 'pervious') + -OUS.

im·pe·ti·go /ˌimpiˈtīgō, -ˈtē-/ ▶ **n.** a contagious bacterial skin infection forming pustules and yellow, crusty sores. ● This disease is caused by the bacteria *Streptococcus pyogenes* or *S. aureus.*
– ORIGIN late Middle English: from Latin, from *impetere* 'to assail, attack.'

im·pe·trate /ˈimpəˌtrāt/ ▶ **v.** [with obj.] archaic beseech or beg for: *a slight testimonial which I thought fit to impetrate from that worthy nobleman.*
– ORIGIN late 15th cent.: from Latin *impetrat-* 'brought to pass,' from the verb *impetrare* (based on *patrare* 'bring to pass').

im·pet·u·ous /imˈpecHo͞oəs/ ▶ **adj.** acting or done quickly and without thought or care: *her friend was headstrong and impetuous.* ■ moving forcefully or rapidly: *an impetuous but controlled flow of water.*
– DERIVATIVES **im·pet·u·os·i·ty** /-ˌpecHo͞oˈäsitē/ **n.**, **im·pet·u·ous·ly** **adv.**, **im·pet·u·ous·ness** **n.**
– ORIGIN late Middle English: from Old French *impetueux*, from late Latin *impetuosus*, from *impetere* 'to assail, attack.'

im·pe·tus /ˈimpitəs/ ▶ **n.** the force or energy with which a body moves: *hit the booster coil before the flywheel loses all its impetus.* ■ the force that makes something happen or happen more quickly: *the crisis of the 1860s provided the original* ***impetus for*** *the settlements.*
– ORIGIN mid 17th cent.: from Latin, 'assault, force,' from *impetere* 'assail,' from *in-* 'toward' + *petere* 'seek.'

Imp·hal /ˈimˌpəl/ a city in northeastern India, the capital of the state of Manipur, that lies close to the border with Burma (Myanmar); pop. 236,400 (est. 2009). It was the scene of an important victory in 1944 by Anglo-Indian forces over the Japanese.

im·pi /ˈimpē/ ▶ **n.** (pl. **impis**) a body of Zulu warriors. ■ an armed band of Zulus involved in urban or rural conflict.
– ORIGIN mid 19th cent.: Zulu, literally 'regiment, armed band.'

im·pi·e·ty /imˈpī-itē/ ▶ **n.** (pl. **impieties**) lack of piety or reverence, esp. for a god: *he blamed the fall of the city on the impiety of the people* | *one impiety will cost me my eternity in Paradise.*
– ORIGIN Middle English: from Old French *impiete* or Latin *impietas*, from *impius* 'impious.'

im·pinge /imˈpinj/ ▶ **v.** (**impinges, impinging, impinged**) [no obj.] have an effect or impact, esp. a negative one: *Nora was determined that the tragedy would impinge as little as possible* ***on*** *Constance's life.* ■ advance over an area belonging to someone or something else; encroach: *the site* ***impinges on*** *a greenbelt area.* ■ (**impinge on/upon**) Physics strike: *the gases impinge on the surface of the liquid.*
– DERIVATIVES **im·pinge·ment** **n.**, **im·ping·er** **n.**
– ORIGIN mid 16th cent.: from Latin *impingere* 'drive something in or at,' from *in-* 'into' + *pangere* 'fix, drive.' The word originally meant 'thrust at forcibly,' then 'come into forcible contact'; hence 'encroach on' (mid 18th cent).

im·pi·ous /ˈimpēəs, imˈpī-/ ▶ **adj.** not showing respect or reverence, esp. for a god: *the emperor's impious attacks on the Church.* ■ (of a person or act) wicked: *impious villains.*
– DERIVATIVES **im·pi·ous·ly** **adv.**, **im·pi·ous·ness** **n.**
– ORIGIN mid 16th cent.: from Latin *impius* (from *in-* 'not' + *pius*: see PIOUS) + -OUS.

imp·ish /ˈimpisH/ ▶ **adj.** inclined to do slightly naughty things for fun; mischievous: *he had an impish look about him.*
– DERIVATIVES **imp·ish·ly** **adv.**, **imp·ish·ness** **n.**

im·plac·a·ble /imˈplakəbəl/ ▶ **adj.** unable to be placated: *he was an implacable enemy of Ted's.* ■ relentless; unstoppable: *the implacable advance of the enemy.*
– DERIVATIVES **im·plac·a·bil·i·ty** /-ˌplakəˈbilitē/ **n.**, **im·plac·a·bly** /-blē/ **adv.**
– ORIGIN late Middle English: from Latin *implacabilis*, from *in-* 'not' + *placabilis* (see PLACABLE).

im·plant ▶ **v.** /imˈplant/ [with obj.] insert or fix (tissue or an artificial object) in a person's body, esp. by surgery: *electrodes had been* ***implanted in*** *his brain.* ■ (**implant someone/something with**) provide someone or something with (something) by such insertion: *rats implanted with amphetamine pellets.* ■ [no obj.] (of a fertilized egg) become attached to the wall of the uterus. ■ establish or fix (an idea) in a person's mind.
▶ **n.** /ˈimˌplant/ a thing implanted in something else, esp. a piece of tissue, prosthetic device, or other object implanted in the body: *a silicone breast implant.*
– ORIGIN late Middle English: from late Latin *implantare* 'engraft,' from Latin *in-* 'into' + *plantare* 'to plant.'

im·plant·able /imˈplantəbəl/ ▶ **adj.** capable of or designed for being implanted in living tissue: *an implantable defibrillator.*

im·plan·ta·tion /ˌimplanˈtāSHən/ ▶ **n.** the action of implanting or state of being implanted. ■ Zoology & Medicine (in a mammal) the attachment of the fertilized egg or blastocyst to the wall of the uterus at the start of pregnancy, often delayed in some mammals by several months. Also called NIDATION.
– ORIGIN late 16th cent.: from French, from *implanter* 'to implant.'

im·plau·si·ble /imˈplôzəbəl/ ▶ **adj.** (of an argument or statement) not seeming reasonable or probable; failing to convince: *this is a blatantly implausible claim.*
– DERIVATIVES **im·plau·si·bil·i·ty** /-ˌplôzəˈbilitē/ **n.**, **im·plau·si·bly** /-blē/ **adv.**

im·ple·ment ▶ **n.** /ˈimpləmənt/ a tool, utensil, or other piece of equipment, esp. as used for a particular purpose: *agricultural implements.*
▶ **v.** /-ˌment/ [with obj.] put (a decision, plan, agreement, etc.) into effect: *the regulations implement a 1954 treaty.*
– DERIVATIVES **im·ple·ment·er** (also **implementor** /-ˌmentər/) **n.**
– ORIGIN late Middle English (in the sense 'article of furniture, equipment, or dress'): partly from medieval Latin *implementa* (plural), partly from late Latin *implementum* 'filling up, fulfillment,' both from Latin *implere* 'fill up' (later 'employ'), from *in-* 'in' + *plere* 'fill.' The verb dates from the early 18th cent.

im·ple·men·ta·tion /ˌimpləmənˈtāsʜən/ ▶ **n.** the process of putting a decision or plan into effect; execution: *she was responsible for the implementation of the plan.*

im·pli·cate /ˈimpliˌkāt/ ▶ **v.** [with obj.] **1** show (someone) to be involved in a crime: *police claims implicated him in many more killings.* ■ (**be implicated in**) bear some of the responsibility for (an action or process, esp. a criminal or harmful one): *the team believes he is heavily implicated in the bombing* | *a chemical implicated in ozone depletion.* ■ involve (something) in a necessary way: *cable franchise activities plainly implicate First Amendment interests.*
2 [with clause] convey (a meaning or intention) indirectly through what one says, rather than stating it explicitly; imply: *by saying that coffee would keep her awake, Mary implicated that she didn't want any.*
▶ **n.** chiefly Logic a thing implied.
– DERIVATIVES **im·pli·ca·tive** /ˈimpliˌkātiv, imˈplikətiv/ **adj.**, **im·pli·ca·tive·ly adv.**
– ORIGIN late Middle English: from Latin *implicatus* 'folded in,' past participle of *implicare* (see IMPLY). The original sense was 'entwine, entangle'; compare with EMPLOY and IMPLY. The earliest modern sense (sense 2 of the verb) dates from the early 17th cent., but appears earlier in IMPLICATION.

im·pli·ca·tion /ˌimpliˈkāsʜən/ ▶ **n.** **1** the conclusion that can be drawn from something, although it is not explicitly stated: *the implication is that no one person at the bank is responsible.* ■ a likely consequence of something: *a victory that had important political implications.*
2 the action or state of being involved in something: *our implication in the problems.*
– PHRASES **by implication** by what is implied or suggested rather than by formal expression: *he criticized her and, by implication, her country.*
– DERIVATIVES **im·pli·ca·tion·al** /-sʜənl/ **adj.**
– ORIGIN late Middle English (in the sense 'entwining, being entwined'): from Latin *implicatio(n-)*, from the verb *implicare* (see IMPLICATE).

im·pli·ca·ture /ˈimplikəcʜər/ ▶ **n.** the action of implying a meaning beyond the literal sense of what is explicitly stated, e.g., saying *the frame is nice* and implying *I don't like the picture in it.* ■ a meaning so implied.

im·plic·it /imˈplisit/ ▶ **adj.** **1** implied though not plainly expressed: *comments seen as implicit criticism of the policies.* ■ [predic.] (**implicit in**) essentially or very closely connected with; always to be found in: *the values implicit in the school ethos.*
2 with no qualification or question; absolute: *an implicit faith in God.*
3 Mathematics (of a function) not expressed directly in terms of independent variables.
– DERIVATIVES **im·plic·it·ness n.**
– ORIGIN late 16th cent.: from French *implicite* or Latin *implicitus*, later form of *implicatus* 'entwined,' past participle of *implicare* (see IMPLY).

im·plic·it·ly /imˈplisitlē/ ▶ **adv.** **1** in a way that is not directly expressed; tacitly: *she implicitly suggested that he was responsible for the error.*
2 without qualification: absolutely: *he trusted Sarah implicitly.*

im·plied /imˈplīd/ ▶ **adj.** suggested but not directly expressed; implicit: *she was aware of his implied criticism.*
– DERIVATIVES **im·pli·ed·ly** /-ˈplī-idlē/ **adv.**

im·plode /imˈplōd/ ▶ **v.** **1** collapse or cause to collapse violently inward: [no obj.] *the windows on both sides of the room had imploded* | [with obj.] *these forces would implode the pellet to a density 100 times higher than that of lead.*
2 [with obj.] Phonetics utter or pronounce (a consonant) with a sharp intake of air.
– DERIVATIVES **im·plo·sion** /-zʜən/ **n.**
– ORIGIN late 19th cent.: from IN-² 'within' + Latin *plodere, plaudere* 'to clap,' on the pattern of *explode.*

im·plore /imˈplôr/ ▶ **v.** [reporting verb] beg someone earnestly or desperately to do something: [with obj. and infinitive] *he implored her to change her mind* | [with direct speech] *"Please don't talk that way," Ellen implored.* ■ [with obj.] archaic beg earnestly for: *I implore mercy.*
– DERIVATIVES **im·plor·ing·ly adv.**
– ORIGIN early 16th cent.: from French *implorer* or Latin *implorare* 'invoke with tears.'

im·plo·sive /imˈplōsiv/ ▶ **adj.** formed by implosion; tending to implode. ■ Phonetics denoting a type of consonant produced in the glottis with an ingressive air flow.

im·ply /imˈplī/ ▶ **v.** (**implies, implying, implied**) [with obj.] strongly suggest the truth or existence of (something not expressly stated): *the salesmen who uses jargon to imply his superior knowledge* | [with clause] *the report implies that two million jobs might be lost.* ■ (of a fact or occurrence) suggest (something) as a logical consequence: *the forecasted traffic increase implied more roads and more air pollution.*
– ORIGIN late Middle English: from Old French *emplier*, from Latin *implicare*, from *in-* 'in' + *plicare* 'to fold.' The original sense was 'entwine, entangle'; in the 16th and 17th centuries the word also meant 'employ' Compare with EMPLOY and IMPLICATE.

> **USAGE** Imply and infer do not mean the same thing and should not be used interchangeably: see usage at INFER.

im·pol·der /imˈpōldər/ ▶ **v.** [with obj.] make (an area of the seabed) into a polder by reclaiming it from the sea.
– ORIGIN late 19th cent.: from Dutch *impolderen.*

im·po·lite /ˌimpəˈlīt/ ▶ **adj.** not having or showing good manners; rude: *it would have been impolite to refuse.*
– DERIVATIVES **im·po·lite·ly adv.**, **im·po·lite·ness n.**
– ORIGIN early 17th cent. (in the sense 'unpolished'): from Latin *impolitus*, from *in-* 'not' + *politus* (see POLITE).

im·pol·i·tic /imˈpäliˌtik/ ▶ **adj.** failing to possess or display prudence; unwise: *it was impolitic to pay the slightest tribute to the enemy.*
– DERIVATIVES **im·pol·i·tic·ly adv.**

im·pon·der·a·ble /imˈpändərəbəl/ ▶ **n.** a factor that is difficult or impossible to estimate or assess: *there are too many imponderables for an overall prediction.*
▶ **adj.** **1** difficult or impossible to estimate, assess, or answer: *an imponderable problem of metaphysics.*
2 archaic or literary very light.
– DERIVATIVES **im·pon·der·a·bil·i·ty** /-ˌpändərəˈbilitē/ **n.**, **im·pon·der·a·bly** /-blē/ **adv.**

im·port ▶ **v.** /imˈpôrt/ [with obj.] **1** bring (goods or services) into a country from abroad for sale: *Japan's reluctance to import more cars.* ■ introduce (an idea) from a different place or context: *new beliefs were often imported by sailors.* ■ Computing transfer (data) into a file or document.
2 archaic indicate or signify: *having thus seen, what is imported in a Man's trusting his Heart.* ■ express or make known: [with clause] *they passed a resolution importing that they relied on His Majesty's gracious promise.*
▶ **n.** /ˈimˌpôrt/ **1** (usu. **imports**) a commodity, article, or service brought in from abroad for sale. ■ (**imports**) sales of goods or services brought in from abroad, or the revenue from such sales: *this surplus pushes up the yen, which ought to boost imports.* ■ the action or process of importing goods or services: *the import of live cattle from Canada.*
2 [in sing.] the meaning or significance of something, esp. when not directly stated: *the import of her message is clear.* ■ great significance; importance: *pronouncements of world-shaking import.*
– DERIVATIVES **im·port·a·ble adj.**, **im·por·ta·tion** /ˌimpôrˈtāsʜən/ **n.**, **im·port·er n.**
– ORIGIN late Middle English (in the sense 'signify'): from Latin *importare* 'bring in' (in medieval Latin 'imply, mean, be of consequence'), from *in-* 'in' + *portare* 'carry.'

im·por·tance /imˈpôrtns/ ▶ **n.** the state or fact of being of great significance or value: *the importance of democracy* | *the relative importances of the external and internal causes.*
– PHRASES **full of one's own importance** having a very high opinion of oneself; self-important.
– ORIGIN early 16th cent.: from French, from medieval Latin *importantia*, from *important-* 'being of consequence,' from the verb *importare* (see IMPORT).

im·por·tant /imˈpôrtnt/ ▶ **adj.** of great significance or value; likely to have a profound effect on success, survival, or well-being: *important habitats for wildlife* | *it is important to avoid monosyllabic answers* | [sentence adverb] *the speech had passion and, more important, compassion.* ■ (of a person) having high rank or status. ■ (of an artist or artistic work) significantly original and influential.
– ORIGIN late Middle English: from medieval Latin *important-* 'being of consequence,' from the verb *importare* (see IMPORT).

im·por·tant·ly /imˈpôrtnt-lē/ ▶ **adv.** **1** [sentence adverb] used to emphasize a significant point or matter: *a nondrinking, nonsmoking, and, importantly, nonpolitical sportsman.*
2 in a manner designed to draw attention to one's importance: *Kruger strutted forward importantly.*

im·por·tu·nate /imˈpôrcʜənit/ ▶ **adj.** persistent, esp. to the point of annoyance or intrusion: *importunate creditors.*
– DERIVATIVES **im·por·tu·nate·ly adv.**, **im·por·tu·ni·ty** /ˌimpôrˈt(y)o͞onitē/ **n.** (pl. **importunities**).
– ORIGIN early 16th cent.: from Latin *importunus* 'inconvenient, unseasonable,' based on *Portunus*, the name of the god who protected harbors (from *portus* 'harbor'); compare with OPPORTUNE.

im·por·tune /ˌimpôrˈt(y)o͞on, imˈpôrcʜən/ ▶ **v.** [with obj.] ask (someone) pressingly and persistently for or to do something: *if he were alive now, I should importune him with my questions.* ■ approach (someone) to offer one's services as a prostitute.
– ORIGIN mid 16th cent.: from French *importuner* or medieval Latin *importunari*, from Latin *importunus* 'inconvenient, unseasonable' (see IMPORTUNATE).

im·pose /imˈpōz/ ▶ **v.** **1** [with obj.] force (something unwelcome or unfamiliar) to be accepted or put in place: *the decision was theirs and was not imposed on them by others.* ■ forcibly put (a restriction) in place: *sanctions imposed on South Africa.* ■ require (a duty, charge, or penalty) to be undertaken or paid. ■ (**impose oneself**) exert firm control over something: *the director was unable to **impose himself** on the production.*
2 [no obj.] take advantage of someone by demanding their attention or commitment: *she realized that she had **imposed on** Miss Hatherby's kindness.*
3 [with obj.] Printing arrange (pages of type) so that they will be in the correct order after printing and folding.
– ORIGIN late 15th cent. (in the sense 'impute'): from French *imposer*, from Latin *imponere* 'inflict, deceive' (from *in-* 'in, upon' + *ponere* 'put'), but influenced by *impositus* 'inflicted' and Old French *poser* 'to place.'

im·pos·ing /imˈpōziɴɢ/ ▶ **adj.** grand and impressive in appearance: *an imposing 17th-century manor house.*
– DERIVATIVES **im·pos·ing·ly adv.**

im·po·si·tion /ˌimpəˈzisʜən/ ▶ **n.** **1** the action or process of imposing something or of being imposed: *the imposition of martial law.*
2 a thing that is imposed, in particular an unfair or unwelcome demand or burden: *I'd like to see you, if that wouldn't be too much of an imposition.* ■ a tax or duty. ■ Christian Church the laying-on of hands, as in blessing or ordination.
3 Printing the imposing of pages of type. ■ a particular arrangement of imposed pages: *some samples of 16-page impositions.*
– ORIGIN late Middle English: from Latin *impositio(n-)*, from the verb *imponere* (see IMPOSE).

im·pos·si·bil·ism /imˈpäsəbəˌlizəm/ ▶ **n.** belief in ideas or policy, esp. on social reform, that are held to be unrealizable or impractical.
– DERIVATIVES **im·pos·si·bil·ist n.**

im·pos·si·bil·i·ty /imˌpäsəˈbilitē/ ▶ **n.** (pl. **impossibilities**) the state or fact of being impossible: *the impossibility of walking anywhere in this jungle.* ■ an impossible thing or situation: *they believe that a world at peace is an impossibility.*
– ORIGIN late Middle English: from French *impossibilité* or Latin *impossibilitas*, from *impossibilis*, from *in-* 'not' + *possibilis* (see POSSIBLE).

im·pos·si·ble /imˈpäsəbəl/ ▶ **adj.** not able to occur, exist, or be done: *a seemingly impossible task* | [with infinitive] *it was almost impossible to keep up with him.* ■ very difficult to deal with: *she was in an impossible situation.* ■ informal (of a person) very unreasonable: *"Impossible woman!" the doctor complained.*
– ORIGIN Middle English: from Old French, or from Latin *impossibilis*, from *in-* 'not' + *possibilis* (see POSSIBLE).

im·pos·si·bly /imˈpäsəblē/ ▶ **adv.** [sentence adverb] used to describe an event or action that is so difficult or unlikely one would not expect it to be possible: *he held her and, impossibly, she fell asleep.* ■ [as submodifier] so as to be impossible: *impossibly high standards.* ■ [as submodifier] possessing the specified

i

quality to an unbelievably high degree: *impossibly blond hair.*

im·post¹ /ˈimˌpōst/ ▶ **n.** a tax or similar compulsory payment. ■ Horse Racing the weight carried by a horse as a handicap.
– ORIGIN mid 16th cent.: from French (earlier form of *impôt*), from medieval Latin *impostus*, from Latin *impositus*, past participle of *imponere* (see IMPOSE).

im·post² ▶ **n.** Architecture the top course of a pillar that supports an arch.
– ORIGIN late 15th cent.: from Italian *imposta*, feminine past participle of *imporre*, from Latin *imponere* (see IMPOSE).

im·pos·tor /imˈpästər/ (also **imposter**) ▶ **n.** a person who pretends to be someone else in order to deceive others, esp. for fraudulent gain.
– ORIGIN late 16th cent. (in early use spelled *imposture*, and sometimes confused with IMPOSTURE in meaning): from French *imposteur*, from late Latin *impostor*, contraction of *impositor*, from Latin *imponere* (see IMPOSE).

im·pos·ture /imˈpäsCHər/ ▶ **n.** an instance of pretending to be someone else in order to deceive others.
– ORIGIN mid 16th cent.: via French from late Latin *impostura*, from Latin *imposit-* 'imposed upon,' from the verb *imponere* (see IMPOSE).

im·po·tent /ˈimpətnt/ ▶ **adj. 1** unable to take effective action; helpless or powerless: *he was seized with an impotent anger.*
2 (of a man) abnormally unable to achieve a sexual erection. ■ (of a male animal) unable to copulate.
– DERIVATIVES **im·po·tence** n., **im·po·ten·cy** n., **im·po·tent·ly** adv.
– ORIGIN late Middle English: via Old French from Latin *impotent-* 'powerless,' from *in-* 'not' + *potent-* (see POTENT¹).

im·pound /imˈpound/ ▶ **v.** [with obj.] **1** seize and take legal custody of (something, esp. a vehicle, goods, or documents) because of an infringement of a law or regulation: *vehicles parked where they cause an obstruction will be impounded.*
2 shut up (domestic animals) in a pound or enclosure. ■ (of a dam) hold back or confine (water).
– DERIVATIVES **im·pound·a·ble** adj., **im·pound·er** n., **im·pound·ment** n.

im·pov·er·ish /imˈpäv(ə)riSH/ ▶ **v.** [with obj.] make (a person or area) poor: *they discourage investment and impoverish their people* | (as adj. **impoverished**) *impoverished peasant farmers.* ■ exhaust the strength, vitality, or natural fertility of: *the soil was impoverished by annual burning* | (as adj. **impoverished**) figurative *an impoverished and debased language.*
– DERIVATIVES **im·pov·er·ish·ment** n.
– ORIGIN late Middle English (formerly also as *empoverish*): from Old French *empoveriss-*, lengthened stem of *empoverir*, based on *povre* 'poor.'

im·prac·ti·ca·ble /imˈpraktikəbəl/ ▶ **adj.** (of a course of action) impossible in practice to do or carry out: *it was impracticable to widen the road here.*
– DERIVATIVES **im·prac·ti·ca·bil·i·ty** /-ˌpraktikəˈbilitē/ n., **im·prac·ti·ca·bly** /-blē/ adv.

> **USAGE** Impracticable and impractical are sometimes confused. **Impracticable** means 'impossible to carry out' and is normally used of a specific procedure or course of action: *poor visibility made the task difficult, even* **impracticable**. **Impractical**, on the other hand, tends to be used in more general senses, often to mean simply 'unrealistic' or 'not sensible': *in windy weather an umbrella is impractical.*

im·prac·ti·cal /imˈpraktikəl/ ▶ **adj. 1** (of an object or course of action) not adapted for use or action; not sensible or realistic: *impractical high heels* | *his impractical romanticism.* ■ (of a person) not skilled or interested in practical matters: *Paul was impractical and dreamy.*
2 impossible to do; impracticable.
– DERIVATIVES **im·prac·ti·cal·i·ty** /-ˌpraktiˈkalitē/ n., **im·prac·ti·cal·ly** /-ik(ə)lē/ adv.

> **USAGE** On the differences in the use of **impractical** and **impracticable**, see usage at IMPRACTICABLE.

im·pre·cate /ˈimpriˌkāt/ ▶ **v.** [with obj.] archaic utter (a curse) or invoke (evil) against someone or something.
– ORIGIN early 17th cent.: from Latin *imprecat-* 'invoked,' from the verb *imprecari*.

im·pre·ca·tion /ˌimpriˈkāSHən/ ▶ **n.** formal a spoken curse: *she hurled her imprecations at anyone who might be listening.*
– DERIVATIVES **im·pre·ca·to·ry** /ˈimprikəˌtôrē/ adj.
– ORIGIN late Middle English: from Latin *imprecatio(n-)*, from *imprecari* 'invoke (evil),' from *in-* 'toward' + *precari* 'pray.'

im·pre·cise /ˌimpriˈsīs/ ▶ **adj.** lacking exactness and accuracy of expression or detail: *the witness could give only vague and imprecise descriptions.*
– DERIVATIVES **im·pre·cise·ly** adv., **im·pre·cise·ness** n., **im·pre·ci·sion** /-ˈsiZHən/ n.

im·preg·na·ble /imˈpregnəbəl/ ▶ **adj.** (of a fortified position) unable to be captured or broken into: *an impregnable wall of solid sandstone* | figurative *the companies are impregnable to takeovers.* ■ unable to be defeated or destroyed; unassailable: *the case against Hastings would have been almost impregnable.*
– DERIVATIVES **im·preg·na·bil·i·ty** /-ˌpregnəˈbilitē/ n., **im·preg·na·bly** /-blē/ adv.
– ORIGIN late Middle English: from Old French *imprenable*, from *in-* 'not' + *prendre* 'take' (from Latin *prehendere*). The current spelling arose in the 16th cent., perhaps influenced by Old French variants.

im·preg·nate /imˈpregˌnāt/ ▶ **v.** [with obj.] **1** make (a woman or female animal) pregnant. ■ Biology fertilize (a female reproductive cell or ovum).
2 (usu. **be impregnated with**) soak or saturate (something) with a substance: *wood that had been impregnated with preservative.* ■ imbue with feelings or qualities: *an atmosphere impregnated with tension.*
– DERIVATIVES **im·preg·na·tion** /ˌimpregˈnāSHən/ n.
– ORIGIN early 17th cent. (in the sense 'fill'): from late Latin *impregnat-* 'made pregnant,' from the verb *impregnare*.

im·pre·sa·ri·o /ˌimprəˈsärēˌō, -ˈse(ə)r-/ ▶ **n.** (pl. **impresarios**) a person who organizes and often finances concerts, plays, or operas. ■ chiefly historical the manager of a musical, theatrical, or operatic company.
– ORIGIN mid 18th cent.: from Italian, from *impresa* 'undertaking.'

im·pre·scrip·ti·ble /ˌimpriˈskriptəbəl/ ▶ **adj.** Law (of rights) unable to be taken away by prescription or by lapse of time.
– ORIGIN late 16th cent.: from medieval Latin *imprescriptibilis*, from *in-* 'not' + Latin *praescript-* (from *praescribere* 'prescribe').

im·press¹ ▶ **v.** /imˈpres/ [with obj.] **1** make (someone) feel admiration and respect: *they immediately impressed the judges* | [no obj.] *he has to put on an act to impress.*
2 make a mark or design on (an object) using a stamp or seal; imprint: *she impressed the damp clay with her seal.* ■ apply (a mark) to something with pressure: *a revenue stamp was embossed or impressed on the instrument.*
3 (**impress something on**) fix an idea in (someone's mind): *nobody impressed on me the need to save.*
4 apply (an electric current or potential) from an external source.
▶ **n.** /ˈimˌpres/ [in sing.] an act of making an impression or mark: *bluish marks made by the impress of his fingers.* ■ a mark made by a seal or stamp. ■ the characteristic mark or quality of a person or attribute: *his desire to put his own impress on the films he made.*
– DERIVATIVES **im·press·i·ble** adj.
– ORIGIN late Middle English (in the sense 'apply with pressure'): from Old French *empresser*, from *em-* 'in' + *presser* 'to press,' influenced by Latin *imprimere* (see IMPRINT). Sense 1 of the verb dates from the mid 18th cent.

im·press² ▶ **v.** [with obj.] historical force (someone) to serve in an army or navy: *a number of Poles, impressed into the German army.* ■ commandeer (goods or equipment) for public service.
– DERIVATIVES **im·press·ment** n.
– ORIGIN late 16th cent.: from IN-² 'into' + PRESS².

im·pres·sion /imˈpreSHən/ ▶ **n. 1** an idea, feeling, or opinion about something or someone, esp. one formed without conscious thought or on the basis of little evidence: *his first impressions of Manchester were very positive* | *they give the impression that all is sweetness and light.* ■ an effect produced on someone: *her courtesy and quick wit had made a good impression.* ■ a difference made by the action or presence of someone or something: *the floor was too dirty for the mop to make much impression.*
2 an imitation of a person or thing, esp. one done to entertain: *he did an impression of Frank Sinatra.* ■ a graphic or pictorial representation of someone or something: *the police have issued an artist's impression of the attacker.*
3 a mark impressed on a surface by something: *the impression of his body on the leaves.* ■ Dentistry a negative copy of the teeth or mouth made by pressing them into a soft substance.
4 the printing of a number of copies of a book, periodical, or picture for issue at one time. ■ [usu. with adj.] a particular printed version of a book or other publication, esp. one reprinted from existing type, plates, or film with no or only minor alteration. Compare with EDITION. ■ a print taken from an engraving.
5 an instance of a pop-up or other Web advertisement being seen on computer users' screens.
– PHRASES **under the impression that** believing, mistakenly or on the basis of little evidence, that something is the case: *he was under the impression that they had become friends.*
– DERIVATIVES **im·pres·sion·al** /-SHənl/ adj.
– ORIGIN late Middle English: via Old French from Latin *impressio(n-)*, from *impress-* 'pressed in,' from the verb *imprimere* (see IMPRINT).

im·pres·sion·a·ble /imˈpreSH(ə)nəbəl/ ▶ **adj.** easily influenced because of a lack of critical ability: *a girl of eighteen is highly impressionable.*
– DERIVATIVES **im·pres·sion·a·bil·i·ty** /-ˌpreSH(ə)nəˈbilitē/ n., **im·pres·sion·a·bly** /-blē/ adv.
– ORIGIN mid 19th cent.: from French, from *impressionner*, from Latin *impressio(n-)*, from the verb *imprimere* 'press into' (see IMPRINT).

Im·pres·sion·ism /imˈpreSHəˌnizəm/ ▶ **n.** a style or movement in painting originating in France in the 1860s, characterized by a concern with depicting the visual impression of the moment, esp. in terms of the shifting effect of light and color. ■ a literary or artistic style that seeks to capture a feeling or experience rather than to achieve accurate depiction. ■ Music a style of composition (associated esp. with Debussy) in which clarity of structure and theme is subordinate to harmonic effects, characteristically using the whole-tone scale.

> The Impressionist painters repudiated both the precise academic style and the emotional concerns of Romanticism, and their interest in objective representation, esp. of landscape, was influenced by early photography. Impressionism met at first with suspicion and scorn, but soon became deeply influential. Its chief exponents included Monet, Renoir, Pissarro, Cézanne, Degas, and Sisley.

– ORIGIN from French *impressionnisme*, from *impressionniste*, originally applied unfavorably with reference to Monet's painting *Impression: Soleil levant* (1872).

Im·pres·sion·ist /imˈpreSHənist/ ▶ **n.** a painter, writer, or composer who is an exponent of Impressionism.
▶ **adj.** of or relating to Impressionism or its exponents.

im·pres·sion·ist /imˈpreSHənist/ ▶ **n.** an entertainer who impersonates famous people.

im·pres·sion·is·tic /imˌpreSHəˈnistik/ ▶ **adj. 1** based on subjective reactions presented unsystematically: *a personal and impressionistic view of the war.*
2 (**Impressionistic**) in the style of Impressionism: *an Impressionistic portrait.*
– DERIVATIVES **im·pres·sion·is·ti·cal·ly** /-ik(ə)lē/ adv.

im·pres·sive /imˈpresiv/ ▶ **adj.** evoking admiration through size, quality, or skill: grand, imposing, or awesome: *an impressive view of the mountains* | *impressive achievements in science.*
– DERIVATIVES **im·pres·sive·ly** adv., **im·pres·sive·ness** n.

im·prest /ˈimˌprest/ ▶ **n.** a fund used by a business for small items of expenditure and restored to a fixed amount periodically. ■ a sum of money advanced to a person for a particular purpose.
– ORIGIN mid 16th cent.: from the earlier phrase *in prest* 'as a loan,' influenced by Italian or medieval Latin *imprestare* 'lend.'

im·pri·ma·tur /ˌimprəˈmätər, -ˈmātər/ ▶ **n.** an official license by the Roman Catholic Church to print an ecclesiastical or religious book. ■ [in sing.] a person's acceptance or guarantee that something is of a good standard: *the original LP enjoyed the imprimatur of the composer.*
– ORIGIN mid 17th cent.: from Latin, 'let it be printed' from the verb *imprimere* (see IMPRINT).

im·print ▶ **v.** /imˈprint/ **1** [with obj.] impress or stamp (a mark or outline) on a surface or body: *tire marks were imprinted in the snow.* ■ make an impression or mark on (something): *clothes imprinted with the logos of sports teams.* ■ fix (an idea) firmly in someone's mind: *he would always have this ghastly image imprinted on his mind.*
2 [no obj.] (**imprint on**) Zoology (of a young animal) come to recognize (another animal, person, or thing) as a parent or other object of habitual trust.
▶ **n.** /ˈimprint/ **1** a mark made by pressing something onto a softer substance so that its outline is reproduced: *he made imprints of the keys in bars of*

soap. ■ a lasting impression or effect: *years in the colonies had left their imprint.*
2 a printer's or publisher's name, address, and other details in a book or other printed item. ■ a brand name under which books are published, typically the name of a former publishing house that is now part of a larger group.
– ORIGIN late Middle English (originally as *emprint*): from Old French *empreinter*, based on Latin *imprimere*, from *in-* 'into' + *premere* 'to press.'

im·pris·on /im'prizən/ ▶ **v.** [with obj.] put or keep in prison or a place like a prison: *he was imprisoned for six months for contempt of court.*
– ORIGIN Middle English *emprison*, from Old French *emprisoner*, from *em-* 'in' + *prison*.

im·pris·oned /im'prizənd/ ▶ **adj.** kept in prison: captive: *an imprisoned dissident.*

im·pris·on·ment /im'prizənmənt/ ▶ **n.** the state of being imprisoned; captivity: *he was sentenced to two months' imprisonment.*

im·prob·a·bil·i·ty /im,präbə'bilitē/ ▶ **n.** (pl. **improbabilities**) the quality of being improbable; unlikelihood: *his belief in the improbability of war in Europe.* ■ an improbable event: *the film is full of improbabilities.*

im·prob·a·ble /im'präbəbəl/ ▶ **adj.** not likely to be true or to happen: *this account of events was seen by the jury as most improbable.* ■ unexpected and apparently inauthentic: *the characters have improbable names.*
– DERIVATIVES **im·prob·a·bly** /-blē/ **adv.**
– ORIGIN late 16th cent.: from French, or from Latin *improbabilis* 'hard to prove,' from *in-* 'not' + *probabilis* (see **PROBABLE**).

im·pro·bi·ty /im'prōbitē/ ▶ **n.** formal wickedness or dishonesty.
– ORIGIN late 16th cent.: from Latin *improbitas*, from *improbus* 'wicked,' from *in-* 'not' + *probus* 'good.' Compare with **PROBITY**.

im·promp·tu /im'präm(p),t(y)o͞o/ ▶ **adj. & adv.** done without being planned, organized, or rehearsed: [as adj.] *an impromptu press conference* | [as adv.] *he spoke impromptu.*
▶ **n.** (pl. **impromptus**) a short piece of instrumental music, esp. a solo, that is reminiscent of an improvisation.
– ORIGIN mid 17th cent. (as an adverb): from French, from Latin *in promptu* 'in readiness,' from *promptus* (see **PROMPT**).

im·prop·er /im'präpər/ ▶ **adj.** not in accordance with accepted rules or standards, esp. of morality or honesty: *he was accused of improper behavior in his business dealings.* ■ lacking in modesty or decency: *it was thought improper for elderly women to wear bright colors.*
– DERIVATIVES **im·prop·er·ly adv.**
– ORIGIN late Middle English: from French *impropre* or Latin *improprius*, from *in-* 'not' + *proprius* 'one's own, proper.'

im·prop·er frac·tion ▶ **n.** a fraction in which the numerator is greater than the denominator, such as $^5/_4$.

im·pro·pri·ate /im'prōprē,āt/ ▶ **v.** [with obj.] (usu. as adj. **impropriated**) grant (an ecclesiastical benefice) to a corporation or person as their property. ■ place (tithes or ecclesiastical property) in lay hands.
– DERIVATIVES **im·pro·pri·a·tion** /-,prōprē'āsHən/ **n.**
– ORIGIN early 16th cent.: from Anglo-Latin *impropriat-* 'appropriated,' from the verb *impropriare*, based on Latin *proprius* 'one's own, proper.'

im·pro·pri·a·tor /im'prōprē,ātər/ ▶ **n.** a person to whom a benefice is granted as their property.

im·pro·pri·e·ty /,imprə'prī-itē/ ▶ **n.** (pl. **improprieties**) a failure to observe standards or show due honesty or modesty; improper language, behavior, or character: *she was scandalized at the impropriety of the question* | *there are no demonstrable legal improprieties.*
– ORIGIN early 17th cent. (also in the sense 'inaccuracy, incorrectness'): from French *impropriété* or Latin *improprietas*, from *improprius* (see **IMPROPER**).

im·prov /'im,präv/ ▶ **n.** informal improvisation, esp. as a theatrical technique.

im·prove /im'pro͞ov/ ▶ **v.** make or become better: [with obj.] *we've used technology to improve relations with customers* | (as adj. **improved**) *improved road and rail links* | [no obj.] *his condition improved after glass was removed from his arm.* ■ [with obj.] develop or increase in mental capacity by education or experience: *I subscribed to two magazines to improve my mind.* ■ [no obj.] (**improve on/upon**) achieve or produce something better than: *they are trying to improve on the tired old style.*
– DERIVATIVES **im·prov·a·bil·i·ty** /-,pro͞ovə'bilitē/ **n.**, **im·prov·a·ble adj.**, **im·prov·er n.**
– ORIGIN early 16th cent. (as *emprowe* or *improwe*): from Anglo-Norman French *emprower* (based on Old French *prou* 'profit,' ultimately from Latin *prodest* 'is of advantage'); *-owe* was changed to *-ove* under the influence of **PROVE**. The original sense was 'make a profit, increase the value of'; subsequently 'make greater in amount or degree.'

im·prove·ment /im'pro͞ovmənt/ ▶ **n.** an example or instance of improving or being improved: *an improvement in East–West relations.* ■ the action of improving or being improved: *there's still room for improvement.* ■ a thing that makes something better or is better than something else: *home improvements* | *it's an improvement on the last cake I made.*
– ORIGIN late Middle English *emprowement* (in the sense 'profitable management or use; profit'), from Anglo-Norman French, from *emprower* (see **IMPROVE**).

im·prov·i·dent /im'prävidənt/ ▶ **adj.** not having or showing foresight; spendthrift or thoughtless: *improvident and undisciplined behavior.*
– DERIVATIVES **im·prov·i·dence n.**, **im·prov·i·dent·ly adv.**

im·prov·i·sa·tion /im,prävi'zāsHən/ ▶ **n.** the action of improvising. ■ something that is improvised, esp. a piece of music, drama, etc., created without preparation: *free-form jazz improvisations.*
– DERIVATIVES **im·prov·i·sa·tion·al adj.**

im·pro·vise /'imprə,vīz/ ▶ **v.** [with obj.] create and perform (music, drama, or verse) spontaneously or without preparation: *the ability to improvise operatic arias in any given style* | [no obj.] *he was improvising to a backing of guitar chords.* ■ produce or make (something) from whatever is available: *I improvised a costume for myself out of an old blue dress.*
– DERIVATIVES **im·pro·vi·sa·to·ry** /im'prävizə,tôrē/ **adj.**, **im·pro·vis·er n.**
– ORIGIN early 19th cent.: from French *improviser* or its source, Italian *improvvisare*, from *improvviso* 'extempore,' from Latin *improvisus* 'unforeseen,' based on *provisus*, past participle of *providere* 'make preparation for.'

im·pro·vised /'imprə,vīzd/ ▶ **adj.** created and performed spontaneously or without preparation; impromptu: *an improvised short speech.* ■ done or made using whatever is available; makeshift: *we slept on improvised beds.*

im·pru·dent /im'pro͞odnt/ ▶ **adj.** not showing care for the consequences of an action; rash: *it would be imprudent to leave her winter coat behind.*
– DERIVATIVES **im·pru·dence n.**, **im·pru·dent·ly adv.**
– ORIGIN late Middle English: from Latin *imprudent-* 'not foreseeing,' from *in-* 'not' + *prudent-* (see **PRUDENT**).

im·pu·dence /'impyəd(ə)ns/ ▶ **n.** the quality of being impudent; impertinence: *his arrogance and impudence had offended many.*

im·pu·dent /'impyəd(ə)nt/ ▶ **adj.** not showing due respect for another person; impertinent: *he could have strangled this impudent upstart.*
– DERIVATIVES **im·pu·dent·ly adv.**
– ORIGIN late Middle English (in the sense 'immodest, indelicate'): from Latin *impudent-*, from *in-* 'not' + *pudent-* 'ashamed, modest' (from *pudere* 'be ashamed').

im·pu·dic·i·ty /,impyə'disitē/ ▶ **n.** formal lack of modesty.
– ORIGIN early 16th cent.: from French *impudicité*, from Latin *impudicitia*, from *impudicus* 'shameless,' from *in-* 'not' + *pudere* 'be ashamed.'

im·pugn /im'pyo͞on/ ▶ **v.** [with obj.] dispute the truth, validity, or honesty of (a statement or motive); call into question: *the father does not impugn her capacity as a good mother.*
– DERIVATIVES **im·pugn·a·ble adj.**, **im·pugn·ment n.**
– ORIGIN late Middle English (also in the sense 'assault, attack physically'): from Latin *impugnare* 'assail,' from *in-* 'toward' + *pugnare* 'fight.'

im·pu·is·sant /im'pwisənt, -'pyo͞o-isənt/ ▶ **adj.** literary unable to take effective action; powerless.
– DERIVATIVES **im·pu·is·sance n.**
– ORIGIN early 17th cent.: French, from *im-* 'not' + *puissant* 'powerful.'

im·pulse /'im,pəls/ ▶ **n. 1** a sudden strong and unreflective urge or desire to act: *I had an almost irresistible impulse to giggle.* ■ the tendency to act in this way: *he was a man of impulse, not premeditation.*
2 a driving or motivating force; an impetus: *an added impulse to this process of renewal.*
3 a pulse of electrical energy; a brief current: *nerve impulses* | *a spiral is used to convert radio waves into electrical impulses.*
4 Physics a force acting briefly on a body and producing a finite change of momentum. ■ a change of momentum so produced, equivalent to the average value of the force multiplied by the time during which it acts.
– PHRASES **on impulse** (or **on an impulse**) suddenly and without forethought; impulsively.
– ORIGIN early 17th cent. (as a verb in the sense 'give an impulse to'): the verb from Latin *impuls-* 'driven on,' the noun from *impulsus* 'impulsion, outward pressure,' both from the verb *impellere* (see **IMPEL**).

im·pulse buy·ing ▶ **n.** the buying of goods without planning to do so in advance, as a result of a sudden whim or impulse.

im·pul·sion /im'pəlsHən/ ▶ **n.** a strong urge to do something; an impulse: *the impulsion of the singers to govern the pace.* ■ the force or motive behind an action or process: *attitudes changed under the impulsion of humanitarian considerations.*
– ORIGIN late Middle English (in the sense 'the act or an instance of impelling'): via Old French from Latin *impulsio(n-)*, from the verb *impellere* (see **IMPEL**).

im·pul·sive /im'pəlsiv/ ▶ **adj. 1** acting or done without forethought: *they had married as young impulsive teenagers* | *perhaps he's regretting his impulsive offer.*
2 Physics acting as an impulse.
– DERIVATIVES **im·pul·sive·ly adv.**, **im·pul·sive·ness n.**, **im·pul·siv·i·ty** /,im,pəl'sivitē/ **n.**
– ORIGIN late Middle English (in the sense 'tending to impel'): from French *impulsif, -ive* or late Latin *impulsivus*, from Latin *impuls-* 'driven onward' (see **IMPULSE**). Sense 1 dates from the mid 18th cent.

im·pu·ni·ty /im'pyo͞onitē/ ▶ **n.** exemption from punishment or freedom from the injurious consequences of an action: *the impunity enjoyed by military officers implicated in civilian killings* | *protesters burned flags on the streets with impunity.*
– ORIGIN mid 16th cent.: from Latin *impunitas*, from *impunis* 'unpunished,' from *in-* 'not' + *poena* 'penalty' or *punire* 'punish.'

im·pure /im'pyo͝or/ ▶ **adj. 1** mixed with foreign matter; adulterated: *bullets cast from an impure lead.* ■ dirty: *a parasite that thrives in impure water.* ■ (of a color) mixed with another color.
2 morally wrong, esp. in sexual matters: *citizens suspected of harboring impure thoughts.* ■ defiled or contaminated according to ritual prescriptions: *the perception of woman as impure.*
– DERIVATIVES **im·pure·ly adv.**, **im·pure·ness n.**
– ORIGIN late Middle English (in the sense 'dirty, containing offensive matter'): from Latin *impurus*, from *in-* 'not' + *purus* 'pure.'

im·pu·ri·ty /im'pyo͝oritē/ ▶ **n.** (pl. **impurities**) the quality or condition of being impure. ■ a thing or constituent that impairs the purity of something: *aluminum and lead are impurities frequently found in tap water.* ■ Electronics a trace element deliberately added to a semiconductor; a dopant.
– ORIGIN late Middle English: from French *impurité* or Latin *impuritas*, from *impurus* (see **IMPURE**).

im·pute /im'pyo͞ot/ ▶ **v.** [with obj.] represent (something, esp. something undesirable) as being done, caused, or possessed by someone; attribute: *the crimes imputed to Richard.* ■ Finance assign (a value) to something by inference from the value of the products or processes to which it contributes: (as adj. **imputed**) *recovering the initial outlay plus imputed interest.* ■ Theology ascribe (righteousness, guilt, etc.) to someone by virtue of a similar quality in another: *Christ's righteousness has been imputed to us.*
– DERIVATIVES **im·put·a·ble adj.**, **im·pu·ta·tion** /,impyə'tāsHən/ **n.**
– ORIGIN late Middle English: from Old French *imputer*, from Latin *imputare* 'enter in the account,' from *in-* 'in, toward' + *putare* 'reckon.'

Im·roz /əm'rôz/ Turkish name of **IMBROS**.

IN ▶ **abbr.** Indiana (in official postal use).

In ▶ **symbol** the chemical element indium.

in /in/ ▶ **prep. 1** expressing the situation of something that is or appears to be enclosed or surrounded by something else: *living in Deep River* | *dressed in their Sunday best* | *soak it in warm soapy water* | *she saw it in the rearview mirror.* ■ expressing motion with the result that something ends up within or surrounded by something else: *don't put dye in the bathtub* | *he got in his car and drove off.*
2 expressing a period of time during which an event takes place or a situation remains the case: *they met in 1885* | *at one o'clock in the morning* | *I hadn't seen him in years.*

i

3 expressing the length of time before a future event is expected to take place: *I'll see you in fifteen minutes.*
4 (often followed by a noun without a determiner) expressing a state or condition: *to be in love | I've got to put my affairs in order | a woman in her thirties | laid out in a straight line.* ■ indicating the quality or aspect with respect to which a judgment is made: *no discernible difference in quality.*
5 expressing inclusion or involvement: *I read it in a book | acting in a film.*
6 indicating someone's occupation or profession: *she works in publishing.*
7 indicating the language or medium used: *say it in Polish | put it in writing.* ■ indicating the key in which a piece of music is written: *Mozart's Piano Concerto in E flat.*
8 [with verbal noun] as an integral part of (an activity): *in planning public expenditure it is better to be prudent.*
▶ **adv. 1** expressing movement with the result that someone or something becomes enclosed or surrounded by something else: *come in | bring it in | presently the admiral breezed in.*
2 expressing the situation of being enclosed or surrounded by something: *we were locked in.*
3 expressing arrival at a destination: *the train got in very late.*
4 (of the tide) rising or at its highest level.
5 Baseball (of an infielder or outfielder) playing closer to home plate than usual: *looking for a force, they brought the infield in.* ■ (of a pitch) very close to the batter: *he threw a fastball in and up a little.*
▶ **adj. 1** [predic.] (of a person) present at one's home or office: *we knocked at the door but there was no one in.*
2 informal fashionable: *pastels and light colors are in this year | the in thing to do.*
3 [predic.] (of the ball in tennis and similar games) landing within the designated playing area.
▶ **n.** a position of influence: *he would ensure an in with the nominee.*
– PHRASES **be in for** have good reason to expect (typically something unpleasant): *it looks as if we're in for a storm.* ■ (**be in for it**) have good reason to expect trouble or retribution. **have it in for someone** see HAVE. **in all** see ALL. **in and out of** being a frequent visitor to (a house) or frequent inmate of (an institution): *he was in and out of jail for most of his twenties.* **in on** privy to (a secret): *they were in on the conspiracy.* **in so far as** see INSOFAR. **in that** for the reason that (used to specify the respect in which a statement is true): *I was fortunate in that I had friends.* **in with** informal enjoying friendly relations with: *I was in demand because I was in with the right people.* **the ins and outs** informal all the details (of something).
– ORIGIN Old English *in* (preposition), *inn, inne* (adverb), of Germanic origin; related to Dutch and German *in* (preposition), German *ein* (adverb), from an Indo-European root shared by Latin *in* and Greek *en.*

in. ▶ **abbr.** inch(es).

in-[1] ▶ **prefix 1** (added to adjectives) not: *inanimate | intolerant.*
2 (added to nouns) without; lacking: *inadvertence | inappreciation.*
– ORIGIN from Latin.

in-[2] ▶ **prefix** in; into; toward; within: *induce | influx | inborn.*
– ORIGIN representing IN or the Latin preposition *in.*

-in[1] ▶ **suffix** Chemistry forming names of organic compounds, pharmaceutical products, proteins, etc.: *insulin | penicillin | dioxin.*
– ORIGIN alteration of -INE[4].

-in[2] ▶ **comb. form** denoting a gathering of people having a common purpose, typically as a form of protest: *sit-in | sleep-in | love-in.*

-ina ▶ **suffix 1** denoting feminine names and titles: *czarina.*
2 denoting names of musical instruments: *concertina.*
3 denoting names of plant and animal groups: *globigerina.*
– ORIGIN from Italian, Spanish, or Latin.

in·a·bil·i·ty /ˌinəˈbilitē/ ▶ **n.** [with infinitive] the state of being unable to do something: *his inability to accept new ideas | the inability of the soldiers to understand an alien culture.*

in ab·sen·tia /ˌin abˈsensн(ē)ə/ ▶ **adv.** while not present at the event being referred to: *two foreign suspects will be tried in absentia.*
– ORIGIN late 19th cent.: Latin, literally 'in absence.'

in·ac·ces·si·ble /ˌinakˈsesəbəl/ ▶ **adj. 1** unable to be reached: *a remote and inaccessible cave.* ■ unable to be used: *such costs would make litigation inaccessible to private individuals.*
2 (of language or an artistic work) difficult to understand or appreciate.
3 (of a person) not open to advances or influence; unapproachable.
– DERIVATIVES **in·ac·ces·si·bil·i·ty** n., **in·ac·ces·si·bly** adv.
– ORIGIN late Middle English: from French, or from late Latin *inaccessibilis*, from *in-* 'not' + *accessibilis* (see ACCESSIBLE).

in·ac·cu·ra·cy /inˈakyərəsē/ ▶ **n.** (pl. **inaccuracies**) the quality or state of not being accurate: *a weapon of notorious inaccuracy.* ■ an aspect of something that is not accurate: *reference works full of inaccuracies.*

in·ac·cu·rate /inˈakyərit/ ▶ **adj.** not accurate: *false or inaccurate descriptions of goods | a forecast that proved wildly inaccurate.*
– DERIVATIVES **in·ac·cu·rate·ly** adv.

in·ac·tion /inˈaksнən/ ▶ **n.** lack of action where some is expected or appropriate: *future generations will condemn us for inaction.*

in·ac·ti·vate /inˈaktəˌvāt/ ▶ **v.** [with obj.] make inactive or inoperative: *household bleach does not inactivate the virus* | (as adj. **inactivated**) *an inactivated polio vaccine.*
– DERIVATIVES **in·ac·ti·va·tion** /-ˌaktəˈvāsнən/ n., **in·ac·ti·va·tor** /-ˌvātər/ n.

in·ac·tive /inˈaktiv/ ▶ **adj.** not engaging in or involving any or much physical activity: *an inactive lifestyle.* ■ not working; inoperative: *the device remains inactive while the computer is started up.* ■ not engaging in political or other activity: *an inactive Russian spy.* ■ having no chemical or biological effect: *the inactive X chromosome.* ■ (of a disease) not exhibiting symptoms.
– DERIVATIVES **in·ac·tive·ly** adv.

in·ac·tiv·i·ty /inakˈtivitē/ ▶ **n.** the state of being inactive; idleness: *don't suddenly take up vigorous exercise after years of inactivity.* ■ reluctance to take action; apathy: *people are frustrated with government inactivity.*

in·ad·e·qua·cy /inˈadikwəsē/ ▶ **n.** the state or quality of being inadequate; lack of the quantity or quality required: *the inadequacy of available resources.* ■ inability to deal with a situation or with life: *her feelings of personal inadequacy.*

in·ad·e·quate /inˈadikwət/ ▶ **adj.** lacking the quality or quantity required; insufficient for a purpose: *these labels prove to be wholly inadequate | inadequate funding.* ■ (of a person) unable to deal with a situation or with life: *a sad, solitary, inadequate man | I felt like a fraud,* ***inadequate to*** *the task.*
– DERIVATIVES **in·ad·e·quate·ly** adv.

in·ad·mis·si·ble /inədˈmisəbəl/ ▶ **adj. 1** (esp. of evidence in court) not accepted as valid.
2 not to be allowed or tolerated: *an inadmissible interference in the affairs of the Church.*
– DERIVATIVES **in·ad·mis·si·bil·i·ty** n., **in·ad·mis·si·bly** adv.

in·ad·vert·ent /ˌinədˈvərtnt/ ▶ **adj.** not resulting from or achieved through deliberate planning: *many French leaders cannot accept at all that American dominance is inadvertent.*
– DERIVATIVES **in·ad·vert·ence** n., **in·ad·vert·en·cy** n.
– ORIGIN mid 17th cent.: from IN-[1] 'not' + Latin *advertent-* 'turning the mind to' (from the verb *advertere*). The noun *inadvertence* dates from late Middle English.

in·ad·vert·ent·ly /ˌinədˈvərtntli/ ▶ **adv.** without intention; accidentally: *his name had been inadvertently omitted from the list.*

in·ad·vis·a·ble /inədˈvīzəbəl/ ▶ **adj.** likely to have unfortunate consequences; unwise: [with infinitive] *it would be inadvisable to involve more than one architect.*
– DERIVATIVES **in·ad·vis·a·bil·i·ty** n.

in·al·ien·a·ble /inˈālēənəbəl/ ▶ **adj.** unable to be taken away from or given away by the possessor: *freedom of religion, the most inalienable of all human rights.*
– DERIVATIVES **in·al·ien·a·bil·i·ty** /-ˌālēənəˈbilitē/ n., **in·al·ien·a·bly** /-blē/ adv.

in·al·ter·a·ble /inˈôltərəbəl/ ▶ **adj.** unable to be changed.
– DERIVATIVES **in·al·ter·a·bil·i·ty** /-ˌôltərəˈbilitē/ n., **in·al·ter·a·bly** /-blē/ adv.

in·am·o·ra·ta /inˌaməˈrätə/ ▶ **n.** a person's female lover.
– ORIGIN mid 17th cent.: Italian, literally 'enamored,' feminine of *inamorato* (see INAMORATO).

in·am·o·ra·to /inˌaməˈräˌtō/ ▶ **n.** (pl. **inamoratos**) a person's male lover.
– ORIGIN late 16th cent.: Italian, literally 'enamored,' past participle of the verb *inamorare* (now *innamorare*), based on Latin *amor* 'love.'

in-and-out ▶ **adj.** informal **1** involving inward and outward movement, esp. rapid entrance and exit: *smuggling drugs was a quick in-and-out operation.*
2 inconsistent and unreliable: *this horse is a notoriously in-and-out performer.*

in·ane /iˈnān/ ▶ **adj.** silly; stupid: *don't constantly badger people with inane questions.*
– DERIVATIVES **in·ane·ly** adv., **in·ane·ness** n., **in·an·i·ty** /iˈnanitē/ n. (pl. **inanities**).
– ORIGIN mid 16th cent.: from Latin *inanis* 'empty, vain.'

in·an·i·mate /inˈanəmit/ ▶ **adj.** not alive, esp. not in the manner of animals and humans: *inanimate objects like stones.* ■ showing no sign of life; lifeless: *he was completely inanimate, and it was difficult to see if he was breathing.*
– DERIVATIVES **in·an·i·mate·ly** adv.
– ORIGIN late Middle English: from late Latin *inanimatus* 'lifeless,' from *in-* 'not' + *animatus* (see ANIMATE).

in·a·ni·tion /ˌinəˈnisнən/ ▶ **n.** lack of mental or spiritual vigor and enthusiasm: *she was thinking that old age bred inanition.* ■ exhaustion caused by lack of nourishment.
– ORIGIN late Middle English: from late Latin *inanitio(n-)*, from Latin *inanire* 'make empty,' from *inanis* 'empty, vain.'

in·ap·par·ent /ˌinəˈparənt, -ˈpe(ə)r-/ ▶ **adj.** Medicine causing no noticeable signs or symptoms: *clinically inapparent hepatitis.*

in·ap·pe·tence /inˈapətəns/ ▶ **n.** chiefly Veterinary Medicine lack of appetite.
– DERIVATIVES **in·ap·pe·tent** adj.

in·ap·pli·ca·ble /inˈaplikəbəl, ˌinəˈplik-/ ▶ **adj.** not relevant or appropriate: *the details are likely to be inapplicable to other designs.*
– DERIVATIVES **in·ap·pli·ca·bil·i·ty** /-ˌaplikəˈbilitē/ n., **in·ap·pli·ca·bly** /-blē/ adv.

in·ap·po·site /inˈapəzit/ ▶ **adj.** out of place; inappropriate: *the Shakespearean allusions are inapposite.*
– DERIVATIVES **in·ap·po·site·ly** adv., **in·ap·po·site·ness** n.

in·ap·pre·ci·a·ble /ˌinəˈprēsн(ē)əbəl/ ▶ **adj. 1** too small or insignificant to be valued or perceived: *they are few in number and those numbers are inappreciable.*
2 archaic too valuable to be properly estimated.
– DERIVATIVES **in·ap·pre·ci·a·bly** adv.

in·ap·pre·ci·a·tive /ˌinəˈprēsн(ē)ətiv/ ▶ **adj.** another term for UNAPPRECIATIVE.
– DERIVATIVES **in·ap·pre·ci·a·tion** n.

in·ap·pro·pri·ate /ˌinəˈprōprē-it/ ▶ **adj.** not suitable or proper in the circumstances: *there are penalties for inappropriate behavior | it would be inappropriate for me to comment.*
– DERIVATIVES **in·ap·pro·pri·ate·ly** adv., **in·ap·pro·pri·ate·ness** n.

in·apt /iˈnapt/ ▶ **adj.** not suitable or appropriate in the circumstances: *a more inapt name I cannot imagine.*
– DERIVATIVES **in·ap·ti·tude** n., **in·apt·ly** adv.

in·arch /inˈärcн/ ▶ **v.** [with obj.] Horticulture graft (a plant) by connecting a growing branch without separating it from its parent stock.
– ORIGIN early 17th cent. (formerly also as *enarch*): from EN-[1], IN-[2] 'into' + the verb ARCH[1].

in·ar·gu·a·ble /ˌinˈärgyo͞oəbəl/ ▶ **adj.** another term for UNARGUABLE.
– DERIVATIVES **in·ar·gu·a·bly** adv.

in·ar·tic·u·late /ˌinärˈtikyəlit/ ▶ **adj. 1** unable to speak distinctly or express oneself clearly: *he was inarticulate with abashment and regret.* ■ not clearly expressed or pronounced: *inarticulate complaints of inadequate remuneration.* ■ not expressed; unspoken: *mention of her mother filled her with inarticulate irritation.*
2 without joints or articulations. ■ Zoology denoting a brachiopod in which the valves of the shell have no hinge and are held together by muscles.
– DERIVATIVES **in·ar·tic·u·la·cy** /-ləsē/ n., **in·ar·tic·u·late·ly** adv., **in·ar·tic·u·late·ness** n.
– ORIGIN early 17th cent.: from IN-[1] 'not' + the adjective ARTICULATE; the sense 'not clearly pronounced' corresponds to that of late Latin *inarticulatus.*

in·ar·tis·tic /ˌinärˈtistik/ ▶ **adj.** having or showing a lack of skill or talent in art.
– DERIVATIVES **in·ar·tis·ti·cal·ly** adv.

in·as·much /ˌinəzˈməcн/ ▶ **adv.** (**inasmuch as**) to the extent that; insofar as: *these provisions apply only inasmuch as trade between Member States is affected.* ■ considering that; since (used to specify the respect in which a statement is true): *it was not really a still life inasmuch as all the objects were in motion.*

–ORIGIN Middle English: originally as *in as much*, translating Old French *en tant (que)* 'in so much (as).'

in·at·ten·tion /ˌinəˈtenCHən/ ▶ n. lack of attention; distraction: *a moment of inattention that could have cost lives.*

in·at·ten·tive /ˌinəˈtentiv/ ▶ adj. not paying attention to something: *a particularly dull and inattentive student.* ■ failing to attend to the comfort or wishes of others: *I was disappointed by the food and the inattentive service.*
–DERIVATIVES **in·at·ten·tive·ly** adv., **in·at·ten·tive·ness** n.

in·au·di·ble /inˈôdəbəl/ ▶ adj. unable to be heard: *inaudible pulses of high-frequency sound.*
–DERIVATIVES **in·au·di·bil·i·ty** n., **in·au·di·bly** adv.
–ORIGIN late Middle English: from late Latin*inaudibilis*, from *in-* 'not' +*audibilis* (see AUDIBLE).

in·au·gu·ral /inˈôg(y)ərəl/ ▶ adj. [attrib.] marking the beginning of an institution, activity, or period of office: *his inaugural concert as music director.*
▶ n. an inaugural speech, esp. one made by an incoming US president. ■ an inaugural ceremony: *the ball before the inaugural.*
–ORIGIN late 17th cent.: from French (from *inaugurer* 'inaugurate,' from Latin *inaugurare*) + -AL.

in·au·gu·rate /inˈôg(y)əˌrāt/ ▶ v. [with obj.] begin or introduce (a system, policy, or period): *he inaugurated a new policy of trade and exploration.* ■ admit (someone) formally to public office: *the new president will be inaugurated on January 20.* ■ mark the beginning or first public use of (an organization or project): *the museum was inaugurated on September 12.*
–DERIVATIVES **in·au·gu·ra·tor** n., **in·au·gu·ra·to·ry** /-əˌtôrē/ adj.
–ORIGIN late 16th cent.: from Latin *inaugurat-* 'interpreted as omens (from the flight of birds),' based on *augurare* 'to augur.'

in·au·gu·ra·tion /iˌnôg(y)əˈrāSHən/ ▶ n. the beginning or introduction of a system, policy, or period: *the inauguration of an independent prosecution service.* ■ the formal admission of someone to office: *Truman's second presidential inauguration.* ■ a ceremony to mark the beginning of something: *the inauguration of the Modern Art Museum.*

in·aus·pi·cious /ˈinôˈspiSHəs/ ▶ adj. not conducive to success; unpromising: *it was an inauspicious beginning to the long and complex entanglement.* ■ unlucky.
–DERIVATIVES **in·aus·pi·cious·ly** adv., **in·aus·pi·cious·ness** n.

in·au·then·tic /ˌinôˈTHentik/ ▶ n. not in fact what it is said to be: *the Holy Shroud of Turin is thought to have been proved inauthentic by radiocarbon dating.* ■ not genuinely belonging to a style or period: *baroque harpsichord pieces played on the decidedly inauthentic modern Steinway.* ■ lacking full reality or sincerity: *people close to death could not waste time being inauthentic.*
–DERIVATIVES **in·au·then·ti·cal·ly** /-ik(ə)lē/ adv., **in·au·then·tic·i·ty** /-ôTHənˈtisitē/ n.

inbd. ▶ abbr. inboard.

in-be·tween informal ▶ adj. situated somewhere between two extremes or recognized categories; intermediate: *I am not unconscious, but in some in-between state.*
▶ n. an intermediate thing: *successes, failures and in-betweens.*
–DERIVATIVES **in-be·tween·er** n.

in·board /ˈinˌbôrd/ ▶ adv. & adj. within a ship, aircraft, or vehicle: [as adv.] *the spray was coming inboard now* | [as adj.] *the uncovered inboard engine.* ■ toward the center of a ship, aircraft, or vehicle: [as adv.] *move the clew inboard along the boom* | [as adj.] *the inboard ailerons on the wings were dead.*
▶ n. a boat's engine housed inside its hull. ■ a boat with such an engine.

in·born /ˈinˈbôrn/ ▶ adj. existing from birth: *an inborn defect in the formation of collagen.* ■ natural to a person or animal: *people think doctors have inborn compassion.*

in·bound /ˈinˌbound/ ▶ adj. & adv. traveling toward a particular place, esp. when returning to the original point of departure: [as adj.] *inbound traffic* | [as adv.] *we have three enemy planes inbound on bearing two ninety.*
▶ v. [with obj.] Basketball throw (the ball) from out of bounds, putting it into play.

in·bounds /ˈinˌboundz/ ▶ adj. Basketball denoting or relating to a throw that puts the ball into play from out of bounds: *an inbounds pass.*

inbox /ˈinˌbäks/ ▶ n. a box or tray on a person's desk for letters and documents that have to be dealt with. ■ a folder in which e-mails received by an individual are held.

in·breathe /ˈinˈbrēTH/ ▶ v. [with obj.] literary breathe in or absorb: *he felt himself inbreathing power from on high.*

in·bred /ˈinˌbred/ ▶ adj. **1** produced by inbreeding: *a classic inbred Englishman.*
2 existing in a person, animal, or plant from birth; congenital: *inbred disease resistance in crops.*

in·breed /ˈinˌbrēd/ ▶ v. (past and past participle **inbred**) [no obj.] (often as noun **inbreeding**) breed from closely related people or animals, esp. over many generations: *persistent inbreeding has produced an unusually high frequency of sufferers from this disease.*

in·built /ˈinˌbilt/ ▶ adj. existing as an original or essential part of something or someone: *the body's inbuilt ability to heal itself.*

Inc. /iNGk/ ▶ abbr. ■ incorporated: *Northeast Airlines Inc.* ■ (also **inc.**) incomplete.

In·ca /ˈiNGkə/ ▶ n. **1** a member of a South American Indian people living in the central Andes before the Spanish conquest.

> The Incas arrived in the Cuzco valley in Peru C.AD 1200. When the Spanish invaded in the early 1530s, the Inca empire covered most of modern Ecuador and Peru, much of Bolivia, and parts of Argentina and Chile. Inca technology and architecture were highly developed. Their descendants, speaking Quechua, still make up about half of Peru's population.

2 the supreme ruler of this people.
–DERIVATIVES **In·ca·ic** /inˈkāik, iNG-/ adj., **In·can** adj.
–ORIGIN late 16th cent.: the name in Quechua, literally 'lord, royal person.'

in·ca /ˈiNGkə/ ▶ n. a South American hummingbird having mainly blackish or bronze-colored plumage with one or two white breast patches. ● Genus *Coeligena*, family Trochilidae: four species.

in·cal·cu·la·ble /inˈkalkyələbəl, iNG-/ ▶ adj. **1** too great to be calculated or estimated: *an archive of incalculable value.*
2 not able to be calculated or estimated: *the cost is incalculable but colossal.* ■ (of a person or their character) unpredictable: *under the pressure of anxiety his temper became incalculable.*
–DERIVATIVES **in·cal·cu·la·bil·i·ty** /-ˌkalkyələˈbilitē/ n., **in·cal·cu·la·bly** /-blē/ adv.

in cam·er·a ▶ adv. see CAMERA².

in·can·desce /ˌinkənˈdes/ ▶ v. [no obj.] glow with heat: *the lights of the town lay incandescing across the prairie.*
–ORIGIN late 19th cent.: back-formation from INCANDESCENT.

in·can·des·cent /ˌinkənˈdesənt/ ▶ adj. **1** emitting light as a result of being heated: *plumes of incandescent liquid rock.* ■ (of an electric light) containing a filament that glows white-hot when heated by a current passed through it.
2 passionate or brilliant: *Mravinsky's incandescent performance of Siegfried's Funeral March.* ■ extremely angry: *she was incandescent at the way the IRS acted.*
–DERIVATIVES **in·can·des·cence** n., **in·can·des·cent·ly** adv.
–ORIGIN late 18th cent.: from French, from Latin *incandescent-* 'glowing,' from the verb *incandescere*, from *in-* (expressing intensive force) + *candescere* 'become white' (from *candidus* 'white').

in·cant /inˈkant/ ▶ v. [with obj.] chant or intone: *priests were incanting psalms around her body.*
–ORIGIN mid 16th cent. (in the sense 'use enchantment on'): from Latin *incantare* 'to chant, charm,' from *in-* (expressing intensive force) + *cantare* 'sing.' The current sense dates from the mid 20th cent.

in·can·ta·tion /ˌinkanˈtāSHən/ ▶ n. a series of words said as a magic spell or charm: *an incantation to raise the dead.* ■ the use of such words: *there was no magic in such incantation* | *incantations of old slogans.*
–DERIVATIVES **in·can·ta·to·ry** /-ˈkantəˌtôrē/ adj.
–ORIGIN late Middle English: via Old French from late Latin *incantatio(n-)*, from *incantare* 'chant, bewitch' (see INCANT).

in·ca·pa·ble /inˈkāpəbəl/ ▶ adj. **1** (**incapable of**) unable to do or achieve (something): *Wilson blushed and was incapable of speech.* ■ not allowing the possibility of (a particular action): *with the battery removed, the car was incapable of being driven.* ■ (of a person) too caring or moral to do (something): *a man incapable of any kind of prejudice.*
2 unable to behave rationally or manage one's affairs: *the pilot may become incapable from the lack of oxygen.*
–DERIVATIVES **in·ca·pa·bil·i·ty** n., **in·ca·pa·bly** adv.
–ORIGIN late 16th cent.: from French, or from late Latin *incapabilis*, from *in-* 'not' +*capabilis* (see CAPABLE).

in·ca·pac·i·tate /ˌinkəˈpasiˌtāt/ ▶ v. [with obj.] prevent from functioning in a normal way: *he was incapacitated by a heart attack.* ■ Law deprive (someone) of their legal capacity.
–DERIVATIVES **in·ca·pac·i·tant** /-ˈpasətnt/ n., **in·ca·pac·i·ta·tion** /-ˌpasiˈtāSHən/ n.
–ORIGIN mid 17th cent.: from INCAPACITY + -ATE³.

in·ca·pac·i·tat·ed /ˌinkəˈpasiˌtātid/ ▶ adj. deprived of strength or power; debilitated: *Richard was temporarily incapacitated.*

in·ca·pac·i·ty /ˌinkəˈpasitē/ ▶ n. (pl. **incapacities**) physical or mental inability to do something or to manage one's affairs: *they can be fired only for incapacity or misbehavior.* ■ legal disqualification: *they are not subject to any legal incapacity.*
–ORIGIN early 17th cent.: from French *incapacité* or late Latin *incapacitas*, from *in-* (expressing negation) + *capacitas* (see CAPACITY).

in·car·cer·ate /inˈkärsəˌrāt/ ▶ v. [with obj.] imprison or confine: *many are incarcerated for property offenses.*
–DERIVATIVES **in·car·cer·a·tor** /-ˌrātər/ n.
–ORIGIN mid 16th cent.: from medieval Latin *incarcerat-* 'imprisoned,' from the verb *incarcerare*, from *in-* 'into' + Latin *carcer* 'prison.'

in·car·cer·a·tion /inˌkärsəˈrāSHən/ ▶ n. the state of being confined in prison; imprisonment: *the public would not be served by her incarceration.*

in·car·na·dine /inˈkärnəˌdīn, -ˌdēn/ literary ▶ n. a bright crimson or pinkish-red color.
▶ adj. of a crimson or pinkish-red color.
▶ v. [with obj.] color (something) a bright crimson or pinkish-red.
–ORIGIN late 16th cent.: from French *incarnadin(e)*, from Italian *incarnadino*, variant of *incarnatino* 'flesh color,' based on Latin *incarnare* (see INCARNATE).

in·car·nate ▶ adj. /inˈkärnit, -ˌnāt/ [often postpositive] (esp. of a deity or spirit) embodied in flesh; in human form: *God incarnate* | *he chose to be incarnate as a man.* ■ [postpositive] represented in the ultimate or most extreme form: *here is capitalism incarnate.*
▶ v. /-ˌnāt/ [with obj.] embody or represent (a deity or spirit) in human form: *the idea that God incarnates himself in man.* ■ put (an idea or other abstract concept) into concrete form: *a desire to make things which will incarnate their personality.* ■ (of a person) be the living embodiment of (a quality): *the man who incarnates the suffering which has affected every single Mozambican.*
–ORIGIN late Middle English: from ecclesiastical Latin *incarnat-* 'made flesh,' from the verb *incarnare*, from *in-* 'into' + *caro, carn-* 'flesh.'

in·car·na·tion /ˌinkärˈnāSHən/ ▶ n. **1** a person who embodies in the flesh a deity, spirit, or abstract quality: *Rama was Vishnu's incarnation on earth.* ■ (**the Incarnation**) (in Christian theology) the embodiment of God the Son in human flesh as Jesus Christ.
2 (with reference to reincarnation) one of a series of lifetimes that a person spends on earth: *in my next incarnation, I'd like to be the Secretary of Fun.* ■ the form in which a person spends such a lifetime.
–ORIGIN Middle English (as a term in Christian theology): via Old French from ecclesiastical Latin *incarnatio(n-)*, from the verb *incarnare* (see INCARNATE).

in·case ▶ v. variant spelling of ENCASE.

in·cau·tious /inˈkôSHəs/ ▶ adj. heedless of potential problems or risks: *he blames incautious borrowing during the boom.*
–DERIVATIVES **in·cau·tion** n., **in·cau·tious·ly** adv., **in·cau·tious·ness** n.
–ORIGIN mid 17th cent.: on the pattern of Latin *incautus*.

in·cen·di·ar·y /inˈsendēˌerē/ ▶ adj. (of a device or attack) designed to cause fires: *incendiary grenades.* ■ tending to stir up conflict: *incendiary rhetoric* | *an incendiary slogan.* ■ very exciting: *an incendiary live performer.*
▶ n. (pl. **incendiaries**) an incendiary bomb or device. ■ a person who starts fires, esp. in a military context. ■ a person who stirs up conflict.
–DERIVATIVES **in·cen·di·a·rism** /-dēəˌrizəm/ n.
–ORIGIN late Middle English: from Latin *incendiarius*, from *incendium* 'conflagration,' from *incendere* 'set fire to.'

in·cense¹ ▶ n. /ˈinˌsens/ a gum, spice, or other substance that is burned for the sweet smell it produces. ■ the smoke or perfume of such a substance.

▶ **v.** /inˈsens/ [with obj.] perfume with incense or a similar fragrance: *the aroma of cannabis incensed the air.*
– DERIVATIVES **in·cen·sa·tion** /ˌinsenˈsāsʜən/ **n.**
– ORIGIN Middle English (originally as *encense*): from Old French *encens* (noun), *encenser* (verb), from ecclesiastical Latin *incensum* 'something burned, incense,' neuter past participle of *incendere* 'set fire to,' from *in-* 'in' + the base of *candere* 'to glow.'

in·cense² /inˈsens/ ▶ **v.** [with obj.] make (someone) very angry: *she was incensed by the accusations.*
– ORIGIN late Middle English (in the general sense 'inflame or excite someone with a strong feeling'): from Old French *incenser*, from Latin *incendere* 'set fire to.'

in·cense ce·dar ▶ **n.** a columnar cedar with scalelike leaves that smell of turpentine when crushed, found chiefly in mountainous areas of California and Oregon and grown as an ornamental in Europe. ● *Calocedrus decurrens*, family Cupressaceae.

in·censed /inˈsenst/ ▶ **adj.** very angry; enraged: *I was absolutely incensed.*

in·cen·so·ry /inˈsensərē/ ▶ **n.** (pl. **incensories**) another term for **CENSER**.
– ORIGIN early 17th cent. (denoting a burnt offering, or an altar for it): from medieval Latin *incensorium*, from *incensum* (see **INCENSE¹**).

in·cen·ter /ˈinˌsentər/ (Brit. **incentre**) ▶ **n.** Geometry the center of the incircle of a triangle or other figure.

in·cen·tive /inˈsentiv/ ▶ **n.** a thing that motivates or encourages one to do something: *there is no incentive for customers to conserve water.* ■ a payment or concession to stimulate greater output or investment: *tax incentives for investing in depressed areas* | [as modifier] *incentive payments.*
– ORIGIN late Middle English: from Latin *incentivum* 'something that sets the tune or incites,' from *incantare* 'to chant or charm.'

in·cen·tiv·ize /inˈsentəˌvīz/ ▶ **v.** [with obj.] provide (someone) with an incentive for doing something: *this is likely to incentivize management to find savings.*

in·cept /inˈsept/ ▶ **v.** [no obj.] Brit. historical graduate from a university with an academic degree.
– DERIVATIVES **in·cep·tor** /-tər/ **n.**
– ORIGIN mid 16th cent. (in the sense 'undertake, begin'): from Latin *incept-* 'begun,' from the verb *incipere*. The current sense dates from the mid 19th cent.

in·cep·tion /inˈsepsʜən/ ▶ **n.** [in sing.] the establishment or starting point of an institution or activity: *she has been on the board since its inception two years ago.*
– ORIGIN late Middle English: from Latin *inceptio(n-)*, from *incipere* 'begin.'

in·cep·ti·sol /inˈseptiˌsôl, -ˌsäl/ ▶ **n.** Soil Science a soil of an order comprising freely draining soils in which the formation of distinct horizons is not far advanced, such as brown earth.
– ORIGIN 1960s: from Latin *inceptum* 'beginning' (from the verb *incipere*) + **-SOL**.

in·cep·tive /inˈseptiv/ ▶ **adj.** relating to or marking the beginning of something; initial. ■ Grammar (of a verb) expressing the beginning of an action; inchoative.
▶ **n.** Grammar an inceptive verb.
– ORIGIN early 17th cent. (as a noun): from late Latin *inceptivus*, from *incept-* 'begun,' from the verb *incipere*.

in·cer·ti·tude /inˈsərtiˌt(y)o͞od/ ▶ **n.** a state of uncertainty or hesitation: *some schools broke down under the stresses of policy incertitude.*
– ORIGIN late Middle English: from Old French, or from late Latin *incertitudo*, from *in-* (expressing negation) + *certitudo* (see **CERTITUDE**).

in·ces·sant /inˈsesənt/ ▶ **adj.** (of something regarded as unpleasant) continuing without pause or interruption: *the incessant beat of the music.*
– DERIVATIVES **in·ces·san·cy n.**, **in·ces·sant·ness n.**
– ORIGIN late Middle English: via Old French from late Latin *incessant-*, from *in-* 'not' + Latin *cessant-* 'ceasing' (from the verb *cessare*).

in·ces·sant·ly /inˈsesəntlē/ ▶ **adv.** without interruption; constantly: *she talked about him incessantly.*

in·cest /ˈinˌsest/ ▶ **n.** sexual relations between people classed as being too closely related to marry each other. ■ the crime of having sexual intercourse with a parent, child, sibling, or grandchild.
– ORIGIN Middle English: from Latin *incestus*, *incestum* 'unchastity, incest,' from *in-* 'not' + *castus* 'chaste.'

in·ces·tu·ous /inˈsesʜo͞oəs/ ▶ **adj. 1** involving or guilty of incest: *the child of an incestuous relationship.*
2 (of human relations generally) excessively close and resistant to outside influence: *the incestuous nature of literary journalism.*
– DERIVATIVES **in·ces·tu·ous·ly adv.**, **in·ces·tu·ous·ness n.**
– ORIGIN early 16th cent.: from late Latin *incestuosus*, from Latin *incestus* (see **INCEST**).

inch¹ /insʜ/ ▶ **n. 1** a unit of linear measure equal to one twelfth of a foot (2.54 cm): *the toy train is four inches long* | *eighteen inches of thread.* (Symbol: **″**) ■ [often with negative] a very small amount or distance: *I had no intention of budging an inch.*
2 a unit used to express other quantities, in particular: ■ (as a unit of rainfall) a quantity that would cover a horizontal surface to a depth of one inch. ■ (also **inch of mercury**) (as a unit of atmospheric pressure) an amount that would support a column of mercury one-inch high in a barometer (equal to 33.86 millibars, 29.5 inches being equal to one bar).
▶ **v.** [no obj.] move slowly and carefully in a specified direction: *the 2,000 mourners inched along narrow country lanes* | figurative *the stock market inched ahead today.* ■ [with obj.] cause (something) to move in this manner: *he inched the car forward.*
– PHRASES **by inches 1** only just: *the shot missed her by inches.* **2** very slowly and gradually; bit by bit: *you can't let him die by inches like this.* **every inch 1** the whole surface, distance, or area: *between them they know every inch of the country.* **2** entirely; very much so: *he's every inch the gentleman.* **give someone an inch and he** (or **she**) **will take a mile** proverb once concessions have been made to someone they will demand a great deal. **inch by inch** gradually; bit by bit: *inch by inch he crept along the wall.* **within an inch of** very close to: *her mouth was within an inch of his chin.* (**to**) **within an inch of one's life** almost to the point of death: *he was beaten within an inch of his life.*
– ORIGIN late Old English *ynce*, from Latin *uncia* 'twelfth part,' from *unus* 'one' (probably denoting a unit). Compare with **OUNCE¹**.

inch² ▶ **n.** [in place names] chiefly Scottish a small island or a small area of high land: *Inchkeith.*
– ORIGIN Middle English: from Scottish Gaelic *innis*.

inch·meal /ˈinsʜˌmēl/ ▶ **adv.** by inches; little by little: *inchmeal he advanced up the slope.*
– ORIGIN mid 16th cent.: from **INCH¹** + *-meal* from Old English *mǣlum*, in the sense 'measure, quantity taken at one time.'

in·cho·ate /inˈkō-it, -āt/ ▶ **adj.** just begun and so not fully formed or developed; rudimentary: *a still inchoate democracy.* ■ Law (of an offense, such as incitement or conspiracy) anticipating a further criminal act.
– DERIVATIVES **in·cho·ate·ly adv.**, **in·cho·ate·ness n.**
– ORIGIN mid 16th cent.: from Latin *inchoatus*, past participle of *inchoare*, variant of *incohare* 'begin.'

in·cho·a·tive /inˈkō-itiv/ ▶ **adj.** Grammar denoting an aspect of a verb expressing the beginning of an action, typically one occurring of its own accord. In many English verbs, inchoative uses alternate systematically with causative uses. Compare with **ERGATIVE**.
▶ **n.** an inchoative verb.

In·chon /ˈinˈcʜän/ a port on the western coast of South Korea, on the Yellow Sea, near Seoul; pop. 2,741,200 (est. 2008). It was the site of a successful invasion by US troops in 1950 that enabled them to return Seoul to South Korea.

inch·worm /ˈinsʜˌwərm/ ▶ **n.** a caterpillar of a geometrid moth, which moves forward by arching and straightening its body. Also called **LOOPER**, **MEASURING WORM**, or **SPANWORM**.

in·ci·dence /ˈinsidəns/ ▶ **n. 1** the occurrence, rate, or frequency of a disease, crime, or something else undesirable: *an increased incidence of cancer.* ■ the way in which the burden of a tax falls upon the population: *the entire incidence falls on the workers.*
2 Physics the intersection of a line, or something moving in a straight line, such as a beam of light, with a surface. See also **ANGLE OF INCIDENCE**.
– ORIGIN late Middle English (denoting a casual or subordinate event or circumstance): from Old French, or from medieval Latin *incidentia*, from Latin *incidere* 'fall upon, happen to' (see **INCIDENT**). Sense 1 dates from the early 19th cent.

in·ci·dent /ˈinsidənt/ ▶ **n.** an event or occurrence: *several amusing incidents.* ■ a violent event, such as a fracas or assault: *one person was stabbed in the incident.* ■ a hostile clash between forces of rival countries. ■ (**incident of**) a case or instance of something happening: *a single incident of rudeness does not support a finding of contemptuous conduct.* ■ the occurrence of dangerous or exciting things: *the winter passed without incident.* ■ a distinct piece of action in a play or a poem.
▶ **adj. 1** [predic.] (**incident to**) likely to happen because of; resulting from: *the changes incident to economic development.* ■ Law attaching to: *the costs properly incident to a suit for foreclosure or redemption.*
2 (esp. of light or other radiation) falling on or striking something: *when an ion beam is incident on a surface.* ■ of or relating to incidence: *the incident angle.*
– ORIGIN late Middle English: via Old French from Latin *incident-* 'falling upon, happening to,' from the verb *incidere*, from *in-* 'upon' + *cadere* 'to fall.'

in·ci·den·tal /ˌinsiˈdentl/ ▶ **adj. 1** accompanying but not a major part of something: *for the fieldworker who deals with real problems, paperwork is incidental* | *incidental expenses.* ■ occurring by chance in connection with something else: *the incidental catch of dolphins in the pursuit of tuna.*
2 [predic.] (**incidental to**) liable to happen as a consequence of (an activity): *the ordinary risks incidental to a fireman's job.*
▶ **n.** (usu. **incidentals**) an incidental detail, expense, event, etc.: *an allowance to cover meals, taxis, and other incidentals.*
– ORIGIN early 17th cent.: originally from medieval Latin *incidentalis*, from Latin *incident-* 'falling upon, happening to' (from the verb *incidere*).

in·ci·den·tal·ly /ˌinsiˈdent(ə)lē/ ▶ **adv. 1** [sentence adverb] used when a person has something more to say, or is about to add a remark unconnected to the current subject; by the way: *incidentally, it was many months before the whole truth was discovered.*
2 in an incidental manner; as a chance occurrence: *the infection was discovered only incidentally at a postmortem examination.*

in·ci·den·tal mu·sic ▶ **n.** music used in a film or play as a background to create or enhance a particular atmosphere.

in·cin·er·ate /inˈsinəˌrāt/ ▶ **v.** [with obj.] destroy (something, esp. waste material) by burning: *such garbage must be incinerated at the hospital.*
– DERIVATIVES **in·cin·er·a·tion** /-ˌsinəˈrāsʜən/ **n.**
– ORIGIN late 15th cent.: from medieval Latin *incinerat-* 'burned to ashes,' from the verb *incinerare*, from *in-* 'into, toward' + *cinis, ciner-* 'ashes.'

in·cin·er·a·tor /inˈsinəˌrātər/ ▶ **n.** an apparatus for burning waste material, esp. industrial waste, at high temperatures until it is reduced to ash.

in·cip·i·ent /inˈsipēənt/ ▶ **adj.** in an initial stage; beginning to happen or develop: *he could feel incipient anger building up* | *an incipient black eye.* ■ (of a person) developing into a specified type or role: *we seemed more like friends than incipient lovers.*
– DERIVATIVES **in·cip·i·ence n.**, **in·cip·i·en·cy n.**, **in·cip·i·ent·ly adv.**
– ORIGIN late 16th cent. (as a noun denoting a beginner): from Latin *incipient-* 'undertaking, beginning,' from the verb *incipere*, from *in-* 'into, toward' + *capere* 'take.'

in·ci·pit /ˈinsipit/ ▶ **n.** the opening words of a text, manuscript, early printed book, or chanted liturgical text. Compare with **EXPLICIT**.
– ORIGIN late 19th cent.: Latin, literally '(here) begins.'

in·cir·cle /ˈinˌsərkəl/ ▶ **n.** Geometry a circle inscribed in a triangle or other figure so as to touch (but not cross) each side.

in·cise /inˈsīz/ ▶ **v.** [with obj.] (usu. **be incised**) mark or decorate (an object or surface) with a cut or a series of cuts: *a button incised with a skull.* ■ cut (a mark or decoration) into a surface: *figures incised on upright stones.* ■ cut (skin or flesh) with a surgical instrument: *the wound was incised and drained.*
– ORIGIN mid 16th cent.: from French *inciser*, from Latin *incis-* 'cut into, engraved,' from the verb *incidere*, from *in-* 'into' + *caedere* 'to cut.'

in·cised me·an·der ▶ **n.** Geology a river meander that has been cut abnormally deeply into the landscape because uplift of the land has led to renewed downward erosion by the river.

in·ci·sion /inˈsizʜən/ ▶ **n.** a surgical cut made in skin or flesh: *an abdominal incision.* ■ a mark or decoration cut into a surface: *a block of marble delicately decorated with incisions.* ■ the action or process of cutting into something: *the method is associated with less blood loss during incision.*
– DERIVATIVES **in·ci·sion·al** /-zʜənl/ **adj.**
– ORIGIN late Middle English: from late Latin *incisio(n-)*, from Latin *incidere* 'cut into' (see **INCISE**).

in·ci·sive /inˈsīsiv/ ▶ **adj.** (of a person or mental process) intelligently analytical and clear-thinking: *she was an incisive critic.* ■ (of an account) accurate and sharply focused: *the songs offer incisive pictures of American ways.*
– DERIVATIVES **in·ci·sive·ly adv.**, **in·ci·sive·ness n.**
– ORIGIN late Middle English (in the sense 'cutting, penetrating'): from medieval Latin *incisivus*, from Latin *incidere* 'cut into' (see **INCISE**).

in·ci·sor /inˈsīzər/ ▶ **n.** (also **incisor tooth**) a narrow-edged tooth at the front of the mouth, adapted for cutting. In humans there are four incisors in each jaw.
– ORIGIN late 17th cent.: from medieval Latin, literally 'cutter,' from Latin *incis-* (see INCISE).

in·cis·ure /inˈsizHər, -ˈsī-/ (also **incisura** /ˌinˌsīˈzHŏŏrə/) ▶ **n.** (pl. **incisures** or **incisurae** /-ˈsizHərē/) Anatomy a deep indentation or notch in an edge or surface.

in·cite /inˈsīt/ ▶ **v.** [with obj.] encourage or stir up (violent or unlawful behavior): *the offense of inciting racial hatred.* ■ urge or persuade (someone) to act in a violent or unlawful way: *he incited loyal subjects to rebellion.*
– DERIVATIVES **in·ci·ta·tion** /ˌinsīˈtāsHən/ **n.**, **in·cit·er** **n.**
– ORIGIN late 15th cent.: from French *inciter*, from Latin *incitare*, from *in-* 'toward' + *citare* 'rouse.'

in·cite·ment /inˈsītmənt/ ▶ **n.** [often with infinitive] the action of provoking unlawful behavior or urging someone to behave unlawfully: *this amounted to an incitement to commit murder.*

in·ci·vil·i·ty /insəˈvilətē/ ▶ **n.** (pl. **incivilities**) rude or unsociable speech or behavior: *absenteeism and incivility were not tolerated.* ■ (often **incivilities**) an impolite or offensive comment.
– ORIGIN mid 16th cent.: from French *incivilité* or late Latin *incivilitas*, from Latin *incivilis*, from *in-* 'not' +*civilis* 'of a citizen' (see CIVIL).

incl. ▶ **abbr.** ■ including. ■ inclusive.

in·clem·ent /inˈklemənt/ ▶ **adj.** (of the weather) unpleasantly cold or wet.
– DERIVATIVES **in·clem·en·cy** **n.** (pl. **inclemencies**).
– ORIGIN early 17th cent.: from French *inclément* or Latin *inclement-*, from *in-* 'not' + *clement-* 'clement.'

in·cli·na·tion /ˌinkləˈnāsHən, ˌiNGklə-/ ▶ **n.** **1** a person's natural tendency or urge to act or feel in a particular way; a disposition or propensity: *John was a scientist by training and inclination | he was free to follow his inclinations.* ■ (**inclination for/to/toward**) an interest in or liking for (something): *Burger King and Wendy's didn't show any inclination to jump into a price war with McDonald's.*
2 a slope or slant: *changes in inclination of the line on the graph.* ■ a bending of the body or head in a bow: *the questioner's inclination of his head.* ■ the dip of a magnetic needle.
3 the angle at which a straight line or plane is inclined to another. ■ Astronomy the angle between the orbital plane of a planet, comet, etc., and the ecliptic, or between the orbital plane of a satellite and the equatorial plane of its primary. ■ Astronomy the angle between the axis of an astronomical object and a fixed reference angle.
– ORIGIN late Middle English: from Latin *inclinatio(n-)*, from *inclinare* 'bend toward' (see INCLINE).

in·cline ▶ **v.** /inˈklīn/ **1** (**be inclined to/toward/to do something**) feel willing or favorably disposed toward (an action, belief, or attitude): *he was inclined to accept the offer | Lucy was inclined to a belief in original sin.* ■ [with infinitive] (esp. as a polite formula) tend toward holding a specified opinion: *I'm inclined to agree with you.* ■ [with obj.] make (someone) willing or disposed to do something: *his prejudice inclines him to overlook obvious facts.* ■ [no obj.] feel favorably disposed to someone or something: *I incline to the view that this conclusion is untenable.*
2 (**be inclined to/to do something**) have a tendency to do something: *she's inclined to gossip with complete strangers.* ■ [with adverbial] have a specified disposition or talent: *some people are very mathematically inclined.*
3 [no obj.] lean or turn away from a given plane or direction, esp. the vertical or horizontal: *the bunker doors incline outward | (as adj.* **inclined**) *an inclined ramp.* ■ [with obj.] bend (one's head) forward and downward.
▶ **n.** /ˈinˌklīn/ an inclined surface or plane; a slope, esp. on a road or railway: *the road climbs a long incline through a forest.*
– DERIVATIVES **in·clin·a·ble** **adj.**, **in·clin·er** **n.**
– ORIGIN Middle English (originally in the sense 'bend (the head, the body, or oneself) toward something'; formerly also as *encline*): from Old French *encliner*, from Latin *inclinare*, from *in-* 'toward' + *clinare* 'to bend.'

in·clined plane ▶ **n.** a plane inclined at an angle to the horizontal. ■ a sloping ramp up which heavy loads can be raised by ropes or chains.

in·cli·nom·e·ter /ˌinkləˈnämitər/ ▶ **n.** a device for measuring the angle of inclination of something, esp. from the horizontal.
– ORIGIN mid 19th cent.: from Latin *inclinare* 'to incline' + -METER.

in·close ▶ **v.** variant spelling of ENCLOSE.

in·clo·sure ▶ **n.** variant spelling of ENCLOSURE.

in·clude /inˈklo͞od/ ▶ **v.** [with obj.] **1** comprise or contain as part of a whole: *the price includes dinner, bed, and breakfast | other changes included the abolition of the death penalty.*
2 make part of a whole or set: *we have included some hints for beginners in this section.* ■ allow (someone) to share in an activity or privilege: *there were doubts as to whether she was included in the invitation.*
– ORIGIN late Middle English (also in the sense 'shut in'): from Latin *includere*, from *in-* 'into' + *claudere* 'to shut.'

> **USAGE** Include has a broader meaning than **comprise**. In the sentence *the accommodations comprise two bedrooms, bathroom, kitchen, and living room,* the word **comprise** implies that there are no accommodations other than those listed. **Include** can be used in this way too, but it is also used in a nonrestrictive way, implying that there may be other things not specifically mentioned that are part of the same category, as in *the price includes a special welcome pack.* Careful writers will avoid superfluous uses of 'including . . . and more,' commonly imitated from advertising. The 'and more' is superfluous because **including** or **includes** implies that there is more than what is listed.

in·clud·ed /inˈklo͞odid/ ▶ **adj.** [postpositive] contained as part of a whole being considered: *all of Europe (Russia included) | service tax included.* ■ Botany (of a style or stamen) not protruding beyond the corolla.

in·clud·ing /inˈklo͞odiNG/ ▶ **prep.** containing as part of the whole being considered: *languages including Welsh, Cornish, and Breton | weapons were recovered from the house, including a shotgun.*

in·clu·sion /inˈklo͞ozHən/ ▶ **n.** **1** the action or state of including or of being included within a group or structure: *federal legislation now mandates the inclusion of students who are English language learners.* ■ a person or thing that is included within a larger group or structure: *the exhibition features such inclusions as the study of the little girl.*
2 Biology, Geology, & Metallurgy a body or particle recognizably distinct from the substance in which it is embedded.
– ORIGIN early 17th cent.: from Latin *inclusio(n-)*, from *includere* 'shut in.'

in·clu·sion·a·ry /inˈklo͞ozHəˌnerē/ ▶ **adj.** designed or intended to accommodate diversity in age, income, race, or some other category: *several clubs prefer not to adhere to the new, inclusionary policies.*
– ORIGIN on the pattern of *exclusionary*.

in·clu·sive /inˈklo͞osiv/ ▶ **adj.** including or covering all the services, facilities, or items normally expected or required: *the price is inclusive, with few incidentals.* ■ [predic.] (**inclusive of**) containing (a specified element) as part of a whole: *all prices are inclusive of taxes.* ■ [postpositive] with the inclusion of the extreme limits stated: *between the ages of 55 and 59 inclusive.* ■ not excluding any section of society or any party involved in something: *only an inclusive peace process will end the conflict.* ■ (of language) deliberately nonsexist, esp. avoiding the use of masculine pronouns to refer to both men and women.
– DERIVATIVES **in·clu·sive·ly** **adv.**, **in·clu·sive·ness** **n.**
– ORIGIN late 16th cent.: from medieval Latin *inclusivus*, from Latin *includere* (see INCLUDE).

in·clu·sive fit·ness ▶ **n.** Genetics the ability of an individual organism to pass on its genes to the next generation, taking into account the shared genes passed on by the organism's close relatives.

in·clu·siv·i·ty /ˌinklo͞oˈsivitē/ ▶ **n.** an intention or policy of including people who might otherwise be excluded or marginalized, such as those who are handicapped or learning-disabled, or racial and sexual minorities: *you will need a thorough understanding of inclusivity and the needs of special education pupils.*
– ORIGIN on the pattern of *exclusivity*.

in·cog /inˈkäg/ ▶ **adj.**, **adv.**, & **n.** informal, dated short for INCOGNITO.

in·cog·ni·to /ˌinkägˈnētō, inˈkägniˌtō/ ▶ **adj. & adv.** (of a person) having one's true identity concealed: [as adj.] *in order to observe you have to be incognito* | [as adv.] *he is now operating incognito.*
▶ **n.** (pl. **incognitos**) an assumed or false identity.
– ORIGIN mid 17th cent.: from Italian, literally 'unknown,' from Latin *incognitus*, from *in-* 'not' + *cognitus* (past participle of *cognoscere* 'know').

in·cog·ni·zant /inˈkägnəzənt/ ▶ **adj.** formal lacking knowledge or awareness: *before my arrest, I was incognizant of the prison-industrial complex.*
– DERIVATIVES **in·cog·ni·zance** **n.**

in·co·her·ent /ˌinkōˈhi(ə)rənt, ˌiNG-, -ˈher-/ ▶ **adj.** **1** (of spoken or written language) expressed in an incomprehensible or confusing way; unclear: *he screamed some incoherent threat.* ■ (of a person) unable to speak intelligibly: *I splutter several more times before becoming incoherent.* ■ (of an ideology, policy, or system) internally inconsistent; illogical: *the film is ideologically incoherent.*
2 Physics (of waves) having no definite or stable phase relationship.
– DERIVATIVES **in·co·her·ence** **n.**, **in·co·her·en·cy** **n.** (pl. **incoherencies**), **in·co·her·ent·ly** **adv.**

in·com·bus·ti·ble /ˌinkəmˈbəstəbəl/ ▶ **adj.** (esp. of a building material or component) consisting or made of material that does not burn if exposed to fire.
– DERIVATIVES **in·com·bus·ti·bil·i·ty** /-ˌbəstəˈbilitē/ **n.**
– ORIGIN late 15th cent.: from medieval Latin *incombustibilis*, from *in-* 'not' + *combustibilis* (see COMBUSTIBLE).

in·come /ˈinˌkəm, ˈiNG-/ ▶ **n.** money received, esp. on a regular basis, for work or through investments: *he has a nice home and an adequate income | figures showed an overall increase in income this year.*
– ORIGIN Middle English (in the sense 'entrance, arrival,' now only Scots): in early use from Old Norse *innkoma*, later from IN + COME. The current sense dates from the late 16th cent.

in·come group ▶ **n.** a section of the population classified according to their level of income.

in·come tax ▶ **n.** tax levied by a government directly on income, esp. an annual tax on personal income.

in·com·ing /ˈinˌkəmiNG/ ▶ **adj.** in the process of coming in; arriving: *incoming passengers | the incoming tide.* ■ (of a message or communication) being received rather than sent: *an incoming call.* ■ (of an official or administration) having just been elected or appointed to succeed another: *the incoming president.*
▶ **n.** (**incomings**) revenue; income: *keep an account of your incomings and outgoings.*

in·com·men·su·ra·ble /ˌinkəˈmensərəbəl, -sHər-/ ▶ **adj.** **1** not able to be judged by the same standard as something; having no common standard of measurement: *the two types of science are incommensurable.*
2 Mathematics (of numbers) in a ratio that cannot be expressed as a ratio of integers. ■ irrational.
▶ **n.** (usu. **incommensurables**) an incommensurable quantity.
– DERIVATIVES **in·com·men·su·ra·bil·i·ty** /-ˌmensərəˈbilitē, -sHər-/ **n.**, **in·com·men·su·ra·bly** **adv.**
– ORIGIN mid 16th cent. (in the mathematical sense): from late Latin *incommensurabilis*, from *in-* 'not' + *commensurabilis* (see COMMENSURABLE).

in·com·men·su·rate /ˌinkəˈmensərit, -sHə-/ ▶ **adj.** **1** [predic.] (**incommensurate with**) out of keeping or proportion with: *man's influence on the earth's surface seems incommensurate with his scale.*
2 another term for INCOMMENSURABLE (sense 1 of the adjective).
– DERIVATIVES **in·com·men·su·rate·ly** **adv.**, **in·com·men·su·rate·ness** **n.**

in·com·mode /ˌinkəˈmōd/ ▶ **v.** [with obj.] formal inconvenience (someone): *they are incommoded by the traffic.*
– ORIGIN late 16th cent.: from French *incommoder* or Latin *incommodare*, from *in-* 'not' + *commodus* 'convenient.'

in·com·mo·di·ous /ˌinkəˈmōdēəs/ ▶ **adj.** formal or dated causing inconvenience or discomfort.
– DERIVATIVES **in·com·mo·di·ous·ly** **adv.**, **in·com·mo·di·ous·ness** **n.**

in·com·mu·ni·ca·ble /ˌinkəˈmyo͞onikəbəl/ ▶ **adj.** not able to be communicated to others: *the pain of separation took the form of an incommunicable depression.*
– DERIVATIVES **in·com·mu·ni·ca·bil·i·ty** /-ˌmyo͞onikəˈbilitē/ **n.**, **in·com·mu·ni·ca·ble·ness** **n.**, **in·com·mu·ni·ca·bly** **adv.**
– ORIGIN mid 16th cent. (in the sense 'incommunicative'): from late Latin *incommunicabilis* 'not to be imparted,' from *in-* 'not' + *communicabilis* (see COMMUNICABLE).

in·com·mu·ni·ca·do /ˌinkəˌmyo͞oniˈkädō/ ▶ **adj.** not able, wanting, or allowed to communicate with other people: *they were separated and detained incommunicado.*
– ORIGIN mid 19th cent.: from Spanish *incomunicado*, past participle of *incomunicar* 'deprive of communication.'

in·com·mu·ni·ca·tive /ˌinkəˈmyo͞onəkətiv/ ▶ **adj.** another term for UNCOMMUNICATIVE.

PRONUNCIATION KEY ə *ago, up*; ər *over, fur*; a *hat*; ā *ate*; ä *car*; e *let*; ē *see*; i *fit*; ī *by*; NG *sing*; ō *go*; ô *law, for*; oi *toy*; o͝o *good*; o͞o *goo*; ou *out*; TH *thin*; T̲H̲ *then*; ZH *vision*

in·com·mut·a·ble /ˌinkəˈmyo͞otəbəl/ ▶ **adj.** not capable of being changed or exchanged.
– DERIVATIVES **in·com·mut·a·bly** /-blē/ **adv.**
– ORIGIN late Middle English: from Latin *incommutabilis*, from *in-* 'not' + *commutabilis* (see **COMMUTABLE**).

in·com·pa·ny ▶ **adj.** occurring or existing within a company: *in-company training programs.*

in·com·pa·ra·ble /inˈkämp(ə)rəbəl/ ▶ **adj.**
1 without an equal in quality or extent; matchless: *the incomparable beauty of Venice.*
2 unable to be compared; totally different in nature or extent: *censorship still exists, but now it's absolutely incomparable with what it was.*
– DERIVATIVES **in·com·pa·ra·bil·i·ty** /-ˌkämp(ə)rəˈbilitē/ **n.**
– ORIGIN late Middle English: via Old French from Latin *incomparabilis*, from *in-* 'not' + *comparabilis* (see **COMPARABLE**).

in·com·pa·ra·bly /inˈkämp(ə)rəblē/ ▶ **adv.** [as submodifier] immeasurably; by far: *this beach is incomparably superior to the others on the island.*

in·com·pat·i·ble /ˌinkəmˈpatəbəl, ˌiNG-/ ▶ **adj.** (of two things) so opposed in character as to be incapable of existing together: *cleverness and femininity were seen as incompatible.* ■ (of two people) unable to live together harmoniously. ■ [predic.] (**incompatible with**) (of one thing or person) not consistent or able to coexist with (another): *long hours are simply incompatible with family life.* ■ (of equipment, machinery, computer programs, etc.) not capable of being used in combination: *all four prototype camcorders used special tapes and were incompatible with one another.*
– DERIVATIVES **in·com·pat·i·bil·i·ty** /-ˌpatəˈbilitē/ **n.**, **in·com·pat·i·bly** /-blē/ **adv.**
– ORIGIN late Middle English: from medieval Latin *incompatibilis*, from *in-* 'not' + *compatibilis* (see **COMPATIBLE**).

in·com·pe·tence /inˈkämpətəns, iNG-/ ▶ **n.** inability to do something successfully; ineptitude: *allegations of professional incompetence.*
– DERIVATIVES **in·com·pe·ten·cy** **n.**

in·com·pe·tent /inˈkämpətənt, iNG-/ ▶ **adj.** not having or showing the necessary skills to do something successfully: *a forgetful and utterly incompetent assistant.* ■ Law not qualified to act in a particular capacity: *the patient is deemed legally incompetent.* ■ Medicine (esp. of a valve or sphincter) not able to perform its function.
▶ **n.** an incompetent person.
– DERIVATIVES **in·com·pe·tent·ly** **adv.**
– ORIGIN late 16th cent. (in the sense 'not legally competent'): from French, or from late Latin *incompetent-*, from *in-* 'not' + Latin *competent-* 'being fit or proper' (see **COMPETENT**).

in·com·plet·a·ble /ˌinkəmˈplētəbəl, ˌiNG-/ ▶ **adj.** rare unable to be completed.

in·com·plete /ˌinkəmˈplēt, ˌiNG-/ ▶ **adj.** not having all the necessary or appropriate parts: *the records are patchy and incomplete.* ■ not full or finished: *the analysis remains incomplete.*
– DERIVATIVES **in·com·plete·ly** **adv.**, **in·com·plete·ness** **n.**
– ORIGIN late Middle English: from late Latin *incompletus*, from Latin *in-* 'not' + *completus* 'filled, finished' (see **COMPLETE**).

in·com·plete·ness the·o·rem (also **Gödel's incompleteness theorem**) ▶ **n.** Logic the theorem that in any sufficiently powerful, logically consistent formulation of logic or mathematics there must be true formulas that are neither provable nor disprovable. The theorem entails the corollary that the consistency of a logical system cannot be proved within that system.

in·com·ple·tion /ˌinkəmˈplēsHən, ˌiNG-/ ▶ **n.** **1** the state of lacking something or of having failed to complete something: *humans with their profound sense of incompletion.*
2 Football a forward pass that is not completed.

in·com·pre·hen·si·ble /ˌinˌkämpriˈhensəbəl/ ▶ **adj.** not able to be understood; not intelligible: *a language that is incomprehensible to anyone outside the office.*
– DERIVATIVES **in·com·pre·hen·si·bil·i·ty** **n.**, **in·com·pre·hen·si·ble·ness** **n.**, **in·com·pre·hen·si·bly** **adv.**
– ORIGIN late Middle English (earlier than *comprehensible*): from Latin *incomprehensibilis*, from *in-* 'not' +*comprehensibilis* (see **COMPREHENSIBLE**).

in·com·pre·hen·sion /ˌinkämprəˈhensHən, inˌkäm-/ ▶ **n.** failure to understand something: *they gave him a look of complete incomprehension.*

in·com·press·i·ble /ˌinkəmˈpresəbəl/ ▶ **adj.** not able to be compressed.
– DERIVATIVES **in·com·press·i·bil·i·ty** /-ˌpresəˈbilitē/ **n.**

in·com·put·a·ble /ˌinkəmˈpyo͞otəbəl/ ▶ **adj.** rare unable to be calculated or estimated: *some probabilities are incomputable.*
– ORIGIN early 17th cent.: from **IN-**[1] 'not' +Latin *computabilis* 'able to be counted' (see **COMPUTE**).

in·con·ceiv·a·ble /ˌinkənˈsēvəbəl/ ▶ **adj.** not capable of being imagined or grasped mentally; unbelievable: [with clause] *it seemed inconceivable that the president had been unaware of what was going on | they behaved with inconceivable cruelty.*
– DERIVATIVES **in·con·ceiv·a·bil·i·ty** /-ˌsēvəˈbilitē/ **n.**, **in·con·ceiv·a·ble·ness** **n.**, **in·con·ceiv·a·bly** /-blē/ **adv.** [as submodifier] *a crisis of inconceivably devastating proportions.*

in·con·clu·sive /ˌinkənˈklo͞osiv, ˌiNG-/ ▶ **adj.** not leading to a firm conclusion; not ending doubt or dispute: *the medical evidence is inconclusive.*
– DERIVATIVES **in·con·clu·sive·ly** **adv.**, **in·con·clu·sive·ness** **n.**

In·co·nel /ˈiNGkəˌnel/ ▶ **n.** trademark an alloy of nickel containing chromium and iron, resistant to corrosion at high temperatures.
– ORIGIN 1930s: apparently from *I(nternational) N(ickel) Co(mpany)*, on the pattern of *nickel.*

in·con·gru·ent /inˈkäNGgro͞oənt, ˌinkənˈgro͞o-/ ▶ **adj.** incongruous; incompatible. ■ Chemistry (of melting, dissolution, or other process) affecting the components of an alloy or other substance differently.
– DERIVATIVES **in·con·gru·ence** **n.**, **in·con·gru·ent·ly** **adv.**
– ORIGIN late Middle English: from Latin *incongruent-*, from *in-* 'not' + *congruent-* 'meeting together' (see **CONGRUENT**).

in·con·gru·i·ty /ˌinkənˈgro͞o-itē, ˌiNG-, -käNG-/ ▶ **n.** (pl. **incongruities**) the state of being incongruous or out of keeping: *the incongruity of his fleshy face and skinny body disturbed her.*

in·con·gru·ous /inˈkäNGgro͞oəs/ ▶ **adj.** not in harmony or keeping with the surroundings or other aspects of something: *the duffel coat looked incongruous with the black dress she wore underneath.*
– DERIVATIVES **in·con·gru·ous·ly** **adv.**
– ORIGIN early 17th cent.: from Latin *incongruus* (from *in-* 'not' + *congruus* 'agreeing, suitable,' from the verb *congruere*) + **-OUS**.

in·con·nu /ˌinkəˈn(y)o͞o, aNkôˈnY/ ▶ **n.** **1** an unknown person or thing.
2 (pl. **same**) an edible predatory freshwater whitefish that is related to the salmon. It lives in Eurasian and North American lakes close to the Arctic Circle. ● *Stenodus leucichthys*, family Salmonidae.
– ORIGIN early 19th cent.: French, literally 'unknown.'

in·con·se·quent /inˈkänsəˌkwent, -ˌkwənt/ ▶ **adj.** not connected or following logically; irrelevant: *people say the most stupid, inconsequent things when surprised.* ■ another term for **INCONSEQUENTIAL**.
– DERIVATIVES **in·con·se·quence** **n.**, **in·con·se·quent·ly** **adv.**
– ORIGIN late 16th cent.: from Latin *inconsequent-*, from *in-* 'not' + *consequent-* 'overtaking, following closely' (see **CONSEQUENT**).

in·con·se·quen·tial /ˌinkänsəˈkwencHəl/ ▶ **adj.** not important or significant: *they talked about inconsequential things.*
– DERIVATIVES **in·con·se·quen·ti·al·i·ty** /-ˌkwencHēˈalitē/ **n.** (pl. **inconsequentialities**), **in·con·se·quen·tial·ly** **adv.**, **in·con·se·quen·tial·ness** **n.**

in·con·sid·er·a·ble /ˌinkənˈsidərəbəl/ ▶ **adj.** [usu. with negative] of small size, amount, or extent: *a not inconsiderable amount of money.* ■ unimportant or insignificant: *a not inconsiderable artist.*
– ORIGIN late 16th cent. (in the sense 'impossible to imagine'): from French, or from late Latin *inconsiderabilis*, from *in-* 'not' + *considerabilis* 'worthy of consideration' (see **CONSIDERABLE**).

in·con·sid·er·ate /ˌinkənˈsidərit/ ▶ **adj.** thoughtlessly causing hurt or inconvenience to others: *it's inconsiderate of her to go away without telling us.*
– DERIVATIVES **in·con·sid·er·ate·ly** **adv.**, **in·con·sid·er·ate·ness** **n.**, **in·con·sid·er·a·tion** /-ˌsidəˈrāsHən/ **n.**
– ORIGIN late Middle English (originally in the sense 'not properly considered'): from Latin *inconsideratus*, from *in-* 'not' + *consideratus* 'examined, considered' (see **CONSIDERATE**).

in·con·sist·en·cy /ˌinkənˈsistənsē/ ▶ **n.** (pl. **inconsistencies**) the fact or state of being inconsistent: *inconsistency between his expressed attitudes and his actual behavior.* ■ an inconsistent element or an instance of being inconsistent: *the single glaring inconsistency in the argument.*
– ORIGIN mid 17th cent.: from **INCONSISTENT**, on the pattern of *consistency.*

in·con·sist·ent /ˌinkənˈsistənt/ ▶ **adj.** not staying the same throughout: *police interpretation of the law was often inconsistent.* ■ acting at variance with one's own principles or former conduct: *parents can become inconsistent and lacking in control over their children.* ■ (**inconsistent with**) not compatible or in keeping with: *he had done nothing inconsistent with his morality.*
– DERIVATIVES **in·con·sist·ent·ly** **adv.**

in·con·sol·a·ble /ˌinkənˈsōləbəl/ ▶ **adj.** (of a person or their grief) not able to be comforted or alleviated: *his widow, Jane, was inconsolable.*
– DERIVATIVES **in·con·sol·a·bil·i·ty** /-ˌsōləˈbilitē/ **n.**, **in·con·sol·a·bly** /-blē/ **adv.**
– ORIGIN late 16th cent.: from French, or from Latin *inconsolabilis*, from *in-* 'not' + *consolabilis* 'able to be consoled,' from the verb *consolari* (see **CONSOLE**[1]).

in·con·so·nant /inˈkänsənənt/ ▶ **adj.** rare not in agreement or harmony; not compatible.
– DERIVATIVES **in·con·so·nance** **n.**, **in·con·so·nant·ly** **adv.**

in·con·spic·u·ous /ˌinkənˈspikyo͞oəs/ ▶ **adj.** not clearly visible or attracting attention; not conspicuous: *an inconspicuous red-brick building.*
– DERIVATIVES **in·con·spic·u·ous·ly** **adv.**, **in·con·spic·u·ous·ness** **n.**
– ORIGIN early 17th cent. (in the sense 'invisible, indiscernible'): from Latin *inconspicuus* (from *in-* 'not' + *conspicuus* 'clearly visible') + **-OUS**.

in·con·stant /inˈkänstənt/ ▶ **adj.** frequently changing; variable or irregular: *their exact dimensions aren't easily measured since they are inconstant.* ■ (of a person or their behavior) not faithful and dependable.
– DERIVATIVES **in·con·stan·cy** **n.** (pl. **inconstancies**), **in·con·stant·ly** **adv.**
– ORIGIN late Middle English: via Old French from Latin *inconstant-*, from *in-* 'not' + *constant-* 'standing firm' (see **CONSTANT**).

in·con·test·a·ble /ˌinkənˈtestəbəl/ ▶ **adj.** not able to be disputed.
– DERIVATIVES **in·con·test·a·bil·i·ty** /-ˌtestəˈbilitē/ **n.**, **in·con·test·a·bly** /-blē/ **adv.**
– ORIGIN late 17th cent.: from French, or from medieval Latin *incontestabilis*, from *in-* 'not' + *contestabilis* 'able to be called upon in witness,' from the verb *contestari* (see **CONTEST**).

in·con·ti·nent /inˈkäntənənt, -ˈkäntn-ənt/ ▶ **adj.**
1 having no or insufficient voluntary control over urination or defecation.
2 lacking self-restraint; uncontrolled: *the incontinent hysteria of the fans.*
– DERIVATIVES **in·con·ti·nence** **n.**, **in·con·ti·nent·ly** **adv.**
– ORIGIN late Middle English (sense 2): from Old French, or from Latin *incontinent-*, from *in-* 'not' + *continent-* 'holding together' (see **CONTINENT**[2]). Sense 1 dates from the early 19th cent.

in·con·tro·vert·i·ble /inˌkäntrəˈvərtəbəl/ ▶ **adj.** not able to be denied or disputed: *incontrovertible proof.*
– DERIVATIVES **in·con·tro·vert·i·bil·i·ty** /-ˌvərtəˈbilitē/ **n.**, **in·con·tro·vert·i·bly** /-blē/ **adv.**

in·con·ven·ience /ˌinkənˈvēn-yəns/ ▶ **n.** trouble or difficulty caused to one's personal requirements or comfort: *the inconvenience of having to change trains.* ■ a cause or instance of such trouble: *the inconveniences of life in a remote city.*
▶ **v.** [with obj.] cause such trouble or difficulty to: *noise and fumes from traffic would inconvenience residents.*
– ORIGIN late Middle English (originally in the sense 'incongruity, inconsistency,' also in the general sense 'unsuitability'): via Old French from late Latin *inconvenientia* 'incongruity, inconsistency,' from *in-* 'not' + Latin *convenient-* 'agreeing, fitting' (see **CONVENIENT**).

in·con·ven·ient /ˌinkənˈvēn-yənt/ ▶ **adj.** causing trouble, difficulties, or discomfort: *she telephoned frequently, usually at inconvenient times.*
– DERIVATIVES **in·con·ven·ient·ly** **adv.**
– ORIGIN late Middle English (originally in the sense 'incongruous' or 'unsuitable'): via Old French from Latin *inconvenient-*, from *in-* 'not' + *convenient-* 'agreeing, fitting' (see **CONVENIENT**). Current senses date from the mid 17th cent.

in·con·vert·i·ble /ˌinkənˈvərtəbəl/ ▶ **adj.** not able to be changed in form, function, or character. ■ (of currency) not able to be converted into another form on demand.
– DERIVATIVES **in·con·vert·i·bil·i·ty** /-ˌvərtəˈbilitē/ **n.**, **in·con·vert·i·bly** /-blē/ **adv.**
– ORIGIN mid 17th cent.: from French, or from late Latin *inconvertibilis*, from *in-* 'not' + *convertibilis* (see **CONVERTIBLE**).

in·co·or·di·na·tion /ˌinkōˌôrdnˈāsHən/ ▶ **n.** technical lack of coordination, esp. the inability to use different parts of the body together smoothly and efficiently.

in·cor·po·rate ▶ **v.** /inˈkôrpəˌrāt/ [with obj.] **1** take in or contain (something) as part of a whole; include: *he has **incorporated in** his proposals a large number of measures* | *territories that had been **incorporated into** the Japanese Empire.* ■ combine (ingredients) into one substance: *add the cheeses and butter and process briefly to incorporate them.*
2 constitute (a company, city, or other organization) as a legal corporation.
▶ **adj.** /-ˈkôrp(ə)rit/ archaic **1** another term for INCORPORATED.
2 literary having a bodily form; embodied.
– DERIVATIVES **in·cor·po·ra·tion** /-ˌkôrpəˈrāshən/ **n.**, **in·cor·po·ra·tor** /-ˌrātər/ **n.**
– ORIGIN late Middle English: from late Latin *incorporat-* 'embodied,' from the verb *incorporare*, from *in-* 'into' + Latin *corporare* 'form into a body' (from *corpus, corpor-* 'body').

in·cor·po·rat·ed /inˈkôrpəˌrātid/ ▶ **adj.** (of a company or other organization) formed into a legal corporation: *the Incorporated Society of Musicians* | [postpositive] *Adobe Systems Incorporated.*

in·cor·po·ra·tive /inˈkôrpəˌrātiv/ ▶ **adj.** tending to incorporate or include things.

in·cor·po·re·al /ˌinkôrˈpôrēəl/ ▶ **adj.** not composed of matter; having no material existence: *ghostly presences and incorporeal beings.* ■ Law having no physical existence.
– DERIVATIVES **in·cor·po·re·al·i·ty** /-ˌpôrēˈalitē/ **n.**, **in·cor·po·re·al·ly adv.**, **in·cor·po·re·i·ty** /-pəˈrēitē/ **n.**
– ORIGIN late Middle English: from Latin *incorporeus*, from *in-* 'not' + *corporeus* (from *corpus, corpor-* 'body') + -AL.

in·cor·rect /ˌinkəˈrekt/ ▶ **adj.** **1** not in accordance with fact; wrong: *the doctor gave you incorrect advice.*
2 not in accordance with particular standards or rules: *strictly speaking, the form of address was incorrect.*
– DERIVATIVES **in·cor·rect·ly adv.**, **in·cor·rect·ness n.**
– ORIGIN late Middle English: from Latin *incorrectus*, from *in-* 'not' + 'made straight, amended' (see CORRECT). Originally in the general sense 'uncorrected,' the word was later applied specifically to a book containing many errors because it had not been corrected for the press.

in·cor·ri·gi·ble /inˈkôrijəbəl, -ˈkär-/ ▶ **adj.** (of a person or their tendencies) not able to be corrected, improved, or reformed: *she's an incorrigible flirt.*
▶ **n.** a person of this type.
– DERIVATIVES **in·cor·ri·gi·bil·i·ty** /-ˌkôrijəˈbilitē, -ˌkär-/ **n.**, **in·cor·ri·gi·ble·ness n.**, **in·cor·ri·gi·bly** /-blē/ **adv.** [as submodifier] *the incorrigibly macho character of news-gathering operations.*
– ORIGIN Middle English: from Old French, or from Latin *incorrigibilis*, from *in-* 'not' + *corrigibilis* (see CORRIGIBLE).

in·cor·rupt /ˌinkəˈrəpt/ ▶ **adj.** rare (esp. of a human body) not having undergone decomposition.
– ORIGIN late Middle English: from Latin *incorruptus*, from *in-* 'not' + *corruptus* 'destroyed, marred' (see CORRUPT).

in·cor·rupt·i·ble /ˌinkəˈrəptəbəl/ ▶ **adj.** **1** not susceptible to corruption, esp. by bribery.
2 not subject to death or decay; everlasting.
– DERIVATIVES **in·cor·rupt·i·bil·i·ty** /-ˌrəptəˈbilitē/ **n.**, **in·cor·rupt·i·bly** /-blē/ **adv.**
– ORIGIN Middle English: from Old French, or from ecclesiastical Latin *incorruptibilis*, from *in-* 'not' + *corruptibilis* 'corruptible, liable to decay.'

in-coun·try ▶ **adj. & adv.** in a country rather than operating from outside but in relation to it: [as adv.] *the people we're putting in-country will get instructions from satellite radios.*

incr. ▶ **abbr.** increase or increased or increasing.

in·cras·sate /inˈkrasit, -ˌsāt/ ▶ **adj.** rare thickened in form or consistency.
– DERIVATIVES **in·cras·sat·ed adj.**
– ORIGIN late 15th cent.: from late Latin *incrassatus* 'made thick,' past participle of *incrassare*.

in·crease ▶ **v.** /inˈkrēs/ become or make greater in size, amount, intensity, or degree: [no obj.] *car use is increasing at an alarming rate* | [with obj.] *we are aiming to increase awareness of social issues* | (as adj. **increasing**) *the increasing numbers of students.*
▶ **n.** /ˈinˌkrēs/ an instance of growing or making greater: *an increase from sixteen to eighteen clubs* | *some increase in inflation.*
– PHRASES **on the increase** becoming greater, more common, or more frequent.
– DERIVATIVES **in·creas·a·ble adj.**
– ORIGIN Middle English (formerly also as *encrease*): from Old French *encreistre*, from Latin *increscere*, from *in-* 'into' + *crescere* 'grow.'

in·creas·ing·ly /inˈkrēsiNGlē, iŋ-/ ▶ **adv.** to an increasing extent; more and more: [sentence adverb] *increasingly, attention is paid to health* | [as submodifier] *an increasingly difficult situation.*

in·cre·ate /ˌinkrēˈāt, inˈkrē-it/ ▶ **adj.** literary not yet created.
– ORIGIN late Middle English: from ecclesiastical Latin *increatus*, from Latin *in-* 'not' + *creatus* (past participle of *creare* 'create').

in·cred·i·ble /inˈkredəbəl/ ▶ **adj.** **1** impossible to believe: *an almost incredible tale of triumph and tragedy.*
2 difficult to believe; extraordinary: *the noise from the crowd was incredible.* ■ informal amazingly good or beautiful: *I was mesmerized: she looked so incredible.*
– DERIVATIVES **in·cred·i·bil·i·ty** /-ˌkredəˈbilitē/ **n.**
– ORIGIN late Middle English: from Latin *incredibilis*, from *in-* 'not' + *credibilis* (see CREDIBLE).

> **USAGE** Believability is at the heart of both **incredible** and **incredulous**, but there is an important distinction in the respective uses of these two adjectives. **Incredible** means 'unbelievable' or 'not convincing' and can be applied to a situation, statement, policy, or threat to a person: *I find this testimony incredible.* **Incredulous** means 'disinclined to believe, skeptical'—the opposite of *credulous, gullible*—and is usually applied to a person's attitude: *you shouldn't be surprised that I'm incredulous after all your lies.*

in·cred·i·bly /inˈkredəblē/ ▶ **adv.** **1** [as submodifier] to a great degree; extremely or unusually: *Michele was incredibly brave.*
2 [sentence adverb] used to introduce a statement that is hard to believe; strangely: *incredibly, he was still alive.*

in·cre·du·li·ty /ˌinkrəˈd(y)o͞olitē/ ▶ **n.** the state of being unwilling or unable to believe something: *he stared down the street in incredulity.*

in·cred·u·lous /inˈkrejələs/ ▶ **adj.** (of a person or their manner) unwilling or unable to believe something: *an incredulous gasp.*
– DERIVATIVES **in·cred·u·lous·ly adv.**, **in·cred·u·lous·ness n.**
– ORIGIN late 16th cent.: from Latin *incredulus* (from *in-* 'not' + *credulus* 'believing, trusting,' from *credere* 'believe') + -OUS.

> **USAGE** See usage at INCREDIBLE.

in·cre·ment /ˈiNGkrəmənt, ˈin-/ ▶ **n.** an increase or addition, esp. one of a series on a fixed scale: *the inmates' pay can escalate in five-cent increments to a maximum of 90 cents an hour.* ■ a regular increase in salary on such a scale. ■ Mathematics a small positive or negative change in a variable quantity or function.
▶ **v.** [with obj.] chiefly Computing cause a discrete increase in (a numerical quantity).
– DERIVATIVES **in·cre·men·tal** /ˌiNGkrəˈmentl, ˌin-/ **adj.**, **in·cre·men·tal·ly** /ˌiNGkrəˈmentl-ē, ˌin-/ **adv.**
– ORIGIN late Middle English: from Latin *incrementum*, from the stem of *increscere* 'grow' (see INCREASE).

in·cre·men·tal back·up ▶ **n.** Computing a security copy that contains only those files that have been altered since the last full backup.

in·cre·men·tal·ism /ˌiNGkrəˈmentlˌizəm, ˌin-/ ▶ **n.** belief in or advocacy of change by degrees; gradualism.
– DERIVATIVES **in·cre·men·tal·ist n. & adj.**

in·crim·i·nate /inˈkriməˌnāt/ ▶ **v.** [with obj.] make (someone) appear guilty of a crime or wrongdoing; strongly imply the guilt of (someone): *he refused to answer questions in order not to incriminate himself* | (as adj. **incriminating**) *incriminating evidence.*
– DERIVATIVES **in·crim·i·na·tion** /-ˌkriməˈnāshən/ **n.**, **in·crim·i·na·to·ry** /-nəˌtôrē/ **adj.**
– ORIGIN mid 18th cent.: from late Latin *incriminat-* 'accused,' from the verb *incriminare*, from *in-* 'into, toward' + Latin *crimen* 'crime.'

in-crowd ▶ **n.** (**the in-crowd**) informal a small group of people perceived by others to be particularly fashionable, informed, or popular.

in·crust ▶ **v.** variant spelling of ENCRUST.

in·crus·ta·tion ▶ **n.** variant spelling of ENCRUSTATION.

in·cu·bate /ˈinkyəˌbāt, ˈiNG-/ ▶ **v.** [with obj.] (of a bird) sit on (eggs) in order to keep them warm and bring them to hatching. ■ (esp. in a laboratory) keep (eggs, cells, bacteria, embryos, etc.) at a suitable temperature so that they develop: *the samples were incubated at 80°C for three minutes.* ■ (**be incubating something**) have an infectious disease developing inside one before symptoms appear: *the possibility that she was incubating early syphilis.* ■ [no obj.] develop slowly without outward or perceptible signs: *unfortunately the BSE bug incubates for around three years.*
– ORIGIN mid 17th cent.: from Latin *incubat-* 'lain on,' from the verb *incubare*, from *in-* 'upon' + *cubare* 'to lie.'

in·cu·ba·tion /ˌinkyəˈbāshən, ˌiNG-/ ▶ **n.** the process of incubating eggs, cells, bacteria, a disease, etc.: *the chick hatches after a month's incubation.*
– DERIVATIVES **in·cu·ba·tive** /ˈinkyəˌbātiv, ˈiNG-/ **adj.**, **in·cu·ba·to·ry** /inˈkyo͞obəˌtôrē, iNG-/ **adj.**
– ORIGIN early 17th cent.: from Latin *incubatio(n-)* 'brooding,' from the verb *incubare* (see INCUBATE).

in·cu·ba·tion pe·ri·od ▶ **n.** the period over which eggs, cells, etc., are incubated. ■ the period between exposure to an infection and the appearance of the first symptoms.

in·cu·ba·tor /ˈinkyəˌbātər, ˈiNG-/ ▶ **n.** an enclosed apparatus providing a controlled environment for the care and protection of premature or unusually small babies. ■ an apparatus used to hatch eggs or grow microorganisms under controlled conditions. ■ a place, esp. with support staff and equipment, made available at low rent to new small businesses.

in·cu·bous /ˈiNGkyo͞obəs/ ▶ **adj.** Botany (of a liverwort) having leaves that point forward so that their upper edges overlap the lower edges of the leaves above. Often contrasted with SUCCUBOUS.
– ORIGIN mid 19th cent.: from Latin *incubare* 'lie on' + -OUS.

in·cu·bus /ˈiNGkyəbəs, ˈin-/ ▶ **n.** (pl. **incubi** /-ˌbī/) a male demon believed to have sexual intercourse with sleeping women. ■ a cause of distress or anxiety: *debt is a big incubus in developing countries.* ■ archaic a nightmare.
– ORIGIN Middle English: late Latin form of Latin *incubo* 'nightmare,' from *incubare* 'lie on' (see INCUBATE).

in·cu·des /inˈkyo͞oˌdēz/ plural form of INCUS.

in·cul·cate /inˈkəlˌkāt, ˈinkəl-/ ▶ **v.** [with obj.] instill (an attitude, idea, or habit) by persistent instruction: *the failures of the churches to inculcate a sense of moral responsibility.* ■ teach (someone) an attitude, idea, or habit by such instruction: *they will try to inculcate you with a respect for culture.*
– DERIVATIVES **in·cul·ca·tion** /ˌinkəlˈkāshən/ **n.**, **in·cul·ca·tor** /-ˌkātər/ **n.**
– ORIGIN mid 16th cent.: from Latin *inculcat-* 'pressed in,' from the verb *inculcare*, from *in-* 'into' + *calcare* 'to tread' (from *calx, calc-* 'heel').

in·cul·pate /inˈkəlˌpāt, ˈinkəl-/ ▶ **v.** [with obj.] archaic accuse or blame. ■ incriminate: *someone placed the pistol in your room in order to inculpate you.*
– DERIVATIVES **in·cul·pa·tion** /ˌinkəlˈpāshən/ **n.**, **in·cul·pa·to·ry** /inˈkəlpəˌtôrē/ **adj.**
– ORIGIN late 18th cent.: from late Latin *inculpat-* 'made culpable,' from the verb *inculpare*, from *in-* 'upon, toward' + *culpare* 'to blame' (from *culpa* 'fault').

in·cul·tu·ra·tion ▶ **n.** variant spelling of ENCULTURATION.

in·cum·ben·cy /inˈkəmbənsē/ ▶ **n.** (pl. **incumbencies**) the holding of an office or the period during which one is held.

in·cum·bent /inˈkəmbənt/ ▶ **adj.** **1** [predic.] (**incumbent on/upon**) necessary for (someone) as a duty or responsibility: *it is incumbent on all decent people to concentrate on destroying this evil.*
2 [attrib.] (of an official or regime) currently holding office: *the incumbent president had been defeated.*
▶ **n.** the holder of an office or post. ■ Christian Church the holder of an ecclesiastical benefice.
– ORIGIN late Middle English (as a noun): from Anglo-Latin *incumbens, incumbent-*, from Latin *incumbere* 'lie or lean on,' from *in-* 'upon' + a verb related to *cubare* 'lie.'

in·cu·na·ble /inˈkyo͞onəbəl/ ▶ **n.** one book in a collection of incunabula.

in·cu·nab·u·la /ˌinkəˈnab-yələ, ˌiNG-/ ▶ **n.** (sing. **incunabulum** /ˌinkəˈnabyələm, ˌiNG-/ or **incunable** /inˈkyo͞onəbəl/) early printed books, esp. those printed before 1501. ■ archaic the early stages of the development of something.
– DERIVATIVES **in·cu·nab·u·list** /-list/ **n.**
– ORIGIN early 19th cent.: Latin (neuter plural), 'swaddling clothes, cradle,' from *in-* 'into' + *cunae* 'cradle.'

in·cur /inˈkər, iNG-/ ▶ **v.** (**incurs, incurring, incurred**) [with obj.] become subject to (something unwelcome or unpleasant) as a result of one's own behavior or actions: *I will pay any expenses incurred.*
– DERIVATIVES **in·cur·rence** /-əns/ **n.**
– ORIGIN late Middle English: from Latin *incurrere*, from *in-* 'toward' + *currere* 'run.'

in·cur·a·ble /inˈkyo͝orəbəl/ ▶ adj. (of a sick person or a disease) not able to be cured. ■ (of a person or behavior) unable to be changed: *an incurable optimist.*
▶ n. a person who cannot be cured.
– DERIVATIVES **in·cur·a·bil·i·ty** n., **in·cur·a·bly** adv. [as submodifier] *incurably ill patients.*
– ORIGIN Middle English: from Old French, or from late Latin *incurabilis*, from *in-* 'not' + *curabilis* (see CURABLE).

in·cu·ri·ous /inˈkyo͝orēəs/ ▶ adj. (of a person or their manner) not eager to know something; lacking curiosity.
– DERIVATIVES **in·cu·ri·os·i·ty** /-ˌkyo͝orēˈäsitē/ n., **in·cu·ri·ous·ly** adv., **in·cu·ri·ous·ness** n.
– ORIGIN late 16th cent. (in the sense 'careless'): partly from Latin *incuriosus* 'careless, indifferent,' from *in-* 'not' + *curiosus* 'careful' (see CURIOUS); partly from IN-[1] 'not' + CURIOUS.

in·cur·rent /inˈkərənt, -ˈkə-rənt/ ▶ adj. chiefly Zoology (of a vessel or opening) conveying fluid inward. The opposite of EXCURRENT.
– ORIGIN late 16th cent. (in the sense 'falling within (a period)'): from Latin *incurrent-* 'running in,' from the verb *incurrere* (see INCUR).

in·cur·sion /inˈkərZHən/ ▶ n. an invasion or attack, esp. a sudden or brief one: *incursions into enemy territory.*
– DERIVATIVES **in·cur·sive** /-siv/ adj.
– ORIGIN late Middle English (formerly also as *encursion*): from Latin *incursio(n-)*, from the verb *incurrere* (see INCUR).

in·cur·vate /inˈkərˌvāt, ˈinkər-/ ▶ v. [no obj.] (usu. as adj. **incurvated**) curve inward.
▶ adj. curved inward.
– DERIVATIVES **in·cur·va·tion** /ˌinkərˈvāSHən/ n.
– ORIGIN late Middle English (as an adjective): from Latin *incurvat-* 'bent into a curve,' from the verb *incurvare*.

in·curve /inˈkərv/ ▶ v. [no obj.] (usu. as adj. **incurved**) curve inward: *incurved horns.*
– ORIGIN late Middle English: from Latin *incurvare*, from *in-* 'in, toward' + *curvare* 'to curve.'

in·cus /ˈiNGkəs/ ▶ n. (pl. **incudes** /inˈkyo͞oˌdēz/) Anatomy a small anvil-shaped bone in the middle ear, transmitting vibrations between the malleus and stapes.
– ORIGIN mid 17th cent.: from Latin, literally 'anvil.'

in·cuse /inˈkyo͞oz, -ˈkyo͞os/ ▶ n. an impression hammered or stamped on a coin.
▶ v. [with obj.] mark (a coin) with a figure by impressing it with a stamp.
▶ adj. hammered or stamped on a coin.
– ORIGIN early 19th cent.: from Latin *incusus* 'forged with a hammer,' past participle of *incudere*, from *in-* 'into' + *cudere* 'to forge.'

Ind. ▶ abbr. ■ Independent. ■ India. ■ Indian. ■ Indiana.

in·debt·ed /inˈdetid/ ▶ adj. owing money: *heavily indebted countries.* ■ owing gratitude for a service or favor: *I am indebted to her for her help in indexing my book.*
– DERIVATIVES **in·debt·ed·ness** n.
– ORIGIN Middle English *endetted*, from Old French *endette* 'involved in debt,' past participle of *endetter*. The spelling change in the 16th cent. was due to association with medieval Latin *indebitare* (based on Latin *debitum* 'debt').

in·de·cen·cy /inˈdēsənsē/ ▶ n. (pl. **indecencies**) indecent behavior: *a law governing indecency on cable television.* ■ an indecent act, gesture, or expression.

in·de·cent /inˈdēsənt/ ▶ adj. not conforming with generally accepted standards of behavior or propriety; obscene: *the film was grossly indecent.* ■ not appropriate or fitting: *they leaped on the suggestion with indecent haste.*
– DERIVATIVES **in·de·cent·ly** adv.
– ORIGIN late 16th cent.: from French *indécent* or Latin *indecent-*, from *in-* 'not' + *decent-* 'being fitting' (see DECENT).

in·de·cent as·sault ▶ n. sexual assault that does not involve rape.

in·de·cent ex·po·sure ▶ n. the crime of intentionally showing one's sexual organs in public. ■ the act of outraging public decency by being naked in a public place.

in·de·ci·pher·a·ble /ˌindiˈsīfərəbəl/ ▶ adj. not able to be read or understood: *indecipherable scrawls.*
– DERIVATIVES **in·de·ci·pher·a·bil·i·ty** n., **in·de·ci·pher·a·bly** adv.

in·de·ci·sion /ˌindiˈsiZHən/ ▶ n. the inability to make a decision quickly.
– ORIGIN mid 18th cent.: from French *indécision*, from *in-* (expressing negation) + *décision*, from Latin *decisio(n-)*, from the verb *decidere* (see DECIDE).

in·de·ci·sive /ˌindiˈsīsiv/ ▶ adj. **1** not settling an issue: *these experimental results are indecisive.*
2 (of a person) not having or showing the ability to make decisions quickly and effectively.
– DERIVATIVES **in·de·ci·sive·ly** adv., **in·de·ci·sive·ness** n.

in·de·clin·a·ble /ˌindiˈklīnəbəl/ ▶ adj. Grammar (of a noun, pronoun, or adjective in a highly inflected language) having no inflections.
– ORIGIN late Middle English: via French from Latin *indeclinabilis*, from *in-* 'not' + *declinabilis* 'able to be inflected' (see DECLINE).

in·de·com·pos·a·ble /ˌindēkəmˈpōzəbəl/ ▶ adj. Mathematics unable to be expressed as a product of factors or otherwise decomposed into simpler elements.

in·dec·o·rous /inˈdekərəs/ ▶ adj. not in keeping with good taste and propriety; improper.
– DERIVATIVES **in·dec·o·rous·ly** adv., **in·dec·o·rous·ness** n.
– ORIGIN late 17th cent.: from Latin *indecorus* (from *in-* 'not' + *decorus* 'seemly') + -OUS.

in·de·co·rum /ˌindiˈkôrəm/ ▶ n. failure to conform to good taste, propriety, or etiquette.
– ORIGIN late 16th cent. (denoting an indecorous act): from Latin, neuter of *indecorus* 'not seemly.'

in·deed /inˈdēd/ ▶ adv. **1** used to emphasize a statement or response confirming something already suggested: *it was not expected to last long, and indeed it took less than three weeks | "She should have no trouble hearing him." "No indeed."* ■ used to emphasize a description, typically of a quality or condition: *it was a very good buy indeed | thank you very much indeed.*
2 used to introduce a further and stronger or more surprising point: *the idea is attractive to many men and indeed to many women.*
3 used in a response to express interest, incredulity, or contempt: *"His neck was broken." "Indeed?" | Nice boys, indeed—they were going to smash his head in!* ■ expressing interest of an ironical kind with repetition of a question just asked: *"Who'd believe it?" "Who indeed?"*
– ORIGIN Middle English: originally as *in deed.*

in·deed·y /inˈdēdē/ ▶ adv. informal term for INDEED (sense 1): *Yes, indeedy! That was a good question.*

indef. ▶ abbr. indefinite.

in·de·fat·i·ga·ble /ˌindəˈfatigəbəl/ ▶ adj. (of a person or their efforts) persisting tirelessly: *an indefatigable defender of human rights.*
– DERIVATIVES **in·de·fat·i·ga·bil·i·ty** /-ˌfatigəˈbilitē/ n., **in·de·fat·i·ga·bly** /-blē/ adv.
– ORIGIN early 17th cent.: from French, or from Latin *indefatigabilis*, from *in-* 'not' + *de-* 'away, completely' + *fatigare* 'wear out.'

in·de·fea·si·ble /ˌindəˈfēzəbəl/ ▶ adj. chiefly Law & Philosophy not able to be lost, annulled, or overturned: *an indefeasible right.*
– DERIVATIVES **in·de·fea·si·bil·i·ty** /-ˌfēzəˈbilitē/ n., **in·de·fea·si·bly** /-blē/ adv.

in·de·fect·i·ble /ˌindəˈfektəbəl/ ▶ adj. rare not liable to fail, end, or decay. ■ perfect; faultless.

in·de·fen·si·ble /ˌindəˈfensəbəl/ ▶ adj. **1** not justifiable by argument: *the policy of apartheid was morally indefensible.*
2 not able to be protected against attack: *the towns were tactically indefensible.*
– DERIVATIVES **in·de·fen·si·bil·i·ty** /-ˌfensəˈbilitē/ n., **in·de·fen·si·bly** /-blē/ adv.

in·de·fin·a·ble /ˌindiˈfīnəbəl/ ▶ adj. not able to be defined or described exactly: *she reminds me, in some indefinable way, of my grandmother.*
– DERIVATIVES **in·de·fin·a·bly** adv. [as submodifier] *his indefinably foreign accent.*

in·def·i·nite /inˈdefənit/ ▶ adj. lasting for an unknown or unstated length of time: *they may face indefinite detention.* ■ not clearly expressed or defined; vague: *their status remains indefinite.* ■ Grammar (of a word, inflection, or phrase) not determining the person, thing, time, etc., referred to.
– DERIVATIVES **in·def·i·nite·ness** n.
– ORIGIN mid 16th cent.: from Latin *indefinitus*, from *in-* 'not' + *definitus* 'defined, set within limits' (see DEFINITE).

in·def·i·nite ar·ti·cle ▶ n. Grammar a determiner (*a* and *an* in English) that introduces a noun phrase and implies that the thing referred to is nonspecific (as in *she bought me a book*; *government is an art*; *he went to a public school*). Typically, the indefinite article is used to introduce new concepts into a discourse. Compare with DEFINITE ARTICLE.

in·def·i·nite in·te·gral ▶ n. Mathematics an integral expressed without limits, and so containing an arbitrary constant.

in·def·i·nite·ly /inˈdefənitlē/ ▶ adv. for an unlimited or unspecified period of time: *talks cannot go on indefinitely.* ■ [as submodifier] to an unlimited or unspecified degree or extent: *an indefinitely large number of channels.*

in·def·i·nite pro·noun ▶ n. Grammar a pronoun that does not refer to any person, amount, or thing in particular, e.g., *anything, something, anyone, everyone.*

in·de·his·cent /ˌindiˈhisənt/ ▶ adj. Botany (of a pod or fruit) not splitting open to release the seeds when ripe.
– DERIVATIVES **in·de·his·cence** n.

in·del·i·ble /inˈdeləbəl/ ▶ adj. (of ink or a pen) making marks that cannot be removed. ■ not able to be forgotten or removed: *his story made an indelible impression on me.*
– DERIVATIVES **in·del·i·bil·i·ty** /-ˌdeləˈbilitē/ n., **in·del·i·bly** /-blē/ adv.
– ORIGIN late 15th cent. (as *indeleble*): from French, or from Latin *indelebilis*, from *in-* 'not' + *delebilis* (from *delere* 'efface, delete'). The ending was altered under the influence of -IBLE.

in·del·i·ca·cy /inˈdelikəsī/ ▶ n. (pl. **indelicacies**) **1** a lack of sensitive understanding or tact: *the magazine printed the photographs with manifest indelicacy for commercial ends.*
2 the quality of being slightly indecent: *the play's cynicism and sexual indelicacy | such crude indelicacies.*

in·del·i·cate /inˈdelikit/ ▶ adj. **1** having or showing a lack of sensitive understanding or tact: *forgive me asking an indelicate question, but how are you for money?*
2 slightly indecent: *an earthy, often indelicate sense of humor.*
– DERIVATIVES **in·del·i·cate·ly** adv.

in·dem·ni·fy /inˈdemnəˌfī/ ▶ v. (**indemnifies, indemnifying, indemnified**) [with obj.] compensate (someone) for harm or loss: *the amount of insurance that may be carried to indemnify the owner in the event of a loss.* ■ secure (someone) against legal responsibility for their actions: *the newspaper could not be forced to indemnify the city for personal-injury liability.*
– DERIVATIVES **in·dem·ni·fi·ca·tion** /-ˌdemnəfiˈkāSHən/ n., **in·dem·ni·fi·er** n.
– ORIGIN early 17th cent.: from Latin *indemnis* 'unhurt, free from loss or damage,' from *in-* (expressing negation) + *damnum* 'loss, damage.'

in·dem·ni·ty /inˈdemnitē/ ▶ n. (pl. **indemnities**) security or protection against a loss or other financial burden: *no indemnity will be given for loss of cash.* ■ security against or exemption from legal responsibility for one's actions: *a deed of indemnity | even warranties and indemnities do not provide complete protection.* ■ a sum of money paid as compensation, esp. a sum exacted by a victor in war as one condition of peace.
– ORIGIN late Middle English: from French *indemnite*, from late Latin *indemnitas*, from *indemnis* 'unhurt, free from loss.'

in·de·mon·stra·ble /ˌindəˈmänstrəbəl, inˈdemən-/ ▶ adj. not able to be proved or demonstrated. ■ Philosophy (of a truth) axiomatic and hence unprovable.

in·dene /ˈinˌdēn/ ▶ n. Chemistry a colorless liquid hydrocarbon, obtained from coal tar and used in making synthetic resins. ● A bicyclic aromatic compound; chem. formula: C_9H_8.
– ORIGIN late 19th cent.: from INDOLE + -ENE.

in·dent[1] ▶ v. /inˈdent/ [with obj.] **1** start (a line of text) or position (a block of text, table, etc.) further from the margin than the main part of the text.
2 form deep recesses or notches in (a line or surface): *a coastline indented by many fjords.*
3 [no obj.] Brit. make a requisition or written order for something.
4 historical divide (a document drawn up in duplicate) into its two copies with a zigzag line, thus ensuring identification. ■ draw up (a legal document) in exact duplicate.
▶ n. /inˈdent, ˈinˌdent/ **1** a space left by indenting a line or block of text.
2 an indentation: *every indent in the coastline.*
3 Brit. an official order or requisition for specified goods or stores.
4 an indenture.
– DERIVATIVES **in·den·tor** /-tər/ n.
– ORIGIN late Middle English (as a verb in the sense 'give a zigzag outline to, divide by a zigzag line'): from Anglo-Norman French *endenter* or medieval Latin *indentare*, from *en-*, *in-* 'into' + Latin *dens, dent-* 'tooth.'

in·dent[2] ▶ v. [with obj.] make a dent or impression in (something): *his chin was firm and slightly indented.*

in·den·ta·tion /ˌindenˈtāSHən/ ▶ n. **1** the action of indenting or the state of being indented: *paragraphs are marked off by indentation | an indentation for each change of speaker.*

2 a deep recess or notch on the edge or surface of something: *the indentation between the upper lip and the nose.*

in·den·ta·tion test ▶ n. a test for determining the hardness of a solid by making an indentation in a sample under standard conditions and measuring the size of the indentation or the distance moved by the indenter.

in·dent·ed /inˈdentid/ ▶ adj. Heraldry divided or edged with a zigzag line.

in·dent·er /inˈdentər/ ▶ n. a small hard object used for producing an indentation in a solid in an indentation test.

in·den·tion /inˈdenCHən/ ▶ n. archaic term for INDENTATION.

in·den·ture /inˈdenCHər/ ▶ n. a formal legal agreement, contract, or document, in particular: ■ historical a deed of contract of which copies were made for the contracting parties with the edges indented for identification. ■ a formal list, certificate, or inventory. ■ an agreement binding an apprentice to a master: *the 30 apprentices have received their indentures on completion of their training.* ■ historical a contract by which a person agreed to work for a set period for a landowner in a British colony in exchange for passage to the colony. ■ the fact of being bound to service by such an agreement: *men in their first year after **indenture to** the Company of Watermen and Lightermen.*
▶ v. [with obj.] (usu. **be indentured to**) chiefly historical bind (someone) by an indenture as an apprentice or laborer: (as adj. **indentured**) *landowners tried to get their estates cultivated by indentured laborers.*
– DERIVATIVES **in·den·ture·ship** /-ˌSHip/ n.
– ORIGIN late Middle English *endenture*, via Anglo-Norman French from medieval Latin *indentura*, from *indentatus*, past participle of *indentare* (see INDENT[1]).

In·de·pend·ence /ˌindəˈpendəns/ a historic city in northwestern Missouri, east of Kansas City; pop. 110,440 (est. 2008).

in·de·pend·ence /ˌindəˈpendəns/ ▶ n. the fact or state of being independent: *Argentina gained independence from Spain in 1816 | I've always valued my independence.*
– ORIGIN mid 17th cent.: from INDEPENDENT, partly on the pattern of French *indépendance.*

In·de·pend·ence Day ▶ n. another term for FOURTH OF JULY. ■ a day celebrating the anniversary of national independence.

In·de·pend·ence Hall a building in Philadelphia where the US Declaration of Independence was proclaimed and outside which the Liberty Bell is kept.

in·de·pend·en·cy /ˌindəˈpendənsē/ ▶ n. (pl. **independencies**) **1** rare an independent or self-governing state.
2 archaic term for INDEPENDENCE.

in·de·pend·ent /ˌindəˈpendənt/ ▶ adj. **1** free from outside control; not depending on another's authority: *the study is totally **independent of** central government | Canada's largest independent investment firm.* ■ (of a country) self-governing: *India became independent in 1947.* ■ not belonging to or supported by a political party: *the independent candidate.* ■ (of broadcasting, a school, etc.) not supported by public funds. ■ not influenced or affected by others; impartial: *a thorough and independent investigation of the case.* ■ (**Independent**) historical Congregational.
2 not depending on another for livelihood or subsistence: *I wanted to remain independent in old age.* ■ capable of thinking or acting for oneself: *advice for independent travelers.* ■ (of income or resources) making it unnecessary to earn one's living: *a woman of independent means.*
3 not connected with another or with each other; separate: *we need two independent witnesses to testify | the legislature and the judicature are **independent of** each other.* ■ not depending on something else for strength or effectiveness; freestanding: *an independent electric shower.* ■ Mathematics (of one of a set of axioms, equations, or quantities) incapable of being expressed in terms of, or derived or deduced from, the others.
▶ n. an independent person or body. ■ an independent political candidate, voter, etc. ■ (**Independent**) historical a Congregationalist.
– ORIGIN early 17th cent. (as an adjective): partly on the pattern of French *indépendant.*

in·de·pend·ent·ly /ˌindəˈpendəntlī/ ▶ adv. **1** in a way that is free from outside control or influence: *the government must prove its ability to govern independently.*
2 without outside help; unaided: *disabled people living independently in their own homes.*
3 in a way that is not connected with another; individually: *decisions are made **independently of** consumers.*

in·de·pend·ent sus·pen·sion ▶ n. a form of vehicle suspension in which each wheel is supported independently of the others.

in·de·pend·ent var·i·a·ble ▶ n. Mathematics a variable (often denoted by *x*) whose variation does not depend on that of another.

in-depth ▶ adj. comprehensive and thorough: *in-depth interviews.*

in·de·scrib·a·ble /ˌindiˈskrībəbəl/ ▶ adj. too unusual, extreme, or indefinite to be adequately described: *most prisoners suffered indescribable hardship.*
– DERIVATIVES **in·de·scrib·a·bil·i·ty** /-ˌskrībəˈbilitē/ n., **in·de·scrib·a·bly** /-blē/ adv.

in·de·struct·i·ble /ˌindiˈstrəktəbəl/ ▶ adj. not able to be destroyed: *indestructible plastic containers.*
– DERIVATIVES **in·de·struct·i·bil·i·ty** /-ˌstrəktəˈbilitē/ n., **in·de·struct·i·bly** /-blē/ adv.

in·de·ter·mi·na·ble /ˌindiˈtərmənəbəl/ ▶ adj. not able to be definitely ascertained, calculated, or identified: *a woman of indeterminable age.* ■ (of a dispute or difficulty) not able to be resolved.
– DERIVATIVES **in·de·ter·mi·na·bly** /-blē/ adv.
– ORIGIN late 15th cent. (in the sense 'unable to be limited'): from late Latin *indeterminabilis*, from *in-* 'not' + *determinabilis* (see DETERMINABLE).

in·de·ter·mi·na·cy prin·ci·ple /ˌindiˈtərmənəsē/ ▶ n. another term for UNCERTAINTY PRINCIPLE.

in·de·ter·mi·nate /ˌindiˈtərmənit/ ▶ adj. not exactly known, established, or defined: *the date of manufacture is indeterminate.* ■ (of a judicial sentence) such that the convicted person's conduct determines the date of release. ■ Mathematics (of a quantity) having no definite or definable value. ■ Medicine (of a condition) from which a diagnosis of the underlying cause cannot be made: *indeterminate colitis.* ■ Botany (of a plant shoot) not having all the axes terminating in a flower bud and so producing a shoot of indefinite length.
– DERIVATIVES **in·de·ter·mi·na·cy** /-nəsē/ n., **in·de·ter·mi·nate·ly** adv., **in·de·ter·mi·nate·ness** n.
– ORIGIN early 17th cent.: from late Latin *indeterminatus*, from *in-* 'not' + Latin *determinatus* 'limited, determined' (see DETERMINATE).

in·de·ter·mi·nate vow·el ▶ n. Phonetics the vowel heard in "*a moment ago*"; a schwa.

in·de·ter·mi·na·tion /ˌindiˌtərməˈnāSHən/ ▶ n. the state of being uncertain or undecided.

in·de·ter·min·ism /ˌindiˈtərməˌnizəm/ ▶ n.
1 Philosophy the doctrine that not all events are wholly determined by antecedent causes.
2 the state of being uncertain or undecided.
– DERIVATIVES **in·de·ter·min·ist** n., **in·de·ter·min·is·tic** /-ˌtərməˈnistik/ adj.

in·dex /ˈinˌdeks/ ▶ n. (pl. **indexes** or esp. in technical use **indices** /-dəˌsēz/) **1** an alphabetical list of names, subjects, etc., with references to the places where they occur, typically found at the end of a book. ■ an alphabetical list by title, subject, author, or other category of a collection of books or documents, e.g., in a library. ■ Computing a set of items each of which specifies one of the records of a file and contains information about its address.
2 an indicator, sign, or measure of something: *exam results may serve as an **index of** the teacher's effectiveness.* ■ a figure in a system or scale representing the average value of specified prices, shares, or other items as compared with some reference figure: *the hundred-shares index closed down 9.3.* ■ a pointer on an instrument, showing a quantity, a position on a scale, etc. ■ [with modifier] a number giving the magnitude of a physical property or another measured phenomenon in terms of a standard: *the oral hygiene index was calculated as the sum of the debris and calculus indices.*
3 Mathematics an exponent or other superscript or subscript number appended to a quantity.
4 Printing a symbol shaped like a pointing hand, typically used to draw attention to a note.
5 (**the Index**) short for INDEX LIBRORUM PROHIBITORUM.
▶ v. [with obj.] **1** record (names, subjects, etc.) in an index: *the list indexes theses under regional headings.* ■ provide an index to.
2 link the value of (prices, wages, or other payments) automatically to the value of a price index: *legislation **indexing** wages **to** prices.*
3 [no obj.] (often as noun **indexing**) (of a machine or part of one) rotate or otherwise move from one predetermined position to another in order to carry out a sequence of operations.
– DERIVATIVES **in·dex·a·ble** adj., **in·dex·a·tion** /ˌindekˈsāSHən/ n., **in·dex·er** n., **in·dex·i·ble** adj.
– ORIGIN late Middle English: from Latin *index*, *indic-* 'forefinger, informer, sign,' from *in-* 'toward' + a second element related to *dicere* 'say' or *dicare* 'make known'; compare with INDICATE. The original sense 'index finger' (with which one points) came to mean 'pointer' (late 16th cent.), and figuratively something that serves to point to a fact or conclusion; hence a list of topics in a book ("pointing" to their location).

in·dex card ▶ n. a small card on which information is recorded, typically stored alphabetically with others in a card index.

in·dex case ▶ n. Medicine the first identified case in a group of related cases of a particular communicable or heritable disease.

in·dex fin·ger ▶ n. the finger next to the thumb; the forefinger.

in·dex fos·sil ▶ n. Geology a fossil that is useful for dating and correlating the strata in which it is found.

in·dex·i·cal /inˈdeksikəl/ Linguistics ▶ adj. another term for DEICTIC.
▶ n. an indexical word or expression.
– ORIGIN early 20th cent.: coined in this sense by the American philosopher C. S. Peirce.

In·dex Li·bro·rum Pro·hib·i·to·rum /ˈinˌdeks līˈbrôrəm ˌprōhibəˈtôrəm/ an official list of books that Roman Catholics were forbidden to read or that were to be read only in expurgated editions, as contrary to Catholic faith or morals. The first Index was issued in 1557; it was revised at intervals until abolished in 1966.
– ORIGIN Latin, 'index of forbidden books.'

In·di·a /ˈindēə/ a country in southern Asia that occupies the greater part of the Indian subcontinent; pop. 1,156,897,800 (est. 2009); capital, New Delhi; official languages, Hindi and English (14 other languages are recognized as official in certain regions; of these, Bengali, Gujarati, Marathi, Tamil, Telugu, and Urdu have the most first-language speakers). Hindi name BHARAT. ■ a code word representing the letter I, used in radio communication.

> Much of India was united under a Muslim sultanate based around Delhi from the 12th century until incorporated in the Mogul empire in the 16th century. Colonial intervention began in the late 17th century, particularly by the British; in 1765, the East India Company acquired the right to administer Bengal. In 1858, after the Indian Mutiny, Britain took over the company's authority, and in 1876 Queen Victoria was proclaimed Empress of India. Independence was won in 1947, at which time India was partitioned, and Pakistan was created from mainly Muslim territories in the northeast (now Bangladesh) and the northwest. A member of the Commonwealth of Nations, India is the second most populous country in the world.

– ORIGIN via Latin from Greek *India*, from *Indos*, the name of the Indus River, from Persian *Hind*, from Sanskrit *sindhu* 'river,' specifically 'the Indus,' also 'the region around the Indus' (compare with SINDHI). Both the Greeks and the Persians extended the name to include all the country east of the Indus. Compare with HINDI and HINDU.

In·di·a ink ▶ n. deep black ink containing dispersed carbon particles, used esp. in drawing and technical graphics.
– ORIGIN mid 17th cent.: originally applied to Chinese and Japanese pigments prepared in solid blocks and imported to Europe via India.

In·di·a·man /ˈindēəmən/ ▶ n. (pl. **Indiamen**) historical a ship engaged in trade with India or the East or West Indies, esp. an East Indiaman.
– ORIGIN early 18th cent.: from INDIA + *-man* from MAN-OF-WAR.

In·di·an /ˈindēən/ ▶ adj. **1** of or relating to the indigenous peoples of America.
2 of or relating to India or to the subcontinent comprising India, Pakistan, and Bangladesh.
▶ n. **1** an American Indian.
2 a native or inhabitant of India, or a person of Indian descent.
– DERIVATIVES **In·di·an·i·za·tion** /ˌindēəniˈzāSHən/ n., **In·di·an·ize** /-ˌnīz/ v., **In·di·an·ness** n.

> **USAGE** Indian, meaning 'native of America before the arrival of Europeans,' is objected to by many who now favor **Native American**. There are others (including many members of these ethnic groups), however, who see nothing wrong with **Indian** or **American Indian**, which are long-established terms, although the preference where possible is to refer to specific peoples, as **Apache**, **Delaware**, and so on. The terms **Amerind** and **Amerindian**, once proposed as alternatives to **Indian**, are used in linguistics and anthropology, but have never gained widespread use. Newer

alternatives, not widely used or established, include **First Nation** (especially in Canada) and the more generic **aboriginal peoples**. It should be noted that **Indian** is held by many not to include some American groups—for example, Aleuts and Eskimos. A further consideration is that **Indian** also (and in some contexts, primarily) refers to inhabitants of India or their descendants, who may be referred to as 'Asian Indians' to prevent misunderstanding. See also usage at **AMERICAN INDIAN.**

In·di·an·a /ˌindēˈanə/ a state in the eastern central US; pop. 6,376,792 (est. 2008); capital, Indianapolis; statehood, Dec. 11, 1816 (19). It was colonized by the French in the early 1700s and ceded to Britain in 1763. It passed to the US in 1783 by the Treaty of Paris.
– DERIVATIVES **In·di·an·an** n. & adj.

In·di·an·ap·o·lis /ˌindēəˈnapələs/ the capital of Indiana, in the central part of the state; pop. 798,382 (est. 2008). The city hosts the Indy 500, an annual 500-mile (804.5-km) car race.

In·di·an bi·son ▶ n. another term for **GAUR.**

In·di·an burn ▶ n. informal an act of placing both hands on a person's arm and then twisting it with a wringing motion to produce a burning sensation.

In·di·an club ▶ n. each of a pair of bottle-shaped clubs swung to exercise the arms in gymnastics or to perform juggling tricks.

In·di·an co·bra ▶ n. another term for **SPECTACLED COBRA.**

In·di·an corn ▶ n. any primitive corn with colorful variegated kernels, dried and used for decoration. ■ another term for **CORN**[1].

In·di·an de·fense ▶ n. [usu. with adj.] Chess a defense in which Black responds to White's advance of the queen's pawn by moving the king's knight to the *f*6 square, usually following with a fianchetto.

In·di·an el·e·phant ▶ n. the elephant of southern Asia, which is smaller than the African elephant, with smaller ears and only one lip to the trunk. It is often tamed as a beast of burden in India. Also called **ASIAN ELEPHANT.** ● *Elephas maximus*, family Elephantidae.

In·di·an file ▶ n. another term for **SINGLE FILE.**
– ORIGIN mid 18th cent.: so called because it was believed that North American Indians usually marched in this order.

In·di·an hemp ▶ n. see **HEMP.**

In·di·an ink ▶ n. British term for **INDIA INK.**

In·di·an·ism /ˈindēəˌnizəm/ ▶ n. **1** devotion to or adoption of the customs and culture of North American Indians.
2 a word or idiom characteristic of Indian English or North American Indians.

In·di·an meal ▶ n. meal ground from corn.

In·di·an Mu·ti·ny a revolt of Indians against British rule, 1857–58. Also called **SEPOY MUTINY.**

Discontent with British administration resulted in widespread mutinies in British garrison towns, with accompanying massacres of white soldiers and inhabitants. After a series of sieges (most notably that of Lucknow) and battles, the revolt was put down; it was followed by the institution of direct rule by the British Crown in place of the East India Company administration.

In·di·an Na·tion·al Con·gress a broad-based political party in India, founded in 1885 and the principal party in government since independence in 1947. Following splits in the party, the Indian National Congress (I), formed by Indira Gandhi as a breakaway group (the I standing for Indira), was confirmed in 1981 as the official Congress Party.

In·di·an O·cean an ocean south of India that extends from the eastern coast of Africa to the East Indies and Australia.

In·di·an paint·brush ▶ n. see **PAINTBRUSH** (sense 2).

In·di·an pipe ▶ n. a plant with a yellowish stem that bears a single drooping flower, native to North America and northeastern Asia. It lacks chlorophyll and obtains nourishment via symbiotic fungi in its roots. ● *Monotropa uniflora*, family Monotropaceae.

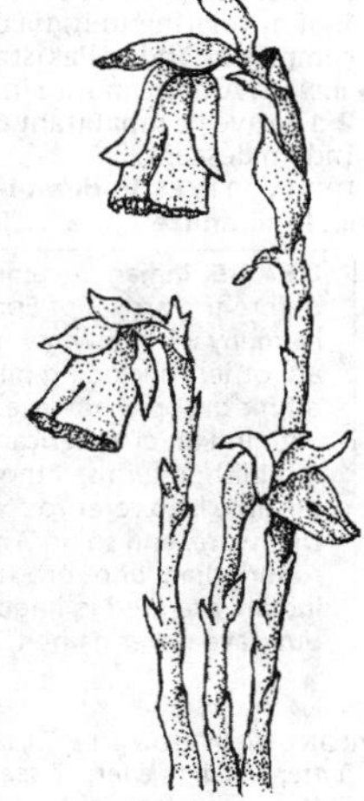
Indian pipe

In·di·an poke ▶ n. see **POKE**[3] (sense 2).

In·di·an red ▶ n. a red ferric oxide pigment made typically by roasting ferrous salts.

In·di·an rhi·noc·er·os ▶ n. a large one-horned rhinoceros with prominent skin folds and a prehensile upper lip, found in northeastern India and Nepal. ● *Rhinoceros unicornis*, family Rhinocerotidae.

In·di·an rope-trick ▶ n. the supposed feat of climbing an upright, unsupported length of rope.

In·di·an run·ner ▶ n. a duck of a slender upright breed, typically with white or yellowish-brown plumage, kept for egg laying.

In·di·an shot ▶ n. see **CANNA.**

In·di·an sign ▶ n. dated a magic spell or curse.

In·di·an sub·con·ti·nent the part of Asia south of the Himalayas that forms a peninsula, which extends into the Indian Ocean between the Arabian Sea and the Bay of Bengal. Historically forming the whole territory of greater India, the region is now divided among India, Pakistan, and Bangladesh.

In·di·an sum·mer ▶ n. a period of unusually dry, warm weather occurring in late autumn. ■ a period of happiness or success occurring late in life.

In·di·an yel·low ▶ n. an orange-yellow pigment originally obtained from the urine of cows fed on mango leaves.

In·di·a pa·per ▶ n. soft, absorbent paper, originally imported from China and used for proofs of engravings. ■ very thin, tough, opaque printing paper, used esp. for Bibles.

In·di·a rub·ber ▶ n. natural rubber.

In·di·a rub·ber tree ▶ n. another term for **RUBBER TREE.**

In·dic /ˈindik/ ▶ adj. relating to or denoting the group of Indo-European languages comprising Sanskrit and the modern Indian languages that are its descendants.
▶ n. this language group.
– ORIGIN via Latin from Greek *Indikos*, from *India* (see **INDIA**).

indic. ▶ abbr. ■ indicating. ■ indicative. ■ indicator.

in·di·can /ˈindiˌkan/ ▶ n. Biochemistry a potassium salt present in urine, in which it occurs as a product of the metabolism of indole. ● Alternative name: **potassium indoxylsulphate**; chem. formula $C_8H_6NOSO_2OH$.
– ORIGIN mid 19th cent.: from Latin *indicum* 'indigo' (because of its early use denoting an indoxyl glucoside occurring in the leaves of indigo plants) + **-AN.**

in·di·cant /ˈindikənt/ ▶ n. a thing that indicates something.
– ORIGIN early 17th cent.: from Latin *indicant-* 'pointing out,' from the verb *indicare* (see **INDICATE**).

in·di·cate /ˈindiˌkāt/ ▶ v. [with obj.] **1** point out; show: *dotted lines indicate the text's margins.* ■ be a sign or symptom of; strongly imply: *sales indicate a growing market for such art* | [with clause] *his tone indicated that he didn't hold out much hope.* ■ admit to or state briefly: *the president indicated his willingness to use force against the rebels.* ■ (of a person) direct attention to (someone or something) by means of a gesture: *he indicated Cindy with a brief nod of the head.* ■ (of a gauge or meter) register a reading of (a quantity, dimension, etc.).
2 suggest as a desirable or necessary course of action: *the treatment is likely to be indicated in severely depressed patients.*
– ORIGIN early 17th cent.: from Latin *indicat-* 'pointed out,' from the verb *indicare*, from *in-* 'toward' + *dicare* 'make known.'

in·di·cat·ed horse·pow·er ▶ n. the power produced in a reciprocating engine by the working of the cylinders.

in·di·ca·tion /ˌindiˈkāsʜən/ ▶ n. a sign or piece of information that indicates something: *the visit was an indication of the improvement in relations between the countries.* ■ a reading given by a gauge or meter. ■ a symptom that suggests certain medical treatment is necessary: *heavy bleeding is a common indication for hysterectomy.*

in·dic·a·tive /inˈdikətiv/ ▶ adj. **1** serving as a sign or indication of something: *having recurrent dreams is not necessarily indicative of any psychological problem.*
2 Grammar denoting a mood of verbs expressing simple statement of a fact. Compare with **SUBJUNCTIVE.**
▶ n. Grammar a verb in the indicative mood. ■ (**the indicative**) the indicative mood.
– DERIVATIVES **in·dic·a·tive·ly** adv.

in·di·ca·tor /ˈindiˌkātər/ ▶ n. **1** a thing, esp. a trend or fact, that indicates the state or level of something: *car ownership is frequently used as an indicator of affluence.*
2 a device providing specific information on the state or condition of something, in particular: ■ [usu. with modifier] a gauge or meter of a specified kind: *a speed indicator.* ■ Brit. a turn signal.
3 Chemistry a compound that changes color at a specific pH value or in the presence of a particular substance and can be used to monitor acidity, alkalinity, or the progress of a reaction.
4 (also **indicator species**) an animal or plant species that can be used to infer conditions in a particular habitat.

in·di·ca·tor di·a·gram ▶ n. a diagram of the variation of pressure and volume within a cylinder of a reciprocating engine.

in·dic·a·to·ry /inˈdikəˌtôrē/ ▶ adj. rare term for **INDICATIVE.**

in·dic·a·trix /ˈindiˌkātriks, inˈdikə-/ (also **optical indicatrix**) ▶ n. (pl. **indicatrices** /-triˌsēz/) Crystallography an imaginary ellipsoidal surface whose axes represent the refractive indices of a crystal for light following different directions with respect to the crystal axes.
– ORIGIN late 19th cent.: modern Latin, feminine of Latin *indicator* 'something that points out.'

in·di·ces /ˈindiˌsēz/ plural form of **INDEX.**

in·di·ci·a /inˈdisʜ(ē)ə/ ▶ plural n. formal signs, indications, or distinguishing marks: *learned footnotes and other indicia of scholarship.* ■ markings used on address labels or bulk mail as a substitute for stamps.
– ORIGIN early 17th cent.: plural of Latin *indicium*, from *index, indic-* 'informer, sign.'

in·dic·o·lite /inˈdikəˌlīt/ ▶ n. an indigo-blue gem variety of lithium-bearing tourmaline.
– ORIGIN early 19th cent.: from Latin *indicum* 'indigo' + **-LITE.**

in·dict /inˈdīt/ ▶ v. [with obj.] formally accuse of or charge with a serious crime: *his former manager was indicted for fraud.*
– DERIVATIVES **in·dict·ee** /ˌindīˈtē/ n., **in·dict·er** n.
– ORIGIN Middle English *endite, indite*, from Anglo-Norman French *enditer*, based on Latin *indicere* 'proclaim, appoint,' from *in-* 'toward' + *dicere* 'pronounce, utter.'

in·dict·a·ble /inˈdītəbəl/ ▶ adj. (of an offense) rendering the person who commits it liable to be charged with a serious crime that warrants a trial by jury. ■ (of a person) liable to be charged with a crime.

in·dic·tion /inˈdiksʜən/ ▶ n. historical a fiscal period of fifteen years used as a means of dating events and transactions in the Roman Empire and in the papal and some royal courts. The system was instituted by the Emperor Constantine in AD 313 and was used until the 16th century in some places. ■ [with numeral] a particular year in such a period.
– ORIGIN from Latin *indiction-*, from the verb *indicere* (see **INDICT**).

in·dict·ment /inˈdītmənt/ ▶ n. **1** Law a formal charge or accusation of a serious crime: *an indictment for conspiracy.* ■ the action of indicting or being indicted: *the indictment of twelve people who had imported cocaine.*
2 a thing that serves to illustrate that a system or situation is bad and deserves to be condemned: *these rapidly escalating crime figures are an indictment of our society.*
– ORIGIN Middle English *enditement, inditement*, from Anglo-Norman French *enditement*, from *enditer* (see **INDICT**).

in·die /ˈindē/ ▶ adj. (of a pop group, record label, or film company) not belonging to or affiliated with a major record or film company. ■ characteristic of the deliberately unpolished or uncommercial style of small independent pop groups.
▶ n. a pop group, record label, or film company of this type. ■ indie music regarded as a genre.
– ORIGIN 1920s (first used with reference to film production): abbreviation of **INDEPENDENT.**

in·dif·fer·ence /inˈdif(ə)rəns/ ▶ n. lack of interest, concern, or sympathy: *she shrugged, feigning indifference.* ■ unimportance: *it cannot be regarded as a matter of indifference.*
– ORIGIN late Middle English (in the sense 'being neither good nor bad'): from Latin *indifferentia*, from *in-* 'not' + *different-* 'differing, deferring' (from the verb *differre*).

in·dif·fer·ence curve ▶ n. Economics a curve on a graph (the axes of which represent quantities of two commodities) linking those combinations of quantities that the consumer regards as of equal value.

in·dif·fer·ent /inˈdif(ə)rənt/ ▶ adj. **1** having no particular interest or sympathy; unconcerned: *they all seemed indifferent rather than angry* | *most workers were indifferent to foreign affairs.*
2 neither good nor bad; mediocre: *attempts to distinguish between good, bad, and indifferent*

work. ■ not especially good; fairly bad: *a pair of indifferent watercolors.*
3 neutral in respect of some specified physical property. ■ Biology, archaic not specialized; undifferentiated.
– DERIVATIVES **in·dif·fer·ent·ly** adv.
– ORIGIN late Middle English (in the sense 'having no partiality for or against'): via Old French from Latin *indifferent-* 'not making any difference,' from *in-* 'not' + *different-* 'differing' (see DIFFERENT).

in·dif·fer·ent·ism /in'dif(ə)rən,tizəm/ ▶ n. the belief that differences of religious belief are of no importance.
– DERIVATIVES **in·dif·fer·ent·ist** n.

in·di·gence /'indijəns/ ▶ n. a state of extreme poverty: *he did valuable work toward the relief of indigence.*

in·di·gene /'indi,jēn/ ▶ n. an indigenous person.
– ORIGIN late 16th cent.: from French *indigène,* from Latin *indigena,* from *indi-* (strengthened form of *in-* 'into') + an element related to *gignere* 'beget.'

in·dig·e·nize /in'dijə,nīz/ ▶ v. [with obj.] bring (something) under the control, dominance, or influence of the people native to an area: *English has been indigenized in different parts of the world.*
– DERIVATIVES **in·dig·e·ni·za·tion** /-,dijəni'zāsHən/ n.

in·dig·e·nous /in'dijənəs/ ▶ adj. originating or occurring naturally in a particular place; native: *the indigenous peoples of Siberia | coriander is indigenous to southern Europe.*
– DERIVATIVES **in·di·ge·ne·i·ty** /in,dijə'nēitē/ n., **in·dig·e·nous·ly** adv., **in·dig·e·nous·ness** n.
– ORIGIN mid 17th cent.: from Latin *indigena* 'a native' (see INDIGENE) + -OUS.

in·di·gent /'indijənt/ ▶ adj. poor; needy.
▶ n. a needy person.
– ORIGIN late Middle English: via Old French from late Latin *indigent-* 'lacking,' from the verb *indigere,* from *indi-* (strengthened form of *in-* 'into') + *egere* 'to need.'

in·di·gest·i·ble /,indi'jestəbəl/ ▶ adj. **1** (of food) difficult or impossible to digest.
2 too complex or awkward to read or understand easily: *a turgid and indigestible book.*
– DERIVATIVES **in·di·gest·i·bil·i·ty** /-,jestə'bilitē/ n., **in·di·gest·i·bly** /-blē/ adv.
– ORIGIN late 15th cent.: via French from late Latin *indigestibilis,* from *in-* 'not' + *digestibilis* (see DIGESTIBLE).

in·di·ges·tion /,indi'jescHən, -dī-/ ▶ n. pain or discomfort in the stomach associated with difficulty in digesting food.
– DERIVATIVES **in·di·ges·tive** /-tiv/ adj.
– ORIGIN late Middle English: from late Latin *indigestio(n-),* from *in-* (expressing negation) + *digestio* (see DIGESTION).

In·di·gir·ka /,ində'girkə/ a river in eastern Siberia in Russia that flows north for 1,112 miles (1,779 km) to the Arctic Ocean, where it forms a wide delta.

in·dig·nant /in'dignənt/ ▶ adj. feeling or showing anger or annoyance at what is perceived as unfair treatment: *he was indignant at being the object of suspicion.*
– DERIVATIVES **in·dig·nant·ly** adv.
– ORIGIN late 16th cent.: from Latin *indignant-* 'regarding as unworthy,' from the verb *indignari,* from *in-* 'not' + *dignus* 'worthy.'

in·dig·na·tion /,indig'nāsHən/ ▶ n. anger or annoyance provoked by what is perceived as unfair treatment: *the letter filled Lucy with indignation.*
– ORIGIN late Middle English (also in the sense 'disdain, contempt'): from Latin *indignatio(n-),* from *indignari* 'regard as unworthy.'

in·dig·ni·ty /in'dignitē/ ▶ n. (pl. **indignities**) treatment or circumstances that cause one to feel shame or to lose one's dignity: *the indignity of needing financial help | he was subjected to all manner of indignities.*
– ORIGIN late 16th cent.: from French *indignité* or Latin *indignitas,* from *indignari* 'regard as unworthy.'

in·di·go /'indi,gō/ ▶ n. (pl. **indigos** or **indigoes**) **1** a tropical plant of the pea family, which was formerly widely cultivated as a source of dark blue dye.
● Genus *Indigofera,* family Leguminosae: several species, in particular *I. tinctoria.*
2 the dark blue dye obtained from this plant. ■ a color between blue and violet in the spectrum.
– ORIGIN mid 16th cent.: from Portuguese *índigo,* via Latin from Greek *indikon,* from *indikos* 'Indian (dye)' (see INDIC).

in·di·go bunt·ing ▶ n. see BUNTING[1].

in·di·goid /'indi,goid/ ▶ adj. (of a dye) related to indigotin in molecular structure.

in·di·go snake ▶ n. a large, harmless American snake that typically has bluish-black skin that may be patterned. Also called CRIBO, BLUE GOPHER SNAKE (see GOPHER SNAKE). ● *Drymarchon corais,* family Colubridae.

in·dig·o·tin /in'digətin, ,ində'gōtn/ ▶ n. Chemistry a dark blue crystalline compound that is the main constituent of the dye indigo. ● Chem. formula: $(C_8H_6NO)_2$.
– ORIGIN mid 19th cent.: from INDIGO + *-t-* (for ease of pronunciation) + -IN[1].

In·di·o[1] /'indē,ō/ a desert city in southern California, southeast of Palm Springs; pop. 84,443 (est. 2008).

In·di·o[2] ▶ n. (pl. **Indios**) a member of any of the indigenous peoples of America or eastern Asia in areas formerly subject to Spain or Portugal.
– ORIGIN mid 19th cent.: from Spanish and Portuguese, literally 'Indian.'

in·di·rect /,ində'rekt/ ▶ adj. **1** not directly caused by or resulting from something: *full employment would have an indirect effect on wage levels.* ■ not done directly; conducted through intermediaries: *the nature of the threat can be pieced together only from indirect evidence.* ■ (of costs) deriving from overhead charges or subsidiary work. ■ (of taxation) levied on goods and services rather than income or profits.
2 (of a route) not straight; not following the shortest way. ■ (of lighting) from a concealed source and diffusely reflected. ■ Soccer denoting a free kick from which a goal may not be scored directly.
3 avoiding direct mention or exposition of a subject: *an indirect attack on the Senator.*
– DERIVATIVES **in·di·rect·ness** n.
– ORIGIN late Middle English (in the sense 'not in full grammatical concord'): from medieval Latin *indirectus,* from *in-* 'not' + *directus* (see DIRECT).

in·di·rec·tion /,ində'reksHən/ ▶ n. indirectness or lack of straightforwardness in action, speech, or progression: *his love of intrigue and sly indirection.*
– ORIGIN late 16th cent.: from INDIRECT, on the pattern of *direction.*

in·di·rect·ly /,ində'rektli/ ▶ adv. **1** in a way that is not directly caused by something; incidentally: *the losses indirectly affect us all.*
2 without having had direct experience; at second hand: *I heard of the damage indirectly.*
3 through implication; obliquely: *both writers refer, if only indirectly, to a wealth of other art.*

in·di·rect ob·ject ▶ n. Grammar a noun phrase referring to someone or something that is affected by the action of a transitive verb (typically as a recipient), but is not the primary object (e.g., *him* in *give him the book*). Compare with DIRECT OBJECT.

in·di·rect ques·tion ▶ n. Grammar a question in reported speech, e.g., *they asked who I was.*

in·di·rect rule ▶ n. a system of government of one nation by another in which the governed people retain certain administrative, legal, and other powers.

in·di·rect speech ▶ n. another term for REPORTED SPEECH.

in·dis·cern·i·ble /indi'sərnəbəl/ ▶ adj. impossible to see or clearly distinguish.
– DERIVATIVES **in·dis·cern·i·bil·i·ty** n., **in·dis·cern·i·bly** adv.

in·dis·ci·pline /in'disəplin/ ▶ n. lack of discipline.

in·dis·creet /,indi'skrēt/ ▶ adj. having, showing, or proceeding from too great a readiness to reveal things that should remain secret or private: *they have been embarrassed by indiscreet friends.*
– DERIVATIVES **in·dis·creet·ly** adv.
– ORIGIN late Middle English (originally as *indiscrete* in the sense 'lacking discernment or judgment'): from late Latin *indiscretus* 'not separate or distinguishable' (in medieval Latin 'careless, indiscreet'), from *in-* 'not' + *discretus* 'separate' (see DISCREET). Compare with INDISCRETE.

in·dis·crete /,indi'skrēt/ ▶ adj. rare not divided into distinct parts.
– ORIGIN early 17th cent. (in the sense 'not separate or distinguishable'; originally as *indiscreet*): from Latin *indiscretus,* from *in-* 'not' + *discretus* 'separate' (see DISCREET). Compare with INDISCREET.

in·dis·cre·tion /,indi'skresHən/ ▶ n. behavior or speech that is indiscreet or displays a lack of good judgment: *he knew himself all too prone to indiscretion | sexual indiscretions.*
– ORIGIN Middle English: from late Latin *indiscretio(n-),* from *in-* (expressing negation) + *discretio* 'separation' (in late Latin 'discernment'), from *discernere* 'separate out, discern.'

in·dis·crim·i·nate /,indi'skrimənit/ ▶ adj. done at random or without careful judgment: *the indiscriminate killing of civilians.* ■ (of a person) not using or exercising discrimination: *she was indiscriminate with her affections.*
– DERIVATIVES **in·dis·crim·i·nate·ly** adv., **in·dis·crim·i·nate·ness** n., **in·dis·crim·i·na·tion** /-,skrimə'nāsHən/ n.
– ORIGIN late 16th cent. (in the sense 'haphazard, not selective'): from IN-[1] 'not' + Latin *discriminatus,* past participle of *discriminare* (see DISCRIMINATE).

in·dis·crim·i·nat·ing /,indi'skrimə,nātiNG/ ▶ adj. making no distinctions; indiscriminate.

in·dis·pen·sa·ble /,indi'spensəbəl/ ▶ adj. absolutely necessary: *he made himself* ***indispensable to*** *the parish priest.*
– DERIVATIVES **in·dis·pen·sa·bil·i·ty** /-,spensə'bilitē/ n., **in·dis·pen·sa·ble·ness** n., **in·dis·pen·sa·bly** /-blē/ adv.
– ORIGIN mid 16th cent. (in the sense 'not to be allowed or provided for by ecclesiastical dispensation'): from medieval Latin *indispensabilis,* from *in-* 'not' + *dispensabilis* (see DISPENSABLE).

in·dis·pose /,indi'spōz/ ▶ v. [with obj.] archaic **1** make (someone) unfit for or unable to do something.
2 make (someone) averse to something: *the miseries of the revolution had totally indisposed the people toward any interference with politics.*

in·dis·posed /,indi'spōzd/ ▶ adj. **1** slightly unwell: *my mother is indisposed.*
2 averse; unwilling: *the potential audience seemed* ***indisposed to*** *attend.*
– ORIGIN late Middle English: from IN-[1] 'not' + DISPOSED, or past participle of *indispose* 'make unwell or unwilling.'

in·dis·po·si·tion /,indispə'zisHən/ ▶ n. **1** mild illness: *she was chiefly confined by indisposition to her bedroom.*
2 lack of enthusiasm or inclination; reluctance: *indisposition to motion, exertion or change | an utter indisposition to do anything whatever.*

in·dis·put·a·ble /indis'pyo͞otəbəl/ ▶ adj. unable to be challenged or denied: *a far from indisputable fact.*
– DERIVATIVES **in·dis·put·a·bil·i·ty** n., **in·dis·put·a·bly** adv.
– ORIGIN mid 16th cent.: from late Latin *indisputabilis,* from *in-* 'not' + *disputabilis* (see DISPUTABLE).

in·dis·so·ci·a·ble /'indi'sōsHəbəl/ ▶ adj. unable to be dissociated: *the three fundamental and indissociable features of market capitalism.*

in·dis·sol·u·ble /,indi'sälyəbəl/ ▶ adj. unable to be destroyed; lasting: *an indissoluble friendship.*
– DERIVATIVES **in·dis·sol·u·bil·i·ty** /-,sälyə'bilitē/ n., **in·dis·sol·u·bly** /-blē/ adv.
– ORIGIN late 15th cent.: from Latin *indissolubilis,* from *in-* 'not' + *dissolubilis* (see DISSOLUBLE).

in·dis·tinct /'indis'tiNGkt/ ▶ adj. not clear or sharply defined: *his speech was slurred and indistinct.*
– DERIVATIVES **in·dis·tinct·ly** adv., **in·dis·tinct·ness** n.
– ORIGIN mid 16th cent.: from Latin *indistinctus,* from *in-* 'not' + *distinctus* 'separated, distinguished' (see DISTINCT).

in·dis·tinc·tive /'indis'tiNGktiv/ ▶ adj. not having a distinctive character or features.
– DERIVATIVES **in·dis·tinc·tive·ly** adv., **in·dis·tinc·tive·ness** n.

in·dis·tin·guish·a·ble /'indis'tiNGgwisHəbəl/ ▶ adj. not able to be identified as different or distinct: *the counterfeit bills were virtually* ***indistinguishable from*** *the real thing.*
– DERIVATIVES **in·dis·tin·guish·a·bly** adv.

in·dite /in'dīt/ ▶ v. [with obj.] archaic write; compose: *he indites the wondrous tale of Our Lord.*
– ORIGIN Middle English *endite,* from Old French *enditier,* based on Latin *indicere* (see INDICT).

in·di·um /'indēəm/ ▶ n. the chemical element of atomic number 49, a soft silvery-white metal occurring naturally in association with zinc and some other metals. (Symbol: **In**)
– ORIGIN mid 19th cent.: from INDIGO (because there are two characteristic indigo lines in its spectrum) + -IUM.

in·di·vid·u·al /,ində'vijəwəl/ ▶ adj. **1** [attrib.] single; separate: *individual tiny flowers.*
2 of or for a particular person: *the individual needs of the children.* ■ designed for use by one person: *individual serving dishes.* ■ characteristic of a particular person or thing: *individual traits of style.* ■ having a striking or unusual character; original: *she creates her own, highly individual, landscapes.*
▶ n. a single human being as distinct from a group, class, or family: *boat trips for parties and individuals.* ■ a single member of a class: *they live in a group or as individuals, depending on the species.* ■ [with adj.]

informal a person of a specified kind: *the most selfish, egotistical individual I have ever met.* ▪ a distinctive or original person.
– ORIGIN late Middle English (in the sense 'indivisible'): from medieval Latin *individualis*, from Latin *individuus*, from *in-* 'not' + *dividuus* 'divisible' (from *dividere* 'to divide').

in·di·vid·u·al·ism /ˌində'vijo͞oəˌlizəm/ ▶ **n.** **1** the habit or principle of being independent and self-reliant. ▪ self-centered feeling or conduct; egoism. **2** a social theory favoring freedom of action for individuals over collective or state control.
– DERIVATIVES **in·di·vid·u·al·ist n. & adj.**

in·di·vid·u·al·is·tic /ˌindivijo͞oə'listik/ ▶ **adj.** **1** characterized by individualism; independent and self-reliant. **2** marked by or expressing individuality; unconventional: *her work is quirky and genuinely individualistic.*
– DERIVATIVES **in·di·vid·u·al·is·ti·cal·ly adv.**

in·di·vid·u·al·i·ty /ˌindəˌvijə'walitē/ ▶ **n.** **1** the quality or character of a particular person or thing that distinguishes them from others of the same kind, esp. when strongly marked: *clothes with real style and individuality.* ▪ **(individualities)** individual characteristics. **2** separate existence: *anything but individuality, anything but aloneness.*
– ORIGIN early 17th cent.: in early use from medieval Latin *individualitas*.

in·di·vid·u·al·ize /ˌində'vijo͞oəˌlīz/ ▶ **v.** [with obj.] give an individual character to: *have your shirt individualized with your own club name.* ▪ (usu. as adj. **individualized**) tailor (something) to suit the individual: *an individualized learning program.*
– DERIVATIVES **in·di·vid·u·al·i·za·tion** /-ˌvijo͞oələ'zāsHən/ **n.**

in·di·vid·u·al·ly /ˌində'vijəwəlē/ ▶ **adv.** **1** one by one; singly; separately: *individually wrapped cheeses.* ▪ in a distinctive manner: *each sign is individually designed and crafted.* **2** personally; in an individual capacity: *partnerships and individually owned firms.*

in·di·vid·u·ate /ˌində'vijo͞oˌāt/ ▶ **v.** [with obj.] distinguish from others of the same kind; single out: *it is easy to individuate and enumerate the significant elements.*
– DERIVATIVES **in·di·vid·u·a·tion** /-ˌvijo͞o'āsHən/ **n.**
– ORIGIN early 17th cent.: from medieval Latin *individuat-* 'singled out,' from the verb *individuare*, from Latin *individuus*, from *in-* 'into' + *dividuus* 'divisible' (from *dividere* 'to divide').

in·di·vis·i·ble /ˌindi'vizəbəl/ ▶ **adj.** unable to be divided or separated: *privilege was indivisible from responsibility.* ▪ (of a number) unable to be divided by another number exactly without leaving a remainder.
– DERIVATIVES **in·di·vis·i·bil·i·ty n., in·di·vis·i·bly adv.**
– ORIGIN late Middle English: from late Latin *indivisibilis*, from *in-* 'not' + *divisibilis* (see DIVISIBLE).

indn. ▶ **abbr.** indication.

Indo- /'indō/ ▶ **comb. form** (used commonly in linguistic and ethnological terms) Indian; Indian and ...: *Indo-Iranian.* ▪ relating to India.
– ORIGIN from Latin *Indus*, from Greek *Indos* 'Indian.'

In·do-Ar·y·an ▶ **adj.** **1** relating to or denoting an Indo-European people who invaded northwestern India in the 2nd millennium BC. See ARYAN. **2** another term for INDIC.

In·do-Chi·na (also **Indochina**) a peninsula in Southeast Asia that consists of Burma (Myanmar), Thailand, Malaya, Laos, Cambodia, and Vietnam; esp. the part of this area that includes Laos, Cambodia, and Vietnam.
– DERIVATIVES **In·do-Chi·nese** /CHī'nēz, -'nēs/ **adj. & n.**

in·do·chin·ite /ˌindō'CHīˌnīt/ ▶ **n.** Geology a tektite from the strewn field in Indo-China.
– ORIGIN 1940s: from INDO-CHINA + -ITE[1].

in·doc·ile /in'däsəl/ ▶ **adj.** difficult to teach or discipline; not submissive.
– DERIVATIVES **in·do·cil·i·ty** /ˌindä'silitē/ **n.**
– ORIGIN early 17th cent.: from French, or from Latin *indocilis*, from *in-* 'not' + *docilis* (see DOCILE).

in·doc·tri·nate /in'däktrəˌnāt/ ▶ **v.** [with obj.] teach (a person or group) to accept a set of beliefs uncritically: *broadcasting was a vehicle for indoctrinating the masses.* ▪ archaic teach or instruct (someone): *he indoctrinated them in systematic theology.*
– DERIVATIVES **in·doc·tri·na·tion** /-ˌdäktrə'nāsHən/ **n., in·doc·tri·na·tor** /-ˌnātər/ **n., in·doc·tri·na·to·ry** /-nəˌtôrē/ **adj.**
– ORIGIN early 17th cent. (formerly also as *endoctrinate*): from EN-[1], IN-[2] 'into' + DOCTRINE + -ATE[3], or from obsolete *indoctrine* (verb), from French *endoctriner*, based on *doctrine* 'doctrine.'

In·do-Eu·ro·pe·an ▶ **adj.** of or relating to the family of languages spoken over the greater part of Europe and Asia as far as northern India. ▪ another term for PROTO-INDO-EUROPEAN.

> The Indo-European languages have a history of over 3,000 years. Their unattested, reconstructed ancestor, Proto-Indo-European, is believed to have been spoken well before 4000 BC in a region somewhere to the north or south of the Black Sea. The family comprises twelve branches: Indic (including Sanskrit and its descendants), Iranian, Anatolian (an extinct group including Hittite and other languages), Armenian, Hellenic (Greek), Albanian (possibly descended from Illyrian), Italic (including Latin and the Romance languages), Celtic, Tocharian (an extinct group from central Asia), Germanic (including English, German, Dutch, Gothic, and the Scandinavian languages), Baltic, and Slavic (including Russian, Czech, Bulgarian, Serbian, and Croatian).

▶ **n.** **1** the ancestral Proto-Indo-European language. ▪ the Indo-European family of languages. **2** a speaker of an Indo-European language, esp. Proto-Indo-European.

In·do-Ger·man·ic ▶ **adj. & n.** former term for INDO-EUROPEAN.

In·do-I·ra·ni·an ▶ **adj.** relating to or denoting a subfamily of Indo-European languages spoken in northern India and Iran.
▶ **n.** the Indo-Iranian subfamily of languages, divided into the Indic group and the Iranian group. Also called ARYAN.

in·dole /'inˌdōl/ ▶ **n.** Chemistry a crystalline organic compound with an unpleasant odor, present in coal tar and in feces. ● A heteroaromatic compound with fused benzene and pyrrole rings; chem. formula: C_8H_7N.
– ORIGIN mid 19th cent.: blend of INDIGO (because obtained artificially from indigo blue) and Latin *oleum* 'oil.'

in·dole·a·ce·tic ac·id /ˌindōlə'sētik, -'setik/ ▶ **n.** Biochemistry a compound that is an acetic acid derivative of indole, esp. one found as a natural growth hormone (auxin) in plants. ● Chem. formula: $C_8H_6(CH_3COOH)N$; seven isomers; auxin is **indole-3-acetic acid**.

in·do·lence /'indələns/ ▶ **n.** avoidance of activity or exertion; laziness: *my failure is probably due to my own indolence.*

in·do·lent /'indələnt/ ▶ **adj.** **1** wanting to avoid activity or exertion; lazy. **2** Medicine (of a disease condition) causing little or no pain. ▪ (esp. of an ulcer) slow to develop, progress, or heal; persistent.
– DERIVATIVES **in·do·lent·ly adv.**
– ORIGIN mid 17th cent.: from late Latin *indolent-*, from *in-* 'not' + *dolere* 'suffer or give pain.' The sense 'idle' arose in the early 18th cent.

In·dol·o·gy /in'däləjē/ ▶ **n.** the study of Indian history, literature, philosophy, and culture.
– DERIVATIVES **In·dol·o·gist** /-jist/ **n.**

In·do-Ma·lay·sian (also **Indo-Malayan**) ▶ **adj.** of or relating to both India and Malaya, in particular: ▪ denoting an ethnological region comprising Sri Lanka, the Malay peninsula, and the Malaysian islands. ▪ (also **Indo-Malesian**) Biology denoting a major biogeographical region comprising Malesia and East, South, and Southeast Asia.

in·do·meth·a·cin /ˌindō'meTHəsin/ ▶ **n.** Medicine a compound with anti-inflammatory, antipyretic, and analgesic properties, used chiefly to treat rheumatoid arthritis and gout. ● Chem. formula: $C_{19}H_{16}NO_4Cl$.
– ORIGIN 1960s: from *indo(le)* + *meth(yl)* + *ac(etic)* + -IN[1].

in·dom·i·ta·ble /in'dämitəbəl/ ▶ **adj.** impossible to subdue or defeat: *a woman of indomitable spirit.*
– DERIVATIVES **in·dom·i·ta·bil·i·ty** /-ˌdämitə'bilitē/ **n., in·dom·i·ta·ble·ness n., in·dom·i·ta·bly** /-blē/ **adv.**
– ORIGIN mid 17th cent. (in the sense 'untamable'): from late Latin *indomitabilis*, from *in-* 'not' + Latin *domitare* 'to tame.'

In·do·ne·sia /ˌində'nēZHə/ a country in Southeast Asia that consists of many islands in the Malay Archipelago; pop. 240,271,500 (est. 2009); capital, Jakarta (on Java); languages, Indonesian (official), Dutch, English, Malay, Balinese, Chinese, Javanese, and others. Former name (until 1949) DUTCH EAST INDIES.

> Indonesia consists of the territories of the former Dutch East Indies, of which the largest are Java, Sumatra, southern Borneo, western New Guinea, the Moluccas, and Sulawesi. The Dutch established control over the area in the 17th century. Independence was won in 1949, although Irian Jaya (now the province of Papua) was not handed over until 1963. An attempted communist coup was crushed by the army in 1965 and East Timor was annexed in 1976. The end of the 20th century saw the introduction of democratic elections and the gaining of full independence by East Timor. In 2004 more than 200,000 people were killed when an earthquake off the coast of Sumatra led to a tsunami that caused devastation in many countries around the Indian Ocean.

– ORIGIN from INDO- + Greek *nēsos* 'island.'

In·do·ne·sian /ˌində'nēZHən/ ▶ **adj.** of or relating to Indonesia, Indonesians, or their languages.
▶ **n.** **1** a native or inhabitant of Indonesia, or a person of Indonesian descent. **2** the group of Austronesian languages, closely related to Malay, that are spoken in Indonesia and neighboring islands. ▪ another term for BAHASA INDONESIA.

in·door /'inˌdôr/ ▶ **adj.** [attrib.] situated, conducted, or used within a building or under cover: *indoor sports.* ▪ of or relating to sports played indoors: *the national indoor champion.*
– ORIGIN early 18th cent. (superseding earlier *within-door*): from IN (as a preposition) + DOOR. Compare with INDOORS.

in·doors /in'dôrz/ ▶ **adv.** into or within a building: *they went indoors and explored the building.*
▶ **n.** the area or space inside a building: *the rain makes indoors feel so warm and safe.*
– ORIGIN late 18th cent. (superseding earlier *within doors*): from INDOOR.

In·do-Pa·cif·ic ▶ **adj.** of or relating to the Indian Ocean and the adjacent parts of the Pacific. ▪ another term for AUSTRONESIAN.
▶ **n.** the Indo-Pacific seas or ocean.

In·dore /'inˌdôr/ a city in central India, in Madhya Pradesh; pop. 1,811,500 (est. 2009).

in·dorse ▶ **v.** variant spelling of ENDORSE.

in·dorse·ment ▶ **n.** variant spelling of ENDORSEMENT.

in·dox·yl /in'däksəl/ ▶ **n.** [as modifier] Chemistry of or denoting the radical $-ONC_8H_6$, derived from a hydroxy derivative of indole and present in indigotin.

In·dra /'indrə/ Hinduism the warrior king of the heavens, god of war and storm, to whom many of the prayers in the Rig Veda are addressed.

in·draft /'inˌdraft/ (Brit. **indraught**) ▶ **n.** the drawing in of something. ▪ an inward flow or current, esp. of air.

in·drawn /'inˌdrôn/ ▶ **adj.** **1** [attrib.] (of breath) taken in. **2** (of a person) shy and introspective.

in·dri /'indrē/ ▶ **n.** (pl. **indris** /'indrēz/) a large, short-tailed Madagascan lemur that jumps from tree to tree in an upright position and rarely comes to the ground. ● *Indri indri*, family Indriidae.
– ORIGIN mid 19th cent.: from Malagasy *indry!* 'behold!' or *indry izy!* 'there he is!,' mistaken for its name. The Malagasy name is *babakoto*.

in·dri·co·there /'indrikōTHe(ə)r/ ▶ **n.** a large ungulate fossil mammal of the Oligocene epoch, related to the rhinoceros. ● Family Hyracodontidae, order Paraceratheriinae.
– ORIGIN 1960s: from modern Latin *Indricotherium* (genus name), from Russian *indrik* 'giant mythical animal' + Greek *thērion* 'wild beast.'

in·du·bi·ta·ble /in'd(y)o͞obitəbəl/ ▶ **adj.** impossible to doubt; unquestionable: *an indubitable truth.*
– DERIVATIVES **in·du·bi·ta·bly** /-blē/ **adv.** [sentence adverb] *indubitably, liberalism parades under many guises.*
– ORIGIN late Middle English: from Latin *indubitabilis*, from *in-* 'not' + *dubitabilis* (see DUBITABLE).

in·duce /in'd(y)o͞os/ ▶ **v.** [with obj.] **1** succeed in persuading or influencing (someone) to do something: [with obj. and infinitive] *the pickets induced many workers to stay away.* **2** bring about or give rise to: *none of these measures induced a change of policy.* ▪ produce (an electric charge or current or a magnetic state) by induction. ▪ (usu. as adj. **induced**) Physics cause (radioactivity) by bombardment with radiation. **3** Medicine bring on (childbirth or abortion) artificially, typically by the use of drugs. ▪ bring on childbirth in (a pregnant woman) in this way. ▪ bring on the birth of (a baby) in this way. **4** Logic derive by inductive reasoning.
– DERIVATIVES **in·duc·er n., in·duc·i·ble adj.**
– ORIGIN late Middle English (formerly also as *enduce*): from Latin *inducere* 'lead in,' from *in-* 'into' + *ducere* 'to lead,' or from French *enduire*. Compare with ENDUE.

in·duced drag ▶ **n.** Aeronautics that part of the drag on an airfoil that arises from the development of lift.

in·duce·ment /inˈd(y)o͞osmənt/ ▶ **n.** a thing that persuades or influences someone to do something: *companies were prepared to build only in return for massive inducements* | [with infinitive] *there is no inducement to wait for payment.* ■ a bribe. ■ Law introductory statements in a pleading explaining the matter in dispute.

in·duct /inˈdəkt/ ▶ **v.** [with obj.] **1** admit (someone) formally to a position or organization: *each worker, if formally inducted into the Mafia, is known as a "soldier."* ■ formally introduce (a member of the clergy) into possession of a benefice. ■ enlist (someone) for military service. ■ (**induct someone in/into**) introduce someone to (a difficult or obscure subject): *my master inducted me into the skills of magic.*
2 archaic install in a seat or room.
– DERIVATIVES **in·duc·tee** /ˌindəkˈtē/ **n.**
– ORIGIN late Middle English: from Latin *induct-* 'led into,' from the verb *inducere* (see **INDUCE**).

in·duc·tance /inˈdəktəns/ ▶ **n.** Physics the property of an electric conductor or circuit that causes an electromotive force to be generated by a change in the current flowing: *the inductance of the winding* | *an inductance of 40 mH.* ■ a component with this property.
– ORIGIN late 19th cent.: from **INDUCTION** + **-ANCE**.

in·duc·tion /inˈdəkSHən/ ▶ **n. 1** the action or process of inducting someone to a position or organization: *the league's induction into the Baseball Hall of Fame.* ■ [usu. as modifier] a formal introduction to a new job or position: *an induction course.* ■ enlistment into military service.
2 the process or action of bringing about or giving rise to something: *isolation, starvation, and other forms of stress induction.* ■ Medicine the process of bringing on childbirth or abortion by artificial means, typically by the use of drugs.
3 Logic the inference of a general law from particular instances. Often contrasted with **DEDUCTION**. ■ (**induction of**) the production of (facts) to prove a general statement. ■ (also **mathematical induction**) Mathematics a means of proving a theorem by showing that if it is true of any particular case, it is true of the next case in a series, and then showing that it is indeed true in one particular case.
4 Physics the production of an electric or magnetic state by the proximity (without contact) of an electrified or magnetized body. See also **MAGNETIC INDUCTION**. ■ the production of an electric current in a conductor by varying the magnetic field applied to the conductor.
5 the stage of the working cycle of an internal combustion engine in which the fuel mixture is drawn into the cylinders.
– ORIGIN late Middle English: from Latin *inductio(n-)*, from the verb *inducere* 'lead into' (see **INDUCE**).

in·duc·tion coil ▶ **n.** a coil for generating intermittent high voltage from a direct current.

in·duc·tion hard·en·ing ▶ **n.** Metallurgy a process for hardening steel surfaces by induction heating followed by quenching.

in·duc·tion heat·ing ▶ **n.** heating of a material by inducing an electric current within it.

in·duc·tion loop ▶ **n.** a sound system in which a loop of wire around an area in a building, such as a theater, produces an electromagnetic signal received directly by hearing aids used by the partially deaf.

in·duc·tive /inˈdəktiv/ ▶ **adj. 1** characterized by the inference of general laws from particular instances: *instinct rather than inductive reasoning marked her approach to life.*
2 of, relating to, or caused by electric or magnetic induction. ■ possessing inductance.
– DERIVATIVES **in·duc·tive·ly adv.**, **in·duc·tive·ness n.**
– ORIGIN late Middle English (in the sense 'leading to'): from Old French *inductif, -ive* or late Latin *inductivus* 'hypothetical' (later 'inducing, leading to'), from Latin *inducere* (see **INDUCE**). Sense 1 dates from the mid 18th cent.

in·duc·tiv·ism /inˈdəktəˌvizəm/ ▶ **n.** the use of or preference for inductive methods of reasoning, esp. in science.
– DERIVATIVES **in·duc·tiv·ist n. & adj.**

in·duc·tor /inˈdəktər/ ▶ **n. 1** a component in an electric or electronic circuit that possesses inductance.
2 a substance that promotes an equilibrium reaction by reacting with one of the substances produced.
– ORIGIN mid 17th cent. (in the sense 'a person who inducts or initiates'): from late Latin, from Latin *inducere* (see **INDUCE**), or from **INDUCT** + **-OR**[1]. Current senses date from the early 20th cent.

in·due ▶ **v.** variant spelling of **ENDUE**.

in·dulge /inˈdəlj/ ▶ **v.** [no obj.] (**indulge in**) allow oneself to enjoy the pleasure of: *we indulged in some hot fudge sundaes.* ■ become involved in (an activity, typically one that is undesirable or disapproved of): *I don't indulge in idle gossip.* ■ informal allow oneself to enjoy a particular pleasure, esp. that of alcohol: *I only indulge on special occasions.* ■ [with obj.] satisfy or yield freely to (a desire or interest): *she was able to indulge a growing passion for literature.* ■ [with obj.] allow (someone) to enjoy a desired pleasure: *I spent time indulging myself with secret feasts.*
– DERIVATIVES **in·dulg·er n.**
– ORIGIN early 17th cent. (in the sense 'treat with excessive kindness'): from Latin *indulgere* 'give free rein to.'

in·dul·gence /inˈdəljəns/ ▶ **n. 1** the action or fact of indulging: *indulgence in self-pity.* ■ the state or attitude of being indulgent or tolerant: *she regarded his affairs with a casual, slightly amused indulgence.* ■ a thing that is indulged in; a luxury: *Claire collects shoes—it is her indulgence.*
2 chiefly historical (in the Roman Catholic Church) a grant by the pope of remission of the temporal punishment in purgatory still due for sins after absolution. The unrestricted sale of indulgences by pardoners was a widespread abuse during the later Middle Ages.
3 an extension of the time in which a bill or debt has to be paid.
– ORIGIN late Middle English: via Old French from Latin *indulgentia*, from the verb *indulgere* (see **INDULGE**).

in·dul·gent /inˈdəljənt/ ▶ **adj.** having or indicating a tendency to be overly generous to or lenient with someone: *indulgent parents.* ■ self-indulgent: *a slightly adolescent, indulgent account of a love affair.*
– DERIVATIVES **in·dul·gent·ly adv.**
– ORIGIN early 16th cent.: from French, or from Latin *indulgent-* 'giving free rein to,' from the verb *indulgere.*

in·du·line /ˈind(y)əˌlēn, -lin/ ▶ **n.** any of a group of insoluble blue azine dyes.
– ORIGIN late 19th cent.: from *indo-* (denoting indigo) + **-ULE** + **-INE**[4].

in·dult /inˈdəlt/ ▶ **n.** (in the Roman Catholic Church) a license granted by the pope authorizing an act that the common law of the Church does not sanction.
– ORIGIN late 15th cent.: from French, from late Latin *indultum* 'grant, concession,' neuter past participle of Latin *indulgere* 'indulge.'

in·du·men·tum /ˌind(y)əˈmentəm/ ▶ **n.** (pl. **indumenta** /-tə/) Botany & Zoology a covering of hairs (or feathers) on an animal or plant.
– ORIGIN mid 19th cent.: from Latin, literally 'garment,' from *induere* 'put on, don.'

in·du·rate /ˈind(y)əˌrāt/ ▶ **v.** [with obj.] (usu. as adj. **indurated**) harden: *a bed of indurated clay.*
– DERIVATIVES **in·du·ra·tion** /ˌind(y)əˈrāSHən/ **n.**, **in·du·ra·tive** /-ˌrātiv/ **adj.**
– ORIGIN mid 16th cent.: from Latin *indurat-* 'made hard,' from the verb *indurare* (based on *durus* 'hard').

In·dus[1] /ˈindəs/ a river in southern Asia, about 1,800 miles (2,900 km) long, that flows from Tibet through Kashmir and Pakistan to the Arabian Sea. Along its valley an early civilization flourished from *c.*2600 to 1760 BC.

In·dus[2] /ˈindəs/ Astronomy an inconspicuous southern constellation (the Indian), between Capricornus and Pavo. ■ (as genitive **Indi** /ˈindī/) used with a preceding letter or numeral to designate a star in this constellation: *the star Alpha Indi.*
– ORIGIN Latin.

indus. ▶ **abbr.** industrial or industry.

in·du·si·um /inˈd(y)o͞ozHēəm, -zēəm/ ▶ **n.** (pl. **indusia** /-zHēə, -zēə/) chiefly Botany a thin membranous covering, esp. a shield covering a sorus on a fern frond.
– ORIGIN early 18th cent.: from Latin, literally 'tunic,' from *induere* 'put on, don.'

in·dus·tri·al /inˈdəstrēəl/ ▶ **adj.** of, relating to, or characterized by industry: *a small industrial town.* ■ having highly developed industries: *the major industrial nations.* ■ designed or suitable for use in industry: *industrial heating oil.* ■ (of a disease or injury) contracted or sustained in the course of employment, esp. in a factory. ■ relating to or denoting a type of harsh, uncompromising rock music incorporating sounds resembling those produced by industrial machinery.
▶ **n.** (**industrials**) shares in industrial companies.
– DERIVATIVES **in·dus·tri·al·ly adv.**
– ORIGIN late 15th cent.: from **INDUSTRY** + **-AL**; in later use influenced by French *industriel.*

in·dus·tri·al ar·chae·ol·o·gy ▶ **n.** the study of equipment and buildings formerly used in industry.

in·dus·tri·al dia·mond ▶ **n.** a small diamond, not of gem quality, used in abrasives and in cutting and drilling tools.

in·dus·tri·al es·pi·o·nage ▶ **n.** spying directed toward discovering the secrets of a rival manufacturer or other industrial company.

in·dus·tri·al es·tate ▶ **n.** British term for **INDUSTRIAL PARK**.

in·dus·tri·al·ism /inˈdəstrēəˌlizəm/ ▶ **n.** a social or economic system built on manufacturing industries.

in·dus·tri·al·ist /inˈdəstrēəlist/ ▶ **n.** a person involved in the ownership and management of industry.

in·dus·tri·al·ize /inˈdəstrēəˌlīz/ ▶ **v.** [with obj.] (often as adj. **industrialized**) develop industries in (a country or region) on a wide scale: *the industrialized nations.* ■ [no obj.] (of a country or region) build up a system of industries: *the country needs to industrialize to create both exports and jobs.*
– DERIVATIVES **in·dus·tri·al·i·za·tion** /inˌdəstrēəliˈzāSHən/ **n.**

in·dus·tri·al mel·a·nism ▶ **n.** Zoology the prevalence of dark-colored varieties of animals (esp. moths) in industrial areas where they are better camouflaged against predators than paler forms.

in·dus·tri·al park ▶ **n.** an area of land developed as a site for factories and other industrial businesses.

in·dus·tri·al re·la·tions ▶ **plural n.** the relations between management and workers in industry.

In·dus·tri·al Rev·o·lu·tion the rapid development of industry that occurred in Britain in the late 18th and 19th centuries, brought about by the introduction of machinery. It was characterized by the use of steam power, the growth of factories, and the mass production of manufactured goods.

in·dus·tri·al-strength ▶ **adj.** very strong or powerful: *an industrial-strength cleaner.*

in·dus·tri·al un·ion /inˈdəstrēəl ˈyo͞onyən/ ▶ **n.** see **VERTICAL UNION**.

In·dus·tri·al Work·ers of the World (abbr.: **IWW**) a radical US labor movement, founded in Chicago in 1905 and, as part of the syndicalist movement, dedicated to the overthrow of capitalism. Its popularity declined after World War I, and by 1925 its membership was insignificant. Also called the **WOBBLIES**.

in·dus·tri·ous /inˈdəstrēəs/ ▶ **adj.** diligent and hard-working.
– DERIVATIVES **in·dus·tri·ous·ly adv.**, **in·dus·tri·ous·ness n.**
– ORIGIN late 15th cent. (in the sense 'skillful, clever, ingenious'): from French *industrieux* or late Latin *industriosus*, from Latin *industria* 'diligence.'

in·dus·try /ˈindəstrē/ ▶ **n.** (pl. **industries**)
1 economic activity concerned with the processing of raw materials and manufacture of goods in factories: *the competitiveness of American industry.* ■ [with adj. or noun modifier] a particular form or branch of economic or commercial activity: *the car industry* | *the tourist industry.* ■ [with adj. or noun modifier] informal an activity or domain in which a great deal of time or effort is expended: *the Shakespeare industry.*
2 hard work: *the kitchen became* **a hive of industry**.
– ORIGIN late Middle English (sense 2): from French *industrie* or Latin *industria* 'diligence.'

in·dwell /inˈdwel/ ▶ **v.** (past and past participle **indwelt**)
1 [with obj.] be permanently present in (someone's soul or mind); possess spiritually: *the Holy Spirit descended to indwell the believers.*
2 (as adj. **indwelling**) Medicine (of a catheter, needle, etc.) fixed in a person's body for a long period of time.
– DERIVATIVES **in·dwell·er n.**
– ORIGIN late Middle English: originally translating Latin *inhabitare.*

In·dy /ˈindē/ ▶ **n.** a form of auto racing in which specially constructed cars are driven around a banked, regular, typically oval circuit, which allows for exceptionally high speeds.
– ORIGIN 1950s: named after **INDIANAPOLIS**, where the principal Indy race is held.

In·dy car ▶ **n.** a type of car used in Indy racing.
▶ **adj.** of or relating to Indy or Indy cars.

-ine[1] ▶ **suffix 1** (forming adjectives) belonging to; resembling in nature: *Alpine* | *canine.*
2 forming adjectives from taxonomic names (such as *bovine* from the genus *Bos*).
– ORIGIN from French *-in, -ine*, or from Latin *-inus.*

-ine[2] ▶ **suffix** forming adjectives from the names of minerals, plants, etc.: *crystalline* | *hyacinthine.*
– ORIGIN from Latin *-inus*, from Greek *-inos.*

-ine[3] ▶ suffix forming feminine common nouns and proper names such as *heroine, Josephine.*
– ORIGIN from French, via Latin *-ina* from Greek *-inē,* or from German *-in.*

-ine[4] ▶ suffix **1** forming chiefly abstract nouns and diminutives such as *doctrine, medicine, figurine.*
2 Chemistry forming names of alkaloids, halogens, amines, amino acids, and other substances: *cocaine | chlorine | thymine.*
– ORIGIN from French, from the Latin feminine form *-ina.*

in·e·bri·ant /i'nēbrēənt/ ▶ adj. (of a substance) intoxicating: *beware of inebriant concoctions disguised as ordinary punch.*
▶ n. an inebriating substance or agent; an intoxicant: *the seedpod is a powerful inebriant.*

in·e·bri·ate formal or humorous ▶ v. /i'nēbrē,āt/ [with obj.] (often as adj. **inebriated**) make (someone) drunk; intoxicate.
▶ n. /-brē-it/ a drunkard.
▶ adj. /-brē-it/ drunk; intoxicated.
– DERIVATIVES **in·e·bri·e·ty** /,ini'brī-itē/ n.
– ORIGIN late Middle English (as an adjective): from Latin *inebriatus,* past participle of *inebriare* 'intoxicate' (based on *ebrius* 'drunk').

in·e·bri·a·tion /i,nēbrē'āsHən/ ▶ n. formal or humorous drunkenness; intoxication: *they were in an advanced state of inebriation.*

in·ed·i·ble /in'edəbəl/ ▶ adj. not fit or suitable for eating: *an inedible variety of mushroom.*
– DERIVATIVES **in·ed·i·bil·i·ty** n.

in·ed·it·ed /in'editid/ ▶ adj. not edited or published. ■ published without editorial emendation.

in·ed·u·ca·ble /in'ejəkəbəl/ ▶ adj. considered incapable of being educated, esp. (formerly) as a result of mental disability.
– DERIVATIVES **in·ed·u·ca·bil·i·ty** n.

in·ef·fa·ble /in'efəbəl/ ▶ adj. too great or extreme to be expressed or described in words: *the ineffable natural beauty of the Everglades.* ■ not to be uttered: *the ineffable Hebrew name that gentiles write as Jehovah.*
– DERIVATIVES **in·ef·fa·bil·i·ty** /-efə'bilitē/ n., **in·ef·fa·bly** /-blē/ adv.
– ORIGIN late Middle English: from Old French, or from Latin *ineffabilis,* from *in-* 'not' + *effabilis* (see EFFABLE).

in·ef·face·a·ble /,ini'fāsəbəl/ ▶ adj. unable to be erased or forgotten.
– DERIVATIVES **in·ef·face·a·bil·i·ty** /-,fāsə'bilitē/ n., **in·ef·face·a·bly** /-blē/ adv.

in·ef·fec·tive /'ini'fektiv/ ▶ adj. not producing any significant or desired effect: *the legal sanctions against oil spills are virtually ineffective | a weak and ineffective president.*
– DERIVATIVES **in·ef·fec·tive·ly** adv., **in·ef·fec·tive·ness** n.

in·ef·fec·tu·al /,ini'fekcHo͞oəl/ ▶ adj. not producing any or the desired effect: *an ineffectual campaign.* ■ (of a person) lacking the ability or qualities to cope with a role or situation: *she was neglectful and ineffectual as a parent.*
– DERIVATIVES **in·ef·fec·tu·al·i·ty** /-fekcHo͞o'alitē/ n., **in·ef·fec·tu·al·ly** adv., **in·ef·fec·tu·al·ness** n.
– ORIGIN late Middle English: from medieval Latin *ineffectualis,* from *in-* 'not' + *effectualis,* from Latin *effectus* (see EFFECT); in later use from IN-[1] 'not' + EFFECTUAL.

in·ef·fi·ca·cious /'inefi'kāsHəs/ ▶ adj. not producing the desired effect.
– DERIVATIVES **in·ef·fi·ca·cy** n., **in·ef·fi·ca·cious·ly** adv.

in·ef·fi·cient /,ini'fisHənt/ ▶ adj. not achieving maximum productivity; wasting or failing to make the best use of time or resources: *an old, inefficient factory | the government was both inefficient and corrupt.*
– DERIVATIVES **in·ef·fi·cien·cy** n., **in·ef·fi·cient·ly** adv.

in·e·gal·i·tar·i·an /,ini,gali'te(ə)rēən/ ▶ adj. characterized by or promoting inequality between people.

in·e·las·tic /'ini'lastik/ ▶ adj. **1** (of a substance or material) not elastic.
2 Economics (of demand or supply) insensitive to changes in price or income.
3 Physics (of a collision) involving an overall loss of translational kinetic energy.
– DERIVATIVES **in·e·las·ti·cal·ly** adv., **in·e·las·ti·ci·ty** n.

in·el·e·gant /in'eligənt/ ▶ adj. having or showing a lack of physical grace, elegance, or refinement: *he came skidding to an inelegant halt | an inelegant bellow of laughter.*
– DERIVATIVES **in·el·e·gance** n., **in·el·e·gant·ly** adv.
– ORIGIN early 16th cent.: from French *inélégant,* from Latin *inelegant-,* from *in-* 'not' + *elegant-* 'fastidious, refined' (see ELEGANT).

in·el·i·gi·ble /'in'eləjəbəl/ ▶ adj. legally or officially unable to be considered for a position or benefit: *they were ineligible for jury duty.* ■ dated not suitable or desirable, esp. as a marriage partner: *as a son-in-law he was quite ineligible.*
– DERIVATIVES **in·el·i·gi·bil·i·ty** n., **in·el·i·gi·bly** adv.

in·e·lim·i·na·ble /ini'liminəbl/ ▶ adj. incapable of being removed or excluded from consideration: *an ineliminable feature of the human condition.*

in·e·luc·ta·ble /,ini'ləktəbəl/ ▶ adj. unable to be resisted or avoided; inescapable: *the ineluctable facts of history.*
– DERIVATIVES **in·e·luc·ta·bil·i·ty** /-,ləktə'bilitē/ n., **in·e·luc·ta·bly** /-blē/ adv.
– ORIGIN early 17th cent.: from Latin *ineluctabilis,* from *in-* 'not' + *eluctari* 'struggle out.'

in·ept /i'nept/ ▶ adj. having or showing no skill; clumsy: *the inept handling of the threat.*
– DERIVATIVES **in·ept·i·tude** /-ti,t(y)o͞od/ n., **in·ept·ly** adv., **in·ept·ness** n.
– ORIGIN mid 16th cent. (in the sense 'not apt, unsuitable'): from Latin *ineptus,* from *in-* 'not' + *aptus* (see APT).

in·e·qual·i·ty /,ini'kwälitē/ ▶ n. (pl. **inequalities**) difference in size, degree, circumstances, etc.; lack of equality: *social inequality | the widening inequalities in income.* ■ archaic lack of smoothness or regularity in a surface: *the inequality of the ground hindered their footing.* ■ Mathematics the relation between two expressions that are not equal, employing a sign such as ≠ "not equal to," > "greater than," or < "less than." ■ Mathematics a symbolic expression of the fact that two quantities are not equal.
– ORIGIN late Middle English: from Old French *inequalité,* or from Latin *inaequalitas,* from *in-* 'not' + *aequalis* (see EQUAL).

in·eq·ui·ta·ble /in'ekwitəbəl/ ▶ adj. unfair; unjust: *the present taxes are inequitable.*
– DERIVATIVES **in·eq·ui·ta·bly** /-blē/ adv.

in·eq·ui·ty /in'ekwitē/ ▶ n. (pl. **inequities**) lack of fairness or justice: *policies aimed at redressing racial inequity | inequities in school financing.*

in·e·qui·valve /in'ēkwə,valv/ ▶ adj. Zoology (of a bivalve shell) having the valves of different sizes.

in·e·rad·i·ca·ble /,inə'radikəbəl/ ▶ adj. unable to be destroyed or removed: *ineradicable hostility.*
– DERIVATIVES **in·e·rad·i·ca·bly** /-blē/ adv.

in·er·rant /in'erənt/ ▶ adj. incapable of being wrong.
– DERIVATIVES **in·er·ran·cy** n., **in·er·ran·tist** /-tist/ n.
– ORIGIN mid 19th cent.: from Latin *inerrant-* 'fixed,' from *in-* 'not' + *errant-* 'erring' (see ERRANT).

in·ert /i'nərt/ ▶ adj. lacking the ability or strength to move: *she lay inert in her bed.* ■ lacking vigor: *an inert political system.* ■ chemically inactive.
– DERIVATIVES **in·ert·ly** adv., **in·ert·ness** n.
– ORIGIN mid 17th cent.: from Latin *iners, inert-* 'unskilled, inactive,' from *in-* (expressing negation) + *ars, art-* 'skill, art.'

in·ert gas ▶ n. another term for NOBLE GAS.

in·er·tia /i'nərsHə/ ▶ n. **1** a tendency to do nothing or to remain unchanged: *the bureaucratic inertia of government.*
2 Physics a property of matter by which it continues in its existing state of rest or uniform motion in a straight line, unless that state is changed by an external force. See also MOMENT OF INERTIA. ■ [with adj.] resistance to change in some other physical property: *the thermal inertia of the oceans will delay the full rise in temperature for a few decades.*
– DERIVATIVES **in·er·tia·less** adj.
– ORIGIN early 18th cent. (sense 2): from Latin, from *iners, inert-* (see INERT).

in·er·tial /i'nərsHəl/ ▶ adj. chiefly Physics of, relating to, or arising from inertia. ■ (of navigation or guidance) depending on internal instruments that measure a craft's acceleration and compare the calculated position with stored data. ■ (of a frame of reference) in which bodies continue at rest or in uniform straight motion unless acted on by a force.

in·er·tia reel ▶ n. a reel device that allows a vehicle seat belt to unwind freely but locks under force of impact or rapid deceleration.

in·es·cap·a·ble /,ini'skāpəbəl/ ▶ adj. unable to be avoided or denied.
– DERIVATIVES **in·es·cap·a·bil·i·ty** /-,skāpə'bilitē/ n., **in·es·cap·a·bly** /-blē/ adv.

in·es·cutch·eon /,ine'skəcHən/ ▶ n. Heraldry a small shield placed within a larger one.

-iness ▶ suffix forming nouns corresponding to adjectives ending in *-y* (such as *clumsiness* corresponding to *clumsy*).
– ORIGIN see -Y[1], -NESS.

in es·se /in 'esē, 'ese/ ▶ adv. in actual existence.
– ORIGIN late 16th cent.: Latin, literally 'in being' (the infinitive used as a noun in an oblique case).

in·es·sen·tial /,ini'sencHəl/ ▶ adj. not absolutely necessary.
▶ n. (usu. **inessentials**) a thing that is not absolutely necessary.

in·es·ti·ma·ble /in'estəməbəl/ ▶ adj. too great to calculate: *a treasure of inestimable value.*
– DERIVATIVES **in·es·ti·ma·bly** /-blē/ adv.
– ORIGIN late Middle English: via Old French from Latin *inaestimabilis,* from *in-* 'not' + *aestimabilis* (see ESTIMABLE).

in·ev·i·ta·ble /in'evitəbəl/ ▶ adj. certain to happen; unavoidable: *war was inevitable.* ■ informal so frequently experienced or seen that it is completely predictable: *the inevitable letter from the bank.*
▶ n. (**the inevitable**) a situation that is unavoidable.
– DERIVATIVES **in·ev·i·ta·bil·i·ty** /-,evitə'bilitē/ n.
– ORIGIN late Middle English: from Latin *inevitabilis,* from *in-* 'not' + *evitabilis* 'avoidable' (from *evitare* 'avoid').

in·ev·i·ta·bly /in'evitəblē/ ▶ adv. [often as sentence adverb] as is certain to happen; unavoidably: *inevitably some details are already out of date | war inevitably has casualties.* ■ informal as one would expect; predictably: *inevitably, the phone started to ring just as we sat down.*

in·ex·act /'inig'zakt/ ▶ adj. not quite accurate or correct: *an inexact description.*
– DERIVATIVES **in·ex·ac·ti·tude** n., **in·ex·act·ly** adv., **in·ex·act·ness** n.

in·ex·cus·a·ble /,inik'skyo͞ozəbəl/ ▶ adj. too bad to be justified or tolerated: *Matt's behavior was inexcusable.*
– DERIVATIVES **in·ex·cus·a·bly** /-blē/ adv.
– ORIGIN late Middle English: from Latin *inexcusabilis,* from *in-* 'not' + *excusabilis* 'able to be excused' (see EXCUSE).

in·ex·haust·i·ble /,inig'zôstəbəl/ ▶ adj. (of an amount or supply of something) unable to be used up because existing in abundance: *his inexhaustible energy.*
– DERIVATIVES **in·ex·haust·i·bil·i·ty** /-,zôstə'bilitē/ n., **in·ex·haust·i·bly** /-blē/ adv.

in·ex·o·ra·ble /in'eksərəbəl/ ▶ adj. impossible to stop or prevent: *the seemingly inexorable march of new technology.* ■ (of a person) impossible to persuade by request or entreaty: *the doctors were inexorable, and there was nothing to be done.*
– DERIVATIVES **in·ex·o·ra·bil·i·ty** /-,eksərə'bilitē/ n., **in·ex·o·ra·bly** /-blē/ adv.
– ORIGIN mid 16th cent.: from French, or from Latin *inexorabilis,* from *in-* 'not' + *exorabilis* (from *exorare* 'entreat').

in·ex·pe·di·ent /'inik'spēdēənt/ ▶ adj. not practical, suitable, or advisable.
– DERIVATIVES **in·ex·pe·di·en·cy** n.

in·ex·pen·sive /'inik'spensiv/ ▶ adj. not costing a great deal; cheap: *a simple and inexpensive solution.*
– DERIVATIVES **in·ex·pen·sive·ly** adv., **in·ex·pen·sive·ness** n.

in·ex·pe·ri·ence /,inik'spi(ə)rēəns/ ▶ n. lack of experience, knowledge, or skill.
– ORIGIN late 16th cent.: from French *inexpérience,* from late Latin *inexperientia,* from *in-* (expressing negation) + *experientia* 'experience.'

in·ex·pe·ri·enced /,inik'spi(ə)rēənst/ ▶ adj. having little knowledge or experience of a particular thing: *an inexperienced driver.*

in·ex·pert /in'ekspərt/ ▶ adj. having or showing a lack of experience, skill, or knowledge: *an inexpert transcription from the real music.*
– DERIVATIVES **in·ex·pert·ly** adv.
– ORIGIN late Middle English (in the sense 'inexperienced'): via Old French from Latin *inexpertus,* from *in-* 'not' + *expertus* (see EXPERT).

in·ex·pi·a·ble /in'ekspēəbəl/ ▶ adj. (of an offense or feeling) so bad as to be impossible to expiate.
– DERIVATIVES **in·ex·pi·a·bly** /-blē/ adv.
– ORIGIN late Middle English: from Latin *inexpiabilis,* from *in-* 'not' + *expiabilis* 'able to be appeased' (from *expiare* 'expiate').

in·ex·pli·ca·ble /,inek'splikəbəl, in'eksplikəbəl/ ▶ adj. unable to be explained or accounted for: *for some inexplicable reason her mind went completely blank.*
– DERIVATIVES **in·ex·pli·ca·bil·i·ty** /'inek,splikə'bilitē/ n., **in·ex·pli·ca·bly** /-blē/ adv. [sentence adverb] *inexplicably, the pumps started to malfunction.*
– ORIGIN late Middle English: from French, or from Latin *inexplicabilis* 'that cannot be unfolded,' from *in-* 'not' + *explicabilis* (see EXPLICABLE).

in·ex·plic·it /'inik'splisit/ ▶ adj. not definitely or clearly expressed or explained.
– DERIVATIVES **in·ex·plic·it·ly** adv.

in·ex·press·i·ble /ˌinikˈspresəbəl/ ▶ **adj.** (of a feeling) too strong to be described or conveyed in words: *inexpressible joy.*
– DERIVATIVES **in·ex·press·i·bly** /-blē/ **adv.**

in·ex·pres·sive /ˌinikˈspresiv/ ▶ **adj.** showing no expression: *an inexpressive face.*
– DERIVATIVES **in·ex·pres·sive·ly** /ˈˌinikˈspresəvlē, ˈˌinekˈspresəvlē/ **adv.**, **in·ex·pres·sive·ness n.**

in·ex·pug·na·ble /ˌinekˈspəgnəbəl, -ˈspyo͞onəbəl/ ▶ **adj.** archaic term for IMPREGNABLE.
– ORIGIN late Middle English: via Old French from Latin *inexpugnabilis*, from *in-* 'not' + *expugnabilis* 'able to be taken by assault.'

in·ex·ten·si·ble /inikˈstensibəl/ ▶ **adj.** unable to be stretched or drawn out in length.

in ex·ten·so /ˌin əkˈstensō/ ▶ **adv.** in full; at length: *the paper covered their speeches in extenso.*
– ORIGIN Latin, from *in* 'in' + *extensus*, past participle of *extendere* 'stretch out.'

in·ex·tin·guish·a·ble /ˌinikˈstiNGgwiSHəbəl/ ▶ **adj.** unable to be extinguished or quenched: *a small inextinguishable candle* | figurative *inextinguishable good humor.*

in ex·tre·mis /ˌin ekˈstrāmēs, ikˈstrēmis/ ▶ **adv.** in an extremely difficult situation: *they suddenly find themselves in extremis 20 miles out to sea.* ■ at the point of death.
– ORIGIN Latin, from *in* 'in' + *extremis*, ablative plural of *extremus* 'outermost.'

in·ex·tri·ca·ble /ˌinikˈstrikəbəl, inˈekstri-/ ▶ **adj.** impossible to disentangle or separate: *the past and the present are inextricable.* ■ impossible to escape from: *an inextricable situation.*
– DERIVATIVES **in·ex·tri·ca·bil·i·ty** /ˌinikˌstrikəˈbilitē/ **n.**, **in·ex·tri·ca·bly** /-blē/ **adv.**
– ORIGIN mid 16th cent.: from Latin *inextricabilis*, from *in-* 'not' + *extricare* 'unravel' (see EXTRICATE).

INF ▶ **abbr.** intermediate-range nuclear force(s).

inf. ▶ **abbr.** ■ infantry. ■ inferior. ■ infield or infielder. ■ infinitive. ■ infinity. ■ infirmary. ■ information. ■ after; below. [from Latin *infra.*] ■ (in prescriptions) infuse. ■ an infusion.

in·fall /ˈinˌfôl/ ▶ **n.** Astronomy the falling of small objects or other matter onto or into a larger body.

in·fal·li·bil·i·ty /inˌfaləˈbilitē/ ▶ **n.** the quality of being infallible; the inability to be wrong: *his judgment became impaired by faith in his own infallibility.* ■ (also **papal infallibility**) (in the Roman Catholic Church) the doctrine that in specified circumstances the pope is incapable of error in pronouncing dogma.
– ORIGIN early 17th cent.: from obsolete French *infallibilité* or medieval Latin *infallibilitas* (based on Latin *fallere* 'deceive').

in·fal·li·ble /inˈfaləbəl/ ▶ **adj.** incapable of making mistakes or being wrong: *doctors are not infallible.* ■ never failing; always effective: *infallible cures.* ■ (in the Roman Catholic Church) credited with papal infallibility: *for an encyclical to be infallible the pope must speak ex cathedra.*
– DERIVATIVES **in·fal·li·bly** /-blē/ **adv.**
– ORIGIN late 15th cent.: from French *infaillible* or late Latin *infallibilis*, from *in-* 'not' + Latin *fallere* 'deceive.'

in·fa·mous /ˈinfəməs/ ▶ **adj.** well known for some bad quality or deed: *an infamous war criminal.* ■ wicked; abominable: *the medical council disqualified him for infamous misconduct.* ■ Law, historical (of a person) deprived of all or some citizens' rights as a consequence of conviction for a serious crime.
– DERIVATIVES **in·fa·mous·ly adv.**
– ORIGIN late Middle English: from medieval Latin *infamosus*, from Latin *infamis* (based on *fama* 'fame').

in·fa·my /ˈɪnfəmē/ ▶ **n.** (pl. **infamies**) the state of being well known for some bad quality or deed: *a day that will live in infamy.* ■ an evil or wicked act: *one of history's greatest infamies.*

in·fan·cy /ˈinfənsē/ ▶ **n.** the state or period of early childhood or babyhood: *a son who died in infancy.* ■ the early stage in the development or growth of something: *opinion polls were in their infancy.* ■ Law the condition of being a minor.
– ORIGIN late Middle English: from Latin *infantia* 'childhood, inability to speak,' from *infans, infant-* (see INFANT).

in·fang·thief /ˈinfaNGˌTHēf/ ▶ **n.** historical the right of the lord of a manor to try and punish a thief caught within the limits of his demesne.
– ORIGIN Old English *infangentheōf* 'thief seized within.'

in·fant /ˈinfənt/ ▶ **n.** a very young child or baby. ■ [as modifier] denoting something in an early stage of its development: *the infant science of bioelectrical medicine.* ■ Law a person who has not attained legal majority.
– ORIGIN late Middle English: from Old French *enfant*, from Latin *infant-* 'unable to speak,' from *in-* 'not' + *fant-* 'speaking' (from the verb *fari*).

in·fan·ta /inˈfantə/ ▶ **n.** historical a daughter of the ruling monarch of Spain or Portugal, esp. the eldest daughter who was not heir to the throne.
– ORIGIN late 16th cent.: Spanish and Portuguese, feminine of INFANTE.

in·fan·te /inˈfantā/ ▶ **n.** historical the second son of the ruling monarch of Spain or Portugal.
– ORIGIN mid 16th cent.: Spanish and Portuguese, from Latin *infans, infant-* (see INFANT).

in·fan·ti·cide /inˈfantiˌsīd/ ▶ **n. 1** the crime of killing a child within a year of birth. ■ the practice in some societies of killing unwanted children soon after birth.
2 a person who kills an infant, esp. their own child.
– DERIVATIVES **in·fan·ti·cid·al** /-ˌfantiˈsīdl/ **adj.**
– ORIGIN mid 17th cent.: via French from late Latin *infanticidium*, from Latin *infant-* (see INFANT) + *-cidium* (see -CIDE).

in·fan·tile /ˈinfənˌtīl, ˈinfənt-il/ ▶ **adj.** of or occurring among babies or very young children: *infantile colic.* ■ derogatory childish: *infantile jokes.*
– DERIVATIVES **in·fan·til·i·ty** /ˌinfənˈtilitē/ **n.** (pl. **infantilities**).
– ORIGIN late Middle English: from French, or from Latin *infantilis*, from *infans, infant-* (see INFANT).

in·fan·tile pa·ral·y·sis ▶ **n.** dated poliomyelitis.

in·fan·til·ism /ˈinfəntlˌizəm, inˈfan-/ ▶ **n.** childish behavior. ■ Psychology the persistence of infantile characteristics or behavior in adult life.

in·fan·til·ize /ˈinfəntlˌīz, inˈfan-/ ▶ **v.** [with obj.] treat (someone) as a child or in a way that denies their maturity in age or experience: *seeing yourself as a victim infantilizes you.*
– DERIVATIVES **in·fan·til·i·za·tion** /ˌinfəntl-iˈzāSHən, inˌfan-/ **n.**

in·fan·tine /ˈinfənˌtīn, -ˌtēn/ ▶ **adj.** archaic term for INFANTILE.
– ORIGIN early 17th cent.: from obsolete French *infantin*, variant of Old French *enfantin*, from Latin *infans, infant-* (see INFANT).

in·fant mor·tal·i·ty ▶ **n.** the death of children under the age of one year.

in·fan·try /ˈinfəntrē/ ▶ **n.** soldiers marching or fighting on foot; foot soldiers collectively.
– ORIGIN late 16th cent.: from French *infanterie*, from Italian *infanteria*, from *infante* 'youth, infantryman,' from Latin *infant-* (see INFANT).

in·fan·try·man /ˈinfəntrēmən/ ▶ **n.** (pl. **infantrymen**) a soldier belonging to an infantry unit.

in·farct /ˈinˌfärkt/ ▶ **n.** Medicine a small localized area of dead tissue resulting from failure of blood supply.
– ORIGIN late 19th cent.: from modern Latin *infarctus*, from *infarcire* 'stuff into or with,' from *in-* 'into' + Latin *farcire* 'to stuff.'

in·farc·tion /inˈfärkSHən/ ▶ **n.** the obstruction of the blood supply to an organ or region of tissue, typically by a thrombus or embolus, causing local death of the tissue.

in·fat·u·ate /inˈfaCHo͞oˌāt/ ▶ **v.** (**be infatuated with**) be inspired with an intense but short-lived passion or admiration for: *she is infatuated with a handsome police chief.*
– ORIGIN mid 16th cent.: from Latin *infatuat-* 'made foolish,' from the verb *infatuare*, from *in-* 'into' + *fatuus* 'foolish.'

in·fat·u·a·tion /inˌfaCHo͞oˈāSHən/ ▶ **n.** an intense but short-lived passion or admiration for someone or something: *he had developed an infatuation with the girl.*

in·fau·na /ˈinˌfônə/ ▶ **n.** Ecology the animals living in the sediments of the ocean floor or river or lake beds. Compare with EPIFAUNA.
– DERIVATIVES **in·fau·nal** /-ˈfônl/ **adj.**

in·fea·si·ble /inˈfēzəbəl/ ▶ **adj.** not possible to do easily or conveniently; impracticable.
– DERIVATIVES **in·fea·si·bil·i·ty n.**

in·fect /inˈfekt/ ▶ **v.** [with obj.] affect (a person, organism, cell, etc.) with a disease-causing organism: *there is no evidence that the virus can infect humans.* ■ contaminate (air, water, etc.) with harmful organisms. ■ Computing affect with a virus. ■ (of a negative feeling or idea) take hold of or be communicated to (someone): *the panic in his voice infected her.*
– DERIVATIVES **in·fec·tor** /-ˈfektər/ **n.**
– ORIGIN late Middle English: from Latin *infect-* 'tainted,' from the verb *inficere*, from *in-* 'into' + *facere* 'put, do.'

in·fec·tion /inˈfekSHən/ ▶ **n.** the process of infecting or the state of being infected: *strict hygiene will limit the risk of infection.* ■ an infectious disease: *a chest infection.* ■ Computing the presence of a virus in, or its introduction into, a computer system.
– ORIGIN late Middle English: from late Latin *infectio(n-)*, from Latin *inficere* 'dip in, taint' (see INFECT).

in·fec·tious /inˈfekSHəs/ ▶ **adj.** (of a disease or disease-causing organism) likely to be transmitted to people, organisms, etc., through the environment. ■ likely to spread infection: *the dogs may still be infectious.* ■ likely to spread or influence others in a rapid manner: *her enthusiasm is infectious.*
– DERIVATIVES **in·fec·tious·ly adv.**, **in·fec·tious·ness n.**

> **USAGE** On the differences in meaning between **infectious** and **contagious**, see usage at CONTAGIOUS.

in·fec·tious mon·o·nu·cle·o·sis ▶ **n.** an infectious viral disease characterized by swelling of the lymph glands and prolonged lassitude. Also called GLANDULAR FEVER.

in·fec·tive /inˈfektiv/ ▶ **adj.** capable of causing infection. ■ dated infectious: *infective hepatitis.*
– DERIVATIVES **in·fec·tive·ness n.**
– ORIGIN late Middle English: from Latin *infectivus*, from *inficere* 'to taint' (see INFECT).

in·fe·cund /inˈfēkənd, -ˈfek-/ ▶ **adj.** Medicine & Zoology (of a woman or female animal) having low or zero fecundity; unable to bear children or young.
– DERIVATIVES **in·fe·cun·di·ty** /ˌinfiˈkənditē/ **n.**
– ORIGIN late Middle English: from Latin *infecundus*, from *in-* 'not' + *fecundus* 'fecund.'

in·feed /ˈinˌfēd/ ▶ **n.** the action or process of supplying material to a machine. ■ a mechanism that does this.

in·fe·lic·i·tous /ˌinfəˈlisitəs/ ▶ **adj.** unfortunate; inappropriate: *his illustration is singularly infelicitous.*
– DERIVATIVES **in·fe·lic·i·tous·ly adv.**

in·fe·lic·i·ty /ˌinfəˈlisitē/ ▶ **n.** (pl. **infelicities**) a thing that is inappropriate, esp. a remark or expression: *she winced at their infelicities and at the clumsy way they talked.* ■ archaic unhappiness; misfortune.
– ORIGIN late Middle English (in the sense 'unhappiness'): from Latin *infelicitas*, from *infelix, infelic-* 'unhappy,' from *in-* 'not' + *felix* 'happy.'

in·fer /inˈfər/ ▶ **v.** (**infers, inferring, inferred**) [with obj.] deduce or conclude (information) from evidence and reasoning rather than from explicit statements: [with clause] *from these facts we can infer that crime has been increasing.*
– DERIVATIVES **in·fer·a·ble** (also **inferrable**) **adj.**
– ORIGIN late 15th cent. (in the sense 'bring about, inflict'): from Latin *inferre* 'bring in, bring about' (in medieval Latin 'deduce'), from *in-* 'into' + *ferre* 'bring.'

> **USAGE** There is a distinction in meaning between **infer** and **imply**. In the sentence *the speaker **implied** that the general had been a traitor*, the word **implied** means that something in the speaker's words 'suggested' that this man was a traitor (although nothing so explicit was actually stated). However, in *we **inferred** from his words that the general had been a traitor*, the word **inferred** means that something in the speaker's words enabled the listeners to 'deduce' that the man was a traitor. The two words **infer** and **imply** can describe the same event, but from different angles. Mistakes occur when **infer** is used to mean **imply**, as in *are you **inferring** that I'm a liar?* (instead of *are you **implying** that I'm a liar?*).

in·fer·ence /ˈinf(ə)rəns/ ▶ **n.** a conclusion reached on the basis of evidence and reasoning. ■ the process of reaching such a conclusion: *his emphasis on order and health, and by **inference** cleanliness.*
– DERIVATIVES **in·fer·en·tial** /ˌinfəˈrenCHəl/ **adj.**, **in·fer·en·tial·ly** /ˌinfəˈrenCHəlē/ **adv.**
– ORIGIN late 16th cent.: from medieval Latin *inferentia*, from *inferent-* 'bringing in,' from the verb *inferre* (see INFER).

in·fe·ri·or /inˈfi(ə)rēər/ ▶ **adj. 1** lower in rank, status, or quality: *schooling in inner-city areas was **inferior to** that in the rest of the country.* ■ of low standard or quality: *inferior goods.* ■ Law (of a court or tribunal) able to have its decisions overturned by a higher court. ■ Economics denoting goods or services that are in greater demand during a recession than in a boom, e.g., secondhand clothes.
2 chiefly Anatomy low or lower in position: *ulcers located in the inferior and posterior wall of the duodenum.* ■ (of a letter, figure, or symbol) written or printed below the line. ■ Botany (of the ovary of

i

a flower) situated below the sepals and enclosed in the receptacle.
▶ **n.** **1** a person lower than another in rank, status, or ability: *her social and intellectual inferiors.*
2 Printing an inferior letter, figure, or symbol.
– DERIVATIVES **in·fe·ri·or·ly** **adv.** (sense 2 of the adjective).
– ORIGIN late Middle English (sense 2 of the adjective): from Latin, comparative of *inferus* 'low.'

in·fe·ri·or con·junc·tion ▶ **n.** Astronomy a conjunction of Mercury or Venus with the sun, in which the planet and the earth are on the same side of the sun.

in·fe·ri·or·i·ty /in,fi(ə)rē'ôritē, -'äritē/ ▶ **n.** the condition of being lower in status or quality than another or others.
– ORIGIN late 16th cent.: probably from medieval Latin *inferioritas*, from Latin *inferior* 'lower.'

in·fe·ri·or·i·ty com·plex ▶ **n.** an unrealistic feeling of general inadequacy caused by actual or supposed inferiority in one sphere, sometimes marked by aggressive behavior in compensation.

in·fe·ri·or plan·et ▶ **n.** Astronomy either of the two planets Mercury and Venus, whose orbits are closer to the sun than the earth's. Compare with SUPERIOR PLANET.

in·fer·nal /in'fərnl/ ▶ **adj.** **1** of, relating to, or characteristic of hell or the underworld: *the infernal regions | the infernal heat of the forge.*
2 [attrib.] informal irritating and tiresome (used for emphasis): *you're an infernal nuisance.*
– DERIVATIVES **in·fer·nal·ly** **adv.**
– ORIGIN late Middle English: from Old French, from Christian Latin *infernalis*, from Latin *infernus* 'below, underground,' used by Christians to mean 'hell,' on the pattern of *inferni* (masculine plural) 'the shades' and *inferna* (neuter plural) 'the lower regions.'

in·fer·no /in'fərnō/ ▶ **n.** (pl. **infernos**) **1** a large fire that is dangerously out of control.
2 (usu. **Inferno**) hell (with reference to Dante's *Divine Comedy*).
– ORIGIN mid 19th cent.: from Italian, from Christian Latin *infernus* (see INFERNAL).

in·fer·tile /in'fərtl/ ▶ **adj.** (of a person, animal, or plant) unable to reproduce. ■ (of land) unable to sustain crops or vegetation.
– DERIVATIVES **in·fer·til·i·ty** /,infər'tilitē/ **n.**
– ORIGIN late 16th cent.: from French, or from late Latin *infertilis*, from *in-* 'not' + *fertilis* (see FERTILE).

in·fest /in'fest/ ▶ **v.** [with obj.] (usu. **be infested**) (of insects or animals) be present (in a place or site) in large numbers, typically so as to cause damage or disease: *the house is **infested with** cockroaches* | [as adj., in combination] (**-infested**) *shark-infested waters.*
– DERIVATIVES **in·fes·ta·tion** /,infe'stāsʜən/ **n.**
– ORIGIN late Middle English (in the sense 'torment, harass'): from French *infester* or Latin *infestare* 'assail,' from *infestus* 'hostile.' The current sense dates from the mid 16th cent.

in·feu·da·tion /,infyo͞o'dāsʜən/ ▶ **n.** historical under the feudal system, the action of putting someone into possession of a fee or fief.
– ORIGIN late 15th cent.: from medieval Latin *infeudatio(n-)*, from *infeudare* 'enfeoff' (based on *feudum* 'fee').

in·fib·u·late /in'fibyə,lāt/ ▶ **v.** (usu. as adj. **infibulated**) perform infibulation on (a girl or woman).
– ORIGIN early 17th cent.: from Latin *infibulat-* 'fastened with a clasp,' from the verb *infibulare*, from *in-* 'into' + *fibula* 'brooch.'

in·fib·u·la·tion /in,fibyə'lāsʜən/ ▶ **n.** the practice of excising the clitoris and labia of a girl or woman and stitching together the edges of the vulva to prevent sexual intercourse. It is traditional in some northeastern African cultures but is highly controversial.

in·fi·del /'infədl, -,del/ ▶ **n.** chiefly archaic a person who does not believe in religion or who adheres to a religion other than one's own: (as plural noun **the infidel**) *they wanted to secure the Holy Places from the infidel.*
▶ **adj.** adhering to a religion other than one's own: *the infidel foe.*
– ORIGIN late 15th cent.: from French *infidèle* or Latin *infidelis*, from *in-* 'not' + *fidelis* 'faithful' (from *fides* 'faith,' related to *fidere* 'to trust'). The word originally denoted a person of a religion other than one's own, specifically a Muslim (to a Christian), a Christian (to a Muslim), or a Gentile (to a Jew).

in·fi·del·i·ty /,infi'delitē/ ▶ **n.** (pl. **infidelities**) **1** the action or state of being unfaithful to a spouse or other sexual partner: *her infidelity continued after her marriage | I ought not to have tolerated his infidelities.*
2 unbelief in a particular religion, esp. Christianity.
– ORIGIN late Middle English (in the senses 'lack of faith' and 'disloyalty'): from Old French *infidelite* or Latin *infidelitas*, from *infidelis* 'not faithful' (see INFIDEL).

in·field /'in,fēld/ ▶ **n.** **1** the inner part of the field of play in various sports, in particular: ■ Baseball the area within and near the four bases. ■ Cricket the part of the field closer to the wicket. ■ the players stationed in the infield, collectively.
2 Brit. the land around or near a farmstead, esp. arable land.
▶ **adv.** into or toward the inner part of the field of play.
– DERIVATIVES **in·field·er** **n.** (sense 1 of the noun).

in·fight·ing /'in,fītiɴɢ/ ▶ **n.** hidden conflict or competitiveness within an organization. ■ boxing closer to an opponent than at arm's length.
– DERIVATIVES **in·fight·er** **n.**

in·fill /'in,fil/ ▶ **n.** material that fills or is used to fill a space or hole. ■ buildings constructed to occupy the space between existing ones.
▶ **v.** [with obj.] fill or block up (a space or hole). ■ construct new buildings between (existing structures).

in·fil·trate /'infil,trāt, in'fil-/ ▶ **v.** [with obj.] **1** enter or gain access to (an organization, place, etc.) surreptitiously and gradually, esp. in order to acquire secret information: *other areas of the establishment were infiltrated by fascists.* ■ permeate or become a part of (something) in this way: *computing has infiltrated most professions now.* ■ Medicine (of a tumor, cells, etc.) spread into or invade (a tissue or organ).
2 (of a liquid) permeate (something) by filtration: *virtually no water infiltrates deserts such as the Sahara.* ■ introduce (a liquid) into something in this way: *lignocaine was **infiltrated into** the wound.*
▶ **n.** Medicine an infiltrating substance or a number of infiltrating cells.
– DERIVATIVES **in·fil·tra·tion** /,infil'trāsʜən/ **n.**, **in·fil·tra·tor** /-,trātər/ **n.**

infin. ▶ **abbr.** infinitive.

in fine /in 'fīnē/ ▶ **adv.** finally; in short; to sum up.
– ORIGIN mid 16th cent.: Latin, literally 'in the end.'

in·fi·nite /'infənit/ ▶ **adj.** **1** limitless or endless in space, extent, or size; impossible to measure or calculate: *the infinite mercy of God | the infinite number of stars in the universe.* ■ very great in amount or degree: *he bathed the wound with infinite care.* ■ Mathematics greater than any assignable quantity or countable number. ■ Mathematics (of a series) able to be continued indefinitely.
2 Grammar another term for NONFINITE.
▶ **n.** (**the infinite**) a space or quantity that is infinite. ■ (**the Infinite**) God.
– DERIVATIVES **in·fi·nite·ly** **adv.** [as submodifier] *the pay is infinitely better*, **in·fi·nite·ness** **n.**
– ORIGIN late Middle English: from Latin *infinitus*, from *in-* 'not' + *finitus* 'finished, finite' (see FINITE).

in·fi·nite re·gress ▶ **n.** chiefly Logic a sequence of reasoning or justification that can never come to an end.

in·fin·i·tes·i·mal /,infini'tes(ə)məl/ ▶ **adj.** extremely small: *an infinitesimal pause.*
▶ **n.** Mathematics an indefinitely small quantity; a value approaching zero.
– DERIVATIVES **in·fin·i·tes·i·mal·ly** **adv.**
– ORIGIN mid 17th cent.: from modern Latin *infinitesimus*, from Latin *infinitus* (see INFINITE), on the pattern of *centesimal*.

> **USAGE** Although this long word is commonly assumed to refer to large numbers, **infinitesimal** describes only very small size. While there may be an *infinite* number of grains of sand on the beach, a single grain may be said to be *infinitesimal*.

in·fin·i·tes·i·mal cal·cu·lus ▶ **n.** see CALCULUS (sense 1).

in·fin·i·tive /in'finitiv/ ▶ **n.** the basic form of a verb, without an inflection binding it to a particular subject or tense (e.g., *see* in *we came to see, let him see*).
▶ **adj.** having or involving such a form.
– DERIVATIVES **in·fin·i·ti·val** /-fini'tīvəl/ **adj.**, **in·fin·i·ti·val·ly** /-,fini'tīvəlē/ **adv.**
– ORIGIN late Middle English (as an adjective): from Latin *infinitivus*, from *infinitus* (see INFINITE). The noun dates from the mid 16th cent.

in·fin·i·tude /in'fini,t(y)o͞od/ ▶ **n.** the state or quality of being infinite or having no limit: *the infinitude of the universe.*
– ORIGIN mid 17th cent.: from Latin *infinitus* (see INFINITE), on the pattern of *magnitude*.

in·fin·i·ty /in'finitē/ ▶ **n.** (pl. **infinities**) **1** the state or quality of being infinite: *the infinity of space.* ■ an infinite or very great number or amount: *an infinity of combinations.* ■ a point in space or time that is or seems infinitely distant: *the lawns stretched into infinity.*
2 Mathematics a number greater than any assignable quantity or countable number (symbol ∞).
– ORIGIN late Middle English: from Old French *infinite* or Latin *infinitas*, from *infinitus* (see INFINITE).

in·fin·i·ty pool ▶ **n.** a swimming pool whose positioning gives the impression that it merges into the ocean or other surrounding landscape.

in·firm /in'fərm/ ▶ **adj.** not physically or mentally strong, esp. through age or illness. ■ archaic (of a person or their judgment) weak; irresolute: *he was infirm of purpose.*
– DERIVATIVES **in·firm·ly** **adv.**
– ORIGIN late Middle English (in the general sense 'weak, frail'): from Latin *infirmus*, from *in-* 'not' + *firmus* 'firm.'

in·fir·mar·er /in'fərmərər/ ▶ **n.** historical a person in charge of the infirmary in a medieval monastery.
– ORIGIN late Middle English: from Old French *enfermerier*, from *enfermerie* 'infirmary,' based on Latin *infirmus* (see INFIRM).

in·fir·ma·ry /in'fərm(ə)rē/ ▶ **n.** (pl. **infirmaries**) a place in a large institution for the care of those who are ill: *the prison infirmary.* ■ a hospital.
– ORIGIN late Middle English: from medieval Latin *infirmaria*, from Latin *infirmus* (see INFIRM).

in·fir·mi·ty /in'fərmitē/ ▶ **n.** (pl. **infirmities**) physical or mental weakness: *old age and infirmity come to men and women alike | the infirmities of old age.*

in·fix ▶ **v.** /in'fiks/ [with obj.] **1** implant or insert firmly in something.
2 Grammar insert (a formative element) into the body of a word.
▶ **n.** /'in,fiks/ Grammar a formative element inserted in a word.
– DERIVATIVES **in·fix·a·tion** /,infik'sāsʜən/ **n.** (sense 2 of the verb).
– ORIGIN early 16th cent.: from Latin *infix-* 'fixed in,' from the verb *infigere*, from *in-* 'into' + *figere* 'fasten,' reinforced by IN-[2] 'into' + FIX. The noun is on the pattern of *prefix* and *suffix*.

infl. ▶ **abbr.** influence or influenced.

in fla·gran·te de·lic·to /,in flə'grāntā də'liktō, flə'grantē/ (also informal **in flagrante**) ▶ **adv.** in the very act of wrongdoing, esp. in an act of sexual misconduct: *he had been caught **in flagrante** with the wife of the association's treasurer.*
– ORIGIN late 18th cent.: Latin, literally 'in blazing crime.'

in·flame /in'flām/ ▶ **v.** [with obj.] **1** provoke or intensify (strong feelings, esp. anger) in someone: *high fines further inflamed public feelings.* ■ provoke (someone) to strong feelings: *her sister was inflamed with jealousy.* ■ make (a situation) worse.
2 cause inflammation in (a part of the body): *the finger joints were inflamed with rheumatoid arthritis* | (as adj. **inflamed**) *inflamed eyes and lips.*
3 literary light up with or as if with flames: *the torches inflame the night to the eastward.*
– DERIVATIVES **in·flam·er** **n.**
– ORIGIN Middle English *enflaume*, *inflaume*, from Old French *enflammer*, from Latin *inflammare*, from *in-* 'into' + *flamma* 'flame.'

in·flam·ma·ble /in'flaməbəl/ ▶ **adj.** easily set on fire: *inflammable and poisonous gases.*
– DERIVATIVES **in·flam·ma·bil·i·ty** /-,flamə'bilitē/ **n.**, **in·flam·ma·ble·ness** **n.**, **in·flam·ma·bly** /-blē/ **adv.**
– ORIGIN early 17th cent.: from French, or from Latin *inflammare* (see INFLAME).

> **USAGE** The words **inflammable** and **flammable** both have the same meaning, 'easily set on fire.' This might seem surprising, given that the prefix **in-** normally has a negative meaning (as in **indirect** and **insufficient**), and so it might be expected that **inflammable** would mean the opposite of **flammable**, i.e., 'not easily set on fire.' In fact, **inflammable** is formed using a different Latin prefix **in-**, which has the meaning 'into' and here has the effect of intensifying the meaning of the word in English. **Flammable** is a far commoner word than **inflammable** and carries less risk of confusion.

in·flam·ma·tion /,inflə'māsʜən/ ▶ **n.** a localized physical condition in which part of the body becomes reddened, swollen, hot, and often painful, esp. as a reaction to injury or infection: *chronic inflammation of the nasal cavities.*
– ORIGIN late Middle English: from Latin *inflammatio(n-)*, from the verb *inflammare* (see INFLAME).

in·flam·ma·to·ry /in'flamə,tôrē/ ▶ **adj.** **1** relating to or causing inflammation of a part of the body.

2 (esp. of speech or writing) arousing or intended to arouse angry or violent feelings: *inflammatory slogans.*

in·flat·a·ble /inˈflātəbəl/ ▶ **adj.** capable of being filled with air: *an inflatable mattress.*
▶ **n.** a plastic or rubber object that must be filled with air before use: *three sailors manned the inflatable.*

in·flate /inˈflāt/ ▶ **v.** [with obj.] **1** fill (a balloon, tire, or other expandable structure) with air or gas so that it becomes distended. ■ [no obj.] become distended in this way.
2 increase (something) by a large or excessive amount: *objectives should be clearly set out so as not to duplicate work and inflate costs.* ■ exaggerate: *numbers have been grossly inflated by the local press.* ■ bring about inflation of (a currency) or in (an economy).
– DERIVATIVES **in·fla·tor** /-ˈflātər/ (also **inflater**) **n.**
– ORIGIN late Middle English: from Latin *inflat-* 'blown into,' from the verb *inflare*, from *in-* 'into' + *flare* 'to blow.'

in·flat·ed /inˈflātid/ ▶ **adj. 1** distended through being filled with air or gas: *a partially inflated balloon.*
2 excessively or unreasonably high: *inflated salaries.* ■ exaggerated: *you have a very inflated opinion of your worth.*

in·fla·tion /inˈflāsHən/ ▶ **n. 1** the action of inflating something or the condition of being inflated: *the inflation of a balloon | the gross inflation of salaries.* ■ Astronomy (in some theories of cosmology) a very brief exponential expansion of the universe postulated to have interrupted the standard linear expansion shortly after the Big Bang.
2 Economics a general increase in prices and fall in the purchasing value of money: *policies aimed at controlling inflation* | [as modifier] *high inflation rates.*
– DERIVATIVES **in·fla·tion·ism** /-ˌnizəm/ **n.**, **in·fla·tion·ist** /-nist/ **n. & adj.**
– ORIGIN Middle English (in the sense 'the condition of being inflated with a gas'): from Latin *inflatio(n-)*, from *inflare* 'blow in to' (see **INFLATE**). Sense 2 dates from the mid 19th cent.

in·fla·tion·ar·y /inˈflāsHəˌnerē/ ▶ **adj. 1** of, characterized by, or tending to cause monetary inflation.
2 Astronomy of, relating to, or involving inflation.

in·flect /inˈflekt/ ▶ **v.** [with obj.] **1** Grammar change the form of (a word) to express a particular grammatical function or attribute, typically tense, mood, person, number, case, and gender. ■ [no obj.] (of a word or a language containing such words) undergo such change.
2 vary the intonation or pitch of (the voice), esp. to express mood or feeling. ■ influence or color (music or writing) in tone or style. ■ vary the pitch of (a musical note).
3 technical bend or deflect (something), esp. inward.
– DERIVATIVES **in·flec·tive** /-tiv/ **adj.**
– ORIGIN late Middle English (sense 3): from Latin *inflectere*, from *in-* 'into' + *flectere* 'to bend.'

in·flec·tion /inˈfleksHən/ (chiefly Brit. also **inflexion**) ▶ **n. 1** Grammar a change in the form of a word (typically the ending) to express a grammatical function or attribute such as tense, mood, person, number, case, and gender. ■ the process or practice of inflecting words.
2 the modulation of intonation or pitch in the voice: *she spoke slowly and without inflection | the variety of his vocal inflections.* ■ the variation of the pitch of a musical note.
3 chiefly Mathematics a change of curvature from convex to concave at a particular point on a curve.
– DERIVATIVES **in·flec·tion·al** /-sHənl/ **adj.**, **in·flec·tion·al·ly** /-sHənl-ē/ **adv.**, **in·flec·tion·less adj.**
– ORIGIN late Middle English (in the sense 'the action of bending inward'): from Latin *inflexio(n-)*, from the verb *inflectere* 'bend in, curve' (see **INFLECT**).

in·flec·tion point ▶ **n. 1** (also **point of inflection**) Mathematics a point of a curve at which a change in the direction of curvature occurs.
2 (in business) a time of significant change in a situation; a turning point.

in·flexed /inˈflekst/ ▶ **adj.** technical bent or curved inward.

in·flex·i·ble /inˈfleksəbəl/ ▶ **adj. 1** unwilling to change or compromise: *once she had made up her mind, she was inflexible.* ■ not able to be changed or adapted to particular circumstances: *inflexible rules.*
2 not able to be bent; stiff: *the heavy inflexible armor of the beetles.*
– DERIVATIVES **in·flex·i·bil·i·ty** /-ˌfleksəˈbilitē/ **n.**, **in·flex·i·bly** /-blē/ **adv.**
– ORIGIN late Middle English: from Latin *inflexibilis*, from *in-* 'not' + *flexibilis* 'flexible.'

in·flict /inˈflikt/ ▶ **v.** [with obj.] cause (something unpleasant or painful) to be suffered by someone or something: *they inflicted serious injuries on three other men.* ■ (**inflict something on**) impose something unwelcome on: *she is wrong to inflict her beliefs on everyone else.*
– DERIVATIVES **in·flict·a·ble adj.**, **in·flict·er n.**
– ORIGIN mid 16th cent. (in the sense 'afflict, trouble'): from Latin *inflict-* 'struck against,' from the verb *infligere*, from *in-* 'into' + *fligere* 'to strike.'

in·flic·tion /inˈfliksHən/ ▶ **n.** the action of inflicting something unpleasant or painful on someone or something: *the repeated infliction of pain.* ■ informal, dated a nuisance: *what an infliction he must be!*

in·flight /ˈinˌflīt/ ▶ **adj.** occurring or provided during an aircraft flight: *inflight entertainment.*

in·flo·res·cence /ˌinflôˈresəns, -flə-/ ▶ **n.** Botany the complete flower head of a plant including stems, stalks, bracts, and flowers. ■ the arrangement of the flowers on a plant. ■ the process of flowering.
– ORIGIN mid 18th cent. (denoting the arrangement of a plant's flowers): from modern Latin *inflorescentia*, from late Latin *inflorescere* 'come into flower,' from Latin *in-* 'into' + *florescere* 'begin to flower.'

in·flow /ˈinˌflō/ ▶ **n.** a large amount of money, people, or water, that moves or is transferred into a place: *some enclosed seas are subject to large inflows of fresh water | the firm experienced two years of cash inflow.*
– DERIVATIVES **in·flow·ing n. & adj.**

in·flu·ence /ˈinflo͝oəns/ ▶ **n.** the capacity to have an effect on the character, development, or behavior of someone or something, or the effect itself: *the influence of television violence | I was still* **under the influence** *of my parents | their friends are having a bad* **influence on** *them.* ■ the power to shape policy or ensure favorable treatment from someone, esp. through status, contacts, or wealth: *the institute has considerable influence with teachers.* ■ a person or thing with such a capacity or power: *Frank was a good* **influence on** *her.* ■ Physics, archaic electrical or magnetic induction.
▶ **v.** [with obj.] have an influence on: *social forces influencing criminal behavior.*
– PHRASES **under the influence** informal affected by alcoholic drink; drunk: *he was charged with driving under the influence.*
– DERIVATIVES **in·flu·ence·a·ble adj.**, **in·flu·enc·er n.**
– ORIGIN late Middle English: from Old French, or from medieval Latin *influentia* 'inflow,' from Latin *influere*, from *in-* 'into' + *fluere* 'to flow.' The word originally had the general sense 'an influx, flowing matter,' also specifically (in astrology) 'the flowing in of ethereal fluid (affecting human destiny).' The sense 'imperceptible or indirect action exerted to cause changes' was established in Scholastic Latin by the 13th cent., but not recorded in English until the late 16th cent.

in·flu·ence ped·dling ▶ **n.** the use of position or political influence on someone's behalf in exchange for money or favors.
– DERIVATIVES **in·flu·ence ped·dler n.**

in·flu·ent /ˈinflo͝oənt/ ▶ **adj.** flowing in: *the influent lines were relocated while waste water was still flowing.*
▶ **n.** a stream, esp. a tributary, that flows into another stream or lake. ■ Ecology a nondominant organism that has a major effect on the balance of a plant or animal community.
– ORIGIN late Middle English (as an adjective): from Latin *influent-* 'flowing in,' from *influere* (see **INFLUENCE**). The noun is recorded from the mid 19th cent.

in·flu·en·tial /ˌinflo͞oˈencHəl/ ▶ **adj.** having great influence on someone or something: *her work is influential in feminist psychology.*
▶ **n.** (usu. **influentials**) an influential person.
– DERIVATIVES **in·flu·en·tial·ly adv.**
– ORIGIN late 16th cent. (referring to astral influence): from medieval Latin *influentia* (see **INFLUENCE**).

in·flu·en·za /ˌinflo͞oˈenzə/ ▶ **n.** a highly contagious viral infection of the respiratory passages causing fever, severe aching, and catarrh, and often occurring in epidemics. Also called **FLU**.
– DERIVATIVES **in·flu·en·zal adj.**
– ORIGIN mid 18th cent.: from Italian, literally 'influence,' from medieval Latin *influentia* (see **INFLUENCE**). The Italian word also has the sense 'an outbreak of an epidemic,' hence 'epidemic.' It was applied specifically to an influenza epidemic that began in Italy in 1743, later adopted in English as the name of the disease.

in·flux /ˈinˌfləks/ ▶ **n. 1** an arrival or entry of large numbers of people or things: *a massive influx of refugees from front-line areas.*
2 an inflow of water into a river, lake, or the sea.
– ORIGIN late 16th cent. (denoting an inflow of liquid, gas, or light): from late Latin *influxus*, from *influere* 'flow in' (see **INFLUENCE**).

in·fo /ˈinfō/ ▶ **n.** informal information.
– ORIGIN early 20th cent.: abbreviation.

in·fold /inˈfōld/ ▶ **v.** [with obj.] **1** turn or fold inward; invaginate: (as adj. **infolded**) *an ovary formed from the infolded carpel.*
2 dated variant spelling of **ENFOLD**.
– DERIVATIVES **in·fold·ing n.** *an infolding of mesodermal tissues.*

in·fo·me·di·ar·y /ˌinfōˈmēdēˌerē/ ▶ **n.** an Internet company that gathers and links information on particular subjects on behalf of commercial organizations and their potential customers.
– ORIGIN 1980s: from *info(rmation)* + *-mediary*, on the pattern of *intermediary*.

in·fo·mer·cial /ˈinfōˌmərsHəl/ ▶ **n.** a television program that promotes a product in an informative and supposedly objective way.
– ORIGIN 1980s: blend of **INFORMATION** and **COMMERCIAL**.

in·form /inˈfôrm/ ▶ **v. 1** [reporting verb] give (someone) facts or information; tell: [with obj.] *he wrote to her, informing her of the situation* | [with obj. and clause] *they were informed that no risk was involved* | [no obj.] *the role of television is to inform and entertain.* ■ [no obj.] give incriminating information about someone to the police or other authority: *people called a confidential hotline to inform on friends, neighbors, and family members.*
2 [with obj.] give an essential or formative principle or quality to: *the relationship of the citizen to the state is informed by the democratic ideal.*
– ORIGIN Middle English *enforme, informe* 'give form or shape to,' also 'form the mind of, teach,' from Old French *enfourmer*, from Latin *informare* 'shape, fashion, describe,' from *in-* 'into' + *forma* 'a form.'

in·for·mal /inˈfôrməl/ ▶ **adj.** having a relaxed, friendly, or unofficial style, manner, or nature: *an informal atmosphere | an informal agreement between the two companies.* ■ of or denoting a style of writing or conversational speech characterized by simple grammatical structures, familiar vocabulary, and use of idioms, e.g., *tu* in French. ■ (of dress) casual; suitable for everyday wear.
– DERIVATIVES **in·for·mal·ly adv.**

in·for·mal·i·ty /ˌinfôrˈmalitē/ ▶ **n.** relaxed, friendly, or unofficial style or nature; absence of formality: *he enjoyed the informality of the occasion.*

in·form·ant /inˈfôrmənt/ ▶ **n.** a person who gives information to another. ■ another term for **INFORMER**. ■ a person from whom a linguist or anthropologist obtains information about language, dialect, or culture.

in·for·mat·ics /ˌinfərˈmatiks/ ▶ **plural n.** [treated as sing.] Computing the science of processing data for storage and retrieval; information science.
– ORIGIN 1960s: from **INFORMATION** + **-ICS**, translating Russian *informatika*.

in·for·ma·tion /ˌinfərˈmāsHən/ ▶ **n. 1** facts provided or learned about something or someone: *a vital piece of information.* ■ Law a formal criminal charge lodged with a court or magistrate by a prosecutor without the aid of a grand jury: *the tenant may lay an information against his landlord.*
2 what is conveyed or represented by a particular arrangement or sequence of things: *genetically transmitted information.* ■ Computing data as processed, stored, or transmitted by a computer. ■ (in information theory) a mathematical quantity expressing the probability of occurrence of a particular sequence of symbols, impulses, etc., as contrasted with that of alternative sequences.
– DERIVATIVES **in·for·ma·tion·al** /-sHənl/ **adj.**, **in·for·ma·tion·al·ly** /-sHənl-ē/ **adv.**
– ORIGIN late Middle English (also in the sense 'formation of the mind, teaching'), via Old French from Latin *informatio(n-)*, from the verb *informare* (see **INFORM**).

in·for·ma·tion re·triev·al ▶ **n.** Computing the tracing and recovery of specific information from stored data.

in·for·ma·tion rev·o·lu·tion ▶ **n.** the proliferation of the availability of information and the accompanying changes in its storage and dissemination owing to the use of computers.

in·forma·tion scent ▶ **n.** visual or textual cues provided on a website to suggest what information it or its links may contain. ■ the perceived usefulness of a page based on such information.

in·for·ma·tion sci·ence ▶ **n.** Computing the study of processes for storing and retrieving information, esp. scientific or technical information.

in·for·ma·tion su·per·high·way ▶ **n.** see **SUPERHIGHWAY** (sense 2).

i

in·for·ma·tion tech·nol·o·gy (abbr.: **IT**) ▶ **n.** the study or use of systems (esp. computers and telecommunications) for storing, retrieving, and sending information.

in·for·ma·tion the·o·ry ▶ **n.** the mathematical study of the coding of information in the form of sequences of symbols, impulses, etc., and of how rapidly such information can be transmitted, e.g., through computer circuits or telecommunications channels.

in·for·ma·tive /inˈfôrmətiv/ ▶ **adj.** providing useful or interesting information: *a thought-provoking, informative article.*
– DERIVATIVES **in·for·ma·tive·ly** adv., **in·for·ma·tive·ness** n.
– ORIGIN late Middle English (in the sense 'formative, giving life or shape'): from medieval Latin *informativus*, from Latin *informare* 'give form to, instruct' (see INFORM).

in·formed /inˈfôrmd/ ▶ **adj.** having or showing knowledge of a particular subject or situation: *an informed readership.* ■ (of a decision or judgment) based on an understanding of the facts of the situation: *twenty-six young adults participated after giving informed consent.*
– DERIVATIVES **in·form·ed·ly** /-m(i)dlē/ adv., **in·form·ed·ness** /-m(i)dnis/ n.

in·form·er /inˈfôrmər/ ▶ **n.** a person who informs on another person to the police or other authority.

in·fo·tain·ment /ˌinfōˈtānmənt/ ▶ **n.** broadcast material that is intended both to entertain and to inform.
– ORIGIN 1980s (originally US): blend of INFORMATION and ENTERTAINMENT.

in·fo·tech /ˈinfōˌtek/ ▶ **n.** short for INFORMATION TECHNOLOGY.

in·fo·war /ˈinfōˌwôr/ ▶ **n. 1** hostile actions against an enemy's information infrastructure.
2 a propaganda war waged via electronic media.

in·fra /ˈinfrə/ ▶ **adv.** (in a written document) below; further on: *see note, infra.*
– ORIGIN late 19th cent.: Latin, 'below.'

infra- ▶ **prefix** below: *infrared* | *infrasonic.* ■ Anatomy below or under a part of the body: *infrarenal.*
– ORIGIN from Latin *infra* 'below.'

in·fra·class /ˈinfrəˌklas/ ▶ **n.** Biology a taxonomic category that ranks below a subclass.

in·frac·tion /inˈfrakSHən/ ▶ **n.** a violation or infringement of a law, agreement, or set of rules.
– DERIVATIVES **in·frac·tor** /-tər/ n.
– ORIGIN late Middle English: from Latin *infractio(n-)*, from the verb *infringere* (see INFRINGE).

in·fra·di·an /inˈfrādēən/ ▶ **adj.** Physiology (of a rhythm or cycle) having a period of recurrence longer than a day; occurring less than once a day. Compare with ULTRADIAN.
– ORIGIN mid 20th cent.: from INFRA- 'below' (i.e., expressing a lower frequency), on the pattern of *circadian.*

in·fra dig ▶ **adj.** [predic.] informal beneath one; demeaning: *it was somewhat infra dig for a man in his position to be found drinking.*
– ORIGIN early 19th cent.: abbreviation of Latin *infra dignitatem* 'beneath (one's) dignity.'

in·fra·lap·sar·i·an /ˌinfrəlapˈse(ə)rēən/ Theology ▶ **n.** a Calvinist holding the view that God's election of only some to everlasting life was not originally part of the divine plan, but a consequence of the Fall of Man.
▶ **adj.** of or relating to the infralapsarians or their doctrine.
– ORIGIN mid 18th cent.: from INFRA- 'below' + Latin *lapsus* 'fall' + -ARIAN.

in·fran·gi·ble /inˈfranjəbəl/ ▶ **adj.** formal unbreakable; inviolable.
– DERIVATIVES **in·fran·gi·bil·i·ty** /-ˌfranjəˈbilitē/ n., **in·fran·gi·bly** /-blē/ adv.
– ORIGIN late 16th cent.: from French, or from medieval Latin *infrangibilis*, from *in-* 'not' + *frangibilis* (see FRANGIBLE).

in·fra·or·der /ˈinfrəˌôrdər/ ▶ **n.** Biology a taxonomic category that ranks below a suborder.

in·fra·red /ˌinfrəˈred/ ▶ **adj.** (of electromagnetic radiation) having a wavelength just greater than that of the red end of the visible light spectrum but less than that of microwaves. Infrared radiation has a wavelength from about 800 nm to 1 mm, and is emitted particularly by heated objects. ■ (of equipment or techniques) using or concerned with this radiation: *infrared cameras.*
▶ **n.** the infrared region of the spectrum; infrared radiation.

in·fra·re·nal /ˌinfrəˈrēnl/ ▶ **adj.** Anatomy below the kidney.

in·fra·son·ic /ˌinfrəˈsänik/ ▶ **adj.** relating to or denoting sound waves with a frequency below the lower limit of human audibility.

in·fra·sound /ˈinfrəˌsound/ ▶ **n.** sound waves with frequencies below the lower limit of human audibility.

in·fra·spe·cif·ic /ˌinfrəspəˈsifik/ ▶ **adj.** Biology at a taxonomic level below that of species, e.g., subspecies, variety, cultivar, or form. In botany, Latin names at this level usually require the addition of a term denoting the rank. ■ occurring within a species: *infraspecific variation.*

in·fra·struc·ture /ˈinfrəˌstrəkCHər/ ▶ **n.** the basic physical and organizational structures and facilities (e.g., buildings, roads, and power supplies) needed for the operation of a society or enterprise.
– DERIVATIVES **in·fra·struc·tur·al** /ˌinfrəˈstrəkCHərəl/ adj.
– ORIGIN early 20th cent.: from French (see INFRA-, STRUCTURE).

in·fre·quent /inˈfrēkwənt/ ▶ **adj.** not occurring often; rare: *her visits were so infrequent.*
– DERIVATIVES **in·fre·quen·cy** n., **in·fre·quent·ly** adv.
– ORIGIN mid 16th cent. (in the sense 'little used, seldom done, uncommon'): from Latin *infrequent-*, from *in-* 'not' + *frequent-* 'frequent.'

in·fringe /inˈfrinj/ ▶ **v.** (**infringes, infringing, infringed**) [with obj.] actively break the terms of (a law, agreement, etc.): *making an unauthorized copy would infringe copyright.* ■ act so as to limit or undermine (something); encroach on: *his legal rights were being infringed* | [no obj.] *I wouldn't infringe on his privacy.*
– DERIVATIVES **in·fring·er** n.
– ORIGIN mid 16th cent.: from Latin *infringere*, from *in-* 'into' + *frangere* 'to break.'

in·fringe·ment /inˈfrinjmənt/ ▶ **n. 1** the action of breaking the terms of a law, agreement, etc.; violation: *copyright infringement* | *an infringement of the rules.*
2 the action of limiting or undermining something: *this bill is an infringement of our civil liberties.*

in·fruc·tes·cence /ˌinfrəkˈtesəns/ ▶ **n.** Botany an aggregate fruit.
– ORIGIN late 19th cent.: from IN-² 'in' + Latin *fructus* 'fruit,' on the pattern of *inflorescence.*

in·fu·la /ˈinfyələ/ ▶ **n.** (pl. **infulae** /-lē/) (in the Christian Church) either of the two ribbons on a bishop's miter.
– ORIGIN early 17th cent.: from Latin, denoting a woolen fillet worn by a priest or placed on the head of a sacrificial victim.

in·fun·dib·u·lum /ˌinfənˈdibyələm/ ▶ **n.** (pl. **infundibula** /-lə/) Anatomy & Zoology a funnel-shaped cavity or structure. ■ the hollow stalk that connects the hypothalamus and the posterior pituitary gland.
– DERIVATIVES **in·fun·dib·u·lar** /-lər/ adj.
– ORIGIN mid 16th cent.: from Latin, 'funnel,' from *infundere* 'pour in.'

in·fu·ri·ate /inˈfyo͝orēˌāt/ ▶ **v.** [with obj.] make (someone) extremely angry and impatient: *her silences infuriated him.*
– ORIGIN mid 17th cent.: from medieval Latin *infuriat-* 'made angry,' from the verb *infuriare*, from *in-* 'into' + Latin *furia* 'fury.'

in·fu·ri·at·ing /inˈfyo͝orēˌātiNG/ ▶ **adj.** making one extremely angry and impatient; very annoying: *that infuriating half-smile on his face.*
– DERIVATIVES **in·fu·ri·at·ing·ly** adv. [as submodifier] *the truth is infuriatingly hard to pin down.*

in·fuse /inˈfyo͞oz/ ▶ **v.** [with obj.] **1** fill; pervade: *her work is **infused with** an anger born of pain and oppression.* ■ instill (a quality) in someone or something: *he did his best to **infuse** good humor **into** his voice.* ■ Medicine allow (a liquid) to flow into a patient, vein, etc.: *saline was **infused into** the aorta.*
2 soak (tea, herbs, etc.) in liquid to extract the flavor or healing properties: *infuse the dried flowers in boiling water.* ■ [no obj.] (of tea, herbs, etc.) be soaked in this way: *allow the mixture to infuse for 15 minutes.*
– DERIVATIVES **in·fus·er** n.
– ORIGIN late Middle English: from Latin *infus-* 'poured in,' from the verb *infundere*, from *in-* 'into' + *fundere* 'pour.'

in·fu·si·ble /inˈfyo͞ozəbəl/ ▶ **adj.** (of a substance) not able to be melted or fused.

in·fu·sion /inˈfyo͞oZHən/ ▶ **n. 1** a drink, remedy, or extract prepared by soaking the leaves of a plant or herb in liquid. ■ the process of preparing such a drink, remedy, or extract.
2 the introduction of a new element or quality into something: *the infusion of $6.3 million for improvements* | *an infusion of youthful talent.* ■ Medicine the slow injection of a substance into a vein or tissue.
– ORIGIN late Middle English (denoting the pouring in of a liquid): from Latin *infusio(n-)*, from the verb *infundere* (see INFUSE).

in·fu·so·ri·a /ˌinfyəˈzôrēə/ ▶ **plural n.** Zoology, dated single-celled organisms of the former group Infusoria, which consisted mainly of ciliate protozoans.
– ORIGIN modern Latin, from Latin *infundere* (see INFUSE); so named because they were originally found in infusions of decaying organic matter.

-ing¹ /iNG/ ▶ **suffix 1** denoting a verbal action, an instance of this, or its result: *fighting* | *outing* | *building.* ■ denoting a verbal action relating to an occupation, skill, etc.: *banking* | *ice skating* | *welding.*
2 denoting material used for or associated with a process, etc.: *cladding* | *piping.* ■ denoting something involved in an action or process but with no corresponding verb: *scaffolding.*
3 forming the gerund of verbs (such as *painting* as in *I love painting*).
– ORIGIN Old English *-ung, -ing*, of Germanic origin.

-ing² ▶ **suffix 1** forming the present participle of verbs: *doing* | *calling.* ■ forming present participles used as adjectives: *charming.*
2 forming adjectives from nouns: *hulking.*
– ORIGIN Middle English: alteration of earlier *-ende*, later *-inde.*

-ing³ ▶ **suffix** (used esp. in names of coins and fractional parts) a thing belonging to or having the quality of: *farthing* | *riding.*
– ORIGIN Old English, of Germanic origin.

in·gath·er /ˈinˌgaT͟Hər/ ▶ **v.** [with obj.] formal gather (something) in or together: *it may not be possible to ingather that information within the time.*

Inge /iNG/, William (Motter) (1913–73) US playwright. He wrote *Come Back, Little Sheba* (1950), *Picnic* (1953), *Bus Stop* (1955), and *The Dark at the Top of the Stairs* (1957).

in·gem·i·nate /inˈjeməˌnāt/ ▶ **v.** [with obj.] archaic repeat or reiterate (a word or statement), typically for emphasis.
– ORIGIN late 16th cent. (originally as *engeminate*): from Latin *ingeminat-* 'redoubled,' from the verb *ingeminare*, from *in-* (expressing intensive force) + *geminare* (see GEMINATE).

Ing·en·housz /ˈiNGənˌhous/, Jan (1730–99), Dutch scientist. He is noted for his work on photosynthesis, in which he discovered that green plants placed in sunlight produce oxygen.

in·gen·ious /inˈjēnyəs/ ▶ **adj.** (of a person) clever, original, and inventive: *he was ingenious enough to overcome the limited budget.* ■ (of a machine or idea) cleverly and originally devised and well suited to its purpose.
– DERIVATIVES **in·gen·ious·ly** adv., **in·gen·ious·ness** n.
– ORIGIN late Middle English: from French *ingénieux* or Latin *ingeniosus*, from *ingenium* 'mind, intellect'; compare with ENGINE.

> **USAGE** **Ingenious** and **ingenuous** are often confused. **Ingenious** means 'clever, skillful, resourceful' (*an ingenious device*), while **ingenuous** means 'artless, frank' (*charmed by the ingenuous honesty of the child*).

in·gé·nue /ˈanjəˌno͞o, ˈänZH-/ ▶ **n.** an innocent or unsophisticated young woman. ■ a part of this type in a play. ■ an actress who plays such a part.
– ORIGIN French, feminine of *ingénu* 'ingenuous,' from Latin *ingenuus* (see INGENUOUS).

in·ge·nu·i·ty /ˌinjəˈn(y)o͞oitē/ ▶ **n.** the quality of being clever, original, and inventive.
– ORIGIN late 16th cent. (also in the senses 'nobility' and 'ingenuousness'): from Latin *ingenuitas* 'ingenuousness,' from *ingenuus* 'inborn.' The current meaning arose by confusion of INGENUOUS with INGENIOUS.

in·gen·u·ous /inˈjenyo͞oəs/ ▶ **adj.** (of a person or action) innocent and unsuspecting.
– DERIVATIVES **in·gen·u·ous·ly** adv., **in·gen·u·ous·ness** n.
– ORIGIN late 16th cent.: from Latin *ingenuus*, literally 'native, inborn,' from *in-* 'into' + an element related to *gignere* 'beget.' The original sense was 'noble, generous,' giving rise to 'honorably straightforward, frank,' hence 'innocently frank' (late 17th cent).

> **USAGE** On the difference between **ingenuous** and **ingenious**, see usage at INGENIOUS.

in·gest /inˈjest/ ▶ **v.** [with obj.] take (food, drink, or another substance) into the body by swallowing or absorbing it. ■ absorb (information): *he spent his days ingesting the contents of the library.*
– DERIVATIVES **in·ges·tion** /-ˈjesCHən/ n., **in·ges·tive** /-ˈjestiv/ adj.

–ORIGIN early 17th cent.: from Latin *ingest-* 'brought in,' from the verb *ingerere*, from *in-* 'into' + *gerere* 'carry.'

in·ges·ta /in'jestə/ ▶ **plural n.** Medicine & Zoology substances taken into the body as nourishment; food and drink.
–ORIGIN early 18th cent.: from Latin, 'things brought in.'

-ing form ▶ **n.** Grammar the form of an English verb ending in *-ing*, which can function as a noun, as an adjective, and in the formation of progressive tenses. See also PARTICIPLE, GERUND.

in·gle /'iNGgəl/ ▶ **n.** chiefly dialect a domestic fire or fireplace. ■ an inglenook.
–ORIGIN early 16th cent. (originally Scots): perhaps from Scottish Gaelic *aingeal* 'light, fire,' Irish *aingeal* 'live ember.'

in·gle·nook /'iNGgəl,no͝ok/ ▶ **n.** a space on either side of a large fireplace.
–ORIGIN late 18th cent.: from Scots INGLE + NOOK.

In·gle·wood /'iNGgəl,wo͝od/ a city in southwestern California, southwest of downtown Los Angeles; pop. 112,714 (est. 2008).

in·glo·ri·ous /in'glôrēəs/ ▶ **adj.** (of an action or situation) causing shame or a loss of honor: *the events are inglorious and culminate in a vicious gang crime.* ■ not famous or renowned.
–DERIVATIVES **in·glo·ri·ous·ly** adv., **in·glo·ri·ous·ness** n.
–ORIGIN mid 16th cent.: from Latin *inglorius* (from *in-* (expressing negation) + *gloria* 'glory') + -OUS.

in·go·ing /'in,gōiNG/ ▶ **adj.** [attrib.] going into or toward a particular place: *the paths of ingoing and outgoing rays.*

in·got /'iNGgət/ ▶ **n.** a block of steel, gold, silver, or other metal, typically oblong in shape.
–ORIGIN late Middle English (denoting a mold in which metal is cast): perhaps from IN + Old English *goten*, past participle of *geotan* 'pour, cast.'

in·graft ▶ **v.** variant spelling of ENGRAFT.

in·grain ▶ **v.** /in'grān/ (also **engrain**) [with obj.] firmly fix or establish (a habit, belief, or attitude) in a person.
▶ **adj.** /'in,grān/ (of a textile) composed of fibers that have been dyed different colors before being woven.
–ORIGIN late Middle English (originally as *engrain* in the sense 'dye with cochineal or in fast colors'): from EN-[1], IN-[2] (as an intensifier) + the verb GRAIN. The adjective is from *in grain* 'fast-dyed,' from the old use of *grain* meaning 'kermes, cochineal.'

in·grain car·pet ▶ **n.** a reversible carpet in which the pattern appears on both sides.

in·grained /in'grānd/ ▶ **adj.** (also **engrained**) **1** (of a habit, belief, or attitude) firmly fixed or established; difficult to change: *his deeply ingrained Catholic convictions.*
2 (of dirt or a stain) deeply embedded and thus difficult to remove: *the ingrained dirt on the flaking paintwork.*

in·grate /'in,grāt/ ▶ **n.** an ungrateful person.
▶ **adj.** literary ungrateful.
–ORIGIN late Middle English (as an adjective): from Latin *ingratus*, from *in-* 'not' + *gratus* 'grateful.'

in·gra·ti·ate /in'grāshē,āt/ ▶ **v.** (**ingratiate oneself**) bring oneself into favor with someone by flattering or trying to please them: *a social climber who had tried to* **ingratiate herself with** *the city gentry.*
–DERIVATIVES **in·gra·ti·a·tion** /-,grāshē'āshən/ n.
–ORIGIN early 17th cent.: from Latin *in gratiam* 'into favor,' on the pattern of obsolete Italian *ingratiare*, earlier form of *ingraziare*.

in·gra·ti·at·ing /in'grāshē,ātiNG/ ▶ **adj.** intended to gain approval or favor; sycophantic: *an ingratiating manner.*
–DERIVATIVES **in·gra·ti·at·ing·ly** adv.

in·grat·i·tude /in'grati,t(y)o͞od/ ▶ **n.** a discreditable lack of gratitude: *she returned her daughter's care with ingratitude and unkindness.*
–ORIGIN Middle English: from Old French, or from late Latin *ingratitudo*, from Latin *ingratus* 'ungrateful' (see INGRATE).

in·gra·ves·cent /,ingrə'vesənt/ ▶ **adj.** Medicine, rare (of a condition or symptom) gradually increasing in severity.
–DERIVATIVES **in·gra·ves·cence** n.
–ORIGIN early 19th cent.: from Latin *ingravescent-* 'growing heavy or worse,' from the verb *ingravescere* (based on *gravis* 'heavy').

in·gre·di·ent /in'grēdēənt, iNG-/ ▶ **n.** any of the foods or substances that are combined to make a particular dish: *pork is an important ingredient in many stir-fried dishes.* ■ a component part or element of something: *the affair contains all the ingredients of an insoluble mystery.*
–ORIGIN late Middle English: from Latin *ingredient-* 'entering,' from the verb *ingredi*, from *in-* 'into' + *gradi* 'walk.'

In·gres /'aNGgrə/, Jean Auguste Dominique (1780–1867), French painter. He vigorously upheld neoclassicism in opposition to romanticism. Notable works: *Ambassadors of Agamemnon* (1801) and *The Bather* (1808).

in·gress /'in,gres/ ▶ **n. 1** a place or means of access; an entrance. ■ the action or fact of going in or entering. ■ the capacity or right of entrance. ■ chiefly Brit. the unwanted introduction of water, foreign bodies, contaminants, etc. into something.
2 Astronomy & Astrology the arrival of the sun, the moon, or a planet in a specified constellation or part of the sky. ■ the beginning of a transit.
–DERIVATIVES **in·gres·sion** /-'greshən/ n.
–ORIGIN late Middle English (in the sense 'an entrance or beginning'): from Latin *ingressus*, from the verb *ingredi* 'enter.'

in·gres·sive /in'gresiv/ ▶ **adj. 1** of or relating to ingress; having the quality or character of entering.
2 Phonetics (of a speech sound) made with an intake of air rather than an exhalation. Compare with EGRESSIVE. ■ (of an airflow) inward.
▶ **n.** an ingressive sound, e.g., a click.

in-group ▶ **n.** an exclusive, typically small, group of people with a shared interest or identity.

in·grow·ing /'in,grōiNG/ ▶ **adj.** growing inward or within something, esp. (of a toenail) growing abnormally so as to press into the flesh.

in·grown /'in,grōn/ ▶ **adj.** growing or having grown within a thing; innate: *as Greek instinct or ingrown habit would have dictated.* ■ (of a toenail) having grown abnormally so as to press into the flesh. ■ preoccupied with oneself; inward-looking: *direct mail is a clubby, ingrown world in which everybody knows everybody.* ■ Geology (of an incised meander) asymmetric in cross section due to lateral erosion.

in·growth /'in,grōTH/ ▶ **n.** a thing that has grown inward or within something. ■ the action of growing inward: *blocked by tumor ingrowth.*

in·gui·nal /'iNGgwənəl/ ▶ **adj.** [attrib.] Anatomy of the groin: *inguinal lymph nodes.*
–DERIVATIVES **in·gui·nal·ly** adv.
–ORIGIN late Middle English: from Latin *inguinalis*, from *inguen*, *inguin-* 'groin.'

in·gulf ▶ **v.** archaic spelling of ENGULF.

in·gur·gi·tate /in'gərji,tāt/ ▶ **v.** [with obj.] literary swallow (something) greedily.
–DERIVATIVES **in·gur·gi·ta·tion** /-,gərji'tāshən/ n.
–ORIGIN late 16th cent.: from Latin *ingurgitat-* 'poured in, drenched,' from the verb *ingurgitare*, from *in-* 'into' + *gurges*, *gurgit-* 'whirlpool, gulf.'

In·gush /in'go͞osh/ ▶ **n.** (pl. **same** or **Ingushes**) **1** a member of a people living mainly in Ingushetia in the central Caucasus.
2 the North Caucasian language of this people.
▶ **adj.** of or relating to the Ingush or their language.
–ORIGIN Russian.

In·gu·she·ti·a /ingo͞o'sHetēə/ an autonomous republic in the central Caucasus in SW Russia, between Chechnya and North Ossetia; pop. 506,600 (est. 2009). Also called **Ingush Republic**.

INH ▶ **abbr.** isonicotinic acid hydrazide.

in·hab·it /in'habit/ ▶ **v.** (**inhabits**, **inhabiting**, **inhabited**) [with obj.] (of a person, animal, or group) live in or occupy (a place or environment): *a bird that inhabits North America | urban centers inhabited by more than 10 million people* | (as adj. **inhabited**) *the loneliest inhabited place on Earth.*
–DERIVATIVES **in·hab·i·ta·tion** /-,habi'tāshən/ n.
–ORIGIN late Middle English *inhabite*, *enhabite*, from Old French *enhabiter* or Latin *inhabitare*, from *in-* 'in' + *habitare* 'dwell' (from *habere* 'have').

in·hab·it·a·ble /in'habitəbəl/ ▶ **adj.** suitable to live in; habitable: *soon we will run out of inhabitable space on the planet.*
–DERIVATIVES **in·hab·it·a·bil·i·ty** /-,habitə'bilitē/ n.

in·hab·it·an·cy /in'habitn-sē/ (also **inhabitance**) ▶ **n.** archaic living in a certain place as an inhabitant, esp. during a specified period so as to acquire certain rights.

in·hab·it·ant /in'habitnt/ ▶ **n.** a person or animal that lives in or occupies a place. ■ a person who fulfills the requirements for legal residency.
–ORIGIN late Middle English: from Old French, from Latin *inhabitare* 'inhabit.'

in·hal·ant /in'hālənt/ ▶ **n.** a medicinal preparation for inhaling. ■ a solvent or other material producing vapor inhaled by drug abusers.
▶ **adj.** [attrib.] chiefly Zoology serving for inhalation: *inhalant canals.*

in·ha·la·tion /,inhə'lāshən/ ▶ **n.** the action of inhaling or breathing in: *the inhalation of airborne particles | with every inhalation air passes over the vocal cords.* ■ Medicine the inhaling of medicines or anesthetics in the form of a gas or vapor. ■ Medicine a preparation to be inhaled in the form of a vapor or spray.
–ORIGIN early 17th cent.: from medieval Latin *inhalatio(n-)*, from *inhalare* 'inhale.'

in·ha·la·tor /'inhə,lātər/ ▶ **n.** a device for inhaling something, esp. oxygen; a respirator; an inhaler.

in·hale /in'hāl/ ▶ **v.** breathe in (air, gas, smoke, etc.): [with obj.] *they were taken to the hospital after inhaling fumes* | [no obj.] *she inhaled deeply on another cigarette.* ■ [with obj.] informal eat (food) greedily or rapidly: *later on I inhaled a box of chocolate cookies while watching cable TV.*
–ORIGIN early 18th cent.: from Latin *inhalare* 'breathe in,' from *in-* 'in' + *halare* 'breathe.'

in·hal·er /in'hālər/ ▶ **n.** a portable device for administering a drug that is to be breathed in, used for relieving asthma and other bronchial or nasal congestion.

in·har·mon·ic /,inhär'mänik/ ▶ **adj.** chiefly Music not harmonic.
–DERIVATIVES **in·har·mo·nic·i·ty** /-mə'nisitē/ n.

in·har·mo·ni·ous /,inhär'mōnēəs/ ▶ **adj.** not forming or contributing to a pleasing whole; discordant: *an inharmonious, negative state of mind.*
–DERIVATIVES **in·har·mo·ni·ous·ly** adv.

in·here /in'hi(ə)r/ ▶ **v.** [no obj.] (**inhere in/within**) formal exist essentially or permanently in: *the potential for change that inheres within the adult education world.* ■ Law (of rights, powers, etc.) be vested in a person or group or attached to the ownership of a property: *the rights inhering in the property they owned.*
–ORIGIN mid 16th cent. (in the sense 'stick, cling to'): from Latin *inhaerere* 'stick to.'

in·her·ent /in'hi(ə)rənt, -'her-/ ▶ **adj.** existing in something as a permanent, essential, or characteristic attribute: *any form of mountaineering has its inherent dangers | the symbolism inherent in all folk tales.* ■ Law vested in (someone) as a right or privilege: *the president's inherent foreign affairs power.*
–DERIVATIVES **in·her·ence** n., **in·her·ent·ly** adv.
–ORIGIN late 16th cent.: from Latin *inhaerent-* 'sticking to,' from the verb *inhaerere*, from *in-* 'in, toward' + *haerere* 'to stick.'

in·her·it /in'herit/ ▶ **v.** (**inherits**, **inheriting**, **inherited**) [with obj.] receive (money, property, or a title) as an heir at the death of the previous holder: *she inherited a fortune from her father.* ■ derive (a quality, characteristic, or predisposition) genetically from one's parents or ancestors: *she had inherited the beauty of her grandmother.* ■ receive or be left with (a situation, object, etc.) from a predecessor or former owner: *spending commitments inherited from previous administrations.* ■ come into possession of (belongings) from someone else: *she inherits all her clothes from her older sisters.* ■ archaic come into possession of (something) as a right (esp. in biblical translations and allusions): *master, what must I do to inherit eternal life?*
–ORIGIN Middle English *enherite* 'receive as a right,' from Old French *enheriter*, from late Latin *inhereditare* 'appoint as heir,' from Latin *in-* 'in' + *heres*, *hered-* 'heir.'

in·her·it·a·ble /in'heritəbəl/ ▶ **adj.** capable of being inherited: *these characteristics are inheritable | inheritable property.*
–DERIVATIVES **in·her·it·a·bil·i·ty** /-,heritə'bilitē/ n.
–ORIGIN late Middle English (formerly also as *enheritable*): from Anglo-Norman French *enheritable* 'able to be made heir,' from Old French *enheriter* (see INHERIT).

in·her·it·ance /in'heritəns/ ▶ **n.** a thing that is inherited: *he came into a comfortable inheritance.* ■ the action of inheriting: *the inheritance of traits.*
–ORIGIN late Middle English (formerly also as *enheritance*): from Anglo-Norman French *enheritaunce* 'being admitted as heir,' from Old French *enheriter* (see INHERIT).

in·her·it·ance tax ▶ **n.** a tax imposed on someone who inherits property or money. Also called DEATH TAX.

in·her·i·tor /in'heritər/ ▶ **n.** a person who inherits something; an heir: *we are the inheritors of these cultural traditions.*

in·he·sion /in'hēZHən/ ▶ **n.** formal the action or state of inhering in something.
–ORIGIN mid 17th cent.: from late Latin *inhaesio(n-)*, from Latin *inhaerere* 'stick to.'

in·hib·in /in'hibin/ ▶ **n.** Biochemistry a gonadal hormone that inhibits the secretion of follicle-stimulating hormone, under consideration as a potential male contraceptive.
–ORIGIN 1930s: from Latin *inhibere* 'hinder' + -IN[1].

in·hib·it /in'hibit/ ▶ **v.** (**inhibits, inhibiting, inhibited**) [with obj.] **1** hinder, restrain, or prevent (an action or process): *cold inhibits plant growth.* ■ prevent or prohibit (someone) from doing something: *the earnings rule **inhibited** some retired people **from** working.* ■ Psychology voluntarily or involuntarily restrain the direct expression of (an instinctive impulse). ■ chiefly Physiology & Biochemistry (chiefly of a drug or other substance) slow down or prevent (a process, reaction, or function) or reduce the activity of (an enzyme or other agent).
2 make (someone) self-conscious and unable to act in a relaxed and natural way: *his mother's strictures would always inhibit him.*
3 (in ecclesiastical law) forbid (a member of the clergy) to exercise clerical functions.
– DERIVATIVES **in·hib·i·tive** /-tiv/ **adj.**, **in·hib·i·to·ry** /-,tôrē/ **adj.**
– ORIGIN late Middle English (in the sense 'forbid (a person) to do something'): from Latin *inhibere* 'hinder,' from *in-* 'in' + *habere* 'hold.'

in·hib·it·ed /in'hibitid/ ▶ **adj.** unable to act in a relaxed and natural way because of self-consciousness or mental restraint: *I could never appear nude, I'm far too inhibited.*

in·hi·bi·tion /,in(h)i'bisHən/ ▶ **n.** a feeling that makes one self-conscious and unable to act in a relaxed and natural way: *the children, at first shy, soon lost their inhibitions | a powerful tranquilizer that causes lack of inhibition.* ■ Psychology a voluntary or involuntary restraint on the direct expression of an instinct. ■ the action of inhibiting, restricting, or hindering a process. ■ the slowing or prevention of a process, reaction, or function by a particular substance.
– ORIGIN late Middle English (in the sense 'forbidding, a prohibition'): from Latin *inhibitio(n-)*, from the verb *inhibere* (see INHIBIT).

in·hib·i·tor /in'hibitər/ ▶ **n.** a thing that inhibits someone or something. ■ a substance that slows down or prevents a particular chemical reaction or other process, or that reduces the activity of a particular reactant, catalyst, or enzyme. ■ Genetics a gene whose presence prevents the expression of some other gene at a different locus.

in-home ▶ **adj.** [attrib.] (of a service or activity) provided or taking place within a person's home: *the best in in-home entertainment.*

in·ho·mo·ge·ne·ous /in,hōmə'jēnēəs, -,hämə-/ ▶ **adj.** not uniform in character or content; diverse. ■ Mathematics consisting of terms that are not all of the same degree or dimensions.
– DERIVATIVES **in·ho·mo·ge·ne·i·ty** /-,hōməjə'nē-itē, -'nā-itē, -,hämə-/ **n.**

in·hos·pi·ta·ble /,inhä'spitəbəl, in'häs-/ ▶ **adj.** (of an environment) harsh and difficult to live in: *the inhospitable landscape.* ■ (of a person) unfriendly and unwelcoming toward people.
– DERIVATIVES **in·hos·pi·ta·ble·ness** **n.**, **in·hos·pi·ta·bly** /-blē/ **adv.**, **in·hos·pi·tal·i·ty** /in,häspi'talitē, ,inhäs-/ **n.**
– ORIGIN late 16th cent.: French, from *in-* 'not' + *hospitable* (see HOSPITABLE).

in-house ▶ **adj.** [attrib.] done or existing within an organization: *in-house publications.*
▶ **adv.** without assistance from outside an organization; internally: *services previously provided in-house are being contracted out.*

in·hu·man /in'(h)yōōmən/ ▶ **adj. 1** lacking human qualities of compassion and mercy; cruel and barbaric.
2 not human in nature or character: *the inhuman scale of the dinosaurs.*
– DERIVATIVES **in·hu·man·ly** **adv.**
– ORIGIN late Middle English (originally as *inhumane*): from Latin *inhumanus*, from *in-* 'not' + *humanus* (see HUMAN).

in·hu·mane /'inhyōō'mān/ ▶ **adj.** without compassion for misery or suffering; cruel: *confining wild horses is inhumane.*
– DERIVATIVES **in·hu·mane·ly** **adv.**
– ORIGIN late Middle English (in the sense 'inhuman, brutal'): originally a variant of INHUMAN (rare after 1700); in modern use from IN-[1] 'not' + HUMANE (the current sense dating from the early 19th cent.).

in·hu·man·i·ty /,in(h)yōō'manitē/ ▶ **n.** (pl. **inhumanities**) extremely cruel and brutal behavior: *a justification for further cruelty and inhumanity.*
– ORIGIN late 15th cent.: from Old French *inhumanite* or Latin *inhumanitas*, from *inhumanus* 'inhuman.'

in·hume /in'(h)yōōm/ ▶ **v.** [with obj.] bury: *no hand his bones shall gather or inhume.*
– DERIVATIVES **in·hu·ma·tion** /,in(h)yōō'māsHən/ **n.**
– ORIGIN early 17th cent.: from Latin *inhumare*, from *in-* 'into' + *humus* 'ground.'

in·im·i·cal /i'nimikəl/ ▶ **adj.** tending to obstruct or harm: *actions **inimical to** our interests.* ■ unfriendly; hostile: *an inimical alien power.*
– DERIVATIVES **in·im·i·cal·ly** /-ik(ə)lē/ **adv.**
– ORIGIN early 16th cent.: from late Latin *inimicalis*, from Latin *inimicus* (see ENEMY).

in·im·i·ta·ble /i'nimitəbəl/ ▶ **adj.** so good or unusual as to be impossible to copy; unique: *the inimitable ambience of Hawaii.*
– DERIVATIVES **in·im·i·ta·bil·i·ty** /i,nimitə'bilitē/ **n.**, **in·im·i·ta·bly** /-blē/ **adv.**
– ORIGIN late 15th cent.: from French, or from Latin *inimitabilis*, from *in-* 'not' + *imitabilis* (from *imitari* 'imitate').

in·i·on /'inēən/ ▶ **n.** Anatomy the projecting part of the occipital bone at the base of the skull.
– ORIGIN early 19th cent.: from Greek, literally 'nape of the neck.'

in·iq·ui·tous /ɪ'nɪkwitəs/ ▶ **adj.** grossly unfair and morally wrong: *an iniquitous tax.*
– DERIVATIVES **in·iq·ui·tous·ly** /-witəslē/ **adv.**, **in·iq·ui·tous·ness** /-witəsnəs/ **n.**

in·iq·ui·ty /i'nikwitē/ ▶ **n.** (pl. **iniquities**) immoral or grossly unfair behavior: *a den of iniquity | a liberal lawyer could uncover the iniquities committed on his own doorstep.*
– ORIGIN Middle English: from Old French *iniquite*, from Latin *iniquitas*, from *iniquus*, from *in-* 'not' + *aequus* 'equal, just.'

in·i·tial /i'nisHəl/ ▶ **adj.** [attrib.] existing or occurring at the beginning: *our initial impression was favorable.* ■ (of a letter) at the beginning of a word.
▶ **n.** (usu. **initials**) the first letter of a name or word, typically a person's name or a word forming part of a phrase: *they carved their initials into the tree trunk.*
▶ **v.** (**initials, initialing, initialed**; Brit. **initials, initialling, initialled**) [with obj.] mark or sign (a document) with one's initials, esp. in order to authorize or validate it. ■ agree to or ratify (a treaty or contract) by signing it.
– ORIGIN early 16th cent.: from Latin *initialis*, from *initium* 'beginning,' from *inire* 'go in,' from *in-* 'into' + *ire* 'go.'

in·i·tial·ese /i,nisHə'lēz/ ▶ **n.** informal the use of abbreviations formed by using initial letters.

in·i·tial·ism /i'nisHə,lizəm/ ▶ **n.** an abbreviation consisting of initial letters pronounced separately (e.g., *CPU*).

in·i·tial·ize /i'nisHə,līz/ ▶ **v.** [with obj.] Computing **1** (often **be initialized to**) set to the value or put in the condition appropriate to the start of an operation: *the counter is initialized to one.*
2 format (a computer disk).
– DERIVATIVES **in·i·tial·i·za·tion** /i,nisHəli'zāsHən/ **n.**

in·i·tial·ly /i'nisHəlē/ ▶ **adv.** [usu. sentence adverb] at first: *initially, he thought the new concept was nonsense.*

in·i·tial pub·lic of·fer·ing ▶ **n.** a company's flotation on the stock exchange.

in·i·ti·and /i'nisHē,and/ ▶ **n.** a person about to be initiated.
– ORIGIN early 20th cent.: from Latin *initiandus*, from *initiare* 'to initiate.'

in·i·ti·ate ▶ **v.** /i'nisHē,āt/ [with obj.] **1** cause (a process or action) to begin: *he proposes to initiate discussions on planning procedures.*
2 admit (someone) into a secret or obscure society or group, typically with a ritual: *she had been formally **initiated into** the sorority.* ■ (as plural noun **the initiated**) a small group of people who share obscure knowledge: *he flies over an airway marker beacon, known as a "fix" to the initiated.*
■ (**initiate someone in/into**) introduce someone to (a particular activity or skill), esp. a difficult or obscure one: *they were initiated into the mysteries of trigonometry.*
▶ **n.** /i'nisHēit/ a person who has been initiated into an organization or activity, typically recently: *initiates of the Shiva cult* | [as modifier] *the initiate Marines.*
– DERIVATIVES **in·i·ti·a·to·ry** /-ə,tôrē/ **adj.**
– ORIGIN mid 16th cent. (sense 2 of the verb): from Latin *initiat-* 'begun,' from the verb *initiare*, from *initium* 'beginning.'

in·i·ti·a·tion /i,nisHē'āsHən/ ▶ **n. 1** the action of admitting someone into a secret or obscure society or group, typically with a ritual: *rituals of initiation* | [as modifier] *an initiation ceremony.* ■ the introduction of someone to a particular activity or skill: *his initiation into the world of martial arts.*
2 the action of beginning something: *the initiation of criminal proceedings.*

in·i·ti·a·tive /i'nisH(ē)ətiv/ ▶ **n. 1** the ability to assess and initiate things independently: *use your initiative, imagination, and common sense.*
2 [in sing.] the power or opportunity to act or take charge before others do: *we have lost the initiative and allowed our opponents to dictate the subject.*
3 an act or strategy intended to resolve a difficulty or improve a situation; a fresh approach to something: *a new initiative against car crime.* ■ a proposal made by one nation to another in an attempt to improve relations: *diplomatic initiatives to end the war | a peace initiative aimed at reducing tensions.*
4 (**the initiative**) (esp. in some US states and Switzerland) the right of citizens outside the legislature to originate legislation.
– PHRASES **on one's own initiative** without being prompted by others. **take** (or **seize**) **the initiative** be the first to take action in a particular situation: *antihunting groups have seized the initiative in the dispute.*
– ORIGIN late 18th cent.: from French, from Latin *initiare*, from *initium* 'beginning.'

in·i·ti·a·tor /i'nisHē,ātər/ ▶ **n.** a person or thing that initiates someone or something. ■ Chemistry a substance that starts a chain reaction. ■ an explosive or device used to detonate a larger one.

inj. ▶ **abbr.** injection.

in·ject /in'jekt/ ▶ **v.** [with obj.] **1** drive or force (a liquid, esp. a drug or vaccine) into a person or animal's body with a syringe or similar device: *the doctor injected a painkilling drug.* ■ administer a drug or medicine to (a person or animal) in this way: *he **injected** himself **with** a drug overdose.* ■ [no obj.] inject oneself with a narcotic drug, esp. habitually: *people who want to stop injecting.* ■ introduce (something) into a passage, cavity, or solid material under pressure: *inject the foam and allow it to expand.* ■ Physics introduce or feed (a current, beam of particles, etc.) into a substance or device. ■ place (a spacecraft or other object) into an orbit or trajectory: *many meteoroids are **injected into** hyperbolic orbits.*
2 introduce (a new or different element) into something, esp. as a boost or interruption: *she tried to **inject** scorn **into** her tone.* ■ (**inject something with**) imbue something with (a new element): *he injected his voice with a confidence he didn't feel.*
– DERIVATIVES **in·ject·a·ble** **adj. & n.**
– ORIGIN late 16th cent. (in the sense 'throw or cast on something'): from Latin *inject-* 'thrown in,' from the verb *inicere*, from *in-* 'into' + *jacere* 'throw.'

in·jec·tion /in'jeksHən/ ▶ **n. 1** an instance of injecting or being injected: *painkilling injections | an injection of capital was needed.* ■ a thing that is injected: *a morphine injection.* ■ the action of injecting: *sometimes a polio vaccine is given by injection.* ■ short for FUEL INJECTION.
2 the entry or placing of a spacecraft or other object into an orbit or trajectory.
– ORIGIN late Middle English: from Latin *injectio(n-)*, from the verb *inicere* (see INJECT).

in·jec·tion mold·ing ▶ **n.** the shaping of rubber or plastic articles by injecting heated material into a mold.
– DERIVATIVES **in·jec·tion-mold·ed** **adj.**

in·jec·tor /in'jektər/ ▶ **n.** a person or thing that injects something. ■ (also **fuel injector**) (in an internal combustion engine) the nozzle and valve through which fuel is sprayed into a combustion chamber. ■ (in a steam engine) a system of nozzles that uses steam to inject water into a pressurized boiler.

in·je·ra /in'ji(ə)rə/ ▶ **n.** a white leavened Ethiopian bread made from teff flour, similar to a crepe.
– ORIGIN Amharic.

in-joke ▶ **n.** a joke that is shared exclusively by a small group of people.

in·ju·di·cious /'injōō'disHəs/ ▶ **adj.** showing very poor judgment; unwise: *I took a few injudicious swigs of potent cider.*
– DERIVATIVES **in·ju·di·cious·ly** **adv.**, **in·ju·di·cious·ness** **n.**

In·jun /'injən/ ▶ **n.** informal, offensive an American Indian.
– PHRASES **honest Injun** dated honestly; really: *I won't run away, honest Injun.*
– ORIGIN late 17th cent.: alteration of INDIAN.

in·junc·tion /in'jəNG(k)sHən/ ▶ **n.** an authoritative warning or order. ■ Law a judicial order that restrains a person from beginning or continuing an action threatening or invading the legal right of another, or that compels a person to carry out a certain act, e.g., to make restitution to an injured party.
– DERIVATIVES **in·junc·tive** /-'jəNG(k)tiv/ **adj.**
– ORIGIN late Middle English: from late Latin *injunctio(n-)*, from Latin *injungere* 'enjoin, impose.'

in·jure /'injər/ ▶ **v.** [with obj.] do physical harm or damage to (someone): *the explosion injured several people.* ■ suffer physical harm or damage to (a part of one's body): *he injured his back.* ■ harm or impair (something): *a libel calculated to injure the company's reputation.* ■ archaic do injustice or wrong to (someone).
– DERIVATIVES **in·jur·er** **n.**

–ORIGIN late Middle English: back-formation from INJURY.

in·jured /'injərd/ ▶ adj. 1 harmed, damaged, or impaired: *a road accident left him severely injured.* 2 offended: *his injured pride.*

in·ju·ri·ous /in'jo͝orēəs/ ▶ adj. causing or likely to cause damage or harm: *high temperature is injurious to mangoes.* ■ (of language) maliciously insulting; libelous.
–DERIVATIVES **in·ju·ri·ous·ly** adv., **in·ju·ri·ous·ness** n.
–ORIGIN late Middle English: from French *injurieux* or Latin *injuriosus*, from *injuria* 'a wrong' (see INJURY).

in·ju·ry /'injərē/ ▶ n. (pl. **injuries**) an instance of being injured: *she suffered an injury to her back | an ankle injury.* ■ the fact of being injured; harm or damage: *all escaped without serious injury.* ■ (**injury to**) offense to: *the possible injury to the feelings of others.*
–PHRASES **do oneself an injury** informal suffer physical harm or damage.
–ORIGIN late Middle English: from Anglo-Norman French *injurie*, from Latin *injuria* 'a wrong,' from *in-* (expressing negation) + *jus, jur-* 'right.'

in·ju·ry time ▶ n. (in soccer and other sports) extra playing time allowed by a referee to compensate for time lost in dealing with injuries.

in·jus·tice /in'jəstis/ ▶ n. lack of fairness or justice: *the injustice of the death penalty.* ■ an unjust act or occurrence: *brooding over life's injustices.*
–PHRASES **do someone an injustice** judge a person unfairly.
–ORIGIN late Middle English: from Old French, from Latin *injustitia*, from *in-* 'not' + *justus* 'just, right.'

ink /iNGk/ ▶ n. a colored fluid used for writing, drawing, printing, or duplicating: *the names are written in ink | a picture executed in colored inks.* ■ informal publicity in the written media: *the story got lots of ink and plenty of air time.* ■ Zoology a black liquid ejected by a cuttlefish, octopus, or squid to confuse a predator.
▶ v. 1 [with obj.] mark (words or a design) with ink: *the cork has the name of the château inked onto the side.* ■ cover (type or a stamp) with ink before printing: *a raised image is inked to produce an impression.* ■ (**ink something in**) fill in writing or a design with ink: *she inked in a cloud of dust.* ■ (**ink something out**) obliterate something, esp. writing, with ink: *he carefully inked out each word.*
2 informal sign (a contract): *she's just inked a deal to host her own talk show.* ■ secure the services of (someone) with a contract: *he has been inked as host for next year's ceremony.*
–DERIVATIVES **ink·er** n.
–ORIGIN Middle English *enke, inke*, from Old French *enque*, via late Latin from Greek *enkauston*, denoting the purple ink used by Roman emperors for signatures, from *enkaiein* 'burn in.'

In·ka·tha /in'kätə/ (in full **Inkatha Freedom Party**) (abbr.: **IFP**) a mainly Zulu political party and organization in South Africa, founded in 1928 and revived in 1975 by Chief Buthelezi. It has a professed aim of racial equality and universal franchise in South Africa, but progress toward political reform was obstructed by violent clashes between Inkatha factions and members of the rival ANC.
–ORIGIN from Zulu *inkhata* 'crown of woven grass,' a tribal emblem symbolizing the force unifying the Zulu nation.

ink·ber·ry /'iNGk,berē/ ▶ n. (pl. **inkberries**) 1 another term for LOW GALLBERRY (see GALLBERRY). 2 another term for POKEWEED.

ink·blot test /'iNGk,blät/ ▶ n. another term for RORSCHACH TEST.

ink·horn /'iNGk,hôrn/ ▶ n. historical a small portable container for ink. ■ [as modifier] denoting pedantic words or expressions used only in academic writing: *I will avoid many of the inkhorn terms coined by the narratologists.*

ink-jet print·er ▶ n. a printer in which the characters are formed by minute jets of ink.

in·kle /'iNGkəl/ ▶ n. a kind of linen tape formerly used to make laces, or the linen yarn from which this is manufactured.
–ORIGIN mid 16th cent.: of unknown origin.

ink·ling /'iNGkliNG/ ▶ n. a slight knowledge or suspicion; a hint: *the records give us an inkling of how people saw the world.*
–ORIGIN late Middle English (in the sense 'a mention in an undertone, a hint'): from the rare verb *inkle* 'utter in an undertone,' of unknown origin.

ink pad ▶ n. an ink-soaked pad in a shallow box, used for inking a rubber stamp or taking fingerprints.

ink·stand /'iNGk,stand/ ▶ n. a stand for one or more ink bottles, typically incorporating a pen tray.

ink·well /'iNGk,wel/ ▶ n. a container for ink typically housed in a hole in a desk.

ink·y /'iNGkē/ ▶ adj. (**inkier, inkiest**) 1 as dark as ink: *the cold inky blackness of a Mexican cave.* 2 stained with ink: *bureaucrats with inky fingers.*
–DERIVATIVES **ink·i·ness** n.

ink·y cap ▶ n. a widely distributed mushroom with a tall, narrow cap and slender white stem, turning into a black liquid after the spores are shed. ● Genus *Coprinus*, family Coprinaceae, class Hymenomycetes: several species, including the **common ink cap** (*C. atramentarius*). See also SHAGGY MANE.

in·laid /'in,lād/ past and past participle of INLAY.

in·land /'in,land, -lənd/ ▶ adj. situated in the interior of a country rather than on the coast: *the deserts of inland Australia.* ■ [attrib.] chiefly Brit. carried on within the limits of a country; domestic: *a network of waterways that allowed inland trade.*
▶ adv. in or toward the interior of a country: *the path turned inland and met the road.*
▶ n. (**the inland**) the parts of a country remote from the sea or borders; the interior.
–DERIVATIVES **in·land·er** n.

In·land Em·pire ▶ n. an area of the Pacific Northwest including parts of Washington, Oregon, Idaho, and Montana, which shares many geographic and economic features. ■ any of various other areas so designated by their residents, esp. the older, eastern part of greater Los Angeles.

in·land nav·i·ga·tion ▶ n. transportation by canals, rivers, and lakes.

In·land Sea an almost landlocked arm of the Pacific Ocean that is surrounded by the Japanese islands of Honshu, Shikoku, and Kyushu. Its chief port is Hiroshima.

in·land sea ▶ n. an entirely landlocked large body of salt or fresh water.

in-law ▶ n. a relative by marriage.

in·lay ▶ v. /,in'lā/ (past and past participle **inlaid**) [with obj.] (usu. **be inlaid**) ornament (an object) by embedding pieces of a different material in it, flush with its surface: *mahogany paneling **inlaid with** rosewood.* ■ embed (something) in an object in this way: *a small silver crown was inlaid in the wood.* ■ insert (a page, an illustration, etc.) in a space cut in a larger thicker page.
▶ n. /'in,lā/ 1 a design, pattern, or piece of material inlaid in something: *ivory inlays that decorated wooden furnishings.* ■ a material or substance that is inlaid. ■ inlaid work: *the cathedral was decorated with mosaic and inlay.* ■ the technique of inlaying material.
2 a filling shaped to fit a tooth cavity.
3 chiefly Brit. a printed card or paper insert supplied with a CD, video, etc.: [as modifier] *an inlay card.*
–DERIVATIVES **in·lay·er** n.
–ORIGIN mid 16th cent. (in the sense 'lay something in a place in order to hide or preserve it'): from IN-[2] 'into' + LAY[1].

in·let /'in,let, -lit/ ▶ n. 1 a small arm of the sea, a lake, or a river.
2 a place or means of entry: *an air inlet.*
3 (chiefly in tailoring and dressmaking) an inserted piece of material.
–ORIGIN Middle English (denoting admission): from IN + the verb LET[1].

in·li·er /'in,līər/ ▶ n. Geology an older rock formation isolated among newer rocks.
–ORIGIN mid 19th cent.: from IN, on the pattern of *outlier*.

in-line ▶ adj. 1 having parts arranged in a line: *a 24-valve in-line 6-cylinder engine.*
2 constituting an integral part of a continuous sequence of operations or machines: *a two-stream in-line fuel-oil blender.* ■ constituting an integral part of a computer program: *the parameters can be set up as in-line code.*

in-line en·gine ▶ n. a type of internal combustion engine used chiefly in aircraft, having its cylinders arranged in a row.

in-lin·er ▶ n. an in-line skater. ■ an in-line skate.

in-line skate ▶ n. a roller skate in which the wheels are fixed in a single line along the sole of the boot.
–DERIVATIVES **in-line skat·er** n., **in-line skat·ing** n.

in-line skate

in lo·co pa·ren·tis /in ,lōkō pə'rentis/ ▶ adv. & adj. (of a teacher or other adult responsible for children) in the place of a parent: [as adv.] *he was used to acting in loco parentis* | [as adj.] *they adhered to an in loco parentis approach when dealing with students.*
–ORIGIN early 19th cent.: Latin.

in·ly /'inlē/ ▶ adv. literary inwardly: *inly stung with anger and disdain.*
–ORIGIN Old English *innlīce* (see IN, -LY[2]).

In·man /'inmən/, Henry (1801–46) US artist. A leading portraitist, he painted many well-known people of his time. He also helped to found the National Academy of Design 1826.

In·mar·sat /'inmär,sat/ an international organization founded in 1978 that provides telecommunication services, as well as distress and safety communication services, to the world's shipping, aviation, and offshore industries.
–ORIGIN from initials of *International Maritime Satellite Organization.*

in·mate /'in,māt/ ▶ n. a person confined to an institution such as a prison or hospital. ■ archaic one of several occupants of a house.
–ORIGIN late 16th cent. (denoting a person who shared a house, specifically a lodger or subtenant): probably originally from INN + MATE[1], later associated with IN.

in me·di·as res /in 'mēdēəs 'res, 'mādē,äs/ ▶ adv. into the middle of a narrative; without preamble: *having begun his story in medias res, he then interrupts it.* ■ into the midst of things.
–ORIGIN late 18th cent.: Latin, literally 'into the middle of things.'

in me·mo·ri·am /,in mə'môrēəm/ ▶ n. [often as modifier] an article written in memory of a dead person; an obituary: *in memoriam notices in the paper.*
▶ prep. in memory of (a dead person): *an openly revolutionary work in memoriam Che Guevara.*
–ORIGIN mid 19th cent.: Latin, literally 'to the memory (of).'

in·most /'in,mōst/ ▶ adj. literary innermost.
–ORIGIN Old English *innemest* (see IN, -MOST).

In·mut·too·yah·lat·lat /in,mo͞oto͞oyä'lät,lät/ see JOSEPH[2].

inn /in/ ▶ n. an establishment providing accommodations, food, and drink, esp. for travelers. ■ [usu. in names] a restaurant or bar, typically one in the country, in some cases providing accommodations: *the Waterside Inn.*
–ORIGIN Old English (in the sense 'dwelling place, lodging'): of Germanic origin; related to IN. In Middle English the word was used to translate Latin *hospitium* (see HOSPICE), denoting a house of residence for students: this sense is preserved in the names of some buildings formerly used for this purpose, notably *Gray's Inn* and *Lincoln's Inn*, two of the INNS OF COURT. The current sense dates from late Middle English.

in·nards /'inərdz/ ▶ plural n. informal entrails. ■ internal workings (of a device or machine).
–ORIGIN early 19th cent.: representing a dialect pronunciation of INWARDS, used as a noun.

in·nate /i'nāt/ ▶ adj. inborn; natural: *her innate capacity for organization.* ■ Philosophy originating in the mind.
–DERIVATIVES **in·nate·ly** adv., **in·nate·ness** n.
–ORIGIN late Middle English: from Latin *innatus*, past participle of *innasci*, from *in-* 'into' + *nasci* 'be born.'

in·ner /'inər/ ▶ adj. [attrib.] 1 situated inside or further in; internal: *an inner courtyard | the inner thigh.* ■ close to the center: *the inner solar system.* ■ close to the center of power: *the inner cabinet.*
2 mental or spiritual: *a test of inner strength.* ■ (of thoughts or feelings) private and not expressed or discernible. ■ denoting a concealed or unacknowledged part of a person's personality: *it's time to get in touch with your inner geek | join a choir and give voice to that inner diva who has been hidden away too long.*
▶ n. the inner part of something: *using his rock shoes as inners for his double boots.* ■ (in archery and shooting) a division of the target next to the bull's-eye. ■ a shot that strikes the inner.
–DERIVATIVES **in·ner·ly** adv. (literary), **in·ner·ness** n. (literary).
–ORIGIN Old English *innerra, innra*, comparative of IN.

in·ner child ▶ n. a person's supposed original or true self, esp. when regarded as damaged or concealed by negative childhood experiences.

in·ner cir·cle ▶ n. an exclusive group close to the center of power of an organization or movement, regarded as elitist and secretive.

in·ner cit·y ▶ n. the area near the center of a city, esp. when associated with social and economic problems: [as modifier] *beleaguered inner-city schools.*

in·ner-di·rect·ed ▶ adj. Psychology (of a person or their behavior) governed by standards formed in childhood.

in·ner ear ▶ n. the semicircular canals and cochlea, which form the organs of balance and hearing and are embedded in the temporal bone.

in·ner light ▶ n. [in sing.] personal spiritual revelation; a source of enlightenment within oneself.
– ORIGIN mid 19th cent.: originally in Quaker doctrine.

in·ner man ▶ n. [in sing.] a man's soul or mind: *the complexities of the inner man.* ■ humorous a man's stomach: *the inner man was well catered for with pizza.*

In·ner Mon·go·li·a /mäNG'gōlēə/ an autonomous region in northern China, on the border with Mongolia; capital, Hohhot.

in·ner·most /'inər,mōst/ ▶ adj. [attrib.] **1** (of thoughts or feelings) most private and deeply felt: *innermost beliefs and convictions.*
2 furthest in; closest to the center: *the innermost layer.*

in·ner plan·et ▶ n. a planet whose orbit lies within the asteroid belt, i.e., Mercury, Venus, Earth, or Mars.

in·ner prod·uct ▶ n. Mathematics a scalar function of two vectors, equal to the product of their magnitudes and the cosine of the angle between them. Also called DOT PRODUCT or SCALAR PRODUCT. Compare with VECTOR PRODUCT. ● Written as **a.b** or **ab**.

in·ner sanc·tum ▶ n. the most sacred place in a temple or church. ■ a private or secret place to which few other people are admitted: *he walked into the inner sanctum of the editor's office.*

in·ner space ▶ n. **1** the region between the earth and outer space. ■ the region below the surface of the sea.
2 the part of the mind not normally accessible to consciousness.

in·ner speech ▶ n. the silent expression of conscious thought to oneself in a coherent linguistic form.

in·ner·spring /'inər,spriNG/ ▶ adj. (of a mattress) with internal springs.

in·ner tube ▶ n. a separate inflatable tube inside a pneumatic tire.

in·ner·vate /i'nər,vāt, 'inər-/ ▶ v. [with obj.] Anatomy & Zoology supply (an organ or other body part) with nerves.
– DERIVATIVES **in·ner·va·tion** /,inər'vāSHən/ n.
– ORIGIN late 19th cent.: from IN-[2] 'into' + NERVE + -ATE[3].

in·ner wom·an ▶ n. [in sing.] a woman's soul or mind: *to behave as her inner woman prompts.* ■ humorous a woman's stomach: *after refreshing the inner woman, I was all for trying again.*

In·ness /'inis/, George (1825–94) US artist. His early work, such as *Peace and Plenty* (1865), was related to the Hudson River School. Later, he painted in a more impressionistic style such as in *The Home of the Heron* (1893).

in·ning /'iniNG/ ▶ n. Baseball a division of a game during which the two teams alternate as offense and defense and during which each team is allowed three outs while batting. ■ a single turn at bat for a team until three outs are made. ■ a similar division of play in other games, such as horseshoes. ■ a period during which a person or group can achieve something: *she thought that now her inning had come.*
– ORIGIN Old English *innung* 'a putting or getting in,' related to IN. The current sense dates from the mid 19th cent.

in·nings /'iniNGz/ ▶ n. (pl. **same** or informal **inningses** /'iniNGziz/) **1** Cricket each of two or four divisions of a game during which one side has a turn at batting. ■ a player's turn at batting. ■ the score achieved during a player's turn at batting.
2 a period during which a person or group is active or effective.
– PHRASES **someone had a good innings** Brit. informal someone had a long and fulfilling life or career (said at or before their death or retirement).

in·nit /'init/ Brit. informal ▶ **contraction** isn't it.

inn·keep·er /'in,kēpər/ ▶ n. a person who runs an inn.

in·no·cence /'inəsəns/ ▶ n. the state, quality, or fact of being innocent of a crime or offense: *they must prove their innocence.* ■ lack of guile or corruption; purity: *the healthy bloom in her cheeks gave her an aura of innocence.* ■ used euphemistically to refer to a person's virginity: *they'd avenge assaults on her innocence by others.*
– PHRASES **in all innocence** without knowledge of something's significance or possible consequences: *she knew the gift had been chosen in all innocence.*
– DERIVATIVES **in·no·cen·cy** n. (archaic).
– ORIGIN Middle English: from Old French, from Latin *innocentia*, from *innocent-* 'not harming' (based on *nocere* 'injure').

in·no·cent /'inəsənt/ ▶ adj. **1** not guilty of a crime or offense: *the arbitrary execution of an innocent man* | *he was innocent of any fraud.* ■ [predic.] **(innocent of)** without; lacking: *a street quite innocent of bookstores.* ■ [predic.] **(innocent of)** without experience or knowledge of: *a man innocent of war's cruelties.*
2 [attrib.] not responsible for or directly involved in an event yet suffering its consequences: *an innocent bystander.*
3 free from moral wrong; not corrupted: *an innocent child.* ■ simple; naive: *she is a poor, innocent young creature.*
4 not intended to cause harm or offense; harmless: *an innocent mistake.*
▶ n. an innocent person, in particular: ■ a pure, guileless, or naive person: *she was an innocent compared with this man.* ■ a person involved by chance in a situation, esp. a victim of crime or war: *they are prepared to kill or maim innocents in pursuit of a cause.* ■ **(the Innocents)** the young children killed by Herod after the birth of Jesus (Matt. 2:16).
– DERIVATIVES **in·no·cent·ly** adv.
– ORIGIN Middle English: from Old French, or from Latin *innocent-* 'not harming,' from *in-* 'not' + *nocere* 'to hurt.'

> **USAGE** **Innocent** properly means 'harmless,' but it has long been extended in general language to mean 'not guilty.' The jury (or judge) in a criminal trial does not, strictly speaking, find a defendant 'innocent.' Rather, a defendant may be *guilty* or *not guilty* of the charges brought. In common use, however, owing perhaps to the concept of the *presumption of innocence*, which instructs a jury to consider a defendant free of wrongdoing until proven guilty on the basis of evidence, 'not guilty' and 'innocent' have come to be thought of as synonymous. See also usage at PLEAD.

In·no·cen·tia /,inə'senCHə/, Sister Maria, see HUMMEL.

In·no·cents' Day (also **Holy Innocents' Day**) ▶ n. a Christian festival commemorating the massacre of the Innocents, December 28.

in·noc·u·ous /i'näkyo͞oəs/ ▶ adj. not harmful or offensive: *it was an innocuous question.*
– DERIVATIVES **in·noc·u·ous·ly** adv., **in·noc·u·ous·ness** n.
– ORIGIN late 16th cent.: from Latin *innocuus*, from *in-* 'not' + *nocuus* 'injurious' (see NOCUOUS).

Inn of Court ▶ n. (in the UK) each of the four legal societies having the exclusive right of admitting people to the English bar. ■ any of the sets of buildings in London occupied by these societies.

in·nom·i·nate /i'nämənit/ ▶ adj. not named or classified.
– ORIGIN mid 17th cent.: from late Latin *innominatus*, from *in-* 'not' + *nominatus* 'named' (past participle of *nominare*).

in·nom·i·nate ar·ter·y ▶ n. Anatomy a large artery that branches from the aortic arch and divides into the right common carotid and right subclavian arteries.

in·nom·i·nate bone ▶ n. Anatomy the bone formed from the fusion of the ilium, ischium, and pubis; the hipbone.

in·nom·i·nate vein ▶ n. Anatomy either of two large veins of the neck formed by the junction of the external jugular and subclavian veins.

in·no·vate /'inə,vāt/ ▶ v. [no obj.] make changes in something established, esp. by introducing new methods, ideas, or products: *the company's failure to diversify and innovate competitively.* ■ [with obj.] introduce (something new, esp. a product): *innovating new products, developing existing ones.*
– DERIVATIVES **in·no·va·to·ry** /-və,tôrē/ adj.
– ORIGIN mid 16th cent.: from Latin *innovat-* 'renewed, altered,' from the verb *innovare*, from *in-* 'into' + *novare* 'make new' (from *novus* 'new').

in·no·va·tion /,inə'vāSHən/ ▶ n. the action or process of innovating. ■ a new method, idea, product, etc.: *technological innovations designed to save energy.*
– DERIVATIVES **in·no·va·tion·al** /-SHənl/ adj.
– ORIGIN late Middle English: from Latin *innovatio(n-)*, from the verb *innovare* (see INNOVATE).

in·no·va·tive /'inə,vātiv/ ▶ adj. (of a product, idea, etc.) featuring new methods; advanced and original: *innovative designs* | *innovative ways to help unemployed people.* ■ (of a person) introducing new ideas; original and creative in thinking: *an innovative thinker.*
– DERIVATIVES **in·no·va·tive·ly** adv., **in·no·va·tive·ness** n.

in·no·va·tor /'inə,vātər/ ▶ n. a person who introduces new methods, ideas, or products: *he was one of the great innovators in jazz.*

Inn Riv·er /in/ a river in western Europe that rises in the Rhaetian Alps of Switzerland and flows for 320 miles (508 km) through the Austrian Tyrol past Innsbruck into southern Germany where it flows into the Danube River at Passau.

Inns·bruck /'inz,bro͝ok/ a city in western Austria, capital of Tyrol; pop. 116,239 (2006). The Winter Olympic Games took place here in 1964 and 1976.

Inns of Court ▶ plural n. see INN OF COURT.

in·nu·en·do /,inyo͞o'endō/ ▶ n. (pl. **innuendoes** or **innuendos**) an allusive or oblique remark or hint, typically a suggestive or disparaging one: *she's always making sly innuendoes* | *a constant torrent of innuendo, gossip, lies, and half-truths.*
– ORIGIN mid 16th cent. (as an adverb in the sense 'that is to say, to wit,' used in legal documents to introduce an explanation): Latin, 'by nodding at, by pointing to,' ablative gerund of *innuere*, from *in-* 'toward' + *nuere* 'to nod.' The noun dates from the late 17th cent.

in·nu·mer·a·ble /i'n(y)o͞omərəbəl/ ▶ adj. too many to be counted (often used hyperbolically): *innumerable flags of all colors.*
– DERIVATIVES **in·nu·mer·a·bil·i·ty** /i,n(y)o͞omərə'bilitē/ n., **in·nu·mer·a·bly** /-blē/ adv.
– ORIGIN Middle English: from Latin *innumerabilis*, from *in-* 'not' + *numerabilis* (see NUMERABLE).

in·nu·mer·ate /i'n(y)o͞omərit/ ▶ adj. without a basic knowledge of mathematics and arithmetic.
▶ n. a person lacking such knowledge.
– DERIVATIVES **in·nu·mer·a·cy** /-rəsē/ n.

in·nu·tri·tion /,i(n)n(y)o͞o'triSHən/ ▶ n. rare lack of nourishment.

in·nu·tri·tious /,i(n)n(y)o͞o'triSHəs/ ▶ adj. (of food) lacking in nutrients; not nourishing.

in·ob·serv·ance /,inəb'zərvəns/ ▶ n. dated failure to observe or notice; inattention. ■ failure to keep or observe a law, custom, promise, etc.
– ORIGIN early 17th cent.: from French, or from Latin *inobservantia*, from *in-* (expressing negation) + *observantia* 'observance' (from *observare* 'observe').

in·oc·u·lant /i'näkyələnt/ ▶ n. a substance suitable for inoculating.

in·oc·u·late /i'näkyə,lāt/ ▶ v. [with obj.] treat (a person or animal) with a vaccine to produce immunity against a disease: *he inoculated his tenants against smallpox.* Compare with VACCINATE. ■ introduce (an infective agent) into an organism: *it can be inoculated into laboratory animals.* ■ introduce (cells or organisms) into a culture medium.
– DERIVATIVES **in·oc·u·la·ble** /-ləbəl/ adj., **in·oc·u·la·tor** /-,lātər/ n.
– ORIGIN late Middle English (in the sense 'graft a bud or shoot into a plant of a different type'): from Latin *inoculat-* 'engrafted,' from the verb *inoculare*, from *in-* 'into' + *oculus* 'eye, bud.' The sense 'vaccinate' dates from the early 18th cent.

in·oc·u·la·tion /i,näkyə'lāSHən/ ▶ n. the action of inoculating or of being inoculated; vaccination: *inoculation against flu was readily available* | *a course of inoculations.*

in·oc·u·lum /i'näkyələm/ ▶ n. (pl. **inocula** /-lə/) Medicine a substance used for inoculation.
– ORIGIN early 20th cent.: modern Latin, from Latin *inoculare* (see INOCULATE), on the pattern of the pair *coagulate, coagulum.*

in·o·dor·ous /in'ōdərəs/ ▶ adj. having no smell; odorless.
– ORIGIN mid 17th cent.: from Latin *inodorus*, from *in-* 'not' + *odorus* 'odorous,' or from IN-[1] 'not' + ODOROUS.

in·of·fen·sive /,inə'fensiv/ ▶ adj. not objectionable or harmful: *the water ouzel is an agile, inoffensive creature* | *inoffensive wallpaper.*
– DERIVATIVES **in·of·fen·sive·ly** adv., **in·of·fen·sive·ness** n.

in·op·er·a·ble /in'äp(ə)rəbəl/ ▶ adj. **1** Medicine not able to be suitably operated on: *inoperable cancer of the pancreas.*
2 not able to be operated: *the airfield was bombed and made inoperable.*
3 impractical; unworkable: *the procedures were inoperable.*
– DERIVATIVES **in·op·er·a·bil·i·ty** /-,äp(ə)rə'bilitē/ n., **in·op·er·a·bly** /-blē/ adv.

in·op·er·a·tive /in'äp(ə)rətiv/ ▶ adj. not working or taking effect: *the telescope is substantially inoperative due to an equipment failure.*

in·op·por·tune /in,äpər't(y)o͞on/ ▶ **adj.** occurring at an inconvenient or inappropriate time: *a storm blew up at an inopportune moment.*
– DERIVATIVES **in·op·por·tune·ly** adv., **in·op·por·tune·ness** n.
– ORIGIN early 16th cent.: from Latin *in opportunus*, from *in-* 'not' + *opportunus* (see **OPPORTUNE**).

in·or·di·nate /i'nôrdn-it/ ▶ **adj.** unusually or disproportionately large; excessive: *a case that had taken up an inordinate amount of time.* ■ archaic (of a person) unrestrained in feelings or behavior; disorderly.
– DERIVATIVES **in·or·di·nate·ly** adv. [as submodifier] *an inordinately expensive business.*
– ORIGIN late Middle English: from Latin *inordinatus*, from *in-* 'not' + *ordinatus* 'arranged, set in order' (past participle of *ordinare*).

in·or·gan·ic /,inôr'ganik/ ▶ **adj. 1** not consisting of or deriving from living matter. ■ without organized physical structure.
2 Chemistry of, relating to, or denoting compounds that are not organic (broadly, compounds not containing carbon).
3 Linguistics not explainable by the normal processes of etymology.
– DERIVATIVES **in·or·gan·i·cal·ly** /-ik(ə)lē/ adv.

in·or·gan·ic chem·is·try ▶ **n.** the branch of chemistry that deals with inorganic compounds.

in·os·cu·late /in'äskyə,lāt/ ▶ **v.** [no obj.] formal join by intertwining or fitting closely together.
– DERIVATIVES **in·os·cu·la·tion** /in,äskyə'lāsHən/ n.
– ORIGIN late 17th cent.: from **IN-**[2] 'into' + Latin *osculare* 'provide with a mouth or outlet' (from *osculum*, diminutive of *os* 'mouth'), on the pattern of Greek *anastomoun*, in the same sense.

in·o·sine /'inə,sēn, -sin/ ▶ **n.** Biochemistry a compound that is an intermediate in the metabolism of purine and is used in kidney transplantation to provide a temporary source of sugar. It is a nucleoside consisting of hypoxanthine linked to ribose.
– ORIGIN early 20th cent.: from Greek *is, in-* 'fiber, muscle' + **-OSE**[2] + **-INE**[4].

in·o·si·tol /i'nōsi,tôl, -,täl, ī'nō-/ ▶ **n.** Biochemistry a simple carbohydrate that occurs in animal and plant tissue and is a vitamin of the B group. ● Alternative name: **hexahydroxycyclohexane**; chem. formula: $C_6H_{12}O_6$.
– ORIGIN late 19th cent.: from the earlier name *inosite* + **-OL**.

i·no·trop·ic /,ēnə'träpik, -'trō-, ,īnə-/ ▶ **adj.** Physiology modifying the force or speed of contraction of muscles.

INP ▶ **abbr.** International News Photo.

in·pa·tient /'in,pāsHənt/ ▶ **n.** a patient who stays in a hospital while under treatment.

in per·so·nam /,in pər'sōnəm/ ▶ **adj. & adv.** Law made or availing against or affecting a specific person only; imposing a personal liability: [as postpositive adj.] *rights and duties in personam* | [as adv.] *the view that trusts operate in personam.* Compare with **IN REM**.
– ORIGIN late 18th cent.: Latin, literally 'against a person.'

in-phase ▶ **adj.** of or relating to electrical signals that are in phase.

in po·ten·ti·a /,in pō'tensHēə/ ▶ **adv.** as a possibility; potentially.
– ORIGIN early 17th cent.: Latin, literally 'in potentiality.'

in·pour·ing /'in,pôriNG/ ▶ **n.** the action of pouring something in; an infusion: *vast inpouring of public money.*

in pro·pri·a per·so·na /,in 'prōprēə pər'sōnə/ ▶ **adv.** in his or her own person: *many people find him, both in his verse and in propria persona, too loud and pushy.*
– ORIGIN mid 17th cent.: Latin.

in·put /'in,po͝ot/ ▶ **n. 1** what is put in, taken in, or operated on by any process or system: *perceptions and sensory input.* ■ a contribution of work, information, or material: *there is little input from other professional members of the team.* ■ energy supplied to a device or system; an electrical signal: *the input is a low-frequency signal.* ■ the action or process of putting or feeding something in: *the input of data to the system.* ■ the information fed into a computer or computer program: *pen-based computers take input from a stylus.*
2 Electronics a place where, or a device through which, energy or information enters a system: *the signal being fed through the main input.*
▶ **v.** (**inputs, inputting**; past and past participle **input** or **inputted**) [with obj.] put (data) into a computer.
– DERIVATIVES **in·put·ter** /-,po͝otər/ n.

in·put-out·put (abbr.: **I/O**) ▶ **adj.** [attrib.] Electronics of, relating to, or for both input and output.

inq. ▶ **abbr.** inquiry.

in·quest /'in,kwest, 'iNG-/ ▶ **n.** Law a judicial inquiry to ascertain the facts relating to an incident, such as a death.
– ORIGIN Middle English: from Old French *enqueste*, based on Latin *inquirere* (see **INQUIRE**).

in·qui·e·tude /in'kwīə,t(y)o͞od/ ▶ **n.** physical or mental restlessness or disturbance.
– ORIGIN late Middle English (in the sense 'disturbance of one's quietness or rest'): from Old French, or from late Latin *inquietudo*, from Latin *inquietus*, from *in-* 'not' + *quietus* 'quiet.'

in·qui·line /'inkwə,līn, -lin/ ▶ **n.** Zoology an animal exploiting the living space of another, e.g., an insect that lays its eggs in a gall produced by another.
– ORIGIN mid 17th cent.: from Latin *inquilinus* 'temporary resident,' from *in-* 'into' + *colere* 'dwell.'

in·quire /in'kwīr, iNG-/ (also chiefly Brit. **enquire**) ▶ **v.**
1 [reporting verb] ask for information from someone: [with direct speech] *"How well do you know Berlin?" he* ***inquired of*** *Hencke* | [with clause] *I inquired where he lived* | [no obj.] ***he inquired about*** *cottages for sale.* ■ [no obj.] (**inquire after**) ask about the health and well-being of (someone): *Annie inquired after her parents.* ■ [no obj.] (**inquire for**) ask to see or speak to (someone): *that was Mr. Paul inquiring for you—I told him he couldn't come in.*
2 [no obj.] (**inquire into**) investigate; look into: *the task of political sociology is to inquire into the causes of political events.*
– DERIVATIVES **in·quir·er** n., **in·quir·ing·ly** adv.
– ORIGIN Middle English *enquere* (later *inquere*), from Old French *enquerre*, from a variant of Latin *inquirere*, based on *quaerere* 'seek.' The spelling with *in-*, influenced by Latin, dates from the 15th cent.

> **USAGE** **Inquire** (and **inquiry**) are the usual US spellings; **enquire** and **enquiry** are the standard forms in Britain. Some American speakers put the stress on the first syllable of the noun **inquiry**, but the dominant pronunciation stresses the second.

in·quir·ing /in'kwīriNG, iNG-/ (also chiefly Brit. **enquiring**) ▶ **adj.** showing an interest in learning new things: *an open, inquiring mind.* ■ (of a look or expression) suggesting that information is sought: *he sent her an inquiring glance.*
– DERIVATIVES **in·quir·ing·ly** adv.

in·quir·y /in'kwī(ə)rē, 'in,kwī(ə)rē, 'inkwərē, 'iNG-/ (also chiefly Brit. **enquiry**) ▶ **n.** (pl. **inquiries**) an act of asking for information: *the deluge of phone inquiries after a crash* | *they were following a definite line of inquiry.* ■ an official investigation.

> **USAGE** See usage at **INQUIRE**.

in·qui·si·tion /,inkwi'zisHən, ,iNG-/ ▶ **n. 1** a period of prolonged and intensive questioning or investigation: *she relented in her determined inquisition and offered help.* ■ historical a judicial or official inquiry. ■ the verdict or finding of an official inquiry.
2 (**the Inquisition**) an ecclesiastical tribunal established by Pope Gregory IX *c.*1232 for the suppression of heresy. It was active chiefly in northern Italy and southern France, becoming notorious for the use of torture. In 1542 the papal Inquisition was re-established to combat Protestantism, eventually becoming an organ of papal government. See also **SPANISH INQUISITION**.
– DERIVATIVES **in·qui·si·tion·al** /-sHənl/ adj.
– ORIGIN late Middle English (denoting a searching examination): via Old French from Latin *inquisitio(n-)* 'examination,' from the verb *inquirere* (see **INQUIRE**).

in·quis·i·tive /in'kwizitiv, iNG-/ ▶ **adj.** curious or inquiring: *he was very chatty and inquisitive about everything.* ■ unduly curious about the affairs of others; prying: *I didn't want to seem inquisitive.*
– DERIVATIVES **in·quis·i·tive·ly** adv., **in·quis·i·tive·ness** n.
– ORIGIN late Middle English: from Old French *inquisitif, -ive*, from late Latin *inquisitivus*, from the verb *inquirere* (see **INQUIRE**).

in·quis·i·tor /in'kwizitər/ ▶ **n.** a person making an inquiry, esp. one seen to be excessively harsh or searching: *the professional inquisitors of the press.* ■ historical an officer of the Inquisition.
– ORIGIN late Middle English: from French *inquisiteur*, from Latin *inquisitor*, from the verb *inquirere* (see **INQUIRE**).

in·quis·i·tor-gen·er·al ▶ **n.** the head of the Spanish Inquisition.

in·quis·i·to·ri·al /in,kwizi'tôrēəl/ ▶ **adj.** of or like an inquisitor. ■ offensively prying. ■ Law (of a trial or legal procedure) in which the judge has an examining or inquiring role: *administration is accompanied by a form of inquisitorial justice.* Compare with **ACCUSATORIAL, ADVERSARIAL**.
– DERIVATIVES **in·quis·i·to·ri·al·ly** adv.
– ORIGIN mid 18th cent.: from medieval Latin *inquisitorius* (from Latin *inquisitor*, from *inquirere* 'inquire') + **-AL**.

in·quo·rate /in'kwô,rāt, -,rit/ ▶ **adj.** Brit. (of an assembly) unable to proceed effectively because not enough members are present to make up a quorum: *they had boycotted the debate, leaving the house inquorate.*

in re /,in 'rā/ ▶ **prep.** in the legal case of; with regard to: *In re Mancet's Estate.*
– ORIGIN early 17th cent.: Latin, 'in the matter of.'

in rem /,in 'rem/ ▶ **adj.** [often postpositive] Law made or availing against or affecting a thing, and therefore other people generally; imposing a general liability: *it confers a right in rem.* Compare with **IN PERSONAM**.
– ORIGIN mid 18th cent.: Latin, 'against a thing.'

INRI ▶ **abbr.** Jesus of Nazareth, King of the Jews (a traditional representation in art of the inscription over Christ's head at the Crucifixion).
– ORIGIN from the initials of Latin *Iesus Nazarenus Rex Iudaeorum.*

in·ro /'inrō/ ▶ **n.** (pl. **same** or **inros**) an ornamental box with compartments for items such as seals and medicines, worn suspended from a waist sash as part of traditional Japanese dress.
– ORIGIN early 17th cent.: from Japanese *inrō*, from *in* 'seal' + *rō* 'basket.'

in·road /'in,rōd/ ▶ **n. 1** [usu. in pl.] (**inroads**) progress; an advance: *an important way to* ***make inroads in*** *reducing spending.* ■ an instance of something being affected, encroached on, or destroyed by something else: *serious* ***inroads*** *had now been* ***made into*** *my pitiful cash reserves.*
2 a hostile attack; a raid.
– ORIGIN mid 16th cent. (sense 2): from **IN** + **ROAD** (from an early use in the sense 'riding').

in·rush /'in,rəsH/ ▶ **n.** [in sing.] the sudden arrival or entry of something: *a great inrush of water occurred.*
– DERIVATIVES **in·rush·ing** adj. & n.

INS ▶ **abbr.** Immigration and Naturalization Service.

in·sa·la·ta /,insä'lätə/ ▶ **n.** an Italian-style salad: *insalata verde.*
– ORIGIN Italian, 'salad.'

in·sa·lu·bri·ous /,insə'lo͞obrēəs/ ▶ **adj.** formal (esp. of a climate or locality) not salubrious; unhealthy.
– DERIVATIVES **in·sa·lu·bri·ty** /-britē/ n.
– ORIGIN mid 17th cent.: from Latin *insalubris* (from *in-* 'not' + *salubris* 'salubrious') + **-OUS**.

in·sane /in'sān/ ▶ **adj.** in a state of mind that prevents normal perception, behavior, or social interaction; seriously mentally ill: *certifying patients as clinically insane* | *he had gone insane.* ■ (of an action or quality) characterized or caused by madness: *charging headlong in an insane frenzy* | *his eyes glowing with insane fury.* ■ in a state of extreme annoyance or distraction: *a fly whose buzzing had been driving me insane.* ■ (of an action or policy) extremely foolish; irrational or illogical: *she had an insane desire to giggle.*
– DERIVATIVES **in·sane·ly** adv.
– ORIGIN mid 16th cent.: from Latin *insanus*, from *in-* 'not' + *sanus* 'healthy.'

in·san·i·tar·y /in'sani,terē/ ▶ **adj.** so dirty or ridden with germs as to be a danger to health: *insanitary conditions.*

in·san·i·ty /in'sanitē/ ▶ **n.** the state of being seriously mentally ill; madness: *he suffered from bouts of insanity* | [as complement] *he attempted to plead insanity.* ■ extreme foolishness or irrationality: *it might be pure insanity to take this loan* | *the insanities of our time.*
– ORIGIN late 16th cent.: from Latin *insanitas*, from *insanus* (see **INSANE**).

in·sa·tia·ble /in'sāsHəbəl/ ▶ **adj.** (of an appetite or desire) impossible to satisfy: *an insatiable hunger for success.* ■ (of a person) having an insatiable appetite or desire for something, esp. sex.
– DERIVATIVES **in·sa·tia·bil·i·ty** /-,sāsHə'bilitē/ n., **in·sa·tia·bly** /-blē/ adv.
– ORIGIN late Middle English: from Old French *insaciable* or Latin *insatiabilis*, from *in-* 'not' + *satiare* 'fill, satisfy' (see **SATIATE**).

in·sa·ti·ate /in'sāsHē-it/ ▶ **adj.** literary never satisfied: *your strong desire is insatiate.*
– ORIGIN late Middle English: from Latin *insatiatus*, from *in-* 'not' + *satiatus* 'filled, satisfied,' past participle of *satiare* (see **SATIATE**).

in·scape /'in,skāp/ ▶ **n.** literary the unique inner nature of a person or object as shown in a work of art, esp. a poem.

PRONUNCIATION KEY ə *ago, up*; ər *over, fur*; a *hat*; ā *ate*; ä *car*; e *let*; ē *see*; i *fit*; ī *by*; NG *sing*; ō *go*; ô *law, for*; oi *toy*; o͝o *good*; o͞o *goo*; ou *out*; TH *thin*; T͟H *then*; ZH *vision*

– ORIGIN mid 19th cent. (originally in the poetic theory of Gerard Manley Hopkins): perhaps from IN-² 'within' + -SCAPE.

in-school ▶ adj. [attrib.] denoting an activity or process that takes place during school hours or on school premises: *an in-school method of assessment.*

in·scribe /in'skrīb/ ▶ v. [with obj.] (usu. **be inscribed**) **1** write or carve (words or symbols) on something, esp. as a formal or permanent record: *his name was inscribed on the new silver trophy.* ■ mark (an object) with characters: *the memorial is* ***inscribed*** *with ten names* | (as adj. **inscribed**) *an inscribed watch.* ■ write an informal dedication to someone in or on (a book): *he inscribed the first copy "To my dearest grandmother."* ■ archaic enter the name of (someone) on a list or in a book; enroll.
2 Geometry draw (a figure) within another so that their boundaries touch but do not intersect: *a regular polygon inscribed in a circle.* Compare with CIRCUMSCRIBE.
– DERIVATIVES **in·scrib·a·ble** adj., **in·scrib·er** n.
– ORIGIN late Middle English: from Latin *inscribere*, from *in-* 'into' + *scribere* 'write.'

in·scrip·tion /in'skripSHən/ ▶ n. words inscribed, as on a monument or in a book: *the inscription on her headstone.* ■ the action of inscribing something: *the inscription of memorable utterances on durable materials.*
– DERIVATIVES **in·scrip·tion·al** /-SHənl/ adj., **in·scrip·tive** /-'skriptiv/ adj.
– ORIGIN late Middle English (denoting a short descriptive or dedicatory passage at the beginning of a book): from Latin *inscriptio(n-)*, from the verb *inscribere* (see INSCRIBE).

in·scru·ta·ble /in'skrōōtəbəl/ ▶ adj. impossible to understand or interpret: *Guy looked blankly inscrutable.*
– DERIVATIVES **in·scru·ta·bil·i·ty** /-ˌskrōōtə'bilitē/ n., **in·scru·ta·bly** /-blē/ adv.
– ORIGIN late Middle English: from ecclesiastical Latin *inscrutabilis*, from *in-* 'not' + *scrutari* 'to search' (see SCRUTINY).

in·seam /'inˌsēm/ ▶ n. the seam in a pair of pants from the crotch to the bottom of the leg, or the length of this.

in·sect /'inˌsekt/ ▶ n. a small arthropod animal that has six legs and generally one or two pairs of wings. ■ informal any small invertebrate animal, esp. one with several pairs of legs.

> Insects are usually placed in the class Insecta (see also HEXAPODA). The body of a typical adult insect is divided into head, thorax (bearing the legs and wings), and abdomen. The class includes many familiar forms, such as flies, bees, wasps, moths, beetles, grasshoppers, and cockroaches. Insects are the most numerous animals in both numbers of individuals and of different kinds, with more than a million species in all habitats except the sea, and they are of enormous economic importance as pests and carriers of disease, and also as pollinators.

– ORIGIN early 17th cent. (originally denoting any small cold-blooded creature with a segmented body): from Latin (*animal*) *insectum* 'segmented (animal)' (translating Greek *zōion entomon*), from *insecare* 'cut up or into,' from *in-* 'into' + *secare* 'to cut.'

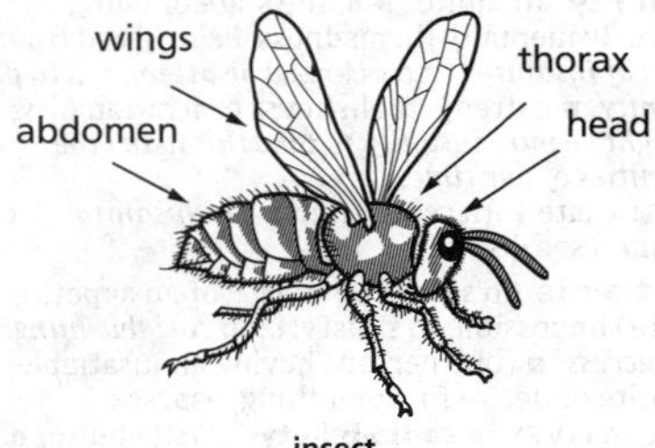

insect

in·sec·tan /in'sektən/ ▶ adj. [attrib.] Zoology of or relating to insects: *the insectan orders.*

in·sec·tar·i·um /ˌinsek'te(ə)rēəm/ (also **insectary** /'insekˌterē, in'sektə-/) ▶ n. (pl. **insectariums** also **insectaries** /'insekˌterēz/) a place where insects are kept, exhibited, and studied.

in·sec·ti·cide /in'sektiˌsīd/ ▶ n. a substance used for killing insects.
– DERIVATIVES **in·sec·ti·cid·al** /-ˌsekti'sīdl/ adj.

in·sec·tile /in'sektl, -ˌtīl/ ▶ adj. resembling or reminiscent of an insect or insects: *he folded his insectile hands.*

In·sec·tiv·o·ra /ˌinsek'tivərə/ Zoology an order of mammals that comprises the shrews, moles, hedgehogs, tenrecs, moonrats, and solenodons. They are distinguished by mainly terrestrial habits and an insectivorous diet.

in·sec·ti·vore /in'sektəˌvôr/ ▶ n. an insectivorous animal or plant. ■ Zoology a mammal of the order Insectivora.
– ORIGIN mid 19th cent.: from modern Latin *insectivorus*, from *insectum* (see INSECT) + *-vorus* 'devouring,' on the pattern of Latin *carnivorus* 'carnivorous.'

in·sec·tiv·o·rous /ˌinˌsek'tivərəs/ ▶ adj. (of an animal) feeding on insects, worms, and other invertebrates. ■ (of a plant such as the Venus flytrap) able to capture and digest insects.

in·se·cure /ˌinsi'kyŏŏr/ ▶ adj. **1** (of a person) not confident or assured; uncertain and anxious: *a top model who is notoriously insecure about her looks* | *a rather gauche, insecure young man.*
2 (of a thing) not firm or set; unsafe. ■ (of a job or position) from which removal or expulsion is always possible. ■ not firmly fixed; liable to give way or break: *an insecure footbridge.* ■ able to be broken into or illicitly accessed: *an insecure computer system.*
– DERIVATIVES **in·se·cure·ly** adv.
– ORIGIN mid 17th cent.: from medieval Latin *insecurus* 'unsafe,' from *in-* 'not' + Latin *securus* 'free from care,' or from IN-¹ 'not' + SECURE.

in·se·cu·ri·ty /ˌinsi'kyŏŏritē/ ▶ n. (pl. **insecurities**) **1** uncertainty or anxiety about oneself; lack of confidence: *she had a deep sense of insecurity* | *he's plagued with insecurities.*
2 the state of being open to danger or threat; lack of protection: *growing job insecurity* | *the insecurity of wireless networks.*

in·sel·berg /'insəlbərg/ ▶ n. Geology an isolated hill or mountain rising abruptly from a plain.
– ORIGIN early 20th cent.: from German, from *Insel* 'island' + *Berg* 'mountain.'

in·sem·i·nate /in'seməˌnāt/ ▶ v. [with obj.] introduce semen into (a woman or a female animal) by natural or artificial means.
– DERIVATIVES **in·sem·i·na·tion** /-ˌsemə'nāSHən/ n.
– ORIGIN early 17th cent.: from Latin *inseminat-* 'sown,' from the verb *inseminare*, from *in-* 'into' + *seminare* 'plant, sow' (from *semen, semin-* 'seed, semen').

in·sem·i·na·tor /in'seməˌnātər/ ▶ n. a man or male animal inseminating a female. ■ a person who performs artificial insemination of farm animals.

in·sen·sate /in'senˌsāt, -sit/ ▶ adj. lacking physical sensation: *a patient who was permanently unconscious and insensate.* ■ lacking sympathy or compassion; unfeeling: *a positively insensate hatred.* ■ completely lacking sense or reason: *insensate jabbering.*
– DERIVATIVES **in·sen·sate·ly** adv.
– ORIGIN late 15th cent.: from ecclesiastical Latin *insensatus*, from *in-* 'not' + *sensatus* 'having senses' (see SENSATE).

in·sen·si·bil·i·ty /inˌsensə'bilitē/ ▶ n. unconsciousness: *I flogged him into insensibility.* ■ inability to feel something, esp. to be moved emotionally. ■ lack of awareness or concern; indifference: *your* ***insensibility to*** *the extreme importance of the mission we are on.*
– ORIGIN late Middle English: partly from Old French *insensibilite* or late Latin *insensibilitas* (from *in-* 'not' + Latin *sensibilis* 'sensible,' from *sensus* 'sense'), partly from IN-¹ 'without, lacking' + SENSIBILITY.

in·sen·si·ble /in'sensəbəl/ ▶ adj. **1** [usu. as complement] without one's mental faculties, typically a result of violence or intoxication; unconscious: *they knocked each other insensible with their fists* | *insensible with drink.* ■ (esp. of a body or bodily extremity) numb; without feeling: *the horny and insensible tip of the beak.*
2 [predic.] (**insensible of/to**) unaware of; indifferent to: *they slept on, insensible to the headlight beams.* ■ without emotion; callous.
3 too small or gradual to be perceived; inappreciable: *varying by insensible degrees.*
– DERIVATIVES **in·sen·si·bly** /-blē/ adv.
– ORIGIN late Middle English (also in the senses 'unable to be perceived' and 'incapable of physical sensation'): partly from Old French *insensible* (from Latin *insensibilis*, from *in-* 'not' + *sensibilis*, from *sensus* 'sense'), partly from IN-¹ 'not' + SENSIBLE.

in·sen·si·tive /in'sensitiv/ ▶ adj. showing or feeling no concern for others' feelings: *an insensitive remark.* ■ not sensitive to a physical sensation: *she was remarkably insensitive to pain.* ■ not aware of or able to respond to something: *both were in many ways* ***insensitive to*** *painting.*
– DERIVATIVES **in·sen·si·tive·ly** adv., **in·sen·si·tive·ness** n., **in·sen·si·tiv·i·ty** /-ˌsensi'tivitē/ n.

in·sen·ti·ent /in'senSH(ē)ənt/ ▶ adj. incapable of feeling or understanding things; inanimate: *it's arrogant to presume animals to be insentient.*
– DERIVATIVES **in·sen·ti·ence** n.

in·sep·a·ra·ble /in'sep(ə)rəbəl/ ▶ adj. unable to be separated or treated separately: *research and higher education seem inseparable.* ■ (of one or more people) unwilling to be separated; usually seen together: *they met 18 months ago and have been inseparable ever since.* ■ Grammar (of a prefix) not used as a separate word or (in German) not separated from the base verb when inflected.
▶ n. a person or thing inseparable from another.
– DERIVATIVES **in·sep·a·ra·bil·i·ty** /-ˌsep(ə)rə'bilitē/ n., **in·sep·a·ra·bly** /-blē/ adv.
– ORIGIN late Middle English: from Latin *inseparabilis*, from *in-* 'not' + *separabilis* (see SEPARABLE).

in·sert ▶ v. /in'sərt/ [with obj.] **1** place, fit, or thrust (something) into another thing, esp. with care: *a steel rod was inserted into the small hole* | *he pulled out a small cassette recorder and inserted a new tape.* ■ add (text) to a piece of writing: *he immediately inserted a clause into later contracts* | *the objection has been inserted in the minutes.* ■ place (a spacecraft or satellite) into an orbit or trajectory. ■ Biology incorporate (a piece of genetic material) into a chromosome.
2 (**be inserted**) Anatomy & Zoology (of a muscle or other organ) be attached to a part, esp. that which is moved: *the muscle that raises the wing* ***is inserted on*** *the dorsal surface of the humerus.*
▶ n. /'inˌsərt/ a thing that has been inserted, in particular: ■ a loose page or section, typically one carrying an advertisement, in a magazine or other publication. ■ an ornamental section of cloth or needlework inserted into the plain material of a garment. ■ a shot inserted into a movie or video.
– DERIVATIVES **in·sert·a·ble** adj., **in·sert·er** n.
– ORIGIN late 15th cent. (in the sense 'include (text) in a piece of writing'): from Latin *insert-* 'put in,' from the verb *inserere*, from *in-* 'into' + *serere* 'to join.'

in·ser·tion /in'sərSHən/ ▶ n. **1** the action of inserting something: *the insertion of a line or two into the script.* ■ the placing of a spacecraft or satellite into an orbit or trajectory.
2 a thing that is inserted, in particular: ■ an amendment or addition inserted in a text. ■ each appearance of an advertisement in a newspaper or periodical. ■ an ornamental section of cloth or needlework inserted into the plain material of a garment.
3 Anatomy & Zoology the manner or place of attachment of an organ: *close to the point of leaf insertion.* ■ the manner or place of attachment of a muscle to the part that it moves: *the names of the muscles and their* ***insertions on*** *the eyeball.*
4 Biology the addition of extra DNA or RNA into a section of genetic material.
– ORIGIN mid 16th cent. (sense 2): from late Latin *insertio(n-)*, from Latin *inserere* (see INSERT).

in-serv·ice ▶ adj. (of training) intended for those actively engaged in the profession or activity concerned: *in-service training of library staff.*

in·set ▶ n. /'inˌset/ a thing that is put in or inserted: *a pair of doors with their original stained-glass insets.* ■ a small picture or map inserted within the border of a larger one. ■ a section of fabric or needlework inserted into the material of a garment: *elastic insets in the waistband.* ■ an insert in a magazine or similar publication.
▶ v. /in'set/ (**insets, insetting**; past and past participle **inset** or **insetted**) put in (something, esp. a small picture or map) as an inset: *type in the text to be inset.* ■ decorate with an inset: *tables inset with ceramic tiles.*
– DERIVATIVES **in·set·ter** n.

in·shal·lah /in'SHälə/ ▶ exclam. if Allah wills it.
– ORIGIN from Arabic *in šā' Allāh*.

in·shore /'in'SHôr/ ▶ adj. at sea but close to the shore: *both mackerel and bluefish have returned to inshore waters by now.* ■ used at sea but close to the shore: *an inshore lifeboat.*
▶ adv. toward or closer to the shore: *birds heading inshore to their breeding sites.*
– PHRASES **inshore of** nearer to shore than.

in·side ▶ n. /'in'sīd/ **1** [usu. in sing.] the inner side or surface of a thing: *she ran a finger around the inside of the bowl.* ■ the side of a bend or curve where the edge or surface is shorter: *the inside of the bend.* ■ the side of a racetrack nearer to the center, where the lanes are shorter: *he was blocked on the inside at the furlong marker.*
2 the inner part; the interior: *the inside of the car was like an oven* | *these boats are built of very thin cedar, with ribs on the inside.* ■ (usu. **insides**) informal the stomach and bowels: *my insides are out of order.*

3 (**the inside**) informal a position affording private information: *will you be my spy on the inside?*
▶ **adj.** /ˌinˈsīd, ˈinˌsīd/ [attrib.] situated on or in, or derived from, the inside: *an inside pocket.* ■ (in some team sports) denoting positions nearer to the center of the field: *possibly the best inside linebacker in the country.* ■ (of a pitch in baseball) passing between the batter and the strike zone: *an inside pitch to a right-handed hitter.*
▶ **prep. & adv.** /ˌinˈsīd/ **1** situated within the confines of (something): [as prep.] *a radio was playing inside the apartment* | *he fitted a light inside the cupboard* | [as adv.] *Mr. Jackson is waiting for you inside.* ■ moving so as to end up within (something): [as prep.] *Anatoly reached inside his shirt and brought out a map* | [as adv.] *we walked inside.* ■ within (the body or mind of a person), typically with reference to sensations of self-awareness: [as prep.] *she felt a stirring of life inside her* | *I just roll the phrases around inside my head* | [as adv.] *I was screaming inside.* ■ informal in prison: *sentenced to three years inside.* ■ Baseball close to the batter. ■ (in basketball, soccer, and other sports) closer to the center of the field than (another player): [as prep.] *he went inside Graves and scored near the post* | [as adv.] *he does an excellent job of getting the ball inside to Randall.*
2 [prep.] in less than (the period of time specified): *the oven will have paid for itself inside 18 months.*
– PHRASES **inside of** informal within: *something inside of me wanted to believe him.* ■ in less than (the period of time specified): *rerigging a ship for a voyage inside of a week.*
– ORIGIN late Middle English (denoting the interior of the body): from IN + SIDE.

in·side in·for·ma·tion ▶ **n.** information only available to those within an organization.

in·side job ▶ **n.** informal a crime committed by or with the assistance of a person living or working on the premises where it occurred.

in·side out ▶ **adv.** with the inner surface turned outward: *we made a very quick change, and her dress was put on inside out.*
▶ **adj.** in such a condition: *inside-out clothes.*
– PHRASES **know something inside out** know something very thoroughly: *managers who know the business inside out.* **turn something inside out** turn the inner surface of something outward: *she played with her leather gloves, turning each finger inside out.* ■ change something utterly: *it is not so easy to turn your whole life inside out.* ■ informal cause utter confusion in; defeat totally: *he turned the defender inside out.*

In·side Pas·sage a water route from Seattle in Washington to Alaska that passes through islands in Washington, British Columbia, and southeastern Alaska.

in·sid·er /inˈsīdər/ ▶ **n.** a person within a group or organization, esp. someone privy to information unavailable to others: *political insiders.*

in·sid·er trad·ing (Brit. also **insider dealing**) ▶ **n.** the illegal practice of trading on the stock exchange to one's own advantage through having access to confidential information.

in·side track ▶ **n.** the inner, shorter track of a racecourse. ■ a position of advantage: *he always had the inside track for the starring role.*

in·sid·i·ous /inˈsidēəs/ ▶ **adj.** proceeding in a gradual, subtle way, but with harmful effects: *sexually transmitted diseases can be insidious and sometimes without symptoms.* ■ treacherous; crafty: *tangible proof of an insidious alliance.*
– DERIVATIVES **in·sid·i·ous·ly** adv., **in·sid·i·ous·ness** n.
– ORIGIN mid 16th cent.: from Latin *insidiosus* 'cunning,' from *insidiae* 'an ambush or trick,' from *insidere* 'lie in wait for,' from *in-* 'on' + *sedere* 'sit.'

in·sight /ˈinˌsīt/ ▶ **n.** the capacity to gain an accurate and deep intuitive understanding of a person or thing: *this paper is alive with sympathetic insight into Shakespeare.* ■ an understanding of this kind: *the signals would give marine biologists new insights into the behavior of whales.* ■ Psychiatry new understanding by a mentally ill person of the causes of their disorder.
– ORIGIN Middle English (in the sense 'inner sight, mental vision, wisdom'): probably of Scandinavian and Low German origin and related to Swedish *insikt*, Danish *indsigt*, Dutch *inzicht*, and German *Einsicht*.

in·sight·ful /ˈinˌsītfəl/ ▶ **adj.** having or showing an accurate and deep understanding; perceptive: *thank you for all the insightful comments.*
– DERIVATIVES **in·sight·ful·ly** /ˈinˌsītfəlē/ adv.

in·sight med·i·ta·tion ▶ **n.** a form of Buddhist mediation that employs concentration sharply focused on bodily sensations and mental events, practiced with the intention of gaining insight into reality.

in·sig·ni·a /inˈsignēə/ ▶ **n.** (pl. **same** or **insignias**) a badge or distinguishing mark of military rank, office, or membership of an organization; an official emblem: *a khaki uniform with colonel's insignia on the collar.* ■ a distinguishing mark or token of something: *they left eternally inert blooms, the insignia of melancholy.*
– ORIGIN mid 17th cent.: from Latin, plural of *insigne* 'sign, badge of office,' neuter of *insignis* 'distinguished (as if by a mark),' from *in-* 'toward' + *signum* 'sign.'

in·sig·nif·i·cant /ˌinsigˈnifikənt/ ▶ **adj.** too small or unimportant to be worth consideration: *the amount required was insignificant compared with military spending* | *no detail is insignificant.* ■ (of a person) without power or influence. ■ meaningless: *insignificant yet enchanting phrases.*
– DERIVATIVES **in·sig·nif·i·cance** n., **in·sig·nif·i·can·cy** n., **in·sig·nif·i·cant·ly** adv.

in·sin·cere /ˌinsinˈsi(ə)r/ ▶ **adj.** not expressing genuine feelings: *she flashed him an insincere smile.*
– DERIVATIVES **in·sin·cere·ly** adv., **in·sin·cer·i·ty** /-ˈseritē/ n. (pl. **insincerities**).
– ORIGIN mid 17th cent.: from Latin *insincerus*, from *in-* 'not' + *sincerus* 'sincere.'

in·sin·u·ate /inˈsinyəˌwāt/ ▶ **v.** [with obj.] **1** suggest or hint (something bad or reprehensible) in an indirect and unpleasant way: [with clause] *he was insinuating that she had slept her way to the top.*
2 (**insinuate oneself into**) maneuver oneself into (a position of favor or office) by subtle manipulation: *she seemed to be taking over, insinuating herself into the family.* ■ slide (oneself or a thing) slowly and smoothly into a position: *the bugs insinuate themselves between one's skin and clothes.*
– DERIVATIVES **in·sin·u·at·ing·ly** adv., **in·sin·u·a·tor** /-ˌwātər/ n.
– ORIGIN early 16th cent. (used in legal contexts in the sense 'enter (a document) in the official register'): from Latin *insinuat-* 'introduced tortuously,' from the verb *insinuare*, from *in-* 'in' + *sinuare* 'to curve.'

in·sin·u·a·tion /inˌsinyo͞oˈāsнən/ ▶ **n.** an unpleasant hint or suggestion of something bad: *I've done nothing to deserve all your vicious insinuations* | *a piece of filthy insinuation.*
– ORIGIN mid 16th cent.: from Latin *insinuatio(n-)*, from *insinuare* (see INSINUATE).

in·sip·id /inˈsipid/ ▶ **adj.** lacking flavor: *mugs of insipid coffee.* ■ lacking vigor or interest: *many artists continued to churn out insipid, shallow works.*
– DERIVATIVES **in·si·pid·i·ty** /ˌinsəˈpiditē/ n., **in·sip·id·ly** adv., **in·sip·id·ness** n.
– ORIGIN early 17th cent.: from French *insipide* or late Latin *insipidus*, from *in-* 'not' + *sapidus* (see SAPID).

in·sist /inˈsist/ ▶ **v.** [no obj.] demand something forcefully, not accepting refusal: *she insisted on carrying her own bag* | *I'll call him and cancel it, if you insist.* ■ (**insist on**) demand forcefully to have something: *he insisted on answers to his allegations.* ■ (**insist on**) persist in doing something even though it is annoying or odd: *the heavy studded boots she insisted on wearing.* ■ [reporting verb] maintain or put forward a statement positively and assertively: [with clause] *the chairman insisted that all was not doom and gloom* | [with direct speech] *"I really am all right now," Isabel insisted.*
– ORIGIN late 16th cent. (in the sense 'persist, persevere'): from Latin *insistere* 'persist,' from *in-* 'upon' + *sistere* 'stand.'

in·sist·ence /inˈsistəns/ ▶ **n.** the fact or quality of insisting that something is the case or should be done: *his insistence on unilateral nuclear disarmament.*
– DERIVATIVES **in·sis·ten·cy** n.

in·sist·ent /inˈsistənt/ ▶ **adj.** insisting or demanding something; not allowing refusal: *Tony's soft, insistent questioning* | [with clause] *she was very insistent that I call her.* ■ regular and repeated, and demanding attention: *a telephone started ringing, loud and insistent.*
– DERIVATIVES **in·sis·tent·ly** adv.

in si·tu /ˌin ˈsītoo, ˈsē-/ ▶ **adv. & adj.** in its original place: [as adv.] *mosaics and frescoes have been left in situ* | [as adj.] *a collection of in situ pumping engines.* ■ in position: [as adv.] *her guests were all in situ.*
– ORIGIN mid 18th cent.: Latin.

in·so·bri·e·ty /ˌinsəˈbrī-itē/ ▶ **n.** drunkenness.

in·so·far /ˌinsōˈfär/ (also **in so far**) ▶ **adv.** (**insofar as**) to the extent that: *he decided that philosophy spoke of personal problems only insofar as they illustrated general ones.*

insol. ▶ **abbr.** insoluble.

in·so·la·tion /ˌinsōˈlāsнən/ ▶ **n.** technical exposure to the sun's rays. ■ the amount of solar radiation reaching a given area.
– ORIGIN early 17th cent.: from Latin *insolatio(n-)*, from the verb *insolare*, from *in-* 'toward' + *sol* 'sun.'

in·sole /ˈinˌsōl/ ▶ **n.** a removable sole worn in a shoe for warmth, as a deodorizer, or to improve the fit. ■ the fixed inner sole of a boot or shoe.

in·so·lence /ˈinsələns/ ▶ **n.** rude and disrespectful behavior: *she was sacked for insolence.*

in·so·lent /ˈinsələnt/ ▶ **adj.** showing a rude and arrogant lack of respect: *she hated the insolent tone of his voice.*
– DERIVATIVES **in·so·lent·ly** adv.
– ORIGIN late Middle English (also in the sense 'extravagant, going beyond acceptable limits'): from Latin *insolent-* 'immoderate, unaccustomed, arrogant,' from *in-* 'not' + *solent-* 'being accustomed' (from the verb *solere*).

in·sol·u·ble /inˈsälyəbəl/ ▶ **adj.** **1** impossible to solve: *the problem is not insoluble.*
2 (of a substance) incapable of being dissolved: *once dry, the paints become insoluble in water.*
– DERIVATIVES **in·sol·u·bil·i·ty** /-ˌsälyəˈbilitē/ n., **in·sol·u·bil·ize** /-ˌlīz/ v., **in·sol·u·bly** /-blē/ adv.
– ORIGIN late Middle English: from Old French, or from Latin *insolubilis*, from *in-* 'not' + *solubilis* (see SOLUBLE).

in·solv·a·ble /inˈsälvəbəl/ ▶ **adj.** rare term for INSOLUBLE.

in·sol·ven·cy /inˈsälvənsi/ ▶ **n.** (pl. **insolvencies**) the state of being insolvent; inability to pay one's debts: *the club was facing insolvency* | *insolvencies in the media sector rose by 8%.*

in·sol·vent /inˈsälvənt/ ▶ **adj.** unable to pay debts owed: *the company became insolvent.* ■ relating to insolvency: *insolvent liquidation.*
▶ **n.** an insolvent person.

in·som·ni·a /inˈsämnēə/ ▶ **n.** habitual sleeplessness; inability to sleep.
– DERIVATIVES **in·som·ni·ac** /-nēˌak/ n. & adj.
– ORIGIN early 17th cent.: from Latin, from *insomnis* 'sleepless,' from *in-* (expressing negation) + *somnus* 'sleep.'

in·so·much /ˌinsōˈməcн/ ▶ **adv.** **1** (**insomuch that**) to such an extent that: *self is the source of evil insomuch that the purity of the soul increases as it loses selfhood.*
2 (**insomuch as**) inasmuch as: *I'm dwelling on their accessories only insomuch as it has a direct bearing on the rest of the story.*
– ORIGIN late Middle English: originally as *in so much*, translating French *en tant (que)* 'in so much (as).'

in·sou·ci·ance /inˈso͞osēəns, ˌansōoˈsyäns/ ▶ **n.** casual lack of concern; indifference: *an impression of boyish insouciance.*
– ORIGIN late 18th cent.: French, from *insouciant*, from *in-* 'not' + *souciant* 'worrying' (present participle of *soucier*).

in·sou·ci·ant /inˈso͞osēənt, ˌansōoˈsyänt/ ▶ **adj.** showing a casual lack of concern; indifferent: *an insouciant shrug.*
– DERIVATIVES **in·sou·ci·ant·ly** adv.

in·sourc·ing /ˈinˌsôrsing/ ▶ **n.** the practice of using an organization's own personnel or other resources to accomplish a task: *offshore insourcing of expense reporting processing.*
– DERIVATIVES **in·source** v.
– ORIGIN on the pattern of *outsourcing*.

insp. ▶ **abbr.** inspector.

in·span /inˈspan/ ▶ **v.** (**inspans, inspanning, inspanned**) [with obj.] S. African yoke (draft animals, typically oxen) in a team to a vehicle.
– ORIGIN early 19th cent.: from Dutch *inspannen* 'to stretch,' from *in-* 'in' + *spannen* 'to span.'

in·spect /inˈspekt/ ▶ **v.** [with obj.] look at (someone or something) closely, typically to assess their condition or to discover any shortcomings: *they were inspecting my outside paintwork for cracks and flaws.* ■ examine (someone or something) to ensure that they reach an official standard: *customs officers came aboard to inspect our documents.*
– ORIGIN early 17th cent.: from Latin *inspect-* 'looked into, examined,' from the verb *inspicere* (from *in-* 'in' + *specere* 'look at'), or from its frequentative, *inspectare*.

in·spec·tion /inˈspeksнən/ ▶ **n.** careful examination or scrutiny: *on closer inspection it looked like a fossil* | *we carry out regular safety inspections.*

in·spec·tor /inˈspektər/ ▶ **n.** **1** an official employed to ensure that official regulations are obeyed, esp. in public services: *a prison inspector.* ■ Brit. an official

i

PRONUNCIATION KEY ə *ago, up*; ər *over, fur*; a *hat*; ā *ate*; ä *car*; e *let*; ē *see*; i *fit*; ī *by*; NG *sing*; ō *go*; ô *law, for*; oi *toy*; o͝o *good*; o͞o *goo*; ou *out*; TH *thin*; TH *then*; ZH *vision*

who examines bus or train tickets to check that they are valid.
2 a police officer ranking below a superintendent or police chief: [as title] *Inspector Simmons.*
– DERIVATIVES **in·spec·to·ri·al** /ˌinspekˈtôrēəl/ **adj.**, **in·spec·tor·ship** /-ˌSHip/ **n.**

in·spec·tor·ate /inˈspektərit/ ▶ **n.** a body that ensures that the official regulations applying to a particular type of institution or activity are obeyed: *the factory inspectorate.*

in·spec·tor gen·er·al (abbr.: **IG**) ▶ **n.** (pl. **inspectors general**) an official in charge of inspecting a particular institution or activity: *a report by the Pentagon's inspector general.* ■ Military a staff officer responsible for conducting inspections and investigations.

in·spi·ra·tion /ˌinspəˈrāSHən/ ▶ **n. 1** the process of being mentally stimulated to do or feel something, esp. to do something creative: *Helen had one of her flashes of inspiration | the history of fashion has provided designers with invaluable inspiration.* ■ the quality of having been so stimulated, esp. when evident in something: *a rare moment of inspiration in an otherwise dull display.* ■ a person or thing that stimulates in this way: *he is an inspiration to everyone.* ■ a sudden brilliant, creative, or timely idea: *then I had an inspiration.* ■ the divine influence believed to have led to the writing of the Bible.
2 the drawing in of breath; inhalation. ■ an act of breathing in; an inhalation.
– ORIGIN Middle English (in the sense 'divine guidance'): via Old French from late Latin *inspiratio(n-)*, from the verb *inspirare* (see **INSPIRE**).

in·spi·ra·tion·al /ˌinspəˈrāSHənl/ ▶ **adj.** providing or showing creative or spiritual inspiration: *the team's inspirational captain.*

in·spir·a·to·ry /inˈspīrəˌtôrē/ ▶ **adj.** Physiology relating to the act of breathing in.

in·spire /inˈspīr/ ▶ **v.** [with obj.] **1** fill (someone) with the urge or ability to do or feel something, esp. to do something creative: [with obj. and infinitive] *his passion for romantic literature inspired him to begin writing.* ■ create (a feeling, esp. a positive one) in a person: *their past record does not inspire confidence.* ■ (**inspire someone with**) animate someone with (such a feeling): *he inspired his students with a vision of freedom.* ■ give rise to: *the movie was successful enough to inspire a sequel.*
2 breathe in (air); inhale.
– DERIVATIVES **in·spir·er n.**
– ORIGIN Middle English *enspire*, from Old French *inspirer*, from Latin *inspirare* 'breathe or blow into,' from *in-* 'into' + *spirare* 'breathe.' The word was originally used of a divine or supernatural being, in the sense 'impart a truth or idea to someone.'

in·spired /inˈspīrd/ ▶ **adj. 1** of extraordinary quality, as if arising from some external creative impulse: *they had to thank the goalie for some inspired saves.* ■ (of a person) exhibiting such a creative impulse in the activity specified: *she was an inspired gardener.*
2 (of air or another substance) that is breathed in: *inspired air must be humidified.*
– DERIVATIVES **in·spir·ed·ly adv.**

in·spir·ing /inˈspīriNG/ ▶ **adj.** having the effect of inspiring someone: *he was an inspiring teacher | the scenery is not very inspiring.*
– DERIVATIVES **in·spir·ing·ly adv.**

in·spir·it /inˈspirit/ ▶ **v.** (**inspirits, inspiriting, inspirited**) [with obj.] (usu. as adj. **inspiriting**) encourage and enliven (someone): *the inspiriting beauty of Gothic architecture.*
– DERIVATIVES **in·spir·it·ing·ly adv.**

in·spis·sate /ˈinspiˌsāt, inˈspisˌāt/ ▶ **v.** [with obj.] (usu. as adj. **inspissated**) thicken or congeal: *inspissated secretions.*
– DERIVATIVES **in·spis·sa·tion** /ˌinspiˈsāSHən/ **n.**
– ORIGIN early 17th cent.: from late Latin *inspissat-* 'made thick,' from the verb *inspissare* (based on Latin *spissus* 'thick, dense').

in·spis·sa·tor /ˈinspiˌsātər, inˈspisˌātər/ ▶ **n.** a heating device for thickening or congealing a liquid.

inst. ▶ **abbr.** ■ dated (in business letters) instant: *we are pleased to acknowledge receipt of your letter of 14 inst.* ■ institute; institution: *the Southwest Research Inst.*

in·sta·bil·i·ty /ˌinstəˈbilitē/ ▶ **n.** (pl. **instabilities**) lack of stability; the state of being unstable: *political and economic instability.* ■ tendency to unpredictable behavior or erratic changes of mood: *she showed increasing signs of mental instability.*
– ORIGIN late Middle English: from French *instabilité*, from Latin *instabilitas*, from *instabilis*, from *in-* 'not' + *stabilis* (see **STABLE**[1]).

in·stall /inˈstôl/ (Brit. also **instal**) ▶ **v.** (**installs** or Brit. **instals, installing, installed**) [with obj.] **1** place or fix (equipment or machinery) in position ready for use: *we're planning to install a new shower.*
2 place (someone) in a new position of authority, esp. with ceremony: *he was installed as music director at the Cathedral of St. Barbara in Cracow.* ■ establish (someone) in a new place, condition, or role: *Ashley installed herself behind her table.*
– DERIVATIVES **in·stall·er n.**
– ORIGIN late Middle English (sense 2): from medieval Latin *installare*, from *in-* 'into' + *stallum* 'place, stall.' Sense 1 dates from the mid 19th cent.

in·stal·la·tion /ˌinstəˈlāSHən/ ▶ **n. 1** the action or process of installing someone or something, or of being installed: *the installation of a central air-conditioning system.*
2 a thing installed, in particular: ■ a large piece of equipment installed for use: *computer installations.* ■ a military or industrial establishment: *nuclear installations.* ■ an art exhibit constructed within a gallery: *a video installation.*

in·stall·ment /inˈstôlmənt/ (chiefly Brit. **instalment**) ▶ **n. 1** a sum of money due as one of several equal payments for something, spread over an agreed period of time: *the first installment of a grant for housing | the purchase price is paid in installments.*
2 any of several parts of something that are published, broadcast, or made public in sequence at intervals: *filming the final installment in his Vietnam trilogy.*
3 the process of installing something; installation: *installment will begin early next year.*
– ORIGIN mid 18th cent. (denoting the arrangement of payment by installments): alteration of obsolete *estalment* (probably by association with **INSTALLATION**), from Anglo-Norman French *estalement*, from Old French *estaler* 'to fix.'

in·stall·ment plan ▶ **n.** an arrangement for payment by installments.

in·stance /ˈinstəns/ ▶ **n. 1** an example or single occurrence of something: *a serious instance of corruption | the search finds every instance where the word appears.* ■ a particular case: *in this instance it mattered little.*
2 Law, rare the institution of a legal suit.
▶ **v.** [with obj.] cite (a fact, case, etc.) as an instance or example: *here he instances in particular the work of Bach.*
– PHRASES **at first instance** Law at the first court hearing concerning a case. **at the instance of** formal at the request or instigation of: *prosecution at the instance of the police.* **for instance** as an example: *take Canada, for instance.* **in the first** (or **second**, etc.) **instance** in the first (or second, etc.) place; at the first (or second, etc.) stage of a proceeding: *a tribunal should be formed, in the first instance to document these and other charges.*
– ORIGIN Middle English: via Old French from Latin *instantia* 'presence, urgency,' from *instare* 'be present, press upon,' from *in-* 'upon' + *stare* 'to stand.' The original sense was 'urgency, urgent entreaty,' surviving in *at the instance of*. In the late 16th cent. the word denoted a particular case cited to disprove a general assertion, derived from medieval Latin *instantia* 'example to the contrary' (translating Greek *enstasis* 'objection'); hence the meaning 'single occurrence.'

in·stan·cy /ˈinstənsē/ ▶ **n.** archaic urgency: *he told his servants to press the message with greater instancy.*
– ORIGIN early 16th cent.: from Latin *instantia* (see **INSTANCE**).

in·stant /ˈinstənt/ ▶ **adj. 1** happening or coming immediately: *the offense justified instant dismissal.* ■ (of a person) becoming a specified thing immediately or very suddenly: *become an instant millionaire.* ■ (of food) processed to allow quick preparation: *instant coffee.* ■ prepared quickly and with little effort: *we can't promise instant solutions.*
2 urgent; pressing: *an instant desire to blame others when things go wrong.*
3 [postpositive] dated (in business letters) of the current month: *your letter of the 6th instant.* Compare with **PROXIMO, ULTIMO.**
4 archaic of the present moment.
▶ **n. 1** a precise moment of time: *come here this instant! | at that instant the sun came out.*
2 a very short space of time; a moment: *for an instant the moon disappeared.*
3 informal instant coffee.
– ORIGIN late Middle English (sense 2 of the adjective, sense 3 of the adjective, and sense 4 of the adjective): via Old French from Latin *instant-* 'being at hand,' from the verb *instare*, from *in-* 'in, at' + *stare* 'to stand.'

in·stan·ta·ne·i·ty /inˌstantnˈē-itē/ ▶ **n.** the quality of being instant or immediate.

in·stan·ta·ne·ous /ˌinstənˈtānēəs/ ▶ **adj.**
1 occurring or done in an instant or instantly: *her reaction was almost instantaneous | modern methods of instantaneous communication.*
2 Physics existing or measured at a particular instant: *measurement of the instantaneous velocity.*
– DERIVATIVES **in·stan·ta·ne·ous·ly adv.**, **in·stan·ta·ne·ous·ness n.**
– ORIGIN mid 17th cent.: from medieval Latin *instantaneus*, from Latin *instant-* 'being at hand' (from the verb *instare*), on the pattern of ecclesiastical Latin *momentaneus*.

in·stant cam·er·a ▶ **n.** a camera of a type with internal processing that produces a finished print rapidly after each exposure.

in·stan·ter /inˈstantər/ ▶ **adv.** at once; immediately: *we sealed the bargain instanter.*
– ORIGIN late 17th cent.: Latin.

in·stan·ti·ate /inˈstanCHēˌāt/ ▶ **v.** [with obj.] represent as or by an instance: *a study of two groups who seemed to instantiate productive aspects of this.* ■ (**be instantiated**) Philosophy (of a universal or abstract concept) have an instance; be represented by an actual example.
– DERIVATIVES **in·stan·ti·a·tion** /-ˌstanCHēˈāSHən/ **n.**
– ORIGIN 1940s: from Latin *instantia* (see **INSTANCE**) + **-ATE**[3].

in·stant·ly /ˈinstəntlē/ ▶ **adv. 1** at once; immediately: *she fell asleep almost instantly.*
2 archaic urgently or persistently.

in·stant mes·sage (abbr.: **IM**) ▶ **n.** a message sent via the Internet that appears on the recipient's screen as soon as it is transmitted.
▶ **v.** (**instant-message**) [with obj.] send (someone) an instant message.
– DERIVATIVES **in·stant mes·sag·ing n.**

in·stant re·play ▶ **n.** an immediate playback of part of a television broadcast, typically one in slow motion showing an incident in a sports event.

in·star /ˈinˌstär/ ▶ **n.** Zoology a phase between two periods of molting in the development of an insect larva or other invertebrate animal.
– ORIGIN late 19th cent.: from Latin, literally 'form, likeness.'

in·state /inˈstāt/ ▶ **v.** [with obj.] (usu. **be instated**) set up in position; install or establish: *the restoration of those very authoritarian forms against which democracy had been instated.*
– ORIGIN early 17th cent. (formerly also as *enstate*): from **EN-**[1], **IN-**[2] 'into' + the noun **STATE**. Compare with earlier **REINSTATE**.

in·stau·ra·tion /ˌinstôˈrāSHən/ ▶ **n.** formal the action of restoring or renewing something.
– DERIVATIVES **in·stau·ra·tor** /ˈinstəˌrātər/ **n.**
– ORIGIN early 17th cent.: from Latin *instauratio(n-)*, from *instaurare* 'renew,' from *in-* 'in, toward' + *staur-* (a stem also found in *restaurare* 'restore').

in·stead /inˈsted/ ▶ **adv.** as an alternative or substitute: *do not use lotions, but put on a clean dressing instead | she never married, preferring instead to remain single.* ■ (**instead of**) as a substitute or alternative to; in place of: *walk to work instead of going by car.*
– ORIGIN Middle English (originally as two words): from **IN** + **STEAD**.

in·step /ˈinˌstep/ ▶ **n.** the part of a person's foot between the ball and the ankle. ■ the part of a shoe that fits over or under this part of a foot. ■ a thing shaped like the inner arch of a foot.
– ORIGIN late Middle English: of unknown origin; compare with West Frisian *ynstap* 'opening in a shoe for insertion of the foot.'

in·sti·gate /ˈinstiˌgāt/ ▶ **v.** [with obj.] bring about or initiate (an action or event): *they instigated a reign of terror | instigating legal proceedings.* ■ (**instigate someone to do something**) incite someone to do something, esp. something bad: *instigating men to refuse allegiance to the civil powers.*
– ORIGIN mid 16th cent. (in the sense 'urge on'): from Latin *instigat-* 'urged, incited,' from the verb *instigare*, from *in-* 'toward' + *stigare* 'prick, incite.'

in·sti·ga·tion /ˌinstiˈgāSHən/ ▶ **n.** the action or process of instigating an action or event: *he was deported in 1891 for his instigation and support of the protest.*
– ORIGIN late Middle English (in the sense 'incitement'): from Old French, or from Latin *instigatio(n-)*, from the verb *instigare* (see **INSTIGATE**).

in·sti·ga·tor /ˈinstiˌgātər/ ▶ **n.** a person who brings about or initiates something: *he was not the instigator of the incident.*

in·still /inˈstil/ (Brit. also **instil**) ▶ **v.** [with obj.]
1 gradually but firmly establish (an idea or attitude, esp. a desirable one) in a person's mind: *how do we instill a sense of rightness in today's youth?*
2 put (a substance) into something in the form of liquid drops: *she was told how to instill eye drops.*
– DERIVATIVES **in·stil·la·tion** /ˌinstəˈlāSHən/ **n.**, **in·still·ment n.**
– ORIGIN late Middle English (sense 2): from Latin *instillare*, from *in-* 'into' + *stillare* 'to drop' (from *stilla* 'a drop').

in·stinct ▸ **n.** /ˈinstiNGkt/ an innate, typically fixed pattern of behavior in animals in response to certain stimuli: *birds have an instinct to build nests* | *maternal instincts.* ■ a natural or intuitive way of acting or thinking: *they retain their old authoritarian instincts.* ■ a natural propensity or skill of a specified kind: *his instinct for making the most of his chances.* ■ the fact or quality of possessing innate behavior patterns: *instinct told her not to ask the question.*
▸ **adj.** /inˈstiNGkt/ [predic.] (**instinct with**) formal imbued or filled with (a quality, esp. a desirable one): *these canvases are instinct with passion.*
– DERIVATIVES **in·stinc·tu·al** /insˈtiNGkCHo͞oəl/ **adj.**, **in·stinc·tu·al·ly adv.**
– ORIGIN late Middle English (also in the sense 'instigation, impulse'): from Latin *instinctus* 'impulse,' from the verb *instinguere*, from *in-* 'toward' + *stinguere* 'to prick.'

in·stinc·tive /inˈstiNG(k)tiv/ ▸ **adj.** relating to or prompted by instinct; apparently unconscious or automatic: *an instinctive distaste for conflict.* ■ (of a person) doing or being a specified thing apparently naturally or automatically: *an instinctive writer.*
– DERIVATIVES **in·stinc·tive·ly adv.**

in·sti·tute /ˈinstiˌt(y)o͞ot/ ▸ **n.** [usu. in names] **1** a society or organization having a particular object or common factor, esp. a scientific, educational, or social one: *the Institute for Advanced Studies* | *a research institute.*
2 (usu. **institutes**) archaic a commentary, treatise, or summary of principles, esp. concerning law.
▸ **v.** [with obj.] **1** set in motion or establish (something, esp. a program, system, or inquiry): *the Illinois Department of Conservation instituted a hunt to remove deer* | *the award was instituted in 1900.* ■ begin (legal proceedings) in a court.
2 appoint (someone) to a position, esp. as a cleric: *his sons were **instituted to** his benefice in 1986* | [with complement] *a testator who has instituted his daughter heir.*
– ORIGIN Middle English (sense 2 of the verb): from Latin *institut-* 'established,' from the verb *instituere*, from *in-* 'in, toward' + *statuere* 'set up.' The noun is from Latin *institutum* 'something designed, precept,' neuter past participle of *instituere*; sense 1 of the noun dates from the early 19th cent.

in·sti·tu·tion /ˌinstiˈt(y)o͞osHən/ ▸ **n. 1** a society or organization founded for a religious, educational, social, or similar purpose: *a certificate from a professional institution.* ■ an organization providing residential care for people with special needs: *an institution for the mentally ill.* ■ an established official organization having an important role in the life of a country, such as a bank, church, or legislature: *the institutions of democratic government.* ■ a large company or other organization involved in financial trading: *the interest rate financial institutions charge one another.*
2 an established law, practice, or custom: *the **institution of** marriage.* ■ informal a well-established and familiar person, custom, or object: *he soon became something of a national institution.*
3 the action of instituting something: *a delay in the institution of proceedings.*
– ORIGIN late Middle English (sense 2 and sense 3): via Old French from Latin *institutio(n-)*, from the verb *instituere* (see INSTITUTE). Sense 1 dates from the early 18th cent.

in·sti·tu·tion·al /ˌinstiˈt(y)o͞osHənl/ ▸ **adj.** of, in, or like an institution or institutions: *institutional care* | *an institutional investor.* ■ unappealing or unimaginative: *institutional chocolate-colored paint.* ■ expressed or organized in the form of institutions: *institutional religion.* ■ (of advertising) intended to create prestige rather than immediate sales.
– DERIVATIVES **in·sti·tu·tion·al·ism** /-ˌizəm/ **n.**, **in·sti·tu·tion·al·ly adv.**

in·sti·tu·tion·al in·ves·tor ▸ **n.** Finance a large organization, such as a bank, pension fund, labor union, or insurance company, that makes substantial investments on the stock exchange.

in·sti·tu·tion·al·ize /ˌinstiˈt(y)o͞osHənlˌīz/ ▸ **v.** [with obj.] **1** establish (something, typically a practice or activity) as a convention or norm in an organization or culture: *a system that institutionalizes bad behavior.*
2 (usu. **be institutionalized**) place or keep (someone) in a residential institution: *these adolescents had more contacts with the police and were charged and institutionalized more often.*
– DERIVATIVES **in·sti·tu·tion·al·i·za·tion** /ˌinstiˌt(y)o͞osHənl-iˈzāsHən/ **n.**

in·sti·tu·tion·al·ized /ˌinstiˈt(y)o͞osHənlˌīzd/ ▸ **adj. 1** established in practice or custom: *the danger of discrimination becoming institutionalized.*
2 established as part of an official organization: *one of the most insidious byproducts of the Cold War, institutionalized secrecy.*
3 (of a person, esp. a long-term patient or prisoner) made apathetic and dependent after a long period in an institution.

in-store ▸ **adj. & adv.** within a store: [as adj.] *an in-store bakery* | [as adv.] *the goods are promoted in-store.*

instr. ▸ **abbr.** ■ instructor. ■ instrument or instrumental.

in·struct /inˈstrəkt/ ▸ **v. 1** [reporting verb] direct or command someone to do something, esp. as an official order: [with obj. and infinitive] *she instructed him to wait* | [with direct speech] *"Look at me," he instructed* | [with clause] *I instructed that she be given hot, sweet tea.*
2 [with obj.] teach (someone) a subject or skill: *he **instructed** them **in** the use of firearms* | [with obj. and clause] *instructing electors how to record their votes.*
3 [with obj.] Law give a person direction, information, or authorization, in particular: ■ (of a judge) give information, esp. clarification of legal principles, to (a jury). ■ inform (someone) of a fact or situation: [with clause] *the bank was instructed that the money from the savings account was now held by the company.*
– ORIGIN late Middle English (sense 2): from Latin *instruct-* 'constructed, equipped, taught,' from the verb *instruere*, from *in-* 'upon, toward' + *struere* 'pile up.'

in·struc·tion /inˈstrəksHən/ ▸ **n. 1** (often **instructions**) a direction or order: *he issued instructions to the sheriff* | *he was acting on my instructions.* ■ (**instructions**) Law directions to a lawyer or to a jury. ■ Computing a code or sequence in a computer program that defines an operation and puts it into effect.
2 (**instructions**) detailed information telling how something should be done, operated, or assembled: *always study the instructions supplied.*
3 teaching; education: *the school offers personalized instruction in a variety of skills.*
– DERIVATIVES **in·struc·tion·al** /-sHənl/ **adj.**
– ORIGIN late Middle English: via Old French from late Latin *instructio(n-)*, from the verb *instruere* (see INSTRUCT).

in·struc·tion set ▸ **n.** Computing the complete set of all the instructions in machine code that can be recognized and executed by a central processing unit.

in·struc·tive /inˈstrəktiv/ ▸ **adj.** useful and informative: *it is instructive to compare the two projects.*
– DERIVATIVES **in·struc·tive·ly adv.**, **in·struc·tive·ness n.**

in·struc·tor /inˈstrəktər/ ▸ **n.** a person who teaches something: *a driving instructor.* ■ a college teacher ranking below assistant professor.
– DERIVATIVES **in·struc·tor·ship** /-ˌsHip/ **n.**

in·stru·ment /ˈinstrəmənt/ ▸ **n. 1** a tool or implement, esp. one for delicate or scientific work: *a surgical instrument* | *writing instruments.* ■ a thing used in pursuing an aim or policy; a means: *drama as an **instrument of** learning.* ■ a person who is exploited or made use of: *he was a mere instrument acting under coercion.*
2 a measuring device used to gauge the level, position, speed, etc., of something, esp. a motor vehicle or aircraft.
3 (also **musical instrument**) an object or device for producing musical sounds: *a percussion instrument.*
4 a formal document, esp. a legal one: *execution involves signature and unconditional delivery of the instrument.*
▸ **v.** [with obj.] equip (something) with measuring instruments.
– ORIGIN Middle English: from Old French, or from Latin *instrumentum* 'equipment, implement,' from the verb *instruere* 'construct, equip.'

in·stru·men·tal /ˌinstrəˈmentl/ ▸ **adj. 1** serving as an instrument or means in pursuing an aim or policy: *the society was **instrumental in** bringing about legislation.* ■ relating to something's function as an instrument or means to an end: *a very instrumental view of education and how it relates to their needs.*
2 (of music) performed on instruments, not sung: *a largely instrumental piece.* ■ relating to musical instruments: *brilliance of instrumental color.*
3 of or relating to an implement or measuring device: *instrumental error* | *instrumental delivery of a baby.*
4 Grammar denoting or relating to a case of nouns and pronouns (and words in grammatical agreement with them) indicating a means or instrument.
▸ **n. 1** a piece of (usually nonclassical) music performed solely by instruments, with no vocals.
2 (**the instrumental**) Grammar the instrumental case. ■ a noun in the instrumental case.
– DERIVATIVES **in·stru·men·tal·ly adv.**

in·stru·men·tal con·di·tion·ing ▸ **n.** Psychology a learning process in which behavior is modified by the reinforcing or inhibiting effects of the resulting consequences.

in·stru·men·tal·ism /ˌinstrəˈmentlˌizəm/ ▸ **n. 1** a pragmatic philosophical approach that regards an activity (such as science, law, or education) chiefly as an instrument or tool for some practical purpose, rather than in more absolute or ideal terms, in particular: ■ Philosophy the pragmatic philosophy of John Dewey that supposes that thought is an instrument for solving practical problems and that truth is not fixed but changes as the problems change. ■ (esp. in Marxist theory) the view that the state and social organizations are tools that are exploited by the ruling class or by individuals in their own interests.
2 Music, rare instrumental technique.

in·stru·men·tal·ist /ˌinstrəˈmentl-ist/ ▸ **n. 1** a player of a musical instrument.
2 an adherent of instrumentalism.
▸ **adj.** of or in terms of instrumentalism.

in·stru·men·tal·i·ty /ˌinstrəmənˈtalitē, -men-/ ▸ **n.** (pl. **instrumentalities**) the fact or quality of serving as an instrument or means to an end; agency: *a corporate body can act only through the instrumentality of human beings.* ■ a thing that serves as an instrument or means to an end.

in·stru·men·ta·tion /ˌinstrəmənˈtāsHən, -men-/ ▸ **n. 1** the particular instruments used in a piece of music; the manner in which a piece is arranged for instruments: *Telemann's specified instrumentation of flute, violin, and continuo.* ■ the arrangement or composition of a piece of music for particular musical instruments: *an experiment in instrumentation.*
2 measuring instruments regarded collectively: *the controls and instrumentation of an aircraft.* ■ the design, provision, or use of measuring instruments.

in·stru·ment pan·el (also **instrument board**) ▸ **n.** a surface in front of a driver's or pilot's seat, on which the vehicle's or aircraft's instruments are situated.

in·sub·or·di·nate /ˌinsəˈbôrdn-it/ ▸ **adj.** defiant of authority; disobedient to orders: *an insubordinate attitude.*
– DERIVATIVES **in·sub·or·di·nate·ly adv.**

in·sub·or·di·na·tion /ˌinsəˌbôrdnˈāsHən/ ▸ **n.** defiance of authority; refusal to obey orders: *he was dismissed for insubordination.*

in·sub·stan·tial /ˌinsəbˈstancHəl/ ▸ **adj.** lacking strength and solidity: *the huts are relatively few and insubstantial* | *insubstantial evidence.* ■ not solid or real; imaginary: *the flickering light made her face seem insubstantial.*
– DERIVATIVES **in·sub·stan·ti·al·i·ty** /-ˌstancHēˈalitē/ **n.**, **in·sub·stan·tial·ly adv.**
– ORIGIN early 17th cent.: from late Latin *insubstantialis*, from *in-* 'not' + *substantialis* (see SUBSTANTIAL).

in·suf·fer·a·ble /inˈsəf(ə)rəbəl/ ▸ **adj.** too extreme to bear; intolerable: *the heat would be insufferable by July.* ■ having or showing unbearable arrogance or conceit: *an insufferable bully* | *insufferable French chauvinism.*
– DERIVATIVES **in·suf·fer·a·ble·ness n.**, **in·suf·fer·a·bly** /-blē/ **adv.**
– ORIGIN late Middle English: perhaps via French (now dialect) *insouffrable*, based on Latin *suffere* 'endure' (see SUFFER).

in·suf·fi·cien·cy /ˌinsəˈfisHənsē/ ▸ **n.** (pl. **insufficiencies**) the condition of being insufficient: *insufficiency of adequate housing* | *there have been demands to redress such insufficiencies.* ■ Medicine the inability of an organ to perform its normal function: *renal insufficiency.*
– ORIGIN early 16th cent. (in the sense 'incompetence, inability'): from late Latin *insufficientia*, from *in-* 'not' + Latin *sufficere* 'be sufficient.'

in·suf·fi·cient /ˈinsəˈfisHənt/ ▸ **adj.** not enough; inadequate: *there was insufficient evidence to convict him.*
– DERIVATIVES **in·suf·fi·cient·ly adv.**
– ORIGIN late Middle English (in the sense 'incapable, incompetent'): via Old French from late Latin *insufficient-* 'not sufficing,' from *in-* 'not' + Latin *sufficere* (see SUFFICE).

in·suf·flate /ˈinsəˌflāt/ ▸ **v.** [with obj.] **1** Medicine blow (air, gas, or powder) into a cavity of the body. ■ blow something into (a part of the body) in this way.
2 Theology blow or breathe on (someone) to symbolize spiritual influence.
– DERIVATIVES **in·suf·fla·tion** /ˌinsəˈflāsHən/ **n.**

–ORIGIN late 17th cent.: from late Latin *insufflat-* 'blown into,' from the verb *insufflare*, from *in-* 'into' + *sufflare* 'blow' (from *sub-* 'from below' + *flare* 'to blow'). Sense 2 dates from the early 20th cent.

in·suf·fla·tor /ˈinsəˌflātər/ ▶ **n. 1** a device for blowing powder onto a surface in order to make fingerprints visible.
2 an instrument for medical insufflation.

in·su·la /ˈins(y)ələ/ ▶ **n.** (pl. **insulae** /-ˌlē/) Anatomy a region of the brain deep in the cerebral cortex.
–ORIGIN mid 19th cent.: Latin, literally 'island.'

in·su·lant /ˈins(y)ələnt/ ▶ **n.** an insulating material.

in·su·lar /ˈins(y)ələr/ ▶ **adj. 1** ignorant of or uninterested in cultures, ideas, or peoples outside one's own experience: *a stubbornly insular farming people.* ■ lacking contact with other people: *people living restricted and sometimes insular existences.*
2 of, relating to, or from an island: *the movement of goods of insular origin.* ■ of or relating to the art and craftwork of Britain and Ireland in the early Middle Ages, esp. a form of Latin handwriting: *insular illumination of the 6th century.* ■ (of climate) equable because of the influence of the sea.
3 Anatomy of or relating to the insula of the brain.
–DERIVATIVES **in·su·lar·ly adv.**
–ORIGIN mid 16th cent. (as a noun denoting an islander): from late Latin *insularis*, from *insula* 'island.'

in·su·lar·i·ty /ˌins(y)əˈlaritē, -ˈler-/ ▶ **n.** ignorance of or lack of interest in cultures, ideas, or peoples outside one's own experience: *an example of British insularity.*

in·su·late /ˈins(y)əˌlāt/ ▶ **v.** [with obj.] **1** protect (something) by interposing material that prevents the loss of heat or the intrusion of sound: *the room was heavily **insulated against** all outside noise.* ■ prevent the passage of electricity to or from (something) by covering it in nonconducting material: *the case is carefully insulated to prevent short circuits.* ■ protect from the unpleasant effects or elements of something: *he claims that the service is complacent and **insulated from** outside pressures.*
2 archaic make (land) into an island: *the village was insulated by every flood of the river.*
–ORIGIN mid 16th cent. (sense 2): from Latin *insula* 'island' + **-ATE**[3].

in·su·lat·ing tape ▶ **n.** another term for **FRICTION TAPE**.

in·su·la·tion /ˌins(y)əˈlāSHən/ ▶ **n.** the action of insulating something or someone: *keep your home warmer through insulation | heat insulation.* ■ the state of being insulated: *his comparative insulation from the world.* ■ material used to insulate something, esp. a building: *fit insulation to all exposed pipes.*

in·su·la·tor /ˈins(y)əˌlātər/ ▶ **n.** a thing or substance used for insulation, in particular: ■ a substance that does not readily allow the passage of heat or sound: *cotton is a poor insulator.* ■ a substance or device that does not readily conduct electricity. ■ a block of material, typically glass or ceramic, enclosing a wire carrying an electric current where it crosses a support.

in·su·lin /ˈinsələn/ ▶ **n.** Biochemistry a hormone produced in the pancreas by the islets of Langerhans that regulates the amount of glucose in the blood. The lack of insulin causes a form of diabetes. ■ an animal-derived or synthetic form of this substance used to treat diabetes.
–ORIGIN early 20th cent.: from Latin *insula* 'island' + **-IN**[1].

in·su·lin shock ▶ **n.** Medicine an acute physiological condition resulting from excess insulin in the blood, involving low blood sugar, weakness, convulsions, and potentially coma.

in·su·li·tis /ˌinsəˈlītis/ ▶ **n.** Medicine disease of the pancreas caused by the infiltration of lymphocytes.

in·sult ▶ **v.** /inˈsəlt/ [with obj.] speak to or treat with disrespect or scornful abuse: *you're insulting the woman I love.*
▶ **n.** /ˈinˌsəlt/ **1** a disrespectful or scornfully abusive remark or action: *he hurled insults at us | he saw the book as a deliberate **insult to** the Church.* ■ a thing so worthless or contemptible as to be offensive: *the present offer is an absolute insult.*
2 Medicine an event or occurrence that causes damage to a tissue or organ: *the movement of the bone causes a severe tissue insult.*
–PHRASES **add insult to injury** act in a way that makes a bad or displeasing situation worse.
–DERIVATIVES **in·sult·er n.**
–ORIGIN mid 16th cent. (as a verb in the sense 'exult, act arrogantly'): from Latin *insultare* 'jump or trample on,' from *in-* 'on' + *saltare*, from *salire* 'to leap.' The noun (in the early 17th cent. denoting an attack) is from French *insulte* or ecclesiastical Latin *insultus*. The main current senses date from the 17th cent., the medical use dating from the early 20th cent.

in·sult·ing /inˈsəltiNG/ ▶ **adj.** disrespectful or scornfully abusive: *insulting remarks | their language is insulting to women.*
–DERIVATIVES **in·sult·ing·ly adv.**

in·su·per·a·ble /inˈso͞op(ə)rəbəl/ ▶ **adj.** (of a difficulty or obstacle) impossible to overcome: *insuperable financial problems.*
–DERIVATIVES **in·su·per·a·bil·i·ty** /-ˌso͞op(ə)rəˈbilitē/ **n., in·su·per·a·bly** /-blē/ **adv.**
–ORIGIN Middle English (in the general sense 'invincible'): from Old French, or from Latin *insuperabilis*, from *in-* 'not' + *superabilis* (from *superare* 'overcome').

in·sup·port·a·ble /ˌinsəˈpôrtəbəl/ ▶ **adj. 1** unable to be supported or justified: *he had arrived at a wholly insupportable conclusion.*
2 unable to be endured; intolerable: *the heat was insupportable.*
–DERIVATIVES **in·sup·port·a·bly** /-blē/ **adv.**
–ORIGIN mid 16th cent.: from French, from *in-* 'not' + *supportable* (from *supporter* 'to support').

in·sur·ance /inˈSHo͝orəns/ ▶ **n. 1** a practice or arrangement by which a company or government agency provides a guarantee of compensation for specified loss, damage, illness, or death in return for payment of a premium: *many new borrowers take out **insurance against** unemployment or sickness.* ■ the business of providing such an arrangement: *Howard is in insurance.* ■ money paid for this: *my insurance has gone up.* ■ money paid out as compensation under such an arrangement: *when will I be able to collect the insurance?*
2 a thing providing protection against a possible eventuality: *adherence to high personal standards of conduct is excellent **insurance against** personal problems | young people are not an insurance against loneliness in old age.*
–ORIGIN late Middle English (originally as *ensurance* in the sense 'ensuring, assurance, a guarantee'): from Old French *enseurance*, from *enseurer* (see **ENSURE**). Sense 1 dates from the mid 17th cent.

in·sur·ance ad·just·er ▶ **n.** another term for **CLAIMS ADJUSTER**.

in·sur·ance a·gent ▶ **n.** a person employed to sell insurance policies.

in·sur·ance car·ri·er ▶ **n.** an insurer; an insurance company.

in·sur·ance pol·i·cy ▶ **n.** a document detailing the terms and conditions of a contract of insurance.

in·sure /inˈSHo͝or/ ▶ **v.** [with obj.] **1** arrange for compensation in the event of damage to or loss of (property), or injury to or the death of (someone), in exchange for regular advance payments to a company or government agency: *the table should be **insured for** $2,500 | the company had **insured** itself **against** a fall of the dollar | [no obj.] businesses can **insure against** exchange rate fluctuations.* ■ provide insurance coverage with respect to: *subsidiaries set up to insure the risks of a group of companies.*
2 (**insure someone against**) secure or protect someone against (a possible contingency): *by appeasing Celia they might insure themselves against further misfortune | [no obj.] such changes could insure against further violence and unrest.*
–DERIVATIVES **in·sur·a·bil·i·ty** /-ˌSHo͝orəˈbilitē/ **n., in·sur·a·ble adj.**
–ORIGIN late Middle English (in the sense 'assure someone of something'): alteration of **ENSURE**.

USAGE There is considerable overlap between the meaning and use of **insure** and **ensure**. In both US and British English, the primary meaning of **insure** is the commercial sense of providing financial compensation in the event of damage to property; **ensure** is not used at all in this sense. For the more general senses, **ensure** is more likely to be used, but **insure** and **ensure** are often interchangeable, particularly in US English: *bail is posted to **insure** that the defendant appears for trial | the system is run to **ensure** that a good quality of service is maintained.*

in·sured /inˈSHo͝ord/ ▶ **adj.** covered by insurance: *the insured car | a privately insured patient | an insured risk.*
▶ **n.** (**the insured**) (pl. **same**) a person or organization covered by insurance.

in·sur·er /inˈSHo͝orər/ ▶ **n.** a person or company that underwrites an insurance risk; the party in an insurance contract undertaking to pay compensation.

in·sur·gent /inˈsərjənt/ ▶ **adj.** [attrib.] rising in active revolt: *alleged links with insurgent groups.* ■ of or relating to rebels: *a series of insurgent attacks.*
▶ **n.** a rebel or revolutionary: *an attack by armed insurgents.*
–DERIVATIVES **in·sur·gence n., in·sur·gen·cy n.** (pl. **insurgencies**).
–ORIGIN mid 18th cent. (as a noun): via French from Latin *insurgent-* 'arising,' from the verb *insurgere*, from *in-* 'into, toward' + *surgere* 'to rise.'

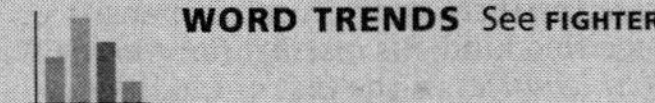

WORD TRENDS See **FIGHTER**.

in·sur·mount·a·ble /ˌinsərˈmountəbəl/ ▶ **adj.** too great to be overcome: *an insurmountable problem.*
–DERIVATIVES **in·sur·mount·a·bly adv.**

in·sur·rec·tion /ˌinsəˈrekSHən/ ▶ **n.** a violent uprising against an authority or government: *the insurrection was savagely put down | opposition to the new regime led to armed insurrection.*
–DERIVATIVES **in·sur·rec·tion·ar·y adj., in·sur·rec·tion·ist n. & adj.**
–ORIGIN late Middle English: via Old French from late Latin *insurrectio(n-)*, from *insurgere* 'rise up.'

in·sus·cep·ti·ble /ˈinsəˈseptəbəl/ ▶ **adj.** not likely to be affected: *the larvae are insusceptible to most treatments.*
–DERIVATIVES **in·sus·cep·ti·bil·i·ty n.**

int. ▶ **abbr.** ■ interior. ■ internal. ■ international.

in·tact /inˈtakt/ ▶ **adj.** [often as complement] not damaged or impaired in any way; complete: *the church was almost in ruins, but its tower remained intact.*
–DERIVATIVES **in·tact·ness n.**
–ORIGIN late Middle English: from Latin *intactus*, from *in-* 'not' + *tactus* (past participle of *tangere* 'touch').

in·tact fam·i·ly ▶ **n.** a nuclear family in which membership has remained constant, in the absence of divorce or other divisive factors.

in·ta·gliat·ed /inˈtalēˌātid, -ˈtälē-/ ▶ **adj.** archaic carved or engraved on the surface.
–ORIGIN late 18th cent.: from Italian *intagliato* 'engraved,' past participle of *intagliare*, from *in-* 'into' + *tagliare* 'to cut.'

in·ta·glio /inˈtalyō, -ˈtäl-/ ▶ **n.** (pl. **intaglios**) a design incised or engraved into a material: *the dies bore a design in intaglio.* ■ a gem with an incised design. ■ any printing process in which the type or design is etched or engraved, such as photogravure or dry point.
▶ **v.** (**intaglioes, intaglioed**) [with obj.] (usu. as adj. **intaglioed**) engrave or represent by an engraving: *a carved box with little intaglioed pineapples on it.*
–ORIGIN mid 17th cent.: Italian, from *intagliare* 'engrave.'

in·take /ˈinˌtāk/ ▶ **n. 1** an amount of food, air, or another substance taken into the body: *your daily intake of calories | his alcohol intake.* ■ an act of taking something into the body: *she heard his sharp **intake of breath** | a protective factor is the intake of cereal fiber.*
2 a location or structure through which something is taken in, e.g., water into a channel or pipe from a river, fuel or air into an engine or machine, commodities into a place, etc.: *cut rectangular holes for the air intake.* ■ the action of taking something in: *facilities for the intake of grain by road.*
–ORIGIN Middle English (originally Scots and northern English): from **IN** + **TAKE**.

in·tan·gi·ble /inˈtanjəbəl/ ▶ **adj.** unable to be touched or grasped; not having physical presence: *my companions do not care about cyberspace or anything else so intangible.* ■ difficult or impossible to define or understand; vague and abstract: *the rose symbolized something intangible about their relationship.* ■ (of an asset or benefit) not constituting or represented by a physical object and of a value not precisely measurable: *intangible business property like trademarks and patents.*
▶ **n.** (usu. **intangibles**) an intangible thing: *intangibles like self-confidence and responsibility.*
–DERIVATIVES **in·tan·gi·bil·i·ty** /-ˌtanjəˈbilitē/ **n., in·tan·gi·bly** /-blē/ **adv.**
–ORIGIN early 17th cent. (as an adjective): from French, or from medieval Latin *intangibilis*, from *in-* 'not' + late Latin *tangibilis* (see **TANGIBLE**).

in·tar·si·a /inˈtärsēə/ ▶ **n.** [often as modifier] **1** a method of knitting with a number of colors, in which a separate length or ball of yarn is used for each area of color (as opposed to different yarns being carried at the back of the work): *an intarsia design.*
2 an elaborate form of marquetry using inlays in wood, esp. as practiced in 15th-century Italy. ■ similar inlaid work in stone, metal, or glass.
–ORIGIN from Italian *intarsio*; sense 2 superseding earlier *tarsia* (from Italian, 'marquetry'); the knitting term dates from the mid 19th cent.

in·te·ger /ˈintijər/ ▶ **n. 1** a whole number; a number that is not a fraction.
2 a thing complete in itself.
–ORIGIN early 16th cent. (as an adjective meaning 'entire, whole'): from Latin, 'intact, whole,' from

in- (expressing negation) + the root of *tangere* 'to touch.' Compare with ENTIRE, also with INTEGRAL, INTEGRATE, and INTEGRITY.

in·te·gral /ˈintigrəl, inˈteg-/ ▶ **adj.** **1** necessary to make a whole complete; essential or fundamental: *games are an integral part of the school's curriculum | systematic training should be integral to library management.* ■ [attrib.] included as part of the whole rather than supplied separately: *the unit comes complete with integral pump and heater.* ■ [attrib.] having or containing all parts that are necessary to be complete: *the first integral recording of the ten Mahler symphonies.*
2 Mathematics of or denoted by an integer. ■ involving only integers, esp. as coefficients of a function.
▶ **n.** Mathematics a function of which a given function is the derivative, i.e., which yields that function when differentiated, and which may express the area under the curve of a graph of the function. See also DEFINITE INTEGRAL, INDEFINITE INTEGRAL. ■ a function satisfying a given differential equation.
– DERIVATIVES **in·te·gral·i·ty** /ˌintiˈgralitē/ **n.**, **in·te·gral·ly adv.**
– ORIGIN mid 16th cent.: from late Latin *integralis*, from *integer* 'whole' (see INTEGER). Compare with INTEGRATE and INTEGRITY.

in·te·gral cal·cu·lus ▶ **n.** a branch of mathematics concerned with the determination, properties, and application of integrals. Compare with DIFFERENTIAL CALCULUS.

in·te·grand /ˈintigrənd/ ▶ **n.** Mathematics a function that is to be integrated.
– ORIGIN late 19th cent.: from Latin *integrandus*, gerundive of *integrare* (see INTEGRATE).

in·te·grant /ˈintigrənt/ ▶ **adj.** (of parts) making up or contributing to a whole; constituent.
▶ **n.** a component.
– ORIGIN mid 17th cent. (as an adjective): from French *intégrant*, from the verb *intégrer*, from Latin *integrare* (see INTEGRATE).

in·te·grate /ˈintiˌgrāt/ ▶ **v.** [with obj.] **1** combine (one thing) with another so that they become a whole: *transportation planning should be* **integrated with** *energy policy.* ■ combine (two things) so that they become a whole: *the problem of integrating the two approaches.* ■ [no obj.] (of a thing) combine with another to form a whole: *the stone will blend with the environment and* **integrate into** *the landscape.*
2 bring (people or groups with particular characteristics or needs) into equal participation in or membership of a social group or institution: **integrating** *children with special needs* **into** *ordinary schools.* ■ [no obj.] come into equal participation in or membership of society or an institution or body: *she was anxious to* **integrate** *well* **into** *her husband's family.* ■ desegregate (a school, neighborhood, etc.), esp. racially: *there was a national campaign under way to integrate the lunch counters* | [no obj.] *cities' efforts to integrate across urban-suburban lines.*
3 Mathematics find the integral of.
– DERIVATIVES **in·te·gra·bil·i·ty** /ˌintigrəˈbilitē/ **n.**, **in·te·gra·ble** /-grəbəl/ **adj.**
– ORIGIN mid 17th cent.: from Latin *integrat-* 'made whole,' from the verb *integrare*, from *integer* 'whole' (see INTEGER). Compare with INTEGRAL and INTEGRITY.

in·te·grat·ed /ˈintiˌgrātid/ ▶ **adj.** having been integrated, in particular: ■ (of an institution, body, etc.) desegregated, esp. racially: *integrated education.* ■ with various parts or aspects linked or coordinated: *an integrated and high-quality public transportation system.* ■ chiefly Physics indicating the mean value or total sum of (temperature, an area, etc.): *integrated electron density along the line of sight.*

in·te·grat·ed cir·cuit ▶ **n.** an electronic circuit formed on a small piece of semiconducting material, performing the same function as a larger circuit made from discrete components.

in·te·grat·ed serv·ic·es dig·it·al net·work (abbr.: **ISDN**) ▶ **n.** a telecommunications network through which sound, images, and data can be transmitted as digitized signals.

in·te·grat·ing /ˈintiˌgrātiNG/ ▶ **adj.** (of an instrument) indicating the mean value or total sum of a measured quantity.

in·te·gra·tion /ˌintiˈgrāSHən/ ▶ **n.** **1** the action or process of integrating: *economic and political integration | integration of individual countries into trading blocs.* ■ the intermixing of people or groups previously segregated: *integration is the best hope for both black and white Americans.*
2 Mathematics the finding of an integral or integrals: *integration of an ordinary differential equation | mathematical integrations.*
3 Psychology the coordination of processes in the nervous system, including diverse sensory information and motor impulses: *visuomotor integration.* ■ Psychoanalysis the process by which a well-balanced psyche becomes whole as the developing ego organizes the id, and the state that results or that treatment seeks to create or restore by countering the fragmenting effect of defense mechanisms.
– DERIVATIVES **in·te·gra·tion·ist** /-nist/ **n.**

in·te·gra·tive /-ˌgrātiv/ ▶ **adj.** serving or intending to unify separate things: *an integrative approach to learning.* ■ Medicine combining allopathic and complementary therapies: *a database for the integrative physician | integrative medicine.*

in·te·gra·tor /ˈintiˌgrātər/ ▶ **n.** a person or thing that integrates, in particular: ■ (also **system integrator** or **systems integrator**) Computing a company that markets commercial integrated software and hardware systems. ■ Electronics a computer chip or circuit that performs mathematical integration. ■ an instrument for indicating or registering the total amount or mean value of some physical quality such as area or temperature.

in·teg·ri·ty /inˈtegritē/ ▶ **n.** **1** the quality of being honest and having strong moral principles; moral uprightness: *he is known to be a man of integrity.*
2 the state of being whole and undivided: *upholding territorial integrity and national sovereignty.* ■ the condition of being unified, unimpaired, or sound in construction: *the structural integrity of the novel.* ■ internal consistency or lack of corruption in electronic data: [as modifier] *integrity checking.*
– ORIGIN late Middle English (sense 2): from French *intégrité* or Latin *integritas*, from *integer* 'intact' (see INTEGER). Compare with ENTIRETY, INTEGRAL, and INTEGRATE.

in·teg·u·ment /inˈtegyəmənt/ ▶ **n.** a tough outer protective layer, esp. that of an animal or plant.
– DERIVATIVES **in·teg·u·men·tal** /-ˌtegyəˈmentl/ **adj.**, **in·teg·u·men·ta·ry** /-ˌtegyəˈmentərē/ **adj.**
– ORIGIN early 17th cent. (denoting a covering or coating): from Latin *integumentum*, from the verb *integere*, from *in-* 'in' + *tegere* 'to cover.'

in·tel /ˈinˌtel/ ▶ **n.** [often as modifier] informal military intelligence; information: *prewar intel.*
– ORIGIN 1980s: shortening.

in·tel·lect /ˈintlˌekt/ ▶ **n.** the faculty of reasoning and understanding objectively, esp. with regard to abstract or academic matters: *he was a man of action rather than of intellect.* ■ the understanding or mental powers of a particular person: *his keen intellect.* ■ an intelligent or intellectual person: *sapping our country of some of its brightest intellects.*
– ORIGIN late Middle English: from Latin *intellectus* 'understanding,' from *intellegere* 'understand' (see INTELLIGENT).

in·tel·lec·tion /ˌintlˈekSHən/ ▶ **n.** the action or process of understanding, as opposed to imagination.
– DERIVATIVES **in·tel·lec·tive** /-tiv/ **adj.**

in·tel·lec·tu·al /ˌintlˈekCHo͞oəl/ ▶ **adj.** of or relating to the intellect: *children need intellectual stimulation.* ■ appealing to or requiring use of the intellect: *the movie wasn't very intellectual, but it caught the mood of the times.* ■ possessing a highly developed intellect: *you are an intellectual girl, like your mother.*
▶ **n.** a person possessing a highly developed intellect.
– DERIVATIVES **in·tel·lec·tu·al·i·ty** /ˌintlˌekCHo͞oˈalitē/ **n.**, **in·tel·lec·tu·al·ly adv.**
– ORIGIN late Middle English: from Latin *intellectualis*, from *intellectus* 'understanding,' from *intellegere* 'understand' (see INTELLIGENT).

in·tel·lec·tu·al·ism /ˌintlˈekCHo͞oəˌlizəm/ ▶ **n.** the exercise of the intellect at the expense of the emotions. ■ Philosophy the theory that knowledge is wholly or mainly derived from pure reason; rationalism.
– DERIVATIVES **in·tel·lec·tu·al·ist n.**
– ORIGIN early 19th cent. (as a term in philosophy): from INTELLECTUAL, on the pattern of German *Intellektualismus*.

in·tel·lec·tu·al·ize /ˌintlˈekCHo͞oəˌlīz/ ▶ **v.** [with obj.] **1** give an intellectual character to: *belief was a gut feeling—it couldn't be intellectualized.*
2 [no obj.] talk, write, or think intellectually: *people who* **intellectualize about** *fashion.*
– DERIVATIVES **in·tel·lec·tu·al·i·za·tion** /-ˌekCHo͞oələˈzāSHən/ **n.**

in·tel·lec·tu·al prop·er·ty ▶ **n.** Law a work or invention that is the result of creativity, such as a manuscript or a design, to which one has rights and for which one may apply for a patent, copyright, trademark, etc.

in·tel·li·gence /inˈtelijəns/ ▶ **n.** **1** the ability to acquire and apply knowledge and skills: *an eminent man of great intelligence | they underestimated her intelligence.* ■ a person or being with this ability: *extraterrestrial intelligences.*
2 the collection of information of military or political value: *the chief of military intelligence |* [as modifier] *the intelligence department.* ■ people employed in the collection of military or political information: *French intelligence has been able to secure numerous local informers.* ■ information collected in this way: *the gathering of intelligence.* ■ archaic information in general; news.
– DERIVATIVES **in·tel·li·gen·tial** /inˌteləˈjenCHəl/ **adj.** (archaic).
– ORIGIN late Middle English: via Old French from Latin *intelligentia*, from *intelligere* 'understand' (see INTELLIGENT).

in·tel·li·gence quo·tient (abbr.: **IQ**) ▶ **n.** a number representing a person's reasoning ability (measured using problem-solving tests) as compared to the statistical norm or average for their age, taken as 100.

in·tel·li·genc·er /inˈtelijənsər, -jen-/ ▶ **n.** archaic a person who gathers intelligence, esp. an informer, spy, or secret agent.

in·tel·li·gence test ▶ **n.** a test designed to measure the ability to think and reason rather than acquired knowledge.

in·tel·li·gent /inˈtelijənt/ ▶ **adj.** having or showing intelligence, esp. of a high level: *Annabelle is intelligent and hardworking | an intelligent guess.* ■ (of a device, machine, or building) able to vary its state or action in response to varying situations, varying requirements, and past experience. ■ (esp. of a computer terminal) incorporating a microprocessor and having its own processing capability. Often contrasted with DUMB.
– DERIVATIVES **in·tel·li·gent·ly adv.**
– ORIGIN early 16th cent.: from Latin *intelligent-* 'understanding,' from the verb *intelligere*, variant of *intellegere* 'understand,' from *inter* 'between' + *legere* 'choose.'

in·tel·li·gent de·sign ▶ **n.** the theory that life, or the universe, cannot have arisen by chance and was designed and created by some intelligent entity.

in·tel·li·gent·si·a /inˌteliˈjentsēə/ ▶ **n.** (usu. **the intelligentsia**) [treated as sing. or pl.] intellectuals or highly educated people as a group, esp. when regarded as possessing culture and political influence.
– ORIGIN early 20th cent.: from Russian *intelligentsiya*, from Polish *inteligencja*, from Latin *intelligentia* (see INTELLIGENCE).

in·tel·li·gi·bil·i·ty /inˌtelijəˈbilitē/ ▶ **n.** the state or quality of being intelligible: *being able to see a speaker can improve intelligibility.*

in·tel·li·gi·ble /inˈtelijəbəl/ ▶ **adj.** able to be understood; comprehensible: *this would make the system more intelligible to the general public.* ■ Philosophy able to be understood only by the intellect, not by the senses.
– DERIVATIVES **in·tel·li·gi·bly** /-blē/ **adv.**
– ORIGIN late Middle English (also in the sense 'capable of understanding'): from Latin *intelligibilis*, from *intelligere* 'understand' (see INTELLIGENT).

In·tel·sat /ˈintelˌsat/ an international organization of more than 100 countries, formed in 1964, that owns and operates the worldwide commercial communications satellite system.
– ORIGIN from *In(ternational) Tel(ecommunications) Sat(ellite Consortium)*.

in·tem·per·ance /inˈtemp(ə)rəns/ ▶ **n.** lack of moderation or restraint: *his occasional intemperance of tone.* ■ excessive indulgence, esp. in alcohol.

in·tem·per·ate /inˈtemp(ə)rit/ ▶ **adj.** having or showing a lack of self-control; immoderate: *intemperate outbursts concerning global conspiracies.* ■ given to or characterized by excessive indulgence, esp. in alcohol: *an intemperate social occasion.*
– DERIVATIVES **in·tem·per·ate·ly adv.**, **in·tem·per·ate·ness n.**
– ORIGIN late Middle English (in the sense 'inclement'): from Latin *intemperatus*, from *in-* 'not' + *temperatus* (see TEMPERATE).

in·tend /inˈtend/ ▶ **v.** [with obj.] **1** have (a course of action) as one's purpose or objective; plan: [with infinitive] *the company intends to cut about 4,500 jobs* | [with clause] *it is intended that coverage shall be worldwide.* ■ plan that (something) function in a particular way: *a series of questions intended as a checklist.* ■ plan that speech should have (a particular meaning): *no offense was intended, I assure you.*
2 design or destine (someone or something) for a particular purpose or end: *pigs* **intended for** *human consumption* | [with infinitive] *a one-room cottage intended to accommodate a family.* ■ (**be intended for**) be meant or designed for (a particular person

or group) to have or use: *this benefit is intended for people incapable of work.*
– DERIVATIVES **in·tend·er** n.
– ORIGIN Middle English *entend* (in the sense 'direct the attention to'), from Old French *entendre*, from Latin *intendere* 'intend, extend, direct,' from *in-* 'toward' + *tendere* 'stretch, tend.'

in·tend·ant /in'tendənt/ ▶ **n. 1** chiefly historical a title given to a high-ranking official or administrator, esp. in France, Spain, Portugal, or one of their colonies.
2 the administrator of an opera house or theater.
– DERIVATIVES **in·tend·an·cy** /-dənsē/ **n.**
– ORIGIN mid 17th cent.: from French, from Latin *intendere* 'to direct' (see INTEND).

in·tend·ed /in'tendid/ ▶ **adj.** [attrib.] planned or meant: *the intended victim escaped.*
▶ **n.** (**one's intended**) informal the person one intends to marry; one's fiancé or fiancée.
– DERIVATIVES **in·tend·ed·ly adv.**

in·tend·ing /in'tendiNG/ ▶ **adj.** [attrib.] (of a person) planning or meaning to do or be the specified thing: *an intending client.*

in·tend·ment /in'tendmənt/ ▶ **n.** Law the sense in which the law understands or interprets something, such as the true intention of a piece of legislation.
– ORIGIN late Middle English (denoting an intended meaning): from Old French *entendement*, from *entendre* 'intend.'

in·tense /in'tens/ ▶ **adj. 1** of extreme force, degree, or strength: *the job demands intense concentration* | *the heat was intense* | *an intense blue.* ■ (of an action) highly concentrated: *a phase of intense activity.*
2 having or showing strong feelings or opinions; extremely earnest or serious: *an intense young woman, passionate about her art* | *a burning and intense look.*
– DERIVATIVES **in·tense·ly adv.**, **in·tense·ness n.**
– ORIGIN late Middle English: from Old French, or from Latin *intensus* 'stretched tightly, strained,' past participle of *intendere* (see INTEND).

> **USAGE** **Intense** and **intensive** are similar in meaning, but they differ in emphasis. **Intense** tends to relate to subjective responses—emotions and how we feel—while **intensive** tends to relate to objective descriptions. Thus *an intensive course of instruction* simply describes the type of course: one that is designed to cover a lot of ground in a short time. On the other hand, in *the course was intense*, the word **intense** describes how someone felt about taking the course.

in·ten·si·fi·ca·tion /in,tensəfi'kāSHən/ ▶ **n.** the action of making or becoming more intense: *the intensification of the conflict.*

in·ten·si·fi·er /in'tensə,fīər/ ▶ **n.** a person or thing that intensifies, in particular: ■ Photography a chemical used to intensify a negative. ■ Grammar an adverb used to give force or emphasis, for example, *really* in *my feet are really cold.* ■ short for IMAGE INTENSIFIER.

in·ten·si·fy /in'tensə,fī/ ▶ **v.** (**intensifies, intensifying, intensified**) **1** become or make more intense: [no obj.] *the dispute began to intensify* | [with obj.] *they had intensified their military campaign.*
2 [with obj.] Photography increase the opacity of (a negative) using a chemical: *the negative may be intensified with bichloride.*
– ORIGIN early 19th cent.: coined by Coleridge.

in·ten·sion /in'tenSHən/ ▶ **n. 1** Logic the internal content of a concept. Often contrasted with EXTENSION (sense 5).
2 archaic resolution or determination.
– DERIVATIVES **in·ten·sion·al** /-SHənl/ **adj.**, **in·ten·sion·al·ly** /-SHənl-ē/ **adv.**
– ORIGIN early 17th cent. (also in the sense 'straining, stretching'): from Latin *intensio(n-)*, from *intendere* (see INTEND). Sense 1 dates from the mid 19th cent.

in·ten·si·ty /in'tensitē/ ▶ **n.** (pl. **intensities**) **1** the quality of being intense: *gazing into her face with disconcerting intensity* | *the pain grew in intensity.* ■ an instance or degree of this: *an intensity that frightened her.*
2 chiefly Physics the measurable amount of a property, such as force, brightness, or a magnetic field: *hydrothermal processes of low intensity* | *different light intensities.*

in·ten·sive /in'tensiv/ ▶ **adj. 1** concentrated on a single area or subject or into a short time; very thorough or vigorous: *she undertook an intensive Arabic course* | *eight days of intensive arms talks.* ■ (of agriculture) aiming to achieve the highest possible level of production within a limited area, esp. by using chemical and technological aids: *intensive farming.* Often contrasted with EXTENSIVE (sense 2). ■ [usu. in combination] (typically in business and economics) concentrating on or making much use of a specified thing: *computer-intensive methods.*
2 Grammar (of an adjective, adverb, or particle) expressing intensity; giving force or emphasis.
3 denoting a property that is measured in terms of intensity (e.g., concentration) rather than of extent (e.g., volume), and so is not simply increased by addition of one thing to another.
▶ **n.** Grammar an intensive adjective, adverb, or particle; an intensifier.
– DERIVATIVES **in·ten·sive·ly adv.**, **in·ten·sive·ness n.**
– ORIGIN late Middle English (in the sense 'vehement, intense'): from French *intensif, -ive* or medieval Latin *intensivus*, from *intendere* (see INTEND).

> **USAGE** On the difference between **intensive** and **intense**, see usage at INTENSE.

in·ten·sive care ▶ **n.** special medical treatment of a dangerously ill patient, with constant monitoring: [as modifier] *she's in the intensive-care unit.*

in·tent /in'tent/ ▶ **n.** intention or purpose: *with alarm she realized his intent* | *a real intent to cut back on social programs.*
▶ **adj. 1** [predic.] (**intent on/upon**) resolved or determined to do (something): *the administration was intent on achieving greater efficiency.* ■ attentively occupied with: *Jill was intent on her gardening magazine.*
2 (esp. of a look) showing earnest and eager attention: *a curiously intent look on her face.*
– PHRASES **to** (or **for**) **all intents and purposes** in all important respects: *a man who was to all intents and purposes illiterate.* **with intent** Law with the intention of committing a specified crime: *he denied arson with intent to endanger life* | *charges of wounding with intent.*
– DERIVATIVES **in·tent·ness n.**
– ORIGIN Middle English: from Old French *entent, entente*, based on Latin *intendere* (see INTEND). The adjective is from Latin *intentus*, past participle of *intendere.*

in·ten·tion /in'tenCHən/ ▶ **n. 1** a thing intended; an aim or plan: *she was full of good intentions* | [with infinitive] *the Ukraine and Kazakhstan have both declared their intention to be nuclear-free.* ■ the action or fact of intending: *intention is just one of the factors that will be considered.* ■ (**one's intentions**) a person's designs, esp. a man's, in respect to marriage: *if his intentions aren't honorable, I never want to see him again.*
2 Medicine the healing process of a wound. See FIRST INTENTION, SECOND INTENTION.
– DERIVATIVES **in·ten·tioned adj.** [in combination] *a well-intentioned remark.*
– ORIGIN late Middle English: from Old French *entencion*, from Latin *intentio(n-)* 'stretching, purpose,' from *intendere* (see INTEND).

in·ten·tion·al /in'tenCHənl/ ▶ **adj.** done on purpose; deliberate: *intentional wrongdoing and harm.*
– ORIGIN mid 16th cent. (in the sense 'existing only in intention'): from French *intentionnel* or medieval Latin *intentionalis*, from Latin *intentio(n-)*, from *intendere* (see INTEND).

in·ten·tion·al fal·la·cy ▶ **n.** (**the intentional fallacy**) (in literary theory) the fallacy of basing an assessment of a work on the author's intention rather than on one's response to the actual work.

in·ten·tion·al·ism /in'tenCHənl,izəm/ ▶ **n.** the theory that a literary work should be judged in terms of the author's intentions.

in·ten·tion·al·i·ty /in,tenCHə'nalitē/ ▶ **n.** the fact of being deliberate or purposive. ■ Philosophy the quality of mental states (e.g., thoughts, beliefs, desires, hopes) that consists in their being directed toward some object or state of affairs.

in·ten·tion·al·ly /in'tenCHənlē/ ▶ **adv.** deliberately; on purpose: *I didn't do it intentionally.*

in·ten·tion trem·or ▶ **n.** a trembling of a part of the body when attempting a precise movement, associated esp. with disease of the cerebellum.

in·tent·ly /in'tentlē/ ▶ **adv.** with earnest and eager attention: *he gazed at her intently.*

in·ter /in'tər/ ▶ **v.** (**inters, interring, interred**) [with obj.] (usu. **be interred**) place (a corpse) in a grave or tomb, typically with funeral rites: *he was interred with the military honors due to him.*
– ORIGIN Middle English: from Old French *enterrer*, based on Latin *in-* 'into' + *terra* 'earth.'

inter. ▶ **abbr.** intermediate.

inter- ▶ **prefix 1** between; among: *interagency* | *interblend.*
2 mutually; reciprocally: *interactive.*
– ORIGIN from Old French *entre-* or Latin *inter* 'between, among.'

in·ter·act /,intər'akt/ ▶ **v.** [no obj.] act in such a way as to have an effect on another; act reciprocally: *all the stages in the process interact* | *the user interacts directly with the library.*
– DERIVATIVES **in·ter·ac·tant** /-tənt/ **adj. & n.**

in·ter·ac·tion /,intər'akSHən/ ▶ **n.** reciprocal action or influence: *ongoing interaction between the two languages.* ■ Physics a particular way in which matter, fields, and atomic and subatomic particles affect one another, e.g., through gravitation or electromagnetism.
– DERIVATIVES **in·ter·ac·tion·al** /-SHənl/ **adj.**

in·ter·ac·tion·ism /,intər'akSHə,nizəm/ ▶ **n.** Philosophy the theory that there are two entities, mind and body, each of which can have an effect on the other.
– DERIVATIVES **in·ter·ac·tion·ist n. & adj.**

in·ter·ac·tive /,intər'aktiv/ ▶ **adj.** (of two people or things) influencing or having an effect on each other: *fully sighted children in interactive play with others with defective vision.* ■ (of a computer or other electronic device) allowing a two-way flow of information between it and a user, responding to the user's input: *interactive video.*
– DERIVATIVES **in·ter·ac·tive·ly adv.**, **in·ter·ac·tiv·i·ty** /-ak'tivitē/ **n.**
– ORIGIN mid 19th cent.: from INTERACT, on the pattern of *active.*

in·ter·ac·tive white·board ▶ **n.** see WHITEBOARD.

in·ter·a·gen·cy /,intər'ājənsē/ ▶ **adj.** taking place between different agencies: *yesterday's interagency decision.* ■ constituted from more than one agency: *an interagency crisis-management team.*

in·ter a·li·a /'intər 'ālēə, 'äleə/ ▶ **adv.** among other things: *the study includes, inter alia, computers, aircraft, and pharmaceuticals.*
– ORIGIN mid 17th cent.: Latin.

in·ter a·li·os /'intər 'ālē,ōs, 'älē,ōs/ ▶ **adv.** among other people: *instruction to be given to them by, inter alios, a volunteer retired teacher.*
– ORIGIN mid 17th cent.: Latin.

in·ter·al·lied /,intərə'līd/ ▶ **adj.** [attrib.] of or relating to two or more states formally cooperating for military purposes.

In·ter-A·mer·i·can High·way the name for the section of the PAN-AMERICAN HIGHWAY between the US-Mexico border at Nuevo Laredo in Mexico and Panama City in Panama.

in·ter·ar·tic·u·lar /,intərär'tikyələr/ ▶ **adj.** Anatomy existing or acting between the adjacent surfaces of a joint.

in·ter·a·tom·ic /,intərə'tämik/ ▶ **adj.** Physics existing or acting between atoms.

in·ter·bank /'intər,baNGk/ ▶ **adj.** [attrib.] agreed, arranged, or operating between banks: *trading opportunities in the interbank market.*

in·ter·bed /'intər,bed/ ▶ **v.** (**interbeds, interbedding, interbedded**) (**be interbedded**) Geology (of a stratum) be embedded among or between others.

in·ter·breed /,intər'brēd/ ▶ **v.** (past and past participle **interbred**) (with reference to an animal) breed or cause to breed with another of a different race or species. [no obj.] *wolves and dogs can interbreed.* ■ [no obj.] (of an animal) inbreed: (as noun **interbreeding**) *their energy and physique had been sapped by interbreeding.*

in·ter·ca·lar·y /in'tərkə,lerē, ,intər'kalərē/ ▶ **adj. 1** (of a day or a month) inserted in the calendar to harmonize it with the solar year, e.g., February 29 in leap years. ■ of the nature of an insertion: *elaborate intercalary notes and footnotes.*
2 Botany (of the meristem of a plant) located between its daughter cells, esp. (in a grass) at or near the base of a leaf.
– ORIGIN early 17th cent.: from Latin *intercalarius*, from INTERCALARE (see INTERCALATE).

in·ter·ca·late /in'tərkə,lāt/ ▶ **v.** [with obj.] **1** interpolate (an intercalary period) in a calendar.
2 (usu. **be intercalated**) insert (something) between layers in a crystal lattice, geological formation, or other structure.
– DERIVATIVES **in·ter·ca·la·tion** /-,tərkə'lāSHən/ **n.**
– ORIGIN early 17th cent.: from Latin *intercalat-* 'proclaimed as inserted in the calendar,' from the verb *intercalare*, from *inter-* 'between' + *calare* 'proclaim solemnly.'

in·ter·cede /,intər'sēd/ ▶ **v.** [no obj.] intervene on behalf of another: *I begged him to intercede for Theresa, but he never did a thing.*
– DERIVATIVES **in·ter·ced·er n.**
– ORIGIN late 16th cent.: from French *intercéder* or Latin *intercedere* 'intervene,' from *inter-* 'between' + *cedere* 'go.'

in·ter·cel·lu·lar /,intər'selyələr/ ▶ **adj.** Biology located or occurring between cells: *intercellular spaces.*

in·ter·cept /,intər'sept/ ▶ **v.** [with obj.] obstruct (someone or something) so as to prevent them from

continuing to a destination: *intelligence agencies intercepted a series of telephone calls | I intercepted Ed on his way to work.* ■ Football (of a defensive player) catch a forward pass. ■ chiefly Physics cut off or deflect (light or other electromagnetic radiation). ■ Mathematics (of a line or surface) mark or cut off (part of a space, line, or surface).
▶ **n.** an act or instance of intercepting something: *he read the file of radio intercepts.* ■ Mathematics the point at which a given line cuts a coordinate axis; the value of the coordinate at that point.
– DERIVATIVES **in·ter·cep·tive** /-tiv/ **adj.**
– ORIGIN late Middle English (in the senses 'contain between limits' and 'halt (an effect)'): from Latin *intercept-* 'caught between,' from the verb *intercipere*, from *inter-* 'between' + *capere* 'take.'

in·ter·cep·tion /,intər'sepSHən/ ▶ **n.** an act or instance of intercepting something, particularly: ■ Football an act of a defensive player catching a forward pass: *Oliver forced a fumble and had three interceptions, two of which were returned for touchdowns.* ■ an act or instance of receiving electronic transmissions before they reach the intended recipient: *designed for the clandestine interception of other people's telephone calls.*

in·ter·cep·tor /,intər'septər/ ▶ **n.** a person or thing that stops or catches (someone or something) going from one place to another. ■ a fast aircraft for stopping or repelling hostile aircraft.

in·ter·ces·sion /,intər'seSHən/ ▶ **n.** the action of intervening on behalf of another: *through the intercession of friends, I was able to obtain her a sinecure.* ■ the action of saying a prayer on behalf of another person: *prayers of intercession.*
– DERIVATIVES **in·ter·ces·so·ry** /-'sesərē/ **adj.**
– ORIGIN late Middle English: from Latin *intercessio(n-)*, from the verb *intercedere* (see INTERCEDE).

in·ter·ces·sor /'intər,sesər/ ▶ **n.** a person who intervenes on behalf of another, esp. by prayer.

in·ter·chain /'intər,CHān/ ▶ **adj.** Chemistry existing between different polymer chains: *interchain hydrogen bonds.*

in·ter·change ▶ **v.** /,intər'CHānj/ [with obj.] (of two or more people) exchange (things) with each other: *superior and subordinates freely interchange ideas and information.* ■ put each of (two things) in the other's place: *the terms are often interchanged.* ■ [no obj.] (of a thing) be able to be exchanged with another: *diesel units will interchange with the gasoline ones.*
▶ **n.** /'intər,CHānj/ **1** the action of interchanging things, esp. information: *the interchange of ideas | a free-market interchange of goods and services.* ■ an exchange of words: *listening in shock to this venomous interchange.*
2 alternation: *the interchange of woods and meadows.*
3 a road junction designed on several levels so that traffic streams do not intersect.
– ORIGIN late Middle English: from Old French *entrechangier*, from *entre-* 'between' + *changier* 'to change.'

in·ter·change·a·ble /,intər'CHānjəbəl/ ▶ **adj.** (of two things) able to be interchanged: *eyepieces are interchangeable and one can use any eyepiece with any telescope | the V8 engines are all* ***interchangeable with*** *each other.* ■ apparently identical; very similar: *the cast includes a lot of interchangeable faces.*
– DERIVATIVES **in·ter·change·a·bil·i·ty** /,intər,CHānjə'bilitē/ **n.**, **in·ter·change·a·ble·ness n.**, **in·ter·change·a·bly** /-blē/ **adv.**

in·ter·cit·y /,intər'sitē/ ▶ **adj.** [attrib.] existing or traveling between cities.

in·ter·class /,intər'klas/ ▶ **adj.** existing or conducted between different classes.

in·ter·col·le·giate /,intərkə'lēj(ē)it/ ▶ **adj.** existing or conducted between colleges or universities: *intercollegiate sports.*

in·ter·co·lum·ni·a·tion /,intərkə,ləmnē'āSHən/ ▶ **n.** Architecture the distance between two adjacent columns.
– DERIVATIVES **in·ter·co·lum·nar** /-'ləmnər/ **adj.**

in·ter·com /'intər,käm/ ▶ **n.** an electrical device allowing one-way or two-way communication.
– ORIGIN World War II: abbreviation of INTERCOMMUNICATION.

in·ter·com·mu·ni·cate /,intərkə'myo͞oni,kāt/ ▶ **v.** [no obj.] **1** engage in two-way communication: *Dr. Haber gazed at this while intercommunicating with his receptionist.*
2 (of two rooms) have a common connecting door: *there were two apartments on the next floor, intercommunicating.*
– ORIGIN late 16th cent.: from Anglo-Latin *intercommunicat-* 'mutually communicated,' from the verb *intercommunicare.*

in·ter·com·mu·ni·ca·tion /,intərkə,myo͞oni'kāSHən/ ▶ **n.** the action of engaging in two-way communication.

in·ter·com·mun·ion /,intərkə'myo͞onyən/ ▶ **n.** participation in Holy Communion or other services by members of different religious denominations.

in·ter·con·nect /,intərkə'nekt/ ▶ **v.** [no obj.] connect with each other: *the way human activities* ***interconnect with*** *the environment* | [with obj.] *a high-speed data service can interconnect the hundreds of thousands of host computers and workstations.*
▶ **n.** a device used to connect two things together.
– DERIVATIVES **in·ter·con·nect·ed adj.**, **in·ter·con·nec·tion** /-'nekSHən/ **n.**

in·ter·con·ti·nen·tal /,intər,käntn'entl/ ▶ **adj.** relating to or traveling between continents: *an intercontinental flight | intercontinental ballistic missiles.*
– DERIVATIVES **in·ter·con·ti·nen·tal·ly adv.**

in·ter·con·vert /,intərkən'vərt/ ▶ **v.** [with obj.] (usu. **be interconverted**) cause (two things) to be converted into each other: *estrogens and androgens are easily interconverted in the laboratory.*
– DERIVATIVES **in·ter·con·ver·sion** /-'vərZHən/ **n.**, **in·ter·con·vert·i·ble adj.**

in·ter·cool·er /,intər'ko͞olər/ ▶ **n.** an apparatus for cooling gas between successive compressions, esp. in a supercharged vehicle engine.
– DERIVATIVES **in·ter·cool v.**

in·ter·cor·re·la·tion /,intər,kôrə'lāSHən/ ▶ **n.** a mutual relationship or connection between two or more things: *analyses showing intercorrelations between sets of variables.*
– DERIVATIVES **in·ter·cor·re·late** /-'kôrə,lāt/ **v.**

in·ter·cos·tal /,intər'kästəl/ Anatomy ▶ **adj.** situated between the ribs: *the fifth left intercostal space.*
▶ **n.** a muscle in this position.
– DERIVATIVES **in·ter·cos·tal·ly adv.**

in·ter·course /'intər,kôrs/ ▶ **n.** communication or dealings between individuals or groups: *everyday social intercourse.* ■ short for SEXUAL INTERCOURSE.
– ORIGIN late Middle English (denoting communication or dealings): from Old French *entrecours* 'exchange, commerce,' from Latin *intercursus*, from *intercurrere* 'intervene,' from *inter-* 'between' + *currere* 'run.' The specifically sexual use arose in the late 18th cent.

in·ter·crop ▶ **v.** /,intər'kräp/ (**intercrops, intercropping, intercropped**) [with obj.] (often as noun **intercropping**) grow (a crop) among plants of a different kind, usually in the space between rows: *lettuce is particularly good for intercropping among young Brussels sprouts.*
▶ **n.** /'intər,kräp/ a crop grown in such a way.

in·ter·cross /,intər'krôs/ ▶ **v.** (with reference to animals or plants of different breeds or varieties) interbreed or cause to interbreed.
▶ **n.** an instance of intercrossing of animals or plants. ■ an animal or plant resulting from this.

in·ter·cru·ral /,intər'kro͞orəl/ ▶ **adj.** between the legs.

in·ter·cur·rent /,intər'kərənt, -'kə-rənt/ ▶ **adj.** **1** Medicine (of a disease) occurring during the progress of another disease: *complicated by intercurrent infection with other microbes.*
2 rare (of a time or event) intervening.
– ORIGIN early 17th cent.: from Latin *intercurrent-* 'intervening,' from the verb *intercurrere.*

in·ter·cut /,intər'kət/ ▶ **v.** (**intercuts, intercutting**; past and past participle **intercut**) [with obj.] alternate (scenes or shots) with contrasting scenes or shots to make one composite scene in a film: *pieces of archive film are intercut with brief interviews* | [no obj.] *the action intercuts between the time periods.*

in·ter·de·nom·i·na·tion·al /,intərdi,nämə'nāSHənl/ ▶ **adj.** of or relating to more than one religious denomination: *an interdenominational Thanksgiving service.*
– DERIVATIVES **in·ter·de·nom·i·na·tion·al·ly adv.**

in·ter·den·tal /,intər'dentl/ ▶ **adj.** situated or placed between teeth or the teeth. ■ Phonetics (of a consonant) pronounced by placing the tip of the tongue between the teeth, such as the "th" sounds in the English words "thaw" and "though."
▶ **n.** Phonetics a consonant pronounced in this way.
– DERIVATIVES **in·ter·den·tal·ly adv.**

in·ter·de·part·men·tal /,intərdi,pärt'mentl, -,dēpärt-/ ▶ **adj.** of or relating to more than one department.
– DERIVATIVES **in·ter·de·part·men·tal·ly adv.**

in·ter·de·pend·ent /,intərdi'pendənt/ ▶ **adj.** (of two or more people or things) dependent on each other: *the increasingly global nature of human society, with interdependent economies.*
– DERIVATIVES **in·ter·de·pend v.**, **in·ter·de·pend·ence n.**, **in·ter·de·pend·en·cy n.**

in·ter·dict ▶ **n.** /'intər,dikt/ an authoritative prohibition: *an interdict against marriage of those of close kin.* ■ (in the Roman Catholic Church) a sentence barring a person, or esp. a place, from ecclesiastical functions and privileges: *a papal interdict.*
▶ **v.** /,intər'dikt/ [with obj.] **1** prohibit or forbid (something): *society will never interdict sex.* ■ (**interdict someone from**) prohibit someone from (doing something): *I have not been interdicted from consuming or holding alcoholic beverages.*
2 intercept and prevent the movement of (a prohibited commodity or person): *the police established roadblocks throughout the country for interdicting drugs.* ■ Military impede (an enemy force), esp. by aerial bombing of lines of communication or supply.
– DERIVATIVES **in·ter·dic·tion** /,intər'dikSHən/ **n.**
– ORIGIN Middle English *entredite* (in the ecclesiastical sense), from Old French *entredit*, from Latin *interdictum*, past participle of *interdicere* 'interpose, forbid by decree,' from *inter-* 'between' + *dicere* 'say.' The spelling change in the 16th cent. was due to association with the Latin form.

in·ter·dic·tor /,intər'diktər/ ▶ **n.** Military an aircraft designed to interrupt enemy supply operations by aerial bombing.

in·ter·dig·it·al /,intər'dijitl/ ▶ **adj.** between the fingers or toes.

in·ter·dig·i·tate /,intər'diji,tāt/ ▶ **v.** [no obj.] (of two or more things) interlock like the fingers of two clasped hands: (as adj. **interdigitating**) *interdigitating metal bars.*
– ORIGIN mid 19th cent.: from INTER- 'between' + DIGIT + -ATE[3].

in·ter·dis·ci·pli·nar·y /,intər'disəpli,nerē/ ▶ **adj.** of or relating to more than one branch of knowledge: *an interdisciplinary research program.*

in·ter·est /'int(ə)rist/ ▶ **n.** **1** the state of wanting to know or learn about something or someone: *she looked about her with interest.* ■ (**an interest in**) a feeling of wanting to know or learn about (something): *he developed an interest in art.* ■ the quality of exciting curiosity or holding the attention: *a tale full of interest.* ■ a subject about which one is concerned or enthusiastic: *my particular interest is twentieth-century poetry.*
2 money paid regularly at a particular rate for the use of money lent, or for delaying the repayment of a debt: *the monthly rate of interest* | [as modifier] *interest payments.*
3 the advantage or benefit of a person or group: *the merger is not contrary to the public interest | we are acting in the best interests of our customers.* ■ archaic the selfish pursuit of one's own welfare; self-interest.
4 a stake, share, or involvement in an undertaking, esp. a financial one: *holders of voting rights must disclose their interests | he must have no personal* ***interest in*** *the outcome of the case.* ■ a legal concern, title, or right in property: *third parties having an interest in a building.*
5 (usu. **interests**) a group or organization having a specified common concern, esp. in politics or business: *the regulation of national interests in India, Brazil, and Africa.*
▶ **v.** [with obj.] excite the curiosity or attention of (someone): *I thought the book might interest Eric.* ■ (**interest someone in**) cause someone to undertake or acquire (something): *efforts were made to interest her in a purchase.*
– PHRASES **declare an** (or **one's**) **interest** make known one's financial interests in an undertaking before it is discussed. **in the interests** (or **interest**) **of something** for the benefit of: *in the interests of security we are keeping the information confidential.* **of interest** interesting: *much of it is of interest to historians.* **with interest** with interest charged or paid: *loans that must be paid back with interest.* ■ (of an action) reciprocated with more force or vigor than the original one: *he may have a reputation for getting even, with interest.*
– ORIGIN late Middle English (originally as *interess*): from Anglo-Norman French *interesse*, from Latin *interesse* 'differ, be important,' from *inter-* 'between' + *esse* 'be.' The *-t* was added partly by association with Old French *interest* 'damage, loss,' apparently from Latin *interest* 'it is important.' The original sense was 'the possession of a share in or a right to something'; hence sense 4 of the noun. Sense 1 of the noun and the verb arose in the 18th cent. Sense 2 of the noun was influenced by medieval Latin *interesse* 'compensation for a debtor's defaulting.'

i

in·ter·est·ed /ˈint(ə)ristid, ˈintəˌrestid/ ▶ **adj.** **1** showing curiosity or concern about something or someone; having a feeling of interest: *I had always been interested in history.* **2** [attrib.] having an interest or involvement; not impartial or disinterested: *seeking views from all interested parties.*
– DERIVATIVES **in·ter·est·ed·ly** adv., **in·ter·est·ed·ness** n.

in·ter·est-free ▶ **adj. & adv.** with no interest charged on money that has been borrowed: [as adj.] *interest-free credit* | [as adv.] *he lent the money interest-free.*

in·ter·est·ing /ˈint(ə)ristiNG, ˈintəˌrestiNG/ ▶ **adj.** arousing curiosity or interest; holding or catching the attention: *an interesting debate* | *it will be very interesting to see what they come up with.*
– DERIVATIVES **in·ter·est·ing·ly** adv. *he talked interestingly and learnedly* | [sentence adverb] *interestingly, the researchers did notice a link.* **in·ter·est·ing·ness** n.

in·ter·face /ˈintərˌfās/ ▶ **n.** **1** a point where two systems, subjects, organizations, etc., meet and interact: *the interface between accountancy and the law.* ■ chiefly Physics a surface forming a common boundary between two portions of matter or space, e.g., between two immiscible liquids: *the surface tension of a liquid at its air/liquid interface.* **2** Computing a device or program enabling a user to communicate with a computer. ■ a device or program for connecting two items of hardware or software so that they can be operated jointly or communicate with each other.
▶ **v.** [no obj.] (**interface with**) **1** interact with (another system, person, organization, etc.): *his goal is to get people interfacing with each other.* **2** Computing connect with (another computer or piece of equipment) by an interface.

in·ter·fa·cial /ˌintərˈfāSHəl/ ▶ **adj.** **1** included between two faces of a crystal or other solid. **2** of, relating to, or forming a common boundary between two portions of matter or space.

in·ter·fac·ing /ˈintərˌfāsiNG/ ▶ **n.** a moderately stiff material, esp. buckram, typically used between two layers of fabric in collars and facings.

in·ter·faith /ˈintərˈfāTH/ ▶ **adj.** [attrib.] of, relating to, or between different religions or members of different religions: *action to encourage interfaith dialogue.*

in·ter·fere /ˌintərˈfi(ə)r/ ▶ **v.** [no obj.] **1** (**interfere with**) prevent (a process or activity) from continuing or being carried out properly: *a job would interfere with his studies.* ■ (of a thing) strike against (something) when working; get in the way of: *the rotors are widely separated and do not interfere with one another.* ■ handle or adjust (something) without permission, esp. so as to cause damage: *he admitted interfering with a van.* ■ Law attempt to bribe or intimidate (a witness). **2** take part or intervene in an activity without invitation or necessity: *she tried not to interfere in her children's lives.* **3** Physics (of light or other electromagnetic waveforms) mutually act upon each other and produce interference: *light pulses interfere constructively in a fiber to emit a pulse.* ■ cause interference to a broadcast radio signal. **4** (**interfere with**) Brit. sexually molest or assault (someone, esp. a child or young person) (used euphemistically). **5** (of a horse) knock one foot against the fetlock of another leg.
– DERIVATIVES **in·ter·fer·er** n.
– ORIGIN late Middle English: from Old French *s'entreferir* 'strike each other,' from *entre-* 'between' + *ferir* (from Latin *ferire* 'to strike').

in·ter·fer·ence /ˌintərˈfi(ə)rəns/ ▶ **n.** **1** the action of interfering or the process of being interfered with: *he denied that there had been any interference in the country's internal affairs* | *an unwarranted interference with personal liberty.* ■ Football the action of illegally interfering with an opponent's ability to catch a passed or kicked ball. ■ Football the legal blocking of an opponent or opponents to clear a way for the ballcarrier. ■ Baseball any of various forms of hindering a player's ability to make a play, run, hit, etc. ■ (in ice hockey and other sports) the illegal hindering of an opponent not in possession of the puck or ball. **2** Physics the combination of two or more electromagnetic waveforms to form a resultant wave in which the displacement is either reinforced or canceled. ■ the fading or disturbance of received radio signals caused by unwanted signals from other sources, such as unshielded electrical equipment, or broadcasts from other stations or channels.
– PHRASES **run interference** Football move in such a way as to provide legal interference (sense 1). ■ informal intervene on someone's behalf, typically so as to protect them from distraction or annoyance: *Elizabeth was quick to run interference and said that the professor would be very busy.*
– DERIVATIVES **in·ter·fe·ren·tial** /-fəˈrenCHəl/ adj.
– ORIGIN mid 18th cent.: from INTERFERE, on the pattern of words such as *difference.*

in·ter·fer·ence fit ▶ **n.** a fit between two parts in which the external dimension of one part slightly exceeds the internal dimension of the part into which it has to fit.

in·ter·fer·ing /ˌintərˈfi(ə)riNG/ ▶ **adj.** (of a person) tending to interfere in other people's affairs: *interfering busybodies.*
– DERIVATIVES **in·ter·fer·ing·ly** adv.

in·ter·fer·o·gram /ˌintərˈfi(ə)rəˌgram/ (Brit. also **interferogramme**) ▶ **n.** Physics a pattern formed by wave interference, esp. one represented in a photograph or diagram.

in·ter·fer·om·e·ter /ˌintərfəˈrämitər/ ▶ **n.** Physics an instrument in which wave interference is employed to make precise measurements of length of displacement in terms of the wavelength.
– DERIVATIVES **in·ter·fer·o·met·ric** /-ˌfi(ə)rəˈmetrik/ adj., **in·ter·fer·o·met·ri·cal·ly** adv., **in·ter·fer·om·e·try** /-trē/ n.

in·ter·fer·on /ˌintərˈfi(ə)rˌän/ ▶ **n.** Biochemistry a protein released by animal cells, usually in response to the entry of a virus, that has the property of inhibiting virus replication.
– ORIGIN 1950s: from INTERFERE + -ON.

in·ter·file /ˌintərˈfīl/ ▶ **v.** [with obj.] file (two or more sequences) together: *the index interfiles books and their authors in one alphabetical sequence.* ■ file (one or more items) into an existing sequence: *this index is interfiled with the main card catalog.*

in·ter·flow /ˌintərˈflō/ ▶ **v.** [no obj.] literary mix or mingle: *the thousand varying shades interflowing.*

in·ter·fluve /ˈintərˌflo͞ov/ ▶ **n.** Geology a region between the valleys of adjacent watercourses, esp. in a dissected upland.
– DERIVATIVES **in·ter·flu·vi·al** /ˌintərˈflo͞ovēəl/ adj.
– ORIGIN early 20th cent.: back-formation from *interfluvial.*

in·ter·fuse /ˌintərˈfyo͞oz/ ▶ **v.** [with obj.] literary join or mix (two or more things) together: *nowhere do art and life seem so interfused.*
– DERIVATIVES **in·ter·fu·sion** /-ˈfyo͞oZHən/ n.
– ORIGIN late 16th cent.: from Latin *interfus-* 'poured among,' from the verb *interfundere,* from *inter-* 'between' + *fundere* 'pour.'

in·ter·ga·lac·tic /ˌintərgəˈlaktik/ ▶ **adj.** of, relating to, or situated between two or more galaxies: *intergalactic gas.*
– DERIVATIVES **in·ter·ga·lac·ti·cal·ly** /-ik(ə)lē/ adv.

in·ter·gen·er·a·tion·al /ˌintərˌjenəˈrāSHənl/ ▶ **adj.** relating to, involving, or affecting several generations: *the intergenerational conflict and political turmoil of the 1960s.*

in·ter·ge·ner·ic /ˌintərjəˈnerik/ ▶ **adj.** Biology existing between or obtained from different genera: *intergeneric differences* | *an intergeneric hybrid.*

in·ter·gla·cial /ˌintərˈglāSHəl/ Geology ▶ **adj.** of or relating to a period of milder climate between two glacial periods. Compare with INTERSTADIAL.
▶ **n.** an interglacial period.

in·ter·gov·ern·men·tal /ˌintərˌgəvər(n)ˈmentl/ ▶ **adj.** of, relating to, or conducted between two or more governments: *an intergovernmental conference.*
– DERIVATIVES **in·ter·gov·ern·men·tal·ly** adv.

in·ter·grade ▶ **v.** /ˌintərˈgrād/ [no obj.] Biology pass into another form by a series of intervening forms: *they have several forms that intergrade with each other.*
▶ **n.** /ˈintərˌgrād/ an intervening form of this kind.
– DERIVATIVES **in·ter·gra·da·tion** /-grāˈdāSHən/ n.

in·ter·grow /ˌintərˈgrō/ ▶ **v.** (past **intergrew**; past participle **intergrown**) [no obj.] (usu. as adj. **intergrown**) (chiefly of crystals) grow into each other: *finely intergrown siderite.*

in·ter·growth /ˈintərˌgrōTH/ ▶ **n.** a thing produced by intergrowing, esp. of mineral crystals in rock.

in·ter·im /ˈintərəm/ ▶ **n.** the intervening time: *in the interim I'll just keep my fingers crossed.*
▶ **adj.** in or for the intervening period; provisional or temporary: *an interim arrangement.* ■ chiefly Brit. relating to less than a full year's business activity: *an interim dividend* | *interim profit.*
▶ **adv.** archaic meanwhile.
– ORIGIN mid 16th cent. (denoting a temporary or provisional arrangement, originally for the adjustment of religious differences between the German Protestants and the Roman Catholic Church): from Latin, 'meanwhile.'

in·te·ri·or /inˈti(ə)rēər/ ▶ **adj.** **1** situated within or inside; relating to the inside; inner: *the interior lighting is not adequate.* ■ [predic.] (**interior to**) chiefly technical situated further in or within: *the layer immediately interior to the epidermis.* ■ drawn, photographed, etc., within a building: *a light that is ideal for every interior shot.* **2** [attrib.] remote from the coast or frontier; inland: *the interior jungle regions.* ■ relating to internal or domestic affairs: *the Interior Department.* **3** existing or taking place in the mind or soul; mental: *an interior monologue.*
▶ **n.** (usu. **the interior**) **1** the inner or indoor part of something, esp. a building; the inside: *six men painting the outside of her house and three men painting the interior.* ■ an artistic representation of the inside of a building or room: *a few still lifes, interiors, and landscapes.* **2** the inland part of a country or region: *the plains of the interior.* ■ the internal affairs of a country: *the Department of the Interior.*
– DERIVATIVES **in·te·ri·or·ize** /-ˌrīz/ v., **in·te·ri·or·ly** adv.
– ORIGIN late 15th cent.: from Latin, 'inner,' comparative adjective from *inter* 'within.'

in·te·ri·or an·gle ▶ **n.** the angle between adjacent sides of a rectilinear figure.

in·te·ri·or dec·o·ra·tion (also **interior decorating**) ▶ **n.** the decoration of the interior of a building or room, esp. with regard to color combination and artistic effect.
– DERIVATIVES **in·te·ri·or dec·o·ra·tor** n.

in·te·ri·or de·sign ▶ **n.** the art or process of designing the interior decoration of a room or building.
– DERIVATIVES **in·te·ri·or de·sign·er** n.

in·te·ri·or·i·ty /inˌti(ə)rēˈôritē, -ˈär-/ ▶ **n.** the quality of being interior or inward. ■ inner character or nature; subjectivity: *the profound interiority of faith.*
– ORIGIN early 18th cent.: from medieval Latin *interioritas,* from Latin *interior* 'inner.'

in·te·ri·or mon·o·logue ▶ **n.** a piece of writing expressing a character's inner thoughts.

interj. ▶ **abbr.** interjection.

in·ter·ject /ˌintərˈjekt/ ▶ **v.** [with obj.] say (something) abruptly, esp. as an aside or interruption: *she interjected the odd question here and there* | [no obj.] *Christine felt bound to interject before there was open warfare.*
– DERIVATIVES **in·ter·jec·to·ry** /-t(ə)rē/ adj.
– ORIGIN late 16th cent.: from Latin *interject-* 'interposed,' from the verb *interjicere,* from *inter-* 'between' + *jacere* 'to throw.'

in·ter·jec·tion /ˌintərˈjekSHən/ ▶ **n.** an abrupt remark, made esp. as an aside or interruption. ■ an exclamation, esp. as a part of speech, e.g., *ah!* or *dear me!*
– DERIVATIVES **in·ter·jec·tion·al** /-SHənl/ adj.
– ORIGIN late Middle English: via Old French from Latin *interjectio(n-),* from the verb *interjicere* (see INTERJECT).

in·ter·lace /ˌintərˈlās/ ▶ **v.** cross or be crossed intricately together; interweave: [with obj.] *Jane interlaced her fingers to form a cup.* | (as adj. **interlacing**) *interlacing bundles of smooth muscle fibers.* ■ [with obj.] (**interlace something with**) mingle or intersperse something with: *buttercups interlacing their gold with the silver of the daisies* | *discussion interlaced with esoteric mathematics.* ■ [with obj.] Electronics scan (a video image) in such a way that alternate lines form one sequence that is followed by the other lines in a second sequence: (as adj. **interlaced**) *interlaced displays.*
– DERIVATIVES **in·ter·lace·ment** n.
– ORIGIN late Middle English: from Old French *entrelacier,* from *entre-* 'between' + *lacier* 'to lace.'

in·ter·lan·guage /ˈintərˌlaNGgwij/ ▶ **n.** a language or form of language having features of two others, typically a pidgin or a version produced by a foreign learner.

in·ter·lard /ˌintərˈlärd/ ▶ **v.** [with obj.] (**interlard something with**) intersperse or embellish speech or writing with different material: *a compendium of advertisements and reviews, interlarded with gossip.*
– ORIGIN late Middle English (in the sense 'mix with alternate layers of fat'): from French *entrelarder,* from *entre-* 'between' + *larder* 'to lard.'

in·ter·lay ▶ **v.** /ˌintərˈlā/ (past and past participle **interlaid**) [with obj.] lay between or among; interpose: *strips of granite are interlaid with creamy Sardinian sard.*
▶ **n.** /ˈintərˌlā/ an inserted layer: *remember to use interlay under foam-backed carpets.* ■ Printing a sheet or piece of paper placed between a letterpress printing plate and its base to give increased pressure on certain areas.

in·ter·lay·er /ˈintərˌlāər/ ▶ **n.** a layer sandwiched between two others.
▶ **adj.** [attrib.] situated or occurring between two layers.

in·ter·leaf /ˈintərˌlēf/ ▶ **n.** (pl. **interleaves**) an extra page, typically a blank one, between the leaves of a book.

in·ter·leave /ˌintərˈlēv/ ▶ **v.** [with obj.] **1** insert pages, typically blank ones, between the pages of (a book): *books of maps **interleaved with** tracing paper.* ■ place something between the layers of (something): *pasta interleaved with strips of zucchini and carrot.*
2 Telecommunications & Computing mix (two or more digital signals) by alternating between them. ■ Computing divide (memory or processing power) between a number of tasks by allocating segments of it to each task in turn.

in·ter·leu·kin /ˈintərˌlo͞okin/ ▶ **n.** Biochemistry any of a class of glycoproteins produced by leukocytes for regulating immune responses.
– ORIGIN 1970s: from **INTER-** 'occurring between' + *leukocyte* (variant of **LEUKOCYTE**) + **-IN**[1].

in·ter·li·brar·y loan /ˌintərˈlīˌbrerē/ ▶ **n.** a system in which one library borrows a book from another library for the use of an individual.

in·ter·line[1] /ˌintərˈlīn/ ▶ **v.** [with obj.] insert words between the lines of (a document or other text): *the writing was overwritten and interlined by many hands.* ■ insert (words) in this way.
– ORIGIN late Middle English: from medieval Latin *interlineare*, from *inter-* 'between' + Latin *linea* 'line.'

in·ter·line[2] ▶ **v.** [with obj.] put an extra lining between the ordinary lining and the fabric of (a garment, curtain, etc.), typically to provide extra strength.

in·ter·lin·e·ar /ˌintərˈlinēər/ ▶ **adj.** written or printed between the lines of a text: *interlinear glosses.* ■ (of a book) having the same text in different languages printed on alternate lines.
– ORIGIN late Middle English: from medieval Latin *interlinearis*, from *inter-* 'between' + Latin *linearis* (from *linea* 'line').

in·ter·lin·e·ate /ˌintərˈlinēˌāt/ ▶ **v.** another term for **INTERLINE**[1].
– DERIVATIVES **in·ter·lin·e·a·tion** /-ˌlinēˈāSHən/ **n.**
– ORIGIN late 17th cent.: from medieval Latin *interlineat-* 'interlined,' from the verb *interlineare*.

in·ter·lin·gua /ˌintərˈliNGgwə/ ▶ **n.** an artificial language, devised for machine translation, that makes explicit the distinctions necessary for successful translation into a target language even where they are not present in the source language. ■ (**Interlingua**) an artificial international language formed of elements common to the Romance languages, designed primarily for scientific and technical use.
– ORIGIN early 20th cent.: from **INTER-** 'between' + Latin *lingua* 'tongue.'

in·ter·lin·gual /ˌintərˈliNGgwəl/ ▶ **adj.** between or relating to two languages: *interlingual dictionaries.* ■ of or relating to an interlingua or artificial interlanguage.

in·ter·lin·ing /ˈintərˌlīniNG/ ▶ **n.** material used as an extra lining between the ordinary lining and the fabric of a garment, curtain, etc.

in·ter·link /ˌintərˈliNGk/ ▶ **v.** [with obj.] join or connect (two or more things) together: *agreement has been reached to interlink the airport's two baggage systems.*
– DERIVATIVES **in·ter·link·age** /-ˈliNGkij/ **n.**

in·ter·lob·u·lar /ˌintərˈläbyələr/ ▶ **adj.** Anatomy situated between lobes (e.g., of the kidney or liver).

in·ter·lock ▶ **v.** /ˌintərˈläk/ [no obj.] (of two or more things) engage with each other by overlapping or by the fitting together of projections and recesses: *their fingers interlocked.*
▶ **n.** /ˈintərˌläk/ **1** a device or mechanism for connecting or coordinating the function of different components.
2 (also **interlock fabric**) a fabric knitted with closely interlocking stitches that allow it to stretch, typically used in underwear.
– DERIVATIVES **in·ter·lock·er** **n.**

in·ter·loc·u·tor /ˌintərˈläkyətər/ ▶ **n.** formal a person who takes part in a dialogue or conversation.
– DERIVATIVES **in·ter·lo·cu·tion** /-ləˈkyo͞oSHən/ **n.**
– ORIGIN early 16th cent.: modern Latin, from Latin *interlocut-* 'interrupted (by speech),' from the verb *interloqui*, from *inter-* 'between' + *loqui* 'speak.'

in·ter·loc·u·to·ry /ˌintərˈläkyəˌtôrē/ ▶ **adj.** **1** Law (of a decree or judgment) given provisionally during the course of a legal action.
2 rare of or relating to dialogue or conversation.
– ORIGIN late 15th cent.: from medieval Latin *interlocutorius*, from Latin *interloqui* 'interrupt' (see **INTERLOCUTOR**).

in·ter·lop·er /ˈintərˌlōpər, ˌintərˈlōpər/ ▶ **n.** a person who becomes involved in a place or situation where they are not wanted or are considered not to belong.
– DERIVATIVES **in·ter·lope** /ˈintərˌlōp, ˌintərˈlōp/ **v.**
– ORIGIN late 16th cent. (denoting an unauthorized trader trespassing on the rights of a trade monopoly): from **INTER-** 'amid' + *-loper* as in archaic *landloper* 'vagabond' (from Middle Dutch *landlooper*).

in·ter·lude /ˈintərˌlo͞od/ ▶ **n.** **1** an intervening period of time: *enjoying a lunchtime interlude.* ■ a pause between the acts of a play.
2 something performed during a theater intermission: *an orchestral interlude.* ■ a piece of music played between other pieces or between the verses of a hymn. ■ a temporary amusement or source of entertainment that contrasts with what goes before or after: *the romantic interlude withered rapidly once he was back in town.*
– ORIGIN Middle English (originally denoting a light dramatic entertainment): from medieval Latin *interludium*, from *inter-* 'between' + *ludus* 'play.'

in·ter·mar·riage /ˌintərˈmarij/ ▶ **n.** marriage between people of different races, castes, or religions: *the main reason for the increase in intermarriage is probably greater religious and ethnic tolerance.* ■ marriage between close relations.

in·ter·mar·ry /ˌintərˈmarē/ ▶ **v.** (**intermarries, intermarrying, intermarried**) [no obj.] (of people belonging to different races, castes, or religions) become connected by marriage: *over the centuries the Greeks **intermarried with** the natives.* ■ (of close relations) marry each other.

in·ter·me·di·ar·y /ˌintərˈmēdēˌerē/ ▶ **n.** (pl. **intermediaries**) a person who acts as a link between people in order to try to bring about an agreement or reconciliation; a mediator: ***intermediaries between** lenders and borrowers.*
▶ **adj.** intermediate: *an intermediary stage.*
– ORIGIN late 18th cent.: from French *intermédiaire*, from Italian *intermediario*, from Latin *intermedius* (see **INTERMEDIATE**).

in·ter·me·di·ate /ˌintərˈmēdē-it/ ▶ **adj.** coming between two things in time, place, order, character, etc.: *an intermediate stage of development* | *a cooled liquid **intermediate between** liquid and solid.* ■ having or suitable for a level of knowledge or skill between basic and advanced: *intermediate skiers* | *an intermediate course.*
▶ **n.** an intermediate thing. ■ a person at an intermediate level of knowledge or skill. ■ a chemical compound formed by one reaction and then taking part in another, esp. during synthesis.
▶ **v.** [no obj.] act as intermediary; mediate: *the theory said that by intermediating between buyers and sellers, middlemen lower the costs of transactions.*
– DERIVATIVES **in·ter·me·di·a·cy** /-əsē/ **n.**, **in·ter·me·di·ate·ly** **adv.**, **in·ter·me·di·ate·ness** **n.**, **in·ter·me·di·a·tion** /-ˌmēdēˈāSHən/ **n.**, **in·ter·me·di·a·tor** /-ˌātər/ **n.**
– ORIGIN late Middle English: from medieval Latin *intermediatus*, from Latin *intermedius*, from *inter-* 'between' + *medius* 'middle.'

in·ter·me·di·ate fre·quen·cy ▶ **n.** the frequency to which a radio signal is converted during heterodyne reception.

in·ter·me·di·ate host ▶ **n.** Biology an organism that supports the immature or nonreproductive forms of a parasite. Compare with **DEFINITIVE HOST**.

in·ter·me·di·ate tech·nol·o·gy ▶ **n.** technology suitable for use in developing countries, typically making use of locally available resources.

in·ter·me·din /ˌintərˈmēdn/ ▶ **n.** Physiology another term for **MELANOCYTE-STIMULATING HORMONE**.
– ORIGIN 1930s: from modern Latin (*pars*) *intermedia* 'intermediate part (of the pituitary)' + **-IN**[1].

in·ter·me·di·um /ˌintərˈmēdēəm/ ▶ **n.** (pl. **intermedia** /-dēə/) Zoology (in tetrapods) a carpal in the center of the wrist joint, or a tarsal in the center of the ankle joint.
– ORIGIN late 16th cent. (denoting an intervening action or performance): from late Latin, neuter (used as a noun) of Latin *intermedius* 'intermediate.'

in·ter·ment /inˈtərmənt/ ▶ **n.** the burial of a corpse in a grave or tomb, typically with funeral rites: *the day of interment* | *interments took place in the churchyard.*

USAGE **Interment**, which means 'burial,' should not be confused with **internment**, which means 'imprisonment.'

in·ter·mesh /ˌintərˈmeSH/ ▶ **v.** [no obj.] (of two or more things) mesh with one another.

in·ter·mez·zo /ˌintərˈmetsō/ ▶ **n.** (pl. **intermezzi** /-ˈmetsē/ or **intermezzos**) a short connecting instrumental movement in an opera or other musical work. ■ a similar piece performed independently. ■ a short piece for a solo instrument. ■ a light dramatic, musical, or other performance inserted between the acts of a play.
– ORIGIN late 18th cent.: from Italian, from Latin *intermedium* 'interval,' neuter of *intermedius* (see **INTERMEDIATE**).

in·ter·mi·na·ble /inˈtərmənəbəl/ ▶ **adj.** endless (often used hyperbolically): *we got bogged down in interminable discussions.*
– DERIVATIVES **in·ter·mi·na·bil·i·ty** /-ˌtərmənəˈbilitē/ **n.**, **in·ter·mi·na·ble·ness** **n.**, **in·ter·mi·na·bly** /-blē/ **adv.**
– ORIGIN late Middle English: from Old French, or from late Latin *interminabilis*, from *in-* 'not' + *terminare* (see **TERMINATE**).

in·ter·min·gle /ˌintərˈmiNGgəl/ ▶ **v.** mix or mingle together: [no obj.] *daisies **intermingled with** huge expanses of gorse and foxgloves* | [with obj.] *Riesling grapes were always intermingled with other varieties.*

in·ter·mis·sion /ˌintərˈmiSHən/ ▶ **n.** a pause or break: *he was granted an intermission in his studies* | *the daily work goes on without intermission.* ■ an interval between parts of a play, movie, or concert.
– ORIGIN late Middle English: from Latin *intermissio(n-)*, from the verb *intermittere* (see **INTERMIT**).

in·ter·mit /ˌintərˈmit/ ▶ **v.** (**intermits, intermitting, intermitted**) [with obj.] suspend or discontinue (an action or practice) for a time: *he was urged to intermit his application.* ■ [no obj.] (esp. of a fever or pulse) cease or stop for a time.
– ORIGIN mid 16th cent.: from Latin *intermittere*, from *inter-* 'between' + *mittere* 'let go.'

in·ter·mit·tent /ˌintərˈmitnt/ ▶ **adj.** occurring at irregular intervals; not continuous or steady: *intermittent rain.*
– DERIVATIVES **in·ter·mit·tence** **n.**, **in·ter·mit·ten·cy** **n.**, **in·ter·mit·tent·ly** **adv.**
– ORIGIN mid 16th cent.: from Latin *intermittent-* 'ceasing,' from the verb *intermittere* (see **INTERMIT**).

in·ter·mit·tent clau·di·ca·tion ▶ **n.** see **CLAUDICATION**.

in·ter·mix /ˌintərˈmiks/ ▶ **v.** mix together: [with obj.] *the ore had to be handled so that it was not inadvertently **intermixed with** other material* | [no obj.] *along its southern edge low trees intermix with the shrubs.*
– DERIVATIVES **in·ter·mix·a·ble** **adj.**, **in·ter·mix·ture** /-ˈmiksCHər/ **n.**
– ORIGIN mid 16th cent. (originally as the past participle *intermixt*): from Latin *intermixtus*, past participle of *intermiscere* 'mix together,' from *inter-* 'between' + *miscere* 'to mix.'

in·ter·mod·al /ˌintərˈmōdl/ ▶ **adj.** involving two or more different modes of transportation in conveying goods.

in·ter·mo·lec·u·lar /ˌintərməˈlekyələr/ ▶ **adj.** existing or taking place between molecules.

In·ter·mon·tane Re·gion /ˌintərˈmänˌtān/ (also **Intermountain Region**) a term for the mountain and basin regions lying between the Rocky Mountains and the mountains of the US western coast.

in·tern ▶ **n.** /ˈinˌtərn/ a student or trainee who works, sometimes without pay, at a trade or occupation in order to gain work experience. ■ a recent medical graduate receiving supervised training in a hospital and acting as an assistant physician or surgeon. Compare with **RESIDENT**.
▶ **v.** **1** /inˈtərn/ [with obj.] confine (someone) as a prisoner, esp. for political or military reasons.
2 /ˈinˌtərn/ [no obj.] serve as an intern.
– DERIVATIVES **in·tern·ment** **n.**, **in·tern·ship** /-ˌSHip/ **n.**
– ORIGIN early 16th cent. (as an adjective in the sense 'internal'): from French *interne* (adjective), *interner* (verb), from Latin *internus* 'inward, internal.' Current senses date from the 19th cent.

USAGE See usage at **INTERMENT**.

in·ter·nal /inˈtərnl/ ▶ **adj.** of or situated on the inside: *the tube had an internal diameter of 1.1 mm.* ■ inside the body: *internal bleeding.* ■ existing or occurring within an organization: *an internal telephone system.* ■ relating to affairs and activities within a country rather than with other countries; domestic: *the government's internal policies* | *internal flights.* ■ experienced in one's mind; inner rather than expressed: *internal feelings.* ■ of the inner nature of a thing; intrinsic: *he creates a dialogue **internal to** his work.*
▶ **plural n.** (**internals**) inner parts or features: *all the weapon's internals are well finished and highly polished.*
– DERIVATIVES **in·ter·nal·i·ty** /ˌintərˈnalitē/ **n.**, **in·ter·nal·ly** **adv.**

PRONUNCIATION KEY ə *ago, up*; ər *over, fur*; a *hat*; ā *ate*; ä *car*; e *let*; ē *see*; i *fit*; ī *by*; NG *sing*; ō *go*; ô *law, for*; oi *toy*; o͝o *good*; o͞o *goo*; ou *out*; TH *thin*; T̲H̲ *then*; ZH *vision*

– ORIGIN early 16th cent. (in the sense 'intrinsic'): from modern Latin *internalis*, from Latin *internus* 'inward, internal.'

in·ter·nal clock ▶ n. a person's innate sense of time. ■ another term for BIOLOGICAL CLOCK.

in·ter·nal com·bus·tion en·gine ▶ n. an engine that generates motive power by the burning of gasoline, oil, or other fuel with air inside the engine, the hot gases produced being used to drive a piston or do other work as they expand.

in·ter·nal en·er·gy ▶ n. Physics the energy in a system arising from the relative positions and interactions of its parts.

in·ter·nal ev·i·dence ▶ n. evidence derived from the contents of the thing discussed.

in·ter·nal ex·ile ▶ n. penal banishment from a part of one's own country.

in·ter·nal·ize /inˈtərnl,īz/ ▶ v. [with obj.] **1** Psychology make (attitudes or behavior) part of one's nature by learning or unconscious assimilation. ■ acquire knowledge of (the rules of a language).
2 Economics incorporate (costs) as part of a pricing structure, esp. social costs resulting from the manufacture and use of a product.
– DERIVATIVES **in·ter·nal·i·za·tion** /in,tərnl-iˈzāsHən/ n.

in·ter·nal mar·ket ▶ n. another term for SINGLE MARKET.

in·ter·nal rhyme ▶ n. a rhyme involving a word in the middle of a line and another at the end of the line or in the middle of the next.

i

in·ter·na·tion·al /,intərˈnasHənl/ ▶ adj. existing, occurring, or carried on between two or more nations: *international trade*. ■ agreed on by all or many nations: *a violation of international law*. ■ used by people of many nations: *large international hotels*.
▶ n. **1** Brit. a game or contest between teams representing different countries in a sport. ■ a player who has taken part in such a game or contest.
2 (**International**) any of four associations founded (1864–1936) to promote socialist or communist action. ■ a member of any of these.

> The First International was formed by Karl Marx in London in 1864 as an international working men's association. The Second International was formed in Paris in 1889 to celebrate the 100th anniversary of the French Revolution and still survives as a loose association of social democrats. The Third International, also known as the Comintern, was formed by the Bolsheviks in 1919 to further the cause of world revolution. It was abolished in 1943. The Fourth International, a body of Trotskyist organizations, was formed in 1938 in opposition to the policies of the Stalin-dominated Third International.

– DERIVATIVES **in·ter·na·tion·al·i·ty** /-,nasHəˈnalitē/ n., **in·ter·na·tion·al·ly** adv.

In·ter·na·tion·al A·tom·ic En·er·gy A·gen·cy (abbr.: **IAEA**) an international organization set up in 1957 to promote research into and the development of atomic energy for peaceful purposes.

In·ter·na·tion·al Bank for Re·con·struc·tion and De·vel·op·ment (abbr.: **IBRD**) an agency of the United Nations that constitutes the main part of the World Bank. It was established in 1945, and its headquarters are in Washington, DC. See also WORLD BANK.

In·ter·na·tion·al Bri·gade a group of volunteers that was raised internationally by foreign communist parties and that fought on the Republican side in the Spanish Civil War.

in·ter·na·tion·al can·dle ▶ n. see CANDLE.

In·ter·na·tion·al Civ·il A·vi·a·tion Or·gan·i·za·tion an agency of the United Nations, founded in 1947 to study problems of international civil aviation and to establish standards and regulations. Its headquarters are in Montreal.

In·ter·na·tion·al Court of Jus·tice a judicial court of the United Nations, formed in 1945, that meets at The Hague.

In·ter·na·tion·al Date Line ▶ n. see DATE LINE.

In·ter·na·tion·al De·vel·op·ment As·so·ci·a·tion (abbr.: **IDA**) an affiliate of the International Bank for Reconstruction and Development (World Bank) established in 1960 to provide assistance primarily in the poorer developing countries.

In·ter·na·tio·nale /,intər,nasHəˈnal, -ˈnäl/ **1** (**the Internationale**) a revolutionary song composed in France in the late 19th century. It was adopted by French socialists and subsequently by others, and was the official anthem of the former Soviet Union until 1944.
2 variant spelling of INTERNATIONAL (sense 2 of the noun).
– ORIGIN French, feminine of *international* 'international.'

In·ter·na·tion·al En·er·gy A·gen·cy (abbr.: **IEA**) an agency founded in 1974, within the framework of the OECD, to coordinate energy supply and demand worldwide. Its headquarters are in Paris.

In·ter·na·tion·al Fi·nance Cor·po·ra·tion (abbr.: **IFC**) an affiliate of the International Bank for Reconstruction and Development (World Bank) established in 1956 to assist developing member countries by promoting the growth of the private sector of their economies.

In·ter·na·tion·al Fund for Ag·ri·cul·tur·al De·vel·op·ment (abbr.: **IFAD**) an agency of the United Nations whose purpose is to mobilize additional funds for agricultural and rural development in developing countries through programs that directly benefit the poorest rural populations. It began operations in 1977.

in·ter·na·tion·al·ism /,intərˈnasHənl,izəm/ ▶ n.
1 the state or process of being international: *the internationalism of popular music*. ■ the advocacy of cooperation and understanding between nations.
2 (**Internationalism**) the principles of any of the four Internationals.
– DERIVATIVES **in·ter·na·tion·al·ist** n.

in·ter·na·tion·al·ize /,intərˈnasHənl,īz/ ▶ v. [with obj.] **1** make (something) international.
2 bring (a place) under the protection or control of two or more nations: (as adj. **internationalized**) *an internationalized city*.
– DERIVATIVES **in·ter·na·tion·al·i·za·tion** /-,nasHənl-iˈzāsHən/ n.

In·ter·na·tion·al La·bor Or·gan·i·za·tion (abbr.: **ILO**) an organization established in 1919 whose aim is to encourage lasting peace through social justice, awarded the Nobel Peace Prize in 1969.

in·ter·na·tion·al law ▶ n. a body of rules established by custom or treaty and recognized by nations as binding in their relations with one another.

In·ter·na·tion·al Mon·e·tar·y Fund (abbr.: **IMF**) an international organization established in 1945 that aims to promote international trade and monetary cooperation and the stabilization of exchange rates. Member countries contribute in gold and in their own currencies to provide a reserve on which they may draw to meet foreign obligations during periods of deficit in their international balance of payments. Payments are usually made on the basis of the country's acceptance of stipulated measures for economic correction, which often entail cuts in public expenditure and an increased cost of living, and have frequently caused controversy. It is affiliated with the United Nations, with headquarters in Washington, DC.

In·ter·na·tion·al Or·gan·i·za·tion for Stand·ard·i·za·tion an organization founded in 1946 to standardize measurements for international industrial, commercial, and scientific purposes.

In·ter·na·tion·al Pho·net·ic Al·pha·bet (abbr.: **IPA**) an internationally recognized set of phonetic symbols developed in the late 19th century, based on the principle of strict one-to-one correspondence between sounds and symbols.

In·ter·na·tion·al So·ci·e·ty for Krish·na Con·scious·ness see HARE KRISHNA.

In·ter·na·tion·al Style ▶ n. a functional style of 20th-century architecture, so called because it crossed national and cultural barriers. It is characterized by the use of steel and reinforced concrete, wide windows, uninterrupted interior spaces, simple lines, and strict geometric forms.

In·ter·na·tion·al Sys·tem of U·nits ▶ n. a system of physical units (**SI Units**) based on the meter, kilogram, second, ampere, kelvin, candela, and mole, together with a set of prefixes to indicate multiplication or division by a power of ten.
– ORIGIN translating French *Système International d'Unités*.

In·ter·na·tion·al Tel·e·com·mu·ni·ca·tions Un·ion (abbr.: **ITU**) an organization whose purpose is to promote international cooperation in the use and improvement of telecommunications of all kinds. Founded in Paris in 1865 as the International Telegraph Union, it became an agency of the United Nations in 1947.

in·ter·na·tion·al u·nit ▶ n. a unit of activity or potency for vitamins, hormones, or other substances, defined individually for each substance in terms of the activity of a standard quantity or preparation.

in·terne ▶ n. rare spelling of INTERN.

in·ter·ne·cine /,intərˈnesēn, -ˈnēsēn, -sin/ ▶ adj. destructive to both sides in a conflict: *the region's history of savage internecine warfare*. ■ of or relating to conflict within a group or organization: *the party shrank from the trauma of more internecine strife*.
– ORIGIN mid 17th cent. (in the sense 'deadly, characterized by great slaughter'): from Latin *internecinus*, based on *inter-* 'among' + *necare* 'to kill.'

in·tern·ee /,intərˈnē/ ▶ n. a person who is confined as a prisoner, esp. for political or military reasons.

in·ter·neg·a·tive /,intərˈnegətiv/ ▶ n. Photography a second negative of an image made from the original negative.

In·ter·net /ˈintər,net/ a global computer network providing a variety of information and communication facilities, consisting of interconnected networks using standardized communication protocols.
– ORIGIN 1970s (denoting a computer network connecting two or more smaller networks): from INTER- 'reciprocal, mutual' + NETWORK.

In·ter·net ap·pli·ance ▶ n. a small computer designed especially to provide easy access to the Internet.

In·ter·net ca·fe (also **Internet café**) ▶ n. another term for CYBERCAFE.

In·ter·net Pro·to·col ▶ n. Computing a set of rules governing the format of data sent over the Internet or other network.

in·ter·neu·ron /,intərˈn(y)o͝or,än/ (Brit. also **inter-neurone** /-,rōn/) ▶ n. Anatomy & Physiology a neuron that transmits impulses between other neurons, esp. as part of a reflex arc.
– DERIVATIVES **in·ter·neu·ro·nal** /-ˈn(y)o͝orənl, -n(y)o͞oˈrōnl/ adj.
– ORIGIN 1930s: from INTERNUNCIAL + NEURON.

in·tern·ist /inˈtərnist, ˈintər-/ ▶ n. Medicine a specialist in internal medicine.
– ORIGIN early 20th cent.: from INTERNAL + -IST.

in·ter·node /ˈintər,nōd/ ▶ n. a slender part between two nodes or joints, in particular: ■ Botany a part of a plant stem between two of the nodes from which leaves emerge. ■ Anatomy a stretch of a nerve cell axon sheathed in myelin, between two nodes of Ranvier.
– ORIGIN mid 17th cent.: from Latin *internodium*, from *inter-* 'between' + *nodus* 'knot.'

in·ter·nu·cle·ar /,intərˈn(y)o͞oklēər/ ▶ adj. between nuclei (esp. of atoms).

in·ter·nun·cial /,intərˈnənsēəl, -sHəl/ ▶ adj. [attrib.] Anatomy & Physiology (of neurons) forming connections between other neurons in the central nervous system.
– ORIGIN mid 19th cent.: from Latin *internuntius* (from *inter-* 'between' + *nuntius* 'messenger') + -AL.

in·ter·o·ce·an·ic /,intər,ōsHēˈanik/ ▶ adj. between or connecting two oceans.

in·ter·o·cep·tive /,intərōˈseptiv/ ▶ adj. Physiology relating to stimuli produced within an organism, esp. in the gut and other internal organs. Compare with EXTEROCEPTIVE.
– ORIGIN early 20th cent.: from INTERIOR + RECEPTIVE.

in·ter·o·cep·tor /,intərōˈseptər/ ▶ n. Physiology a sensory receptor that receives stimuli from within the body, esp. from the gut and other internal organs. Compare with EXTEROCEPTOR.

in·ter·op·er·a·ble /,intərˈäp(ə)rəbəl/ ▶ adj. (of computer systems or software) able to exchange and make use of information.
– DERIVATIVES **in·ter·op·er·a·bil·i·ty** /-,äp(ə)rəˈbilitē/ n.

in·ter·os·se·ous /,intərˈäsēəs/ ▶ adj. situated between bones, in particular: ■ of or denoting certain muscles of the hand and foot. ■ of or denoting certain arteries of the forearm.

interp. ▶ abbr. interpreter.

in·ter·pel·late /,intərˈpelāt, inˈtərpə,lāt/ ▶ v. [with obj.] **1** (in certain parliamentary systems) interrupt the order of the day by demanding an explanation from (the minister concerned).
2 Philosophy (of an ideology or discourse) bring into being or give identity to (an individual or category). [from the works of Althusser.]
– DERIVATIVES **in·ter·pel·la·tion** /,intərpəˈlāsHən/ n., **in·ter·pel·la·tor** /-,lātər/ n.
– ORIGIN late 16th cent. (in the sense 'interrupt'): from Latin *interpellat-* 'interrupted (by speech),' from the verb *interpellare*, from *inter-* 'between' + *pellere* 'to drive.' Sense 1 dates from the late 19th cent.

in·ter·pen·e·trate /,intərˈpeni,trāt/ ▶ v. mix or merge together: [no obj.] *the two concepts interpenetrate in interesting ways* | [with obj.] *fibers of meaning interpenetrate every strand of sound*.

– DERIVATIVES **in·ter·pen·e·tra·tion** /-ˌpeniˈtrāSHən/ **n.**, **in·ter·pen·e·tra·tive** /-ˌtrātiv/ **adj.**

in·ter·per·son·al /ˌintərˈpərsənəl/ ▶ **adj.** [attrib.] of or relating to relationships or communication between people: *you will need good interpersonal skills.*
– DERIVATIVES **in·ter·per·son·al·ly** **adv.**

in·ter·phase /ˈintərˌfāz/ ▶ **n.** Biology the resting phase between successive mitotic divisions of a cell, or between the first and second divisions of meiosis.

in·ter·plan·e·tar·y /ˌintərˈplaniˌterē/ ▶ **adj.** situated or traveling between planets: *interplanetary missions.*

in·ter·plant /ˌintərˈplant/ ▶ **v.** [with obj.] (usu. **be interplanted**) plant (a crop or plant) together with another crop or plant. ■ plant (land) with a mixture of crops or plants.

in·ter·play /ˈintərˌplā/ ▶ **n.** the way in which two or more things have an effect on each other: *the **interplay between** inheritance and learning.*

in·ter·plead·er /ˌintərˈplēdər/ ▶ **n.** Law a suit pleaded between two parties to determine a matter of claim or right to property held by a third party.
– ORIGIN mid 16th cent.: from Anglo-Norman French *enterpleder*, from *enter-* 'between' + *pleder* 'to plead.'

In·ter·pol /ˈintərˌpôl, -ˌpäl/ an organization based in Paris that coordinates investigations made by the police forces of member countries into crimes with an international dimension.
– ORIGIN originally the address for telegrams sent to the International Criminal Police Commission, founded in 1923; from *Inter(national) pol(ice)*.

in·ter·po·late /inˈtərpəˌlāt/ ▶ **v.** [with obj.] insert (something) between fixed points: *illustrations were interpolated in the text.* ■ insert (words) in a book or other text, esp. in order to give a false impression as to its date. ■ make such insertions in (a book or text). ■ interject (a remark) in a conversation: [with direct speech] *"I dare say," interpolated her employer.* ■ Mathematics insert (an intermediate value or term) into a series by estimating or calculating it from surrounding known values.
– DERIVATIVES **in·ter·po·la·tion** /-ˌtərpəˈlāSHən/ **n.**, **in·ter·po·la·tive** /-ˌlātiv/ **adj.**
– ORIGIN early 17th cent.: from Latin *interpolat-* 'refurbished, altered,' from the verb *interpolare*, from *inter-* 'between' + *-polare* (related to *polire* 'to polish').

in·ter·po·la·tor /inˈtərpəˌlātər/ ▶ **n.** a person who interpolates something. ■ a device or apparatus that guides a tool through a smooth curve when provided with a set of points defining the curve.

in·ter·pole /ˈintərˌpōl/ ▶ **n.** an auxiliary pole of a commutator placed between the main poles to increase its efficiency.

in·ter·pose /ˌintərˈpōz/ ▶ **v. 1** [with obj.] place or insert between one thing and another: *he **interposed himself between** her and the top of the stairs.*
2 [no obj.] intervene between parties: [with infinitive] *the legislature interposed to suppress these amusements.* ■ [with obj.] say (words) as an interruption: *if I might interpose a personal remark here.* ■ [with obj.] exercise or advance (a veto or objection) so as to interfere: *the memo interposes no objection to issuing a discharge.*
– ORIGIN late 16th cent.: from French *interposer*, from Latin *interponere* 'put in' (from *inter-* 'between' + *ponere* 'put'), but influenced by *interpositus* 'inserted' and Old French *poser* 'to place.'

in·ter·po·si·tion /ˌintərpəˈziSHən/ ▶ **n.** the action of interposing someone or something: *the interposition of members between tiers of management.* ■ interference: *prevented from taking your life by the interposition of your wife.*
– ORIGIN late Middle English: from Latin *interpositio(n-)*, from the verb *interponere* (see INTERPOSE).

in·ter·pret /inˈtərprit/ ▶ **v.** (**interprets, interpreting, interpreted**) [with obj.] **1** explain the meaning of (information, words, or actions): *the evidence is difficult to interpret.* ■ [no obj.] translate orally or into sign language the words of a person speaking a different language: *I agreed to interpret for Jean-Claude.* ■ perform (a dramatic role or piece of music) in a particular way that conveys one's understanding of the creator's ideas.
2 understand (an action, mood, or way of behaving) as having a particular meaning or significance: *her self-confidence was often **interpreted as** brashness.*
– DERIVATIVES **in·ter·pret·a·bil·i·ty** /-ˌtərpritəˈbilitē/ **n.**, **in·ter·pret·a·ble** **adj.**, **in·ter·pre·ta·tive** /-ˌtātiv/ **adj.**, **in·ter·pre·ta·tive·ly** /-ˌtātivlē/ **adv.**, **in·ter·pre·tive** /-ˈtərpritiv/ **adj.**, **in·ter·pre·tive·ly** /-ˈtərpritivlē/ **adv.**
– ORIGIN late Middle English: from Old French *interpreter* or Latin *interpretari* 'explain, translate,' from *interpres, interpret-* 'agent, translator, interpreter.'

> **USAGE** **Interpretative**, which means 'serving to interpret or explain,' dates back to around 1560, but the shorter form **interpretive**, about a hundred years younger, is steadily pressing it out of employment. They mean the same thing, and both are correct. The traditional **interpretative** is still the preferred form in Britain, but in American usage, **interpretive** is far more common.

in·ter·pre·tant /inˈtərpritənt/ ▶ **n.** (in Peirce's philosophy of language) the effect of a proposition or sign series on the person who interprets it.

in·ter·pre·ta·tion /inˌtərpriˈtāSHən/ ▶ **n.** the action of explaining the meaning of something: *the interpretation of data.* ■ an explanation or way of explaining: *this action is open to a number of interpretations.* ■ a stylistic representation of a creative work or dramatic role: *two differing interpretations, both bearing the distinctive hallmarks of each writer's perspective.*
– DERIVATIVES **in·ter·pre·ta·tion·al** /-SHənl/ **adj.**
– ORIGIN late Middle English: from Old French *interpretation* or Latin *interpretatio(n-)*, from the verb *interpretari* (see INTERPRET).

in·ter·pret·er /inˈtərpritər/ ▶ **n.** a person who interprets, esp. one who translates speech orally. ■ Computing a program that can analyze and execute a program line by line.
– ORIGIN late Middle English: from Old French *interpreteur*, from late Latin *interpretator*, from Latin *interpretari* (see INTERPRET).

in·ter·pro·vin·cial /ˌintərprəˈvinSHəl/ ▶ **adj.** existing or carried on between provinces of the same country.
▶ **n.** (usu. **interprovincials**) a sports tournament between different provinces of the same country. ■ a member of a team competing in such a tournament.

in·ter·quar·tile /ˌintərˈkwôrˌtīl, -ˈkwôrtl/ ▶ **adj.** Statistics situated between the first and third quartiles of a distribution.

in·ter·ra·cial /ˌintərˈrāSHəl/ ▶ **adj.** existing between or involving different races: *interracial conflict.*
– DERIVATIVES **in·ter·ra·cial·ly** **adv.**

in·ter·reg·num /ˌintərˈregnəm/ ▶ **n.** (pl. **interregnums** or **interregna** /-nə/) a period when normal government is suspended, esp. between successive reigns or regimes. ■ an interval or pause: *the interregnum between the discovery of radioactivity and its detailed understanding.*
– ORIGIN late 16th cent. (denoting temporary rule between reigns or during suspension of normal government): from Latin, from *inter-* 'between' + *regnum* 'reign.'

in·ter·re·late /ˌintərəˈlāt/ ▶ **v.** relate or connect to one another: [no obj.] *each component interrelates with all the others* | [with obj.] *shared values and mechanisms that interrelate peoples in all corners of the world.*
– DERIVATIVES **in·ter·re·lat·ed·ness** **n.**

in·ter·re·la·tion·ship /ˌintərəˈlāSHənˌSHip/ ▶ **n.** the way in which each of two or more things is related to the other or others: *the **interrelationship between** the comprehension and production of early vocabulary.*
– DERIVATIVES **in·ter·re·la·tion** **n.**

interrog. ▶ **abbr.** interrogative.

in·ter·ro·gate /inˈterəˌgāt/ ▶ **v.** [with obj.] ask questions of (someone, esp. a suspect or a prisoner) closely, aggressively, or formally. ■ Computing obtain data from (a computer file, database, storage device, or terminal). ■ (of an electronic device) transmit a signal to (another device, esp. one on a vehicle) to obtain a response giving information about identity, condition, etc.
– DERIVATIVES **in·ter·ro·ga·tor** /-ˌgātər/ **n.**
– ORIGIN late 15th cent.: from Latin *interrogat-* 'questioned,' from the verb *interrogare*, from *inter-* 'between' + *rogare* 'ask.'

in·ter·ro·ga·tion /inˌterəˈgāSHən/ ▶ **n.** the action of interrogating or the process of being interrogated: *would he keep his mouth shut **under interrogation**?* | *he had conducted hundreds of criminal interrogations.*
– DERIVATIVES **in·ter·ro·ga·tion·al** /-SHənl/ **adj.**

in·ter·ro·ga·tion point (also **interrogation mark**) ▶ **n.** another term for QUESTION MARK.

in·ter·rog·a·tive /ˌintəˈrägətiv/ ▶ **adj.** having or conveying the force of a question: *a hard, interrogative stare.* ■ Grammar used in questions: *an interrogative adverb.* Contrasted with AFFIRMATIVE and NEGATIVE.
▶ **n.** a word used in questions, such as *how* or *what.* ■ a construction that has the force of a question.
– DERIVATIVES **in·ter·rog·a·tive·ly** **adv.**
– ORIGIN early 16th cent.: from late Latin *interrogativus*, from Latin *interrogare* (see INTERROGATE).

in·ter·rog·a·to·ry /ˌintəˈrägəˌtôrē/ ▶ **adj.** conveying the force of a question; questioning: *the guard moves away with an interrogatory stare.*
▶ **n.** (pl. **interrogatories**) Law a written question that is formally put to one party in a case by another party and that must be answered.
– ORIGIN mid 16th cent.: the noun from medieval Latin *interrogatoria*, plural of *interrogatorium*; the adjective from late Latin *interrogatorius*, based on Latin *interrogare* (see INTERROGATE).

in·ter·rupt /ˌintəˈrəpt/ ▶ **v.** [with obj.] **1** stop the continuous progress of (an activity or process): *the buzzer interrupted his thoughts.* ■ stop (someone speaking) by saying or doing something: *"Of course ..." Shepherd began, but his son interrupted him* | [with direct speech] *"Hold on," he interrupted.*
2 break the continuity of (a line or surface): *the coastal plain is interrupted by chains of large lagoons.* ■ obstruct (something, esp. a view).
– DERIVATIVES **in·ter·rupt·i·ble** **adj.**, **in·ter·rup·tive** /-tiv/ **adj.**
– ORIGIN late Middle English: from Latin *interrupt-* 'broken, interrupted,' from the verb *interrumpere*, from *inter-* 'between' + *rumpere* 'to break.'

in·ter·rupt·ed /ˌintəˈrəptid/ ▶ **adj. 1** Botany (of a compound leaf, inflorescence, or other plant organ) made discontinuous by smaller interposed leaflets or intervals of bare stem.
2 Music (of a cadence) having a penultimate dominant chord that is followed not by the expected tonic chord but by another chord, usually the submediant.

in·ter·rupt·er /ˌintəˈrəptər/ (also **interruptor**) ▶ **n.** a person or thing that interrupts. ■ a device that automatically breaks an electric circuit if a fault develops.

in·ter·rup·tion /ˌintəˈrəpSHən/ ▶ **n.** the action of interrupting or being interrupted: *a chance to study without interruption.* ■ an act, utterance, or period that interrupts someone or something: *she ignored the interruption and carried on* | *students returning to education after an interruption in their career.*

in·ter se /ˈintər ˈsē, ˈsā/ ▶ **adv.** between or among themselves: *agreements entered into by all the shareholders inter se.*
– ORIGIN mid 19th cent.: Latin.

in·ter·sect /ˌintərˈsekt/ ▶ **v.** [with obj.] divide (something) by passing or lying across it: *occasionally the water table intersects the earth's surface, forming streams and lakes* | *the area is intersected only by minor roads.* ■ [no obj.] (of two or more things) pass or lie across each other: *lines of latitude and longitude intersect at right angles.*
– ORIGIN early 17th cent.: from Latin *intersect-* 'cut, intersected,' from the verb *intersecare*, from *inter-* 'between' + *secare* 'to cut.'

in·ter·sec·tion /ˌintərˈsekSHən/ ▶ **n.** a point or line common to lines or surfaces that intersect: *the intersection of a plane and a cone.* ■ a point at which two or more things intersect, esp. roads: *red and green lights at the nearby intersection.* ■ an action of intersecting: *his course is on a direct intersection with ours.*
– DERIVATIVES **in·ter·sec·tion·al** /-SHənl/ **adj.**
– ORIGIN mid 16th cent.: from Latin *intersectio(n-)*, from *intersecare* (see INTERSECT).

in·ter·seg·men·tal /ˌintərsegˈmentl/ ▶ **adj.** chiefly Zoology situated or occurring between segments.
– DERIVATIVES **in·ter·seg·men·tal·ly** **adv.**

in·ter·sep·tal /ˌintərˈseptl/ ▶ **adj.** Anatomy & Zoology situated between septa or partitions.

in·ter·sex /ˈintərˌseks/ ▶ **n.** the abnormal condition of being intermediate between male and female; hermaphroditism. ■ an individual in this condition; a hermaphrodite.

in·ter·sex·u·al /ˌintərˈsekSHo͞oəl/ ▶ **adj. 1** existing or occurring between the sexes: *intersexual selection, or mate choice, was, to Darwin, the job of females.*
2 relating to or having the condition of being intermediate between male and female.
– DERIVATIVES **in·ter·sex·u·al·i·ty** /-ˌsekSHo͞oˈalitē/ **n.**

in·ter·space ▶ **n.** /ˈintərˌspās/ a space between objects: *volcanic rock that has been crushed into fragments and the interspaces filled with turquoise and oxide of iron.*
▶ **v.** /ˌintərˈspās/ [with obj.] (usu. **be interspaced**) put or occupy a space between: *the great four-story houses **were interspaced with** the ramshackle cottages of the workmen.*

PRONUNCIATION KEY ə **ago, up**; ər **over, fur**; a **hat**; ā **ate**; ä **car**; e **let**; ē **see**; i **fit**; ī **by**; NG **sing**; ō **go**; ô **law, for**; oi **toy**; o͝o **good**; o͞o **goo**; ou **out**; TH **thin**; T͟H **then**; ZH **vision**

in·ter·spe·cif·ic /ˌintərspiˈsifik/ ▶ **adj.** Biology existing or occurring between different species: *interspecific differences.*
– DERIVATIVES **in·ter·spe·cif·i·cal·ly** /-ik(ə)lē/ **adv.**

in·ter·sperse /ˌintərˈspərs/ ▶ **v.** [with obj.] scatter among or between other things; place here and there: ***interspersed between** tragic stories are a few songs supplying comic relief.* ■ diversify (a thing or things) with other things at intervals: *a patchwork of open fields **interspersed with** copses of pine.*
– DERIVATIVES **in·ter·sper·sion** /-ˈspərZHən/ **n.**
– ORIGIN mid 16th cent. (in the sense 'diversify (something) by introducing other things at intervals'): from Latin *interspers-* 'scattered between,' from *interspergere*, from *inter-* 'between' + *spargere* 'scatter.'

in·ter·spi·nal /ˌintərˈspīnl/ ▶ **adj.** Anatomy situated between the spines or spinous protuberances of the vertebrae.
– DERIVATIVES **in·ter·spi·nous** /-ˈspīnəs/ **adj.**

in·ter·sta·di·al /ˌintərˈstādēəl/ Geology ▶ **adj.** of or relating to a minor period of less cold climate during a glacial period. Compare with **INTERGLACIAL.**
▶ **n.** an interstadial period.
– ORIGIN early 20th cent.: from **INTER-** 'between' + *stadial* from Latin *stadialis*, from *stadium* 'stage.'

in·ter·state /ˈintərˌstāt/ ▶ **adj.** [attrib.] existing or carried on between states: *interstate travel.* ■ in a different state from one referred to or understood: *their interstate rivals.*
▶ **n.** (also **interstate highway**) one of a system of expressways covering the 48 contiguous states: *a picnic area just off the interstate | Interstate 65 runs generally parallel to Route 31.*

in·ter·stel·lar /ˌintərˈstelər/ ▶ **adj.** occurring or situated between stars: *interstellar travel.*

in·ter·stice /inˈtərstis/ ▶ **n.** (usu. **interstices**) an intervening space, esp. a very small one: *sunshine filtered through the interstices of the arching trees.*
– ORIGIN late Middle English: from Latin *interstitium*, from *intersistere* 'stand between,' from *inter-* 'between' + *sistere* 'to stand.'

in·ter·sti·tial /ˌintərˈstiSHəl/ ▶ **adj.** of, forming, or occupying interstices: *the interstitial space.* ■ Ecology (of minute animals) living in the spaces between individual sand grains in the soil or aquatic sediments: *the interstitial fauna of marine sands.*
– DERIVATIVES **in·ter·sti·tial·ly adv.**

in·ter·sub·jec·tive /ˌintərsəbˈjektiv/ ▶ **adj.** Philosophy existing between conscious minds; shared by more than one conscious mind.
– DERIVATIVES **in·ter·sub·jec·tive·ly adv., in·ter·sub·jec·tiv·i·ty** /-ˌsəbjekˈtivitē/ **n.**

in·ter·tex·tu·al·i·ty /ˌintərˌteksCHo͞oˈalitē/ ▶ **n.** the relationship between texts, esp. literary ones: *every text is a product of intertextuality.*
– DERIVATIVES **in·ter·tex·tu·al** /-ˈteksCHo͞oəl/ **adj., in·ter·tex·tu·al·ly adv.**

in·ter·ti·dal /ˌintərˈtīdl/ ▶ **adj.** Ecology of or denoting the area of a seashore that is covered at high tide and uncovered at low tide.

in·ter·trib·al /ˌintərˈtrībəl/ ▶ **adj.** existing or occurring between different tribes: *intertribal conflict.* ■ involving members of more than one tribe: *an intertribal group.*

in·ter·tri·go /ˌintərˈtrīgō/ ▶ **n.** Medicine inflammation caused by the rubbing of one area of skin on another.
– ORIGIN early 18th cent.: from Latin, 'a sore place caused by rubbing,' from *interterere* 'rub against each other.'

in·ter·trop·i·cal con·ver·gence zone /ˌintərˈträpikəl/ ▶ **n.** a narrow zone near the equator where northern and southern air masses converge, typically producing low atmospheric pressure.

in·ter·twine /ˌintərˈtwīn/ ▶ **v.** twist or twine together: [with obj.] *a net made of cotton **intertwined with** other natural fibers* | [no obj.] *the coils **intertwine with** one another like strands of spaghetti.* ■ [with obj.] connect or link (two or more things) closely: *Dickens has been very clever to intertwine all these aspects and ideas.*
– DERIVATIVES **in·ter·twine·ment n.**

in·ter·val /ˈintərvəl/ ▶ **n. 1** an intervening time or space: *after his departure, there was an interval of many years without any meetings | the intervals between meals were very short.*
2 a pause; a break in activity: *an interval of mourning.* ■ Brit. an intermission separating parts of a theatrical or musical performance. ■ Brit. a break between the parts of an athletic contest: *leading 3-0 at the interval.*
3 a space between two things; a gap. ■ the difference in pitch between two musical sounds.
– PHRASES **at intervals 1** with time between, not continuously: *the light flashed at intervals.* **2** with spaces between: *the path is marked with rocks at intervals.*
– DERIVATIVES **in·ter·val·lic** /ˌintərˈvalik/ **adj.**
– ORIGIN Middle English: from Old French *entrevalle*, based on Latin *intervallum* 'space between ramparts, interval,' from *inter-* 'between' + *vallum* 'rampart.'

in·ter·val es·ti·mate ▶ **n.** Statistics an interval within which the value of a parameter of a population has a stated probability of occurring. Compare with **POINT ESTIMATE.**

in·ter·val·om·e·ter /ˌintərvəˈlämitər/ ▶ **n.** Photography an attachment or facility on a camera that operates the shutter regularly at set intervals over a period. On a movie camera the device is used for time-lapse photography.

in·ter·val train·ing ▶ **n.** training in which an athlete alternates between two activities, typically requiring different rates of speed, degrees of effort, etc.

in·ter·vene /ˌintərˈvēn/ ▶ **v.** [no obj.] **1** come between so as to prevent or alter a result or course of events: *he acted outside his authority when he intervened in the dispute* | [with infinitive] *their forces intervened to halt the attack.* ■ (of an event or circumstance) occur as a delay or obstacle to something being done: *Christmas intervened, and the investigation was suspended.* ■ interrupt verbally: [with direct speech] *"It's true!" he intervened.* ■ Law interpose in a lawsuit as a third party.
2 (usu. as adj. **intervening**) occur in time between events: *to occupy the intervening months, she took a job in a hospital.* ■ be situated between things: *they heard the sound of distant gunfire, muffled by the intervening trees.*
– DERIVATIVES **in·ter·ven·er n., in·ter·ven·ient** /-ˈvēnyənt/ **adj., in·ter·ve·nor** /-ˈvēnər/ **n.**
– ORIGIN late 16th cent. (in the sense 'come in as an extraneous factor or thing'): from Latin *intervenire*, from *inter-* 'between' + *venire* 'come.'

in·ter·ven·tion /ˌintərˈvenCHən/ ▶ **n.** the action or process of intervening: *they are plants that grow naturally without human intervention.* ■ interference by a country in another's affairs: *the administration was reported to be considering military intervention.* ■ action taken to improve a situation, esp. a medical disorder: *two patients were referred for surgical intervention.* ■ a meeting in which people confront an addicted, or otherwise troubled, individual in order to persuade the individual to seek help.
– DERIVATIVES **in·ter·ven·tion·al** /-SHənl/ **adj.**
– ORIGIN late Middle English: from Latin *interventio(n-)*, from the verb *intervenire* (see **INTERVENE**).

in·ter·ven·tion·ist /ˌintərˈvenSHənist/ ▶ **adj.** favoring intervention, esp. by a government in its domestic economy or by one country in the affairs of another.
▶ **n.** a person who favors intervention of this kind.
– DERIVATIVES **in·ter·ven·tion·ism** /-ˌnizəm/ **n.**

in·ter·ver·te·bral /ˌintərˈvərtəbrəl/ ▶ **adj.** [attrib.] situated between vertebrae: *intervertebral joints.*

in·ter·ver·te·bral disk ▶ **n.** see **DISK** (sense 3 of the noun).

in·ter·view /ˈintərˌvyo͞o/ ▶ **n.** a meeting of people face to face, esp. for consultation. ■ a conversation between a journalist or radio or television presenter and a person of public interest, used as the basis of a broadcast or publication. ■ an oral examination of an applicant for a job, college admission, etc.: *I am pleased to advise you that you have been selected for an interview.*
▶ **v.** [with obj.] hold an interview with (someone): *he arrived to be interviewed by a local TV station about the level of unemployment.* ■ question (someone) to discover their opinions or experience: *in a survey more than half the women interviewed hated the label "housewife."* ■ orally examine (an applicant for a job, college admission, etc.): *he came to be interviewed for a top job* | [no obj.] *I was interviewing all last week.* ■ [no obj.] perform (well or badly) at an interview.
– DERIVATIVES **in·ter·view·ee** /ˌintərˌvyo͞oˈē/ **n., in·ter·view·er n.**
– ORIGIN early 16th cent. (formerly also as *enterview*): from French *entrevue*, from *s'entrevoir* 'see each other,' from *voir* 'to see,' on the pattern of *vue* 'a view.'

in·ter vi·vos /ˈintər ˈvēˌvōs, ˈvīˌvōs/ ▶ **adv. & adj.** (esp. of a gift as opposed to a legacy) between living people: [as adv.] *gifts made inter vivos* | [as postpositive adj.] *a gift inter vivos.*
– ORIGIN Latin.

in·ter·vo·cal·ic /ˌintərvōˈkalik/ ▶ **adj.** Phonetics occurring between vowels: *in intervocalic position.*
– DERIVATIVES **in·ter·vo·cal·i·cal·ly** /-ik(ə)lē/ **adv.**

in·ter·war /ˌintərˈwôr/ ▶ **adj.** [attrib.] existing in the period between two wars, esp. the two world wars (i.e., between 1918 and 1939).

in·ter·weave /ˌintərˈwēv/ ▶ **v.** (past **interwove**; past participle **interwoven**) weave or become woven together: [with obj.] *the rugs are made by tightly interweaving the strands* | [no obj.] *the branches met and interwove above his head.* ■ [with obj.] blend closely: *Wordsworth's political ideas are often interwoven with his philosophical and religious beliefs.*

In·ter·web /ˈintərweb/ ▶ **n.** humorous the Internet.

in·ter·wind /ˌintərˈwīnd/ ▶ **v.** (past and past participle **interwound** /-ˈwound/) [with obj.] (usu. as adj. **interwound**) wind together: *a transformer consists of two interwound coils.*

in·ter·work /ˌintərˈwərk/ ▶ **v.** [no obj.] Computing (of items of hardware or software) be able to connect, communicate, or exchange data: *servers running new and old versions of the software will interwork.*

in·tes·tate /inˈtestāt, -tit/ ▶ **adj.** [predic.] not having made a will before one dies: *he died intestate* | [postpositive] *in the event of his death intestate.* ■ [attrib.] of or relating to a person who dies without having made a will: *his brother's posthumous children are admissible as intestate heirs.*
▶ **n.** a person who has died without having made a will.
– DERIVATIVES **in·tes·ta·cy** /-təsē/ **n.**
– ORIGIN late Middle English: from Latin *intestatus*, from *in-* 'not' + *testatus* 'testified, witness' (see **TESTATE**).

in·tes·ti·nal /inˈtestinəl/ ▶ **adj.** relating to or affecting the intestine: *the intestinal tract.*

in·tes·ti·nal flo·ra /inˈtestənl ˈflôrə/ ▶ **plural n.** [usu. treated as sing.] the symbiotic bacteria occurring naturally in the intestine.

in·tes·tine /inˈtestən/ (also **intestines**) ▶ **n.** (in vertebrates) the lower part of the alimentary canal from the end of the stomach to the anus: *the contents of the intestine | loops of intestine.* See also **LARGE INTESTINE, SMALL INTESTINE.** ■ (esp. in invertebrates) the whole alimentary canal from the mouth downward.
– ORIGIN late Middle English: from Latin *intestinum*, neuter of *intestinus*, from *intus* 'within.'

in·thrall /inˈTHrôl/ ▶ **v.** archaic spelling of **ENTHRALL.**

in·ti /ˈintē/ ▶ **n.** (pl. **same** or **intis** /ˈintēz/) a former basic monetary unit of Peru, equal to 100 centimos.

in·ti·fa·da /ˌintəˈfādə/ ▶ **n.** the Palestinian uprising against Israeli occupation of the West Bank and Gaza Strip, beginning in 1987.
– ORIGIN from Arabic *intifāḍa* 'an uprising' (literally 'a jumping up as a reaction to something'), from *intifaḍa* 'be shaken, shake oneself.'

in·ti·ma /ˈintəmə/ ▶ **n.** (pl. **intimae** /-ˌmē/) Anatomy & Zoology the innermost coating or membrane of a part or organ, esp. of a vein or artery.
– DERIVATIVES **in·ti·mal** /-məl/ **adj.**
– ORIGIN late 19th cent.: shortening of modern Latin *tunica intima* 'innermost sheath.'

in·ti·ma·cy /ˈintəməsē/ ▶ **n.** (pl. **intimacies**) close familiarity or friendship; closeness: *the intimacy between a husband and wife.* ■ a private cozy atmosphere: *the room had a peaceful sense of intimacy about it.* ■ an intimate act, esp. sexual intercourse. ■ an intimate remark: *here she was sitting swapping intimacies with a stranger.* ■ [in sing.] closeness of observation or knowledge of a subject: *he acquired an intimacy with Swahili literature.*

in·ti·mate[1] /ˈintəmit/ ▶ **adj. 1** closely acquainted; familiar, close: *intimate friends | they are on intimate terms.* ■ (of a place or setting) having or creating an informal friendly atmosphere: *an intimate little Italian restaurant.* ■ [predic.] used euphemistically to indicate that a couple is having a sexual relationship: *he was sickened by the thought of others having been **intimate with** her.* ■ involving very close connection: *their intimate involvement with their community.*
2 private and personal: *going into intimate details of his sexual encounters | intimate correspondence.*
3 (of knowledge) detailed; thorough: *an intimate knowledge of the software.*
▶ **n.** a very close friend: *his circle of intimates.*
– DERIVATIVES **in·ti·mate·ly adv.**
– ORIGIN early 17th cent. (as a noun): from late Latin *intimatus*, past participle of Latin *intimare* 'impress, make familiar,' from *intimus* 'inmost.'

in·ti·mate[2] /ˈintəˌmāt/ ▶ **v.** [with obj.] imply or hint: [with clause] *he had already intimated that he might not be able to continue.* ■ state or make known: *Mr. Hutchison has intimated his decision to retire.*
– ORIGIN early 16th cent. (earlier (late Middle English) as *intimation*): from late Latin *intimat-* 'made known,' from the verb *intimare* (see **INTIMATE[1]**).

in·ti·ma·tion /ˌintəˈmāSHən/ ▶ **n.** an indication or hint: *the first intimations of trouble | no one gave any intimation that there had been any problems.* ■ the action of making something known, esp. in an indirect way.

in·tim·i·date /inˈtimiˌdāt/ ▶ v. frighten or overawe (someone), esp. in order to make them do what one wants: *he tries to intimidate his rivals* | (as adj. **intimidating**) *the intimidating defense lawyer.*
– DERIVATIVES **in·tim·i·dat·ing·ly** adv., **in·tim·i·da·tor** /-ˌdātər/ n., **in·tim·i·da·to·ry** /-dəˌtôrē/ adj.
– ORIGIN mid 17th cent.: from medieval Latin *intimidat-* 'made timid,' from the verb *intimidare* (based on *timidus* 'timid').

in·tim·i·da·tion /inˌtimiˈdāsHən/ ▶ n. the action of intimidating someone, or the state of being intimidated: *the intimidation of witnesses and jurors.*

in·ti·mism /ˈintəˌmizəm/ ▶ n. a style of painting showing intimate views of domestic interiors using Impressionist techniques, used by artists such as Bonnard in the early 20th century.
– DERIVATIVES **in·ti·mist** adj. & n.
– ORIGIN early 20th cent.: from French *intimisme*, from Latin *intimus* 'innermost.'

in·tinc·tion /inˈtiNG(k)sHən/ ▶ n. the action of dipping the bread in the wine at a Eucharist so that a communicant receives both together.
– ORIGIN mid 16th cent.: from late Latin *intinctio(n-)*, from Latin *intingere*, from *in-* 'into' + *tingere* 'dip.' The word originally denoted the general action of dipping, esp. into something colored; compare with TINGE. The current sense dates from the late 19th cent.

in·tit·ule /inˈticHo͝ol/ ▶ v. [with obj.] Brit. give a specified title to (a legislative act).
– ORIGIN late 15th cent. (formerly also as *entitule*): from Old French *entituler*, *intituler* (see ENTITLE).

intl. ▶ abbr. international.

in·to /ˈinto͞o/ ▶ prep. **1** expressing movement or action with the result that someone or something becomes enclosed or surrounded by something else: *cover the bowl and put it into the fridge* | *Sara got into her car and shut the door* | figurative *he walked into a trap sprung by the opposition.*
2 expressing movement or action with the result that someone or something makes physical contact with something else: *he crashed into a parked car.*
3 indicating a route by which someone or something may arrive at a particular destination: *the narrow road that led down into the village.*
4 indicating the direction toward which someone or something is turned when confronting something else: *with the wind blowing into your face* | *sobbing into her skirt.*
5 indicating an object of attention or interest: *a clearer insight into what is involved* | *an inquiry into the squad's practices.*
6 expressing a change of state: *a peaceful protest which turned into a violent confrontation* | *the fruit can be made into jam.*
7 expressing the result of an action: *they forced the club into a humiliating and expensive special general meeting.*
8 expressing division: *three into twelve equals four.*
9 informal (of a person) taking a lively and active interest in (something): *he's into surfing.*
– ORIGIN Old English *intō* (see IN, TO).

in·tol·er·a·ble /inˈtälərəbəl/ ▶ adj. unable to be endured: *the intolerable pressures of his work.*
– DERIVATIVES **in·tol·er·a·bil·i·ty** /-ˌtäləraˈbilitē/ n., **in·tol·er·a·ble·ness** n., **in·tol·er·a·bly** /-blē/ adv.
– ORIGIN late Middle English: from Old French, or from Latin *intolerabilis*, from *in-* 'not' + *tolerabilis* (see TOLERABLE).

in·tol·er·ance /inˈtälərəns/ ▶ n. unwillingness to accept views, beliefs, or behavior that differ from one's own: *a struggle against religious intolerance.* ■ an inability to eat a food or take a drug without adverse effects: *young children with lactose intolerance.*

in·tol·er·ant /inˈtälərənt/ ▶ adj. not tolerant of views, beliefs, or behavior that differ from one's own: *he was intolerant of ignorance.* ■ unable to be given (a medicine or other treatment) or to eat (a food) without adverse effects: *intolerant of aspirin* | [in combination] *these patients were lactose-intolerant.* ■ (of a plant or animal) unable to survive exposure to (physical influence).
– DERIVATIVES **in·tol·er·ant·ly** adv.
– ORIGIN mid 18th cent.: from Latin *intolerant-*, from *in-* 'not' + *tolerant-* 'enduring' (see TOLERANT).

in·to·nate /ˈintəˌnāt/ ▶ v. intone.
– ORIGIN late 18th cent.: from medieval Latin *intonat-* 'intoned,' from the verb *intonare* (see INTONE).

in·to·na·tion /ˌintəˈnāsHən, -tō-/ ▶ n. **1** the rise and fall of the voice in speaking: *she spoke English with a German intonation.* ■ the action of intoning or reciting in a singing voice.
2 accuracy of pitch in playing or singing, or on a stringed instrument such as a guitar: *poor woodwind intonation at the opening.*
3 the opening phrase of a plainsong melody.
– DERIVATIVES **in·to·na·tion·al** /-sHənl/ adj.
– ORIGIN early 17th cent. (sense 3): from medieval Latin *intonatio(n-)*, from *intonare* (see INTONE).

in·tone /inˈtōn/ ▶ v. [with obj.] say or recite with little rise and fall of the pitch of the voice: *he intoned a short Latin prayer* | [with direct speech] *"All rise," intoned the usher.*
– DERIVATIVES **in·ton·er** n.
– ORIGIN late 15th cent. (originally as *entone*): from Old French *entoner* or medieval Latin *intonare*, from *in-* 'into' + Latin *tonus* 'tone.'

in to·to /ˌin ˈtōtō/ ▶ adv. as a whole: *such proposals should be subjected to specific criticism rather than rejected in toto.* ■ [sentence adverb] in all; overall: *there was, in toto, an increase in legal regulation and public surveillance.*
– ORIGIN Latin.

in·tox·i·cant /inˈtäksikənt/ ▶ n. an intoxicating substance.

in·tox·i·cate /inˈtäksiˌkāt/ ▶ v. [with obj.] (usu. as adj. **intoxicated**) **1** (of alcoholic drink or a drug) cause (someone) to lose control of their faculties or behavior. ■ excite or exhilarate: *the team was intoxicated by the prospect of another victorious season.*
2 archaic poison (someone).
– ORIGIN late Middle English (in the sense 'poison'): from medieval Latin *intoxicare*, from *in-* 'into' + *toxicare* 'to poison,' from Latin *toxicum* (see TOXIC).

in·tox·i·cat·ing /inˈtäksiˌkātiNG/ ▶ adj. (of alcoholic drink or a drug) liable to cause intoxication. ■ exhilarating or exciting: *the intoxicating touch of freedom.*
– DERIVATIVES **in·tox·i·cat·ing·ly** adv.

in·tox·i·ca·tion /inˌtäksiˈkāsHən/ ▶ n. the state of being intoxicated, esp. by alcohol: *signs of intoxication.*

in·tox·im·e·ter /inˈtäksəˌmētər/ ▶ n. a nonportable instrument for measuring the alcohol content of a person's breath, esp. in cases of suspected drunk driving, usually sited at a police station.
– ORIGIN 1950s: from *intoxication* (see INTOXICATE) + -METER.

intr. ▶ abbr. ■ intransitive. ■ introduce or introduced or introducing or introduction or introductory.

intra- ▶ prefix (added to adjectives) on the inside; within: *intramural* | *intrauterine.*
– ORIGIN from Latin *intra* 'inside.'

in·tra·cel·lu·lar /ˌintrəˈselyələr/ ▶ adj. Biology located or occurring within a cell or cells: *an increase in intracellular calcium.*
– DERIVATIVES **in·tra·cel·lu·lar·ly** adv.

in·tra·cra·ni·al /ˌintrəˈkrānēəl/ ▶ adj. within the skull: *intracranial hemorrhage.*
– DERIVATIVES **in·tra·cra·ni·al·ly** adv.

in·trac·ta·ble /inˈtraktəbəl/ ▶ adj. hard to control or deal with: *intractable economic problems* | *intractable pain.* ■ (of a person) difficult; stubborn.
– DERIVATIVES **in·trac·ta·bil·i·ty** /-ˌtraktəˈbilitē/ n., **in·trac·ta·ble·ness** n., **in·trac·ta·bly** /-blē/ adv.
– ORIGIN late 15th cent.: from Latin *intractabilis*, from *in-* 'not' + *tractabilis* (see TRACTABLE).

in·tra·day /ˈintrəˌdā/ ▶ adj. [attrib.] Stock Market occurring within one day: *the dollar slipped from an intraday high of 104.*

in·tra·dos /ˈintrəˌdäs, -ˌdōs, inˈtrā-/ ▶ n. (pl. **same** or **intradoses**) Architecture the lower or inner curve of an arch. Often contrasted with EXTRADOS.
– ORIGIN late 18th cent.: from French, from *intra-* 'on the inside' + *dos* 'the back' (from Latin *dorsum*).

in·tra·mo·lec·u·lar /ˌintrəməˈlekyələr/ ▶ adj. existing or taking place within a molecule.
– DERIVATIVES **in·tra·mo·lec·u·lar·ly** adv.

in·tra·mu·ral /ˌintrəˈmyo͝orəl/ ▶ adj. situated or done within the walls of a building: *both intramural and churchyard graves.* ■ taking place within a single educational institution: *recreational intramural games.* ■ forming part of normal university or college studies. ■ Medicine & Biology situated within the wall of a hollow organ or a cell: *an intramural hematoma.* ■ situated or done within a community: *an intramural social symbol within the tribe.*
– DERIVATIVES **in·tra·mu·ral·ly** adv.
– ORIGIN mid 19th cent.: from INTRA- 'within' + Latin *murus* 'wall' + -AL.

in·tra·mus·cu·lar /ˌintrəˈməskyələr/ ▶ adj. situated or taking place within, or administered into, a muscle: *an intramuscular injection.*
– DERIVATIVES **in·tra·mus·cu·lar·ly** adv.

in·tra·net /ˈintrəˌnet/ (also **Intranet**) ▶ n. Computing a local or restricted communications network, esp. a private network created using World Wide Web software.

in·tran·si·gent /inˈtransijənt, -zi-/ ▶ adj. unwilling or refusing to change one's views or to agree about something.
▶ n. an intransigent person.
– DERIVATIVES **in·tran·si·gence** n., **in·tran·si·gen·cy** n., **in·tran·si·gent·ly** adv.
– ORIGIN late 19th cent.: from French *intransigeant*, from Spanish *los intransigentes* (a name adopted by the extreme republicans in the Cortes, 1873–74); based on Latin *in-* 'not' + *transigere* 'come to an understanding.'

in·tran·si·tive /inˈtransitiv, -zi-/ ▶ adj. (of a verb or a sense or use of a verb) not taking a direct object, e.g., *look* in *look at the sky*. The opposite of TRANSITIVE.
▶ n. an intransitive verb.
– DERIVATIVES **in·tran·si·tive·ly** adv., **in·tran·si·tiv·i·ty** /-ˌtransiˈtivitē, -zi-/ n.
– ORIGIN early 17th cent.: from late Latin *intransitivus* 'not passing over,' from *in-* 'not' + *transitivus* (see TRANSITIVE).

in·tra·pre·neur /ˌintrəprəˈnər, -ˈno͝or/ ▶ n. a manager within a company who promotes innovative product development and marketing.
– DERIVATIVES **in·tra·pre·neu·ri·al** /-ēəl/ adj.
– ORIGIN 1970s (originally US): from INTRA- 'within' + a shortened form of ENTREPRENEUR.

in·tra·spe·cif·ic /ˌintrəspəˈsifik/ ▶ adj. Biology produced, occurring, or existing within a species or between individuals of a single species: *intraspecific competition.*

in·tra·the·cal /ˌintrəˈTHēkəl/ ▶ adj. Medicine occurring within or administered into the spinal theca: *intrathecal injection.*
– DERIVATIVES **in·tra·the·cal·ly** adv.

in·tra·u·ter·ine /ˌintrəˈyo͞otərin, -rīn/ ▶ adj. within the uterus.

in·tra·u·ter·ine de·vice (abbr.: **IUD**) ▶ n. a contraceptive device fitted inside the uterus and physically preventing the implantation of fertilized ova.

in·tra·vas·cu·lar /ˌintrəˈvaskyələr/ ▶ adj. Medicine & Biology situated or occurring within a vessel or vessels of an animal or plant, esp. within a blood vessel or blood vascular system.
– DERIVATIVES **in·tra·vas·cu·lar·ly** adv.

in·tra·ve·nous /ˌintrəˈvēnəs/ (abbr.: **IV**) ▶ adj. existing or taking place within, or administered into, a vein or veins: *an intravenous drip.*
– DERIVATIVES **in·tra·ve·nous·ly** adv.

in·tra·zon·al /ˌintrəˈzōnl/ ▶ adj. Soil Science (of a soil) having a well-developed structure different from that expected for its climatic and vegetational zone owing to the overriding influence of relief, parent material, or some other local factor.

in·trench ▶ v. variant spelling of ENTRENCH.

in·trep·id /inˈtrepid/ ▶ adj. fearless; adventurous (often used for rhetorical or humorous effect): *our intrepid reporter.*
– DERIVATIVES **in·tre·pid·i·ty** /ˌintrəˈpiditē/ n., **in·trep·id·ly** adv., **in·trep·id·ness** n.
– ORIGIN late 17th cent.: from French *intrépide* or Latin *intrepidus*, from *in-* 'not' + *trepidus* 'alarmed.'

in·tri·ca·cy /ˈintrikəsē/ ▶ n. (pl. **intricacies**) the quality of being intricate: *the exquisite intricacy of Indian silverwork.* ■ (**intricacies**) details, esp. of an involved or perplexing subject: *the intricacies of economic policymaking.*

in·tri·cate /ˈintrikit/ ▶ adj. very complicated or detailed: *an intricate network of canals.*
– DERIVATIVES **in·tri·cate·ly** adv.
– ORIGIN late Middle English: from Latin *intricat-* 'entangled,' from the verb *intricare*, from *in-* 'into' + *tricae* 'tricks, perplexities.'

in·tri·gant /ˈintriˌgənt, ANtrēˈgäN/ (also **intriguant**) ▶ n. a person who makes secret plans to do something illicit or detrimental to someone else.
– ORIGIN late 18th cent.: variant of French *intriguant*, from *intriguer* 'to intrigue.'

in·tri·gante /ˈintriˌgənt, ANtrēˈgänt/ ▶ n. a female intrigant.
– ORIGIN early 19th cent.: variant of French *intriguante*, from *intriguer* 'to intrigue.'

in·trigue ▶ v. /inˈtrēg/ (**intrigues**, **intriguing**, **intrigued**) **1** [with obj.] arouse the curiosity or interest of; fascinate: *I was intrigued by your question.*
2 [no obj.] make secret plans to do something illicit or detrimental to someone: *the delegates were intriguing for their own gains.*
▶ n. /ˈinˌtrēg/ **1** the secret planning of something illicit or detrimental to someone: *the cabinet was*

a nest of intrigue | the intrigues of local government officials. ■ a secret love affair.
2 a mysterious or fascinating quality: *within the region's borders is a wealth of interest and intrigue.*
– DERIVATIVES **in·tri·guer** n.
– ORIGIN early 17th cent. (in the sense 'deceive, cheat'): from French *intrigue* 'plot,' *intriguer* 'to tangle, to plot,' via Italian from Latin *intricare* (see INTRICATE). Sense 1 of the verb, which was influenced by a later French sense 'to puzzle, make curious,' arose in the late 19th cent.

in·trigu·ing /in'trēgiNG/ ▶ adj. arousing one's curiosity or interest; fascinating: *an intriguing story.*
– DERIVATIVES **in·tri·guing·ly** adv. *the album is intriguingly titled "The Revenge of the Goldfish."*

in·trin·sic /in'trinzik, -sik/ ▶ adj. belonging naturally; essential: *access to the arts is intrinsic to a high quality of life.* ■ (of a muscle) contained wholly within the organ on which it acts.
– DERIVATIVES **in·trin·si·cal·ly** /-ik(ə)lē/ adv.
– ORIGIN late 15th cent. (in the general sense 'interior, inner'): from French *intrinsèque*, from late Latin *intrinsecus*, from the earlier adverb *intrinsecus* 'inwardly, inward.'

in·trin·sic fac·tor ▶ n. Biochemistry a substance secreted by the stomach that enables the body to absorb vitamin B_{12}. It is a glycoprotein.

in·tro /'intrō/ ▶ n. (pl. **intros**) informal an introduction.
– ORIGIN early 19th cent.: abbreviation.

intro. ▶ abbr. introduce or introduced or introducing or introduction or introductory.

i

intro- ▶ prefix into; inward: *introgression | introvert.*
– ORIGIN from Latin *intro* 'to the inside.'

in·tro·duce /,intrə'd(y)o͞os/ ▶ v. [with obj.] **1** bring (something, esp. a product, measure, or concept) into use or operation for the first time: *various new taxes were introduced | measures were introduced to help families with children.* ■ (**introduce something to**) bring a subject to the attention of (someone) for the first time: *the program is a bid to introduce opera to the masses.* ■ present (a new piece of legislation) for debate in a legislative assembly. ■ bring (a new plant, animal, or disease) to a place and establish it there: *a cold-resistant strain of sugar cane was* **introduced to** *Louisiana.*
2 make (someone) known by name to another in person, esp. formally: *I hope to introduce Jenny to them very soon.*
3 insert or bring into something: *a device that introduces chlorine into the pool automatically.*
4 occur at the start of; open: *a longer, more lyrical opening that introduces her first solo.* ■ (of a person) provide an opening explanation or announcement for (a television or radio program, book, etc.).
– DERIVATIVES **in·tro·duc·er** n.
– ORIGIN late Middle English (in the sense 'bring (a person) into a place or group'): from Latin *introducere*, from *intro-* 'to the inside' + *ducere* 'to lead.'

in·tro·duc·tion /,intrə'dəksHən/ ▶ n. **1** the action of introducing something: *issues arising from the introduction of new technology | the introduction of muskrats into central Europe.* ■ a thing newly brought into use or introduced to a place for the first time: *these grains are valuable introductions from Sweden.*
2 (often **introductions**) a formal presentation of one person to another, in which each is told the other's name: *he returned to his desk, leaving Michael to make the introductions | a letter of introduction.*
3 a thing preliminary to something else, esp. an explanatory section at the beginning of a book, report, or speech: *your talk will need an introduction that states clearly what you are talking about and why.* ■ a preliminary section in a piece of music, often thematically different from the main section. ■ a book or course of study intended to introduce a subject to a person: *it is a simple introduction to Euclidean geometry.* ■ [in sing.] a person's first experience of a subject or thing: *my introduction to drama was through an amateur dramatic society.*
– ORIGIN late Middle English: from Latin *introductio(n-)*, from the verb *introducere* (see INTRODUCE).

in·tro·duc·to·ry /,intrə'dəktərē/ ▶ adj. serving as an introduction to a subject or topic; basic or preliminary: *an introductory course in Russian.* ■ intended to persuade someone to purchase something for the first time: *we are making a special introductory offer of a reduced subscription.*
– ORIGIN late Middle English (as a noun denoting an introductory text): from late Latin *introductorius*, from Latin *introducere* (see INTRODUCE).

in·tro·gres·sion /,intrə'gresHən/ ▶ n. Biology the transfer of genetic information from one species to another as a result of hybridization between them and repeated backcrossing.
– DERIVATIVES **in·tro·gres·sive** /-'gresiv/ adj.
– ORIGIN mid 17th cent.: from Latin *introgredi* 'step in,' from *intro-* 'to the inside' + *gradi* 'proceed, walk,' on the pattern of *egression, ingression.*

in·tro·it /'in,trō-it, -,troit/ ▶ n. a psalm or antiphon sung or said while the priest approaches the altar for the Eucharist.
– ORIGIN late Middle English (denoting an entrance or the action of going in): via Old French from Latin *introitus*, from *introire* 'enter,' from *intro-* 'to the inside' + *ire* 'go.'

in·tro·jec·tion /,intrə'jeksHən/ ▶ n. Psychoanalysis the unconscious adoption of the ideas or attitudes of others.
– DERIVATIVES **in·tro·ject** /-'jekt/ v.
– ORIGIN mid 19th cent.: from INTRO- 'into,' on the pattern of *projection.*

in·tro·mis·sion /,intrə'misHən/ ▶ n. the action or process of inserting the penis into the vagina in sexual intercourse.

in·tro·mit·tent or·gan /,intrə'mitnt/ ▶ n. Zoology the male copulatory organ of an animal.
– ORIGIN mid 19th cent.: *intromittent* from Latin *intromittent-* 'introducing,' from the verb *intromittere*, from *intro-* 'to the inside' + *mittere* 'send.'

in·tron /'in,trän/ ▶ n. Biochemistry a segment of a DNA or RNA molecule that does not code for proteins and interrupts the sequence of genes. Compare with EXON.
– DERIVATIVES **in·tron·ic** /in'tränik/ adj.
– ORIGIN 1970s: from INTRA- 'within' + -GENIC + -ON.

in·trorse /'in,trôrs/ ▶ adj. Botany & Zoology turned inward. The opposite of EXTRORSE. ■ (of anthers) releasing their pollen toward the center of the flower.
– DERIVATIVES **in·trorse·ly** adv.
– ORIGIN mid 19th cent.: from Latin *introrsus*, from *introversus* 'turned inward.'

in·tro·scan /'intrō,skan/ ▶ n. a facility on some CD players that allows the first few seconds of each track to be played in turn in order to identify the required track.

in·tro·spect /,intrə'spekt/ ▶ v. [no obj.] examine one's own thoughts or feelings: *what they don't do is introspect much about the reasons for their plight.*
– ORIGIN late 17th cent.: from Latin *introspect-* 'looked into,' from the verb *introspicere*, or from *introspectare* 'keep looking into.'

in·tro·spec·tion /,intrə'speksHən/ ▶ n. the examination or observation of one's own mental and emotional processes: *quiet introspection can be extremely valuable.*

in·tro·spec·tive /,intrə'spektiv/ ▶ adj. characterized by or given to introspection: *he grew withdrawn and introspective.*
– DERIVATIVES **in·tro·spec·tive·ly** /-'spektiv-lē/ adv., **in·tro·spec·tive·ness** /-'spektivnis/ n.

in·tro·vert /'intrə,vərt/ ▶ n. a shy, reticent, and typically self-centered person. ■ Psychology a person predominantly concerned with their own thoughts and feelings rather than with external things. Compare with EXTROVERT.
▶ adj. another term for INTROVERTED.
– DERIVATIVES **in·tro·ver·sion** /-,vərZHən/ n., **in·tro·ver·sive** /-,vərsiv/ adj.
– ORIGIN mid 17th cent. (as a verb in the general sense 'turn one's thoughts inward [in spiritual contemplation]'): from modern Latin *introvertere*, from *intro-* 'to the inside' + *vertere* 'to turn.' Its use as a term in psychology dates from the early 20th cent.

in·tro·vert·ed /'intrə,vərtid/ ▶ adj. **1** of, denoting, or typical of an introvert. ■ (of a community, company, or other group) concerned principally with its own affairs; inward-looking or parochial.
2 Anatomy & Zoology (of an organ or other body part) turned or pushed inward on itself.

in·trude /in'tro͞od/ ▶ v. **1** [no obj.] put oneself deliberately into a place or situation where one is unwelcome or uninvited: *he had no right to* **intrude into** *their lives | she felt awkward at* **intruding on** *private grief.* ■ enter with disruptive or adverse effect: *politics quickly* **intrude into** *the booklet.* ■ [with obj.] introduce into a situation with disruptive or adverse effect: *to* **intrude** *political criteria* **into** *military decisions risks reducing efficiency.*
2 [with obj.] Geology (of igneous rock) be forced or thrust into (a preexisting formation): *the granite may have intruded these rock layers.* ■ (usu. **be intruded**) force or thrust (igneous rock) into a preexisting formation.
– ORIGIN mid 16th cent. (in the sense 'usurp an office or right'; originally as *entrude*): from Latin *intrudere*, from *in-* 'into' + *trudere* 'to thrust.'

in·trud·er /in'tro͞odər/ ▶ n. a person who intrudes, esp. into a building with criminal intent.

in·tru·sion /in'tro͞oZHən/ ▶ n. **1** the action of intruding: *he was furious about this intrusion into his private life | unacceptable intrusions of privacy.* ■ a thing that intrudes: *they oppose the excavations as an intrusion on their heritage.*
2 Geology the action or process of forcing a body of igneous rock between or through existing formations, without reaching the surface. ■ a body of igneous rock that has intruded the surrounding strata.
– ORIGIN late Middle English (in the sense 'invasion, usurpation'): from medieval Latin *intrusio(n-)*, from Latin *intrudere* 'thrust in' (see INTRUDE).

in·tru·sive /in'tro͞osiv/ ▶ adj. **1** causing disruption or annoyance through being unwelcome or uninvited: *that was an intrusive question | tourist attractions that are environmentally intrusive.*
2 Phonetics (of a sound) pronounced between words or syllables to facilitate pronunciation, such as an *r* in *saw a movie*, which occurs in the speech of some eastern New Englanders and metropolitan New Yorkers.
3 Geology of, relating to, or formed by intrusion.
– DERIVATIVES **in·tru·sive·ly** adv., **in·tru·sive·ness** n.

in·trust /in'trəst/ ▶ v. archaic spelling of ENTRUST.

in·tu·bate /'int(y)o͝o,bāt/ ▶ v. [with obj.] Medicine insert a tube into (a person or a body part, esp. the trachea for ventilation).
– DERIVATIVES **in·tu·ba·tion** /,int(y)o͝o'bāsHən/ n.
– ORIGIN late 19th cent.: from IN-² 'into' + Latin *tuba* 'tube' + -ATE³.

in·tu·it /in't(y)o͞o-it/ ▶ v. [with obj.] understand or work out by instinct: *I intuited his real identity.*
– DERIVATIVES **in·tu·it·a·ble** adj.
– ORIGIN late 18th cent. (in the sense 'instruct, teach'): from Latin *intuit-* 'contemplated,' from the verb *intueri*, from *in-* 'upon' + *tueri* 'to look.'

in·tu·i·tion /,int(y)o͞o'isHən/ ▶ n. the ability to understand something immediately, without the need for conscious reasoning: *we shall allow our intuition to guide us.* ■ a thing that one knows or considers likely from instinctive feeling rather than conscious reasoning: *your insights and intuitions as a native speaker are positively sought.*
– DERIVATIVES **in·tu·i·tion·al** /-'isHənl/ adj., **in·tu·i·tion·al·ly** /-'isHənl-ē/ adv.
– ORIGIN late Middle English (denoting spiritual insight or immediate spiritual communication): from late Latin *intuitio(n-)*, from Latin *intueri* 'consider' (see INTUIT).

in·tu·i·tion·ism /,int(y)o͞o'isHə,nizəm/ (also **intuitionalism** /-'isHənl,izəm/) ▶ n. Philosophy the theory that primary truths and principles (esp. those of ethics and metaphysics) are known directly by intuition. ■ the theory that mathematical knowledge is based on intuition and mental construction, rejecting certain modes of reasoning and the notion of independent mathematical objects.
– DERIVATIVES **in·tu·i·tion·ist** n. & adj.

in·tu·i·tive /in't(y)o͞oitiv/ ▶ adj. using or based on what one feels to be true even without conscious reasoning; instinctive: *I had an intuitive conviction that there was something unsound in him.* ■ (chiefly of computer software) easy to use and understand.
– DERIVATIVES **in·tu·i·tive·ly** adv., **in·tu·i·tive·ness** n.
– ORIGIN late 15th cent. (originally used of sight, in the sense 'accurate, unerring'): from medieval Latin *intuitivus*, from Latin *intueri* (see INTUIT).

in·tu·mesce /,int(y)o͝o'mes/ ▶ v. [no obj.] rare swell up.
– DERIVATIVES **in·tu·mes·cence** /-'mesəns/ n.
– ORIGIN late 18th cent.: from Latin *intumescere*, from *in-* 'into' + *tumescere* 'begin to swell' (from *tumere* 'swell').

in·tu·mes·cent /,int(y)o͝o'mesənt/ ▶ adj. (of a coating or sealant) swelling up when heated, thus protecting the material underneath or sealing a gap in the event of a fire: *intumescent fire-retardant paints.*

in·tus·sus·cep·tion /,intəsə'sepsHən/ ▶ n. **1** Medicine the inversion of one portion of the intestine within another.
2 Botany the growth of a cell wall by the deposition of cellulose: *the area of the surface increases uniformly by intussusception.*
– ORIGIN early 18th cent. (in the sense 'absorption'): from modern Latin *intussusceptio(n-)*, from Latin *intus* 'within' + *susceptio(n-)* (from *suscipere* 'take up').

in·twine /in'twīn/ ▶ v. archaic spelling of ENTWINE.

In·u·it /'in(y)o͞o-it/ ▶ n. **1** (pl. **same** or **Inuits**) a member of an indigenous people of northern Canada and parts of Greenland and Alaska.
2 the family of languages of this people, one of the three branches of the Eskimo-Aleut language family. It is also known, esp. to its speakers, as **Inuktitut**.

▶ **adj.** of or relating to the Inuit or their language.
– ORIGIN Inuit, plural of *inuk* 'person.'

USAGE The peoples inhabiting the regions from northwestern Canada to western Greenland speak **Inuit** languages (**Inuit** in Canada, **Greenlandic** in Greenland) and call themselves **Inuit** (not **Eskimo**). **Inuit** has official status in Canada, and is used in the US as a general synonym for **Eskimo**. This, however, is inaccurate because the **Inuit** are not among native Alaskans (who speak **Inupiaq**, or **Yupik**, which is also spoken in Siberia). Since neither **Inupiaq** nor **Yupik** is in common US usage, only **Eskimo** includes all of these peoples and their languages. See also usage at **ESKIMO**.

I·nuk·ti·tut /i'n(y)ŏŏkti,tŏŏt/ (also **Inuktituk** /-tŏŏk/) ▶ **n.** the Inuit language spoken in the central and eastern Canadian arctic.
– ORIGIN Inuit, literally 'the Inuk way,' used as the title of a periodical.

in·u·lin /'inyəlin/ ▶ **n.** Biochemistry a complex of sugar present in the roots of various plants and used medically to test kidney function. It is a polysaccharide based on fructose.
– ORIGIN early 19th cent.: from Latin *inula* (identified by medieval herbalists with elecampane) + **-IN**[1].

in·unc·tion /i'nəNG(k)SHən/ ▶ **n.** chiefly Medicine the rubbing of ointment or oil into the skin.
– ORIGIN late 15th cent.: from Latin *inunctio(n-)*, from *inunguere* 'smear on.'

in·un·date /'inən,dāt/ ▶ **v.** [with obj.] **1** overwhelm (someone) with things or people to be dealt with: *we've been* **inundated with** *complaints from listeners.* **2** flood: *the islands may be the first to be inundated as sea levels rise.*
– ORIGIN late 16th cent.: from Latin *inundat-* 'flooded,' from the verb *inundare*, from *in-* 'into, upon' + *undare* 'to flow' (from *unda* 'a wave').

in·un·da·tion /,inən'dāSHən/ ▶ **n. 1** an overwhelming abundance of people or things: *we see an inundation of campaign posters.* **2** flooding: *the annual inundation of the Nile | areas at risk of inundation.*

I·nu·pi·aq /i'n(y)ŏŏpē,ak/ (also **Inupiat** /-,at/, **Inupik** /i'n(y)ŏŏpik/) ▶ **n.** (pl. Inupiat) **1** a member of a group of the Eskimo people inhabiting northwestern Alaska. **2** the language of this people.
▶ **adj.** of or relating to this people or their language.
– ORIGIN Inupiaq, from *inuk* 'person' + *piaq* 'genuine.'

USAGE See usage at **INUIT**.

in·ure /i'n(y)ŏŏr/ (also **enure**) ▶ **v. 1** [with obj.] (usu. **be inured to**) accustom (someone) to something, esp. something unpleasant: *these children have been inured to violence.* **2** [no obj.] (**inure for/to**) Law come into operation; take effect: *a release given to one of two joint contractors inures to the benefit of both.*
– DERIVATIVES **in·ure·ment** n.
– ORIGIN late Middle English *inure, enure*, from an Anglo-Norman French phrase meaning 'in use or practice,' from *en* 'in' + Old French *euvre* 'work' (from Latin *opera*).

in·urn /in'ərn/ (also **enurn**) ▶ **v.** [with obj.] place or bury (something, esp. ashes after cremation) in an urn.
– DERIVATIVES **in·urn·ment** n.

in u·ter·o /in 'yŏŏtərō/ ▶ **adv. & adj.** in a woman's uterus; before birth: [as adv.] *this damage may occur in utero* | [as adj.] *the in utero development of the gastrointestinal tract.*
– ORIGIN Latin.

in·u·tile /in'yŏŏtl, -'yŏŏ,tīl/ ▶ **adj.** useless; pointless.
– DERIVATIVES **in·u·til·i·ty** /,inyŏŏ'tilitē/ n.
– ORIGIN late Middle English: from Old French, from Latin *inutilis*, from *in-* 'not' + *utilis* 'useful.'

inv. ▶ **abbr.** ■ invent or invented or invention or inventor. ■ inventory. ■ investment. ■ invoice.

in·vac·u·ate /in'vakyŏŏ,āt/ ▶ **v.** [with obj.] confine (people) to a space in an emergency: *these buildings can now invacuate tenants to safe havens within the building.*
– DERIVATIVES **in·vac·u·a·tion** /in,vakyŏŏ'āSHən/ n.
– ORIGIN on the pattern of *evacuate*.

in vac·u·o /in 'vakyə,wō/ ▶ **adv.** in a vacuum: *the hydrochloric acid was removed by evaporation in vacuo.* ■ away from or without the normal context or environment: *instead of dealing with individual aspects of lifestyle in vacuo, social factors are taken into account.*
– ORIGIN Latin.

in·vade /in'vād/ ▶ **v.** [with obj.] (of an armed force or its commander) enter (a country or region) so as to subjugate or occupy it: *it was all part of a grander French plan to invade Ireland* | [no obj.] *they would invade at dawn.* ■ enter (a place, situation, or sphere of activity) in large numbers, esp. with intrusive effect: *demonstrators invaded the presidential palace.* ■ (of a parasite or disease) spread into (an organism or bodily part). ■ (of a person or emotion) encroach or intrude on: *he felt his privacy was being invaded.*
– ORIGIN late Middle English (in the sense 'attack or assault [a person]'): from Latin *invadere*, from *in-* 'into' + *vadere* 'go.'

in·vad·er /in'vādər/ ▶ **n.** a person or group that invades a country, region, or other place: *it is a country that has repelled all invaders.*

in·vag·i·nate /in'vajə,nāt/ ▶ **v.** (**be invaginated**) chiefly Anatomy & Biology be turned inside out or folded back on itself to form a cavity or pouch.
– ORIGIN mid 17th cent.: back-formation from **INVAGINATION**.

in·vag·i·na·tion /in,vajə'nāSHən/ ▶ **n.** chiefly Anatomy & Biology the action or process of being turned inside out or folded back on itself to form a cavity or pouch. ■ a cavity or pouch so formed.
– ORIGIN mid 17th cent.: from modern Latin *invaginatio(n-)*, based on **IN-**[2] 'into' + Latin *vagina* 'sheath.'

in·va·lid[1] /'invəlid/ ▶ **n.** a person made weak or disabled by illness or injury: [as modifier] *an invalid husband.*
▶ **v.** (**invalids, invaliding, invalided**) [with obj.] remove (someone) from active service in the armed forces because of injury or illness: *he was badly wounded and* **invalided out of** *the infantry.* ■ disable (someone) by injury or illness.
– DERIVATIVES **in·va·lid·ism** /-,izəm/ n.
– ORIGIN mid 17th cent. (as an adjective in the sense 'infirm or disabled'): a special sense of **INVALID**[2], with a change of pronunciation.

in·val·id[2] /in'valid/ ▶ **adj.** not valid, in particular: ■ (esp. of an official document or procedure) not legally recognized and therefore void because contravening a regulation or law: *the vote was declared invalid due to a technicality.* ■ (esp. of an argument, statement, or theory) not true because based on erroneous information or unsound reasoning: *a comparison is invalid if we are not comparing like with like.* ■ (of computer instructions, data, etc.) not conforming to the correct format or specifications.
– DERIVATIVES **in·val·id·ly** adv.
– ORIGIN mid 16th cent. (earlier than *valid*): from Latin *invalidus*, from *in-* 'not' + *validus* 'strong' (see **VALID**).

in·val·i·date /in'vali,dāt/ ▶ **v.** [with obj.] **1** make (an argument, statement, or theory) unsound or erroneous. **2** deprive (an official document or procedure) of legal efficacy because of contravention of a regulation or law: *a technical flaw in her papers invalidated her nomination.*
– DERIVATIVES **in·val·i·da·tion** /-,vali'dāSHən/ n., **in·val·i·da·tor** /-,dātər/ n.
– ORIGIN mid 17th cent.: from medieval Latin *invalidat-* 'annulled,' from the verb *invalidare* (based on Latin *validus* 'strong').

in·va·lid·i·ty /,invə'liditē/ ▶ **n. 1** the fact of not being valid: *the invalidity of their independence declaration.* **2** chiefly Brit. the condition of being an invalid.

in·val·u·a·ble /in'valyŏŏəbəl/ ▶ **adj.** extremely useful; indispensable: *an invaluable source of information.*
– DERIVATIVES **in·val·u·a·ble·ness** n., **in·val·u·a·bly** /-blē/ adv.

In·var /'in,vär/ ▶ **n.** trademark an alloy of iron and nickel with a negligible coefficient of expansion, used in the making of clocks and scientific instruments.
– ORIGIN early 20th cent.: abbreviation of **INVARIABLE**.

in·var·i·a·ble /in've(ə)rēəbəl/ ▶ **adj.** never changing: *disillusion was the almost invariable result.* ■ (of a noun in an inflected language) having the same form in both the singular and the plural, e.g., *sheep*. ■ Mathematics (of a quantity) constant.
– DERIVATIVES **in·var·i·a·bil·i·ty** /-,ve(ə)rēə'bilitē/ n., **in·var·i·a·ble·ness** n.
– ORIGIN late Middle English: from French, or from late Latin *invariabilis*, from *in-* 'not' + *variabilis* (see **VARIABLE**).

in·var·i·a·bly /in've(ə)rēəblē/ ▶ **adv.** in every case or on every occasion; always: *the meals here are invariably big and hearty.*

in·var·i·ant /in've(ə)rēənt/ ▶ **adj.** never changing: *the pattern of cell divisions was found to be invariant.*
▶ **n.** Mathematics a function, quantity, or property that remains unchanged when a specified transformation is applied.
– DERIVATIVES **in·var·i·ance** n.

in·va·sion /in'vāZHən/ ▶ **n.** an instance of invading a country or region with an armed force: *the Allied invasion of Normandy | in 1546 England had to be defended from invasion.* ■ an incursion by a large number of people or things into a place or sphere of activity: *stadium guards are preparing for another invasion of fans.* ■ an unwelcome intrusion into another's domain: *random drug testing of employees is an unwarranted invasion of privacy.*
– ORIGIN late Middle English: from late Latin *invasio(n-)*, from the verb *invadere* (see **INVADE**).

in·va·sive /in'vāsiv/ ▶ **adj.** (esp. of plants or a disease) tending to spread prolifically and undesirably or harmfully. ■ (esp. of an action or sensation) tending to intrude on a person's thoughts or privacy: *the sound of the piano was invasive.* ■ (of medical procedures) involving the introduction of instruments or other objects into the body or body cavities: *minimally invasive surgery.*
– DERIVATIVES **in·va·sive·ly** adv., **in·va·sive·ness** n.
– ORIGIN late Middle English: from obsolete French *invasif, -ive* or medieval Latin *invasivus*, from Latin *invadere* (see **INVADE**).

in·vect·ed /in'vektid/ ▶ **adj.** [usu. postpositive] Heraldry having convex semicircular projections along the edge. Compare with **ENGRAILED**.

in·vec·tive /in'vektiv/ ▶ **n.** insulting, abusive, or highly critical language: *he let out a stream of invective.*
– ORIGIN late Middle English (originally as an adjective meaning 'reviling, abusive'): from Old French *invectif, -ive*, from late Latin *invectivus* 'attacking,' from *invehere* (see **INVEIGH**). The noun is from late Latin *invectiva (oratio)* 'abusive or censorious (language).'

in·veigh /in'vā/ ▶ **v.** [no obj.] (**inveigh against**) speak or write about (something) with great hostility: *nationalists inveighed against those who worked with the British.*
– ORIGIN late 15th cent. (in the sense 'carry in, introduce'; formerly also as *enveigh*): from Latin *invehere* 'carry in,' *invehi* 'be carried into, assail,' from *in-* 'into' + *vehere* 'carry.'

in·vei·gle /in'vāgəl/ ▶ **v.** [with obj.] persuade (someone) to do something by means of deception or flattery: *we cannot inveigle him into putting pen to paper.* ■ (**inveigle oneself** or **one's way into**) gain entrance to (a place) by using such methods.
– DERIVATIVES **in·vei·gle·ment** n.
– ORIGIN late 15th cent. (in the sense 'beguile, deceive'; formerly also as *enveigle*): from Anglo-Norman French *envegler*, alteration of Old French *aveugler* 'to blind,' from *aveugle* 'blind.'

in·vent /in'vent/ ▶ **v.** [with obj.] create or design (something that has not existed before); be the originator of: *he invented an improved form of the steam engine.* ■ make up (an idea, name, story, etc.), esp. so as to deceive: *I did not have to invent any tales about my past.*
– ORIGIN late 15th cent. (in the sense 'find out, discover'): from Latin *invent-* 'contrived, discovered,' from the verb *invenire*, from *in-* 'into' + *venire* 'come.'

in·ven·tion /in'venSHən/ ▶ **n.** the action of inventing something, typically a process or device: *the invention of printing in the 15th century.* ■ something, typically a process or device, that has been invented: *medieval inventions included spectacles for reading and the spinning wheel.* ■ creative ability: *his powers of invention were rather limited.* ■ something fabricated or made up: *you know my story is an invention.* ■ used as a title for a short piece of music: *Bach's two-part Inventions.*
– ORIGIN Middle English (in the sense 'finding out, discovery'): from Latin *inventio(n-)*, from *invenire* 'discover' (see **INVENT**).

in·ven·tive /in'ventiv/ ▶ **adj.** (of a person) having the ability to create or design new things or to think originally: *she is the most inventive painter around.* ■ (of a product, process, action, etc.) showing creativity or original thought: *methods of communication during the war were diverse and inventive.*
– DERIVATIVES **in·ven·tive·ly** adv.
– ORIGIN late Middle English: from French *inventif, -ive* or medieval Latin *inventivus*, from Latin *invenire* 'discover' (see **INVENT**).

in·ven·tive·ness /in'ventivnis/ ▶ **n.** the quality of being inventive; creativity: *the inventiveness of the staging.*

PRONUNCIATION KEY ə *ago, up*; ər *over, fur*; a *hat*; ā *ate*; ä *car*; e *let*; ē *see*; i *fit*; ī *by*; NG *sing*; ō *go*; ô *law, for*; oi *toy*; ŏŏ *good*; ōō *goo*; ou *out*; TH *thin*; TH *then*; ZH *vision*

in·ven·tor /inˈventər/ ▶ **n.** a person who invented a particular process or device or who invents things as an occupation.

in·ven·to·ry /ˈinvənˌtôrē/ ▶ **n.** (pl. **inventories**) a complete list of items such as property, goods in stock, or the contents of a building. ■ a quantity of goods held in stock: *in our warehouse you'll find a large inventory of new and used bicycles.* ■ (in accounting) the entire stock of a business, including materials, components, work in progress, and finished products.
▶ **v.** (**inventories, inventoried**) [with obj.] make a complete list of. ■ enter in a list: *about forty possible sites were inventoried.*
– ORIGIN late Middle English: from medieval Latin *inventorium*, alteration of late Latin *inventarium*, literally 'a list of what is found,' from Latin *invenire* 'come upon.'

in·ve·rac·i·ty /ˌinvəˈrasitē/ ▶ **n.** (pl. **inveracities**) a lie. ■ untruthfulness.

In·ver·ness¹ /ˌinvərˈnes/ a city in Scotland, at the mouth of the Ness River; pop. 41,200 (est. 2009).

In·ver·ness² ▶ **n.** a sleeveless cloak with a removable cape.

Inverness[2]

in·verse /ˈinvərs, inˈvərs/ ▶ **adj.** [attrib.] opposite or contrary in position, direction, order, or effect: *the well-observed inverse relationship between disability and social contact.* ■ chiefly Mathematics produced from or related to something else by a process of inversion.
▶ **n.** [usu. in sing.] something that is the opposite or reverse of something else: *his approach is the inverse of most research.* ■ Mathematics a reciprocal quantity, mathematical expression, geometric figure, etc., that is the result of inversion. ■ Mathematics an element that, when combined with a given element in an operation, produces the identity element for that operation.
– DERIVATIVES **in·verse·ly adv.**
– ORIGIN late Middle English: from Latin *inversus*, past participle of *invertere* (see INVERT).

in·verse pro·por·tion (also **inverse ratio**) ▶ **n.** a relation between two quantities such that one increases in proportion as the other decreases.

in·verse square law ▶ **n.** Physics a law stating that the intensity of an effect such as illumination or gravitational force changes in inverse proportion to the square of the distance from the source.

in·ver·sion /inˈvərZHən/ ▶ **n. 1** the action of inverting something or the state of being inverted: *the inversion of the normal domestic arrangement.* ■ reversal of the normal order of words, typically for rhetorical effect but also found in the regular formation of questions in English. ■ Music the process of inverting an interval, chord, or phrase. ■ Music an inverted interval, chord, or phrase. ■ Physics (also **population inversion**) a transposition in the relative numbers of atoms, molecules, etc., occupying particular energy levels. ■ Chemistry a reaction causing a change from one optically active configuration to the opposite configuration, esp. the hydrolysis of dextrose to give a levorotatory solution of fructose and glucose. ■ Physics the conversion of direct current into alternating current.
2 (also **temperature inversion** or **thermal inversion**) a reversal of the normal decrease of air temperature with altitude, or of water temperature with depth. ■ (also **inversion layer**) a layer of the atmosphere in which temperature increases with height.
3 Mathematics the process of finding a quantity, function, etc., from a given one such that the product of the two under a particular operation is the identity. ■ the interchanging of numerator and denominator of a fraction, or antecedent and consequent of a ratio. ■ the process of finding the expression that gives a given expression under a given transformation. ■ Geometry a transformation in which each point of a given figure is replaced by another point on the same straight line from a fixed point, esp. in such a way that the product of the distances of the two points from the center of inversion is constant.
4 (also **sexual inversion**) Psychology, dated the adoption of behavior typical of the opposite sex; homosexuality.
– DERIVATIVES **in·ver·sive** /-ˈvərsiv/ **adj.**
– ORIGIN mid 16th cent. (as a term in rhetoric, denoting the turning of an argument against the person who put it forward): from Latin *inversio(n-)*, from the verb *invertere* (see INVERT).

in·vert ▶ **v.** /inˈvərt/ [with obj.] put upside down or in the opposite position, order, or arrangement: *invert the mousse onto a serving plate.* ■ Music modify (a phrase) by reversing the direction of pitch changes. ■ Music alter (an interval or triad) by changing the relative position of the notes in it. ■ chiefly Mathematics subject to inversion; transform into its inverse.
▶ **n.** /ˈinvərt/ **1** an arch constructed in an upside-down position to provide lateral support, e.g., in a tunnel. ■ the concave lower surface of a sewer or drain.
2 Psychology, dated a person showing sexual inversion; a homosexual.
3 Philately a postage stamp printed with an error such that part of its design is upside down.
– DERIVATIVES **in·vert·i·bil·i·ty** /inˌvərtəˈbilitē/ **n.**, **in·vert·i·ble adj.**
– ORIGIN mid 16th cent. (in the sense 'turn back to front'): from Latin *invertere*, literally 'turn inside out,' from *in-* 'into' + *vertere* 'to turn.'

in·vert·ase /inˈvərtās, ˈinvərˌtās, -ˌtāz/ ▶ **n.** Biochemistry an enzyme produced by yeast that catalyzes the hydrolysis of sucrose, forming invert sugar. Also called SUCRASE.

in·ver·te·brate /inˈvərtəbrit, -ˌbrāt/ ▶ **n.** an animal lacking a backbone, such as an arthropod, mollusk, annelid, coelenterate, etc. The invertebrates constitute an artificial division of the animal kingdom, comprising 95 percent of animal species and about 30 different phyla. Compare with VERTEBRATE.
▶ **adj.** of, relating to, or belonging to this division of animals. ■ humorous irresolute; spineless: *so invertebrate is today's Congress regarding foreign policy responsibilities.*
– ORIGIN early 19th cent. (as a noun): from modern Latin *invertebrata* (plural) 'the invertebrates' (former taxonomic group), from French *invertébrés*, from *in-* 'without' + Latin *vertebra* (see VERTEBRA).

in·vert·ed com·ma ▶ **n.** chiefly Brit. another term for QUOTATION MARK.

in·vert·ed snob·ber·y ▶ **n.** derogatory the attitude of seeming to despise anything associated with wealth or social status, while at the same time elevating those things associated with lack of wealth and social position.
– DERIVATIVES **in·vert·ed snob n.**

in·vert·er /inˈvərtər/ ▶ **n. 1** an apparatus that converts direct current into alternating current.
2 Electronics a device that converts either of the two binary digits or signals into the other.

in·vert sug·ar ▶ **n.** a mixture of glucose and fructose obtained by the hydrolysis of sucrose.
– ORIGIN late 19th cent.: *invert* from *inverted*, because of the reversal of optical activity involved in its formation (see the chemical sense of INVERSION.).

in·vest /inˈvest/ ▶ **v. 1** [no obj.] expend money with the expectation of achieving a profit or material result by putting it into financial schemes, shares, or property, or by using it to develop a commercial venture: *getting workers to invest in private pension funds* | [with obj.] *the company is to invest $12 million in its new manufacturing site.* ■ [with obj.] devote (one's time, effort, or energy) to a particular undertaking with the expectation of a worthwhile result: *politicians who have invested so much time in the Constitution would be crestfallen.* ■ [no obj.] (**invest in**) informal buy (something) whose usefulness will repay the cost.
2 [with obj.] (**invest someone/something with**) provide or endow someone or something with (a particular quality or attribute): *the passage of time has invested the words with an unintended humor.* ■ endow someone with (a rank or office). ■ (**invest something in**) establish a right or power in.
3 [with obj.] archaic clothe or cover with a garment: *he stands before you invested in the full canonicals of his calling.*
4 [with obj.] archaic surround (a place) in order to besiege or blockade it: *Fort Pulaski was invested and captured.*
– DERIVATIVES **in·vest·a·ble adj.**, **in·vest·i·ble adj.**, **in·ves·tor** /-ˈvestər/ **n.**
– ORIGIN mid 16th cent. (in the senses 'clothe,' 'clothe with the insignia of a rank,' and 'endow with authority'): from French *investir* or Latin *investire*, from *in-* 'into, upon' + *vestire* 'clothe' (from *vestis* 'clothing'). Sense 1 (early 17th cent.) is influenced by Italian *investire*.

in·ves·ti·ga·ble /inˈvestigəbəl/ ▶ **adj.** open to investigation, inquiry, or research.
– ORIGIN late 16th cent.: from late Latin *investigabilis*, from *investigare* (see INVESTIGATE).

in·ves·ti·gate /inˈvestiˌgāt/ ▶ **v.** [with obj.] carry out a systematic or formal inquiry to discover and examine the facts of (an incident, allegation, etc.) so as to establish the truth: *police are investigating the alleged beating.* ■ carry out research or study into (a subject, typically one in a scientific or academic field) so as to discover facts or information: [with clause] *future studies will investigate whether long-term use of the drugs could prevent cancer.* ■ make inquiries as to the character, activities, or background of (someone): *everyone with a possible interest in your brother's death must be thoroughly investigated.* ■ [no obj.] make a check to find out something: *when you didn't turn up, I thought I'd better come back to investigate.*
– DERIVATIVES **in·ves·ti·ga·to·ry** /-gəˌtôrē/ **adj.**
– ORIGIN early 16th cent.: from Latin *investigat-* 'traced out,' from the verb *investigare*, from *in-* 'into' + *vestigare* 'track, trace out.'

in·ves·ti·ga·tion /inˌvestiˈgāSHən/ ▶ **n.** the action of investigating something or someone; formal or systematic examination or research: *he is under investigation for receiving illicit funds.* ■ a formal inquiry or systematic study: *an investigation has been launched into the potential impact of the oil spill.*
– DERIVATIVES **in·ves·ti·ga·tion·al** /-SHənl/ **adj.**
– ORIGIN late Middle English: from Latin *investigatio(n-)*, from the verb *investigare* (see INVESTIGATE).

in·ves·ti·ga·tive /inˈvestiˌgātiv/ (also **investigatory** /-gəˌtôrē/) ▶ **adj.** of or concerned with investigating something: *a special investigative committee to look into the strikers' demands.* ■ (of journalism or a journalist) inquiring intensively into and seeking to expose malpractice, the miscarriage of justice, or other controversial issues.

in·ves·ti·ga·tor /inˈvestiˌgātər/ ▶ **n.** a person who carries out a formal inquiry or investigation: *accident investigators are at the crash site.*

in·ves·ti·ture /inˈvestiCHər, -ˌCHo͝or/ ▶ **n.** the action of formally investing a person with honors or rank: *the investiture of bishops.* ■ a ceremony at which honors or rank are formally conferred on a particular person.
– ORIGIN late Middle English: from medieval Latin *investitura*, from *investire* (see INVEST).

in·vest·ment /inˈves(t)mənt/ ▶ **n. 1** the action or process of investing money for profit or material result: *a debate over private investment in road-building* | *a total investment of $50,000.* ■ a thing that is worth buying because it may be profitable or useful in the future: *a used car is rarely a good investment.* ■ an act of devoting time, effort, or energy to a particular undertaking with the expectation of a worthwhile result: *the time spent in attending a one-day seminar is an investment in our professional futures.*
2 archaic the surrounding of a place by a hostile force in order to besiege or blockade it.

in·vest·ment bank ▶ **n.** a bank that purchases large holdings of newly issued shares and resells them to investors.
– DERIVATIVES **in·vest·ment bank·er n.**, **in·vest·ment bank·ing n.**

in·vest·ment cast·ing ▶ **n.** technical a technique for making small, accurate castings in refractory alloys using a mold formed around a pattern of wax or similar material which is then removed by melting.

in·vest·ment grade ▶ **n.** a level of credit rating for stocks regarded as carrying a minimal risk to investors.

in·vest·ment trust ▶ **n.** a limited company whose business is the investment of shareholders' funds, the shares being traded like those of any other public company.

in·vet·er·ate /inˈvetərit/ ▶ **adj.** [attrib.] having a particular habit, activity, or interest that is long-established and unlikely to change: *he was an inveterate gambler.* ■ (of a feeling or habit) long-established and unlikely to change.
– DERIVATIVES **in·vet·er·a·cy** /-rəsē/ **n.**, **in·vet·er·ate·ly adv.**
– ORIGIN late Middle English (referring to disease, in the sense 'of long standing, chronic'): from Latin *inveteratus* 'made old,' past participle of *inveterare* (based on *vetus, veter-* 'old').

in·vi·a·ble /inˈvīəbəl/ ▶ **adj.** not viable.
– DERIVATIVES **in·vi·a·bil·i·ty n.**

in·vid·i·ous /inˈvidēəs/ ▶ **adj.** (of an action or situation) likely to arouse or incur resentment or anger in others: *she'd put herself in an invidious position.* ■ (of a comparison or distinction) unfairly discriminating; unjust: *it seems invidious to make special mention of one aspect of his work.*
– DERIVATIVES **in·vid·i·ous·ly adv.**, **in·vid·i·ous·ness n.**
– ORIGIN early 17th cent.: from Latin *invidiosus*, from *invidia* (see ENVY).

in·vig·i·late /inˈvijəˌlāt/ ▶ **v.** [no obj.] Brit. supervise candidates during an examination.

– DERIVATIVES **in·vig·i·la·tion** /-ˌvijəˈlāSHən/ **n.**, **in·vig·i·la·tor** /-ˌlātər/ **n.**
– ORIGIN mid 16th cent. (in the general sense 'watch over, keep watch'): from Latin *invigilat-* 'watched over,' from the verb *invigilare*, from *in-* 'upon, toward' + *vigilare* 'watch' (from *vigil* 'watchful').

in·vig·or·ate /inˈvigəˌrāt/ ▶ **v.** [with obj.] give strength or energy to: *the shower had invigorated her.*
– DERIVATIVES **in·vig·or·a·tion** **n.**, **in·vig·or·a·tor** /-ˌrātər/ **n.**
– ORIGIN mid 17th cent.: from medieval Latin *invigorat-* 'made strong,' from the verb *invigorare*, from *in-* 'toward' + Latin *vigorare* 'make strong' (from *vigor* 'vigor').

in·vig·or·at·ing /inˈvigəˌrātiNG/ ▶ **adj.** making one feel strong, healthy, and full of energy: *a brisk, invigorating walk.*
– DERIVATIVES **in·vig·or·at·ing·ly** **adv.**

in·vin·ci·ble /inˈvinsəbəl/ ▶ **adj.** too powerful to be defeated or overcome: *an invincible warrior.*
– DERIVATIVES **in·vin·ci·bil·i·ty** /-ˌvinsəˈbilitē/ **n.**, **in·vin·ci·bly** /-blē/ **adv.**
– ORIGIN late Middle English (earlier than *vincible*): via Old French from Latin *invincibilis*, from *in-* 'not' + *vincibilis* (see VINCIBLE).

in vi·no ve·ri·tas /in ˈvēnō ˈveriˌtäs, ˈvīnō ˈveriˌtas/ ▶ **exclam.** under the influence of alcohol, a person tells the truth.
– ORIGIN Latin, literally 'truth in wine.'

in·vi·o·la·ble /inˈvīələbəl/ ▶ **adj.** never to be broken, infringed, or dishonored: *an inviolable rule of chastity | the Polish–German border was inviolable.*
– DERIVATIVES **in·vi·o·la·bil·i·ty** /-ˌvīələˈbilitē/ **n.**, **in·vi·o·la·bly** /-blē/ **adv.**
– ORIGIN late Middle English: from French, or from Latin *inviolabilis*, from *in-* 'not' + *violabilis* 'able to be violated' (from the verb *violare*).

in·vi·o·late /inˈvīəlit/ ▶ **adj.** free or safe from injury or violation: *an international memorial which must remain inviolate.*
– DERIVATIVES **in·vi·o·la·cy** /-ləsē/ **n.**, **in·vi·o·late·ly** **adv.**
– ORIGIN late Middle English: from Latin *inviolatus*, from *in-* 'not' + *violare* 'violate.'

in·vis·cid /inˈvisid/ ▶ **adj.** Physics having no or negligible viscosity.

in·vis·i·ble /inˈvizəbəl/ ▶ **adj.** unable to be seen; not visible to the eye: *this invisible gas is present to some extent in every home.* ■ concealed from sight; hidden: *he lounged in a doorway, invisible in the dark.* ■ treated as if unable to be seen; ignored or not taken into consideration: *before 1971, women artists were pretty well invisible.* ■ Economics relating to or denoting earnings that a country makes from the sale of services or other items not constituting tangible commodities: *tourism is the most important of our invisible exports.*
▶ **n.** (**invisibles**) invisible exports and imports.
– DERIVATIVES **in·vis·i·bil·i·ty** /-ˌvizəˈbilitē/ **n.**, **in·vis·i·bly** /-blē/ **adv.**
– ORIGIN Middle English: from Old French, or from Latin *invisibilis*, from *in-* 'not' + *visibilis* (see VISIBLE).

in·vis·i·ble ink ▶ **n.** a type of ink used to produce writing that cannot be seen until the paper is heated or otherwise treated.

in·vi·ta·tion /ˌinviˈtāSHən/ ▶ **n.** a written or verbal request inviting someone to go somewhere or to do something: *a wedding invitation.* ■ the action of inviting someone to go somewhere or to do something: *a club with membership by invitation only | an herb garden where guests can go only at the invitation of the chef.* ■ [in sing.] a situation or action that tempts someone to do something or makes a particular outcome likely: *tactics like those of the colonel would have been an invitation to disaster.*
– ORIGIN late Middle English: from French, or from Latin *invitatio(n-)*, from *invitare* (see INVITE).

in·vi·ta·tion·al /ˌinviˈtāSHənl/ ▶ **adj.** (esp. of a competition) open only to those invited.
▶ **n.** a competition of such a type.

in·vi·ta·tor·y /inˈvītəˌtôrē/ ▶ **adj.** containing or conveying an invitation. ■ (in the Christian Church) denoting a psalm or versicle acting as an invitation to worshipers, esp. Psalm 95.
– ORIGIN Middle English: from late Latin *invitatorius*, from Latin *invitare* (see INVITE).

in·vite ▶ **v.** /inˈvīt/ [with obj.] make a polite, formal, or friendly request to (someone) to go somewhere or to do something: *we were invited to a dinner at the embassy* | [with obj. and infinitive] *she invited Patrick to sit down.* ■ make a formal or polite request for (something, esp. an application for a job or opinions on a particular topic) from someone. ■ (of an action or situation) tend to elicit (a particular reaction or response) or to tempt (someone) to do something: *his use of the word did little but invite criticism.*
▶ **n.** /ˈinˌvīt/ informal an invitation.
– DERIVATIVES **in·vi·tee** /ˌinvīˈtē/ **n.**, **in·vit·er** /inˈvītər/ **n.**
– ORIGIN mid 16th cent.: from Old French *inviter*, or from Latin *invitare*.

in·vit·ing /inˈvītiNG/ ▶ **adj.** offering the promise of an attractive or enjoyable experience: *the sea down there looks so inviting.*
– DERIVATIVES **in·vit·ing·ly** **adv.**

in vi·tro /in ˈvēˌtrō/ ▶ **adj. & adv.** Biology (of processes or reactions) taking place in a test tube, culture dish, or elsewhere outside a living organism: [as adj.] *in vitro fertilization.* The opposite of IN VIVO.
– ORIGIN Latin, literally 'in glass.'

in vi·vo /in ˈvēvō/ ▶ **adv. & adj.** Biology (of processes) taking place in a living organism. The opposite of IN VITRO.
– ORIGIN Latin, 'in a living thing.'

in·vo·ca·tion /ˌinvəˈkāSHən/ ▶ **n.** the action of invoking something or someone for assistance or as an authority: *the invocation of new disciplines and methodologies.* ■ the summoning of a deity or the supernatural: *his invocation of the ancient mystical powers.* ■ an incantation used for this. ■ (in the Christian Church) a form of words such as "In the name of the Father" introducing a prayer, sermon, etc.
– DERIVATIVES **in·voc·a·to·ry** /inˈväkəˌtôrē/ **adj.**
– ORIGIN late Middle English: via Old French from Latin *invocatio(n-)*, from the verb *invocare* (see INVOKE).

in·voice /ˈinˌvois/ ▶ **n.** a list of goods sent or services provided, with a statement of the sum due for these; a bill.
▶ **v.** [with obj.] send an invoice to (someone). ■ send an invoice for (goods or services provided).
– ORIGIN mid 16th cent.: originally the plural of obsolete *invoy*, from obsolete French *envoy*, from *envoyer* 'send' (see ENVOY).

in·voke /inˈvōk/ ▶ **v.** [with obj.] cite or appeal to (someone or something) as an authority for an action or in support of an argument: *the antiquated defense of insanity is rarely invoked today.* ■ call on (a deity or spirit) in prayer, as a witness, or for inspiration. ■ call earnestly for: *she invoked his help against this attack.* ■ summon (a spirit) by charms or incantation. ■ give rise to; evoke: *how could she explain how the accident happened without invoking his wrath?* ■ Computing cause (a procedure) to be carried out.
– DERIVATIVES **in·vok·er** **n.**
– ORIGIN late 15th cent.: from French *invoquer*, from Latin *invocare*, from *in-* 'upon' + *vocare* 'to call.'

in·vol·a·tile /inˈvälətl/ ▶ **adj.** not volatile; unable to be vaporized.

in·vo·lu·cre /ˈinvəˌlo͝okər/ (also **involucrum** /-krəm/) ▶ **n.** Botany a whorl or rosette of bracts surrounding an inflorescence (esp. a capitulum) or at the base of an umbel.
– DERIVATIVES **in·vo·lu·cral** /ˌinvəˈlo͝okrəl/ **adj.**
– ORIGIN late 16th cent.: from French, or from Latin *involucrum*, from *involvere* 'roll in, envelop' (see INVOLVE).

in·vol·un·tar·y /inˈvälənˌterē/ ▶ **adj. 1** done without will or conscious control: *she gave an involuntary shudder.* ■ (esp. of muscles or nerves) concerned in bodily processes that are not under the control of the will.
2 done against someone's will; compulsory: *a policy of involuntary repatriation.*
– DERIVATIVES **in·vol·un·tar·i·ly** /inˌvälənˈte(ə)rəlē, -ˈvälənˌter-/ **adv.**, **in·vol·un·tar·i·ness** **n.**

in·vo·lute /ˈinvəˌlo͞ot/ ▶ **adj. 1** formal involved; intricate: *the art novel has grown increasingly involute.*
2 technical curled spirally. ■ Zoology (of a shell) having the whorls wound closely around the axis. ■ Botany (of a leaf or the cap of a fungus) rolled inward at the edges.
▶ **n.** Geometry the locus of a point considered as the end of a taut string being unwound from a given curve in the plane of that curve. Compare with EVOLUTE.
▶ **v.** [no obj.] become involute; curl up.
– ORIGIN mid 17th cent.: from Latin *involutus*, past participle of *involvere* (see INVOLVE).

in·vo·lut·ed /ˈinvəˌlo͞otid/ ▶ **adj.** complicated; abstruse: *his involuted prose.*

in·vo·lu·tion /ˌinvəˈlo͞oSHən/ ▶ **n. 1** Physiology the shrinkage of an organ in old age or when inactive, e.g., of the uterus after childbirth.
2 Mathematics a function, transformation, or operator that is equal to its inverse, i.e., which gives the identity when applied to itself.
3 formal the process of involving or complicating, or the state of being involved or complicated: *periods of artistic involution.*
– DERIVATIVES **in·vo·lu·tion·al** /-SHənl/ **adj.**, **in·vo·lu·tion·ar·y** /-ˌnerē/ **adj.**
– ORIGIN late Middle English (in the sense '[part] curling inward'): from Latin *involutio(n-)*, from *involvere* (see INVOLVE).

in·volve /inˈvälv/ ▶ **v.** [with obj.] (of a situation or event) include (something) as a necessary part or result: *his transfer to another school would involve a lengthy assessment procedure.* ■ cause (a person or group) to experience or participate in an activity or situation: *what kind of organizations will be* **involved** *in setting up these projects?*
– ORIGIN late Middle English (in the senses 'enfold' and 'entangle'; formerly also as *envolve*): from Latin *involvere*, from *in-* 'into' + *volvere* 'to roll.'

in·volved /inˈvälvd/ ▶ **adj. 1** [predic.] connected or concerned with someone or something, typically on an emotional or personal level: *Angela told me that she was* **involved with** *someone else.*
2 difficult to comprehend; complicated: *a long, involved conversation.*

in·volve·ment /inˈvälvmənt/ ▶ **n.** the fact or condition of being involved with or participating in something: *he was imprisoned for his involvement in a plot to overthrow the government.* ■ emotional or personal association with someone.

in·vul·ner·a·ble /inˈvəlnərəbəl/ ▶ **adj.** impossible to harm or damage.
– DERIVATIVES **in·vul·ner·a·bil·i·ty** /-ˌvəlnərəˈbilitē/ **n.**, **in·vul·ner·a·bly** /-blē/ **adv.**
– ORIGIN late 16th cent. (earlier than *vulnerable*): from Latin *invulnerabilis*, from *in-* 'not' + *vulnerabilis* (see VULNERABLE).

-in-wait·ing ▶ **comb. form 1** awaiting a turn, confirmation of a process, etc.: *a political administration-in-waiting.* ■ about to happen: *an explosion-in-waiting.*
2 denoting a position as attendant to a royal personage: *lady-in-waiting.*

in·wale /ˈinˌwāl/ ▶ **n.** a longitudinal structural piece on the inside of a boat; an internal gunwale.

in·ward /ˈinwərd/ ▶ **adj.** [attrib.] directed or proceeding toward the inside; coming in from outside: *the inward rush of air | a graceful inward movement of her wrist.* ■ existing within the mind, soul, or spirit, and often not expressed: *she felt an inward sense of release.*
▶ **adv.** (also **inwards**) toward the inside: *the door began to swing inward.* ■ into or toward the mind, spirit, or soul: *people must look inward to gain insight into their own stress.*
– ORIGIN Old English *inweard*, *inneweard*, *innanweard* (see IN, -WARD).

in·ward-look·ing ▶ **adj.** not interested in or taking account of other people or groups: *an isolated and inward-looking community.*

in·ward·ly /ˈinwərdlē/ ▶ **adv.** (of a particular thought, feeling, or action) registered or existing in the mind but not expressed to others: *inwardly seething, he did as he was told.*
– ORIGIN Old English *inweardlīce* (see INWARD, -LY[2]).

in·ward·ness /ˈinwərdnəs/ ▶ **n.** preoccupation with one's inner self; concern with spiritual or philosophical matters rather than externalities.

in·wards /ˈinwərdz/ ▶ **adv.** variant of INWARD.

in·wrought /inˈrôt/ ▶ **adj.** literary (of a fabric or garment) intricately embroidered with a particular pattern or decoration: *robes inwrought with gold.*

In·yo Moun·tains /ˈinyō/ a range in east central California that includes Mount Whitney at 14,495 feet (4,418 m), the highest point in the US outside Alaska.

in-your-face ▶ **adj.** informal blatantly aggressive or provocative; impossible to ignore or avoid: *hard-boiled, in-your-face action thrillers.*
– ORIGIN 1970s: from *in your face*, used as a derisive insult.

I·o /ˈī-ō, ˈē-ō/ **1** Greek Mythology a priestess of Hera who was loved by Zeus. Trying to protect her from the jealousy of Hera, Zeus turned Io into a heifer. Hera sent a gadfly to torture the heifer, which then fled across the world and finally reached Egypt, where Zeus turned her back into human form.
2 Astronomy one of the Galilean moons of Jupiter, the fifth closest satellite to the planet. It is actively volcanic, colored red and yellow with sulfur compounds, and has a diameter of 2,526 miles (3,630 km).

I/O ▶ **abbr.** Electronics input-output.

IOC ▶ **abbr.** International Olympic Committee.

iod- ▶ **comb. form** variant spelling of IODO- shortened before a vowel (as in *iodic*).

i

i·od·ic ac·id /īˈädik/ ▶ **n.** Chemistry a crystalline acid with strong oxidizing properties, made by oxidation of iodine. ● Chem. formula: HIO_3.
– DERIVATIVES **i·o·date** /ˈīəˌdāt/ **n.**

i·o·dide /ˈīəˌdīd/ ▶ **n.** Chemistry a compound of iodine with another element or group, esp. a salt of the anion I^-.

i·o·din·ate /ˈīədnˌāt/ ▶ **v.** [with obj.] (usu. as adj. **iodinated**) Chemistry introduce iodine into (a compound).
– DERIVATIVES **i·o·din·a·tion** /ˌīədnˈāsHən/ **n.**

i·o·dine /ˈīəˌdīn/ ▶ **n.** the chemical element of atomic number 53, a nonmetallic element forming black crystals and a violet vapor. (Symbol: **I**) ■ a solution of this in alcohol, used as a mild antiseptic.

> A member of the halogen group, iodine occurs chiefly as salts in seawater and brines. As a constituent of thyroid hormones, it is required in small amounts in the body, and deficiency can lead to goiter.

– ORIGIN early 19th cent.: from French *iode* (from Greek *iōdēs* 'violet-colored,' from *ion* 'violet' + *-eidēs* 'like') + -INE[4].

i·o·dism /ˈīəˌdizəm/ ▶ **n.** Medicine iodine poisoning, causing thirst, diarrhea, weakness, and convulsions.

i·o·dize /ˈīəˌdīz/ ▶ **v.** [with obj.] (usu. as adj. **iodized**) treat or impregnate with iodine: *iodized salt*.
– DERIVATIVES **i·o·di·za·tion** /ˌīədiˈzāsHən/ **n.**

iodo- (usu. **iod-** before a vowel) ▶ **comb. form** Chemistry representing IODINE.

i

i·o·do·form /īˈōdəˌfôrm, īˈädə-/ ▶ **n.** a volatile pale yellow sweet-smelling crystalline organic compound of iodine, with antiseptic properties. ● Alternative name: **triiodomethane**; chem. formula: CHI_3.
– ORIGIN mid 19th cent.: from IODINE, on the pattern of *chloroform*.

i·o·dom·e·try /īəˈdämitrē/ ▶ **n.** Chemistry the quantitative analysis of a solution of an oxidizing agent by adding an iodide that reacts to form iodine, which is then titrated.
– DERIVATIVES **i·o·do·met·ric** /ˌī-ōdəˈmetrik/ **adj.**

i·o·do·phor /īˈōdəˌfôr/ ▶ **n.** any of a group of disinfectants containing iodine in combination with a surfactant.

IOM ▶ **abbr.** Isle of Man.

I·o moth ▶ **n.** a large, mainly yellow North American moth of the silkworm moth family, with prominent eyespots on the hind wings. ● *Automeris io*, family Saturniidae.
– ORIGIN late 19th cent.: named after the Greek priestess **Io**.

Io moth

i·on /ˈīən, ˈīˌän/ ▶ **n.** an atom or molecule with a net electric charge due to the loss or gain of one or more electrons. See also CATION, ANION.
– ORIGIN mid 19th cent.: from Greek, neuter present participle of *ienai* 'go.'

Ion. ▶ **abbr.** Ionic.

-ion ▶ **suffix** forming nouns denoting verbal action: *communion*. ■ denoting an instance of this: *a rebellion*. ■ denoting a resulting state or product: *oblivion* | *opinion*.
– ORIGIN via French from Latin *-ion-*.

I·o·na /īˈōnə/ a small island in the Inner Hebrides, off the western coast of Mull. It is the site of a monastery founded by St. Columba in about 563.

I·o·nes·co /yôˈneskō, ēəˈneskō/, Eugène (1912–94), French playwright; born in Romania; a leading exponent of the theater of the absurd. Notable plays: *The Bald Soprano* (1949), *Rhinoceros* (1959), and *Exit the King* (1962).

i·on ex·change ▶ **n.** the exchange of ions of the same charge between an insoluble solid and a solution in contact with it, used in water-softening and other purification and separation processes.

i·on ex·chang·er ▶ **n.** a solid used in ion exchange, typically a special cross-linked synthetic resin or a zeolite.

I·o·nia /īˈōnēə/ in classical times, the central part of the west coast of Asia Minor, which had long been inhabited by Hellenic people (the Ionians) and was again colonized by Greeks from the mainland from about the 8th century BC.

I·o·ni·an /īˈōnēən/ ▶ **n.** a member of an ancient Hellenic people inhabiting Attica, parts of western Asia Minor, and the Aegean islands in preclassical and classical times. They also colonized the islands that became known as the Ionian Islands. ■ a native or inhabitant of the Ionian Islands.
▶ **adj.** of or relating to the Ionians, Ionia, or the Ionian Islands.

I·o·ni·an Is·lands a chain of about 40 Greek islands off the western coast of mainland Greece, in the Ionian Sea.

I·o·ni·an mode ▶ **n.** Music the mode represented by the natural diatonic scale C–C (the major scale).

I·o·ni·an Sea the part of the Mediterranean Sea between western Greece and southern Italy, at the mouth of the Adriatic Sea.

I·on·ic /īˈänik/ ▶ **adj. 1** relating to or denoting a classical order of architecture characterized by a column with scroll shapes (volutes) on either side of the capital.
2 another term for IONIAN.
▶ **n. 1** the Ionic order of architecture.
2 the ancient Greek dialect used in Ionia.
– ORIGIN late 16th cent.: via Latin from Greek *Iōnikos*, from *Iōnia* (see IONIA).

i·on·ic /īˈänik/ ▶ **adj.** of, relating to, or using ions. ■ (of a chemical bond) formed by the electrostatic attraction of oppositely charged ions. Often contrasted with COVALENT.
– DERIVATIVES **i·on·i·cal·ly** /-ik(ə)lē/ **adv.**

i·on·ic strength ▶ **n.** Chemistry a quantity representing the strength of the electric field in a solution, equal to the sum of the molalities of each type of ion present multiplied by the square of their charges.

i·on·i·za·tion cham·ber /ˌīəniˈzāsHən/ ▶ **n.** an instrument for detecting ionizing radiation.

i·on·ize /ˈīəˌnīz/ ▶ **v.** [with obj.] (usu. **be ionized**) convert (an atom, molecule, or substance) into an ion or ions, typically by removing one or more electrons. ■ [no obj.] become converted into an ion or ions in this way.
– DERIVATIVES **i·on·iz·a·ble adj.**, **i·on·i·za·tion** /ˌīəniˈzāsHən/ **n.**

i·on·iz·er /ˈīəˌnīzər/ ▶ **n.** a device that produces ionization, esp. one used to improve the quality of the air in a room.

i·on·iz·ing ra·di·a·tion ▶ **n.** radiation consisting of particles, X-rays, or gamma rays with sufficient energy to cause ionization in the medium through which it passes.

i·on·o·mer /īˈänəmər/ ▶ **n.** any of a class of polymer materials consisting of thermoplastic resins stabilized by ionic cross-linkages, used to make dental cement and sealants.

i·on·o·pause /īˈänəˌpôz/ ▶ **n.** Astronomy the upper boundary of the ionosphere of a planet, comet, or other celestial object.

i·on·o·phore /īˈänəˌfôr/ ▶ **n.** Biochemistry a substance that is able to transport particular ions across a lipid membrane in a cell.

i·on·o·sphere /īˈänəˌsfi(ə)r/ ▶ **n.** the layer of the earth's atmosphere that contains a high concentration of ions and free electrons and is able to reflect radio waves. It lies above the mesosphere and extends from about 50 to 600 miles (80 to 1,000 km) above the earth's surface. ■ a similar region above the surface of another planet.
– DERIVATIVES **i·on·o·spher·ic** /īˌänəˈsfi(ə)rik, -ˈsfer-/ **adj.**

i·on·to·pho·re·sis /īˌäntəfəˈrēsis/ ▶ **n.** Medicine a technique of introducing ionic medicinal compounds into the body through the skin by applying a local electric current.
– DERIVATIVES **i·on·to·pho·ret·ic** /-ˈretik/ **adj.**, **i·on·to·pho·ret·i·cal·ly** /-ˈretik(ə)lē/ **adv.**
– ORIGIN early 20th cent.: from ION, on the pattern of *electrophoresis*.

IOOF ▶ **abbr.** Independent Order of Odd Fellows.

-ior ▶ **suffix** forming adjectives in the comparative degree: *anterior* | *junior* | *senior*.
– ORIGIN from Latin.

i·o·ta /īˈōtə/ ▶ **n. 1** the ninth letter of the Greek alphabet (Ι, ι), transliterated as 'i.' ■ (**Iota**) [followed by Latin genitive] Astronomy the ninth star in a constellation: *Iota Piscium*.
2 [in sing., usu. with negative] an extremely small amount: *nothing she said seemed to make an iota of difference*. [*iota* being the smallest letter of the Greek alphabet. Compare with JOT.]

IOU ▶ **n.** a signed document acknowledging a debt.
– ORIGIN late 18th cent.: representing the pronunciation of *I owe you*.

-ious ▶ **suffix** (forming adjectives) characterized by; full of: *cautious* | *vivacious*.
– ORIGIN from French *-ieux*, from Latin *-iosus*.

I·o·wa /ˈīəwə/ a state in the northern central US, on the western banks of the Mississippi River; pop. 3,002,555 (est. 2008); capital, Des Moines; statehood, Dec. 28, 1846 (29). It was acquired as part of the Louisiana Purchase in 1803.
– DERIVATIVES **I·o·wan adj. & n.**

I·o·wa Cit·y a city in eastern Iowa, south of Cedar Rapids; pop. 67,831 (est. 2008).

IP ▶ **abbr.** Computing Internet protocol, the method by which information is sent between any two Internet computers on the Internet.

IPA ▶ **abbr.** ■ India pale ale, a type of light-colored beer similar to bitter. [said to have been brewed originally for the British colonies.] ■ International Phonetic Alphabet.

IP ad·dress ▶ **n.** Computing a unique string of numbers separated by periods that identifies each computer using the Internet Protocol to communicate over a network.
– ORIGIN *IP*, abbreviation of INTERNET PROTOCOL.

ip·e·cac /ˈipikak/ (also **ipecacuanha** /ˌipiˌkak(y)ōōˈan(y)ə, ēˌpākə-/) ▶ **n. 1** the dried rhizome of a South American shrub, or a drug prepared from this, used as an emetic and expectorant.
2 the shrub of the bedstraw family that produces this rhizome, native to Brazil and cultivated elsewhere. ● *Cephaelis ipecacuanha*, family Rubiaceae.
■ used in names of other plants with similar uses, e.g., **American ipecac** (*Gillenia trifoliata*, family Rosaceae).
– ORIGIN early 17th cent.: from Portuguese, from Tupi-Guarani *ipekaaguéne* 'emetic creeper,' from *ipe* 'small' + *kaa* 'leaves' + *guéne* 'vomit.'

Iph·i·ge·ni·a /ˌifijəˈnīə, -ˈnēə/ Greek Mythology the daughter of Agamemnon, who was obliged to offer her as a sacrifice to Artemis when the Greek fleet was becalmed at Aulis on its way to the Trojan War. In some versions of the story, Artemis saved her life and took her to Tauris in the Crimea, where she became a priestess until rescued by her brother Orestes.

I·pi·ros Greek name for EPIRUS.

ipm (also **i.p.m.**) ▶ **abbr.** inches per minute.

IPO ▶ **abbr.** initial public offering.

i·Pod /ˈīpäd/ ▶ **n.** trademark a portable electronic device for playing and storing digital audio and video files.

I·poh /ˈēpō/ a city in western Malaysia, the capital of the state of Perak; pop. 702,500 (est. 2009).

ip·o·moe·a /ˌipəˈmēə/ ▶ **n.** a plant of the genus *Ipomoea* in the family Convolvulaceae, esp. a morning glory.
– ORIGIN modern Latin, from Greek *ips* 'worm' + *homoios* 'like.'

ip·pon /ˈipˌän/ ▶ **n.** a full point scored in judo, karate, and other martial sports.
– ORIGIN Japanese.

IPR ▶ **abbr.** intellectual property rights.

i·pro·ni·a·zid /ˌīprōˈnīəˌzid/ ▶ **n.** Medicine a synthetic compound used as a drug to treat depression. ● A derivative of isoniazid; chem. formula: $(CH_3)_2CHNHNHCOC_5H_4N$.
– ORIGIN mid 20th cent.: from *i(so)pro(pyl)* + *(iso) niazid*.

ip·se dix·it /ˈipsē ˈdiksit/ ▶ **n.** a dogmatic and unproven statement.
– ORIGIN Latin, literally 'he himself said it,' translating Greek *autos epha*, a phrase used of Pythagoras by his followers.

ip·si·lat·er·al /ˌipsəˈlatərəl/ ▶ **adj.** belonging to or occurring on the same side of the body.
– DERIVATIVES **ip·si·lat·er·al·ly adv.**
– ORIGIN early 20th cent.: formed irregularly from Latin *ipse* 'self' + LATERAL.

ip·sis·si·ma ver·ba /ipˈsisəmə ˈvərbə/ ▶ **plural n.** the precise words.
– ORIGIN Latin.

ip·so fac·to /ˈipsō ˈfaktō/ ▶ **adv.** by that very fact or act: *the enemy of one's enemy may be ipso facto a friend*.
– ORIGIN Latin.

Ips·wich /ˈipswicH/ a town in southeastern England, the county town of Suffolk, a port on the estuary of the Orwell River; pop. 145,700 (est. 2009).

IQ ▶ **abbr.** intelligence quotient.

i.q. ▶ **abbr.** the same as.
– ORIGIN from Latin *idem quod*.

Iq·bal /ˈikˌbäl/, Sir Muhammad (1875–1938), Indian poet and philosopher; generally regarded as the father of Pakistan.

-ique ▶ **suffix** archaic spelling of -IC.

I·qui·tos /ēˈkētôs/ a city in northeastern Peru, a port on the west bank of the Amazon River; pop. 371,000 (est. 2007).

IR ▶ abbr. infrared.

Ir ▶ symbol the chemical element iridium.

ir- ▶ prefix variant spelling of IN-¹, IN-² assimilated before *r* (as in *irrelevant, irradiate*).

IRA ▶ abbr. ■ individual retirement account. ■ Irish Republican Army.

I·rá·kli·on /i'räklē,ôn/ Greek name for **HERAKLION**.

I·ran /i'rän, i'ran, ī'ran/ a country in the Middle East, between the Caspian Sea and the Persian Gulf; pop. 66,429,300 (est. 2009); capital, Tehran; languages, Farsi (Persian) (official), Turkish, Kurdish, Arabic, and others.

> Previously known as Persia, the country adopted the name of Iran in 1935. Iran was a monarchy until 1979, when the shah was overthrown in a popular uprising that was headed by Ayatollah Khomeini. Soon after, Iran was established as an Islamic republic. From 1980 until 1988, it was at war with its neighbor Iraq. See also **PERSIA, IRAN–IRAQ WAR**.

I·ran–Con·tra af·fair n. a political scandal of 1987 involving the covert sale by the US of arms to Iran. The proceeds of the arms sales were used by officials to give arms to the anticommunist Contras in Nicaragua, despite congressional prohibition. Also called **IRANGATE**.

> The sale occurred during the presidency of Ronald Reagan, at a time when official relations between the countries were suspended (and while Iran was at war with Iraq), and was followed by the release of American hostages held in the Middle East.

I·ran·gate /i'ran,gāt, i'rän-/ another term for the **IRAN–CONTRA AFFAIR**.

I·ra·ni·an /i'rānēən, i'rä-/ ▶ adj. of or relating to Iran or its people. ■ relating to or denoting the group of Indo-European languages that includes Persian (Farsi), Pashto, Avestan, and Kurdish.
▶ n. a native or inhabitant of Iran, or a person of Iranian descent.

I·ran–I·raq War the war of 1980–88 between Iran and Iraq in the general area of the Persian Gulf. It ended inconclusively after great hardship and loss of life on both sides. Also called **GULF WAR**.

I·raq /i'räk, i'rak, ī'rak/ a country in the Middle East, with an outlet on the Persian Gulf; pop. 28,945,600 (est. 2009); capital, Baghdad; official language, Arabic.

> Iraq is traversed by the Tigris and Euphrates rivers, whose valley was the site of the ancient civilizations of Mesopotamia. It was conquered by Arabia in the 7th century and from 1534 formed part of the Ottoman Empire. After World War I, a kingdom was established, although the country was under British administration until 1932. Saddam Hussein came to power as president in 1979. From 1980 to 1988, the country was at war with Iran, its eastern neighbor. In 1990, Iraq invaded Kuwait; it was driven back by an international coalition of forces in the Gulf War of 1991. In 2003 the country was invaded and occupied by US-led forces in response to its failure to comply fully with a UN resolution that it should disarm. Sovereignty was transferred to an interim government in June 2004, but US forces remained in the country.

I·ra·qi /i'räkē, i'rakē/ ▶ adj. of or relating to Iraq, its people, or their language.
▶ n. (pl. **Iraqis**) **1** a native or inhabitant of Iraq, or a person of Iraqi descent.
2 the form of Arabic spoken in Iraq.

IRAS /'ī,ras/ a satellite launched in 1983 to map the distribution of infrared radiation in the sky.
– ORIGIN abbreviation of *Infrared Astronomical Satellite*.

i·ras·ci·ble /i'rasəbəl/ ▶ adj. having or showing a tendency to be easily angered: *an irascible man*.
– DERIVATIVES **i·ras·ci·bil·i·ty** /i,rasə'bilitē/ n., **i·ras·ci·bly** /-blē/ adv.
– ORIGIN late Middle English: via French from late Latin *irascibilis*, from Latin *irasci* 'grow angry,' from *ira* 'anger.'

i·rate /ī'rāt/ ▶ adj. feeling or characterized by great anger: *a barrage of irate letters*.
– DERIVATIVES **i·rate·ly** adv., **i·rate·ness** n.
– ORIGIN mid 19th cent.: from Latin *iratus*, from *ira* 'anger.'

IRC ▶ abbr. Internet Relay Chat.

ire /ī(ə)r/ ▶ n. anger: *the plans provoked the ire of conservationists*.
– DERIVATIVES **ire·ful** /-fəl/ adj.
– ORIGIN Middle English: via Old French from Latin *ira*.

Ire·dell /'ī(ə)r,del/, James (1751–99) US Supreme Court associate justice 1790–99; born in England. Appointed to the Court by President Washington, he was a Federalist.

Ire·land /'īrlənd/ an island in the British Isles that lies west of Great Britain. Approximately four fifths of the area of Ireland constitutes the Republic of Ireland, with the remaining one fifth belonging to Northern Ireland. After an unsuccessful rebellion in 1798, union of Britain and Ireland followed in 1801. Ireland was divided into two self-governing areas after World War I. For later history see **IRELAND, REPUBLIC OF** and **NORTHERN IRELAND**.

Ire·land, Republic of a country that comprises approximately four fifths of Ireland; pop. 4,203,200 (est. 2009); capital, Dublin; languages, Irish (official) and English. Also called **IRISH REPUBLIC**.

> Ireland was partitioned by the Government of Ireland Act (1920), which divided the island into two self-governing areas. The Anglo-Irish Treaty, signed in 1921, gave Southern Ireland dominion status as the Irish Free State. The treaty was followed by civil war between the Free State government and the republicans, led by Eamon de Valera, who rejected partition. The war ended in victory for the government in 1923. A new constitution as a sovereign state (Eire) was adopted in 1937. Eire remained neutral during World War II; in 1949 it left the Commonwealth of Nations and became fully independent as the Republic of Ireland.

Ire·nae·us, St. /,īrə'nēəs/ (*c.* AD 130–*c.*200), Greek theologian. He wrote *Against Heresies* (*c.*180), a detailed attack on Gnosticism. Feast day (Eastern Church) August 23; (Western Church) June 28.

i·ren·ic /ī'renik, ī'rē-/ (also **eirenic**) ▶ adj. formal aiming or aimed at peace.
▶ n. (**irenics**) a part of Christian theology concerned with reconciling different denominations and sects.
– DERIVATIVES **i·ren·i·cal** adj., **i·ren·i·cal·ly** /-ik(ə)lē/ adv., **i·ren·i·cism** /-ni,sizəm/ n.
– ORIGIN mid 19th cent.: from Greek *eirēnikos*, from *eirēnē* 'peace.'

Ir·gun /ir'go͞on/ a right-wing Zionist organization founded in 1931. During the period when it was active (1937–48), it carried out violent attacks on Arabs and Britons in its campaign to establish a Jewish state; it was disbanded after the creation of Israel in 1948.
– ORIGIN from modern Hebrew *'irgūn (sĕbā'ī lĕ'ummī)* '(national military) organization.'

I·ri·an Ja·ya /'irē,än 'jīə/ former name for **PAPUA** (sense 1).

irid. ▶ abbr. iridescent.

ir·i·da·ceous /,iri'dāsнəs/ ▶ adj. Botany of, relating to, or denoting plants of the iris family (Iridaceae), which grow from bulbs, corms, or rhizomes.
– ORIGIN mid 19th cent.: from modern Latin *Iridaceae* (plural), based on Greek *iris, irid-* 'rainbow,' + **-OUS**.

ir·i·dec·to·my /,iri'dektəmē/ ▶ n. (pl. **iridectomies**) a surgical procedure to remove part of the iris.

ir·i·des·cent /,iri'desənt/ ▶ adj. showing luminous colors that seem to change when seen from different angles.
– DERIVATIVES **ir·i·des·cence** n., **ir·i·des·cent·ly** adv.
– ORIGIN late 18th cent.: from Latin *iris, irid-* 'rainbow' + **-ESCENT**.

i·rid·i·um /i'ridēəm/ ▶ n. the chemical element of atomic number 77, a hard, dense silvery-white metal. (Symbol: **Ir**)
– ORIGIN early 19th cent.: modern Latin, from Latin *iris, irid-* 'rainbow' (so named because it forms compounds of various colors).

ir·i·dol·o·gy /,iri'däləjē/ ▶ n. (in alternative medicine) diagnosis by examination of the iris of the eye.
– DERIVATIVES **ir·i·dol·o·gist** /-jist/ n.
– ORIGIN early 20th cent.: from Greek *iris, irid-* 'iris' + **-LOGY**.

i·rie /'īrē/ ▶ adj. black English nice, good, or pleasing (used as a general term of approval): *the place is jumping with irie vibes* | *I'm feeling irie*.
▶ exclam. used by Rastafarians as a friendly greeting.
– ORIGIN perhaps representing a pronunciation of *all right*.

I·ris /'īris/ Greek Mythology the goddess of the rainbow, who acted as a messenger of the gods.

i·ris /'īris/ ▶ n. **1** a flat, colored, ring-shaped membrane behind the cornea of the eye, with an adjustable circular opening (pupil) in the center. ■ (also **iris diaphragm**) an adjustable diaphragm of thin overlapping plates for regulating the size of a central hole, esp. for the admission of light to a lens.
2 a plant with sword-shaped leaves and showy flowers, typically purple, yellow, or white. Native to both Eurasia and North America, it is widely cultivated as an ornamental. ● Genus *Iris*, family Iridaceae (the **iris family**): many species and numerous hybrids, including the **crested dwarf iris** (*I. cristata*) and the **sweet iris** (*I. pallida*). The iris family also includes the gladioli, crocuses, and freesias.
3 a rainbow or a rainbowlike appearance.
▶ v. [no obj.] (of an aperture, typically that of a lens) open or close in the manner of an iris or iris diaphragm.
– ORIGIN modern Latin, via Latin from Greek *iris* 'rainbow, iris.'

iris 2

I·rish /'īrisн/ ▶ adj. of or relating to Ireland, its people, or the Goidelic language traditionally and historically spoken there.
▶ n. **1** (also **Irish Gaelic**) the Goidelic language that is the first official language of the Republic of Ireland.
2 (as plural noun **the Irish**) the people of Ireland; Irish people collectively.
– PHRASES **get one's Irish up** cause one to become angry: *if someone tries to make me do something I don't want to do, it gets my Irish up*.
– DERIVATIVES **I·rish·ness** n.
– ORIGIN Middle English: from Old English *Īr-* (stem of *Īras* 'the Irish' and *Īrland* 'Ireland,' obscurely related to **HIBERNIAN**) + **-ISH**¹.

I·rish cof·fee ▶ n. coffee mixed with a dash of Irish whiskey and served with cream on top.

I·rish elk ▶ n. an extinct giant European and North African deer of the Pleistocene epoch, with massive antlers up to 10 feet (3 m) across. Also called **GIANT DEER**. ● *Megaloceros giganteus*, family Cervidae.

I·rish·man /'īrisнmən/ ▶ n. (pl. **Irishmen**) a native or inhabitant of Ireland, or a person of Irish descent, esp. a man.

I·rish moss ▶ n. another term for **CARRAGEEN**.

I·rish Na·tion·al Lib·er·a·tion Ar·my (abbr.: **INLA**) a small paramilitary organization seeking union between Northern Ireland and the Republic of Ireland. It was formed in the early 1970s, probably as an offshoot of the Provisional IRA.

I·rish Re·pub·lic see **IRELAND, REPUBLIC OF**.

I·rish Re·pub·li·can Ar·my (abbr.: **IRA**) the military arm of Sinn Fein, aiming for union between the Republic of Ireland and Northern Ireland.

> The IRA was formed during the struggle for independence from Britain in 1916–21; in 1969 it split into Official and Provisional wings. The Official IRA became virtually inactive, while the Provisional IRA stepped up the level of violence against military and civilian targets in Northern Ireland, Britain, and Europe. The IRA declared a ceasefire in 1994 and another in 1997, and in 2005 announced that it had ended its armed campaign.

I·rish Sea the sea that separates Ireland from England and Wales.

I·rish set·ter ▶ n. a dog of a breed of setter with a long, silky dark red coat and a long feathered tail.

I·rish stew ▶ n. a stew made with mutton or other meat, potatoes, and onions.

I·rish ter·ri·er ▶ n. a terrier of a rough-haired light reddish-brown breed.

I·rish wolf·hound ▶ n. a large, typically grayish hound of a rough-coated breed.

I·rish·wom·an /'īrisн,wo͝omən/ ▶ n. (pl. **Irishwomen**) a female native or inhabitant of Ireland, or a woman of Irish descent.

i·ri·tis /ī'rītis/ ▶ n. Medicine inflammation of the iris of the eye.
– DERIVATIVES **i·rit·ic** /ī'ritik/ adj.

irk /ərk/ ▶ v. [with obj.] irritate; annoy: *it irks her to think of the runaround she received*.
– ORIGIN Middle English (in the sense 'be annoyed or disgusted'): perhaps from Old Norse *yrkja* 'to work.'

irk·some /'ərksəm/ ▶ adj. irritating; annoying.
– DERIVATIVES **irk·some·ly** adv., **irk·some·ness** n.

Ir·kutsk /ir'ko͞otsk/ the chief city of Siberia in eastern Russia, on the western shore of Lake Baikal; pop. 575,800 (est. 2008).

i·ron /'īərn/ ▶ n. **1** a strong, hard magnetic silvery-gray metal, the chemical element of atomic number 26, much used as a material for construction and manufacturing, esp. in the form of steel. (Symbol: **Fe**)

■ compounds of this metal, esp. as a component of the diet: *serve liver as it's a good source of iron* | [as modifier] *how are your iron levels?* ■ used figuratively as a symbol or type of firmness, strength, or resistance: *her father had a will of iron* | [as modifier] *the iron grip of religion on minority cultures.*

Iron is widely distributed as ores such as hematite, magnetite, and siderite, and the earth's core is believed to consist largely of metallic iron and nickel. Besides steel, other important forms of the metal are cast iron and wrought iron. Chemically a transition element, iron is a constituent of some biological molecules, notably hemoglobin.

2 a tool or implement now or originally made of iron: *a caulking iron.* ■ **(irons)** fetters or handcuffs. ■ informal a handgun.
3 a handheld implement with a flat steel base that is heated (typically with electricity) to smooth clothes, sheets, etc.
4 a golf club with a metal head (typically with a numeral indicating the degree to which the head is angled in order to loft the ball).
5 Astronomy (also **iron meteorite**) a meteorite containing a high proportion of iron.
▶ v. [with obj.] smooth (clothes, sheets, etc.) with an iron.
– PHRASES **have many** (or **other**) **irons in the fire** have many (or a range of) options or courses of action available or be involved in many activities or commitments at the same time. **in irons 1** having the feet or hands fettered. **2** (of a sailing vessel) stalled head to wind and unable to come about or tack either way. **iron hand** (or **fist**) used to refer to firmness or ruthlessness of attitude or behavior: *Fascism's iron hand.* **an iron hand** (or **fist**) **in a velvet glove** firmness or ruthlessness cloaked in outward gentleness.
– PHRASAL VERBS **iron something out** solve or settle difficulties or problems: *they had ironed out their differences.*
– DERIVATIVES **i·ron·er** n., **i·ron·like** /-ˌlīk/ adj.
– ORIGIN Old English *īren, īsen, īsern*, of Germanic origin; related to Dutch *ijzer* and German *Eisen*, and probably ultimately from Celtic.

I·ron Age 1 a period that followed the Bronze Age, when weapons and tools came to be made of iron.

The Iron Age is conventionally taken as beginning in the early 1st millennium BC, but iron-working began with the Hittites in Anatolia in c.1400 BC. In much of Europe it ended at the Roman period, but outside the Roman Empire it continued to the 4th–6th centuries AD.

2 (in Greek and Roman mythology) the last and worst age of the world, a time of wickedness and oppression.

i·ron·bark /ˈīərnˌbärk/ ▶ n. an Australian eucalyptus tree with thick, solid bark and hard, dense, durable timber. ● Genus *Eucalyptus*, family Myrtaceae: several species.

i·ron·bound /ˈīərnˈbound/ ▶ adj. bound with iron: *a massive ironbound chest.* ■ rigorous; inflexible: *ironbound rules.* ■ archaic (of a coast) faced or enclosed with rocks.

I·ron Chan·cel·lor see **BISMARCK**[2].

i·ron·clad /ˈīərnˌklad/ ▶ adj. covered or protected with iron. ■ impossible to contradict, weaken, or change: *an ironclad guarantee.*
▶ n. historical a 19th-century warship with armor plating.

I·ron Cross ▶ n. the highest German military decoration for bravery, instituted in 1813.

I·ron Cur·tain ▶ n. the notional barrier separating the former Soviet bloc and the West prior to the decline of communism that followed the political events in eastern Europe in 1989.

I·ron Duke see **WELLINGTON**[2].

I·ron Gate a gorge through which a section of the Danube River flows and forms part of the boundary between Romania and Serbia. Navigation was improved by means of a ship canal constructed through it in 1896. Romanian name **PORŢILE DE FIER**, Serbian name **GVOZDENA VRATA**.

i·ron gray ▶ n. a dark gray color. ■ a horse of this color.

I·ron Guard a fascist Romanian political party that was founded in 1927 and ceased to exist after World War II.

i·ron horse ▶ n. literary a steam locomotive. ■ **(Iron Horse)** see **GEHRIG**.

i·ron·ic /īˈränik/ ▶ adj. using or characterized by irony: *his mouth curved into an ironic smile.* ■ happening in the opposite way to what is expected, and typically causing wry amusement because of this: [with clause] *it was ironic that now that everybody had plenty of money for food, they couldn't obtain it because everything was rationed.*
– DERIVATIVES **i·ron·i·cal** adj.
– ORIGIN mid 17th cent.: from French *ironique* or late Latin *ironicus*, from Greek *eirōnikos* 'dissembling, feigning ignorance,' from *eirōneia* (see **IRONY**[1]).

i·ron·i·cal·ly /īˈränik(ə)lē/ ▶ adv. in an ironic manner. ■ used to denote a paradoxical, unexpected, or coincidental situation: [sentence adverb] *ironically, the rescue craft that saved her was the boat she was helping to pay for.*

i·ron·ing /ˈīərniNG/ ▶ n. the task of ironing clothes, sheets, etc. ■ clothes, sheets, etc., that need to be or have just been ironed.

i·ron·ing board ▶ n. a long, narrow board covered with soft material and having folding legs, on which clothes, sheets, etc., are ironed.

i·ro·nist /ˈīrənist, ˈīərnist/ ▶ n. a person who uses irony.
– ORIGIN early 18th cent.: from Greek *eirōn* 'dissembler' + **-IST**.

i·ro·nize /ˈīrəˌnīz, īərˈnīz/ ▶ v. [with obj.] use ironically: *this novel also follows and yet ironizes many of the conventions of the picaresque narrative.*

i·ron lung ▶ n. a rigid case fitted over a patient's body, used for administering prolonged artificial respiration by means of mechanical pumps.

i·ron maid·en ▶ n. (in historical contexts) an instrument of torture consisting of a coffin-shaped box lined with iron spikes.

i·ron man (also **ironman**) ▶ n. (esp. in sporting contexts) an exceptionally strong or robust man. ■ [often as modifier] a multi-event sporting contest demanding stamina, in particular a consecutive triathlon of swimming, cycling, and running.

i·ron mold ▶ n. a spot caused by rust or an ink stain, esp. on fabric.

i·ron·mon·ger /ˈīərnˌməNGgər, -ˌmäNGgər/ ▶ n. Brit. a person or store selling hardware such as tools and household implements.
– DERIVATIVES **i·ron·mon·ger·y** /-g(ə)rē/ n. (pl. **ironmongeries**).

i·ron-on ▶ adj. [attrib.] able to be fixed to the surface of a fabric by ironing: *T-shirts with iron-on transfers.*

i·ron ore ▶ n. a rock or mineral from which iron can be profitably extracted.

I·ron·sides /ˈīərnˌsīdz/ ▶ n. **1** a nickname for Oliver Cromwell.
2 **(ironsides)** historical an ironclad.

i·ron·stone /ˈīərnˌstōn/ ▶ n. **1** sedimentary rock containing a substantial proportion of iron compounds.
2 [usu. as modifier] a kind of dense, opaque stoneware.

i·ron·ware /ˈīərnˌwer/ ▶ n. articles made of iron, typically domestic implements.

i·ron·wood /ˈīərnˌwo͝od/ ▶ n. **1** any of a number of trees that produce very hard timber, in particular: ● a southern African tree of the olive family (*Olea laurifolia*, family Oleaceae). ● another term for the **AMERICAN HORNBEAM** and the **EASTERN HORNBEAM** (see **HORNBEAM**).
2 see **TITI**[2].

i·ron·work /ˈīərnˌwərk/ ▶ n. articles or parts made of iron.
– DERIVATIVES **i·ron·work·ing** n.

i·ron·works /ˈīərnˌwərks/ ▶ n. [treated as sing. or pl.] a place where iron is smelted or iron goods are made.

i·ro·ny[1] /ˈīrənē, ˈīərnē/ ▶ n. (pl. **ironies**) the expression of one's meaning by using language that normally signifies the opposite, typically for humorous or emphatic effect: *"Don't go overboard with the gratitude," he rejoined with heavy irony.* ■ a state of affairs or an event that seems deliberately contrary to what one expects and is often amusing as a result: [with clause] *the irony is that I thought he could help me.* ■ (also **dramatic** or **tragic irony**) a literary technique, originally used in Greek tragedy, by which the full significance of a character's words or actions are clear to the audience or reader although unknown to the character.
– ORIGIN early 16th cent. (also denoting Socratic irony): via Latin from Greek *eirōneia* 'simulated ignorance,' from *eirōn* 'dissembler.'

i·ro·ny[2] /ˈīərnē/ ▶ adj. of or like iron: *an irony gray color.*

Ir·o·quoi·an /ˌirəˈkwoiən/ ▶ n. a language family of eastern North America, including the languages of the Five Nations, Tuscarora, Huron, Wyandot, and Cherokee. With the exception of Cherokee, all its members are extinct or nearly so.
▶ adj. of or relating to the Iroquois people or the Iroquoian language family.

Ir·o·quois /ˈirəˌkwoi/ ▶ n. (pl. **same**) **1** a member of a former confederacy of North American Indian peoples originally comprising the Cayuga, Mohawk, Oneida, Onondaga, and Seneca peoples (known as the **FIVE NATIONS**), and later including also the Tuscarora (thus forming the **SIX NATIONS**).
2 any of the Iroquoian languages.
▶ adj. of or relating to the Iroquois or their languages.
– ORIGIN mid 17th cent.: French, perhaps a term from a Basque-Algonquian pidgin *h)irokoa* 'killer people,' from Basque *((h)ilo* 'kill' + *koa* 'person.'

ir·ra·di·ance /iˈrādēəns/ ▶ n. **1** Physics the flux of radiant energy per unit area (normal to the direction of flow of radiant energy through a medium).
2 literary the fact of shining brightly.

ir·ra·di·ant /iˈrādēənt/ ▶ adj. literary shining brightly.
– ORIGIN early 16th cent.: from Latin *irradiant-* 'shining upon,' from the verb *irradiare* (based on *radius* 'ray').

ir·ra·di·ate /iˈrādēˌāt/ ▶ v. [with obj.] **1** expose to radiation. ■ expose (food) to gamma rays to kill microorganisms.
2 illuminate (something) by or as if by shining light on it: *sunlight streamed down through stained glass, irradiating the faces of family and friends.*
– DERIVATIVES **ir·ra·di·a·tor** /-ˌātər/ n.
– ORIGIN late 16th cent. (in the sense 'emit rays, shine upon'): from Latin *irradiat-* 'shone upon,' from the verb *irradiare*, from *in-* 'upon' + *radiare* 'to shine' (from *radius* 'ray').

ir·ra·di·a·tion /iˌrādēˈāSHən/ ▶ n. **1** the process or fact of irradiating or being irradiated.
2 Optics the apparent extension of the edges of an illuminated object seen against a dark background.

ir·ra·tion·al /iˈraSHənl/ ▶ adj. **1** not logical or reasonable. ■ not endowed with the power of reason.
2 Mathematics (of a number, quantity, or expression) not expressible as a ratio of two integers, and having an infinite and nonrecurring expansion when expressed as a decimal. Examples of irrational numbers are the number π and the square root of 2.
▶ n. Mathematics an irrational number.
– DERIVATIVES **ir·ra·tion·al·i·ty** /iˌraSHəˈnalitē/ n., **ir·ra·tion·al·ize** /-ˌīz/ v., **ir·ra·tion·al·ly** adv.
– ORIGIN late Middle English: from Latin *irrationalis*, from *in-* 'not' + *rationalis* (see **RATIONAL**).

ir·ra·tion·al·ism /iˈraSHənlˌizəm/ ▶ n. a system of belief or action that disregards or contradicts rational principles.
– DERIVATIVES **ir·ra·tion·al·ist** n. & adj.

Ir·ra·wad·dy /ˌirəˈwädē/ the principal river of Burma (Myanmar), 1,300 miles (2,090 km) long. It flows through a large delta into the eastern part of the Bay of Bengal.

ir·re·claim·a·ble /ˌiriˈklāməbəl/ ▶ adj. not able to be reclaimed or reformed.
– DERIVATIVES **ir·re·claim·a·bly** /-blē/ adv.

ir·rec·on·cil·a·ble /iˌrekənˈsīləbəl, iˈrekənˌsī-/ ▶ adj. (of ideas, facts, or statements) representing findings or points of view that are so different from each other that they cannot be made compatible: *these two views of the early medieval economy are irreconcilable.* ■ (of people) implacably hostile to each other.
▶ n. (usu. **irreconcilables**) any of two or more ideas, facts, or statements that cannot be made compatible.
– DERIVATIVES **ir·rec·on·cil·a·bil·i·ty** /-ˌsīləˈbilitē/ n., **ir·rec·on·cil·a·bly** /-blē/ adv.

ir·re·cov·er·a·ble /ˌiriˈkəvərəbəl/ ▶ adj. not able to be recovered, regained, or remedied: *his liquid assets had to be written off as irrecoverable.*
– DERIVATIVES **ir·re·cov·er·a·bly** /-blē/ adv.

ir·re·cu·per·a·ble /ˌiriˈk(y)o͞opərəbəl/ ▶ adj. rare unable to be recovered from.
– ORIGIN late Middle English: from Old French, from late Latin *irrecuperabilis*, from Latin *in-* 'not' + *recuperare* (see **RECUPERATE**).

ir·re·cu·sa·ble /ˌiriˈkyo͞ozəbəl/ ▶ adj. rare (of evidence or a statement) not able to be challenged or rejected.
– ORIGIN late 18th cent.: via French from late Latin *irrecusabilis*, from *in-* 'not' + *recusabilis* 'that should be refused' (from the verb *recusare*).

ir·re·deem·a·ble /ˌiriˈdēməbəl/ ▶ adj. **1** not able to be saved, improved, or corrected: *so many irredeemable mistakes have been made.*
2 (of paper currency) for which the issuing authority does not undertake to pay coin.
– DERIVATIVES **ir·re·deem·a·bil·i·ty** /-ˌdēməˈbilitē/ n., **ir·re·deem·a·bly** /-blē/ adv.

ir·re·den·tist /ˌiriˈdentist/ ▶ n. [usu. as modifier] a person advocating the restoration to their country of any territory formerly belonging to it. ■ historical (in 19th-century Italian politics) an advocate of the return to Italy of all Italian-speaking districts subject to other countries.
– DERIVATIVES **ir·re·den·tism** /-ˌtizəm/ n.
– ORIGIN from Italian *irredentista*, from *(Italia) irredenta* 'unredeemed (Italy).'

ir·re·duc·i·ble /ˌiri'd(y)o͞osəbəl/ ▶ **adj.** not able to be reduced or simplified. ■ not able to be brought to a certain form or condition: *the imagery remains irreducible to textual structures.*
– DERIVATIVES **ir·re·duc·i·bil·i·ty** /-ˌd(y)o͞osə'bilitē/ **n.**, **ir·re·duc·i·bly** /-blē/ **adv.**

ir·re·flex·ive /ˌirə'fleksiv/ ▶ **adj.** Logic denoting a relation that never holds between a term and itself.

ir·re·form·a·ble /ˌirə'fôrməbəl/ ▶ **adj.** (chiefly of religious dogma) unable to be revised or altered.

ir·ref·ra·ga·ble /i'refrəgəbəl/ ▶ **adj.** not able to be refuted or disproved; indisputable.
– DERIVATIVES **ir·ref·ra·ga·bly** /-blē/ **adv.**
– ORIGIN mid 16th cent.: from late Latin *irrefragabilis*, from *in-* 'not' + *refragari* 'oppose.'

ir·re·fu·ta·ble /ˌirə'fyo͞otəbəl, i'refyə-/ ▶ **adj.** impossible to deny or disprove: *irrefutable evidence.*
– DERIVATIVES **ir·ref·u·ta·bil·i·ty** /-ˌfyo͞otə'bilitē, iˌrefyətə-/ **n.**, **ir·ref·u·ta·bly** /-blē/ **adv.**
– ORIGIN early 17th cent.: from late Latin *irrefutabilis*, from *in-* 'not' + *refutabilis* (from *refutare* 'repel, rebut').

irreg. ▶ **abbr.** irregular or irregularly.

ir·re·gard·less /ˌiri'gärdlis/ ▶ **adj. & adv.** informal regardless.
– ORIGIN early 20th cent.: probably a blend of IRRESPECTIVE and REGARDLESS.

> **USAGE** Irregardless is widely heard, perhaps arising under the influence of such perfectly correct forms as *irrespective*, but should be avoided by careful users of English. Use **regardless** to mean 'without regard or consideration for' or 'nevertheless'.

ir·reg·u·lar /i'regyələr/ ▶ **adj.** **1** not even or balanced in shape or arrangement: *her features were too irregular.* ■ occurring at uneven or varying rates or intervals: *an irregular heartbeat.* ■ Botany (of a flower) having the petals differing in size and shape; zygomorphic.
2 contrary to the rules or to that which is normal or established: *they were questioned about their involvement in irregular financial dealings.* ■ [attrib.] (of troops) not belonging to regular or established army units. ■ Grammar (of a verb or other word) having inflections that do not conform to the usual rules.
▶ **n.** (usu. **irregulars**) **1** a member of an irregular military force.
2 an imperfect piece of merchandise sold at a reduced price.
– DERIVATIVES **ir·reg·u·lar·ly** **adv.**
– ORIGIN late Middle English (in the sense 'not conforming to rule [esp. that of the Church]'): via Old French from medieval Latin *irregularis*, from *in-* 'not' + *regularis* (see REGULAR).

ir·reg·u·lar·i·ty /iˌregyə'laritē/ ▶ **n.** (pl. **irregularities**) the state or quality of being irregular: *there is evidence that fraud and irregularity continue on a large scale.* ■ (usu. **irregularities**) a thing that is irregular in form or nature: *irregularities of the heartbeat | financial irregularities.*
– ORIGIN Middle English: from Old French *irregularite*, from late Latin *irregularitas*, from *irregularis* (see IRREGULAR).

ir·rel·a·tive /i'relətiv/ ▶ **adj.** rare unconnected; unrelated. ■ irrelevant.
– DERIVATIVES **ir·rel·a·tive·ly** **adv.**

ir·rel·e·vance /i'reləvəns/ ▶ **n.** the quality or state of being irrelevant: *the document was withheld on grounds of irrelevance.* ■ a person or thing that is irrelevant: *he regarded religion as an irrelevance.*
– DERIVATIVES **irrelevancy** **n.** (pl. **irrelevancies**).

ir·rel·e·vant /i'reləvənt/ ▶ **adj.** not connected with or relevant to something.
– DERIVATIVES **ir·rel·e·vant·ly** **adv.**

> **USAGE** See usage at IMMATERIAL.

ir·re·li·gious /ˌiri'lijəs/ ▶ **adj.** indifferent or hostile to religion: *an irreligious world.*
– DERIVATIVES **ir·re·li·gion** /-'lijən/ **n.**, **ir·re·li·gious·ly** **adv.**, **ir·re·li·gious·ness** **n.**
– ORIGIN late Middle English: from Latin *irreligiosus*, from *in-* 'not' + *religiosus* (see RELIGIOUS).

ir·re·me·di·a·ble /ˌiri'mēdēəbəl/ ▶ **adj.** impossible to cure or put right.
– DERIVATIVES **ir·re·me·di·a·bly** /-blē/ **adv.**
– ORIGIN late Middle English: from Latin *irremediabilis*, from *in-* 'not' + *remediabilis* 'curable' (from *remedium* 'remedy').

ir·re·mis·si·ble /ˌiri'misəbəl/ ▶ **adj.** **1** (of a crime) unpardonable.
2 (of an obligation or duty) binding.
– ORIGIN late Middle English: from Old French, or from ecclesiastical Latin *irremissibilis*, from *in-* 'not' + *remissibilis* (from *remittere* 'remit').

ir·re·mov·a·ble /ˌiri'mo͞ovəbəl/ ▶ **adj.** incapable of being removed: *the irremovable taint of corruption.* ■ (of an official) unable to be displaced from office.
– DERIVATIVES **ir·re·mov·a·bil·i·ty** /-ˌmo͞ovə'bilitē/ **n.**, **ir·re·mov·a·bly** /-blē/ **adv.**

ir·rep·a·ra·ble /i'rep(ə)rəbəl/ ▶ **adj.** (of an injury or loss) impossible to rectify or repair: *they were doing irreparable damage to my heart and lungs.*
– DERIVATIVES **ir·rep·a·ra·bil·i·ty** /iˌrep(ə)rə'bilitē/ **n.**, **ir·rep·a·ra·bly** /-blē/ **adv.**
– ORIGIN late Middle English: via Old French from Latin *irreparabilis*, from *in-* 'not' + *reparabilis* (see REPARABLE).

ir·re·place·a·ble /iri'plāsəbəl/ ▶ **adj.** impossible to replace if lost or damaged.
– DERIVATIVES **ir·re·place·a·bly** /-blē/ **adv.**

ir·re·press·i·ble /ˌiri'presəbəl/ ▶ **adj.** not able to be controlled or restrained: *a great shout of irrepressible laughter.*
– DERIVATIVES **ir·re·press·i·bil·i·ty** /-ˌpresə'bilitē/ **n.**, **ir·re·press·i·bly** /-blē/ **adv.**

ir·re·proach·a·ble /ˌiri'prōchəbəl/ ▶ **adj.** beyond criticism; faultless: *his private life was irreproachable.*
– DERIVATIVES **ir·re·proach·a·bil·i·ty** /-ˌprōchə'bilitē/ **n.**, **ir·re·proach·a·bly** /-blē/ **adv.**
– ORIGIN mid 17th cent.: from French *irréprochable*, from *in-* 'not' + *reprochable* (from *reprocher* 'to reproach').

ir·re·sist·i·ble /ˌiri'zistəbəl/ ▶ **adj.** too attractive and tempting to be resisted: *he found the delicious-looking cakes irresistible.* ■ too powerful or convincing to be resisted: *she felt an irresistible urge to object.*
– DERIVATIVES **ir·re·sist·i·bil·i·ty** /-ˌzistə'bilitē/ **n.**, **ir·re·sist·i·bly** /-blē/ **adv.**
– ORIGIN late 16th cent.: from medieval Latin *irresistibilis*, from *in-* 'not' + *resistibilis* (from *resistere* 'resist').

ir·res·o·lute /i(r)'rezəˌlo͞ot/ ▶ **adj.** showing or feeling hesitancy; uncertain: *she stood irresolute outside his door.*
– DERIVATIVES **ir·res·o·lute·ly** **adv.**, **ir·res·o·lute·ness** **n.**
– ORIGIN late 16th cent.: from Latin *irresolutus* 'not loosened,' or from IN-[1] + RESOLUTE.

ir·res·o·lu·tion /i(r)ˌrezə'lo͞oshən/ ▶ **n.** hesitancy; uncertainty: *a moment of irresolution.*

ir·re·solv·a·ble /ˌiri'zälvəbəl/ ▶ **adj.** (of a problem or dilemma) impossible to solve or settle.

ir·re·spec·tive /ˌiri'spektiv/ ▶ **adj.** [predic.] (**irrespective of**) not taking (something) into account; regardless of: *child benefit is paid irrespective of income levels.*
– DERIVATIVES **ir·re·spec·tive·ly** **adv.**

ir·re·spon·si·ble /ˌiri'spänsəbəl/ ▶ **adj.** (of a person, attitude, or action) not showing a proper sense of responsibility: [with infinitive] *it would have been irresponsible just to drive on.*
– DERIVATIVES **ir·re·spon·si·bil·i·ty** /-ˌspänsə'bilitē/ **n.**, **ir·re·spon·si·bly** /-blē/ **adv.**

ir·re·spon·sive /ˌiri'spänsiv/ ▶ **adj.** not responsive to someone or something.
– DERIVATIVES **ir·re·spon·sive·ness** **n.**

ir·re·triev·a·ble /ˌiri'trēvəbəl/ ▶ **adj.** not able to be retrieved or put right: *the irretrievable breakdown of their marriage.*
– DERIVATIVES **ir·re·triev·a·bil·i·ty** /-ˌtrēvə'bilitē/ **n.**, **ir·re·triev·a·bly** /-blē/ **adv.**

ir·rev·er·ence /i'rev(ə)rəns/ ▶ **n.** a lack of respect for people or things that are generally taken seriously: *an attitude of irreverence toward politicians.*

ir·rev·er·ent /i'rev(ə)rənt/ ▶ **adj.** showing a lack of respect for people or things that are generally taken seriously: *she is irreverent about the whole business of politics.*
– DERIVATIVES **ir·rev·er·en·tial** /iˌrevə'renshəl/ **adj.**, **ir·rev·er·ent·ly** **adv.**
– ORIGIN late Middle English: from Latin *irreverent-* 'not revering,' from *in-* 'not' + *reverent-* 'revering' (see REVERENT).

ir·re·vers·i·ble /ˌiri'vərsəbəl/ ▶ **adj.** not able to be undone or altered: *she suffered irreversible damage to her health.*
– DERIVATIVES **ir·re·vers·i·bil·i·ty** /-ˌvərsə'bilitē/ **n.**, **ir·re·vers·i·bly** /-blē/ **adv.**

ir·re·vers·i·ble bi·no·mi·al ▶ **n.** Grammar a noun phrase consisting of two nouns joined by a conjunction, in which the conventional order is fixed. Examples include *bread and butter* and *kith and kin.*

ir·rev·o·ca·ble /ˌi'revəkəbəl/ ▶ **adj.** not able to be changed, reversed, or recovered; final: *an irrevocable step.*
– DERIVATIVES **ir·rev·o·ca·bil·i·ty** /iˌrevəkə'bilitē/ **n.**, **ir·rev·o·ca·bly** /-blē/ **adv.**
– ORIGIN late Middle English: from Old French, or from Latin *irrevocabilis*, from *in-* 'not' + *revocabilis* 'able to be revoked' (from the verb *revocare*).

ir·ri·gate /'irigāt/ ▶ **v.** [with obj.] supply water to (land or crops) to help growth, typically by means of channels. ■ (of a river or stream) supply (land) with water. ■ Medicine apply a continuous flow of water or liquid medication to (an organ or wound).
– DERIVATIVES **ir·ri·ga·ble** /-gəbəl/ **adj.**, **ir·ri·ga·tion** /ˌiri'gāshən/ **n.**, **ir·ri·ga·tor** /-ˌgātər/ **n.**
– ORIGIN early 17th cent.: from Latin *irrigat-* 'moistened,' from the verb *irrigare*, from *in-* 'into' + *rigare* 'moisten, wet.'

ir·ri·ta·bil·i·ty /ˌiritə'bilitē/ ▶ **n.** the quality or state of being irritable: *symptoms include insomnia and irritability.*

ir·ri·ta·ble /'iritəbəl/ ▶ **adj.** having or showing a tendency to be easily annoyed or made angry: *she was tired and irritable.* ■ Medicine (of a bodily part or organ) abnormally sensitive. ■ Medicine (of a condition) caused by such sensitivity. ■ Biology (of a living organism) having the property of responding actively to physical stimuli.
– DERIVATIVES **ir·ri·ta·bly** /-blē/ **adv.**
– ORIGIN mid 17th cent.: from Latin *irritabilis*, from the verb *irritare* (see IRRITATE).

ir·ri·ta·ble bow·el syn·drome (abbr.: **IBS**) ▶ **n.** a widespread condition involving recurrent abdominal pain and diarrhea or constipation, often associated with stress, depression, anxiety, or previous intestinal infection.

ir·ri·tant /'iritənt/ ▶ **n.** **1** a substance that causes slight inflammation or other discomfort to the body.
2 a thing that is continually annoying or distracting: *in 1966, Vietnam was becoming an irritant to the government.*
▶ **adj.** causing slight inflammation or other discomfort to the body.
– DERIVATIVES **ir·ri·tan·cy** **n.**

ir·ri·tate /'iriˌtāt/ ▶ **v.** [with obj.] make (someone) annoyed, impatient, or angry: *his tone irritated her* | [no obj.] *his voice tends to irritate.* ■ cause inflammation or other discomfort in (a part of the body). ■ Biology stimulate (an organism, cell, or organ) to produce an active response.
– DERIVATIVES **ir·ri·ta·tive** /-ˌtātiv/ **adj.**, **ir·ri·ta·tor** /-ˌtātər/ **n.**
– ORIGIN mid 16th cent. (in the sense 'excite, provoke'): from Latin *irritat-* 'irritated,' from the verb *irritare.*

ir·ri·tat·ed /'iriˌtātid/ ▶ **adj.** showing or feeling slight anger; annoyed: *the irritated look on Alec's face.*
– DERIVATIVES **ir·ri·tat·ed·ly** **adv.**

ir·ri·tat·ing /'iriˌtātiNG/ ▶ **adj.** **1** causing annoyance, impatience, or mild anger: *an irritating child.*
2 causing irritation to a body part: *the substance may be irritating to eyes and skin.*
– DERIVATIVES **ir·ri·tat·ing·ly** **adv.**

ir·ri·ta·tion /ˌiri'tāshən/ ▶ **n.** the state of feeling annoyed, impatient, or angry. ■ a cause of this: *the minor irritations of life.* ■ the production of inflammation or other discomfort in a bodily part or organ. ■ Biology the stimulation of an organism, cell, or organ to produce an active response.
– ORIGIN late Middle English: from Latin *irritatio(n-)*, from the verb *irritare* (see IRRITATE).

ir·ro·ta·tion·al /irō'tāshənl/ ▶ **adj.** Physics (esp. of fluid motion) not rotational; having no rotation.

ir·rupt /i'rəpt/ ▶ **v.** [no obj.] enter forcibly or suddenly: *the specter of social revolution once again irrupted into a confident capitalist world.* ■ (of a bird or other animal) migrate into an area in abnormally large numbers.
– DERIVATIVES **ir·rup·tion** /-shən/ **n.**, **ir·rup·tive** /-tiv/ **adj.**
– ORIGIN mid 19th cent.: from Latin *irrupt-* 'broken into,' from the verb *irrumpere*, from *in-* 'into' + *rumpere* 'break.'

IRS ▶ **abbr.** Internal Revenue Service.

Ir·tysh /ir'tish, ər-/ a river in central Asia that rises in the Altai Mountains in northern China and flows west into northeastern Kazakhstan, where it turns northwest to join the Ob River near its mouth in Russia. Its length is 2,655 miles (4,248 km).

Ir·vine /'ərvīn/ a planned city in southwestern California; pop. 207,500 (est. 2008).

Ir·ving[1] /'ərviNG/ an industrial city in northeastern Texas, between Dallas and Fort Worth; pop. 201,358 (est. 2008).

Ir·ving[2], John (Winslow) (1942–) US writer and teacher; born John Wallace Blunt, Jr. His works such

PRONUNCIATION KEY ə *ago, up;* ər *over, fur;* a *hat;* ā *ate;* ä *car;* e *let;* ē *see;* i *fit;* ī *by;* NG *sing;* ō *go;* ô *law, for;* oi *toy;* o͝o *good;* o͞o *goo;* ou *out;* TH *thin;* T͟H *then;* ZH *vision*

as *The World According to Garp* (1978) combine tragedy with comedy. He also wrote *The Hotel New Hampshire* (1981), *The Cider House Rules* (1985), and *Last Night in Twisted River* (2009).

Ir·ving[3], Washington (1783–1859), US writer. He is best known for *The Sketch Book of Geoffrey Crayon, Gent.* (1819–20), which contains such tales as "Rip Van Winkle" and "The Legend of Sleepy Hollow."

Ir·ving·ton /ˈərviNGtən/ an industrial and residential township in northeastern New Jersey, west of Newark; pop. 56,299 (est. 2008).

is /iz/ third person singular present of **BE**.

Is. ▶ **abbr.** ■ (also **Isa.**) Bible Isaiah. ■ Island(s). ■ Isle(s).

ISA ▶ **abbr.** Computing industry standard architecture, a standard for connecting computers and their peripherals: [as adj.] *an ISA expansion slot*.

I·saac /ˈīˌzək/ (in the Bible) a Hebrew patriarch, son of Abraham and Sarah and father of Jacob and Esau.

I·sa·bel·la /ˌizəˈbelə/ ▶ **n.** another term for **FOX GRAPE**. ■ a wine made from this grape.

Is·a·bel·la I (1451–1504), queen of Castile 1474–1504 and of Aragon 1479–1504. Her marriage in 1469 to Ferdinand of Aragon marked the beginning of the unification of Spain. They instituted the Spanish Inquisition in 1478 and supported the explorations of Christopher Columbus in 1492.

Is·a·bel·la of France (1292–1358), daughter of Philip IV of France and wife of Edward II of England 1308–27. She left England to return to France in 1325, where she and her lover, Roger de Mortimer, organized an invasion of England in 1326. They murdered Edward and replaced him with Isabella's son, Edward III.

i·sa·gog·ics /ˌīsəˈgäjiks/ ▶ **plural n.** [treated as sing.] introductory study, esp. of the literary and external history of the Bible prior to exegesis.
– DERIVATIVES **i·sa·gog·ic** /-jik/ **adj.**
– ORIGIN mid 19th cent.: plural of *isagogic*, via Latin from Greek *eisagōgikos*, from *eisagōgē* 'introduction,' from *eis* 'into' + *agein* 'to lead.'

I·sa·iah /īˈzāə/ a major Hebrew prophet of Judah in the 8th century BC, who taught the supremacy of the God of Israel and emphasized the moral demands on worshipers. ■ a book of the Bible containing his prophecies and, it is generally thought, those of at least one later prophet.

is·al·lo·bar /īˈsaləˌbär/ ▶ **n.** Meteorology a line on a map connecting points at which the atmospheric pressure has changed by an equal amount during a specified time.
– DERIVATIVES **is·al·lo·bar·ic** /īˌsaləˈbärik/ **adj.**
– ORIGIN early 20th cent.: from **ISO-** 'equal' + **ALLO-** 'other' + **BAR**[2].

i·sa·tin /ˈīsətin/ ▶ **n.** Chemistry a red crystalline compound used in the manufacture of dyes. ● An indole derivative; chem. formula: $C_8H_5NO_2$.
– ORIGIN mid 19th cent.: from Latin *isatis* 'woad' (from Greek) + **-IN**[1].

ISBN ▶ **abbr.** international standard book number, a ten-digit number assigned to every book before publication, recording such details as language, provenance, and publisher.

is·che·mi·a /isˈkēmēə/ (Brit. **ischaemia**) ▶ **n.** Medicine an inadequate blood supply to an organ or part of the body, esp. the heart muscles.
– DERIVATIVES **is·che·mic** /-mik/ **adj.**
– ORIGIN late 19th cent. (denoting the stanching of bleeding): modern Latin, from Greek *iskhaimos* 'stopping blood,' from *iskhein* 'keep back' + *haima* 'blood.'

Is·chi·a /ˈiskēə/ an island in the Tyrrhenian Sea off the western coast of Italy, about 16 miles (26 km) west of Naples.

is·chi·um /ˈiskēəm/ ▶ **n.** (pl. **ischia** /-kēə/) the curved bone forming the base of each half of the pelvis.
– DERIVATIVES **is·chi·ad·ic** /ˌiskēˈadik/ **adj.**, **is·chi·al** /-kēəl/ **adj.**
– ORIGIN early 17th cent.: from Latin, from Greek *iskhion* 'hip joint,' later 'ischium.'

ISDN ▶ **abbr.** integrated services digital network.

Ise /ˈēsā/ a city in Japan, on the central part of the island of Honshu, on Ise Bay; pop. 134,573 (2007). Former name (until 1956) **UJIYAMADA**.

-ise[1] ▶ **suffix** chiefly British variant spelling of **-IZE**.

> **USAGE** There are some verbs that must be spelled **-ise** and are not variants of the **-ize** ending. Most reflect a French influence: they include *advertise*, *televise*, *compromise*, and *improvise*. For more details, see usage at **-IZE**.

-ise[2] ▶ **suffix** forming nouns of quality, state, or function: *expertise* | *franchise* | *merchandise*.
– ORIGIN from Old French *-ise*, from Latin *-itia*, *-itium*.

is·en·trop·ic /ˌīsənˈträpik, -ˈtrōpik/ ▶ **adj.** Physics having equal entropy.

I·seult[1] /iˈsōōlt, iˈzōōlt/ (also **Isolde**) a princess in medieval legend; known as **Iseult the Fair**. She was the daughter of the king of Ireland. Tristram was sent to seek her hand on behalf of his uncle, King Mark of Cornwall. En route back to Cornwall Tristram and Iseult mistakenly drank the love potion intended for the wedding night of Iseult and Mark and fell hopelessly in love. Iseult was bound to marry King Mark, but she and Tristram continued their affair until Mark became suspicious and Tristram had to flee. The tragic story is part of the body of Arthurian literature. Versions of the legend were told by Thomas of Brittany (*fl.* 12th cent.), Gottfried von Strassburg (*fl.* 12th–13th cent.), Alfred, Lord Tennyson, and Richard Wagner in his opera *Tristan*.

I·seult[2] /iˈsōōlt, iˈzōōlt/ a princess in medieval legend; known as **Iseult of the White Hands**. She was the daughter of the king of Brittany and, in some versions of the legend, married Tristram after he was banished from Cornwall because of his love for Iseult the Fair.

Is·fa·han /ˌisfəˈhän/ (also **Esfahan** /ˌesfə-/, **Ispahan** /ˌispə-/) an industrial city in central Iran; pop. 1,602,110 (2006). It was the capital of Persia 1598–1722.

-ish[1] /isH/ ▶ **suffix** forming adjectives: **1** (from nouns) having the qualities or characteristics of: *apish* | *girlish*. ■ of nationality or religious or ethnic group: *Swedish* | *Amish* | *Flemish*.
2 (from adjectives) somewhat: *yellowish*. ■ informal denoting an approximate age or time of day: *sixish*.
– ORIGIN Old English *-isc*, of Germanic origin; related to Old Norse *-iskr*, German and Dutch *-isch*, also to Greek *-iskos* (suffix forming diminutive nouns).

-ish[2] ▶ **suffix** forming verbs such as *abolish*, *establish*.
– ORIGIN from French *-iss-* (from stems of verbs ending in *-ir*), from Latin *-isc-* (suffix forming inceptive verbs); compare with **-ISH**[1].

Ish·er·wood /ˈisHərˌwo͝od/, Christopher (William Bradshaw) (1904–86), US novelist; born in Britain. Notable works: *Mr. Norris Changes Trains* (1935) and *Goodbye to Berlin* (1939; movie version: *Cabaret*, 1972).

Ishi·gu·ro /ˌisHiˈgo͞oˌrō/, Kazuo (1954–), British novelist; born in Japan. Notable works: *An Artist of the Floating World* (1986), *The Remains of the Day* (1989), and *Never Let Me Go* (2005).

Ish·i·ha·ra test /ˌisHēˈhärə/ ▶ **n.** a test for color-blindness in which the subject is asked to distinguish numbers or pathways printed in colored spots on a background of spots of a different color or colors.
– ORIGIN early 20th cent.: named after Shinobu *Ishihara* (1879–1963), Japanese ophthalmologist.

Ish·ma·el /ˈisHmēəl, -mā-/ (in the Bible) a son of Abraham, by his wife Sarah's maid, Hagar, driven away with his mother after the birth of Sarah's son Isaac (Gen. 16:12). Ishmael (or Ismail) is also important in Islamic belief as the traditional ancestor of Muhammad and of the Arab peoples.
– DERIVATIVES **Ish·ma·el·ite** /-ˌlīt/ **n.**

Ish·tar /ˈisHˌtär/ Near Eastern Mythology a Babylonian and Assyrian goddess of love and war whose name and functions correspond to those of the Phoenician goddess Astarte.

Is·i·dore of Se·ville, St. /ˈizəˌdôr əv səˈvil/ (*c.*560–636), Spanish archbishop and doctor of the Church; also called **Isidorus Hispalensis**. He is noted for *Etymologies*, an encyclopedic work used by many medieval authors. Feast day, April 4.

i·sin·glass /ˈīzənˌglas, ˈīziNG-/ ▶ **n.** a kind of gelatin obtained from fish, esp. sturgeon, and used in making jellies, glue, etc., and for clarifying ale. ■ mica or a similar material in thin transparent sheets.
– ORIGIN mid 16th cent.: alteration (by association with **GLASS**) of obsolete Dutch *huysenblas* 'sturgeon's bladder,' from *huysen* 'sturgeon' + *blas* 'bladder.'

I·sis /ˈīsis/ Egyptian Mythology a goddess of fertility, wife of Osiris and mother of Horus. Her worship spread to western Asia, Greece, and Rome, where she was identified with various local goddesses.

Is·ken·de·run /isˌkendəˈro͞on/ a port and naval base in southern Turkey, on the Mediterranean coast; pop. 177,300 (est. 2007).

isl. (also **Isl.**) ▶ **abbr.** island or isle.

Is·lam /isˈläm, iz-/ ▶ **n.** the religion of the Muslims, a monotheistic faith regarded as revealed through Muhammad as the Prophet of Allah. ■ the Muslim world: *the most enormous complex of fortifications in all Islam*.

> Founded in the Arabian peninsula in the 7th century AD, Islam is now the professed faith of more than a billion people worldwide, particularly in North Africa, the Middle East, and parts of Asia. The ritual observances and moral code of Islam were said to have been given to Muhammad as a series of revelations, which were codified in the Koran. Islam is regarded by its adherents as the last of the revealed religions, and Muhammad is seen as the last of the prophets, building on and perfecting the examples and teachings of Abraham, Moses, and Jesus. There are two major branches in Islam: Sunni and Shia.

– DERIVATIVES **Is·lam·i·za·tion** /isˌlämiˈzāsHən, iz-/ **n.**, **Is·lam·ize** /ˈisləˌmīz, ˈiz-/ **v.**
– ORIGIN from Arabic *'islām* 'submission,' from *'aslama* 'submit (to God).'

Is·lam·a·bad /isˈläməˌbäd, izˈlaməˌbad/ the capital of Pakistan, a modern planned city in the north of the country; pop. 673,800 (est. 2009). It replaced Rawalpindi as the capital in 1967.

Is·lam·ic /isˈlämik, iz-/ ▶ **adj.** relating to Islam: *the Islamic world* | *Islamic law*.
– DERIVATIVES **Is·lam·i·ci·za·tion** /isˌlämisiˈzāsHən, iz-/ **n.**, **Is·lam·i·cize** /isˈlämiˌsīz, iz-/ **v.**

Is·lam·ic Ji·had /isˈlämik jiˈhad, -ˈhäd, iz-/ (also **Jehad**) a Muslim fundamentalist group within the Shiite Hezbollah association.

Is·la·mism /isˈlämizəm/ (also **Islamicism**) ▶ **n.** Islamic militancy or fundamentalism.
– DERIVATIVES **Is·la·mist n. & adj.**

Is·lam·o·pho·bi·a /isˌläməˈfōbēə, iz-/ ▶ **n.** a hatred or fear of Islam or Muslims, esp. when feared as a political force.
– DERIVATIVES **Is·lam·o·phobe n.**, **Is·lam·o·pho·bic adj.**
– ORIGIN from *Islam* + *-o-* + *phobia*.

Is·land /ˈēˌslän(t)/ Icelandic name for **ICELAND**.

is·land /ˈīlənd/ ▶ **n. 1** a piece of land surrounded by water. ■ a thing resembling an island, esp. in being isolated, detached, or surrounded in some way: *the university is the last island of democracy in this country*. ■ a freestanding kitchen cupboard unit with a countertop, allowing access from all sides.
2 Anatomy a detached portion of tissue or group of cells. Compare with **ISLET**.
▶ **v.** [with obj.] literary make into or like an island; place or enclose on or as on an island; isolate: *islanded among the new stores, these houses were valuable property*.
– ORIGIN Old English *īegland*, from *īeg* 'island' (from a base meaning 'watery, watered') + **LAND**. The change in the spelling of the first syllable in the 16th cent. was due to association with the unrelated word **ISLE**.

is·land arc ▶ **n.** Geology a curved chain of volcanic islands located at a tectonic plate margin, typically with a deep ocean trench on the convex side.

is·land·er /ˈīləndər/ ▶ **n.** a native or inhabitant of an island.

is·land-hop ▶ **v.** [no obj.] (usu. as noun **island-hopping**) travel from one island to another, esp. as a tourist in an area of small islands.

Is·lands of the Bless·ed (in classical mythology) a land, typically located near the place where the sun sets, to which the souls of the good were taken to enjoy a life of eternal bliss.

isle /īl/ ▶ **n.** chiefly literary an island or peninsula, esp. a small one: *Crusoe's fabled isle* | [in place names] *the British Isles*.
– ORIGIN Middle English *ile*, from Old French, from Latin *insula*. The spelling with *s* (also in 15th-cent. French) is influenced by Latin.

Isle of Man /man/ an island in the Irish Sea that is a British Crown colony with home rule; pop. 82,800 (2009); capital, Douglas. Its ancient language, Manx, is still occasionally used for ceremonial purposes.

Isle of Wight /wīt/ an island in England, off the southern coast, a county since 1974; pop. 131,700 (est. 2009); administrative center, Newport.

Isle Roy·ale /ˈroiəl/ an island in Michigan, in western Lake Superior, near Grand Portage in Minnesota. Part of a national park, it is noted for its wildlife.

is·let /ˈīlət/ ▶ **n. 1** a small island.
2 Anatomy a portion of tissue structurally distinct from surrounding tissues. ■ (**islets**) short for **ISLETS OF LANGERHANS**.
– ORIGIN mid 16th cent.: from Old French, diminutive of *isle* (see **ISLE**).

is·lets of Lang·er·hans /ˈlaNGərˌhanz, ˈläNGərˌhäns/ (also **islands of Langerhans**) ▶ **plural n.** groups of pancreatic cells secreting insulin and glucagon.
– ORIGIN late 19th cent.: named after Paul *Langerhans* (1847–88), the German anatomist who first described them.

I·slip /ˈīˌslip/ a town on the south shore of Long Island, New York; pop. 336,292 (est. 2008).

ism /ˈizəm/ ▶ **n.** informal, chiefly derogatory a distinctive practice, system, or philosophy, typically a political ideology or an artistic movement: *of all the isms, fascism is the most repressive.*
– DERIVATIVES **ist n.**
– ORIGIN late 17th cent.: independent usage of **-ISM**.

-ism ▶ **suffix** forming nouns: **1** denoting an action or its result: *baptism | exorcism.* ■ denoting a state or quality: *barbarism.*
2 denoting a system, principle, or ideological movement: *Anglicanism | feminism | hedonism.* ■ denoting a basis for prejudice or discrimination: *racism.*
3 denoting a peculiarity in language: *colloquialism | Canadianism.*
4 denoting a pathological condition: *alcoholism.*
– ORIGIN from French *-isme*, via Latin from Greek *-ismos, -isma.*

Is·ma·il /ˌismäˈēl/ Arabic spelling of **ISHMAEL**.

Is·ma·il·i /ˌismäˈēlē/ ▶ **n.** (pl. **Ismailis**) a member of a branch of Shiite Muslims that seceded from the main group in the 8th century because of their belief that Ismail, the son of the sixth Shiite imam, should have become the seventh imam.

Is·mail Sa·ma·ni Peak /ˈismīl səˈmänē/ one of the principal peaks in the Pamir Mountains of Tajikistan, rising to 24,590 feet (7,495 m). It was the highest mountain in the former Soviet Union. Former names: **Mount Garmo** (until 1933), **Stalin Peak** (1933–62), **Communism Peak** (1962–98).
– ORIGIN named after the 9th-century founder of the Tajik nation.

is·n't /ˈizənt/ ▶ **contraction** is not.

ISO ▶ **abbr.** International Organization for Standardization.

iso- ▶ **comb. form** equal: *isochron | isosceles.* ■ Chemistry (chiefly of hydrocarbons) isomeric: *isooctane.*
– ORIGIN from Greek *isos* 'equal.'

i·so·ag·glu·ti·na·tion /ˌīsōəglo͞otnˈāSHən/ ▶ **n.** Physiology agglutination of sperms, erythrocytes, or other cells of an individual caused by a substance from another individual of the same species.

i·so·bar /ˈīsəˌbär/ ▶ **n. 1** Meteorology a line on a map connecting points having the same atmospheric pressure at a given time or on average over a given period. ■ Physics a curve or formula representing a physical system at constant pressure.
2 Physics each of two or more isotopes of different elements, with the same atomic weight.
– DERIVATIVES **i·so·bar·ic** /ˌīsəˈbarik, -ˈbär-/ **adj.**
– ORIGIN mid 19th cent.: from Greek *isobaros* 'of equal weight,' from *isos* 'equal' + *baros* 'weight.'

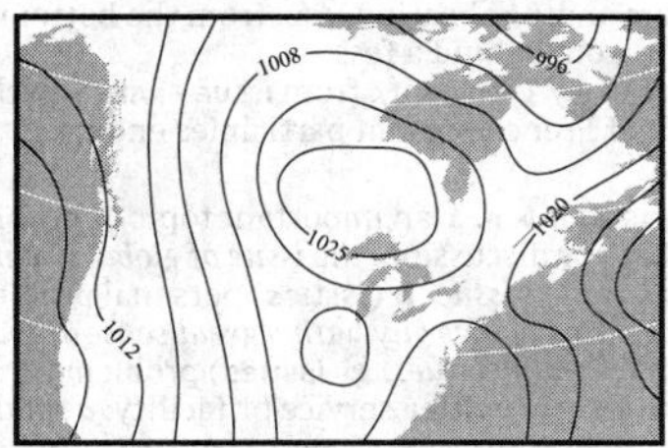

isobar 1

i·so·bu·tane /ˌīsəˈbyo͞otān, -byo͞oˈtān/ ▶ **n.** Chemistry a gaseous hydrocarbon isomeric with butane. ● Chem. formula: $CH_3CH(CH_3)_2$.

i·so·bu·tyl·ene /ˌīsəˈbyo͞otlˌēn/, ▶ **n.** Chemistry an easily liquefied hydrocarbon gas, $(CH_3)_2C{=}CH_2$, used in the making of butyl rubber.

i·so·cheim /ˈīsəˌkīm/ ▶ **n.** Meteorology a line on a map connecting points having the same average temperature in winter.
– ORIGIN mid 19th cent.: from **ISO-** 'equal' + Greek *kheima* 'winter weather.'

i·so·chro·mat·ic /ˌīsəkrəˈmatik/ ▶ **adj.** of a single color.

i·so·chron /ˈīsəˌkrän/ ▶ **n.** chiefly Geology a line on a diagram or map connecting points relating to the same time or equal times.
– ORIGIN late 17th cent. (as an adjective in the sense 'isochronous'): from Greek *isokhronos*, from *isos* 'equal' + *khronos* 'time.'

i·soch·ro·nous /īˈsäkrənəs/ ▶ **adj.** occurring at the same time. ■ occupying equal time.
– DERIVATIVES **i·soch·ro·nous·ly adv.**
– ORIGIN early 18th cent. (in the sense 'equal in duration or in frequency'): from modern Latin *isochronus* (from Greek *isokhronos*, from *isos* 'equal' + *khronos* 'time') + **-OUS**.

i·so·cli·nal /ˌīsəˈklīnl/ ▶ **adj.** Geology denoting a fold of strata so acute that the two limbs are parallel.
– ORIGIN mid 19th cent. (denoting 'equal magnetic inclination'): from **ISO-** 'equal' + Greek *klinein* 'to lean, slope' + **-AL**.

i·so·cline /ˈīsəˌklīn/ ▶ **n.** a line on a diagram or map connecting points of equal gradient or inclination.
– DERIVATIVES **i·so·clin·ic** /ˌīsəˈklinik/ **adj.**
– ORIGIN late 19th cent. (denoting an isoclinal line or fold): from Greek *isoklinēs* 'equally balanced,' from *klinein* 'to lean, slope.'

i·so·clin·ic line /ˌīsəˈklinik/ ▶ **n.** a line on a map connecting points where the dip of the earth's magnetic field is the same.

i·so·crat·ic /ˌīsəˈkratik/ ▶ **adj.** Chemistry (of a chromatographic method) involving a mobile phase whose composition is kept constant and uniform.
– ORIGIN early 19th cent.: from Greek *isokratia* 'equality of power' (from *isos* 'equal' + *kratos* 'strength') + **-IC**.

i·so·di·a·met·ric /ˌīsōˌdīəˈmetrik/ ▶ **adj.** chiefly Botany (of a cell, spore, etc.) roughly spherical or polyhedral.

i·so·dy·nam·ic /ˌīsədīˈnamik/ ▶ **adj.** Geography indicating or connecting points on the earth's surface at which the intensity of the magnetic force is the same.

i·so·e·lec·tric /ˌīsō-iˈlektrik/ ▶ **adj.** having or involving no net electric charge or difference in electrical potential.

i·so·e·lec·tric fo·cus·ing ▶ **n.** Biochemistry a technique of electrophoresis in which the resolution is improved by maintaining a pH gradient between the electrodes.

i·so·e·lec·tron·ic /ˌīsō-ilekˈtränik, -ˌēlek-/ ▶ **adj.** Chemistry having the same numbers of electrons or the same electronic structure.

i·so·en·zyme /ˌīsōˈenzīm/ ▶ **n.** Biochemistry another term for **ISOZYME**.

i·sog·a·my /īˈsägəmē/ ▶ **n.** Biology sexual reproduction by the fusion of similar gametes. Compare with **ANISOGAMY**.
– DERIVATIVES **i·so·gam·ete** /ˌīsēˈgamēt, īsōgəˈmēt/ **n.**, **i·sog·a·mous** /-məs/ **adj.**
– ORIGIN late 19th cent.: from **ISO-** 'equal' + Greek *-gamia* (from *gamos* 'marriage').

i·so·gen·ic /ˌīsəˈjenik/ ▶ **adj.** Biology (of organisms) having the same or closely similar genotypes.

i·so·ge·o·therm /ˌīsəˈjēəˌTHərm/ ▶ **n.** Geography a line or surface on a diagram connecting points representing those in the interior of the earth having the same temperature.
– DERIVATIVES **i·so·ge·o·ther·mal** /-ˌjēəˈTHərməl/ **adj.**
– ORIGIN mid 19th cent.: from **ISO-** 'equal' + **GEO-** 'earth' + Greek *thermē* 'heat.'

i·so·gloss /ˈīsəˌglôs, -ˌgläs/ ▶ **n.** Linguistics a line on a dialect map marking the boundary between linguistic features.
– DERIVATIVES **i·so·glos·sal** /ˌīsəˈglôsəl, -ˈgläsəl/ **adj.**
– ORIGIN early 20th cent.: from **ISO-** 'equal' + Greek *glōssa* 'tongue, word.'

i·so·gon·ic /ˌīsəˈgänik/ (also **isogonal** /īˈsägənl/) ▶ **adj.** Geography indicating or connecting points of the earth's surface at which the magnetic declination is the same.
– ORIGIN mid 19th cent.: from Greek *isogōnios* 'equiangular' + **-IC**.

i·so·hel /ˈīsəˌhel/ ▶ **n.** Meteorology a line on a map connecting points having the same duration of sunshine.
– ORIGIN early 20th cent.: from **ISO-** 'equal' + Greek *hēlios* 'sun.'

i·so·hy·et /ˌīsəˈhī-it/ ▶ **n.** Meteorology a line on a map connecting points having the same amount of rainfall in a given period.
– ORIGIN late 19th cent.: from **ISO-** 'equal' + Greek *huetos* 'rain.'

i·so·ki·net·ic /ˌīsōkəˈnetik/ ▶ **adj.** characterized by or producing a constant speed. ■ Physiology of or relating to muscular action with a constant rate of movement.

i·so·late ▶ **v.** /ˈīsəˌlāt/ [with obj.] cause (a person or place) to be or remain alone or apart from others: *a country that is isolated from the rest of the world.* ■ identify (something) and examine or deal with it separately: *you can't isolate stress from the management context.* ■ Chemistry & Biology obtain or extract (a compound, microorganism, etc.) in a pure form. ■ cut off the electrical or other connection to (something, esp. a part of a supply network). ■ place (a person or animal) in quarantine as a precaution against infectious or contagious disease.
▶ **n.** /-lit/ a person or thing that has been or become isolated: *social isolates often become careless of their own welfare.* ■ Biology a culture of microorganisms isolated for study.
– DERIVATIVES **i·so·la·ble** /-ləbəl/ **adj.**, **i·so·lat·a·ble adj.**, **i·so·la·tor** /-ˌlātər/ **n.**
– ORIGIN early 19th cent. (as a verb): back-formation from **ISOLATED**.

i·so·lat·ed /ˈīsəˌlātid/ ▶ **adj.** far away from other places, buildings, or people; remote: *isolated farms and villages.* ■ having minimal contact or little in common with others: *he lived a very isolated existence.* ■ single; exceptional: *they were isolated incidents.*
– ORIGIN mid 18th cent.: from French *isolé*, from Italian *isolato*, from late Latin *insulatus* 'made into an island,' from Latin *insula* 'island.'

i·so·lat·ing /ˈīsəˌlātiNG/ ▶ **adj.** (of a language) tending to have each element as an independent word without inflections.

i·so·la·tion /ˌīsəˈlāSHən/ ▶ **n.** the process or fact of isolating or being isolated: *the isolation of older people.* ■ an instance of isolating something, esp. a compound or microorganism. ■ [as modifier] denoting a hospital or ward for patients with contagious or infectious diseases.
– PHRASES **in isolation** without relation to other people or things; separately: *environmental problems must not be seen in isolation from social ones.*
– ORIGIN mid 19th cent.: from **ISOLATE**, partly on the pattern of French *isolation.*

i·so·la·tion·ism /ˌīsəˈlāSHəˌnizəm/ ▶ **n.** a policy of remaining apart from the affairs or interests of other groups, esp. the political affairs of other countries.
– DERIVATIVES **i·so·la·tion·ist n.**

I·solde /iˈsōld, iˈsōldə, ēˈzôldə/ another name for **ISEULT**[2].

i·so·leu·cine /ˌīsəˈlo͞osēn, -sin/ ▶ **n.** Biochemistry a hydrophobic amino acid that is a constituent of most proteins. It is an essential nutrient in the diet of vertebrates. ● Chem. formula: $CH_3CH_2CH(CH_3)CH(NH_2)COOH$.

i·so·line /ˈīsəˌlīn/ ▶ **n.** another term for **ISOPLETH**.

i·so·mer /ˈīsəmər/ ▶ **n. 1** Chemistry each of two or more compounds with the same formula but a different arrangement of atoms in the molecule and different properties.
2 Physics each of two or more atomic nuclei that have the same atomic number and the same mass number but different energy states.
– DERIVATIVES **i·so·mer·ic** /ˌīsəˈmerik/ **adj.**, **i·som·er·ism** /īˈsäməˌrizəm/ **n.**, **i·som·er·ize** /īˈsäməˌrīz/ **v.**
– ORIGIN mid 19th cent.: from Greek *isomerēs* 'sharing equally,' from *isos* 'equal' + *meros* 'a share.'

i·som·er·ase /īˈsäməˌrās, -ˌrāz/ ▶ **n.** Biochemistry an enzyme that catalyzes the conversion of a specified compound to an isomer.

i·som·er·ous /īˈsämərəs/ ▶ **adj.** Biology having or composed of parts that are similar in number or position.
– ORIGIN mid 19th cent.: from Greek *isomerēs* (see **ISOMER**) + **-OUS**.

i·so·met·ric /ˌīsəˈmetrik/ ▶ **adj. 1** of or having equal dimensions.
2 Physiology of, relating to, or denoting muscular action in which tension is developed without contraction of the muscle.
3 (in technical or architectural drawing) incorporating a method of showing projection or perspective in which the three principal dimensions are represented by three axes 120° apart.
4 Mathematics (of a transformation) without change of shape or size.
– DERIVATIVES **i·so·met·ri·cal·ly** /-ik(ə)lē/ **adv.**, **i·som·e·try** /īˈsämitrē/ **n.** (sense 4).
– ORIGIN mid 19th cent.: from Greek *isometria* 'equality of measure' (from *isos* 'equal' + *-metria* 'measuring') + **-IC**.

i·so·met·rics /ˌīsəˈmetriks/ ▶ **plural n.** a system of physical exercises in which muscles are caused to act against each other or against a fixed object. Also called **isometric exercise**.

i·so·mor·phic /ˌīsəˈmôrfik/ (also **isomorphous** /-fəs/) ▶ **adj.** corresponding or similar in form and relations. ■ having the same crystalline form.
– DERIVATIVES **i·so·mor·phism** /-ˌfizəm/ **n.**

-ison ▶ **suffix** (forming nouns) equivalent to **-ATION** (as in *comparison, jettison*).
– ORIGIN from Old French *-aison, -eison*, etc., from Latin *-atio(n)-*.

i·so·ni·a·zid /ˌīsəˈnīəzid/ ▶ **n.** Medicine a synthetic compound used as a bacteriostatic drug, chiefly to treat tuberculosis. ● A derivative of nicotinic acid and hydrazine; chem. formula: $C_5H_4NCONHNH_2$.

PRONUNCIATION KEY ə *ago, up*; ər *over, fur*; a *hat*; ā *ate*; ä *car*; e *let*; ē *see*; i *fit*; ī *by*; NG *sing*; ō *go*; ô *law, for*; oi *toy*; o͝o *good*; o͞o *goo*; ou *out*; TH *thin*; T͟H *then*; ZH *vision*

– ORIGIN 1950s: from **iso-** 'equal' + *ni(cotinic)* + *(hydr)azine* + **-ide**.

i·so·oc·tane /ˌīsōˈäktān/ ▶ **n.** Chemistry a liquid hydrocarbon present in petroleum. It serves as a standard in the system of octane numbers. ● Chem. formula: $(CH_3)_3CCH_2CH(CH_3)CH_3$.

i·so·pach /ˈīsəˌpak/ ▶ **n.** Geology a line on a map or diagram connecting points beneath which a particular stratum or group of strata has the same thickness.
– ORIGIN early 20th cent.: from **iso-** 'equal' + Greek *pakhus* 'thick.'

i·so·pleth /ˈīsəpleTH/ ▶ **n.** Meteorology a line on a map connecting points having equal incidence of a specified meteorological feature.
– ORIGIN early 20th cent.: from Greek *isoplēthēs* 'equal in quantity,' from *isos* 'equal' + *plēthos* 'multitude, quantity.'

i·so·pod /ˈīsəˌpäd/ ▶ **n.** Zoology a crustacean of the order Isopoda, such as a wood louse.

I·sop·o·da /īˈsäpədə/ Zoology an order of crustaceans that includes the terrestrial wood lice and several marine and freshwater parasites. They have a flattened segmented body with seven similar pairs of legs.
– ORIGIN modern Latin (plural), from Greek *isos* 'equal' + *pous, pod-* 'foot.'

i·so·pre·na·line /ˌīsəˈprenlˌēn/ ▶ **n.** another term for **isoproterenol**.
– ORIGIN 1950s: from elements of the systematic name *N-isopropylnoradrenaline*.

i·so·prene /ˈīsəˌprēn/ ▶ **n.** Chemistry a volatile liquid hydrocarbon obtained from petroleum, whose molecule forms the basic structural unit of natural and synthetic rubbers. ● Chem. formula: $CH_2{:}C(CH_3)CH{:}CH_2$.
– ORIGIN mid 19th cent.: apparently from **iso-** 'equal' + *pr(opyl)ene*.

i·so·pro·pa·nol /ˌīsəˈprōpəˌnôl, -ˌnäl/ ▶ **n.** Chemistry a liquid alcohol, used as a solvent and in the industrial production of acetone. ● Chem. formula: $CH_3CHOHCH_3$.

i·so·pro·pyl /ˌīsəˈprōpəl/ ▶ **n.** [as modifier] Chemistry of or denoting the alkyl radical $-CH(CH_3)_2$, derived from propane by removal of a hydrogen atom from the middle carbon atom.

i·so·pro·pyl al·co·hol ▶ **n.** Chemistry another term for **isopropanol**.

i·so·pro·ter·e·nol /ˌīsəprōˈterəˌnôl, -ˌnäl/ ▶ **n.** Medicine a synthetic derivative of adrenaline, used for the relief of bronchial asthma and pulmonary emphysema.
– ORIGIN 1950s: from elements of the semisystematic name *N-isopropylarterenol*.

I·sop·ter·a /īˈsäptərə/ Entomology an order of insects that comprises the termites.
– DERIVATIVES **i·sop·te·ran n. & adj.**
– ORIGIN modern Latin (plural), from Greek *isos* 'equal' + *pteron* 'wing.'

i·so·pyc·nal /ˌīsəˈpiknl/ ▶ **adj.** Oceanography (esp. of an imaginary line or surface on a map or chart) connecting points in the ocean where the water has the same density.
– ORIGIN early 20th cent.: from **iso-** 'equal' + Greek *puknos* 'dense' + **-al**.

i·so·pyc·nic /ˌīsəˈpiknik/ ▶ **adj.** Biochemistry of or denoting ultracentrifugal separation techniques making use of differences in density between the components of a mixture.
– ORIGIN late 19th cent.: from **iso-** 'equal' + Greek *puknos* 'dense' + **-ic**.

i·so·rhyth·mic /ˌīsəˈriT͟Hmik/ ▶ **adj.** Music (of a composition or part) in which the rhythm is often repeated but the pitch of the notes is varied each time.

i·sos·bes·tic point /ˌīsəsˈbestik/ ▶ **n.** Chemistry a wavelength at which the absorption of light by a mixed solution remains constant as the equilibrium between the components in the solution changes.
– ORIGIN early 20th cent.: *isosbestic* from **iso-** 'equal' + Greek *sbestos* 'extinguished' (from *sbennunai* 'quench') + **-ic**.

i·sos·ce·les /īˈsäsəˌlēz/ ▶ **adj.** (of a triangle) having two sides of equal length.
– ORIGIN mid 16th cent.: via late Latin from Greek *isoskelēs*, from *isos* 'equal' + *skelos* 'leg.'

i·so·seis·mal /ˌīsəˈsīzməl/ ▶ **adj.** Geology relating to or denoting lines on a map connecting places where an earthquake was experienced with equal strength.
– DERIVATIVES **i·so·seis·mic** /-mik/ **adj.**

i·sos·mot·ic /ˌīsäzˈmätik, -säs-/ ▶ **adj.** Biology having the same osmotic pressure.

i·so·spin /ˈīsəˌspin/ ▶ **n.** Physics a vector quantity or quantum number assigned to subatomic particles and atomic nuclei and having values such that similar particles differing only in charge-related properties (independent of the strong interaction between particles) can be treated as different states of a single particle.
– ORIGIN 1960s: contraction of *isotopic spin, isobaric spin*.

i·sos·ta·sy /īˈsästəsē/ ▶ **n.** Geology the equilibrium that exists between parts of the earth's crust, which behaves as if it consists of blocks floating on the underlying mantle, rising if material (such as an ice cap) is removed and sinking if material is deposited.
– DERIVATIVES **i·so·stat·ic** /ˌīsəˈstatik/ **adj.**
– ORIGIN late 19th cent.: from **iso-** 'equal' + Greek *stasis* 'station.'

i·so·tac·tic /ˌīsəˈtaktik/ ▶ **adj.** Chemistry (of a polymer) in which all the repeating units have the same stereochemical configuration.
– ORIGIN 1950s: from **iso-** 'equal' + Greek *taktos* 'arranged' + **-ic**.

i·so·there /ˈīsəˌTHir/ ▶ **n.** Meteorology a line on a map connecting points having the same average temperature in summer.
– ORIGIN mid 19th cent.: from French *isothère*, from Greek *isos* 'equal' + *theros* 'summer.'

i·so·therm /ˈīsəˌTHərm/ ▶ **n.** a line on a map connecting points having the same temperature at a given time or on average over a given period. ■ Physics a curve on a diagram joining points representing states or conditions of equal temperature.
– DERIVATIVES **i·so·ther·mal** /ˌīsəˈTHərməl/ **adj. & n.**, **i·so·ther·mal·ly** /ˌīsəˈTHərməlē/ **adv.**
– ORIGIN mid 19th cent.: from French *isotherme*, from Greek *isos* 'equal' + *thermē* 'heat.'

i·so·thi·o·cy·a·nate /ˌīsōˌTHī-ōˈsīənāt, -nit/ ▶ **n.** a family of organic compounds found in tangy herbs such as horseradish, mustard, and onions. They have several patented applications including use as a pesticide, and their presence in the diet is thought to help prevent cancer in humans.

i·so·ton·ic /ˌīsəˈtänik/ ▶ **adj.** Physiology **1** (of muscle action) taking place with normal contraction.
2 denoting or relating to a solution having the same osmotic pressure as some other solution, esp. one in a cell or a body fluid. ■ (of a drink) containing essential salts and minerals in the same concentration as in the body and intended to replace those lost as a result of sweating during vigorous exercise.
– DERIVATIVES **i·so·ton·i·cal·ly** /-ik(ə)lē/ **adv.**, **i·so·to·nic·i·ty** /-təˈnisitē/ **n.**
– ORIGIN early 19th cent. (as a musical term designating a system of tuning, characterized by equal intervals): from Greek *isotonos*, from *isos* 'equal' + *tonos* 'tone.'

i·so·tope /ˈīsəˌtōp/ ▶ **n.** Chemistry each of two or more forms of the same element that contain equal numbers of protons but different numbers of neutrons in their nuclei, and hence differ in relative atomic mass but not in chemical properties; in particular, a radioactive form of an element.
– DERIVATIVES **i·so·top·ic** /ˌīsəˈtäpik/ **adj.**, **i·so·top·i·cal·ly** /ˌīsəˈtäpik(ə)lē/ **adv.**, **i·sot·o·py** /ˈīsəˌtōpē, īˈsätəpē/ **n.**
– ORIGIN 1913: coined by F. Soddy, from **iso-** 'equal' + Greek *topos* 'place' (because the isotopes occupy the same place in the periodic table of elements).

i·so·trop·ic /ˌīsəˈträpik, -ˈtrōpik/ ▶ **adj.** Physics (of an object or substance) having a physical property that has the same value when measured in different directions. Often contrasted with **anisotropic**. ■ (of a property or phenomenon) not varying in magnitude according to the direction of measurement.
– DERIVATIVES **i·so·trop·i·cal·ly** /-ik(ə)lē/ **adv.**, **i·sot·ro·py** /īˈsätrəpē/ **n.**
– ORIGIN mid 19th cent.: from **iso-** 'equal' + Greek *tropos* 'a turn' + **-ic**.

i·so·zyme /ˈīsəˌzīm/ ▶ **n.** Biochemistry each of two or more enzymes with identical function but different structure.

ISP ▶ **abbr.** Internet Service Provider.

Is·pa·han variant spelling of **Isfahan**.

I spy ▶ **n.** a children's game in which one player specifies the first letter of an object they can see, the other players then having to guess the identity of this object.

Is·ra·el[1] /ˈizrēəl, ˈizˌrāl/ **1** (also **children of Israel**) the Hebrew nation or people. According to tradition, they are descended from the patriarch Jacob (also named Israel), whose twelve sons became founders of the twelve tribes of ancient Israel. See also **Tribes of Israel**.
2 the northern kingdom of the Hebrews (*c.*930–721 BC), formed after the reign of Solomon, whose inhabitants were carried away to captivity in Assyria. See also **Judah** (sense 2).
– ORIGIN from Hebrew *Yiśrā'ēl* 'he that strives with God' (see Gen. 32:28).

Is·ra·el[2] a country in the Middle East, on the Mediterranean Sea; pop. 7,233,700 (est. 2009); capital (not recognized as such by the United Nations), Jerusalem; languages, Hebrew (official), English, and Arabic.

> The modern state of Israel was established as a Jewish homeland in 1948, on land that was at that time part of the British mandated territory of Palestine. Israel was immediately attacked by the surrounding Arab states, which it defeated. The continuing conflict with the neighbouring Arabs, mainly over the rights of the Palestinians displaced from their homes or living under Israeli rule, has caused continual tension and intermittent terrorist and military activity. Further wars occurred in 1956, 1967, and 1973, which resulted in Israeli occupation of eastern Jerusalem, the West Bank, the Gaza Strip, and the Golan Heights. In 1993, Israel and the Palestine Liberation Organization signed an agreement for limited Palestinian autonomy in the West Bank and the Gaza Strip, but this proved unsuccessful in bringing about an end to conflict. See also **Palestine**.

Is·rae·li /izˈrālē/ ▶ **adj.** of or relating to the modern country of Israel.
▶ **n.** (pl. **Israelis**) a native or inhabitant of Israel, or a person of Israeli descent.

Is·ra·el·ite /ˈizrēəˌlīt/ ▶ **n.** a member of the ancient Hebrew nation, esp. in the period from the Exodus to the Babylonian Captivity (*c.*12th to 6th centuries BC). ■ old-fashioned and sometimes offensive term for **Jew**.
▶ **adj.** of or relating to the Israelites.
– ORIGIN via late Latin from Greek *Israēlitēs*.

Is·ra·fil /ˈizrəˌfēl/ (in Muslim tradition) the angel of music, who will sound the trumpet on Judgment Day.

Is·sa /ˈēˌsä, iˈsä/ ▶ **n.** (pl. **same** or **Issas**) a member of a Somali people living in Djibouti.
▶ **adj.** of or relating to the Issa.
– ORIGIN the name in Somali.

Is·sa·char /ˈisəˌkär/ (in the Bible) a Hebrew patriarch, son of Jacob and Leah (Gen. 30:18). ■ the tribe of Israel traditionally descended from him.

is·sei /ˈē(s)ˌsā/ ▶ **n.** (pl. **same**) a Japanese immigrant to North America. Compare with **nisei** and **sansei**.
– ORIGIN Japanese, literally 'first generation.'

ISSN ▶ **abbr.** international standard serial number, an eight-digit number assigned to many serial publications such as newspapers, magazines, annuals, and series of books.

is·su·ant /ˈisHo͞oənt/ ▶ **adj.** [predic. or postpositive] Heraldry (of the upper part of an animal) shown rising up or out from another bearing, esp. from the bottom of a chief or from behind a fess.
– ORIGIN early 17th cent.: from **issue** + **-ant** (on the pattern of French present participles ending in *-ant*).

is·sue /ˈisHo͞o/ ▶ **n. 1** an important topic or problem for debate or discussion: *the issue of global warming* | *money is not an issue*. ■ (**issues**) personal problems or difficulties: *a nice guy with a great sense of humor and not too many issues*. ■ (**issues**) problems or difficulties, esp. with a service or facility: *a small number of users are experiencing connectivity issues*.
2 the action of supplying or distributing an item for use, sale, or official purposes: *the issue of promissory notes by the bank*. ■ each of a regular series of publications: *the December issue of the magazine*. ■ a number or set of items distributed at one time: *a share issue has been launched*.
3 formal or Law children of one's own: *he died without male issue*.
4 the action of flowing or coming out: *the point of issue* | *an issue of blood*.
5 dated a result or outcome of something: *the chance of carrying such a scheme to a successful issue was small*.
▶ **v.** (**issues, issued, issuing**) **1** [with obj.] supply or distribute (something): *licenses were issued indiscriminately to any company*. ■ (**issue someone with**) supply someone with (something). ■ formally send out or make known: *the minister issued a statement*. ■ put (something) on sale or into general use: *Christmas stamps to be issued in November*.
2 [no obj.] (**issue from**) come, go, or flow out from: *exotic smells issued from a nearby building*. ■ result or be derived from: *the struggles of history issue from the divided heart of humanity*.
– PHRASES **at issue** under discussion; in dispute. **make an issue of** treat too seriously or as a problem. **take issue with** disagree with; challenge: *she takes issue with the notion of crime as unique to contemporary society*.
– DERIVATIVES **is·su·a·ble adj.**, **is·su·ance** /-əns/ **n.**, **is·sue·less adj.**, **is·su·er n.**

– ORIGIN Middle English (in the sense 'outflowing'): from Old French, based on Latin *exitus*, past part. of *exire* 'go out.'

> **WORD TRENDS** To say that someone has **issues** is to imply that they suffer from emotional or psychological difficulties: *she's got issues from her childhood | he has serious issues with monogamy.* This use of the term is a euphemistic way of avoiding the word **problem**, which is seen as negative and stigmatizing. The exact nature of the issues is generally left vague and mysterious, even when narrowed down by a modifier (*intimacy issues, emotional issues, mental issues*). More generally, **issues** are problems or difficulties, particularly with the provision of a service (*devices on the company's network are experiencing performance issues*): again, the word has a euphemistic feel, perhaps implying that what is occurring is not so serious or specific as to amount to an actual problem. See also **SOLUTION**.

IST ▶ **abbr.** insulin shock therapy.

-ist /əst, ist/ ▶ **suffix** [forming personal nouns and some related adjectives:] **1** denoting an adherent of a system of beliefs, principles, etc., expressed by nouns ending in *-ism*: *hedonist | Buddhist.* See **-ISM** (sense 2). ■ denoting a person who subscribes to a prejudice or practices discrimination: *sexist.* **2** denoting a member of a profession or business activity: *dentist | dramatist | florist.* ■ denoting a person who uses a thing: *flutist | motorist.* ■ denoting a person who does something expressed by a verb ending in *-ize*: *plagiarist.*
– ORIGIN from Old French *-iste*, Latin *-ista*, from Greek *-istēs.*

-ista ▶ **suffix** informal forming nouns denoting a person associated with a particular activity, often with a humorous intent: *fashionista.*
– ORIGIN from the Spanish suffix *-ista*, as in *Sandinista.*

Is·tan·bul /ˌistəmˈbo͞ol, -ˌtän-, -ˌtan-, -ˈbo͝ol/ a port in Turkey on the Bosporus that straddles Europe and Asia; pop. 10,757,300 (est. 2007). Formerly the Roman city of Constantinople 330–1453, it was built on the site of the ancient Greek city of Byzantium. It was captured by the Ottoman Turks in 1453 and was the capital of Turkey from that time until 1923.
– ORIGIN Turkish, from Greek *eis tēn polin* 'into the city.'

isth. (also **Isth.**) ▶ **abbr.** isthmus.

isth·mi·an /ˈismēən/ ▶ **adj.** of or relating to an isthmus. ■ (**Isthmian**) of or relating to the Isthmus of Corinth in southern Greece or the Isthmus of Panama.

isth·mus /ˈisməs/ ▶ **n.** (pl. **isthmuses**) a narrow strip of land with sea on either side, forming a link between two larger areas of land. ■ (pl. **isthmi** /-mī/) Anatomy a narrow organ, passage, or piece of tissue connecting two larger parts.
– ORIGIN mid 16th cent.: via Latin from Greek *isthmos.*

is·tle /ˈis(t)lē/ ▶ **n.** variant spelling of **IXTLE**.

ISV ▶ **abbr.** ■ independent software vendor. ■ International Scientific Vocabulary.

IT ▶ **abbr.** information technology.

it ▶ **pron.** [third person singular] **1** used to refer to a thing previously mentioned or easily identified: *a room with two beds in it | this approach is refreshing because it breaks down barriers.* ■ referring to an animal or child of unspecified sex: *she was holding the baby, cradling it and smiling into its face.* ■ referring to a fact or situation previously mentioned, known, or happening: *stop it, you're hurting me.* **2** used to identify a person: *it's me | it's a boy!* **3** used in the normal subject position in statements about time, distance, or weather: *it's half past five | it was two miles to the island | it is raining.* **4** used in the normal subject or object position when a more specific subject or object is given later in the sentence: *it is impossible to assess the problem | she found it interesting to learn about their strategy.* **5** [with clause] used to emphasize a following part of a sentence: *it is the child who is the victim.* **6** the situation or circumstances; things in general: *no one can stay here—it's too dangerous now | he would like to see you right away if it's convenient.* **7** exactly what is needed or desired: *they thought they were it | you've either got it or you haven't.* **8** (usu. **"it"**) informal sex appeal: *he's still got "it."* ■ sexual intercourse. **9** (usu. **"it"**) (in children's games) the player who has to catch the others.
– PHRASES **at it** see **AT**[1]. **that's it 1** that is the main point or difficulty: *"Is she going?" "That's just it—she can't make up her mind."* **2** that is enough or the end: *okay, that's it, you've cried long enough.* **this is it 1** the expected event is about to happen: *this is it—the big sale.* **2** this is enough or the end: *this is it, I'm going.* **3** this is the main point or difficulty.
– ORIGIN Old English *hit*, neuter of **HE**, of Germanic origin; related to Dutch *het.*

ital. ▶ **abbr.** italic (used as an instruction for a typesetter).

I·tal·ian /iˈtalyən/ ▶ **adj.** of or relating to Italy, its people, or their language.
▶ **n. 1** a native or inhabitant of Italy, or a person of Italian descent. **2** the Romance language of Italy, also one of the official languages of Switzerland.
– DERIVATIVES **I·tal·ian·ize** /-ˌnīz/ **v.**
– ORIGIN late Middle English: from Italian *italiano*, from *Italia* 'Italy.'

I·tal·ian·ate /iˈtalyəˌnāt/ ▶ **adj.** Italian in character or appearance: *an Italianate staircase with triple loggia.*
– ORIGIN late 16th cent.: from Italian *italianato*, from *Italia* 'Italy.'

I·tal·ian·ism /iˈtalyəˌnizəm/ ▶ **n. 1** an Italian characteristic, expression, or custom. **2** attachment to Italy or Italian ideas or practices.

I·tal·ian pars·ley ▶ **n.** another term for **FLAT-LEAFED PARSLEY**.

I·tal·ic /iˈtalik, īˈtal-/ ▶ **adj.** relating to or denoting the branch of Indo-European languages that includes Latin, Oscan, Umbrian, and the Romance languages.
▶ **n.** the Italic group of languages.
– ORIGIN late 19th cent.: via Latin from Greek *Italikos*, from *Italia* 'Italy.'

i·tal·ic /iˈtalik, īˈtal-/ ▶ **adj.** Printing of the sloping kind of typeface used esp. for emphasis or distinction and in foreign words. ■ (of handwriting) modeled on 16th-century Italian handwriting, typically cursive and sloping and with elliptical or pointed letters.
▶ **n.** (also **italics**) an italic typeface or letter: *the key words are in italics.*
– ORIGIN late Middle English (in the general sense 'Italian'): via Latin from Greek *Italikos*, from *Italia* 'Italy.' Senses relating to writing date from the early 17th cent.

i·tal·i·cize /iˈtaliˌsīz, īˈtal-/ ▶ **v.** [with obj.] print (text) in italics: *she italicized the title* | [no obj.] *use this key to italicize.*
– DERIVATIVES **i·tal·i·ci·za·tion** /iˌtalisiˈzāsʜən/ **n.**

Italo- ▶ **comb. form** Italian; Italian and ...: *Italophile | Italo-Grecian.* ■ relating to Italy.

It·a·ly /ˈitl-ē/ a country in southern Europe; pop. 58,126,200 (est. 2009); capital, Rome; official language, Italian. Italian name **Italia**.

> Successor to Rome, Italy achieved unification in the 19th century. It entered World War I on the Allied side in 1915. In 1922, the country was taken over by Fascist dictator Mussolini; participation in support of Germany during World War II resulted in defeat and Mussolini's downfall. Italy was a founding member of the EEC.

ITAR-Tass /ˌētär ˈtäs/ the official news agency of Russia, founded in 1925 in Leningrad as Tass, and renamed in 1992.
– ORIGIN from the initials of Russian *Informatsionnoe telegrafnoe agentstvo Rossii* 'Information Telegraph Agency of Russia,' + **TASS**.

itch /icʜ/ ▶ **n.** [usu. in sing.] an uncomfortable sensation on the skin that causes a desire to scratch. ■ informal a restless or strong desire: [with infinitive] *the itch to write fiction.* ■ [usu. with modifier] a skin disease or condition of which itching is a symptom. ■ (**the itch**) informal scabies.
▶ **v.** [no obj.] be the site of or cause an itch: *the bite itched like crazy.* ■ (of a person) experience an itch. ■ informal feel a restless or strong desire to do something: [with infinitive] *your hands itch to take the wheel.*
– PHRASES **an itching palm** informal an avaricious nature.
– ORIGIN Old English *gycce* (noun), *gyccan* (verb); related to Dutch *jeuk* (noun) and Dutch *jeuken*, German *jucken* (verb).

itch mite ▶ **n.** a parasitic mite that burrows under the skin, causing scabies in humans and sarcoptic mange in animals. ● *Sarcoptes scabiei*, family Sarcoptidae.

itch·y /ˈicʜē/ ▶ **adj.** (**itchier, itchiest**) having or causing an itch: *dry, itchy skin | an itchy rash.*
– PHRASES **get** (or **have**) **itchy feet** informal have or develop a strong urge to travel or move from place to place. **an itchy palm** informal an avaricious nature.
– DERIVATIVES **itch·i·ness** **n.**

it'd /ˈitid/ ▶ **contraction** it had: *it'd been there for years.* ■ it would: *it'd be great to see you.*

-ite[1] ▶ **suffix 1** forming names denoting natives of a country: *Israelite | Samnite.* ■ often derogatory denoting followers of a movement, doctrine, etc.: *Luddite | Jacobite.* **2** used in scientific and technical terms. ■ forming names of fossil organisms: *ammonite.* ■ forming names of minerals: *graphite.* ■ forming names of constituent parts of a body or organ: *somite.* ■ forming names of explosives and other commercial products: *dynamite | vulcanite.* ■ Chemistry forming names of salts or esters of acids ending in *-ous*: *sulfite.*
– ORIGIN from French *-ite*, via Latin *-ita* from Greek *-itēs.*

-ite[2] ▶ **suffix 1** forming adjectives such as *composite, erudite.* **2** forming nouns such as *appetite.* **3** forming verbs such as *unite.*
– ORIGIN from Latin *-itus*, past participle of verbs ending in *-ere* and *-ire.*

i·tem /ˈītəm/ ▶ **n.** an individual article or unit, esp. one that is part of a list, collection, or set: *the items on the agenda | an item of clothing.* ■ a piece of news or information. ■ an entry in an account.
▶ **adv.** archaic used to introduce each item in a list: *item two statute books ... item two drums.*
– PHRASES **be an item** informal (of a couple) be involved in an established romantic or sexual relationship.
– ORIGIN late Middle English (as an adverb): from Latin, 'in like manner, also.' The noun sense arose (late 16th cent.) from the use of the adverb to introduce each statement in a list.

i·tem·ize /ˈītəˌmīz/ ▶ **v.** [with obj.] present as a list of individual items: *I have itemized the morning's tasks.* ■ break down (a whole) into its constituent parts: (as adj. **itemized**) *an itemized bill.* ■ specify (an individual item or items).
– DERIVATIVES **i·tem·i·za·tion** /ˌītəmiˈzāsʜən/ **n.**, **i·tem·iz·er** **n.**

it·er·ate /ˈitəˌrāt/ ▶ **v.** [with obj.] perform or utter repeatedly. ■ [no obj.] make repeated use of a mathematical or computational procedure, applying it each time to the result of the previous application; perform iteration.
▶ **n.** Mathematics a quantity arrived at by iteration.
– ORIGIN mid 16th cent.: from Latin *iterat-* 'repeated,' from the verb *iterare*, from *iterum* 'again.'

it·er·a·tion /ˌitəˈrāsʜən/ ▶ **n.** the repetition of a process or utterance. ■ repetition of a mathematical or computational procedure applied to the result of a previous application, typically as a means of obtaining successively closer approximations to the solution of a problem. ■ a new version of a piece of computer hardware or software.
– ORIGIN late Middle English: from Latin *iteratio(n-)*, from the verb *iterare* (see **ITERATE**).

it·er·a·tive /ˈitəˌrātiv, -rətiv/ ▶ **adj.** relating to or involving iteration, esp. of a mathematical or computational process. ■ Linguistics denoting a grammatical rule that can be applied repeatedly. ■ Grammar another term for **FREQUENTATIVE**.
– DERIVATIVES **it·er·a·tive·ly** **adv.**
– ORIGIN late 15th cent.: from French *itératif, -ive*, from Latin *iterare* 'to repeat'; the grammar term is from late Latin *iterativus.*

It girl ▶ **n.** a young woman who has achieved celebrity because of her socialite lifestyle.
– ORIGIN coined by American screenwriter Elinor Glyn (1864–1943), with reference to American actress and sex symbol Clara Bow (1905–65), who starred in Glyn's romantic comedy *It* (1927). The current usage dates from the 1960s.

Ith·a·ca /ˈitʜikə/ **1** an island off the western coast of Greece in the Ionian Sea, the legendary home of Odysseus. **2** an academic city in central New York, at the southern end of Cayuga Lake, home to Cornell University and Ithaca College; pop. 29,763 (est. 2008).

I-Thou ▶ **adj.** [attrib.] (of a personal relationship, esp. one with God) formed by personal encounter.

ith·y·phal·lic /ˌitʜəˈfalik/ ▶ **adj.** (esp. of a statue of a deity or other carved figure) having an erect penis.
– ORIGIN early 17th cent. (as a noun denoting a sexually explicit poem): via late Latin from Greek *ithuphallikos*, from *ithus* 'straight' + *phallos* 'phallus.'

-itic ▶ **suffix** forming adjectives and nouns corresponding to nouns ending in *-ite* (such as *Semitic* corresponding to *Semite*). ■ corresponding to nouns ending in *-itis* (such as *arthritic* corresponding to *arthritis*). ■ from other bases: *syphilitic.*

PRONUNCIATION KEY ə *ago, up*; ər *over, fur*; a *hat*; ā *ate*; ä *car*; e *let*; ē *see*; i *fit*; ī *by*; NG *sing*; ō *go*; ô *law, for*; oi *toy*; o͝o *good*; o͞o *goo*; ou *out*; TH *thin*; T͟H *then*; ZH *vision*

– ORIGIN from French *-itique*, via Latin *-iticus* from Greek *-itikos*.

i·tin·er·ant /ī'tinərənt, i'tin-/ ▶ **adj.** traveling from place to place: *itinerant traders*.
▶ **n.** a person who travels from place to place.
– DERIVATIVES **i·tin·er·a·cy** /-rəsē/ **n.**, **i·tin·er·an·cy n.**, **i·tin·er·ant·ly adv.**
– ORIGIN late 16th cent. (used to describe a judge traveling on a circuit): from late Latin *itinerant-* 'traveling,' from the verb *itinerari*, from Latin *iter, itiner-* 'journey, road.'

i·tin·er·ar·y /ī'tinə,rerē, i'tin-/ ▶ **n.** (pl. **itineraries**) a planned route or journey. ■ a travel document recording these.
– ORIGIN late Middle English: from late Latin *itinerarium*, neuter of *itinerarius* 'of a journey or roads,' from Latin *iter, itiner-* 'journey, road.'

i·tin·er·ate /ī'tinə,rāt, i'tin-/ ▶ **v.** [no obj.] (esp. of a church minister or a judge) travel from place to place to perform one's professional duty.
– DERIVATIVES **i·tin·er·a·tion** /ī,tinə'rāsHən, i,tin-/ **n.**
– ORIGIN early 17th cent.: from late Latin *itinerat-* 'traveled,' from the verb *itinerari* (see ITINERANT).

-ition ▶ **suffix** (forming nouns) equivalent to -ATION (as in *audition, rendition*).
– ORIGIN from French, or from Latin *-itio(n)-*.

-itious[1] ▶ **suffix** forming adjectives corresponding to nouns ending in *-ition* (such as *ambitious* corresponding to *ambition*).
– ORIGIN from Latin *-itiosus*.

-itious[2] ▶ **suffix** (forming adjectives) related to; having the nature of: *fictitious | suppositious*.
– ORIGIN from late Latin *-itius*, alteration of Latin *-icius*.

-itis ▶ **suffix** forming names of inflammatory diseases: *cystitis | hepatitis*. ■ informal used with reference to a tendency or state of mind that is compared to a disease: *creditcarditis*.
– ORIGIN from Greek feminine form of adjectives ending in *-itēs* (combined with *nosos* 'disease' implied).

-itive ▶ **suffix** (forming adjectives) equivalent to -ATIVE (as in *genitive, positive*).
– ORIGIN from French *-itif, -itive* or Latin *-itivus* (from past participial stems ending in *-it*).

it'll /'itl/ ▶ **contraction** it shall; it will.

I·to /'ētō/, Prince Hirobumi (1841–1909), Japanese statesman; premier 1885–88, 1892–96, 1898, 1900–01. He helped to draft the Japanese constitution 1889 and to establish a bicameral national diet 1890. He was assassinated by a member of the Korean independence movement.

-itous ▶ **suffix** forming adjectives corresponding to nouns ending in *-ity* (such as *calamitous* corresponding to *calamity*).
– ORIGIN from French *-iteux*, from Latin *-itosus*.

its /its/ ▶ **possessive determiner** belonging to or associated with a thing previously mentioned or easily identified: *turn the camera on its side | he chose the area for its atmosphere*. ■ belonging to or associated with a child or animal of unspecified sex: *a baby in its mother's womb*.

> **USAGE** Its is the possessive form of *it* (*the dog licked its paw*), while **it's** is the contraction of *it is* (*look, it's a dog licking its paw*) or *it has* (*it's been too long*). The apostrophe in **it's** never denotes a possessive. The confusion is understandable, since other possessive forms (singular nouns) do take an apostrophe + *s*, as in *the girl's bike* or *the president's smile*.

it's /its/ ▶ **contraction** it is: *it's my fault*. ■ it has: *it's been a hot day*.

> **USAGE** See usage at ITS.

it·self /it'self/ ▶ **pron.** [third person singular] **1** [reflexive] used as the object of a verb or preposition to refer to a thing or animal previously mentioned as the subject of the clause: *his horse hurt itself | wisteria was tumbling over itself*.
2 [emphatic] used to emphasize a particular thing or animal mentioned: *the roots are several inches long, though the plant itself is only a foot tall*. ■ used after a quality to emphasize what a perfect example of that quality someone or something is: *Mrs. Vincent was kindness itself*.
– PHRASES **by itself** see BY ONESELF at BY. **in itself** viewed in its essential qualities; considered separately from other things: *some would say bringing up a family was a full-time job in itself*.
– ORIGIN Old English (see IT, SELF).

it·ty-bit·ty /,itē 'bitē/ (also **itsy-bitsy** /,itsē 'bitsē/) ▶ **adj.** informal very small; tiny.
– ORIGIN 1930s: from a child's form of LITTLE + BITTY.

ITU ▶ **abbr.** International Telecommunication Union.

ITV (also **iTV**) ▶ **abbr.** interactive television.

-ity ▶ **suffix** forming nouns denoting quality or condition: *humility | probity*. ■ denoting an instance or degree of this: *a profanity*.
– ORIGIN from French *-ité*, from Latin *-itas, -itatis*.

IU ▶ **abbr.** international unit.

IUCN ▶ **abbr.** International Union for the Conservation of Nature.

IUD ▶ **abbr.** ■ intrauterine death (of the fetus before birth). ■ intrauterine device.

-ium ▶ **suffix 1** forming nouns adopted unchanged from Latin (such as *alluvium*) or based on Latin or Greek words (such as *euphonium*).
2 (also **-um**) forming names of metallic elements: *cadmium | magnesium*.
3 denoting a region of the body: *pericardium*.
4 denoting a biological structure: *mycelium*.
– ORIGIN modern Latin in sense 2, sense 3, and sense 4 via Latin from Greek *-ion*.

IUPAC ▶ **abbr.** International Union of Pure and Applied Chemistry.

IV ▶ **abbr.** intravenous(ly).
▶ **n.** an intravenous drip feed: *they put an IV in me*.

I·van /'īvən/ the name of six rulers of Russia.
■ **Ivan I** (*c.*1304–41), grand duke of Muscovy 1328–40. He strengthened and enlarged the duchy, making Moscow the ecclesiastical capital in 1326.
■ **Ivan II** (1326–59), grand duke of Muscovy 1353–59; known as **Ivan the Red**. ■ **Ivan III** (1440–1505), grand duke of Muscovy 1462–1505; known as **Ivan the Great**. He consolidated and enlarged his territory, defending it against a Tartar invasion in 1480. ■ **Ivan IV** (1530–84), grand duke of Muscovy 1533–47 and first tsar of Russia 1547–84; known as **Ivan the Terrible**. In 1581, Ivan killed his eldest son, Ivan, in a fit of rage; the succession passed to his mentally handicapped second son, **Fyodor**. ■ **Ivan V** (1666–96), nominal tsar of Russia 1682–96. ■ **Ivan VI** (1740–64), infant tsar of Russia 1740–41.

I've /īv/ ▶ **contraction** I have.

-ive ▶ **suffix** (forming adjectives, also nouns derived from them) tending to; having the nature of: *active | corrosive | palliative*.
– ORIGIN from French *-if, -ive*, from Latin *-ivus*.

-ively ▶ **suffix** forming adverbs corresponding to adjectives ending in *-ive* (such as *corrosively* corresponding to *corrosive*).
– ORIGIN see -IVE, -LY[2].

-iveness ▶ **suffix** forming nouns corresponding to adjectives ending in *-ive* (such as *corrosiveness* corresponding to *corrosive*).
– ORIGIN see -IVE, -NESS.

i·ver·mec·tin /,īvər'mektin/ ▶ **n.** a compound used as an anthelmintic in veterinary medicine and as a treatment for river blindness.

Ives[1], Charles (Edward) (1874–1954), US composer, noted for his use of polyrhythms, polytonality, quarter-tones, and aleatoric techniques. Notable works: *The Unanswered Question* (1906), *Three Places in New England* (1903–14), and *Concord* (1915).

Ives[2], James Merritt (1824–1907) US publisher and artist who partnered with Nathaniel Currier to establish the company of Currier & Ives in 1857.

IVF ▶ **abbr.** in vitro fertilization.

i·vied /'īvēd/ ▶ **adj.** covered in ivy: *an ivied church*. ■ of or relating to the academic institutions of the Ivy League: *the ivied eastern schools and colleges*.

IVM ▶ **abbr.** in vitro maturation, a fertility treatment in which immature eggs are extracted from a woman's body and matured in a laboratory before being fertilized.

I·vo·ri·an /ī'vôrēən/ ▶ **adj.** relating to Côte d'Ivoire (Ivory Coast) or its people: *Ivorian protests*.
▶ **n.** a native or inhabitant of Côte d'Ivoire: *a call for all Ivorians to participate*.

I·vo·ry /'īvərē/, James (1928–), US movie director. He made a number of movies in partnership with producer Ismail Merchant, including *Heat and Dust* (1983), *A Room with a View* (1985), *Howards End* (1992), and *The Remains of the Day* (1993).

i·vo·ry /'īv(ə)rē/ ▶ **n.** (pl. **ivories**) **1** a hard creamy-white substance composing the main part of the tusks of an elephant, walrus, or narwhal, often (esp. formerly) used to make ornaments and other articles: [as modifier] *a knife with an ivory handle*. ■ an object made of ivory. ■ (**the ivories**) informal the keys of a piano. ■ (**ivories**) informal a person's teeth.
2 a creamy-white color.
– DERIVATIVES **i·vo·ried** /-rēd/ **adj.**
– ORIGIN Middle English: from Anglo-Norman French *ivurie*, based on Latin *ebur*.

i·vo·ry black ▶ **n.** a black carbon pigment made from charred ivory or (now usually) bone, used in drawing and painting.

I·vo·ry Coast see CÔTE D'IVOIRE.

i·vo·ry nut ▶ **n.** the seed of a tropical American palm, which, when hardened, is a source of vegetable ivory. Also called TAGUA NUT. ● The palm is *Phytelephas macrocarpa*, family Palmae.

i·vo·ry tow·er ▶ **n.** a state of privileged seclusion or separation from the facts and practicalities of the real world: *the ivory tower of academia*.
– ORIGIN early 20th cent.: translating French *tour d'ivoire*, used by the writer Sainte-Beuve (1804–69).

i·vy /'īvē/ ▶ **n.** a woody evergreen Eurasian climbing plant, typically having shiny, dark green five-pointed leaves. ● Genus *Hedera*, family Araliaceae: several species, in particular the common **English ivy** (*H. helix*), which is often seen climbing on tree trunks and walls.
■ used in names of similar climbing plants, e.g., **poison ivy, Boston ivy**.
– ORIGIN Old English *īfig*, of Germanic origin; related to the first elements of Dutch *eiloof* and German *Efeu*.

English ivy

I·vy League ▶ **n.** a group of long-established colleges and universities in the eastern US having high academic and social prestige. It includes Harvard, Yale, Princeton, Columbia, Dartmouth, Cornell, Brown, and the University of Pennsylvania: [as modifier] *an Ivy League school*.
– DERIVATIVES **I·vy Lea·guer n.**
– ORIGIN with reference to the ivy traditionally growing over the walls of these establishments.

IW ▶ **abbr.** ■ index word. ■ isotopic weight.

i.w. ▶ **abbr.** ■ inside width. ■ isotopic weight.

IWC ▶ **abbr.** International Whaling Commission.

I·wo Ji·ma /,ēwə 'jēmə, ,ēwō/ a small volcanic island, the largest of the Volcano Islands in the western Pacific Ocean, 760 miles (1,222 km) south of Tokyo. During World War II, it was a heavily fortified site of a Japanese airbase, and its attack and capture in 1944–45 was one of the most severe US campaigns. It was returned to Japan in 1968.

IWW ▶ **abbr.** Industrial Workers of the World.

ix·i·a /'iksēə/ ▶ **n.** a South African plant of the iris family that bears showy six-petaled starlike flowers on tall wiry stems and has sword-shaped leaves.
● Genus *Ixia*, family Iridaceae: and many cultivars.
– ORIGIN modern Latin, from Latin, denoting a kind of thistle, from Greek.

Ix·i·on /ik'sīən, 'iksē, än/ Greek Mythology a king who, by Zeus's command, was pinned to a fiery wheel that revolved unceasingly through the underworld, as punishment for his alleged seduction of Hera.

ix·nay /'iks,nā/ informal ▶ **exclam.** (**ixnay on/to**) used in rejecting something specified: *a nice place to paddle, but ixnay on the swimming*.
▶ **v.** [with obj.] cancel or stop: *he ought to ixnay with the moral exhibitionism and get into the entertainment biz*.
– ORIGIN 1930s: pig Latin for *nix*.

ix·tle /'ikstl-ē, 'is(t)-/ (also **istle**) ▶ **n.** (in Mexico and Central America) a plant fiber used for cordage, nets, and carpets. ● This fiber is obtained chiefly from *Agave* species (family Agavaceae), in particular *A. funkiana* and *A. lecheguilla*.
– ORIGIN late 19th cent.: via American Spanish from Nahuatl *ixtli*.

I·yen·gar /ē'yeNGgär/ ▶ **n.** a type of ashtanga yoga focusing on the correct alignment of the body, making use of straps, wooden blocks, etc. as aids to achieving the correct postures.
– ORIGIN named after the Indian yoga teacher B. K. S. *Iyengar* (1918–), who devised the method.

Iy·yar /'ē,yär, ē'yär/ (also **Iyar**) ▶ **n.** (in the Jewish calendar) the eighth month of the civil and second of the religious year, usually coinciding with parts of April and May.
– ORIGIN from Hebrew *'iyyār*.

iz·ard /'izərd/ ▶ **n.** (in the Pyrenees) a chamois.
– ORIGIN late 18th cent.: from French *isard* or Gascon *isart*, of unknown origin.

-ization ▶ **suffix** forming nouns corresponding to adjectives ending in *-ize* (such as *fossilization* corresponding to *fossilize*).
– ORIGIN see -IZE, -ATION.

-ize ▶ **suffix** forming verbs meaning: **1** make or become: *fossilize | privatize*. ■ cause to resemble: *Americanize*.
2 treat in a specified way: *pasteurize*. ■ treat or cause to combine with a specified substance: *carbonize | oxidize*.
3 follow a specified practice: *agonize | theorize*.
■ subject to a practice: *hospitalize*.

– ORIGIN from French *-iser*, via late Latin *-izare* from Greek verbs ending in *-izein*.

USAGE 1 The form **-ize** has been in use in English since the 16th century. The alternative spelling **-ise** (reflecting a French influence) is in common use, especially in British English. It is obligatory in certain cases: first, where it forms part of a larger word element, such as **-mise** (= sending) in **compromise**, and **-prise** (= taking) in **surprise**; and second, in verbs corresponding to nouns with **-s-** in the stem, such as **televise** (from *television*). 2 Adding **-ize** to a noun or adjective has been a standard way of forming new verbs for centuries, and verbs such as **characterize**, **terrorize**, and **sterilize** were all formed in this way hundreds of years ago. Some traditionalists object to recent formations of this type: during the 20th century, objections were raised against **prioritize, finalize,** and **hospitalize**, among others. There doesn't seem to be any coherent reason for this, except that verbs formed from nouns tend, inexplicably, to be criticized as vulgar formations. Despite objections, it is clear that **-ize** forms are an accepted part of the standard language.

-izer ▶ **suffix** forming agent nouns corresponding to adjectives ending in *-ize* (such as *theorizer* corresponding to *theorize*).
– ORIGIN see **-IZE, -ER**¹.

I·zhevsk /'ē,ZHefsk/ an industrial city in central Russia, capital of the republic of Udmurtia; pop. 612,400 (est. 2009). Former name (1984–87) **USTINOV**.

Iz·mir /iz'mi(ə)r/ a seaport and naval base in western Turkey, on an inlet of the Aegean Sea; pop. 2,606,300 (est. 2007). Former name **SMYRNA**.

Iz·mit /iz'mit/ a city in northwestern Turkey, on the Gulf of Izmit; pop. 248,400 (est. 2007).

Iz·ves·ti·a /iz'vestēə/ (also **Izvestiya**) a Russian daily newspaper founded in 1917 as the official organ of the Soviet government. It has continued to be published independently since the collapse of communist rule and the breakup of the Soviet Union.
– ORIGIN from Russian *izvestiya* 'news.'

iz·zat /'izət/ ▶ **n.** Indian honor, reputation, or prestige: *the izzat of the household was at stake.*
– ORIGIN Persian and Urdu, from Arabic *'izza* 'glory.'

i

PRONUNCIATION KEY ə *ago, up;* ər *over, fur;* a *hat;* ā *ate;* ä *car;* e *let;* ē *see;* i *fit;* ī *by;* NG *sing;* ō *go;* ô *law, for;* oi *toy;* o͝o *good;* o͞o *goo;* ou *out;* TH *thin;* T͟H *then;* ZH *vision*

Jj

j

J[1] /jā/ (also **j**) ▶ **n.** (pl. **Js** or **J's** /jāz/) **1** the tenth letter of the alphabet. ■ denoting the next after I (or H if I is omitted) in a set of items, categories, etc.
2 (**J**) a shape like that of a capital J.
3 archaic used instead of I as the Roman numeral for one in final position: *between ij and iij of the clock.*

J[2] ▶ **abbr.** ■ jack (used in describing play in card games). ■ Physics joule(s). ■ (in titles) Journal (of): *J. Biol. Chem.* ■ Judge. ■ Justice.

j ▶ **symbol** (*j*) (in electrical engineering and electronics) the imaginary quantity equal to the square root of minus one. Compare with **I**.

jab /jab/ ▶ **v.** (**jabs, jabbing, jabbed**) [with obj.] poke (someone or something) roughly or quickly, esp. with something sharp or pointed: *she jabbed him in his ribs* | [no obj.] *he **jabbed at** the air with his finger.* ■ poke someone or something roughly or quickly with (a sharp or pointed object or a part of the body): *she jabbed the fork into the earth.*
▶ **n.** a quick, sharp blow, esp. with the fist: *fast jabs to the face.* ■ informal a hypodermic injection, esp. a vaccination: *an anti-tetanus jab.* ■ a sharp painful sensation or feeling: *the jabs of pain up my spine* | *a jab of envy.*
– ORIGIN early 19th cent. (originally Scots): variant of **JOB**[2].

Ja·bal·pur /ˈjəbəlˌpo͝or/ an industrial city and military post in central India, in Madhya Pradesh; pop. 1,067,000 (est. 2009).

jab·ber /ˈjabər/ ▶ **v.** [no obj.] talk rapidly and excitedly but with little sense: *he **jabbered away** to his friends.*
▶ **n.** fast, excited talk that makes little sense: *stop your jabber.*
– ORIGIN late 15th cent.: imitative.

jab·ber·wock·y /ˈjabərˌwäkē/ ▶ **n.** (pl. **jabberwockies**) invented or meaningless language; nonsense.
– ORIGIN early 20th cent.: from the title of a nonsense poem in Lewis Carroll's *Through the Looking Glass* (1871).

jab·i·ru /ˈjabəˌro͞o/ (also **jabiru stork**) ▶ **n.** a large Central and South American stork with a black neck, mainly white plumage, and a large black upturned bill. ● *Jabiru mycteria*, family Ciconiidae. ■ either of two related storks found in Asia, Australasia, and Africa.
– ORIGIN late 18th cent.: from Tupi-Guarani *jabirú*, from *j* 'that which has' + *abirú* 'swollen' (suggested by the bird's large neck).

Ja·bo·a·tão /ˌZHäbwäˈtoun/ a commercial city in northeastern Brazil, west of Recife; pop. 665,400 (est. 2007).

jab·o·ran·di /ˌjabəˈrandē/ ▶ **n.** **1** a drug made from the dried leaves of certain South American plants that contain the alkaloid pilocarpine and promote salivation when chewed.
2 any of the plants that yield this drug. ● Several genera and species, in particular *Pilocarpus jaborandi* (family Rutaceae).
– ORIGIN early 17th cent.: from Tupi-Guarani *jaburandi*, literally 'a person who spits.'

ja·bot /ZHaˈbō, ja-/ ▶ **n.** an ornamental frill or ruffle on the front of a shirt or blouse, typically made of lace.
– ORIGIN early 19th cent. (denoting a frill on a man's shirt): French, originally 'crop of a bird.'

ja·cal /häˈkäl/ ▶ **n.** (pl. **jacales** /-ˈkäläs/) (in Mexico and the southwestern US) a thatched wattle-and-daub hut.
– ORIGIN Mexican Spanish, from Nahuatl *xacalli*, contraction of *xamitl calli* 'adobe house.'

jac·a·mar /ˈjakəˌmär/ ▶ **n.** an insectivorous bird of tropical American forests, with a long pointed bill, a long tail, and plumage that is typically iridescent green above. ● Family Galbulidae: several genera and species.
– ORIGIN early 19th cent.: from French, apparently from Tupi.

ja·ca·na /ˌZHäkəˈnä, jä-/ (also **jaçana** /ˌZHäsəˈnä, ˌjä-/) ▶ **n.** a small tropical wading bird with greatly elongated toes and claws that enable it to walk on floating vegetation. Also called **LILY-TROTTER**. ● FamilyJacanidae: several genera and species.
– ORIGIN mid 18th cent.: from Portuguese *jaçanã*, from Tupi-Guarani *jasanã*.

jac·a·ran·da /ˌjakəˈrandə/ ▶ **n.** a tropical American tree that has blue trumpet-shaped flowers, fernlike leaves, and fragrant timber. ● Genus *Jacaranda*, family Bignoniaceae.
– ORIGIN mid 18th cent.: from Portuguese, from Tupi-Guarani *jakaraʹnda*.

ja·cinth /ˈjāsənTH, ˈjas-/ ▶ **n.** a reddish-orange gem variety of zircon.
– ORIGIN Middle English: from Old French *iacinte* or medieval Latin *iacintus*, alteration of Latin *hyacinthus* (see **HYACINTH**).

jack[1] /jak/ ▶ **n.** **1** a device for lifting heavy objects, esp. one for raising the axle of a motor vehicle off the ground so that a wheel can be changed or the underside inspected.
2 a playing card bearing a representation of a soldier, page, or knave, normally ranking next below a queen.
3 a socket with two or more pairs of terminals, designed to receive a jack plug.
4 (also **jackstone**) a small round pebble or star-shaped piece of metal used in tossing and catching games. ■ (**jacks**) a game played by tossing and catching such pebbles or pieces of metal.
5 in lawn bowling, the small ball at which the players aim.
6 (**Jack**) informal used as a form of address to a man whose name is not known. [familiar form of the given name *John*.] ■ informal a lumberjack. ■ archaic a steeplejack. ■ the figure of a man striking the bell on a clock.
7 a small version of a national flag flown at the bow of a vessel in harbor to indicate its nationality.
8 informal, dated money.
9 a device for turning a spit.
10 a part of the mechanism in a spinet or harpsichord that connects a key to its corresponding string and causes the string to be plucked when the key is pressed down.
11 a marine fish that is typically laterally compressed with a row of large spiky scales along each side. Jacks are important in many places as food or game fish. Also called **POMPANO, SCAD**. [originally a West Indian term.] ● Family Carangidae (the **jack family**): many genera and numerous species. The jack family also includes the horse mackerel, pilotfish, kingfishes, and trevallies.
12 the male of some animals, esp. a merlin or an ass.
13 used in names of animals that are smaller than similar kinds, e.g., **jacksnipe**.
14 short for **JACKRABBIT**.
15 informal short for **JACK SHIT**.
– PHRASES **before one can say Jack Robinson** informal very quickly or suddenly. **every man jack** informal, dated each and every person (used for emphasis): *they're spies, every man jack of them.* **jack of all trades** (**and master of none**) a person who can do many different types of work but who is not necessarily very competent at any of them.
– PHRASAL VERBS **jack someone around** informal cause someone inconvenience or problems, esp. by acting unfairly or indecisively. **jack in** (or **into**) informal log into or connect up (a computer or electronic device). **jack off** vulgar slang masturbate. **jack up** informal inject oneself with a narcotic drug. **jack something up** raise something, esp. a vehicle, with a jack. ■ informal increase something by a considerable amount: *France jacked up its key bank interest rate.*
– ORIGIN late Middle English: from *Jack*, nickname for the given name *John*. The term was used originally to denote an ordinary man (sense 6), also

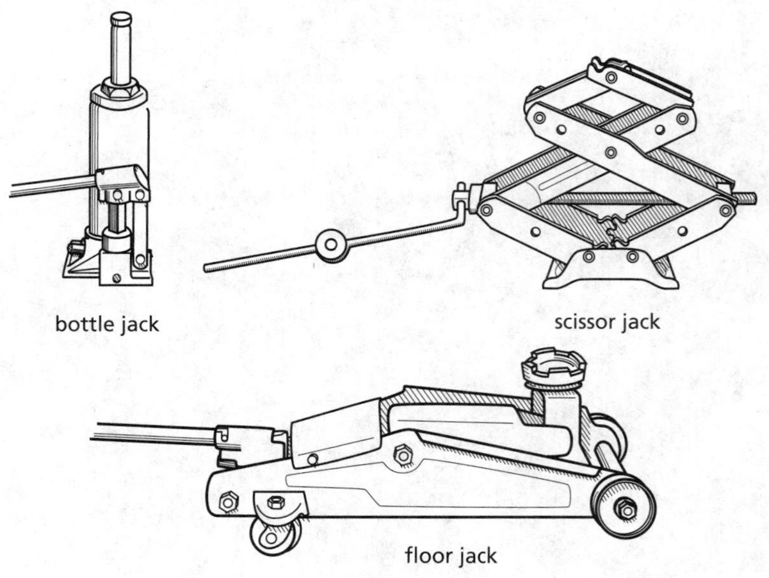

jacks

a youth (mid 16th cent.), hence the 'knave' in cards and 'male animal.' The word also denoted various devices saving human labor, as though one had a helper (sense 1, sense 3, sense 9, and sense 10, and in compounds such as JACKHAMMER and JACKKNIFE); the general sense 'laborer' arose in the early 18th cent. and survives in CHEAPJACK, LUMBERJACK, STEEPLEJACK, etc. Since the mid 16th cent. a notion of 'smallness' has arisen, hence sense 4, sense 5, sense 7, and sense 13.

jack² ▶ n. historical **1** another term for BLACKJACK (sense 4).
2 a sleeveless padded tunic worn by foot soldiers. [late Middle English: from Old French *jaque*; origin uncertain, perhaps based on Arabic.]

jack³ /jak/ ▶ v. [with obj.] informal take (something) illicitly; steal: *his MO in the studio remains the same—jack other people's tracks and present them in a new context.* ■ rob (someone): *they jacked him for his car.*
– ORIGIN 1990s: from *hijack*.

jack·al /ˈjakəl/ ▶ n. a slender, long-legged wild dog that feeds on carrion, game, and fruit and often hunts cooperatively, found in Africa and southern Asia. ● Genus *Canis*, family Canidae: four species, including the **golden jackal** (*C. aureus*) and the **black-backed jackal** (*C. mesomelas*).
– ORIGIN early 17th cent.: from Turkish *çakal*, from Persian *šagāl*. The change in the first syllable was due to association with JACK¹.

black-backed jackal

jack·a·napes /ˈjakəˌnāps/ ▶ n. **1** dated an impertinent person.
2 archaic a tame monkey.
– ORIGIN early 16th cent. (originally as *Jack Napes*): perhaps from a playful name for a tame ape, the initial *n-* by elision of *an ape* (compare with NEWT), and the final *-s* as in surnames such as *Hobbes*: hence applied to a person whose behavior resembled that of an ape.

jack arch ▶ n. a small arch only one brick in thickness, esp. as used in numbers to support a floor.

jack·a·roo /ˌjakəˈro͞o/ ▶ n. & v. variant spelling of JACKEROO.

jack·ass /ˈjakˌas/ ▶ n. **1** a stupid person.
2 a male ass or donkey.

jack bean ▶ n. a tropical American climbing plant of the pea family, which yields an edible bean and pod and is widely grown for fodder in tropical countries. ● Genus *Canavalia*, family Leguminosae: in particular *C. ensiformis*. ■ the seed of this plant.

jack·boot /ˈjakˌbo͞ot/ ▶ n. a large leather military boot reaching to the knee. ■ [in sing.] used as a symbol of cruel or authoritarian behavior or rule: *a country **under the jackboot** of colonialism.*
– DERIVATIVES **jack·boot·ed** adj.

Jack cheese ▶ n. another term for MONTEREY JACK.

jack·daw /ˈjakˌdô/ ▶ n. a small, gray-headed crow that typically nests in tall buildings and chimneys, noted for its inquisitiveness. ● Genus *Corvus*, family Corvidae: two species, in particular the Eurasian *C. monedula*.

jack·e·roo /ˌjakəˈro͞o/ (also **jackaroo**) Austral. informal ▶ n. a young man working on a sheep or cattle station to gain experience.
▶ v. [no obj.] work as a jackeroo.
– ORIGIN late 19th cent.: alteration of an Aboriginal (Queensland) term *dhugai-iu* 'wandering white man,' by blending JACK¹ and KANGAROO.

jack·et /ˈjakit/ ▶ n. an outer garment extending either to the waist or the hips, typically having sleeves and a fastening down the front. ■ an outer covering, esp. one placed around a tank or pipe to insulate it. ■ a metal casing for a bullet. ■ the skin of a potato: *potatoes cooked in their jackets.* ■ the dust jacket of a book. ■ a record sleeve. ■ a steel frame fixed to the seabed, forming the support structure of an oil production platform.
▶ v. (**jackets, jacketing, jacketed**) [with obj.] cover with a jacket.
– ORIGIN late Middle English: from Old French *jaquet*, diminutive of *jaque* (see JACK²).

jack·et po·ta·to ▶ n. Brit. a baked potato served with the skin on.

jack·fish /ˈjakˌfish/ ▶ n. (pl. **same** or **jackfishes**) a pike or sauger, esp. the northern pike.

Jack Frost ▶ n. a personification of frost: *the seedlings battled with Jack Frost.*

jack·fruit /ˈjakˌfro͞ot/ ▶ n. a fast-growing tropical Asian tree related to the breadfruit. ● *Artocarpus heterophyllus*, family Moraceae. ■ the very large edible fruit of this tree, resembling a breadfruit and important as food in the tropics.
– ORIGIN late 16th cent.: from Portuguese *jaca* (from Malayalam *chakka*) + FRUIT.

jack·ham·mer /ˈjakˌhamər/ ▶ n. a portable pneumatic hammer or drill.
▶ v. [with obj.] beat or hammer heavily or loudly and repeatedly.

jack-in-the-box ▶ n. a toy consisting of a box containing a figure on a spring that pops up when the lid is opened.

jack-in-the-pul·pit ▶ n. any of several small plants of the arum family, in particular: ● a North American arum with a green or purple-brown spathe. Genus *Arisaema*, family Araceae: three species, the **woodland jack-in-the-pulpit** (*A. atrorubens*), the **small** (or **swamp**) **jack-in-the-pulpit** (*A. triphyllum*), and the **northern jack-in-the-pulpit** (*A. stewardsonii*). ● another term for CUCKOOPINT.
– ORIGIN mid 19th cent.: so named because the erect spadix overarched by the spathe resembles a person in a pulpit.

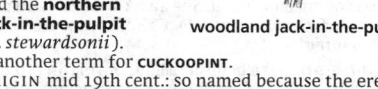

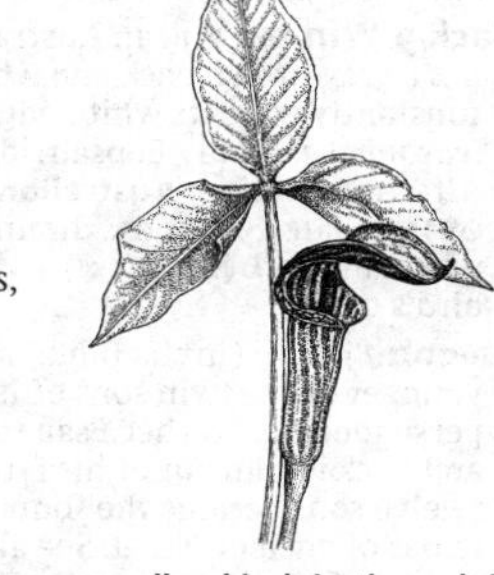
woodland jack-in-the-pulpit

jack·knife /ˈjakˌnīf/ ▶ n. (pl. **jackknives**) **1** a knife with a folding blade.
2 a dive in which the body is first bent at the waist and then straightened.
3 Statistics a method of assessing the variability of data by repeating a calculation on the sets of data obtained by removing one value from the complete set.
▶ v. (**jackknifed, jackknifing**) [with obj.] move (one's body) into a bent or doubled-up position: *the Major jackknifed his thin body at the waist* | [no obj.] *she jackknifed into a sitting position.* ■ [no obj.] (of an articulated vehicle) bend into a V-shape in an uncontrolled skidding movement. ■ [no obj.] (of a diver) perform a jackknife.

jack·knife clam ▶ n. another term for RAZOR CLAM.

jack·knife fish ▶ n. a strikingly marked fish with a long, upright dorsal fin that lives among rocks and corals in the warm waters of the western Atlantic. ● *Equetus lanceolatus*, family Sciaenidae.

jack·leg /ˈjakˌleg/ ▶ n. informal an incompetent, unskillful, or dishonest person: [as modifier] *a jackleg carpenter.*

jack·light /ˈjakˌlīt/ ▶ n. a portable light, esp. one used for hunting or fishing at night.

jack mack·er·el ▶ n. a game fish of the jack family, occurring in the eastern Pacific. ● *Trachurus symmetricus*, family Carangidae.

Jack Mor·mon ▶ n. informal **1** a Mormon who is not strictly observant: *the only thing that's going to end up happening is me doing homework on Sundays and drinking Pepsi and being just another Jack Mormon.*
2 a sympathetic non-Mormon living among Mormons.

jack-o'-lan·tern /ˈjak əˌlantərn/ ▶ n. **1** a lantern made from a hollowed-out pumpkin in which holes are cut to represent facial features, typically made at Halloween.
2 archaic an ignis fatuus.

jack pine ▶ n. a small, hardy North American pine with very short needles, found chiefly in Canada. ● *Pinus banksiana*, family Pinaceae.

jack plane ▶ n. a medium-sized plane for use in carpentry.

jack plug ▶ n. a plug consisting of a single shaft used to make a connection that transmits a signal, typically used in sound equipment.

jack·pot /ˈjakˌpät/ ▶ n. a large cash prize in a game or lottery, esp. one that accumulates until it is won.
– PHRASES **hit the jackpot** informal **1** win a jackpot.
2 have great or unexpected success, esp. in making a lot of money quickly: *the theater hit the jackpot with its first musical.*
– ORIGIN late 19th cent.: from JACK¹ + POT¹. The term was originally used in a form of poker, where the pool or pot accumulated until a player could open the bidding with two jacks or better.

jack·rab·bit /ˈjakˌrabət/ ▶ n. a hare found in open country in western North America. ● Genus *Lepus*, family Leporidae: several species, including the **blacktail jackrabbit** (*L. californicus*).
– ORIGIN mid 19th cent.: abbreviation of *jackass-rabbit*, because of its long ears.

black-tailed jackrabbit

Jack Rus·sell /ˈrəsəl/ (also **Jack Russell terrier**) ▶ n. a terrier of a small working breed with short legs.
– ORIGIN early 20th cent.: named after John (*Jack*) *Russell* (1795–1883), an English clergyman famed in fox-hunting circles as a breeder of such terriers.

jack screw ▶ n. a screw that can be turned to adjust the position of an object into which it fits. ■ a vehicle jack worked by a screw device. Also called SCREW JACK.

jack·shaft /ˈjakˌSHaft/ ▶ n. a small auxiliary or intermediate shaft in machinery.

jack shit ▶ n. [usu. with negative] vulgar slang anything at all.

jack·snipe /ˈjakˌsnīp/ ▶ n. a small dark Eurasian snipe. ● *Lymnocryptes minima*, family Scolopacidae. ■ any similar wader, e.g., the pectoral sandpiper or the common snipe.

Jack·son¹ /ˈjaksən/ **1** the capital of Mississippi, an industrial and commercial city in the central part of the state, on the Pearl River; pop. 173,861 (est. 2008).
2 a commercial city in western Tennessee; pop. 63,158 (est. 2008).

Jack·son², Andrew (1767–1845) 7th president of the US 1829–37; known as **Old Hickory**. A Tennessee Democrat, he served in the US House of Representatives 1796–97 and as a US Senator 1797–98, 1823–25. As a general in the US Army during the War of 1812, he became known for his successful defense of New Orleans. As president, he vetoed the renewal of the charter of the Bank of the United States, opposed the nullification issue in South Carolina, and initiated the spoils system. During his administration, the national debt was paid off completely, the Wisconsin Territory was organized, Michigan was admitted as the 26th state, and the independence of Texas was recognized.

Andrew Jackson

Jack·son[3], Howell Edmunds (1832–95) US Supreme Court associate justice 1893–95. He also served as a US Senator 1881–86.

Jack·son[4], Jesse (Louis) (1941–), US civil rights activist, politician, and clergyman. After working with Martin Luther King, Jr., in the civil rights struggle, he campaigned for but failed to win the Democratic Party's 1984 and 1988 presidential nominations. His son, **Jesse Jackson, Jr.** (1965–), a Democrat from Illinois, was elected to the US House of Representatives in 1995.

Jack·son[5], Mahalia (1911–72), US gospel singer and musician. She came into her own in the mid 1940s, when her recording of "Move Up a Little Higher" sold over a million copies. She was a featured performer at President Kennedy's inaugural ceremony.

Jack·son[6], Michael (1958–2009), US singer, the top-selling pop artist of the 1980s. His hit albums include *Thriller* (1982), *Bad* (1987), *Dangerous* (1991), and *HIStory* (1995).

Michael Jackson

Jack·son[7], Reggie (1946–) US baseball player; full name *Reginald Martinez Jackson*; known as **Mr. October**. An outfielder, he played for the Kansas City A's (later Oakland Athletics) 1967–75, the Baltimore Orioles 1976, and the New York Yankees 1977–87. Baseball Hall of Fame (1993).

Jack·son[8], Robert Houghwout (1892–1954) US Supreme Court associate justice 1941–54. He was the chief prosecutor for the US at the Nuremberg war crimes tribunal 1945–46.

Jack·son[9], Thomas Jonathan (1824–63), Confederate general; known as **Stonewall Jackson**. The commander of the Shenandoah campaign 1861–62, he was mortally wounded by one of his own sharpshooters at Chancellorsville in 1863.

Thomas "Stonewall" Jackson

Jack·son Heights a commercial and residential section of northern Queens in New York City.

Jack·son Hole a valley on the Snake River in northwestern Wyoming, partly in Grand Teton National Park, home to a fashionable resort.

Jack·so·ni·an /jak'sōnēən/ ▶ **adj.** Medicine relating to or denoting a form of epilepsy in which seizures begin at one site (typically a digit or the angle of the mouth).
– ORIGIN late 19th cent.: from the name of John H. *Jackson* (1835–1911), English physician and neurologist, + **-IAN**.

Jack·son·ville /'jaksən,vil/ **1** an industrial city and port in northeastern Florida; pop. 807,815 (est. 2008).
2 a city in southeastern North Carolina, a service town for nearby Camp Lejeune and other military facilities; pop. 76,233 (est. 2008).

jack·staff /'jak,staf/ ▶ **n.** a short flagpole at a ship's bow, on which a jack is flown.

jack·stay /'jak,stā/ ▶ **n.** Nautical a rope, bar, or batten placed along a ship's yard to bend the head of a square sail to.

jack·stone /'jak,stōn/ ▶ **n.** see **JACK**[1] (sense 4).

jack·straws /'jak,strôz/ ▶ **plural n.** [treated as sing.] a game played with a heap of small rods of wood, bone, or plastic, in which players try to remove one at a time without disturbing the others.

Jack tar ▶ **n.** Brit. informal or dated a sailor.

Jack the Lad ▶ **n.** Brit. informal a brash, cocky young man.
– ORIGIN nickname of *Jack Sheppard*, an 18th-cent. thief.

Jack the Rip·per an unidentified 19th-century English murderer. In 1888, at least six London prostitutes were brutally killed. Authorities received taunting notes from a person called Jack the Ripper, who claimed to be the murderer, but the cases remain unsolved.

jack-up (also **jack-up rig**) ▶ **n.** an offshore drilling rig the legs of which are lowered to the seabed from the operating platform.

Jack·y liz·ard /'jakē/ ▶ **n.** a brownish southeastern Australian lizard that becomes paler as the temperature rises. When threatened, it puffs itself up and opens its orange mouth. • *Amphibolus muricatus*, family Agamidae.

Jack·y Win·ter ▶ **n.** an Australasian flycatcher that has a gray-brown back and whitish underside and constantly wags its white-edged tail. • *Microeca leucophaea*, family Eopsaltridae (or Muscicapidae). Alternative name: **Australian brown flycatcher**.
– ORIGIN late 19th cent.: diminutive form of the nickname *Jack* (see **JACK**[1]) + *Winter* (imitative of the bird's cry).

Ja·cob /'jākəb/ (in the Bible) a Hebrew patriarch, the younger of the twin sons of Isaac and Rebecca, who persuaded his brother Esau to sell him his birthright and tricked him out of his father's blessing. Jacob's twelve sons became the founders of the twelve tribes of ancient Israel. See also **TRIBES OF ISRAEL**.
– ORIGIN from Hebrew *ya'aqōb* 'following after, supplanter.'

Jac·o·be·an /,jakə'bēən/ ▶ **adj.** of or relating to the reign of James I of England: *a Jacobean mansion*. ■ (of furniture) in the style prevalent during the reign of James I, esp. being the color of dark oak.
▶ **n.** a person who lived during this period.
– ORIGIN mid 19th cent. (in use earlier with reference to St. James): from modern Latin *Jacobaeus* (from ecclesiastical Latin *Jacobus* 'James,' from Greek *Iakōbos* 'Jacob') + **-AN**.

Jac·o·be·than /,jakə'bēTHən/ ▶ **adj.** (esp. of architecture) displaying a combination of Elizabethan and Jacobean styles.
– ORIGIN mid 20th cent.: blend of **JACOBEAN** and **ELIZABETHAN**.

Ja·co·bi /jə'kōbē/, Karl Gustav Jacob (1804–51), German mathematician. He worked on the theory of elliptic functions, in competition with Niels Abel.

Jac·o·bi·an /jə'kōbēən/ Mathematics ▶ **adj.** of or relating to the work of the mathematician K. G. J. Jacobi.
▶ **n.** a determinant whose constituents are the derivatives of a number of functions $(u, v, w, ...)$ with respect to each of the same number of variables $(x, y, z, ...)$.

Jac·o·bin /'jakəbən/ ▶ **n. 1** historical a member of a democratic club established in Paris in 1789. The Jacobins were the most radical and ruthless of the political groups formed in the wake of the French Revolution, and in association with Robespierre they instituted the Terror of 1793–4. ■ an extreme political radical.
2 chiefly historical a Dominican friar.
3 (**jacobin**) a pigeon of a breed with reversed feathers on the back of its neck like a cowl.
4 (**jacobin**) a mainly green Central and South American hummingbird, with blue feathers on the head. • *Florisuga mellivora* and *Melanotrichilus fuscus*, family Trochilidae.
– DERIVATIVES **Jac·o·bin·ic** /,jakə'binik/ **adj.**, **Jac·o·bin·i·cal** /,jakə'binikəl/ **adj.**, **Jac·o·bin·ism** /-,nizəm/ **n.**
– ORIGIN Middle English (sense 2): from Old French, from medieval Latin *Jacobinus*, from ecclesiastical Latin *Jacobus* 'James.' The term was applied to the Dominicans in Old French from their church in Paris, St. Jacques, near which they built their first convent; the convent eventually became the headquarters of the French revolutionary group.

Jac·o·bite[1] /'jakə,bīt/ ▶ **n.** a supporter of the deposed James II and his descendants in their claim to the British throne after the Revolution of 1688. Drawing most of their support from Catholic clans of the Scottish Highlands, Jacobites made attempts to regain the throne in 1689–90, 1715, 1719, and 1745–46, finally being defeated at the Battle of Culloden.
– DERIVATIVES **Jac·o·bit·i·cal** /,jakə'bitikəl/ **adj.**, **Jac·o·bit·ism** /-bīt,izəm/ **n.**
– ORIGIN from Latin *Jacobus* 'James' (see **JACOBEAN**) + **-ITE**[1].

Jac·o·bite[2] ▶ **n.** a member of the Syrian Orthodox Church (Monophysite).
– ORIGIN early 15th cent.: from medieval Latin *Jacobita*, from the name of *Jacobus* Baradaeus, a 6th-cent. Syrian monk.

Ja·cob's lad·der ▶ **n. 1** a plant of the northeastern US with loose clusters of purplish-blue flowers and slender pointed leaves, rows of which are said to resemble a ladder. • *Polemonium van-bruntiae*, family Polemoniaceae.
2 a rope ladder with wooden rungs, esp. for access to a ship up the side.
– ORIGIN mid 18th cent.: with biblical allusion to Jacob's dream of a ladder reaching to heaven (Gen. 28:12).

Ja·cob·son's or·gan /'jākəbsənz/ ▶ **n.** Zoology a scent organ consisting of a pair of sacs or tubes typically in the roof of the mouth. Such organs are present in many vertebrates, notably snakes and lizards.
– ORIGIN mid 19th cent.: named after Ludwig L. *Jacobson* (1783–1843), Danish anatomist.

Ja·cob's staff ▶ **n.** a rod with a sliding cursor formerly used for measuring distances and heights, esp. in navigation.
– ORIGIN mid 16th cent. (denoting a pilgrim's staff): alluding to St. James (*Jacobus* in ecclesiastical Latin), whose symbols are a pilgrim's staff and a scallop shell.

jac·o·net /'jakə,net/ ▶ **n.** a lightweight cotton cloth with a smooth and slightly stiff finish.
– ORIGIN mid 18th cent.: from Hindi *Jagannāth(purī)* (now *Puri*) in India, its place of origin; see also **JUGGERNAUT**.

Ja·co·po del·la Quer·cia see **DELLA QUERCIA**.

jac·quard /'ja,kärd, jə'kärd/ ▶ **n.** an apparatus with perforated cards, fitted to a loom to facilitate the weaving of figured and brocaded fabrics. ■ a fabric made on a loom with such a device, with an intricate variegated pattern.
– ORIGIN early 19th cent.: named after Joseph M. *Jacquard* (1787–1834), French weaver and inventor.

jac·que·rie /ZHäk'rē/ ▶ **n.** a communal uprising or revolt.
– ORIGIN early 16th cent. (referring to the 1357 peasants' revolt against the nobles in northern France): from Old French, literally 'villeins,' from *Jacques*, a given name used in the sense 'peasant.'

jac·ti·ta·tion /,jakti'tāSHən/ ▶ **n.** Medicine the restless tossing of the body in illness. ■ the twitching of a limb or muscle. [expressive extension of *jactation* 'restless tossing,' from Latin *jactare* 'to throw.']
– PHRASES **jactitation of marriage** archaic false declaration that one is married to a specified person. [*jactitation* in the sense 'public bragging,' from medieval Latin *jactitatio(n-)* 'false declaration,' from Latin *jactitare* 'to boast.']

Ja·cuz·zi /jə'ko͞ozē/ ▶ **n.** (pl. **Jacuzzis**) trademark a large bath with a system of underwater jets of water to massage the body.
– ORIGIN 1960s: named after Candido *Jacuzzi* (*c.*1903–86), Italian-born American inventor.

jade[1] /jād/ ▶ **n.** a hard, typically green stone used for ornaments and implements and consisting of the minerals jadeite or nephrite. ■ an ornament made of this. ■ (also **jade green**) a light bluish-green: [as modifier] *a baggy jade T-shirt*.
– ORIGIN late 16th cent.: from French *le jade* (earlier *l'ejade*), from Spanish *piedra de ijada* 'stone of the flank' (i.e., stone for colic, which it was believed to cure).

jade[2] ▶ **n.** archaic **1** a bad-tempered or disreputable woman.
2 an inferior or worn-out horse.
– ORIGIN late Middle English: of unknown origin.

jad·ed /'jādid/ ▶ **adj.** tired, bored, or lacking enthusiasm, typically after having had too much of something: *meals to tempt the most jaded appetites*.
– DERIVATIVES **jad·ed·ly adv.**, **jad·ed·ness n.**
– ORIGIN late 16th cent. (in the sense 'disreputable'): from **JADE**[2].

jade·ite /'jād,īt/ ▶ **n.** a green, blue, or white mineral that is one of the forms of jade. It is a silicate of sodium, aluminum, and iron and belongs to the pyroxene group.

j'a·doube /ZHä'do͞ob/ ▶ **exclam.** Chess a declaration by a player intending to adjust the placing of a chessman without making a move with it.
– ORIGIN French, literally 'I adjust.'

jae·ger /'yāgər/ ▶ **n.** any of the smaller kinds of Arctic-breeding skuas. • Genus *Stercorarius*, family

Stercorariidae: three species, e.g., the **parasitic jaeger** or Arctic skua (*S. parasiticus*).
– ORIGIN mid 19th cent. (applied to any predatory seabird): from German *Jäger* 'hunter,' from *jagen* 'to hunt.'

Jaf·fa /ˈjäfə, ˈjafə/ a city and port on the Mediterranean coast of Israel, a southern suburb of Tel Aviv and since 1949 united with Tel Aviv; pop. (with Tel Aviv) 392,500 (est. 2008). Hebrew name **Yafo**; biblical name **Joppa**.

Jaff·na /ˈjäfnə/ a city and port on the Jaffna peninsula at the northern tip of Sri Lanka; pop. 151,600 (est. 2007).

JAG ▶ **abbr.** judge advocate general.

Jag /jag/ ▶ **n.** informal a Jaguar car: *an E-type Jag.*
– ORIGIN 1950s: abbreviation.

jag[1] /jag/ ▶ **n.** a sharp projection.
▶ **v.** (**jags, jagging, jagged** /ˈjagd/) [with obj.] stab, pierce, or prick: *she jagged herself in the mouth.*
– DERIVATIVES **jag·ger n.**
– ORIGIN late Middle English (in the sense 'stab, pierce'): perhaps symbolic of sudden movement or unevenness (compare with **jam**[1] and **rag**[1]).

jag[2] ▶ **n.** informal **1** a bout of unrestrained activity or emotion, esp. drinking, crying, or laughing: *an incredible crying jag.*
2 dialect a bundle: *a jag of hay.*
– ORIGIN late 16th cent. (sense 2): of unknown origin. In the late 18th cent. the sense was 'portion, quantity,' later 'as much alcohol as one can hold,' hence 'a binge.' Sense 1 dates from the early 20th cent.

Jag·an·na·tha /ˌjəgəˈnät-hə/ Hinduism the form of Krishna worshipped in Puri, Orissa, where in the annual festival his image is dragged through the streets on a heavy chariot; devotees are said formerly to have thrown themselves under its wheels. Formerly called **Juggernaut**.
– ORIGIN via Hindi from Sanskrit *Jagannātha* 'Lord of the world.'

jag·ged /ˈjagid/ ▶ **adj.** having rough, sharp points protruding: *the jagged edges gashed their fingers* | figurative *soothing her jagged nerves.*
– DERIVATIVES **jag·ged·ly adv., jag·ged·ness n.**
– ORIGIN late Middle English: from **jag**[1].

Jag·ger /ˈjagər/, Mick (1943–), English rock singer and songwriter; full name *Sir Michael Philip Jagger.* He formed the Rolling Stones *c.*1962 with guitarist **Keith Richards** (1943–).

Mick Jagger

jag·ger·y /ˈjagərē/ ▶ **n.** a coarse dark brown sugar made in India by evaporation of the sap of palm trees.
– ORIGIN late 16th cent.: from Portuguese *xagara, jag(a)ra*, from Malayalam *cakkarā*, from Sanskrit *śarkarā* 'sugar.'

jag·gy /ˈjagē/ ▶ **adj.** (**jaggier, jaggiest**) jagged.
▶ **plural n.** (**jaggies**) Computing, informal another term for **aliasing** (sense 2).

jag·uar /ˈjagˌwär/ ▶ **n.** a large, heavily built cat that has a yellowish-brown coat with black spots, found mainly in the dense forests of Central and South America. ● *Panthera onca*, family Felidae.
– ORIGIN early 17th cent.: from Portuguese, from Tupi-Guarani *yaguára.*

jaguar

ja·gua·run·di /ˌjagwəˈrəndē/ ▶ **n.** (pl. **jaguarundis**) a small American wildcat with a uniform red or gray coat, slender body, and short legs, found from Arizona to Argentina. ● *Felis yagouaroundi*, family Felidae.
– ORIGIN mid 19th cent.: from Portuguese, from Tupi-Guarani, from *yaguára* 'jaguar' + *undi* 'dark.'

Jah /jä, yä/ ▶ **n.** the Rastafarian name of God.
– ORIGIN representing Hebrew *Yāh*, abbreviation of **Yahweh**. The current use was popularized in the mid 20th cent.

jai a·lai /ˈhī (ə)ˌlī/ ▶ **n.** a game like pelota played with large, curved wicker baskets.
– ORIGIN Spanish, from Basque *jai* 'festival' + *alai* 'merry.'

jail /jāl/ (Brit. also **gaol**) ▶ **n.** a place for the confinement of people accused or convicted of a crime: *he spent 15 years in jail* | [as modifier] *a jail sentence.* ■ confinement in a jail: *she was sentenced to three months' jail.*
▶ **v.** [with obj.] (usu. **be jailed**) put (someone) in jail: *the driver was jailed for two years.*
– ORIGIN Middle English: based on Latin *cavea* (see **cage**). The word came into English in two forms, *jaiole* from Old French and *gayole* from Anglo-Norman French *gaole* (surviving in the spelling *gaol*), originally pronounced with a hard *g*, as in *gale.*

jail·bait /ˈjālˌbāt/ ▶ **n.** [treated as sing. or pl.] informal a young woman, or young women collectively, considered in sexual terms but under the age of consent.

jail·bird /ˈjālˌbərd/ ▶ **n.** informal a person who is or has been in prison, esp. a criminal who has been jailed repeatedly.

jail·break /ˈjālˌbrāk/ ▶ **n.** an escape from jail.

jail·er /ˈjālər/ (also **jailor** or Brit. **gaoler**) ▶ **n.** a person in charge of a jail or of the prisoners in it.

jail·house /ˈjālˌhous/ ▶ **n.** a prison.

Jain /jān/ ▶ **n.** an adherent of Jainism.
▶ **adj.** of or relating to Jainism.
– ORIGIN via Hindi from Sanskrit *jaina* 'of or concerning a *Jina*' (a great Jain teacher or holy man, literally 'victor'), from *ji-* 'conquer' or *jyā-* 'overcome.'

Jain·ism /ˈjāˌnizəm/ ▶ **n.** a nontheistic religion founded in India in the 6th century BC by the Jina Vardhamana Mahavira as a reaction against the teachings of orthodox Brahmanism, and still practiced there. The Jain religion teaches salvation by perfection through successive lives, and noninjury to living creatures, and is noted for its ascetics. See also **Svetambara** and **Digambara**.
– DERIVATIVES **Jain·ist n.**

Jai·pur /ˈjīˌpŏŏr/ a city in western India, the capital of Rajasthan; pop. 3,102,800 (est. 2009).

Ja·kar·ta /jəˈkärtə/ (also **Djakarta**) the capital of Indonesia, in northwestern Java; pop. 9,125,000 (est. 2009). Former name (until 1949) **Batavia**.

jake /jāk/ ▶ **adj.** [predic.] informal all right; satisfactory: *everything was jake again.*
– ORIGIN early 20th cent.: of unknown origin.

jakes /jāks/ ▶ **n.** a toilet, esp. an outdoor one.
– ORIGIN mid 16th cent.: perhaps from the given name *Jacques*, or as the genitive of the nickname *Jack* (see **jack**[1]).

Ja·kob·son /ˈyäkəbsən/, Roman (Osipovich) (1896–1982), US linguist; born in Russia. He taught Slavic languages and literature and general linguistics at Harvard University from 1949 to 1967. His most influential work described universals in phonology.

Ja·lal ad-Din ar-Ru·mi /jəˈläl əˌdēn əˈrōōmē/ (1207–73), Persian poet and Sufi mystic; founder of the order of whirling dervishes; also called **Mawlana**.

Ja·lan·dhar /ˈjələndər/ (also **Jullundur**) a city in northwestern India, in Punjab; pop. 880,500 (est. 2009).

jal·ap /ˈjäləp, ˈjal-/ ▶ **n.** a purgative drug obtained chiefly from the tuberous roots of a Mexican climbing plant. ● This drug is obtained from *Ipomoea purga*, family Convolvulaceae.
– ORIGIN mid 17th cent.: from French, from Spanish (*purga de*) *Jalapa* (see **Jalapa**).

Ja·la·pa /häˈläpä/ a city in eastern central Mexico, capital of the state of Veracruz; pop. 387,879 (2005). Full name **Jalapa Enríquez**.

ja·la·pe·ño /ˌhäləˈpānyō, -ˈpē-/ (also **jalapeño pepper**) ▶ **n.** (pl. **jalapeños**) a very hot green chili pepper, used esp. in Mexican-style cooking.
– ORIGIN 1940s (originally US): from Mexican Spanish (*chile*) *jalapeño.*

ja·le·o /häˈlā-ō/ ▶ **n.** (pl. **jaleos**) a lively dance of Andalusian origin, or the music or handclapping that accompanies it. ■ a fast instrumental chorus in merengue music.
– ORIGIN mid 19th cent.: Spanish, literally 'halloo.'

jal·fre·zi /jälˈfrāzē/ ▶ **n.** (pl. **jalfrezis**) a medium-hot Indian dish consisting of chicken or lamb with fresh chili peppers, tomatoes, and onions.
– ORIGIN 1980s: from Bengali *jalfrezi*, from *jal* 'hot.'

Ja·lis·co /häˈlēskō/ a state in western central Mexico, on the Pacific coast; capital, Guadalajara.

ja·lop·y /jəˈläpē/ ▶ **n.** (pl. **jalopies**) informal an old car in a dilapidated condition.
– ORIGIN 1920s (originally US): of unknown origin.

jal·ou·sie /ˈjaləˌsē/ ▶ **n.** a blind or shutter made of a row of angled slats.
– ORIGIN mid 18th cent.: French, literally 'jealousy,' from Italian *geloso* 'jealous,' also (by extension) 'screen,' associated with the screening of women from view in the Middle East.

jam[1] /jam/ ▶ **v.** (**jams, jamming, jammed**) **1** [with obj.] squeeze or pack tightly into a specified space: *four of us were jammed in one compartment* | *people jammed their belongings into cars* | [no obj.] *75,000 refugees jammed into a stadium today to denounce the accord.* ■ push (something) roughly and forcibly into position or a space: *he jammed his hat on.* ■ crowd onto (a road) so as to block it: *the roads were jammed with traffic.* ■ cause (telephone lines) to be continuously busy with a large number of calls: *listeners jammed WBOQ's switchboard with calls.*
2 become or make unable to move or work due to a part seizing or becoming stuck: [no obj.] *the photocopier jammed* | [with obj.] *the doors were jammed open.* ■ [with obj.] make (a radio transmission) unintelligible by causing interference.
3 [no obj.] informal improvise with other musicians, esp. in jazz or blues: *the opportunity to jam with Atlanta blues musicians.*
▶ **n. 1** an instance of a machine or thing seizing or becoming stuck: *paper jams.* ■ informal an awkward situation or predicament: *I'm in a jam.* ■ short for **traffic jam**. ■ [often with adj.] Climbing a handhold obtained by stuffing a part of the body such as a hand or foot into a crack in the rock.
2 (also **jam session**) an informal gathering of musicians improvising together, esp. in jazz or blues.
– PHRASES **jam on the brakes** operate the brakes of a vehicle suddenly and forcibly, typically in an emergency.
– ORIGIN early 18th cent.: probably symbolic; compare with **jag**[1] and **cram**.

jam[2] ▶ **n.** a sweet spread or preserve made from fruit and sugar boiled to a thick consistency.
– ORIGIN mid 18th cent.: perhaps from **jam**[1].

Jam. ▶ **abbr.** ■ Jamaica. ■ Bible James.

Ja·mai·ca /jəˈmākə/ **1** an island country in the Caribbean Sea, southeast of Cuba; pop. 2,825,900 (est. 2009); official capital, Kingston; language, English.

> Visited by Columbus in 1494, Jamaica was colonized by the Spanish, who enslaved or killed the native people. Both the Spanish and the British, who took the island by force in 1655, imported slaves, mainly to work on sugar plantations. Self-government was achieved in 1944, and Jamaica became an independent Commonwealth of Nations state in 1962.

2 a commercial and residential section of east central Queens in New York City.
– DERIVATIVES **Ja·mai·can adj. & n.**

Ja·mai·can sat·in·wood ▶ **n.** see **satinwood**.

jamb /jam/ ▶ **n.** a side post or surface of a doorway, window, or fireplace. ■ a columnar mass or pillar in a mine or quarry.
– ORIGIN Middle English: from Old French *jambe* 'leg, vertical support,' based on Greek *kampē* 'joint.'

jam·ba·lay·a /ˌjəmbəˈlīə/ ▶ **n.** a Cajun dish of rice with shrimp, chicken, and vegetables.
– ORIGIN Louisiana French, from Provençal *jambalaia.*

jam·beau /ˈjambō/ ▶ **n.** (pl. **jambeaux** /-bōz/ or **jambeaus**) historical a piece of armor for the leg.
– ORIGIN late Middle English: apparently an Anglo-Norman French derivative of French *jambe* 'leg.'

Jam·bi /ˈjämbē/ (also **Djambi**) a commercial city in Indonesia, on southern Sumatra, on the Hari River; pop. 409,200 (est. 2005).

jam·bo·ree /ˌjambəˈrē/ ▶ **n.** a large celebration or party, typically a lavish and boisterous one: *the film industry's annual jamboree in Cannes.* ■ a large rally of Boy Scouts or Girl Scouts.
– ORIGIN mid 19th cent. (originally US slang): of unknown origin.

James¹ /jāmz/ the name of two kings of England. ■ **James I** (1566–1625), king of England and Ireland 1603–25; as **James VI** king of Scotland (1567–1625). He was the son of Mary Stuart and the father of Charles I. A major accomplishment during his reign was the translation of the King James Bible (1611). ■ **James II** (1633–1701), king of England, Ireland, and Scotland (1685–88). The son of Charles I, he escaped to the Continent in 1648 and returned to England at the Restoration in 1660. He became king on the death of his brother Charles II in 1685, but his conversion to Catholicism made him extremely unpopular. William of Orange and his wife, Mary, James's daughter, were invited to England by Whig and Tory leaders in 1688, and James was allowed to escape to France.

James², Henry (1843–1916), US novelist and critic, resident in England from 1896. Notable works: *Portrait of a Lady* (1881), *The Wings of the Dove* (1902), and *The Golden Bowl* (1904). He was the brother of William James.

James³, Jesse Woodson (1847–82) US outlaw. With brother **Frank** (1843–1915), he was a member of a notorious gang of train and bank robbers.

James⁴, P. D., Baroness James of Holland Park (1920–), English detective novelist; full name *Phyllis Dorothy James*. Her novels feature the detective Adam Dalgliesh and include *An Unsuitable Job for a Woman* (1972), *A Certain Justice* (1997), and *Death in Holy Orders* (2001).

James⁵, William (1842–1910), US psychologist and philosopher. A leading exponent of pragmatism, he sought a functional definition of truth, and in psychology he is credited with introducing the concept of the stream of consciousness. He was the brother of Henry James.

j

James, St.¹ /jāmz/, an Apostle; son of Zebedee and brother of John; known as **St. James the Great**. He was put to death by Herod Agrippa I. Feast day, July 25.

James, St.², an Apostle; known as **St. James the Less**. Feast day (Eastern Church) October 9; (Western Church) May 1.

James, St.³ leader of the early Christian Church at Jerusalem; known as **St. James the Just** or **the Lord's brother**. He was put to death by the Sanhedrin. Feast day, May 1. ■ the epistle of the New Testament traditionally ascribed to St. James.

James Bay a shallow southern arm of Hudson Bay, between Quebec and Ontario provinces in Canada.
– ORIGIN named after Captain Thomas *James* (*c.*1593–*c.*1635), who explored the region in 1631.

James Riv·er 1 a river that flows for 700 miles (1,100 km) from North Dakota through South Dakota into the Missouri River. Also called **DAKOTA RIVER**.
2 a river that flows for 340 miles (550 km) across eastern Virginia, past Richmond, and into the Tidewater region into Hampton Roads. Colonial Jamestown was on its estuary.

James·town /ˈjāmzˌtoun/ a British settlement established on the James River in Virginia in 1607, abandoned when the colonial capital was moved to Williamsburg at the end of the 17th century.

jam·mer /ˈjamər/ ▶ **n.** a transmitter used for jamming signals.

Jam·mu /ˈjəmo͞o/ a town in northwestern India; pop. 542,200 (est. 2009). It is the winter capital of Jammu and Kashmir.

Jam·mu and Kash·mir /ˈkashˌmi(ə)r, ˈkazh-/ a mountainous state in northwestern India, at the western end of the Himalayas, formerly part of Kashmir; capitals, Srinagar (in summer) and Jammu (in winter).

jam·my /ˈjamē/ ▶ **adj.** (**jammier, jammiest**) covered with, filled with, or resembling jam: *a jammy doughnut.*

Jam·na·gar /jämˈnəgər/ a port and walled city in western India, in the state of Gujarat; pop. 529,600 (est. 2009).

jam-packed ▶ **adj.** informal extremely crowded or full to capacity: *rutabagas are jam-packed with nutrients.*

jam ses·sion ▶ **n.** see **JAM¹** (sense 2 of the noun).

Jam·shed·pur /ˈjämshedˌpo͝or/ an industrial city in northeastern India, in the state of Jharkhand; pop. 666,700 (est. 2009).

Jam·shid /jamˈshid/ a legendary early king of Persia, reputed inventor of the arts of medicine, navigation, and ironworking.

Jan. ▶ **abbr.** January.

jane /jān/ ▶ **n.** informal a woman.
– PHRASES **plain Jane** an unattractive girl or woman.
– ORIGIN early 20th cent.: from the given name *Jane*.

Jane Doe /ˈjān ˈdō/ ▶ **n.** Law an anonymous female party, typically the plaintiff, in a legal action. ■ informal a hypothetical average woman. See also **JOHN DOE**.

Janes·ville /ˈjānzˌvil/ an industrial city in southern Wisconsin, on the Rock River; pop. 62,516 (est. 2008).

jan·gle /ˈjaNGgəl/ ▶ **v.** make or cause to make a ringing metallic sound, typically a discordant one: [no obj.] *a bell jangled loudly* | [with obj.] *Ryan stood on the terrace jangling his keys.* ■ [with obj.] (with reference to nerves) set on edge: *a thirty-eight point game that jangled the nerves.*
▶ **n.** [in sing.] a ringing metallic sound: *the jangle of a telephone.*
– DERIVATIVES **jan·gly adj.**
– ORIGIN Middle English (in the sense 'talk excessively or noisily, squabble'): from Old French *jangler*, of unknown origin.

jan·is·sar·y /ˈjaniˌserē/ (also**janizary** /-ˌzerē/) ▶ **n.** (pl. **janissaries**) historical a member of the Turkish infantry forming the Sultan's guard between the 14th and 19th centuries. ■ a devoted follower or supporter.
– ORIGIN early 16th cent.: from French *janissaire*, based on Turkish *yeniçeri*, from *yeni* 'new' + *çeri* 'troops.'

jan·i·tor /ˈjanitər/ ▶ **n.** a person employed as a caretaker of a building; a custodian. ■ archaic a doorman or doorkeeper.
– DERIVATIVES **jan·i·to·ri·al** /ˌjaniˈtôrēəl/ **adj.**
– ORIGIN mid 16th cent.: from Latin, from *janua* 'door.'

Jan·ja·weed /ˈjanjəwēd/ a grouping of Arabic-speaking fighters in conflict with rebel groups in the Darfur region of western Sudan.

Jan·sen /ˈjansən, ˈyänsən/, Cornelius Otto (1585–1638), Flemish theologian; founder of Jansenism. A Roman Catholic, he strongly opposed the Jesuits and proposed reform of Christianity through a return to the teachings of St. Augustine.

Jan·sen·ism /ˈjansəˌnizəm/ ▶ **n.** a Christian movement of the 17th and 18th centuries, based on Jansen's writings and characterized by moral rigor and asceticism.
– DERIVATIVES **Jan·sen·ist n.**

Jan·sens /ˈyänsən/ (also **Janssen van Ceulen** /vän ˈkələn/) variant spelling of **JOHNSON³**.

Jan·u·ar·y /ˈjanyo͞oˌerē/ ▶ **n.** (pl. **Januaries**) the first month of the year, in the northern hemisphere usually considered the second month of winter: *Sophie was two in January* | [as modifier] *the January sales.*
– ORIGIN Old English, from Latin *Januarius* (*mensis*) '(month) of *Janus*' (see **JANUS**), the Roman god who presided over doors and beginnings.

Ja·nus /ˈjānəs/ **1** Roman Mythology an ancient Italian deity, guardian of doorways and gates and protector of the state in time of war. He is usually represented with two faces, so that he looks both forward and backward.
2 Astronomy a moon of Saturn, sixth closest to the planet, discovered in 1966, and having a diameter of 118 miles (190 km).

Ja·nus-faced ▶ **adj.** having two sharply contrasting aspects or characteristics: *the Janus-faced nature of American society.* ■ insincere or deceitful: *a Janus-faced politician.*
– ORIGIN suggestive of the Roman deity **JANUS**.

Jap /jap/ ▶ **n. & adj.** informal, offensive short for **JAPANESE**.

Ja·pan /jəˈpan/ a country in eastern Asia that occupies a chain of islands in the Pacific Ocean roughly parallel with the eastern coast of the Asiatic mainland; pop. 127,078,700 (est. 2009); capital, Tokyo; official language, Japanese. Japanese name **NIPPON**.

> From the late 19th century Japan began a modernizing process that eventually made it into a major world power. It fought wars against China 1894–95 and Russia 1904–05, and after World War I occupied Manchuria 1931 and invaded China 1937. Japan entered World War II on the Axis side with a surprise attack on Pearl Harbor in 1941. The country surrendered in 1945 after the US dropped the atom bombs on Hiroshima and Nagasaki. Japan is now a highly industrialized country and the leading economic power in the region.

– ORIGIN rendering of Chinese *Riben*.

ja·pan /jəˈpan/ ▶ **n.** a hard, dark, enamellike varnish containing asphalt, used to give a black gloss to metal objects. ■ a kind of varnish in which pigments are ground, typically used to imitate lacquer on wood. ■ articles made in a Japanese style, esp. when decorated with lacquer or enamellike varnish.
▶ **v.** (**japans, japanning, japanned**) [with obj.] cover (something) with a hard black varnish: (as adj. **japanned**) *a japanned tin tray.*
– ORIGIN late 17th cent.: from **JAPAN**.

Ja·pan, Sea of the sea between Japan and mainland Asia.

Ja·pan Cur·rent another name for **KUROSHIO**.

Jap·a·nese /ˌjapəˈnēz, -ˈnēs/ ▶ **adj.** of or relating to Japan or its language, culture, or people.
▶ **n.** (pl. **same**) **1** a native or inhabitant of Japan, or a person of Japanese descent.
2 the language of Japan, spoken by almost all of its population.

> Japanese is possibly related to Korean. It has many Chinese loanwords, and is usually written in vertical columns using Chinese characters (kanji) supplemented by two sets of syllabic characters (kana).

Jap·a·nese a·nem·o·ne ▶ **n.** an autumn-flowering anemone with large pink or white flowers. It is native to China and naturalized in Japan, and several cultivars have been developed. ● *Anemone hupehensis* var. *japonica*, family Ranunculaceae.

Jap·a·nese bee·tle ▶ **n.** a metallic green and copper chafer that is a pest of fruit and foliage as an adult and of grass roots as a larva. It is native to Japan but has spread elsewhere. ● *Popillia japonica*, family Scarabaeidae.

Jap·a·nese ce·dar ▶ **n.** another term for **CRYPTOMERIA**.

Ja·pan·ese Cur·rent another name for **KUROSHIO**.

Jap·a·nese knot·weed ▶ **n.** a tall fast-growing Japanese plant of the dock family, with bamboolike stems and small white flowers. It has been grown as an ornamental but tends to become an aggressive weed. Also called **MEXICAN BAMBOO**. ● *Reynoutria japonica*, family Polygonaceae.

Jap·a·nese lan·tern ▶ **n.** another term for **CHINESE LANTERN** (sense 1).

Jap·a·nese pa·per ▶ **n.** paper of a kind traditionally handmade in Japan, typically from vegetable fibers such as mulberry bark and without being sized, used for art and craft work.

Jap·a·nese per·sim·mon ▶ **n.** see **PERSIMMON**.

Jap·a·nese quince ▶ **n.** another term for **FLOWERING QUINCE**.

Jap·a·nese stilt grass ▶ **n.** an annual grass of Asian origin that is established as an invasive ecological threat in the eastern and southern US. ● *Microstegium vimineum*, family Poaceae.

Jap·an·i·ma·tion /japˌanəˈmāshən/ ▶ **n.** another term for **ANIME**.
– ORIGIN 1980s: blend of **JAPAN** and **ANIMATION**.

jape /jāp/ ▶ **n.** a practical joke: *the childish jape of depositing a stink bomb in her locker.*
▶ **v.** [no obj.] say or do something in jest or mockery.
– DERIVATIVES **jap·er·y** /ˈjāp(ə)rē/ **n.**
– ORIGIN Middle English: apparently combining the form of Old French *japer* 'to yelp, yap' with the sense of Old French *gaber* 'to mock.'

Ja·pheth /ˈjāfeth/ (in the Bible) a son of Noah, traditional ancestor of the peoples living around the Mediterranean. His name is probably to be connected with that of Iapetus, a Titan in Greek mythology.

Jap·lish /ˈjaplish/ ▶ **n.** informal a blend of Japanese and English, either Japanese speech that makes liberal use of English expressions or unidiomatic English spoken by a Japanese person.

ja·pon·i·ca /jəˈpänikə/ ▶ **n. 1** another term for **COMMON CAMELLIA** (see **CAMELLIA**).
2 another term for **FLOWERING QUINCE**.
– ORIGIN early 19th cent.: modern Latin, feminine of *japonicus* 'Japanese.'

Ja·pu·rá Riv·er /ˌzhäpo͞oˈrä/ (Colombian name *Caquetá*) a river that flows for 1,750 miles (2,815 km) from southwestern Colombia into Brazil to join the Amazon River.

Jaques-Dal·croze /ˌjäk dalˈkrōz/, Émile (1865–1950), Swiss music teacher and composer; born in Austria. He developed the eurhythmics method for teaching music and dance and established a school for eurhythmics instruction in 1910.

jar¹ /jär/ ▶ **n.** a wide-mouthed, cylindrical container made of glass or pottery, esp. one used for storing food. ■ the contents of such a container: *jars of mustard.*
– DERIVATIVES **jar·ful** /-ˌfo͝ol/ **n.** (pl. **jarfuls**).
– ORIGIN late 16th cent.: from French *jarre*, from Arabic *jarra*.

jar² ▶ **v.** (**jars, jarring, jarred**) **1** [with obj.] send a painful or damaging shock through (something, esp. a part of the body): *he jarred his knee in training.* ■ [no obj.] strike against something with an unpleasant vibration or jolt: *the stick jarred on the bottom of the pond.*

2 [no obj.] have an unpleasant, annoying, or disturbing effect: *a laugh that **jarred on the ears** | the difference in their background began to jar.* ■ be incongruous in a striking or shocking way: *the play's symbolism **jarred with** the realism of its setting.*
▶ n. a physical shock or jolt. ■ archaic discord; disagreement.
– ORIGIN late 15th cent. (as a noun in the sense 'disagreement, dispute'): probably imitative.

jar·di·niere /ˌjärdn'i(ə)r, ˌZHärdn'ye(ə)r/ (also **jardinière**) ▶ n. 1 an ornamental pot or stand for the display of growing plants.
2 a garnish of mixed vegetables.
– ORIGIN mid 19th cent.: from French *jardinière*, literally 'female gardener.'

jar·gon[1] /'järgən/ ▶ n. special words or expressions that are used by a particular profession or group and are difficult for others to understand: *legal jargon.* ■ a form of language regarded as barbarous, debased, or hybrid.
– DERIVATIVES **jar·gon·is·tic** /ˌjärgə'nistik/ adj., **jar·gon·ize** /-ˌnīz/ v.
– ORIGIN late Middle English (originally in the sense 'twittering, chattering,' later 'gibberish'): from Old French *jargoun*, of unknown origin. The main modern sense dates from the mid 17th cent.

jar·gon[2] /'järgän/ (also **jargoon** /jär'go͞on/) ▶ n. a translucent, colorless, or smoky gem variety of zircon.
– ORIGIN mid 18th cent.: from French, from Italian *giargone*; probably ultimately related to **ZIRCON**.

Jar·gon·elle /ˌjärgə'nel/ ▶ n. Brit. a pear of an early ripening variety.
– ORIGIN late 17th cent.: from French, diminutive of **JARGON[2]** (with reference to the color).

jar·head /'järˌhed/ ▶ n. military slang a US Marine.

jarl /yärl/ ▶ n. historical a Norse or Danish chief.
– ORIGIN Old Norse, literally 'man of noble birth'; related to **EARL**.

Jarls·berg /'yärlzbərg/ ▶ n. trademark a kind of hard yellow Norwegian cheese with many holes and a mild, nutty flavor.
– ORIGIN named after the town of *Jarlsberg*, Norway.

jar·rah /'jarə/ ▶ n. a eucalyptus tree native to western Australia, yielding durable timber. ● *Eucalyptus marginata*, family Myrtaceae.
– ORIGIN mid 19th cent.: from Nyungar *djarryl, jerrhyl*.

jar·ring /'järiNG/ ▶ adj. 1 incongruous in a striking or shocking way; clashing: *the telephone **struck a jarring note** in those Renaissance surroundings.*
2 causing a physical shock, jolt, or vibration: *the truck came to a jarring halt.*
– DERIVATIVES **jar·ring·ly** adv.

Jar·ry /ZHä'rē/, Alfred (1873–1907), French playwright. His satirical farce *Ubu Roi* (1896) anticipated surrealism and the Theater of the Absurd.

Ja·ru·zel·ski /ˌyärə'zelskē/, Wojciech (1923–), Polish general and statesman; prime minister 1981–85; head of state 1985–89, and president 1989–90. Upon the rise of Solidarity, he imposed martial law and banned labor union activities; after Solidarity's victory in the 1989 elections, he supervised Poland's transition to a democracy.

Jar·vik /'järvik/, Robert Koffler (1946–) US biomedical research scientist. He patented an artificial heart driven by compressed air in 1979.

Jas. ▶ abbr. James (in biblical references and generally).

jas·mine /'jazmən/ (also **jessamine** /'jesəmin/) ▶ n. an Old World shrub or climbing plant that bears fragrant flowers used in perfumery or tea. It is popular as an ornamental. ● Genus *Jasminum*, family Oleaceae: many species, including the **winter jasmine**. ■ used in names of other shrubs or climbers with fragrant flowers, e.g., **Cape jasmine**, **yellow jasmine**.
– ORIGIN mid 16th cent.: from French *jasmin* and obsolete French *jessemin*, from Arabic *yāsamīn*, from Persian *yāsamīn*.

jas·mine tea ▶ n. a tea perfumed with dried jasmine blossoms.

Ja·son /'jāsən/ Greek Mythology the son of the king of Iolcos in Thessaly, and leader of the Argonauts in the quest for the Golden Fleece.

jas·pé /ZHa'spā/ ▶ adj. randomly mottled or variegated, like jasper.
– ORIGIN mid 19th cent.: French, past participle of *jasper* 'to marble,' from *jaspe* (see **JASPER**).

jas·per /'jaspər/ ▶ n. 1 an opaque reddish-brown variety of chalcedony.
2 a kind of hard fine porcelain invented by Josiah Wedgwood and used for Wedgwood cameos and other delicate work.
– ORIGIN Middle English (originally denoting any bright-colored chalcedony other than carnelian): from Old French *jasp(r)e*, from Latin *iaspis*, from Greek, of Asian origin.

Jas·sy /'yäsē/ German name for **IAȘI**.

Jat /jät/ ▶ n. a member of a people widely scattered throughout the northwest of India and Pakistan.
– ORIGIN Hindi *Jāṭ*.

Ja·ta·ka /'jätəkə/ ▶ n. any of the various stories of the former lives of the Buddha found in Buddhist literature.
– ORIGIN from Sanskrit *jātaka* 'born under.'

ja·to /'jātō/ ▶ n. (pl. **jatos**) Aeronautics jet-assisted takeoff. ■ an auxiliary power unit providing extra thrust at takeoff.
– ORIGIN World War II (originally US): acronym.

ja·tro·pha /'jatrəfə/ ▶ n. any of various plants or shrubs of the genus *Jatropha* (family Euphorbiaceae), one species of which (*Jatropha curcas*) produces seeds that are used in the production of biodiesel.
– ORIGIN mid 18th cent.: modern Latin (genus name), from Greek *iatros* 'physician' + *trophē* 'nourishment.'

jaun·dice /'jôndis/ ▶ n. a medical condition with yellowing of the skin or whites of the eyes, arising from excess of the pigment bilirubin and typically caused by obstruction of the bile duct, by liver disease, or by excessive breakdown of red blood cells. ■ bitterness, resentment, or envy.
– ORIGIN Middle English *jaunes*, from Old French *jaunice* 'yellowness,' from *jaune* 'yellow.' The sense 'bitterness' (late 16th cent.) arose from the traditional association of the color yellow with jealousy.

jaun·diced /'jôndist/ ▶ adj. having or affected by jaundice, in particular unnaturally yellow in complexion. ■ affected by bitterness, resentment, or envy: *they looked on politicians with a jaundiced eye.*

jaunt /jônt/ ▶ n. a short excursion or journey for pleasure: *her little jaunt in France was over.*
▶ v. [no obj.] make such an excursion or journey: *they went jaunting through Ireland.*
– ORIGIN late 16th cent.: of unknown origin. Originally depreciatory, early senses included 'tire a horse out by riding it up and down,' 'traipse around,' and (as a noun) 'troublesome journey.' The current positive sense dates from the mid 17th cent.

jaunt·ing car ▶ n. historical a light two-wheeled horse-drawn vehicle formerly used in Ireland.

jaun·ty /'jôntē/ ▶ adj. (**jauntier**, **jauntiest**) having or expressing a lively, cheerful, and self-confident manner: *there was no mistaking that jaunty walk.*
– DERIVATIVES **jaun·ti·ly** /-tl-ē/ adv., **jaun·ti·ness** n.
– ORIGIN mid 17th cent. (in the sense 'well-bred, genteel'): from French *gentil* (see **GENTLE**, **GENTEEL**).

Jav. ▶ abbr. Javanese.

Ja·va[1] /'jävə, 'javə/ a large island in the Malay Archipelago that forms part of Indonesia; pop. 120,000,000 (est. 2008).
– DERIVATIVES **Ja·van** n. & adj.

Ja·va[2] /'jävə/ ▶ n. trademark a general-purpose computer programming language designed to produce programs that will run on any computer system.
– ORIGIN 1990s: with allusion to **JAVA**.

ja·va /'jävə, 'javə/ ▶ n. informal coffee.
– ORIGIN mid 19th cent.: originally referring to coffee from **JAVA[1]**.

Ja·va man ▶ n. a fossil hominid of the middle Pleistocene epoch, whose remains were found in Java in 1891. ● An early form of *Homo erectus* (formerly *Pithecanthropus*), family Hominidae.

Jav·a·nese /ˌjävə'nēz, -'nēs/ ▶ n. (pl. **same**) 1 a native or inhabitant of Java, or a person of Javanese descent.
2 the Indonesian language of central Java.
▶ adj. of or relating to Java, its people, or their language.

Ja·van rhi·noc·er·os /'jävən/ ▶ n. a rare, one-horned rhinoceros that is now confined to the lowland rain forests of Java. ● *Rhinoceros sondaicus*, family Rhinocerotidae.

Ja·va·ri Riv·er /ˌZHävä'rē/ (Peruvian name *Yavari*) a river that flows northeast for 500 miles (810 km) from eastern Peru, along the Peru-Brazil border, to the Amazon River.

Ja·va Sea a sea in the Malay Archipelago in southeastern Asia that is surrounded by the islands of Borneo, Java, and Sumatra.

Ja·va spar·row ▶ n. a waxbill with a large red bill and black-and-white head, native to Java and Bali but introduced widely elsewhere and popular as a pet bird. ● *Padda oryzivora*, family Estrildidae.

jave·lin /'jav(ə)lən/ ▶ n. a light spear thrown in a competitive sport or as a weapon. ■ (**the javelin**) the athletic event or sport of throwing the javelin: *his nearest rival in the javelin.*
– ORIGIN late Middle English: from Old French *javeline*, of Celtic origin.

ja·ve·li·na /ˌhävə'lēnə/ ▶ n. another term for **PECCARY**.
– ORIGIN early 19th cent.: from Spanish *jabalina*, from the feminine form of *jabalí* 'wild boar,' from Arabic *jabali* 'mountaineer.'

jaw /jô/ ▶ n. each of the upper and lower bony structures in vertebrates forming the framework of the mouth and containing the teeth. ■ the lower movable bone of such a structure or the part of the face containing it: *she suffered a broken jaw.* ■ (**jaws**) the mouth with its bones and teeth. ■ (**jaws**) the grasping, biting, or crushing mouthparts of an invertebrate. ■ (**jaws**) used to suggest the notion of being in danger from something such as death or defeat: *victory was snatched **from the jaws of defeat**.* ■ (usu. **jaws**) the gripping parts of a tool or machine, such as a wrench or vise. ■ (**jaws**) an opening likened to a mouth: *a passenger stepping from the jaws of a ferry.* ■ informal talk or gossip, esp. when lengthy or tedious: *committee work is just endless jaw | we ought to have a jaw.*
▶ v. [no obj.] informal talk at length; chatter: *he could still hear men **jawing away about** the vacuum cleaners.*
– DERIVATIVES **jawed** adj. [in combination] *square-jawed young men*, **jaw·less** adj.
– ORIGIN late Middle English: from Old French *joe* 'cheek, jaw,' of unknown origin.

jaw·bone /'jôˌbōn/ ▶ n. a bone of the jaw, esp. that of the lower jaw (the mandible), or either half of this.
▶ v. [with obj.] attempt to persuade or pressure by the force of one's position of authority: *the Federal Reserve Board Vice Chairman jawboned the dollar higher by calling its recent steep decline a purely speculative phenomenon* | [no obj.] *an analyst jawboning about the industry.*

jaw·break·er /'jôˌbrākər/ ▶ n. 1 informal a word that is very long or hard to pronounce.
2 a large, hard, spherical candy.

jaw-drop·ping ▶ adj. informal amazing: *jaw-dropping displays of genius.*
– DERIVATIVES **jaw-drop·ping·ly** adv.

jaw·fish /'jôˌfiSH/ ▶ n. (pl. **same** or **jawfishes**) a small fish with very large jaws that lives in shallow tropical seas. It often inhabits a burrow in the sand, the walls of which are lined with pieces of shell and stone. ● Family Opistognathidae: several genera and species.

jaw·line /'jôˌlīn/ ▶ n. the contour of the lower edge of a person's jaw: *he had a dark, unshaven jawline.*

Jaws of Life ▶ n. trademark a hydraulic apparatus used to pry apart the wreckage of crashed vehicles in order to free people trapped inside.

Jay /jā/, John (1745–1829) US chief justice 1789–95 and statesman. With James Madison and Alexander Hamilton, he was the author of the *Federalist* 1787–88. He served as the first chief justice of the US and was responsible for Jay's Treaty 1794–95 that settled outstanding disputes with Britain.

John Jay

jay /jā/ ▶ n. 1 a bird of the crow family with boldly patterned plumage, typically having blue feathers in the wings or tail. ● Family Corvidae: several genera and numerous species, in particular the Eurasian *Garrulus glandarius*, with a crest, mainly pinkish-brown plumage, and a harsh screech.
2 archaic a person who chatters impertinently.
– ORIGIN late 15th cent.: via Old French from late Latin *gaius*, *gaia*, perhaps from the Latin given name *Gaius*.

PRONUNCIATION KEY ə ago, up; ər over, fur; a hat; ā ate; ä car; e let; ē see; i fit; ī by; NG sing; ō go; ô law, for; oi toy; o͝o good; o͞o goo; ou out; TH thin; T͟H then; ZH vision

j

Jay·cee /ˌjāˈsē/ ▶ **n.** a member of a Junior Chamber of Commerce, a civic organization for business and community leaders.
– ORIGIN 1940s: representing the initials of *Junior Chamber*.

Jay·hawk State /ˈjāˌhôk/ a nickname for the state of KANSAS.

jay·walk /ˈjāˌwôk/ ▶ **v.** [no obj.] cross or walk in the street or road unlawfully or without regard for approaching traffic.
– DERIVATIVES **jay·walk·er n.**
– ORIGIN early 20th cent.: from JAY in the colloquial sense 'silly person' + WALK.

jazz /jaz/ ▶ **n.** a type of music of black American origin characterized by improvisation, syncopation, and usually a regular or forceful rhythm, emerging at the beginning of the 20th century. Brass and woodwind instruments and piano are particularly associated with jazz, although guitar and occasionally violin are also used; styles include Dixieland, swing, bebop, and free jazz. ■ informal enthusiastic or lively talk, esp. when considered exaggerated or insincere: *all this jazz about how they can't afford it is preposterous.*
▶ **v.** [no obj.] dated play or dance to jazz music.
– PHRASES **and all that jazz** informal and such similar things: *oh, love, life, and all that jazz.*
– PHRASAL VERBS **jazz something up** make something more lively or cheerful: *jazz up an all-white kitchen with red tiles.*
– DERIVATIVES **jazz·er n.**
– ORIGIN early 20th cent.: of unknown origin.

Jazz Age the 1920s in the US characterized as a period of carefree hedonism, wealth, freedom, and youthful exuberance, reflected in the novels of writers such as F. Scott Fitzgerald.

jazz·bo /ˈjazbō/ ▶ **n.** (pl. **jazzbos**) informal **1** a jazz musician or jazz enthusiast.
2 archaic a person, esp. a black man.
– ORIGIN early 20th cent.: of unknown origin.

Jazz·er·cise /ˈjazərˌsīz/ ▶ **n.** trademark a type of fitness training combining aerobic exercise and dancing to jazz music.
– ORIGIN 1970s: blend of JAZZ and EXERCISE.

jazz funk ▶ **n.** a style of popular dance music incorporating elements of jazz and funk: [as modifier] *a jazz-funk ensemble.*

jazz·man /ˈjazmən, -ˌman/ ▶ **n.** (pl. **jazzmen**) a male jazz musician.

jazz·y /ˈjazē/ ▶ **adj.** (**jazzier, jazziest**) of, resembling, or in the style of jazz: *a jazzy piano solo.* ■ bright, colorful, and showy: *jazzy ties.*
– DERIVATIVES **jazz·i·ly** /ˈjazəlē/ **adv., jazz·i·ness n.**

JCD ▶ **abbr.** ■ Doctor of Canon Law. [from modern Latin *Juris Canonici Doctor*.] ■ Doctor of Civil Law. [from Latin *Juris Civilis Doctor*.]

JCL ▶ **abbr.** ■ Computing job control language. ■ Licentiate in Canon Law.

JCS ▶ **abbr.** Joint Chiefs of Staff, the chief military advisory body to the president of the US.

jct. ▶ **abbr.** junction.

JD ▶ **abbr.** ■ informal juvenile delinquency or juvenile delinquent. ■ Doctor of Law. [from Latin *juris doctor*.]

jeal·ous /ˈjeləs/ ▶ **adj.** feeling or showing envy of someone or their achievements and advantages: *he grew jealous of her success.* ■ feeling or showing suspicion of someone's unfaithfulness in a relationship: *a jealous boyfriend.* ■ fiercely protective or vigilant of one's rights or possessions: *Howard is still a little jealous of his authority* | *they kept a jealous eye over their interests.* ■ (of God) demanding faithfulness and exclusive worship.
– DERIVATIVES **jeal·ous·ly adv.**
– ORIGIN Middle English: from Old French *gelos*, from medieval Latin *zelosus* (see ZEALOUS).

jeal·ous·y /ˈjeləsē/ ▶ **n.** (pl. **jealousies**) the state or feeling of being jealous: *a sharp pang of jealousy* | *resentments and jealousies festered.*
– ORIGIN Middle English: from Old French *gelosie*, from *gelos* (see JEALOUS).

jean /jēn/ ▶ **n.** heavy twilled cotton cloth, esp. denim: [as modifier] *a jean jacket.* ■ (in commercial use) a pair of jeans: *a button-fly jean.*
– ORIGIN late 15th cent. (as an adjective): from Old French *Janne* (now *Gênes*), from medieval Latin *Janua* 'Genoa,' the place of original production. The noun sense comes from *jean fustian*, literally 'fustian from Genoa,' used in the 16th cent. to denote a heavy twilled cotton cloth.

jeans /jēnz/ ▶ **plural n.** hard-wearing trousers made of denim or other cotton fabric, for informal wear. See also BLUE JEANS.
– ORIGIN mid 19th cent.: plural of JEAN.

jeb·el /ˈjebəl/ (also **djebel**) ▶ **n.** (in the Middle East and North Africa) a mountain or hill, or a range of hills.
– ORIGIN colloquial Arabic form of *jabal* 'mountain.'

Jed·dah /ˈjedə/ variant spelling of JIDDAH.

Jed·i /ˈjedˌī/ (also **Jedi knight** or **Jedi warrior**) ▶ **n.** (pl. **same** or **Jedis**) a member of the mystical knightly order in the *Star Wars* films, trained to guard peace and justice in the universe. ■ anyone with special privileges or supernormal powers reminiscent of a Jedi: *these guys hang out in places mere mortal lobbyists who were not Jedi warriors cannot go.*

jeep /jēp/ ▶ **n.** trademark a small, sturdy motor vehicle with four-wheel drive, esp. one used by the military.
– ORIGIN World War II: from the initials *GP*, standing for *general purpose*, influenced by 'Eugene the Jeep,' a creature of great resourcefulness and power represented in the *Popeye* comic strip.

jee·pers /ˈjēpərz/ (also **jeepers creepers**) ▶ **exclam.** informal used to express surprise or alarm: *Jeepers! Do you think she saw?*
– ORIGIN 1920s: alteration of JESUS.

jeer /ji(ə)r/ ▶ **v.** [no obj.] make rude and mocking remarks, typically in a loud voice: *some of the younger men jeered at him* | (as adj. **jeering**) *the jeering crowds.* ■ [with obj.] shout such remarks at (someone): *the performers were jeered and heckled.*
▶ **n.** a rude and mocking remark.
– DERIVATIVES **jeer·ing·ly adv.**
– ORIGIN mid 16th cent.: of unknown origin.

jeet kune do /ˈjēt ˌko͞on ˈdō/ ▶ **n.** a modern martial art incorporating elements of kung fu, fencing, and boxing, devised by American actor Bruce Lee (1940–73).
– ORIGIN 1990s: from Cantonese, literally 'the way of the intercepting fist.'

jeez /jēz/ (also**geez**) ▶ **exclam.** informal a mild expression used to show surprise or annoyance.
– ORIGIN 1920s: abbreviation of JESUS.

je·fe /ˈhefā/ ▶ **n.** informal a boss or leader; a person in charge of something.
– ORIGIN late 19th cent.: Spanish from French *chef* 'chief.'

Jef·fers /ˈjefərz/, (John) Robinson (1887–1962) US poet. His poetry is collected in *Tamar and Other Poems* (1924), *The Women at Point Sur* (1927), and *Hungerfield and Other Poems* (1954).

Jef·fer·son /ˈjefərsən/, Thomas (1743–1826), 3rd president of the US 1801–09. A Democratic-Republican from Virginia, he played a key role in leadership during the American Revolution and was the principal drafter of the Declaration of Independence 1776. While president, he secured the Louisiana Purchase 1803 and authorized the Lewis-Clark expedition to explore this territory. Re-elected to a second term, his poor handling of US shipping and maritime policy made a third term impossible. He chartered the University of Virginia 1819 and served as its head.
– DERIVATIVES **Jef·fer·so·ni·an** /ˌjefərˈsōnēən/ **adj. & n.**

Thomas Jefferson

Jef·fer·son Cit·y the capital of Missouri, in the central part of the state; pop. 40,771 (est. 2008).

je·had ▶ **n.** variant spelling of JIHAD.

Je·hosh·a·phat /jəˈhäsHəˌfat, -ˈhäs-/ (also **Jehosaphat**) a king of Judah in the mid 9th century BC. ■ [as exclamation] (also **jumping Jehoshaphat**) a mild expletive: *Jehoshaphat! That would be ghastly.* [probably a euphemism for JESUS.]

Je·ho·vah /jəˈhōvə/ ▶ **n.** a form of the Hebrew name of God used in some translations of the Bible.
– ORIGIN from medieval Latin *Iehouah, Iehoua*, from Hebrew *YHWH* or *JHVH*, the consonants of the name of God, with the inclusion of vowels taken from *'ăḏōnāy* 'my lord'; see also YAHWEH.

Je·ho·vah's Wit·ness ▶ **n.** a member of a Christian movement (the Watch Tower Bible and Tract Society) founded in the US by Charles Taze Russell (1852–1916). Jehovah's Witnesses deny many traditional Christian doctrines (including the divinity of Christ). and refuse military service and blood transfusion on religious grounds.

Je·ho·vist /jəˈhōvist/ ▶ **n.** another name for YAHWIST.

je·june /jiˈjo͞on/ ▶ **adj. 1** naive, simplistic, and superficial: *their entirely predictable and usually jejune opinions.*
2 (of ideas or writings) dry and uninteresting: *the poem seems to me rather jejune.*
– DERIVATIVES **je·june·ly adv., je·june·ness n.**
– ORIGIN early 17th cent.: from Latin *jejunus* 'fasting, barren.' The original sense was 'without food,' hence 'not intellectually nourishing.'

je·ju·no·i·le·al /jiˌjo͞onōˈilēəl/ ▶ **adj.** Medicine of or involving the jejunum and the ileum, usually with reference to a bypass operation in which they are connected.

je·ju·num /jiˈjo͞onəm/ ▶ **n.** [in sing.] Anatomy the part of the small intestine between the duodenum and ileum.
– DERIVATIVES **je·ju·nal** /ˈjo͞onl/ **adj.**
– ORIGIN mid 16th cent.: from medieval Latin, neuter of *jejunus* 'fasting' (because it is usually found to be empty after death).

Jek·yll /ˈjekəl/, Dr., the central character of Robert Louis Stevenson's story *The Strange Case of Dr. Jekyll and Mr. Hyde* (1886). He discovers a drug that creates a separate personality (appearing in the character of Mr. Hyde) into which Jekyll's evil impulses are channeled.
– PHRASES **a Jekyll and Hyde** a person alternately displaying opposing good and evil personalities.

Je·li·nek /ˈyeləˌnek/, Elfriede (1946–), Austrian novelist, poet, and playwright. Her novels include *Women as Lovers* (1975), *Wonderful, Wonderful Times* (1980), *The Piano Teacher* (1983), and *Lust* (1989). Nobel Prize for Literature (2004).

jell /jel/ ▶ **v.** [no obj.] (of jelly or a similar substance) set or become firmer: *the stew is jelling.* ■ (of a project or idea) take a definite shape; begin to work well: *everything seemed to jell for the magazine.* ■ (of people) relate well to one another: *it's gratifying seeing everybody jelling.*
– ORIGIN mid 18th cent.: back-formation from JELLY.

jel·la·ba ▶ **n.** variant spelling of DJELLABA.

jell·o /ˈjelō/ (also trademark **Jell-O**) ▶ **n.** a fruit-flavored gelatin dessert made from a commercially prepared powder.

Jell·o shot (also **jello shot**) ▶ **n.** an alcoholic beverage consisting of liquor incorporated into sweetened gelatin dessert and chilled in a small container.
– ORIGIN from JELL-O, the proprietary name of a gelatin dessert.

jel·ly /ˈjelē/ ▶ **n.** (pl. **jellies**) a sweet, clear, semisolid, somewhat elastic spread or preserve made from fruit juice and sugar boiled to a thick consistency. ■ used figuratively and in similes to refer to sensations of fear or strong emotion: *her legs felt like jelly.* ■ a similar clear preparation made with fruit or other ingredients as a condiment: *roast pheasant with red currant jelly.* ■ a gelatinous savory preparation made by boiling meat and bones. ■ any substance of a gelatinous consistency: *spermicidal jellies* | *frogs lay eggs coated in jelly.* ■ chiefly Brit. a sweet, fruit-flavored gelatin dessert. ■ (**jellies**) jelly shoes.
▶ **v.** (**jellies, jellied**) [with obj.] (usu. as adj. **jellied**) set (food) as or in a jelly: *jellied cranberry sauce* | *jellied eels.*
– DERIVATIVES **jel·li·fi·ca·tion** /ˌjeləfiˈkāsHən/ **n., jel·li·fy** /ˈjeləˌfī/ **v., jel·ly·like** /-ˌlīk/ **adj.**
– ORIGIN late Middle English: from Old French *gelée* 'frost, jelly,' from Latin *gelata* 'frozen,' from *gelare* 'freeze,' from *gelu* 'frost.'

jel·ly bean (also **jellybean**) ▶ **n.** a bean-shaped candy with a jellylike center and a firm sugar coating.

jel·ly·fish /ˈjelēˌfisH/ ▶ **n.** (pl. **same** or **jellyfishes**) **1** a free-swimming marine coelenterate with a jellylike bell- or saucer-shaped body that is typically transparent and has stinging tentacles around the edge. ● Classes Scyphozoa and Cubozoa.
2 informal a feeble or weak-willed person.

jel·ly roll ▶ **n.** a cylindrical cake with a spiral cross section, made from a flat sponge cake spread with a filling such as jam and rolled up. ■ vulgar slang a woman's genitals, or sexual intercourse.

jel·ly shoe ▶ **n.** a sandal made from brightly colored or translucent molded plastic.

Je·mez Moun·tains /ˈhāmes/ a range in northern New Mexico, northwest of Santa Fe, the site of an enormous caldera called Valle Grande. Chicoma Peak (11,950 feet; 3,642 m) is the high point.

jem·my /ˈjemē/ ▶ **n. & v.** British spelling of **JIMMY**.

Je·na /ˈyānə/ a university town in central Germany, in Thuringia; pop. 102,500 (est. 2006).

je ne sais quoi /ˌZHə nə sā ˈkwä/ ▶ **n.** a quality that cannot be described or named easily: *that je ne sais quoi that makes a professional.*
– ORIGIN French, literally 'I do not know what.'

Jen·kins /ˈjeNGkinz/, Roy (Harris), Baron Jenkins of Hillhead (1920–2003), English politician and scholar. He was a member of Parliament 1948–76 and 1982–87 and then served as chancellor of Oxford University. Notable works: *Mr. Attlee* (1948), *Truman* (1986), and *Gladstone* (1995).

Jen·kins's Ear, War of a war between England and Spain (1739). It was precipitated by a British sea captain, **Robert Jenkins**, who appeared before Parliament to produce what he claimed was his ear, cut off by the Spanish while they were carrying out a search of his ship in the Caribbean.

Jen·ner /ˈjenər/, Edward (1749–1823), British physician; the pioneer of vaccination. He deliberately infected people with small amounts of cowpox because he believed it would protect them from catching the disease. The practice led to the widespread use of vaccination against disease.

jen·net /ˈjenit/ ▶ **n. 1** a female donkey.
2 (also **genet**) a kind of small Spanish horse.
– ORIGIN late Middle English: via French from Spanish *jinete* 'light horseman,' from Spanish Arabic *Zenāta*, the name of a Berber people famous for horsemanship.

jen·ny /ˈjenē/ ▶ **n.** (pl. **jennies**) **1** a female donkey or ass.
2 short for **SPINNING JENNY**.
– ORIGIN early 17th cent. (used to denote a female mammal or bird): nickname for the given name *Janet* (compare with **JACK**[1]).

jen·ny wren ▶ **n.** Brit. informal a wren.

jeon /ˈjēˌän/ ▶ **n.** (pl. **same**) a monetary unit of South Korea, equal to one hundredth of a won.
– ORIGIN Korean.

jeop·ard·ize /ˈjepərˌdīz/ ▶ **v.** [with obj.] put (someone or something) into a situation in which there is a danger of loss, harm, or failure: *a devaluation of the dollar would jeopardize New York's position as a financial center.*

jeop·ard·y /ˈjepərdē/ ▶ **n.** danger of loss, harm, or failure: *Michael's job was not in jeopardy.* ■ Law danger arising from being on trial for a criminal offense.
– ORIGIN Middle English *iuparti*, from Old French *ieu parti* '(evenly) divided game.' The term was originally used in chess and other games to denote a problem, or a position in which the chances of winning or losing were evenly balanced, hence 'a dangerous situation.'

Jeph·thah /ˈjefTHə, yifˈtäKH/ (in the Bible) a judge of Israel who sacrificed his daughter in consequence of a vow that if victorious in battle he would sacrifice the first living thing that met him on his return.

je·quir·i·ty /jəˈkwiritē/ (also **jequirity bean**) ▶ **n.** another term for **ROSARY PEA**.
– ORIGIN late 19th cent.: from French *jéquirity*, from Tupi-Guarani *jekiriti.*

Jer. ▶ **abbr.** Bible Jeremiah.

jer·bo·a /jərˈbōə/ ▶ **n.** a desert-dwelling rodent with very long hind legs that enable it to walk upright and perform long jumps, found from North Africa to central Asia. ● Family Dipodidae: several genera and species, including the **rough-legged** (or **northern three-toed**) **jerboa** (*Dipus sagitta*).
– ORIGIN mid 17th cent.: modern Latin, from Arabic *yarbū'*.

rough-legged jerboa

jer·e·mi·ad /ˌjerəˈmīəd, -ˌad/ ▶ **n.** a long, mournful complaint or lamentation; a list of woes.
– ORIGIN late 18th cent.: from French *jérémiade*, from *Jérémie* 'Jeremiah,' from ecclesiastical Latin *Jeremias*, with reference to the Lamentations of Jeremiah in the Old Testament.

Jer·e·mi·ah /ˌjerəˈmīə/, (*c.*650–*c.*585 BC) a Hebrew prophet. He foresaw the fall of Assyria, the conquest of his country by Egypt and Babylon, and the destruction of Jerusalem. The biblical Lamentations are traditionally ascribed to Jeremiah. ■ a book of the Bible containing his prophecies. ■ (as noun **a Jeremiah**) a person who complains continually or foretells disaster.

Je·rez /hāˈres, -ˈreTH/ a town in southwestern Spain, in Andalusia; pop. 205,364 (2008). It is the center of a sherry-making industry. Full name **Jerez de la Frontera**.

Jer·i·cho /ˈjeriˌkō/ a town in Palestine, on the West Bank, north of the Dead Sea. According to the Bible, Jericho was a Canaanite city destroyed by the Israelites after they crossed the Jordan River into the Promised Land. Occupied by the Israelis since the Six Day War of 1967, it was the first area given partial autonomy under the PLO–Israeli peace accord in 1994.

jerk[1] /jərk/ ▶ **n. 1** a quick, sharp, sudden movement: *he gave a sudden jerk of his head.* ■ a spasmodic muscular twitch. ■ [in sing.] Weightlifting the raising of a barbell above the head from shoulder level by an abrupt straightening of the arms and legs, typically as the second part of a clean and jerk.
2 informal a contemptibly obnoxious person.
▶ **v.** [with obj.] move or cause to move with a jerk: [no obj.] *the van jerked forward* | [with obj.] *she jerked her chin up* | figurative *the thud jerked her back to reality.* ■ Weightlifting raise (a weight) from shoulder level to above the head.
– PHRASAL VERBS **jerk someone around** informal deal with someone dishonestly or unfairly. **jerk off** vulgar slang masturbate.
– DERIVATIVES **jerk·er n.**
– ORIGIN mid 16th cent. (denoting a stroke with a whip): probably imitative.

jerk[2] ▶ **v.** [with obj.] (usu. as adj. **jerked**) prepare (meat) by marinating it in spices and drying or barbecuing it over a wood fire: *jerked beef.*
▶ **n.** meat cooked in this way: *fiery Jamaican jerk* | [as modifier] *jerk chicken.*
– ORIGIN early 18th cent.: from Latin American Spanish *charquear*, from *charqui*, from Quechua *echarqui* 'dried flesh.'

jer·kin /ˈjərkin/ ▶ **n.** a sleeveless jacket. ■ historical a man's close-fitting jacket, typically made of leather.
– ORIGIN early 16th cent.: of unknown origin.

jerkin

jer·kin head ▶ **n.** Architecture the end of a roof that is hipped for only part of its height, leaving a truncated gable.
– ORIGIN mid 19th cent.: perhaps from an alteration of *jerking* (from the verb **JERK**[1]) + **HEAD**; compare also with earlier *kirkin-head* (apparently arbitrarily formed from **KIRK**) in the same sense.

jerk·wa·ter /ˈjərkˌwôtər, -ˌwätər/ ▶ **adj.** [attrib.] informal of or associated with small, remote, and insignificant rural settlements: *some jerkwater town.*
– ORIGIN mid 19th cent.: from **JERK**[1] + **WATER**, from the need for early railroad engines to be supplied with water in remote areas, by dipping a bucket into a stream and "jerking" it out by rope.

jerk·y[1] /ˈjərkē/ ▶ **adj.** (**jerkier, jerkiest**)
1 characterized by abrupt stops and starts: *shallow, jerky, irregular breathing.*
2 informal contemptibly foolish: *he makes mischief with his jerky pals.*
– DERIVATIVES **jerk·i·ly** /-kəlē/ **adv.**, **jerk·i·ness n.**

jerk·y[2] ▶ **n.** meat that has been cured by being cut into long, thin strips and dried: *beef jerky.*
– ORIGIN mid 19th cent.: from American Spanish *charqui*, from Quechua.

jer·o·bo·am /ˌjerəˈbōəm/ ▶ **n.** a wine bottle with a capacity four times larger than that of an ordinary bottle.
– ORIGIN early 19th cent.: named after *Jeroboam*, a king of Israel, "who made Israel to sin" (1 Kings 11:28, 14:16).

Je·rome, St. /jəˈrōm/ (*c.*342–420), doctor of the Church. He is noted for his compilation of the Vulgate Bible. Feast day, September 30.

jer·ry-built ▶ **adj.** badly or hastily built with materials of poor quality.
– DERIVATIVES **jer·ry-build·er n.**, **jer·ry-build·ing n.**
– ORIGIN mid 19th cent.: origin unknown; sometimes said to be from the name of a firm of builders in Liverpool, or to allude to the walls of Jericho, which fell down at the sound of Joshua's trumpets (Josh. 6:20).

jer·ry·can /ˈjerēˌkan/ (also **jerry can, jerrican**) ▶ **n.** a large, flat-sided metal container for storing or transporting liquids, typically gasoline or water.
– ORIGIN World War II: from *Jerry* 'a German' (probably an alteration of **GERMAN**) + **CAN**[2], because such containers were first used in Germany.

Jer·sey /ˈjərzē/ the largest of the Channel Islands; pop. 91,900 (est. 2009).

jer·sey /ˈjərzē/ ▶ **n.** (pl. **jerseys**) **1** a knitted garment with long sleeves worn over the upper body. ■ a distinctive shirt worn by a player or competitor in certain sports. ■ a soft, fine knitted fabric.
2 (**Jersey**) an animal of a breed of light brown dairy cattle from Jersey.
– ORIGIN late 16th cent. (denoting woolen worsted fabric made in Jersey): from **JERSEY**.

Jer·sey Cit·y an industrial city in northeastern New Jersey, on the Hudson River, opposite New York City; pop. 241,114 (est. 2008).

Je·ru·sa·lem /jəˈro͞os(ə)ləm, -ˈro͞oz-/ the holy city of the Jews, sacred also to Christians and Muslims, that lies in the Judaean hills about 20 miles (32 km) from the Jordan River; pop. 763,600 (est. 2008). From 1947, the city was divided between the states of Israel and Jordan until the Israelis occupied the whole city in June 1967 and proclaimed it the capital of Israel although it is not accepted as such by the United Nations. It is revered by Christians as the place of Christ's death and resurrection and by Muslims as the site of the Dome of the Rock.

Je·ru·sa·lem ar·ti·choke ▶ **n. 1** a knobby edible tuber with white flesh, eaten as a vegetable.
2 the tall North American plant, closely related to the sunflower, that produces this tuber. ● *Helianthus tuberosus*, family Compositae.
– ORIGIN early 17th cent.: *Jerusalem*, alteration of Italian *girasole* 'sunflower.'

Je·ru·sa·lem Bi·ble ▶ **n.** a modern English translation of the Bible by mainly Roman Catholic scholars, published in 1966 and revised (as the **New Jerusalem Bible**) in 1985.

Je·ru·sa·lem cross ▶ **n.** a cross with arms of equal length each ending in a bar; a cross potent.

Je·ru·sa·lem thorn ▶ **n. 1** a thorny tropical American tree of the pea family, grown as an ornamental. ● *Parkinsonia aculeata*, family Leguminosae.
2 see **CHRIST'S THORN**.

Jer·vis /ˈjərvəs/, John, Earl St. Vincent (1735–1823), British admiral. In 1797, as commander of the British fleet, he defeated a Spanish fleet off the coast of Portugal.

Jer·vis Bay Ter·ri·to·ry /ˈjärvəs/ a territory on Jervis Bay on the southeastern coast of Australia.

Jes·per·sen /ˈyespərsən/ Otto (1860–1943), Danish philologist, grammarian, and educationist; full name *Jens Otto Harry Jespersen*. He promoted the use of the "direct method" in language teaching. Notable works: *How to Teach a Foreign Language* (1904) and *Modern English Grammar* (1909–49).

jess /jes/ Falconry ▶ **n.** (usu. **jesses**) a short leather strap that is fastened around each leg of a hawk, usually also having a ring or swivel to which a leash may be attached.
▶ **v.** [with obj.] put such straps on (a hawk).
– ORIGIN Middle English: from Old French *ges*, based on Latin *jactus* 'a throw,' from *jacere* 'to throw.'

jes·sa·mine /ˈjesəmin/ ▶ **n.** variant spelling of **JASMINE**.

Jes·se /ˈjesē/ (in the Bible) the father of David, represented as the first in the genealogy of Jesus Christ.

Jes·sel /ˈjesəl/, George Albert (1898–1981) US entertainer; known as America's "toastmaster general." He was best known as a master of ceremonies.

Jes·se tree ▶ **n.** a representation usually in carving or stained glass of the genealogy of Jesus as a tree with Jesse at the base and intermediate descendants on branching scrolls of foliage.

Jes·se win·dow ▶ **n.** a church window showing Jesus' descent from Jesse, typically in the form of a Jesse tree.

jest /jest/ ▶ **n.** a thing said or done for amusement; a joke: *there are jests about administrative gaffes* | *it*

j

was said *in jest*. ■ archaic an object of derision: *lowly virtue is the jest of fools*.
▶ v. [no obj.] speak or act in a joking manner: *you jest, surely?* | [with direct speech] *"I don't know about maturing," jests William*.
– ORIGIN late Middle English: from earlier *gest*, from Old French *geste*, from Latin *gesta* 'actions, exploits,' from *gerere* 'do.' The original sense was 'exploit, heroic deed,' hence 'a narrative of such deeds' (originally in verse); later the term denoted an idle tale, hence a joke (mid 16th cent).

jest·er /ˈjestər/ ▶ n. historical a professional joker or "fool" at a medieval court, typically wearing a cap with bells on it and carrying a mock scepter. ■ a person who habitually plays the fool.

Je·su /ˈjāzo͞o, ˈjē-, ˈyā-/ archaic form of **Jesus**.
– ORIGIN Middle English: from Old French. *Jesus* became the usual spelling in the 16th cent., but *Jesu* was often retained in translations of the Bible, reflecting Latin vocative use.

Jes·u·it /ˈjezHo͞oit, ˈjez(y)o͞o-/ ▶ n. a member of the Society of Jesus, a Roman Catholic order of priests founded by St. Ignatius Loyola, St. Francis Xavier, and others in 1534, to do missionary work. The order was zealous in opposing the Reformation. Despite periodic persecution it has retained an important influence in Catholic thought and education.
– ORIGIN from French *jésuite* or modern Latin *Jesuita*, from Christian Latin *Iesus* (see **Jesus**).

Jes·u·it·i·cal /ˌjezHo͞oˈitikəl, ˌjez(y)o͞o-/ ▶ adj. of or concerning the Jesuits. ■ dissembling or equivocating, in the manner associated with Jesuits.
– DERIVATIVES **Jes·u·it·i·cal·ly** adv.

Jes·u·its' bark ▶ n. archaic cinchona bark.

Je·sus /ˈjēzəs/ (also **Jesus Christ** or **Jesus of Nazareth**) the central figure of the Christian religion. Jesus conducted a mission of preaching and healing (with reported miracles) in Palestine in about AD 28–30, which is described in the Gospels. His followers considered him to be the Christ or Messiah and the Son of God, and belief in his resurrection from the dead is the central tenet of Christianity.

Je·sus freak ▶ n. informal, chiefly derogatory a fervent evangelical Christian.

jet[1] /jet/ ▶ n. **1** a rapid stream of liquid or gas forced out of a small opening: *a high-pressure shower with pulsating jets*. ■ a nozzle or narrow opening for sending out such a stream: *Agnes turned up the gas jet*.
2 an aircraft powered by one or more jet engines: *a private jet* | [as modifier] *a jet plane*. ■ a jet engine.
▶ v. (**jets, jetting, jetted**) [no obj.] **1** travel by jet aircraft: *the newlyweds jetted off for a honeymoon in New York*.
2 spurt out in jets: *blood jetted from his nostrils*.
– ORIGIN late 16th cent. (as a verb meaning 'jut out'): from French *jeter* 'to throw,' based on Latin *jactare*, frequentative of *jacere* 'to throw.'

jet[2] ▶ n. a hard black semiprecious variety of lignite, capable of being carved and highly polished. ■ a glossy black color: [as modifier] *the gloss of her jet hair* | *jet black*.
– ORIGIN Middle English: from Old French *jaiet*, from Latin *Gagates*, from Greek *gagatēs* 'from *Gagai*,' a town in Asia Minor.

je·té /ZHəˈtā/ ▶ n. Ballet a jump in which a dancer springs from one foot to land on the other with one leg extended outward from the body while in the air. See also **grand jeté, petit jeté**.
– ORIGIN French, past participle of *jeter* 'to throw.'

jet en·gine ▶ n. an engine using jet propulsion for forward thrust, mainly used for aircraft.

jet·foil /ˈjetˌfoil/ ▶ n. a type of passenger-carrying hydrofoil.
– ORIGIN 1970s: blend of **jet**[1] and **hydrofoil**.

jet lag ▶ n. extreme tiredness and other physical effects felt by a person after a long flight across several time zones.
– DERIVATIVES **jet-lagged** adj.

jet·lin·er /ˈjetˌlīnər/ ▶ n. a large jet aircraft carrying passengers.
– ORIGIN 1940s: blend of **jet**[1] and **airliner**.

jet pipe ▶ n. the exhaust duct of a jet engine.

jet-pro·pelled ▶ adj. moved by jet propulsion.

jet pro·pul·sion ▶ n. propulsion by the backward ejection of a high-speed jet of gas or liquid.

jet·sam /ˈjetsəm/ ▶ n. unwanted material or goods that have been thrown overboard from a ship and washed ashore, esp. material that has been discarded to lighten the vessel. Compare with **flotsam**.
– ORIGIN late 16th cent. (as *jetson*): contraction of **jettison**.

jet set ▶ n. (**the jet set**) informal wealthy and fashionable people who travel widely and frequently for pleasure: [as modifier] *the jet-set lifestyle*.
– DERIVATIVES **jet-set·ter** n., **jet-set·ting** adj.

jet ski ▶ n. trademark a small, jet-propelled vehicle that skims across the surface of water and typically is ridden like a motorcycle.
▶ v. (**jet-ski**) [no obj.] (often as noun **jet-skiing**) ride on such a vehicle.
– DERIVATIVES **jet-ski·er** n.

jet stream ▶ n. **1** a narrow, variable band of very strong, predominantly westerly air currents encircling the globe several miles above the earth. There are typically two or three jet streams in each of the northern and southern hemispheres.
2 a flow of exhaust gasses from a jet engine.

jet·ti·son /ˈjetisən, -zən/ ▶ v. [with obj.] throw or drop (something) from an aircraft or ship: *six aircraft jettisoned their loads in the sea*. ■ abandon or discard (someone or something that is no longer wanted): *individuals are often forced to jettison certain attitudes and behaviors*.
▶ n. the action of jettisoning something.
– ORIGIN late Middle English (as a noun denoting the throwing of goods overboard to lighten a ship in distress): from Old French *getaison*, from Latin *jactatio(n-)*, from *jactare* 'to throw' (see **jet**[1]). The verb dates from the mid 19th cent.

jet·ton /ˈjetn/ ▶ n. Brit. a counter or token used as a gambling chip or to operate slot machines.
– ORIGIN mid 18th cent.: from French *jeton*, from *jeter* 'throw, add up accounts' (see **jet**[1]); so named because the term was formerly used in accounting.

jet·ty /ˈjetē/ ▶ n. (pl. **jetties**) a landing stage or small pier at which boats can dock or be moored. ■ a breakwater constructed to protect or defend a harbor, stretch of coast, or riverbank.
– ORIGIN late Middle English: from Old French *jetee*, feminine past participle of *jeter* 'to throw' (see **jet**[1]).

jet·way /ˈjetˌwā/ ▶ n. trademark (in the UK) a portable bridge put against an aircraft door to allow passengers to embark or disembark.

jeu d'es·prit /ˌZHə dəˈsprē, ˌZHœ/ ▶ n. (pl. **jeux d'esprit** pronunc. **same**) a lighthearted display of wit and cleverness, esp. in a work of literature.
– ORIGIN French, literally 'game of the mind.'

jeu·nesse do·rée /ZHəˌnes dôˈrā/ ▶ n. [treated as sing. or pl.] young people of wealth, fashion, and flair.
– ORIGIN mid 19th cent.: French, literally 'gilded youth.'

Jew /jo͞o/ ▶ n. a member of the people and cultural community whose traditional religion is Judaism and who trace their origins through the ancient Hebrew people of Israel to Abraham.
– PHRASES **jew someone down** offensive bargain with someone in a miserly or petty way.
– ORIGIN Middle English: from Old French *juiu*, via Latin from Greek *Ioudaios*, via Aramaic from Hebrew *yĕhūḏī*, from *yĕhūḏāh* 'Judah' (see **Judah**).

jew·el /ˈjo͞oəl/ ▶ n. a precious stone, typically a single crystal or a piece of a hard lustrous or translucent mineral, cut into shape with flat facets or smoothed and polished for use as an ornament. ■ (usu. **jewels**) an ornament or piece of jewelry containing such a stone or stones. ■ a hard precious stone used as a bearing in a watch, compass, or other device. ■ a very pleasing or valued person or thing; a very fine example: *she was a jewel of a nurse*.
– PHRASES **the jewel in the** (or **one's**) **crown** the most valuable or successful part of something: *science is the brightest jewel in the crown of our civilization*.
– ORIGIN Middle English: from Old French *joel*, from *jeu* 'game, play,' from Latin *jocus* 'jest.'

jew·el bee·tle ▶ n. a chiefly tropical beetle that has bold metallic colors and patterns. The larvae are mainly wood-borers and can be serious pests of timber. ● Family Buprestidae: numerous genera.

jew·el box ▶ n. a storage box for a compact disc.

jew·eled /ˈjo͞oəld/ (Brit. **jewelled**) ▶ adj. adorned, set with, or made from jewels: *a jeweled dagger*.

jew·el·er /ˈjo͞o(ə)lər/ (Brit. **jeweller**) ▶ n. a person or company that makes or sells jewels or jewelry.
– ORIGIN Middle English: from Old French *juelier*, from *joel* (see **jewel**).

jew·el·er's rouge ▶ n. finely ground ferric oxide, used as a polish for metal and optical glass.

jew·el·fish /ˈjo͞oəlˌfisH/ ▶ n. (pl. **same** or **jewelfishes**) a scarlet and green tropical freshwater cichlid. ● *Hemichromis bimaculatus*, family Cichlidae.

jew·el·ry /ˈjo͞o(ə)lrē/ (Brit. **jewellery**) ▶ n. personal ornaments, such as necklaces, rings, or bracelets, that are typically made from or contain jewels and precious metal.
– ORIGIN late Middle English: from Old French *juelerie*, from *juelier* 'jeweler,' from *joel* (see **jewel**).

USAGE Avoid the pronunciation /ˈjo͞oləreˉ/, widely regarded as uneducated.

jew·el·weed another term for **touch-me-not**.

Jew·ess /ˈjo͞o-is/ ▶ n. often offensive a Jewish woman or girl.

Jew·ett /ˈjo͞oət/, Sarah Orne (1849–1909) US writer and poet; full name *Theodora Sarah Orne Jewett* Her pen names include **A. D. Eliot, Alice Eliot,** and **Sarah C. Sweet**. Notable works: *The King of Folly Island* (1888) and *The Country of the Pointed Firs* (1896).

jew·fish /ˈjo͞oˌfisH/ ▶ n. (pl. **same** or **jewfishes**) a large sporting or food fish of warm coastal waters. ● a fish of the Atlantic and Pacific coasts of North America (*Epinephelus itajara*, family Serranidae). ● a fish of the Indo-Pacific (family Sciaenidae: several species), in particular the mulloway.

Jew·ish /ˈjo͞o-isH/ ▶ adj. relating to, associated with, or denoting Jews or Judaism: *the Jewish people*.
– DERIVATIVES **Jew·ish·ly** adv., **Jew·ish·ness** n.

Jew·ish cal·en·dar ▶ n. a complex ancient calendar in use among the Jews.

It is a lunar calendar adapted to the solar year, normally consisting of twelve months but having thirteen months in leap years, which occur seven times in every cycle of nineteen years. The years are reckoned from the Creation (which is placed at 3761 BC); the months are Nisan, Iyyar, Sivan, Thammuz, Ab, Elul, Tishri, Hesvan, Kislev, Tebet, Sebat, and Adar, with an intercalary month (First Adar) being added in leap years. The religious year begins with Nisan and ends with Adar; the civil year begins with Tishri and ends with Elul.

Jew·ish New Year ▶ n. another term for **Rosh Hashanah**.

Jew·i·son /ˈjo͞o-isən/, Norman (1926–), Canadian movie director and producer. He is known for the drama *In the Heat of the Night* (1967), which won five Academy Awards; the musical *Fiddler on the Roof* (1971); and the romantic comedy *Moonstruck* (1987).

Jew·ry /ˈjo͞orē/ ▶ n. (pl. **Jewries**) **1** Jews collectively.
2 historical a Jewish quarter in a town or city.
– ORIGIN Middle English: from Old French *juierie*, from *juiu* (see **Jew**).

Jew's ear ▶ n. a common fungus with a brown, rubbery, cup-shaped fruiting body, growing on dead or dying trees in both Eurasia and North America. ● *Auricularia auricula-judae*, family Auriculariaceae, class Hymenomycetes.
– ORIGIN mid 16th cent.: a mistranslation of medieval Latin *auricula Judae* 'Judas's ear,' from its shape, and because it grows on the elder, which was said to be the tree from which Judas Iscariot hanged himself.

Jew's harp ▶ n. a small, lyre-shaped musical instrument held between the teeth and struck with a finger. It can produce only one note, but harmonics are sounded by the player altering the shape of the mouth cavity.

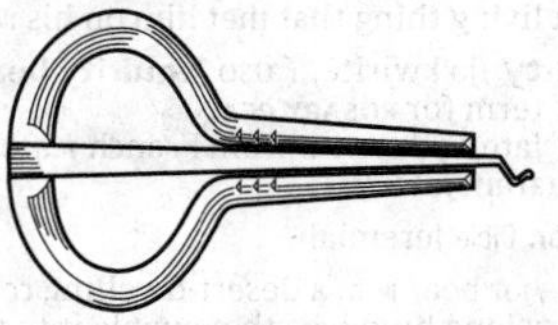
Jew's harp

Je·ze·bel /ˈjezəˌbel, -bəl/ (*fl.* 9th century BC), a Phoenician princess, traditionally the great-aunt of Dido and in the Bible the wife of **Ahab**, king of Israel. She was denounced by Elijah for introducing the worship of Baal into Israel (1 Kings 16:31, 21:5–15, 2 Kings 9:30–7). ■ (as noun **a Jezebel**) a shameless or immoral woman.

jg ▶ abbr. junior grade.

Jg. ▶ abbr. Bible Judges.

Jhab·va·la /ˈjubwələ, -vələ/, Ruth Prawer (1927–), US screenwriter and novelist; born in Germany. Her writing career began in India, where she lived 1951–75. Working with James Ivory and Ismail Merchant, she adapted for the screen *A Room with a View* (1986), *Howards End* (1992), and *The Remains of the Day* (1993).

Jhan·si /ˈjänsē/ a city in northern India, in the state of Uttar Pradesh; pop. 442,400 (est. 2009).

Jhar·khand /ˈjärˌkand/ a state in northeastern India, formed in 2000 from the southern part of Bihar; capital, Ranchi.

Jhe·lum /'jāləm/ a river that rises in the Himalayas and flows through the Vale of Kashmir into Punjab, where it meets the Chenab River. About 450 miles (720 km) long, it is one of the five rivers that gave Punjab its name. In ancient times it was called the Hydaspes.

JHVH ▶ **abbr.** YHVH.

Jia·mu·si /jē'ä'mo͞o'sē, 'jyä'mY'sē/ a city in Heilongjiang province, in northeastern China, on the Sungari River, northeast of Harbin; pop. 599,300 (est. 2006).

Jiang Jie Shi /,jäNG jē 'SHē/ variant form of CHIANG KAI-SHEK.

Jiang·su /jē'äNG'so͞o/ (also **Kiangsu**) a province in eastern China; capital, Nanjing. It includes much of the Yangtze delta.

Jiang·xi /jē'äNG'SHē/ (also **Kiangsi**) a province in southeastern China; capital, Nanchang.

jiao /jyou/ ▶ **n.** (pl. **same**) a monetary unit of China, equal to one tenth of a yuan.
– ORIGIN from Chinese *jiǎo*.

Jia·xing /jē'ä'SHiNG/ (formerly *Kashing*) a city in Zhejiang province, in eastern China, on the Grand Canal, southwest of Shanghai; pop. 363,200 (est. 2006).

jib[1] /jib/ ▶ **n.** **1** Sailing a triangular staysail set forward of the forwardmost mast.
2 the projecting arm of a crane.
– ORIGIN mid 17th cent.: of unknown origin.

jib[2] ▶ **v.** (**jibs, jibbing, jibbed**) [no obj.] (of an animal, esp. a horse) stop and refuse to go on: *he jibbed at the final fence.* ■ (of a person) be unwilling to do or accept something: *he jibs at paying large bills.*
– DERIVATIVES **jib·ber** **n.**
– ORIGIN early 19th cent.: perhaps related to French *regimber* (earlier *regiber*) 'to buck, rear'; compare with JIBE[1].

jib·ba /'jibə/ (also **jibbah, djibba,** or **djibbah**) ▶ **n.** a long coat worn by Muslim men.
– ORIGIN mid 19th cent.: Egyptian variant of Arabic *jubba*.

jib boom ▶ **n.** Sailing a spar run out forward as an extension of the bowsprit.

jibe[1] /jīb/ ▶ **n. & v.** variant spelling of GIBE.

jibe[2] (Brit. **gybe**) Sailing ▶ **v.** [no obj.] change course by swinging a fore-and-aft sail across a following wind: *they jibed, and the boat turned over.* ■ [with obj.] swing (a sail or boom) across the wind in such a way. ■ (of a sail or boom) swing or be swung across the wind: (as adj. **jibing**) *the skipper was hit by a jibing boom.*
▶ **n.** an act or instance of jibing.
– ORIGIN late 17th cent.: from obsolete Dutch *gijben*.

jibe[3] ▶ **v.** [no obj.] informal be in accord; agree: *the verdict does not jibe with the medical evidence.*
– ORIGIN early 19th cent.: of unknown origin.

jib sheet ▶ **n.** Sailing a rope by which a jib is trimmed.

ji·ca·ma /'hikəmə, 'hē-/ ▶ **n.** the crisp, white-fleshed, edible tuber of a Central American climbing plant of the pea family (*Pachyrhizus erosus*, family Leguminosae), cultivated since pre-Columbian times and used esp. in Mexican cooking.
– ORIGIN early 17th cent.: from Mexican Spanish *jícama*, from Nahuatl *xicama*.

Ji·ca·ril·la /,hēkə'rēə, -'rēlyə/ ▶ **n.** (pl. **same** or **Jicarillas**) **1** (also **Jicarilla Apache**) a member of an Apache people of northern New Mexico.
2 the Athabaskan language of this people.
▶ **adj.** of or relating to this people or their language.
– ORIGIN Mexican Spanish: probably diminutive of *jícara* 'chocolate-cup' (from the shape of a local hill); perhaps from Nahuatl *xicalli* 'drinking vessel, gourd.'

Ji·ca·ril·la Moun·tains /,hēkə'rēə/ a range in south central New Mexico that reaches 8,200 feet (2,500 m) at Jicarilla Mountain.

Jid·dah /'jidə/ (also **Jidda, Jeddah,** or **Jedda** /'jedə/) a seaport on the Red Sea coast of Saudi Arabia, near Mecca; pop. 3,012,000 (est. 2007).

jif·fy /'jifē/ (also **jiff**) ▶ **n.** [in sing.] informal a moment: *we'll be back in a jiffy.*
– ORIGIN late 18th cent.: of unknown origin.

jig /jig/ ▶ **n.** **1** a lively dance with leaping movements. ■ a piece of music for such a dance, typically in compound time.
2 a device that holds a piece of work and guides the tools operating on it.
3 Fishing a type of artificial bait that is jerked up and down through the water.
▶ **v.** (**jigs, jigging, jigged**) **1** [no obj.] dance a jig. ■ [with adverbial] move up and down with a quick jerky motion: *we were jigging about in our seats.*
2 [with obj.] equip (a factory or workshop) with a jig or jigs.
3 [no obj.] fish with a jig: *a man jigged for squid.*
– PHRASES **in jig time** informal extremely quickly; in a very short time. **the jig is up** informal the scheme or deception is revealed or foiled.
– ORIGIN mid 16th cent.: of unknown origin.

jig·a·boo /'jigə,bo͞o/ ▶ **n.** informal, offensive a black person.
– ORIGIN early 20th cent.: related to slang *jig* (in the same sense); compare with the pair *bug, bugaboo*.

jig·ger[1] /'jigər/ ▶ **n.** **1** a machine or vehicle with a part that rocks or moves back and forth, e.g., a jigsaw.
2 a person who dances a jig.
3 a small fore-and-aft sail set at the stern of a ship. ■ a small tackle consisting of a double and single block or two single blocks with a rope.
4 a measure or small glass of spirits or wine.
5 Golf, dated a metal golf club with a narrow face.
6 used to refer to a thing whose name one does not know or does not wish to mention: *see them little jiggers?*
▶ **v.** [with obj.] informal rearrange or tamper with.
– PHRASES **well, I'll be** (or **I'm**) **jiggered** used to express one's astonishment.
– ORIGIN mid 16th cent. (originally a slang word for a door): from the verb JIG (the relationship with which is obscure in certain senses).

jig·ger[2] ▶ **n.** variant spelling of CHIGGER.

jig·ger·y-pok·er·y /,jigərē 'pōkərē/ ▶ **n.** informal, chiefly Brit. deceitful or dishonest behavior.
– ORIGIN late 19th cent.: probably a variant of Scots *joukery-pawkery*, from *jouk* 'dodge, skulk,' of unknown origin.

jig·gle /'jigəl/ ▶ **v.** [no obj.] move about lightly and quickly from side to side or up and down: *his head jiggles up and down as he speaks.* ■ [with obj.] shake (something) lightly up and down or from side to side: *he was jiggling his car keys in his hand.*
▶ **n.** [in sing.] a quick light shake: *give that rack a jiggle.*
– DERIVATIVES **jig·gly** /'jig(ə)lē/ **adj.**
– ORIGIN mid 19th cent.: partly an alteration of JOGGLE[1], reinforced by JIG.

jig·gy /'jigē/ ▶ **adj.** (**jiggier, jiggiest**) informal
1 uninhibited, esp. in a sexual manner: *the script required her to get jiggy with Leonardo.*
2 trembling or nervous, esp. as the result of drug withdrawal.
– ORIGIN 1930s: from *jig* + *-y*.

jig·saw /'jig,sô/ ▶ **n.** **1** (also **jigsaw puzzle**) a puzzle consisting of a picture printed on cardboard or wood and cut into various pieces of different shapes that have to be fitted together. ■ a mystery that can only be resolved by assembling various pieces of information: *help the police put all the pieces of the jigsaw together.*
2 a machine saw with a fine blade enabling it to cut curved lines in a sheet of wood, metal, or plastic.

ji·had /ji'häd/ ▶ **n.** (among Muslims) a war or struggle against unbelievers. ■ (also **greater jihad**) Islam the spiritual struggle within oneself against sin.
– DERIVATIVES **ji·had·ism** **n.**, **ji·had·ism** **n.**
– ORIGIN from Arabic *jihād*, literally 'effort,' expressing, in Muslim thought, struggle on behalf of God and Islam.

ji·had·i /ji'hädē/ (also **jehadi**) ▶ **n.** (pl. **jihadis**) a person involved in a jihad; an Islamic militant.
– ORIGIN from Arabic *jihādī*, from *jihād*.

ji·had·ist /ji'hädist/ ▶ **n.** a jihadi.

jil·bab /jil'bäb/ ▶ **n.** a full-length outer garment, traditionally covering the head and hands, worn in public by some Muslim women.
– ORIGIN Persian *jilbāb*, from Arabic, 'garment, dress, veil.'

Ji·lin /jē'lin/ (also **Kirin**) a province in northeastern China; capital, Changchun. ■ an industrial city in Jilin province; pop. 1,263,900 (est. 2006).

jill /jil/ ▶ **n.** variant spelling of GILL[4].

jill·er·oo /'jilə,ro͞o/ (also **jillaroo**) ▶ **n.** Austral. informal a young woman working on a sheep or cattle station to gain experience.
– ORIGIN 1940s: from the given name *Jill*, on the pattern of *jackeroo*.

jil·lion /'jilyən/ ▶ **cardinal number** informal an extremely large number: *they ran jillions of ads.*
– ORIGIN 1940s: fanciful formation on the pattern of *billion* and *million*.

jilt /jilt/ ▶ **v.** [with obj.] suddenly reject or abandon (a lover): *he was jilted at the altar by his bride-to-be.*
▶ **n.** archaic a person, esp. a woman, who capriciously rejects a lover.
– ORIGIN mid 17th cent. (in the sense 'deceive, trick'): of unknown origin.

Jim Crow /'jim 'krō/ ▶ **n.** **1** the former practice of segregating black people in the US: [as modifier] *Jim Crow laws.* ■ offensive a black person.
2 an implement for straightening steel bars or bending rails by screw pressure.
– DERIVATIVES **Jim Crow·ism** /'krō,izəm/ **n.**
– ORIGIN mid 19th cent.: the name of a black character in a 19th-cent. plantation song.

jim-dan·dy /,jim 'dandē/ informal ▶ **adj.** fine, outstanding, or excellent.
▶ **n.** an excellent or notable person or thing.
– ORIGIN late 19th cent.: from the given name *Jim* (nickname for *James*) + DANDY.

Ji·mé·nez de Cis·ne·ros /hē'mānəs dā sis'nerōs/ (also **Ximenes de Cisneros**), Francisco (1436–1517), Spanish cardinal and statesman; regent of Spain 1516–17. He was Grand Inquisitor for Castile and Léon from 1507 to 1517, during which time he undertook a massive campaign against heresy and had about 2,500 alleged heretics put to death.

Jim·i·ny /'jimənē/ ▶ **exclam.** used in phrases as an expression of surprise: *by Jiminy, she was right* | *Jiminy Cricket!*
– ORIGIN early 19th cent.: alteration of GEMINI used as a mild oath in the mid 17th cent., a euphemistic form of *Jesus* (*Christ*).

jim-jams /'jim ,jamz/ ▶ **plural n.** informal a fit of depression or nervousness: *prerace jim-jams.*
– ORIGIN mid 16th cent.
(originally denoting a small article or knickknack): fanciful reduplication. The current sense dates from the late 19th cent.

Jim·mu /'jēmo͞o/ the legendary first emperor of Japan (660 BC), descendant of the sun goddess Amaterasu and founder of the imperial dynasty.

jim·my /'jimē/ (Brit. **jemmy** /'jemē/) ▶ **n.** (pl. **jimmies**) a short crowbar used by a burglar to force open a window or door.
▶ **v.** (**jimmies, jimmying, jimmied**) [with obj.] informal force open (a window or door) with a jimmy.
– ORIGIN early 19th cent.: pet form of the given name *James* (compare with JACK[1]).

jim·son weed /'jimsən/ (also **jimpson weed**) ▶ **n.** a strong-smelling poisonous datura with large, trumpet-shaped white flowers and toothed leaves, which has become a weed of waste ground in many countries. ● *Datura stramonium*, family Solanaceae. ■ the prickly fruit of this plant, which resembles that of a horse chestnut.
– ORIGIN late 17th cent. (originally as *Jamestown weed*): named after JAMESTOWN in Virginia.

jimson weed

Jin /jin/ (also **Chin**) **1** a dynasty that ruled China AD 265–420, commonly divided into **Western Jin** (265–317) and **Eastern Jin** (317–420).
2 a dynasty that ruled Manchuria and northern China AD 1115–1234.

Ji·na /'jēnə/ ▶ **n.** (in Jainism) a great teacher who has attained liberation from karma.
– ORIGIN from Sanskrit (see also JAIN).

Ji·nan /'jē'nän/ (also **Tsinan**) a city in eastern China, the capital of Shandong province; pop. 2,726,400 (est. 2006).

jin·gle /'jiNGgəl/ ▶ **n.** **1** [in sing.] a light ringing sound such as that made by metal objects being shaken together.
2 a short slogan, verse, or tune designed to be easily remembered, esp. as used in advertising.
3 (also **jingle shell**) a bivalve mollusk with a fragile, slightly translucent shell, the lower valve of which has a hole through which pass byssus threads for

anchorage. ● Family Anomidae: *Anomia* and other genera.
▶ **v.** make or cause to make a light metallic ringing sound: [no obj.] *her bracelets were jingling* | [with obj.] *he jingled the coins in his pocket.* ■ [no obj.] (of writing) be full of alliteration or rhymes.
– DERIVATIVES **jin·gler n.**, **jin·gly** /'jiNG(ə)lē/ **adj.**
– ORIGIN late Middle English: imitative.

jin·go /'jiNGgō/ ▶ **n.** (pl. **jingoes**) dated, chiefly derogatory a vociferous supporter of policy favoring war, esp. in the name of patriotism.
– PHRASES **by jingo!** an exclamation of surprise.
– ORIGIN late 17th cent. (originally a conjuror's word): *by jingo* (and the noun sense) come from a popular song adopted by those supporting the sending of a British fleet into Turkish waters to resist Russia in 1878. The chorus ran: "We don't want to fight, yet by Jingo! if we do, We've got the ships, we've got the men, and got the money too."

jin·go·ism /'jiNGgō,izəm/ ▶ **n.** chiefly derogatory extreme patriotism, esp. in the form of aggressive or warlike foreign policy.
– DERIVATIVES **jin·go·ist n.**, **jin·go·is·tic** /,jiNGgō'istik/ **adj.**

jink /jiNGk/ ▶ **v.** [no obj.] change direction suddenly and nimbly, as when dodging a pursuer: *she was too quick for him and jinked away every time.*
▶ **n.** a sudden quick change of direction.
– ORIGIN late 17th cent. (originally Scots as *high jinks*, denoting antics at drinking parties): probably symbolic of nimble motion. Current senses date from the 18th cent.

jinn /jin/ (also **djinn** or **jinni** /ji'nē, 'jinē/) ▶ **n.** (pl. **same** or **jinns**) (in Arabian and Muslim mythology) an intelligent spirit of lower rank than the angels, able to appear in human and animal forms and to possess humans. Compare with GENIE.
– ORIGIN from Arabic *jinnī*, plural *jinn*.

Jin·nah /'jinə/, Muhammad Ali (1876–1948), Indian statesman and founder of Pakistan. He headed the Muslim League in its struggle with the Hindu-oriented Indian National Congress over Indian independence. In 1947, he became the first governor general and president of Pakistan.

jin·rik·i·sha /jin'riksHô, -sHä/ (also **jinricksha**) ▶ **n.** another term for RICKSHA.
– ORIGIN Japanese, from *jin* 'man' + *riki* 'strength' + *sha* 'vehicle.'

Jin·sha /'jin'sHä/ see YANGTZE.

jinx /jiNGks/ ▶ **n.** a person or thing that brings bad luck.
▶ **v.** [with obj.] (usu. **be jinxed**) bring bad luck to; cast an evil spell on: *the play is jinxed.*
– ORIGIN early 20th cent. (originally US): probably a variant of *jynx* 'wryneck' (because the bird was used in witchcraft).

Jin·zhou /'jin'jō/ a city in Liaoning province, in northeastern China, near the Gulf of Liaodong at the northern end of the Bo Hai; pop. 721,500 (2006).

jird /jərd/ ▶ **n.** a long-tailed burrowing rodent related to the gerbils, found in deserts and steppes from North Africa to China. ● Genus *Meriones*, family Muridae: several species, in particular *M. unguiculatus*, popular as a pet.
– ORIGIN from Berber *(a)gherda*.

jir·ga /'jərgə/ ▶ **n.** (in Afghanistan) a tribal council. A grand tribal council (**loya jirga**) presently has a legislative function in the country.
– ORIGIN mid 19th cent.: Pashto, 'council, assembly.' *Loya jirga* is from Pashto, from *loya* 'great, grand' and *jirga*.

jism /'jizəm/ ▶ **n.** vulgar slang semen.
– ORIGIN mid 19th cent.: of unknown origin.

JIT ▶ **abbr.** (of manufacturing systems) just-in-time.

jit·ney /'jitnē/ ▶ **n.** (pl. **jitneys**) informal a bus or other vehicle carrying passengers for a low fare.
– ORIGIN early 20th cent. (originally denoting a five-cent piece): of unknown origin.

jit·ter /'jitər/ informal ▶ **n. 1** (**jitters**) feelings of extreme nervousness: *a bout of the jitters.*
2 slight irregular movement, variation, or unsteadiness, esp. in an electrical signal or electronic device.
▶ **v.** [no obj.] act nervously: *an anxious student who jittered at any provocation.* ■ (of a signal or device) suffer from jitter.
– ORIGIN 1920s: of unknown origin.

jit·ter·bug /'jitər,bəg/ ▶ **n. 1** a fast dance popular in the 1940s, performed chiefly to swing music. ■ dated a person fond of dancing such a dance.
2 informal, dated a nervous person.
▶ **v.** (**jitterbugs, jitterbugging, jitterbugged**) [no obj.] dance the jitterbug.
– ORIGIN 1930s (originally US): from the verb JITTER + BUG.

jit·ter·y /'jɪtəri/ ▶ **adj.** informal nervous or unable to relax: *caffeine makes me jittery.*
– DERIVATIVES **jit·ter·i·ness** /-rēnis/ **n.** /-rēnis/ **n.**

jiu·jit·su /jo͞o'jitso͞o/ ▶ **n.** variant spelling of JUJITSU.

Ji·va·ro /'hēvə,rō/ ▶ **n.** (pl. **same** or **Jivaros**) **1** a member of an indigenous people of the eastern slopes of the Andes in Ecuador and Peru.
2 any of the group of languages spoken by this people.
▶ **adj.** of or relating to this people or their languages.
– DERIVATIVES **Ji·va·ro·an** /,hēvə'rōən/ **adj.** & **.n.**
– ORIGIN from Spanish *jíbaro*, probably from the local name *Shuara, Shiwora*.

jive /jīv/ ▶ **n. 1** a lively style of dance popular esp. in the 1940s and 1950s, performed to swing music or rock and roll. ■ swing music. ■ a style of dance music popular in South Africa: *township jive.*
2 (also **jive talk**) a form of slang associated with black American jazz musicians. ■ informal a thing, esp. talk, that is deceptive or worthless: *a single image says more than any amount of blather and jive.*
▶ **v.** informal **1** [no obj.] perform the jive or a similar dance to popular music: *people were jiving in the aisles.*
2 [with obj.] informal taunt or sneer at: *Willy kept jiving him until Jimmy left.* ■ [no obj.] talk nonsense: *he wasn't jiving about that bartender.*
▶ **adj.** informal deceitful or worthless.
– DERIVATIVES **jiv·er n.**, **jiv·ey adj.**
– ORIGIN 1920s (originally US denoting meaningless or misleading speech): of unknown origin; the later musical sense 'jazz' gave rise to 'dance performed to jazz' (1940s).

Ji·xi /'jē'sHē/ a city in Heilongjiang province, in northeastern China, on the Muling River, east of Harbin; pop. 740,500 (est. 2006).

jizz /jiz/ ▶ **n.** Brit. informal (among birdwatchers and naturalists) the characteristic impression given by a particular species of animal or plant.
– ORIGIN 1920s: of unknown origin.

JJ ▶ **abbr.** ■ Judges. ■ Justices.

Jn ▶ **abbr.** ■ Bible an epistle of John. ■ the Gospel of John.

Jnr ▶ **abbr.** chiefly Brit. Junior (in names).

jnt. ▶ **abbr.** joint.

Jo·a·chim /'jōəkim/ see RITZ BROTHERS.

Jo·a·chim, St. /'yōəkim, 'jō-/ (in Christian tradition) the husband of St. Anne and father of the Virgin Mary. He is first mentioned in an apocryphal work of the 2nd century, and then rarely referred to until much later in time.

Joan of Arc, St. /,jōn əv 'ärk/ (*c.*1412–31), French national heroine; known as **the Maid of Orleans**; French name **Jeanne d'Arc**. She led the French armies against the English in the Hundred Years War, relieving besieged Orleans in 1429 and ensuring that Charles VII could be crowned in Reims. Captured by the Burgundians in 1430, she was handed over to the English, convicted of heresy, and burned at the stake. Canonized in 1920, her feast day is May 30.

João Pes·soa /,ZHwoun pes'ōə/ a city in northeastern Brazil, on the Atlantic coast, capital of the state of Paraíba; pop. 674,762 (2007).

Job /jōb/ (in the Bible) a prosperous man whose patience and piety were tried by undeserved misfortunes, and who, in spite of his bitter lamentations, remained confident in the goodness and justice of God. ■ a book of the Bible telling of Job.

job[1] /jäb/ ▶ **n. 1** a paid position of regular employment: *jobs are created in the private sector, not in Washington* | *a part-time job.*
2 a task or piece of work, esp. one that is paid: *she wants to be left alone to get on with the job* | *you did a good job of explaining.* ■ a responsibility or duty: *it's our job to find things out.* ■ [in sing.] informal a difficult task: *we thought you'd have a job getting there.* ■ [with modifier] informal a procedure to improve the appearance of something, esp. an operation involving plastic surgery: *she's had a nose job* | *someone had done a skillful paint job.* ■ [with adj. or noun modifier] informal a thing of a specified nature: *the car was a blue malevolent-looking job.* ■ informal a crime, esp. a robbery: *a series of daring bank jobs.* ■ Computing an operation or group of operations treated as a single and distinct unit.
▶ **v.** (**jobs, jobbing, jobbed**) **1** [no obj.] (usu. as adj. **jobbing**) do casual or occasional work: *a jobbing builder.*
2 [with obj.] buy and sell (stocks) as a broker-dealer, esp. on a small scale.
3 [with obj.] informal cheat; betray.
4 [no obj.] archaic turn a public office or a position of trust to private advantage.
– PHRASES **do the job** informal achieve the required result: *a piece of board will do the job.* **do a job on someone** informal do something that harms or defeats an opponent: *I go out and do a job on anyone who is giving our top scorers a hard time.* **a good job** informal, chiefly Brit. a fortunate fact or circumstance: *it was a good job she hadn't brought the car.* **on the job** while working; at work. **out of a job** unemployed.
– PHRASAL VERBS **job something out** assign separate elements of a piece of work to different companies, contractors, or workers: *all the work done by the middleman can be jobbed out at a much lower cost.*
– ORIGIN mid 16th cent.(sense 2 of the noun): of unknown origin.

job[2] archaic ▶ **v.** (**jobs, jobbing, jobbed**) [with obj.] prod or stab: *he prepared to job the huge brute.* ■ thrust (something pointed) at or into something.
▶ **n.** an act of prodding, thrusting, or wrenching.
– ORIGIN late Middle English: apparently symbolic of a brief forceful action (compare with JAB).

job·ber /'jäbər/ ▶ **n. 1** a wholesaler.
2 a person who does casual or occasional work.
3 historical (in the UK) a principal or wholesaler who dealt only on the Stock Exchange with brokers, not directly with the public.
– ORIGIN late 17th cent. (in the sense 'broker, middleman,' originally not derogatory): from JOB[1].

job·ber·y /'jäbərē/ ▶ **n.** the practice of using a public office or position of trust for one's own gain or advantage.

job·bie /'jäbē/ ▶ **n.** [with adj. or noun modifier] informal an object or product of a specified kind: *the room was a no-frills jobbie.*

job con·trol lan·guage ▶ **n.** Computing a language enabling the user to define the tasks to be undertaken by the operating system.

job cre·a·tion ▶ **n.** the provision of new opportunities for paid employment, esp. for those who are unemployed.

job de·scrip·tion ▶ **n.** a formal account of an employee's responsibilities.

job-hunt ▶ **v.** [no obj.] (usu. as noun **job-hunting**) informal seek employment.
– DERIVATIVES **job-hunt·er n.**

job·less /'jäbləs/ ▶ **adj.** unemployed.
– DERIVATIVES **job·less·ness n.**

job lot ▶ **n.** a miscellaneous group of articles, esp. when sold or bought together: *a job lot of stuff I bought from a demolition firm.*

job ro·ta·tion ▶ **n.** the practice of moving employees between different tasks to promote experience and variety.

Jobs /jäbz/, Steven (Paul) (1955–), US computer entrepreneur. He set up the Apple computer company in 1976 with **Steve Wozniak** and served as chairman until 1985, returning in 1997 as CEO. He is also the former CEO of the Pixar animation studio.

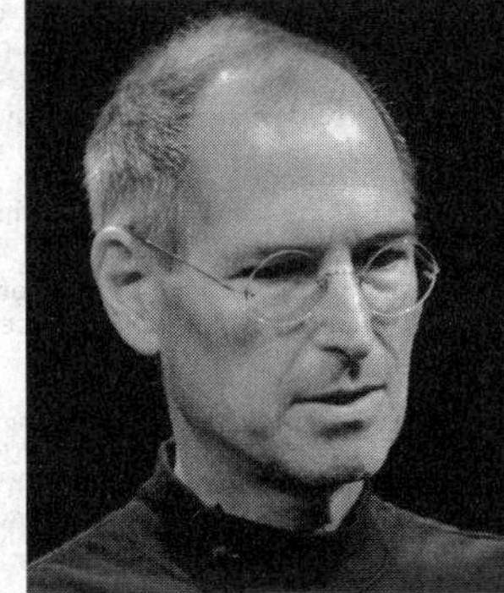

Steve Jobs

Job's com·fort·er /jōbz/ ▶ **n.** a person who aggravates distress under the guise of giving comfort.
– ORIGIN mid 18th cent.: alluding to the biblical story (Job 16:2) of JOB.

job seek·er (also **jobseeker**) ▶ **n.** a person who is unemployed and looking for work.

job-share ▶ **v.** [no obj.] (of two part-time employees) jointly do a full-time job, sharing the remuneration.
▶ **n.** an arrangement of such a kind.
– DERIVATIVES **job-shar·er n.**

Job's tears /'jōbz 'ti(ə)rz/ ▶ **plural n.** a widely cultivated Southeast Asian grass that bears its seeds inside hollow, pear-shaped receptacles, which are gray and shiny and sometimes used as beads. ● *Coix lacryma-jobi*, family Gramineae.
– ORIGIN late 16th cent.: named after the patriarch JOB.

Jo·burg /'jō,bərg/ a nickname for JOHANNESBURG.

Jo·cas·ta /jō'kastə/ Greek Mythology a Theban woman, the wife of Laius and mother and later wife of Oedipus.

jock[1] /jäk/ ▶ **n.** informal **1** a disc jockey. **2** an enthusiast or participant in a specified activity: *a computer jock*.
– ORIGIN late 18th cent.: abbreviation.

jock[2] ▶ **n.** informal another term for JOCKSTRAP. ■ an enthusiastic athlete or sports fan, esp. one with few other interests.
– DERIVATIVES **jock·ish** **adj.**

jock[3] ▶ **n.** informal a pilot or astronaut.
– ORIGIN late 20th cent.: probably an abbreviation of JOCKEY, from its informal use in combinations such as *jet jockey, plow jockey*, where "operation" or "control" of equipment is involved.

jock·ey /'jäkē/ ▶ **n.** (pl. **jockeys**) a person who rides in horse races, esp. as a profession. ■ an enthusiast or participant in a specified activity: *a car jockey*.
▶ **v.** (**jockeys, jockeyed**) [no obj.] struggle by every available means to gain or achieve something: *both men will be jockeying for the two top jobs*. ■ [with obj.] handle or manipulate (someone or something) in a skillful manner: *Jason jockeyed his machine into a dive*.
– DERIVATIVES **joc·key·ship** /-,SHip/ **n.**
– ORIGIN late 16th cent.: diminutive of *Jock* 'ordinary man; a rustic,' Scots form of the given name *Jack*. The word came to mean 'mounted courier,' hence the current sense (late 17th cent). Another early use 'horse dealer' (long a byword for dishonesty) probably gave rise to the verb sense 'manipulate,' whereas the main verb sense probably relates to the behavior of jockeys maneuvering for an advantageous position during a race.

jock·ey cap ▶ **n.** a strengthened cap with a long visor of a kind worn by jockeys.

jock·ey shorts (also **Jockey shorts** or **Jockeys**) ▶ **plural n.** trademark men's close-fitting underpants with a short leg.

jock itch ▶ **n.** informal a fungal infection of the groin area.
– ORIGIN 1970s: *jock* from JOCKSTRAP.

jocks /jäks/ ▶ **plural n.** informal jockey shorts.

jock·strap /'jäk,strap/ ▶ **n.** a support or protection for the male genitals, worn esp. by athletes.
– ORIGIN late 19th cent.: from slang *jock* 'genitals' (of unknown origin) + STRAP.

jo·cose /jō'kōs/ ▶ **adj.** formal playful or humorous: *a jocose allusion*.
– DERIVATIVES **jo·cose·ly** **adv.**, **jo·cose·ness** **n.**, **jo·cos·i·ty** /-'käsitē/ **n.** (pl. **jocosities**).
– ORIGIN late 17th cent.: from Latin *jocosus*, from *jocus* (see JOKE).

joc·u·lar /'jäkyələr/ ▶ **adj.** fond of or characterized by joking; humorous or playful: *she sounded in a jocular mood* | *his voice was jocular*.
– DERIVATIVES **joc·u·lar·i·ty** /,jäkyə'laritē/ **n.**, **joc·u·lar·ly** **adv.**
– ORIGIN early 17th cent.: from Latin *jocularis*, from *joculus*, diminutive of *jocus* (see JOKE).

joc·und /'jäkənd, 'jō-/ ▶ **adj.** formal cheerful and lighthearted: *a jocund wedding party*.
– DERIVATIVES **jo·cun·di·ty** /jō'kənditē/ **n.** (pl. **jocundities**), **joc·und·ly** **adv.**
– ORIGIN late Middle English: via Old French from Latin *jocundus*, variant (influenced by *jocus* 'joke') of *jucundus* 'pleasant, agreeable,' from *juvare* 'to delight.'

Jodh·pur /'jädpər, -,po͝or/ **1** a city in western India, in Rajasthan; pop. 1,006,700 (est. 2009). **2** a former princely state in India, now part of Rajasthan.

jodh·purs /'jädpərz/ ▶ **plural n.** full-length trousers, worn for horseback riding, that are close-fitting below the knee and have reinforced patches on the inside of the leg.
– ORIGIN late 19th cent.: named after JODHPUR, where similar garments are worn by Indian men as part of everyday dress.

jodhpurs

joe /jō/ ▶ **n.** informal **1** coffee. [1940s: of unknown origin.] **2** an ordinary man: *the average joe*. [mid 19th cent.: nickname for the given name *Joseph*; compare with JOE BLOW.]

Joe Bloggs /blägz/ ▶ **n.** British term for JOE BLOW.

Joe Blow /blō/ ▶ **n.** informal a name for a hypothetical average man.

Jo·el /jō(ə)l/ a Hebrew minor prophet of the 5th or possibly 9th century BC. ■ a book of the Bible containing his prophecies.

Joe Pub·lic ▶ **n.** British term for JOHN Q. PUBLIC.

joe-pye weed /,jō 'pī/ (also **joe pye weed**) ▶ **n.** a tall North American perennial plant of the daisy family that bears clusters of small purple flowers. ● Genus *Eupatorium*, family Compositae, several species, in particular **sweet joe-pye weed** *E. purpureum* and **spotted joe-pye weed** *E. maculatum*.
– ORIGIN early 19th cent.: of unknown origin.

Joe Schmoe /SHmō/ (also **Joe Schmo**) ▶ **n.** (pl. **Joe Schmoes**) informal a hypothetical ordinary man: *a lot of Joe Schmoes make it to the big leagues*.
– ORIGIN 1940s: alteration of *schmuck*.

Joe Six·pack /'siks,pak/ ▶ **n.** a name for a hypothetical ordinary working man.
– ORIGIN 1970s: from *Joe*, familiar abbreviation of the given name *Joseph*, used to denote any ordinary man; see also SIX-PACK.

jo·ey[1] /'jō-ē/ ▶ **n.** (pl. **joeys**) Austral. a young kangaroo, wallaby, or possum. ■ informal a baby or young child.
– ORIGIN from Aboriginal *joè*.

jo·ey[2] ▶ **n.** Brit. & historical a silver threepenny bit.
– ORIGIN 1930s: diminutive of the nickname *Joe*: the derivation remains unknown. The term (originally slang in London, England) denoted a fourpenny piece in the 19th cent.

Jof·fre /'jôfrə/, Joseph Jacques Césaire (1852–1931), French marshal; commander in chief of the French army on the western front during World War I.

Jof·frey /'jäfrē/, Robert (1930–88) US ballet dancer and choreographer; born *Abdullah Jaffa Anver Bey Khan*. He founded the Joffrey Ballet in 1966.

jog /jäg/ ▶ **v.** (**jogs, jogging, jogged**) **1** [no obj.] run at a steady gentle pace, esp. on a regular basis as a form of physical exercise: *he began to jog along the road* | (as noun **jogging**) *try cycling or gentle jogging*. ■ (of a horse) move at a slow trot. ■ move in an unsteady way, typically slowly: *the bus jogged and jolted*. ■ (**jog along/on**) continue in a steady, uneventful way: *our marriage worked, and we jogged along*. **2** [with obj.] nudge or knock slightly: *a hand jogged his elbow*.
▶ **n.** **1** a spell of jogging: *his morning jog*. ■ [in sing.] a gentle running pace: *he set off along the bank at a jog*. **2** a slight push or nudge.
– PHRASES **jog someone's memory** cause someone to remember something suddenly.
– DERIVATIVES **jog·ger** **n.**
– ORIGIN late Middle English (in the sense 'stab, pierce'): variant of JAG[1].

jog·gle[1] /'jägəl/ ▶ **v.** move or cause to move with repeated small bobs or jerks: [no obj.] *the car bounced and joggled on the rough road*.
▶ **n.** a bobbing or jerking movement.
– ORIGIN early 16th cent.: frequentative of JOG.

jog·gle[2] ▶ **n.** a joint between two pieces of stone, concrete, or timber consisting of a projection in one of the pieces fitting into a notch in the other or a small piece let in between the two.
▶ **v.** [with obj.] join (pieces of stone, concrete, or timber) in such a way.
– ORIGIN early 18th cent.: perhaps related to JAG[1].

Jog·ja·kar·ta /,jägjə'kärtə/ variant spelling of YOGYAKARTA.

jog trot ▶ **n.** dated a slow trot.

Jo·han·nes·burg /jō'hänəs,bərg, -'han-/ a city in South Africa, the capital of the province of Gauteng; pop. 2,023,500 (est. 2009). It is the largest city in South Africa and the center of its gold-mining industry.

Jo·han·nine /jō'hanən, -īn/ ▶ **adj.** relating to the Apostle St. John the Evangelist, or to the Gospel or epistles of John in the New Testament.
– ORIGIN mid 19th cent.: from the medieval Latin given name *Johannes* 'John' + -INE[1].

Jo·han·nis·berg /jō'hanisbərg/ (also **Johannisberg Riesling**) ▶ **n.** the chief variety of the Riesling wine grape, originating in Germany and widely grown in California and elsewhere. ■ a white wine made from this grape.
– ORIGIN from the name of a castle and village on the Rhine, Germany, where it was originally produced.

Jo·han·nis·berg·er /jō'hanis,bərgər/ ▶ **n.** variant of JOHANNISBERG.

John[1] /jän/ (1165–1216), son of Henry II and Eleanor of Aquitaine; king of England 1199–1216; known as **John Lackland**. He lost most of his French possessions to Phillip II of France. In 1209, he was excommunicated for refusing to accept Stephen Langton as the archbishop of Canterbury. Forced to sign the Magna Carta by his barons in 1215, he ignored its provisions and civil war broke out.

John[2] the name of six kings of Portugal. ■ **John I** (1357–1433), reigned 1385–1433; known as **John the Great**. Reinforced by an English army, he defeated the Castilians at Aljubarrota in 1385 and won independence for Portugal. ■ **John II** (1455–95), reigned 1481–95. ■ **John III** (1502–57), reigned 1521–57. ■ **John IV** (1604–56), reigned 1640–56; known as **John the Fortunate**. The founder of the Braganza dynasty, he expelled a Spanish usurper and proclaimed himself king. ■ **John V** (1689–1750), reigned 1706–50. ■ **John VI** (1767–1826), reigned 1816–26.

John[3], Sir Elton (Hercules) (1947–), English singer, pianist, and songwriter; born *Reginald Kenneth Dwight*. His hit songs include "Your Song" (1970), "Nikita" (1985), and "Don't Let the Sun Go Down on Me" (1991). His "Candle in the Wind" (1997) tribute to Diana, Princess of Wales, became the highest-selling single in history.

john /jän/ ▶ **n.** informal **1** a toilet. **2** a prostitute's client.
– ORIGIN early 20th cent. (sense 2): from the given name *John*, used from late Middle English as a form of address to a man, or to denote various occupations, including that of priest (late Middle English) and policeman (mid 17th cent).

John III (1624–96), king of Poland 1674–96; known as **John Sobieski**. In 1683, he relieved Vienna when it was besieged by the Turks and became a hero in the Christian world.

John, St. an Apostle; son of Zebedee and brother of James; known as **St. John the Evangelist** or **St. John the Divine**. He is traditionally credited with having written the fourth Gospel, Revelation, and three epistles of the New Testament. Feast day, December 27. ■ the fourth Gospel (see GOSPEL (sense 2)). ■ any of the three epistles of the New Testament attributed to St. John.

John Bar·ley·corn /'bärlē,kôrn/ ▶ **n.** a personification of barley, or of malt liquor.

john·boat /'jän,bōt/ ▶ **n.** a small flat-bottomed boat with square ends, used chiefly on inland waterways.

John Bull ▶ **n.** a personification of England or the typical Englishman, represented as a stout, red-faced farmer in a top hat and high boots.
– ORIGIN late 18th cent.: from the name of a character representing the English nation in John Arbuthnot's satire *Law is a Bottomless Pit; or, the History of John Bull* (1712).

John Chrys·os·tom, St. see CHRYSOSTOM, ST. JOHN.

John Day Riv·er /'jän 'dā/ a river that flows for 280 miles (450 km) across northern Oregon to join the Columbia River east of The Dalles.

John Doe /dō/ ▶ **n.** Law an anonymous party, typically the plaintiff, in a legal action. ■ informal a hypothetical average man.
– ORIGIN mid 18th cent.: originally in legal use as a name of a fictitious plaintiff, corresponding to *Richard Roe*, used to represent the defendant.

John Do·ry /'dôrē/ ▶ **n.** (pl. **John Dories**) an edible dory (fish) of the eastern Atlantic and Mediterranean, with a black oval mark on each side. ● *Zeus faber*, family Zeidae.

Joh·ne's dis·ease /'yōniz/ ▶ **n.** a form of chronic enteritis in cattle and sheep, caused by a mycobacterium.
– ORIGIN early 20th cent.: named after Heinrich A. Johne (1839–1910), German veterinary surgeon.

john·ny /'jänē/ ▶ **n.** (pl. **johnnies**) informal **1** a short gown fastened in the back, worn by hospital patients. **2** Brit. used as a name for an unknown man, often suggesting that he is unimportant or insignificant: *the security johnny insists that you sign the visitors' book*.
– ORIGIN late 17th cent. (sense 2): nickname for the given name *John*.

john·ny cake (also **johnnycake**) ▶ **n.** **1** a flat cornmeal cake typically baked or fried on a griddle. **2** Austral./NZ a small, thin unleavened wheat loaf baked in wood ashes.
– ORIGIN early 18th cent.: also referred to as *journey cake*, which may be the original form.

john·ny-come-late·ly ▶ **n.** informal a newcomer to or late starter at a particular place or sphere of activity.

John·ny-on-the-spot ▶ **n.** informal, dated a person who is at hand whenever needed.

John·ny Reb ▶ **n.** another term for REB[2].

John of Da·mas·cus, St. (c.675–c.749), Syrian theologian and doctor of the Church. He wrote the influential encyclopedic work on Christian theology *The Fount of Wisdom*. Feast day, December 4.

PRONUNCIATION KEY ə *ago, up*; ər *over, fur*; a *hat*; ā *ate*; ä *car*; e *let*; ē *see*; i *fit*; ī *by*; NG *sing*; ō *go*; ô *law, for*; oi *toy*; o͝o *good*; o͞o *goo*; ou *out*; TH *thin*; T̲H̲ *then*; ZH *vision*

John of Gaunt /gônt/ (1340–99), son of Edward III. He was the effective ruler of England during the final years of his father's reign and during the minority of Richard II. His son Henry Bolingbroke later became King Henry IV.

John of the Cross, St. (1542–91), Spanish mystic and poet; born *Juan de Yepis y Alvarez*. A Carmelite monk and priest, he founded, with St. Teresa of Ávila, the "discalced" Carmelite order in 1568. Feast day, December 14.

John Paul II (1920–2005), Polish cleric; pope 1978–2005; born *Karol Jozef Wojtyla*. The first non-Italian pope since 1522, he traveled abroad extensively during his papacy and upheld the Roman Catholic Church's traditional opposition to artificial contraception and abortion, homosexuality, the ordination of women, and the relaxation of the rule of celibacy for priests.

John Q. Pub·lic ▶ n. informal a name for a hypothetical representative member of the general public, or the general public personified.

Johns /jänz/, Jasper (1930–), US painter, sculptor, and printmaker. A key figure in the development of pop art, he depicted commonplace and universally recognized images. His *Flags*, *Targets*, and *Numbers* series from the mid-1950s are among his best-known works.

John·son[1] /ˈjänsən/, Andrew (1808–75), 17th president of the US 1865–69. As vice president 1865, he succeeded to the presidency upon the assassination of President Lincoln. During his administration, Alaska was purchased from Russia. His lenient policy toward the southern states after the Civil War and his refusal to cooperate with Congress led him to be the first president ever to be impeached. He was acquitted by one vote short of the two-thirds majority required.

John·son[2], Benj. F., see **RILEY**[3].

John·son[3] (also **Jansens** or **Janssen van Ceulen**), Cornelius (1593–*c.*1661), Dutch portrait painter; born in England. He painted for the court of Charles I; in 1643, after the outbreak of the English Civil War, he emigrated to Holland.

John·son[4], Earvin (1959–), US basketball player; known as **Magic Johnson**. He played for the Los Angeles Lakers from 1979 to 1991. He played on the US basketball team that won a gold medal at the 1992 Olympic games and then returned briefly to the Lakers.

John·son[5], Jack (1878–1946), US boxer. He was the first black world heavyweight champion 1908–15.

John·son[6], James Weldon (1871–1938) US writer, songwriter, and social activist. Originally a song lyricist and then a part of the US consular service, he began writing and made many contributions to the Harlem Renaissance. He edited *The Book of American Negro Poetry* in 1922 and wrote his autobiography, *Along This Way*, in 1933.

John·son[7], Lyndon Baines (1908–73), 36th president of the US 1963–69; known as **LBJ**. Before becoming vice president 1961–64, he was a US senator 1949–61. He succeeded to the presidency upon the assassination of President Kennedy and was elected for four more years in 1964. His domestic programs, such as those for civil rights, were labeled the Great Society. During his administration, US involvement in Vietnam increased, undermining his popularity, and he did not seek re-election.

Lyndon Baines Johnson

John·son[8], Philip Courtelyou (1906–2005), US architect and writer. He designed many buildings in New York City, including Lincoln Center, the AT&T headquarters building (now the Sony building), and the Bobst Library at New York University. He co-authored *The International Style* (1932).

John·son[9], Robert (1911–38), US blues singer and guitarist. Despite his mysterious early death, he was very influential on the 1960s blues movement. Notable songs: "I Was Standing at the Crossroads," "Love In Vain," and "I Believe I'll Dust My Broom."

John·son[10], Samuel (1709–84), British lexicographer, writer, critic, and conversationalist; known as **Dr. Johnson**. A leading figure in the literary London of his day, he is noted particularly for his *Dictionary of the English Language* (1755), his edition of Shakespeare (1765), and *The Lives of the English Poets* (1777). James Boswell's biography of Johnson records details of his life and conversation.
– DERIVATIVES **John·so·ni·an** /jänˈsōnēən/ **adj.**

John·son[11], Thomas (1732–1819) US Supreme Court associate justice 1791–93. A chief judge in Maryland's court system, he was appointed to the Court by President Washington.

John·son[12], Walter Perry (1887–1946) US baseball player; known as the **Big Train**. He pitched for the Washington Senators 1907–27 and had a record 113 career shutouts and led the American League in strikeouts for 12 seasons. Baseball Hall of Fame (1936).

John·son[13], William (1771–1834) US Supreme Court associate justice 1804–34. A Democrat-Republican, he was appointed to the Court by President Jefferson.

Andrew Johnson

John·son Cit·y an industrial city in northeastern Tennessee, part of a complex with Bristol and Kingsport; pop. 61,990 (est. 2008).

John·ston, Joseph Eggleston (1807–91), Confederate officer and US politician. A Confederate general, he was defeated by Grant at Vicksburg and surrendered to Sherman in 1865. From Virginia, he later served in the US House of Representatives 1879–81.

John·ston Atoll /ˈjänstən/ an atoll in the central Pacific Ocean, southwest of Hawaii, that is controlled by the US and used for military operations.

John the Bap·tist, St., Jewish preacher and prophet; a contemporary of Jesus. In c.AD 27 he preached and baptized on the banks of the Jordan River. Among those whom he baptized was Jesus Christ. He was beheaded by Herod Antipas after denouncing the latter's marriage to **Herodias**, the wife of Herod's brother **Philip** (Matt. 14:1–12). Feast day, June 24.

John the E·van·ge·list, St. (also **John the Divine**) see **JOHN, ST.**

John the For·tu·nate, John IV of Portugal (see **JOHN**[2]).

John the Great, John I of Portugal (see **JOHN**[2]).

Jo·hor /jəˈhôr/ (also **Johore**) a state in Malaysia, at the most southern point of mainland Asia, connected to Singapore by a causeway; capital, Johor Baharu.

Jo·hor Ba·ha·ru /bəˈhäro͞o/ a city in southwestern Malaysia, the capital of the state of Johor, opposite the island of Singapore; pop. 895,500 (est. 2009).

joie de vi·vre /ˌZHwä də ˈvēvrə/ ▶ n. exuberant enjoyment of life.
– ORIGIN French, literally 'joy of living.'

join /join/ ▶ v. [with obj.] link; connect: *the tap was joined to a pipe* | *join the paragraphs together.* ■ become linked or connected to: *where the River Drave joins the Danube.* ■ connect (points) with a line: *join up the points in a different color.* ■ [no obj.] unite to form one entity or group: *they joined up with local environmentalists* | *countries join together to abolish restrictions on trade.* ■ become a member or employee of: *she joined the department last year.* ■ take part in: *I joined the demonstration* | [no obj.] *I joined in and sang along.* ■ [no obj.] (**join up**) become a member of the armed forces: *her brothers joined up in 1914.* ■ come into the company of: *after the show we were joined by Jessica's sister.* ■ support (someone) in an activity: *I am sure you will join me in wishing him every success.*
▶ n. a place or line where two or more things are connected or fastened together.
– PHRASES **join battle** formal begin fighting. **join the club** see **CLUB**[1]. **join forces** combine efforts. **join hands** hold each other's hands. ■ work together: *education has been shy to join hands with business.*
– DERIVATIVES **join·a·ble adj.**
– ORIGIN Middle English: from Old French *joindre*, from Latin *jungere* 'to join.'

join·der /ˈjoindər/ ▶ n. Law the action of bringing parties together; union.
– ORIGIN late Middle English: from Anglo-Norman French, from Old French *joindre* 'to join.'

joined-up ▶ adj. chiefly Brit. (of handwriting) written with the characters joined; cursive. ■ (esp. of a policy) characterized by coordination and coherence of thought; integrated: *a joined-up approach to rural poverty, public services, and employment.*

join·er /ˈjoinər/ ▶ n. **1** a person who constructs the wooden components of a building, such as stairs, doors, and door and window frames.
2 informal a person who readily joins groups or campaigns: *a compulsive joiner of revolutionary movements.*
– ORIGIN Middle English: from Old French *joigneor*, from *joindre* 'to join.'

join·er·y /ˈjoinərē/ ▶ n. the wooden components of a building, such as stairs, doors, and door and window frames, viewed collectively.

joint /joint/ ▶ n. **1** a point at which parts of an artificial structure are joined. ■ Geology a break or fracture in a mass of rock, with no relative displacement of the parts. ■ a piece of flexible material forming the hinge of a book cover.
2 a structure in the human or animal body at which two parts of the skeleton are fitted together. ■ each of the distinct sections of a body or limb between the places at which they are connected: *the top two joints of his index finger.* ■ Brit. a large piece of meat cooked whole or ready for cooking: *a joint of ham.* ■ the part of a stem of a plant from which a leaf or branch grows. ■ a section of a plant stem between such parts; an internode.
3 informal an establishment of a specified kind, esp. one where people meet for eating, drinking, or entertainment: *a burger joint.* ■ (**the joint**) prison.
4 informal a marijuana cigarette.
▶ adj. [attrib.] shared, held, or made by two or more people, parties, or organizations together: *the companies issued a joint statement* | *a joint session of Congress.* ■ sharing in a position, achievement, or activity: *a joint winner.* ■ Law applied or regarded together. Often contrasted with **SEVERAL**.
▶ v. [with obj.] **1** provide or fasten (something) with joints: (as adj. **jointed**) *jointed lever arms.* ■ fill up the joints of (masonry or brickwork) with mortar; point. ■ prepare (a board) for being joined to another by planing its edge.
2 cut (the body of an animal) into joints.
– PHRASES **out of joint** (of a joint of the body) out of position; dislocated: *he put his hip out of joint.* ■ in a state of disorder or disorientation: *time was thrown completely out of joint.*
– DERIVATIVES **joint·less adj.**
– ORIGIN Middle English: from Old French, past participle of *joindre* 'to join' (see **JOIN**).

joint ac·count ▶ n. a bank account held by more than one person, each individual having the right to deposit and withdraw funds.

joint and sev·er·al ▶ adj. (of a legal obligation) undertaken by two or more people, each individual having liability for the whole.

Joint Chiefs of Staff ▶ n. the chiefs of staff of the US Army and Air Force, the commandant of the US Marine Corps, and the chief of US Naval Operations. This group's chairman, selected from one of the branches, is the highest-ranking military adviser to the president of the US.

joint·er /ˈjointər/ ▶ n. a plane used for preparing a wooden edge for fixing or joining to another. ■ a tool used for pointing masonry and brickwork.

joint·ly /ˈjointlē/ ▶ adv. with another person or people; together: *a report prepared jointly by Harvard and Yale universities.*

joint·ress /ˈjointrəs/ ▶ n. Law, dated a widow who holds a jointure.
– ORIGIN early 17th cent.: feminine of obsolete *jointer* 'joint owner.'

joint-stock com·pa·ny ▶ n. Finance a company whose stock is owned jointly by the shareholders.

joint ten·an·cy ▶ n. the holding of an estate or property jointly by two or more parties, the share of each passing to the other or others on death.
– DERIVATIVES **joint ten·ant n.**

join·ture /ˈjoinCHər/ ▶ **n.** Law an estate settled on a wife for the period during which she survives her husband, in lieu of a dower.
– ORIGIN Middle English (in the sense 'junction, joint'): from Old French, from Latin *junctura* (see JUNCTURE). In late Middle English the term denoted the joint holding of property by a husband and wife for life, whence the current sense.

joint ven·ture ▶ **n.** a commercial enterprise undertaken jointly by two or more parties that otherwise retain their distinct identities.

joist /joist/ ▶ **n.** a length of timber or steel supporting part of the structure of a building, typically arranged in parallel series to support a floor or ceiling.
– DERIVATIVES **joist·ed adj.**
– ORIGIN late Middle English *giste*, from Old French, 'beam supporting a bridge,' based on Latin *jacere* 'lie down.'

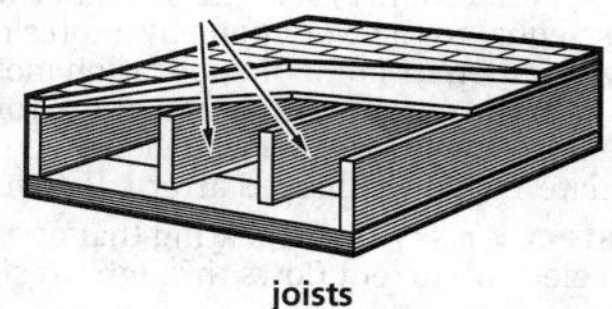

joists

jo·jo·ba /hōˈhōbə/ ▶ **n. 1** (also **jojoba oil**) an oil extracted from the seeds of an American shrub, widely used in cosmetics.
2 the leathery-leaved evergreen shrub or small tree that produces these seeds, native chiefly to the southwestern US. It is grown to prevent desertification as well as for its seeds. ● *Simmondsia chinensis*, the only member of the family Simmondsiaceae.
– ORIGIN early 20th cent.: from Mexican Spanish.

joke /jōk/ ▶ **n.** a thing that someone says to cause amusement or laughter, esp. a story with a funny punchline: *she was in a mood to tell jokes.* ■ a trick played on someone for fun. ■ [in sing.] informal a person or thing that is ridiculously inadequate: *the transportation system is a joke.*
▶ **v.** [no obj.] make jokes; talk humorously or flippantly: *she could laugh and joke with her colleagues* | [with direct speech] *"It's OK, we're not related," she joked.* ■ [with obj.] archaic poke fun at: *he was pretending to joke his daughter.*
– PHRASES **be no joke** informal be a serious matter or difficult undertaking: *trying to shop with three children in tow is no joke.* **can** (or **can't**) **take a joke** be able (or unable) to receive humorous remarks or tricks in the spirit in which they are intended: *if you can't take a joke, you should never have joined.* **the joke is on someone** informal someone looks foolish, esp. after trying to make someone else look so. **make a joke of** laugh or be humorous about (something that is not funny in itself).
– DERIVATIVES **jok·ing·ly adv.**
– ORIGIN late 17th cent. (originally slang): perhaps from Latin *jocus* 'jest, wordplay.'

jok·er /ˈjōkər/ ▶ **n. 1** a person who is fond of joking. ■ informal a foolish or inept person: *a bunch of jokers.*
2 a playing card, typically bearing the figure of a jester, used in some games as a wild card.
3 a clause unobtrusively inserted in a bill or document and affecting its operation in a way not immediately apparent.
– PHRASES **the joker in the pack** a person or factor likely to have an unpredictable effect on events.

jok·ey /ˈjōkē/ (also **joky**) ▶ **adj.** (**jokier, jokiest**) not serious; teasing or humorous: *a brief exchange of jokey comments.*
– DERIVATIVES **jok·i·ly** /-kəlē/ **adv.**, **jok·i·ness n.**

jol·ie laide /ˈZHōlē ˈled/ ▶ **n.** (pl. **jolies laides** pronunc. **same**) a woman whose face is attractive despite having ugly features.
– ORIGIN French, from *jolie* 'pretty' and *laide* 'ugly,' feminine adjectives.

Jo·li·et /ˌjōlēˈet/ an industrial and commercial city in northeastern Illinois; pop. 146,125 (est. 2008).

Jo·liot /ˈjōlyō/, Jean-Frédéric (1900–58), French nuclear physicist. As Marie Curie's assistant at the Radium Institute, he worked with her daughter **Irène** (1897–1956), whom he married (taking the name **Joliot-Curie**); together they discovered artificial radioactivity. Nobel Prize for Chemistry (1935), shared with his wife.

jo·li·o·ti·um /ˌjōlēˈōSH(ē)əm/ ▶ **n.** the name proposed by IUPAC for the chemical element of atomic number 105, now called **dubnium**.
– ORIGIN late 20th cent.: modern Latin, from the name of J. F. JOLIOT.

Jol·liet /ZHōlˈye, ZHōlēˈet/, Louis (1645–1700) French–Canadian explorer. With Jacques Marquette, he explored the upper Mississippi River 1673–74.

jol·li·fi·ca·tion /ˌjäləfiˈkāSHən/ ▶ **n.** lively celebration with others; merrymaking.

jol·li·ty /ˈjälitē/ ▶ **n.** (pl. **jollities**) lively and cheerful activity or celebration: *a night of riotous jollity.* ■ the quality of being cheerful: *he was full of false jollity.*
– ORIGIN Middle English: from Old French *jolite*, from *joli* (see JOLLY¹).

jol·lof rice /ˈjäləf/ ▶ **n.** a West African stew made with rice, chili peppers, and meat or fish.
– ORIGIN *jollof*, variant of WOLOF.

jol·ly¹ /ˈjälē/ ▶ **adj.** (**jollier, jolliest**) happy and cheerful: *he was a jolly man full of jokes.* ■ informal or dated lively and entertaining: *we had a very jolly time.*
▶ **v.** (**jollies, jollied**) [with obj.] informal encourage (someone) in a friendly way: *he jollied people along* | *they were trying to jolly her out of her torpor.* ■ (**jolly someone/something up**) make someone or something more lively or cheerful: *ideas to jolly up a winter's party.*
▶ **adv.** [as submodifier] Brit. informal very; extremely: *that's a jolly good idea.*
▶ **n.** (pl. **jollies**) Brit. informal a party or celebration.
– PHRASES **get one's jollies** informal have fun or find pleasure. **jolly well** Brit. informal used for emphasis, esp. when one is angry or irritated: *I'm going to keep on eating as much sugar as I jolly well like.*
– DERIVATIVES **jol·li·ly** /ˈjäləlē/ **adv.**, **jol·li·ness n.**
– ORIGIN Middle English: from Old French *jolif*, an earlier form of *joli* 'pretty,' perhaps from Old Norse *jól* (see YULE).

jol·ly² (also **jolly boat**) ▶ **n.** (pl. **jollies**) a lapstraked ship's boat that is smaller than a cutter, typically hoisted at the stern of the ship.
– ORIGIN early 18th cent.: perhaps related to YAWL.

Jol·ly Rog·er /ˈjälē ˈräjər/ ▶ **n.** a pirate's flag with a white skull and crossbones on a black background.
– ORIGIN late 18th cent.: of unknown origin.

Jolly Roger

Jol·son /ˈjōlsən/, Al (1886–1950), US singer, movie actor, and comedian; born *Asa Yoelson* in Russia. He made the Gershwin song "Swanee" his trademark and appeared in the first full-length talking movie, *The Jazz Singer*, in 1927.

jolt /jōlt/ ▶ **v.** [with obj.] push or shake (someone or something) abruptly and roughly: *a surge in the crowd behind him jolted him forward.* ■ give a surprise or shock to (someone) in order to make them act or change: *she tried to jolt him out of his depression.* ■ [no obj.] move with sudden lurches: *the train jolted into motion.*
▶ **n.** an abrupt rough or violent movement. ■ a surprise or shock, esp. of an unpleasant kind and often manifested physically: *that information gave her a severe jolt.*
– DERIVATIVES **jolt·y adj.**
– ORIGIN late 16th cent.: of unknown origin.

Jon. ▶ **abbr.** ■ Bible Jonah. ■ Jonathan.

Jon·a·gold /ˈjänəˌgōld/ ▶ **n.** a dessert apple of a variety with greenish-gold skin and crisp flesh.
– ORIGIN 1960s: blend of JONATHAN² and GOLDEN DELICIOUS.

Jo·nah /ˈjōnə/ (in the Bible) a Hebrew minor prophet. He was called by God to preach in Nineveh, but disobeyed and attempted to escape by sea; in a storm he was thrown overboard as a bringer of bad luck and swallowed by a great fish, only to be saved and finally succeed in his mission. ■ a book of the Bible telling of Jonah.

Jon·a·than¹ /ˈjänəTHən/ (in the Bible) a son of Saul, noted for his friendship with David and killed at the battle of Mount Gilboa.

Jon·a·than² ▶ **n.** a cooking apple of a red-skinned variety first grown in the US.
– ORIGIN mid 19th cent.: named after *Jonathan* Hasbrouck (died 1846), American lawyer.

Jones¹ /jōnz/, Bobby (1902–71), US golfer; full name *Robert Tyre Jones*. In a short competitive career 1923–30, and as an amateur, he won thirteen major competitions, including four US and three British open championships.

Jones², Inigo (1573–1652), British architect and stage designer. He introduced the Palladian style to Britain in buildings such as the Queen's House at Greenwich (1616) and the Banqueting Hall at Whitehall (1619).

Jones³, James (1921–77), US writer. His novel *From Here to Eternity* (1951) was made into a movie in 1953. He also wrote *The Thin Red Line* (1962). *Whistle*, which he did not complete, was published posthumously in 1978.

Jones⁴, John Paul (1747–92), American naval officer; born *John Paul* in Scotland. Noted for his raids off the northern coasts of Britain during the American Revolution, he is said to have stated "I have not yet begun to fight!" after victory in a 1779 battle between the Americans and the British.

Jones⁵, Quincy (Delight, Jr.) (1933–), US composer, conductor, and jazz trumpeter. He founded his own recording label, Qwest Records, in 1975. He also wrote television scores, such as the theme for *The Bill Cosby Show* and movie scores, such as for *The Color Purple* (1985).

jones /jōnz/ informal ▶ **n.** a fixation on or compulsive desire for someone or something, typically a drug; an addiction: *a two-year amphetamine jones.*
▶ **v.** [no obj.] (**jones on/for**) have a fixation on; be addicted to: *Palmer was jonesing for some coke again.*
– ORIGIN 1960s: said to come from *Jones* Alley, in Manhattan, associated with drug addicts.

Jones·bo·ro /ˈjōnzˌbərō/ a city in northeastern Arkansas; pop. 63,960 (est. 2008).

Jones·es /ˈjōnziz/ ▶ **n.** (usu. **the Joneses**) a person's neighbors or social equals.
– PHRASES **keep up with the Joneses** try to emulate or not be outdone by one's neighbors.
– ORIGIN late 19th cent.: from *Jones*, a commonly found British surname.

Jones·town /ˈjōnzˌtoun/ a former religious settlement in the jungle of Guyana, established by Reverend Jim Jones with about 1,000 followers, almost all of whom died in a mass suicide in late 1978.

Jong /ˈyôNG/, Erica (Mann) (1942–), US novelist and poet. She is best known for her picaresque novels *Fear of Flying* (1973), recounting the sexual exploits of heroine Isadora Wing, and *Fanny* (1980), written in a pseudo-18th-century style.

jon·gleur /ZHôNˈglər, ˈjäNGglər/ ▶ **n.** historical an itinerant minstrel.
– ORIGIN French, variant of *jougleur* 'juggler,' earlier *jogleor* 'pleasant, smiling,' from Latin *joculator* 'joker.'

Jön·kö·ping /ˈyœnˌCHœpiNG/ an industrial city in southern Sweden, at the southern end of Lake Vättern; pop. 125,154 (2008).

jon·quil /ˈjänkwəl/ ▶ **n.** a widely cultivated narcissus with clusters of small fragrant yellow flowers and cylindrical leaves, native to southern Europe and northeastern Africa. ● *Narcissus jonquilla*, family Liliaceae (or Amaryllidaceae).
– ORIGIN early 17th cent.: from modern Latin *jonquilla* or French *jonquille*, from Spanish *junquillo*, diminutive of *junco*, from Latin *juncus* 'rush, reed.'

Jon·son /ˈjänsən/, Ben (1572–1637), British playwright and poet; full name *Benjamin Jonson*. With his play *Every Man in His Humour* (1598), he established his "comedy of humors," whereby each character is dominated by a particular obsession. Other notable works: *Volpone* (1606) and *Bartholomew Fair* (1614).
– DERIVATIVES **Jon·so·ni·an** /jänˈsōnēən/ **adj.**

jook /jo͝ok, jo͞ok/ ▶ **n.** another term for JUKE JOINT.

Jop·lin¹ /ˈjäplin/ an industrial and commercial city in southwestern Missouri; pop. 49,775 (est. 2008).

Jop·lin² /ˈjäplən/, Janis (1943–70), US rock and blues singer. She became a vocalist with Big Brother and the Holding Company, and gave a raw, powerful performance at the Monterey pop festival in 1967. She died from a heroin overdose just before her most successful album, *Pearl*, and her number-one single "Me and Bobby McGee" were released in 1970.

Jop·lin³, Scott (1868–1917), US pianist and composer. He was the first of the creators of ragtime to write down his compositions. Notable works: "Maple Leaf Rag" (1899), "The Entertainer" (1902), and "Gladiolus Rag" (1907).

Jop·pa biblical name for JAFFA.

Jor·daens /ˈyôrˌdäns/, Jacob (1593–1678), Flemish painter. Influenced by Rubens, he is noted for his boisterous peasant scenes.

Jor·dan¹ /ˈjôrdən/ **1** a country in the Middle East, east of the Jordan River; pop. 6,269,300 (est. 2009); capital, Amman; official language, Arabic. Official name HASHEMITE KINGDOM OF JORDAN.

Romans, Arabs, Crusaders, and Turks dominated the area successively until it was made a British protectorate in 1916 and achieved independence in 1946. During the war of 1948–49 that followed

j

the establishment of the state of Israel, Jordan took over the area of the West Bank; this was recovered by Israel in the Six Day War of 1967, after which many Palestinian refugees entered the country. A peace treaty with Israel was signed in 1994, ending an official state of war between the two countries.

2 a river that flows south for 200 miles (320 km) from the Anti-Lebanon Mountains through the Sea of Galilee into the Dead Sea. John the Baptist baptized Jesus Christ in the Jordan River. It is regarded as sacred not only by Christians but also by Jews and Muslims.
– DERIVATIVES **Jor·da·ni·an** /jôr'dānēən/ **adj. & n.**

Jor·dan², Barbara (Charline) (1936–96) US lawyer, educator, and politician. She was the first black woman to serve in the Texas Senate (1967–72), before being elected to the US House of Representatives 1973–79.

Jor·dan³, Michael (Jeffrey) (1963–), US basketball player. Playing for the Chicago Bulls 1984–93 and 1995–98, he led them to six titles and was the NBA's most valuable player five times. He later played for the Washington Wizards 2001–03.

Michael Jordan

jor·dan al·mond /'jôrdn/ ▶ **n.** a high-quality almond of a variety grown chiefly in southeastern Spain.
– ORIGIN late Middle English: *jordan* apparently from French or Spanish *jardin* 'garden.'

Jor·na·da del Muer·to /hôr'nädə del 'mwertō/ a desert region in southern New Mexico, near White Sands, known as the "journey of death" for the difficulties early travelers endured.

jo·rum /'jôrəm/ ▶ **n.** historical a large bowl or jug used for serving drinks such as tea or punch.
– ORIGIN early 18th cent.: perhaps from *Joram* (2 Sam. 8:10), who "brought with him vessels of silver, and vessels of gold" to King David.

Jos. ▶ **abbr.** ■ Joseph. ■ Josiah. ■ Bible Joshua.

Jo·seph¹ /'jōzəf, -səf/ (in the Bible) a Hebrew patriarch, son of Jacob and oldest son of Rachel. He was given a coat of many colors by his father, but was then sold by his jealous brothers into captivity in Egypt, where he attained high office.

Jo·seph², Chief (c.1840–1904) American Indian chief; Indian name **Inmuttooyahlatlat**. As chief of the Nez Percé tribe, he defied the efforts of the US government to move his people from Oregon until he was captured in 1877.

Chief Joseph

Jo·seph, St., husband of the Virgin Mary. A carpenter of Nazareth, he was betrothed to Mary at the time of the Annunciation. Feast day, March 19.

Jo·se·phine /'jōzə,fēn, ,jōzə'fēn/ (1763–1814), empress of France 1804–09; full name *Marie Joséphine Rose Tascher de la Pagerie*. She married Napoleon in 1796. Their marriage proved childless, and she was divorced by Napoleon in 1809.

Jo·seph of Ar·i·ma·the·a, St /,arəmə'THēə/ a member of the council at Jerusalem who, after the Crucifixion, asked Pilate for Jesus' body, which he buried. He is also known from the medieval story that he came to England with the Holy Grail and built the first church at Glastonbury. Feast day, 17 March.

Jo·seph·son junc·tion /'jōzəfsən, -səf-/ ▶ **n.** Physics an electrical device in which two superconducting metals are separated by a thin layer of insulator, across which an electric current may flow in the absence of a potential difference. The current may be made to oscillate in proportion to an applied potential difference.
– ORIGIN 1960s: named after Brian D. *Josephson* (born 1940), British physicist.

Jo·se·phus /jō'sēfəs/, Flavius (*c.*37–*c.*100), Jewish historian, general, and Pharisee; born *Joseph ben Matthias*. His *Jewish War* gives an eyewitness account of the events that led up to the Jewish revolt against the Romans in 66, in which he was a leader.

josh /jäsh/ informal ▶ **v.** [with obj.] tease (someone) in a playful way: *he loved to josh people*. ■ [no obj.] engage in joking or playful talk with others.
▶ **n.** good-natured banter.
– DERIVATIVES **josh·er n.**
– ORIGIN mid 19th cent. (as a verb): of unknown origin.

Josh. ▶ **abbr.** Bible Joshua.

Josh·u·a /'jäsHōōə/ (*fl. c.*13th century BC), Israelite leader who succeeded Moses and led his people into the Promised Land. ■ the sixth book of the Bible, telling of the conquest of Canaan and its division among the twelve tribes of Israel.

Josh·u·a tree ▶ **n.** a yucca that grows as a tree and has clusters of spiky leaves, native to arid regions of southwestern North America. ● *Yucca brevifolia*, family Agavaceae.
– ORIGIN mid 19th cent.: apparently from **JOSHUA** (Josh. 8:18), the plant being likened to a man brandishing a spear.

Joshua tree

Josh·u·a Tree Na·tion·al Park /'jäsHōōə/ a national preserve in southern California, noted for its desert plant and animal life.

joss /jäs/ ▶ **n.** a Chinese religious statue or idol.
– ORIGIN early 18th cent.: from Javanese *dejos*, from obsolete Portuguese *deos*, from Latin *deus* 'god.'

jos·ser /'jäsər/ ▶ **n.** informal **1** Brit. a man, typically an old man or one regarded with some contempt: *an old josser*.
2 Austral. a clergyman.
– ORIGIN late 19th cent.: from **JOSS** + **-ER¹**.

joss house ▶ **n.** a Chinese temple.

joss stick ▶ **n.** a thin stick consisting of a substance that burns slowly and with a fragrant smell, used as incense.

jos·tle /'jäsəl/ ▶ **v.** [with obj.] push, elbow, or bump against (someone) roughly, typically in a crowd: *passengers arriving and departing, jostling one another* | [no obj.] *people jostled against us*. ■ [no obj.] **(jostle for)** struggle or compete forcefully for: *a jumble of images jostled for attention*.
▶ **n.** the action of jostling.
– ORIGIN late Middle English *justle*, from *just*, an earlier form of **JOUST**. The original sense was 'have sexual intercourse with'; current senses date from the mid 16th cent.

jot /jät/ ▶ **v.** **(jots, jotting, jotted)** [with obj.] write (something) quickly: *when you've found the answers, jot them down*.
▶ **n.** [usu. with negative] a very small amount: *you didn't care a jot* | *I have yet to see* ***one jot of*** *evidence*.
– ORIGIN late 15th cent. (as a noun): via Latin from Greek *iōta*, the smallest letter of the Greek alphabet (see **IOTA**).

jo·ta /'hōtə/ ▶ **n.** a folk dance from northern Spain, danced in couples in fast triple time.
– ORIGIN Spanish.

jot·ting /'jätiNG/ ▶ **n.** (usu. **jottings**) a brief note.

Jo·tun /'yôtōōn/ ▶ **n.** Scandinavian Mythology a member of the race of giants, enemies of the gods.
– ORIGIN from Old Norse *jǫtunn*, related to Old English *eoten*, of Germanic origin.

jou·al /zhōō'al, -'äl/ ▶ **n.** a nonstandard form of popular Canadian French, influenced by English vocabulary and grammar.
– ORIGIN Canadian French dialect, from French *cheval* 'horse,' apparently from the way *cheval* is pronounced in rural areas of Quebec.

jougs /jōōgz/ ▶ **plural n.** historical a hinged iron collar chained to a wall or post, used in medieval Scotland as an instrument of punishment.
– ORIGIN late 16th cent.: from French *joug* or Latin *jugum* 'yoke.'

jou·is·sance /zhwē'säNs/ ▶ **n.** formal physical or intellectual pleasure, delight, or ecstasy.
– ORIGIN French, from *jouir* 'enjoy.'

Joule /jōōl/, James Prescott (1818–89), British physicist. He established that all forms of energy were basically the same and interchangeable—the first law of thermodynamics. The Joule–Thomson effect, discovered with William Thomson (later Lord Kelvin) in 1852, led to the development of the refrigerator and to the science of cryogenics.

joule /jōōl, joul/ (abbr.: **J**) ▶ **n.** the SI unit of work or energy, equal to the work done by a force of one newton when its point of application moves one meter in the direction of action of the force, equivalent to one 3600th of a watt-hour.
– ORIGIN late 19th cent.: named after J. P. **JOULE**.

Joule ef·fect ▶ **n.** Physics the heating that occurs when an electric current flows through a resistance.

Joule's law Physics a law stating that the heat produced by an electric current i flowing through a resistance R for a time t is proportional to i^2Rt.

Joule–Thom·son ef·fect ▶ **n.** Physics the change of temperature of a gas when it is allowed to expand without doing any external work. The gas becomes cooler if it was initially below a certain temperature (the **inversion temperature**), or hotter if initially above it.

jounce /jouns/ ▶ **v.** jolt or bounce: [no obj.] *the car jounced wildly* | [with obj.] *the pilot jounced the plane through turbulence*.
– ORIGIN late Middle English: probably symbolic; compare with **BOUNCE**.

jour. ▶ **abbr.** ■ journal. ■ journeyman.

jour·nal /'jərnl/ ▶ **n.** **1** a newspaper or magazine that deals with a particular subject or professional activity: *medical journals* | [in names] *the Wall Street Journal*.
2 a daily record of news and events of a personal nature; a diary. ■ Nautical a logbook. ■ **(the Journals)** a record of the daily proceedings in the British Houses of Parliament. ■ (in bookkeeping) a daily record of business transactions with a statement of the accounts to which each is to be debited and credited.
3 Mechanics the part of a shaft or axle that rests on bearings.
– ORIGIN late Middle English (originally denoting a book containing the appointed times of daily prayers): from Old French *jurnal*, from late Latin *diurnalis* (see **DIURNAL**).

jour·nal box ▶ **n.** Mechanics a box that houses a journal and its bearing.

jour·nal·ese /,jərnl'ēz/ ▶ **n.** informal a hackneyed style of writing supposedly characteristic of newspapers and magazines.

jour·nal·ism /'jərnl,izəm/ ▶ **n.** the activity or profession of writing for newspapers or magazines or of broadcasting news on radio or television. ■ the product of such activity: *an art critic whose essays and journalism are never dull*.

jour·nal·ist /'jərnl-ist/ ▶ **n.** a person who writes for newspapers or magazines or prepares news to be broadcast on radio or television.
– DERIVATIVES **jour·nal·is·tic** /,jərnl'istik/ **adj.**, **jour·nal·is·ti·cal·ly** /,jərnl'istik(ə)lē/ **adv.**

jour·nal·ize /'jərnl,īz/ ▶ **v.** [with obj.] dated enter (notes or information) in a journal or account book: *I would gladly journalize some of my proceedings*.

jour·ney /'jərnē/ ▶ **n.** (pl. **journeys**) an act of traveling from one place to another: *she went on a long journey*. ■ a long and often difficult process of personal change and development: *her spiritual journey towards Roman Catholicism* | *I was excited with my character's journey in the film*.
▶ **v.** **(journeys, journeyed)** [no obj.] travel somewhere: *they journeyed south*.
– DERIVATIVES **jour·ney·er n.**
– ORIGIN Middle English: from Old French *jornee* 'day, a day's travel, a day's work' (the earliest senses in English), based on Latin *diurnum* 'daily portion,' from *diurnus* (see **DIURNAL**).

jour·ney·man /'jərnēmən/ ▶ **n.** (pl. **journeymen**) a trained worker who is employed by someone else. ■ a worker or sports player who is reliable but not outstanding: [as modifier] *a solid journeyman professional*.
– ORIGIN late Middle English: from **JOURNEY** (in the obsolete sense 'day's work') + **MAN**; so named

because the journeyman was no longer bound by indentures but was paid by the day.

jour·no /ˈjərnō/ ▶ **n.** (pl. **journos**) informal a journalist.
– ORIGIN 1960s (originally an Australian usage): abbreviation.

joust /joust/ ▶ **v.** [no obj.] **1** (often as noun **jousting**) historical (of a medieval knight) engage in a sports contest in which two opponents on horseback fight with lances.
2 compete closely for superiority: *the guerrillas jousted for supremacy.*
▶ **n.** a medieval sports contest in which two opponents on horseback fought with lances.
– DERIVATIVES **joust·er n.**
– ORIGIN Middle English (originally in the sense 'join battle, engage'): from Old French *jouster* 'bring together,' based on Latin *juxta* 'near.'

J'Ou·vert /ZHōōˈver/ ▶ **n.** (in the Caribbean) the official start of carnival, at dawn on the Monday preceding Lent.
– ORIGIN French Creole, from French *jour ouvert* 'day opened.'

Jove /jōv/ another name for JUPITER.
– PHRASES **by Jove** dated an exclamation indicating surprise or used for emphasis: *by Jove, that's a cold wind.*
– ORIGIN from Latin *Jov-*, stem of Old Latin *Jovis*, replaced later by *Jupiter*. The exclamation *by Jove* dates from the late 16th cent.

jo·vi·al /ˈjōvēəl/ ▶ **adj.** cheerful and friendly: *she was in a jovial mood.*
– DERIVATIVES **jo·vi·al·i·ty** /jōvēˈalitē/ **n., jo·vi·al·ly adv.**
– ORIGIN late 16th cent.: from French, from late Latin *jovialis* 'of Jupiter' (see JOVE), with reference to the supposed influence of the planet Jupiter on those born under it.

Jo·vi·an /ˈjōvēən/ ▶ **adj. 1** (in Roman mythology) of or like the god Jove (or Jupiter).
2 of or relating to the planet Jupiter or the class of giant planets to which Jupiter belongs.
▶ **n.** a hypothetical or fictional inhabitant of the planet Jupiter.

jowl /joul/ ▶ **n.** (often **jowls**) the lower part of a person's or animal's cheek, esp. when it is fleshy or drooping: *she had a large nose and heavy jowls.* ■ the cheek of a pig used as meat. ■ the loose fleshy part of the neck of certain animals, such as the dewlap of cattle or the wattle of birds.
– DERIVATIVES **jowled adj.** [in combination] *ruddy-jowled*, **jowl·y adj.**
– ORIGIN Old English *ceole* (related to German *Kehle* 'throat, gullet'), partly merged with Old English *ceafl* 'jaw' (related to Dutch *kevels* 'cheekbones').

joy /joi/ ▶ **n.** a feeling of great pleasure and happiness: *tears of joy | the joy of being alive.* ■ a thing that causes joy: *the joys of Manhattan.*
▶ **v.** [no obj.] literary rejoice: *I felt shame that I had ever joyed in his discomfiture or pain.*
– ORIGIN Middle English: from Old French *joie*, based on Latin *gaudium*, from *gaudere* 'rejoice.'

Joyce /jois/, James (Augustine Aloysius) (1882–1941), Irish writer. An important writer of the modernist movement, he first became known for his short stories in *Dubliners* (1914). His novel *Ulysses* (1922) revolutionized the structure of the modern novel and developed the stream-of-consciousness technique. Other notable novels: *A Portrait of the Artist as a Young Man* (1914–15) and *Finnegans Wake* (1939).
– DERIVATIVES **Joyc·e·an** /ˈjoisēən/ **adj. & n.**

joy·ful /ˈjoifəl/ ▶ **adj.** feeling, expressing, or causing great pleasure and happiness: *joyful music.*
– DERIVATIVES **joy·ful·ly adv., joy·ful·ness n.**

joy·less /ˈjoilis/ ▶ **adj.** not giving or feeling any pleasure or satisfaction; grim or dismal: *she had to face the thought of a joyless future.*
– DERIVATIVES **joy·less·ly adv.**

Joy·ner–Ker·see /ˈjoinər ˈkərsē/, Jackie (1962–) US track and field athlete. She won gold medals in the heptathlon in the 1988 and 1992 Olympic Games.

joy·ous /ˈjoiəs/ ▶ **adj.** chiefly literary full of happiness and joy: *scenes of joyous celebration.*
– DERIVATIVES **joy·ous·ly adv., joy·ous·ness n.**

joy·pad /ˈjoiˌpad/ ▶ **n.** an input device for a computer games console which uses buttons to control the motion of an image on the screen.
– ORIGIN late 20th cent.: blend of JOYSTICK and KEYPAD.

joy·ride /ˈjoiˌrīd/ ▶ **n.** informal a fast and dangerous ride, esp. one taken in a stolen vehicle: *kids stealing cars for a Saturday night joyride.*
– DERIVATIVES **joy·rid·er** /-ˌrīdər/ **n.**

joy·rid·ing /ˈjoiˌrīdiNG/ ▶ **n.** the action or practice of driving fast and dangerously in a stolen car for enjoyment.

joy·stick /ˈjoiˌstik/ ▶ **n.** informal the control column of an aircraft. ■ a lever that can be moved in several directions to control the movement of an image on a computer or similar display screen.

JP ▶ **abbr.** Justice of the Peace.

JPEG /ˈjāˌpeg/ ▶ **n.** Computing a format for compressing image files: [as modifier] *a JPEG image.* ■ a file in this format.
– ORIGIN 1990s: abbreviation of *Joint Photographic Experts Group*.

Jr. ▶ **abbr.** junior (in names): *John Smith Jr.*

JRC ▶ **abbr.** Junior Red Cross.

JSD ▶ **abbr.** Doctor of the Science of Law (Doctor of Juristic Science).

Juan Car·los /(h)wän ˈkärlōs/ (1938–), king of Spain 1975–; full name *Juan Carlos Victor María de Borbón y Borbón*; grandson of Alfonso XIII. Franco's chosen successor, he became king after Franco's death. His reign has seen Spain's increasing liberalization and its entry into NATO and the European Community.

Juan de Fu·ca Strait /ˈ(h)wän də ˈfyōōkə/ an ocean passage between Vancouver Island in British Columbia and the Olympic Peninsula in Washington.

Juan Fer·nan·dez Is·lands /ˈ(h)wän fərˈnandəs/ a group of three almost uninhabited islands in the Pacific Ocean, 400 miles (640 km) west of Chile.

Juá·rez /(h)wäˈrez, ˈ(h)wärəs/, Benito Pablo (1806–72), Mexican statesman; president 1861–64 and 1867–72. Between 1864 and 1867, he was replaced as emperor by Maximilian, who was supported by the French.

Ju·ba /ˈjōōbə/ the capital of the southern region of Sudan, on the White Nile River; pop. 250,000 (est. 2005).

ju·ba /ˈjōōbə/ ▶ **n.** a dance originating among plantation slaves in the southern US, featuring rhythmic handclapping and slapping of the thighs.
– ORIGIN late 19th cent.: of unknown origin.

Jub·ba /ˈjōōbə/ a river in East Africa that rises in the highlands of central Ethiopia and flows south for about 1,000 miles (1,600 km) through Somalia to the Indian Ocean.

ju·bi·lant /ˈjōōbələnt/ ▶ **adj.** feeling or expressing great happiness and triumph.
– DERIVATIVES **ju·bi·lance n., ju·bi·lant·ly adv.**
– ORIGIN mid 17th cent. (originally in the sense 'making a joyful noise'): from Latin *jubilant-* 'calling, hallooing,' from the verb *jubilare* (see JUBILATE).

Ju·bi·la·te /ˌjōōbəˈlātē, ˌyōōbəˈlätā/ ▶ **n.** [in sing.] Psalm 100 (99 in the Vulgate), beginning *Jubilate deo* "rejoice in God," esp. as used as a canticle in the Anglican service of matins. ■ a musical setting of this.
– ORIGIN Latin, 'shout for joy!,' imperative of *jubilare* (see JUBILATE).

ju·bi·late /ˈjōōbəˌlāt/ ▶ **v.** [no obj.] archaic show great happiness; rejoice: *sing and jubilate aloud.*
– ORIGIN mid 17th cent.: from Latin *jubilat-* 'called out,' from the verb *jubilare*, used by Christian writers to mean 'shout for joy.'

ju·bi·la·tion /ˌjōōbəˈlāSHən/ ▶ **n.** a feeling of great happiness and triumph.

ju·bi·lee /ˈjōōbəˌlē, ˌjōōbəˈlē/ ▶ **n.** a special anniversary of an event, esp. one celebrating twenty-five or fifty years of a reign or activity: [as modifier] *jubilee celebrations.* ■ Judaism (in Jewish history) a year of emancipation and restoration, celebrated every fifty years. ■ (in full **Jubilee Year**) a period of remission from the penal consequences of sin, granted by the Roman Catholic Church under certain conditions for a year, usually at intervals of twenty-five years.
▶ **adj.** [postpositive] (of desserts) flambé: *cherries jubilee.*
– ORIGIN late Middle English: from Old French *jubile*, from late Latin *jubilaeus* (*annus*) '(year) of jubilee,' based on Hebrew *yōbēl*, originally 'ram's-horn trumpet,' with which the jubilee year was proclaimed.

Jud. ▶ **abbr.** Bible ■ Judges. ■ Judith.

Ju·dae·a /jōōˈdēə, -ˈdāə/ the southern part of ancient Palestine that corresponds to the former kingdom of Judah.
– DERIVATIVES **Ju·dae·an adj.**

Judaeo- ▶ **comb. form** chiefly Brit. alternate spelling of JUDEO-.

Ju·dah /ˈjōōdə/ **1** (in the Bible) a Hebrew patriarch, the fourth son of Jacob and Leah. ■ the tribe of Israel traditionally descended from him, the most powerful of the twelve tribes of Israel.
2 the southern part of ancient Palestine, occupied by the tribe of Judah. After the reign of Solomon (*c.*930 BC) it formed a separate kingdom from Israel. Later known as JUDAEA.

Ju·da·ic /jōōˈdāik/ ▶ **adj.** of or relating to Judaism or the ancient Jews: *tenets of Judaic law.*
– ORIGIN early 17th cent.: from Latin *Judaicus*, from Greek *Ioudaikos*, from *Ioudaios* (see JEW).

Ju·da·ism /ˈjōōdēˌizəm, -dā-/ ▶ **n.** the monotheistic religion of the Jews. ■ the Jews collectively.

> For its origins Judaism looks to the biblical covenant made by God with Abraham, and to the laws revealed to Moses and recorded in the Torah (supplemented by the rabbinical Talmud), which established the Jewish people's special relationship with God. Since the destruction of the Temple in Jerusalem in AD 70, the rituals of Judaism have centered on the home and the synagogue, the chief day of worship being the Sabbath (sunset on Friday to sunset on Saturday), and the annual observances including Yom Kippur and Passover.

– DERIVATIVES **Ju·da·ist n.**
– ORIGIN from late Latin *Judaismus*, from Greek *Ioudaïsmos*, from *Ioudaios* (see JEW).

Ju·da·ize /ˈjōōdēˌīz, -dā-/ ▶ **v.** [with obj.] make Jewish; convert to Judaism. ■ [no obj.] follow Jewish customs or religious rites.
– DERIVATIVES **Ju·da·i·za·tion** /ˌjōōdē-iˈzāSHən, -dā-/ **n., Ju·da·iz·er n.**
– ORIGIN late 16th cent.: from Christian Latin *judaizare*, from Greek *ioudaizein*, from *Ioudaios* (see JEW).

Ju·das[1] /ˈjōōdəs/ an Apostle; full name *Judas Iscariot*. He betrayed Jesus to the Jewish authorities in return for thirty pieces of silver; the Gospels leave his motives uncertain. Overcome with remorse, he later committed suicide. ■ (as noun, usu. **a Judas**) a person who betrays a friend or comrade.

Ju·das[2] see JUDE, ST.

ju·das /ˈjōōdəs/ (also **judas hole**) ▶ **n.** a peephole in a door.
– ORIGIN mid 19th cent.: from *Judas* Iscariot (see JUDAS[1]), because of his association with betrayal.

Ju·das kiss ▶ **n.** an act of betrayal, esp. one disguised as a gesture of friendship.
– ORIGIN early 15th cent.: with biblical allusion (Matt. 26:48) to the betrayal of Jesus Christ by Judas Iscariot.

Ju·das Mac·ca·bae·us /ˌmakəˈbēəs/ (died *c.*161 BC), Jewish leader. As the leader of a Jewish revolt in Judaea against Antiochus IV Epiphanes from around 167, he recovered Jerusalem and rededicated the Temple. He is the hero of the two books of the Maccabees in the Apocrypha.

Ju·das tree ▶ **n.** a Mediterranean tree of the pea family, with purple flowers that typically appear before the rounded leaves. ● *Cercis siliquastrum*, family Leguminosae.

jud·der /ˈjədər/ ▶ **v.** [no obj.] chiefly Brit. (esp. of something mechanical) shake and vibrate rapidly and with force: *the steering wheel juddered in his hand.*
▶ **n.** an instance of rapid and forceful shaking and vibration: *the car gave a judder.*
– DERIVATIVES **jud·der·y adj.**
– ORIGIN 1930s: imitative; compare with SHUDDER.

Jude, St. /jōōd/ an Apostle; supposedly the brother of James; also known as **Judas**. Thaddaeus is traditionally identified with him. According to tradition, he was martyred in Persia with St. Simon. Feast day (with St. Simon), October 28. ■ the last epistle of the New Testament, ascribed to St. Jude.

Ju·den·rat /ˈyōōdnˌrät/ ▶ **n.** (pl. **Judenrate** /-ˌrätə/) a council representing a Jewish community, esp. in German-occupied territory during World War II.
– ORIGIN German, 'Jewish council.'

ju·den·rein /ˈjōōdnˌrīn/ ▶ **adj.** from which Jews are excluded (originally with reference to organizations in Nazi Germany).
– ORIGIN German, 'free of Jews.'

Judeo- (also chiefly Brit. **Judaeo-**) ▶ **comb. form** Jewish; Jewish and ...: *Judeo-Christian.* ■ relating to Judaea.
– ORIGIN from Latin *Judaeus* 'Jewish.'

Ju·dez·mo /jōōˈdezmō/ ▶ **n.** another term for LADINO.

Judg. ▶ **abbr.** Bible Judges.

judge /jəj/ ▶ **n.** a public official appointed to decide cases in a court of law. ■ a person who decides the results of a competition or watches for infractions of the rules. ■ a person able or qualified to give an opinion on something: *she was a good judge of character.* ■ a leader having temporary authority in

ancient Israel in the period between Joshua and the kings. See also JUDGES.
▶ v. [with obj.] form an opinion or conclusion about: *scientists were judged according to competence* | [with clause] *it is hard to judge whether such opposition is justified* | [no obj.] *judging from his letters home, Monty was in good spirits.* ■ decide (a case) in court: *other cases were judged by tribunal.* ■ [with obj. and complement] give a verdict on (someone) in court: *she was judged innocent of murder.* ■ decide the results of (a competition).
– DERIVATIVES **judge·ship** /-ˌSHip/ n.
– ORIGIN Middle English: from Old French *juge* (noun), *juger* (verb), from Latin *judex, judic-*, from *jus* 'law' + *dicere* 'to say.'

judge ad·vo·cate ▶ n. Law a lawyer who advises a court-martial on points of law and sums up the case.

judge ad·vo·cate gen·er·al ▶ n. an officer in supreme control of the courts-martial of one of the armed forces.

judge-made ▶ adj. Law constituted by judicial decisions rather than explicit legislation.

judge·ment ▶ n. variant spelling of JUDGMENT.

judge·men·tal ▶ adj. variant spelling of JUDGMENTAL.

Judg·es /ˈjəjiz/ the seventh book of the Bible, describing the conquest of Canaan under the leaders called "judges" in an account that is parallel to that of the Book of Joshua. The book includes the stories of Deborah, Gideon, Jephthah, and Samson.

judg·ment /ˈjəjmənt/ (also **judgement**) ▶ n. **1** the ability to make considered decisions or come to sensible conclusions: *an error of judgment* | *that is not, in my judgment, the end of the matter.* ■ an opinion or conclusion: *they make subjective judgments about children's skills.* ■ a decision of a court or judge: *the Supreme Court upheld the judgment of the Alberta Court of Appeal.*
2 a misfortune or calamity viewed as a divine punishment: *the crash had been a judgment on the parents for wickedness.*
– PHRASES **against one's better judgment** contrary to what one believes to be wise or sensible. **pass judgment** (of a court or judge) give a decision concerning a defendant or legal matter: *he passed judgment on the accused.* ■ criticize or condemn someone from a position of assumed moral superiority. **reserve judgment** delay the process of judging or giving one's opinion. **sit in judgment** assume the right to judge someone, esp. in a critical manner.
– ORIGIN Middle English: from Old French *jugement*, from *juger* 'to judge.'

> **USAGE** In British English, the normal spelling in general contexts is **judgement**. However, the spelling **judgment** is conventional in legal contexts, and standard in North American English.

judg·men·tal /jəjˈmentl/ (also **judgemental**) ▶ adj. of or concerning the use of judgment: *judgmental errors.* ■ having or displaying an excessively critical point of view: *I don't like to sound judgmental, but it was a big mistake.*
– DERIVATIVES **judg·men·tal·ly** adv.

Judg·ment Day ▶ n. the time of the Last Judgment; the end of the world.

judg·ment in de·fault ▶ n. Law judgment awarded to the plaintiff on the defendant's failure to plead.

Judg·ment of Sol·o·mon (in the Bible) the arbitration of King Solomon over a baby claimed by two women. He proposed cutting the baby in half, and then gave it to the woman who showed concern for its life.

ju·di·ca·ture /ˈjo͞odikəˌCHo͝or, -ˌkāCHər/ ▶ n. the administration of justice. ■ (**the judicature**) judges collectively; the judiciary.
– DERIVATIVES **ju·di·ca·to·ry** /-kəˌtôrē/ adj.
– ORIGIN mid 16th cent.: from medieval Latin *judicatura*, from Latin *judicare* 'to judge.'

ju·di·cial /jo͞oˈdiSHəl/ ▶ adj. of, by, or appropriate to a court or judge: *a judicial inquiry into the allegations* | *a judicial system.*
– DERIVATIVES **ju·di·cial·ly** adv.
– ORIGIN late Middle English: from Latin *judicialis*, from *judicium* 'judgment,' from *judex* (see JUDGE).

> **USAGE** **Judicial** means 'relating to judgment and the administration of justice': *the judicial system; judicial robes.* Do not confuse it with **judicious**, which means 'prudent, reasonable': *getting off the highway the minute you felt tired was a judicious choice.* **Judiciary** refers to the judicial branch of government, the court system, or judges collectively.

ju·di·cial re·view ▶ n. review by the US Supreme Court of the constitutional validity of a legislative act. ■ (in the UK) a procedure by which a court can review an administrative action by a public body and (in England) secure a declaration, order, or award.

ju·di·cial sep·a·ra·tion ▶ n. another term for LEGAL SEPARATION (sense 1).

ju·di·ci·ar·y /jo͞oˈdiSHēˌerē, -ˈdiSHərē/ ▶ n. (pl. **judiciaries**) (usu. **the judiciary**) the judicial authorities of a country; judges collectively.
– ORIGIN early 19th cent.: from Latin *judiciarius*, from *judicium* 'judgment.'

> **USAGE** See usage at JUDICIAL.

ju·di·cious /jo͞oˈdiSHəs/ ▶ adj. having, showing, or done with good judgment or sense: *the efficient and judicious use of pesticides.*
– DERIVATIVES **ju·di·cious·ly** adv., **ju·di·cious·ness** n.
– ORIGIN late 16th cent.: from French *judicieux*, from Latin *judicium* 'judgment' (see JUDICIAL).

> **USAGE** See usage at JUDICIAL.

Ju·dith /ˈjo͞odəTH/ (in the Apocrypha) a rich Israelite widow who saved the town of Bethulia from Nebuchadnezzar's army by seducing the besieging general Holofernes and cutting off his head while he slept. ■ a book of the Apocrypha recounting the story of Judith.

ju·do /ˈjo͞odō/ ▶ n. a sport of unarmed combat derived from jujitsu and intended to train the body and mind. It involves using holds and leverage to unbalance the opponent.
– DERIVATIVES **ju·do·ist** /-ist/ n.
– ORIGIN late 19th cent.: Japanese, from *jū* 'gentle' + *dō* 'way.'

ju·do·ka /ˈjo͞odōˌkä, ˌjo͞odōˈkä/ ▶ n. a person who practices or is an expert in judo.
– ORIGIN Japanese, from JUDO + *-ka* 'person, profession.'

Ju·dy /ˈjo͞odē/ ▶ n. (pl. **Judies**) the wife of Punch in the Punch and Judy show.
– ORIGIN early 19th cent.: nickname for the given name *Judith*.

jug /jəg/ ▶ n. **1** a large container for liquids, with a narrow mouth and typically a stopper or cap. ■ the contents of such a container: *she gave us a big jug of water.*
2 (**the jug**) informal prison: *three months in the jug.*
3 (**jugs**) vulgar slang a woman's breasts.
4 (also **jug handle**) Climbing a secure hold that is cut into rock for climbing.
▶ v. (**jugs, jugged, jugging**) [with obj.] **1** (usu. as adj. **jugged**) stew or boil (a hare or rabbit) in a covered container: *jugged hare.*
2 informal prosecute and imprison (someone).
– DERIVATIVES **jug·ful** /-ˌfo͝ol/ n. (pl. **jugfuls**).
– ORIGIN mid 16th cent.: perhaps from *Jug*, nickname for the given names *Joan, Joanna*, and *Jenny*.

ju·gal /ˈjo͞ogəl/ ▶ adj. **1** Anatomy of or relating to the zygoma (the bony arch of the cheek).
2 Entomology of or relating to the jugum of an insect's forewing.
– ORIGIN late 16th cent.: from Latin *jugalis*, from *jugum* 'yoke.'

jug band ▶ n. a group of jazz, blues, or folk musicians using simple or improvised instruments such as jugs and washboards.

Ju·gend·stil /ˈyo͞ogəntˌSHtēl/ ▶ n. German term for ART NOUVEAU.
– ORIGIN German, from *Jugend* 'youth' + *Stil* 'style.'

Jug·ger·naut /ˈjəgərˌnôt/ old-fashioned name for JAGANNATHA.

jug·ger·naut /ˈjəgərˌnôt/ ▶ n. a huge, powerful, and overwhelming force or institution: *a juggernaut of secular and commercial culture.*
– ORIGIN mid 19th cent.: extension of JUGGERNAUT.

jug·gle /ˈjəgəl/ ▶ v. [with obj.] continuously toss into the air and catch (a number of objects) so as to keep at least one in the air while handling the others, typically for the entertainment of others. ■ cope with by adroitly balancing: *she works full time, juggling her career with raising children.* ■ organize (information or figures) in order to give a particular impression: *defense chiefs juggled the figures on bomb tests.*
▶ n. [in sing.] an act of juggling.
– DERIVATIVES **jug·gler** /ˈjəg(ə)lər/ n., **jug·gler·y** /ˈjəglərē/ n.
– ORIGIN late Middle English (in the sense 'entertain with jesting, tricks, etc'): back-formation from *juggler*, or from Old French *jogler*, from Latin *joculari* 'to jest,' from *joculus*, diminutive of *jocus* 'jest.' Current senses date from the late 19th cent.

jug·u·lar /ˈjəgyələr/ ▶ adj. **1** of the neck or throat.
2 Zoology (of fish's pelvic fins) located in front of the pectoral fins.
▶ n. short for JUGULAR VEIN.
– PHRASES **go for the jugular** be aggressive or unrestrained in making an attack.
– ORIGIN late 16th cent.: from late Latin *jugularis*, from Latin *jugulum* 'collarbone, throat,' diminutive of *jugum* 'yoke.'

jug·u·lar vein ▶ n. any of several large veins in the neck, carrying blood from the head and face.

ju·gu·late /ˈjəgyəˌlāt/ ▶ v. [with obj.] archaic kill (someone) by cutting the throat.
– ORIGIN early 17th cent.: from Latin *jugulat-* 'slain by a cut to the throat,' from the verb *jugulare*, from *jugulum* 'throat' (see JUGULAR).

ju·gum /ˈjo͞ogəm/ ▶ n. (pl. **juga** /-gə/) chiefly Zoology a connecting ridge or projection. ■ Entomology a lobe on the forewing of some moths which interlocks with the hind wing in flight.
– ORIGIN mid 19th cent.: from Latin, literally 'yoke.'

Ju·gur·tha /jo͞oˈgərTHə/ (died 104 BC), joint king of Numidia *c.*118–104. His attacks on his royal partners prompted intervention by Rome and led to the outbreak of the Jugurthine War (112–105). Eventually captured by the Roman general Marius, he was executed in Rome.
– DERIVATIVES **Ju·gur·thine** /-ˈgərTHən/ adj.

juice /jo͞os/ ▶ n. the liquid obtained from or present in fruit or vegetables: *add the juice of a lemon.* ■ a drink made from such a liquid: *a carton of orange juice.* ■ (**juices**) fluid secreted by the body, esp. in the stomach to help digest food. ■ (**juices**) the liquid that comes from meat or other food when cooked. ■ informal electrical energy: *the batteries have run out of juice.* ■ informal gasoline: *he ran out of juice on the last lap.* ■ informal alcoholic drink. ■ (**juices**) a person's vitality or creative faculties: *it saps the creative juices.*
▶ v. [with obj.] **1** extract the juice from (fruit or vegetables): *juice one orange at a time.*
2 (**juice something up**) informal liven something up: *they juiced it up with some love interest.*
3 (as adj. **juiced**) informal drunk.
– DERIVATIVES **juice·less** adj.
– ORIGIN Middle English: via Old French from Latin *jus* 'broth, vegetable juice.'

juic·er /ˈjo͞osər/ ▶ n. **1** an appliance for extracting juice from fruit and vegetables.
2 informal a person who drinks alcoholic beverages excessively.

juic·y /ˈjo͞osē/ ▶ adj. (**juicier, juiciest**) (of food) full of juice; succulent: *a juicy apple* | *a juicy steak.* ■ informal interestingly scandalous: *juicy gossip.* ■ informal temptingly appealing: *the promise of juicy returns.*
– DERIVATIVES **juic·i·ly** /-səlē/ adv., **juic·i·ness** n.

Juil·li·ard /ˈjo͞olēˌärd/, Augustus D. (1840–1919), US merchant and patron of music. In 1920 he founded the Juilliard Musical Foundation, which became the Juilliard School of Music in 1926.

ju·jit·su /jo͞oˈjitso͞o/ (also **jiujitsu** or **jujutsu** /jo͞oˈjət-/) ▶ n. a Japanese system of unarmed combat and physical training. Compare with JUDO.
– ORIGIN Japanese *jūjutsu*, from *jū* 'gentle' + *jutsu* 'skill.'

ju·ju[1] /ˈjo͞oˌjo͞o/ ▶ n. a style of music popular among the Yoruba in Nigeria and characterized by the use of guitars and variable-pitch drums.
– ORIGIN perhaps from Yoruba *jo jo* 'dance.'

ju·ju[2] ▶ n. a charm or fetish, esp. of a type used by some West African peoples. ■ supernatural power attributed to such a charm or fetish: *juju and witchcraft.*
– ORIGIN early 17th cent.: of West African origin, perhaps from French *joujou* 'toy.'

ju·jube /ˈjo͞oˌjo͞ob/ ▶ n. **1** the edible berrylike fruit of a Eurasian plant, formerly taken as a cough cure. ■ a jujube-flavored lozenge or gumdrop.
2 (also **jujube bush**) the shrub or small tree that produces this fruit, native to the warmer regions of Eurasia. ● *Ziziphus jujuba*, family Rhamnaceae.
– ORIGIN late Middle English: from French, or from medieval Latin *jujuba*, based on Greek *zizuphos*.

juke /jo͞ok/ informal ▶ n. **1** short for JUKE JOINT.
2 short for JUKEBOX.
▶ v. [no obj.] **1** dance, esp. to the music of a jukebox: *a middle-aged couple juked to the music.*
2 move in a zigzag fashion: *I juked down an alley.*
– ORIGIN 1930s: related to Gullah *juke* 'disorderly.'

juke·box /ˈjo͞okˌbäks/ ▶ n. a machine that automatically plays a selected musical recording when a coin is inserted. ■ Computing a device that

stores several computer disks in such a way that data can be read from any of them.
– ORIGIN 1930s: from *juke* 'roadhouse' (related to Gullah *juke* 'disorderly') + BOX[1].

juke joint ▶ **n.** a bar featuring music on a jukebox and typically having an area for dancing: *she would slip out of the house with tall country boys . . . going out to good-time, finger popping juke joints.*

ju·ku /ˈjo͝oko͞o/ ▶ **n.** (pl. **same**) (in Japan) a private school or college attended in addition to an ordinary educational institution.
– ORIGIN Japanese.

Jul. ▶ **abbr.** July.

ju·lep /ˈjo͞oləp/ ▶ **n.** a sweet flavored drink made from a sugar syrup, sometimes containing alcohol or medication. ■ short for MINT JULEP.
– ORIGIN late Middle English: from Old French, from medieval Latin *julapium*, via Arabic from Persian *gulāb*, from *gul* 'rose' + *āb* 'water.'

jul·ia /ˈjo͞olyə/ ▶ **n.** an orange and black American butterfly with long narrow forewings, found chiefly in tropical regions. ● *Dryas julia*, subfamily Heliconiinae, family Nymphalidae.

Jul·ian[1] /ˈjo͞olyən, -lēən/ ▶ **adj.** of or associated with Julius Caesar.
– ORIGIN from Latin *Julianus*, from the given name *Julius*.

Jul·ian[2] (*c.*AD 331–363), Roman emperor 360–363; nephew of Constantine; full name *Flavius Claudius Julianus*; known as **the Apostate**. He restored paganism as the state cult in place of Christianity, but this was reversed after his death.

Ju·li·an·a /jo͞olēˈanə, -ˈänə/ (1909–2004), queen of the Netherlands 1948–80; full name *Juliana Louise Emma Marie Wilhelmina*. She was the daughter of Queen Wilhelmina and the mother of Queen Beatrix, in whose favor she abdicated.

Ju·lian Alps an Alpine range in western Slovenia and northeastern Italy. The highest peak is Triglav.

Jul·ian cal·en·dar ▶ **n.** a calendar introduced by the authority of Julius Caesar in 46 BC, in which the year consisted of 365 days, every fourth year having 366 days. It was superseded by the Gregorian calendar though it is still used by some Orthodox Churches. Dates in the Julian calendar are sometimes designated "Old Style."

Jul·ian of Nor·wich (*c.*1342–*c.*1413), English mystic. She is said to have lived as a recluse outside St. Julian's Church in Norwich and is chiefly associated with the *Revelations of Divine Love* (*c.*1393), a description of a series of visions.

Jul·ia set /ˈjo͞olyə/ ▶ **n.** Mathematics a set of complex numbers that do not converge to any limit when a given mapping is repeatedly applied to them. In some cases the result is a connected fractal set.
– ORIGIN 1970s: named after Gaston M. *Julia* (1893–1978), Algerian-born French mathematician.

ju·li·enne /ˌjo͞olēˈen/ ▶ **n.** a portion of food cut into short, thin strips: *a julienne of vegetables* | [as modifier] *julienne leeks.*
▶ **v.** [with obj.] cut (food) into short, thin strips.
– ORIGIN early 18th cent. (originally as an adjective designating soup made of chopped vegetables, esp. carrots): French, from the male given names *Jules* or *Julien*, of obscure development.

Ju·li·et /ˌjo͞olēˈet, ˈjo͞olyət/ ▶ **n.** a code word representing the letter J, used in radio communication.

Ju·li·et bal·co·ny ▶ **n.** a very shallow balcony with a safety railing on an upper story of a building.

Ju·li·et cap ▶ **n.** a type of women's small ornamental cap, typically made of lace or net and often worn by brides.
– ORIGIN early 20th cent.: so named because it forms part of the traditional costume of the heroine of Shakespeare's *Romeo and Juliet*.

Jul·ius Cae·sar /ˈjo͞olyəs/ see CAESAR[1].

Jul·lun·dur /ˈjələndər/ variant spelling of JALANDHAR.

Ju·ly /jo͝oˈlī/ ▶ **n.** (pl. **Julys**) the seventh month of the year, in the northern hemisphere usually considered the second month of summer: *I had a letter from him in July* | [as modifier] *one hot July afternoon in 1981.*
– ORIGIN Middle English: from Latin *Julius* (*mensis*) '(month) of July,' named after Julius Caesar.

ju·mar /ˈjo͞omər, -ˌmär/ Climbing ▶ **n.** a clamp that is attached to a fixed rope and automatically tightens when weight is applied and relaxes when it is removed.
▶ **v.** (**jumars, jumaring, jumared**) [no obj.] climb with the aid of such a clamp.
– ORIGIN 1960s: originally in Swiss use, of unknown origin.

jum·bie /ˈjəmbē/ ▶ **n.** W. Indian a spirit of a dead person, typically an evil one.
– ORIGIN from Kikongo *zumbi* 'fetish.'

jum·bie bird ▶ **n.** W. Indian a bird of ill omen, esp. a pygmy owl. ● *Glaucidium brasilianum*, family Strigidae. Alternative name: **ferruginous pygmy owl**.

jum·ble /ˈjəmbəl/ ▶ **n.** an untidy collection or pile of things: *the books were in a chaotic jumble.* ■ Brit. articles collected for a jumble sale.
▶ **v.** [with obj.] mix up in a confused or untidy way: *a drawer full of letters jumbled together.*
– ORIGIN early 16th cent.: probably symbolic.

jum·ble sale ▶ **n.** Brit. a rummage sale.

jum·bo /ˈjəmbō/ informal ▶ **n.** (pl. **jumbos**) a very large person or thing. ■ (also **jumbo jet**) a very large airliner (originally and specifically a Boeing 747).
▶ **adj.** [attrib.] very large: *a jumbo pad.*
– ORIGIN early 19th cent. (originally of a person): probably the second element of MUMBO JUMBO. Originally denoting a large and clumsy person, the term was popularized as the name of an elephant at London Zoo, sold in 1882 to the Barnum and Bailey circus.

Jum·bo·tron /ˈjəmbōˌträn/ ▶ **n.** trademark a large-screen television designed to accommodate a very large venue, such as a sports stadium.
– ORIGIN 1980s: created as *JumboTron* by the original manufacturer, Sony Corporation.

Jum·na /ˈjəmnə/ a river in northern India that rises in the Himalayas and flows more than 850 miles (1,370 km) in a large arc south and southeast, through Delhi, before joining the Ganges River below Allahabad. Its source (Yamunotri River) and its confluence with the Ganges River are both Hindu holy places. Hindi name YAMUNA.

jump /jəmp/ ▶ **v. 1** [no obj.] push oneself off a surface and into the air by using the muscles in one's legs and feet: *the cat jumped off his lap* | *he jumped twenty-five feet to the ground.* ■ [with obj.] pass over (an obstacle or barrier) in such a way. ■ [with adverbial] (of an athlete or horse) perform in a competition involving such action: *his horse jumped well and won by five lengths.* ■ (esp. of prices or figures) rise suddenly and by a large amount: *exports jumped by 500 percent during the decade.* ■ informal (of a place) be full of lively activity: *the bar is jumping on Fridays and Saturdays.* ■ [with obj.] informal (of driver or a vehicle) fail to stop at (a red traffic light). ■ [with obj.] get on or off (a train or other vehicle) quickly, typically illegally or dangerously. ■ [with obj.] take summary possession of (a mining concession or other piece of land) after alleged abandonment or forfeiture by the former occupant.
2 [no obj.] (of a person) move suddenly and quickly in a specified way: *Juliet jumped to her feet* | *they jumped back into the car and drove off.* ■ (of a person) make a sudden involuntary movement in reaction to something that causes surprise or shock: *an owl hooted nearby, making her jump.* ■ pass quickly or abruptly from one idea, subject, or state to another: *she jumped backward and forward in her narrative.* ■ [with obj.] omit or skip over (part of something) and pass on to a further point or stage. ■ (of a machine or device) move or jerk suddenly and abruptly: *the vibration can cause the needle to jump.* ■ (of a person) make a sudden, impulsive rush to do something: *Gordon jumped to my defense.* ■ [with obj.] (in checkers) capture (an opponent's piece) by jumping over it. ■ Bridge make a bid that is higher than necessary, in order to signal a strong hand: *East jumped to four spades.* ■ [with obj.] informal attack (someone) suddenly and unexpectedly. ■ [with obj.] vulgar slang have sexual intercourse with (someone).
3 [with obj.] informal start (a vehicle) using jumper cables: *I jumped his Camry from my Civic.*
▶ **n. 1** an act of jumping from a surface by pushing upward with one's legs and feet: *in making the short jump across the gully he lost his balance.* ■ an obstacle to be jumped, esp. by a horse and rider in an equestrian competition. ■ an act of descending from an aircraft by parachute. ■ a sudden dramatic rise in amount, price, or value: *a 51 percent jump in annual profits.* ■ a large or sudden transition or change: *the jump from mass-market to luxury goods.* ■ (in checkers) the act of capturing an opponent's piece by jumping over it. ■ Bridge a bid that is higher than necessary, signaling strength. ■ vulgar slang, dated an act of sexual intercourse.
2 a sudden involuntary movement caused by shock or surprise: *I woke up with a jump.* ■ (**the jumps**) informal extreme nervousness or anxiety.
– PHRASES **be jumping up and down** informal be very angry, upset, or excited. **get** (or **have**) **the jump on someone** informal get (or have) an advantage over someone as a result of one's prompt action. **jump bail** see BAIL[1]. **jump someone's bones** vulgar slang have sexual intercourse with someone. **jump down someone's throat** informal respond to what someone has said in a sudden and angrily critical way. **jump for joy** be ecstatically happy: *I'm not exactly jumping for joy at the prospect.* **jump the gun** see GUN. **jump into bed with** informal engage readily in sexual intercourse with. **jump in with both feet** get started enthusiastically. **jump on the bandwagon** see BANDWAGON. **jump out of one's skin** informal be extremely startled. **jump the queue** Brit. cut in line. **jump the shark** informal (of a television series or movie) reach a point at which far-fetched events are included merely for the sake of novelty, indicative of a decline in quality. [an allusion to the television series *Happy Days*, in which a central character (the Fonz) jumps over a shark in a waterskiing stunt.] **jump ship** (of a sailor) leave the ship on which one is serving without having obtained permission to do so: *he jumped ship in Cape Town* | figurative *three producers jumped ship two weeks after the show's debut.* **jump through hoops** go through an elaborate or complicated procedure in order to achieve an objective. **jump** (or **leap**) **to conclusions** (or **the conclusion**) form an opinion hastily, before one has learned or considered all the facts. **jump to it!** informal used to exhort someone to prompt or immediate action. **jump the track** (of a train) become derailed. **one jump ahead** one step or stage ahead of someone else and so having the advantage over them: *the Americans were **one jump ahead** of the British in this.*
– PHRASAL VERBS **jump at** accept (an opportunity or offer) eagerly: *he **jumped at** the chance to start his own company.* **jump off** (of a military campaign) begin: *the air-attack phase will continue before the ground attack jumps off.* **jump on** informal attack or take hold of (someone) suddenly. ■ criticize (someone) suddenly and severely. ■ seize on (something) eagerly; give sudden (typically critical) attention to: *the paper jumped on the inconsistencies of his stories.* **jump out** have a strong visual or mental impact; be very striking: *advertising posters that really **jump out** at you.*
– DERIVATIVES **jump·a·ble** **adj.**
– ORIGIN early 16th cent. (in the sense 'be moved or thrown with a sudden jerk'): probably imitative of the sound of feet coming into contact with the ground.

jump ball ▶ **n.** Basketball a ball put in play by the referee, who throws it up between two opposing players.

jump blues ▶ **n.** a style of popular music combining elements of swing and blues.

jump cut ▶ **n.** (in film or television) an abrupt transition from one scene to another.
▶ **v.** (**jump-cut**) [no obj.] make such a transition.

jumped-up ▶ **adj.** informal, chiefly Brit. denoting someone who considers themselves to be more important than they really are, or who has suddenly and undeservedly risen in status: *she's not really a journalist, more a jumped-up PR woman.*

jump·er[1] /ˈjəmpər/ ▶ **n. 1** a collarless sleeveless dress, typically worn over a blouse. **2** Brit. a sweater. **3** historical a loose outer jacket worn by sailors.
– ORIGIN mid 19th cent. (sense 3): probably from dialect *jump* 'short coat,' perhaps from Scots *jupe* 'a man's (later also a woman's) loose jacket or tunic,' via Old French from Arabic *jubba*. Compare with JIBBA.

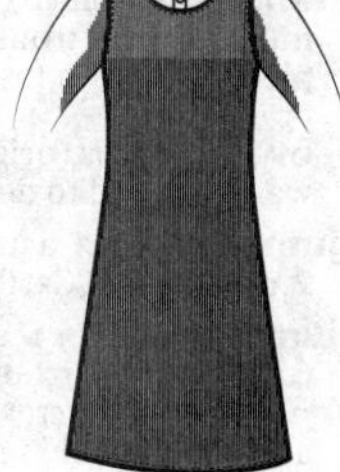
jumper[1] 1

jump·er[2] ▶ **n. 1** a person or animal that jumps.
2 (also **jumper wire**) a short wire used to complete an electric circuit or bypass a break in a circuit.
3 Basketball another term for JUMP SHOT.
4 Nautical a rope made fast to keep a yard or mast from jumping.
5 a heavy chisel-ended steel bar for drilling blast holes.

jump·er ca·ble ▶ **n.** each of a pair of thick electric cables fitted with clips at either end, used for starting a vehicle by connecting its dead battery to the battery of another vehicle.

jump·ing bean ▶ **n.** a plant seed that jumps as a result of the movement of a moth larva that is developing inside it. ● Affected seeds are found in several plants of the family Euphorbiaceae, in particular the Mexican plant *Sebastiana pavoniana*,

PRONUNCIATION KEY ə *ago, up*; ər *over, fur*; a *hat*; ā *ate*; ä *car*; e *let*; ē *see*; i *fit*; ī *by*; NG *sing*; ō *go*; ô *law, for*; oi *toy*; o͝o *good*; o͞o *goo*; ou *out*; TH *thin*; T͟H *then*; ZH *vision*

j

the seeds of which can contain larvae of the moth *Cydia saltitans*.

jump·ing gene ▶ n. informal term for TRANSPOSON.

jump·ing jack ▶ n. 1 a calisthenic jump done from a standing position with legs together and arms at the sides to a position with the legs apart and the arms over the head.
2 a toy figure of a man, with movable limbs.

jump·ing Je·hosh·a·phat ▶ exclam. see JEHOSHAPHAT.

jump·ing mouse ▶ n. a mouselike rodent that has long back feet and typically moves in short hops, found in North America and China. ● Family Zapodidae: three genera, in particular *Zapus*, and several species.

jump·ing-off place (also **jumping-off point**) ▶ n. the point from which something is begun.

jump·ing spi·der ▶ n. a large-eyed spider that hunts prey by stalking and pouncing on it. ● Family Salticidae, order Araneae.

jump in·struc·tion ▶ n. Computing an instruction in a computer program that causes processing to move to a different place in the program sequence.

jump jet ▶ n. a jet aircraft that can take off and land vertically, without need of a runway.

jump lead /lēd/ ▶ n. British term for JUMPER CABLE.

jump-off ▶ n. a deciding round in a show-jumping competition.

jump ring ▶ n. a wire ring made by bringing the two ends together without soldering or welding.

jump rope ▶ n. (also **jumprope**) a length of rope used for jumping by swinging it over the head and under the feet.
▶ v. [no obj.] play or exercise using a jump rope.

jump seat ▶ n. an extra seat, esp. in a car or taxicab, that folds back when not in use.

jump shift ▶ n. Bridge a bid that is both in a different suit from that bid by oneself or one's partner and at a higher level than necessary, typically indicating a strong hand.

jump shot ▶ n. 1 Basketball a shot made while jumping.
2 Billiards a shot in which the cue ball is made to jump over another ball.
– DERIVATIVES **jump shoot·er** n.

jump-start ▶ v. [with obj.] start (a car with a dead battery) with jumper cables or by a sudden release of the clutch while it is being pushed. ■ give an added impetus to (something that is proceeding slowly or is at a standstill): *she suggests ways to jump-start the sluggish educational system.*
▶ n. an act of starting a car in such a way. ■ an added impetus.

jump·sta·tion /ˈjəmp ˌstāsHən/ ▶ n. Computing a site on the World Wide Web containing a collection of hypertext links, usually to pages on a particular topic.

jump·suit /ˈjəm(p)ˌso͞ot/ ▶ n. a garment incorporating trousers and a sleeved top in one piece, worn as a fashion item, protective garment, or uniform.
– ORIGIN 1940s (originally US): so named because it was first used to denote a parachutist's garment.

jump-up ▶ n. 1 a jump in an upward direction.
2 an informal Caribbean dance or celebration.

jump·y /ˈjəmpē/ ▶ adj. (**jumpier**, **jumpiest**) informal (of a person) anxious and uneasy: *he was tired and jumpy.* ■ characterized by abrupt stops and starts or an irregular course: *a jumpy pulse.*
– DERIVATIVES **jump·i·ly** /-pəlē/ adv., **jump·i·ness** n.

jun /CHən/ ▶ n. (pl. **same**) a monetary unit of North Korea, equal to one hundredth of a won.
– ORIGIN Korean.

Jun. ▶ abbr. ■ June. ■ Junior (in names): *John Smith Jun.*

Junc. ▶ abbr. Junction.

jun·co /ˈjəNGkō/ ▶ n. (pl. **juncos**) a North American songbird related to the buntings, with mainly gray and brown plumage. See also SNOWBIRD. ● Genus *Junco*, family Emberizidae (subfamily Emberizinae): three or four species.
– ORIGIN early 18th cent.: from Spanish, from Latin *juncus* 'rush, reed.'

junc·tion /ˈjəNGksHən/ ▶ n. 1 a point where two or more things are joined: *the junction of the two rivers.* ■ a place where two or more roads or railroad lines meet.
2 Electronics a region of transition in a semiconductor between a part where conduction is mainly by electrons and a part where it is mainly by holes.
3 the action or fact of joining or being joined.
– DERIVATIVES **junc·tion·al** /-sHənl/ adj.
– ORIGIN early 18th cent. (sense 3): from Latin *junctio(n-)*, from *jungere* 'to join.'

junc·tion box ▶ n. a box containing a junction of electric wires or cables.

junc·ture /ˈjəNGkCHər/ ▶ n. a particular point in events or time: *it is difficult to say at this juncture whether this upturn can be sustained.* ■ a place where things join: *the plane crashed at the juncture of two mountains.* ■ Phonetics the set of features in speech that enable a hearer to detect a word or phrase boundary, e.g., distinguishing *I scream* from *ice cream*.
– ORIGIN late Middle English (in the sense 'act of joining'): from Latin *junctura* 'joint,' from *jungere* 'to join.'

June /jo͞on/ ▶ n. the sixth month of the year, in the northern hemisphere usually considered the first month of summer: *the roses flower in June* | [as modifier] *a June afternoon.*
– ORIGIN Middle English: from Old French *juin*, from Latin *Junius (mensis)* '(month) of June,' variant of *Junonius* 'sacred to Juno.'

Ju·neau /ˈjo͞onō/ the capital of Alaska, a seaport on an inlet of the Pacific Ocean, in the southern part of the state; pop. 30,988 (est. 2008).
– ORIGIN named after Joseph *Juneau*, who discovered gold there in 1880.

june·ber·ry /ˈjo͞onˌberē/ (also **Juneberry**) ▶ n. (pl. **juneberries**) a North American shrub of the rose family, some kinds of which are grown for their showy white flowers and bright autumn colors. ● Genus *Amelanchier*, family Rosaceae: many species, including the **smooth juneberry** (*A. laevis*) and the **inland juneberry** (*A. interior*). ■ the black edible berry of this plant.

June bug (also **June beetle**) ▶ n. a large brown scarab beetle that appears in late spring and early summer. Also called MAY BEETLE. ● Genus *Phyllophaga*, family Scarabaeidae: several species, esp. the **northern June bug** (*P. fusca*).

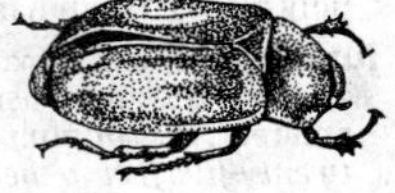
northern June bug

June·teenth /ˌjo͞onˈtēnTH/ ▶ n. a festival held annually on the nineteenth of June by African Americans (esp. in the southern states), to commemorate emancipation from slavery in Texas on that day in 1865.
– ORIGIN 1930s: blend of *June* and *(nine)teenth*.

June War Arab name for SIX DAY WAR.

Jung /yo͝oNG/, Carl (Gustav) (1875–1961), Swiss psychologist. He originated the concept of introvert and extrovert personality and of the four psychological functions of sensation, intuition, thinking, and feeling.
– DERIVATIVES **Jung·i·an** /ˈyo͝oNGgēən/ adj. & n.

jun·gle /ˈjəNGgəl/ ▶ n. 1 an area of land overgrown with dense forest and tangled vegetation, typically in the tropics: *we set off into the jungle* | *the lakes are hidden in dense jungle.* ■ a wild tangled mass of vegetation or other things: *the garden was a jungle of bluebells.* ■ a situation or place of bewildering complexity or brutal competitiveness: *it's a jungle out there.* ■ (also **hobo jungle**) informal a hobo camp.
2 (also **jungle music**) a style of dance music incorporating elements of ragga, hip-hop, and hard core and consisting almost exclusively of very fast electronic drum tracks and slower synthesized bass lines, originating in Britain in the early 1990s. Compare with DRUM AND BASS.
– PHRASES **the law of the jungle** the principle that those who are strong and apply ruthless self-interest will be most successful.
– DERIVATIVES **jun·gled** adj., **jun·gly** adj.
– ORIGIN late 18th cent.: via Hindi from Sanskrit *jāṅgala* 'rough and arid (terrain).'

jun·gle cat ▶ n. a small wildcat that has a yellowish or grayish coat with dark markings on the legs and tail, living in dry forests from Egypt to Southeast Asia. ● *Felis chaus*, family Felidae.

jun·gle fe·ver ▶ n. a severe form of malaria.

jun·gle fowl ▶ n. (pl. **same**) a southern Asian game bird related to the domestic fowl, typically frequenting forested country. ● Genus *Gallus*, family Phasianidae: four species, in particular the **red jungle fowl** (*G. gallus*), which is the ancestor of the domestic fowl.

jun·gle gym ▶ n. a structure of joined bars or logs for children to climb on.
– ORIGIN 1920s: formerly a US trademark.

jun·gle juice ▶ n. informal powerful or roughly prepared alcoholic liquor.

jun·glist ▶ n. a performer or enthusiast of jungle music.
▶ adj. of or relating to jungle music: *he's at the forefront of junglist innovation.*

jun·ior /ˈjo͞onyər/ ▶ adj. 1 of, for, or denoting young or younger people: *junior tennis.* ■ of or for students in the third year of a course lasting four years in college or high school: *his junior year in college.* ■ (often **Junior**) [postpositive in names] denoting the younger of two who have the same name in a family, esp. a son as distinct from his father: *John F. Kennedy Junior.* ■ Brit. of, for, or denoting schoolchildren between the ages of 7 and 11.
2 low or lower in rank or status: *Virginia's junior senator* | *part of my function is to supervise those junior to me.*
▶ n. 1 a person who is a specified number of years younger than someone else: *he's five years her junior.* ■ a student in the third year of college or high school. ■ (in sports) a young competitor, typically under sixteen or eighteen. ■ informal used as a nickname or form of address for one's son.
2 a person with low rank or status compared with others.
3 a size of clothing for teenagers or slender women.
– DERIVATIVES **jun·ior·i·ty** /jo͞onˈyôritē, -ˈyär-/ n.
– ORIGIN Middle English (as an adjective following a family name): from Latin, comparative of *juvenis* 'young.'

jun·ior bar·ris·ter ▶ n. (in the UK) a barrister who has not taken silk, i.e., is not a Queen's (or King's) Counsel.

jun·ior col·lege ▶ n. a college offering courses for two years beyond high school, either as a complete training or in preparation for completion at a four-year college.

jun·ior com·mon room ▶ n. Brit. a room used for social purposes by the undergraduates of a college.

jun·ior high school ▶ n. another term for MIDDLE SCHOOL.

jun·ior light·weight ▶ n. a weight in professional boxing of 125–130 pounds (57.1–59 kg). ■ a professional boxer of this weight.

jun·ior mid·dle·weight ▶ n. a weight in professional boxing of 146–154 pounds (66.7–69.8 kg). ■ a professional boxer of this weight.

jun·ior school ▶ n. Brit. a school for children aged between about 7 and 11.

jun·ior wel·ter·weight ▶ n. a weight in professional boxing of 135–140 pounds (61.2–63.5 kg). ■ a professional boxer of this weight.

ju·ni·per /ˈjo͞onəpər/ ▶ n. an evergreen shrub or small tree that bears berrylike cones, widely distributed throughout Eurasia and North America. Many kinds have aromatic cones or foliage. ● Genus *Juniperus*, family Cupressaceae: many species, including the shrubby **common juniper** (*J. communis*), the berries of which are used for flavoring gin.
– ORIGIN late Middle English: from Latin *juniperus*.

junk[1] /jəNGk/ ▶ n. 1 informal old or discarded articles that are considered useless or of little value. ■ worthless writing, talk, or ideas: *I can't write this kind of junk.* ■ Finance junk bonds.
2 informal heroin.
3 the lump of oily fibrous tissue in a sperm whale's head, containing spermaceti.
▶ v. [with obj.] informal discard or abandon unceremoniously: *sort out what could be sold off and junk the rest.*
– ORIGIN late Middle English (denoting an old or inferior rope): of unknown origin. Sense 1 of the noun dates from the mid 19th cent.

junk[2] ▶ n. a flat-bottomed sailing vessel typical in China and the East Indies, with a prominent stem, a high stern, and lugsails.
– ORIGIN mid 16th cent.: from obsolete French *juncque* or Portuguese *junco*, from Malay *jong*, reinforced by Dutch *jonk*.

junk[2]

Junk·a·noo /ˈjəNGkəˌno͞o/ ▶ n. (chiefly in Jamaica, Belize, and the Bahamas) a masquerade held at Christmas, consisting of a street procession of characters in traditional costumes and dancing to drums, bells, and whistles.

junk bond ▶ n. a high-yield, high-risk security, typically issued by a company seeking to raise capital quickly in order to finance a takeover.

junk DNA ▶ **n.** genomic DNA that does not encode proteins, and whose function, if it has one, is not well understood.

Jun·ker /ˈyo͝oNGkər/ (also **junker**) ▶ **n.** historical a German nobleman or aristocrat, esp. a member of the Prussian aristocracy.
– DERIVATIVES **jun·ker·dom** /-dəm/ **n.**, **jun·ker·ism** /-ˌizəm/ **n.**
– ORIGIN German, earlier *Junkher*, from Middle High German *junc* 'young' + *herre* 'lord.'

jun·ket /ˈjəNGkit/ ▶ **n. 1** a dish of sweetened and flavored curds of milk, often served with fruit. **2** informal an extravagant trip or celebration, in particular one enjoyed by a government official at public expense.
▶ **v.** (**junkets, junketing, junketed**) [no obj.] (often as noun **junketing**) informal attend or go on such a trip or celebration.
– DERIVATIVES **jun·ke·teer** /ˌjəNGkiˈti(ə)r/ **n.**
– ORIGIN late Middle English: from Old French *jonquette* 'rush basket,' from *jonc* 'rush,' from Latin *juncus*. Originally denoting a rush basket, esp. one for fish (remaining in dialect use), the term also denoted a cream cheese, formerly made in a rush basket or served on a rush mat. A later extended sense, 'feast, merrymaking,' gave rise to sense 2 of the noun.

junk food ▶ **n.** food that has low nutritional value, typically produced in the form of packaged snacks needing little or no preparation.

junk·ie /ˈjəNGkē/ (also **junky**) ▶ **n.** informal a drug addict. ■ [with modifier] a person with a compulsive habit or obsessive dependency on something: *power junkies*.
– ORIGIN 1920s (originally US): from **JUNK**[1].

junk mail ▶ **n.** informal unsolicited advertising or promotional material received through the mail and e-mail.

junk sci·ence ▶ **n.** untested or unproven theories when presented as scientific fact, esp. in a court of law.

junk shop ▶ **n.** informal a shop selling secondhand goods or inexpensive antiques.

junk·y /ˈjəNGkē/ informal ▶ **adj.** useless or of little value.
▶ **n.** (pl. **junkies**) variant spelling of **JUNKIE**.

junk·yard /ˈjəNGkˌyärd/ ▶ **n.** a place where scrap is collected before being discarded, reused, or recycled.

Ju·no /ˈjo͞oˌnō/ **1** Roman Mythology the most important goddess of the Roman state, wife of Jupiter. She was originally an ancient Italian goddess. Greek equivalent **HERA**.
2 Astronomy asteroid 3, discovered in 1804 (diameter 244 km).

Ju·no·esque /ˌjo͞onōˈesk/ ▶ **adj.** (of a woman) imposingly tall and shapely.
– ORIGIN mid 19th cent.: from **JUNO** + **-ESQUE**.

Junr ▶ **abbr.** Junior (in names).

jun·ta /ˈho͝ontə, ˈjəntə/ ▶ **n. 1** a military or political group that rules a country after taking power by force: *the country's ruling military junta*.
2 historical a deliberative or administrative council in Spain or Portugal.
– ORIGIN early 17th cent. (sense 2): from Spanish and Portuguese, from Latin *juncta*, feminine past participle of *jungere* 'to join.'

jun·to /ˈjəntō/ ▶ **n.** (pl. **juntos**) historical a political grouping or faction, esp. in 17th- and 18th-century Britain.
– ORIGIN alteration of **JUNTA**, on the pattern of Spanish nouns ending in *-o*.

Ju·pi·ter /ˈjo͞opitər/ **1** Roman Mythology the chief god of the Roman state religion, originally a sky god associated with thunder and lightning. His wife was Juno. Also called **JOVE**. Greek equivalent **ZEUS**. [Latin, from *Jovis pater*, literally 'Father Jove.']
2 Astronomy the largest planet in the solar system, a gas giant that is the fifth in order from the sun and one of the brightest objects in the night sky.

> Jupiter orbits between Mars and Saturn at an average distance of 484 million miles (778 million km) from the sun. Although it has an equatorial diameter of 88,846 miles (142,984 km), the planet rotates in less than ten hours. Its upper atmosphere consists mainly of hydrogen with swirling clouds of ammonia and methane, with a circulation system that results in a number of distinct latitudinal bands. There are at least sixteen satellites, four of which (the Galilean moons) are visible through binoculars, and a faint ring system.

Ju·ra[1] /ˈjo͝orə, ZHYˈrä/ a system of mountain ranges on the border of France and Switzerland. It has given its name to the Jurassic period, when most of its rocks were laid down.

Jura[2] an island of the Inner Hebrides, north of Islay and south of Mull, separated from the west coast of Scotland by the Sound of Jura.

ju·ral /ˈjo͝orəl/ ▶ **adj.** formal of or relating to the law. ■ Philosophy of or relating to rights and obligations.
– ORIGIN mid 17th cent.: from Latin *jus, jur-* 'law, right' + **-AL**.

Ju·ras·sic /jəˈrasik/ ▶ **adj.** Geology of, relating to, or denoting the second period of the Mesozoic era, between the Triassic and Cretaceous periods. ■ (as noun **the Jurassic**) the Jurassic period or the system of rocks deposited during it.

> The Jurassic lasted from about 208 million to 146 million years ago. Large reptiles, including the largest known dinosaurs, were dominant on both land and sea. Ammonites were abundant, and the first birds (including Archaeopteryx) appeared.

– ORIGIN mid 19th cent.: from French *jurassique*; named after the *Jura* Mountains (see **JURA**[1]).

ju·rat /ˈjo͝orat/ ▶ **n.** Law **1** chiefly historical a person who has taken an oath or who performs a duty on oath, e.g., a juror.
2 a statement on an affidavit of when, where, and before whom it was sworn.
– ORIGIN late Middle English: based on Latin *juratus* 'sworn,' past participle of *jurare*.

ju·rid·i·cal /jo͞oˈridikəl/ ▶ **adj.** Law of or relating to judicial proceedings and the administration of the law.
– DERIVATIVES **ju·rid·i·cal·ly** **adv.**
– ORIGIN early 16th cent.: from Latin *juridicus* (from *jus, jur-* 'law' + *dicere* 'say') + **-AL**.

ju·ris·con·sult /ˌjo͝orisˈkänˌsəlt, -kənˈsəlt/ ▶ **n.** Law, chiefly historical an expert on law.
– ORIGIN early 17th cent.: from Latin *jurisconsultus*, from *jus, jur-* 'law' + *consultus* 'skilled' (from *consulere* 'take counsel').

ju·ris·dic·tion /ˌjo͝orisˈdikSHən/ ▶ **n.** the official power to make legal decisions and judgments: *federal courts had no* ***jurisdiction over*** *the case* | *the District of Columbia was placed under the* ***jurisdiction of*** *Congress*. ■ the extent of this power: *the claim will be* ***within the jurisdiction*** *of the industrial tribunal*. ■ a system of law courts; a judicature: *in some jurisdictions there is a mandatory death sentence for murder*. ■ the territory or sphere of activity over which the legal authority of a court or other institution extends: *several different tax jurisdictions*.
– DERIVATIVES **ju·ris·dic·tion·al** **adj.**
– ORIGIN Middle English: from Old French *juredicion*, from Latin *jurisdictio(n-)*, from *jus, jur-* 'law' + *dictio* 'saying' (from *dicere* 'say').

ju·ris doc·tor /ˈjo͝oris ˈdäktər/ ▶ **n.** Law see **JD**.

ju·ris·pru·dence /ˌjo͝orisˈpro͞odns/ ▶ **n.** the theory or philosophy of law. ■ a legal system: *American jurisprudence*.
– DERIVATIVES **ju·ris·pru·dent** **adj.** & **n.**, **ju·ris·pru·den·tial** /-pro͞oˈdenCHəl/ **adj.**
– ORIGIN early 17th cent.: from late Latin *jurisprudentia*, from Latin *jus, jur-* 'law' + *prudentia* 'knowledge.'

ju·rist /ˈjo͝orist/ ▶ **n.** an expert in or writer on law. ■ a lawyer or a judge.
– DERIVATIVES **ju·ris·tic** /jo͞oˈristik/ **adj.**
– ORIGIN late 15th cent. (in the sense 'lawyer'): from French *juriste*, medieval Latin *jurista*, from *jus, jur-* 'law.'

ju·ror /ˈjo͝orər, -ôr/ ▶ **n.** a member of a jury. ■ historical a person taking an oath, esp. one of allegiance. Compare with **NONJUROR**.
– ORIGIN late Middle English: from Old French *jureor*, from Latin *jurator*, from *jurare* 'swear,' from *jus, jur-* 'law.'

Ju·ruá Riv·er /ˌZHo͞oro͞oˈä/ a river that flows for 1,500 miles (2,400 km) from eastern Peru through northwestern Brazil into the Amazon River.

ju·ry[1] /ˈjo͝orē/ ▶ **n.** (pl. **juries**) a body of people (typically twelve in number) sworn to give a verdict in a legal case on the basis of evidence submitted to them in court: *the jury returned unanimous guilty verdicts*. ■ a body of people selected to judge a competition.
▶ **v.** (**juries, juried**) [with obj.] (usu. **be juried**) judge (an art or craft exhibition or exhibit): *the exhibition was juried by a tapestry artist* | (as adj. **juried**) *the juried show*.
– PHRASES **the jury is still out** a decision has not yet been reached on a controversial subject: *the jury is still out on whether self-regulation by doctors is adequate*.
– ORIGIN late Middle English: from Old French *juree* 'oath, inquiry,' from Latin *jurata*, feminine past participle of *jurare* 'swear' (see **JUROR**).

ju·ry[2] ▶ **adj.** [attrib.] Nautical (of a mast or other fitting) improvised or temporary: *we need to get that jury rudder fixed*.
– ORIGIN early 19th cent.: independent usage of the first element of early 17th-cent. *jury-mast* 'temporary mast,' of uncertain origin (compare with **JURY-RIGGED**).

ju·ry box ▶ **n.** a segregated area in which the jury sits in a court of law.

ju·ry-rigged ▶ **adj.** (of a ship) having temporary makeshift rigging. ■ makeshift; improvised: *jury-rigged classrooms in gymnasiums*.
– DERIVATIVES **ju·ry-rig** **v.**
– ORIGIN late 18th cent.: *jury* perhaps based on Old French *ajurie* 'aid.'

jus /ZHo͞o(s), jo͞os/ ▶ **n.** (esp. in French cuisine) a thin gravy or sauce made from meat juices: *chicken with a rich game jus*.
– ORIGIN French.

jus co·gens /ˈjəs ˈkōjənz/ ▶ **n.** Law the principles that form the norms of international law that cannot be set aside.
– ORIGIN Latin, literally 'compelling law.'

jus gen·ti·um /ˈjəs ˈjenSHēəm/ ▶ **n.** Law international law.
– ORIGIN Latin, literally 'law of nations.'

Jus·sieu /jo͞oˈSHo͞o/, Antoine Laurent de (1748–1836), French botanist. He developed the system on which modern plant classification is based.

jus·sive /ˈjəsiv/ ▶ **adj.** Grammar (of a form of a verb) expressing a command.
– ORIGIN mid 19th cent.: from Latin *juss-* 'commanded' (from the verb *jubere*) + **-IVE**.

just /jəst/ ▶ **adj.** based on or behaving according to what is morally right and fair: *a just and democratic society* | *fighting for a just cause*. ■ (of treatment) deserved or appropriate in the circumstances: *we all get our just deserts*. ■ (of an opinion or appraisal) well founded; justifiable: *these simplistic approaches have been the subject of just criticism*.
▶ **adv. 1** exactly: *that's just what I need* | *you're a human being, just like everyone else* | *conditions were* ***just as*** *bad* | *you can have it, but* ***not just yet***. ■ exactly or almost exactly at this or that moment: *she's just coming* | *we were just finishing breakfast*.
2 very recently; in the immediate past: *I've just seen the local paper*.
3 barely; by a little: *I got here* ***just after*** *nine* | *inflation fell to* ***just over*** *4 percent* | *I* ***only just*** *caught the train*.
4 simply; only; no more than: *they were just interested in making money*. ■ really; absolutely (used for emphasis): *they're just great*. ■ used as a polite formula for giving permission or making a request: *just help yourselves*. ■ [with modal] possibly (used to indicate a slight chance of something happening or being true): *it might just help*.
5 Brit. expressing agreement: *"Simon really messed things up." "Didn't he just?"*
– PHRASES **just about** informal almost exactly; nearly: *he can do just about anything*. **just as well** a good or fortunate thing: *it was just as well I didn't know at the time*. **just in case** as a precaution. **just a minute, moment, second, etc.** used to ask someone to wait or pause for a short time. ■ used to interrupt someone, esp. in protest or disagreement. **just now 1** at this moment: *it's pretty hectic just now*. **2** a little time ago: *she was talking to me just now*. **just on** Brit. (with reference to time and numbers) exactly: *it was just on midnight*. **just the same** nevertheless: *I put on my raincoat and big straw hat. But we got soaked just the same*. **just so 1** arranged or done very neatly and carefully: *polishing the furniture and making everything just so*. **2** Brit. formal used to express agreement.
– DERIVATIVES **just·ness** **n.**
– ORIGIN late Middle English: via Old French from Latin *justus*, from *jus* 'law, right.'

juste mi·lieu /ˈZHYst mēˈlyə/ ▶ **n.** the happy medium; judicious moderation.
– ORIGIN French, literally 'correct mean.'

jus·tice /ˈjəstis/ ▶ **n. 1** just behavior or treatment: *a concern for justice, peace, and genuine respect for people*. ■ the quality of being fair and reasonable: *the justice of his case*. ■ the administration of the law or authority in maintaining this: *a tragic miscarriage of justice*. ■ (**Justice**) the personification of justice, usually a blindfolded woman holding scales and a sword.
2 a judge or magistrate, in particular a judge of the supreme court of a country or state.
– PHRASES **bring someone to justice** arrest someone for a crime and ensure that they are tried in court. **do oneself justice** perform as well as one is able to. **do someone/something justice** (or **do justice to**

someone/something) do, treat, or represent with due fairness or appreciation: *the brief menu does not do justice to the food.* **in justice to** out of fairness to: *I say this in justice to both of you.* **rough justice** see ROUGH.
– DERIVATIVES **jus·tice·ship** /-,sHip/ **n.** (sense 2).
– ORIGIN late Old English *iustise* 'administration of the law,' via Old French from Latin *justitia*, from *justus* (see JUST).

jus·tice of the peace ▶ **n.** a magistrate appointed to hear minor cases, perform marriages, grant licenses, etc., in a town, county, or other local district.

jus·ti·ci·a·ble /jə'stisH(ē)əbəl/ ▶ **adj.** Law (of a state or action) subject to trial in a court of law.
– DERIVATIVES **jus·ti·ci·a·bil·i·ty n.**
– ORIGIN late Middle English: from Old French, from *justicier* 'bring to trial,' from medieval Latin *justitiare*, from Latin *justitia* 'equity,' from *justus* (see JUST).

jus·ti·ci·ar /jə'stisH(ē)ər/ ▶ **n.** historical an administrator of justice, in particular: ■ a regent and deputy presiding over the court of a Norman or early Plantagenet king of England. ■ either of two supreme judges in medieval Scotland.
– ORIGIN late 15th cent.: from medieval Latin *justitiarius* (see JUSTICIARY).

jus·ti·ci·ar·y /jə'stisHē,erē/ ▶ **n.** (pl. **justiciaries**) the administration of justice: [as modifier] *justiciary cases.* ■ chiefly Scottish an administrator of justice.
– ORIGIN mid 16th cent.: from medieval Latin *justitiarius*, from Latin *justitia*, from *justus* (see JUST).

jus·ti·fi·a·ble /'jəstə,fīəbəl, ,jəstə'fī-/ ▶ **adj.** able to be shown to be right or reasonable; defensible: *it is not financially justifiable | their justifiable fears.*
– DERIVATIVES **jus·ti·fi·a·bil·i·ty** /,jəstə,fīə'bilitē/ **n.**, **jus·ti·fi·a·ble·ness n.**, **jus·ti·fi·a·bly** /-blē/ **adv.** *he was justifiably angry.*
– ORIGIN early 16th cent. (in the sense 'justiciable'): from French, from *justifier* 'to justify.'

jus·ti·fi·a·ble hom·i·cide ▶ **n.** the killing of a person in circumstances that allow the act to be regarded in law as without criminal guilt.

jus·ti·fi·ca·tion /,jəstəfi'kāsHən/ ▶ **n. 1** the action of showing something to be right or reasonable: *the justification of revolutionary action | he made a speech in justification of his career.* ■ good reason for something that exists or has been done: *there is no justification for an increase in charges | all these incidents were used again as a justification for my dismissal.*
2 Theology the action of declaring or making righteous in the sight of God.
3 Printing the action or manner of justifying a line of type or piece of text.

jus·ti·fied /'jəstə,fīd/ ▶ **adj. 1** having, done for, or marked by a good or legitimate reason: *the doctors were justified in treating her.*
2 Theology declared or made righteous in the sight of God.
3 Printing having been adjusted so that the print fills a space evenly or forms a straight line at one or both margins: [in combination] *the text is left-justified.*

jus·ti·fy /'jəstə,fī/ ▶ **v.** (**justifies, justifying, justified**) [with obj.] **1** show or prove to be right or reasonable: *the person appointed has fully justified our confidence.* ■ be a good reason for: *the situation was grave enough to justify further investigation.*
2 Theology declare or make righteous in the sight of God.
3 Printing adjust (a line of type or piece of text) so that the print fills a space evenly or forms a straight edge at one or both margins.
– DERIVATIVES **jus·tif·i·ca·to·ry** /jə'stifəkə,tôrē, ,jəstəfi'kātôrē/ **adj.**, **jus·ti·fi·er n.**
– ORIGIN Middle English (in the senses 'administer justice to' and 'inflict a judicial penalty on'): from Old French *justifier*, from Christian Latin *justificare* 'do justice to,' from Latin *justus* (see JUST).

Jus·tin, St. /'jəstən/ (*c.*100–165), Christian philosopher; known as **St. Justin the Martyr**. According to tradition, he was martyred in Rome together with some of his followers. He is remembered for his *Apologia* (*c.*150). Feast day, June 1.

Jus·tin·i·an /jə'stinēən/ (483–565), Byzantine emperor 527–565; Latin name *Flavius Petrus Sabbatius Justinianus.* He regained North Africa from the Vandals, Italy from the Ostrogoths, and Spain from the Visigoths. He codified Roman law 529.

just-in-time ▶ **adj.** [attrib.] denoting a manufacturing system in which materials or components are delivered immediately before they are required in order to minimize inventory costs.

just·ly /'jəstlē/ ▶ **adv.** according to what is morally right or fair; fairly: *we deal justly with complaints.* ■ in a way that is well founded; justifiably: *we can justly be proud of our achievements.*

just war ▶ **n.** a war that is deemed to be morally or theologically justifiable.
– ORIGIN translation of Latin 'bellum justum.'

jut /jət/ ▶ **v.** (**juts, jutting, jutted**) [no obj.] extend out, over, or beyond the main body or line of something: *a rock jutted out from the side of the bank.* ■ [with obj.] cause (something, such as one's chin) to protrude: *she put up her head and jutted out her chin with determination.*
▶ **n.** a point that sticks out.
– ORIGIN mid 16th cent.: variant of JET[1].

Jute /jo͞ot/ ▶ **n.** a member of a Germanic people that may have come from Jutland and, according to the Venerable Bede, joined the Angles and Saxons in invading Britain in the 5th century, settling in a region including Kent and the Isle of Wight.
– DERIVATIVES **Jut·ish adj.**
– ORIGIN Old English *Eotas, Iotas*, influenced later in spelling by medieval Latin *Jutae, Juti.*

jute /jo͞ot/ ▶ **n. 1** rough fiber made from the stems of a tropical Old World plant, used for making twine and rope or woven into sacking or matting.
2 the herbaceous plant that is cultivated for this fiber, with edible young shoots. ● Genus *Corchorus*, family Tiliaceae: several species, in particular *C. capsularis* of China and *C. olitorius* of India. ■ used in names of other plants that yield fiber, e.g., **Chinese jute**.
– ORIGIN mid 18th cent.: from Bengali *jhuto*, from Prakrit *justi.*

Jut·land /'jətlənd/ a peninsula in northwestern Europe that includes the mainland of Denmark as well as the northern German state of Schleswig-Holstein. Danish name JYLLAND.

Jut·land, Bat·tle of a major naval battle in World War I, fought between the British Grand Fleet under Admiral Jellicoe and the German High Seas Fleet in the North Sea west of Jutland on May 31, 1916. Although the battle was indecisive, the German fleet never again sought a full-scale engagement, and the Allies retained control of the North Sea.

juv. ▶ **abbr.** juvenile.

Ju·ve·nal /'jo͞ovənl/ (*c.*60–*c.*140), Roman satirist; Latin name *Decimus Junius Juvenalis.* He wrote 16-verse satires that savagely attacked the vices and follies of Roman society, chiefly during the reign of Domitian.

ju·ve·nes·cence /,jo͞ovə'nesəns/ ▶ **n.** formal the state or period of being young.
– DERIVATIVES **ju·ve·nes·cent adj.**
– ORIGIN early 19th cent.: from Latin *juvenescent-* 'reaching the age of youth,' from the verb *juvenescere*, from *juvenis* 'young.'

ju·ve·nile /'jo͞ovə,nīl, -vənl/ ▶ **adj.** of, for, or relating to young people: *juvenile crime.* ■ childish; immature: *she's bored with my juvenile conversation.* ■ of or denoting a theatrical or film role representing a young person: *the romantic juvenile lead.* ■ of or relating to young birds or other animals.
▶ **n.** a young person. ■ Law a person below the age at which ordinary criminal prosecution is possible (18 in most countries). ■ a young bird or other animal. ■ an actor who plays juvenile roles.
– DERIVATIVES **ju·ve·nil·i·ty** /,jo͞ovə'nilitē/ **n.**
– ORIGIN early 17th cent.: from Latin *juvenilis*, from *juvenis* 'young, a young person.'

ju·ve·nile court ▶ **n.** a court of law responsible for the trial or legal supervision of children under a specified age (18 in most countries).

ju·ve·nile de·lin·quen·cy ▶ **n.** the habitual committing of criminal acts or offenses by a young person, esp. one below the age at which ordinary criminal prosecution is possible.
– DERIVATIVES **ju·ve·nile de·lin·quent n.**

ju·ve·nile hor·mone ▶ **n.** Entomology any of a number of hormones regulating larval development in insects and inhibiting metamorphosis.

ju·ve·nile of·fend·er ▶ **n.** a person below a specific age (18 in most countries) who has committed a crime.

ju·ve·nil·i·a /,jo͞ovə'nilēə/ ▶ **plural n.** works produced by an author or artist while still young.
– ORIGIN early 17th cent.: from Latin, neuter plural of *juvenilis* (see JUVENILE).

ju·ve·nil·ize /'jo͞ovənl,īz/ ▶ **v.** [with obj.] make or keep young or youthful; arrest the development of. ■ (as adj. **juvenilized**) Entomology (of an insect or part of one) having a juvenile appearance or physiology; showing arrested or reversed development.

Ju·ven·tud, Isla de la /'ēslä dā lä ,ho͞ovän'to͞od/ (English name *Isle of Youth*; formerly *Isle of Pines*) an island off southwestern Cuba, in the Caribbean Sea; pop. 71,000. Long a source of jurisdictional disputes between Cuba and the US, it has been a resort and a prison colony. Renamed in 1978, it has many facilities dedicated to youth.

ju·vie /'jo͞ovē/ ▶ **n.** (pl. **juvies**) informal a juvenile delinquent.
– ORIGIN 1940s: abbreviation of JUVENILE.

jux·ta·glo·mer·u·lar /,jəkstəglä'meryələr, -glə-/ ▶ **adj.** Anatomy denoting a group of structures secreting regulatory hormones into the arteriole that leads into a glomerulus in the kidney.
– ORIGIN 1930s: from Latin *juxta* 'near to' + *glomerular* (see GLOMERULUS).

jux·ta·pose /'jəkstə,pōz, ,jəkstə'pōz/ ▶ **v.** [with obj.] place or deal with close together for contrasting effect: *black-and-white photos of slums were starkly juxtaposed with color images.*
– ORIGIN mid 19th cent.: from French *juxtaposer*, from Latin *juxta* 'next' + French *poser* 'to place.'

jux·ta·po·si·tion /,jəkstəpə'zisHən/ ▶ **n.** the fact of two things being seen or placed close together with contrasting effect: *the juxtaposition of these two images.*
– DERIVATIVES **jux·ta·po·si·tion·al** /,jəkstəpə'zisHənl/ **adj.**

JV ▶ **abbr.** ■ joint venture. ■ junior varsity.

jwlr. ▶ **abbr.** jeweler.

Jyl·land /'yo͞o,län/ Danish name for JUTLAND.

Kk

K[1] /kā/ (also **k**) ▶ **n.** (pl. **Ks** or **K's**) the eleventh letter of the alphabet. ■ denoting the next after J in a set of items, categories, etc.

K[2] ▶ **abbr.** ■ kelvin(s). ■ Computing kilobyte(s). ■ kilometer(s). ■ kindergarten. ■ king (used esp. in describing play in card games and recording moves in chess): *declarer overruffed with ♦K and led another spade* | *18.Ke2.* ■ knit (as an instruction in knitting patterns): *K 42 rows.* ■ Köchel (catalog of Mozart's works): *the Sinfonia Concertante, K364.* ■ (also **k**) informal thousand (used chiefly in expressing salaries or other sums of money). [from **KILO-** 'thousand.'] ■ Baseball strikeout. ▶ **symbol** the chemical element potassium. [from modern Latin *kalium*.]

k ▶ **abbr.** ■ karat. ■ [in combination] (in units of measurement) kilo-: *a distance of 700 kpc.* ■ kopeck(s). ▶ **symbol** ■ a constant in a formula or equation. ■ Chemistry Boltzmann's constant.

K2 the highest mountain in the Karakoram range, on the border between Pakistan and China. The second highest peak in the world, it rises to 28,250 feet (8,611 m). It was discovered in 1856 and named K2 because it was the second peak to be surveyed in the Karakoram range. It was formerly known as Mount Godwin-Austen after **Col. H. H. Godwin-Austen** (1834–1923), who first surveyed it. Also called **DAPSANG.**

Kaa·ba /ˈkäbə/ (also **Caaba**) a square stone building in the center of the Great Mosque at Mecca, the site most holy to Muslims and toward which they must face when praying. It stands on the site of a pre-Islamic shrine said to have been built by Abraham.
– ORIGIN from Arabic (*al-*)*ka'ba*, literally '(the) square house.'

ka·ba·ka /kəˈbäkə/ ▶ **n.** the traditional ruler of the Baganda people of Uganda.
– ORIGIN a local title.

Ka·ba·le·ga Falls /ˌkäbəˈlāgə/ a waterfall on the lower Victoria Nile River near Lake Albert, in northwestern Uganda. Former name **MURCHISON FALLS.**

Kab·ar·di·no-Bal·kar·i·a /ˌkabərˌdēnō ˌbôlˈkarēə/ an autonomous republic in southwestern Russia, on the border with Georgia; pop. 893,100 (est. 2009); capital, Nalchik. Also called **Kabarda-Balkar Republic.**

Kab·ba·lah /ˈkabələ, kəˈbä-/ (also **Kabbala, Cabala, Cabbala,** or **Qabalah**) ▶ **n.** the ancient Jewish tradition of mystical interpretation of the Bible, first transmitted orally and using esoteric methods (including ciphers). It reached the height of its influence in the later Middle Ages and remains significant in Hasidism.
– DERIVATIVES **Kab·ba·lism** /ˈkabəˌlizəm/ **n.**, **Kab·ba·list** /-list/ **n.**, **Kab·ba·lis·tic** /ˌkabəˈlistik/ **adj.**
– ORIGIN from medieval Latin *cabala, cabbala*, from Rabbinical Hebrew *qabbālāh* 'tradition,' from *qibbēl* 'receive, accept.'

Ka·bi·la /kəˈbēlə/, Laurent (1937–2001), African statesman; president of the Democratic Republic of the Congo (formerly Zaire) 1997–2001. His forces overthrew President Mobutu in 1997. He was assassinated in January 2001 and was succeeded as president by his son **Joseph Kabila** (1971–).

Ka·bi·nett /ˌkabiˈnet/ ▶ **n.** a wine of German origin or style of superior or reserve quality, esp. one made from a specified quality of grape must, without added sugar.
– ORIGIN from German *Kabinettwein*, literally 'chamber wine.'

ka·bloo·ey (also **kablooie** /kəˈblo͞oē/) ▶ **adj.** informal destroyed or ruined: *the amp will go kablooey since you will be sending an input signal far too strong for it.*
▶ **exclam.** used to convey that something has happened in an abrupt way: *and, kablooey! The whole damn thing exploded!*

ka·bob ▶ **n.** variant spelling of **KEBAB.**

ka·boo·dle ▶ **n.** variant spelling of **CABOODLE.**

ka·boom /kəˈbo͞om/ ▶ **exclam.** used to represent the sound of a loud explosion.

ka·bu·ki /kəˈbo͝okē/ ▶ **n.** a form of traditional Japanese drama with highly stylized song, mime, and dance, now performed only by male actors, using exaggerated gestures and body movements to express emotions, and including historical plays, domestic dramas, and dance pieces.
– ORIGIN Japanese, originally as a verb meaning 'act dissolutely,' later interpreted as if from *ka* 'song' + *bu* 'dance' + *ki* 'art.'

Ka·bul /ˈkäbəl, kəˈbo͞ol/ the capital of Afghanistan; pop. 2,536,300 (est. 2006). It is situated in the northeastern part of the country, with a strategic position commanding the mountain passes through the Hindu Kush, esp. the Khyber Pass. Capital of the Mogul empire 1504–1738, it replaced Kandahar as capital of an independent Afghanistan in 1773.

Ka·bwe /ˈkäbwā/ a town in central Zambia, north of Lusaka; pop. 211,500 (est. 2009). It is the site of a cave that has yielded human fossils associated with the Upper Pleistocene period. Former name (1904–65) **BROKEN HILL.**

Ka·byle /kəˈbīl/ ▶ **n. 1** a member of a Berber people inhabiting northern Algeria.
2 the Berber dialect of this people.
▶ **adj.** of or relating to this people or their language.
– ORIGIN probably from Arabic *ḳabā'il*, plural of *ḳabīla* 'tribe.'

Ka·chin /kəˈCHin/ ▶ **n. 1** a member of an indigenous people living in northern Burma (Myanmar) and adjacent parts of China and India.
2 the Tibeto-Burman language of this people.
▶ **adj.** of or relating to this people or their language.

ka·chi·na /kəˈCHēnə/ (also **katsina** /kətˈsēnə/) ▶ **n.** (pl. **kachinas**) a deified ancestral spirit in the mythology of Pueblo Indians. ■ (also **kachina dancer**) a person who represents such a spirit in ceremonial dances. ■ (also **kachina doll**) a small carved figure representing such a spirit.
– ORIGIN from Hopi *kacina* 'supernatural,' of Keres origin.

ka-ching /kəˈCHiNG/ (also **ker-ching** /kə(r)ˈCHiNG/) ▶ **n.** used to represent the sound of a cash register, esp. with reference to making money: *they likely have assets beyond the ka-ching of the cash register.*
– ORIGIN early 1990s: imitative.

Ká·dár /ˈkäˌdär/, János (1912–89), Hungarian statesman; first secretary of the Hungarian Socialist Workers' Party 1956–88 and prime minister 1956–58 and 1961–65. After crushing the Hungarian uprising of 1956, he consistently supported the former Soviet Union. His policy of "consumer socialism" made Hungary the most affluent state in Eastern Europe.

Kad·dish /ˈkädisH/ ▶ **n.** an ancient Jewish prayer sequence regularly recited in the synagogue service, including thanksgiving and praise and concluding with a prayer for universal peace. ■ a form of this prayer sequence recited for the dead.
– ORIGIN from Aramaic *qaddîš* 'holy.'

ka·di ▶ **n.** (pl. **kadis**) variant spelling of **CADI.**

Ka·di·köy /käˈdikœi, -koi/ Turkish name for **CHALCEDON.**

Kae·song /ˈkāˈsôNG/ a commercial and industrial city in southern North Korea, on the 38th Parallel (the South Korean border), the scene of armistice talks at the end of the Korean War; pop. 354,800 (est. 2009).

kaf·fee·klatsch /ˈkäfēˌkläCH, -ˌklaCH, ˈkôfē-/ ▶ **n.** an informal social gathering at which coffee is served. ■ talking or gossip at such gatherings.
– ORIGIN German, from *Kaffee* 'coffee' + *Klatsch* 'gossip.'

Kaf·fir /ˈkafər/ ▶ **n.** chiefly S. African, offensive an insulting and contemptuous term for a black African.
– ORIGIN from Arabic *kāfir* 'infidel,' from *kafara* 'not believe.'

Kaf·fir lil·y ▶ **n.** either of two South African plants with straplike leaves and stems bearing a number of red, pink, or orange flowers. ● a plant with star-shaped flowers (*Schizostylis coccinea*, family Iridaceae). ● another term for **CLIVIA.**

Kaf·fir lime /ˈkafər/ ▶ **n.** a citrus tree of southeast Asia with green fruit and aromatic leaves that are used in Thai and Indonesian cooking. ● *Citrus hystrix*, family Rutaceae.

kaf·fi·yeh /kəˈfē(y)ə/ (also **keffiyeh**) ▶ **n.** a Bedouin Arab's kerchief worn as a headdress.
– ORIGIN early 19th cent.: from Arabic *keffiyya, kūfiyya.*

kaffiyeh

Kaf·ir /ˈkafər/ ▶ **n.** a member of a people of the Hindu Kush mountains of northeastern Afghanistan.
– DERIVATIVES **Kaf·i·ri** /ˈkafərē, kəˈfi(ə)rē/ **adj. & n.**
– ORIGIN from Arabic *kāfir* (see **KAFFIR**).

kaf·ir /ˈkafər/ ▶ **n.** a person who is not a Muslim (used chiefly by Muslims).
– ORIGIN from Arabic *kāfir* 'infidel, unbeliever.' Compare with **KAFFIR.**

Kaf·ka /ˈkäfkə/, Franz (1883–1924), Czech novelist, who wrote in German. His work is characterized by its portrayal of an enigmatic and nightmarish reality where the individual is perceived as lonely, perplexed, and threatened. Notable works: *The Metamorphosis* (1917), *The Trial* (1925), and *The Castle* (1926).

Kaf·ka·esque /ˌkäfkəˈesk/ ▶ **adj.** characteristic or reminiscent of the oppressive or nightmarish qualities of Franz Kafka's fictional world.

kaf·tan /ˈkaftən, -ˌtan/ (also **caftan**) ▶ **n.** a man's long belted tunic, worn in countries of the Near East. ■ a woman's long loose dress. ■ a loose shirt or top.
– ORIGIN late 16th cent.: from Turkish, from Persian *kaftān*, partly influenced by French *cafetan.*

Ka·go·shi·ma /ˌkägəˈSHēmə, käˈgôSHēmə/ a city and port in Japan; pop. 601,122 (2007). Situated on the southern coast of Kyushu island, on the Satsuma Peninsula, it is noted for Satsuma ware, a type of porcelain.

Ka·ha·na·mo·ku /kəˌhänəˈmōko͞o/, Duke Paoa (1890–1968) US swimmer and surfer. The developer of the flutter kick, he won the 100-yard freestyle gold medals in the 1912 and 1920 Olympic Games, as well as the 800-meter relay gold medal in the 1920 games.

ka·hi·ka·te·a /ˌkīkəˈtēə/ ▶ **n.** a tall coniferous New Zealand tree used for its timber and resin. Its seeds, which are borne on conspicuous red stems, were formerly eaten by the Maoris. Also called **WHITE PINE.** ● *Podocarpus* (or *Dacrycarpus*) *dacrydioides*, family Podocarpaceae.
– ORIGIN early 19th cent.: from Maori.

Kah·lo /ˈkälō/, Frida (1907–54), Mexican painter. She is noted for her brightly colored self-portraits, which were influenced by Mexican primitive art. She was married to Diego Rivera.

Kah·lú·a /kəˈlo͞oə/ ▶ **n.** trademark a coffee-flavored liqueur.

Ka·ho·o·la·we /kä,hō-ōˈläwā/ an island in Hawaii, southwest of Maui, formerly used as a military range.

Ka·hu·lu·i /ˌkähōōˈlo͞o-ē/ a city in Hawaii, on northern Maui Island; pop. 20,146 (2000).

ka·hu·na /kəˈho͞onə/ ▶ **n.** (in Hawaii) a wise man or shaman. ■ informal an important person; the person in charge: *one big kahuna runs the whole show.* ■ informal (in surfing) a very large wave.
– ORIGIN Hawaiian.

Kai·bab Plateau /ˈkīˌbab/ a highland region in northwestern Arizona, north of the Grand Canyon, that adjoins southern Utah.

Kai·feng /ˈkīˈfeNG/ a city in eastern China, in Henan province, on the Yellow River; pop. 591,300 (est. 2006). Established in the 4th century BC, it is one of the oldest cities in China.

Kai·lua /kīˈlo͞oə/ a community in southeastern Oahu on the island of Hawaii, in the Pacific Ocean, northeast of Honolulu; pop. 36,513 (2000).

kai·nic ac·id /ˈkīnik/ ▶ **n.** Medicine an organic acid extracted from a red alga, used to kill intestinal worms. ● Chem. formula: $C_{10}H_{15}NO_4$.
– ORIGIN mid 20th cent.: *kainic* from Japanese *kainin* (from *kainin-sō*, name of the alga *Digenea simplex* from which it is extracted) + **-IC.**

kai·nite /ˈkīˌnīt, ˈkā-/ ▶ **n.** a white mineral consisting of a double salt of hydrated magnesium sulfate and potassium chloride.
– ORIGIN mid 19th cent.: from German *Kainit*, from Greek *kainos* 'new, recent,' because of the mineral's recent formation.

Kai·pa·ro·wits Plateau /kīˈpärō-its/ a highland region in south central Utah, north of Lake Powell.

kai·ro·mone /ˈkīrəˌmōn/ ▶ **n.** Biology a chemical substance emitted by an organism and detected by another of a different species that gains advantage from this, e.g., a parasite seeking a host.
– ORIGIN late 20th cent.: from Greek *kairos* 'advantage, opportunity,' on the pattern of *pheromone*.

kai·ros /ˈkīräs/ ▶ **n.** [in sing.] chiefly Theology a propitious moment for decision or action.
– ORIGIN mid 20th cent.: Greek, literally 'opportunity.'

Kair·ouan /kerˈwän/ a city in northeastern Tunisia; pop. 117,900 (est. 2004). It is a Muslim holy city and a place of pilgrimage.

kai·se·ki /ˈkīsekē/ ▶ **n.** a style of traditional Japanese cuisine in which a series of very small, intricate dishes are prepared.
– ORIGIN Japanese, from *kai* (from *kaichu* 'kimono pocket') + *seki* 'stone.'

Kai·ser /ˈkīzər/, Georg (1878–1945), German playwright. He is best known for his expressionist plays *The Burghers of Calais* (1914), *Gas I* (1918), and *Gas II* (1920); the last two provide a gruesome vision of futuristic science and end with the extinction of all life by poisonous gas.

kai·ser /ˈkīzər/ ▶ **n. 1** historical the German emperor, the emperor of Austria, or the head of the Holy Roman Empire: [as title] *Kaiser Wilhelm*.
2 see **KAISER ROLL.**
– PHRASES **the Kai·ser's War** dated World War I.
– DERIVATIVES **kai·ser·ship** /-ˌSHip/ **n.**
– ORIGIN Middle English *cayser*, from Old Norse *keisari*, based on Latin *Caesar* (see **CAESAR**[1]), and later reinforced by Middle Dutch *keiser*. The modern English form (early 19th cent.) derives from German *Kaiser*.

ka·iser roll ▶ **n.** a round, soft bread roll with a crisp crust, made by folding the corners of a square of dough into the center, resulting in a pinwheel shape when baked.

Kai·sers·lau·tern /ˌkīzərzˈloutərn/ a city in western Germany, in Rhineland-Palatinate; pop. 98,000 (est. 2006).

Kai·ser Wil·helm, Wilhelm II of Germany (see **WILHELM II**).

k

kai·zen /ˈkīzən/ ▶ **n.** a Japanese business philosophy of continuous improvement of working practices, personal efficiency, etc.
– ORIGIN Japanese, literally 'improvement.'

ka·ka /ˈkäkə/ ▶ **n.** a large New Zealand parrot with olive-brown and dull green upper parts and reddish underparts. ● *Nestor meridionalis*, family Psittacidae.
– ORIGIN late 18th cent.: from Maori.

ka·ka·po /ˈkäkəˌpō/ ▶ **n.** (pl. **kakapos**) a large flightless New Zealand parrot with greenish plumage. Now endangered, it is nocturnal and ground-dwelling. Also called **OWL PARROT.** ● *Strigops habroptilus*, family Psittacidae.
– ORIGIN mid 19th cent.: from Maori, literally 'night kaka.'

ka·ke·mo·no /ˌkäkəˈmōnō/ ▶ **n.** (pl. **kakemonos**) a Japanese unframed painting made on paper or silk and displayed as a wall hanging.
– ORIGIN late 19th cent.: Japanese, from *kake-* 'hang, suspend' + *mono* 'thing.'

ka·ki /ˈkäkē/ ▶ **n.** the Japanese persimmon.
– ORIGIN early 18th cent.: from Japanese.

Ka·laal·lit Nu·naat /käˈlätlēt no͞oˈnät, -ˈlälēt/ Inuit name for **GREENLAND.**

ka·la-a·zar /ˌkälə əˈzär/ ▶ **n.** a form of the disease leishmaniasis marked by emaciation, anemia, fever, and enlargement of the liver and spleen. ● This is caused by *Leishmania donovani*, phylum Kinetoplastida, kingdom Protista.
– ORIGIN late 19th cent.: from Assamese, from *kālā* 'black' + *āzār* 'disease' (because of the bronzing of the skin often associated with it).

Ka·la·ha·ri Des·ert /ˌkäləˈhärē/ a high, vast, arid plateau in southern Africa north of the Orange River. It comprises most of Botswana with parts in Namibia and South Africa.

Kal·a·ma·zoo /ˌkaləməˈzo͞o/ an industrial and commercial city in southwestern Michigan; pop. 72,179 (est. 2008).

kal·an·cho·e /ˌkalənˈkō-ē, kəˈlaNGkō-ē/ ▶ **n.** a tropical succulent plant with clusters of tubular flowers, sometimes producing miniature plants along the edges of the leaves and grown as an indoor or greenhouse plant. ● Genus *Kalanchoe*, family Crassulaceae.
– ORIGIN mid 19th cent.: modern Latin, from French, based on Chinese *gāláncài*.

Ka·lash·ni·kov /kəˈläSHnəˌkôf, -ˌkôv/ ▶ **n.** a type of rifle or submachine gun made in Russia, esp. the AK-47 assault rifle.
– ORIGIN 1970s: named after Mikhail T. *Kalashnikov* (born 1919), the Russian designer of the weapons.

kale /kāl/ ▶ **n. 1** a hardy cabbage of a variety that produces erect stems with large leaves and no compact head. See also **CURLY KALE.**
2 informal, dated money.
– ORIGIN Middle English: northern English form of **COLE.**

ka·lei·do·scope /kəˈlīdəˌskōp/ ▶ **n.** a toy consisting of a tube containing mirrors and pieces of colored glass or paper, whose reflections produce changing patterns that are visible through an eyehole when the tube is rotated. ■ a constantly changing pattern or sequence of objects or elements: *the dancers moved in a kaleidoscope of color.*
– ORIGIN early 19th cent.: from Greek *kalos* 'beautiful' + *eidos* 'form' + **-SCOPE.**

ka·lei·do·scop·ic /kəˌlīdəˈskäpik/ ▶ **adj.** having complex patterns of colors; multicolored: *kaleidoscopic diamond patterns.* ■ made up of a complex mix of elements; multifaceted: *a kaleidoscopic range of topics.*
– DERIVATIVES **ka·lei·do·scop·i·cal·ly** /-ˌlīdəˈskäpik(ə)lē/ **adv.**

kal·ends ▶ **plural n.** variant spelling of **CALENDS.**

Ka·le·va·la /ˌkäliˈvälə/ a collection of Finnish legends transmitted orally until published in the 19th century, and now regarded as the Finnish national epic.
– ORIGIN of Karelian origin.

Kale·yard School /ˈkālˌyärd/ a group of late 19th-century fiction writers, including J. M. Barrie, who described local town life in Scotland in a romantic vein and with much use of the vernacular.
– ORIGIN from Scots *kaleyard*, literally 'kitchen garden.'

Kal·gan /ˈkälˈgän, ˈkalˈgan/ Mongolian name for **ZHANGJIAKOU.**

Ka·li /ˈkälē/ Hinduism the most terrifying goddess, wife of Shiva, often identified with Durga, and in her benevolent aspect with Parvati. She is typically depicted as black, naked, old, and hideous.
– ORIGIN from Sanskrit *Kālī* 'black.'

Ka·li·man·tan /ˌkäləˈmänˌtän/ a region of Indonesia that is located on the southern part of the island of Borneo.

ka·lim·ba /kəˈlimbə/ ▶ **n.** a type of African thumb piano.
– ORIGIN 1950s: a local word; related to **MARIMBA.**

Ka·li·nin[1] /kəˈlēnən, kəlˈyēnyēn/ former name (1931–91) of **TVER.**

Ka·li·nin[2] /kəˈlēnin/, Mikhail (Ivanovich) (1875–1946), Soviet statesman; head of state 1919–46. He founded the newspaper *Pravda* 1912.

Ka·li·nin·grad /kəˈlēninˌgrät, kəlˈyēnyēn-/ **1** a port on the Baltic coast of eastern Europe, capital of the Russian region of Kaliningrad; pop. 421,700 (est. 2008). It was known by its German name of Königsberg until 1946 when it was ceded to the former Soviet Union under the Potsdam Agreement and renamed in honor of Kalinin. Its port is ice-free all year round and is an important naval base for the Russian fleet.
2 a region of Russia, an enclave situated on the Baltic coast of eastern Europe; capital, Kaliningrad.

Ka·lisz /ˈkäleSH/ a city in central Poland; pop. 108,311 (2007).

Kal·mar, Un·ion of the treaty that unified the crowns of Denmark, Sweden, and Norway in 1397, dissolved in 1523.

Kal·mar Sound /ˈkälmär/ a narrow strait between the mainland of southeastern Sweden and the island of Öland in the Baltic Sea.

kal·mi·a /ˈkalmēə/ ▶ **n.** an evergreen leathery-leaved shrub of the heath family, bearing large clusters of pink, white, or red flowers. It is native to North America and Cuba and widely grown as an ornamental. ● Genus *Kalmia*, family Ericaceae.
– ORIGIN modern Latin, named after Pehr *Kalm* (1716–79), Swedish botanist.

Kal·muck /ˈkalˌmək, kalˈmək/ (also **Kalmyk**) ▶ **n.** (pl. **same** or **Kalmucks** also **Kalmyks** /-miks/) **1** a member of a mainly Buddhist people of Mongolian origin living chiefly in Kalmykia.
2 the Altaic language of this people.
▶ **adj.** of or relating to this people or their language.
– ORIGIN from Russian *kalmyk*.

Kal·myk·ia /kalˈmikēə/ an autonomous republic in southwestern Russia, on the Caspian Sea; pop. 285,800 (est. 2009); capital, Elista. Official name **REPUBLIC OF KALMYKIA-KHALMG TANGCH.**

ka·long /ˈkälôNG, -läNG/ ▶ **n.** a flying fox found in Southeast Asia and Indonesia. ● Genus *Pteropus*, family Pteropodidae, in particular the large flying fox (*P. vampyrus*).
– ORIGIN early 19th cent.: from Javanese.

kal·so·mine ▶ **n. & v.** variant spelling of **CALCIMINE.**

Ka·lu·ga /kəˈlo͞ogə/ an industrial city and river port in Russia, on the Oka River, southwest of Moscow; pop. 326,900 (est. 2008).

Kal·yan /kəlˈyän/ a city on the west coast of India, in the state of Maharashtra, northeast of Mumbai (Bombay); pop. 1,328,000 (est. 2009).

Ka·ma /ˈkämə/ Hinduism the god of love, typically represented as a youth with a bow of sugar cane, a bowstring of bees, and arrows of flowers.

kam·a·cite /ˈkaməˌsīt/ ▶ **n.** an alloy of iron and nickel occurring in some meteorites.
– ORIGIN late 19th cent.: from Greek *kamax, kamak-* 'vine pole' (because of the occurrence of the alloy in bar-shaped masses) + **-ITE**[1].

Ka·ma Riv·er /ˈkämə/ a river in Russia that flows for 1,128 miles (1,805 km) from the central Ural Mountains to the Volga River near Kazan.

Ka·ma Su·tra /ˈkämə ˈso͞otrə/ an ancient Sanskrit treatise on the art of love and sexual technique.
– ORIGIN Sanskrit, from *kāma* 'love' + *sūtra* 'thread.'

Kam·ba /ˈkämbə/ ▶ **n.** (pl. **same**, **Kambas**, or **Wakamba** /wäˈkämbə/) **1** a member of a people of central Kenya, ethnically related to the Kikuyu.
2 the Bantu language of this people.
▶ **adj.** of or relating to this people or their language.
– ORIGIN a local name.

Kam·chat·ka /kämˈCHätkə/ a mountainous peninsula on the northeast coast of Siberia in Russia that separates the Sea of Okhotsk from the Bering Sea; chief port, Petropavlovsk.

kame /kām/ ▶ **n.** Geology a steep-sided mound of sand and gravel deposited by a melting ice sheet.
– ORIGIN late 18th cent.: Scots form of **COMB.**

Ka·me·ha·me·ha I /kəˌmäəˈmäə/ (1758?–1819), king of the Hawaiian islands 1795–1819, known as *Kamehameha the Great*. He united all the islands under his rule.

Ka·men·sko·ye /ˈkäminskəyə/ former name (until 1936) for **DNIPRODZERZHINSK.**

Ka·mensk-Ural·sky /ˌkäminsk o͝or'älsk(y)ē/ an industrial city in central Russia, in the eastern foothills of the Urals; pop. 180,900 (est. 2008).

Ka·mer·lingh On·nes /'kämərliNG 'ônəs/, Heike (1853–1926), Dutch physicist. During his studies of cryogenic phenomena, he succeeded in liquefying helium. He also discovered the phenomenon of superconductivity in 1911. Nobel Prize for Physics (1913).

ka·mi /'kämē/ ▶ **n.** (pl. **same**) a divine being in the Shinto religion.
– ORIGIN Japanese.

ka·mi·ka·ze /ˌkämi'käzē/ ▶ **n.** (in World War II) a Japanese aircraft loaded with explosives and making a deliberate suicidal crash on an enemy target. ■ the pilot of such an aircraft.
▶ **adj.** [attrib.] of or relating to such an attack or pilot. ■ reckless or potentially self-destructive: *he made a kamikaze run across three lanes of traffic.*
– ORIGIN Japanese, from *kami* 'divinity' + *kaze* 'wind,' originally referring to the gale that, in Japanese tradition, destroyed the fleet of invading Mongols in 1281.

Ka·mi·la·roi /'kämēˌläroi/ ▶ **n.** (pl. **same**) **1** a member of a group of Australian Aboriginal peoples of northeastern New South Wales.
2 the language of these peoples, now extinct.
▶ **adj.** of or relating to the Kamilaroi or their language.
– ORIGIN the name in Kamilaroi.

Kam·pa·la /käm'pälə/ the capital of Uganda, in the southern part of the country on the northern shores of Lake Victoria; pop. 1,533,600 (est. 2009). It replaced Entebbe as the capital when Uganda became independent in 1963.

kam·pong /'kämpôNG, -päNG/ ▶ **n.** a Malaysian enclosure or village.
– ORIGIN Malay; compare with COMPOUND².

Kam·pu·che·a /ˌkämpə'CHēə/ former name (1976–89) for **CAMBODIA**.
– DERIVATIVES **Kam·pu·che·an** n. & adj.

Kan. ▶ **abbr.** Kansas.

ka·na /'känə/ ▶ **n.** the system of syllabic writing used for Japanese, having two forms, hiragana and katakana. Compare with KANJI.
– ORIGIN Japanese.

ka·nak·a /kə'näkə/ ▶ **n.** a native of Hawaii. ■ historical a Pacific Islander employed as an indentured laborer in Australia, esp. in the sugar and cotton plantations of Queensland.
– ORIGIN Hawaiian, literally 'man.'

kan·al /'kanl/ ▶ **n.** a land measure used in Pakistan, standardized under British rule to equal one-eighth acre: *seventeen kanals of agricultural land.*

kan·a·my·cin /ˌkanə'mīsin/ ▶ **n.** Medicine a broad-spectrum antibiotic obtained from a strain of bacteria.
– ORIGIN mid 20th cent.: from modern Latin *Streptomyces kanamyceticus*, the name of the source bacterium (see also -MYCIN).

Ka·na·rese /ˌkänə'rēz, -'rēs/ ▶ **n.** (pl. **same**) **1** a member of a people living mainly in Kanara, a district in southwestern India.
2 another term for **KANNADA**.
▶ **adj.** of or relating to Kanara, its people, or their language.

Ka·na·wha Riv·er /kə'nô-wə, kə'noi/ a river in west central West Virginia that connects the New River with the Ohio River. Charleston and other industrial centers lie along it.

kan·ban /'känˌbän/ ▶ **n.** (also **kanban system**) a Japanese manufacturing system in which the supply of components is regulated through the use of a card displaying a sequence of specifications and instructions, sent along the production line. ■ a card of this type.
– ORIGIN late 20th cent.: Japanese, literally 'billboard, sign.'

Kan·chen·jun·ga /ˌkənCHən'jəNGgə, -'jo͝oNGgə/ (also **Kangchenjunga** or **Kinchinjunga**) a mountain in the Himalayas, on the border between Nepal and Sikkim. Rising to a height of 28,209 feet (8,598 m), it is the world's third highest mountain.
– ORIGIN Tibetan, literally 'the five treasures of the snows,' referring to the five separate peaks of the summit.

Kan·da·har /ˌkəndə'här, 'kəndəˌhär/ a city in southern Afghanistan; pop. 324,800 (est. 2006). It was Afghanistan's capital 1773–78.

Kan·din·sky /kən'dinskē/, Wassily (1866–1944), Russian painter and theorist. A pioneer of abstract art, he cofounded the Munich-based *Blaue Reiter* group of artists in 1911.

Kan·dy /'kandē/ a city in Sri Lanka; pop. 121,300 (est. 2007). It contains one of the most sacred Buddhist shrines, the Dalada Maligava, which means Temple of the Tooth.
– DERIVATIVES **Kan·dy·an** /-dēən/ **adj.**

Ka·ne·o·he /ˌkänä'ōhā, ˌkänē'ō-ē/ a community on eastern Oahu Island in Hawaii, northeast of Honolulu; pop. 34,970 (2000).

kan·ga·roo /ˌkaNGgə'ro͞o/ ▶ **n.** a large plant-eating marsupial with a long powerful tail and strongly developed hind limbs that enable it to travel by leaping, found only in Australia and New Guinea. ● Genus *Macropus*, family Macropodidae: several species.
– ORIGIN late 18th cent.: the name of a specific kind of kangaroo in an extinct language of northern Queensland, Australia.

kangaroo

kan·ga·roo care ▶ **n.** a method of caring for premature babies in which the infants are held skin-to-skin with a parent, usually the mother, for as many hours as possible every day.

kan·ga·roo court ▶ **n.** an unofficial court held by a group of people in order to try someone regarded, esp. without good evidence, as guilty of a crime or misdemeanor.

kan·ga·roo paw ▶ **n.** an Australian plant that has long straplike leaves and tubular flowers with woolly outer surfaces. ● Genera *Anigozanthos* and *Macropidia*, family Haemodoraceae: several species, in particular **Mangles' kangaroo paw** (*A. manglesii*), which is the floral emblem of Western Australia.

kan·ga·roo rat ▶ **n.** a seed-eating hopping rodent with large cheek pouches and long hind legs, found from Canada to Mexico. ● Genus *Dipodomys*, family Heteromyidae: several species.

Kang·chen·jun·ga /ˌkäNGCHən'jo͝oNGgə/ variant spelling of **KANCHENJUNGA**.

kan·ji /'känjē/ ▶ **n.** a system of Japanese writing using Chinese characters. Compare with KANA.
– ORIGIN Japanese, from *kan* 'Chinese' + *ji* 'character.'

Kan·na·da /'känədə/ ▶ **n.** a Dravidian language related to Telugu and using a similar script. It is spoken by about 24 million people, mainly in Kanara and Karnataka in southwestern India. Also called **KANARESE**.
▶ **adj.** of or relating to this language.
– ORIGIN the name in Kannada.

Ka·no /'känō/ a city in northern Nigeria; pop. 2,359,200 (est. 2009).

Kan·pur /'känˌpo͝or/ a city in Uttar Pradesh, in northern India, on the Ganges River; pop. 3,144,300 (est. 2009). Former name **CAWNPORE**.

Kans. ▶ **abbr.** Kansas.

Kan·sa /'kanzə, -sə/ ▶ **n.** a North American people of eastern Kansas. ■ the language of this people. Also called **KAW**.

Kan·sas /'kanzəs/ a state in the central US; pop. 2,802,134 (est. 2008); capital, Topeka; statehood, Jan. 29, 1861 (34). It was acquired by the US as part of the Louisiana Purchase in 1803.
– DERIVATIVES **Kan·san** /-zən/ **adj. & n.**

Kan·sas Cit·y each of two adjacent cities in the US, situated at the junction of the Missouri and Kansas rivers. One is in northeastern Kansas; pop. 142,562 (est. 2008), and the other is in northwestern Missouri; pop. 451,572 (est. 2008).

Kan·su /'kanˌso͞o, 'gän'so͞o/ variant of **GANSU**.

Kant /känt/, Immanuel (1724–1804), German philosopher. In the *Critique of Pure Reason* (1781) he countered Hume's skeptical empiricism by arguing that any affirmation or denial regarding the ultimate nature of reality ("noumenon") makes no sense. His *Critique of Practical Reason* (1788) affirms the existence of an absolute moral law—the categorical imperative.
– DERIVATIVES **Kant·i·an** /'käntēən/ **adj. & n.**, **Kant·i·an·ism** /-ˌnizəm/ **n.**

Kao·hsiung /'gousHē'o͝oNG, -'SHo͝oNG/ the chief port of Taiwan, on the southwestern coast; pop. 1,520,600 (est. 2007).

kao·li·ang /ˌkoulē'aNG/ ▶ **n.** sorghum of a variety grown in China and used to make dough and alcoholic drinks. ● *Sorghum bicolor* var. *nervosum*, family Gramineae.
– ORIGIN early 20th cent.: from Chinese *gāoliang*, from *gāo* 'high' + *liáng* 'fine grain.'

ka·o·lin /'kāəlin/ ▶ **n.** a fine, soft white clay, resulting from the natural decomposition of other clays or feldspar. It is used for making porcelain and china, as a filler in paper and textiles, and in medicinal absorbents. Also called **CHINA CLAY**.
– DERIVATIVES **ka·o·lin·ize** /-ˌnīz/ **v.**
– ORIGIN early 18th cent.: from French, from Chinese *gāolǐ ng*, literally 'high hill,' the name of a mountain in Jiangxi province where the clay is found.

ka·o·lin·ite /'kāələˌnīt/ ▶ **n.** a white or gray clay mineral that is the chief constituent of kaolin.

ka·on /'kāˌän/ ▶ **n.** Physics a meson having a mass several times that of a pion.
– ORIGIN 1950s: from *ka* representing the letter *K* (as a symbol for the particle) + -ON.

ka·pell·meis·ter /kə'pelˌmīstər/ ▶ **n.** the leader or conductor of an orchestra or choir. ■ historical a leader of a chamber ensemble or orchestra attached to a German court.
– ORIGIN mid 19th cent.: German, from *Kapelle* 'court orchestra' (from medieval Latin *capella* 'chapel') + *Meister* 'master.'

ka·pok /'kāˌpäk/ ▶ **n.** a fine, fibrous cottonlike substance that grows around the seeds of the ceiba tree, used as stuffing for cushions, soft toys, etc. ■ (also **kapok tree**) another term for **CEIBA**.
– ORIGIN mid 18th cent.: from Malay *kapuk*.

Ka·po·si's sar·co·ma /kə'pōsēz sär'kōmə, 'kapəˌsēz, 'käpōˌsHēz/ ▶ **n.** Medicine a form of cancer involving multiple tumors of the lymph nodes or skin, occurring chiefly in people with depressed immune systems, e.g., as a result of AIDS.
– ORIGIN late 19th cent.: named after Moritz K. *Kaposi* (1837–1902), Hungarian dermatologist.

kap·pa /'kapə/ ▶ **n.** the tenth letter of the Greek alphabet (Κ, κ), transliterated in the traditional Latin style as 'c' (as in *Socrates*) or in the modern style as 'k' (as in *kyanite* and in the etymologies of this dictionary). ■ **(Kappa)** [followed by Latin genitive] Astronomy the tenth star in a constellation: *Kappa Orionis*. ■ [as modifier] Biochemistry denoting one of the two types of light polypeptide chain present in all immunoglobulin molecules (the other being lambda).

ka·pu /'käpō/ ▶ **n.** (in Hawaiian traditional culture and religion) a set of rules and prohibitions for everyday life.
– ORIGIN Hawaiian.

ka·put /kə'po͝ot, kä-/ ▶ **adj.** [predic.] informal broken and useless; no longer working or effective.
– ORIGIN late 19th cent.: from German *kaputt*, from French *(être) capot* '(be) without tricks in a card game.'

kar·a·bi·ner ▶ **n.** variant spelling of **CARABINER**.

Ka·ra·chai /ˌkarə'CHī/ ▶ **n. 1** a member of an indigenous people living in Karachai-Cherkessia.
2 (also **Karachai-Balkar**) the Turkic language of this people.
▶ **adj.** of or relating to this people or their language.

Ka·ra·chai-Cher·kes·sia /ˌkarəˌCHī CHir'kesēə/ an autonomous republic in the northern Caucasus, in southwestern Russia; pop. 427,100 (est. 2009); capital, Cherkessk. Official name **Karachai-Cherkess Republic**.

Ka·ra·chi /kə'räCHē/ a major city and port in Pakistan, capital of Sind province; pop. 12,827,900 (est. 2009). Situated by the Arabian Sea, it was the capital of Pakistan 1947–59 before being replaced by Rawalpindi.

Ka·ra·gan·da /ˌkärə'gändə/ Russian name for **QARAGHANDY**.

Kar·a·ite /'karəˌīt/ ▶ **n.** a member of a Jewish sect founded in the 8th century and located chiefly in the Crimea and nearby areas, and in Israel, which rejects rabbinical interpretation in favor of a literal interpretation of the scriptures.
– ORIGIN early 18th cent.: from Hebrew *Qārā'īm* 'Scripturalists' (from *qārā'* 'read') + -ITE¹.

Ka·raj /kä'räj/ a city in northern Iran, west of Tehran; pop. 1,386,030 (2006).

Ka·ra·jan /'kärəˌyän/, Herbert von (1908–89), Austrian conductor. He was the principal conductor of the Berlin Philharmonic Orchestra 1955–89.

Ka·ra·kal·pak /ˌkärəkäl'päk, kəˌräkəl'päk/ ▶ **n.** **1** a member of an indigenous people living in the

Karakalpak Autonomous Republic of Russia, south of the Aral Sea.
2 the Turkic language of this people.
▶ **adj.** of or relating to this people or their language.

Ka·ra·ko·ram /ˌkarəˈkôrəm/ a mountain system in central Asia that extends more than 300 miles (480 km) southeast from Afghanistan to Kashmir and that forms part of the borders of India and Pakistan with China. One of the highest mountain systems in the world, it consists of a group of parallel ranges that form a westward continuation of the Himalayas, with many peaks over 26,000 feet (7,900 m), the highest being K2.

kar·a·kul /ˈkarəkəl/ (also **caracul**) ▶ **n.** a sheep of an Asian breed with a dark, curled fleece when young. ■ cloth or fur made from or resembling the fleece of such a sheep.
– ORIGIN mid 19th cent.: from Russian, from the name of an oasis in Uzbekistan and of two lakes in Tadjikistan, based on Turkic.

Ka·ra Kum /ˌkarə ˈko͝om, ˌkärə/ a desert in central Asia, east of the Caspian Sea, that covers much of Turkmenistan. Russian name **Karakumy**.

kar·a·o·ke /ˌkarēˈōkē/ ▶ **n.** a form of entertainment, offered typically by bars and clubs, in which people take turns singing popular songs into a microphone over prerecorded backing tracks.
– ORIGIN 1970s: from Japanese, literally 'empty orchestra.'

Ka·ra Sea /ˈkarə, ˈkärə/ an arm of the Arctic Ocean off the northern coast of Russia, bounded on the east by the islands of Severnaya Zemlya and on the west by those of Novaya Zemlya.

kar·at /ˈkarət/ (chiefly Brit. also **carat**) ▶ **n.** a measure of the purity of gold, pure gold being 24 karats: *an ounce of 24-karat gold.*

ka·ra·te /kəˈrätē/ ▶ **n.** an Asian system of unarmed combat using the hands and feet to deliver and block blows, widely practiced as a sport. It was formalized in Okinawa in the 17th century and popularized via Japan after about 1920. Karate is performed barefoot in loose padded clothing, with a colored belt indicating the level of skill, and involves mental as well as physical training.
– ORIGIN Japanese, from *kara* 'empty' + *te* 'hand.'

ka·ra·te chop ▶ **n.** a sharp downward blow or movement executed with the side of the hand.
– DERIVATIVES **ka·ra·te-chop v.**

ka·ra·te·ka /kəˈrätēˌkä/ ▶ **n.** (pl. **same** or **karatekas**) a practitioner of karate.

Kar·ba·la /ˈkärbələ/ a city in southern Iraq; pop. 475,000 (est. 2003). A holy city for Shiite Muslims, it is the site of the tomb of **Husayn**, grandson of Muhammad, who was killed here in AD 680.

ka·rel·a /kəˈrelə/ ▶ **n.** Indian name for **BITTER MELON**.

Ka·re·lia /kəˈrēlēə/ a region of northeastern Europe on the border between Russia and Finland. Following Finland's declaration of independence in 1917, part of Karelia became a region of Finland and part an autonomous republic of the Soviet Union. After the Russo-Finnish war of 1939–40, the greater part of Finnish Karelia was ceded to the former Soviet Union. The remaining part of Karelia constitutes a province of eastern Finland.
– DERIVATIVES **Ka·re·li·an adj. & n.**

Ka·ren /kəˈren/ ▶ **n.** (pl. **same** or **Karens**) **1** a member of an indigenous people of eastern Burma (Myanmar) and western Thailand.
2 the language of this people, probably Sino-Tibetan.
▶ **adj.** of or relating to this people or their language.
– ORIGIN from Burmese *ka-reng* 'wild unclean man.'

Ka·ren State a state in southeastern Burma (Myanmar), on the border with Thailand; capital, Pa-an. Inaugurated in 1954 as an autonomous state of Burma, it was given the traditional Karen name of Kawthoolay in 1964, but reverted to Karen after the 1974 constitution limited its autonomy. The people are engaged in armed conflict with the government in an attempt to gain independence. Also called **KAWTHOOLAY**.

Ka·ri·ba, Lake /kəˈrēbə/ a large man-made lake on the Zambia–Zimbabwe border in central Africa. Created by damming the Zambezi River with the Kariba Dam, it is the chief source of hydroelectric power for Zimbabwe and Zambia.

Ka·ri·ba Dam a concrete arch dam on the Zambezi River on the Zambia-Zimbabwe border, 240 miles (385 km) downstream from Victoria Falls. Built in 1955–59, it created Lake Kariba and provided a bridge over the river between Zambia and Zimbabwe.

Karl-Marx-Stadt /kärl ˈmärks ˌshtät/ former name (1953–90) for **CHEMNITZ**.

Kar·loff /ˈkärˌlôf/, Boris (1887–1969), US actor, born in England; born *William Henry Pratt.* He appeared mostly in horror movies, such as *Frankenstein* (1931) and *The Body Snatcher* (1945).

Kar·lo·vy Va·ry /ˈkärlôvē ˈvärē/ a spa town in the western Czech Republic; pop. 50,940 (2007). It is noted for its alkaline thermal springs. German name **Karlsbad**.

Karls·ru·he /ˈkärlzˌro͞oə/ an industrial town and port on the Rhine River in western Germany; pop. 286,300 (est. 2006).

kar·ma /ˈkärmə/ ▶ **n.** (in Hinduism and Buddhism) the sum of a person's actions in this and previous states of existence, viewed as deciding their fate in future existences. ■ informal destiny or fate, following as effect from cause.
– DERIVATIVES **kar·mic** /-mik/ **adj.**, **kar·mi·cal·ly** /-mik(ə)lē/ **adv.**
– ORIGIN from Sanskrit *karman* 'action, effect, fate.'

kar·ma yo·ga ▶ **n.** Hinduism the discipline of selfless action as a way to perfection.

Kar·nak /ˈkärˌnak/ a village in Egypt on the Nile River, now largely amalgamated with Luxor. It is the site of the northern complex of monuments of ancient Thebes, including the great temple of Amun.

Kar·na·ta·ka /kärˈnätəkə/ a state in southwestern India; capital, Bangalore. Former name (until 1973) **MYSORE**.

Kar·naugh map /ˈkärˌnô/ (also **Karnaugh diagram**) ▶ **n.** Mathematics & Electronics a diagram consisting of a rectangular array of squares, each representing a different combination of the variables of a Boolean function.
– DERIVATIVES **Kar·naugh map·ping n.**
– ORIGIN mid 20th cent.: named after US physicist Maurice *Karnaugh* (1924–).

Kar·oo /kəˈro͞o/ (also **Karroo**) an elevated semidesert plateau in South Africa. ■ (as noun **a karoo**) S. African a tract of semidesert land.
– ORIGIN from Khoikhoi, literally 'hard, dry.'

ka·ro·shi /käˈrōshē, ˈkärˌō-/ ▶ **n.** (in Japan) death caused by overwork or job-related exhaustion.
– ORIGIN Japanese, from *ka* 'excess' + *rō* 'labor' + *shi* 'death.'

ka·ross /kəˈräs/ ▶ **n.** S. African a rug or blanket of sewn animal skins, formerly worn as a garment by African people, now used as a bed or floor covering.
– ORIGIN South African Dutch, from Khoikhoi *karos.*

Kar·pov /ˈkärˌpôf/, Anatoli (Yevgenevich) (1951–), Russian chess player. He was world champion from 1975 until defeated by Gary Kasparov in 1985.

kar·ri /ˈkarē/ ▶ **n.** (pl. **karris**) a tall Australian eucalyptus with hard red wood. ● *Eucalyptus diversicolor*, family Myrtaceae.
– ORIGIN late 19th cent.: from Nyungar.

Kar·roo variant spelling of **KAROO**.

karst /kärst/ ▶ **n.** Geology landscape underlain by limestone that has been eroded by dissolution, producing ridges, towers, fissures, sinkholes, and other characteristic landforms.
– DERIVATIVES **kars·tic** /ˈkärstik/ **adj.**, **kars·ti·fi·ca·tion** /ˌkärstəfiˈkāshən/ **n.**, **kars·ti·fy** /ˈkärstəˌfī/ **v.** (**karstifies, karstifying, karstified**).
– ORIGIN late 19th cent.: from German *der Karst*, the name of a limestone region in Slovenia.

kart /kärt/ ▶ **n.** a small unsprung racing vehicle typically having four wheels and consisting of a tubular frame with a rear-mounted engine.
– DERIVATIVES **kart·ing n.**
– ORIGIN mid 20th cent.: shortening of **GO-KART**.

Kart·ve·lian /kärtˈvēlēən/ ▶ **adj.** another term for **SOUTH CAUCASIAN** (see **CAUCASIAN** (sense 3 of the adjective)).
– ORIGIN from Georgian *Kartvelebi* 'Georgians' + **-IAN**.

karyo- ▶ **comb. form** Biology denoting the nucleus of a cell: *karyotype.*
– ORIGIN from Greek *karuon* 'kernel.'

kar·y·o·ki·ne·sis /ˌkarēˌōkəˈnēsis/ ▶ **n.** Biology division of a cell nucleus during mitosis.
– ORIGIN late 19th cent.: from **KARYO-** 'cell nucleus' + Greek *kinēsis* 'movement' (from *kinein* 'to move').

kar·y·ol·y·sis /ˌkarēˈäləsis/ ▶ **n.** Biology dissolution of a cell nucleus, esp. during mitosis.

kar·y·o·type /ˈkarēəˌtīp/ ▶ **n.** Biology & Medicine the number and visual appearance of the chromosomes in the cell nuclei of an organism or species.
– DERIVATIVES **kar·y·o·typ·ic** /ˌkarēəˈtipik/ **adj.**

kar·y·o·typ·ing /ˈkarēəˌtīpiNG/ ▶ **n.** Biology & Medicine the determination of a karyotype, e.g., to detect chromosomal abnormalities.

Ka·sai Riv·er /käˈsī/ (also **Cassai**) a river that flows for 1,100 miles (1,800 km) from central Angola through southern and central Democratic Republic of the Congo (formerly Zaire) into the Congo River. On its lower 500 miles (800 km), it is an important trade route.

kas·bah /ˈkäzbä/ ▶ **n.** variant spelling of **CASBAH**.

Kash·a /ˈkashə/ ▶ **n.** trademark a soft, napped fabric of wool and hair. ■ a kind of cotton flannel used as a lining material.
– ORIGIN early 20th cent.: of unknown origin.

ka·sha /ˈkäshə/ ▶ **n.** a soft food made from cooked buckwheat or similar grain. ■ uncooked buckwheat groats.
– ORIGIN Russian.

Kash·mir /ˈkashˌmi(ə)r, ˈkazh-/ a region on the northern border of India and in northeastern Pakistan. Formerly a state of India, it has been disputed between India and Pakistan since partition in 1947. The northwestern part is controlled by Pakistan, most of it forming the state of Azad Kashmir, while the remainder is incorporated into the Indian state of Jammu and Kashmir.

Kash·mir goat ▶ **n.** a goat of a Himalayan breed, yielding fine, soft wool that is used to make cashmere.

Kash·mir·i /ˌkashˈmi(ə)rē, ˌkazh-/ ▶ **adj.** of or relating to Kashmir, its people, or their language.
▶ **n. 1** a native or inhabitant of Kashmir.
2 the Dardic language of Kashmir, written in both Devanagari and Arabic script.

kash·ruth /ˈkäshrəth, -ro͞ot, käshˈro͞ot/ (also **kashrut**) ▶ **n.** the body of Jewish religious laws concerning the suitability of food, the fitness for use of ritual objects, etc. ■ the observance of these laws.
– ORIGIN Hebrew, literally 'legitimacy (in religion)'; see also **KOSHER**.

Kas·pa·rov /ˈkäspəˌrôf, kəˈspäˌrôf/, Garry (1963–), Azerbaijani chess player; born *Gary Weinstein*. In 1985, at the age of 22, he defeated Anatoli Karpov to become the youngest-ever world chess champion. In 1997, he was beaten in a match with the IBM computer Deeper Blue, a loss that did not affect his world championship title.

Kas·sel /ˈkäsəl/ a city in central Germany, in Hesse; pop. 193,500 (est. 2006). It was the capital of the kingdom of Westphalia 1807–13 and of the Prussian province of Hesse-Nassau 1866–1944.

Kas·ser·ine Pass /ˈkäsəˌrēn/ a historic site near the village of al-Qasrayn in north central Tunisia. A gap in an extension of the Atlas Mountains, it was fought over by German and US forces in 1943 during World War II.

Ka·sur /kəˈso͝or/ a city in northeastern Pakistan, in Punjab province; pop. 322,000 (est. 2009).

ka·ta /ˈkätə/ ▶ **n.** a system of individual training exercises for practitioners of karate and other martial arts. ■ (pl. **same** or **katas**) an individual exercise of this kind.
– ORIGIN Japanese.

kat·a·bat·ic /ˌkatəˈbatik/ ▶ **adj.** Meteorology (of a wind) caused by local downward motion of cool air. Compare with **ANABATIC**.
– ORIGIN late 19th cent.: from Greek *katabatikos*, from *katabainein* 'go down.'

Ka·tah·din, Mount /kəˈtädn/ (also **Ktaadn**) a peak in north central Maine, in Baxter State Park, 5,267 feet (1,606 m), the highest point in the state, site of the northern end of the Appalachian Trail.

ka·ta·ka·na /ˌkätəˈkänə/ ▶ **n.** the more angular form of kana (syllabic writing) used in Japanese, primarily used for words of foreign origin. Compare with **HIRAGANA**.
– ORIGIN early 18th cent.: Japanese, literally 'side kana.'

ka·ta·na /kəˈtänə/ ▶ **n.** a long, single-edged sword used by Japanese samurai.
– ORIGIN early 17th cent.: Japanese.

Ka·tan·ga /kəˈtäNGgə, -ˈtaNGgə/ former name (until 1972) for **SHABA**.

Kat·ang·ese /ˌkatäNGˈgēz, -ˈgēs, -aNG-/ ▶ **n.** (pl. **same**) a native or inhabitant of Shaba (before 1972 called Katanga).
▶ **adj.** of or relating to the Katangese.

ka·tha·re·vou·sa /ˌkäTHəˈrevo͞osä/ ▶ **n.** the purist form of modern Greek used in traditional literary writing, as opposed to the form that is spoken and used in everyday writing (called demotic).
– ORIGIN early 20th cent.: modern Greek, literally 'purifying,' feminine of *kathareuōn*, present active participle of Greek *kathareuein* 'be pure,' from *katharos* 'pure.'

Ka·thi·a·war /ˌkätēəˈwär/ a peninsula on the western coast of India, in the state of Gujarat, that separates the gulfs of Kutch and Cambay.

Kath·man·du /ˌkätmänˈdo͞o, ˌkatˌman-/ (also **Katmandu**) the capital of Nepal, in the east central part of the country; pop. 895,000 (est. 2007). It is located in the Himalayas at an altitude of 4,450 feet (1,370 m).

Kat·mai Na·tion·al Park /ˈkatˌmī/ a national preserve in southwestern Alaska, on the Alaska Peninsula, noted for its volcanic activity and wildlife.

Ka·to·wi·ce /ˌkätəˈvētsə/ a city in southwestern Poland; pop. 313,461 (2007). It is the industrial center of the Silesian coal-mining region.

kat·si·na /kəˈCHēnə, kətˈsēnə/ ▶ **n.** (pl. **katsinam** /-nəm/ or **katsinas**) variant of **KACHINA**.

kat·suo·bu·shi /ˌkätswōˈbo͝oSHē, -ˈbo͞o-/ ▶ **n.** dried fish prepared in hard blocks from the skipjack tuna and used in Japanese cooking.
– ORIGIN Japanese.

kat·su·ra /ˈkätsərə/ ▶ **n.** an ornamental eastern Asian tree that has leaves that resemble those of the Judas tree and light, fine-grained timber. ● *Cercidiphyllum japonicum*, the only member of the family Cercidiphyllaceae.
– ORIGIN early 20th cent.: from Japanese.

Kat·te·gat /ˈkätəˌgät, ˈkatəˌgat/ a strait, 140 miles (225 km) long, between Sweden and Denmark. It is linked to the North Sea by the Skagerrak and to the Baltic Sea by the Øresund.

ka·ty·did /ˈkātēˌdid/ ▶ **n.** a large, typically green, long-horned grasshopper native to North America. The male makes a characteristic sound that resembles the name. ● *Microcentrum* and other genera, family Tettigoniidae.

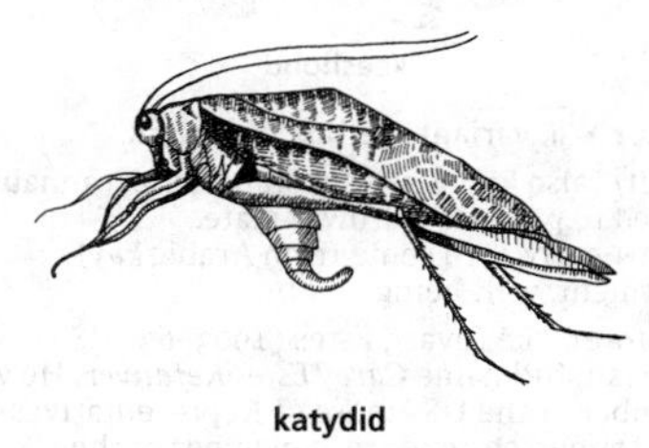

katydid

katz·en·jam·mer /ˈkatsənˌjamər/ ▶ **n.** informal, dated confusion; uproar. ■ a hangover; a severe headache resulting from a hangover.
– ORIGIN mid 19th cent.: from German *Katzen* (combining form of *Katze* 'cat') + *Jammer* 'distress'; popularized by the cartoon *Katzenjammer Kids*, drawn by Rudolf Dirks (1877–1968) in 1897 for the *New York Journal*, featuring two incorrigible children.

Kau·ai /ˈkouˌī/ an island in Hawaii, separated from Oahu by the Kauai Channel; chief town, Lihue.

Kauf·man /ˈkôfmən/, George S. (1889–1961) US journalist, playwright, and director; full name *George Simon Kaufman*. He collaborated with George Gershwin to write *Of Thee I Sing* (1931) and with Moss Hart to write *You Can't Take It with You* (1936) and *The Man Who Came to Dinner* (1939).

Kau·nas /ˈkounəs, -ˌnäs/ an industrial city and river port in southern Lithuania, at the confluence of the Viliya and Neman rivers; pop. 352,279 (2009).

Ka·un·da /kəˈo͞ondə/, Kenneth (David) (1924–), Zambian statesman; first president of independent Zambia 1964–91.

kau·ri /ˈkourē/ ▶ **n.** (pl. **kauris**) (also **kauri pine**) a tall coniferous forest tree that has broad leathery leaves and produces valuable timber and dammar resin. It grows in warm countries from Malaysia to New Zealand. ● Genus *Agathis*, family Araucariaceae: several species, in particular *A. australis* of New Zealand.
– ORIGIN early 19th cent.: from Maori.

kau·ri res·in (also **kauri gum**) ▶ **n.** the resin of the kauri tree, used as a varnish, and often also found in fossilized form where the tree formerly grew.

ka·va /ˈkävə/ (also **kava-kava**) ▶ **n. 1** a narcotic sedative drink made in Polynesia from the crushed roots of a plant of the pepper family.
2 the Polynesian shrub from which this root is obtained. ● *Piper methysticum*, family Piperaceae.
– ORIGIN late 18th cent.: from Tongan.

Ka·ver·i variant spelling of **CAUVERY**.

Kaw /käw/ ▶ **n.** another name for **KANSA**.

Ka·wa·ba·ta /ˌkäwəˈbätə/, Yasunari (1899–1972), Japanese novelist. At first an experimental writer, he reverted to traditional Japanese novel forms during the 1930s. Notable works: *The Izu Dancer* (1925) and *The Sound of the Mountain* (1949–54). Nobel Prize for Literature (1968).

ka·waii /kəˈwī/ ▶ **adj.** (in the context of Japanese popular culture) cute: *she paints elephants that are extremely kawaii.*
▶ **n.** the quality of being cute, or items that are cute.
– ORIGIN Japanese.

Ka·wa·sa·ki /ˌkäwəˈsäkē, ˌkouə-/ an industrial city in eastern Japan, on the southeastern coast of the island of Honshu; pop. 1,316,006 (2007).

Ka·wa·sa·ki dis·ease ▶ **n.** a disease of unknown cause, occurring primarily in young children and giving rise to a rash, glandular swelling, and sometimes damage to the heart.
– ORIGIN 1960s: named after Tomisaku *Kawasaki*, Japanese physician.

Kaw·thoo·lay /ˌkôTHo͞oˈlā/ (also **Kawthulei**) former name (1964–74) for **KAREN STATE**.

kay·ak /ˈkīˌak/ ▶ **n.** a canoe of a type used originally by the Inuit, made of a light frame with a watertight covering having a small opening in the top to sit in.
▶ **v.** (**kayaks, kayaking, kayaked**) [no obj.] (usu. as noun **kayaking**) travel in or use a kayak.
– DERIVATIVES **kay·ak·er n.**
– ORIGIN mid 18th cent.: from Inuit *qayaq*.

kayak

Kay·an /ˈkīən/ ▶ **n.** (pl. **same** or **Kayans**) **1** a member of an indigenous people of Sarawak and Borneo.
2 the Indonesian language of this people.
▶ **adj.** of or relating to this people or their language.
– ORIGIN the name in Kayan.

kay·o /ˈkāˈō/ Boxing, informal ▶ **n.** (pl. **kayos**) a knockout.
▶ **v.** (**kayoes, kayoing, kayoed**) [with obj.] knock (someone) out.
– ORIGIN 1920s: representing the pronunciation of *KO*.

Kay·se·ri /ˌkīsəˈrē/ a city in central Turkey; pop. 696,800 (est. 2007).

ka·za·chok /kəzäˈCHôk/ ▶ **n.** a Slavic dance with a fast and typically quickening tempo, featuring a step in which a squatting dancer kicks out each leg alternately to the front.
– ORIGIN early 20th cent.: Russian, diminutive of *kazak* 'Cossack.'

Ka·zakh /kəˈzäk/ ▶ **n. 1** a member of a people living chiefly in Kazakhstan. Traditionally nomadic, Kazakhs are predominantly Sunni Muslims.
2 the Turkic language of this people.
▶ **adj.** of or relating to this people or their language.
– ORIGIN Russian, from Turkic; see **COSSACK**.

Ka·zakh·stan /kəzäkˈstän, -zakˈstan/ a republic in central Asia, south of Russia, that extends east from the Caspian Sea to the Altai Mountains and China; pop. 15,399,400 (est. 2009); capital, Astana; languages, Kazakh (official) and Russian.

> The Turkic tribes of Kazakhstan were overrun by the Mongols in the 13th century, and the region was eventually absorbed into the Russian empire. Kazakhstan formed a constituent republic of the former Soviet Union and became an independent republic within the Commonwealth of Independent States in 1991.

Ka·zan¹ /kəˈzän(yə)/ a port in western Russia, situated on the Volga River to the east of Nizhni Novgorod, capital of the autonomous republic of Tatarstan; pop. 1,120,200 (est. 2008).

Ka·zan² /kəˈzan/, Elia (1909–2003), US movie and theater director, born in Turkey; born *Elia Kazanjoglous*. In 1947, he cofounded the Actors' Studio, a leading center of method acting. He directed *A Streetcar Named Desire* (stage, 1947; movie, 1953). Other notable movies: *On the Waterfront* (1954) and *East of Eden* (1955).

ka·zil·lion /kəˈzilyən/ ▶ **cardinal number** informal another term for **GAZILLION**.

ka·zoo /kəˈzo͞o/ ▶ **n.** a small, simple musical instrument consisting of a hollow pipe with a hole in it, over which is a thin covering that vibrates and produces a buzzing sound when the player sings or hums into the pipe.
– ORIGIN late 19th cent.: apparently imitative of the sound produced.

KB ▶ **abbr.** ■ (also **Kb**) kilobyte(s). ■ (in the UK) King's Bench.

kb ▶ **abbr.** Biochemistry kilobase(s).

Kbps ▶ **abbr.** kilobits per second.

kbyte /ˈkāˌbīt/ ▶ **abbr.** kilobyte(s).

KC ▶ **abbr.** ■ Kansas City. ■ (in the UK) King's Counsel.

kc ▶ **abbr.** kilocycle(s).

kcal ▶ **abbr.** kilocalorie(s).

kcl ▶ **abbr.** kilocalorie.

kc/s ▶ **abbr.** kilocycles per second.

KD ▶ **abbr.** ■ kiln-dried. ■ knocked-down.

KE ▶ **abbr.** kinetic energy.

ke·a /kēə/ ▶ **n.** a New Zealand mountain parrot with a long, narrow bill and mainly olive-green plumage. ● *Nestor notabilis*, family Psittacidae.
– ORIGIN mid 19th cent.: from Maori, imitative of its call.

Kear·ney /ˈkärnē/ a city in southern Nebraska, on the north shore of the Platte River, southwest of Grand Island; pop. 30,417 (est. 2008).

Kea·ton /ˈkētn/, Buster (1895–1966), US actor and director; born *Joseph Francis Keaton*. Noted for his deadpan face and acrobatic skills, he starred in and directed movies such as *The Navigator* (1924), and *The General* (1926).

Keats¹ /kēts/, Ezra Jack (1916–83) US illustrator and author of children's books; born *Jacob Ezra Katz*. Some of his books in which the main character was a little boy named Peter included *The Snowy Day* (1962), *Whistle for Willie* (1964), *Goggles!* (1969), and *Pet Show* (1972).

Keats², John (1795–1821), English poet. A principal figure of the romantic movement, he wrote most of his best-known poems, including "La Belle Dame sans Merci," "Ode to a Nightingale," and "Ode on a Grecian Urn," in 1818; they were published in 1820.
– DERIVATIVES **Keats·i·an** /ˈkētsēən/ **adj.**

ke·bab /kəˈbäb/ (also **kabob**) ▶ **n.** a dish of pieces of meat, fish, or vegetables roasted or grilled on a skewer or spit.
– ORIGIN late 17th cent.: from Arabic *kabāb*, partly via Urdu, Persian, and Turkish.

ke·bay·a /kəˈbäyə/ ▶ **n.** a light, loose tunic worn by women in Malaysia, Indonesia, and other Southeast Asian countries.
– ORIGIN Malay, ultimately of Persian or Arabic origin.

Ke·ble /ˈkēbəl/, John (1792–1866), English churchman; a founder of the Oxford Movement in 1833 with John Henry Newman and Edward Pusey.

k

keck /kek/ ▶ **v.** [no obj.] informal, chiefly Brit. feel as if one is about to vomit; retch.
– ORIGIN early 17th cent.: imitative.

kedge /kej/ ▶ **v.** [with obj.] move (a ship or boat) by hauling in a hawser attached to a small anchor dropped at some distance. ■ [no obj.] (of a ship or boat) move in such a way.
▶ **n.** (also **kedge anchor**) a small anchor used for such a purpose.
– ORIGIN late 15th cent.: perhaps a specific use of dialect *cadge* 'bind, tie.'

ked·ger·ee /ˈkejəˌrē/ ▶ **n. 1** an Indian dish consisting chiefly of rice, lentils, onions, and eggs.
2 a European dish consisting chiefly of fish, rice, and hard-boiled eggs.
– ORIGIN from Hindi *khichṛī*, from Sanskrit *khiccā*, a dish of rice and sesame.

keek /kēk/ Scottish ▶ **v.** [no obj.] peep surreptitiously: *he keeked through the window.*
▶ **n.** [in sing.] a surreptitious glance.
– ORIGIN late Middle English: perhaps related to Dutch *kijken* 'have a look.'

keel¹ /kēl/ ▶ **n.** the longitudinal structure along the centerline at the bottom of a vessel's hull, on which the rest of the hull is built, in some vessels extended downward as a blade or ridge to increase stability. ■ Zoology a ridge along the breastbone of many birds to which the flight muscles are attached; the carina. ■ Botany a prow-shaped pair of petals present in flowers of the pea family. ■ literary a ship.
▶ **v.** [no obj.] (**keel over**) (of a boat or ship) turn over on its side; capsize. ■ informal (of a person or thing) fall over; collapse.
– DERIVATIVES **keeled adj.** [in combination] *a deep-keeled yacht*, **keel·less adj.**
– ORIGIN Middle English: from Old Norse *kjǫlr*, of Germanic origin.

keel² ▶ **n.** Brit. a flat-bottomed freight boat; a keelboat.
– ORIGIN Middle English: from Middle Low German *kēl*, Middle Dutch *kiel* 'ship, boat.'

keel·boat /ˈkēlˌbōt/ ▶ **n. 1** a yacht built with a permanent keel rather than a centerboard.
2 a large, flat freight boat used on rivers.

keel·haul /ˈkēlˌhôl/ ▶ **v.** [with obj.] historical punish (someone) by dragging them through the water under the keel of a ship, either across the width or from bow to stern. ■ often humorous punish or reprimand severely.
– ORIGIN mid 17th cent.: from Dutch *kielhalen*.

Kee·ling Is·lands /ˈkēliNG/ another name for **Cocos Islands.**

keel·son /ˈkēlsən/ (also **kelson**) ▶ **n.** a centerline structure running the length of a ship and fastening the transverse members of the floor to the keel below.
– ORIGIN Middle English *kelswayn*, related to Low German *kielswīn*, from *kiel* 'keel of a ship' + *swīn* 'swine' (used as the name of a timber).

Kee·lung /ˈkēˈlo͝oNG/ see **Chilung.**

Kee·mun /ˈkēˈmo͞on, ˈkā-/ ▶ **n.** a black tea grown in Keemun, China.

keen[1] /kēn/ ▶ **adj. 1** having or showing eagerness or enthusiasm: *keen believers in the monetary system* | *a keen desire to learn.* ■ [predic.] (**keen on**) interested in or attracted by (someone or something): *Bob makes it obvious he's keen on her.*
2 sharp or penetrating, in particular: ■ (of a sense) highly developed: *I have keen eyesight.* ■ (of mental faculties) quick to understand or function: *her keen intellect.* ■ (of the air or wind) extremely cold; biting. ■ (of the edge or point of a blade) sharp. ■ literary (of a smell, light, or sound) penetrating; clear.
3 [predic.] informal, dated excellent: *I would soon fly to distant stars—how keen!*
4 Brit. (of prices) very low; competitive.
– DERIVATIVES **keen·ly adv.**
– ORIGIN Old English *cēne* 'wise, clever,' also 'brave, daring,' of Germanic origin; related to Dutch *koen* and German *kühn* 'bold, brave.' Current senses date from Middle English.

keen[2] ▶ **v.** [no obj.] wail in grief for a dead person; sing a keen. ■ (usu. as noun **keening**) make an eerie wailing sound: *the keening of the cold night wind.*
▶ **n.** an Irish funeral song accompanied by wailing in lamentation for the dead.
– ORIGIN mid 19th cent.: from Irish *caoinim* 'I wail.'

k

keen·er /ˈkēnər/ ▶ **n. 1** a person who keens for someone who has died.
2 Canadian informal a person who is who is extremely eager, zealous, or enthusiastic: *keeners who spent most of high school buried in homework.*

keen·ness /ˈkēnˈnis/ ▶ **n.** the quality of being eager or enthusiastic; eagerness: *he has expressed his keenness to retain his job.*

keep /kēp/ ▶ **v.** (past and past participle **kept** /kept/) [with obj.] **1** have or retain possession of: *my father would keep the best for himself* | *she had trouble keeping her balance.* ■ retain or reserve for use in the future: *return one copy to me, keeping the other for your files.* ■ put or store in a regular place: *the stand where her umbrella was kept.* ■ retain one's place in or on (a seat or saddle, the ground, etc.) against opposition or difficulty: *are you able to keep your saddle?* ■ delay or detain; cause to be late: *I won't keep you; I know you've got a busy evening.*
2 continue or cause to continue in a specified condition, position, course, etc.: [no obj.] *she could have had some boyfriend she kept quiet about* | *keep left along the wall* | [with obj. and complement] *she might be kept alive artificially by machinery.* ■ [no obj.] continue doing or do repeatedly or habitually: *he keeps going on about the murder.* ■ [no obj.] (of a perishable commodity) remain in good condition: *fresh ginger does not keep well.* ■ make (someone) do something for a period of time: *I have kept her waiting too long.* ■ archaic continue to follow (a way, path, or course): *the friars and soldiers removed, keeping their course toward Jericho.*
3 provide for the sustenance of (someone): *he had to keep his large family in the manner he had chosen.* ■ provide (someone) with a regular supply of a commodity: *the money should* **keep him in** *cigarettes for a week.* ■ own and look after (an animal) for pleasure or profit. ■ own and manage (a shop or business). ■ guard; protect: *his only thought is to* **keep** *the boy* **from** *harm.* ■ support (someone, esp. a woman) financially in return for sexual favors: [as adj.] *a kept woman.* ■ [no obj.] act as a goalkeeper.
4 honor or fulfill (a commitment or undertaking): *I'll keep my promise, naturally.* ■ observe (a religious occasion) in the prescribed manner: *today's consumers do not keep the Sabbath.* ■ pay due regard to (a law or custom).
5 make written entries in (a diary) on a regular basis: *the master kept a weekly journal.* ■ write down as (a record): *keep a note of the whereabouts of each item.*
▶ **n. 1** food, clothes, and other essentials for living: *working overtime to* **earn his keep.** ■ the cost of such items.
2 archaic charge; control: *if from shepherd's keep a lamb strayed far.*
3 the strongest or central tower of a castle, acting as a final refuge.
– PHRASES **you can't keep a good man** (or **woman**) **down** informal a competent person will always recover well from setbacks or problems. **for keeps** informal permanently; indefinitely. **keep one's feet** manage not to fall. **keep going** make an effort to live normally when in a difficult situation. **keep open house** provide general hospitality. **keep to oneself** avoid contact with others. **keep something to oneself** refuse to disclose or share something. **keep up with the Joneses** try to maintain the same social and material standards as one's friends or neighbors.
– PHRASAL VERBS **keep someone after** make a student stay at school after normal hours as a punishment. **keep at** (or **keep someone at**) persist (or force someone to persist) with: *it was the best part of a day's work, but I kept at it.* **keep away** (or **keep someone away**) stay away (or make someone stay away): *keep away from the edge of the cliff.* **keep back** (or **keep someone/something back**) remain (or cause someone or something to remain) at a distance: *he had kept back from the river when he could.* **keep someone back** make a student repeat a year at school because of poor grades. **keep something back** retain or withhold something: *the father kept back $5 for himself.* ■ decline to disclose something. ■ prevent tears from flowing. **keep down** stay hidden by crouching or lying down: *Keep down! There's someone coming.* **keep someone down** hold someone in subjection: *but others doubted the injury would keep him down that long.* **keep something down 1** cause something to remain at a low level: *the population of aphids is normally kept down by other animals.* **2** retain food or drink in one's stomach without vomiting. **keep from** (or **keep someone from**) avoid (or cause someone to avoid) doing something: *Dinah bit her lips to keep from screaming* | *he could hardly keep himself from laughing.* **keep something from 1** cause something to remain a secret from (someone). **2** cause something to stay out of: *she could not keep the dismay from her voice.* **keep someone in** confine someone indoors or in a particular place: *he should be kept in overnight for a second operation.* **keep something in** restrain oneself from expressing a feeling: *he wanted to make me mad, but I kept it all in.* **keep off 1** avoid encroaching on or touching. ■ avoid consuming or smoking: *the first thing was to keep off alcohol.* ■ avoid (a subject). **2** (of bad weather) fail to occur. **keep someone/something off** prevent someone or something from encroaching on or touching: *keep your hands off me.* **keep on** continue to do (something): *they would have preferred to keep on working.* **keep on about** speak about (something) repeatedly. **keep someone/something on** continue to use or employ someone or something. **keep out** (or **keep someone/something out**) remain (or cause someone or something to remain) outside: *cover with cheesecloth to keep out flies.* **keep to** avoid leaving (a path, road, or place). ■ adhere to (a schedule). ■ observe (a promise). ■ confine or restrict oneself to: *nothing is more irritating than people who do not keep to the point.* **keep someone under** hold a person or group in subjection: *the local people are kept under by the army.* **keep up** move or progress at the same rate as someone or something else: *often they had to pause to allow him to keep up.* ■ meet a commitment to pay or do something regularly: *if you do not* **keep up with** *the payments, the loan company can make you sell your home.* **keep up with** learn about or be aware of (current events or developments). ■ continue to be in contact with (someone). **keep someone up** prevent someone from going to bed or to sleep. **keep something up** maintain or preserve something in the existing state; continue a course of action: *keep up the good work.* ■ keep something in an efficient or proper state: *the new owners could not afford to keep up the grounds.* ■ make something remain at a high level: *he was whistling to keep up his spirits.*
– DERIVATIVES **keep·a·ble adj.**
– ORIGIN late Old English *cēpan* 'seize, take in,' also 'care for, attend to,' of unknown origin.

keep·er /ˈkēpər/ ▶ **n. 1** a person who manages or looks after something or someone: *I would not stop him—I'm his wife, not his keeper.* ■ a guard at a prison or a museum. ■ short for **zookeeper.** ■ short for **gamekeeper.** ■ short for **goalkeeper.**
2 [with adj.] a food or drink that remains in a specified condition if stored: *hazelnuts are good keepers.*
3 a fish large enough to be kept when caught.
■ informal a person or thing that is valuable and to be cherished: *this disc is a keeper and one that belongs on every serious DVD collector's shelf* | *if he's a good communicator and a great listener, he's a keeper.*
4 an object that keeps another in place, or protects something more fragile or valuable, in particular: ■ a ring worn to keep a more valuable one on the finger. ■ a bar of soft iron placed across the poles of a horseshoe magnet to maintain its strength.
5 Football a play in which the quarterback runs with the ball instead of handing it off or passing it.
– DERIVATIVES **keep·er·ship** /-ˌSHip/ **n.**

keep·ing /ˈkēpiNG/ ▶ **n.** the action of owning, maintaining, or protecting something: *the keeping of dogs* | [in combination] *careful record-keeping is needed.*
– PHRASES **in someone's keeping** in someone's care or custody. **in** (or **out of**) **keeping with** in (or out of) harmony or conformity with: *the cuisine is in keeping with the hotel's Edwardian character.*

keep·sake /ˈkēpˌsāk/ ▶ **n.** a small item kept in memory of the person who gave it or originally owned it.

kees·hond /ˈkāsˌhänd, -ˌhônt/ ▶ **n.** a dog of a Dutch breed with long thick gray hair resembling a large Pomeranian.
– ORIGIN 1920s: Dutch, from *Kees* (nickname for the given name *Cornelius*) + *hond* 'dog.'

keeshond

kees·ter ▶ **n.** variant spelling of **keister.**

kef /kef/ (also **kif**) ▶ **n.** a substance, esp. cannabis, smoked to produce a drowsy state.
– ORIGIN early 19th cent.: from Arabic *kayf* 'enjoyment, well-being.'

Ke·fau·ver /ˈkēˌfôvər/, Estes (1903–63) US politician; full name *Carey Estes Kefauver.* He was a member of the US House of Representatives from Tennessee 1939–49, a member of the US Senate 1949–63, and a Democratic vice presidential candidate 1956. As a senator, he conducted hearings 1950–51 to investigate organized crime in interstate commerce.

kef·fi·yeh ▶ **n.** variant spelling of **kaffiyeh.**

ke·fir /kəˈfi(ə)r/ ▶ **n.** a sour-tasting drink make from cow's milk fermented with certain bacteria.
– ORIGIN from Russian.

Kef·la·vik /ˈkefləˌvēk, ˈkyeblə-/ a fishing port in southwestern Iceland; pop. 14,183 (2009). Iceland's international airport is located nearby.

kef·te·des /kefˈtedēz, -ˈteTHes/ ▶ **plural n.** (in Greek cooking) small meatballs made with herbs and onions.
– ORIGIN from Greek *kephtedes*, plural of *kephtes*, via Turkish from Persian *koftah.*

keg /keg/ ▶ **n. 1** a small barrel, esp. one of less than 30 gallons or (in the UK) 10 gallons.
2 a unit of weight equal to 100 lb (45 kg), used for nails.
– ORIGIN early 17th cent.: variant of Scots and US dialect *cag*, from Old Norse *kaggi.*

Ke·gel ex·er·cise /ˈkēgəl, ˈkeg-/ ▶ **n.** an exercise to strengthen the pelvic floor muscles, in which the levator muscles are squeezed and held for five seconds, then released for five seconds, for a number of repetitions. They are used to treat urinary incontinence, or to prepare for or recover from childbirth.
– ORIGIN from California physician Dr. Arnold *Kegel*, who advocated such exercises from the late 1940s.

keg·ger /ˈkegər/ ▶ **n.** informal (also **keg party**) a party at which beer is served, typically from kegs. ■ a keg of beer.

Keil·lor /ˈkēlər/, Garrison (Edward) (1942–), US writer and radio entertainer. He created the radio program *A Prairie Home Companion* (1974–87, 1993–) and wrote fictional works such as *Happy to Be Here* (1982), *Lake Wobegon Days* (1985), and *Wobegon Boy* (1996). In 2004 he published *Homegrown Democrat: A Few Plain Thoughts from the Heart of America.*

kei·ret·su /kāˈretso͞o/ ▶ **n.** (pl. **same**) (in Japan) a conglomeration of businesses linked together by cross-shareholdings to form a robust corporate structure.
– ORIGIN Japanese, from *kei* 'systems' + *retsu* 'tier.'

kei·rin /ˈkāˈrin/ ▶ **n.** a racing event in which cyclists ride several laps around an indoor track behind a motorized pacesetter before sprinting to the finish.
– ORIGIN 1950s: Japanese, literally 'bicycle race.'

keis·ter /ˈkēstər/ (also **keester**) ▶ **n. 1** informal a person's buttocks.
2 dated a suitcase, bag, or box for carrying possessions or merchandise.

–ORIGIN late 19th cent. (in the sense 'suitcase, bag'): of unknown origin.

kei·tai /ˈkātī/ ▶ **n.** (pl. **same** or **keitais**) (in Japan) a cellular phone.
–ORIGIN Japanese, literally 'portable,' short for *keitai denwa* 'cell phone.'

Ke·ku·lé /ˈkekəˌlā/, Friedrich August, (1829–96), German chemist; full name *Friedrich August Kekulé von Stradonitz*. One of the founders of structural organic chemistry, he is best known for discovering the ring structure of benzene.

Kel·ler /ˈkelər/, Helen (Adams) (1880–1968), US writer, social reformer, and academic. Blind and deaf from an early age, she learned how to read, type, and speak with the help of her tutor, **Anne Sullivan** (1866–1936).

Kel·logg Pact /ˈkelôg, -äg/ (also **Kellogg–Briand Pact**) a treaty renouncing war as an instrument of national policy, signed in Paris in 1928 by representatives of fifteen nations. It grew out of a proposal made by the French Premier **Aristide Briand** (1862–1932) to **Frank B. Kellogg** (1856–1937), US Secretary of State.

Kells, Book of /kelz/ an illuminated manuscript of the Gospels, perhaps made by Irish monks in Iona in the 8th or early 9th century, now kept at Trinity College, Dublin.
–ORIGIN *Kells*, the name of a town in County Meath, Ireland, where the manuscript was formerly kept.

Kel·ly[1] /ˈkelē/, Emmett Lee (1898–1979), US entertainer. He played Weary Willie, the mournful tramp clown, with Ringling Brothers and Barnum and Bailey Circus from 1942 until 1957.

Kel·ly[2], Gene (1912–96), US dancer and choreographer; full name *Eugene Curran Kelly*. He performed in and choreographed many movie musicals, including *An American in Paris* (1951) and *Singin' in the Rain* (1952).

Kel·ly[3], Grace (Patricia) (1928–82), US movie actress; also called (from 1956) **Princess Grace of Monaco**. She starred in such movies as *High Noon* (1952), *The Country Girl* (1954), and *To Catch a Thief* (1955) before retiring from the industry in 1956 to marry Monaco's **Prince Rainier III** (1923–2005).

Kel·ly[4], Ned (1855–80), Australian outlaw; full name *Edward Kelly*; leader of a band of horse and cattle thieves and bank robbers.

ke·loid /ˈkēˌloid/ ▶ **n.** Medicine an area of irregular fibrous tissue formed at the site of a scar or injury.
–ORIGIN mid 19th cent.: via French from Greek *khēlē* 'crab's claw' + **-OID**.

kelp /kelp/ ▶ **n.** a large brown seaweed that typically has a long, tough stalk with a broad frond divided into strips. Some kinds grow to a very large size and form underwater "forests" that support a large population of animals. ● Family Laminariaceae, class Phaeophyceae, including the genera *Laminaria* (used in some areas as manure) and *Macrocystis* (harvested in the US as a source of algin). ■ the calcined ashes of seaweed, used as a source of various salts.
–ORIGIN late Middle English: of unknown origin.

kelp·fish /ˈkelpˌfisH/ ▶ **n.** (pl. **same** or **kelpfishes**) any of a number of fish that live among kelp or other marine algae, in particular: ● a small fish with the dorsal fin running the length of the body, of the Pacific coast of North America (*Gibbonsia* and other genera, family Clinidae). ● an Australian fish that lives among seagrass and algae (family Chironemidae: several genera).

kel·pie /ˈkelpē/ ▶ **n. 1** a water spirit of Scottish folklore, typically taking the form of a horse, reputed to delight in the drowning of travelers. **2** a sheepdog of an Australian breed with a smooth coat, originally bred from a Scottish collie.
–ORIGIN late 17th cent.: perhaps from Scottish Gaelic *cailpeach, colpach* 'bullock, colt.' Sense 2 apparently comes from the name of a particular bitch, *King's Kelpie* (*c.*1879).

kel·son /ˈkelsən/ ▶ **n.** variant spelling of **KEELSON**.

kelt /kelt/ ▶ **n.** a salmon or sea trout after spawning and before returning to the sea.
–ORIGIN Middle English: of unknown origin.

Kel·vin /ˈkelvən/, William Thomson, 1st Baron (1824–1907), British physicist and natural philosopher. He introduced the absolute scale of temperature and restated the second law of thermodynamics. He was involved in the laying of the first Atlantic cable, for which he invented several instruments.

kel·vin /ˈkelvən/ (abbr.: **K**) ▶ **n.** (pl. **same** or **kelvins**) the SI base unit of thermodynamic temperature, equal in magnitude to the degree Celsius.
–ORIGIN late 19th cent.: named after Lord **KELVIN**.

Kel·vin scale ▶ **n.** a scale of temperature with absolute zero as zero, and the triple point of water as exactly 273.16 degrees.

Ke·mal Pa·sha /keˈmäl ˈpäsHə, kəˈmäl/ see **ATATÜRK**.

Ke·me·ro·vo /ˈkyemirəvə, -əˌvō/ an industrial city in south central Russia, to the east of Novosibirsk; pop. 515,100 (est. 2009).

kemp /kemp/ ▶ **n.** a coarse hair or fiber in wool.
–DERIVATIVES **kemp·y adj.**
–ORIGIN late Middle English (originally denoting a coarse human hair): from Old Norse *kampr* 'beard, whisker.'

Kem·pis /ˈkempəs/, Thomas à, see **THOMAS À KEMPIS**.

kempt /kem(p)t/ ▶ **adj.** chiefly Brit. (of a person or a place) maintained in a neat and clean condition; well cared for: *she was looking as thoroughly kempt as ever*.
–ORIGIN Old English *cemd-*, past participle of *cemban* 'to comb,' of Germanic origin; related to **COMB**. The Middle English form *kemb* survives in dialect.

ken /ken/ ▶ **n.** [in sing.] one's range of knowledge or sight: *such determination is beyond my ken*.
▶ **v.** (**kens, kenning**; past and past participle **kenned** or **kent** /kent/) [with obj.] Scottish & N. English know: *d'ye ken anyone who can boast of that?* ■ recognize; identify: *that's him—d'ye ken him?*
–ORIGIN Old English *cennan* 'tell, make known,' of Germanic origin; related to Dutch and German *kennen* 'know, be acquainted with,' from an Indo-European root shared by **CAN**[1] and **KNOW**. Current senses of the verb date from Middle English; the noun from the mid 16th cent.

ke·naf /kəˈnaf/ ▶ **n.** a tropical plant of the mallow family that yields a jutelike fiber. ● *Hibiscus cannabinus*, family Malvaceae. ■ the brown fiber of this plant, used to make paper, ropes, and coarse cloth.
–ORIGIN late 19th cent.: from Persian, variant of *kanab* 'hemp.'

Ke·nai Peninsula /ˈkēˌnī/ a region in southern Alaska, in the Gulf of Alaska, south of Anchorage.

Ken·dal Green /ˈkendl/ ▶ **n.** a kind of rough green woolen cloth. ■ the green color of this cloth.

Ken·dall /ˈkendl/, Edward Calvin (1886–1972), US biochemist. He isolated crystalline thyroxine from the thyroid gland, and he also discovered cortisone. Nobel Prize for Physiology or Medicine (1950), shared with Philip S. Hench (1896–1965) and Tadeus Reichstein (1897–1996).

ken·do /ˈkenˌdō/ ▶ **n.** a Japanese form of fencing with two-handed bamboo swords, originally developed as a safe form of sword training for samurai.
–DERIVATIVES **ken·do·ist** /-dōist/ **n.**
–ORIGIN Japanese, from *ken* 'sword' + *dō* 'way.'

Ke·neal·ly /kəˈnēlē/, Thomas (Michael) (1935–), Australian novelist. He is best known for his novel *Schindler's List* (1982; movie, 1993), the true story of German industrialist Oskar Schindler, who helped more than 1,200 Jews escape death in Nazi concentration camps.

Ken·nan /ˈkenən/, George Frost (1904–2005) US writer and diplomat. He held ambassadorships to the former Soviet Union 1952 and to Yugoslavia 1961–63. He wrote *Russia Leaves the War* (1956), *Decision to Intervene* (1958), *Memoirs: 1925–1950* (1967), *Memoirs: 1950–1963* (1972), and *Cloud of Danger* (1977).

Ken·ne·bec Riv·er /ˈkenəˌbek/ a river that flows for 150 miles (240 km) through west central Maine to the Atlantic Ocean. Waterville, Augusta, and Bath lie on it.

Ken·ne·dy[1] /ˈkenidē/ the name of a US family of Democratic politicians, including: ■ **John Fitzgerald** (1917–63), 35th president of the US 1961–63; known as **JFK**. The youngest person to be elected to the presidency, he was a popular advocate of civil rights. In foreign affairs he recovered from the Bay of Pigs fiasco to demand successfully the withdrawal of Soviet missiles from Cuba during the Cuban Missile Crisis, October 18–29, 1962. On November 22, 1963, he was assassinated while riding in a motorcade through Dallas, Texas. Lee Harvey Oswald was charged with his murder. ■ **Robert (Francis)** (1925–68), US attorney general 1961–64; brother of John and Edward; known as **Bobby** and **RFK**. He closely assisted his brother John in domestic policy and was also a champion of the civil rights movement. He was assassinated during his campaign to become the 1968 Democratic presidential nominee. ■ **Edward (Moore)** (1932–2009), US senator from Massachusetts 1962–2009; brother of John and Robert; known as **Ted**. As one of the longest serving senators in US history, he was a leading influence in the passage of much social reform legislation.

John F. Kennedy

Ken·ne·dy[2], Anthony McLeod (1935–) US Supreme Court associate justice 1988– . Appointed to the Court by President Reagan, he maintained a generally conservative stance.

Ken·ne·dy[3], Joseph Patrick (1888–1969) US businessman and diplomat; father of John Fitzgerald, Robert Francis, and Edward Moore Kennedy. He made his fortune in banking, the stock market, shipbuilding, and movies.

Ken·ne·dy[4], William (Joseph) (1928–) US writer. His novels include *Ironweed* (1983), *Quinn's Book* (1988), *Very Old Bones* (1992), and *Roscoe* (2002).

Ken·ne·dy, Cape former name (1963–73) for **CANAVERAL, CAPE**.

ken·nel /ˈkenl/ ▶ **n.** a small shelter for a dog or cat. ■ a boarding or breeding establishment for dogs or cats.
▶ **v.** (**kennels, kenneling, kenneled**; chiefly Brit. **kennels, kennelling, kennelled**) [with obj.] put (a dog or cat) in a kennel.
–ORIGIN Middle English: from an Old Northern French variant of Old French *chenil*, from Latin *canis* 'dog.'

Ken·nel·ly /ˈkenəlē/, Arthur Edwin (1861–1939), US electrical engineer. He worked on the theory of alternating currents, and, independently of Oliver Heaviside, he also discovered the layer in the atmosphere responsible for reflecting radio waves back to the earth.

Ken·nel·ly lay·er (also **Kennelly–Heaviside layer** /ˈhevēˌsīd/) ▶ **n.** another name for **E LAYER**.

Ken·ner /ˈkenər/ a city in southeastern Louisiana, west of New Orleans; pop. 66,942 (est. 2008).

Ken·neth I /ˈkeniTH/ (d.858), king of Scotland *c.*844–858; known as **Kenneth MacAlpin**. He is traditionally viewed as the founder of the kingdom of Scotland, which was established following his defeat of the Picts in about 844.

Ken·ne·wick /ˈkenəwik/ a city in southeastern Washington, on the Columbia River; pop. 63,216 (est. 2008).

ken·ning /ˈkeniNG/ ▶ **n.** a compound expression in Old English and Old Norse poetry with metaphorical meaning, e.g., *oar-steed* = ship.
–ORIGIN late 19th cent.: from Old Norse, from *kenna* 'know, perceive'; related to **KEN**.

ke·no /ˈkēnō/ ▶ **n.** a game of chance similar to lotto, based on the drawing of numbers that must correspond with selected numbers on cards.
–ORIGIN early 19th cent.: from French *kine*, denoting a set of five winning lottery numbers.

Ke·no·sha /kəˈnōsHə/ an industrial port city in southeastern Wisconsin, on Lake Michigan; pop. 96,950 (est. 2008).

ke·no·sis /kəˈnōsis/ ▶ **n.** (in Christian theology) the renunciation of the divine nature, at least in part, by Christ in the Incarnation.
–DERIVATIVES **ke·not·ic** /-ˈnätik/ **adj.**
–ORIGIN late 19th cent.: from Greek *kenōsis* 'an emptying,' from *kenoun* 'to empty,' from *kenos* 'empty,' with biblical allusion (Phil. 2:7) to Greek *heauton ekenōse*, literally 'emptied himself.'

Ken·sing·ton /ˈkenziNGtən/ a fashionable residential district in central London, England. Part of the borough of Kensington and Chelsea, it contains Kensington palace and gardens and the Victoria and Albert, Natural History, and Science museums.

k

PRONUNCIATION KEY ə ago, up; ər over, fur; a hat; ā ate; ä car; e let; ē see; i fit; ī by; NG sing; ō go; ô law, for; oi toy; o͝o good; o͞o goo; ou out; TH thin; T͟H then; ZH vision

ken·speck·le /ˈkenˌspekəl/ ▶ **adj.** Scottish easily recognizable; conspicuous.
– ORIGIN mid 16th cent.: of Scandinavian origin, probably based on Old Norse *kenna* 'know, perceive' and *spak-*, *spek-* 'wise or wisdom.'

Kent[1] /kent/ a county on the southeastern coast of England; county town, Maidstone.
– DERIVATIVES **Kent·ish** adj.
– ORIGIN from Latin *Cantium*, of Celtic origin.

Kent[2] **1** a city in northeastern Ohio, home to Kent State University; pop. 27,983 (est. 2008).
2 a city in western Washington, on the Naches River, a southern suburb of Seattle; pop. 83,978 (est. 2008).

kent /kent/ past and past participle of **KEN**.

ken·te /ˈkentə, -tē/ ▶ **n.** a brightly colored, banded material made in Ghana. ■ a long garment made from this material, worn loosely around the shoulders and waist.
– ORIGIN mid 20th cent.: from Twi, 'cloth.'

ken·ti·a palm /ˈkentēə/ (also **kentia**) ▶ **n.** an Australasian palm tree that is popular as a houseplant while it is young. ● *Howeia* (or *Howea*) *forsteriana* (formerly *Kentia forsteriana*), family Palmae.
– ORIGIN late 19th cent.: modern Latin, named after William *Kent* (died 1828), botanical collector.

Ken·ton /ˈkentn/, Stan (1912–79), US bandleader, composer, and arranger; born *Stanley Newcomb*. He formed his own orchestra in 1940 and is particularly associated with the big-band jazz style of the 1950s. Notable works: "Artistry in Rhythm" (1941) and "Eager Beaver" (1943).

Ken·tuck·y /kənˈtəkē/ a state in the southeastern US; pop. 4,269,245 (est. 2008); capital, Frankfort; statehood, June 1, 1792 (15). Ceded by the French to the British in 1763 and then to the US in 1783 by the Treaty of Paris, it was explored by Daniel Boone.
– DERIVATIVES **Ken·tuck·i·an** /-ēən/ adj.

Ken·tuck·y colo·nel ▶ **n.** an honorary commission given by the state of Kentucky to individuals noted for their public service and their work for the advancement of Kentucky.

Ken·tuck·y Der·by ▶ **n.** an annual horse race for three-year-olds at Louisville, Kentucky. First held in 1875, it is the oldest horse race in the US It is the first race of horse racing's Triple Crown.

Ken·ya /ˈkenyə, ˈkēnyə/ a country in East Africa, on the Indian Ocean; pop. 39,002,800 (est. 2009); capital, Nairobi; languages, Swahili (official), English (official), and Kikuyu.

> Populated largely by Bantu-speaking peoples, Kenya became a British Crown Colony in 1920. The demands made on land by European settlers led to the Mau Mau rebellion of the 1950s. Kenya became an independent state within the Commonwealth of Nations in 1963, and a republic was established the following year.

– DERIVATIVES **Ken·yan** adj. & n.

Ken·ya, Mount a mountain in central Kenya, just south of the equator, that rises to a height of 17,058 feet (5,200 m). The second highest mountain in Africa, it gave its name to the country of Kenya.

Ken·yat·ta /kenˈyätə/, Jomo (*c.*1891–1978), Kenyan statesman; prime minister 1963 and president 1964–78.

kep·i /ˈkāpē, ˈkepē/ ▶ **n.** (pl. **kepis**) a French military cap with a flat top and horizontal brim.
– ORIGIN mid 19th cent.: from French *képi*, from Swiss German *Käppi*, diminutive of *Kappe* 'cap.'

kepi

Kep·ler /ˈkeplər/, Johannes (1571–1630), German astronomer. He discovered the three laws that govern orbital motion.
– DERIVATIVES **Kep·ler·i·an** /kepˈli(ə)rēən/ adj.

Kep·ler's laws three theorems describing orbital motion. The first law states that planets move in elliptical orbits with the sun at one focus. The second states that the radius vector of a planet sweeps out equal areas in equal times. The third law relates the distances of the planets from the sun to their orbital periods.

kept /kept/ past and past participle of **KEEP**.

Ke·ra·la /ˈkerələ/ a state on the southwestern coast of India; capital, Thiruvananthapuram. It was created in 1956 from the former state of Travancore-Cochin and part of Madras.
– DERIVATIVES **Ke·ra·lite** /-ˌlīt/ adj. & n.

kerat- ▶ **comb. form** variant spelling of **KERATO-** shortened before a vowel (as in *keratectomy*).

ker·a·tec·to·my /ˌkerəˈtektəmē/ ▶ **n.** surgical removal of a section or layer of the cornea, usually performed using a laser to correct myopia.

ker·a·tin /ˈkerətin/ ▶ **n.** a fibrous protein forming the main structural constituent of hair, feathers, hoofs, claws, horns, etc.
– DERIVATIVES **ker·at·i·nous** /kəˈratn-əs/ adj.
– ORIGIN mid 19th cent.: from Greek *keras*, *kerat-* 'horn' + **-IN**[1].

ker·a·tin·ize /ˈkerətnˌīz/ ▶ **v.** Biology change or become changed into a form containing keratin: [with obj.] *the products of the epidermal line are ultimately keratinized* | [no obj.] *the cells keratinize under estrogenic action.*
– DERIVATIVES **ker·a·tin·i·za·tion** /ˌkerətn-iˈzāsHən/ **n.**
– ORIGIN late 19th cent.: from Greek *keratinos* 'horny' + **-IZE**.

ker·a·tin·o·cyte /kəˈratn-əˌsīt/ ▶ **n.** Biology an epidermal cell that produces keratin.

ker·a·ti·tis /ˌkerəˈtītis/ ▶ **n.** Medicine inflammation of the cornea of the eye.

kerato- ▶ **comb. form** (also **kerat-**) **1** relating to keratin or horny tissue.
2 relating to the cornea.
– ORIGIN from Greek *keras*, *kerat-* 'horn.'

ker·a·to·mi·leu·sis /ˌkerətōmiˈlo͞osis/ ▶ **n.** the surgical reshaping of the cornea, carried out in order to correct a refractive error.
– ORIGIN 1990s: from *kerato-* 'of the cornea' + Greek *smileusis* 'carving.'

ker·a·to·plas·ty /ˈkerətəˌplastē/ ▶ **n.** surgery carried out on the cornea, esp. corneal transplantation.

ker·a·tose /ˈkerəˌtōs/ ▶ **adj.** Zoology (of certain sponges) composed of a horny substance.
– ORIGIN mid 19th cent.: from Greek *keras*, *kerat-* 'horn' + **-OSE**[1].

ker·a·to·sis /ˌkerəˈtōsis/ ▶ **n.** (pl. **keratoses** /-sēz/) Medicine a horny growth, esp. on the skin.

ker·a·tot·o·my /ˌkerəˈtätəmē/ ▶ **n.** a surgical operation involving cutting into the cornea of the eye. The most common form is **radial keratotomy**, performed to correct myopia.

kerb /kərb/ ▶ **n.** British spelling of **CURB**.

Kerch /kercH/ a city in southern Ukraine, the chief port and industrial center of the Crimea, at the eastern end of the Kerch peninsula; pop. 148,100 (est. 2009).

ker·chief /ˈkərcHəf, -ˌcHēf/ ▶ **n.** a piece of fabric used to cover the head, or worn tied around the neck. ■ a handkerchief.
– DERIVATIVES **ker·chiefed** adj.
– ORIGIN Middle English *kerchef*, from Old French *cuevrechief*, from *couvrir* 'to cover' + *chief* 'head.'

Ke·res /ˈkāˌrās/ ▶ **n.** (pl. **same**) **1** a member of a Pueblo Indian people of New Mexico.
2 the language of this people, of unknown affinity.
▶ **adj.** of or relating to this people or their language.
– DERIVATIVES **Ker·e·san** /ˈkerisən/ adj.
– ORIGIN from American Spanish *Queres*, from American Indian.

kerf /kərf/ ▶ **n.** **1** a slit made by cutting, esp. with a saw.
2 the cut end of a felled tree.
– DERIVATIVES **kerfed** adj.
– ORIGIN Old English *cyrf* 'cutting, a cut'; related to **CARVE**.

ker·fuf·fle /kərˈfəfəl/ ▶ **n.** [in sing.] informal, chiefly Brit. a commotion or fuss, esp. one caused by conflicting views: *there was a kerfuffle over the chairmanship.*
– ORIGIN early 19th cent.: perhaps from Scots *curfuffle* (probably from Scottish Gaelic *car* 'twist, bend' + imitative Scots *fuffle* 'to disorder'), or related to Irish *cior thual* 'confusion, disorder.'

Ker·gue·len Is·lands /ˈkərgələn, ˌkərgəˈlen/ a group of islands in the southern Indian Ocean that comprise the island of Kerguelen and some 300 small islets, part of the French Southern and Antarctic Territories. The only settlement is a scientific base.
– ORIGIN named after the Breton navigator Yves-Joseph de *Kerguélen*-Trémarec, who discovered the islands in 1772.

Kér·ki·ra /ˈkerki(ə)rə/ modern Greek name for **CORFU**.

Ker·mad·ec Is·lands /kərˈmadik/ a group of uninhabited islands in the western South Pacific Ocean, north of New Zealand, administered by New Zealand since 1887.

ker·mes /ˈkərmēz/ ▶ **n.** **1** a red dye used, esp. formerly, for coloring fabrics and manuscripts. ■ the dried bodies of a female scale insect, which are crushed to yield this dye.
2 (**oak kermes**) the scale insect that is used for this dye, forming berrylike galls on the kermes oak. ● *Kermes ilicis*, family Eriococcidae, suborder Homoptera.
– ORIGIN late 16th cent. (denoting the kermes oak): from French *kermès*, from Arabic *ḳirmiz*; related to **CRIMSON**.

ker·mes oak ▶ **n.** a very small evergreen Mediterranean oak that sometimes remains a shrub. It has prickly hollylike leaves and was formerly prized as a host plant for the insect kermes. ● *Quercus coccifera*, family Fagaceae.

ker·mis /ˈkərmis/ ▶ **n.** a summer fair held in towns and villages in the Netherlands. ■ a fair or carnival, esp. one held to raise money for a charity.
– ORIGIN late 16th cent.: Dutch, originally denoting a mass on the anniversary of the dedication of a church, when a fair was held, from *kerk* 'church' + *mis* 'Mass.'

Kern /kərn/, Jerome (David) (1885–1945), US composer. A major influence in the development of the musical, he wrote several musical comedies, including *Showboat* (1927), which featured the song "Ol' Man River."

kern[1] /kərn/ Printing ▶ **v.** [with obj.] **1** (usu. as noun **kerning**) adjust the spacing between (letters or characters) in a piece of text to be printed. ■ make (letters) overlap.
2 design (metal type) with a projecting part beyond the body or shank.
▶ **n.** the part of a metal type projecting beyond its body or shank.
– ORIGIN late 17th cent.: perhaps from French *carne* 'corner,' from Latin *cardo*, *cardin-* 'hinge.'

kern[2] (also **kerne**) ▶ **n.** **1** historical a light-armed Irish foot soldier.
2 archaic a peasant; a rustic.
– ORIGIN late Middle English: from Irish *ceithearn*, from Old Irish *ceithern* 'band of foot soldiers.'

ker·nel /ˈkərnl/ ▶ **n.** a softer, usually edible part of a nut, seed, or fruit stone contained within its hard shell. ■ the seed and hard husk of a cereal, esp. wheat. ■ [in sing.] the central or most important part of something: *this is the kernel of the argument.* ■ the most basic level or core of an operating system of a computer, responsible for resource allocation, file management, and security. ■ [as modifier] Linguistics denoting a basic unmarked linguistic string.
– ORIGIN Old English *cyrnel*, diminutive of **CORN**[1].

kern·ite /ˈkərnīt/ ▶ **n.** a transparent crystalline mineral that consists of hydrated sodium borate.
– ORIGIN early 20th cent.: from *Kern* (the name of the California county where it was discovered) + **-ITE**[1].

ker·o·gen /ˈkerəjən/ ▶ **n.** a complex fossilized organic material, found in oil shale and other sedimentary rock, that is insoluble in common organic solvents and yields petroleum products on distillation.
– ORIGIN early 20th cent.: from Greek *kēros* 'wax' + **-GEN**.

ker·o·sene /ˈkerəˌsēn, ˈkar-, ˌkerəˈsēn, ˌkar-/ (also chiefly Brit. **kerosine**) ▶ **n.** a light fuel oil obtained by distilling petroleum, used esp. in jet engines and domestic heaters and lamps and as a cleaning solvent.
– ORIGIN mid 19th cent.: from Greek *kēros* 'wax' (because the solid form of paraffin is waxlike) + **-ENE**.

Ker·ou·ac /ˈkero͞oˌak/, Jack (1922–69), US novelist and poet; born *Jean-Louis Lebris de Kérouac*. A leading figure of the beat generation, he is best known for his semiautobiographical novel *On the Road* (1957). Other notable works: *Doctor Sax* (1959) and *Big Sur* (1962).

Kerr ef·fect /kər ɪˈfekt, kär/ ▶ **n.** Physics **1** the rotation of the plane of polarization of light when reflected from a magnetized surface.
2 the production of double refraction in a substance by an electric field.
– ORIGIN early 20th cent.: named after John *Kerr* (1824–1907), the Scottish physicist who studied these effects.

ker·ri·a /ˈkerēə/ ▶ **n.** an eastern Asian shrub of the rose family, cultivated for its yellow flowers, esp. the double-flowered variety. ● *Kerria japonica*, family Rosaceae.
– ORIGIN early 19th cent.: modern Latin, named after William *Ker(r)* (died 1814), English botanical collector.

Ker·ry /ˈkerē/ a county of the Republic of Ireland, on the southwestern coast in the province of Munster; county town, Tralee.

Ker·ry blue (also **Kerry blue terrier**) ▶ **n.** a terrier of a breed with a silky blue-gray coat.

ker·sey /ˈkərzē/ ▶ **n.** a kind of coarse, ribbed cloth with a short nap, woven from short-stapled wool.

– ORIGIN late Middle English: probably from *Kersey*, a town in Suffolk, England, where woolen cloth was made.

ker·sey·mere /ˈkərzē,mi(ə)r/ ▶ n. a fine twilled woolen cloth.
– ORIGIN late 18th cent.: alteration of *cassimere*, variant of CASHMERE, changed by association with KERSEY.

Ker·u·len Riv·er /ˈkerə,len/ a river in northeastern Mongolia and northeastern China that rises in the Hentiyn Nuruu range northeast of Ulaanbaatar in Mongolia and flows south and east for 785 miles (1,263 km) to Hulun Lake in China's Heilongjiang Province. Also called HERLEN.

Ke·sey /ˈkēzē/, Ken (Elton) (1935–2001), US novelist. His best-known novel, *One Flew over the Cuckoo's Nest* (1962; movie 1975), is based on his experiences as a ward attendant in a mental hospital.

kes·trel /ˈkestrəl/ ▶ n. a small falcon that hovers with rapidly beating wings while searching for prey on the ground. ● Genus *Falco*, family Falconidae: several species, in particular the **common kestrel** (*F. tinnunculus*) of Eurasia and Africa, and the **American kestrel** (*F. sparverius*).
– ORIGIN late Middle English *castrel*, perhaps from *casserelle*, dialect variant of Old French *crecerelle*, perhaps imitative of its call.

ke·ta·mine /ˈketə,mēn, -min/ ▶ n. a synthetic compound used as an anesthetic and analgesic drug and also (illicitly) as a hallucinogen. ● Chem. formula: $C_{13}H_{16}NOCl$.
– ORIGIN mid 20th cent.: blend of KETONE and AMINE.

ketch /kecH/ ▶ n. a two-masted, fore-and-aft-rigged sailboat with a mizzenmast stepped forward of the rudder and smaller than the foremast.
– ORIGIN mid 17th cent.: later form of obsolete *catch*, probably from CATCH.

Ketch·i·kan /ˈkecHi,kan/ a city in southeastern Alaska, on Revillagigedo Island, in the Alexander Archipelago; pop. 7,280 (est. 2008).

ketch·up /ˈkecHəp/ (also **catsup** /ˈkecHəp, ˈkacHəp, ˈkatsəp/) ▶ n. a spicy sauce made chiefly from tomatoes and vinegar, used as a condiment.
– ORIGIN late 17th cent.: perhaps from Chinese (Cantonese dialect) *k'ē chap* 'tomato juice.'

ke·tene /ˈkē,tēn/ ▶ n. Chemistry a pungent colorless reactive gas, used as an intermediate in chemical synthesis. ● Chem. formula: C_2H_2O. ■ any substituted derivative of this.
– ORIGIN early 20th cent.: from KETONE + -ENE.

ke·to ac·id /ˈkētō/ ▶ n. Chemistry a compound whose molecule contains both a carboxyl group (–COOH) and a ketone group (–CO–).

ke·tone /ˈkē,tōn/ ▶ n. Chemistry an organic compound containing a carbonyl group (C=O) bonded to two hydrocarbon groups, made by oxidizing secondary alcohols. The simplest such compound is acetone.
– DERIVATIVES **ke·ton·ic** /kēˈtänik/ adj.
– ORIGIN mid 19th cent.: from German *Keton*, alteration of *Aketon* 'acetone.'

ke·tone bod·y ▶ n. Biochemistry any of three related compounds (acetone, acetoacetic acid, beta-hydroxybutyric acid) produced during the metabolism of fats.

ke·to·ne·mi·a /,kētəˈnēmēə/ (Brit. **ketonaemia**) ▶ n. Medicine the presence of an abnormally high concentration of ketone bodies in the blood.

ke·to·nu·ri·a /,kētōˈn(y)o͝orēə/ ▶ n. Medicine the excretion of abnormally large amounts of ketone bodies in the urine, characteristic of diabetes mellitus, starvation, or other medical conditions.

ke·to·sis /kēˈtōsis/ ▶ n. Medicine a condition characterized by raised levels of ketone bodies in the body, associated with abnormal fat metabolism and diabetes mellitus.
– DERIVATIVES **ke·tot·ic** /-ˈtätik/ adj.

Ket River /ˈket/ a river in Russia that flows west for 842 miles (1,355 km) from Krasnoyarsk into the Ob River at Kolpashevo.

Ket·ter·ing[1] /ˈketəriNG/ a city in southwestern Ohio, southeast of Dayton; pop. 53,708 (est. 2008).

Ket·ter·ing[2], Charles Franklin (1876–1958), US automobile engineer. He developed the electric starter in 1912 and went on to discover tetraethyl lead as an anti-knock agent and to define the octane rating of fuels.

ket·tle /ˈketl/ ▶ n. a vessel, usually made of metal and with a handle, used for boiling liquids or cooking foods. ■ a teakettle.
– PHRASES **a different kettle of fish** informal a completely different type of person or thing from the one previously mentioned: *the new office is a rather different kettle of fish*. **the pot calling the kettle black** see POT[1]. **a fine** (or **pretty**) **kettle of fish** informal an awkward state of affairs.
– DERIVATIVES **ket·tle·ful** /-,fo͝ol/ n. (pl. **kettlefuls**).
– ORIGIN Old English *cetel*, *cietel*, of Germanic origin, based on Latin *catillus*, diminutive of *catinus* 'deep container for cooking or serving food.' In Middle English the word's form was influenced by Old Norse *ketill*.

ket·tle·bell /ˈketl,bel/ ▶ n. Weightlifting a large cast-iron ball-shaped weight with a single handle.

ket·tle corn ▶ n. popcorn that is sweetened with sugar during cooking.

ket·tle·drum /ˈketl,drəm/ ▶ n. a large drum shaped like a bowl, with a membrane adjustable for tension (and so pitch) stretched across. Also collectively called TIMPANI.
– DERIVATIVES **ket·tle·drum·mer** n.

kettledrum

ket·tle hole ▶ n. Geology a hollow, typically filled by a lake, resulting from the melting of a mass of ice trapped in glacial deposits.

ket·tling /ˈketl-iNG/ ▶ n. a method used by police to maintain order during a large demonstration by confining demonstrators to a small area.

keV ▶ abbr. kiloelectronvolt(s).

Kev·lar /ˈkevlär/ ▶ n. trademark a synthetic fiber of high tensile strength used esp. as a reinforcing agent in the manufacture of tires and other rubber products and protective gear such as helmets and vests.

Kew Gar·dens /kyo͞o/ the Royal Botanic Gardens at Kew, in Richmond, London. They were developed by the mother of George III with the aid of Sir Joseph Banks.

kew·pie /ˈkyo͞opē/ (also **kewpie doll**) ▶ n. trademark a type of doll characterized by a large head, big eyes, chubby cheeks, and a curl or topknot on top of its head.
– ORIGIN early 20th cent. (originally US): from CUPID + -IE.

Key /kē/, Francis Scott (1779–1843) US lawyer and poet. A witness to the successful US defense against the British bombardment of Fort McHenry in Baltimore in September 1814, he wrote the poem "Defence of Fort M'Henry." The poem was later set to music, renamed "The Star-Spangled Banner," and, in 1931, adopted as the US national anthem.

key[1] /kē/ ▶ n. (pl. **keys**) **1** a small piece of shaped metal with incisions cut to fit the wards of a particular lock, and that is inserted into a lock and turned to open or close it. ■ a similar implement for operating a switch in the form of a lock, esp. one operating the ignition of a motor vehicle. ■ short for KEY CARD. ■ an instrument for grasping and turning a screw, peg, or nut, esp. one for winding a clock or turning a valve. ■ a pin, bolt, or wedge inserted between other pieces, or fitting into a hole or space designed for it, so as to lock parts together.
2 each of several buttons on a panel for operating a computer, typewriter, or telephone. ■ a lever depressed by the finger in playing an instrument such as the organ, piano, flute, or concertina. ■ a lever operating a mechanical device for making or breaking an electric circuit, for example, in telegraphy.
3 a thing that provides a means of gaining access to or understanding something: *the key to Jack's behavior may lie submerged in his unhappy past*. ■ an explanatory list of symbols used in a map, table, etc. ■ a set of answers to exercises or problems. ■ a word or system for solving a cipher or code. ■ the first move in the solution of a chess problem. ■ Computing a field in a record that is used to identify that record uniquely.
4 Music a group of notes based on a particular note and comprising a scale, regarded as forming the tonal basis of a piece or passage of music: *the key of E minor*. ■ the tone or pitch of someone's voice: *his voice had changed to a lower key*. ■ the prevailing tone or tenor of a piece of writing, situation, etc.: *it was like the sixties all over again, in a new, more austerely intellectual key*. ■ the prevailing range of tones or intensities in a painting: *these mauves, lime greens, and saffron yellows recall the high key of El Greco's palette*.
5 the dry winged fruit of an ash, maple, or sycamore maple, typically growing in bunches; a samara.
6 Brit. the part of a first coat of wall plaster that passes between the laths and so secures the rest. ■ [in sing.] the roughness of a surface, helping the adhesion of plaster or other material.
7 Basketball the keyhole-shaped area marked on the court near each basket, comprising the free-throw circle and the foul line.
▶ adj. of paramount or crucial importance: *she became a key figure in the suffragette movement*.
▶ v. (**keys, keying, keyed** /kēd/) [with obj.] **1** enter or operate on (data) by means of a computer keyboard or telephone keypad: *she* **keyed in** *a series of commands* | [no obj.] *a hacker caused considerable disruption after* **keying into** *a vital database*.
2 (usu. **be keyed**) fasten (something) in position with a pin, wedge, or bolt: *the coils may be keyed into the slots by fiber wedges*.
3 Brit. roughen (a surface) to help the adhesion of plaster or other material.
4 word (an advertisement in a particular periodical), typically by varying the form of the address given, so as to identify the publication generating particular responses.
5 informal be the crucial factor in achieving: *Ewing keyed a 73–35 advantage on the boards with twenty rebounds*.
6 vandalize a car by scraping the paint from it with a key: *somebody could key your car and not get punished*.
– PHRASES **in** (or **out of**) **key** in (or out of) harmony: *this vaguely uplifting conclusion is out of key with the body of his book*. **under lock and key** see LOCK[1].
– PHRASAL VERBS **key someone/something into** (or **in with**) cause someone or something to be in harmony with: *to those who are keyed into his lunatic sense of humor, the arrival of any Bergman movie is a major comic event*. **key something to** make something fit in with or be linked to: *this optimism is keyed to the possibility that the US might lead in the research field*. **be keyed up** be nervous, tense, or excited, esp. before an important event.
– DERIVATIVES **keyed** adj., **key·er** n., **key·less** adj.
– ORIGIN Old English *cǣg*, *cǣge*, of unknown origin.

key[2] ▶ n. a low-lying island or reef, esp. in the Caribbean. Compare with CAY.
– ORIGIN late 17th cent.: from Spanish *cayo* 'shoal, reef,' influenced by QUAY.

key·board /ˈkē,bôrd/ ▶ n. **1** a panel of keys that operate a computer or typewriter.
2 a set of keys on a piano or similar musical instrument. ■ an electronic musical instrument with keys arranged as on a piano: *she plays keyboard and guitar*.
▶ v. [with obj.] enter (data) by means of a keyboard.
– DERIVATIVES **key·board·er** n. (sense 1 of the noun), **key·board·ist** /-ist/ n. (sense 2 of the noun).

key card (also **card key**) ▶ n. a small plastic card that can be used instead of a door key, bearing magnetically encoded data that can be read and processed by an electronic device.

key·chain drive /ˈkē,cHān/ ▶ n. Computing another term for **USB** FLASH DRIVE.

key grip ▶ n. the person in a film crew who is in charge of the camera equipment.

key·hole /ˈkē,hōl/ ▶ n. a hole in a lock into which the key is inserted. ■ a circle cut out of a garment as a decorative effect, typically at the front or back neckline of a dress.

key·hole saw ▶ n. a saw with a long, narrow blade for cutting small holes such as keyholes.

key·hole sur·ger·y ▶ n. informal minimally invasive surgery carried out through a very small incision, with special instruments and techniques including fiber optics.

Key Lar·go /ˈkē ˈlärgō/ a resort island off the southern coast of Florida, the northernmost and the longest of the Florida Keys.

key light ▶ n. the main source of light in a photograph or film.

Key lime ▶ n. a small yellowish lime with a sharp flavor.
– ORIGIN named after the Florida *Keys*.

Key lime pie ▶ n. a custard pie made with the juice of Key limes.

key·log·ging /ˈkē,lôgiNG/ ▶ n. the use of a computer program to record every keystroke made by a computer user, esp. in order to gain fraudulent access to passwords and other confidential information.
– DERIVATIVES **key·log·ger** n.

key mon·ey ▶ n. informal money paid to a landlord as an inducement by a person wishing to rent a property.

Keynes /kānz/, John Maynard, 1st Baron (1883–1946), English economist. He laid the foundations of modern macroeconomics with *The General Theory of Employment, Interest and Money* (1936).

– DERIVATIVES **Keynes·i·an** /ˈkānzēən/ **adj. & n.**, **Keynes·i·an·ism** /ˈkānzēəˌnizəm/ **n.**

key·note /ˈkēˌnōt/ ▶ **n. 1** a prevailing tone or central theme, typically one set or introduced at the start of a conference: *individuality is the keynote of the Nineties* | [as modifier] *he delivered the keynote address at the launch.*
2 Music the note on which a key is based.
– DERIVATIVES **key·not·er n.**

key·pad /ˈkēˌpad/ ▶ **n.** a miniature keyboard or set of buttons for operating a portable electronic device, telephone, or other equipment.

key·pal /ˈkēˌpal/ ▶ **n.** informal (esp. among students) a person with whom one becomes friendly by exchanging e-mails.
– ORIGIN 1990s: from *key* + *pal*, by analogy with *pen pal.*

key·punch /ˈkēˌpənCH/ ▶ **n.** a device for transferring data by means of punching holes or notches on a series of cards or paper tape.
▶ **v.** [with obj.] put into the form of punched cards or paper tape by means of such a device.
– DERIVATIVES **key·punch·er n.**

key ring ▶ **n.** a metal ring onto which keys may be threaded in order to keep them together.

key sig·na·ture ▶ **n.** Music any of several combinations of sharps or flats after the clef at the beginning of each stave indicating the key of a composition.

key·stone /ˈkēˌstōn/ ▶ **n.** a central stone at the summit of an arch, locking the whole together. ■ [usu. in sing.] the central principle or part of a policy, system, etc., on which all else depends: *cooperation remains the keystone of the government's security policy.*

keystone

key·stone spe·cies ▶ **n.** (pl. **same**) a species on which other species in an ecosystem largely depend, such that if it were removed the ecosystem would change drastically.

Key·stone State a nickname for the state of **PENNSYLVANIA**.

key·stroke /ˈkēˌstrōk/ ▶ **n.** a single depression of a key on a keyboard, esp. as a measure of work.

key·stroke log·ging ▶ **n.** another term for **KEYLOGGING**.

key·way /ˈkēˌwā/ ▶ **n.** a slot cut in a part of a machine or an electrical connector to ensure correct orientation with another part that is fitted with a key. ■ a keyhole for a flat key.

Key West a city in southern Florida, on Key West Island, at the southern tip of the Florida Keys; pop. 22,364 (est. 2008). It is the southernmost city in the continental US.

key·word /ˈkēˌwərd/ ▶ **n.** a word or concept of great significance: *homes and jobs are the keywords in the campaign.* ■ a word that acts as the key to a cipher or code. ■ an informative word used in an information retrieval system to indicate the content of a document. ■ a significant word mentioned in an index.

KG ▶ **abbr.** (in the UK) Knight of the Order of the Garter.

kg ▶ **abbr.** ■ keg(s). ■ kilogram(s).

KGB the state security police (1954–91) of the former Soviet Union with responsibility for external espionage, internal counterintelligence, and internal "crimes against the state."
– ORIGIN Russian, abbreviation of *Komitet gosudarstvennoĭ bezopasnosti* 'Committee of State Security.'

kgf ▶ **abbr.** kilogram force.

Kgs ▶ **abbr.** Bible Kings.

Kha·ba·rovsk /KHəˈbärəfsk/ an administrative territory on the eastern coast of Siberia in Russia. ■ its capital, a city on the Amur River, on the Chinese border; pop. 577,300 (est. 2008).

kha·di /ˈkädē/ (also **khaddar** /ˈkädər/) ▶ **n.** an Indian homespun cotton cloth.
– ORIGIN from Punjabi, from Hindi *khādī.*

Kha·kas·sia /KHəˈkäsyə/ an autonomous republic in south central Russia; pop. 533,000 (est. 2009); capital, Abakan.

khak·i /ˈkakē/ ▶ **n.** (pl. **khakis**) a textile fabric of a dull brownish-yellow color, in particular a strong cotton fabric used in military clothing. ■ a dull brownish-yellow color: [as modifier] *the pale khaki sand.* ■ (**khakis**) clothing, esp. pants, of this fabric and color.
– ORIGIN mid 19th cent.: from Urdu *khākī* 'dust-colored,' from *khāk* 'dust,' from Persian.

Khak·i Camp·bell /ˈkakē ˈkambəl/ ▶ **n.** a duck of a light brown breed, kept for egg laying.

Khalistan /ˌKHäliˈstän, ˌkäl-, -ˈstan/ the name given by Sikh nationalists to a proposed independent Sikh state.
– ORIGIN compare with Arabic *khālsa* 'pure, real, proper.'

Khal·kha /ˈkalkə/ ▶ **n. 1** a member of a section of the Mongolian people, constituting the bulk of the population of Mongolia.
2 the language of these people, a demotic form of Mongolian adopted as the official language of Mongolia.
▶ **adj.** of or relating to this people or their language.
– ORIGIN of unknown origin.

Khal·sa /ˈkälsə/ ▶ **n.** the body or company of fully initiated Sikhs, to which devout orthodox Sikhs are ritually admitted at puberty. The Khalsa was founded in 1699 by the last Guru (Gobind Singh). Members show their allegiance by five signs (called the five Ks): kangha (comb), kara (steel bangle), kesh (uncut hair, covered by a turban, and beard), kirpan (short sword), and kuccha (short trousers, originally for riding).
– ORIGIN via Urdu from Persian, from the feminine form of Arabic *kāliṣ* 'pure, belonging to.'

Kha·ma /ˈkämə/, Sir Seretse (1921–80), Botswanan statesman; prime minister of Bechuanaland 1965 and first president of Botswana 1966–80.

Kham·bhat, Gulf of /ˈkəmbət/ (also **Gulf of Khambat**) another name for **CAMBAY, GULF OF**.

kham·sin /kämˈsēn/ ▶ **n.** an oppressive, hot southerly or southeasterly wind blowing in Egypt in spring.
– ORIGIN late 17th cent.: from Arabic *khamsīn*, from *khamsūn* 'fifty' (being the approximate duration in days).

Khan /kän/, Ayub, see **AYUB KHAN**.

khan¹ /kän/ ▶ **n.** a title given to rulers and officials in central Asia, Afghanistan, and certain other Muslim countries. ■ any of the successors of Genghis Khan, supreme rulers of the Turkish, Tartar, and Mongol peoples and emperors of China in the Middle Ages.
– DERIVATIVES **khan·ate** /ˈkänāt/ **n.**
– ORIGIN late Middle English: from Old French *chan*, medieval Latin *canus, caanus*, from Turkic *ḵān* 'lord, prince.'

khan² ▶ **n.** (in the Middle East) an inn for travelers, built around a central courtyard.
– ORIGIN from Persian *ḵān.*

khan·da /ˈkandə/ ▶ **n.** an emblem of Sikhism, representing a vertical two-edged sword with its blade surrounded by a circle and its hilt intersected by the crossing hilts of two single-edged swords.
– ORIGIN from Persian *khanjar* 'dagger.'

khan·sa·ma /ˈkänsəˌmä/ ▶ **n.** Indian a male cook, who often also assumes the role of house steward.
– ORIGIN from Urdu and Persian *ḵānsāmān*, from *ḵān* 'master' + *sāmān* 'household goods.'

Kharg Is·land /kärg, KHärg/ a small island at the head of the Persian Gulf, site of Iran's principal deep-water oil terminal.

Khar·kiv /ˈKHärkif, ˈkärˌkôf/ an industrial city in northeastern Ukraine, in the Donets basin; pop. 1,456,000 (est. 2009). Russian name **Kharkov**.

Khar·toum /kärˈto͞om/ the capital of Sudan, situated at the junction of the Blue Nile and the White Nile rivers; pop. 2,737,500 (est. 2007). It was the capital of the Anglo-Egyptian government of Sudan until 1956, when it became the capital of the independent Republic of Sudan.

khat /kät/ (also **qat**) ▶ **n. 1** the leaves of an Arabian shrub, which are chewed (or drunk as an infusion) as a stimulant.
2 the shrub that produces these leaves, growing in mountainous regions and often cultivated. ● *Catha edulis*, family Celastraceae.
– ORIGIN mid 19th cent.: from Arabic *ḳāt.*

Khay·e·lit·sa /kīəˈlitsə/ a township 25 miles (40 km) southeast of Cape Town, South Africa; pop. 2,100,000 (est. 2009). Designed to accommodate 250,000 people, it was built in 1983 for black Africans from the squatter camps of Crossroads, Langa, and KTC.

Kha·zar /kəˈzär/ ▶ **n.** a member of a Turkic people who occupied a large part of southern Russia from the 6th to the 11th centuries and who converted to Judaism in the 8th century.
▶ **adj.** of or relating to the Khazars.
– ORIGIN of unknown origin.

khe·dive /kəˈdēv/ ▶ **n.** the title of the viceroy of Egypt under Turkish rule (1867–1914).
– DERIVATIVES **khe·div·al** /-ˈdēvəl/ **adj.**, **khe·div·i·al** /-ˈdēvēəl/ **adj.**
– ORIGIN via French from Ottoman Turkish *ḳediv*, from Persian *ḳadiw* 'prince' (variant of *ḳudaiw* 'minor god,' from *ḳudā* 'god').

Kher·son /KHerˈsôn, ker-/ a port on the coast of Ukraine, on the Dnieper estuary; pop. 306,600 (est. 2009).

Khe Sanh /ˈkāˈsän/ a site in north central Vietnam of one of the costliest battles of the Vietnam War.

khi·mar /kiˈmär/ ▶ **n.** a head covering or veil worn in public by some Muslim women, typically covering the head, neck, and shoulders.
– ORIGIN Arabic *khimār.*

Khi·os /ˈKHēˌôs, ˈkē-/ Greek name for **CHIOS**.

Khi·tai /ˈkēˈtī/ variant of **CATHAY**.

Khmer /kəˈme(ə)r, kme(ə)r/ ▶ **n. 1** an ancient kingdom in Southeast Asia that reached the peak of its power in the 11th century, when it ruled the entire Mekong River valley from the capital at Angkor. It was destroyed by Thai conquests in the 12th and 14th centuries.
2 a native or inhabitant of the ancient Khmer kingdom.
3 a native or inhabitant of Cambodia.
4 the Mon-Khmer language that is the official language of Cambodia. Also called **CAMBODIAN**.
▶ **adj.** of, relating to, or denoting the Khmers or their language.
– ORIGIN the name in Khmer.

Khmer Re·pub·lic former official name (1970–75) for **CAMBODIA**.

Khmer Rouge /ˈro͞oZH/ a communist guerrilla organization that opposed the Cambodian government in the 1960s and waged a civil war from 1970, taking power in 1975.

> Under Pol Pot the Khmer Rouge forced the reconstruction of Cambodian society with mass deportations from the towns to the countryside and mass executions. More than two million died before the regime was overthrown by the Vietnamese in 1979. Khmer Rouge forces have continued a program of guerrilla warfare from bases in Thailand.

– ORIGIN from **KHMER** + French *rouge* 'red.'

Khoi·khoi /ˈkoiˌkoi/ (also **Khoi-khoin** /-ˌkoi-in/, **Khoi**) ▶ **n.** (pl. **same**) a member of a group of indigenous peoples of South Africa and Namibia, traditionally nomadic hunter-gatherers, including the Nama people and the ancestors of the Griquas.
▶ **adj.** of or relating to this people or their languages.
– ORIGIN Nama, literally 'men of men.'

> **USAGE** See usage at **HOTTENTOT**.

Khoi·san /ˈkoiˌsän/ ▶ **n. 1** [usu. treated as pl.] a collective term for the Khoikhoi (Hottentot) and San (Bushmen) peoples of southern Africa.
2 a language family of southern Africa, including the languages of the Khoikhoi and San, notable for the use of clicks as consonants.
▶ **adj.** of or relating to these languages or their speakers.
– ORIGIN blend of **KHOIKHOI** and **SAN**.

Kho·mei·ni /kōˈmānē, KHō-, ˌKHōmāˈnē/, Ruhollah (1900–89), Iranian Shiite Muslim leader; known as **Ayatollah Khomeini**. He returned from exile in 1979 to lead an Islamic revolution that overthrew the shah. He established Iran as a fundamentalist Islamic republic and relentlessly pursued the Iran–Iraq War 1980–88.

Khon·su /ˈKHänˌso͞o/ Egyptian Mythology a moon god worshiped esp. at Thebes, a member of a triad as the divine son of Amun and Mut.

Khor·ram·shahr /ˌKHôrəmˈSHähər, ˌkôr-/ an oil port on the Shatt al-Arab waterway in western Iran. It was almost totally destroyed during the Iran–Iraq War of 1980–88. Former name (until 1924) **MOHAMMERAH**.

khoum /ko͞om, ko͝om/ ▶ **n.** a monetary unit of Mauritania, equal to one fifth of an ouguiya.
– ORIGIN from Arabic *ḳums* 'one fifth.'

Khru·shchev /ˈkro͞oSHˌCHev, -ˌCHôf, KHro͞oSHˈCHyôf/, Nikita (Sergeevich) (1894–1971), Soviet statesman; premier 1958–64. He came close to war with the US over the Cuban Missile Crisis in 1962 and also clashed with China, which led to his being ousted by Brezhnev and Kosygin.
– DERIVATIVES **Khru·shchev·i·an** /kro͞oSHˈCHevēən/ **adj.**

Khu·fu /ˈko͞oˌfo͞o/ see **CHEOPS**.

Khul·na /ˈko͞olnə/ an industrial city in southern Bangladesh, on the Ganges delta; pop. 855,650 (2008).

Khun·jer·ab Pass /ˈko͞onjəˌräb/ a high-altitude pass through the Himalayas, on the Karakoram highway at a height of 16,088 feet (4,900 m), that links China and Pakistan.

khus-khus /ˈkəs kəs/ ▶ **n.** another term for VETIVER.
– ORIGIN early 19th cent.: from Urdu and Persian *kaskas*.

Khy·ber Pass /ˈkībər/ a mountain pass in the Hindu Kush, on the border between Pakistan and Afghanistan, at a height of 3,520 feet (1,067 m). It was for long of great commercial and strategic importance, the route by which successive invaders entered India, and it was garrisoned by the British intermittently between 1839 and 1947.

kHz ▶ **abbr.** kilohertz.

ki ▶ **n.** variant spelling of QI.

KIA (also **K.I.A.**) ▶ **abbr.** killed in action.

ki·ang /kēˈäNG/ ▶ **n.** an animal of a large race of the Asian wild ass with a thick furry coat, native to the Tibetan plateau. ● *Equus hemionus kiang*, family Equidae; sometimes treated as a separate species. Compare with ONAGER.
– ORIGIN mid 19th cent.: from Tibetan *kyang*.

Kiang·si /ˈkyäNGˈsē, ˈgyäNG-/ variant of JIANGXI.

Kiang·su /ˈkyäNGˈso͞o, ˈgyäNG-/ variant of JIANGSU.

ki·a·su /ˈkēəˌso͞o/ ▶ **n.** SE Asian a grasping, selfish attitude.
▶ **adj.** (of a person) very anxious not to miss out on an opportunity; grasping.
– ORIGIN from Chinese, 'scared to lose.'

kib·beh /ˈkibē/ ▶ **n.** a Middle Eastern dish of ground lamb with bulgar wheat and seasonings, eaten cooked or raw.
– ORIGIN from Egyptian Arabic *kubba* 'ball, lump.'

kib·ble[1] /ˈkibəl/ ▶ **v.** [with obj.] (usu. as adj. **kibbled**) grind or chop (beans, grain, etc.) coarsely.
▶ **n.** ground meal shaped into pellets, esp. for pet food.
– ORIGIN late 18th cent.: of unknown origin.

kib·ble[2] ▶ **n.** Brit. an iron hoisting bucket used in mines.
– ORIGIN late Middle English: from Middle High German *kübel*, from medieval Latin *cupellus* 'wheat measure, cask,' diminutive of *cuppa* 'cup.'

kib·butz /kiˈbo͝ots/ ▶ **n.** (pl. **kibbutzim** /kiˌbo͝otˈsēm/) a communal settlement in Israel, typically a farm.
– ORIGIN 1930s: from modern Hebrew *qibbūṣ* 'gathering.'

kib·butz·nik /kiˈbo͝otsnik/ ▶ **n.** a member of a kibbutz.

kibe /kīb/ ▶ **n.** an ulcerated chilblain, esp. one on the heel.
– ORIGIN late Middle English: of unknown origin.

kib·itz /ˈkibits/ ▶ **v.** [no obj.] informal look on and offer unwelcome advice, esp. at a card game. ■ speak informally; chat: *she kibitzed with friends*.
– DERIVATIVES **kib·itz·er n.**
– ORIGIN 1920s: Yiddish, from colloquial German, from German *Kiebitz* 'interfering onlooker' (literally 'lapwing').

kib·lah ▶ **n.** variant spelling of QIBLAH.

ki·bosh /ˈkəˈbäsH, ˈkīˌbäsH/ ▶ **n.** (in phrase **put the kibosh on**) informal put an end to; dispose of decisively: *he put the kibosh on the deal*.
– ORIGIN mid 19th cent.: of unknown origin.

kick[1] /kik/ ▶ **v. 1** [with obj.] strike or propel forcibly with the foot: *police kicked down the door | he kicked the door open*. ■ [no obj.] strike out or flail with the foot or feet: *she kicked out at him* | [with obj. and complement] *he kicked his feet free of a vine*. ■ (**kick oneself**) be annoyed with oneself for doing something foolish or missing an opportunity. ■ (in football, rugby, etc.) score (a goal) by a kick. ■ [no obj.] (of a gun) recoil when fired.
2 [with obj.] informal succeed in giving up (a habit or addiction).
▶ **n. 1** a blow or forceful thrust with the foot: *a kick in the head*. ■ (in sports) an instance of striking the ball with the foot: *Ball blasted the kick wide*. ■ the recoil of a gun when discharged. ■ a sudden forceful jolt: *the shuttle accelerated with a kick*.
2 [in sing.] informal the sharp stimulant effect of something, esp. alcohol. ■ a thrill of pleasurable, often reckless excitement: *rich kids turning to crime just for kicks | I get such a kick out of driving a race car*. ■ [with modifier] a specified temporary interest or enthusiasm: *the jogging kick*.
– PHRASES **kick (some) ass** (or **butt**) vulgar slang act in a forceful or aggressive manner. **kick someone's ass** (or **butt**) vulgar slang beat, dominate, or defeat someone. **kick the bucket** informal die. **a kick in the pants** (or **up the backside**) informal an unwelcome surprise that prompts or forces fresh effort: *the competition will be healthy, but we needed a kick in the pants*. **a kick in the teeth** informal a grave setback or disappointment: *this broken promise is a kick in the teeth for football*. **kick someone in the teeth** informal cause someone a grave setback or disappointment. **kick someone/something to the curb** informal reject someone or something: *things get complicated for Alfie when he's kicked to the curb by his girlfriend*. **kick someone when they are down** cause further misfortune to someone who is already in a difficult situation. **kick up a fuss** (or **a stink**) informal object loudly or publicly to something. **kick up one's heels** see HEEL[1]. **kick someone upstairs** informal remove someone from an influential position in a business by giving them an ostensible promotion.
– PHRASAL VERBS **kick against** express resentment at or frustration with (an institution or restriction). **kick around** (or **about**) (of a thing) lie unwanted or unexploited: *the idea has been kicking around for more than a year now*. ■ (of a person) drift idly from place to place: *I kicked around picking up odd jobs*. **kick someone around** (or **about**) treat someone roughly or without respect. **kick something around** (or **about**) discuss an idea casually or idly. **kick back** informal be at leisure; relax. **kick in** (esp. of a device or drug) become activated; come into effect. **kick something in** informal contribute something, esp. money: *if you subscribe now we'll kick in a bonus*. **kick off** (of a football game, soccer game, etc.) be started or resumed after a score by a player kicking the ball from a designated spot. ■ (of a team or player) begin or resume a game in this way. ■ informal (of an event) begin. **kick something off 1** remove something, esp. shoes, by striking out vigorously with the foot or feet. **2** informal begin something: *the presidential primary kicks off the political year*. **kick someone out** informal expel or dismiss someone.
– DERIVATIVES **kick·a·ble adj.**
– ORIGIN late Middle English: of unknown origin.

kick[2] ▶ **n.** archaic an indentation in the bottom of a glass bottle, diminishing the internal capacity.
– ORIGIN mid 19th cent.: of unknown origin.

Kick·a·poo /ˈkikəˌpo͞o/ ▶ **n.** (pl. **same** or **Kickapoos**) **1** a member of an American Indian people formerly living in Wisconsin, and now in Kansas, Oklahoma, and north central Mexico.
2 the Algonquian language of this people.
▶ **adj.** of or relating to this people or their language.
– ORIGIN from Kickapoo *kiikaapoa*.

kick-ass ▶ **adj.** [attrib.] informal forceful, vigorous, and aggressive: *he's a kick-ass guy who takes no prisoners | a kick-ass foreign policy*.

kick·back /ˈkikˌbak/ ▶ **n. 1** a sudden forceful recoil: *the kickback from the gun punches your shoulder*.
2 informal a payment made to someone who has facilitated a transaction or appointment, esp. illicitly.

kick·ball /ˈkikˌbôl/ ▶ **n.** an informal game combining elements of baseball and soccer, in which an inflated ball is thrown to a person who kicks it and proceeds to run the bases.

kick-box·ing (also **kickboxing**) ▶ **n.** a form of martial art that combines boxing with elements of karate, in particular kicking with bare feet.
– DERIVATIVES **kick-box·er n.**

kick drum ▶ **n.** informal a bass drum played using a pedal.

kick·er /ˈkikər/ ▶ **n. 1** a person or animal that kicks. ■ the player in a team who scores by kicking or who kicks to gain positional advantage.
2 informal an unexpected and often unpleasant discovery or turn of events: *the kicker was you couldn't get a permit*. ■ an extra clause in a contract: *Hale added a kicker to the mortgage*.
3 informal a small outboard motor.
4 (in poker) a high third card retained in the hand with a pair at the draw.

kick·flip /ˈkikflip/ ▶ **n.** (in skateboarding) a maneuver in which the board is manipulated by the feet during a jump so that it spins sideways through 360 degrees before landing.

kick·ing /ˈkikiNG/ ▶ **n.** a punishment or assault in which the victim is kicked repeatedly: *they gave him a good kicking*.
▶ **adj.** informal (esp. of music) lively and exciting: *their seriously kicking debut, "Paradise."*

kick·ing strap ▶ **n.** a strap used to prevent a horse from kicking.

kick·off /ˈkikˌôf/ ▶ **n.** the start or resumption of a football game, in which a player kicks the ball from the center of the field: *three minutes before kickoff*. ■ informal a start of an event or activity.

kick plate ▶ **n.** a metal plate at the base of a door or panel to protect it from damage or wear.

kick pleat ▶ **n.** an inverted pleat in a narrow skirt to allow freedom of movement.

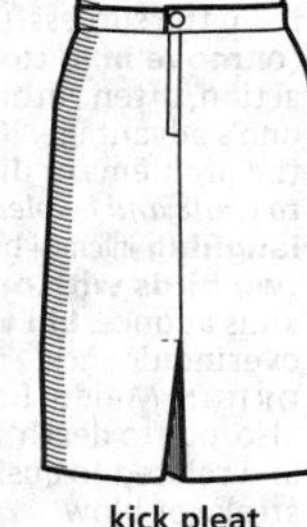
kick pleat

kick·shaw /ˈkikˌSHô/ ▶ **n.** archaic a fancy but insubstantial cooked dish, esp. one of foreign origin. ■ an elegant but insubstantial trinket.
– ORIGIN late 16th cent.: from French *quelque chose* 'something.' The French spelling was common in the 17th cent.; the present form results from interpretation of *quelque chose* as plural.

kick·stand /ˈkikˌstand/ ▶ **n.** a metal rod attached to a bicycle or motorcycle, lying horizontally when not in use, that may be kicked into a vertical position to support the vehicle when it is stationary.

kick-start ▶ **v.** [with obj.] start (an engine on a motorcycle) with a downward thrust of a pedal. ■ provide the initial impetus to: *they need to kick-start the economy*.
▶ **n.** (also **kick start** or **kick starter**) a device to start an engine by the downward thrust of a pedal, as in older motorcycles. ■ an act of starting an engine in this way. ■ an impetus given to get a process or thing started or restarted: *new investment will provide the kick-start needed to escape from recession*.

kick turn ▶ **n.** Skiing a turn carried out while stationary by lifting first one and then the other ski through 180°. ■ (in skateboarding) a turn performed with the front wheels lifted off the ground.
– DERIVATIVES **kick-turn v.**

kick·y /ˈkikē/ ▶ **adj.** informal exciting or fashionable: *kicky high-heeled boots*.

kid[1] /kid/ ▶ **n. 1** informal a child or young person. ■ used as an informal form of address: *get going, kid!*
2 a young goat. ■ leather made from a young goat's skin: [as modifier] *white kid gloves*.
▶ **v.** (**kids, kidding, kidded**) [no obj.] (of a goat) give birth.
– PHRASES **kids'** (also **kid**) **stuff** informal a thing regarded as childishly simple or naive: *all this was kids' stuff though, compared to the directing*.
– ORIGIN Middle English (sense 2 of the noun): from Old Norse *kith*, of Germanic origin; related to German *Kitze*.

> **USAGE** Kid, meaning 'child,' although widely seen in informal contexts, should, like its casual relatives *mom* and *dad*, be avoided in formal writing.

kid[2] ▶ **v.** (**kids, kidding, kidded**) [with obj.] informal deceive (someone) in a playful or teasing way: *you're kidding me!* | [no obj.] *we were just kidding around*. ■ [with obj. and clause] deceive or fool (someone): *he likes to kid everyone he's the big macho tough guy | they kid themselves that it's still the same*.
– PHRASES **no kidding** used to emphasize the truth of a statement: *no kidding, she's gone*.
– DERIVATIVES **kid·der n., kid·ding·ly adv.**
– ORIGIN early 19th cent.: perhaps from KID[1], expressing the notion 'make a child or goat of.'

kid broth·er ▶ **n.** informal a younger brother.

Kidd /kid/, William (1645–1701), Scottish pirate; known as **Captain Kidd**. In 1699, he went to Boston in the hope of obtaining a pardon, but was arrested and later hanged in London.

Kid·der·min·ster car·pet /ˈkidərˌminstər/ ▶ **n.** a reversible carpet made of two cloths of different colors woven together.
– ORIGIN late 17th cent.: named after Kidderminster, England, a center of carpet-making.

kid·die /ˈkidē/ (also **kiddy**) ▶ **n.** (pl. **kiddies**) informal a young child.

kid·die tax ▶ **n.** informal tax on a child's investment income, which is taxed at the parents' rate under certain conditions.

kid·do /ˈkidō/ ▶ **n.** (pl. **kiddos** or **kiddoes**) informal used as a friendly or slightly condescending form of address.

kid·dush /ˈkidəsH, kēˈdo͝osH/ ▶ **n.** [in sing.] a ceremony of prayer and blessing over wine, performed by the head of a Jewish household at the meal ushering in the Sabbath (on a Friday night) or a holy day, or at the lunch preceding it.
– ORIGIN mid 18th cent.: from Hebrew *qiddûš* 'sanctification.'

kid gloves ▶ **plural n.** gloves made of fine kid leather. ■ (also **kid-glove**) [as modifier] used in reference to careful and delicate treatment of a person or situation: *the star is getting kid-glove treatment*.
– PHRASES **handle** (or **treat**) **someone or something with kid gloves** deal with someone or something very carefully or tactfully.

PRONUNCIATION KEY ə *ago, up*; ər *over, fur*; a *hat*; ā *ate*; ä *car*; e *let*; ē *see*; i *fit*; ī *by*; NG *sing*; ō *go*; ô *law, for*; oi *toy*; o͝o *good*; o͞o *goo*; ou *out*; TH *thin*; TH *then*; ZH *vision*

kid·nap /ˈkidˌnap/ ▶ **v.** (**kidnaps, kidnapping, kidnapped**; also **kidnaping, kidnaped**) [with obj.] take (someone) away illegally by force, typically to obtain a ransom.
▶ **n.** the action of kidnapping someone: *they were arrested for robbery and kidnap.*
– DERIVATIVES **kid·nap·per n.**
– ORIGIN late 17th cent.: back-formation from *kidnapper*, from KID[1] + slang *nap* 'nab, seize.'

kid·ney /ˈkidnē/ ▶ **n.** (pl. **kidneys**) each of a pair of organs in the abdominal cavity of mammals, birds, and reptiles, excreting urine. ■ the kidney of a sheep, ox, or pig as food. ■ temperament, nature, or kind: *I hoped that he would not prove of similar kidney.*

> The kidneys' main function is to purify the blood by removing nitrogenous waste products and excreting them in the urine. They also control the fluid and ion levels in the body by excreting any excesses. The kidneys were anciently thought to control disposition and temperament.

– ORIGIN Middle English: of obscure origin.

kid·ney bean ▶ **n.** a kidney-shaped bean, esp. a dark red variety of the common bean plant *Phaseolus vulgaris.*

kid·ney di·al·y·sis ▶ **n.** see DIALYSIS.

kid·ney stone ▶ **n.** a hard mass formed in the kidneys, typically consisting of insoluble calcium compounds; a renal calculus.

kid·ney tu·bule ▶ **n.** Anatomy each of the long, fine, convoluted tubules conveying urine from the glomeruli to the renal pelvis in the vertebrate kidney. Water and salts are reabsorbed into the blood along their length. Also called RENAL TUBULE, URINIFEROUS TUBULE.

kid sis·ter ▶ **n.** informal a younger sister.

kid·skin /ˈkidˌskin/ ▶ **n.** another term for KID[1] (sense 2 of the noun).

kid·ult /ˈkidəlt, ˈkidˌəlt/ ▶ **n.** informal an adult with childish tastes.
– ORIGIN blend of *kid* and *adult*.

Kiel /kēl/ a naval port in northern Germany, capital of Schleswig-Holstein, on the Baltic Sea coast at the eastern end of the Kiel Canal; pop. 235,400 (est. 2006).

kiel·ba·sa /kilˈbäsə, kēl-/ ▶ **n.** a type of highly seasoned Polish sausage, typically containing garlic.
– ORIGIN Polish, literally 'sausage.'

Kiel Ca·nal a man-made waterway, 61 miles (98 km) in length, in northwestern Germany, that runs westward from Kiel to Brunsbüttel at the mouth of the Elbe River. It connects the North Sea with the Baltic Sea and was constructed in 1895 to provide the German navy with a shorter route between these two seas.

Kiel·ce /ˈkyeltsə/ an industrial city in southern Poland; pop. 206,796 (2007).

kier /ki(ə)r/ ▶ **n.** a vat.
– ORIGIN late 16th cent.: from Old Norse *ker* 'container, tub.'

Kier·ke·gaard /ˈki(ə)rkiˌgärd, -ˌgôr/, Søren (Aabye) (1813–55), Danish philosopher. A founder of existentialism, he affirmed the importance of individual experience and choice and believed that one could know God only through a "leap of faith," not through doctrine.
– DERIVATIVES **Kier·ke·gaard·i·an** /ˌki(ə)rkiˈgärdēən/ **adj.**

kie·sel·guhr /ˈkēzelgər/ ▶ **n.** a form of diatomaceous earth used in various manufacturing and laboratory processes, chiefly as a filter, filler, or insulator.
– ORIGIN late 19th cent.: from German, from *Kiesel* 'gravel' + dialect *Guhr* (literally 'yeast') used to denote a loose earthy deposit, found in the cavities of rocks.

kie·ser·ite /ˈkēzəˌrit/ ▶ **n.** a fine-grained white mineral consisting of hydrated magnesium sulfate, occurring often in salt mines in Europe and India.
– ORIGIN mid 19th cent.: from the name of Dietrich G. *Kieser* (1779–1862), German physician, + -ITE[1].

Ki·ev /ˈkēˌ(y)ef, -ˌ(y)ev/ the capital of Ukraine, an industrial city and port on the Dnieper River; pop. 2,765,500 (est. 2009). Founded in the 8th century, it became capital of the Ukrainian Soviet Socialist Republic in 1934 and of independent Ukraine in 1991. Ukrainian name KYIV.

kif /kif/ ▶ **n. & adj.** variant spelling of KEF.

Ki·ga·li /kiˈgälē/ the capital of Rwanda, located in the central part of the country; pop. 860,000 (est. 2007).

kike /kīk/ ▶ **n.** informal, offensive a Jewish person.
– ORIGIN early 20th cent.: of unknown origin.

Ki·klá·dhes /kiˈklä<u>TH</u>is/ Greek name for CYCLADES.

ki·koi /kiˈkoi/ ▶ **n.** (pl. **kikois**) a distinctive East African striped cloth with an end fringe. ■ a garment made of this cloth, worn around the waist.
– ORIGIN mid 20th cent.: from Kiswahili.

Ki·kon·go /kēˈkäNGgō/ ▶ **n.** either of two similar Bantu languages spoken in Congo, the Democratic Republic of the Congo (Zaire), and adjacent areas.
▶ **adj.** of or relating to this language.
– ORIGIN the name in Kikongo.

Ki·ku·yu /kiˈkoōyoō/ ▶ **n.** (pl. **same** or **Kikuyus**) **1** a member of the largest ethnic group in Kenya.
2 the Bantu language of this people.
3 (**kikuyu, kikuyu grass**) a creeping perennial grass native to Kenya and cultivated elsewhere as a lawn and fodder grass. ● *Pennisetum clandestinum*, family Gramineae.
▶ **adj.** of or relating to the Kikuyu people or their language.
– ORIGIN a local name.

Ki·lau·ea /ˌkiləˈwāə, ˌkēˌlouˈāə/ an active volcano with a crater roughly 5 miles (8 km) long and 3 miles (5 km) wide on the island of Hawaii, situated on the eastern flank of Mauna Loa at an altitude of 4,090 feet (1,247 m).

Kil·dare /kilˈde(ə)r/ a county in the Republic of Ireland, in the east, in the province of Leinster; county town, Naas.

kil·der·kin /ˈkildərkin/ ▶ **n.** a cask for liquids or other substances, holding 16 or 18 gallons. ■ this amount as a unit of measurement.
– ORIGIN late Middle English: from Middle Dutch *kinderkin*, variant of *kinerkijn*, diminutive of *kintal* (see QUINTAL).

ki·lim /kēˈlēm, ˈkiləm/ ▶ **n.** a flat-woven carpet or rug made in Turkey, Kurdistan, and neighboring areas.
– ORIGIN late 19th cent.: via Turkish from Persian *gelīm*.

Kil·i·man·ja·ro, Mount /ˌkiləmənˈjärō/ an extinct volcano in northern Tanzania. It has twin peaks, the higher of which, Kibo (19,340 feet; 5,895 m), is the highest mountain in Africa.

Kil·ken·ny /kilˈkenē/ a county of the Republic of Ireland, in the southeast, in the province of Leinster. ■ its county town; pop. 8,661 (2006).

kill[1] /kil/ ▶ **v.** [with obj.] **1** cause the death of (a person, animal, or other living thing): *her father was killed in a car crash* | [no obj.] *a robber armed with a shotgun who kills in cold blood.* ■ (**kill someone/something off**) get rid of or destroy completely, esp. in large numbers: *there is every possibility all river life would be killed off for generations.* ■ (**kill someone off**) (of a writer) bring about the "death" of a fictional character.
2 put an end to or cause the failure or defeat of (something): *the committee voted to kill the project.* ■ stop (a computer program or process). ■ informal switch off (a light or engine). ■ informal delete (a line, paragraph, or file) from a document or computer. ■ informal consume the entire contents of (a bottle containing an alcoholic drink). ■ (in tennis and similar games) hit (the ball) so forcefully that it cannot be returned. ■ (in soccer or other ball games) make (the ball) stop. ■ neutralize or subdue (an effect or quality): *the sauce would kill the taste of the herbs.*
3 informal overwhelm (someone) with an emotion: *the suspense is killing me.* ■ (**kill oneself**) overexert oneself: *I killed myself carrying those things home.* ■ used hyperbolically to indicate that someone will be extremely angry with (another person): *my parents will kill me if they catch me out here.* ■ cause pain or anguish to: *my feet are killing me.*
4 pass (time, or a specified amount of it), typically while waiting for a particular event: *when he reached the station, he found he actually had an hour to kill.*
▶ **n.** [usu. in sing.] an act of killing, esp. of one animal by another: *a lion has made a kill.* ■ an animal or animals killed, either by a hunter or by another animal: *the vulture is able to survey the land and locate a fresh kill.* ■ informal an act of destroying or disabling an enemy aircraft, submarine, tank, etc. ■ (in tennis and similar games) a very forceful shot that cannot be returned.
– PHRASES **be in at the kill** be present at or benefit from the successful conclusion of an enterprise. **go** (or **move in** or **close in**) **for the kill** take decisive action, often ruthlessly, to turn a situation to one's advantage. **if it kills one** informal whatever the problems or difficulties involved: *we are going to smile and be pleasant if it kills us.* **kill oneself laughing** informal be overcome with laughter. **kill two birds with one stone** proverb achieve two aims at once. **kill with** (or **by**) **kindness** spoil with overindulgence.
– ORIGIN Middle English (in the sense 'strike, beat,' also 'put to death'): probably of Germanic origin and related to QUELL. The noun originally denoted a stroke or blow.

kill[2] ▶ **n.** (in place names, esp. in New York, New Jersey, and Pennsylvania) a stream, creek, or tributary: *Kill Van Kull.*
– ORIGIN mid 17th cent.: from Dutch *kil*, from Middle Dutch *kille* 'riverbed, channel.'

Kil·lar·ney /kilˈärnē/ a town in southwestern Republic of Ireland, in County Kerry, noted for the beauty of the nearby lakes and mountains; pop. 13,497 (2006).

kill·deer /ˈkilˌdi(ə)r/ (also **killdeer plover**) ▶ **n.** a widespread American plover with a plaintive call that resembles its name. ● *Charadrius vociferus*, family Charadriidae.
– ORIGIN mid 18th cent.: imitative of its call.

killdeer

Kil·leen /kiˈlēn/ a city in east central Texas, near Fort Hood; pop. 116,934 (est. 2008).

kill·er /ˈkilər/ ▶ **n.** a person, animal, or thing that kills: *police are still searching for the killer* | [as modifier] *a killer virus.* ■ informal a formidable or excellent person or thing: *that wind's a killer* | *they make a killer salsa.* ■ informal a hilarious joke.

kill·er app ▶ **n.** informal a feature, function, or application of a new technology or product that is presented as virtually indispensable or much superior to rival products.
– ORIGIN from *killer* and *app*, a shortening of *application.*

kill·er bee ▶ **n.** informal an Africanized honeybee. See AFRICANIZE (sense 2).

kill·er cell ▶ **n.** Physiology a white blood cell (a type of lymphocyte) that destroys infected or cancerous cells.

kill·er in·stinct ▶ **n.** a ruthless determination to succeed or win.

kill·er whale ▶ **n.** another term for ORCA.

kil·lick /ˈkilik/ ▶ **n.** a heavy stone used by small craft as an anchor. ■ any anchor, esp. a small one.
– ORIGIN mid 17th cent.: of unknown origin.

kil·li·fish /ˈkilēˌfish/ ▶ **n.** (pl. **same** or **killifishes**) a small carplike fish of fresh, brackish, or salt water, typically brightly colored. They are mainly native to America and include many popular aquarium fishes. ● Families Fundulidae and Cyprinodontidae, which include numerous genera of egg-laying killifishes.
– ORIGIN early 19th cent.: apparently from KILL[2] and FISH[1].

kill·ing /ˈkiliNG/ ▶ **n.** an act of causing death, esp. deliberately.
▶ **adj.** causing death: [in combination] *weed-killing.* ■ informal exhausting; unbearable: *the suspense will be killing.* ■ dated overwhelmingly funny.
– PHRASES **make a killing** have a great financial success: *they're a safe investment, you can make a killing overnight.*
– DERIVATIVES **kill·ing·ly adv.**

kill·ing field ▶ **n.** (usu. **killing fields**) a place where a heavy loss of life has occurred, typically as the result of massacre or genocide during a time of warfare or violent civil unrest.

kill·joy /ˈkilˌjoi/ ▶ **n.** a person who deliberately spoils the enjoyment of others through resentful or overly sober behavior.

Kil·ly /ˈkēyē/, Jean-Claude (1943–) French alpine skier. He won three gold medals at the 1968 Olympic games and was a three-time world champion 1966, 1967, 1968; winner of the World Cup 1967, 1968; and professional world champion 1973.

kill zone (also **killing zone**) ▶ **n. 1** the area of a military engagement with a high concentration of fatalities.
2 the area of the human body where entry of a projectile would kill, esp. as indicated on a target for shooting practice.

Kil·mer /ˈkilmər/, Joyce (1888–1918) US poet; full name *Alfred Joyce Kilmer*. He was killed in action during World War I. His poetry is collected in *Summer of Love* (1911) and *Trees and Other Poems* (1914).

kiln /kiln, kil/ ▶ **n.** a furnace or oven for burning, baking, or drying, esp. one for calcining lime or firing pottery.
▶ **v.** [with obj.] burn, bake, or dry in a kiln.
– ORIGIN Old English *cylene*, from Latin *culina* 'kitchen, cooking stove.'

k

kiln-dry ▶ v. [with obj.] (usu. as noun **kiln-drying**) dry (a material such as wood or sand) in a kiln.

ki·lo /ˈkēlō/ ▶ n. (pl. **kilos**) **1** a kilogram.
2 rare a kilometer.
3 a code word representing the letter K, used in radio communication.
– ORIGIN late 19th cent.: from French, abbreviation of *kilogramme, kilomètre.*

kilo- ▶ comb. form (used commonly in units of measurement) denoting a factor of 1,000: *kilojoule | kiloliter.*
– ORIGIN via French from Greek *khilioi* 'thousand.'

kil·o·base /ˈkiləˌbās/ (abbr.: **kb**) ▶ n. Biochemistry (in expressing the lengths of nucleic acid molecules) 1,000 bases.

kil·o·bit /ˈkiləˌbit/ ▶ n. a unit of computer memory or data equal to 1,024 (2^{10}) bits.

kil·o·byte /ˈkiləˌbīt/ (abbr.: **Kb** or **KB**) ▶ n. Computing a unit of memory or data equal to 1,024 (2^{10}) bytes.

kil·o·cal·o·rie /ˈkiləˌkalərē/ ▶ n. a unit of energy of 1,000 calories (equal to 1 large calorie).

kil·o·cy·cle /ˈkiləˌsīkəl/ (abbr.: **kc**) ▶ n. a former measure of frequency, equivalent to 1 kilohertz.

kil·o·gram /ˈkiləˌgram/ (Brit. also **kilogramme**) (abbr.: **kg**) ▶ n. the SI unit of mass, equivalent to the international standard kept at Sèvres near Paris (approximately 2.205 lb).
– ORIGIN late 18th cent.: from French *kilogramme* (see KILO-, GRAM[1]).

kil·o·hertz /ˈkiləˌhərts/ (abbr.: **kHz**) ▶ n. a measure of frequency equivalent to 1,000 cycles per second.

kil·o·li·ter /ˈkiləˌlētər/ (Brit. **kilolitre**) (abbr.: **kl**) ▶ n. 1,000 liters (equivalent to 220 imperial gallons).

kil·o·me·ter /kiˈlämitər, ˈkiləˌmētər/ (Brit. **kilometre**) (abbr.: **km**) ▶ n. a metric unit of measurement equal to 1,000 meters (approximately 0.62 miles).
– DERIVATIVES **kil·o·met·ric** /ˌkiləˈmetrik/ adj.
– ORIGIN late 18th cent.: from French *kilomètre* (see KILO-, METER[1]).

kil·o·ton /ˈkiləˌtən/ (Brit. also **kilotonne**) ▶ n. a unit of explosive power equivalent to 1,000 tons of TNT.

kil·o·volt /ˈkiləˌvōlt/ (abbr.: **kV**) ▶ n. 1,000 volts.

kil·o·watt /ˈkiləˌwät/ (abbr.: **kW**) ▶ n. a measure of 1,000 watts of electrical power.

kil·o·watt-hour (abbr.: **kWh**) ▶ n. a measure of electrical energy equivalent to a power consumption of 1,000 watts for 1 hour.

Kil·roy /ˈkilˌroi/ a mythical person, popularized by American servicemen in World War II, who left such inscriptions as "Kilroy was here" on walls all over the world.

kilt /kilt/ ▶ n. a knee-length skirt of pleated tartan cloth, traditionally worn by men as part of Scottish Highland dress and now also worn by women and girls.
▶ v. [with obj.] gather (a garment or material) in vertical pleats: (as adj. **kilted**) *kilted skirts.*
– DERIVATIVES **kilt·ed** adj.
– ORIGIN Middle English (as a verb in the sense 'tuck up around the body'): of Scandinavian origin; compare with Danish *kilte (op)* 'tuck (up)' and Old Norse *kilting* 'a skirt.' The noun dates from the mid 18th cent.

kilt

kil·ter /ˈkiltər/ ▶ n. (in phrase **out of kilter**) out of harmony or balance: *daylight savings throws everybody's body clock out of kilter.*
– ORIGIN early 17th cent.: of unknown origin.

kilt·ie /ˈkiltē/ (also **kilty**) ▶ n. **1** informal a person who wears a kilt (often used as a humorous or slightly derogatory term for a Scot).
2 a casual or sports shoe with a fringed tongue that covers the lacing.

Kim·ber·ley /ˈkimbərlē/ **1** a city in South Africa, in the province of Northern Cape; pop. 183,000 (est. 2009). It has been a diamond-mining center since the early 1870s.
2 (also **the Kimberleys**) a plateau region in the far north of Western Australia. A mining and cattle-rearing region, it was the scene of a gold rush in 1885.

kim·ber·lite /ˈkimbərˌlīt/ ▶ n. Geology a rare, blue-tinged, coarse-grained intrusive igneous rock sometimes containing diamonds, found esp. in South Africa and Siberia. Also called BLUE GROUND.
– ORIGIN late 19th cent.: from KIMBERLEY + -ITE[1].

Kim·bun·du /kimˈbo͝ondo͞o/ see MBUNDU.

Kim·chaek /ˈkēmˈCHak/ (formerly *Songjin*) an industrial port city in eastern North Korea, on the Sea of Japan; pop. 198,000 (est. 2009).

kim·chi /ˈkimCHē/ (also **kimchee**) ▶ n. spicy pickled cabbage, the national dish of Korea.
– ORIGIN Korean.

Kim Dae-jung /kim dīˈjo͝oNG/ (1925–2009) Korean politician. Long a voice for democracy in Korea, he served as president of South Korea 1997–2003 and worked to reunify North and South Korea and to achieve peace in Asia. Nobel Peace Prize (2000).

Kim Il-sung /kim ilˈso͝oNG, ˈsəNG/ (1912–94), Korean communist statesman; first premier of North Korea 1948–72 and president 1972–94; born *Kim Song-ju.* He maintained a one-party state and created a personality cult around himself and his family. He was succeeded by his son **Kim Jong-il** (1942–).

ki·mo·no /kəˈmōnō, -nə/ ▶ n. (pl. **kimonos**) a long, loose robe with wide sleeves and tied with a sash, originally worn as a formal garment in Japan and now also used elsewhere as a robe.
– DERIVATIVES **ki·mo·noed** /-nōd, -nəd/ adj.
– ORIGIN mid 17th cent.: Japanese, from *ki* 'wearing' + *mono* 'thing.'

kimono

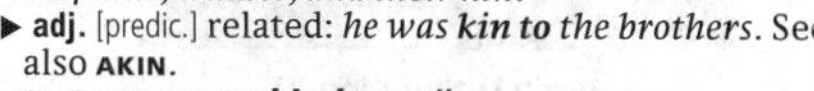

Ki-moon see BAN KI-MOON.

kin /kin/ ▶ n. [treated as pl.] one's family and relations: *he is expected to make a payment to his wife's kin.* ■ animals or plants that are related to a particular species or kind: *dolphins, whales, and their kin.*
▶ adj. [predic.] related: *he was kin to the brothers.* See also AKIN.
– DERIVATIVES **kin·less** adj.
– ORIGIN Old English *cynn,* of Germanic origin; related to Dutch *kunne,* from an Indo-European root meaning 'give birth to,' shared by Greek *genos* and Latin *genus* 'race.'

-kin ▶ suffix forming diminutive nouns such as *bumpkin, catkin.*
– ORIGIN from Middle Dutch *-kijn, -ken,* Middle Low German *-kīn.*

ki·na ▶ n. (pl. **same**) the basic monetary unit of Papua New Guinea, equal to 100 toea.
– ORIGIN Papuan.

Ki·na·ba·lu, Mount /ˌkinəbəˈlo͞o/ a mountain in eastern Malaysia, on the northern coast of Borneo. Rising to 13,431 feet (4,094 m), it is the highest peak in Borneo and in Southeast Asia.

kin·aes·the·sia ▶ n. British spelling of KINESTHESIA.

ki·nase /ˈkīˌnās, ˈkināś/ ▶ n. [usu. with modifier] Biochemistry an enzyme that catalyzes the transfer of a phosphate group from ATP to a specified molecule.
– ORIGIN early 20th cent.: from Greek *kinein* 'to move' + -ASE.

Kin·chin·jun·ga /ˌkinCHənˈjo͝oNGgə/ variant of KANCHENJUNGA.

kind[1] /kīnd/ ▶ n. a group of people or things having similar characteristics: *all kinds of music | a new kind of education | more data of this kind would be valuable.* ■ character; nature: *the trials were different* ***in kind*** *from any that preceded them |* ***true to kind.*** ■ each of the elements (bread and wine) of the Eucharist: ***communion in both kinds.*** ■ (of cards) having the same face value but of a different suit. ■ a hand consisting of such cards.
– PHRASES **in kind** in the same way; with something similar: *if he responded positively, they would respond in kind.* ■ (of payment) in goods or services as opposed to money. **one's (own) kind** people with whom one has a great deal in common: *we stick with our own kind.* **someone's kind** used to express disapproval of a certain type of person: *I don't apologize to her kind ever.* **kind of** informal rather; to some extent (often expressing vagueness or used as a meaningless filler): *it got kind of cozy.* **a kind of** something resembling (used to express vagueness or moderate a statement): *teaching based on a kind of inspired guesswork.* **nothing of the kind** not at all like the thing in question: *my son had done nothing of the kind before.* ■ used to express an emphatic denial: *"He made you do that?" "He did nothing of the kind."* **of its kind** within the limitations of its class: *this new building was no doubt excellent of its kind.* **of a kind** used to indicate that something is not as good as it might be expected to be: *there is tribute, of a kind, in such popularity.* **one of a kind** unique. **something of the kind** something like the thing in question: *they had always suspected something of the kind.* **two** (or **three, four, etc.**) **of a kind** the same or very similar: *she and her sister were two of a kind.*
– ORIGIN Old English *cynd(e), gecynd(e),* of Germanic origin; related to KIN. The original sense was 'nature, the natural order,' also 'innate character, form, or condition' (compare with KIND[2]); hence 'a class or race distinguished by innate characteristics.'

> **USAGE 1** Kind of is sometimes used to be deliberately vague: *it was kind of a big evening; I was kind of hoping you'd call.* More often it reveals an inability to speak clearly: *he's kind of, like, inarticulate, you know?* Used precisely, it means 'sort' or 'type': *a maple is a kind of tree.*
> **2** The plural of kind often causes difficulty. With *this* or *that,* speaking of one kind, use a singular construction: *this kind of cake is my favorite; that kind of fabric doesn't need ironing.* With *these* or *those,* speaking of more than one kind, use a plural construction: *these kinds of guitars are very expensive; those kinds of animals ought to be left in the wild.* Although often encountered, sentences such as *I don't like these kind of things* are incorrect. The same recommendations apply to sort and sorts.

kind[2] ▶ adj. having or showing a friendly, generous, and considerate nature: *she was a good, kind woman | he was very* ***kind to*** *me.* ■ [predic.] used in a polite request: ***would you be kind enough to repeat what you said?*** ■ [predic.] (**kind to**) (of a consumer product) gentle on (a part of the body): *look for rollers that are kind to hair.* ■ archaic affectionate; loving.
– ORIGIN Old English *gecynde* 'natural, native'; in Middle English the earliest sense is 'well born or well bred,' whence 'well disposed by nature, courteous, gentle, benevolent.'

kind·a /ˈkīndə/ informal ▶ contraction kind of: *I think it's kinda funny.*
– ORIGIN early 20th cent. (originally US): alteration.

kin·der·gar·ten /ˈkindərˌgärtn, -ˌgärdn/ ▶ n. a school or class that prepares children for first grade. A child in kindergarten is typically 5 or 6 years old.
– DERIVATIVES **kin·der·gar·ten·er** /-ˌgärtnər, -ˌgärd-/ (also **kindergartner**) n.
– ORIGIN mid 19th cent.: from German, literally 'children's garden.'

kind·heart·ed /ˈkīndˈhärtid/ ▶ adj. having a kind and sympathetic nature.
– DERIVATIVES **kind·heart·ed·ly** adv., **kind·heart·ed·ness** n.

kin·dle[1] /ˈkindl/ ▶ v. [with obj.] light or set on fire. ■ arouse or inspire (an emotion or feeling): *a love of art was kindled in me.* ■ [no obj.] (of an emotion) be aroused: *she hesitated, suspicion kindling within her.* ■ [no obj.] become impassioned or excited: *the young man kindled at once.*
– DERIVATIVES **kin·dler** n.
– ORIGIN Middle English: based on Old Norse *kynda,* influenced by Old Norse *kindill* 'candle, torch.'

kin·dle[2] ▶ v. [no obj.] (of a hare or rabbit) give birth.
– ORIGIN Middle English: apparently a frequentative of KIND[1].

kind·li·ness /ˈkīn(d)lēnis/ ▶ n. the quality of being kind, warmhearted, or gentle; kindness.

kin·dling /ˈkindliNG/ ▶ n. **1** easily combustible small sticks or twigs used for starting a fire.
2 (in neurology) a process by which a seizure or other brain event is both initiated and its recurrence made more likely.

kind·ly /ˈkīn(d)lē/ ▶ adv. in a kind manner: *"Never mind," she said kindly.* ■ please (used in a polite request or demand, often ironically): *will you kindly sign the enclosed copy of this letter.*
▶ adj. (**kindlier, kindliest**) **1** kind; warmhearted; gentle: *he was a quiet, kindly man.*
2 archaic native-born.
– PHRASES **look kindly on** regard (someone or something) sympathetically. **not take kindly to** not welcome or be pleased by (someone or something). **take something kindly** like or be pleased by something. **thank someone kindly** thank someone very much.
– ORIGIN Old English *gecyndelīce* 'naturally, characteristically' (see KIND[2], -LY[2]).

kind·ness /ˈkīn(d)nis/ ▶ n. the quality of being friendly, generous, and considerate. ■ a kind act: *it is a kindness I shall never forget.*

kin·dred /ˈkindrid/ ▶ n. [treated as pl.] one's family and relations. ■ relationship by blood: *ties of kindred.*
▶ adj. [attrib.] similar in kind; related: *books on kindred subjects.*

PRONUNCIATION KEY ə **ago, up**; ər **over, fur**; a **hat**; ā **ate**; ä **car**; e **let**; ē **see**; i **fit**; ī **by**; NG **sing**; ō **go**; ô **law, for**; oi **toy**; o͝o **good**; o͞o **goo**; ou **out**; TH **thin**; T͟H **then**; ZH **vision**

k

–ORIGIN Middle English: from **KIN** + *-red* (from Old English *rǣden* 'condition'), with insertion of *-d-* in the modern spelling through phonetic development (as in *thunder*).

kin·dred spir·it ▶ n. a person whose interests or attitudes are similar to one's own: *I longed to find a kindred spirit.*

kine /kīn/ ▶ **plural n.** archaic cows collectively.

kin·e·mat·ics /ˌkinəˈmatiks/ ▶ **plural n.** [usu. treated as sing.] the branch of mechanics concerned with the motion of objects without reference to the forces that cause the motion. Compare with **DYNAMICS**. ■ [usu. treated as pl.] the features or properties of motion in an object, regarded in such a way.
–DERIVATIVES **kin·e·mat·ic** adj., **kin·e·mat·i·cal·ly** /-ˈmatik(ə)lē/ adv.
–ORIGIN mid 19th cent.: from Greek *kinēma, kinēmat-* 'motion' (from *kinein* 'to move') + **-ICS**.

kin·e·mat·o·graph /ˌkinəˈmatəˌgraf/ ▶ n. variant spelling of **CINEMATOGRAPH**.

kin·e·scope /ˈkinəˌskōp/ ▶ n. a television picture tube. ■ a film recording of a television broadcast.
–ORIGIN mid 20th cent.: originally a proprietary name, from Greek *kinēsis* 'movement' + **-SCOPE**.

ki·ne·sics /kəˈnēsiks, -ziks/ ▶ **plural n.** [usu. treated as sing.] the study of the way in which certain body movements and gestures serve as a form of nonverbal communication. ■ [usu. treated as pl.] certain body movements and gestures regarded in such a way.
–ORIGIN 1950s: from Greek *kinēsis* 'motion' (from *kinein* 'to move') + **-ICS**.

ki·ne·si·ol·o·gy /kəˌnēsēˈäləjē, -zē-/ ▶ n. the study of the mechanics of body movements.
–DERIVATIVES **ki·ne·si·o·log·i·cal** /-sēəˈläjikəl, -zēə-/ adj., **ki·ne·si·ol·o·gist** /-jist/ n.
–ORIGIN late 19th cent.: from Greek *kinēsis* 'movement' (from *kinein* 'to move') + **-LOGY**.

ki·ne·sis /kəˈnēsis/ ▶ n. (pl. **kineses** /-ˌsēz/) movement; motion. ■ Biology an undirected movement of a cell, organism, or part in response to an external stimulus. Compare with **TAXIS**. ■ Zoology mobility of the bones of the skull, as in some birds and reptiles.
–ORIGIN early 17th cent.: from Greek *kinēsis* 'movement,' from *kinein* 'to move.'

kin·es·the·sia /ˌkinəsˈTHēZHə/ (Brit. **kinaesthesia**) ▶ n. awareness of the position and movement of the parts of the body by means of sensory organs (proprioceptors) in the muscles and joints.
–DERIVATIVES **kin·es·thet·ic** /-ˈTHetik/ adj.
–ORIGIN late 19th cent.: from Greek *kinein* 'to move' + *aisthēsis* 'sensation.'

ki·net·ic /kəˈnetik/ ▶ adj. of, relating to, or resulting from motion. ■ (of a work of art) depending on movement for its effect.
–DERIVATIVES **ki·net·i·cal·ly** /-ik(ə)lē/ adv.
–ORIGIN mid 19th cent.: from Greek *kinētikos*, from *kinein* 'to move.'

ki·net·ic art ▶ n. a form of art that depends on movement for its effect. The term was coined by artists Naum Gabo (1890–1977) and his brother Antoine Pevsner (1886–1962) in 1920 and is associated with the mobiles of artist Alexander Calder.

ki·net·ic en·er·gy ▶ n. Physics energy that a body possesses by virtue of being in motion. Compare with **POTENTIAL ENERGY**.

ki·net·ics /kəˈnetiks/ ▶ **plural n.** [usu. treated as sing.] the branch of chemistry or biochemistry concerned with measuring and studying the rates of reactions. ■ [usu. treated as pl.] the rates of chemical or biochemical reaction. ■ Physics the study of forces acting on mechanisms.

ki·net·ic the·o·ry ▶ n. the body of theory that explains the physical properties of matter in terms of the motions of its constituent particles.

ki·ne·tin /ˈkīnətin/ ▶ n. Biochemistry & Botany a synthetic compound similar to kinin, used to stimulate cell division in plants.
–ORIGIN 1950s: from Greek *kinētos* 'movable' (from *kinein* 'to move') + **-IN**[1].

kineto- ▶ comb. form relating to movement.
–ORIGIN from Greek *kinētos* 'movable.'

ki·ne·to·chore /kəˈnetəˌkôr, -ˈnētə-/ ▶ n. another term for **CENTROMERE**.
–ORIGIN mid 20th cent.: from **KINETO-** 'of movement' + Greek *khōros* 'place.'

ki·ne·to·plast /kəˈnetəˌplast, -ˈnētə-/ ▶ n. Biology a mass of mitochondrial DNA lying close to the nucleus in some flagellate protozoa.

ki·ne·to·scope /kəˈnetəˌskōp, -ˈnē-/ ▶ n. an early motion-picture device in which the images were viewed through a peephole.

ki·ne·to·some /kəˈnetəˌsōm, -ˈnētə-, kī-/ ▶ n. another term for **BASAL BODY**.

kin·folk /ˈkinˌfōk/ (also **kinsfolk** /ˈkinz-/ or **kinfolks**) ▶ **plural n.** (in anthropological or formal use) a person's blood relations, regarded collectively. ■ a group of people related by blood: *a set of kinfolk.* ■ a

King[1] /kiNG/, B. B. (1925–), US blues singer and guitarist; born *Riley B. King*. An established blues performer, he came to the notice of a wider audience in the late 1960s, when his style of guitar playing was imitated by rock musicians.

King[2], Billie Jean (1943–), US tennis player. She won a record 20 Wimbledon titles, including 6 singles titles (1966–68, 1972–73, and 1975), 10 doubles titles, and 4 mixed doubles titles. She retired in 1983.

King[3], Martin Luther, Jr. (1929–68), US Baptist minister and civil rights leader. A noted orator, he opposed discrimination against blacks by organizing nonviolent resistance and peaceful mass demonstrations. He was assassinated in Memphis, Tennessee. Nobel Peace Prize (1964). His birthday, January 15, is a national holiday.

Martin Luther King, Jr.

King[4], Stephen (Edwin) (1947–) US writer; pseudonym Richard Bachman. He is best known for his writings of horror and suspense, such as *Carrie* (1974, movie 1976), *The Shining* (1977, movie 1980), *The Green Mile* (1996, movie 1999), *The Plant* (2000), and *Cell* (2006).

King[5], William Lyon Mackenzie (1874–1950), Canadian Liberal statesman; prime minister 1921–26, 1926–30, and 1935–48.

king /kiNG/ ▶ n. **1** the male ruler of an independent state, esp. one who inherits the position by right of birth: [as title] *King Henry VIII.* ■ a person or thing regarded as the finest or most important in its sphere or group: *a country where football is king | the king of rock.* ■ (**the King**) dated (in the UK) the national anthem when there is a male sovereign. ■ [attrib.] used in names of animals and plants that are particularly large, e.g., **king cobra**.
2 the most important chess piece, of which each player has one, which the opponent has to checkmate in order to win. The king can move in any direction, including diagonally, to any adjacent square that is not attacked by an opponent's piece or pawn. ■ a piece in the game of checkers with extra capacity for moving, made by crowning an ordinary piece that has reached the opponent's baseline. ■ a playing card bearing a representation of a king, normally ranking next below an ace.
▶ v. [with obj.] archaic make (someone) king. ■ (**king it**) dated act in an unpleasantly superior and domineering manner: *he kings it over the natives on his atoll.*
–PHRASES **a king's ransom** see **RANSOM**. **live like a king** (or **queen**) live in great comfort and luxury.
–DERIVATIVES **king·hood** /-ˌhŏŏd/ n., **king·less** adj., **king·like** /-ˌlīk/ adj., **king·ship** /-ˌSHip/ n.
–ORIGIN Old English *cyning, cyng*, of Germanic origin; related to Dutch *koning* and German *König*, also to **KIN**.

king·bird /ˈkiNGˌbərd/ ▶ n. a large American tyrant flycatcher, typically with a gray head and back and yellowish or white underparts. ● Genus *Tyrannus*, family Tyrannidae: several species.

king bo·lete ▶ n. another term for **CEP**.

king·bolt /ˈkiNGˌbōlt/ ▶ n. a kingpin in a mechanical structure.

King Charles span·iel ▶ n. a spaniel of a small breed, typically with a white, black, and tan coat.

king co·bra ▶ n. a brownish cobra with an orange-cream throat patch, native to southern Asia. It is the largest of all venomous snakes. Also called **HAMADRYAD**. ● *Ophiophagus hannah*, family Elapidae.

king crab ▶ n. **1** an edible crab of the North Pacific, resembling a spider crab. ● Genus *Paralithodes*, family Lithodidae.
2 another term for **HORSESHOE CRAB**.

king·craft /ˈkiNGˌkraft/ ▶ n. archaic the art of ruling as a king, esp. with reference to the use of clever or crafty diplomacy in dealing with subjects.

king·cup /ˈkiNGˌkəp/ ▶ n. British term for **MARSH MARIGOLD**.

king·dom /ˈkiNGdəm/ ▶ n. **1** a country, state, or territory ruled by a king or queen. ■ a realm associated with or regarded as being under the control of a particular person or thing: *the kingdom of dreams.*
2 the spiritual reign or authority of God. ■ the rule of God or Christ in a future age. ■ heaven as the abode of God and of the faithful after death.
3 each of the three traditional divisions (animal, vegetable, and mineral) in which natural objects have conventionally been classified. ■ Biology the highest category in taxonomic classification.
–PHRASES **come into** (or **to**) **one's kingdom** achieve recognition or supremacy. **till** (or **until**) **kingdom come** informal forever. **to kingdom come** informal into the next world: *the truck was blown to kingdom come.*
–ORIGIN Old English *cyningdōm* 'kingship' (see **KING**, **-DOM**).

king·fish /ˈkiNGˌfiSH/ ▶ n. (pl. **same** or **kingfishes**)
1 any of a number of large sporting fish, many of which are edible. ■ a fish of the jack family (Carangidae), including the **yellowtail kingfish** (*Seriola grandis*) of the South Pacific. ■ (**northern kingfish**) a fish of the drum family (*Menticirrhus saxatilis*, family Sciaenidae), of the east coast of North America. ■ a western Atlantic fish of the mackerel family (*Scomberomorus cavalla*, family Scombridae).
2 informal a person regarded as an authority figure; an influential leader or boss.

king·fish·er /ˈkiNGˌfiSHər/ ▶ n. an often brightly colored bird with a large head and long sharp beak, typically diving for fish from a perch. Many of the tropical kinds live in forests and feed on terrestrial prey such as insects and lizards. ● Family Alcedinidae: many genera and numerous species, esp. the **belted kingfisher** (*Ceryle alcyon*), with blue-gray and white plumage and a shaggy crest, found throughout North America.

belted kingfisher

King James Bi·ble (also **King James Version**) ▶ n. an English translation of the Bible made in 1611 at the order of King James I and still widely used. Also called **AUTHORIZED VERSION**, chiefly in the UK.

king·let /ˈkiNGlit/ ▶ n. **1** chiefly derogatory a minor king.
2 a very small greenish bird with a bright orange or yellow crown. ● Genus *Regulus*, family Sylviidae: several species, e.g., the American **golden-crowned kinglet** (*R. satrapa*).

king·ly /ˈkiNGlē/ ▶ adj. (**kinglier**, **kingliest**) associated with or typical of a king; regal: *his kingly duties.*
–DERIVATIVES **king·li·ness** n.

king·mak·er /ˈkiNGˌmākər/ ▶ n. a person who brings leaders to power through the exercise of political influence.
–ORIGIN used originally with reference to the Earl of Warwick (see **WARWICK**[2]).

king of beasts ▶ n. chiefly literary the lion (used in reference to the animal's perceived grandeur).

King of Kings ▶ n. used as a name or form of address for God. ■ (in the Christian Church) used as a name or form of address for Jesus Christ. ■ a title assumed by certain kings who rule over lesser kings.

king of the hill ▶ n. a children's game in which the object is to beat one's rivals to the top of a mound or other high place, and to keep possession of the place. ■ one who is in command or successful: *your daddy brags about you—you're king of the hill with him.*

king pen·guin ▶ n. a large penguin native to Antarctic islands as well as the Falklands and other subantarctic islands. ● *Aptenodytes patagonica*, family Spheniscidae.

King Phil·ip's War (1675–77) the first large-scale military action in the American colonies, pitting various Indian tribes against New England colonists and their Indian allies. Marked by heavy slaughters on both sides (including killings of women and children), the war cost thousands of lives.

king·pin /ˈkiNG,pin/ ▶ **n.** a main or large bolt in a central position. ■ a vertical bolt used as a pivot. ■ a person or thing that is essential to the success of an organization or operation: *the kingpins of the television industry*.

king post ▶ **n.** an upright post in the center of a roof truss, extending from the tie beam to the apex of the truss.

kin group ▶ **n.** a group of people related by blood or marriage.

Kings /kiNGz/ the name of two books of the Bible, recording the history of Israel from the accession of Solomon to the destruction of the Temple in 586 BC.

King's Bench ▶ **n.** (in the UK) in the reign of a king, the term for QUEEN'S BENCH.

Kings Can·yon Na·tion·al Park a national park in the Sierra Nevada, in south central California, north of Sequoia National Park. Established in 1940, it preserves groves of ancient sequoia trees, including some of the largest in the world.

King's Coun·sel (abbr.: **KC**) ▶ **n.** (in the UK) in the reign of a king, the term for QUEEN'S COUNSEL.

King's Eng·lish ▶ **n.** another term for QUEEN'S ENGLISH.

king's e·vil ▶ **n.** (usu. **the king's evil**) historical scrofula, formerly held to be curable by the royal touch.

king·side /ˈkiNG,sīd/ ▶ **n.** Chess the half of the board on which both kings stand at the start of a game (the right-hand side for White, left for Black).

king-sized (also **king-size**) ▶ **adj.** (esp. of a commercial product) of a larger size than the standard; very large: *a king-sized bed*.

Kings·ley /ˈkiNGzlē/, Charles (1819–75), English novelist and clergyman. He is remembered for his historical novel *Westward Ho!* (1855) and for his classic children's story *The Water-Babies* (1863).

king snake ▶ **n.** a large, smooth-scaled North American constrictor that typically has shiny dark brown or black skin with lighter markings. ● Genus *Lampropeltis*, family Colubridae: several species, in particular *L. getulus*. Compare with MILK SNAKE.

king's pawn ▶ **n.** Chess the pawn occupying the square immediately in front of each player's king at the start of a game.

Kings·port /ˈkiNGz,pôrt/ an industrial city in northeastern Tennessee, part of a complex with Johnson City and Bristol; pop. 44,473 (est. 2008).

king's shil·ling ▶ **n.** a shilling formerly given to a recruit when enlisting in the army during the reign of a king.

Kings·ton /ˈkiNGstən/ **1** a port in southeastern Canada, on Lake Ontario, at the head of the St. Lawrence River; pop. 117,207 (2006).
2 the capital and chief port of Jamaica; pop. 580,000 (est. 2007).
3 a historic city in southeastern New York, on the Hudson River; pop. 22,441 (est. 2008).

Kings·ton up·on Hull official name for HULL¹.

Kings·town /ˈkiNGz,toun/ the capital and chief port of St. Vincent and the Grenadines in the Caribbean; pop. 26,000 (est. 2007).

ki·nin /ˈkīnin/ ▶ **n.** **1** Biochemistry any of a group of substances formed in body tissue in response to injury. They are polypeptides and cause vasodilation and smooth muscle contraction.
2 Botany a compound that promotes cell division and inhibits aging in plants. Also called CYTOKININ.
– ORIGIN 1950s: from Greek *kinein* 'to move' + -IN¹.

kink /kiNGk/ ▶ **n.** **1** a sharp twist or curve in something that is otherwise straight: *a kink in the road*. ■ a flaw or obstacle in a plan, operation, etc.: *though the system is making some headway, there are still some kinks to iron out*. ■ a quirk of character or behavior. ■ informal a person's unusual sexual preference.
2 a stiffness in the neck, back, etc.; crick: *it takes the kinks out of stiff necks*.
▶ **v.** form or cause to form a sharp twist or curve: [no obj.] *the river kinks violently in a right angle* | [with obj.] *when the spine gets kinked, the muscles react with pain*.
– ORIGIN late 17th cent.: from Middle Low German *kinke*, probably from Dutch *kinken* 'to kink.'

kin·ka·jou /ˈkiNGkə,jo͞o/ ▶ **n.** an arboreal nocturnal fruit-eating mammal with a prehensile tail and a long tongue, found in the tropical forests of Central and South America. ● *Potos flavus*, family Procyonidae.
– ORIGIN late 18th cent.: from French *quincajou*, alteration of CARCAJOU.

kink·y /ˈkiNGkē/ ▶ **adj.** (**kinkier**, **kinkiest**) **1** informal involving or given to unusual sexual behavior. ■ (of clothing) sexually provocative in an unusual way: *kinky underwear*.
2 having kinks or twists: *long and kinky hair*.
– DERIVATIVES **kink·i·ly** /-kilē/ **adv.**, **kink·i·ness** **n.**
– ORIGIN mid 19th cent. (sense 2): from KINK + -Y¹.

Kin·ner·et, Lake /kēˈneret/ another name for Sea of Galilee (see GALILEE, SEA OF).

kin·ni·kin·nick /,kinikiˈnik/ (also **kinnikinnic** or **kinnikinnik**) ▶ **n.** a smoking mixture used by North American Indians as a substitute for tobacco or for mixing with it, typically consisting of dried sumac leaves and the inner bark of willow or dogwood. ■ the bearberry, which was also sometimes used in this mixture.
– ORIGIN late 18th cent.: from a Delaware (Unami) word meaning 'mixture.'

ki·no /ˈkēnō/ ▶ **n.** a gum obtained from certain tropical trees by tapping, used locally as an astringent in medicine and in tanning. ● The trees belong to genera in various families, in particular *Pterocarpus* and *Butea* (family Leguminosae).
– ORIGIN late 18th cent.: apparently from a West African language.

Kin·o·rhyn·cha /,kinəˈriNGkə, ,kē-/ Zoology a small phylum of minute marine invertebrates that have a spiny body and burrow in sand or mud.
– DERIVATIVES **kin·o·rhynch** /ˈkinə,riNGk, ˈkē-/ **n.**
– ORIGIN modern Latin (plural), from Greek *kinein* 'set in motion' + *rhunkos* 'snout.'

-kins ▶ **suffix** equivalent to -KIN, often expressing endearment.

kin se·lec·tion ▶ **n.** Zoology natural selection in favor of behavior by individuals that may decrease their chance of survival but increases that of their kin (who share a proportion of their genes).

Kin·sey /ˈkinzē/, Alfred Charles (1894–1956), US zoologist and sex researcher. He carried out pioneering studies on sexual behavior by interviewing large numbers of people. His best-known work, *Sexual Behavior in the Human Male* (1948, also known as the *Kinsey Report*), was controversial but highly influential.

kins·folk /ˈkinz,fōk/ ▶ **plural n.** another term for KINFOLK.

Kin·sha·sa /kinˈSHäsə/ the capital of the Democratic Republic of the Congo (formerly Zaire), a port on the Congo River, in the southwestern part of the country; pop. 7,273,900 (est. 2004). Founded in 1881 by explorer Sir Henry Morton Stanley, it became capital of the Republic of Zaire in 1960. Former name (until 1966) LÉOPOLDVILLE.

kin·ship /ˈkin,SHip/ ▶ **n.** blood relationship. ■ a sharing of characteristics or origins: *they felt a kinship with architects*.

kin·ship group ▶ **n.** Anthropology a family, clan, or other group based on kinship.

kins·man /ˈkinzmən/ ▶ **n.** (pl. **kinsmen**) (in anthropological or formal use) one of a person's blood relations, esp. a male.

kins·wom·an /ˈkinz,wo͝omən/ ▶ **n.** (pl. **kinswomen**) (in anthropological or formal use) one of a person's female blood relations.

ki·osk /ˈkē,äsk/ ▶ **n.** a small open-fronted hut or cubicle from which newspapers, refreshments, tickets, etc., are sold. ■ a small structure in a public area used for providing information or displaying advertisements, often incorporating an interactive display screen or screens. ■ (usu. **telephone kiosk**) Brit. a telephone booth. ■ archaic (in Turkey and Iran) a light open pavilion or summerhouse.
– ORIGIN early 17th cent. (in the sense 'pavilion'): from French *kiosque*, from Turkish *köşk* 'pavilion,' from Persian *kuš*.

Ki·o·wa /ˈkīəwə/ ▶ **n.** (pl. **same** or **Kiowas**) **1** a member of an American Indian people of the southern plains of the US, now living mainly in Oklahoma.
2 the language of this people, related to the Tanoan group.
3 (in full **Kiowa Apache**) an Athabaskan (Apache) language of western Oklahoma and neighboring areas.
▶ **adj.** of or relating to this people or these languages.
– ORIGIN from American Spanish *Caygua*, perhaps from Caddoan *káˑhiwa* 'Kiowa.'

kip¹ /kip/ ▶ **n.** (in leather-making) the hide of a young or small animal. ■ a set or bundle of such hides.
– ORIGIN late Middle English: perhaps related to Middle Dutch *kip*, *kijp* 'bundle (of hides).'

kip² ▶ **n.** (pl. **same** or **kips**) the basic monetary unit of Laos, equal to 100 ats.
– ORIGIN Thai.

kip³ ▶ **n.** a unit of weight equal to 1,000 lb (453.6 kg).
– ORIGIN early 20th cent.: probably from *ki-* in KILO- + *p-* in POUND¹.

kip⁴ informal ▶ **n.** Brit. a sleep; a nap: *I might have a little kip | he was trying to get some kip*. ■ chiefly Scottish a bed.
▶ **v.** (**kips**, **kipping**, **kipped**) [no obj.] Brit. sleep: *they kipped down for the night*.
– ORIGIN mid 18th cent. (in the sense 'brothel'): perhaps related to Danish *kippe* 'hovel, tavern.'

Kip·ling /ˈkipliNG/, Rudyard (1865–1936), British novelist, short-story writer, and poet, born in India; full name *Joseph Rudyard Kipling*. He is known for his poems, such as "If" and "Gunga Din," and for his children's tales, notably *The Jungle Book* (1894) and the *Just So Stories* (1902). Nobel Prize for Literature (1907).
– DERIVATIVES **Kip·ling·esque** /,kipliNGˈesk/ **adj.**

kip·pa /kēˈpä/ (also **kippah**) ▶ **n.** another term for YARMULKE.
– ORIGIN mid 20th cent.: from modern Hebrew *kippāh*.

kip·per /ˈkipər/ ▶ **n.** **1** a kippered fish, esp. a herring.
2 a male salmon in the spawning season.
▶ **v.** [with obj.] (usu. as adj. **kippered**) cure (a herring or other fish) by splitting it open and salting and drying it in the open air or in smoke.
– ORIGIN Old English *cypera* (sense 2 of the noun), of Germanic origin; related to Old Saxon *kupiro*, perhaps also to COPPER¹.

Kir /ki(ə)r/ (also **kir**) ▶ **n.** trademark a drink made from dry white wine and crème de cassis.
– ORIGIN 1960s: named after Canon Félix *Kir* (1876–1968), a mayor of Dijon, France, who is said to have invented the recipe.

Kirch·hoff /ˈki(ə)r,KHôf/, Gustav Robert (1824–87), German physicist; a pioneer in spectroscopy. He developed the concept of black-body radiation and discovered the elements cesium and rubidium.

Kir·ghiz /ki(ə)rˈgēz/ (also **Kyrgyz**) ▶ **n.** (pl. **same**) **1** a member of an indigenous people of central Asia, living chiefly in Kyrgyzstan.
2 the Turkic language of this people.
▶ **adj.** of or relating to this people or their language.
– ORIGIN the name in Kirghiz.

Kir·ghi·zia /ki(ə)rˈgēZHə, -ˈgēzēə/ another name for KYRGYZSTAN.

Ki·ri·ba·ti /ˈki(ə)rə,bas/ a country in the southwestern Pacific Ocean that includes the Gilbert, Line, and Phoenix islands, as well as Banaba (Ocean Island); pop. 112,900 (est. 2009); capital, Bairiki (on Tarawa); official languages, English and I-Kiribati (a local Austronesian language).

> Inhabited by Micronesian people, the islands were sighted by the Spaniards in the mid 16th century. Britain declared a protectorate over the Gilbert and Ellice Islands in 1892, and they became a colony in 1915. British links with the Ellice Islands (now Tuvalu) ended in 1975, and Kiribati became an independent republic within the Commonwealth of Nations in 1979.

Ki·rin /ˈkēˈrin/ variant of JILIN.

Ki·riti·mati /kəˈrismәs, ˈkris-/ an island in the Pacific Ocean, one of the Line Islands of Kiribati; pop. 5,115 (2005). The largest atoll in the world, it was discovered by Captain James Cook on Christmas Eve 1777 and was British until it became part of an independent Kiribati in 1979. Former name (until 1981) CHRISTMAS ISLAND.

kirk /kərk/ ▶ **n.** Scottish & N. English **1** a church.
2 (**the Kirk** or **the Kirk of Scotland**) the Church of Scotland as distinct from the Church of England or from the Episcopal Church in Scotland.
– ORIGIN Middle English: from Old Norse *kirkja*, from Old English *cirice* (see CHURCH).

Kirk·land /ˈkərklənd/ a city in west central Washington, northeast of Seattle; pop. 47,303 (est. 2008).

Kir·kuk /kirˈko͝ok/ an industrial city in northern Iraq, center of the oil industry in that region; pop. 600,000 (est. 2003).

Kirk·wall /kərˈkwôl/ a port in the Orkney Islands; pop. 6,600 (2009). Situated on Mainland, it is the chief town of the islands.

Kir·li·an pho·tog·ra·phy /ˈki(ə)rlēən/ ▶ **n.** a technique for recording photographic images of corona discharges and hence, supposedly, the auras of living creatures.
– ORIGIN late 20th cent.: from the name of Semyon D. and Valentina K. *Kirlian*, Russian electricians.

Kir·man /kir'män/ ▶ **n.** a carpet of a kind typically having soft, delicate coloring and naturalistic designs.
– ORIGIN late 19th cent.: from *Kirman*, the name of a province and town in southeastern Iran.

Ki·rov /'ki(ə)r,ôf, -əf/ former name (1934–92) for **VYATKA**.

Ki·ro·va·bad /,kērəf'bät/ former name (1935–89) for **GÄNCÄ**.

Kir roy·al (also **Kir royale**) ▶ **n.** a drink made from champagne or sparkling white wine and crème de cassis.
– ORIGIN French, literally 'royal Kir.'

kirsch /ki(ə)rsH/ (also **kirschwasser** /-,väsər/) ▶ **n.** brandy distilled from the fermented juice of cherries.
– ORIGIN German, abbreviation of *Kirschenwasser*, from *Kirsche* 'cherry' + *Wasser* 'water.'

kir·tle /'kərtl/ ▶ **n.** archaic a woman's gown or outer petticoat. ■ a man's tunic or coat.
– ORIGIN Old English *cyrtel*, of Germanic origin, probably based on Latin *curtus* 'short.'

ki·san /ki'sän/ ▶ **n.** Indian an agricultural worker; a peasant.
– ORIGIN 1930s: Hindi *kisān*, from Sanskrit *kṛṣāṇa* 'person who plows.'

Ki·san·ga·ni /,kēsäNG'gänē, kē'säNG,gänē/ a city in northern Democratic Republic of the Congo (formerly Zaire), on the Congo River; pop. 682,600 (est. 2004). Former name (until 1966) **STANLEYVILLE**.

Ki·shi·nev /'kisHə,nef, -,nev/ Russian name for **CHIŞINĂU**.

Ki·shi·nyov /'kisHə,nef, -,nev, kyisHə'nyôf/ Russian name for **CHIŞINĂU**.

kish·ke /'kisHkə/ ▶ **n.** a beef intestine stuffed with a seasoned filling. ■ (usu. **kishkes**) informal a person's guts.
– ORIGIN mid 20th cent.: Yiddish, from Polish *kiszka* or Ukrainian *kishka*.

kis·ka·dee /'kiskə,dē/ ▶ **n.** a large tyrant flycatcher with a black-and-white-striped head and bright yellow breast, found mainly in tropical America. ● The **greater kiskadee** (*Pitangus sulphuratus*) and the **lesser kiskadee** (*Philohydor lictor*), family Tyrannidae.
– ORIGIN late 19th cent.: imitative of its call.

Kis·ka Is·land /'kiskə/ an island in the Aleutian Islands, in southwestern Alaska. It was occupied by the Japanese during World War II.

Kis·lev /'kisləv, kēs'lev/ ▶ **n.** (in the Jewish calendar) the third month of the civil and ninth of the religious year, usually coinciding with parts of November and December.
– ORIGIN from Hebrew *kislēw*.

kis·met /'kizmit, -,met/ ▶ **n.** destiny; fate: *what chance did I stand against kismet?*
– ORIGIN early 19th cent.: from Turkish, from Arabic *kismat* 'division, portion, lot,' from *ḳasama* 'to divide.'

kiss /kis/ ▶ **v.** [with obj.] touch with the lips as a sign of love, sexual desire, reverence, or greeting: *he kissed her on the lips* | [with obj. and complement] *she kissed the children goodnight* | [no obj.] *we started kissing.* ■ Billiards (of a ball) lightly touch (another ball) in passing.
▶ **n. 1** a touch with the lips in kissing. ■ Billiards a slight touch of a ball against another ball. ■ used to express affection at the end of a letter (conventionally represented by the letter X): *she sent lots of love and a whole line of kisses.*
2 a small cake or cookie, typically a meringue. ■ a small candy, esp. one made of chocolate.
– PHRASES **kiss and make up** become reconciled. **kiss and tell** recount one's sexual exploits, esp. to the media concerning a famous person: [as adj.] *this isn't a kiss-and-tell book.* **kiss someone's ass** vulgar slang behave obsequiously toward someone. **kiss ass** vulgar slang behave in an obsequious or sycophantic way. **kiss something good-bye** (or **kiss good-bye to something**) informal accept the certain loss of something: *I could kiss my career good-bye.* **kiss something to make it better** informal comfort a sick or injured person, esp. a child, by kissing the sore or injured part of their body as a gesture of removing pain. **kiss of death** an action or event that causes certain failure for an enterprise: *it would be the kiss of death for the company if it could be proved that the food was unsafe.* **kiss of life** mouth-to-mouth resuscitation. ■ an action or event that revives a failing enterprise: *good ratings gave the program the kiss of life.* **kiss of peace** a ceremonial kiss given or exchanged as a sign of unity, esp. during the Christian Eucharist. **kiss the rod** accept punishment submissively.
– PHRASAL VERBS **kiss someone/something off** informal dismiss someone rudely; end a relationship abruptly. **kiss up to** informal behave sycophantically or obsequiously toward (someone) in order to obtain something.
– DERIVATIVES **kiss·a·ble** adj.
– ORIGIN Old English *cyssan* (verb), of Germanic origin; related to Dutch *kussen* and German *küssen*.

kiss-and-tell ▶ **adj.** revealing private or confidential information: *a kiss-and-tell article by the actor's former girlfriend.*

kiss-ass ▶ **adj.** vulgar slang having or showing an obsequious or sycophantic eagerness to please.
▶ **n.** a person who behaves in such a way.

kiss-curl ▶ **n.** British term for **SPIT CURL**.

kis·sel /'kisəl/ ▶ **n.** a dessert made from fruit juice or purée, boiled with sugar and water and thickened with potato or cornstarch.
– ORIGIN from Russian *kisel'*, from a base shared by *kislyĭ* 'sour.'

kiss·er /'kisər/ ▶ **n. 1** [usu. with adj.] a person who kisses someone: *he's a good kisser.* [mid 16th cent.: from the verb **KISS** + **-ER**¹.]
2 informal a person's mouth: *I belted him one, right on the kisser.* [mid 19th cent.: originally boxing slang.]

Kis·sim·mee /ki'simē/ a resort and agricultural city in central Florida; pop. 62,291 (est. 2008).

kiss·ing bug ▶ **n.** a bloodsucking North American assassin bug that can inflict a painful bite on humans and often attacks the face.

kiss·ing cous·in ▶ **n.** a relative known well enough to be given a kiss in greeting.

kiss·ing dis·ease ▶ **n.** informal a disease transmitted by contact with infected saliva, esp. infectious mononucleosis.

Kis·sin·ger /'kisənjər/, Henry (Alfred) (1923–), US statesman and diplomat; born in Germany; secretary of state 1973–77. In 1973, he helped to negotiate the withdrawal of US troops from South Vietnam. His numerous trips to foster Middle East negotiations led to the term "shuttle diplomacy." Nobel Peace Prize (1973).

kiss-off ▶ **n.** informal a rude or abrupt dismissal, esp. from a job or romantic relationship.

kiss·o·gram /'kisə,gram/ ▶ **n.** a novelty greeting or message delivered by a man or woman who accompanies it with a kiss, arranged as a humorous surprise for the recipient.

kiss·y /'kisē/ ▶ **adj.** informal characterized by or given to kissing; amorous: *Dean and I were just getting kissy.*

kiss·y-face ▶ **n.** informal a puckering of the lips as if to kiss someone: ***she made kissy-face when she saw me.***
– PHRASES **play kissy-face** (or **kissy-kissy**) engage in kissing or petting, esp. in public. ■ behave in an excessively friendly way in order to gain favor.

kist /kist/ ▶ **n. 1** chiefly Scottish & S. African a chest used for storing clothes and linen.
2 variant spelling of **CIST**.
– ORIGIN Middle English: northern English form of **CHEST**.

Ki·swa·hi·li /,kiswä'hēlē/ ▶ **n.** another term for **SWAHILI** (sense 1 of the noun).
– ORIGIN from the Bantu prefix *ki-* (used in names of languages) + **SWAHILI**.

kit¹ /kit/ ▶ **n. 1** a set of articles or equipment needed for a specific purpose: *a first-aid kit.* ■ a set of all the parts needed to assemble something: *an aircraft kit.* ■ Brit. the clothing and other items belonging to a soldier or used in an activity such as a sport: *boys in football kit.*
2 chiefly Brit. a large basket, box, or other container, esp. for fish.
▶ **v.** [with obj.] (**kit someone/something out/up**) (usu. **be kitted out/up**) chiefly Brit. provide someone or something with the appropriate clothing or equipment: *we were all kitted out in life jackets.*
– ORIGIN Middle English: from Middle Dutch *kitte* 'wooden vessel,' of unknown origin. The original sense 'wooden tub' was later applied to other containers; the use denoting a soldier's equipment (late 18th cent.) probably arose from the idea of a set of articles packed in a container.

kit² ▶ **n.** the young of certain animals, such as the beaver, fox, ferret, and mink. ■ informal term for **KITTEN**.

kit³ ▶ **n.** historical a small violin, esp. one used by a dancing master.
– ORIGIN early 16th cent.: perhaps from Latin *cithara* (see **CITTERN**).

Ki·ta·kyu·shu /,kētä'kyōōsHōō/ a port in southern Japan, on the northern coast of Kyushu island; pop. 986,755 (2007).

kit bag (also **kitbag**) ▶ **n.** a rectangular canvas bag, used esp. for carrying a soldier's clothes and personal possessions.

kitch·en /'kicHən/ ▶ **n. 1** a room or area where food is prepared and cooked. ■ a set of fixtures, cabinets, and appliances that are sold together and installed in such a room or area: *a complete kitchen at a bargain price.* ■ cuisine: *the dried shrimp pastes of the Thai kitchen.*
2 informal the percussion section of an orchestra.
3 [as modifier] (of a language) in an uneducated or domestic form: *kitchen Swahili.*
– ORIGIN Old English *cycene*; related to Dutch *keuken* and German *Küche*, based on Latin *coquere* 'to cook.'

kitch·en cab·i·net ▶ **n.** a group of unofficial advisers to the holder of an elected office who are considered to be unduly influential.

Kitch·e·ner¹ /'kicH(ə)nər/ a city in Ontario, southern Canada; pop. 204,668 (2006). Settled as Dutch Sand Hills by German Mennonites in 1806, it was renamed Berlin in 1830 and Kitchener in 1916, in honor of Field Marshal Kitchener.

Kitch·e·ner², Herbert (1850–1916), British soldier and statesman, born in Ireland; full name *Horatio Herbert Kitchener, 1st Earl Kitchener*. He served as secretary of state for war during World War I.

kitch·en·ette /,kicHə'net/ ▶ **n.** a small kitchen or part of a room equipped as a kitchen.

kitch·en gar·den ▶ **n.** a garden or area where vegetables, fruit, or herbs are grown for domestic use.

kitch·en mid·den ▶ **n.** a prehistoric refuse heap that marks an ancient settlement, chiefly containing bones, shells, and stone implements.

kitch·en po·lice ▶ **n.** [usu. treated as pl.] military slang enlisted personnel detailed to help the cook by washing dishes, peeling vegetables, and performing other kitchen duties.

kitch·en sink ▶ **n.** a sink in a kitchen, used for washing dishes and preparing food: ***the traditional view of women as dedicated housewives tied to the kitchen sink is all but extinct.*** ■ [as modifier] (in art forms) characterized by great realism in the depiction of drab or sordid subjects: *a kitchen-sink drama.*
– PHRASES **everything but the kitchen sink** humorous everything imaginable.

kitch·en·ware /'kicHən,we(ə)r/ ▶ **n.** the utensils used in a kitchen.

kite /kīt/ ▶ **n. 1** a toy consisting of a light frame with thin material stretched over it, flown in the wind at the end of a long string. ■ Sailing, informal a spinnaker or other high, light sail.
2 a medium to large long-winged bird of prey that typically has a forked tail and frequently soars on updrafts of air. ● *Ictinia*, *Elanoides*, and other genera, family Accipitridae: many species, including the **American swallow-tailed kite** (*E. forficatus*) and the **Mississippi kite** (*I. mississippiensis*).
3 informal a fraudulent check, bill, or receipt. ■ an illicit or surreptitious letter or note. ■ archaic a person who exploits or preys on others.
4 Geometry a quadrilateral figure having two pairs of equal adjacent sides, symmetrical only about its diagonals.
▶ **v. 1** [no obj.] (usu. as noun **kiting**) fly a kite. ■ [with adverbial of direction] fly; move quickly: *he kited into England on the Concorde.*
2 [with obj.] informal write or use (a check, bill, or receipt) fraudulently.
– PHRASES (**as**) **high as a kite** informal intoxicated with drugs or alcohol.
– ORIGIN Old English *cȳta* (in sense 2 of the noun); probably of imitative origin and related to German *Kauz* 'screech owl.' The toy was so named because it hovers in the air like the bird.

American swallow-tailed kite

kite·board·ing /'kīt,bôrdiNG/ ▶ **n.** another term for **KITESURFING**.
– DERIVATIVES **kite·board·er** n.

kite-fly·ing ▶ **n.** the action of flying a kite on a string. ■ the action of trying something out to test public opinion. ■ informal the fraudulent writing or using of a check, bill, or receipt.

kite·surf·ing /'kīt,sərfiNG/ ▶ **n.** the sport or pastime of riding on a modified surfboard while holding

on to a specially designed kite, using the wind for propulsion. Also called KITEBOARDING.
– DERIVATIVES **kite·surf·er** n.

kit fox ▶ n. a small nocturnal fox with a yellowish-gray back and large, close-set ears, found in the deserts and plains of the southwestern US. ● *Vulpes macrotis*, family Canidae.
– ORIGIN early 19th cent.: *kit* probably from KIT[2] (because of its small size).

kith /kiTH/ ▶ n. (in phrase **kith and kin** or **kith or kin**) one's friends, acquaintances, and relations: *a widow without kith or kin.*
– ORIGIN Old English *cȳth*, of Germanic origin; related to COUTH. The original senses were 'knowledge,' 'one's native land,' and 'friends and neighbors' The phrase *kith and kin* originally denoted one's country and relatives; later one's friends and relatives.

kith·a·ra /'kiTHərə/ ▶ n. variant spelling of CITHARA.

kitsch /kiCH/ ▶ n. art, objects, or design considered to be in poor taste because of excessive garishness or sentimentality, but sometimes appreciated in an ironic or knowing way: *the lava lamp is an example of sixties kitsch* | [as modifier] *kitsch decor.*
– DERIVATIVES **kitsch·i·ness** n., **kitsch·y** adj.
– ORIGIN 1920s: German.

kit·ten /'kitn/ ▶ n. **1** a young cat. ■ the young of several other animals, such as the rabbit and beaver. **2** a stout furry gray and white moth, the caterpillar of which resembles that of the puss moth. ● Genus *Furcula*, family Notodontidae.
▶ v. [no obj.] (of a cat or certain other animals) give birth.
– PHRASES **have kittens** informal be extremely nervous or upset.
– ORIGIN late Middle English *kitoun, ketoun*, from an Anglo-Norman French variant of Old French *chitoun*, diminutive of *chat* 'cat.'

kit·ten heel ▶ n. a type of curvy heel, typically between 1 and 2 inches in height.

kit·ten·ish /'kitn-isH/ ▶ adj. playful, lively, or flirtatious: *her voice had that kittenish quality.*
– DERIVATIVES **kit·ten·ish·ly** adv., **kit·ten·ish·ness** n.

kit·ti·wake /'kitē,wāk/ ▶ n. a small gull that nests in colonies on sea cliffs, having a loud call that resembles its name. ● Genus *Rissa*, family Laridae: two species, in particular the black-legged *Rissa tridactyla* of the North Atlantic and North Pacific.
– ORIGIN early 17th cent. (originally Scots): imitative of its call.

kit·tle /'kitl/ ▶ adj. archaic difficult to deal with; prone to erratic behavior.
– ORIGIN mid 16th cent.: from *kittle* 'to tickle' (now Scots and dialect), probably from Old Norse *kitla*.

kit·ty[1] /'kitē/ ▶ n. (pl. **kitties**) a fund of money for communal use, made up of contributions from a group of people. ■ a pool of money in some gambling card games.
– ORIGIN early 19th cent. (denoting a jail): of unknown origin.

kit·ty[2] ▶ n. (pl. **kitties**) a pet name or a child's name for a kitten or cat.

kit·ty-cor·ner ▶ adj. & adv. another term for CATER-CORNERED.

Kit·ty Hawk /'kitē ,hôk/ a town on a narrow sand peninsula on the Atlantic Ocean coast of North Carolina. It was there that, in 1903, the Wright brothers made the first powered airplane flight.

Kit·we /'kē,twā/ a city in the Copperbelt mining region of northern Zambia; pop. 508,700 (est. 2009).

ki·va /'kēvə/ ▶ n. a chamber, built wholly or partly underground, used by male Pueblo Indians for religious rites.
– ORIGIN late 19th cent.: from Hopi *kíva*.

Ki·vu, Lake /'kēvo͞o/ a lake in central Africa, on the Democratic Republic of the Congo (formerly Zaire)–Rwanda frontier.

Ki·wa·nis /kə'wänis/ (in full **Kiwanis Club**) ▶ n. a North American society of business and professional people formed to maintain commercial ethics and as a social and charitable organization.
– DERIVATIVES **Ki·wa·ni·an** /-nēən/ n. & adj.
– ORIGIN early 20th cent.: of unknown origin.

ki·wi /'kēwē/ ▶ n. (pl. **kiwis**) **1** a flightless New Zealand bird with hairlike feathers, having a long down-curved bill with sensitive nostrils at the tip. ● Family Apterygidae and genus *Apteryx*: three species, including the **brown kiwi** (*A. australis*). **2** (**Kiwi**) informal a New Zealander, esp. a soldier or member of a national sports team.

brown kiwi

3 KIWI FRUIT: *a bowl of cherries and kiwis.*
– ORIGIN mid 19th cent.: from Maori.

ki·wi fruit (also **kiwifruit**) ▶ n. (pl. **same**) a fruit with a thin hairy skin, green flesh, and black seeds. Also called CHINESE GOOSEBERRY. ● This fruit is obtained from the eastern Asian climbing plant *Actinidia chinensis* (family Actinidiaceae).

Ki·zil Ir·mak /ki'zil ir'mäk/ (ancient name *Halys*) the longest river in Turkey that flows for 715 miles (1,150 km) in a great curve through central Anatolia to the Black Sea.

kJ ▶ abbr. kilojoule(s).

KJV ▶ abbr. King James Version.

KKK ▶ abbr. Ku Klux Klan.

Kkt ▶ abbr. Chess king's knight.

KL ▶ abbr. informal Kuala Lumpur.

kl ▶ abbr. kiloliter(s).

Klai·pe·da /'klīpədə/ a city and port in Lithuania, on the Baltic Sea; pop. 183,433 (2009). Former name (1918–23 and 1941–44, when under German control) MEMEL.

Klam·ath /'klaməTH/ ▶ n. (pl. **same** or **Klamaths**) **1** a member of an American Indian people of southern Oregon and northern California. **2** the language of this people.
▶ adj. of or relating to this people or their language.
– ORIGIN from the Chinook name *łámał* 'those of the river.'

Klam·ath Moun·tains /'klaməTH/ a range in southwestern Oregon and northern California, through which the ***Klamath River*** flows to the Pacific Ocean.

Klan /klan/ ▶ n. the Ku Klux Klan or a large organization within it.
– DERIVATIVES **Klans·man** /'klanzmən/ n. (pl. **Klansmen**), **Klans·wom·an** /'klanz,wo͝omən/ n. (pl. **Klanswomen**).

Klap·roth /'kläp,rōt/, Martin Heinrich (1743–1817), German chemist; one of the founders of analytical chemistry.

klatch /kläCH, klaCH/ (also **klatsch**) ▶ n. a social gathering, esp. for coffee and conversation.
– ORIGIN mid 20th cent.: from German *Klatsch* 'gossip.'

Klau·sen·burg /'klouzən,bo͝ork, -,bərg/ German name for CLUJ-NAPOCA.

klax·on /'klaksən/ ▶ n. trademark an electric horn or a similar loud warning device.
– ORIGIN early 20th cent.: from the name of the manufacturing company.

kleb·si·el·la /,klebzē'elə, ,klepsē-/ ▶ n. a bacterium that causes respiratory, urinary, and wound infections. ● Genus *Klebsiella*; nonmotile Gram-negative rods.
– ORIGIN modern Latin, from the name *Klebs*.

Klee /klā/, Paul (1879–1940), Swiss painter who lived in Germany from 1906–33. He joined the *Blaue Reiter* group in 1912 and later taught at the Bauhaus (1920–33).

Kleen·ex /'klē,neks/ ▶ n. (pl. **same** or **Kleenexes**) trademark an absorbent disposable paper tissue.

Klein[1] /klīn/, Calvin (Richard) (1942–), US fashion designer.

Klein[2], Melanie (1882–1960), Austrian psychoanalyst. She was the first psychologist to specialize in the psychoanalysis of small children.

Klein bot·tle ▶ n. Mathematics a closed surface with only one side, formed by passing one end of a tube through the side of the tube and joining it to the other end.
– ORIGIN 1940s.: named after Felix *Klein* (1849–1925), the German mathematician who first described it.

Klein bottle

Klem·per·er /'klempərər/, Otto (1885–1973), US conductor and composer; born in Germany. He conducted the Los Angeles Symphony Orchestra 1933–39.

klepht /kleft/ ▶ n. **1** a Greek independence fighter, esp. one who fought the Turks in the 15th century or during the war of independence (1821–28). **2** a Greek brigand or bandit.
– ORIGIN from modern Greek *klephtēs*, from Greek *kleptēs* 'thief.' The original klephts led an outlaw existence in the mountains; those who maintained this after the war of independence became mere bandits.

klep·to·crat /'kleptə,krat/ ▶ n. a ruler who uses political power to steal his or her country's resources.
– DERIVATIVES **klep·toc·ra·cy** /klep'täkrəsē/ n., **klep·to·crat·ic** /,kleptə'kratik/ adj.
– ORIGIN 1960s: from Greek *kleptēs* 'thief' + *-crat*.

klep·to·ma·ni·a /,kleptə'mānēə, -'mānyə/ ▶ n. a recurrent urge to steal, typically without regard for need or profit.
– DERIVATIVES **klep·to·ma·ni·ac** /-'mānē,ak/ n. & adj.
– ORIGIN mid 19th cent.: from Greek *kleptēs* 'thief' + -MANIA.

klep·to·par·a·site /,kleptə'parə,sīt/ ▶ n. Zoology a bird, insect, or other animal that habitually robs animals of other species of food.
– DERIVATIVES **klep·to·par·a·sit·ic** /-,parə'sitik/ adj., **klep·to·par·a·sit·ism** /-si,tizəm, -sī-/ n.
– ORIGIN late 20th cent.: from Greek *kleptēs* 'thief' + PARASITE.

Klerk, F. W. de, see DE KLERK.

Klerks·dorp /'klerks,dôrp/ a city in South Africa, southwest of Johannesburg; pop. 174,900 (est. 2009).

klez·mer /'klezmər/ ▶ n. (pl. **klezmorim** /klez'môrim, ,klezmə,rēm/) (also **klezmer music**) traditional eastern European Jewish music. ■ a musician who plays this kind of music.
– ORIGIN mid 20th cent.: Yiddish, contraction of Hebrew *kĕlē zemer* 'musical instruments.'

klick /klik/ (also **click**) ▶ n. informal a kilometer: *about 200 klicks northwest of Moscow.*
– ORIGIN mid 20th cent.: of unknown origin; the term was originally used in the Vietnam War.

klieg /klēg/ (usu. **klieg light**) ▶ n. a powerful electric lamp used in filming.
– ORIGIN 1920s: named after the American brothers, Anton T. *Kliegl* (1872–1927) and John H. *Kliegl* (1869–1959), who invented it.

Klimt /klimt/, Gustav (1862–1918), Austrian painter and designer. Cofounder of the Vienna Secession (1897), he is known for his decorative and allegorical paintings and his portraits of women.

Kline·fel·ter's syn·drome /'klīn,feltərz/ ▶ n. Medicine a syndrome affecting males in which the cells have an extra X chromosome (in addition to the normal XY), characterized by a tall thin physique, small infertile testes, and enlarged breasts.
– ORIGIN mid 20th cent.: named after Harry F. *Klinefelter* (born 1912), American physician.

Kling·on /'kliNG,än/ ▶ n. **1** a member of a warlike humanoid alien species in the television series *Star Trek* and its derivatives and sequels. **2** the language of the Klingons: *the site is also available in synthetic languages like Esperanto and Klingon.*
– ORIGIN 1960s: invented name.

klip·spring·er /'klip,spriNGər/ ▶ n. a small rock-dwelling antelope with a yellowish-gray coat, an arched back, and a stiff bouncing gait, native to southern Africa. ● *Oreotragus oreotragus*, family Bovidae.
– ORIGIN late 18th cent.: from Afrikaans, from Dutch *klip* 'rock' + *springer* 'jumper.'

Klon·dike /'klän,dīk/ **1** a tributary of the Yukon River, in Yukon Territory, northwestern Canada, that rises in the Ogilvie Mountains and flows west for 100 miles (160 km) to join the Yukon at Dawson. It gave its name to the surrounding region, which became famous when gold was found in nearby Bonanza Creek in 1896. ■ [as noun] a source of valuable material. **2** [as noun] a form of the card game patience or solitaire.

klong /klôNG, kläNG/ ▶ n. (in Thailand) a canal.
– ORIGIN Thai.

kloof /klo͞of/ ▶ n. S. African a steep-sided, wooded ravine or valley.
– ORIGIN Afrikaans, from Middle Dutch *clove* 'cleft.'

kludge /klo͞oj/ (also **kluge**) informal ▶ n. an ill-assorted collection of parts assembled to fulfill a particular purpose. ■ Computing a machine, system, or program that has been badly put together.
▶ v. [with obj.] use ill-assorted parts to make (something): *Hugh had to kludge something together.*
– ORIGIN 1960s (originally US): invented word, perhaps symbolic. Compare with FUDGE.

klutz /kləts/ ▶ n. informal a clumsy, awkward, or foolish person.
– DERIVATIVES **klutz·i·ness** n., **klutz·y** adj.
– ORIGIN 1960s: from Yiddish *klots* 'wooden block.'

Klux·er /'kləksər/ ▶ n. informal a member of the Ku Klux Klan.

klys·tron /'klī,strän/ ▶ n. Physics an electron tube that generates or amplifies microwaves by velocity modulation.
– ORIGIN 1930s: from Greek *kluzein, klus-* 'wash over' + -TRON.

PRONUNCIATION KEY ə *ago, up*; ər *over, fur*; a *hat*; ā *ate*; ä *car*; e *let*; ē *see*; i *fit*; ī *by*; NG *sing*; ō *go*; ô *law, for*; oi *toy*; o͝o *good*; o͞o *goo*; ou *out*; TH *thin*; TH *then*; ZH *vision*

k

km ▶ **abbr.** kilometer(s).

K-me·son ▶ **n.** another term for KAON.
– ORIGIN 1950s: from *K* (for KAON) + MESON.

km/h (also **kmph**) ▶ **abbr.** kilometers per hour.

kmps ▶ **abbr.** kilometers per second.

KN ▶ **abbr.** Chess king's knight.

kn ▶ **abbr.** knot(s).

knack /nak/ ▶ **n.** [in sing.] an acquired or natural skill at performing a task: *she got the knack of it in the end.* ■ a tendency to do something: *the band has a knack of warping classic soul songs.*
– ORIGIN late Middle English (originally denoting a clever or deceitful trick): probably related to obsolete *knack* 'sharp blow or sound,' of imitative origin (compare with Dutch *knak* 'crack, snap').

knack·er /ˈnakər/ Brit. ▶ **n.** a person whose business is the disposal of dead or unwanted animals, esp. those whose flesh is not fit for human consumption.
▶ **v.** [with obj.] (often as adj. **knackered**) informal tire (someone) out; exhaust: *you look absolutely knackered.* ■ damage severely.
– ORIGIN late 16th cent. (originally denoting a harness-maker, then a slaughterer of horses): possibly from obsolete *knack* 'trinket' The word also had the sense 'old worn-out horse' (late 18th cent). It is unclear whether the verb represents a figurative use of 'slaughter,' from the noun sense, or of 'castrate,' from a slang sense of the noun, 'testicles.'

knack·wurst /ˈnäkˌwərst/ (also **knockwurst**) ▶ **n.** a type of short, fat, highly seasoned German sausage.
– ORIGIN mid 20th cent.: from German *Knackwurst*, from *knacken* 'make a cracking noise' + *Wurst* 'sausage.'

knai·del /ˈk(ə)nādl/ (also **kneidel**) ▶ **n.** (pl. **knaidlach** /ˈk(ə)nādˌläkʜ/) (usu. **knaidlach**) a type of dumpling eaten esp. in Jewish households during Passover.
– ORIGIN from Yiddish *kneydel*.

knap[1] /nap/ ▶ **n.** archaic the crest of a hill.
– ORIGIN Old English *cnæpp*, *cnæp*.

knap[2] ▶ **v.** (**knaps, knapping, knapped**) [with obj.] Architecture & Archaeology shape (a piece of stone, typically flint) by striking it so as to make stone tools or weapons or to give a flat-faced stone for building walls: (as adj. **knapped**) *buildings made of knapped flint.* ■ archaic strike with a hard short sound; knock.
– DERIVATIVES **knap·per** **n.**
– ORIGIN late Middle English (in the sense 'to knock, rap'): imitative; compare with Dutch and German *knappen* 'crack, crackle.'

knap·sack /ˈnapˌsak/ ▶ **n.** a bag with shoulder straps, carried on the back, and typically made of canvas or other weatherproof material.
– ORIGIN early 17th cent.: from Middle Low German, from Dutch *knapzack*, probably from German *knappen* 'to bite' + *zak* 'sack.'

knap·weed /ˈnapˌwēd/ ▶ **n.** a tough-stemmed plant of the daisy family that typically has purple thistlelike flower heads, occurring typically in grassland and on roadsides. ● Genus *Centaurea*, family Compositae: several species, including the widespread **black knapweed** (*C. nigra*) (also called HARDHEADS).
– ORIGIN late Middle English (originally as *knopweed*): from KNOP (because of its hard rounded involucre or "head") + WEED.

knar /när/ (also **knur** /nər/) ▶ **n.** archaic a knot or protuberance on a tree trunk or root.
– ORIGIN Middle English *knarre* (denoting a rugged rock or stone); related to Middle Low German *knarre* 'knobbly protuberance'; compare with KNUR.

knave /nāv/ ▶ **n.** archaic a dishonest or unscrupulous man. ■ another term for JACK[1] in cards.
– DERIVATIVES **knav·er·y** /-vərē/ **n.** (pl. **knaveries**).
– ORIGIN Old English *cnafa* 'boy, servant'; related to German *Knabe* 'boy.'

knav·ish /ˈnāvish/ ▶ **adj.** archaic dishonest or unscrupulous: *his knavish tricks will be frustrated.*
– DERIVATIVES **knav·ish·ly** **adv.**, **knav·ish·ness** **n.**

knawel /nôl/ ▶ **n.** a low-growing inconspicuous plant of the pink family, growing in temperate regions of the northern hemisphere. ● Genus *Scleranthus*, family Caryophyllaceae.
– ORIGIN late 16th cent.: from German *Knauel*, *Knäuel* 'knotgrass.'

knead /nēd/ ▶ **v.** [with obj.] work (moistened flour or clay) into dough or paste with the hands. ■ make (bread or pottery) by such a process. ■ massage or squeeze with the hands: *she kneaded his back.*
– DERIVATIVES **knead·a·ble** **adj.**, **knead·er** **n.**
– ORIGIN Old English *cnedan*, of Germanic origin; related to Dutch *kneden* and German *kneten*.

knee /nē/ ▶ **n.** the joint between the thigh and the lower leg in humans. ■ the corresponding or analogous joint in other animals. ■ the upper surface of someone's thigh when sitting; a person's lap: *they were eating their supper on their knees.* ■ the part of a garment covering the knee. ■ an angled piece of wood or metal frame used to connect and support the beams and timbers of a wooden vessel; a triangular plate serving the same purpose in a modern vessel. ■ an abrupt obtuse or approximately right-angled bend in a graph between parts where the slope varies smoothly.
▶ **v.** (**knees, kneeing, kneed**) [with obj.] hit (someone) with one's knee: *she kneed him in the groin.*
– PHRASES **at one's mother's** (or **father's**) **knee** at an early age. **bend** (or **bow**) **the** (or **one's**) **knee** (**to**) kneel in submission; submit. **bring someone/something to their/its knees** reduce someone or something to a state of weakness or submission. **fall** (or **drop**, **sink**, etc.) **to one's knees** assume a kneeling position. **on bended knee(s)** kneeling, esp. in entreaty or worship: *did he propose on bended knee?* **on one's knees** in a kneeling position. ■ on the verge of collapse: *when they took over, the newspaper was on its knees.* **weak at the knees** overcome by a strong feeling, typically desire.
– ORIGIN Old English *cnēow*, *cnēo*, of Germanic origin; related to Dutch *knie* and German *Knie*, from an Indo-European root shared by Latin *genu* and Greek *gonu*.

knee ac·tion ▶ **n.** a form of independent front-wheel suspension in a motor vehicle: [as modifier] *knee-action wheels.*

knee bend ▶ **n.** an act of bending the knee, esp. as a physical exercise in which the body is raised and lowered without the use of the hands.

knee·board /ˈnēˌbôrd/ ▶ **n.** a short board for surfing or waterskiing in a kneeling position.
– DERIVATIVES **knee·board·er** **n.**, **knee·board·ing** **n.**

knee breech·es ▶ **plural n.** archaic short trousers worn by men and fastened at or just below the knee.

knee·cap /ˈnēˌkap/ ▶ **n.** the convex bone in front of the knee joint; the patella.
▶ **v.** (**kneecaps, kneecapping, kneecapped**) [with obj.] shoot (someone) in the knee or leg as a form of punishment: (as noun **kneecapping**) *petty crimes are punished by kneecapping.*

knee-deep ▶ **adj.** immersed up to the knees: *we were knee-deep in snow.* ■ having more than one needs or wants of something: *we shall soon be knee-deep in conflicting legal views.* ■ so deep as to reach the knees: *the water was knee-deep on Main Street.*
▶ **adv.** so as to be immersed up to the knees: *I plodded knee-deep through the mud.*

knee-high ▶ **adj. & adv.** so high as to reach the knees: [as adj.] *knee-high boots* | [as adv.] *they were wading knee-high in the water.*
▶ **n.** (usu. **knee-highs**) a sock or nylon stocking with an elasticized top that reaches to a person's knee.
– PHRASES **knee-high to a grasshopper** informal very small or very young.

knee·hole /ˈnēˌhōl/ ▶ **n.** a space for the knees, esp. one under a desk: [as modifier] *a kneehole desk.*

knee-jerk ▶ **adj.** [attrib.] (of a response) automatic and unthinking: *a knee-jerk reaction.* ■ (of a person) responding in this way: *knee-jerk radicals.*
▶ **n.** a sudden involuntary reflex kick caused by a blow on the tendon just below the knee.

kneel /nēl/ ▶ **v.** (past and past participle **knelt** /nelt/ also **kneeled**) [no obj.] be in or assume a position in which the body is supported by a knee or the knees, as when praying or showing submission: *they knelt down and prayed.*
– ORIGIN Old English *cnēowlian*, from *cnēow* (see KNEE).

knee-length ▶ **adj.** (esp. of an item of clothing) reaching the knees: *knee-length boots.*

kneel·er /ˈnēlər/ ▶ **n.** a person who kneels, esp. in prayer. ■ a cushion or bench for kneeling on.

knee·pan /ˈnēˌpan/ ▶ **n.** old-fashioned term for KNEECAP.

knee-slap·per ▶ **n.** informal an uproariously funny joke.
– DERIVATIVES **knee-slap·ping** **adj.**

knees-up ▶ **n.** [in sing.] Brit. informal a lively party or gathering: *we had a bit of a knees-up last night.*

knee-trem·bler ▶ **n.** informal an act of sexual intercourse between people in a standing position.

knei·del /ˈk(ə)nādl/ ▶ **n.** (pl. **kneidlach** /ˈk(ə)nādˌläkʜ/) variant spelling of KNAIDEL.

knell /nel/ literary ▶ **n.** the sound of a bell, esp. when rung solemnly for a death or funeral. ■ used in reference to an announcement, event, or sound that warns of the end of something: *the decision will probably toll the knell for the facility.*
▶ **v.** [no obj.] (of a bell) ring solemnly, esp. for a death or funeral. ■ [with obj.] proclaim (something) by or as if by a knell.
– ORIGIN Old English *cnyll* (noun), *cnyllan* (verb); related to Dutch *knal* (noun), *knallen* (verb) 'bang, pop, crack.' The current spelling (dating from the 16th cent.) is perhaps influenced by BELL[1].

knelt /nelt/ past and past participle of KNEEL.

Knes·set /k(ə)ˈneset/ the parliament of modern Israel, established in 1949. It consists of 120 members elected every four years.
– ORIGIN Hebrew, literally 'gathering.'

knew /n(y)o͞o/ past of KNOW.

knick·er·bock·er /ˈnikərˌbäkər/ ▶ **n.**
1 (**knickerbockers**) see KNICKERS.
2 (**Knickerbocker**) a New Yorker. ■ a descendant of the original Dutch settlers in New York.
– DERIVATIVES **knick·er·bock·ered** **adj.**
– ORIGIN mid 19th cent. (sense 2): named after Diedrich *Knickerbocker*, pretended author of W. Irving's *History of New York* (1809). Sense 1 is said to have arisen from the resemblance of knickerbockers to the breeches worn by Dutchmen in Cruikshank's illustrations in Irving's book.

knick·ers /ˈnikərz/ ▶ **plural n.** **1** (also **knickerbockers**) loose-fitting trousers gathered at the knee or calf.
2 Brit. a woman's or girl's underpants.
– PHRASES **get one's knickers in a twist** Brit. informal become upset or angry.
– DERIVATIVES **knick·ered** **adj.**
– ORIGIN late 19th cent. (sense 1): abbreviation of *knickerbockers* (see KNICKERBOCKER).

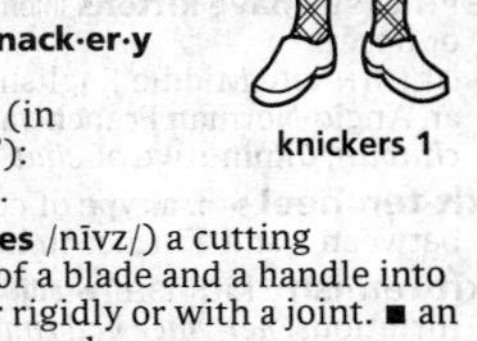

knickers 1

knick·knack /ˈnikˌnak/ ▶ **n.** (usu. **knickknacks**) a small worthless object, esp. a household ornament.
– DERIVATIVES **knick·knack·er·y** /-ˌnakərē/ **n.**
– ORIGIN late 16th cent. (in the sense 'a petty trick'): reduplication of KNACK.

knife /nīf/ ▶ **n.** (pl. **knives** /nīvz/) a cutting instrument composed of a blade and a handle into which it is fixed, either rigidly or with a joint. ■ an instrument such as this used as a weapon. ■ a cutting blade forming part of a machine.
▶ **v.** [with obj.] stab (someone) with a knife. ■ [no obj.] cut like a knife: *a shard of steel knifed through the mainsail.*
– PHRASES **before you can say knife** informal very quickly; almost instantaneously. (**so thick that**) **you could cut** (**it**) **with a knife** (of an accent, atmosphere, or sentiment) very obvious: *the patriotism was so thick that you could cut it with a knife* | *a southern accent you could cut with a knife.* **stick** (or **get**) **the knife into** (or **in**) **someone** informal do something hostile or aggressive to someone. **go** (or **be**) **under the knife** informal have surgery. **the knives are out** (**for someone**) informal there is open hostility (toward someone). **like a** (**hot**) **knife through butter** very easily; without any resistance or difficulty: *antiaircraft fire would slice through the car like a hot knife through butter.* **twist** (or **turn**) **the knife** (**in the wound**) deliberately make someone's sufferings worse.
– DERIVATIVES **knife·like** /-ˌlīk/ **adj.**, **knif·er** **n.**
– ORIGIN late Old English *cnīf*, from Old Norse *knífr*, of Germanic origin.

knife block ▶ **n.** a block of wood or other solid material, containing long grooves in which kitchen knives of various sizes can be inserted up to the handle.

knife edge ▶ **n.** the edge of a knife. ■ [as modifier] (of creases or pleats in a garment) very fine: *knife-edge creases.* ■ [in sing.] a tense or uncertain situation, esp. one finely balanced between success and failure: *they have been living on a knife edge since his libel action.* ■ a steel wedge on which a pendulum or other device oscillates or is balanced. ■ a narrow, sharp ridge; an arête.

knife pleat ▶ **n.** a sharp, narrow pleat on a skirt made in one direction and typically overlapping another.

knife·point /ˈnīfˌpoint/ ▶ **n.** the pointed end of a knife.
– PHRASES **at knifepoint** under threat of injury from a knife: *he was mugged at knifepoint.*

knife-throw·ing ▶ **n.** a circus act or other entertainment in which knives are thrown at a target.
– DERIVATIVES **knife-throw·er** **n.**

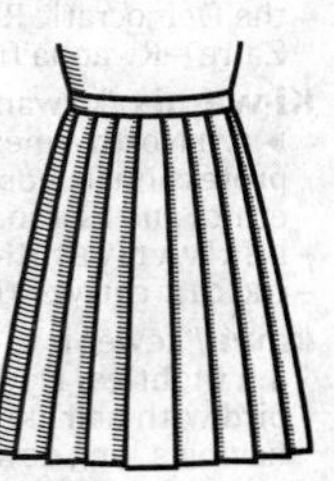

knife pleats

Knight, John Shively (1894–1981) US newspaper publisher. He merged his newspapers in Detroit, Chicago, New York, and other large cities with the Ridder Publications chain in 1974 to form Knight–Ridder Newspapers, Inc.

knight /nīt/ ▶ **n. 1** (in the Middle Ages) a man who served his sovereign or lord as a mounted soldier in armor. ■ (in the Middle Ages) a man raised by a sovereign to honorable military rank after service as a page and squire. ■ literary a man devoted to the service of a woman or a cause: *in all your quarrels I will be your knight.* ■ dated (in ancient Rome) a member of the class of equites. ■ (in ancient Greece) a citizen of the second class in Athens.
2 (in the UK) a man awarded a nonhereditary title by the sovereign in recognition of merit or service and entitled to use the honorific "Sir" in front of his name.
3 a chess piece, typically with its top shaped like a horse's head, that moves by jumping to the opposite corner of a rectangle two squares by three.
▶ **v.** [with obj.] (usu. **be knighted**) invest (someone) with the title of knight.
– PHRASES **knight in shining armor** (or **knight on a white charger**) an idealized or chivalrous man who comes to the rescue of a woman in a difficult situation. **knight of the road** informal a man who frequents the roads, for example, a traveling salesman, a vagrant, or (formerly) a highwayman.
– ORIGIN Old English *cniht* 'boy, youth, servant'; related to Dutch *knecht* and German *Knecht*. Sense 2 of the noun dates from the mid 16th cent.; the uses relating to Greek and Roman history derive from comparison with medieval knights.

knight bach·e·lor ▶ **n.** (pl. **knights bachelor**) a knight not belonging to any particular order.

knight er·rant ▶ **n.** (pl. **knights errant**) a medieval knight wandering in search of chivalrous adventures.
– DERIVATIVES **knight-er·rant·ry n.**

knight·hood /ˈnītˌhŏŏd/ ▶ **n.** the title, rank, or status of a knight: *he received a knighthood* | *the basis of feudal knighthood.*

knight·ly /ˈnītlē/ ▶ **adj.** (**knightlier, knightliest**) associated with or typical of a knight; chivalrous: *a knightly quest.*
– DERIVATIVES **knight·li·ness n.**

Knights·bridge /ˈnītsˌbrij/ a district in the West End of London, to the south of Hyde Park, noted for its fashionable and expensive shops.

Knights Hos·pi·tal·ler a military and religious order founded as the Knights of the Order of the Hospital of St. John of Jerusalem in the 11th century.

Knights Tem·plar a religious and military order for the protection of pilgrims to the Holy Land, founded as the Poor Knights of Christ and of the Temple of Solomon in 1118.

knish /k(ə)ˈnisн/ ▶ **n.** a dumpling of dough that is stuffed with a filling and baked or fried.
– ORIGIN Yiddish, from Russian *knish, knysh*, denoting a kind of bun or dumpling.

knit /nit/ ▶ **v.** (**knits, knitting**; past and past participle **knitted** or (esp. in sense 2) **knit**) **1** [with obj.] make (a garment, blanket, etc.) by interlocking loops of wool or other yarn with knitting needles or on a machine. ■ make (a stitch or row of stitches) in such a way. ■ knit with a knit stitch: *knit one, purl one.*
2 unite or cause to unite: [no obj.] *disparate regions had begun to **knit together** under the king* | [with obj.] *he **knitted together** a squad of players other clubs had disregarded* | [as adj., with submodifier] (**knit**) *a closely knit family.* ■ [no obj.] (of parts of a broken bone) become joined during healing.
3 [with obj.] tighten (one's brow or eyebrows) in a frown of concentration, disapproval, or anxiety.
▶ **adj.** denoting or relating to a knitting stitch made by putting the needle through the front of the stitch from left to right. Compare with PURL[1].
▶ **n.** a knitted fabric: *a machine-washable knit.* ■ a garment made of such fabric: *an array of casual knits.*
– DERIVATIVES **knit·ter n.**
– ORIGIN Old English *cnyttan*; related to German dialect *knütten*, also to KNOT[1]. The original sense was 'tie in or with a knot,' hence 'join, unite' (sense 2 of the verb); an obsolete Middle English sense 'knot string to make a net' gave rise to sense 1 of the verb.

knit·bone /ˈnitˌbōn/ ▶ **n.** another term for COMFREY.

knit·ting /ˈnitiNG/ ▶ **n.** the craft or action of knitting. ■ material that is in the process of being knitted: *I put down my knitting.*
– PHRASES **stick** (or **tend**) **to the** (or **one's**) **knitting** informal (of a person or an organization) concentrate on a familiar area of activity rather than diversify; mind one's own business.

knit·ting ma·chine ▶ **n.** a machine with a bank of needles on which garments can be knitted.

knit·ting nee·dle ▶ **n.** a long, thin, pointed rod used as part of a pair for knitting by hand.

knit·wear /ˈnitˌwe(ə)r/ ▶ **n.** knitted garments.

knives /nīvz/ plural form of KNIFE.

knob /näb/ ▶ **n.** a rounded lump or ball, esp. at the end or on the surface of something. ■ a handle on a door or drawer shaped like a ball. ■ a rounded button for adjusting or controlling a machine. ■ a small lump of a substance: *add a knob of butter or margarine.* ■ a prominent round hill. ■ vulgar slang a penis.
– PHRASES **with (brass) knobs on** Brit. informal and something more: *it's evocative, with knobs on.* [with allusion to the addition of decorative knobs to an object as an embellishment.]
– DERIVATIVES **knobbed adj., knob·by adj., knob·like** /-ˌlīk/ **adj.**
– ORIGIN late Middle English: from Middle Low German *knobbe* 'knot, knob, bud.'

knob·bly /ˈnäblē/ ▶ **adj.** (**knobblier, knobbliest**) chiefly Brit. having lumps that give a misshapen appearance: *knobbly potatoes.*

knob·ker·rie /ˈnäbˌkerē/ (also **knobkierie**) ▶ **n.** a short stick with a knobbed head, traditionally used as a weapon by the indigenous peoples of South Africa.
▶ **v.** [with obj.] beat with such a stick.
– ORIGIN mid 19th cent.: from KNOB + *-kerrie* (from Nama *kieri* 'knobkerrie'), suggested by Afrikaans *knopkierie.*

knock /näk/ ▶ **v. 1** [no obj.] strike a surface noisily to attract attention, esp. when waiting to be let in through a door: *I **knocked on** the kitchen door.* ■ strike or thump together or against something: *my knees were knocking and my lips quivering.* ■ (of a motor or other engine) make a regular thumping or rattling noise because of improper ignition.
2 [with obj.] collide with (someone or something), giving them a hard blow: *he deliberately ran into her, knocking her shoulder* | [no obj.] *he **knocked into** an elderly man.* ■ force to move or fall with a deliberate or accidental blow or collision: *he'd **knocked over** a glass of water.* ■ injure or damage by striking: *she knocked her knee painfully on the table* | figurative *you have had a setback that has knocked your self-esteem.* ■ make (a hole or a dent) in something by striking it forcefully: *he suggests we knock a hole through the wall into the broom closet.* ■ demolish the barriers between (rooms or buildings): *two of the downstairs rooms had been **knocked into one**.* ■ informal talk disparagingly about; criticize.
▶ **n. 1** a sudden short sound caused by a blow, esp. on a door to attract attention or gain entry. ■ a continual thumping or rattling sound made by an engine because of improper ignition.
2 a blow or collision: *the casing is tough enough to withstand knocks.* ■ an injury caused by a blow or collision. ■ a discouraging experience; a setback: *the region's industries have taken a severe knock.* ■ informal a critical comment.
– PHRASES **knock someone's block off** informal hit someone very hard in anger. **knock the bottom out of** see BOTTOM. **knock someone dead** informal greatly impress someone. **knock someone for six** see SIX. **knock someone for a loop** see LOOP. **knock people's heads together** see KNOCK at BANG[1]. **knock something into a cocked hat** see COCKED HAT. **knock someone into the middle of next week** informal hit someone very hard. **knock someone/something into shape** see SHAPE. **knock it off** informal used to tell someone to stop doing something that one finds annoying or foolish. **knock someone on the head** stun or kill someone by a blow on the head. **knock on wood** see WOOD. **knock someone's socks off** see SOCK. **the school of hard knocks** painful or difficult experiences that are seen to be useful in teaching someone about life. **you could have knocked me** (or **her, him, etc.**) **down** (or **over**) **with a feather** informal used to express great surprise.
– PHRASAL VERBS **knock around** (or **about**) informal travel without a specific purpose: *for a couple of years she and I knocked around the Mediterranean.* ■ happen to be present: *it gets confusing when there are too many people knocking about.* ■ chiefly Brit. spend time with someone: *she **knocked around with** artists.* **knock someone/something about** (or **around**) injure or damage someone or something by rough treatment. **knock something back** informal consume a drink quickly and entirely: *we knocked back a few beers.* **knock someone down** chiefly Brit. (of a person or vehicle) strike or collide with someone so as to cause them to fall to the ground. **knock something down 1** demolish a building. ■ take machinery or furniture to pieces for transportation. **2** (at an auction) confirm the sale of an article to a bidder by a knock with a hammer. ■ informal reduce the price of an article. **3** informal earn a specified sum as a wage. **knock off** informal stop work. **knock someone off 1** informal kill someone. **2** Brit. vulgar slang have sexual intercourse with a woman. **knock something off 1** informal produce a piece of work quickly and easily, esp. to order. **2** informal deduct an amount from a total: *when the bill came, they knocked off $600 because of a little scratch.* **3** Brit. informal steal something. ■ informal make an illegal copy of a product. **knock someone out** make a person unconscious, typically with a blow to the head. ■ knock down (a boxer) for a count of ten, thereby winning the contest. ■ (**knock oneself out**) informal work so hard that one is exhausted. ■ informal astonish or greatly impress someone. **knock something out 1** destroy a machine or damage it so that it stops working. ■ destroy or disable enemy installations or equipment. **2** informal produce work at a steady fast rate: *if you knock out a thousand words a day you'll soon have it finished.* **3** empty a tobacco pipe by tapping it against a surface. **knock someone over** another way of saying KNOCK SOMEONE DOWN. **knock something over** informal rob a store or similar establishment: *they knocked over a liquor store.* **knock someone sideways** informal astonish someone. **knock something together** assemble something in a hasty and makeshift way. **knock someone up 1** vulgar slang make a woman pregnant. **2** Brit. knock at someone's door.
– ORIGIN Old English *cnocian*, of imitative origin.

knock·a·bout /ˈnäkəˌbout/ ▶ **adj. 1** denoting a rough, slapstick comic performance.
2 (of clothes) suitable for rough use.
▶ **n. 1** a rough, slapstick comic performance.
2 a tramp or vagrant.
3 a small yacht or dinghy.

knock·down /ˈnäkˌdoun/ ▶ **adj.** [attrib.] **1** informal (of a price) very low. [used earlier to refer to reserve prices set at an auction.]
2 capable of knocking down or overwhelming someone or something: *repeated knockdown blows.* ■ (of furniture) easily dismantled and reassembled.
▶ **n.** Boxing an act of knocking an opponent down. ■ (also **knockdown pitch**) Baseball a pitch aimed so close to the body that the batter must drop to the ground to avoid being hit: *the catcher gave the sign for a knockdown pitch.* ■ Sailing an instance of a vessel being knocked on its side by the force of the wind.

knock-down-drag-out ▶ **n.** informal a free-for-all fight: [as modifier] *knock-down-drag-out fights.*

knock·er /ˈnäkər/ ▶ **n. 1** short for DOOR KNOCKER.
2 informal a person who continually finds fault.
3 (**knockers**) vulgar slang a woman's breasts.

knock knees ▶ **plural n.** a condition in which the legs curve inward so that the feet are apart when the knees are touching.
– DERIVATIVES **knock-kneed adj.**

knock·off /ˈnäkˌôf/ ▶ **n.** informal a copy or imitation, esp. of an expensive or designer product: [as modifier] *knockoff merchandise.*

knock·out /ˈnäkˌout/ ▶ **n.** an act of knocking someone out, esp. in boxing: [as modifier] *a knockout blow.* ■ informal an extremely attractive or impressive person or thing: *he must have been a knockout when he was young.* ■ Brit. a tournament in which the loser in each round is eliminated.

knock·out drops ▶ **plural n.** a drug in liquid form added to a drink to cause unconsciousness.

knock·out mouse ▶ **n.** Genetics a mouse whose DNA has been genetically engineered so that it does not express particular proteins.

knock·wurst /ˈnäkˌwərst/ ▶ **n.** variant spelling of KNACKWURST.

Knole so·fa /nōl/ ▶ **n.** a sofa with adjustable sides allowing conversion into a bed.
– ORIGIN mid 20th cent.: named after *Knole* Park, Kent, England, site of the original sofa (*c.*1605–20) from which others were designed.

knoll[1] /nōl/ ▶ **n.** a small hill or mound.
– ORIGIN Old English *cnoll* 'hilltop,' of Germanic origin; related to German *Knolle* 'clod, lump, tuber' and Dutch *knol* 'tuber, turnip.'

knoll[2] ▶ **v. & n.** archaic form of KNELL.
– ORIGIN Middle English: probably an imitative alteration of KNELL.

knop /näp/ ▶ **n.** a knob, esp. an ornamental one, for example in the stem of a wine glass. ■ an ornamental loop or tuft in yarn.
– ORIGIN Middle English: from Middle Low German and Middle Dutch *knoppe.*

Knopf /(kə)ˈnäpf/, Alfred A. (1892–1984) US publisher. He founded Alfred A. Knopf, a publishing firm, in 1915.

Knos·sos /ˈnäsəs/ the principal city of Minoan Crete, the remains of which are situated on the northern coast of Crete. The city site was occupied from Neolithic times until *c.*1200 BC. Excavations by Sir Arthur Evans from 1899 revealed the remains of a luxurious palace, which he called the Palace of Minos.

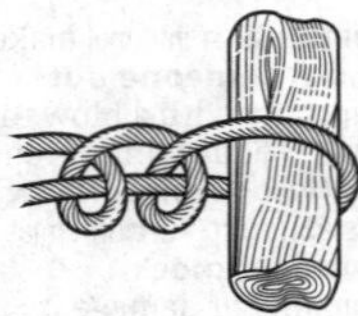
two half hitches

timber hitch

cow hitch

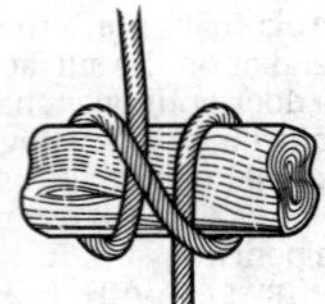
clove hitch

rolling hitch

slip knot

square knot

granny knot

bowline

overhand knot

figure-eight knot

barrel knot

knots

knot[1] /nät/ ▸ **n. 1** a fastening made by tying a piece of string, rope, or something similar: *tie a knot at the end of the cord* | figurative *a complicated knot of racial politics and pride.* ■ a particular method of tying a knot: *you need to master two knots, the clove hitch and the sheet bend.* ■ a tied or folded ribbon, worn as an ornament.
2 a tangled mass in something such as hair.
3 a knob, protuberance, or node in a stem, branch, or root. ■ a hard mass formed in a tree trunk at the intersection with a branch, resulting in a round cross-grained piece in timber when cut through. ■ a hard lump of tissue in an animal or human body.
4 an unpleasant feeling of tightness or tension in a part of the body: *her stomach was* **in knots** *as she unlocked the door.*
5 a small tightly packed group of people: *the little knot of people clustered around the doorway.*
6 a unit of speed equivalent to one nautical mile per hour, used esp. of ships, aircraft, and winds. ■ chiefly historical a length marked by knots on a log line, as a measure of speed: *some days the vessel logged 12* **knots**.
▸ **v.** (**knots, knotting, knotted**) [with obj.] **1** fasten with a knot: *the scarves were knotted loosely around their throats.* ■ make (a carpet or other decorative item) with knots.
2 make (something, esp. hair) tangled.
3 cause (a muscle) to become tense and hard.
■ [no obj.] (of the stomach) tighten as a result of nervousness or tension.
– PHRASES **tie someone (up) in knots** informal make someone completely confused: *they* **tied themselves in knots** *over what to call the country.* **tie the knot** informal get married.
– DERIVATIVES **knot·less** adj., **knot·ter** n.
– ORIGIN Old English *cnotta*; related to Dutch *knot*.

knot[2] ▸ **n.** (pl. **same** or **knots**) a small, relatively short-billed sandpiper, with a reddish-brown or blackish breast in the breeding season. ● Genus *Calidris*, family Scolopacidae: two species, in particular the **red knot** (*C. canutus*), which breeds in the Arctic and winters in the southern hemisphere.
– ORIGIN late Middle English: of unknown origin.

knot gar·den ▸ **n.** a formal garden laid out in an intricate design.

knot·grass /ˈnät,gras/ ▸ **n.** a common Eurasian plant of the dock family, with jointed creeping stems and small pink flowers. It is a serious weed in some areas. ● Genus *Polygonum*, family Polygonaceae: several species, in particular *P. aviculare*. ■ any of a number of other plants, esp. grasses, with jointed stems.

knot·hole /ˈnät,hōl/ ▸ **n.** a hole in a piece of timber where a knot has fallen out, or in a tree trunk where a branch has decayed.

knot·ting /ˈnätiNG/ ▸ **n.** the action or craft of tying knots in yarn or string to make carpets or other decorative items. ■ the knots tied in a carpet or other item.

knot·ty /ˈnätē/ ▸ **adj.** (**knottier, knottiest**) full of knots: *the room was paneled in knotty pine.* ■ (of a problem or matter) extremely difficult or intricate.
– DERIVATIVES **knot·ti·ly** /ˈnätəlē/ adv., **knot·ti·ness** n.

knot·weed /ˈnät,wēd/ ▸ **n.** a plant of the dock family that typically has sheaths where the leaves join the stems. It is often an invasive weed. ● *Polygonum* and other genera, family Polygonaceae: several species, in particular **Japanese knotweed**. ■ knotgrass.

knout /nout/ ▸ **n.** (in imperial Russia) a whip used to inflict punishment, often causing death.
▸ **v.** [with obj.] flog (someone) with such a whip.
– ORIGIN mid 17th cent.: via French from Russian *knut*, from Old Norse *knútr*; related to KNOT[1].

know /nō/ ▸ **v.** (past **knew** /n(y)o͞o/; past participle **known** /nōn/) **1** [with clause] be aware of through observation, inquiry, or information: *most people know that CFCs can damage the ozone layer* | *I know what I'm doing.* ■ [with obj.] have knowledge or information concerning: *I would write to him if I knew his address* | [no obj.] *I* **know of** *one local who shot himself.* ■ be absolutely certain or sure about something: *I just knew it was something I wanted to do* | [with obj.] *I knew it!*
2 [with obj.] have developed a relationship with (someone) through meeting and spending time with them; be familiar or friendly with: *he knew and respected Laura.* ■ have a good command of (a subject or language). ■ recognize (someone or something): *Isabel couldn't hear the words clearly, but she knew the voice.* ■ be familiar or acquainted with (something): *a little restaurant she knew near Times Square.* ■ have personal experience of (an emotion or situation): *a man who had known better times.* ■ (usu. **be known as**) regard or perceive as having a specified characteristic: *he is also known as an amateur painter.* ■ (usu. **be known as**) give (someone or something) a particular name or title: *the doctor was universally known as "Hubert."* ■ (**know someone/something from**) be able to distinguish one person or thing from (another): *you are convinced you know your own baby from any other in the world.*
3 [with obj.] archaic have sexual intercourse with (someone). [a Hebraism that has passed into modern languages; compare with German *erkennen*, French *connaître*.]
– PHRASES **all one knows** used to emphasize the limited nature of one's knowledge concerning something: *all I knew was that she was a schoolteacher.* ■ used to emphasize the importance or significance of the following fact or facts: *all she knew was that she was cold and hungry and thirsty.* **and one knows it** said to emphasize that someone is well aware of a fact although they might pretend otherwise: *the senator's priorities do not add up and he knows it.* **—— as we know it** as is familiar or customary in the present: *by the year 2000 management as we know it will not exist.* **before one knows where one is** (or **before one knows it**) informal with baffling speed. **be in the know** be aware of something known only to a few people: *he had a tip from a friend in the know: the horse was a sure bet.* **be not to know** have no way of being aware of: *you weren't to know he was about to die.* **don't I know it!** informal used as an expression of rueful assent or agreement. **don't you know** informal used to emphasize what one has just said or is about to say: *I was, don't you know, a great automobile enthusiast in those days.* **for all someone knows** used to express the limited scope or extent of one's information: *she could be dead for all I know.* **God** (or **goodness** or **heaven**) **knows 1** used to emphasize that one does not know something: *God knows what else they might find.* **2** used to emphasize the truth of a statement: *God knows, we deserve a glass of bubbly after all these years.* **I know 1** I agree: *"It's not the same without Rosie." "I know."* **2** (also **I know what**) I have a new idea or suggestion: *I know what, let's do it now.* **know best** have better knowledge or more appropriate skills. **know better than** be wise or polite enough to avoid doing a particular thing: *you ought to know better than to ask that.* **know someone by sight** recognize someone by their appearance without knowing their name or being so well acquainted as to talk to them. **know different** (or **otherwise**) be aware of information or evidence to the contrary. **know something for a fact** be aware of something that is irrefutable or beyond doubt: *I know for a fact that he can't speak a word of Japanese.* **know someone in the biblical sense** informal, humorous have sexual intercourse with someone. **know no bounds** have no limits: *their courage knows no bounds.* **know one's own mind** be decisive and certain. **know one's way around** be familiar with (an area, procedure, or subject). **know the ropes** have experience of the appropriate procedures. [with reference to ropes used in sailing.] **know what's what** informal be experienced and competent in a particular area. **know who's who** be aware of the identity and status of each person. **let it be** (or **make something**) **known** ensure that people are informed about something, esp. via a third party: [with clause] *the commissioner let it be known that he was not seeking reappointment.* **not know from nothing** informal be totally ignorant, either generally or concerning something in particular: *she shakes her head while you talk, as if to say you don't know from nothing.* **not know the first thing about** have not the slightest idea about (something). **not know that** informal used to express one's doubts about one's ability to do something: *I don't know that I can sum up my meaning on paper.* **not know what to do with oneself** be at a loss as to know what to do, typically through boredom, embarrassment, or anxiety. **not know where** (or **which way**) **to look** feel great embarrassment and not know how to react. **not want to know** informal refuse to react or take notice: *they just didn't want to know when I gave my side of the story.* **what does —— know?** informal used to indicate that someone knows nothing about the subject in question: *what does he know about football, anyway?* **what do you know (about that)?** informal used as an expression of surprise. **wouldn't you like to know?** informal used to express the speaker's firm intention not to reveal something in spite of a questioner's curiosity: *"You're dating him, aren't you?" "Wouldn't you like to know?"* **you know** informal used to imply that what is being referred to is known to or understood by the listener: *when in Rome, you know.* ■ used as a gap-filler in conversation: *well, you know, I was wondering if you had any jobs for me.* **you know something** (or **what**)**?** informal used to indicate that one is going to say something interesting or surprising: *you know what? I believed her.* **you never know** informal you can never be certain; it's impossible to predict.
– DERIVATIVES **know·a·ble** adj., **know·er** n.
– ORIGIN Old English *cnāwan* (earlier *gecnāwan*) 'recognize, identify,' of Germanic origin; from an Indo-European root shared by Latin (*g*)*noscere*, Greek *gignōskein*, also by CAN[1] and KEN.

know·bot /ˈnō,bät/ ▸ **n.** Computing, trademark a program on a network (esp. the Internet) that operates independently and has reasoning and decision-making capabilities.
– ORIGIN late 20th cent.: from *knowledgeable robot*.

know-how ▸ **n.** practical knowledge or skill; expertise: *technical know-how.*

know·ing /ˈnōiNG/ ▸ **adj. 1** showing or suggesting that one has knowledge or awareness that is secret or known to only a few people: *a knowing smile.* ■ chiefly derogatory experienced or shrewd, esp. excessively or prematurely so: *today's society is too knowing, too corrupt.*
2 done in full awareness or consciousness: *a knowing breach of the order by the appellants.*
▸ **n.** the state of being aware or informed.
– PHRASES **there is no knowing** no one can tell.
– DERIVATIVES **know·ing·ness** n.

know·ing·ly /ˈnōiNGlē/ ▸ **adv. 1** in a way that suggests one has secret knowledge or awareness: *Amy looked at me knowingly.*

2 in full awareness or consciousness; deliberately: *when a journalist knowingly misleads the readers.*

know-it-all ▶ **n.** informal a person who behaves as if they know everything.

knowl·edge /ˈnälij/ ▶ **n. 1** facts, information, and skills acquired by a person through experience or education; the theoretical or practical understanding of a subject: *a thirst for knowledge | her considerable knowledge of antiques.* ■ what is known in a particular field or in total; facts and information: *the transmission of knowledge.* ■ Philosophy true, justified belief; certain understanding, as opposed to opinion.
2 awareness or familiarity gained by experience of a fact or situation: *the program had been developed without his knowledge | he denied all knowledge of the overnight incidents.*
– PHRASES **come to one's knowledge** become known to one. **to (the best of) my knowledge 1** so far as I know. **2** as I know for certain.
– ORIGIN Middle English (originally as a verb in the sense 'acknowledge, recognize,' later as a noun): from an Old English compound based on *cnāwan* (see **KNOW**).

knowl·edge·a·ble /ˈnälijəbəl/ (also **knowledgable**) ▶ **adj.** intelligent and well informed: *she is very knowledgeable about livestock and pedigrees.*
– DERIVATIVES **know·ledge·a·bil·i·ty** /ˌnälijəˈbilitē/ **n.**, **know·ledge·a·bly** /-blē/ **adv.**

knowl·edge base ▶ **n. 1** a store of information or data that is available to draw on.
2 the underlying set of facts, assumptions, and rules that a computer system has available to solve a problem.

knowl·edge e·con·o·my ▶ **n.** an economy in which growth is dependent on the quantity, quality, and accessibility of the information available, rather than on the means of production.

knowl·edge man·age·ment /ˈnälij ˌmanijmənt/ ▶ **n.** efficient handling of information and resources within a commercial organization.

knowl·edge work·er ▶ **n.** Computing a person whose job involves handling or using information.

known /nōn/ past participle of **KNOW**.
▶ **adj.** recognized, familiar, or within the scope of knowledge: *bivalved crustaceans little known to nonprofessionals | the known world.* ■ [attrib.] publicly acknowledged to be: *a known criminal.* ■ Mathematics (of a quantity or variable) having a value that can be stated.

know-noth·ing ▶ **n. 1** an ignorant person.
2 (**Know-Nothing**) historical a member of a political party in the US, prominent from 1853 to 1856, that was antagonistic toward Roman Catholics and recent immigrants and whose members preserved its secrecy by denying its existence.
– DERIVATIVES **know-no·thing·ism n.**

Knox[1] /näks/, Henry (1750–1806) American military officer. He served in the American Revolution and then became the first US secretary of war 1785–94.

Knox[2], John (*c.*1505–72), Scottish Protestant reformer. He played an important part in the establishment of the Church of Scotland within a Scottish Protestant state.

Knox·ville /ˈnäksˌvil, -vəl/ a port on the Tennessee River, in eastern Tennessee; pop. 184,802 (est. 2008). Twice the state capital (1796–1812 and 1817–19), it is now the headquarters of the Tennessee Valley Authority.

Knt. ▶ **abbr.** Knight.

knuck·le /ˈnəkəl/ ▶ **n.** a part of a finger at a joint where the bone is near the surface, esp. where the finger joins the hand: *Charlotte rapped on the window with her knuckles.* ■ a projection of the carpal or tarsal joint of a quadruped. ■ a cut of meat consisting of such a projection together with the adjoining parts: *a knuckle of pork.*
▶ **v.** [with obj.] rub or press (something, esp. the eyes) with the knuckles.
– PHRASAL VERBS **knuckle down 1** apply oneself seriously to a task. **2** (also **knuckle under**) give in; submit.
– DERIVATIVES **knuck·ly adj.**
– ORIGIN Middle English *knokel* (originally denoting the rounded shape when a joint such as the elbow or knee is bent), from Middle Low German, Middle Dutch *knökel*, diminutive of *knoke* 'bone.' In the mid 18th cent. the verb *knuckle (down)* expressed setting the knuckles down to shoot the taw in a game of marbles, hence the notion of applying oneself with concentration.

knuck·le·ball /ˈnəkəlˌbôl/ (also **knuckler**) ▶ **n.** Baseball a slow pitch that has virtually no spin and moves erratically, typically made by releasing the ball from between the thumb and the knuckles of the first joints of the index and middle finger.
– DERIVATIVES **knuck·le·ball·er n.**

knuck·le·bone /ˈnəkəlˌbōn/ ▶ **n. 1** a bone forming or corresponding to a knuckle. ■ a knuckle of meat.
2 (**knucklebones**) animal knucklebones used in the game of jacks. ■ the game of jacks.

knuck·le-drag·ger ▶ **n.** informal a stupid or loutish person.
– DERIVATIVES **knuck·le-drag·ging adj.**

knuck·le-dust·er /ˈnəkəlˌdəstər/ ▶ **n.** a metal guard worn over the knuckles in fighting to increase the effect of blows.

knuck·le·head /ˈnəkəlˌhed/ ▶ **n.** informal a stupid person.

knuck·le joint ▶ **n.** a joint connecting two parts of a mechanism, in which a projection in one fits into a recess in the other.

knuck·le sand·wich ▶ **n.** informal a punch in the mouth.

knur /nər/ ▶ **n.** variant form of **KNAR**.

knurl /nərl/ ▶ **n.** a small projecting knob or ridge, esp. in a series around the edge of something.
– DERIVATIVES **knurled adj.**
– ORIGIN early 17th cent.: apparently a derivative of **KNUR**.

Knut /kəˈno͞ot/ variant spelling of **CANUTE**.

KO /ˌkāˈō/ Boxing, informal ▶ **n.** a knockout in a boxing match. See also **KAYO**.
▶ **v.** (**KO's, KO'ing, KO'd**) [with obj.] knock (an opponent) out in a boxing match.
– ORIGIN 1920s: abbreviation.

ko·a /ˈkōə/ ▶ **n.** a large Hawaiian forest tree that yields dark red timber. ● *Acacia koa*, family Leguminosae.
– ORIGIN early 19th cent.: from Hawaiian.

ko·a·la /kōˈälə/ ▶ **n.** a bearlike arboreal Australian marsupial that has thick gray fur and feeds on eucalyptus leaves. Also called **NATIVE BEAR** in Australia. ● *Phascolarctos cinereus*, the only member of the family Phascolarctidae.
– ORIGIN early 19th cent.: from Dharuk.

koala

USAGE In nontechnical contexts, **koala bear** (as opposed to **koala**) is widely used. Zoologists, however, regard this form as incorrect on the grounds that, despite appearances, koalas are completely unrelated to bears.

ko·an /ˈkōˌän/ ▶ **n.** a paradoxical anecdote or riddle, used in Zen Buddhism to demonstrate the inadequacy of logical reasoning and to provoke enlightenment.
– ORIGIN Japanese, literally 'matter for public thought,' from Chinese *gōngàn* 'official business.'

kob /käb, kōb/ ▶ **n.** (pl. **same**) an antelope with a reddish coat and lyre-shaped horns, found on the savannas of southern Africa. ● *Kobus kob*, family Bovidae.
– ORIGIN late 18th cent.: from Wolof *kooba*.

Ko·be /ˈkōbā, -bē/ a port in central Japan, on the island of Honshu; pop. 1,502,772 (2007). The city was severely damaged by an earthquake in 1995.

ko·bo /ˈkōbō/ ▶ **n.** (pl. **same**) a monetary unit of Nigeria, equal to one hundredth of a naira.
– ORIGIN corruption of **COPPER**[1].

ko·bold /ˈkōˌbōld/ ▶ **n.** Germanic Mythology a spirit that haunts houses or lives underground in caves or mines.
– ORIGIN German *Kobold*.

Koch /kôkʜ/, Robert (1843–1910), German bacteriologist. He identified the organisms that cause anthrax, tuberculosis, and cholera. Nobel Prize for Physiology or Medicine (1905).

Kö·chel num·ber /ˈkərsʜəl, -kəl, ˈkœkʜəl/ ▶ **n.** Music a number given to each of Mozart's compositions in the complete catalog of his works compiled by the Austrian scientist Ludwig von Köchel (1800–77) and his successors.

Ko·chi /kōˈcʜē/ a seaport and naval base on the Malabar Coast of southwestern India, in the state of Kerala; pop. 254,500 (est. 2009). Former name **COCHIN**[1].

ko·chi·a /ˈkōkēə/ ▶ **n.** a shrubby Eurasian plant of the goosefoot family, grown for its decorative foliage, which turns deep fiery red in the autumn. Also called **BURNING BUSH, SUMMER CYPRESS**. ● *Bassia* (formerly *Kochia*) *scoparia*, family Chenopodiaceae.
– ORIGIN late 19th cent.: named after Wilhelm D. J. *Koch* (1771–1849), German botanist.

Ko·dá·ly /kōˈdī(yə), ˈkōdī/, Zoltán (1882–1967), Hungarian composer. He was deeply involved in the collection and publication of Hungarian folk songs. His works include *Psalmus Hungaricus* (1923) and the opera *Háry János* (1925–27).

Ko·di·ak bear /ˈkōdēˌak/ ▶ **n.** an animal of a large race of the North American brown bear or grizzly, found on islands to the south of Alaska. ● *Ursus arctos middendorffi*, family Ursidae.
– ORIGIN late 19th cent.: named after *Kodiak* Island, Alaska.

Ko·di·ak Is·land /ˈkōdēˌak/ an island in the Gulf of Alaska, in southwestern Alaska, noted for its wildlife and sites of early European settlement.

ko·el /ˈkōəl/ ▶ **n.** an Asian and Australasian cuckoo with a call that resembles its name, the male typically having all-black plumage. ● Genus *Eudynamys*, family Cuculidae: one or two species, in particular *E. scolopacea*.
– ORIGIN early 19th cent.: from Hindi *koēl*, from Sanskrit *kokila* in the same sense.

K of C ▶ **abbr.** Knights of Columbus.

K of P ▶ **abbr.** Knights of Pythias.

kof·ta /ˈkôftə/ ▶ **n.** (pl. **same** or **koftas**) (in Middle Eastern and Indian cooking) a spiced meatball.
– ORIGIN from Urdu and Persian, literally 'pounded meat.'

ko·hen /ˈkōhən, ˈkōən, kōˈhān/ (also **cohen**) ▶ **n.** (pl. **kohanim** /kōˈhänim, ˌkôhäˈnēm/ or **cohens**) Judaism a member of the priestly class, having certain rights and duties in the synagogue.
– ORIGIN from Hebrew, literally 'priest.'

Ko·hi·ma /ˈkōhēmə/ a city in far northeastern India, capital of the state of Nagaland; pop. 103,200 (est. 2009).

Koh-i-noor /ˈkō ə ˌno͝or/ a famous Indian diamond that has a history going back to the 14th century. It passed into British possession on the annexation of Punjab in 1849 and was set in the queen's state crown for the coronation of George VI (1937).
– ORIGIN from Persian *kōh-i nūr* 'mountain of light.'

Kohl /kōl/, Helmut (1930–), German statesman; chancellor of the Federal Republic of Germany 1982–90, and of Germany 1990–98. As chancellor, he showed a strong commitment to NATO and to closer ties within the EU.

kohl /kōl/ ▶ **n.** a black powder, usually antimony sulfide or lead sulfide, used as eye makeup esp. in Eastern countries.
– ORIGIN late 18th cent.: from Arabic *kuḥl*.

kohl·ra·bi /kōlˈräbē/ ▶ **n.** (pl. **kohlrabies**) a cabbage of a variety with an edible turniplike swollen stem.
– ORIGIN early 19th cent.: via German from Italian *cavoli rape*, plural of *cavolo rapa*, from medieval Latin *caulorapa*, from Latin *caulis* (see **COLE**) + *rapum, rapa* 'turnip'; compare with French *chou-rave*.

kohlrabi

koi /koi/ (also **koi carp**) ▶ **n.** (pl. **same**) a common carp of a large ornamental variety, originally bred in Japan.
– ORIGIN early 18th cent.: from Japanese, 'carp.'

koi·ne /koiˈnā, ˈkoinā/ ▶ **n.** the common language of the Greeks from the close of the classical period to the Byzantine era. ■ a common language shared by various peoples; a lingua franca.
– ORIGIN late 19th cent.: from Greek *koinē (dialektos)* 'common (language).'

koi·no·ni·a /ˌkoinəˈnēə/ ▶ **n.** Theology Christian fellowship or communion, with God or, more commonly, with fellow Christians.
– ORIGIN early 20th cent.: from Greek *koinōnia* 'fellowship.'

ko·kan·ee /kōˈkanē/ ▶ **n.** (pl. **same** or **kokanees**) a sockeye salmon of a dwarf variety that lives in landlocked lakes in western North America.
– ORIGIN late 19th cent.: from Interior Salish.

Ko·ko·mo /ˈkōkəˌmō/ an industrial city in north central Indiana; pop. 45,694 (est. 2008).

Ko·ko·pel·li /ˌkōkəˈpeli/ a fertility god of the southwestern Native American culture. Depicted as a hunchbacked flute player, he is known as a playful prankster and storyteller.

Kokopelli

PRONUNCIATION KEY ə *ago, up*; ər *over, fur*; a *hat*; ā *ate*; ä *car*; e *let*; ē *see*; i *fit*; ī *by*; NG *sing*; ō *go*; ô *law, for*; oi *toy*; o͝o *good*; o͞o *goo*; ou *out*; TH *thin*; T͟H *then*; ZH *vision*

ko·la /ˈkōlə/ ▶ **n.** variant spelling of COLA (sense 2).

Ko·la Pen·in·su·la /ˈkōlə/ a peninsula on the northwestern coast of Russia, that separates the White Sea from the Barents Sea. The port of Murmansk lies on its north coast.

Kol·ha·pur /ˈkōlə,po͝or/ an industrial city in the state of Maharashtra, in western India; pop. 562,000 (est. 2009).

ko·lin·sky /kəˈlinskē/ ▶ **n.** (pl. **kolinskies**) a dark brown weasel with a bushy tail, found from Siberia to Japan. ● *Mustela sibirica*, family Mustelidae. Alternative name: **Siberian weasel**. ■ the fur of this animal.
– ORIGIN mid 19th cent.: from the place name *Kola*, a port in northwestern Russia, + the pseudo-Russian ending *-insky*.

Kol·ka·ta /kälˈkätə, -ˈkətə/ a port and industrial center in eastern India, capital of the state of West Bengal, the second largest city in India; pop. 5,080,500 (est. 2009). It is situated on the banks of the Hooghly River near the Bay of Bengal. Former name (until 2000) CALCUTTA.
– DERIVATIVES **Kol·kat·an** /-ˈkətn/ **n. & adj.**

Kol·khis /ˈkôlkēs/ Greek name for COLCHIS.

kol·khoz /kəlˈkôz, -ˈKHôz/ ▶ **n.** (pl. **same** or **kolkhozes** or **kolkhozy** /-ˈKHôzē/) a collective farm in the former Soviet Union.
– ORIGIN 1920s: Russian, from *kol(lektivnoe) khoz(yaĭstvo)* 'collective farm.'

Köln /kœln/ German name for COLOGNE.

Kol Ni·dre /kôl ˈnidrā, ˈnidrə, ˌkôl nēˈdrā/ ▶ **n.** an Aramaic prayer annulling vows made before God, sung by Jews at the opening of the Day of Atonement service on the eve of Yom Kippur.
– ORIGIN from Aramaic *kol nidrē* 'all vows' (the opening words of the prayer).

ko·lo /ˈkōlō/ ▶ **n.** (pl. **kolos**) a Slavic dance performed in a circle.
– ORIGIN late 18th cent.: Croatian, literally 'wheel.'

Ko·lozs·vár /ˈkōlōZH,vär/ Hungarian name for CLUJ-NAPOCA.

Ko·ly·ma /kəˈlēmə/ a river in far eastern Siberia, which flows approximately 1,500 miles (2,415 km) north to the Arctic Ocean.

Ko·man·dor·ski Is·lands /ˌkəmənˈdôrskyē/ an island group in extreme eastern Russia, off the eastern Kamchatka Peninsula. US naval forces defeated the Japanese nearby in 1943.

ko·mat·ik /kōˈmatik/ ▶ **n.** a sled drawn by dogs, used by the people of Labrador.
– ORIGIN early 19th cent.: from Inuit *qamutik*.

Ko·ma·ti Riv·er /kəˈmätē/ (also **Rio Incomati**) a river that flows for 500 miles (800 km) from the Drakensberg Range in South Africa, through Swaziland, South Africa, and Mozambique, to the Indian Ocean north of Maputo.

kom·bu·cha /kômˈbo͞oCHə/ ▶ **n.** a food supplement prepared from a symbiotic colony of yeast and bacteria that is added to tea for its alleged health benefits.
– ORIGIN Japanese, 'tea sponge.'

Ko·mi /ˈkōmē/ an autonomous republic in northwestern Russia; pop. 959,500 (est. 2009); capital, Syktyvkar.

Ko·mo·do /kəˈmōdō/ a small island in Indonesia, in the Lesser Sunda Islands, situated between the islands of Sumbawa and Flores. It is home to the Komodo dragon.

Ko·mo·do drag·on ▶ **n.** a heavily built monitor lizard that captures large prey such as pigs by ambush. Occurring only on Komodo and neighboring Indonesian islands, it is the largest living lizard. ● *Varanus komodoensis*, family Varanidae.

Ko·mon·dor /ˈkōmən,dôr, ˈkäm-/ ▶ **n.** a powerful sheepdog of a white breed with a dense matted or corded coat.
– ORIGIN Hungarian.

Komondor

Kom·so·mol /ˈkämsə,môl, ˌkəmsəˈmôl/ historical an organization for communist youth in the former Soviet Union.
– ORIGIN Russian, from *Kommunisticheskiĭ Soyuz Molodëzhi* 'Communist League of Youth.'

Kom·so·molsk /ˌkämsəˈmôlsk/ an industrial city in far eastern Russia, on the Amur River; pop. 272,400 (est. 2008). It was built in 1932 by members of the Komsomol on the site of the village of Permskoe. Also called **Komsomolsk-on-Amur**.

Ko·na Coast /ˈkōnə/ the name for part of the southwestern coast of the island of Hawaii, noted for its resorts and coffee production.

Kon·go /ˈkäNGgō/ ▶ **n.** (pl. **same** or **Kongos**) **1** a member of an indigenous people inhabiting the region of the Congo River in west central Africa. **2** the Bantu language of this people; Kikongo.
▶ **adj.** of or relating to this people or their language.
– ORIGIN the name in Kikongo.

kon·go·ni /käNGˈgōnē/ ▶ **n.** (pl. **same**) a hartebeest, in particular one of a pale yellowish-brown race found in Kenya and Tanzania. ● *Alcelaphus buselaphus cokii*, family Bovidae.
– ORIGIN early 20th cent.: from Kiswahili.

Kö·nig·grätz /ˈkœniKH,grets/ German name for HRADEC KRÁLOVÉ.

Kö·nigs·berg /ˈkœniKHs,berk/ German name for KALININGRAD.

ko·nim·e·ter /kōˈnimitər/ ▶ **n.** an instrument that measures the amount of dust in the air by directing a measured volume of air onto a greased slide to which any dust present will stick.
– ORIGIN early 20th cent.: from Greek *konis* 'dust' + -METER.

Kon·ka·ni /ˈkôNGkə,nē, ˈkäNG-/ ▶ **n.** an Indic language that is the main language of Goa and adjacent parts of Maharashtra. Also called GOANESE (see GOA).
▶ **adj.** of or relating to this language.
– ORIGIN from Marathi and Hindi *koṅkaṇī*, from Sanskrit *koṅkaṇa* 'Konkan' (a coastal region of western India).

Kon-Ti·ki /ˌkän ˈtēkē/ the raft made of balsa logs in which Thor Heyerdahl sailed from the western coast of Peru to the islands of Polynesia in 1947.
– ORIGIN named after an Inca god.

Kon·ya /ˈkôn,yä, kônˈyä/ a city in southwest central Turkey; pop. 967,100 (est. 2007). An ancient Phrygian settlement, it became the capital of the Seljuk sultans toward the end of the 11th century.

kook /ko͞ok/ ▶ **n.** informal a crazy or eccentric person.
– ORIGIN 1960s: probably from CUCKOO.

kook·a·bur·ra /ˈko͝okə,bərə/ ▶ **n.** a very large Australasian kingfisher that feeds on terrestrial prey such as reptiles and birds. ● Genus *Dacelo*, family Alcedinidae: two species, the **laughing kookaburra** (*D. gigas* or D. novaeguineae), which has a loud cackling call, and the **blue-winged kookaburra** (*D. leachii*).
– ORIGIN late 19th cent.: from Wiradhuri *gugubarra*.

laughing kookaburra

kook·y /ˈko͞okē/ ▶ **adj.** (**kookier**, **kookiest**) informal strange or eccentric: *I like kooky foreign films.*
– DERIVATIVES **kook·i·ly** /-kəlē/ **adv.**, **kook·i·ness n.**

Koon·ing, Willem de, see DE KOONING.

Koop /ko͞op/, C. Everett (1916–) US physician and government official; full name *Charles Everett Koop*. As the US surgeon general 1981–89, he campaigned vigorously against the tobacco industry and sought to impress upon the public the dangers of smoking.

Koo·te·nai Riv·er /ˈko͞otn-ˌā/ (also **Kootneya**) a river that flows for 450 miles (720 km) from southeastern British Columbia into Montana and Idaho and then back into British Columbia, where it joins the Columbia River.

ko·pek /ˈkōpek/ (also **copeck** or **kopeck**) ▶ **n.** a monetary unit of Russia and some other countries of the former Soviet Union, equal to one hundredth of a ruble.
– ORIGIN from Russian *kopeĭka*, diminutive of *kop'ë* 'lance' (from the figure on the coin (1535) of Tsar Ivan IV, bearing a lance instead of a sword).

ko·piy·ka /kôˈpēkə/ ▶ **n.** a monetary unit of Ukraine, equal to one-hundredth of a hryvna.
– ORIGIN 1990s: Ukrainian, from Russian *kopeĭka* 'kopek.'

kop·je /ˈkäpē/ (also **koppie**) ▶ **n.** S. African a small hill in a generally flat area.
– ORIGIN from Afrikaans *koppie*, from Dutch *kopje*, diminutive of *kop* 'head.'

ko·ra /ˈkôrə/ ▶ **n.** a West African musical instrument shaped like a lute, with 21 strings passing over a high bridge, and played like a harp.
– ORIGIN late 18th cent.: a local word.

Ko·ran /kəˈrän, kô-, ˈkôrän/ (also **Qur'an** or **Quran**) ▶ **n.** the Islamic sacred book, believed to be the word of God as dictated to Muhammad by the archangel Gabriel and written down in Arabic. The Koran consists of 114 units of varying lengths, known as *suras*; the first sura is said as part of the ritual prayer. These touch upon all aspects of human existence, including matters of doctrine, social organization, and legislation.
– DERIVATIVES **Ko·ran·ic** /-ˈränik/ **adj.**
– ORIGIN from Arabic *qur'ān* 'recitation,' from *qara'a* 'read, recite.'

Kor·but /ˈkôrbət/, Olga (1955–), Soviet gymnast, born in Belarus. She won two individual gold medals at the 1972 Olympic Games.

ko·re /ˈkôrē, ˈkôrā/ ▶ **n.** (pl. **korai** /ˈkôrī/) an archaic Greek statue of a young woman, standing and clothed in long loose robes.
– ORIGIN from Greek *korē* 'maiden.'

Ko·re·a /kəˈrēə/ a region in eastern Asia that forms a peninsula between the East Sea and the Yellow Sea, now divided into the countries of North Korea and South Korea.

> The first Korean state was established in the 1st century ad, and Korea was unified under the Silla dynasty in the 7th century. The country was ruled by the Joseon dynasty from the 14th century until its annexation by Japan in 1910. Following the Japanese surrender at the end of the Second World War, Korea was partitioned along the 38th parallel in 1948.

Ko·re·a, Dem·o·crat·ic Peo·ple's Re·pub·lic of official name for NORTH KOREA.

Ko·re·a, Re·pub·lic of official name for SOUTH KOREA.

Ko·re·an /kəˈrēən, kô-/ ▶ **adj.** of or relating to North or South Korea or its people or language.
▶ **n. 1** a native or inhabitant of North or South Korea, or a person of Korean descent.
2 the language of Korea, which has has its own writing system and may be distantly related to Japanese.

Ko·re·an War the war of 1950–53 between North and South Korea.

> UN troops, dominated by US forces, countered the invasion of South Korea by North Korean forces by invading North Korea, while China intervened on the side of the North. Peace negotiations were begun in 1951, and the war ended two years later with the restoration of previous boundaries.

Kó·rin·thos /ˈkôrin,THôs/ Greek name for CORINTH.

kor·ma /ˈkôrmə/ ▶ **n.** a mildly spiced Indian curry dish of meat or fish marinated in yogurt or curds.
– ORIGIN from Urdu *kormā*, from Turkish *kavurma*.

Kor·sa·koff's syn·drome /ˈkôrsə,kôfs/ (also **Korsakoff's psychosis**) ▶ **n.** Psychiatry a serious mental illness, typically the result of chronic alcoholism, characterized by disorientation and a tendency to invent explanations to cover a loss of memory of recent events.
– ORIGIN early 20th cent.: named after Sergei S. *Korsakoff* (1854–1900), Russian psychiatrist.

ko·ru·na /ˈkôrənə/ ▶ **n.** the basic monetary unit of the Czech Republic, equal to 100 halers.
– ORIGIN Czech, literally 'crown.'

Kos·ci·us·ko /ˌkäskēˈəskō, ˌkäse-, kôSHˈCHo͞oSHkō/, Thaddeus (1746–1817), Polish soldier and patriot; Polish name *Tadeusz Andrzej Bonawentura Kościuszko*. After fighting for the Americans during the American Revolution, he led a nationalist uprising against Russia in Poland in 1794.

Kos·ci·us·ko, Mount /ˌkäzēˈəskō/ a mountain in southeastern Australia, in the Great Dividing Range. Rising to a height of 7,234 feet (2,228 m), it is the highest mountain in Australia.
– ORIGIN named by the explorer Sir Paul Edmund de Strzelecki (1797–1873) in honor of T. KOSCIUSKO.

ko·sher /ˈkōSHər/ ▶ **adj. 1** (of food, or premises in which food is sold, cooked, or eaten) satisfying the requirements of Jewish law: *a kosher kitchen.* ■ (of a person) observing Jewish food laws. ■ (of ritual objects) fit for use according to Jewish laws.
2 genuine and legitimate: *she consulted lawyers to make sure everything was kosher.*

> Restrictions on the foods suitable for Jews are derived from rules in the books of Leviticus and Deuteronomy. Animals must be slaughtered and prepared in the prescribed way, in which the blood is drained from the body, while certain creatures, notably pigs and shellfish, are forbidden altogether. Meat and milk must not be cooked or consumed together, and separate utensils must be kept for each. Strict observance of these rules is today confined mainly to Orthodox Jews.

▶ v. [with obj.] prepare (food) according to the requirements of Jewish law.
– PHRASES **keep** (or **eat**) **kosher** observe the Jewish food regulations (kashruth).
– ORIGIN mid 19th cent.: from Hebrew *kāšēr* 'proper.'

Ko·ši·ce /'kôsHētse/ an industrial city in southern Slovakia; pop. 234,237 (2007).

Ko·sin·ski /kə'zinskē/, Jerzy (Nikodem) (1933–91) US writer; born in Poland. His many works include *Steps* (1968), *Being There* (1971), *The Devil Tree* (1973), *Blind Date* (1977), and *The Hermit of 69th Street* (1988).

Ko·so·vo /'kôsə,vō, 'käs-/ an autonomous area in the Balkans, formerly a part of Yugoslavia; pop. 1,804,800 (est. 2009); capital, Priština. It borders on Albania and the majority of the people are of Albanian descent. In 1998, Kosovo was attacked by Serbian forces intent on expelling the Albanian population; the aggression was halted by NATO bombing in 1999, and Kosovo was put under UN administration. In 2008, it declared itself independent.
– DERIVATIVES **Ko·so·van** n. & adj., **Ko·so·var** n.

Ko·stro·ma /kəsträ'mä/ an industrial city in western Russia, situated on the Volga River, northwest of Nizhni Novgorod; pop. 271,700 (est. 2008).

Ko·sy·gin /kə'sēgin, -gyin/, Aleksei (Nikolaevich) (1904–80), Soviet statesman; premier 1964–80. He devoted most of his attention to internal economic affairs, being gradually eased out of the leadership by Brezhnev.

Ko·ta /'kōtə/ an industrial city in Rajasthan state, in northwestern India, on the Chambal River; pop. 827,400 (est. 2009).

Ko·ta Ba·ha·ru /'kōtə 'bähə,rōō/ a city in Malaysia, on the eastern coast of the Malay Peninsula; pop. 277,300 (est. 2009).

Ko·ta Ki·na·ba·lu /'kōtə ,kinəbə'lōō/ a port in Malaysia, on the northern coast of Borneo; pop. 579,300 (est. 2009).

ko·to /'kōtō/ ▶ n. (pl. **kotos**) a Japanese zither about six feet long, with thirteen silk strings passed over small movable bridges.
– ORIGIN late 18th cent.: Japanese.

Kou·fax /'kōfaks/, Sandy (1935–) US baseball player; born *Sanford Braun*. A pitcher, he played for the Brooklyn (later Los Angeles) Dodgers 1955–66. He was the first three-time Cy Young Award winner, having won unanimously in 1963, 1965, and 1966. Baseball Hall of Fame (1972).

kou·miss /kōō'mis, 'kōōmis/ (also **kumiss** or **kumis**) ▶ n. a drink made from fermented mare's milk, used also as a medicine by Asian nomads.
– ORIGIN late 16th cent.: based on Tartar *kumiz*.

kou·ros /'kōōräs/ ▶ n. (pl. **kouroi** /'kōōroi/) an archaic Greek statue of a young man, standing and often naked.
– ORIGIN Ionic form of Greek *koros* 'boy.'

Kow·loon /'kou'lōōn/ a densely populated peninsula on the southeastern coast of China that forms part of Hong Kong. It is separated from Hong Kong Island by Hong Kong Harbor.

kow·tow /'kou'tou/ ▶ v. [no obj.] **1** act in an excessively subservient manner: *she didn't have to kowtow to a boss*.
2 historical kneel and touch the ground with the forehead in worship or submission as part of Chinese custom.
▶ n. historical an act of kowtowing as part of Chinese custom.
– DERIVATIVES **kow·tow·er** n.
– ORIGIN early 19th cent.: from Chinese *kētóu*, from *kē* 'knock' + *tóu* 'head.'

Ko·zhi·kode /'kōzHi,kōd/ a seaport in the state of Kerala in southwestern India, on the Malabar Coast; pop. 440,900 (est. 2009). Formerly called **Calicut**.

KP ▶ abbr. kitchen police.

kph ▶ abbr. kilometers per hour.

KR ▶ abbr. Chess king's rook.

Kr ▶ symbol the chemical element krypton.

kr. ▶ abbr. ■ krona. ■ krone.

Kra, Isthmus of /krä/ the narrowest part of the Malay Peninsula, forming part of southern Thailand.

kraal /kräl/ S. African ▶ n. a traditional African village of huts, typically enclosed by a fence. ■ another term for **homestead** (sense 3). ■ an enclosure for cattle or sheep.
▶ v. [with obj.] drive (cattle or sheep) into an enclosure: *they kraal their sheep every night*. ■ restrict or separate (people) to a particular area or into groups.
– ORIGIN Dutch, from Portuguese *curral* (see **corral**).

kraft /kraft/ (also **kraft paper**) ▶ n. a kind of strong, smooth brown wrapping paper.
– ORIGIN early 20th cent.: from Swedish, literally 'strength,' used to form the term *kraftpapper* 'kraft paper.'

Kra·gu·je·vac /'krägōōyə,väts/ a city in central Serbia; pop. 145,400 (est. 2008). It was the capital of Serbia 1818–39.

krait /krīt/ ▶ n. a highly venomous Asian snake of the cobra family. ● Genus *Bungarus*, family Elapidae: several species, including the black and yellow **banded krait** (*B. fasciatus*). See also **sea krait**.
– ORIGIN late 19th cent.: from Hindi *karait*.

Kra·ka·toa /,krakə'tōə, ,kräk-/ a small volcanic island in Indonesia that lies between Java and Sumatra. It was the scene of a great eruption in 1883 that destroyed most of the island.

kra·ken /'kräkən/ ▶ n. an enormous mythical sea monster said to appear off the coast of Norway.
– ORIGIN Norwegian.

Kra·ków /'krä,kōōf/ Polish name for **Cracow**.

Kras·no·dar /,kräsnə'där/ an administrative territory in the northern Caucasus Mountains, on the Black Sea, in southern Russia. ■ its capital, a port on the lower Kuban River; pop. 705,500 (est. 2009). Until 1922, it was known as Yekaterinodar (Ekaterinodar).

Kras·no·yarsk /,kräsnə'yärsk/ an administrative territory in south central Russia. ■ its capital, a port on the Yenisei River; pop. 936,400 (est. 2008).

kraut /krout/ ▶ n. informal sauerkraut. ■ (also **Kraut**) informal, offensive a German.
– ORIGIN World War I: shortening of **sauerkraut**.

Kraut·rock /'krout,räk/ ▶ n. an experimental style of rock music associated with German groups of the 1970s, characterized by improvisation and strong, hypnotic rhythms.
– DERIVATIVES **Kraut·rock·er** n.

Krav Ma·ga /'kräv mə'gä/ ▶ n. a form of self-defense and physical training, first developed by the Israeli army in the 1940s, based on the use of reflexive responses to threatening situations.
– ORIGIN 1990s: from Hebrew, 'contact combat.'

Krebs cy·cle /krebz/ ▶ n. Biochemistry the sequence of reactions by which most living cells generate energy during the process of aerobic respiration. It takes place in the mitochondria, consuming oxygen, producing carbon dioxide and water as waste products, and converting ADP to energy-rich ATP.
– ORIGIN 1940s: named after Sir Hans A. *Krebs* (1900–81), German-born British biochemist.

Kre·feld /'krā,felt/ an industrial town and port on the Rhine River in western Germany, in North Rhine–Westphalia; pop. 237,100 (est. 2006).

Kreis·ler /'krīslər/, Fritz (1875–1962), US violinist and composer, born in Austria. In 1910, he gave the first performance of Elgar's violin concerto, which was dedicated to him.

Kre·men·chuk /,krimin'CHōōk/ an industrial city in east central Ukraine, on the Dnieper River; pop. 228,500 (est. 2009). Russian name **Kremenchug**.

krem·lin /'kremlin/ ▶ n. a citadel within a Russian town. ■ (**the Kremlin**) the citadel in Moscow. ■ the Russian or (formerly) Soviet government.
– ORIGIN mid 17th cent.: via French from Russian *kreml'* 'citadel.'

Krem·lin·ol·o·gy /,kremlə'näləjē/ ▶ n. the study and analysis of Soviet or Russian policies.
– DERIVATIVES **Krem·lin·ol·o·gist** /-jist/ n.

krep·lach /'krepläKH/ ▶ plural n. (in Jewish cooking) triangular noodles filled with chopped meat or cheese and served with soup.
– ORIGIN from Yiddish *kreplekh*, plural of *krepel*, from German dialect *Kräppel* 'fritter.'

krieg·spiel /'krēg,sHpēl, -,spēl/ ▶ n. a war game in which blocks representing armies or other military units are moved about on maps. ■ a form of chess in which each player has a separate board and can only infer the position of the opponent's forces from limited information given by an umpire who disallows illegal moves.
– ORIGIN late 19th cent.: from German, from *Krieg* 'war' + *Spiel* 'game.'

Kriem·hild /'krēmhilt/ (in the Nibelungenlied) a Burgundian princess, wife of Siegfried and later of Etzel (Attila the Hun).

krill /kril/ ▶ n. a small shrimplike planktonic crustacean of the open seas. It is eaten by a number of larger animals, notably the baleen whales. ● *Meganyctiphanes norvegica*, class Malacostraca.
– ORIGIN early 20th cent.: from Norwegian *kril* 'young fry of fish.'

krim·mer /'krimər/ ▶ n. tightly curled gray or black fur made from the wool of young Crimean lambs.
– ORIGIN mid 19th cent.: from German, from *Krim* 'Crimea.'

Krin·gle /'kriNGgəl/ ▶ n., Kris (or Kriss). Another name for **Santa Claus**.

Kri·o /'krēō/ ▶ n. an English-based Creole language of Sierra Leone. It is the first language of about 350,000 people and is used as a lingua franca by over 3 million.
▶ adj. of or relating to this language.
– ORIGIN probably an alteration of **Creole**.

kris /krēs/ (also archaic **creese**) ▶ n. a Malay or Indonesian dagger with a wavy blade.
– ORIGIN late 16th cent.: based on Malay *keris*.

Krish·na /'krisHnə/ Hinduism one of the most popular gods, the eighth and most important avatar or incarnation of Vishnu.

> He is worshiped in several forms: as the child god whose miracles and pranks are extolled in the Puranas; as the divine cowherd whose erotic exploits, esp. with his favorite, Radha, have produced both romantic and religious literature; and as the divine charioteer who preaches to Arjuna on the battlefield in the Bhagavadgita.

– ORIGIN from Sanskrit *Kṛṣṇa*, literally 'black.'

Krish·na Riv·er a river that rises in the Western Ghats of southern India and flows generally east for 805 miles (1,288 km) to the Bay of Bengal.

Kris·tall·nacht /'kristl,näkt, -,näKHt/ the occasion of concerted violence by Nazis throughout Germany and Austria against Jews and their property on the night of November 9–10, 1938.
– ORIGIN German, literally 'night of crystal,' referring to the broken glass produced by the smashing of store windows.

Kris·ti·an·i·a variant spelling of **Christiania**.

Krí·ti /'krētē/ Greek name for **Crete**.

Kri·voi Rog /kri'voi 'rōg, 'rôk/ (also **Krivoy Rog**) Russian name for **Kryvyi Rih**.

Kroc /kräk/, Ray (1902–84) US entrepreneur and philanthropist; full name *Raymond Albert Kroc*. In 1955, he founded the franchise empire of McDonald's fast-food restaurants.

kro·na /'krōnə/ ▶ n. **1** (pl. **kronor** /-nôr/) the basic monetary unit of Sweden, equal to 100 öre. [Swedish, 'crown.']
2 (pl. **kronur** /-nər/) the basic monetary unit of Iceland, equal to 100 aurar. [from Old Norse *króna* 'crown.']

Kro·ne /'krōnə/, Julie (1963–) US jockey. She was the first woman to capture a Triple Crown horse-racing title 1993. She retired from racing in 1999.

kro·ne /'krōnə/ ▶ n. (pl. **kroner** /-nər/) the basic monetary unit of Denmark and Norway, equal to 100 øre.
– ORIGIN Danish and Norwegian, literally 'crown.'

Kro·nos variant spelling of **Cronus**.

Kron·stadt /'krän,stät/ German name for **Brașov**.

kroon /krōōn/ ▶ n. (pl. **kroons** or **krooni** /'krōōnē/) the basic monetary unit of Estonia, equal to 100 senti.
– ORIGIN Estonian, literally 'crown'; compare with **krona, krone**.

Kru /krōō/ ▶ n. (pl. **same**) **1** a member of a seafaring people of the coast of Liberia and Côte d'Ivoire (Ivory Coast).
2 the Niger–Congo language of this people.
▶ adj. of or relating to the Kru or their language.
– ORIGIN from a West African language.

Kru Coast a section of the coast of Liberia to the northwest of Cape Palmas, inhabited by the Kru people.

Kru·ger /'krōōgər, 'kryər/, Stephanus Johannes Paulus (1825–1904), South African soldier and statesman; president of Transvaal 1883–99. He led the Afrikaners to victory in the First Boer War in 1881.

Kru·ger·rand /'krōōgə,rand/ (also **krugerrand** or **Kruger**) ▶ n. a South African gold coin with a portrait of President Kruger on the obverse.
– ORIGIN 1967: from the name of S. J. P. **Kruger** + **rand**¹.

krumm·holz /'krōōmhōlts/ ▶ n. stunted windblown trees growing near the tree line on mountains.
– ORIGIN early 20th cent.: from German, literally 'crooked wood.'

krumm·horn /'krōōm,hôrn/ (also **crumhorn**) ▶ n. a medieval wind instrument with an enclosed double

reed and an upward-curving end, producing an even, nasal sound.
– ORIGIN from German, from *krumm* 'crooked' + *Horn* 'horn.'

Kru·pa /'kro͞opə/, Gene (1909–73) US jazz drummer and bandleader. He was the first major popular drum soloist.

Krupp /krəp, kro͞op/, Alfred (1812–87), German arms manufacturer. His company was a major arms producer for Germany from the 1840s through the end of World War II.

kryp·ton /'krip,tän/ ▶ **n.** the chemical element of atomic number 36, a member of the noble gas series. It is obtained by distillation of liquid air and is used in some kinds of electric light. (Symbol: **Kr**)
– ORIGIN late 19th cent.: from Greek *krupton*, neuter of *kruptos* 'hidden.'

kry·tron /'krī,trän/ ▶ **n.** Physics a high-speed solid-state switching device that is triggered by a pulse of coherent light and is used in the triggers of nuclear devices.
– ORIGIN late 20th cent.: first element of obscure derivation + **-TRON**.

Kry·vyi Rih /kri'vi 'riKH/ an industrial city in southern Ukraine, at the center of an iron-ore mining region; pop. 675,600 (est. 2009). Russian name **KRIVOI ROG**.

KS ▶ **abbr.** ■ Kansas (in official postal use). ■ Kaposi's sarcoma.

Kshat·ri·ya /k(ə)'SHätrēə/ ▶ **n.** a member of the second of the four great Hindu castes, the military caste. The traditional function of the Kshatriyas is to protect society by fighting in wartime and governing in peacetime.
– ORIGIN late 18th cent.: from Sanskrit *kṣatriya*, from *kṣhatra* 'rule, authority.'

KT ▶ **abbr.** Knight Templar.

Kt ▶ **abbr.** Knight.

kt. ▶ **abbr.** ■ karat(s). ■ kiloton(s). ■ knot(s): *a cruising speed of 240 kt.*

K/T bound·a·ry short for **CRETACEOUS–TERTIARY BOUNDARY**.
– ORIGIN late 20th cent.: *K/T*, from the symbols for *Cretaceous* and *Tertiary*.

Ku ▶ **symbol** the chemical element kurchatovium.

Kua·la Lum·pur /,kwälə 'lo͝om,po͝or, lo͝om'po͝or/ the capital of Malaysia, in the southwestern part of the Malay Peninsula; pop. 1,469,000 (est. 2009).

Kua·la Treng·ga·nu /,kwälə treNG'gäno͞o/ (also **Kuala Terengganu** /,tereNG-/) a city in Malaysia, on the east coast of the Malay Peninsula at the mouth of the Trengganu River; pop. 286,400 (est. 2009).

Kuan·tan /'kwän,tän/ a city in Malaysia, on the east coast of the Malay Peninsula; pop. 407,800 (est. 2009).

Ku-band /'kā'yo͞o ,band/ ▶ **n.** a microwave frequency band used for satellite communication and broadcasting, using frequencies of about 12 gigahertz for terrestrial reception and 14 gigahertz for transmission.
– ORIGIN 1990s: from *Ku* (arbitrary serial designation) + *band*.

Ku·blai Khan /'ko͞oblə 'kän, 'ko͞oblī/ (1215–94), Mongol emperor of China; grandson of Genghis Khan. With his brother **Mangu** (then Mongol Khan), he conquered southern China (1252–59). After Mangu's death in 1259, he completed the conquest of China, founded the Yuan dynasty, and established his capital on the site of modern Beijing.

Kübler-Ross, Elisabeth (1926–2004), US psychiatrist, born in Switzerland. She was a pioneer in the field of palliative care and revolutionized attitudes toward treatment of the terminally ill. Among her many books was the influential *On Death and Dying* (1969).

Ku·brick /'ko͞obrik/, Stanley (1928–99), US movie director, producer, and writer. Notable movies: *Dr. Strangelove* (1964), *2001: A Space Odyssey* (1968) and *A Clockwork Orange* (1971).

ku·chen /'ko͞okən, -KHən/ ▶ **n.** (pl. **same**) a cake, esp. one eaten with coffee.
– ORIGIN from German *Kuchen*.

Ku·ching /'ko͞oCHiNG/ a port in Malaysia, on the Sarawak River near the northwestern coast of Borneo; pop. 658,600 (est. 2009).

ku·dos /'k(y)o͞o,dōs, -,dōz, -,däs/ ▶ **n.** praise and honor received for an achievement. ■ informal compliments or congratulations: *kudos to everyone who put the event together.*
– ORIGIN late 18th cent.: Greek.

> **USAGE** **Kudos** comes from Greek and means 'glory.' Despite appearances, it is not a plural form. This means that there is no singular form **kudo** and that use as a plural, as in the following sentence, is incorrect: *he received* **many kudos** *for his work* (correct use is *he received* **much kudos** *for his work*).

ku·du /'ko͞odo͞o/ ▶ **n.** (pl. **same** or **kudus**) an African antelope that has a grayish or brownish coat with white vertical stripes, and a short bushy tail. The male has long spirally curved horns. ● Genus *Tragelaphus*, family Bovidae: the **greater kudu** (*T. strepsiceros*) and the **lesser kudu** (*T. imberbis*).
– ORIGIN late 18th cent.: from Afrikaans *koedoe*, from Xhosa *i-qudu*.

kud·zu /'ko͝odzo͞o/ (also **kudzu vine**) ▶ **n.** a quick-growing eastern Asian climbing plant with reddish-purple flowers, used as a fodder crop and for erosion control. It has become a pest in the southeastern US. ● *Pueraria lobata*, family Leguminosae.
– ORIGIN late 19th cent.: from Japanese *kuzu*.

Ku·fic /'k(y)o͞ofik/ ▶ **n.** an early angular form of the Arabic alphabet found chiefly in decorative inscriptions.
▶ **adj.** of or in this type of script.
– ORIGIN early 18th cent.: from the name *Kufa*, a city south of Baghdad, Iraq (because it was attributed to the city's scholars), + **-IC**.

ku·gel /'ko͞ogəl, 'ko͞o-/ ▶ **n.** (in Jewish cooking) a kind of sweet or savory pudding of noodles or potatoes.
– ORIGIN Yiddish, literally 'ball.'

Kui·by·shev /'kwēbə,SHef/ former name (1935–91) of **SAMARA**.

Kui·per belt /'kīpər ,belt/ ▶ **n.** a region of the solar system beyond the orbit of Neptune, believed to contain many comets, asteroids, and other small bodies made largely of ice.
– ORIGIN 1990s: named after Gerard P. *Kuiper* (1905–73), Dutch-born US astronomer.

Ku Klux Klan /'ko͞o ,kləks 'klan/ (abbr.: **KKK**) an extremist right-wing secret society in the US.

> The Ku Klux Klan was originally founded in the southern states after the Civil War to oppose social change and black emancipation by using violence and terrorism. Although disbanded twice, it re-emerged in the 1950s and 1960s and continues at a local level. Members disguise themselves in white robes and hoods and often use a burning cross as a symbol of their organization.

– DERIVATIVES **Ku Klux·er n.**, **Ku Klux Klans·man** /'klanzmən/ **n.** (pl. **Ku Klux Klansmen**).
– ORIGIN perhaps from Greek *kuklos* 'circle' and **CLAN**.

kuk·ri /'ko͝okrē/ ▶ **n.** (pl. **kukris**) a curved knife broadening toward the point, used by Gurkhas.
– ORIGIN early 19th cent.: from Nepalese *khukuri*.

ku·la /'ko͞olə/ ▶ **n.** (in some Pacific communities) an interisland system of ceremonial gift exchange as a prelude to or at the same time as regular trading.
– ORIGIN Melanesian.

ku·lak /ko͞o'lak, -'läk/ ▶ **n.** historical a peasant in Russia wealthy enough to own a farm and hire labor. Emerging after the emancipation of serfs in the 19th century, the kulaks resisted Stalin's forced collectivization, but millions were arrested, exiled, or killed.
– ORIGIN Russian, literally 'fist, tightfisted person,' from Turkic *ḳol* 'hand.'

kul·cha /'ko͝olCHə/ ▶ **n.** a small, round Indian bread made from flour, milk, and butter, typically stuffed with meat or vegetables.
– ORIGIN from Persian *kulīca*.

kul·fi /'ko͝olfē/ ▶ **n.** a type of Indian ice cream, typically served in the shape of a cone.
– ORIGIN from Hindi *kulfī*.

Kul·tur /ko͝ol'to͝or/ ▶ **n.** German civilization and culture (sometimes used derogatorily to suggest elements of racism, authoritarianism, or militarism).
– ORIGIN German, from Latin *cultura* or French *culture* (see **CULTURE**).

Kul·tur·kampf /ko͝ol'to͝or,käm(p)f/ a conflict from 1872 to 1887 between the German government (headed by Bismarck) and the papacy for the control of schools and Church appointments, in which Bismarck was forced to concede to the Catholic Church.
– ORIGIN German, from **KULTUR** + *Kampf* 'struggle.'

Kum variant spelling of **QOM**.

Ku·ma·mo·to /,ko͞omə'mōtō/ a city in southern Japan, on the western coast of Kyushu Island; pop. 662,565 (2007).

Ku·ma·si /ko͞o'mäsē, -'masē/ a city in southern Ghana; pop. 1,517,000 (est. 2005). It is the capital of the Ashanti region.

Ku·may·ri /ko͞o,mīrē/ Russian name for **GYUMRI**.

Kumbh Me·la /,ko͝om 'mälä/ ▶ **n.** a Hindu festival and assembly, held once every twelve years at four locations in India, at which pilgrims bathe in the waters of the Ganges and Jumna rivers for the purification of sin.
– ORIGIN from Sanskrit, literally 'pitcher festival,' from *kumbh* 'pitcher' + *melā* 'assembly.'

ku·mis (also **kumiss**) ▶ **n.** variant spelling of **KOUMISS**.

ku·mite /'ko͞omi,tā/ ▶ **n.** (in martial arts) freestyle fighting.
– ORIGIN Japanese, literally 'sparring.'

kum·kum /'ko͝om,ko͝om/ ▶ **n.** a red powder used ceremonially and cosmetically, esp. by Hindu women to make a small distinctive mark on the forehead.
– ORIGIN mid 20th cent.: from Sanskrit *kuṅkuma* 'saffron.'

küm·mel /'kiməl/ ▶ **n.** a sweet liqueur flavored with caraway and cumin seeds.
– ORIGIN from German, from Old High German *kumil*, variant of *kumîn* (see **CUMIN**).

Ku·mon /'ko͞omən, -män/ ▶ **n.** trademark a tutoring program, originating in Japan, in which children improve their skills in a subject (esp. mathematics) by completing worksheets of increasing difficulty, led by a special instructor.
– ORIGIN from the name of Tru *Kumon* (1914-95), the Japanese mathematics teacher who invented the method.

kum·quat /'kəm,kwät/ (also **cumquat**) ▶ **n.** **1** an orangelike fruit related to the citruses, with an edible sweet rind and acid pulp. It is eaten raw or used in preserves.
2 the eastern Asian shrub or small tree that yields this fruit and that hybridizes with citrus trees.
● Genus *Fortunella*, family Rutaceae.
– ORIGIN late 17th cent.: from Chinese (Cantonese dialect) *kam kwat* 'little orange.'

Ku·na /'ko͞onə/ (also **Cuna**) ▶ **n.** (pl. **same** or **Kunas**) **1** a member of an American Indian people of the isthmus of Panama.
2 the Chibchan language of this people.
▶ **adj.** of or relating to the Kunas or their language.
– ORIGIN the name in Kuna.

ku·na /'ko͞onə/ ▶ **n.** (pl. **kune** /-nā/) the basic monetary unit of Croatia, equal to 100 lipa.
– ORIGIN Croatian, literally 'marten' (the fur of the marten was formerly a medium of exchange).

kun·da·li·ni /,ko͝ondl'ēnē/ ▶ **n.** (in yoga) latent female energy believed to lie coiled at the base of the spine. ■ (also **kundalini yoga**) a system of meditation directed toward the release of such energy.
– ORIGIN Sanskrit, literally 'snake.'

Kun·de·ra /'ko͝ondərə, ,kən'derə/, Milan (1929–), Czech novelist. He emigrated to France in 1975 after his books were condemned in Czechoslovakia following the Soviet military invasion of 1968. Notable works: *The Book of Laughter and Forgetting* (1979) and *The Unbearable Lightness of Being* (1984).

Kung /ko͝oNG/ ▶ **n.** **1** (pl. **same**) a member of a San (Bushman) people of the Kalahari Desert in southern Africa.
2 the Khoisan language of this people.
▶ **adj.** of or relating to the Kung or their language.
– ORIGIN Khoikhoi *!Kung*, literally 'people.'

kung fu /'kəNG 'fo͞o, 'ko͝oNG/ ▶ **n.** a primarily unarmed Chinese martial art resembling karate.
– ORIGIN from Chinese *gōngfú*, from *gōng* 'merit' + *fú* 'master.'

K'ung Fu-tzu /'ko͝oNG ,fo͞o 'dzə/ see **CONFUCIUS**.

Ku·nitz /'ko͞onits/, Stanley Jasspon (1905–2006), US poet and editor. His *Selected Poems: 1928–58* (1958) received the Pulitzer Prize for Poetry. In 2000, he was named US poet laureate, a post he had held 1974–76, when it was called "consultant in poetry to the Library of Congress".

Kun·lun Shan /ko͞on'lo͞on 'SHän/ a range of mountains in western China, on the northern edge of the Tibetan plateau, that extends east for more than 1,000 miles (1,600 km) from the Pamir Mountains. The highest peak is Muztag, which rises to 25,338 feet (7,723 m).

Kun·ming /ko͞on'miNG/ a city in southwestern China, capital of Yunnan province; pop. 1,700,200 (est. 2006).

kunz·ite /'ko͝ont,sīt/ ▶ **n.** a lilac-colored gem variety of spodumene that fluoresces or changes color when irradiated.
– ORIGIN early 20th cent.: from the name of George F. *Kunz* (1856–1932), American gemologist, + **-ITE**.

Kuo·min·tang /'kwō'min'taNG, -'täNG, 'gwô-/ (also **Guomindang** /'gwō'min'däNG/) a nationalist party founded in China under Sun Yat-sen in 1912, and led by Chiang Kai-shek from 1925. It held power from 1928 until the Communist Party took power in October 1949, and it subsequently formed the central administration of Taiwan.
– ORIGIN from Chinese, 'national people's party.'

Kupf·fer cell /ˈko͝opfər/ ▶ **n.** Anatomy a phagocytic cell that forms the lining of the sinusoids of the liver and is involved in the breakdown of red blood cells.
– ORIGIN early 20th cent.: named after Karl Wilhelm von *Kupffer* (1829–1902), Bavarian anatomist.

Ku·ra Riv·er /kəˈrä, ˈko͝orə/ a river that flows for 940 miles (1,510 km) from northeastern Turkey through Georgia and Azerbaijan into the Caspian Sea.

kur·cha·tov·i·um /ˌkərchəˈtōvēəm/ ▶ **n.** historical a name proposed in the former Soviet Union for the artificial radioactive element of atomic number 104, now called **rutherfordium**.
– ORIGIN 1960s: named after Igor V. *Kurchatov* (1903–60), Russian nuclear physicist.

Kurd /kərd/ ▶ **n.** a member of a mainly pastoral Islamic people living in Kurdistan.
– ORIGIN the name in Kurdish.

Kurd·ish /ˈkərdisн/ ▶ **adj.** of or relating to the Kurds or their language.
▶ **n.** the Iranian language of the Kurds.

Kur·di·stan /ˌkərdəˈstän, ˌko͝or-, -ˈstan/ a region in the Middle East, south of the Caucasus Mountains, the traditional home of the Kurdish people.
The area includes large parts of eastern Turkey, northern Iraq, western Iran, eastern Syria, Armenia, and Azerbaijan. Following persecution of the Kurds by Iraq in the aftermath of the Gulf War of 1991, certain areas designated safe havens were established for the Kurds in northern Iraq.

Ku·re /ˈko͝orā/ a city in southern Japan, on the southern coast of the island of Honshu, near Hiroshima; pop. 250,345 (2007).

Kur·gan /ko͝orˈgän/ a city in central Russia, commercial center for an agricultural region; pop. 324,100 (est. 2008).

kur·gan /ko͝orˈgän, -ˈgan/ ▶ **n.** Archaeology a prehistoric burial mound or barrow of a type found in southern Russia and Ukraine. ■ (**Kurgan**) a member of the ancient people who built such burial mounds.
▶ **adj.** of or relating to the ancient Kurgans.
– ORIGIN Russian, of Turkic origin; compare with Turkish *kurgan* 'castle.'

Ku·ril Is·lands /ˈk(y)o͝orˌēl, k(y)o͝oˈrēl/ (also **Kurile Islands** or **the Kurils**) a chain of 56 islands between the Sea of Okhotsk and the North Pacific Ocean, stretching from the southern tip of the Kamchatka peninsula to the northeastern corner of the Japanese island of Hokkaido. They are the subject of dispute between Russia and Japan.

Ku·ro·sa·wa /ˌko͝orəˈsäwə/, Akira (1910–98), Japanese movie director. Notable movies: *Rashomon* (1950) and *Ran* (1985).

Ku·ro·shi·o /ˌko͝orōˈsнē-ō/ a warm current in the Pacific Ocean that flows northeast past Japan and toward Alaska. Also called **Japanese Current**, **Japan Current**.
– ORIGIN late 19th cent.: Japanese, from *kuro* 'black' + *shio* 'tide.'

kur·ra·jong /ˈkərəˌjôNG, -ˌjäNG/ (also **currajong**) ▶ **n.** an Australian plant that produces useful tough fiber. ● Several species, in particular a small tree with shiny pointed leaves and boat-shaped leathery seed cases (*Brachychiton populneus*, family Sterculiaceae).
– ORIGIN early 19th cent.: from Dharuk *garrajung* 'fiber fishing line.'

Kursk /ko͝orsk/ an industrial city in southwestern Russia; pop. 408,100 (est. 2008). It was the scene of an important Soviet victory in World War II.

kur·ta /ˈkərtə/ ▶ **n.** a loose collarless shirt worn by people from South Asia.
– ORIGIN from Urdu and Persian *kurtah*.

kur·to·sis /kərˈtōsis/ ▶ **n.** Statistics the sharpness of the peak of a frequency-distribution curve.
– ORIGIN early 20th cent.: from Greek *kurtōsis* 'a bulging,' from *kurtos* 'bulging, convex.'

ku·ru /ˈko͝oro͞o/ ▶ **n.** Medicine a fatal disease of the brain occurring in some peoples in New Guinea and thought to be caused by a viruslike agent such as a prion.
– ORIGIN 1950s: a local word.

ku·rus /kəˈro͞osн/ ▶ **n.** (pl. **same**) a monetary unit of Turkey, equal to one hundredth of a Turkish lira.
– ORIGIN from Turkish *kuruş*.

Ku·shan /ˈko͞oˌsнän/ ▶ **n.** (pl. **same** or **Kushans**) a member of an Iranian dynasty that invaded the Indian subcontinent and established a powerful empire in the northwest between the 1st and 3rd centuries AD.
▶ **adj.** of or relating to this people or their dynasty.
– ORIGIN from Prakrit *kuṣāṇa* (adjective), from Iranian.

Ku·ta·i·si /ˌko͞otäˈēsē/ an industrial city in central Georgia; pop. 186,000 (est. 2002). One of the oldest cities in Transcaucasia, it has been the capital of various kingdoms, including Colchis and Abkhazia.

Kutch, Gulf of /kəcн/ an inlet of the Arabian Sea on the west coast of India.

Kutch, Rann of /ˈkəcн, ˈrän əv/ a vast salt marsh on the shores of the Arabian Sea, that extends over the boundary between southeastern Pakistan and the state of Gujarat in northwestern India.

Ku·te·nai /ˈko͞otn,ā/ (also **Kutenay**) ▶ **n.** (pl. **same** or **Kutenais**) **1** a member of an American Indian people of the Rocky Mountains in British Columbia, Idaho, and Montana.
2 the language of this people, of unknown affinity.
▶ **adj.** of or relating to the Kutenai or their language.
– ORIGIN from Blackfoot *Kotonáai-*.

Ku·wait /kəˈwāt/ a country on the northwestern coast of the Persian Gulf; pop. 2,692,500 (est. 2009); capital, Kuwait City; official language, Arabic.

> With a history as a fishing and trading sheikhdom, Kuwait, since the 1930s, has become one of the world's leading oil producers. Iraqi claims on the area led to the 1990–91 occupation and resulting Gulf War.

– DERIVATIVES **Ku·wai·ti** /-ˈwātē/ **adj. & n.**

Ku·wait Cit·y a port on the Persian Gulf, the capital city of Kuwait; pop. 32,400 (est. 2005).

Kuz·bass /ko͝ozˈbäs/ another name for **Kuznets Basin**.

Kuz·nets Ba·sin /kəzˈnyets/ (also **Kuznetsk** /-ˈnyetsk/) an industrial region in southern Russia, situated in the valley of the Tom River, between Tomsk and Novokuznetsk. It is rich in iron and coal deposits. Also called **Kuzbass**.

kV ▶ **abbr.** kilovolt(s).

kvass /k(ə)ˈväs, kfäs/ ▶ **n.** (esp. in Russia) a fermented drink, low in alcohol, made from rye flour or bread with malt.
– ORIGIN from Russian *kvas*.

kvell /k(ə)vel/ ▶ **v.** [no obj.] informal feel happy and proud: *my mom was kvelling—bursting with pride.*
– ORIGIN 1960s: from Yiddish *kveln*, from Middle High German, literally 'well up.'

kvetch /k(ə)vecн, kfecн/ informal ▶ **n.** a person who complains a great deal. ■ a complaint.
▶ **v.** [no obj.] complain.
– ORIGIN 1960s: from Yiddish *kvetsh* (noun), *kvetshn* (verb), from Middle High German *quetschen*, literally 'crush.'

kW ▶ **abbr.** kilowatt(s).

Kwa /kwä/ ▶ **n.** a major branch of the Niger–Congo family of languages, spoken from Côte d'Ivoire (Ivory Coast) to Nigeria and including Ibo and Yoruba.
▶ **adj.** of or relating to this group of languages.
– ORIGIN the name in Kwa.

kwa·cha /ˈkwächə/ ▶ **n.** the basic monetary unit of Zambia and Malawi, equal to 100 ngwee in Zambia and 100 tambala in Malawi.
– ORIGIN previously used as a Zambian nationalist slogan calling for a new "dawn" of freedom, later applied to the currency of the newly independent state.

Kwa·ja·lein /ˈkwäjələn, -ˌlān/ the largest atoll in the Marshall Islands, in the west central Pacific Ocean, fought over by US and Japanese forces during World War II.

Kwa·ki·u·tl /ˌkwäkēˈo͞otl/ ▶ **n.** (pl. **same** or **Kwakiutls**) **1** a member of an American Indian people of the northwestern Pacific coast, living mainly on Vancouver Island.
2 the Wakashan language of this people.
▶ **adj.** of or relating to the Kwakiutl or their language.
– ORIGIN the name in Kwakiutl.

Kwang·chow /ˈkwäNGˈcнō, ˈgwäNGˈjō/ variant of **Guangzhou**.

Kwang·ju /ˈgwôNGˈjo͞o/ a city in southwestern South Korea; pop. 1,434,600 (est. 2008).

Kwang·si Chuang /ˈkwäNGˌsē ˈcнwäNG, ˈgwäNGˌsē/ variant of **Guangxi Zhuang**.

Kwang·tung /ˈkwäNGˈto͝oNG, ˈgwäNGˈdo͝oNG/ variant of **Guangdong**.

kwan·za /ˈkwänzə/ ▶ **n.** (pl. **same** or **kwanzas**) the basic monetary unit of Angola, equal to 100 lwei.
– ORIGIN perhaps from a Swahili word meaning 'first.'

Kwan·zaa /ˈkwänzə/ ▶ **n.** a secular festival observed by many African Americans from December 26 to January 1 as a celebration of their cultural heritage and traditional values.
– ORIGIN from Kiswahili *matunda ya kwanza*, literally 'first fruits (of the harvest),' from *kwanza* 'first.'

kwash·i·or·kor /ˌkwäsнēˈôrkôr, -kər/ ▶ **n.** a form of malnutrition caused by protein deficiency in the diet, typically affecting young children in the tropics.
– ORIGIN 1930s: a local word in Ghana.

Kwa·Zu·lu-Na·tal /kwäˌzo͞olo͞o näˈtäl/ a province of eastern South Africa, on the Indian Ocean; capital, Pietermaritzburg. Formerly called Natal, it became one of the new provinces of South Africa following the democratic elections of 1994. See also **Natal**.

Kwei·chow /ˈkwāˈcнou, -ˈcнō, ˈgwāˈjō/ variant of **Guizhou**.

Kwei·lin /ˈkwāˈlin, ˈgwā-/ variant of **Guilin**.

Kwei·sui /ˈkwāˈswā, ˈgwā-/ former name (until 1954) of **Hohhot**.

Kwei·yang /ˈkwāˈyäNG, ˈgwā-/ variant of **Guiyang**.

kWh ▶ **abbr.** kilowatt-hour(s).

kW-hr ▶ **abbr.** kilowatt-hour.

KWIC /kwik/ ▶ **n.** [as modifier] Computing keyword in context, denoting a database search in which the keyword is shown highlighted in the middle of the display, with the text forming its context on either side.
– ORIGIN 1950s: abbreviation.

KY ▶ **abbr.** Kentucky (in official postal use).

Ky. ▶ **abbr.** Kentucky.

ky·a·nite /ˈkīəˌnīt/ (also **cyanite** /ˈsīə-/) ▶ **n.** a blue or green crystalline mineral consisting of aluminum silicate, used in heat-resistant ceramics.
– DERIVATIVES **ky·a·nit·ic** /ˌkīəˈnitik/ **adj.**
– ORIGIN late 18th cent.: from Greek *kuanos*, *kuaneos* 'dark blue' + **-ite**[1].

ky·an·ize /ˈkīəˌnīz/ ▶ **v.** [with obj.] treat (wood) with a solution of mercuric chloride to prevent decay.
– ORIGIN mid 19th cent.: named after John H. *Kyan* (1774–1850), the Irish inventor who patented the process in 1832.

kyat /kēˈ(y)ät, kyät, cнät/ ▶ **n.** (pl. **same** or **kyats**) the basic monetary unit of Burma (Myanmar), equal to 100 pyas.
– ORIGIN Burmese.

Kyd /kid/, Thomas (1558–94), English playwright. His anonymously published *The Spanish Tragedy* (1592), an early example of revenge tragedy, was very popular on the Elizabethan stage.

Kyiv /ˈkēyif/ Ukrainian name for **Kiev**.

ky·lix /ˈkīliks, ˈkiliks/ ▶ **n.** (pl. **kylikes** /kīliˌkēz, kili-/ or **kylixes**) an ancient Greek cup with a shallow bowl and a tall stem.
– ORIGIN from Greek *kulix*.

ky·mo·graph /ˈkīməˌgraf/ ▶ **n.** an instrument for recording variations in pressure, e.g., in sound waves or in blood within blood vessels, by the trace of a stylus on a rotating cylinder.
– DERIVATIVES **ky·mo·graph·ic** /ˌkīməˈgrafik/ **adj.**
– ORIGIN mid 19th cent.: from Greek *kuma* 'wave' + **-graph**.

Kyo·to /kēˈōtō/ an industrial city in central Japan, on the island of Honshu; pop. 1,389,595 (2007). Founded in the 8th century, it was the imperial capital from 794 until 1868.

ky·pho·plas·ty /ˈkīfōˌplastē/ ▶ **n.** (pl. **kyphoplasties**) the surgical filling of an injured or collapsed vertebra. This procedure restores original shape and configuration and relieves pain from spinal compression.

ky·pho·sis /kīˈfōsis/ ▶ **n.** Medicine excessive outward curvature of the spine, causing hunching of the back. Compare with **lordosis**.
– DERIVATIVES **ky·phot·ic** /-ˈfätik/ **adj.**
– ORIGIN mid 19th cent.: from Greek *kuphōsis*, from *kuphos* 'bent, hunchbacked.'

Kyr·gyz /kirˈgēz/ ▶ **n. & adj.** variant spelling of **Kirghiz**.

Kyr·gyz·stan /ˌki(ə)rgiˈstän, -ˈstan, ˌkər-/ a mountainous country in central Asia, on the northwestern border of China; pop. 5,431,700 (est. 2009); capital, Bishkek; official languages, Kyrgyz and Russian (since 2001). Also called **Kyrgyz Republic**. **Kirghizia**.

> The region was annexed by Russia in 1864 and became a constituent republic of the Soviet Union. When the Soviet Union broke up in 1991, Kyrgyzstan became an independent republic within the Commonwealth of Independent States.

Kyr·i·e /ˈki(ə)rēˌā/ (also **Kyrie eleison** /iˈlā-iˌsän, -sən/) ▶ **n.** a short repeated invocation (in Greek or in translation) used in many Christian liturgies, esp. at the beginning of the Eucharist or as a response in a litany.
– ORIGIN from Greek *Kurie eleēson* 'Lord, have mercy.'

Kyu·shu /kēˈo͞osho͞o/ the most southerly of the four main islands of Japan, constituting an administrative region; pop. 13,232,000 (est. 2006); capital, Fukuoka.

Ky·zyl /kəˈzil/ a city in south central Russia, on the Yenisei River, capital of the republic of Tuva; pop. 108,100 (est. 2008).

Ky·zyl Kum /kəˈzil ˈko͞om/ an arid desert region in central Asia that extends east from the Aral Sea to the Pamir Mountains and covers part of Uzbekistan and southern Kazakhstan.

k

Ll

L¹ /el/ (also **l**) ▶ **n.** (pl. **Ls** or **L's**) **1** the twelfth letter of the alphabet. ■ denoting the next after K in a set of items, categories, etc.
2 (**L**) a shape like that of a capital L: [in combination] *a four-story L-shaped building.*
3 the Roman numeral for 50. [originally a symbol identified with the letter *L*, because of coincidence of form. In ancient Roman notation, *L* with a stroke above denoted 50,000.]

L² ▶ **abbr.** ■ (in tables of sports results) games lost. ■ Chemistry levorotatory: *L-tryptophan.* ■ (**L.**) Lake, Loch, or Lough (chiefly on maps): *L. Ontario.* ■ large (as a clothes size). ■ Latin. ■ Liberal. ■ (**L.**) Linnaeus (as the source of names of animal and plant species): *Swallowtail Butterfly Papilio machaon* (*L., 1758*). ■ lire. ▶ **symbol** ■ Chemistry Avogadro's number. ■ Physics inductance.

l ▶ **abbr.** ■ (giving position or direction) left: *l to r: Gordon, Anthony, Jerry, and Mark.* ■ (chiefly in horse racing) length(s): *distances 5 l, 3 l.* ■ (**l.**) (in textual references) line: *l. 648.* ■ Chemistry liquid. ■ liter(s). ■ (**l.**) archaic pound(s): *a salary of 4l. a week.* ▶ **symbol** (in mathematical formulas) length.

LA ▶ **abbr.** ■ Library Association. ■ Los Angeles. ■ Louisiana (in official postal use).

La ▶ **symbol** the chemical element lanthanum.

la /lä/ (Brit. also **lah**) ▶ **n.** Music (in solmization) the sixth note of a major scale. ■ the note A in the fixed-do system.
– ORIGIN Middle English: representing (as an arbitrary name for the note) the first syllable of Latin *labii*, taken from a Latin hymn (see SOLMIZATION).

La. ▶ **abbr.** Louisiana.

laa·ger /ˈlägər/ ▶ **n. 1** S. African historical a camp or encampment formed by a circle of wagons.
2 an entrenched position or viewpoint that is defended against opponents: *an educational laager, isolated from the outside world.*
▶ **v.** [with obj.] S. African historical form (vehicles) into a laager. ■ [no obj.] make camp.
– ORIGIN South African Dutch, from Dutch *leger, lager* 'camp.' Compare with LAGER and LAIR.

Laa·youne /läˈyo͞on/ (also **La'youn**) the capital of Western Sahara; pop. 200,000 (est. 2007). Arabic name EL-AAIÚN.

Lab /lab/ ▶ **abbr.** a Labrador dog.

lab /lab/ ▶ **n.** informal a laboratory: *a science lab.*
– ORIGIN late 19th cent.: abbreviation.

La·ban /ˈlābən/, Rudolf von (1879–1958), Hungarian choreographer and dancer. In 1920, he published the first of several volumes outlining Labanotation, his system of dance notation.

la Bar·ca, Pe·dro Cal·de·rón de see CALDERÓN DE LA BARCA.

lab·a·rum /ˈlabərəm/ ▶ **n.** rare a banner or flag bearing symbolic motifs. ■ historical Constantine the Great's imperial standard, which bore Christian symbolic imagery fused with the military symbols of the Roman Empire.
– ORIGIN early 17th cent.: from late Latin, of unknown origin.

lab coat ▶ **n.** a white protective coat worn by workers in a laboratory.

lab·da·num /ˈlabdənəm/ (also **ladanum** /ˈlädn-əm, ˈladnəm/) ▶ **n.** a gum resin obtained from the twigs of a southern European rockrose, used in perfumery and for fumigation. ● The rockrose is usually *Cistus ladanifer*, family Cistaceae.
– ORIGIN mid 16th cent.: via Latin from Greek *ladanon, lēdanon*, from *lēdon* 'mastic.'

lab·e·fac·tion /ˌlabəˈfaksHən/ ▶ **n.** archaic deterioration or downfall.
– ORIGIN early 17th cent.: from Latin *labefactio(n-)*, from *labefacere* 'weaken,' from *labi* 'to fall' + *facere* 'make.'

la·bel /ˈlābəl/ ▶ **n. 1** a small piece of paper, fabric, plastic, or similar material attached to an object and giving information about it. ■ a piece of fabric sewn inside a garment and bearing the brand name, size, or instructions for care. ■ the piece of paper in the center of a phonograph record giving the artist and title. ■ a company that produces recorded music: *independent labels.* ■ the name or trademark of a fashion company: *she plans to launch her own designer clothes label.* ■ a classifying phrase or name applied to a person or thing, esp. one that is inaccurate or restrictive: *my reluctance to stick a label on myself politically.* ■ (in a dictionary entry) a word or words used to specify the subject area, register, or geographical origin of the word being defined. ■ Computing a string of characters used to refer to a particular instruction in a program. ■ Biology & Chemistry a radioactive isotope, fluorescent dye, or enzyme used to make something identifiable for study.
2 Heraldry a narrow horizontal strip, typically with three downward projections, that is superimposed on a coat of arms by an eldest son during the life of his father.
3 Architecture another term for DRIPSTONE.
▶ **v.** (**labels, labeling, labeled**; Brit. **labels, labelling, labelled**) [with obj.] attach a label to (something): *she labeled the parcels neatly, writing the addresses in capital letters.* ■ assign to a category, esp. inaccurately or restrictively: *children were labeled as bullies* | [with obj. and complement] *the critics labeled him a loser.* ■ Biology & Chemistry make (a substance, molecule, or cell) identifiable or traceable by replacing an atom with one of a distinctive radioactive isotope, or by attaching a fluorescent dye, enzyme, or other molecule.
– DERIVATIVES **la·bel·er n.**
– ORIGIN Middle English (denoting a narrow strip or band): from Old French, 'ribbon,' probably of Germanic origin and related to LAP¹.

La Belle Prov·ince /lä ˌbel prəˈväNs/ nickname for QUEBEC.
– ORIGIN French, literally 'the Beautiful Province.'

la·bel·lum /ləˈbeləm/ ▶ **n.** (pl. **labella** /-ˈbelə/)
1 Entomology each of a pair of lobes at the tip of the proboscis in some insects.
2 Botany a central petal at the base of an orchid flower, typically larger than the other petals and of a different shape.
– ORIGIN early 19th cent.: from Latin, diminutive of *labrum* 'lip.'

la·bel·mate /ˈlāblˌmāt/ ▶ **n.** a musician, group, or singer that is signed to the same record label as another.

la·bi·a /ˈlābēə/ ▶ **plural n. 1** Anatomy the inner and outer folds of the vulva, at either side of the vagina.
2 plural form of LABIUM.

la·bi·al /ˈlābēəl/ ▶ **adj. 1** chiefly Anatomy of or relating to the lips. ■ Dentistry (of the surface of a tooth) adjacent to the lips. ■ Zoology of, resembling, or serving as a lip, liplike part, or labium.
2 Phonetics (of a consonant) requiring complete or partial closure of the lips (e.g., *p, b, f, v, m, w*), or (of a vowel) requiring rounded lips (e.g., *oo* in *moon*).
▶ **n.** Phonetics a labial sound.
– DERIVATIVES **la·bi·al·ize** /-ˌlīz/ **v.** (sense 2 of the adjective), **la·bi·al·ly adv.**
– ORIGIN late 16th cent.: from medieval Latin *labialis*, from Latin *labium* 'lip.'

la·bi·a ma·jo·ra /məˈjôrə/ ▶ **plural n.** Anatomy the larger outer folds of the vulva.

la·bi·a mi·no·ra /məˈnôrə/ ▶ **plural n.** Anatomy the smaller inner folds of the vulva.

la·bi·ate /ˈlābē-it, -ˌāt/ ▶ **n.** Botany a plant of the mint family (Labiatae) with a distinctive two-lobed flower.
▶ **adj. 1** Botany of, relating to, or denoting plants of the mint family.
2 Botany & Zoology resembling or possessing a lip or labium.
– ORIGIN early 18th cent. (as an adjective in the sense 'two-lipped,' describing a corolla or calyx): from modern Latin *labiatus*, from *labium* 'lip.'

la·bile /ˈlāˌbīl, -bəl/ ▶ **adj.** technical liable to change; easily altered. ■ of or characterized by emotions that are easily aroused or freely expressed, and that tend to alter quickly and spontaneously; emotionally unstable. ■ Chemistry easily broken down or displaced.
– DERIVATIVES **la·bil·i·ty** /lāˈbilətē, lə-/ **n.**
– ORIGIN late Middle English (in the sense 'liable to err or sin'): from late Latin *labilis*, from *labi* 'to fall.'

labio- /ˈlābēō/ ▶ **comb. form** of or relating to the lips: *labiodental.*
– ORIGIN from Latin *labium* 'lip.'

la·bi·o·den·tal /ˌlābēōˈdentl/ ▶ **adj.** Phonetics (of a sound) made with the lips and teeth, for example *f* and *v*.
▶ **n.** Phonetics a labiodental sound.

la·bi·o·ve·lar /ˌlābēōˈvēlər/ ▶ **adj.** Phonetics (of a sound) made with the lips and soft palate, for example *w*.
▶ **n.** Phonetics a labiovelar sound.

la·bi·um /ˈlābēəm/ ▶ **n.** (pl. **labia** /-bēə/) **1** Entomology a fused mouthpart that forms the floor of the mouth of an insect.
2 Botany the lower lip of the flower of a plant of the mint family.
– ORIGIN late 16th cent. (in the general sense 'lip, liplike structure'): from Latin, 'lip'; related to LABRUM.

lab·lab /ˈlabˌlab/ ▶ **n.** another term for HYACINTH BEAN.
– ORIGIN early 19th cent.: from Arabic *lablāb*.

la·bor /ˈlābər/ (Brit. **labour**) ▶ **n. 1** work, esp. hard physical work: *the price of repairs includes labor and parts* | *manual labor.* ■ workers, esp. manual workers, considered collectively: *nonunion casual labor.* ■ such workers considered as a social class or political force: [as modifier] *the labor movement.* ■ (**Labor**) a department of government concerned with a nation's workforce: *Secretary of Labor.*
2 the process of childbirth, esp. the period from the start of uterine contractions to delivery: *his wife is in labor.*
3 (**Labour**) [treated as sing. or pl.] (in the UK or Canada) the Labour Party.
▶ **v.** [no obj.] work hard; make great effort: *they labored from dawn to dusk in two shifts* | *it now looks as if the reformers had labored in vain.* ■ work at an unskilled manual occupation: *he was eking out an existence by laboring.* ■ have difficulty in doing something despite working hard: *Coley labored against confident opponents.* ■ (of an engine) work noisily and with difficulty: *the wheels churned, the engine laboring.* ■ [with adverbial of direction] move or proceed with trouble or difficulty: *they labored up a steep, tortuous track.* ■ (of a ship) roll or pitch heavily. ■ [with obj.] archaic till (the ground): *the land belonged to him who labored it.*
– PHRASES **a labor of Hercules** see HERCULES. **a labor of love** a task done for pleasure, not reward. **labor**

the point explain or discuss something at excessive or unnecessary length.
– PHRASAL VERBS **labor under 1** carry (a heavy load or object) with difficulty. **2** be deceived or misled by (a mistaken belief): *you've been laboring under a misapprehension.*
– ORIGIN Middle English *labo(u)r*, from Old French *labour* (noun), *labourer* (verb), both from Latin *labor* 'toil, trouble.'

lab·o·ra·to·ry /ˈlabrəˌtôrē/ ▶ **n.** (pl. **laboratories**) a room or building equipped for scientific experiments, research, or teaching, or for the manufacture of drugs or chemicals: *pepsin can be extracted in the laboratory | a film processing laboratory* | [as modifier] *a laboratory technician.* ■ [as modifier] (of an animal) bred for or used in experiments in laboratories: *studies on laboratory rats.*
– ORIGIN early 17th cent.: from medieval Latin *laboratorium*, from Latin *laborare* 'to labor.'

la·bor camp ▶ **n.** a prison camp in which a regime of hard labor is enforced.

La·bor Day ▶ **n.** a public holiday or day of festivities held in honor of working people, in the US and Canada on the first Monday in September, in many other countries on May 1.

la·bored /ˈlābərd/ (Brit. **laboured**) ▶ **adj.** done with great effort and difficulty: *his breathing was becoming less labored.* ■ (esp. of humor or a performance) not spontaneous or fluent: *one of Arthur's labored jokes.*

la·bor·er /ˈlāb(ə)rər/ (Brit. **labourer**) ▶ **n.** a person doing unskilled manual work for wages: *a farm laborer.*

la·bor force ▶ **n.** all the members of a particular organization or population who are able to work, viewed collectively.

la·bor-in·ten·sive ▶ **adj.** (of a form of work) needing a large workforce or a large amount of work in relation to output: *the labor-intensive task of tagging each item in the store.*

la·bo·ri·ous /ləˈbôrēəs/ ▶ **adj.** (esp. of a task, process, or journey) requiring considerable effort and time: *years of laborious training | the work is very slow and laborious.* ■ (esp. of speech or writing style) showing obvious signs of effort and lacking in fluency: *his slow, laborious style.*
– DERIVATIVES **la·bo·ri·ous·ly** **adv.**, **la·bo·ri·ous·ness** **n.**
– ORIGIN late Middle English (also in the sense 'industrious, assiduous'): from Old French *laborieux*, from Latin *laboriosus*, from *labor* 'labor.'

La·bor·ite /ˈlābəˌrīt/ (Brit. **Labourite**) ▶ **n.** a member or supporter of a labor party.

la·bor mar·ket ▶ **n.** the supply of available workers in relation to available work: *a diverse workforce in a tight labor market.*

la·bor pain ▶ **n.** [usu. in pl.] one of the recurrent pains felt by a woman during childbirth. Also called **BIRTH PANG.**

la·bor par·ty ▶ **n.** a political party formed to represent the interests of ordinary working people. ■ (**the Labor Party**) a major party in Israel, Australia, and certain other countries. ■ variant spelling of **LABOUR PARTY.**

La·bor Par·ty, Aus·tral·ian see **AUSTRALIAN LABOR PARTY.**

la·bor-sav·ing ▶ **adj.** [attrib.] (of an appliance) designed to reduce the amount of work needed to complete a task.

la·bor un·ion ▶ **n.** an organized association of workers, often in a trade or profession, formed to protect and further their rights and interests.

la·bour ▶ **n.** British spelling of **LABOR.**

La·bour Par·ty ▶ **n.** a major left-of-center British party that since World War II has been in power 1945–51, 1964–70, 1974–79, and since 1997. Arising from the trade union movement at the end of the 19th century, it replaced the Liberals as the country's second party after World War I.

la·bra /ˈlābrə, ˈlabrə/ plural form of **LABRUM.**

lab·ra·doo·dle /ˈlabrəˌdo͞odl/ ▶ **n.** a dog resulting from a cross between a Labrador and a standard poodle.

Lab·ra·dor[1] /ˈlabrəˌdôr/ a coastal region of eastern Canada that forms the mainland part of the province of Newfoundland and Labrador.

Lab·ra·dor[2] (also **Labrador retriever**) ▶ **n.** a retriever of a breed that predominantly has a black or yellow coat, widely used as a gun dog or as a guide for a blind person.
– ORIGIN early 20th cent.: named after the **LABRADOR PENINSULA**, where the breed was developed. The name *Labrador dog* had been applied in the 19th cent. to a much larger breed, similar to the Newfoundland.

Labrador retriever

Lab·ra·dor Cur·rent a cold ocean current that flows south from the Arctic Ocean along the northeastern coast of North America. It meets the warm Gulf Stream in an area off the coast of Newfoundland that is noted for dense fogs.

lab·ra·dor·ite /ˈlabrədôˌrīt/ ▶ **n.** a mineral of the plagioclase feldspar group, found in many igneous rocks.
– ORIGIN early 19th cent.: from **LABRADOR PENINSULA**, where it was found, + **-ITE**[1].

Lab·ra·dor Pen·in·su·la a broad peninsula in eastern Canada, between Hudson Bay, the Atlantic Ocean, and the Gulf of St. Lawrence. Consisting of the Ungava Peninsula and Labrador, it contains most of Quebec and the mainland part of the province of Newfoundland and Labrador. Also called **Labrador-Ungava.**

Lab·ra·dor Sea a section of the Atlantic Ocean between Labrador and southern Greenland, noted for its icebergs.

Lab·ra·dor tea ▶ **n.** a low-growing northern shrub of the heath family, with fragrant leathery evergreen leaves that are sometimes used as a tea substitute. ● *Ledum groenlandicum*, family Ericaceae.

la·bret /ˈlābret, -brit/ ▶ **n.** an object such as a small piece of shell, bone, or stone inserted into the lip as an ornament in some cultures.
– ORIGIN mid 19th cent.: diminutive of **LABRUM.**

la·brum /ˈlābrəm, ˈlabrəm/ ▶ **n.** (pl. **labra** /ˈlābrə, ˈlabrə/) Zoology a structure corresponding to a lip, esp. the upper border of the mouthparts of a crustacean or insect.
– DERIVATIVES **la·bral** /ˈlābrəl/ **adj.**
– ORIGIN early 18th cent.: from Latin, literally 'lip'; related to **LABIUM.**

la·bru·sca /ləˈbrəskə/ ▶ **n.** another term for **FOX GRAPE**: [as modifier] *labrusca grapes.* ■ a wine made from this grape.
– ORIGIN from Latin *labrusca*, denoting a wild vine.

La·bu·an /ləˈbo͞oən/ a small Malaysian island off the northern coast of Borneo; pop. 85,000 (2009); capital, Victoria.

la·bur·num /ləˈbərnəm/ ▶ **n.** a small European tree that has hanging clusters of yellow flowers succeeded by slender pods containing poisonous seeds. The hard timber is sometimes used as an ebony substitute. Native to Central and Southern Europe, laburnums have been widely planted as ornamentals. ● Genus *Laburnum*, family Leguminosae.
– ORIGIN modern Latin.

lab·y·rinth /ˈlab(ə)ˌrinTH/ ▶ **n. 1** a complicated irregular network of passages or paths in which it is difficult to find one's way; a maze: ***a labyrinth of passages and secret chambers.*** ■ an intricate and confusing arrangement: ***a labyrinth of*** *conflicting laws and regulations.*
2 Anatomy a complex structure in the inner ear that contains the organs of hearing and balance. It consists of bony cavities (the **bony labyrinth**) filled with fluid and lined with sensitive membranes (the **membranous labyrinth**). ■ Zoology an organ of intricate structure, in particular the accessory respiratory organs of certain fishes.
– DERIVATIVES **lab·y·rin·thi·an** /ˌlabəˈrinTHēən/ **adj.**
– ORIGIN late Middle English (referring to the maze constructed by Daedalus to house the Minotaur): from French *labyrinthe* or Latin *labyrinthus*, from Greek *laburinthos*.

labyrinth 1

lab·y·rinth fish ▶ **n.** a freshwater fish with poorly developed gills and a labyrinthine accessory breathing organ, native to Africa and Asia. ● Suborder Anabantoidei: Belontiidae and related families, with many species, including such popular aquarium fishes as the gouramis and the fighting fish.

lab·y·rin·thine /ˌlabəˈrinˌTHēn, -ˈrinTHin, -ˈrinˌTHīn/ ▶ **adj.** (of a network) like a labyrinth; irregular and twisting: *labyrinthine streets and alleys.* ■ (of a system) intricate and confusing: *labyrinthine plots and counterplots.*

lab·y·rin·thi·tis /ˌlabərənˈTHītis/ ▶ **n.** Medicine inflammation of the labyrinth or inner ear.

lab·y·rin·tho·dont /ˌlabəˈrinTHəˌdänt/ ▶ **adj.** Zoology (of teeth) having the enamel deeply folded to form a labyrinthine structure. ■ Paleontology of or relating to a group of large fossil amphibians of the late Devonian to early Triassic periods having such teeth.
▶ **n.** a labyrinthodont amphibian. ● Former subclass Labyrinthodontia: several families, but no longer considered to be a single group.
– ORIGIN mid 19th cent.: from modern Latin *Labyrinthodontia*, from Greek *laburinthos* 'labyrinth' + *odous, odont-* 'tooth.'

lac[1] /lak/ ▶ **n.** a resinous substance secreted as a protective covering by the lac insect, used to make varnish, shellac, sealing wax, dyes, etc.
– ORIGIN late Middle English: from medieval Latin *lac, lac(c)a*, from Portuguese *laca*, based on Hindi *lākh* or Persian *lāk*.

lac[2] ▶ **adj.** [attrib.] Biology denoting the ability of normal strains of the bacterium *E. coli* to metabolize lactose, or the genetic factors involved in this ability (which is lost in some mutant strains).
– ORIGIN 1940s: abbreviation of **LACTOSE.**

lac[3] ▶ **n.** variant spelling of **LAKH.**

La·can /läˈkän/, Jacques (1901–81), French psychoanalyst and writer. A notable poststructuralist, he reinterpreted Freudian psychoanalysis, esp. the theory of the unconscious, in the light of structural linguistics and anthropology.
– DERIVATIVES **La·can·i·an** /ləˈkānēən, -ˈkan-/ **adj. & n.**, **La·can·i·an·ism** /ləˈkānēəˌnizəm, -ˈkan-/ **n.**

Lac·ca·dive Is·lands /ˈlakəˌdīv/ one of the groups of islands that form the Indian Union Territory of Lakshadweep in the Indian Ocean.

lac·co·lith /ˈlakəˌliTH/ ▶ **n.** Geology a mass of igneous rock, typically lens-shaped, that has been intruded between rock strata causing uplift in the shape of a dome.
– ORIGIN late 19th cent.: from Greek *lakkos* 'reservoir' + **-LITH.**

lace /lās/ ▶ **n. 1** a fine open fabric, typically one of cotton or silk, made by looping, twisting, or knitting thread in patterns and used esp. for trimming garments. ■ braid used for trimming, esp. on military dress uniforms.
2 (usu. **laces**) a cord or leather strip passed through eyelets or hooks on opposite sides of a shoe or garment and then pulled tight and fastened.
▶ **v.** [with obj.] **1** fasten or tighten (a shoe or garment) by tying its laces: *he put the shoes on and **laced them up.*** ■ (**lace someone into**) fasten someone into (a garment) by tightening the laces: *Morris laced Bill and David into boxing gloves.* ■ (**lace something through**) pass a lace or cord through (a hole). ■ compress the waist of (someone) with a laced corset: *Rosina **laced her up tight** to show off her neat, pretty waist.* ■ [no obj.] (of a garment or shoe) be fastened by means of laces: *the shoes laced at the front.*
2 entwine or tangle (things, esp. fingers) together: *he laced his fingers together and sat back.*
3 (usu. **be laced with**) add an ingredient, esp. alcohol, to (a drink or dish) to enhance its flavor or strength: *he gave us coffee laced with brandy* | figurative *his voice was laced with derision.*
4 hit (something, esp. a baseball) hard: *he laced a double down the first-base line.*
– PHRASAL VERBS **lace into** informal assail or tackle (something): *Marion laced into her opponent with a blistering criticism.*
– ORIGIN Middle English: from Old French *laz, las* (noun), *lacier* (verb), based on Latin *laqueus* 'noose' (also an early sense in English). Compare with **LASSO.**

lace·bark /ˈlāsˌbärk/ ▶ **n.** any of a number of trees or shrubs that possess a lacy bark or inner bark, in particular: ● an evergreen Caribbean shrub with a lacy inner bark that is used ornamentally (*Lagetta lagetto*, family Thymelaeaceae). ● a small ornamental New Zealand tree (genus *Hoheria*, family Malvaceae).

lace bug ▶ **n.** a small plant-eating bug that has a raised netlike pattern on the wings and upper surface. ● Family Tingidae, suborder Heteroptera: several genera.

lace-cur·tain ▶ **adj.** informal having social pretensions; self-consciously genteel: *the fancy sons of lace-curtain Boston lawyers.*

-laced /lāst/ ▶ **adj.** [in combination] contaminated with a substance (usually harmful or toxic) present in small amounts: *dioxin-laced sludge | anthrax-laced letters.*

Lac·e·dae·mo·ni·an /ˌlasədəˈmōnēən/ ▶ **n.** a native or inhabitant of Lacedaemon, an area of ancient Greece comprising the city of Sparta and its surroundings.
▶ **adj.** of Lacedaemon or its inhabitants; Spartan.

lace·mak·ing /ˈlās,mākiNG/ ▶ **n.** the activity of making lace.
– DERIVATIVES **lace·mak·er** /-ˌmākər/ **n.**

lace pil·low ▶ **n.** a hard cushion placed on the lap to provide support in lacemaking.

lac·er·ate /ˈlasə,rāt/ ▶ **v.** [with obj.] tear or deeply cut (something, esp. flesh or skin): *the point had lacerated his neck* | (as adj. **lacerated**) *his badly lacerated hands and knees* | figurative *an assertion calculated to lacerate nobody's feelings.*
– ORIGIN late Middle English: from Latin *lacerat-* 'mangled,' from the verb *lacerare,* from *lacer* 'mangled, torn.'

lac·er·a·tion /ˌlasəˈrāSHən/ ▶ **n.** a deep cut or tear, esp. in skin; a gash: *he suffered lacerations to his head and face.* ■ the action of making such a cut.

La·cer·ta /ləˈsərtə/ Astronomy a small and inconspicuous northern constellation (the Lizard), on the edge of the Milky Way between Cygnus and Andromeda. ■ (as genitive **Lacertae** /ləˈsərtē/) used with a preceding letter or numeral to designate a star in this constellation: *the star Alpha Lacertae.*
– ORIGIN Latin.

la·cer·tid /ləˈsərtid/ ▶ **n.** Zoology a lizard of a large family (Lacertidae) to which most European lizards belong.
– ORIGIN late 19th cent.: from modern Latin *Lacertidae* (plural), from Latin *lacerta* 'lizard.'

Lac·er·til·i·a /ˌlasərˈtilēə, -ˈtilyə/ Zoology a group of reptiles that comprises the lizards. Also called SAURIA. ● Suborder Lacertilia (or Sauria), order Squamata.
– ORIGIN modern Latin (plural), from Latin *lacerta* 'lizard.'

lac·er·til·i·an /ˌlasərˈtilēən, -ˈtilyən/ Zoology ▶ **n.** a reptile of the suborder Lacertilia; a lizard.
▶ **adj.** relating to or denoting lacertilians.

lace-up ▶ **adj.** (of a shoe or garment) fastened with laces: *flat lace-up shoes.*
▶ **n.** chiefly Brit. a shoe or boot that is fastened with laces: *brown leather lace-ups.*

lace·wing /ˈlās,wiNG/ ▶ **n.** a slender, delicate insect with large clear membranous wings. Both the adults and larvae are typically predators of aphids. ● Several families in the order Neuroptera, in particular Chrysopidae (the **green lacewings**).

lace·wood /ˈlās,wo͝od/ ▶ **n.** the timber of the plane tree.

lace·work /ˈlās,wərk/ ▶ **n.** lace fabric and other items made of lace viewed collectively. ■ the process of making lace.

lach·es /ˈlaCHiz/ ▶ **n.** Law unreasonable delay in making an assertion or claim, such as asserting a right, claiming a privilege, or making an application for redress, which may result in refusal.
– ORIGIN late Middle English (in the sense 'slackness, negligence'): from Old French *laschesse,* from *lasche* 'loose, lax,' based on Latin *laxus.* The current sense dates from the late 16th cent.

Lach·e·sis /ˈlakəsis/ Greek Mythology one of the three Fates.
– ORIGIN Greek, literally 'obtaining by lot.'

Lach·lan /ˈläklən/ a river of New South Wales in Australia that rises in the Great Dividing Range and flows about 920 miles (1,472 km) northwest and then southwest to join the Murrumbidgee River near the border with Victoria.
– ORIGIN named after *Lachlan* Macquarie (1761–1824), the governor of New South Wales 1809–21.

lach·ry·mal /ˈlakrəməl/ (also **lacrimal** or **lacrymal**) ▶ **adj. 1** formal or literary connected with weeping or tears.
2 (usu. **lacrimal**) Physiology & Anatomy concerned with the secretion of tears: *lacrimal cells.*
▶ **n. 1** (usu. **lacrimal** or **lacrimal bone**) Anatomy a small bone forming part of the eye socket.
2 short for LACHRYMAL VASE.
– ORIGIN late Middle English (in sense 2 of the adjective): from medieval Latin *lachrymalis,* from Latin *lacrima* 'tear.'

lach·ry·mal vase ▶ **n.** historical a vial holding the tears of mourners at a funeral.

lach·ry·ma·tion /ˌlakrəˈmāSHən/ (also **lacrimation** or **lacrymation**) ▶ **n.** literary or Medicine the flow of tears.
– ORIGIN late 16th cent.: from Latin *lacrimatio(n-),* from *lacrimare* 'weep,' from *lacrima* 'tear.'

lach·ry·ma·tor /ˈlakrə,mātər/ (also **lacrimator**) ▶ **n.** chiefly Medicine a substance that irritates the eyes and causes tears to flow.

lach·ry·ma·to·ry /ˈlakrəmə,tôrē/ (also **lacrimatory**) ▶ **adj.** technical or literary relating to, tending to cause, or containing tears: *a lachrymatory secretion.*
▶ **n.** (pl. **lachrymatories**) a vial of a kind found in ancient Roman tombs and thought to be a lachrymal vase.
– ORIGIN mid 17th cent. (as a noun denoting a vial): from Latin *lacrima,* on the pattern of *chrismatory.*

lach·ry·mose /ˈlakrə,mōs, -,mōz/ ▶ **adj.** formal or literary tearful or given to weeping: *she was pink-eyed and lachrymose.* ■ inducing tears; sad: *a lachrymose children's classic.*
– DERIVATIVES **lach·ry·mose·ly adv., lach·ry·mos·i·ty** /ˌlakrəˈmäsətē/ **n.**
– ORIGIN mid 17th cent. (in the sense 'like tears; liable to exude in drops'): from Latin *lacrimosus,* from *lacrima* 'tear.'

lac·ing /ˈlāsiNG/ ▶ **n. 1** the laced fastening of a shoe or garment. ■ lace trimming, esp. on a uniform.
2 a dash of liquor added to a drink: *coffee to which he added a liberal lacing of brandy.*

la·cin·i·ate /ləˈsinē,āt, -ē-it/ (also **laciniated** /-,ātid/) ▶ **adj.** Botany & Zoology divided into deep narrow irregular segments.
– ORIGIN mid 18th cent.: from Latin *lacinia* 'fringe, hem, flap of a garment' + -ATE[2].

lac in·sect /ˈlak ˈin,sekt/ ▶ **n.** an Asian scale insect that lives on trees and produces secretions that are used in the production of shellac. ● *Laccifer lacca,* family Lacciferidae, suborder Homoptera.

lack /lak/ ▶ **n.** the state of being without or not having enough of something: *the case was dismissed **for lack of** evidence | there is **no lack of** entertainment aboard ship* | [in sing.] *there is a lack of parking space in the town.*
▶ **v.** [with obj.] be without or deficient in: *the novel lacks imagination* | [no obj.] *she **lacks in** patience | Sam did not **lack for** friends.*
– ORIGIN Middle English: corresponding to, and perhaps partly from, Middle Dutch and Middle Low German *lak* 'deficiency,' Middle Dutch *laken* 'lack, blame.'

lack·a·dai·si·cal /ˌlakəˈdāzikəl/ ▶ **adj.** lacking enthusiasm and determination; carelessly lazy: *a lackadaisical defense left the Spurs adrift in the second half.*
– DERIVATIVES **lack·a·dai·si·cal·ly adv.**
– ORIGIN mid 18th cent. (also in the sense 'feebly sentimental'): from the archaic interjection *lackaday, lackadaisy* (see ALACK) + -ICAL.

lack·a·day /ˈlakə,dā/ ▶ **exclam.** archaic an expression of surprise, regret, or grief.
– ORIGIN late 17th cent.: shortening of *alack-a-day.*

Lack·a·wan·na /lakəˈwänə/ an industrial city in western New York, on Lake Erie, west of Buffalo; pop. 17,588 (est. 2008).

lack·ey /ˈlakē/ ▶ **n.** (pl. **lackeys**) a servant, esp. a liveried footman or manservant. ■ derogatory a person who is obsequiously willing to obey or serve another person or group of people.
▶ **v.** (also **lacquey**) (**lackeys, lackeying, lackeyed**) [with obj.] archaic behave servilely to; wait upon as a lackey.
– ORIGIN early 16th cent.: from French *laquais,* perhaps from Catalan *alacay,* from Arabic *al-kā'id* 'the chief.'

lack·ing /ˈlakiNG/ ▶ **adj.** [predic.] not available or in short supply: *adequate resources and funds are both sadly lacking at present.* ■ (of a quality) missing or absent: *there was something lacking in our marriage.* ■ deficient or inadequate: *the students are not **lacking in** intellectual ability | workers were asked in what way they **found** their managers **lacking.***

lack·lus·ter /ˈlak,ləstər/ (Brit. **lacklustre**) ▶ **adj.** lacking in vitality, force, or conviction; uninspired or uninspiring: *no excuses were made for the team's lackluster performance.* ■ (of the hair or the eyes) not shining; dull.

Lac Lé·man /läk leˈmän/ French name for Lake Geneva (see GENEVA, LAKE).

La·co·ni·a /ləˈkōnēə, -ˈkōnyə/ (also **Lakonia**) a modern department and an ancient region of Greece, in the southeastern Peloponnese. Throughout the classical period the region was dominated by its capital, Sparta.
– DERIVATIVES **La·co·ni·an adj. & n.**

la·con·ic /ləˈkänik/ ▶ **adj.** (of a person, speech, or style of writing) using very few words: *his laconic reply suggested a lack of interest in the topic.*
– DERIVATIVES **la·con·i·cal·ly** /-(ə)lē/ **adv., la·con·i·cism** /ləˈkänə,sizəm/ **n., lac·o·nism** /ˈlakə,nizəm/ **n.**
– ORIGIN mid 16th cent. (in the sense 'Laconian'): via Latin from Greek *Lakōnikos,* from *Lakōn* 'Laconia, Sparta,' the Spartans being known for their terse speech.

La Co·ru·ña /ˌlä kəˈro͞onyə/ Spanish name for CORUNNA.

lac·quer /ˈlakər/ ▶ **n. 1** a liquid made of shellac dissolved in alcohol, or of synthetic substances, that dries to form a hard protective coating for wood, metal, etc. ■ (also **hair lacquer**) British term for HAIR SPRAY.
2 the sap of the lacquer tree used to varnish wood or other materials. ■ decorative objects made of wood coated with lacquer: [as modifier] *a small lacquer box.*
▶ **v.** [with obj.] (often as adj. **lacquered**) coat with lacquer: *choose from brushed or lacquered copper.*
– DERIVATIVES **lac·quer·er n.**
– ORIGIN late 16th cent. (denoting lac): from obsolete French *lacre* 'sealing wax,' from Portuguese *laca* (see LAC[1]).

lac·quer tree ▶ **n.** an eastern Asian tree with white sap that turns dark on exposure to air, producing a hard-wearing varnish traditionally used in lacquerware. ● *Rhus verniciflua,* family Anacardiaceae.

lac·quer·ware /ˈlakər,we(ə)r/ ▶ **n.** articles that have a decorative lacquer coating, viewed collectively.

lac·quer·work /ˈlakər,wərk/ ▶ **n.** lacquerware. ■ the design, construction, or finish of lacquerware.

lac·quey ▶ **n. & v.** archaic spelling of LACKEY.

lac·ri·mal ▶ **adj. & n.** variant spelling of LACHRYMAL.

lac·ri·ma·tion ▶ **n.** variant spelling of LACHRYMATION.

lac·ri·ma·tor ▶ **n.** variant spelling of LACHRYMATOR.

lac·ri·ma·to·ry ▶ **adj. & n.** variant spelling of LACHRYMATORY.

la·crosse /ləˈkrôs, -ˈkräs/ ▶ **n.** a team game, originally played by North American Indians, in which the ball is thrown, caught, and carried with a long-handled stick having a curved L-shaped or triangular frame at one end with a piece of shallow netting in the angle.
– ORIGIN mid 19th cent.: from French (*le jeu de*) *la crosse* '(the game of) the hooked stick.' Compare with CROSSE.

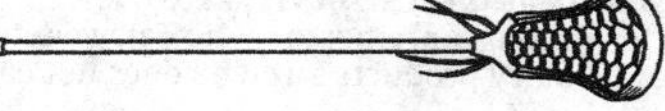

lacrosse stick

La Crosse /lə ˈkrôs, ˈkräs/ an industrial and commercial city in western Wisconsin, on the Mississippi River; pop. 50,902 (est. 2008).

lac·ry·mal ▶ **adj. & n.** variant spelling of LACHRYMAL.

lac·ry·ma·tion ▶ **n.** variant spelling of LACHRYMATION.

lac·tal·bu·min /ˌlak,talˈbyo͞omin/ ▶ **n.** Biochemistry a protein or mixture of similar proteins occurring in milk, obtained after the removal of casein and soluble in a salt solution.
– ORIGIN late 19th cent.: from LACTO- 'of milk' + ALBUMIN.

lac·tam /ˈlak,tam/ ▶ **n.** Chemistry an organic compound containing an amide group –NHCO– as part of a ring.
– ORIGIN late 19th cent.: blend of LACTONE and AMIDE.

lac·tar·i·us /lakˈte(ə)rēəs/ ▶ **n.** a large woodland mushroom with a concave cap, the flesh exuding a white or colored milky fluid when cut. ● Genus *Lactarius,* family Russulaceae, class Hymenomycetes: several species, including the edible **orange milk lactarius** (*L. deliciosus*).

lac·tase /ˈlak,tās, -tāz/ ▶ **n.** Biochemistry an enzyme that catalyzes the hydrolysis of lactose to glucose and galactose.
– ORIGIN late 19th cent.: from LACTOSE + -ASE.

lac·tate[1] /ˈlak,tāt/ ▶ **v.** [no obj.] (of a female mammal) secrete milk.
– ORIGIN late 19th cent.: back-formation from LACTATION.

lac·tate[2] ▶ **n.** Chemistry a salt or ester of lactic acid.
– ORIGIN late 18th cent.: from LACTIC + -ATE[1].

lac·ta·tion /lakˈtāSHən/ ▶ **n.** the secretion of milk by the mammary glands. ■ the suckling of young.
– DERIVATIVES **lac·ta·tion·al** /-ˈtāSHənl/ **adj.**
– ORIGIN mid 17th cent.: from Latin *lactatio(n-),* from *lactare* 'suckle,' from *lac, lact-* 'milk.'

lac·te·al /ˈlaktēəl/ ▶ **adj.** of milk. ■ Anatomy (of a vessel) conveying chyle or other milky fluid.

PRONUNCIATION KEY ə *ago, up;* ər *over, fur;* a *hat;* ā *ate;* ä *car;* e *let;* ē *see;* i *fit;* ī *by;* NG *sing;* ō *go;* ô *law, for;* oi *toy;* o͝o *good;* o͞o *goo;* ou *out;* TH *thin;* T͟H *then;* ZH *vision*

▶ plural n. (**lacteals**) Anatomy the lymphatic vessels of the small intestine that absorb digested fats.
– ORIGIN mid 17th cent.: from Latin *lacteus* (from *lac, lact-* 'milk') + **-AL**.

lac·tes·cent /lak'tesənt/ ▶ adj. milky in appearance. ■ Botany yielding a milky latex.
– ORIGIN mid 17th cent.: from Latin *lactescent-* 'being milky,' from the verb *lactere,* from *lac, lact-* 'milk.'

lac·tic /'laktik/ ▶ adj. of, relating to, or obtained from milk.
– ORIGIN late 18th cent.: from Latin *lac, lact-* 'milk' + **-IC**.

lac·tic ac·id ▶ n. Biochemistry a colorless syrupy organic acid formed in sour milk and produced in the muscle tissues during strenuous exercise. • Chem. formula: $CH_3CH(OH)COOH$.

lac·tif·er·ous /lak'tif(ə)rəs/ ▶ adj. chiefly Anatomy forming or conveying milk or milky fluid: *lactiferous ducts*.
– ORIGIN late 17th cent.: from Latin *lac, lact-* 'milk' + **-FEROUS**.

lacto- ▶ comb. form **1** of or relating to milk: *lactometer*.
2 from or relating to lactic acid or lactose: *lactobacillus*.
– ORIGIN from Latin *lac, lact-* 'milk.'

lac·to·ba·cil·lus /ˌlaktōbə'siləs/ ▶ n. (pl. **lactobacilli** /-'siˌlī, -'siˌlē/) Biology a rod-shaped bacterium that produces lactic acid from the fermentation of carbohydrates. • Genus *Lactobacillus*; nonmotile Gram-postive bacteria.

lac·to·fer·rin /ˌlaktō'ferin, -tə-/ ▶ n. Biochemistry a protein present in milk and other secretions, with bactericidal and iron-binding properties.

lac·to·fla·vin /ˌlaktō'flāvin, 'laktōˌflāvin/ ▶ n. Brit. another term for **RIBOFLAVIN**.

lac·to·gen·ic /ˌlaktə'jenik/ ▶ adj. Physiology (of a hormone or other substance) inducing the secretion of milk.

lac·to·glob·u·lin /ˌlaktō'gläbyəlin/ ▶ n. Biochemistry a protein or mixture of similar proteins occurring in milk, obtained after the removal of casein and precipitated in a salt solution.

lac·tom·e·ter /lak'tämətər/ ▶ n. an instrument for measuring the density of milk.

lac·tone /'lakˌtōn/ ▶ n. Chemistry an organic compound containing an ester group –OCO– as part of a ring.

lac·to-o·vo-veg·e·tar·i·an /ˌlaktōˌōvō-ˌvejə'te(ə)rēən/ ▶ n. a person who eats vegetables, eggs, and dairy products but who does not eat meat.

lac·to·pro·tein /ˌlaktō'prōˌtēn/ ▶ n. the protein component of milk.

lac·tose /'lakˌtōs, -ˌtōz/ ▶ n. Chemistry a sugar present in milk. It is a disaccharide containing glucose and galactose units.

lac·to·veg·e·tar·i·an /'laktōˌvejə'te(ə)rēən/ ▶ n. a person who abstains from eating meat and eggs, but who eats dairy products.

lac·tu·lose /'lakt(y)əˌlōs, -ˌlōz/ ▶ n. Chemistry a synthetic sugar with laxative properties. It is a disaccharide consisting of glucose and fructose units.
– ORIGIN 1930s: from **LACTO-** 'of milk,' perhaps on the pattern of *cellulose*.

la·cu·na /lə'k(y)o͞onə/ ▶ n. (pl. **lacunae** /-nī, -nē/ or **lacunas**) an unfilled space or interval; a gap: *the journal has filled a lacuna in Middle Eastern studies*. ■ a missing portion in a book or manuscript. ■ Anatomy a cavity or depression, esp. in bone.
– DERIVATIVES **la·cu·nal** /lə'k(y)o͞onl/ adj., **la·cu·nar·y** /'lakyəˌnerē, lə'k(y)o͞onərē/ adj., **la·cu·nate** /'lakyəˌnāt, -nit/ adj., **la·cu·nose** /'lakyəˌnōs, -ˌnōz/ adj.
– ORIGIN mid 17th cent.: from Latin, 'pool,' from *lacus* 'lake.'

la·cu·nar¹ /lə'k(y)o͞onər/ ▶ adj. of or relating to a lacuna.

la·cu·nar² ▶ n. a vault or ceiling consisting of recessed panels. ■ a panel in such a vault or ceiling.

la·cus·trine /lə'kəstrin/ ▶ adj. technical or literary of, relating to, or associated with lakes.
– ORIGIN early 19th cent.: from Latin *lacus* 'lake' (the stem *lacustr-* influenced by Latin *palustris* 'marshy') + **-INE¹**.

lac·y /'lāsē/ ▶ adj. (**lacier, laciest**) made of, resembling, or trimmed with lace: *a lacy petticoat*.
– DERIVATIVES **lac·i·ly** /-səlē/ adv., **lac·i·ness** n.

lad /lad/ ▶ n. **1** informal a boy or young man (often as a form of address): *I read that book when I was a lad* | *come in, lad, and shut the door*. ■ (**lads**) chiefly Brit. a group of men sharing recreational, working, or other interests: *she wouldn't let him go out with **the lads** anymore*. ■ Brit. a man who is boisterously macho in his behavior or actions, esp. one who is interested in sexual conquest: *Tony was **a bit of a lad**—always had an eye for the women*.
2 Brit. a stable worker (regardless of age or sex).
– ORIGIN Middle English: of unknown origin.

La·dakh /lə'däk/ a high-altitude region in northwestern India, Pakistan, and China that contains the Ladakh and Karakoram mountain ranges and the upper Indus valley.

La·da·khi /lə'däkē/ ▶ n. (pl. **Ladakhis**) **1** a native or inhabitant of Ladakh.
2 the Tibetan dialect of this people.
▶ adj. of or relating to Ladakh, the Ladakhis, or their language.
– ORIGIN the name in Ladakhi.

lad·a·num /'ladn-əm, 'ladnəm/ ▶ n. variant spelling of **LABDANUM**.

lad·der /'ladər/ ▶ n. **1** a structure consisting of a series of bars or steps between two upright lengths of wood, metal, or rope, used for climbing up or down something. ■ a series of ascending stages by which someone or something may advance or progress: *employees on their way up the career ladder*.
2 Brit. (in tights or stockings) a run.
▶ v. Brit. (with reference to tights or stockings) develop or cause to develop a run.
– ORIGIN Old English *hlǣd(d)er,* of West Germanic origin; related to Dutch *leer* and German *Leiter*.

lad·der-back (also **ladder-back chair**) ▶ n. an upright chair with a back resembling a ladder.

lad·der stitch ▶ n. a stitch in embroidery consisting of transverse bars.

lad·der tour·na·ment ▶ n. a sporting contest in which the participants are listed in ranking order and can move up by defeating the contestant above.

lad·die /'ladē/ ▶ n. informal, chiefly Scottish a boy or young man (often as a form of address): *he's just a wee laddie*.

lad·dish /'ladisн/ ▶ adj. Brit. characteristic of a young man who behaves in a boisterously macho manner.
– DERIVATIVES **lad·dish·ness** n.

lad·du /'lədo͞o/ ▶ n. (pl. **laddus**) an Indian confection, typically made from flour, sugar, and shortening, that is shaped into a ball.
– ORIGIN from Hindi *laḍḍū*.

lade /lād/ ▶ v. (past participle **laden** /'lādn/) [with obj.] archaic load (a ship or other vessel). ■ ship (goods) as cargo. ■ [no obj.] (of a ship) take on cargo.
– ORIGIN Old English *hladan,* of West Germanic origin; related to Dutch and German *laden* 'to load,' also to **LADLE** and perhaps to **LATHE**.

lad·en /'lādn/ ▶ adj. heavily loaded or weighed down: *a tree laden with apples* | [in combination] *the moisture-laden air*.
– ORIGIN late 16th cent.: past participle of **LADE**.

lad·ette /la'det/ ▶ n. Brit. informal a young woman who behaves in a boisterously assertive or crude manner and engages in heavy drinking.
– ORIGIN 1990s: from *lad* + *-ette*.

la-di-da /ˌlä dē 'dä/ (also **lah-di-dah** or **la-de-da**) informal ▶ adj. pretentious or snobbish, esp. in manner or speech: *do I really look or sound like a la-di-da society lawyer?*
– ORIGIN late 19th cent.: imitative of an affected manner of speech.

la·dies /'lādēz/ plural form of **LADY**.

la·dies chain ▶ n. a figure in a square dance or other dance.

la·dies' man (also **lady's man**) ▶ n. [in sing.] informal a man who enjoys spending time and flirting with women.

la·dies' night ▶ n. a time at a bar or nightclub when women are charged less or admitted free. ■ a function at a men's institution or club to which women are invited.

la·dies' room ▶ n. a restroom for women in a public or institutional building.

la·dies' tress·es (also **lady's tresses**) ▶ plural n. [usu. treated as sing.] a short orchid with small white flowers arranged in a single or double spiral, growing chiefly in north temperate regions. • Genus *Spiranthes* (and *Goodyera*), family Orchidaceae: several species, including the **slender ladies' tresses** (*S. gracilis*) of North America.

La·din /lə'dēn/ ▶ n. the Rhaeto-Romanic dialect of the Engadine in Switzerland.
– ORIGIN mid 19th cent.: from Latin *Latinus* (see **LATIN**).

lad·ing /'lādiNG/ ▶ n. archaic the action or process of loading a ship or other vessel with cargo. ■ a cargo.

La·di·no /lə'dēnō/ ▶ n. (pl. **Ladinos**) **1** the language of some Sephardic Jews, esp. formerly in Mediterranean countries. It is based on medieval Spanish, with an admixture of Hebrew, Greek, and Turkish words, and is written in modified Hebrew characters. Also called **JUDEZMO**.
2 a mestizo or Spanish-speaking white person in Central America.
– ORIGIN Spanish, from Latin *Latinus* (see **LATIN**).

la·di·no /lə'dīnō, -'dēnō/ ▶ n. (pl. **ladinos**) a white clover of a large variety native to Italy and cultivated for fodder in North America.
– ORIGIN 1920s: from Italian.

Lad·is·laus I /'lädisˌlôs/ (*c*.1040–95), king of Hungary 1077–95; canonized as **St. Ladislaus**. He extended Hungarian power and advanced the spread of Christianity. Feast day, June 27.

Lad·is·laus II (*c*.1351–1434), king of Poland 1386–1434; Polish name **Władysław**. As grand duke of Lithuania, he came to the Polish throne upon his marriage to the Polish monarch, **Queen Jadwiga**, thus uniting Lithuania and Poland.

la·dle /'lādl/ ▶ n. a large long-handled spoon with a cup-shaped bowl, used for serving soup, stew, or sauce. ■ a vessel for transporting molten metal in a foundry.
▶ v. [with obj.] serve (soup, stew, or sauce) with a ladle: *she ladled out onion soup*. ■ provide (information, advice, etc.) lavishly or overgenerously: *he was **ladling out** his personal philosophy of life*.
– DERIVATIVES **la·dle·ful** /-ˌfo͝ol/ n. (pl. **ladlefuls**), **la·dler** n.
– ORIGIN Old English *hlædel,* from *hladan* (see **LADE**).

Lad·o·ga, Lake /'lädəgə, 'lad-/ a lake in northwestern Russia, northeast of St. Petersburg, near the border with Finland. It is the largest lake in Europe, with an area of 6,837 square miles (17,700 sq km).

lad's love ▶ n. another term for **SOUTHERNWOOD**.

la·dy /'lādē/ ▶ n. (pl. **ladies**) **1** a woman (used as a polite or old-fashioned form of reference): *I spoke to the lady at the travel agency* | [as modifier] *a lady doctor*. ■ (**the Ladies**) Brit. a women's public toilet. ■ an informal, often brusque, form of address to a woman: *I'm sorry, lady, but you have the wrong number*.
2 a woman of superior social position, esp. one of noble birth: *lords and ladies and royalty were once entertained at the house*. ■ a courteous, decorous, or genteel woman: *his wife was a real lady, with such nice manners*. ■ (**Lady**) (in the UK) a title used by peeresses, female relatives of peers, the wives and widows of knights, etc.: *Lady Caroline Lamb*.
3 (**one's lady**) dated a man's wife: *welcoming the vice president and his lady*. ■ (also **lady friend**) a woman with whom a man is romantically or sexually involved: *the young man bought a rose for his lady*. ■ historical a woman to whom a man, esp. a knight, is chivalrously devoted.
– PHRASES **it isn't over till the fat lady sings** used to convey that there is still time for a situation to change. [by association with the final aria in tragic opera.] **ladies who lunch** informal or often derogatory women with both the means and the free time to meet each other socially for lunch in expensive restaurants. **Lady Bountiful** a woman who engages in ostentatious acts of charity, more to impress others than out of a sense of concern for those in need. [early 19th cent.: from the name of a character in Farquhar's *The Beaux' Stratagem* (1707).] **Lady Luck** chance personified as a controlling power in human affairs: *it seemed Lady Luck was still smiling on them*. **Lady Muck** Brit. informal a haughty or pretentious woman (often as a mocking form of address). **lady of the house** a woman at the head of a household: *he always asked the lady of the house the shade of paint she would like*. **My Lady** a polite form of address to certain noblewomen.
– DERIVATIVES **la·dy·hood** /-ˌho͝od/ n.
– ORIGIN Old English *hlǣfdīge* (denoting a woman to whom homage or obedience is due, such as the wife of a lord or the mistress of a household, also specifically the Virgin Mary), from *hlāf* 'loaf' + a Germanic base meaning 'knead,' related to **DOUGH**; compare with **LORD**. In **LADY DAY** and other compounds where it signifies possession, it represents the Old English genitive *hlǣfdīgan* '(Our) Lady's.'

la·dy·bird /'lādēˌbərd/ ▶ n. chiefly Brit. another term for **LADYBUG**.

la·dy·boy /'lādēˌboi/ ▶ n. (esp. in Thailand) a transvestite.

la·dy·bug /'lādēˌbəg/ ▶ n. a small beetle with a domed back, typically red or yellow with black spots. Both the adults and larvae are important predators of aphids. • Family Coccinellidae: several genera and species, including the familiar **convergent ladybug** (*Hippodamia convergens*).

convergent ladybug

La·dy chap·el ▶ **n.** a chapel in a church or cathedral dedicated to the Virgin Mary.

La·dy Day ▶ **n.** March 25, the feast of the Annunciation.
– ORIGIN with reference to *Our Lady*, the Virgin Mary.

la·dy fern ▶ **n.** a tall, graceful fern of worldwide distribution that favors moist shady habitats. ● *Athyrium* and other genera, family Woodsiaceae: several species, in particular *A. filix-femina.*

la·dy·fin·ger /ˈlādēˌfiNGgər/ ▶ **n.** a small finger-shaped sponge cake.

la·dy·fish /ˈlādēˌfisH/ ▶ **n.** (pl. **same** or **ladyfishes**) any of a number of marine fishes of warm, coastal waters, several of which are popular with anglers. ■ the tenpounder. ■ a bonefish.

la·dy-in-wait·ing ▶ **n.** (pl. **ladies-in-waiting**) a woman who attends a queen or princess.

la·dy·kill·er /ˈlādēˌkilər/ ▶ **n.** informal a charming man who is very attractive to women.

la·dy·like /ˈlādēˌlīk/ ▶ **adj.** appropriate for or typical of a well-bred, decorous woman or girl: *it wasn't ladylike to be too interested in men.*
– DERIVATIVES **la·dy·like·ness n.**

la·dy·love /ˈlādēˌləv/ ▶ **n.** dated a female lover or sweetheart: *he could not legally marry his ladylove.*

la·dy of the night ▶ **n.** used euphemistically to refer to a prostitute.

la·dy·ship /ˈlādēˌsHip/ ▶ **n.** (**Her/Your Ladyship**) a respectful form of reference or address to a woman who has a title: *the car is outside, Your Ladyship.* ■ ironic a form of reference or address to a woman thought to be acting in a pretentious or snobbish way: *bow everyone, Her Ladyship's actually gracing us with her presence!*

la·dy's maid ▶ **n.** chiefly historical a maid who attended to the personal needs of her mistress.

la·dy's man ▶ **n.** variant spelling of LADIES' MAN.

la·dy's-slip·per (also **lady's slipper**) ▶ **n.** an orchid of north temperate regions, the flower of which has a lip that is a conspicuous slipper-shaped pouch. ● Genus *Cypripedium*, family Orchidaceae: several species, in particular the large-pouched **showy lady's-slipper** (*C. reginae*), with bicolored (white and rose) flowers, and the **pink lady's-slipper** (*C. acaule*), with a deeply cleft dark pink or (rarely) white pouch.

showy lady's-slipper

la·dy's tress·es ▶ **n.** variant spelling of LADIES' TRESSES.

Laen·nec's cir·rho·sis /läˈneks/ ▶ **n.** Medicine a type of cirrhosis of the liver characterized by a nodular appearance of the liver surface, associated with alcoholism.
– ORIGIN early 19th cent.: named after René T. H. *Laënnec* (1781–1826), the French physician who described the condition.

La·e·trile /ˈlāəˌtril, -trəl/ ▶ **n.** trademark a compound extracted from amygdalin, formerly used controversially to treat cancer.
– ORIGIN 1950s: from a blend of *laevorotatory* (a variant of LEVOROTATORY) and NITRILE.

laevo- ▶ **comb. form** chiefly Brit. alternate spelling of LEVO-.
– ORIGIN from Latin *laevus* 'left.'

lae·vo·ro·ta·to·ry ▶ **adj.** British spelling of LEVOROTATORY.

laev·u·lose ▶ **n.** British spelling of LEVULOSE.

La Farge /lə ˈfärzH, ˈfärj/, John (1835–1910), US artist. He was noted for his panels in St. Thomas' Church in New York City and for the stained glass at the Second Presbyterian Church in Chicago. His paintings include "Manua Our Boatman" (1891). He invented opaline glass.

La·fa·yette[1] /ˌläfēˈet/ **1** an industrial and commercial city in northwestern Indiana; pop. 64,049 (est. 2008).
2 a city in southern Louisiana, an oil industry center in Cajun country; pop. 113,656 (est. 2008).

La·fa·yette[2] /ˌlafēˈet, ˌlafī-, ˌläf-/ (also **La Fayette**), Marie Joseph Paul Yves Roch Gilbert du Motier, Marquis de (1757–1834), French soldier and statesman. He fought alongside the colonists in the American Revolution and commanded the French national guard 1789–91 in the French Revolution.

Laf·fer curve /ˈlafər/ ▶ **n.** Economics a supposed relationship between economic activity and the rate of taxation that suggests the existence of an optimum tax rate that maximizes tax revenue.
– ORIGIN 1970s: named after Arthur *Laffer* (born 1940), American economist.

La Fon·taine /lä fänˈtān, fônˈten/, Jean de (1621–95), French poet. He is chiefly known for *Fables* (1668–94), drawn from oriental, classical, and contemporary sources.

lag[1] /lag/ ▶ **v.** (**lags, lagging, lagged**) [no obj.] **1** fall behind in movement, progress, or development; not keep pace with another or others: *they stopped to wait for one of the children who was lagging behind.*
2 [no obj.] Billiards determine the order of play by striking the cue ball from balk to rebound off the top cushion, first stroke going to the player whose ball comes to rest nearer the bottom cushion.
▶ **n. 1** (also **time lag**) a period of time between one event or phenomenon and another: *there was a time lag between the commission of the crime and its reporting to the police.*
2 Physics a retardation in an electric current or movement.
– DERIVATIVES **lag·ger n.**
– ORIGIN early 16th cent. (as a noun in the sense 'hindmost person (in a game, race, etc.),' also 'dregs'): related to the dialect adjective *lag* (perhaps from a fanciful distortion of LAST[1], or of Scandinavian origin: compare with Norwegian dialect *lagga* 'go slowly').

lag[2] ▶ **v.** (**lags, lagging, lagged**) [with obj.] (usu. **be lagged**) enclose or cover (a boiler, pipes, etc.) with material that provides heat insulation: (as adj. **lagged**) *a lagged hot-water tank.*
▶ **n.** the non-heat-conducting cover of a boiler, pipes, etc.; lagging. ■ a piece of this.
– DERIVATIVES **lag·ger n.**
– ORIGIN late 19th cent.: from earlier *lag* 'piece of insulating cover.'

lag[3] Brit. informal ▶ **n.** a person who has been frequently convicted and sent to prison: *both old lags were sentenced to ten years' imprisonment.*
▶ **v.** (**lags, lagging, lagged**) [with obj.] archaic arrest or send to prison.
– ORIGIN late 16th cent. (as a verb in the sense 'carry off, steal'): of unknown origin. Current senses date from the 19th cent.

lag·an /ˈlagən/ ▶ **n.** archaic (in legal contexts) goods or wreckage lying on the bed of the sea.
– ORIGIN mid 16th cent.: from Old French, perhaps of Scandinavian origin and related to LAY[1].

la·gar /ləˈgär/ ▶ **n.** (pl. **lagares** /-ˈgärās/) (in Spain and Portugal) a large, typically stone trough in which grapes are trod.
– ORIGIN Spanish, from Latin *lacus*, denoting a vat for freshly pressed wine.

lag bolt ▶ **n.** another term for LAG SCREW.

Lag b'O·mer /ˈläg bəˈōmər, ˈbōmər/ ▶ **n.** a Jewish festival held on the 33rd day of the Omer (the period between Passover and Pentecost), traditionally regarded as celebrating the end of a plague in the 2nd century.
– ORIGIN from Hebrew *lāg* (pronunciation of the letters L (*lamed*) and G (*gimel*) symbolizing 33) + *bā* 'in the' + *'ōmer* (see OMER).

la·ge·na /ləˈjēnə/ ▶ **n.** (pl. **lagenae** /-ˈjēˌnē/) Zoology an extension of the saccule of the ear in some vertebrates, corresponding to the cochlear duct in mammals.
– ORIGIN late 19th cent.: from Latin, literally 'flagon,' from Greek *lagunos.*

la·ger /ˈlägər/ ▶ **n.** a kind of beer, effervescent and light in color and body.
– ORIGIN mid 19th cent.: from German *Lagerbier* 'beer brewed for keeping,' from *Lager* 'storehouse.' Compare with LAAGER and LAIR.

La·ger·löf /ˈlägərˌlov, -ˌlœf/, Selma (Ottiliana Lovisa) (1858–1940), Swedish novelist. She became known with the publication of *Gösta Berlings Saga* in 1891. Nobel Prize for Literature (1909).

la·ger lout ▶ **n.** Brit. informal a young man who regularly behaves in an offensive way, typically as a result of excessive drinking.

lag·gard /ˈlagərd/ ▶ **n.** a person who makes slow progress and falls behind others: *there was no time for laggards.*
▶ **adj.** slower than desired or expected: *a bell to summon laggard children to school.*
– DERIVATIVES **lag·gard·ly adj. & adv., lag·gard·ness n.**
– ORIGIN early 18th cent. (as an adjective): from LAG[1].

lagged /lagd/ ▶ **adj.** Economics showing a delayed effect: *a lagged measure of unemployment.*

lag·ging /ˈlagiNG/ ▶ **n.** material providing heat insulation for a boiler, pipes, etc.
– ORIGIN mid 19th cent.: from LAG[2].

La Gio·con·da /ˌlä jōˈkôndə, jōˈkändə/ another name for MONA LISA.

la·gniappe /ˌlanˈyap, ˈlanˌyap/ ▶ **n.** something given as a bonus or extra gift.
– ORIGIN Louisiana French, from Spanish *la ñapa.*

lag·o·morph /ˈlagəˌmôrf/ Zoology ▶ **n.** a mammal of the order Lagomorpha; a hare, rabbit, or pika.
▶ **adj.** relating to or denoting lagomorphs.

Lag·o·mor·pha /ˌlagəˈmôrfə/ Zoology an order of mammals that comprises the hares, rabbits, and pikas. They are distinguished by the possession of double incisor teeth, and were formerly placed with the rodents.
– ORIGIN modern Latin (plural), from Greek *lagōs* 'hare' + *morphē* 'form.'

la·goon /ləˈgo͞on/ ▶ **n.** a stretch of salt water separated from the sea by a low sandbank or coral reef. ■ a small freshwater lake near a larger lake or river. ■ an artificial pool for the treatment of effluent or to accommodate surface water that overflows drains during heavy rain.
– DERIVATIVES **la·goon·al** /-ˈgo͞onl/ **adj.**
– ORIGIN early 17th cent.: from Italian and Spanish *laguna*, from Latin *lacuna* (see LACUNA).

La·gos /ˈläˌgōs, ˈläˌgäs, ˈlägəs/ the chief city of Nigeria, a port on the Gulf of Guinea; pop. 7,439,300 (est. 2007). Originally a slave trade center, it became capital of the newly independent Nigeria in 1960, but was replaced by Abuja in 1991.

La Grande Riv·er /lə ˈgränd, ˈgrand/ a river that flows for 500 miles (800 km) across central Quebec to Hudson Bay.

La·grange /ləˈgränj/, Joseph Louis, Comte de (1736–1813), French mathematician, born in Italy. He proved that every positive integer can be expressed as a sum of at most four square and worked on mechanics and its application to the description of planetary and lunar motion.

La·gran·gi·an point /ləˈgranjēən, -ˈgrän-/ ▶ **n.** one of five points in the plane of orbit of one body around another (e.g., the moon around the earth) at which a small third body can remain stationary with respect to both.

lag screw ▶ **n.** a heavy wood screw with a square or hexagonal head. Also called COACH SCREW, LAG BOLT.
▶ **v.** [with obj.] (**lag-screw**) fasten with a lag screw.

La Guar·di·a /lə ˈgwärdēə/, Fiorello (Henry) (1882–1947), US politician; nickname the **Little Flower.** He served in the US House of Representatives from New York 1917–21 before he became a corruption-fighting mayor of New York City 1933–45.

La Ha·ba·na /ˌlä äˈbänä/ Spanish name for HAVANA[1].

La Ha·bra /lə ˈhäbrə/ a city in southwestern California, southeast of Los Angeles; pop. 59,155 (est. 2008).

la·har /ˈläˌhär/ ▶ **n.** Geology a destructive mudflow on the slopes of a volcano.
– ORIGIN 1920s: from Javanese.

lah-di-dah ▶ **adj.** variant spelling of LA-DI-DA.

Lahn·da /ˈländə/ ▶ **n.** an Indic language of the western Punjab and adjacent areas of Pakistan, sometimes classified as a dialect of Punjabi.
▶ **adj.** of or relating to this language.
– ORIGIN early 20th cent.: from Punjabi *lahandā*, literally 'western.'

La·hore /ləˈhôr/ the capital of Punjab province and second largest city in Pakistan, situated near the border with India; pop. 6,926,600 (est. 2009).

Lai·bach /ˈlīˌbäk, -ˌbäkH/ German name for LJUBLJANA.

la·ic /ˈlāik/ formal ▶ **adj.** nonclerical; lay.
▶ **n.** a layperson; a noncleric.
– DERIVATIVES **la·i·cal** /-ikəl/ **adj., la·i·cal·ly** /-ik(ə)lē/ **adv.**
– ORIGIN mid 16th cent.: from late Latin *laicus* (see LAY[2]).

la·ic·i·ty /lāˈisətē/ ▶ **n.** formal the principles, status, or influence of the laity.

la·i·cize /ˈlāəˌsīz/ ▶ **v.** [with obj.] formal withdraw clerical character, control, or status from (someone or something); secularize: *when his priestly vocation no longer satisfied him, he had asked to be laicized.*
– DERIVATIVES **la·i·cism** /-ˌsizəm/ **n., la·i·ci·za·tion** /ˌlāəsəˈzāsHən/ **n.**

laid /lād/ past and past participle of LAY[1].

laid-back ▶ **adj.** informal relaxed and easygoing: *a shaggy dog with an engaging, laid-back temperament.*

laid pa·per ▶ **n.** paper that has a finely ribbed appearance. Compare with WOVE PAPER.

lain /lān/ past participle of LIE[1].

PRONUNCIATION KEY ə *ago, up*; ər *over, fur*; a *hat*; ā *ate*; ä *car*; e *let*; ē *see*; i *fit*; ī *by*; NG *sing*; ō *go*; ô *law, for*; oi *toy*; o͝o *good*; o͞o *goo*; ou *out*; TH *thin*; T̲H̲ *then*; ZH *vision*

Laing /laNG/, R. D. (1927–89), Scottish psychiatrist; full name *Ronald David Laing*. He was known for his controversial views on insanity and, in particular, on schizophrenia.

lair /le(ə)r/ ▶ **n.** a wild animal's resting place, esp. one that is well hidden. ■ a secret or private place in which a person seeks concealment or seclusion.
– ORIGIN Old English *leger* 'resting place, bed,' of Germanic origin; related to Dutch *leger* 'bed, camp' and German *Lager* 'storehouse,' also to LIE[1]. Compare with LAAGER and LAGER.

laird /le(ə)rd/ ▶ **n.** (in Scotland) a person who owns a large estate.
– DERIVATIVES **laird·ship** /-,SHip/ **n.**
– ORIGIN late Middle English: Scots form of LORD.

lair·y /'le(ə)rē/ ▶ **adj.** (**lairier, lairiest**) Brit. informal
1 cunning or conceited.
2 ostentatiously attractive; flashy: *the former Hollywood bad girl is putting her lairy Tinseltown past behind her.*
3 aggressive or rowdy: *a couple of lairy people pushed me around.*
– ORIGIN mid 19th cent. (originally Cockney slang): alteration of *leery*. Sense 2 was originally Australian slang and dates from the early 20th cent.

lais·sez-faire /,lesā 'fe(ə)r, ,lezā/ ▶ **n.** a policy or attitude of letting things take their own course, without interfering. ■ Economics abstention by governments from interfering in the workings of the free market: [as modifier] *laissez-faire capitalism.*
– DERIVATIVES **lais·sez-faire·ism** /'fe(ə)r,izəm/ **n.**
– ORIGIN French, literally 'allow to do.'

lais·sez-pas·ser /,lesā pa'sā, ,lezā/ ▶ **n.** a document allowing the holder to pass; a permit.
– ORIGIN French, literally 'allow to pass.'

la·i·ty /'lāətē/ ▶ **n.** (usu. treated as pl. **the laity**) lay people, as distinct from the clergy. ■ ordinary people, as distinct from professionals or experts.
– ORIGIN late Middle English: from LAY[2] + -ITY.

La·ius /'lāəs/ Greek Mythology a king of Thebes, the father of Oedipus and husband of Jocasta.

La Jol·la /lə 'hoiə/ a resort section of northern San Diego in California, on the Pacific Ocean. A number of well-known research institutions are in the area.

lake[1] /lāk/ ▶ **n.** a large body of water surrounded by land: *boys were swimming in the lake* | [in names] *Lake Superior.* ■ a pool of liquid: *the fish was served in a bright lake of spicy carrot sauce.*
– DERIVATIVES **lake·let** /-lit/ **n.**
– ORIGIN late Old English (denoting a pond or pool), from Old French *lac*, from Latin *lacus* 'basin, pool, lake.'

lake[2] ▶ **n.** [often with modifier] an insoluble pigment made by combining a soluble organic dye and an insoluble mordant. ■ a purplish-red pigment of this kind, originally one made with lac, used in dyes, inks, and paints.
– ORIGIN early 17th cent.: variant of LAC[1].

Lake Al·bert, Lake Bai·kal, etc. see ALBERT, LAKE; BAIKAL, LAKE, etc.

lake·bed /'lāk,bed/ ▶ **n.** the floor or bottom of a lake.

Lake Charles /CHärlz/ an industrial port city in southwestern Louisiana, on the Calcasieu River; pop. 71,061 (est. 2008).

Lake Dis·trict a region of lakes and mountains in northwestern England, long associated with English poets, such as Wordsworth, Southey, and Coleridge.

lake dwell·ing ▶ **n.** a prehistoric hut built on piles driven into the bed or shore of a lake.
– DERIVATIVES **lake dwell·er n.**

lake ef·fect snow ▶ **n.** snow falling on the lee side of a lake, generated by cold dry air passing over warmer water, esp. in the Great Lakes region.

lake·front /'lāk,frənt/ ▶ **n.** the land along the edge of a lake.
▶ **adj.** located along the edge of a lake.

Lake Ha·va·su Cit·y /'hava,soo/ a city in western Arizona, on the eastern shore of Lake Havasu; pop. 56,553 (est. 2008). It is home to the reconstructed 19th-century London Bridge.

Lake·hurst /'lākhərst/ a borough in east central New Jersey, associated with the 1937 explosion and crash of the dirigible *Hindenburg*.

Lake·land /'lāklənd/ a city in central Florida, noted for its resorts and its citrus industry; pop. 93,333 (est. 2008).

Lake·land ter·ri·er ▶ **n.** a small, stocky terrier originating in the Lake District of England.

Lake Lou·ise /loo'ēz/ a resort in southwestern Alberta, in the Rocky Mountains, noted for the beauty of the lake that gives it its name.

Lake of the O·zarks a lake in central Missouri, a well-known recreational area created by a dam built in 1931.

Lake of the Woods a lake on the border between Canada and the US, west of the Great Lakes.

Lake Plac·id /'plasid/ a resort village in the Adirondack Mountains, in northeastern New York, site of Olympic competition in 1932 and 1980; pop. 2,750 (est. 2008).

Lake Po·ets (also **Lake School**) the poets Samuel Taylor Coleridge, Robert Southey, and William Wordsworth, who lived in and were inspired by the Lake District.

lak·er /'lākər/ ▶ **n.** informal **1** a lake trout.
2 a ship constructed for carrying cargo on the Great Lakes.

lake·shore /'lāk,SHôr/ ▶ **n.** another term for LAKEFRONT.

lake·side /'lāk,sīd/ ▶ **n.** the land adjacent to a lake: *this road hugs the flat land by the lakeside* | [as modifier] *beautiful lakeside cabins.*

lake trout ▶ **n.** any of a number of fishes of the salmon family that live in large lakes and are highly prized as a game fish and as food. ● a North American char (*Salvelinus namaycush*, family Salmonidae). ● a European brown trout of a large race.

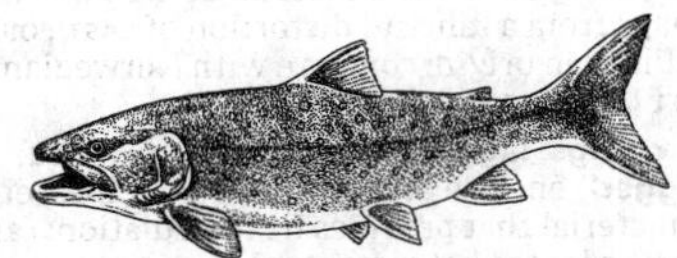

North American lake trout

Lake·wood /'lāk,wood/ **1** a city in southwestern California, southeast of Los Angeles; pop. 78,444 (est. 2008).
2 a city in north central Colorado, west of Denver; pop. 140,989 (est. 2008).
3 a city in northeastern Ohio, west of Cleveland, on Lake Erie; pop. 50,704 (est. 2008).
4 a city in northwestern Washington, a southwestern suburb of Tacoma; pop. 56,983 (est. 2008).

lakh /läk, lak/ ▶ **n.** (pl. **same** or **lakhs**) Indian a hundred thousand: *they fixed the price at five lakhs of rupees.*
– ORIGIN via Hindi from Sanskrit *lakṣa*.

La·ko·ni·a variant spelling of LACONIA.

La·ko·ta /lə'kōtə/ ▶ **n.** (pl. **same** or **Lakotas**) **1** a member of an American Indian people of western South Dakota. Also called TETON SIOUX (see TETON).
2 the Siouan language of this people.
▶ **adj.** of or relating to this people or their language.
– ORIGIN the name in Lakota, related to the word DAKOTA[1].

lak·sa /'läksə/ ▶ **n.** a Malaysian dish of Chinese origin, consisting of rice noodles served in a curry sauce or hot soup.
– ORIGIN Malay.

Lak·shad·weep /lək'SHäd,wēp/ a Union Territory in India that consists of a group of islands off the Malabar Coast of southwestern India; pop. 67,400 (est. 2009); capital, Kavaratti. The group consists of the Laccadive, Minicoy, and Amindivi Islands.

Laksh·mi /'ləksHmē/ Hinduism the goddess of prosperity, consort of Vishnu. She assumes different forms (e.g., Radha, Sita) in order to accompany her husband in his various incarnations.

la-la land /'lä,lä/ ▶ **n.** informal Los Angeles or Hollywood, esp. with regard to the lifestyle and attitudes of those living there or associated with it. ■ a fanciful state or dreamworld.
– ORIGIN *la-la*, reduplication of LA (i.e., Los Angeles).

la·la·pa·loo·za ▶ **n.** variant spelling of LOLLAPALOOZA.

La Le·che League /lə ,lā'CHā/ ▶ **n.** an international nonprofit breastfeeding advocacy group. Local chapters hold meetings to provide breastfeeding information and support.

La·lique /lä'lēk/, René (1860–1945), French jeweler, known for his art nouveau brooches and combs and for his decorative glassware.

Lal·lans /'lalənz/ ▶ **n.** a distinctive Scottish literary form of English, based on standard older Scots.
▶ **adj.** of, in, or relating to this language.
– ORIGIN early 18th cent. (also, as an adjective, *Lallan*): Scots variant of *Lowlands*, with reference to a central Lowlands dialect.

lal·ly·gag ▶ **v.** variant spelling of LOLLYGAG.

lam[1] /lam/ ▶ **v.** (**lams, lamming, lammed**) [with obj.] informal hit (someone) hard: *I'll come over and lam you in the mouth in a minute.* ■ [no obj.] (**lam into**) attack: *they surged up and down in their riot gear, lamming into anyone in their path.*
– ORIGIN late 16th cent.: perhaps of Scandinavian origin and related to Norwegian and Danish *lamme* 'paralyze.'

lam[2] informal ▶ **n.** (in phrase **on the lam**) in flight, esp. from the police: *he went on the lam and is living under a false name.*
▶ **v.** (**lams, lamming, lammed**) [no obj.] escape; flee.
– ORIGIN late 19th cent.: from LAM[1].

Lam. ▶ **abbr.** Bible Lamentations.

la·ma /'lämə/ ▶ **n. 1** an honorific title applied to a spiritual leader in Tibetan Buddhism, whether a reincarnate lama (such as the Dalai Lama) or one who has earned the title in life.
2 a Tibetan or Mongolian Buddhist monk.
– ORIGIN mid 17th cent.: from Tibetan *bla-ma* (the initial *b* being silent), literally 'superior one.'

La·ma·ism /'lämə,izəm/ ▶ **n.** the system of doctrine and observances inculcated and maintained by lamas; Tibetan Buddhism.
– DERIVATIVES **La·ma·ist n. & adj., La·ma·is·tic** /,lämə'istik/ **adj.**

La·mar[1] /lə'mär/, Joseph Rucker (1857–1916), US Supreme Court associate justice 1911–16. A former associate justice in Georgia's supreme court, he was appointed to the Court by President Taft.

La·mar[2], Lucius Quintus Cincinnatus (1825–93), US Supreme Court associate justice 1888–93. A US senator 1877–85 and secretary of the interior 1885–88, he was appointed to the Court by President Cleveland. During the Civil War, he served the Confederacy in various capacities.

La·marck /lä'märk/, Jean Baptiste de (1744–1829), French naturalist. He was an early proponent of organic evolution, although his theory is not widely accepted today.
– DERIVATIVES **La·marck·i·an** /lə'märkēən/ **n. & adj., La·marck·ism** /lə'mär,kizəm/ **n.**

La·mar·tine /lämär'tēn/, Alphonse Marie Louis de (1790–1869), French poet, statesman, and historian. He served as minister of foreign affairs in the provisional government following the Revolution of 1848.

la·ma·ser·y /'lämə,serē/ ▶ **n.** (pl. **lamaseries**) a monastery of lamas.

La·maze /lə'mäz/ ▶ **adj.** [attrib.] relating to a method of childbirth involving exercises and breathing control to give pain relief without drugs.
– ORIGIN 1950s: from the name of Fernand Lamaze (1891–1957), French physician.

Lamb[1] /lam/, Charles (1775–1834), English essayist and critic. The author of *Essays of Elia* (1823), he wrote *Tales from Shakespeare* (1807) with his sister Mary (1764–1847).

Lamb[2], Wally (1950–), US writer and teacher. His works include *She's Come Undone* (1992), *I Know This Much Is True* (1998), and *The Hour I First Believed* (2008).

lamb /lam/ ▶ **n.** a young sheep. ■ the flesh of such young sheep as food. ■ used figuratively as a symbol of meekness, gentleness, or innocence: *to her amazement, he accepted her decision like a lamb.* ■ used to describe or address someone regarded with affection or pity, esp. a young child: *the poor lamb is very upset.* ■ (**the Lamb**) short for LAMB OF GOD.
▶ **v.** [no obj.] (of a ewe) give birth to lambs. ■ [with obj.] tend (ewes) at lambing time.
– PHRASES **like a lamb to (the) slaughter** as a helpless victim.
– DERIVATIVES **lamb·er n., lamb·like** /-,līk/ **adj.**
– ORIGIN Old English, of Germanic origin; related to Dutch *lam* and German *Lamm*.

lam·ba·da /lam'bädə/ ▶ **n.** a fast, erotic Brazilian dance that couples perform with their stomachs touching.
– ORIGIN 1980s: Portuguese, literally 'a beating,' from *lambar* 'to beat.'

lam·baste /lam'bāst, -'bast/ (also **lambast** /-'bast/) ▶ **v.** [with obj.] criticize (someone or something) harshly: *they lambasted the report as a gross distortion of the truth.*
– ORIGIN mid 17th cent. (in the sense 'beat, thrash'): from LAM[1] + BASTE[3]. The current sense dates from the late 19th cent.

lamb·da /'lamdə/ ▶ **n.** the eleventh letter of the Greek alphabet (Λ, λ), transliterated as 'l.' ■ (**Lambda**) [followed by Latin genitive] Astronomy the eleventh star in a constellation: *Lambda Tauri.* ■ Biology a type of bacteriophage virus used in genetic research: [as modifier] *lambda phage.* ■ Anatomy the point at the back of the skull where the parietal bones and the occipital bone meet. ■ [as modifier] Biochemistry denoting one of the two types of light polypeptide chain present in all immunoglobulin molecules (the other being kappa). ▶ **symbol** ■ (λ) wavelength. ■ (λ) Astronomy celestial longitude.

lamb·doid /'lam,doid/ ▶ **adj.** resembling the Greek letter lambda in form. ■ Anatomy of or denoting the

suture near the back of the skull that connects the parietal bones with the occipital.
– DERIVATIVES **lamb·doi·dal** /lam'doidl/ **adj.**

lam·bent /'lambənt/ ▶ **adj.** literary (of light or fire) glowing, gleaming, or flickering with a soft radiance: *the magical, lambent light of the north.*
– DERIVATIVES **lam·ben·cy** /-bənsē/ **n.**, **lam·bent·ly adv.**
– ORIGIN mid 17th cent.: from Latin *lambent-* 'licking,' from the verb *lambere.*

lam·bert /'lambərt/ ▶ **n.** a former unit of luminance, equal to the emission or reflection of one lumen per square centimeter.
– ORIGIN early 20th cent.: named after Johann H. *Lambert* (1728–77), German physicist.

Lam·beth Con·fer·ence /'lambeth/ ▶ **n.** an assembly of bishops from the Anglican Communion, usually held every ten years (since 1867) at Lambeth Palace and presided over by the Archbishop of Canterbury.

Lam·beth Pal·ace a palace in the London borough of Lambeth, the residence of the Archbishop of Canterbury since 1197.

lam·bic /'lambik/ ▶ **n.** a strong, sweet Belgian beer.
– ORIGIN French.

lamb·ing /'lamiNG/ ▶ **n.** the birth of lambs on a farm: *lambing begins in mid-January.*

lamb·kin /'lamkin/ ▶ **n.** a small or young lamb. ■ used as a term of endearment for a young child.

Lamb of God ▶ **n.** a title of Jesus (see John 1:29). Compare with AGNUS DEI.

lam·bre·quin /'lambərkin, -brə-/ ▶ **n. 1** a short piece of decorative drapery hung over the top of a door or window or draped from a shelf or mantelpiece.
2 a piece of cloth covering the back of a medieval knight's helmet, represented in heraldry as the mantling.
– ORIGIN early 18th cent. (sense 2): from French, from the Dutch diminutive of *lamper* 'veil.'

Lam·bru·sco /lam'brōōskō, -'brōōs-/ ▶ **n.** a variety of wine grape grown in the Emilia-Romagna region of northern Italy. ■ a sparkling red wine made from this grape. ■ a red or white wine of a similar kind produced elsewhere.
– ORIGIN Italian, literally 'grape of the wild vine.'

lamb's ears ▶ **plural n.** [usu. treated as sing.] a southwestern Asian plant of the mint family that has gray-green woolly leaves and is cultivated as an ornamental, particularly for ground cover. ● *Stachys byzantina*, family Labiatae.

lamb·skin /'lam,skin/ ▶ **n.** prepared skin from a lamb, either with the wool on or as leather: [as modifier] *lambskin gloves.*

lamb's let·tuce ▶ **n.** another term for CORN SALAD.

lamb's-quar·ters ▶ **n.** a herbaceous plant with mealy, edible leaves, often considered to be a weed. Also called PIGWEED. ● *Chenopodium album*, family Chenopodiaceae.

lamb's tongue ▶ **n.** another term for LAMB'S EARS.

lambs·wool /'lamz,wōōl/ ▶ **n.** fine wool from a young sheep, used to make knitted garments, blankets, etc., with a soft texture.

lame /lām/ ▶ **adj. 1** (of a person or animal) unable to walk normally because of an injury or illness affecting the leg or foot: *his horse went lame.* ■ (of a leg or foot) affected in this way.
2 (of an explanation or excuse) unconvincingly feeble: *it was a lame statement and there was no excusing his behavior.* ■ (of something intended to be entertaining) uninspiring and dull. ■ (of a person) naive or inept, esp. socially: *anyone who doesn't know that is obviously lame.* ■ (of verse or metrical feet) halting; metrically defective.
▶ **v.** [with obj.] make (a person or animal) lame: *somebody lamed him with a stone.*
– DERIVATIVES **lame·ly adv.**, **lame·ness n.**
– ORIGIN Old English *lama*, of Germanic origin, related to Dutch *lam* and German *lahm.*

la·mé /la'mā, lä-/ ▶ **n.** fabric with interwoven gold or silver threads.
▶ **adj.** (of fabric or a garment) having such threads.
– ORIGIN 1920s: French, from Latin *lamina* (see LAMINA).

lame·brain /'lām,brān/ ▶ **n.** informal a stupid person.
– DERIVATIVES **lame·brained adj.**

lame duck ▶ **n.** an official (esp. the president) in the final period of office, after the election of a successor: *as a lame duck, the president had nothing to lose by approving the deal* | [as modifier] *a lame-duck governor.* ■ an ineffectual or unsuccessful person or thing.

la·mel·la /lə'melə/ ▶ **n.** (pl. **lamellae** /-'melē, -'melī/) a thin layer, membrane, scale, or platelike tissue or part, esp. in bone tissue. ■ Botany a membranous fold in a chloroplast.
– DERIVATIVES **la·mel·lar** /-'melər/ **adj.**, **la·mel·late** /'lamәlit, lə'melit, 'lamə,lāt/ **adj.**, **la·mel·li·form** /-'melə,fôrm/ **adj.**, **la·mel·lose** /-,lōs, -,lōz/ **adj.**
– ORIGIN late 17th cent.: from Latin, diminutive of *lamina* 'thin plate.'

la·mel·li·branch /lə'melə,braNGk/ ▶ **n.** another term for BIVALVE.
– ORIGIN mid 19th cent.: from modern Latin *Lamellibranchia* (former class name), from Latin *lamella* (diminutive of *lamina* 'thin plate') + Greek *brankhia* 'gills.'

la·mel·li·corn /lə'melə,kôrn/ ▶ **n.** former term for SCARABAEOID.
– ORIGIN mid 19th cent.: from modern Latin *Lamellicornia* (former taxonomic name), from Latin *lamella* 'thin plate' + *cornu* 'horn.'

la·mel·li·po·di·um /lə,melə'pōdēəm/ ▶ **n.** (pl. **lamellipodia** /-dēə/) Zoology a flattened extension of a cell, by which it moves over or adheres to a surface.
– DERIVATIVES **la·mel·li·po·di·al** /-dēəl/ **adj.**
– ORIGIN 1970s: from LAMELLA, on the pattern of *pseudopodium.*

la·ment /lə'ment/ ▶ **n.** a passionate expression of grief or sorrow: *his mother's night-long laments for his father* | *a song full of lament and sorrow.* ■ a song, piece of music, or poem expressing such emotions. ■ an expression of regret or disappointment; a complaint: *there were constant laments about the conditions of employment.*
▶ **v.** [with obj.] mourn (a person's loss or death): *he was lamenting the death of his infant daughter.* ■ [no obj.] (**lament for/over**) express one's deep grief about. ■ [reporting verb] express regret or disappointment over something considered unsatisfactory, unreasonable, or unfair: [with obj.] *she lamented the lack of shops in the town* | [with direct speech] *Thomas Jefferson later lamented, "Heaven remained silent."*
– DERIVATIVES **la·ment·er n.**
– ORIGIN late Middle English (as a verb): from French *lamenter* or Latin *lamentari*, from *lamenta* (plural) 'weeping, wailing.'

lam·en·ta·ble /lə'mentəbəl, 'laməntəbəl/ ▶ **adj.**
1 (of circumstances or conditions) deplorably bad or unsatisfactory: *the facilities provided were lamentable, not merely basic but squalid.* ■ (of an event, action, or attitude) unfortunate; regrettable: *her open prejudice showed lamentable immaturity.*
2 archaic full of or expressing sorrow or grief.
– DERIVATIVES **la·men·ta·bly** /-əblē/ **adv.** [as submodifier] *she was lamentably ignorant.*
– ORIGIN late Middle English (in the sense 'mournful,' also 'pitiable, regrettable'): from Old French, or from Latin *lamentabilis*, from the verb *lamentari* (see LAMENT).

lam·en·ta·tion /,lamən'tāSHən/ ▶ **n.** the passionate expression of grief or sorrow; weeping: *scenes of lamentation.* ■ (**Lamentations** or **Lamentations of Jeremiah**) a book of the Bible telling of the desolation of Judah after the fall of Jerusalem in 586 BC.

la·ment·ed /lə'mentid/ ▶ **adj.** (often **the late lamented**) a conventional way of describing someone who has died or something that has been lost or that has ceased to exist: *the late and much lamented Leonard Bernstein.*

la·mi·a /'lāmēə/ ▶ **n.** (pl. **lamias** or **lamiae** /-mē,ē/) a mythical monster, with the body of a woman or with the head and breasts of a woman and the body of a snake, said to prey on human beings and suck the blood of children.
– ORIGIN via Latin from Greek, denoting a carnivorous fish or mythical monster.

lam·i·na /'lamənə/ ▶ **n.** (pl. **laminae** /-,nē, -,nī/) technical a thin layer, plate, or scale of sedimentary rock, organic tissue, or other material.
– DERIVATIVES **lam·i·nose** /-,nōs, -,nōz/ **adj.**
– ORIGIN mid 17th cent.: from Latin.

lam·i·nal /'lamənl/ ▶ **adj.** Phonetics (of a consonant) formed with the blade of the tongue touching the alveolar ridge (e.g., *n, s, t*).
▶ **n.** Phonetics a laminal sound.
– ORIGIN 1950s: from LAMINA + -AL.

lam·i·na pro·pri·a /'prōprēə/ ▶ **n.** technical term for BASEMENT MEMBRANE.

lam·i·nar /'lamənər/ ▶ **adj. 1** consisting of laminae.
2 Physics (of a flow) taking place along constant streamlines; not turbulent.

lam·i·nate ▶ **v.** /'lamə,nāt/ [with obj.] (often as adj. **laminated**) overlay (a flat surface, esp. paper) with a layer of plastic or some other protective material. ■ manufacture by placing layer on layer. ■ split into layers or leaves. ■ beat or roll (metal) into thin plates.
▶ **n.** /-nit, -,nāt/ a laminated structure or material, esp. one made of layers fixed together to form a hard, flat, or flexible material.
▶ **adj.** /-nit, -,nāt/ in the form of a lamina or laminae.
– DERIVATIVES **lam·i·na·ble** /-nəbəl/ **adj.**, **lam·i·na·tion** /,lamə'nāSHən/ **n.**, **lam·i·na·tor** /-,nātər/ **n.**
– ORIGIN mid 17th cent.: from LAMINA + -ATE[2].

lam·i·nec·to·my /,lamə'nektəmē/ ▶ **n.** (pl. **laminectomies**) a surgical operation to remove the back of one or more vertebrae, usually to give access to the spinal cord or to relieve pressure on nerves.

lam·i·nin /'lamənin/ ▶ **n.** Biochemistry a fibrous protein present in the basal lamina of the epithelia.

lam·i·ni·tis /,lamə'nītis/ ▶ **n.** inflammation of sensitive layers of tissue (laminae) inside the hoof in horses and other animals. It is particularly prevalent in ponies feeding on rich spring grass and can cause extreme lameness.

Lam·mas /'laməs/ (also **Lammas Day**) ▶ **n.** the first day of August, formerly observed in Britain as a harvest festival, during which bread baked from the first crop of wheat was blessed.
– ORIGIN Old English *hlāfmæsse* (see LOAF[1], MASS), later interpreted as if it were from LAMB + MASS.

lam·mer·gei·er /'lamər,gīər/ (also **lammergeyer**) ▶ **n.** a large Old World vulture of mountainous country, with a wingspan of 10 feet (3 m) and dark beardlike feathers, noted for its habit of dropping bones from a height to break them. Also called BEARDED VULTURE. ● *Gypaetus barbatus*, family Accipitridae.
– ORIGIN early 19th cent.: from German *Lämmergeier*, from *Lämmer* (plural of *Lamm* 'lamb') + *Geier* 'vulture.'

lamp /lamp/ ▶ **n.** a device for giving light, either one consisting of an electric bulb together with its holder and shade or cover, or one burning gas or a liquid fuel and consisting of a wick or mantle and a glass shade: *a table lamp.* ■ an electrical device producing ultraviolet, infrared, or other radiation, used for therapeutic purposes. ■ literary a source of spiritual or intellectual inspiration.
– DERIVATIVES **lamp·er n.**, **lamp·less adj.**
– ORIGIN Middle English: via Old French from late Latin *lampada*, from Latin *lampas, lampad-* 'torch,' from Greek.

lam·pas[1] /'lampəs/ (also **lampers** /-pərz/) ▶ **n.** a condition of horses, in which there is swelling of the fleshy lining of the roof of the mouth behind the front teeth.
– ORIGIN early 16th cent.: from French, probably via French dialect from the Germanic base of the verb LAP[3].

lam·pas[2] ▶ **n.** a patterned drapery and upholstery fabric similar to brocade, made of silk, cotton, or rayon, originally imitating textiles from India and later imported from China, Iran, and France.
– ORIGIN mid 19th cent.: from French *lampas, lampasse*, of unknown origin.

lamp·black /'lamp,blak/ ▶ **n.** a black pigment made from soot.

lamp chim·ney ▶ **n.** a glass cylinder positioned over the wick of an oil lamp or candlestick to encircle and provide a draft for the flame.

lamp·light /'lamp,līt/ ▶ **n.** the light cast from a lamp: *he was working in the stables by lamplight.*
– DERIVATIVES **lamp·lit** /-,lit/ **adj.**

lamp·light·er /'lamp,lītər/ ▶ **n.** historical a person employed to light street gaslights by hand.

lam·poon /lam'pōōn/ ▶ **v.** [with obj.] publicly criticize (someone or something) by using ridicule, irony, or sarcasm: *the senator made himself famous as a pinch-penny watchdog of public spending, lampooning dubious federal projects.*
▶ **n.** a speech or text criticizing someone or something in this way: *does this sound like a lampoon of student life?*
– DERIVATIVES **lam·poon·er n.**, **lam·poon·ist** /-ist/ **n.**
– ORIGIN mid 17th cent.: from French *lampon*, said to be from *lampons* 'let us drink' (used as a refrain), from *lamper* 'gulp down,' nasalized form of *laper* 'to lap (liquid).'

lamp·post /'lam(p),pōst/ ▶ **n.** a tall pole with a light at the top; a street light.

lam·prey /'lamprē, -prā/ ▶ **n.** (pl. **lampreys**) an eellike aquatic jawless vertebrate that has a sucker mouth with horny teeth and a rasping tongue. The adult is often parasitic, attaching itself to other fish and sucking their blood. ● Family Petromyzonidae: several genera and species.
– ORIGIN Middle English: from Old French *lampreie*, from medieval Latin *lampreda*, probably from Latin *lambere* 'to lick' + *petra* 'stone' (because the lamprey attaches itself to stones by its mouth).

lam·pro·phyre /ˈlamprəˌfīr/ ▶ **n.** Geology a porphyritic igneous rock consisting of a fine-grained feldspathic groundmass with phenocrysts chiefly of biotite.
– ORIGIN late 19th cent.: from Greek *lampros* 'bright, shining' + *porphureos* 'purple.'

lamp·shade /ˈlampˌshād/ ▶ **n.** a cover for a lamp, used to soften or direct its light.

lamp shell ▶ **n.** a marine invertebrate that superficially resembles a bivalve mollusk but has two or more arms of ciliated tentacles (lophophores) that are extended for filter feeding. Lamp shells are common as fossils. Also called **BRACHIOPOD**. ● Phylum Brachiopoda: numerous groups in the Paleozoic era but few surviving to the present day.
– ORIGIN mid 19th cent.: from its resemblance to an ancient oil lamp.

LAN /lan/ ▶ **abbr.** local area network.

La·nai /ləˈnī/ an island in Hawaii, west of Maui, primarily agricultural, with some resorts.

la·na·i /ləˈnäē, ləˈnī/ ▶ **n.** (pl. **lanais**) a porch or veranda.
– ORIGIN Hawaiian.

Lan·cas·ter[1] /ˈlaNGˌkastər, -kəstər, ˈlan-/ **1** a city in western England, north of Liverpool, on the estuary of the Lune River; pop. 44,500 (est. 2009).
2 a city in southwestern California, northeast of Los Angeles, on the edge of the Mojave Desert; pop. 145,469 (est. 2008).
3 a city in southeastern Pennsylvania, primarily a commercial center for the Pennsylvania Dutch Country; pop. 54,626 (est. 2008).

Lan·cas·ter[2] /ˈlanˌkastər, ˈlaNG-/, Burt (1913–94), US movie actor; full name *Burton Stephen Lancaster*. He made his debut in *The Killers* (1946) and was often cast in "tough guy" roles. Notable movies: *From Here to Eternity* (1953), *Elmer Gantry* (1960), and *Field of Dreams* (1989).

Lan·cas·ter, House of the English royal house descended from John of Gaunt, Duke of Lancaster, that ruled England from 1399 (Henry IV) until 1461 (the deposition of Henry VI) and again on Henry VI's brief restoration in 1470–71. With the red rose as its emblem, it fought the Wars of the Roses with the House of York; Lancaster's descendants, the Tudors, eventually prevailed through Henry VII's accession to the throne in 1485.

Lan·cas·ter House A·gree·ment an agreement that brought about the establishment of the independent state of Zimbabwe, reached in September 1979 at Lancaster House in London.

Lan·cas·tri·an /laNGˈkastrēən/ ▶ **n. 1** a native of Lancashire or Lancaster in England.
2 historical a follower of the British House of Lancaster, esp. during the Wars of the Roses.
▶ **adj.** of or relating to Lancashire or Lancaster, or the House of Lancaster.

lance /lans/ ▶ **n. 1** a long weapon for thrusting, having a wooden shaft and a pointed steel head, formerly used by a horseman in charging. ■ a weapon resembling a lance used in hunting fish or whales. ■ another term for **LANCER** (sense 1).
2 [usu. with modifier] a metal pipe supplying a jet of oxygen to a furnace or to a hot flame for cutting.
3 a rigid tube at the end of a hose for pumping or spraying liquid.
▶ **v.** [with obj.] Medicine prick or cut open with a lancet or other sharp instrument: *abscesses should not be lanced until there is a soft spot in the center* | figurative *the governor made it one of his priorities to lance the boil of corruption.* ■ pierce with or as if with a lance: *the teenager had been lanced by a wooden splinter* | [no obj.] figurative *his eyes lanced right through her.* ■ [no obj.] move suddenly and quickly: *pain lanced through her.* ■ literary fling; launch: *he affirms to have lanced darts at the sun.*
– ORIGIN Middle English: from Old French *lance* (noun), *lancier* (verb), from Latin *lancea* (noun).

lance cor·po·ral ▶ **n.** an enlisted person in the US Marine Corps ranking above private first class and below corporal.
– ORIGIN late 18th cent.: on the analogy of obsolete *lancepesade*, the lowest grade of noncommissioned officer, based on Italian *lancia spezzata* 'broken lance.'

lance·let /ˈlanslit/ ▶ **n.** a small elongated marine invertebrate that resembles a fish but lacks jaws and obvious sense organs. Lancelets possess a notochord and are among the most primitive chordates. ● Subphylum Cephalochordata, phylum Chordata: several species, including amphioxus.
– ORIGIN mid 19th cent.: from the noun **LANCE** (because of its long narrow form) + **-LET**.

Lan·ce·lot /ˈlansəˌlät, ˈlän-, -s(ə)lət/ (also **Launcelot**) (in Arthurian legend) the most famous of Arthur's knights, lover of Queen Guinevere and father of Galahad.

lan·ce·o·late /ˈlansēəlit, -ˌlāt/ ▶ **adj.** technical shaped like the head of a lance; of a narrow oval shape tapering to a point at each end: *the leaves are lanceolate.*
– ORIGIN mid 18th cent.: from late Latin *lanceolatus*, from Latin *lanceola*, diminutive of *lancea* 'a lance.'

lanc·er /ˈlansər/ ▶ **n. 1** historical a soldier of a cavalry regiment armed with lances.
2 (**lancers**) [treated as sing.] a quadrille for eight or sixteen pairs.
– ORIGIN late 16th cent.: from French *lancier*, from *lance* 'a lance.'

lan·cet /ˈlansit/ ▶ **n. 1** a small, broad, two-edged surgical knife or blade with a sharp point.
2 a lancet arch or window. ■ [as modifier] shaped like a lancet arch: *a lancet clock.*
– DERIVATIVES **lan·cet·ed** adj.
– ORIGIN late Middle English (also denoting a small lance): from Old French *lancette*, diminutive of *lance* 'a lance.'

lan·cet arch ▶ **n.** an arch with an acutely pointed head.

lan·cet win·dow ▶ **n.** a high and narrow window with an acutely pointed head.

lance·wood /ˈlansˌwo͝od/ ▶ **n.** any of a number of hardwood trees with tough elastic timber, in particular: ● a Caribbean tree (*Oxandra lanceolata*, family Annonaceae). ● a New Zealand tree (*Pseudopanax crassifolius*, family Araliaceae).

Lan·chow /ˌlänˈjō, ˈlänˈchou/ variant of **LANZHOU**.

Land[1] /länt, länd/ ▶ **n.** (pl. **Länder** /ˈlendər/) (in Germany or Austria) a state.
– ORIGIN German, literally 'land.'

Land[2] /land/, Edwin (1909–91), US inventor. He developed a new polarizing filter with wide use in optical instruments. In 1937, he founded the Polaroid Corporation and introduced the first Polaroid Land camera in 1947.

land /land/ ▶ **n. 1** the part of the earth's surface that is not covered by water, as opposed to the sea or the air: *the reptiles lay their eggs on land* | *after four weeks at sea we sighted land.* ■ [as modifier] living or traveling on land rather than in water or the air: *a land mammal.* ■ an expanse of land; an area of ground, esp. in terms of its ownership or use: *the land north of the village* | (**lands**) *the Indians were wiped out as gold prospectors invaded their lands.* ■ (**the land**) ground or soil used as a basis for agriculture: *my family had worked the land for many years.*
2 a country: *the valley is one of the most beautiful in the land* | *the lands of the Middle East* | *America, the land of political equality.* ■ a conceptual realm or domain: *you are living in a fantasy land.*
3 the space between the rifling grooves in a gun.
▶ **v. 1** [with obj.] put (someone or something) on land from a boat: *the lifeboat landed the survivors safely ashore.* ■ [no obj.] go ashore; disembark: *the marines landed at a small fishing jetty.* ■ bring (a fish) to land, esp. with a net or hook: *I landed a scrappy three-pound walleye.* ■ informal succeed in obtaining or achieving (something desirable), esp. in the face of strong competition: *she landed the starring role in a new film.*
2 [no obj.] come down through the air and alight on the ground: *planes landing at the rate of two a minute.* ■ [with obj.] bring (an aircraft or spacecraft) to the ground or the surface of water, esp. in a controlled way: *the copilot landed the plane.* ■ reach the ground after falling or jumping: *he leaped over the fence and landed nimbly on his feet.* ■ [with adverbial of place] (of an object) come to rest after falling or being thrown: *the plate landed in her lap.* ■ informal (of something unpleasant or unexpected) arrive suddenly: *there seemed to be more problems than ever landing on her desk this week.*
3 [with obj.] (**land someone in**) informal cause someone to be in (a difficult or unwelcome situation): *his exploits always landed him in trouble.* ■ (**land someone with**) inflict (an unwelcome task or a difficult situation) on someone: *the mistake landed the company with a massive bill.*
4 [with obj.] informal inflict (a blow) on someone: *I won the fight without landing a single punch* | [with two objs.] *I landed him one.*
– PHRASES **how the land lies** what the state of affairs is: *let's keep it to ourselves until we see how the land lies.* **in the land of the living** humorous alive or awake. **the land of Nod** humorous a state of sleep. [punningly, with biblical allusion to the place name *Nod* (Gen. 4:16).] **land on one's feet** have good luck or success, esp. after risk or trial: *after some ups and downs, he has finally landed on his feet.* **live off the land** live on whatever food one can obtain by hunting, gathering, or subsistence farming.
– PHRASAL VERBS **land up** reach a place or situation; end up: *I landed up in prison.*
– ORIGIN Old English, of Germanic origin; related to Dutch *land* and German *Land*.

-land /land, lənd/ ▶ **comb. form** forming nouns denoting a particular sphere of activity or group of people: *the blunt, charmless climate of technoland.*

Lan·dau /ˈlanˌdou, lənˈdou/, Lev (Davidovich) (1908–68), Soviet theoretical physicist. Active in many fields, Landau was noted for his work on the superfluidity and thermal conductivity of liquid helium. Nobel Prize for Physics (1962).

lan·dau /ˈlanˌdou/ ▶ **n.** a horse-drawn four-wheeled enclosed carriage with a removable front cover and a back cover that can be raised and lowered.
– ORIGIN mid 18th cent.: named after *Landau*, near Karlsruhe in Germany, where it was first made.

landau

lan·dau·let /ˌlandôˈlet/ ▶ **n.** a small landau. ■ chiefly historical a car with a folding hood over the rear seats.

land bank ▶ **n. 1** a bank whose main function is to provide loans for land purchase, esp. by farmers.
2 a large body of land held by a public or private organization for future development or disposal.

land·bank·ing /ˈlandˌbaNGkiNG/ (also **land banking**) ▶ **n.** the practice of buying land as an investment, holding it for future use, and making no specific plans for its development.

land breeze ▶ **n.** a breeze blowing toward the sea from the land, esp. at night, owing to the relative warmth of the sea. Compare with **SEA BREEZE**.

land bridge ▶ **n.** a connection between two landmasses, esp. a prehistoric one that allowed humans and animals to colonize new territory before being cut off by the sea, as across the Bering Strait and the English Channel.

land crab ▶ **n.** a crab that lives in burrows inland and migrates in large numbers to the sea to breed. ● Family Gecarcinidae: *Cardisoma* and other genera.

land·ed /ˈlandid/ ▶ **adj.** [attrib.] owning much land, esp. through inheritance: *the landed aristocracy.* ■ consisting of, including, or relating to such land: *the decline of landed estates* | *landed income.*

land·er /ˈlandər/ ▶ **n.** a spacecraft designed to land on the surface of a planet or moon: *a lunar lander.* Compare with **ORBITER**.

Län·der /ˈlendər/ plural form of **LAND**[1].

Lan·ders /ˈlanderz/, Ann (1918–2002), US journalist; born *Esther Pauline Friedman*. Author of the "Ann Landers" advice column from 1955, she competed with her twin sister, Abigail Van Buren, who wrote a similar column.

land·fall /ˈlan(d)ˌfôl/ ▶ **n. 1** an arrival at land on a sea or air journey.
2 a collapse of a mass of land, esp. one that blocks a route.
– DERIVATIVES **land·fall·ing** adj.

land·fill /ˈlan(d)ˌfil/ ▶ **n.** a place to dispose of refuse and other waste material by burying it and covering it over with soil, esp. as a method of filling in or extending usable land. ■ waste material used to reclaim ground in this way. ■ an area filled in by this process.
▶ **v.** [with obj.] bury in a landfill: *the Florida school intends to landfill its old computers* | [as adj.] *landfilled waste.*

land·form /ˈlan(d)ˌfôrm/ ▶ **n.** a natural feature of the earth's surface.

land-grab·ber ▶ **n.** a person who seizes and possesses land in an unfair or illegal manner.
– DERIVATIVES **land-grab** n., **land-grab·bing** n.

land grant ▶ **n.** a grant of public land, esp. to an institution, organization, or to particular groups of people.

land·grave /ˈlan(d)ˌgrāv/ ▶ **n.** historical a count having jurisdiction over a territory. ■ the title of certain German princes.
– ORIGIN late Middle English: from Middle Low German, from *land* 'land' + *grave* 'count' (used as a title).

land·hold·er /ˈlandˌhōldər/ ▶ **n.** a person who owns land, esp. one who either makes a living from it or rents it out to others.

land·hold·ing /ˈlandˌhōldiNG/ ▶ **n.** a piece of land owned or rented. ■ possession or rental of land.

land·ing /ˈlandiNG/ ▶ **n. 1** an instance of coming or bringing something to land, either from the air or from water: *we made a perfect landing at the* *airstrip* | *the landing of men on the moon.* ■ (also **landing place**) a place where people and goods can be landed from a boat or ship: *the ferry landing.* **2** a level area at the top of a staircase or between one flight of stairs and another.

land·ing craft ▶ **n.** a boat specially designed for putting troops and military equipment ashore on a beach.

land·ing gear ▶ **n.** the undercarriage of an aircraft, including the wheels or pontoons on which it rests while not in the air.

land·ing light ▶ **n.** (usu. **landing lights**) a bright lamp on an aircraft that is switched on before landing. ■ a light of a kind that is arranged in rows along each side of an aircraft runway.

land·ing net ▶ **n.** a net for landing a large fish that has been hooked.

land·ing pad ▶ **n.** a small area designed for helicopters to land on and take off from.

land·ing stage ▶ **n.** a platform, typically a floating one, onto which passengers from a boat or ship disembark or cargo is unloaded.

land·ing strip ▶ **n.** an airstrip.

land·la·dy /ˈlan(d),lādē/ ▶ **n.** (pl. **landladies**) a woman who rents land, a building, or an apartment to a tenant. ■ a woman who owns or runs a boarding house, inn, or similar establishment.

länd·ler /ˈlendlər/ ▶ **n.** an Austrian folk dance in triple time, a precursor of the waltz.
– ORIGIN late 19th cent.: German, from *Landl* 'Upper Austria.'

land·less /ˈlan(d)lis/ ▶ **adj.** (esp. of an agricultural worker) owning no land.
– DERIVATIVES **land·less·ness n.**

land·line /ˈlan(d),līn/ ▶ **n.** a conventional telecommunications connection by cable laid across land, typically either on poles or buried underground.

land·locked /ˈlan(d),läkt/ ▶ **adj.** (esp. of a country) almost or entirely surrounded by land; having no coastline or seaport: *a midget state landlocked in the mountains.* ■ (of a lake) enclosed by land and having no navigable route to the sea. ■ (of a fish, esp. a North American salmon) cut off from the sea in the past and now confined to fresh water.

land·lord /ˈlan(d),lôrd/ ▶ **n.** a person, esp. a man, who rents land, a building, or an apartment to a tenant. ■ a person who owns or runs a boarding house, inn, or similar establishment.

land·lord·ism /ˈlan(d)lôr,dizəm/ ▶ **n.** the system whereby land (or property) is owned by landlords to whom tenants pay a fixed rent.

land·lub·ber /ˈlan(d),ləbər/ ▶ **n.** informal a person unfamiliar with the sea or sailing.

land·mark /ˈlan(d),märk/ ▶ **n.** **1** an object or feature of a landscape or town that is easily seen and recognized from a distance, esp. one that enables someone to establish their location: *the spire was once a landmark for ships sailing up the river.* ■ historical the boundary of an area of land, or an object marking this. **2** an event, discovery, or change marking an important stage or turning point in something: *the birth of a child is an important landmark in the lives of all concerned* | [as modifier] *a landmark decision.*

land·mass /ˈlan(d),mas/ (also **land mass**) ▶ **n.** a continent or other large body of land.

land mine ▶ **n.** an explosive mine laid on or just under the surface of the ground.

land of·fice ▶ **n.** a government office recording dealings in public land.
– PHRASES **do a land-office business** informal do a lot of successful business: *the open-air air show did a land-office business.*

Land of Hi·a·wath·a a nickname for the UPPER PENINSULA of Michigan.

Land of Lin·coln a nickname for the state of ILLINOIS.

Land of Stead·y Hab·its a nickname for the state of CONNECTICUT.

Land of the Da·ko·tas a nickname for the state of NORTH DAKOTA.

Land of the Mid·night Sun a nickname for the state of ALASKA.

Land of the Ris·ing Sun ▶ **n.** a poetic name for Japan.

land·own·er /ˈlan,dōnər/ ▶ **n.** a person who owns land, esp. a large amount of land.
– DERIVATIVES **land·own·er·ship** /-dōnər,SHip/ **n.**, **land·own·ing** /-dōniNG/ **adj. & n.**

land·race /ˈland,rās/ ▶ **n.** a local cultivar or animal breed that has been improved by traditional agricultural methods.

land rail ▶ **n.** another term for CORNCRAKE.

land re·form ▶ **n.** the statutory division of agricultural land and its reallocation to landless people.

Land·sat /ˈlan(d),sat/ a series of artificial satellites that monitor the earth's resources by photographing the surface at different wavelengths. The resulting images provide information about agriculture, geology, ecological changes, etc.

land·scape /ˈlan(d),skāp/ ▶ **n.** **1** all the visible features of an area of countryside or land, often considered in terms of their aesthetic appeal: *the giant cacti that dominate this landscape* | *a bleak urban landscape.* ■ a picture representing an area of countryside: [as modifier] *a landscape painter.* ■ the genre of landscape painting. ■ the distinctive features of a particular situation or intellectual activity: *the event transformed the political landscape.* **2** [as modifier] (of a page, book, or illustration, or the manner in which it is set or printed) wider than it is high. Compare with PORTRAIT (sense 2).
▶ **v.** [with obj.] (usu. **be landscaped**) improve the aesthetic appearance of (a piece of land) by changing its contours, adding ornamental features, or planting trees and shrubs: *the site has been tastefully landscaped* | (as noun **landscaping**) *the company spent $15,000 on landscaping.*
– DERIVATIVES **land·scap·er n.**, **land·scap·ist** /-,skāpist/ **n.**
– ORIGIN late 16th cent. (denoting a picture of natural scenery): from Middle Dutch *lantscap*, from *land* 'land' + *scap* (equivalent of -SHIP).

land·scape ar·chi·tec·ture ▶ **n.** the art and practice of designing the outdoor environment, esp. designing parks or gardens together with buildings and roads.
– DERIVATIVES **land·scape ar·chi·tect n.**

land·scape gar·den·ing ▶ **n.** the art and practice of laying out grounds in a way that is ornamental or that imitates natural scenery.
– DERIVATIVES **land·scape gar·den·er n.**

land scrip ▶ **n.** see SCRIP[1] (sense 2).

Land's End a rocky promontory in southwestern Cornwall that is England's westernmost point.

lands·knecht /ˈlänts,kneKHt/ ▶ **n.** historical a member of a class of mercenary soldiers in the German and other continental armies in the 16th and 17th centuries.
– ORIGIN from German *Landsknecht*, literally 'soldier of the land.'

land·slide /ˈlan(d),slīd/ ▶ **n.** **1** the sliding down of a mass of earth or rock from a mountain or cliff. **2** an overwhelming majority of votes for one party in an election: *winning the election **by a landslide*** | [as modifier] *a landslide victory.*

land·slip /ˈlan(d),slip/ ▶ **n.** chiefly Brit. another term for LANDSLIDE (sense 1).

Lands·mål /ˈlänts,môl/ ▶ **n.** another term for NYNORSK.
– ORIGIN Norwegian, literally 'language of the land.'

lands·man /ˈlan(d)zmən/ ▶ **n.** **1** (pl. **landsmen**) a person unfamiliar with the sea or sailing. **2** a fellow countryman.

Land·stei·ner /ˈlan(d),stīnər, ˈlänt,SHtīnər/, Karl (1868–1943), US physician, born in Austria. In 1930, he devised the ABO system of classifying blood. He was also the first to describe the Rhesus factor in blood. Nobel Prize for Physiology or Medicine (1930).

land·ward /ˈlan(d)wərd/ ▶ **adv.** (also **landwards** /-wərdz/) toward land: *the ship turned landward.*
▶ **adj.** facing toward land as opposed to sea: *the landward side of the road.*

land yacht ▶ **n.** a wind-powered wheeled vehicle with sails, used for recreation and competition. ■ informal a large car: *the bechromed land yachts of the 1950s.*

lane /lān/ ▶ **n.** **1** a narrow road, esp. in a rural area: *she drove along the winding lane.* ■ (in place names) a street: *Park Lane.* ■ Astronomy a dark streak or band that shows up against a bright background, esp. in a spiral galaxy or emission nebula. **2** a division of a road marked off with painted lines and intended to separate single lines of traffic according to speed or direction: *the car accelerated and moved into the outside lane.* ■ each of a number of parallel strips of track or water for runners, rowers, or swimmers in a race: *she went into the final in lane three.* ■ a path or course prescribed for or regularly followed by ships or aircraft: *the shipping lanes of the South Atlantic.* ■ (in basketball) a 12-foot-wide area extending from the free-throw line to below the basket. ■ (in bowling) a long narrow strip of floor down which the ball is bowled. ■ Biochemistry each of a number of notional parallel strips in the gel of an electrophoresis plate, occupied by a single sample.
– ORIGIN Old English, related to Dutch *laan*; of unknown ultimate origin.

Lang /laNG/, Fritz (1890–1976), Austrian movie director, who worked in the US from 1933. He made the transition from silent to sound movies in 1931 with the thriller *M*. Later works include *The Big Heat* (1953).

lang. ▶ **abbr.** language.

Lange /laNG/, Dorothea (1895–1965), US photographer. She was known for her documentary photographs of the Great Depression, including "White Angel Breadline" (1932), and those of the Japanese-American internment camps around 1942. Many of her later photoessays were published in *Life* magazine.

Lang·land /ˈlaNGlənd/, William (*c.*1330–*c.*1400), English poet. He is best known for *Piers Plowman* (*c.*1367–70), a long allegorical poem that is in the form of a spiritual pilgrimage.

lang·lauf /ˈläNG,louf/ ▶ **n.** cross-country skiing: [as modifier] *langlauf skiers.*
– ORIGIN 1920s: from German, literally 'long run.'

Lang·ley[1] /ˈlaNGlē/ a community in northeastern Virginia, northwest of Washington, DC, home to the Central Intelligence Agency.

Lang·ley[2], Samuel Pierpoint (1834–1906), US astronomer and aviation pioneer. He invented the bolometer (1879–81) and contributed to the design of early aircraft.

Lang·muir /ˈlaNG,myo͝or/, Irving (1881–1957), US chemist and physicist. His principal work was in surface chemistry, esp. applied to catalysis. He also worked on high-temperature electrical discharges in gases and studied atomic structure.

Lang·muir–Blod·gett film /ˈbläjit/ ▶ **n.** Chemistry a monomolecular layer of an organic material that can be used to build extremely small electronic devices.
– ORIGIN named after I. LANGMUIR, and Katherine B. *Blodgett* (1898–1979), US physicist and chemist.

lan·gos·ta /laNGˈgästə/ ▶ **n.** another term for LANGOUSTE.
– ORIGIN Spanish.

lan·gouste /läNGˈgo͞ost/ ▶ **n.** a spiny lobster, esp. in French cuisine.
– ORIGIN French, from Old Provençal *lagosta*, based on Latin *locusta* 'locust,crustacean.'

lan·gous·tine /ˈlaNGgə,stēn/ ▶ **n.** a large, commercially important prawn. ● *Nephrops norvegicus*, class Malacostraca.
– ORIGIN French, from *langouste* (see LANGOUSTE).

lang syne /,laNG ˈzīn, ˈsīn/ Scottish archaic ▶ **adv.** in the distant past; long ago: *we talked of races run lang syne.*
▶ **n.** times gone by; the old days, esp. in the phrase, "auld lang syne."
– ORIGIN early 16th cent.: from *lang*, Scots variant of LONG[1] + SYNE.

Lang·ton /ˈlaNGtən/, Stephen (*c.*1150–1228), English prelate; archbishop of Canterbury 1207–15 and 1218–28. A champion of the English Church, he was involved in the negotiations leading to the signing of Magna Carta.

Lang·try /ˈlaNGtrē/, Lillie (1853–1929), British actress; born *Emilie Charlotte le Breton*. She was the mistress of the Prince of Wales, who later became Edward VII.

lan·guage /ˈlaNGgwij/ ▶ **n.** **1** the method of human communication, either spoken or written, consisting of the use of words in a structured and conventional way: *a study of the way children learn language* | [as modifier] *language development.* ■ any nonverbal method of expression or communication: *a language of gesture and facial expression.* **2** the system of communication used by a particular community or country: *the book was translated into twenty-five languages.* ■ Computing a system of symbols and rules for writing programs or algorithms: *a new programming language.* **3** the manner or style of a piece of writing or speech: *he explained the procedure in simple, everyday language.* ■ the phraseology and vocabulary of a certain profession, domain, or group of people: *legal language.* ■ (usu. as **bad/strong language**) coarse, crude, or offensive language: *strong language.*
– PHRASES **speak the same language** understand one another as a result of shared opinions or values.
– ORIGIN Middle English: from Old French *langage*, based on Latin *lingua* 'tongue.'

lan·guage ar·e·a ▶ **n. 1** Physiology the area of the cerebral cortex thought to be particularly involved in the processing of language: *the language areas of the left cerebral hemisphere.*
2 a region where a particular language is spoken.

lan·guage arts ▶ **n.** the study of grammar, composition, spelling, and (sometimes) public speaking, typically taught as a single subject in elementary and middle school.

lan·guage en·gi·neer·ing ▶ **n.** any of a variety of computing procedures that use tools such as machine-readable dictionaries and sentence parsers in order to process natural languages for industrial applications such as speech recognition and speech synthesis.

lan·guage lab·o·ra·to·ry (also **language lab**) ▶ **n.** a room equipped with audio and visual equipment, such as tape and video recorders, for learning a foreign language.

lan·guage of flow·ers ▶ **n.** a set of symbolic meanings attached to different flowers when they are given or arranged.

langue /läNG(g)/ ▶ **n.** (pl. **same**) Linguistics a language viewed as an abstract system used by a speech community, in contrast to the actual linguistic behavior of individuals. Contrasted with PAROLE.
– ORIGIN 1920s: French, from Latin *lingua* 'language, tongue.'

langued /laNGd/ ▶ **adj.** Heraldry having the tongue of a specified tincture.
– ORIGIN late Middle English: from French *langué* 'tongued' + -ED[2].

langue d'oc /ˌläNG(gə)ˈ dôk/ ▶ **n.** the form of medieval French spoken south of the Loire, generally characterized by the use of *oc* to mean 'yes,' and forming the basis of modern Provençal. Compare with OCCITAN.
– ORIGIN from Old French *langue* 'language' (from Latin *lingua* 'tongue'), *d'* (from *de* 'of'), and *oc* (from Latin *hoc*) 'yes.' Compare with LANGUE D'OÏL.

Langue·doc-Rous·sil·lon /ˌläNGdôk ˌro͞oseˈyôN/ a region of southern France, on the Mediterranean coast, extending from the Rhône delta to the border with Spain.

langue d'oïl /ˌläNG(gə) ˈdoi(l)/ ▶ **n.** the form of medieval French spoken north of the Loire, generally characterized by the use of *oïl* to mean 'yes,' and forming the basis of modern French.
– ORIGIN from Old French *langue* 'language' (from Latin *lingua* 'tongue'), *d'* (from *de* 'of'), and *oïl* (from Latin *hoc ille*) 'yes.' Compare with LANGUE D'OC.

lan·guid /ˈlaNGgwid/ ▶ **adj. 1** (of a person, manner, or gesture) displaying or having a disinclination for physical exertion or effort; slow and relaxed: *they turned with languid movements from back to front so as to tan evenly.* ■ (of an occasion or period of time) pleasantly lazy and peaceful: *the terrace was perfect for languid days in the Italian sun.*
2 weak or faint from illness or fatigue: *she was pale, languid, and weak, as if she had delivered a child.*
– DERIVATIVES **lan·guid·ly** adv., **lan·guid·ness** n.
– ORIGIN late 16th cent. (sense 2): from French *languide* or Latin *languidus*, from *languere* (see LANGUISH).

lan·guish /ˈlaNGgwiSH/ ▶ **v.** [no obj.] **1** (of a person or other living thing) lose or lack vitality; grow weak or feeble: *plants may appear to be languishing simply because they are dormant.* ■ fail to make progress or be successful: *foreign stocks are still languishing.* ■ archaic pine with love or grief: *she still languished after Richard.* ■ archaic assume or display a sentimentally tender or melancholy expression or tone: *when a visitor comes in, she smiles and languishes.*
2 suffer from being forced to remain in an unpleasant place or situation: *he has been languishing in jail since 1974.*
– DERIVATIVES **lan·guish·er** n., **lan·guish·ing·ly** adv., **lan·guish·ment** n. (archaic).
– ORIGIN Middle English (in the sense 'become faint, feeble, or ill'): from Old French *languiss-*, lengthened stem of *languir* 'languish,' from a variant of Latin *languere*, related to *laxus* 'loose, lax.'

lan·guor /ˈlaNG(g)ər/ ▶ **n. 1** the state or feeling, often pleasant, of tiredness or inertia: *he remembered the languor and warm happiness of those golden afternoons.*
2 an oppressive stillness of the air: *the afternoon was hot, quiet, and heavy with languor.*
– DERIVATIVES **lan·guor·ous** /-g(ə)rəs, ˈlaNGərəs/ adj., **lan·guor·ous·ly** /-g(ə)rəslē, ˈlaNGərəslē/ adv.
– ORIGIN Middle English: via Old French from Latin, from *languere* (see LANGUISH). The original sense was 'illness, disease, distress,' later 'faintness, lassitude'; current senses date from the 18th cent., when such lassitude became associated with a sometimes rather self-indulgent romantic yearning.

lan·gur /läNGˈgo͝or/ ▶ **n.** a long-tailed arboreal Asian monkey with a characteristic loud call. ● *Presbytis* and other genera, family Cercopithecidae: several species. Compare with LEAF MONKEY.
– ORIGIN early 19th cent.: via Hindi from Sanskrit *lāṅgūla*.

La Ni·ña /lä ˈnēnyə/ ▶ **n.** a cooling of the water in the equatorial Pacific that occurs at irregular intervals and is associated with widespread changes in weather patterns complementary to those of El Niño, but less extensive and damaging in their effects.
– ORIGIN Spanish, literally 'the girl child,' after *El Niño*.

lank /laNGk/ ▶ **adj.** (of hair) long, limp, and straight. ■ (of a person) lanky.
– DERIVATIVES **lank·ly** adv., **lank·ness** n.
– ORIGIN Old English *hlanc* 'thin, not filled out,' of Germanic origin; related to High German *lenken* 'to bend, turn,' also to FLINCH[1] and LINK[1].

lank·y /ˈlaNGkē/ ▶ **adj.** (**lankier**, **lankiest**) (of a person) ungracefully thin and tall.
– DERIVATIVES **lank·i·ly** /-kəlē/ adv., **lank·i·ness** n.

lan·ner /ˈlanər/ (also **lanner falcon**) ▶ **n.** a falcon with a dark brown back and buff cap, found in southeastern Europe, the Middle East, and Africa. ● *Falco biarmicus*, family Falconidae.
– ORIGIN late Middle English: from Old French *lanier*, perhaps a noun use of *lanier* 'cowardly,' from a derogatory use of *lanier* 'wool merchant,' from Latin *lanarius*, from *lana* 'wool.'

lan·o·lin /ˈlanl-in, ˈlanələn/ ▶ **n.** a fatty substance found naturally on sheep's wool. It is extracted as a yellowish viscous mixture of esters and used as a base for ointments.
– ORIGIN late 19th cent.: coined in German from Latin *lana* 'wool' + *oleum* 'oil' + -IN[1].

Lan·sing /ˈlansiNG/ the capital of Michigan, in the southern part of the state; pop. 113,968 (est. 2008). First settled in 1847, it expanded rapidly after the establishment of the automobile industry there in 1887.

lans·que·net /ˌlanskəˈnet/ ▶ **n. 1** historical a gambling game of German origin involving betting on cards turned up by the dealer.
2 archaic variant of LANDSKNECHT.
– ORIGIN early 17th cent. (sense 2): via French from German *Landsknecht* (see LANDSKNECHT).

lan·ta·na /lanˈtanə, -ˈtänə/ ▶ **n.** a tropical evergreen shrub of the verbena family, several kinds of which are cultivated as ornamentals. ● Genus *Lantana*, family Verbenaceae: many species, in particular the South American scrambler *L. camara*, grown as an ornamental and sometimes becoming an invasive weed.
– ORIGIN modern Latin, from the specific name of the wayfaring tree *Viburnum lantana*, which it resembles superficially.

Lan·tau /ˈlänˈdou/ an island of Hong Kong, situated to the west of Hong Kong Island and forming part of the New Territories. Chinese name TAI YUE SHAN.

lan·tern /ˈlantərn/ ▶ **n. 1** a lamp with a transparent case protecting the flame or electric bulb, and typically having a handle by which it can be carried or hung: *a paper lantern.* ■ the light chamber at the top of a lighthouse. ■ short for MAGIC LANTERN.
2 a square, curved, or polygonal structure on the top of a dome or a room, with the sides glazed or open, so as to admit light.
– ORIGIN Middle English: from Old French *lanterne*, from Latin *lanterna*, from Greek *lamptēr* 'torch, lamp,' from *lampein* 'to shine.'

Lan·tern Fes·ti·val ▶ **n.** another name for BON.

lan·tern fish ▶ **n.** (pl. **same** or **fishes**) a deep-sea fish that has organs on its body that emit light, seen chiefly when it rises to the surface at night. ● Family Myctophidae: several genera and species.

lan·tern jaw ▶ **n.** a long, thin jaw and prominent chin.
– DERIVATIVES **lan·tern-jawed** adj.

lan·tern slide ▶ **n.** historical a mounted photographic transparency for projection by a magic lantern.

lan·tha·nide /ˈlanTHəˌnīd/ ▶ **n.** Chemistry any of the series of fifteen metallic elements from lanthanum to lutetium in the periodic table. See also RARE EARTH.
– ORIGIN 1920s: from LANTHANUM + -IDE.

lan·tha·num /ˈlanTHənəm/ ▶ **n.** the chemical element of atomic number 57, a silvery-white rare earth metal. (Symbol: **La**)
– ORIGIN mid 19th cent.: from Greek *lanthanein* 'escape notice' (because it was long undetected in cerium oxide) + -UM.

la·nu·go /ləˈn(y)o͞ogō/ ▶ **n.** Anatomy fine, soft hair, esp. that which covers the body and limbs of a human fetus or newborn.
– ORIGIN late 17th cent.: from Latin, 'down,' from *lana* 'wool.'

La·nús /läˈno͞os/ a city in eastern Argentina, south of Buenos Aires; pop. 463,000 (est. 2008).

lan·yard /ˈlanyərd/ ▶ **n.** a rope threaded through a pair of deadeyes, used to adjust the tension in the rigging of a sailing vessel. ■ a cord passed around the neck, shoulder, or wrist for holding a knife, whistle, or similar object.
– ORIGIN late Middle English *lanyer*, in the general sense 'a short length of rope or line for securing something,' from Old French *laniere*. The change in the ending in the 17th cent. was due to association with YARD[1].

Lan·za /ˈlänzə, lan-/, Mario (1921–59), US tenor; born *Alfredo Arnold Cocozza*. He became an international star as the portrayer of Enrico Caruso in the movies *The Great Caruso* (1951) and *The Seven Hills of Rome* (1958).

Lan·zhou /ˈlänjō/ (also **Lanchow**) a city in northern China, on the upper Yellow River, capital of Gansu province; pop. 1,708,200 (est. 2006).

Lao /lou/ ▶ **n.** (pl. **same** or **Laos** /louz/) **1** a member of an indigenous people of Laos and northeastern Thailand.
2 the Tai language of this people, closely related to Thai. Also called LAOTIAN.
▶ **adj.** of or relating to the Lao or their language.
– ORIGIN the name in Lao.

La·oc·o·on /lāˈäkōˌän/ Greek Mythology a Trojan priest who, with his two sons, was crushed to death by two great sea serpents as a penalty for warning the Trojans against drawing the wooden horse of the Greeks into Troy.

La·od·i·ce·an /ˌlāˌädəˈsēən/ archaic ▶ **adj.** lukewarm or halfhearted, esp. with respect to religion or politics.
▶ **n.** a person with such an attitude.
– ORIGIN early 17th cent.: from Latin *Laodicea* in Asia Minor, with reference to the early Christians there (Rev. 3:16), + -AN.

lao·gai /ˌlouˈgī/ ▶ **n.** (**the laogai**) (in China) a system of labor camps, many of whose inmates are political dissidents.
– ORIGIN Chinese, 'reform through labor.'

Laois /lāSH, lēSH/ (also **Laoighis**, **Leix**) a county of the Republic of Ireland, in the province of Leinster; county town, Portlaoise. Former name QUEEN'S COUNTY.

Laos /ˈlä-ōs, lous, ˈlāˌäs/ a landlocked country in Southeast Asia; pop. 6,834,300 (est. 2009); capital, Vientiane; official language, Laotian.

> Part of French Indo-China, Laos became independent in 1953, but for most of the next 25 years was torn by civil strife between the communist Pathet Lao movement and government supporters. In 1975, the Pathet Lao achieved total control, and a communist republic was established. The end of the 20th century saw a gradual return to free enterprise.

– DERIVATIVES **La·o·tian** /lāˈōSHən/ adj. & n.

Lao-tzu /ˌlä-ō ˈtso͞o, ˈdzə/ (also **Laoze** /ˈtsä, ˈdzä/) (*fl.* 6th century BC), Chinese philosopher traditionally regarded as the founder of Taoism and author of the Tao-te-Ching, its most sacred scripture.
– ORIGIN Chinese, literally 'Lao the Master.'

lap[1] /lap/ ▶ **n. 1** (usu. **one's lap**) the flat area between the waist and knees of a seated person: *come and sit on my lap.* ■ the part of an item of clothing, esp. a skirt, covering the lap.
2 archaic a hanging flap on a garment or a saddle.
– PHRASES **fall** (or **drop**) **into someone's lap** (of something unexpected) come someone's way without any effort having been made: *not many reporters are lucky enough to have stories fall into their laps.* **in someone's lap** as someone's responsibility: *she dumped the problem in my lap.* **in the lap of luxury** in conditions of great comfort and wealth.
– DERIVATIVES **lap·ful** /-ˌfo͝ol/ n. (pl. **lapfuls**).
– ORIGIN Old English *læppa*, of Germanic origin; related to Dutch *lap*, German *Lappen* 'piece of cloth.' The word originally denoted a fold or flap of a garment (compare with LAPEL), later specifically one that could be used as a pocket or pouch, or the front of a skirt when held up to catch or carry something (Middle English), hence the area between the waist and knees as a place where a child could be nursed or an object held.

lap[2] ▶ **n. 1** one circuit of a track or racetrack. ■ a stage in a swim consisting of two lengths of a pool. ■ a section of a journey or other undertaking: *we caught a cab for the last lap of our journey.*
2 an overlapping or projecting part. ■ the amount by which one thing overlaps or covers a part of another. ■ Metallurgy a defect formed in rolling when a projecting part is accidentally folded over

and pressed against the surface of the metal. ■ (in a steam engine) the distance by which the valve overlaps the steam port (or the exhaust port).
3 a single turn of rope, thread, or cable around a drum or reel. ■ a layer or sheet, typically wound on a roller, into which cotton or wool is formed during its manufacture.
4 (in a lapping machine) a rotating disk with a coating of fine abrasive for polishing. ■ a polishing tool of a special shape, coated or impregnated with an abrasive.
▶ **v.** (**laps, lapping, lapped**) **1** [with obj.] overtake (a competitor in a race) to become one or more laps ahead: *she lapped all of her rivals in the 3,000 meters.* ■ [no obj.] (of a competitor or vehicle in a race) complete a lap, esp. in a specified time: *he lapped two tenths of a second faster than anyone else.*
2 [with obj.] (**lap someone/something in**) literary enfold or swathe a person or thing, esp. a part of the body, in (something soft): *he was lapped in blankets* | figurative *I was accustomed to being lapped in luxury.*
3 [no obj.] project beyond or overlap something: *the water lapped over the edges.*
4 [with obj.] polish (a gem or a metal or glass surface) with a lapping machine.
– ORIGIN Middle English (as a verb in the sense 'coil, fold, or wrap'): from LAP[1]. Sense 1 of the noun and verb date from the mid 19th cent.

lap[3] ▶ **v.** (**laps, lapping, lapped**) [with obj.] **1** (of an animal) take up (liquid) with the tongue in order to drink: *the cat was lapping up a saucer of milk.* ■ (**lap something up**) accept something eagerly and with obvious pleasure: *she's lapping up the attention.*
2 (of water) wash against (something) with a gentle rippling sound: *the waves lapped the shore* | [no obj.] *the sound of the river lapping against the banks.*
▶ **n.** [in sing.] the action of water washing gently against something: *listening to the comfortable lap of the waves against the shore.*
– DERIVATIVES **lap·per** n.
– ORIGIN Old English *lapian*, of Germanic origin; related to Middle Low German and Middle Dutch *lapen.*

lap·a·ros·co·py /ˌlapəˈräskəpē/ ▶ **n.** (pl. **laparoscopies**) a surgical procedure in which a fiber-optic instrument is inserted through the abdominal wall to view the organs in the abdomen or to permit a surgical procedure.
– DERIVATIVES **lap·a·ro·scope** /ˈlap(ə)rəˌskōp/ n., **lap·a·ro·scop·ic** /ˌlap(ə)rəˈskäpik/ adj., **lap·a·ro·scop·i·cal·ly** adv.
– ORIGIN mid 19th cent.: from Greek *lapara* 'flank' + -SCOPY.

lap·a·rot·o·my /ˌlapəˈrätəmē/ ▶ **n.** (pl. **laparotomies**) a surgical incision into the abdominal cavity, for diagnosis or in preparation for surgery.
– ORIGIN mid 19th cent.: from Greek *lapara* 'flank' + -TOMY.

La Paz /lä ˈpäz, ˈpäs/ **1** the capital of Bolivia, in the northwestern part of the country, near the border with Peru; pop. 835,301 (2009). Situated in the Andes at an altitude of 12,000 feet (3,660 m), it is the highest capital city in the world.
2 a city in Mexico, near the southern tip of the Baja California peninsula, capital of the state of Baja California Sur; pop. 189,176 (2005).

lap belt ▶ **n.** a seat belt worn across the lap.

lap dance ▶ **n.** an erotic dance or striptease performed close to, or sitting on the lap of, a paying customer.
– DERIVATIVES **lap danc·er** n., **lap danc·ing** n.

lap desk ▶ **n.** a portable writing case or surface, esp. one for use on the lap.

lap dis·solve ▶ **n.** a fade-out of a scene in a movie that overlaps with a fade-in of a new scene, so that one appears to dissolve into the other.

lap·dog /ˈlapˌdôg, -ˌdäg/ (also **lap dog**) ▶ **n.** a small dog kept as a pet. ■ a person or organization that is influenced or controlled by another: *the government and its media lapdogs.*

la·pel /ləˈpel/ ▶ **n.** the part on each side of a coat or jacket immediately below the collar that is folded back on either side of the front opening.
– DERIVATIVES **la·pelled** adj. [in combination] *a narrow-lapelled suit.*
– ORIGIN mid 17th cent.: diminutive of LAP[1].

lap·i·dar·y /ˈlapəˌderē/ ▶ **adj.** (of language) engraved on or suitable for engraving on stone and therefore elegant and concise: *a lapidary statement.* ■ of or relating to stone and gems and the work involved in engraving, cutting, or polishing.
▶ **n.** (pl. **lapidaries**) a person who cuts, polishes, or engraves gems.
– ORIGIN Middle English (as a noun): from Latin *lapidarius* (in late Latin 'stonecutter'), from *lapis, lapid-* 'stone.' The adjective dates from the early 18th cent.

la·pil·li /ləˈpiˌlī/ ▶ **plural n.** Geology rock fragments ejected from a volcano.
– ORIGIN mid 18th cent. (in the general sense 'stones, pebbles'): via Italian from Latin, plural of *lapillus*, diminutive of *lapis* 'stone.'

lap·is laz·u·li /ˈlapis ˈlazəlē, ˈlaZHəˌlī, ˈlazyəlē/ (also **lapis**) ▶ **n.** a bright blue metamorphic rock consisting largely of lazurite, used for decoration and in jewelry. ■ a bright blue pigment formerly made by crushing this, being the original ultramarine. ■ the color ultramarine.
– ORIGIN late Middle English: from Latin *lapis* 'stone' and medieval Latin *lazuli*, genitive of *lazulum*, from Persian *lāžward* 'lapis lazuli.' Compare with AZURE.

Lap·ith /ˈlapiTH/ ▶ **n.** Greek Mythology a member of a Thessalian people who fought and defeated the centaurs.
– ORIGIN via Latin from Greek *Lapithai* (plural).

lap joint ▶ **n.** a joint made with two pieces of metal, timber, etc., by halving the thickness of each member at the joint and fitting them together.

La·place /läˈpläs/, Pierre Simon, Marquis de (1749–1827), French applied mathematician and theoretical physicist. His treatise *Mécanique céleste* (1799–1825) is an extensive mathematical analysis of geophysical matters and of planetary and lunar motion.

Lap·land /ˈlapˌland, -lənd/ a region in northern Europe that extends from the Norwegian Sea to the White Sea and lies mainly within the Arctic Circle. It consists of the northern parts of Norway, Sweden, and Finland, as well as the Kola Peninsula of Russia.
– DERIVATIVES **Lap·land·er** n.
– ORIGIN late 16th cent.: from Swedish *Lappland*, from *Lapp* (see LAPP) + *land* 'land.'

La Pla·ta /lə ˈplätə, lä ˈplätä/ a port in Argentina, on the Plate River (Río de la Plata) southeast of Buenos Aires; pop. 654,800 (est. 2008).

Lapp /lap/ ▶ **n. 1** a member of an indigenous people of far northern Scandinavia, traditionally associated with the herding of reindeer.
2 the Finno-Ugric language of this people, with nine distinct dialects.
▶ **adj.** of or relating to the Lapps or their language.
– ORIGIN Swedish, perhaps originally a term of contempt and related to Middle High German *lappe* 'simpleton.'

USAGE Although the term **Lapp** is still widely used and is the most familiar term to many, the people themselves prefer to be called **Sami**.

lap·pet /ˈlapit/ ▶ **n. 1** a small flap or fold, in particular: ■ a fold or hanging piece of flesh in some animals. ■ a loose or overlapping part of a garment.
2 (also **lappet moth**) a brownish moth, the hairy caterpillars of which have fleshy lappets along each side of the body. ● Several species in the family Lasiocampidae: including *Phyllodesma americana.*
– DERIVATIVES **lap·pet·ed** adj.
– ORIGIN late Middle English (denoting a lobe of the ear, liver, etc.): diminutive of LAP[1].

lap·ping ma·chine ▶ **n.** a machine with a rotating abrasive disk for polishing gems, metal, and optical glass.

Lap·pish /ˈlapiSH/ ▶ **adj.** of or relating to the Lapps (Sami) or their language.
▶ **n.** the Lapp language.

lap pool ▶ **n.** a swimming pool specially designed or designated for swimming laps.

lap robe ▶ **n.** a thick blanket or pelt used for warming the lap and legs while traveling or sitting outdoors.

lap·sang sou·chong /ˈlapˌsaNG ˈso͞oˌCHäNG, ˈläpˌsäNG, ˈso͞oˌSHäNG/ ▶ **n.** a variety of souchong tea with a smoky flavor.
– ORIGIN late 19th cent.: from an invented first element + SOUCHONG.

lapse /laps/ ▶ **n. 1** a temporary failure of concentration, memory, or judgment: *a lapse of concentration in the second set cost her the match.* ■ a weak or careless decline from previously high standards: *tracing his lapse into petty crime.* ■ Law the termination of a right or privilege through disuse or failure to follow appropriate procedures.
2 an interval or passage of time: *there was a considerable lapse of time between the two events.*
▶ **v.** [no obj.] **1** (of a right, privilege, or agreement) become invalid because it is not used, claimed, or renewed; expire: *my membership to the gym has lapsed.* ■ (of a state or activity) fail to be maintained; come to an end: *if your diet has lapsed it's time you revived it.* ■ (of an adherent to a particular religion or doctrine) cease to follow the rules and practices of that religion or doctrine.
2 (**lapse into**) pass gradually into (an inferior state or condition): *the country has lapsed into chaos.* ■ revert to (a previous or more familiar style of speaking or behavior): *the girls lapsed into French.*
– ORIGIN late Middle English: from Latin *lapsus*, from *labi* 'to glide, slip, or fall'; the verb reinforced by Latin *lapsare* 'to slip or stumble.'

lapsed /lapst/ ▶ **adj.** no longer valid; expired: *a lapsed insurance policy.* ■ no longer following the rules and practices of a religion or doctrine; nonpracticing: *a lapsed Catholic.*

lapse rate ▶ **n.** the rate at which air temperature falls with increasing altitude.

lap steel (also **lap steel guitar**) ▶ **n.** another term for PEDAL STEEL.

lap·strake /ˈlapˌsträk/ ▶ **n.** a clinker-built boat.
▶ **adj.** (also **lapstraked**) clinker-built.

lap·sus ca·la·mi /ˈlapsəs ˈkaləˌmī, -ˌmē/ ▶ **n.** (pl. **same**) formal a slip of the pen.
– ORIGIN Latin.

lap·sus lin·guae /ˈlapsəs ˈliNGˌgwī, -ˌgwē/ ▶ **n.** (pl. **same**) formal a slip of the tongue.
– ORIGIN Latin.

Lap·tev Sea /ˈlapˌtev, -ˌtef/ a part of the Arctic Ocean that lies to the north of Russia between the Taimyr Peninsula and the New Siberian Islands.

lap·top /ˈlapˌtäp/ (also **laptop computer**) ▶ **n.** a computer that is portable and suitable for use while traveling.

lap-weld ▶ **v.** [with obj.] weld (something) with the edges overlapping.
▶ **n.** (**lap weld**) a weld made in this way.

lap·wing /ˈlapˌwiNG/ ▶ **n.** a large plover, typically having a black and white head and underparts and a loud call. ● Genus *Vanellus*, family Charadriidae: several species, in particular the **northern lapwing** (*V. vanellus*) of Eurasia (also called GREEN PLOVER or PEWIT), which has a dark green back and a crest.
– ORIGIN Old English *hlēapewince*, from *hlēapan* 'to leap' and a base meaning 'move from side to side' (whence also WINK); so named because of the way it flies. The spelling was changed in Middle English by association with LAP[1] and WING.

Lar·a·mie /ˈlarəmē/ a city in southeastern Wyoming; pop. 27,664 (est. 2008). It was first settled in 1868 during the construction of the Union Pacific Railroad.

lar·board /ˈlärˌbôrd, -bərd/ ▶ **n.** Nautical archaic term for PORT[3].
– ORIGIN Middle English *ladebord* (see LADE, BOARD), referring to the side on which cargo was put aboard. The change to *lar-* in the 16th cent. was due to association with STARBOARD.

lar·ce·ny /ˈlärs(ə)nē/ ▶ **n.** (pl. **larcenies**) theft of personal property. See also GRAND LARCENY, PETTY LARCENY.
– DERIVATIVES **lar·ce·ner** /-nər/ n. (archaic), **lar·ce·nist** /-nist/ n., **lar·ce·nous** /-nəs/ adj.
– ORIGIN late 15th cent.: from Old French *larcin*, from Latin *latrocinium*, from *latro(n-)* 'robber,' earlier 'mercenary soldier,' from Greek *latreus.*

larch /lärCH/ ▶ **n.** a coniferous tree with bunches of deciduous bright green needles, found in cool regions of the northern hemisphere. It is grown for its tough timber and its resin (which yields turpentine). See also TAMARACK. ● Genus *Larix*, family Pinaceae: several species, including the **common** (or **European**) **larch** (*L. decidua*).
– ORIGIN mid 16th cent.: from Middle High German *larche*, based on Latin *larix.*

lard /lärd/ ▶ **n.** fat from the abdomen of a pig that is rendered and clarified for use in cooking. ■ informal excess human fat that is seen as unhealthy and unattractive.
▶ **v.** [with obj.] **1** insert strips of fat or bacon in (meat) before cooking. ■ smear or cover (a foodstuff) with lard or fat, typically to prevent it from drying out during storage.
2 (usu. **be larded with**) embellish (talk or writing) with a variety of expressions: *his conversation is larded with quotations from Coleridge.* ■ cover or fill thickly or excessively: *the pages were larded with corrections and crossings-out.*
– DERIVATIVES **lard·y** adj.
– ORIGIN Middle English (also denoting bacon fat): from Old French, 'bacon,' from Latin *lardum, laridum*, related to Greek *larinos* 'fat.'

lard·ass /ˈlärˌdas/ ▶ **n.** informal, derogatory a fat person, esp. one with large buttocks or who is regarded as lazy.

lard·er /ˈlärdər/ ▶ **n.** a room or large cupboard for storing food.
– ORIGIN Middle English (denoting a store of meat): from Old French *lardier*, from medieval Latin *lardarium*, from *laridum* (see LARD).

lar·der bee·tle ▶ **n.** a brownish scavenging beetle that is a pest of stored products, esp. meat and hides. ● *Dermestes lardarius*, family Dermestidae.

Lard·ner /ˈlärdnər/, Ring (1885–1933), US writer and journalist; full name *Ringgold Wilmer Lardner*. He wrote *You Know Me Al: A Busher's Letters* (1914), *Treat 'Em Rough* (1918), and *The Real Dope* (1919), all collections of his stories that feature his best-known character, baseball pitcher Jack Keefe.

lar·don /ˈlärdn/ (also **lardoon** /lärˈdo͞on/) ▶ **n.** a piece of bacon used to lard meat.
– ORIGIN late Middle English: from French, from *lard* 'bacon' (see **LARD**).

La·re·do /ləˈrādō/ an industrial port city in southern Texas, across the Rio Grande from Nuevo Laredo in Mexico; pop. 221,659 (est. 2008).

lar·es /ˈlāˌrēz, ˈle(ə)rēz/ ▶ **plural n.** gods of the household worshiped in ancient Rome. See also **PENATES**.
– PHRASES **lares and penates** the home.
– ORIGIN Latin.

large /lärj/ ▶ **adj. 1** of considerable or relatively great size, extent, or capacity: *add a large clove of garlic | the concert attracted large crowds | the sweater comes in small, medium, and large sizes.* ■ pursuing an occupation or commercial activity on a significant scale: *many large investors are likely to take a different view.*
2 of wide range or scope: *we can afford to take a larger view of the situation.*
3 Sailing another term for **FREE** (sense 8 of the adjective).
▶ **adv.** Sailing another term for **FREE** (sense 2 of the adverb).
– PHRASES **at large 1** (esp. of a criminal or dangerous animal) at liberty; escaped or not yet captured: *the fugitive was still at large.* **2** as a whole; in general: *there has been a loss of community values in society at large.* **3** (also **at-large**) in a general way; without particularizing: *the magazine's editor at large.* **4** dated at length; in great detail: *writing at large on the policies he wished to pursue.* **in large measure** (or **part**) to a great extent: *the success of the conference was due in large part to its organizers.* **(as) large as life** see **LIFE**. **larger than life** see **LIFE**.
– DERIVATIVES **large·ness n.**, **larg·ish** /-jisʜ/ **adj.** (sense 1 of the adjective).
– ORIGIN Middle English (in the sense 'liberal in giving, lavish, ample in quantity'): via Old French from Latin *larga*, feminine of *largus* 'copious.'

large cal·o·rie ▶ **n.** see **CALORIE**.

large-cap ▶ **adj.** Finance denoting or relating to the stock of a company with a large capitalization.

large-heart·ed ▶ **adj.** sympathetic and generous.

large in·tes·tine ▶ **n.** Anatomy the cecum, colon, and rectum collectively.

large·ly /ˈlärjlē/ ▶ **adv.** [sentence adverb] to a great extent; on the whole; mostly: *he was soon arrested, largely through the efforts of Tom Poole* | [as submodifier] *their efforts were largely unsuccessful.*

large-mind·ed ▶ **adj.** open to and tolerant of other people's ideas; liberal.

large·mouth /ˈlärjˌmoutʜ/ ▶ **n.** the largemouth bass (see **BLACK BASS**).

large-scale ▶ **adj. 1** involving large numbers or a large area; extensive: *large-scale commercial farming.*
2 (of a map or model) made to a scale large enough to show certain features in detail.

lar·gesse /lärˈzʜes, -ˈjes/ (also **largess**) ▶ **n.** generosity in bestowing money or gifts upon others: *dispensing his money with such largesse.* ■ money or gifts given generously: *the distribution of largesse to the local population.*
– ORIGIN Middle English: from Old French, from Latin *largus* 'copious.'

lar·ghet·to /lärˈgetō/ Music ▶ **adv. & adj.** (esp. as a direction) in a fairly slow tempo.
▶ **n.** (pl. **larghettos**) a passage or movement marked to be performed in this way.
– ORIGIN Italian, diminutive of *largo* 'broad.'

lar gib·bon /ˈlär/ ▶ **n.** another term for **WHITE-HANDED GIBBON**.

Lar·go /ˈlärˌgō/ a resort city in west central Florida, southwest of Clearwater; pop. 72,732 (est. 2008).

lar·go /ˈlärgō/ Music ▶ **adv. & adj.** (esp. as a direction) in a slow tempo and dignified in style.
▶ **n.** (often **Largo**) (pl. **largos**) a passage, movement, or composition marked to be performed in this way.
– ORIGIN Italian, from Latin *largus* 'copious, abundant.'

la·ri /ˈlärē/ ▶ **n.** (pl. **same** or **laris**) a monetary unit of the Maldives, equal to one hundredth of a rufiyaa.
– ORIGIN from Persian.

Lar·i·am /ˈlarēəm/ ▶ **n.** trademark for **MEFLOQUINE**.
– ORIGIN 1980s: probably from partial rearrangement of **MALARIA**.

lar·i·at /ˈlarēət/ ▶ **n.** a rope used as a lasso or for tethering.
– ORIGIN mid 19th cent.: from Spanish *la reata*, from *la* 'the' and *reatar* 'tie again' (based on Latin *aptare* 'adjust,' from *aptus* 'apt, fitting').

La Rio·ja /lä rēˈōhä/ an autonomous region of northern Spain, in the wine-producing valley of the Ebro River; capital, Logroño.

La·ris·sa /ləˈrisə/ a city in east central Greece; pop. 134,100 (est. 2009). Greek name **Lárisa**.

lark¹ /lärk/ ▶ **n.** a small ground-dwelling songbird, typically with brown streaky plumage, a crest, and elongated hind claws, and with a song that is delivered in flight. ● Family Alaudidae: many genera and numerous species, e.g., the **skylark**. ■ used in names of similar birds of other families, e.g., the **meadowlark**.
– ORIGIN Old English *lāferce*, *lǣwerce*; related to Dutch *leeuwerik* and German *Lerche*; of unknown ultimate origin.

lark² informal ▶ **n.** something done for fun, esp. something mischievous or daring; an amusing adventure or escapade: *I only went along for a lark.* ■ [usu. with modifier] chiefly Brit. used to suggest that an activity is foolish or a waste of time: *he's serious about this music lark.*
▶ **v.** [no obj.] enjoy oneself by behaving in a playful and mischievous way: *he jumped the fence to go larking the rest of the day.*
– DERIVATIVES **lark·ish adj.**, **lark·y adj.**
– ORIGIN early 19th cent.: perhaps from dialect *lake* 'play,' from Old Norse *leika*, but compare with **SKYLARK** in the same sense, which is recorded earlier.

lark·spur /ˈlärkˌspər/ ▶ **n.** an annual Mediterranean plant of the buttercup family that bears spikes of spurred flowers. It is closely related to the delphiniums, with which it has been bred to produce a number of cultivated hybrids. ● Genus *Consolida* (formerly *Delphinium*), family Ranunculaceae.

larn /lärn/ ▶ **v.** dialect form of **LEARN**.

La·rousse /ləˈro͞os, lä-/, Pierre (1817–75), French lexicographer and encyclopedist. He edited the 15-volume *Grand dictionnaire universel du XIXe siècle* (1866–76) and cofounded the publishing house of Larousse in 1852.

lar·rup /ˈlarəp/ ▶ **v.** (**larrups, larruping, larruped**) [with obj.] informal thrash or whip (someone).
– ORIGIN early 19th cent. (originally dialect): perhaps related to **LATHER** or **LEATHER**.

Lar·son /ˈlärsən/, Gary (1950–), US cartoonist and writer. His one-panel comic "The Far Side," which he began in 1984 and retired in 1995, was syndicated in more than 900 newspapers.

lar·va /ˈlärvə/ ▶ **n.** (pl. **larvae** /-vē, -ˌvī/) the active immature form of an insect, esp. one that differs greatly from the adult and forms the stage between egg and pupa, e.g., a caterpillar or grub. Compare with **NYMPH** (sense 2). ■ an immature form of other animals that undergo some metamorphosis, e.g., a tadpole.
– DERIVATIVES **lar·val** /-vəl/ **adj.**, **lar·vi·cide** /-ˌsīd/ **n.**
– ORIGIN mid 17th cent. (denoting a disembodied spirit or ghost): from Latin, literally 'ghost, mask.'

Lar·va·ce·a /lärˈvāsʜēə/ Zoology a class of minute transparent planktonic animals related to the sea squirts. They have a body that is typically enclosed in a gelatinous "house" that is regularly shed and replaced.
– DERIVATIVES **lar·va·ce·an adj. & n.**
– ORIGIN modern Latin (plural), from **LARVA**.

la·ryn·ge·al /ləˈrinj(ē)əl, ˌlarənˈjēəl/ ▶ **adj.** of or relating to the larynx: *the laryngeal artery.* ■ Phonetics (of a speech sound) made in the larynx with the vocal cords partly closed and partly vibrating (producing, in English, the so-called "creaky voice" sound): *laryngeal consonants.*
▶ **n.** Phonetics a laryngeal sound.
– ORIGIN late 18th cent.: from modern Latin *laryngeus* 'relating to the larynx' + **-AL**.

la·ryn·ges /ləˈrinˌjēz/ plural form of **LARYNX**.

lar·yn·gi·tis /ˌlarənˈjītis/ ▶ **n.** inflammation of the larynx, typically resulting in huskiness or loss of the voice, harsh breathing, and a painful cough.
– DERIVATIVES **lar·yn·git·ic** /-ˈjitik/ **adj.**

lar·yn·gol·o·gy /ˌlarəɴGˈgäləjē/ ▶ **n.** the branch of medicine that deals with the larynx and its diseases.
– DERIVATIVES **lar·yn·gol·o·gist** /-jist/ **n.**

la·ryn·go·scope /ləˈriɴGgəˌskōp, -ˈrinjə-/ ▶ **n.** an instrument for examining the larynx, or for inserting a tube through it.
– DERIVATIVES **lar·yn·gos·co·py** /ˌlarənˈgäskəpē, ˌlarəɴGˈgä-/ **n.**

lar·yn·got·o·my /ˌlarənˈgätəmē, ˌlarəɴGˈgä-/ ▶ **n.** surgical incision into the larynx, typically to provide an air passage when breathing is obstructed.

lar·ynx /ˈlariɴGks, ˈler-/ ▶ **n.** (pl. **larynges** /ləˈrinˌjēz/ or **larynxes**) Anatomy the hollow muscular organ forming an air passage to the lungs and holding the vocal cords in humans and other mammals; the voice box.
– ORIGIN late 16th cent.: modern Latin, from Greek *larunx*.

la·sa·gna /ləˈzänyə/ (also **lasagne**) ▶ **n.** pasta in the form of wide strips. ■ a baked Italian dish consisting of this cooked and layered with meat or vegetables, cheese, and tomato sauce.
– ORIGIN Italian, plural of *lasagna*, based on Latin *lasanum* 'chamber pot,' perhaps also 'cooking pot.'

La Salle /lə ˈsal, lä ˈsäl/, René-Robert Cavelier, Sieur de (1643–87), French explorer. He sailed from Canada down the Ohio and Mississippi rivers to the Gulf of Mexico in 1682, naming the Mississippi basin Louisiana in honor of Louis XIV. In 1684, he led an expedition to establish a French colony on the Gulf of Mexico, but was murdered when his followers mutinied.

La Sca·la /lä ˈskälə/ an opera house in Milan built 1776–78 on the site of the church of Santa Maria della Scala.

las·car /ˈlaskər/ ▶ **n.** dated a sailor from India or Southeast Asia.
– ORIGIN early 17th cent.: from Portuguese *lascari*, from Urdu and Persian *laškarī* 'soldier,' from *laškar* 'army.'

Las·caux /läsˈkō, las-/ the site of a cave in the Dordogne, France, which is richly decorated with Paleolithic wall paintings of animals dated to the Magdalenian period.

las·civ·i·ous /ləˈsivēəs/ ▶ **adj.** (of a person, manner, or gesture) feeling or revealing an overt and often offensive sexual desire: *he gave her a lascivious wink.*
– DERIVATIVES **las·civ·i·ous·ly adv.**, **las·civ·i·ous·ness n.**
– ORIGIN late Middle English: from late Latin *lasciviosus*, from Latin *lascivia* 'lustfulness,' from *lascivus* 'lustful, wanton.'

Las Cru·ces /läs ˈkro͞osəs/ a city in southern New Mexico, on the Rio Grande; pop. 91,865 (est. 2008).

lase /lāz/ ▶ **v.** [no obj.] (of a substance, esp. a gas or crystal) undergo the physical processes employed in a laser; function as or in a laser.
– ORIGIN 1960s: back-formation from **LASER**, interpreted as an agent noun.

la·ser /ˈlāzər/ ▶ **n.** a device that generates an intense beam of coherent monochromatic light (or other electromagnetic radiation) by stimulated emission of photons from excited atoms or molecules. Lasers are used in drilling and cutting, alignment and guidance, and in surgery; the optical properties are exploited in holography, reading bar codes, and in recording and playing compact discs.
– ORIGIN 1960s: acronym from *light amplification by stimulated emission of radiation*, on the pattern of *maser*.

la·ser·disc /ˈlāzərˌdisk/ (also **laser disc**) ▶ **n.** a disk resembling a larger CD but able to store video, now generally replaced by the DVD.

la·ser gun ▶ **n.** a handheld device incorporating a laser beam, used typically for reading a bar code or for determining the distance or speed of an object. ■ (in science fiction) a weapon that uses a powerful laser beam.

la·ser point·er ▶ **n.** a pen-shaped pointing device that contains a small diode laser that emits an intense beam of light, used to direct attention during presentations.

la·ser print·er ▶ **n.** a printer, linked to a computer, producing good-quality printed material by using a laser to form a pattern of electrostatically charged dots on a light-sensitive drum, which attract toner (or dry ink powder). The toner is transferred to a piece of paper and fixed by a heating process.

la·ser tweez·ers ▶ **plural n.** another term for **OPTICAL TWEEZERS**.

lash /lasʜ/ ▶ **v.** [with obj.] **1** strike (someone) with a whip or stick: *they lashed him repeatedly about the head.* ■ beat forcefully against (something): *waves lashed the coast.* ■ (**lash someone into**) drive someone into (a particular state or condition): *fear lashed him into a frenzy.*
2 (of an animal) move (a part of the body, esp. the tail) quickly and violently: *the cat was lashing its tail back and forth.* ■ [no obj.] (of a part of the body) move in this way.

3 fasten (something) securely with a cord or rope: *the hatch was securely **lashed down** | he lashed the flag to the mast.*
▶ **n. 1** a sharp blow or stroke with a whip or rope, typically given as a form of punishment: *he was sentenced to fifty lashes for his crime* | figurative *she felt the lash of my tongue.* ■ the flexible leather part of a whip, used for administering such blows. ■ **(the lash)** punishment in the form of a beating with a whip or rope: *they were living under the threat of the lash.*
2 (usu. **lashes**) an eyelash: *she fluttered her long dark lashes.*
– PHRASAL VERBS **lash down** (of rain) fall very heavily: *torrential rain was lashing down.* **lash out 1** hit or kick out at someone or something: *sticks with which to lash out and strike the prisoner.* ■ attack verbally: *he used his thank-you speech to **lash out** at critics.* **2** Brit. spend money extravagantly: *let's **lash out** on a taxi.*
– DERIVATIVES **lash·er n., lash·less adj.**
– ORIGIN Middle English (in the sense 'make a sudden movement'): probably imitative.

lashed¹ /lasHt/ ▶ **adj.** [in combination] having eyelashes of a specified kind: *long-lashed eyes.*

lashed² /lasHt/ ▶ **adj.** Brit. informal very drunk: *they were all eager to get lashed and start their working week off with a hangover.*

lash·ing /ˈlasHiNG/ ▶ **n. 1** an act or instance of whipping: *I threatened to give him a good lashing!* | figurative *he was on the receiving end of a verbal lashing yesterday.*
2 (usu. **lashings**) a cord used to fasten something securely.

lash·ings /ˈlasHiNGz/ ▶ **plural n.** Brit. informal a copious amount of something, esp. food or drink: *chocolate cake with lashings of cream.*

lash-up ▶ **n.** chiefly Brit. a makeshift, improvised structure or arrangement.

LASIK /ˈlāzik/ ▶ **n.** eye surgery to correct vision in which a laser reshapes the inner cornea.
– ORIGIN from *l(aser)-as(sisted) i(n-situ) k(eratomileusis).*

Las Pal·mas /läs ˈpälməs/ a port and resort on the north coast of the island of Gran Canaria, capital of the Canary Islands; pop. 381,123 (2008). Full name **Las Palmas de Gran Canaria**.

La Spe·zia /lä ˈspetsēə/ an industrial port in northwestern Italy; pop. 95,372 (2008). From 1861, it was Italy's chief naval station.

lass /las/ ▶ **n.** chiefly Scottish & N. English a girl or young woman: *he married a lass from Yorkshire.*
– ORIGIN Middle English: based on Old Norse *laskura* (feminine adjective) 'unmarried.'

Las·sa fe·ver /ˈläsə, ˈlasə/ ▶ **n.** an acute and often fatal viral disease, with fever, occurring chiefly in West Africa. It is usually acquired from infected rats.
– ORIGIN 1970s: named after the village of *Lassa*, in northwestern Nigeria, where it was first reported.

las·si /ˈlasē/ ▶ **n.** a sweet or savory Indian drink made from a yogurt or buttermilk base with water.
– ORIGIN from Hindi *lassī.*

las·sie /ˈlasē/ ▶ **n.** chiefly Scottish & N. English another term for **LASS**.

las·si·tude /ˈlasəˌt(y)o͞od/ ▶ **n.** a state of physical or mental weariness; lack of energy: *she was overcome by lassitude and retired to bed | a patient complaining of lassitude and inability to concentrate.*
– ORIGIN late Middle English: from French, from Latin *lassitudo*, from *lassus* 'tired.'

las·so /ˈlasō, ˈlaso͞o, laˈso͞o/ ▶ **n.** (pl. **lassos** or **lassoes**) a rope with a noose at one end, used esp. in North America for catching cattle or horses.
▶ **v. (lassoes, lassoing, lassoed)** [with obj.] catch (an animal) with a lasso: *at last his father lassoed the horse.*
– DERIVATIVES **las·so·er n.**
– ORIGIN mid 18th cent.: representing a Spanish American pronunciation of Spanish *lazo*, based on Latin *laqueus* 'noose.' Compare with **LACE**.

Las·sus /ˈläsəs/, Orlande de (*c.*1532–94), Flemish composer; Italian name *Orlando di Lasso.* He wrote over 2,000 secular and sacred works.

last¹ /last/ ▶ **adj.** [attrib.] **1** coming after all others in time or order; final: *they caught the last bus.* ■ met with or encountered after any others: *the last house in the village.* ■ the lowest in importance or rank: *finishing in last place* | [as complement] *he came last in the race.* ■ **(the last)** the least likely or suitable: *addicts are often the last people to face up to their problems | **the last thing she needed** was a husband.*
2 most recent in time; latest: *last year* | [postpositive] *your letter of Sunday last.* ■ immediately preceding in order; previous in a sequence or enumeration: *their last album | this last point is critical.*
3 only remaining: *it's our last hope.*
▶ **adv. 1** on the last occasion before the present; previously: *he looked much older than when I'd last seen him.*
2 [in combination] after all others in order or sequence: *the two last-mentioned classes.*
3 (esp. in enumerating points) finally; in conclusion: *and last, I'd like to thank you all for coming.*
▶ **n.** (pl. **same**) the last person or thing; the one occurring, mentioned, or acting after all others: *the last of their guests had gone | eating as if every mouthful were his last.* ■ **(the last of)** the only part of something that remains: *they drank the last of the wine.* ■ [in sing.] last position in a race, contest, or ranking: *he came from last in a slowly run race.* ■ **(the last)** the end or last moment, esp. death: *she did love me **to the last**.* ■ **(the last)** the last mention or sight of someone or something: *that was the last we saw of her.*
– PHRASES **at last** (or **at long last**) after much delay: *you've come back to me at last!* **as a last resort** see **RESORT**. —— **one's last** do something for the last time: *the dying embers sparked their last.* **last but not least** last in order of mention or occurrence but just as important. **last call** (in a bar) an expression used to inform customers that closing time is approaching and that any further drinks should be purchased immediately: *the hours were 11:00 last call and drink up by 11:15.* **one's** (or **the**) **last gasp** see **GASP**. **the last straw** see **STRAW**. **on one's last legs** see **LEG**.
– ORIGIN Old English *latost* (adverb) 'after all others in a series,' of Germanic origin; related to Dutch *laatst, lest* and German *letzt*, also to **LATE**.

last² ▶ **v.** [no obj.] **1** [with adverbial] (of a process, activity, or state of things) continue for a specified period of time: *the guitar solo lasted for twenty minutes | childhood seems to last forever.*
2 continue to function well or to be in good condition for a considerable or specified length of time: *the car is built to last | a lip pencil lasts longer than lipstick.* ■ (of a person) manage to continue in a job or course of action: *how long does he think he'll last as manager?* ■ survive or endure: *his condition is so serious that he won't last the night.* ■ [with obj.] (of provisions or resources) be adequate or sufficient for (someone), esp. for a specified length of time: *he filled the freezer with enough food to last him for three months.*
– ORIGIN Old English *lǣstan*, of Germanic origin, related to German *leisten* 'afford, yield,' also to **LAST³**.

last³ ▶ **n.** a shoemaker's model for shaping or repairing a shoe or boot.
– ORIGIN Old English *lǣste*, of Germanic origin, from a base meaning 'follow'; related to Dutch *leest* and German *Leisten*.

last-born ▶ **adj.** last in order of birth; youngest.
▶ **n.** a youngest or last-born child.

last-ditch ▶ **adj.** denoting a final, often desperate attempt to achieve something: *a last-ditch effort to break the deadlock.*

Last Fron·tier a nickname for the state of **ALASKA**.

last-gasp ▶ **adj.** informal done at the last possible moment, typically in desperation: *his current appeal is a last-gasp effort to try to overturn the conviction.*

last hur·rah ▶ **n.** a final act, performance, or effort: *"This is my last hurrah in newsprint," said Mr. Evans.*

last·ing /ˈlastiNG/ ▶ **adj.** enduring or able to endure over a long period of time: *they left a lasting impression | a lasting, happy marriage.*
– DERIVATIVES **last·ing·ly adv., last·ing·ness n.**

Last Judg·ment ▶ **n.** the judgment of humankind expected in some religious traditions to take place at the end of the world.

last·ly /ˈlastlē/ ▶ **adv.** in the last place (used to introduce the last of a series of points or actions): *lastly, I would like to thank my parents.*

last min·ute (also **last moment**) ▶ **n.** the latest possible time before an event: *the visit was canceled at the last minute* | [as modifier] *a last-minute change of plans.*

last name ▶ **n.** a surname.

last post ▶ **n.** (in the British armed forces) the second of two bugle calls giving notice of the hour of retiring at night, played also at military funerals and acts of remembrance.

last rites ▶ **plural n.** (in the Christian Church) rites administered to a person who is about to die.

Last Sup·per the supper eaten by Jesus and his disciples on the night before the Crucifixion, as recorded in the New Testament and commemorated by Christians in the Eucharist. ■ an artistic representation based on this event.

last trump ▶ **n.** the trumpet blast that in some religious beliefs is thought will wake the dead on Judgment Day.

last word ▶ **n. 1** a final or definitive pronouncement on or decision about a subject: *he's always determined to **have the last word**.*
2 the finest or most modern, fashionable, or advanced example of something: *the spa **is the last word** in luxury and efficiency.*

Las Ve·gas /läs ˈvāgəs/ a city in southern Nevada; pop. 558,383 (est. 2008). It is noted for its casinos and nightclubs.

lat¹ /lat, lät/ ▶ **n.** (pl. **lati** /ˈlätē/ or **lats**) the basic monetary unit of Latvia, equal to 100 santims.
– ORIGIN from the first syllable of *Latvija* 'Latvia.'

lat² /lat/ ▶ **n.** (usu. **lats**) informal (in bodybuilding) a latissimus muscle.
– ORIGIN mid 20th cent.: abbreviation.

lat. ▶ **abbr.** latitude: *between approximately 40° and 50° S. lat.*

Lat·a·ki·a /ˌlatəˈkēə/ a seaport on the coast of western Syria, opposite the northeastern tip of Cyprus; pop. 366,600 (est. 2009).

latch /lacH/ ▶ **n.** a metal bar with a catch and lever used for fastening a door or gate. ■ a spring lock for an outer door that catches when the door is closed and can only be opened from the outside with a key. ■ Electronics a circuit that retains whatever output state results from a momentary input signal until reset by another signal. ■ the part of a knitting machine needle that closes or opens to hold or release the wool.
▶ **v.** [with obj.] fasten (a door or gate) with a latch: *she latched the door carefully.* ■ [no obj.] Electronics (of a device) become fixed in a particular state.
– PHRASAL VERBS **latch onto** informal attach oneself to (someone) as a constant and usually unwelcome companion: *a knack for latching onto people with greater initiative and enterprise.* ■ take up (an idea or trend) enthusiastically: *the media have latched onto the snappy "Generation X" catchphrase.* ■ (of one substance) cohere with (another).
– ORIGIN Old English *læccan* 'take hold of, grasp (physically or mentally),' of Germanic origin.

latch·et /ˈlacHit/ ▶ **n.** archaic a narrow thong or lace for fastening a shoe or sandal.
– ORIGIN late Middle English: from Old French *lachet*, variant of *lacet*, from *laz* 'lace.'

latch·key /ˈlacHˌkē/ ▶ **n.** (pl. **latchkeys**) a key of an outer door of a house.

latch·key child (also informal **latchkey kid**) ▶ **n.** a child who is at home without adult supervision for some part of the day, esp. after school until a parent returns from work.

late /lāt/ ▶ **adj. 1** doing something or taking place after the expected, proper, or usual time: *his late arrival | she was half an hour **late for** her lunch appointment.*
2 belonging or taking place near the end of a particular time or period: *they won the game with a late goal.* ■ [attrib.] denoting or belonging to the advanced stage of a historical period or cultural movement: *the late 1960s | late Gothic style.* ■ far on into the day or night: *I'm sorry the call is so late | it's too late for lunch.* ■ flowering or ripening toward the end of the season: *the last late chrysanthemums.*
3 **(the/one's late)** (of a specified person) no longer alive: *the late William Jennings Bryan | her late husband's grave.* ■ no longer having the specified status; former: *a late colleague of mine.*
4 **(latest)** of recent date: *the latest news.*
▶ **adv. 1** after the expected, proper, or usual time: *she arrived late.*
2 toward the end of a period: *it happened late in 1984.* ■ at or until a time far into the day or night: *now I'm old enough to stay up late.* ■ **(later)** at a time in the near future; afterward: *I'll see you later | later on it will be easier.*
3 **(late of)** formerly but not now living or working in a specified place or institution: *Captain Falconer, late of the British army.*
▶ **n. (the latest)** the most recent news or fashion: *have you heard the latest?*
– PHRASES **at the latest** no later than the time specified: *all new cars will be required to meet this standard by 1997 at the latest.* **late in the game** (or **day**) at a late stage in proceedings, esp. too late to be useful. **of late** recently: *she'd been drinking too much of late.*
– ORIGIN Old English *læt* (adjective; also in the sense 'slow, tardy'), *late* (adverb), of Germanic origin;

related to German *lass*, from an Indo-European root shared by Latin *lassus* 'weary,' LET[1], and LET[2].

late·com·er /ˈlātˌkəmər/ ▶ **n.** a person who arrives late: *latecomers were not admitted before the intermission* | figurative *he was a latecomer to modernism.*

la·teen /ləˈtēn, la-/ ▶ **n.** (also **lateen sail**) a triangular sail on a long yard at an angle of 45° to the mast. ■ a ship rigged with such a sail.
– ORIGIN mid 16th cent.: from French (*voile*) *Latine* 'Latin (sail),' so named because it was common in the Mediterranean.

lateen

late-gla·cial (also **late glacial**) ▶ **adj.** Geology of or relating to the later stages of the final glaciation, from the beginning of the rise in temperature about 15,000 years ago to about 10,000 years ago. Compare with POSTGLACIAL.

late Lat·in ▶ **n.** Latin of about AD 200–600.

late·ly /ˈlātlē/ ▶ **adv.** recently; not long ago: *she hasn't been looking too well lately.*
– ORIGIN Old English *lætlīce* 'slowly, tardily' (see LATE, -LY[2]).

late-mod·el ▶ **adj.** (esp. of a car) recently made or of a recent design.

la·ten·cy /ˈlātn-sē/ ▶ **n.** another term for LATENT PERIOD.

La Tène /lə ˈten/ ▶ **n.** [usu. as modifier] Archaeology the second cultural phase of the European Iron Age, following the Halstatt period (c.480 BC) and lasting until the coming of the Romans. This culture represents the height of Celtic power.
– ORIGIN late 19th cent.: named after a district in Switzerland, where remains of the culture were first identified.

late·ness /ˈlātnis/ ▶ **n. 1** the fact or quality of happening or arriving after the expected or usual time; unpunctuality: *she wouldn't tolerate lateness in her class.*
2 the fact of being far on in the day or night: *she noticed the lateness of the hour.*

la·tent /ˈlātnt/ ▶ **adj.** (of a quality or state) existing but not yet developed or manifest; hidden; concealed: *discovering her latent talent for diplomacy.* ■ Biology (of a bud, resting stage, etc.) lying dormant or hidden until circumstances are suitable for development or manifestation. ■ (of a disease) in which the usual symptoms are not yet manifest. ■ (of a microorganism, esp. a virus) present in the body without causing disease, but capable of doing so at a later stage or when transmitted to another body.
– DERIVATIVES **la·tent·ly** adv.
– ORIGIN late Middle English: from Latin *latent-* 'being hidden,' from the verb *latere.*

la·tent heat ▶ **n.** Physics the heat required to convert a solid into a liquid or vapor, or a liquid into a vapor, without change of temperature.

la·tent im·age ▶ **n.** Photography an image on an exposed film or print that has not yet been made visible by developing.

la·tent pe·ri·od ▶ **n. 1** Medicine (also **latency period**) the period between infection with a virus or other microorganism and the onset of symptoms, or between exposure to radiation and the appearance of a cancer.
2 Physiology (also **latency**) the delay between the receipt of a stimulus by a sensory nerve and the response to it.

lat·er /ˈlātər/ ▶ **adj. & adv.** comparative of LATE.
▶ **exclam.** informal goodbye for the present; see you later.

-later ▶ **comb. form** denoting a person who worships a specified thing: *idolater.*
– ORIGIN from Greek *-latrēs* 'worshiper.'

lat·er·al /ˈlatərəl, ˈlatrəl/ ▶ **adj.** of, at, toward, or from the side or sides: *the plant takes up water through its lateral roots.* ■ Anatomy & Zoology situated on one side or other of the body or of an organ, esp. in the region furthest from the median plane. The opposite of MEDIAL. ■ Medicine (of a disease or condition) affecting the side or sides of the body, or confined to one side of the body. ■ Physics acting or placed at right angles to the line of motion or of strain. ■ Phonetics (of a consonant, esp. *l*, or its articulation) formed by or involving partial closure of the air passage by the tongue, which is so placed as to allow the breath to flow on one or both sides of the point of contact.
▶ **n. 1** a side part of something, esp. a shoot or branch growing out from the side of a stem.
2 Phonetics a lateral consonant.
3 Football (also **lateral pass**) a pass thrown either sideways or backward from the position of the passer.
▶ **v.** [with obj.] throw (a football) in a sideways or backward direction: *he tried to lateral a kick return but fumbled.* ■ [no obj.] throw a lateral: *he got the ball back on a handoff and then lateraled to a halfback.*
– DERIVATIVES **lat·er·al·ly** adv.
– ORIGIN late Middle English: from Latin *lateralis*, from *latus, later-* 'side.'

lat·er·al bud ▶ **n.** another term for AXILLARY BUD.

lat·er·al·i·ty /ˌlatəˈralətē/ ▶ **n.** dominance of one side of the brain in controlling particular activities or functions, or of one of a pair of organs such as the eyes or hands.

lat·er·al·ize /ˈlatərəˌlīz, ˈlatrə-/ ▶ **v.** (**be lateralized**) (of the brain) show laterality. ■ [with adverbial] (of an organ, function, or activity) be largely under the control of one side of the brain: *this is a function that is usually lateralized on the right.* ■ [with adverbial] Medicine (of a lesion or pathological process) be diagnosed as localized to one or the other side of the brain.
– DERIVATIVES **lat·er·al·i·za·tion** /ˌlatərəliˈzāshən, ˌlatrə-, -ˌlīˈzā/ **n.**

lat·er·al line ▶ **n.** Zoology a visible line along the side of a fish consisting of a series of sense organs that detect pressure and vibration.

lat·er·al ven·tri·cle ▶ **n.** Anatomy each of the first and second ventricles in the center of each cerebral hemisphere of the brain.

Lat·er·an /ˈlatərən/ the site in Rome containing the cathedral church of Rome (a basilica dedicated to St. John the Baptist and St. John the Evangelist) and the Lateran Palace, where the popes resided until the 14th century.

Lat·er·an Coun·cil any of five general councils of the Western Church held in the Lateran Palace in 1123, 1139, 1179, 1215, and 1512–17. The council of 1215 condemned the Albigenses as heretical and clarified the Church doctrine on transubstantiation, the Trinity, and the Incarnation.

Lat·er·an Trea·ty a concordat signed in 1929 in the Lateran Palace between the kingdom of Italy (represented by Mussolini) and the Holy See (represented by **Pope Pius XI**), which recognized the papal state as fully sovereign and independent under the name Vatican City.

lat·er·ite /ˈlatəˌrīt/ ▶ **n.** a reddish clayey material, hard when dry, forming a topsoil in some tropical or subtropical regions and sometimes used for building. ■ Geology a clayey soil horizon rich in iron and aluminum oxides, formed by weathering of igneous rocks in moist warm climates.
– DERIVATIVES **lat·er·it·ic** /ˌlatəˈritik/ **adj.**
– ORIGIN early 19th cent.: from Latin *later* 'brick' + -ITE[1].

la·tex /ˈlāˌteks/ ▶ **n.** (pl. **latexes** or **latices** /ˈlatəˌsēz/) a milky fluid found in many plants, such as poppies and spurges, that exudes when the plant is cut and coagulates on exposure to the air. The latex of the rubber tree is the chief source of natural rubber. ■ a synthetic product resembling this, consisting of a dispersion in water of polymer particles, used to make paints, coatings, and other products. ■ (also **latex paint**) a type of paint used for walls, consisting of pigment bound in synthetic latex that forms an emulsion with water.
– ORIGIN mid 17th cent. (denoting various bodily fluids, esp. the watery part of blood): from Latin, literally 'liquid, fluid.'

lath /laTH/ ▶ **n.** (pl. **laths** /laT͟Hz, laTHs/) a thin flat strip of wood, esp. one of a series forming a foundation for the plaster of a wall or the tiles of a roof, or made into a trellis or fence. ■ laths collectively as a building material, esp. as a foundation for supporting plaster.
▶ **v.** [with obj.] cover (a wall or ceiling) with laths.
– ORIGIN Old English *lætt*, of Germanic origin; related to Dutch *lat* and German *Latte*, also to LATTICE.

lathe /lāT͟H/ ▶ **n.** a machine for shaping wood, metal, or other material by means of a rotating drive that turns the piece being worked on against changeable cutting tools.
▶ **v.** [with obj.] shape with a lathe.
– ORIGIN Middle English: probably from Old Danish *lad* 'structure, frame,' perhaps from Old Norse *hlath* 'pile, heap,' related to *hlatha* (see LADE).

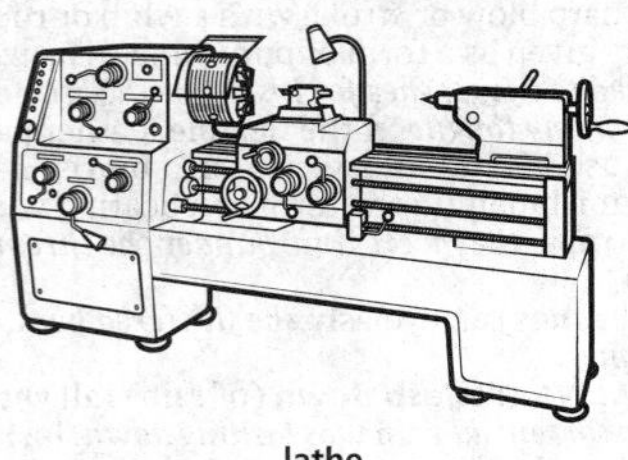
lathe

lath·er /ˈlaT͟Hər/ ▶ **n.** a frothy white mass of bubbles produced by soap or a similar cleansing substance when mixed with water. ■ heavy sweat visible on a horse's coat as a white foam. ■ (**a lather**) informal a state of agitation or nervous excitement: *Larry was worked into a lather and shouted at the mayor.*
▶ **v. 1** ■ (with reference to soap or a similar cleansing substance) form or cause to form a frothy white mass of bubbles .[no obj.] *soap will not lather in hard water.* ■ [with obj.] rub soap onto (a part of the body) until a lather is produced: *she was lathering herself languidly beneath the shower.* ■ cause (a horse) to become covered with sweat: *his horse was lathered up by the end of the day.* ■ (**lather something with**) cover something liberally with (a substance): *she lathered a slice of toast with butter.*
2 [with obj.] informal thrash (someone).
– DERIVATIVES **lath·er·y** adj.
– ORIGIN Old English *lēathor* (denoting washing soda or its froth), *lēthran* (verb), of Germanic origin; related to Old Norse *lauthr* (noun), from an Indo-European root shared by Greek *loutron* 'bath.'

lath·y·rism /ˈlaTHəˌrizəm/ ▶ **n.** a tropical disease marked by tremors, muscular weakness, and paraplegia, esp. prevalent in South Asia. It is commonly attributed to continued consumption of the seeds of the grass pea.
– ORIGIN late 19th cent.: from modern Latin *Lathyrus* (genus name of various leguminous plants) + -ISM.

lat·i·ces /ˈlatəˌsēz/ plural form of LATEX.

la·tic·i·fer /lāˈtisəfər/ ▶ **n.** Botany a cell, tissue, or vessel that contains or conducts latex.
– DERIVATIVES **lat·i·cif·er·ous** /ˌlatəˈsif(ə)rəs/ **adj.**
– ORIGIN mid 19th cent.: from Latin *latex, latic-* 'fluid' + *-fer* 'bearing.'

lat·i·fun·di·um /ˌlatəˈfəndēəm/ ▶ **n.** (pl. **latifundia** /-dēə/) a large landed estate or ranch in ancient Rome or more recently in Spain or Latin America, typically worked by slaves.
– ORIGIN mid 17th cent.: from Latin, from *latus* 'broad' + *fundus* 'landed estate,' partly via Spanish.

Lat·in /ˈlatn/ ▶ **n. 1** the language of ancient Rome and its empire, widely used historically as a language of scholarship and administration.

> Latin is a member of the Italic branch of the Indo-European family of languages. After the decline of the Roman Empire, it continued to be a medium of communication among educated people throughout the Middle Ages in Europe and remained the liturgical language of the Roman Catholic Church until the reforms of the Second Vatican Council (1962–65); it is still used for scientific names in biology and astronomy. The Romance languages are derived from it.

2 a native or inhabitant of a country whose language developed from Latin, esp. a Latin American. ■ music of a kind originating in Latin America, characterized by dance rhythms and extensive use of indigenous percussive instruments.
▶ **adj.** of, relating to, or in the Latin language: *Latin poetry.* ■ of or relating to the countries or peoples using languages, esp. Spanish, that developed from Latin. ■ of, relating to, or characteristic of Latin American music or dance: *snapping his fingers to a Latin beat.* ■ of or relating to the Western or Roman Catholic Church (as historically using Latin for its rites): *the Latin patriarch of Antioch.* ■ historical of or relating to ancient Latium or its inhabitants.
– DERIVATIVES **Lat·in·ism** /-ˌizəm/ **n.**, **Lat·in·ist** /-ist/ **n.**
– ORIGIN from Latin *Latinus* 'of Latium' (see LATIUM).

La·ti·na /ləˈtēnə, la-/ ▶ **n.** a female Latin American inhabitant of the United States.
▶ **adj.** of or relating to these inhabitants.
– ORIGIN Latin American Spanish, feminine of *Latino* (see LATINO).

Lat·in A·mer·i·ca the parts of the American continents where Spanish or Portuguese is the main national language (i.e., Mexico and, in effect, the whole of Central and South America including many of the Caribbean islands).
– DERIVATIVES **Lat·in A·mer·i·can** **n. & adj.**

Lat·in·ate /ˈlatn,āt/ ▶ **adj.** (of language) having the character of Latin: *Latinate suffixes.*

Lat·in Church the Christian Church that originated in the Western Roman Empire, giving allegiance to the pope of Rome, and historically using Latin for the liturgy; the Roman Catholic Church as distinguished from Orthodox and Uniate Churches.

Lat·in cross ▶ **n.** a plain cross in which the vertical part below the horizontal is longer than the other three parts.

La·tin·i·ty /ləˈtinətē, la-/ ▶ **n.** the use of Latin style or words of Latin origin.

Lat·in·ize /ˈlatn,īz/ ▶ **v.** [with obj.] **1** give a Latin or Latinate form to (a word): *his name was Latinized into Confucius.* ■ archaic translate into Latin. ■ [no obj.] archaic use Latin forms or idiom.
2 make (a people or culture) conform to the ideas and customs of the ancient Romans, the Latin peoples, or the Latin Church.
– DERIVATIVES **Lat·in·i·za·tion** /,latn-əˈzāSHən/ **n.**, **Lat·in·iz·er n.**
– ORIGIN late 16th cent.: from late Latin *Latinizare*, from Latin *Latinus* (see **LATIN**).

Lat·in lov·er ▶ **n.** a Latin male popularly characterized as having a romantic, passionate temperament and great sexual prowess.

La·ti·no /ləˈtēnō, la-/ ▶ **n.** (pl. **Latinos**) a Latin American inhabitant of the United States.
▶ **adj.** of or relating to these inhabitants.
– ORIGIN Latin American Spanish, probably a special use of Spanish *latino* (see **LATIN**).

Lat·in square ▶ **n.** an arrangement of letters or symbols that each occur *n* times, in a square array of n^2 compartments so that no letter appears twice in the same row or column. ■ such an arrangement used as the basis of experimental procedures in which it is desired to control or allow for two sources of variability while investigating a third.

lat·ish /ˈlātiSH/ ▶ **adj. & adv.** fairly late: [as adv.] *Margaret came in latish.*

la·tis·si·mus /ləˈtisəməs/ (also **latissimus dorsi** /ˈdôrsī/) ▶ **n.** (pl. **latissimi** /-,mī, -,mē/) Anatomy either of a pair of large, roughly triangular muscles covering the lower part of the back, extending from the sacral, lumbar, and lower thoracic vertebrae to the armpits.
– ORIGIN early 17th cent.: modern Latin, from *musculus latissimus dorsi*, literally 'broadest muscle of the back.'

lat·i·tude /ˈlatə,t(y)o͞od/ ▶ **n. 1** the angular distance of a place north or south of the earth's equator, or of a celestial object north or south of the celestial equator, usually expressed in degrees and minutes: *at a latitude of 51° N | lines of latitude.* ■ (**latitudes**) regions, esp. with reference to their temperature and distance from the equator: *temperate latitudes | northern latitudes.* ■ Astronomy see **CELESTIAL LATITUDE.**
2 scope for freedom of action or thought: *journalists have considerable latitude in criticizing public figures.* ■ Photography the range of exposures for which an emulsion or printing paper will give acceptable contrast: *a film with a latitude that is outstanding.*
– DERIVATIVES **lat·i·tu·di·nal** /,latəˈt(y)o͞odn-əl/ **adj.**, **lat·i·tu·di·nal·ly** /,latəˈt(y)o͞odn-əlē/ **adv.**
– ORIGIN late Middle English: from Latin *latitudo* 'breadth,' from *latus* 'broad.'

latitude 1

lat·i·tu·di·nar·i·an /,latə,t(y)o͞odnˈerēən/ ▶ **adj.** allowing latitude, esp. in religion; showing no preference among varying creeds and forms of worship.
▶ **n.** a person with a latitudinarian attitude.
– DERIVATIVES **lat·i·tu·di·nar·i·an·ism** /-,nizəm/ **n.**
– ORIGIN mid 17th cent.: from Latin *latitudo* 'breadth' (see **LATITUDE**) + **-ARIAN.**

La·ti·um /ˈlāSH(ē)əm/ an ancient region in west central Italy, west of the Apennines and south of the Tiber River. Settled during the early part of the 1st millennium BC by a branch of the Indo-European people known as the Latini, it was dominated by Rome by the end of the 4th century BC.

lat·ke /ˈlätkə/ ▶ **n.** (in Jewish cooking) a pancake, esp. one made with grated potato.
– ORIGIN Yiddish.

La·to·na /ləˈtōnə/ Roman Mythology Roman name for **LETO.**

la·tri·a /ləˈtrīə/ ▶ **n.** (in the Roman Catholic Church) supreme worship allowed to God alone. Compare with **DULIA.**
– ORIGIN early 16th cent.: from late Latin, from Greek *latreia* 'worship,' from *latreuein* 'serve.'

la·trine /ləˈtrēn/ ▶ **n.** a toilet, esp. a communal one in a camp or barracks.
– ORIGIN Middle English (rare before the mid 19th cent.): via French from Latin *latrina*, contraction of *lavatrina*, from *lavare* 'to wash.'

La·trobe /ləˈtrōb/, Benjamin Henry (1764–1820), US architect; born in England. He designed the south wing of the US Capitol in Washington, DC, and rebuilt the Capitol after its destruction by the British in 1815–17.

-latry ▶ **comb. form** denoting worship of a specified thing: *idolatry.*
– ORIGIN from Greek *-latreia* 'worship.'

lat·te /ˈlä,tā/ ▶ **n.** a drink made by adding a shot of espresso to a glass or cup of frothy steamed milk.
– ORIGIN from Italian (*caffè*) *latte*, literally '(milk) coffee.'

lat·ten /ˈlatn/ ▶ **n.** historical an alloy of copper and zinc resembling brass, hammered into thin sheets and used to make monumental brasses and church ornaments.
– ORIGIN Middle English: from Old French *laton*, of unknown origin.

lat·ter /ˈlatər/ ▶ **adj.** [attrib.] **1** situated or occurring nearer to the end of something than to the beginning: *the latter half of 1989 | heart disease dogged his latter years.* ■ recent: *the project had low cash flows in its latter years.*
2 (**the latter**) denoting the second or second mentioned of two people or things: *the Russians could advance into either Germany or Austria—they chose the latter option.*
– ORIGIN Old English *lætra* 'slower,' comparative of *læt* (see **LATE**).

> **USAGE** Latter means 'the second-mentioned of two.' Its use to mean 'the last-mentioned of three or more' is common, but is considered incorrect by some because **latter** means 'later' rather than 'latest.' *Last* or *last-mentioned* is preferred where three or more things are involved. See also usage at **FORMER'**.

lat·ter-day ▶ **adj.** [attrib.] modern or contemporary, esp. when mirroring some person or thing of the past: *the book is built around the story of the Flood and a latter-day Noah.*

Lat·ter-Day Saints (abbr.: **LDS**) ▶ **plural n.** another name for the Mormons.

lat·ter·ly /ˈlatərlē/ ▶ **adv.** recently: *latterly, his painting has shown a new freedom of expression.* ■ in the later stages of a period of time, esp. of a person's life: *he worked on the paper for fifty years, latterly as its political editor.*

lat·tice /ˈlatis/ ▶ **n.** a structure consisting of strips of wood or metal crossed and fastened together with square or diamond-shaped spaces left between, used typically as a screen or fence or as a support for climbing plants. ■ an interlaced structure or pattern resembling this: *the lattice of branches above her.* ■ Physics a regular repeated three-dimensional arrangement of atoms, ions, or molecules in a metal or other crystalline solid.
– ORIGIN Middle English: from Old French *lattis*, from *latte* 'lath,' of Germanic origin.

lattice

lat·ticed /ˈlatist/ ▶ **adj.** decorated with or in the form of a lattice: *a latticed screen.*

lat·tice en·er·gy ▶ **n.** Chemistry a measure of the energy contained in the crystal lattice of a compound, equal to the energy that would be released if the component ions were brought together from infinity.

lat·tice frame (also **lattice girder**) ▶ **n.** an iron or steel structure consisting of two horizontal beams connected by diagonal struts.

lat·tice win·dow ▶ **n.** a window with small panes set in diagonally crossing strips of wood, vinyl, or metal.

lat·tice·work /ˈlatis,wərk/ ▶ **n.** interlacing strips of wood, metal, or other material forming a lattice.

lat·ti·ci·nio /,latiˈCHēnyō/ (also **latticino** /-ˈCHēnō/) ▶ **n.** an opaque white glass used in threads to decorate clear Venetian glass.
– ORIGIN Italian, literally 'dairy produce,' from medieval Latin *lacticinium.*

Lat·via /ˈlatvēə/ a country on the eastern shore of the Baltic Sea, between Estonia and Lithuania; pop. 2,231,500 (est. 2009); capital, Riga; languages, Latvian (official), Russian, Lithuanian.

> Latvia was annexed by Russia in the 18th century after periods of Polish and Swedish rule. It was proclaimed an independent republic in 1918, but in 1940 was annexed by the Soviet Union as a constituent republic. In 1991, on the breakup of the Soviet Union, Latvia became an independent republic once again. It joined both NATO and the EU in 2004.

Lat·vi·an /ˈlatvēən/ ▶ **adj.** of or relating to Latvia, its people, or its language.
▶ **n. 1** a native or citizen of Latvia, or a person of Latvian descent.
2 the Baltic language of Latvia.

lau·an /ˈlo͞o-än/ ▶ **n.** another term for **PHILIPPINE MAHOGANY.**

Laud /lôd/, William (1573–1645), English prelate; archbishop of Canterbury 1633–45. His attempts to restore pre-Reformation practices in England and Scotland contributed to the causes of the English Civil War. He was executed for treason.

laud /lôd/ ▶ **v.** [with obj.] formal praise (a person or their achievements) highly, esp. in a public context: *the obituary lauded him as a great statesman and soldier* | [as adj., with submodifier] (**lauded**) *her much lauded rendering of Lady Macbeth.*
▶ **n.** archaic praise: *all glory, laud, and honor to Thee.*
– ORIGIN late Middle English: the noun from Old French *laude*, the verb from Latin *laudare*, both from Latin *laus, laud-* 'praise' (see also **LAUDS**).

laud·a·ble /ˈlôdəbəl/ ▶ **adj.** (of an action, idea, or goal) deserving praise and commendation: *laudable though the aim might be, the results have been criticized.*
– DERIVATIVES **laud·a·bil·i·ty** /,lôdəˈbilətē/ **n.**, **laud·a·bly** /-blē/ **adv.**
– ORIGIN late Middle English: from Latin *laudabilis*, from *laus, laud-* 'praise.'

lau·da·num /ˈlôdn-əm, ˈlôdnəm/ ▶ **n.** an alcoholic solution containing morphine, prepared from opium and formerly used as a narcotic painkiller.
– ORIGIN mid 16th cent. (applied to various preparations containing opium): modern Latin, the name given by Paracelsus to a costly medicament of which opium was believed to be the active ingredient; perhaps a variant of Latin *ladanum* (see **LABDANUM**).

lau·da·tion /lôˈdāSHən/ ▶ **n.** formal praise; commendation.
– ORIGIN late Middle English: from Latin *laudatio(n-)*, from the verb *laudare* (see **LAUD**).

laud·a·to·ry /ˈlôdə,tôrē/ ▶ **adj.** (of speech or writing) expressing praise and commendation.
– ORIGIN mid 16th cent.: from late Latin *laudatorius*, from *laudat-* 'praised,' from the verb *laudare* (see **LAUD**).

lauds /lôdz/ ▶ **n.** a service of morning prayer in the Divine Office of the Western Christian Church, traditionally said or chanted at daybreak, though historically it was often held with matins on the previous night.
– ORIGIN Middle English: from the frequent use, in Psalms 148–150, of the Latin imperative *laudate!* 'praise ye!' (see also **LAUD**).

laugh /laf/ ▶ **v.** [no obj.] make the spontaneous sounds and movements of the face and body that are the instinctive expressions of lively amusement and sometimes also of contempt or derision: *she couldn't help laughing at his jokes | he laughed out loud* | [with direct speech] *she laughed, "Not a chance."* ■ (**laugh at**) ridicule; scorn. ■ (**laugh something off**) dismiss something embarrassing, unfortunate, or potentially serious by treating it in a lighthearted way or making a joke of it. ■ (**be laughing**) informal be in a fortunate or successful position: *if next year's model is as successful, Ford will be laughing.*
▶ **n. 1** an act of laughing: *she gave a loud, silly laugh.*
2 (**a laugh**) informal a thing that causes laughter; a source of fun, amusement, or derision: *that's a*

PRONUNCIATION KEY ə *ago, up;* ər *over, fur;* a *hat;* ā *ate;* ä *car;* e *let;* ē *see;* i *fit;* ī *by;* NG *sing;* ō *go;* ô *law, for;* oi *toy;* o͝o *good;* o͞o *goo;* ou *out;* TH *thin;* T͟H *then;* ZH *vision*

laugh, the idea of you cooking a meal! | *she decided to play along with him* ***for a laugh.*** ■ a person who is good fun or amusing company: *I like Peter—he's* ***a good laugh.***
– PHRASES **be laughing all the way to the bank** informal be making a great deal of money very easily. **have the last laugh** be finally vindicated, thus confounding earlier skepticism. **laugh one's head off** laugh heartily or uncontrollably. **laugh in someone's face** show open contempt for someone by laughing rudely at them in their presence: figurative *vandals and muggers who laugh in the face of the law.* **the laugh is on me** (or **you**, **him**, etc.) the tables are turned and now the other person is the one who appears ridiculous: *all the critics had laughed at him—well, the laugh was on them now.* **laugh like a drain** Brit. informal laugh raucously. **a laugh a minute** very funny: *it's a laugh a minute when Lois gets together with her dad.* **laugh out of the other side of one's mouth** be discomfited after feeling satisfaction or confidence about something: *you'd be laughing out the other side of your mouth if we were sitting in jail right now.* **laugh someone/something out of court** dismiss with contempt as being obviously ridiculous. **laugh oneself silly** (or **sick**) laugh uncontrollably or for a long time. **laugh something to scorn** dated ridicule something. **laugh up one's sleeve** be secretly or inwardly amused. **no laughing matter** something serious that should not be joked about: *heavy snoring is no laughing matter.* **play something for laughs** (of a performer) try to arouse laughter in an audience, esp. in inappropriate circumstances.
– ORIGIN Old English *hlæhhan, hliehhan*, of Germanic origin; related to Dutch and German *lachen*, also to LAUGHTER.

laugh·a·ble /ˈlafəbəl/ ▶ **adj.** so ludicrous as to be amusing: *if it didn't make me so angry it would be laughable.*
– DERIVATIVES **laugh·a·bly** /-blē/ **adv.** [as submodifier] *his antics were laughably pretentious.*

laugh·er /ˈlafər/ ▶ **n. 1** a person who laughs. **2** informal a sports contest or other competition that is so easily won by one team or competitor that it seems absurd.

I

laugh·ing gas ▶ **n.** nontechnical term for NITROUS OXIDE.

laugh·ing hy·e·na ▶ **n.** another term for SPOTTED HYENA.

laugh·ing jack·ass ▶ **n.** Austral. the laughing kookaburra. See KOOKABURRA.

laugh·ing·ly /ˈlafiNGlē/ ▶ **adv.** with amused ridicule or ludicrous inappropriateness: *we finally reached what we laughingly called civilization.* ■ in an amused way; with laughter.

laugh·ing·stock /ˈlafiNG,stäk/ ▶ **n.** [in sing.] a person subjected to general mockery or ridicule.

laugh·ing thrush ▶ **n.** a gregarious thrushlike babbler of South and Southeast Asia, typically with dark gray or brown plumage and a boldly marked head, and having a cackling call. ● Genus *Garrulax*, family Timaliidae: many species.

Laugh·lin /ˈläklən, ˈläflən/ a community in southern Nevada, across the Colorado River from Bullhead City; pop. 7,076 (2000).

laugh·ter /ˈlaftər/ ▶ **n.** the action or sound of laughing: *he roared with laughter.*
– ORIGIN Old English *hleahtor*, of Germanic origin; related to German *Gelächter*, also to LAUGH.

Laugh·ton /ˈlôtn/, Charles (1899–1962), US actor, born in England. He is remembered for character roles such as Henry VIII (*The Private Life of Henry VIII*, 1933) and Captain Bligh (*Mutiny on the Bounty*, 1935); he also played Quasimodo in *The Hunchback of Notre Dame* (1939).

launce /lôns, läns/ ▶ **n.** another term for SAND EEL.
– ORIGIN early 17th cent.: early variant of LANCE (because of its shape).

Laun·ce·lot /ˈlônsə,lät, ˈlän-, -lət/ variant spelling of LANCELOT.

launch[1] /lônCH, länCH/ ▶ **v.** [with obj.] **1** set (a boat) in motion by pushing it or allowing it to roll into the water: *the town's lifeboat was launched to rescue the fishermen.* ■ set (a newly built ship or boat) afloat for the first time, typically as part of an official ceremony: *King Gustav II Adolph of Sweden launched a huge new warship.* ■ send (a missile, satellite, or spacecraft) on its course or into orbit: *they launched two Scud missiles.* ■ hurl (something) forcefully: *she launched a tortoiseshell comb.* ■ [with adverbial of direction] (**launch oneself**) (of a person) make a sudden energetic movement: *I launched myself out of bed.* ■ utter (criticism or a threat) vehemently: *scores of customers launched a volley of complaints.* **2** start or set in motion (an activity or enterprise): *she was launching a campaign against ugly architecture.* ■ introduce (a new product or publication) to the public for the first time: *the company has launched a software package specifically for the legal sector.*
▶ **n.** an act or an instance of launching something: *the launch of a new campaign against drinking and driving.* ■ an occasion at which a new product or publication is introduced to the public: *a book launch.*
– PHRASAL VERBS **launch into** begin (something) energetically and enthusiastically: *he launched into a two-hour sales pitch.* **launch out** make a start on a new and challenging enterprise: *she wasn't brave enough to launch out by herself.*
– ORIGIN Middle English (in the sense 'hurl a missile, discharge with force'): from Anglo-Norman French *launcher*, variant of Old French *lancier* (see LANCE).

launch[2] ▶ **n.** a large motorboat, used esp. for short trips. Also called MOTOR LAUNCH. ■ historical the largest boat carried on a man-of-war.
– ORIGIN late 17th cent. (denoting the longboat of a man-of-war): from Spanish *lancha* 'pinnace,' perhaps from Malay *lancharan*, from *lanchar* 'swift, nimble.'

launch·er /ˈlônCHər, ˈlän-/ ▶ **n.** a structure that holds a rocket or missile, typically one used as a weapon, during launching: *a rocket launcher* | *a grenade launcher.* ■ a rocket that is used to convey a satellite or spacecraft into orbit.

launch pad (also **launching pad**) ▶ **n.** the area on which a rocket stands for launching, typically consisting of a platform with a supporting structure.

launch ve·hi·cle ▶ **n.** a rocket-powered vehicle used to send artificial satellites or spacecraft into space.

laun·der /ˈlôndər, ˈlän-/ ▶ **v.** [with obj.] wash, or wash and iron, (clothes or linens): *he wasn't used to laundering his own bed linens* | [as adj., with submodifier] (**laundered**) *freshly laundered sheets.* ■ conceal the origins of (money obtained illegally) by transfers involving foreign banks or legitimate businesses. ■ alter (information) to make it appear more acceptable: *we began to notice attempts to launder the data retrospectively.*
▶ **n.** a trough for holding or conveying water, esp. (in mining) one used for washing ore. ■ a channel for conveying molten metal from a furnace or container to a ladle or mold.
– DERIVATIVES **laun·der·er n.**
– ORIGIN Middle English (as a noun denoting a person who washes linen): contraction of *lavender*, from Old French *lavandier*, based on Latin *lavanda* 'things to be washed,' from *lavare* 'to wash.'

laun·der·ette /,lôndəˈret, ,län-/ (also **laundrette**) ▶ **n.** a laundromat.

laun·dress /ˈlôndrəs, ˈlän-/ ▶ **n.** a woman who is employed to launder clothes and linens.

Laun·dro·mat /ˈlôndrə,mat, ˈlän-/ (also **laundromat**) ▶ **n.** trademark an establishment with coin-operated washing machines and dryers for public use.
– ORIGIN 1940s (originally US, as the proprietary name of a washing machine): blend of LAUNDER and AUTOMATIC.

laun·dry /ˌlôndrē, ˈlän-/ ▶ **n.** (pl. **laundries**) **1** clothes and linens that need to be washed or that have been newly washed: *piles of dirty laundry.* ■ the action or process of washing such items: *I talked her into letting me help Ben with the rest of the laundry.* **2** a room in a house, hotel, or institution where clothes and linens can be washed and ironed. ■ a business that washes and irons clothes and linens commercially.
– ORIGIN early 16th cent.: contraction of Middle English *lavendry*, from Old French *lavanderie*, from *lavandier* 'person who washes linen' (see LAUNDER).

laun·dry list ▶ **n.** a long or exhaustive list of people or things: *there's* ***a laundry list of*** *possible triggers for migraines.*

laun·dry·man /ˈlôndrēmən, ˈlän-/ ▶ **n.** (pl. **laundrymen**) a man who is employed to launder clothes and linens, or deliver them to customers.

Laur·a·sia /lôˈrāZHə/ a vast continental area believed to have existed in the northern hemisphere and to have resulted from the breakup of Pangaea in Mesozoic times. It comprised the present North America, Greenland, Europe, and most of Asia north of the Himalayas.

lau·re·ate /ˈlôrē-it, ˈlär-/ ▶ **n.** a person who is honored with an award for outstanding creative or intellectual achievement: *a Nobel laureate.* ■ short for POET LAUREATE.
▶ **adj.** literary wreathed with laurel as a mark of honor. ■ (of a crown or wreath) consisting of laurel.
– DERIVATIVES **lau·re·ate·ship** /-,SHip/ **n.**
– ORIGIN late Middle English (as an adjective): from Latin *laureatus*, from *laurea* 'laurel wreath,' from *laurus* 'laurel.'

lau·rel /ˈlôrəl, ˈlär-/ ▶ **n. 1** any of a number of shrubs and other plants with dark green glossy leaves, in particular: ■ the MOUNTAIN LAUREL ■ the CHERRY LAUREL ■ the bay tree. See BAY[2]. **2** an aromatic evergreen shrub related to the bay tree, several kinds of which form forests in tropical and warm countries. ● Family Lauraceae: many genera and species. **3** (usu. **laurels**) the foliage of the bay tree woven into a wreath or crown and worn on the head as an emblem of victory or mark of honor in classical times. ■ honor or praise for an achievement: *she has rightly won laurels for this brilliantly perceptive first novel.*
▶ **v.** (**laurels**, **laureling**, **laureled**; Brit. **laurelling**, **laurelled**) [with obj.] adorn with or as if with a laurel: *they banish our anger forever when they laurel the graves of our dead.*
– PHRASES **look to one's laurels** be careful not to lose one's superior position to a rival. **rest on one's laurels** be so satisfied with what one has already achieved that one makes no further effort.
– ORIGIN Middle English *lorer*, from Old French *lorier*, from Provençal *laurier*, from earlier *laur*, from Latin *laurus*.

Lau·rel and Har·dy /ˈlôrəl and ˈhärdē/ US comedy duo that consisted of **Stan Laurel** (born *Arthur Stanley Jefferson*) (1890–1965) and **Oliver Hardy** (1892–1957). British-born Laurel played the scatterbrained and often tearful innocent; Hardy played his pompous, overbearing, and frequently exasperated friend. They brought their distinctive slapstick comedy to many movies from 1927.

Stan Laurel and Oliver Hardy

Lau·ren·tian Pla·teau /lôˈrensHən/ another name for CANADIAN SHIELD.
– ORIGIN *Laurentian* from Latin *Laurentius* 'Lawrence' (from St. *Lawrence* River) + -AN.

Lau·ri·er /ˈlôrē,ā, lôrˈyā/, Sir Wilfrid (1841–1919), Canadian Liberal statesman; prime minister 1896–1911. He was Canada's first French-Canadian and first Roman Catholic prime minister.

lau·rus·ti·nus /,lôˈrə-stīnəs, ,lä-, -ˈstē-/ ▶ **n.** an evergreen winter-flowering viburnum with dense glossy green leaves and white or pink flowers, native to the Mediterranean area and cultivated elsewhere. ● *Viburnum tinus*, family Caprifoliaceae.
– ORIGIN early 17th cent.: modern Latin, from Latin *laurus* 'laurel' + *tinus* 'wild laurel.'

Lau·sanne /lōˈzän/ a town in southwestern Switzerland, on the north shore of Lake Geneva; pop. 119,180 (2007).

Lau·sit·zer Neis·se /ˈlouzitsər ˈnīsə/ German name for NEISSE (sense 1).

lav /lav/ ▶ **n.** informal a lavatory.
– ORIGIN early 20th cent.: abbreviation.

la·va /ˈlävə, ˈlavə/ ▶ **n.** hot molten or semifluid rock erupted from a volcano or fissure, or solid rock resulting from cooling of this.
– ORIGIN mid 18th cent.: from Italian (Neapolitan dialect), denoting the lava stream from Vesuvius, but originally denoting a stream caused by sudden rain, from *lavare* 'to wash,' from Latin.

la·va·bo /ləˈväbō, -ˈvābō/ ▶ **n.** (pl. **lavaboes**) (in the Roman Catholic Church) a towel or basin used for the ritual washing of the celebrant's hands at the offertory of the Mass. ■ ritual washing of this type. ■ dated a washbasin. ■ a washing trough in a monastery.
– ORIGIN mid 18th cent.: from Latin, literally 'I will wash,' in *Lavabo inter innocentes manus meas* 'I will wash my hands among the innocent' (Ps. 26:6), which was recited at the washing of hands in the Roman rite.

la·va dome ▶ **n.** a mound of viscous lava that has been extruded from a volcanic vent.

la·va flow ▶ **n.** a mass of flowing or solidified lava.

la·vage /ləˈväZH, ˈlavij/ ▶ **n.** Medicine washing out of a body cavity, such as the colon or stomach, with water or a medicated solution.
– ORIGIN late 18th cent. (in the general sense 'washing, a wash'): from French, from *laver* 'to wash.'

la·va lamp ▶ **n.** a transparent electric lamp containing a viscous liquid in which a brightly colored waxy substance is suspended, rising and falling in irregular and constantly changing shapes.

la·vash /ləˈväsн/ ▶ **n.** a crisp Middle Eastern flatbread.
– ORIGIN Armenian, from Turkish.

lav·a·to·ri·al /ˌlavəˈtôrēəl/ ▶ **adj.** of or relating to lavatories, in particular: ■ (of conversation or humor) characterized by undue reference to toilets and their use: *the comic's lavatorial schoolboy humor.* ■ resembling the style or architecture supposed to typify public lavatories: *the lavatorial utility that was a feature of subway design.*

lav·a·to·ry /ˈlavəˌtôrē/ ▶ **n.** (pl. **lavatories**) a room or compartment with a toilet and washbasin; a bathroom. ■ a sink or washbasin in a bathroom. ■ Brit. a flush toilet.
– ORIGIN late Middle English: from late Latin *lavatorium* 'place for washing,' from Latin *lavare* 'to wash.' The word originally denoted something in which to wash, such as a bath or piscina, later (mid 17th cent.) a room with washing facilities; the current sense dates from the 19th cent.

la·va tube ▶ **n.** a natural tunnel within a solidified lava flow, formerly occupied by flowing molten lava.

lave /lāv/ ▶ **v.** [with obj.] literary wash: *she ran cold water in the basin, laving her face and hands.* ■ (of water) wash against or over (something): *the sea below laved the shore with small, agitated waves.*
– DERIVATIVES **la·va·tion** /ləˈvāsнən/ **n.**
– ORIGIN Old English *lafian*, from Latin *lavare* 'to wash'; reinforced in Middle English by Old French *laver.*

lav·en·der /ˈlavəndər/ ▶ **n. 1** a small aromatic evergreen shrub of the mint family, with narrow leaves and bluish-purple flowers. Lavender has been widely used in perfumery and medicine since ancient times. ● Genus *Lavandula*, family Labiatae. ■ the flowers and stalks of such a shrub dried and used to give a pleasant smell to clothes and bed linens. ■ (also **lavender oil**) a scented oil distilled from lavender flowers. ■ dated used in reference to refinement or gentility: [as modifier] *she had a certain lavender charm.*
2 a pale blue color with a trace of mauve.
▶ **v.** [with obj.] perfume with lavender.
– ORIGIN Middle English: from Anglo-Norman French *lavendre*, based on medieval Latin *lavandula.*

lav·en·der cot·ton (chiefly Brit. also **cotton lavender**) ▶ **n.** a small aromatic shrubby plant of the daisy family, with silvery or greenish lavenderlike foliage and yellow button flowers. Native to the Mediterranean area, it has insecticidal properties and is widely cultivated for garden plantings. ● Genus *Santolina*, family Compositae: several species, in particular *S. chamaecyparissus.*

lav·en·der wa·ter ▶ **n.** a perfume made from distilled lavender, alcohol, and ambergris.

La·ver /ˈlāvər/, Rod (1938–), Australian tennis player; full name *Rodney George Laver.* Twice he won all four Grand Slam singles titles in the same year (1962, 1969).

la·ver¹ /ˈlāvər, ˈlävər/ (also **purple laver**) ▶ **n.** an edible seaweed with thin sheetlike fronds of a reddish-purple and green color that becomes black when dry. Laver typically grows on exposed shores, but in Japan it is cultivated in estuaries. ● *Porphyra umbilicaulis*, division Rhodophyta.
– ORIGIN late Old English (as the name of a water plant mentioned by Pliny), from Latin. The current sense dates from the early 17th cent.

la·ver² /ˈlāvər/ ▶ **n.** archaic or literary a basin or similar container used for washing oneself. ■ (in biblical use) a large brass bowl for the ritual ablutions of Jewish priests.
– ORIGIN Middle English: from Old French *laveoir*, from late Latin *lavatorium* 'place for washing' (see **LAVATORY**).

lav·ish /ˈlavisн/ ▶ **adj.** sumptuously rich, elaborate, or luxurious: *a lavish banquet.* ■ (of a person) very generous or extravagant: *he was lavish with his hospitality.* ■ spent or given in profusion: *lavish praise.*
▶ **v.** [with obj.] (**lavish something on**) bestow something in generous or extravagant quantities upon: *the media couldn't lavish enough praise on the film.* ■ (**lavish something with**) cover something thickly or liberally with: *she lavished our son with kisses.*
– DERIVATIVES **lav·ish·ly adv.**, **lav·ish·ness n.**
– ORIGIN late Middle English (as a noun denoting profusion): from Old French *lavasse* 'deluge of rain,' from *laver* 'to wash,' from Latin *lavare.*

La·voi·sier /ləˈvwäzyā, lävwäˈzyā/, Antoine Laurent (1743–94), French scientist. He is regarded as the father of modern chemistry.

law /lô/ ▶ **n. 1** (often **the law**) the system of rules that a particular country or community recognizes as regulating the actions of its members and may enforce by the imposition of penalties: *they were taken to court for breaking the law | a license is required by law |* [as modifier] *law enforcement.* ■ an individual rule as part of such a system: *an initiative to tighten up the laws on pornography.* ■ such systems as a subject of study or as the basis of the legal profession: *he was still practicing law |* [as modifier] *a law firm.* Compare with **JURISPRUDENCE**. ■ a thing regarded as having the binding force or effect of a formal system of rules: *what he said was law.* ■ (**the law**) informal the police: *he'd never been in trouble with the law in his life.* ■ statutory law and the common law. Compare with **EQUITY**. ■ a rule defining correct procedure or behavior in a sport: *the laws of the game.*
2 a statement of fact, deduced from observation, to the effect that a particular natural or scientific phenomenon always occurs if certain conditions are present: *the second law of thermodynamics.* ■ a generalization based on a fact or event perceived to be recurrent: *the first law of American corporate life is that dead wood floats.*
3 the body of divine commandments as expressed in the Bible or other religious texts. ■ (**the Law**) the Pentateuch as distinct from the other parts of the Hebrew Bible (the Prophets and the Writings). ■ (also **the Law of Moses**) the precepts of the Pentateuch. Compare with **TORAH**.
– PHRASES **at** (or **in**) **law** according to or concerned with the laws of a country: *an agreement enforceable at law | an attorney-at-law.* **be a law unto oneself** behave in a manner that is not conventional or predictable. **go to law** resort to legal action in order to settle a matter. **law and order** a situation characterized by respect for and obedience to the rules of a society. **the law of the jungle** see **JUNGLE**. **lay down the law** issue instructions to other people in an authoritative or dogmatic way. **take the law into one's own hands** punish someone for an offense according to one's own ideas of justice, esp. in an illegal or violent way. **take someone to law** initiate legal proceedings against someone. **there's no law against it** informal used in spoken English to assert that one is doing nothing wrong, esp. in response to an actual or implied criticism: *I can laugh, can't I? There's no law against it.*
– ORIGIN Old English *lagu*, from Old Norse *lag* 'something laid down or fixed,' of Germanic origin and related to **LAY¹**.

law-a·bid·ing ▶ **adj.** obedient to the laws of society: *a law-abiding citizen.*
– DERIVATIVES **law-a·bid·ing·ness n.**

law·break·er /ˈlôˌbrākər/ ▶ **n.** a person who violates the law.
– DERIVATIVES **law·break·ing** /-ˌbrākiNG/ **n. & adj.**

law clerk ▶ **n.** an assistant to a judge, typically a recent law-school graduate, whose function is to do legal research, help write opinions, and provide general assistance.

law court ▶ **n.** a court of law.

law·ful /ˈlôfəl/ ▶ **adj.** conforming to, permitted by, or recognized by law or rules: *it is an offense to carry a weapon in public without lawful authority.* ■ dated (of a child) born within a lawful marriage.
– DERIVATIVES **law·ful·ly adv.**, **law·ful·ness n.**

law·giv·er /ˈlôˌgivər/ ▶ **n.** a person who draws up and enacts laws.

law·less /ˈlôləs/ ▶ **adj.** not governed by or obedient to laws; characterized by a lack of civic order: *it was a lawless, anarchic city.*
– DERIVATIVES **law·less·ly adv.**, **law·less·ness n.**

law·mak·er /ˈlôˌmākər/ ▶ **n.** a legislator.
– DERIVATIVES **law·mak·ing** /-ˌmākiNG/ **adj. & n.**

law·man /ˈlôˌmən, -man/ ▶ **n.** (pl. **lawmen**) a law-enforcement officer, esp. a sheriff.

lawn¹ /lôn/ ▶ **n.** an area of short, mown grass in a yard, garden, or park.
– DERIVATIVES **lawned adj.**
– ORIGIN mid 16th cent.: alteration of dialect *laund* 'glade, pasture,' from Old French *launde* 'wooded district, heath,' of Celtic origin. The current sense dates from the mid 18th cent.

lawn² ▶ **n.** a fine linen or cotton fabric used for making clothes.
– DERIVATIVES **lawn·y adj.**
– ORIGIN Middle English: probably from *Laon*, the name of a city in France important for linen manufacture.

lawn bowl·ing (Brit. **bowls**) ▶ **n.** a game played with heavy balls, the object of which is to propel one's ball so that it comes to rest as close as possible to a previously bowled small ball (the jack). Lawn bowling is played chiefly outdoors (although an indoor version is also popular in Britain) on a closely trimmed lawn called a green.

lawn chair ▶ **n.** a folding chair for use outdoors.

lawn fla·min·go ▶ **n.** a pink plastic flamingo used as a lawn decoration.

lawn mow·er ▶ **n.** a machine for cutting the grass on a lawn.

lawn par·ty ▶ **n.** a garden party.

lawn ten·nis ▶ **n.** dated or formal the standard form of tennis, played with a soft ball on an open court. Compare with **COURT TENNIS**.

law of av·er·ag·es ▶ **n.** the principle that supposes most future events are likely to balance any past deviation from a presumed average.

law of·fice ▶ **n.** a lawyer's office.

law of mass ac·tion ▶ **n.** Chemistry the principle that the rate of a chemical reaction is proportional to the masses of the reacting substances.

law of na·tions ▶ **n.** Law international law.

law of na·ture ▶ **n. 1** another term for **NATURAL LAW**.
2 informal a regularly occurring or apparently inevitable phenomenon observable in human society: *it's a law of nature—however much space you have, you fill it.*

law of par·si·mo·ny ▶ **n.** see **PARSIMONY**.

law of suc·ces·sion ▶ **n.** the law regulating the inheritance of property. ■ the law regulating the appointment of a new monarch or head of state.

Law·rence¹ /ˈlôrəns, ˈlär-/ **1** a city in northeastern Kansas, home to the University of Kansas, the scene of fierce fighting before and during the Civil War; pop. 90,520 (est. 2008).
2 a city in northeastern Massachusetts, northeast of Lowell; pop. 70,014 (est. 2008).

Law·rence² /ˈlôrəns, ˈlär-/, D. H. (1885–1930), English novelist, poet, and essayist; full name *David Herbert Lawrence.* His work is characterized by its condemnation of industrial society and its frank exploration of sexual relationships. Notable works: *Sons and Lovers* (1913), *The Rainbow* (1915), and *Lady Chatterley's Lover* (1928).

Law·rence³, Ernest Orlando (1901–58), US physicist. He developed the first circular particle accelerator, later called a cyclotron, and opened the way for high-energy physics. He also worked on providing fissionable material for the atom bomb. Nobel Prize for Physics (1939).

Law·rence⁴, Jacob (1917–2000), US artist and educator. He is noted for *Migration* (1941–42), a series of 60 murals that depict the migration of black Americans northward in hopes of finding employment. He wrote *Harriet and the Promised Land* (1993) for children.

Law·rence⁵, T. E. (1888–1935), British soldier and writer; full name *Thomas Edward Lawrence*; known as **Lawrence of Arabia**. From 1916, he helped to organize the Arab revolt against the Turks in the Middle East, contributing to General Allenby's eventual victory in Palestine in 1918. He described this in *The Seven Pillars of Wisdom* (1926).

Law·rence, St. (died 258), Roman martyr and deacon of Rome; Latin name *Laurentius.* According to tradition, when Lawrence offered the poor people of Rome as the treasure of the Church to the prefect of Rome, he was roasted to death on a gridiron. Feast day, August 10.

law·ren·ci·um /lôˈrensēəm/ ▶ **n.** the chemical element of atomic number 103, a radioactive metal of the actinide series. Lawrencium does not occur naturally and was first made by bombarding californium with boron nuclei. (Symbol: **Lr**)
– ORIGIN 1960s: modern Latin, named after Ernest O. **LAWRENCE³**, who founded the laboratory in which it was produced.

laws of war ▶ **plural n.** international rules and conventions that limit belligerents' action.

Law·son cy·press /ˈlôsən/ ▶ **n.** another term for **PORT ORFORD CEDAR**.
– ORIGIN mid 19th cent.: named after Peter *Lawson* (died 1820) and his son Charles (1794–1873), the Scottish nurserymen who first cultivated it.

law·suit /ˈlôˌso͞ot/ ▶ **n.** a claim or dispute brought to a court of law for adjudication: *his lawyer filed a lawsuit against Los Angeles city.*

Law·ton /ˈlôtn/ a city in southwestern Oklahoma; pop. 90,091 (est. 2008).

law·yer /ˈloi-ər, ˈlôyər/ ▶ **n.** a person who practices or studies law; an attorney or a counselor.
▶ **v.** [no obj.] practice law; work as a lawyer: (as noun **lawyering**) *lawyering is a craft that takes a long time to become proficient at.* ■ [with obj.] (of a lawyer) work on the legal aspects of (a contract, lawsuit, etc.):

there is always a danger that the deal will be lawyered to death.
– DERIVATIVES **law·yer·ly** adj.

law·yer·ing /ˈloi-əriNG, ˈlôyər-/ ▶ n. the work of practicing law: *although he holds a law degree, he lets his hired guns do the real lawyering.*

lax /laks/ ▶ adj. **1** not sufficiently strict, severe, or careful: *lax security arrangements at the airport | he'd been a bit lax about discipline in school lately.*
2 (of the limbs or muscles) relaxed. ■ (of the bowels) loose. ■ Phonetics (of a speech sound, esp. a vowel) pronounced with the vocal muscles relaxed. The opposite of TENSE[1].
– DERIVATIVES **lax·i·ty** /ˈlaksətē/ n., **lax·ly** adv., **lax·ness** n.
– ORIGIN late Middle English (in the sense 'loose,' said of the bowels): from Latin *laxus*.

lax·a·tive /ˈlaksətiv/ ▶ adj. (chiefly of a drug or medicine) tending to stimulate or facilitate evacuation of the bowels.
▶ n. a medicine that has such an effect.
– ORIGIN late Middle English: via Old French *laxatif, -ive* or late Latin *laxativus*, from Latin *laxare* 'loosen' (from *laxus* 'loose').

lay[1] /lā/ ▶ v. (past and past participle **laid** /lād/) **1** [with obj.] put down, esp. gently or carefully: *she laid the baby in his crib.* ■ prevent (something) from rising off the ground: *there may have been the odd light shower just to lay the dust.*
2 [with obj.] put down and set in position for use: *it is advisable to have your carpet laid by a professional |* figurative *the groundwork for change had been laid.* ■ set cutlery, crockery, and mats on (a table) in preparation for a meal: *she laid the table for the evening meal.* ■ (often **be laid with**) cover (a surface) with objects or a substance: *the floor was laid with tiles.* ■ make ready (a trap) for someone: *she wouldn't put it past him to lay a trap for her.* ■ put the material for (a fire) in place and arrange it. ■ work out (an idea or suggestion) in detail ready for use or presentation: *I'd like more time to lay my plans.* ■ (**lay something before**) present information or suggestions to be considered and acted upon by (someone): *he laid before the House proposals for the establishment of the committee.* ■ (usu. **be laid**) locate (an episode in a play, novel, etc.) in a certain place: *no one who knew the area could be in doubt where the scene was laid.* ■ Nautical follow (a specified course). ■ [no obj.] Nautical go or come: *they had to lay aloft.* ■ [with obj.] stake (an amount of money) in a wager: *she suspected he was pulling her leg, but she wouldn't have laid money on it.*
3 [with obj.] used with an abstract noun so that the phrase formed has the same meaning as the verb related to the noun used, e.g., "lay the blame on" means 'to blame': *she* **laid** *great stress* **on** *little courtesies.*
4 [with obj.] (of a female bird, insect, reptile, or amphibian) produce (an egg) from inside the body: *flamingos lay only one egg |* [no obj.] *the hens were laying at the same rate as usual.*
5 [with obj.] vulgar slang have sexual intercourse with.
▶ n. **1** [in sing.] the general appearance of an area, including the direction of streams, hills, and similar features: *the lay of the surrounding countryside.* ■ the position or direction in which something lies: *roll the carpet against the lay of the nap.* ■ the direction or amount of twist in rope strands.
2 vulgar slang an act of sexual intercourse. ■ [with adj.] a person with a particular ability or availability as a sexual partner.
3 the laying of eggs or the period during which they are laid.
– PHRASES **lay something at someone's door** see DOOR. **lay something bare** bring something out of concealment; expose something: *the sad tale of failure was laid bare.* **lay a charge** make an accusation: *we could lay a charge of gross negligence.* **lay claim to something** assert that one has a right to something: *four men laid claim to the leadership.* ■ assert that one possesses a skill or quality: *she has never laid claim to medical knowledge.* **lay down one's arms** (or **weapons**) cease fighting: *they renounced violence and laid down their arms.* **lay down the law** see LAW. **lay down one's life** sacrifice one's life for a cause: *he laid down his life for his country.* **lay eyes on** see EYE. **lay a** (or **the**) **ghost** exorcise a ghost. ■ get rid of a distressing, frightening, or worrying memory or thought: *we need to lay the ghost of the past and move ahead.* **lay hands on 1** find and take possession of: *they huddled, trying to keep warm under anything they could lay hands on.* **2** place one's hands on or over, esp. in confirmation, ordination, or spiritual healing. **lay** (or **put**) **one's hands on** find and acquire: *I would read every book I could lay my hands on.* **lay hold of** (or **on**) catch or gain possession of: *he was afraid she might vanish if he did not lay hold of her.* **lay it on the line** see LINE[1]. **the lay** (Brit. **lie**) **of the land** the way in which the features or characteristics of an area present themselves. ■ the current situation or state of affairs: *she was beginning to see the lay of the land with her in-laws.* **lay someone low** (of an illness) reduce someone to inactivity. ■ bring to an end the high position or good fortune formerly enjoyed by someone: *she reflected on how quickly fate can lay a person low.* **lay something on the table** see TABLE. **lay something on thick** (or **with a trowel**) informal grossly exaggerate or overemphasize something. **lay someone open to** expose someone to the risk of (something): *his position could lay him open to accusations of favoritism.* **lay over** break one's journey: *Steven and I will lay over in New York, then fly to London.* **lay siege to** see SIEGE. **lay store by** see STORE. **lay someone/something to rest** bury a body in a grave. ■ soothe and dispel fear, anxiety, grief, or a similar unpleasant emotion: *suspicion will be laid to rest by fact rather than hearsay.* **lay something** (**to**) **waste** see WASTE.
– PHRASAL VERBS **lay about (someone)** beat or attack (someone) violently: *they weren't against laying about you with sticks and stones.* ■ strike out wildly on all sides: *the mare laid about her with her front legs and teeth.* **lay something aside** put something to one side: *he laid aside his book |* figurative *the situation gave them a good reason to lay aside their differences.* ■ reserve money for the future or for a particular cause: *he begged them to lay something aside toward the cause.* **lay something down 1** put something down: *she finished her eclair and laid down her fork.* **2** formulate and enforce or insist on a rule or principle: *stringent criteria have been laid down.* **3** begin to construct a ship or railroad. ■ (usu. **be laid down**) build up a deposit of a substance: *these cells lay down new bone tissue.* **4** store wine in a cellar. **5** pay or wager money. **6** informal record a piece of music: *he was invited to the studio to lay down some backing vocals.* **lay something in/up** build up a stock of something in case of need. **lay into** informal attack violently with words or blows: *three youths laid into him.* **lay off** informal give up or stop doing something: *I laid off smoking for seven years.* **lay someone off** discharge a worker, esp. temporarily because of a shortage of work. **lay something on** informal require (someone) to endure or deal with a responsibility or difficulty: *this is an absurdly heavy guilt trip to lay on anyone.* **lay someone out 1** prepare someone for burial after death. **2** informal knock someone unconscious: *he was lucky that the punch didn't lay him out.* **lay something out 1** spread something out to its full extent, esp. so that it can be seen: *the police were insisting that suitcases should be opened and their contents laid out.* **2** construct or arrange buildings or gardens according to a plan: *they proceeded to lay out a new town.* ■ arrange and present material for printing and publication: *the brochure is beautifully laid out.* ■ explain something clearly and carefully: *we need a paper laying out our priorities.* **3** informal spend a sum of money: *look at the money I had to lay out for your uniform.* **lay up** Golf hit the ball deliberately to a lesser distance than possible, typically in order to avoid a hazard. **lay someone up** put someone out of action through illness or injury: *he was laid up with his familiar fever.* **lay something up 1** see LAY SOMETHING IN/UP above. **2** take a ship or other vehicle out of service: *our boats were laid up during the winter months.* **3** assemble layers in the arrangement required for the manufacture of plywood or other laminated material.
– ORIGIN Old English *lecgan*, of Germanic origin; related to Dutch *leggen* and German *legen*, also to LIE[1].

> **USAGE** The verb **lay** means, broadly, 'put something down': *they are going to* **lay** *the carpet.* The past tense and the past participle of **lay** is **laid**: *they* **laid** *the groundwork; she had* **laid** *careful plans.* The verb **lie**, on the other hand, means 'assume a horizontal or resting position': *why don't you* **lie** *on the floor?* The past tense of **lie** is **lay**: *he* **lay** *on the floor earlier in the day.* The past participle of **lie** is **lain**: *she had* **lain** *on the bed for hours.* In practice, many speakers inadvertently get the **lay** forms and the **lie** forms into a tangle of right and wrong usage. Here are some examples of typical incorrect usage: *have you been* **laying** *on the sofa all day?* (should be **lying**); *he* **lay** *the books on the table* (should be **laid**); *I had* **laid** *in this position so long, my arm was stiff* (should be **lain**). See also usage at LIE[1].

lay[2] ▶ adj. [attrib.] **1** not ordained into or belonging to the clergy: *a lay preacher.*
2 not having professional qualifications or expert knowledge, esp. in law or medicine: *lay and professional views of medicine.*
– ORIGIN Middle English: from Old French *lai*, via late Latin from Greek *laïkos*, from *laos* 'people.' Compare with LAIC.

lay[3] ▶ n. a short lyric or narrative poem meant to be sung. ■ literary a song: *on his lips there died the cheery lay.*
– ORIGIN Middle English: from Old French *lai*, corresponding to Provençal *lais*, of unknown origin.

lay[4] past of LIE[1].

lay·a·bout /ˈlāəˌbout/ ▶ n. derogatory a person who habitually does little or no work.

lay·a·way /ˈlāəˌwā/ (also **layaway plan**) ▶ n. a system of paying a deposit to secure an item for later purchase: *she picked up a coat she had* **on layaway.**

lay·back /ˈlāˌbak/ ▶ n. Climbing a method of climbing a crack in rock by leaning back and pulling with the hands on one face, with the feet against the other face.

lay broth·er ▶ n. a man who has taken the vows of a religious order but is not ordained or obliged to take part in the full cycle of liturgy and is employed in ancillary or manual work.

lay-by ▶ n. (pl. **lay-bys**) an area at the side of a road where vehicles may pull off the road and stop. ■ a similar arrangement on a canal, or in a river or harbor.

lay·er /ˈlāər/ ▶ n. **1** a sheet, quantity, or thickness of material, typically one of several, covering a surface or body: *bears depend on* **a layer of** *blubber to keep them warm in the water |* figurative *a larger missile would provide a layer of defense at higher altitudes.* ■ a level of seniority in the hierarchy of an organization: *a managerial layer.*
2 [in combination] a person or thing that lays something: *the worms are prolific egg-layers.*
3 a shoot fastened down to take root while attached to the parent plant.
▶ v. [with obj.] (often as adj. **layered**) **1** arrange in a layer or layers: *the current trend for layered clothes.* ■ cut (hair) in overlapping layers: *her layered, shoulder-length hair.*
2 propagate (a plant) as a layer: *a layered shoot.*
– ORIGIN Middle English (denoting a mason): from LAY[1] + -ER[1]. The sense 'stratum of material covering a surface' (early 17th cent.) may represent a respelling of an obsolete agricultural use of LAIR denoting quality of soil.

lay·er cake ▶ n. a cake of two or more layers with icing or another filling between them.

lay·er·ing /ˈlāəriNG/ ▶ n. **1** the action of arranging something in layers. ■ Geology the presence or formation of layers in sedimentary or igneous rock.
2 the method or activity of propagating a plant by producing layers.

lay·ette /lāˈet/ ▶ n. a set of clothing, linens, and sometimes toiletries for a newborn child.
– ORIGIN mid 19th cent.: from French, diminutive of Old French *laie* 'drawer,' from Middle Dutch *laege*.

lay fig·ure ▶ n. a dummy or jointed manikin of a human body used by artists, esp. for arranging drapery on.
– ORIGIN late 18th cent.: from obsolete *layman*, from Dutch *leeman*, from obsolete *led*, earlier form of *lid* 'joint.'

lay figure

lay·man /ˈlāmən/ ▶ n. (pl. **laymen**) **1** a nonordained member of a church.
2 a person without professional or specialized knowledge in a particular subject: *the book seems well suited to the interested layman.*

lay·off /ˈlāˌôf, -ˌäf/ ▶ n. **1** a discharge, esp. temporary, of a worker or workers. ■ a period when this is in force.
2 a period during which someone does not take part in a customary sport or other activity: *they needed to rehabilitate injuries or just brush up after long layoffs.*

La'youn variant spelling of LAAYOUNE.

lay·out /ˈlāˌout/ ▶ n. the way in which the parts of something are arranged or laid out: *changing the layout of the ground floor.* ■ the way in which text or pictures are set out on a page: *the layout is uncluttered and the illustrations are helpful.* ■ the process of setting out material on a page or in a work: *doing layout for newspapers and magazines.* ■ a thing arranged or set out in a particular way: *a model railroad layout.* ■ Diving & Gymnastics a position in which the body is extended, the head upright, the legs held straight and together, and the arms held out to the sides.

lay·o·ver /ˈlā,ōvər/ ▶ **n.** a period of rest or waiting before a further stage in a journey.

lay·per·son /ˈlā,pərsən/ ▶ **n.** (pl. **laypeople**) a nonordained member of a church. ■ a person without professional or specialized knowledge in a particular subject.

lay read·er ▶ **n.** (in the Anglican Church) a layperson licensed to preach and to conduct some religious services, but not licensed to celebrate the Eucharist.

lay·shaft /ˈlā,SHaft/ ▶ **n.** chiefly Brit. a second or intermediate transmission shaft in a machine.

lay sis·ter ▶ **n.** a woman who has taken the vows of a religious order but is not obliged to take part in the full cycle of liturgy and is employed in ancillary or manual work.

Lay·ton /ˈlātn/ a city in northern Utah, south of Ogden; pop. 65,514 (est. 2008).

lay·up /ˈlāəp/ ▶ **n. 1** Basketball a one-handed shot made from near the basket, esp. one that rebounds off the backboard.
2 (also **lay-up**) the state or action of something, esp. a ship, being laid up.

lay·wom·an /ˈlā,wo͝omən/ ▶ **n.** (pl. **laywomen**) a nonordained female member of a church.

laz·ar /ˈlazər, ˈlāzər/ ▶ **n.** archaic a poor and diseased person, esp. one afflicted by a feared, contagious disease such as leprosy.
– ORIGIN Middle English: from medieval Latin *lazarus*, with biblical allusion to *Lazarus*, the name of a beggar covered in sores (Luke 16:20).

laz·a·rette /,lazəˈret/ (also **lazaret**) ▶ **n. 1** a small compartment below the deck in the after end of a vessel, used for stores.
2 a lazaretto.
– ORIGIN early 17th cent. (denoting an isolation hospital): from French *lazaret*, from Italian *lazaretto* (see LAZARETTO).

laz·a·ret·to /,lazəˈretō/ ▶ **n.** (pl. **lazarettos**) chiefly historical an isolation hospital for people with infectious diseases, esp. leprosy or plague. ■ a building (or ship) used for quarantine. ■ a military or prison hospital.
– ORIGIN mid 16th cent.: from Italian, diminutive of *lazzaro* 'beggar,' from medieval Latin *lazarus* (see LAZAR).

Laz·a·rist /ˈlazərist/ ▶ **n.** another name for VINCENTIAN.
– ORIGIN from French *Lazariste*, from the biblical name *Lazarus* (see LAZAR).

Laz·a·rus /ˈlazərəs/, Emma (1849–87), US poet. She is best known as the author of "The New Colossus" (1883), her sonnet to the Statue of Liberty, which is engraved on a plaque inside the statue.

laze /lāz/ ▶ **v.** [no obj.] spend time in a relaxed, lazy manner: *she spent the day at home, reading the papers and generally lazing around.* ■ [with obj.] (**laze something away**) pass time in such a way: *laze away a long summer day.*
▶ **n.** [in sing.] a spell of acting in such a way.
– ORIGIN late 16th cent.: back-formation from LAZY.

la·zi·ness /ˈlāzēnis/ ▶ **n.** the quality of being unwilling to work or use energy; idleness: *it was sheer laziness on my part.*

laz·u·li ▶ **n.** short for LAPIS LAZULI.

laz·u·lite /ˈlazyo͞o,līt, ˈlazə-/ ▶ **n.** an azure-blue mineral with a glasslike luster. ● Chem. formula: $(FeMg)Al_2P_2O_8(OH)_2$.

laz·u·rite /ˈlaz(y)ə,rīt, ˈlaZHə-/ ▶ **n.** a bright blue mineral that is the main constituent of lapis lazuli and consists chiefly of a silicate and sulfate of sodium and aluminum.

la·zy /ˈlāzē/ ▶ **adj.** (**lazier, laziest**) **1** unwilling to work or use energy: *I'm very lazy by nature* | *he was too lazy to cook.* ■ characterized by lack of effort or activity: *lazy summer days.* ■ showing a lack of effort or care: *lazy writing.* ■ (of a river) slow-moving.
2 (of a livestock brand) placed on its side rather than upright: *a logo with a lazy E.*
– DERIVATIVES **la·zi·ly** /-zəlē/ **adv.**
– ORIGIN mid 16th cent.: perhaps related to Low German *lasich* 'languid, idle.'

la·zy·bones /ˈlāzē,bōnz/ ▶ **n.** (pl. **same**) informal a lazy person (often as a form of address).

la·zy dai·sy stitch ▶ **n.** an embroidery stitch in the form of a flower petal.

la·zy eye ▶ **n.** an eye with poor vision that is mainly caused by underuse, esp. the unused eye in strabismus.

la·zy Su·san /ˈso͞ozən/ ▶ **n.** a revolving stand or tray on a table, used esp. for holding condiments.

la·zy tongs ▶ **n.** a set of extending tongs for grasping objects at a distance, with several connected pairs of levers pivoted like scissors.

lb. ▶ **abbr.** pound(s) (in weight). [from Latin *libra*.]

LBD ▶ **n.** (pl. **LBDs**) informal little black dress: *you can't go wrong with an LBD for premières or parties.*
– ORIGIN abbreviation.

LBO ▶ **abbr.** leveraged buyout.

LC ▶ **abbr.** ■ landing craft. ■ Library of Congress.

l.c. ▶ **abbr.** ■ in the passage cited. [from Latin *loco citato*.] ■ letter of credit. ■ lower case.

L/C (also **l.c.**) ▶ **abbr.** letter of credit.

LCD ▶ **abbr.** ■ Electronics & Computing liquid crystal display. ■ Mathematics lowest (or least) common denominator.

LCL ▶ **abbr.** less-than-carload lot.

LCM ▶ **abbr.** Mathematics lowest (or least) common multiple.

LCpl ▶ **abbr.** lance corporal.

LCS ▶ **abbr.** ■ landing craft support. ■ liquid crystal shutter.

LCT ▶ **abbr.** ■ land conservation trust. ■ landing craft, tank. ■ local civil time.

LD ▶ **abbr.** ■ learning disabled. ■ lethal dose (of a toxic compound, drug, or pathogen). It is usually written with a following numeral indicating the percentage of a group of animals or cultured cells or microorganisms killed by such a dose, typically standardized at 50 percent (**LD_{50}**).

Ld. ▶ **abbr.** Lord: *Ld. Lothian.*

ld. ▶ **abbr.** ■ lead. ■ load.

LDC ▶ **abbr.** less-developed country.

LDL ▶ **abbr.** Biochemistry low-density lipoprotein.

L-do·pa /,el ˈdōpə/ ▶ **n.** Biochemistry the levorotatory form of dopa, used to treat Parkinson's disease. Also called LEVODOPA.

LDS ▶ **abbr.** Latter-Day Saints.

LE ▶ **abbr.** language engineering.

-le[1] ▶ **suffix 1** forming names of appliances or instruments: *bridle* | *thimble.*
2 forming names of animals and plants: *beetle.*
– ORIGIN Old English, of Germanic origin.

-le[2] (also **-el**) ▶ **suffix** forming nouns having or originally having a diminutive sense: *mantle* | *battle* | *castle.*
– ORIGIN Middle English *-el*, *-elle*, partly from Old English and partly from Old French (based on Latin forms).

-le[3] ▶ **suffix** (forming adjectives from an original verb) apt to; liable to: *brittle* | *nimble.*
– ORIGIN Middle English: from earlier *-el*, of Germanic origin.

-le[4] ▶ **suffix** forming verbs, chiefly those expressing repeated action or movement (as in *babble, dazzle*), or having diminutive sense (as in *nestle*).
– ORIGIN Old English *-lian*, of Germanic origin.

lea /lē/ ▶ **n.** literary an open area of grassy or arable land: *the lowing herd winds slowly o'er the lea.*
– ORIGIN Old English *lēa(h)*, of Germanic origin; related to Old High German *loh* 'grove,' from an Indo-European root shared by Sanskrit *lokás* 'open space,' Latin *lucus* 'grove,' and perhaps also LIGHT[1].

lea. ▶ **abbr.** league.

leach /lēCH/ ▶ **v.** (with reference to a soluble chemical or mineral) drain away from soil, ash, or similar material by the action of percolating liquid, esp. rainwater: [with obj.] *the nutrient is quickly leached away* | [no obj.] *pesticides that leach into rivers.* ■ [with obj.] subject (soil, ash, etc.) to this process.
– ORIGIN Old English *leccan* 'to water,' of West Germanic origin. The current sense dates from the mid 19th cent.

leach·ate /ˈlē,CHāt/ ▶ **n.** technical water that has percolated through a solid and leached out some of the constituents.

Lea·cock /ˈlē,käk/, Stephen (Butler) (1869–1949), Canadian humorist and economist. He is known for his many humorous short stories, parodies, and essays. Notable works: *Sunshine Sketches of a Little Town* (1912) and *Arcadian Adventures with the Idle Rich* (1914).

lead[1] /lēd/ ▶ **v.** (past and past participle **led** /led/) [with obj.] **1** cause (a person or animal) to go with one by holding them by the hand, a halter, a rope, etc., while moving forward: *she emerged leading a bay horse.* ■ show (someone or something) the way to a destination by going in front of or beside them: *she stood up and led her friend to the door.* ■ be a reason or motive for (someone): *nothing that I have read about the case **leads me to the conclusion that** anything untoward happened* | [with obj. and infinitive] *a fascination for art led him to start a collection of paintings.* ■ [no obj.] be a route or means of access to a particular place or in a particular direction: *a door leading to a better-lit corridor.* ■ [no obj.] (**lead to**) culminate in (a particular event): *closing the plant will lead to the loss of 300 jobs.*
2 be in charge or command of: *a military delegation was led by the Chief of Staff.* ■ organize and direct: *the conference included sessions led by people with personal knowledge of the area.* ■ set (a process) in motion: *they are waiting for an expansion of world trade to lead a recovery.* ■ be the principal player of (a group of musicians): *since the forties he has led his own big bands.* ■ [no obj.] (**lead with**) assign the most important position to (a particular news item): *the news on the radio led with the murder.*
3 be superior to (competitors or colleagues): *there will be specific areas or skills in which other nations **lead the world**.* ■ have the first place in (a competition); be ahead of (competitors): *the veteran jockey was leading the field.* ■ [no obj.] have the advantage in a race or game: *Dallas was fortunate to lead 85-72.*
4 have or experience (a particular way of life): *she's led a completely sheltered life.*
5 initiate (action in a game or contest), in particular: ■ (in card games) play (the first card) in a trick or round of play. ■ [no obj.] (**lead with**) Boxing make an attack with (a particular punch or fist): *Adam led with a left.* ■ [no obj.] Baseball (of a base runner) advance one or more steps from the base one occupies while the pitcher has the ball: *the runner leads from first.*
▶ **n. 1** the initiative in an action; an example for others to follow: *The US is now **taking the** environmental **lead**.* ■ a clue to be followed in the resolution of a problem: *detectives investigating the murder are chasing new leads.* ■ (in card games) an act or right of playing first in a trick or round of play: *it's your lead.* ■ the card played first in a trick or round.
2 (**the lead**) a position of advantage in a contest; first place: *they were beaten 5-3 after twice being **in the lead**.* ■ an amount by which a competitor is ahead of the others: *the team held a slender one-goal lead.* ■ Baseball an advance of one or more steps taken by a base runner from the base they occupy while the pitcher has the ball.
3 the chief part in a play or film: *she had the lead in a new film* | [as modifier] *the lead role.* ■ the person playing the chief part: *he still looked like a romantic lead.* ■ [usu. as modifier] the chief performer or instrument of a specified type: *that girl will be your lead dancer.* ■ [often as modifier] the item of news given the greatest prominence in a newspaper or magazine: *the lead story.*
4 a leash for a dog or other animal.
5 a wire that conveys electric current from a source to an appliance, or that connects two points of a circuit together.
6 the distance advanced by a screw in one turn.
7 a channel, in particular: ■ an artificial watercourse leading to a mill. ■ a channel of water in an ice field.
– PHRASES **lead someone astray** cause someone to act or think foolishly or wrongly. **lead someone by the nose** informal control someone totally, esp. by deceiving them. **lead someone a dance** see DANCE. **lead from the front** take an active role in what one is urging and directing others to do. **lead someone up** (or **down**) **the garden path** informal give someone misleading clues or signals. **lead the way** see WAY. **lead with one's chin** informal (of a boxer) leave one's chin unprotected. ■ behave or speak incautiously.
– PHRASAL VERBS **lead off** start: *the newsletter leads off with a report on tax bills.* ■ Baseball bat first in a game or inning. **lead someone on** mislead or deceive someone, esp. into believing that one is in love with or attracted to them. **lead up to** immediately precede: *the weeks leading up to the elections.* ■ result in: *fashioning a policy appropriate to the situation entails understanding the forces that led up to it.*
– ORIGIN Old English *lǣdan*, of Germanic origin; related to Dutch *leiden* and German *leiten*, also to LOAD and LODE.

lead[2] /led/ ▶ **n. 1** a heavy, bluish-gray, soft, ductile metal, the chemical element of atomic number 82. It has been used in roofing, plumbing, ammunition, storage batteries, radiation shields, etc., and its compounds have been used in crystal glass, as an antiknock agent in gasoline, and (formerly) in paints. (Symbol: **Pb**)
2 an item or implement made of lead, in particular: ■ Nautical a lead casting suspended on a line to determine the depth of water. ■ bullets.

3 graphite used as the part of a pencil that makes a mark.
4 Printing a blank space between lines of print. [originally with reference to the metal strip used to create this space.]
– PHRASES **get the lead out** informal move or work more quickly.
– ORIGIN Old English *lēad*, of West Germanic origin; related to Dutch *lood* 'lead' and German *Lot* 'plummet, solder.'

lead-ac·id /led/ ▶ **adj.** denoting a secondary cell or battery in which the electrodes are plates or grids of lead (or lead alloy) immersed in dilute sulfuric acid. The anode is coated with lead dioxide and the cathode with spongy lead.

lead ar·ti·cle /lēd/ ▶ **n.** the principal article in a newspaper or magazine.

lead bal·loon /led/ ▶ **n.** (in phrase **go over like a lead balloon**) informal (of something said or written) be poorly received: *Jenkins' book has gone over like a lead balloon.*

lead crys·tal /led/ ▶ **n.** another term for LEAD GLASS.

lead·ed /'ledid/ ▶ **adj.** **1** (of windowpanes or a roof) framed, covered, or weighted with lead: *Georgian-style leaded windows.*
2 (of gasoline) containing tetraethyl lead: *leaded fuel.*
3 Printing (of print) having the lines separated by spaces.

lead·en /'ledn/ ▶ **adj.** dull, heavy, or slow: *his eyelids were leaden with sleep.* ■ of the color of lead; dull gray: *the snow fell from a leaden sky.* ■ archaic made of lead: *a leaden coffin.*
– DERIVATIVES **lead·en·ly adv.**, **lead·en·ness n.**
– ORIGIN Old English *lēaden* (see LEAD[2], -EN[2]).

lead·en seal ▶ **n.** chiefly historical a seal made of lead, used esp. for papal documents.

lead·er /'lēdər/ ▶ **n.** **1** the person who leads or commands a group, organization, or country: *the leader of a protest group.* ■ an organization or company that is the most advanced or successful in a particular area: *a leader in the use of video conferencing.* ■ (also **Leader of the House**) Brit. a member of the government officially responsible for initiating business in Parliament.
2 the principal player in a music group. ■ a conductor of a band or small musical group. ■ Brit. the principal first violinist in an orchestra.
3 Brit. a leading article or editorial in a newspaper.
4 a short strip of nonfunctioning material at each end of a reel of film or recording tape for connection to the spool. ■ a length of filament attached to the end of a fishing line to carry the hook or fly.
5 a shoot of a plant at the apex of a stem or main branch.
6 (**leaders**) Printing a series of dots or dashes across the page to guide the eye, esp. in tabulated material.
– DERIVATIVES **lead·er·less adj.**

lead·er board ▶ **n.** a scoreboard showing the names and current scores of the leading competitors, esp. in a golf tournament.

lead·er·ship /'lēdər,SHip/ ▶ **n.** the action of leading a group of people or an organization: *different styles of leadership.* ■ the state or position of being a leader: *the leadership of the party.* ■ [treated as sing. or pl.] the leaders of an organization, country, etc.: *a change of leadership had become desirable.*

lead foot /led/ ▶ **n.** [in sing.] informal a tendency to drive fast: *she drives with a lead foot.*

lead-foot·ed /led/ ▶ **adj.** informal **1** slow; clumsy: *the most lead-footed guy can try aerobic moves.*
2 tending to drive too quickly.

lead-free /led/ ▶ **adj.** (of gasoline) unleaded.

lead glass /led/ ▶ **n.** glass containing a substantial proportion of lead oxide, making it more refractive. Also called LEAD CRYSTAL.

lead-in /lēd/ ▶ **n.** **1** an introduction or preamble that allows one to move smoothly on to the next part of something: [as modifier] *the lead-in note.*
2 a wire leading in from outside, esp. from an antenna to a receiver or transmitter.

lead·ing[1] /'lēdiNG/ ▶ **adj.** [attrib.] most important: *a number of leading politicians.*
▶ **n.** guidance or leadership, esp. in a spiritual context. ■ an instance of such guidance: *the leadings of the Holy Spirit.*

lead·ing[2] /'lediNG/ ▶ **n.** the amount of blank space between lines of print.

lead·ing ar·ti·cle /'lēdiNG/ ▶ **n.** Brit. the chief editorial or article in a newspaper.

lead·ing edge /'lēdiNG/ ▶ **n.** the front edge of something, in particular: ■ Aeronautics the foremost edge of an airfoil, esp. a wing or propeller blade. ■ Electronics the part of a pulse in which the amplitude increases. ■ the forefront or vanguard, esp. of technological development: [as modifier] *leading-edge research.*

lead·ing la·dy /'lēdiNG/ ▶ **n.** the actress playing the principal female part in a movie, play, or television show.

lead·ing light /'lēdiNG/ ▶ **n.** a person who is prominent or influential in a particular field or organization: *Glass is one of the leading lights in modern music.*

lead·ing man /'lēdiNG/ ▶ **n.** the actor playing the principal male part in a movie, play, or television show.

lead·ing note /'lēdiNG/ ▶ **n.** Music another term for SUBTONIC.

lead·ing ques·tion /'lēdiNG/ ▶ **n.** a question that prompts or encourages the desired answer.

lead·ing rein /'lēdiNG/ ▶ **n.** a rein used to lead a horse along, esp. when ridden by an inexperienced rider.

lead·ing tone /'lēdiNG/ ▶ **n.** Music another term for SUBTONIC.

lead-off /'lēd/ ▶ **adj.** (of an action) beginning a series or a process: *the album's lead-off track.* ■ (**leadoff**) Baseball denoting the first batter in a lineup or of an inning.

lead pen·cil /led/ ▶ **n.** a pencil of graphite enclosed in wood.

lead poi·son·ing /led/ ▶ **n.** acute or chronic poisoning due to the absorption of lead into the body. Also called PLUMBISM.

lead shot /led/ ▶ **n.** another term for SHOT[1] (sense 3).

lead tet·ra·eth·yl /led/ ▶ **n.** Chemistry another term for TETRAETHYL LEAD.

lead time /lēd/ ▶ **n.** the time between the initiation and completion of a production process.

lead-up /lēd/ ▶ **n.** [in sing.] an event, point, or sequence that leads up to something else: ***the lead-up to the elections.***

Lead·ville /'led,vil/ a historic mining city in central Colorado, the highest US city at 10,190 feet (3,108 m); pop. 2,743 (est. 2008).

lead·wort /'led,wərt, -,wôrt/ ▶ **n.** another term for PLUMBAGO (sense 2).

leaf /lēf/ ▶ **n.** (pl. **leaves** /lēvz/) **1** a flattened structure of a higher plant, typically green and bladelike, that is attached to a stem directly or via a stalk. Leaves are the main organs of photosynthesis and transpiration. Compare with COMPOUND LEAF, LEAFLET. ■ any of a number of similar plant structures, e.g., bracts, sepals, and petals. ■ foliage regarded collectively. ■ the state of having leaves: *the trees are still* ***in leaf.*** ■ the leaves of tobacco or tea: [as modifier] *leaf tea.*
2 a thing that resembles a leaf in being flat and thin, typically something that is one of two or more similar items forming a set or stack. ■ a single thickness of paper, esp. in a book with each side forming a page. ■ [with modifier] gold, silver, or other specified metal in the form of very thin foil. ■ the hinged part or flap of a door, shutter, or table. ■ an extra section inserted to extend a table. ■ the inner or outer part of a cavity wall or double-glazed window. ■ any of the stacked metal strips that form a leaf spring.
▶ **v.** [no obj.] **1** (of a plant, esp. a deciduous one in spring) put out new leaves.
2 (**leaf through**) turn over (the pages of a book or the papers in a pile), reading them quickly or casually: *he leafed through the stack of notes.*
– PHRASES **shake** (or **tremble**) **like a leaf** (of a person) tremble greatly, esp. from fear. **take a leaf out of someone's book** see BOOK. **turn over a new leaf** see TURN.
– DERIVATIVES **leaf·age** /'lēfij/ **n.**, **leaf·less adj.**, **leaf·like** /-līk/ **adj.**
– ORIGIN Old English *lēaf*, of Germanic origin; related to Dutch *loof* and German *Laub.*

leaf bee·tle ▶ **n.** a small beetle that feeds chiefly on leaves and typically has bright metallic coloring. Some kinds are serious crop pests. ● Family Chrysomelidae: numerous species.

leaf·bird /'lēf,bərd/ ▶ **n.** a tree-dwelling songbird of South and Southeast Asia with mainly green plumage and a black bill, the male typically having a black throat. ● Genus *Chloropsis*, family Irenidae (or Chloropseidae): several species.

leaf curl ▶ **n.** a plant condition distinguished by the presence of curling leaves, caused by environmental stress or disease.

leaf·cut·ter ant /'lēf,kətər/ ▶ **n.** a tropical ant that cuts pieces from leaves and carries them back to the nest for use as a culture medium for growing food fungi. ● Genus *Atta*, family Formicidae.

leaf·cut·ter bee ▶ **n.** a solitary bee that cuts pieces from leaves, typically of roses, and uses them to construct cells in its nest. ● Genus *Megachile*, family Megachilidae.

leafed /lēfd/ ▶ **adj.** another term for LEAVED.

leaf fat ▶ **n.** dense fat occurring in layers around the kidneys of some animals, esp. pigs.

leaf fish ▶ **n.** a small, deep-bodied, predatory freshwater fish, with mottled brownish-green coloration that gives it a leaflike appearance. ● Two species in the family Nandidae: *Monocirrhus polyacanthus* of South America, and *Polycentropsis abbreviata* of Africa.

leaf green ▶ **n.** a bright, deep green color.

leaf·hop·per /'lēf,häpər/ ▶ **n.** a small plant bug that is typically brightly colored and leaps when disturbed. It can be a serious crop pest in warm regions. ● Family Cicadellidae, suborder Homoptera: numerous genera.

leaf in·sect ▶ **n.** a large, slow-moving tropical insect related to the stick insects, with a flattened body that is leaflike in shape and color. ● Family Phylliidae, order Phasmida: *Phyllium* and other genera.

leaf lard ▶ **n.** lard prepared from the leaf fat of a hog.

leaf·let /'lēflit/ ▶ **n.** **1** a printed sheet of paper, sometimes folded, containing information or advertising and usually distributed free.
2 Botany each of the leaflike structures that together make up a compound leaf, such as in the ash and horse chestnut. ■ (in general use) a young leaf.
▶ **v.** (**leaflets, leafleting, leafleted**) [with obj.] distribute leaflets to (people or an area): *I won't be leafleting neighborhoods* | [no obj.] *the union has leafleted, protested, and staged petition drives.*

leaf lit·ter ▶ **n.** see LITTER (sense 3 of the noun).

leaf·love /'lēf,ləv/ ▶ **n.** an African bulbul that frequents dense thickets, with mainly drab brown plumage and a loud bubbling call. ● The **leaflove** (*Phyllastrephus scandens*) and the **yellow-throated leaflove** (*Chlorocichla flavicollis*), family Pycnonotidae.

leaf min·er ▶ **n.** a small fly, moth, beetle, or sawfly whose larvae burrow between the two surfaces of a leaf.

leaf mold (also **leafmold**) ▶ **n.** **1** soil consisting chiefly of decayed leaves.
2 a fungal disease of plants in which mold develops on the leaves. ● The fungus is *Fulvia fulva* (formerly *Cladosporium fulvum*), subdivision Deuteromycotina.

leaf mon·key ▶ **n.** a leaf-eating, arboreal Asian monkey that is related to the langurs. ● Genus *Presbytis*, family Cercopithecidae: several species.

leaf-nosed bat ▶ **n.** a bat with a leaflike appendage on the snout. ● Families Hipposideridae (Old

lobed

toothed

clasping

ovate

lanceolate
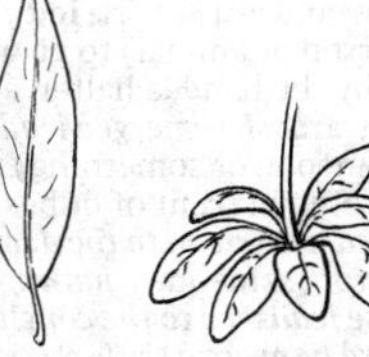

basal

alternate

opposite
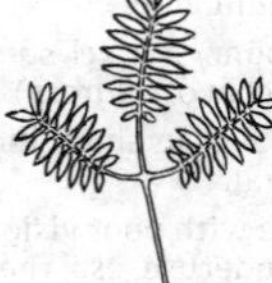
pinnate

palmate

leaf types

World) and Phyllostomatidae (New World): numerous species.

leaf-nosed bat

leaf peep·er ▶ **n.** informal a person who visits particular areas, esp. in New England, to view the autumn foliage.
– DERIVATIVES **leaf peep·ing n.**

leaf spot ▶ **n.** [usu. with modifier] any of a large number of fungal, bacterial, or viral plant diseases that cause leaves to develop discolored spots.

leaf spring ▶ **n.** a spring made of a number of strips of metal curved slightly upward and clamped together one above the other.

leaf·stalk /'lēf,stôk/ ▶ **n.** a petiole.

leaf-tailed geck·o ▶ **n.** a gecko with a wide, flat, leaf-shaped tail and skin color that blends with its surroundings. ● Genus *Phyllurus* (four Australian species), family Pygopodidae, and *Uroplatus* (several Madagascan species), family Gekkonidae.

leaf trace ▶ **n.** Botany a strand of conducting vessels extending from the stem to the base of a leaf.

leaf war·bler ▶ **n.** a small, slender Old World songbird with a brown or greenish back and whitish or yellowish underparts. ● Genus *Phylloscopus*, family Sylviidae: many species, including the chiffchaff.

leaf·y /'lēfē/ ▶ **adj.** (**leafier, leafiest**) having many leaves or much foliage: *leafy bushes* | *a remote, leafy glade.* ■ (of a plant) producing or grown for its broad-bladed leaves: *green leafy vegetables.* ■ resembling a leaf or leaves: *a three-pointed leafy bract.*
– DERIVATIVES **leaf·i·ness n.**

leaf·y spurge ▶ **n.** a perennial Eurasian herb that produces a flat-topped cluster of yellow bracts bearing small flowers. It is a noxious weed in prairie and grassland areas of the US, where it aggressively displaces native plants. ● *Euphorbia esula*, family Euphorbiaceae.

league[1] /lēg/ ▶ **n. 1** a collection of people, countries, or groups that combine for a particular purpose, typically mutual protection or cooperation: *the League of Nations.* ■ an agreement to combine in this way.
2 a group of sports clubs that play each other over a period for a championship. ■ the contest for the championship of such a league: *the year we won the league.*
3 a class or category of quality or excellence: *the two men were not in the same league* | *Jack's in a league of his own.*
▶ **v.** (**leagues, leaguing, leagued**) [no obj.] join in a league or alliance: *Oscar had **leagued with** other construction firms.*
– PHRASES **in league** conspiring with another or others: *he is **in league with** the devil.*
– ORIGIN late Middle English (denoting a compact for mutual protection or advantage): via French from Italian *lega*, from *legare* 'to bind,' from Latin *ligare*.

league[2] ▶ **n.** a former measure of distance by land, usually about three miles.
– ORIGIN late Middle English: from late Latin *leuga*, *leuca*, late Greek *leugē*, or from Provençal *lega* (modern French *lieue*).

League of Na·tions an association of countries established in 1919 by the Treaty of Versailles to promote international cooperation and achieve international peace and security. It was powerless to stop Italian, German, and Japanese expansionism leading to World War II and was replaced by the United Nations in 1945.

lea·guer /'lēgər/ ▶ **n.** [with adj. or noun modifier] a member of a particular league, esp. a sports player: *minor leaguers in spring training.*

leak /lēk/ ▶ **v.** [no obj.] **1** (of a container or covering) accidentally lose or admit contents, esp. liquid or gas, through a hole or crack: *the roof leaked* | (as adj. **leaking**) *a leaking gutter* | [with obj.] *the drums were leaking an unidentified liquid.* ■ (of liquid, gas, etc.) pass in or out through a hole or crack in such a way: *water kept leaking in.*
2 (of secret information) become known: *the news **leaked out**.* ■ [with obj.] intentionally disclose (secret information): *who had a motive to leak the story?* | (as adj. **leaked**) *a leaked government document.*
▶ **n. 1** a hole in a container or covering through which contents, esp. liquid or gas, may accidentally pass: *I checked all of the pipes for leaks.* ■ the action of leaking in such a way: *the leak of fluid may occur* | *a gas leak.*
2 an intentional disclosure of secret information: *one of the employees was responsible for the leak.*
– PHRASES **take a leak** informal urinate.
– DERIVATIVES **leak·er n.**
– ORIGIN late Middle English: probably of Low German or Dutch origin and related to LACK.

leak·age /'lēkij/ ▶ **n.** the accidental admission or escape of a fluid or gas through a hole or crack: *we're saving water by reducing leakage* | *there have been no leakages of radioactive material.* ■ Physics the gradual escape of an electric charge or current, or magnetic flux. ■ deliberate disclosure of confidential information.

Lea·key /'lēkē/ the name of a family of Kenyan archaeologists and anthropologists. ■ **Louis (Seymour Bazett)** (1903–72), born in Kenya of British parents. He pioneered the investigation of human origins in East Africa. In excavations at Olduvai Gorge, he and his wife discovered the remains of early hominids, including *Australopithecus* (or *Zinjanthropus*) *boisei*, and their implements in 1959. ■ **Mary (Douglas)** (1913–96), Louis's wife, born in England. She discovered *Homo habilis* and *Homo erectus* at Olduvai in 1960. ■ **Richard (Erskine)** (1944–), the son of Louis and Mary, born in Kenya. He was director of the Kenya Wildlife Service 1989–94 and is noted for his efforts against elephant poaching. (1984).

leak·proof /'lēk,pro͞of/ ▶ **adj.** designed or constructed to prevent leakage.

leak·y /'lēkē/ ▶ **adj.** (**leakier, leakiest**) having a leak or leaks: *a leaky roof.*
– DERIVATIVES **leak·i·ness n.**

leal /lēl/ ▶ **adj.** Scottish archaic loyal and honest: *his leal duty to the King.*
– ORIGIN Middle English: from Old French *leel*, earlier form of *loial* (see LOYAL).

Lean /lēn/, Sir David (1908–91), English movie director. His many movies include *The Bridge on the River Kwai* (1957), *Lawrence of Arabia* (1962), *Doctor Zhivago* (1965), and *A Passage to India* (1984).

lean[1] /lēn/ ▶ **v.** (past and past participle **leaned** /lēnd/ or chiefly Brit. **leant** /lent/) [no obj.] be in or move into a sloping position: *he leaned back in his chair.* ■ (**lean against/on**) incline from the perpendicular and rest for support on or against (something): *a man was leaning against the wall.* ■ [with obj.] (**lean something against/on**) cause something to rest on or against: *he leaned his elbows on the table.*
▶ **n.** a deviation from the perpendicular; an inclination: *the vehicle has a definite lean to the left.*
– PHRASAL VERBS **lean on 1** rely on or derive support from: *they have learned to lean on each other for support.* **2** put pressure on (someone) to act in a certain way: *a determination not to allow the majority to lean on the minority.* **lean to/toward** incline or be partial to (a view or position): *I now lean toward sabotage as the cause of the crash.*
– ORIGIN Old English *hleonian*, *hlinian*, of Germanic origin; related to Dutch *leunen* and German *lehnen*, from an Indo-European root shared by Latin *inclinare* and Greek *klinein*.

lean[2] /lēn/ ▶ **adj. 1** (of a person or animal) thin, esp. healthily so; having no superfluous fat: *his lean, muscular body.* ■ (of meat) containing little fat: *lean bacon.* ■ (of an industry or company) efficient and with no waste: *he made leaner government a campaign theme.*
2 (of an activity or a period of time) offering little reward, substance, or nourishment; meager: *the lean winter months* | *keep a small reserve to tide you over **the lean years**.*
3 (of a vaporized fuel mixture) having a high proportion of air: *lean air-to-fuel ratios.*
▶ **n.** the lean part of meat.
– DERIVATIVES **lean·ly adv.**, **lean·ness n.**
– ORIGIN Old English *hlǣne*, of Germanic origin.

lean-burn ▶ **adj.** of or relating to an internal combustion engine designed to run on a lean mixture to reduce pollution: *lean-burn technology.*

Le·an·der /lē'andər/ Greek Mythology a young man, the lover of the priestess Hero. He was drowned swimming across the Hellespont to visit her.

lean·ing /'lēniNG/ ▶ **n.** (often **leanings**) a tendency or partiality of a particular kind: *despite his liberal leanings, he had little sympathy for the individuals concerned.*

lean-to ▶ **n.** (pl. **lean-tos**) a building sharing one wall with a larger building, and having a roof that leans against that wall: [as modifier] *a lean-to garage.* ■ a temporary shelter, either supported or freestanding.

leap /lēp/ ▶ **v.** (past or past participle **leaped** /lēpt/ or **leapt** /lept/) [no obj.] jump or spring a long way, to a great height, or with great force: *I leaped across the threshold* | figurative *Fabia's heart leapt excitedly.* ■ move quickly and suddenly: *Polly leapt to her feet.* ■ [with obj.] jump across or over: *a coyote leaped the fence.* ■ make a sudden rush to do something; act eagerly and suddenly: *it was time for me to leap into action.* ■ (**leap at**) accept (an opportunity) eagerly: *they leapt at the opportunity to combine fun with fund-raising.* ■ (of a price or figure) increase dramatically: *sales leaped 40 percent during the Christmas season.* ■ (**leap out**) (esp. of writing) be conspicuous; stand out: *amid the notes, a couple of items leap out.*
▶ **n.** a forceful jump or quick movement: *she came downstairs in a series of flying leaps.* ■ a dramatic increase in price, amount, etc.: *a leap of 75 percent in two years.* ■ a sudden, abrupt change or transition: *a leap of faith.* ■ (in place names) a thing to be leaped over or from: *Lover's Leap.*
– PHRASES **a leap in the dark** a daring step or enterprise whose consequences are unpredictable. **by** (or **in**) **leaps and bounds** with startlingly rapid progress: *productivity improved in leaps and bounds.* **leap to the eye** (or **to mind**) be immediately apparent: *one dire question leaped to our minds.*
– DERIVATIVES **leap·er n.**
– ORIGIN Old English *hlēapan* (verb), *hlȳp* (noun), of Germanic origin; related to Dutch *lopen*, German *laufen* (verb), and Dutch *loop*, German *Lauf* (noun), all meaning 'run,' also to LOPE.

leap day ▶ **n.** the intercalary day in a leap year; February 29.

leap·frog /'lēp,frôg, -,fräg/ ▶ **n.** a game in which players in turn vault with parted legs over the backs of others who are bending down.
▶ **v.** (**leapfrogs, leapfrogging, leapfrogged**) [no obj.] perform such a vault: *they leapfrogged around the courtyard.* ■ (of a person or group) surpass or overtake another to move into a leading or dominant position: *she leapfrogged into a sales position.* ■ [with obj.] pass over (a stage or obstacle): *attempts to leapfrog the barriers of class.*

leap sec·ond /'sekənd/ ▶ **n.** a second that is occasionally inserted into the atomic scale of reckoning time in order to bring it into line with solar time. It is indicated by an additional beep in the time signal at the end of some years.

leap year ▶ **n.** a year, occurring once every four years, that has 366 days including February 29 as an intercalary day.
– ORIGIN late Middle English: probably from the fact that feast days after February in such a year fell two days later than in the previous year, rather than one day later as in other years, and could be said to have "leaped" a day.

Lear[1] /li(ə)r/ a legendary early king of Britain, the central figure in Shakespeare's tragedy *King Lear.* He is mentioned by the chronicler Geoffrey of Monmouth.

Lear[2], Edward (1812–88), English humorist and illustrator. He wrote *A Book of Nonsense* (1845) and *Laughable Lyrics* (1877). He published *Illustrations of the Family of the Psittacidae* (1832), as well as illustrated accounts of his travels around the Mediterranean.

learn /lərn/ ▶ **v.** (past and past participle **learned** /lərnd/ or chiefly Brit. **learnt** /lərnt/) [with obj.] **1** gain or acquire knowledge of or skill in (something) by study, experience, or being taught: *they'd started learning French* | [with infinitive] *she is learning to play the piano* | [no obj.] *we learn from experience.* ■ commit to memory: *I'd learned too many grim poems in school.* ■ become aware of (something) by information or from observation: [with clause] *I learned that they had eaten already* | [no obj.] *the military **learned of** a plot to attack the presidential compound.*
2 archaic, informal teach (someone): *"That'll learn you," he chuckled* | [with obj. and infinitive] *we'll have to learn you to milk cows.*
– PHRASES **learn one's lesson** see LESSON.
– DERIVATIVES **learn·a·bil·i·ty** /,lərnə'bilətē/ **n.**, **learn·a·ble adj.**
– ORIGIN Old English *leornian* 'learn' (in Middle English also 'teach'), of West Germanic origin; related to German *lernen*, also to LORE[1].

USAGE In modern standard English, it is wrong to use **learn** to mean **teach**, as in *that'll learn you* (correct use is *that'll teach you*). This meaning has been recorded since the 13th century and has been used by writers such as Spenser, Bunyan, and Samuel Johnson, but it fell into disfavor in the early 19th century and is now found only in nonstandard and dialect use.

learn·ed /ˈlərnid/ ▶ **adj.** (of a person) having much knowledge acquired by study. ■ showing, requiring, or characterized by learning; scholarly: *an article in a learned journal*.
– DERIVATIVES **learn·ed·ly** /-nidlē/ **adv.**, **learn·ed·ness** /-nidnis/ **n.**
– ORIGIN Middle English: from LEARN, in the sense 'teach.'

learned help·less·ness /lərnd/ ▶ **n.** Psychiatry a condition in which a person suffers from a sense of powerlessness, arising from a traumatic event or persistent failure to succeed. It is thought to be one of the underlying causes of depression.

learn·er /ˈlərnər/ ▶ **n.** a person who is learning a subject or skill: *a fast learner*.

learn·fare /ˈlərn,fe(ə)r/ ▶ **n.** a public assistance program in which attendance at school, college, or a training program is necessary to receive benefits.

learn·ing /ˈlərniNG/ ▶ **n.** the acquisition of knowledge or skills through experience, practice, or study, or by being taught: *these children experienced difficulties in learning* | [as modifier] *an important learning process*. ■ knowledge acquired in this way: *I liked to parade my learning in front of my sisters*.
– ORIGIN Old English *leornung* (see LEARN, -ING[1]).

learn·ing curve ▶ **n.** the rate of a person's progress in gaining experience or new skills: *the latest software packages have a steep learning curve*.

learn·ing dis·a·bil·i·ty ▶ **n.** a condition giving rise to difficulties in acquiring knowledge and skills to the level expected of those of the same age, esp. when not associated with a physical handicap.
– DERIVATIVES **learn·ing-dis·a·bled adj.**

> **USAGE** The phrase **learning disability** became prominent in the 1980s. It is broad in scope, covering general conditions such as Down syndrome as well as more specific cognitive or neurological conditions such as dyslexia and attention deficit disorder. In emphasizing the difficulty experienced rather than any perceived 'deficiency,' it is considered less discriminatory and more positive than other terms such as **mentally handicapped**, and is now the standard accepted term in official contexts. See also usage at HANDICAPPED.

Leary /ˈli(ə)rē/, Timothy (Francis) (1920–96), US psychologist. After experimenting with consciousness-altering drugs, including LSD, he was dismissed from his teaching job at Harvard University in 1963 and became a figurehead for the hippie drug culture.

lease /lēs/ ▶ **n.** a contract by which one party conveys land, property, services, etc., to another for a specified time, usually in return for a periodic payment.
▶ **v.** [with obj.] grant (property) on lease; let: *she **leased** the site **to** a local company*. ■ take (property) on lease; rent: *land was **leased from** the city*.
– PHRASES **a new lease on life** a substantially improved chance to lead a happy or successful life.
– DERIVATIVES **leas·a·ble adj.**
– ORIGIN late Middle English: from Old French *lais*, *leis*, from *lesser*, *laissier* 'let, leave,' from Latin *laxare* 'make loose,' from *laxus* 'loose, lax.'

lease·back /ˈlēs,bak/ ▶ **n.** [often as modifier] the leasing of a property back to the vendor: *leaseback agreements*.

lease·hold /ˈlēs,hōld/ ▶ **n.** the holding of property by lease: *a form of leasehold* | [as modifier] *leasehold premises*. Often contrasted with FREEHOLD. ■ a property held by lease.
– DERIVATIVES **lease·hold·er n.**
– ORIGIN early 18th cent.: from LEASE, on the pattern of *freehold*.

leash /lēsH/ ▶ **n.** a strap or cord for restraining and guiding a dog or other animal. ■ Falconry a thong or string attached to the jesses of a hawk, used for tying it to a perch or a creance. ■ a restraint: *her bristling temper was kept **on a leash*** | *the state needs to let business **off the leash***.
▶ **v.** [with obj.] put a leash on (a dog). ■ restrain: *his violence was barely leashed*.
– PHRASES **strain at the leash** be eager to begin or do something.
– ORIGIN Middle English: from Old French *lesse*, *laisse*, from *laissier* in the specific sense 'let run on a slack lead' (see LEASE).

least /lēst/ ▶ **determiner & pron.** (usu. **the least**) smallest in amount, extent, or significance: [as determiner] *who has the least money?* | *he never had the least idea what to do about it* | [as pronoun] *how others see me is **the least of** my worries* | *it's the least I can do*.
▶ **adv.** to the smallest extent or degree: *my best number was the one I had practiced **the least*** | *turning up when he was least expected* | *only the least expensive lot sold* | *I never hid the truth, **least of all** from you*.
▶ **adj.** used in names of very small animals and plants, e.g., **least shrew**.
– PHRASES **at least 1** not less than; at the minimum: *clean the windows at least once a week*. **2** if nothing else (used to add a positive comment about a generally negative situation): *the options aren't complete, but at least they're a start*. **3** anyway (used to modify something just stated): *they seldom complained—officially at least*. **at the least** (or **very least**) **1** (used after amounts) not less than; at the minimum: *stay ten days at the least*. **2** taking the most pessimistic or unfavorable view: *a program that is, at the very least, excellent PR for the hospital*. **least said, soonest mended** proverb a difficult situation will be resolved more quickly if there is no more discussion of it. **not in the least** not in the smallest degree; not at all: *he was not in the least taken aback*. **not least** in particular; notably: *there is a great deal at stake, not least in relation to the environment*. **to say the least** used as an understatement (implying the reality is more extreme, usually worse): *his performance was disappointing to say the least*.
– ORIGIN Old English *lǣst*, *lǣsest*, of Germanic origin; related to LESS.

> **USAGE** On the punctuation of least in compound adjectives, see usage at WELL[1].

least com·mon de·nom·i·na·tor ▶ **n.** another term for LOWEST COMMON DENOMINATOR.

least com·mon mul·ti·ple ▶ **n.** another term for LOWEST COMMON MULTIPLE.

least sig·nif·i·cant bit (abbr.: **LSB**) ▶ **n.** Computing the bit in a binary number that is of the lowest numerical value.

least squares ▶ **n.** a method of estimating a quantity or fitting a graph to data so as to minimize the sum of the squares of the differences between the observed values and the estimated values.

least·ways /ˈlēst,wāz/ (also **leastwise** /-,wīz/) ▶ **adv.** dialect or informal at least: *there is no place like our home, leastways not this side of hell*.

leath·er /ˈleTHər/ ▶ **n. 1** a material made from the skin of an animal by tanning or a similar process: [as modifier] *a leather jacket*.
2 a thing made of leather, in particular: ■ a piece of leather as a polishing cloth. ■ short for STIRRUP LEATHER. ■ (**leathers**) leather clothes, esp. those worn by a motorcyclist.
▶ **v.** [with obj.] **1** (usu. as adj. **leathered**) cover with leather: *dancers in leathered costumes*.
2 beat or thrash (someone): *he caught me and leathered me black and blue* | (as noun **leathering**) *go, before you get a leathering*.
– ORIGIN Old English *lether*, of Germanic origin; related to Dutch *leer* and German *Leder*, from an Indo-European root shared by Irish *leathar* and Welsh *lledr*.

leath·er·back /ˈleTHər,bak/ (also **leatherback turtle**) ▶ **n.** a very large black turtle with a thick leathery shell, living chiefly in tropical seas.
● *Dermochelys coriacea*, the only member of the family Dermochelyidae.

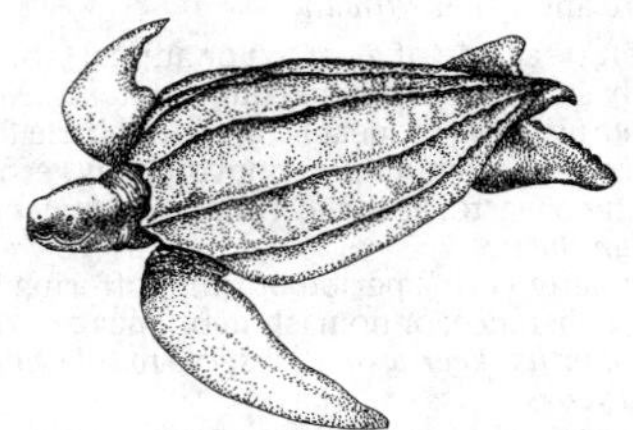

leatherback

leath·er-bound ▶ **adj.** (esp. of a book) covered or held together by leather.

leath·er carp ▶ **n.** a carp of a variety that lacks scales.

leath·er·ette /,leTHəˈret/ ▶ **n.** imitation leather.

leath·er-hard ▶ **adj.** (of unfired pottery) dried and hardened enough to be trimmed or decorated with slip but not hard enough to be fired.

leath·er·jack·et /ˈleTHər,jakit/ ▶ **n. 1** any of a number of tough-skinned marine fishes, in particular: ● a fish of the jack family (Carangidae), in particular a slender fish of American coastal waters, with a greenish back and a bright yellow tail (*Oligoplites saurus*). ● a filefish or triggerfish (family Balistidae).
2 the tough-skinned larva of a large crane fly. It lives in the soil, where it feeds on plant matter and can seriously damage the roots of grasses and crops.
● Genus *Tipula*, family Tipulidae.

leath·er·leaf /ˈleTHər,lēf/ ▶ **n.** a low-growing evergreen shrub of the heath family, found in north temperate regions. ● *Chamaedaphne calyculata*, family Ericaceae.

leath·ern /ˈleTHərn/ ▶ **adj.** archaic made of leather.

leath·er·neck /ˈleTHər,nek/ ▶ **n.** informal a US marine.
– ORIGIN late 19th cent.: with allusion to the leather lining inside the collar of a marine's uniform.

leath·er·wear /ˈleTHər,wer/ ▶ **n.** articles of clothing made of leather.

leath·er·wood /ˈleTHər,wo͝od/ ▶ **n. 1** see TITI[2].
2 a North American shrub with yellow flowers and very short leafstalks. Its tough, pliant bark was formerly used by American Indians for making baskets, fishing lines, and bowstrings. ● *Dirca palustris*, family Thymelaeaceae.

leath·er·work /ˈleTHər,wərk/ ▶ **n.** work or decoration done in leather. ■ an article or articles made of leather.

leath·er·y /ˈleTH(ə)rē/ ▶ **adj.** having a tough, hard texture: *brown, leathery skin*.
– DERIVATIVES **leath·er·i·ness n.**

leave[1] /lēv/ ▶ **v.** (past and past participle **left** /left/) [with obj.] **1** go away from: *she left New York on June 6* | [no obj.] *we were almost the last to leave* | *the Bruins left **for** Toronto on Monday*. ■ depart from permanently: *at the age of sixteen he left home*. ■ cease attending (a school or college) or working for (an organization): *she is leaving NBC after 20 years*.
2 allow to remain: *the parts he disliked he would alter, and the parts he didn't dislike he'd leave*. ■ (**be left**) remain to be used or dealt with: *we've even got one of the plum puddings **left over** from last year* | *a retired person with no mortgage left to pay*. ■ go away from a place without taking (someone or something): *we had not **left** any of our belongings **behind*** | figurative *women had been left behind in the struggle for pay equality*. ■ abandon (a spouse or partner): *her boyfriend **left** her **for** another woman*. ■ have as (a surviving relative) after one's death: *he leaves a wife and three children*. ■ bequeath: *he left $500 to the Police Athletic League* | *Harry had left her $5,000 a year for life*.
3 cause (someone or something) to be in a particular state or position: *he'll leave you in no doubt about what he thinks* | *I'll leave the door open* | *the children were **left with** feelings of loss*. ■ let (someone) do or deal with something without offering help or assistance: *infected people are often rejected by family and friends, leaving them to face this chronic condition alone*. ■ cause to remain as a trace or record: *dark fruit that would leave purple stains on the table napkins* | figurative *they leave the impression that they can be bullied*. ■ deposit or entrust to be kept, collected, or attended to: *she left a note for me*. ■ (**leave something to**) entrust a decision, choice, or action to (someone else, esp. someone considered better qualified): *the choice of which link to take is generally **left up to** the reader*.
▶ **n.** (in pool, billiards, snooker, croquet, and other games) the position of the balls after a shot.
– PHRASES **be left at the post** be beaten from the start of a race or competition. **be left for dead** be abandoned as being almost dead or certain to die. **be left to oneself** be allowed to do what one wants: *women, left to themselves, would make the world a beautiful place to live in*. ■ be in the position of being alone or solitary: *left to himself, he removed his shirt and tie*. **leave someone/something alone** see ALONE. **leave someone be** refrain from disturbing or interfering with someone. **leave someone cold** fail to interest someone: *the Romantic poets left him cold*. **leave hold of** cease holding. **leave it at that** abstain from further comment or action: *if you are not sure of the answers, say so, and leave it at that*. **leave much** (or **a lot**) **to be desired** be highly unsatisfactory.
– PHRASAL VERBS **leave off** discontinue (an activity): *the dog left off chasing the sheep*. ■ come to an end: *he resumed the other story at the point where the previous author had left off*. **leave something off** omit to put on: *a bolt may have been left off the plane's forward door during production*. **leave someone/something out** fail to include: *it seemed unkind to leave Daisy out; so she was invited, too* | (as adj. **left out**) *Janet was feeling rather left out*.
– DERIVATIVES **leav·er n.**
– ORIGIN Old English *lǣfan* 'bequeath,' also 'allow to remain, leave in place,' of Germanic origin; related to German *bleiben* 'remain.'

leave[2] ▶ **n. 1** (also **leave of absence**) time when one has permission to be absent from work or from duty in the armed forces: *Joe was home **on leave*** | *he took a leave of absence last year*.
2 [often with infinitive] permission: *he is seeking leave to appeal the injunction*.
– PHRASES **by** (or **with**) **your leave** with your permission: *with your leave, I will send him your address*. **take one's leave** formal say goodbye: *he*

went to take his leave of his hostess. **take leave of one's senses** see **SENSE**.
– ORIGIN Old English *lēaf* 'permission'; related to **LIEF** and **LOVE**.

leave[3] ▸ **v.** put forth leaves.

leaved /lēvd/ (also **leafed**) ▸ **adj.** [in combination] having a leaf or leaves of a particular kind or number: *broadleaved evergreens | red-leafed lettuce.*

leav·en /'levən/ ▸ **n. 1** a substance, typically yeast, that is added to dough to make it ferment and rise. ■ dough that is reserved from an earlier batch in order to start a later one fermenting.
2 a pervasive influence that modifies something or transforms it for the better: *they acted as an intellectual leaven to the warriors who dominated the city.*
▸ **v.** [with obj.] **1** (usu. as adj. **leavened**) cause (dough or bread) to ferment and rise by adding leaven: *leavened breads are forbidden during Passover.*
2 permeate and modify or transform (something) for the better: *the proceedings should be leavened by humor* | (as noun **leavening**) *companies of militia volunteers with a leavening of regular soldiers.*
– ORIGIN Middle English: from Old French *levain*, based on Latin *levamen* 'relief' (literally 'means of raising'), from *levare* 'to lift.'

Leav·en·worth /'levən,wərTH/ a city in northeastern Kansas, on the Missouri River, home to several prisons and also military facilities; pop. 34,729 (est. 2008).

leave of ab·sence ▸ **n.** see **LEAVE**[2] (sense 1).

leaves /lēvz/ plural form of **LEAF**.

leave-tak·ing ▸ **n.** an act of saying goodbye: *the leave-taking was restrained, with none of her earlier displays of emotion.*

leav·ings /'lēviNGz/ ▸ **plural n.** things that have been left as worthless: *she dropped her lunch leavings into the trash.*

Leb·a·non /'lebə,nän, -,nən/ **1** a country in the Middle East, with a coastline on the Mediterranean Sea; pop. 4,017,100 (est. 2009); capital, Beirut; official language, Arabic.

> Part of the Ottoman Empire from the early 16th century, Lebanon became a French mandate after World War I and achieved independence in 1943. Until the mid 1970s the country prospered, but conflict between the Christian and Muslim communities, the influx of Palestinian refugees, and repeated Middle Eastern wars destabilized the country. The first general elections in 20 years were held in 1992.

2 an industrial city in southeastern Pennsylvania, in Pennsylvania Dutch country; pop. 24,097 (est. 2008).
– DERIVATIVES **Leb·a·nese** /,lebə'nēz, -'nēs/ **adj. & n.**

Leb·a·non Moun·tains a range of mountains in Lebanon that runs parallel to the Mediterranean coast. It rises to a height of 10,022 feet (3,087 m) at Qornet es Saouda and is separated from the Anti-Lebanon Mountains, on the border with Syria, by the Bekaa valley.

Le·bens·raum /'lābəns,roum, -bənz-/ ▸ **n.** the territory that a state or nation believes is needed for its natural development, esp. associated with Nazi Germany.
– ORIGIN German, literally 'living space' (originally with reference to Germany).

leb·kuch·en /'lābko͞oKHən/ ▸ **n.** (pl. **same**) a type of cookie with a cakelike texture, typically frosted and containing spices and honey.
– ORIGIN German *Lebkuchen*, from Kuchen 'cake'; the origin of the first element is uncertain.

Le·blanc /lə'bläNGk, -'blän/, Nicolas (1742–1806), French surgeon and chemist. He developed a process for making soda ash (sodium carbonate) from common salt, which enabled the large-scale manufacture of glass, soap, paper, and other chemicals.

Le·brun /lə'brœN/, Charles (1619–90), French painter, designer, and decorator.

Le Car·ré /lə ka'rā/, John (1931–), English novelist; pseudonym of *David John Moore Cornwell*. His unromanticized and thoughtful spy novels, which often feature British agent George Smiley, include *The Spy Who Came in from the Cold* (1963), *Tinker, Tailor, Soldier, Spy* (1974), and *A Most Wanted Man* (2008).

lech /leCH/ informal, derogatory ▸ **n.** a lecher. ■ a lecherous urge or desire: *I think he has a kind of lech for you.*
▸ **v.** [no obj.] act in a lecherous or lustful manner: *businessmen leching after bimbos.*
– ORIGIN late 18th cent. (denoting a strong desire, particularly sexually): back-formation from **LECHER**.

Le Cha·te·lier's prin·ci·ple /lə 'shätl,yāz/ Chemistry a principle stating that if a constraint (such as a change in pressure, temperature, or concentration of a reactant) is applied to a system in equilibrium, the equilibrium will shift so as to tend to counteract the effect of the constraint.
– ORIGIN early 20th cent.: named after Henri *le Chatelier* (1850–1936), French chemist.

lech·er /'leCHər/ ▸ **n.** a lecherous man.
– ORIGIN Middle English: from Old French *lichiere, lecheor*, from *lechier* 'live in debauchery or gluttony,' ultimately of West Germanic origin and related to **LICK**.

lech·er·ous /'leCH(ə)rəs/ ▸ **adj.** having or showing excessive or offensive sexual desire: *she ignored his lecherous gaze.*
– DERIVATIVES **lech·er·ous·ly adv., lech·er·ous·ness n.**
– ORIGIN Middle English: from Old French *lecheros*, from *lecheor* (see **LECHER**).

lech·er·y /'leCH(ə)rē/ ▸ **n.** excessive or offensive sexual desire; lustfulness.
– ORIGIN Middle English: from Old French *lecherie*, from *lecheor* (see **LECHER**).

lech·u·guil·la /,leCHə'gēə/ ▸ **n.** a succulent desert plant (*Agave lecheguilla*) of Mexico, with pointed basal leaves and a tall flower spike. It is a principal source of ixtle.

le·chwe /'leCHwē, -,wā/ ▸ **n.** (pl. **same**) a rough-coated grazing antelope with pointed hooves and long horns, found in swampy grassland in southern Africa and the Sudan. ● Genus *Kobus*, family Bovidae: two species, in particular *K. leche*.
– ORIGIN mid 19th cent.: from Setswana.

lec·i·thin /'lesəTHin/ ▸ **n.** Biochemistry a substance widely distributed in animal tissues, egg yolk, and some higher plants, consisting of phospholipids linked to choline.
– ORIGIN mid 19th cent.: from Greek *lekithos* 'egg yolk' + **-IN**[1].

lec·i·thin·ase /'lesəTHi,nās, -,nāz/ ▸ **n.** Biochemistry another term for **PHOSPHOLIPASE**.

Le·clan·ché cell /lə'klänsHā/ ▸ **n.** a primary electrochemical cell having a zinc cathode in contact with zinc chloride, ammonium chloride (as a solution or a paste) as the electrolyte, and a carbon anode in contact with a mixture of manganese dioxide and carbon powder.
– ORIGIN late 19th cent.: named after Georges *Leclanché* (1839–82), French chemist.

Le Cor·bu·sier /lə ,kôrbə'zyā, -by'zyā/ (1887–1965), French architect and city planner, born in Switzerland; born *Charles Édouard Jeanneret*. A pioneer of the international style, he developed theories on functionalism, the use of new materials and industrial techniques, and a modular system of standard-sized units (Modulor).

lect. ▸ **abbr.** lecture.

lec·tern /'lektərn/ ▸ **n.** a tall stand with a sloping top to hold a book or notes, and from which someone, typically a preacher or lecturer, can read while standing up.
– ORIGIN Middle English: from Old French *letrun*, from medieval Latin *lectrum*, from *legere* 'to read.'

lectern

lec·tin /'lektin/ ▸ **n.** Biochemistry any of a class of proteins, chiefly of plant origin, that bind specifically to certain sugars and so cause agglutination of particular cell types.
– ORIGIN 1950s: from Latin *lect-* 'chosen' (from the verb *legere*) + **-IN**[1].

lec·tion /'leksHən/ ▸ **n.** archaic a reading of a text found in a particular copy or edition.
– ORIGIN Middle English (in the sense 'election'): from Latin *lection-* 'choosing, reading,' from the verb *legere*. The current sense dates from the mid 17th cent.

lec·tion·ar·y /'leksHə,nerē/ ▸ **n.** (pl. **lectionaries**) a list or book of portions of the Bible appointed to be read at a church service.
– ORIGIN late 18th cent.: from medieval Latin *lectionarium*, from Latin *lect-* 'chosen, read,' from the verb *legere*.

lec·tor /'lektər, -,tôr/ ▸ **n. 1** a reader, esp. someone who reads lessons in a church service.
2 a lecturer, esp. one employed in a foreign university to teach in their native language.
– ORIGIN late Middle English: from Latin, from *lect-* 'read, chosen,' from the verb *legere*.

lectr. ▸ **abbr.** lecturer.

lec·ture /'lekCHər/ ▸ **n.** an educational talk to an audience, esp. to students in a university or college. ■ a long, serious speech, esp. one given as a scolding or reprimand: *the usual lecture on table manners.*
▸ **v.** [no obj.] deliver an educational lecture or lectures: *she was lecturing to her class of eighty students.* ■ [with obj.] give a lecture to (a class or other audience): *he was lecturing future generations of health-service professionals.* ■ [with obj.] talk seriously or reprovingly to (someone): *don't lecture me!*
– ORIGIN late Middle English (in the sense 'reading, a text to read'): from Old French, or from medieval Latin *lectura*, from Latin *lect-* 'read, chosen,' from the verb *legere*.

lec·tur·er /'lekCHərər/ ▸ **n.** a person who gives lectures, esp. as a profession. ■ a member of a college or university faculty, esp. one without tenure or one that ranks below assistant professor.

lec·ture·ship /'lekCHər,SHip/ ▸ **n.** a post as a lecturer: *a three-year lectureship in English literature.*

LED ▸ **abbr.** light-emitting diode, a semiconductor diode that glows when a voltage is applied.

led /led/ past and past participle of **LEAD**[1].

Le·da /'lēdə/ Greek Mythology the wife of Tyndareus, king of Sparta. She was loved by Zeus, who visited her in the form of a swan; among her children were the Dioscuri, Helen, and Clytemnestra.

Led·bet·ter /'led,betər/, Huddie (1885–1949) US blues singer and composer; known as **Leadbelly**. His many recordings include "Good Morning, Blues" (1940), and his compositions include "Good Night, Irene" (1943).

le·der·ho·sen /'lādər,hōzən/ ▸ **plural n.** leather shorts with H-shaped suspenders, traditionally worn by men in Alpine regions such as Bavaria.
– ORIGIN from German, from *Leder* 'leather' + *Hosen* 'trousers.'

ledge /lej/ ▸ **n. 1** a narrow horizontal surface projecting from a wall, cliff, or other surface: *he heaved himself up over a ledge.*
2 an underwater ridge, esp. of rocks beneath the sea near the shore.
3 Mining a stratum of metal- or ore-bearing rock; a vein of quartz or other mineral.
– DERIVATIVES **ledg·y** /'lejē/ **adj.**
– ORIGIN Middle English (denoting a strip of wood or other material fixed across a door, gate, etc.): perhaps from an early form of **LAY**[1]. Sense 1 dates from the mid 16th cent.

ledg·er /'lejər/ ▸ **n. 1** a book or other collection of financial accounts of a particular type: *the total balance of the purchases ledger.*
2 a flat stone slab covering a grave.
3 a horizontal scaffolding pole, parallel to the face of a building.
– ORIGIN late Middle English *legger, ligger* (denoting a large bible or breviary), probably from variants of **LAY**[1] and **LIE**[1], influenced by Dutch *legger* and *ligger*. Current senses date from the 16th cent.

ledg·er line (also **leger line**) ▸ **n.** Music a short line added for notes above or below the range of a staff.

Lee[1] /lē/, Ann (1736–84) US religious leader; born in England; known as **Mother Ann**. A Shaker leader, she founded the first Shaker colony in the US at Watervliet, New York, in 1776.

Lee[2], Bruce (1941–73), US actor; born *Lee Yuen Kam*. An expert in kung fu, he starred in a number of martial arts movies, such as *Fists of Fury* (1972) and *Enter the Dragon* (1973).

Lee[3], Francis Lightfoot (1734–97) American statesman. He was a delegate to the Continental Congress 1775–79 and a signer of the Declaration of Independence in 1776.

Lee[4], Gypsy Rose (1914–70), US striptease artist; born *Rose Louise Hovick*. In the 1930s, she became famous on Broadway for her sophisticated striptease act. Her autobiography, *Gypsy* (1957), was made into a movie in 1962.

Lee[5], Harper (1926–), US novelist; full name *Nelle Harper Lee*. She won a Pulitzer Prize for her only novel, *To Kill a Mockingbird* (1960), about the trial of a black man falsely charged with raping a white woman.

Lee[6], Henry (1756–1818) American soldier and politician; known as **Light-Horse Harry**; father of Robert E. Lee. Noted as a brilliant cavalry commander in the American Revolution, he later became governor of Virginia 1792–95 and a member of the US House of Representatives 1799–1801.

Lee[7], Robert E. (1807–70), Confederate general; full name *Robert Edward Lee*. He was the commander of the Confederate Army of Northern Virginia for most of the Civil War. A noted tactician and strategist, his invasion of the North was repulsed at the Battle of Gettysburg (1863), and he surrendered in 1865.

Robert E. Lee

Lee[8], Spike (1957–), US filmmaker; born *Shelton Jackson Lee*. His work is noted for its treatment of controversial social issues. Movies for which he was writer, director, producer, and actor include *She's Gotta Have It* (1986), *Do the Right Thing* (1989), *Mo' Better Blues* (1990), *Malcolm X* (1992), *Crooklyn* (1994), and *Summer of Sam* (1998).

lee /lē/ ▶ **n.** shelter from wind or weather given by a neighboring object, esp. nearby land: *we pitch our tents in the lee of a rock.* ■ (also **lee side**) the sheltered side; the side away from the wind: *ducks were taking shelter on the lee of the island.* Contrasted with WEATHER.
– ORIGIN Old English *hlēo, hlēow* 'shelter,' of Germanic origin; probably related to *luke-* in LUKEWARM.

lee·board /ˈlēˌbôrd/ ▶ **n.** a plate or board fixed to the side of a flat-bottomed boat and let down into the water to reduce drift to the leeward side.

leech[1] /lēCH/ ▶ **n. 1** an aquatic or terrestrial annelid worm with suckers at both ends. Many species are bloodsucking parasites, esp. of vertebrates, and others are predators. ● Class Hirudinea: many species. See also MEDICINAL LEECH.
2 a person who extorts profit from or sponges on others: *they are leeches feeding off the hardworking majority.*
▶ **v.** [no obj.] habitually exploit or rely on: *he's leeching off the kindness of others.*
– ORIGIN Old English *lǣce, lȳce*; related to Middle Dutch *lake, lieke*.

leech[2] ▶ **n.** archaic a doctor or healer.
– ORIGIN Old English *lǣce*, of Germanic origin.

leech[3] ▶ **n.** Sailing the after or leeward edge of a fore-and-aft sail, the leeward edge of a spinnaker, or a vertical edge of a square sail.
– ORIGIN late 15th cent.: probably of Scandinavian origin and related to Swedish *lik*, Danish *lig*, denoting a rope sewn round the edge of a sail to stop the canvas from tearing.

leech·craft /ˈlēCHˌkraft/ ▶ **n.** archaic the art of healing.
– ORIGIN Old English *lǣcecræft* (see LEECH[2], CRAFT).

Leeds /lēdz/ an industrial city in northern England; pop. 441,100 (est. 2009). It developed as a wool town in the Middle Ages and became a clothing center during the Industrial Revolution.

Lee–En·field /ˌlē ˈenfēld/ (also **Lee–Enfield rifle**) ▶ **n.** a bolt-action rifle of a type formerly used by the British army.

lee helm ▶ **n.** Sailing the tendency of a vessel to turn its bow to leeward.

leek /lēk/ ▶ **n.** a plant related to the onion, with flat overlapping leaves forming an elongated cylindrical bulb that together with the leaf bases is eaten as a vegetable. It is used as a Welsh national emblem. ● *Allium porrum*, family Liliaceae (or Alliaceae).
– ORIGIN Old English *lēac*, of Germanic origin; related to Dutch *look* and German *Lauch*.

leek

leer /li(ə)r/ ▶ **v.** [no obj.] look or gaze in an unpleasant, malicious, or lascivious way: *bystanders were leering at the nude painting* | (as adj. **leering**) *every leering eye in the room was on her.*
▶ **n.** an unpleasant, malicious, or lascivious look.
– DERIVATIVES **leer·ing·ly** adv.
– ORIGIN mid 16th cent. (in the general sense 'look sideways or askance'): perhaps from obsolete *leer* 'cheek,' from Old English *hlēor*, as though the sense were 'to glance over one's cheek.'

leer·y /ˈli(ə)rē/ ▶ **adj.** (**leerier, leeriest**) informal cautious or wary due to realistic suspicions: *a city leery of gang violence.*
– DERIVATIVES **leer·i·ness n.**
– ORIGIN late 17th cent.: from obsolete *leer* 'looking askance,' from LEER + -Y[1].

lees /lēz/ ▶ **plural n.** the sediment of wine in the barrel. ■ the most worthless part or parts of something: *the lees of the Venetian underworld.*
– ORIGIN late Middle English: plural of obsolete *lee* in the same sense, from Old French *lie*, from medieval Latin *liae* (plural), of Gaulish origin.

lee shore ▶ **n.** a shore lying on the leeward side of a ship (and onto which a ship could be blown in foul weather).

lee side ▶ **n.** see LEE.

Lee's Summit /lēz/ an industrial city in northwestern Missouri, southeast of Kansas City; pop. 84,208 (est. 2008).

leet[1] /lēt/ ▶ **n.** historical (in England) a yearly or half-yearly court of record that the lords of certain manors held.
– ORIGIN Middle English: from Anglo-Norman French *lete* or Anglo-Latin *leta*, of unknown origin.

leet[2] /lēt/ (also **leetspeak**) ▶ **n.** an informal language or code used on the Internet, in which standard letters are often replaced by numerals or special characters.
– ORIGIN early 21st cent.: from *leet*, representing a pronunciation of ELITE (+ -SPEAK).

Lee·u·wen·hoek /ˈlāvənˌho͝ok, ˈlāYən-/, Antoni van (1632–1723), Dutch naturalist. He developed a lens for scientific purposes and was the first to observe bacteria, protozoa, and yeast. He accurately described red blood cells, capillaries, striated muscle fibers, spermatozoa, and the crystalline lens of the eye.

lee·ward /ˈlēwərd, ˈlo͞oərd/ ▶ **adj. & adv.** on or toward the side sheltered from the wind or toward which the wind is blowing; downwind: [as adj.] *the leeward side of the house* | [as adv.] *we pitched our tents leeward of a hill.* Contrasted with WINDWARD.
▶ **n.** the side sheltered or away from the wind: *the ship was drifting to leeward.*

Lee·ward Is·lands /ˈlēwərd/ a group of islands in the Caribbean Sea that constitutes the northern part of the Lesser Antilles. The group includes Guadeloupe, Antigua, St. Kitts, and Montserrat.
– ORIGIN *Leeward* with reference to the islands' situation further downwind (in terms of the prevailing southeasterly winds) than the Windward Islands.

lee wave ▶ **n.** a standing atmospheric wave generated on the sheltered side of a mountain by an air current passing over or around it, and often made visible by the formation of clouds.

lee·way /ˈlēˌwā/ ▶ **n. 1** the amount of freedom to move or act that is available: *the government had several months' leeway to introduce reforms.* ■ margin of safety: *there is little leeway if anything goes wrong.*
2 the sideways drift of a ship or an aircraft to leeward of the desired course: *the leeway is only about 2°.*

left[1] /left/ ▶ **adj. 1** on, toward, or relating to the side of a human body or of a thing that is to the west when the person or thing is facing north: *her left eye* | *the left side of the road.*
2 of or relating to a person or group favoring liberal, socialist, or radical views: *Left politics.* [see LEFT WING.]
▶ **adv.** on or to the left side: *turn left here* | *keep left.*
▶ **n. 1** (**the left**) the left-hand part, side, or direction: *a turn to the left* | (**one's left**) *the general sat to his left.* ■ (in soccer or a similar sport) the left-hand half of the field when facing the opponents' goal: *a free kick from the left.* ■ (**left**) Baseball short for LEFT FIELD: *a sacrifice fly to left.* ■ the left wing of an army: *a token attack on the Russian left.*
2 (often **the Left**) [treated as sing. or pl.] a group or party favoring liberal, socialist, or radical views: *the Left is preparing to fight presidential elections* | *he is on the left of the party.*
3 a thing on the left-hand side or done with the left hand, in particular: ■ a left turn: *take a left here.* ■ a road, entrance, etc., on the left: *my road's the first left.* ■ a person's left fist, esp. a boxer's: *a dazzler with the left.* ■ a blow given with this: *a left to the body.*
– PHRASES **have two left feet** be clumsy or awkward. **left, right, and center** (also **left and right** or **right and left**) on all sides: *deals were being done left, right, and center.*
– DERIVATIVES **left·ish adj.**
– ORIGIN Old English *lyft, left* 'weak' (the left-hand side being regarded as the weaker side of the body).

left[2] past and past participle of LEAVE[1].

Left Bank a district of Paris, France, situated on the left bank of the Seine River, to the south of the river. It is an area noted for its intellectual and artistic life.

left bank ▶ **n.** the bank of a river on the left as one faces downstream.

left brain ▶ **n.** the left-hand side of the human brain, which is believed to be associated with linear and analytical thought.
– DERIVATIVES **left-brained** /ˈleft ˌbrānd/ **adj.**

left-click ▶ **v.** [no obj.] Computing click on a link or other screen object by depressing the left-hand button of the mouse: *left-click on any of the thumbnails to see a photo.*

left coast ▶ **n.** the West Coast of the US, esp. California: *America's left coast should be on everyone's vacation list.*

left face ▶ **exclam.** (**left face!**) (in military contexts) a command to turn 90 degrees to the left.

left field ▶ **n. 1** Baseball the part of the outfield to the left of center field from the perspective of home plate: *a high fly to left field.* ■ the position of the defensive player stationed in left field: *I played left field a lot against him.*
2 a surprising or unconventional position or style: *seldom do so many witty touches come out of left field.* ■ a position of ignorance, error, or confusion: *he's so far out in left field that even his followers are embarrassed.*
– DERIVATIVES **left field·er n.**

left-foot·ed ▶ **adj.** (of a person) using one's left foot more naturally than the right. ■ (esp. of a kick) done with a person's left foot: *he drove a left-footed shot into the net.*

left hand ▶ **n.** the hand of a person's left side. ■ the region or direction on the left side of a person or thing: *there was a vast forest on the left hand.*
▶ **adj.** [attrib.] on or toward the left side of a person or thing: *his left-hand pocket.* ■ done with or using the left hand: *an excellent left-hand catch.*

left-hand·ed ▶ **adj. 1** (of a person) using the left hand more naturally than the right: *a left-handed batter.* ■ (of a tool or item of equipment) made to be used with the left hand: *left-handed golf clubs.* ■ made or performed with the left hand: *my left-handed scrawl.*
2 turning to the left; toward the left, in particular: ■ (of a screw) advanced by turning counterclockwise. ■ Biology (of a spiral shell or helix) sinistral. ■ (of a racecourse) turning counterclockwise.
3 perverse: *we take a left-handed pleasure in our errors.* ■ (esp. of a compliment) ambiguous.
▶ **adv.** with the left hand: *a significant number play the game left-handed.*
– DERIVATIVES **left-hand·ed·ly adv., left-hand·ed·ness n.**

left-hand·er ▶ **n.** a left-handed person, esp. a left-handed baseball pitcher. ■ a blow struck with a person's left hand.

left·ie ▶ **n.** variant spelling of LEFTY.

left·ist /ˈleftist/ ▶ **n.** a person who supports the political views or policies of the left.
▶ **adj.** supportive of the political views or policies of the left: *leftist radicals.*
– DERIVATIVES **left·ism** /-ˌtizəm/ **n.**

left-lean·ing ▶ **adj.** sympathetic to or tending toward the left in politics: *a left-leaning professor.*

left·most /ˈlef(t)ˌmōst/ ▶ **adj.** [attrib.] farthest to the left: *the leftmost edge of the screen.*

left·o·ver /ˈleftˌōvər/ ▶ **n.** (usu. **leftovers**) something, esp. food, remaining after the rest has been used or consumed.
▶ **adj.** [attrib.] remaining; surplus: *yesterday's leftover bread.*

left turn ▶ **n.** a turn that brings a person's front to face the way their left side did before: *take a left turn onto Paramus Road.*

left·ward /ˈleftwərd/ ▶ **adv.** (also **leftwards** /-wərdz/) toward the left.
▶ **adj.** going toward or facing the left: *they moved their eyes in a leftward direction.*

left wing ▶ **n.** (**the left wing**) **1** the liberal, socialist, or radical section of a political party or system. [with reference to the National Assembly in France (1789–91), where the nobles sat to the president's right and the commons to the left.]
2 the left side of a team on the field in soccer, rugby, and field hockey: *his usual position on the left wing.* ■ the left side of an army: *the Allied left wing.*
▶ **adj.** (**left-wing**) liberal, socialist, or radical: *left-wing activists.*
– DERIVATIVES **left-wing·er n.**

left·y /ˈleftē/ (also **leftie**) ▶ **n.** (pl. **lefties**) informal **1** a left-handed person.
2 a leftist.

leg /leg/ ▶ **n. 1** each of the limbs on which a person or animal walks and stands: *Adams broke his leg | he was off as fast as his legs would carry him* | [as modifier] *a leg injury.* ■ a leg of an animal or bird as food: *a roast leg of lamb.* ■ a part of a garment covering a leg or part of a leg: *his trouser leg.* ■ (**legs**) informal used to refer to the sustained popularity or success of a product or idea: *some books have legs; others don't.*
2 each of the supports of a chair, table, or other piece of furniture: *table legs.* ■ a long, thin support or prop: *the house was set on legs.*
3 a section or stage of a journey or process: *the return leg of his journey.* ■ Sailing a run made on a single tack. ■ (in soccer and other sports) each of two games constituting a round of a competition. ■ a section of a relay or other race done in stages: *one leg of its race around the globe.* ■ a single game in a darts match.
4 a branch of a forked object.
5 (also **leg side**) Cricket the half of the field (as divided lengthways through the pitch) away from which the batsman's feet are pointed when standing to receive the ball. The opposite of OFF.
6 archaic an obeisance made by drawing back one leg and bending it while keeping the front leg straight.
▶ **v.** (**legs, legging, legged** /'legd/) **1** (**leg it**) [no obj.] informal travel by foot; walk. ■ run away: *he legged it after someone shouted at him.*
2 [with obj.] chiefly historical propel (a boat) through a tunnel on a canal by pushing with one's legs against the tunnel roof or sides.
– PHRASES **feel** (or **find**) **one's legs** become able to stand or walk. **leg up** help to mount a horse or high object: *give me a leg up over the wall.* ■ help to improve one's position: *the council is to provide a financial leg up for the club.* **not have** (**the**) **legs** (of a ball, esp. in golf) not have sufficient momentum to reach the desired point. **not have a leg to stand on** have no facts or sound reasons to support one's argument or justify one's actions. **on one's last legs** near the end of life, usefulness, or existence: *the foundry business was on its last legs.*
– DERIVATIVES **leg·ged** /'legid/ **adj.** [in combination] *a four-legged animal*, **leg·ger n.** [in combination] *a three-legger.*
– ORIGIN Middle English (superseding SHANK): from Old Norse *leggr* (compare with Danish *læg* 'calf (of the leg)'), of Germanic origin.

leg. ▶ **abbr.** ■ legal. ■ legate. ■ Music legato. ■ legend. ■ legislation or legislative or legislature.

leg·a·cy /'legəsē/ ▶ **n.** (pl. **legacies**) an amount of money or property left to someone in a will. ■ a thing handed down by a predecessor: *the legacy of centuries of neglect.*
▶ **adj.** Computing denoting software or hardware that has been superseded but is difficult to replace because of its wide use.
– ORIGIN late Middle English (also denoting the function or office of a deputy, esp. a papal legate): from Old French *legacie*, from medieval Latin *legatia* 'legateship,' from *legatus* 'person delegated' (see LEGATE).

le·gal /'lēgəl/ ▶ **adj. 1** [attrib.] of, based on, or concerned with the law: *the American legal system.* ■ appointed or required by the law: *a legal requirement.* ■ of or relating to theological legalism. ■ Law recognized by common or statutory law, as distinct from equity. ■ (of paper) measuring 8 ½ by 14 inches.
2 permitted by law: *he claimed that it had all been legal.*
– DERIVATIVES **le·gal·ly adv.** [sentence adverb] *legally, we're still very much married.*
– ORIGIN late Middle English (in the sense 'to do with Mosaic law'): from French, or from Latin *legalis*, from *lex, leg-* 'law.' Compare with LOYAL.

le·gal age ▶ **n.** the age at which a person takes on the rights and responsibilities of an adult.

le·gal aid ▶ **n.** free legal advice or representation for a person who cannot afford it.

le·gal ca·pac·i·ty ▶ **n.** a person's authority under law to engage in a particular undertaking or maintain a particular status.

le·gal clin·ic ▶ **n.** a place where one can obtain legal advice and assistance, paid for by legal aid.

le·gal ea·gle (also **legal beagle**) ▶ **n.** informal a lawyer, esp. one who is keen and astute.

le·gal·ese /ˌlēgə'lēz, -'lēs/ ▶ **n.** informal the formal and technical language of legal documents that is often hard to understand.

le·gal fic·tion ▶ **n.** an assertion accepted as true, though probably fictitious, to achieve a particular goal in a legal matter.

le·gal hol·i·day ▶ **n.** a public holiday established by law.

le·gal·ism /'lēgəˌlizəm/ ▶ **n.** excessive adherence to law or formula. ■ Theology dependence on moral law rather than on personal religious faith.
– DERIVATIVES **le·gal·ist n. & adj., le·gal·is·tic** /ˌlēgə'listik/ **adj., le·gal·is·ti·cal·ly** /ˌlēgə'listik(ə)lē/ **adv.**

le·gal·i·ty /lə'galətē/ ▶ **n.** (pl. **legalities**) the quality or state of being in accordance with the law: *documentation testifying to the legality of the arms sale.* ■ (**legalities**) obligations imposed by law.
– ORIGIN late Middle English: from French *légalité* or medieval Latin *legalitas* 'relating to the law,' from Latin *legalis* (see LEGAL).

le·gal·ize /'lēgəˌlīz/ ▶ **v.** [with obj.] make (something that was previously illegal) permissible by law: *a measure legalizing gambling in Deadwood.*
– DERIVATIVES **le·gal·i·za·tion** /-ˌlēgələ'zāSHən, -ˌlī'zā-/ **n.**

le·gal pad ▶ **n.** a ruled writing tablet, often yellow, that measures 8½ by 14 inches. ■ a ruled pad of paper: *premium legal pads with recycled paper, 5 x 8, white.*

le·gal per·son ▶ **n.** Law an individual, company, or other entity that has legal rights and is subject to obligations.

le·gal sep·a·ra·tion ▶ **n. 1** an arrangement by which a husband or wife remain married but live apart, following a court order. Also called JUDICIAL SEPARATION.
2 an arrangement by which a child lives apart from a natural parent and with the other natural parent or a foster parent, following a court order.

le·gal-size ▶ **adj.** (of paper) measuring 8 ½ by 14 inches. ■ designed to hold paper of this size.

le·gal ten·der ▶ **n.** coins or banknotes that must be accepted if offered in payment of a debt.

leg·ate /'legit/ ▶ **n. 1** a member of the clergy, esp. a cardinal, representing the pope. ■ archaic an ambassador or messenger.
2 a general or governor of an ancient Roman province, or their deputy: *the Roman legate of Syria.*
– DERIVATIVES **leg·ate·ship** /-ˌSHip/ **n., leg·a·tine** /'legəˌtēn, -ˌtīn/ **adj.**
– ORIGIN late Old English, from Old French *legat*, from Latin *legatus*, past participle of *legare* 'depute, delegate, bequeath.'

le·gate a la·te·re /'legit ä 'lätəˌrā/ ▶ **n.** a papal legate of the highest class, with full powers.
– ORIGIN early 16th cent.: from LEGATE + Latin *a latere* 'from the (pope's) side.'

leg·a·tee /ˌlegə'tē/ ▶ **n.** a person who receives a legacy.
– ORIGIN late 17th cent.: from 15th-cent. *legate* 'bequeath' (from Latin *legare* 'delegate, bequeath') + -EE.

le·ga·tion /li'gāSHən/ ▶ **n. 1** a diplomatic minister, esp. one below the rank of ambassador, and their staff. ■ the official residence of a diplomatic minister.
2 archaic the position or office of legate; a legateship. ■ the sending of a legate, esp. a papal legate, on a mission.
– ORIGIN late Middle English (denoting the sending of a papal legate; also the mission itself): from Latin *legatio(n-)*, from *legare* 'depute, delegate, bequeath.'

le·ga·to /li'gätō/ ▶ **adv. & adj.** Music in a smooth, flowing manner, without breaks between notes. Compare with STACCATO.
▶ **n.** (pl. **legatos**) a piece or passage marked to be performed legato.
– ORIGIN Italian, literally 'bound.'

le·ga·tor /li'gātər/ ▶ **n.** rare a testator, esp. one who leaves a legacy.
– ORIGIN mid 17th cent.: from Latin, from *legat-* 'deputed, delegated, bequeathed,' from the verb *legare.*

leg·end /'lejənd/ ▶ **n. 1** a traditional story sometimes popularly regarded as historical but unauthenticated: *the legend of King Arthur | according to legend he banished all the snakes from Ireland.*
2 an extremely famous or notorious person, esp. in a particular field: *the man was **a living legend** | a Wall Street legend.*
3 an inscription, esp. on a coin or medal. ■ a caption: *a picture of a tiger with the legend, "Go ahead, make my day."* ■ the wording on a map or diagram explaining the symbols used: *see legend under Fig. 1.*
4 historical the story of a saint's life: *the mosaics illustrate the legends of the saints.*
▶ **adj.** very well known: *his speed and ferocity in attack were legend.*
– ORIGIN Middle English (sense 4 of the noun): from Old French *legende*, from medieval Latin *legenda* 'things to be read,' from Latin *legere* 'read.' Sense 1 of the noun dates from the early 17th cent.

leg·end·ar·y /'lejənˌderē/ ▶ **adj. 1** of, described in, or based on legends: *a legendary British king of the 4th century.*
2 remarkable enough to be famous; very well known: *her wisdom in matters of childbirth was legendary.*
– DERIVATIVES **leg·end·ar·i·ly** /-ˌderəlē, ˌlejən'de(ə)r-/ **adv.**
– ORIGIN early 16th cent. (as a noun denoting a collection of legends, esp. of saints' lives): from medieval Latin *legendarius*, from *legenda* 'things to be read' (see LEGEND).

Lé·ger /lā'ZHā/, Fernand (1881–1955), French painter. His works include the *Contrast of Forms* series (1913).

leg·er·de·main /ˌlejərdə'mān, 'lejərdəˌmān/ ▶ **n.** skillful use of one's hands when performing conjuring tricks. ■ deception; trickery.
– ORIGIN late Middle English: from French *léger de main* 'dexterous,' literally 'light of hand.'

leg·er line /'lejər/ ▶ **n.** Music variant spelling of LEDGER LINE.
– ORIGIN late 19th cent.: *leger*, variant of LEDGER.

leg·gings /'leginGz/ ▶ **plural n.** tight-fitting stretch pants worn by women and children. ■ protective coverings for the legs.

leg·gy /'legē/ ▶ **adj.** (**leggier, leggiest**) **1** (of a woman) having attractively long legs: *a leggy redhead.* ■ long-legged: *a leggy type of collie.*
2 (of a plant) having an excessively long and straggly stem: *tulips may grow tall and leggy.*
– DERIVATIVES **leg·gi·ness n.**

leg·hold trap /'legˌhōld/ ▶ **n.** a type of trap with a mechanism that catches and holds an animal by one of its legs.

Leg·horn /'legˌhôrn/ another name for LIVORNO.

leg·horn /'legˌhôrn, 'legərn/ ▶ **n. 1** fine plaited straw. ■ (also **leghorn hat**) a hat made of this.
2 (**Leghorn** /'legərn, -ˌhôrn/) a chicken of a small hardy breed.
– ORIGIN mid 18th cent.: anglicized from the Italian name *Leghorno* (now LIVORNO), from where the straw and fowls were imported.

leg·i·bil·i·ty /ˌlejə'bilətē/ ▶ **n.** the quality of being clear enough to read: *we've increased the type size for greater legibility.*

leg·i·ble /'lejəbəl/ ▶ **adj.** (of handwriting or print) clear enough to read: *the original typescript is scarcely legible.*
– DERIVATIVES **leg·i·bly** /-blē/ **adv.**
– ORIGIN late Middle English: from late Latin *legibilis*, from *legere* 'to read.'

le·gion /'lējən/ ▶ **n. 1** a unit of 3,000–6,000 men in the ancient Roman army. ■ (**the Legion**) the Foreign Legion. ■ (**the Legion**) any of the national associations of former servicemen and servicewomen instituted after World War I, such as the American Legion.
2 (**a legion/legions of**) a vast host, multitude, or number of people or things: *legions of photographers and TV cameras.*
▶ **adj.** great in number: *her fans are legion.*
– ORIGIN Middle English: via Old French from Latin *legion-*, from *legere* 'choose, levy.' The adjective dates from the late 17th cent., in early use often in the phrase *my, their, etc., name is legion*, i.e., 'we, they, etc., are many' (Mark 5:9).

le·gion·ar·y /'lējəˌnerē/ ▶ **n.** (pl. **legionaries**) a soldier in a Roman legion.
▶ **adj.** [attrib.] of an ancient Roman legion: *the legionary fortress of Isca.*
– ORIGIN late Middle English: from Latin *legionarius*, from *legio(n-)* (see LEGION).

le·gioned /'lējənd/ ▶ **adj.** literary arrayed in legions.

le·gion·el·la /ˌlējə'nelə/ ▶ **n.** (pl. **legionellae** /ˌlējə'nelē, -'nelˌī/) the bacterium that causes legionnaires' disease, flourishing in air conditioning and central heating systems. ● *Legionella pneumophila*, a motile, aerobic, rod-shaped (or filamentous) Gram-negative bacterium. ■ informal legionnaires' disease.
– ORIGIN late 20th cent.: modern Latin, from LEGION + the diminutive suffix *-ella.*

le·gion·naire /ˌlējə'ner/ ▶ **n.** a member of a legion, in particular an ancient Roman legion or the French Foreign Legion.
– ORIGIN early 19th cent.: from French *légionnaire*, from *légion* 'legion,' from Latin *legio* (see LEGION).

le·gion·naires' dis·ease ▶ **n.** a form of bacterial pneumonia first identified after an outbreak at an American Legion meeting in 1976. It is spread

I

chiefly by water droplets through air conditioning and similar systems. See also LEGIONELLA.

Le·gion of Hon·or a French order of distinction founded in 1802.
– ORIGIN translation of French *Légion d'honneur*.

Le·gion of Mer·it ▶ n. (abbr.: **LM**) a US military decoration, ranking below the Silver Star and above the Distinguished Flying Cross, awarded for exceptional performance of services to the US.

leg i·ron ▶ n. (usu. **leg irons**) a metal band or chain placed around a prisoner's ankle as a restraint.

legis. ▶ abbr. ■ legislation. ■ legislative. ■ legislature.

leg·is·late /ˈlejəˌslāt/ ▶ v. [no obj.] make or enact laws: *he didn't want to name anyone to the Court who would legislate from the bench.* ■ [with obj.] cover, affect, or create by making or enacting laws: *Congress must legislate strong new laws.*
– ORIGIN early 18th cent.: back-formation from LEGISLATION.

leg·is·la·tion /ˌlejəˈslāSHən/ ▶ n. laws, considered collectively: *tax legislation.*
– ORIGIN mid 17th cent. (denoting the enactment of laws): from late Latin *legis latio(n-)*, literally 'proposing of a law,' from *lex* 'law' and *latus* 'raised' (past participle of *tollere*).

leg·is·la·tive /ˈlejəˌslātiv/ ▶ adj. having the power to make laws: *the country's supreme legislative body.* ■ of or relating to laws or the making of them: *legislative proposals.* Often contrasted with EXECUTIVE. ■ of or relating to a legislature: *legislative elections.*
– DERIVATIVES **leg·is·la·tive·ly** adv.

leg·is·la·tor /ˈlejəˌslātər/ ▶ n. a person who makes laws; a member of a legislative body.
– ORIGIN late 15th cent.: from Latin *legis lator*, literally 'proposer of a law,' from *lex* 'law' and *lator* 'proposer, mover' (see also LEGISLATION).

leg·is·la·ture /ˈlejəˌslāCHər/ ▶ n. the legislative body of a country or state.
– ORIGIN late 17th cent.: from LEGISLATION, on the pattern of *judicature*.

le·git /liˈjit/ ▶ adj. informal legal; conforming to the rules: *is this car legit?* ■ (of a person) not engaging in illegal activity or attempting to deceive; honest: *to see if he's legit, I call up the business.*
– PHRASES **go legit** begin to behave honestly after a period of illegal activity.
– ORIGIN early 20th cent.: abbreviation of LEGITIMATE.

le·git·i·mate ▶ adj. /liˈjitəmit/ conforming to the law or to rules: *his claims to legitimate authority.* ■ able to be defended with logic or justification: *a legitimate excuse for being late.* ■ (of a child) born of parents lawfully married to each other. ■ (of a sovereign) having a title based on strict hereditary right: *the last legitimate Anglo-Saxon king.* ■ constituting or relating to serious drama as distinct from musical comedy, revue, etc.: *the legitimate theater.*
▶ v. /-ˌmāt/ [with obj.] make legitimate; justify or make lawful: *the regime was not legitimated by popular support.*
– DERIVATIVES **le·git·i·ma·cy** /-məsē/ n., **le·git·i·mate·ly** /-mitlē/ adv., **le·git·i·ma·tion** /liˌjitəˈmāSHən/ n., **le·git·i·ma·tize** /-məˌtīz/ v.
– ORIGIN late Middle English (in the sense 'born of parents lawfully married to each other'): from medieval Latin *legitimatus* 'made legal,' from the verb *legitimare*, from Latin *legitimus* 'lawful,' from *lex, leg-* 'law.'

le·git·i·mism /liˈjitəˌmizəm/ ▶ n. support for a ruler whose claim to a throne is based on direct descent.
– DERIVATIVES **le·git·i·mist** n. & adj.
– ORIGIN late 19th cent.: from French *légitimisme*, from *légitime*, from Latin *legitimus* (see LEGITIMATE).

le·git·i·mize /liˈjitəˌmīz/ ▶ v. [with obj.] make legitimate: *voters legitimize the government through the election of public officials.*
– DERIVATIVES **le·git·i·mi·za·tion** /liˌjitəməˈzāSHən/ n.

leg·less liz·ard /ˈlegləs/ ▶ n. a lizard that lacks legs and has a snakelike or wormlike appearance, in particular: ● an Australian lizard of a group that includes the scalyfoots (several genera in the family Pygopodidae). ● a North American lizard of California and Baja California (genus *Anniella*, family Anniellidae).

leg·man /ˈlegˌman/ ▶ n. (pl. **legmen**) a reporter whose job it is to gather information about news stories at the scene of the event or from an original source. ■ a person employed to do simple tasks such as running errands or collecting information from outside their workplace.

Le·go /ˈlegō/ ▶ n. trademark a construction toy consisting of interlocking plastic building blocks.
– ORIGIN 1950s: from Danish *leg godt* 'play well,' from *lege* 'to play.'

leg-of-mut·ton sleeve ▶ n. a sleeve that is full and loose on the upper arm but close-fitting on the forearm and wrist.

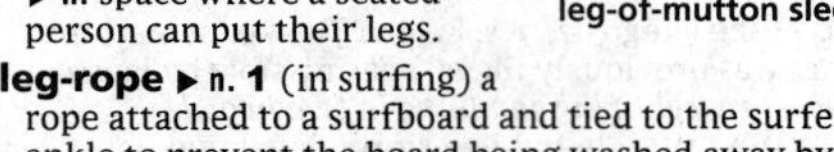

leg-of-mutton sleeve

leg-pull ▶ n. informal a trick or practical joke.
– DERIVATIVES **leg-pull·er** n., **leg-pull·ing** n.

leg rest ▶ n. a support for a seated person's leg.

leg·room /ˈlegˌro͞om, -ˌro͝om/ ▶ n. space where a seated person can put their legs.

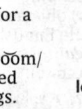

leg-rope ▶ n. **1** (in surfing) a rope attached to a surfboard and tied to the surfer's ankle to prevent the board being washed away by the surf.
2 a rope secured to a horse's leg, used to prepare the horse for a rider.

leg show ▶ n. informal, dated a theatrical production in which dancing girls display their legs.

Le Guin /lə ˈgwin/, Ursula (Kroeber) (1929–), US writer. She has written science fiction for children and adults, as well as other novels and poetry. Her science fiction includes five *Earthsea* novels for children (1968–2001) and the Hainish Cycle novels, which include *Rocannon's World* (1966) and *The Left Hand of Darkness* (1969).

leg·ume /ˈlegˌyo͞om, ləˈgyo͞om/ ▶ n. a leguminous plant, esp. one grown as a crop. ■ a seed, pod, or other edible part of a leguminous plant used as food. ■ Botany the long seedpod of a leguminous plant.
– ORIGIN mid 17th cent. (denoting the edible portion of the plant): from French *légume*, from Latin *legumen*, from *legere* 'to pick' (because the fruit may be picked by hand).

le·gu·mi·nous /liˈgyo͞omənəs/ ▶ adj. Botany of, relating to, or denoting plants of the pea family (Leguminosae). They have seeds in pods, distinctive flowers, and typically root nodules containing symbiotic bacteria able to fix nitrogen. Compare with PAPILIONACEOUS.
– ORIGIN late Middle English (in the sense 'relating to pulses'): from medieval Latin *leguminosus*, from *legumen* (see LEGUME).

leg warm·ers ▶ plural n. a pair of tubular knitted garments designed to cover the leg from ankle to knee or thigh, esp. worn by dancers during rehearsal.

leg·work /ˈlegˌwərk/ ▶ n. work that involves much traveling to collect information, esp. when such work is difficult but boring.

Le·hár /ˈlāˌhär/, Franz (Ferencz) (1870–1948), Hungarian composer. He is known for his operettas, of which the best-known is *The Merry Widow* (1905).

Le Ha·vre /lə ˈhäv(rə)/ a port in northern France, on the English Channel at the mouth of the Seine River; pop. 185,311 (2006).

Le·high Riv·er /ˈlēˌhī/ a river that flows for 103 miles (166 km) through eastern Pennsylvania to the Delaware River. Bethlehem and Allentown are among its centers.

Leh·mann /ˈlāmən/, Lotte (1888–1976), US lyric soprano; born in Germany. She was known for her interpretations of Strauss and other great composers.

lei[1] /lā/ ▶ n. a Polynesian garland of flowers.
– ORIGIN Hawaiian.

lei[2] plural form of LEU.

Leib·niz /ˈlībˌnits, ˈlīp-/, Gottfried Wilhelm (1646–1716), German rationalist philosopher, mathematician, and logician. He argued that the world is composed of single units (monads) and also devised a method of calculus independently of Newton.
– DERIVATIVES **Leib·niz·i·an** /lībˈnitsēən/ adj. & n.

Lei·bo·vitz /ˈlēbəˌvits/, Annie (1949–), US photographer. She was chief photographer of *Rolling Stone* magazine 1973–83 before moving to *Vanity Fair*. She has produced portraits of many celebrities and has had numerous exhibitions, including that at the Smithsonian National Portrait Gallery in Washington, DC, in 1991.

Leices·ter[1] /ˈlestər/ a city in central England, on the Soar River; pop. 294,900 (est. 2009).

Leices·ter[2], Earl of, see DUDLEY[2].

Leices·ter[3] ▶ n. **1** (also **Red Leicester**) a kind of mild, firm cheese, typically orange-colored and originally made in Leicestershire.
2 (also **Border Leicester**) a sheep of a breed often crossed with other breeds to produce lambs for the meat industry.

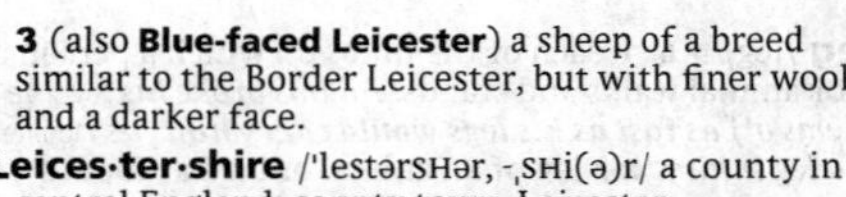

3 (also **Blue-faced Leicester**) a sheep of a breed similar to the Border Leicester, but with finer wool and a darker face.

Leices·ter·shire /ˈlestərSHər, -ˌSHi(ə)r/ a county in central England; county town, Leicester.

Lei·den /ˈlīdn, ˈlādn/ (also **Leyden**) a city in the western Netherlands, 9 miles (15 km) northeast of The Hague; pop. 116,878 (2008).

Leif Er·ics·son /ˌlēf ˈeriksən/ see ERICSSON[2].

Leigh[1] /lē/, Janet (1927–2004), US actress. Best known for her role in Alfred Hitchcock's *Psycho* (1960), she appeared in more than fifty other films, including *Little Women* (1949) and *The Manchurian Candidate* (1962).

Leigh[2], Vivien (1913–67), British actress, born in India; born *Vivian Mary Hartley*. She won Academy Awards for her performances in *Gone with the Wind* (1939) and *A Streetcar Named Desire* (1951). She was married to Laurence Olivier from 1940 to 1961.

Lein·ster /ˈlenstər/ a province of the Republic of Ireland, in the southeastern part of the country.

lei·o·thrix /ˈlī-ōˌTHriks/ ▶ n. an Asian bird of the babbler family, with orange-yellow underparts and a melodious song, popular as a pet bird. Also called **Pekin robin, red-billed leiothrix**. ● *Leiothrix lutea*, family Timaliidae.
– ORIGIN modern Latin, from Greek *leios* 'smooth' + *thrix* 'hair.'

Leip·zig /ˈlīpsig, -sik/ an industrial city in east central Germany; pop. 506,600 (est. 2006).

leish·man·i·a /lēSHˈmānēə, -ˈmanēə/ ▶ n. (pl. **same** or **leishmanias** or **leishmaniae** /-ˈmānē-ē, -ˈman-, -ēˌī/) a single-celled parasitic protozoan that spends part of its life cycle in the gut of a sandfly and part in the blood and other tissues of a vertebrate. ● Genus *Leishmania*, phylum Kinetoplastida, kingdom Protista.
– ORIGIN modern Latin, from the name of William B. *Leishman* (1856–1926), British pathologist.

leish·man·i·a·sis /ˌlēSHməˈnīəsəs/ ▶ n. a tropical and subtropical disease caused by leishmania and transmitted by the bite of sandflies. It affects either the skin or the internal organs.

leis·ter /ˈlēstər/ ▶ n. a pronged spear used for catching fish.
▶ v. [with obj.] spear (a fish) with a leister.
– ORIGIN mid 16th cent.: from Old Norse *ljóstr*, from *ljósta* 'to strike.'

lei·sure /ˈlēZHər, ˈleZHər/ ▶ n. free time. ■ use of free time for enjoyment: *increased opportunities for leisure* | [as modifier] *leisure activities.* ■ (**leisure for/to do something**) opportunity afforded by free time to do something: *writers with enough leisure to practice their art.*
– PHRASES **at leisure 1** not occupied; free: *the rest of the day can be spent at leisure.* **2** in an unhurried manner: *the poems were left for others to read at leisure.* **at one's leisure** at one's ease or convenience. **lady** (or **man** or **gentleman**) **of leisure** a woman or man of independent means or whose time is free from obligations to others. **leisure class** a social class that is independently wealthy or has much leisure.
– ORIGIN Middle English: from Old French *leisir*, based on Latin *licere* 'be allowed.'

lei·sured /ˈlēZHərd, ˈleZHərd/ ▶ adj. having ample leisure, esp. through being rich: *the leisured classes.* ■ leisurely: *a new, more leisured lifestyle.*

lei·sure·ly /ˈlēZHərlē, ˈleZHər-/ ▶ adj. acting or done at leisure; unhurried or relaxed: *a leisurely breakfast at our hotel.*
▶ adv. without hurry: *couples strolled leisurely along.*
– DERIVATIVES **lei·sure·li·ness** n.

lei·sure suit ▶ n. a man's casual suit, consisting of pants and a matching shirtlike jacket, often in pastel colors.

lei·sure·wear /ˈlēZHərˌwe(ə)r, ˈleZHər-/ ▶ n. casual clothes designed to be worn for leisure activities, particularly sweatsuits and other sportswear.

leit·mo·tif /ˈlītmōˌtēf/ (also **leitmotiv**) ▶ n. a recurrent theme throughout a musical or literary composition, associated with a particular person, idea, or situation.
– ORIGIN late 19th cent.: from German *Leitmotiv*, from *leit-* 'leading' (from *leiten* 'to lead') + *Motiv* 'motive.'

Lei·trim /ˈlētrəm/ a county of the Republic of Ireland, in the province of Connacht.

Leix variant spelling of LAOIS.

lek[1] /lek/ ▶ n. the basic monetary unit of Albania, equal to 100 qintars.
– ORIGIN Albanian.

lek[2] ▶ n. a patch of ground used for communal display in the breeding season by the males of certain birds and mammals, esp. black grouse. Each

male defends a small territory in order to attract females for mating.
▶ v. [no obj.] (usu. as adj. **lekking**) take part in such a display: *antelopes mate in lekking grounds.*
– ORIGIN late 19th cent.: perhaps from Swedish *leka* 'to play.'

LEM /lem/ ▶ abbr. lunar excursion module.

lem·an /'lemən/ ▶ n. (pl. **lemans**) archaic a lover or sweetheart. ■ an illicit lover, esp. a mistress.
– ORIGIN Middle English *lēofman*, from *lēof* (see LIEF) + MAN.

Le Mans /lə mäN/ an industrial city in northwestern France; pop. 148,169 (2006). It is the site of a race car track on which a 24-hour endurance race, established in 1923, is held each summer.

Le May /lə 'mā/, Curtis Emerson (1906–90), US air force officer; known as **Old Iron Pants**. After serving in World War II, he directed the Berlin Airlift in 1948. He was the commanding general of the US Strategic Air Command 1948–57 and Air Force chief of staff 1961–65.

Lem·berg /'lembərg, -bərk/ German name for LVIV.

Le·mieux /lə'myōō, lə'myœ/, Mario (1965–), Canadian hockey player. He played for the Pittsburgh Penguins 1984–97. Hockey Hall of Fame (1997).

lem·ma[1] /'lemə/ ▶ n. (pl. **lemmas** or **lemmata** /'lemətə/) **1** a subsidiary or intermediate theorem in an argument or proof.
2 a heading indicating the subject or argument of a literary composition, an annotation, or a dictionary entry.
– ORIGIN late 16th cent.: via Latin from Greek *lēmma* 'something assumed'; derived from *lambanein* 'take.'

lem·ma[2] ▶ n. (pl. **lemmas** or **lemmata**) Botany the lower bract of the floret of a grass. Compare with PALEA.
– ORIGIN mid 18th cent. (denoting the husk or shell of a fruit): from Greek, from *lepein* 'to peel.'

lem·ma·tize /'leməˌtīz/ ▶ v. [with obj.] sort words by grouping inflected or variant forms of the same word.
– DERIVATIVES **lem·ma·ti·za·tion** /ˌlemətə'zāSHən/ n.

lem·me /'lemē/ ▶ contraction informal let me: *lemme ask you something.*

lem·ming /'lemiNG/ ▶ n. a small, short-tailed, thickset rodent related to the voles, found in the Arctic tundra. ● *Lemmus, Dicrostonyx*, and other genera, family Muridae: several species, in particular the **Norway lemming** (*L. lemmus*), noted for its fluctuating populations and periodic mass migrations, which in popular belief sometimes culminate in the animals jumping off cliffs into the sea. ■ a person who unthinkingly joins a mass movement, esp. a headlong rush to destruction: *the flailings of the lemmings on Wall Street.*
– ORIGIN early 18th cent.: from Norwegian and Danish; related to Old Norse *lómundr*.

Lem·mon /'lemən/, Jack (1925–2001), US actor; born *John Uhler Lemmon III*. Acclaimed for both comedy and drama, he appeared in such movies as *Mr. Roberts* (1955), *Some Like It Hot* (1959), *The Apartment* (1960), *The Odd Couple* (1968), and *Save the Tiger* (1973).

Lem·nitz·er /'lemˌnitsər/, Lyman Louis (1899–1988) US army officer. He played a key role in the Allied invasions of Africa in World War II and in the negotiated surrender of Italy. Later he served as commander of UN forces in Korea 1955–57, as chairman of the US joint chiefs of staff 1960–62, and as supreme allied commander in Europe 1962–69.

Lem·nos /'lemˌnäs, 'lemnəs/ a Greek island in the northern Aegean Sea. Greek name LÍMNOS.

lem·on /'lemən/ ▶ n. **1** a yellow, oval citrus fruit with thick skin and fragrant, acidic juice. ■ a drink made from or flavored with lemon juice: *a port and lemon* | [as modifier] *lemon tea.*
2 (also **lemon tree**) the evergreen citrus tree that produces this fruit, widely cultivated in warm climates. ● *Citrus limon*, family Rutaceae.
3 a pale yellow color: [as modifier] *lemon yellow* | *a lemon T-shirt.*
4 informal a person or thing, esp. an automobile, regarded as unsatisfactory, disappointing, or feeble.
– DERIVATIVES **lem·on·y** adj.
– ORIGIN Middle English: via Old French *limon* (in modern French denoting a lime) from Arabic *līmūn* (a collective term for fruits of this kind); compare with LIME[2].

lem·on·ade /ˌlemə'nād, 'leməˌnād/ ▶ n. a drink made from lemon juice and sweetened water.
– ORIGIN mid 17th cent.: from French *limonade*, from *limon* 'lemon.'

lem·on balm ▶ n. see BALM (sense 3).

lem·on curd ▶ n. a preserve with a thick consistency made from lemons, butter, eggs, and sugar.

LeMond /lə'môn(d)/, Greg (1961–), US cyclist. In 1986, he became the first American to win the Tour de France bicycle race, a feat he repeated in 1989 and 1990.

lem·on drop ▶ n. a yellow, lemon-flavored hard candy.

lem·on ge·ra·ni·um ▶ n. a pelargonium that contains aromatic oil that smells of lemon. ● *Pelargonium crispum*, family Geraniaceae.

lem·on·grass /'leməngras/ (also **lemon grass**) ▶ n. a fragrant tropical grass that yields an oil that smells of lemon. It is widely used in Asian cooking and in perfumery and medicine. ● *Cymbopogon citratus*, family Gramineae.

lem·on sole ▶ n. a common European flatfish of the plaice family. It is an important food fish. ● *Microstomus kitt*, family Pleuronectidae.
– ORIGIN mid 19th cent.: *lemon* from French *limande*, of unknown origin.

lem·on thyme ▶ n. thyme of a hybrid variety having lemon-scented leaves. ● *Thymus × citriodorus*, family Labiatae.

lem·on ver·be·na ▶ n. a South American shrub of the verbena family, with lemon-scented leaves that are used as flavoring and to make a sedative tea. ● *Aloysia triphylla*, family Verbenaceae.

lem·on·wood /'lemənˌwŏŏd/ ▶ n. the light-colored wood of any of several tropical American trees, esp. the Cuban *Calycophyllum candidissimum* of the madder family (Rubiaceae).

lem·pi·ra /lem'pi(ə)rə/ ▶ n. the basic monetary unit of Honduras, equal to 100 centavos.
– ORIGIN named after *Lempira*, a 16th-cent. Indian chieftain who opposed the Spanish conquest of Honduras.

le·mur /'lēmər/ ▶ n. an arboreal primate with a pointed snout and typically a long tail, found only in Madagascar. Compare with FLYING LEMUR. ● Lemuridae and other families, suborder Prosimii; includes also the sifaka, indri, and aye-aye.
– ORIGIN late 18th cent.: modern Latin, from Latin *lemures* (plural) 'spirits of the dead' (from its specterlike face).

lem·u·res /'leməˌrās, 'lemyəˌrēz/ ▶ plural n. the family spirits of the dead in ancient Rome, considered frightening or troublesome, that must be exorcised or appeased through certain household rituals.

Le·na /'lānə, 'lē-/ a river in Siberia, Russia, that rises in the mountains on the western shore of Lake Baikal and flows for 2,750 miles (4,400 km) into the Laptev Sea. It is noted for the goldfields in its basin.

Len·a·pe ▶ n. see LENNI LENAPE.

lend /lend/ ▶ v. (past and past participle **lent** /lent/) [with obj.] **1** grant to (someone) the use of (something) on the understanding that it shall be returned: *Stewart asked me to lend him my car* | *the pictures were lent to each museum in turn.* ■ allow (a person or organization) the use of (a sum of money) under an agreement to pay it back later, typically with interest: *no one would lend him the money* | [no obj.] *the bank lends only to its current customers* | (as noun **lending**) *balance sheets weakened by unwise lending.*
2 contribute or add (something, esp. a quality) to: *the smile lent his face a boyish charm.*
3 (**lend oneself to**) accommodate or adapt oneself to: *John stiffly lent himself to her enthusiastic embraces.* ■ (**lend itself to**) (of a thing) be suitable for: *bay windows lend themselves to blinds.*
– PHRASES **lend an ear** (or **one's ears**) listen sympathetically or attentively: *the Samaritans lend their ears to those in crisis.* **lend a hand** (or **a helping hand**) see GIVE A HAND at HAND. **lend one's name to** allow oneself to be publicly associated with: *he lent his name and prestige to the organizers of the project.*
– DERIVATIVES **lend·a·ble** adj.
– ORIGIN Old English *lǣnan*, of Germanic origin; related to Dutch *lenen*, also to LOAN. The addition of the final *-d* in late Middle English was due to association with verbs such as *bend* and *send.*

lend·er /'lendər/ ▶ n. an organization or person that lends money: *a mortgage lender.*

lend·ing li·brar·y ▶ n. a public library from which books may be borrowed and taken away for a short time.

Len·dl /'lendl/, Ivan (1960–), US tennis player, born in Czechoslovakia. During 1984–90, he won the men's singles title at two Australian Open, three French Open, and three US Open tournaments.

Lend-Lease historical an arrangement made in 1941 whereby the US supplied military equipment and armaments to the UK and its allies, originally as a loan in return for the use of British-owned military bases.

Le·nex·a /lə'neksə/ a city in eastern Kansas, a southwestern suburb of Kansas City; pop. 46,822 (est. 2008).

L'Enfant /länfäN(t)/, Pierre Charles (1754–1825), US architect and soldier; born in France. In 1791, he submitted plans that were followed in the design of the city of Washington, DC.

L'Engle /'leNGgəl/, Madeleine (Camp) (1918–2007), US writer. She wrote mainly children's fiction, including *A Wrinkle in Time* (1962), the first of a quartet that also included *A Wind in the Door* (1973), *A Swiftly Tilting Planet* (1978), and *Many Waters* (1986).

length /leNG(k)TH, lenth/ ▶ n. **1** the measurement or extent of something from end to end; the greater of two or the greatest of three dimensions of a body: *it can reach over two feet in length* | *the length of the airport terminal.* ■ the amount of time occupied by something: *delivery must be within a reasonable length of time.* ■ the quality of being long: *the length of the waiting list.* ■ the full distance that a thing extends for: *the muscles running the length of my spine.* ■ the extent of a garment in a vertical direction when worn: *the length of her skirt.* ■ Prosody & Phonetics the metrical quantity or duration of a vowel or syllable.
2 the extent of something, esp. as a unit of measurement, in particular: ■ the length of a swimming pool as a measure of the distance swum: *fifty lengths of the pool.* ■ the length of a horse, boat, etc., as a measure of the lead in a race: *the mare won the race last year by seven lengths.* ■ (**one's length**) the full extent of one's body: *he awkwardly lowered his length into the small car.*
3 (in bridge or whist) the number of cards of a suit held in one's hand, esp. when five or more.
4 a stretch or piece of something: *a stout length of wood.*
5 a degree or extreme to which a course of action is taken: *they go to great lengths to avoid the press.*
– PHRASES **at length 1** in detail; fully: *these aspects have been discussed at length.* **2** after a long time: *at length she laid down the pencil.* **the length and breadth of** the whole extent of: *women from the length and breadth of Russia.*
– ORIGIN Old English *lengthu*, of Germanic origin; related to Dutch *lengte*, also to LONG[1].

-length ▶ comb. form reaching up to or down to the place specified: *knee-length.* ■ of the size, duration, or extent specified: *full-length* | *medium-length* | *feature-length.*

length·en /'leNG(k)THən, 'len-/ ▶ v. make or become longer: [with obj.] *she lengthened her stride to catch up* | [no obj.] *in the spring when the days are lengthening* | (as adj. **lengthening**) *the lengthening shadows.* ■ [with obj.] Prosody & Phonetics make (a vowel or syllable) long.

length·ways /'leNG(k)THˌwāz, 'lenTH-/ ▶ adv. lengthwise.

length·wise /'leNG(k)THˌwīz, 'lenTH-/ ▶ adv. in a direction parallel with a thing's length: *halve the potatoes lengthwise.*
▶ adj. [attrib.] lying or moving lengthwise: *a lengthwise crack.*

length·y /'leNG(k)THē, 'len-/ ▶ adj. (**lengthier, lengthiest**) (esp. in reference to time) of considerable or unusual length, esp. so as to be tedious: *lengthy delays* | *a lengthy book.*
– DERIVATIVES **length·i·ly** /-THəlē/ adv., **length·i·ness** n.

le·nien·cy /'lēnēənsē, 'lēnyən(t)sē/ ▶ n. the fact or quality of being more merciful or tolerant than expected; clemency: *the court could show leniency.*
– DERIVATIVES **le·ni·ence** n.

le·ni·ent /'lēnēənt, 'lēnyənt/ ▶ adj. **1** (of punishment or a person in authority) permissive, merciful, or tolerant: *judges were far too lenient with petty criminals.*
2 archaic emollient.
– DERIVATIVES **le·ni·ent·ly** adv.
– ORIGIN mid 17th cent. (in sense 2): from Latin *lenient-* 'soothing,' from the verb *lenire*, from *lenis* 'mild, gentle.'

Le·nin /'lenən, 'lyenyin/, Vladimir Ilich (1870–1924), the principal figure in the Russian Revolution and first premier of the former Soviet Union 1918–24; born *Vladimir Ilich Ulyanov*. He was the first political leader to attempt to put Marxist principles into practice. In 1917 he established Bolshevik control after the overthrow of the tsar and in 1918 became head of state.

Vladimir Lenin

Le·nin·a·kan /li,nēnə'kän/ former name (1924–91) for **Gyumri**.

Len·in·grad /'lenən,grad/ former name (1924–91) for **St. Petersburg**.

Le·nin·ism /'lenə,nizəm/ ▶ **n.** Marxism as interpreted and applied by Lenin.
– DERIVATIVES **Le·nin·ist n. & adj.**, **Le·nin·ite** /-,nīt/ **n. & adj.**
– ORIGIN early 20th cent.: named after **Lenin**.

le·nis /'lēnis, 'lā-/ Phonetics ▶ **adj.** (of a consonant, in particular a voiced consonant) weakly articulated, esp. denoting the less or least strongly articulated of two or more similar consonants. The opposite of **fortis**.
▶ **n.** (pl. **lenes** /-nēz/) a consonant of this type.
– ORIGIN early 20th cent.: from Latin, literally 'mild, gentle.'

le·nite /'lē,nīt, li'nīt/ ▶ **v.** (**be lenited**) (of a consonant) be pronounced with lenition.
– ORIGIN early 20th cent.: back-formation from **lenition**.

le·ni·tion /li'nisHən/ ▶ **n.** the process or result of weakened articulation of a consonant, causing the consonant to become voiced, spirantized, or lost.
– ORIGIN early 20th cent.: from Latin *lenis* 'soft' + **-ition**, suggested by German *Lenierung*.

len·i·tive /'lenətiv/ Medicine, archaic ▶ **adj.** (of a medicine) laxative.
▶ **n.** a medicine of this type.
– ORIGIN late Middle English: from medieval Latin *lenitivus*, from *lenit-* 'softened,' from the verb *lenire*.

len·i·ty /'lenətē/ ▶ **n.** literary kindness; gentleness.
– ORIGIN late Middle English: from Old French *lenite*, or from Latin *lenitas*, from *lenis* 'gentle.'

Len·ni Len·a·pe /'lenē 'lenəpē, lə'näpē/ ▶ **n. 1** a group of North American Indian peoples who formerly occupied the Delaware and Hudson River valleys, with existing populations in Oklahoma, Kansas, Wisconsin, and Ontario. ■ a member of one of the Delaware peoples.
2 the Eastern Algonquian language spoken by any of the Delaware peoples.

Len·non /'lenən/, John (1940–80), English pop and rock singer, guitarist, and songwriter. A founding member of the Beatles, he wrote most of their songs in collaboration with Paul McCartney. After the group broke up in 1970, he continued recording material, such as *Imagine* (1971), some with his second wife, Yoko Ono. He was fatally shot by a mentally disturbed fan outside his home in New York City.

John Lennon

le·no /'lēnō/ ▶ **n.** (pl. **lenos**) an openwork fabric with the warp threads twisted in pairs before weaving.
– ORIGIN late 18th cent.: from French *linon*, from *lin* 'flax,' from Latin *linum*. Compare with **linen**.

Le Nô·tre /lə 'nôtrə/, André (1613–1700), French landscape gardener. He designed many formal gardens, including the parks of Vaux-le-Vicomte and Versailles.

Len·ox /'lenəks/ a resort town in western Massachusetts, in the Berkshire Hills, site of the summer music complex called Tanglewood; pop. 5,095 (est. 2008).

lens /lenz/ ▶ **n.** a piece of glass or other transparent substance with curved sides for concentrating or dispersing light rays, used singly (as in a magnifying glass) or with other lenses (as in a telescope).
■ the light-gathering device of a camera, typically containing a group of compound lenses. ■ Physics an object or device that focuses or otherwise modifies the direction of movement of light, sound, electrons, etc. ■ Anatomy short for **crystalline lens**.
■ short for **contact lens**.
– DERIVATIVES **lensed adj.**, **lens·less adj.**
– ORIGIN late 17th cent.: from Latin, 'lentil' (because of the similarity in shape).

lens hood ▶ **n.** a tube or ring attached to the front of a camera lens to prevent unwanted light from reaching the film.

lens·man /'lenzmən, -,man/ ▶ **n.** (pl. **lensmen**) a professional photographer or cameraman.

Lent /lent/ ▶ **n.** the period preceding Easter that in the Christian Church is devoted to fasting, abstinence, and penitence in commemoration of Christ's fasting in the wilderness. In the Western Church it runs from Ash Wednesday to Holy Saturday and so includes forty weekdays.
– ORIGIN Middle English: abbreviation of **Lenten**.

lent /lent/ past and past participle of **lend**.

-lent ▶ **suffix** (forming adjectives) full of; characterized by: *pestilent* | *violent*. Compare with **-ulent**.

len·tan·do /len'tändō/ ▶ **adv. & adj.** Music (as a direction) slowing gradually.

Lent·en /'lent(ə)n/ ▶ **adj.** [attrib.] of, in, or appropriate to Lent: *Lenten food*.
– ORIGIN Old English *lencten* 'spring, Lent,' of Germanic origin, related to **long**[1] (perhaps with reference to the lengthening of the day in spring); now interpreted as being from **Lent** + **-en**[2].

len·tic /'lentik/ ▶ **adj.** Ecology (of organisms or habitats) inhabiting or situated in still, fresh water. Compare with **lotic**.
– ORIGIN mid 20th cent.: from Latin *lentus* 'calm, slow' + **-ic**.

len·ti·cel /'lentə,sel/ ▶ **n.** Botany one of many raised pores in the stem of a woody plant that allows gas exchange between the atmosphere and the internal tissues.
– ORIGIN mid 19th cent.: from modern Latin *lenticella*, diminutive of Latin *lens*, *lent-* 'lentil.'

len·tic·u·lar /len'tikyələr/ ▶ **adj. 1** shaped like a lentil, esp. by being biconvex: *lenticular lenses*.
2 of or relating to the lens of the eye.
– ORIGIN late Middle English: from Latin *lenticularis*, from *lenticula*, diminutive of *lens*, *lent-* 'lentil.'

len·ti·form nu·cle·us /'lentə,fôrm/ ▶ **n.** Anatomy the lower of the two gray nuclei of the corpus striatum.
– ORIGIN early 18th cent.: *lentiform* from Latin *lens*, *lent-* 'lentil' + **-iform**.

len·ti·go /len'tīgō, -'tē-/ ▶ **n.** (pl. **lentigines** /-'tijə,nēz/) a condition marked by small brown patches on the skin, typically in elderly people.
– ORIGIN late Middle English (denoting a freckle or pimple): from Latin, from *lens*, *lent-* 'lentil.'

len·til /'lent(ə)l/ ▶ **n. 1** a high-protein pulse that is dried and then soaked and cooked before eating. There are several varieties of lentils, including green ones and smaller orange ones, which are typically sold split.
2 the plant that yields this pulse, native to the Mediterranean and Africa and grown also for fodder. ● *Lens culinaris*, family Leguminosae.
– ORIGIN Middle English: from Old French *lentille*, from Latin *lenticula*, diminutive of *lens*, *lent-* 'lentil.'

len·tisk /'len,tisk/ (also **lentisc**) ▶ **n.** the mastic tree.
– ORIGIN late Middle English: from Latin *lentiscus*.

len·tis·si·mo /len'tisi,mō, -'tēsē-/ ▶ **adj. & adv.** Music (as a direction) at a very slow tempo.

len·ti·vi·rus /'lentə,vīrəs/ ▶ **n.** Medicine any of a group of retroviruses producing illnesses characterized by a delay in the onset of symptoms after infection.
– ORIGIN 1970s: from Latin *lentus* 'slow' + **virus**.

len·to /'lentō/ ▶ **adv. & adj.** Music (esp. as a direction) slow or slowly.
▶ **n.** (pl. **lentos**) a passage or movement marked to be performed in this way.
– ORIGIN Italian.

len·toid /'len,toid/ ▶ **adj.** another term for **lenticular** (sense 1).
– ORIGIN late 19th cent.: from Latin *lens*, *lent-* 'lentil' + **-oid**.

Lenz's law /'lentsiz, 'lenziz/ Physics a law stating that the direction of an induced current is always such as to oppose the change in the circuit or the magnetic field that produces it.
– ORIGIN mid 19th cent.: named after Heinrich F. E. *Lenz* (1804–65), German physicist.

Le·o[1] /'lēō/ the name of 13 popes, notably: ■ **Leo I** (died 461), pope from 440 and doctor of the Church; known as **Leo the Great**; canonized as **St. Leo I**. He defined the doctrine of the Incarnation at the Council of Chalcedon (451) and extended the power of the Roman see to Africa, Spain, and Gaul. Feast day (Eastern Church) February 18; (Western Church) April 11. ■ **Leo X** (1475–1521), pope from 1513; born *Giovanni de' Medici*. He excommunicated Martin Luther and bestowed the title of Defender of the Faith on Henry VIII of England. He was a noted patron of learning and of the arts.

Le·o[2] **1** Astronomy a large constellation (the Lion), said to represent the lion slain by Hercules. It contains the bright stars Regulus and Denebola and numerous galaxies. ■ (as genitive **Leonis** /lē'ōnis/) used with a preceding letter or numeral to designate a star in this constellation: *the star Omicron Leonis*.
2 Astrology the fifth sign of the zodiac, which the sun enters about July 23. ■ (**a Leo**) (pl. **Leos**) a person born when the sun is in this sign.
– DERIVATIVES **Le·on·i·an** /lē'ōnēən/ **n. & adj.** (sense 2).
– ORIGIN Latin.

Le·o III (*c.*680–741), Byzantine emperor 717–741. He repulsed several Muslim invasions and carried out an extensive series of reforms. In 726, he banned icons and other religious images; the resulting iconoclastic controversy led to more than a century of political and religious turmoil.

Le·o Mi·nor Astronomy a small and inconspicuous northern constellation (the Little Lion), immediately north of Leo. ■ (as genitive **Leonis Minoris** /lē'ōnis mī'nôris/) used with a preceding letter or numeral to designate a star in this constellation: *the star Alpha Leonis Minoris*.
– ORIGIN Latin.

Leom·in·ster /'lemənstər/ an industrial city in north central Massachusetts; pop. 41,055 (est. 2008).

Le·ón /lā'ôn/ **1** an industrial city in central Mexico; pop. 1,137,465 (2005).
2 a city in western Nicaragua, the second largest city in the country; pop. 174,051 (2006).
3 a city in northern Spain; pop. 135,119 (2008). It is the capital of the province and former kingdom of León, now part of the Castilla-León region.

Leon·ard[1] /'lenərd/, Elmore (1925–), US writer; full name *Elmore John Leonard, Jr.* Noted for their gritty realism, his works include *Unknown Man No. 89* (1977), *Freaky Deaky* (1988), *Get Shorty* (1990), and *Road Dogs* (2009).

Leon·ard[2], Sugar Ray (1956–), US boxer; full name *Ray Charles Leonard*. He won world championship titles in four different weight divisions: welterweight in 1979, middleweight in 1987, and super middleweight and light heavyweight in 1988.

Le·o·nar·do da Vin·ci /,lēə'närdō də 'vinCHē, ,lā-/ (1452–1519), Italian painter, scientist, and engineer. His paintings are notable for their use of the technique of *sfumato* and include *The Virgin of the Rocks* (1483–85), *The Last Supper* (1498), and the *Mona Lisa* (1504–05). He devoted himself to a wide range of other subjects, from anatomy and biology to mechanics and hydraulics: his 19 notebooks include studies of the human circulatory system and plans for a type of aircraft and a submarine.

Le·on·berg·er /'lēən,bərgər/ ▶ **n.** a large dog of a breed typically having a golden coat, produced by crossing a St. Bernard and a Newfoundland.
– ORIGIN early 20th cent.: named after a town in southwestern Germany.

le·one /lē'ōn/ ▶ **n.** the basic monetary unit of Sierra Leone, equal to 100 cents.

Le·o·nids /'lēənidz/ Astronomy an annual meteor shower with a radiant in the constellation Leo, reaching a peak about November 17.
– ORIGIN late 19th cent.: from Latin *leo*, *leon-* (see **Leo**[2]) + **-id**[3].

Le·o·nine /'lēə,nīn/ ▶ **adj. 1** of or relating to one of the popes named Leo, esp. Leo IV and the part of Rome that he fortified.
2 Prosody (of medieval Latin verse) in hexameter or elegiac meter with internal rhyme. ■ (of English verse) with internal rhyme.
▶ **plural n.** (**Leonines**) Prosody verse of this type.
– ORIGIN late Middle English: from the name *Leo*, from Latin *leo* 'lion.' Sense 2 of the adjective may be from the name of a medieval poet, but his identity is not known.

le·o·nine /'lēə,nīn/ ▶ **adj.** of or resembling a lion or lions: *a handsome, leonine profile*.

L

–ORIGIN late Middle English: from Old French, or from Latin *leoninus*, from *leo, leon-* 'lion.'

Le·o·nine Cit·y /'lēə,nīn/ the part of Rome in which the Vatican stands, walled and fortified by **Pope Leo IV**.

Le·on·ti·ef /lē'(y)ôn,tyef/, Wassily (1906–99), US economist, educator, and writer; born in Germany to Russian parents. His most significant published work is *The Structure of the American Economy 1919–1929* (1941). Nobel Prize for Economics (1973).

leop·ard /'lepərd/ ▶ **n.** a large, solitary cat that has a yellowish-brown or brown coat with black spots and usually hunts at night, widespread in the forests of Africa and southern Asia. Also called **PANTHER.** ● *Panthera pardus*, family Felidae. See also **BLACK PANTHER.** ■ Heraldry the spotted leopard as a heraldic device; also, a lion passant guardant as in the arms of England. ■ [as modifier] spotted like a leopard: *a leopard-print outfit.*
–PHRASES **a leopard can't change his spots** proverb people can't change their basic nature.
–ORIGIN Middle English: via Old French from late Latin *leopardus*, from late Greek *leopardos*, from *leōn* 'lion' + *pardos* (see **PARD**).

leop·ard cat ▶ **n.** a small eastern Asian wild cat that has a yellowish-brown coat with black spots and often lives near water. ● *Felis bengalensis*, family Felidae.

leop·ard·ess /'lepərdis/ ▶ **n.** a female leopard.

leop·ard frog ▶ **n.** a common greenish-brown North American frog that has dark leopardlike spots with a pale border. ● *Rana pipiens*, family Ranidae.

leop·ard lil·y ▶ **n.** a lily resembling a tiger lily, native to the southwestern US. ● *Lilium pardalinum*, family Liliaceae.

leop·ard moth ▶ **n.** a large white European moth with black spots, the larvae of which tunnel into trees and can cause damage. ● *Zeuzera pyrina*, family Cossidae.

leop·ard's bane ▶ **n.** a herbaceous Eurasian plant of the daisy family, with large yellow flowers that typically bloom early in the spring. ● Genus *Doronicum*, family Compositae.

leop·ard seal ▶ **n.** a large, gray Antarctic seal that has leopardlike spots and preys on penguins and other seals. ● *Hydrurga leptonyx*, family Phocidae.

leop·ard-skin ▶ **adj.** (of a garment) made of a fabric resembling the spotted skin of a leopard: *leopard-skin pedal pushers.*

Le·o·pold I /'lēə,pōld/ (1790–1865), first king of Belgium 1831–65. The fourth son of the Duke of Saxe-Coburg-Saalfield, he was an uncle of Britain's Queen Victoria.

Lé·o·pold·ville /'lēə,pōld,vil, 'lā-/ former name (until 1966) of **KINSHASA**.

le·o·tard /'lēə,tärd/ ▶ **n.** a close-fitting one-piece garment, made of a stretchy fabric, that covers a person's body from the shoulders to the top of the thighs and typically the arms, worn by dancers or people exercising indoors. ■ **(leotards)** close-fitting leggings or tights, esp. those worn by dancers.
–ORIGIN early 20th cent.: named after Jules *Léotard* (1839–70), French trapeze artist.

Le·o the Great Pope Leo I (see **LEO**[1]).

Le·pan·to, Bat·tle of /li'pantō, 'lepän,tō/ a naval battle fought in 1571 close to the port of Lepanto at the entrance to the Gulf of Corinth. The Christian forces of Rome, Venice, and Spain defeated a large Turkish fleet, ending for the time being Turkish naval domination in the eastern Mediterranean.

Le·pan·to, Gulf of another name for the Gulf of Corinth (see **CORINTH, GULF OF**).

Lep·cha /'lepchə/ ▶ **n. 1** a member of a people living mainly in mountain valleys in the Indian state of Sikkim, western Bhutan, and parts of Nepal and West Bengal.
2 the Tibeto-Burman language of this people.
▶ **adj.** of or relating to the Lepchas or their language.
–ORIGIN from Nepali *lāpche*.

lep·er /'lepər/ ▶ **n.** a person suffering from leprosy. ■ a person who is avoided or rejected by others for moral or social reasons: *the story made her out to be a social leper.*
–ORIGIN late Middle English: probably from an attributive use of *leper* 'leprosy,' from Old French *lepre*, via Latin from Greek *lepra*, feminine of *lepros* 'scaly,' from *lepos, lepis* 'scale.'

lep·i·do·cro·cite /,lepədō'krō,sīt/ ▶ **n.** a red to reddish-brown mineral consisting of ferric hydroxide, typically occurring as scaly or fibrous crystals.

le·pid·o·lite /li'pidl,īt/ ▶ **n.** a mineral of the mica group containing lithium, typically gray or lilac in color.
–ORIGIN late 18th cent.: from Greek *lepis, lepid-* 'scale' + **-LITE**.

Lep·i·dop·ter·a /,lepə'däptərə/ Entomology an order of insects that comprises the butterflies and moths. They have four large scale-covered wings that bear distinctive markings, and larvae that are caterpillars. ■ **(lepidoptera)** [as plural noun] insects of this order.
–DERIVATIVES **lep·i·dop·ter·an adj. & n., lep·i·dop·ter·ous** /-tərəs/ **adj.**
–ORIGIN modern Latin (plural), from Greek *lepis, lepid-* 'scale' + *pteron* 'wing.'

lep·i·dop·ter·ist /,lepə'däptərist/ ▶ **n.** a person who studies or collects butterflies and moths.

Lep·i·dus /'lepidəs/, Marcus Aemilius (died c.13 BC), Roman statesman and triumvir. A supporter of Julius Caesar in the civil war against Pompey, he was elected consul in 46 and was appointed one of the Second Triumvirate with Octavian and Antony in 43.

Le·pon·tic /lə'päntik/ ▶ **n.** an ancient Celtic language, possibly a variant of Gaulish, spoken at one time in parts of Switzerland and northern Italy.

lep·o·rine /'lepə,rīn, -rin/ ▶ **adj.** of or resembling a hare or hares.
–ORIGIN mid 17th cent.: from Latin *leporinus*, from *lepus, lepor-* 'hare.'

lep·o·spon·dyl /,lepə'spändl/ ▶ **n.** an extinct, early amphibian of the Carboniferous and Permian periods, distinguished by vertebrae shaped liked hourglasses. ● Microsauria and related orders, formerly placed in the subclass Lepospondyli.
–ORIGIN 1930s: from modern Latin *Lepospondyli* (plural), from Greek *lepos* 'husk' + *spondulos* 'vertebra.'

lep·re·chaun /'leprə,kän, -,kôn/ ▶ **n.** (in Irish folklore) a small, mischievous sprite.
–ORIGIN early 17th cent.: from Irish *leipreachán*, based on Old Irish *luchorpán*, from *lu* 'small' + *corp* 'body.'

le·prom·a·tous /li'prämətəs, -'prōmə-/ ▶ **adj.** Medicine relating to or denoting the more severe of the two principal forms of leprosy, marked by thickening of the skin and nerves, the formation of lumps on the skin, and often severe loss of feeling and paralysis leading to disfigurement. Compare with **TUBERCULOID.**

lep·ro·sar·i·um /,leprə'se(ə)rēəm/ ▶ **n.** a hospital for people with leprosy.
–ORIGIN mid 19th cent.: from late Latin *leprosus* 'leprous' + **-ARIUM**.

lep·ro·sy /'leprəsē/ ▶ **n.** a contagious disease that affects the skin, mucous membranes, and nerves, causing discoloration and lumps on the skin and, in severe cases, disfigurement and deformities. Leprosy is now mainly confined to tropical Africa and Asia. Also called **HANSEN'S DISEASE.** ● Leprosy is caused by the bacterium *Mycobacterium leprae*, which is Gram-positive, nonmotile, and acid-fast.
–ORIGIN mid 16th cent. (superseding Middle English *lepry*): from **LEPROUS** + **-Y**[3].

lep·rous /'leprəs/ ▶ **adj. 1** suffering from leprosy. ■ relating to or resembling leprosy: *leprous growths.* **2** covered with scales; scaly.
–ORIGIN Middle English: via Old French from late Latin *leprosus*, from Latin *lepra* 'scaly' (see **LEPER**).

lep·ta /'leptə/ plural form of **LEPTON**[1].

lep·tin /'leptin/ ▶ **n.** Biochemistry a protein produced by fatty tissue and believed to regulate fat storage in the body.
–ORIGIN 1990s: from Greek *leptos* 'fine, thin' + **-IN**[1].

lepto- ▶ **comb. form** small; narrow: *leptocephalic.*
–ORIGIN from Greek *leptos* 'fine, thin, delicate.'

lep·to·kur·tic /,leptə'kərtik/ ▶ **adj.** Statistics (of a frequency distribution or its graphical representation) having greater kurtosis than the normal distribution; more concentrated about the mean. Compare with **PLATYKURTIC, MESOKURTIC.**
–DERIVATIVES **lep·to·kur·to·sis** /-tō,kər'tōsis/ **n.**
–ORIGIN early 20th cent.: from **LEPTO-** 'narrow' + Greek *kurtos* 'bulging' + **-IC**.

lep·to·me·nin·ges /,leptōmə'nin,jēz/ ▶ **plural n.** Anatomy the inner two meninges, the arachnoid and the pia mater, between which circulates the cerebrospinal fluid.
–DERIVATIVES **lep·to·me·nin·ge·al** /-,menən'jēəl/ **adj.**

lep·ton[1] /'lep,tän/ ▶ **n.** (pl. **lepta** /-tə/) a monetary unit of Greece until the introduction of the euro, worth one hundredth of a drachma (used only in calculations).
–ORIGIN from Greek *lepton*, neuter of *leptos* 'small.'

lep·ton[2] ▶ **n.** Physics a subatomic particle, such as an electron, muon, or neutrino, that does not take part in the strong interaction.
–DERIVATIVES **lep·ton·ic** /lep'tänik/ **adj.**
–ORIGIN 1940s: from Greek *leptos* 'small' + **-ON**.

lep·ton num·ber ▶ **n.** Physics a quantum number assigned to subatomic particles that is ±1 for leptons and 0 for other particles and is conserved in all known interactions.

lep·to·spi·ro·sis /,leptə,spī'rōsis/ ▶ **n.** an infectious bacterial disease that occurs in rodents, dogs, and other mammals and can be transmitted to humans. See also **WEIL'S DISEASE.** ● The bacterium is a spirochete of the genus *Leptospira*.
–ORIGIN 1920s: from **LEPTO-** 'narrow' + Greek *speira* 'coil' + **-OSIS**.

lep·to·tene /'leptə,tēn/ ▶ **n.** Biology the first stage of the prophase of meiosis, during which each chromosome becomes visible as two fine threads (chromatids).
–ORIGIN early 20th cent.: from **LEPTO-** 'narrow, fine' + Greek *tainia* 'band, ribbon.'

Lep·us /'lepəs, 'lēpəs/ Astronomy a small constellation (the Hare) at the foot of Orion, said to represent the hare pursued by him. ■ (as genitive **Leporis** /'lepəris/) used with a preceding letter or numeral to designate a star in this constellation: *the star R Leporis.*
–ORIGIN Latin.

Ler·ner /'lərnər/, Alan Jay (1918–86), US lyricist and playwright. See also **LOEWE**.

Ler·wick /'lərwik/ the capital of the Shetland Islands, on the island of Mainland; pop. 6,200 (2009). The most northerly town in the British Isles, it is a fishing center and a service port for the oil industry.

les /lez/ (also **lez**) ▶ **n.** informal, usu. offensive a lesbian.

Les·bi·an /'lezbēən/ ▶ **adj.** from or relating to the island of Lesbos.

les·bi·an /'lezbēən/ ▶ **n.** a homosexual woman. ▶ **adj.** of or relating to homosexual women or to homosexuality in women: *a lesbian relationship.*
–DERIVATIVES **les·bi·an·ism** /-,nizəm/ **n.**
–ORIGIN late 19th cent.: via Latin from Greek *Lesbios*, from **LESBOS**, home of Sappho, who expressed affection for women in her poetry, + **-IAN**.

les·bi·gay /'lezbi'gā/ ▶ **adj.** relating to lesbians, bisexuals, and male homosexuals.
–ORIGIN from from *les(bian)*, *bi(sexual)*, and *gay*.

les·bo /'lezbō/ ▶ **n.** (pl. **lesbos**) informal, usu. offensive a lesbian.
–ORIGIN 1940s: abbreviation.

Les·bos /'lez,bäs, 'lezbəs/ a Greek island in the eastern Aegean Sea, off the coast of northwestern Turkey. Its artistic golden age of the late 7th and early 6th centuries BC produced the poets Alcaeus and Sappho. Greek name **LÉSVOS**.

Lesch–Ny·han syn·drome /'lesʜ 'nīən/ ▶ **n.** a rare hereditary disease that affects young boys, usually causing early death. It is marked by compulsive self-mutilation of the head and hands, together with mental retardation and involuntary muscular movements.
–ORIGIN 1960s: named after Michael *Lesch* (1939–2008) and William L. *Nyhan* (1926–), US physicians.

lèse-maj·es·té /,lez ,mäjə'stā, ,lēz, 'majəstē/ ▶ **n.** the insulting of a monarch or other ruler; treason.
–ORIGIN late Middle English: from French *lèse-majesté*, from Latin *laesa majestas* 'injured sovereignty.'

le·sion /'lēzʜən/ ▶ **n.** chiefly Medicine a region in an organ or tissue that has suffered damage through injury or disease, such as a wound, ulcer, abscess, tumor, etc.
–ORIGIN late Middle English: via Old French from Latin *laesio(n-)*, from *laedere* 'injure.'

Le·so·tho /lə'sōōtōō, lə'sōtō/ a landlocked mountainous country that forms an enclave in South Africa; pop. 2,130,800 (est. 2009); capital, Maseru; official languages, Sesotho and English.

The region was settled by the Sotho people in the 16th century and came under British rule (as Basutoland) in 1868. It became an independent kingdom within the Commonwealth of Nations in 1966, changing its name to Lesotho.

less /les/ ▶ **determiner & pron.** a smaller amount of; not as much: [as determiner] *the less time spent there, the better* | [as pronoun] *storage is less of a problem than it used to be* | *ready in less than an hour.* ■ fewer in number: [as pronoun] *a population of less than 200,000.*

PRONUNCIATION KEY ə *ago, up*; ər *over, fur*; a *hat*; ā *ate*; ä *car*; e *let*; ē *see*; i *fit*; ī *by*; NG *sing*; ō *go*; ô *law, for*; oi *toy*; ŏŏ *good*; ōō *goo*; ou *out*; TH *thin*; TH *then*; ZH *vision*

▶ **adj.** archaic of lower rank or importance: *James the Less.*
▶ **adv.** to a smaller extent; not so much: *he listened less to the answer than to Kate's voice | that this is a positive stereotype makes it* **no less** *a stereotype.* ■ (**less than**) far from; certainly not: *Mitch looked less than happy | the data was less than ideal.*
▶ **prep.** before subtracting (something); minus: *$900,000 less tax.*
– PHRASES **in less than no time** informal very quickly or soon. **less and less** at a continually decreasing rate. **less is more** used to express the view that a minimalist approach to artistic or aesthetic matters is more effective. **much** (or **still**) **less** used to introduce something as being even less likely or suitable than something else already mentioned: *what woman would consider a date with him, much less a marriage?* **no less** used to suggest, often ironically, that something is surprising or impressive: *Peter cooked dinner—fillet steak and champagne, no less.* ■ (**no less than**) used to emphasize a surprisingly large amount.
– ORIGIN Old English *lǣssa*, of Germanic origin; related to Old Frisian *lēssa*, from an Indo-European root shared by Greek *loisthos* 'last.'

> **USAGE** In standard English, **less** should be used only with uncountable things (*less money; less time*). With countable things, it is incorrect to use **less**: thus, *less people* and *less words* should be corrected to *fewer people* and *fewer words*. See also usage at **FEW**.

-less ▶ **suffix** forming adjectives and adverbs: **1** (from nouns) not having; without; free from: *flavorless | skinless.*
2 (from verbs) not affected by or not carrying out the action of the verb: *fathomless | tireless.*
– ORIGIN Old English *-lēas*, from *lēas* 'devoid of.'

less-de·vel·oped coun·try ▶ **n.** a nonindustrialized or Third World country.

les·see /le'sē/ ▶ **n.** a person who holds the lease of a property; a tenant.
– DERIVATIVES **les·see·ship** /-ˌSHip/ **n.**
– ORIGIN late 15th cent.: from Old French *lesse*, past participle of *lesser* 'to let, leave,' + **-EE**.

I

less·en /'lesən/ ▶ **v.** make or become less; diminish: [with obj.] *the years have lessened the gap in age between us* | [no obj.] *the warmth of the afternoon lessened.*

Les·seps /'lesəps, lə'seps/, Ferdinand Marie, Vicomte de (1805–94), French diplomat. From 1854, while in the consular service in Egypt, he devoted himself to the Suez Canal project. In 1881, as the head of a private company, he embarked on the building of the Panama Canal, but the project was abandoned in 1889.

less·er /'lesər/ ▶ **adj.** [attrib.] not so great or important as the other or the rest: *he was convicted of a lesser assault charge | they nest mostly in Alaska and* **to a lesser extent** *in Siberia.* ■ lower in terms of rank or quality: *the lesser aristocracy | you're looking down your nose at us lesser mortals.* ■ used in names of animals and plants that are smaller than similar kinds, e.g., **lesser spotted woodpecker**, **lesser celandine**.
– PHRASES **a/the lesser evil** (or **the lesser of two evils**) the less harmful or unpleasant of two bad choices or possibilities: *authoritarianism may seem a lesser evil than abject poverty.*
– ORIGIN Middle English: a double comparative, from **LESS** + **-ER**[2].

> **USAGE** On the punctuation of lesser in compound adjectives, see usage at **WELL**[1].

Less·er An·til·les see **ANTILLES**.

less·er cel·an·dine ▶ **n.** see **CELANDINE**.

less·er-known ▶ **adj.** not as well or widely known as others of the same kind.

less·er pan·da ▶ **n.** another term for **RED PANDA**.

Less·er Sun·da Is·lands see **SUNDA ISLANDS**.

Les·sing /'lesiNG/, Doris (May) (1919–), British novelist and short-story writer, brought up in Rhodesia. Notable novels: *The Grass is Singing* (1950), *The Golden Notebook* (1962), and *Canopus in Argos: Archives* (science-fiction quintet, 1979–83). Nobel Prize for Literature (2007).

Les Six /lā 'sēs/ (also **the Six**) a group of six Parisian composers (Louis Durey, Arthur Honegger, Darius Milhaud, Germaine Tailleferre, Georges Auric, and Francis Poulenc) formed after World War I, whose music represents a reaction against Romanticism and Impressionism.
– ORIGIN French, literally 'the Six.'

-lessly ▶ **suffix** forming adverbs corresponding to adjectives ending in *-less.*
– ORIGIN see **-LESS**, **-LY**[2].

-lessness ▶ **suffix** forming nouns corresponding to adjectives ending in *-less.*
– ORIGIN see **-LESS**, **-NESS**.

les·son /'lesən/ ▶ **n. 1** an amount of teaching given at one time; a period of learning or teaching: *an advanced lesson in math | a driving lesson.* ■ a thing learned or to be learned by a student. ■ a thing learned by experience: *the tragedy is a lesson in disappointment.* ■ an occurrence, example, or punishment that serves or should serve to warn or encourage: *let that be a lesson to you!*
2 a passage from the Bible read aloud during a church service, esp. either of two readings at morning and evening prayer in the Anglican Church.
▶ **v.** [with obj.] archaic instruct or teach (someone). ■ admonish or rebuke (someone).
– PHRASES **learn one's lesson** acquire a greater understanding of the world through a particular unpleasant or stressful experience. **teach someone a lesson** punish or hurt someone as a deterrent: *they were teaching me a lesson for daring to complain.*
– ORIGIN Middle English: from Old French *leçon*, from Latin *lectio* (see **LECTION**).

les·sor /'lesˌôr, le'sôr/ ▶ **n.** a person who leases or lets a property to another; a landlord.
– ORIGIN late Middle English: from Anglo-Norman French, from Old French *lesser* 'let, leave.'

lest /lest/ ▶ **conj.** formal with the intention of preventing (something undesirable); to avoid the risk of: *he spent whole days in his room, headphones on lest he disturb anyone.* ■ (after a clause indicating fear) because of the possibility of something undesirable happening; in case: *she sat up late worrying lest he be held up on the way home.*
– ORIGIN Old English *thȳ lǣs the* 'whereby less that,' later *the lǣste.*

> **USAGE** There are very few contexts in English where the subjunctive mood is, strictly speaking, required: **lest** remains one of them. Thus the standard use is *she was worrying* **lest** *he* **be** *attacked* (not **lest** *he was attacked*), or *she is using headphones* **lest** *she* **disturb** *anyone* (not **lest** *she* **disturbs** *anyone*). See also **SUBJUNCTIVE**.

Lés·vos /'lezˌvôs/ Greek name for **LESBOS**.

let[1] /let/ ▶ **v.** (**lets**, **letting**; past and past participle **let**)
1 [with obj. and infinitive] not prevent or forbid; allow: *my boss let me leave early | you mustn't let yourself get so involved.* ■ [with obj.] allow to pass in a particular direction: *could you let the dog out? | a tiny window that let in hardly any light.*
2 [with obj. and infinitive] used in the imperative to formulate various expressions. ■ (**let us** or **let's**) used as a polite way of making or responding to a suggestion, giving an instruction, or introducing a remark: *let's have a drink | "Shall we go?" "Yes, let's."* ■ (**let me** or **let us**) used to make a polite offer of help: *"Here, let me," offered Bruce.* ■ used to express one's strong desire for something to happen or be the case: *"Dear God," Jessica prayed, "let him be all right."* ■ used as a way of expressing defiance or challenge: *if he wants to walk out, well, let him!* ■ used to express an assumption upon which a theory or calculation is to be based: *let A and B stand for X and Y, respectively.*
3 [with obj.] allow someone to have the use of (a room or property) in return for regular payments; rent: *homeowners will be able to let rooms to lodgers without having to pay tax | they've* **let out** *their apartment.*
4 [with obj.] award (a contract for a particular project) to an applicant: *preliminary contracts were let and tunneling work started.*
– PHRASES **let alone** used to indicate that something is far less likely, possible, or suitable than something else already mentioned: *he was incapable of leading a bowling team, let alone a country.* **let someone/something alone** see **ALONE**. **let someone/something be** stop disturbing or interfering with: *let him be—he knows what he wants.* **let someone down gently** seek to give someone bad news in a way that avoids causing them too much distress or humiliation. **let something drop** (or **fall**) casually reveal a piece of information: *from the things he let drop, I think there was a woman in his life.* **let fall** Geometry draw (a perpendicular) from an outside point to a line. **let fly** attack, either physically or verbally: *the troops let fly with tear gas.* **let oneself go 1** act in an unrestrained or uninhibited way: *you need to unwind and let yourself go.* **2** become careless or untidy in one's habits or appearance: *he's really let himself go since my mother died.* **let someone/something go 1** allow someone or something to escape or go free: *they let the hostages go.* ■ dismiss an employee. **2** (also **let go** or **let go of**) relinquish one's grip on someone or something: *Adam let go of the reins* | figurative *you must let the past go.* **let someone have it** informal attack someone physically or verbally: *I really let him have it for worrying me so much.* **let in** (or **out**) **the clutch** engage (or release) the clutch of a vehicle by releasing pressure on (or applying it to) the clutch pedal. **let it drop** (or **rest**) say or do no more about a matter or problem. **let it go** (or **pass**) choose not to react to an action or remark: *the decision worried us, but we let it go.* **let someone know** inform someone: *let me know what you think of him.* **let someone/something loose** release someone or something: *let the dog loose for a minute.* ■ allow someone freedom of action in a particular place or situation: *people are only* **let loose on** *the system once they have received sufficient training.* ■ suddenly utter a sound or remark: *he let loose a stream of abuse.* **let me see** (or **think**) used when one is pausing, trying to remember something, or considering one's next words: *now let me see, where did I put it?* **let me tell you** used to emphasize a statement: *let me tell you, I was very scared!* **let off steam** see **STEAM**. **let rip** see **RIP**[1]. **let's face it** (or **let's be honest**) informal used to convey that one must be realistic about an unwelcome fact or situation: *let's be honest, your taste in men is famously bad.* **let slip** see **SLIP**[1]. **let's pretend** a game or set of circumstances in which one behaves as though a fictional or unreal situation were a real one. **let's say** (or **let us say**) used as a way of introducing a hypothetical or possible situation: *let's say we agreed to go our separate ways.* **to let** chiefly Brit. (of a room or property) available for rent.
– PHRASAL VERBS **let down** (of an aircraft or a pilot) descend before making a landing. **let someone down** fail to support or help someone as they had hoped or expected. ■ (**let someone/something down**) have a detrimental effect on the overall quality or success of someone or something: *the whole machine is let down by the tacky keyboard.* **let something down 1** lower something slowly or in stages: *they let down a basket on a chain.* **2** make a garment longer, esp. by lowering the hem. **let someone in** admit someone to a room, building, or area: *I had to wake up my roommate to let me in.* **let oneself in for** informal involve oneself in (something likely to be difficult or unpleasant): *I didn't know what I was letting myself in for.* **let someone in on/into** allow someone to know or share (something secret or confidential): *I'll let you into a secret.* **let something into** set something back into (the surface to which it is fixed), so that it does not project from it: *the basin is partly let into the wall.* **let someone off 1** punish someone lightly or not at all for a misdemeanor or offense: *he was let off with a warning.* **2** excuse someone from a task or obligation: *he let me off work for the day.* **let something off** cause a gun, firework, or bomb to fire or explode. **let on** informal **1** reveal or divulge information to someone: *she knows a lot more than she lets on* | [with clause] *I never let on that he made me feel anxious.* **2** pretend: [with clause] *they all let on that they didn't hear me.* **let out** (of lessons at school, a meeting, or an entertainment) finish, so that those attending are able to leave: *his classes let out at noon.* **let someone out** release someone from obligation or suspicion: *they've started looking for motives—that lets me out.* **let something out 1** utter a sound or cry: *he let out a sigh of happiness.* **2** make a garment looser or larger, typically by adjusting a seam. **3** reveal a piece of information: [with clause] *she let out that he'd given her a ride home.* **let up** informal (of something undesirable) become less intense or severe: *the rain's letting up—it'll be clear soon.* ■ relax one's efforts: *she was so far ahead that she could afford to let up a bit.* ■ (**let up on**) informal treat or deal with in a more lenient manner: *she didn't let up on Cunningham.*
– ORIGIN Old English *lǣtan* 'leave behind, leave out,' of Germanic origin; related to Dutch *laten* and German *lassen*, also to **LATE**.

let[2] ▶ **n.** (in racket sports) a play that is nullified and has to be played again, esp. when a served ball touches the top of the net.
▶ **v.** (**lets**, **letting**; past and past participle **letted** or **let**) [with obj.] archaic hinder: *pray you let us not; we fain would greet our mother.*
– PHRASES **let or hindrance** formal obstruction or impediment: *the passport opened frontiers to the traveler without let or hindrance.* **play a let** (in tennis, squash, etc.) play a point again because the ball or one of the players has been obstructed.
– ORIGIN Old English *lettan* 'hinder,' of Germanic origin; related to Dutch *letten*, also to **LATE**.

-let ▶ **suffix 1** (forming nouns) denoting a smaller or lesser kind: *booklet | starlet.*
2 denoting articles of ornament or dress: *anklet | bracelet.*
– ORIGIN originally corresponding to French *-ette* added to nouns ending in *-el.*

let·down /'letˌdoun/ ▶ **n. 1** a disappointment or a feeling of disappointment: *the election was a bit of*

a letdown. ■ a decrease in size, volume, or force: *letdowns in sales have been frequent and widespread.*
2 the release of milk in a nursing mother or lactating animal.
3 Aeronautics the descent of an aircraft or spacecraft before landing.

le·thal /ˈlēTHəl/ ▶ **adj.** sufficient to cause death: *a lethal cocktail of alcohol and pills.* ■ harmful or destructive: *the Krakatoa eruption was the most lethal on record.*
– DERIVATIVES **le·thal·i·ty** /lēˈTHalətē/ **n.**, **le·thal·ly adv.**
– ORIGIN late 16th cent. (in the sense 'causing spiritual death'): from Latin *lethalis*, from *lethum*, a variant (influenced by Greek *lēthē* 'forgetfulness') of *letum* 'death.'

le·thal cham·ber ▶ **n.** an enclosed space in which animals may be killed with gas.

le·thal gene ▶ **n.** a gene that is capable of causing the death of an organism, usually during the development of the embryo. Also called **lethal factor**, **lethal mutation**.

le·thal in·jec·tion ▶ **n.** an injection administered for the purposes of euthanasia or as a means of capital punishment.

le·thar·gic /ləˈTHärjik/ ▶ **adj.** affected by lethargy; sluggish and apathetic: *I felt tired and a little lethargic.*
– DERIVATIVES **le·thar·gi·cal·ly** /-jik(ə)lē/ **adv.**
– ORIGIN late Middle English: via Latin from Greek *lēthargikos*, from *lēthargos* 'forgetful.'

leth·ar·gy /ˈleTHərjē/ ▶ **n.** a lack of energy and enthusiasm: *periods of weakness and lethargy* | [in sing.] *she might have sunk into a lethargy.* ■ Medicine a pathological state of sleepiness or deep unresponsiveness and inactivity.
– ORIGIN late Middle English: via Old French from late Latin *lethargia*, from Greek *lēthargia*, from *lēthargos* 'forgetful,' from the base of *lanthanesthai* 'forget.'

Le·the /ˈlēTHē, liˈTHē-/ Greek Mythology a river in Hades whose water when drunk made the souls of the dead forget their life on earth.
– DERIVATIVES **Le·the·an** /ˈlēTHēən/ **adj.**
– ORIGIN via Latin from Greek *lēthē* 'forgetfulness,' from the base of *lanthanesthai* 'forget.'

Le·to /ˈlētō/ Greek Mythology the daughter of a Titan, mother (by Zeus) of Artemis and Apollo. Roman name **Latona**.

let's /lets/ ▶ **contraction** let us: *let's meet for a drink sometime.*

let·ter /ˈletər/ ▶ **n. 1** a character representing one or more of the sounds used in speech; any of the symbols of an alphabet: *a capital letter.* ■ a school or college initial as a mark of proficiency, esp. in sports: *I earned a varsity letter in tennis* | [as modifier] *a letter jacket.*
2 a written, typed, or printed communication, esp. one sent in an envelope by mail or messenger: *he sent a letter to Mrs. Falconer.* ■ (**letters**) a legal or formal document of this kind.
3 the precise terms of a statement or requirement; the strict verbal interpretation: *we must be seen to keep the spirit of the law as well as the letter.*
4 (**letters**) literature: *the world of letters.* ■ archaic scholarly knowledge; erudition.
5 Printing a style of typeface.
▶ **v. 1** [with obj.] inscribe letters or writing on: *her name was lettered in gold.* ■ classify with letters: *he numbered and lettered the paragraphs.*
2 [no obj.] informal be given a school or college initial as a mark of proficiency in sports: *juniors who lettered in soccer, basketball, or softball.*
– PHRASES **to the letter** with adherence to every detail: *the method was followed to the letter.*
– ORIGIN Middle English: from Old French *lettre*, from Latin *litera*, *littera* 'letter of the alphabet,' (plural) 'epistle, literature, culture.'

let·ter bomb ▶ **n.** an explosive device hidden in a small package and sent to someone with the intention of harming or killing them.

let·ter·box /ˈletərˌbäks/ ▶ **n.** (chiefly in the UK) a mailbox. ■ [usu. as modifier] a format for presenting widescreen films on a standard television screen in which the image is displayed in approximately its original proportions across the middle of the screen, leaving horizontal black bands above and below: *this uncut version is presented in letterbox format.*
▶ **v.** [with obj.] record (a widescreen film) onto video in letterbox format.

let·ter car·ri·er ▶ **n.** a mail carrier.

let·tered /ˈletərd/ ▶ **adj.** dated formally educated: *though not lettered, he read widely.*

let·ter·form /ˈletərˌfôrm/ ▶ **n.** the graphic form of a letter of the alphabet, either as written or in a particular type font.

let·ter·head /ˈletərˌhed/ ▶ **n.** a printed heading on stationery stating a person's or organization's name and address. ■ a sheet of paper with such a heading.

let·ter·ing /ˈletəriNG/ ▶ **n.** the letters inscribed on something, esp. decorative ones.

let·ter·man /ˈletərˌman, -mən/ ▶ **n.** a high school or college student who has earned a letter in an interscholastic or intercollegiate activity, esp. a sport.

let·ter mis·sive (also **letters missive**) ▶ **n.** in the Anglican church, a letter from a monarch to a dean and chapter nominating a person to be elected bishop.

let·ter of cred·it ▶ **n.** a letter issued by a bank to another bank (typically in a different country) to serve as a guarantee for payments made to a specified person under specified conditions.

let·ter of in·tent ▶ **n.** a document containing a declaration of the intentions of the writer.

let·ter of marque /märk/ ▶ **n.** (usu. **letters of marque**) historical a license to fit out an armed vessel and use it in the capture of enemy merchant shipping and to commit acts that would otherwise have constituted piracy. ■ a ship carrying such a license.
– ORIGIN late Middle English: Law French *marque*, from Old French *marque* 'right of reprisal.'

let·ter-per·fect ▶ **adj.** (of an actor or speaker) knowing by heart the words for one's part or speech. ■ accurate to the smallest verbal detail: *when he delivered a manuscript, it was letter-perfect.*

let·ter·press /ˈletərˌpres/ ▶ **n. 1** printing from a hard, raised image under pressure, using viscous ink.
2 Brit. printed text as opposed to illustrations.

let·ter·set /ˈletərˌset/ ▶ **n.** a method of printing in which ink is transferred from a raised surface to a blanket wrapped around a cylinder and from that to the paper.
– ORIGIN 1960s: blend of **letterpress** and **offset**.

let·ters mis·sive ▶ **n.** variant of **letter missive**.

let·ters of ad·min·is·tra·tion ▶ **plural n.** Law authority to administer the estate of someone who has died without making a will.

let·ters pat·ent /ˈpatnt/ ▶ **plural n.** an open document issued by a monarch or government conferring a patent or other right.
– ORIGIN late Middle English: from medieval Latin *litterae patentes*, literally 'letters lying open.'

let·ters rog·a·to·ry /ˈrōgəˌtôrē, ˈrägə-/ ▶ **plural n.** Law documents making a request through a foreign court for the obtaining of information or evidence from a specified person within the jurisdiction of that court.
– ORIGIN mid 19th cent.: *rogatory* from medieval Latin *rogatorius* 'interrogatory.'

let·ters tes·ta·men·ta·ry ▶ **plural n.** Law a document issued by a court or public official authorizing the executor of a will to take control of a deceased person's estate.

let·tuce /ˈletis/ ▶ **n. 1** a cultivated plant of the daisy family, with edible leaves that are a usual ingredient of salads. Many varieties of lettuce have been developed with a range of form, texture, and color. ● *Lactuca sativa*, family Compositae. ■ used in names of other plants with edible green leaves, e.g., **lamb's lettuce**, **sea lettuce**.
2 informal paper money; greenbacks.
– ORIGIN Middle English: from Old French *letues*, *laitues*, plural of *laitue*, from Latin *lactuca*, from *lac*, *lact-* 'milk' (because of its milky juice).

let·up /ˈletˌəp/ ▶ **n.** [in sing.] informal a pause or reduction in the intensity of something dangerous, difficult, or tiring: *there had been no letup in the eruption.*

Letz·e·burg·esch /ˈletseˌbo͝orgəsh/ (also **Letzebuergesch**) ▶ **n. & adj.** another term for **Luxemburgish**.
– ORIGIN from a local name for **Luxembourg** + *-esch* (equivalent of **-ish**[1]).

le·u /ˈlā(y)o͞o/ ▶ **n.** (pl. **lei** /lā/) the basic monetary unit of Romania, equal to 100 bani.
– ORIGIN Romanian, literally 'lion.'

leu·cine /ˈlo͞oˌsēn, -sin/ ▶ **n.** Biochemistry a hydrophobic amino acid that is a constituent of most proteins. It is an essential nutrient in the diet of vertebrates. ● Chem. formula: $(CH_3)_2CHCH_2CH(NH_2)COOH$.
– ORIGIN early 19th cent.: coined in French from Greek *leukos* 'white' + **-ine**[4].

leu·cite /ˈlo͞oˌsīt/ ▶ **n.** a gray or white potassium aluminosilicate, typically found in alkali volcanic rocks.
– DERIVATIVES **leu·cit·ic** /lo͞oˈsitik/ **adj.**

leuco- ▶ **comb. form** chiefly Brit. variant spelling of **leuko-**.
– ORIGIN from Greek *leukos* 'white.'

leu·co·der·ma /ˌlo͞okəˈdərmə/ (also **leukoderma**) ▶ **n.** another term for **vitiligo**.

leu·con /ˈlo͞oˌkän/ ▶ **n.** Zoology a sponge of the most complex structure, composed of a mass of flagellated chambers and water canals. Compare with **ascon** and **sycon**.
– DERIVATIVES **leu·co·noid** /-kəˌnoid/ **adj.**

leu·co·plast /ˈlo͞okəˌplast/ ▶ **n.** Botany a colorless organelle found in plant cells, used for the storage of starch or oil.

leu·ke·mi·a /lo͞oˈkēmēə/ (Brit. **leukaemia**) ▶ **n.** a malignant progressive disease in which the bone marrow and other blood-forming organs produce increased numbers of immature or abnormal leukocytes. These suppress the production of normal blood cells, leading to anemia and other symptoms.
– DERIVATIVES **leu·ke·mic** /-ˈkēmik/ **adj.**
– ORIGIN mid 19th cent.: coined in German from Greek *leukos* 'white' + *haima* 'blood.'

leu·ke·mo·gen·ic /lo͞oˌkēməˈjenik/ (Brit. **leukaemogenic**) ▶ **adj.** Medicine relating to or promoting the development of leukemia.
– DERIVATIVES **leu·ke·mo·gen** /-ˈkēməjən, -ˌjen/ **n.**, **leu·ke·mo·gen·e·sis** /-ˌkēməˈjenəsis/ **n.**

leuko- (also chiefly Brit. **leuco-**) ▶ **comb. form 1** white: *leukoma.*
2 representing **leukocyte**.

leu·ko·cyte /ˈlo͞okəˌsīt, -kō-/ (Brit. also **leucocyte**) ▶ **n.** Physiology a colorless cell that circulates in the blood and body fluids and is involved in counteracting foreign substances and disease; a white (blood) cell. There are several types, all ameboid cells with a nucleus, including lymphocytes, granulocytes, monocytes, and macrophages.
– DERIVATIVES **leu·ko·cyt·ic** /ˌlo͞okəˈsitik/ **adj.**

leu·ko·cy·to·sis /ˌlo͞okəsīˈtōsis, -kō-/ (Brit. also **leucocytosis**) ▶ **n.** Medicine an increase in the number of white cells in the blood, esp. during an infection.
– DERIVATIVES **leu·ko·cy·tot·ic** /-ˈtätik/ **adj.**

leu·ko·der·ma /ˌlo͞okəˈdərmə/ (also **leucoderma**) ▶ **n.** another term for **vitiligo**.

leu·ko·ma /lo͞oˈkōmə/ ▶ **n.** Medicine a white opacity in the cornea of the eye.
– ORIGIN early 18th cent.: modern Latin, from Greek *leukōma*.

leu·ko·pe·ni·a /ˌlo͞okəˈpēnēə/ (Brit. also **leucopenia**) ▶ **n.** Medicine a reduction in the number of white cells in the blood, typical of various diseases.
– DERIVATIVES **leu·ko·pe·nic** /-nik/ **adj.**
– ORIGIN late 19th cent.: from Greek *leukos* 'white' + *penia* 'poverty.'

leu·ko·pla·ki·a /ˌlo͞okəˈplākēə/ (also **leucoplakia**) ▶ **n.** a mucous membrane disorder characterized by white patches, esp. on the cheek, tongue, vulva, or penis. Also called **leukoplasia**.

leu·ko·pla·sia /ˌlo͞okəˈplāZHə, -ZHēə, -zēə/ (also **leucoplasia**) ▶ **n.** another term for **leukoplakia**.

leu·kor·rhe·a /ˌlo͞okəˈrēə/ (also **leucorrhea**, Brit. **leucorrhoea**) ▶ **n.** a whitish or yellowish discharge of mucus from the vagina.

leu·ko·sis /lo͞oˈkōsis/ (Brit. also **leucosis**) ▶ **n.** a leukemic disease of animals, esp. one of a group of malignant viral diseases of poultry or cattle.
– DERIVATIVES **leu·kot·ic** /-ˈkätik/ **adj.**

leu·kot·o·my /lo͞oˈkätəmē/ ▶ **n.** (pl. **leukotomies**) the surgical cutting of white nerve fibers within the brain, esp. prefrontal lobotomy, formerly used to treat mental illness.

leu·ko·tri·ene /ˌlo͞okəˈtrīˌēn/ ▶ **n.** Biochemistry any of a group of biologically active compounds, originally isolated from leukocytes. They are metabolites of arachidonic acid, containing three conjugated double bonds.

lev /lev, lef/ ▶ **n.** the basic monetary unit of Bulgaria, equal to 100 stotinki.
– ORIGIN Bulgarian, variant of *lăv* 'lion.'

Lev. ▶ **abbr.** Bible Leviticus.

Le·val·lois /ləˌvalˈwä, -ˈvalˌwä/ ▶ **n.** [usu. as modifier] Archaeology a flint-working technique associated with the Mousterian culture of the Neanderthals, in which a flint is trimmed so that a flake of predetermined size and shape can be struck from it.
– DERIVATIVES **Le·val·loi·si·an** /ˌlevəˈloizēən, ləˌvalˈwäzēən/ **adj.**
– ORIGIN early 20th cent.: named after a suburb of northern Paris.

le·va·mi·sole /ləˈvaməˌsōl/ ▶ **n.** Medicine a synthetic compound used as an anthelmintic drug (esp. in

animals) and in cancer chemotherapy. ● A polycyclic imidazole derivative; chem. formula: $C_{11}H_{12}N_2S$.
– ORIGIN 1960s: from LEVO- (it being a levorotatory isomer) + (*tetra*)*misole*, the name of an anthelmintic drug.

Le·vant /lə'vant, lə'vänt/ archaic the eastern part of the Mediterranean with its islands and neighboring countries.
– ORIGIN late 15th cent.: from French, literally 'rising,' present participle of *lever* 'to lift' used as a noun in the sense 'point of sunrise, east.'

le·vant /lə'vant/ ▶ v. [no obj.] Brit. archaic run away, typically leaving unpaid debts.
– ORIGIN early 17th cent.: perhaps from LEVANT: compare with French *faire voile en Levant* 'be stolen or spirited away,' literally 'set sail for the Levant.'

le·vant·er[1] /lə'vantər/ ▶ n. a strong easterly wind in the Mediterranean region.

le·vant·er[2] ▶ n. archaic a person who runs away leaving unpaid debts.

Le·van·tine /'levən,tīn, -,tēn, lə'vantin/ chiefly archaic ▶ adj. of or trading to the Levant: *the Levantine coast.*
▶ n. a person who lives in or comes from the Levant.

Le·vant mo·roc·co (also **Levant**) ▶ n. high-grade, large-grained morocco leather.

Le·vant worm·seed ▶ n. see WORMSEED.

le·va·tor /lə'vātər/ (also **levator muscle**) ▶ n. Anatomy a muscle whose contraction causes the raising of a part of the body.
– ORIGIN early 17th cent.: from Latin, literally 'a person who lifts,' from *levare* 'raise, lift.'

lev·ee[1] /'levē/ ▶ n. an embankment built to prevent the overflow of a river. ■ a ridge of sediment deposited naturally alongside a river by overflowing water. ■ a landing place; a quay. ■ a ridge of earth surrounding a field to be irrigated.
– ORIGIN early 18th cent. (originally US): from French *levée*, feminine past participle of *lever* 'to lift.'

lev·ee[2] ▶ n. a reception or assembly of people, in particular: ■ a formal reception of visitors or guests. ■ historical an afternoon assembly for men held by the British monarch or their representative. ■ archaic a reception of visitors just after rising from bed.
– ORIGIN late 17th cent. (denoting a reception of visitors after rising from bed): from French *levé*, variant of *lever* 'rising,' from the verb *lever*.

lev·el /'levəl/ ▶ n. **1** a position on a real or imaginary scale of amount, quantity, extent, or quality: *a high level of unemployment | debt rose to unprecedented levels.* ■ a social, moral, or intellectual standard: *at six he could play chess at an advanced level.* ■ a position in a real or notional hierarchy: *a fairly junior level of management.*
2 a height or distance from the ground or another stated or understood base: *storms caused river levels to rise.*
3 a device consisting of a sealed glass tube partially filled with alcohol or other liquid, containing an air bubble whose position reveals whether a surface is perfectly level or plumb. Also called SPIRIT LEVEL, BUBBLE LEVEL. ■ Surveying an instrument for giving a horizontal line of sight.
4 a flat tract of land: *flooded levels.*
▶ adj. **1** having a flat and even surface without slopes or bumps: *we had reached level ground.* ■ at the same height as someone or something else: *his eyes were level with hers.* ■ having the same relative position; not in front of or behind: *the car braked suddenly, then backed rapidly until it was level with me.* ■ (of a quantity of a dry substance) with the contents not rising above the brim of the measure: *a level teaspoon of salt.* ■ unchanged; not having risen or fallen: *earnings were level at 57 cents a share.*
2 calm and steady: *"Adrian," she said in her most level voice.*
▶ v. (**levels, leveling, leveled**; also chiefly Brit. **levels, levelling, levelled**) **1** [with obj.] give a flat and even surface to: *contractors started leveling the ground for the new power station.* ■ Surveying ascertain differences in the height of (land). ■ demolish (a building or town): *bulldozers are now waiting to level their home.*
2 [no obj.] (**level off/out**) begin to fly horizontally after climbing or diving. ■ (of a path, road, or incline) cease to slope upward or downward: *the track leveled out, and there below us was the bay.* ■ cease to fall or rise in number, amount, or quantity: *inflation has leveled out at an acceptable rate.* ■ [with obj.] (**level something up/down**) increase or reduce the amount, number, or quantity of something in order to remove a disparity.
3 [with obj.] aim (a weapon): *he leveled a long-barreled pistol at us.* ■ direct (a criticism or accusation): *accusations of corruption had been leveled against him.*
4 [no obj.] (**level with**) informal be frank or honest with (someone): *when are you going to level with me?*
– PHRASES **do one's level best** do one's utmost; make all possible efforts. **find its (own) level** (of a liquid) reach the same height in containers that are interconnected. ■ reach a stable level, value, or position without interference. **find one's (own) level** (of a person) reach a position or competency that seems appropriate and natural in relation to one's associates. **a level playing field** a situation in which everyone has a fair and equal chance of succeeding. **on the level** informal honest; truthful: *Eddie said my story was on the level.* **on a level with** in the same horizontal plane as. ■ equal with: *they were treated as menials, on a level with cooks.*
– DERIVATIVES **lev·el·ly** adv. (sense 2 of the adjective), **lev·el·ness** n.
– ORIGIN Middle English (denoting an instrument to determine whether a surface is horizontal): from Old French *livel*, based on Latin *libella*, diminutive of *libra* 'scales, balance.'

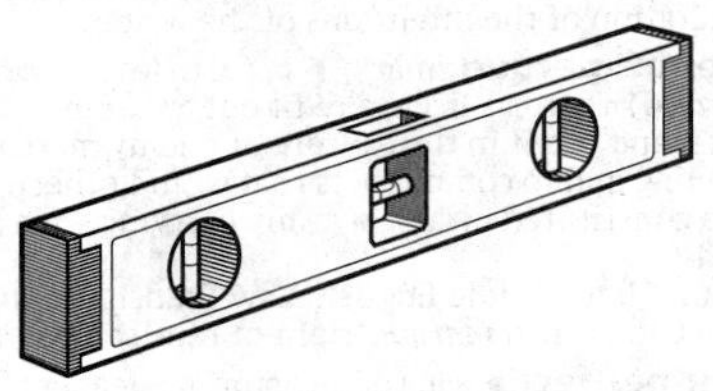
level 3

lev·el cross·ing ▶ n. British term for GRADE CROSSING.

lev·el·er /'lev(ə)lər/ (Brit. **leveller**) ▶ n. **1** a person who advocates the abolition of social distinctions. ■ (**Leveller**) an extreme radical dissenter in the English Civil War (1642–49), calling for the abolition of the monarchy, social and agrarian reforms, and religious freedom.
2 a person or thing that levels something.

lev·el·head·ed /'levəl'hedid/ ▶ adj. calm and sensible.
– DERIVATIVES **lev·el·head·ed·ly** adv., **lev·el·head·ed·ness** n.

lev·el·ing rod ▶ n. a graduated pole with a movable marker, held upright and used with a surveying instrument to measure differences in elevation. Also called **leveling pole, leveling staff**.

lev·el·ing screw ▶ n. a screw for adjusting part of a machine or instrument to a precise level.

lev·er /'levər, 'lēvər/ ▶ n. a rigid bar resting on a pivot, used to help move a heavy or firmly fixed load with one end when pressure is applied to the other. ■ a projecting arm or handle that is moved to operate a mechanism: *she pulled a lever at the base of the cage.* ■ a means of exerting pressure on someone to act in a particular way: *rich countries increasingly use foreign aid as a lever to promote political pluralism.*
▶ v. [with obj.] lift or move with a lever: *she levered the lid off the pot with a screwdriver.* ■ move (someone or something) with a concerted physical effort: *she levered herself up against the pillows.* ■ [no obj.] use a lever: *the men got hold of the coffin and levered at it with crowbars.* ■ pressurize (someone) to do something: *another sticking point is the money that will be required to lever the unions into accepting a deal.*
– ORIGIN Middle English: from Old French *levier*, *leveor*, from *lever* 'to lift.'

lever

lev·er·age /'lev(ə)rij, 'lēv(ə)rij/ ▶ n. **1** the exertion of force by means of a lever or an object used in the manner of a lever: *my spade hit something solid that wouldn't respond to leverage.* ■ mechanical advantage gained in this way: *use a metal bar to increase the leverage.* ■ the power to influence a person or situation to achieve a particular outcome: *the right wing had lost much of its political leverage in the Assembly.*
2 Finance the ratio of a company's loan capital (debt) to the value of its common stock (equity). ■ the use of credit or borrowed capital to increase the earning potential of stock.
▶ v. [with obj.] **1** (usu. as adj. **leveraged**) use borrowed capital for (an investment), expecting the profits made to be greater than the interest payable: *a leveraged takeover bid.*
2 use (something) to maximum advantage: *the organization needs to leverage its key resources.*

lev·er·aged buy·out ▶ n. the purchase of a controlling share in a company by its management, using outside capital.

lev·er es·cape·ment ▶ n. a mechanism in a watch connecting the escape wheel and the balance wheel with two levers.

lev·er·et /'lev(ə)rit/ ▶ n. a young hare in its first year.
– ORIGIN late Middle English: from Anglo-Norman French, diminutive of *levre*, from Latin *lepus, lepor-* 'hare.'

Le·ver·hulme /'levər,hyōōm/, 1st Viscount (1851–1925), English industrialist and philanthropist; born *William Hesketh Lever*. He and his brother founded Lever Bros., the company that later formed the basis of the international corporation Unilever. He founded the model village Port Sunlight for his company's workers.

Le·ver·ku·sen /'lāvər,kōōzən/ an industrial city in western Germany, in North Rhine–Westphalia, on the Rhine River north of Cologne; pop. 161,300 (est. 2006).

Le Ver·ri·er /lə ver'yā/, Urbain (1811–77), French mathematician. His analysis of the motions of the planets suggested that an unknown body was disrupting the orbit of Uranus. Le Verrier prompted the German astronomer **Johann Galle** (1812–1910) to investigate, and the planet Neptune was discovered in 1846.

Le·vi[1] /'lē,vī/ (in the Bible) a Hebrew patriarch, third son of Jacob and Leah. ■ the tribe of Israel traditionally descended from him.

Le·vi[2] /'levē/, Primo (1919–87), Italian writer and chemist. His experiences as a survivor of Auschwitz are recounted in his first book, *If This Is a Man* (1947).

le·vi·a·than /lə'vīəTHən/ ▶ n. (in biblical use) a sea monster, identified in different passages with the whale and the crocodile (e.g., Job 41, Ps. 74:14), and with the Devil (after Isa. 27:1). ■ a very large aquatic creature, esp. a whale: *the great leviathans of the deep.* ■ a thing that is very large or powerful, esp. a ship. ■ an autocratic monarch or state. [with allusion to Hobbes' *Leviathan* (1651).]
– ORIGIN via late Latin from Hebrew *liwyāṯān*.

lev·i·gate /'levə,gāt/ ▶ v. [with obj.] reduce (a substance) to a fine powder or smooth paste.
– DERIVATIVES **lev·i·ga·tion** /,levə'gāSHən/ n.
– ORIGIN mid 16th cent.: from Latin *levigat-* 'made smooth, polished,' from the verb *levigare*, from *levis* 'smooth.'

lev·in /'levin/ ▶ n. archaic lightning; thunderbolts.
– ORIGIN Middle English: probably of Scandinavian origin.

lev·i·rate /'levərit, -,rāt/ ▶ n. (usu. **the levirate**) a custom of the ancient Hebrews and other peoples by which a man may be obliged to marry his brother's widow: [as modifier] *levirate marriages.*
– ORIGIN early 18th cent.: from Latin *levir* 'brother-in-law' + -ATE[1].

Le·vi's /'lē,vīz/ ▶ plural n. trademark a brand of denim jeans.
– ORIGIN 1920s: named after *Levi* Strauss, original US manufacturer in the 1860s.

Lé·vi-Strauss /,lāvē 'strous/, Claude (1908–2009), French social anthropologist. He regarded language as an essential common denominator underlying cultural phenomena.

lev·i·tate /'levə,tāt/ ▶ v. rise or cause to rise and hover in the air, esp. by means of supernatural or magical power: [no obj.] *he seems to levitate about three inches off the ground* | [with obj.] *he was focused on levitating the backpack.*
– DERIVATIVES **lev·i·ta·tion** /,levə'tāSHən/ n., **lev·i·ta·tor** /-,tātər/ n.
– ORIGIN late 17th cent.: from Latin *levis* 'light,' on the pattern of *gravitate*.

Le·vite /'lē,vīt/ ▶ n. a member of the Hebrew tribe of Levi, esp. of that part of it that provided assistants to the priests in the worship in the Jewish temple.
– ORIGIN Middle English: from late Latin *levita*, from Greek *leuitēs*, from Hebrew *Lēwī* 'Levi.'

Le·vit·i·cal /lə'vitikəl/ ▶ adj. **1** of or relating to the Levites or the tribe of Levi: *a Levitical priest.*
2 Judaism (of rules concerning codes of conduct, temple rituals, etc.) derived from the biblical Book of Leviticus: *a Levitical edict.*
– ORIGIN mid 16th cent.: via late Latin from Greek *levitikos*, from *Levi* (see LEVITE), + -AL.

Le·vit·i·cus /lə'vitikəs/ the third book of the Bible, containing details of law and ritual.

Lev·it·town /'levət,toun/ a village in central Long Island in New York, noted for its "cookie-cutter" houses, developed after World War II; pop. 53,067

(2000). There are also Levittowns in New Jersey, Pennsylvania, and Puerto Rico.

lev·i·ty /ˈlevətē/ ▶ **n.** humor or frivolity, esp. the treatment of a serious matter with humor or in a manner lacking due respect: *as an attempt to introduce a note of levity, the words were a disastrous flop.*
– ORIGIN mid 16th cent.: from Latin *levitas*, from *levis* 'light.'

levo- (also chiefly Brit. **laevo-**) ▶ **comb. form** on or to the left: *levorotatory*.

le·vo·do·pa /ˌlevəˈdōpə, ˌlēvə/ (also **levodopamine** /-ˈdōpəmēn/) ▶ **n.** another term for **L-DOPA**.

le·vo·nor·ges·trel /ˌlēvənôrˈjestrəl/ ▶ **n.** Biochemistry a synthetic steroid hormone that has a similar effect to progesterone and is used in some contraceptive pills.
– ORIGIN 1970s: from **LEVO-** (it being a levorotatory isomer) + *norgestrel*, a synthetic steroid hormone.

le·vo·ro·ta·to·ry /ˌlevəˈrōtəˌtôrē/ (Brit. **laevorotatory**) ▶ **adj.** Chemistry (of a compound) having the property of rotating the plane of a polarized light ray to the left, i.e., counterclockwise facing the oncoming radiation. The opposite of **DEXTROROTATORY**.
– DERIVATIVES **le·vo·ro·ta·tion** /-rōˈtāSHən/ **n.**

lev·u·lose /ˈlevyəˌlōs, -ˌlōz/ (Brit. **laevulose**) ▶ **n.** Chemistry another term for **FRUCTOSE**.

le·vy /ˈlevē/ ▶ **v.** (**levies, levying, levied**) [with obj.] **1** impose (a tax, fee, or fine): *a new tax could be levied on industry to pay for cleaning up contaminated land.* ■ impose a tax, fee, or fine on: *there will be powers to levy the owner.* ■ [no obj.] (**levy on/upon**) seize (property) to satisfy a legal judgment: *there were no goods to levy upon.*
2 archaic enlist (someone) for military service: *he sought to levy one man from each parish for service.* ■ begin to wage (war).
▶ **n.** (pl. **levies**) **1** an act of levying a tax, fee, or fine: *union members were hit with a 2 percent levy on all pay.* ■ a tax so raised. ■ a sum collected for a specific purpose, esp. as a supplement to an existing subscription. ■ an item or set of items of property seized to satisfy a legal judgment.
2 historical an act of enlisting troops. ■ (usu. **levies**) a body of troops that have been enlisted: *lightly armed local levies.*
– DERIVATIVES **lev·i·a·ble adj.**
– ORIGIN Middle English (as a noun): from Old French *levee*, feminine past participle of *lever* 'raise,' from Latin *levare*, from *levis* 'light.'

lewd /lo͞od/ ▶ **adj.** crude and offensive in a sexual way: *she began to gyrate to the music and sing a lewd song.*
– DERIVATIVES **lewd·ly adv.**, **lewd·ness n.**
– ORIGIN Old English *lǣwede*, of unknown origin. The original sense was 'belonging to the laity'; in Middle English, 'belonging to the common people, vulgar,' and later 'worthless, vile, evil,' leading to the current sense.

Lew·is[1] /ˈlo͞o-is/, Cecil Day, see **DAY LEWIS**.

Lew·is[2], C. S. (1898–1963), British novelist, religious writer, and literary scholar; full name *Clive Staples Lewis*. He broadcast and wrote on religious and moral issues and created the imaginary land of Narnia for a series of children's books. Notable works: *The Screwtape Letters* (1942) and *The Lion, the Witch, and the Wardrobe* (1950).

Lew·is[3], Carl (1961–), US track and field athlete; full name *Frederick Carleton Lewis*. He won Olympic gold medals in 1984, 1988, 1992, and 1996 (his ninth) for sprinting and the long jump and broke the world record for the 100 meters on several occasions.

Lew·is[4], Jerry (1926–), US actor, comedian, and director; born *Joseph Levitch*. He was known initially for his act with Dean Martin 1946–1956 but then appeared on his own on the stage and in films and also worked as a director.

Lew·is[5], Jerry Lee (1935–), US rock-and-roll singer and pianist. In 1957, he had hits with "Whole Lotta Shakin' Goin' On" and "Great Balls of Fire." His career was interrupted when his marriage to his 14-year-old cousin caused a public outcry.

Lew·is[6], John Llewellyn (1880–1969), US labor leader. He headed the United Mine Workers 1920–60 and organized the Committee for Industrial Organization 1935, which became the Congress of Industrial Organizations (CIO). He served as its president until 1940.

Lew·is[7], Meriwether (1774–1809), US explorer. Together with William Clark, he led an expedition to explore the newly acquired Louisiana Purchase (1804–06). They traveled from St. Louis to the Pacific Northwest and back. He then served as governor of Louisiana Territory 1807–09.

Lew·is[8], Sinclair (1885–1951), US novelist; full name *Harry Sinclair Lewis*. His satirical works include *Main Street* (1920), *Babbitt* (1922), and *Elmer Gantry* (1927). Nobel Prize for Literature (1930).

lew·is /ˈlo͞o-is/ ▶ **n.** a steel device for gripping heavy blocks of stone or concrete for lifting, consisting of three pieces arranged to form a dovetail, the outside pieces being fixed in a dovetail mortise by the insertion of the middle piece.
– ORIGIN late Middle English: probably from Old French *lous*, plural of *lou(p)* 'wolf,' the name of a kind of siege engine.

Lew·is ac·id ▶ **n.** Chemistry a compound or ionic species that can accept an electron pair from a donor compound.
– ORIGIN 1940s: named after Gilbert N. *Lewis* (1875–1946), US chemist.

Lew·is and Clark Trail the route of the Lewis and Clark expedition that explored the Louisiana Purchase from St. Louis in Missouri to the Pacific coast from 1804 until 1806. Official name **Lewis and Clark National Historic Trail**.

Lew·is base ▶ **n.** Chemistry a compound or ionic species that can donate an electron pair to an acceptor compound.
– ORIGIN 1960s: named after G. N. *Lewis* (see **LEWIS ACID**).

Lew·is gun ▶ **n.** chiefly historical a light, air-cooled machine gun with a magazine operated by gas from its own firing, used mainly in World War I.
– ORIGIN early 20th cent.: named after its inventor, Isaac N. *Lewis* (1858–1931), a colonel in the US Army.

lew·is·ite /ˈlo͞oəˌsīt/ ▶ **n.** a dark, oily liquid producing an irritant gas that causes blisters, developed for use in chemical warfare. ● An organic compound of arsenic; chem. formula: $ClCH{=}CHAsCl_2$.
– ORIGIN 1920s: named after Winford L. *Lewis* (1878–1943), US chemist.

Lew·is·ton an industrial city in southwestern Maine, on the Androscoggin River, opposite Auburn; pop. 35,131 (est. 2008).

lex /leks/ ▶ **n.** (pl. **leges** /ˈlējēz, ˈleges/) **LAW**.
– ORIGIN Latin, literally 'law.'

lex. ▶ **abbr.** ■ lexical. ■ lexicon.

Lex·an /ˈlekˌsan/ ▶ **n.** trademark a transparent plastic (polycarbonate) of high impact strength, used for cockpit canopies, bulletproof screens, etc.
– ORIGIN 1950s: an invented name.

lex·eme /ˈlekˌsēm/ ▶ **n.** Linguistics a basic lexical unit of a language, consisting of one word or several words, considered as an abstract unit, and applied to a family of words related by form or meaning.
– ORIGIN 1940s: from **LEXICON** + **-EME**.

lex fo·ri /ˈleks ˈfôrˌī, ˈfôrˌē/ ▶ **n.** Law the law of the country in which an action is brought.
– ORIGIN Latin, 'law of the court.'

lex·i·cal /ˈleksikəl/ ▶ **adj.** of or relating to the words or vocabulary of a language: *lexical analysis.* ■ relating to or of the nature of a lexicon or dictionary: *a lexical entry.*
– DERIVATIVES **lex·i·cal·ly** /-ik(ə)lē/ **adv.**
– ORIGIN mid 19th cent.: from Greek *lexikos* 'of words' (from *lexis* 'word') + **-AL**.

lex·i·cal mean·ing ▶ **n.** the meaning of a word considered in isolation from the sentence containing it and regardless of its grammatical context, e.g., of *love* in or as represented by *loves, loved, loving*, etc.

lex·i·cog·ra·pher /ˌleksəˈkägrəfər/ ▶ **n.** a person who compiles dictionaries.

lex·i·cog·ra·phy /ˌleksəˈkägrəfē/ ▶ **n.** the practice of compiling dictionaries.
– DERIVATIVES **lex·i·co·graph·ic** /-kəˈgrafik/ **adj.**, **lex·i·co·graph·i·cal** /-kəˈgrafikəl/ **adj.**, **lex·i·co·graph·i·cal·ly** /-kəˈgrafik(ə)lē/ **adv.**

lex·i·col·o·gy /ˌleksəˈkäləjē/ ▶ **n.** the study of the form, meaning, and use of words.
– DERIVATIVES **lex·i·co·log·i·cal** /-kəˈläjikəl/ **adj.**, **lex·i·co·log·i·cal·ly** /-kəˈläjik(ə)lē/ **adv.**

lex·i·con /ˈleksiˌkän, -kən/ ▶ **n.** (pl. **lexicons** or **lexica** /-kə/) the vocabulary of a person, language, or branch of knowledge: *the size of the English lexicon.* ■ a dictionary, esp. of Greek, Hebrew, Syriac, or Arabic: *a Greek–Latin lexicon.*
– ORIGIN early 17th cent.: modern Latin, from Greek *lexikon (biblion)* '(book) of words,' from *lexis* 'word,' from *legein* 'speak.'

lex·i·gram /ˈleksiˌgram/ ▶ **n.** a symbol representing a word, esp. one used in learning a language.

Lex·ing·ton /ˈleksiNGtən/ **1** a city in central Kentucky; pop. 282,114 (est. 2008). It is a noted horse-breeding center.
2 a residential town in northeastern Massachusetts, northwest of Boston; pop. 30,272 (est. 2008). In 1775, it was the scene of the first battle in the American Revolution.

lex·is /ˈleksis/ ▶ **n.** the total stock of words in a language: *a notable loss of English lexis.* ■ the level of language consisting of vocabulary, as opposed to grammar or syntax.
– ORIGIN 1950s (denoting the wording, as opposed to other elements, in a piece of writing): from Greek, literally 'word' (see **LEXICON**).

lex lo·ci /ˈleks ˈlōsī, -ˌsē, -ˌkē, -ˌkī/ ▶ **n.** Law the law of the country in which a transaction is performed, a tort is committed, or a property is situated.
– ORIGIN Latin, 'law of the place.'

lex ta·li·o·nis /ˈleks ˌtālēˈōnis, ˌtalē-/ ▶ **n.** the law of retaliation, whereby a punishment resembles the offense committed in kind and degree.
– ORIGIN Latin, from *lex* 'law' and *talio(n-)* 'retaliation' (from *talis* 'such').

Ley·den /ˈlīdn/ variant spelling of **LEIDEN**.

Ley·den jar ▶ **n.** an early form of capacitor consisting of a glass jar with layers of metal foil on the outside and inside.
– ORIGIN mid 18th cent.: named after *Leyden* (see **LEIDEN**), where it was invented (1745).

Ley·land cy·press /ˈlālənd, ˈlē-/ ▶ **n.** a fast-growing hybrid conifer that is narrowly conical with a dense growth of shoots bearing scalelike leaves, widely grown as a screening plant or for shelter. ● × *Cupressocyparis leylandii*, family Cupressaceae; a hybrid between the Nootka cypress and the Monterey cypress (macrocarpa).
– ORIGIN 1930s: named after Christopher J. *Leyland* (1849–1926), British horticulturist.

Ley·te /ˈlāˌtē, -ˌtā/ an island in the central Philippines; pop. 1,790,400 (est. 2009); chief town, Tacloban.

Ley·te Gulf an inlet of the Philippine Sea, in the eastern Philippines, between Leyte and Samar islands, scene of the destruction of a Japanese fleet in 1944, during World War II.

lez ▶ **n.** variant spelling of **LES**.

lez·zy /ˈlezē/ ▶ **n.** (pl. **lezzies**) informal, usu. offensive a lesbian.

LF ▶ **abbr.** low frequency.

lg. ▶ **abbr.** ■ large. ■ long.

LGBT ▶ **abbr.** lesbian, gay, bisexual, or transgendered.

lge. ▶ **abbr.** large.

LH ▶ **abbr.** Biochemistry luteinizing hormone.

l.h. ▶ **abbr.** left hand.

Lha·sa /ˈläsə/ the capital of Tibet; pop. 140,000. It is situated in the northern Himalayas at an altitude of *c.*11,800 feet (3,600 m) on a tributary of the Brahmaputra River. Known as the Forbidden City until the 20th century because it was closed to foreign visitors, it was the seat of the Dalai Lama until 1959.

Lha·sa ap·so /ˈläsə ˈäpsō, ˈlasə, ˈap-/ ▶ **n.** (pl. **Lhasa apsos**) a dog of a small, long-coated breed, typically gold or gray and white, originating at Lhasa.
– ORIGIN mid 20th cent.: from **LHASA** + Tibetan *a-sob*.

Lhasa apso

LHRH ▶ **abbr.** luteinizing hormone-releasing hormone.

LI ▶ **abbr.** Long Island.

Li ▶ **symbol** the chemical element lithium.

li /lē/ ▶ **n.** (pl. **same**) a Chinese unit of distance, equal to about 0.6 km (0.4 mile).

li·a·bil·i·ty /ˌlīəˈbilətē/ ▶ **n.** (pl. **liabilities**) **1** the state of being responsible for something, esp. by law: *the partners accept unlimited liability for any risks they undertake.* ■ (usu. **liabilities**) a thing for which someone is responsible, esp. a debt or financial obligation: *valuing the company's liabilities and assets.*
2 [usu. in sing.] a person or thing whose presence or behavior is likely to cause embarrassment or put

one at a disadvantage: *he has become a political liability.*

li·a·ble /ˈlī(ə)bəl/ ▶ **adj. 1** responsible by law; legally answerable: *the supplier of goods or services can become* ***liable for*** *breach of contract in a variety of ways.*
2 likely to do or to be something: *patients were liable to faint if they stood up too suddenly.* ■ **(liable to)** likely to experience (something undesirable): *areas liable to flooding.*
– ORIGIN late Middle English: perhaps from Anglo-Norman French, from French *lier* 'to bind,' from Latin *ligare.*

li·aise /lēˈāz/ ▶ **v.** [no obj.] establish a working relationship, typically in order to cooperate on a matter of mutual concern: *she will* ***liaise with*** *teachers across the country.*
– ORIGIN 1920s (originally British military slang): back-formation from LIAISON.

li·ai·son /ˈlēəˌzän, lēˈā-/ ▶ **n. 1** communication or cooperation that facilitates a close working relationship between people or organizations: *the head porter works in close* ***liaison with*** *the reception office.* ■ a person who acts as a link to assist communication or cooperation between groups of people: *he's our liaison with a number of interested parties.* ■ a sexual relationship, esp. one that is secret and involves unfaithfulness to a partner.
2 the binding or thickening agent of a sauce, often based on egg yolks.
3 Phonetics (in French and other languages) the sounding of a consonant that is normally silent at the end of a word because the next word begins with a vowel.
– ORIGIN mid 17th cent. (as a culinary term): from French, from *lier* 'to bind.'

li·ai·son of·fi·cer ▶ **n.** a person who is employed to form a working relationship between two organizations to their mutual benefit.

li·a·na /lēˈänə, -ˈanə/ (also **liane** /-ˈän, -ˈan/) ▶ **n.** a woody climbing plant that hangs from trees, esp. in tropical rain forests. ■ the free-hanging stem of such a plant.
– ORIGIN late 18th cent.: from French *liane* 'clematis, liana,' of unknown origin.

Liao[1] /lēˈou/ a river in northeastern China that rises in Inner Mongolia and flows about 900 miles (1,450 km) east and then south to the Gulf of Liaodong at the head of the Gulf of Bo Hai.

Liao[2] /liˈou/ a dynasty that ruled much of Manchuria and part of northeastern China AD 947–1125.

Liao·dong Pen·in·su·la /lēˈouˈdo͝oNG/ a peninsula in northeastern China that extends south into the Yellow Sea between Bo Hai and Korea Bay.

Liao·ning /lēˈouˈniNG/ a province in northeastern China, bordered on the east by North Korea; capital, Shenyang.

li·ar /ˈlīər/ ▶ **n.** a person who tells lies.
– ORIGIN Old English *lēogere* (see LIE[2], -AR[4]).

Li·ard Riv·er /ˈlēˌärd, lēˈärd/ a river that flows for 570 miles (920 km) from the Yukon Territory through British Columbia and the Northwest Territories to the Mackenzie River.

Li·as /ˈlīəs/ ▶ **n.** **(the Lias)** Geology the earliest epoch of the Jurassic period, lasting from about 208 to 178 million years ago. ■ the system of rocks deposited during this epoch, consisting of shales and limestones rich in fossils.
– DERIVATIVES **li·as·sic** /līˈasik/ **adj.**
– ORIGIN late Middle English (denoting blue lias): from Old French *liais* 'hard limestone,' probably from *lie* (see LEES).

li·a·tris /līˈatris/ ▶ **n.** (pl. **same**) a plant of a genus that includes the blazing stars of the daisy family.
● Genus *Liatris,* family Compositae.
– ORIGIN modern Latin, of unknown origin.

lib /lib/ ▶ **n.** informal (in the names of political movements) liberation: *I'm all for* ***women's lib.***
– ORIGIN 1970s: abbreviation.

Lib. ▶ **abbr.** Liberal.

li·ba·tion /līˈbāSHən/ ▶ **n.** a drink poured out as an offering to a deity. ■ the pouring out of such a drink-offering: *gin was poured in libation.* ■ humorous a drink: *they steadily worked their way through free food and the occasional libation.*
– ORIGIN late Middle English: from Latin *libatio(n-),* from *libare* 'pour as an offering.'

lib·ber /ˈlibər/ ▶ **n.** [usu. with modifier] informal a member or advocate of a movement calling for the liberation of people or animals: *a women's libber.*

li·bel /ˈlībəl/ ▶ **n. 1** Law a published false statement that is damaging to a person's reputation; a written defamation. Compare with SLANDER. ■ the action or crime of publishing such a statement: *a councilor who sued two national newspapers for libel* | [as modifier] *a libel action.* ■ a false and malicious statement about a person. ■ a thing or circumstance that brings undeserved discredit on a person by misrepresentation.
2 (in admiralty and ecclesiastical law) a plaintiff's written declaration.
▶ **v.** (**libels, libeling, libeled**; Brit. **libels, libelling, libelled**) [with obj.] **1** Law defame (someone) by publishing a libel: *she alleged the magazine had libeled her.* ■ make a false and malicious statement about.
2 (in admiralty and ecclesiastical law) bring a suit against (someone).
– DERIVATIVES **li·bel·er n.**
– ORIGIN Middle English (in the general sense 'a document, a written statement'): via Old French from Latin *libellus,* diminutive of *liber* 'book.'

li·bel·ous /ˈlībələs/ (Brit. **libellous**) ▶ **adj.** containing or constituting a libel: *a libelous newspaper story.*
– DERIVATIVES **li·bel·ous·ly adv.**

Lib·e·ra·ce /ˌlibəˈräCHē/ (1919–87), US pianist and entertainer; full name *Wladziu Valentino Liberace.* He was known for his romantic arrangements of popular piano classics and for his flamboyant costumes. He appeared on his own television show from 1952 to 1957.

lib·er·al /ˈlib(ə)rəl/ ▶ **adj. 1** open to new behavior or opinions and willing to discard traditional values: *they have more liberal views toward marriage and divorce than some people.* ■ favorable to or respectful of individual rights and freedoms: *liberal citizenship laws.* ■ (in a political context) favoring maximum individual liberty in political and social reform: *a liberal democratic state.* ■ **(Liberal)** of or characteristic of Liberals or a Liberal Party. ■ **(Liberal)** (in the UK) of or relating to the Liberal Democrat Party: *the Liberal leader.* ■ Theology regarding many traditional beliefs as dispensable, invalidated by modern thought, or liable to change.
2 [attrib.] (of education) concerned mainly with broadening a person's general knowledge and experience, rather than with technical or professional training.
3 (esp. of an interpretation of a law) broadly construed or understood; not strictly literal or exact: *they could have given the 1968 Act a more liberal interpretation.*
4 given, used, or occurring in generous amounts: *liberal amounts of wine had been consumed.* ■ (of a person) giving generously: *Sam was too* ***liberal with*** *the wine.*
▶ **n.** a person of liberal views. ■ **(Liberal)** a supporter or member of a Liberal Party.
– DERIVATIVES **lib·er·al·ism** /-ˌlizəm/ **n.**, **lib·er·al·ist** /-rəlist/ **n.**, **lib·er·al·is·tic** /ˌlib(ə)rəˈlistik/ **adj.**, **lib·er·al·ly adv.**, **lib·er·al·ness n.**
– ORIGIN Middle English: via Old French from Latin *liberalis,* from *liber* 'free (man).' The original sense was 'suitable for a free man,' hence 'suitable for a gentleman' (one not tied to a trade), surviving in *liberal arts.* Another early sense, 'generous' (sense 4 of the adjective), gave rise to an obsolete meaning 'free from restraint,' leading to sense 1 of the adjective (late 18th cent).

lib·er·al arts ▶ **plural n.** academic subjects such as literature, philosophy, mathematics, and social and physical sciences as distinct from professional and technical subjects. ■ historical the medieval trivium and quadrivium.
– ORIGIN *liberal,* as distinct from *servile* or *mechanical* (i.e., involving manual labor) and originally referring to arts and sciences considered "worthy of a free man"; later the word related to general intellectual development rather than vocational training.

lib·er·al·i·ty /ˌlibəˈralətē/ ▶ **n. 1** the quality of giving or spending freely.
2 the quality of being open to new ideas and free from prejudice: *liberality toward bisexuality.*
– ORIGIN Middle English: from Old French *liberalite,* or from Latin *liberalitas,* from *liberalis* (see LIBERAL).

lib·er·al·ize /ˈlib(ə)rəˌlīz/ ▶ **v.** [with obj.] remove or loosen restrictions on (something, typically an economic or political system): *several agreements to liberalize trade were signed.*
– DERIVATIVES **lib·er·al·i·za·tion** /ˌlib(ə)rələˈzāSHən, -ˌlīˈzā-/ **n.**, **lib·er·al·iz·er n.**

Lib·er·al Par·ty ▶ **n.** a political party advocating liberal policies, in particular a British party that emerged in the 1860s from the old Whig Party and until World War I was one of the two major parties in Britain. The name was discontinued in official use in 1988 when the party regrouped with elements of the Social Democratic Party to form the Social and Liberal Democrats, now known as the Liberal Democrats.

lib·er·ate /ˈlibəˌrāt/ ▶ **v.** [with obj.] set (someone) free from a situation, esp. imprisonment or slavery, in which their liberty is severely restricted: *the serfs had been liberated.* ■ free (a country, city, or people) from enemy occupation: *twelve months earlier Paris had been liberated.* ■ release (someone) from a state or situation that limits freedom of thought or behavior: *the use of computers can* ***liberate*** *students* ***from*** *the constraints of disabilities* | (as adj. **liberating**) *the arts can have a liberating effect on people.* ■ free (someone) from rigid social conventions, esp. those concerned with accepted sexual roles: *ways of working politically that liberate women.* ■ informal steal (something): *the drummer's wearing a beret he's liberated from Lord knows where.* ■ Chemistry & Physics release (gas, energy, etc.) as a result of chemical reaction or physical decomposition: *energy liberated by the annihilation of matter.*
– ORIGIN late 16th cent.: from Latin *liberat-* 'freed,' from the verb *liberare,* from *liber* 'free.'

lib·er·at·ed /ˈlibəˌrātid/ ▶ **adj. 1** (of a person) showing freedom from social conventions or traditional ideas, esp. with regard to sexual roles: *the modern image of the independent, liberated woman.*
2 (of a place or people) freed from imprisonment, slavery, or enemy occupation: *liberated areas of the country.*

lib·er·a·tion /ˌlibəˈrāSHən/ ▶ **n.** the act of setting someone free from imprisonment, slavery, or oppression; release: *the liberation of all political prisoners.* ■ freedom from limits on thought or behavior: *the struggle for women's liberation.*
– DERIVATIVES **lib·er·a·tion·ist** /ˌlibəˈrāSHənist/ **n.**

lib·er·a·tion the·ol·o·gy ▶ **n.** a movement in Christian theology, developed mainly by Latin American Roman Catholics, that emphasizes liberation from social, political, and economic oppression as an anticipation of ultimate salvation.

Lib·er·a·tion Ti·gers of Tam·il Ee·lam /ˈtaməl ˈēˌlam/ another name for TAMIL TIGERS.

lib·er·a·tor /ˈlibəˌrātər/ ▶ **n.** a person who liberates a person or place from imprisonment or oppression: *they saw themselves not as conquerors but as liberators.*

Li·be·ri·a /līˈbi(ə)rēə/ a country on the Atlantic coast of West Africa; pop. 3,441,800 (est. 2009); capital, Monrovia; languages, English (official) and English-based pidgin.

> Liberia was founded in 1822 as a settlement for freed slaves from the US and was proclaimed independent in 1847. Indigenous peoples form the majority of the population. In 1980, the predominant Liberian-American elite was overthrown in a coup, and a civil war began in 1990, ending with a ceasefire in 1996. A second civil war (1999–2003) resulted in a transitional government backed by the UN.

– DERIVATIVES **Li·be·ri·an adj. & n.**
– ORIGIN from Latin *liber* 'free.'

li·be·ro /ˈlēbəˌrō, ˈlibəˌrō/ ▶ **n.** (pl. **liberos**) the rearmost, roaming defensive player in volleyball or soccer.

lib·er·tar·i·an /ˌlibərˈte(ə)rēən/ ▶ **n. 1** an adherent of libertarianism: [as modifier] *libertarian philosophy.* ■ a person who advocates civil liberty.
2 Philosophy a person who believes in the doctrine of free will.
– ORIGIN late 18th cent. (sense 2): from LIBERTY, on the pattern of words such as *unitarian.*

lib·er·tar·i·an·ism /ˌlibərˈte(ə)rēəˌnizəm/ ▶ **n.** an extreme laissez-faire political philosophy advocating only minimal state intervention in the lives of citizens.

> The adherents of libertarianism believe that private morality is not the state's affair and that therefore activities such as drug use and prostitution, which arguably harm no one but the participants, should not be illegal. Libertarianism shares elements with anarchism, although it is generally associated more with the political right (chiefly in the US). Unlike traditional liberalism, libertarianism lacks a concern with social justice.

lib·er·tine /ˈlibərˌtēn/ ▶ **n. 1** a person, esp. a man, who behaves without moral principles or a sense of responsibility, esp. in sexual matters.
2 a person who rejects accepted opinions in matters of religion; a freethinker.
▶ **adj. 1** characterized by a disregard of morality, esp. in sexual matters: *his more libertine impulses.*
2 freethinking in matters of religion.
– DERIVATIVES **lib·er·tin·age** /-ˌtēnij/ **n.**, **lib·er·tin·ism** /-ˌnizəm/ **n.**
– ORIGIN late Middle English (denoting a freed slave or the son of one): from Latin *libertinus* 'freedman,' from *liber* 'free.' In the mid 16th cent., imitating French *libertin,* the term denoted a member of any of various antinomian sects in France; hence sense 2 of the noun.

lib·er·ty /ˈlibərtē/ ▶ **n.** (pl. **liberties**) **1** the state of being free within society from oppressive restrictions imposed by authority on one's way

of life, behavior, or political views: *compulsory retirement would interfere with individual liberty.* ■ (usu. **liberties**) an instance of this; a right or privilege, esp. a statutory one: *the Bill of Rights was intended to secure basic civil liberties.* ■ the state of not being imprisoned or enslaved: *people who have lost property or liberty without due process.* ■ (**Liberty**) the personification of liberty as a female figure.
2 the power or scope to act as one pleases: *individuals should enjoy the liberty to pursue their own interests and preferences.* ■ Philosophy a person's freedom from control by fate or necessity. ■ informal a presumptuous remark or action: *how did he know what she was thinking?—it was a liberty!* ■ Nautical shore leave granted to a sailor.
– PHRASES **at liberty 1** not imprisoned: *he was at liberty for three months before he was recaptured.* **2** allowed or entitled to do something: *competent adults are generally **at liberty to** refuse medical treatment.* **take liberties 1** behave in an unduly familiar manner toward a person: *you've taken too many liberties with me.* **2** treat something freely, without strict faithfulness to the facts or to an original: *the scriptwriter has **taken** few **liberties** with the original narrative.* **take the liberty** venture to do something without first asking permission: *I have **taken the liberty of** submitting an idea to several of their research departments.*
– ORIGIN late Middle English: from Old French *liberte*, from Latin *libertas*, from *liber* 'free.'

Lib·er·ty, Statue of see STATUE OF LIBERTY.

Lib·er·ty Bell ▶ **n.** a bell in Philadelphia first rung on July 8, 1776, to celebrate the first public reading of the Declaration of Independence. It bears the legend "Proclaim liberty throughout all the land unto all the inhabitants thereof" (Leviticus 25:10).

Liberty Bell

lib·er·ty cap ▶ **n. 1** a common small European toadstool that has a grayish-brown cap with a distinct boss and a long thin stem, containing the hallucinogen psilocybin. See also MAGIC MUSHROOM. ● *Psilocybe semilanceata*, family Strophariaceae, class Hymenomycetes.
2 another term for CAP OF LIBERTY.

Lib·er·ty Is·land an island in New York Bay, off Jersey City in New Jersey, site (since 1885) of the Statue of Liberty.

Lib·er·ty ship ▶ **n.** historical a prefabricated US-built freighter of World War II.

li·bid·i·nous /lə'bidn-əs/ ▶ **adj.** showing excessive sexual drive; lustful.
– DERIVATIVES **li·bid·i·nous·ly adv.**, **li·bid·i·nous·ness n.**
– ORIGIN late Middle English: from Latin *libidinosus*, from *libido* 'desire, lust.'

li·bi·do /lə'bēdō/ ▶ **n.** (pl. **libidos**) sexual desire: *loss of libido* | *a deficient libido.* ■ Psychoanalysis the energy of the sexual drive as a component of the life instinct.
– DERIVATIVES **li·bid·i·nal** /-'bidn-əl/ **adj.**, **li·bid·i·nal·ly** /-'bidn-əlē/ **adv.**
– ORIGIN early 20th cent.: from Latin, literally 'desire, lust.'

Li Bo /'lē 'bō, 'bô/ variant of LI PO.

Li·bra /'lēbrə, 'lī-/ **1** Astronomy a small constellation (the Scales or Balance), said to represent the balance that is the symbol of justice. It contains no bright stars. ■ (as genitive **Librae** /'lēbrē, 'lī-/) used with a preceding letter or numeral to designate a star in this constellation: *the star Alpha Librae.*
2 Astrology the seventh sign of the zodiac, which the sun enters at the northern autumnal equinox (about September 23). ■ (**a Libra**) a person born when the sun is in this sign.
– DERIVATIVES **Li·bran n. & adj.** (sense 2).
– ORIGIN Latin.

li·bra /'lēbrə, 'lī-/ ▶ **n.** (pl. **librae** /-ˌbrī, -ˌbrē/) (in ancient Rome) a unit of weight, equivalent to 12 ounces (0.34 kg). It was the forerunner of the pound.
– ORIGIN Latin, 'pound, balance.'

li·brar·i·an /lī'bre(ə)rēən/ ▶ **n.** a person, typically with a degree in library science, who administers or assists in a library.
– DERIVATIVES **li·brar·i·an·ship** /-ˌship/ **n.**
– ORIGIN late 17th cent. (denoting a scribe or copyist): from Latin *librarius* 'relating to books,' (used as a noun) 'bookseller, scribe,' + -AN.

li·brar·y /'līˌbrerē, -brərē/ ▶ **n.** (pl. **libraries**) a building or room containing collections of books, periodicals, and sometimes films and recorded music for people to read, borrow, or refer to: *a school library* | [as modifier] *a library book.* ■ a collection of books and periodicals held in such a building or room: *the Institute houses an outstanding library of 35,000 volumes on the fine arts.* ■ a collection of films, recorded music, genetic material, etc., organized systematically and kept for research or borrowing: *a record library.* ■ a series of books, recordings, etc., issued by the same company and similar in appearance. ■ a room in a private house where books are kept. ■ (also **software library**) Computing a collection of programs and software packages made generally available, often loaded and stored on disk for immediate use.
– ORIGIN late Middle English: via Old French from Latin *libraria* 'bookshop,' feminine (used as a noun) of *librarius* 'relating to books,' from *liber, libr-* 'book.'

li·brar·y e·di·tion ▶ **n.** an edition of a book that is of large size and has good-quality print and binding, esp. the standard edition of a writer's works.

Li·brar·y of Con·gress the US national library, in Washington, DC.

li·brar·y school ▶ **n.** a graduate school of a university teaching library science.

li·brar·y sci·ence ▶ **n.** the study of collecting, preserving, cataloging, and making available books and other documents in libraries.

li·bra·tion /lī'brāshən/ ▶ **n.** Astronomy an apparent or real oscillation of the moon, by which parts near the edge of the disc that are often not visible from the earth sometimes come into view.
– DERIVATIVES **li·brate** /'līˌbrāt/ **v.**
– ORIGIN early 17th cent. (denoting an oscillating motion, or equilibrium): from Latin *libratio(n-)*, from the verb *librare*, from *libra* 'a balance.'

li·bret·to /lə'bretō/ ▶ **n.** (pl. **libretti** /-'bretē/ or **librettos**) the text of an opera or other long vocal work.
– DERIVATIVES **li·bret·tist** /-'bretist/ **n.**
– ORIGIN mid 18th cent.: from Italian, diminutive of *libro* 'book,' from Latin *liber.*

Li·bre·ville /'lēbrəˌvil/ the capital of Gabon, a port on the Atlantic coast at the mouth of the Gabon River; pop. 576,000 (est. 2007).

Lib·ri·um /'librēəm/ ▶ **n.** trademark for CHLORDIAZEPOXIDE.
– ORIGIN 1960s: of unknown origin.

Lib·y·a /'libēə/ a country in North Africa, in the Sahara Desert, with a coastline on the Mediterranean Sea; pop. 6,324,400 (est. 2009); capital, Tripoli; official language, Arabic. ■ ancient northern Africa west of Egypt.

> The area came under Turkish domination in the 16th century, was annexed by Italy in 1912, and became an independent kingdom in 1951. The monarchy was overthrown in 1969, and the country emerged with a radical revolutionary leadership. In 2003, the government announced it would cease its program to develop weapons of mass destruction. Libya has major oil deposits.

– DERIVATIVES **Lib·y·an adj. & n.**

Lib·y·an Des·ert the name for the northeastern Sahara Desert, west of the Nile in Egypt, Libya, and northwestern Sudan. Also called WESTERN DESERT (in Egypt).

lice /līs/ plural form of LOUSE.

li·cense /'līsəns/ ▶ **n.** (Brit. **licence**) a permit from an authority to own or use something, do a particular thing, or carry on a trade (esp. in alcoholic beverages): *a gun license* | [as modifier] *vehicle license fees.* ■ formal or official permission to do something: *logging is permitted under license from the Forest Service.* ■ a writer's or artist's freedom to deviate from fact or from conventions such as grammar, meter, or perspective, for effect: *artistic license.* ■ freedom to behave as one wishes, esp. in a way that results in excessive or unacceptable behavior: *the government was criticized for giving the army too much license.* ■ (**a license to do something**) a reason or excuse to do something wrong or excessive: *police say that the lenient sentence is a license to assault.*
▶ **v.** (Brit. also **licence**) [with obj.] grant a license to (someone or something) to permit the use of something or to allow an activity to take place: *brokers must be licensed to sell health-related insurance* | [with obj. and infinitive] *he ought not to have been licensed to fly a plane* | (as adj. **licensing**) *a licensing authority.* ■ authorize the use, performance, or release of (something): *the drug is already licensed for human use* | *he was required to delete certain scenes before the film could be licensed for showing.* ■ dated give permission to (someone) to do something: [with obj. and infinitive] *he was licensed to do no more than send a message.*
– PHRASES **license to print money** a very lucrative commercial activity, typically one perceived as requiring little effort.
– DERIVATIVES **li·cens·a·ble adj.**, **li·cens·er n.**, **li·cen·sor** /-sər, ˌlīsən'sôr/ **n.**
– ORIGIN late Middle English: via Old French from Latin *licentia* 'freedom, licentiousness' (in medieval Latin 'authority, permission'), from *licere* 'be lawful or permitted.'

li·censed /'līsənst/ ▶ **adj.** having an official license: *a licensed taxi operator.*

li·cen·see /ˌlīsən'sē/ ▶ **n.** the holder of a license.

li·cense num·ber ▶ **n.** the series of letters or numbers identifying a vehicle, displayed on a license plate.

li·cense plate ▶ **n.** a sign affixed to a vehicle displaying a series of letters or numbers indicating that the vehicle has been registered with the state.

li·cen·sure /'līsənshər, -ˌshŏŏr/ ▶ **n.** the granting or regulation of licenses, as for professionals: *licensure for respiratory therapists.*
– ORIGIN mid 19th cent.: from LICENSE + -URE.

li·cen·ti·ate /lī'sensh(ē)it/ ▶ **n.** the holder of a certificate of competence to practice a certain profession. ■ (in certain universities, esp. in Europe) a degree between that of bachelor and master or doctor. ■ the holder of such a degree.
– DERIVATIVES **li·cen·ti·ate·ship** /-ˌship/ **n.**
– ORIGIN late 15th cent.: from medieval Latin, noun use of *licentiatus* 'having freedom,' based on *licentia* 'freedom.'

li·cen·tious /lī'senshəs/ ▶ **adj. 1** promiscuous and unprincipled in sexual matters.
2 archaic disregarding accepted rules or conventions, esp. in grammar or literary style.
– DERIVATIVES **li·cen·tious·ly adv.**, **li·cen·tious·ness n.**
– ORIGIN late Middle English: from Latin *licentiosus*, from *licentia* 'freedom.'

li·chee ▶ **n.** variant spelling of LITCHI.

li·chen /'līkən/ ▶ **n. 1** a simple slow-growing plant that typically forms a low crustlike, leaflike, or branching growth on rocks, walls, and trees.

> Lichens are composite plants consisting of a fungus that contains photosynthetic algal cells. Their classification is based upon that of the fungal partner, which in most cases belongs to the subdivision Ascomycotina, and the algal partners are either green algae or cyanobacteria. Lichens obtain their water and nutrients from the atmosphere and can be sensitive indicators of atmospheric pollution.

2 [usu. with modifier] a skin disease in which small pimples or bumps occur close together.
– DERIVATIVES **li·chened adj.** (sense 1), **li·chen·ol·o·gy** /ˌlīkə'näləjē/ **n.** (sense 1), **li·chen·ous** /-nəs/ **adj.** (sense 2).
– ORIGIN early 17th cent.: via Latin from Greek *leikhēn.*

licht /likHt/ ▶ **n. adj., & v.** Scottish variant of LIGHT[1], LIGHT[2].

Lich·ten·stein /'liktənˌstēn/, Roy (1923–97), US painter and sculptor. A leading exponent of pop art, he became known for paintings inspired by comic strips. Notable works: *Whaam!* (1963) and *Big Painting VI* (1965).

-licious ▶ **comb. form** informal forming adjectives denoting someone or something as delightful or extremely attractive: *babelicious* | *bootylicious.*
– ORIGIN 1950s: from DELICIOUS.

lic·it /'lisit/ ▶ **adj.** not forbidden; lawful: *licit and illicit drugs.*
– DERIVATIVES **lic·it·ly adv.**
– ORIGIN late 15th cent.: from Latin *licitus* 'allowed,' from the verb *licere.*

lick /lik/ ▶ **v.** [with obj.] **1** pass the tongue over (something), typically in order to taste, moisten, or clean it: *he licked the stamp and stuck it on the*

envelope | [no obj.] *he licked at his damaged hand with his tongue.* ■ [no obj.] (of a flame, wave, or breeze) move lightly and quickly like a tongue: *the flames licked around the wood.*
2 informal defeat (someone) comprehensively: *all right, Mary, I know when I'm licked.* ■ thrash: *she stands tall and could lick any man in the place.*
▶ **n. 1** an act of licking something with the tongue: *Sammy gave his fingers a long lick.* ■ a movement of flame, water, etc., resembling this.
2 informal a light coating or quick application of something, esp. paint: *all she'd need to do to the kitchen was give it a lick of paint.* ■ [in sing.] [usu. with negative] an extremely small amount of something abstract: *there's not a lick of suspense in the entire plot.*
3 (often **licks**) informal a short phrase or solo in jazz or popular music: *cool guitar licks.*
4 informal a smart blow: *his mother gave him several licks for daring to blaspheme.*
– PHRASES **at a lick** informal at a fast pace; with considerable speed. **a lick and a promise** informal a hasty performance of a task, esp. of cleaning something. **lick someone's boots** (or vulgar slang **ass**) be excessively obsequious toward someone, esp. to gain favor from them. **lick someone/something into shape** see SHAPE. **lick one's lips** (or **chops**) look forward to something with eager anticipation. **lick one's wounds** retire to recover one's strength or confidence after a defeat or humiliating experience: *the political organization he worked for was licking its wounds after electoral defeat.* **not be able to do something a lick** informal be totally incompetent at a specified activity: *I couldn't sing a lick.*
– DERIVATIVES **lick·er n.** [usu. in combination].
– ORIGIN Old English *liccian*; related to Dutch *likken* and German *lecken*, from an Indo-European root shared by Greek *leikhein* and Latin *lingere*.

lick·er·ish /ˈlik(ə)risH/ ▶ **adj.** lecherous: *a barrage of lickerish grins and dirty jokes.*
– DERIVATIVES **lick·er·ish·ly adv.**
– ORIGIN late 15th cent.: alteration of obsolete *lickerous*, in the same sense, from an Anglo-Norman French variant of Old French *lecheros* (see LECHEROUS).

lick·e·ty-split /ˌlikətē ˈsplit/ ▶ **adv.** informal as quickly as possible; immediately: *I took off lickety-split across the lawn.*
– ORIGIN early 19th cent. (in the phrase *as fast as lickety* 'at full speed'): from a fanciful extension of LICK + the verb SPLIT.

lick·ing /ˈlikiNG/ ▶ **n.** informal a severe defeat or beating.

lick·spit·tle /ˈlikˌspitl/ ▶ **n.** a person who behaves obsequiously to those in power.

lic·o·rice /ˈlik(ə)risH, -ris/ (Brit. **liquorice**) ▶ **n. 1** a sweet, chewy, aromatic black substance made by evaporation from the juice of a root and used as a candy and in medicine. ■ a candy flavored with such a substance: [as modifier] *licorice gumdrops.*
2 the widely distributed plant of the pea family from which this product is obtained. ● Genus *Glycyrrhiza*, family Leguminosae; many species are used locally to obtain licorice, the chief commercial source being the cultivated *G. glabra*.
– ORIGIN Middle English: from Old French *licoresse*, from late Latin *liquiritia*, from Greek *glukurrhiza*, from *glukus* 'sweet' + *rhiza* 'root.'

lic·o·rice stick ▶ **n.** a stick of licorice candy. ■ dated, informal a clarinet.

lic·tor /ˈliktər/ ▶ **n.** (in ancient Rome) an officer attending the consul or other magistrate, bearing the fasces, and executing sentences on offenders.
– ORIGIN Latin, perhaps related to *ligare* 'to bind.'

lid /lid/ ▶ **n.** a removable or hinged cover for the top of a container: *a large frying pan with a lid* | *a garbage can lid.* ■ (usu. **lids**) an eyelid: *eyes now hooded beneath heavy lids.* ■ Botany the operculum of a moss capsule. ■ informal a hat.
– PHRASES **blow** (or **take**) **the lid off** informal reveal unwelcome secrets about: *prosecutors have taken the lid off a multimillion-dollar payoff scandal.* **keep a** (or **the**) **lid on** informal keep (an emotion or process) from going out of control: *she was no longer able to keep the lid on her simmering anger.* ■ keep secret: *she keeps a very tight lid on her own private life.* **put a** (or **the**) **lid on** informal put a stop to or be the culmination of: *it's time to put the lid on all the talk.*
– DERIVATIVES **lid·ded adj.**, **lid·less adj.**
– ORIGIN Old English *hlid*, of Germanic origin, from a base meaning 'cover'; related to Dutch *lid*.

li·dar /ˈlīdär/ ▶ **n.** a detection system that works on the principle of radar, but uses light from a laser.
– ORIGIN 1960s: blend of LIGHT[1] and RADAR.

Lid·dell /ˈlidl, liˈdel/, Eric (Henry) (1902–45), British runner and missionary, born in China. In the 1924 Olympic Games, he won the 400 meters in world record time. His exploits were celebrated in the movie *Chariots of Fire* (1981).

Li·do /ˈlēdō/ an island reef off the coast of northeastern Italy, in the northern Adriatic. It separates the Lagoon of Venice from the Gulf of Venice. Full name **Lido di Malamocco**.

li·do /ˈlēdō/ ▶ **n.** (pl. **lidos**) a public, open-air swimming pool or beach.
– ORIGIN late 17th cent.: from Italian *Lido*, from *lido* 'shore,' from Latin *litus*.

li·do·caine /ˈlīdəˌkān/ ▶ **n.** Medicine a synthetic compound used as a local anesthetic, e.g., for dental surgery, and in treating abnormal heart rhythms. ● An aromatic amide; chem. formula: $C_{14}H_{22}N_2O$.
– ORIGIN 1940s: from *(acetani)lid(e)* + *-caine* (from COCAINE).

Lie /lē/, Trygve Halvdan (1896–1968), Norwegian politician; first secretary general of the United Nations 1946–53.

lie[1] /lī/ ▶ **v.** (**lies**, **lying** /ˈlī-iNG/; past **lay** /lā/; past participle **lain** /lān/) [no obj.] **1** (of a person or animal) be in or assume a horizontal or resting position on a supporting surface: *the man lay face downward on the grass* | *I had to lie down for two hours because I was groggy* | *Lily lay back on the pillows and watched him.* ■ (of a thing) rest flat on a surface: *a book lay open on the table.* ■ (of a dead person) be buried in a particular place.
2 be, remain, or be kept in a specified state: *the church lies in ruins today* | *putting homeless families into apartments that would otherwise lie empty.* ■ (of something abstract) reside or be found: *the solution lies in a return to "traditional family values."*
3 (of a place) be situated in a specified position or direction: *the small town of Swampscott lies about ten miles north of Boston.* ■ (of a scene) extend from the observer's viewpoint in a specified direction: *stand here, and all of Amsterdam lies before you.*
4 Law (of an action, charge, or claim) be admissible or sustainable.
▶ **n.** (usu. **the lie**) the way, direction, or position in which something lies. ■ Golf the position in which a golf ball comes to rest, esp. as regards the ease of the next shot. ■ the lair or place of cover of an animal or a bird.
– PHRASES **let something lie** take no action regarding a controversial or problematic matter. **lie heavy on one** cause one to feel troubled or uncomfortable. **lie in state** (of the corpse of a person of national importance) be laid in a public place of honor before burial. **lie in wait** conceal oneself, waiting to surprise, attack, or catch someone. **lie low** (esp. of a criminal) keep out of sight; avoid detection or attention: *at the time of the murder, he appears to have been lying low in a barn.* **take something lying down** [usu. with negative] accept an insult, setback, rebuke, etc., without reacting or protesting.
– PHRASAL VERBS **lie ahead** be going to happen; be in store: *I'm excited by what lies ahead.* **lie around/about** (of an object) be left carelessly out of place: *there were pills and potions lying around in every corner of the house.* ■ (of a person) pass the time lazily or aimlessly: *you all just lay around all day on your backsides, didn't you?* **lie behind** be the real, often hidden, reason for (something): *a subtle strategy lies behind such silly claims.* **lie in** Brit. remain in bed after the normal time for getting up. ■ archaic (of a pregnant woman) go to bed to give birth. **lie off** Nautical (of a ship) stand some distance from shore or from another ship. **lie to** Nautical (of a ship) come almost to a stop with its head toward the wind. **lie with 1** (of a responsibility or problem) be attributable to (someone): *the ultimate responsibility for the violence lies with the country's president.* **2** archaic have sexual intercourse with.
– ORIGIN Old English *licgan*, of Germanic origin; related to Dutch *liggen* and German *liegen*, from an Indo-European root shared by Greek *lektron*, *lekhos* and Latin *lectus* 'bed.'

> **USAGE** The verb lie ('assume a horizontal or resting position') is often confused with the verb **lay** ('put something down'), giving rise to incorrect uses such as *he is laying on the bed* (correct use is *he is lying on the bed*) or *why don't you lie the suitcase on the bed?* (correct use is *why don't you lay the suitcase on the bed?*). The confusion is only heightened by the fact that **lay** is not only the base form of **to lay**, but is also the past tense of **to lie**, so while *he is laying on the bed* is incorrect, *he lay on the bed yesterday* is quite correct. For more discussion of these **lie** and **lay** verb forms, see usage at LAY[1].

lie[2] ▶ **n.** an intentionally false statement: *Mungo felt a pang of shame at* ***telling*** *Alice* ***a lie*** | *the whole thing* ***is a pack of lies.*** ■ used with reference to a situation involving deception or founded on a mistaken impression: *all their married life she had been living a lie.*
▶ **v.** (**lies**, **lying** /ˈlī-iNG/, **lied**) [no obj.] tell a lie or lies: *why had Wesley lied about his visit to Philadelphia?* | [with direct speech] *"I am sixty-five," she lied.* ■ (**lie one's way into/out of**) get oneself into or out of a situation by lying: *you lied your way on to this voyage by implying you were an experienced sailor.* ■ (of a thing) present a false impression; be deceptive: *the camera cannot lie.*
– PHRASES **give the lie to** serve to show that (something seemingly apparent or previously stated or believed) is not true: *these figures give the lie to the notion that Britain is excessively strike-ridden.* **I tell a lie** (or **that's a lie**) informal an expression used to correct oneself immediately when one realizes that one has made an incorrect remark: *I never used to dream—I tell a lie, I did dream when I was little.* **lie through one's teeth** informal tell an outright lie without remorse.
– ORIGIN Old English *lyge* (noun), *lēogan* (verb), of Germanic origin; related to Dutch *liegen* and German *lügen*.

Lieb·chen /ˈlēbCHən, ˈlēp-, -SHən, -KHən/ ▶ **n.** a person who is very dear to another (often used as a term of endearment).
– ORIGIN German, diminutive of *lieb* 'dear.'

Lieb·frau·milch /ˈlēbˌfrouˌmilCH, ˈlēp-, -ˌmilk, -ˌmilKH/ ▶ **n.** a light white wine from the Rhine region.
– ORIGIN German, from *lieb* 'dear' + *Frau* 'lady' (referring to the Virgin Mary, patroness of the convent where it was first made) + *Milch* 'milk.'

Lie·big /ˈlēbig, -bIKH/, Justus von, Baron (1803–73), German chemist and teacher. With Friedrich Wöhler, he discovered the benzoyl radical and demonstrated that such radicals were groups of atoms that remained unchanged in many chemical reactions.

Liech·ten·stein /ˈliktənˌstīn, -ˌSHtīn/ a small independent principality in the Alps, between Switzerland and Austria; pop. 34,800 (est. 2009); capital, Vaduz; official language, German.

> The principality was created in 1719 within the Holy Roman Empire and became independent of the German confederation in 1866. Liechtenstein is economically integrated with Switzerland.

– DERIVATIVES **Lich·ten·stein·er n.**

lied /lēd, lēt/ ▶ **n.** (pl. **lieder** /ˈlēdər/) a type of German song, esp. of the Romantic period, typically for solo voice with piano accompaniment.
– ORIGIN from German *Lied*.

lie de·tec·tor ▶ **n.** an instrument for determining whether a person is telling the truth by testing for physiological changes considered to be associated with lying. Compare with POLYGRAPH.

lief /lēf/ ▶ **adv.** (**as lief**) archaic as happily; as gladly: *he would just as lief eat a pincushion.*
– ORIGIN Old English *lēof* 'dear, pleasant,' of Germanic origin: related to LEAVE[2] and LOVE.

liege /lēj, lēZH/ historical ▶ **adj.** [attrib.] concerned with or relating to the relationship between a feudal superior and a vassal: *an oath of fealty and liege homage.*
▶ **n.** (also **liege lord**) a feudal superior or sovereign. ■ a vassal or subject: *the king's lieges.*
– ORIGIN Middle English: via Old French *lige*, *liege* from medieval Latin *laeticus*, probably of Germanic origin.

Liège /lēˈeZH/ a province of eastern Belgium. Formerly ruled by independent prince-bishops, it became a part of the Netherlands in 1815 and of Belgium in 1830. Flemish name **LUIK**. ■ its capital city, situated at the junction of the Meuse and Ourthe rivers; pop. 190,102 (2008).

liege·man /ˈlējˌman, -mən/ ▶ **n.** (pl. **liegemen**) historical a vassal who owes feudal service or allegiance to a nobleman.

lien /ˈlē(ə)n/ ▶ **n.** Law a right to keep possession of property belonging to another person until a debt owed by that person is discharged.
– DERIVATIVES **lien·or n.**
– ORIGIN mid 16th cent.: from French, via Old French *loien* from Latin *ligamen* 'bond,' from *ligare* 'to bind.'

li·erne /lēˈərn/ ▶ **n.** [usu. as modifier] Architecture (in vaulting) a short rib connecting the bosses and intersections of the principal ribs: *a fine lierne vault.*
– ORIGIN late Middle English: from French, perhaps a transferred use of dialect *lierne* (standard French *liane*) 'clematis.'

lieu /lo͞o/ ▶ **n.** (in phrase **in lieu**) instead: *the company issued additional shares to shareholders in lieu of a cash dividend.*
– ORIGIN Middle English: via French from Latin *locus* 'place.'

Lieut. ▶ **abbr.** lieutenant.

lieu·ten·ant /lo͞o'tenənt/ ▸ **n.** a deputy or substitute acting for a superior: *he accepted his top lieutenant's resignation with deep regret.* ■ see FIRST LIEUTENANT, SECOND LIEUTENANT. ■ a naval officer of a high rank, in particular a commissioned officer in the US Navy or Coast Guard ranking above lieutenant junior grade and below lieutenant commander. ■ a police or fire department officer next in rank below captain.
– DERIVATIVES **lieu·ten·an·cy** /-'tenənsē/ **n.** (pl. **lieutenancies**).
– ORIGIN late Middle English: from Old French (see LIEU, TENANT).

> **USAGE** In the normal British pronunciation of **lieutenant**, the first syllable sounds like **lef**. In the standard US pronunciation, the first syllable, in contrast, sounds like **loo**. It is difficult to explain where the **f** in the British pronunciation comes from. Probably, at some point before the 19th century, the **u** at the end of Old French **lieu** was read and pronounced as a **v**, and the **v** later became an **f**.

lieu·ten·ant colo·nel ▸ **n.** a commissioned officer in the US Army, Air Force, or Marine Corps ranking above major and below colonel.

lieu·ten·ant com·man·der ▸ **n.** a commissioned officer in the US Navy or Coast Guard ranking above lieutenant and below commander.

lieu·ten·ant gen·er·al ▸ **n.** a commissioned officer in the US Army, Air Force, or Marine Corps ranking above major general and below general.

lieu·ten·ant gov·er·nor ▸ **n.** the executive officer of a state who is next in rank to a governor and who takes the governor's place in case of disability or death. ■ the executive officer of a Canadian province, appointed by the governor general.
– DERIVATIVES **lieu·ten·ant gov·er·nor·ship n.**

lieu·ten·ant jun·ior grade ▸ **n.** a commissioned officer in the US Navy or Coast Guard ranking above ensign and below lieutenant.

life /līf/ ▸ **n.** (pl. **lives** /līvz/) **1** the condition that distinguishes animals and plants from inorganic matter, including the capacity for growth, reproduction, functional activity, and continual change preceding death: *the origins of life.* ■ living things and their activity: *some sort of life existed on Mars | lower forms of life | the ice-cream vendors were the only signs of life.* ■ [with adj. or noun modifier] a particular type or aspect of people's existence: *an experienced teacher will help you settle into school life | revelations about his private life | his father decided to start a new life in California.* ■ vitality, vigor, or energy: *she was beautiful and full of life.*
2 the existence of an individual human being or animal: *a disaster that claimed the lives of 266 Americans | she didn't want to die; she loved life.* ■ a biography: *a life of Shelley.* ■ either of the two states of a person's existence separated by death (as in Christianity and some other religious traditions): *too much happiness in this life could reduce the chances of salvation in the next.* ■ any of a number of successive existences in which a soul is held to be reincarnated (as in Hinduism and some other religious traditions). ■ a chance to live after narrowly escaping death (esp. with reference to the nine lives traditionally attributed to cats).
3 (usu. **one's life**) the period between the birth and death of a living thing, esp. a human being: *she has lived all her life in the country | I want to be with you for the rest of my life | they became friends* ***for life.*** ■ the period during which something inanimate or abstract continues to exist, function, or be valid: *underlay helps to prolong the life of a carpet.* ■ informal a sentence of imprisonment for life.
4 (in art) the depiction of a subject from a real model, rather than from an artist's imagination: *the pose and clothing were sketched* ***from life*** | [as modifier] *life drawing.* See also STILL LIFE.
– PHRASES **bring** (or **come**) **to life** regain or cause to regain consciousness or return as if from death: *all this was of great interest to her, as if she were coming to life after a long sleep.* ■ (with reference to a fictional character or inanimate object) cause or seem to be alive or real: *he brings the character of MacDonald to life with power and precision | all the puppets came to life again.* ■ make or become active, lively, or interesting: *soon, with the return of the peasants and fishermen, the village comes to life again | you can bring any room to life with these coordinating cushions.* **do anything for a quiet life** make any concession to avoid being disturbed. **for dear** (or **one's**) **life** as if or in order to escape death: *I clung to the tree for dear life | Sue struggled free and ran for her life.* **for the life of me** informal however hard I try; even if my life depended on it: *I can't for the life of me understand what it is you see in that place.* **frighten the life out of** terrify. **get a life** [often in imperative] informal start living a fuller or more interesting existence: *if he's a lout, then get yourself out of there and get a life.* **give one's life for** die for. (**as**) **large as life** informal used to emphasize that a person is conspicuously present: *he was standing nearby, large as life.* **larger than life** seeming disproportionately important, interesting, etc.; attracting much attention: *your problems seem larger than life at that time of night.* **life and limb** see LIMB¹. **the life of the party** a vivacious and sociable person. **life in the fast lane** informal an exciting and eventful lifestyle, esp. one bringing wealth and success. **one's life's work** the work (esp. that of an academic or artistic nature) accomplished in or pursued throughout someone's lifetime. **lose one's life** be killed: *he lost his life in a car accident.* **a matter of life and death** a matter of vital importance. **not on your life** informal said to emphasize one's refusal to comply with a request: *"I want to see Clare alone." "Not on your life," said Buzz.* **save someone's** (or **one's own**) **life** prevent someone's (or one's own) death: *the driver of the truck managed to save his life by leaping out of the cab.* ■ informal provide much-needed relief from boredom or a difficult situation. **see life** gain a wide experience of the world, esp. its more pleasurable aspects. **take one's life in one's own hands** risk being killed. **take someone's** (or **one's own**) **life** kill someone (or oneself). **that's life** an expression of one's acceptance of a situation, however difficult: *we'll miss each other, but still, that's life.* **this is the life** an expression of contentment with one's present circumstances: *Ice cubes clinked in crystal glasses. "This is the life," she said.* **to the life** exactly like the original: *there he was, Nathan to the life, sitting at a table.* **to save one's life** [with modal and negative] even if one's life were to depend on it: *she couldn't stop crying now to save her life.*
– ORIGIN Old English *līf*, of Germanic origin; related to Dutch *lijf*, German *Leib* 'body,' also to LIVE¹.

life-and-death (also **life-or-death**) ▸ **adj.** deciding whether someone lives or dies; vitally important: *life-and-death decisions.*

life·belt /'līf,belt/ ▸ **n.** a life preserver in the shape of a belt.

life·blood /'līf,bləd/ ▸ **n.** the blood, as being necessary to life. ■ the indispensable factor or influence that gives something its strength and vitality: *my family was the lifeblood of the church.*

life·boat /'līf,bōt/ ▸ **n.** a specially constructed boat launched from land to rescue people in distress at sea. ■ a small boat kept on a ship for use in emergency, typically one of a number on deck or suspended from davits.
– DERIVATIVES **life·boat·man** /-mən/ **n.** (pl. **lifeboatmen**).

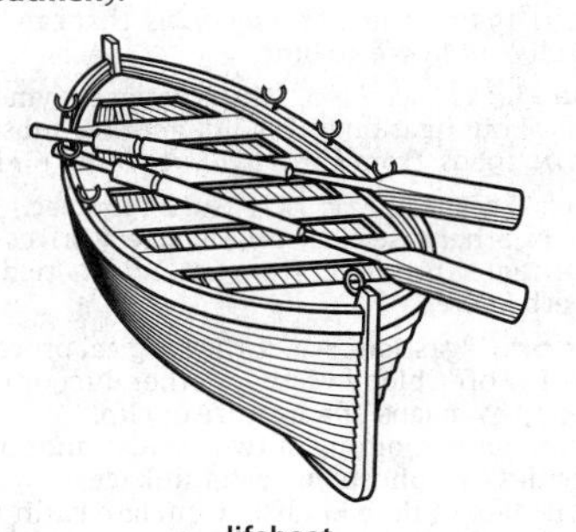
lifeboat

life·bu·oy /'līf,bo͞o-ē, -,boi/ ▸ **n.** a life preserver, esp. one in the shape of a ring.

life coach /'līf ,kōCH/ ▸ **n.** a person who counsels and encourages clients on matters having to do with careers or personal challenges.
– DERIVATIVES **life coach·ing n.**

life cy·cle ▸ **n.** the series of changes in the life of an organism, including reproduction.

life ex·pec·tan·cy ▸ **n.** the average period that a person may expect to live.

life force ▸ **n.** the force or influence that gives something its vitality or strength: *the passionate life force of the symphony.* ■ the spirit or energy that animates living creatures; the soul.

life form ▸ **n.** any living thing.

life-giv·ing ▸ **adj.** sustaining or revitalizing life: *the life-giving water of baptism.*

life·guard /'līf,gärd/ ▸ **n.** an expert swimmer employed to rescue people who get into difficulty in a swimming pool or at the beach.
– DERIVATIVES **life·guard·ing n.**

Life Guards ▸ **plural n.** (in the UK) a regiment of the Household Cavalry.

life his·to·ry ▸ **n.** the series of changes undergone by an organism during its lifetime. ■ the story of a person's life, esp. when told at tedious length.

life in·stinct ▸ **n.** Psychoanalysis an innate desire for self-preservation, manifest in hunger, self-defensive aggression, and the sexual instincts. Compare with DEATH INSTINCT.

life in·sur·ance ▸ **n.** insurance that pays out a sum of money either on the death of the insured person or after a set period.

life in·ter·est ▸ **n.** Law a right to property that a person holds for life but cannot dispose of further.

life jack·et ▸ **n.** a sleeveless buoyant or inflatable jacket for keeping a person afloat in water.

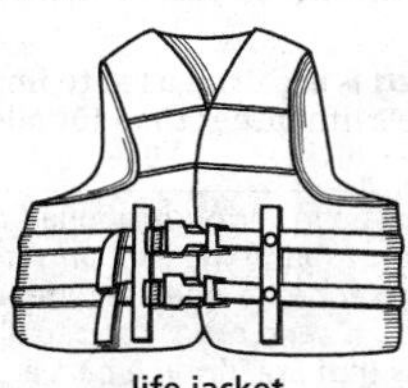
life jacket

life·less /'līflis/ ▸ **adj.** dead or apparently dead: *his lifeless body was taken from the river.* ■ lacking vigor, vitality, or excitement: *my hair always seems to look lifeless.* ■ devoid of living things: *the moon is lifeless.*
– DERIVATIVES **life·less·ly adv.**, **life·less·ness n.**
– ORIGIN Old English *līflēas* (see LIFE, -LESS).

life·like /'līf,līk/ ▸ **adj.** very similar to the person or thing represented: *an etching of a lifelike horse.*
– DERIVATIVES **life·like·ness n.**

life·line /'līf,līn/ ▸ **n. 1** a rope or line used for life-saving, typically one thrown to rescue someone in difficulties in water or one used by sailors to secure themselves to a boat. ■ a line used by a diver for sending signals to the surface.
2 a thing on which someone or something depends or which provides a means of escape from a difficult situation: *fertility treatment can seem like a lifeline to childless couples.*
3 (in palmistry) a line on the palm of a person's hand, regarded as indicating how long they will live.
– PHRASES **throw a lifeline to** (or **throw someone a lifeline**) provide (someone) with a means of escaping from a difficult situation.

life list ▸ **n.** Ornithology a list of all the kinds of birds observed by a person during his or her life.

life·long /'līf,lôNG, -,läNG/ ▸ **adj.** lasting or remaining in a particular state throughout a person's life: *the two men were to remain lifelong friends | a lifelong conservative.*

life mem·ber ▸ **n.** a person who has lifelong membership in a society.
– DERIVATIVES **life mem·ber·ship n.**

life-or-death ▸ **adj.** see LIFE-AND-DEATH.

life part·ner ▸ **n.** a person with whom one is in a long-term monogamous relationship.

life peer ▸ **n.** (in the UK) a peer whose title cannot be inherited.
– DERIVATIVES **life peer·age n.**

life peer·ess ▸ **n.** (in the UK) a woman holding a life peerage.

life pre·serv·er ▸ **n. 1** a device made of buoyant or inflatable material, such as a life jacket, to keep someone afloat in water.
2 Brit. a short club with a heavily weighted end, used as a weapon; a blackjack.

lif·er /'līfər/ ▸ **n.** informal **1** a person serving a life sentence in prison.
2 a person who spends their life in a particular career, esp. in one of the armed forces.

life raft ▸ **n.** a raft, typically inflatable, for use in an emergency at sea.

life·sav·er /'līf,sāvər/ ▸ **n. 1** informal a thing that saves one from serious difficulty: *a microwave oven could be a lifesaver this Christmas.*
2 a ring-shaped life preserver.

life sci·enc·es ▸ **plural n.** the sciences concerned with the study of living organisms, including biology, botany, zoology, microbiology, physiology, biochemistry, and related subjects. Often contrasted with PHYSICAL SCIENCES.
– DERIVATIVES **life sci·en·tist n.**

life sen·tence ▸ **n.** a punishment for a felon of imprisonment for life.

life-size (also **life-sized**) ▸ **adj.** of the same size as the person or thing represented: *a life-size statue of a discus-thrower.*

life skill ▶ n. (usu. **life skills**) a skill that is necessary or desirable for full participation in everyday life: *sharing with a sibling can help children learn important life skills.*

life span (also **lifespan**) ▶ n. the length of time for which a person or animal lives or a thing functions: *the human life span.*

life·style /ˈlīfˌstīl/ ▶ n. the way in which a person or group lives: *the benefits of a healthy lifestyle.* ■ [as modifier] denoting advertising or products designed to appeal to a consumer by association with a desirable lifestyle.

life·style drug ▶ n. a drug used to improve the quality of one's life rather than for alleviating pain or curing disease.

> This term has been variously applied to drugs used for cosmetic reasons (e.g., for hair replacement), drugs used to enhance one's sex life (e.g., for erectile dysfunction), and drugs used to alleviate medical problems that are in some part attributable to lifestyle choices (e.g., for obesity). Some objections have been raised to the use of this term, as it may trivialize serious health problems.

life sup·port ▶ n. Medicine maintenance of the vital functions of a critically ill or comatose person or a person undergoing surgery: [as modifier] *a life-support machine.* ■ informal equipment in a hospital used for this: *a patient on life support.*

life ta·ble ▶ n. a table of statistics relating to life expectancy and mortality for a given category of people. ■ Zoology a similar table for a population of animals divided into cohorts of given age.

life·time /ˈlīfˌtīm/ ▶ n. the duration of a person's life: *a reward for a lifetime's work.* ■ the duration of a thing's existence or usefulness: *a plan to extend the lifetime of satellites.* ■ informal used to express the view that a period is very long: *five weeks was a lifetime, and anything could have happened.*
– PHRASES **of a lifetime** (of a chance or experience) such as does not occur more than once in a person's life: *because of Frankie she had rejected the opportunity of a lifetime.*

life·work /ˈlīfwərk/ ▶ n. the entire or principal work, labor, or task of a person's lifetime.

life·world /ˈlifˌwərld/ ▶ n. Philosophy all the immediate experiences, activities, and contacts that make up the world of an individual or corporate life.
– ORIGIN 1940s: translating German *Lebenswelt*.

Lif·fey /ˈlifē/ a river in eastern Ireland that flows for 50 miles (80 km) from the Wicklow Mountains to Dublin Bay. The city of Dublin is situated at its mouth.

Lif·ford /ˈlifərd/ the county town of Donegal, in the Republic of Ireland; pop. 1,448 (2006).

LIFO /ˈlīfō/ ▶ abbr. last in, first out (chiefly with reference to methods of stock valuation and data storage). Compare with **FIFO**.

lift /lift/ ▶ v. [with obj.] **1** raise to a higher position or level: *he lifted his trophy over his head.* ■ move (one's eyes or face) to face upward and look at someone or something: *he lifted his eyes from the paper for an instant.* ■ increase the volume or pitch of (one's voice): *Willie sang boldly, lifting up his voice.* ■ increase (a price or amount): *higher than expected oil prices lifted Oklahoma's revenue.* ■ transport by air: *a helicopter lifted 11 crew members to safety from the ship.* ■ hit or kick (a ball) high into the air. ■ [no obj.] move upward; be raised: *Thomas's eyelids drowsily lifted | their voices lifted in wails and cries.* ■ [no obj.] (of a cloud, fog, etc.) move upward or away: *the factory smoke hung low, never lifted | the gray weather lifted on the following Wednesday.* ■ perform cosmetic surgery on (esp. the face or breasts) to reduce sagging: *surgeons lift and remove excess skin from the face and neck.*
2 pick up and move to a different position: *he lifted her down from the pony's back.* ■ enable (someone or something) to escape from an unpleasant situation: *two billion barrels of oil that could lift this nation out of chronic poverty.*
3 raise (a person's spirits or confidence); encourage or cheer: *we heard inspiring talks that lifted our spirits.* ■ [no obj.] (of a person's mood) become happier: *suddenly his heart lifted, and he could have wept with relief.*
4 formally remove or end (a legal restriction, decision, or ban): *the European Community lifted its oil embargo against South Africa.*
5 informal steal (something, esp. a minor item of property): *the shirt she had lifted from a supermarket.* ■ use (a person's work or ideas) without permission or acknowledgment; plagiarize: *this is a hackneyed adventure lifted straight from a vintage Lassie episode.*
▶ n. **1** something that is used for lifting, in particular: ■ British term for **ELEVATOR**. ■ a device incorporating a moving cable for carrying people, typically skiers, up or down a mountain. ■ a built-up heel or device worn in a boot or shoe to make the wearer appear taller or to correct shortening of a leg.
2 an act of lifting: *weightlifters attempting a particularly heavy lift.* ■ a rise in price or amount: *the company has already produced a 10 percent lift in profits.* ■ informal an instance of stealing or plagiarizing something. ■ an upward force that counteracts the force of gravity, produced by changing the direction and speed of a moving stream of air: *it had separate engines to provide lift and generate forward speed.* ■ the maximum weight that an aircraft can raise.
3 a free ride in another person's vehicle: *Miss Green is giving me a lift back to school.*
4 a feeling of encouragement or increased cheerfulness: *winning this game has given everyone on the team **a lift**.*
– PHRASES **lift a finger** (or **hand**) [usu. with negative] make the slightest effort to do something, esp. to help someone: *he never once lifted a finger to get Jimmy released from prison.* **lift his** (or **its**) **leg** informal (of a male dog) urinate.
– PHRASAL VERBS **lift off** (of an aircraft, spacecraft, or rocket) rise from the ground or a launch pad, esp. vertically.
– DERIVATIVES **lift·a·ble** adj., **lift·er** n.
– ORIGIN Middle English: from Old Norse *lypta*, of Germanic origin; related to **LOFT**.

lift·off /ˈliftˌôf, -ˌäf/ ▶ n. takeoff, esp. the vertical takeoff of a rocket or helicopter.

lift pump ▶ n. a simple pump consisting of a piston moving in a cylinder, both parts incorporating a valve.

lig·a·ment /ˈligəmənt/ ▶ n. Anatomy a short band of tough, flexible, fibrous connective tissue that connects two bones or cartilages or holds together a joint. ■ a membranous fold that supports an organ and keeps it in position. ■ any similar connecting or binding structure. ■ archaic a bond of union.
– DERIVATIVES **lig·a·men·tal** /ˌligəˈmentl/ adj., **lig·a·men·ta·ry** /ˌligəˈment(ə)rē/ adj., **lig·a·men·tous** /ˌligəˈmentəs/ adj.
– ORIGIN late Middle English: from Latin *ligamentum* 'bond,' from *ligare* 'to bind.'

li·gand /ˈligənd, ˈlī-/ ▶ n. Chemistry an ion or molecule attached to a metal atom by coordinate bonding. ■ Biochemistry a molecule that binds to another (usually larger) molecule.
– ORIGIN 1950s: from Latin *ligandus* 'that can be tied,' gerundive of *ligare* 'to bind.'

li·gase /ˈlīˌgās, -ˌgāz/ ▶ n. Biochemistry an enzyme that brings about ligation of DNA or another substance.
– ORIGIN 1960s: from Latin *ligare* 'to bind' + **-ASE**.

li·gate /ˈlīˌgāt/ ▶ v. [with obj.] (usu. **be ligated**) Surgery tie up or otherwise close off (an artery or vessel).
– ORIGIN late 16th cent.: from Latin *ligat-* 'tied,' from the verb *ligare*.

li·ga·tion /līˈgāsʜən/ ▶ n. **1** the surgical procedure of closing off a blood vessel or other duct or tube in the body by means of a ligature or clip.
2 Biochemistry the joining of two DNA strands or other molecules by a phosphate ester linkage.
– ORIGIN late Middle English: from late Latin *ligatio(n-)*, from the verb *ligare* (see **LIGATE**).

li·ga·ture /ˈligəcʜər, -ˌcʜo͝or/ ▶ n. **1** a thing used for tying or binding something tightly. ■ a cord or thread used in surgery, esp. to tie up a bleeding artery.
2 Music a slur or tie.
3 Printing a character consisting of two or more joined letters, e.g., æ, *fl*. ■ a stroke that joins adjacent letters in writing or printing.
▶ v. [with obj.] bind or connect with a ligature.
– ORIGIN Middle English: via late Latin *ligatura* from Latin *ligat-* 'bound,' from the verb *ligare*.

li·ger /ˈlīgər/ ▶ n. the hybrid offspring of a male lion and a tigress. Compare with **TIGON**.
– ORIGIN 1930s: blend of **LION** and **TIGER**.

Li·ge·ti /ˈligətē/, György Sándor (1923–2006), Hungarian composer. His orchestral works *Apparitions* (1958–59) and *Atmosphères* (1961) dispense with the formal elements of melody, harmony, and rhythm.

light[1] /līt/ ▶ n. **1** the natural agent that stimulates sight and makes things visible: *the light of the sun |* [in sing.] *the street lamps shed a faint light into the room.* ■ a source of illumination, esp. an electric lamp: *a light came on in his room.* ■ (**lights**) decorative illuminations: *Christmas lights.* ■ a traffic light: *turn right at the light.* ■ [in sing.] an expression in someone's eyes indicating a particular emotion or mood: *a shrewd light entered his eyes.* ■ the amount or quality of light in a place: *the plant requires good light | in some lights she could look beautiful.*

> Visible light is electromagnetic radiation whose wavelength falls within the range to which the human retina responds, i.e., between about 390 nm (violet light) and 740 nm (red). White light consists of a roughly equal mixture of all visible wavelengths, which can be separated to yield the colors of the spectrum, as was first demonstrated conclusively by Newton. In the 20th century it has become apparent that light consists of energy quanta called photons that behave partly like waves and partly like particles. The velocity of light in a vacuum is 299,792 km per second.

2 understanding of a problem or mystery; enlightenment: *she saw light dawn on the woman's face.* ■ spiritual illumination by divine truth. ■ (**lights**) a person's opinions, standards, and abilities: *leaving the police to do the job **according to their lights**.*
3 an area of something that is brighter or paler than its surroundings: *sunshine will brighten the natural lights in your hair.*
4 a device that makes something start burning, as a match, lighter, or flame: *he asked me for a light.*
5 a window or opening in a wall to let light in. ■ any of the perpendicular divisions of a mullioned window. ■ any of the panes of glass forming the roof or side of a greenhouse or the top of a cold frame.
6 a person notable or eminent in a particular sphere of activity or place: *such lights of liberalism as the historian Goldwin Smith.*
▶ v. (past **lit** /lit/; past participle **lit** or **lighted**) [with obj.] **1** provide with light or lighting; illuminate: *the room was lighted by a number of small lamps | lightning suddenly lit up the house.* ■ switch on (an electric light): *only one of the table lamps was lit.* ■ [no obj.] (**light up**) become illuminated: *the sign to fasten seat belts lit up.*
2 make (something) start burning; ignite: *Allen gathered sticks and lit a fire |* (as adj. **lighted** or **lit**) *a lighted cigarette.* ■ [no obj.] begin to burn; be ignited: *the gas wouldn't light properly.* ■ (**light something up**) ignite a cigarette, cigar, or pipe and begin to smoke it: *she lit up a cigarette and puffed on it serenely |* [no obj.] *workers who light up in prohibited areas face dismissal.*
▶ adj. **1** having a considerable or sufficient amount of natural light; not dark: *the bedrooms are light and airy | it was almost light outside.*
2 (of a color) pale: *her eyes were light blue.*
– PHRASES **bring** (or **come**) **to light** make (or become) widely known or evident: *an investigation to bring to light examples of extravagant expenditure.* **go out like a light** informal fall asleep or lose consciousness suddenly. **in a —— light** in the way specified; so as to give a specified impression: *the audit portrayed the company in a very favorable light.* **in (the) light of** drawing knowledge or information from; taking (something) into consideration: *the exorbitant prices are explainable in the light of the facts.* **light a fire under someone** see **FIRE**. **light at the end of the tunnel** a long-awaited indication that a period of hardship or adversity is nearing an end. **light the fuse** see **FUSE**[2]. **the light of day** daylight. ■ general public attention: *bringing old family secrets into the light of day.* **the light of someone's life** a much loved person. **lights out** bedtime in a school dormitory, military barracks, or other institution, when lights should be switched off. **lit up** informal, dated drunk. **see the light** understand or realize something after prolonged thought or doubt. ■ undergo religious conversion. **see the light of day** be born. ■ come into existence; be made public, visible, or available: *this software first saw the light of day back in 1993.* **shed** (or **throw** or **cast**) **light on** help to explain (something) by providing further information about it.
– PHRASAL VERBS **light up** (or **light something up**) (with reference to a person's face or eyes) suddenly become or cause to be animated with liveliness or joy: *his eyes lit up and he smiled | a smile of delight lit up her face.*
– DERIVATIVES **light·ish** adj., **light·less** adj., **light·ness** n.
– ORIGIN Old English *lēoht*, *līht* (noun and adjective), *līhtan* (verb), of Germanic origin; related to Dutch *licht* and German *Licht*, from an Indo-European root shared by Greek *leukos* 'white' and Latin *lux* 'light.'

light[2] ▶ adj. **1** of little weight; easy to lift: *they are very light and portable | you're **as light as a feather**.* ■ deficient in weight, esp. by a specified amount: *the sack of potatoes is 5 pounds light.* ■ not strongly or heavily built or constructed; small of its kind: *light, impractical clothes | light armor.* ■ carrying or suitable for small loads: *light commercial vehicles.* ■ carrying only light armaments: *light infantry.*

■ (of a vehicle, ship, or aircraft) traveling unladen or with less than a full load. ■ (of food or a meal) small in quantity and easy to digest: *a light supper.* ■ (of a foodstuff) low in fat, cholesterol, sugar, or other rich ingredients: *stick to a light diet.* ■ (of drink) not too sweet or rich in flavor or strongly alcoholic: *a glass of light Hungarian wine.* ■ (of food, esp. pastry or sponge cake) fluffy or well aerated during cooking. ■ (of soil) friable, porous, and workable. ■ (of an isotope) having not more than the usual mass; (of a compound) containing such an isotope.
2 relatively low in density, amount, or intensity: *passenger traffic was light | light summer breezes | trading was light for most of the day.* ■ (of sleep or a sleeper) easily disturbed. ■ easily borne or done: *he received a relatively light sentence | some light housework.*
3 gentle or delicate: *she planted a light kiss on his cheek | my breathing was steady and light.* ■ (of type) having thin strokes; not bold.
4 (of entertainment) requiring little mental effort; not profound or serious: *pop is thought of as light entertainment | some light reading.* ■ not serious or solemn: *his tone was light.* ■ free from worry or unhappiness; cheerful: *I left the island with a light heart.*
5 archaic (of a woman) unchaste; promiscuous.
– PHRASES **be light on** be rather short of: *light on hard news.* **be light on one's feet** (of a person) be quick or nimble. **a** (or **someone's**) **light touch** the ability to deal with something delicately, tactfully, or in an understated way: *a novel that handles its tricky subject with a light touch.* **make light of** treat as unimportant: *I didn't mean to make light of your problems.* **make light work of** accomplish (a task) quickly and easily. **travel light** travel with a minimum load or minimum luggage.
– DERIVATIVES **light·ish** adj., **light·ness** n.
– ORIGIN Old English *lēocht, līht* (noun), *lēohte* (adverb), of Germanic origin; related to Dutch *licht* and German *leicht*, from an Indo-European root shared by LUNG.

light[3] ▶ v. (past and past participle **lit** /lit/ or **lighted**) [no obj.] **1** (**light on/upon**) come upon or discover by chance: *he lit on a possible solution.*
2 archaic descend: *from the horse he lit down.* ■ (**light on**) fall and settle or land on (a surface): *a feather just lighted on the ground.*
– PHRASAL VERBS **light into** informal criticize severely; attack: *he lit into him for his indiscretion.* **light out** informal depart hurriedly.
– ORIGIN Old English *līhtan* (sense 2; also 'lessen the weight of'), from LIGHT[2]; compare with ALIGHT[1].

light air ▶ n. a wind of force 1 on the Beaufort scale (1–3 knots or 1–3.5 mph).

light box ▶ n. a flat box with a side of translucent glass or plastic and containing an electric light, so as to provide an evenly lighted flat surface or even illumination, such as in an art or photography studio.

light breeze ▶ n. a wind of force 2 on the Beaufort scale (4–6 knots or 4.5-7 mph).

Light Bri·gade, Charge of the see CHARGE OF THE LIGHT BRIGADE.

light bulb (also **lightbulb**) ▶ n. a glass bulb inserted into a lamp or a socket in a ceiling, that provides light by passing an electric current through a pocket of inert gas.

light chain ▶ n. Biochemistry a protein subunit that, as one of a pair, forms part of the main antigen-binding region of an immunoglobulin molecule.

light cone ▶ n. Physics a surface in space-time, represented as a cone in three dimensions, comprising all the points from which a light signal would reach a given point (at the apex) simultaneously, and that therefore appear simultaneous to an observer at the apex.

light curve ▶ n. Astronomy a graph showing the variation in the light received over a period of time from a variable star or other varying celestial object.

light-emit·ting di·ode ▶ n. see **LED**.

light·en[1] /ˈlītn/ ▶ v. make or become lighter in weight, pressure, or severity: [with obj.] *efforts to lighten the burden of regulation* | [no obj.] *the strain had lightened.* ■ make or become more cheerful or less serious: [with obj.] *she attempted a joke to lighten the atmosphere* | [no obj.] *Robbie felt her spirits lighten a little.*

light·en[2] ▶ v. **1** make or become lighter or brighter: [no obj.] *the sky began to lighten in the east* | [with obj.] *she had lightened her hair.* ■ [with obj.] archaic enlighten spiritually: *now the Lord lighten thee, thou art a great fool.*
2 [no obj.] (**it lightens, it is lightening**, etc.) rare emit flashes of lightning; flash with lightning: *it thundered and lightened.*

USAGE Years ago, the phrase **it is lightening** (as in 'thundering and lightening') was contracted to **it is light'ning**, which eventually became further shortened to **it is lightning**. In modern use, the word **lightning** stands on its own as a noun (*did you see that lightning?*) and a verb (*it looks as if it's going to start lightning*). Today, in the context of electrical storms, **lightening** would likely be considered a misspelling of **lightning**, rather than a variant spelling.

light en·gine ▶ n. a railroad locomotive running with no vehicles attached.
▶ adv. (of a locomotive) running with no vehicles attached: *75069 returned light engine.*

light·en·ing /ˈlītn-iNG, ˈlītniNG/ ▶ n. a drop in the level of the uterus during the last weeks of pregnancy as the head of the fetus engages in the pelvis.

light·er[1] /ˈlītər/ ▶ n. a device that produces a small flame, typically used to light cigarettes.

light·er[2] ▶ n. a flat-bottomed barge or other unpowered boat used to transfer cargo to and from ships in harbor.
▶ v. [with obj.] transport (goods) in a lighter: *they lightered their cargo ashore.*
– DERIVATIVES **light·er·man** /-mən/ n. (pl. **lightermen**).
– ORIGIN late Middle English: from LIGHT[2] (in the sense 'unload'), or from Middle Low German *luchter*.

light·er·age /ˈlītərij/ ▶ n. the transfer of cargo by means of a lighter; the charge levied for such transfer.

light·er-than-air ▶ adj. [attrib.] relating to or denoting a balloon or other aircraft weighing less than the air it displaces, and so flying as a result of its own buoyancy.

light·face /ˈlītˌfās/ ▶ n. typeface or font characterized by light, thin lines.

light·fast /ˈlītˌfast/ ▶ adj. (of a dye or pigment) not prone to discolor when exposed to light.
– DERIVATIVES **light·fast·ness** n.

light-fin·gered ▶ adj. **1** prone to steal: *light-fingered shoplifters.*
2 having or showing delicate skill with the hands: *it is played with an irresistibly light-fingered spontaneity.*

light fly·weight ▶ n. the lowest weight in amateur boxing, ranging up to 106 pounds (48 kg). ■ an amateur boxer of this weight.

light-foot·ed ▶ adj. fast, nimble, or stealthy on one's feet: *a light-footed leap.*
– DERIVATIVES **light-foot·ed·ly** adv.

light gun ▶ n. Computing a handheld gunlike photosensitive device used chiefly in computer games, held to the display screen for passing information to the computer.

light·head·ed /ˈlītˌhedid/ ▶ adj. dizzy and slightly faint: *I was lightheaded from fear.*
– DERIVATIVES **light·head·ed·ly** adv., **light·head·ed·ness** n.

light·heart·ed /ˈlītˌhärtid/ ▶ adj. cheerful and carefree: *excited, lighthearted chatter.*
– DERIVATIVES **light·heart·ed·ly** adv., **light·heart·ed·ness** n.

light heav·y·weight ▶ n. a weight in boxing and other sports intermediate between middleweight and heavyweight. In the amateur boxing scale it ranges from 165 to 178 pounds (75 to 81 kg). ■ a boxer or other competitor of this weight.

light·house /ˈlītˌhous/ ▶ n. a tower or other structure containing a beacon light to warn or guide ships at sea.

lighthouse

light in·dus·try ▶ n. the manufacture of small or light articles.

light·ing /ˈlītiNG/ ▶ n. equipment in a home, workplace, studio, theater, or street for producing light: *the heartless glare of strip lighting.* ■ the arrangement or effect of lights: *the lighting was very flat.*

light·ing cam·er·a·man ▶ n. (in filmmaking) a person in charge of the lighting of sets being filmed.

light·ly /ˈlītlē/ ▶ adv. **1** gently, delicately or softly: *she placed her hand lightly on my shoulder.*
2 in relatively small amounts or in low density; sparingly: *it was snowing lightly.*
3 in a way that is not serious or solemn; carelessly: *it is not something that should be taken lightly.*
4 without severe punishment; leniently: *some people are let off lightly.*

light ma·chine gun ▶ n. any air-cooled machine gun with a caliber no greater than .30 inch (7.6 mm).

light me·ter ▶ n. an instrument for measuring the intensity of light, used chiefly to show the correct exposure when taking a photograph. Also called EXPOSURE METER.

light mid·dle·weight ▶ n. a weight in amateur boxing ranging from 148 to 156 pounds (67 to 71 kg). ■ an amateur boxer of this weight.

light·ning /ˈlītniNG/ ▶ n. the occurrence of a natural electrical discharge of very short duration and high voltage between a cloud and the ground or within a cloud, accompanied by a bright flash and typically also thunder: *a tremendous flash of lightning.* ■ literary a flash or discharge of this kind: *the sky was a mass of black cloud out of which lightnings flashed.*
▶ adj. [attrib.] very quick: *a lightning cure for his hangover | galloping across the country at lightning speed.*
– PHRASES **lightning never strikes twice in the same place** proverb an unusual situation or event is unlikely to happen again in exactly the same circumstances or to the same person. **like (greased) lightning** very quickly.
– ORIGIN Middle English: special use of *lightening* (verbal noun from LIGHTEN[2]).

USAGE See usage at LIGHTEN[2].

light·ning bug ▶ n. another term for FIREFLY.

light·ning rod ▶ n. a metal rod or wire fixed to an exposed part of a building or other tall structure to divert lightning harmlessly into the ground. ■ a person or thing that attracts a lot of criticism, esp. in order to divert attention from more serious issues or to allow a more important public figure to appear blameless.

Light on the Moun·tain a nickname for the state of IDAHO.

light op·er·a ▶ n. another term for OPERETTA.

light pen ▶ n. **1** Computing a handheld, penlike photosensitive device held to the display screen of a computer terminal for passing information to the computer.
2 a handheld, light-emitting device used for reading bar codes.

light pol·lu·tion ▶ n. brightening of the night sky that inhibits the observation of stars and planets, caused by street lights and other man-made sources.

light·proof /ˈlītˌpro͞of/ ▶ adj. able to block out light completely.

light rail ▶ n. a railroad constructed for light traffic.

light re·ac·tion ▶ n. **1** the reaction of something, esp. the iris of the eye, to different intensities of light.
2 (**the light reaction**) Biochemistry the reaction that occurs as the first phase of photosynthesis, in which energy in the form of light is absorbed and converted to chemical energy in the form of ATP.

lights /līts/ ▶ plural n. the lungs of sheep or pigs used as food, esp. for pets.
– ORIGIN Middle English: use of LIGHT[2] as a noun (so named because of their lightness). Compare with LUNG.

light scoop ▶ n. an architectural feature that captures natural light and draws it into parts of a building.

light-sen·si·tive ▶ adj. (of a surface or substance) changing physically or chemically when exposed to light. ■ Biology (of a cell, organ, or tissue) able to detect the presence or intensity of light.

light·ship /ˈlītˌSHip/ ▶ n. a moored or anchored vessel with a beacon light to warn or guide ships at sea.

light show ▶ n. a spectacle of colored lights that move and change, esp. at a pop concert.

light·some /ˈlītsəm/ ▶ adj. chiefly literary **1** merry and carefree.
2 gracefully nimble: *lightsome, high-flying dancers.*
– DERIVATIVES **light·some·ly** adv., **light·some·ness** n.

light ta·ble ▶ n. a horizontal or tilted surface of translucent glass or plastic with a light behind it, used as a light box for drawing or viewing transparencies or negatives.

light trap ▶ n. **1** Zoology an illuminated trap for attracting and catching nocturnal animals, esp. moths and other flying insects.

2 Photography a device for excluding light from a darkroom without preventing entry into it.

light wa·ter ▶ **n. 1** water containing the normal proportion (or less) of deuterium oxide, i.e., about 0.02 percent, esp. to distinguish it from heavy water. **2** foam formed by water and a fluorocarbon surfactant, which floats on flammable liquids lighter than water and is used in firefighting.

light·weight /ˈlītˌwāt/ ▶ **n. 1** a weight in boxing and other sports intermediate between featherweight and welterweight. In the amateur boxing scale it ranges from 125 to 132 pounds (57 to 60 kg). ■ a boxer or other competitor of this weight.
2 a person or thing that is lightly built or constructed. ■ a person of little importance or influence, esp. in a particular sphere: *he was regarded as a political lightweight.*
▶ **adj. 1** of thin material or build and weighing less than average: *a lightweight gray suit.*
2 containing little serious matter: *the newspaper is lightweight and trivial.*

light well ▶ **n.** an open area or vertical shaft in the center of a building, typically roofed with glass, bringing natural light to the lower floors or basement.

light wel·ter·weight ▶ **n.** a weight in amateur boxing ranging from 132 to 140 pounds (60 to 63.5 kg). ■ an amateur boxer of this weight.

light·wood /ˈlītˌwo͝od/ ▶ **n.** firewood that burns easily and with a bright flame, esp. dry, resinous pine.

light year ▶ **n.** Astronomy a unit of astronomical distance equivalent to the distance that light travels in one year, which is 9.4607×10^{12} km (nearly 6 trillion miles). ■ (**light years**) informal a long distance or great amount: *the new range puts them light years ahead of the competition.*

lig·ne·ous /ˈlignēəs/ ▶ **adj.** made, consisting of, or resembling wood; woody.
– ORIGIN early 17th cent.: from Latin *ligneus* 'relating to wood' + **-OUS**.

ligni- ▶ **comb. form** relating to wood: *lignify.*
– ORIGIN from Latin *lignum* 'wood.'

lig·ni·fy /ˈlignəˌfī/ ▶ **v.** (**lignifies, lignifying, lignified**) [with obj.] (usu. as adj. **lignified**) Botany make rigid and woody by the deposition of lignin in cell walls.
– DERIVATIVES **lig·ni·fi·ca·tion** /ˌlignəfəˈkāsHən/ **n.**

lig·nin /ˈlignin/ ▶ **n.** Botany a complex organic polymer deposited in the cell walls of many plants, making them rigid and woody.
– ORIGIN early 19th cent.: from **LIGNI-** 'of wood' + **-IN**[1].

lig·nite /ˈligˌnīt/ ▶ **n.** a soft brownish coal showing traces of plant structure, intermediate between bituminous coal and peat.
– DERIVATIVES **lig·nit·ic** /ligˈnitik/ **adj.**
– ORIGIN early 19th cent.: coined in French from Latin *lignum* 'wood' + **-ITE**[1].

ligno- ▶ **comb. form** relating to wood: *lignotuber.* ■ representing **LIGNIN**: *lignocellulose.*
– ORIGIN from Latin *lignum* 'wood.'

lig·no·caine /ˈlignəˌkān/ ▶ **n.** another term for **LIDOCAINE**.
– ORIGIN 1950s: from **LIGNO-** (Latin equivalent of **XYLO-**, used in the earlier name *xylocaine* and reflecting chemical similarity to **XYLENE**) + *-caine* (from **COCAINE**).

lig·no·cel·lu·lose /ˌlignōˈselyəˌlōs, -ˌlōz/ ▶ **n.** Botany a complex of lignin and cellulose present in the cell walls of woody plants.

lig·no·tu·ber /ˈlignōˌt(y)o͞obər/ ▶ **n.** Botany a rounded woody growth at or below ground level on some shrubs and trees that grow in areas subject to fire or drought, containing a mass of buds and food reserves.

lig·num vi·tae /ˈlignəm ˈvīˌtē, ˈvēˌtī/ ▶ **n.** another term for **GUAIACUM**.
– ORIGIN Latin, 'wood of life.'

lig·ro·in /ˈligrō-in/ ▶ **n.** Chemistry a volatile hydrocarbon mixture obtained from petroleum and used as a solvent.
– ORIGIN late 19th cent.: of unknown origin.

lig·u·la /ˈligyələ/ ▶ **n.** (pl. **ligulae** /-ˌlē, -ˌlī/) Entomology the strap-shaped terminal part of an insect's labium, typically lobed.
– DERIVATIVES **lig·u·lar adj.**
– ORIGIN mid 18th cent.: from Latin, 'strap.'

lig·u·late /ˈligyəˌlāt, -lit/ ▶ **adj.** chiefly Botany strap-shaped, such as the ray florets of plants of the daisy family. ■ (of a plant) having ray florets or ligules.

lig·ule /ˈligˌyo͞ol/ ▶ **n.** Botany a narrow strap-shaped part of a plant, esp., in most grasses and sedges, a membranous scale on the inner side of the leaf sheath at its junction with the blade.
– ORIGIN early 19th cent.: from Latin *ligula* 'strap.'

Li·gu·ri·a /liˈg(y)o͞orēə/ a coastal region of northwestern Italy that extends along the Mediterranean coast from Tuscany to the border with France; capital, Genoa. In ancient times, Liguria extended as far as the Atlantic Ocean.
– DERIVATIVES **Li·gu·ri·an adj. & n.**
– ORIGIN from Latin *Ligur* 'Ligurian,' from Greek *Ligus.*

Li·gu·ri·an Sea /liˈg(y)o͞orēən/ a part of the northern Mediterranean Sea, between Corsica and the northwestern coast of Italy.

li·gus·trum /liˈgəstrəm/ ▶ **n.** a plant of a genus that comprises the privets. ● Genus *Ligustrum*, family Oleaceae.
– ORIGIN mid 17th cent.: from Latin.

lik·a·ble /ˈlīkəbəl/ (also **likeable**) ▶ **adj.** (esp. of a person) pleasant, friendly, and easy to like.
– DERIVATIVES **lik·a·bil·i·ty** /ˌlīkəˈbilətē/ **n.**, **lik·a·ble·ness n.**, **lik·a·bly** /-blē/ **adv.**

like[1] /līk/ ▶ **prep. 1** having the same characteristics or qualities as; similar to: *there were other suits like mine in the shop* | *they were like brothers* | *she looked nothing like Audrey Hepburn.* ■ in the manner of; in the same way or to the same degree as: *he was screaming like a banshee* | *you must run like the wind.* ■ in a way appropriate to: *students were angry at being treated like children.* ■ such as one might expect from; characteristic of: *just like you to put a damper on people's enjoyment.* ■ used in questions to ask about the characteristics or nature of someone or something: *What is it like to be a tuna fisherman?* | *What's she like?*
2 used to draw attention to the nature of an action or event: *I apologize for coming over unannounced like this* | *why are you talking about me like that?*
3 such as; for example: *the cautionary vision of works like Animal Farm and 1984.*
▶ **conj.** informal **1** in the same way that; as: *people who change countries like they change clothes.*
2 as though; as if: *I felt like I'd been kicked by a camel.*
▶ **n.** used with reference to a person or thing of the same kind as another: *the quotations could be arranged to put* **like with like** | *I know him—him and his like.* ■ (**the like**) a thing or things of the same kind (often used to express surprise or for emphasis): *did you ever hear the like?* | *a church interior* **the like of which** *he had never seen before.*
▶ **adj.** (of a person or thing) having similar qualities or characteristics to another person or thing: *I responded in like manner* | *the grouping of children of like ability together.* ■ (Brit.) (of a portrait or other image) having a faithful resemblance to the original: *"Who painted the dog's picture? It's very like."*
▶ **adv. 1** informal used in speech as a meaningless filler or to signify the speaker's uncertainty about an expression just used: *there was this funny smell—sort of dusty like.*
2 informal used to convey a person's reported attitude or feelings in the form of direct speech (whether or not representing an actual quotation): *so she comes into the room and she's like "Where is everybody?"*
3 (**like as/to**) archaic in the manner of: *like as a ship with dreadful storm long tossed.*
– PHRASES **and the like** and similar things; et cetera. **like anything** informal to a great degree: *they would probably worry like anything.* **(as) like as not** probably: *she would be in bed by now, like as not.* **like enough** (or **most like**) archaic probably: *he'll have lost a deal of blood, I dare say, and like enough he's still losing it.* **like ——, like ——** as —— is, so is ——: *like father, like son.* **like so** informal in this manner: *the votive candles are arranged like so.* **the likes of** informal used of someone or something regarded as a type: *she didn't want to associate with the likes of me.* **more like** informal nearer to (a specified number or description) than one previously given: *he believes the figure should be more like $10 million.* ■ (**more like it**) nearer to what is required or expected; more satisfactory. **of (a) like mind** (of a person) sharing the same opinions or tastes.
– ORIGIN Middle English: from Old Norse *líkr*; related to **ALIKE**.

> **USAGE** The use of like as a conjunction meaning 'as' or 'as if' (*I don't have a wealthy set of in-laws like you do; they sit up like they're begging for food*) is considered by many to be incorrect. Although like has been used as a conjunction in this way since the 15th century by many respected writers, it is still frowned upon and considered unacceptable in formal English. In more precise use, like is a preposition, used before nouns and pronouns: *to fly like a bird; a town like ours.* See also usage at **GO**[1].

like[2] ▶ **v.** [with obj.] **1** find agreeable, enjoyable, or satisfactory: *I like all Angela Carter's stories* | *people who don't like reading books* | *I like to be the center of attention.*
2 wish for; want: *would you like a cup of coffee?* | *I'd like to rent a car* | [with obj. and infinitive] *I'd like you to stay* | [no obj.] *we would like for you to work for us.* ■ (**would like to do something**) used as a polite formula: *we would like to apologize for the late running of this service.* ■ (**not like doing/to do something**) feel reluctant to do something: *I don't like leaving her on her own too long.* ■ choose to have (something); prefer: *how do you like your coffee?* ■ [in questions] feel about or regard (something): *how would you like it if it happened to you?*
▶ **n.** (**likes**) the things one likes or prefers: *a wide variety of likes, dislikes, tastes, and income levels.*
– PHRASES **if you like 1** if it suits or pleases you: *we could go riding if you like.* **2** used when expressing something in a new or unusual way: *it's a whole new branch of chemistry, a new science if you like.* **I like that!** used as an exclamation expressing affront. **like it or not** informal used to indicate that someone has no choice in a matter: *you're celebrating with us, like it or not.* **not like the look** (or **sound**) **of** find worrying or alarming: *I don't like the look of that head injury.* **what's not to like?** informal used as a rhetorical expression of approval or satisfaction: *cleaner air, cooler temperatures, and mountain views—what's not to like?*
– ORIGIN Old English *līcian* 'be pleasing,' of Germanic origin; related to Dutch *lijken.*

-like ▶ **comb. form** (added to nouns) similar to; characteristic of: *pealike* | *crustlike.*

like·a·ble ▶ **adj.** variant spelling of **LIKABLE**.

like·li·hood /ˈlīklēˌho͝od/ ▶ **n.** the state or fact of something's being likely; probability: *young people who can see no likelihood of finding employment* | [in sing.] *situations where there is* **a likelihood of** *violence.*
– PHRASES **in all likelihood** very probably.

like·ly /ˈlīklē/ ▶ **adj.** (**likelier, likeliest**) **1** such as well might happen or be true; probable: *the likely effects of the drought on sugar beet yields* | *it was likely that he would make a televised statement* | *sales are likely to drop further.*
2 apparently suitable; promising: *a likely-looking spot.*
▶ **adv.** probably: *we will most likely go to a bar.*
– PHRASES **a likely story** used to express disbelief in an account or excuse: *Gone running, has he? A likely story!* **as likely as not** probably: *I won't take their pills because as likely as not they'd poison me.* **not likely!** informal certainly not; I refuse: *"Are you going home?" "Not likely!"*
– DERIVATIVES **like·li·ness n.**
– ORIGIN Middle English: from Old Norse *líkligr*, from *líkr* (see **LIKE**[1]).

like-mind·ed ▶ **adj.** having similar tastes or opinions: *a small group of like-minded friends.*
– DERIVATIVES **like-mind·ed·ness n.**

lik·en /ˈlīkən/ ▶ **v.** [with obj.] (**liken someone/something to**) point out the resemblance of someone or something to: *they likened the reigning emperor to a god.*
– ORIGIN Middle English: from **LIKE**[1] + **-EN**[1].

like·ness /ˈlīknis/ ▶ **n.** the fact or quality of being alike; resemblance: *her likeness to him was astonishing* | *a family likeness can be seen among all the boys.* ■ the semblance, guise, or outward appearance of: *humans are described as being made in God's likeness.* ■ a portrait or representation: *the only known likeness of Dorothy as a young woman.*
– ORIGIN Old English *gelīknes* (see **ALIKE**, **-NESS**).

like·wise /ˈlīkˌwīz/ ▶ **adv. 1** in the same way; also: *the dream of young people is to grow old, and it is likewise the dream of their parents to relive youth.* ■ used to introduce a point similar or related to one just made: *you will forget the bad things that have happened in the past. Likewise, I will forget what you have done to me.*
2 in a like manner; similarly: *I stuck out my tongue and Frankie* **did likewise**.
– ORIGIN late Middle English: from the phrase *in like wise.*

lik·ing /ˈlīkiNG/ ▶ **n.** [in sing.] a feeling of regard or fondness: *Mrs. Parsons had a liking for gin and tonic* | *she'd taken an instant liking to Arnie's new girlfriend.*
– PHRASES **for one's liking** to suit one's taste or wishes: *he is a little too showy for my liking.* **to one's liking** to one's taste; pleasing: *his coffee was just to his liking.*
– ORIGIN Old English *līcung* (see **LIKE**[2], **-ING**[1]).

Li·kud /liˈko͞od, -ˈko͝od/ a coalition of right-wing Israeli political parties, formed in 1973. Likud returned to power in 1996 under Benjamin Netanyahu.
– ORIGIN Hebrew, literally 'consolidation, unity.'

li·lac /ˈlīˌläk, -ˌlak, -ˌlək/ ▶ **n.** a Eurasian shrub or small tree of the olive family, that has fragrant violet, pink, or white blossoms and is widely cultivated as an ornamental. ● Genus *Syringa*, family Oleaceae;

several species, in particular the **common lilac** (*S. vulgaris*), with many cultivars. ■ a pale pinkish-violet color.
▶ **adj.** of a pale pinkish-violet color.
– ORIGIN early 17th cent.: from obsolete French, via Spanish and Arabic from Persian *līlak*, variant of *nīlak* 'bluish,' from *nīl* 'blue.'

li·lan·ge·ni /ˌliläNGˈgenē/ ▶ **n.** (pl. **emalangeni** /ˌeməläNGˈgenē/) the basic monetary unit of Swaziland, equal to 100 cents.
– ORIGIN from the Bantu prefix *li-* (used to denote a singular) + *-langeni* 'member of a royal family.'

lil·i·a·ceous /ˌlilēˈāsHəs/ ▶ **adj.** Botany of, relating to, or denoting plants of the lily family (Liliaceae). These have elongated leaves that grow from a corm, bulb, or rhizome.
– ORIGIN mid 18th cent.: from modern Latin *Liliaceae* (plural), based on Latin *lilium* 'lily,' + **-OUS**.

Lil·i·en·thal /ˈlilēənˌTHôl, -ˌtäl/, Otto (1848–96), German pioneer in the design and flying of gliders. Working with his brother, he made over 2,000 flights in various gliders before being killed in a crash.

Lil·ith /ˈliliTH/ a female demon of Jewish folklore, who tries to kill newborn children. In the Talmud she is the first wife of Adam, dispossessed by Eve.

Li·li·u·o·ka·la·ni /lī,lēə,wäkəˈlänē/ (1838–1917), Hawaiian queen; also known as **Lydia Paki Liliuokalani**. The last reigning queen of the Hawaiian Islands 1891–93, she ascended the throne in 1891. As queen, she fought for the independence of Hawaii. She was deposed by US marines in 1893 and formally renounced her royal claim in 1895.

Lille /lēl/ an industrial city in northern France, near the border with Belgium; pop. 232,432 (2006).

Lil·le·ham·mer /ˈlilə,hämər/ a resort town and capital of Oppland county, in southern Norway, site of the 1994 Winter Olympics; pop. 19,992 (2008).

Lil·li·pu·tian /ˌliləˈpyo͞osHən/ ▶ **adj.** trivial or very small: *America's banks no longer look Lilliputian in comparison with Japan's*.
▶ **n.** a trivial or very small person or thing.
– ORIGIN early 18th cent.: from the imaginary country of *Lilliput* in Swift's *Gulliver's Travels*, inhabited by people 6 inches (15 cm) high, + **-IAN**.

Li·lon·gwe /liˈlôNGwā/ the capital of Malawi, founded in 1975; pop. 669,021 (2008).

lilt /lilt/ ▶ **n.** a characteristic rising and falling of the voice when speaking; a pleasant gentle accent: *he spoke with a faint but recognizable Irish lilt*. ■ a pleasant, gently swinging rhythm in a song or tune: *the lilt of the Hawaiian music*. ■ archaic, chiefly Scottish a cheerful tune.
▶ **v.** [no obj.] (often as adj. **lilting**) speak, sing, or sound with a lilt: *a lilting Welsh accent*.
– ORIGIN late Middle English *lulte* (in the senses 'sound an alarm' or 'lift up the voice'), of unknown origin.

lil·y /ˈlilē/ ▶ **n.** (pl. **lilies**) **1** a bulbous plant with large trumpet-shaped, typically fragrant, flowers on a tall, slender stem. Lilies have long been cultivated, some kinds being of symbolic importance and some used in perfumery. ● Genus *Lilium*, family Liliaceae (the **lily family**). This family includes many flowering bulbs, such as bluebells, hyacinths, and tulips. Several plants are often placed in different families, esp. the Alliaceae (onions and their relatives), Aloaceae (aloes), and Amaryllidaceae (amaryllis, daffodils, jonquil), and as many as 38 families are sometimes recognized. ■ short for **WATER LILY**. ■ used in names of other plants with similar flowers or leaves, e.g., **arum lily**.
2 a heraldic fleur-de-lis.
– DERIVATIVES **lil·ied** /ˈlilēd/ **adj.**
– ORIGIN Old English *lilie*, from Latin *lilium*, from Greek *leirion*.

lil·y-liv·ered ▶ **adj.** weak and cowardly.

lil·y-of-the-Nile ▶ **n.** another term for **AGAPANTHUS**.

lil·y of the val·ley ▶ **n.** a widely cultivated European plant of the lily family, with broad leaves and arching stems of fragrant, bell-shaped white flowers. ● *Convallaria majalis*, family Liliaceae.

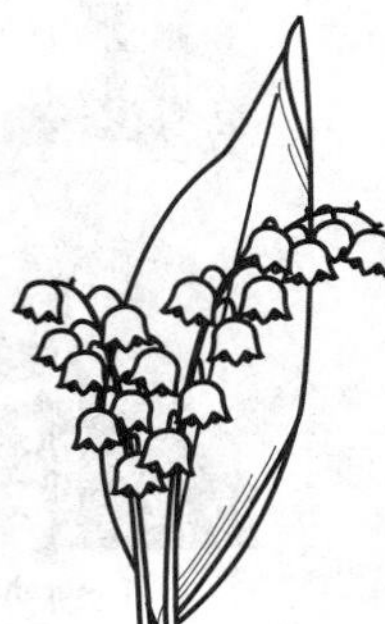
lily of the valley

lil·y pad ▶ **n.** a round, floating leaf of a water lily.

lil·y-trot·ter ▶ **n.** (esp. in Africa) a jacana.

lil·y-white ▶ **adj.** pure or ideally white. ■ without fault or corruption; totally innocent or immaculate: *they want me to conform, to be lily-white*.

lim. ▶ **abbr.** limit.

Li·ma /ˈlēmə/ the capital of Peru; pop. 7,605,700 (est. 2007). Founded in 1535 by Francisco Pizarro, it was the capital of the Spanish colonies in South America until the 19th century. ■ a code word representing the letter L, used in radio communication.

li·ma bean /ˈlīmə/ ▶ **n.** **1** an edible flat whitish bean. See also **BUTTER BEAN**.
2 the tropical American plant that yields this bean. ● *Phaseolus lunatus* (or **limensis**), family Leguminosae.
– ORIGIN mid 18th cent.: *lima* from the name of the Peruvian capital **LIMA**.

Li·mas·sol /ˌlēməˈsôl/ a port on the south coast of Cyprus, on Akrotiri Bay; pop. 179,900 (est. 2005).

limb¹ /lim/ ▶ **n.** an arm or leg of a person or four-legged animal, or a bird's wing. ■ a large branch of a tree. ■ a projecting landform such as a spur of a mountain range, or each of two or more such projections as in a forked peninsula or archipelago. ■ a projecting section of a building. ■ a branch of a cross. ■ each half of an archery bow.
– PHRASES **life and limb** life and all bodily faculties: *a reckless disregard for life and limb*. **out on a limb** in or into a dangerous or uncompromising position, where one is not joined or supported by anyone else; vulnerable: *she's prepared to **go out on a limb** and do something different*. **tear someone limb from limb** violently dismember someone.
– DERIVATIVES **limbed adj.** [in combination] *long-limbed*, **limb·less adj.**
– ORIGIN Old English *lim* (also in the sense 'organ or part of the body'), of Germanic origin.

limb² ▶ **n.** **1** Astronomy the edge of the disk of a celestial object, esp. the sun or moon.
2 Botany the blade or broad part of a leaf or petal. ■ the spreading upper part of a tube-shaped flower.
3 the graduated arc of a quadrant or other scientific instrument, used for measuring angles.
– ORIGIN late Middle English: from French *limbe* or Latin *limbus* 'hem, border.'

Lim·ba /ˈlimbə/ ▶ **n.** (pl. **same** or **Limbas**) **1** a member of a people of Sierra Leone and Guinea.
2 the Niger–Congo language of this people.
▶ **adj.** of or relating to the Limbas or their language.
– ORIGIN the name in Limba.

lim·ber¹ /ˈlimbər/ ▶ **adj.** (of a person or body part) lithe; supple. ■ (of a thing) flexible: *limber graphite fishing rods*.
▶ **v.** [no obj.] warm up in preparation for exercise or activity, esp. sports: *the acrobats were **limbering up** for the big show*.
– DERIVATIVES **lim·ber·ness n.**
– ORIGIN mid 16th cent. (as an adjective): perhaps from **LIMBER²** in the dialect sense 'cart shaft,' with allusion to a to-and-fro motion.

lim·ber² ▶ **n.** the detachable front part of a gun carriage, consisting of two wheels and an axle, a pole, and a frame holding one or more ammunition boxes.
▶ **v.** [with obj.] attach a limber to (a gun).
– ORIGIN Middle English *lymour*, apparently related to medieval Latin *limonarius* from *limo, limon-* 'shaft.'

lim·ber·neck /ˈlimbər,nek/ ▶ **n.** a kind of botulism affecting poultry.

lim·ber pine ▶ **n.** a small pine tree with tough pliant branches, native to the Rocky Mountains. ● *Pinus flexilis*, family Pinaceae.

lim·bi /ˈlim,bī, -,bē/ plural form of **LIMBUS**.

lim·bic sys·tem /ˈlimbik/ ▶ **n.** a complex system of nerves and networks in the brain, involving several areas near the edge of the cortex concerned with instinct and mood. It controls the basic emotions (fear, pleasure, anger) and drives (hunger, sex, dominance, care of offspring).
– ORIGIN late 19th cent.: *limbic* from French *limbique*, from Latin *limbus* 'edge.'

lim·bo¹ /ˈlimbō/ ▶ **n.** **1** (also **Limbo**) (in some Christian beliefs) the supposed abode of the souls of unbaptized infants, and of the just who died before Christ's coming.
2 an uncertain period of awaiting a decision or resolution; an intermediate state or condition: *the fate of the Contras is now **in limbo***. ■ a state of neglect or oblivion: *children left in an emotional limbo*.
– ORIGIN late Middle English: from the medieval Latin phrase *in limbo*, from *limbus* 'hem, border, limbo.'

lim·bo² ▶ **n.** (pl. **limbos**) a West Indian dance in which the dancer bends backward to pass under a horizontal bar that is progressively lowered to a position just above the ground.
▶ **v.** [no obj.] dance in such a way.
– ORIGIN 1950s: from **LIMBER¹**.

Lim·burg·er /ˈlim,bərgər/ ▶ **n.** a soft white cheese with a characteristic strong smell, originally made in Limburg, a former duchy of Lorraine.

lim·bus /ˈlimbəs/ ▶ **n.** (pl. **limbi** /-,bī, -,bē/) Anatomy the border or margin of a structure, esp. the junction of the cornea and sclera in the eye.
– ORIGIN late Middle English (denoting limbo): from Latin, 'edge, border.' The current sense dates from the late 17th cent.

lime¹ /līm/ ▶ **n.** (also **quicklime**) a white caustic alkaline substance consisting of calcium oxide, obtained by heating limestone. ■ (also **slaked lime**) a white alkaline substance consisting of calcium hydroxide, made by adding water to quicklime. ■ (in general use) any of a number of calcium compounds, esp. calcium hydroxide, used as an additive to soil or water. ■ archaic birdlime.
▶ **v.** [with obj.] **1** treat (soil or water) with lime to reduce acidity and improve fertility or oxygen levels. ■ (often as adj. **limed**) give (wood) a bleached appearance by treating it with lime: *limed oak dining furniture*.
2 archaic catch (a bird) with birdlime.
– DERIVATIVES **lim·y** (also **limey**) /ˈlīmē/ **adj.** (**limier, limiest**).
– ORIGIN Old English *līm*, of Germanic origin; related to Dutch *lijm*, German *Leim*, also to **LOAM**.

lime² ▶ **n.** **1** a rounded citrus fruit similar to a lemon but greener, smaller, and with a distinctive acid flavor.
2 (also **lime tree**) the evergreen citrus tree that produces this fruit, widely cultivated in warm climates. ● *Citrus aurantifolia*, family Rutaceae.
3 a bright light green color like that of a lime: [as modifier] *day-glo orange, pink, or lime green*.
– ORIGIN mid 17th cent.: from French, from modern Provençal *limo*, Spanish *lima*, from Arabic *līma*; compare with **LEMON**.

lime³ (also **lime tree**) ▶ **n.** another term for **LINDEN**, esp. the European linden.
– ORIGIN early 17th cent.: alteration of obsolete *line*, from Old English *lind* (see **LINDEN**).

lime·ade /ˌlīmˈād, ˈlīm,ād/ ▶ **n.** a drink made from lime juice and water sweetened with sugar.

lime·burn·er /ˈlīm,bərnər/ ▶ **n.** historical a person whose job was burning limestone in order to obtain lime.

lime·kiln /ˈlīm,kil(n)/ ▶ **n.** a kiln in which limestone is burned or calcined to produce quicklime.

lime·light /ˈlīm,līt/ ▶ **n.** intense white light obtained by heating a cylinder of lime, formerly used in theaters. ■ (**the limelight**) the focus of public attention: *the works that brought the artists into the limelight*.

li·men /ˈlīmən/ ▶ **n.** (pl. **limens** or **limina** /ˈlimənə/) Psychology a threshold below which a stimulus is not perceived or is not distinguished from another.
– ORIGIN mid 17th cent.: from Latin, 'threshold.'

lim·er·ence /ˈlimərəns/ ▶ **n.** Psychology the state of being infatuated or obsessed with another person, typically experienced involuntarily and characterized by a strong desire for reciprocation of one's feelings but not primarily for a sexual relationship.
– DERIVATIVES **lim·e·rent adj.**
– ORIGIN 1970s: from *limer-* (apparently an arbitrary syllable) + **-ENCE**.

Lim·er·ick /ˈlim(ə)rik/ a county in the Republic of Ireland, in the western part of the province of Munster. ■ its county town, on the Shannon River; pop. 52,539 (2006).

lim·er·ick /ˈlim(ə)rik/ ▶ **n.** a humorous, frequently bawdy, verse of three long and two short lines rhyming *aabba*, popularized by Edward Lear.
– ORIGIN late 19th cent.: said to be from the chorus "Will you come up to Limerick?," sung between improvised verses at a gathering.

lime·scale /ˈlīm,skāl/ ▶ **n.** chiefly Brit. a whitish deposit on the inside of pipes, pots, and kettles, caused by minerals leeched from the water.

lime·stone /ˈlīm,stōn/ ▶ **n.** a hard sedimentary rock, composed mainly of calcium carbonate or dolomite, used as building material and in the making of cement.

lime sul·fur ▶ **n.** an insecticide and fungicide containing calcium polysulfides, made by boiling lime and sulfur in water.

lime·wa·ter /ˈlīm,wôtər, -,wätər/ ▶ **n.** Chemistry a solution of calcium hydroxide in water, which is alkaline and turns milky in the presence of carbon dioxide.

Lim·ey /ˈlīmē/ ▶ n. (pl. **Limeys**) chiefly derogatory a British person.
– ORIGIN late 19th cent.: from LIME[2] + -Y[1], because of the former enforced consumption of lime juice to prevent scurvy in the British navy.

lim·i·na /ˈlimənə/ plural form of LIMEN.

lim·i·nal /ˈlimənl/ ▶ adj. technical **1** of or relating to a transitional or initial stage of a process.
2 occupying a position at, or on both sides of, a boundary or threshold.
– DERIVATIVES **lim·i·nal·i·ty** /ˌliməˈnalətē/ n.
– ORIGIN late 19th cent.: from Latin *limen, limin-* 'threshold' + -AL.

lim·it /ˈlimit/ ▶ n. **1** a point or level beyond which something does not or may not extend or pass: *the limits of presidential power | the 10-minute* ***limit on speeches*** *| there was* ***no limit to*** *his imagination.* ■ (often **limits**) the terminal point or boundary of an area or movement: *the city limits | the upper limit of the tidal reaches.* ■ the furthest extent of one's physical or mental endurance: *Mary Ann tried everyone's patience* ***to the limit*** *| other horses were reaching their limit.*
2 a restriction on the size or amount of something permissible or possible: *an age limit | a weight limit.* ■ a speed limit: *a 30 mph limit.* ■ (in card games) an agreed maximum stake or bet. ■ (also **legal limit**) the maximum concentration of alcohol in the blood that the law allows in the driver of a motor vehicle: *the risk of drinkers inadvertently going* ***over the limit***.
3 Mathematics a point or value that a sequence, function, or sum of a series can be made to approach progressively, until it is as close to the point or value as desired.
▶ v. (**limits, limiting, limited**) [with obj.] set or serve as a limit to: *try to limit the amount you drink | class sizes are* ***limited to*** *a maximum of 10* | (as adj. **limiting**) *a limiting factor.*
– PHRASES **be the limit** informal be intolerably troublesome or irritating. **off limits** out of bounds: *they declared the site off limits.* ■ not to be mentioned or discussed: *it was apparent that the whole topic was off limits.* **within limits** moderately; up to a point. **without limit** with no restriction.
– DERIVATIVES **lim·i·ta·tive** /ˈliməˌtātiv/ adj.
– ORIGIN late Middle English: from Latin *limes, limit-* 'boundary, frontier.' The verb is from Latin *limitare*, from *limes*.

lim·i·tar·y /ˈliməˌterē/ ▶ adj. rare of, relating to, or subject to restriction.

lim·i·ta·tion /ˌliməˈtāsʜən/ ▶ n. **1** (often **limitations**) a limiting rule or circumstance; a restriction: *severe* ***limitations on*** *water use.* ■ a condition of limited ability; a defect or failing: *she knew her limitations better than she knew her worth.* ■ the action of limiting something: *the limitation of local authorities' powers.*
2 (also **limitation period**) Law a legally specified period beyond which an action may be defeated or a property right is not to continue. See also STATUTE OF LIMITATIONS.
– ORIGIN late Middle English: from Latin *limitatio(n-)*, from the verb *limitare* (see LIMIT).

lim·it bid ▶ n. Bridge a bid showing that the value of the bidder's hand is within a narrow range, typically ten or eleven points.

lim·it·ed /ˈlimitid/ ▶ adj. restricted in size, amount, or extent; few, small, or short: *a limited number of places are available | special offers available for a limited period | the legislation has had a limited effect.* ■ (of a monarchy or government) exercised under limitations of power prescribed by a constitution. ■ (of a person) not great in ability or talents: *I think he is a very limited man.* ■ (of a train or other vehicle of public transportation) making few intermediate stops; express. ■ (**Limited**) Brit. denoting a company whose owners are legally responsible for its debts only to the extent of the amount of capital they invested (used after a company name): *Times Newspapers Limited.*
– DERIVATIVES **lim·it·ed·ness** n.

lim·it·ed ed·i·tion ▶ n. an edition of a book, or reproduction of a print or object, limited to a specific number of copies.

lim·it·ed part·ner ▶ n. a partner in a company or venture who receives limited profits from the business and whose liability toward its debts is legally limited to the extent of his or her investment.
– DERIVATIVES **lim·it·ed part·ner·ship** n.

lim·it·ed war ▶ n. a war in which the weapons used, the nations or territory involved, or the objectives pursued are restricted in some way, in particular one in which the use of nuclear weapons is avoided.

lim·it·er /ˈlimitər/ ▶ n. a person or thing that limits something, in particular: ■ Electronics a circuit whose output is restricted to a certain range of values irrespective of the size of the input. Also called CLIPPER. ■ a device that prevents a vehicle from being driven above a specified speed. Also called SPEED LIMITER.

lim·it·less /ˈlimitlis/ ▶ adj. without end, limit, or boundary: *our resources are not limitless.*
– DERIVATIVES **lim·it·less·ly** adv., **lim·it·less·ness** n.

lim·it point ▶ n. Mathematics a point for which every neighborhood contains at least one point belonging to a given set.

lim·it switch ▶ n. a switch preventing the travel of an object in a mechanism past some predetermined point, mechanically operated by the motion of the object itself.

limn /lim/ ▶ v. [with obj.] literary depict or describe in painting or words. ■ suffuse or highlight (something) with a bright color or light: *a crescent moon limned each shred with white gold.*
– ORIGIN late Middle English (in the sense 'illuminate a manuscript'): alteration of obsolete *lumine* 'illuminate,' via Old French *luminer* from Latin *luminare* 'make light.'

lim·ner /ˈlim(n)ər/ ▶ n. chiefly historical a painter, esp. of portraits or miniatures.

lim·nol·o·gy /limˈnäləjē/ ▶ n. the study of the biological, chemical, and physical features of lakes and other bodies of fresh water.
– DERIVATIVES **lim·no·log·i·cal** /ˌlimnəˈläjikəl/ adj., **lim·nol·o·gist** /-jist/ n.
– ORIGIN late 19th cent.: from Greek *limnē* 'lake' + -LOGY.

Lím·nos /ˈlimˌnôs/ Greek name for LEMNOS.

lim·o /ˈlimō/ ▶ n. (pl. **limos**) short for LIMOUSINE.

Li·moges /lēˈmōzʜ/ a city in west central France; pop. 139,026 (2006). Famous in the late Middle Ages for enamel work, it has been noted since the 18th century for the production of porcelain.

li·mon·cel·lo /ˌlimənˈcʜelō/ ▶ n. (pl. **limoncellos**) a lemon-flavored Italian liqueur.
– ORIGIN Italian, from *limone* 'lemon' + the diminutive suffix '-cello.'

lim·o·nene /ˈliməˌnēn/ ▶ n. Chemistry a colorless liquid hydrocarbon with a lemonlike scent, present in lemon oil, orange oil, and similar essential oils.
● A terpene; chem. formula: $C_{10}H_{16}$.

li·mo·nite /ˈlīməˌnīt/ ▶ n. an amorphous brownish secondary mineral consisting of a mixture of hydrous ferric oxides, important as an iron ore.
– DERIVATIVES **li·mo·nit·ic** /ˌlīməˈnitik/ adj.
– ORIGIN early 19th cent.: from German *Limonit*, probably from Greek *leimōn* 'meadow' (suggested by the earlier German name *Wiesenerz*, literally 'meadow ore').

lim·ou·sine /ˈliməˌzēn, ˌliməˈzēn/ ▶ n. a large, luxurious automobile, esp. one driven by a chauffeur who is separated from the passengers by a partition. ■ a passenger vehicle carrying people to and from an airport.
– ORIGIN early 20th cent.: from French, feminine adjective meaning 'of Limousin,' originally denoting a caped cloak worn in *Limousin*: the car originally had a roof that protected the outside driving seat.

lim·ou·sine lib·er·al ▶ n. derogatory a wealthy liberal.

limp[1] /limp/ ▶ v. [no obj.] walk with difficulty, typically because of a damaged or stiff leg or foot: *he limped heavily as he moved* | [with adverbial of direction] *he limped off during Saturday's game.* ■ [with adverbial of direction] (of a damaged ship, aircraft, or vehicle) proceed with difficulty: *the badly damaged aircraft limped back to Sicily.*
▶ n. a tendency to limp; a gait impeded by injury or stiffness: *he walked with a limp.*
– ORIGIN late Middle English (in the sense 'fall short of'): related to obsolete *limphalt* 'lame,' and probably of Germanic origin.

limp[2] ▶ adj. lacking internal strength or structure; not stiff or firm: *she let her whole body go limp | the flags hung limp and still.* ■ having or denoting a book cover that is not stiffened with board. ■ without energy or will: *he was feeling too limp to argue | a limp handshake.*
– DERIVATIVES **limp·ly** adv., **limp·ness** n.
– ORIGIN early 18th cent.: of unknown origin; perhaps related to LIMP[1], having the basic sense 'hanging loose.'

lim·pet /ˈlimpit/ ▶ n. a marine mollusk with a shallow conical shell and a broad muscular foot, noted for the way it clings tightly to rocks.
● Patellidae, Fissurellidae (the keyhole limpets), and other families, class Gastropoda: numerous species, including the **common limpet** (*Patella vulgata*).
– ORIGIN Old English *lempedu*, from medieval Latin *lampreda* 'limpet, lamprey.'

lim·pet mine ▶ n. a mine designed to be attached magnetically to a ship's hull and set to explode after a certain time.

lim·pid /ˈlimpid/ ▶ adj. (of a liquid) free of anything that darkens; completely clear. ■ (of a person's eyes) unclouded; clear. ■ (esp. of writing or music) clear and accessible or melodious: *the limpid notes of a recorder.*
– DERIVATIVES **lim·pid·i·ty** /limˈpidətē/ n., **lim·pid·ly** adv.
– ORIGIN late Middle English: from Latin *limpidus*; perhaps related to LYMPH.

limp·kin /ˈlim(p)kin/ ▶ n. a wading marsh bird related to the rails, with long legs and a long bill, found in the southeastern US and tropical America.
● *Aramus guarauna*, the only member of the family Aramidae.
– ORIGIN late 19th cent.: from LIMP[1] (with reference to the bird's limping gait) + -KIN.

Lim·po·po /limˈpōpō/ a river in southeastern Africa. Rising as the Crocodile River near Johannesburg, it flows 1,100 miles (1,770 km) in a sweeping curve to the north and east to meet the Indian Ocean north of Maputo, Mozambique. For much of its course it forms South Africa's boundary with Botswana and Zimbabwe.

limp-wrist·ed ▶ adj. informal **1** weak; ineffectual.
2 derogatory (of a man, esp. a homosexual) effeminate.

lim·u·lus /ˈlimyələs/ ▶ n. (pl. **limuli** /-ˌlī, -ˌlē/) an arthropod of a genus that comprises the North American horseshoe crab and its extinct relatives.
● Genus *Limulus*, class Merostomata.
– ORIGIN modern Latin, from Latin *limulus* 'somewhat oblique,' from *limus* 'oblique.'

Lin /lin/, Maya (1959–) US architect. She designed the Vietnam Veterans' Memorial in Washington, DC, which was dedicated in 1982, and the Civil Rights Memorial at the Southern Poverty Law Center in Montgomery, Alabama in 1989.

lin. ▶ abbr. ■ lineal or linear. ■ liniment.

lin·ac /ˈlinˌak/ ▶ n. short for LINEAR ACCELERATOR.

Lin·a·cre /ˈlinəkər/, Thomas (*c.*1460–1524), English physician and classical scholar. In 1518, he founded the College of Physicians in London and became its first president.

lin·age /ˈlīnij/ ▶ n. the number of lines in printed or written matter, esp. when used to calculate payment.

Lin Biao /ˈlin ˈbyou/ (also **Lin Piao**) (1908–71), Chinese communist statesman and general. Having been nominated to become Mao's successor in 1969, he staged an unsuccessful coup in 1971 and was reported to have been killed in a plane crash while fleeing to the former Soviet Union.

linch·pin /ˈlincʜˌpin/ (also **lynchpin**) ▶ n. **1** a pin passed through the end of an axle to keep a wheel in position.
2 a person or thing vital to an enterprise or organization: *regular brushing is the linchpin of all good dental hygiene.*
– ORIGIN late Middle English: from Old English *lynis* (in the sense 'linchpin') + PIN.

Lin·coln[1] /ˈlinɢkən/ **1** the state capital of Nebraska; pop. 251,624 (est. 2008). Founded as Lancaster in 1856, it was made the state capital in 1867 and renamed in honor of Abraham Lincoln.
2 a city in eastern England, the county town of Lincolnshire; pop. 86,800 (est. 2009). It was founded by the Romans as Lindum Colonia.

Lin·coln[2], Abraham (1809–65), 16th president of the US 1861–65. A Republican, his election to the presidency on an anti-slavery platform helped to precipitate the Civil War, which was fought during his administration. He was assassinated shortly after the war ended and before he could fulfill his campaign promise to reconcile the North and the South. He was noted for his succinct, eloquent speeches, including the Gettysburg Address of 1863.
– DERIVATIVES **Lin·coln·esque** /ˌlinɢkəˈnesk/ adj.

Abraham Lincoln

Lin·coln green ▶ n. historical bright green woolen cloth originally made at Lincoln, England.

Lin·coln Me·mo·ri·al a monument in Washington, DC, to Abraham Lincoln, designed by **Henry Bacon** (1866–1924). Built in the form of a Greek temple, the monument houses a large statue of Lincoln.

Lincoln Memorial

Lin·coln·shire /ˈliNGkənSHər, -ˌSHi(ə)r/ a county on the eastern coast of England; county town, Lincoln.

Lin·coln's Inn one of the Inns of Court in London.

Lind[1] /lind/, James (1716–94), Scottish physician. He laid the foundations for the discovery of vitamins by performing experiments on scurvy in sailors. After his death, the Royal Navy officially adopted the practice of giving lime juice to sailors.

Lind[2], Jenny (1820–87), Swedish soprano; born *Johanna Maria Lind Goldschmidt*. She was known as "the Swedish nightingale" for the purity and agility of her voice.

lin·dane /ˈlinˌdān/ ▶ **n.** a synthetic organochlorine insecticide, now generally restricted in use due to its toxicity and persistence in the environment. Also called **GAMMA-HCH**. ● An isomer of benzene hexachloride; chem. formula: $C_6H_{12}Cl_6$.
– ORIGIN 1940s: named after Teunis van der *Linden*, 20th-cent. Dutch chemist.

Lind·bergh[1] /ˈlin(d)bərg/, Anne Morrow (1906–2001), US writer; the wife of Charles Lindbergh. Her writings, such as *North to the Orient* (1935), *Gift from the Sea* (1955), and *War Within and Without* (1980), told of her life experiences, esp. those regarding aviation, the kidnapping and murder of her two-year-old son, the political climate of the times, and her general philosophy.

Lind·bergh[2], Charles (Augustus) (1902–74), US aviator. In 1927, he made the first solo transatlantic flight in a single-engined monoplane, *Spirit of St. Louis*. Known thereafter as "Lucky Lindy," he moved to Europe with his wife, Anne Morrow Lindbergh, to escape the publicity surrounding the kidnapping and murder of their two-year-old son in 1932. He recounted his historic flight of 1927 in *The Spirit of St. Louis* (1953).

Lin·den /ˈlindən/ an industrial city in northeastern New Jersey, south of Elizabeth, noted for its oil refineries; pop. 39,162 (est. 2008).

lin·den /ˈlindən/ ▶ **n.** a deciduous tree with heart-shaped leaves and fragrant yellowish blossoms, native to north temperate regions. The pale soft timber is used for carving and furniture. See also **BASSWOOD**. ● Genus *Tilia*, family Tiliaceae: many species, including the **American linden** (*T. americana*) and the **European linden** (*T. europaea*).
– ORIGIN Old English (as an adjective in the sense 'made of wood from the lime tree'): from *lind* 'lime tree' (compare with **LIME**[3]) + **-EN**[2], reinforced by obsolete Dutch *lindenboom* and German *Lindenbaum*.

Lind·say /ˈlinzē/, Vachel (1879–1931), US poet; full name *Nicholas Vachel Lindsay*. His works are collected in *General Booth Enters into Heaven and Other Poems* (1913), *The Congo and Other Poems* (1914), and *Every Soul Is a Circus* (1929).

line[1] /līn/ ▶ **n. 1** a long, narrow mark or band: *a row of closely spaced dots will look like a continuous line* | *I can't draw a straight line.* ■ Mathematics a straight or curved continuous extent of length without breadth. ■ a positioning or movement of a thing or things that creates or appears to follow such a line: *her mouth set in an angry line* | *the ball rose in a straight line.* ■ a furrow or wrinkle in the skin of the face or hands. ■ a contour or outline considered as a feature of design or composition: *crisp architectural lines* | *the artist's use of clean line and color.* ■ (on a map or graph) a curve connecting all points having a specified common property. ■ a line marking the starting or finishing point in a race. ■ a line marked on a field or court that relates to the rules of a game or sport. ■ Football the line of scrimmage. ■ (**the Line**) the equator. ■ a notional limit or boundary: *the issue of peace cut across class lines* | *television blurs the line between news and entertainment.* ■ each of the very narrow horizontal sections forming a television picture. ■ Physics a narrow range of the spectrum noticeably brighter or darker than the adjacent parts. ■ (**the line**) the level of the base of most letters, such as *h* and *x*, in printing and writing. ■ [as modifier] Printing & Computing denoting an illustration or graphic consisting of lines and solid areas, with no gradation of tone: *a line block* | *line art.* ■ each of (usually five) horizontal lines forming a staff in musical notation. ■ a sequence of notes or tones forming an instrumental or vocal melody: *a powerful melodic line.* ■ a dose of a powdered narcotic or hallucinatory drug, esp. cocaine or heroin, laid out in a line.
2 a length of cord, rope, wire, or other material serving a particular purpose: *wring the clothes and hang them on the line* | *a telephone line.* ■ a telephone connection: *she had a crank on the line.* ■ a railroad track. ■ a branch or route of a railroad system: *the Philadelphia to Baltimore line.* ■ a company that provides ships, aircraft, or buses on particular routes on a regular basis: *a major shipping line.*
3 a horizontal row of written or printed words. ■ a part of a poem forming one such row: *each stanza has eight lines.* ■ (**lines**) the words of an actor's part in a play or film. ■ (**lines**) Brit. an amount of text or number of repetitions of a sentence written out as a school punishment.
4 a row of people or things: *a line of acolytes proceeded down the aisle.* ■ a row or sequence of people or vehicles awaiting their turn to be attended to or to proceed. ■ a connected series of people following one another in time (used esp. of several generations of a family): *we follow the history of a family through the male line.* ■ (in football, hockey, etc.) a set of players in the forwardmost positions for offense or defense. ■ Football one of the positions on the line of scrimmage. ■ a series of related things: *the bill is the latest in a long line of measures to protect society from criminals.* ■ a range of commercial goods: *the company intends to hire more people and expand its product line.* ■ informal a false or exaggerated account or story: *he feeds me a line about this operation.* ■ the point spread for sports events on which bets may be made.
5 an area or branch of activity: *the stresses unique to their line of work.* ■ a direction, course, or channel: *lines of communication* | *he opened another line of attack.* ■ (**lines**) a manner of doing or thinking about something: *you can't run a business on these lines* | *the superintendent was thinking along the same lines.* ■ an agreed-upon approach; a policy: *the official line is that there were no chemical attacks on allied troops.*
6 a connected series of military fieldworks or defenses facing an enemy force: *raids behind enemy lines.* ■ an arrangement of soldiers or ships in a column or line formation; a line of battle. ■ (**the line**) regular army regiments (as opposed to auxiliary forces or household troops).
▶ **v.** [with obj.] **1** stand or be positioned at intervals along: *a processional route lined by people waving flags.*
2 (usu. as adj. **lined**) mark or cover with lines: *a thin woman with a lined face* | *lined paper.*
3 Baseball hit a line drive.
– PHRASES **above the line 1** Finance denoting or relating to money spent on items of current expenditure. **2** Bridge denoting bonus points and penalty points, which do not count toward the game. **all (the way) down** (or **along**) **the line** at every point or stage: *the mistakes were caused by lack of care all down the line.* **along** (or **down**) **the line** at a further, later, or unspecified point: *I knew that somewhere down the line there would be an inquest.* **below the line 1** Finance denoting or relating to money spent on items of capital expenditure. **2** Bridge denoting points for tricks bid and won, which count toward the game. **bring someone/something into line** cause someone or something to conform: *the change in the law will bring Britain into line with Europe.* **come down to the line** (of a race) be closely fought right until the end. **come into line** conform: *Britain has come into line with other Western democracies in giving the vote to its citizens living abroad.* **the end of the line** the point at which further effort is unproductive or one can go no further. **get a line on** informal learn something about. **in line 1** under control: *that threat kept a lot of people in line.* **2** in a row waiting to proceed: *I always peer at other people's shopping carts as we stand in line.* **in line for** likely to receive: *she might be in line for a cabinet post.* **in the line of duty** while one is working (used mainly of police officers, firefighters, or soldiers). **in** (or **out of**) **line with** in (or not in) alignment or accordance with: *remuneration is in line with comparable international organizations.* **lay** (or **put**) **it on the line** speak frankly. (**draw**) **a line in the sand** (state that one has reached) a point beyond which one will not go. **line of communications** see **COMMUNICATION**. **line of credit** an amount of credit extended to a borrower. **line of fire** the expected path of gunfire or a missile: *residents within line of fire were evacuated from their homes.* **line of flight** the route taken through the air. **line of force** an imaginary line that represents the strength and direction of a magnetic, gravitational, or electric field at any point. **the line of least resistance** see **RESISTANCE**. **line of march** the route taken in marching. **line of sight** a straight line along which an observer has unobstructed vision: *a building that obstructs our line of sight.* **line of vision** the straight line along which an observer looks: *Jimmy moved forward into Len's line of vision.* **on the line 1** at serious risk: *their careers were on the line.* **2** (of a picture in an exhibition) hung with its center about level with the spectator's eye. **out of line** informal behaving in a way that breaks the rules or is considered disreputable or inappropriate: *he had never stepped out of line with her before.*
– PHRASAL VERBS **line out** Baseball be put out by hitting a line drive that is caught. **line something out** transplant seedlings from beds into nursery lines, where they are grown before being moved to their permanent position. **line someone/something up 1** arrange a number of people or things in a straight row. ■ (**line up**) (of a number of people or things) be arranged in this way: *we would line up across the parade ground, shoulder to shoulder.* **2** have someone or something ready or prepared: *have you got any work lined up?*
– ORIGIN Old English *line* 'rope, series,' probably of Germanic origin, from Latin *linea* (*fibra*) 'flax (fiber),' from *linum* 'flax,' reinforced in Middle English by Old French *ligne*, based on Latin *linea*.

line[2] ▶ **v.** [with obj.] cover the inside surface of (a container or garment) with a layer of different material: *a basket lined with polyethylene.* ■ form a layer on the inside surface of (an area); cover as if with a lining: *hundreds of telegrams lined the walls.*
– PHRASES **line one's pockets** make money, esp. by dishonest means.
– ORIGIN late Middle English: from obsolete *line* 'flax,' with reference to the common use of linen for linings.

lin·e·age /ˈlinē-ij/ ▶ **n. 1** lineal descent from an ancestor; ancestry or pedigree. ■ Anthropology a social group tracing its descent from a single ancestor.
2 Biology a sequence of species each of which is considered to have evolved from its predecessor: *the chimpanzee and gorilla lineages.* ■ a sequence of cells in the body that developed from a common ancestral cell: *the myeloid lineage.*
– ORIGIN Middle English: from Old French *lignage*, from Latin *linea* 'a line' (see **LINE**[1]).

lin·e·al /ˈlinēəl/ ▶ **adj. 1** in a direct line of descent or ancestry: *a lineal descendant.*
2 of, relating to, or consisting of lines; linear.
– DERIVATIVES **lin·e·al·ly adv.**
– ORIGIN late Middle English: via Old French from late Latin *linealis*, from *linea* 'a line' (see **LINE**[1]).

lin·e·a·ment /ˈlin(ē)əmənt/ ▶ **n. 1** (usu. **lineaments**) literary a distinctive feature or characteristic, esp. of the face.
2 Geology a linear feature on the earth's surface, such as a fault.
– ORIGIN late Middle English: from Latin *lineamentum*, from *lineare* 'make straight,' from *linea* 'a line' (see **LINE**[1]).

lin·e·ar /ˈlinēər/ ▶ **adj. 1** arranged in or extending along a straight or nearly straight line: *linear arrangements* | *linear in shape* | *linear movement.* ■ consisting of or predominantly formed using lines or outlines: *simple linear designs.* ■ involving one dimension only: *linear elasticity.* ■ Mathematics able to be represented by a straight line on a graph; involving or exhibiting directly proportional change in two related quantities: *linear functions* | *linear relationship.*
2 progressing from one stage to another in a single series of steps; sequential: *a linear narrative.*
– DERIVATIVES **lin·e·ar·i·ty** /ˌlinēˈaritē/ **n.**, **lin·e·ar·ly adv.**
– ORIGIN mid 17th cent.: from Latin *linearis*, from *linea* 'a line' (see **LINE**[1]).

Lin·e·ar A the earlier of two related forms of writing discovered at Knossos in Crete between 1894 and

PRONUNCIATION KEY ə *ago, up*; ər *over, fur*; a *hat*; ā *ate*; ä *car*; e *let*; ē *see*; i *fit*; ī *by*; NG *sing*; ō *go*; ô *law, for*; oi *toy*; o͝o *good*; o͞o *goo*; ou *out*; TH *thin*; T͟H *then*; ZH *vision*

1901, found on tablets and vases dating from *c.*1700 to 1450 BC and still largely unintelligible.

lin·e·ar ac·cel·er·a·tor ▶ n. Physics an accelerator in which particles travel in straight lines, not in closed orbits.

Lin·e·ar B a form of Bronze Age writing discovered on tablets in Crete, dating from *c.*1400 to 1200 BC. In 1952, it was shown to be a syllabic script composed of linear signs, derived from Linear A and older Minoan scripts, representing a form of Mycenaean Greek.

lin·e·ar e·qua·tion ▶ n. an equation between two variables that gives a straight line when plotted on a graph.

lin·e·ar·ize /ˈlinēəˌrīz/ ▶ v. [with obj.] technical make linear; represent in or transform into a linear form.
– DERIVATIVES **lin·e·ar·i·za·tion** /ˌlinēərəˈzāSHən/ n., **lin·e·ar·iz·er** n.

lin·e·ar mo·tor ▶ n. an electric induction motor that produces straight-line motion (as opposed to rotary motion) by means of a linear stator and rotor placed in parallel. It has been used to drive streetcars and monorails, where one part of the motor is on the underside of the vehicle and the other is in the track.

lin·e·ar per·spec·tive ▶ n. a type of perspective used by artists in which the relative size, shape, and position of objects are determined by drawn or imagined lines converging at a point on the horizon.

lin·e·ar pro·gram·ming ▶ n. a mathematical technique for maximizing or minimizing a linear function of several variables, such as output or cost.

lin·e·a·tion /ˌlinēˈāSHən/ ▶ n. the action or process of drawing lines or marking with lines. ■ a line or linear marking; an arrangement or group of lines: *magnetic lineations.* ■ a contour or outline. ■ the division of text into lines: *the punctuation and lineation are reproduced accurately.*
– ORIGIN late Middle English: from Latin *lineatio(n-)*, from *lineare* 'make straight.'

line·back·er /ˈlīnˌbakər/ ▶ n. Football a defensive player normally positioned behind the line of scrimmage, but in front of the safeties.

line breed·ing ▶ n. the selective breeding of animals for a desired feature by mating them within a closely related line.

line cut ▶ n. an engraving from a drawing consisting of solid blacks and whites, without gradations of color.

line danc·ing ▶ n. a type of country and western dancing in which dancers line up in a row without partners and follow a choreographed pattern of steps to music.
– DERIVATIVES **line dance** n., **line-dance** v., **line danc·er** n.

line draw·ing ▶ n. a drawing done using only narrow lines, the variation of which, in width and density, produce such effects as tone and shading.

line drive ▶ n. Baseball a powerfully hit ball that travels in the air and relatively close to and parallel with the ground.

line en·grav·ing ▶ n. the art or technique of engraving by lines incised on the plate, as distinguished from etching and mezzotint. ■ an engraving executed in this manner.
– DERIVATIVES **line-en·graved** adj., **line en·grav·er** n.

line feed ▶ n. the action of advancing paper in a printing machine by the space of one line. ■ Computing the analogous movement of text on a computer screen.

line in·te·gral ▶ n. Mathematics the integral, taken along a line, of any function that has a continuously varying value along that line.

Line Is·lands a group of 11 islands in the central Pacific Ocean that straddle the equator south of Hawaii. Eight of the islands, including Kiritimati (Christmas Island), form part of Kiribati; the remaining three are uninhabited dependencies of the US.

line i·tem ▶ n. an entry that appears on a separate line in a bookkeeping ledger or a fiscal budget. ■ a single item in a legislative appropriations bill.

line-i·tem ve·to ▶ n. (also **item veto**) the power of a president, governor, or other elected executive to reject individual provisions of a bill.

line·man /ˈlīnmən/ ▶ n. (pl. **linemen**) **1** a person employed in laying and maintaining railroad track. ■ a person employed for the repair and maintenance of telephone or electricity power lines.
2 Football a player normally positioned on the line of scrimmage.

line man·ag·er ▶ n. chiefly Brit. a person with direct managerial responsibility for a particular employee.
– DERIVATIVES **line man·age·ment** n.

lin·en /ˈlinin/ ▶ n. cloth woven from flax. ■ garments or other household articles such as sheets made, or originally made, of linen.
– ORIGIN Old English *līnen* (as an adjective in the sense 'made of flax'); related to Dutch *linnen*, German *Leinen*, also to obsolete *line* 'flax.'

lin·en·fold /ˈlininˌfōld/ ▶ n. carved or molded ornaments, esp. on a panel, representing folds or scrolls of linen.

line of bat·tle ▶ n. a disposition of troops for action in battle. ■ historical a battle formation of warships in line ahead (one behind another).

line of scrim·mage ▶ n. Football the imaginary line separating the teams at the beginning of a play.

line print·er ▶ n. a machine that prints output from a computer a line at a time rather than character by character.

lin·er[1] /ˈlīnər/ ▶ n. **1** (also **ocean liner**) a large luxurious passenger ship of a type formerly used on a regular line.
2 a fine paintbrush used for painting thin lines and for outlining. ■ a cosmetic used for outlining or accentuating a facial feature, or a brush or pencil for applying this.
3 informal another term for LINE DRIVE.

lin·er[2] ▶ n. a lining in an appliance, device, or container, esp. a removable one, in particular: ■ the lining of a garment. ■ (also **cylinder liner**) a replaceable metal sleeve placed within the cylinder of an engine, forming a durable surface to withstand wear from the piston.

-liner ▶ comb. form informal denoting a text of a specified number, usually a small number, of lines, such as an advertisement or a spoken passage in a play, dialogue, etc.: *two-liner.*

lin·er note ▶ n. (usu. **liner notes**) the text printed on a paper insert issued as part of the packaging of a compact disc or on the sleeve of a phonograph record.

line score ▶ n. a summary of the scoring in a game displayed in a horizontal table, esp. an inning-by-inning record of the runs, hits, and errors in a baseball game.

lines·man /ˈlīnzmən/ ▶ n. (pl. **linesmen**) (in games played on a field or court) an official who assists the referee or umpire from the sideline, esp. in deciding on whether the ball is out of play.

line spec·trum ▶ n. Physics an emission spectrum consisting of separate isolated lines. ■ an emission (of light, sound, or other radiation) composed of a number of discrete frequencies or energies.

line squall ▶ n. Meteorology a violent local storm occurring as one of a number along a cold front.

line-up /ˈlīnˌəp/ ▶ n. **1** a group of people or things brought together in a particular context, esp. the members of a sports team or a group of musicians or other entertainers: *a talented batting lineup.* ■ the schedule of television programs for a particular period: *NBC's Thursday lineup of hit comedies.*
2 a line of people or things. ■ a group of people including a suspect for a crime assembled for the purpose of having an eyewitness identify the suspect from among them.

line work ▶ n. **1** drawings or designs carried out with a pen or pencil, as opposed to wash or similar techniques.
2 work on lines, esp. as a lineman or a production-line worker.

ling[1] /liNG/ ▶ n. any of a number of long-bodied edible marine fishes. ● a large eastern Atlantic fish related to the cod (genus *Molva*, family Gadidae), in particular *M. molva*, which is of commercial importance. ● a related Australian fish (*Lotella callarias*, family Gadidae). ● a similar but unrelated Australian fish (*Genypterus blacodes*, family Ophidiidae).
– ORIGIN Middle English *lenge*, probably from Middle Dutch; related to LONG[1].

ling[2] ▶ n. the common heather of Eurasia.
– ORIGIN Middle English: from Old Norse *lyng*, of unknown origin.

ling. ▶ abbr. linguistics.

-ling ▶ suffix **1** forming nouns from nouns, adjectives, and verbs (such as *hireling, youngling*).
2 forming nouns from adjectives and adverbs (such as *darling, sibling, underling*).
3 forming diminutive words: *gosling | sapling.* ■ often with depreciatory reference: *princeling.*
– ORIGIN Old English; sense 3 from Old Norse.

Lin·ga·la /liNGˈgälə/ ▶ n. a Bantu language used by over 8 million people as a lingua franca in northern parts of Congo and the Democratic Republic of the Congo (formerly Zaire).
– ORIGIN a local name.

lin·gam /ˈliNGgəm/ (also **linga** /-gə/) ▶ n. Hinduism a symbol of divine generative energy, esp. a phallus or phallic object worshiped as a symbol of Shiva. Compare with YONI.
– ORIGIN from Sanskrit *liṅga*, literally 'mark, (sexual) characteristic.'

ling·cod /ˈliNGˌkäd/ ▶ n. (pl. **same**) a large slender greenling that has large teeth and is greenish-brown with golden spots. It lives along the Pacific coast of North America, where it is a valuable commercial and sport fish. ● *Ophiodon elongatus*, family Hexagrammidae.

lin·ger /ˈliNGgər/ ▶ v. [no obj.] stay in a place longer than necessary, typically because of a reluctance to leave: *she lingered in the yard, enjoying the warm sunshine | she let her eyes linger on him suggestively.* ■ (**linger over**) spend a long time over (something): *she lingered over her meal.* ■ be slow to disappear or die: *the tradition seems to linger on | we are thankful that she didn't linger on and suffer.*
– DERIVATIVES **lin·ger·er** n.
– ORIGIN Middle English (in the sense 'dwell, abide'): frequentative of obsolete *leng* 'prolong,' of Germanic origin; related to German *längen* 'make long(er),' also to LONG[1].

lin·ge·rie /ˌlänZHəˈrā, -jə-/ ▶ n. women's underwear and nightclothes.
– ORIGIN mid 19th cent.: from French, from *linge* 'linen.'

lin·ger·ing /ˈliNG(ə)riNG/ ▶ adj. lasting for a long time or slow to end: *there are still some lingering doubts in my mind | a painful and lingering death.*
– DERIVATIVES **lin·ger·ing·ly** adv.

lin·go /ˈliNGgō/ ▶ n. (pl. **lingos** or **lingoes**) informal, often humorous a foreign language or local dialect: *they were unable to speak a word of the local lingo.* ■ the vocabulary or jargon of a particular subject or group of people: *fat, known in medical lingo as adipose tissue.*
– ORIGIN mid 17th cent.: probably via Portuguese *lingoa* from Latin *lingua* 'tongue.'

ling·on·ber·ry /ˈliNGənˌberē/ ▶ n. (pl. **lingonberries**) another term for the mountain cranberry, esp. in Scandinavia, where the berries are much used in cooking.
– ORIGIN 1950s: from Swedish *lingon* 'mountain cranberry' + BERRY.

lin·gua fran·ca /ˈliNGgwə ˈfraNGkə/ ▶ n. (pl. **lingua francas**) a language that is adopted as a common language between speakers whose native languages are different. ■ historical a mixture of Italian with French, Greek, Arabic, and Spanish, formerly used in the Levant.
– ORIGIN late 17th cent.: from Italian, literally 'Frankish tongue.'

lin·gual /ˈliNGgwəl/ ▶ adj. technical **1** Anatomy relating to, near, or on the side toward the tongue. ■ Phonetics (of a sound) formed by the tongue.
2 of or relating to speech or language: *his demonstrations of lingual dexterity.*
▶ n. Phonetics a lingual sound.
– DERIVATIVES **lin·gual·ly** adv.
– ORIGIN mid 17th cent.: from medieval Latin *lingualis*, from Latin *lingua* 'tongue, language.'

lin·gui·ne /liNGˈgwēnē/ (also **linguini**) ▶ n. pasta in the form of narrow ribbons.
– ORIGIN Italian, plural of *linguina*, diminutive of *lingua* 'tongue.'

lin·guist /ˈliNGgwist/ ▶ n. **1** a person skilled in foreign languages.
2 a person who studies linguistics.
– ORIGIN late 16th cent.: from Latin *lingua* 'language' + -IST.

lin·guis·tic /liNGˈgwistik/ ▶ adj. of or relating to language or linguistics.
– DERIVATIVES **lin·guis·ti·cal·ly** /tik(ə)lē/ adv.

lin·guis·tic com·pe·tence ▶ n. see COMPETENCE (sense 2).

lin·guis·tic per·for·mance ▶ n. see PERFORMANCE (sense 2).

lin·guis·tic pro·fil·ing ▶ n. the analysis of a person's speech or writing, esp. to assist in identifying or characterizing an individual or particular subgroup: *linguistic profiling revealed that the bomber was probably an uneducated Southerner.*

lin·guis·tics /liNGˈgwistiks/ ▶ plural n. [treated as sing.] the scientific study of language and its structure, including the study of morphology, syntax, phonetics, and semantics. Specific branches of linguistics include sociolinguistics, dialectology, psycholinguistics, computational linguistics, historical-comparative linguistics, and applied linguistics.
– DERIVATIVES **lin·guis·ti·cian** /ˌliNGgwəˈstiSHən/ n.

lin·gu·late /ˈliNGgyəˌlāt/ ▶ adj. Botany & Zoology tongue-shaped. ■ Zoology denoting a type of

burrowing brachiopod with an inarticulate shell and a long pedicle.
– ORIGIN mid 19th cent.: from Latin *lingulatus*, based on *lingua* 'tongue,' from *lingere* 'to lick.'

lin·i·ment /ˈlinəmənt/ ▶ **n.** a liquid or lotion, esp. one made with oil, for rubbing on the body to relieve pain.
– ORIGIN late Middle English: from late Latin *linimentum*, from Latin *linire* 'to smear.'

lin·ing /ˈlīniNG/ ▶ **n.** a layer of different material covering the inside surface of something: *a lining of fireproof insulation* | [as modifier] *lining paper.* ■ an additional layer of different material attached to the inside of a garment or curtain to make it warmer or hang better: *leather gloves with fur linings.*

link[1] /liNGk/ ▶ **n. 1** a relationship between two things or situations, esp. where one thing affects the other: *investigating a link between pollution and forest decline.* ■ a social or professional connection between people or organizations: *he retained strong links with the media.* ■ something that enables communication between people: *sign language interpreters represent a vital link between the deaf and hearing communities.* ■ a means of contact, travel, or transport between two points or places: *they set up a satellite link with Tokyo* | *a rail link from Newark to Baltimore.* ■ Computing a code or instruction that connects one part of a program or an element in a list to another. ■ short for HYPERLINK.
2 a ring or loop in a chain. ■ a unit of measurement of length equal to one hundredth of a surveying chain (7.92 inches).
▶ **v.** make, form, or suggest a connection with or between: [with obj.] *rumors that linked his name with Judith* | *foreign and domestic policy are linked* | [no obj.] *she was linked up with an artistic group.* ■ connect or join physically: [with obj.] *a network of routes linking towns and villages* | *the cows are linked up to milking machines* | [no obj.] *three different groups, each linking with the other.* ■ [with obj.] clasp; intertwine: *once outside he linked arms with her.*
– ORIGIN late Middle English (denoting a loop; also as a verb in the sense 'connect physically'): from Old Norse *hlekkr*, of Germanic origin; related to German *Gelenk* 'joint.'

link[2] ▶ **n.** historical a torch of pitch and tow for lighting the way in dark streets.
– ORIGIN early 16th cent.: perhaps from medieval Latin *li(n)chinus* 'wick,' from Greek *lukhnos* 'light.'

link·age /ˈliNGkij/ ▶ **n.** the action of linking or the state of being linked. ■ a system of links: *a complex linkage of nerves.* ■ the linking of different issues in political negotiations. ■ Genetics the tendency of groups of genes on the same chromosome to be inherited together.

linked list ▶ **n.** Computing an ordered set of data elements, each containing a link to its successor (and sometimes its predecessor).

link·er /ˈliNGkər/ ▶ **n.** a thing that links other things, in particular: ■ Computing a program used with a compiler or assembler to provide links to the libraries needed for an executable program. ■ an attachment on a knitting machine for linking two pieces of knitting.

link·ing /ˈliNGkiNG/ ▶ **adj.** connecting or joining something to something else. ■ Phonetics denoting a consonant that is sounded at a boundary between two words or morphemes where two vowels would otherwise be adjacent, as in *law(r) and order.* See also LIAISON.

Lin·kö·ping /ˈlin,CHŏŏpiNG, -,CHœ-/ an industrial town in southeastern Sweden; pop. 141,863 (2008). It was a noted cultural and ecclesiastical center during the Middle Ages.

links /liNGks/ (also **golf links**) ▶ **plural n.** [treated as sing. or pl.] a golf course.
– ORIGIN Old English *hlinc* 'rising ground,' perhaps related to LEAN[1].

links·land /ˈliNGksland/ ▶ **n.** Scottish level or undulating sandy ground covered by coarse grass and near the sea.
– ORIGIN 1920s: from Scots *links* 'rising ground' (see LINKS) + LAND.

link·up /ˈliNGk,əp/ ▶ **n.** an instance of two or more people or things connecting or joining. ■ a connection enabling two or more people or machines to communicate with each other: *a live satellite linkup.*

link·work /ˈliNGk,wərk/ ▶ **n.** something made of links, as a chain. ■ a kind of gearing that transmits motion by a series of links rather than by wheels or bands.

linn /lin/ ▶ **n.** Scottish archaic a waterfall. ■ the pool below a waterfall. ■ a steep precipice.
– ORIGIN early 16th cent.: from Scottish Gaelic *linne*, Irish *linn*, related to Welsh *llyn* 'lake.'

Lin·nae·us /liˈnēəs/, Carolus (1707–78), Swedish botanist; founder of modern systematic botany and zoology; Latinized name of *Carl von Linné.* He devised an authoritative classification system for flowering plants involving binomial Latin names (later superseded by that of Antoine Jussieu) and also a classification method for animals.
– DERIVATIVES **Lin·nae·an** /-ˈnēən, -ˈnā-/ (also **Linnean**) **adj. & n.**

lin·net /ˈlinit/ ▶ **n.** a mainly brown and gray finch with a reddish breast and forehead. ● Genus *Acanthis*, family Fringillidae: three species, in particular the Eurasian *A. cannabina.*
– ORIGIN early 16th cent.: from Old French *linette*, from *lin* 'flax' (because the bird feeds on flaxseeds).

li·no /ˈlīnō/ ▶ **n.** (pl. **linos**) chiefly Brit. informal term for LINOLEUM.

li·no·cut /ˈlīnō,kət/ ▶ **n.** a design or form carved in relief on a block of linoleum. ■ a print made from such a block.
– DERIVATIVES **li·no·cut·ting n.**

lin·o·le·ic ac·id /,linəˈlēik, -ˈlā-, ləˈnōlēik/ ▶ **n.** Chemistry a polyunsaturated fatty acid present as a glyceride in linseed oil and other oils and essential in the human diet. ● Chem. formula: $C_{17}H_{31}COOH$.
– DERIVATIVES **li·no·le·ate** /ləˈnōlē,āt/ **n.**
– ORIGIN mid 19th cent.: from Latin *linum* 'flax' + OLEIC ACID.

lin·o·le·nic ac·id /,linəˈlēnik, -ˈlenik/ ▶ **n.** Chemistry a polyunsaturated fatty acid (with one more double bond than linoleic acid) present as a glyceride in linseed and other oils and essential in the human diet. ● Chem. formula: $C_{17}H_{29}COOH$; several isomers, notably **gamma-linolenic acid**, present in evening primrose oil.
– DERIVATIVES **lin·o·le·nate** /-ˈlē,nāt, -ˈlen,āt/ **n.**
– ORIGIN late 19th cent.: from German *Linolensaüre*, from *Linolsaüre* 'linoleic acid,' with the insertion of *-en-* (from -ENE).

li·no·le·um /ləˈnōlēəm/ ▶ **n.** a material consisting of a canvas backing thickly coated with a preparation of linseed oil and powdered cork, used esp. as a floor covering.
– DERIVATIVES **li·no·le·umed adj.**
– ORIGIN late 19th cent.: from Latin *linum* 'flax' + *oleum* 'oil.'

Li·no·type /ˈlīnə,tīp/ ▶ **n.** Printing, trademark a composing machine producing lines of words as single strips of metal, used chiefly for newspapers. It is now rarely used.
– ORIGIN late 19th cent.: alteration of the phrase *line o' type.*

Lin Piao variant of LIN BIAO.

lin·sang /ˈlin,saNG/ ▶ **n.** a small secretive relation of the civet, with a spotted or banded coat and a long tail, found in the forests of Southeast Asia and West Africa. ● Family Viverridae: genera *Prionodon* (two Asian species) and *Poiana* (one African species).
– ORIGIN early 19th cent.: via Javanese from Malay.

lin·seed /ˈlin,sēd/ ▶ **n.** the seeds of the flax plant, which are the source of linseed oil and linseed cake. Also called FLAXSEED. ■ the flax plant, esp. when grown for linseed oil.
– ORIGIN Old English *linsǣd*, from *līn* 'flax' + *sǣd* 'seed.'

lin·seed oil ▶ **n.** a pale yellow oil extracted from linseed, used esp. in paint and varnish.

lin·sey-wool·sey /,linzē ˈwŏŏlzē/ ▶ **n.** a strong, coarse fabric with a linen or cotton warp and a woolen weft.
– ORIGIN late 15th cent.: from *linsey*, originally denoting a coarse linen fabric (probably from *Lindsey*, a village in Suffolk, England, where the material was first made) + WOOL + *-sey* as a rhyming suffix.

lin·stock /ˈlin,stäk/ ▶ **n.** historical a long pole used to hold a match for firing a cannon.
– ORIGIN late 16th cent.: from earlier *lintstock*, from Dutch *lontstok*, from *lont* 'match' + *stok* 'stick.' The change in the first syllable was due to association with LINT.

lint /lint/ ▶ **n.** short, fine fibers that separate from the surface of cloth or yarn, esp. during processing. ■ a fabric, originally of linen, with a raised nap on one side, used for dressing wounds. ■ the fibrous material of a cotton boll. ■ chiefly Scottish flax fibers prepared for spinning.
– DERIVATIVES **lint·y adj.**
– ORIGIN late Middle English *lynnet* 'flax prepared for spinning,' perhaps from Old French *linette* 'linseed,' from *lin* 'flax.'

lin·tel /ˈlintl/ ▶ **n.** a horizontal support of timber, stone, concrete, or steel across the top of a door or window.
– DERIVATIVES **lin·teled** (Brit. **lintelled**) **adj.**
– ORIGIN Middle English: from Old French, based on late Latin *liminare*, from Latin *limen* 'threshold.'

lint·er /ˈlintər/ ▶ **n.** a machine for removing the short fibers from cotton seeds after ginning. ■ (**linters**) fibers of this kind.

Lin·ux /ˈlinəks/ ▶ **n.** Computing, trademark an open-source operating system modelled on UNIX.
– ORIGIN 1990s: from the name of *Linus* Benedict Torvalds (born 1969), a Finnish software engineer who wrote the first version of the system, + *-x*, as in *Unix.*

lin·y /ˈlīnē/ ▶ **adj.** (**linier, liniest**) informal marked with lines; wrinkled.

Linz /lin(t)s/ an industrial city in northern Austria, on the Danube River; pop. 188,430 (2006).

li·on /ˈlīən/ ▶ **n. 1** a large tawny-colored cat that lives in prides, found in Africa and northwestern India. The male has a flowing shaggy mane and takes little part in hunting, which is done cooperatively by the females. ● *Panthera leo*, family Felidae. ■ (**the Lion**) the zodiacal sign or constellation Leo. ■ a brave or strong person. ■ an influential or celebrated person: *a literary lion.* ■ the lion as an emblem (e.g., of English or Scottish royalty) or as a charge in heraldry.
2 (**Lion**) a member of a Lions Club.
– PHRASES **throw someone to the lions** cause someone to be in an extremely dangerous or unpleasant situation. [with reference to the throwing of Christians to the lions in Roman times.]
– DERIVATIVES **li·on·like** /-,līk/ **adj.**
– ORIGIN Middle English: from Anglo-Norman French *liun*, from Latin *leo*, *leon-*, from Greek *leōn*, *leont-*.

lion

li·on dance ▶ **n.** a traditional Chinese dance in which the dancers are masked and costumed to resemble lions.

li·on·ess /ˈlīənəs/ ▶ **n.** a female lion.

li·on·heart·ed /ˈlīən,härtid/ ▶ **adj.** brave and determined.

li·on·ize /ˈlīə,nīz/ ▶ **v.** [with obj.] give a lot of public attention and approval to (someone); treat as a celebrity: *modern athletes are lionized.*
– DERIVATIVES **li·on·i·za·tion** /,līənəˈzāSHən/ **n.**, **li·on·iz·er n.**

Li·ons Club ▶ **n.** a worldwide charitable society devoted to social and international service, taking its membership primarily from business and professional groups.

li·on's paw ▶ **n.** a large Caribbean bivalve mollusk with a thick reddish fan-shaped shell that bears coarse radial ribs. ● *Chlamys nodosus*, family Pectinidae.

li·on's share ▶ **n.** the biggest or greatest part: *William was appointed editor, which meant that he did the lion's share of the work.*

li·on tam·a·rin ▶ **n.** a rare tamarin with a golden or black and golden coat and an erect mane, found only in Brazil. ● Genus *Leontopithecus*, family Callitrichidae (or Callithricidae): the **golden lion tamarin** (*L. rosalia*), and three other species that have been recently recognized or discovered.

golden lion tamarin

lip /lip/ ▶ **n. 1** either of the two fleshy parts that form the upper and lower edges of the opening of

the mouth: *he kissed her on the lips.* ■ (**lips**) used to refer to a person's speech or to current topics of conversation: *downsizing is on everyone's lips at the moment.* ■ another term for LABIUM (sense 1 and sense 2). ■ another term for LABELLUM.
2 the edge of a hollow container or an opening: *drawing her finger around the lip of the cup.* ■ a rounded, raised, or extended piece along an edge.
3 informal impudent talk: *don't give me any of your lip!*
▶ **v.** (**lips, lipping, lipped**) [with obj.] (of water) lap against: *beaches lipped by the surf rimming the Pacific.* ■ Golf hit the rim of (a hole) but fail to go in.
– PHRASES **bite one's lip** repress an emotion; stifle laughter or a retort: *she bit her lip to stop the rush of bitter words.* **curl one's lip** raise a corner of one's upper lip to show contempt; sneer. **lick** (or **smack**) **one's lips** look forward to something with relish; show one's satisfaction. **my** (or **his**, etc.) **lips are sealed** see SEAL[1]. **pass one's lips** be eaten, drunk, or spoken. **pay lip service to** express approval of or support for (something) without taking any significant action.
– DERIVATIVES **lip·less adj.**, **lip·like** /-līk/ **adj.**, **lipped adj.** *her pale-lipped mouth.*
– ORIGIN Old English *lippa*, of Germanic origin; related to Dutch *lip* and German *Lippe*, from an Indo-European root shared by Latin *labia, labra* 'lips.'

li·pa /'lē,pä, -pə/ ▶ **n.** (pl. **same** or **lipas**) a monetary unit of Croatia, equal to one hundredth of a kuna.
– ORIGIN Croatian, literally 'lime tree.'

Lip·a·ri Is·lands /'lipərē/ a group of seven volcanic islands in the Tyrrhenian Sea, off the northeastern coast of Sicily, in Italian possession. Believed by the ancient Greeks to be the home of Aeolus, they were formerly known as the Aeolian Islands.

li·pase /'lip,ās, 'lī,pās/ ▶ **n.** Biochemistry a pancreatic enzyme that catalyzes the breakdown of fats to fatty acids and glycerol or other alcohols.
– ORIGIN late 19th cent.: from Greek *lipos* 'fat' + -ASE.

lip balm ▶ **n.** a preparation, typically in stick form, to prevent or relieve chapped lips.

Lip·chitz /'lipsHits/, Jacques (1891–1973), French sculptor, born in Lithuania; born *Chaim Jacob Lipchitz*. After producing cubist works such as *Sailor with a Guitar* (1914), he explored the interpenetration of solids and voids in his series of "transparent" sculptures of the 1920s.

lip·ec·to·my /li'pektəmē, lī-/ ▶ **n.** the surgical removal of fatty tissue, esp. from the abdomen in obese people.

li·pe·mi·a /li'pēmēə/ (also **lipaemia**) ▶ **n.** Medicine the presence in the blood of an abnormally high concentration of emulsified fat.
– ORIGIN late 19th cent.: from Greek *lipos* 'fat' + -EMIA.

Li·petsk /'li,pitsk/ an industrial city in southwestern Russia, on the Voronezh River; pop. 502,500 (est. 2008).

lip gloss (also **lipgloss**) ▶ **n.** a cosmetic applied to the lips to provide a glossy finish, often tinted.

lip·id /'lipid/ ▶ **n.** Chemistry any of a class of organic compounds that are fatty acids or their derivatives and are insoluble in water but soluble in organic solvents. They include many natural oils, waxes, and steroids.
– ORIGIN early 20th cent.: from French *lipide*, based on Greek *lipos* 'fat.'

li·pi·do·sis /,lipə'dōsis/ ▶ **n.** (pl. **lipidoses** /-,sēz/) Medicine a disorder of lipid metabolism in the body tissues.

Lip·iz·za·ner /'lipə,zänər, ,lipə'tsänər/ (also **Lippizaner**) ▶ **n.** a horse of a fine white breed used esp. in displays of dressage.
– ORIGIN early 20th cent.: from German, from *Lippiza*, site of the former Austrian Imperial stud near Trieste.

lip·lin·er /'lip,līnər/ ▶ **n.** a cosmetic applied to the outline of the lips, mainly to prevent the unwanted spreading of lipstick or lipgloss.

lipo- ▶ **comb. form** relating to fat or other lipids: *liposuction | lipoprotein.*
– ORIGIN from Greek *lipos* 'fat.'

Li Po /'lē 'pō, 'bō/ (also **Li Bo** /'lē 'bō/ or **Li T'ai Po** /'lē 'tī 'bō/) (AD 701–62), Chinese poet.

li·po·dys·tro·phy syn·drome /,līpə'distrəfē, ,lipə-/ ▶ **n.** a metabolic disease in which fat distribution in the body becomes abnormal, often as a result of taking protease inhibitor drugs. Fat is lost from the face, arms, and legs, and is built up in other places, esp. the breasts, abdomen, and back of the neck.

lip·o·gen·e·sis /,lipō'jenəsis, ,lī-/ ▶ **n.** Physiology the metabolic formation of fat.
– DERIVATIVES **li·po·gen·ic** /-'jenik/ **adj.**

lip·o·gram /'lipə,gram, 'lī-/ ▶ **n.** a composition from which the writer systematically omits a certain letter or certain letters of the alphabet.
– DERIVATIVES **lip·o·gram·mat·ic** /,lipōgrə'matik, ,lī-/ **adj.**
– ORIGIN early 18th cent.: back-formation from Greek *lipogrammatos* 'lacking a letter,' from *lip-* (stem of *leipein* 'to leave (out)') + *gramma* 'letter.'

lip·oid /'lip,oid, 'lī,poid/ ▶ **adj.** (also **lipoidal**) Biochemistry relating to or resembling fat.
▶ **n.** a fatlike substance; a lipid.
– ORIGIN late 19th cent.: from Greek *lipos* 'fat' + -OID.

li·pol·y·sis /li'päləsis, lī-/ ▶ **n.** Physiology the breakdown of fats and other lipids by hydrolysis to release fatty acids.
– DERIVATIVES **li·po·lyt·ic** /,lipə'litik, ,lī-/ **adj.**

li·po·ma /li'pōmə/ ▶ **n.** (pl. **lipomas** or **lipomata** /-mətə/) Medicine a benign tumor of fatty tissue.
– DERIVATIVES **li·pom·a·tous** /-mətəs/ **adj.**

lip·o·phil·ic /,lipə'filik, ,lī-/ ▶ **adj.** Biochemistry tending to combine with or dissolve in lipids or fats.

lip·o·pol·y·sac·cha·ride /'lipō,pälē'sakə,rīd, 'lī-/ ▶ **n.** Biochemistry a complex molecule containing both lipid and polysaccharide parts.

lip·o·pro·tein /,lipə'prō,tēn, ,lī-/ ▶ **n.** Biochemistry any of a group of soluble proteins that combine with and transport fat or other lipids in the blood plasma.

lip·o·sculp·ture /'lipō,skəlpCHər, 'līpō-/ ▶ **n.** the use of liposuction to accentuate specific bodily features.

lip·o·some /'lipə,sōm, 'lī-/ ▶ **n.** Biochemistry a minute spherical sac of phospholipid molecules enclosing a water droplet, esp. as formed artificially to carry drugs or other substances into the tissues.

lip·o·suc·tion /'lipō,səksHən, 'lī-/ ▶ **n.** a technique in cosmetic surgery for removing excess fat from under the skin by suction.

lip·o·tro·pin /,lipə'trōpin, ,lipə-/ (also **lipotrophin** /-'trōfən/) ▶ **n.** Biochemistry a hormone secreted by the anterior pituitary gland. It promotes the release of fat reserves from the liver into the bloodstream.

Lip·pes loop /'lipēz/ ▶ **n.** a type of intrauterine contraceptive device made of inert plastic in a double S-shape, which can be left in place for long periods.
– ORIGIN 1960s: named after Jack *Lippes* (born 1924), American obstetrician.

Lip·pi·zan·er /'lipə,zänər, ,lipə'tsänər/ ▶ **n.** variant spelling of LIPIZZANER.

Lipp·mann[1] /'lipmən/, Gabriel Jonas (1845–1921), French physicist. He is best known for his production of the first fully orthochromatic color photograph in 1893.

Lipp·mann[2], Walter (1899–1974), US journalist and essayist. He was a founder and associate editor of *The New Republic* (1914–17) and a columnist for the *New York Herald Tribune* (1931–67). Notable works: *A Preface to Morals* (1929), *The Good Society* (1937), and *Western Unity and the Common Market* (1962). His excellence in news analysis was recognized in 1958 by a Pulitzer Prize Special Citation.

lip·py /'lipē/ informal ▶ **adj.** (**lippier, lippiest**)
1 insolent; impertinent.
2 having prominent lips.

lip-read /'lip ,rēd/ (also **lipread**) ▶ **v.** [no obj.] (of a deaf person) understand speech from observing a speaker's lip movements.
– DERIVATIVES **lip-read·er n.**

lip·slide /'lipslīd/ ▶ **n.** (in skateboarding and snowboarding) a maneuver in which the board slides along a rail, ledge, edge of a ramp, etc., on the underside of the lip of the board at either the front or the back.

lip·stick /'lip,stik/ ▶ **n.** colored cosmetic applied to the lips from a small solid stick.

lip·stick les·bi·an ▶ **n.** informal a lesbian who favors a glamorous, traditionally feminine style.

lip-sync /'lip ,siNGk/ (also **lip-synch**) ▶ **v.** [no obj.] (of an actor or singer) move the lips silently in synchronization with a recorded soundtrack: [with obj.] *several singers were alleged to have lip-synched their songs.*
– DERIVATIVES **lip-sync·er n.**

Lip·ton /'liptən/, Sir Thomas Johnstone (1850–1931), Scottish merchant and yachtsman. He worked at a number of jobs in the US before he developed a chain of food stores in Scotland. He then invested in tea and coffee and had some of it packed in the US. Also noted for his yachts, he entered five of them in the America's Cup races.

liq. ▶ **abbr.** ■ liquid. ■ liquor. ■ (in prescriptions) solution. [from Latin *liquor*.]

li·quate /'lī,kwāt, 'lik,wāt/ ▶ **v.** [with obj.] Metallurgy separate or purify (a metal) by melting it.
– DERIVATIVES **li·qua·tion** /lī'kwāsHən, li-/ **n.**
– ORIGIN mid 19th cent.: from Latin *liquat-* 'made liquid,' from the verb *liquare*; related to LIQUOR.

liq·ue·fied pet·ro·le·um gas (abbr.: **LPG**) ▶ **n.** a mixture of light gaseous hydrocarbons (ethane, propane, butane, etc.) made liquid by pressure and used as fuel.

liq·ue·fy /'likwə,fī/ (also **liquify**) ▶ **v.** (**liquefies, liquefying, liquefied**) make or become liquid: [with obj.] *the minimum pressure required to liquefy a gas* | [no obj.] *as the fungus ripens, the cap turns black and liquefies.*
– DERIVATIVES **liq·ue·fac·tion** /,likwə'faksHən/ **n.**, **liq·ue·fac·tive** /,likwə'faktiv/ **adj.**, **liq·ue·fi·a·ble** /,likwə'fīəbəl/ **adj.**, **liq·ue·fi·er n.**
– ORIGIN late Middle English: from French *liquéfier*, from Latin *liquefacere* 'make liquid,' from *liquere* 'be liquid.'

li·ques·cent /li'kwesənt/ ▶ **adj.** literary becoming or apt to become liquid.
– DERIVATIVES **li·ques·cence n.**
– ORIGIN early 18th cent.: from Latin *liquescent-* 'becoming liquid,' from the verb *liquescere* (see LIQUEFY).

li·queur /li'kər, -'k(y)o͝or/ ▶ **n.** a strong, sweet flavored alcoholic liquor, usually drunk after a meal.
– ORIGIN mid 18th cent.: from French, 'liquor.'

liq·uid /'likwid/ ▶ **adj.** **1** having a consistency like that of water or oil, i.e., flowing freely but of constant volume. ■ having the clear shimmer of water: *looking into those liquid dark eyes.* ■ denoting a substance normally a gas that has been liquefied by cold or pressure: *liquid oxygen.* ■ not fixed or stable; fluid.
2 (of a sound) clear, pure, and flowing; harmonious: *the liquid song of the birds.*
3 Phonetics (of a consonant, typically *l* and *r*) produced by allowing the airstream to flow over the sides of the tongue and able to be prolonged like a vowel.
4 (of assets) held in cash or easily converted into cash. ■ having ready cash or liquid assets. ■ (of a market) having a high volume of activity.
▶ **n. 1** a liquid substance: *drink plenty of liquids.*
2 Phonetics a liquid consonant.
– DERIVATIVES **liq·uid·ly adv.**, **liq·uid·ness n.**
– ORIGIN late Middle English: from Latin *liquidus*, from *liquere* 'be liquid.'

liq·uid·am·bar /,likwid'ambər/ ▶ **n.** a deciduous North American and Asian tree with maplelike leaves and bright autumn colors, yielding aromatic resinous balsam. ● Genus *Liquidambar*, family Hamamelidaceae: several species, including *L. orientalis* of Asia, which yields liquid storax, and the sweet gum of North America. ■ liquid balsam obtained chiefly from the Asian liquidambar tree, used medicinally and in perfume. Also called STORAX.
– ORIGIN late 16th cent.: modern Latin, apparently formed irregularly from Latin *liquidus* 'liquid' + medieval Latin *ambar* 'amber.'

liq·ui·date /'likwə,dāt/ ▶ **v.** [with obj.] **1** wind up the affairs of (a company or firm) by ascertaining liabilities and apportioning assets. ■ [no obj.] (of a company) undergo such a process. ■ convert (assets) into cash: *a plan to liquidate $10,000,000 worth of property over seven years.* ■ pay off (a debt).
2 eliminate, typically by violent means; kill.
– DERIVATIVES **liq·ui·da·tion** /,likwə'dāsHən/ **n.**
– ORIGIN mid 16th cent. (in the sense 'set out (accounts) clearly'): from medieval Latin *liquidat-* 'made clear,' from the verb *liquidare*, from Latin *liquidus* (see LIQUID). Sense 1 was influenced by Italian *liquidare* and French *liquider*, sense 2 by Russian *likvidirovat'*.

liq·ui·da·tor /'likwə,dātər/ ▶ **n.** a person appointed to wind up the affairs of a company or firm.

liq·uid crys·tal ▶ **n.** a substance that flows like a liquid but has some degree of ordering in the arrangement of its molecules.

liq·uid crys·tal dis·play ▶ **n.** a form of visual display used in electronic devices in which a layer of a liquid crystal is sandwiched between two transparent electrodes. The application of an electric current to a small area of the layer alters the alignment of its molecules, which affects its reflectivity or its transmission of polarized light and makes it opaque.

liq·uid·i·ty /li'kwidətē/ ▶ **n.** Finance the availability of liquid assets to a market or company. ■ liquid assets; cash. ■ a high volume of activity in a market.
– ORIGIN early 17th cent.: from French *liquidité* or medieval Latin *liquiditas*, from Latin *liquidus* (see LIQUID).

li·quid·i·ty ra·tio ▶ **n.** Finance the ratio between the liquid assets and the liabilities of a bank or other institution.

liq·uid·ize /ˈlikwəˌdīz/ ▶ **v.** [with obj.] Brit. another term for LIQUEFY.
– DERIVATIVES **liq·uid·iz·er n.**

liq·uid lunch ▶ **n.** informal, humorous a drinking session at lunchtime sometimes taking the place of a meal.

liq·uid meas·ure ▶ **n.** a unit for measuring the volume of liquids.

liq·uid par·af·fin ▶ **n.** chiefly Brit. a colorless, odorless oily liquid consisting of a mixture of hydrocarbons obtained from petroleum, used as a laxative.

liq·uid sto·rax ▶ **n.** see STORAX (sense 1).

liq·ui·dus /ˈlikwidəs/ ▶ **n.** (pl. **liquidi** /-ˌdī/) (also **liquidus curve**) Chemistry a curve in a graph of the temperature and composition of a mixture, above which the substance is entirely liquid.
– ORIGIN Latin, literally 'liquid.'

liq·ui·fy /ˈlikwəˌfī/ ▶ **v.** variant spelling of LIQUEFY.

liq·uor /ˈlikər/ ▶ **n. 1** alcoholic drink, esp. distilled spirits.
2 a liquid produced or used in a process of some kind, in particular: ■ water used in brewing. ■ liquid in which something has been steeped or cooked. ■ liquid that drains from food during cooking. ■ the liquid from which a substance has been crystallized or extracted.
– PHRASAL VERBS **liquor up** (or **liquor someone up**) informal get (or make someone) drunk.
– ORIGIN Middle English (denoting liquid or something to drink): from Old French *lic(o)ur*, from Latin *liquor*; related to *liquare* 'liquefy,' *liquere* 'be fluid.'

liq·uo·rice /ˈlik(ə)risн, -ris/ ▶ **n.** British spelling of LICORICE.

liq·uor·ish /ˈlik(ə)risн/ ▶ **adj.** archaic form of LICKERISH.
– DERIVATIVES **liq·uor·ish·ness n.**

li·ra /ˈli(ə)rə/ ▶ **n.** (pl. **lire** /ˈli(ə)rā, ˈli(ə)rə/) **1** the basic monetary unit of Italy (until replaced by the euro in 2002), notionally equal to 100 centesimos. **2** the basic monetary unit of Turkey, equal to 100 kurus.
– ORIGIN Italian, from Provençal *liura*, from Latin *libra* 'pound.'

lir·i·o·den·dron /ˌli(ə)rēəˈdendrən/ ▶ **n.** a tree of a small genus that includes the tulip tree. ● Genus *Liriodendron*, family Magnoliaceae.
– ORIGIN modern Latin, from Greek *leirion* 'lily' + *dendron* 'tree.'

lir·i·pipe /ˈli(ə)rəˌpīp/ ▶ **n.** a long tail hanging from the back of a hood, esp. in medieval or academic dress.
– ORIGIN early 17th cent.: from medieval Latin *liripipium* 'tippet of a hood, cord,' of unknown origin.

Lis·bon /ˈlizbən/ the capital and chief port of Portugal, on the Atlantic coast at the mouth of the Tagus River; pop. 499,700 (2007). Portuguese name **Lisboa**.

li·sen·te /liˈsentē/ plural form of SENTE.

lisle /līl/ (also **lisle thread**) ▶ **n.** a fine, smooth cotton thread used esp. for hosiery.
– ORIGIN mid 16th cent.: from *Lisle*, former spelling of LILLE, the original place of manufacture.

Lisp /lisp/ (also **LISP**) ▶ **n.** a high-level computer programming language devised for list processing.
– ORIGIN 1950s: from *lis(t) p(rocessor)*.

lisp /lisp/ ▶ **n.** a speech defect in which *s* is pronounced like *th* in *thick* and *z* is pronounced like *th* in *this*.
▶ **v.** [no obj.] speak with a lisp.
– DERIVATIVES **lisp·er n.**, **lisp·ing·ly adv.**
– ORIGIN Old English *wlispian* (recorded in *āwlyspian*), from *wlisp* (adjective) 'lisping,' of imitative origin; compare with Dutch *lispen* and German *lispeln*.

lis pen·dens /ˈlis ˈpenˌdenz/ ▶ **n.** Law a pending legal action, or a formal notice of this.
– ORIGIN Latin.

Lis·sa·jous fig·ure /ˈlēsəˌzнo͞o, ˌlēsəˈzнo͞o/ ▶ **n.** Mathematics any of a number of characteristic looped or curved figures traced out by a point undergoing two independent simple harmonic motions at right angles with frequencies in a simple ratio.
– ORIGIN late 19th cent.: named after Jules A. *Lissajous* (1822–80), French physicist.

lis·some /ˈlisəm/ (also chiefly Brit. **lissom**) ▶ **adj.** (of a person or their body) thin, supple, and graceful.
– DERIVATIVES **lis·some·ness n.**
– ORIGIN late 18th cent.: contraction, from LITHE + -SOME[1].

list[1] /list/ ▶ **n. 1** a number of connected items or names written or printed consecutively, typically one below the other: *consult the list of drugs on page 326 | writing a shopping list* | figurative *tourism is at the top of the list of potential job creators.* ■ Computing a formal structure analogous to a list by which items of data can be stored or processed in a definite order. [late 16th cent.: from French *liste*, of Germanic origin.]
2 (**lists**) historical barriers enclosing an area for a jousting tournament. ■ the scene of a contest or combat. [late Middle English: from Old French *lisse*.]
3 a selvage of a piece of fabric. [Middle English, from Old English *liste* 'border,' of Germanic origin; related to Dutch *lijst* and German *Leiste*.]
▶ **v.** [with obj.] **1** make a list of: *I have listed four reasons below.* ■ include or enter in a list: *93 men were still listed as missing.* ■ [no obj.] (**list at/for**) be on a list of products at (a specified price): *the bottom-of-the-line Mercedes lists for $52,050.*
2 archaic enlist for military service.
– PHRASES **enter the lists** issue or accept a challenge.
– DERIVATIVES **list·a·ble adj.**

list[2] ▶ **v.** [no obj.] (of a ship) lean to one side, typically because of a leak or unbalanced cargo. Compare with HEEL[2].
▶ **n.** an instance of a ship leaning over in such a way.
– ORIGIN early 17th cent.: of unknown origin.

list[3] archaic ▶ **v.** [no obj.] want; like: *let them think what they list.*
▶ **n.** desire; inclination: *I have little list to write.*
– ORIGIN Old English *lystan* (verb), of Germanic origin, from a base meaning 'pleasure.'

list·box /ˈlis(t)ˌbäks/ ▶ **n.** Computing a box on the screen that contains a list of options, only one of which can be selected.

list·ed /ˈlistid/ ▶ **adj. 1** admitted for trading on a stock exchange: *listed securities.*
2 represented in a telephone directory.

lis·tel /ˈlistəl/ ▶ **n.** Architecture a narrow strip with a flat surface running between moldings. Also called FILLET.
– ORIGIN late 16th cent.: from Italian *listello*, diminutive of *lista* 'strip, band.'

lis·ten /ˈlisən/ ▶ **v.** [no obj.] give one's attention to a sound: *evidently he was not listening | sit and listen to the radio.* ■ take notice of and act on what someone says; respond to advice or a request: *I told her over and over again, but she wouldn't listen.* ■ make an effort to hear something; be alert and ready to hear something: *they listened for sounds from the baby's room.* ■ (also **listen up**) [in imperative] used to urge someone to pay attention to what one is going to say: *listen, I've got an idea.*
▶ **n.** [in sing.] an act of listening to something.
– PHRASAL VERBS **listen in** listen to a private conversation, often secretly. ■ use a radio receiving set to listen to a broadcast or conversation.
– ORIGIN Old English *hlysnan* 'pay attention to,' of Germanic origin.

lis·ten·a·ble /ˈlisənəbəl/ ▶ **adj.** easy or pleasant to listen to.
– DERIVATIVES **lis·ten·a·bil·i·ty** /ˌlis(ə)nəˈbilitē/ **n.**

lis·ten·er /ˈlis(ə)nər/ ▶ **n.** a person who listens, esp. someone who does so in an attentive manner. ■ a person listening to a radio station or program.

lis·ten·ing post ▶ **n.** a station for intercepting electronic communications. ■ a point near an enemy's lines for detecting movements by sound.

Lis·ter /ˈlistər/, Joseph, 1st Baron (1827–1912), English surgeon, inventor of antiseptic techniques in surgery. He realized the significance of Louis Pasteur's germ theory in connection with sepsis, and in 1865 he used carbolic acid dressings on patients who had undergone surgery.

list·er /ˈlistər/ ▶ **n.** a plow with a double moldboard.
– ORIGIN late 19th cent.: from late 18th-cent. *list* 'prepare land for a crop' (see LIST[1], -ER[1]).

lis·te·ri·a /liˈstirēə/ ▶ **n.** a type of bacterium that infects humans and other warm-blooded animals through contaminated food. ● *Listeria monocytogenes*; motile aerobic Gram-positive rods. ■ informal food poisoning or other disease caused by infection with listeria; listeriosis.
– ORIGIN 1940s: modern Latin, named after Joseph LISTER.

lis·te·ri·o·sis /liˌsti(ə)rēˈōsis/ ▶ **n.** disease caused by infection with listeria.

list·ing /ˈlistiNG/ ▶ **n. 1** a list or catalog. ■ the drawing up of a list. ■ an entry in a list or register.
2 a selvage of fabric.

list·less /ˈlis(t)lis/ ▶ **adj.** (of a person or their manner) lacking energy or enthusiasm: *bouts of listless depression.*
– DERIVATIVES **list·less·ly adv.**, **list·less·ness n.**
– ORIGIN Middle English: from obsolete *list* 'appetite, desire' + -LESS.

Lis·ton /ˈlistən/, Sonny (1932–70), US heavyweight boxing champion; born *Charles Liston*. He defeated Floyd Patterson for the world heavyweight championship in 1962 but lost the title to Muhammad Ali (then Cassius Clay) in 1964.

list price ▶ **n.** the price of an article as shown in a list issued by the manufacturer or by the general body of manufacturers of the particular class of goods.

list proc·ess·ing ▶ **n.** Computing the manipulation of data organized as lists.

LIST·SERV /ˈlis(t)ˌsərv/ ▶ **n.** trademark an electronic mailing list of people who wish to receive information about or discuss a specific topic. ■ (also **listserv**) any similar application.

Liszt /list/, Franz (1811–86), Hungarian composer and pianist. He was a key figure in the romantic movement; many of his piano compositions combine lyricism with great technical complexity, while his 12 symphonic poems 1848–58 created a new musical form.
– DERIVATIVES **Liszt·i·an** /-tēən/ **adj. & n.**

lit[1] /lit/ past and past participle of LIGHT[1], LIGHT[3].

lit[2] ▶ **adj.** informal drunk.

lit. ▶ **abbr.** ■ liter or liters. ■ literal or literally. ■ literary or literature.

Li T'ai Po /ˈlē ˈtī ˈbō, ˈpō/ variant of LI PO.

lit·a·ny /ˈlitn-ē/ ▶ **n.** (pl. **litanies**) a series of petitions for use in church services or processions, usually recited by the clergy and responded to in a recurring formula by the people. ■ a tedious recital or repetitive series: *a litany of complaints.*
– ORIGIN Middle English: from Old French *letanie*, via ecclesiastical Latin from Greek *litaneia* 'prayer,' from *litē* 'supplication.'

li·tas /ˈlēˌtäs/ ▶ **n.** (pl. **same**) the basic monetary unit of Lithuania, equal to 100 centas.

LitB ▶ **abbr.** ■ Bachelor of Letters. ■ Bachelor of Literature.
– ORIGIN from Latin *Literarum Baccalaureus*.

li·tchi /ˈlēcнē/ (also **lychee** or **lichee**) ▶ **n. 1** a small rounded fruit with sweet white scented flesh, a large central stone, and a thin rough skin. Also called **litchi nut** when dried.
2 the Chinese tree that bears this fruit. ● *Nephelium litchi* (or *Litchi chinensis*), family Sapindaceae.
– ORIGIN late 16th cent.: from Chinese *lìzhī*.

lit crit /ˈlit ˌkrit/ ▶ **abbr.** literary criticism.

LitD ▶ **abbr.** ■ Doctor of Letters. ■ Doctor of Literature.
– ORIGIN from modern Latin *Literarum Doctor*.

lite /līt/ ▶ **adj.** of or relating to low-fat or low-sugar versions of manufactured food or drink products: *lite beer.* ■ informal denoting a simpler or less challenging version of a particular thing or person: *a sort of newspaper lite – a snappy tabloid filled with shorter news pieces and extra sports and entertainment.*
▶ **n.** beer with relatively few calories.
– ORIGIN 1950s: a commercial respelling of LIGHT[1], LIGHT[2].

-lite ▶ **suffix** forming names of rocks, minerals, and fossils: *rhyolite | zeolite.*
– ORIGIN from French, from Greek *lithos* 'stone.'

li·ter /ˈlētər/ (Brit. **litre**) (abbr.: **l**) ▶ **n.** a metric unit of capacity, formerly defined as the volume of 1 kilogram of water under standard conditions, now equal to 1,000 cubic centimeters (about 1.75 pints).
– ORIGIN late 18th cent.: from French *litre*, alteration of *litron* (an obsolete measure of capacity), via medieval Latin from Greek *litra*, a Sicilian monetary unit.

lit·er·a·cy /ˈlitərəsē, ˈlitrə-/ ▶ **n.** the ability to read and write. ■ competence or knowledge in a specified area: *wine literacy can't be taught in three hours.*
– ORIGIN late 19th cent.: from LITERATE, on the pattern of *illiteracy*.

Li·te·rae Hu·ma·ni·o·res /ˈlitəˌrī hyo͞oˌmanēˈōˌrāz, ˈlitərē, -ˈôrˌēz/ ▶ **plural n.** [treated as sing.] the honors course in classics, philosophy, and ancient history at Oxford University.
– ORIGIN Latin, literally 'the more humane studies.'

lit·er·al /ˈlitərəl, ˈlitrəl/ ▶ **adj. 1** taking words in their usual or most basic sense without metaphor or allegory: *dreadful in its literal sense, full of dread.* ■ free from exaggeration or distortion: *you shouldn't take this as a literal record of events.* ■ informal absolute (used to emphasize that a strong expression is deliberately chosen to convey one's feelings): *fifteen years of literal hell.*
2 (of a translation) representing the exact words of the original text. ■ (of a visual representation) exactly copied; realistic as opposed to abstract or impressionistic.

3 (also **literal-minded**) (of a person or performance) lacking imagination; prosaic.
4 of, in, or expressed by a letter or the letters of the alphabet: *literal mnemonics*.
▶ **n.** Brit. Printing a misprint of a letter.
– DERIVATIVES **lit·er·al·i·ty** /ˌlitəˈralətē/, **lit·er·al·ize** /-ˌlīz/ **v.**, **lit·er·al·ness n.**
– ORIGIN late Middle English: from Old French, or from late Latin *litteralis*, from Latin *littera* (see LETTER).

USAGE See usage at LITERALLY.

lit·er·al·ism /ˈlitərəˌlizəm, ˈlitrə-/ ▶ **n.** the interpretation of words in their usual or most basic sense: *biblical literalism*. ■ literal representation in literature or art.
– DERIVATIVES **lit·er·al·ist n.**, **lit·er·al·is·tic** /ˌlitərəˈlistik, ˌlitrə-/ **adj.**

lit·er·al·ly /ˈlitərəlē, ˈlitrə-/ ▶ **adv.** in a literal manner or sense; exactly: *the driver took it literally when asked to go straight across the traffic circle | tiramisu, literally translated "pick me up."* ■ informal used for emphasis or to express strong feeling while not being literally true: *I have received literally thousands of letters.*

USAGE In its standard use, **literally** means 'in a literal sense, as opposed to a nonliteral or exaggerated sense': *I told him I never wanted to see him again, but I didn't expect him to take it literally.* In recent years, an extended use of **literally** (and also **literal**) has become very common, where **literally** (or **literal**) is used deliberately in nonliteral contexts, for added effect: *they bought the car and literally ran it into the ground.* This use can lead to unintentional humorous effects (*we were literally killing ourselves laughing*) and is not acceptable in formal English.

lit·er·ar·y /ˈlitəˌrerē/ ▶ **adj. 1** [attrib.] concerning the writing, study, or content of literature, esp. of the kind valued for quality of form: *the great literary works of the nineteenth century*. ■ concerned with literature as a profession: *it was signed by such literary figures as Maya Angelou.*
2 (of language) associated with literary works or other formal writing; having a marked style intended to create a particular emotional effect.
– DERIVATIVES **lit·er·ar·i·ly** /ˌlitəˈre(ə)rəlē/ **adv.**, **lit·er·ar·i·ness n.**
– ORIGIN mid 17th cent. (in the sense 'relating to the letters of the alphabet'): from Latin *litterarius*, from *littera* (see LETTER).

lit·er·ar·y a·gent ▶ **n.** a professional agent who acts on behalf of an author in dealing with publishers and others involved in promoting the author's work.

lit·er·ar·y crit·i·cism ▶ **n.** the art or practice of judging and commenting on the qualities and character of literary works.

Modern critics tend to pass over the concerns of earlier centuries, such as formal categories or the place of moral or aesthetic value; some analyze texts as self-contained entities, in isolation from external factors, while others discuss them in terms of spheres such as biography, history, Marxism, or feminism. Since the 1950s, the concepts of meaning and authorship have been explored or questioned by structuralism, poststructuralism, postmodernism, and deconstruction.

– DERIVATIVES **lit·er·ar·y crit·ic n.**

lit·er·ar·y ex·ec·u·tor ▶ **n.** a person entrusted with a dead writer's papers and copyrighted and unpublished works.

lit·er·ate /ˈlitərit/ ▶ **adj.** (of a person) able to read and write. ■ having or showing education or knowledge, typically in a specified area: *we need people who are economically and politically literate.*
▶ **n.** a literate person.
– DERIVATIVES **lit·er·ate·ly adv.**
– ORIGIN late Middle English: from Latin *litteratus*, from *littera* (see LETTER).

lit·e·ra·ti /ˌlitəˈrätē/ ▶ **plural n.** well-educated people who are interested in literature.
– ORIGIN early 17th cent.: from Latin, plural of *literatus* 'acquainted with letters,' from *littera* (see LETTER).

lit·e·ra·tim /ˌlitəˈrätim, -ˈrät-/ ▶ **adv.** formal (of the copying of a text) letter by letter.
– ORIGIN from medieval Latin.

lit·er·a·ture /ˈlit(ə)rəCHər, -ˌCHo͝or, -ˌt(y)o͝or/ ▶ **n.** written works, esp. those considered of superior or lasting artistic merit: *a great work of literature.* ■ books and writings published on a particular subject: *the literature on environmental epidemiology.* ■ leaflets and other printed matter used to advertise products or give advice.
– ORIGIN late Middle English (in the sense 'knowledge of books'): via French from Latin *litteratura*, from *littera* (see LETTER).

lith /liTH/ ▶ **n.** photographic film with a very thin coat of emulsion, producing images of high contrast and density.
– ORIGIN mid 20th cent.: abbreviation of LITHOGRAPHY, LITHOGRAPHIC.

-lith ▶ **suffix** denoting types of stone: *laccolith | monolith.*
– ORIGIN from Greek *lithos* 'stone.'

lith·arge /ˈliTHˌärj, liˈTHärj/ ▶ **n.** lead monoxide, esp. a red form used as a pigment and in glass and ceramics. ● Chem. formula: PbO.
– ORIGIN Middle English: from Old French *litarge*, via Latin from Greek *litharguros*, from *lithos* 'stone' + *arguros* 'silver.'

lithe /līT͟H/ (also **lithesome**) ▶ **adj.** (esp. of a person's body) thin, supple, and graceful.
– DERIVATIVES **lithe·ly adv.**, **lithe·ness n.**
– ORIGIN Old English *līthe* 'gentle, meek,' also 'mellow,' of Germanic origin; related to German *lind* 'soft, gentle.'

lith·i·a /ˈliTHēə/ ▶ **n.** Chemistry lithium oxide, a white alkaline solid. ● Chem. formula: Li_2O.
– ORIGIN early 19th cent.: modern Latin, alteration of earlier *lithion*, from Greek, neuter of *litheios*, from *lithos* 'stone,' on the pattern of words such as *soda*.

li·thi·a·sis /liˈTHīəsis/ ▶ **n.** Medicine the formation of stony concretions (calculi) in the body, most often in the gallbladder or urinary system.
– ORIGIN mid 17th cent.: from medieval Latin, based on Greek *lithos* 'stone.'

lith·ic /ˈliTHik/ ▶ **adj. 1** chiefly Archaeology & Geology of the nature of or relating to stone.
2 Medicine, dated relating to calculi.
– ORIGIN late 18th cent.: from Greek *lithikos*, from *lithos* 'stone.'

lith·i·fy /ˈliTHəˌfī/ ▶ **v.** (**lithifies**, **lithifying**, **lithified**) [with obj.] chiefly Geology transform (a sediment or other material) into stone.
– DERIVATIVES **lith·i·fi·ca·tion** /ˌliTHəfiˈkāSHən/ **n.**
– ORIGIN late 19th cent.: from Greek *lithos* 'stone' + -FY.

lith·i·um /ˈliTHēəm/ ▶ **n.** the chemical element of atomic number 3, a soft silver-white metal. It is the lightest of the alkali metals. (Symbol: **Li**) ■ lithium carbonate or another lithium salt, used as a mood-stabilizing drug.
– ORIGIN early 19th cent.: from LITHIA + -IUM.

lith·o /ˈliTHō, ˈlīTHō/ informal ▶ **n.** (pl. **lithos**) short for LITHOGRAPHY or LITHOGRAPH.
▶ **adj.** short for LITHOGRAPHIC.
▶ **v.** (**lithoes**, **lithoing**, **lithoed**) short for LITHOGRAPH.

litho- ▶ **comb. form 1** of or relating to stone: *lithosol.*
2 relating to a calculus: *lithotomy.*
– ORIGIN from Greek *lithos* 'stone.'

lithog. ▶ **abbr.** ■ lithograph. ■ lithography.

lith·o·graph /ˈliTHəˌgraf/ ▶ **n.** a lithographic print.
▶ **v.** [with obj.] print by lithography: (as adj. **lithographed**) *a set of lithographed drawings.*
– ORIGIN early 19th cent.: back-formation from LITHOGRAPHY.

lith·o·graph·ic /ˌliTHəˈgrafik/ ▶ **adj.** of, relating to, or produced by lithography: *lithographic prints.*
– DERIVATIVES **lith·o·graph·i·cal·ly** /-ik(ə)lē/ **adv.**

li·thog·ra·phy /liˈTHägrəfē/ ▶ **n.** the process of printing from a flat surface treated so as to repel the ink except where it is required for printing. ■ Electronics an analogous method for making printed circuits.

The earliest forms of lithography used greasy ink to form an image on a piece of limestone that was then etched with acid and treated with gum arabic. In a modern press, rollers transfer ink to a thin aluminum plate wrapped around a cylinder. In **offset lithography** the image is transferred to an intermediate rubber-covered cylinder before being printed.

– DERIVATIVES **li·thog·ra·pher** /-fər/ **n.**
– ORIGIN early 19th cent.: from German *Lithographie* (see LITHO-, -GRAPHY).

li·thol·o·gy /liˈTHäləjē/ ▶ **n.** the study of the general physical characteristics of rocks. Compare with PETROLOGY. ■ the general physical characteristics of a rock or the rocks in a particular area: *the lithology of South Dakota.*
– DERIVATIVES **lith·o·log·ic** /ˌliTHəˈläjik/ **adj.**, **lith·o·log·i·cal** /ˌliTHəˈläjikəl/ **adj.**, **lith·o·log·i·cal·ly** /ˌliTHəˈläjik(ə)lē/ **adv.**

lith·o·phyte /ˈliTHəˌfīt/ ▶ **n. 1** Botany a plant that grows on bare rock or stone.
2 Zoology a polyp with a calcareous skeleton; a stony coral.
– DERIVATIVES **lith·o·phyt·ic** /ˌliTHəˈfitik/ **adj.**

lith·o·pone /ˈliTHəˌpōn/ ▶ **n.** a white pigment made from zinc sulfide and barium sulfate.
– ORIGIN late 19th cent.: from LITHO- 'stone, crystals' + Greek *ponos* '(thing) produced by work.'

lith·o·sphere /ˈliTHəˌsfi(ə)r/ ▶ **n.** Geology the rigid outer part of the earth, consisting of the crust and upper mantle.
– DERIVATIVES **lith·o·spher·ic** /ˌliTHəˈsferik, -ˈsfi(ə)r-/ **adj.**

li·thot·o·my /liˈTHätəmē/ ▶ **n.** surgical removal of a calculus (stone) from the bladder, kidney, or urinary tract.
– DERIVATIVES **li·thot·o·mist** /-mist/ **n.**
– ORIGIN mid 17th cent.: via late Latin from Greek *lithotomia* (see LITHO-, -TOMY).

li·thot·o·my po·si·tion ▶ **n.** a supine position of the body with the legs separated, flexed, and supported in raised stirrups, originally used for lithotomy and later also for childbirth.

lith·o·trip·sy /ˈliTHəˌtripsē/ ▶ **n.** Surgery a treatment, typically using ultrasound shock waves, by which a kidney stone or other calculus is broken into small particles that can be passed out by the body.
– DERIVATIVES **lith·o·trip·ter** /-ˌtriptər/ **n.**, **lith·o·trip·tic** /ˌliTHəˈtriptik/ **adj.**
– ORIGIN mid 19th cent.: from LITHO- 'of stone' + Greek *tripsis* 'rubbing,' from *tribein* 'to rub.'

li·thot·ri·ty /liˈTHätrətē/ ▶ **n.** Surgery a surgical procedure involving the mechanical breaking down of gallstones or other calculi.
– ORIGIN early 19th cent.: from LITHO- 'of stone' + Latin *tritor* 'thing that rubs' + -Y[3].

Lith·u·a·ni·a /ˌliTHəˈwānēə, -nyə/ a country on the southeastern shore of the Baltic Sea; pop. 3,555,200 (est. 2009); capital, Vilnius; languages, Lithuanian (official), Russian, Polish.

Lithuania was absorbed into the Russian empire in 1795, having been united with Poland from 1386. It was declared an independent republic in 1918, but in 1940 was annexed by the Soviet Union as a constituent republic. In 1991, on the breakup of the Soviet Union, Lithuania became an independent republic once again. In 2004 it joined both NATO and the EU.

Lith·u·a·ni·an /ˌliTHəˈwānēən/ ▶ **adj.** of or relating to Lithuania or its people or language.
▶ **n. 1** a native or citizen of Lithuania, or a person of Lithuanian descent.
2 the Baltic language of Lithuania.

lit·i·gant /ˈlitəgənt/ ▶ **n.** a person involved in a lawsuit.
▶ **adj.** [postpositive] archaic involved in a lawsuit: *the parties litigant.*
– ORIGIN mid 17th cent.: from French, from Latin *litigant-* 'carrying on a lawsuit,' from the verb *litigare* (see LITIGATE).

lit·i·gate /ˈlitəˌgāt/ ▶ **v.** [no obj.] go to law; be a party to a lawsuit. ■ [with obj.] take (a claim or a dispute) to a court of law.
– DERIVATIVES **lit·i·ga·tor** /-ˌgātər/ **n.**
– ORIGIN early 17th cent.: from Latin *litigat-* 'disputed in a lawsuit,' from the verb *litigare*, from *lis, lit-* 'lawsuit.'

lit·i·ga·tion /ˌlitəˈgāSHən/ ▶ **n.** the process of taking legal action: *the company wishes to avoid litigation.*
– DERIVATIVES **lit·i·ga·tive** /ˈlitəˌgātiv/ **adj.**

li·ti·gious /ləˈtijəs/ ▶ **adj.** concerned with lawsuits or litigation. ■ unreasonably prone to go to law to settle disputes. ■ suitable to become the subject of a lawsuit.
– DERIVATIVES **li·ti·gious·ly adv.**, **li·ti·gious·ness n.**
– ORIGIN late Middle English: from Old French *litigieux* or Latin *litigiosus*, from *litigium* 'litigation,' from *lis, lit-* 'lawsuit.'

lit·mus /ˈlitməs/ ▶ **n.** a dye obtained from certain lichens that is red under acid conditions and blue under alkaline conditions.
– ORIGIN Middle English: from Old Norse *lit-mosi*, from *litr* 'dye' + *mosi* 'moss.'

lit·mus pa·per ▶ **n.** paper stained with litmus, used to indicate the acidity or alkalinity of a substance.

lit·mus test ▶ **n.** Chemistry a test for acidity or alkalinity using litmus. ■ a decisively indicative test: *opposition to the nomination became a litmus test for political support of candidates.*

li·top·tern /līˈtäpˌtərn/ ▶ **n.** an extinct South American hoofed mammal resembling a horse or camel, found from the Paleocene to the Pleistocene epochs. ● Order Litopterna: several families.
– ORIGIN early 20th cent.: from modern Latin *Litopterna*, from Greek *litos* 'smooth' + *pternē* 'heel bone.'

li·to·tes /ˈlītəˌtēz, ˈlit-, līˈtōtēz/ ▶ **n.** Rhetoric ironical understatement in which an affirmative is expressed by the negative of its contrary (e.g., *you won't be sorry*, meaning *you'll be glad*).

–ORIGIN late 16th cent.: via late Latin from Greek *litotēs*, from *litos* 'plain, meager.'

li·tre ▶ **n.** British spelling of LITER.

LittB ▶ **abbr.** ■ Bachelor of Letters. ■ Bachelor of Literature.
–ORIGIN from Latin *Literarum Baccalaureus*.

LittD ▶ **abbr.** ■ Doctor of Letters. ■ Doctor of Literature.
–ORIGIN from Latin *Litterarum Doctor*.

lit·ter /ˈlitər/ ▶ **n.** **1** trash, such as paper, cans, and bottles, that is left lying in an open or public place: *fines for dropping litter.* ■ [in sing.] an untidy collection of things lying about: *a litter of sleeping bags on the floor.*
2 the group of young animals born to an animal at one time: *a litter of five kittens.*
3 material forming a surface-covering layer, in particular: ■ (also **cat litter**) granular absorbent material lining a tray where a cat can urinate and defecate when indoors. ■ straw or other plant matter used as bedding for animals. ■ (also **leaf litter**) decomposing but recognizable leaves and other debris forming a layer on top of the soil, esp. in forests.
4 historical a vehicle containing a bed or seat enclosed by curtains and carried on men's shoulders or by animals. ■ a stretcher, for transporting the sick and wounded.
▶ **v.** [with obj.] **1** make (a place) untidy with rubbish or a large number of objects left lying about: *clothes and newspapers littered the floor.* ■ (usu. **be littered**) leave (rubbish or a number of objects) lying untidily in a place: *there was broken glass littered about.* ■ (usu. **be littered with**) fill (a text, history, etc.) with examples of something unpleasant: *news pages have been littered with doom and gloom about company collapses.*
2 archaic provide (a horse or other animal) with litter as bedding.
–DERIVATIVES **lit·ter·er n.**
–ORIGIN Middle English (sense 4 of the noun): from Old French *litiere*, from medieval Latin *lectaria*, from Latin *lectus* 'bed.' Sense 1 of the noun dates from the mid 18th cent.

litter 4

lit·té·ra·teur /ˌlitərəˈtər/ ▶ **n.** a person who is interested in and knowledgeable about literature.
–ORIGIN early 19th cent.: French.

lit·ter box ▶ **n.** a box or tray containing granular absorbent material into which a cat can urinate or defecate.

lit·ter·bug /ˈlitərˌbəg/ ▶ **n.** informal a person who carelessly drops litter in a public place.

lit·ter·mate /ˈlitərˌmāt/ ▶ **n.** one member of a pair or group of animals born in the same litter.

lit·tle /ˈlitl/ ▶ **adj.** small in size, amount, or degree (often used to convey an appealing diminutiveness or express an affectionate or condescending attitude): *the plants will grow into little bushes | a little puppy dog | a boring little man | he's a good little worker.* ■ (of a person) young or younger: *my little brother | when she was little she was always getting into scrapes.* ■ denoting something, esp. a place, that is named after a similar larger one: *New York's Little Italy.* ■ used in names of animals and plants that are smaller than related kinds, e.g., little grebe. ■ of short distance or duration: *stay for a little while | we climbed up a little way.* ■ relatively unimportant; trivial (often used ironically): *we have a little problem | I can't remember every little detail.*
▶ **determiner & pron.** **1** (**a little**) a small amount of: [as determiner] *we got a little help from my sister |* [as pronoun] *you only see a little of what he can do.* ■ [pronoun] a short time or distance: *after a little, the rain stopped.*
2 used to emphasize how small an amount is: [as determiner] *I have little doubt of their identity | there was very little time to be lost |* [as pronoun] *he ate and drank very little | the ruble is worth so little these days.*
▶ **adv.** (**less** /les/, **least** /lēst/) **1** (**a little**) to a small extent: *he reminded me a little of my parents | I was always a little afraid of her.*
2 (used for emphasis) only to a small extent; not much or often: *he was little known in this country | he had slept little these past weeks.* ■ hardly or not at all: *little did he know what he was putting into motion.*
–PHRASES **in little** archaic on a small scale; in miniature. **little by little** by degrees; gradually: *little by little the money dried up.* **little or nothing** hardly anything. **make little of** treat as unimportant: *they made little of their royal connection.* **no little** considerable: *a factor of no little importance.* **not a little** a great deal (of); much: *not a little consternation was caused.* ■ very: *it was not a little puzzling.* **quite a little** a fairly large amount of: *some spoke quite a little English.* ■ a considerable: *it turned out to be quite a little bonanza.*
–DERIVATIVES **lit·tle·ness n.**
–ORIGIN Old English *lȳtel*, of Germanic origin; related to Dutch *luttel*, German dialect *lützel*.

Lit·tle Ar·a·rat see ARARAT, MOUNT.

lit·tle auk ▶ **n.** British term for DOVEKIE.

Lit·tle Bear the constellation Ursa Minor.

Lit·tle Big·horn, Bat·tle of /ˈbigˌhôrn/ a battle in which General George Custer and his forces were defeated by Sioux and Cheyenne warriors on June 25, 1876, popularly known as Custer's Last Stand. It took place in the valley of the Little Bighorn River in Montana.

Lit·tle Big·horn Riv·er a river in northern Wyoming and southeastern Montana, scene of the 1876 defeat of George Custer's cavalry by Cheyenne and Sioux warriors.

Lit·tle Cor·po·ral a nickname for Napoleon.

Lit·tle Dip·per the seven bright stars of the constellation Ursa Minor.

Lit·tle Eng·land·er /ˈiNG(g)ləndər/ ▶ **n.** a person who opposes an international role or policy for Britain.
–DERIVATIVES **Lit·tle Eng·land·ism** /-ˌdizəm/ **n.**

lit·tle fin·ger ▶ **n.** the smallest finger, at the outer end of the hand, farthest from the thumb.
–PHRASES **twist** (or **wrap** or **wind**) **someone around one's little finger** have the ability to make someone do whatever one wants.

lit·tle grebe ▶ **n.** a small, puffy-looking Old World grebe with a short neck and bill and a trilling call. ● Genus *Tachybaptus*, family Podicipedidae: three species, in particular the widespread *T. ruficollis* (also called DABCHICK).

lit·tle hours ▶ **plural n.** (in the Roman Catholic Church) the offices of prime, terce, sext, and none.

Lit·tle Ice Age ▶ **n.** a comparatively cold period occurring between major glacial periods, in particular one such period that reached its peak during the 17th century.

Lit·tle League ▶ **n.** youth baseball or softball under the auspices of an organization founded in 1939, for children up to age 12.
–DERIVATIVES **Lit·tle Lea·guer n.**

Lit·tle Lord Faunt·le·roy see FAUNTLEROY.

lit·tle man ▶ **n.** a person who conducts business or life on a small or ordinary scale; an average person. ■ dated used as a form of address to a young boy.

Lit·tle Minch see MINCH.

Lit·tle Mis·sou·ri Riv·er a river that flows for 560 miles (900 km) from Wyoming, through Montana and the Dakotas, to the Missouri River.

Lit·tle Ouse another name for OUSE (sense 4).

lit·tle owl ▶ **n.** a small owl with speckled plumage, native to Eurasia and Africa. ● *Athene noctua*, family Strigidae.

lit·tle peo·ple ▶ **plural n.** **1** the ordinary people in a country, organization, etc., who do not have much power.
2 small supernatural creatures such as fairies and leprechauns.

Lit·tle Rock the capital of Arkansas, located in the central part of the state, on the Arkansas River; pop. 189,515 (est. 2008).

Lit·tle Rus·sian ▶ **n. & adj.** former term for UKRAINIAN.

Lit·tle St. Ber·nard Pass see ST. BERNARD PASS.

lit·tle the·a·ter ▶ **n.** a small independent theater used for experimental or avant-garde drama, or for noncommercial, community productions.

Lit·tle Ti·bet another name for BALTISTAN.

lit·tle toe ▶ **n.** the smallest toe, on the outer side of the foot.

Lit·tle·ton /ˈlitl-tən/ an industrial city in north central Colorado, south of Denver, scene of a shooting at Columbine High School in April 1999 in which 15 (including the two student gunmen) died and 21 were wounded; pop. 40,777 (est. 2008).

Lit·tle Tur·tle (c.1752–1812), chief of the Miami Indians. He led raids on settlers in the Northwest Territory and was successful until several defeats forced him to sign the Treaty of Greenville in 1795.

lit·to·ral /ˈlitərəl/ ▶ **adj.** of, relating to, or situated on the shore of the sea or a lake: *the littoral states of the Indian Ocean.* ■ Ecology of, relating to, or denoting the zone of the seashore between high- and low-water marks, or the zone near a lake shore with rooted vegetation: *limpets and other littoral mollusks.*
▶ **n.** a region lying along a shore: *irrigated regions of the Mediterranean littoral.* ■ Ecology the littoral zone.
–ORIGIN mid 17th cent.: from Latin *littoralis*, from *litus, litor-* 'shore.'

Lit·tré /lēˈtrā/, Émile (1801–81), French lexicographer and philosopher. He was the author of the major *Dictionnaire de la langue française* (1863–77). A follower of Auguste Comte, he became the leading exponent of positivism after Comte's death.

li·tur·gi·cal /liˈtərjikəl/ ▶ **adj.** of or relating to liturgy or public worship.
–DERIVATIVES **li·tur·gi·cal·ly adv.**
–ORIGIN mid 17th cent.: via medieval Latin from Greek *leitourgikos* (see LITURGY) + -AL.

li·tur·gics /liˈtərjiks/ ▶ **plural n.** [treated as sing.] the study of liturgies.

li·tur·gi·ol·o·gy /liˌtərjēˈäləjē/ ▶ **n.** another term for LITURGICS.
–DERIVATIVES **li·tur·gi·o·log·i·cal** /-jēəˈläjikəl/ **adj.**, **li·tur·gi·ol·o·gist n.**

lit·ur·gy /ˈlitərjē/ ▶ **n.** (pl. **liturgies**) **1** a form or formulary according to which public religious worship, esp. Christian worship, is conducted. ■ a religious service conducted according to such a form or formulary. ■ (**the Liturgy**) the Eucharistic service of the Eastern Orthodox Church (also called **the Divine Liturgy**).
2 (in ancient Athens) a public office or duty performed voluntarily by a rich Athenian.
–DERIVATIVES **lit·ur·gist n.**
–ORIGIN mid 16th cent.: via French or late Latin from Greek *leitourgia* 'public service, worship of the gods,' from *leitourgos* 'minister,' from *lēitos* 'public' + *-ergos* 'working.'

Liu·zhou /liˈyo͝oˈjō/ (also **Liuchow**) an industrial city in southern China, in Guangxi Zhuang province, northeast of Nanning; pop. 871,600 (est. 2006).

liv·a·ble /ˈlivəbəl/ (also **liveable**) ▶ **adj.** worth living; enjoyable: *fatherhood makes life more livable.* ■ (of an environment or climate) fit to live in: *one of the most livable cities in the world.*
–DERIVATIVES **liv·a·bil·i·ty** /ˌlivəˈbilətē/ **n.**

live[1] /liv/ ▶ **v.** **1** [no obj.] remain alive: *the doctors said she had only six months to live | both cats lived to a ripe age.* ■ be alive at a specified time: *he lived four centuries ago.* ■ spend one's life in a particular way or under particular circumstances: *people are living in fear in the wake of the shootings |* [with obj.] *he was living a life of luxury in Australia.* ■ supply oneself with the means of subsistence: *they live by hunting and fishing.* ■ survive in someone's mind; be remembered: *only the name lived on.* ■ have an exciting or fulfilling life: *he couldn't wait to get out of school and really start living.*
2 [no obj.] make one's home in a particular place or with a particular person: *I've lived in New England all my life | they lived with his grandparents.*
–PHRASES **as I live and breathe** used, esp. in spoken English, to express one's surprise at coming across someone or something: *good Lord, Jack Stone, as I live and breathe!* **be living on borrowed time** see BORROW. **live and breathe something** be extremely interested in or enthusiastic about a particular subject or activity and so devote a great deal of one's time to it: *they live and breathe Italy and all things Italian.* **live and let live** proverb you should tolerate the opinions and behavior of others so that they will similarly tolerate your own. **live by one's wits** see WIT[1]. **live dangerously** do something risky, esp. on a habitual basis. **live for the moment** see MOMENT. **live in hope** be or remain optimistic about something. **live in the past** have old-fashioned or outdated ideas and attitudes. ■ dwell on or reminisce at length about past events. **live in sin** see SIN[1]. **live it up** informal spend one's time in an extremely enjoyable way, typically by spending a great deal of money or engaging in an exciting social life. **live off** (or **on**) **the fat of the land** see FAT. **live off the land** see LAND. **live out of a suitcase** live or stay somewhere on a temporary basis and with only a limited selection of one's belongings, typically

because one's occupation requires a great deal of traveling. **live one's own life** follow one's own plans and principles independent of others. **live rough** live and sleep outdoors as a consequence of having no proper home. **live to fight another day** survive a particular experience or ordeal. **live to regret something** come to wish that one had not done something: *those who put work before their family life often live to regret it.* **live to tell the tale** survive a dangerous experience and be able to tell others about it. **live with oneself** be able to retain one's self-respect as a consequence of one's actions: *taking money from children—how can you live with yourself?* **long live ——!** said to express loyalty or support for a specified person or thing: *long live the Queen!* **where one lives** informal at, to, or in the right, vital, or most vulnerable spot: *it gets me where I live.* **you haven't lived** used, esp. in spoken English, as a way of enthusiastically recommending something to someone who has not experienced it: *you haven't lived until you've tasted their lobster ravioli.* **you** (or **we**) **live and learn** used, esp. in spoken English, to acknowledge that a fact is new to one.

– PHRASAL VERBS **live something down** succeed in making others forget something embarrassing that has happened. **live for** regard as the purpose or most important aspect of one's life: *Tony lived for his painting.* **live in** (of an employee or student) reside at the place where one works or studies. **live off** (or **on**) depend on (someone or something) as a source of income or support: *if you think you're going to live off me for the rest of your life, you're mistaken.* ■ have (a particular amount of money) with which to buy food and other necessities. ■ subsist on (a particular type of food). ■ (of a person) eat, or seem to eat, only (a particular type of food): *she used to live on bacon and tomato sandwiches.* **live out** (of an employee or student) reside away from the place where one works or studies. **live something out 1** do in reality that which one has thought or dreamed about: *your wedding day is the one time that you can live out your most romantic fantasies.* **2** spend the rest of one's life in a particular place or particular circumstances: *he lived out his days as a happy family man.* **live through** survive (an unpleasant experience or period): *both men lived through the Depression.* **live together** (esp. of a couple not married to each other) share a home and have a sexual relationship. **live up to** fulfill (expectations). ■ fulfill (an undertaking): *the president lived up to his promise to set America swiftly on a new path.* **live with 1** share a home and have a sexual relationship with (someone to whom one is not married). **2** accept or tolerate (something unpleasant): *our marriage was a failure—you have to learn to live with that fact.*

– ORIGIN Old English *libban, lifian*, of Germanic origin; related to Dutch *leven* and German *leben*, also to LIFE and LEAVE[1].

live[2] /līv/ ▶ **adj. 1** not dead or inanimate; living: *live animals | the number of live births and deaths.* ■ (of a vaccine) containing viruses or bacteria that are living but of a mild or attenuated strain. ■ (of yogurt) containing the living microorganisms by which it is formed.
2 relating to a musical performance given in concert, not on a recording: *there is traditional live music played most nights | a live album.* ■ (of a broadcast) transmitted at the time of occurrence, not from a recording: *live coverage of the match.*
3 (of a wire or device) connected to a source of electric current. ■ of, containing, or using undetonated explosive: *live ammunition.* ■ (of coals) burning; glowing. ■ (of a match) unused. ■ (of a wheel or axle in machinery) moving or imparting motion. ■ (of a ball in a game) in play, esp. in contrast to being foul or out of bounds.
4 (of a question or subject) of current or continuing interest and importance: *the future organization of Europe has become a live issue.*
▶ **adv.** as or at an actual event or performance: *the match will be televised live.*
– PHRASES **go live** Computing (of a system) become operational.
– ORIGIN mid 16th cent.: shortening of ALIVE.

live·a·ble /'livəbəl/ ▶ **adj.** variant spelling of LIVABLE.

live ac·tion /līv/ ▶ **n.** (in filmmaking) action involving real people or animals, as contrasted with animation or computer-generated effects: [as modifier] *a live-action version of the cartoon.*

live·bear·er /'līv,be(ə)rər/ ▶ **n.** a small, chiefly freshwater, carplike American fish that has internal fertilization and gives birth to live young. Many livebearers, including the guppy, swordtail, mollies, platyfish, and gambusias, are very popular in aquariums. ● Family Poeciliidae: many genera and species.

live·bear·ing /'līv,be(ə)riNG/ ▶ **adj.** (of an animal) bearing live young rather than laying eggs; viviparous or ovoviviparous.

live birth /līv/ ▶ **n.** a birth at which a child is born alive.

lived-in ▶ **adj.** (of a room or building) showing comforting signs of wear and habitation. ■ informal (of a person's face) marked by experience.

live-in /'liv ,in/ ▶ **adj.** (of a domestic employee) resident in an employer's house: *a live-in housekeeper.* ■ (of a person) living with another in a sexual relationship: *a live-in lover.* ■ residential: *a live-in treatment program.*
▶ **n.** informal a person who shares another's living accommodations as a sexual partner or as an employee.

live·li·hood /'līvlē,ho͝od/ ▶ **n.** a means of securing the necessities of life: *people whose livelihoods depend on the rain forest.*
– ORIGIN Old English *liflād* 'way of life,' from *līf* 'life' + *lād* 'course' (see LODE). The change in the word's form in the 16th cent. was due to association with LIVELY and -HOOD.

live load /līv/ ▶ **n.** the weight of people or goods in a building or vehicle. Often contrasted with DEAD LOAD.

live·long /'liv,lôNG, -,läNG/ ▶ **adj.** literary (of a period of time) entire: *all this livelong day I lay in the sun.*
– ORIGIN late Middle English *leve longe* 'dear long' (see LIEF, LONG[1]). The change in spelling of the first word was due to association with LIVE[1].

live·ly /'līvlē/ ▶ **adj.** (**livelier**, **liveliest**) full of life and energy; active and outgoing: *she joined a lively team of reporters.* ■ (of a place or atmosphere) full of activity and excitement: *Barcelona's many lively bars.* ■ intellectually stimulating or perceptive: *a lively discussion | her lively mind.* ■ (of a vessel) buoyant and responsive in a sea.
– PHRASES **look lively** (or **alive**) [usu. in imperative] informal move more quickly and energetically: *"Look lively, men!" Charlie shouted.*
– DERIVATIVES **live·li·ly** /-ləlē/ **adv.**, **live·li·ness n.**
– ORIGIN Old English *līflīc* 'living, animate' (see LIFE, -LY[1]).

liv·en /'līvən/ ▶ **v.** make or become more lively or interesting: [with obj.] ***liven up** bland foods with a touch of mustard* | [no obj.] *the match didn't **liven up** until the second half.*

live oak /līv/ ▶ **n.** a large, spreading oak of the southern US that has leathery, elliptical evergreen leaves. Live oaks typically support a large quantity of Spanish moss and other epiphytes. ● *Quercus virginiana*, family Fagaceae.

liv·er[1] /'livər/ ▶ **n.** a large lobed glandular organ in the abdomen of vertebrates, involved in many metabolic processes. ■ a similar organ in other animals. ■ the flesh of an animal's liver as food: *slices of calf's liver* | [as modifier] *liver pâté | chicken livers.* ■ (also **liver color**) a dark reddish brown.

> The liver's main role is in the processing of the products of digestion into substances useful to the body. It also neutralizes harmful substances in the blood, secretes bile for the digestion of fats, synthesizes plasma proteins, and stores glycogen and some minerals and vitamins. It was anciently supposed to be the seat of love and violent emotion.

– ORIGIN Old English *lifer*, of Germanic origin; related to German *Leber*, Dutch *lever*.

liv·er[2] ▶ **n.** [with adj.] a person who lives in a specified way: *a clean liver | high livers.*

liv·er chest·nut ▶ **n.** a horse of a dark chestnut color.

liv·er fluke ▶ **n.** a fluke that has a complex life cycle and is of medical and veterinary importance. The adult lives within the liver tissues of a vertebrate, and the larva within one or more secondary hosts such as a snail or fish. ● Many species in the subclass Digenea, class Trematoda, including the **Chinese liver fluke** (*Opisthorchis sinensis*), which infests humans, and *Fasciola hepatica*, which infests sheep and cattle.

liv·er·ish /'liv(ə)risH/ ▶ **adj. 1** slightly ill, as though having a disordered liver. ■ unhappy and bad-tempered.
2 resembling liver in color: *a liverish red.*
– DERIVATIVES **liv·er·ish·ly adv.**, **liv·er·ish·ness n.**

Liv·er·more /'livər,môr/ a city in north central California, east of Oakland; pop. 80,188 (est. 2008).

Liv·er·pool[1] /'livər,po͞ol/ a city and seaport in northwestern England, on the eastern side of the mouth of the Mersey River; pop. 454,700 (est. 2009).

Liv·er·pool[2], Robert Banks Jenkinson, 2nd Earl of (1770–1828), British statesman; prime minister 1812–27.

Liv·er·pud·li·an /,livər'pədlēən/ ▶ **n.** a native of Liverpool. ■ the dialect or accent of people from Liverpool.
▶ **adj.** of or relating to Liverpool.
– ORIGIN mid 19th cent.: humorous formation from LIVERPOOL[1] + PUDDLE.

liv·er spot ▶ **n.** a small brown spot on the skin, esp. as caused by a skin condition such as lentigo.
– DERIVATIVES **liv·er-spot·ted adj.**

liv·er·wort /'livər,wərt, -,wôrt/ ▶ **n.** a small flowerless green plant with leaflike stems or lobed leaves, occurring in moist habitats. Liverworts lack true roots and reproduce by means of spores released from capsules. ● Class Hepaticae, division Bryophyta.
– ORIGIN late Old English, from LIVER[1] + WORT, translating medieval Latin *hepatica*.

liv·er·wurst /'livər,wərst/ ▶ **n.** a seasoned meat paste in the form of a sausage containing cooked liver, or a mixture of liver and pork.
– ORIGIN mid 19th cent.: partial translation of German *Leberwurst* 'liver sausage.'

liv·er·y[1] /'liv(ə)rē/ ▶ **n.** (pl. **liveries**) **1** special uniform worn by a servant or official. ■ a special design and color scheme used on the vehicles, aircraft, or products of a particular company.
2 short for LIVERY STABLE.
3 (in the UK) the members of a livery company collectively.
4 historical a provision of food or clothing for servants.
– PHRASES **at livery** (of a horse) kept for the owner and fed and cared for at a fixed charge.
– DERIVATIVES **liv·er·ied** /'liv(ə)rēd/ **adj.** (sense 1).
– ORIGIN Middle English: from Old French *livree* 'delivered,' feminine past participle of *livrer*, from Latin *liberare* 'liberate' (in medieval Latin 'hand over'). The original sense was 'the dispensing of food, provisions, or clothing to servants'; hence sense 4, also 'allowance of provender for horses,' surviving in the phrase *at livery* and in LIVERY STABLE. Sense 1 arose because medieval nobles provided matching clothes to distinguish their servants from others'.

liv·er·y[2] ▶ **adj.** resembling liver in color or consistency: *he was short with livery lips.* ■ informal liverish: *port always makes you livery.*

liv·er·y com·pa·ny ▶ **n.** (in the UK) any of a number of companies of the City of London descended from the medieval trade guilds. They are now largely social and charitable organizations.
– ORIGIN mid 18th cent.: so named because of the distinctive costume formerly used for special occasions.

liv·er·y·man /'liv(ə)rēmən/ ▶ **n.** (pl. **liverymen**) **1** an owner of or attendant in a livery stable.
2 (in the UK) a member of a livery company.

liv·er·y sta·ble (also **livery yard**) ▶ **n.** a stable where horses are kept at livery or let out for hire.

lives /līvz/ plural form of LIFE.

live·stock /'līv,stäk/ ▶ **n.** farm animals regarded as an asset: *markets for the trading of livestock.*

live·ware /'līv,we(ə)r/ ▶ **n.** informal working personnel, esp. computer personnel, as distinct from the inanimate or abstract things they work with.

live weight /līv/ ▶ **n.** the weight of an animal before it has been slaughtered and prepared as a carcass.

live wire /līv/ ▶ **n.** informal an energetic and unpredictable person.

live-work /'liv ,wərk/ ▶ **adj.** denoting or relating to property that combines residential living space with commercial or manufacturing space: *housing on the site might include live-work units for small businesses.*

liv·id /'livid/ ▶ **adj. 1** furiously angry: *he was livid at being left out.*
2 dark bluish gray in color: *livid bruises | his face went livid, then purple.*
– DERIVATIVES **li·vid·i·ty** /lə'vidətē/ **n.**, **liv·id·ly adv.**, **liv·id·ness n.**
– ORIGIN late Middle English (in the sense 'of a bluish leaden color'): from French *livide* or Latin *lividus*, from *livere* 'be bluish.' The sense 'furiously angry' dates from the early 20th cent.

liv·ing /'liviNG/ ▶ **n. 1** [usu. in sing.] an income sufficient to live on or the means of earning it: *she was struggling to **make a living** as a dancer | what does he **do for a living**?* ■ Brit. (in church use) a position as a vicar or rector with an income or property.
2 [with adj. or noun modifier] the pursuit of a lifestyle of the specified type: *the benefits of country living.*
▶ **adj.** alive: *living creatures* | (as plural noun **the living**) *flowers were for the living.* ■ (of a place) used for living rather than working in: *the living quarters of the ship.* ■ (of a language) still spoken and used. ■ literary (of water) perennially flowing: *streams of living water.*

–PHRASES **be (the) living proof that** (or **of**) show by one's existence and qualities that something is the case: *she is living proof that hard work need not be aging.* **in** (or **within**) **living memory** within or during a time that is remembered by people still alive: *the worst recession in living memory.* **the living image of** an exact copy or likeness of.

liv·ing death ▶ **n.** [in sing.] a state of existence that is very difficult; a life of hopeless and unbroken misery.

liv·ing rock ▶ **n.** rock that is not detached but still forms part of the earth: *a chamber cut out of the living rock.*

liv·ing room ▶ **n.** a room in a house for general and informal everyday use.

Liv·ing·ston /ˈliviNGstən/, Henry Brockholst (1757–1823), US Supreme Court associate justice 1806–23. A Democratic-Republican, he was appointed to the Court by President Jefferson.

liv·ing stone ▶ **n.** a small succulent southern African plant that resembles a pebble in appearance. It consists of two fleshy cushionlike leaves divided by a slit through which a daisylike flower emerges. ● Genus *Lithops*, family Aizoaceae.

liv·ing wage ▶ **n.** [in sing.] a wage that is high enough to maintain a normal standard of living.

liv·ing will ▶ **n.** a written statement detailing a person's desires regarding their medical treatment in circumstances in which they are no longer able to express informed consent, esp. an advance directive.

Li·vo·nia /liˈvōnēə, -yə/ **1** a region on the eastern coast of the Baltic Sea, north of Lithuania, that comprises most of present-day Latvia and Estonia. German name **Livland**.
2 an industrial city in southeastern Michigan, west of Detroit; pop. 91,220 (est. 2008).
–DERIVATIVES **Li·vo·ni·an adj. & n.**

Li·vor·no /lēˈvôrnō/ a port in northwestern Italy, in Tuscany, on the Ligurian Sea; pop. 161,095 (2008). Also called **LEGHORN**.

Liv·y /ˈlivē/ (59 BC–AD 17), Roman historian; Latin name *Titus Livius*. His history of Rome from its foundation to his own time filled 142 books, of which 35 survive.

lix·iv·i·ate /likˈsivēˌāt/ ▶ **v.** [with obj.] Chemistry, archaic separate (a substance) into soluble and insoluble constituents by the percolation of liquid.
–DERIVATIVES **lix·iv·i·a·tion** /-ˌsivēˈāSHən/ **n.**
–ORIGIN mid 17th cent.: from modern Latin *lixiviat-* 'impregnated with lye,' from the verb *lixiviare*, from *lixivius* 'made into lye,' from *lix* 'lye.'

Liz·ard /ˈlizərd/ a promontory in southwestern England, in Cornwall. Its southern tip, Lizard Point, is the southernmost point of the British mainland.

liz·ard /ˈlizərd/ ▶ **n.** a reptile that typically has a long body and tail, four legs, movable eyelids, and a rough, scaly, or spiny skin. ● Suborder Lacertilia (or Sauria), order Squamata: many families.
–ORIGIN late Middle English: from Old French *lesard(e)*, from Latin *lacertus* 'lizard, sea fish,' also 'muscle.'

liz·ard·fish /ˈlizərdˌfiSH/ ▶ **n.** (pl. **same** or **lizardfishes**) a fish of lizardlike appearance with a broad bony head, pointed snout, and heavy shiny scales. It lives in warm shallow seas, where it often rests on the bottom propped up on its pelvic fins. ● Family Synodontidae: several genera and species, including the widespread *Trachinocephalus myops* (also called **SNAKEFISH**).

liz·ard's tail ▶ **n.** a North American bog plant with long tapering, drooping spikes of fragrant white flowers. ● *Saururus cernuus*, family Saururaceae.

Lju·blja·na /lēˌo͞obləˈänə, lēˈo͞obləəˌnä/ the capital of Slovenia; pop. 267,760 (2007). It was founded as Emona by the Romans in 34 BC. German name **LAIBACH**.

Lk ▶ **abbr.** Bible the Gospel of Luke.

ll. ▶ **abbr.** (in textual references) lines.

'll ▶ **contraction** shall; will: *I'll get the food on.*

lla·ma /ˈlämə/ ▶ **n.** a domesticated pack animal of the camel family found in the Andes, valued for its soft woolly fleece. ● *Lama glama*, family Camelidae, probably descended from the wild guanaco. ■ the wool of the llama. ■ cloth made from such wool.
–ORIGIN early 17th cent.: from Spanish, probably from Quechua.

llama

lla·no /ˈlänō, ˈyä-/ ▶ **n.** (pl. **llanos**) (in South America) a treeless grassy plain.
–ORIGIN Spanish, from Latin *planum* 'plain.'

LLB ▶ **abbr.** Bachelor of Laws.
–ORIGIN from Latin *legum baccalaureus*.

LLD ▶ **abbr.** Doctor of Laws.
–ORIGIN from Latin *legum doctor*.

Llew·e·lyn /lo͝oˈ(w)elən/ (died 1282), prince of Gwynedd in North Wales; also known as **Llywelyn ap Gruffydd**. Proclaiming himself prince of all Wales in 1258, he was recognized by Henry III in 1265. His refusal to pay homage to Edward I led the latter to subjugate Wales 1277–84; Llewelyn died in an unsuccessful rebellion.

LLM ▶ **abbr.** Master of Laws.
–ORIGIN from Latin *legum magister*.

Llo·sa, Mario Vargas, see **VARGAS LLOSA**.

Lloyd /loid/, Harold (Clayton) (1893–1971), US movie comedian. Performing his own hair-raising stunts, he used physical danger as a source of comedy in silent movies such as *High and Dizzy* (1920), *Safety Last* (1923), and *The Freshman* (1925).

Lloyd George, David, 1st Earl Lloyd-George of Dwyfor (1863–1945), British statesman; prime minister 1916–22. His coalition government was threatened by economic problems and trouble in Ireland. He resigned when the Conservatives withdrew their support in 1922.

Lloyd's /loidz/ an incorporated society of insurance underwriters in London, made up of private syndicates. Founded in 1871, Lloyd's originally dealt only in marine insurance.
–ORIGIN named after the coffeehouse of Edward *Lloyd* (*fl.* 1688–1726), in which underwriters and merchants congregated and where *Lloyd's List* was started in 1734.

Lloyd Web·ber /ˈwebər/, Sir Andrew (1948–), English composer. His many musicals, several of them written in collaboration with lyricist Sir Tim Rice, include *Jesus Christ Superstar* (1970), *Cats* (1981), and *The Phantom of the Opera* (1986).

Ly·wel·yn ap Gruff·ydd /(h)lo͞oˈelin äp ˈgrifiTH/ see **LLEWELYN**.

LM ▶ **abbr.** ■ long meter. ■ lunar module.

lm ▶ **abbr.** lumen(s).

LMAO ▶ **abbr.** vulgar slang laughing my ass off.

ln ▶ **abbr.** Mathematics natural logarithm.
–ORIGIN from modern Latin *logarithmus naturalis*.

LNB ▶ **abbr.** low noise blocker, a circuit on a satellite dish that selects the required signal from the transmission.

LNG ▶ **abbr.** liquefied natural gas.

lo /lō/ ▶ **exclam.** archaic used to draw attention to an interesting or amazing event: *and lo, the star, which they saw in the east, went before them.*
–PHRASES **lo and behold** used to present a new scene, situation, or turn of events, often with the suggestion that although surprising, it could in fact have been predicted: *you took me out and, lo and behold, I got home to find my house had been ransacked.*
–ORIGIN natural exclamation: first recorded as *lā* in Old English; reinforced in Middle English by a shortened form of *loke* 'look!,' imperative of **LOOK**.

lo·a /lōˈä/ ▶ **n.** (pl. **same** or **loas**) a god in the voodoo cult of Haiti.
–ORIGIN Haitian Creole.

loach /lōCH/ ▶ **n.** a small elongated bottom-dwelling freshwater fish with several barbels near the mouth, found in Eurasia and northwestern Africa. ● Families Cobitidae and Homalopteridae (or Balitoridae): several genera and numerous species.
–ORIGIN Middle English: from Old French *loche*, of unknown origin.

load /lōd/ ▶ **n. 1** a heavy or bulky thing that is being carried or is about to be carried: *in addition to their own food, they must carry a load of up to eighty pounds.* ■ the total number or amount that can be carried in something, esp. a vehicle of a specified type: *a tractor-trailer **load** of new appliances.* ■ the material carried along by a stream, glacier, ocean current, etc. ■ an amount of items washed or to be washed in a washing machine or dishwasher at one time: *I do at least six **loads** of washing a week.*
2 a weight or source of pressure borne by someone or something: *the increased **load** on the heart caused by a raised arterial pressure | the arch has hollow spandrels to lighten the **load** on the foundations.* ■ the amount of work to be done by a person or machine: *Arthur has a light teaching load.* ■ a burden of responsibility, worry, or grief: *consumers will find it difficult to service their heavy load of debt.*
3 (**a load of**) informal a lot of (often used to express one's disapproval or dislike of something): *she was talking **a load of** garbage.* ■ (**a load/loads**) informal plenty: *she spends **loads** of money on clothes | there's loads to see here, even when it rains.*
4 the amount of power supplied by a source; the resistance of moving parts to be overcome by a motor. ■ the amount of electricity supplied by a generating system at any given time. ■ Electronics an impedance or circuit that receives or develops the output of a transistor or other device.
▶ **v.** [with obj.] **1** put a load or large amount of something on or in (a vehicle, ship, container, etc.): *they **load up** their dugout canoes.* ■ place (a load or large quantity of something) on or in a vehicle, ship, container, etc.: *stolen property from a burglary was **loaded into** a taxi.* ■ [no obj.] (of a ship or vehicle) take on a load: *when we came to the quay the ship was still loading.* ■ [no obj.] (**load up on**) take, buy, or consume a large amount of: *I just went down to the store and loaded up on beer.*
2 make (someone or something) carry or hold a large or excessive amount of heavy things: *Elaine was **loaded down with** bags full of shopping.* ■ (**load someone/something with**) supply someone or something with (something) in overwhelming abundance or to excess: *the King and Queen loaded Columbus with wealth and honors.* ■ (usu. **be loaded**) bias toward a particular outcome: *the odds were loaded against them before the match.*
3 charge (a firearm) with ammunition. ■ insert something into (a device) so that it can be operated: *load your camera before you start.* ■ insert (something) into a device so that it will operate: *load the cassette into the camcorder.* ■ Computing transfer (a program or data) into memory, or into the central processor from storage.
4 add an extra charge to (an insurance premium) in the case of a poorer risk.
–PHRASES **get a load of** informal used to draw attention to someone or something: *get a load of what we've just done.* **get** (or **have**) **a load on** informal become drunk. **load the bases** Baseball (of the team at bat) fill all three bases with runners; (of a pitcher) allow all three bases to be occupied by runners. **load the dice against/in favor of someone** put someone at a disadvantage or advantage. **take a** (or **the**) **load off one's feet** sit or lie down. **take a load off someone's mind** bring someone relief from anxiety.
–ORIGIN Old English *lād* 'way, journey, conveyance,' of Germanic origin; related to German *Leite*, also to **LEAD**[1]; compare with **LODE**. The verb dates from the late 15th cent.

load-bear·ing ▶ **adj.** (esp. of a wall) supporting much of the weight of the overlying parts of a building or other structure. ■ relating to the carrying of a load: *the road's load-bearing capacity.*

load dis·place·ment ▶ **n.** the weight of water displaced by a ship when laden.

load·ed /ˈlōdid/ ▶ **adj. 1** carrying or bearing a load, esp. a large one: *a heavily loaded freight train.* ■ (of a firearm) charged with ammunition: *a loaded gun.* ■ (**loaded with**) containing in abundance or to excess: *your average chocolate bar is loaded with fat.* ■ informal having a lot of money; wealthy: *she doesn't really have to work—they're loaded.* ■ informal having had too much alcohol; drunk: *man, did I **get loaded** after I left his house.* ■ informal (of a car) equipped with many optional extras; deluxe: *1989 Ford 250 LXT: low miles, loaded.*
2 weighted or biased toward a particular outcome: *a trick like the one with the loaded dice.* ■ (of a word, statement, or question) charged with an underlying meaning or implication: *avoid politically loaded terms like "nation" | "Anything else?" It was a loaded question and Kelly knew it.*
–PHRASES **loaded for bear** see **BEAR**[2].

load·er /ˈlōdər/ ▶ **n. 1** a machine or person that loads something. ■ an attendant who loads guns at a shoot.
2 [in combination] a gun, machine, or truck that is loaded in a specified way: *a front-loader.*

load fac·tor ▶ **n.** the ratio of the average or actual amount of some quantity and the maximum possible or permissible. ■ the ratio between the lift and the weight of an aircraft.

load·ing /ˈlōdiNG/ ▶ **n. 1** the application of a mechanical load or force to something. ■ the amount of electric current or power delivered to a device. ■ the maximum electric current or power taken by an appliance. ■ the provision of extra electrical inductance to improve the properties of a transmission wire or antenna.
2 the application of an extra amount of something to balance some other factor. ■ an increase in an insurance premium due to a factor increasing the risk involved.

PRONUNCIATION KEY ə *ago, up*; ər *over, fur*; a *hat*; ā *ate*; ä *car*; e *let*; ē *see*; i *fit*; ī *by*; NG *sing*; ō *go*; ô *law, for*; oi *toy*; o͝o *good*; o͞o *goo*; ou *out*; TH *thin*; T͟H *then*; ZH *vision*

l

▶ **adj.** [in combination] (of a gun, machine, or truck) loaded in a specified way: *a front-loading dishwasher.*

load·ing coil ▶ **n.** a coil used to provide additional inductance in an electric circuit in order to reduce distortion and attenuation of transmitted signals or to reduce the resonant frequency of an aerial.

load·ing dock ▶ **n.** see DOCK[1].

load line ▶ **n.** another term for **PLIMSOLL LINE.**

load·mas·ter /ˈlōdˌmastər/ ▶ **n.** the member of an aircraft's crew responsible for the cargo.

load-shed·ding ▶ **n.** action to reduce the load on something, esp. the interruption of an electricity supply to avoid excessive load on the generating plant.

load·space /ˈlōdˌspās/ ▶ **n.** the space in a motor vehicle for carrying a load.

load·stone ▶ **n.** archaic spelling of **LODESTONE.**

loaf[1] /lōf/ ▶ **n.** (pl. **loaves** /lōvz/) a quantity of bread that is shaped and baked in one piece and usually sliced before being eaten: *a loaf of bread | two loaves in the oven.* ■ an item food formed into an oblong shape and sliced into portions.
– PHRASES **half a loaf is better than none** proverb it is better to accept less than one wants or expects than to have nothing at all.
– ORIGIN Old English *hlāf*, of Germanic origin; related to German *Laib*.

loaf[2] ▶ **v.** [no obj.] idle one's time away, typically by aimless wandering or loitering: *don't let him see you loafing around with your hands in your pockets.*
– ORIGIN mid 19th cent.: probably a back-formation from **LOAFER.**

loaf·er /ˈlōfər/ ▶ **n. 1** a person who idles time away. **2** trademark a leather shoe shaped like a moccasin, with a low flat heel.
– ORIGIN mid 19th cent.: perhaps from German *Landläufer* 'tramp,' from *Land* 'land' + *laufen* (dialect *lofen*) 'to run.'

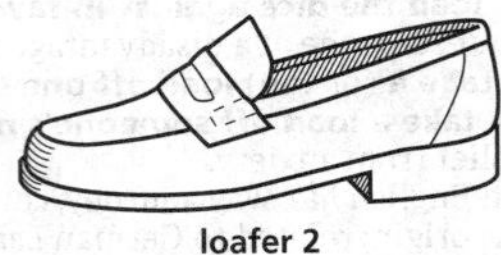
loafer 2

loam /lōm/ ▶ **n.** a fertile soil of clay and sand containing humus. ■ Geology a soil with roughly equal proportions of sand, silt, and clay. ■ a paste of clay and water with sand, chopped straw, etc., used in making bricks and plastering walls.
– DERIVATIVES **loam·i·ness n., loamy adj.**
– ORIGIN Old English *lām* 'clay'; related to Dutch *leem* and German *Lehm*, also to **LIME**[1].

loan /lōn/ ▶ **n.** a thing that is borrowed, esp. a sum of money that is expected to be paid back with interest: *borrowers can take out a loan for $84,000.* ■ an act of lending something to someone: *she offered to buy him dinner in return for the loan of the car.* ■ short for **LOANWORD.**
▶ **v.** [with obj.] borrow (a sum of money or item of property): *the word processor was loaned to us by the theater | he knew Rob would not loan him money.*
– PHRASES **on loan** (of a thing) being borrowed: *the painting is at present on loan to the gallery.* ■ (of a worker or sports player) released to another organization or team, typically for an agreed fixed period.
– DERIVATIVES **loan·a·ble adj., loan·ee** /ˌlōˈnē/ **n., loan·er n.**
– ORIGIN Middle English (also denoting a gift from a superior): from Old Norse *lán*, of Germanic origin; related to Dutch *leen*, German *Lehn*, also to **LEND.**

loan shark ▶ **n.** informal, derogatory a moneylender who charges extremely high rates of interest, typically under illegal conditions.
– DERIVATIVES **loan-shark·ing** /ˈlōnˌSHärkiNG/ **n.**

loan trans·la·tion ▶ **n.** an expression adopted by one language from another in a more or less literally translated form. Also called **CALQUE.**

loan·word /ˈlōnˌwərd/ ▶ **n.** a word adopted from a foreign language with little or no modification.

loath /lōTH, lōT͟H/ (also **loth**) ▶ **adj.** reluctant; unwilling: *I was loath to leave.*
– ORIGIN Old English *lāth* 'hostile, spiteful,' of Germanic origin; related to Dutch *leed*, German *Leid* 'sorrow.'

> **USAGE** Although different in meaning, **loath** and **loathe** are often confused. **Loath** (also spelled **loth**, although not commonly) is an adjective meaning 'reluctant or unwilling,' as in *I was loath to leave*, whereas **loathe** is a verb meaning 'feel intense dislike or disgust for,' as in *she loathed him on sight*.

loathe /lōT͟H/ ▶ **v.** [with obj.] feel intense dislike or disgust for: *she loathed him on sight.*
– DERIVATIVES **loath·er n.**
– ORIGIN Old English *lāthian*, of Germanic origin; related to **LOATH.**

loath·ing /ˈlōT͟HiNG/ ▶ **n.** a feeling of intense dislike or disgust; hatred: *the thought filled him with loathing.*

loath·some /ˈlōTHsəm, ˈlōT͟H-/ ▶ **adj.** causing hatred or disgust; repulsive: *this loathsome little swine.*
– DERIVATIVES **loath·some·ly adv., loath·some·ness n.**
– ORIGIN Middle English: from archaic *loath* 'disgust, loathing' + **-SOME**[1].

loaves /lōvz/ plural form of **LOAF**[1].

lob /läb/ ▶ **v. (lobs, lobbing, lobbed)** [with obj.] throw or hit (a ball or missile) in a high arc: *he lobbed the ball over their heads.* ■ (in tennis) hit the ball over (an opponent) in such a way.
▶ **n.** (chiefly in tennis) a ball hit in a high arc over an opponent.
– ORIGIN late 16th cent. (in the senses 'cause or allow to hang heavily' and 'behave like a lout'): from the archaic noun *lob* 'lout,' 'pendulous object,' probably from Low German or Dutch (compare with modern Dutch *lubbe* 'hanging lip'). The current sense dates from the mid 19th cent.

Lo·ba·chev·sky /ˌlōbəˈCHefskē, ləbəˈCHyefskyē/, Nikolai Ivanovich (1792–1856), Russian mathematician. At about the same time as Gauss and **János Bolyai** (1802–60), he independently discovered non-Euclidean geometry.

lo·bar /ˈlōˌbär, -bər/ ▶ **adj.** chiefly Anatomy & Medicine of, relating to, or affecting a lobe, esp. a whole lobe of a lung.

lo·bate /ˈlōˌbāt/ ▶ **adj.** Biology having a lobe or lobes: *lobate oak leaves.*
– DERIVATIVES **lo·ba·tion** /lōˈbāSHən/ **n.**

lob·by /ˈläbē/ ▶ **n.** (pl. **lobbies**) **1** a room providing a space out of which one or more other rooms or corridors lead, typically one near the entrance of a public building. **2** a group of people seeking to influence politicians or public officials on a particular issue: *members of the anti-abortion lobby* | [as modifier] *lobby groups.* ■ [in sing.] an organized attempt by members of the public to influence politicians or public officials: *a recent lobby of Congress by retirees.*
▶ **v. (lobbies, lobbying, lobbied)** [with obj.] seek to influence (a politician or public official) on an issue: *it is recommending that booksellers lobby their representatives* | [no obj.] *a group lobbying for better rail services.*
– DERIVATIVES **lob·by·ist** /-ist/ **n.**
– ORIGIN mid 16th cent. (in the sense 'monastic cloister'): from medieval Latin *lobia, lobium* 'covered walk, portico.' The verb sense derives from the practice of frequenting the lobby of a house of legislature to influence its members into supporting a cause.

lobe /lōb/ ▶ **n.** a roundish and flattish part of something, typically each of two or more such parts divided by a fissure, and often projecting or hanging. See also **EARLOBE.** ■ each of the parts of the cerebrum of the brain.
– DERIVATIVES **lobed adj., lobe·less adj.**
– ORIGIN late Middle English: via late Latin from Greek *lobos* 'lobe, pod.'

lo·bec·to·my /lōˈbektəmē/ ▶ **n.** (pl. **lobectomies**) surgical removal of a lobe of an organ such as the thyroid gland, lung, or liver.

lobe-finned fish (also **lobefin**) ▶ **n.** a fish of a largely extinct group having fleshy lobed fins, including the probable ancestors of the amphibians. Compare with **RAY-FINNED FISH.** ● Subclass Crossopterygia (or Actinistia or Coelacanthimorpha): the only living representative is the coelacanth.

lo·bel·ia /lōˈbēlēə, -ˈbēlyə/ ▶ **n.** a chiefly tropical or subtropical plant of the bellflower family, in particular an annual widely grown as a bedding plant. Some kinds are aquatic, and some grow as thick-trunked shrubs or trees on African mountains. ● Genus *Lobelia*, family Campanulaceae: many species, including the popular blue-flowered *L. erinus*.
– ORIGIN modern Latin, named after Matthias de *Lobel* (1538–1616), Flemish botanist to James I.

Lo·bi·to /lōˈbētō/ a seaport and natural harbor on the Atlantic coast of Angola; pop. 128,600 (est. 2004).

lob·lol·ly /ˈläbˌlälē/ ▶ **n.** (pl. **loblollies**) **1** (also **loblolly pine**) a pine tree of the southern US that has very long slender needles and is an important source of timber. ● *Pinus taeda*, family Pinaceae. **2** (also **loblolly bay**) a small evergreen tree of the tea family, with baylike leaves and white camellialike flowers, native to the southeastern US. ● *Gordonia lasianthus*, family Theaceae. **3** a marshy patch of ground. **4** Cooking, dated a thick mush or gruel.
– ORIGIN late 16th cent. (denoting thick gruel): the reason for the application of the word to the two plants, and the word's origin, are unknown.

lo·bo /ˈlōbō/ ▶ **n.** (pl. **lobos**) (in the southwestern US and Mexico) a timber wolf.
– ORIGIN mid 19th cent.: from Spanish, from Latin *lupus* 'wolf.'

lo·bo·la /lōbələ/ (also **lobolo** /ləˈbōlō/) ▶ **n.** (among southern African peoples) a bride price, esp. one paid with cattle. ■ the practice of making such a payment.
– ORIGIN Zulu and Xhosa.

lo·bo·pod /ˈlōbəˌpäd/ ▶ **n.** Zoology the lobopodium of an onychophoran. ■ an onychophoran: [as modifier] *a lobopod animal.*

lo·bo·po·di·um /ˌlōbəˈpōdēəm/ ▶ **n.** (pl. **lobopodia** /-dēə/) Zoology a blunt limb, or an organ resembling a limb, in particular: ■ the primitive leg of an onychophoran. ■ a lobelike pseudopodium in an ameba.
– DERIVATIVES **lo·bo·po·di·al** /-dēəl/ **adj.**
– ORIGIN early 20th cent.: from modern Latin *lobosus* 'having many lobes, large-lobed' + **PODIUM.**

lo·bot·o·mize /ləˈbätəˌmīz/ ▶ **v.** [with obj.] Surgery perform a lobotomy on. ■ informal reduce the mental or emotional capacity or ability to function of: *couples we knew who had been lobotomized by the birth of their children.*
– DERIVATIVES **lo·bot·o·mi·za·tion** /-ˌbätəməˈzāshən/ **n.**

lo·bot·o·my /ləˈbätəmē/ ▶ **n.** (pl. **lobotomies**) a surgical operation involving incision into the prefrontal lobe of the brain, formerly used to treat mental illness.

lob·scouse /ˈläbˌskous/ ▶ **n.** a stew formerly eaten by sailors, consisting of meat, vegetables, and hardtack.
– ORIGIN early 18th cent.: of unknown origin; compare with Dutch *lapskous*, Danish and Norwegian *lapskaus*, and German *Lapskaus*.

lob·ster /ˈläbstər/ ▶ **n.** a large marine crustacean with a cylindrical body, stalked eyes, and the first of its five pairs of limbs modified as pincers. ● *Homarus* and other genera, class Malacostraca: several species, in particular the **American lobster** (*H. americanus*). ■ the flesh of this animal as food. ■ a deep red color typical of a cooked lobster. ■ any of various similar crustaceans, esp. certain crayfish whose claws are eaten as food.
▶ **v.** [no obj.] catch lobsters.
– ORIGIN Old English *lopustre*, alteration of Latin *locusta* 'crustacean, locust.'

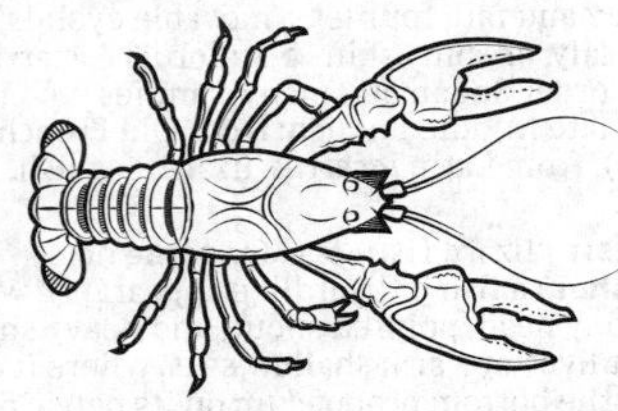
American lobster

lob·ster claw ▶ **n.** a tropical American plant with brightly colored flowers that resemble a lobster claw, each being composed of boat-shaped bracts. ● *Heliconia bihai*, family Heliconiaceae.

lob·ster·man /ˈläbstərmən/ ▶ **n.** a person whose occupation is trapping lobsters.

lob·ster pot (also **lobster trap**) ▶ **n.** a cratelike or basketlike trap in which lobsters are caught.

lob·ster ther·mi·dor /ˈTHərməˌdôr/ ▶ **n.** a dish of lobster cooked in a cream sauce, returned to its shell, sprinkled with cheese, and browned under the grill.
– ORIGIN *thermidor* from **THERMIDOR.**

lob·ule /ˈläbˌyo͞ol/ ▶ **n.** chiefly Anatomy a small lobe.
– DERIVATIVES **lob·u·lar** /-yələr/ **adj., lob·u·late** /-yəˌlāt/ **adj., lob·u·lat·ed** /-yəˌlātid/ **adj.**
– ORIGIN late 17th cent.: from **LOBE,** on the pattern of words such as *globule*.

lob·worm /ˈläbˌwərm/ ▶ **n.** another term for **LUGWORM.**
– ORIGIN mid 17th cent.: from **LOB** in the obsolete sense 'pendulous object.'

lo·cal /ˈlōkəl/ ▶ **adj.** belonging or relating to a particular area or neighborhood, typically exclusively so: *researching local history | the local post office.* ■ denoting a telephone call made to a nearby place and charged at a relatively low rate. ■ denoting a train or bus serving a particular district, with frequent stops: *the town has an excellent local bus service.* Compare with **EXPRESS**[2].

■ (in technical use) relating to a particular region or part, or to each of any number of these: *a local infection | migration can regulate the local density of animals.* ■ Computing denoting a variable or other entity that is only available for use in one part of a program. ■ Computing denoting a device that can be accessed without the use of a network. Compare with REMOTE.
▶ n. a local person or thing, in particular: ■ an inhabitant of a particular area or neighborhood: *the street was full of locals and tourists.* ■ Brit. informal a pub convenient to a person's home: *a pint in the local.* ■ a local train or bus service: *catch the local into New Delhi.* ■ a local branch of an organization, esp. a labor union. ■ short for LOCAL ANESTHESIA. ■ Stock Exchange, slang a floor trader who trades on their own account, rather than on behalf of other investors.
– DERIVATIVES **lo·cal·ly** adv., **lo·cal·ness** n.
– ORIGIN late Middle English: from late Latin *localis*, from Latin *locus* 'place.'

lo·cal an·es·the·sia ▶ n. anesthesia that affects a restricted area of the body. Compare with GENERAL ANESTHESIA.

lo·cal ar·e·a net·work (abbr.: **LAN**) ▶ n. a computer network that links devices within a building or group of adjacent buildings. Compare with WIDE AREA NETWORK.

lo·cal bus ▶ n. Computing a high-speed data connection directly linking peripheral devices to the processor and memory, allowing activities that require high data transmission rates such as video display.

lo·cal col·or ▶ n. **1** the customs, manner of speech, dress, or other typical features of a place or period that contribute to its particular character: *reporters in search of local color and gossip.*
2 Art the natural color of a thing in ordinary daylight, uninfluenced by the proximity of other colors.

lo·cale /lō'kal/ ▶ n. a place where something happens or is set, or that has particular events associated with it: *her summers were spent in a variety of exotic locales.*
– ORIGIN late 18th cent.: from French *local* (noun), respelled to indicate stress on the final syllable; compare with MORALE.

lo·cal gov·ern·ment ▶ n. the administration of a particular town, county, or district, with representatives elected by those who live there.

Lo·cal Group Astronomy the cluster of galaxies of which the Milky Way is a member.

lo·cal·ism /'lōkə,lizəm/ ▶ n. preference for a locality, particularly for one's own area or region. ■ derogatory the limitation of ideas and interests resulting from this. ■ a characteristic of a particular locality, such as a local idiom or custom.
– DERIVATIVES **lo·cal·ist** n. & adj.

lo·cal·i·ty /lō'kalətē/ ▶ n. (pl. **localities**) the position or site of something: *the rock's size and locality.* ■ an area or neighborhood, esp. as regarded as a place occupied by certain people or as the scene of particular activities: *the results of other schools in the locality | a working-class locality.*
– ORIGIN early 17th cent.: from French *localité* or late Latin *localitas*, from *localis* 'relating to a place' (see LOCAL).

lo·cal·ize /'lōkə,līz/ ▶ v. [with obj.] (often as adj. **localized**) restrict (something) to a particular place: *symptoms include localized pain and numbness.* ■ make (something) local in character: *there'd now be a more localized news service.* ■ assign (something) to a particular place: *most vertebrates localize sounds by orienting movements.*
– DERIVATIVES **lo·cal·iz·a·ble** adj., **lo·cal·i·za·tion** /,lōkələ'zāsHən/ n.

lo·cal op·tion ▶ n. a choice available to a local administration to accept or reject national legislation (e.g., concerning the sale of alcoholic liquor).

lo·cal time ▶ n. time as reckoned in a particular region or time zone. ■ time at a particular place as measured from the sun's transit over the meridian at that place, defined as noon.

lo·carb /'lō,kärb/ ▶ n. variant spelling of LOW-CARB.

Lo·car·no /lō'kärnō/ a resort in southern Switzerland, at the northern end of Lake Maggiore; pop. 14,909 (2007).

lo·cate /'lō,kāt, lō'kāt/ ▶ v. [with obj.] discover the exact place or position of: *engineers were working to locate the fault.* ■ (usu. **be located**) situate in a particular place: *these popular apartments are centrally located.* ■ place within a particular context: *they locate their policies in terms of wealth creation.* ■ [no obj.] establish oneself or one's business in a specified place: *his marketing strategy has been to locate in small towns.*
– DERIVATIVES **lo·cat·a·ble** /-,kātəbəl, lō'kāt-/ adj.
– ORIGIN early 16th cent.: from Latin *locat-* 'placed,' from the verb *locare*, from *locus* 'place.' The original sense was as a legal term meaning 'rent out,' later (late 16th cent.) 'assign to a particular place,' then 'establish in a place.' The sense 'discover the exact position of' dates from the late 19th cent.

lo·ca·tion /lō'kāsHən/ ▶ n. a particular place or position: *the property is set in a convenient location.* ■ an actual place or natural setting in which a film or broadcast is made, as distinct from a simulation in a studio: *the movie was filmed entirely **on location**.* ■ the action or process of placing someone or something in a particular position: *the location of new housing beyond the existing built-up areas.* ■ a position or address in computer memory.
– DERIVATIVES **lo·ca·tion·al** /-sHənl, -sHnəl/ adj.
– ORIGIN late 16th cent.: from Latin *locatio(n-)*, from the verb *locare* (see LOCATE).

loc·a·tive /'läkətiv/ Grammar ▶ adj. relating to or denoting a case, in some languages, of nouns, pronouns, and adjectives, expressing location.
▶ n. (**the locative**) the locative case. ■ a word in the locative case.
– ORIGIN early 19th cent.: from LOCATE, on the pattern of *vocative*.

lo·ca·tor /'lō,kātər, lō'kā-/ ▶ n. a device or system for locating something, typically by means of radio signals.

lo·ca·vore /'lōkə,vôr/ ▶ n. a person whose diet consists only or principally of locally grown or produced food.
– ORIGIN early 21st cent.: on the pattern of *carnivore*, *herbivore*, etc.

loc. cit. ▶ abbr. in the passage already cited.
– ORIGIN from Latin *loco citato*.

loch /läk, läKH/ ▶ n. Scottish a lake. ■ (also **sea loch**) an arm of the sea, esp. when narrow or partially landlocked.
– ORIGIN late Middle English: from Scottish Gaelic.

lo·chi·a /'lōkēə, 'läk-/ ▶ n. Medicine the normal discharge from the uterus after childbirth.
– DERIVATIVES **lo·chi·al** adj.
– ORIGIN late 17th cent.: modern Latin, from Greek *lokhia*, neuter plural (used as a noun) of *lokhios* 'of childbirth.'

Loch Ness /läk 'nes, läKH/ a deep lake in northwestern Scotland, in the Great Glen. Forming part of the Caledonian Canal, it is 24 miles (38 km) long, with a maximum depth of 755 feet (230 m). The lake has long been rumored to be the home of the Loch Ness monster.

Loch Ness mon·ster a large creature alleged to live in the deep waters of Loch Ness. Reports of its existence date from the time of St. Columba (6th century); despite recent scientific expeditions, there is still no proof of its existence.

lo·ci /'lō,sī, -,sē, -,kē, -,kī/ plural form of LOCUS.

lo·ci clas·si·ci /'lō,sī 'klasə,sī, 'lō,sē 'klasə,sē, 'lō,kē 'klasi,kē, 'lō,kī 'klasi,kī/ plural form of LOCUS CLASSICUS.

lock[1] /läk/ ▶ n. **1** a mechanism for keeping a door, lid, etc., fastened, typically operated only by a key of a particular form: *the key turned firmly in the lock.* ■ a similar device used to prevent the operation or movement of a vehicle or other machine: *a bicycle lock.* ■ (in wrestling and martial arts) a hold that prevents an opponent from moving a limb. ■ [in sing.] archaic a number of interlocked or jammed items: *a street closed by a lock of carriages.*
2 a short confined section of a canal or other waterway in which the water level can be changed by the use of gates and sluices, used for raising and lowering vessels between two gates. ■ an airlock.
3 (**a lock**) informal a person or thing that is certain to succeed; a certainty.
4 historical a mechanism for exploding the charge of a gun.
▶ v. **1** [with obj.] fasten or secure (something) with a lock: *she closed and locked her desk* | (as adj. **locked**) *behind locked doors.* ■ enclose or shut in by locking or fastening a door, lid, etc.: *the prisoners are **locked in** overnight | Phil **locked away** the takings every night.* ■ [no obj.] (of a door, window, box, etc.) become or be able to be secured through activation of a lock: *the door will automatically lock behind you.*
2 make or become rigidly fixed or immovable: [with obj.] *he locked his hands behind her neck | the vessel was **locked in** ice* | [no obj.] *their gaze locked for several long moments.*
3 [no obj.] go through a lock on a canal: *we locked through at Moore Haven.*
– PHRASES **have a lock on** informal have an unbreakable hold on or total control over. **lock horns** engage in conflict. **lock, stock, and barrel** including everything; completely: *the place is owned lock, stock, and barrel by an oil company.* [referring to the complete mechanism of a firearm.] **under lock and key** securely locked up.
– PHRASAL VERBS **lock someone down** confine a prisoner to their cell, esp. so as to gain control. **lock someone/something in** (or **into**) involve or entangle someone or something in (an embrace or struggle): *they were locked in a legal battle.* ■ oblige a person or company to abide by the terms of a contract for a specific period. **lock onto** locate (a target) by radar or similar means and then track. **lock someone out 1** keep someone out of a room or building by locking the door. **2** (of an employer) subject employees to a lockout. **lock someone out of** exclude someone from: *those now locked out of the job market.* **lock someone up** (or **away**) imprison someone. **lock something up** (also **lock up**) shut and secure something, esp. a building, by fastening its doors with locks: *the diplomatic personnel locked up their building and walked off | you could lock up for me when you leave.* ■ (also **lock something away**) invest money in something so that it is not easily accessible: *vast sums of money locked up in pension funds.*
– DERIVATIVES **lock·a·ble** adj., **lock·less** adj.
– ORIGIN Old English *loc*, of Germanic origin; related to German *Loch* 'hole.'

lock[2] ▶ n. a piece of a person's hair that coils or hangs together: *she pushed back **a lock of hair**.* ■ (**locks**) chiefly literary a person's hair: *flowing locks and a long white beard.* ■ a tuft of wool or cotton. ■ (**locks**) short for DREADLOCKS.
– DERIVATIVES **locked** adj. *his curly-locked comrades.*
– ORIGIN Old English *locc*, of Germanic origin; related to Dutch *lok*, German *Locke*, possibly also to LOCK[1].

lock·age /'läkij/ ▶ n. the construction or use of locks on waterways. ■ the amount of rise and fall of water levels resulting from the use of locks. ■ money paid as a toll for the use of a lock.

lock·box /'läk,bäks/ ▶ n. **1** a box that locks, usually for storing money or valuables.
2 a service provided by a bank, whereby the bank receives, processes, and deposits all of a company's receivables.
3 any of various computerized devices or services intended to prevent the unauthorized distribution or copying of digitally stored or transmitted data.

lock·down /'läk,doun/ ▶ n. the confining of prisoners to their cells, typically after an escape or to regain control during a riot. ■ a state of isolation or restricted access instituted as a security measure: *the university is **on lockdown** and nobody has been able to leave.*

Locke /läk/, John (1632–1704), English philosopher; a founder of empiricism and political liberalism. His *Two Treatises of Government* (1690) argues that the authority of rulers has a human origin and is limited. In *An Essay concerning Human Understanding* (1690) he argued that all knowledge is derived from sense-experience.
– DERIVATIVES **Lock·e·an** /'läkēən/ adj.

lock·er /'läkər/ ▶ n. **1** a small lockable closet or compartment, typically as one of a number placed together for public or general use, e.g., in schools, gymnasiums, or train stations. ■ a chest or compartment on a ship or boat for clothes, stores, equipment, or ammunition.
2 a device that locks something.
– ORIGIN late Middle English: probably related to Flemish *loker*.

Lock·er·bie /'läkərbē/ a town in southwestern Scotland; pop. 4,500 (est. 2004). In 1988, a US airliner, destroyed by a terrorist bomb, crashed on the town and killed all those on board as well as 11 people on the ground.

lock·er room ▶ n. a room containing lockers for the storage of personal belongings, esp. in schools or gymnasiums.
▶ adj. regarded as characteristic of or suited to a men's locker room, esp. as being coarse or ribald: *locker-room humor.*

lock·et /'läkit/ ▶ n. **1** a small ornamental case, typically made of gold or silver, worn around a person's neck on a chain and used to hold things of sentimental value, such as a photograph or lock of hair.
2 a metal plate or band on a scabbard.
– ORIGIN late Middle English (sense 2): from Old French *locquet*, diminutive of *loc* 'latch, lock,' of Germanic origin; related to LOCK[1]. Sense 1 dates from the late 17th cent.

l

lock-in ▶ **n. 1** an arrangement according to which a person or company is obliged to deal only with a specific company.
2 a protest demonstration in which a group locks itself within an office or factory.

lock·jaw /ˈläkˌjô/ ▶ **n.** nontechnical term for **TRISMUS**.

lock·knit ▶ **adj.** (of a fabric) knitted with an interlocking stitch.

lock·nut /ˈläkˌnət/ ▶ **n.** a nut screwed down on another to keep it tight. ■ a nut designed so that, once tightened, it cannot be accidentally loosened.

lock·out /ˈläkˌout/ ▶ **n. 1** the exclusion of employees by their employer from their place of work until certain terms are agreed to.
2 a device used to ensure that machines remain inoperable while repairs or adjustments are made.

Lock·port /ˈläkˌpôrt/ a city in western New York, northeast of Buffalo, on the Erie Canal; pop. 20,630 (est. 2008).

lock·set /ˈläkˌset/ ▶ **n.** a complete locking system, including knobs, plates, and a locking mechanism, esp. for a door.

lock·smith /ˈläkˌsmiTH/ ▶ **n.** a person who makes and repairs locks.

lock·step /ˈläkˌstep/ ▶ **n.** a way of marching with each person as close as possible to the one in front: *the trio marched **in lockstep*** | [as adv.] *hundreds of shaven-headed youths march lockstep into the stadium.* ■ close adherence to and emulation of another's actions: *they raised prices **in lockstep with** those of foreign competitors* | [as modifier] *the party touted a lockstep unity.*

lock·stitch ▶ **n.** a stitch made by a sewing machine by firmly linking together two threads or stitches.

lock·up /ˈläkˌəp/ ▶ **n. 1** a jail, esp. a temporary one.
2 the locking up of premises for the night. ■ the time of doing this: *hurrying back to their dorms before lockup.*
3 the action of becoming fixed or immovable: *anti-lock braking helps prevent wheel lockup.*
4 an investment in assets that cannot readily be realized or sold in the short term.

Lock·yer /ˈläkyər/, Norman (1836–1920), English astronomer; full name *Sir Joseph Norman Lockyer.* His spectroscopic analysis of the sun led to his discovery of a new element, which he named *helium.*

lo·co /ˈlōkō/ ▶ **adj.** informal crazy.
– ORIGIN late 19th cent.: from Spanish, 'insane.'

lo·co·mo·tion /ˌlōkəˈmōSHən/ ▶ **n.** movement or the ability to move from one place to another: *the muscles that are concerned with locomotion* | *he preferred walking to other forms of locomotion.*
– ORIGIN mid 17th cent.: from Latin *loco,* ablative of *locus* 'place' + *motio* 'motion' (see **MOTION**).

lo·co·mo·tive /ˌlōkəˈmōtiv/ ▶ **n.** a powered rail vehicle used for pulling trains: *a diesel locomotive.*
▶ **adj.** of, relating to, or effecting locomotion: *locomotive power.* ■ archaic (of a machine, vehicle, or animal) having the power of progressive motion: *locomotive bivalves have the strongest hinges.*
– ORIGIN early 17th cent. (as an adjective): from modern Latin *locomotivus,* from Latin *loco* (ablative of *locus* 'place') + late Latin *motivus* 'motive,' suggested by medieval Latin *in loco moveri* 'move by change of position.'

lo·co·mo·tor /ˌlōkəˈmōtər/ ▶ **adj.** chiefly Biology of or relating to locomotion: *locomotor organs.*
– ORIGIN early 19th cent.: from **LOCOMOTION** + **MOTOR**.

lo·co·mo·tor a·tax·i·a ▶ **n.** another term for **TABES DORSALIS**.

lo·co·mo·to·ry /ˌlōkəˈmōtərē/ ▶ **adj.** chiefly Zoology relating to or having the power of locomotion: *locomotory cilia.*

lo·co·weed /ˈlōkōˌwēd/ ▶ **n. 1** a widely distributed plant of the pea family that, if eaten by livestock, can cause a brain disorder, the symptoms of which include unpredictable behavior and loss of coordination. ● Genus *Astragalus* (and *Oxytropis*), family Leguminosae.
2 informal cannabis.

Lo·cri·an mode /ˈlōkrēən, ˈläkrē-/ ▶ **n.** Music the mode represented by the natural diatonic scale B–B (containing a minor 2nd, 3rd, 6th, and 7th, and a diminished 5th).
– ORIGIN late 19th cent.: *Locrian* from Greek *Locris,* a division of ancient Greece, + **-IAN**; named after an ancient Greek mode but not identifiable with it.

loc·ule /ˈläkˌyo͞ol/ ▶ **n.** chiefly Botany each of a number of small separate cavities, esp. in an ovary.
– DERIVATIVES **loc·u·lar** /-yələr/ **adj.**

loc·u·lus /ˈläkyələs/ ▶ **n.** (pl. **loculi** /-ˌlī, -ˌlē/) another term for **LOCULE**.
– ORIGIN mid 19th cent.: from Latin, 'compartment,' diminutive of *locus* 'place.'

lo·cum /ˈlōkəm/ ▶ **n.** Brit. a person who stands in temporarily for someone else of the same profession, esp. a cleric or doctor.
– ORIGIN early 20th cent.: short for **LOCUM TENENS**.

lo·cum te·nens /ˈlōkəm ˈtenənz, ˈtēˌnenz/ ▶ **n.** (pl. **locum tenentes** /təˈnentēz/) full form of **LOCUM**.
– DERIVATIVES **lo·cum te·nen·cy** /ˈtenənsē, ˈtēnən-/ **n.**
– ORIGIN mid 17th cent.: from medieval Latin, literally 'one holding a place' (see **LOCUS, TENANT**).

lo·cus /ˈlōkəs/ ▶ **n.** (pl. **loci** /ˈlōˌsī, -ˌsē, -ˌkē, -ˌkī/)
1 technical a particular position, point, or place: *it is impossible to specify the exact locus in the brain of these neural events.* ■ the effective or perceived location of something abstract: *the real locus of power is the informal council.* ■ Genetics the position of a gene or mutation on a chromosome.
2 Mathematics a curve or other figure formed by all the points satisfying a particular equation of the relation between coordinates, or by a point, line, or surface moving according to mathematically defined conditions.
– ORIGIN early 18th cent.: from Latin, 'place.'

lo·cus clas·si·cus /ˈlōkəs ˈklasikəs/ ▶ **n.** (pl. **loci classici** /ˈlōˌsī ˈklasəˌsī, ˈlōˌsē ˈklasəˌsē, ˈlōˌkē ˈklasiˌkē, ˈlōˌkī ˈklasiˌkī/) a passage considered to be the best known or most authoritative on a particular subject.
– ORIGIN Latin, literally 'classical place.'

lo·cust /ˈlōkəst/ ▶ **n. 1** a large and mainly tropical grasshopper with strong powers of flight. It is usually solitary, but from time to time there is a population explosion, and it migrates in vast swarms that cause extensive damage to crops. ● Several species in the family Acrididae, including the **migratory locust** (*Locusta migratoria*), which is sometimes seen in Europe. ■ (also **seventeen-year locust**) the periodical cicada.
2 (also **locust bean**) the large edible pod of some plants of the pea family, in particular the carob bean, which is said to resemble a locust.
3 (also **locust tree**) any of a number of pod-bearing trees of the pea family, in particular the carob tree and the black locust.
– ORIGIN Middle English: via Old French *locuste* from Latin *locusta* 'locust, crustacean.'

lo·cu·tion /lōˈkyo͞oSHən/ ▶ **n. 1** a word or phrase, esp. with regard to style or idiom. ■ a person's style of speech: *his impeccable locution.*
2 an utterance regarded in terms of its intrinsic meaning or reference, as distinct from its function or purpose in context. Compare with **ILLOCUTION, PERLOCUTION**. ■ language regarded in terms of locutionary rather than illocutionary or perlocutionary acts.
– DERIVATIVES **lo·cu·tion·ar·y** /-ˌnerē/ **adj.**
– ORIGIN late Middle English: from Old French, or from Latin *locutio(n-),* from *loqui* 'speak.'

lode /lōd/ ▶ **n.** a vein of metal ore in the earth. ■ [in sing.] a rich source of something: *a rich lode of scandal and alleged crime.*
– ORIGIN Old English *lād* 'way, course,' variant of **LOAD**. The term denoted a watercourse in late Middle English and a lodestone in the early 16th cent. The current sense dates from the early 17th cent.

lo·den /ˈlōdn/ ▶ **n.** a thick waterproof woolen cloth. ■ the dark green color in which such cloth is often made.
– ORIGIN early 20th cent.: from German *Loden.*

lode·star /ˈlōdˌstär/ ▶ **n.** a star that is used to guide the course of a ship, esp. Polaris: figurative *she was his intellectual lodestar.*
– ORIGIN Middle English: from **LODE** in the obsolete sense 'way, course' + **STAR**.

lode·stone /ˈlōdˌstōn/ ▶ **n.** a piece of magnetite or other naturally magnetized mineral, able to be used as a magnet. ■ a mineral of this kind; magnetite. ■ a thing that is the focus of attention or attraction.

Lodge[1] /läj/, David (John) (1935–), English novelist and academic. Notable works: *Changing Places* (1975), *Small World* (1984), and *Therapy* (1995).

Lodge[2], Henry Cabot (1850–1924), US politician and writer. He was a member of the US House of Representatives 1887–93 and the US Senate 1893–1924 as a Republican from Massachusetts. He opposed accepting the peace treaty that ended World War I and that was linked to the US entry into the League of Nations. He was the grandfather of Henry Cabot Lodge.

Lodge[3], Henry Cabot (1902–85), US politician and diplomat. He was a Republican vice presidential candidate in 1960 and served as ambassador to South Vietnam 1963–64, 1965–67. The grandson of Henry Cabot Lodge, he was the US representative to the United Nations 1953–60.

lodge /läj/ ▶ **n. 1** a small house at the gates of a park or in the grounds of a large house, typically occupied by a gatekeeper, gardener, or other employee. ■ a small country house occupied in season for sports such as hunting, shooting, fishing, and skiing: *a hunting lodge.* ■ a large house or hotel: *Cumberland Lodge.* ■ a porter's quarters at the main entrance of a college or other large building. ■ the residence of a head of a college, esp. at Cambridge. ■ an American Indian hut. ■ a beaver's den.
2 a branch or meeting place of an organization such as the Freemasons.
▶ **v. 1** [with obj.] present (a complaint, appeal, claim, etc.) formally to the proper authorities: *he has 28 days in which to lodge an appeal.* ■ (**lodge something in/with**) leave money or a valuable item in (a place) or with (someone) for safekeeping.
2 make or become firmly fixed or embedded in a particular place: [with obj.] *they had to remove a bullet lodged near his spine* | [no obj.] figurative *the image had lodged in her mind.*
3 [no obj.] stay or sleep in another person's house, paying money for one's accommodations: *the man who lodged in the room next door.* ■ [with obj.] provide (someone) with a place to sleep or stay in return for payment.
4 [with obj.] (of wind or rain) flatten (a standing crop): (as adj. **lodged**) *rain that soaks standing or lodged crops.* ■ [no obj.] (of a crop) be flattened in such a way.
– ORIGIN Middle English *loge,* via Old French *loge* 'arbor, hut' from medieval Latin *laubia, lobia* (see **LOBBY**), of Germanic origin; related to German *Laube* 'arbor.'

lodge·pole pine /ˈläjiˌpōl/ ▶ **n.** a straight-trunked pine tree that grows in the mountains of western North America, widely grown for timber and traditionally used by some American Indians in the construction of lodges. ● *Pinus contorta* var. *latifolia,* family Pinaceae.

lodg·er /ˈläjər/ ▶ **n.** a roomer.

lodg·ing /ˈläjiNG/ ▶ **n.** a place in which someone lives or stays temporarily: *they found a cheap lodging in a backstreet* | *a fee for **board and lodging**.* ■ (**lodgings**) a room or rooms rented out to someone, usually in the same residence as the owner.

lodg·ing house ▶ **n.** a rooming house.

lodg·ment /ˈläjmənt/ (also **lodgement**) ▶ **n. 1** chiefly literary a place in which a person or thing is located, deposited, or lodged: *they found a lodgment for the hook in the crumbling parapet.*
2 the depositing of money in a particular bank, account, etc.
3 Military a temporary defensive work made on a captured part of an enemy's fortifications to secure a position and provide protection.
– ORIGIN late 16th cent.: from French *logement* 'dwelling,' from Old French *loge* 'arbor' (see **LODGE**).

Lo·di /ˈlōˌdī/ a city in north central California, north of Stockton, in the San Joaquin Valley; pop. 61,301 (est. 2008).

lod·i·cule /ˈlädəˌkyo͞ol/ ▶ **n.** Botany a small green or white scale below the ovary of a grass flower.
– ORIGIN mid 19th cent.: from Latin *lodicula,* diminutive of *lodix* 'coverlet.'

Łódź /lädz, wo͞oCH/ an industrial city in central Poland, southwest of Warsaw, the second largest city in the country; pop. 756,666 (2007).

lo·ess /les, ləs, ˈlōˌes/ ▶ **n.** Geology a loosely compacted yellowish-gray deposit of windblown sediment of which extensive deposits occur, e.g., in eastern China and the American Midwest.
– DERIVATIVES **lo·ess·i·al** /ˈlesēəl, ˈlə-, lōˈes-/ **adj.**, **lo·ess·ic** /ˈlesik, ˈlə-, lōˈes-/ **adj.**
– ORIGIN mid 19th cent.: from German *Löss,* from Swiss German *lösch* 'loose.'

Loewe /lō/, Frederick (1901–88), US composer; born in Austria. The collaboration he began with lyricist Alan Jay Lerner in 1942 became one of the most successful in the history of musical theater. Their Broadway hits include *Brigadoon* (1947), *My Fair Lady* (1956) and *Camelot* (1960).

Loe·wi /ˈlō-ē/, Otto (1873–1961), US pharmacologist and physiologist, born in Germany. He showed that a chemical neurotransmitter (acetylcholine) is produced at the junction of a parasympathetic nerve and a muscle. Nobel Prize for Physiology or Medicine (1936), shared with Sir Henry Dale.

lo-fi /ˈlōˌfī/ (also **low-fi**) ▶ **adj.** of or employing sound reproduction of a lower quality than hi-fi: *defiantly lo-fi recording techniques.* ■ (of popular music) recorded and produced with basic equipment and thus having a raw and unsophisticated sound.
▶ **n.** sound reproduction or music of such a kind.
– ORIGIN 1950s: from an alteration of **LOW**[1] + *-fi* on the pattern of *hi-fi.*

Lo·fo·ten Is·lands /ˈlōˌfōtn/ a group of islands off the northwestern coast of Norway. They are situated within the Arctic Circle in the Norwegian Sea.

loft /lôft, läft/ ▶ **n. 1** a room or space directly under the roof of a house or other building, which may be used for accommodations or storage. ■ a gallery in a church or hall: *a choir loft.* ■ short for ORGAN LOFT. ■ a large, open area over a shop, warehouse, or factory, sometimes converted into living space. ■ a pigeon house.
2 Golf upward inclination given to the ball in a stroke. ■ backward slope of the head of a club, designed to give upward inclination to the ball.
3 the thickness of insulating matter in an object such as a sleeping bag or a padded coat.
▶ **v.** [with obj.] kick, hit, or throw (a ball or missile) high up: *he lofted the ball over the infield.* ■ (**lofted**) give backward slope to the head of (a golf club): *a lofted metal club.*
– ORIGIN late Old English, from Old Norse *lopt* 'air, sky, upper room,' of Germanic origin; related to Dutch *lucht* and German *Luft*.

loft·er /'lôftər, 'läf-/ ▶ **n.** Golf, dated a nine-iron or similar lofted club. [late 19th cent.: from the verb LOFT.]

loft·y /'lôftē, 'läf-/ ▶ **adj.** (**loftier, loftiest**) **1** of imposing height: *the elegant square was shaded by lofty palms.* ■ of a noble or exalted nature: *an extraordinary mixture of harsh reality and lofty ideals.* ■ proud, aloof, or self-important: *lofty intellectual disdain.*
2 (of wool and other textiles) thick and resilient.
– DERIVATIVES **loft·i·ly** /-təlē/ **adv.**, **loft·i·ness n.**
– ORIGIN Middle English: from LOFT, influenced by ALOFT.

log[1] /lôg, läg/ ▶ **n. 1** a part of the trunk or a large branch of a tree that has fallen or been cut off.
2 (also **logbook**) an official record of events during the voyage of a ship or aircraft: *a ship's log.* ■ a regular or systematic record of incidents or observations: *keep a detailed log of your activities.*
3 an apparatus for determining the speed of a ship, originally consisting of a float attached to a knotted line wound on a reel, the distance run out in a certain time being used as an estimate of the vessel's speed.
▶ **v.** (**logs, logging, logged**) [with obj.] **1** enter (an incident or fact) in the log of a ship or aircraft or in another systematic record: *the incident has to be logged | the red book where we log our calls.* ■ (of a ship, aircraft, or pilot) achieve (a certain distance, speed, or time): *she had logged more than 12,000 miles since she had been launched.* ■ make a systematic recording of (events, observations, or measurements): *the virus can log keystrokes that you make when you access all sorts of services.*
2 cut down (an area of forest) in order to exploit the timber commercially.
– PHRASES (**as**) **easy as falling off a log** informal very easy.
– PHRASAL VERBS **log in** (or **on**) go through the procedures to begin use of a computer, database, or system. **log off** (or **out**) go through the procedures to conclude use of a computer, database, or system.
– ORIGIN Middle English (in the sense 'bulky mass of wood'): of unknown origin; perhaps symbolic of the notion of heaviness. Sense 3 of the noun originally denoted a thin quadrant of wood loaded to float upright in the water, whence 'ship's journal' in which information from the log board was recorded.

> **WORD TRENDS** The verb **log** has become part of the vocabulary of modern paranoia. As the Oxford English Corpus shows, the word is now primarily associated with technology, in particular that used for surveillance: *the spyware secretly records your keystrokes, logging sensitive information such as online banking passwords.* Hackers are not the only ones responsible for the logging of information. Increasingly, those in authority are accused of systematically recording people's details without reason or permission: *the government is logging details of every man, woman and child in 'Big Brother' computers.*

log[2] ▶ **n.** short for LOGARITHM: [as modifier] *log tables* | [prefixed to a number or algebraic symbol] *log x*.

log. ▶ **abbr.** logic.

-log ▶ **comb. form** variant spelling of -LOGUE.

log_e ▶ **symbol** natural logarithm (a logarithm to the base *e*).

Lo·gan[1] /'lōgən/ a city in northern Utah; pop. 48,657 (est. 2008).

Lo·gan[2] /'lōgən/, Joshua Lockwood, III (1908–88), US director and playwright. He directed Broadway shows, including *Annie Get Your Gun* (1946), *Mister Roberts* (1948), *South Pacific* (1949) and *Fanny* (1954), as well as motion pictures, including *Picnic* (1955), *Bus Stop* (1956), *South Pacific* (1958), and *Camelot* (1967). He wrote or cowrote several of these and other titles, and in 1950 shared the Pulitzer Prize for Drama with his *South Pacific* cowriters Richard Rodgers and Oscar Hammerstein II.

Lo·gan, Mount /'lōgən/ a mountain in southwestern Yukon Territory, Canada, near the border with Alaska. Rising to 19,850 feet (6,054 m), it is the highest peak in Canada and the second-highest peak in North America.

lo·gan·ber·ry /'lōgən,berē/ ▶ **n.** (pl. **loganberries**) **1** an edible dull-red soft fruit, considered to be a hybrid of a raspberry and an American dewberry.
2 the scrambling blackberrylike plant that bears this fruit. ● *Rubus loganobaccus*, family Rosaceae.
– ORIGIN late 19th cent.: from the name of John H. *Logan* (1841–1928), American horticulturalist, + BERRY.

log·a·rithm /'lôgə,riTHəm, 'lägə-/ (abbr.: **log**) ▶ **n.** a quantity representing the power to which a fixed number (the base) must be raised to produce a given number.

> Logarithms can be used to simplify calculations because the addition and subtraction of logarithms is equivalent to multiplication and division, although the use of printed tables of logarithms for this has declined with the spread of electronic calculators. They also allow a geometric relationship to be represented conveniently by a straight line. The base of a **common logarithm** is 10, and that of a **natural logarithm** is the number e (2.71828 ...).

– ORIGIN early 17th cent.: from modern Latin *logarithmus*, from Greek *logos* 'reckoning, ratio' + *arithmos* 'number.'

log·a·rith·mic /,lôgə'riT͟Hmik, ,lägə-/ ▶ **adj.** of, relating to, or expressed in terms of logarithms. ■ (of a scale) constructed so that successive points along an axis, or graduations that are an equal distance apart, represent values that are in an equal ratio. ■ (of a curve) forming a straight line when plotted on a logarithmic scale; exponential.
– DERIVATIVES **log·a·rith·mi·cal·ly** /-mik(ə)lē/ **adv.**

log·a·rith·mic spi·ral ▶ **n.** Geometry a spiral such that the angle between the tangent and the radius vector is the same for all points of the spiral. Also called EQUIANGULAR SPIRAL.

log·book /'lôg,bo͝ok, 'läg-/ ▶ **n.** another term for LOG[1] (sense 2 of the noun).

loge /lōZH/ ▶ **n.** a private box or enclosure in a theater. ■ the front section of the first balcony in a theater. ■ a similar section in an arena or stadium.
– ORIGIN mid 18th cent.: from French.

-loger ▶ **comb. form** equivalent to -LOGIST.
– ORIGIN on the pattern of words such as (*astro*)*loger*.

log·ger /'lôgər, 'lägər/ ▶ **n. 1** a person who fells trees for timber; a lumberjack.
2 a device or computer program for making a systematic recording of events, observations, or measurements.

log·ger·head /'lôgər,hed, 'lägər-/ ▶ **n. 1** (also **loggerhead turtle**) a reddish-brown turtle with a very large head, occurring chiefly in warm seas. ● *Caretta caretta*, family Cheloniidae.
2 (also **loggerhead shrike**) a widespread North American shrike, having mainly gray plumage with a black eyestripe, wings, and tail. ● *Lanius ludovicianus*, family Laniidae.
3 archaic a foolish person.
– PHRASES **at loggerheads** in stubborn dispute or disagreement: *council was at loggerheads with the government over the grant allocation.* [possibly a use of *loggerhead* in the late 17th-cent. sense 'long-handled iron instrument for heating liquids and tar,' perhaps wielded as a weapon.]
– ORIGIN late 16th cent. (sense 3): from dialect *logger* 'block of wood for hobbling a horse' + HEAD.

loggerhead turtle

log·gia /'lōj(ē)ə, 'lô-/ ▶ **n.** a gallery or room with one or more open sides, esp. one that forms part of a house and has one side open to the garden. ■ an open-sided extension to a house.
– ORIGIN mid 18th cent.: from Italian, 'lodge.'

log·ging /'lôgiNG, 'lägiNG/ ▶ **n.** the activity or business of felling trees and cutting and preparing the timber.

lo·gi·a /'lōgēə, -jēə/ plural form of LOGION.

log·ic /'läjik/ ▶ **n. 1** reasoning conducted or assessed according to strict principles of validity: *experience is a better guide to this than deductive logic | he explains his move with simple logic | the logic of the argument is faulty.* ■ a particular system or codification of the principles of proof and inference: *Aristotelian logic.* ■ the systematic use of symbolic and mathematical techniques to determine the forms of valid deductive argument. ■ the quality of being justifiable by reason: *there's no logic in telling her not to hit people when that's what you're doing.* ■ (**logic of**) the course of action or line of reasoning suggested or made necessary by: *if the logic of capital is allowed to determine events.*
2 a system or set of principles underlying the arrangements of elements in a computer or electronic device so as to perform a specified task. ■ logical operations collectively.
– DERIVATIVES **lo·gi·cian** /lə'jisHən, lō-/ **n.**
– ORIGIN late Middle English: via Old French *logique* and late Latin *logica* from Greek *logikē* (*tekhnē*) '(art) of reason,' from *logos* 'word, reason.'

-logic ▶ **comb. form** equivalent to -LOGICAL (as in *pharmacologic*).
– ORIGIN from Greek *-logikos*.

log·i·cal /'läjikəl/ ▶ **adj.** of or according to the rules of logic or formal argument: *a logical impossibility.* ■ characterized by or capable of clear, sound reasoning: *the information is displayed in a simple and logical fashion | her logical mind.* ■ (of an action, development, decision, etc.) natural or sensible given the circumstances: *it is a logical progression from the job before.*
– DERIVATIVES **log·i·cal·i·ty** /,läjə'kalətē/ **n.**, **log·i·cal·ly** /-ik(ə)lē/ **adv.** *such a situation is logically impossible.*
– ORIGIN late Middle English: from medieval Latin *logicalis*, from late Latin *logica* (see LOGIC).

-logical ▶ **comb. form** in adjectives corresponding chiefly to nouns ending in *-logy* (such as *pharmacological* corresponding to *pharmacology*).

log·i·cal em·pir·i·cism ▶ **n.** see LOGICAL POSITIVISM.

log·i·cal form ▶ **n.** Logic the abstract form in which an argument or proposition may be expressed in logical terms, as distinct from its particular content.

log·i·cal ne·ces·si·ty ▶ **n.** that state of things that obliges something to be as it is because no alternative is logically possible. ■ a thing that logically must be so.

log·i·cal op·er·a·tion ▶ **n.** an operation of the kind used in logic, e.g., conjunction or negation. ■ Computing an operation that acts on binary numbers to produce a result according to the laws of Boolean logic (e.g., the AND, OR, and NOT functions).

log·i·cal op·er·a·tor ▶ **n.** Computing a programming-language symbol that denotes a logical operation.

log·i·cal pos·i·tiv·ism ▶ **n.** a form of positivism, developed by members of the Vienna Circle, that considers that the only meaningful philosophical problems are those that can be solved by logical analysis. Also called LOGICAL EMPIRICISM.

log·ic bomb ▶ **n.** Computing a set of instructions secretly incorporated into a program so that if a particular condition is satisfied they will be carried out, usually with harmful effects.

log·ic cir·cuit ▶ **n.** Electronics a circuit for performing logical operations on input signals.

log·in /'lôg,in, 'läg-/ (also **logon**) ▶ **n.** an act of logging in to a computer, database, or system.

lo·gi·on /'lōgē,än, -jē-/ ▶ **n.** (pl. **logia** /-gēə, -jēə/) a saying attributed to Jesus Christ, esp. one not recorded in the canonical Gospels.
– ORIGIN late 19th cent.: from Greek, 'oracle,' from *logos* 'word.'

-logist ▶ **comb. form** indicating a person skilled or involved in a branch of study denoted by a noun ending in *-logy* (such as *biologist* corresponding to *biology*).

lo·gis·tic /lə'jistik, lō-/ ▶ **adj.** of or relating to logistics: *logistic problems.*
– DERIVATIVES **lo·gis·ti·cal** /-tikəl/ **adj.**, **lo·gis·ti·cal·ly** /-tik(ə)lē/ **adv.**

lo·gis·tics /lə'jistiks, lō-/ ▶ **plural n.** [treated as sing. or pl.] the detailed coordination of a complex operation involving many people, facilities, or supplies: *the logistics and costs of a vaccination campaign.* ■ Military the organization of moving, housing, and supplying troops and equipment. ■ the commercial activity of transporting goods to customers: [as modifier] *Germany's largest beverage logistics organization.*
– ORIGIN late 19th cent. (in the sense 'movement and supplying of troops and equipment'): from French *logistique*, from *loger* 'lodge.'

PRONUNCIATION KEY ə *ago, up*; ər *over, fur*; a *hat*; ā *ate*; ä *car*; e *let*; ē *see*; i *fit*; ī *by*; NG *sing*; ō *go*; ô *law, for*; oi *toy*; o͝o *good*; o͞o *goo*; ou *out*; TH *thin*; T͟H *then*; ZH *vision*

l

log·jam /ˈlôg,jam, ˈläg-/ ▶ **n.** **1** a crowded mass of logs blocking a river.
2 a situation that seems irresolvable: *the president can use the power of the White House to* ***break the logjam*** *over this issue.* ■ a backlog: *keeping a diary may ease the logjam of work considerably.*

log-log ▶ **adj.** Mathematics denoting a graph or graph paper having or using a logarithmic scale along both axes.

log-nor·mal ▶ **adj.** Statistics of or denoting a set of data in which the logarithm of the variate is distributed according to a normal distribution.
– DERIVATIVES **log-nor·mal·i·ty** **n.**, **log-nor·mal·ly** **adv.**

LOGO /ˈlō,gō/ ▶ **n.** Computing a high-level programming language used to teach computer programming to children.
– ORIGIN from Greek *logos* 'word,' spelled as if an acronym.

lo·go /ˈlōgō/ ▶ **n.** (pl. **logos**) a symbol or other design adopted by an organization to identify its products, uniform, vehicles, etc.: *the Olympic logo was emblazoned across their jackets.*
– DERIVATIVES **lo·goed** **adj.**
– ORIGIN 1930s: abbreviation of LOGOGRAM or LOGOTYPE.

lo·go·cen·tric /,lôgəˈsentrik, ,lägə-/ ▶ **adj.** regarding words and language as a fundamental expression of an external reality (esp. applied as a negative term to traditional Western thought by postmodernist critics).
– DERIVATIVES **logocentrism** /-,trizəm/ **n.**
– ORIGIN 1930s: from Greek *logos* 'word, reason' + -CENTRIC.

log·off /ˈlôg,ôf, ˈläg-, -,äf/ ▶ **n.** another term for LOGOUT.

log·o·gram /ˈlôgə,gram, ˈlägə-/ ▶ **n.** a sign or character representing a word or phrase, such as those used in shorthand and some writing systems.
– ORIGIN mid 19th cent.: from Greek *logos* 'word' + -GRAM[1].

log·o·graph /ˈlôgə,graf, ˈlägə-/ ▶ **n.** another term for LOGOGRAM.
– DERIVATIVES **log·o·graph·ic** /,lôgəˈgrafik, ,lägə-/ **adj.**

log·o·griph /ˈlôgə,grif, ˈlägə-/ ▶ **n.** a puzzle involving anagrams, esp. one in which a number of words that can be spelled using a group of letters are to be identified from their synonyms introduced into a set of verses.
– ORIGIN late 16th cent.: from Greek *logos* 'word' + *griphos* 'fishing basket, riddle.'

lo·gom·a·chy /lōˈgäməkē/ ▶ **n.** (pl. **logomachies**) rare an argument about words.
– ORIGIN mid 16th cent.: from Greek *logomakhia*, from *logos* 'word' + *-makhia* 'fighting.'

log·on /ˈlôg,än, ˈläg-, -,ôn/ ▶ **n.** another term for LOGIN.

log·o·phile /ˈlôgə,fīl, ˈlägə-/ ▶ **n.** a lover of words.

log·or·rhe·a /,lôgəˈrēə, ,lägə-/ (Brit. **logorrhoea**) ▶ **n.** a tendency to extreme loquacity.
– DERIVATIVES **log·or·rhe·ic** /-ˈrēik/ **adj.**
– ORIGIN early 20th cent.: from Greek *logos* 'word' + *rhoia* 'flow.'

Lo·gos /ˈlō,gōs, -,gäs/ ▶ **n.** Theology the Word of God, or principle of divine reason and creative order, identified in the Gospel of John with the second person of the Trinity incarnate in Jesus Christ. ■ (in Jungian psychology) the principle of reason and judgment, associated with the animus. Often contrasted with EROS.
– ORIGIN Greek, 'word, reason.'

lo·go·type /ˈlôgə,tīp, ˈlägə-/ ▶ **n.** Printing a single piece of type that prints a word or group of separate letters. ■ a single piece of type that prints a logo or emblem. ■ a logo.
– ORIGIN early 19th cent.: from Greek *logos* 'word' + TYPE.

log·out /ˈlôg,out, ˈläg-/ (also **logoff**) ▶ **n.** an act of exiting a computer system or program.

log·roll·ing /ˈlôg,rōliNG, ˈläg-/ ▶ **n.** **1** informal the practice of exchanging favors, esp. in politics by reciprocal voting for each other's proposed legislation. [from the phrase *you roll my log and I'll roll yours.*]
2 a sport in which two contestants stand on a floating log and try to knock each other off by spinning it with their feet.
– DERIVATIVES **log·roll·er** /-lər/ **n.**

Lo·gro·ño /ləˈgrōnyō/ a market town in northern Spain, on the Ebro River; pop. 150,071 (2008).

-logue (also **-log**) ▶ **comb. form** **1** denoting discourse of a specified type: *dialogue.*
2 denoting compilation: *catalogue.*
3 equivalent to -LOGIST.
– ORIGIN from French *-logue*, from Greek *-logos*, *-logon.*

log·wood /ˈlôg,wo͝od, ˈläg-/ ▶ **n.** a spiny Caribbean tree of the pea family, the dark heartwood of which yields hematoxylin and other dyes. ● *Haematoxylon campechianum*, family Leguminosae.

lo·gy /ˈlōgē/ ▶ **adj.** (**logier**, **logiest**) dull and heavy in motion or thought; sluggish.
– ORIGIN mid 19th cent.: of uncertain origin; compare with Dutch *log* 'heavy, dull.'

-logy ▶ **comb. form** **1** (usu. as **-ology**) denoting a subject of study or interest: *psychology.*
2 denoting a characteristic of speech or language: *eulogy.* ■ denoting a type of discourse: *trilogy.*
– ORIGIN from French *-logie* or medieval Latin *-logia*, from Greek.

Lo·hen·grin /ˈlōən,grin/ (in medieval French and German romances) the son of Perceval (Parsifal). He was summoned from the temple of the Holy Grail and taken in a boat to Antwerp, where he consented to marry Elsa of Brabant on condition that she not ask who he was. Elsa broke this condition, and he was carried away again in the boat.

lo·i·a·sis /lōˈīəsis/ ▶ **n.** a tropical African disease caused by infestation with eye worms that cause transient subcutaneous swellings, often accompanied by pain or fever.
– ORIGIN early 20th cent.: modern Latin, from *loa* (a local Angolan word for the parasite) + -IASIS.

loin /loin/ ▶ **n.** (usu. **loins**) the part of the body on both sides of the spine between the lowest (false) ribs and the hipbones. ■ (**loins**) chiefly literary the region of the sexual organs, esp. when regarded as the source of erotic or procreative power: *he felt a stirring in his loins at the thought.* ■ (**loin**) a large cut of meat that includes the vertebrae of the loins: *loin of pork with potatoes.*
– PHRASES **gird (up) one's loins** see GIRD[1].
– ORIGIN Middle English: from Old French *loigne*, based on Latin *lumbus.*

loin·cloth /ˈloin,klôTH, -,kläTH/ ▶ **n.** a single piece of cloth wrapped round the hips, typically worn by men in some hot countries as their only garment.

Loire /l(ə)ˈwär/ a river in west central France. The country's longest river, it rises in the Massif Central and flows 630 mi. (1,015 km.) north and west to the Atlantic Ocean at the town of Saint-Nazaire.

loi·ter /ˈloitər/ ▶ **v.** [no obj.] stand or wait around idly or without apparent purpose: *she saw Mary loitering near the cloakrooms.* ■ travel indolently and with frequent pauses: *they loitered along in the sunshine, stopping at the least excuse.*
– DERIVATIVES **loi·ter·er** **n.**
– ORIGIN late Middle English: perhaps from Middle Dutch *loteren* 'wag around.'

Lo·ki /ˈlōkē/ Scandinavian Mythology a mischievous and sometimes evil god who contrived the death of Balder and was punished by being bound to a rock.

Lok Sab·ha /ˈläk ˈsäbə, ˈlôk/ ▶ **n.** the lower house of the Indian Parliament. Compare with RAJYA SABHA.
– ORIGIN from Hindi *lok* 'the public' and *sabhā* 'assembly.'

LOL ▶ **abbr.** laughing (or laugh) out loud.

Lo·li·ta /lōˈlētə/ ▶ **n.** a sexually precocious young girl.
– ORIGIN from the name of a character in the novel *Lolita* (1958) by Vladimir Nabokov.

loll /läl/ ▶ **v.** [no obj.] sit, lie, or stand in a lazy, relaxed way: *the two girls lolled in their chairs.* ■ hang loosely; droop: *he slumped against a tree trunk, his head lolling back | her tongue was* ***lolling out*** *between her teeth.* ■ [with obj.] stick out (one's tongue) so that it hangs loosely out of the mouth: *the boy lolled out his tongue.*
– ORIGIN late Middle English: probably symbolic of dangling.

lol·la·pa·loo·za /,läləpəˈlo͞ozə/ (also **lalapalooza** or **lollapaloosa**) ▶ **n.** informal a person or thing that is particularly impressive or attractive: *it's a lollapalooza, just like your other books.*
– ORIGIN late 19th cent.: of fanciful formation.

Lol·lard /ˈlälərd/ ▶ **n.** a follower of John Wycliffe. The Lollards believed that the church should aid people to live a life of evangelical poverty and imitate Jesus Christ. Their ideas influenced the thought of John Huss, who in turn influenced Martin Luther.
– DERIVATIVES **Lol·lard·ism** /-,dizəm/ **n.**, **Lol·lard·y** **n.**
– ORIGIN originally a derogatory term, derived from a Dutch word meaning 'mumbler,' based on *lollen* 'to mumble.'

lol·li·pop /ˈlälē,päp/ ▶ **n.** a flat, rounded candy on the end of a stick.
– ORIGIN late 18th cent.: perhaps from dialect *lolly* 'tongue' + POP[1].

lol·lop /ˈläləp/ ▶ **v.** (**lollops**, **lolloping**, **lolloped**) [no obj.] move in an ungainly way in a series of clumsy paces or bounds: *the bear lolloped along the path.*
– ORIGIN mid 18th cent.: probably from LOLL, associated with TROLLOP.

lol·ly /ˈlälē/ ▶ **n.** (pl. **lollies**) informal **1** chiefly Brit. a lollipop.
2 Brit. money: *you've done brilliantly raising all that lovely lolly.*
– ORIGIN mid 19th cent.: abbreviation. Sense 2 dates from the 1940s.

lol·ly·gag /ˈlälē,gag/ (also **lallygag**) ▶ **v.** (**lollygags**, **lollygagging**, **lollygagged**) [no obj.] informal spend time aimlessly; idle: *he sends her to Arizona every January to lollygag in the sun.* ■ dawdle: *we're lollygagging along.*
– ORIGIN mid 19th cent.: of unknown origin.

lo·ma·ti·um /lōˈmāSH(ē)əm/ ▶ **n.** a perennial herb of the parsley family, found throughout western North America It has various folk-medicine applications (mainly antibiotic) and is eaten as a survival food. ● (genus *Lomatium*; numerous species).

Lomb /läm/, Henry (1828–1908) US optician; born in Germany. He cofounded Bausch & Lomb Optical Company in 1853.

Lom·bard /ˈläm,bärd, -bərd/ ▶ **n.** **1** a member of a Germanic people who invaded Italy in the 6th century.
2 a native of Lombardy in northern Italy.
3 the Italian dialect of Lombardy.
▶ **adj.** of or relating to Lombardy, or to the Lombards or their language.
– DERIVATIVES **Lom·bar·dic** /lämˈbärdik/ **adj.** (sense 1 of the noun).
– ORIGIN from Italian *lombardo*, representing late Latin *Langobardus*, of Germanic origin, from the base of LONG[1] + the ethnic name *Bardi.*

Lom·bar·di /lämˈbärdē, ,ləm-/, Vince (1913–70), US football coach; full name *Vincent Thomas Lombardi.* The legendary coach of the Green Bay Packers 1959–67, he led them to five NFL championships between 1961 and 1967 and two Super Bowl titles 1967, 1968. During 1969, he coached the Washington Redskins.

Lom·bar·do /lämˈbärdō, ,ləm-/, Guy (1902–77), US bandleader; born in Canada; full name *Gaetano Alberto Lombardo.* His dance band, formed in 1920 and named the Royal Canadians in 1927, played the "sweetest music this side of heaven," and his New Year's Eve broadcasts from New York City's Waldorf Astoria hotel became a national tradition.

Lom·bard Street /ˈläm,bärd, -bərd/ a street in the city of London that contains many of the principal London banks.
– ORIGIN so named because formerly occupied by bankers from *Lombardy.*

Lom·bar·dy /ˈläm,bärdē, -bərdē/ a region of central northern Italy, between the Alps and the Po River; capital, Milan. Italian name **Lombardia**.

Lom·bard·y pop·lar ▶ **n.** a black poplar of a variety that has a distinctive tall, slender columnar form. It arose as a mutation in Italy and is widely cultivated. ● *Populus nigra* var. *italica*, family Salicaceae.

Lom·bok /ˈläm,bäk/ a volcanic island of the Lesser Sunda group in Indonesia, between Bali and Sumbawa; pop. 2,950,100 (est. 2005); chief town, Mataram.

Lo·mé /lōˈmā/ the capital and chief port of Togo, on the Gulf of Guinea; pop. 1,452,000 (est. 2007).

lo·ment /ˈlōmənt, -,ment/ (also **lomentum** /lōˈmentəm/) ▶ **n.** Botany the pod of some leguminous plants, breaking up when mature into one-seeded joints.
– ORIGIN mid 19th cent.: from Latin, literally 'bean meal' (originally used as a cosmetic), from *lavare* 'to wash.'

Lo·mond, Loch /ˈlōmənd/ a lake in west central Scotland, northwest of Glasgow. It is the largest freshwater lake in Scotland.

Lon·don[1] /ˈləndən/ **1** the capital of the United Kingdom, in southeastern England on the Thames River; pop. 7,619,800 (est. 2008). London, called Londinium, was settled as a river port and trading center shortly after the Roman invasion of AD 43 and has been a flourishing center since the Middle Ages. It is divided administratively into the City of London, which is the country's financial center, and 32 boroughs.
2 an industrial city in southwestern Ontario, Canada, north of Lake Erie; pop. 353,395 (2006).
– DERIVATIVES **Lon·don·er** **n.**

Lon·don[2], Jack (1876–1916), US novelist; pseudonym of *John Griffith Chaney.* The Klondike gold rush of 1897 provided the material for his works, which depict the struggle for survival. Notable works: *The Call of the Wild* (1903) and *White Fang* (1906).

Lon·don broil ▶ n. a grilled steak served cut diagonally in thin slices.

Lon·don·der·ry /ˈləndən,derē, ˌləndənˈderē/ one of the six counties of Northern Ireland, formerly an administrative area. ■ its chief town, a city and port on the Foyle River near its outlet on the north coast; pop. 89,900 (est. 2009). It was formerly called Derry, a name still used by many. In 1613 it was granted to the City of London for colonization and became known as Londonderry.

Lon·don pride ▶ n. a European saxifrage with rosettes of fleshy leaves and stems of pink starlike flowers. ● *Saxifraga* × urbium, family Saxifragaceae.

lone /lōn/ ▶ adj. having no companions; solitary or single: *I approached a lone drinker across the bar* | *we sheltered under a lone tree.* ■ lacking the support of others; isolated: *I am by no means a lone voice.* ■ literary (of a place) unfrequented and remote: *houses in lone rural settings.*
– ORIGIN late Middle English: shortening of ALONE.

lone hand ▶ n. (in euchre or quadrille) a hand played against the rest, or a player playing such a hand.
– PHRASES **play a lone hand** act on one's own without help.

lone·li·ness /ˈlōnlēnis/ ▶ n. **1** sadness because one has no friends or company: *feelings of depression and loneliness.* ■ the fact of being without companions; solitariness: *the loneliness of a sailor's life.*
2 (of a place) the quality of being unfrequented and remote; isolation: *the loneliness of the farm.*

lone·ly /ˈlōnlē/ ▶ adj. (**lonelier**, **loneliest**) sad because one has no friends or company: *lonely old people whose families do not care for them.* ■ without companions; solitary: *passing long lonely hours looking onto the street.* ■ (of a place) unfrequented and remote: *a lonely stretch of country lane.*

lone·ly heart ▶ n. [usu. as modifier] a person looking for a lover or friend by advertising in a newspaper: *a lonely hearts column.*
– DERIVATIVES **lone·ly-heart·ed** adj.

lon·er /ˈlōnər/ ▶ n. a person who prefers not to associate with others.

lone·some /ˈlōnsəm/ ▶ adj. solitary or lonely: *she felt lonesome and out of things.* ■ remote and unfrequented: *a lonesome, unfriendly place.*
– PHRASES **by one's lonesome** informal all alone.
– DERIVATIVES **lone·some·ness** n.

Lone Star State a nickname for the state of TEXAS.

lone wolf ▶ n. a person who prefers to act or be alone.

Long[1] /lôNG/, Huey Pierce (1893–1935) US politician; known as the **Kingfish**. A Democrat, he served as governor of Louisiana 1928–31 and as a US senator 1932–35 and was known as a dictatorial demagogue with politically radical ideas, most notably his "Share the Wealth" program. Not long after he announced his plans to run for the US presidency, he was assassinated.

Long[2], Stephen Harriman (1784–1864), US Army officer and explorer. His expeditions included the upper Mississippi in 1817 and the Rocky Mountain region in 1820. Longs Peak in Colorado is named for him.

long[1] /lôNG, läNG/ ▶ adj. (**longer** /ˈlôNGgər, ˈläNG-/, **longest** /lôNGgist, ˈläNG-/) **1** measuring a great distance from end to end: *a long corridor* | *long black hair* | *the line for tickets was long.* ■ (after a measurement and in questions) measuring a specified distance from end to end: *a boat 150 feet long* | *how long is the leash?* ■ (of a journey) covering a great distance: *I went for a long walk.* ■ (of a garment or sleeves on a garment) covering the whole of a person's legs or arms: *a sweater with long sleeves.* ■ of elongated shape: *shaped like a torpedo, long and thin.* ■ (of a ball in sports) traveling a great distance, or further than expected or intended: *he threw a long ball to the catcher.* ■ informal (of a person) tall.
2 lasting or taking a great amount of time: *a long and distinguished career* | *she took a long time to dress.* ■ (after a noun of duration and in questions) lasting or taking a specified amount of time: *the debates will be 90 minutes long.* ■ seeming to last more time than is the case; lengthy or tedious: *serving long hours on the committee.* ■ (of a person's memory) retaining things for a great amount of time.
3 relatively great in extent: *write a long report* | *a long list of candidates.* ■ (after a noun of extent and in questions) having a specified extent: *the statement was three pages long.*
4 Phonetics (of a vowel) categorized as long with regard to quality and length (e.g., in standard American English, the vowel in *food* is long, as distinct from the short vowel in *good*). ■ Prosody (of a vowel or syllable) having the greater of the two recognized durations.
5 (of odds or a chance) reflecting or representing a low level of probability: *winning against long odds* | *you're taking a long chance.*
6 Finance (of shares, bonds, or other assets) bought in advance, with the expectation of a rise in price. ■ (of a broker or their position in the market) buying or based on long stocks. ■ (of a security) maturing at a distant date.
7 (**long on**) informal well-supplied with: *an industry that seems long on ideas but short on cash.*
▶ n. **1** a long interval or period: *see you before long* | *it will not be for long.*
2 a long sound such as a long signal in Morse code or a long vowel or syllable: *two longs and a short.*
3 (**longs**) Finance long-dated securities, esp. gilt-edged securities. ■ assets held in a long position.
▶ adv. (**longer**; **longest**) **1** for a long time: *we hadn't known them long* | *an experience they will long remember* | *his long-awaited Grand Prix debut.* ■ in questions about a period of time: ***how long** have you been working?* ■ at a time distant from a specified event or point of time: *it was abandoned long ago* | *the work was compiled long after his death.* ■ after an implied point of time: *he could not wait any longer.* ■ (after a noun of duration) throughout a specified period of time: *it rained all day long.*
2 (with reference to the ball in sports) at, to, or over a great distance, or further than expected or intended: *the quarterback dropped back and threw the ball long.* ■ beyond the point aimed at; too far: *he threw the ball long.*
– PHRASES **as** (or **so**) **long as 1** during the whole time that: *they have been there as long as anyone can remember.* **2** provided that: *as long as you fed him, he would be cooperative.* **be long** take a long time to happen or arrive: *it won't be long before you're hooked* | *sit down, tea won't be long.* **in the long run** over or after a long period of time; eventually: *it saves money in the long run.* **the long and the short of it** all that can or need be said: *the long and short of it is that he got himself mugged.* **long in the tooth** rather old. [originally said of horses, from the receding of the gums with age.] **long time no see** informal it's a long time since we last met (used as a greeting). [in humorous imitation of broken English spoken by an American Indian.] **not by a long shot** by no means: *we're not there yet, not by a long shot.* **take the long view** think beyond the current situation; plan for the future.
– DERIVATIVES **long·ish** adj.
– ORIGIN Old English *lang*, *long* (adjective), *lange*, *longe* (adverb), of Germanic origin; related to Dutch and German *lang.*

long[2] ▶ v. [no obj.] have a strong wish or desire: *she **longed for** a little more excitement* | [with infinitive] *we are longing to see the new baby.*
– ORIGIN Old English *langian* 'grow long, prolong,' also 'dwell in thought, yearn,' of Germanic origin; related to Dutch *langen* 'present, offer' and German *langen* 'reach, extend.'

long. ▶ abbr. longitude.

-long ▶ comb. form (added to nouns) for the duration of: *lifelong.*

long-act·ing ▶ adj. (chiefly of a drug) having effects that last for a long time.

lon·gan /ˈlôNGgən, ˈläNG-/ ▶ n. an edible juicy fruit from a plant related to the litchi, cultivated in Southeast Asia. ● The plant is *Dimocarpus longan*, family Sapindaceae.
– ORIGIN mid 18th cent.: from Chinese *lóngyǎn*, literally 'dragon's eye.'

long-a·wait·ed ▶ adj. having been hoped for or expected for a long time: *their long-awaited debut album.*

Long Beach a port and resort in southwestern California, on the Pacific Ocean, south of Los Angeles; pop. 463,789 (est. 2008).

long·board /ˈlôNG,bôrd, ˈläNG-/ ▶ n. a type of long surfboard.

long·boat /ˈlôNG,bōt, ˈläNG-/ ▶ n. a large boat that may be launched from a sailing ship. ■ another term for LONGSHIP.

long·bow /ˈlôNG,bō, ˈläNG-/ ▶ n. a large bow drawn by hand and shooting a long feathered arrow. It was the chief weapon of English armies from the 14th century until the introduction of firearms.

Long Branch a city in east central New Jersey, on the Atlantic Ocean, long a noted summer resort; pop. 32,622 (est. 2008).

long·case clock ▶ n. another term for GRANDFATHER CLOCK.

long-day ▶ adj. (of a plant) needing a long period of light each day to initiate flowering, which therefore happens naturally as the days lengthen in the spring.

long dis·tance ▶ adj. (usu. **long-distance**) traveling or operating between distant places: *a long-distance truck driver* | *long-distance phone calls.*
▶ adv. between distant places: *traveling long distance.*
▶ n. [often as modifier] Track & Field a race distance of 6 miles or 10,000 meters (6 miles 376 yds), or longer: *a long-distance runner.*

long di·vi·sion ▶ n. arithmetical division in which the divisor has two or more figures, and a series of steps is made as successive groups of digits of the dividend are divided by the divisor, to avoid excessive mental calculation.

long·dog /ˈlôNG,dôg, ˈläNG,däg/ ▶ n. informal a greyhound or other hound of similar body shape.

long doz·en ▶ n. (**a long dozen**) thirteen.

long-drawn (often **long-drawn-out**) ▶ adj. continuing for a long time, esp. for longer than is necessary: *long-drawn-out negotiations.*

longe /lənj/ (also **lunge**) ▶ n. a long rein on which a horse is held and made to move in a circle around its trainer.
▶ v. (**longes**, **longeing**, **longed**) [with obj.] exercise (a horse or rider) on a longe.
– ORIGIN early 18th cent.: French, from *allonge* 'lengthening out.'

long-eared bat ▶ n. an insectivorous bat with ears that are very long in proportion to the body. ● *Plecotus* and other genera, family Vespertilionidae: several species, in particular the **common** (or **brown**) **long-eared bat** (*P. auritus*) of Eurasia.

lon·ge·ron /ˈlänjərən, -ˌrän/ ▶ n. a longitudinal structural component of an aircraft's fuselage.
– ORIGIN early 20th cent.: from French, literally 'girder.'

lon·gev·i·ty /lônˈjevətē, län-/ ▶ n. long life: *the greater longevity of women compared with men.* ■ long existence or service: *her longevity in office now appeared as a handicap to the party.*
– ORIGIN early 17th cent.: from late Latin *longaevitas*, from Latin *longus* 'long' + *aevum* 'age.'

long face ▶ n. an unhappy or disappointed expression.
– DERIVATIVES **long-faced** adj.

Long·fel·low /ˈlôNG,felō/, Henry Wadsworth (1807–82), US poet. He is known for "The Wreck of the Hesperus" and "The Village Blacksmith" (both 1841) and for narrative poems such as *Evangeline* (1847), *The Song of Hiawatha* (1855), and *Paul Revere's Ride* (1861).

long·hair /ˈlôNG,he(ə)r, ˈläNG-/ ▶ n. **1** a person with long hair or characteristics associated with it, such as a hippie or intellectual. ■ a devotee of classical music.
2 a cat of a long-haired breed.

long·hand /ˈlôNG,hand, ˈläNG-/ ▶ n. ordinary handwriting (as opposed to shorthand, typing, or printing): *he wrote out the reply in longhand* | [as modifier] *a longhand draft.*

long haul ▶ n. a long distance (in reference to the transport of freight or passengers): [as modifier] *a long-haul flight.* ■ a prolonged and difficult effort or task: *getting the proposal passed is likely to be a long haul* | *we're **in for the long haul**.*
– PHRASES **over the long haul** over an extended period of time.

long-head·ed ▶ adj. **1** having a long head; dolichocephalic.
2 dated having or showing foresight and good judgment.
– DERIVATIVES **long-head·ed·ness** n.

long·horn /ˈlôNG,hôrn, ˈläNG-/ ▶ n. **1** an animal of a breed of cattle with long horns.
2 (also **longhorn beetle**) an elongated beetle with long antennae, the larva of which typically bores in wood and can be a pest of timber. ● Family Cerambycidae (formerly in the superfamily Longicornia).

long-horned grass·hop·per ▶ n. an insect related to the grasshoppers, with very long antennae and a mainly carnivorous diet. Many kinds live among shrubby vegetation, active mainly at dusk and in the night. ● Family Tettigoniidae: many genera.

long·house /ˈlôNG,hous, ˈläNG-/ ▶ n. historical the traditional dwelling of the Iroquois and other North American Indians. ■ a large communal village house in parts of Malaysia and Indonesia.

long hun·dred·weight ▶ n. see HUNDREDWEIGHT.

lon·gi·corn /ˈlänjə,kôrn/ ▶ n. former term for LONGHORN (sense 2).
– ORIGIN mid 19th cent.: from modern Latin *longicornis*, from Latin *longus* 'long' + *cornu* 'horn.'

l

long·ing /ˈlôNGiNG/ ▶ **n.** a yearning desire: *Miranda felt a wistful longing for the old days* | [with infinitive] *a longing to be free* | *his tale of love and longing.*
▶ **adj.** having or showing such desire: *her longing eyes.*
– DERIVATIVES **long·ing·ly** adv.

Lon·gi·nus /länˈjīnəs/ (*fl.* 1st century AD), Greek scholar. He is the supposed author of a Greek literary treatise *On the Sublime*, concerned with the moral function of literature.

Long Is·land an island on the coast of New York State. Its western tip, comprising the New York boroughs of Brooklyn and Queens, is separated from Manhattan and the Bronx by the East River and is linked to Manhattan by the several bridges.

Long Is·land Cit·y a section of Queens in New York City, across the East River from Manhattan.

lon·gi·tude /ˈlänjiˌt(y)o͞od, ˈlôn-/ ▶ **n.** the angular distance of a place east or west of the meridian at Greenwich, England, or west of the standard meridian of a celestial object, usually expressed in degrees and minutes: *at a longitude of 2° W* | *lines of longitude.* ■ Astronomy see CELESTIAL LONGITUDE.
– ORIGIN late Middle English (also denoting length and tallness): from Latin *longitudo*, from *longus* 'long.'

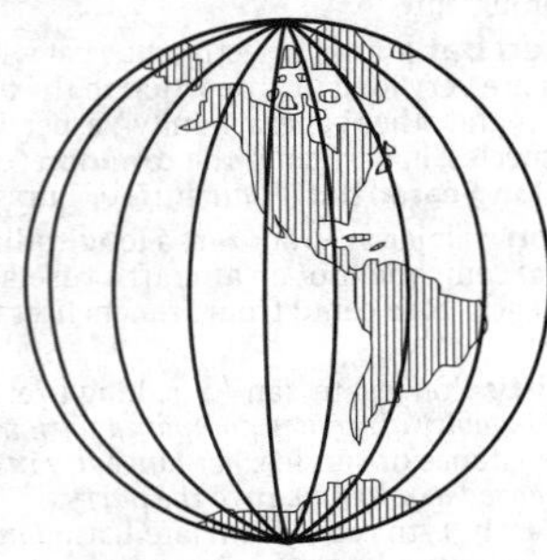
longitude

lon·gi·tu·di·nal /ˌlänjəˈt(y)o͞odn-əl, ˌlôn-, -ˈt(y)o͞odnəl/ ▶ **adj. 1** running lengthwise rather than across: *longitudinal muscles* | *longitudinal stripes* | *longitudinal extent.* ■ (of research or data) involving information about an individual or group gathered over a long period of time.
2 of or relating to longitude; measured from east to west: *longitudinal positions.*
– DERIVATIVES **lon·gi·tu·di·nal·ly** adv.

lon·gi·tu·di·nal wave ▶ **n.** Physics a wave vibrating in the direction of propagation.

long johns ▶ **plural n.** informal underwear with closely fitted legs that extend to the wearer's ankles, often with a long-sleeved top.

long jump ▶ **n.** (**the long jump**) an athletic event in which competitors jump as far as possible along the ground in one leap.
– DERIVATIVES **long jump·er** n.

long-last·ing ▶ **adj.** enduring or having endured for a long period of time: *long-lasting effects* | *a long-lasting friendship.*

long·leaf pine /ˈlôNGˌlēf, ˈläNG-/ ▶ **n.** a large pine tree of the southeastern US with very long needles and cones. It was formerly an important source of turpentine. ● *Pinus palustris*, family Pinaceae.

long·line /ˈlôNGˌlīn, ˈläNG-/ ▶ **n.** a type of deep-sea fishing gear consisting of a long main line anchored to the bottom to which shorter lines with baited hooks are fastened at intervals: [as modifier] *a longline fishing boat.*

long·lin·er /ˈlôNGˌlīnər, ˈläNG-/ ▶ **n.** a person or fishing vessel that uses longlines.

long-lived /livd/ ▶ **adj.** living or lasting a long time.

long-lost ▶ **adj.** lost or absent for a long time: *a long-lost friend* | *his long-lost youth.*

Long March the epic withdrawal of the Chinese communists from southeastern to northwestern China in 1934–35, over a distance of 6,000 miles (9,600 km). 100,000 people, led by Mao Zedong, left the communist rural base after it was almost destroyed by the Kuomintang; 20,000 people survived the journey.

long me·ter (abbr.: **LM**) ▶ **n.** (also **long measure**)
1 a metrical pattern for hymns in which the stanzas have four lines with eight syllables each.
2 Prosody a quatrain of iambic tetrameters with alternate lines rhyming.

Long·mont /ˈlôNGˌmänt/ a city in northern Colorado; pop. 85,928 (est. 2008).

long·neck /ˈlôNGˌnek, ˈläNG-/ ▶ **n.** informal a beer bottle with a long, narrow neck: *he smashed the bottom of his longneck on the bar.*

Long Par·lia·ment the English Parliament that sat from November 1640 to March 1653, was restored for a short time in 1659, and finally voted its own dissolution in 1660. It was summoned by Charles I and sat through the English Civil War and on into the interregnum that followed.

long pig ▶ **n.** a translation of a term formerly used in some Pacific Islands for human flesh as food.

long-play·ing ▶ **adj.** (of a phonograph record) designed to be played at 33$^1/_3$ revolutions per minute.

long-range ▶ **adj. 1** (esp. of vehicles or missiles) able to be used or be effective over long distances: *long-range bombers.*
2 relating to a period of time that extends far into the future: *long-range forecasts* | *long-range plans.*

long-run·ning ▶ **adj.** continuing for a long time: *a long-running dispute* | *a long-running soap opera.*

long s ▶ **n.** an obsolete form of lower-case s, written or printed as ſ. It was used in initial and medial but not final position in a word and was generally abandoned in English-language printing shortly before 1800.

long·ship /ˈlôNGˌSHip, ˈläNG-/ ▶ **n.** a long, narrow warship, powered by both oar and sail, used by the Vikings and other northern European peoples.

longship

long·shore /ˈlôNGˌSHôr, ˈläNG-/ ▶ **adj.** existing on, frequenting, or moving along the seashore: *longshore currents.*
– ORIGIN early 19th cent.: from *along shore.*

long·shore drift ▶ **n.** the movement of material along a coast by waves that approach at an angle to the shore but recede directly away from it.

long·shore·man /ˈlôNGˌSHôrmən, ˈläNG-/ ▶ **n.** (pl. **longshoremen**) a person employed in a port to load and unload ships.

long shot ▶ **n.** a venture or guess that has only the slightest chance of succeeding or being accurate: *it's a long shot, but well worth trying.*
– PHRASES **(not) by a long shot** informal (not) by far or at all: *she had not told Tony everything, not by a long shot.*

long·sight·ed /ˈlôNGˌsītid, ˈläNG-/ ▶ **adj.** British term for FARSIGHTED.
– DERIVATIVES **long·sight·ed·ly** adv., **long·sight·ed·ness** n.

long·spur /ˈlôNGˌspər, ˈläNG-/ ▶ **n.** a mainly Canadian songbird related to the buntings, with brownish plumage and a boldly marked head in the male. ● Genus *Calcarius*, family Emberizidae (subfamily Emberizinae): three or four species.

long-stand·ing (also **longstanding**) ▶ **adj.** having existed or continued for a long time: *a long-standing tradition.*

Long·street /ˈlôNGˌstrēt/, James (1821–1904) Confederate army officer. He was sometimes thought to be overcautious as a commander. He surrendered with Robert E. Lee at Appomattox and recounted his experiences in *From Manassas to Appomattox* (1896).

long-suf·fer·ing ▶ **adj.** having or showing patience in spite of troubles, esp. those caused by other people: *his long-suffering wife.*
– DERIVATIVES **long-suf·fer·ing·ly** adv.

long suit ▶ **n.** (in bridge or whist) a holding of several cards of one suit in a hand, typically 5 or more out of the 13. ■ [usu. with negative] an outstanding personal quality or achievement: *tact was not his long suit.*

long-term ▶ **adj.** occurring over or relating to a long period of time: *the long-term unemployed* | *the long-term effects of smoking.*

long·time /ˈlôNGˌtīm, ˈläNG-/ ▶ **adj.** (esp. of a person) having had a specified role or identity for a long time: *his longtime friend and colleague.*

long tom ▶ **n.** informal, historical **1** a large cannon with a long range.
2 a trough for washing gold-bearing deposits.

long ton ▶ **n.** see TON¹.

lon·gueur /lôNGˈgər, läNG-/ ▶ **n.** a tedious passage in a book or other work: *its brilliant comedy passages do not cancel out the occasional longueurs* | *the last act is sometimes marred by longueur.*
– ORIGIN French, literally 'length.'

Long·view /ˈlôNGˌvyo͞o, ˈläNG-/ a city in eastern Texas; pop. 77,211 (est. 2008).

long waist ▶ **n.** a low waist on a dress or a person's body.
– DERIVATIVES **long-waist·ed** adj.

long wave ▶ **n.** a radio wave of a wavelength above one kilometer (and a frequency below 300 kHz): [as modifier] *long-wave radio.* ■ broadcasting using radio waves of 1 to 10 km wavelength: *listening to news radio on long wave.*

long-wind·ed /ˈwindid/ ▶ **adj.** (of speech or writing) continuing at length and in a tedious way: *his good wishes were long-winded but sincere.* ■ archaic capable of doing something for a long time without needing a rest.
– DERIVATIVES **long-wind·ed·ly** adv., **long-wind·ed·ness** n.

long·wise /ˈlôNGˌwīz, ˈläNG-/ (also **longways** /-ˌwāz/) ▶ **adv.** lengthwise: *it has been sliced longwise to show the internal structure.*

loo¹ /lo͞o/ ▶ **n.** Brit. informal a toilet.
– ORIGIN 1940s: many theories have been put forward about the word's origin: one suggests the source is *Waterloo*, a trade name for iron cisterns in the early part of the century; the evidence remains inconclusive.

loo² ▶ **n.** a gambling card game, popular from the 17th to the 19th centuries, in which a player who fails to win a trick must pay a sum to a pool.
– ORIGIN late 17th cent.: abbreviation of obsolete *lanterloo*, from French *lanturlu*, a meaningless song refrain.

loo·ey /ˈlo͞o-ē/ (also **looie**) ▶ **n.** (pl. **looeys** or **looies**) military slang short for LIEUTENANT.

loo·fah /ˈlo͞ofə/ (also **loofa, luffa**) ▶ **n. 1** a coarse, fibrous cylindrical object used like a bath sponge for washing. It consists of the dried fibrous matter of the fluid-transport system of a marrowlike fruit.
2 the tropical Old World climbing plant of the gourd family that produces these fruits, which are also edible. ● *Luffa cylindrica*, family Cucurbitaceae.
– ORIGIN late 19th cent.: from Egyptian Arabic *lūfa*, denoting the plant.

look /lo͝ok/ ▶ **v.** [no obj.] **1** direct one's gaze toward someone or something or in a specified direction: *people were looking at him* | *they looked up as he came quietly into the room.* ■ (of a building or room) have a view or outlook in a specified direction: *the principal rooms look out over Nahant Bay.* ■ (**look through**) ignore (someone) by pretending not to see them: *he glanced up once but looked right through me.* ■ [with obj.] dated express or show (something) by one's gaze: *Poirot looked a question.* ■ (**look something over**) inspect something quickly with a view to establishing its merits: *they looked over a property on Ryer Avenue.* ■ (**look through**) peruse (a book or other written material): *we looked through all the books, and this was still the one we liked best.* ■ (**look round/around**) move around (a place or building) in order to view whatever it might contain that is of interest: *he spent the morning and afternoon looking around Cambridge.* ■ (**look at/on**) think of or regard in a specified way: *I look at tennis differently from some coaches.* ■ (**look at**) examine (a matter, esp. a problem) and consider what action to take: *a committee is looking at the financing of PBS.* ■ (**look into**) investigate: *the police looked into his business dealings.* ■ (**look for**) attempt to find: *Howard has been looking for you.* ■ [with clause] ascertain with a quick glance: *people finishing work don't look where they're going.*
2 have the appearance or give the impression of being: *her father looked unhappy* | *the home looked like a prison* | [as adj., in combination] (**-looking**) *a funny-looking guy.* ■ (**look like**) informal show a likelihood of: *it doesn't look like you'll be moving to Brooklyn.* ■ (**look oneself**) appear one's normal, healthy self: *he just didn't look himself at all.*
3 (**look to**) rely on to do or provide something: *she will look to you for help.* ■ [with infinitive] hope or expect to do something: *universities are looking to expand their intakes.* ■ archaic take care; make sure: *Look ye obey the masters of the craft.*
▶ **n. 1** an act of directing one's gaze in order to see someone or something: *let me get a closer look.* ■ an expression of a feeling or thought by such an act: *Brenton gave me a funny look.* ■ a scrutiny or examination: *the government should be taking a look at the amount of grant the council receives.*
2 the appearance of someone or something, esp. as expressing a particular quality: *the bedraggled look of the village.* ■ (**looks**) a person's facial appearance considered aesthetically: *he had charm, good looks, and an amusing insouciance.* ■ a style or fashion: *Italian designers unveiled their latest look.*
▶ **exclam.** (also **look here!**) used to call attention to what one is going to say: *"Look, this is ridiculous."*

–PHRASES **look one's age** appear to be as old as one really is. **look alive** see LIVELY. **look before you leap** proverb one shouldn't act without first considering the possible consequences or dangers. **look daggers at** see DAGGER. **look down one's nose at** another way of saying LOOK DOWN ON. **look for trouble** see TROUBLE. **look someone in the eye** (or **face**) look directly at someone without showing embarrassment, fear, or shame. **look lively** see LIVELY. **look the other way** deliberately ignore wrongdoing by others: *they do look the other way at corrupt practices here.* **look sharp** be quick. **look small** see SMALL. **look to the future** consider and plan for what is in the future, rather than worrying about the past or present. **look someone up and down** scrutinize someone carefully.

–PHRASAL VERBS **look after** take care of: *women who stay at home to look after children.* **look back 1** think of the past: *don't waste time looking back on things that have caused you distress.* **2** [with negative] suffer a setback or interrupted progress: *she launched her own company in 1981 and has never looked back.* **look down on** regard (someone) with a feeling of superiority. **look forward to** await eagerly: *we look forward to seeing you.* **look in** make a short visit or call: *I will look in on you tomorrow.* **look on** watch without getting involved: *Cameron was looking on and making no move to help.* **look out** [usu. in imperative] be vigilant and take notice: *"Look out!" warned Billie, seeing a movement from the room beyond | look out for the early warning signals.* **look something out** Brit. search for and produce something: *I've got a catalog somewhere and I'll look it out if you're interested.* **look up** (of a situation) improve: *things seemed to be looking up at last.* **look someone up** informal make social contact with someone. **look something up** search for and find a piece of information in a reference book. **look up to** have a great deal of respect for (someone): *he needed a model, someone to look up to.*

–ORIGIN Old English *lōcian* (verb); related to German dialect *lugen*.

look-a-like (also **lookalike**) ▶ n. a person or thing that closely resembles another, esp. someone who looks very similar to a famous person: *an Elvis Presley look-alike.*

look-and-say ▶ n. [as modifier] denoting a method of teaching reading based on the visual recognition of words rather than by the association of sounds and letters. Compare with PHONIC.

look·book /ˈlo͝ok,bo͝ok/ ▶ n. a set of photographs displaying a fashion designer's new collection, assembled for marketing purposes.

look·er /ˈlo͝okər/ ▶ n. **1** a person who looks: *the percentage of lookers who actually buy is pretty low.* **2** [with adj.] a person with a specified appearance: *a tough looker is not necessarily a tough fighter.* ■ informal a very attractive person, esp. a woman: *he shook his head in admiration—she was some looker.*

look·er-on ▶ n. (pl. **lookers-on**) a person who is a spectator rather than a participant in a situation.

look-in ▶ n. **1** Football a short pass pattern in which the receiver runs diagonally toward the center of the field.
2 Brit. informal a chance to take part or succeed in something: *they didn't let the other side get a look-in in the semifinal.*

look·ing glass ▶ n. a mirror: *she stared at her reflection in the looking glass.* ■ [as modifier] being or involving the opposite of what is normal or expected: *a looking-glass land | looking-glass logic.*

look·ism /ˈlo͝ok,izəm/ ▶ n. construction of a standard for beauty and attractiveness, and judgments made about people on the basis of how well or poorly they meet the standard.

look·it /ˈlo͝okit/ informal ▶ v. phonetic spelling of "look at": *Hey, lookit that!*
▶ exclam. used to draw attention to what one is about to say: *lookit, Pete, this is serious.*

look·out /ˈlo͝ok,out/ ▶ n. a place from which to keep watch or view landscape. ■ a person stationed to keep watch for danger or trouble: *they acted as lookouts at the post office.* ■ archaic a view over a landscape. ■ (**one's lookout**) informal a person's own concern: *everyone's life is his own lookout.* ■ [in sing.] informal, chiefly Brit. used to indicate whether a likely outcome is good or bad: *"What if he gets sick?" "It's a bad lookout in that case."*

–PHRASES **be on the lookout** (or **keep a lookout**) **for** be alert to (danger or trouble): *he told them to be on the lookout for dangerous gas.* ■ keep searching for (something that is wanted): *we kept a sharp lookout for animals.*

Look·out Moun·tain /ˈlo͝ok,out/ an Appalachian ridge, on the Cumberland Plateau in Alabama, Georgia, and Tennessee, near Chattanooga. It was the site of a November 1863 Civil War battle.

look-see ▶ n. informal a brief look or inspection: *we are just about to take a little look-see around the hotel.*
–ORIGIN late 19th cent.: from, or in imitation of, pidgin English.

look·up /ˈlo͝ok,əp/ ▶ n. [usu. as modifier] the action of or a facility for systematic electronic information retrieval. a facility for lookup: *you need an online dictionary with fast phonetic lookup.*

look·y /ˈlo͝okē/ (also **lookie**) ▶ exclam. informal used to draw attention to what one is about to say: *Looky there! You've gone and broken it.*

loom[1] /lo͞om/ ▶ n. an apparatus for making fabric by weaving yarn or thread.
–ORIGIN Old English *gelōma* 'tool,' shortened to *lome* in Middle English.

loom[1]

loom[2] ▶ v. [no obj.] appear as a shadowy form, esp. one that is large or threatening: *vehicles loomed out of the darkness.* ■ (of an event regarded as ominous or threatening) seem about to happen: *there is a crisis looming | higher mortgage rates **loomed large** last night.*
▶ n. [in sing.] a vague and often exaggerated first appearance of an object seen in darkness or fog, esp. at sea: *the loom of the land ahead.* ■ the dim reflection by cloud or haze of a light that is not directly visible, e.g., from a lighthouse over the horizon.
–ORIGIN mid 16th cent.: probably from Low German or Dutch; compare with East Frisian *lōmen* 'move slowly,' Middle High German *lüemen* 'be weary.'

loon[1] /lo͞on/ ▶ n. informal a silly or foolish person.
–ORIGIN late 19th cent.: from LOON[2] (referring to the bird's actions when escaping from danger), perhaps influenced by LOONY.

loon[2] ▶ n. a large diving waterbird with a sleek black or gray head, a straight pointed bill, and short legs set far back under the body. Loons breed by lakes in northern latitudes and have wailing calls. ● Family Gaviidae and genus *Gavia*: five species, including the **common loon** (*G. immer*) of both Canada and Eurasia.
–ORIGIN mid 17th cent.: probably by alteration of Shetland dialect *loom*, denoting esp. a guillemot or a diver, from Old Norse.

common loon

loon·ey tunes (also **loony-tunes** informal ▶ adj. crazy; deranged: *a looney tunes initiative for easing the parking problem.*
▶ n. crazy or deranged people.
–ORIGIN 1980s: from *Looney Tunes*, the name of an animated cartoon series that began in the 1930s, featuring Bugs Bunny and other characters.

loon·ie /ˈlo͞onē/ ▶ n. (pl. **loonies**) Canadian informal a Canadian one-dollar coin, introduced in 1987.

loon·y /ˈlo͞onē/ informal ▶ n. (pl. **loonies**) a crazy or silly person: *she was working with a bunch of loonies.*
▶ adj. (**loonier, looniest**) crazy or silly: *loony drivers.*
–DERIVATIVES **loon·i·ness** n.
–ORIGIN mid 19th cent.: abbreviation of LUNATIC.

loon·y bin ▶ n. informal, offensive a home or hospital for people who are mentally ill.

loop /lo͞op/ ▶ n. **1** a shape produced by a curve that bends around and crosses itself. ■ a length of thread, rope, or similar material, doubled or crossing itself, typically used as a fastening or handle. ■ a curved stroke forming part of a letter (e.g., *b, p*). ■ (also **loop-the-loop**) a maneuver in which an aircraft describes a vertical circle in the air. ■ Skating a maneuver describing a curve that crosses itself, made on a single edge. ■ (**the Loop**) informal name for the commercial district in downtown Chicago.
2 a structure, series, or process the end of which is connected to the beginning. ■ an endless strip of tape or film allowing continuous repetition. ■ a complete circuit for an electric current. ■ Computing a programmed sequence of instructions that is repeated until or while a particular condition is satisfied.
▶ v. form (something) into a loop or loops; encircle: *she looped her arms around his neck.* ■ follow a course that forms a loop or loops: *the canal loops for two miles through the city.* ■ put into or execute a loop of tape, film, or computing instructions: *the program loops back on reaching a RETURN statement.* ■ (also **loop the loop**) circle an aircraft vertically in the air.
–PHRASES **in** (or **out of**) **the loop** informal aware (or unaware) of information known to only a privileged few. **throw** (or **knock**) **someone for a loop** informal surprise or astonish someone; catch someone off guard.
–ORIGIN late Middle English: of unknown origin; compare with Scottish Gaelic *lùb* 'loop, bend.'

loop di·u·ret·ic ▶ n. Medicine a powerful diuretic that inhibits resorption of water and sodium from the loop of Henle.

loop·er /ˈlo͞opər/ ▶ n. **1** another term for INCHWORM.
2 Baseball a fly ball that becomes a hit by dropping out of the reach of the infielders.

loop·hole /ˈlo͞op,(h)ōl/ ▶ n. **1** an ambiguity or inadequacy in the law or a set of rules: *they exploited tax loopholes.*
2 historical an arrow slit in a wall.
▶ v. [with obj.] make arrow slits in (a wall or building).
–ORIGIN late 16th cent. (denoting an arrow slit): from obsolete *loop* 'embrasure' + HOLE.

loop of Hen·le /ˈhenlē/ ▶ n. Anatomy the part of a kidney tubule that forms a long loop in the medulla of the kidney, from which water and salts are resorbed into the blood.
–ORIGIN mid 19th cent.: named after Friedrich G. J. *Henle* (1809–85), German anatomist.

loop stitch ▶ n. a method of sewing or knitting in which each stitch incorporates a free loop of thread for ornament or to give a thick pile.
–DERIVATIVES **loop-stitched** adj., **loop stitch·ing** n.

loop·y /ˈlo͞opē/ ▶ adj. (**loopier, loopiest**) **1** informal crazy or silly: *the author comes across as a bit loopy.*
2 having many loops: *a big, loopy signature.*
–DERIVATIVES **loop·i·ness** n.

Loos /lo͞os/, Anita (1893–1981) US writer. She wrote stories collected in *Gentlemen Prefer Blondes* (1925) that involved the character Lorelei Lee and that were later adapted for the stage and the screen.

loose /lo͞os/ ▶ adj. **1** not firmly or tightly fixed in place; detached or able to be detached: *a loose tooth | the truck's trailer came loose.* ■ not held or tied together; not packaged or placed in a container: *wear your hair loose | pockets bulging with loose change.* ■ (of a person or animal) free from confinement; not bound or tethered: *the bull was loose with cattle in the field | the tethered horses **broke loose**.* ■ not strict or exact: *a loose interpretation.* ■ not close or compact in structure: *a loose weave* | figurative *a loose federation of political and industrial groups.* ■ typical of diarrhea: *many patients report loose bowel movements.*
2 (of a garment) not fitting tightly or closely: *she slipped into a loose T-shirt and shorts.*
3 relaxed; physically slack: *she swung back into her easy, loose stride.* ■ careless and indiscreet in what is said: *there is too much loose talk about the situation.* ■ dated promiscuous; immoral: *she ran the risk of being called a loose woman.* ■ (of the ball in a game) in play but not in any player's possession.
▶ v. [with obj.] set free; release: *the hounds have been loosed.* ■ untie; unfasten: *the ropes were loosed.* ■ relax (one's grip): *he loosed his grip suddenly.*
–PHRASES **hang** (or **stay**) **loose** [often as imperative] informal be relaxed; refrain from taking anything too seriously: *hang loose, baby!* **on the loose** having escaped from confinement: *a serial killer is on the loose.*
–DERIVATIVES **loose·ly** adv., **loose·ness** n.
–ORIGIN Middle English *loos* 'free from bonds,' from Old Norse *lauss*, of Germanic origin; related to Dutch and German *los*.

USAGE The adjective **loose**, meaning 'not tight,' should not be confused with the verb **loose**, which means 'let go': *they loosed the reins and let the horse gallop.* This verb in turn should not be confused with the verb **lose**, which means 'be deprived of, fail to keep': *I will lose my keys if I don't mend the hole in my pocket.*

loose can·non ▶ n. an unpredictable or uncontrolled person who is likely to cause unintentional damage.

loose con·struc·tion ▶ n. Law a broad interpretation of a statute or document by a court.
– DERIVATIVES **loose con·struc·tion·ist** n.

loose end ▶ n. a detail not yet settled or explained: *Mark arrived back at his office to tie up any loose ends.*
– PHRASES **be at loose ends** have nothing specific to do: *he dropped out of school and found himself alone and at loose ends.*

loose-joint·ed ▶ adj. having or characterized by easy, free movement; limber. ■ having loose joints. ■ loosely built, badly put together.

loose-knit ▶ adj. connected in a tenuous or ill-defined way; not closely linked: *a loose-knit grouping of independent states.*

loose-leaf (also **looseleaf**) ▶ adj. (of a notebook or folder) having each sheet of paper separate and removable.

loose-limbed ▶ adj. supple and physically relaxed: *his loose-limbed, athletic body exudes fitness and energy.*

loos·en /ˈlo͞osən/ ▶ v. [with obj.] make (something tied, fastened, or fixed in place) less tight or firm: *loosen your collar and tie.* ■ make more lax: *his main mistake was to loosen monetary policy* | (as noun **loosening**) *a loosening of the benefit rules.* ■ relax (one's grip or muscles): *he loosened his hold so she could pull her arms free.* ■ [no obj.] become relaxed or less tight: *the stiffness in his shoulders had loosened.* ■ make (a connection or relationship) less strong: *he wanted to strengthen rather than loosen union links.* ■ (with reference to the bowels) make or become relaxed before excretion: [no obj.] *his bowels loosened in terror.*
– PHRASES **loosen someone's tongue** make someone talk freely.
– PHRASAL VERBS **loosen up** warm up in preparation for an activity: *arrive early to loosen up and hit some practice shots.* ■ make or become relaxed: *they taught me to have fun at work and loosen up* | (**loosen someone up**) *the beer is loosening him up.*
– DERIVATIVES **loos·en·er** n.

l

loose·strife /ˈlo͞o(s)ˌstrīf/ ▶ n. any of various tall plants that bear upright spikes of flowers. ● several plants of the genus *Lythrum* (family Lythraceae), in particular the **purple loosestrife** (*L. salicaria*) of the Old World, now well established in North America. ● several yellow-flowered plants of the genus *Lysimachia* (family Primulaceae), in particular the **garden loosestrife** (*L. vulgaris*) of Eurasia and North America.
– ORIGIN mid 16th cent.: from LOOSE + STRIFE, taking the Greek name *lusimakheion* (actually from *Lusimakhos*, the name of its discoverer) to be directly from *luein* 'undo' + *makhē* 'battle.'

loos·ey-goos·ey /ˌlo͞osē ˈgo͞osē/ ▶ adj. informal relaxed or loose: *other guys can goof around, be all loosey-goosey before a game* | *a loosey-goosey interpretation of traditional doctrine.*
– ORIGIN rhyming formation from the expression *loose as a goose.*

loot /lo͞ot/ ▶ n. goods, esp. private property, taken from an enemy in war. ■ stolen money or valuables: *two men wearing stocking masks, each swinging a bag of loot.* ■ informal money; wealth: *the thief made off with $5 million in loot.*
▶ v. [with obj.] steal goods from (a place), typically during a war or riot: *police confronted the rioters who were looting shops.* ■ steal (goods) in such circumstances: *tons of food aid awaiting distribution had been looted.*
– DERIVATIVES **loot·er** n.
– ORIGIN early 19th cent. (as a verb): from Hindi *lūṭ*, from Sanskrit *lunṭh-* 'rob.'

lop[1] /läp/ ▶ v. (**lops, lopping, lopped**) [with obj.] cut off (a branch, limb, or other protrusion) from the main body of a tree: *they* **lopped off** *more branches to save the tree.* ■ informal remove (something regarded as unnecessary or burdensome): *it lops an hour off commuting time.* ■ remove branches from (a tree).
▶ n. branches and twigs lopped off trees.
– ORIGIN late Middle English (as a noun denoting branches and twigs of trees).

lop[2] ▶ v. (**lops, lopping, lopped**) [no obj.] hang loosely or limply; droop: *a stomach that lopped over his belt.* ■ move in a loping or slouching way: *he lopped toward the plane.* ■ archaic dawdle.
– ORIGIN late 16th cent.: probably symbolic of limpness; compare with LOB.

lope /lōp/ ▶ v. [no obj.] run or move with a long bounding stride: *the dog was loping along by his side* | (as adj. **loping**) *a loping stride.*
▶ n. [in sing.] a long bounding stride: *they set off at a fast lope.*
– ORIGIN Middle English: variant of Scots *loup*, from Old Norse *hlaupa* 'leap.'

lop-eared ▶ adj. (of an animal) having ears that droop down by the sides of the head: *a lop-eared mule.*

lo·per·a·mide /lōˈperəˌmīd/ ▶ n. Medicine a synthetic drug of the opiate class that inhibits peristalsis and is used to treat diarrhea.
– ORIGIN 1970s: probably from *(ch)lo(ro-)* + *(pi) per(idine)* + AMIDE.

lopho- ▶ comb. form Zoology crested: *lophodont.*
– ORIGIN from Greek *lophos* 'crest.'

loph·o·dont /ˈläfəˌdänt, ˈlōfə-/ ▶ adj. Zoology (of molar teeth) having transverse ridges on the grinding surfaces, characteristic of some ungulates. ■ (of an ungulate) having such teeth.
– ORIGIN late 19th cent.: from LOPHO- 'crest' + Greek *odous, odont-* 'tooth.'

lo·phoph·o·rate /ləˈfäfəˌrāt, ˌlōfəˈfôrˌāt/ Zoology ▶ adj. of or relating to small aquatic invertebrates belonging to a group of phyla characterized by the possession of lophophores. They include bryozoans, brachiopods, and phoronids.
▶ n. a lophophorate animal.

loph·o·phore /ˈläfəˌfôr, ˈlōfə-/ ▶ n. Zoology a horseshoe-shaped structure bearing ciliated tentacles around the mouth in certain small marine invertebrates.

Lop Nor /lôp no͝or/ (also **Lop Nur**) a dried-up salt lake in the arid basin of the Tarim River in northwestern China, used since 1964 for nuclear testing.

lop·pers /ˈläpərz/ ▶ plural n. a cutting tool, esp. for pruning trees: *a good pair of loppers.*

lop·sid·ed /ˈläpˌsīdid/ ▶ adj. with one side lower or smaller than the other: *a lopsided grin.* ■ disproportionately weighted in favor of one side over another: *a lopsided competition.*
– DERIVATIVES **lop·sid·ed·ly** adv., **lop·sid·ed·ness** n.
– ORIGIN early 18th cent.: from LOP[2] + SIDE + -ED[1].

lo·qua·cious /lōˈkwāsHəs/ ▶ adj. tending to talk a great deal; talkative.
– DERIVATIVES **lo·qua·cious·ly** adv., **lo·qua·cious·ness** n.
– ORIGIN mid 17th cent.: from Latin *loquax, loquac-* (from *loqui* 'talk') + -IOUS.

lo·quac·i·ty /lōˈkwasətē/ ▶ n. the quality of talking a great deal; talkativeness: *he was renowned for loquacity.*

lo·quat /ˈlōˌkwät/ ▶ n. **1** a small yellow egg-shaped acidic fruit.
2 the evergreen eastern Asian tree of the rose family that bears this fruit, cultivated in subtropical regions both for its fruit and as an ornamental. ● *Eriobotrya japonica*, family Rosaceae.
– ORIGIN early 19th cent.: from Chinese dialect *luh kwat* 'rush orange.'

lo·qui·tur /ˈläkwitər, ˈlōkwi-/ (abbr.: **loq.**) ▶ v. (he or she) speaks (with the speaker's name following, as a stage direction or to inform the reader).
– ORIGIN Latin, from *loqui* 'talk, speak.'

Lo·rain /lôˈrān/ a port city in north central Ohio, on Lake Erie, west of Cleveland; pop. 70,239 (est. 2008).

lo·ran /ˈlôrˌan/ (also **Loran**) ▶ n. a system of long-distance navigation in which position is determined from the intervals between signal pulses received from widely spaced radio transmitters.
– ORIGIN 1940s: from *lo(ng-)ra(nge) n(avigation).*

lor·az·e·pam /lôˈrazəˌpam, -ˈrāzə-/ ▶ n. Medicine a drug of the benzodiazepine group, used esp. to treat anxiety.
– ORIGIN 1960s: from *(ch)lor(o-)* (as in 'chlorine') + *-azepam*, on the pattern of words such as *diazepam.*

Lor·ca /ˈlôrkə/, Federico García (1898–1936), Spanish poet and playwright. His works include *Gypsy Ballads* (1928), *Blood Wedding* (1933), and *The House of Bernada Alba* (1936).

lord /lôrd/ ▶ n. someone or something having power, authority, or influence; a master or ruler: *lord of the sea* | *lords of the jungle* | *our lord the king.* ■ (in the UK) a man of noble rank or high office; a peer. ■ (**Lord**) (in the UK) a title given formally to a baron, and less formally to a marquess, earl, or viscount (prefixed to a family or territorial name): *Lord Derby.* ■ (**the Lords**) (in the UK) the House of Lords, or its members collectively. ■ (**Lord**) (in the UK) a courtesy title given to a younger son of a duke or marquess (prefixed to a Christian name): *Lord John Russell.* ■ (in the UK) in compound titles of other people of authority: *Lord High Executioner.* ■ historical a feudal superior, esp. the proprietor of a manor house. ■ (**Lord**) a name for God or Christ: *give thanks to the Lord.*
▶ exclam. (**Lord**) used in exclamations expressing surprise or worry, or for emphasis: *Lord, I'm cold!*
▶ v. **1** [with obj.] archaic confer the title of Lord upon.
2 (**lord it over**) act in a superior and domineering manner toward (someone).
– PHRASES **live like a lord** live sumptuously. **Lord** (**God**) **of hosts** God as Lord over earthly or heavenly armies. **lord of the manor** the owner of a manor house (formerly the master of a feudal manor). **Lord of Misrule** historical a person presiding over Christmas games and revelry in a wealthy household. **the Lord's Day** Sunday. **the Lord's Prayer** the prayer taught by Jesus to his disciples, beginning "Our Father." **the Lord's Supper** the Eucharist; Holy Communion (esp. in Protestant use). **My Lord** (in the UK) a polite form of address to judges, bishops, and certain noblemen. **Our Lord** Christ.
– DERIVATIVES **lord·less** adj., **lord·like** /-ˌlīk/ adj.
– ORIGIN Old English *hlāford*, from *hlāfweard* 'bread-keeper,' from a Germanic base (see LOAF[1], WARD). Compare with LADY.

Lord Chan·cel·lor (also **Lord High Chancellor**) ▶ n. (in the UK) the highest officer of the Crown, responsible for the efficient functioning and independence of the courts, and formerly presiding over the House of Lords, the Chancery Division, or the Court of Appeal. ■ historical an officer of state acting as head of the judiciary and administrator of the royal household.

Lord Faunt·le·roy see FAUNTLEROY.

Lord High Ad·mi·ral a title of the British monarch, originally the title of an officer who governed the Royal Navy and had jurisdiction over maritime causes.

lord·ling /ˈlôrdliNG/ ▶ n. archaic, chiefly derogatory a minor lord.

lord·ly /ˈlôrdlē/ ▶ adj. (**lordlier, lordliest**) of, characteristic of, or suitable for a lord: *lordly titles* | *they were putting on lordly airs.*
– DERIVATIVES **lord·li·ness** n.
– ORIGIN Old English *hlāfordlic* (see LORD, -LY[1]).

lord may·or ▶ n. the title of the mayor in London and some other large British cities.

lor·do·sis /lôrˈdōsis/ ▶ n. Medicine excessive inward curvature of the spine. Compare with KYPHOSIS. ■ a posture assumed by some female mammals during mating, in which the back is arched downward.
– DERIVATIVES **lor·dot·ic** /-ˈdätik/ adj.
– ORIGIN early 18th cent.: modern Latin, from Greek *lordōsis*, from *lordos* 'bent backward.'

Lord Pro·tec·tor ▶ n. see PROTECTOR (sense 2).

lords-and-la·dies ▶ n. another term for CUCKOOPINT.

lord·ship /ˈlôrdˌsHip/ ▶ n. **1** supreme power or rule: *his lordship over the other gods.* ■ archaic the authority or state of being a lord. ■ historical a piece of land or territory belonging to or under the jurisdiction of a lord: *lands including the lordship of Denbigh.*
2 (**His/Your**, etc., **Lordship**) in the UK, a respectful form of reference or address to a judge, a bishop, or a man with a title: *if Your Lordship pleases.*
– ORIGIN Old English *hlāfordscipe* (see LORD, -SHIP).

Lords spir·it·u·al ▶ plural n. the bishops in the House of Lords.

Lords tem·po·ral ▶ plural n. the members of the House of Lords other than the bishops.

Lord·y /ˈlôrdē/ ▶ exclam. informal used to express surprise or dismay: *Lordy! Whatever happened?*

lore[1] /lôr/ ▶ n. a body of traditions and knowledge on a subject or held by a particular group, typically passed from person to person by word of mouth: *the jinns of Arabian lore* | *baseball lore.*
– ORIGIN Old English *lār* 'instruction,' of Germanic origin: related to Dutch *leer*, German *Lehre*, also to LEARN.

lore[2] ▶ n. Zoology the surface on each side of a bird's head between the eye and the upper base of the beak, or between the eye and nostril in snakes.
– ORIGIN early 19th cent.: from Latin *lorum* 'strap.'

Lo·ren /ləˈren/, Sophia (1934–), Italian actress; born *Sofia Scicolone*. She starred in both Italian and US movies, including *The Millionairess* (1960), *Marriage Italian Style* (1964), *Two Women* (1961), *Arabesque* (1966) and *Grumpier Old Men* (1995).

Lo·rentz /ˈlôrənts/, Hendrik Antoon (1853–1928), Dutch theoretical physicist. He worked on the forces affecting electrons and realized that electrons and cathode rays were the same thing. Nobel Prize for Physics (1902), shared with Pieter Zeeman (1865–1943).

Lo·rentz con·trac·tion ▶ n. Physics the shortening of a moving body in the direction of its motion, esp. at speeds close to that of light.

Lo·rentz force ▶ n. Physics the force that is exerted by a magnetic field on a moving electric charge.

Lo·rentz trans·for·ma·tion ▶ n. Physics the set of equations that, in Einstein's special theory of relativity, relate the space and time coordinates of one frame of reference to those of another.

Lo·renz /ˈlôrənz, -rents/, Konrad (Zacharias) (1903–89), Austrian zoologist. He pioneered the science of ethology, emphasizing innate rather than learned behavior or conditioned reflexes. Notable works: *King Solomon's Ring* (1952) and *On Aggression* (1966). Nobel Prize for Physics (1973), shared with Karl von Frisch and Nikolaas Tinbergen.

Lo·renz at·trac·tor ▶ **n.** Mathematics a strange attractor in the form of a two-lobed figure formed by a trajectory that spirals around the two lobes, passing randomly between them.
– ORIGIN 1970s: named after Edward N. *Lorenz* (born 1917), American meteorologist.

Lo·renz curve ▶ **n.** Economics a graph on which the cumulative percentage of total national income (or some other variable) is plotted against the cumulative percentage of the corresponding population (ranked in increasing size of share). The extent to which the curve sags below a straight diagonal line indicates the degree of inequality of distribution.
– ORIGIN early 20th cent.: named after Max O. *Lorenz*, the American statistician who devised the curve.

Lo·ren·zo de' Me·di·ci /ləˈrenzō də ˈmedicHē, lôˈrentsō/ (1449–92), Italian statesman and scholar. A patron of the arts and humanist learning, he supported Botticelli, Leonardo da Vinci, and Michelangelo, among others.

lo·res /ˈlōˈrez/ ▶ **adj.** variant spelling of LOW-RES.

lor·gnette /lôrnˈyet/ (also **lorgnettes**) ▶ **n.** a pair of glasses or opera glasses held in front of a person's eyes by a long handle at one side.
– ORIGIN early 19th cent.: from French, from *lorgner* 'to squint.'

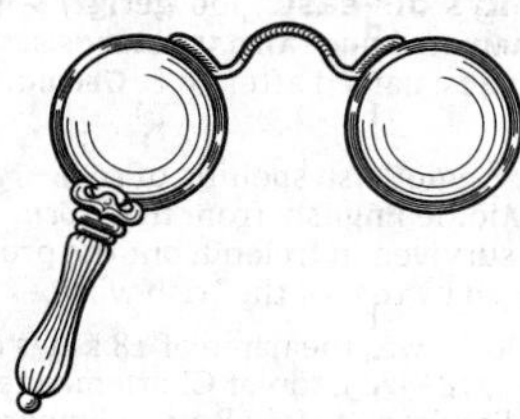

lorgnette

lo·ri·ca /ləˈrīkə/ ▶ **n.** (pl. **loricae** /-ˌkē, -ˌsē/ or **loricas**) **1** historical a Roman corselet or cuirass of leather. **2** Zoology the rigid case or shell of some rotifers and protozoans.
– ORIGIN Latin, literally 'breastplate.'

lor·i·cate /ˈlôrəˌkāt/ ▶ **adj.** Zoology (of an animal) having a protective covering of plates or scales. ■ having a lorica.
– ORIGIN early 19th cent.: from Latin *loricatus*, from *lorica* 'breastplate,' from *lorum* 'strap.'

Lor·i·cif·er·a /ˌlôriˈsifərə/ Zoology a minor phylum of minute marine invertebrates (genus *Nanaloricus*), resembling rotifers and living in gravel.
– DERIVATIVES **lor·i·cif·er·an** **n. & adj.**
– ORIGIN modern Latin (plural), from Latin *lorica* 'breastplate' + *ferre* 'to bear.'

lor·i·keet /ˈlôrəˌkēt, ˈlär-/ ▶ **n.** a small bird of the lory family, found chiefly in New Guinea. ● *Charmosyna* and other genera, family Loridae (or Psittacidae): several species.
– ORIGIN late 18th cent.: diminutive of LORY, on the pattern of *parakeet*.

lo·ris /ˈlôris/ ▶ **n.** (pl. **lorises**) a small, slow-moving nocturnal primate with a short or absent tail, living in dense vegetation in southern Asia. ● Genera *Loris* and *Nycticebus*, family Lorisidae, suborder Prosimii: the **slender loris** (*L. tardigradus*) of southern India and Sri Lanka, and the **slow loris** (genus *Nycticebus*, two species) of Southeast Asia.
– ORIGIN late 18th cent.: from French, perhaps from obsolete Dutch *loeris* 'clown.'

lorn /lôrn/ ▶ **adj.** literary lonely and abandoned; forlorn.
– ORIGIN Middle English: past participle of obsolete *lese* from Old English *lēosan* 'lose.'

Lor·rain, Claude see CLAUDE LORRAIN.

Lor·raine /ləˈrān, lô-/ a region of northeastern France, between Champagne and the Vosges mountains. The modern region corresponds to the southern part of the medieval kingdom of Lorraine, which extended from the North Sea to Italy.
– ORIGIN from Latin *Lotharingia*, from *Lothair*, the name of a king (825–869).

Lor·raine cross ▶ **n.** a cross with one vertical and two horizontal bars. It was the symbol of Joan of Arc, and in World War II it was adopted by the Free French forces of General de Gaulle.

lor·ry /ˈlôrē, ˈlärē/ ▶ **n.** (pl. **lorries**) Brit. a large, heavy motor vehicle for transporting goods or troops; a truck.
– ORIGIN mid 19th cent.: perhaps from the given name *Laurie*.

lo·ry /ˈlôrē/ ▶ **n.** (pl. **lories**) a small Australasian and Southeast Asian parrot with a brush-tipped tongue for feeding on nectar and pollen, having mainly green plumage with patches of bright color. ● Family Loridae (or Psittacidae): several genera and species, e.g., the brightly colored **rainbow lory** or **rainbow lorikeet** (*Trichoglossus haematodus*).
– ORIGIN late 17th cent.: from Malay *lūrī*.

LOS ▶ **abbr.** ■ law of the sea. ■ length of stay. ■ line of scrimmage. ■ line of sight. ■ loss of signal.

Los Al·a·mos /lôs ˈaləˌmōs, läs/ a town in northern New Mexico; pop. 11,909 (2000). It is a center for nuclear research.

Los An·ge·le·no /lôs ˌanjəˈlēnō, läs/ ▶ **n.** variant of ANGELENO.

Los An·ge·les /lôs ˈanjələs, läs, -ˌlēz/ a city on the Pacific coast of southern California; pop. 3,833,995 (est. 2008). It is a major center of industry, filmmaking, and television.

lose /lo͞oz/ ▶ **v.** (past and past participle **lost** /lôst, läst/) [with obj.] **1** be deprived of or cease to have or retain (something): *I've lost my appetite | Linda was very upset about losing her job | the company may find itself losing customers to cheaper rivals.* ■ cause (someone) to fail to gain or retain (something): *you lost me my appointment at the university.* ■ be deprived of (a close relative or friend) through their death or as a result of the breaking off of a relationship: *she lost her husband in the fire.* ■ (of a pregnant woman) miscarry (a baby) or suffer the death of (a baby) during childbirth. ■ (**be lost**) be destroyed or killed, esp. through accident or as a result of military action: *a fishing disaster in which 19 local men were lost.* ■ decrease in (body weight); undergo a reduction of (a specified amount of weight): *she couldn't eat and began to lose weight.* ■ waste or fail to take advantage of (time or an opportunity): *they lost every chance to score in the first inning | he* **lost no time** *in attacking his opponent's tax proposals.* ■ (of a watch or clock) become slow by (a specified amount of time): *this clock will neither gain nor lose a second.* ■ (**lose it**) informal lose control of one's temper or emotions: *in the end I completely lost it—I was screaming at them.* **2** become unable to find (something or someone): *I've lost the car keys.* ■ cease or become unable to follow (the right route): *the clouds came down, and we lost the path.* ■ evade or shake off (a pursuer): *he came after me waving his revolver, but I easily lost him.* ■ informal get rid of (an undesirable person or thing): *lose that creep!* ■ informal cause (someone) to be unable to follow an argument or explanation: *sorry, Tim, you've lost me there.* ■ (**lose oneself in/be lost in**) be or become deeply absorbed in (something): *he had been lost in thought.* **3** fail to win (a game or contest): *the Bears lost the final game of the series* | [no obj.] *they lost by one vote* | (as adj. **losing**) *the losing side.* ■ cause (someone) to fail to win (a game or contest): *that shot lost him the championship.* **4** earn less (money) than one is spending or has spent: *the paper is losing $500,000 a month* | [no obj.] *he lost heavily on box-office flops.*
– PHRASES **have nothing to lose** be in a situation that is so bad that even if an action or undertaking is unsuccessful, it cannot make it any worse. **lose face** come to be less highly respected: *he was trying to work out how he could go back home without losing face.* **lose heart** become discouraged. **lose one's heart to** see HEART. **lose height** (of an aircraft) descend to a lower level in flight. **lose one's mind** (or **one's marbles**) informal go insane. **lose sleep** [usu. with negative] worry about something: *no one is losing any sleep over what he thinks of us.* **lose one's** (or **the**) **way** become lost; fail to reach one's destination. ■ no longer have a clear idea of one's purpose or motivation in an activity or business: *the company has lost its way and should pull out of general insurance.* **you can't lose** used to express the conviction that someone must inevitably profit from an action or undertaking: *we're offering them for only $5.00—you can't lose!*
– PHRASAL VERBS **lose out** be deprived of an opportunity to do or obtain something; be disadvantaged: *youngsters who were* **losing out on** *regular schooling.* ■ be beaten in competition or replaced by: *they were disappointed at losing out to Chicago in the playoffs.*
– ORIGIN Old English *losian* 'perish, destroy,' also 'become unable to find,' from *los* 'loss.'

USAGE See usage at LOOSE.

lo·sel /ˈlōzəl/ ▶ **n.** archaic or dialect a worthless person. ▶ **adj.** archaic or dialect good-for-nothing; worthless.
– ORIGIN late Middle English: apparently from *los-*, stem of obsolete *lese* 'lose,' + -EL.

los·er /ˈlo͞ozər/ ▶ **n.** a person or thing that loses or has lost something, esp. a game or contest. ■ a person who accepts defeat with good or bad grace, as specified: *we won fair and square—they should concede that and be good losers.* ■ a person or thing that is put at a disadvantage by a particular situation or course of action: *children are the losers when politicians keep fiddling around with education.* ■ informal a person who fails frequently or is generally unsuccessful in life: *a ragtag community of rejects and losers.* ■ Bridge a card that is expected to be part of a losing trick.

los·ing bat·tle ▶ **n.** [in sing.] a struggle that seems certain to end in failure: *the police force is fighting a losing battle against a rising tide of crime.*

los·ing·est /ˈlo͞ozINGist/ ▶ **adj.** informal losing more often than others of its kind; least successful.

loss /lôs, läs/ ▶ **n.** the fact or process of losing something or someone: *avoiding loss of time | funding cuts will lead to job losses.* ■ an amount of money lost by a business or organization: *insurance can protect you against financial loss | we have incurred huge losses* | [in combination] *loss-making industries.* ■ the state or feeling of grief when deprived of someone or something of value: *I feel a terrible sense of loss.* ■ [in sing.] a person or thing that is badly missed when lost: *he will be* **a great loss** *to many people.* ■ Physics a reduction of power within or among circuits, measured as a ratio of power input to power output.
– PHRASES **at a loss 1** puzzled or uncertain what to think, say, or do: [with infinitive] *she became popular, and was at a loss to know why | he was* **at a loss for** *words.* **2** making less money than is spent buying, operating, or producing something: *a railroad running at a loss.*
– ORIGIN Old English *los* 'destruction,' of Germanic origin; related to Old Norse *los* 'breaking up of the ranks of an army' and LOOSE; later probably a back-formation from *lost*, past participle of LOSE.

loss-lead·er ▶ **n.** a product sold at a loss to attract customers.

loss·less /ˈlôsləs, ˈläs-/ ▶ **adj.** having or involving no dissipation of electrical or electromagnetic energy. ■ Computing of or relating to data compression without loss of information.

loss-mak·ing ▶ **adj.** (esp. of a business) losing money, rather than making a profit.
– DERIVATIVES **loss-mak·er** **n.**

loss ra·tio ▶ **n.** the ratio of the claims paid by an insurer to the premiums earned, usually for a one-year period.

loss·y /ˈlôsē, ˈläsē/ ▶ **adj.** having or involving the dissipation of electrical or electromagnetic energy. ■ Computing of or relating to data compression in which unnecessary information is discarded.

lost /lôst, läst/ past and past participle of LOSE. ▶ **adj. 1** unable to find one's way; not knowing one's whereabouts: *Help! We're lost! | they* **got lost** *in the fog.* ■ unable to be found: *he turned up with my lost golf clubs.* ■ (of a person) very confused or insecure or in great difficulties: *she stood there clutching a drink, feeling completely lost | I'd* **be lost without** *her.* **2** denoting something that has been taken away or cannot be recovered: *if only one could recapture one's lost youth!* ■ (of time or an opportunity) not used advantageously; wasted: *the decision meant a lost opportunity to create 200 jobs.* ■ having perished or been destroyed: *a memorial to the lost crewmen.* **3** (of a game or contest) in which a defeat has been sustained: *the lost election of 1994.*
– PHRASES **all is not lost** used to suggest that there is still some chance of success or recovery. **be lost for words** be so surprised, confused, or upset that one cannot think what to say. **be lost on** fail to influence or be noticed or appreciated by (someone): *the significance of his remarks was not lost on Scott.* **be lost to** be no longer affected by or accessible to: *once a vital member of the community, he is now lost to the world.* **get lost** [often in imperative] informal go away (used as an expression of anger or impatience): *Why don't you leave me alone? Go on, get lost!* **give someone up for lost** stop expecting that a missing person will be found alive. **make up for lost time** do something faster or more often in order to compensate for not having done it quickly or often enough before.

lost-and-found ▶ **n.** a place where lost items are kept to await reclaiming by their owners.

PRONUNCIATION KEY ə *ago, up*; ər *over, fur*; a *hat*; ā *ate*; ä *car*; e *let*; ē *see*; i *fit*; ī *by*; NG *sing*; ō *go*; ô *law, for*; oi *toy*; o͝o *good*; o͞o *goo*; ou *out*; TH *thin*; T͟H *then*; ZH *vision*

lost cause ▶ **n.** a person or thing that can no longer hope to succeed or be changed for the better.

lost gen·er·a·tion ▶ **n.** the generation reaching maturity during and just after World War I, a high proportion of whose men were killed during those years. ■ an unfulfilled generation coming to maturity during a period of instability.
– ORIGIN phrase applied by Gertrude Stein to disillusioned young American writers, such as Ernest Hemingway, F. Scott Fitzgerald, and Ezra Pound, who went to live in Paris in the 1920s.

Lost Tribes (also **Ten Lost Tribes of Israel**) the ten tribes of Israel taken away *c.*720 BC by Sargon II to captivity in Assyria, from which they are believed never to have returned while the tribes of Benjamin and Judah remained. See also **TRIBES OF ISRAEL**.

lost wax ▶ **n.** a method of bronze casting using a clay core and a wax coating placed in a mold. The wax is melted in the mold and drained out, and bronze poured into the space left, producing a hollow bronze figure when the core is discarded. Also called **CIRE PERDUE**.

Lot[1] /lät/ a river in southern France that flows 300 miles (480 km) west to meet the Garonne River southeast of Bordeaux.

Lot[2] (in the Bible) the nephew of Abraham, who was allowed to escape from the destruction of Sodom. His wife, who disobeyed orders and looked back, was turned into a pillar of salt.

lot /lät/ ▶ **pron.** (**a lot** or **lots**) informal a large number or amount; a great deal: *there are **a lot of** actors in the cast | they took **a lot of** abuse | a lot can happen in eight months | we had **lots of** fun.* ■ (**the lot** or **the whole lot**) the whole number or quantity that is involved or implied: *you might as well take the whole lot.*
▶ **adv.** (**a lot** or **lots**) informal a great deal; much: *my life is a lot better now | he played tennis a lot last year | thanks a lot | I feel **a whole lot** better.*
▶ **n. 1** [treated as sing. or pl.] informal a particular group, collection, or set of people or things: *it's just one lot of rich people stealing from another.* ■ a group or a person of a particular kind (generally used in a derogatory or dismissive way): *an inefficient lot, our town council | he was known as a bad lot | **you lot** think you're clever, don't you?*
2 an article or set of articles for sale at an auction: *nineteen lots failed to sell | the picture is lot 16.*
3 one of a set of objects such as straws, stones, or pieces of paper that are randomly selected as part of a decision-making process: *they **drew lots** to determine the order in which they asked questions.* ■ the making of a decision by such random selection: *officers were elected rather than selected **by lot**.* ■ [in sing.] the choice resulting from such a process: *eventually the lot fell on the king's daughter.*
4 [in sing.] a person's luck or condition in life, particularly as determined by fate or destiny: *plans to improve the lot of the disadvantaged.*
5 a plot of land assigned for sale or for a particular use: *a vacant lot | a fenced-off back lot.* ■ short for **PARKING LOT**. ■ an area of land near a television or movie studio where outside filming may be done. ■ the area at a car dealership where cars for sale are kept.
▶ **v.** (**lots, lotting, lotted**) [with obj.] divide (items) into lots for sale at an auction: *the contents have already been lotted up, and the auction takes place on Monday.*
– PHRASES **all over the lot** informal in a state of confusion or disorganization. **fall to someone's lot** become someone's task or responsibility: *they accepted the burden of domestic responsibilities that fell to their lot.* **throw in one's lot with** decide to ally oneself closely with and share the fate of (a person or group).
– ORIGIN Old English *hlot* (noun), of Germanic origin; related to Dutch *lot*, German *Los*. The original meanings were sense 3 of the noun and (by extension) the sense 'a portion assigned to someone'; the latter gave rise to the other noun senses. The pronoun and adverb uses date from the early 19th cent.

> **USAGE** 1 The expressions **a lot of** and **lots of** are used before nouns to mean 'a large number or amount of.' In common with other words denoting quantities, **lot** itself does not normally function as a head noun, meaning that it does not itself determine whether the following verb is singular or plural. Thus, although **lot** is singular in *a lot of people*, the verb that follows is not singular. In this case, the word **people** acts as the head noun and, being plural, ensures that the following verb is also plural: *a lot of people* **were** *assembled* (not *a lot of people* **was** *assembled*). See also usage at **NUMBER**. 2 **A lot of** and **lots of** are very common in speech and writing, but they still have a distinctly informal feel and are generally not considered acceptable for formal English, where alternatives such as **many** or **a large number** are used instead. 3 Written as one word, **alot** is incorrect, although not uncommon.

lo·ta /ˈlōtə/ ▶ **n.** Indian a round water pot, typically of polished brass.
– ORIGIN from Hindi *loṭā*.

lo-tech ▶ **adj.** & **n.** variant spelling of **LOW-TECH**.

loth ▶ **adj.** variant spelling of **LOATH**.

Lo·thar·i·o /lōˈᴛʜe(ə)rēˌō, -ˈᴛʜär-/ ▶ **n.** (pl. **Lotharios**) a man who behaves selfishly and irresponsibly in his sexual relationships with women.
– ORIGIN from a character in Rowe's *Fair Penitent* (1703).

lo·ti /ˈlōtē/ ▶ **n.** (pl. **maloti** /məˈlōtē/) the basic monetary unit of Lesotho, equal to 100 lisente.
– ORIGIN Sesotho.

lo·tic /ˈlōtik/ ▶ **adj.** Ecology (of organisms or habitats) inhabiting or situated in rapidly moving fresh water. Compare with **LENTIC**.
– ORIGIN early 20th cent.: from Latin *lotus* 'washing' + **-IC**.

lo·tion /ˈlōsʜən/ ▶ **n.** a thick, smooth liquid preparation designed to be applied to the skin for medicinal or cosmetic purposes.
– ORIGIN late Middle English: from Old French, or from Latin *lotio(n-)*, from *lot-* 'washed,' from the verb *lavare*.

lot·ta /ˈlätə/ (also **lotsa** /ˈlätsə/) informal ▶ **contraction** lots of (representing nonstandard use): *I saw a lotta courage out there, and a lotta hard work.*

lot·ter·y /ˈlätərē/ ▶ **n.** (pl. **lotteries**) a means of raising money by selling numbered tickets and giving prizes to the holders of numbers drawn at random. ■ [in sing.] a process or thing whose success or outcome is governed by chance: *the lottery of life.*
– ORIGIN mid 16th cent.: probably from Dutch *loterij*, from *lot* 'lot.'

Lot·to /ˈlätō/, Lorenzo (*c.*1480–1556), Italian painter. He painted religious subjects as well as a number of notable portraits.

lot·to /ˈlätō/ ▶ **n.** a lottery game similar to bingo.
– ORIGIN late 18th cent.: from Italian.

lo·tus /ˈlōtəs/ ▶ **n. 1** any of a number of large water lilies, in particular: ● (also **sacred lotus**) a lily of Asia and northern Australia, typically with dark pink or white-and-pink flowers (*Nelumbo nucifera*, family Nelumbonaceae). ● (also **American lotus**) a yellow-flowered North American lily with bowl-shaped leaves (*Nelumbo lutea*, family Nelumbonaceae).
● (also **Egyptian lotus**) a lily regarded as sacred in ancient Egypt (the white-flowered *Nymphaea lotus* and the blue-flowered *N. caerulea*, family Nymphaeaceae).
2 (in Greek mythology) a legendary plant whose fruit induces a dreamy forgetfulness and an unwillingness to depart. ■ the flower of the sacred lotus as a symbol in Asian art and religion. ■ short for **LOTUS POSITION**.
– ORIGIN late 15th cent. (denoting a type of clover or trefoil, described by Homer as food for horses): via Latin from Greek *lōtos*, of Semitic origin. The term was used by classical writers to denote various trees and plants; the legendary plant (sense 2) mentioned by Homer was thought by later Greek writers to be *Ziziphus lotus*, a relative of the jujube.

American lotus

lo·tus-eat·er ▶ **n.** a person who spends time indulging in pleasure and luxury rather than dealing with practical concerns.
– DERIVATIVES **lo·tus-eat·ing adj.**
– ORIGIN mid 19th cent.: from the people in Homer's *Odyssey* who lived on the fruit of the lotus, which was said to cause a dreamy forgetfulness in those who ate it.

lo·tus·land /ˈlōtəsˌland/ ▶ **n.** a place or state concerned solely with, or providing, idle pleasure and luxury: *a lush lotusland where you can shed your inhibitions.*

lo·tus po·si·tion ▶ **n.** a cross-legged position for meditation, with the feet resting on the thighs.

Lo·tus Su·tra /ˈlōtəs ˈso͞otrə/ ▶ **n.** Buddhism one of the most important texts in Mahayana Buddhism, significant particularly in China and Japan and given special veneration by the Nichiren sect.

Louang·phra·bang /ləˈwäNGprəˈbäNG/ variant spelling of **LUANG PRABANG**.

louche /lo͞osʜ/ ▶ **adj.** disreputable or sordid in a rakish or appealing way: *the louche world of the theater.*
– DERIVATIVES **louche·ness n.**
– ORIGIN early 19th cent.: from French, literally 'squinting.'

loud /loud/ ▶ **adj.** producing or capable of producing much noise; easily audible: *they were kept awake by loud music | she had a loud voice.* ■ strong or emphatic in expression: *there were loud protests from the lumber barons.* ■ vulgarly obtrusive; flashy: *a man in a loud checked suit.*
▶ **adv.** with a great deal of volume: *they shouted as loud as they could.*
– PHRASES **out loud** aloud; audibly: *she laughed out loud.*
– DERIVATIVES **loud·en** /ˈloudn/ **v.**, **loud·ly adv.**, **loud·ness n.**
– ORIGIN Old English *hlūd*; related to Dutch *luid*, German *laut*, from an Indo-European root meaning 'hear,' shared by Greek *kluein* 'hear,' *klutos* 'famous' and Latin *cluere* 'be famous.'

loud·hail·er /ˌloudˈhālər/ ▶ **n.** chiefly Brit. another term for **BULLHORN**.

loud·mouth /ˈloudˌmouᴛʜ/ ▶ **n.** informal a person who tends to talk too much in an offensive or tactless way.
– DERIVATIVES **loud·mouthed** /ˈloudˌmouᴛʜd, -ˌmouᴛʜt/ (also **loud-mouthed**) **adj.**

loud·speak·er /ˈloudˌspēkər/ ▶ **n.** an apparatus that converts electrical impulses into sound, typically as part of a public address system or stereo equipment.

Lou·ga·nis /lo͞oˈgānis/, Greg (1960–), US diver; full name *Gregory Efthimios Louganis*. He won two gold medals each at the 1984 and 1988 Olympic Games.

Lou Gehr·ig's dis·ease /ˌlo͞o ˈgerigz/ ▶ **n.** another term for **AMYOTROPHIC LATERAL SCLEROSIS**.
– ORIGIN 1940s: named after H. L. **GEHRIG**, who died from it.

lough ▶ **n.** Anglo-Irish spelling of **LOCH**.
– ORIGIN Middle English: from Irish *loch*. The spelling *lough* survived in Ireland, but the pronunciation was replaced by that of the Irish word.

Lou·is[1] /ˈlo͞o-ē, lwē/ the name of 18 kings of France.
■ **Louis I** (778–840), son of Charlemagne; king of the West Franks and Holy Roman Emperor 814–840.
■ **Louis II** (846–879), reigned 877–879. ■ **Louis III** (863–882), son of Louis II; reigned 879–882.
■ **Louis IV** (921–954), reigned 936–954. ■ **Louis V** (967–987), reigned 979–987.
■ **Louis VI** (1081–1137), reigned 1108–37.
■ **Louis VII** (1120–80), reigned 1137–80.
■ **Louis VIII** (1187–1226), reigned 1223–26.
■ **Louis IX** (1214–70), son of Louis VIII; reigned 1226–70; canonized as **St. Louis**. He conducted two unsuccessful crusades, dying of plague in Tunis during the second. Feast day, August 25.
■ **Louis X** (1289–1316), reigned 1314–16.
■ **Louis XI** (1423–83), son of Charles VII; reigned 1461–83. He continued his father's work in laying the foundations of a united France ruled by an absolute monarchy. ■ **Louis XII** (1462–1515), reigned 1498–1515. ■ **Louis XIII** (1601–43), son of Henry IV of France; reigned 1610–43. During his minority the country was ruled by his mother Marie de Médicis. From 1624, he was heavily influenced in policymaking by his chief minister Cardinal Richelieu. ■ **Louis XIV** (1638–1715), son of Louis XIII; reigned 1643–1715; known as **the Sun King**. His reign represented the high point of the Bourbon dynasty and of French power in Europe. His almost constant wars of expansion united Europe against him, however, and gravely weakened France's financial position. ■ **Louis XV** (1710–74), great-grandson and successor of Louis XIV; reigned 1715–74. He led France into the Seven Years War (1756–63). ■ **Louis XVI** (1754–93), grandson and successor of Louis XV; reigned 1774–92. His minor concessions and reforms in the face of the emerging French Revolution proved disastrous. As the revolution became more extreme, he was executed with his wife, Marie Antoinette, and the monarchy was abolished. ■ **Louis XVII** (1785–95), son of Louis XVI; titular king who died in prison during the revolution. ■ **Louis XVIII** (1755–1824), brother of Louis XVI; reigned 1814–24. After his nephew Louis XVII's death, he became titular king in exile until the fall of Napoleon in 1814, when he returned to Paris on the summons of Talleyrand and was officially restored to the throne.

Lou·is[2] /ˈlo͞o-is/, Joe (1914–81), US heavyweight boxing champion; born *Joseph Louis Barrow*; known as the **Brown Bomber**. He was heavyweight champion of the world 1937–49, defending his title 25 times during that period.

lou·is /'lo͞o-ē/ (also **louis d'or** /dôr/) ▶ **n.** (pl. **same**) a gold coin issued in France between 1640 and 1793. ■ another term for **NAPOLEON** (sense 2).
– ORIGIN from *Louis*, the name of many kings of France.

Lou·is I /'lo͞o-is, 'lo͞o-ē/ (1326–82), king of Hungary 1342–82 and of Poland 1370–82; known as **Louis the Great**. Under his rule, Hungary became a powerful state; he fought two successful wars against Venice (1357–58; 1378–81), and the rulers of Serbia, Wallachia, Moldavia, and Bulgaria became his vassals.

Lou·is, St., Louis IX of France (see **LOUIS**[1]).

Lou·i·si·an·a /lo͞o,ēzē'anə/ a state in the southern US, on the Gulf of Mexico; pop. 4,410,796 (est. 2008); capital, Baton Rouge; statehood, Apr. 30, 1812 (18). It was sold by the French to the US as part of the Louisiana Purchase in 1803.
– DERIVATIVES **Lou·i·si·an·an** (also **Louisianian** /-nēən/) **adj. & n.**
– ORIGIN named in honor of *Louis* XIV.

Lou·i·si·an·a French ▶ **n.** French as spoken in Louisiana, esp. by the descendants of the original French settlers; Cajun.

Lou·i·si·an·a Pur·chase the territory sold by France to the US in 1803, comprising the western part of the Mississippi valley and including the modern state of Louisiana. The area had been explored by France, ceded to Spain in 1762, and returned to France in 1800.

Lou·is Phi·lippe /'lo͞o-ē fē'lēp/ (1773–1850), king of France 1830–48. After the restoration of the Bourbons, he was made king, replacing **Charles X**. His regime was eventually overthrown.

Lou·is the Great, Louis I of Hungary (see **LOUIS I**).

Lou·is·ville /'lo͞oē,vil, 'lo͞owəvəl/ an industrial city and river port in northern Kentucky, on the Ohio River just south of the border with Indiana; since a 2003 merger, is part of Louisville–Jefferson County; consolidated pop. 713,877 (est. 2008). It is the site of the annual Kentucky Derby.

lounge /lounj/ ▶ **v.** [no obj.] lie, sit, or stand in a relaxed or lazy way: *several students were lounging about reading papers.*
▶ **n.** **1** a public room, as in a hotel, theater, or club, in which to sit and relax. ■ a spacious area in an airport with seats for waiting passengers: *the departure lounge.* ■ short for **COCKTAIL LOUNGE**.
2 a couch or sofa, esp. a backless one having a headrest at one end.
– ORIGIN early 16th cent. (in the sense 'move indolently'): perhaps symbolic of slow movement. Sense 1 of the noun dates from the late 19th cent.

lounge liz·ard ▶ **n.** informal an idle person who spends time in lounges and nightclubs.

loung·er /'lounjər/ ▶ **n.** a person spending their time lazily or in a relaxed way. ■ chiefly Brit. another term for **CHAISE LONGUE**.

lounge suit ▶ **n.** chiefly Brit. a man's business suit.

lounge·wear /'lounj,we(ə)r/ ▶ **n.** casual, comfortable clothing suitable for wearing at home.

loupe /lo͞op/ ▶ **n.** a small magnifying glass used by jewelers and watchmakers.
– ORIGIN late 19th cent.: from French.

lour ▶ **v. & n.** variant spelling of **LOWER**[3].

Lourdes /lo͝ord(z)/ a town in southwestern France, at the foot of the Pyrenees; pop. 15,698 (2006). It has been a major place of Roman Catholic pilgrimage since 1858 when a young peasant girl, Marie Bernarde Soubirous (St. Bernadette), claimed to have had a series of visions of the Virgin Mary.

Lou·ren·ço Mar·ques /lə'rensō ,mär'kes/ former name, until 1976, of **MAPUTO**.

louse /lous/ ▶ **n.** **1** (pl. **lice** /līs/) a small, wingless, parasitic insect that lives on the skin of mammals and birds. ● (**sucking louse**) an insect with piercing mouthparts, found only on mammals (order Anoplura or Siphunculata). See also **BODY LOUSE, HEAD LOUSE** ● (**biting louse**) an insect with a large head and jaws, found chiefly on birds (order Mallophaga). ■ used in names of small invertebrates that parasitize aquatic animals or infest plants, e.g., **fish louse**.
2 (pl. **louses**) informal a contemptible or unpleasant person.
▶ **v.** [with obj.] **1** (**louse something up**) informal spoil or ruin something: *he loused up my promotion chances.*
2 archaic remove lice from.
– ORIGIN Old English *lūs*, (plural) *lȳs*, of Germanic origin; related to Dutch *luis*, German *Laus*.

louse fly ▶ **n.** a flattened bloodsucking fly that may have reduced or absent wings and typically spends much of its life on one individual of the host species. ● Family Hippoboscidae: several genera.

louse·wort /'lous,wərt, -,wôrt/ ▶ **n.** a partially parasitic herbaceous plant of the figwort family, typically favoring damp habitats. It is native to both Eurasia and North America and was formerly reputed to harbor lice. ● Genus *Pedicularis*, family Scrophulariaceae: several species, including **wood betony** (*P. canadensis*) and **swamp lousewort** (*P. lanceolata*).

lous·y /'louzē/ ▶ **adj.** (**lousier, lousiest**) **1** informal very poor or bad; disgusting: *the service is usually lousy* | *lousy weather.* ■ ill; in poor physical condition: *she felt lousy.*
2 infested with lice. ■ [predic.] (**lousy with**) informal teeming with (something regarded as bad or undesirable): *the town is lousy with tourists.*
– DERIVATIVES **lous·i·ly** /-zəlē/ **adv.**, **lous·i·ness n.**

lout /lout/ ▶ **n.** an uncouth or aggressive man or boy: *drunken louts.*
– ORIGIN mid 16th cent.: perhaps from archaic *lout* 'to bow down,' of Germanic origin.

Louth /louTH, louTH/ a county of the Republic of Ireland, on the eastern coast in the province of Leinster; county town, Dundalk.

lout·ish /'loutisH/ ▶ **adj.** (of a man or boy) uncouth and aggressive.
– DERIVATIVES **lout·ish·ly adv.**, **lout·ish·ness n.**

lou·var /'lo͞o,vär/ ▶ **n.** a large, brightly colored fish with a distinctive high forehead. It lives in warm open seas, feeding on jellyfishes and comb jellies. ● *Luvarus imperialis*, the only member of the family Luvaridae.
– ORIGIN alteration of Latin name.

lou·ver /'lo͞ovər/ (also **louvre**) ▶ **n.** **1** each of a set of angled slats or flat strips fixed or hung at regular intervals in a door, shutter, or screen to allow air or light to pass through.
2 a domed structure on a roof, with side openings for ventilation.
– DERIVATIVES **lou·vered adj.**
– ORIGIN Middle English (sense 2): from Old French *lover, lovier* 'skylight,' probably of Germanic origin and related to **LODGE**.

louver 1

Louvre /'lo͞ov(rə)/ the principal museum and art gallery of France, in Paris, housed in the former royal palace built by Francis I. The Louvre holds the Mona Lisa and the Venus de Milo.

lov·a·ble /'ləvəbəl/ (also **loveable**) ▶ **adj.** inspiring or deserving love or affection.
– DERIVATIVES **lov·a·bil·i·ty** /,ləvə'bilətē/ **n.**, **lov·a·ble·ness n.**, **lov·a·bly** /-blē/ **adv.**

lov·age /'ləvij/ ▶ **n.** a large, edible, white-flowered plant of the parsley family. ● Several species in the family Umbelliferae, in particular a Mediterranean herb (*Levisticum officinale*), which is chiefly used for flavoring liqueurs.
– ORIGIN Middle English *loveache*, alteration (as if from **LOVE** + obsolete *ache* 'parsley') of Old French *luvesche, levesche*, via late Latin *levisticum* from Latin *ligusticum*, neuter of *ligusticus* 'Ligurian.'

lov·at /'ləvət/ ▶ **n.** a muted green color used esp. in tweed and woolen garments.
– ORIGIN early 20th cent.: from *Lovat*, a place name in Highland Scotland.

love /ləv/ ▶ **n.** **1** an intense feeling of deep affection: *babies fill parents with intense feelings of love* | *their love for their country.* ■ a deep romantic or sexual attachment to someone: *it was love at first sight* | *they were both* **in love with** *her* | *we were slowly* **falling in love**. ■ (**Love**) a personified figure of love, often represented as Cupid. ■ a great interest and pleasure in something: *his love for football* | *we share a love of music.* ■ affectionate greetings conveyed to someone on one's behalf. ■ a formula for ending an affectionate letter: *take care, lots of love, Judy.*
2 a person or thing that one loves: *she was the love of his life* | *their two great loves are tobacco and whiskey.* ■ Brit. informal a friendly form of address: *it's all right, love.* ■ (**a love**) Brit. informal used to express affectionate approval for someone: *don't fret, there's a love.*
3 (in tennis, squash, and some other sports) a score of zero; nil: *love fifteen* | *he was down two sets to love.* [apparently from the phrase *play for love* (i.e., the love of the game, not for money); folk etymology has connected the word with French *l'oeuf* 'egg,' from the resemblance in shape between an egg and a zero.]
▶ **v.** [with obj.] feel a deep romantic or sexual attachment to (someone): *do you love me?* ■ like very much; find pleasure in: *I'd love a cup of tea, thanks* | *I just love dancing* | [as adj., in combination] (**-loving**) *a fun-loving girl.*
– PHRASES **for love** for pleasure not profit: *he played for the love of the game.* **for the love of God** used to express annoyance, surprise, or urgent pleading: *for the love of God, get me out of here!* **for the love of Mike** informal used to accompany an exasperated request or to express dismay. **love me, love my dog** proverb if you love someone, you must accept everything about them, even their faults or weaknesses. **make love 1** have sexual intercourse. **2** (**make love to**) dated pay amorous attention to (someone). **not for love or money** informal not for any inducement or in any circumstances: *they'll not return for love or money.* **there's no** (or **little** or **not much**) **love lost between** there is mutual dislike between (two or more people mentioned).
– DERIVATIVES **love·wor·thy** /-,wərTHē/ **adj.**
– ORIGIN Old English *lufu*, of Germanic origin; from an Indo-European root shared by Sanskrit *lubhyati* 'desires,' Latin *libet* 'it is pleasing,' *libido* 'desire,' also by **LEAVE**[2] and **LIEF**.

love·a·ble /'ləvəbəl/ ▶ **adj.** variant spelling of **LOVABLE**.

love af·fair ▶ **n.** a romantic or sexual relationship between two people, esp. one that is outside marriage. ■ an intense enthusiasm or liking for something: *the great American love affair with the automobile.*

love ap·ple ▶ **n.** an old-fashioned term for a tomato.

love beads ▶ **n.** a necklace of small beads, esp. as worn by hippies in the 1960s as a symbol of peace and goodwill.

love·bird /'ləv,bərd/ ▶ **n.** **1** a very small African and Madagascan parrot with mainly green plumage and typically a red or black face, noted for the affectionate behavior of mated birds. ● Genus *Agapornis*, family Psittacidae: several species.
2 (**lovebirds**) informal an openly affectionate couple.

love bite ▶ **n.** a temporary red mark on a person's skin caused by a lover biting or sucking it as a sexual act; a hickey.

Love Ca·nal /'ləv/ a section of Niagara Falls in New York that was evacuated after 1970s exposure that chemical wastes were buried in its residential neighborhood. It has been partially reoccupied.

love child ▶ **n.** dated a child born to parents who are not married to each other.

love feast ▶ **n.** historical a feast in token of fellowship among early Christians; an agape. ■ a religious service or gathering imitating this, esp. among early Methodists.

love game ▶ **n.** (in tennis and similar sports) a game in which the loser makes no score.

love han·dles ▶ **plural n.** informal deposits of excess fat at the sides of a person's waistline.

love-hate ▶ **adj.** (of a relationship) characterized by ambivalent feelings of love and hate felt by one or each of two or more parties.

love-in ▶ **n.** informal a gathering or party at which people are encouraged to express feelings of friendship and physical attraction, associated with the hippies of the 1960s.
– ORIGIN 1960s: originally with reference to Californian hippie gatherings.

love-in-a-mist ▶ **n.** a Mediterranean plant of the buttercup family that bears blue flowers surrounded by delicate threadlike green bracts, giving a hazy appearance to the flowers. ● *Nigella damascena*, family Ranunculaceae.

love-in-i·dle·ness ▶ **n.** another term for **HEARTSEASE**.

love in·ter·est ▶ **n.** a theme or subsidiary plot in a story or film in which the main element is the affection of lovers. ■ an actor whose role is chiefly concerned with this.

Love·lace[1] /'ləvlās/, Ada Augusta Byron King, Countess of (1815–52), English mathematician. The daughter of Lord Byron, she worked with Charles Babbage on his "analytical engine," a mechanical computer. The Ada standardized computer language was named for her in 1980.

Love·lace[2] Richard (1618–57), English poet. A Royalist, he was imprisoned in 1642, when he probably wrote "To Althea, from Prison."

Love·land /ˈləvlənd/ a city in north central Colorado, between Denver and Fort Collins; pop. 65,587 (est. 2008).

love·less /ˈləvlis/ ▶ **adj.** having no feelings of love: *a young wife trapped in a loveless marriage.*
– DERIVATIVES **love·less·ly adv.**, **love·less·ness n.**

love-lies-bleed·ing ▶ **n.** a South American plant with long, drooping tassels of crimson flowers. Cultivated today as an ornamental, it was formerly an important cereal-type crop in the Andes.
● *Amaranthus caudatus*, family Amaranthaceae.

love life ▶ **n.** the area of a person's life concerning their relationships with lovers.

Love·lock /ˈləvläk, -lək/, James (Ephraim) (1919–), English scientist. He is best known for the Gaia hypothesis, first presented by him in 1972 and discussed in several popular books, including *Gaia* (1979).

love·lock /ˈləvˌläk/ ▶ **n.** archaic a curl of hair worn on the temple or forehead.

love·lorn /ˈləvˌlôrn/ ▶ **adj.** unhappy because of unrequited love.

love·ly /ˈləvlē/ ▶ **adj.** (**lovelier**, **loveliest**) exquisitely beautiful: *you have lovely eyes | lovely views.* ■ informal very pleasant or enjoyable; delightful: *we've had a lovely day | she's a lovely person.*
▶ **n.** (pl. **lovelies**) informal a glamorous woman or girl: *a bevy of rock lovelies.*
– DERIVATIVES **love·li·ly** /-ləlē/ **adv.**, **love·li·ness n.**
– ORIGIN Old English *luflic* (see **LOVE**, **-LY**[1]).

love·mak·ing /ˈləvˌmākiNG/ ▶ **n.** sexual activity between lovers, esp. sexual intercourse. ■ archaic courtship.

love match ▶ **n.** a marriage based on the mutual love of the couple rather than social or financial considerations.

love nest ▶ **n.** informal a place where two lovers spend time together, esp. in secret.

lov·er /ˈləvər/ ▶ **n.** a person having a sexual or romantic relationship with someone, often outside marriage. ■ a person who likes or enjoys something specified: *he was a great lover of cats | music lovers.*
– DERIVATIVES **lov·er·less adj.**

lov·ers' rock ▶ **n.** a gentle, melodic style of reggae incorporating elements of soul and usually featuring lyrics with a romantic theme.

love seat ▶ **n.** a small sofa for two people, in the past designed in an S-shape so that the couple could face each other.

love·sick /ˈləvˌsik/ ▶ **adj.** in love, or missing the person one loves, so much that one is unable to act normally: *a lovesick teenager.*
– DERIVATIVES **love·sick·ness n.**

love·some /ˈləvsəm/ ▶ **adj.** literary lovely or lovable.

love vine ▶ **n.** the dodder, which is sometimes used medicinally and in herbal lore as a love charm.

love·ware /ˈləvˌwe(ə)r/ ▶ **n.** informal computer software that is distributed freely, with the developer asking for the users to think kindly of the developer or of a dedicatee in lieu of payment.

lov·ey /ˈləvē/ ▶ **n.** (pl. **loveys**) Brit. informal used as an affectionate form of address: *Ruth, lovey, are you there?*
▶ **adj.** Brit. informal short for **LOVEY-DOVEY**.

lov·ey-dove·y /ˌləvē ˈdəvē/ ▶ **adj.** informal very affectionate or romantic, esp. excessively so: *a lovey-dovey couple.*

lov·ing /ˈləviNG/ ▶ **adj.** feeling or showing love or great care: *a kind and loving father.*
▶ **n.** the demonstration of love or great care.
– DERIVATIVES **lov·ing·ly adv.**, **lov·ing·ness n.**

lov·ing cup ▶ **n.** a large two-handled cup, passed around at banquets for each guest to drink from in turn.

lov·ing·kind·ness /ˌləviNGˈkīn(d)nis/ ▶ **n.** tenderness and consideration toward others.
– ORIGIN from usage in Coverdale's translation of the Psalms.

Low /lō/, Juliette Gordon (1860–1927) US youth leader. She founded the Girl Scouts of America in 1912, first calling them Girl Guides as they were known in England.

low[1] /lō/ ▶ **adj. 1** of less than average height from top to bottom or to the top from the ground: *the school is a long, low building | a low table.* ■ situated not far above the ground, the horizon, or sea level: *the sun was low in the sky.* ■ located at or near the bottom of something: *low back pain | there were stunted trees* ***low down*** *on the ridge.* ■ Baseball (of a pitched ball) below a certain level, such as the batter's knees, as it comes across home plate, and thus outside the strike zone. ■ (of a river or lake) below the usual water level; shallow. ■ (of latitude) near the equator. ■ (of women's clothing) cut so as to reveal the neck and the upper part of the breasts: *the low neckline of her blouse |* [in combination] *a low-cut black dress.* ■ Phonetics (of a vowel) pronounced with the tongue held low in the mouth; open. ■ (of a sound or voice) not loud or high: *his low, husky voice | they were told to keep the volume very low.*
2 below average in amount, extent, or intensity; small: *bringing up children on a low income | shops with low levels of staff and service | cook over low heat.* ■ (of a substance or food) containing smaller quantities than usual of a specified ingredient: *vegetables are* ***low in*** *calories |* [in combination] *low-fat spreads.* ■ (of a supply) small or reduced in quantity: *food and ammunition were* ***running low.*** ■ having a small or reduced quantity of a supply: *they were* ***low on*** *fuel.*
3 ranking below other people or things in importance or class: *jobs with low status | training will be given low priority.* ■ (of art or culture) considered to be inferior in quality and refinement: *the dual traditions of high and low art.* ■ less good than is expected or desired; inferior: *the standard of living is low.* ■ unscrupulous or dishonest: *practice a little low cunning | low tricks.* ■ (of an opinion) unfavorable: *he had a low opinion of himself.*
4 depressed or lacking in energy: *I was feeling low.*
▶ **n.** a low point, level or figure: *his popularity ratings are at an all-time low.* ■ a particularly bad or difficult moment: *the highs and lows of an actor's life.* ■ informal a state of depression or low spirits. ■ an area of low atmospheric pressure; a depression.
▶ **adv. 1** in or into a low position or state: *she pressed on, bent low to protect her face.*
2 in a low voice or at a low pitch: *we were talking low so we wouldn't wake Dean.*
– PHRASES **the lowest of the low** the people regarded as the most immoral or socially inferior of all.
– DERIVATIVES **low·ness n.**
– ORIGIN Middle English: from Old Norse *lágr*, of Germanic origin; related to Dutch *laag*, also to **LIE**[1].

low[2] ▶ **v.** [no obj.] (of a cow) make a characteristic deep sound: (as noun **lowing**) *the lowing of cattle.*
▶ **n.** a sound made by cattle; a moo.
– ORIGIN Old English *hlōwan*, of Germanic origin; related to Dutch *loeien*, from an Indo-European root shared by Latin *clamare* 'to shout.'

low·ball /ˈlōˌbôl/ ▶ **adj.** informal (of an estimate, bid, etc.) deceptively or unrealistically low.
▶ **v.** [with obj.] offer a deceptively or unrealistically low estimate, bid, etc.: *are you being lowballed by someone who hopes to make money on extras later?*
– DERIVATIVES **low·ball·ing n.**

low beam ▶ **n.** an automobile headlight providing short-range illumination, used on lit roads and when visible to oncoming traffic.

low blow ▶ **n.** Boxing an illegal blow that strikes below an opponent's waist. ■ an unfair or unsportsmanlike comment.

low-born ▶ **adj.** born to a family that has a low social status.

low·boy /ˈlōˌboi/ ▶ **n.** a low chest or table with drawers and short legs. Compare with **HIGHBOY**.

low·bred /ˈlōˈbred/ ▶ **adj.** characterized by coarse behavior or vulgar breeding.

low·brow /ˈlōˌbrou/ ▶ **adj.** not highly intellectual or cultured: *lowbrow tabloids.*
▶ **n.** a person of such a type.

low-carb (also **lo-carb**) ▶ **adj.** low in carbohydrates.

Low Church ▶ **adj.** of or adhering to a tradition within the Anglican Church (and some other denominations) that is Protestant in outlook and gives relatively little emphasis to ritual, sacraments, and the authority of the clergy. Compare with **HIGH CHURCH**, **BROAD CHURCH**.
▶ **n.** [treated as sing. or pl.] the principles or adherents of this tradition.
– DERIVATIVES **Low Church·man n.** (pl. **Low Churchmen**).

low-class ▶ **adj.** of a low or inferior standard, quality, or social class: *low-class places of amusement.*

low com·e·dy ▶ **n.** comedy in which the subject and the treatment border on farce.

low-cost ▶ **adj.** relatively inexpensive; cheap: *a low-cost airline.*

Low Coun·tries the region of northwestern Europe that includes the Netherlands, Belgium, and Luxembourg.

low-den·si·ty ▶ **adj.** having a low concentration.

low-den·si·ty lip·o·pro·tein (abbr.: **LDL**) ▶ **n.** the form of lipoprotein in which cholesterol is transported in the blood.

low·down /ˈlōˌdoun/ informal ▶ **adj.** mean and unfair: *dirty lowdown tricks.*
▶ **n.** (**the lowdown**) the true facts or relevant information about something: *get the lowdown on the sit-in.*

Low·ell[1] /ˈlōəl/ a city in northeastern Massachusetts, on the Concord and Merrimack rivers, developed after 1822 as a planned industrial community based on textile manufacturing; pop. 103,615 (est. 2008).

Low·ell[2], Amy (Lawrence) (1874–1925), US poet. She is known for her polyphonic prose and sensuous imagery. Notable works: *A Critical Fable* (1922) and *What's O'Clock* (1925).

Low·ell[3], James Russell (1819–91), US poet and critic. His works include the satirical *Biglow Papers* (1848 and 1867) and volumes of essays including *Among My Books* (1870) and *My Study Window* (1871).

Low·ell[4], Percival (1855–1916), US astronomer. He inferred the existence of a ninth planet beyond Neptune. When it was eventually discovered in 1930, it was given the name Pluto, with a symbol that also included his initials. He was the brother of poet Amy Lowell.

Low·ell[5], Robert (Traill Spence) (1917–77), US poet. His poetry, often describing his manic depression, is notable for its intense confessional nature and for its complex imagery. Notable works: *Lord Weary's Castle* (1946), *Life Studies* (1959), and *The Dolphin* (1973).

low-end ▶ **adj.** denoting the cheaper products of a range, esp. of audio or computer equipment.

low·er[1] /ˈlōər/ ▶ **adj. 1** comparative of **LOW**[1].
2 less high: *the lower levels of the building | managers lower down the hierarchy.* ■ (of an animal or plant) showing relatively primitive or simple characteristics. ■ (often **Lower**) Geology & Archaeology denoting an older (and hence usually deeper) part of a stratigraphic division or archaeological deposit or the period in which it was formed or deposited: *Lower Cretaceous | Lower Paleolithic.*
3 (in place names) situated on less high land or to the south or toward the sea: *the sweatshops of the Lower East Side.*
▶ **adv.** in or into a lower position: *the sun sank lower.*
– DERIVATIVES **low·er·most** /-ˌmōst/ **adj.**

low·er[2] /ˈlōər/ ▶ **v.** [with obj.] move (someone or something) in a downward direction: *he watched the coffin being lowered into the ground.* ■ make or become less in amount, intensity, or degree: [with obj.] *traffic speeds must be lowered | she lowered her voice to a whisper |* [no obj.] *temperatures lowered.* ■ (**lower oneself**) behave in a way that is perceived as unworthy or debased.
– PHRASES **lower the boom on** informal treat or reprimand (someone) severely. ■ put a stop to (an activity): *let's lower the boom on high-level corruption.*

low·er[3] /ˈlou(ə)r/ (also **lour**) ▶ **v.** [no obj.] look angry or sullen; frown: *the lofty statue lowers at patients in the infirmary.* ■ (of the sky, weather, or landscape) look dark and threatening: (as adj. **lowering**) *a day of lowering clouds.*
▶ **n.** a scowl. ■ a dark and gloomy appearance of the sky, weather or landscape.
– DERIVATIVES **low·er·ing·ly adv.**
– ORIGIN Middle English: of unknown origin.

low·er an·i·mals /ˈlōər/ ▶ **plural n.** animals of relatively simple or primitive characteristics as contrasted with humans or with more advanced animals such as mammals or vertebrates.

Low·er Cal·i·for·nia another name for **BAJA CALIFORNIA**.

Low·er Can·a·da the mainly French-speaking region of Canada around the lower St. Lawrence River, in what is now southern Quebec.

low·er·case /ˈlōərˌkās/ (also **lower case**) ▶ **n.** small letters as opposed to capital letters (uppercase): *the name may be typed in lowercase |* [as modifier] *lowercase letters.*
– ORIGIN referring originally to the lower of two cases of type positioned on an angled stand for use by a compositor (see **UPPERCASE**).

low·er cham·ber /ˈlōər/ ▶ **n.** another term for **LOWER HOUSE**.

low·er class /ˈlōər/ ▶ **n.** [treated as sing. or pl.] the social group that has the lowest status; the working class.
▶ **adj.** of, relating to, or characteristic of people belonging to such a group: *a lower-class area.*

low·er court /ˈlōər/ ▶ **n.** Law a court whose decisions may be overruled by another court on appeal.

low·er crit·i·cism /ˈlōər/ ▶ **n.** dated another term for TEXTUAL CRITICISM (esp. as applied to the Bible, in contrast to HIGHER CRITICISM).

low·er deck /ˈlōər/ ▶ **n.** the deck of a ship situated immediately above the hold.

Low·er East Side a district of southeastern Manhattan in New York City, noted as home to immigrants from the 1880s through the early 20th century.

Low·er Forty-eight (States) a term for the 48 contiguous US states, excluding Alaska and Hawaii.

low·er house /ˈlōər/ ▶ **n.** the larger of two sections of a bicameral legislature or parliament, typically with elected members and having the primary responsibility for legislation. ■ **(the Lower House)** (in the UK) the House of Commons.

Low·er Mer·i·on /ˈmerēən/ a township in southeastern Pennsylvania that contains many suburban communities northwest of Philadelphia; pop. 57,203 (est. 2008).

low·er or·ders /ˈlōər/ ▶ **plural n.** dated the lower classes of society.

low·er plants /ˈlōər/ ▶ **plural n.** plants of relatively simple or primitive characteristics, esp. those that are not vascular plants, i.e., algae, mosses, liverworts, and sometimes fungi.

low·er re·gions /ˈlōər/ ▶ **plural n.** archaic hell or the underworld.

Low·er Sax·o·ny a state of northwestern Germany; capital, Hanover. It corresponds to the northwestern part of the former kingdom of Saxony. German name NIEDERSACHSEN.

low·er school /ˈlōər/ ▶ **n.** the section of a larger school that educates younger students, esp. those below the fifth grade.

low·est com·mon de·nom·i·na·tor ▶ **n.** Mathematics the lowest common multiple of the denominators of several fractions. ■ derogatory the level of the least discriminating audience or consumer group: *they were accused of pandering to the lowest common denominator of public taste.*

low·est com·mon mul·ti·ple (abbr.: **LCM**) ▶ **n.** Mathematics the lowest quantity that is a multiple of two or more given quantities (e.g., 12 is the lowest common multiple of 2, 3, and 4).

low-fi ▶ **adj.** variant spelling of LO-FI.

low fre·quen·cy ▶ **n.** (in radio) 30–300 kilohertz.

low gear ▶ **n.** a gear that causes a wheeled vehicle to move slowly, because of a low ratio between the speed of the wheels and that of the mechanism driving them.

Low Ger·man ▶ **n.** a vernacular language spoken in much of northern Germany, more closely related to Dutch than to standard German. Also called PLATTDEUTSCH.

low-grade ▶ **adj.** of low quality or strength: *low-grade steel | low-grade fuels.* ■ at a low level in a salary or employment structure: *low-grade clerical jobs.* ■ (of a medical condition) of a less serious kind; minor: *a low-grade fever.*

low-hang·ing fruit ▶ **n.** informal a thing or person that can be won, obtained, or persuaded with little effort: *we know mining our own customer base is low-hanging fruit.*

low-im·pact /ˈimˌpakt/ ▶ **adj.** [attrib.] **1** denoting exercises, typically aerobics, designed to put little or no harmful stress on the body.
2 (of an activity, industry, or product) affecting or altering the environment as little as possible.

low-key (also **low-keyed**) ▶ **adj.** not elaborate, showy, or intensive; modest or restrained: *their wedding was a very quiet, low-key affair | a simple, low-keyed style.* ■ Art & Photography having a predominance of dark or muted tones.

low·land /ˈlōlənd, -ˌland/ ▶ **n.** (also **lowlands**) low-lying country: *economic power gravitated toward the lowlands* | [as modifier] *lowland farming.* ■ **(the Lowlands)** the region of Scotland lying south and east of the Highlands.
–DERIVATIVES **low·land·er** (also **Lowlander**) **n.**

Low Lat·in ▶ **n.** medieval and later forms of Latin.

low lat·i·tudes ▶ **plural n.** regions near the equator.

low-lev·el ▶ **adj.** situated relatively near or below ground level: *low-level flying was banned.* ■ of or showing a small degree of some measurable quantity, for example radioactivity: *the dumping of low-level waste.* ■ of relatively little importance, scope, or prominence; basic: *opportunities to progress beyond low-level jobs.* ■ Computing of or relating to programming languages or operations that are relatively close to machine code in form.

low·life /ˈlōˌlīf/ (also **low life**) ▶ **n.** people or activities characterized as being disreputable and often criminal: *crackheads, loafers, and general nineties low life.*
–DERIVATIVES **low·lif·er n.**

low·light /ˈlōˌlīt/ ▶ **n.** informal a particularly disappointing or dull event or feature.
–ORIGIN early 20th cent.: from LOW[1], suggested by HIGHLIGHT.

low·ly /ˈlōlē/ ▶ **adj.** (**lowlier, lowliest**) low in status or importance; humble: *she was too good for her lowly position.* ■ (of an organism) primitive or simple.
▶ **adv.** to a low degree; in a low manner: *lowly paid workers.*
–DERIVATIVES **low·li·ly** /ˈlōləˌlē/ **adv.**, **low·li·ness n.**

low-ly·ing ▶ **adj.** at low altitude above sea level: *flooding problems in low-lying areas.*

low-main·te·nance ▶ **adj.** requiring little work to keep in good condition: *low-maintenance lawns.* ■ informal (of a person) not demanding a great deal of attention; independent.

Low Mass ▶ **n.** (in the Roman Catholic Church) formerly, a Mass with no music and a minimum of ceremony.

low-mind·ed ▶ **adj.** vulgar or sordid in mind or character.
–DERIVATIVES **low-mind·ed·ness n.**

low-necked ▶ **adj.** (of a dress or garment) cut so as to leave the neck and shoulders exposed; décolleté.

low·pass /ˈlōˌpas/ ▶ **adj.** Electronics (of a filter) transmitting all frequencies below a certain value.

low-pitched ▶ **adj. 1** (of a sound or voice) deep or relatively quiet.
2 (of a roof) having only a slight slope.

low post ▶ **n.** Basketball an offensive position on the court close to the basket.

low-pres·sure ▶ **n.** a condition of the atmosphere in which the pressure is below average (e.g., in a depression).
▶ **adj. 1** involving a small or limited degree of physical force: *a low-pressure nozzle is recommended.*
2 involving a low level of activity or exertion; nonstressful: *her low-pressure style of teaching.* ■ (of a salesperson or sales pitch) employing a low degree of coercion: *a seminar in low-pressure sales tactics.*

low pro·file ▶ **n.** [in sing.] a position of avoiding or not attracting much attention or publicity: *he's not the sort of politician to **keep a low profile**.*
▶ **adj. 1** avoiding attention or publicity: *a low-profile campaign.*
2 (of an object) lower or slimmer than is usual for objects of its type. ■ (of a motor vehicle tire) of smaller diameter and greater width than usual, for high-performance use.

low-rank·ing ▶ **adj.** having a low rank or position in a particular hierarchy: *low-ranking police officers.*

low re·lief ▶ **n.** Sculpture another term for BAS-RELIEF (see RELIEF (sense 4)).

low-rent ▶ **adj.** (of a property) costing relatively little to rent: *a low-rent apartment.* ■ informal having little prestige; inferior or shoddy: *low-rent reality shows.*

low-res /ˈlōˌrez/ ▶ **adj.** informal (of a display or an image) showing a small amount of detail.
–ORIGIN late 20th cent.: from *low-resolution.*

low-res·o·lu·tion ▶ **adj.** Computing of or relating to a visual output device, such as a CRT or a printer, whose images are not sharply defined. ■ of or relating to an image that lacks sharp focus or fine detail.

low·rid·er /ˈlōˌrīdər/ ▶ **n.** a customized vehicle with hydraulic jacks that allow the chassis to be lowered nearly to the road.
–DERIVATIVES **low·rid·ing** /-ˌrīdiNG/ **n.**

low-rise ▶ **adj. 1** (of a building) having few stories: *low-rise apartment blocks.*
2 (of pants) cut so as to fit low on the hips rather than on the waist.
▶ **n.** a building having few stories.

low road ▶ **n.** informal a behavior or approach that is unscrupulous or immoral.

low-slung ▶ **adj. 1** lower in height or closer to the ground than usual: *a low-slung Mercedes with blacked-out windows.*
2 (of clothes, esp. pants) cut to fit low on the hips rather than the waist: *a pair of low-slung jeans.*

low-spir·it·ed ▶ **adj.** sad and despondent; depressed: *he was a bit low-spirited.*
–DERIVATIVES **low-spir·it·ed·ness n.**

low spir·its ▶ **plural n.** a feeling of sadness and despondency: *he was in low spirits.*

Low Sun·day ▶ **n.** the Sunday after Easter.
–ORIGIN perhaps so named in contrast to the high days of Holy Week and Easter.

low-tech /ˌlōˈtek/ (also **lo-tech**) ▶ **adj.** involved in, employing, or requiring only low technology: *low-tech solar heating systems.*
▶ **n.** (**low tech**) short for LOW TECHNOLOGY.

low tech·nol·o·gy ▶ **n.** less advanced or relatively unsophisticated technological development or equipment.

low ten·sion (also **low voltage**) ▶ **n.** an electrical potential not large enough to cause injury or damage if diverted.

low tide ▶ **n.** the state of the tide when at its lowest level: *islets visible at low tide.*

low wa·ter ▶ **n.** another term for LOW TIDE.

low-wa·ter mark ▶ **n.** the lowest level reached by the sea at low tide, or by a lake or river during a drought or dry season. ■ a minimum recorded level or value: *the market was approaching its low-water mark.*

Low Week ▶ **n.** the week that begins with Low Sunday.

low-yield ▶ **adj.** producing little; giving a low return: *low-yield investment.* ■ (of a nuclear weapon) having a relatively low explosive force.

lox[1] /läks/ (also **LOX**) ▶ **n.** liquid oxygen.
–ORIGIN early 20th cent.: acronym from *l(iquid) o(xygen) (e)x(plosive)*, later interpreted as being from *l(iquid) ox(ygen)*.

lox[2] ▶ **n.** smoked salmon.
–ORIGIN 1940s: from Yiddish *laks*.

lox·o·drome /ˈläksəˌdrōm/ ▶ **n.** another term for RHUMB (sense 1).

Loy /loi/, Myrna (1905–93) US actress; born *Myrna Williams*. She played Nora Charles in the six comedy-crime *Thin Man* movies (1934–47). Other notable movies include *The Best Years of Our Lives* (1946), *Mr. Blanding Builds His Dream House* (1948), and *Cheaper by the Dozen* (1950).

loy·a jir·ga /ˈloiə/ ▶ **n.** see JIRGA.

loy·al /ˈloiəl/ ▶ **adj.** giving or showing firm and constant support or allegiance to a person or institution: *he remained **loyal to** the government | loyal service.*
–DERIVATIVES **loy·al·ly adv.**
–ORIGIN mid 16th cent.: from French, via Old French *loial* from Latin *legalis* (see LEGAL).

loy·al·ist /ˈloiəlist/ ▶ **n.** a person who remains loyal to the established ruler or government, esp. in the face of a revolt. ■ **(Loyalist)** a colonist of the American revolutionary period who supported the British cause. ■ **(Loyalist)** a supporter of union between Great Britain and Northern Ireland.
–DERIVATIVES **loy·al·ism** /-ˌlizəm/ **n.**

loy·al·ty /ˈloiəltē/ ▶ **n.** (pl. **loyalties**) the quality of being loyal to someone or something: *her **loyalty to** her husband of 34 years.* ■ (often **loyalties**) a strong feeling of support or allegiance: *fights with in-laws are distressing because they cause **divided loyalties**.*

Loy·al·ty Is·lands a group of islands in the southwestern Pacific Ocean that forms part of the French overseas territory of New Caledonia; pop. 22,080 (2004).

loz·enge /ˈläzənj/ ▶ **n.** a rhombus or diamond shape. ■ a small medicinal tablet, originally of this shape, taken for sore throats and dissolved in the mouth: *throat lozenges.* ■ Heraldry a charge in the shape of a solid diamond, in particular one on which the arms of an unmarried or widowed woman are displayed.
–ORIGIN Middle English: from Old French *losenge*, probably derived from the base of Spanish *losa*, Portuguese *lousa* 'slab,' late Latin *lausiae (lapides)* 'stone slabs.'

LP ▶ **abbr.** ■ long-playing (phonograph record): *two LP records | a collection of LPs.* ■ low pressure.

l.p. ▶ **abbr.** low pressure.

LPG ▶ **abbr.** liquefied petroleum gas.

LPGA ▶ **abbr.** Ladies' Professional Golf Association.

LPM (also **lpm**) ▶ **abbr.** lines per minute.

LPN ▶ **abbr.** Licensed Practical Nurse. See PRACTICAL NURSE.

LR ▶ **abbr.** ■ living room. ■ lower right. ■ low rate.

Lr ▶ **symbol** the chemical element lawrencium.

L/R ▶ **abbr.** left/right.

LRV ▶ **abbr.** lunar roving vehicle.

LSAT ▶ **abbr.** Law School Admission Test.

LSB ▶ **abbr.** Computing least significant bit.

LSD ▶ **n.** a synthetic crystalline compound, lysergic acid diethylamide, that is a potent hallucinogenic drug. ● Chem. formula: $C_{20}H_{26}N_2O$.
– ORIGIN mid 20th cent.: abbreviation.

LSI ▶ **abbr.** large-scale integration.

Lt. ▶ **abbr.** ■ lieutenant. ■ (also **lt**) light.

lt. ▶ **abbr.** light.

l.t. ▶ **abbr.** ■ Football left tackle. ■ local time. ■ long ton.

Lt. Col. (also **LTC**) ▶ **abbr.** lieutenant colonel.

Lt. Comdr. (also **Lt. Com.**) ▶ **abbr.** lieutenant commander.

Ltd. ▶ **abbr.** (after a company name) Limited.

Lt. Gen. (also **LTG**) ▶ **abbr.** lieutenant general.

Lt. Gov. ▶ **abbr.** lieutenant governor.

LTJG ▶ **abbr.** lieutenant junior grade.

LTP ▶ **abbr.** long-term potentiation. See **POTENTIATION**.

LTR ▶ **abbr.** (in personal ads) long-term relationship.

Lu ▶ **symbol** the chemical element lutetium.

Lu·a·la·ba /ˌlo͞oəˈläbə/ a river in central Africa that rises near the southern border of the Democratic Republic of the Congo (formerly Zaire) and flows north for about 400 miles (640 km) before it joins the Lomami River to form the Congo River.

Lu·an·da /lo͞oˈändə/ the capital of Angola, a port on the Atlantic coast; pop. 1,729,500 (est. 2006).

Luang Pra·bang /lo͞oˌäNG prəˈbäNG/ (also **Louangphrabang**) a city in northwestern Laos, on the Mekong River; pop. 60,800 (est. 2009). It was the royal residence and Buddhist religious center of Laos until the end of the monarchy in 1975.

lu·au /ˈlo͞oˌou/ ▶ **n.** (pl. **same** or **luaus**) a Hawaiian party or feast, esp. one accompanied by entertainment.
– ORIGIN from Hawaiian *lu'au*.

Lu·ba /ˈlo͞obə/ ▶ **n.** (pl. **same** or **Lubas**) **1** a member of a people living mainly in southeastern Democratic Republic of the Congo (formerly Zaire).
2 the Bantu language of this people. Also called **CHILUBA**.
▶ **adj.** of or relating to the Luba or their language.
– ORIGIN a local name.

Lu·ba·vitch·er /ˈlo͞obəˌviCHər, lo͞oˈbäviCHər/ ▶ **n.** a member of a Hasidic community founded in the 1700s by Rabbi Shneour Zalman.

lub·ber /ˈləbər/ ▶ **n. 1** archaic or dialect a big, clumsy person.
2 short for **LANDLUBBER**.
– DERIVATIVES **lub·ber·like** /-ˌlīk/ **adj.**, **lub·ber·ly adj. & adv.**
– ORIGIN late Middle English: perhaps via Old French *lobeor* 'swindler, parasite' from *lober* 'deceive.'

lub·ber's line (also **lubber line**) ▶ **n.** a line marked on the compass in a ship or aircraft, showing the direction straight ahead.

Lub·bock /ˈləbək/ a city in northwestern Texas; pop. 220,483 (est. 2008).

lube /lo͞ob/ informal ▶ **n.** a lubricant. ■ lubrication: [as modifier] *a lube job*.
▶ **v.** [with obj.] lubricate (something).
– ORIGIN 1930s: abbreviation.

Lü·beck /ˈlo͞oˌbek, ˈlʏ-/ a port in northern Germany, on the Baltic coast in Schleswig-Holstein, northeast of Hamburg; pop. 211,200 (est. 2006). Between the 14th and 19th centuries it was an important city within the Hanseatic League.

Lu·bian·ka variant spelling of **LUBYANKA**.

Lub·lin /ˈlo͞oblən, ˈlo͞oˌblēn/ a manufacturing city in eastern Poland; pop. 352,786 (2007).

lu·bri·cant /ˈlo͞obrəkənt/ ▶ **n.** a substance, such as oil or grease, used for minimizing friction, esp. in an engine or component.
▶ **adj.** lubricating: *a thin lubricant film*.
– ORIGIN early 19th cent.: from Latin *lubricant-* 'making slippery,' from the verb *lubricare* (see **LUBRICATE**).

lu·bri·cate /ˈlo͞obrəˌkāt/ ▶ **v.** [with obj.] apply a substance such as oil or grease to (an engine or component) to minimize friction and allow smooth movement: *remove the nut and lubricate the thread* | (as adj. **lubricating**) *lubricating oils*. ■ make (a process) run smoothly: *the availability of credit lubricated the channels of trade*. ■ informal make (someone) convivial, esp. with alcohol: *men lubricated with alcohol speak their true feelings*.
– DERIVATIVES **lu·bri·ca·tion** /ˌlo͞obrəˈkāSHən/ **n.**, **lu·bri·ca·tor** /-ˌkātər/ **n.**
– ORIGIN early 17th cent.: from Latin *lubricat-* 'made slippery,' from the verb *lubricare*, from *lubricus* 'slippery.'

lu·bri·cious /lo͞oˈbriSHəs/ (also **lubricous** /ˈlo͞obrikəs/) ▶ **adj. 1** offensively displaying or intended to arouse sexual desire.
2 smooth and slippery with oil or a similar substance.
– DERIVATIVES **lu·bri·cious·ly adv.**, **lu·bric·i·ty** /-ˈbrisitē/ **n.**
– ORIGIN late 16th cent.: from Latin *lubricus* 'slippery' + **-IOUS**.

Lu·bum·ba·shi /ˌlo͞obo͝omˈbäSHē/ a city in southeastern Democratic Republic of the Congo (formerly Zaire), near the border with Zambia, capital of the region of Shaba; pop. 1,283,400 (est. 2004). Former name (until 1966) **ELISABETHVILLE**.

Lu·byan·ka /lo͞oˈbyäNGkə/ (also **Lubianka**) a building in Moscow used as a prison and as the headquarters of the KGB and other Russian secret police organizations since the Russian Revolution.

Lucan[1] /ˈlo͞okən/ (AD 39–65), Roman poet, born in Spain; Latin name *Marcus Annaeus Lucanus*. He was forced to commit suicide after joining a conspiracy against Nero. His major work is *Pharsalia*, an epic in ten books dealing with the civil war between Julius Caesar and Pompey.

Lu·can[2] ▶ **adj.** of or relating to St. Luke.
– ORIGIN via ecclesiastical Latin from Greek *Loukas* 'Luke' + **-AN**.

Lu·cas /ˈlo͞okəs/, George (1944–), US movie director, producer, and screenwriter. He wrote, directed, and produced the science-fiction movie *Star Wars* (1977) and then went on to write and produce *The Empire Strikes Back* (1980), *Return of the Jedi* (1983), and *Star Wars: Episode I: The Phantom Menace* (1999). He also wrote and produced the "Indiana Jones" series of movies (1981–2008).

Luce[1] /lo͞os/, Clare Boothe (1903–87), US playwright and public official; wife of Henry Robinson Luce. After a stint as managing editor of the magazine *Vanity Fair* 1929–34, she wrote the plays *The Women* (1936), *Kiss the Boys Goodbye* (1938), and *Margin for Error* (1939). She was a war correspondent during World War II, served in the US House of Representatives 1943–46 as a Republican from Connecticut, and was US ambassador to Italy 1953–57. Presidential Medal of Freedom (1983).

Luce[2], Henry Robinson (1898–1967) US publisher and editor; born in China of US parents; husband of Clare Boothe Luce. He cofounded *Time*, a weekly news magazine, in 1924. He later launched several other magazines: *Fortune* (1929), *Life* (1936), *House and Home* (1952), and *Sports Illustrated* (1954).

luce /lo͞os/ ▶ **n.** (pl. **same**) a pike (fish), esp. when full-grown.
– ORIGIN late Middle English: via Old French *lus, luis* from late Latin *lucius*.

lu·cent /ˈlo͞osənt/ ▶ **adj.** literary glowing with or giving off light: *the moon was lucent in the background*.
– DERIVATIVES **lu·cen·cy n.**
– ORIGIN late Middle English: from Latin *lucent-* 'shining,' from the verb *lucere* (see **LUCID**).

Lu·cerne /lo͞oˈsərn/ a resort on the western shore of Lake Lucerne, in central Switzerland; pop. 58,381 (2007). German name **Luzern**.

lu·cerne /lo͞oˈsərn/ ▶ **n.** chiefly Brit. another term for **ALFALFA**.
– ORIGIN mid 17th cent.: from French *luzerne*, from modern Provençal *luzerno* 'glowworm' (with reference to its shiny seeds).

Lu·cerne, Lake a lake in central Switzerland, surrounded by the four cantons of Lucerne, Nidwalden, Uri, and Schwyz. Also called **FOUR CANTONS, LAKE OF THE**; German name **VIERWALDSTÄTTERSEE**.

lu·cid /ˈlo͞osid/ ▶ **adj. 1** expressed clearly; easy to understand: *a lucid account* | *write in a clear and lucid style*. ■ showing ability to think clearly, esp. in the intervals between periods of confusion or insanity: *he has a few lucid moments every now and then*. ■ Psychology (of a dream) experienced with the dreamer feeling awake, aware of dreaming, and able to control events consciously.
2 literary bright or luminous: *birds dipped their wings in the lucid flow of air*.
– DERIVATIVES **lu·cid·i·ty** /lo͞oˈsiditē/ **n.**, **lu·cid·ly adv.**, **lu·cid·ness n.**
– ORIGIN late 16th cent. (sense 2): from Latin *lucidus* (perhaps via French *lucide* or Italian *lucido*), from *lucere* 'shine,' from *lux, luc-* 'light.'

Lu·ci·fer /ˈlo͞osəfər/ ▶ **n. 1** another name for **SATAN**. [by association with the 'son of the morning' (Isa. 14:12), believed by Christian interpreters to be a reference to Satan.]
2 literary the planet Venus when it rises in the morning.
3 (**lucifer**) archaic a match struck by rubbing it on a rough surface.
– ORIGIN Old English, from Latin, 'light-bringing, morning star,' from *lux, luc-* 'light' + *-fer* 'bearing.'

lu·cif·u·gous /lo͞oˈsifyəgəs/ ▶ **adj.** chiefly Zoology shunning the light.
– ORIGIN mid 17th cent.: from Latin *lucifugus* (from *lux, luc-* 'light' + *fugere* 'to fly') + **-OUS**.

lu·cine /ˈlo͞oˌsīn/ ▶ **n.** a bivalve mollusk that typically has a rounded white shell with radial and concentric ridges, found in tropical and temperate seas.
● Family Lucinidae: *Lucina* and other genera.

Lu·cite /ˈlo͞oˌsīt/ (also **lucite**) ▶ **n.** trademark a solid transparent plastic made of polymethyl methacrylate (the same material as Perspex or Plexiglas).
– ORIGIN 1930s: from Latin *lux, luc-* 'light' + **-ITE**[1].

luck /lək/ ▶ **n.** success or failure apparently brought by chance rather than through one's own actions: *it was just luck that the first kick went in* | *this charm was supposed to bring* ***good luck***. ■ chance considered as a force that causes good or bad things to happen: *luck was with me*. ■ something regarded as bringing about or portending good or bad things: *I don't like Friday—it's* ***bad luck***.
▶ **v.** [no obj.] (**luck into/onto**) informal chance to find or acquire: *he lucked into a disc-jockey job*. ■ (**luck out**) achieve success or advantage by good luck: *I lucked out and found a wonderful woman*.
– PHRASES **as luck would have it** used to indicate the fortuitousness of a situation: *as luck would have it, his route took him very near where they lived*. **tough luck** informal used to express a lack of sympathy: *tough luck if they complain*. **be in** (or **out of**) **luck** be fortunate (or unfortunate). **for luck** to bring good fortune: *I wear this crystal under my costume for luck*. **good** (or **the best of**) **luck** used to express wishes for success: ***good luck*** *with your studies!* **the luck of the draw** the outcome of chance rather than something one can control: *quality of care depends largely on the luck of the draw*. **no such luck** informal used to express disappointment that something has not happened or is unlikely to happen. **try one's luck** do something that involves risk or luck, hoping to succeed: *he thought he'd try his luck at farming in Canada*. **with** (**any** or **a little** or **a bit of**) **luck** expressing the hope that something will happen in the way described: *with luck we should be there in time for breakfast*. **worse luck** Brit. informal used to express regret about something: *I have to go to secretarial school, worse luck*.
– ORIGIN late Middle English (as a verb): perhaps from Middle Low German or Middle Dutch *lucken*. The noun use (late 15th cent.) is from Middle Low German *lucke*, related to Dutch *geluk*, German *Glück*, of West Germanic origin and possibly related to **LOCK**[1].

luck·i·ly /ˈləkəlē/ ▶ **adv.** [sentence adverb] it is fortunate that: *luckily they didn't recognize me* | ***luckily for me*** *it's worked out*.

luck·less /ˈləkləs/ ▶ **adj.** having bad luck; unfortunate.
– DERIVATIVES **luck·less·ly adv.**, **luck·less·ness n.**

Luck·now /ˈləkˌnou/ a city in northern India, capital of the state of Uttar Pradesh; pop. 2,685,500 (est. 2009). In 1857, during the Indian Mutiny, its British residents were besieged by Indian insurgents twice.

luck·y /ˈləkē/ ▶ **adj.** (**luckier**, **luckiest**) having, bringing, or resulting from good luck: *you had a very lucky escape* | *three's my lucky number*.
– PHRASES **you** (or **he** etc.) **should be so lucky** used to imply in an ironic or resigned way that someone's wishes or expectations are unlikely to be fulfilled: *"Moving in?" "You should be so lucky."* **lucky devil** (or **lucky you**, **her**, etc.) used to express envy at someone else's good fortune.
– DERIVATIVES **luck·i·ness n.**

luck·y dip ▶ **n.** British term for **GRAB BAG**.

lu·cra·tive /ˈlo͞okrətiv/ ▶ **adj.** producing a great deal of profit: *a lucrative career as a stand-up comedian*.
– DERIVATIVES **lu·cra·tive·ly adv.**, **lu·cra·tive·ness n.**
– ORIGIN late Middle English: from Latin *lucrativus*, from *lucrat-* 'gained,' from the verb *lucrari*, from *lucrum* (see **LUCRE**).

lu·cre /ˈlo͞okər/ ▶ **n.** money, esp. when regarded as sordid or distasteful or gained in a dishonorable way: *officials getting their hands grubby with* ***filthy lucre***.
– ORIGIN late Middle English: from French *lucre* or Latin *lucrum*; the phrase *filthy lucre* is with biblical allusion to Tit. 1:11.

Lu·cre·tia /lo͞oˈkrēSHə/ (in Roman legend) a woman who was raped by a son of Tarquinius Superbus and took her own life; this led to the expulsion of the Tarquins from Rome by a rebellion under Brutus.

Lu·cre·tius /lo͞oˈkrēSHəs/ (*c.*94–*c.*55 BC), Roman poet and philosopher; full name *Titus Lucretius Carus*. His didactic epic poem *On the Nature of Things* is an exposition of the materialist atomist physics of Epicurus.

lu·cu·brate /ˈlo͝ok(y)əˌbrāt/ ▶ **v.** [no obj.] archaic discourse learnedly in writing.
– DERIVATIVES **lu·cu·bra·tor** /-ˌbrātər/ **n.**
– ORIGIN early 17th cent.: from Latin *lucubrat-* '(having) worked by lamplight,' from the verb *lucubrare.*

lu·cu·bra·tion /ˌlo͝ok(y)əˈbrāsHən/ ▶ **n.** formal study; meditation: *after sixteen years' lucubration he produced this account.* ■ (usu. **lucubrations**) a piece of writing, typically a pedantic or overelaborate one.
– ORIGIN late 16th cent.: from Latin *lucubratio(n-)*, from the verb *lucubrare* (see LUCUBRATE).

Lu·cul·lan /lo͞oˈkələn/ ▶ **adj.** (esp. of food) extremely luxurious: *Lucullan feasts.*
– ORIGIN mid 19th cent.: from the name of Licinius *Lucullus*, Roman general of the 1st cent. BC, famous for giving lavish banquets, + -AN.

Lu·cy /ˈlo͞osē/ the nickname of a partial female skeleton of a fossil hominid found in Ethiopia in 1974, about 3.2 million years old and 3 feet 8 inches (1.1 m) in height. ● *Australopithecus afarensis*, family Hominidae. This species is regarded by many as the ancestor of all subsequent *Australopithecus* and *Homo* species.

Lu·da /ˈlo͞oˈdä/ an industrial center and port in northeastern China, in the province of Liaoning at the southeastern tip of the Liaodong Peninsula; pop. 2,407,300 (est. 2006). It consists of the cities of Lushun and Dalian.

Lud·dite /ˈlədˌīt/ ▶ **n.** a member of any of the bands of English workers who destroyed machinery, esp. in cotton and woolen mills, that they believed was threatening their jobs (1811–16). ■ a person opposed to increased industrialization or new technology: *a small-minded Luddite resisting progress.*
– DERIVATIVES **Lud·dism** /-ˌizəm/ **n.**, **Lud·dit·ism** /-ītˌizəm/ **n.**
– ORIGIN perhaps named after Ned *Lud*, a participant in the destruction of machinery, + -ITE[1].

Lu·den·dorff /ˈlo͞odnˌdôrf/, Erich (1865–1937), German general; chief of staff to General von Hindenburg during World War I.

lu·der·ick /ˈlo͞od(ə)rik/ ▶ **n.** (pl. **same**) an edible, herbivorous fish of Australasian coastal waters and estuaries. Also called BLACKFISH. ● *Girella tricuspidata*, family Kyphosidae.
– ORIGIN late 19th cent.: from Ganay (an Aboriginal language) *ludarag.*

Lu·dhi·a·na /ˌlo͞odēˈänə/ a city in northwestern India, in Punjab southeast of Amritsar; pop. 1,701,200 (est. 2009).

lu·dic /ˈlo͞odik/ ▶ **adj.** formal showing spontaneous and undirected playfulness.
– ORIGIN 1940s: from French *ludique*, from Latin *ludere* 'to play,' from *ludus* 'sport.'

lu·di·crous /ˈlo͞odəkrəs/ ▶ **adj.** so foolish, unreasonable, or out of place as to be amusing; ridiculous: *it's ludicrous that I have been fined | every night he wore a ludicrous outfit.*
– DERIVATIVES **lu·di·crous·ly** **adv.** *a ludicrously inadequate army*, **lu·di·crous·ness** **n.**
– ORIGIN early 17th cent. (in the sense 'sportive, intended as a jest'): from Latin *ludicrus* (probably from *ludicrum* 'stage play') + -OUS.

Lud·lum /ˈlədləm/, Robert (1927–2001) US writer; pen names **Jonathan Ryder**, **Michael Shepherd**. He wrote suspense novels, including *The Bourne Identity* (1980), *The Matarese Countdown* (1997), and *The Prometheus Deception* (2000).

Lud·wig /ˈlədwig, ˈlo͞od-, ˈlo͞otviKH/ the name of three kings of Bavaria. ■ **Ludwig I** (1786–1868), reigned 1825–48. He became unpopular due to his reactionary policies, lavish expenditures, and his domination by the dancer Lola Montez. He was forced to abdicate in favor of his son, Maximilian II. ■ **Ludwig II** (1845–86), reigned 1864–86. Son of Maximilian II and a patron of the arts, he became a recluse and built a series of elaborate castles. He was declared insane and deposed in 1886. ■ **Ludwig III** (1845–1921), reigned 1913–18. Succeeding his deposed cousin, Ludwig II, he became the last king of Bavaria.

Lud·wigs·ha·fen /ˌlo͞odviksˈhäfən/ an industrial river port in west central Germany, southwest of Mannheim, on the Rhine River in the state of Rhineland-Palatinate; pop. 163,600 (est. 2006).

lu·es /ˈlo͞oˌēz/ (also **lues venerea** /vəˈni(ə)rēə/) ▶ **n.** dated a serious infectious disease, particularly syphilis.
– DERIVATIVES **lu·et·ic** /lo͞oˈetik/ **adj.**
– ORIGIN mid 17th cent.: from Latin *lues (venerea)*, literally '(venereal) plague.'

luff /ləf/ ▶ **n.** the edge of a fore-and-aft sail next to the mast or stay.
▶ **v.** [with obj.] steer (a sailing vessel) nearer the wind to the point at which the sails just begin to flap: *I came aft and luffed her for the open sea.* ■ obstruct (an opponent in yacht racing) by sailing closer to the wind.
– ORIGIN Middle English: from Old French *lof*, probably from Low German.

luf·fa /ˈləfə, ˈlo͞ofə/ ▶ **n.** variant spelling of LOOFAH.

Luft·waf·fe /ˈlo͞oftˌwäfə, -ˌväfə/ the German air force.
– ORIGIN German, from *Luft* 'air' + *Waffe* 'weapon.'

lug[1] /ləg/ ▶ **v.** (**lugs, lugging, lugged**) [with obj.] carry or drag (a heavy or bulky object) with great effort: *she began to lug her suitcase down the stairs.* ■ be encumbered with: *he had lugged his poor wife around for so long.*
▶ **n.** a box or crate used for transporting fruit.
– ORIGIN late Middle English: probably of Scandinavian origin: compare with Swedish *lugga* 'pull a person's hair' (from *lugg* 'forelock').

lug[2] ▶ **n. 1** a projection on an object by which it may be carried or fixed in place: *mount the fitting directly to the lugs at each side of the box.*
2 informal an uncouth, aggressive man: *a hood who, despite his fancy clothes, remains a lug.* [contemptuous use, perhaps from the 19th-cent. term denoting the lowest grade of tobacco.]
3 (usu. **lugs**) Scottish or informal a person's ear.
– ORIGIN late 15th cent. (denoting the earflap of a hat): probably of Scandinavian origin: compare with Swedish *lugg* 'forelock, nap of cloth.'

lug[3] ▶ **n.** short for LUGWORM.

lug[4] ▶ **n.** short for LUGSAIL.

Lu·gan·da /lo͞oˈgändə, -ˈgan-/ ▶ **n.** the Bantu language of the Baganda people, widely used in Uganda.
▶ **adj.** of or relating to this language.

Lu·ga·no /lo͞oˈgänō/ a town in southern Switzerland, on the northern shore of Lake Lugano; pop. 50,603 (2007). It is a center of international finance and a health and recreational resort.

Lu·gansk /lo͞oˈgänsk/ Russian name for LUHANSK.

Lug·du·num /ləgˈdo͞onəm/ Roman name for LYONS.

luge /lo͞ozH/ ▶ **n.** a light toboggan for one or two people, ridden in a sitting or supine position. ■ a sport in which competitors make a timed descent of a course riding such toboggans.
▶ **v.** [no obj.] ride on a luge.
– ORIGIN late 19th cent. (as a verb): from Swiss French.

Lu·ger /ˈlo͞ogər/ ▶ **n.** trademark a type of German automatic pistol.
– ORIGIN early 20th cent.: named after George *Luger* (1849–1923), German firearms expert.

lug·ga·ble /ˈləgəbəl/ ▶ **adj.** (esp. of computer equipment) portable but only with difficulty.

lug·gage /ˈləgij/ ▶ **n.** suitcases or other bags in which to pack personal belongings for traveling.
– ORIGIN late 16th cent. (originally denoting inconveniently heavy baggage): from LUG[1] + -AGE.

lug·ger /ˈləgər/ ▶ **n.** a small sailing ship with two or three masts and a lugsail on each.
– ORIGIN mid 18th cent.: from LUGSAIL + -ER[1].

lug nut ▶ **n.** a large rounded nut that fits over a heavy bolt, used esp. to attach the wheel of a vehicle to its axle.

Lu·go·si /ləˈgōsē/, Bela (born *Béla Ferenc Blasko*) (1884–1956), US actor, born in Hungary. He was known for his roles in horror movies such as *Dracula* (1931), *Mark of the Vampire* (1935), and *The Wolf Man* (1940).

lug·sail /ˈləgsəl, -ˌsāl/ ▶ **n.** an asymmetrical four-sided sail that is hoisted on a steeply inclined yard.
– ORIGIN late 17th cent.: probably from LUG[2] + the noun SAIL.

lu·gu·bri·ous /ləˈg(y)o͞obrēəs/ ▶ **adj.** looking or sounding sad and dismal.
– DERIVATIVES **lu·gu·bri·ous·ly** **adv.**, **lu·gu·bri·ous·ness** **n.**
– ORIGIN early 17th cent.: from Latin *lugubris* (from *lugere* 'mourn') + -OUS.

lug·worm /ˈləgˌwərm/ ▶ **n.** a bristle worm that lives in muddy sand. It is widely used as bait for fishing. ● Genus *Arenicola*, class Polychaeta: several species, including the **northern lugworm**, *A. marina*, which leaves characteristic worm casts on lower shores.
– ORIGIN early 19th cent.: from earlier *lug* 'lugworm' (of unknown origin) + WORM.

Lu·hansk /lo͞oˈhänsk/ an industrial city in eastern Ukraine, in the Donets Basin; pop. 438,000 (est. 2009). Former name VOROSHILOVGRAD (1935–58 and 1970–91). Russian name LUGANSK.

Luik /loik/ Flemish name for LIÈGE.

Luke, St. /lo͞ok/ an evangelist, closely associated with St. Paul and traditionally the author of the third Gospel and the Acts of the Apostles. Feast day, October 18. ■ the third Gospel (see GOSPEL (sense 2)).

luke·warm /ˈlo͞okˈwôrm/ ▶ **adj.** (of liquid or food that should be hot) only moderately warm; tepid: *they drank bitter lukewarm coffee.* ■ (of a person, attitude, or action) unenthusiastic: *the universities were lukewarm about the proposal from the start.*
– DERIVATIVES **luke·warm·ly** **adv.**, **luke·warm·ness** **n.**
– ORIGIN late Middle English: from dialect *luke* (probably from dialect *lew* 'lukewarm' and related to LEE) + WARM.

lull /ləl/ ▶ **v.** [with obj.] calm or send to sleep, typically with soothing sounds or movements: *the rhythm of the boat lulled her to sleep.* ■ cause (someone) to feel deceptively secure or confident: *the rarity of earthquakes there has lulled people into a false sense of security.* ■ allay (a person's doubts, fears, or suspicions), typically by deception. ■ [no obj.] (of noise or a storm) abate or fall quiet: *conversation lulled for an hour.*
▶ **n.** a temporary interval of quiet or lack of activity: *for two days there had been a lull in the fighting.*
– PHRASES **the lull before the storm** see STORM.
– ORIGIN Middle English: imitative of sounds used to calm a child; compare with Latin *lallare* 'sing to sleep,' Swedish *lulla* 'hum a lullaby,' and Dutch *lullen* 'talk nonsense.' The noun (first recorded in the sense 'soothing drink') dates from the mid 17th cent.

lull·a·by /ˈləlәˌbī/ ▶ **n.** (pl. **lullabies**) a quiet, gentle song sung to send a child to sleep.
▶ **v.** (**lullabies, lullabying, lullabied**) [with obj.] rare sing to (someone) to get them to go to sleep: *she lullabied us, she fed us.*
– ORIGIN mid 16th cent.: from LULL + *bye-bye*, a sound used as a refrain in lullabies.

Lul·ly /ˈlo͞olē, lYˈlē/, Jean-Baptiste (1632–87), French composer, born in Italy; Italian name *Giovanni Battista Lulli.* His operas, which include *Alceste* (1674) and *Armide* (1686), mark the beginning of the French operatic tradition.

lu·lu /ˈlo͞oˌlo͞o/ ▶ **n.** informal an outstanding example of a particular type of person or thing: *as far as nightmares went, this one was a lulu.*
– ORIGIN late 19th cent.: perhaps from *Lulu*, nickname for the given name *Louise.*

lu·ma /ˈlo͞omə/ ▶ **n.** (pl. **same** or **lumas**) a monetary unit of Armenia, equal to one hundredth of a dram.

lum·ba·go /ˌləmˈbāgō/ ▶ **n.** pain in the muscles and joints of the lower back.
– ORIGIN late 17th cent.: from Latin, from *lumbus* 'loin.'

lum·bar /ˈləmbər, -ˌbär/ ▶ **adj.** relating to the lower part of the back: *backache in the lumbar region.*
– ORIGIN mid 17th cent.: from medieval Latin *lumbaris*, from Latin *lumbus* 'loin.'

lum·bar punc·ture ▶ **n.** Medicine the procedure of taking fluid from the spine in the lower back through a hollow needle, usually done for diagnostic purposes.

lum·ber[1] /ˈləmbər/ ▶ **v.** [no obj.] move in a slow, heavy, awkward way: *a truck filled his mirror and lumbered past.*
– ORIGIN late Middle English *lomere*, perhaps symbolic of clumsy movement.

lum·ber[2] ▶ **n. 1** timber sawn into rough planks or otherwise partly prepared.
2 chiefly Brit. articles of furniture or other household items that are no longer useful and inconveniently take up storage space: [as modifier] *a lumber room.*
▶ **v. 1** [no obj.] (usu. as noun **lumbering**) cut and prepare forest timber for transport and sale: *the traditional resource industries of the nation, chiefly fishing and lumbering.*
2 [with obj.] (usu. **be lumbered with**) Brit. informal burden (someone) with an unwanted responsibility, task, or set of circumstances.
– ORIGIN mid 16th cent.: perhaps from LUMBER[1]; later associated with obsolete *lumber* 'pawnbroker's shop.'

lum·ber·er /ˈləmbərər/ ▶ **n.** a person engaged in the lumber trade, esp. a lumberjack.

lum·ber·ing /ˈləmbəriNG/ ▶ **adj.** moving in a slow, heavy, awkward way: *Bob was the big, lumbering, gentle sort | figurative a lumbering bureaucracy.*

L

lum·ber·jack /ˈləmbərˌjak/ ▶ **n.** a person who fells trees, cuts them into logs, or transports them to a sawmill. Also called **LUMBERMAN**.

lum·ber·jack·et /ˈləmbərˌjakit/ ▶ **n.** a warm, thick jacket, typically in a bright color with a check pattern, of the kind worn by lumberjacks.

lum·ber·man /ˈləmbərmən/ ▶ **n.** (pl. **lumbermen** /-mən/) another term for **LUMBERJACK**.

lum·ber·yard /ˈləmbərˌyärd/ ▶ **n.** a place that sells lumber and other building materials, usu. outdoors.

lu·men[1] /ˈlo͞omən/ (abbr.: **lm**) ▶ **n.** Physics the SI unit of luminous flux, equal to the amount of light emitted per second in a unit solid angle of one steradian from a uniform source of one candela.
– ORIGIN late 19th cent.: from Latin, literally 'light.'

lu·men[2] ▶ **n.** (pl. **lumina** /-mənə/) Anatomy the central cavity of a tubular or other hollow structure in an organism or cell.
– DERIVATIVES **lu·mi·nal** /-mənl/ **adj.**
– ORIGIN late 19th cent.: from Latin, literally 'opening.'

Lu·mière /ˌlo͞omēˈe(ə)r, lymˈyer/, Auguste Marie Louis Nicholas (1862–1954) and Louis Jean (1864–1948), French inventors and movie pioneers. In 1895, the brothers patented their "Cinématographe," which combined a movie camera and projector. They also invented the improved "autochrome" process of color photography.

lu·mi·naire /ˌlo͞oməˈner/ ▶ **n.** a complete electric light unit (used esp. in technical contexts).
– ORIGIN early 20th cent.: from French.

lu·mi·nance /ˈlo͞omənəns/ ▶ **n.** Physics the intensity of light emitted from a surface per unit area in a given direction. ■ the component of a television signal that carries information on the brightness of the image.
– ORIGIN late 19th cent. (as a general term meaning 'light, brightness'): from Latin *luminant-* 'illuminating' (from the verb *luminare*) + **-ANCE**.

lu·mi·nar·i·a /ˌlo͞oməˈne(ə)rēə/ ▶ **n.** **1** a Christmas lantern consisting of a votive candle set in a small paper bag weighted with sand and typically placed with others along a driveway, sidewalk, or rooftop as a holiday decoration. Also called **FAROLITO**.
2 (in New Mexico) a Christmas Eve bonfire.

lu·mi·nar·y /ˈlo͞oməˌnerē/ ▶ **n.** (pl. **luminaries**) **1** a person who inspires or influences others, esp. one prominent in a particular sphere: *one of the luminaries of child psychiatry.*
2 an artificial light. ■ literary a natural light-giving body, esp. the sun or moon.
– ORIGIN late Middle English: from Old French *luminarie* or late Latin *luminarium*, from Latin *lumen, lumin-* 'light.'

lu·mi·nesce /ˌlo͞oməˈnes/ ▶ **v.** [no obj.] emit light by luminescence.
– ORIGIN late 19th cent.: back-formation from **LUMINESCENCE**.

lu·mi·nes·cence /ˌlo͞oməˈnesəns/ ▶ **n.** the emission of light by a substance that has not been heated, as in fluorescence and phosphorescence.
– DERIVATIVES **lu·mi·nes·cent adj.**
– ORIGIN late 19th cent.: from Latin *lumen, lumin-* 'light' + *-escence* (denoting a state).

lu·mi·nif·er·ous /ˌlo͞oməˈnif(ə)rəs/ ▶ **adj.** producing or transmitting light.

lu·mi·nos·i·ty /ˌlo͞oməˈnäsətē/ ▶ **n.** (pl. **luminosities**) luminous quality: *acrylic colors retain freshness and luminosity.* ■ Astronomy the intrinsic brightness of a celestial object (as distinct from its apparent brightness diminished by distance). ■ Physics the rate of emission of radiation, visible or otherwise.

lu·mi·nous /ˈlo͞omənəs/ ▶ **adj.** full of or shedding light; bright or shining, esp. in the dark: *the luminous dial on his watch | a luminous glow* | figurative *her eyes were* **luminous with** *joy.* ■ (of a color) very bright; harsh to the eye: *he wore luminous green socks.* ■ Physics relating to light as it is perceived by the eye, rather than in terms of its actual energy.
– DERIVATIVES **lu·mi·nous·ly adv.**, **lu·mi·nous·ness n.**
– ORIGIN late Middle English: from Old French *lumineux* or Latin *luminosus*, from *lumen, lumin-* 'light.'

lum·mox /ˈləməks/ ▶ **n.** informal a clumsy, stupid person: *watch it, you great lummox!*
– ORIGIN early 19th cent.: of unknown origin.

lump[1] /ləmp/ ▶ **n.** a compact mass of a substance, esp. one without a definite or regular shape: *there was a lump of ice floating in the milk.* ■ a swelling under the skin, esp. one caused by injury or disease: *he was unhurt apart from a huge lump on his head.* ■ a small cube of sugar. ■ informal a heavy, ungainly, or slow-witted person: *I wouldn't stand a chance against a big lump like you.*
▶ **v. 1** [with obj.] put in an indiscriminate mass or group; treat as alike without regard for particulars: *Hong Kong and Bangkok tend to* **be lumped together** *in travel brochures | he tends to* **be lumped in with** *the crowd of controversial businessmen.* ■ [no obj.] (in taxonomy) classify plants or animals in relatively inclusive groups, disregarding minor variations.
2 [no obj.] (**lump along**) proceed heavily or awkwardly: *I came lumping along behind him.*
– PHRASES **a lump in the throat** a feeling of tightness or dryness in the throat caused by strong emotion, esp. sadness: *there was a lump in her throat as she gazed down at her uncle's gaunt features.* **take** (or **get**) **one's lumps** informal suffer punishment; be attacked or defeated.
– ORIGIN Middle English: perhaps from a Germanic base meaning 'shapeless piece'; compare with Danish *lump* 'lump,' Norwegian and Swedish dialect *lump* 'block, log,' and Dutch *lomp* 'rag.'

lump[2] ▶ **v.** [with obj.] (**lump it**) informal accept or tolerate a disagreeable situation whether one likes it or not: *you can like it or lump it but I've got to work.*
– ORIGIN late 16th cent. (in the sense 'look sulky'): symbolic of displeasure; compare with words such as *dump* and *grump*. The current sense dates from the early 19th cent.

lump·ec·to·my /ˌləmˈpektəmē/ ▶ **n.** (pl. **lumpectomies**) a surgical operation in which a lump is removed from the breast, typically when cancer is present but has not spread.

lum·pen /ˈləmpən, ˈlo͝om-/ ▶ **adj.** (in Marxist contexts) uninterested in revolutionary advancement: *the lumpen public is enveloped in a culture of dependency.* ■ boorish and stupid: *growing ranks of lumpen, uninhibited, denim-clad youth.*
▶ **plural n.** (**the lumpen**) the lumpenproletariat.
– ORIGIN mid 20th cent.: back-formation from **LUMPENPROLETARIAT**.

lum·pen·pro·le·tar·i·at /ˈləmpənˌprōləˈte(ə)rēət, ˈlo͝om-/ ▶ **n.** (esp. in Marxist terminology) the unorganized and unpolitical lower orders of society who are not interested in revolutionary advancement.
– ORIGIN early 20th cent.: from German (a term originally used by Karl Marx), from *Lumpen* 'rag, rogue' + **PROLETARIAT**.

lump·er /ˈləmpər/ ▶ **n. 1** a laborer who unloads cargo.
2 a person (esp. a taxonomist) who attaches more importance to similarities than to differences in classification. Contrasted with **SPLITTER**.

lump·fish /ˈləmpˌfisʜ/ ▶ **n.** (pl. **same** or **lumpfishes**) a North Atlantic lumpsucker, the roe of which is sometimes used as a substitute for caviar.
● *Cyclopterus lumpus*, family Cyclopteridae.
– ORIGIN early 17th cent.: from Middle Low German *lumpen*, Middle Dutch *lompe* + **FISH**[1].

lump·ish /ˈləmpisʜ/ ▶ **adj.** roughly or clumsily formed or shaped: *those large and lumpish hands could produce exquisitely fine work.* ■ (of a person) stupid and lethargic.
– DERIVATIVES **lump·ish·ly adv.**, **lump·ish·ness n.**

lump·suck·er /ˈləmpsəkər/ ▶ **n.** a globular fish of cooler northern waters, typically having a ventral sucker and spiny fins; a lumpfish. ● Family Cyclopteridae: several genera and species.

lump sum ▶ **n.** a single payment made at a particular time, as opposed to a number of smaller payments or installments.

lump·y /ˈləmpē/ ▶ **adj.** (**lumpier**, **lumpiest**) full of or covered with lumps: *he lay on the lumpy mattress.* ■ Nautical (of water) formed by the wind into small waves: *a large lumpy sea.*
– DERIVATIVES **lump·i·ly** /-pəlē/ **adv.**, **lump·i·ness n.**

lump·y jaw ▶ **n.** infection of the jaw with actinomycete bacteria, common in cattle.

Lu·na /ˈlo͞onə/ a series of Soviet moon probes launched in 1959–76. They made the first hard and soft landings on the moon (1959 and 1966).

lu·na·cy /ˈlo͞onəsē/ ▶ **n.** (pl. **lunacies**) the state of being a lunatic; insanity (not in technical use): *it has been suggested that originality demands a degree of lunacy.* ■ extreme folly or eccentricity: *such an economic policy would be sheer lunacy.*
– ORIGIN mid 16th cent. (originally referring to insanity of an intermittent kind attributed to changes of the moon): from **LUNATIC** + **-ACY**.

lu·na moth /ˈlo͞onə/ ▶ **n.** a very large North American moth that has pale green wings with long tails and transparent eyespots bearing crescent-shaped markings. ● *Actias luna*, family Saturniidae.
– ORIGIN late 19th cent.: *luna* from Latin *luna* 'moon' (from its markings).

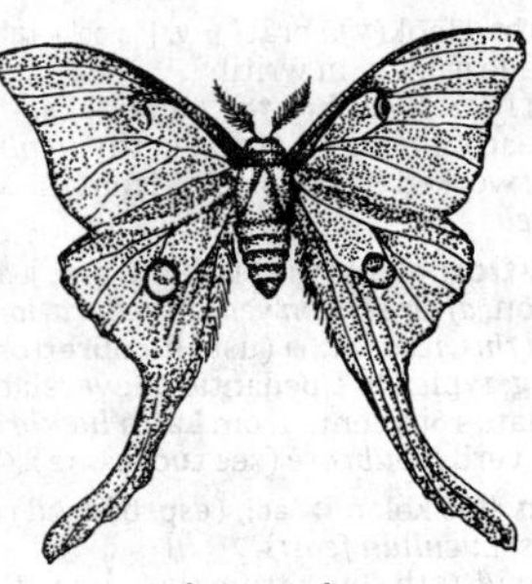
luna moth

lu·nar /ˈlo͞onər/ ▶ **adj.** of, determined by, relating to, or resembling the moon: *a lunar landscape.*
– ORIGIN late Middle English: from Latin *lunaris*, from *luna* 'moon.'

lu·nar caus·tic ▶ **n.** Chemistry, archaic silver nitrate, esp. fused in the form of a stick.
– ORIGIN early 19th cent.: *lunar* in the sense 'containing silver.'

lu·nar cy·cle ▶ **n.** another term for **METONIC CYCLE**.

lu·nar day ▶ **n. 1** the interval of time between two successive crossings of the earth's meridian by the moon (roughly 24 hours and 50 minutes).
2 rare the interval of time between two successive sunrises as seen from the moon.

lu·nar dis·tance ▶ **n.** the angular distance of the moon from the sun, a planet, or a star, used in finding longitude at sea.

lu·nar e·clipse ▶ **n.** an eclipse in which the moon appears darkened as it passes into the earth's shadow.

Lu·nar·i·an /lo͞oˈne(ə)rēən/ ▶ **n.** (in science fiction) an imagined inhabitant of the moon.

lu·nar mod·ule (abbr.: **LM**) ▶ **n.** a small craft used for traveling between the moon's surface and an orbiting spacecraft (formerly known as **lunar excursion module** or **LEM**).

lu·nar month ▶ **n.** a month measured between successive new moons (roughly 29½ days). ■ (in general use) a period of four weeks.

lu·nar node ▶ **n.** Astronomy each of the two points at which the moon's orbit cuts the ecliptic.

lu·nar ob·ser·va·tion ▶ **n. 1** a measurement of the position of the moon in order to calculate longitude from lunar distance.
2 observational study of the moon.

lu·nar rov·ing ve·hi·cle (abbr.: **LRV**) (also **lunar rover**) ▶ **n.** a vehicle designed for use by astronauts on the moon's surface, used on the last three missions of the Apollo project. Also called **MOON BUGGY**.

lu·nar year ▶ **n.** a period of twelve lunar months (approximately 354 days).

lu·nate /ˈlo͞oˌnāt/ ▶ **adj.** crescent-shaped.
▶ **n.** (also **lunate bone**) Anatomy a crescent-shaped carpal bone situated in the center of the wrist and articulating with the radius.
– ORIGIN late 18th cent.: from Latin *lunatus*, from *luna* 'moon.'

lu·na·tic /ˈlo͞onəˌtik/ ▶ **n.** a mentally ill person (not in technical use). ■ an extremely foolish or eccentric person: *this lunatic just accelerated out of the side of the road.*
▶ **adj.** mentally ill (not in technical use). ■ extremely foolish, eccentric, or absurd: *he would be asked to acquiesce in some lunatic scheme.*
– ORIGIN Middle English: from Old French *lunatique*, from late Latin *lunaticus*, from Latin *luna* 'moon' (from the belief that changes of the moon caused intermittent insanity).

lu·na·tic fringe ▶ **n.** an extreme or eccentric minority within society or a group.

lu·na·tion /lo͞oˈnāsʜən/ ▶ **n.** Astronomy another term for **LUNAR MONTH**.
– ORIGIN late Middle English: from medieval Latin *lunatio(n-)*, from Latin *luna* 'moon.'

lunch /ləncʜ/ ▶ **n.** a meal eaten in the middle of the day, typically one that is lighter or less formal than an evening meal: *a vegetarian lunch | do join us for lunch.*
▶ **v.** [no obj.] eat lunch: *he told his wife he was lunching with a client.* ■ [with obj.] take (someone) out for lunch: *public relations people lunch their clients there.*
– PHRASES **do lunch** informal meet for lunch. **out to lunch** informal unaware of or inattentive to present conditions. **there's no such thing as a free lunch** proverb it isn't possible to get something for nothing.

–DERIVATIVES **lunch·er** n.
–ORIGIN early 19th cent.: abbreviation of LUNCHEON.

lunch·box /ˈlənCH,bäks/ ▶ n. a container in which to carry a packed meal. ■ a portable computer slightly larger than a laptop.

lunch·eon /ˈlənCHən/ ▶ n. a formal lunch, or a formal word for lunch.
–ORIGIN late 16th cent. (in the sense 'thick piece, hunk'): possibly an extension of obsolete *lunch* 'thick piece, hunk,' from Spanish *lonja* 'slice.'

lunch·eon·ette /,lənCHəˈnet/ ▶ n. a small, informal restaurant serving lunches.

lunch·meat /ˈlənCH,mēt/ (also **luncheon meat**) ▶ n. meat sold in slices for sandwiches; cold cuts.

lunch pail ▶ n. a lunchbox.
▶ adj. (**lunch-pail**) informal working-class; blue-collar: *lunch-pail labourers.*

lunch·room /ˈlənCH,ro͞om, -,ro͝om/ ▶ n. a room or establishment in which lunch is served or in which it may be eaten; a school or office cafeteria.

lunch·time /ˈlənCH,tīm/ ▶ n. the time in the middle of day when lunch is eaten.

Lund /lo͝ond/ a city in southwestern Sweden, just northeast of Malmö; pop. 107,351 (2008). Its university was founded in 1666.

Lun·da /ˈlo͝ondə, ˈlo͞on-/ ▶ n. (pl. **same** or **Balunda** /bəˈlo͝ondə, -ˈlo͞on-/ or **Lundas**) **1** a member of any of several peoples living mainly in northern Zambia and adjoining parts of the Democratic Republic of the Congo (formerly Zaire) and Angola. From the 16th to 19th centuries, they established a substantial empire in the region.
2 any of several Bantu languages of these peoples, esp. one spoken mainly in northwestern Zambia.
▶ adj. of, relating to, or denoting this people or their language.
–ORIGIN a local name.

Lun·dy /ˈləndē/ **1** a granite island in the Bristol Channel, off the coast of northern Devon.
2 a shipping forecast area covering the Bristol Channel and the eastern Celtic Sea.

lune /lo͞on/ ▶ n. a crescent-shaped figure formed on a sphere or plane by two arcs intersecting at two points. ■ a filled pasta case made from a circle of pasta dough folded over.
–ORIGIN early 18th cent.: from French, from Latin *luna* 'moon.'

lu·nette /lo͞oˈnet/ ▶ n. something crescent-shaped, in particular: ■ an arched aperture or window, esp. one in a domed ceiling. ■ a crescent-shaped or semicircular alcove containing something such as a painting or statue. ■ a fortification with two faces forming a projecting angle, and two flanks. ■ Christian Church a holder for the consecrated host in a monstrance.
–ORIGIN late 16th cent. (denoting a semicircular horseshoe): from French, diminutive of *lune* 'moon,' from Latin *luna.*

lung /ləNG/ ▶ n. each of the pair of organs situated within the rib cage, consisting of elastic sacs with branching passages into which air is drawn, so that oxygen can pass into the blood and carbon dioxide be removed. Lungs are characteristic of vertebrates other than fish, though similar structures are present in some other animal groups.
–DERIVATIVES **lunged** /ləNGd/ adj. [in combination] *strong-lunged*, **lung·ful** /-,fo͝ol/ n. (pl. **lungfuls**), **lung·less** adj.
–ORIGIN Old English *lungen*, of Germanic origin; related to Dutch *long* and German *Lunge*, from an Indo-European root shared by LIGHT²; compare with LIGHTS.

lunge¹ /lənj/ ▶ n. a sudden forward thrust of the body, typically with an arm outstretched to attack someone or seize something: *he made a lunge at her.* ■ the basic attacking move in fencing, in which the leading foot is thrust forward with the knee bent while the back leg remains straightened. ■ an exercise or gymnastic movement resembling the lunge of a fencer.
▶ v. (**lunges, lungeing** or **lunging, lunged**) [no obj.] make a lunge: *the sequined guests lunged at the food* | *John lunged forward and grabbed him by the throat.* ■ [with obj.] make a sudden forward thrust with (a part of the body or a weapon): *Billy lunged his spear at the fish.*
–ORIGIN mid 18th cent.: from earlier *allonge*, from French *allonger* 'lengthen.'

lunge² ▶ n. variant of LONGE.

lunge³ ▶ n. short for MUSKELLUNGE.

lunge·ing cav·es·son ▶ n. another term for CAVESSON.

lung·fish /ˈləNG,fiSH/ ▶ n. (pl. **same** or **lungfishes**) an elongated freshwater fish with one or two sacs that function as lungs, enabling it to breathe air. It lives in poorly oxygenated water and can estivate in mud for long periods to survive drought. ● Subclass Dipnoi: families Ceratodontidae (one Australian species), Lepidosirenidae (one South American species), and Protopteridae (four African species).

lun·gi /ˈlo͝oNGgē/ ▶ n. (pl. **lungis**) a length of cotton cloth worn as a loincloth in India or as a skirt in Burma (Myanmar), where it is the national dress for both sexes.
–ORIGIN Urdu.

lung·worm /ˈləNG,wərm/ ▶ n. a parasitic nematode worm found in the lungs of mammals, esp. farm and domestic animals. ● *Dictyocaulus* and other genera, class Phasmida.

lung·wort /ˈləNG,wərt, -,wôrt/ ▶ n. a bristly herbaceous European plant of the borage family, typically having white-spotted leaves and pink flowers that turn blue as they age. [so named because the leaves were said to have the appearance of a diseased lung.] ● Genus *Pulmonaria*, family Boraginaceae: several species, in particular *P. officinalis.*

lu·ni·so·lar /,lo͞oniˈsōlər/ ▶ adj. of or concerning the combined motions or effects of the sun and moon. ■ of or employing a calendar year divided according to the phases of the moon, but adjusted in average length to fit the length of the solar cycle. ■ of or denoting a 532-year period over which both the lunar months and the days of the week return to the same point in relation to the solar year.
–ORIGIN late 17th cent.: from Latin *luna* 'moon' + SOLAR¹.

lu·ni·tid·al /,lo͞oniˈtīdl/ ▶ adj. denoting the interval between the time at which the moon crosses a meridian and the time of high tide at that meridian.

lunk /ləNGk/ ▶ n. short for LUNKHEAD.

lun·ker /ˈləNGkər/ ▶ n. informal an exceptionally large specimen of something, in particular (among anglers) a fish.
–ORIGIN early 20th cent.: of unknown origin.

lunk·head /ˈləNGk,(h)ed/ ▶ n. informal a slow-witted person.
–DERIVATIVES **lunk·head·ed** adj.
–ORIGIN mid 19th cent.: probably from an alteration of LUMP¹ + HEAD.

lu·nu·la /ˈlo͞onyələ/ ▶ n. (pl. **lunulae** /-,lē, -,lī/) a crescent-shaped object or mark, in particular: ■ the white area at the base of a fingernail. ■ Printing one of a pair of parentheses.
–DERIVATIVES **lu·nu·lar** /-lər/ adj., **lu·nu·late** /-,lāt, -lit/ adj.
–ORIGIN late 16th cent. (denoting a crescent-shaped geometric figure): from Latin, diminutive of *luna* 'moon.'

lu·nule /ˈlo͞on,yo͞ol/ ▶ n. a crescent-shaped or oval part or marking, in particular: ■ an oval depression in front of the beak on the outside of many clams. ■ a small area above the antennae on the front of some kinds of flies.

Lu·o /ˈlo͞o,ō/ ▶ n. (pl. **same** or **Luos**) **1** a member of an East African people of Kenya and the upper Nile valley.
2 the Nilotic language of this people.
▶ adj. of or relating to the Luo or their language.
–ORIGIN the name in Luo.

Luo·yang /ˈlo͞oˈyäNG/ an industrial city in east central China, in Henan province, on the Luo River; pop. 1,065,100 (est. 2006). Between the 4th and 6th centuries AD, the construction of cave temples to the south of the city made it an important Buddhist center. Former name HONAN.

Lu·per·ca·li·a /,lo͞opərˈkālēə, -ˈkālyə/ (also in sing. **Lupercal** /ˈlo͞opər,kal/) ▶ plural n. [usu. treated as sing.] an ancient Roman festival of purification and fertility, held annually on February 15.
–DERIVATIVES **Lu·per·ca·li·an** adj.
–ORIGIN Latin, neuter plural of *lupercalis* 'relating to *Lupercus*,' Roman equivalent of the Greek god Pan.

lu·pine¹ /ˈlo͞opin/ ▶ n. a plant of the pea family, with deeply divided leaves and tall, colorful, tapering spikes of flowers. ● Genus *Lupinus*, family Leguminosae: several species, in particular the popular cultivar **Russell lupine**.
–ORIGIN late Middle English: from Latin *lupinus.*

lu·pine² /ˈlo͞o,pīn/ ▶ adj. of, like, or relating to a wolf or wolves.
–ORIGIN mid 17th cent.: from Latin *lupinus*, from *lupus* 'wolf.'

Lu·pi·no /ləˈpēnō, lo͞o-/, Ida (1918–95), US actress and director; born in England. She starred in *They Drive by Night* (1940), *The Sea Wolf* (1936), and *The Big Knife* (1955). Movies that she both acted in and directed include *The Bigamist* (1953).

lu·pu·lin /ˈlo͞opyəlin/ ▶ n. a bitter, yellowish powder found on glandular hairs beneath the scales of the flowers of the female hop plant.
–ORIGIN early 19th cent.: from the modern Latin use as an epithet of Latin *lupulus* (as in *Humulus lupulus*), a plant mentioned by Pliny and perhaps denoting 'wild hops,' + -IN¹.

Lu·pus /ˈlo͞opəs/ Astronomy a southern constellation (the Wolf), lying partly in the Milky Way between Scorpius and Centaurus. ■ (as genitive **Lupi** /ˈlo͞opī/) used with a preceding letter or numeral to designate a star in this constellation: *the star Delta Lupi.*
–ORIGIN Latin.

lu·pus /ˈlo͞opəs/ ▶ n. any of various diseases or conditions marked by inflammation of the skin, esp. lupus vulgaris or lupus erythematosus.
–DERIVATIVES **lu·poid** /-,poid/ adj., **lu·pous** /-pəs/ adj.
–ORIGIN late 16th cent.: from Latin, literally 'wolf.'

lu·pus er·y·the·ma·to·sus /,erə,THēməˈtōsəs/ ▶ n. an inflammatory autoimmune disease causing scaly red patches on the skin, esp. on the face, and sometimes affecting connective tissue in the internal organs.
–ORIGIN from LUPUS + modern Latin *erythematosus*, from Greek *eruthēma* 'reddening.'

lu·pus vul·ga·ris /,vəlˈge(ə)ris/ ▶ n. chronic direct infection of the skin with tuberculosis, causing dark red patches.
–ORIGIN 1940s: from LUPUS + Latin *vulgaris* 'common.'

lurch¹ /lərCH/ ▶ n. [usu. in sing.] an abrupt uncontrolled movement, esp. an unsteady tilt or roll: *the boat gave a violent lurch, and he missed his footing.*
▶ v. [no obj.] make an abrupt, unsteady, uncontrolled movement or series of movements; stagger: *the car lurched forward* | *Stuart lurched to his feet* | figurative *he was lurching from one crisis to the next.*
–ORIGIN late 17th cent. (as a noun denoting the sudden leaning of a ship to one side): of unknown origin.

lurch² ▶ n. (in phrase **leave someone in the lurch**) leave an associate or friend abruptly and without assistance or support in a difficult situation.
–ORIGIN mid 16th cent. (denoting a state of discomfiture): from French *lourche*, the name of a game resembling backgammon, used in the phrase *demeurer lourche* 'be discomfited.'

lurch·er /ˈlərCHər/ ▶ n. **1** a crossbred dog, typically a retriever, collie, or sheepdog crossed with a greyhound, of a kind originally used for hunting and by poachers for catching rabbits.
2 archaic a prowler, swindler, or petty thief.
–ORIGIN early 16th cent. (sense 2): from obsolete *lurch* 'remain in a place furtively,' variant of LURK.

lur·dan /ˈlərdn/ (also **lurdane**) archaic ▶ n. an idle or incompetent person.
▶ adj. lazy; good-for-nothing.
–ORIGIN Middle English: from Old French *lourdin*, from *lourd* 'heavy,' *lort* 'foolish,' from Latin *luridus* 'lurid.'

lure /lo͝or/ ▶ v. [with obj.] tempt (a person or an animal) to do something or to go somewhere, esp. by offering some form of reward: *the child was lured into a car but managed to escape.*
▶ n. something that tempts or is used to tempt a person or animal to do something: *the film industry always has been a glamorous lure for young girls.* ■ the strongly attractive quality of a person or thing: *the lure of a better-paid job.* ■ a type of bait used in fishing or hunting. ■ Falconry a bunch of feathers with a weighted object attached to a long string, swung around the head of the falconer to recall a hawk.
–ORIGIN Middle English: from Old French *luere*, of Germanic origin; probably related to German *Luder* 'bait.'

Lur·ex /ˈlo͝or,eks/ (also **lurex**) ▶ n. trademark a type of yarn or fabric that incorporates a glittering metallic thread.
–ORIGIN 1940s: of unknown origin.

lu·rid /ˈlo͝orid/ ▶ adj. very vivid in color, esp. so as to create an unpleasantly harsh or unnatural effect: *lurid food colorings* | *a pair of lurid shorts.* ■ (of a description) presented in vividly shocking or sensational terms, esp. giving explicit details of crimes or sexual matters: *the more lurid details of the massacre were too frightening for the children.*
–DERIVATIVES **lu·rid·ly** adv., **lu·rid·ness** n.
–ORIGIN mid 17th cent. (in the sense 'pale and dismal in color'): from Latin *luridus*; related to *luror* 'wan or yellow color.'

lurk /lərk/ ▶ v. [no obj.] (of a person or animal) be or remain hidden so as to wait in ambush for someone or something: *a ruthless killer still lurked in the*

darkness. ■ (of an unpleasant quality) be present in a latent or barely discernible state, although still presenting a threat: *fear lurks beneath the surface* | (as adj. **lurking**) *he lives with a lurking fear of exposure as a fraud.* ■ informal read the postings on an Internet message board or in a chat room without making any contribution oneself.
– ORIGIN Middle English: perhaps from LOUR + the frequentative suffix *-k* (as in *talk*).

lurk·er /ˈlərkər/ ▶ n. a person who lurks, in particular a user of an Internet message board or chat room who does not participate.

Lur·ton /ˈlərtn/, Horace Harmon (1844–1914), US Supreme Court associate justice 1909–14. A judge in the US Court of Appeals 1893–1909, he was appointed to the Court by President Taft.

Lu·sa·ka /lo͞oˈsäkə/ the capital of Zambia; pop. 1,420,000 (est. 2009).

Lu·sa·tian /lo͞oˈsāsHən/ ▶ adj. & n. another term for SORBIAN.

lus·cious /ˈləsHəs/ ▶ adj. (of food or wine) having a pleasingly rich, sweet taste: *a luscious and fragrant dessert wine.* ■ richly verdant or opulent. ■ (of a woman) very sexually attractive.
– DERIVATIVES **lus·cious·ly** adv., **lus·cious·ness** n.
– ORIGIN late Middle English: perhaps an alteration of obsolete *licious*, shortened form of DELICIOUS.

lush[1] /ləsH/ ▶ adj. (of vegetation) growing luxuriantly: *lush greenery and cultivated fields.* ■ very rich and providing great sensory pleasure: *lush orchestrations.* ■ (of a woman) very sexually attractive: *Marianne, with her lush body and provocative green eyes.*
– DERIVATIVES **lush·ly** adv., **lush·ness** n.
– ORIGIN late Middle English: perhaps an alteration of obsolete *lash* 'soft, lax,' from Old French *lasche* 'lax,' by association with LUSCIOUS.

lush[2] informal ▶ n. a heavy drinker, esp. a habitual one. ▶ v. [with obj.] dated make (someone) drunk: *Mr. Hobart got so lushed up he was spilling drinks down his shirt.*
– ORIGIN late 18th cent.: perhaps a humorous use of LUSH[1].

l

Lu·shai /lo͞oˈsHī, ˈlo͞o,sHī/ ▶ n. another name for MIZO (sense 2 of the noun).

Lu·shun /ˈlo͞oˈsHo͝on, ˈlY-/ a port on the Liaodong Peninsula in northeastern China, now part of the urban complex of Luda. It was leased by Russia for use as a Pacific naval port 1898–1905, when it was known as Port Arthur.

Lu·si·ta·ni·a[1] /,lo͞osəˈtānēə, -nyə/ an ancient Roman province on the Iberian peninsula that corresponds to modern Portugal.
– DERIVATIVES **Lu·si·ta·ni·an** adj. & n.

Lu·si·ta·ni·a[2] a Cunard liner that was sunk by a German submarine in the Atlantic in May 1915 with the loss of over 1,000 lives.

lust /ləst/ ▶ n. very strong sexual desire: *he knew that his lust for her had returned.* ■ [in sing.] a passionate desire for something: *a lust for power.* ■ (usu. **lusts**) chiefly Theology a sensual appetite regarded as sinful: *lusts of the flesh.*
▶ v. [no obj.] have a very strong sexual desire for someone: *he really lusted after me in those days.* ■ feel a strong desire for something: *pregnant women lusting for pickles and ice cream.*
– ORIGIN Old English (also in the sense 'pleasure, delight'), of Germanic origin; related to Dutch *lust* and German *Lust.*

lus·ter[1] /ˈləstər/ (Brit. **lustre**) ▶ n. **1** a gentle sheen or soft glow, esp. that of a partly reflective surface: *the luster of the Milky Way* | *she couldn't eat, and her hair lost its luster.* ■ the manner in which the surface of a mineral reflects light. ■ glory or distinction: *a celebrity player to add luster to the lineup.*
2 a thin coating containing unoxidized metal that gives an iridescent glaze to ceramics. ■ ceramics with such a glaze; lusterware: [as modifier] *luster jugs.*
3 a fabric or yarn with a sheen or gloss. ■ Brit. a thin dress material with a cotton warp, woolen weft, and a glossy surface.
4 a prismatic glass pendant on a chandelier or other ornament. ■ a cut-glass chandelier or candelabra.
– ORIGIN early 16th cent.: from French *lustre*, from Italian *lustro*, from the verb *lustrare*, from Latin *lustrare* 'illuminate.'

lus·ter[2] (Brit. **lustre**) ▶ n. another term for LUSTRUM.

lus·tered /ˈləstərd/ ▶ adj. (esp. of ceramics) having an iridescent surface; shining.

lus·ter·less /ˈləstərlis/ (Brit. **lustreless**) ▶ adj. not bright or shiny; dull: *a lusterless complexion.*

lus·ter·ware /ˈləstər,wer/ (Brit. **lustreware**) ▶ n. ceramic articles with an iridescent metallic glaze.

lust·ful /ˈləs(t)fəl/ ▶ adj. having or showing strong feelings of sexual desire: *lustful glances.*
– DERIVATIVES **lust·ful·ly** /-(t)fəlē/ adv., **lust·ful·ness** /-(t)fəlnəs/ n.

lust·i·ly /ˈləstəlē/ ▶ adv. in a strong, healthy, vigorous way; heartily: *fans cheered lustily.*

lus·tra /ˈləstrə/ plural form of LUSTRUM.

lus·tral /ˈləstrəl/ ▶ adj. relating to or used in ceremonial purification.
– ORIGIN mid 16th cent.: from Latin *lustralis*, from *lustrum* (see LUSTRUM).

lus·trate /ˈləs,trāt/ ▶ v. [with obj.] rare purify by expiatory sacrifice, ceremonial washing, or some other ritual action: *a soul lustrated in the baptismal waters.*
– DERIVATIVES **lus·tra·tion** /,ləsˈtrāsHən/ n.
– ORIGIN early 17th cent.: from Latin *lustrat-* 'purified by lustral rites,' from the verb *lustrare*, from *lustrum* (see LUSTRUM).

lus·tre /ˈləstər/ ▶ n. British spelling of LUSTER[1], LUSTER[2].

lus·tre·ware /ˈləstər,wer/ ▶ n. British spelling of LUSTERWARE.

lust·ring /ˈləstriNG/ ▶ n. variant spelling of LUTESTRING.

lus·trous /ˈləstrəs/ ▶ adj. having luster; shining: *large, lustrous eyes.*
– DERIVATIVES **lus·trous·ly** adv., **lus·trous·ness** n.

lus·trum /ˈləstrəm/ ▶ n. (pl. **lustra** /-trə/ or **lustrums**) chiefly literary historical a period of five years.
– ORIGIN late 16th cent.: from Latin, originally denoting a purificatory sacrifice after a quinquennial census.

lust·y /ˈləstē/ ▶ adj. (**lustier, lustiest**) healthy and strong; full of vigor: *the other farms had lusty young sons to work the land* | *lusty singing.*
– DERIVATIVES **lust·i·ness** n.
– ORIGIN Middle English: from LUST (in the early sense 'vigor') + -Y[1].

lu·sus na·tu·rae /ˈlo͞osəs nəˈt(y)o͝orē, -ˈt(y)o͝or,ī/ ▶ n. (pl. **same** or **lususes naturae**) rare a freak of nature.
– ORIGIN Latin, literally 'a sport of nature.'

lu·ta·nist ▶ n. variant spelling of LUTENIST.

lute[1] /lo͞ot/ ▶ n. a plucked stringed instrument with a long neck bearing frets and a rounded body with a flat front that is shaped like a halved egg.
– ORIGIN Middle English: from Old French *lut, leut*, probably via Provençal from Arabic *al-ʿūd.*

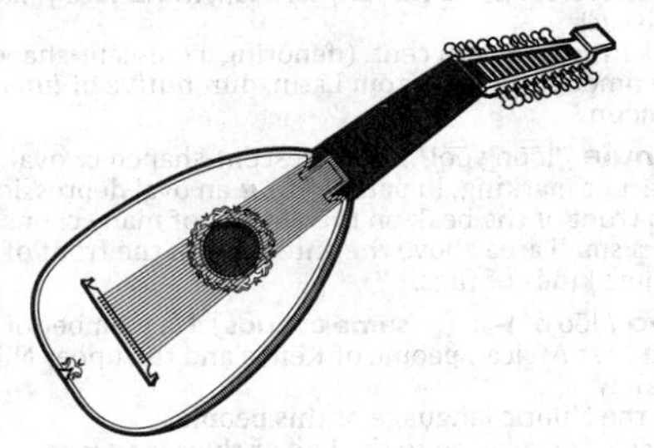

lute[1]

lute[2] ▶ n. (also **luting**) liquid clay or cement used to seal a joint, coat a crucible, or protect a graft.
▶ v. [with obj.] seal, join, or coat with lute.
– ORIGIN late Middle English: from Old French *lut* or medieval Latin *lutum*, a special use of Latin *lutum* 'potter's clay.'

lu·te·al /ˈlo͞otēəl/ ▶ adj. Anatomy of or relating to the corpus luteum.

lu·te·fisk /ˈlo͞otə,fisk/ ▶ n. a Scandinavian dish prepared by soaking dried cod in lye to tenderize it, then skinning, boning, and boiling the fish to a gelatinous consistency.

lu·te·in /ˈlo͞otēən, ˈlo͞o,tēn/ ▶ n. Biochemistry a deep yellow pigment of the xanthophyll class, found in the leaves of plants, in egg yolk, and in the corpus luteum.
– ORIGIN mid 19th cent.: from Latin *luteum* 'yolk of egg' (neuter of *luteus* 'yellow') + -IN[1].

lu·te·in·iz·ing hor·mone /ˈlo͞otēə,nīziNG, ˈlo͞otn,īziNG/ ▶ n. Biochemistry a hormone secreted by the anterior pituitary gland that stimulates ovulation in females and the synthesis of androgen in males.

lu·te·nist /ˈlo͞otn-ist, ˈlo͞otnist/ (also **lutanist**) ▶ n. a lute player.
– ORIGIN early 17th cent.: from medieval Latin *lutanista*, from *lutana* 'lute.'

luteo- ▶ comb. form **1** orange-colored: *luteofulvous.* **2** relating to the corpus luteum: *luteotrophic.*
– ORIGIN from Latin *luteus* (or neuter *luteum*) 'yellow.'

lu·te·o·trop·ic hor·mone /,lo͞otēəˈtrōpik, -ˈträpik/ (also **luteotrophic hormone** /-ˈträfik, -ˈtrō-/) ▶ n. another term for PROLACTIN.

lute·string /ˈlo͞ot,striNG/ (also **lustrine** /ˈləstrēn/ or **lustring** /ˈləstriNG/) ▶ n. historical a glossy silk fabric, or a satin-weave fabric resembling it.
– ORIGIN late 17th cent.: from French *lustrine* or from Italian *lustrino*, from *lustro* 'luster.'

Lu·te·tia /lo͞oˈtēsH(ē)ə/ Roman name for PARIS[1].

lu·te·ti·um /lo͞oˈtēsH(ē)əm/ ▶ n. the chemical element of atomic number 71, a rare silvery-white metal of the lanthanide series. (Symbol: **Lu**)
– ORIGIN early 20th cent.: from French *lutécium*, from Latin *Lutetia*, the ancient name of Paris, the home of its discoverer.

Lu·ther /ˈlo͞oTHər/, Martin (1483–1546), German theologian; the principal figure of the German Reformation. He preached the doctrine of justification by faith rather than by works and railed against the sale of indulgences and papal authority.

Martin Luther

Lu·ther·an /ˈlo͞oTH(ə)rən/ ▶ n. a follower of Martin Luther. ■ a member of the Lutheran Church.
▶ adj. of or characterized by the theology of Martin Luther. ■ of or relating to the Lutheran Church.
– DERIVATIVES **Lu·ther·an·ism** /-,nizəm/ n., **Lu·ther·an·ize** /-,nīz/ v.

Lu·ther·an Church the Protestant Church accepting the Augsburg Confession of 1530, with justification by faith alone as a cardinal doctrine. The Lutheran Church is the largest Protestant body worldwide, with substantial membership in Germany, Scandinavia, and the US.

lu·thern /ˈlo͞oTHərn/ ▶ n. old-fashioned term for DORMER.
– ORIGIN mid 17th cent.: perhaps an alteration of earlier *lucarne* 'skylight,' from Old French.

lu·thi·er /ˈlo͞otēər/ ▶ n. a maker of stringed instruments such as violins or guitars.
– ORIGIN late 19th cent.: from French, from *luth* 'lute.'

Lu·thu·li /lo͞oˈto͞olē/ (also **Lutuli**), Albert John (*c.*1898–1967), South African political leader. His presidency of the African National Congress 1952–60 was marked by a program of civil disobedience. Nobel Peace Prize (1960).

lut·ing /ˈlo͞otiNG/ ▶ n. see LUTE[2].

lu·ti·no /lo͞oˈtēnō/ ▶ n. (pl. **lutinos**) [often as modifier] a bird (esp. a bird of the parrot family that is often kept as a pet) with more yellow in the plumage than is usual for the species.
– ORIGIN early 20th cent.: from Latin *luteus* 'yellow' + *-ino*, on the pattern of *albino.*

lut·ist /ˈlo͞otist/ ▶ n. a lute player. ■ a maker of lutes; a luthier.

Lu·ton /ˈlo͞otn/ an industrial town northwest of London; pop. 167,000.

Lutsk /lo͞otsk/ (Polish name **Łuck**) a river port and industrial city in northwestern Ukraine, on the Styr River; pop. 209,300 (est. 2009).

Lut·yens[1] /ˈlətyenz/, Sir Edwin Landseer (1869–1944), English architect. He is particularly known for his open garden-city layout in New Delhi in 1912 and for the Cenotaph in London (1919–21).

Lut·yens[2] Elisabeth (1906–83), English composer; full name *Agnes Elisabeth Lutyens*; the daughter of Sir Edwin Lutyens. She was one of the first English composers to use the 12-note system.

lutz /ləts, lo͞ots/ (also **Lutz**) ▶ n. Figure Skating a jump with a backward takeoff from the backward outside edge of one skate to the backward outside edge of the other, with one or more full turns in the air.
– ORIGIN 1930s: probably from the name of Gustave *Lussi* (born 1898), who invented it.

luv /ləv/ ▶ **n. & v.** nonstandard spelling of LOVE (representing informal or dialect use).

Lu·va·le /lo͞oˈvälā/ ▶ **n.** (pl. **same**) **1** a member of a people living mainly in eastern Angola and western Democratic Republic of the Congo (formerly Zaire).
2 the Bantu language of this people, with around 600,000 speakers. Also called LWENA.
▶ **adj.** of or relating to this people or their language.

luv·vy /ˈləvē/ (also **luvvie**) ▶ **n.** (pl. **luvvies**) Brit. informal, often derogatory an actor or actress, esp. one who is particularly effusive or affected.

Lu·wi·an /ˈlo͞o-ēən/ (also **Luvian** /-vēən/) ▶ **n.** an Anatolian language of the 2nd millennium BC. It is recorded in both cuneiform and hieroglyphic scripts and may have been the language spoken in Troy at the time of the Homeric war.
– ORIGIN from *Luwia*, part of Asia Minor, + -AN.

lux /ləks/ (abbr.: **lx**) ▶ **n.** (pl. **same**) the SI unit of illuminance, equal to one lumen per square meter.
– ORIGIN late 19th cent.: from Latin, literally 'light.'

lux·ate /ˈlək,sāt/ ▶ **v.** [with obj.] Medicine dislocate.
– DERIVATIVES **lux·a·tion** /,ləkˈsāsнən/ **n.**
– ORIGIN early 17th cent.: from Latin *luxat-* 'dislocated,' from the verb *luxare*, from *luxus* 'out of joint.'

luxe /ləks, lo͝oks/ ▶ **adj.** expensive and of high quality; luxurious: *the luxe 65-room Four Seasons hotel.*
▶ **n.** luxury.
– ORIGIN mid 16th cent.: from French, from Latin *luxus* 'abundance.'

Lux·em·bourg /ˈləksəmbərg, ˈlo͝oksəm,bo͝ork/ a country in western Europe, between Belgium and Germany and north of France; pop. 491,800 (est. 2009); capital, Luxembourg; official languages, Luxemburgish, French, and German. ■ the capital of the Grand Duchy of Luxembourg; pop. 88,600 (est. 2009). It is the seat of the European Court of Justice. ■ a province in southeastern Belgium; capital, Arlon.

> Annexed by France in 1795, Luxembourg became an independent grand duchy as a result of the Treaty of Vienna in 1815. It formed a customs union with Belgium in 1922, which was extended in 1948 into the Benelux Customs Union with the Netherlands. It was a founding member of the EEC in 1957.

– DERIVATIVES **Lux·em·bourg·er n.**

Lux·em·burg /ˈləksəmbərg, ˈlo͝oksəm,bo͝ork/, Rosa (1871–1919), German revolutionary leader, born in Poland. Together with the German socialist **Karl Liebknecht** /ˈlēpknekнt/ (1871–1919), she founded the Spartacus League in 1916 and the German Communist Party in 1918.

Lux·em·burg·ish /ˈləksəm,bərgisн, ˈlo͝oksəm,bo͝or-/ ▶ **n.** the local language of Luxembourg, a form of German with a strong admixture of French. Also called LETZEBURGESCH.

Lux·or /ˈlək,sôr, ˈlo͝ok-/ a city in eastern Egypt, on the eastern bank of the Nile River; pop. 202,200 (est. 2006). The site of ancient Thebes, it contains the ruins of a temple built by Amenhotep III and of monuments erected by Ramses II. Arabic name EL-UQSUR.
– ORIGIN from Arabic *al-uqṣur* 'the castles.'

lux·u·ri·ant /,ləgˈzно͝orēənt, ,ləkˈsно͝or-/ ▶ **adj.** (of vegetation) rich and profuse in growth; lush: *forests of dark, luxuriant foliage* | figurative *luxuriant prose.* ■ (of hair) thick and healthy.
– DERIVATIVES **lux·u·ri·ance n., lux·u·ri·ant·ly adv.**
– ORIGIN mid 16th cent.: from Latin *luxuriant-* 'growing rankly,' from the verb *luxuriare*, from *luxuria* 'luxury, rankness.'

> **USAGE** See usage at LUXURIOUS.

lux·u·ri·ate /,ləgˈzно͝orē,āt, ,ləkˈsно͝or-/ ▶ **v.** [no obj.] (often **luxuriate in**) enjoy oneself in a luxurious way; take self-indulgent delight: *she was luxuriating in a long bath.*
– ORIGIN early 17th cent.: from Latin *luxuriat-* 'grown in abundance,' from the verb *luxuriare*.

lux·u·ri·ous /,ləgˈzно͝orēəs, ,ləkˈsно͝or-/ ▶ **adj.** extremely comfortable, elegant, or enjoyable, esp. in a way that involves great expense: *the bedrooms have luxurious marble bathrooms* | *many of the leadership led relatively luxurious lives.* ■ giving self-indulgent or sensuous pleasure: *a luxurious wallow in a scented bath.*
– DERIVATIVES **lux·u·ri·ous·ly adv., lux·u·ri·ous·ness n.**
– ORIGIN Middle English (in the sense 'lascivious'): from Old French *luxurios*, from Latin *luxuriosus*, from *luxuria* 'luxury.'

> **USAGE** Luxuriant and luxurious are sometimes confused. **Luxuriant** means 'lush, profuse, prolific': *forests of dark luxuriant foliage; luxuriant black eyelashes.* **Luxurious**, a much more common word, means 'supplied with luxuries, extremely comfortable': *a luxurious mansion.*

lux·u·ry /ˈləksн(ə)rē, ˈləgzн(ə)-/ ▶ **n.** (pl. **luxuries**) the state of great comfort and extravagant living: *he lived a life of luxury.* ■ an inessential, desirable item that is expensive or difficult to obtain: *luxuries like raspberry vinegar and state-of-the-art CD players* | *he considers bananas a luxury.*
▶ **adj.** luxurious or of the nature of a luxury: *a luxury yacht* | *luxury goods.*
– ORIGIN Middle English (denoting lechery): from Old French *luxurie, luxure*, from Latin *luxuria*, from *luxus* 'excess.' The earliest current sense dates from the mid 17th cent.

Lu·zon /lo͞oˈzän/ the largest and most northern island in the Philippines. Its chief towns are Quezon City and Manila, which is the country's capital.

lv. ▶ **abbr.** leave or leaves.

Lviv /ləˈvēf, ləˈvēo͞o/ an industrial city in western Ukraine, near the border with Poland; pop. 734,500 (est. 2009). Russian name **Lvov**. Polish name **Lwów**. German name LEMBERG.

LVN ▶ **abbr.** licensed vocational nurse.

lwei /ləˈwā/ ▶ **n.** (pl. **same**) a monetary unit of Angola, equal to one hundredth of a kwanza.
– ORIGIN a local word.

Lwe·na /ləˈwānə/ ▶ **n.** another term for LUVALE.

LWM ▶ **abbr.** low-water mark.

L-word ▶ **n.** informal, humorous used in place of such words as "liberal," "lesbian," and "love," in contexts where the word is regarded as having negative or taboo connotations.
– ORIGIN on the pattern of *F-word*.

Lwów /ləˈvôf, -ˈvôv/ Polish name for LVIV.

LWV ▶ **abbr.** League of Women Voters.

lx ▶ **abbr.** Physics lux.

LXX ▶ **symbol** Septuagint.
– ORIGIN special use of the Roman numeral for 70.

-ly[1] /lē/ ▶ **suffix** forming adjectives meaning: **1** having the qualities of: *brotherly* | *rascally.*
2 recurring at intervals of: *hourly* | *quarterly.*
– ORIGIN Old English *-līc*, of Germanic origin; related to LIKE[1].

-ly[2] ▶ **suffix** forming adverbs from adjectives, chiefly denoting manner or degree: *greatly* | *happily* | *pointedly.*
– ORIGIN Old English *-līce*, of Germanic origin.

Lyall·pur /ˈlīl,po͝or/ former name (until 1979) for FAISALABAD.

ly·ase /ˈlī,ās, -,āz/ ▶ **n.** Biochemistry an enzyme that catalyzes the joining of specified molecules or groups by a double bond.

ly·cae·nid /līˈsēnid/ ▶ **n.** Entomology a small butterfly of a family (Lycaenidae) that includes the blues, coppers, hairstreaks, and arguses.
– ORIGIN late 19th cent.: from modern Latin *Lycaenidae* (plural), from the genus name *Lycaena*, apparently from Greek *lukaina* 'she-wolf.'

ly·can·thrope /ˈlīkən,тнrōp/ ▶ **n.** a werewolf.
– ORIGIN early 17th cent.: from modern Latin *lycanthropus*, from Greek *lukanthrōpos* 'wolf man' (see LYCANTHROPY).

ly·can·thro·py /līˈkanтнrəpē/ ▶ **n.** the supernatural transformation of a person into a wolf, as recounted in folk tales. ■ archaic a form of madness involving the delusion of being an animal, usually a wolf, with correspondingly altered behavior.
– DERIVATIVES **ly·can·throp·ic** /,līkənˈтнräpik/ **adj.**
– ORIGIN late 16th cent. (as a supposed form of madness): from modern Latin *lycanthropia*, from Greek *lukanthrōpia*, from *lukos* 'wolf' + *anthrōpos* 'human being, man.'

ly·cée /lēˈsā/ ▶ **n.** (pl. pronunc. **same**) a secondary school in France that is funded by the government.
– ORIGIN French, from Latin *lyceum* (see LYCEUM).

Ly·ce·um /līˈsēəm/ the garden at Athens in which Aristotle taught philosophy. ■ (**the Lyceum**) Aristotelian philosophy and its followers. ■ (**a lyceum**) archaic a literary institution, lecture hall, or teaching place.
– ORIGIN via Latin from Greek *Lukeion*, neuter of *Lukeios*, epithet of Apollo (from whose neighboring temple the Lyceum was named).

ly·chee /ˈlēcнē/ ▶ **n.** variant spelling of LITCHI.

lych·gate /ˈlicн,gāt/ (also **lichgate**) ▶ **n.** a roofed gateway to a churchyard, formerly used during burials for sheltering a coffin until the clergyman's arrival.
– ORIGIN late 15th cent.: from Old English *līc* 'body' + GATE.

lych·nis /ˈliknis/ ▶ **n.** a plant of a genus that includes the campions and a number of cultivated ornamental flowers. ● Genus *Lychnis*, family Caryophyllaceae.
– ORIGIN modern Latin, via Latin from Greek *lukhnis*, denoting a red flower, from *lukhnos* 'lamp.'

Ly·cia /ˈlisн(ē)ə/ an ancient region on the coast of southwestern Asia Minor, between Caria and Pamphylia.
– DERIVATIVES **Ly·ci·an adj. & n.**

ly·co·pene /ˈlīkə,pēn/ ▶ **n.** Biochemistry a red carotenoid pigment present in tomatoes and many berries and fruits.
– ORIGIN 1930s: from the variant *lycopin* (from modern Latin *Lycopersicon*, a genus name including the tomato) + -ENE.

ly·co·pod /ˈlīkə,päd/ ▶ **n.** Botany a club moss, esp. a lycopodium. Giant lycopods the size of trees were common in the Carboniferous period. ● Class Lycopsida: several families.
– ORIGIN mid 19th cent.: anglicized form of LYCOPODIUM.

ly·co·po·di·um /,līkəˈpōdēəm/ ▶ **n.** a plant of a genus that includes the common club mosses. ● Genus *Lycopodium*, family Lycopodiaceae. ■ (usu. **lycopodium powder** or **lycopodium seed**) a fine, flammable powder consisting of club moss spores, formerly used as an absorbent in surgery, in experiments in the physical sciences, and in making fireworks.
– ORIGIN modern Latin, from Greek *lukos* 'wolf' + *pous, pod-* 'foot' (because of the clawlike shape of the root).

Ly·cop·si·da /līˈkäpsədə/ Botany a class of pteridophyte plants that comprises the club mosses and their extinct relatives.
– DERIVATIVES **ly·cop·sid** /-sid/ **n. & adj.**
– ORIGIN modern Latin (plural), from Greek *lukos* 'wolf' + *opsis* 'appearance.'

Ly·cra /ˈlīkrə/ ▶ **n.** trademark an elastic polyurethane fiber or fabric used esp. for close-fitting sports clothing.

Ly·cur·gus /līˈkərgəs/ (9th century BC), Spartan lawmaker. He is traditionally held to have been the founder of the constitution and military regime of ancient Sparta.

lydd·ite /ˈlid,īt/ ▶ **n.** chiefly historical a high explosive containing picric acid, used chiefly by the British during World War I.
– ORIGIN late 19th cent.: named after *Lydd*, a town in Kent, England, where the explosive was first tested, + -ITE[1].

Lyd·gate /ˈlid,gāt, -git/, John (*c.*1370–*c.*1450), English poet and monk.

Lyd·i·a /ˈlidēə/ an ancient region of western Asia Minor, south of Mysia and north of Caria. It became a powerful kingdom in the 7th century BC but in 546 Croesus, its last king, was defeated by Cyrus and it was absorbed into the Persian empire.

Lyd·i·an /ˈlidēən/ ▶ **n.** **1** a native or inhabitant of Lydia.
2 the Anatolian language of the Lydians, of which some inscriptions and other texts have survived in a version of the Greek alphabet.
▶ **adj.** of or relating to the Lydians or their language.

Lyd·i·an mode ▶ **n.** Music the mode represented by the natural diatonic scale F–F (containing an augmented 4th).

lye /lī/ ▶ **n.** a strongly alkaline solution, esp. of potassium hydroxide, used for washing or cleansing.
– ORIGIN Old English *lēag*, of Germanic origin: related to Dutch *loog*, German *Lauge*, also to LATHER.

Ly·ell /ˈlī(ə)l/, Sir Charles (1797–1875), Scottish geologist. He held that the Earth's features were shaped over a long period of time by natural processes.

ly·ing[1] /ˈlī-ing/ present participle of LIE[1].

ly·ing[2] present participle of LIE[2].
▶ **adj.** not telling the truth: *he's a lying, cheating, snake in the grass.*
– DERIVATIVES **ly·ing·ly adv.**

ly·ing-in ▶ **n.** archaic seclusion before and after childbirth; confinement.

Ly·ly /ˈlilē/, John (*c.*1554–1606), English prose writer and playwright. His prose romance in two parts, *Euphues, The Anatomy of Wit* (1578) and *Euphues and His England* (1580), was written in a style that became known as *euphuism*.

Ly·man se·ries /ˈlīmən/ Physics a series of lines in the ultraviolet spectrum of atomic hydrogen, between 122 and 91 nanometers.
– ORIGIN early 20th cent.: named after Theodore *Lyman* (1874–1954), American physicist.

Lyme /līm/ a town in southeastern Connecticut, on the Connecticut River, that gave its name to Lyme disease. Pop. 2,077 (est. 2008).

Lyme dis·ease /līm/ ▶ **n.** an inflammatory disease characterized at first by a rash, headache, fever, and chills, and later by possible arthritis and neurological and cardiac disorders, caused by bacteria that are transmitted by ticks. ● Lyme disease is caused by the spirochete *Borrelia burgdorferi*.
– ORIGIN 1970s: named after *Lyme*, Connecticut, where an outbreak occurred.

lymph /limf/ ▶ **n. 1** Physiology a colorless fluid containing white blood cells, that bathes the tissues and drains through the lymphatic system into the bloodstream. ■ fluid exuding from a sore or inflamed tissue.
2 literary pure water.
– DERIVATIVES **lymph·ous** /-fəs/ **adj.**
– ORIGIN late 16th cent. (sense 2): from French *lymphe* or Latin *lympha*, *limpa* 'water.'

lymph- ▶ **comb. form** variant spelling of LYMPHO- shortened before a vowel, as in *lymphangiography*.

lym·phad·e·ni·tis /ˌlimˌfadnˈītis/ ▶ **n.** Medicine inflammation of the lymph nodes.

lym·phad·e·nop·a·thy /ˌlimˌfadnˈäpəTHē/ ▶ **n.** Medicine a disease affecting the lymph nodes.

lym·phan·gi·og·ra·phy /ˌlimˌfanjēˈägrəfē/ ▶ **n.** Medicine X-ray examination of the vessels of the lymphatic system after injection of a substance opaque to X-rays.
– DERIVATIVES **lym·phan·gi·o·gram** /limˈfanjēəˌgram/ **n.**, **lym·phan·gi·o·graph·ic** /-jēəˈgrafik/ **adj.**

lym·phan·gi·tis /ˌlimˌfanˈjītis/ ▶ **n.** Medicine inflammation of the walls of the lymphatic vessels.

lym·phat·ic /limˈfatik/ ▶ **adj. 1** [attrib.] Physiology of or relating to lymph or its secretion: *lymphatic vessels* | *lymphatic drainage*.
2 archaic (of a person) pale, flabby, or sluggish.
▶ **n.** Anatomy a veinlike vessel conveying lymph in the body.
– ORIGIN mid 17th cent. (in the sense 'frenzied, mad'): from Latin *lymphaticus* 'mad,' from Greek *numpholēptos* 'seized by nymphs'; now associated with LYMPH, on the pattern of words such as *spermatic*.

lym·phat·ic sys·tem ▶ **n.** the network of vessels through which lymph drains from the tissues into the blood.

lymph gland ▶ **n.** less technical term for LYMPH NODE.

lymph node ▶ **n.** Physiology each of a number of small swellings in the lymphatic system where lymph is filtered and lymphocytes are formed.

lympho- (also **lymph-** before a vowel) ▶ **comb. form** representing LYMPH: *lymphocyte*.

lym·pho·blast /ˈlimfəˌblast/ ▶ **n.** Medicine an abnormal cell resembling a large lymphocyte, produced in large numbers in a form of leukemia.
– DERIVATIVES **lym·pho·blas·tic** /ˌlimfəˈblastik/ **adj.**

lym·pho·cyte /ˈlimfəˌsīt/ ▶ **n.** Physiology a form of small leukocyte (white blood cell) with a single round nucleus, occurring esp. in the lymphatic system.
– DERIVATIVES **lym·pho·cyt·ic** /ˌlimfəˈsitik/ **adj.**

lym·phog·ra·phy /limˈfägrəfē/ ▶ **n.** short for LYMPHANGIOGRAPHY.

lym·phoid /ˈlimˌfoid/ ▶ **adj.** Anatomy & Medicine of, relating to, or denoting the tissue responsible for producing lymphocytes and antibodies. This tissue occurs in the lymph nodes, thymus, tonsils, and spleen, and dispersed elsewhere in the body.

lym·pho·kine /ˈlimfəˌkīn/ ▶ **n.** Physiology a substance produced by lymphocytes, such as interferon, that acts upon other cells of the immune system, e.g., by activating macrophages.
– ORIGIN 1960s: from LYMPHO- + Greek *kinein* 'to move.'

lym·pho·ma /limˈfōmə/ ▶ **n.** (pl. **lymphomas** or **lymphomata** /-mətə/) Medicine cancer of the lymph nodes.

lym·pho·re·tic·u·lar /ˌlimfōriˈtikyələr/ ▶ **adj.** another term for RETICULOENDOTHELIAL.

lym·pho·tox·in /ˌlimfəˈtäksin/ ▶ **n.** Immunology a lymphokine that causes the destruction of certain cells, esp. tumor cells.

lynch /linCH/ ▶ **v.** [with obj.] (of a mob) kill (someone), esp. by hanging, for an alleged offense with or without a legal trial.
– DERIVATIVES **lynch·er n.**
– ORIGIN mid 19th cent.: from *Lynch's law*, early form of *lynch law* 'the practice of killing an alleged criminal by lynching,' named after Capt. William *Lynch*, head of a self-constituted judicial tribunal in Virginia *c.*1780.

Lynch·burg /ˈlinCHˌbərg/ a city in west central Virginia, near the Blue Ridge Mountains; pop. 72,596 (est. 2008).

lynch mob ▶ **n.** a band of people intent on lynching someone.

lynch·pin /ˈlinCHˌpin/ ▶ **n.** variant spelling of LINCHPIN.

Lynn¹ /lin/ a city in northeastern Massachusetts, on Massachusetts Bay, northeast of Boston; pop. 86,957 (est. 2008).

Lynn², Loretta (1935–), US country singer and songwriter; born *Loretta Webb*. She had hits with songs such as "Honky Tonk Girl" (1960), "Don't Come Home A-Drinkin' (With Loving on Your Mind)" (1966), and "Coal Miner's Daughter" (1970). Her life was recounted in the movie *Coal Miner's Daughter* (1980). Country Music Hall of Fame (1988).

Lynx /liNGks/ Astronomy an inconspicuous northern constellation (the Lynx), between Ursa Major and Gemini. ■ (as genitive **Lyncis** /ˈlinsis/) used with a preceding letter or numeral to designate a star in this constellation: *the star Alpha Lyncis*.
– ORIGIN via Latin from Greek *lunx*.

lynx /liNGks/ ▶ **n.** a wild cat with yellowish-brown fur (sometimes spotted), a short tail, and tufted ears, found chiefly in the northern latitudes of North America and Eurasia. ● Genus *Felis*, family Felidae: the **Eurasian lynx** (*L. lynx*) and the **Canadian lynx** (*L. canadensis* or *L. lynx*). ■ the fur of the lynx.
■ **(African lynx)** see CARACAL.
– ORIGIN Middle English: via Latin from Greek *lunx*.

Eurasian lynx

lynx-eyed ▶ **adj.** keen-sighted.

ly·o·cell /ˈlīəˌsel/ ▶ **n.** trademark a strong synthetic fiber made from reconstituted cellulose, used in carpets and in apparel when blended with other fibers.
– ORIGIN 1990s: probably from Greek *luein* 'loosen' + *cell* as in CELLULOSE.

Ly·on /ˈlīən/, Mary Mason (1797–1849), US educator. She founded Mount Holyoke Female Seminary (later Mount Holyoke College) in South Hadley, Massachusetts, in 1837 and served as its first president 1837–49.

ly·on·naise /ˌlīəˈnāz/ ▶ **adj.** (of food, esp. sliced potatoes) cooked with onions or with a white wine and onion sauce.
– ORIGIN French, 'characteristic of the city of Lyons.'

Ly·ons /lēˈôN, ˈlīənz/ an industrial city and river port in southeastern France, situated at the confluence of the Rhône and Saône rivers; pop. 480,778 (2006). Founded by the Romans in AD 43 as Lugdunum, it was an important city of Roman Gaul. French name LYON.

ly·o·phil·ic /ˌlīəˈfilik/ ▶ **adj.** Chemistry (of a colloid) readily dispersed by a solvent and not easily precipitated.
– ORIGIN early 20th cent.: from Greek *luein* 'loosen, dissolve' + *philos* 'loving.'

ly·oph·i·lize /līˈäfəˌlīz/ ▶ **v.** [with obj.] technical freeze-dry (a substance).
– DERIVATIVES **ly·oph·i·li·za·tion** /-ˌäfələˈzāshən, -ˌlīˈzā-/ **n.**

ly·o·pho·bic /ˌlīəˈfōbik/ ▶ **adj.** Chemistry (of a colloid) not lyophilic.

Lyo·tard /ˌlēəˈtär/, Jean-François (1924–1998), French philosopher and literary critic. He outlined his "philosophy of desire," based on the politics of Nietzsche, in *L'Économie libidinale* (1974). In later works, he adopted a postmodern quasi-Wittgensteinian linguistic philosophy.

lyr. ▶ **abbr.** lyric.

Ly·ra /ˈlīrə/ Astronomy a small northern constellation (the Lyre), said to represent the lyre invented by Hermes. It contains the bright star Vega. ■ (as genitive **Lyrae** /ˈlīrē/) used with a preceding letter or numeral to designate a star in this constellation: *the star Beta Lyrae*.
– ORIGIN Latin.

lyre /līr/ ▶ **n.** a stringed instrument like a small U-shaped harp with strings fixed to a crossbar, used esp. in ancient Greece. Modern instruments of this type are found mainly in East Africa.
– ORIGIN Middle English: via Old French *lire* and Latin *lyra* from Greek *lura*.

lyre

lyre·bird /ˈlīrˌbərd/ ▶ **n.** a large Australian songbird, the male of which has a long, lyre-shaped tail and is noted for his remarkable song and display.
● Family Menuridae and genus *Menura*: two species, in particular the **superb lyrebird** (*M. novaehollandiae*).

lyr·ic /ˈlirik/ ▶ **adj. 1** (of poetry) expressing the writer's emotions, usually briefly and in stanzas or recognized forms. ■ (of a poet) writing in this manner.
2 (of a singing voice) using a light register: *a lyric soprano with a light, clear timbre*.
▶ **n.** (usu. **lyrics**) **1** a lyric poem or verse. ■ lyric poetry as a literary genre.
2 the words of a song: *she has published both music and lyrics for a number of songs*.
– ORIGIN late 16th cent.: from French *lyrique* or Latin *lyricus*, from Greek *lurikos*, from *lura* 'lyre.'

lyr·i·cal /ˈlirikəl/ ▶ **adj. 1** (of literature, art, or music) expressing the writer's emotions in an imaginative and beautiful way: *the poet's combination of lyrical and descriptive power*. ■ (of poetry or a poet) lyric: *Wordsworth's Lyrical Ballads*.
2 of or relating to the words of a popular song: *the lyrical content of his songs*.
– PHRASES **wax lyrical** talk in a highly enthusiastic and effusive way: *waxing lyrical about his splendid son-in-law*.
– DERIVATIVES **lyr·i·cal·ly** /-ik(ə)lē/ **adv.**

lyr·i·cism /ˈlirəˌsizəm/ ▶ **n.** an artist's expression of emotion in an imaginative and beautiful way; the quality of being lyrical.

lyr·i·cist /ˈlirəsist/ ▶ **n.** a person who writes the words to a popular song or musical.

lyr·i·cize /ˈlirəˌsīz/ ▶ **v.** [no obj.] Music write or sing lyrics. ■ write in a lyric style. ■ [with obj.] treat in a lyric style or put into lyric form.

lyr·ist /ˈlīrist/ ▶ **n. 1** a person who plays the lyre.
2 a lyric poet.
– ORIGIN mid 17th cent.: from Latin *lyrista*, from Greek *luristēs*, from *lura* 'lyre.'

Ly·san·der /līˈsandər/ (died 395 BC) Spartan general. He defeated the Athenian navy in 405 and captured Athens in 404, bringing the Peloponnesian War to an end.

ly·sate /ˈlīˌsāt/ ▶ **n.** Biology a preparation containing the products of lysis of cells.

lyse /līs, līz/ ▶ **v.** Biology undergo or cause to undergo lysis.
– ORIGIN early 20th cent.: back-formation from LYSIS.

Ly·sen·ko /līˈsenkō, liˈsyenkə/, Trofim Denisovich (1898–1976), Soviet biologist and geneticist. An adherent of Lamarck's theory of evolution by the inheritance of acquired characteristics, he dominated Soviet genetics for many years.
– DERIVATIVES **Ly·sen·ko·ism** /-kōˌizəm/ **n.**, **Ly·sen·ko·ist** /-kōˌist/ **adj.** & **n.**

ly·ser·gic ac·id /līˈsərjik, li-/ ▶ **n.** Chemistry a crystalline compound prepared from natural ergot alkaloids or synthetically, from which the drug LSD (**lysergic acid diethylamide**) can be made. ● A tetracyclic acid; chem. formula: $C_{16}H_{16}N_2O_2$.
– ORIGIN 1930s: *lysergic* from (*hydro*)*lys*(*is*) + *erg*(*ot*) + -IC.

ly·sin /ˈlīsin/ ▶ **n.** Biology an antibody or other substance able to cause lysis of cells (esp. bacteria).
– ORIGIN early 20th cent.: from German *Lysine*.

ly·sine /ˈlīˌsēn/ ▶ **n.** Biochemistry a basic amino acid that is a constituent of most proteins. It is an essential nutrient in the diet of vertebrates. ● Chem. formula: $NH_2(CH_2)_4CH(NH_2)COOH$.
– ORIGIN late 19th cent.: from German *Lysin*, based on LYSIS.

ly·sis /ˈlīsis/ ▶ **n.** **1** Biology the disintegration of a cell by rupture of the cell wall or membrane. **2** the gradual decline of disease symptoms.
– ORIGIN early 19th cent.: from Latin, from Greek *lusis* 'loosening,' from *luein* 'loosen.'

-lysis ▶ **comb. form** denoting disintegration or decomposition. ■ in nouns specifying an agent: *hydrolysis*. ■ in nouns specifying a reactant: *hemolysis*. ■ in nouns specifying the nature of the process: *autolysis*.
– ORIGIN via Latin from Greek *lusis* 'loosening.'

ly·so·gen /ˈlīsəjən, -ˌjen/ ▶ **n.** a lysogenic bacterium or bacterial strain.

Ly·sol /ˈlīˌsôl, -ˌsäl/ ▶ **n.** trademark a disinfectant consisting of a mixture of cresols and soft soap.
– ORIGIN late 19th cent.: from LYSIS + -OL.

ly·so·some /ˈlīsəˌsōm/ ▶ **n.** Biology an organelle in the cytoplasm of eukaryotic cells containing degradative enzymes enclosed in a membrane.
– DERIVATIVES **ly·so·so·mal** /ˌlīsəˈsōməl/ **adj.**

ly·so·zyme /ˈlīsəˌzīm/ ▶ **n.** Biochemistry an enzyme that catalyzes the destruction of the cell walls of certain bacteria, occurring notably in tears and egg white.
– ORIGIN early 20th cent.: from LYSIS + a shortened form of ENZYME.

lyt·ic /ˈlitik/ ▶ **adj.** Biology of, relating to, or causing lysis: *the lytic activity of bile acids*.
– DERIVATIVES **lyt·i·cal·ly** /ik(ə)lē/ **adv.**

-lytic ▶ **comb. form** in adjectives corresponding to nouns ending in *-lysis* (such as *hydrolytic* corresponding to *hydrolysis*).
– ORIGIN from Greek *-lutikos* 'able to loosen.'

Lyt·ton /ˈlitn/, 1st Baron (1803–73), British novelist, playwright, and statesman; born *Edward George Earle Bulwer-Lytton*. He wrote *Pelham* (1828), a novel of fashionable society, and also wrote historical romances, such as *The Last Days of Pompeii* (1834), and plays.

LZ ▶ **abbr.** landing zone.

M¹ /em/ (also **m**) ▶ **n.** (pl. **Ms** or **M's**) **1** the thirteenth letter of the alphabet. See also **EM**. ■ denoting the next after L in a set of items, categories, etc.
2 (**M**) a shape like that of a capital M.
3 the Roman numeral for 1,000. [from Latin *mille*.]

M² ▶ **abbr.** ■ Majesty. ■ male. ■ Manitoba. ■ markka; markkas. ■ Marquis. ■ Music measure. ■ medicine. ■ medium (as a clothes size). ■ [in combination] (in units of measurement) mega-: *8 Mbytes of memory*. ■ meridian. ■ Astronomy Messier (catalog of nebulae): *the galaxy M33*. ■ Chemistry (with reference to solutions) molar: *0.15 M NaCl solution*. ■ Monday. ■ Monsieur: *M Chirac*. ■ money, when used with a following numeral in measures of money supply: *broad money, M3, grew by an annualized 9.7%*. ■ mountain. ■ noon. [from Latin *meridies*.]

M³ ▶ **symbol** Physics mutual inductance.

m ▶ **abbr.** ■ mare. ■ (in Germany) mark; marks. ■ married: *m twice; two d.* ■ masculine. ■ Physics mass. ■ (*m-*) [in combination] Chemistry meta-: *m-xylene*. ■ meter(s). ■ middle. ■ mile(s). ■ [in combination] (in units of measurement) milli-: *100 mA*. ■ million(s): *$5 m*. ■ minute(s). ■ (in prescriptions) mix. ■ modification of. ■ modulus. ■ molar. ■ month. ■ moon. ■ morning. ■ mouth. ■ noon. [from Latin *meridies*.] ▶ **symbol** Physics mass: $E = mc^2$.

m' /mə, mə/ ▶ **possessive adj.** Brit. short for **MY** (representing the pronunciation used by lawyers in court to refer to or address the judge or a fellow barrister on the same side): *he can't hold the Bible, m'lud*.

'm¹ ▶ **abbr.** informal am: *I'm a doctor*.

'm² ▶ **n.** informal madam: *yes'm*.

M-1 ▶ **n.** a .30-caliber semiautomatic clip-fed rifle capable of firing eight rounds before reloading, the standard rifle used by US troops in World War II and the Korean War.

M-16 ▶ **n.** a lightweight, fully automatic assault rifle that shoots small-caliber bullets at an extremely high velocity, used by US troops after 1966.

MA ▶ **abbr.** ■ Massachusetts (in official postal use). ■ Master of Arts: *David Jones, MA*. ■ Psychology mental age. ■ Military Academy.

ma /mä/ ▶ **n.** informal one's mother: *I didn't want to make trouble for my ma*.
– ORIGIN early 19th cent.: abbreviation of **MAMA**.

ma'am /mam/ ▶ **n.** a term of respectful or polite address used for a woman: *excuse me, ma'am*. ■ a term of address for a ranking female officer in the police or armed forces. ■ Brit. a term of address for female royalty.
– ORIGIN mid 17th cent.: contraction of **MADAM**.

maar /mär/ ▶ **n.** Geology a broad, shallow crater, typically filled by a lake, formed by a volcanic explosion with little lava.
– ORIGIN early 19th cent.: from German dialect, originally denoting a kind of crater lake in the Eifel district of Germany.

Maas /mäs/ Dutch name for **MEUSE**.

Maa·sai ▶ **n. & adj.** variant spelling of **MASAI**.

Maas·tricht /'mäs,trikt, -,trikHt/ an industrial city in the Netherlands, situated on the Maas River near the Belgian and German borders; pop. 118,004 (2008). The treaty of the European Union was signed here in 1992.

Ma·at /mät/ Egyptian Mythology the goddess of truth, justice, and cosmic order, daughter of Ra. She is depicted as a young and beautiful woman, standing or seated, with a feather on her head.

Ma Bell ▶ **n.** informal a nickname for the American Telephone and Telegraph Corporation.

Mab·i·no·gi·on /,mabə'nôgēən, -'nōgēən/ a collection of Welsh tales of the 11th–13th centuries, dealing with Celtic legends and mythology.
– ORIGIN from Welsh *Mabinogi* 'instruction for young bards.'

Mac¹ /mak/ ▶ **n.** trademark a type of personal computer.
– ORIGIN 1980s: from *Macintosh*, the brand name of a range of computers manufactured by Apple Computer Inc.; the range was named after a variety of dessert apple (see **MCINTOSH**).

Mac² /mak/ ▶ **n.** informal a form of address for a man whose name is unknown to the speaker.
– ORIGIN early 17th cent. (originally a form of address to a Scotsman): from *Mac-*, a patronymic prefix in many Scots and Irish surnames.

mac /mak/ (also **mack**) ▶ **n.** informal, chiefly Brit. a mackintosh.
– ORIGIN early 20th cent.: abbreviation.

ma·ca·bre /mə'käbrə, -'käb/ ▶ **adj.** disturbing and horrifying because of involvement with or depiction of death and injury: *a macabre series of murders*.
– ORIGIN late 19th cent.: from French *macabre*, from *Danse Macabre* 'dance of death,' from Old French, perhaps from *Macabé* 'a Maccabee,' with reference to a miracle play depicting the slaughter of the Maccabees.

mac·ad·am /mə'kadəm/ ▶ **n.** broken stone of even size used in successively compacted layers for surfacing roads and paths, and typically bound with tar or bitumen.
– DERIVATIVES **mac·ad·amed adj.**
– ORIGIN early 19th cent.: named after John L. *McAdam* (1756–1836), the British surveyor who advocated using this material.

mac·a·da·mi·a /,makə'dāmēə/ ▶ **n.** an Australian tree with slender, glossy evergreen leaves and globular edible nuts. ● Genus *Macadamia*, family Proteaceae: several species, esp. *M. integrifolia* and *M. tetraphylla*, which are cultivated for their nuts. ■ (also **macadamia nut**) the edible nut of this tree.
– ORIGIN modern Latin, named after John *Macadam* (1827–65), Australian chemist.

mac·ad·am·ize /mə'kadə,mīz/ ▶ **v.** [with obj.] make or cover with macadam: (as adj. **macadamized**) *macadamized roads*.

Mc·Al·len /mi'kalən/ a city in southern Texas, in the Rio Grande valley; pop. 129,776 (est. 2008).

Mac·Al·pin /mə'kalpən/, Kenneth, see **KENNETH I**.

Ma·cao /mə'kou/ a special administrative region on the southeastern coast of China, formerly a Portuguese dependency, comprising the Macao peninsula and the islands of Taipa and Cologne; pop. 433,700 (est. 2006); capital, Macao City. Visited by Vasco da Gama in 1497, Macao was developed by the Portuguese as a trading post and became the chief center of trade between Europe and China in the 18th century. In 1999, Macao passed to China, as agreed upon in 1987. Portuguese name **MACAU**.
– DERIVATIVES **Mac·a·nese** /,makə'nēz, -'nēs/ **adj. & n.**

Ma·ca·pá /,mäkə'pä/ a town in northern Brazil, on the Amazon delta; pop. 344,153 (2007).

Ma·ca·pa·gal-Ar·roy·o /mäkäpä'gäl-ə'roi,ō/ see **ARROYO**.

ma·caque /mə'käk, -'kak/ ▶ **n.** (also **macaque monkey**) a medium-sized, chiefly forest-dwelling Old World monkey that has a long face and cheek pouches for holding food. ● Genus *Macaca*, family Cercopithecidae: several species, including the rhesus monkey and the Barbary ape.
– ORIGIN late 17th cent.: via French and Portuguese; based on the Bantu morpheme *ma* (denoting a plural) + *kaku* 'monkey.'

Ma·ca·re·na /,mäkə'rānə/ ▶ **n.** a dance performed with exaggerated hip motion to a fast Latin rhythm.
– ORIGIN apparently from the title of a song by the Spanish duo Los del Río (1993).

Mac·a·ro·ne·sia /,makərə'nēZHə/ Botany a phytogeographical region comprising the Azores, Madeira, Canary Islands, and Cape Verde Islands in the eastern North Atlantic.
– DERIVATIVES **Mac·a·ro·ne·sian** /-'nēZHēən/ **adj.**
– ORIGIN from Greek *makarōn nēsoi* 'islands of the Blessed' (mythical islands later associated with the Canaries).

mac·a·ro·ni /,makə'rōnē/ ▶ **n.** (pl. **macaronies**) **1** a variety of pasta formed in narrow tubes.
2 an 18th-century British dandy affecting Continental fashions.
– ORIGIN late 16th cent.: from Italian *maccaroni* (now usually spelled *maccheroni*), plural of *maccarone*, from late Greek *makaria* 'food made from barley.'

mac·a·ron·ic /,makə'ränik/ ▶ **adj.** denoting language, esp. burlesque verse, containing words or inflections from one language introduced into the context of another.
▶ **n.** (usu. **macaronics**) macaronic verse, esp. that which mixes the vernacular with Latin.
– ORIGIN early 17th cent. (in the sense 'characteristic of a jumble or medley'): from modern Latin *macaronicus*, from obsolete Italian *macaronico*, a humorous formation from *macaroni* (see **MACARONI**).

mac·a·ro·ni pen·guin ▶ **n.** a penguin with an orange crest, breeding on islands in the Antarctic. ● *Eudyptes chrysolophus*, family Spheniscidae.
– ORIGIN early 19th cent.: so named because the orange crest was thought to resemble the hairstyle of dandies known as *macaronies* (see **MACARONI**).

mac·a·roon /,makə'rōōn/ ▶ **n.** a light cookie made with egg white, sugar, and usually ground almonds or coconut.
– ORIGIN late 16th cent.: from French *macaron*, from Italian *maccarone* (see **MACARONI**).

Mac·Ar·thur /mə'kärTHər/, Douglas (1880–1964), US general. Commander of US (later Allied) forces in the southwestern Pacific during World War II, he accepted Japan's surrender in 1945 and administered the ensuing Allied occupation. He was in charge of UN forces in Korea 1950–51, before being forced to relinquish command by President Truman.

Ma·cas·sar /mə'kasər/ ▶ **n. 1** (also **Macassar oil**) a kind of oil formerly used, esp. by men, to make one's hair shine and lie flat.
2 variant spelling of **MAKASSAR**.
– ORIGIN mid 17th cent.: earlier form of **MAKASSAR**. The oil was originally represented as consisting of ingredients from Makassar.

Ma·cau /mə'kou/ Portuguese name for **MACAO**.

Ma·cau·lay /mə'kôlē/, Thomas Babington, 1st Baron (1800–59), English historian, essayist, and philanthropist. Notable works: *The Lays of Ancient Rome* (1842) and *History of England* (1849–61).

ma·caw /mə'kô/ ▶ **n.** a large long-tailed parrot with brightly colored plumage, native to Central and South America. ● *Ara* and related genera, family Psittacidae: several species.
– ORIGIN early 17th cent.: from Portuguese *macao*, of unknown origin.

Mac·beth /mək'beTH, ˌmak-/ (c.1005–57), king of Scotland 1040–57. He came to the throne after killing his cousin **Duncan I** in battle and was himself defeated and killed by Malcolm III.

Macc. ▶ **abbr.** Maccabees (Apocrypha) (in biblical references).

Mac·ca·bae·us, Judas, see **Judas Maccabaeus**.

Mac·ca·bees /'makəˌbēz/ ▶ **plural n.** historical the members or followers of the family of the Jewish leader Judas Maccabaeus. ■ (in full **the Books of the Maccabees**) four books of Jewish history and theology, of which the first and second are in the Apocrypha and feature Judas Maccabaeus.
– DERIVATIVES **Mac·ca·be·an** /ˌmakə'bēən/ **adj.**
– ORIGIN late Middle English: from Latin *Maccabaeus*, an epithet applied to Judas, perhaps from Hebrew *maqqebet* 'hammer' (by association with the religious revolt led by Judas).

Mc·Cain /mə'kān/, John Sidney III (1936–), US politician, an Arizona senator since 1987. He ran as the Republican presidential candidate in 2008, losing to Democrat Barack Obama.

Mc·Car·thy[1] /mə'kärTHē/, Joseph (Raymond) (1909–57), US politician; a US senator from Wisconsin 1947–57. Between 1950 and 1954, he was the instigator of widespread investigations into alleged communist infiltration in US public life. Eventually discredited, he was censured by the Senate in 1954.

Mc·Car·thy[2], Mary (Therese) (1912–89), US novelist and critic. Her novels are satirical social commentaries that draw on her experience with intellectual circles and academic life. Notable novels: *The Groves of Academe* (1952) and *The Group* (1963).

Mc·Car·thy·ism /mə'kärTHēˌizəm/ ▶ **n.** a vociferous campaign against alleged communists in the US government and other institutions carried out under Senator Joseph McCarthy in the period 1950–54. Many of the accused were blacklisted or lost their jobs, although most did not in fact belong to the Communist Party. ■ any similar practice that endorses the use of unfair allegations and investigations: *he practiced McCarthyism long before there was a McCarthy.*
– DERIVATIVES **Mc·Car·thy·ist adj. & n.**, **Mc·Car·thy·ite** /-THēˌīt/ **adj. & n.**

Mc·Cart·ney, Sir Paul (1942–), English pop and rock musician; full name *James Paul McCartney*. A founding member of the Beatles, he wrote most of their songs in collaboration with John Lennon. After the group broke up in 1970, he formed the band Wings.

Paul McCartney

mac·chi·a·to /ˌmäkē'ätō/ ▶ **n.** (pl. **macchiatos**) espresso with a dash of frothy steamed milk.
– ORIGIN 1970s: from Italian (*caffè*) *macchiato*, literally 'stained, marked (coffee),' from *macchiare* 'stain, mark.'

Mc·Clel·lan /mə'klelən/, George Brinton (1826–85), US army officer; known as **Little Mac**. He became general in chief of the US Army 1861 during the Civil War. Although the victor at Antietam 1862, he was removed from command due to a lack of military aggressiveness. The Democratic presidential candidate in 1864, he was defeated by incumbent Abraham Lincoln. He later served as governor of New Jersey 1878–81.

Mc·Clin·tock /mə'klinˌtäk/, Barbara (1902–92), US geneticist. The discovery of DNA vindicated her earlier findings of transposable genetic elements 1951. Nobel Prize for Physiology or Medicine (1983).

Mc·Cor·mack /mə'kôrmək/, John (1884–1945), US opera singer; born in Ireland. A tenor, he sang with various opera groups, including the Chicago and Metropolitan opera companies. He was also popular for his renderings of Irish folk songs.

Mc·Cor·mick /mə'kôrmək/, Cyrus Hall (1809–84), US inventor and industrialist. His patented reaper 1834 was the cornerstone of his harvesting machinery company, and the innovative deferred-payment plans and guarantees that he offered customers became a model in US consumerism.

Mc·Court /mə'kôrt/, Frank (1930–2009), US writer. He wrote the award-winning *Angela's Ashes* (1996), a memoir about his impoverished childhood, some of which was spent in Ireland. Other works include *'Tis* (1999), also based on his past experiences.

Mc·Coy /mə'koi/ ▶ **n.** (in phrase **the real McCoy**) informal the real thing; the genuine article: *the apparent fake turned out to be the real McCoy.*
– ORIGIN mid 19th cent.: first appears as *the real MacKay*, in which *real* may be a corruption of the name of the Reay branch of the Scottish MacKay family.

Mc·Cul·lers /mə'kələrz/, Carson (1917–67), US writer; born *Lula Carson Smith*. Her work deals sensitively with loneliness and the plight of the eccentric. Notable works: *The Heart Is a Lonely Hunter* (1940), *The Member of the Wedding* (1946), and *The Ballad of the Sad Cafe* (1951).

Mc·Cul·lough /mə'kələ(k)/, Colleen (1937–), Australian writer. Her novels include *Tim* (1974), *The Thorn Birds* (1977) *The Song of Troy* (1998), and *Morgan's Run* (2000).

Mac·Don·ald /mək'dänəld/, Ramsay (1866–1937), British statesman, born in Scotland; full name James Ramsay MacDonald. He became Britain's first Labour prime minister in 1924 and headed the second Labour government 1929–31. When the cabinet split over proposed cuts in unemployment benefits, he led a coalition "National" government 1931–35.

Mac·don·ald /mək'dänəld/, Sir John Alexander (1815–91), Canadian Liberal-Conservative statesman, born in Scotland; prime minister 1867–73 and 1878–91. He played a leading role in the confederation of the Canadian provinces and was appointed the first prime minister of the Dominion of Canada.

Mac·Don·nell Rang·es /mək'dänl/ a series of mountain ranges extending west from Alice Springs in Northern Territory, Australia. The highest peak is Mount Zeil, which rises to a height of 5,023 feet (1,531 m).
– ORIGIN named after Sir Richard *MacDonnell*, governor of South Australia when John McDouall Stuart explored the ranges in 1860.

Mace /mās/ ▶ **n.** trademark an irritant chemical used in an aerosol to disable attackers.
▶ **v.** (also **mace**) [with obj.] spray (someone) with Mace.
– ORIGIN 1960s (originally US): probably from **mace**[1].

mace[1] /mās/ ▶ **n. 1** historical a heavy club, typically having a metal head and spikes.
2 a ceremonial staff of office.
– ORIGIN Middle English: from Old French *masse* 'large hammer.'

mace[2] ▶ **n.** the reddish fleshy outer covering of the nutmeg, dried as a spice.
– ORIGIN Middle English *macis* (taken as plural), via Old French from Latin *macir*.

mac·é·doine /ˌmäsə'dwän/ ▶ **n. 1** a mixture of vegetables or fruit cut into small pieces and served as a salad.
2 a medley or jumble: *a macédoine of disjointed detail.*
– ORIGIN French, literally 'Macedonia,' with reference to the mixture of peoples in the Macedonian Empire of Alexander the Great.

Mac·e·do·ni·a /ˌmasə'dōnēə, -nyə/ **1** a landlocked republic in the Balkans; pop. 2,066,700 (est. 2009); capital, Skopje; official language, Macedonian. Formerly a constituent republic of Yugoslavia, Macedonia became independent after a 1991 referendum. Also called **Former Yugoslav Republic of Macedonia**.
2 (also **Macedon** /'masədən, -ˌdän/) an ancient country in southeastern Europe, north of Greece. In classical times it was a kingdom that became a world power under Philip II and Alexander the Great. The region is now divided between Greece, Bulgaria, and the republic of Macedonia.
3 a region in northeastern Greece; capital, Thessaloníki.

Mac·e·do·ni·an /ˌmasə'dōnēən/ ▶ **n. 1** a native or inhabitant of the Former Yugoslav Republic of Macedonia.
2 a native of ancient Macedonia. ■ a native or inhabitant of the region of Macedonia in modern Greece.
3 the South Slavic language of the republic of Macedonia and adjacent parts of Bulgaria.
4 the language of ancient Macedonia, possibly a dialect of Greek.
▶ **adj.** of or relating to Macedonia or Macedonian.

Mac·e·do·ni·an Wars a series of four wars between Rome and Macedonia in the 3rd and 2nd centuries BC, which ended in the defeat of Macedonia and its annexation as a Roman province (148 BC).

Ma·ceió /ˌmäsä'ō/ a port in eastern Brazil, on the Atlantic coast; pop. 896,965 (2007).

Mc·En·roe /'makənˌrō/, John (Patrick) (1959–), US tennis player. During 1979–84, he won the men's singles title at three Wimbledon and four US Open tournaments.

mac·er·ate /'masəˌrāt/ ▶ **v. 1** (esp. with reference to food) soften or become softened by soaking in a liquid.
2 archaic cause to grow thinner or waste away, esp. by fasting.
– DERIVATIVES **mac·er·a·tion** /ˌmasə'rāSHən/ **n.**, **mac·er·a·tor** /-ˌrātər/ **n.**
– ORIGIN mid 16th cent.: from Latin *macerat-* 'made soft, soaked,' from the verb *macerare*.

Mc·Graw /mə(k)'grô/, John (Joseph) (1873–1934), US baseball player and manager; nickname **Little Napoleon**. He played for the Baltimore Orioles 1891–99 and then managed the New York Giants 1902–32. Baseball Hall of Fame (1937).

Mc·Guf·fey /mə(k)'gəfē/, William Holmes (1800–1873), US public education reformer. He is best known for his series of *Eclectic Readers*, compiled between 1836 and 1857 and more commonly called *McGuffey Readers*.

Mc·Guf·fin /mə'gəfin/ (also **MacGuffin**) ▶ **n.** chiefly Brit. an object or device in a movie or a book that serves merely as a trigger for the plot.
– ORIGIN 1930s: a Scottish surname, said to have been borrowed by the English film director Alfred Hitchcock, from a humorous story involving such a pivotal factor.

Mach[1] /mäk, mäKH/, Ernst (1838–1916), Austrian physicist and philosopher of science. He did important work on aerodynamics.

Mach[2] (also **Mach number**) ▶ **n.** the ratio of the speed of a body to the speed of sound in the surrounding medium. It is often used with a numeral (as **Mach 1**, **Mach 2**, etc.) to indicate the speed of sound, twice the speed of sound, etc.

mach. ▶ **abbr.** machine or machinery or machinist.

mache /mäsH/ (also **mâche**) ▶ **n.** another term for **corn salad**.
– ORIGIN late 17th cent. (originally as the anglicized plural form *maches*): from French *mâche*.

mach·er /'mäKHər/ ▶ **n.** informal a person who gets things done. ■ derogatory an overbearing person.
– ORIGIN 1930s: from Yiddish *makher*, from Middle High German *macher* 'doer, active person.'

ma·chet·e /mə'sHetē/ ▶ **n.** a broad, heavy knife used as an implement or weapon, originating in Central America and the Caribbean.
– ORIGIN late 16th cent.: from Spanish, from *macho* 'hammer.'

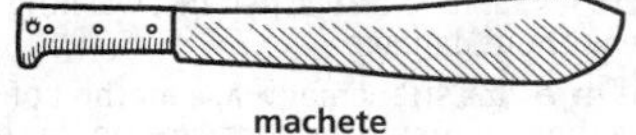

machete

Mach·i·a·vel /'makēəˌvel, 'mäk-/ ▶ **n.** archaic a person compared to Machiavelli for favoring expediency over morality.

Mach·i·a·vel·li /ˌmäkēə'velē, ˌmak-/, Niccolò di Bernardo dei (1469–1527), Italian statesman and political philosopher. His *The Prince* (1532) advises rulers that the acquisition and effective use of power may necessitate unethical methods.

Mach·i·a·vel·li·an /ˌmakēə'velēən, ˌmäk-/ ▶ **adj. 1** cunning, scheming, and unscrupulous, esp. in politics or in advancing one's career.
2 of or relating to Niccolò Machiavelli.
▶ **n.** a person who schemes in such a way.
– DERIVATIVES **Mach·i·a·vel·li·an·ism** /-ˌnizəm/ **n.**

ma·chic·o·late /mə'CHikəˌlāt/ ▶ **v.** [with obj.] (usu. as adj. **machicolated**) provide with machicolations: *a machicolated fortress.*
– ORIGIN late 18th cent.: from Anglo-Latin *machicollare*, based on Provençal *machacol*, from *macar* 'to crush' + *col* 'neck.'

ma·chic·o·la·tion /məˌCHikə'lāSHən/ ▶ **n.** (in medieval fortifications) an opening between the supporting corbels of a projecting parapet or the vault of a gate, through which stones or burning objects could be dropped on attackers. ■ a projecting structure containing a series of such openings.

m

ma·chin·a·ble /məˈsʜēnəbəl/ ▶ **adj.** (of a material) able to be worked by a machine tool.
– DERIVATIVES **ma·chin·a·bil·i·ty** /məˌsʜēnəˈbilətē/ **n.**

mach·i·nate /ˈmakəˌnāt, ˈmasʜə-/ ▶ **v.** [no obj.] engage in plots and intrigues; scheme.
– DERIVATIVES **mach·i·na·tion** /ˌmakəˈnāsʜən, ˌmasʜə-/ **n.**, **mach·i·na·tor** /-ˌnātər/ **n.**
– ORIGIN early 16th cent. (used transitively in the sense 'to plot (a malicious act)'): from Latin *machinat-* 'contrived,' from the verb *machinari*, from *machina* (see MACHINE).

ma·chine /məˈsʜēn/ ▶ **n.** an apparatus using or applying mechanical power and having several parts, each with a definite function and together performing a particular task: *a fax machine* | *a shredding machine.* ■ [usu. with modifier] a coin-operated dispenser: *a candy machine.* ■ technical any device that transmits a force or directs its application. ■ an efficient and well-organized group of powerful people: *his campaign illustrated the continuing strength of a powerful political machine.* ■ a person who acts with the mechanical efficiency of a machine: *comedians are more than just laugh machines.*
▶ **v.** [with obj.] (esp. in manufacturing) make or operate on with a machine: (as adj. **machined**) *a decoratively machined brass rod.*
– ORIGIN mid 16th cent. (originally denoting a structure of any kind): from French, via Latin from Doric Greek *makhana* (Attic Greek *mēkhanē*, from *mēkhos* 'contrivance').

ma·chine code (also **machine language**) ▶ **n.** a computer programming language consisting of binary or hexadecimal instructions that a computer can respond to directly.

ma·chine gun ▶ **n.** an automatic gun that fires bullets in rapid succession for as long as the trigger is pressed.
▶ **v.** (**machine-gun**) [with obj.] shoot with a machine gun.
– DERIVATIVES **ma·chine-gun·ner** **n.**

ma·chine-read·a·ble ▶ **adj.** (of data or text) in a form that a computer can process.

ma·chin·er·y /məˈsʜēn(ə)rē/ ▶ **n.** machines collectively: *farm machinery.* ■ the components of a machine: *the movement of the machinery.* ■ the organization or structure of something: *the machinery of democracy.*

ma·chine screw ▶ **n.** a fastening device similar to a bolt but having a socket in its head that allows it to be turned with a screwdriver.

ma·chine tool ▶ **n.** a nonportable power tool, such as a lathe or milling machine, used for cutting or shaping metal, wood, or other material.
– DERIVATIVES **ma·chine-tooled** **adj.**

ma·chine trans·la·tion ▶ **n.** translation carried out by a computer.

ma·chine wash·a·ble ▶ **adj.** (of clothes or other fabric articles) able to be washed in a washing machine without damage.

ma·chin·i·ma /məˈsʜēnəmə/ ▶ **n.** a method of making animated film using software similar to that designed for making video and computer games. ■ the genre of films created in this way.

ma·chin·ist /məˈsʜēnist/ ▶ **n.** a person who operates a machine, esp. a machine tool. ■ a person who makes or repairs machinery.

ma·chis·mo /məˈcʜēzmō, -ˈkēz-/ ▶ **n.** strong or aggressive masculine pride.
– ORIGIN 1940s: Mexican Spanish, from *macho* 'male' (see MACHO).

Mach·me·ter /ˈmäkˌmētər/ ▶ **n.** an instrument in an aircraft indicating airspeed as a Mach number.

Mach num·ber ▶ **n.** see MACH².

MACHO /ˈmäcʜō, ˈmacʜō/ ▶ **n.** Astronomy a compact object, such as a brown dwarf, a low-mass star, or a black hole, of a kind that is thought by some to constitute part of the dark matter in galactic halos.
– ORIGIN 1990s: acronym from *Massive (Astrophysical) Compact Halo Object.*

ma·cho /ˈmäcʜō/ ▶ **adj.** showing aggressive pride in one's masculinity: *the big macho tough guy.*
▶ **n.** (pl. **machos**) a man who is aggressively proud of his masculinity. ■ machismo.
– ORIGIN 1920s: Mexican Spanish, 'masculine or vigorous,' from Latin *masculus.*

Mach's prin·ci·ple /mäks, mäkʜs/ Physics the hypothesis that a body's inertial mass results from its interaction with the rest of the matter in the universe.

Ma·chu Pic·chu /ˌmäcʜo͞o ˈpi(k)cʜo͞o/ a fortified Inca town in the Andes Mountains in Peru that the invading Spaniards never found. It is noted for its dramatic position, perched high on a steep-sided ridge.

Machu Picchu

Mc·In·tosh /ˈmakənˌtäsʜ/ (also **McIntosh red**) ▶ **n.** a dessert apple of a variety native to North America, with deep red skin.
– ORIGIN late 19th cent.: named after John *McIntosh* (1777–1845 or 1846), the American-born Canadian farmer on whose farm the apple was discovered as a wild variety.

mac·in·tosh ▶ **n.** variant spelling of MACKINTOSH.

Mc·Job /məkˈjäb/ ▶ **n.** a low-paid job with few prospects, typically one taken by an overqualified person.
– ORIGIN 1980s: from *McDonald's*, a fast-food restaurant chain, + JOB.

Mack /mak/, Connie (1862–1956), US baseball player and manager; born *Cornelius Alexander McGillicuddy*. A catcher, he played with various teams from 1886 until 1896. In 1901, he became the manager of the Philadelphia Athletics, a job he held for 50 years. He led the team to nine American League pennants and five World Series championships. Baseball Hall of Fame (1937).

mack ▶ **n. 1** variant spelling of MAC.
2 informal a confident, successful man who has many sexual partners.

Mc·Ken·na /məˈkenə/, Joseph (1843–1926), US Supreme Court associate justice 1898–1925. He was the US attorney general 1897–98 when he was appointed to the Court by President McKinley.

Mac·ken·zie¹ /məˈkenzē/, Sir Alexander (1764–1820), Scottish explorer in Canada. He discovered the Mackenzie River in 1789 and became the first European to reach the Pacific Ocean by land along a northern route in 1793.

Mac·ken·zie² /məˈkenzi/, Sir Alexander (1822–92), Canadian Liberal statesman; prime minister 1873–78.

Mac·ken·zie³, William Lyon (1795–1861), Canadian politician and journalist, born in Scotland. He was involved with the movement for political reform in Canada. In 1837, he led an unsuccessful rebellion in Toronto and fled to New York.

Mac·ken·zie Riv·er /məˈkenzē/ a river that flows northwest for 1,060 miles (1,700 km) from Great Slave Lake to Beaufort Sea, which is a part of the Arctic Ocean. It is the longest river in Canada.

mack·er·el /ˈmak(ə)rəl/ ▶ **n.** (pl. **same** or **mackerels**) a migratory surface-dwelling predatory fish, commercially important as a food fish. ● *Scomber* and other genera, family Scombridae (the **mackerel family**): many species, in particular the **North Atlantic mackerel** (*S. scombrus*). The members of the mackerel family, which includes the tunas, are fast-moving marine predators and often popular as game fish.
– ORIGIN Middle English: from Old French *maquerel*, of unknown origin.

mack·er·el shark ▶ **n.** a shark of the family Lamnidae, esp. the porbeagle or the mako.

mack·er·el sky ▶ **n.** a sky dappled with rows of small white fleecy clouds, typically cirrocumulus, like the pattern on a mackerel's back.

Mack·i·nac, Straits of /ˈmakəˌnô/ a passage between lakes Huron and Michigan, crossed since 1957 by the Mackinac Bridge. The Upper Peninsula of Michigan lies to the north, and historic Mackinac Island lies just to the east.

mack·i·naw /ˈmakəˌnô/ (also **mackinaw coat** or **jacket**) ▶ **n.** a short coat or jacket made of a thick, heavy woolen cloth, typically with a plaid design.
– ORIGIN early 19th cent.: named after *Mackinaw* City, Michigan, formerly an important trading post.

Mc·Kin·ley¹ /məˈkinlē/, John (1780–1852), US Supreme Court associate justice 1837–52. A US senator 1826–31, 1837 and a member of the US House of Representatives 1833–35, he was appointed to the Court by President Van Buren.

Mc·Kin·ley², William (1843–1901), 25th president of the US 1897–1901. A Republican, he favored big business and waged the Spanish–American War of 1898, which resulted in the acquisition of Puerto Rico, Cuba, and the Philippines, as well as the annexation of Hawaii, and brought the US to the forefront of world power. He was assassinated by an anarchist while in Buffalo, New York.

William McKinley

Mc·Kin·ley, Mount /məˈkinlē/ a mountain in south central Alaska. Rising to 20,321 feet (6,194 m), it is the highest mountain in North America. Also called DENALI.

Mc·Kin·ney /məˈkinē/ a city in northeastern Texas, in the northeastern part of the Dallas–Fort Worth metropolitan area; pop. 121,211 (est. 2008). It is noted for its remarkable growth since 1990, when its population was 21,283.

Mack·in·tosh /ˈmakənˌtäsʜ/, Charles Rennie (1868–1928), Scottish architect, designer, and painter. A leading exponent of art nouveau, he pioneered the new concept of functionalism in architecture and interior design.

mack·in·tosh /ˈmakənˌtäsʜ/ (also **macintosh**) ▶ **n.** chiefly Brit. a full-length waterproof coat. ■ [usu. as modifier] cloth waterproofed with rubber.
– ORIGIN mid 19th cent.: named after Charles *Macintosh* (1766–1843), the Scottish inventor who originally patented the cloth.

mack·le /ˈmakəl/ ▶ **n.** a blurred impression in printing.
– ORIGIN late 16th cent.: from French *macule*, from Latin *macula* 'stain.'

Mc·Ku·en /məˈkyo͞oən/, Rod (1933–), US poet, writer, and composer. Some of his poetry is collected in *Stanyan Street and Other Sorrows* (1966) and *Listen to the Warm* (1967). He also wrote many songs and movie scores.

ma·cle /ˈmakəl/ ▶ **n. 1** a diamond or other crystal that is twinned.
2 another term for CHIASTOLITE.
– ORIGIN early 19th cent.: from French, from Anglo-Latin *mascula* 'mesh.'

Mac·lean¹ /məˈklān/, Alistair (1922–87), Scottish novelist. He wrote thrillers including *The Guns of Navarone* (1957; movie, 1961), *Where Eagles Dare* (1967; movie, 1969), and *Bear Island* (1971; movie, 1979).

Mac·lean², Donald (Duart) (1913–83), British foreign office official and Soviet spy. He fled to the former Soviet Union with Guy Burgess in 1951.

Mc·Lean /məˈklēn/, John (1785–1861), US Supreme Court associate justice 1829–61. The US postmaster general 1823–29, he was appointed to the Court by President Jackson.

Mac·Leish /məˈklēsʜ/, Archibald (1892–1982), US poet. His award-winning works include *Conquistador* (1932), *Collected Poems* (1952), and *J.B.* (1958).

Mac·leod /məˈkloud/, John James Rickard (1876–1935), Scottish physiologist. He directed the research on pancreatic extracts by Frederick G. Banting and Charles H. Best that led to the discovery and isolation of insulin. Nobel Prize for Physiology or Medicine (1923), shared with Banting.

Mc·Lu·han /məˈklo͞oən/, Marshall (1911–80), Canadian writer and thinker; full name *Herbert Marshall McLuhan*. He became known in the 1960s for his phrase "the medium is the message" and for his argument that it is the characteristics of a particular medium rather than the information it disseminates that influence and control society.

Mc·Man·sion /məkˈmansʜən/ ▶ **n.** a large modern house that is considered ostentatious and lacking in architectural integrity.
– ORIGIN from *Mc-* + *mansion*, with reference to the name of a restaurant chain.

m

Mac·mil·lan /mək'milən/, Harold (1894–1986), British Conservative statesman; prime minister 1957–63; full name *Maurice Harold Macmillan, 1st Earl of Stockton*. During his term of office, the Test Ban Treaty (1963) with the US and the former Soviet Union was signed, and Britain granted independence to a number of its African colonies. Macmillan resigned on grounds of ill health shortly after the scandal surrounding John Profumo, a member of his government.

Mc·Mur·try /mək'mərtrē/, Larry (Jeff) (1936–), US writer. Included in his works are *The Last Picture Show* (1966), *Terms of Endearment* (1975), *Lonesome Dove* (1985), and *Comanche Moon* (1997).

Mc·Na·mar·a /'maknə,marə/, Robert Strange (1916–2009), US businessman and public official. He was secretary of the US Department of Defense 1961–68 during the Kennedy and Johnson administrations and president of the World Bank 1968–81.

Ma·con /'mākən/ an industrial and commercial city in central Georgia, on the Ocmulgee River; pop. 92,775 (est. 2008).

Mc·Phee /mək'fē/, John (Angus) (1931–), US journalist and writer. He wrote for *The New Yorker* magazine from 1964 and also published such nonfiction works as *Coming into the Country* (1977) and *Basin and Range* (1981).

Mac·quar·ie Riv·er /mə'kwôrē, -'kwärē/ a river in New South Wales, Australia, that rises on the western slopes of the Great Dividing Range and flows northwest for 600 miles (960 km) to join the Darling River, of which it is a headwater.

mac·ra·mé /'makrə,mā/ ▶ **n.** the art of knotting cord or string in patterns to make decorative articles. ■ [usu. as modifier] fabric or articles made in this way.
– ORIGIN mid 19th cent.: French, from Turkish *makrama* 'tablecloth or towel,' from Arabic *mikrama* 'bedspread.'

Mc·Rey·nolds /mək'renəl(d)z/, James Clark (1862–1946), US Supreme Court associate justice 1914–41. The US attorney general 1913–14, he was appointed to the Court by President Wilson.

mac·ro /'makrō/ ▶ **n.** (pl. **macros**) **1** (also **macro instruction**) Computing a single instruction that expands automatically into a set of instructions to perform a particular task.
2 Photography short for MACRO LENS.
▶ **adj. 1** large-scale; overall: *the analysis of social events at the macro level.* Often contrasted with MICRO.
2 Photography relating to or used in macrophotography.
– ORIGIN independent usage of MACRO-.

macro- ▶ **comb. form 1** long; over a long period: *macroevolution.*
2 large; large-scale: *macromolecule* | *macronutrient.* ■ (used in medical terms) large compared with the norm: *macrocephaly.*
– ORIGIN from Greek *makros* 'long, large.'

mac·ro·bi·ot·ic /,makrōbī'ätik/ ▶ **adj.** constituting, relating to, or following a diet of whole pure prepared foods that is based on Taoist principles of the balance of yin and yang.
▶ **plural n.** (**macrobiotics**) [treated as sing.] the use or theory of such a diet.

mac·ro·car·pa /'makrə,kärpə/ ▶ **n.** another term for MONTEREY CYPRESS.
– ORIGIN early 20th cent.: modern Latin, from MACRO- 'large' + Greek *karpos* 'fruit.'

mac·ro·ce·phal·ic /,makrōsə'falik/ (also **macrocephalous** /-'sefələs/) ▶ **adj.** Anatomy having an unusually large head.
– DERIVATIVES **mac·ro·ceph·a·ly** /-'sefəlē/ **n.**

mac·ro·cosm /'makrə,käzəm/ (also **macrocosmos** /-,käzməs, -mōs/) ▶ **n.** the whole of a complex structure, esp. the world or universe, contrasted with a small or representative part of it.
– DERIVATIVES **mac·ro·cos·mic** /,makrə'käzmik/ **adj.**, **mac·ro·cos·mi·cal·ly** /,makrə'käzmik(ə)lē/ **adv.**

mac·ro·cy·clic /,makrō'siklik, -'sīklik/ ▶ **adj.** Chemistry of, relating to, or denoting a ring composed of a relatively large number of atoms, such as occurs in heme, chlorophyll, and several natural antibiotics.
– DERIVATIVES **mac·ro·cy·cle** /'makrō,sīkəl/ **n.**

mac·ro·ec·o·nom·ics /'makrō,ekə'nämiks, -,ēkə-/ ▶ **plural n.** [treated as sing.] the part of economics concerned with large-scale or general economic factors, such as interest rates and national productivity.
– DERIVATIVES **mac·ro·ec·o·nom·ic** **adj.**, **mac·ro·e·con·o·mist** /-i'känəmist/ **n.**

mac·ro·e·con·o·my /'makrō-i'känəmē/ ▶ **n.** a large-scale economic system.

mac·ro·ev·o·lu·tion /,makrō-evə'lo͞oSHən, -,ēvə-/ ▶ **n.** Biology major evolutionary change. The term applies mainly to the evolution of whole taxonomic groups over long periods of time.
– DERIVATIVES **mac·ro·ev·o·lu·tion·ar·y** /-SHə,nerē, -,ēvə-/ **adj.**

mac·ro·gam·ete /,makrōgə'mēt, -'gam,ēt/ ▶ **n.** Biology (esp. in protozoans) the larger of a pair of conjugating gametes, usually regarded as female.

mac·ro lens ▶ **n.** Photography a lens suitable for taking photographs unusually close to the subject.

mac·ro·lep·i·dop·ter·a /'makrō,lepə'däptərə/ ▶ **plural n.** Entomology the butterflies and larger moths, comprising those of interest to the general collector. Compare with MICROLEPIDOPTERA.
– ORIGIN modern Latin (plural), from MACRO- 'large' + LEPIDOPTERA.

mac·ro·lide /'makrə,līd/ ▶ **n.** any of a class of antibiotics containing a lactone ring, of which the first and best known is erythromycin.
– ORIGIN mid 20th cent.: from *macro-* + *l(actone)* + *-ide.*

mac·ro·mol·e·cule /,makrō'mälə,kyo͞ol/ ▶ **n.** Chemistry a molecule containing a very large number of atoms, such as a protein, nucleic acid, or synthetic polymer.
– DERIVATIVES **mac·ro·mo·lec·u·lar** /-mə'lekyələr/ **adj.**

ma·cron /'mā,krän, 'mak-, 'mākrən/ ▶ **n.** a written or printed mark (¯) used to indicate a long vowel in some languages and phonetic transcription systems, or a stressed vowel in verse.
– ORIGIN mid 19th cent.: from Greek *makron*, neuter of *makros* 'long.'

mac·ro·nu·tri·ent /,makrō'no͞otrēənt/ ▶ **n.** Biology a substance required in relatively large amounts by living organisms, in particular: ■ a type of food (e.g., fat, protein, carbohydrate) required in large amounts in the human diet. ■ a chemical element (e.g., potassium, magnesium, calcium) required in large amounts for plant growth and development.

mac·ro·phage /'makrə,fāj/ ▶ **n.** Physiology a large phagocytic cell found in stationary form in the tissues or as a mobile white blood cell, esp. at sites of infection.

mac·ro·pho·tog·ra·phy /,makrōfə'tägrəfē/ ▶ **n.** photography producing photographs of small items larger than life size.

mac·ro·phyte /'makrə,fīt/ ▶ **n.** Botany a plant, esp. an aquatic plant, large enough to be seen by the naked eye.

mac·ro·pod /'makrə,päd/ ▶ **n.** Zoology a plant-eating marsupial mammal of an Australasian family that comprises the kangaroos and wallabies. ● Family Macropodidae: several genera, in particular *Macropus.*
– ORIGIN late 19th cent.: from modern Latin *Macropodidae* (plural), from MACRO- 'large' + Greek *pous, pod-* 'foot.'

mac·ro·scop·ic /,makrə'skäpik/ ▶ **adj.** visible to the naked eye; not microscopic. ■ of or relating to large-scale or general analysis.
– DERIVATIVES **mac·ro·scop·i·cal·ly** /-ik(ə)lē/ **adv.**

Mac·ro-Siou·an /,makrō'so͞oən/ ▶ **n.** a proposed phylum of North American languages including the Siouan, Iroquoian, and Caddoan families and some others.
▶ **adj.** of or relating to this language phylum.

mac·ro·struc·ture /'makrō,strəkCHər/ ▶ **n.** the large-scale or overall structure of something, e.g., an organism, a mechanical construction, or a written text.
– DERIVATIVES **mac·ro·struc·tur·al** /,makrō'strəkCHərəl/ **adj.**

ma·cru·ran /mə'kro͝orən/ ▶ **adj.** Zoology of, relating to, or denoting those decapod crustaceans (such as lobsters and crayfish) that have a relatively long abdomen.
– DERIVATIVES **ma·cru·rous** **adj.**
– ORIGIN mid 19th cent. (as a noun): from modern Latin *Macrura* (former suborder name), from Greek *makros* 'long' + *oura* 'tail,' + -AN.

mac·u·la /'makyələ/ ▶ **n.** (pl. **maculae** /-,lē, -,lī/) a distinct spot, such as a discolored spot on the skin. Also called MACULE. ■ (also **macula lutea**) /'lo͞otēə/ (pl. **maculae luteae** /'lo͞otē,ē, -tē,ī/) Anatomy an oval yellowish area surrounding the fovea near the center of the retina in the eye. It is the region of greatest visual acuity.
– DERIVATIVES **mac·u·lar** /'makyələr/ **adj.**
– ORIGIN late Middle English: from Latin, 'spot.'

mac·u·late /'makyə,lāt/ literary ▶ **adj.** spotted or stained.
▶ **v.** [with obj.] mark with a spot or spots; stain.
– DERIVATIVES **mac·u·la·tion** /,makyə'lāSHən/ **n.**
– ORIGIN late Middle English (as a verb): from Latin *maculat-* 'spotted,' from the verb *maculare*, from *macula* 'spot.'

mac·ule /'mak,yo͞ol/ ▶ **n.** another term for MACULA.
– ORIGIN late 15th cent.: from French, or from Latin *macula* 'spot.'

ma·cum·ba /mə'ko͞ombə/ ▶ **n.** a black religious cult practiced in Brazil, using sorcery, ritual dance, and fetishes.
– ORIGIN Portuguese.

MAD ▶ **abbr.** mutual assured destruction.

mad /mad/ ▶ **adj.** (**madder, maddest**) mentally ill; insane: *he felt as if he were going mad.* ■ (of a person, conduct, or an idea) extremely foolish or ill-advised: *they were all mad to go believing such a cock-and-bull story.* ■ in a frenzied mental or physical state: *she pictured loved ones mad with anxiety about her* | *it was a mad dash to get ready.* ■ informal enthusiastic about someone or something: *I wasn't **mad about** mountain bikes* | [in combination] *a sports-mad nation.* ■ informal very angry: *they were mad at each other.* ■ (of a dog) rabid. ■ Brit. informal very exciting.
▶ **v.** (**mads, madding, madded** /madəd/) [with obj.] archaic make mad or insane.
– PHRASES **like mad** informal with great intensity, energy, or enthusiasm: *I ran like mad.* **(as) mad as a hatter** informal completely crazy. [with reference to Lewis Carroll's character the Mad Hatter in *Alice's Adventures in Wonderland* (1865), the allusion being to the effects of mercury poisoning from the use of mercurous nitrate in the manufacture of felt hats.]
– ORIGIN Old English *gemǣd(e)d* 'maddened,' participial form related to *gemād* 'mad,' of Germanic origin.

Mad·a·gas·car /,madə'gaskər/ an island country in the Indian Ocean, off the eastern coast of Africa; pop. 20,653,600 (est. 2009); capital, Antananarivo; official languages, Malagasy and French.

> Settled by peoples of mixed Indo-Melanesian and African descent, Madagascar was visited by the Portuguese in 1500 but resisted colonization until the French established control in 1896. It regained its independence as the Malagasy Republic in 1960 and changed its name back to Madagascar in 1975. It is the fourth largest island in the world, and many of its plants and animals are unique to the island.

– DERIVATIVES **Mad·a·gas·can** /-'gaskən/ **adj. & n.**

mad·am /'madəm/ ▶ **n.** used to address or refer to a woman in a polite or respectful way: *Can I help you, madam?* ■ (**Madam**) used to address a woman at the start of a formal or business letter: *Dear Madam,* .... ■ (**Madam**) used before a title to address or refer to a female holder of that position: *Madam President.* ■ a woman who runs a brothel.
– ORIGIN Middle English: from Old French *ma dame* 'my lady.'

Mad·ame /mə'däm, -'dam/ ▶ **n.** (pl. **Mesdames** /mā'däm, -'dam/) a title or form of address used of or to a French-speaking woman: *Madame Bovary.* ■ used as a title for women in artistic or exotic occupations, such as musicians or fortune-tellers.
– ORIGIN French; compare with MADAM.

mad·a·ro·sis /,madə'rōsis/ ▶ **n.** Medicine absence or loss of the eyelashes (and sometimes the eyebrows), either as a congenital condition or as a result of an infection.
– ORIGIN late 17th cent.: modern Latin, from Greek, 'baldness,' from *madaros* 'bald.'

mad·cap /'mad,kap/ ▶ **adj.** amusingly eccentric: *a surreal, madcap novel.* ■ done or thought up without considering the consequences; crazy or reckless: *some madcap money-making scheme.*
▶ **n.** an eccentric person.

mad cow dis·ease ▶ **n.** informal bovine spongiform encephalopathy. See BSE.

MADD /mad/ ▶ **abbr.** Mothers Against Drunk Driving.

mad·den /'madn/ ▶ **v.** [with obj.] make (someone) extremely irritated or annoyed: *the audacity of the convicts maddened the governor.* ■ (often as adj. **maddened**) drive (someone) insane: *a maddened crowd.*

mad·den·ing /'madniNG, 'madn-iNG/ ▶ **adj.** extremely annoying; infuriating: *his maddening stories.*
– DERIVATIVES **mad·den·ing·ly** **adv.**

mad·der /'madər/ ▶ **n.** a scrambling or prostrate Eurasian plant of the bedstraw family, with whorls of four to six leaves. ● Genera *Rubia* and *Sherardia*, family Rubiaceae: several species, in particular *R. tinctorum* of southern Europe and western Asia, formerly cultivated for its root, which yields a red dye, and the Eurasian **wild madder** (*R. peregrina*). ■ a red dye or pigment obtained from the root of this plant, or a synthetic dye resembling it.
– ORIGIN Old English *mædere*, of Germanic origin; obscurely related to Dutch *mede*, in the same sense.

mad·ding /'madiNG/ ▶ **adj.** literary **1** acting madly; frenzied.
2 maddening.
– PHRASES **far from the madding crowd** secluded or removed from public notice. [in allusion to use in Gray's *Elegy*, also to the title of one of Thomas Hardy's novels.]

PRONUNCIATION KEY ə *ago, up*; ər *over, fur*; a *hat*; ā *ate*; ä *car*; e *let*; ē *see*; i *fit*; ī *by*; NG *sing*; ō *go*; ô *law, for*; oi *toy*; o͝o *good*; o͞o *goo*; ou *out*; TH *thin*; TH *then*; ZH *vision*

m

made /mād/ past and past participle of MAKE.
▶ **adj.** [usu. in combination] made or formed in a particular place or by a particular process: *a Japanese-made camera | handmade chocolates.*

Ma·dei·ra¹ /mə'di(ə)rə, mə'de(ə)rə/ **1** an island in the Atlantic Ocean off the northwestern coast of Africa, the largest of the Madeiras, a group of islands that constitutes an autonomous region of Portugal; pop. 247,161 (2007); capital, Funchal. Encountered by the Portuguese in 1419, the islands were occupied by the Spanish 1580–1640 and the British 1807–14.
2 a river in northwestern Brazil that rises on the Bolivian border and flows about 900 miles (1,450 km) to meet the Amazon River east of Manaus. It is navigable to large oceangoing vessels as far as Pôrto Velho.
– DERIVATIVES **Ma·dei·ran adj. & n.**
– ORIGIN Portuguese, literally 'timber' (from Latin *materia* 'substance'), because of the island's dense woods.

Ma·dei·ra² (also **Madeira wine**) ▶ **n.** a fortified wine from the island of Madeira.

mad·e·leine /'madl-ən, ˌmadl-'ān/ ▶ **n.** a small rich cake, typically baked in a shell-shaped mold and often decorated with coconut and jam.
– ORIGIN French, probably named after *Madeleine* Paulmier, 19th-cent. French pastry cook.

made man ▶ **n.** a man whose success in life is assured. ■ a man who has been formally inducted as a full member of the Mafia.

Mad·e·moi·selle /ˌmad(ə)m(w)ə'zel, mam'zel/ ▶ **n.** (pl. **Mesdemoiselles** /ˌmād(ə)m(w)ə'zel(z)/) a title or form of address used of or to an unmarried French-speaking woman: *Mademoiselle Rossignol | thank you, Mademoiselle.* ■ (**mademoiselle**) a young Frenchwoman. ■ (**mademoiselle**) dated a French governess. ■ (**mademoiselle**) a female French teacher in an English-speaking school.
– ORIGIN French, from *ma* 'my' + *demoiselle* 'damsel.'

mad·er·i·za·tion /ˌmadərə'zāsʜən/ ▶ **n.** a form of oxidation that gives white wine a brownish color and caramelized flavor like that of Madeira.
– DERIVATIVES **mad·er·ized** /'madəˌrīzd/ **adj.**
– ORIGIN 1950s: from French *madérisation*, from *madériser*, from *Madère* 'Madeira.'

made to meas·ure ▶ **adj.** chiefly Brit. specially made to fit a particular person or space: *bicycles are made to measure.* ■ designed to fulfill a particular set of requirements: *amenities and attractions for a made-to-measure vacation.*

made to or·der ▶ **adj.** specially made according to a customer's specifications: *the kitchen's made-to-order breads.* ■ ideally suited to certain requirements: *a formalism seemingly made to order for the problem at hand.*

made-up ▶ **adj. 1** wearing makeup: *her immaculately made-up face.*
2 invented; not true: *a made-up story.*

mad·house /'madˌhous/ ▶ **n.** historical a mental institution. ■ informal a psychiatric hospital. ■ [in sing.] a scene of extreme confusion or uproar: *this place is a madhouse.*

Ma·dhya Pra·desh /'mədyə prə'desʜ/ a large state in central India, formed in 1956; capital, Bhopal.

Mad·i·son¹ /'madəsən/ the capital of Wisconsin, situated in the central part of the state; pop. 231,916 (est. 2008).
– ORIGIN named after President James *Madison* (see MADISON²).

Mad·i·son², James (1751–1836), 4th president of the US 1809–17. He played a major part in the drafting of the US Constitution 1787, and he proposed the Bill of Rights 1791. A Democratic-Republican, his presidency saw the US emerge successfully from the War of 1812.

James Madison

Mad·i·son³ ▶ **n.** an energetic group dance popular in the 1960s.
– ORIGIN of unknown origin.

Mad·i·son Av·e·nue /ˌmadəsən 'avən(y)o͞o/ a street in New York City, center of the advertising business in the US. ■ used in allusion to the world of advertising: *Madison Avenue's youth-oriented approach.*

mad·ly /'madlē/ ▶ **adv.** in a manner suggesting or characteristic of insanity: *his eyes bulged madly.* ■ informal with extreme intensity: *the boys are all madly in love with you.*

mad·man /'madˌman, -mən/ ▶ **n.** (pl. **madmen**) a man who is mentally ill. ■ an extremely foolish or reckless person: *the car was out of control—some madman going too fast.* ■ used in similes to refer to a person who does something very fast, intensely, or violently: *I was working like a madman.*

mad·ness /'madnəs/ ▶ **n.** the state of being mentally ill, esp. severely. ■ extremely foolish behavior: *it is madness to allow children to roam around after dark.* ■ a state of frenzied or chaotic activity: *from about midnight to three in the morning it's absolute madness in here.*

Ma·don·na¹ /mə'dänə/ ▶ **n.** (**the Madonna**) the Virgin Mary. ■ a picture, statue, or medallion of the Madonna, typically depicted seated and holding the infant Jesus. ■ (usu. **madonna**) an idealized virtuous and beautiful woman.
– ORIGIN late 16th cent. (as a respectful form of address to an Italian woman): Italian, from *ma* (old form of *mia* 'my') + *donna* 'lady' (from Latin *domina*).

Ma·don·na² (1958–), US pop singer and actress; born *Madonna Louise Ciccone.* Albums such as *Like a Virgin* (1984) and her image as a sex symbol brought her international stardom in the mid-1980s.

ma·don·na lil·y ▶ **n.** a tall white-flowered lily with golden pollen. Native to Asia Minor, it is traditionally associated with purity and is often depicted in paintings of the Madonna. ● *Lilium candidum*, family Liliaceae.

Ma·dras /mə'dras, mə'dräs/ **1** former name (until 1995) for CHENNAI.
2 former name (until 1968) of the Indian state of TAMIL NADU.

mad·ras /'madrəs, mə'dras/ ▶ **n.** a strong, fine-textured cotton fabric, typically patterned with colorful stripes or checks.
– ORIGIN mid 19th cent.: by association with MADRAS.

ma·dra·sa /mə'drasə/ (also **madrasah** or **medrese** /-'dresə/) ▶ **n.** a college for Islamic instruction.
– ORIGIN Arabic, from *darasa* 'to study.'

Mad·re·po·rar·i·a /ˌmadrəpə're(ə)rēə, məˌdrepə-/ Zoology another term for SCLERACTINIA.
– DERIVATIVES **mad·re·po·rar·i·an** /-'re(ə)rēən/ **n. & adj.**
– ORIGIN modern Latin (plural), from *Madrepora* (genus name), from Italian, probably from *madre* 'mother,' with reference to the prolific growth of the coral.

mad·re·pore /'madrəˌpôr/ ▶ **n. 1** a stony coral of the genus *Madrepora.*
2 the polyp producing this.
– DERIVATIVES **mad·re·por·ic** /ˌmadrə'pôrik/ **adj.**

mad·re·por·ite /'madrəˌpôˌrīt/ ▶ **n.** Zoology a perforated plate by which the entry of seawater into the vascular system of an echinoderm is controlled.
– ORIGIN early 19th cent.: from *madrepore* (see MADREPORARIA) + -ITE¹.

Ma·drid /mə'drid/ the capital of Spain; pop. 3,213,271 (2008). Situated on a high plateau in the center of the country, it replaced Valladolid as capital in 1561.

mad·ri·gal /'madrigəl/ ▶ **n.** a part-song for several voices, esp. one of the Renaissance period, typically arranged in elaborate counterpoint and without instrumental accompaniment. Originally used of a genre of 14th-century Italian songs, the term now usually refers to English or Italian songs of the late 16th and early 17th c., in a free style strongly influenced by the text.
– DERIVATIVES **mad·ri·gal·i·an** /ˌmadri'gālēən/ **adj.**, **mad·ri·gal·ist** /-ist/ **n.**
– ORIGIN from Italian *madrigale* (from medieval Latin *carmen matricale* 'simple song'), from *matricalis* 'maternal or primitive,' from *matrix* 'womb.'

mad·ri·lene /ˌmadrə'lān, -'len/ ▶ **n.** a clear soup, usually served cold.
– ORIGIN from French (*consommé à la*) *madrilène*, literally 'soup in the Madrid style.'

Mad·ri·le·nian /ˌmadrə'lānēən/ ▶ **adj.** of or relating to Madrid.
▶ **n.** a native or inhabitant of Madrid.
– ORIGIN from MADRILEÑO + -IAN.

Ma·dri·le·ño /ˌmädri'lānyō/ ▶ **n.** (pl. **Madrileños**) (fem. **Madrileña** /ˌmädri'lānyə/) a native or inhabitant of Madrid.
– ORIGIN Spanish.

ma·dro·ne /mə'drōnə/ (also **madroño** /-'drōnyō/) ▶ **n.** an evergreen tree of the heath family with white flowers, red berries, and glossy leaves, native to western North America. Typically, its smooth, thin red bark peels away to reveal a yellowish layer underneath. ● Genus *Arbutus*, family Ericaceae: several species, in particular the **Pacific madrone** (*A. menziesii*).
– ORIGIN mid 19th cent.: from Spanish.

mad·tom /'madˌtäm/ ▶ **n.** a small North American freshwater catfish that has a venom gland at the base of the pectoral fin spines, with which it can inflict a painful wound. ● Genus *Noturus*, family Ictaluridae: numerous species, including the common **tadpole madtom** (*N. gyrinus*).

Ma·du·ra /mə'do͝orə/ an island of Indonesia, off the northeastern coast of Java.

Ma·du·rai /ˌmädə'rī/ a city in Tamil Nadu in southern India; pop. 895,600 (est. 2009).

Mad·u·rese /ˌmadyə'rēz, -'rēs/ ▶ **n.** (pl. **same**) **1** a native or inhabitant of the island of Madura in Indonesia.
2 an Indonesian language spoken in Madura and nearby parts of Java.
▶ **adj.** of or relating to the inhabitants of Madura or their language.

mad·wom·an /'madˌwo͝omən/ ▶ **n.** (pl. **madwomen**) a woman who is mentally ill. ■ used in similes to refer to a woman who does something very fast, intensely, or violently: *she'd driven my father's convertible like a madwoman.*

MAE ▶ **abbr.** ■ Master of Aeronautical Engineering. ■ Master of Art Education. ■ Master of Arts in Education.

Mae·an·der /mē'andər/ ancient name of MENDERES.

M.A.Ed. ▶ **abbr.** Master of Arts in Education.

mael·strom /'mālˌsträm, -strəm/ ▶ **n.** a powerful whirlpool in the sea or a river. ■ a situation or state of confused movement or violent turmoil: *the train station was a maelstrom of crowds.*
– ORIGIN late 17th cent.: from early modern Dutch (denoting a mythical whirlpool supposed to exist in the Arctic Ocean, west of Norway), from *maalen* 'grind, whirl' + *stroom* 'stream.'

mae·nad /'mēˌnad/ ▶ **n.** (in ancient Greece) a female follower of Bacchus, traditionally associated with divine possession and frenzied rites.
– DERIVATIVES **mae·nad·ic** /mē'nadik/ **adj.**
– ORIGIN late 16th cent.: via Latin from Greek *Mainas, Mainad-*, from *mainesthai* 'to rave.'

ma·es·to·so /mī'stōsō, ˌmīe-, -'stōzō/ Music ▶ **adv. & adj.** (esp. as a direction) in a majestic manner.
▶ **n.** (pl. **maestosos**) a movement or passage marked to be performed in this way.
– ORIGIN Italian, 'majestic,' based on Latin *majestas* 'majesty.'

maes·tro /'mīstrō/ ▶ **n.** (pl. **maestri** /'mīstrē/ or **maestros**) a distinguished musician, esp. a conductor of classical music. ■ a great or distinguished figure in any sphere: *a movie maestro.*
– ORIGIN early 18th cent.: Italian, 'master,' from Latin *magister.*

Mae·ter·linck /'metərˌlingk/, Count Maurice (1862–1949), Belgian poet, playwright, and essayist. His prose dramas *La Princesse Maleine* (1889) and *Pelléas et Mélisande* (1892) established him as a leading figure in the symbolist movement. Nobel Prize for Literature (1911).

Mae West /'mā 'west/ ▶ **n.** informal, dated an inflatable life jacket, originally as issued to pilots during World War II.
– ORIGIN 1940s: from the name of the US movie actress *Mae West*, noted for her large bust.

Ma·fi·a /'mäfēə/ ▶ **n.** (**the Mafia**) [treated as sing. or pl.] an organized international body of criminals, operating originally in Sicily and now esp. in Italy and the US and having a complex and ruthless behavioral code. ■ (usu. **mafia**) any similar group using extortion and other criminal methods. ■ (usu. **mafia**) a closed group of people in a particular field, having a controlling influence: *the conservative top tennis mafia.*
– ORIGIN Italian (Sicilian dialect), originally in the sense 'bragging.'

maf·ic /'mafik/ ▶ **adj.** Geology relating to, denoting, or containing a group of dark-colored, mainly ferromagnesian minerals such as pyroxene and olivine. Often contrasted with FELSIC.
– ORIGIN early 20th cent.: blend of MAGNESIUM and a contracted form of FERRIC.

Ma·fi·o·so /ˌmäfē'ōsō, -zō/ (also **mafioso**) ▶ **n.** (pl. **Mafiosi** /-sē, -zē/) a member of the Mafia.
– ORIGIN Italian.

mag /mag/ ▶ **n.** informal **1** a magazine (periodical).
2 a magazine (of ammunition).
3 magnesium or magnesium alloy.
4 a magneto.
5 magnitude (of stars or other celestial objects).

Ma·ga·di, Lake /mə'gädē/ a salt lake in the Great Rift Valley, in southern Kenya, with extensive deposits of sodium carbonate and other minerals.

Mag·a·hi /'mɑgə,hē/ ▶ **n.** a Bihari language spoken in central Bihar and West Bengal.
▶ **adj.** of or relating to this language.
– ORIGIN from Hindi *Magadhī* 'of Magadha.'

mag·a·zine /,magə'zēn, 'magə,zēn/ ▶ **n. 1** a periodical publication containing articles and illustrations, typically covering a particular subject or area of interest: *a car magazine* | *a women's magazine.* ■ a regular television or radio program comprising a variety of topical news or entertainment items.
2 a chamber for holding a supply of cartridges to be fed automatically to the breech of a gun. ■ a similar device feeding a camera, compact disc player, etc.
3 a store for arms, ammunition, explosives, and provisions for use in military operations.
– ORIGIN late 16th cent.: from French *magasin,* from Italian *magazzino,* from Arabic *makzin, makzan* 'storehouse,' from *kazana* 'store up.' The term originally meant 'store' and was often used from the mid 17th cent. in the title of books providing information useful to particular groups of people, whence sense 1 (mid 18th cent). Sense 3, a contemporary specialization of the original meaning, gave rise to sense 2 in the mid 18th cent.

Mag·da·le·na /,magdə'lānə, ,mäg-/ the principal river of Colombia, rising in the Andes and flowing north for about 1,000 miles (1,600 km) to enter the Caribbean Sea at Barranquilla.

mag·da·lene /'magdə,lēn, -,lin/ (also **magdalen**) ▶ **n.** (**the Magdalene**) St. Mary Magdalene. ■ archaic a reformed prostitute. ■ archaic a home for reformed prostitutes.
– ORIGIN late Middle English: via ecclesiastical Latin from Greek (*Maria hē*) *Magdalēnē* '(Mary of) *Magdala*' (to whom Jesus appeared after his resurrection; John 20:1–18), commonly identified (probably wrongly) with the sinner of Luke 8:37.

Mag·da·le·ni·an /,magdə'lēnēən/ ▶ **adj.** Archaeology of, relating to, or denoting the final Paleolithic culture in Europe, following the Solutrean and dated to about 17,000–11,500 years ago. It is characterized by a range of bone and horn tools, and by highly developed cave art. ■ (as noun **the Magdalenian**) the Magdalenian culture or period.
– ORIGIN late 19th cent.: from French *Magdalénien* 'from La Madeleine,' a site in the Dordogne, France, where objects from this culture were found.

Mag·de·burg /'magdəbərg, 'mägdə,bo͝ork/ an industrial city in Germany, the capital of Saxony-Anhalt, situated on the Elbe River and linked to the Rhine and Ruhr rivers by the Mittelland Canal; pop. 229,800 (est. 2006).

mage /māj/ ▶ **n.** archaic or literary a magician or learned person.
– ORIGIN late Middle English: anglicized form of Latin *magus* (see **MAGUS**).

Ma·gel·lan[1] /mə'jelən/ an American space probe launched in 1989 to map the surface of Venus, using radar to penetrate the dense cloud cover. The probe was deliberately burned up in Venus's atmosphere in 1994.

Ma·gel·lan[2], Ferdinand (*c.*1480–1521), Portuguese explorer; Portuguese name *Fernão Magalhães.* In 1519, he sailed from Spain, rounding South America through the strait that now bears his name, and reached the Philippines in 1521. He was killed in a skirmish on Cebu; the survivors sailed back to Spain around Africa, completing the first circumnavigation of the globe in 1522.

Ma·gel·lan, Strait of a passage that separates Tierra del Fuego and other islands from mainland South America. It connects the Atlantic and Pacific oceans.

Mag·el·lan·ic Clouds /,majə'lanik/ Astronomy two diffuse luminous patches in the southern sky, now known to be small irregular galaxies that are the closest to our own. The **Large Magellanic Cloud** is about 169,000 light years away, and the **Small Magellanic Cloud** is about 210,000 light years away.
– ORIGIN named after the Portuguese explorer *Magellan* (see **MAGELLAN**[2]).

Ma·gen Da·vid /mä'gen dä'vēd, 'môgən 'dôvid/ ▶ **n.** another name for **STAR OF DAVID**.
– ORIGIN early 20th cent.: Hebrew, literally 'shield of David,' with reference to David, King of Israel (see **DAVID**[1]).

ma·gen·ta /mə'jentə/ ▶ **n.** a light purplish red that is one of the primary subtractive colors, complementary to green. ■ the dye fuchsin.
– ORIGIN mid 19th cent.: named after *Magenta* in northern Italy, site of a battle (1859) fought shortly before the dye (of bloodlike color) was discovered.

mag·gid /'mägid, mä'gēd/ ▶ **n.** (pl. **maggidim** /mä'gēdim, ,mägē'dēm/) an itinerant Jewish preacher.
– ORIGIN late 19th cent.: from Hebrew *maggīd* 'narrator.'

Mag·gio·re, Lake /mä'jôrā/ the second largest of the lakes of northern Italy. It extends into southern Switzerland.

mag·got /'magət/ ▶ **n. 1** a soft-bodied legless larva, esp. that of a fly found in decaying matter. ■ Fishing bait consisting of a maggot or maggots.
2 archaic a whimsical fancy.
– DERIVATIVES **mag·got·y** adj.
– ORIGIN late Middle English: perhaps an alteration of dialect *maddock,* from Old Norse *mathkr,* of Germanic origin.

Ma·ghrib /'məgrəb/ (also **Maghreb**) a region of north and northwestern Africa between the Atlantic Ocean and Egypt that comprises the coastal plain and Atlas Mountains of Morocco, together with Algeria and Tunisia and sometimes Tripolitania. Compare with **BARBARY**.

Ma·gi /'mā,jī/ (**the Magi**) the "wise men" from the East who brought gifts to the infant Jesus (Matt. 2:1), said in later tradition to be kings named Caspar, Melchior, and Balthasar who brought gifts of gold, frankincense, and myrrh.
– ORIGIN see **MAGUS**.

ma·gi /'mā,jī/ plural form of **MAGUS**.

ma·gi·an /'māj(ē)ən, 'mā,jīən/ (also **Magian**) ▶ **adj.** of or relating to the magi of ancient Persia. ■ of or relating to the Magi who brought gifts to the infant Jesus.
▶ **n.** a magus or Magus.

mag·ic /'majik/ ▶ **n.** the power of apparently influencing the course of events by using mysterious or supernatural forces: *do you believe in magic?* | *suddenly, as if by magic, the doors start to open.* ■ mysterious tricks, such as making things disappear and appear again, performed as entertainment. ■ a quality that makes something seem removed from everyday life, esp. in a way that gives delight: *the magic of the theater.* ■ informal something that has such a quality: *their seaside town is pure magic.*
▶ **adj. 1** used in magic or working by magic; having or apparently having supernatural powers: *a magic wand.* ■ [attrib.] very effective in producing results, esp. desired ones: *confidence is the magic ingredient needed to spark recovery.*
2 informal wonderful; exciting: *what a magic moment.*
▶ **v.** (**magics, magicking, magicked**) [with obj.] move, change, or create by or as if by magic: *he must have been magicked out of the car at the precise second it exploded.*
– PHRASES **like magic** remarkably effectively or rapidly: *it repels rain like magic.*
– ORIGIN late Middle English (also in the sense 'a magical procedure'): from Old French *magique,* from Latin *magicus* (adjective), late Latin *magica* (noun), from Greek *magikē* (*tekhnē*) '(art of) a magus': magi were regarded as magicians.

mag·i·cal /'majikəl/ ▶ **adj. 1** relating to, using, or resembling magic: *he had a gentle, magical touch with the child.*
2 beautiful or delightful in such a way as to seem removed from everyday life: *it was a magical evening of pure nostalgia.*
– DERIVATIVES **mag·i·cal·ly** adv.

mag·i·cal re·al·ism ▶ **n.** another term for **MAGIC REALISM**.

mag·ic bul·let ▶ **n.** informal a medicine or other remedy, esp. an undiscovered or hypothetical one, with wonderful or highly specific properties.

mag·ic eye ▶ **n. 1** informal a photoelectric cell or similar electrical device used for identification, detection, or measurement.
2 a small cathode ray tube in some radio receivers that displays a pattern that enables the radio to be accurately tuned.

ma·gi·cian /mə'jisHən/ ▶ **n.** a person with magical powers. ■ a person who performs magic tricks for entertainment. ■ informal a person with exceptional skill in a particular area: *he was the magician of the fan belt.*
– ORIGIN late Middle English: from Old French *magicien,* from late Latin *magica* (see **MAGIC**).

ma·gick ▶ **n.** chiefly archaic spelling of **MAGIC**.
– DERIVATIVES **ma·gick·al** adj.

mag·ic lan·tern ▶ **n.** historical a simple form of image projector used for showing photographic slides.

Mag·ic Mark·er ▶ **n.** trademark an indelible felt-tip marker, esp. one with a wide tip.

mag·ic mush·room ▶ **n.** informal any toadstool with hallucinogenic properties, esp. the liberty cap and its relatives. ● Genus *Psilocybe,* family Strophariaceae, class Hymenomycetes: several species, including *P. mexicana,* which is traditionally consumed by American Indians in Mexico.

mag·ic num·ber ▶ **n.** a figure regarded as significant or momentous in a particular context. ■ chiefly Baseball the number that, at a late stage in the season, signifies the combination of wins for the first-place team and losses for another team that will allow the former to end the season alone in first place.

mag·ic re·al·ism (also **magical realism**) ▶ **n.** a literary or artistic genre in which realistic narrative and naturalistic technique are combined with surreal elements of dream or fantasy.
– DERIVATIVES **mag·ic re·al·ist** n.

mag·ic square ▶ **n.** a square that is divided into smaller squares, each containing a number, such that the figures in each vertical, horizontal, and diagonal row add up to the same value.

8	18	16
22	14	6
12	10	20

magic square

Ma·gi·not Line /'mazHə,nō, 'maj-/ a line of defensive fortifications constructed by the French along their eastern border, extending from Switzerland to Luxembourg, between 1929 and 1936. In World War II, although the defenses held, the Germans outflanked them, going through Belgium to conquer France. ■ [as noun] (also **Maginot line**) an impressive but often ineffectual means of protection or defense: *the courts are our Maginot Line against industry.*
– ORIGIN named after André *Maginot* (1877–1932), a French minister of war.

mag·is·ter /'majəstər/ ▶ **n.** archaic a title or form of address given to scholars, esp. those qualified to teach in a medieval university.
– ORIGIN late Middle English: from Latin, 'master.'

mag·is·te·ri·al /,majə'sti(ə)rēəl/ ▶ **adj. 1** having or showing great authority: *a magisterial pronouncement.* ■ domineering; dictatorial: *he dropped his somewhat magisterial style of questioning.*
2 relating to or conducted by a magistrate. ■ (of a person) holding the office of a magistrate.
– DERIVATIVES **mag·is·te·ri·al·ly** adv.
– ORIGIN early 17th cent.: from medieval Latin *magisterialis,* from late Latin *magisterius,* from Latin *magister* 'master.'

mag·is·te·ri·um /,majə'sti(ə)rēəm/ ▶ **n.** the teaching authority of the Roman Catholic Church, esp. as exercised by bishops or the pope. ■ the official and authoritative teaching of the Roman Catholic Church.
– ORIGIN mid 19th cent.: Latin, 'the office of master,' from *magister* (see **MAGISTER**).

mag·is·tra·cy /'majəstrəsē/ ▶ **n.** (pl. **magistracies**) the office or authority of a magistrate. ■ (**the magistracy**) magistrates collectively.

mag·is·tral /'majəstrəl/ ▶ **adj.** formal or archaic relating to a master or masters.
– ORIGIN late 16th cent.: from French, or from Latin *magistralis,* from *magister* 'master.'

mag·is·trate /'majə,strāt/ ▶ **n.** a civil officer or lay judge who administers the law, esp. one who conducts a court that deals with minor offenses and holds preliminary hearings for more serious ones.
– DERIVATIVES **mag·is·tra·ture** /-,strāCHər, -strə,CHo͝o(ə)r/ n.
– ORIGIN late Middle English: from Latin *magistratus* 'administrator,' from *magister* 'master.'

mag·lev /'mag,lev/ ▶ **n.** [usu. as modifier] a transportation system in which trains glide above a track, supported by magnetic repulsion and propelled by a linear motor: *maglev trains.*
– ORIGIN late 20th cent.: from *mag(netic) lev(itation).*

mag·ma /'magmə/ ▶ **n.** hot fluid or semifluid material below or within the earth's crust from which lava and other igneous rock is formed by cooling.
– DERIVATIVES **mag·mat·ic** /mag'matik/ adj.

m

–ORIGIN late Middle English (in the sense 'residue of dregs after evaporation or pressing of a semiliquid substance'): via Latin from Greek *magma* (from *massein* 'knead').

mag·ma·tism /ˈmagməˌtizəm/ ▶ n. Geology the motion or activity of magma.

Mag·na Car·ta /ˌmagnə ˈkärtə/ a charter of liberty and political rights obtained from King John of England by his rebellious barons at Runnymede in 1215, which came to be seen as the seminal document of English constitutional practice.
–ORIGIN from medieval Latin, 'great charter.'

mag·na cum lau·de /ˌmagnə ko͝om ˈloudə, ˈloudē/ ▶ adv. & adj. with great distinction (with reference to college degrees and diplomas).
–ORIGIN Latin, literally 'with great praise.'

Mag·na Grae·ci·a /ˌmagnə ˈgrāsHə/ the ancient Greek cities of southern Italy, founded from *c.*750 BC onward by colonists from Euboea, Sparta, and elsewhere in Greece.
–ORIGIN Latin, literally 'Great Greece.'

mag·na·nim·i·ty /ˌmagnəˈnimətē/ ▶ n. the fact or condition of being magnanimous; generosity: *both sides will have to show magnanimity.*

mag·nan·i·mous /magˈnanəməs/ ▶ adj. very generous or forgiving, esp. toward a rival or someone less powerful than oneself.
–DERIVATIVES **mag·nan·i·mous·ly** adv.
–ORIGIN mid 16th cent.: from Latin *magnanimus* (from *magnus* 'great' + *animus* 'soul') + **-OUS**.

mag·nate /ˈmagˌnāt, ˈmagnət/ ▶ n. a wealthy and influential person, esp. in business: *a media magnate.*
–ORIGIN late Middle English: from late Latin *magnas, magnat-* 'great man,' from Latin *magnus* 'great.'

mag·ne·sia /magˈnēZHə, -ˈnēSHə/ ▶ n. Chemistry magnesium oxide. ● Chem. formula: MgO. ■ hydrated magnesium carbonate used as an antacid and laxative.
–ORIGIN late Middle English (referring to a mineral said to be an ingredient of the philosopher's stone): via medieval Latin from Greek *Magnēsia*, denoting a mineral from Magnesia in Asia Minor.

m

mag·ne·sian /magˈnēZHən, -ˈnēSHən/ ▶ adj. (chiefly of rocks and minerals) containing or relatively rich in magnesium.

mag·ne·site /ˈmagnəˌsīt/ ▶ n. a whitish mineral consisting of magnesium carbonate, used as a heat-resistant lining in some furnaces.

mag·ne·si·um /magˈnēzēəm, -ZHəm/ ▶ n. the chemical element of atomic number 12, a silver-white metal of the alkaline earth series. It is used to make strong lightweight alloys, esp. for the aerospace industry, and is also used in flashbulbs and pyrotechnics because it burns with a brilliant white flame. (Symbol: **Mg**)

mag·ne·si·um flare (also **magnesium light**) ▶ n. a brilliant white flare containing metallic magnesium wire or ribbon.

mag·net /ˈmagnət/ ▶ n. a piece of iron (or an ore, alloy, or other material) that has its component atoms so ordered that the material exhibits properties of magnetism, such as attracting other iron-containing objects or aligning itself in an external magnetic field. ■ archaic term for **LODESTONE**. ■ a person or thing that has a powerful attraction: *the beautiful stretch of white sand is a magnet for sun worshipers.*
–ORIGIN late Middle English (denoting a lodestone): from Latin *magnes, magnet-*, from Greek *magnēs lithos* 'lodestone,' probably influenced by Anglo-Norman French *magnete* (from Latin *magnes, magnet-*).

mag·ne·tar /ˈmagniˌtär/ ▶ n. Astronomy a neutron star with an extremely strong magnetic field.
–ORIGIN 1990s: from *magnetic* + *-ar*, on the pattern of *pulsar* and *quasar*.

mag·net·ic /magˈnetik/ ▶ adj. **1** capable of being attracted by or acquiring the properties of a magnet: *steel is magnetic.* ■ relating to or exhibiting magnetism: *an airborne magnetic survey | the clock has a magnetic back to stick to the fridge.* ■ (of a bearing in navigation) measured relative to magnetic north.
2 very attractive or alluring: *his magnetic personality.*
–DERIVATIVES **mag·net·i·cal·ly** /-ik(ə)lē/ adv.
–ORIGIN early 17th cent.: from late Latin *magneticus*, from Latin *magneta* (see **MAGNET**).

mag·net·ic com·pass ▶ n. another term for **COMPASS** (sense 1 of the noun).

mag·net·ic disk ▶ n. see **DISK** (sense 1 of the noun).

mag·net·ic e·qua·tor ▶ n. the irregular imaginary line, passing around the earth near the equator, on which a magnetic needle has no dip (see **DIP** (sense 4 of the noun)).

mag·net·ic field ▶ n. a region around a magnetic material or a moving electric charge within which the force of magnetism acts.

mag·net·ic in·cli·na·tion ▶ n. another term for **DIP** (sense 4 of the noun).

mag·net·ic in·duc·tion ▶ n. **1** magnetic flux or flux density.
2 the process by which an object or material is magnetized by an external magnetic field.

mag·net·ic mine ▶ n. a mine detonated by the proximity of a magnetized body such as a ship or tank.

mag·net·ic mo·ment ▶ n. Physics the property of a magnet that interacts with an applied field to give a mechanical moment.

mag·net·ic nee·dle ▶ n. a piece of magnetized steel used as an indicator on the dial of a compass and in magnetic and electrical apparatus.

mag·net·ic north ▶ n. the direction in which the north end of a compass needle or other freely suspended magnet will point in response to the earth's magnetic field. It deviates from true north over time and from place to place because the earth's magnetic poles are not fixed in relation to its axis.

mag·net·ic pole ▶ n. each of the points near the extremities of the axis of rotation of the earth or another celestial body where a magnetic needle dips vertically. ■ each of the two points or regions of an artificial or natural magnet to and from which the lines of magnetic force are directed.

mag·net·ic res·o·nance im·ag·ing (abbr.: **MRI**) ▶ n. a form of medical imaging that measures the response of the atomic nuclei of body tissues to high-frequency radio waves when placed in a strong magnetic field, and that produces images of the internal organs.

mag·net·ic storm ▶ n. a disturbance of the magnetic field of the earth (or other celestial body).

mag·net·ic tape ▶ n. tape used in recording sound, pictures, or computer data.

mag·net·ic var·i·a·tion ▶ n. see **VARIATION** (sense 1).

mag·net·ism /ˈmagnəˌtizəm/ ▶ n. **1** a physical phenomenon produced by the motion of electric charge, resulting in attractive and repulsive forces between objects.

> All magnetism is due to circulating electric currents. In magnetic materials the magnetism is produced by electrons orbiting within the atoms; in most substances the magnetic effects of different electrons cancel each other out, but in some, such as iron, a net magnetic field can be induced by aligning the atoms.

2 the ability to attract and charm people: *his personal magnetism attracted men to the brotherhood.*
–ORIGIN early 17th cent.: from modern Latin *magnetismus*, from Latin *magneta* (see **MAGNET**).

mag·net·ite /ˈmagnəˌtīt/ ▶ n. a gray-black magnetic mineral that consists of an oxide of iron and is an important form of iron ore.
–ORIGIN mid 19th cent.: from **MAGNET** + **-ITE**¹.

mag·net·ize /ˈmagnəˌtīz/ ▶ v. [with obj.] give magnetic properties to; make magnetic. ■ attract strongly as if by a magnet.
–DERIVATIVES **mag·net·iz·a·ble** adj., **mag·net·i·za·tion** /ˌmagnətəˈzāSHən/ n., **mag·net·iz·er** n.

mag·ne·to /magˈnētō/ ▶ n. (pl. **magnetos**) a small electric generator containing a permanent magnet and used to provide high-voltage pulses, esp. (formerly) in the ignition systems of internal combustion engines.
–ORIGIN late 19th cent.: abbreviation of **MAGNETO-ELECTRIC**.

magneto- ▶ comb. form relating to a magnet or magnetism: *magneto-electric.*

mag·ne·to-e·lec·tric ▶ adj. relating to the electric currents generated in a material by its motion in a magnetic field. ■ (of an electric generator) using permanent magnets.
–DERIVATIVES **mag·ne·to-e·lec·tric·i·ty** n.

mag·ne·to·graph /magˈnētəˌgraf/ ▶ n. an instrument for recording measurements of magnetic forces.

mag·ne·to·hy·dro·dy·nam·ics /magˌnētōˌhīdrōˌdīˈnamiks/ ▶ plural n. [treated as sing.] the branch of physics that studies the behavior of an electrically conducting fluid such as a plasma or molten metal acted on by a magnetic field.
–DERIVATIVES **mag·ne·to·hy·dro·dy·nam·ic** /-ˌhīdrōˌdīˈnamik/ adj.

mag·ne·tom·e·ter /ˌmagnəˈtämətər/ ▶ n. an instrument used for measuring magnetic forces, esp. the earth's magnetism.
–DERIVATIVES **mag·ne·tom·e·try** /-ətrē/ n.

mag·ne·to·mo·tive force /magˌnētōˈmōtiv/ ▶ n. Physics a quantity representing the line integral of the magnetic intensity around a closed line (e.g., the sum of the magnetizing forces along a circuit).

mag·ne·ton /ˈmagnəˌtän/ ▶ n. a unit of magnetic moment in atomic and nuclear physics.
–ORIGIN early 20th cent.: from **MAGNETIC** + **-ON**.

mag·ne·to-op·ti·cal ▶ adj. of, relating to, or employing both optical and magnetic phenomena or technology.

mag·ne·to·pause /magˈnētəˌpôz/ ▶ n. the outer limit of a magnetosphere.

mag·ne·to·re·sist·ance /magˌnētəriˈzistəns/ ▶ n. Physics the dependence of the electrical resistance of a body on an external magnetic field.
–DERIVATIVES **mag·ne·to·re·sist·ive** /magˌnētəriˈzistiv/ adj.

mag·ne·to·sphere /magˈnētəˌsfir/ ▶ n. the region surrounding the earth or another astronomical body in which its magnetic field is the predominant effective magnetic field.
–DERIVATIVES **mag·ne·to·spher·ic** /ˌmagˌnētəˈsfirik/ adj.

mag·ne·to·tail /magˈnētəˌtāl/ ▶ n. Astronomy the broad elongated extension of a planet's magnetosphere on the side away from the sun.

mag·ne·tron /ˈmagnəˌträn/ ▶ n. an electron tube for amplifying or generating microwaves, with the flow of electrons controlled by an external magnetic field.
–ORIGIN early 20th cent.: from **MAGNETIC** + *-tron* from **ELECTRON**.

mag·net school ▶ n. a public school offering special instruction and programs not available elsewhere, designed to attract a more diverse student body from throughout a school district.

Mag·nif·i·cat /magˈnifiˌkät, mänˈyifi-/ ▶ n. a canticle used in Christian liturgy, esp. at vespers and evensong, the text being the hymn of the Virgin Mary (Luke 1:46–55).
–ORIGIN Middle English: Latin, literally 'magnifies' (from the opening words, which translate as 'my soul magnifies the Lord').

mag·ni·fi·ca·tion /ˌmagnəfiˈkāSHən/ ▶ n. the action or process of magnifying something or being magnified, esp. visually: *visible under high magnification.* ■ the degree to which something is or can be magnified: *at this magnification the pixels making up the image become visible.* ■ the magnifying power of an instrument: *this microscope should give a magnification of about 100.* ■ a magnified reproduction of something.

mag·nif·i·cence /magˈnifəsəns/ ▶ n. the quality of being magnificent. ■ (**His, Your,** etc., **Magnificence**) chiefly historical a title given to a monarch or other distinguished person, or used in addressing them.

mag·nif·i·cent /magˈnifəsənt/ ▶ adj. **1** impressively beautiful, elaborate, or extravagant; striking: *a dramatic landscape of magnificent mountains | the interior layout is magnificent.*
2 very good; excellent: *she paid tribute to their magnificent efforts.*
–DERIVATIVES **mag·nif·i·cent·ly** adv.
–ORIGIN late Middle English: via Old French from Latin *magnificent-* 'making great, serving to magnify,' based on *magnus* 'great.'

mag·nif·i·co /magˈnifiˌkō/ ▶ n. (pl. **magnificoes**) informal an eminent, powerful, or illustrious person.
–ORIGIN late 16th cent.: Italian, 'magnificent,' originally used to denote a Venetian magnate.

mag·ni·fy /ˈmagnəˌfī/ ▶ v. (**magnifies, magnifying, magnified**) [with obj.] **1** make (something) appear larger than it is, esp. with a lens or microscope: *the camera's zoom mode can magnify a certain area if required.* ■ increase or exaggerate the importance or effect of: *the risk is magnified if there is any dirty material next to the skin | she tended to magnify the defects of those she disliked.*
2 archaic extol; glorify: *praise the Lord and magnify Him.*
–DERIVATIVES **mag·ni·fi·er** /-ˌfīər/ n.
–ORIGIN late Middle English (in the senses 'show honor to (God)' and 'make greater in size or importance'): from Old French *magnifier* or Latin *magnificare*, based on Latin *magnus* 'great.' Sense 1 dates from the mid 17th cent.

mag·ni·fy·ing glass ▶ n. a lens that produces an enlarged image, typically set in a frame with a handle and used to examine small or finely detailed things such as fingerprints, stamps, and fine print.

mag·nil·o·quence /mag'niləkwəns/ ▶ **n.** use of high-flown language: *there was no trace of magniloquence.*

mag·nil·o·quent /mag'niləkwənt/ ▶ **adj.** using high-flown or bombastic language.
– DERIVATIVES **mag·nil·o·quent·ly** **adv.**
– ORIGIN mid 17th cent.: from Latin *magniloquus* (from *magnus* 'great' + *-loquus* '-speaking') + **-ENT**.

Mag·ni·to·gorsk /mǝg,nētǝ'gôrsk/ an industrial city in southern Russia, on the Ural River close to the border with Kazakhstan; pop. 409,600 (est. 2009).

mag·ni·tude /'magnǝ,to͞od/ ▶ **n. 1** the great size or extent of something: *they may feel discouraged at the magnitude of the task before them.* ■ great importance: *events of tragic magnitude.*
2 size: *electorates of less than average magnitude.* ■ a numerical quantity or value: *the magnitudes of all the economic variables could be determined.*
3 the degree of brightness of a star. The magnitude of an astronomical object is now reckoned as the negative logarithm of the brightness; a decrease of one magnitude represents an increase in brightness of 2.512 times. A star with an apparent magnitude of six is barely visible to the naked eye. See also **APPARENT MAGNITUDE, ABSOLUTE MAGNITUDE**. ■ the class into which a star falls by virtue of its brightness. ■ a difference of one on a scale of brightness, treated as a unit of measurement.
– PHRASES **of the first magnitude** see **FIRST**.
– ORIGIN late Middle English (also in the sense 'greatness of character'): from Latin *magnitudo*, from *magnus* 'great.'

mag·no·lia /mag'nōlyǝ/ ▶ **n.** a tree or shrub with large, typically creamy-pink, waxy flowers. Magnolias are widely grown as ornamental trees. ● Genus *Magnolia*, family Magnoliaceae: numerous species, including *M. campbellii*, native to the Himalayas and from which several varieties have been cultivated in North America.
– ORIGIN modern Latin, named after Pierre *Magnol* (1638–1715), French botanist.

magnolia

Mag·no·lia State a nickname for the state of **MISSISSIPPI**.

mag·no·lia vine ▶ **n.** another term for **SCHIZANDRA**.

mag·num /'magnǝm/ ▶ **n.** (pl. **magnums**) a thing of a type that is larger than normal, in particular: ■ a wine bottle of twice the standard size, normally 1½ liters. ■ (often **Magnum**) [often as modifier] trademark a gun designed to fire cartridges that are more powerful than its caliber would suggest: *his .357 Magnum pistol.*
– ORIGIN late 18th cent.: from Latin, neuter (used as a noun) of *magnus* 'great.'

mag·num o·pus /'magnǝm 'ōpǝs/ ▶ **n.** (pl. **magnum opuses** or **magna opera** /'magnǝ 'ōpǝrǝ, 'äpǝrǝ/) a large and important work of art, music, or literature, esp. one regarded as the most important work of an artist or writer.
– ORIGIN late 18th cent.: from Latin, 'great work.'

Mag·nus ef·fect /'magnǝs/ ▶ **n.** Physics the force exerted on a rapidly spinning cylinder or sphere moving through air or another fluid in a direction at an angle to the axis of spin. This force is responsible for the swerving of balls when hit or thrown with spin.
– ORIGIN 1920s: named after Heinrich G. *Magnus* (1802–70), German scientist.

Ma·gog /mǝ'gäg/ see **GOG AND MAGOG**.

mag·pie /'mag,pī/ ▶ **n.**
1 a long-tailed crow with boldly marked (or green) plumage and a raucous voice. ● Family Corvidae: five genera and several species, in particular the black-and-white **black-billed magpie** (*Pica pica*) of Eurasia and North America.
2 used in similes or comparisons to refer to a person who collects things, esp. things of little use or value, or a person who chatters idly.
– ORIGIN late 16th cent.: probably shortening of dialect *maggot the pie, maggoty-pie*, from *Magot* (Middle English nickname for the given name *Marguerite*) + **PIE²**.

black-billed magpie

M.Agr. ▶ **abbr.** Master of Agriculture.

mag·ret /'māgrā/ ▶ **n.** a fillet of meat cut from a breast of duck.
– ORIGIN French, diminutive of Gascon dialect *magre* 'lean' (as the leanest meat is chosen), corresponding to standard French *maigre*.

Ma·gritte /mǝ'grēt, ma-/, René (François Ghislain) (1898–1967), Belgian surrealist painter. His paintings are startling or amusing juxtapositions of the ordinary, the strange, and the erotic, depicted in a realist manner.

mag·uey /mǝ'gā/ ▶ **n.** an agave plant, esp. one yielding pulque.
– ORIGIN mid 16th cent.: via Spanish from Taino.

ma·gus /'māgǝs/ ▶ **n.** (pl. **magi** /'mā,jī/) a member of a priestly caste of ancient Persia. See also **MAGI**. ■ a sorcerer.
– ORIGIN Middle English: via Latin and Greek from Old Persian *maguš*.

mag wheel /mag/ ▶ **n.** a motor-vehicle wheel made from lightweight magnesium steel, typically having a pattern of holes or spokes around the hub.

Mag·yar /'mag,yär/ ▶ **n. 1** a member of a people who originated in the Urals and migrated westward to settle in what is now Hungary in the 9th century AD.
2 the Uralic language of this people; Hungarian.
▶ **adj.** of or relating to this people or language.
– ORIGIN the name in Hungarian.

Ma·gyar·or·szág /'mädyär,ôr,säg/ Hungarian name for **HUNGARY**.

Mah·a·bad /,mähǝ'bäd/ a city in northwestern Iran, near the Iraqi border, with a chiefly Kurdish population; pop. 135,780 (2006). Between 1941 and 1946 it was the center of a Soviet-supported Kurdish republic.

Ma·ha·bha·ra·ta /,mähǝ'bärǝtǝ/ one of the two great Sanskrit epics of the Hindus, existing in its present form since *c.*AD 400.It describes the civil war waged between the five Pandava brothers and their 100 stepbrothers at Kuruksetra near modern Delhi.
– ORIGIN Sanskrit, literally 'great Bharata,' i.e., the great epic of the Bharata dynasty.

ma·hal /mǝ'häl/ ▶ **n.** Indian **1** a mansion or palace (in names): *the Taj Mahal.*
2 living quarters set aside for a particular group of people: *the servant mahal.*
– ORIGIN early 17th cent.: from Urdu and Persian *maḥal(l)*, from Arabic *maḥall*, from *ḥall*, 'stopping-place, abode.'

ma·hant /mǝ'hǝnt/ ▶ **n.** Hinduism a chief priest of a temple or the head of a monastery.
– ORIGIN Hindi.

ma·ha·ra·ja /,mähǝ'räjǝ, -'räZHǝ/ (also **maharajah**) ▶ **n.** historical an Indian prince.
– ORIGIN from Hindi *mahārājā*, from Sanskrit *mahā* 'great' + *rājan* 'raja.'

ma·ha·ra·ni /,mähǝ'ränē/ (also **maharanee**) ▶ **n.** a maharaja's wife or widow.
– ORIGIN from Hindi *mahārānī*, from Sanskrit *mahā* 'great' + *rājñī* 'ranee.'

Ma·ha·rash·tra /,mä(h)ǝ'räsHtrǝ/ a large state in western India that borders on the Arabian Sea, formed in 1960 from the southeastern part of the former state of Bombay; capital, Mumbai (Bombay).
– DERIVATIVES **Ma·ha·rash·tri·an** /-trēǝn/ **adj. & n.**

Ma·ha·ri·shi /,mähǝ'rēsHē, mǝ'häräsHē/ ▶ **n.** a great Hindu sage or spiritual leader.
– ORIGIN alteration of Sanskrit *maharṣi*, from *mahā* 'great' + *ṛṣi* 'rishi.'

ma·hat·ma /mǝ'hätmǝ, -'hatmǝ/ ▶ **n.** (in South Asia) a person regarded with reverence or loving respect; a holy person or sage. ■ (**the Mahatma**) Mahatma Gandhi. ■ (in some forms of theosophy) a person in India or Tibet said to have supernatural powers.
– ORIGIN from Sanskrit *mahātman*, from *mahā* 'great' + *ātman* 'soul.'

Ma·ha·we·li /,mähǝ'wālē/ the major river in Sri Lanka. Rising in the central highlands, it flows north for 206 miles (330 km) to the Bay of Bengal.

Ma·ha·ya·na /,mähǝ'yänǝ/ (also **Mahayana Buddhism**) ▶ **n.** one of the two major traditions of Buddhism, now practiced in a variety of forms esp. in China, Tibet, Japan, and Korea. The tradition emerged around the 1st century AD and is typically concerned with altruistically oriented spiritual practice as embodied in the ideal of the bodhisattva. Compare with **THERAVADA**.
– ORIGIN from Sanskrit, from *mahā* 'great' + *yāna* 'vehicle.'

Mah·di /'mädē/ ▶ **n.** (pl. **Mahdis**) (in popular Muslim belief) a spiritual and temporal leader who will rule before the end of the world and restore religion and justice. ■ a person claiming to be this leader, notably Muhammad Ahmad of Dongola in Sudan (1843–85), whose revolutionary movement captured Khartoum and overthrew the Egyptian regime. ■ (in Shiite belief) the twelfth imam, who is expected to return and triumph over injustice.
– DERIVATIVES **Mah·dism** /'mä,dizǝm/ **n.**, **Mah·dist** /'mädist/ **n. & adj.**
– ORIGIN from Arabic *(al-)mahdī* 'he who is guided in the right way,' passive participle of *hadā* 'to guide.'

Mah·fouz /mä'fo͞oz/, Naguib (1911–2006), Egyptian novelist and short-story writer. Notable works: *Miramar* (1967), *Wedding Song* (1981), and *The Seventh Heaven* (2005). Nobel Prize for Literature (1988).

Ma·hi·can /mǝ'hēkǝn/ (also **Mohican**) ▶ **n. 1** a member of an American Indian people formerly inhabiting the Upper Hudson Valley in New York. Compare with **MOHEGAN**.
2 the Algonquian language of this people.
▶ **adj.** of or relating to the Mahicans or their language.
– ORIGIN the name in Mahican, meaning 'people of the estuary.'

Ma·hi·lyow /mǝgil'yôf/ an industrial city and railroad center in eastern Belarus, on the Dnieper River; pop. 372,000 (est. 2009). Russian name **MOGILYOV**.

ma·hi·ma·hi /,mähē'mähē/ ▶ **n.** an edible marine fish of warm seas, with silver and bright blue or green coloration when alive. Also called **DOLPHIN** or **DORADO**. ● Family Coryphaenidae and genus *Coryphaena*: two species, in particular the large *C. hippurus*.
– ORIGIN 1940s: from Hawaiian.

mah-jongg /,mä 'ZHäNG, -ZHôNG/ (also **mah-jong**) ▶ **n.** a Chinese game played, usually by four people, with 136 or 144 rectangular pieces called tiles. The object is to collect winning sets of these tiles, as in card games such as gin rummy.
– ORIGIN early 20th cent.: from Chinese dialect *ma-tsiang*, literally 'sparrows.'

Mah·ler /'mälǝr/, Gustav (1860–1911), Austrian composer, conductor, and pianist. His works, which include symphonies and songs, form a link between romanticism and the experimentalism of Schoenberg.
– DERIVATIVES **Mah·ler·i·an** /mä'le(ǝ)rēǝn/ **adj.**

mahl·stick /'môl,stik/ (also **maulstick**) ▶ **n.** a light stick with a padded leather ball at one end, held against work by a painter or signwriter to support and steady the brush hand.
– ORIGIN mid 17th cent.: from Dutch *maalstok*, from *malen* 'to paint' + *stok* 'stick.'

ma·hoe¹ /mǝ'hō, 'mä,hō/ ▶ **n.** a small bushy New Zealand tree of the violet family, with whitish bark and clusters of small greenish flowers. ● *Melicytus ramiflorus*, family Violaceae.
– ORIGIN early 19th cent.: from Maori.

ma·hoe² ▶ **n.** W. Indian any of a number of tropical trees and shrubs yielding bast that is used to make cordage. ● Several species, esp. of the genus *Hibiscus* (family Malvaceae), in particular the widespread *H. tiliaceus* and the Caribbean *H. elatus*.
– ORIGIN from Arawak *maho*.

ma·hog·a·ny /mǝ'hägǝnē/ ▶ **n. 1** hard reddish-brown timber from a tropical tree, used for high-quality furniture. ■ a rich reddish-brown color like that of mahogany wood.
2 the tropical American tree that produces this timber, widely harvested from the wild. ● Genus *Swietenia*, family Meliaceae: three species, esp. *S. mahagoni*. ■ used in names of trees that yield similar timber, e.g., **Philippine mahogany**.
– ORIGIN mid 17th cent.: of unknown origin.

Ma·hon /mǝ'hōn, mä'ōn/ (also **Port Mahon**) the capital of the island of Minorca, a port on the southeastern coast; pop. 30,300 (est. 2009). Spanish name **Mahón**.

ma·ho·ni·a /mǝ'hōnēǝ/ ▶ **n.** an evergreen shrub of the barberry family that produces clusters of small fragrant yellow flowers followed by purple or black berries, native to eastern Asia and North and Central America. ● Genus *Mahonia*, family Berberidaceae.
– ORIGIN modern Latin, named after Bernard *McMahon* (*c.*1775–1816), American botanist.

Ma·hore /mǝ'hôr/ another name for **MAYOTTE**.

m

PRONUNCIATION KEY ǝ *ago, up*; ǝr *over, fur*; a *hat*; ā *ate*; ä *car*; e *let*; ē *see*; i *fit*; ī *by*; NG *sing*; ō *go*; ô *law, for*; oi *toy*; o͝o *good*; o͞o *goo*; ou *out*; TH *thin*; T̲H̲ *then*; ZH *vision*

ma·hout /mə'hout/ ▶ **n.** (in South and Southeast Asia) a person who works with, rides, and tends an elephant.
– ORIGIN from Hindi *mahāvat*.

Mah·rat·ta /mə'rätə/ ▶ **n.** variant spelling of **MARATHA**.

Mah·rat·ti /mə'rätē/ ▶ **n.** variant spelling of **MARATHI**.

ma·hua /'mähwä, -hōōə/ (also **mahwa**) ▶ **n.** an Indian tree that has fleshy edible flowers and yields oil-rich seeds. ● *Madhuca latifolia*, family Sapotaceae. ■ an alcoholic drink produced from the nectar-rich flowers of this tree.
– ORIGIN late 17th cent.: via Hindi from Sanskrit *madhūka*, from *madhu* 'sweet.'

Ma·ia[1] /'mīə/ Greek Mythology the daughter of Atlas and mother of Hermes.

Ma·ia[2] Roman Mythology a goddess associated with Vulcan and also (by confusion with **MAIA[1]**) with Mercury (Hermes). She was worshiped on May 1 and May 15; that month is named after her.

maid /mād/ ▶ **n.** a female domestic servant. ■ archaic or literary a girl or young woman, esp. an unmarried one. ■ archaic or literary a virgin.
– ORIGIN Middle English: abbreviation of **MAIDEN**.

mai·dan /mī'dän/ ▶ **n.** (in South Asia) an open space in or near a town, used as a parade ground or for events such as public meetings and polo matches.
– ORIGIN from Urdu and Persian *maidān*, from Arabic *maydān*.

maid·en /'mādn/ ▶ **n. 1** archaic or literary a girl or young woman, esp. an unmarried one. ■ a virgin.
2 (also **maiden over**) Cricket an over in which no runs are scored.
▶ **adj.** [attrib.] **1** (of a woman, esp. an older one) unmarried: *a maiden aunt*. ■ (of a female animal) unmated.
2 being or involving the first attempt or act of its kind: *the ship's maiden voyage*. ■ denoting a horse that has never won a race, or a race intended for such horses. ■ (of a tree or other fruiting plant) in its first year of growth.
– DERIVATIVES **maid·en·ish adj.**, **maid·en·like** /-,līk/ **adj.**
– ORIGIN Old English *mægden*, from a Germanic diminutive meaning 'maid, virgin'; related to German *Mädchen*, diminutive of *Magd* 'maid,' from an Indo-European root shared by Old Irish *mug* 'boy, servant.'

m

maid·en·hair /'mādn,he(ə)r/ (also **maidenhair fern**) ▶ **n.** a chiefly tropical fern of delicate appearance, having slender-stalked fronds with round or wedge-shaped divided lobes. ● Genus *Adiantum*, family Adiantaceae: several species, in particular *A. capillus-veneris* of Eurasia and North America.

maid·en·hair tree ▶ **n.** the ginkgo, whose leaves resemble those of the maidenhair fern.

maid·en·head /'mādn,hed/ ▶ **n.** virginity. ■ dated the hymen.

maid·en·hood /'mādn,hōōd/ ▶ **n.** the fact or condition of being a young, unmarried woman. ■ a girl's virginity: *she had forsworn that her maidenhood would be kept sacred*.

maid·en·ly /'mādnlē/ ▶ **adj.** relating to or appropriate to a maiden; demure: *maidenly modesty*.

maid·en name ▶ **n.** the surname that a married woman used from birth, prior to its being legally changed at marriage.

maid·en o·ver ▶ **n.** see **MAIDEN** (sense 2 of the noun).

maid of hon·or ▶ **n.** an unmarried woman acting as principal bridesmaid at a wedding. ■ an unmarried woman, typically of noble birth, attending a queen or princess.

maid·serv·ant /'mād,sərvənt/ ▶ **n.** dated a female domestic servant.

Maid·stone /'mād,stōn/ a town in southeastern England, on the Medway River; pop. 91,000 (est. 2009).

ma·ieu·tic /mā'yōōtik/ ▶ **adj.** of or denoting the Socratic mode of inquiry, which aims to bring a person's latent ideas into clear consciousness.
▶ **plural n.** (**maieutics**) [treated as sing.] the maieutic method.
– ORIGIN mid 17th cent.: from Greek *maieutikos*, from *maieuesthai* 'act as a midwife,' from *maia* 'midwife.'

Mai·kop /mī'käp/ a city in southwestern Russia, capital of the republic of Adygea; pop. 153,500 (est. 2008).

mail[1] /māl/ ▶ **n.** letters and packages conveyed by the postal system. ■ the postal system: *you can order by mail | the check is in the mail* | [as modifier] *a mail truck*. ■ [in sing.] a single delivery or collection of mail: *the new magazine that came in the mail today*. ■ Computing e-mail. ■ dated a vehicle, such as a train, carrying mail. ■ archaic a bag of letters to be conveyed by the postal system.
▶ **v.** [with obj.] send (a letter or package) using the postal system: *if you will mail the coupon, we'll send you a free trial package*. ■ Computing send (someone) e-mail.
– DERIVATIVES **mail·a·ble adj.**
– ORIGIN Middle English (in the sense 'traveling bag'): from Old French *male* 'wallet,' of West Germanic origin. The notion 'by post' dates from the mid 17th cent.

mail[2] ▶ **n.** historical armor made of metal rings or plates, joined together flexibly. ■ the protective shell or scales of certain animals.
▶ **v.** [with obj.] clothe or cover with mail: (as adj. **mailed**) *a mailed gauntlet*.
– PHRASES **the mailed fist** the use of physical force to maintain control or impose one's will.
– ORIGIN Middle English (also denoting the individual metal elements composing mail armor): from Old French *maille*, from Latin *macula* 'spot or mesh.'

mail·bag /'māl,bag/ ▶ **n.** a large sack or bag for carrying mail.

mail·boat /'māl,bōt/ (also **mail boat**) ▶ **n.** chiefly historical a ship or boat that carries mail.

mail bomb ▶ **n. 1** another term for **LETTER BOMB**.
2 an overwhelmingly large quantity of e-mail messages sent to one e-mail address.
▶ **v.** (**mail-bomb**) [with obj.] send an overwhelmingly large quantity of e-mail messages to (someone).

mail·box /'māl,bäks/ ▶ **n.** a public box with a slot into which mail is placed for collection by the post office. ■ a private box into which mail is delivered, esp. one mounted on a post at the entrance to a person's property. ■ a computer file in which e-mail messages received by a particular user are stored.

mail call ▶ **n.** Military the distribution of mail to soldiers.

mail car·ri·er ▶ **n.** a person who is employed to deliver and collect letters and parcels.

mail drop ▶ **n. 1** a receptacle for mail, esp. one in which mail is kept until the addressee collects it.
2 Brit. a delivery of mail, advertising leaflets, or other material.

Mail·er /'mālər/, Norman (1923–2007), US novelist and essayist. His novels, in which he frequently deals with the effect of war and violence on human relationships, include *The Naked and the Dead* (1948) and *Ancient Evenings* (1983). His nonfiction works include the prize-winning *The Armies of the Night* (1968) and *The Executioner's Song* (1979).

mail·er /'mālər/ ▶ **n. 1** the sender of a letter or package by mail. ■ a person employed to dispatch newspapers or periodicals by mail. ■ a free advertising pamphlet, brochure, or catalog sent out by mail. ■ a container used for conveying items by mail, esp. a padded envelope or protective tube.
2 Computing a program that sends e-mail messages.

mail·ing /'māliNG/ ▶ **n.** the action or process of sending something by mail. ■ something sent by mail, esp. a piece of mass advertising.

mail·ing list ▶ **n.** a list of the names and addresses of people to whom material such as advertising matter, information, or a magazine may be mailed, esp. regularly.

mail·lot /mī'ō/ ▶ **n.** (pl. **same**) **1** a pair of tights worn for dancing or gymnastics. ■ a woman's tight-fitting one-piece swimsuit.
2 a jersey or top, esp. one worn in sports such as cycling.
– ORIGIN French.

mail·man /'māl,man/ ▶ **n.** (pl. **mailmen**) a person who is employed to deliver and collect letters and parcels.

mail merge ▶ **n.** Computing the automatic addition of names and addresses from a database to letters and envelopes in order to facilitate sending mail, esp. advertising, to many addresses.

mail or·der ▶ **n.** the selling of goods to customers by mail, generally involving selection from a special catalog: *available by mail order only* | [as modifier] *a mail-order distributor of generic drugs*.

mail-out ▶ **n.** chiefly Brit. an instance of sending out by mail a number of promotional brochures or other items at one time.

mail slot ▶ **n.** a slot in the door of a building into which mail is delivered.

maim /mām/ ▶ **v.** [with obj.] wound or injure (someone) so that part of the body is permanently damaged: *100,000 soldiers were killed or maimed*.
– ORIGIN Middle English: from Old French *mahaignier*, of unknown origin.

Mai·mon·i·des /mī'mänidēz/ (1135–1204), Jewish philosopher and rabbinic scholar, born in Spain; born *Moses ben Maimon*. His *Guide for the Perplexed* (1190) attempts to reconcile Talmudic scripture with the philosophy of Aristotle.

Main /mīn/ a river of southwestern Germany that rises in northern Bavaria and flows west for 310 miles (500 km), through Frankfurt to meet the Rhine River at Mainz.

main[1] /mān/ ▶ **adj.** [attrib.] chief in size or importance: *a main road | the main problem is one of resources*.
▶ **n. 1** a principal pipe carrying water or gas to buildings, or taking sewage from them: *a faulty gas main*. ■ Brit. a principal cable carrying electricity.
2 (**the main**) archaic or literary the open ocean.
3 Nautical short for **MAINSAIL** or **MAINMAST**.
– PHRASES **by main force** through sheer strength. **in the main** on the whole; chiefly.
– ORIGIN Middle English: from Old English *mægen* 'physical force,' reinforced by Old Norse *meginn*, *megn* 'strong, powerful,' both from a Germanic base meaning 'have power.'

main[2] ▶ **n. 1** historical a match between fighting cocks.
2 (in the game of hazard) a number (5, 6, 7, 8, or 9) called by a player before dice are thrown.
– ORIGIN late 16th cent.: probably from the phrase *main chance*.

main brace ▶ **n.** one of the braces attached to the main yard of a sailing ship.

main clause ▶ **n.** Grammar a clause that can form a complete sentence standing alone, having a subject and a predicate. Contrasted with **SUBORDINATE CLAUSE**.

main course ▶ **n. 1** the most substantial course of a meal.
2 the mainsail of a square-rigged sailing ship.

main drag ▶ **n.** (usu. **the main drag**) informal the main street of a town.

Maine /mān/ a state in the northeastern US, one of the six New England states, on the Atlantic coast, on the US–Canada border; pop. 1,316,456 (est. 2008); capital, Augusta; statehood, Mar. 15, 1820 (23). Visited by John Cabot in 1498 and colonized by England in the 1600s and 1700s, it was annexed to Massachusetts from 1652 until 1820.
– DERIVATIVES **Main·er n.**

Maine Coon (also **Maine Coon cat**) ▶ **n.** a large, powerful domestic cat of a long-haired breed, native to America.
– ORIGIN 1970s: so named because of partial resemblance to the raccoon.

Maine Coon

main·frame /'mān,frām/ ▶ **n. 1** a large high-speed computer, esp. one supporting numerous workstations or peripherals.
2 the central processing unit and primary memory of a computer.

Main·land /'mānlənd, -,land/ **1** the largest island in the Orkney Islands.
2 the largest island in the Shetland Islands.

main·land /'mān,land, -lənd/ ▶ **n.** a large continuous extent of land that includes the greater part of a country or territory, as opposed to offshore islands and detached territories.
– DERIVATIVES **main·land·er n.**

Main Line a popular name for a series of affluent suburbs west of Philadelphia in Pennsylvania, along the old Pennsylvania Railroad main line.

main line ▶ **n.** a chief railroad line: [as modifier] *a main-line station*. ■ a chief road or street. ■ informal a principal vein as a site for a drug injection.
▶ **v.** (**mainline**) [with obj.] informal inject (a drug) intravenously: *Mariella mainlines cocaine five to seven times a day*.
– DERIVATIVES **main·lin·er n.**

main·ly /'mānlē/ ▶ **adv.** more than anything else: *he is mainly concerned with fiction*. ■ for the most part: *the west will be mainly dry*.

main man ▶ **n.** informal a close and trusted male friend.

main·mast /'mān,mast/ ▶ **n.** the principal mast of a ship, typically the second mast in a sailing ship of three or more masts.

main·plane /ˈmānˌplān/ ▶ **n.** a principal supporting surface of an aircraft (typically a wing), as opposed to a horizontal stabilizer.

main·sail /ˈmānsəl, -ˌsāl/ ▶ **n.** the principal sail of a ship, esp. the lowest sail on the mainmast in a square-rigged vessel. ■ the sail set on the after side of the mainmast in a fore-and-aft-rigged vessel.

main se·quence ▶ **n.** Astronomy a series of star types to which most stars belong, represented on a Hertzsprung–Russell diagram as a continuous band extending from the upper left (hot, bright stars) to the lower right (cool, dim stars).

main·sheet /ˈmānˌsHēt/ ▶ **n.** a sheet used for controlling the mainsail of a sailing vessel.

main·spring /ˈmānˌspriNG/ ▶ **n. 1** the principal spring in a watch, clock, or other mechanism.
2 something that plays a principal part in motivating or maintaining a movement, process, or activity: *innovation is the mainspring of the new economy.*

main·stay /ˈmānˌstā/ ▶ **n. 1** a stay that extends from the maintop to the foot of the foremast of a sailing ship.
2 a thing on which something else is based or depends: *farming is the mainstay of the rural economy.*

main stor·age ▶ **n.** Computing the total memory available to executing programs, equivalent to RAM on modern computers.

main·stream /ˈmānˌstrēm/ ▶ **n.** (**the mainstream**) the ideas, attitudes, or activities that are regarded as normal or conventional; the dominant trend in opinion, fashion, or the arts: *companies that are bringing computers to the mainstream of American life.* ■ (also **mainstream jazz**) jazz that is neither traditional nor modern, based on the 1930s swing style and consisting esp. of solo improvisation on chord sequences.
▶ **adj.** belonging to or characteristic of the mainstream: *mainstream politics | a mixture of mainstream and avant-garde artists.* ■ (of a school or class) for students without special needs: *children with minor handicaps would be able to attend mainstream schools.*
▶ **v.** [with obj.] bring (something) into the mainstream: *vegetarianism has been mainstreamed.* ■ place (a student with special needs) into a mainstream class or school: *the goal is to have the child mainstreamed into a regular classroom.*

main street ▶ **n.** the principal street of a town, traditionally the site of shops, banks, and other businesses: *the money you save on a car can offset some of the higher prices on Main Street.* ■ (**Main Street**) used in reference to the materialism, mediocrity, or parochialism regarded as typical of small-town life. [from the title of a novel (1920) by Sinclair Lewis.]

main·tain /mānˈtān/ ▶ **v.** [with obj.] **1** cause or enable (a condition or state of affairs) to continue: *the need to maintain close links between industry and schools.* ■ keep (something) at the same level or rate: *agricultural prices will have to be maintained.* ■ keep (a building, machine, or road) in good condition or in working order by checking or repairing it regularly.
2 provide with necessities for life or existence: *the allowance covers the basic costs of maintaining a child.* ■ keep (a military unit) supplied with equipment and other requirements. ■ archaic give one's support to; uphold: *the king swears he will maintain the laws of God.*
3 [reporting verb] state something strongly to be the case; assert: [with obj.] *he has always maintained his innocence* | [with clause] *he had persistently maintained that he would not stand against his old friend* | [with direct speech] *"It was not an ideology at all," she maintained.*
– DERIVATIVES **main·tain·a·bil·i·ty** /ˌmānˌtānəˈbilətē/ **n.**, **main·tain·a·ble adj.**
– ORIGIN Middle English (also in the sense 'practice (a good or bad action) habitually'): from Old French *maintenir*, from Latin *manu tenere* 'hold in the hand.'

main·tain·er /mānˈtānər/ ▶ **n.** a person or thing that maintains something, in particular computer software. ■ (also **maintainor**) Law, historical a person guilty of aiding a party in a legal action without lawful cause.

main·te·nance /ˈmānt(ə)nəns, ˈmāntn-əns/ ▶ **n.**
1 the process of maintaining or preserving someone or something, or the state of being maintained: *crucial conditions for the maintenance of democratic government.* ■ the process of keeping something in good condition: *car maintenance* | [as modifier] *essential maintenance work.*
2 the provision of financial support for a person's living expenses, or the support so provided. ■ alimony or child support.
3 Law, historical the former offense of aiding a party in a legal action without lawful cause.
– ORIGIN Middle English (in the sense 'aiding a party in a legal action without lawful cause'): from Old French, from *maintenir* (see **MAINTAIN**).

Main·te·non /ˌmantˈ(ə)nôN/, Françoise d'Aubigné, Marquise de (1635–1719), mistress and later second wife of the French king Louis XIV.

main·top /ˈmānˌtäp/ ▶ **n.** a platform around the head of the lower section of a sailing ship's mainmast.

main·top·mast ▶ **n.** the second section of a sailing ship's mainmast.

main verb ▶ **n.** Grammar **1** the verb in a main clause.
2 the head of a verb phrase, for example *eat* in *might have been going to eat it.*

Mainz /min(t)s/ a city in western Germany, capital of Rhineland-Palatinate, situated at the confluence of the Rhine and Main rivers; pop. 196,400 (est. 2006).

ma·iol·i·ca /mīˈäləkə/ ▶ **n.** fine earthenware with colored decoration on an opaque white tin glaze, originating in Italy during the Renaissance.
– ORIGIN mid 16th cent.: Italian, from *Maiolica* 'Majorca.'

mai·son·ette /ˌmāzəˈnet/ ▶ **n.** a set of rooms for living in, typically on two stories of a larger building and with its own entrance from outside.
– ORIGIN late 18th cent.: from French *maisonnette*, diminutive of *maison* 'house.'

mai tai /ˈmī ˌtī/ ▶ **n.** a cocktail based on light rum,curaçao, and fruit juices.
– ORIGIN Polynesian.

Mai·thi·li /ˈmītilē/ ▶ **n.** a Bihari language spoken in northern Bihar, elsewhere in India, and in Nepal.
– ORIGIN Sanskrit (as an adjective), from *Mithilā*, a place in northern Bihar.

maî·tre d'hô·tel /ˌmātrə dōˈtel, ˌmetrə/ (also **maître d'** /ˌmātrə ˈdē, ˌmātər/) ▶ **n.** (pl. **maîtres d'hôtel** pronunc. **same**; also **maître d's**) the person in a restaurant who oversees the waitpersons and busboys, and who typically handles reservations. ■ the manager of a hotel.
– ORIGIN mid 16th cent.: French, literally 'master of (the) house.'

Mai·tre·ya /mīˈtrāə/ Buddhism the Buddha who will appear in the future.
– ORIGIN Sanskrit, from *mitra* 'friend or friendship.'

maize /māz/ ▶ **n.** technical or chiefly British term for **CORN**[1].
– ORIGIN mid 16th cent.: from Spanish *maíz*, from Taino *mahiz*.

Maj. ▶ **abbr.** Major.

ma·jes·tic /məˈjestik/ ▶ **adj.** having or showing impressive beauty or dignity: *watching majestic eagles soar along the Mississippi.*
– DERIVATIVES **ma·jes·ti·cal·ly** /-(ə)lē/ **adv.**

maj·es·ty /ˈmajəstē/ ▶ **n.** (pl. **majesties**)
1 impressive stateliness, dignity, or beauty: *experience the majesty of the Rockies.*
2 royal power: *the majesty of the royal household.* ■ (**His, Your**, etc., **Majesty**) a title given to a sovereign or a sovereign's wife or widow: *Her Majesty the Queen.* ■ (**Her** or **His Majesty's**) Brit. used in the title of several state institutions: *Her Majesty's Inspectorate of Schools.*
– ORIGIN Middle English (in the sense 'greatness of God'): from Old French *majeste*, from Latin *majestas*, from a variant of *majus*, *major-* (see **MAJOR**).

Maj. Gen. ▶ **abbr.** Major General.

maj·lis /ˈmajlis, majˈlis/ ▶ **n.** the parliament of various North African and Middle Eastern countries, esp. Iran.
– ORIGIN Arabic, literally 'assembly.'

ma·jol·i·ca /məˈjälikə/ ▶ **n.** a kind of earthenware made in imitation of Italian maiolica, esp. in England during the 19th century.
– ORIGIN variant of **MAIOLICA**.

Ma·jor /ˈmājər/, Sir John (1943–), British Conservative statesman; prime minister 1990–97. His premiership saw the negotiations leading to the Maastricht Treaty and progress toward peace in Northern Ireland.

ma·jor /ˈmājər/ ▶ **adj. 1** [attrib.] important, serious, or significant: *the use of drugs is a major problem.* ■ greater or more important; main: *he got the major share of the spoils.* ■ (of a surgical operation) serious or life-threatening: *he had to undergo major surgery.*
2 Music (of a scale) having an interval of a semitone between the third and fourth degrees and the seventh and eighth degrees. Contrasted with **MINOR**. ■ (of an interval) equivalent to that between the tonic and another note of a major scale, and greater by a semitone than the corresponding minor interval. ■ [postpositive] (of a key) based on a major scale, tending to produce a bright or joyful effect: *Prelude in G Major.*
3 Logic (of a term) occurring as the predicate in the conclusion of a categorical syllogism. ■ (of a premise) containing the major term in a categorical syllogism.
4 Brit. dated (appended to a surname in some schools) indicating the elder of two brothers.
▶ **n. 1** an army officer of high rank, in particular (in the US Army, Air Force, and Marine Corps) an officer ranking above captain and below lieutenant colonel. [Shortening of **SERGEANT MAJOR**, formerly a high rank.]
2 Music a major key, interval, or scale. ■ (**Major**) Bell-ringing a system of change-ringing using eight bells.
3 a student's principal subject or course of study. ■ [often with modifier] a student specializing in a specified subject: *a math major.*
4 a major world organization, company, or competition: *it's not unreasonable to believe someone can win all four majors.* ■ (**the majors**) the major leagues.
5 a person of full legal age.
6 Logic a major term or premise.
7 Bridge short for **MAJOR SUIT**.
▶ **v.** [no obj.] (**major in**) specialize in (a particular subject) at a college or university: *I was trying to decide if I should major in drama or English.*
– ORIGIN Middle English: from Latin, comparative of *magnus* 'great'; perhaps influenced by French *majeur*.

ma·jor ar·ca·na ▶ **n.** see **ARCANA**.

ma·jor ax·is ▶ **n.** Geometry the longer axis of an ellipse, passing through its foci.

Ma·jor·ca /məˈjôrkə, mäˈyôrkə/ the largest of the Balearic Islands; pop. 614,000; capital, Palma. Spanish name **Mallorca**.
– DERIVATIVES **Ma·jor·can adj. & n.**

ma·jor-do·mo /ˌmājərˈdōmō/ ▶ **n.** (pl. **major-domos**) the chief steward of a large household.
– ORIGIN late 16th cent.: via Spanish and Italian from medieval Latin *major domus* 'highest official of the household.'

ma·jor·ette /ˌmājəˈret/ ▶ **n.** short for **DRUM MAJORETTE**.

ma·jor gen·er·al ▶ **n.** (pl. **major generals**) an officer in the US Army, Air Force, and Marine Corps ranking above brigadier general and below lieutenant general.
– ORIGIN mid 17th cent.: shortening of *sergeant major general.*

ma·jor his·to·com·pat·i·bil·i·ty com·plex (abbr.: **MHC**) ▶ **n.** a genetic system that allows large proteins in immune system cells to identify compatible or foreign proteins. It allows the matching of potential organ or bone marrow donors with recipients.

ma·jor·i·tar·i·an /mə ˌjôriˈte(ə)rēən, -ˌjär-/ ▶ **adj.** governed by or believing in decision by a majority.
▶ **n.** a person who is governed by or believes in decision by a majority.
– DERIVATIVES **ma·jor·i·tar·i·an·ism** /-ˌnizəm/ **n.**

ma·jor·i·ty /məˈjôrətē, -ˈjär-/ ▶ **n.** (pl. **majorities**)
1 the greater number: *in the majority of cases all will go smoothly* | [as modifier] *it was a majority decision.* ■ the number by which votes for one candidate in an election are more than those for all other candidates combined. ■ Brit. the number by which the votes for one party or candidate exceed those of the next in rank. ■ a party or group receiving the greater number of votes.
2 the age when a person is legally considered a full adult, in most contexts either 18 or 21.
3 the rank or office of a major.
– PHRASES **be in the majority** belong to or constitute the larger group or number: *publishing houses where women are in the majority.*
– ORIGIN mid 16th cent. (denoting superiority): from French *majorité*, from medieval Latin *majoritas*, from Latin *major* (see **MAJOR**).

USAGE **1** Strictly speaking, **majority** should be used with countable nouns to mean 'the greater number': *the majority of cases.* The use of **majority** with uncountable nouns to mean 'the greatest part' (*I spent the majority of the day reading*), although common in informal contexts, is not considered good standard English.
2 Majority means more than half: *fifty-one out of a hundred is a majority.* A **plurality** is the largest number among three or more. Consider the following scenarios: If Anne received 50 votes, Barry received 30, and Carlos received 20, then

PRONUNCIATION KEY ə *ago, up*; ər *over, fur*; a *hat*; ā *ate*; ä *car*; e *let*; ē *see*; i *fit*; ī *by*; NG *sing*; ō *go*; ô *law, for*; oi *toy*; o͝o *good*; o͞o *goo*; ou *out*; TH *thin*; T͟H *then*; ZH *vision*

m

> Anne received a **plurality**, and no candidate won a **majority**. If Anne got 35 votes, Barry 14, and Carlos 51, then Carlos won both the **plurality** and the **majority**.

ma·jor·i·ty lead·er ▶ **n.** the head of the majority party in a legislative body, esp. the US Senate or House of Representatives.

ma·jor·i·ty rule ▶ **n.** the principle that the greater number should exercise greater power.

ma·jor league ▶ **n.** the highest-ranking league in a particular professional sport, esp. baseball: *my dream of pitching in the major leagues* | [as modifier] *future major-league ballplayers.* ■ the highest attainable level in any endeavor or activity: [as modifier] *many of the nation's service companies are major-league corporations.*
– DERIVATIVES **ma·jor-lea·guer n.**

ma·jor·ly /ˈmājərlē/ ▶ **adv.** [as submodifier] informal very; extremely: *I'm majorly depressed.*

ma·jor med·i·cal ▶ **n.** insurance designed to cover medical expenses due to severe or prolonged illness by paying all or most of the bills above a set amount.

ma·jor piece ▶ **n.** Chess a rook or queen.

ma·jor plan·et ▶ **n.** any of the eight planets of the solar system, as distinct from an asteroid or smaller body.

ma·jor proph·et ▶ **n.** any of the prophets after whom the longer prophetic books of the Bible are named; Isaiah, Jeremiah, Ezekiel, or Daniel.

ma·jor suit ▶ **n.** Bridge spades or hearts.
– ORIGIN early 20th cent.: so named because of their higher scoring value.

ma·jor tran·quil·iz·er ▶ **n.** a tranquilizer of the kind used to treat psychotic states.

ma·jus·cule /ˈmajəsˌkyo͞ol/ ▶ **n.** large lettering, either capital or uncial, in which all the letters are usually the same height. ■ a large letter.
– DERIVATIVES **ma·jus·cu·lar** /məˈjəskyələr/ **adj.**
– ORIGIN early 18th cent.: from French, from Latin *majuscula* (*littera*) 'somewhat greater (letter).'

Ma·kar·i·os III /məˈkarēəs, -ˌōs, mäˈkärēˌôs/ (1913–77), Greek Cypriot archbishop and statesman; first president of the republic of Cyprus 1960–77; born *Mikhail Christodolou Mouskos*. He reorganized the movement for enosis (union of Cyprus with Greece) and was exiled 1956–59 by the British for allegedly supporting terrorism.

m

Ma·ka·sar·ese /məˌkasəˈrēz, -ˈrēs/ (also **Makassarese**) ▶ **n.** (pl. **same**) **1** a native or inhabitant of Makassar (now Ujung Pandang) in Indonesia.
2 the Indonesian language of this people.
▶ **adj.** of or relating to this people or their language.

Ma·kas·sar /məˈkasər/ (also **Macassar** or **Makasar**) former name (until 1973) for **UJUNG PANDANG**.

Ma·kas·sar Strait /məˈkasər/ a stretch of water that separates the islands of Borneo and Sulawesi and links the Celebes Sea in the north with the Java Sea in the south.

make /māk/ ▶ **v.** (past and past participle **made** /mād/) [with obj.] **1** form (something) by putting parts together or combining substances; construct; create: *my grandmother made a dress for me* | *the body is* **made from** *four pieces of maple* | *baseball bats are* **made of** *ash.* ■ (**make something into**) alter something so that it forms or constitutes (something else): *buffalo's milk can be made into cheese.* ■ compose, prepare, or draw up (something written or abstract): *she made her will.* ■ prepare (a dish, drink, or meal) for consumption: *she was making lunch for Lucy and Francis* | [with two objs.] *I'll make us both a cup of tea.* ■ arrange bedclothes tidily on (a bed) ready for use. ■ arrange and light materials for (a fire). ■ Electronics complete or close (a circuit).
2 cause (something) to exist or come about; bring about: *the drips had made a pool on the floor.* ■ [with obj. and complement or infinitive] cause to become or seem: *decorative features make brickwork more interesting* | *the best way to disarm your critics is to make them laugh.* ■ carry out, perform, or produce (a specified action, movement, or sound): *Unger made a speech of forty minutes* | *anyone can make a mistake* | *we made a deal.* ■ communicate or express (an idea, request, or requirement): *I tend to* **make** *heavy* **demands on** *people* | [with two objs.] *make him an offer he can't refuse.* ■ chiefly archaic enter into a contract of (marriage): *a marriage made in heaven.* ■ [with obj. and complement] appoint or designate (someone) to a position: *he was made a colonel in the Mexican army.* ■ [with obj. and complement] represent or cause to appear in a specified way: *the sale price and extended warranty make it an excellent value.* ■ cause or ensure the success or advancement of: *the work which really made Wordsworth's reputation.*
3 [with obj. and infinitive] compel (someone) to do something: *she bought me a brandy and made me drink it.*
4 constitute; amount to: *they made an unusual duo.* ■ serve as or become through development or adaptation: *this fern makes a good houseplant.* ■ consider to be; estimate as: *How many are there? I make it sixteen.* ■ agree or decide on (a specified arrangement), typically one concerning a time or place: *let's make it 7:30.*
5 gain or earn (money or profit): *he'd made a lot of money out of hardware.*
6 arrive at (a place) within a specified time or in time for (a train or other transport): *we've got a lot to do if you're going to make the shuttle* | *they didn't always* **make it** *on time.* ■ (**make it**) succeed in something; become successful: *he waited confidently for his band to make it.* ■ achieve a place in: *these dogs seldom make the news* | *they* **made it to** *the semifinals.* ■ achieve the rank of: *he wasn't going to make captain.*
7 [no obj.] go or prepare to go in a particular direction: *he struggled to his feet and* **made toward** *the car.* ■ [with infinitive] act as if one is about to perform an action: *she* **made as if to** *leave the room.*
8 informal induce (someone) to have sexual intercourse with one: *he had been trying to make Cynthia for two years now* | *his alleged quest to* **make it with** *the world's most attractive women.*
9 (in bridge, whist, and similar games) win (a trick). ■ win a trick with (a card). ■ win the number of tricks that fulfills (a contract). ■ shuffle (a pack of cards) for dealing.
10 [no obj.] (of the tide) begin to flow or ebb.
▶ **n. 1** the manufacturer or trade name of a particular product: *the make, model, and year of his car.* ■ the structure or composition of something.
2 the making of electrical contact. ■ the position in which this is made.
– PHRASES **be made of money** [often with negative] informal be very rich. **have (got) it made** informal be in a position where success is certain: *because your dad's a manager, he's got it made.* **make a day** (or **night**) **of it** devote a whole day (or night) to an activity, esp. an enjoyable one. **make someone's day** make an otherwise ordinary or dull day pleasingly memorable for someone. **make do** manage with the limited or inadequate means available: *Dad would have to* **make do with** *an old car.* **make like** informal pretend to be; imitate: *tell the whole group to make like a bird by putting their arms out.* **make or break** be the factor that decides whether (something) will succeed or fail. **make sail** Sailing spread a sail or sails. ■ start a voyage. **make time 1** find an occasion when time is available to do something: *the nurse should make time to talk to the patient.* **2** informal make sexual advances to someone: *I couldn't* **make time with** *Marilyn because she was already a senior.* **make up one's mind** make a decision; decide: *he made up his mind to attend the meeting.* **make way 1** allow room for someone or something else: *the land is due to be bulldozed to* **make way for** *a parking garage.* **2** chiefly Nautical make progress; travel. **on the make** informal intent on gain, typically in an unscrupulous way. ■ looking for a sexual partner. **put the make on** informal make sexual advances to (someone).
– PHRASAL VERBS **make after** archaic pursue (someone). **make away** another way of saying **MAKE OFF**. **make away with** ■ kill (someone) furtively and illicitly: *for all we know she could have been made away with.* **make for 1** move or head toward (a place): *I made for the life raft and hung on for dear life.* ■ approach (someone) to attack them. **2** tend to result in or be received as (a particular thing): *job descriptions never make for exciting reading.* **3** (**be made for**) be eminently suited for (a particular function): *a man made for action.* ■ form an ideal partnership; be ideally suited: *you two were just* **made for each other**. **make something of** give or ascribe a specified amount of attention or importance to: *oddly, he* **makes little of** *America's low investment rates.* ■ understand or derive advantage from: *they stared at the stone but could* **make nothing of** *it.* ■ [with negative or in questions] conclude to be the meaning or character of: *he wasn't sure what to make of Russell.* **make off** leave hurriedly, esp. in order to avoid duty or punishment: *they made off without paying.* **make off with** carry (something) away illicitly: *burglars made off with all their wedding presents.* **make out** informal **1** make progress; fare: *how are you making out, now that the summer's over?* **2** informal engage in sexual activity: *Ernie was* **making out with** *Bernice.* **make someone/something out 1** manage with some difficulty to see or hear something: *in the dim light it was difficult to make out the illustration.* ■ understand the character or motivation of someone: *I can't make her out—she's so inconsistent.* **2** [with infinitive or clause] assert; represent: *I'm not as bad as I'm* **made out to be**. ■ try to give a specified impression; pretend: *he made out he was leaving.* **3** draw up or write out a list or document, esp. an official one: *advice about making out a will* | *send a check* **made out to** *Trinity College.* **make something over 1** transfer the possession of something to someone: *if he dies childless he is to make over his share of the estate to his brother.* **2** completely transform or remodel something, esp. a person's hairstyle, makeup, or clothes. **make up** be reconciled after a quarrel: *let's kiss and make up.* **make someone up** apply cosmetics to oneself or another. **make something up 1** (also **make up for**) serve or act to compensate for something lost, missed, or deficient: *I'll make up the time tomorrow.* ■ (**make it up to**) compensate someone for negligent or unfair treatment: *I'll try to make it up to you in the future.* **2** (**make up**) (of parts) compose or constitute (a whole): *women make up 56 percent of the student body* | *the team is made up of three women and two men.* ■ complete an amount or group: *he brought along a girl to make up a foursome.* **3** put together or prepare something from parts or ingredients: *make up the mortar to a consistency that can be molded in the hands.* ■ get an amount or group together: *he was trying to make up a party to go dancing.* ■ prepare a bed for use with fresh bedclothes. ■ Printing arrange type and illustrations into pages or arrange the type and illustrations on a page. **4** concoct or invent a story, lie, or plan: *she enjoyed making up tall tales.* **make up to** informal attempt to win the favor of (someone) by being pleasant: *you can't go on about morals when you're making up to Adam like that.* **make with** informal proceed to use or supply: *make with the feet, honey—we're late.*
– DERIVATIVES **make·a·ble** /-əbəl/ (also **makable**) **adj.**
– ORIGIN Old English *macian*, from a base meaning 'fitting'; related to **MATCH**[1].

make-and-break ▶ **n.** a switch or other device in which electrical contact is automatically made and broken.

make-be·lieve ▶ **n.** the action of pretending or imagining, typically that things are better than they really are: *she's living in a world of make-believe.*
▶ **adj.** imitating something real; pretend: *he was firing a make-believe gun at the spy planes.*
▶ **v.** pretend; imagine: [with clause] *Brenda rode along, make-believing she was a knight riding to the rescue.*

make-do ▶ **adj.** [attrib.] makeshift, ad hoc, or temporary: *his make-do clothes and borrowed tie.*

make·o·ver /ˈmākˌōvər/ ▶ **n.** a complete transformation or remodeling of something, esp. a person's hairstyle, makeup, or clothes.

mak·er /ˈmākər/ ▶ **n. 1** [usu. in combination] a person or thing that makes or produces something: *a cabinetmaker.*
2 (**our, the,** etc., **Maker**) God; the Creator.
– PHRASES **meet one's Maker** chiefly humorous die.

make·read·y /ˈmākˌredē/ ▶ **n.** (in letterpress printing) final adjustment of a form for printing, with overlays and underlays to achieve the correct pressure over the whole printing area.

make·shift /ˈmākˌsHift/ ▶ **adj.** serving as a temporary substitute; sufficient for the time being: *arranging a row of chairs to form a makeshift bed.*
▶ **n.** a temporary substitute or device.

make·up /ˈmākˌəp/ ▶ **n. 1** cosmetics such as lipstick or powder applied to the face, used to enhance or alter the appearance.
2 the composition or constitution of something: *studying the makeup of ocean sediments.* ■ the combination of qualities that form a person's temperament: *a nastiness that had long been in his makeup.*
3 Printing the arrangement of type, illustrations, etc., on a printed page: *page makeup.*
4 a supplementary test or assignment given to a student who missed or failed the original one: [as modifier] *Tony has a makeup exam.*

make·weight /ˈmākˌwāt/ ▶ **n.** something put on a scale to make up the required weight. ■ an extra person or thing that is only added or included in order to complete something: *use it for casserole toppings or makeweight in meatloaf* | *this suggestion was thrown in as a makeweight.*

make-work ▶ **adj.** denoting an activity that serves mainly to keep someone busy and is of little value in itself: *a make-work scheme for lawyers.*
▶ **n.** work or activity of this kind.

Ma·khach·ka·la /məˌkäCHkəˈlä/ a port in southwestern Russia, on the Caspian Sea, capital of the autonomous republic of Dagestan; pop. 464,200 (est. 2008). Former name (until 1922) **PORT PETROVSK**.

Makh·pi·ya·lu·ta /ˌmäKHˌpēä ˈlo͞otä/ see **RED CLOUD**.

ma·ki /ˈmäkē/ (also **maki zushi** /ˈzo͞osHē/) ▶ **n.** a Japanese dish consisting of sushi and raw vegetables wrapped in seaweed.

–ORIGIN 1970s: Japanese, from *maki-* (combining form of *maku* 'roll up') + *-zushi, sushi.*

mak·ing /'mākiNG/ ▶ **n.** **1** the process of making or producing something: *the making of videos* | [in combination] *glassmaking.*
2 (**makings**) informal money made; earnings or profit.
3 (**makings**) essential qualities or ingredients needed for something: *a film with all the makings of a cinematic success.* ■ (**makings**) informal or dated paper and tobacco for rolling a cigarette.
–PHRASES **be the making of someone** ensure someone's success or favorable development: *this place has been the making of me in many ways.* **in the making** in the process of developing or being made: *a campaign that's been two years in the making.* **of one's (own) making** (of a difficulty) caused by oneself.

Mak·kah /'mak(k)ə, -kä/ Arabic name for **Mecca**.

ma·ko /'mākō, 'mäkō/ (also **mako shark**) ▶ **n.** (pl. **makos**) a large fast-moving oceanic shark with a deep blue back and white underparts. ● Genus *Isurus*, family Lamnidae: two species.
–ORIGIN mid 19th cent.: from Maori.

Ma·kon·de /mə'kändā/ ▶ **n.** (pl. **same** or **Makondes**) **1** a member of a people inhabiting southern Tanzania and northeastern Mozambique.
2 the Bantu language of this people.
▶ **adj.** of or relating to this people or their language.
–ORIGIN the name in Makonde.

Mak·su·tov tel·e·scope /'mäksə,tôv, mäk'sōōt,ôv/ ▶ **n.** a type of catadioptric telescope having a deeply curved meniscus lens and a spheroidal primary mirror. A secondary mirror on the back of the lens brings the light to a focus just behind a hole in the primary mirror.
–ORIGIN mid 20th cent.: named after Dmitri D. *Maksutov* (1896–1964), Soviet astronomer.

Ma·ku·a /'makōōə/ ▶ **n.** (pl. **same** or **Makuas**) **1** a member of a people inhabiting the border regions of Mozambique, Malawi, and Tanzania.
2 the Bantu language of this people.
–ORIGIN a local name.

Mal. ▶ **abbr.** Bible Malachi.

mal- ▶ **comb. form** **1** in an unpleasant degree: *malodorous.*
2 in a faulty manner: *malfunction.* ■ in an improper manner: *malpractice.* ■ in an inadequate manner: *malnourishment.*
3 not: *maladroit.*
–ORIGIN from French *mal,* from Latin *male* 'badly.'

Mal·a·bar Coast /'malə,bär/ the southern part of the western coast of India, including the coastal region of Karnataka and most of the state of Kerala.
–ORIGIN *Malabar* from *Malabars,* the name of an ancient Dravidian people.

Ma·la·bo /mə'läbō/ the capital of Equatorial Guinea, on the island of Bioko; pop. 96,000 (est. 2007).

mal·ab·sorp·tion /,maləb'sôrpsHən, -'zôrp-/ ▶ **n.** imperfect absorption of food material by the small intestine.

Ma·lac·ca variant spelling of **Melaka**.

ma·lac·ca /mə'lakə/ ▶ **n.** brown cane that is widely used for walking sticks and umbrella handles. ● The cane is obtained from the stem of a Malaysian climbing palm (*Calamus scipionum,* family Palmae). ■ a walking stick of malacca cane.
–ORIGIN mid 19th cent.: from the place name **Malacca**.

Ma·lac·ca, Strait of /mə'läkə, -'lakə/ the channel between the Malay Peninsula and the Indonesian island of Sumatra, an important sea passage linking the Indian Ocean to the South China Sea. The ports of Melaka and Singapore lie on this strait.

Mal·a·chi /'malə,kī/ a book of the Bible belonging to a period before Ezra and Nehemiah.
–ORIGIN from Hebrew *mal'ākī,* literally 'my messenger'; *Malachi* is probably not a personal name, though often taken as such.

mal·a·chite /'malə,kīt/ ▶ **n.** a bright green mineral consisting of copper hydroxyl carbonate. It typically occurs in masses and fibrous aggregates with azurite and is capable of taking a high polish.
–ORIGIN late Middle English: from Old French *melochite,* via Latin from Greek *molokhitis,* from *molokhē,* variant of *malakhē* 'mallow.'

malaco- ▶ **comb. form** soft: *malacostracan.*
–ORIGIN from Greek *malakos* 'soft.'

mal·a·col·o·gy /,malə'käləjē/ ▶ **n.** the branch of zoology that deals with mollusks. Compare with **conchology**.
–DERIVATIVES **mal·a·co·log·i·cal** /-kə'läjikəl/ **adj.**, **mal·a·col·o·gist** /-jist/ **n.**

Mal·a·cos·tra·ca /,malə'kästrəkə/ Zoology a large class of crustaceans that includes crabs, shrimps, lobsters, isopods, and amphipods. They have compound eyes, which are typically on stalks.
–ORIGIN modern Latin (plural), from **malaco-** 'soft' + Greek *ostrakon* 'shell.'

mal·a·cos·tra·can /,malə'kästrəkən/ Zoology ▶ **n.** a crustacean of the large class Malacostraca, such as a crab, shrimp, or lobster.
▶ **adj.** relating to or denoting malacostracans.

mal·a·dap·tive /,malə'daptiv/ ▶ **adj.** technical not providing adequate or appropriate adjustment to the environment or situation.
–DERIVATIVES **mal·ad·ap·ta·tion** /-,adəp'tāsHən, -,ad,ap-/ **n.**, **mal·a·dap·ted** /-'daptəd/ **adj.**

mal·ad·just·ed /,malə'jəstid/ ▶ **adj.** failing or unable to cope with the demands of a normal social environment: *maladjusted behavior.*
–DERIVATIVES **mal·ad·just·ment** /-'jəstmənt/ **n.**

mal·ad·min·is·ter /,maləd'ministər/ ▶ **v.** [with obj.] formal manage or administer inefficiently, badly, or dishonestly.

mal·ad·min·is·tra·tion /,maləd,minə'strāsHən/ ▶ **n.** formal inefficient or dishonest administration; mismanagement: *I found no maladministration in the committee's actions.*

mal·a·droit /,malə'droit/ ▶ **adj.** ineffective or bungling; clumsy.
–DERIVATIVES **mal·a·droit·ly** **adv.**, **mal·a·droit·ness** **n.**
–ORIGIN late 17th cent.: French.

mal·a·dy /'malədē/ ▶ **n.** (pl. **maladies**) a disease or ailment: *an incurable malady* | figurative *the nation's maladies.*
–ORIGIN Middle English: from Old French *maladie,* from *malade* 'sick,' based on Latin *male* 'ill' + *habitus* 'having (as a condition).'

ma·la fi·de /,malə 'fīdē, fīdə/ ▶ **adj. & adv.** chiefly Law in bad faith; with intent to deceive: [as adj.] *a mala fide abuse of position.*
–ORIGIN Latin, ablative of **mala fides**.

ma·la fi·des /,malə 'fīdēz, 'fē,däz/ ▶ **n.** chiefly Law bad faith; intent to deceive.
–ORIGIN Latin.

Ma·la·ga[1] /'maləgə, 'mälə,gä/ a seaport on the Andalusian coast of southern Spain; pop. 566,447 (2008). Spanish name **Málaga**.

Mal·a·ga[2] ▶ **n.** a sweet fortified wine from Malaga.

Mal·a·gas·y /,malə'gasē/ ▶ **n.** (pl. **same** or **Malagasies**) **1** a native or inhabitant of Madagascar.
2 the Austronesian language of Madagascar.
▶ **adj.** of or relating to Madagascar or its people or language.
–ORIGIN variant of **Madagascar**; earlier forms included *Malegass, Madegass,* because of dialect division between the sounds *-l-* and *-d-.*

Mal·a·gas·y Re·pub·lic former name (1960–75) for **Madagascar**.

ma·la·gue·ña /,mälə'g(w)ānyə, ,mal-/ ▶ **n.** a Spanish dance similar to the fandango.
–ORIGIN mid 19th cent.: Spanish.

ma·la·guet·ta /,malə'getə/ (also **malaguetta pepper**) ▶ **n.** another term for **grains of paradise**.
–ORIGIN mid 16th cent.: probably from French *malaguette,* perhaps based on a diminutive of Italian *melica* 'millet.'

ma·laise /mə'lāz, -'lez/ ▶ **n.** a general feeling of discomfort, illness, or uneasiness whose exact cause is difficult to identify: *a society afflicted by a deep cultural malaise* | *a general air of malaise.*
–ORIGIN mid 18th cent.: from French, from Old French *mal* 'bad' (from Latin *malus*) + *aise* 'ease.'

Mal·a·mud /'maləməd/, Bernard (1914–86), US novelist and short-story writer. Notable works: *The Natural* (1952; movie version: 1984), *The Fixer* (1967), *Dubin's Lives* (1979), and *Stories of Bernard Malamud* (1983).

mal·a·mute /'malə,myōōt/ (also **malemute**) ▶ **n.** see **Alaskan malamute**.

ma·lan·ga /mə'laNGgə/ ▶ **n.** see **yautia**.
–ORIGIN early 20th cent.: from American Spanish, probably from Kikongo, plural of *elanga* 'water lily.'

mal·a·pert /,malə'pərt/ archaic ▶ **adj.** boldly disrespectful to a person of higher standing.
▶ **n.** an impudent person.
–ORIGIN Middle English: from **mal-** 'improperly' + archaic *apert* 'insolent.'

mal·a·prop /'malə,präp/ (also **malapropism**) ▶ **n.** the mistaken use of a word in place of a similar-sounding one, often with unintentionally amusing effect, as in, for example, "dance a *flamingo*" (instead of *flamenco*).
–ORIGIN mid 19th cent.: from the name of the character Mrs. *Malaprop* in Sheridan's play *The Rivals* (1775) + **-ism**.

mal·ap·ro·pos /,mal,aprə'pō/ formal ▶ **adv.** inopportunely; inappropriately.
▶ **adj.** inopportune; inappropriate: *these terms applied to him seem to me malapropos.*
▶ **n.** (pl. **same**) something inappropriately said or done.
–ORIGIN mid 17th cent.: from French *mal à propos,* from *mal* 'ill' + *à* 'to' + *propos* 'purpose.'

ma·lar /'mālər/ ▶ **adj.** Anatomy & Medicine of or relating to the cheek: *a slight malar flush.*
▶ **n.** (also **malar bone**) another term for **zygomatic bone**.
–ORIGIN late 18th cent.: from modern Latin *malaris,* from Latin *mala* 'jaw.'

Mä·lar·en /'mā,lär,ən/ a lake in southeastern Sweden, extending inland from the Baltic Sea. The city of Stockholm is situated at its outlet.

ma·lar·i·a /mə'le(ə)rēə/ ▶ **n.** an intermittent and remittent fever caused by a protozoan parasite that invades the red blood cells. The parasite is transmitted by mosquitoes in many tropical and subtropical regions. ● The parasite belongs to the genus *Plasmodium* (phylum Sporozoa) and is transmitted by female mosquitoes of the genus *Anopheles.*
–DERIVATIVES **ma·lar·i·al** /-ēəl/ **adj.**, **ma·lar·i·an** /-ēən/ **adj.**, **ma·lar·i·ous** /-ēəs/ **adj.**
–ORIGIN mid 18th cent.: from Italian, from *mal'aria,* contracted form of *mala aria* 'bad air.' The term originally denoted the unwholesome atmosphere caused by the exhalations of marshes, to which the disease was formerly attributed.

ma·lar·key /mə'lärkē/ ▶ **n.** informal meaningless talk; nonsense: *don't give me that malarkey.*
–ORIGIN 1920s: of unknown origin.

mal·a·thi·on /,malə'THī,än/ ▶ **n.** a synthetic organophosphorus compound that is used as an insecticide and is relatively harmless to plants and other animals.
–ORIGIN 1950s: from *(diethyl) mal(eate)* (see **maleic acid**) + **thio-** + **-on**.

Ma·la·wi /mə'läwē/ a landlocked country in southern central Africa, in the Great Rift Valley, on the western shore of Lake Nyasa; pop. 15,028,800 (est. 2009); capital, Lilongwe; official languages, English and Nyanja.

> Malawi was a British protectorate called Nyasaland from 1891 and was a part of the Federation of Rhodesia and Nyasaland from 1891 until 1963. It became an independent Commonwealth state under Hastings Banda in 1964 and a republic in 1966.

–DERIVATIVES **Ma·la·wi·an** /-wēən/ **adj. & n.**

Ma·la·wi, Lake another name for Lake Nyasa (see **Nyasa, Lake**).

Ma·lay /mə'lā, 'mā,lā/ ▶ **n.** **1** a member of a people inhabiting Malaysia and Indonesia. ■ a person of Malay descent.
2 the Austronesian language of the Malays, closely related to Indonesian, that is the official language of Malaysia.
▶ **adj.** of or relating to this people or language.
–ORIGIN from Malay *Malayu* (now *Melayu*).

Ma·la·ya /mə'lāə/ a former country in Southeast Asia that consists of the southern part of the Malay Peninsula and some adjacent islands (originally including Singapore) and that now forms the western part of the federation of Malaysia and is known as West Malaysia. The area was colonized by the Dutch, Portuguese, and the British, who eventually dominated; the several Malay states federated under British control in 1896. The country became independent in 1957, and the federation expanded and became Malaysia in 1963.

Mal·a·ya·lam /mälē'äləm/ ▶ **n.** the Dravidian language of the Indian state of Kerala, closely related to Tamil.
▶ **adj.** of or relating to this language or its speakers.
–ORIGIN early 19th cent.: from Malayalam, from *mala* (Tamil *malai*) 'mountain' + *āḷ* 'man.'

Ma·lay·an /mə'lāən/ ▶ **n.** another term for **Malay**.
▶ **adj.** of or relating to Malays, the Malay language, or Malaya (now part of Malaysia).

Ma·lay·an sun bear ▶ **n.** see **sun bear**.

Ma·lay Ar·chi·pel·a·go a very large group of islands, including Sumatra, Java, Borneo, the Philippines, and New Guinea, that lie between Southeast Asia and Australia. They constitute the bulk of the area formerly known as the East Indies.

Malayo- ▶ **comb. form** Malay; Malay and ...: *Malayo-Polynesian.*

Ma·lay·o-Pol·y·ne·sian /mə,lāō ,pälə'nēzHən/ ▶ **n.** another term for **Austronesian**.

m

Ma·lay Pen·in·su·la a peninsula in Southeast Asia that separates the Indian Ocean from the South China Sea. It extends approximately 700 miles (1,100 km) south from the Isthmus of Kra and comprises the southern part of Thailand and all of Malaya (West Malaysia).

Ma·lay·sia /mə'lāzhə/ a country in Southeast Asia; pop. 25,715,800 (est. 2009); capital, Kuala Lumpur; languages, Malay (official), English, Tamil, Chinese dialects.

> Malaysia is a federation that consists of **East Malaysia** (the northern part of Borneo, including Sabah and Sarawak) and **West Malaysia** (the southern part of the Malay Peninsula, formerly Malaya). The two parts of Malaysia are separated from each other by 400 miles (650 km) of the South China Sea. Malaysia was federated as an independent Commonwealth of Nations state in 1963; Singapore, briefly a part of the federation, withdrew in 1965.

– DERIVATIVES **Ma·lay·sian** adj. & n.

Mal·colm /'malkəm/ the name of four kings of Scotland. ■ **Malcolm I** (died 954), reigned 943–954. ■ **Malcolm II** (*c.*954–1034), reigned 1005–34. ■ **Malcolm III** (*c.*1031–93), son of Duncan I; reigned 1058–93; known as **Malcolm Canmore** (from Gaelic *Ceann-mor*, great head). He came to the throne after killing Macbeth in battle (1057) and was responsible for helping to form Scotland into an organized kingdom. ■ **Malcolm IV** (1141–65), grandson of David I; reigned 1153–65; known as **Malcolm the Maiden**. His reign witnessed a progressive loss of power to Henry II of England.

Mal·colm X /'malkəm 'eks/ (1925–65), US political activist; born *Malcolm Little*. He joined the Nation of Islam in 1946 and became a vigorous campaigner for black rights, initially advocating the use of violence. In 1964, he converted to orthodox Islam and moderated his views on black separatism; he was assassinated the following year.

Malcolm X

mal·con·tent /,malkən'tent, 'malkən,tent/ ▶ n. a person who is dissatisfied and rebellious.
▶ adj. dissatisfied and complaining or making trouble.
– DERIVATIVES **mal·con·tent·ed** adj.
– ORIGIN late 16th cent.: from French, from *mal* 'badly, ill' + *content* 'pleased.'

mal de mer /,mal də 'me(ə)r/ ▶ n. seasickness.
– ORIGIN French.

Mal·den /'môldən/ a city in eastern Massachusetts, north of Boston; pop. 55,597 (est. 2008).

mal·de·vel·op·ment /,maldi'veləpmənt/ ▶ n. chiefly Medicine & Biology faulty or imperfect development.

mal·dis·tri·bu·tion /,mal,distrə'byo͞oshən/ ▶ n. uneven distribution of something, esp. when disadvantageous or unfair: *the maldistribution of wealth.*
– DERIVATIVES **mal·dis·trib·ut·ed** /,maldə'stribyətəd/ adj.

Mal·dives /'môl,dēvz, -,dīvz, 'mäl-/ (also **Maldive Islands**) a country that consists of a chain of coral islands in the Indian Ocean, southwest of Sri Lanka; pop. 396,300 (est. 2009); capital, Male; official language, Maldivian.

> The islands were probably first settled from southern India and Sri Lanka, but later came under Arab influence. A British protectorate from 1887, the Maldives became independent within the Commonwealth of Nations under the rule of a sultan in 1965 and then as a republic in 1968.

– DERIVATIVES **Mal·div·i·an** /môl'divēən, mäl-/ adj. & n.

mal du siè·cle /,mal də sē'ek(lə)/ ▶ n. world-weariness.
– ORIGIN French, literally 'sickness of the century.'

Ma·le /'mälā/ the capital of the Maldives; pop. 111,000 (est. 2007).

male /māl/ ▶ adj. of or denoting the sex that produces small, typically motile gametes, esp. spermatozoa, with which a female may be fertilized or inseminated to produce offspring: *male children.* ■ relating to or characteristic of men or male animals; masculine: *male unemployment | a deep male voice.* ■ (of a plant or flower) bearing stamens but lacking functional pistils. ■ (of parts of machinery, fittings, etc.) designed to enter, fill, or fit inside a corresponding female part.
▶ n. a male person, plant, or animal: *the audience consisted of adult males | the male of the species.*
– DERIVATIVES **male·ness** n.
– ORIGIN late Middle English: from Old French *masle*, from Latin *masculus*, from *mas* 'a male.'

male chau·vin·ism ▶ n. male prejudice against women; the belief that men are superior in terms of ability, intelligence, etc.: *a bastion of male chauvinism.*
– DERIVATIVES **male chau·vin·ist** n. & adj.

male chau·vin·ist pig ▶ n. informal, derogatory a man who believes that men are superior to women.

mal·e·dic·tion /,malə'dikshən/ ▶ n. a magical word or phrase uttered with the intention of bringing about evil or destruction; a curse.
– DERIVATIVES **mal·e·dic·tive** /-'diktiv/ adj., **mal·e·dic·to·ry** /-'diktərē/ adj.
– ORIGIN late Middle English: from Latin *maledictio(n-)*, from *maledicere* 'speak evil of.'

mal·e·fac·tor /'malə,faktər/ ▶ n. formal a person who commits a crime or some other wrong.
– DERIVATIVES **mal·e·fac·tion** /,malə'fakshən/ n.
– ORIGIN late Middle English: from Latin, from *malefact-* 'done wrong,' from the verb *malefacere*, from *male* 'ill' + *facere* 'do.'

male fern ▶ n. a fern with brown scales on the stalks of the fronds, found in wooded areas of the northeastern US, but much more common in Eurasia. ● Genus *Dryopteris*, family Dryopteridaceae: several species, in particular *D. filix-mas.*

ma·lef·ic /mə'lefik/ ▶ adj. literary causing or capable of causing harm or destruction, esp. by supernatural means. ■ Astrology relating to the planets Saturn and Mars, traditionally considered to have an unfavorable influence.
– DERIVATIVES **ma·lef·i·cence** /-'lefəsəns/ n., **ma·lef·i·cent** /-'lefəsənt/ adj.
– ORIGIN mid 17th cent.: from Latin *maleficus*, from *male* 'ill' + *-ficus* 'doing.'

Ma·le·gaon /,mälə'goun/ a city in western India, in Maharashtra, northeast of Mumbai (Bombay); pop. 461,300 (est. 2009).

ma·le·ic ac·id /mə'lēik, -'lā-/ ▶ n. Chemistry a crystalline acid made by distilling malic acid and used in making synthetic resins. ● Alternative name: *cis*-**butenedioic acid**; chem. formula: HOOCCH·CHCOOH.
– DERIVATIVES **mal·e·ate** /mə'lē,āt, -ət/ n.
– ORIGIN mid 19th cent.: from French *maléique*, alteration of *malique* (see MALIC ACID).

male men·o·pause ▶ n. a stage in a middle-aged man's life supposedly corresponding to the menopause of a woman, associated with the loss of sexual potency and a crisis of confidence and identity (not in technical use).

mal·e·mute /'malə,myo͞ot/ ▶ n. variant spelling of MALAMUTE.

Ma·le·sia /mə'lēzhə/ Botany a phytogeographical region comprising Malaysia, Indonesia, New Guinea, the Philippines, and Brunei.
– DERIVATIVES **Ma·le·sian** adj.

Ma·le·vich /məl'yāvich/, Kazimir (Severinovich) (1878–1935), Russian painter and designer. In his abstract works he used only basic geometric shapes and a severely restricted range of color.

ma·lev·o·lence /mə'levələns/ ▶ n. the state or condition of being malevolent: *his eyes were glowing with malevolence.*

ma·lev·o·lent /mə'levələnt/ ▶ adj. having or showing a wish to do evil to others: *the glint of dark, malevolent eyes | some malevolent force of nature.*
– DERIVATIVES **ma·lev·o·lent·ly** adv.
– ORIGIN early 16th cent.: from Latin *malevolent-* 'wishing evil,' from *male* 'ill' + *volent-* 'wishing' (from the verb *velle*).

mal·fat·ti /mäl'fätē/ ▶ plural n. dumplings or gnocchi made with spinach and ricotta.
– ORIGIN 1980s: Italian, from *malfatto* 'badly made' (because they resemble ravioli without their pasta envelopes).

mal·fea·sance /mal'fēzəns/ ▶ n. Law wrongdoing, esp. by a public official.
– DERIVATIVES **mal·fea·sant** /-'fēzənt/ n. & adj.
– ORIGIN late 17th cent.: from Anglo-Norman French *malfaisance*, from *mal-* 'evil' + Old French *faisance* 'activity.' Compare with MISFEASANCE.

mal·for·ma·tion /,malfôr'māshən, -fər-/ ▶ n. a deformity; an abnormally formed part of the body. ■ the condition of being abnormal in shape or form: *malformation of one or both ears.*

mal·formed /mal'fôrmd/ ▶ adj. (of a person or part of the body) abnormally formed; misshapen: *her ribs are malformed.* ■ not conforming to a standard type: *malformed web pages.*

mal·func·tion /mal'fəngkshən/ ▶ v. [no obj.] (of a piece of equipment or machinery) fail to function normally or satisfactorily: *the unit is clearly malfunctioning.*
▶ n. a failure to function in a normal or satisfactory manner.

Ma·li /'mälē/ a landlocked country in West Africa, south of Algeria, in the Sahel except for desert in the north; pop. 13,443,200 (est. 2009); capital, Bamako; languages, French (official) and others mainly of the Mande group. Former name (until 1958) FRENCH SUDAN.

> Conquered by the French in the late 19th century, Mali became part of French West Africa. It was a partner with Senegal in the Federation of Mali in 1959 and achieved full independence a year later, when Senegal withdrew.

– DERIVATIVES **Ma·li·an** /-ēən/ adj. & n.

Mal·i·bu[1] /'malə,bo͞o/ a resort on the Pacific Ocean coast of southern California, west of Los Angeles. It is home to many movie stars.

Mal·i·bu[2] (also **Malibu board**) ▶ n. (pl. **Malibus**) a lightweight surfboard, typically relatively long with a rounded front end.
– ORIGIN 1960s: named after *Malibu* beach (see MALIBU[1]).

mal·ic ac·id /'malik/ ▶ n. Chemistry a crystalline acid present in unripe apples and other fruits. ● Chem. formula: $HOOCCH_2CH(OH)COOH$.
– DERIVATIVES **mal·ate** /'mal,āt, 'mā,lāt/ n.
– ORIGIN late 18th cent.: *malic* from French *malique*, from Latin *malum* 'apple.'

mal·ice /'maləs/ ▶ n. the intention or desire to do evil; ill will: *I bear no malice toward anybody.* ■ Law wrongful intention, esp. as increasing the guilt of certain offenses.
– ORIGIN Middle English: via Old French from Latin *malitia*, from *malus* 'bad.'

mal·ice a·fore·thought ▶ n. Law the intention to kill or harm, which is held to distinguish unlawful killing from murder.

ma·li·cious /mə'lishəs/ ▶ adj. characterized by malice; intending or intended to do harm: *malicious destruction of property | the transmission of malicious software such as computer viruses.*
– DERIVATIVES **ma·li·cious·ly** adv., **ma·li·cious·ness** n.
– ORIGIN Middle English (also in the sense 'wicked'): from Old French *malicios*, from Latin *malitiosus*, from *malitia* (see MALICE).

ma·li·cious mis·chief ▶ n. Law the willful destruction of another person's property for vicious, wanton, or mischievous purposes.

ma·lign /mə'līn/ ▶ adj. evil in nature or effect; malevolent: *she had a strong and malign influence.* ■ archaic (of a disease) malignant.
▶ v. [with obj.] speak about (someone) in a spitefully critical manner: *don't you dare malign her in my presence.*
– DERIVATIVES **ma·lign·er** n., **ma·lig·ni·ty** /-'lignətē/ n., **ma·lign·ly** adv.
– ORIGIN Middle English: via Old French *maligne* (adjective), *malignier* (verb), based on Latin *malignus* 'tending to evil,' from *malus* 'bad.'

ma·lig·nan·cy /mə'lignənsē/ ▶ n. (pl. **malignancies**) **1** the state or presence of a malignant tumor; cancer: *after biopsy, evidence of malignancy was found.* ■ a cancerous growth. ■ a form of cancer: *diffuse malignancies such as leukemia.*
2 the quality of being malign or malevolent: *her eyes sparkled with renewed malignancy.*

ma·lig·nant /mə'lignənt/ ▶ adj. **1** (of a disease) very virulent or infectious. ■ (of a tumor) tending to invade normal tissue or to recur after removal; cancerous. Contrasted with BENIGN.
2 malevolent: *in the hands of malignant fate.*
– DERIVATIVES **ma·lig·nant·ly** adv.
– ORIGIN mid 16th cent. (also in the sense 'likely to rebel against God or authority'): from late Latin *malignant-* 'contriving maliciously,' from the verb *malignare*. The term was used in its early sense to describe those sympathetic to the royalist cause during the English Civil War (1642–49).

ma·lin·ger /mə'linggər/ ▶ v. [no obj.] exaggerate or feign illness in order to escape duty or work.

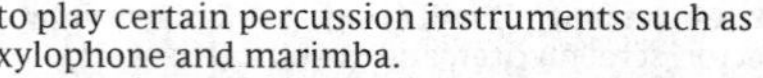

– ORIGIN early 19th cent.: back-formation from *malingerer*, apparently from French *malingre*, perhaps formed as *mal-* 'wrongly, improperly' + *haingre* 'weak,' probably of Germanic origin.

ma·lin·ger·er /mə'liNGgərər/ ▶ **n.** a person who malingers: *the doctor said my son was a malingerer.*

Ma·lin·ke /mə'liNGkä/ ▶ **n.** (pl. **same** or **Malinkes**) **1** a member of a people living mainly in Senegal, Mali, and Côte d'Ivoire (Ivory Coast). **2** the Mande language of this people. ▶ **adj.** of or relating to the Malinke or their language.
– ORIGIN the name in Malinke.

Ma·li·now·ski /ˌmalə'nôfskē, -'näf-, ˌmäl-/, Bronisław Kaspar (1884–1942), Polish anthropologist. He initiated the technique of "participant observation" and developed the functionalist approach to anthropology.

mal·i·son /'maləsən, -zən/ ▶ **n.** archaic a curse.
– ORIGIN Middle English: from Old French.

mall /môl/ ▶ **n. 1** (also **shopping mall**) a large building or series of connected buildings containing a variety of retail stores and typically also restaurants. **2** a sheltered walk or promenade. ■ (also **pedestrian mall**) a section of a street, typically in the downtown area of a city, from which vehicular traffic is excluded. **3** historical another term for the game PALL-MALL. ■ an alley used for this.
– ORIGIN mid 17th cent. (sense 3): probably a shortening of PALL-MALL. Sense 2 derives from *The Mall*, a tree-bordered walk in St. James's Park, London, so named because it was the site of a pall-mall alley. Sense 1 dates from the 1960s.

mal·lard /'malərd/ ▶ **n.** (pl. **same** or **mallards**) the most common duck of the northern hemisphere and the ancestor of most domestic ducks, the male having a dark green head and white collar. ● *Anas platyrhynchos*, family Anatidae.
– ORIGIN Middle English: from Old French 'wild drake,' from *masle* 'male.'

mallard

Malle /mäl/, Louis (1932–95), French movie director. His movies are seminal examples of the French *nouvelle vague*. Notable movies: *Les Amants* (1959), *Pretty Baby* (1978), and *Au Revoir les enfants* (1987).

mal·le·a·ble /'malyəbəl, 'malēə-/ ▶ **adj.** (of a metal or other material) able to be hammered or pressed permanently out of shape without breaking or cracking. ■ easily influenced; pliable: *Anna was shaken enough to be malleable.*
– DERIVATIVES **mal·le·a·bil·i·ty** /ˌmalyə'bilitē, ˌmalēə-/ **n.**, **mal·le·a·bly** /-blē/ **adv.**
– ORIGIN late Middle English (in the sense 'able to be hammered'): via Old French from medieval Latin *malleabilis*, from Latin *malleus* 'a hammer.'

mal·lee /'malē/ ▶ **n.** a low-growing bushy Australian eucalyptus that typically has several slender stems. ● Genus *Eucalyptus*, family Myrtaceae: several species, in particular *E. dumosa*. ■ scrub that is dominated by mallee bushes, typical of some arid parts of Australia.
– ORIGIN mid 19th cent.: from Wuywurung (an Aboriginal language).

mal·lee fowl ▶ **n.** (pl. **same**) a megapode found in the mallee scrub of southern Australia, with pale patterned plumage. ● *Leipoa ocellata*, family Megapodiidae.

mal·le·o·lus /mə'lēələs/ ▶ **n.** (pl. **malleoli** /-ˌlī, -ˌlē/) Anatomy a bony projection with a shape likened to a hammer head, esp. each of those on either side of the ankle.
– DERIVATIVES **mal·le·o·lar** /mə'lēələr/ **adj.**
– ORIGIN late 17th cent.: from Latin, diminutive of *malleus* 'hammer.'

mal·let /'malət/ ▶ **n.** a hammer with a large, usually wooden head, used esp. for hitting a chisel. ■ a long-handled wooden stick with a head like a hammer, used for hitting a croquet or polo ball. ■ Music a wooden or plastic stick with a rounded head, used to play certain percussion instruments such as xylophone and marimba.
– ORIGIN late Middle English: from Old French *maillet*, from *mail* 'hammer,' from Latin *malleus*.

mallet

mal·le·us /'malēəs/ ▶ **n.** (pl. **mallei** /'malēˌī, -ēˌē/) Anatomy a small bone in the middle ear that transmits vibrations of the eardrum to the incus.
– ORIGIN mid 17th cent.: from Latin, literally 'hammer.'

mall·ing /'môliNG/ ▶ **n. 1** the development of shopping malls: *the malling of America.* **2** the action or activity of passing time in a shopping mall: *Jessie had time to go malling.*

Mal·lon /'malən/, Mary (c.1870–1938) US cook; born in Ireland; known as **Typhoid Mary**. Immune to typhoid herself, she spread the disease while working in New York City. She was institutionalized for life from 1914 to protect others.

Mal·loph·a·ga /mə'läfəgə/ Entomology an order of insects that comprises the biting lice. See also PHTHIRAPTERA.
– DERIVATIVES **mal·loph·a·gan** /-gən/ **n. & adj.**
– ORIGIN modern Latin (plural), from Greek *mallos* 'lock of wool' + *-phagos* 'eating.'

Mal·lor·ca /mä'yôrkə/ Spanish name for MAJORCA.

mal·low /'malō/ ▶ **n.** a herbaceous plant with hairy stems, pink or purple flowers, and disk-shaped fruit. Several kinds are grown as ornamentals, and some are edible. ● Genus *Malva*, family Malvaceae (the **mallow family**): many species. This family also includes the hollyhocks, hibiscus, and abutilon. See also MARSH MALLOW, ROSE MALLOW.
– ORIGIN Old English *meal(u)we*, from Latin *malva*; related to Greek *malakhē*; compare with MAUVE.

mall rat ▶ **n.** informal a young person who frequents shopping malls, usually for social purposes.

malm /mä(l)m/ ▶ **n.** a soft, crumbly, chalky rock, or the fertile loamy soil produced as it weathers. ■ (also **malm brick**) a fine-quality brick made originally from malm, marl, or a similar chalky clay.
– ORIGIN Old English *mealm-*, of Germanic origin; related to MEAL[2].

Malmö /'mälˌmō͝o, -ˌmœ/ a port and fortified city in southwestern Sweden, situated on the Øresund opposite Copenhagen; pop. 286,535 (2008).

malm·sey /'mä(l)mzē/ ▶ **n.** a fortified Madeira wine of the sweetest type. ■ historical a strong, sweet white wine imported from Greece and the eastern Mediterranean islands.
– ORIGIN late Middle English: from Middle Dutch *malemeseye*, via Old French from *Monemvasia*, the name of a port in southeastern mainland Greece. Compare with MALVOISIE.

mal·nour·ished /mal'nərisнt, -'nə-risнt/ ▶ **adj.** suffering from malnutrition.
– DERIVATIVES **mal·nourish·ment** /-'nərisнmənt/ **n.**

mal·nu·tri·tion /ˌmaln(y)o͞o'trisнən/ ▶ **n.** lack of proper nutrition, caused by not having enough to eat, not eating enough of the right things, or being unable to use the food that one does eat.

mal·oc·clu·sion /ˌmalə'klo͞ozнən/ ▶ **n.** Dentistry imperfect positioning of the teeth when the jaws are closed.

mal·o·dor /mal'ōdər/ ▶ **n.** a very unpleasant smell.

mal·o·dor·ous /mal'ōdərəs/ ▶ **adj.** smelling very unpleasant.

ma·lo·lac·tic /ˌmalə'laktik, ˌmālə-/ ▶ **adj.** of or denoting bacterial fermentation that converts malic acid to lactic acid, esp. as a secondary process used to reduce the acidity of some wines. ▶ **n.** fermentation of this kind.

ma·lo·nic ac·id /mə'lōnik, -'län-/ ▶ **n.** Chemistry a crystalline acid obtained by the oxidation of malic acid. ● Alternative name: **propane-1,3-dioic acid**; chem. formula: $HOOCCH_2COOH$.
– DERIVATIVES **mal·o·nate** /'maləˌnāt, 'mā-/ **n.**
– ORIGIN mid 19th cent.: *malonic* from French *malonique*, alteration of *malique* 'malic.'

Mal·o·ry /'malərē/, Sir Thomas (died 1471), English writer. His major work, *Le Morte d'Arthur*, which was printed in 1483, is a prose translation of a collection of legends of King Arthur.

ma·lo·ti /mə'lōtē, -'lo͞otē/ plural form of LOTI.

mal·per·for·mance /ˌmalpər'fôrməns/ ▶ **n.** faulty or inadequate performance of a task.

Mal·pi·ghi /mal'pigē, mäl-/, Marcello (c.1628–94), Italian microscopist. He discovered the alveoli and capillaries in the lungs and the fibers and red cells of clotted blood, and he demonstrated the pathway of blood from arteries to veins.

Mal·pigh·i·an lay·er /ˌmal'pigēən, -'pēgē-/ ▶ **n.** Zoology & Anatomy a layer in the epidermis in which skin cells are continually formed by division.

Mal·pigh·i·an tu·bule ▶ **n.** Zoology a tubular excretory organ, numbers of which open into the gut in insects and some other arthropods.

mal·prac·tice /mal'praktəs/ ▶ **n.** improper, illegal, or negligent professional activity or treatment, esp. by a medical practitioner, lawyer, or public official: *victims of medical malpractice | investigations into malpractices and abuses of power.*

mal·pres·en·ta·tion /ˌmalˌprezən'tāsнən/ ▶ **n.** Medicine abnormal positioning of a fetus at the time of delivery.

Mal·raux /mal'rō, mäl-/, André (1901–76), French novelist, politician, and art critic. Involved in the Chinese Communist uprising of 1927 and the Spanish Civil War, he was later appointed the first minister of cultural affairs 1959–69.

MALS ▶ **abbr.** Master of Library Science.

malt /môlt/ ▶ **n.** barley or other grain that has been steeped, germinated, and dried, used esp. for brewing or distilling and vinegar-making. ■ chiefly Brit. short for MALT WHISKEY. ■ short for MALTED MILK. ▶ **v.** [with obj.] convert (grain) into malt: (as noun **malting**) *barley is grown for malting.* ■ [no obj.] (of a seed) become malt when germination is checked by drought.
– DERIVATIVES **malt·i·ness** /-tēnis/ **n.**, **malt·y** **adj.**
– ORIGIN Old English *m(e)alt*, of Germanic origin; related to MELT.

Mal·ta /'môltə/ an island country in the central Mediterranean Sea, about 60 miles (100 km) south of Sicily; pop. 405,200 (est. 2009); capital, Valletta; official languages, Maltese and English.

> Historically of great strategic importance, the island has been held in turn by invaders that have included the Greeks, Arabs, Normans, and Knights Hospitaller. It was annexed by Britain in 1814 and was an important naval base until independence within the Commonwealth of Nations in 1964. Besides the island of Malta, the country includes the islands of Gozo and Comino.

malt·ase /'môlˌtās, -ˌtāz/ ▶ **n.** Biochemistry an enzyme, present in saliva and pancreatic juice, that catalyzes the breakdown of maltose and similar sugars to form glucose.

malt·ed /môltid/ ▶ **adj.** mixed with malt or a malt extract. ▶ **n.** short for MALTED MILK: *they were sipping malteds at the drive-in.*

malt·ed milk ▶ **n.** a drink combining milk, a malt preparation, and ice cream or flavoring.

Mal·tese[1] /môl'tēz/ ▶ **n.** (pl. **same**) **1** a native or inhabitant of Malta or a person of Maltese descent. **2** the national language of Malta, a Semitic language derived from Arabic but much influenced by Italian, Spanish, and Norman French. ▶ **adj.** of or relating to Malta, its people, or their language.

Mal·tese[2] (also **Maltese terrier**) ▶ **n.** a dog of a very small long-haired breed, typically with white hair.

Maltese[2]

Mal·tese cross ▶ **n. 1** a cross with arms of equal length that broaden from the center and have their ends indented in a shallow V-shape. **2** a plant of the pink family (*Lychnis chalcedonica*), with small scarlet petals arranged in the shape of a Maltese cross.
– ORIGIN so named because the cross was formerly worn by the Knights of Malta, a religious order.

malt·house /'môltˌhous/ ▶ **n.** a building in which malt is prepared and stored.

Mal·thus /'malтнəs, 'môl-/, Thomas Robert (1766–1834), English economist and clergyman. In *Essay on Population* (1798) he argued that without the practice of "moral restraint" the population tends to increase at a greater rate than its means of subsistence, resulting in the population checks of war, famine, and epidemic.

– DERIVATIVES **Mal·thu·sian** /mal'TH(y)ōōZHən, môl-/ **adj. & n.**, **Mal·thu·sian·ism** /mal'TH(y)ōōZHə,nizəm, môl-/ **n.**

malt liq·uor ▶ **n.** alcoholic liquor made from malt by fermentation rather than distillation; beer with a relatively high alcohol content.

mal·to·dex·trin /,môltō'dekstrən/ ▶ **n.** dextrin containing maltose, used as a food additive.

malt·ose /'môl,tōs, -,tōz/ ▶ **n.** Chemistry a sugar produced by the breakdown of starch, e.g., by enzymes found in malt and saliva. It is a disaccharide consisting of two linked glucose units.
– ORIGIN mid 19th cent.: from MALT + -OSE².

mal·treat /mal'trēt/ ▶ **v.** [with obj.] treat (a person or animal) cruelly or with violence.
– DERIVATIVES **mal·treat·er n.**
– ORIGIN early 18th cent.: from French *maltraiter*.

mal·treat·ment /mal'trētmənt/ ▶ **n.** cruel or violent treatment of a person or animal; mistreatment: *16 percent of children experience serious maltreatment at the hands of their parents.*

malt whis·key ▶ **n.** whiskey made only from malted barley and not blended with grain whiskey.

Ma·lu·ku Indonesian name for MOLUCCA ISLANDS.

mal·va·ceous /mal'vāSHəs/ ▶ **adj.** Botany of, relating to, or denoting plants of the mallow family (Malvaceae).
– ORIGIN late 17th cent.: from modern Latin *Malvaceae* (plural), based on Latin *malva* 'mallow,' + -OUS.

Mal·va·si·a /mal'vāZHə/ ▶ **n.** a variety of grape used to make white and red wines, esp. in Italy.
– ORIGIN Italian form of the place name *Monemvasia*, in the Peloponnese (see MALMSEY).

mal·ver·sa·tion /,malvər'sāSHən/ ▶ **n.** formal corrupt behavior in a position of trust, esp. in public office: *ineptitude and malversation were major factors in the trouncing of the group's candidates.*
– ORIGIN mid 16th cent.: from French, from *malverser*, from Latin *male* 'badly' + *versari* 'behave.'

Mal·vi·nas, Islas /môl'vēnəs/ the name by which the Falkland Islands are known in Argentina.

mal·voi·sie /,mal,vwä'zē, -,voi-/ ▶ **n.** (in French-speaking regions) any of several grape varieties used to make full-flavored white wines.
– ORIGIN from Old French *malvesie*, from the French form of *Monemvasia* (see MALMSEY).

mal·ware /'mal,we(ə)r/ ▶ **n.** Computing software that is intended to damage or disable computers and computer systems.
– ORIGIN blend of *malicious* and *software*.

mam /mäm/ ▶ **n.** informal **1** chiefly Brit. one's mother: [as name] *it was better when Mam was alive.* [late 16th cent.: perhaps imitative of a child's first syllables (see MAMA).]
2 a term of respectful or polite address used for any woman: *"You all ride them horses down here?" "Yes, mam."* [variant of MA'AM.]

ma·ma /'mämə/ (also **mamma**) ▶ **n. 1** one's mother (esp. as a child's term): [as name] *come and meet Mama.*
2 informal a mature woman: *the ultimate tough blues mama.*
– ORIGIN mid 16th cent.: imitative of a child's first syllables *ma, ma*.

ma·ma-san /'mämə ,sän/ ▶ **n.** (in Japan and East Asia) a woman in a position of authority, esp. one in charge of a geisha house or bar.
– ORIGIN Japanese, from *mama* 'mother' + *san*, an honorific title used as a mark of politeness.

ma·ma's boy ▶ **n.** a boy or man who is excessively influenced by or attached to his mother.

mam·ba /'mämbə/ ▶ **n.** a large, agile, highly venomous African snake. ● Genus *Dendroaspis*, family Elapidae: three species. See also BLACK MAMBA.
– ORIGIN mid 19th cent.: from Zulu *imamba*.

mam·bo /'mämbō/ ▶ **n.** (pl. **mambos**) **1** a Latin American dance similar in rhythm to the rumba.
2 a voodoo priestess.
▶ **v.** (**mamboes, mamboing, mamboed**) [no obj.] dance the mambo.
– ORIGIN 1940s: from American Spanish, probably from Haitian Creole, from Yoruba, literally 'to talk.'

mam·ee /mäm'ē/ ▶ **n.** variant spelling of MAMMEE.

Mam·e·luke /'mamə,lōōk/ ▶ **n.** a member of a regime that formerly ruled parts of the Middle East. Descended from slaves, they ruled Syria (1260–1516) and Egypt (1250–1517), and continued as a ruling military caste in Ottoman Egypt until massacred by the viceroy Muhammad Ali in 1811.
– ORIGIN from French *mameluk*, from Arabic *mamlūk* (passive participle used as a noun meaning 'slave'), from *malaka* 'possess.'

Mam·et /'mamit/, David (1947–), US playwright, director, screenwriter, and novelist. His works include the play *Glengarry Glen Ross* (Pulitzer Prize, 1984; movie version: 1992) and the novel *The Village* (1994).

ma·mey /mäm'ē/ ▶ **n.** variant spelling of MAMMEE.

ma·mil·la /mam'ilə/ ▶ **n.** variant spelling of MAMMILLA.

mam·ma¹ ▶ **n.** variant spelling of MAMA.

mam·ma² /'mamə/ ▶ **n.** (pl. **mammae** /'mamē, 'mam,ī/) a milk-secreting organ of female mammals (in humans, the breast). ■ a corresponding nonsecretory structure in male mammals.
– DERIVATIVES **mam·mi·form** /'mamə,fôrm/ **adj.**
– ORIGIN Old English, from Latin, 'breast.'

mam·mal /'maməl/ ▶ **n.** a warm-blooded vertebrate animal of a class that is distinguished by the possession of hair or fur, the secretion of milk by females for the nourishment of the young, and (typically) the birth of live young.

> The first small mammals evolved from reptiles about 200 million years ago, and the group diversified rapidly after the extinction of the dinosaurs to become the dominant form of land animal, with about 4,000 living species. Mammals belong to the class Mammalia, which contains the subclass Prototheria (monotremes) and the infraclasses Metatheria (marsupials) and Eutheria (placental mammals such as rodents, cats, whales, bats, and humans).

– DERIVATIVES **mam·ma·li·an** /mə'mālēən/ **adj.**
– ORIGIN early 19th cent.: anglicized form (first used in the plural) of modern Latin *mammalia*, neuter plural of Latin *mammalis* (adjective), from *mamma* 'breast' (see MAMMA²).

mam·ma·lif·er·ous /,mamə'lifərəs/ ▶ **adj.** Geology containing mammalian fossil remains.

mam·mal-like rep·tile /'mamə(l),līk/ ▶ **n.** another term for SYNAPSID.

mam·mal·o·gy /mə'maləjē/ ▶ **n.** the branch of zoology concerned with mammals.
– DERIVATIVES **mam·mal·o·gist** /-jist/ **n.**

mam·ma·ry /'mamərē/ ▶ **adj.** [attrib.] denoting or relating to the human female breasts or the milk-secreting organs of other mammals: *mammary tumor viruses.*
▶ **n.** (pl. **mammaries**) informal a breast.
– ORIGIN late 17th cent.: from MAMMA² + -ARY¹.

mam·ma·ry gland ▶ **n.** the milk-producing gland of women or other female mammals.

mam·mee /mä'mā, -'mē/ (also **mamee, mamey**) ▶ **n. 1** (also **mammee apple**) a tropical American tree having large edible red fruit with red rind and sweet yellow flesh. ● *Mammea americana*, family Guttiferae.
2 (also **mammee sapote** /sə'pōtē, -tā/) a Central American tree having edible russet fruit with spicy red flesh. [*sapote* from Spanish *zapote* 'sapodilla.'] ● *Pouteria sapota*, family Sapotaceae.
– ORIGIN late 16th cent.: from Spanish *mamei*, from Taino.

mam·mil·la /mə'milə/ (also **mamilla**) ▶ **n.** (pl. **mammillae** /-'milē, -'mil,ī/) Anatomy the nipple of a woman's breast. ■ the corresponding organ in any mammal. ■ a nipple-shaped structure.
– ORIGIN late 17th cent.: from Latin, diminutive of *mamma* 'breast' (see MAMMA²).

mam·mil·lar·y /'mamə,lerē/ (also **mamillary**) ▶ **adj.** rounded like a breast or nipple, in particular: ■ (of minerals) having several smoothly rounded convex surfaces. ■ Anatomy denoting two rounded bodies in the floor of the hypothalamus in the brain.
– ORIGIN early 17th cent.: from modern Latin *mamillaris*, from *mamilla* (see MAMILLA). The spelling variant of *-mm-* was due to association with MAMMARY.

mam·mil·lat·ed /'mamə,lātid/ (also **mamillated**) ▶ **adj.** technical covered with rounded mounds or lumps. ■ (of minerals) mammillary.
– DERIVATIVES **mam·mil·late** /-,lāt/ **adj.**
– ORIGIN mid 18th cent.: from MAMILLA + the adjectival suffix *-ated*.

mam·mo·gram /'mamə,gram/ ▶ **n.** an image obtained by mammography.

mam·mog·ra·phy /mə'mägrəfē/ ▶ **n.** Medicine a technique using X-rays to diagnose and locate tumors of the breasts.
– ORIGIN 1930s: from MAMMA² + -GRAPHY.

mam·mon /'mamən/ (also **Mammon**) ▶ **n.** wealth regarded as an evil influence or false object of worship and devotion. It was taken by medieval writers as the name of the devil of covetousness, and revived in this sense by Milton.
– DERIVATIVES **mam·mon·ism** /-,izəm/ **n.**, **mam·mon·ist** /-,ist/ **n.**
– ORIGIN late Middle English: via late Latin from New Testament Greek *mamōnas* (see Matt. 6:24, Luke 16:9–13), from Aramaic *māmōn* 'riches.'

mam·moth /'maməTH/ ▶ **n.** a large extinct elephant of the Pleistocene epoch, typically hairy with a sloping back and long curved tusks. ● Genus *Mammuthus*, family Elephantidae: several species.
▶ **adj.** huge: *a mammoth corporation.*
– ORIGIN early 18th cent.: from Russian *mamo(n)t*, probably of Siberian origin.

Mam·moth Cave Na·tion·al Park a national park in west central Kentucky, site of the largest known cave system in the world. It consists of over 300 miles (480 km) of charted passageways and contains some spectacular rock formations.

mam·my /'mamē/ ▶ **n.** (pl. **mammies**) informal one's mother (esp. as a child's word): *he was screaming for his mammy.* ■ offensive (formerly in the southern US) a black nursemaid or nanny in charge of white children.
– ORIGIN early 16th cent.: from MAM + -Y²; compare with MOMMY and MUMMY².

Ma·mout·zu /mä'mōōtsōō/ the capital (since 1977) of Mayotte; pop. 53,000 (est. 2007).

Mam'·selle /mam'zel/ ▶ **n.** short for MADEMOISELLE.

man /man/ ▶ **n.** (pl. **men** /men/) **1** an adult human male. ■ a male worker or employee: *more than 700 men were laid off | CNN's man in India.* ■ a male member of a sports team: *Johnson took the ball past three men and scored.* ■ (**men**) ordinary members of the armed forces as distinct from the officers: *he had a platoon of forty men to prepare for battle.* ■ a husband, boyfriend, or lover: *the two of them lived for a time as man and wife.* ■ [with adj.] a male person associated with a particular place, activity, or occupation: *a Harvard man | I'm a solid union man.* ■ a male pursued or sought by another, esp. in connection with a crime: *Inspector Bull was sure they would find their man.* ■ dated a manservant or valet: *get me a cocktail, my man.* ■ historical a vassal.
2 a human being of either sex; a person: *God cares for all races and all men.* ■ (also **Man**) [in sing.] human beings in general; the human race: *places untouched by the ravages of man.* ■ [in sing.] an individual; one: *a man could buy a lot with eighteen million dollars.* ■ a person with the qualities often associated with males such as bravery, spirit, or toughness: *she was more of a man than any of them.* ■ [in sing.] a type of prehistoric human named after the place where the remains were found: *Cro-Magnon man.*
3 (usu. **the Man**) informal a group or person in a position of authority over others, such as a corporate employer or the police: *it was a vicarious way of powerless people being able to stick it to the Man.* ■ informal white people collectively regarded as the controlling group in society: *he urged that black college athletes boycott the Man's Rose Bowl.*
4 a figure or token used in playing a board game.
▶ **v.** (**mans, manning, manned**) [with obj.] **1** (of personnel) work at, run, or operate (a place or piece of equipment) or defend (a fortification): *the firemen manned the pumps and fought the blaze.* ■ provide someone to fill (a post or office): *the chaplaincy was formerly manned by the cathedral.*
2 archaic fortify the spirits or courage of: *he **manned himself** with dauntless air.*
▶ **exclam.** informal used, irrespective of the sex of the person addressed, to express surprise, admiration, delight, etc., or for emphasis: *man, what a show!*
– PHRASES **as — as the next man** as — as the average person: *I'm as ambitious as the next man.* **as one man** with everyone acting together or in agreement: *the crowd rose to their feet as one man.* **be someone's man** be the person perfectly suited to a particular requirement or task: *for any coloring and perming services, David's your man.* **be man enough for** (or **to do**) be brave enough to do: *who's man enough for the job? | he has not been man enough to face up to his responsibilities.* **every man for himself** proverb everyone should (or does) look after their own interests rather than considering those of others: *when the bottom drops out of the market, it's every man for himself.* **make a man out of someone** (of an experience or person) turn a young man into a mature adult: *I make men out of them and teach them never to let anyone outsmart them.* **man about town** a fashionable male socialite. **man and boy** dated throughout life from youth: *the time when families worked in the fields man and boy.* **the man in the moon** the imagined likeness of a face seen on the surface of a full moon. ■ used, esp. in comparisons, to refer to someone regarded as out of touch with real life: *a kid with no more idea of what to do than the man in the moon.* **the man in** (or **on**) **the street** an ordinary person, often with regard to their opinions, or as distinct from an expert: *it will be interesting to hear what the man in the street has to say about these latest tax cuts.* **man of action** see ACTION. **man of the cloth** a clergyman. **man of God** a clergyman. ■ a holy man or saint. **man of**

honor a man who adheres to what is right or to a high standard of conduct. **man of the house** the male head of a household. **man of letters** a male scholar or author. **man of the moment** a man of importance at a particular time. **man of the world** see WORLD. **man's best friend** an affectionate or approving way of referring to the dog. **a man's man** a man whose personality is such that he is as popular and at ease, or more so, with other men than with women. **man to man** (or **man-to-man**) **1** in a direct and frank way between two men; openly and honestly: *he was able to talk man to man with the delegates* | *a man-to-man chat.* **2** denoting a defensive tactic in a sport such as football or basketball in which each player is responsible for defending against one opponent: *Washington's cornerbacks are fast enough to cover man-to-man.* **men in white coats** medical or laboratory staff, esp. doctors. ■ humorous psychiatrists or psychiatric workers (used to imply that someone is mad or mentally unbalanced): *I wondered how much more stupid I could get before the men in white coats would lead me away.* **separate** (or **sort out**) **the men from the boys** informal show or prove which people in a group are truly competent, brave, or mature. **to a man** without exception: *to a man, we have all taken a keen interest in the business.*

– DERIVATIVES **man·less** adj.

– ORIGIN Old English *man(n)*, (plural) *menn* (noun), *mannian* (verb), of Germanic origin; related to Dutch *man*, German *Mann*, and Sanskrit *manu* 'mankind.'

> **USAGE** Traditionally, the word **man** has been used to refer not only to adult males but also to human beings in general, regardless of sex. There is a historical explanation for this: in Old English, the principal sense of **man** was 'a human being,' and the words **wer** and **wif** were used to refer specifically to 'a male person' and 'a female person,' respectively. Subsequently, **man** replaced **wer** as the normal term for 'a male person,' but at the same time the older sense 'a human being' remained in use. In the second half of the 20th century, the generic use of **man** to refer to 'human beings in general' (as in *reptiles were here long before man appeared on the earth*) became problematic; the use is now often regarded as sexist or old-fashioned. In some contexts, terms such as **the human race** or **humankind** may be used instead of **man** or **mankind**. Certain fixed phrases and sayings, such as *time and tide wait for no man* can be easily rephrased (e.g., *time and tide wait for no one*). Alternatives for other related terms exist as well: the noun **manpower**, for example, can usually be replaced with **staff** or **crew**, and in most cases, the verbal form **to man** can be expressed as **to staff** or **to operate**.

Man. ▶ abbr. Manitoba.

-man ▶ comb. form in nouns denoting. ■ a male of a specified nationality or origin: *Frenchman* | *Yorkshireman.* ■ a man belonging to a distinct specified group: *layman.* ■ a person, esp. a male, having a specified occupation or role: *exciseman* | *chairman* | *oarsman.* ■ a ship of a specified kind: *merchantman.*

> **USAGE** Traditionally, the form **-man** was combined with other words to create a term denoting an occupation or role, as in **fireman, layman, chairman,** and **mailman.** As the role of women in society has changed, with the result that women are now more likely to be in roles previously held exclusively by men, many of these terms ending in **-man** have been challenged as sexist and out of date. As a result, there has been a gradual shift away from **-man** compounds except where referring to a specific male person. Gender-neutral terms such as **firefighter** and **mail carrier** are widely accepted alternatives. And new terms such as **chairperson, layperson,** and **spokesperson,** which only a few decades ago seemed odd or awkward, are common today.

Man, Isle of see ISLE OF MAN.

ma·na /'mänə/ ▶ n. (esp. in Polynesian, Melanesian, and Maori belief) pervasive supernatural or magical power.

– ORIGIN Maori.

man·a·cle /'manikəl/ ▶ n. (usu. **manacles**) a metal band, chain, or shackle for fastening someone's hands or ankles: *the practice of keeping prisoners in manacles.*
▶ v. [with obj.] (usu. **be manacled**) fetter (a person or a part of the body) with manacles: *his hands were manacled behind his back.*

– ORIGIN Middle English: from Old French *manicle* 'handcuff,' from Latin *manicula*, diminutive of *manus* 'hand.'

man·age /'manij/ ▶ v. **1** [with obj.] be in charge of (a company, establishment, or undertaking); administer; run: *their elder son managed the farm.* ■ administer and regulate (resources under one's control): *we manage our cash extremely well.* ■ have the position of supervising (staff) at work: *the skills needed to manage a young, dynamic team.* ■ be the manager of (a sports team or a performer): *he managed five or six bands in his career.* ■ maintain control or influence over (a person or animal): *she manages horses better than anyone I know.* ■ control the use or exploitation of (land): *the forest is managed to achieve maximum growth.*
2 [no obj.] succeed in surviving or in attaining one's aims, esp. against heavy odds; cope: *Catherine* ***managed on*** *five hours' sleep a night.* ■ [with obj.] succeed in doing, achieving, or producing (something, esp. something difficult): *she managed a brave but unconvincing smile* | [with infinitive] *Beth finally managed to hail a cab* | ironic *one fund managed to lose money.* ■ [with obj.] succeed in dealing with or withstanding (something): *there was more stress and anxiety than he could manage.* ■ [with obj.] be free to attend on (a certain day) or at (a certain time): *he could not manage March 24 after all.*

– ORIGIN mid 16th cent. (in the sense 'put (a horse) through the paces of the manège'): from Italian *maneggiare*, based on Latin *manus* 'hand.'

man·age·a·ble /'manijəbəl/ ▶ adj. able to be managed, controlled, or accomplished without great difficulty: *it leaves hair feeling soft and manageable* | *the situation was manageable, if a little nerve-racking.*

– DERIVATIVES **man·age·a·bil·i·ty** /ˌmanijə'bilətē/ n., **man·age·a·ble·ness** n., **man·age·a·bly** /-blē/ adv.

man·aged care ▶ n. a system of health care in which patients agree to visit only certain doctors and hospitals, and in which the cost of treatment is monitored by a managing company.

man·aged cur·ren·cy ▶ n. a currency whose exchange rate is regulated or controlled by the government.

man·aged fund ▶ n. an investment fund run on behalf of an investor by an agent (typically an insurance company).

man·age·ment /'manijmənt/ ▶ n. **1** the process of dealing with or controlling things or people: *the management of elk herds.* ■ the responsibility for and control of a company or similar organization: *the management of a great metropolitan newspaper* | *a successful career in management.* ■ [treated as sing. or pl.] the people in charge of running a company or organization, regarded collectively: *management was extremely cooperative.* ■ Medicine & Psychiatry the treatment or control of diseases, injuries, or disorders, or the care of patients who suffer from them: *the use of combination chemotherapy in the management of breast cancer.*
2 archaic trickery; deceit: *if there has been any management in the business, it has been concealed from me.*

man·age·ment ac·count·ing ▶ n. the provision of financial data and advice to a company for use in the organization and development of its business.

– DERIVATIVES **man·age·ment ac·count·ant** n.

man·age·ment com·pa·ny ▶ n. a company that is set up to manage a group of properties, a mutual fund, an investment fund, etc.

man·age·ment in·for·ma·tion sys·tem ▶ n. (abbr. **MIS**) a computerized information-processing system designed to support the activities of company or organizational management.

man·ag·er /'manijər/ ▶ n. a person responsible for controlling or administering all or part of a company or similar organization: *the manager of a bar* | *the sales manager.* ■ a person who controls the activities, business dealings, and other aspects of the career of an entertainer, athlete, group of musicians, etc.: *she left it to her manager to deal with the canceled concerts.* ■ a person in charge of the activities, tactics, and training of a sports team: *Frank Robinson became baseball's first black manager.* ■ [with modifier] Computing a program or system that controls or organizes a peripheral device or process: *a file manager.*

– DERIVATIVES **man·ag·er·ship** /-ˌship/ n.

man·ag·er·ess /manijə'rəs/ ▶ n. rare a female manager.

man·a·ger·i·al /ˌmanə'ji(ə)rēəl/ ▶ adj. relating to management or managers, esp. of a company or similar organization: *I have a managerial role* | *managerial skills.*

– DERIVATIVES **man·a·ger·i·al·ly** adv.

man·a·ger·i·al·ism /ˌmanə'ji(ə)rēəˌlizəm/ ▶ n. belief in or reliance on the use of professional managers in administering or planning an activity.

– DERIVATIVES **man·a·ger·i·al·ist** n. & adj.

man·ag·ing /'manijiNG/ ▶ adj. [attrib.] having executive or supervisory control or authority: *a managing editor* | *the managing director.*

Ma·na·gua /mə'nägwə/ the capital of Nicaragua; pop. 937,489 (2006). The city was almost completely destroyed by an earthquake in 1972.

man·a·kin /'manəˌkin/ ▶ n. a small tropical American bird with a large head and small bill, the male of which is typically brightly colored. Compare with MANNIKIN. ● Family Pipridae (or Cotingidae, Tyrannidae): several genera and many species.

> **USAGE** See usage at MANNEQUIN.

Ma·na·ma /mə'nämə/ a seaport and the capital of Bahrain; pop. 157,000 (est. 2007).

ma·ña·na /mən'yänə/ ▶ adv. in the indefinite future (used to indicate procrastination): *the exhibition will be ready mañana.*

– ORIGIN Spanish, literally 'tomorrow.'

Ma·nas·seh /mə'nasə/ (in the Bible) a Hebrew patriarch, son of Jacob and Rachel. ■ the tribe of Israel traditionally descended from him.

ma·nat /'manˌat/ ▶ n. (pl. **same**) the basic monetary unit of Azerbaijan and Turkmenistan, equal to 100 gopik in Azerbaijan and 100 tenge in Turkmenistan.

man-at-arms ▶ n. (pl. **men-at-arms**) archaic a soldier, esp. one heavily armed and mounted on horseback.

man·a·tee /'manəˌtē/ ▶ n. an aquatic mammal with a rounded tail flipper, living in shallow coastal waters and adjacent rivers of the tropical Atlantic. ● Family Trichechidae and genus *Trichechus*: three species, all of which are endangered, including the **West Indian manatee** (*T. manatus*).

– ORIGIN mid 16th cent.: from Spanish *manatí*, from Carib *manáti*.

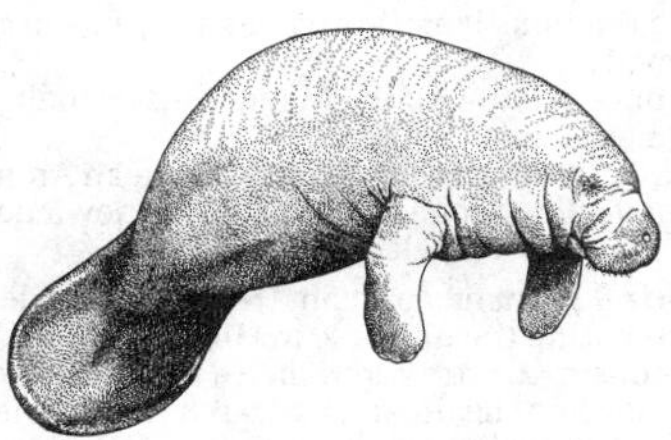

West Indian manatee

Ma·naus /mä'nous/ a city in northwestern Brazil; pop. 1,646,602 (2007). It is the principal commercial center of the upper Amazon region.

man·bag /'manbag/ ▶ n. informal a man's handbag or shoulder bag.

Man·che·go /man'CHāgō/ ▶ n. a Spanish cheese traditionally made with sheep's milk.

– ORIGIN Spanish, from *La Mancha*, the region of Spain where the cheese originates.

Man·ches·ter[1] /'manˌCHestər, 'manCHi-/ **1** an industrial city in northwestern England; pop. 396,300 (est. 2009). Founded in Roman times, it developed in the 18th and 19th centuries as a center of the English cotton industry.
2 a town in central Connecticut, east of Hartford; pop. 56,385 (est. 2008).
3 the largest city in New Hampshire, on the Merrimack River, in the southern part of the state; pop. 108,586 (est. 2008).

Man·ches·ter[2], William (1922–2004), US historian and biographer. His works include *The Death of a President* (1967), *The Last Lion* (2 volumes, 1983, 1988), and *A World Lit Only by Fire* (1992).

Man·ches·ter ter·ri·er ▶ n. a small terrier of a breed with a short black-and-tan coat.

man·chet /'manCHət/ ▶ n. historical a loaf of the finest kind of wheat bread.

– ORIGIN late Middle English: perhaps from obsolete *maine* 'flour of the finest quality' + obsolete *cheat*, denoting a kind of wheaten bread.

man-child ▶ n. an immature man. ■ archaic a male child.

man·chi·neel /ˌmanCHə'nēl/ ▶ n. a Caribbean tree that has acrid applelike fruit and poisonous milky sap that can cause temporary blindness. ● *Hippomane mancinella*, family Euphorbiaceae.

– ORIGIN mid 17th cent.: from French *mancenille*, from Spanish *manzanilla*, diminutive of *manzana* 'apple,' based on Latin *matiana* (*poma*) (neuter plural) denoting a kind of apple.

Man·chu /'manˌCHōō, man'CHōō/ ▶ n. (pl. **same** or **Manchus**) **1** a member of a people originally living in Manchuria who formed the last imperial dynasty of China (1644–1912).
2 the Tungusic language of the Manchus.
▶ adj. of or relating to the Manchu people or their language.

– ORIGIN the name in Manchu, literally 'pure.'

Man·chu·ri·a /man'CHŏŏrēə/ a mountainous region that forms the northeastern portion of China and comprises the provinces of Jilin, Liaoning, and Heilongjiang. In 1932, it was declared

m

an independent state by Japan and renamed Manchukuo; it was restored to China in 1945.

Man·ci·ni /ˌman'sēnē/, Henry (1924–94), US composer and conductor. He wrote many movie scores, including those for *The Pink Panther* (1964) and *Victor/Victoria* (1982). He also wrote "Moon River" for *Breakfast at Tiffany's* (1961).

man·ci·ple /'mansəpəl/ ▶ **n.** chiefly archaic an officer who buys provisions for a college, monastery, or other institution.
– ORIGIN Middle English: via Anglo-Norman French and Old French from Latin *mancipium* 'purchase,' from *manceps* 'buyer,' from *manus* 'hand' + *capere* 'take.'

Man·cu·ni·an /man'kyo͞onēən/ ▶ **n.** a native or inhabitant of Manchester, England.
▶ **adj.** of or relating to Manchester, England.
– ORIGIN early 20th cent.: from *Mancunium*, the Latin name of Manchester, + **-AN**.

-mancy ▶ **comb. form** divination by a specified means: *geomancy*.
– ORIGIN from Old French *-mancie*, via late Latin *-mantia* from Greek *manteia* 'divination.'

Man·dae·an /man'dēən/ (also **Mandean**) ▶ **n. 1** a member of a Gnostic sect surviving in Iraq and southwestern Iran, who regard John the Baptist as the Messiah and stress salvation through knowledge of the divine origin of the soul.
2 the religious language of this sect, a form of Aramaic.
▶ **adj.** of or relating to the Mandaeans or their language.
– ORIGIN late 19th cent.: from Mandaean Aramaic *mandaia* 'Gnostics, those who have knowledge' (from *manda* 'knowledge') + **-AN**.

man·da·la /'mandələ, 'mən-/ ▶ **n.** a geometric figure representing the universe in Hindu and Buddhist symbolism. ■ Psychoanalysis such a symbol in a dream, representing the dreamer's search for completeness and self-unity.
– DERIVATIVES **man·dal·ic** /man'dalik, ˌmən-/ **adj.**
– ORIGIN from Sanskrit *maṇḍala* 'disk.'

Man·da·lay /ˌmandə'lā/ a port on the Irrawaddy River in central Burma (Myanmar); pop. 961,000 (est. 2007). Founded in 1857, it was the capital (until 1885) of the Burmese kingdom. It is an important Buddhist religious center.

m

man·da·mus /man'dāməs/ ▶ **n.** Law a judicial writ issued as a command to an inferior court or ordering a person to perform a public or statutory duty: *a writ of mandamus*.
– ORIGIN mid 16th cent.: from Latin, literally 'we command.'

Man·dan /'mandən, -ˌdan/ ▶ **n.** (pl. **same** or **Mandans**) **1** a member of an American Indian people formerly living on the upper Missouri River in North Dakota.
2 the Siouan language of this people, related to Winnebago.
▶ **adj.** of or relating to this people or their language.
– ORIGIN from Canadian French *Mandane*, probably from Dakota Sioux *mawátąna*.

man·da·rin¹ /'mandərən/ ▶ **n. 1** (**Mandarin**) the standard literary and official form of Chinese based on the Beijing dialect, spoken by over 730 million people: [as modifier] *Mandarin Chinese*.
2 an official in any of the nine top grades of the former imperial Chinese civil service. ■ [as modifier] (esp. of clothing) characteristic or supposedly characteristic of such officials: *a red-buttoned mandarin cap*. ■ an ornament consisting of a nodding figure in traditional Chinese dress, typically made of porcelain. ■ porcelain decorated with Chinese figures dressed as mandarins. ■ a powerful official or senior bureaucrat, esp. one perceived as reactionary and secretive: *a civil service mandarin*.
– ORIGIN late 16th cent. (denoting a Chinese official): from Portuguese *mandarim*, via Malay from Hindi *mantrī* 'counselor.'

man·da·rin² (also **mandarine** /-dəˌrēn/, **mandarin orange**) ▶ **n. 1** a small flattish citrus fruit with a loose skin, esp. a variety with yellow-orange skin. Compare **TANGERINE**.
2 the citrus tree that yields this fruit. ● *Citrus reticulata*, family Rutaceae.
– ORIGIN late 18th cent.: from French *mandarine*; perhaps related to **MANDARIN¹**, the color of the fruit being likened to the official's yellow robes.

man·da·rin col·lar ▶ **n.** a small, close-fitting upright collar.

man·da·rin duck ▶ **n.** a small tree-nesting eastern Asian duck, the male of which has showy plumage with an orange ruff and orange saillike feathers on each side of the body. ● *Aix galericulata*, family Anatidae.

mandarin collar

man·da·rin jack·et ▶ **n.** a plain jacket, typically of embroidered silk, with a mandarin collar.

man·da·tar·y /'mandəˌterē/ ▶ **n.** (pl. **mandataries**) historical a person or country receiving a mandate.
– ORIGIN late 15th cent. (denoting a person appointed by a papal mandate): from late Latin *mandatarius*, from *mandatum* (see **MANDATE**).

man·date /'manˌdāt/ ▶ **n. 1** an official order or commission to do something: *a mandate to seek the release of political prisoners*. ■ Law a commission by which a party is entrusted to perform a service, esp. without payment and with indemnity against loss by that party. ■ Law an order from an appellate court to a lower court to take a specific action. ■ a written authority enabling someone to carry out transactions on another's bank account. ■ historical a commission from the League of Nations to a member state to administer a territory: *the end of the British mandate in Palestine*.
2 the authority to carry out a policy or course of action, regarded as given by the electorate to a candidate or party that is victorious in an election: *a sick leader living beyond his mandate*. ■ Canadian a period during which a government is in power.
▶ **v.** [with obj.] **1** give (someone) authority to act in a certain way: *other colleges have mandated coed fraternities*. ■ require (something) to be done; make mandatory: *the government began mandating better car safety*.
2 historical assign (territory) under a mandate of the League of Nations: (as adj. **mandated**) *mandated territories*.
– ORIGIN early 16th cent.: from Latin *mandatum* 'something commanded,' neuter past participle of *mandare*, from *manus* 'hand' + *dare* 'give.' Sense 2 of the noun has been influenced by French *mandat*.

man·da·to·ry /'mandəˌtôrē/ ▶ **adj.** required by law or rules; compulsory: *wearing helmets was made mandatory for cyclists*. ■ of or conveying a command: *he did not want the guidelines to be mandatory*.
▶ **n.** (pl. **mandatories**) variant spelling of **MANDATARY**.
– DERIVATIVES **man·da·to·ri·ly** /-ˌtôrəlē/ **adv.**
– ORIGIN late 15th cent.: from late Latin *mandatorius*, from Latin *mandatum* 'something commanded.'

man-day ▶ **n.** a day regarded in terms of the amount of work that can be done by one person within this period.

Man·de /'mänˌdā, män'dā/ ▶ **n.** (pl. **same** or **Mandes**) **1** a member of any of a large group of peoples of West Africa.
2 any of the Niger–Congo languages or dialects spoken by these peoples, including Malinke, Mende, and Bambara.
▶ **adj.** of or relating to these peoples or the Mande group of languages.
– ORIGIN the name in Mande.

Man·de·an /man'dēən/ ▶ **n. & adj.** variant spelling of **MANDAEAN**.

Man·de·la /man'delə/, Nelson (Rolihlahla) (1918–), South African statesman, president 1994–99. He was sentenced to life imprisonment in 1964 as an activist for the African National Congress (ANC). Released in 1990, as leader of the ANC, he engaged in talks on the introduction of majority rule with President F. W. de Klerk. He became the country's first democratically elected president in 1994, serving until 1999. Nobel Peace Prize (1993), shared with de Klerk.

Nelson Mandela

Man·del·brot /'mandlˌbrät, -ˌbrō, ˌmändel'brô/, Benoit (1924–), French mathematician, born in Poland. He is known as the pioneer of fractal geometry.

Man·del·brot set ▶ **n.** Mathematics a particular set of complex numbers that has a highly convoluted fractal boundary when plotted.

Man·del·stam /'mändlˌstäm, məndyil'sʜtäm/ (also **Mandelshtam**), Osip (Emilevich) (1891–1938), Russian poet; a member of the Acmeist group. Sent into internal exile in 1934, he died in a prison camp. Notable works: *Stone* (1913) and *Tristia* (1922).

man·di·ble /'mandəbəl/ ▶ **n.** Anatomy & Zoology the jaw or a jawbone, esp. the lower jawbone in mammals and fishes. ■ either of the upper and lower parts of a bird's beak. ■ either half of the crushing organ in an arthropod's mouthparts.
– DERIVATIVES **man·dib·u·lar** /man'dibyələr/ **adj.**, **man·dib·u·late** /man'dibyəˌlāt/ **adj.**
– ORIGIN late Middle English: from Old French, or from late Latin *mandibula*, from *mandere* 'to chew.'

Man·ding /'mandiɴɢ/ (also **Mandingo** /man'diɴɢgō/) ▶ **n. & adj.** another term for **MANDE**.

Man·din·ka /man'diɴɢkə/ ▶ **n.** (pl. **same** or **Mandinkas**) **1** a member of a people living mainly in Senegal, Gambia, and Sierra Leone.
2 the Mande language of this people.
▶ **adj.** of or relating to the Mandinkas or their language.
– ORIGIN the name in Mandinka.

man·do·la /man'dōlə/ ▶ **n.** a large tenor or bass mandolin, used in ensembles and folk groups. ■ (also **mandora** /-'dôrə/) historical an early stringed instrument of the mandolin or cittern type.
– ORIGIN early 18th cent.: from Italian.

man·do·lin /ˌmandə'lin, 'mandələn/ ▶ **n. 1** a musical instrument resembling a lute, having paired metal strings plucked with a plectrum. It is played with a characteristic tremolo on long sustained notes.
2 variant spelling of **MANDOLINE**.
– DERIVATIVES **man·do·lin·ist** /-'linist/ **n.**
– ORIGIN early 18th cent.: from French *mandoline*, from Italian *mandolino*, diminutive of *mandola* (see **MANDOLA**).

mandolin 1

man·do·line /ˌmandə'lin, 'mandələn/ (also **mandolin**) ▶ **n.** a kitchen utensil consisting of a flat frame with adjustable cutting blades for slicing vegetables.

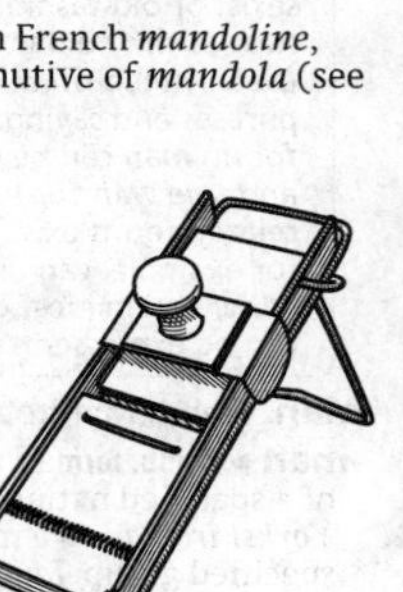

mandoline

man·dor·la /man'dôrlə/ (also **Mandorla**) ▶ **n.** a pointed oval figure used as an architectural feature and as an aureole enclosing figures such as Jesus Christ or the Virgin Mary in medieval art. Also called **VESICA PISCIS**.
– ORIGIN late 19th cent.: from Italian, literally 'almond.'

man·drag·o·ra /man'dragərə/ ▶ **n.** literary the mandrake, esp. when used as a narcotic.
– ORIGIN Old English, via medieval Latin from Latin and Greek *mandragoras*.

man·drake /'manˌdrāk/ ▶ **n. 1** a Mediterranean plant of the nightshade family, with white or purple flowers and large yellow berries. It has a forked fleshy root that supposedly resembles the human form and was formerly widely used in medicine and magic, allegedly shrieking when pulled from the ground. ● *Mandragora officinarum*, family Solanaceae.
2 another term for **MAYAPPLE**.
– ORIGIN Middle English *mandrag(g)e*, from Middle Dutch *mandrag(r)e*, from medieval Latin *mandragora*; associated with **MAN** (because of the shape of its root) + *drake* in the Old English sense 'dragon.'

Man·drax /'manˌdraks/ ▶ **n.** trademark a sedative drug containing methaqualone and diphenhydramine hydrochloride.
– ORIGIN 1960s: of unknown origin.

man·drel /'mandrəl/ ▶ **n. 1** a shaft or spindle in a lathe to which work is fixed while being turned.
2 a cylindrical rod around which metal or other material is forged or shaped.
– ORIGIN early 16th cent.: of unknown origin.

man·drill /'mandrəl/ ▶ **n.** a large West African baboon with a brightly colored red and blue face,

the male having a blue rump. ● *Mandrillus sphinx*, family Cercopithecidae.
– ORIGIN mid 18th cent.: probably from MAN + DRILL[3].

mandrill

man·du·cate /'manjə,kāt/ ▶ v. [with obj.] formal chew or eat.
– DERIVATIVES **man·du·ca·tion** /,manjə'kāsHən/ n., **man·du·ca·to·ry** /-jəkə,tôrē/ adj.
– ORIGIN early 17th cent.: from Latin *manducat-* 'chewed,' from the verb *manducare*, from *manduco* 'guzzler,' from *mandere* 'to chew.'

mane /mān/ ▶ n. a growth of long hair on the neck of a horse, lion, or other animal. ■ a person's long or thick hair: *he had a mane of white hair.*
– DERIVATIVES **maned** adj. [in combination] *a black-maned lion*, **mane·less** adj.
– ORIGIN Old English *manu*, of Germanic origin; related to Dutch *manen*.

man-eat·er ▶ n. 1 an animal that has a propensity for killing and eating humans.
2 informal a dominant woman who has many sexual partners.
– DERIVATIVES **man-eat·ing** adj.

man·eb /'man,eb/ ▶ n. a white compound used as a fungicidal powder on vegetables and fruit. ● Alternative name: **manganese ethylene bisdithiocarbamate**; chem. formula: $C_4H_6N_2S_4Mn$.

maned wolf ▶ n. a large, long-legged, endangered wild dog that has a reddish coat with black hair across the shoulders and large erect ears, native to the grasslands of South America. ● *Chrysocyon brachyurus*, family Canidae.

ma·nège /ma'nezH, mə-/ ▶ n. an arena or enclosed area in which horses and riders are trained. ■ the movements of a trained horse. ■ horsemanship.
– ORIGIN mid 17th cent.: French, from Italian (see MANAGE).

ma·nes /'män,ās, 'mā,nēz/ ▶ plural n. (in Roman mythology) the deified souls of dead ancestors.
– ORIGIN Latin.

Ma·net /mä'nā/, Édouard (1832–83), French painter. He adopted a realist approach that greatly influenced the Impressionists, using pure color to give a direct unsentimental effect. Notable works: *Déjeuner sur l'herbe* (1863), *Olympia* (1865), and *A Bar at the Folies-Bergère* (1882).

Man·e·tho /'mani,THō/ (3rd century BC), Egyptian priest. He wrote a history of Egypt from mythical times to 323, in which he arbitrarily divided the succession of rulers known to him into 30 dynasties, an arrangement that is still followed.

ma·neu·ver /mə'nōōvər/ (Brit. **manoeuvre**) ▶ n. 1 a movement or series of moves requiring skill and care: *spectacular jumps and other daring maneuvers.* ■ a carefully planned scheme or action, esp. one involving deception: *shady financial maneuvers.* ■ the fact or process of taking such action: *the economic policy provided no room for maneuver.*
2 (**maneuvers**) a large-scale military exercise of troops, warships, and other forces: *the Russian vessel was on maneuvers.*
▶ v. (**maneuvers, maneuvering, maneuvered**)
1 move skillfully or carefully: [no obj.] *the truck was unable to maneuver comfortably in the narrow street* | [with obj.] *I'm maneuvering a loaded tray around the floor.*
2 [with obj.] carefully guide or manipulate (someone or something) in order to achieve an end: *they were maneuvering him into a betrayal of his countryman.* ■ [no obj.] carefully manipulate a situation to achieve an end: (as noun **maneuvering**) *two decades of political maneuvering.*
– DERIVATIVES **ma·neu·ver·er** n.
– ORIGIN mid 18th cent. (as a noun in the sense 'tactical movement'): from French *manœuvre* (noun), *manœuvrer* (verb), from medieval Latin *manuoperare*, from Latin *manus* 'hand' + *operari* 'to work.'

ma·neu·ver·a·ble /mə'nōōvərəbəl/ (Brit. **manoeuvrable**) ▶ adj. (esp. of a craft or vessel) able to be maneuvered easily while in motion.
– DERIVATIVES **ma·neu·ver·a·bil·i·ty** /mə,nōōvərə'bilətē/ n.

man Fri·day ▶ n. a male helper or follower.
– ORIGIN from *Friday*, the name of a character in Defoe's novel *Robinson Crusoe* (1719).

man·ful /'manfəl/ ▶ adj. resolute or brave, esp. in the face of adversity: *a manful attempt to smile.*
– DERIVATIVES **man·ful·ness** n.

man·ful·ly /'manfəlē/ ▶ adv. in a manful way; bravely: *his boys strove manfully to accomplish the task.*

man·ga /'manG,gä/ ▶ n. a Japanese genre of cartoons, comic books, and animated films, typically having a science-fiction or fantasy theme and sometimes including violent or sexually explicit material. Compare with ANIME.
– ORIGIN Japanese, from *man* 'indiscriminate' + *ga* 'picture.'

man·ga·bey /'manGgə,bā/ ▶ n. a medium-sized long-tailed monkey native to the forests of western and central Africa. ● Genus *Cercocebus*, family Cercopithecidae: several species.
– ORIGIN late 18th cent.: by erroneous association with *Mangabey*, a region of Madagascar.

man·ga·nate /'manGgə,nāt/ ▶ n. Chemistry a salt in which the anion contains both manganese and oxygen, esp. one of the anion MnO_4 II.

man·ga·nese /'manGgə,nēz, -,nēs/ ▶ n. the chemical element of atomic number 25, a hard gray metal of the transition series. Manganese is an important component of special steels and magnetic alloys. (Symbol: **Mn**) ■ the black dioxide of this as an industrial raw material or additive, esp. in glassmaking.
– ORIGIN late 17th cent.: via French from Italian *manganese*, unexplained alteration of medieval Latin *magnesia* (see MAGNESIA).

man·ga·nese bronze ▶ n. an alloy of copper and zinc with manganese.

man·ga·nese nod·ule ▶ n. a small concretion consisting of manganese and iron oxides, occurring in large numbers in ocean-floor sediment.

man·gan·ic /man'ganik, manG-/ ▶ adj. Chemistry of manganese with a valence of three. Compare with MANGANOUS.

Man·ga·nin /'manGgənin/ ▶ n. Brit. trademark an alloy of copper, manganese, and nickel, used chiefly in electrical apparatus.
– ORIGIN 1920s: from MANGANESE + -IN[1].

man·ga·nite /'manGgə,nīt/ ▶ n. a mineral consisting of manganese oxyhydroxide, typically occurring as steel-gray or black prisms.

man·ga·nous /'manGgənəs/ ▶ adj. Chemistry of manganese with a valence of two. Compare with MANGANIC.

mange /mānj/ ▶ n. a skin disease of mammals caused by parasitic mites and occasionally communicable to humans. It typically causes severe itching, hair loss, and the formation of scabs and lesions. See also DEMODECTIC MANGE, SARCOPTIC MANGE.
– ORIGIN late Middle English: from Old French *mangeue*, from *mangier* 'eat,' from Latin *manducare* 'to chew.'

man·gel /'manGgəl/ (also **mangel-wurzel**) ▶ n. a beet of a variety with a large root, cultivated as feed for livestock. ● *Beta vulgaris* subsp. *crassa*, family Chenopodiaceae.
– ORIGIN mid 19th cent.: from German *Mangoldwurzel*, from *Mangold* 'beet' + *Wurzel* 'root.'

man·ger /'mānjər/ ▶ n. a long open box or trough for horses or cattle to eat from.
– ORIGIN Middle English: from Old French *mangeure*, based on Latin *manducat-* 'chewed' (see MANDUCATE).

man·ger scene ▶ n. another term for NATIVITY SCENE.

man·gey /'mānjē/ ▶ adj. variant spelling of MANGY.

man·gle[1] /'manGgəl/ ▶ v. [with obj.] severely mutilate, disfigure, or damage by cutting, tearing, or crushing: *the car was mangled almost beyond recognition* | figurative *he was mangling Bach on the piano.*
– DERIVATIVES **man·gler** n.
– ORIGIN late Middle English: from Anglo-Norman French *mahangler*, apparently a frequentative of *mahaignier* 'maim.'

man·gle[2] ▶ n. a large machine for ironing sheets or other fabrics, usually when they are damp, using heated rollers. ■ chiefly Brit. a machine having two or more cylinders turned by a handle, between which wet laundry is squeezed (to remove excess moisture) and pressed.
▶ v. [with obj.] press or squeeze with a mangle.
– ORIGIN late 17th cent.: from Dutch *mangel*, from *mangelen* 'to mangle,' from medieval Latin *mango*, *manga*, from Greek *manganon* 'axis, engine.'

man·go /'manGgō/ ▶ n. (pl. **mangoes** or **mangos**)
1 a fleshy yellowish-red tropical fruit that is eaten ripe or used green for pickles or chutneys.
2 (also **mango tree**) the evergreen Indian tree of the cashew family that bears this fruit, widely cultivated in the tropics. ● *Mangifera indica*, family Anacardiaceae; many local varieties.
3 a tropical American hummingbird that typically has green plumage with purple feathers on the wings, tail, or head. ● Genus *Anthracothorax*, family Trochilidae: several species, e.g., the **Jamaican mango** (*A. mango*), which has a dark bronze-green back, purple head, and black underside.
– ORIGIN late 16th cent.: from Portuguese *manga*, from a Dravidian language.

man·gold /'manGgōld/ ▶ n. another term for MANGEL.

man·go·nel /'manGgə,nel/ ▶ n. historical a military device for throwing stones and other missiles.
– ORIGIN Middle English: from Old French *mangonel(le)*, from medieval Latin *manganellus*, diminutive of late Latin *manganum*, from Greek *manganon* 'axis of a pulley.'

man·go·steen /'manGgə,stēn/ ▶ n. 1 a tropical fruit with sweet juicy white segments of flesh inside a thick reddish-brown rind.
2 the slow-growing Malaysian tree that bears this fruit. ● *Garcinia mangostana*, family Guttiferae.
– ORIGIN late 16th cent.: from Malay *manggustan*, dialect variant of *manggis*.

man·grove /'man,grōv, 'manG-/ ▶ n. a tree or shrub that grows in chiefly tropical coastal swamps that are flooded at high tide. Mangroves typically have numerous tangled roots above ground and form dense thickets. ● Genera in several families, in particular *Rhizophora* and related genera (family Rhizophoraceae), and *Avicennia* (family Verbenaceae or Avicenniaceae). ■ (also **mangrove swamp**) a tidal swamp that is dominated by mangroves and associated vegetation.
– ORIGIN early 17th cent.: probably from Portuguese *mangue*, Spanish *mangle*, from Taino. The change in the ending was due to association with GROVE.

man·gy /'mānjē/ (also **mangey**) ▶ adj. (**mangier, mangiest**) having mange. ■ in poor condition; shabby: *a girl in a mangy fur coat.*
– DERIVATIVES **man·gi·ness** /-jēnis/ n.

man·han·dle /'man,handl/ ▶ v. [with obj.] move (a heavy object) by hand with great effort: *seven guys had to manhandle the piano down the stairs.* ■ informal handle (someone) roughly by dragging or pushing: *a drunk had manhandled one of the deputies.*

Man·hat·tan /man'hatn, mən-/ 1 a commercial city in northeastern Kansas; pop. 52,284 (est. 2008).
2 an island near the mouth of the Hudson River that forms part of the city of New York. The site of the original Dutch settlement of New Amsterdam, it is now a borough containing the commercial and cultural center of New York City.
– ORIGIN (sense 2): named after the Algonquin tribe from whom the Dutch settlers claimed to have bought the island in 1626.

man·hat·tan /man'hatn, mən-/ (also **Manhattan**) ▶ n. a cocktail made of whiskey and vermouth, sometimes with a dash of bitters.

Man·hat·tan Pro·ject the code name for the American project set up in 1942 to develop an atom bomb. The project culminated in 1945 with the detonation of the first nuclear weapon, at White Sands in New Mexico.

man·hole /'man,hōl/ ▶ n. a small covered opening in a floor, pavement, or other surface to allow a person to enter, esp. an opening in a city street leading to a sewer.

man·hood /'man,hŏŏd/ ▶ n. the state or period of being a man rather than a child: *boys in the process of growing to manhood.* ■ men, esp. those of a country, regarded collectively: *Germany had lost the best of her young manhood.* ■ qualities traditionally associated with men, such as courage, strength, and sexual potency: *we drank to prove our manhood.* ■ archaic the condition of being human: *the unity of Godhead and manhood in Christ.* ■ (**one's manhood**) informal used euphemistically to refer to a man's genitals.

man-hour ▶ n. an hour regarded in terms of the amount of work that can be done by one person within this period.

man·hunt /'man,hənt/ ▶ n. an organized search for a person, esp. a criminal.

ma·ni·a /'mānēə/ ▶ n. mental illness marked by periods of great excitement, euphoria, delusions,

and overactivity. ■ an excessive enthusiasm or desire; an obsession: *he had a mania for automobiles*.
– ORIGIN late Middle English: via late Latin from Greek, literally 'madness,' from *mainesthai* 'be mad.'

-mania ▶ **comb. form** Psychology denoting a specified type of mental abnormality or obsession: *kleptomania*. ■ denoting extreme enthusiasm or admiration: *Beatlemania*.

ma·ni·ac /'mānē,ak/ ▶ **n.** informal a person exhibiting extreme symptoms of wild behavior, esp. when violent and dangerous: *a homicidal maniac*. ■ [with modifier] an obsessive enthusiast: *a gambling maniac*. ■ Psychiatry, archaic a person suffering from mania.
– DERIVATIVES **ma·ni·a·cal** /mə'nīəkəl/ **adj.**, **ma·ni·a·cal·ly** /mə'nīək(ə)lē/ **adv.**
– ORIGIN early 16th cent. (as an adjective): via late Latin from late Greek *maniakos*, from *mania* (see MANIA).

-maniac ▶ **comb. form** Psychology forming nouns corresponding to words ending in *-mania*: *kleptomaniac* | *Beatlemaniac*.

man·ic /'manik/ ▶ **adj.** showing wild and apparently deranged excitement and energy: *his manic enthusiasm* | *a manic grin*. ■ frenetically busy; frantic: *the pace is utterly manic*. ■ Psychiatry relating to or affected by mania: *the manic interludes in depression*.
– DERIVATIVES **man·i·cal·ly** /-(ə)lē/ **adv.**

man·ic de·pres·sion ▶ **n.** another term, esp. formerly, for BIPOLAR DISORDER.
– DERIVATIVES **man·ic-de·pres·sive adj. & n.**

USAGE The term **manic depression** has largely been replaced with the term **bipolar disorder**, which many feel has a less negative connotation. People with the condition can be referred to simply as **bipolar**, or as **having bipolar disorder**.

Man·i·chae·an /,manə'kēən/ (also **Manichean**) ▶ **adj.** chiefly historical of or relating to Manichaeism. ■ of or characterized by dualistic contrast or conflict between opposites.
▶ **n.** an adherent of Manichaeism.
– DERIVATIVES **Man·i·chae·an·ism** /-'kēə,nizəm/ **n.**

Man·i·chae·ism /'manə,kēizəm/ (also **Manicheism**) ▶ **n.** a dualistic religious system with Christian, Gnostic, and pagan elements, founded in Persia in the 3rd century by **Manes** (*c.*216–*c.*276). The system was based on a supposed primeval conflict between light and darkness. It spread widely in the Roman Empire and in Asia, and survived in Chinese Turkestan until the 13th century. ■ religious or philosophical dualism.
– ORIGIN early 17th cent.: from late Latin *Manichaeus* (from the name *Manes*: see above) + -ISM.

Man·i·chee /'manə,kē/ ▶ **n. & adj.** archaic term for MANICHAEAN.
– ORIGIN Middle English: from late Latin *Manichaei*, plural of *Manichaeus* (see MANICHAEISM).

ma·ni·cot·ti /,manə'kätē/ ▶ **n.** pasta in the shape of large tubes.
– ORIGIN Italian, plural of *manicotto* 'muff.'

man·i·cure /'mani,kyŏŏr/ ▶ **n.** a cosmetic treatment of the hands involving cutting, shaping, and often painting of the nails, removal of the cuticles, and softening of the skin.
▶ **v.** [with obj.] give a manicure to. ■ (usu. as adj. **manicured**) trim neatly: *manicured lawns*.
– ORIGIN late 19th cent.: from French, from Latin *manus* 'hand' + *cura* 'care.'

man·i·cur·ist /'mani,kyŏŏrist/ ▶ **n.** a person who performs manicures professionally.

man·i·fest¹ /'manə,fest/ ▶ **adj.** clear or obvious to the eye or mind: *the system's manifest failings*.
▶ **v.** [with obj.] display or show (a quality or feeling) by one's acts or appearance; demonstrate: *Ray manifested signs of severe depression*. ■ (often **be manifested in**) be evidence of; prove: *bad industrial relations are often manifested in disputes and strikes*. ■ [no obj.] (of an ailment) become apparent through the appearance of symptoms: *a disorder that usually manifests in middle age*. ■ [no obj.] (of a ghost or spirit) appear: *one deity manifested in the form of a bird*.
– DERIVATIVES **man·i·fest·ly adv.**
– ORIGIN late Middle English: via Old French from Latin *manifestus*.

man·i·fest² ▶ **n.** a document giving comprehensive details of a ship and its cargo and other contents, passengers, and crew for the use of customs officers. ■ a list of passengers or cargo in an aircraft. ■ a list of the cars forming a freight train.
▶ **v.** [with obj.] record in such a manifest: *every passenger is manifested at the point of departure*.
– ORIGIN mid 16th cent. (denoting a manifestation): from Italian *manifesto* (see MANIFESTO). The current sense dates from the early 17th cent.

man·i·fes·ta·tion /,manəfə'stāSHən, -,fes'tāSHən/ ▶ **n.** an event, action, or object that clearly shows or embodies something, esp. a theory or an abstract idea: *the first obvious manifestations of global warming*. ■ the action or fact of showing something in such a way: *the manifestation of anxiety over the upcoming exams*. ■ a symptom or sign of an ailment: *a characteristic manifestation of Lyme disease*. ■ a version or incarnation of something or someone: *Purity and Innocence and Young Love in all their gentle manifestations*. ■ an appearance of a ghost or spirit.
– ORIGIN late Middle English: from late Latin *manifestatio(n-)*, from the verb *manifestare* 'make public.'

Man·i·fest Des·ti·ny ▶ **n.** the 19th-century doctrine or belief that the expansion of the US throughout the American continents was both justified and inevitable.

man·i·fes·to /,manə'festō/ ▶ **n.** (pl. **manifestos**) a public declaration of policy and aims, esp. one issued before an election by a political party or candidate.
– ORIGIN mid 17th cent.: from Italian, from *manifestare*, from Latin, 'make public,' from *manifestus* 'obvious' (see MANIFEST¹).

man·i·fold /'manə,fōld/ ▶ **adj.** many and various: *the implications of this decision were manifold*. ■ having many different forms or elements: *the appeal of the crusade was manifold*.
▶ **n. 1** [often with modifier] a pipe or chamber branching into several openings: *the pipeline manifold*. ■ (in an internal combustion engine) the part conveying air and fuel from the carburetor to the cylinders or that leading from the cylinders to the exhaust pipe: *the exhaust manifold*.
2 technical something with many different parts or forms, in particular: ■ Mathematics a collection of points forming a certain kind of set, such as those of a topologically closed surface or an analog of this in three or more dimensions. ■ (in Kantian philosophy) the sum of the particulars furnished by sense before they have been unified by the synthesis of the understanding.
– DERIVATIVES **man·i·fold·ly adv.**, **man·i·fold·ness n.**
– ORIGIN Old English *manigfeald*; current noun senses date from the mid 19th cent.

man·i·kin /'manikən/ (also **mannikin**) ▶ **n. 1** a person who is very small, esp. one not otherwise abnormal or deformed.
2 a jointed model of the human body, used in anatomy or as an artist's lay figure.
– ORIGIN mid 16th cent.: from Dutch *manneken* (Middle Dutch *mannekijn*), diminutive of *man* 'man.'

USAGE See usage at MANNEQUIN.

Ma·nil·a¹ /mə'nilə/ the capital and chief port of the Philippines, on the island of Luzon; pop. 1,660,700 (est. 2007).

Ma·nil·a² (also **Manilla**) ▶ **n. 1** (also **Manila hemp**) the strong fiber of a Philippine plant, used for rope, matting, paper, etc.: [as modifier] *Manila rope*. See also ABACA. ■ (also **Manila paper**) strong brown paper, originally made from Manila hemp.
2 [often as modifier] a cigar or cheroot made in Manila.
– ORIGIN late 17th cent. (as an adjective meaning 'from Manila'): from MANILA¹.

ma·nille /mə'nil/ ▶ **n.** (in the card games ombre and quadrille) the second-best trump or honor.
– ORIGIN late 17th cent.: from French (perhaps influenced by *main* 'hand'), from *malille*, also used as a term in card games, from Spanish *malilla*, diminutive of *mala*, feminine of *malo* 'bad.' Although "bad" because of its low value, the card acquires power when its suit is trumps.

man·i·oc /'manē,äk/ ▶ **n.** another term for CASSAVA.
– ORIGIN mid 16th cent.: from French, from Tupi *manioca*.

man·i·ple /'manəpəl/ ▶ **n. 1** a subdivision of a Roman legion, containing either 120 or 60 men.
2 (in church use) a vestment formerly worn by a priest celebrating the Eucharist, consisting of a strip hanging from the left arm.
– DERIVATIVES **ma·nip·u·lar** /mə'nipyələr/ **adj.** (sense 1).
– ORIGIN late Middle English (sense 2): from Old French *maniple*, from Latin *manipulus* 'handful, troop,' from *manus* 'hand' + the base of *plere* 'fill.'

ma·nip·u·late /mə'nipyə,lāt/ ▶ **v.** [with obj.] **1** handle or control (a tool, mechanism, etc.), typically in a skillful manner: *he manipulated the dials of the set*. ■ alter, edit, or move (text or data) on a computer. ■ examine or treat (a part of the body) by feeling or moving it with the hand: *a system of healing based on manipulating the ligaments of the spine*.
2 control or influence (a person or situation) cleverly, unfairly, or unscrupulously: *the masses were deceived and manipulated by a tiny group*. ■ alter (data) or present (statistics) so as to mislead.
– DERIVATIVES **ma·nip·u·la·bil·i·ty** /-,nipyələ'bilətē/ **n.**, **ma·nip·u·la·ble** /-ləbəl/ **adj.**, **ma·nip·u·lat·a·ble** /-,lātəbəl/ **adj.**, **ma·nip·u·la·tion** /mə,nipyə'lāSHən/ **n.**, **ma·nip·u·la·tor** /-,lātər/ **n.**, **ma·nip·u·la·to·ry** /-lə,tôrē/ **adj.**
– ORIGIN early 19th cent.: back-formation from earlier *manipulation*, from Latin *manipulus* 'handful.'

ma·nip·u·la·tive /mə'nipyələtiv, -,lātiv/ ▶ **adj.**
1 characterized by unscrupulous control of a situation or person: *she was sly, selfish, and manipulative*.
2 of or relating to manipulation of an object or part of the body: *a manipulative skill*.
– DERIVATIVES **ma·nip·u·la·tive·ly adv.**, **ma·nip·u·la·tive·ness n.**

Ma·ni·pur /'manə,pŏŏr, ,mənə'pŏŏr/ a small state in eastern India, east of Assam, on the border with Burma (Myanmar); capital, Imphal.

Man·i·pu·ri /,manə'pŏŏrē/ ▶ **n.** (pl. **same** or **Manipuris**) **1** a native or inhabitant of Manipur.
2 the official language of Manipur, belonging to the Tibeto-Burman family.
▶ **adj.** of or relating to the people of Manipur or their language.

Manit. ▶ **abbr.** Manitoba.

Man·i·to·ba /,manə'tōbə/ a province in central Canada, with a coastline on Hudson Bay; pop. 1,148,401 (2006); capital, Winnipeg. The area was part of Rupert's Land from 1670 until it was transferred to Canada by the Hudson's Bay Company and became a province in 1870.
– DERIVATIVES **Man·i·to·ban adj. & n.**

man·i·tou /'mani,tōō/ ▶ **n.** (among certain Algonquian Indians) a good or evil spirit as an object of reverence.
– ORIGIN late 17th cent.: via French from an Algonquian language.

Man·i·tou·lin Is·land /,mani'tōōlən/ an island in southern Canada, in the province of Ontario, in northern Lake Huron. At 1,068 square miles (2,766 sq km), it is the largest lake island in the world.

Man·kie·wicz /'mankə,wits/, Joseph Leo (1909–93), US movie director, producer, and screenwriter. He wrote and directed *A Letter to Three Wives* (1949) and *All About Eve* (1950).

Man·kil·ler /'man,kilər/, Wilma (Pearl) (1945–), US Cherokee Nation tribal leader 1985–95 and historian. A women's rights activist, she wrote *Mankiller: A Chief and Her People* (1993).

man·kind /,man'kīnd, 'man,kīnd/ ▶ **n. 1** human beings considered collectively; the human race: *research for the benefit of all mankind*.
2 /'man,kīnd/ archaic men, as distinct from women.

USAGE On the use of **mankind** versus that of **humankind** or **the human race**, see usage at MAN.

man·like /'man,līk/ ▶ **adj. 1** resembling a human being: *a manlike creature*.
2 (of a woman) having an appearance or qualities associated with men.

man·li·ness /'manlēnis/ ▶ **n.** the traditional male quality of being brave and strong: *men accustomed to proving their manliness on the streets*. ■ the fact of being typically male; masculinity: *the author's alleged lack of manliness*.

man·ly /'manlē/ ▶ **adj.** (**manlier**, **manliest**) having or denoting those good qualities traditionally associated with men, such as courage and strength: *looking manly and capable in his tennis whites*. ■ (of an activity) befitting a man, esp. in a traditional sense: *the manly art of knife-throwing*.

man-made ▶ **adj.** made or caused by human beings (as opposed to occurring or being made naturally); artificial: *a man-made lake*.

Mann¹ /man/, Horace (1796–1859), US editor and politician. Considered the father of public education, he helped to establish the first state board of education while he was a representative to the Massachusetts state legislature 1827–37. He served as the board's president 1837–48.

Mann² /män/, Thomas (1875–1955), German novelist and essayist. The role and character of the artist in relation to society is a constant theme in his works. Notable works: *Buddenbrooks* (1901), *Death in Venice* (1912), *The Magic Mountain* (1924), and *Dr. Faustus* (1947). Nobel Prize for Literature (1929).

man·na /'manə/ ▶ **n.** (in the Bible) the substance miraculously supplied as food to the Israelites in the wilderness (Exod. 16). ■ an unexpected or gratuitous benefit: *the cakes were manna from heaven*. ■ (in Christian contexts) spiritual nourishment, esp. the Eucharist. ■ a sweet secretion

from the manna ash or a similar plant, used as a mild laxative and as a principal source of mannitol.
– ORIGIN Old English, via late Latin and Greek from Aramaic *mannā*, from Hebrew *mān*, corresponding to Arabic *mann*, denoting an exudation of the tamarisk *Tamarix mannifera*.

man·na ash ▶ n. an ash tree that bears fragrant white flowers and exudes a sweet edible gum (manna) from its branches when they are damaged, native to southern Europe and southwestern Asia. ● *Fraxinus ornus*, family Oleaceae.

Man·nar, Gulf of /məˈnär/ an inlet of the Indian Ocean that lies between northwestern Sri Lanka and the southern tip of India. It is south of Adam's Bridge, which separates it from the Palk Strait.

manned /mand/ ▶ adj. (esp. of an aircraft or spacecraft) having a human crew: *a manned mission to Mars*.

man·ne·quin /ˈmanikən/ ▶ n. a dummy used to display clothes in a store window. ■ chiefly historical a young woman or man employed to show clothes to customers.
– ORIGIN mid 18th cent.: from French, from Dutch (see MANIKIN).

USAGE In English usage, the word **mannequin** occurs much more frequently than any of its relatives **manakin, manikin,** and **mannikin**. The source for all four words is the Middle Dutch *mannekijn* (modern Dutch *manneken*) 'little man,' 'little doll.' **Mannequin** is the French spelling from this Dutch source. One of its French meanings, dating from about 1830, is 'a young woman hired to model clothes' (even though the word means 'little *man*'). This sense—still current, but rare in English—first appeared in 1902. The far more common sense of 'a life-size jointed figure or dummy used for displaying clothes' is first recorded in 1939. **Manikin** has had the sense 'little man' (often contemptuous) since the mid 16th century, when it was sometimes spelled *manakin* (as it appeared in Shakespeare's *Twelfth Night*, as a term of abuse). **Manikin's** sense of 'an artist's lay figure' also dates from the mid 16th century (first recorded with the Dutch spelling *manneken*).To confuse matters further, in modern usage, the words **manakin** and **mannikin** refer to birds of two unrelated families. The history of these bird names is somewhat obscure. **Manakin** may have come from the Portuguese *manaquim* 'mannikin,' a variant of *manequim* 'mannequin.' **Mannikin** may have come directly from the source of the Portuguese words, the Middle Dutch *mannekijn*.

man·ner /ˈmanər/ ▶ n. **1** a way in which a thing is done or happens: *taking notes in an unobtrusive manner*. ■ a style in literature or art: *a dramatic poem in the manner of Goethe*. ■ Grammar a semantic category of adverbs and adverbials that answer the question "how?": *an adverb of manner*. ■ (**manner of**) chiefly literary a kind or sort of: *what manner of man is he?*
2 a person's outward bearing or way of behaving toward others: *his arrogance and pompous manner* | *a shy and diffident manner*.
3 (**manners**) polite or well-bred social behavior: *didn't your mother teach you any manners?* ■ social behavior or habits: *Tim apologized for his son's bad manners*. ■ the way a motor vehicle handles or performs: *I have no complaints about the performance or road manners*.
– PHRASES **all manner of** many different kinds of: *they accuse me of all manner of evil things*. **by no** (or **any**) **manner of means** see MEANS. **in a manner of speaking** in some sense; so to speak. **to the manner born** naturally at ease in a specified job or situation: *she slipped into a more courtly role as if to the manner born*. [with allusion to Shakespeare's *Hamlet* I. iv. 17.] ■ destined by birth to follow a custom or way of life.
– DERIVATIVES **man·ner·less** adj.
– ORIGIN Middle English: from Old French *maniere*, based on Latin *manuarius* 'of the hand,' from *manus* 'hand.'

man·nered /ˈmanərd/ ▶ adj. **1** [in combination] behaving in a specified way: *pleasant-mannered*.
2 (of a writer, artist, or artistic style) marked by idiosyncratic mannerisms; artificial, stilted, and overelaborate in delivery: *inane dialogue and mannered acting*.

man·ner·ism /ˈmanəˌrizəm/ ▶ n. **1** a habitual gesture or way of speaking or behaving; an idiosyncrasy: *learning the great man's speeches and studying his mannerisms*. ■ Psychiatry an ordinary gesture or expression that becomes abnormal through exaggeration or repetition.
2 excessive or self-conscious use of a distinctive style in art, literature, or music: *he seemed deliberately to be stripping his art of mannerism*.
3 (**Mannerism**) a style of 16th-century Italian art preceding the Baroque, characterized by unusual effects of scale, lighting, and perspective, and the use of bright, often lurid colors. It is particularly associated with the work of Pontormo, Vasari,and the later Michelangelo.
– DERIVATIVES **man·ner·ist** n. & adj., **man·ner·is·tic** /ˌmanəˈristik/ adj.

man·ner·ly /ˈmanərlē/ ▶ adj. well-mannered; polite.
– DERIVATIVES **man·ner·li·ness** /-lēnis/ n.

Mann·heim /ˈmanˌhīm, ˈmän-/ an industrial port at the confluence of the Rhine and the Neckar rivers in Baden-Württemberg, in southwestern Germany; pop. 307,900 (est. 2006).

man·ni·kin /ˈmanikən/ ▶ n. **1** a small waxbill of the Old World tropics, typically having brown, black, and white plumage and popular as a pet bird. Compare with MANAKIN. ● Genus *Lonchura*, family Estrildidae: many species.
2 variant spelling of MANIKIN.

USAGE See usage at MANNEQUIN.

man·nish /ˈmanisH/ ▶ adj. often derogatory (of a woman) having characteristics that are stereotypically associated with men and can be considered unbecoming in a woman.
– DERIVATIVES **man·nish·ly** adv., **man·nish·ness** n.
– ORIGIN Old English *mennisc* 'human' (see MAN, -ISH[1]). The current sense dates from late Middle English.

man·ni·tol /ˈmanəˌtôl, -ˌtäl/ ▶ n. Chemistry a colorless sweet-tasting crystalline compound that is found in many plants and is used in various foods and medical products. ● An alcohol; chem. formula: $CH_2OH(CHOH)_4CH_2OH$.
– ORIGIN late 19th cent.: from *mannite*, in the same sense, + -OL.

man·nose /ˈmanˌōs, -ˌōz/ ▶ n. Chemistry a sugar of the hexose class that occurs as a component of many natural polysaccharides.
– ORIGIN late 19th cent.: from *mannite* 'mannitol' + -OSE[2].

man·ny /ˈmanē/ ▶ n. (pl. **mannies**) a male nanny: *my husband would like us to hire a manny for our two boys*.
– ORIGIN 1990s: blend of *man* and *nanny*.

Ma·no /ˈmänō/ a river of West Africa. It rises in northwestern Liberia and flows southwest to the Atlantic Ocean, forming for part of its length the boundary between Liberia and Sierra Leone.

ma·no a ma·no /ˌmänō ä ˈmänō/ informal ▶ adj. (of combat or competition) hand-to-hand: *the exhilaration of the mano-a-mano battle*.
▶ adv. in the manner of hand-to-hand combat or a duel: *they want to settle this mano a mano*.
▶ n. (pl. **mano a manos**) an intense fight or contest between two adversaries; a duel: *a real courtroom mano-a-mano*.
– ORIGIN Spanish, 'hand-to-hand.'

ma·noeu·vre ▶ n. & v. British spelling of MANEUVER.

man of col·or ▶ n. see PERSON OF COLOR.

man-of-war (also **man-o'-war**) ▶ n. (pl. **men-of-war** also **men-o'-war**) historical an armed sailing ship. ■ (also **man-o'-war bird**) another term for FRIGATE BIRD. ■ short for PORTUGUESE MAN-OF-WAR.

man-of-war fish ▶ n. a fish (*Nomeus gronovii*, family Nomeidae) of tropical oceans that is often found among the tentacles of the Portuguese man-of-war, where it sometimes browses on the host's body and tentacles.

ma·nom·e·ter /məˈnämətər/ ▶ n. an instrument for measuring the pressure acting on a column of fluid, esp. one with a U-shaped tube of liquid in which a difference in the pressures acting in the two arms of the tube causes the liquid to reach different heights in the two arms.
– DERIVATIVES **man·o·met·ric** /ˌmanəˈmetrik/ adj., **man·o·met·ri·cal·ly** /ˌmanəˈmetrik(ə)lē/ adv., **ma·nom·e·try** /-trē/ n.
– ORIGIN mid 18th cent.: from French *manomètre*, from Greek *manos* 'thin' + *-mètre* '(instrument) measuring.'

ma non trop·po /ˌmä ˌnôn ˈtrôpō/ ▶ adv. see TROPPO[1].

man·or /ˈmanər/ ▶ n. (also **manor house**) a large country house with lands; the principal house of a landed estate. ■ chiefly historical (esp. in England and Wales) a unit of land, originally a feudal lordship, consisting of a lord's demesne and lands rented to tenants. ■ historical (in North America) an estate or district leased to tenants, esp. one granted by royal charter in a British colony or by the Dutch governors of what is now New York.
– DERIVATIVES **ma·no·ri·al** /məˈnôrēəl/ adj.
– ORIGIN Middle English: from Anglo-Norman French *maner* 'dwelling,' from Latin *manere* 'remain.'

man page ▶ n. Computing a document forming part of the documentation of a computer system.
– ORIGIN short for *manual page*.

man·pow·er /ˈmanˌpouər/ ▶ n. the number of people working or available for work or service: *the police had only limited manpower*.

man·qué /mäNGˈkā/ ▶ adj. [postpositive] having failed to become what one might have been; unfulfilled: *a starlet manqué*.
– ORIGIN late 18th cent.: French, past participle of *manquer* 'to lack.'

Man Ray (1890–1976), US photographer, painter, and filmmaker; born *Emmanuel Radnitsky*. A leading figure in the New York and European Dada movements, he is best known for *Violon d'Ingres* (1924), his photograph in which he made the back of a female nude resemble a violin.

man·rope /ˈmanˌrōp/ ▶ n. a safety rope on a ship's deck, esp. a rope on the side of a ship's gangway or ladder for support in walking or climbing.

man·sard /ˈmanˌsärd, -sərd/ ▶ n. (also **mansard roof**) a roof that has four sloping sides, each of which becomes steeper halfway down. ■ a story or apartment under a mansard roof. ■ Brit. another term for GAMBREL.
– ORIGIN mid 18th cent.: from French *mansarde*, named after F. MANSART.

Man·sart /mänˈsär(t)/, François (1598–1666), French architect. He rebuilt part of the château of Blois, which incorporated the type of roof now named after him.

manse /mans/ ▶ n. the house occupied by a minister of a Presbyterian church. ■ informal a person's house or home: *she has just returned to her mother and the family manse after being expelled from convent school*.
– ORIGIN late 15th cent. (denoting the principal house of an estate): from medieval Latin *mansus* 'house, dwelling,' from *manere* 'remain.'

man·serv·ant /ˈmanˌsərvənt/ ▶ n. (pl. **menservants** /ˈmenˌsərvənts/) a male servant.

Mans·field[1] /ˈmanzˌfēld/ an industrial city in north central Ohio; pop. 49,579 (est. 2008).

Mans·field[2], Katherine (1888–1923), New Zealand short-story writer; pseudonym of *Kathleen Mansfield Beauchamp Murray*. Her stories range from extended impressionistic evocations of family life to short sketches. Notable collections: *In a German Pension* (1911) and *Bliss* (1920).

-manship ▶ suffix (forming nouns) denoting skill in a subject or activity: *marksmanship*.

man·sion /ˈmansHən/ ▶ n. a large, impressive house. ■ a manor house. ■ [in names] Brit. a large building divided into apartments: *Carlyle Mansions*.
– ORIGIN late Middle English (denoting the chief residence of a lord): via Old French from Latin *mansio(n-)* 'place where someone stays,' from *manere* 'remain.'

man-sized (also **man-size**) ▶ adj. large enough to occupy, suit, or satisfy a man: *a man-sized breakfast*.

man·slaugh·ter /ˈmanˌslôtər/ ▶ n. the crime of killing a human being without malice aforethought, or otherwise in circumstances not amounting to murder: *the defendant was convicted of manslaughter*.

Man·son[1] /ˈmansən/, Charles (1934–), US cult leader. He founded a commune based on free love and complete subordination to him. In 1969, its members carried out a series of murders, including that of actress **Sharon Tate** (1943–69), for which he and some followers received the death sentence, which was later commuted to life imprisonment.

Man·son[2], Sir Patrick (1844–1922), Scottish physician; pioneer of tropical medicine. He established that elephantiasis was spread by the bite of a mosquito and suggested a similar role for the mosquito in the spread of malaria.

man·sue·tude /ˈmanswiˌto͞od, manˈso͞oə-/ ▶ n. archaic meekness; gentleness.
– ORIGIN late Middle English: from Old French, or from Latin *mansuetudo*, from *mansuetus* 'gentle, tame,' from *manus* 'hand' + *suetus* 'accustomed.'

man·ta /ˈmantə/ ▶ n. **1** (also **manta ray**) a devil ray that occurs in all tropical seas and may reach very great size. It is sometimes seen leaping high out of the water. ● *Manta birostris*, family Mobulidae.
2 a rough-textured cotton fabric made and used in Spanish America. ■ a shawl made of this fabric.
– ORIGIN late 17th cent.: from Latin American Spanish, literally 'large blanket.'

m

man·teau /man'tō/ ▶ **n.** (pl. **manteaus** or **manteaux** /-'tōz/) historical a loose gown or cloak worn by women.
– ORIGIN late 17th cent.: from French; compare with MANTUA.

Man·te·ca /man'tēkə/ a city in central California, in the San Joaquin Valley; pop. 65,028 (est. 2008).

Man·te·gna /män'tānyə/, Andrea (1431–1506), Italian painter and engraver, noted esp. for his frescoes.

man·tel /'mantl/ (also **mantle**) ▶ **n.** a mantelpiece or mantelshelf.
– ORIGIN mid 16th cent.: specialized use of MANTLE[1].

man·te·let /'mantlət, 'mantl-ət/ (also **mantlet**) ▶ **n.** **1** historical a woman's short, loose, sleeveless cloak or shawl.
2 a bulletproof screen for a soldier.
– ORIGIN late Middle English: from Old French *mantelet*, diminutive of *mantel* 'mantle.'

man·tel·let·ta /,mantl'etə/ ▶ **n.** (pl. **mantellettas** or **mantellette** /-tl'etā/) a sleeveless vestment reaching to the knees, worn by cardinals, bishops, and other high-ranking Roman Catholic ecclesiastics.
– ORIGIN mid 19th cent.: from Italian, from a diminutive of Latin *mantellum* 'mantle.'

man·tel·piece /'mantl,pēs/ (also **mantlepiece**) ▶ **n.** a structure of wood, marble, or stone above and around a fireplace. ■ a mantelshelf.

man·tel·shelf /'mantl,shelf/ (also **mantleshelf**) ▶ **n.** a shelf above a fireplace. ■ Climbing a projecting shelf or ledge of rock. ■ Climbing a move for climbing on such a ledge from below by pressing down on it with the hands to raise the upper body, enabling a foot or knee to reach the ledge.
▶ **v.** [no obj.] Climbing perform a mantelshelf move.

man·tel·tree /'mantl,trē/ (also **mantletree**) ▶ **n.** a beam or arch across the opening of a fireplace, supporting the masonry above.

man·tic /'mantik/ ▶ **adj.** formal of or relating to divination or prophecy.
– ORIGIN mid 19th cent.: from Greek *mantikos*, from *mantis* 'prophet.'

-mantic ▶ **comb. form** in adjectives corresponding to nouns ending in *-mancy* (such as *geomantic* corresponding to *geomancy*).

man·ti·core /'manti,kôr/ ▶ **n.** a mythical beast typically depicted as having the body of a lion, the face of a man, and the sting of a scorpion.
– ORIGIN late Middle English: from Old French, via Latin from Greek *mantikhōras*, corrupt reading in Aristotle for *martikhoras*, from an Old Persian word meaning 'man-eater.'

man·tid /'mantid/ ▶ **n.** another term for MANTIS.

man·til·la /man'tē(y)ə, -'tilə/ ▶ **n.** a lace or silk scarf worn by women over the hair and shoulders, esp. in Spain.
– ORIGIN Spanish, diminutive of *manta* 'mantle.'

mantilla

man·tis /'mantis/ (also **praying mantis**) ▶ **n.** (pl. **same** or **mantises**) a slender predatory insect related to the cockroach. It waits motionless for prey with its large spiky forelegs folded like hands in prayer. ● Suborder Mantodea, order Dictyoptera: Mantidae and other families, and many species, including *Mantis religiosa*, introduced to America from southern Europe and now found commonly in the northeastern US.
– ORIGIN mid 17th cent.: modern Latin, from Greek, literally 'prophet.'

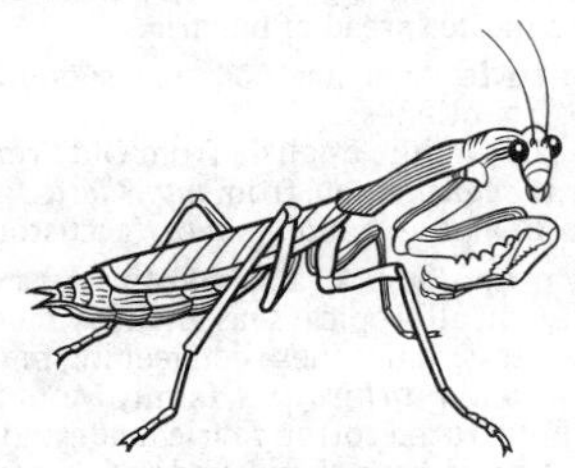

mantis

man·tis·sa /man'tisə/ ▶ **n.** **1** Mathematics the part of a logarithm that follows the decimal point.
2 Computing the part of a floating-point number that represents the significant digits of that number, and that is multiplied by the base raised to the exponent to give the actual value of the number.
– ORIGIN mid 17th cent.: from Latin, literally 'makeweight,' perhaps from Etruscan.

man·tis shrimp ▶ **n.** a predatory marine crustacean with a pair of large spined front legs that resemble those of a mantis and are used for capturing prey. ● Order Stomatopoda: many species, including the European *Squilla desmaresti*.

Man·tle /'mantl/, Mickey (Charles) (1931–95), US baseball player. He played for the New York Yankees 1951–69. His records for most World Series runs, home runs, runs batted in, extra-base hits, walks, and total bases remain unbroken. Baseball Hall of Fame (1974).

man·tle[1] /'mantl/ ▶ **n.** **1** a loose sleeveless cloak or shawl, worn esp. by women. ■ a covering of a specified sort: *the houses were covered with a thick mantle of snow.* ■ (also **gas mantle**) a fragile mesh cover fixed around a gas jet, kerosene wick, etc., to give an incandescent light when heated. ■ Ornithology a bird's back, scapulars, and wing coverts, esp. when of a distinctive color. ■ Zoology an outer or enclosing layer of tissue, esp. (in mollusks, cirripedes, and brachiopods) a fold of skin enclosing the viscera and secreting the substance that produces the shell.
2 an important role or responsibility that passes from one person to another: *the second son has now assumed his father's mantle.* [with allusion to the passing of Elijah's cloak (mantle) to Elisha (2 Kings 2:13).]
3 Geology the region of the earth's interior between the crust and the core, believed to consist of hot, dense silicate rocks (mainly peridotite). ■ the corresponding part of another planetary body: *the lunar mantle.*
▶ **v.** **1** [with obj.] literary clothe in or as if in a mantle; cloak or envelop: *heavy mists mantled the forested slopes.* ■ archaic (of blood) suffuse (the face): *a warm pink mounted to the girl's cheeks and mantled her brow.* ■ [no obj.] (of the face) glow with a blush: *her rich face mantling with emotion.* ■ [no obj.] archaic (of a liquid) become covered with a head or froth.
2 [no obj.] (of a bird of prey on the ground or on a perch) spread the wings and tail, esp. so as to cover captured prey.
– ORIGIN Old English *mentel*, from Latin *mantellum* 'cloak'; reinforced in Middle English by Old French *mantel*.

man·tle[2] ▶ **n.** variant spelling of MANTEL.

man·tle·piece ▶ **n.** variant spelling of MANTELPIECE.

man·tle plume ▶ **n.** see PLUME.

man·tle·shelf ▶ **n.** variant spelling of MANTELSHELF.

mant·let /'mantlət/ ▶ **n.** variant spelling of MANTELET.

man·tle·tree /'mantl,trē/ ▶ **n.** variant spelling of MANTELTREE.

man·tling /'mantling, 'mantl-ing/ ▶ **n.** Heraldry a piece of ornamental drapery depicted issuing from a helmet and surrounding a shield. Compare with LAMBREQUIN (sense 2). ■ drapery of this kind.
– ORIGIN late 16th cent.: from MANTLE[1] + -ING[1].

Man·toux test /man'too/ ▶ **n.** Medicine a test for immunity to tuberculosis using intradermal injection of tuberculin.
– ORIGIN 1930s: named after Charles *Mantoux* (1877–1947), French physician.

man·tra /'mantrə, 'män-/ ▶ **n.** (originally in Hinduism and Buddhism) a word or sound repeated to aid concentration in meditation. ■ a Vedic hymn. ■ a statement or slogan repeated frequently: *the environmental mantra that energy has for too long been too cheap.*
– DERIVATIVES **man·tric** /-trik/ **adj.**
– ORIGIN late 18th cent.: Sanskrit, literally 'instrument of thought,' from *man* 'think.'

man·trap /'man,trap/ ▶ **n.** a trap for catching people, esp. trespassers or poachers.

man·tu·a /'manchooə/ ▶ **n.** a woman's loose gown of a kind fashionable during the 17th and 18th centuries.
– ORIGIN alteration of French *manteau*.

Man·u /'mänoo, 'manoo/ the archetypal first man of Hindu mythology, survivor of the great flood and father of the human race.

man·u·al /'manyə(wə)l/ ▶ **adj.** of or done with the hands: *manual dexterity | manual hauling of boats along the towpath.* ■ (of a machine or device) worked by hand, not automatically or electronically: *a manual typewriter.* ■ [attrib.] using or working with the hands: *a manual laborer.*
▶ **n.** **1** a book of instructions, esp. for operating a machine or learning a subject; a handbook: *a computer manual | a training manual.* ■ a small book: *a pocket-sized manual of the artist's aphorisms.* ■ historical a book of the forms to be used by priests in the administration of the sacraments.
2 a thing operated or done by hand rather than automatically or electronically, in particular: ■ an organ keyboard played with the hands. ■ a vehicle with a manual transmission.
– DERIVATIVES **man·u·al·ly** **adv.**
– ORIGIN late Middle English: from Old French *manuel*, from (and later assimilated to) Latin *manualis*, from *manus* 'hand.'

man·u·al al·pha·bet ▶ **n.** a set of sign-language symbols used in fingerspelling, in which different finger configurations correspond to letters of the alphabet.

man·u·al trans·mis·sion ▶ **n.** an automotive transmission consisting of a system of interlocking gear wheels and a lever that enables the driver to shift gears manually.

ma·nu·bri·um /mə'nōōbrēəm/ ▶ **n.** (pl. **manubria** /-brēə/ or **manubriums**) Anatomy & Zoology a handle-shaped projection or part, in particular: ■ the broad upper part of the sternum of mammals, with which the clavicles and first ribs articulate. ■ the tube that bears the mouth of a coelenterate.
– DERIVATIVES **ma·nu·bri·al** /-brēəl/ **adj.**
– ORIGIN mid 17th cent. (as a rare usage in the sense 'handle'): from Latin, 'haft.'

man·u·code /'manyə,kōd/ ▶ **n.** a bird of paradise of which the male and female have similar blue-black plumage and breed as stable pairs. ● Genus *Manucodia*, family Paradisaeidae: five species, in particular the **trumpet manucode** or trumpet bird (*M. keraudrenii*), the male of which has a loud trumpeting call.
– ORIGIN mid 19th cent.: from French, from modern Latin *manucodiata* (used in the same sense from the mid 16th to 18th centuries), from Malay *manuk dewata* 'bird of the gods.'

Man·u·el·ine /man'wel,in/ ▶ **adj.** denoting a style of Portuguese architecture developed during the reign of Manuel I (1495–1521) and characterized by ornate elaborations of Gothic and Renaissance styles.

manuf. ▶ **abbr.** manufacture or manufacturer or manufacturing.

man·u·fac·to·ry /,manyə'fakt(ə)rē/ ▶ **n.** (pl. **manufactories**) archaic a factory.
– ORIGIN early 17th cent. (denoting a manufactured article): from MANUFACTURE, on the pattern of *factory*.

man·u·fac·ture /,manyə'fakchər/ ▶ **n.** the making of articles on a large scale using machinery: *the manufacture of armored vehicles.* ■ [with modifier] a specified branch of industry: *the porcelain manufacture for which France became justly renowned.* ■ (**manufactures**) manufactured goods or articles: *exports and imports of manufactures.*
▶ **v.** [with obj.] **1** make (something) on a large scale using machinery: *a company that manufactured paint-by-number sets* | (as adj. **manufacturing**) *a manufacturing company.* ■ (of a living thing) produce (a substance) naturally. ■ make or produce (something abstract) in a merely mechanical way: (as adj. **manufactured**) *manufactured love songs.*
2 invent or fabricate (evidence or a story): *the tabloid industry that manufactures epochal discoveries out of thin air.*
– DERIVATIVES **man·u·fac·tur·a·bil·i·ty** /-,fakchərə'bilətē/ **n.**, **man·u·fac·tur·a·ble** **adj.**
– ORIGIN mid 16th cent. (denoting something made by hand): from French (re-formed by association with Latin *manu factum* 'made by hand'), from Italian *manifattura*. Sense 1 of the verb dates from the early 17th cent.

man·u·fac·tured home ▶ **n.** (mainly in advertising) a mobile home.

man·u·fac·tured hous·ing ▶ **n.** prefabricated houses that are constructed in a factory and then assembled at the building site in modular sections.

man·u·fac·tur·er /,manyə'fakchərər/ ▶ **n.** a person or company that makes goods for sale: *the manufacturers supply the goods to the distribution center.*

man·u·mat·ic /,manyə'matik/ ▶ **n.** an automatic car transmission that enables the driver to shift through the gears manually.
– ORIGIN 1990s: blend of *manual* and *automatic*.

man·u·mit /,manyə'mit/ ▶ **v.** (**manumits**, **manumitting**, **manumitted**) [with obj.] historical release from slavery; set free.
– DERIVATIVES **man·u·mis·sion** /-'mishən/ **n.**, **man·u·mit·ter** **n.**
– ORIGIN late Middle English: from Latin *manumittere*, literally 'send forth from the hand,' from *manus* 'hand' + *mittere* 'send.'

ma·nure /mə'n(y)oor/ ▶ **n.** animal dung used for fertilizing land. ■ any compost or artificial fertilizer.

▶ **v.** [with obj.] apply manure to (land): *the ground should be well dug and manured.*
– ORIGIN late Middle English (as a verb in the sense 'cultivate (land)'): from Anglo-Norman French *mainoverer*, Old French *manouvrer* (see MANEUVER). The noun sense dates from the mid 16th cent.

ma·nus /'mānəs, 'mänəs/ ▶ **n.** (pl. **same**) chiefly Zoology the terminal segment of a forelimb, corresponding to the hand and wrist in humans.
– ORIGIN early 19th cent.: from Latin, 'hand.'

man·u·script /'manyə,skript/ ▶ **n.** a book, document, or piece of music written by hand rather than typed or printed: *an illuminated manuscript.* ■ an author's text that has not yet been published: *preparing the final manuscript | her autobiography remained in manuscript.*
– ORIGIN late 16th cent.: from medieval Latin *manuscriptus*, from *manu* 'by hand' + *scriptus* 'written' (past participle of *scribere*).

man·u·script pa·per ▶ **n.** paper printed with staves for writing music on.

Ma·nu·ti·us, Aldus, see **ALDUS MANUTIUS**.

Manx /maNGks/ ▶ **adj.** of or relating to the Isle of Man.
▶ **n. 1** the Goidelic language formerly spoken in the Isle of Man.
2 (**the Manx**) the Manx people collectively.
– DERIVATIVES **Manx·man** /-mən/ **n.** (pl. **Manxmen**), **Manx·wom·an** /-,wŏŏmən/ **n.** (pl. **Manxwomen**).
– ORIGIN from Old Norse, from Old Irish *Manu* 'Isle of Man' + *-skr* (equivalent of **-ISH**¹).

Manx cat ▶ **n.** a cat of a breed having no tail or an extremely short one.

Manx shear·wa·ter ▶ **n.** a dark-backed shearwater that nests on remote islands in the northeastern Atlantic, Mediterranean, and Hawaiian waters.
● *Puffinus puffinus*, family Procellariidae.

man·y /'menē/ ▶ **determiner, pron., & adj.** (**more, most**) a large number of: [as determiner] *many people agreed with her* | [as pronoun] *the solution to many of our problems | many think it is a new craze.*
▶ **n.** (as plural noun **the many**) the majority of people: *music for the many.*
– PHRASES **as many** the same number of: *changing his mind for the third time in as many months.* **a good** (or **great**) **many** a large number: *a good many of us.* **have one too many** informal become slightly drunk. **how many** used to ask what a particular quantity is: *how many books did you sell?* **many a ——** a large number of: *many a good man has been destroyed by booze.* **many's the ——** used to indicate that something happens often: *many's the night we've been wakened by that racket.*
– ORIGIN Old English *manig*, of Germanic origin; related to Dutch *menig* and German *manch*.

man·y·fold /'menē,fōld/ ▶ **adv.** by many times: *the problems would be multiplied manyfold.*
▶ **adj.** involving multiplication by many times: *the manyfold increase in staffing levels.*

man·y-sid·ed ▶ **adj.** having many sides or aspects: *the reasons for poor collaboration are complex and many-sided.*
– DERIVATIVES **man·y-sid·ed·ness n.**

man·za·nil·la /,manzə'nē(y)ə/ ▶ **n.** a pale, very dry Spanish sherry.
– ORIGIN Spanish, literally 'chamomile' (because the flavor is said to be reminiscent of that of chamomile).

man·za·ni·ta /,manzə'nētə/ ▶ **n.** an evergreen dwarf shrub related to the bearberry, native to California.
● Genus *Arctostaphylos*, family Ericaceae: several species, in particular *A. manzanita*.
– ORIGIN mid 19th cent.: from Spanish, diminutive of *manzana* 'apple.'

MAO ▶ **abbr.** Biochemistry monoamine oxidase.

Mao /mou/ ▶ **n.** [as modifier] denoting a jacket or suit of a plain style with a mandarin collar, associated with communist China.
– ORIGIN 1960s: by association with **MAO ZEDONG**.

MAOI ▶ **abbr.** monoamine oxidase inhibitor.

Mao·ism /'mou,izəm/ ▶ **n.** the communist doctrines of Mao Zedong as formerly practiced in China, having as a central idea permanent revolution and stressing the importance of the peasantry, of small-scale industry, and of agricultural collectivization.
– DERIVATIVES **Mao·ist n. & adj.**

Ma·o·ri /'mourē/ ▶ **n.** (pl. **same** or **Maoris**) **1** a member of the aboriginal people of New Zealand.
2 the Polynesian language of this people.
▶ **adj.** of or relating to the Maoris or their language.
– ORIGIN the name in Maori.

mao-tai /'mou 'tī, 'dī/ ▶ **n.** a strong sorghum-based liquor distilled in southwestern China.
– ORIGIN named after a town in southwestern China.

Mao Ze·dong /'mou ,zə'dôNG/ (also **Mao Tse-tung** /,tsə 'tŏŏNG, ,dzə 'dŏŏNG/) (1893–1976), Chinese statesman; chairman of the Communist Party of the Chinese People's Republic 1949–76; head of state 1949–59. A cofounder of the Chinese Communist Party in 1921 and its effective leader from the time of the Long March (1934–35), he eventually defeated both the occupying Japanese and rival Kuomintang nationalist forces to create the People's Republic of China in 1949.

Mao Zedong meets President Richard M. Nixon

MAP ▶ **abbr.** modified American plan (see **AMERICAN PLAN**).

map /map/ ▶ **n. 1** a diagrammatic representation of an area of land or sea showing physical features, cities, roads, etc.: *a street map* | figurative *expansion of the service sector is reshaping the map of employment.* ■ a two-dimensional representation of the positions of stars or other astronomical objects. ■ a diagram or collection of data showing the spatial arrangement or distribution of something over an area: *an electron density map.* ■ Biology a representation of the sequence of genes on a chromosome or of bases in a DNA or RNA molecule. ■ Mathematics another term for **MAPPING**.
2 informal, dated a person's face.
▶ **v.** (**maps, mapping, mapped**) [with obj.] represent (an area) on a map; make a map of: *inaccessible parts will be mapped from the air.* ■ record in detail the spatial distribution of (something): *the project to map the human genome.* ■ associate (a group of elements or qualities) with an equivalent group, according to a particular formula or model: *the transformational rules map deep structures into surface structures.* ■ Mathematics associate each element of (a set) with an element of another set. ■ [no obj.] be associated or linked to something: *it is not obvious that the subprocesses of language will map onto individual brain areas.*
– PHRASES **off the map** (of a place) very distant or remote: *just a hick town, right off the map.* **put something on the map** bring something to prominence: *the exhibition put Cubism on the map.* **wipe something off the map** obliterate something totally.
– PHRASAL VERBS **map something out** plan a route or course of action in detail: *I mapped out a route over familiar country near home.*
– DERIVATIVES **map·less adj.**, **map·pa·ble adj.**, **map·per n.**
– ORIGIN early 16th cent.: from medieval Latin *mappa mundi*, literally 'sheet of the world,' from Latin *mappa* 'sheet, napkin' + *mundi* 'of the world' (genitive of *mundus*).

ma·ple /'māpəl/ ▶ **n.** a tree or shrub with lobed leaves, winged fruits, and colorful autumn foliage, grown as an ornamental or for its timber or syrupy sap. ● Genus *Acer*, family Aceraceae: many species, including the common European **field maple** (*A. campestre*), the North American **sugar maple** (*A. saccharum*), and the **Japanese maple** (*A. palmatum*), which has many cultivars. ■ maple syrup or maple sugar.
– ORIGIN Old English *mapel* (as the first element of *mapeltrēow*, *mapulder* 'maple tree'); used as an independent word from Middle English onward.

Ma·ple Grove a city in southeastern Minnesota, a northwestern suburb of Minneapolis; pop. 61,542 (est. 2008).

ma·ple leaf ▶ **n.** the leaf of the maple, used as an emblem of Canada.

ma·ple sug·ar ▶ **n.** sugar produced by evaporating the sap of certain maples, esp. the sugar maple.

ma·ple syr·up ▶ **n.** syrup produced from the sap of certain maples, esp. the sugar maple.

map·mak·er /'map,mākər/ ▶ **n.** a cartographer.
– DERIVATIVES **map·mak·ing** /-,mākiNG/ **n.**

Map·pa Mun·di /,mapə 'mŏŏndē/ a famous 13th-century map of the world, now in Hereford cathedral, England. The map is round and typical of similar maps of the time in that it depicts Jerusalem at its center.
– ORIGIN from medieval Latin, literally 'sheet of the world.'

map·ping /'mapiNG/ ▶ **n.** Mathematics & Linguistics an operation that associates each element of a given set (the domain) with one or more elements of a second set (the range).

map pro·jec·tion ▶ **n.** see **PROJECTION** (sense 6).

map ref·er·ence ▶ **n.** a set of numbers and letters specifying a location as represented on a map.

map tur·tle ▶ **n.** a small North American freshwater turtle with bold patterns on the shell and head.
● Genus *Graptemys*, family Emydidae: several species, in particular *G. geographica*.

Ma·pu·che /ma'pŏŏCHē/ ▶ **n.** (pl. **same** or **Mapuches**) **1** a member of an American Indian people of central Chile and adjacent parts of Argentina, noted for their resistance to colonial Spanish and later Chilean domination.
2 the Araucanian language of this people.
▶ **adj.** relating to or denoting this people or their language.
– ORIGIN the name in Mapuche, from *mapu* 'land' + *che* 'people.'

Ma·pu·to /mə'pōōtō/ the capital and chief port of Mozambique, on the Indian Ocean in the southern part of the country; pop. 1,099,102 (2007). Former name (until 1976) **LOURENÇO MARQUES**.

ma·quette /ma'ket/ ▶ **n.** a sculptor's small preliminary model or sketch.
– ORIGIN early 20th cent.: from French, from Italian *machietta*, diminutive of *macchia* 'spot.'

ma·qui·la /mə'kēlə/ ▶ **n.** another term for **MAQUILADORA**.

ma·qui·la·do·ra /,makilə'dôrə/ ▶ **n.** a factory in Mexico run by a foreign company and exporting its products to the country of that company.
– ORIGIN Mexican Spanish, from *maquilar* 'assemble.'

ma·quil·lage /,mäkē'(y)äZH/ ▶ **n.** makeup; cosmetics.
– ORIGIN French, from *maquiller* 'to make up,' from Old French *masquiller* 'to stain.'

ma·quis /mä'kē/ ▶ **n.** (pl. **same**) **1** (**the Maquis**) the French resistance movement during the German occupation (1940–45). ■ a member of this movement.
2 dense scrub vegetation consisting of hardy evergreen shrubs and small trees, characteristic of coastal regions in the Mediterranean.
– ORIGIN early 19th cent. (sense 2): from French, 'brushwood,' from Corsican Italian *macchia*.

ma·qui·sard /,mäkē'zär/ ▶ **n.** a member of the Maquis.

mar /mär/ ▶ **v.** (**mars, marring, marred**) [with obj.] impair the appearance of; disfigure: *no wrinkles marred her face.* ■ impair the quality of; spoil: *violence marred a number of New Year celebrations.*
– ORIGIN Old English *merran* 'hinder, damage,' of Germanic origin; probably related to Dutch *marren* 'loiter.'

Mar. ▶ **abbr.** March.

mar·a·bou /'marə,bōō/ ▶ **n.** (also **marabou stork**) a large African stork with a massive bill and large neck pouch, feeding mainly by scavenging.
● *Leptoptilos crumeniferus*, family Ciconiidae.
■ down from the wing or tail of the marabou used as a trimming for hats or clothing, or on a fishing lure.
– ORIGIN early 19th cent.: from French, from Arabic *murābiṭ* 'holy man' (see also **MARABOUT**), the stork being regarded as holy.

mar·a·bout /'marə,bōō/ ▶ **n. 1** a Muslim hermit or monk, esp. in North Africa. ■ a shrine marking the burial place of a Muslim hermit or monk.
2 variant spelling of **MARABOU**.
– ORIGIN early 17th cent.: via French and Portuguese from Arabic *murābiṭ* 'holy man.'

Mar·a·cai·bo /,marə'kībō/ a city and port in northwestern Venezuela, situated on the channel that links the Gulf of Venezuela with Lake Maracaibo; pop. 1,891,800 (est. 2009).

Mar·a·cai·bo, Lake a large lake in northwestern Venezuela, linked by a narrow channel to the Gulf of Venezuela and the Caribbean Sea.

ma·rac·as /mə'räkəz/ ▶ **plural n.** a pair of hollow clublike gourd or gourd-shaped containers filled with beans, pebbles, or similar objects, shaken as a percussion instrument.
– ORIGIN early 17th cent.: from Portuguese *maracá*, from Tupi.

maracas

Ma·ra·do·na /ˌmärə'dônə/, Diego (Armando) (1960–), Argentine soccer player. He captained the Argentine team that won the World Cup in 1986 and aroused controversy when his apparent handball scored a goal in the quarterfinal match against England.

mar·ag·ing steel /'märˌājiNG/ ▶ **n.** a steel alloy, containing up to 25 percent nickel and other metals, strengthened by a process of slow cooling and age hardening.
– ORIGIN 1960s: *maraging* from *mar-* (abbreviation of MARTENSITE, because the process involves conversion of austenite to martensite) + *aging* from the verb AGE.

ma·ran·ta /mə'rantə/ ▶ **n.** a tropical American plant of a genus that includes the prayer plant and the arrowroot. ● Genus *Maranta*, family Marantaceae. ■ a calathea.
– ORIGIN modern Latin, named after Bartollomeo *Maranta*, 16th-cent. Italian herbalist.

Ma·ra·ñón /ˌmärə'nyōn/ a river in northern Peru that rises in the Andes and forms one of the principal headwaters of the Amazon River.

mar·a·schi·no /ˌmarə'SHēˌnō, -'skē-/ ▶ **n.** (pl. **maraschinos**) a strong, sweet liqueur made from a variety of small bitter cherries. ■ a maraschino cherry.
– ORIGIN Italian, from *marasca* (the name of the cherry), from *amaro* 'bitter,' from Latin *amarus*.

mar·a·schi·no cher·ry ▶ **n.** a cherry preserved in maraschino or maraschino-flavored syrup.

ma·ras·mus /mə'razməs/ ▶ **n.** Medicine severe undernourishment causing an infant's or child's weight to be significantly low for their age (e.g., below 60 percent of normal).
– DERIVATIVES **ma·ras·mic** /-mik/ **adj.**
– ORIGIN mid 17th cent.: modern Latin, from Greek *marasmos* 'withering,' from *marainein* 'wither.'

m

Ma·rat /mä'rä/, Jean Paul (1743–93), French revolutionary and journalist. A virulent critic of the moderate Girondists, he was instrumental (with Danton and Robespierre) in their fall from power in 1793. He was murdered in his bath by Girondin supporter Charlotte Corday.

Ma·ra·tha /mə'rätə/ (also **Mahratta**) ▶ **n.** a member of the princely and military castes of the former Hindu kingdom of Maharashtra in central India.
– ORIGIN via Hindi from Sanskrit *Mahārāṣṭra* 'great kingdom.'

Ma·ra·thi /mə'rätē/ (also **Mahratti**) ▶ **n.** the Indic language of the Marathas, spoken by about 60 million people in Maharashtra and elsewhere.

mar·a·thon /'marəˌTHän/ ▶ **n.** a long-distance running race, strictly one of 26 miles and 385 yards (42.195 km). ■ a long-lasting or difficult task or operation of a specified kind: *the last leg of an interview marathon that began this summer* | [as modifier] *marathon workdays*.
– DERIVATIVES **mar·a·thon·er n.**
– ORIGIN late 19th cent.: from *Marathōn* in Greece, the scene of a victory over the Persians in 490 BC; the modern race is based on the tradition that a messenger ran from Marathon to Athens (22 miles) with the news. The original account by Herodotus told of the messenger Pheidippides running 150 miles from Athens to Sparta before the battle, seeking help.

ma·raud /mə'rôd/ ▶ **v.** [no obj.] roam in search of things to steal or people to attack: *war parties crossed the river to maraud*. ■ [with obj.] raid and plunder (a place).
– ORIGIN late 17th cent.: from French *marauder*, from *maraud* 'rogue.'

ma·raud·er /mə'rôdər/ ▶ **n.** a person who marauds; a raider: *a band of English marauders were surprised and overcome*.

ma·raud·ing /mə'rôdiNG/ ▶ **adj.** going about in search of things to steal or people to attack: *marauding gangs of youths*.

mar·a·ve·di /ˌmarə'vādē/ ▶ **n.** (pl. **maravedis**) a medieval Spanish copper coin and monetary unit.
– ORIGIN Spanish, from Arabic *murābiṭīn* 'holy men,' a name applied to the North African Berber rulers of Muslim Spain, from the late 11th cent. to 1145.

Mar·a·vich /'marəˌviCH/, Pete (1947–88), US basketball player; known as **Pistol Pete**. He played for the Atlanta Hawks 1970–74, the New Orleans Jazz (Utah Jazz from 1979) 1974–1980, and the Boston Celtics briefly in 1980. Basketball Hall of Fame (1987).

Mar·bel·la /mär'bāə/ a resort town on the Costa del Sol of southern Spain, in Andalusia; pop. 130,549 (2008).

mar·ble /'märbəl/ ▶ **n. 1** a hard crystalline metamorphic form of limestone, typically white with mottlings or streaks of color, that is capable of taking a polish and is used in sculpture and architecture. ■ used in similes and comparisons with reference to the smoothness, hardness, or color of marble: *her shoulders were as white as marble*. ■ a marble sculpture.
2 a small ball of colored glass or similar material used as a toy. ■ **(marbles)** [treated as sing.] a game in which such balls are rolled along the ground.
3 (one's marbles) informal one's mental faculties: *I thought she'd* **lost her marbles**, *asking a question like that*.
▶ **v.** [with obj.] stain or streak (something) so that it looks like variegated marble: *the low stone walls were marbled with moss and lichen*.
– PHRASES **pick up one's marbles and go home** informal withdraw petulantly from an activity after having suffered a setback: *he doesn't have the guts to take a bad defeat, and is now picking up his marbles and going home*.
– DERIVATIVES **mar·bler n.**, **mar·bly** /-blē, -bəlē/ **adj.**
– ORIGIN Middle English: via Old French (variant of *marbre*) from Latin *marmor*, from Greek *marmaros* 'shining stone,' associated with *marmairein* 'to shine.'

mar·ble cake ▶ **n.** a cake with a streaked appearance, made of light and dark (esp. chocolate) batter.

mar·bled /'märbəld/ ▶ **adj.** having a streaked and patterned appearance like that of variegated marble. ■ (of meat) streaked with alternating layers or swirls of lean and fat.

Mar·ble·head /'märbəlˌhed/ a coastal town in northeastern Massachusetts, a noted yachting and fishing port; pop. 19,951 (est. 2008).

mar·ble·ize /'märbəˌlīz/ ▶ **v.** [with obj.] give a marblelike variegated finish to (an object or material): (as adj. **marbleized**) *an old financial ledger with a marbleized cover*.

mar·bling /'märb(ə)liNG/ ▶ **n.** coloring or marking that resembles variegated marble. ■ streaks of fat in lean meat.

Mar·burg /'märˌbərg/ **1** a city in the state of Hesse in west central Germany; pop. 79,400 (est. 2006). It was the scene in 1529 of a debate between German and Swiss theologians, notably Martin Luther and Ulrich Zwingli, on the doctrine of consubstantiation.
2 German name for MARIBOR.

Mar·burg dis·ease ▶ **n.** an acute, often fatal, form of hemorrhagic fever. It is caused by a filovirus (**Marburg virus**) that normally lives in African monkeys. Also called GREEN MONKEY DISEASE.

marc /märk/ ▶ **n.** the refuse of grapes or other fruit that has been pressed for winemaking. ■ an alcoholic spirit distilled from this.
– ORIGIN early 17th cent.: from French, from *marcher* in the early sense 'to tread or trample.'

Mar·can /'märkən/ (also **Markan**) ▶ **adj.** of or relating to St. Mark or the Gospel ascribed to him.

mar·ca·site /'märkəˌsīt/ ▶ **n.** a semiprecious stone consisting of pyrite. ■ a bronze-yellow mineral consisting of iron disulfide but differing from pyrite in typically forming aggregates of tabular crystals. ■ a piece of polished steel or a similar metal cut as a gem.
– ORIGIN late Middle English: from medieval Latin *marcasita*, from Arabic *markašīṭā*, from Persian.

mar·ca·to /mär'käˌtō/ ▶ **adv. & adj.** Music (esp. as a direction) played with emphasis.
– ORIGIN Italian, 'marked, accented,' of Germanic origin.

Mar·ceau /mär'sō/, Marcel (1923–2007), French mime artist. He was known for appearing as the white-faced Bip, a character he developed from the French Pierrot character.

mar·cel /mär'sel/ dated ▶ **n.** (also **marcel wave**) a deep artificial wave in the hair.
▶ **v.** (**marcels, marcelling, marcelled**) [with obj.] give such a wave to (hair).
– ORIGIN late 19th cent.: named after *Marcel* Grateau (1852–1936), the Parisian hairdresser who invented it.

mar·ces·cent /mär'sesənt/ ▶ **adj.** Botany (of leaves or fronds) withering but remaining attached to the stem.
– DERIVATIVES **mar·ces·cence n.**
– ORIGIN early 18th cent.: from Latin *marcescent-* 'beginning to wither,' from *marcere* 'wither.'

March /märCH/ ▶ **n.** the third month of the year, in the northern hemisphere usually considered the first month of spring: *the work was completed in March* | [as modifier] *the March issue of the magazine*.
– ORIGIN Middle English: from an Old French dialect variant of *marz*, from Latin *Martius* (*mensis*) '(month) of Mars.'

march¹ /märCH/ ▶ **v.** [no obj.] walk in a military manner with a regular measured tread: *three companies of soldiers marched around the field*. ■ walk or proceed quickly and with determination: *without a word she marched from the room*. ■ [with obj.] force (someone) to walk somewhere quickly: *she gripped Rachel's arm and marched her out through the doors*. ■ walk along public roads in an organized procession to protest about something: *antigovernment protesters marched today through major cities* | *they planned to* **march on** *Baton Rouge*. ■ (of something abstract) proceed or advance inexorably: *time marches on*.
▶ **n.** [usu. in sing.] an act or instance of marching: *the relieving force was more than a day's march away*. ■ a piece of music composed to accompany marching or with a rhythmic character suggestive of marching. ■ a procession as a protest or demonstration: *a protest march*. ■ [in sing.] the progress or continuity of something abstract that is considered to be moving inexorably onward: *the inevitable march of history*.
– PHRASES **march to (the beat of) a different drummer** informal consciously adopt a different approach or attitude from the majority of people; be unconventional. **on the march** marching: *the army was on the march at last*.
– ORIGIN late Middle English: from French *marcher* 'to walk' (earlier 'to trample'), of uncertain origin.

march² ▶ **n.** (usu. **Marches**) a frontier or border area between two countries or territories, esp. between England and Wales or (formerly) England and Scotland: *the Welsh Marches*. ■ **(the Marches)** a region of east central Italy, between the Apennines and the Adriatic Sea; capital, Ancona. Italian name **Marche**.
▶ **v.** [no obj.] **(march with)** rare (of a country, territory, or estate) have a common frontier with.
– ORIGIN Middle English: from Old French *marche* (noun), *marchir* (verb), of Germanic origin; related to MARK¹.

mar·chands de vin /mär'SHän də 'vaN/ ▶ **n.** a French wine sauce sauce served hot or cold to accompany grilled or roasted meat.
– ORIGIN French, 'wine merchants.'

Marche /'märkā/ ▶ **n.** a region of east central Italy, between the Apennines and the Adriatic Sea; capital, Ancona. Italian name **Le Marche**.

march·er¹ /'märCHər/ ▶ **n.** a person who marches, esp. one taking part in a protest march.

march·er² ▶ **n.** chiefly historical an inhabitant of a frontier or border district.

mar·che·sa /mär'kāzə/ ▶ **n.** (pl. **marchese** /-'kāzā/) an Italian marchioness.
– ORIGIN Italian, feminine of MARCHESE.

mar·che·se /mär'kāzā/ ▶ **n.** (pl. **marchesi** /-'kāzē/) an Italian marquis.
– ORIGIN Italian.

March hare ▶ **n.** informal a brown hare in the breeding season, noted for its leaping, boxing, and chasing in circles.
– PHRASES **(as) mad as a March hare** (of a person) completely mad or irrational; crazy.

march·ing or·der ▶ **n.** Military equipment for marching: *they stood before their company commander dressed in full marching order*.

march·ing or·ders ▶ **plural n.** instructions from a superior officer for troops to depart. ■ informal a dismissal or sending off: *the ref called me over and gave me my marching orders*.

mar·chion·ess /'märsH(ə)nəs/ ▶ **n.** the wife or widow of a marquess. ■ a woman holding the rank of marquess in her own right.
– ORIGIN late 16th cent.: from medieval Latin *marchionissa*, feminine of *marchio(n-)* 'ruler of a border territory,' from *marcha* 'march' (see MARCH²).

March Mad·ness ▶ **n.** informal the time of the annual NCAA college basketball tournament, generally throughout the month of March.

march·pane /'märCHˌpān/ ▶ **n.** archaic spelling of MARZIPAN.

Mar·ci·a·no /ˌmärsē'änō, -'anō/, Rocky (1923–69), US heavyweight boxing champion; born *Rocco Francis Marchegiano*. He became world heavyweight champion in 1952 and successfully defended his title six times until he retired, undefeated, in 1956.

Mar·co·ni /märˈkōnē/, Guglielmo (1874–1937), Italian electrical engineer; the father of radio. In 1912, Marconi produced a continuously oscillating wave, essential for the transmission of sound. He went on to develop shortwave transmission over long distances. Nobel Prize for Physics (1909), shared with Carl Braun.

Mar·co Po·lo /ˈmärkō ˈpōlō/ (*c.*1254–*c.*1324), Italian traveler. With his father and uncle he traveled to China and the court of Kublai Khan via central Asia (1271–75). He eventually returned home (1292–95) via Sumatra, India, and Persia. His account of his travels spurred the European quest for the riches of the East.

Mar·cos /ˈmär,kōs/, Ferdinand (Edralin) (1917–89), president of the Philippines 1965–86. Amid charges of corruption and political intrigue he was unable to secure his 1986 re-election and was forced into exile after a government takeover in 1986 by a front led by Corazon Aquino, wife of Benigno Aquino (1932–83), who had been assassinated by Marcos forces.

Mar·cus Au·re·li·us /ˈmärkəs ôˈrēlēəs, ôˈrēlyəs/ see **AURELIUS**.

Mar·cu·se /märˈko͞ozə/, Herbert (1898–1979), US philosopher, born in Germany. A member of the Frankfurt School, he argued in *Soviet Marxism* (1958) that revolutionary change can come only from alienated elites such as students.

Mar del Pla·ta /ˌmär dəl ˈplätə/ a fishing port and resort in Argentina, on the Atlantic coast south of Buenos Aires; pop. 620,800 (est. 2008).

Mar·di Gras /ˈmärdē ˌgrä/ ▶ **n.** a carnival held in some countries on Shrove Tuesday, most famously in New Orleans.
– ORIGIN French, literally 'fat Tuesday,' alluding to the last day of feasting before the fast and penitence of Lent.

Mar·duk /ˈmär,do͝ok/ Babylonian Mythology the chief god of Babylon, who became lord of the gods of heaven and earth after conquering Tiamat, the monster of primeval chaos.

Mare, Walter de la, see **DE LA MARE**.

mare[1] /me(ə)r/ ▶ **n.** the female of a horse or other equine animal.
– ORIGIN Old English *mearh* 'horse,' *mere* 'mare,' from a Germanic base with cognates in Celtic languages meaning 'stallion' The sense 'male horse' died out at the end of the Middle English period.

ma·re[2] /ˈmärā/ ▶ **n.** (pl. **maria** /ˈmärēə/) Astronomy a large, level basalt plain on the surface of the moon, appearing dark by contrast with highland areas: [in names] *Mare Imbrium*.
– ORIGIN mid 19th cent.: special use of Latin *mare* 'sea'; these areas were once thought to be seas.

ma·re clau·sum /ˌmärā ˈklousəm, ˈklô-/ ▶ **n.** (pl. **maria clausa** /ˌmärēə ˈklousə, ˈklô-/) Law the sea under the jurisdiction of a particular country.
– ORIGIN Latin, 'closed sea.'

Ma·rek's dis·ease /ˈmariks, ˈmär-/ ▶ **n.** an infectious disease of poultry caused by a herpesvirus that attacks nerves and causes paralysis or initiates widespread tumor formation.
– ORIGIN 1960s: named after Josef *Marek* (died 1952), Hungarian veterinary surgeon.

ma·re li·be·rum /ˌmärā ˈlēbəˌro͝om/ ▶ **n.** (pl. **maria libera** /ˌmärēə ˈlēbərə/) Law the sea open to all nations.
– ORIGIN Latin, literally 'free sea.'

ma·rem·ma /məˈremə/ ▶ **n.** (pl. **maremme** /-ˈremē/) (esp. in Italy) an area of low, marshy land near a seashore.
– ORIGIN mid 19th cent.: Italian, from Latin *maritima*, feminine of *maritimus* (see **MARITIME**).

Ma·ren·go /məˈrenggō/ ▶ **adj.** [postpositive] (of chicken or veal) sautéed in oil, served with a tomato sauce, and traditionally garnished with eggs and crayfish: *chicken Marengo*.
– ORIGIN named after the village of Marengo in northern Italy, scene of a battle in 1800 in which the French were victorious and after which the dish is said to have been served to Napoleon.

mare's nest ▶ **n.** 1 a complex and difficult situation; a muddle: *your desk is usually a mare's nest*.
2 an illusory discovery: *the mare's nest of perfect safety*.
– ORIGIN late 16th cent.: formerly in the phrase *to have found* (or *spied*) *a mare's nest* (i.e., something that does not exist), used in the sense 'to have discovered something amazing.'

mare's tail ▶ **n.** 1 a widely distributed water plant with whorls of narrow leaves around a tall stout stem. ● *Hippuris vulgaris*, family Haloragaceae.
2 (**mare's tails**) long straight streaks of cirrus cloud.

Mar·fan's syn·drome /ˈmärfənz, märˈfänz/ (also **Marfan syndrome**) ▶ **n.** Medicine a hereditary disorder of connective tissue, resulting in abnormally long and thin digits and also frequently in optical and cardiovascular defects.
– ORIGIN 1930s: named after Antonin B. J. *Marfan* (1858–1942), French pediatrician.

marg. ▶ **abbr.** margin or marginal.

Mar·ga·ret, Princess /ˈmärg(ə)rət/, Margaret Rose (1930–2002), member of the British royal family; the only sister of Elizabeth II.

Mar·ga·ret, St. (*c.*1046–93), Scottish queen; wife of Malcolm III. She exerted a strong influence over royal policy during her husband's reign and was instrumental in the reform of the Scottish Church. Feast day, November 16.

mar·ga·rine /ˈmärjərən/ ▶ **n.** a butter substitute made from vegetable oils or animal fats.
– ORIGIN late 19th cent.: from French, from Greek *margaron* 'pearl' (because of the luster of the crystals of margaric acid) + **-INE**[4].

Mar·ga·ri·ta /ˌmärgəˈrētə/ an island in the Caribbean Sea, off the coast of Venezuela. Visited by Columbus in 1498, it was used as a base by Simón Bolívar in 1816 during the struggle for independence from Spanish rule.

mar·ga·ri·ta /ˌmärgəˈrētə/ ▶ **n.** a cocktail made with tequila and citrus fruit juice.
– ORIGIN from the Spanish given name equivalent to *Margaret*.

mar·gate /ˈmärgit, -ˌgāt/ ▶ **n.** a deep-bodied grayish fish that typically occurs in small groups in warm waters of the western Atlantic. ● Two species in the family Pomadasyidae: *Haemulon album*, a large grunt that is an important food fish, and the mainly nocturnal **black margate** (*Anisotremus surinamesis*).
– ORIGIN mid 18th cent.: of unknown origin.

mar·gay /ˈmär,gā, märˈgā/ ▶ **n.** a small South American wild cat with large eyes and a yellowish coat with black spots and stripes. ● *Felis wiedii*, family Felidae.
– ORIGIN late 18th cent.: via French from Tupi *marakaya*.

marge /märj/ ▶ **n.** literary a margin or edge.
– ORIGIN mid 16th cent.: from French, from Latin *margo* 'margin.'

mar·gin /ˈmärjən/ ▶ **n.** 1 the edge or border of something: *the eastern margin of the Indian Ocean* | figurative *they were forced to live on the margins of society*. ■ the blank border on each side of the print on a page. ■ a line ruled on paper to mark off a margin.
2 an amount by which a thing is won or falls short: *they won by a convincing 17-point margin*. ■ an amount of something included so as to be sure of success or safety: *there was no margin for error*. ■ the lower limit of possibility, success, etc.: *the lighting is considerably brighter than before but is still at the margins of acceptability*. ■ a profit margin. ■ Finance a sum deposited with a broker to cover the risk of loss on a transaction or account.
▶ **v.** (**margins, margining, margined**) [with obj.]
1 provide with an edge or border: *its leaves are margined with yellow*. ■ archaic annotate or summarize (a text) in the margins.
2 deposit an amount of money with a broker as security for (an account or transaction): (as adj. **margined**) *a margined transaction*.
– PHRASES **margin of error** an amount (usually small) that is allowed for in case of miscalculation or change of circumstances.
– DERIVATIVES **mar·gined** **adj.** [in combination] *a wide-margined volume*.
– ORIGIN late Middle English: from Latin *margo*, *margin-* 'edge.'

mar·gin·al /ˈmärjənl/ ▶ **adj.** of, relating to, or situated at the edge or margin of something: *marginal notes*. ■ of secondary or minor importance; not central: *it seems likely to make only a marginal difference* | *a marginal criminal element*. ■ (of a decision or distinction) very narrow: *a marginal offside decision*. ■ of or relating to water adjacent to the land's edge or coast: *water lilies and marginal aquatics*. ■ (chiefly of costs or benefits) relating to or resulting from small or unit changes. ■ (of taxation) relating to increases in income. ■ chiefly Brit. (of a parliamentary seat) having a small majority and therefore at risk in an election. ■ close to the limit of profitability, esp. through difficulty of exploitation: *marginal farmland*.
▶ **n.** a plant that grows in water adjacent to the edge of land.
– DERIVATIVES **mar·gin·al·i·ty** /ˌmärjəˈnalətē/ **n.**
– ORIGIN late 16th cent.: from medieval Latin *marginalis*, from *margo*, *margin-* (see **MARGIN**).

mar·gin·al cost ▶ **n.** Economics the cost added by producing one extra item of a product.

mar·gi·na·li·a /ˌmärjəˈnālēə/ ▶ **plural n.** marginal notes.
– ORIGIN mid 19th cent.: from medieval Latin, neuter plural of *marginalis*, from *margo*, *margin-* (see **MARGIN**).

mar·gin·al·ize /ˈmärjənəˌlīz/ ▶ **v.** [with obj.] treat (a person, group, or concept) as insignificant or peripheral: *attempting to marginalize those who disagree* | (as adj. **marginalized**) *members of marginalized cultural groups*.
– DERIVATIVES **mar·gin·al·i·za·tion** /ˌmärjənələˈzāshən/ **n.**

mar·gin·al·ly /ˈmärjənəlē/ ▶ **adv.** to only a limited extent; slightly: *inflation is predicted to drop marginally* | [as submodifier] *he's marginally worse than he was*.

mar·gin·ate Biology ▶ **v.** /ˈmärjəˌnāt/ [with obj.] provide with a margin or border; form a border to.
▶ **adj.** /-nit, ˌnāt/ having a distinct margin or border.
– DERIVATIVES **mar·gin·a·tion** /ˌmärjəˈnāshən/ **n.**

mar·gin call ▶ **n.** Finance a demand by a broker that an investor deposit further cash or securities to cover possible losses.

mar·gin re·lease ▶ **n.** a device on a typewriter allowing a word to be typed beyond the margin normally set.

mar·go·sa /märˈgōsə/ ▶ **n.** another term for **NEEM**.
– ORIGIN Portuguese *amargosa*, feminine of *amargoso* 'bitter.'

mar·gra·vate /ˈmärgrəˌvāt/ (also **margraviate** /märˈgrāvē-it, -ˌāt/) ▶ **n.** the territory ruled by a margrave.

mar·grave /ˈmär,grāv/ ▶ **n.** historical the hereditary title of some princes of the Holy Roman Empire.
– ORIGIN mid 16th cent., from Middle Dutch *markgrave* 'count of a border territory,' from *marke* 'boundary' + *grave* 'count' (used as a title).

mar·gra·vine /ˈmärgrəˌvēn, ˌmärgrəˈvēn/ ▶ **n.** historical the wife of a margrave.
– ORIGIN late 17th cent.: from Dutch *markgravin*, feminine of *markgraaf*, earlier *markgrave* (see **MARGRAVE**).

Mar·gre·the II /märˈgrātə/ (1940–), queen of Denmark since 1972.

mar·gue·rite /ˌmärg(y)əˈrēt/ ▶ **n.** another term for **OXEYE DAISY**.
– ORIGIN early 17th cent.: French equivalent of the given name Margaret.

Ma·ri /ˈmärē/ an ancient city on the western bank of the Euphrates River in Syria. Its period of greatest importance was late 19th–mid-18th centuries BC; the vast palace of the last king, **Zimri-Lin**, has yielded an archive of 25,000 cuneiform tablets, which are the principal source for the history of northern Syria and Mesopotamia at that time.

ma·ri·a /ˈmärēə/ plural form of **MARE**[2].

ma·ri·a·chi /ˌmärēˈächē/ ▶ **n.** (pl. **mariachis**) [as modifier] denoting a type of traditional Mexican folk music, typically performed by a small group of strolling musicians dressed in native costume. ■ a musician in such a group.
– ORIGIN from Mexican Spanish *mariache*, *mariachi* 'street singer.'

Ma·ri·a de' Me·di·ci /mäˈrēä de ˈmedēchē/ see **MARIE DE MÉDICIS**.

ma·riage blanc /märˈyäzh ˈblän/ ▶ **n.** (pl. **mariages blancs** pronunc. **same**) an unconsummated marriage.
– ORIGIN French, literally 'white marriage.'

ma·riage de con·ve·nance /märˈyäzh də ˌkônvəˈnäns/ ▶ **n.** (pl. **mariages de convenance** pronunc. **same**) French term for **MARRIAGE OF CONVENIENCE** (see **MARRIAGE**).

Mar·i·an /ˈme(ə)rēən/ ▶ **adj.** 1 of or relating to the Virgin Mary.
2 of or relating to Queen Mary I of England.

Ma·ri·an·a Is·lands /ˌme(ə)rēˈanə, ˌmarēˈänə/ (also **the Marianas**) a group of islands in the western Pacific comprising Guam and the Northern Marianas. In 1975, the Northern Marianas voted to establish a commonwealth in union with the US and became self-governing three years later.
– ORIGIN translating *Las Marianas*, the name given by Spanish colonists to the islands, in honor of *Maria Anna*, widow of Philip IV.

Ma·ri·an·a Trench an ocean trench to the southeast of the Mariana Islands in the western Pacific Ocean. Its greatest known ocean depth is 36,201 feet (11,034 m) at the Challenger Deep, which was discovered by HMS *Challenger II* in 1948.

PRONUNCIATION KEY ə *ago, up*; ər *over, fur*; a *hat*; ā *ate*; ä *car*; e *let*; ē *see*; i *fit*; ī *by*; NG *sing*; ō *go*; ô *law, for*; oi *toy*; o͝o *good*; o͞o *goo*; ou *out*; TH *thin*; T͟H *then*; ZH *vision*

m

Ma·ri·a The·re·sa /mə'rēə tə'rāsə, -zə/ (1717–80), archduchess of Austria; queen of Hungary and Bohemia 1740–80. The daughter of Emperor Charles VI, she succeeded to the Habsburg dominions in 1740 by virtue of the Pragmatic Sanction. Her accession triggered the War of the Austrian Succession (1740–48), which led in turn to the Seven Years War (1756–63).

Ma·ri Au·ton·o·mous Re·pub·lic another name for **Mari El**.

Ma·ri·bor /'märi,bôr/ an industrial city in northeastern Slovenia, on the Drava River near the border with Austria; pop. 111,340 (2007). German name **Marburg**.

Mar·i·co·pa Coun·ty /,mari'kōpə/ a county in south central Arizona that is home to more than half of all Arizonans. Its seat is Phoenix; pop. 3,954,598 (est. 2008).

mar·i·cul·ture /'mari,kəlCHər/ ▶ **n.** the cultivation of fish or other marine life for food.
– ORIGIN early 20th cent.: from *mare*, *mari-* 'sea' + **culture**, on the pattern of words such as *agriculture*.

Ma·rie An·toi·nette /mə'rē ,ant(w)ə'net, ,äntwä'net/ (1755–93), French queen; wife of Louis XVI. A daughter of Maria Theresa, she married the future Louis XVI of France in 1770. Her extravagant lifestyle led to widespread unpopularity and, like her husband, she was executed during the French Revolution.

Ma·rie Byrd Land /mə'rē bərd/ a region of Antarctica that borders on the Pacific Ocean, between Ellsworth Land and the Ross Sea.
– ORIGIN named after the wife of Richard E. *Byrd*, the US naval commander who explored the region in 1933–34.

Ma·rie Ce·leste /mə'rē sə'lest/ see **Mary Celeste**.

Ma·rie de Mé·di·cis /mä'rē də mādē'sēs/ (1573–1642), queen of France; Italian name *Maria de' Medici*. The second wife of Henry IV of France, she ruled as regent during the minority of her son Louis XIII (1610–17) and retained her influence after her son came to power.

Ma·ri El /'märē 'el/ an autonomous republic in European Russia, north of the Volga River; pop. 700,900 (est. 2009); capital, Yoshkar-Ola. Also called **Mari Autonomous Republic**.

m

Mar·i·et·ta /,marē'etə/ a city in northwestern Georgia, a northwestern suburb of Atlanta; pop. 67,562 (est. 2008).

mar·i·gold /'mari,gōld/ ▶ **n.** a plant of the daisy family, typically with yellow, orange, or copper-brown flowers, that is widely cultivated as an ornamental. ● Genera *Tagetes* (the **French** and **African marigolds**) and *Calendula* (the **common** (or **pot**) **marigold**), family Compositae. ■ used in names of other plants with yellow flowers, e.g., **corn marigold**, **marsh marigold**.
– ORIGIN late Middle English: from the given name *Mary* (probably referring to the Virgin) + dialect *gold*, denoting the corn or garden marigold in Old English.

ma·ri·jua·na /,marə'(h)wänə/ (also **marihuana**) ▶ **n.** cannabis, esp. as smoked in cigarettes.
– ORIGIN late 19th cent.: from Latin American Spanish.

ma·rim·ba /mə'rimbə/ ▶ **n.** a deep-toned xylophone of African origin. The modern form was developed in the US *c.*1910.
– ORIGIN early 18th cent.: from Kimbundu, perhaps via Portuguese.

ma·ri·na /mə'rēnə/ ▶ **n.** a specially designed harbor with moorings for pleasure craft and small boats.
– ORIGIN early 19th cent.: from Italian or Spanish, feminine of *marino*, from Latin *marinus* (see **marine**).

mar·i·nade /,marə'nād/ ▶ **n.** a sauce, typically made of oil, vinegar, spices, and herbs, in which meat, fish, or other food is soaked before cooking in order to flavor or soften it. ■ [with modifier] a dish prepared using such a mixture: *a chicken marinade*.
▶ **v.** also /'marə,nād/ another term for **marinate**.
– ORIGIN late 17th cent. (as a verb): from French, from Spanish *marinada*, via *marinar* 'pickle in brine' from *marino* (see **marina**).

ma·ri·na·ra /,marə'narə, ,märə'närə/ ▶ **n.** [usu. as modifier] (in Italian cooking) a sauce made from tomatoes, onions, and herbs, served esp. with pasta.
– ORIGIN from the Italian phrase *alla marinara* 'sailor-style.'

mar·i·nate /'marə,nāt/ ▶ **v.** [with obj.] soak (meat, fish, or other food) in a marinade: *the beef was marinated in red wine vinegar*. ■ [no obj.] (of food) undergo such a process.
– DERIVATIVES **mar·i·na·tion** /,marə'nāSHən/ **n.**
– ORIGIN mid 17th cent.: from Italian *marinare* 'pickle in brine,' or from French *mariner* (from *marine* 'brine').

Ma·rin Coun·ty /mə'rin/ a county that includes many affluent suburbs in northwestern California, across the Golden Gate from San Francisco; pop. 248,794 (est. 2008).

ma·rine /mə'rēn/ ▶ **adj.** of, found in, or produced by the sea: *marine plants* | *marine biology*. ■ of or relating to shipping or naval matters: *marine insurance*. ■ (of artists or painting) depicting scenes at sea: *marine painters*.
▶ **n.** a member of a body of troops trained to serve on land or at sea, in particular a member of the US Marine Corps.
– PHRASES **tell that** (or **it**) **to the marines** a scornful expression of disbelief. [from the saying *that will do for the marines but the sailors won't believe it*, referring to the *horse marines*, an imaginary corps of cavalrymen employed to serve as marines (thus out of their element).]
– ORIGIN Middle English (as a noun in the sense 'seashore'): from Old French *marin*, *marine*, from Latin *marinus*, from *mare* 'sea.'

Ma·rine Corps /mə'rēn kô(ə)r/ a branch of the US armed services (part of the US Navy), founded in 1775 and trained to operate on land and at sea.

ma·rine i·gua·na ▶ **n.** a large lizard with webbed feet that swims strongly and feeds on marine algae. It is native to the Galapagos Islands and is the only marine lizard. ● *Amblyrhynchus cristatus*, family Iguanidae.

Ma·rine One the helicopter used by the president of the US.

Mar·i·ner /'marənər/ a series of American space probes launched in 1962–77 to investigate the planets Venus, Mars, and Mercury.

mar·i·ner /'marənər/ ▶ **n.** a sailor.
– ORIGIN Middle English: from Old French *marinier*, from medieval Latin *marinarius*, from Latin *marinus* (see **marine**).

ma·rine toad ▶ **n.** another term for **cane toad**.

Ma·ri·net·ti /,marə'netē, ,mär-/, Filippo Tommaso (1876–1944), Italian poet and playwright. He launched the futurist movement with a manifesto in 1909 that exalted technology, glorified war, and demanded revolution in the arts.

Ma·ri·no /mə'rēnō/, Dan (1961–) US football player; full name *Daniel Constantine Marino, Jr.* He was the quarterback for the Miami Dolphins 1983–2000.

Mar·i·ol·a·try /,me(ə)rē'älətrē/ ▶ **n.** idolatrous worship of the Virgin Mary.
– ORIGIN early 17th cent.: from *Maria* (Latin equivalent of 'Mary') + **-latry**, on the pattern of *idolatry*.

Mar·i·ol·o·gy /,me(ə)rē'äləjē/ ▶ **n.** the part of Christian theology dealing with the Virgin Mary.
– DERIVATIVES **Mar·i·o·log·i·cal** /,me(ə)rēə'läjikəl/ **adj.**, **Mar·i·ol·o·gist** /-jist/ **n.**

Mar·i·on, Francis (c.1732–1795), American Revolutionary commander; known as the **Swamp Fox**. He commanded militia troops in South Carolina and evaded the British by hiding in swamps and woods.

mar·i·on·ette /,marēə'net/ ▶ **n.** a puppet worked from above by strings attached to its limbs.
– ORIGIN early 17th cent.: from French *marionnette*, from *Marion*, diminutive of the given name *Marie*.

marionette

mar·i·po·sa lil·y /,marə'pōsə, -'pōzə/ (also **mariposa tulip**) ▶ **n.** a plant of the lily family, with brightly colored cup-shaped flowers, native to Mexico and the western US. Closely related to the **sego**. ● Genus *Calochortus*, family Liliaceae: several species.
– ORIGIN mid 19th cent.: *mariposa* from Spanish, literally 'butterfly.'

Mar·is /'maris/, Roger (Eugene) (1934–85), US baseball player. A New York Yankees right fielder, he broke Babe Ruth's record for most home runs in a season (60 in 1927) by hitting 61 in 1961.

Mar·ist /'me(ə)rəst, 'mar-/ ▶ **n.** **1** (also **Marist Father**) a member of the Society of Mary, a Roman Catholic missionary and teaching congregation. **2** (also **Marist Brother**) a member of the Little Brothers of Mary, a Roman Catholic teaching congregation.
– ORIGIN late 19th cent.: from French *Mariste*, from the given name *Marie*, equivalent of *Mary*.

mar·i·tal /'maritl/ ▶ **adj.** of or relating to marriage or the relations between husband and wife: *marital fidelity*.
– DERIVATIVES **mar·i·tal·ly adv.**
– ORIGIN early 16th cent.: from Latin *maritalis*, from *maritus* 'husband.'

mar·i·tal rape ▶ **n.** sexual intercourse forced on a woman by her husband, knowingly against her will.

mar·i·tal sta·tus ▶ **n.** a person's state of being single, married, separated, divorced, or widowed.

mar·i·time /'mari,tīm/ ▶ **adj.** connected with the sea, esp. in relation to seafaring commercial or military activity: *a maritime museum* | *maritime law*. ■ living or found in or near the sea: *dolphins and other maritime mammals*. ■ bordering on the sea: *two species of Diptera occur in the maritime Antarctic*. ■ denoting a climate that is moist and temperate owing to the influence of the sea.
– ORIGIN mid 16th cent.: from Latin *maritimus*, from *mare* 'sea.'

mar·i·time pine ▶ **n.** a pine tree with long, thick needles and clustered cones, native to the coasts of the Mediterranean and Iberia. ● *Pinus pinaster*, family Pinaceae.

Mar·i·time Prov·inc·es (also **the Maritimes**) the Canadian provinces of New Brunswick, Nova Scotia, and Prince Edward Island, with coastlines on the Gulf of St. Lawrence and the Atlantic Oceans. Compare with **Atlantic Provinces**.

Ma·ri·tsa /mə'rētsə/ a river in southern Europe that rises in southwestern Bulgaria and flows 300 miles (480 km) south to the Aegean Sea. It forms the border between Bulgaria and Greece and between Greece and Turkey. Its ancient name is the Hebros or Hebrus. Turkish name **Meriç**; Greek name **Évros**.

Ma·ri·u·pol /,märē'ōōpəl/ an industrial port on the southern coast of Ukraine, on the Sea of Azov; pop. 472,000 (est. 2009). Former name (1948–89) **Zhdanov**.

Mar·i·us /'me(ə)rēəs, 'mar-/, Gaius (*c.*157–86 BC), Roman general and politician. Elected consul in 107 BC, he defeated Jugurtha and invading Germanic tribes. After a power struggle with Sulla he was expelled from Italy, but returned to take Rome by force in 87 BC.

mar·jo·ram /'märjərəm/ ▶ **n.** (also **sweet marjoram**) an aromatic southern European plant of the mint family, the leaves of which are used as a culinary herb. ● *Origanum majorana*, family Labiatae. ■ (also **wild marjoram**) another term for **oregano**.
– ORIGIN late Middle English: from Old French *majorane*, from medieval Latin *majorana*, of unknown ultimate origin.

mark[1] /märk/ ▶ **n.** **1** a small area on a surface having a different color from its surroundings, typically one caused by accident or damage: *the blow left a red mark down one side of her face*. ■ a spot, area, or feature on a person's or animal's body by which they may be identified or recognized: *he was five feet nine, with no distinguishing marks*.
2 a line, figure, or symbol made as an indication or record of something. ■ a written symbol made on a document in place of a signature by someone who cannot write. ■ a level or stage that is considered significant: *unemployment had passed the two million mark*. ■ a sign or indication of a quality or feeling: *the flag was at half-mast as a mark of respect*. ■ a characteristic property or feature: *it is the mark of a civilized society to treat its elderly members well*. ■ a competitor's starting point in a race. ■ Nautical a piece of material or a knot used to indicate a depth on a sounding line. ■ Telecommunications one of two possible states of a signal in certain systems. The opposite of **space**.
3 a point awarded for a correct answer or for proficiency in an examination or competition: *many candidates lose marks because they don't read the questions carefully* | figurative *full marks to them for highlighting the threat to the rain forest*. ■ a figure or letter representing the total of such points and signifying a person's score: *the highest mark was 98 percent*. ■ (esp. in track and field) a time or distance achieved by a competitor, esp. one which represents a record or personal best.
4 (followed by a numeral) a particular model or type of a vehicle, machine, or device: *a Mark 10 Jaguar*.
5 a target: *few bullets could have missed their mark*. ■ informal a person who is easily deceived or taken advantage of: *they figure I'm an easy mark*.
▶ **v.** [with obj.] **1** make (a visible impression or stain) on: *he fingered the photograph gently, careful not to mark it*. ■ [no obj.] become stained: *it is made from a sort of woven surface which doesn't mark or tear*.

2 write a word or symbol on (an object), typically for identification: *she marked all her possessions with her name* | [with obj. and complement] *an envelope marked "private and confidential."* ■ write (a word or figure) on an object: *she* **marked** *the date* **down** *on a card.* ■ (**mark something off**) put a line by or through something written or printed on paper to indicate that it has passed or been dealt with: *he marked off their names in a ledger.*
3 show the position of: *the top of the pass marks the border between Alaska and the Yukon.* ■ separate or delineate (a particular section or area of something): *you need to* **mark out** *the part of the garden where the sun lingers longest.* ■ (of a particular quality or feature) separate or distinguish (someone or something) from other people or things: *his sword* **marked** *him* **out** *as an officer.* ■ (**mark someone out for**) select or destine someone for (a particular role or condition): *the solicitor general marked him out for government office.* ■ (**mark someone down as**) judge someone to be (a particular type or class of person): *she had marked him down as a liberal.* ■ acknowledge, honor, or celebrate (an important event or occasion) with a particular action: *to mark its fiftieth anniversary, the group held a fashion show.* ■ be an indication of (a significant occasion, stage, or development): *the move to the new Globe theatre marked a new phase in Shakespeare's writing career.* ■ (usu. **be marked**) characterize as having a particular quality or feature: *the reaction to these developments has been marked by a note of hysteria.* ■ chiefly Brit. (of a clock or watch) show (a certain time): *his watch marked five past eight.*
4 (of a teacher or examiner) assess the standard of (a piece of written work) by assigning points for proficiency or correct answers: *the teachers are given adequate time to mark term papers.* ■ (**mark someone/something down**) reduce the number of marks awarded to a student, candidate, or their work: *I was marked down for having skipped the last essay question.*
5 notice or pay careful attention to: *he'll leave you, you mark my words!*
6 (of a player in a team game) stay close to (a particular opponent) in order to prevent them getting or passing the ball.
– PHRASES **be quick** (or **slow**) **off the mark** be fast (or slow) in responding to a situation or understanding something. **get off the mark** get started. **leave** (or **make**) **its** (or **one's** or **a**) **mark** have a lasting or significant effect: *she left her mark on the world of foreign policy.* **make one's mark** attain recognition or distinction. **mark time** (of troops) march on the spot without moving forward. ■ pass one's time in routine activities until a more favorable or interesting opportunity presents itself. **mark you** chiefly Brit. used to emphasize or draw attention to a statement: *I was persuaded, against my better judgment, mark you, to vote for him.* **near** (or **close**) **to the mark** almost accurate: *to say he was their legal adviser would be nearer the mark.* **off** (or **wide of**) **the mark** incorrect or inaccurate: *his solutions are completely off the mark.* **of mark** dated having importance or distinction: *he had been a man of mark.* **on the mark** correct; accurate. **on your marks** used to instruct competitors in a race to prepare themselves in the correct starting position: *on your marks, get set, go!* **up to the mark** of the required standard. ■ [usu. with negative] (of a person) as healthy or in as good spirits as usual: *Johnny's not feeling up to the mark at the moment.*
– PHRASAL VERBS **mark something down** (of a retailer) reduce the indicated price of an item. **mark something up 1** (of a retailer) add a certain amount to the cost of goods to cover overhead and profit: *they mark up the price of imported wines by 66 percent.* **2** annotate or correct text for printing, keying, or typesetting.
– ORIGIN Old English *mearc, gemerce* (noun), *mearcian* (verb), of Germanic origin; from an Indo-European root shared by Latin *margo* 'margin.'

mark[2] ▶ **n. 1** the basic monetary unit of Germany (until the introduction of the euro), equal to 100 pfennigs; a Deutschmark or, formerly, an Ostmark.
2 a former English and Scottish money of account, equal to thirteen shillings and four pence in the currency of the day. ■ a denomination of weight for gold and silver, formerly used throughout western Europe and typically equal to 8 ounces (226.8 grams).
– ORIGIN Old English *marc*, from Old Norse *mǫrk*; probably related to MARK[1].

Mark, St. /märk/ an Apostle; companion of St. Peter and St. Paul; traditional author of the second Gospel. Feast day, April 25. ■ the second Gospel, the earliest in date (see GOSPEL (sense 2).

Mark An·to·ny see ANTONY.

mark·down /ˈmärkˌdoun/ ▶ **n.** a reduction in price.

marked /märkt/ ▶ **adj. 1** having a visible mark: *plants with beautifully marked leaves.* ■ (of playing cards) having distinctive marks on their backs to assist cheating. ■ Linguistics (of words or forms) distinguished by a particular feature: *the word "drake" is semantically marked as masculine; the unmarked form is "duck."*
2 clearly noticeable; evident: *a marked increase in sales.*
– DERIVATIVES **mark·ed·ness** /ˈmärkidnis/ **n.**

mark·ed·ly /ˈmärkidlē/ ▶ **adv.** to an extent that is clearly noticeable; significantly: *new diagnoses have increased markedly since 1998* | [as submodifier] *this advice is markedly different to that last year.*

marked man ▶ **n.** a person who is singled out for special treatment, esp. to be harmed or killed.

mark·er /ˈmärkər/ ▶ **n. 1** an object used to indicate a position, place, or route: *they erected a granite marker at the crash site* | [as modifier] *marker posts* | figurative *the most portable marker of class privilege, the wearing of natural fibers.* ■ a thing serving as a standard of comparison or as an indication of what may be expected: *such studies may provide a unique marker in the quest to understand the brain.* ■ a radio beacon used to guide the pilot of an aircraft. ■ informal a promissory note; an IOU: *Phyllis owed a marker in the neighborhood of $100,000.*
2 a felt-tip pen with a broad tip.
3 (chiefly in soccer) a player who is assigned to mark a particular opponent.
4 Brit. a person who records the score in a game, esp. in snooker or billiards.

mar·ket /ˈmärkit/ ▶ **n. 1** a regular gathering of people for the purchase and sale of provisions, livestock, and other commodities: *farmers* **going to market**. ■ an open space or covered building where vendors convene to sell their goods.
2 an area or arena in which commercial dealings are conducted: *the sale of cruisers in the American market continues to plummet* | *the labor market.* ■ a demand for a particular commodity or service: *there is* **a market for** *ornamental daggers.* ■ the state of trade at a particular time or in a particular context: *the bottom's fallen out of the market.* ■ the free market; the operation of supply and demand: *future development cannot simply be left to the market* | [as modifier] *a market economy.* ■ a stock market.
▶ **v.** (**markets, marketing, marketed**) [with obj.] advertise or promote (something): *the product was marketed under the name "aspirin."* ■ offer for sale: *sheep farmers are still unable to market their lambs.* ■ [no obj.] buy or sell provisions in a market: (as noun **marketing**) *some people liked to do their marketing very early in the morning.*
– PHRASES **be in the market for** wish to buy. **make a market** Finance take part in active dealing in particular shares or other assets. **on the market** available for sale: *he bought every new gadget as it* **came on the market**.
– DERIVATIVES **mar·ket·er n.**
– ORIGIN Middle English, via Anglo-Norman French from Latin *mercatus*, from *mercari* 'buy' (see also MERCHANT).

mar·ket·a·ble /ˈmärkitəbəl/ ▶ **adj.** able or fit to be sold or marketed: *the fish are perfectly marketable.* ■ in demand: *marketable skills.*
– DERIVATIVES **mar·ket·a·bil·i·ty** /ˌmärkitəˈbilətē/ **n.**

mar·ket·eer /ˌmärkəˈti(ə)r/ ▶ **n.** a person who sells goods or services in a market: *a consumer-goods marketeer.* ■ [with adj.] a person who works in or advocates a particular type of market: *free-marketeers.*

mar·ket forc·es ▶ **plural n.** the economic factors affecting the price, demand, and availability of a commodity: *leaving oil prices to be determined purely by market forces.*

mar·ket gar·den ▶ **n.** British term for TRUCK FARM.
– DERIVATIVES **mar·ket gar·den·er n., mar·ket gar·den·ing n.**

mar·ket·ing /ˈmärkitiNG/ ▶ **n.** the action or business of promoting and selling products or services, including market research and advertising.

mar·ket·ing mix ▶ **n.** a combination of factors that can be controlled by a company to influence consumers to purchase its products.

mar·ket·i·za·tion /ˌmärkitəˈzāSHən/ ▶ **n.** the exposure of an industry or service to market forces. ■ the conversion of a national economy from a planned to a market economy: *the marketization of the Russian economy.*
– DERIVATIVES **mar·ket·ize** /ˈmärkiˌtīz/ **v.**

mar·ket lead·er ▶ **n.** the company selling the largest quantity of a particular type of product. ■ a product that outsells its competitors.

mar·ket mak·er ▶ **n.** a dealer in securities or other assets who undertakes to buy or sell at specified prices at all times.

mar·ket·place /ˈmärkətˌplās/ ▶ **n.** an open space where a market is or was formerly held in a town. ■ the arena of competitive or commercial dealings; the world of trade: *the changing demands of the global marketplace.*

mar·ket price ▶ **n.** the price of a commodity when sold in a given market: *the world market price for nonfat dry milk.*

mar·ket re·search ▶ **n.** the action or activity of gathering information about consumers' needs and preferences.
– DERIVATIVES **mar·ket re·search·er n.**

mar·ket share ▶ **n.** the portion of a market controlled by a particular company or product.

mar·ket tim·er ▶ **n.** Finance a person or organization that makes decisions to buy or sell investments based on economic and other factors that might affect the direction of the market.
– DERIVATIVES **mar·ket tim·ing n.**

mar·ket town /ˈmärkət ˌtoun/ ▶ **n.** a town of moderate size in a rural area, where a regular market is held.

mar·ket val·ue ▶ **n.** the amount for which something can be sold on a given market. Often contrasted with BOOK VALUE.

mar·khor /ˈmärˌkôr/ ▶ **n.** a large wild goat with very long twisted horns, native to central Asia. ● *Capra falconeri*, family Bovidae.
– ORIGIN mid 19th cent.: from Persian *mār-ḵwār*, from *mār* 'serpent' + *ḵwār* '-eating.'

mark·ing /ˈmärkiNG/ ▶ **n.** (usu. **markings**) an identification mark, esp. a mark or pattern of marks on an animal's fur, feathers, or skin: *the distinctive black-and-white markings on its head.* ■ Music a word or symbol on a score indicating the correct tempo, dynamic, or other aspect of performance.

mark·ka /ˈmär(k)ˌkä/ ▶ **n.** (pl. **markkaa** /-kä/) the basic monetary unit of Finland (until replaced by the euro), equal to 100 penniä.
– ORIGIN Finnish.

Mar·ko·va /märˈkōvə/, Dame Alicia (1910–2004), British ballet dancer; born *Lilian Alicia Marks*. She made her debut with the Ballets Russes in 1924, established the Markova-Dolin Company in London with Anton Dolin (1904–83) in 1935, and was prima ballerina with the London Festival Ballet 1950–52. She directed the Metropolitan Opera Ballet 1963–69.

Mar·kov chain /ˈmärˌkôf, -ˌkôv/ (also **Markov model**) ▶ **n.** Statistics a stochastic model describing a sequence of possible events in which the probability of each event depends only on the state attained in the previous event.
– ORIGIN mid 20th cent.: named after Andrei A. *Markov* (1856–1922), Russian mathematician.

marks·man /ˈmärksmən/ ▶ **n.** (pl. **marksmen**) a person skilled in shooting, esp. with a pistol or rifle: *a police marksman.*
– DERIVATIVES **marks·man·ship** /-ˌSHip/ **n.**

marks·wom·an /ˈmärksˌwoŏmən/ ▶ **n.** (pl. **markswomen**) a woman skilled in shooting, esp. with a pistol or rifle.

mark-to-mar·ket ▶ **adj.** Finance denoting or relating to a system of valuing assets by the most recent market price.

mark·up /ˈmärˌkəp/ ▶ **n. 1** the amount added to the cost price of goods to cover overhead and profit.
2 the process or result of correcting text in preparation for printing. ■ the process of making the final changes in a legislative bill: *the bill concerning acid rain is* **in markup**.
3 Computing a set of tags assigned to elements of a text to indicate their relation to the rest of the text or dictate how they should be displayed.

marl /märl/ ▶ **n.** an unconsolidated sedimentary rock or soil consisting of clay and lime, formerly used typically as fertilizer.
▶ **v.** [with obj.] apply marl to.
– DERIVATIVES **marl·y adj.**
– ORIGIN Middle English: from Old French *marle*, from medieval Latin *margila*, from Latin *marga*, of Celtic origin.

Marl·bor·ough[1] /ˈmärlˌbərō, -ˌbərə/ an industrial city in east central Massachusetts; pop. 37,932 (est. 2008).

Marl·bor·ough[2], John Churchill, 1st Duke of (1650–1722), British general. He was commander of British and Dutch troops in the War of the Spanish Succession and won a series of victories (notably at Blenheim in 1704) over the French armies of Louis XIV.

m

Mar·ley /ˈmärlē/, Bob (1945–81), Jamaican reggae singer, guitarist, and songwriter; full name *Robert Nesta Marley*. Instrumental in popularizing reggae in the 1970s, his lyrics often reflected his commitment to Rastafarianism.

mar·lin /ˈmärlən/ ▶ **n.** a large edible billfish of warm seas that is a highly prized game fish and typically reaches a great weight. ● Genera *Makaira* and *Tetrapterus*, family Istiophoridae: several species, including the **striped marlin** (*T. audax*).
– ORIGIN early 20th cent.: from MARLINSPIKE (with reference to its pointed snout).

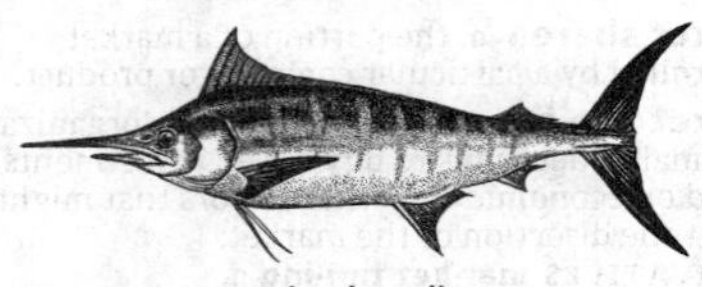
striped marlin

mar·line /ˈmärlən/ ▶ **n.** Nautical light two-stranded rope.
– ORIGIN late Middle English: from Middle Low German *marling*, with the ending influenced by LINE[1].

mar·lin·spike /ˈmärlənˌspīk/ (also **marlinespike**) ▶ **n.** a pointed metal tool used by sailors to separate strands of rope or wire, esp. in splicing.
– ORIGIN early 17th cent. (originally as *marling spike*): from *marling*, present participle of *marl* 'fasten with marline' (from Dutch *marlen* 'keep binding') + SPIKE[1].

Mar·lowe /ˈmärlō/, Christopher (1564–93), English playwright and poet whose work influenced Shakespeare's early historical plays. Notable plays: *Doctor Faustus* (c.1590) and *The Jew of Malta* (1592).

marm /märm/ ▶ **n.** dated variant spelling of MA'AM.

mar·ma·lade /ˈmärməˌlād/ ▶ **n.** a preserve made from citrus fruit, esp. bitter oranges, prepared like jam.
– ORIGIN late 15th cent.: from Portuguese *marmelada* 'quince jam,' from *marmelo* 'quince,' based on Greek *melimēlon* (from *meli* 'honey' + *mēlon* 'apple').

Mar·ma·ra, Sea of /ˈmärmərə/ a small sea in northwestern Turkey. Connected by the Bosporus to the Black Sea and by the Dardanelles to the Aegean Sea, it separates European Turkey from Asian Turkey. In ancient times it was known as the Propontis.

mar·mite /ˈmärˌmīt/ ▶ **n.** an earthenware cooking container.
– ORIGIN early 19th cent.: French, from Old French *marmite* 'hypocritical,' with reference to the hidden contents of the lidded pot, from *marmotter* 'to mutter' + *mite* 'cat.'

mar·mo·re·al /märˈmôrēəl/ ▶ **adj.** literary made of or likened to marble.
– DERIVATIVES **mar·mo·re·al·ly adv.**
– ORIGIN late 18th cent.: from Latin *marmoreus* (from *marmor* 'marble') + -AL.

mar·mo·set /ˈmärməˌset, -ˌzet/ ▶ **n.** a small Central and South American monkey with a silky coat and a long nonprehensile tail. ● Family Callitrichidae (or Callithricidae): genus *Callithrix* (three species), and the **pygmy marmoset** (*Cebuella pygmaea*).
– ORIGIN late Middle English (also in the sense 'grotesque figure'): from Old French *marmouset* 'grotesque image,' of unknown ultimate origin.

mar·mot /ˈmärmət/ ▶ **n.** a heavily built, gregarious, burrowing rodent of both Eurasia and North America, typically living in mountainous country. ● Genus *Marmota*, family Sciuridae: several species.
– ORIGIN early 17th cent.: from French *marmotte*, probably via Romansh *murmont* from late Latin *mus montanus* 'mountain mouse'; compare with French *marmotter* 'mutter through the teeth.'

Marne /märn/ a river in east central France that rises north of Dijon and flows 328 miles (525 km) north and then west to join the Seine River near Paris. Its valley was the scene of two World War I battles. The first (September 1914) halted and repelled the German advance on Paris; the second (July 1918) ended the final German offensive.

mar·o·cain /ˌmärəˈkān/ ▶ **n.** a dress fabric of ribbed crepe, made of silk or wool or both.
– ORIGIN 1920s: from French, literally 'Moroccan,' from *Maroc* 'Morocco.'

Mar·o·nite /ˈme(ə)rəˌnīt/ ▶ **n.** a member of a Christian sect of Syrian origin that is in communion with the Roman Catholic Church and living chiefly in Lebanon.
▶ **adj.** [attrib.] of or relating to the Maronites.
– ORIGIN early 16th cent.: from medieval Latin *Maronita*, from the name of John *Maro*, a 7th-cent. Syrian religious leader, who may have been the first Maronite patriarch.

Ma·roon /məˈroon/ ▶ **n.** a member of any of various communities in parts of the Caribbean who were originally descended from escaped slaves. In the 18th century Jamaican Maroons fought two wars against the British settlers, both of which ended with treaties affirming the independence of the Maroons.
– ORIGIN mid 17th cent.: from French *marron* 'feral,' from Spanish *cimarrón* 'wild,' (as a noun) 'escaped slave'; compare with SEMINOLE.

ma·roon[1] /məˈroon/ ▶ **adj.** of a brownish-crimson color.
▶ **n. 1** a brownish-crimson color.
2 chiefly Brit. a firework that makes a loud bang, used mainly as a signal or warning. [early 19th cent.: so named because the firework makes the noise of a chestnut (see below) bursting in the fire.]
– ORIGIN late 17th cent. (in the sense 'chestnut'): from French *marron* 'chestnut,' via Italian from medieval Greek *maraon*. The sense relating to color dates from the late 18th cent.

ma·roon[2] ▶ **v.** [with obj.] leave (someone) trapped and isolated in an inaccessible place, esp. an island: *a novel about schoolboys marooned on a desert island.*
– ORIGIN early 18th cent.: from MAROON, originally in the form *marooned* 'lost in the wilds.'

Mar·quand /ˌmärˈkwänd/, J. P. (1893–1960), US writer; full name *John Phillips Marquand*. He created the character Mr. Moto, a Japanese detective featured in several of his novels, such as *Last Laugh, Mr. Moto* (1942). His other works include *The Late George Apley* (1937), *Point of No Return* (1949), and *Women and Thomas Harrow* (1958).

marque[1] /märk/ ▶ **n.** a make of car, as distinct from a specific model.
– ORIGIN early 20th cent.: from French, back-formation from *marquer* 'to brand,' of Scandinavian origin.

marque[2] ▶ **n.** see LETTER OF MARQUE.

mar·quee /märˈkē/ ▶ **n. 1** a rooflike projection over the entrance to a theater, hotel, or other building. ■ [as modifier] leading; preeminent: *a marquee player.* [with allusion to the practice of billing the name of an entertainer on the *marquee* (i.e., awning) over the entrance to a theater.]
2 chiefly Brit. a large tent used for social or commercial functions.
– ORIGIN late 17th cent.: from MARQUISE, taken as plural and assimilated to -EE.

mar·que·sa /märˈkāzə/ ▶ **n.** a Spanish marchioness.
– ORIGIN Spanish.

Mar·que·san /märˈkāzən/ ▶ **n. 1** a native or inhabitant of the Marquesas Islands, esp. a member of the aboriginal Polynesian inhabitants.
2 the Polynesian language of this people.
▶ **adj.** of or relating to the Marquesans or their language.

Mar·que·sas Is·lands /ˈmärkēsəz/ a group of volcanic islands in the South Pacific Ocean that forms part of French Polynesia; pop. 8,658 (2007). They were annexed by France in 1842. The largest island, Hiva Oa, is where painter Paul Gauguin spent the last two years of his life.

mar·quess /ˈmärkwəs/ ▶ **n.** a British nobleman ranking above an earl and below a duke. Compare with MARQUIS.
– ORIGIN early 16th cent.: variant of MARQUIS.

mar·que·try /ˈmärkətrē/ (also **marqueterie** or **marquetery**) ▶ **n.** inlaid work made from small pieces of variously colored wood or other materials, used chiefly for the decoration of furniture.
– ORIGIN mid 16th cent.: from French *marqueterie*, from *marqueter* 'to variegate.'

Mar·quette[1] /märˈket/ a port city in the Upper Peninsula in Michigan, on Lake Superior; pop. 20,916 (est. 2008).

Mar·quette[2], Jacques (1637–75), French Jesuit missionary and explorer. Arriving in Canada in 1666, he played a prominent part in the attempt to Christianize the American Indians. He explored the Wisconsin, Mississippi, and Illinois rivers.

Már·quez, Gabriel García, see GARCÍA MÁRQUEZ.

mar·quis /märˈkē, ˈmärkwəs/ ▶ **n.** (in some European countries) a nobleman ranking above a count and below a duke. Compare with MARQUESS. ■ another term for MARQUESS.
– ORIGIN Middle English: from Old French *marchis*, reinforced by Old French *marquis*, both from the base of MARCH[2].

mar·quis·ate /ˈmärkwəsət/ ▶ **n.** the rank or dignity of a marquess or marquis. ■ the territorial lordship or possessions of a marquis or margrave.
– ORIGIN early 16th cent.: from MARQUIS, on the pattern of words such as French *marquisat*, Italian *marchesato*.

Mar·quis de Sade /märˈkē də ˈsäd/ see SADE.

mar·quise /märˈkēz/ ▶ **n. 1** the wife or widow of a marquis. Compare with MARCHIONESS. ■ a woman holding the rank of marquis in her own right.
2 a finger ring set with a pointed oval gem or cluster of gems.
3 archaic term for MARQUEE (sense 2).
4 a chilled dessert similar to a chocolate mousse.
– ORIGIN early 17th cent.: French, feminine of MARQUIS.

mar·qui·sette /ˌmärk(w)əˈzet/ ▶ **n.** a fine light cotton, rayon, or silk gauze fabric, now chiefly used for net curtains.
– ORIGIN early 20th cent.: from French, diminutive of MARQUISE.

Mar·ra·kech /ˌmarəˈkesн, ˈmarəˌkesн, məˈrä-/ (also **Marrakesh**) a city in western Morocco, in the foothills of the High Atlas Mountains; pop. 1,070,838 (2004). It was founded in 1062 as the capital of the Almoravids.

mar·ram grass /ˈmarəm/ (also **marram**) ▶ **n.** a coarse grass of coastal sand dunes that binds the loose sand with its tough rhizomes, found in Europe, North America, and Australia. ● *Ammophila arenaria*, family Gramineae.
– ORIGIN mid 17th cent.: from Old Norse *marálmr*, from *marr* 'sea' + *hálmr* 'haulm.'

Mar·ra·no /məˈränō/ ▶ **n.** (pl. **Marranos**) (in medieval Spain) a Christianized Jew or Moor, esp. one who merely professed conversion in order to avoid persecution.
– ORIGIN Spanish, of unknown origin.

mar·riage /ˈmarij/ ▶ **n. 1** the formal union of a man and a woman, typically recognized by law, by which they become husband and wife: *a happy marriage* | *the children from his first marriage.* ■ the state of being married: *women want equality in marriage.* ■ informal a similar union between partners of the same sex: *gay marriage.*
2 a combination or mixture of two or more elements: *a marriage of jazz, pop, blues, and gospel.* ■ (in pinochle and other card games) a combination of a king and queen of the same suit.
– PHRASES **by marriage** as a result of a marriage: *a distant cousin by marriage.* **in marriage** as husband or wife: *he asked my father for my hand in marriage.* **marriage of convenience** a marriage concluded to achieve a practical purpose.
– ORIGIN Middle English: from Old French *mariage*, from *marier* 'marry.'

mar·riage·a·ble /ˈmarijəbəl/ ▶ **adj.** fit, suitable, or attractive for marriage, esp. in being of the right age.
– DERIVATIVES **mar·riage·a·bil·i·ty** /ˌmarijəˈbilitē/ **n.**

mar·riage bro·ker ▶ **n.** (in a culture where arranged marriages are customary) a person who arranges marriages for a fee.

mar·riage li·cense ▶ **n.** a copy of the record of a legal marriage, with details of names, date, etc.

mar·riage por·tion ▶ **n.** see PORTION.

mar·ried /ˈmarēd/ ▶ **adj.** (of two people) united in marriage: *a married couple.* ■ (of one person) having a husband or wife: *a happily married man.* ■ of or relating to marriage: *married life.* ■ closely combined or linked: *in the seventeenth century, science was still married to religion.*
▶ **plural n.** (**marrieds**) a married person: *we were young marrieds during World War Two.*

Mar·ri·ott /ˈme(ə)rēˌət/, J. Willard (1900–1985), US businessman; full name *John Willard Marriott*. He founded the Marriott hotel chain, which began in 1927 with a Hot Shoppe in Washington, DC. Presidential Medal of Freedom (posthumously, 1988).

mar·ron gla·cé /maˈrôɴ gläˈsā/ ▶ **n.** (pl. **marrons glacés** pronunc. **same**) a chestnut preserved in and coated with sugar.
– ORIGIN French, 'iced chestnut.'

mar·row /ˈmarō/ ▶ **n. 1** (also **bone marrow**) a soft fatty substance in the cavities of bones, in which blood cells are produced (often taken as typifying strength and vitality).
2 (also **vegetable marrow**) Brit. a white-fleshed green-skinned gourd, which is eaten as a vegetable.
– PHRASES **to the marrow** to one's innermost being: *a sight which chilled me to the marrow.*
– DERIVATIVES **mar·row·less adj.**, **mar·row·y adj.**
– ORIGIN Old English *mearg, mærg*, denoting the plant that produces vegetable marrow, of Germanic origin; related to Dutch *merg* and German *Mark*. Sense 1 dates from the early 19th cent.

mar·row·bone /ˈmarōˌbōn/ ▶ **n.** a bone containing edible marrow. ■ (**marrowbones**) dated, humorous the knees.

mar·row·fat pea /ˈmarōˌfat/ ▶ **n.** a pea of a large variety that is processed and sold in cans.

mar·ry[1] /ˈmarē/ ▶ **v.** (**marries, marrying, married**) [with obj.] **1** join in marriage: *I was married in church* |

the priest who married us | he was engaged to get ***married to*** *Ginger.* ■ take (someone) as one's wife or husband in marriage: *Eric asked me to marry him.* ■ [no obj.] enter into marriage: *they had no plans to marry.* ■ [no obj.] (**marry into**) become a member of (a family) by marriage. ■ (of a parent or guardian) give (a son or daughter) in marriage, esp. for reasons of expediency: *her parents married her to a wealthy landowner.*
2 cause to meet or fit together; combine: *the two halves are trimmed and* ***married up*** *| the show* ***marries*** *poetry* ***with*** *art.* ■ [no obj.] meet or blend with something: *most Chardonnays don't* ***marry*** *well* ***with*** *salmon.* ■ Nautical splice (ropes) end to end without increasing their girth.
– PHRASES **marry in haste, repent at leisure** proverb those who rush impetuously into marriage may spend a long time regretting having done so. **marry money** informal marry a rich person.
– ORIGIN Middle English: from Old French *marier*, from Latin *maritare*, from *maritus*, literally 'married,' (as a noun) 'husband.'

mar·ry² ▶ **exclam.** archaic expressing surprise, indignation, or emphatic assertion.
– ORIGIN late Middle English: variant of **Mary¹**.

Mar·ry·at /ˈmarēət/, Frederick (1792–1848), English novelist and naval officer; known as **Captain Marryat**. Notable works: *Peter Simple* (1833), *Mr. Midshipman Easy* (1836), *The Children of the New Forest* (1847).

mar·ry·ing /ˈmarē-iNG/ ▶ **adj.** [attrib.] likely or inclined to marry: *I'm not the marrying kind.*

Mars /märz/ **1** Roman Mythology the god of war and the most important Roman god after Jupiter.The month of March is named after him. Greek equivalent **Ares**.
2 Astronomy a small, reddish planet that is the fourth in order from the sun and is periodically visible to the naked eye.

> Mars orbits between earth and Jupiter at an average distance of 141.6 million miles (228 million km) from the sun, and has an equatorial diameter of 4,208 miles (6,787 km). Its characteristic red color arises from the iron-rich minerals covering its surface. There is a tenuous atmosphere of carbon dioxide, and the seasonal polar caps are mainly of frozen carbon dioxide. Unambiguous evidence of life has yet to be found. There are two small satellites, Phobos and Deimos.

Mar·sa·la /märˈsälə/ ▶ **n.** a dark, sweet, fortified dessert wine that resembles sherry, produced in Sicily.
▶ **adj.** [postpositive] cooked or flavored with Marsala: *chicken Marsala.*
– ORIGIN named after *Marsala*, a town in Sicily where it was originally made.

Mar·sal·is /märˈsalis/, Wynton (1961–) US jazz trumpeter. He formed his own group in 1981 and was the first musician to win Grammy awards for both a jazz and a classical recording 1984. He cofounded Jazz at Lincoln Center and served as its artistic director from 1987. He is the brother of saxophonist Branford Marsalis (1960–).

Mar·sanne /märˈsän/ ▶ **n.** a variety of white wine grape originating in the northern Rhône area of France.
– ORIGIN from *Marsanne*, the name of a town in southern France.

Mar·seil·laise /ˌmärseˈyez/ the national anthem of France, written by **Rouget de Lisle** in 1792.
– ORIGIN French, feminine of *Marseillais* 'of Marseilles.'

Mar·seilles /märˈsā/ a city and port on the Mediterranean coast of southern France; pop. 860,363 (2007). French name **Marseille**.

Mars Glob·al Sur·vey·or see **Global Surveyor**.

marsh /märsH/ ▶ **n.** an area of low-lying land that is flooded in wet seasons or at high tide, and typically remains waterlogged at all times.
– ORIGIN Old English *mer(i)sc* (perhaps influenced by late Latin *mariscus* 'marsh'), of West Germanic origin.

mar·shal /ˈmärsHəl/ ▶ **n. 1** an officer of the highest rank in the armed forces of some countries, including France. ■ chiefly historical a high-ranking officer of state.
2 a federal or municipal law officer. ■ the head of a police department. ■ the head of a fire department.
3 an official responsible for supervising public events, esp. sports events or parades.
▶ **v.** (**marshals, marshaling, marshaled**; chiefly Brit. **marshals, marshalling, marshalled**) [with obj.]
1 arrange or assemble (a group of people, esp. soldiers) in order: *the general marshaled his troops |* figurative *he paused for a moment, as if marshaling his thoughts.* ■ [with obj.] correctly position or arrange (rolling stock). ■ [with obj.] guide or direct the movement of (an aircraft) on the ground at an airport.
2 Heraldry combine (coats of arms), typically to indicate marriage, descent, or the bearing of office.
– DERIVATIVES **mar·shal·er** n., **mar·shal·ship** /-ˌsHip/ n.
– ORIGIN Middle English (denoting a high-ranking officer of state): from Old French *mareschal* 'blacksmith, commander,' from late Latin *mariscalcus*, from Germanic elements meaning 'horse' (compare with **mare¹**) and 'servant.'

Mar·shall¹ /ˈmärsHəl/, George Catlett (1880–1959), US general and statesman. A career army officer, he served as chief of staff 1939–45 during World War II. As secretary of state 1947–49, he initiated the program of economic aid to European countries known as the Marshall Plan. Nobel Peace Prize (1953).

Mar·shall², John (1755–1835), US chief justice 1801–35. He is considered the father of the American system of constitutional law, esp. of the doctrine of judicial review.

Mar·shall³, Thurgood (1908–93), US Supreme Court associate justice 1967–91. The first black justice appointed to the US Supreme Court, he had previously won most of the cases he argued before the Court, including the landmark civil rights case *Brown v. Board of Education* in 1954. Known as a liberal, he championed individual rights and affirmative action.

Thurgood Marshall

Mar·shall·ese /ˌmärsHəˈlēz, -ˈlēs/ ▶ **n.** (pl. **same**) **1** a native or inhabitant of the Marshall Islands.
2 the Micronesian language of the Marshall Islands.
▶ **adj.** of or relating to the Marshall Islands, their inhabitants, or their language.

Mar·shall Is·lands (also **the Marshalls**) a country that consists of two chains of islands in the northwestern Pacific Ocean; pop. 64,500 (est. 2009); capital, Majuro; languages, English (official) and local Austronesian languages.

> The islands were made a German protectorate in 1885. After being under Japanese mandate following World War I, they were administered from 1947 until 1986 by the US as part of the Pacific Islands Trust Territory and then became a republic in free association with the US.

– ORIGIN named after John Marshall, an English adventurer who visited the islands in 1788.

Mar·shall Plan /ˈmärsHəl ˈplan/ a program of financial aid and other initiatives, sponsored by the US, designed to boost the economies of western European countries after World War II. It was originally advocated by Secretary of State George C. Marshall and passed by Congress in 1948. Official name **European Recovery Program**.

mar·shal·sea /ˈmärsHəlsē/ ▶ **n.** (in England) a court held before the marshal of the royal household. It was abolished in 1849. ■ (**the Marshalsea**) a former prison in London, used esp. to incarcerate debtors. It was abolished in 1842.
– ORIGIN late Middle English (earlier *marchalcy*): from Anglo-Norman French *marschalcie*, from late Latin *mariscalcia*, from *mariscalcus* 'marshal.'

Marsh Ar·ab ▶ **n.** a member of a seminomadic Arab people inhabiting marshland in southern Iraq, near the confluence of the Tigris and Euphrates rivers.

marsh fern ▶ **n.** a tall, graceful fern that grows in moist meadows and marshes in North America and Eurasia. ● *Thelypteris palustris*, family Thelypteridaceae.

marsh gas ▶ **n.** methane, esp. as generated by decaying matter in marshes. Also called **swamp gas**.

marsh hawk ▶ **n.** another term for **northern harrier**.

marsh·land /ˈmärsHˌland/ ▶ **n.** (also **marshlands**) land consisting of marshes.

marsh·mal·low /ˈmärsHˌmelō, -ˌmalō/ ▶ **n.** a spongy confection made from a soft mixture of sugar, albumen, and gelatin.

marsh mal·low ▶ **n.** a tall pink-flowered plant that typically grows in brackish marshes. The roots were formerly used to make marshmallow, and it is sometimes cultivated for use in medicine. Introduced from Europe, it is found along the coast from Connecticut to Virginia. ● *Althaea officinalis*, family Malvaceae.

marsh mar·i·gold ▶ **n.** a plant of the buttercup family that has large yellow flowers and grows in damp ground and shallow water, native to north temperate regions. Also called **cowslip**. ● *Caltha palustris*, family Ranunculaceae.

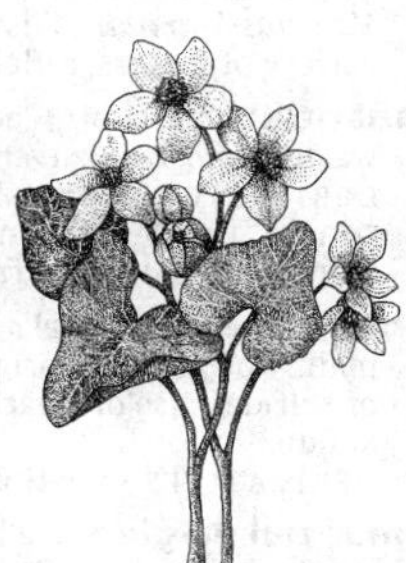
marsh marigold

marsh snail ▶ **n.** any of a number of snails that live in marshy habitats or ponds, in particular: ● an American salt-marsh snail (family Ellobiidae). ● a European freshwater snail (*Galba* (or *Limnaea*) *palustris*, family Limnaeidae).

marsh tread·er /märsH ˈtredər/ ▶ **n.** another term for **water measurer**.

marsh·y /ˈmärsHē/ ▶ **adj.** (**marshier, marshiest**) characteristic of or resembling a marsh; waterlogged: *the marshy ground toward the sea.*
– DERIVATIVES **marsh·i·ness** /ˈmärsHēnis/ n.

Mars Path·find·er see **Pathfinder**.

Mars·ton Moor, Bat·tle of /ˈmärstən/ a battle of the English Civil War, fought in 1644 on Marston Moor near York, in which the Royalists were defeated, fatally weakening Charles I's cause.

mar·su·pi·al /märˈso͞opēəl/ Zoology ▶ **n.** a mammal of an order whose members are born incompletely developed and are typically carried and suckled in a pouch on the mother's belly. Marsupials are found mainly in Australia and New Guinea, although three families, including the opossums, live in America. ● Order Marsupialia and infraclass Metatheria, subclass Theria.
▶ **adj.** of or relating to this order.
– ORIGIN late 17th cent. (in the sense 'resembling a pouch'): from modern Latin *marsupialis*, via Latin from Greek *marsupion* 'pouch' (see **marsupium**).

mar·su·pi·um /märˈso͞opēəm/ ▶ **n.** (pl. **marsupia** /-pēə/) Zoology a pouch that protects eggs, offspring, or reproductive structures, esp. the pouch of a female marsupial mammal.
– ORIGIN mid 17th cent.: via Latin from Greek *marsupion*, diminutive of *marsipos* 'purse.'

Mar·sy·as /ˈmärsēəs/ Greek Mythology a satyr who challenged Apollo to a contest in flute playing and was flayed alive when he lost.

mart /märt/ ▶ **n.** [usu. with modifier] a trade center or market: *Atlanta's downtown apparel marts.*
– ORIGIN late Middle English: from Middle Dutch *mart*, variant of *marct* 'market.'

Mar·ta·ban, Gulf of /ˌmärtəˈbän, -ˈban/ an inlet of the Andaman Sea, a part of the Indian Ocean, on the coast of southeastern Burma (Myanmar) east of Rangoon.

Mar·tel /märˈtel/, Charles, see **Charles Martel**.

Mar·tel·lo /märˈtelō/ (also **Martello tower**) ▶ **n.** (pl. **Martellos**) any of numerous small circular forts that were erected for defense purposes along the southeast coasts of England during the Napoleonic Wars.
– ORIGIN alteration (by association with Italian *martello* 'hammer') of Cape *Mortella* in Corsica, where such a tower proved difficult for the English to capture in 1794.

mar·ten /ˈmärtn/ ▶ **n.** a chiefly arboreal weasellike mammal found in Eurasia and North America, hunted for its fur in many northern countries. ● Genus *Martes*, family Mustelidae: several species. See **pine marten, stone marten**.
– ORIGIN Middle English (frequently in the plural, denoting the fur): from Old French (*peau*) *martrine* 'marten (fur),' from *martre*, of West Germanic origin.

mar·tens·ite /ˈmärtnˌsīt/ ▶ **n.** Metallurgy a hard and very brittle solid solution of carbon in iron that is the main constituent of hardened steel.

PRONUNCIATION KEY ə *ago, up*; ər *over, fur*; a *hat*; ā *ate*; ä *car*; e *let*; ē *see*; i *fit*; ī *by*; NG *sing*; ō *go*; ô *law, for*; oi *toy*; o͝o *good*; o͞o *goo*; ou *out*; TH *thin*; T̲H̲ *then*; ZH *vision*

– DERIVATIVES **mar·ten·sit·ic** /ˌmärtn'sitik/ **adj.**
– ORIGIN late 19th cent.: named after Adolf *Martens* (1850–1914), German metallurgist, + **-ITE**[1].

Mar·tha's Vine·yard /'märTHəz/ an island off the coast of Massachusetts, to the south of Cape Cod. Settled by the English in 1642, it became an important center of fishing and whaling during the 18th and 19th centuries.

Mar·tial /'märSHəl/ (*c.*40–*c.*AD 104), Roman epigrammatist, born in Spain; Latin name *Marcus Valerius Martialis*. His 15 books of epigrams, in a variety of meters, reflect all facets of Roman life.

mar·tial /'märSHəl/ ▶ **adj.** of or appropriate to war; warlike: *martial bravery*.
– DERIVATIVES **mar·tial·ly adv.**
– ORIGIN late Middle English: from Old French, or from Latin *martialis*, from *Mars, Mart-* (see **MARS**).

mar·tial arts ▶ **plural n.** various sports or skills, mainly of Japanese origin, that originated as forms of self-defense or attack, such as judo, karate, and kendo.
– DERIVATIVES **mar·tial art·ist n.**

mar·tial ea·gle ▶ **n.** a brown eagle with a brown-spotted white belly. It is Africa's largest raptor. ● *Polmaetus bellicosus*, family Accipitridae.

mar·tial law ▶ **n.** military government involving the suspension of ordinary law.

Mar·tian /'märSHən/ ▶ **adj.** of or relating to the planet Mars or its supposed inhabitants.
▶ **n.** a hypothetical or fictional inhabitant of Mars.
– ORIGIN late Middle English (in the senses 'subject to Mars's influence' and 'martial'): from Latin *Mars, Mart-* (see **MARS**) + **-IAN**.

Mar·tin[1] /'märtn/, Dean (1917–95), US singer and actor; born *Dino Paul Crocetti*. He became known for his comedy and singing act with Jerry Lewis from 1946. He joined with Frank Sinatra and **Sammy Davis, Jr.** (1925–90) in a number of movies, including *Ocean's Eleven* (1960), and had his own television show 1965–73.

Mar·tin[2], Mary (1913–90), US actress and singer. She starred in the Broadway musicals *South Pacific* (1949), *Peter Pan* (1954), and *The Sound of Music* (1959).

Mar·tin[3], Paul Edgar Philippe (1938–), Canadian Liberal statesman; prime minister 2003–06.

mar·tin /'märtn/ ▶ **n.** a swift-flying, insectivorous songbird of the swallow family, typically having a less strongly forked tail than a swallow. ● Family Hirundinidae: several genera and numerous species, e.g., the **purple martin**.
– ORIGIN late Middle English: probably a shortening of obsolete *martinet*, from French, probably from the name of St. *Martin* of Tours, celebrated at **MARTINMAS**.

Mar·tin, St. (died 397), French priest; bishop of Tours from 371; a patron saint of France. As he was giving half of his cloak to a beggar, he received a vision of Christ and was soon baptized. Feast day, November 11.

mar·ti·net /ˌmärtn'et/ ▶ **n.** a strict disciplinarian, esp. in the armed forces.
– DERIVATIVES **mar·ti·net·ish** (also **martinettish**) **adj.**
– ORIGIN late 17th cent. (denoting the drill system invented by Martinet): named after Jean *Martinet*, 17th-cent. French drillmaster.

Mar·ti·nez /mär'tēnez/ an industrial port in north central California, on Suisun Bay, north of Oakland; pop. 35,145 (est. 2008).

mar·tin·gale /'märtnˌgāl/ ▶ **n. 1** a strap, or set of straps, attached at one end to the noseband (**standing martingale**) or reins (**running martingale**) of a horse and at the other end to the girth. It is used to prevent the horse from raising its head too high.
2 a gambling system of continually doubling the stakes in the hope of an eventual win that must yield a net profit.
– ORIGIN late 16th cent.: from French, from Spanish *almártaga*, from Arabic *al-marta'a* 'the fastening,' influenced by *martingale*, from Occitan *martegal* 'inhabitant of Martigues (in Provence).'

mar·ti·ni /mär'tēnē/ ▶ **n.** a cocktail made from gin and dry vermouth.
– ORIGIN named after *Martini* and Rossi, an Italian firm selling vermouth.

Mar·ti·nique /ˌmärtn'ēk/ a French island in the Caribbean Sea, in the Lesser Antilles group; pop. 399,000 (est. 2007); capital, Fort-de-France.
– DERIVATIVES **Mar·ti·niq·uan** /-'ēkən/ **n. & adj.**

Mar·tin·ist /'märtn-ist, mär'tan-/ ▶ **n.** an adherent of a form of mystical pantheism developed by the French philosopher L.C. de Saint-Martin (1743–1803).
– DERIVATIVES **Mar·tin·ism** /-izəm/ **n.**

Mar·tin·mas /'märtnməs/ ▶ **n.** St. Martin's Day, November 11.

mart·let /'märtlət/ ▶ **n.** Heraldry a bird like a swallow without feet, borne (typically with the wings closed) as a charge or a mark of cadency for a fourth son.
– ORIGIN late Middle English (denoting a swift): from Old French *merlet*, influenced by *martinet* (see **MARTIN**).

mar·tyr /'märtər/ ▶ **n.** a person who is killed because of their religious or other beliefs: *saints, martyrs, and witnesses to the faith.* ■ a person who displays or exaggerates their discomfort or distress in order to obtain sympathy or admiration: *she wanted to play the martyr.* ■ (**martyr to**) a constant sufferer from (an ailment): *I'm a martyr to migraines!*
▶ **v.** [with obj.] (usu. **be martyred**) kill (someone) because of their beliefs: *she was martyred for her faith.* ■ cause great pain or distress to: *there was no need to martyr themselves again.*
– DERIVATIVES **mar·tyr·i·za·tion** /ˌmärtərə'zāSHən/ **n.**, **mar·tyr·ize** /'märtəˌrīz/ **v.**
– ORIGIN Old English *martir*, via ecclesiastical Latin from Greek *martur* 'witness' (in Christian use, 'martyr').

mar·tyr·dom /'märtərdəm/ ▶ **n.** the death or suffering of a martyr. ■ a display of feigned or exaggerated suffering to obtain sympathy or admiration.
– ORIGIN Old English *martyrdōm* (see **MARTYR**, **-DOM**).

mar·tyred /'märtərd/ ▶ **adj.** (of a person) having been martyred: *a martyred saint.* ■ (of an attitude or manner) showing feigned or exaggerated suffering to obtain sympathy or admiration: *he gave Mulder a brief, martyred look.*

mar·tyr·ol·o·gy /ˌmärtə'räləjē/ ▶ **n.** (pl. **martyrologies**) the branch of history or literature that deals with the lives of martyrs. ■ a list or register of martyrs.
– DERIVATIVES **mar·tyr·o·log·i·cal** /-rə'läjikəl/ **adj.**, **mar·tyr·ol·o·gist** /-jist/ **n.**
– ORIGIN late 16th cent.: via medieval Latin from ecclesiastical Greek *marturologion*, from *martur* 'martyr' + *logos* 'account.'

mar·tyr·y /'märtərē/ ▶ **n.** (pl. **martyries**) a shrine or church erected in honor of a martyr.
– ORIGIN Middle English (denoting martyrdom): via medieval Latin from Greek *marturion* 'martyrdom.'

Ma·ruts /'mərōōts/ Hinduism the sons of Rudra. In the Rig Veda they are the storm gods, Indra's helpers. Also called **RUDRAS**.

mar·vel /'märvəl/ ▶ **v.** (**marvels, marveling, marveled**; chiefly Brit. **marvels, marvelling, marvelled**) [no obj.] be filled with wonder or astonishment: *she marveled at Jeffrey's composure* | [with direct speech] *"Isn't this an evening," marveled John.*
▶ **n.** a wonderful or astonishing person or thing: *the marvels of technology* | *Charlie, you're a marvel!*
– DERIVATIVES **mar·vel·er n.**
– ORIGIN Middle English (as a noun): from Old French *merveille*, from late Latin *mirabilia*, neuter plural of Latin *mirabilis* 'wonderful,' from *mirari* 'wonder at.'

Mar·vell /'märvəl/, Andrew (1621–78), English metaphysical poet. Most of his poetry was published posthumously and was not recognized until the 20th century. Notable poems: "To his Coy Mistress" and "An Horatian Ode on Cromwell's Return from Ireland."

mar·vel of Pe·ru ▶ **n.** another term for **FOUR-O'CLOCK**.

mar·vel·ous /'märv(ə)ləs/ (Brit. **marvellous**) ▶ **adj.** causing great wonder; extraordinary: *marvelous technological toys.* ■ extremely good or pleasing; splendid: *you have done a marvelous job* | *it's marvelous to see you.*
– DERIVATIVES **mar·vel·ous·ly adv.**, **mar·vel·ous·ness n.**
– ORIGIN Middle English: from Old French *merveillus*, from *merveille* (see **MARVEL**).

marv·y /'märvē/ ▶ **adj.** informal wonderful; marvelous.

Mar·wa·ri /mər'wärē/ ▶ **n.** a native or inhabitant of Rajasthan in India. the Indic language of Rajasthan.
▶ **adj.** of or relating to the Marwari language or people.
– ORIGIN from Hindi *Mārvār*, from Sanskrit *maru* 'desert.'

Marx /märks/, Karl (Heinrich) (1818–83), German political philosopher and economist, resident of England from 1849. The founder of modern communism with Friedrich Engels, he collaborated with him in the writing of the *Communist Manifesto* (1848) and enlarged it into a series of books, most notably the three-volume *Das Kapital*.
– DERIVATIVES **Marx·i·an adj. & n.**

Karl Marx

Marx Broth·ers the name of a family of US comedians, consisting of brothers **Chico** (Leonard, 1886–1961), **Harpo** (Adolph Arthur, 1888–1964), **Groucho** (Julius Henry, 1890–1977), and **Zeppo** (Herbert, 1901–79). Their movies, characterized by their anarchic humor, include *Horse Feathers* (1932), *Duck Soup* (1933), and *A Night at the Opera* (1935).

Marx·ism /'märkˌsizəm/ ▶ **n.** the political and economic theories of Karl Marx and Friedrich Engels, later developed by their followers to form the basis for the theory and practice of communism.

Central to Marxist theory is an explanation of social change in terms of economic factors, according to which the means of production provide the economic *base*, which influences or determines the political and ideological *superstructure*. Marx and Engels predicted the revolutionary overthrow of capitalism by the proletariat and the eventual attainment of a classless communist society.

– DERIVATIVES **Marx·i·an** /-sēən/ **adj.**, **Marx·ist n. & adj.**

Marx·ism–Le·nin·ism ▶ **n.** the doctrines of Marx as interpreted and put into effect by Lenin in the former Soviet Union and (at first) by Mao Zedong in China.
– DERIVATIVES **Marx·ist–Le·nin·ist n. & adj.**

Mar·y[1] /'me(ə)rē/, mother of Jesus; known as **the (Blessed) Virgin Mary**, or **St. Mary**, or **Our Lady**. According to the Gospels, she was a virgin betrothed to Joseph and conceived Jesus by the power of the Holy Spirit. She has been venerated by Catholic and Orthodox Churches from earliest Christian times. Feast days, January 1 (Roman Catholic Church), March 25 (Annunciation), August 15 (Assumption), September 8 (Nativity), December 8 (Immaculate Conception).

Mar·y[2] the name of two queens of England. ■ **Mary I** (1516–58), daughter of Henry VIII and Catherine of Aragon; reigned 1553–58; known as **Mary Tudor** or **Bloody Mary**. In an attempt to reverse the country's turn toward Protestantism, she instigated the series of religious persecutions by which she earned her nickname. ■ **Mary II** (1662–94), daughter of James II; reigned 1689–94. Having been invited to replace her Catholic father on the throne after his deposition in 1689, she insisted that her husband, William of Orange, be crowned along with her.

Mar·y, Queen of Scots (1542–87), daughter of James V; queen of Scotland 1542–67; queen consort of France 1559–60 as the wife of Francis II; known as **Mary Stuart**. A devout Catholic, she was unable to control her Protestant lords and fled from Scotland to England in 1567. She became the focus of several Catholic plots against Elizabeth I and was eventually beheaded. Her son James VI of Scotland became James I of England.

Mar·y, St. see **MARY**[1].

Mar·y Ce·leste /sə'lest/ an American brig that was found adrift in the North Atlantic in December 1872 in perfect condition but abandoned. The fate of the crew and the reason for the abandonment of the ship remain a mystery. ■ [as noun] (also **Marie Celeste**) a ship, building, or other thing that is deserted, esp. inexplicably. [The variant spelling 'Marie Celeste' was used by Sir Arthur Conan Doyle in his 1884 fictionalized account of the abandoned ship.]

Mar·y Jane /'me(ə)rē 'jān/ ▶ **n. 1** trademark a flat, round-toed shoe for women and girls, with a single strap across the top.
2 informal marijuana.

– ORIGIN 1920s: from the female given name *Mary Jane*.

Mar·y·land /ˈmerələnd/ a state in the eastern US that surrounds Chesapeake Bay, on the Atlantic coast; pop. 5,633,597 (est. 2008); capital, Annapolis; statehood, Apr. 28, 1788 (7). Colonized by England in the 1600s, it was one of the original thirteen states.
– DERIVATIVES **Mary·land·er** /-ˌlandər/ **n.**
– ORIGIN named after Queen Henrietta *Maria* (1609–69), wife of Charles I.

Mar·y Mag·da·lene, St. /ˈmagdəˌlēn, -lən/ (also **the Magdalen** /-lən/) (in the New Testament) a woman of Magdala in Galilee. She was a follower of Jesus, who cured her of evil spirits (Luke 8:2); she is also traditionally identified with the "sinner" of Luke 7:37. Feast day, July 22.

Mar·y Stu·art /ˈst(y)o͞oərt/ see **Mary, Queen of Scots**.

Mar·y Tu·dor /ˈt(y)o͞odər/, Mary I of England (see **Mary**[2]).

mar·zi·pan /ˈmärzəˌpan, ˈmärtsə-/ ▶ **n.** a sweet, yellowish paste of ground almonds, sugar, and egg whites, often colored and used to make small cakes or confections or as an icing for larger cakes. Also called **almond paste**. ■ a confection or cake made of or based on marzipan.
– ORIGIN late 15th cent. (as *marchpane*): from Italian *marzapane*, possibly from Arabic. The form *marchpane* (influenced by **March** and obsolete *pain* 'bread') was more usual until the late 19th cent., when *marzipan* (influenced by German, which has the same spelling) displaced it.

ma·sa /ˈmäsə, ˈmäsä/ ▶ **n.** (in Latin American cuisine) dough made from corn flour and used to make tortillas, tamales, etc.
– ORIGIN Spanish.

Ma·sac·cio /məˈsächē-ō/, (1401–28), Italian painter; born *Tommaso Giovanni di Simone Guidi*. The first artist to apply the laws of perspective to painting, he is known particularly for his frescoes in the Brancacci Chapel in Florence (1424–27).

Ma·sa·da /məˈsädə/ the site of the ruins of a palace and fortification built by Herod the Great on the southwestern shore of the Dead Sea in the 1st century BC.

Ma·sai /ˈmäˌsī, mäˈsī/ (also **Maasai**) ▶ **n.** (pl. **same** or **Masais**) **1** a member of a pastoral people living in Tanzania and Kenya.
2 the Nilotic language of the Masai.
▶ **adj.** of or relating to the Masai or their language.

ma·sa·la /məˈsälə/ ▶ **n.** any of a number of spice mixtures ground into a paste or powder for use in Indian cooking. ■ a dish flavored with this: *chicken masala*.
– ORIGIN from Urdu *maṣālah*, based on Arabic *maṣāliḥ* 'ingredients, materials.'

Ma·san /ˈmäˌsän/ a port city in southeastern South Korea, on an inlet of the Western Channel (the Korea Strait); pop. 414,800 (est. 2008).

Ma·sa·ryk /ˈmäsəˌrik/, Tomáš (Garrigue) (1850–1937), Czech statesman; president 1918–35. He became Czechoslovakia's first president when independence was achieved in 1918.

Mas·ba·te /mäsˈbätē/ an island in the central Philippines; pop. 806,300 (est. 2009).

masc. ▶ **abbr.** masculine.

Mas·ca·gni /məˈskänē, mäˈskänyē/, Pietro (1863–1945), Italian composer and conductor. He is especially known for the opera *Cavalleria Rusticana* (1890).

mas·car·a /maˈskarə/ ▶ **n.** a cosmetic for darkening and thickening the eyelashes.
– DERIVATIVES **mas·car·aed** /-ˈskarəd/ **adj.**
– ORIGIN late 19th cent.: from Italian, literally 'mask,' from Arabic *masḵara* 'buffoon.'

Mas·ca·rene Is·lands /ˌmaskəˈrēn/ (also **the Mascarenes**) a group of three islands—Réunion, Mauritius, and Rodrigues—in the western Indian Ocean, east of Madagascar.

mas·car·po·ne /ˌmäskärˈpōn(e)/ ▶ **n.** a soft, mild Italian cream cheese.

mas·cle /ˈmaskəl/ ▶ **n.** Heraldry a lozenge voided, i.e., with a central lozenge-shaped aperture.
– ORIGIN late Middle English: from Anglo-Norman French, from Anglo-Latin *mascula* 'mesh.'

mas·con /ˈmasˌkän/ ▶ **n.** Astronomy a concentration of denser material below the surface of the moon or other body, causing a local increase in gravitational pull.
– ORIGIN 1960s: from *mas(s) con(centration)*.

mas·cot /ˈmasˌkät, -kət/ ▶ **n.** a person or thing that is supposed to bring good luck or that is used to symbolize a particular event or organization: *the squadron's mascot was a young lion cub.*
– ORIGIN late 19th cent.: from French *mascotte*, from modern Provençal *mascotto*, feminine diminutive of *masco* 'witch.'

mas·cu·line /ˈmaskyələn/ ▶ **adj.** **1** having qualities or appearance traditionally associated with men, esp. strength and aggressiveness: *he is outstandingly handsome and robust, very masculine.* ■ of or relating to men; male: *a masculine voice.*
2 Grammar of or denoting a gender of nouns and adjectives, conventionally regarded as male.
▶ **n.** (**the masculine**) the male sex or gender: *the masculine as the norm.* ■ Grammar a masculine word or form.
– DERIVATIVES **mas·cu·line·ly adv.**
– ORIGIN late Middle English (in grammatical use): via Old French from Latin *masculinus*, from *masculus* 'male.'

mas·cu·line rhyme ▶ **n.** Prosody a rhyme of final stressed syllables (e.g., *blow/flow, confess/redress*). Compare with **feminine rhyme**.

mas·cu·lin·ist /ˈmaskyələˌnist/ (also **masculist** /-list/) ▶ **adj.** characterized by or denoting attitudes or values held to be typical of men: *masculinist language.* ■ of or relating to the advocacy of the rights or needs of men.
▶ **n.** an advocate of the rights or needs of men.

mas·cu·lin·i·ty /ˌmaskyəˈlinitē/ ▶ **n.** possession of the qualities traditionally associated with men: *a need for men to prove their masculinity through domination over women.*

mas·cu·lin·ize /ˈmaskyələˌnīz/ ▶ **v.** [with obj.] induce male physiological characteristics in: *male sex steroids masculinize female hyenas.* ■ cause to appear or seem masculine: (as adj. **masculinized**) *a slightly masculinized swagger.*
– DERIVATIVES **mas·cu·lin·i·za·tion** /ˌmaskyələnəˈzāsʜən/ **n.**

Mase·field /ˈmāsˌfēld/, John (Edward) (1878–1967), English poet and novelist. He was appointed poet laureate in 1930. Notable works: *Salt-Water Ballads* (1902) and *Reynard the Fox* (1919).

ma·ser /ˈmāzər/ ▶ **n.** a device using the stimulated emission of radiation by excited atoms to amplify or generate coherent monochromatic electromagnetic radiation in the microwave range.
– ORIGIN 1950s: acronym from *microwave amplification by the stimulated emission of radiation.*

Ma·se·ru /ˈmäzəˌro͞o, ˈmaz-/ the capital of Lesotho, situated on the Caledon River near the border with the province of Free State in South Africa; pop. 211,000 (est. 2007).

MASH /mash/ ▶ **abbr.** mobile army surgical hospital.

mash /masʜ/ ▶ **n.** a uniform mass made by crushing a substance into a soft pulp, sometimes with the addition of liquid: *pound the garlic to a mash.* ■ bran mixed with hot water given as a warm food to horses or other animals. ■ Brit. informal mashed potatoes. ■ (in brewing) a mixture of powdered malt and hot water, which is stood until the sugars dissolve to form the wort.
▶ **v.** [with obj.] **1** reduce (a food or other substance) to a uniform mass by crushing it: *mash the beans to a paste* | (as adj. **mashed**) *mashed bananas.* ■ crush or smash (something) to a pulp: *he almost had his head mashed by a slamming door.* ■ informal press forcefully on (something): *the worst thing you can do is mash the brake pedal.*
2 (in brewing) mix (powdered malt) with hot water to form wort.
3 Brit. informal (with reference to tea) brew or infuse.
– ORIGIN Old English *māsc* (used as a brewing term); perhaps ultimately related to **mix**.

mashed po·ta·toes ▶ **plural n.** a dish of potatoes that have been boiled and mashed, typically prepared with milk and butter.

mash·er /ˈmasʜər/ ▶ **n.** **1** a utensil for mashing food: *a potato masher.*
2 informal a man who makes unwelcome sexual advances, often in public places and typically to women he does not know. [late 19th cent.: probably a derivative of slang *mash* 'attract sexually,' perhaps from Romany *masherava* 'allure.']

Mash·had /məˈsʜäd/ (also **Meshed** /məˈsʜed/) a city in northeastern Iran, close to the border with Turkmenistan; pop. 2,427,316 (2006). The burial place in AD 809 of the Abbasid caliph Harun ar-Rashid and in 818 of the Shiite leader **Ali ar-Rida**, it is a holy city of the Shiite Muslims. It is the second largest city in Iran.

mash·ie /ˈmasʜē/ ▶ **n.** Golf, dated an iron used for lofting or for medium distances.
– ORIGIN late 19th cent.: perhaps from French *massue* 'club.'

mash note ▶ **n.** informal a letter that expresses infatuation with or gushing admiration of someone.
– ORIGIN late 19th cent.: from slang *mash* 'infatuation' + **note**.

Ma·sho·na /məˈsʜōnə, -ˈsʜänə/ ▶ **n.** the Shona people collectively.
▶ **adj.** of or relating to the Shona people.
– ORIGIN the name in Shona.

Ma·sho·na·land /məˈsʜōnəˌland, -ˈsʜänə-/ an area of northern Zimbabwe that is occupied by the Shona people. A former province of Southern Rhodesia, it is now divided into the three provinces of Mashonaland East, West, and Central.

mash-up ▶ **n.** informal a recording created by digitally combining and synchronizing instrumental tracks with vocal tracks from two or more different songs.

mas·jid /ˈməsjid, ˈmas-/ ▶ **n.** Arabic word for a mosque.

mask /mask/ ▶ **n.** **1** a covering for all or part of the face, in particular: ■ a covering worn as a disguise, or to amuse or terrify other people. ■ a covering made of fiber or gauze and fitting over the nose and mouth to protect against dust or air pollutants, or made of sterile gauze and worn to prevent infection of the wearer or (in surgery) of the patient. ■ a protective covering fitting over the whole face, worn in fencing, ice hockey, and other sports. ■ a respirator used to filter inhaled air or to supply gas for inhalation. ■ (also **masque**) a cosmetic preparation spread over the face and left for some time to cleanse and improve the skin. ■ Entomology the enlarged lower lip of a dragonfly larva, which can be extended to seize prey.
2 a likeness of a person's face in clay or wax, esp. one made by taking a mold from the face. ■ a person's face regarded as having set into a particular expression: *his face was a mask of rage.* ■ a hollow model of a human head worn by ancient Greek and Roman actors. ■ the face or head of an animal, esp. of a fox, as a hunting trophy. ■ archaic a masked person.
3 a manner or expression that hides one's true character or feelings; a pretense: *she let her mask of moderate respectability slip.*
4 Photography a piece of something, such as a card, used to cover a part of an image that is not required when exposing a print. ■ Electronics a patterned metal film used in the manufacture of microcircuits to allow selective modification of the underlying material.
▶ **v.** [with obj.] cover (the face) with a mask. ■ conceal (something) from view: *the poplars masked a factory.* ■ disguise or hide (a sensation or quality): *brandy did not completely mask the bitter taste.* ■ cover (an object or surface) so as to protect it from a process, esp. painting: ***mask off** doors and cupboards with sheets of plastic.*
– DERIVATIVES **masked adj.**
– ORIGIN mid 16th cent.: from French *masque*, from Italian *maschera, mascara*, probably from medieval Latin *masca* 'witch, specter,' but influenced by Arabic *masḵara* 'buffoon.'

masked ball ▶ **n.** a ball at which participants wear masks to conceal their faces.

mask·er /ˈmaskər/ ▶ **n.** **1** a thing that masks or conceals something else.
2 a person taking part in a masquerade or masked ball.

mask·ing tape ▶ **n.** adhesive tape used in painting to cover areas on which paint is not wanted.

mas·ki·nonge /ˈmaskəˌnänj/ ▶ **n.** another term for **muskellunge**.

Mas·low /ˈmazlō/, Abraham (Harold) (1908–70), US psychologist. He was a leader of the humanistic school of psychology, and he postulated a "hierarchy of needs" to explain human motivation. He wrote *Motivation and Personality* (1954).

mas·och·ism /ˈmasəˌkizəm, ˈmaz-/ ▶ **n.** the tendency to derive pleasure, esp. sexual gratification, from one's own pain or humiliation. ■ (in general use) the enjoyment of what appears to be painful or tiresome: *isn't there some masochism involved in taking on this kind of project?*
– DERIVATIVES **mas·och·ist n.**, **mas·och·is·tic** /ˌmasəˈkistik, ˌmaz-/ **adj.**, **mas·och·is·ti·cal·ly** /ˌmasəˈkistik(ə)lē, ˌmaz-/ **adv.**
– ORIGIN late 19th cent.: named after Leopold von Sacher-*Masoch* (1835–95), the Austrian novelist who described it, + **-ism**.

Ma·son /ˈmāsən/, James (Neville) (1909–84), English actor. Notable movies: *A Star is Born* (1954), *Lolita* (1962), *Georgy Girl* (1966), and *The Verdict* (1982).

ma·son /ˈmāsən/ ▶ **n.** **1** a builder and worker in stone.

m

2 (**Mason**) a Freemason.
▶ **v.** [with obj.] build from or strengthen with stone. ■ cut, hew, or dress (stone).
– ORIGIN Middle English: from Old French *masson* (noun), *maçonner* (verb), probably of Germanic origin; perhaps related to MAKE.

ma·son bee ▶ **n.** a solitary bee that nests in cavities within which it constructs cells of sand and other particles glued together with saliva. ● *Osmia* and other genera, family Apidae.

Ma·son–Dix·on line /ˈdiksən/ ▶ **n.** (in the US) the boundary between Maryland and Pennsylvania, taken as the northern limit of the slave-owning states before the abolition of slavery.
– ORIGIN named after Charles *Mason* (1728–1786) and Jeremiah *Dixon* (1733–1779), the English astronomers who surveyed it in 1763–67.

Ma·son·ic /məˈsänik/ ▶ **adj.** of or relating to Freemasons: *a Masonic lodge.*

Ma·son·ite /ˈmāsəˌnīt/ ▶ **n.** trademark a type of hardboard.
– ORIGIN 1920s: from the name of the *Mason* Fibre Co., Laurel, Mississippi, + -ITE[1].

ma·son jar (also **Mason jar**) ▶ **n.** a wide-mouthed glass jar with an airtight screw top, used for preserving fruit and vegetables.
– ORIGIN late 19th cent.: named after John L. *Mason* (died 1902), US inventor.

ma·son·ry /ˈmāsənrē/ ▶ **n. 1** stonework. ■ the work of a mason.
2 (**Masonry**) Freemasonry.

ma·son wasp ▶ **n.** a solitary wasp that nests in a cavity or in a hole in the ground, sealing the nest with mud or similar material. ● Several genera in the family Eumenidae.

Ma·so·rah /məˈsôrə/ (also **Massorah**) ▶ **n.** (**the Masorah**) the collection of information and comment on the text of the traditional Hebrew Bible by the Masoretes. ■ the Masoretic text of the Bible.
– ORIGIN from Hebrew *māsōrāh*, based on *ʾāsar* 'to bind,' later interpreted in the sense 'tradition' (as if from *māsar* 'hand down').

Mas·o·rete /ˈmasəˌrēt/ (also **Massorete**) ▶ **n.** any of the Jewish scholars of the 6th–10th centuries AD who contributed to the establishment of a recognized text of the Hebrew Bible, and to the compilation of the Masorah.
– DERIVATIVES **Mas·o·ret·ic** /ˌmasəˈretik/ **adj.**
– ORIGIN from French *Massoret* and modern Latin *Massoreta*, from Hebrew *māsōreṯ*; related to *māsōrāh* (see MASORAH).

m

masque /mask/ ▶ **n. 1** a form of amateur dramatic entertainment, popular among the nobility in 16th- and 17th-century England, which consisted of dancing and acting performed by masked players.
2 variant spelling of MASK (sense 1 of the noun).
– DERIVATIVES **mas·quer** /ˈmaskər/ **n.**
– ORIGIN early 16th cent. (in the sense 'masquerade or masked ball'): probably a back-formation (with spelling influenced by French *masque* 'mask') from *masker*, from Italian *mascar* 'person wearing a mask.'

mas·quer·ade /ˌmaskəˈrād/ ▶ **n.** a false show or pretense: *his masquerade ended when he was arrested.* ■ the wearing of disguise: *dressing up, role-playing, and masquerade.* ■ a masked ball.
▶ **v.** [no obj.] pretend to be someone one is not: *a journalist **masquerading as** a man in distress.* ■ be disguised or passed off as something else: *the idle gossip that masquerades as news in some local papers.*
– DERIVATIVES **mas·quer·ad·er n.**
– ORIGIN late 16th cent.: from French *mascarade*, from Italian *mascherata*, from *maschera* 'mask.'

Mass /mas/ ▶ **n.** the Christian Eucharist or Holy Communion, esp. in the Roman Catholic Church: *we went to Mass | the Latin Mass.* ■ a celebration of this: *there was a Mass and the whole family was supposed to go.* ■ a musical setting of parts of the liturgy used in the Mass.
– ORIGIN Old English *mæsse*, from ecclesiastical Latin *missa*, from Latin *miss-* 'dismissed,' from *mittere*, perhaps from the last words of the service, *Ite, missa est* 'Go, it is the dismissal.'

mass /mas/ ▶ **n. 1** a coherent, typically large body of matter with no definite shape: *a mass of curly hair | from here the trees were a dark mass.* ■ a large number of people or objects crowded together: ***a mass of** cyclists.* ■ a large amount of material: ***a mass of** conflicting evidence.* ■ (**masses**) informal a large quantity or amount of something: *we get masses of homework.* ■ any of the main portions in a painting or drawing that each have some unity in color, lighting, or some other quality: *the masterly distribution of masses.*
2 (**the mass of**) the majority of: *the great mass of the population had little interest in the project.* ■ (**the masses**) the ordinary people.
3 Physics the quantity of matter that a body contains, as measured by its acceleration under a given force or by the force exerted on it by a gravitational field. ■ (in general use) weight.
▶ **adj.** [attrib.] relating to, done by, or affecting large numbers of people or things: *the movie has mass appeal | a mass exodus of refugees.*
▶ **v.** assemble or cause to assemble into a mass or as one body: [with obj.] *both countries began massing troops in the region* | [no obj.] *clouds massed heavily on the horizon.*
– PHRASES **be a mass of** be completely covered with: *his face was a mass of bruises.* **in the mass** as a whole: *her genuine affection for humanity in the mass.*
– DERIVATIVES **mass·less adj.**
– ORIGIN late Middle English: from Old French *masse*, from Latin *massa*, from Greek *maza* 'barley cake'; perhaps related to *massein* 'knead.'

Mass. ▶ **abbr.** Massachusetts.

mas·sa /ˈmasə/ ▶ **n.** chiefly historical (in representations of black speech) master.

Mas·sa·chu·sett /ˌmasəˈCHo͞osit/ (also **Massachuset**) ▶ **n. 1** (pl. **same** or **Massachusetts**) a member of an extinct North American Indian people, formerly found in eastern Massachusetts.
2 the Algonquian language of this people.

Mas·sa·chu·setts /ˌmasəˈCHo͞osits/ a state in the northeastern US, on the Atlantic coast, one of the six New England states; pop. 6,497,967 (est. 2008); capital, Boston; statehood, Feb. 6, 1788 (6). Settled by the Pilgrims in 1620, it was a center of resistance to the British before becoming one of the original thirteen states.

Mas·sa·chu·setts Bay an inlet of the Atlantic Ocean between Cape Cod and Cape Ann, in eastern Massachusetts, of which Boston Harbor is an inlet.

Mas·sa·chu·setts In·sti·tute of Tech·nol·o·gy (abbr.: **MIT**) a US institute of higher education, famous for scientific and technical research, founded in 1861 in Cambridge, Massachusetts.

mas·sa·cre /ˈmasikər/ ▶ **n.** an indiscriminate and brutal slaughter of people: *the attack was described as a cold-blooded massacre | she says he is an accomplice to massacre.* ■ informal a heavy defeat of a sports team or contestant.
▶ **v.** [with obj.] deliberately and violently kill (a large number of people). ■ informal inflict a heavy defeat on (a sports team or contestant).
– ORIGIN late 16th cent.: from French, of unknown origin.

mas·sage /məˈsäZH, -ˈsäj/ ▶ **n.** the rubbing and kneading of muscles and joints of the body with the hands, esp. to relieve tension or pain: *massage can ease tiredness and jet lag | a massage will help loosen you up.*
▶ **v.** [with obj.] **1** rub and knead (a person or part of the body) with the hands. ■ (**massage something in/into/onto**) rub a substance into (the skin or hair). ■ flatter (someone's ego): *I chose a man who massaged my bruised ego.*
2 manipulate (figures) to give a more acceptable result: *the accounts had been massaged and adjusted to suit the government.*
– DERIVATIVES **mas·sag·er n.**
– ORIGIN late 19th cent.: from French, from *masser* 'knead, treat with massage,' probably from Portuguese *amassar* 'knead,' from *massa* 'dough.'

mas·sage par·lor ▶ **n.** an establishment providing massages. ■ such an establishment that is actually a front for prostitution.

mas·sa·sau·ga /ˌmasəˈsôgə/ ▶ **n.** a small North American rattlesnake of variable color that favors damp habitats. ● *Sistrurus catenatus*, family Viperidae.
– ORIGIN mid 19th cent.: formed irregularly from MISSISSAUGA.

Mas·sa·soit /ˌmasəˈsoit/ (c.1580–1661), chief of the Wampanoag Indians; father of King Philip. He signed a peace treaty with the Pilgrims at Plymouth in 1621 and remained a friend to white settlers.

Mass card ▶ **n.** (in the Roman Catholic Church) a card sent to the family of someone who has died, stating that the sender has arranged for a Mass to be said in memory of the deceased.

mass de·fect ▶ **n.** Physics the difference between the mass of an isotope and its mass number.

mas·sé /maˈsā/ ▶ **n.** [usu. as modifier] Billiards a stroke made with an inclined cue, imparting swerve to the ball: *a massé shot.*
– ORIGIN late 19th cent.: French, past participle of *masser*, describing the action of making such a stroke.

mass en·er·gy ▶ **n.** Physics mass and energy regarded as interconvertible manifestations of the same phenomenon, according to the laws of relativity. ■ the mass of a body regarded relativistically as energy.

mas·se·ter /məˈsētər, ma-/ (also **masseter muscle**) ▶ **n.** Anatomy a muscle that runs through the rear part of the cheek from the temporal bone to the lower jaw on each side and closes the jaw in chewing.
– ORIGIN late 16th cent.: from Greek *masētēr*, from *masasthai* 'to chew.'

mas·seur /maˈsər, mə-/ ▶ **n.** a person, esp. a man, who provides massages professionally.
– ORIGIN French, from *masser* 'to massage.'

mas·seuse /maˈso͞os, mə-, maˈsœz/ ▶ **n.** a female masseur.
– ORIGIN French.

mas·si·cot /ˈmasiˌkät/ ▶ **n.** a yellow form of lead monoxide, used as a pigment.
– ORIGIN late 15th cent.: from French (influenced by Italian *marzacotto* 'unguent'), ultimately from Arabic *martak*.

mas·sif /maˈsēf/ ▶ **n.** a compact group of mountains, esp. one that is separate from other groups.
– ORIGIN early 16th cent. (denoting a large building): French adjective meaning 'massive,' used as a noun. The current sense dates from the late 19th cent.

Mas·sif Cen·tral /mäˈsēf sänˈträl/ a mountainous plateau in south central France. It covers almost one sixth of the country and rises to a height of 6,188 feet (1,887 m) at Puy de Sancy, a mountain in the Auvergne region.

Mas·sine /mäˈsēn/, Léonide Fédorovitch (1895–1979), French choreographer and ballet dancer, born in Russia; born *Leonid Fyodorovich Myasin*. He was the originator of the symphonic ballet, and danced in and choreographed the movie *The Red Shoes* (1948).

mas·sive /ˈmasiv/ ▶ **adj. 1** large and heavy or solid: *a massive rampart of stone.*
2 exceptionally large: *massive crowds are expected.* ■ very intense or severe: *a massive heart attack.* ■ informal particularly successful or influential: *the title song became a massive hit.*
3 Geology (of rocks or beds) having no discernible form or structure. ■ (of a mineral) not visibly crystalline.
– DERIVATIVES **mas·sive·ly adv.** [as submodifier] *a massively complicated network*, **mas·sive·ness n.**
– ORIGIN late Middle English: from French *massif, -ive*, from Old Fre *massis*, based on Latin *massa* (see MASS).

mas·sive·ly par·al·lel ▶ **adj.** (of a computer) consisting of many individual processing units, and thus able to execute many different parts of a program at the same time.

mass mar·ket ▶ **n.** the market for goods that are produced in large quantities.
▶ **v.** (**mass-market**) [with obj.] market (a product) on a large scale.

mass me·di·a ▶ **plural n.** (usu. **the mass media**) [treated as sing. or pl.] the media.

mass noun ▶ **n.** Grammar **1** a noun denoting something that cannot be counted (e.g., a substance or quality), in English usually a noun that lacks a plural in ordinary usage and is not used with the indefinite article, e.g., *luggage, china, happiness.* Contrasted with COUNT NOUN.
2 a noun denoting something that normally cannot be counted but that may be countable when it refers to different units or types, e.g., *coffee, bread* (*drank some coffee, ordered two coffees; ate some bread, several different breads*).

mass num·ber ▶ **n.** Physics the total number of protons and neutrons in a nucleus.

Mas·son /məˈsän, mäˈsôN/, André (1896–1987), French painter and graphic artist. He joined the surrealists in the mid 1920s and pioneered "automatic" drawing, a form of fluid, spontaneous composition intended to express images emerging from the unconscious.

Mas·so·rah /məˈsôrə/ ▶ **n.** variant spelling of MASORAH.

Mas·so·rete /ˈmasəˌrēt/ ▶ **n.** variant spelling of MASORETE.

mass-pro·duce /ˌmas prəˈdo͞os/ ▶ **v.** [with obj.] produce large quantities of (a standardized article) by an automated mechanical process: (as adj. **mass-produced**) *cheap mass-produced goods.*
– DERIVATIVES **mass-pro·duc·er n.**, **mass pro·duc·tion n.**

mass spec·tro·graph ▶ **n.** a mass spectrometer in which the particles are detected photographically.

mass spec·trom·e·ter ▶ **n.** an apparatus for separating isotopes, molecules, and molecular fragments according to mass. The sample is vaporized and ionized, and the ions are accelerated in an electric field and deflected by a magnetic field into a curved trajectory that gives a distinctive mass spectrum.

mass spec·trum ▶ **n.** a distribution of ions shown by the use of a mass spectrograph or mass spectrometer.

mass trans·it ▶ **n.** public transportation, esp. in an urban area.

mass·y /ˈmasē/ ▶ **adj.** literary or archaic consisting of a large mass; bulky; massive: *a round massy table.*

mast[1] /mast/ ▶ **n. 1** a tall upright post, spar, or other structure on a ship or boat, in sailing vessels generally carrying a sail or sails. ■ a similar structure on land, esp. a flagpole or a television or radio transmitter.
2 (in full **captain's mast**) (in the US Navy) a session of court presided over by the captain of a ship, esp. to hear cases of minor offenses.
– PHRASES **before the mast** historical serving as an ordinary seaman in a sailing ship (quartered in the forecastle).
– DERIVATIVES **mast·ed adj.** [in combination] *a single-masted fishing boat.*
– ORIGIN Old English *mæst*; related to Dutch *mast* and German *Mast.*

mast[1] 1

mast[2] ▶ **n.** the fruit of beech, oak, chestnut, and other forest trees, esp. as food for pigs and wild animals.
– ORIGIN Old English *mæst*; probably related to MEAT.

mas·ta·ba /ˈmastəbə/ (also **mastabah**) ▶ **n.**
1 Archaeology an ancient Egyptian tomb rectangular in shape with sloping sides and a flat roof, standing to a height of 17–20 feet (5–6 m), consisting of an underground burial chamber with rooms above it (at ground level) in which to store offerings.
2 (in Islamic countries) a bench, typically of stone, attached to a house.
– ORIGIN from Arabic *maṣṭaba.*

mast cell ▶ **n.** a cell filled with basophil granules, found in numbers in connective tissue and releasing histamine and other substances during inflammatory and allergic reactions.
– ORIGIN late 19th cent.: *mast* from German *Mast* 'fattening, feeding.'

mas·tec·to·my /maˈstektəmē/ ▶ **n.** (pl. **mastectomies**) a surgical operation to remove a breast.
– ORIGIN 1920s: from Greek *mastos* 'breast' + -ECTOMY.

mas·ter[1] /ˈmastər/ ▶ **n. 1** chiefly historical a man who has people working for him, esp. servants or slaves: *he acceded to his master's wishes.* ■ a person who has dominance or control of something: *he was master of the situation.* ■ a machine or device directly controlling another: [as modifier] *a master cylinder.* Compare with SLAVE. ■ dated a male head of a household: *the master of the house.* ■ the owner of a dog, horse, or other domesticated animal.
2 a skilled practitioner of a particular art or activity: *I'm a master of disguise.* ■ a great artist, esp. one belonging to the accepted canon: *the work of the great masters is spread around the art galleries of the world.* ■ a very strong chess or bridge player, esp. one who has qualified for the title at international tournaments: *a chess master.* See also GRAND MASTER. ■ (**Masters**) [treated as sing.] (in some sports) a class for competitors over the usual age for the highest level of competition.
3 a person who holds a second or further degree from a university or other academic institution (only in titles and set expressions): *a master's degree | a Master of Arts.*
4 a man in charge of an organization or group, in particular: ■ chiefly Brit. a male schoolteacher, esp. at a public or prep school. ■ the head of a college or school. ■ the captain of a merchant ship.
5 used as a title prefixed to the name of a boy not old enough to be called "Mr.": *Master James Williams.* ■ archaic a title for a man of high rank or learning. ■ the title of the heir apparent of a Scottish viscount or baron.
6 an original movie, recording, or document from which copies can be made: [as modifier] *the master tape.*
▶ **adj.** [attrib.] **1** having or showing very great skill or proficiency: *a master painter.* ■ denoting a person skilled in a particular trade and able to teach others: *a master bricklayer.*
2 main; principal: *the master bedroom.*
▶ **v.** [with obj.] **1** acquire complete knowledge or skill in (an accomplishment, technique, or art): *I never mastered Latin.*
2 gain control of; overcome: *I managed to master my fears.*
3 make a master copy of (a movie or record).
– DERIVATIVES **mas·ter·dom** /-dəm/ **n.**, **mas·ter·hood** /-ˌho͝od/ **n.**, **mas·ter·less adj.**, **mas·ter·ship** /-ˌSHip/ **n.**
– ORIGIN Old English *mæg(i)ster* (later reinforced by Old French *maistre*), from Latin *magister*; probably related to *magis* 'more' (i.e., 'more important').

mas·ter[2] ▶ **n.** [in combination] a ship or boat with a specified number of masts: *a three-master.*

mas·ter-at-arms ▶ **n.** (pl. **masters-at-arms**) a naval petty officer appointed to carry out or supervise police duties on board a ship.

mas·ter chief pet·ty of·fi·cer ▶ **n.** a noncommissioned officer in the US Navy or Coast Guard ranking above senior chief petty officer and below warrant officer.

mas·ter class (also **masterclass**) ▶ **n.** a class, esp. in music, given by an expert to highly talented students.

mas·ter·ful /ˈmastərfəl/ ▶ **adj. 1** powerful and able to control others: *behind the lace and ruffles was a masterful woman.*
2 performed or performing very skillfully: *a masterful assessment of the difficulties.*
– DERIVATIVES **mas·ter·ful·ly adv.**, **mas·ter·ful·ness n.**

mas·ter gun·ner·y ser·geant ▶ **n.** a noncommissioned officer in the US Marine Corps ranking above master sergeant and below sergeant major.

mas·ter key ▶ **n.** a key that opens several locks, each of which also has its own key: *the custodian has the master key to all the classrooms.*

mas·ter·ly /ˈmastərlē/ ▶ **adj.** performed or performing in a very skillful and accomplished way: *his masterly account of rural France.*

mas·ter ma·son ▶ **n. 1** a skilled mason, esp. one who employs other workers.
2 a fully qualified Freemason.

mas·ter·mind /ˈmastərˌmīnd/ ▶ **n.** a person with an outstanding intellect: *an eminent musical mastermind.* ■ someone who plans and directs an ingenious and complex scheme or enterprise: *the mastermind behind the project.*
▶ **v.** [with obj.] plan and direct (an ingenious and complex scheme or enterprise): *he was accused of masterminding a gold-smuggling racket.*

mas·ter of cer·e·mo·nies ▶ **n.** a person who introduces speakers, players, or entertainers.

mas·ter·piece /ˈmastərˌpēs/ ▶ **n.** a work of outstanding artistry, skill, or workmanship: *a great literary masterpiece | the car was a masterpiece of space-age technology.* ■ an artist's or craftsman's best piece of work: *the painting is arguably Picasso's masterpiece.* ■ historical a piece of work by a craftsman accepted as qualification for membership of a guild as an acknowledged master.

mas·ter plan ▶ **n.** a comprehensive or far-reaching plan of action.

Mas·ters /ˈmastərz/, Edgar Lee (1869–1950), US writer. His verse is collected in such works as *Spoon River Anthology* (1915), *Domesday Book* (1920), and *The New Spoon River* (1924). He also wrote biographies and novels.

mas·ter ser·geant ▶ **n.** a noncommissioned officer in the US armed forces of high rank, in particular (in the Army) an NCO above sergeant first class and below sergeant major, (in the Air Force) an NCO above technical sergeant and below senior master sergeant, or (in the Marine Corps) an NCO above gunnery sergeant and below master gunnery sergeant.

mas·ter·sing·er /ˈmastərˌsiNGər/ ▶ **n.** another term for MEISTERSINGER.

Mas·ters Tour·na·ment /ˈmastərz/ a prestigious US golf competition, held in Augusta, Georgia, in which golfers (chiefly professionals) compete only by invitation on the basis of their past achievements.

mas·ter stroke ▶ **n.** an outstandingly skillful and opportune act; a very clever move.

mas·ter switch ▶ **n.** a switch controlling the supply of electricity or fuel to an entire system. ■ Biology a substance or gene that regulates gene expression or embryonic development, or initiates cancer.

mas·ter·work /ˈmastərˌwərk/ ▶ **n.** a masterpiece.

mas·ter·y /ˈmast(ə)rē/ ▶ **n. 1** comprehensive knowledge or skill in a subject or accomplishment: *she played with some mastery.* ■ the action or process of mastering a subject or accomplishment: *a child's mastery of language.*
2 control or superiority over someone or something: *man's mastery over nature.*
– ORIGIN Middle English: from Old French *maistrie*, from *maistre* 'master.'

mast·head /ˈmastˌhed/ ▶ **n. 1** the highest part of a ship's mast or of the lower section of a mast.
2 the title of a newspaper or magazine at the head of the front or editorial page. ■ the listed details in a newspaper or magazine referring to ownership, advertising rates, etc.
▶ **v.** [with obj.] **1** historical send (a sailor) to the masthead, esp. as a punishment.
2 raise (a flag or sail) to the masthead.

mas·tic /ˈmastik/ ▶ **n. 1** an aromatic gum or resin exuded from the bark of a Mediterranean tree, used in making varnish and chewing gum and as a flavoring.
2 (also **mastic tree**) the bushy evergreen Mediterranean tree of the cashew family that yields mastic and has aromatic leaves and fruit, closely related to the pistachio. ● *Pistacia lentiscus*, family Anacardiaceae.
3 a puttylike waterproof filler and sealant used in building.
– ORIGIN late Middle English: via Old French and Latin from Greek *mastikhē* (perhaps from *mastikhan* 'masticate').

mas·ti·cate /ˈmastiˌkāt/ ▶ **v.** [with obj.] chew (food).
– DERIVATIVES **mas·ti·ca·tion** /ˌmastiˈkāSHən/ **n.**, **mas·ti·ca·tor** /-ˌkātər/ **n.**, **mas·ti·ca·to·ry** /ˈmastikəˌtôrē/ **adj.**
– ORIGIN mid 17th cent.: from late Latin *masticat-* 'chewed,' from the verb *masticare*, from Greek *mastikhan* 'gnash the teeth' (related to *masasthai* 'to chew').

mas·tiff /ˈmastif/ ▶ **n.** a dog of a large, strong breed with drooping ears and pendulous lips.
– ORIGIN Middle English: obscurely representing Old French *mastin*, based on Latin *mansuetus* 'tame.'

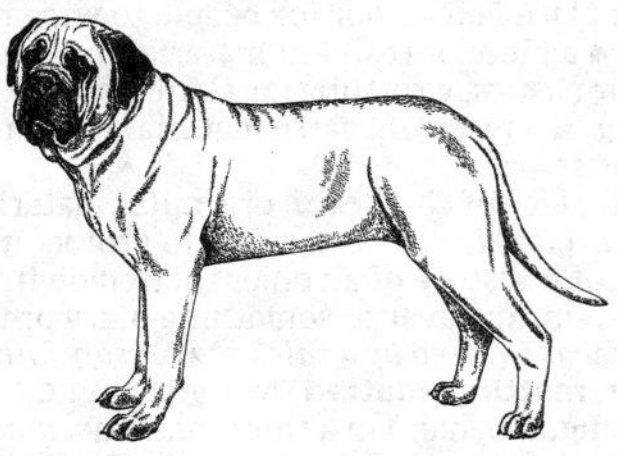

mastiff

mas·tiff bat ▶ **n.** a heavily built, free-tailed bat with a broad muzzle, found mainly in America and Australasia. ● *Eumops*, *Molossus*, and other genera, family Molossidae: several species, including the large **western mastiff bat** (*E. perotis*).

Mas·ti·goph·o·ra /ˌmastiˈgäfərə/ Zoology a group of single-celled animals that includes the protozoal flagellates, which are now generally divided among several phyla of the kingdom Protista. ● Subphylum (or superclass) Mastigophora.
– DERIVATIVES **mas·ti·goph·o·ran** /-ˈgäf(ə)rən/ **n. & adj.**
– ORIGIN modern Latin (plural), from Greek *mastigophoros*, from *mastix, mastig-* 'whip' + *-phoros* 'bearing.'

mas·ti·tis /maˈstītis/ ▶ **n.** inflammation of the mammary gland in the breast or udder, typically due to bacterial infection via a damaged nipple or teat.
– ORIGIN mid 19th cent.: from Greek *mastos* 'breast' + -ITIS.

mas·to·don /ˈmastəˌdän/ ▶ **n.** a large, extinct, elephantlike mammal of the Miocene to Pleistocene epochs, having teeth of a relatively primitive form and number. ● Mammutidae and other families, order Proboscidea: many species, including the **American mastodon** (*Mammut americanum*), which possibly survived to historical times in North America.
– ORIGIN early 19th cent.: modern Latin, from Greek *mastos* 'breast' + *odous, odont-* 'tooth' (with reference to nipple-shaped tubercles on the crowns of its molar teeth).

mastodon

PRONUNCIATION KEY ə *ago, up*; ər *over, fur*; a *hat*; ā *ate*; ä *car*; e *let*; ē *see*; i *fit*; ī *by*; NG *sing*; ō *go*; ô *law, for*; oi *toy*; o͝o *good*; o͞o *goo*; ou *out*; TH *thin*; T͟H *then*; ZH *vision*

mas·toid /ˈmasˌtoid/ ▶ **adj.** Anatomy of or relating to the mastoid process: *mastoid disease.*
▶ **n.** Anatomy the mastoid process. ■ (**mastoids**) [treated as sing.] informal mastoiditis.
– ORIGIN mid 18th cent.: via French and modern Latin from Greek *mastoeidēs* 'breast-shaped,' from *mastos* 'breast.'

mas·toid·i·tis /ˌmasˌtoidˈītis/ ▶ **n.** Medicine inflammation of the mastoid process.

mas·toid proc·ess ▶ **n.** a conical prominence of the temporal bone behind the ear, to which neck muscles are attached, and which has air spaces linked to the middle ear.

mas·tur·bate /ˈmastərˌbāt/ ▶ **v.** [no obj.] stimulate one's own genitals for sexual pleasure. ■ [with obj.] stimulate the genitals of (someone) to give them sexual pleasure.
– DERIVATIVES **mas·tur·ba·tion** /ˌmastərˈbāsʜən/ **n.**, **mas·tur·ba·tor n.**, **mas·tur·ba·to·ry** /-bəˌtôrē/ **adj.**
– ORIGIN mid 19th cent.: from Latin *masturbat-* 'masturbated,' from the verb *masturbari*, of unknown ultimate origin.

Ma·su·ri·a /məˈso͝orēə/ a low-lying forested region in northeastern Poland. Formerly part of East Prussia, it was assigned to Poland after World War II. Also called **Masurian Lakes**.

MAT[1] /mat/ ▶ **n.** a technology that uses chemicals (usually petrolatum, dimethicone, and polyquaternium) to reduce the ability of bacteria to adhere to the skin: *the company is developing MAT-containing soaps.*
– ORIGIN abbr. of *microbial anti-attachment technology.*

MAT[2] ▶ **abbr.** Master of Arts in Teaching.

mat[1] /mat/ ▶ **n. 1** a piece of protective material placed on a floor, in particular: ■ a piece of coarse material placed on a floor for people to wipe their feet on. ■ a piece of resilient material for landing on in gymnastics, wrestling, or similar sports. ■ a small rug. ■ a piece of coarse material for lying on: *a beach mat.*
2 a small piece of cork, card, or similar material placed on a table or other surface to protect it from the heat or moisture of an object placed on it.
3 a thick, untidy layer of something hairy or woolly: *his chest was covered by a thick mat of soft fair hair.*
▶ **v.** (**mats, matting, matted**) [with obj.] tangle (something, esp. hair) in a thick mass: *sweat matted his hair | the fur on its flank was matted with blood.* ■ [no obj.] become tangled.
– PHRASES **go to the mat** informal vigorously engage in an argument or dispute, typically on behalf of a particular person or cause. **on the mat** informal being reprimanded by someone in authority. [with military reference to the orderly room mat, where an accused would stand before the commanding officer.]
– ORIGIN Old English *m(e)att(e)*; related to Dutch *mat* and German *Matte*, from late Latin *matta*, from Phoenician.

mat[2] ▶ **n.** short for MATRIX (sense 2).

mat[3] ▶ **adj., n., & v.** variant spelling of MATTE[1].

mat. ▶ **abbr.** ■ matins. ■ maturity.

Mat·a·be·le /ˌmatəˈbēlē/ ▶ **n.** the Ndebele people collectively, particularly those of Zimbabwe.
– ORIGIN from Sotho *matebele*, singular *letebele*, the name given to this people.

mat·a·dor /ˈmatəˌdôr/ ▶ **n. 1** a bullfighter whose task is to kill the bull.
2 (in ombre, skat, and other card games) any of the highest trumps.
3 a domino game in which halves are matched so as to make a total of seven. ■ any of the dominoes that have seven spots altogether, together with the double blank.
– ORIGIN Spanish, literally 'killer,' from *matar* 'to kill,' from Persian *māt* 'dead'; senses relating to games are extended uses, expressing a notion of dominance or control.

Mat·a·gor·da Bay /ˌmatəˈgôrdə/ an inlet of the Gulf of Mexico in southeastern Texas, at the mouth of the Colorado River.

Ma·ta Ha·ri /ˈmätə ˈhärē, ˈmatə ˈharē/ (1876–1917), Dutch dancer and secret agent; born *Margaretha Geertruida Zelle.* She probably worked for both French and German intelligence services before being executed by the French in 1917. ■ (as noun **a Mata Hari**) a beautiful and seductive female spy.
– ORIGIN from Malay *mata* 'eye' and *hari* 'day,' as a compound meaning 'sun.'

ma·ta·ma·ta /ˌmatəməˈtä/ ▶ **n.** a grotesque South American freshwater turtle that has a broad flat head and neck with irregular projections of skin resembling waterweed. ● *Chelus fimbriatus*, family Chelidae.
– ORIGIN mid 19th cent.: of unknown origin; probably from a South American Indian language.

Mat·a·nus·ka Val·ley /ˌmatəˈno͞oskə/ an agricultural region in south central Alaska, northeast of Anchorage.

match[1] /macʜ/ ▶ **n. 1** a contest in which people or teams compete against each other in a particular sport: *a boxing match.*
2 a person or thing able to contend with another as an equal in quality or strength: *they were **no match for** the trained mercenaries.*
3 a person or thing that resembles or corresponds to another: *the child's identical twin would be a perfect match for organ donation.* ■ Computing a string that fulfills the specified conditions of a computer search. ■ a pair that corresponds or is very similar: *the headdresses and bouquet were a perfect match.* ■ the fact or appearance of corresponding: *stones of a perfect match and color.*
4 a person viewed in regard to their eligibility for marriage, esp. as regards class or wealth: *he was an unsuitable match for any of their girls.* ■ a marriage: *a dynastic match.*
▶ **v.** [with obj.] **1** correspond or cause to correspond in some essential respect; make or be harmonious: [with obj.] *we bought green and blue curtains to match the bedspread | she matched her steps **to** his* | [no obj.] *the jacket and pants do not match.* ■ team (someone or something) with someone or something else appropriate or harmonious: *they **matched** suitably qualified applicants **with** institutions that had vacancies | she was trying to **match** the draperies **to** the couch.*
2 be equal to (something) in quality or strength: *his anger matched her own.* ■ succeed in reaching or equaling (a standard or quality): *he tried to match her nonchalance.* ■ equalize (two coupled electrical impedances) so as to bring about the maximum transfer of power from one to the other.
3 place (a person or group) in contest or competition with another: *the big names were **matched against** nobodies* | (as adj., with submodifier **matched**) *evenly matched teams.*
– PHRASES **make a match** form a partnership, esp. by getting married. **meet one's match** encounter one's equal in strength or ability: *Iris had met her match.* **to match** corresponding in some essential respect with something previously mentioned or chosen: *a new coat and a hat to match.*
– PHRASAL VERBS **match up to** be as good as or equal to: *she matches up to the challenges of the job.* **match someone with** archaic bring about the marriage of someone to: *try if you can to match her with a duke.*
– DERIVATIVES **match·a·ble adj.**
– ORIGIN Old English *gemæcca* 'mate, companion'; related to the base of MAKE.

match[2] ▶ **n.** a short, thin piece of wood or cardboard used to light a fire, being tipped with a composition that ignites when rubbed against a rough surface. ■ historical a piece of wick or cord designed to burn at a uniform rate, used for firing a cannon or lighting gunpowder.
– PHRASES **put a match to** set fire to.
– ORIGIN late Middle English (in the sense 'wick of a candle'): from Old French *meche*, perhaps from Latin *myxa* 'spout of a lamp,' later 'lamp wick.'

match·board /ˈmacʜˌbôrd/ ▶ **n.** any of a set of interlocking boards joined together by a tongue cut along the edge of one board and fitting into a groove along the edge of another. Also called **matched board**.

match·book /ˈmacʜˌbo͝ok/ ▶ **n.** a small cardboard folder of matches with a striking surface on one side.

match·box /ˈmacʜˌbäks/ ▶ **n.** a small box in which matches are sold. ■ [usu. as modifier] something very small, esp. a house, apartment, or room: *her new thimble-sized, matchbox apartment.*

match·ing /ˈmacʜiNG/ ▶ **adj. 1** corresponding in pattern, color, or design; complementary: *a blue jacket and matching skirt.*
2 equal in number or amount; equivalent: *the college will provide matching funds to complete the project.*

match·less /ˈmacʜləs/ ▶ **adj.** unable to be equaled; incomparable: *the Parthenon has a matchless beauty.*
– DERIVATIVES **match·less·ly adv.**

match·lock /ˈmacʜˌläk/ ▶ **n.** historical a type of gun with a lock in which a piece of wick or cord is placed for igniting the powder: [as modifier] *matchlock guns.* ■ a lock of this kind.

match·mak·er /ˈmacʜˌmākər/ ▶ **n.** a person who arranges relationships and marriages between others, either informally or, in certain cultural communities, as a formal occupation. ■ a person or company that brings parties together for commercial purposes.
– DERIVATIVES **match·mak·ing** /-ˌmākiNG/ **n.**

match play ▶ **n.** play in golf in which the score is reckoned by counting the holes won by each side, as opposed to the number of strokes taken. Compare with STROKE PLAY.

match point ▶ **n. 1** (in tennis and other sports) a point that if won by one contestant will also win the match.
2 (**matchpoint**) (in duplicate bridge) a unit of scoring in matches and tournaments: *a convincing margin of 54 matchpoints.*

match·stick /ˈmacʜˌstik/ ▶ **n.** the stem of a match, esp. a wooden one. ■ something likened to a match in being long and thin: *cut the vegetables into matchsticks* | [as modifier] *matchstick legs.*

match·up /ˈmacʜəp/ ▶ **n.** a contest between athletes or sports teams: *a matchup of two twenty-something pitchers wondering what it is like to win in the majors.* ■ Basketball another term for a man-to-man defense. See MAN-TO-MAN at MAN.

match·wood /ˈmacʜˌwo͝od/ ▶ **n.** very small pieces or splinters of wood: *their boat was shattered into matchwood against the rocks.* ■ light wood suitable for making matches.

mate[1] /māt/ ▶ **n. 1** each of a pair of birds or other animals: *a male bird sings to court a mate.* ■ informal a person's husband, wife, or other sexual partner. ■ informal one of a matched pair: *a sock without its mate.*
2 [in combination] a fellow member or joint occupant of a specified thing: *his tablemates.* ■ Brit. informal used as a friendly form of address between men or boys: *"See you then, mate."* ■ Brit. informal a friend or companion: *I was with a mate | my best mate, Steve.*
3 an assistant or deputy, in particular: ■ an assistant to a skilled worker: *a plumber's mate.* ■ a deck officer on a merchant ship subordinate to the master. See also FIRST MATE.
▶ **v. 1** [no obj.] (of animals or birds) come together for breeding; copulate: *successful males may **mate with** many females.* ■ [with obj.] bring (animals or birds) together for breeding. ■ join in marriage or sexual partnership: *people tend to **mate with** others in their own social class.*
2 connect or be connected mechanically. [with obj.] *a four-cylinder engine **mated to** a five-speed gearbox.*
– DERIVATIVES **mate·less adj.**
– ORIGIN late Middle English: from Middle Low German *māt(e)* 'comrade,' of West Germanic origin; related to MEAT (the underlying notion being that of eating together).

mate[2] ▶ **n. & v.** Chess short for CHECKMATE.
– ORIGIN Middle English: the noun from Anglo-Norman French *mat* (from the phrase *eschec mat* 'checkmate'); the verb from Anglo-Norman French *mater* 'to checkmate.'

ma·té /ˈmäˌtā/ (also **yerba maté**) ▶ **n. 1** (also **maté tea**) an infusion of the leaves of a South American shrub, which is high in caffeine and bitter. ■ the leaves of this shrub.
2 the South American shrub of the holly family that produces these leaves. ● *Ilex paraguariensis*, family Aquifoliaceae.
– ORIGIN early 18th cent.: from Spanish *mate*, from Quechua *mati.*

mat·e·las·sé /ˌmatlˌäˈsā, ˌmätlä-/ ▶ **adj.** (of a silk or wool fabric) having a raised design like quilting.
▶ **n.** fabric of this type.
– ORIGIN late 19th cent.: French, literally 'quilted,' past participle of *matelasser*, from *matelas* 'mattress.'

mate·lot /ˌmatlˈō, matˈlō/ ▶ **n.** Brit. informal a sailor.
– ORIGIN mid 19th cent. (nautical slang): from French, variant of *matenot*, from Middle Dutch *mattenoot* 'bed companion,' because sailors had to share hammocks in twos.

mat·e·lote /ˌmatlˈōt, matˈlōt/ ▶ **n.** a dish of fish in a sauce of wine and onions.
– ORIGIN French, from *à la matelote*, literally 'mariner-style,' from *matelot* 'sailor' (see MATELOT).

ma·ter /ˈmātər/ ▶ **n.** Brit. informal or dated mother: *the mater has kept the house in London.*
– ORIGIN Latin.

ma·ter do·lo·ro·sa /ˈmätər ˌdōləˈrōsə, ˈmätər, ˌdäl-/ the Virgin Mary sorrowing for the death of Jesus Christ, esp. as a representation in art.
– ORIGIN from medieval Latin, 'sorrowful mother.'

ma·ter·fa·mil·i·as /ˌmātərfəˈmilēəs, ˌmätər-/ ▶ **n.** (pl. **matresfamilias** /ˌmäˌtrās-, ˌmätərz-/) the female head of a family or household. Compare with PATERFAMILIAS.
– ORIGIN Latin, from *mater* 'mother' + *familias*, old genitive form of *familia* 'family.'

ma·te·ri·al /məˈti(ə)rēəl/ ▶ **n. 1** the matter from which a thing is or can be made: *goats can eat more or less any plant material | materials such as brass | highly flammable materials.* ■ (usu. **materials**) things needed for an activity: *cleaning materials.* ■ [with adj. or noun modifier] a person of a specified

quality or suitability: *he's not really Olympic material.*
2 facts, information, or ideas for use in creating a book or other work: *there is much good material here for priests to use in sermons.* ■ items, esp. songs or jokes, comprising a performer's act: *a band playing original material.*
3 cloth or fabric: *a piece of dark material | dress materials.*
▶ adj. 1 [attrib.] denoting or consisting of physical objects rather than the mind or spirit: *the material world | moral and material support.* ■ concerned with physical needs or desires: *material living standards have risen.* ■ concerned with the matter of reasoning, not its form: *political conflict lacks mathematical or material certitude.*
2 important; essential; relevant: *the insects did not do any material damage to the crop.* ■ chiefly Law (of evidence or a fact) significant, influential, or relevant, esp. to the extent of determining a cause or affecting a judgment: *information that could be material to a murder inquiry.*
– ORIGIN late Middle English (in the sense 'relating to matter'): from late Latin *materialis*, adjective from Latin *materia* 'matter.'

ma·te·ri·al cause ▶ n. Philosophy (in Aristotelian thought) the matter or substance that constitutes a thing.

ma·te·ri·al·ism /məˈti(ə)rēəˌlizəm/ ▶ n. 1 a tendency to consider material possessions and physical comfort as more important than spiritual values.
2 Philosophy the doctrine that nothing exists except matter and its movements and modifications. ■ the doctrine that consciousness and will are wholly due to material agency. See also DIALECTICAL MATERIALISM.
– DERIVATIVES **ma·te·ri·al·ist** n. & adj.

ma·te·ri·al·is·tic /məˌti(ə)rēəˈlistik/ ▶ adj. excessively concerned with material possessions; money-oriented: *we're living in a highly materialistic society.*
– DERIVATIVES **ma·te·ri·al·is·ti·cal·ly** adv.

ma·te·ri·al·i·ty /məˌti(ə)rēˈalitē/ ▶ n. (pl. **materialities**) the quality or character of being material or composed of matter. ■ chiefly Law the quality of being relevant or significant: *the applicant must establish materiality on the balance of probabilities.*

ma·te·ri·al·ize /məˈti(ə)rēəˌlīz/ ▶ v. [no obj.] 1 (of a ghost, spirit, or similar entity) appear in bodily form. ■ [with obj.] cause to appear in bodily or physical form.
2 become actual fact; happen: *the assumed savings may not materialize.* ■ appear or be present: *the train didn't materialize.*
– DERIVATIVES **ma·te·ri·al·i·za·tion** /məˌti(ə)rēələˈzāSHən/ n.

ma·te·ri·al·ly /məˈti(ə)rēəlē/ ▶ adv. 1 [often as submodifier] substantially; considerably: *materially different circumstances.*
2 in terms of wealth or material possessions: *a materially and culturally rich area.*

ma·te·ri·al wit·ness ▶ n. Law a witness whose evidence is likely to be sufficiently important to influence the outcome of a trial.

ma·te·ria med·i·ca /məˈti(ə)rēə ˈmedikə/ ▶ n. the body of remedial substances used in the practice of medicine. ■ the study of the origin and properties of these substances.
– ORIGIN late 17th cent.: modern Latin, translation of Greek *hulē iatrikē* 'healing material' (the title of a work by Dioscorides).

ma·te·ri·el /məˌti(ə)rēˈel/ (also **matériel**) ▶ n. military materials and equipment. Often contrasted with PERSONNEL.
– ORIGIN early 19th cent.: from French *matériel*, adjective (used as a noun).

ma·ter·nal /məˈtərnl/ ▶ adj. of or relating to a mother, esp. during pregnancy or shortly after childbirth: *maternal age | maternal care.* ■ [attrib.] related through the mother's side of the family: *my maternal grandfather.* ■ denoting feelings associated with or typical of a mother; motherly: *maternal instincts.*
– DERIVATIVES **ma·ter·nal·ism** /-ˌizəm/ n., **ma·ter·nal·ist** /-ist/ adj., **ma·ter·nal·is·tic** /məˌtərnlˈistik/ adj., **ma·ter·nal·ly** adv.
– ORIGIN late 15th cent.: from French *maternel*, from Latin *maternus*, from *mater* 'mother.'

ma·ter·ni·ty /məˈtərnətē/ ▶ n. motherhood. ■ [usu. as modifier] the period during pregnancy and shortly after childbirth: *maternity leave | maternity clothes.*
– ORIGIN early 17th cent.: from French *maternité*, from Latin *maternus*, from *mater* 'mother.'

mate·y /ˈmātē/ Brit. informal ▶ n. used as a familiar and sometimes hostile form of address, esp. to a stranger: *"Shove off, matey, she's mine."*
▶ adj. (**matier, matiest**) familiar and friendly; sociable: *a fixed, matey grin.*

math /maTH/ ▶ n. informal mathematics: *she teaches math and science.*
– ORIGIN mid 19th cent.: abbreviation.

math·e·mat·i·cal /ˌmaTH(ə)ˈmatikəl/ (also **mathematic**) ▶ adj. of or relating to mathematics: *mathematical equations.* ■ (of a proof or analysis) rigorously precise: *mathematical thinking | figurative he arranged the meal with mathematical precision on a plate.*
– DERIVATIVES **math·e·mat·i·cal·ly** /-ik(ə)lē/ adv.
– ORIGIN late Middle English: from Latin *mathematicalis*, from Greek *mathēmatikos*, from *mathēma, mathēmat-* 'science,' from the base of *manthanein* 'learn.'

math·e·mat·i·cal in·duc·tion ▶ n. see INDUCTION (sense 3).

math·e·mat·i·cal log·ic ▶ n. the part of mathematics concerned with the study of formal languages, formal reasoning, the nature of mathematical proof, provability of mathematical statements, computability, and other aspects of the foundations of mathematics.

math·e·ma·ti·cian /ˌmaTH(ə)məˈtiSHən/ ▶ n. an expert in or student of mathematics.
– ORIGIN late Middle English: from Old French *mathematicien*, from Latin *mathematicus* 'mathematical,' from Greek *mathēmatikos* (see MATHEMATICAL).

math·e·mat·ics /maTH(ə)ˈmatiks/ ▶ plural n. [usu. treated as sing.] the abstract science of number, quantity, and space. Mathematics may be studied in its own right (**pure mathematics**), or as it is applied to other disciplines such as physics and engineering (**applied mathematics**). ■ [often treated as pl.] the mathematical aspects of something: *the mathematics of general relativity.*
– ORIGIN late 16th cent.: plural of obsolete *mathematic* 'mathematics,' from Old French *mathematique*, from Latin (*ars*) *mathematica* 'mathematical (art),' from Greek *mathēmatikē* (*tekhnē*), from the base of *manthanein* 'learn.'

math·e·ma·tize /ˈmaT͟Hə)məˌtīz/ ▶ v. [with obj.] regard or treat (a subject or problem) in mathematical terms.
– DERIVATIVES **math·e·ma·ti·za·tion** /ˌmaT͟H(ə) mətəˈzāSHən/ n.

Math·er[1] /ˈmaT͟Hər/, Cotton (1663–1728), American minister and writer; son of Increase Mather. Noted for his political writings, he sponsored the Massachusetts charter in 1691 and is thought to have influenced the events that led to the Salem witch trials in 1692.

Math·er[2], Increase (1639–1723), American minister; father of Cotton Mather. A Congregationalist, he was the pastor of North Church in Boston 1664–1723 and the president of Harvard College 1685–1701.

Math·er[3], John Cromwell (1946–), US astrophysicist. His work with George Smoot on the COBE project advanced the study of the Big Bang theory. Nobel Prize for Physics (2006), shared with Smoot.

Math·ew·son /ˈmaTHyo͞osən/, Christy (1880–1925), US baseball player; full name *Christopher Mathewson.* A pitcher for the New York Giants 1900–1916, he won 22 or more games per year for 12 straight years and pitched three shutouts in the 1905 World Series. He later managed the Cincinnati Reds 1916–18 and was president of the Boston Braves 1923–25. Baseball Hall of Fame (1936).

Ma·thi·as /məˈTHīəs/, Bob (1930–2006), US track and field athlete and politician; full name *Robert Bruce Mathias.* At 17, he was the youngest winner of the decathlon with a gold medal in the 1948 Olympic Games and another in the 1952 games. He later served as a Republican member of the US House of Representatives from California 1967–1975.

maths /maTHs/ ▶ plural n. [treated as sing.] Brit. informal mathematics: [as modifier] *her mother was a maths teacher.*
– ORIGIN early 20th cent.: abbreviation.

Ma·til·da[1] /məˈtildə/ (1102–67), English princess; daughter of Henry I and mother of Henry II; known as **the Empress Maud.** Henry's only legitimate child, she was named his heir, but her cousin Stephen seized the throne on Henry's death in 1135. She waged an unsuccessful civil war against Stephen until 1148.

Ma·til·da[2] ▶ n. Austral. informal a bushman's bundle of possessions carried when traveling.
– PHRASES **waltz** (or **walk**) **Matilda** carry such a bundle.
– ORIGIN late 19th cent.: from the given name *Matilda.*

mat·in·al /ˈmatn-l/ ▶ adj. rare relating to or taking place in the morning.
– ORIGIN early 19th cent.: from French, from *matin* 'morning.'

mat·i·nee /ˌmatnˈā/ (also **matinée**) ▶ n. a performance in a theater or a showing of a movie that takes place in the daytime.
– ORIGIN mid 19th cent.: from French *matinée*, literally 'morning (as a period of activity),' from *matin* 'morning.'

mat·i·nee i·dol ▶ n. informal, dated a handsome actor admired chiefly by women.

mat·ing /ˈmātiNG/ ▶ n. the action of animals coming together to breed; copulation: *ovulation occurs only if mating has taken place.*

mat·ins /ˈmatnz/ (Brit. also **mattins**) ▶ n. a service of morning prayer in various churches, esp. the Anglican Church. ■ a service forming part of the traditional Divine Office of the Western Christian Church, originally said (or chanted) at or after midnight, but historically often held with lauds on the previous evening. ■ (also **matin**) literary the morning song of birds.
– ORIGIN Middle English: from Old French *matines*, plural (influenced by ecclesiastical Latin *matutinae* 'morning prayers') of *matin* 'morning,' from Latin *matutinum*, neuter of *matutinus* 'early in the morning,' from *Matuta*, the name of the dawn goddess.

Ma·tisse /məˈtēs, mä-/, Henri (Emile Benoît) (1869–1954), French painter and sculptor. His use of nonnaturalistic color led him to be considered a leader among the Fauvists. His later paintings and sculptures display a trend toward formal simplification and abstraction.

Ma·to Gros·so /ˌmätə ˈgrōso͞o/ a high plateau region in southwestern Brazil that forms a watershed between the Amazon and Plate river systems.
– ORIGIN Portuguese, literally 'dense forest.'

ma·tri·arch /ˈmātrēˌärk/ ▶ n. a woman who is the head of a family or tribe. ■ an older woman who is powerful within a family or organization: *a domineering matriarch.*
– DERIVATIVES **ma·tri·ar·chal** /ˌmātrēˈärkəl/ adj.
– ORIGIN early 17th cent.: from Latin *mater* 'mother,' on the false analogy of *patriarch.*

ma·tri·ar·chate /ˈmātrēˌärˌkāt, -ˌärkət/ ▶ n. a matriarchal form of social organization, esp. in a tribal society.

ma·tri·ar·chy /ˈmātrēˌärkē/ ▶ n. (pl. **matriarchies**) a system of society or government ruled by a woman or women. ■ a form of social organization in which descent and relationship are reckoned through the female line. ■ the state of being an older, powerful woman in a family or group: *she cherished a dream of matriarchy—catered to by grandchildren.*

ma·tri·ces /ˈmātrəˌsēz/ plural form of MATRIX.

mat·ri·cide /ˈmatrəˌsīd, ˈmā-/ ▶ n. the killing of one's mother: *a man suspected of matricide.* ■ a person who kills their mother.
– DERIVATIVES **mat·ri·cid·al** /ˌmatrəˈsīdl, ˌmā-/ adj.
– ORIGIN late 16th cent.: from Latin *matricidium*, from *mater, matr-* 'mother' + *-cidium* (see -CIDE).

ma·tric·u·late /məˈtrikyəˌlāt/ ▶ v. 1 [no obj.] be enrolled at a college or university: *he matriculated at the University of Vermont.* ■ [with obj.] admit (a student) to a college or university.
2 [with obj.] Heraldry, chiefly Scottish record (arms) in an official register.
▶ n. /məˈtrikyəˌlət/ chiefly Indian a person who has matriculated.
– DERIVATIVES **ma·tric·u·la·tion** /məˌtrikyəˈlāSHən/ n.
– ORIGIN late 16th cent.: from medieval Latin *matriculat-* 'enrolled,' from the verb *matriculare*, from late Latin *matricula* 'register,' diminutive of Latin *matrix.*

mat·ri·fo·cal /ˈmatriˌfōkəl, ˈmā-/ ▶ adj. (of a society, culture, etc.) based on the mother as the head of the family or household.
– ORIGIN 1950s: from Latin *mater, matr-* 'mother' + FOCAL.

mat·ri·lin·e·al /ˌmatrəˈlinēəl, ˌmā-/ ▶ adj. of or based on kinship with the mother or the female line.
– DERIVATIVES **mat·ri·lin·e·al·ly** adv.
– ORIGIN early 20th cent.: from Latin *mater, matr-* 'mother' + LINEAL.

mat·ri·lo·cal /ˌmatrəˈlōkəl, ˈmā-/ ▶ adj. of or denoting a custom in marriage whereby the husband goes to live with the wife's community.
– DERIVATIVES **mat·ri·lo·cal·i·ty** /-lōˈkalətē/ n.

m

– ORIGIN early 20th cent.: from Latin *mater, matr-* 'mother' + LOCAL.

mat·ri·mo·ni·al /ˌmatrəˈmōnēəl/ ▶ **adj.** of or relating to marriage or married people: *matrimonial bonds.*
– DERIVATIVES **mat·ri·mo·ni·al·ly** adv.
– ORIGIN late Middle English: via Old French from Latin *matrimonialis*, from *matrimonium* (see MATRIMONY).

mat·ri·mo·ny /ˈmatrəˌmōnē/ ▶ **n.** the state or ceremony of being married; marriage: *a couple joined in matrimony | the sacrament of holy matrimony.*
– ORIGIN late Middle English: via Old French from Latin *matrimonium*, based on *mater, matr-* 'mother.'

ma·tri·osh·ka /ˌmatrēˈäsHkə/ ▶ **n.** variant spelling of MATRYOSHKA.

ma·trix /ˈmātriks/ ▶ **n.** (pl. **matrices** /ˈmātrisēz/ or **matrixes**) **1** an environment or material in which something develops; a surrounding medium or structure: *free choices become the matrix of human life.* ■ a mass of fine-grained rock in which gems, crystals, or fossils are embedded. ■ Biology the substance between cells or in which structures are embedded. ■ fine material: *the matrix of gravel paths is raked regularly.*
2 a mold in which something, such as printing type or a phonograph record, is cast or shaped.
3 Mathematics a rectangular array of quantities or expressions in rows and columns that is treated as a single entity and manipulated according to particular rules. ■ an organizational structure in which two or more lines of command, responsibility, or communication may run through the same individual.
– ORIGIN late Middle English (in the sense 'womb'): from Latin, 'breeding female,' later 'womb,' from *mater, matr-* 'mother.'

ma·tron /ˈmātrən/ ▶ **n. 1** a woman in charge of domestic and medical arrangements at a boarding school or other establishment. ■ a female prison officer.
2 a married woman, esp. a dignified and sober middle-aged one.
– DERIVATIVES **ma·tron·hood** /-ˌho͝od/ n.
– ORIGIN late Middle English (sense 2): from Old French *matrone*, from Latin *matrona*, from *mater, matr-* 'mother.'

m

ma·tron·ly /ˈmātrənlē/ ▶ **adj.** like or characteristic of a matron, esp. in being dignified and staid and typically associated with having a large or plump build: *she was beginning to look matronly.*

ma·tron of hon·or ▶ **n.** a married woman attending the bride at a wedding.

mat·ro·nym·ic /ˌmatrəˈnimik/ (also **metronymic** /ˌme-/) ▶ **n.** a name derived from the name of a mother or female ancestor.
▶ **adj.** (of a name) so derived.
– ORIGIN late 18th cent.: from Latin *mater, matr-* 'mother,' on the pattern of *patronymic.*

ma·try·osh·ka /ˌmatrēˈäsHkə/ (also **matryoshka doll**) ▶ **n.** (pl. **matryoshki** /-kē/) each of a set of brightly painted hollow wooden dolls of varying sizes, designed to nest inside one another. Also called RUSSIAN DOLL.
– ORIGIN 1940s: from Russian *matrëshka.*

mat·su·ri /matˈso͝orē/ ▶ **n.** a solemn festival celebrated periodically at Shinto shrines in Japan.
– ORIGIN Japanese.

Ma·tsu·ya·ma /ˌmätsəˈyämə/ a city in Japan, the capital and largest city of the island of Shikoku; pop. 513,902 (2007).

matt ▶ **adj., n., & v.** variant spelling of MATTE[1].

Matt. ▶ **abbr.** Bible Matthew.

matte[1] /mat/ (also **matt** or **mat**) ▶ **adj.** (of a color, paint, or surface) dull and flat, without a shine: *matte black.*
▶ **n. 1** a matte color, paint, or finish: *the varnishes are available in gloss, satin, and matte.*
2 a sheet of cardboard placed on the back of a picture, either as a mount or to form a border around the picture.
▶ **v.** (**mattes, matting, matted**) [with obj.] give a matte appearance to (something).
– ORIGIN early 17th cent. (as a verb): from French *mat.*

matte[2] ▶ **n.** an impure product of the smelting of sulfide ores, esp. those of copper or nickel.
– ORIGIN mid 19th cent.: from French (in Old French meaning 'curds'), feminine of *mat* (adjective) 'dull, matte,' used as a noun.

matte[3] ▶ **n.** a mask used to obscure part of an image in a film and allow another image to be substituted, combining the two.
– ORIGIN mid 19th cent.: from French, perhaps from *mat* (see MATT).

mat·ted /ˈmatid/ ▶ **adj. 1** (esp. of hair or fur) tangled into a thick mass: *a cardigan of matted gray wool.*
2 covered or furnished with mats: *the matted floor.*

mat·ter /ˈmatər/ ▶ **n. 1** physical substance in general, as distinct from mind and spirit; (in physics) that which occupies space and possesses rest mass, esp. as distinct from energy: *the structure and properties of matter.* ■ a substance or material: *organic matter | vegetable matter | fecal matter.* ■ written or printed material: *reading matter.*
2 an affair or situation under consideration; a topic: *a great deal of work was done on this matter | financial matters.* ■ Law something that is to be tried or proved in court; a case. ■ (**matters**) the present situation or state of affairs: *we can do nothing to change matters.* ■ (**a matter for/of**) something that evokes a specified feeling: *it's a matter of complete indifference to me.* ■ (**a matter for**) something that is the concern of a specified person or agency: *the evidence is a matter for the courts.*
3 [usu. with negative or in questions] (**the matter**) the reason for distress or a problem: *what's the matter? | pretend that nothing's the matter.*
4 the substance or content of a text as distinct from its manner or form. ■ Printing the body of a printed work, as distinct from titles, headings, etc. ■ Logic the particular content of a proposition, as distinct from its form.
▶ **v.** [no obj.] **1** [usu. with negative or in questions] be of importance; have significance: *it doesn't matter what the guests wear | what did it matter to them? | to him, animals mattered more than human beings.* ■ (of a person) be important or influential: *she was trying to get known by the people who matter.*
2 rare (of a wound) secrete or discharge pus.
– PHRASES **for that matter** used to indicate that a subject or category, though mentioned second, is as relevant or important as the first: *I am not sure what value it adds to determining public, or for that matter private, policy.* **in the matter of** as regards: *the British are given preeminence in the matter of tea.* **it is only a matter of time** there will not be long to wait: *it's only a matter of time before the general is removed.* **a matter of 1** no more than (a specified period of time): *they were shown the door in a matter of minutes.* **2** a thing that involves or depends on: *it's a matter of working out how to get something done.* **a matter of course** the natural or expected thing: *the reports are published as a matter of course.* **a matter of form** a point of correct procedure: *they must as a matter of proper form check to see that there is no tax liability.* **a matter of record** see RECORD. **no matter 1** [with clause] regardless of: *no matter what the government calls them, they are cuts.* **2** it is of no importance: *"No matter, I'll go myself."* **to make matters worse** with the result that a bad situation is made worse. **what matter?** Brit. dated why should that worry us?: *what matter if he was a Protestant or not?*
– ORIGIN Middle English: via Old French from Latin *materia* 'timber, substance,' also 'subject of discourse,' from *mater* 'mother.'

Mat·ter·horn /ˈmatərˌhôrn/ a mountain in the Alps that is 14,688 feet (4,477 m) high, on the border between Switzerland and Italy. French name MONT CERVIN; Italian name MONTE CERVINO.

Matterhorn

mat·ter of fact ▶ **n.** something that belongs to the sphere of fact as distinct from opinion or conjecture: *it's a matter of fact that they had a relationship.* ■ Law the part of a judicial inquiry concerned with the truth of alleged facts. Often contrasted with MATTER OF LAW.
▶ **adj.** (**matter-of-fact**) unemotional and practical: *he was characteristically calm and matter-of-fact.* ■ concerned only with factual content rather than style or expression: *the text is written in a breezy matter-of-fact manner.*
– PHRASES **as a matter of fact** in reality (used esp. to correct a falsehood or misunderstanding): *as a matter of fact, I was talking to him this afternoon.*
– DERIVATIVES **mat·ter-of-fact·ly** adv., **mat·ter-of-fact·ness** n.

mat·ter of law ▶ **n.** Law the part of a judicial inquiry concerned with the interpretation of the law. Often contrasted with MATTER OF FACT.

Mat·thau /ˈmaTHou/, Walter (1920–2000), US actor. He starred in The *Odd Couple*, both on Broadway (1965) and in the movie (1968). Among his other movies were *The Fortune Cookie* (1966), *The Sunshine Boys* (1975), *Grumpy Old Men* (1993), and *Hanging Up* (2000).

Mat·thew, St. /ˈmaTHyo͞o/ an Apostle; a tax collector from Capernaum in Galilee; traditional author of the first Gospel. Feast day, September 21. ■ the first Gospel, written after AD 70 and based largely on that of St. Mark.

Mat·thew Par·is (*c.*1199–1259), English chronicler and Benedictine monk; noted for his *Chronica Majora*, a history of the world from the Creation to the mid 13th century.

Mat·thews /ˈmaTHyo͞oz/, Stanley (1824–89), US Supreme Court associate justice 1881–89. He was appointed to the Court by President Garfield. A previous nomination by President Hayes in 1880 had been rejected because it was felt that a conflict of interest existed.

Mat·thi·as, St. /məˈTHīəs/ an Apostle; chosen by lot after the Ascension to replace Judas. Feast day (Western Church) May 14; (Eastern Church) August 9.

Mat·thies·sen /ˈmaTH(y)əsən/, Peter (1927–), US writer. Notable works include the novels *Far Tortuga* (1974) and *Killing Mr. Watson* (1990) and the travel-based nonfiction *The Snow Leopard* (1978) and *East of Lo Monthang* (1995).

mat·ting /ˈmatiNG/ ▶ **n. 1** material used for mats, esp. coarse fabric woven from a natural fiber: *rush matting.*
2 the process of becoming matted.

mat·tins /ˈmatnz/ ▶ **n.** variant spelling of MATINS.

mat·tock /ˈmatək/ ▶ **n.** an agricultural tool shaped like a pickax, with an adze and a chisel edge as the ends of the head.
– ORIGIN Old English *mattuc*, of uncertain origin.

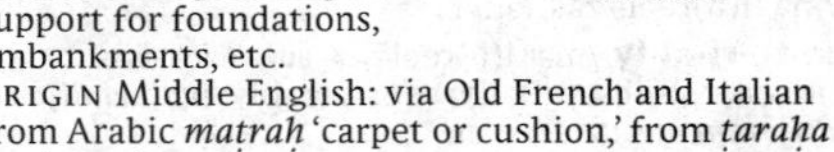
mattock

mat·tress /ˈmatrəs/ ▶ **n.** a fabric case filled with deformable or resilient material, used for sleeping on. ■ Engineering a flat structure of brushwood, concrete, or other material used as strengthening or support for foundations, embankments, etc.
– ORIGIN Middle English: via Old French and Italian from Arabic *matraḥ* 'carpet or cushion,' from *ṭaraḥa* 'to throw.'

mat·u·rate /ˈmaCHəˌrāt/ ▶ **v.** [no obj.] Medicine (of a boil, abscess, etc.) form pus.
– ORIGIN mid 16th cent.: from Latin *maturat-* 'ripened, hastened,' from the verb *maturare*, from *maturus* (see MATURE).

mat·u·ra·tion /ˌmaCHəˈrāSHən/ ▶ **n.** the action or process of maturing: *sexual maturation.* ■ (of wine or other fermented drink) the process of becoming ready for drinking. ■ the ripening of fruit: *pod maturation.* ■ Medicine the development of functional ova or sperm cells. ■ the formation of pus in a boil, abscess, etc.
– DERIVATIVES **mat·u·ra·tion·al** adj., **ma·tur·a·tive** /ˈmaCHəˌrātiv/ adj.
– ORIGIN late Middle English (denoting the formation of pus): from medieval Latin *maturatio(n-)*, from Latin *maturare* (see MATURE).

ma·ture /məˈCHo͝or, -ˈt(y)o͝or/ ▶ **adj.** (**maturer, maturest**) **1** fully developed physically; full-grown: *she was now a mature woman | owls are sexually mature at one year | mature trees.* ■ having reached an advanced stage of mental or emotional development characteristic of an adult: *a young man mature beyond his years.* ■ (of thought or planning) careful and thorough: *on mature reflection he decided they should not go.* ■ used euphemistically to describe someone as being middle-aged or old: *Miss Walker was a mature lady when she married.* ■ (of a style) fully developed: *Van Gogh's mature work.* ■ (of certain foodstuffs or drinks) ready for consumption.
2 denoting an economy, industry, or market that has developed to a point where substantial expansion and investment no longer takes place.
3 (of a bill) due for payment.
▶ **v.** [no obj.] **1** (of an organism) become physically mature: *children mature at different ages | the trees*

*take at least thirty years to mature | she **matured** into a woman.* ■ (of a person) reach an advanced stage of mental or emotional development: *men mature as they grow older.* ■ (with reference to certain foodstuffs or drinks) become or cause to become ready for consumption: [no obj.] *leave the cheese to mature* | [with obj.] *the Scotch is matured for a minimum of three years.*
2 (of an insurance policy, security, etc.) reach the end of its term and hence become payable.
– DERIVATIVES **ma·ture·ly** adv.
– ORIGIN late Middle English: from Latin *maturus* 'timely, ripe'; perhaps related to **MATINS**.

ma·tu·ri·ty /mə'CHo͝orité, mə't(y)o͝or-/ ▶ n. the state, fact, or period of being mature: *their experience, maturity, and strong work ethic | the delicate style of his maturity.* ■ the time when an insurance policy, security, etc., matures. ■ an insurance policy, security, etc., having a fixed maturity date.
– ORIGIN late Middle English: from Latin *maturitas*, from *maturus* (see **MATURE**).

ma·tu·ti·nal /mə't(y)o͞otn-əl, ˌmacHə'tīnl/ ▶ adj. formal of or occurring in the morning.
– ORIGIN mid 16th cent.: from late Latin *matutinalis*, from Latin *matutinus* 'early.'

mat·zo (also **matzoh** or **matzah** /'mätsə/) ▶ n. (pl. **matzos** or **matzoth** /-ˌsōt, -ˌsōs/) a thin, crisp unleavened bread, traditionally eaten by Jews during Passover.
– ORIGIN Yiddish, from Hebrew *maṣṣāh*.

mat·zo ball ▶ n. a small dumpling made of seasoned matzo meal bound together with egg and chicken fat, typically served in chicken soup.

mat·zo meal ▶ n. meal made from ground matzos.

maud /môd/ ▶ n. a gray striped plaid cloak, formerly worn by shepherds in Scotland.
– ORIGIN late 18th cent.: of unknown origin.

maud·lin /'môdlin/ ▶ adj. self-pityingly or tearfully sentimental, often through drunkenness: *the drink made her maudlin | a maudlin ballad.*
– ORIGIN late Middle English (as a noun denoting Mary Magdalen): from Old French *Madeleine*, from ecclesiastical Latin *Magdalena* (see **MAGDALENE**). The sense of the adjective derives from allusion to pictures of Mary Magdalen weeping.

Maugham /môm/, W. Somerset (1874–1965), British novelist, short-story writer, and playwright, born in France; full name *William Somerset Maugham*. Notable novels: *Of Human Bondage* (1915), *The Moon and Sixpence* (1919), and *Cakes and Ale* (1930).

Mau·i /'moueē/ the second largest of the Hawaiian islands, northwest of the island of Hawaii.

maul /môl/ ▶ v. [with obj.] (of an animal) wound (a person or animal) by scratching and tearing: *the herdsmen were mauled by lions.* ■ treat (someone or something) roughly.
▶ n. a tool with a heavy head and a handle, used for tasks such as ramming, crushing, and driving wedges; a beetle.
– DERIVATIVES **maul·er** n.
– ORIGIN Middle English (in the sense 'hammer or wooden club,' also 'strike with a heavy weapon'): from Old French *mail*, from Latin *malleus* 'hammer.'

maul·stick ▶ n. variant of **MAHLSTICK**.

maul·vi ▶ n. variant spelling of **MOULVI**.

Mau Mau /'mou ˌmou/ an African secret society originating among the Kikuyu that in the 1950s used violence and terror to try to expel European settlers and end British rule in Kenya. The British eventually subdued the organization, but Kenya gained independence in 1963. ■ (**mau-mau**) [as verb with obj.] informal terrorize or threaten (someone).
– ORIGIN Kikuyu.

Mau·na Kea /ˌmounə 'kāə, ˌmônə/ an extinct volcano on the island of Hawaii, in the central Pacific. Rising to 13,796 feet (4,205 m), it is the highest peak in the Hawaiian islands. The summit area is the site of several large telescopes.

Mau·na Lo·a /'lōə, ˌmônə/ an active volcano on the island of Hawaii that is 13,678 feet (4,169 m) high, south of Mauna Kea.

maund /mônd/ ▶ n. a varying unit of weight in some Asian countries, esp. an Indian unit of weight equal to 40 seers.

maun·der /'môndər/ ▶ v. [no obj.] talk in a rambling manner: *Dennis **maundered on about** the wine.* ■ [with adverbial] move or act in a dreamy or idle manner: *he maunders through the bank, composing his thoughts.*
– ORIGIN early 17th cent.: perhaps from obsolete *maunder* 'to beg.'

Maun·der min·i·mum /'môndər/ a prolonged minimum in sunspot activity on the sun between about 1645 and 1715, which coincided with the Little Ice Age in the northern hemisphere.
– ORIGIN 1970s: named after Edward W. *Maunder* (1851–1928), English astronomer.

Maun·dy Thurs·day /'môndē/ ▶ n. the Thursday before Easter, observed in the Christian Church as a commemoration of the Last Supper.

Mau·pas·sant /ˌmōpä'säN/, Guy de (1850–93), French novelist and short-story writer; full name *Henri René Albert Guy de Maupassant*. He wrote about 300 short stories and 6 novels in a simple, direct narrative style. Notable novels: *Une Vie* (1883) and *Bel-Ami* (1885).

Mau·re·ta·ni·a /ˌmôri'tānēə, -'tānyə/ an ancient region of North Africa that corresponds to the northern part of Morocco and western and central Algeria.
– DERIVATIVES **Mau·re·ta·ni·an** adj. & n.
– ORIGIN based on Latin *Mauri* 'Moors,' by whom the region was originally occupied.

Mau·riac /ˌmôr'yäk/, François (1885–1970), French novelist, playwright, and critic. His stories show the conflicts of convention, religion, and human passions suffered by prosperous bourgeoisie. Notable works: *Thérèse Desqueyroux* (novel, 1927) and *Asmodée* (play, 1938). Nobel Prize for Literature (1952).

Mau·ri·ta·ni·a /ˌmôri'tānēə, -'tānyə/ a country in West Africa with a coastline on the Atlantic Ocean; pop. 3,129,500 (est. 2009); capital, Nouakchott; languages, Arabic (official), Wolof (official), and French.

> Mauritania was a center of Berber power in the 11th and 12th centuries, at which time Islam was established in the region. Later, nomadic Arab tribes became dominant, while European nations, especially France, established trading posts on the coast. A French protectorate from 1902 and a colony from 1920, Mauritania achieved full independence in 1961.

– DERIVATIVES **Mau·ri·ta·ni·an** adj. & n.

Mau·ri·tius /mô'risHəs/ an island country in the Indian Ocean, about 550 miles (850 km) east of Madagascar; pop. 1,284,300 (est. 2009); capital, Port Louis; languages, English (official), French (official), Creole, and Indian languages. The two main islands are Mauritius and Rodrigues.

> The Portuguese visited uninhabited Mauritius in the early 16th century. It was held by the Dutch 1598–1710 and then by the French until 1810, when it was ceded to Britain. Mauritius became independent as a member of the Commonwealth of Nations in 1968.

– DERIVATIVES **Mau·ri·tian** /-'risHən/ adj. & n.
– ORIGIN named by the Dutch in honor of Prince *Maurice* of Nassau, a stadtholder of the United Provinces.

Mau·ry /'môrē/, Matthew Fontaine (1806–73), US oceanographer. He conducted the first systematic survey of oceanic winds and currents, and published charts of his findings.

Mau·ser /'mouzər/ ▶ n. trademark a make of firearm, esp. a repeating rifle: [as modifier] *a Mauser rifle.*
– ORIGIN late 19th cent.: named after Paul von *Mauser* (1838–1914), German inventor.

mau·so·le·um /ˌmôzə'lēəm, ˌmôsə-/ ▶ n. (pl. **mausolea** /-'lēə/ or **mausoleums**) a building, esp. a large and stately one, housing a tomb or tombs.
– ORIGIN late 15th cent.: via Latin from Greek *Mausōleion*, from *Mausōlos*, the name of a king of Caria (4th cent. BC), to whose tomb in Halicarnassus the name was originally applied.

mauve /mōv, môv/ ▶ adj. of a pale purple color.
▶ n. **1** a pale purple color: *a few pale streaks of mauve were all that remained of the sunset | glowing with soft pastel mauves and pinks.*
2 historical a bright but delicate pale purple aniline dye prepared by William H. Perkin (1838–1907) in 1856. It was the first synthetic dyestuff.
– ORIGIN mid 19th cent.: from French, literally 'mallow,' from Latin *malva*.

ma·ven /'māvən/ ▶ n. [often with modifier] informal an expert or connoisseur: *fashion mavens.*
– ORIGIN 1960s: Yiddish.

mav·er·ick /'mav(ə)rik/ ▶ n. **1** an unorthodox or independent-minded person: *a maverick among Connecticut Republicans.*
2 an unbranded calf or yearling.
▶ adj. unorthodox: *a maverick detective.*
– ORIGIN mid 19th cent.: from the name of Samuel A. *Maverick* (1803–70), a Texas engineer and rancher who did not brand his cattle.

ma·vis /'māvis/ ▶ n. literary a song thrush.
– ORIGIN late Middle English: from Old French *mauvis*, of unknown origin.

maw /mô/ ▶ n. the jaws or throat of a voracious animal: *a gigantic wolfhound with a fearful, gaping maw.* ■ informal the mouth or gullet of a greedy person: *I was cramming large pieces of toast and cheese down my maw.*
– ORIGIN Old English *maga* (in the sense 'stomach'), of Germanic origin; related to Dutch *maag* and German *Magen* 'stomach.'

mawk·ish /'môkisH/ ▶ adj. sentimental in a feeble or sickly way: *a mawkish poem.* ■ archaic or dialect having a faint sickly flavor: *the mawkish smell of warm beer.*
– DERIVATIVES **mawk·ish·ly** adv., **mawk·ish·ness** n.
– ORIGIN mid 17th cent. (in the sense 'inclined to sickness'): from obsolete *mawk* 'maggot,' from Old Norse *mathkr*, of Germanic origin.

Maw·la·na /mou'länä/ another name for **JALAL AD-DIN AR-RUMI**.

Max /maks/, Peter (1937–), US artist; born in Germany. Noted for combining serious art with commercial outlets, his brightly colored works, begun as pop art in the 1960s, have included art for US postage stamps, murals for border stations between the US and Canada and the US and Mexico, posters for Woodstock revivals and the Earth Summit, and an annual series of Statue of Liberty paintings.

max /maks/ ▶ abbr. maximum.
▶ n. informal a maximum amount or setting: *the sound is distorted to the max.*
▶ adv. informal at the most: *our information can be in the commander's hand in half an hour, max.*
▶ v. informal reach or cause to reach the limit of capacity or ability: *job growth in high technology will max out.*

max·i /'maksē/ ▶ n. (pl. **maxis**) a thing that is very large of its kind, in particular: ■ (also **maxiskirt** or **maxicoat**) a skirt or coat reaching to the ankle. ■ (also **maxi-yacht** or **maxi-boat**) a racing yacht of between approximately 15 and 20 meters in length.
– ORIGIN 1960s: abbreviation of **MAXIMUM**, on the pattern of *mini*.

max·il·la /mak'silə/ ▶ n. (pl. **maxillae** /mak'silē, -'silˌī/) Anatomy & Zoology the jaw or jawbone, specifically the upper jaw in most vertebrates. In humans it also forms part of the nose and eye socket. ■ (in many arthropods) each of a pair of mouthparts used in chewing.
– ORIGIN late Middle English: from Latin, 'jaw.'

max·il·lar·y /'maksəˌlerē/ ▶ adj. Anatomy & Zoology of or attached to a jaw or jawbone, esp. the upper jaw: *a maxillary fracture | maxillary teeth.* ■ of or relating to the maxillae of an arthropod.
– ORIGIN early 17th cent.: from **MAXILLA**, probably suggested by Latin *maxillaris*.

max·il·li·ped /mak'siləˌped/ ▶ n. Zoology (in crustaceans) an appendage modified for feeding, situated in pairs behind the maxillae.
– ORIGIN mid 19th cent.: from **MAXILLA** + Latin *pes, ped-* 'foot.'

max·il·lo·fa·cial /makˌsilō'fāsHəl, maksəlō-/ ▶ n. Anatomy of or relating to the jaws and face: *maxillofacial surgery.*
– ORIGIN late 19th cent.: from *maxillo-* (combining form of Latin *maxilla* 'jaw') + **FACIAL**.

max·im /'maksim/ ▶ n. a short, pithy statement expressing a general truth or rule of conduct: *the maxim that actions speak louder than words.*
– ORIGIN late Middle English (denoting an axiom): from French *maxime*, from medieval Latin (*propositio*) *maxima* 'largest or most important (proposition).'

max·i·ma /'maksəmə/ plural form of **MAXIMUM**.

max·i·mal /'maksəməl/ ▶ adj. of or constituting a maximum; the highest or greatest possible: *the maximal speed.*
– DERIVATIVES **max·i·mal·ly** adv.

max·i·mal·ist /'maksəməlist/ ▶ n. (esp. in politics) a person who holds extreme views and is not prepared to compromise.
▶ adj. of or denoting an extreme opinion: *if we demand only maximalist ends, we will get nothing.*
– DERIVATIVES **max·i·mal·ism** /-ˌizəm/ n.
– ORIGIN early 20th cent.: from **MAXIMAL**, on the pattern of Russian *maksimalist*.

max·i·mand /'maksəˌmand/ ▶ n. chiefly Economics a quantity or thing that is to be maximized.
– ORIGIN 1950s: from **MAXIMIZE** + **-AND**.

Max·im gun /'maksim/ ▶ n. the first fully automatic water-cooled machine gun, designed in Britain in 1884 and used esp. in World War I.
– ORIGIN named after Sir Hiram S. *Maxim* (1840–1916), American-born British inventor.

PRONUNCIATION KEY ə *ago, up*; ər *over, fur*; a *hat*; ā *ate*; ä *car*; e *let*; ē *see*; i *fit*; ī *by*; NG *sing*; ō *go*; ô *law, for*; oi *toy*; o͝o *good*; o͞o *goo*; ou *out*; TH *thin*; TH *then*; ZH *vision*

m

Max·i·mil·ian /ˌmaksəˈmilyən/ (1832–67), Austrian emperor of Mexico 1864–67; full name *Ferdinand Maximilian Joseph*. The brother of Franz Josef, he became emperor of Mexico under French auspices in 1864. US pressure forced Napoleon III to withdraw his support in 1867, and Maximilian was executed by a popular uprising led by Mexico's president Benito Juárez.

Max·i·mil·ian II 1811–64, king of Bavaria 1848–64. He became king upon the abdication of his father, Ludwig I. A patron of the arts and education, his liberal objectives went largely unrealized due to an adversarial political climate and his frequent bouts of ill health.

max·i·min /ˈmaksəˌmin, -sē-/ ▶ **n.** Mathematics the largest of a series of minima. Compare with **MINIMAX.** ■ [as modifier] denoting a method or strategy in game theory that maximizes the smallest gain that can be relied on by a participant in a game or other situation of conflict.
– ORIGIN 1950s: blend of **MAXIMUM** and **MINIMUM**, on the pattern of *minimax*.

max·i·mize /ˈmaksəˌmīz/ ▶ **v.** [with obj.] make as large or great as possible: *the company was aiming to maximize profits.* ■ make the best use of: *a rider can maximize a young horse's athletic potential.*
– DERIVATIVES **max·i·mi·za·tion** /ˌmaksəməˈzāsHən/ **n.**, **max·i·miz·er n.**
– ORIGIN early 19th cent.: from Latin *maximus* (see **MAXIMUM**) + **-IZE.**

max·i·mum /ˈmaksəməm/ ▶ **adj.** [attrib.] as great, high, or intense as possible or permitted: *the vehicle's maximum speed | a maximum penalty of ten years' imprisonment.* ■ denoting the greatest or highest point or amount attained: *the maximum depth of the pool is 6 feet.*
▶ **n.** (pl. **maxima** /-mə/ or **maximums**) the greatest or highest amount possible or attained: *the school takes a maximum of 32 students | production levels are near their maximum.* ■ a maximum permitted prison sentence for an offense: *an offense that carries a maximum of 14 years.*
▶ **adv.** at the most: *it has a length of 4 feet maximum.*
– ORIGIN mid 17th cent. (as a noun): from modern Latin, neuter (used as a noun) of the Latin adjective *maximus*, superlative of *magnus* 'great.' The adjective use dates from the early 19th cent.

m

max·i·mum sus·tain·a·ble yield (abbr.: **MSY**) ▶ **n.** (esp. in forestry and fisheries) the maximum level at which a natural resource can be routinely exploited without long-term depletion. ■ Ecology the size of a natural population at which it produces a maximum rate of increase, typically at half the carrying capacity.

max·ixe /mäkˈsēks, mäkˈsHēsHə/ ▶ **n.** a Brazilian dance for couples, resembling the polka and the local tango.
– ORIGIN early 20th cent.: Portuguese.

Max·well[1] /ˈmaksˌwel/, Elsa (1883–1963), US columnist and professional hostess. She was a legendary hostess for high society and royalty from the 1920s and began to write a syndicated gossip column during the 1940s.

Max·well[2], James Clerk (1831–79), Scottish physicist. He extended the ideas of Faraday and Kelvin with his equations of electromagnetism, and he succeeded in unifying electricity and magnetism, identifying the electromagnetic nature of light and postulating the existence of other electromagnetic radiation.

max·well /ˈmaksˌwel, -wəl/ (abbr.: **Mx**) ▶ **n.** Physics a unit of magnetic flux in the centimeter-gram-second system, equal to that induced through one square centimeter by a perpendicular magnetic field of one gauss.
– ORIGIN early 20th cent.: named after J. C. *Maxwell* (see **MAXWELL[2]**).

Max·well–Boltz·mann dis·tri·bu·tion /ˈmakˌswel ˈbōltsmən, ˈmakswəl/ Physics a formula describing the statistical distribution of particles in a system among different energy levels. The number of particles in a given energy level is proportional to exp. $(-E/kT)$, where E is the energy of the level, k is Boltzmann's constant, and T is the absolute temperature.
– ORIGIN 1920s: named after J. C. *Maxwell* (see **MAXWELL[2]**) and L. **BOLTZMANN.**

Max·well's de·mon Physics a hypothetical being imagined as controlling a hole in a partition dividing a gas-filled container into two parts, and allowing only fast-moving molecules to pass in one direction, and slow-moving molecules in the other. This would result in one side of the container becoming warmer and the other cooler, in violation of the second law of thermodynamics.
– ORIGIN late 19th cent.: named after J. C. *Maxwell* (see **MAXWELL[2]**).

Max·well's e·qua·tions Physics a set of four linear partial differential equations that summarize the classical properties of the electromagnetic field.
– ORIGIN early 20th cent.: named after J. C. *Maxwell* (see **MAXWELL[2]**).

May /mā/ ▶ **n.** the fifth month of the year, in the northern hemisphere usually considered the last month of spring: *the new model makes its showroom debut in May* | [as modifier] *a May morning.* ■ (usu. **one's May**) literary one's bloom or prime: *others murmured that their May was passing.*
– ORIGIN late Old English, from Old French *mai*, from Latin *Maius (mensis)* '(month) of the goddess *Maia*.'

may[1] /mā/ ▶ **modal v.** (3rd sing. present **may**; past **might** /mīt/) **1** expressing possibility: *that may be true | he may well win.* ■ used when admitting that something is so before making another, more important point: *they may have been old-fashioned, but they were excellent teachers.*
2 expressing permission: *you may use a sling if you wish | may I ask a few questions?*
3 expressing a wish or hope: *may she rest in peace.*
– PHRASES **be that as it may** despite that; nevertheless. **may as well** another way of saying **MIGHT AS WELL** (see **MIGHT[1]**).
– ORIGIN Old English *mæg*, of Germanic origin, from a base meaning 'have power'; related to Dutch *mogen* and German *mögen*, also to **MAIN[1]** and **MIGHT[2]**.

> **USAGE** Traditionalists insist that one should distinguish between **may** (present tense) and **might** (past tense) in expressing possibility: *I may have some dessert after dinner if I'm still hungry | I might have known that the highway would be closed because of the storm.* In casual use, though, **may** and **might** are generally interchangeable: *they might take a vacation next month | he may have called earlier, but the answering machine was broken.* On the difference in use between **may** and **can**, see usage at **CAN[1]**.

may[2] ▶ **n.** the hawthorn or its blossom.
– ORIGIN late Middle English: from **MAY.**

Ma·ya /ˈmīə/ ▶ **n.** (pl. **same** or **Mayas**) **1** a member of an American Indian people of Yucatán and adjacent areas.
2 the Mayan language of this people.
▶ **adj.** of or relating to this people or their language.

> The Maya civilization developed over an extensive area of southern Mexico, Guatemala, and Belize from the 2nd millennium BC, reaching its peak c.AD 300–c. 900. Its remains include stone temples built on pyramids and ornamented with sculptures. The Mayas had a system of pictorial writing and an extremely accurate calendar system.

– ORIGIN the name in Maya.

ma·ya /ˈmīə, ˈmäyə/ ▶ **n.** Hinduism the supernatural power wielded by gods and demons to produce illusions. ■ Hinduism & Buddhism the power by which the universe becomes manifest; the illusion or appearance of the phenomenal world.
– ORIGIN from Sanskrit *māyā*, from *mā* 'create.'

Ma·ya·kov·sky /ˌmäyəˈkôfskē, -skyē/, Vladimir (Vladimirovich) (1893–1930), Soviet poet and playwright. A fervent futurist, he wrote in a declamatory, aggressive avant-garde style, which he altered to have a comic mass appeal after the Bolshevik revolution.

Ma·yan /ˈmīən/ ▶ **n.** a large family of American Indian languages spoken in Central America and Mexico, of which the chief members are Maya and Quiché.
▶ **adj. 1** denoting, relating to, or belonging to this family of languages.
2 relating to or denoting the Maya people.

may·ap·ple /ˈmāˌapəl/ (also **May apple**) ▶ **n.** an American herbaceous plant of the barberry family with large, deeply divided leaves. The plant, which bears a yellow, egg-shaped edible fruit in May, has long been used medicinally. Also called **MANDRAKE.** ● *Podophyllum peltatum*, family Berberidaceae.

may·be /ˈmābē/ ▶ **adv.** perhaps; possibly: *maybe I won't go back | maybe she'd been wrong to accept this job.*
▶ **n.** a mere possibility or probability: *no ifs, buts, or maybes.*
– ORIGIN late Middle English: from the phrase *it may be (that).*

May bee·tle ▶ **n.** another term for **JUNE BUG.**

May·day /ˈmāˌdā/ (also **mayday**) ▶ **exclam.** an international radio distress signal used by ships and aircraft.
▶ **n.** a distress signal using the word "Mayday": *we sent out a Mayday* | [as modifier] *a Mayday call.*
– ORIGIN 1920s: representing a pronunciation of French *m'aider*, from *venez m'aider* 'come and help me.'

May Day ▶ **n.** May 1, celebrated in many countries as a traditional springtime festival or as an international day honoring workers.

May·er /ˈmāər/, Louis B. (1885–1957), US movie executive, born in Russia; full name *Louis Burt Mayer*; born *Eliezer Mayer*. In 1924, with Samuel Goldwyn, he formed Metro-Goldwyn-Mayer (MGM). He headed the company until 1951.

may·est /ˈmā-ist, māst/ archaic second person singular present of **MAY[1]**.

May·fair /ˈmāˌfe(ə)r/ a fashionable and opulent district in the West End of London.
– ORIGIN originally the site of a fair held annually in May in the 17th and 18th cents.

May·flow·er /ˈmāˌflou(-ə)r/ the ship in which the Pilgrims sailed from England to America in 1620.

may·flow·er /ˈmāˌflou(-ə)r/ ▶ **n.** a name given to several plants that bloom in May, esp. certain hepaticas and anemones and the trailing arbutus.

may·fly /ˈmāˌflī/ ▶ **n.** (pl. **mayflies**) a short-lived, slender insect with delicate, transparent wings and two or three long filaments on the tail. It lives close to water, where the chiefly herbivorous aquatic larvae develop. ● Order Ephemeroptera: several families and many species. ■ an artificial fishing fly that imitates such an insect.

may·hap /ˈmāˌhap/ ▶ **adv.** archaic perhaps; possibly.
– ORIGIN mid 16th cent.: from *it may hap.*

may·hem /ˈmāˌhem/ ▶ **n.** violent or damaging disorder; chaos: *complete mayhem broke out.* ■ Law, chiefly historical the crime of maliciously injuring or maiming someone, originally so as to render the victim defenseless.
– ORIGIN early 16th cent.: from Old French *mayhem* (see **MAIM**). The sense 'disorder, chaos' (originally US) dates from the late 19th cent.

may·ing /ˈmā-iNG/ (also **Maying**) ▶ **n.** archaic celebration of May Day.

may·n't /ˈmā(ə)nt/ rare ▶ **contraction** may not.

Ma·yo[1] /ˈmā-ō/ a county in the Republic of Ireland, in the northwestern part of the province of Connacht; county town, Castlebar.

Ma·yo[2], William Worrall (1819–1911), US physician; born in England. He helped the Sisters of St. Francis found St. Mary's Hospital in Rochester, Minnesota in 1899. His sons **William James** (1861–1939) and **Charles Horace** (1865–1939), both surgeons, developed the Mayo Clinic as a part of the hospital.

may·o /ˈmā-ō/ ▶ **n.** informal short for **MAYONNAISE.**

may·on·naise /ˈmāəˌnāz, ˌmāəˈnāz/ ▶ **n.** a thick, creamy dressing consisting of egg yolks beaten with oil and vinegar and seasoned.
– ORIGIN French, probably from the feminine of *mahonnais* 'of or from Port Mahon,' the capital of Minorca.

may·or /ˈmāər/ ▶ **n.** the elected head of a city, town, or other municipality. ■ the titular head of a municipality that is administered by a city manager.
– DERIVATIVES **may·or·al** /māˈôrəl, ˈmāərəl/ **adj.**, **may·or·ship** /-ˌSHip/ **n.**
– ORIGIN Middle English: from Old French *maire*, from the Latin adjective *major* 'greater,' used as a noun in late Latin.

may·or·al·ty /ˈmāərəltē/ ▶ **n.** (pl. **mayoralties**) the office of mayor: *the party failed to win the mayoralty.* ■ a mayor's period of office.
– ORIGIN late Middle English: from Old French *mairalte*, from *maire* (see **MAYOR**).

may·or·ess /ˈmāərəs/ ▶ **n. 1** the wife of a mayor.
2 a woman holding the office of mayor.

Ma·yotte /mäˈyôt/ an island in the Indian Ocean, east of Comoros; pop. 223,800 (est. 2009); capital, Mamoutzu. When the Comoros became independent in 1974, Mayotte remained an overseas territory of France. Also called **MAHORE.**

may·pole /ˈmāˌpōl/ (also **Maypole**) ▶ **n.** a pole painted and decorated with flowers, around which people traditionally dance on May Day, holding long ribbons that are attached to the top of the pole.

may·pop /ˈmāˌpäp/ ▶ **n.** the yellow edible fruit of a North American passionflower. ● The plant, grown chiefly in the southern US, is *Passiflora incarnata*, family Passifloraceae.

May queen ▶ **n.** a girl or young woman chosen to be crowned in traditional celebrations of May Day.

Mayr /ˈmāər/, Ernst Walter (1904), US zoologist, born in Germany. He argued for a neo-Darwinian approach to evolution in his classic *Animal Species and Evolution* (1963).

Mays /māz/, Willie (Howard, Jr.) (1931–), US baseball player; known as the **Say Hey Kid**. A center fielder, he played for the New York (later San Francisco) Giants 1951–52, 1954–71 and the New York Mets 1971–72. Baseball Hall of Fame (1979).

Willie Mays

mayst /māst/ archaic second person singular present of MAY[1].

may·weed /ˈmāˌwēd/ ▶ **n.** a plant of the daisy family that typically grows as a weed of fields and waste ground. ● Several species in the family Compositae, in particular **stinking mayweed** (*Anthemis cotula*).
– ORIGIN mid 16th cent.: from *maythe(n)*, an earlier name for this plant (in Old English *mægethe, magothe*), + WEED.

Ma·zar-e-Sha·rif /məˌzär ē SHəˈrēf/ a city in northern Afghanistan; pop. 300,600 (est. 2006). Its name means "tomb of the saint," and it is the reputed burial place of Ali, son-in-law of Muhammad.

Maz·a·rin /ˈmäzərin, mäzäˈraN/, Jules (1602–61), French statesman, born in Italy; Italian name *Giulio Mazzarino*. Sent to Paris as the Italian papal legate (1634), he became a naturalized Frenchman and was made a cardinal in 1641 and then chief minister of Louis XIV in 1642.

Ma·za·tlán /ˌmäsətˈlän/ a seaport and resort in Mexico, on the Pacific coast in the state of Sinaloa; pop. 352,471 (2005). Founded in 1531, it developed as a center of trade with the Philippines.

Maz·da·ism /ˈmäzdəˌizəm, maz-/ ▶ **n.** another term for ZOROASTRIANISM.
– DERIVATIVES **Maz·da·ist n. & adj.**
– ORIGIN late 19th cent.: from Avestan *mazdā* (short for AHURA MAZDA) + -ISM.

maze /māz/ ▶ **n.** a network of paths and hedges designed as a puzzle through which one has to find a way. ■ a complex network of paths or passages: *they were trapped in a menacing maze of corridors*. ■ a confusing mass of information: *a maze of petty regulations*.
▶ **v.** (**be mazed**) archaic or dialect be dazed and confused: *she was still mazed with the drug she had taken*.
– ORIGIN Middle English (denoting delirium or delusion): probably from the base of AMAZE, of which the verb is a shortening.

ma·zel tov /ˈmäzəl ˌtôv, ˌtôf/ ▶ **exclam.** a Jewish phrase expressing congratulations or wishing someone good luck.
– ORIGIN from modern Hebrew *mazzāl ṭōḇ*, literally 'good star.'

ma·zer /ˈmāzər/ ▶ **n.** historical a hardwood drinking bowl.
– ORIGIN Middle English: from Old French *masere*, of Germanic origin.

ma·zu·ma /məˈzo͞omə/ ▶ **n.** informal money; cash.
– ORIGIN early 20th cent.: Yiddish, from Hebrew *mĕzummān*, from *zimmēn* 'prepare.'

ma·zur·ka /məˈzərkə, -ˈzo͝or-/ ▶ **n.** a lively Polish dance in triple time.
– ORIGIN early 19th cent.: via German from Polish *mazurka*, denoting a woman of the province Mazovia.

ma·zy /ˈmāzē/ ▶ **adj.** (**mazier, maziest**) like a maze; labyrinthine: *the museum's mazy treasure house*.

maz·zard /ˈmazərd/ ▶ **n.** (in full **mazzard cherry**) a cherry tree native to both Eurasia and North America, commercially important for both its fruit and wood. Also called SWEET CHERRY. ● *Prunus avium*, family Rosaceae.

Maz·zi·ni /məˈzēnē, mädˈzēnē/, Giuseppe (1805–72), Italian nationalist leader. He founded the patriotic movement Young Italy (1831) and was a leader of the Risorgimento.

MB ▶ **abbr.** ■ Bachelor of Medicine. [from Latin *Medicinae Baccalaureus*.] ■ Manitoba (in official postal use). ■ (also **Mb**) Computing megabyte: *a 800 MB hard disk*.

MBA ▶ **abbr.** Master of Business Administration.

Mba·ba·ne /əmbäˈbänä/ the capital of Swaziland, in the northwestern part of the country; pop. 78,000 (est. 2007).

mba·qan·ga /(ə)mbəˈkäNGgə/ ▶ **n.** a rhythmical popular music style of southern Africa.
– ORIGIN from Zulu *umbaqanga*, literally 'steamed cornbread,' used to express the combined notion of the homely cultural sustenance of the townships and the musicians' "daily bread" (coined in this sense by trumpeter Michael Xaba).

m.b.d ▶ **abbr.** (of oil) million barrels per day.

M·bek·i /(ə)mˈbekē/, Thabo (1942–), South African statesman, president 1999–2008.

mbi·ra /(ə)mˈbi(ə)rə/ ▶ **n.** (esp. in southern Africa) another term for THUMB PIANO.
– ORIGIN late 19th cent.: from Shona, probably an alteration of *rimba* 'a note.'

Mbps ▶ **abbr.** Computing ■ millions of bits per second. ■ megabits per second. ■ (**MBps**) megabytes per second.

Mbun·du /(ə)mˈbo͝ondo͞o/ ▶ **n.** (pl. **same**) **1** a member of either of two peoples of western Angola (sometimes distinguished as **Mbundu** and **Ovimbundu**).
2 either of the Bantu languages of these peoples, often distinguished as **Umbundu** (related to Herero) and **Kimbundu** (related to Kikongo).
▶ **adj.** of or relating to these peoples or their languages.

Mbu·ti /(ə)mˈbo͞otē/ ▶ **n.** (pl. **same** or **Mbutis**) a member of a pygmy people of western Uganda and adjacent areas of the Democratic Republic of the Congo (formerly Zaire).
▶ **adj.** of or relating to this people.
– ORIGIN the name in local languages.

Mbyte ▶ **abbr.** megabyte(s).

MC ▶ **abbr.** ■ Master of Ceremonies. ■ (in the US) Member of Congress. ■ (in an astrological chart) the midheaven. [from Latin *Medium Coeli*.] ■ (in the UK) Military Cross. ■ music cassette (of prerecorded audiotape).

Mc ▶ **abbr.** megacycle(s), a unit of frequency equal to one million cycles.

MCAT ▶ **abbr.** Medical College Admissions Test.

MCB ▶ **abbr.** miniature circuit-breaker.

mcf (also **MCF** or **Mcf**) ▶ **abbr.** one thousand cubic feet.

mcg ▶ **abbr.** microgram(s).

mCi ▶ **abbr.** millicurie(s), a quantity of a radioactive substance having one thousandth of a curie of radioactivity: *15 mCi of the radionuclide*.

MCL ▶ **abbr.** ■ Master of Civil Law. ■ Master of Comparative Law.

m-com·merce ▶ **n.** electronic commerce conducted on cellular phones.
– ORIGIN from *m(obile)* + *commerce*.

MCP ▶ **abbr.** informal male chauvinist pig.

MCPO ▶ **abbr.** master chief petty officer.

Mc/s ▶ **abbr.** megacycles per second, a unit of frequency equal to one million cycles per second.

MD ▶ **abbr.** ■ Doctor of Medicine. [from Latin *Medicinae Doctor*.] ■ Brit. Managing Director. ■ Maryland (in official postal use). ■ musical director.

Md ▶ **symbol** the chemical element mendelevium.

Md. ▶ **abbr.** Maryland.

m/d (also **M/D**) ▶ **abbr.** months after date.

MDF ▶ **abbr.** medium density fiberboard.

M.Div. ▶ **abbr.** Master of Divinity.

MDMA ▶ **abbr.** methylenedioxymethamphetamine, the drug Ecstasy.

MDS ▶ **abbr.** Master of Dental Science.

mdse. ▶ **abbr.** merchandise.

MDT ▶ **abbr.** Mountain Daylight Time (see MOUNTAIN TIME).

ME ▶ **abbr.** ■ Maine (in official postal use). ■ medical examiner. ■ Middle English. ■ myalgic encephalitis or myalgic encephalopathy.

Me ▶ **abbr.** ■ Maine. ■ Maître (title of a French advocate).

me /mē/ ▶ **pron.** [first person singular] **1** used by a speaker to refer to himself or herself as the object of a verb or preposition: *do you understand me?* | *wait for me!* Compare with I[2]. ■ used after the verb "to be" and after "than" or "as": *hi, it's me* | *you have more than me*. ■ informal to or for myself: *I've got me a job*.
2 informal used in exclamations: *dear me!* | *silly me!*
– PHRASES **me and mine** /ˈmē ən ˈmīn/ my relatives.
– ORIGIN Old English *mē*, accusative and dative of I[2], of Germanic origin; related to Dutch *mij*, German *mir* (dative), from an Indo-European root shared by Latin *me*, Greek *(e)me*, and Sanskrit *mā*.

> **USAGE 1** Traditional grammar teaches that it is correct to say *between you and* **me** and incorrect to say *between you and I*. For details, see usage at BETWEEN. **2** Which of the following is correct: *you have more than* **me**, or *you have more than I*? See usage at PERSONAL PRONOUN.

me·a cul·pa /ˌmāə ˈko͝olˌpə, -ˌpä/ ▶ **n.** an acknowledgment of one's fault or error: [as exclamation] *"Well, whose fault was that?" "Mea culpa!" Frank said*.
– ORIGIN Latin, 'by my fault.'

Mead /mēd/, Margaret (1901–78), US anthropologist and social psychologist. She worked in Samoa and the New Guinea area and wrote a number of studies of primitive cultures, including *Coming of Age in Samoa* (1928). Her writings made anthropology accessible to a wide readership and demonstrated its relevance to Western society.

mead[1] /mēd/ ▶ **n.** chiefly historical an alcoholic drink of fermented honey and water.
– ORIGIN Old English *me(o)du*, of Germanic origin; related to Dutch *mee* and German *Met*, from an Indo-European root shared by Sanskrit *madhu* 'sweet drink, honey' and Greek *methu* 'wine.'

mead[2] ▶ **n.** literary a meadow.
– ORIGIN Old English *mǣd*, of Germanic origin; related to MOW[1].

Mead, Lake /mēd/ the largest US reservoir, located in southeast Nevada, created after 1933 by the Hoover Dam on the Colorado River.

Meade /mēd/, George Gordon (1815–72), US army officer; born in Spain. The son of American parents, he was a graduate of West Point 1835 and commanded the Army of the Potomac 1863–65 during the Civil War. He is most noted for his victory at Gettysburg in 1863.

mead·ow /ˈmedō/ ▶ **n.** a piece of grassland, esp. one used for hay. ■ a piece of low ground near a river.
– DERIVATIVES **mead·ow·y adj.**
– ORIGIN Old English *mǣdwe*, oblique case of *mǣd* (see MEAD[2]), from the Germanic base of MOW[2].

m

mead·ow fes·cue ▶ **n.** a tall Eurasian fescue that is grown in North America as a pasture and hay grass. ● *Festuca pratensis*, family Gramineae.

mead·ow grass ▶ **n.** a perennial creeping grass that is widely used for fodder and lawns, and for sowing roadside borders. ● Genus *Poa*, family Gramineae: many species, in particular **Kentucky bluegrass** (*P. pratensis*).

mead·ow·land /ˈmedōˌland, ˈmedə-/ ▶ **n.** (also **meadowlands**) land used for the cultivation of grass, esp. for hay.

Mead·ow·lands /ˈmedōˌlandz/ (**the Meadowlands**) an entertainment and sports complex in northeastern New Jersey, in the meadows of the Hackensack River, northwest of New York City.

mead·ow·lark /ˈmedōˌlärk, ˈmedə-/ ▶ **n.** a ground-dwelling songbird of the American blackbird family, with a brown streaky back and typically yellow and black underparts. ● Genus *Sturnella*, family Icteridae: five species, in particular the yellow-breasted **eastern meadowlark** (*S. magna*) and **western meadowlark** (*S. neglecta*).

eastern meadowlark

mead·ow mouse ▶ **n.** another term for MEADOW VOLE.

mead·ow mush·room ▶ **n.** another term for CHAMPIGNON.

mead·ow rue ▶ **n.** a widely distributed plant of the buttercup family that typically has divided leaves and heads of small fluffy flowers or delicate drooping flowers. ● Genus *Thalictrum*, family Ranunculaceae: many species, including the Eurasian **greater meadow rue** (*T. aquilegiifolium*) and the **early meadow rue** (*T. dioicum*) of North American woods.

mead·ow saf·fron ▶ n. a poisonous autumn crocus that produces its flowers, usually lilac, in the autumn while leafless. Native to Europe and North Africa, it is a source of the drug colchicine. ● *Colchicum autumnale*, family Liliaceae.

mead·ow·sweet /ˈmedō,swēt, ˈmedə-/ ▶ n. a tall plant of the rose family (Rosaceae) with clusters of sweet-smelling flowers. ● *Spiraeae latifola* of North American meadows and roadsides, with white or pale pink flowers. ● *Filipendula ulmaria*, native to Eurasia and naturalized in North America, with creamy white flowers and favoring damp meadows.

mead·ow vole ▶ n. a burrowing vole that occurs in grassland and open country in Eurasia and North America. ● Genus *Microtus*, family Muridae: numerous species, in particular *Microtus pennsylvanicus* of the northern US and Canada.

mea·ger /ˈmēgər/ (Brit. **meagre**) ▶ adj. (of something provided or available) lacking in quantity or quality: *they were forced to supplement their meager earnings.* ■ (of a person or animal) lean; thin.
– DERIVATIVES **mea·ger·ly** adv.
– ORIGIN Middle English (in the sense 'lean'): from Old French *maigre*, from Latin *macer*.

mea·ger·ness /ˈmēgərnis/ ▶ n. lack of quantity or quality; inadequacy: *job satisfaction eclipses the meagerness of income.*

meal[1] /mēl/ ▶ n. any of the regular occasions in a day when a reasonably large amount of food is eaten, such as breakfast, lunch, or dinner. ■ the food eaten on such an occasion: *a perfectly cooked meal.*
– PHRASES **meals on wheels** meals delivered to elderly people or invalids who are unable either to prepare meals or have meals otherwise provided.
– ORIGIN Old English *mǣl* (also in the sense 'measure,' surviving in words such as *piecemeal* 'measure taken at one time'), of Germanic origin. The early sense of *meal* involved a notion of fixed time; compare with Dutch *maal* 'meal, (portion of) time' and German *Mal* 'time,' *Mahl* 'meal,' from an Indo-European root meaning 'to measure.'

meal[2] ▶ n. the edible part of any grain or pulse ground to powder, such as cornmeal. ■ any powdery substance made by grinding: *herring meal.*
– ORIGIN Old English *melu, meolo*, of Germanic origin; related to Dutch *meel* and German *Mehl*, from an Indo-European root shared by Latin *molere* 'to grind.'

m

meal·ie /ˈmēlē/ ▶ n. (usu. **mealies**) chiefly S. African corn, esp. sweet corn. ■ corn kernels: [as modifier] *mealie pudding.* ■ an ear of corn.
– ORIGIN early 19th cent.: from Afrikaans *mielie*, from Portuguese *milho* 'corn, millet' from Latin *milium*.

meal tick·et ▶ n. a person or thing that is used as a source of regular income: *the violin was going to be my meal ticket.*

meal·time /ˈmēl,tīm/ ▶ n. the time at which a meal is eaten: *fill up at mealtimes and get out of the habit of snacking | it must be mealtime soon.*

meal·worm /ˈmēl,wərm/ ▶ n. the larva of a darkling beetle (genus *Tenebrio*), which is widely fed to captive birds and other insectivorous animals.

meal·y /ˈmēlē/ ▶ adj. (**mealier, mealiest**) of, like, or containing meal: *a mealy flavor | stomp along through deep, mealy sand.* ■ (of a person's complexion, an animal's muzzle, or a bird's plumage) pale. ■ (of part of a plant or fungus) covered with granules resembling meal.
– DERIVATIVES **meal·i·ness** /-lēnis/ n.

meal·y·bug /ˈmēlē,bəg/ (also **mealy bug**) ▶ n. a small, sap-sucking scale insect that is coated with a white, powdery wax that resembles meal. It forms large colonies and can be a serious pest, esp. in greenhouses. ● Family Pseudococcidae, suborder Homoptera: *Pseudococcus* and other genera.

meal·y-mouthed /ˈmēlē ,mouTHd, -,mouTHt/ (also **mealymouthed**) ▶ adj. afraid to speak frankly or straightforwardly: *mealy-mouthed excuses.*

mean[1] /mēn/ ▶ v. (past and past participle **meant** /ment/) [with obj.] **1** intend to convey, indicate, or refer to (a particular thing or notion); signify: *I don't know what you mean | he was asked to clarify what his remarks meant | I meant you, not Jones.* ■ (of a word) have (something) as its signification in the same language or its equivalent in another language: *its name means "painted rock" in Cherokee.* ■ genuinely intend to convey or express (something): *when she said that before, she meant it.* ■ (**mean something to**) be of some specified importance to (someone), esp. as a source of benefit or object of affection: *animals have always meant more to him than people.*
2 intend (something) to occur or be the case: *they mean no harm* | [with infinitive] *it was meant to be a secret.* ■ (**be meant to do something**) be supposed or intended to do something: *we were meant to go over yesterday.* ■ (often **be meant for**) design or destine for a particular purpose: *the jacket was meant for a much larger person.* ■ (**mean something by**) have as a motive or excuse in explanation: *what do you mean by leaving me out here in the cold?*
3 have as a consequence or result: *the proposals are likely to mean another hundred closures* | [with clause] *heavy rain meant that the ground was waterlogged.* ■ necessarily or usually entail or involve: *coal stoves mean a lot of smoke.*
– PHRASES **I mean** used to clarify or correct a statement or to introduce a justification or explanation: *I mean, it's not as if I owned property.* **mean business** be in earnest. **mean to say** [usu. in questions] really admit or intend to say: *do you mean to say you've uncovered something new?* **mean well** have good intentions, but not always the ability to carry them out.
– ORIGIN Old English *mænan*; related to Dutch *meenen* and German *meinen*, from an Indo-European root shared by **MIND**.

mean[2] ▶ adj. **1** unwilling to give or share things, esp. money; not generous: *she felt mean not giving a tip | they're not mean with the garlic.*
2 unkind, spiteful, or unfair: *it was very mean of me | she is always mean to my little brother.* ■ vicious or aggressive in behavior: *the dogs were considered mean.*
3 (esp. of a place) poor in quality and appearance; shabby: *her home was mean and small.* ■ (of a person's mental capacity or understanding) inferior; poor: *it was obvious to even the meanest intelligence.* ■ dated of low birth or social class: *it was a hat like that worn by the meanest of people.*
4 informal excellent; very skillful or effective: *he's a mean cook | she dances a mean Charleston.*
– PHRASES **no mean ——** denoting something very good of its kind: *it was no mean feat.*
– DERIVATIVES **mean·ly** adv.
– ORIGIN Middle English, shortening of Old English *gemǣne*, of Germanic origin, from an Indo-European root shared by Latin *communis* 'common.' The original sense was 'common to two or more persons,' later 'inferior in rank,' leading to sense 3 and a sense 'ignoble, small-minded,' from which sense 1 and sense 2 (which became common in the 19th cent.) arose.

mean[3] ▶ n. **1** the quotient of the sum of several quantities and their number; an average: *acid output was calculated by taking the mean of all three samples.* See also **ARITHMETIC MEAN, GEOMETRIC MEAN.** ■ the term or one of the terms midway between the first and last terms of a progression.
2 a condition, quality, or course of action equally removed from two opposite (usually unsatisfactory) extremes: *the mean between two extremes.*
▶ adj. [attrib.] **1** (of a quantity) calculated as a mean; average: *by 1989, the mean age at marriage stood at 24.8 for women and 26.9 for men.*
2 equally far from two extremes: *hope is the mean virtue between despair and presumption.*
– ORIGIN Middle English: from Old French *meien*, from Latin *medianus* 'middle' (see **MEDIAN**).

mean a·nom·a·ly ▶ n. Astronomy the angle in an imaginary circular orbit corresponding to a planet's eccentric anomaly.

me·an·der /mēˈandər/ ▶ v. [no obj.] (of a river or road) follow a winding course: *a river that meandered gently through a meadow.* ■ (of a person) wander at random: *kids meandered in and out.* ■ (of a speaker or text) proceed aimlessly or with little purpose: *a stylish offbeat thriller which occasionally meanders.*
▶ n. (usu. **meanders**) a winding curve or bend of a river or road: *the river flows in sweeping meanders.* ■ [in sing.] a circuitous journey, esp. an aimless one: *a leisurely meander around the twisting coastline road.* ■ an ornamental pattern of winding or interlocking lines, e.g., in a mosaic.
– ORIGIN late 16th cent. (as a noun): from Latin *maeander*, from Greek *Maiandros*, the name of a river (see **MENDERES**).

me·an·der·ing /mēˈand(ə)riNG/ ▶ adj. following a winding course: *a meandering lane.* ■ proceeding in a convoluted or undirected fashion: *a brilliant sample of meandering discourse | a florid and rather meandering melody.*
▶ n. (usu. **meanderings**) an act of following a winding course: *oxbow lagoons left by the river's meanderings.* ■ an act of wandering in a leisurely or aimless manner: *in the course of his meanderings through the city.* ■ convoluted or undirected thought or language: *he has a penchant for obscure verbal meanderings.*

mean free path ▶ n. Physics the average distance traveled by a gas molecule or other particle between collisions with other particles.

mean·ie /ˈmēnē/ (also **meany**) ▶ n. (pl. **meanies**) informal a mean or small-minded person.

mean·ing /ˈmēniNG/ ▶ n. what is meant by a word, text, concept, or action: *the meaning of the word "supermarket" | it was as if time had lost all meaning.* ■ implied or explicit significance: *he gave me a look full of meaning.* ■ important or worthwhile quality; purpose: *this can lead to new meaning in the life of older people.*
▶ adj. [attrib.] intended to communicate something that is not directly expressed: *she gave Gabriel a meaning look.*
– PHRASES **not know the meaning of the word** informal behave as if unaware of the concept referred to or implied: *"Humanity?" You don't know the meaning of the word!*
– DERIVATIVES **mean·ing·ly** adv.
– ORIGIN late Middle English: verbal noun from **MEAN**[1].

mean·ing·ful /ˈmēniNGfəl/ ▶ adj. having meaning: *meaningful elements in a language | questions that are* **meaningful to** *students.* ■ having a serious, important, or useful quality or purpose: *making our lives rich and meaningful.* ■ communicating something that is not directly expressed: *meaningful glances and repressed passion.* ■ Logic having a recognizable function in a logical language or other sign system.
– DERIVATIVES **mean·ing·ful·ly** adv., **mean·ing·ful·ness** n.

mean·ing·less /ˈmēniNGlis/ ▶ adj. having no meaning or significance: *the paragraph was a jumble of meaningless words.* ■ having no purpose or reason: *the Great War was an outstanding example of meaningless conflict | rules are* **meaningless to** *a child if they do not have a rationale.*
– DERIVATIVES **mean·ing·less·ly** adv., **mean·ing·less·ness** n.

mean·ness /ˈmēn'nis/ ▶ n. **1** unkindness, spitefulness, or unfairness: *all the hatred and meanness, despair and sorrow surrounding us.* ■ aggressive character; viciousness: *he is also callous, with a streak of meanness.*
2 lack of quality or attractiveness; shabbiness: *the meanness of that existence.*

means /mēnz/ ▶ plural n. **1** [usu. treated as sing.] (often **means of something** or **means to do something**) an action or system by which a result is brought about; a method: *these pledges are a means to avoid prosecution | resolving disputes by peaceful means.*
2 money; financial resources: *a woman of modest but independent means | prospective students without the means to attend Cornell.* ■ resources; capability: *every country in the world has the means to make ethanol.* ■ wealth: *a man of means.*
– PHRASES **beyond** (or **within**) **one's means** beyond (or within) one's budget or income: *the government is living beyond its means.* **by all means** of course; certainly (granting a permission): *"May I make a suggestion?" "By all means."* **by any means** (or **by any manner of means**) (following a negative) in any way; at all: *I'm not poor by any means.* **by means of** with the help or agency of: *supplying water to cities by means of aqueducts.* **by no means** (or **by no manner of means**) not at all; certainly not: *the outcome is by no means guaranteed.* **a means to an end** a thing that is not valued or important in itself but is useful in achieving an aim: *a computer is merely a means to an end.*
– ORIGIN late Middle English: plural of **MEAN**[3], the early sense being 'intermediary.'

mean sea lev·el ▶ n. the sea level halfway between the mean levels of high and low water.

means of production ▶ n. (esp. in a political context) the facilities and resources for producing goods: *in this society, the means of production are communally owned.*

mean so·lar day ▶ n. Astronomy the time between successive passages of the mean sun across the meridian.

mean so·lar time ▶ n. Astronomy time as calculated by the motion of the mean sun. The time shown by an ordinary clock corresponds to mean solar time. Compare with **APPARENT SOLAR TIME.**

mean-spir·it·ed ▶ adj. unkind and ungenerous; unwilling to help others: *the voice of an intolerant scold, narrow and shrill and mean-spirited.*

means test ▶ n. an official investigation into someone's financial circumstances to determine whether they are eligible for a welfare payment or other public funds.
▶ v. (**means-test**) [with obj.] (usu. as adj. **means-tested**) make (a welfare payment, etc.) conditional on a means test: *means-tested benefits.* ■ subject (someone) to a means test.

mean streets ▶ plural n. an area of a city where the poor or socially deprived live or work, or an area that is noted for violence and crime: *the mean streets of the South Bronx.*

mean sun ▶ n. an imaginary sun conceived as moving through the sky throughout the year at a constant speed equal to the mean rate of the real sun, used in calculating mean solar time.

meant /ment/ past and past participle of MEAN[1].

mean·time /'mēn,tīm/ ▶ adv. (also **in the meantime**) meanwhile: *in the meantime, I'll make some inquiries of my own | Mom and Dad, meantime, had learned to confront their differences.*
– ORIGIN Middle English (as a noun): from MEAN[3] + TIME.

mean time ▶ n. another term for MEAN SOLAR TIME. See also GREENWICH MEAN TIME.

mean·while /'mēn,(h)wīl/ ▶ adv. (also **in the meanwhile**) in the intervening period of time: *Julie has meanwhile found herself another dancing partner.* ■ at the same time: *steam for another five minutes; meanwhile, make a white sauce.*
– ORIGIN late Middle English: from MEAN[3] + WHILE.

Mea·ny /'mēnē/, George (1894–1980), US labor leader. He served as president of the AFL-CIO 1955–79.

mean·y /'mēnē/ ▶ n. variant spelling of MEANIE.

meas. ▶ abbr. measurable or measured or measurement.

mea·sles /'mēzəlz/ ▶ plural n. (often **the measles**) [treated as sing.] an infectious viral disease causing fever and a red rash on the skin, typically occurring in childhood. ■ a disease of pigs and other animals caused by the encysted larvae of the human tapeworm.
– ORIGIN Middle English *maseles*, probably from Middle Dutch *masel* 'pustule' (compare with modern Dutch *mazelen* 'measles'). The spelling change was due to association with Middle English *mesel* 'leprous, leprosy.'

mea·sly /'mēzlē/ ▶ adj. (**measlier, measliest**) informal contemptibly small or few: *three measly votes.*
– ORIGIN late 16th cent. (describing a pig or pork infected with measles): from MEASLES + -Y[1]. The current sense dates from the mid 19th cent.

meas·ur·a·ble /'meZH(ə)rəbəl/ ▶ adj. able to be measured: *objectives should be measurable and achievable.* ■ large enough to be measured; noticeable; definite: *a small but measurable improvement in behavior.*
– DERIVATIVES **meas·ur·a·bil·i·ty** /,meZH(ə)rə'bilətē/ n., **meas·ur·a·bly** adv. [as submodifier] *the company's performance was measurably better.*
– ORIGIN Middle English (in the sense 'moderate'): from Old French *mesurable*, from late Latin *mensurabilis*, from Latin *mensurare* 'to measure.'

meas·ure /'meZHər/ ▶ v. [with obj.] **1** ascertain the size, amount, or degree of (something) by using an instrument or device marked in standard units or by comparing it with an object of known size: *the amount of water collected is measured in pints | they will **measure up** the room and install the cabinets.* ■ be of (a specified size or degree): *the fabric measures 45 inches wide.* ■ ascertain the size and proportions of (someone) in order to make or provide clothes for them: *he will be measured for his tuxedo next week.* ■ (**measure something out**) take an exact quantity or fixed amount of something: *she helped to measure out the ingredients.* ■ estimate or assess the extent, quality, value, or effect of (something): *it is hard to measure teaching ability.* ■ (**measure someone/something against**) judge someone or something by comparison with (a certain standard): *she did not need to measure herself against some ideal.* ■ [no obj.] (**measure up**) reach the required or expected standard; fulfill expectations: *I'm afraid we didn't **measure up** to the standards they set.* ■ scrutinize (someone) keenly in order to form an assessment of them: *the two shook hands and silently **measured** each other **up**.*
2 consider (one's words or actions) carefully: *I had better measure my words so as not to embarrass anyone.*
3 archaic travel over (a certain distance or area): *we must measure twenty miles today.*
▶ n. **1** a plan or course of action taken to achieve a particular purpose: *cost-cutting measures | children were evacuated as a precautionary measure.* ■ a legislative bill: *the Senate passed the measure by a 48–30 vote.* ■ archaic punishment or retribution imposed or inflicted on someone: *her husband had dealt out **hard measure** to her.*
2 a standard unit used to express the size, amount, or degree of something: *a furlong is an obsolete measure of length | tables of weights and measures.* ■ a system or scale of such units: *the original dimensions were in imperial measure.* ■ a container of standard capacity used for taking fixed amounts of a substance. ■ a particular amount of something: ***a measure of** egg white as a binding agent.* ■ a standard official amount of an alcoholic drink as served in a licensed establishment. ■ a graduated rod or tape used for ascertaining the size of something. ■ Printing the width of a full line of type or print, typically expressed in picas. ■ Mathematics a quantity contained in another an exact number of times; a divisor.
3 a certain quantity or degree of something: *the states retain a large measure of independence.* ■ an indication or means of assessing the degree, extent, or quality of something: *it was a measure of the team's problems that they were still working after 2 a.m.*
4 the rhythm of a piece of poetry or a piece of music. ■ a particular metrical unit or group: *measures of two or three syllables are more frequent in English prose.* ■ any of the sections, typically of equal time value, into which a musical composition is divided, shown on a score by vertical lines across the staff; bar. ■ archaic a dance, typically one that is grave or stately: *now tread we a measure!*
5 (**measures**) [with modifier] a group of rock strata.
– PHRASES **beyond measure** to a very great extent: *it irritates him beyond measure.* **for good measure** in addition to what has already been done, said, or given: *he added a couple of chili peppers for good measure.* **take** (or **get** or **have**) **the measure of** assess or have assessed the character, nature, or abilities of (someone or something): *he's got her measure—she won't fool him.* **in —— measure** to the degree specified: *his rapid promotion was due in some measure to his friendship with the CEO.*
– ORIGIN Middle English (as a noun in the senses 'moderation,' 'instrument for measuring,' 'unit of capacity'): from Old French *mesure*, from Latin *mensura*, from *mens-* 'measured,' from the verb *metiri*.

meas·ured /'meZHərd/ ▶ adj. having a slow, regular rhythm: *he walks with confident, measured steps.* ■ (of speech or writing) carefully considered; deliberate and restrained: *his measured prose.*
– DERIVATIVES **meas·ured·ly** adv.

meas·ure·less /'meZHərlis/ ▶ adj. having no bounds or limits; unlimited: *Otto had measureless charm.*

meas·ure·ment /'meZHərmənt/ ▶ n. the action of measuring something: *accurate measurement is essential | a telescope with which precise measurements can be made.* ■ the size, length, or amount of something, as established by measuring: *his inseam measurement.* ■ a unit or system of measuring: *a hand is a measurement used for measuring horses.*

meas·ur·ing cup /'meZH(ə)riNG/ ▶ n. a cup marked in graded amounts, used for measuring ingredients in cooking.

meas·ur·ing tape ▶ n. another term for TAPE MEASURE.

meas·ur·ing worm ▶ n. another term for INCHWORM.

meat /mēt/ ▶ n. **1** the flesh of an animal (esp. a mammal) as food: *rabbit meat* | [as modifier] *meat sandwiches | assorted meats.* ■ the flesh of a person's body: *this'll put meat on your bones!* ■ the edible part of fruits or nuts. ■ (**the meat of**) the essence or chief part of something: *he did the meat of the climb on the first day.*
2 archaic food of any kind.
– PHRASES **be meat and drink to** Brit. **1** be a source of great pleasure to: *meat and drink to me, this life is!* **2** be a routine matter or task for: *he should be meat and drink to the English defense.* **meat and potatoes** ordinary but fundamental things; basic ingredients: *the club's meat and potatoes remains blues performers.* **one man's meat is another man's poison** proverb things liked or enjoyed by one person may be distasteful to another.
– DERIVATIVES **meat·less** adj.
– ORIGIN Old English *mete* 'food' or 'article of food' (as in *sweetmeat*), of Germanic origin.

meat·ball /'mēt,bôl/ ▶ n. a ball of ground or chopped meat, usually beef, with added seasonings. ■ informal a dull, stupid, or foolish person.

meat grind·er ▶ n. a machine for mincing meat. ■ a destructive action or process: *trench warfare was the meat grinder that every soldier dreaded.*

Meath /mēTH, mēTH/ a county in the eastern part of the Republic of Ireland, in the province of Leinster; county town, Navan.

meat·head /'mēt,hed/ ▶ n. informal a stupid person.

meat·hook /'mēt,ho͝ok/ ▶ n. a sharp metal hook of a kind used to hang meat carcasses. ■ (**meathooks**) informal a person's hands or arms: *get your big meathooks out of those pies!*

meat loaf (also **meatloaf**) ▶ n. ground or chopped meat, usually beef, with added seasonings, molded into the shape of a loaf and baked.

meat mar·ket ▶ n. informal a meeting place such as a bar or nightclub for people seeking sexual encounters.

meat·space /'mēt,spās/ ▶ n. informal the physical world, as opposed to cyberspace or a virtual environment: *I'd like to know a little more before we talk about a get-together in meatspace.*

me·a·tus /mē'ātəs/ ▶ n. (pl. **same** or **meatuses**) Anatomy a passage or opening leading to the interior of the body: *the urethral meatus.* ■ (also **external auditory meatus**) the passage leading into the ear.
– ORIGIN late Middle English: from Latin, 'passage,' from *meare* 'to flow, run.'

meat wag·on ▶ n. informal an ambulance or hearse.

meat·y /'mētē/ ▶ adj. (**meatier, meatiest**) consisting of or full of meat: *a meaty flavor.* ■ fleshy; brawny: *the tall, meaty young man.* ■ full of substance or interest; satisfying: *the ballet has stayed the course because of the meaty roles it offers.*
– DERIVATIVES **meat·i·ly** /'mētl-ē/ adv., **meat·i·ness** /'mētēnis/ n.

Mec·ca /'mekə/ a city in western Saudi Arabia, an oasis town in the Red Sea region of Hejaz, east of Jiddah, considered by Muslims to be the holiest city of Islam; pop. 1,385,000 (est. 2007). The birthplace in AD 570 of the prophet Muhammad, it was the scene of his early teachings before his emigration to Medina in 622 (the HEGIRA). On Muhammad's return to Mecca in 630 it became the center of the new Muslim faith. Arabic name MAKKAH. ■ (as noun **a Mecca**) a place that attracts people of a particular group or with a particular interest: *Holland is a Mecca for jazz enthusiasts.*
– DERIVATIVES **Mec·can** adj. & n.

mech /mek/ ▶ n. informal a mechanic.
– ORIGIN mid 20th cent.: abbreviation.

me·chan·ic /mə'kanik/ ▶ n. **1** a person who repairs and maintains machinery: *a car mechanic.*
2 archaic a manual laborer or artisan: *the Mechanics' Institute.*
– ORIGIN late Middle English (as an adjective in the sense 'relating to manual labor'): via Old French or Latin from Greek *mēkhanikos*, from *mēkhanē* (see MACHINE).

me·chan·i·cal /mə'kanikəl/ ▶ adj. **1** working or produced by machines or machinery: *a mechanical device.* ■ of or relating to machines or machinery: *a mechanical genius | mechanical failure.*
2 (of a person or action) not having or showing thought or spontaneity; automatic: *she stopped the mechanical brushing of her hair.*
3 relating to physical forces or motion; physical: *the smoothness was the result of mechanical abrasion.* ■ (of a theory) explaining phenomena in terms only of physical processes. ■ of or relating to mechanics as a science.
▶ n. **1** (**mechanicals**) the working parts of a machine, esp. a car.
2 (usu. **mechanicals**) archaic (esp. with allusion to Shakespeare's *A Midsummer Night's Dream*) a manual worker: *rude mechanicals.*
3 Printing a completed assembly of artwork and copy, typically mounted on a sheet of stiff paper.
– DERIVATIVES **me·chan·i·cal·ly** adv., **me·chan·i·cal·ness** n.
– ORIGIN late Middle English (describing an art or occupation concerned with the design or construction of machines): via Latin from Greek *mēkhanikos* (see MECHANIC) + -AL.

me·chan·i·cal ad·van·tage ▶ n. the ratio of the force produced by a machine to the force applied to it, used in assessing the performance of a machine.

me·chan·i·cal draw·ing ▶ n. a scale drawing of a mechanical or architectural structure done with precision instruments. ■ the action or process of making such drawings.

me·chan·i·cal en·gi·neer·ing ▶ n. the branch of engineering dealing with the design, construction, and use of machines.
– DERIVATIVES **me·chan·i·cal en·gi·neer** n.

me·chan·i·cal pen·cil ▶ n. a pencil with a plastic or metal case and a thin replaceable lead that may be extended as the point is worn away by twisting the outer casing.

mech·a·ni·cian /,mekə'niSHən/ ▶ n. a person skilled in the design or construction of machinery.

me·chan·ics /mə'kaniks/ ▶ plural n. **1** [treated as sing.] the branch of applied mathematics dealing with motion and forces producing motion. ■ machinery as a subject; engineering.
2 the machinery or working parts of something: *he looks at the mechanics of a car before the bodywork.* ■ the way in which something is done or operated; the practicalities or details of something: *the mechanics of cello playing.*

m

PRONUNCIATION KEY ə ago, up; ər over, fur; a hat; ā ate; ä car; e let; ē see; i fit; ī by; NG sing; ō go; ô law, for; oi toy; o͝o good; o͞o goo; ou out; TH thin; TH then; ZH vision

mech·an·ism /ˈmekəˌnizəm/ ▶ **n.** **1** a system of parts working together in a machine; a piece of machinery: *the gunner injured his arm in the turret mechanism.*
2 a natural or established process by which something takes place or is brought about: *we have no mechanism for assessing the success of forwarded inquiries | the mechanism by which genes build bodies.* ■ a contrivance in the plot of a literary work: *his Irma La Douce is a musical based on the farce mechanism.*
3 Philosophy the doctrine that all natural phenomena, including life and thought, allow mechanical explanation by physics and chemistry.
– ORIGIN mid 17th cent.: from modern Latin *mechanismus*, from Greek *mēkhanē* (see MACHINE).

mech·a·nist /ˈmekənist/ ▶ **n.** **1** Philosophy a person who believes in the doctrine of mechanism.
2 a person skilled in the design or construction of machinery.

mech·a·nis·tic /ˌmekəˈnistik/ ▶ **adj.** of or relating to theories that explain phenomena in purely physical or deterministic terms: *a mechanistic interpretation of nature.* ■ determined by physical processes alone: *he insisted that animals were entirely mechanistic.*
– DERIVATIVES **mech·a·nis·ti·cal·ly** /-(ə)lē/ **adv.**

mech·a·nize /ˈmekəˌnīz/ ▶ **v.** [with obj.] introduce machines or automatic devices into (a process, activity, or place): *the farm was mechanized in the 1950s.* ■ equip (a military force) with modern weapons and vehicles: (as adj. **mechanized**) *the units comprised tanks and mechanized infantry.* ■ give a mechanical character to: *public virtue cannot be mechanized or formulated.*
– DERIVATIVES **mech·a·ni·za·tion** /ˌmekənəˈzāsHən/ **n.**, **mech·a·niz·er n.**

mechano- ▶ **comb. form** mechanical; relating to a mechanical source: *mechanoreceptor.*
– ORIGIN from Greek *mēkhanē* 'machine.'

mech·a·no·re·cep·tor /ˌmekəˌnōriˈseptər/ ▶ **n.** Zoology a sense organ or cell that responds to mechanical stimuli such as touch or sound.
– DERIVATIVES **mech·a·no·re·cep·tive** /-ˈseptiv/ **adj.**

mech·a·no·sen·sa·tion /ˌmekəˌnōsenˈsāsHən/ ▶ **n.** the process by which mechanical stimuli are translated into neuronal impulses. It is the physiological basis for sense experiences such as touch, hearing, and balance.

mech·a·tron·ics /ˌmekəˈträniks/ ▶ **plural n.** [treated as sing.] technology combining electronics and mechanical engineering.
– DERIVATIVES **mech·a·tron·ic adj.**
– ORIGIN 1980s: blend of MECHANICS and ELECTRONICS.

Mech·lin /ˈmeklin/ (also **Mechlin lace**) ▶ **n.** lace made in the Belgian city of Mechelen (formerly known as Mechlin), characterized by patterns outlined in heavier thread.

Meck·len·burg-West Pom·er·a·ni·a /ˌmeklənbərg ˌwest päməˈrānēə/ a state in northeastern Germany, on the coast of the Baltic Sea; capital, Schwerin.

MEcon ▶ **abbr.** Master of Economics.

me·co·ni·um /miˈkōnēəm/ ▶ **n.** Medicine the dark green substance forming the first feces of a newborn infant.
– ORIGIN early 18th cent.: from Latin, literally 'poppy juice,' from Greek *mēkōnion*, from *mēkōn* 'poppy.'

mec·o·nop·sis /ˌmēkəˈnäpsis, ˌmek-/ ▶ **n.** (pl. **same** or **meconopses** /-sēz/) a Eurasian poppy that is sometimes grown as an ornamental. ● Genus *Meconopsis*, family Papaveraceae: several species, in particular the blue-flowered *M. betonicifolia.*
– ORIGIN modern Latin, from Greek *mēkōn* 'poppy' + *opsis* 'appearance.'

Me·cop·ter·a /miˈkäptərə/ Entomology an order of insects that comprises the scorpionflies.
– DERIVATIVES **me·cop·ter·an** /-tərən/ **n. & adj.**
– ORIGIN modern Latin (plural), from Greek *mēkos* 'length' + *pteron* 'wing.'

MEd ▶ **abbr.** Master of Education.

Med /med/ ▶ **n.** **(the Med)** informal, chiefly Brit. the Mediterranean Sea.
– ORIGIN 1940s: abbreviation.

med ▶ **adj.** informal medical: *med school.*
▶ **plural n.** **(meds)** medicine; medication: *he'd forgotten to take his meds.*

med. ▶ **abbr.** medium.

mé·dail·lon /ˌmādīˈyôN/ ▶ **n.** (pl. **same**) a small flat round or oval cut of meat or fish: *veal médaillons.*
– ORIGIN French, literally 'medallion.'

me·da·ka /məˈdäkə/ (also **medakafish** /məˈdäkə ˌfisH/) ▶ **n.** a small Japanese freshwater fish of variable color that is bred for aquariums and also extensively studied in the sciences. ● *Oryzias latipes*, family Adrianichthyidae.

med·al /ˈmedl/ ▶ **n.** a metal disk with an inscription or design, made to commemorate an event or awarded as a distinction to someone such as a soldier, athlete, or scholar.
▶ **v.** (**medals, medaling, medaled**; also chiefly Brit. **medals, medalling, medalled**) [no obj.] earn a medal, esp. in an athletic contest: *Norwegian athletes medaled in 12 of the 14 events* | [as adj.] *the most medaled swimmer in Olympics history.*
– DERIVATIVES **me·dal·lic** /məˈdalik/ **adj.**
– ORIGIN late 16th cent.: from French *médaille*, from Italian *medaglia*, from medieval Latin *medalia* 'half a denarius,' from Latin *medialis* 'medial.'

med·al·ist /ˈmedl-ist/ (Brit. **medallist**) ▶ **n.** **1** an athlete or other person awarded a medal: *an Olympic gold medalist.*
2 the lowest scorer in a qualifying round of a golf tournament.
3 an engraver or designer of medals.

me·dal·lion /məˈdalyən/ ▶ **n.** a piece of jewelry in the shape of a medal, typically worn as a pendant. ■ an oval or circular painting, panel, or design used to decorate a building or textile. ■ another term for MÉDAILLON.
– ORIGIN mid 17th cent.: from French *médaillon*, from Italian *medaglione*, augmentative of *medaglia* (see MEDAL).

Med·al of Hon·or (also **Congressional Medal of Honor**) ▶ **n.** the highest US military decoration, awarded by Congress to a member of the armed forces for gallantry and bravery in combat at the risk of life above and beyond the call of duty.

med·al play ▶ **n.** Golf another term for STROKE PLAY.

Me·dan /māˈdän/ a city in Indonesia, in northeastern Sumatra near the Strait of Malacca; pop. 1,772,800 (est. 2009). Established as a trading post by the Dutch in 1682, it became a leading commercial center.

Med·a·war /ˈmedəwər/, Sir Peter (Brian) (1915–87), English immunologist. He studied the biology of tissue transplantation and showed that the rejection of grafts was the result of an immune mechanism. Nobel Prize for Physiology or Medicine (1960).

med·dle /ˈmedl/ ▶ **v.** [no obj.] interfere in or busy oneself unduly with something that is not one's concern: *I don't want him meddling in our affairs* | (as noun **meddling**) *bureaucratic meddling.*
■ (**meddle with**) touch or handle (something) without permission: *you have no right to come in here and meddle with my things.*
– DERIVATIVES **med·dler** /ˈmedlər, ˈmedl-ər/ **n.**
– ORIGIN Middle English (in the sense 'mingle, mix'): from Old French *medler*, variant of *mesler*, based on Latin *miscere* 'to mix.'

med·dle·some /ˈmedlsəm/ ▶ **adj.** fond of meddling; interfering: *a gaggle of meddlesome politicians.*
– DERIVATIVES **med·dle·some·ly adv.**, **med·dle·some·ness n.**

Mede /mēd/ ▶ **n.** a member of an Iranian people who inhabited ancient Media, establishing an extensive empire during the 7th century BC, which was conquered by Cyrus the Great of Persia in 550 BC.
– ORIGIN from Latin *Medi*, Greek *Mēdoi*, plural forms.

Me·de·a /miˈdēə/ Greek Mythology a sorceress, daughter of Aeetes king of Colchis, who helped Jason to obtain the Golden Fleece and married him. When Jason deserted her for Creusa, the daughter of King Creon of Corinth, she took revenge by killing Creon, Creusa, and her own children, and fled to Athens.

Me·del·lín /ˈmedəˌyēn, ˌmedəˈyēn/ a city in eastern Colombia, the second largest city in the country; pop. 2,219,861 (2005). A major center of coffee production, it has in recent years gained a reputation as the hub of the Colombian drug trade.

med·e·vac /ˈmediˌvak/ (also **medivac**) ▶ **n.** the evacuation of military or other casualties to the hospital in a helicopter or airplane.
▶ **v.** (**medevacs, medevacking, medevacked**) [with obj.] transport (someone) to the hospital in this way: *the helicopter pilot who medevacked me the day I got shot.*
– ORIGIN 1960s: blend of MEDICAL and EVACUATION.

med·fly /ˈmedˌflī/ ▶ **n.** (pl. **medflies**) another term for MEDITERRANEAN FRUIT FLY.

Med·ford **1** a city in northeastern Massachusetts, northwest of Boston; pop. 55,573 (est. 2008).
2 a commercial city in southwestern Oregon, in an agricultural area near the California border; pop. 73,212 (est. 2008).

Med. Gr. ▶ **abbr.** Medieval Greek.

Me·di·a /ˈmēdēə/ an ancient region of Asia, southwest of the Caspian Sea, corresponding approximately to present-day Azerbaijan, northwestern Iran, and northeastern Iraq.
– DERIVATIVES **Me·di·an adj.**

me·di·a[1] /ˈmēdēə/ ▶ **n.** **1** plural form of MEDIUM.
2 (usu. **the media**) [treated as sing. or pl.] the main means of mass communication (esp. television, radio, newspapers, and the Internet) regarded collectively: [as modifier] *the campaign won media attention.*

> **USAGE** The word **media** comes from the Latin plural of **medium**. The traditional view is that it should therefore be treated as a plural noun in all its senses in English and be used with a plural rather than a singular verb: *the media **have** not followed the reports* (rather than ***has** not followed*). In practice, in the sense 'television, radio, the press, and the Internet, collectively,' **media** behaves as a collective noun (like *staff* or *clergy*, for example), which means that it is now acceptable in standard English for it to take either a singular or a plural verb. The word is also increasingly used in the plural form **medias**, as if it had a conventional singular form **media**, especially when referring to different forms of new media, and in the sense 'the material or form used by an artist': *there were great efforts made by the medias of the involved countries | about 600 works in all genres and medias were submitted for review.*

me·di·a[2] ▶ **n.** (pl. **mediae** /-dēˌē, -dēˌī/) **1** Anatomy an intermediate layer, esp. in the wall of a blood vessel.
2 Phonetics a voiced unaspirated stop; (in Greek) a voiced stop. [mid 19th cent.: from Latin, feminine of *medius* 'middle.']
– ORIGIN late 19th cent.: shortening of modern Latin *tunica* (or *membrana*) *media* 'middle sheath (or layer).'

me·di·a card ▶ **n.** Computing a small cardlike information storage device that holds data in flash memory.

me·di·a·cy /ˈmēdēəsē/ ▶ **n.** the quality of being mediate.

me·di·ae·val ▶ **adj.** variant spelling of MEDIEVAL.

me·di·a e·vent ▶ **n.** an event intended primarily to attract publicity: *a staged media event.*

me·di·a·gen·ic /ˌmēdēəˈjenik/ ▶ **adj.** tending to convey a favorable impression when reported by the media, esp. by television: *the mediagenic politician.*

me·di·al /ˈmēdēəl/ ▶ **adj.** technical situated in the middle, in particular: ■ Anatomy & Zoology situated near the median plane of the body or the midline of an organ. The opposite of LATERAL. ■ Phonetics (of a speech sound) in the middle of a word. ■ Phonetics (esp. of a vowel) pronounced in the middle of the mouth; central.
– DERIVATIVES **me·di·al·ly adv.**
– ORIGIN late 16th cent. (in the sense 'relating to the mean or average'): from late Latin *medialis*, from Latin *medius* 'middle.'

me·di·a mail ▶ **n.** a class of mail for sending books, recordings, and computer media. It is cheaper and usually slower than first-class mail.

me·di·an /ˈmēdēən/ ▶ **adj.** [attrib.] **1** denoting or relating to a value or quantity lying at the midpoint of a frequency distribution of observed values or quantities, such that there is an equal probability of falling above or below it: *the median duration of this treatment was four months.* ■ denoting the middle term of a series arranged in order of magnitude, or (if there is no middle term) the average of the middle two terms. For example, the median number of the series 55, 62, 76, 85, 93 is 76.
2 technical, chiefly Anatomy situated in the middle, esp. of the body: *the median part of the sternum.*
▶ **n.** **1** the median value of a range of values: *acreages ranged from one to fifty-two with a median of twenty-four.*
2 (also **median strip**) the strip of land between the lanes of opposing traffic on a divided highway.
3 Geometry a straight line drawn from any vertex of a triangle to the middle of the opposite side.
– DERIVATIVES **me·di·an·ly adv.**
– ORIGIN late Middle English (denoting a median vein or nerve): from medieval Latin *medianus*, from *medius* 'middle, middle of.'

me·di·ant /ˈmēdēənt/ ▶ **n.** Music the third note of the diatonic scale of any key.
– ORIGIN mid 18th cent.: from French *médiante*, from Italian *mediante* 'coming between,' present participle of obsolete *mediare* 'come between,' from late Latin *mediare* 'be in the middle of.'

me·di·a·scape /ˈmēdēəˌskāp/ ▶ **n.**
1 communications media as a whole: *the rapidly changing mediascape in Belgium.*
2 the world as presented through, or perceived by, the mass media: *the vast, ubiquitous mediascape we inhabit today.*

me·di·as·ti·num /ˌmēdēəˈstīnəm/ ▶ **n.** (pl. **mediastina** /-əˈstīnə/) Anatomy a membranous partition between two body cavities or two parts of an organ, esp. that between the lungs.
– DERIVATIVES **me·di·as·ti·nal** /-ˈstīnl/ **adj.**

–ORIGIN late Middle English: neuter of medieval Latin *mediastinus* 'medial,' based on Latin *medius* 'middle.'

me·di·a stud·ies ▶ **plural n.** [usu. treated as sing.] the study of the mass media, esp. as an academic subject.

me·di·ate ▶ **v.** /ˈmēdēˌāt/ **1** [no obj.] intervene between people in a dispute in order to bring about an agreement or reconciliation: *Wilson attempted to mediate between the powers to end the war.* ■ [with obj.] intervene in (a dispute) to bring about an agreement. ■ [with obj.] bring about (an agreement or solution) by intervening in a dispute: *efforts to mediate a peaceful resolution of the conflict.*
2 [with obj.] technical bring about (a result such as a physiological effect): *the right hemisphere plays an important role in mediating tactile perception of direction.* ■ be a means of conveying: *this important ministry of mediating the power of the word.* ■ form a connecting link between: *structures that mediate gender divisions.*
▶ **adj.** /ˈmēdēət/ connected indirectly through another person or thing; involving an intermediate agency: *public law institutions are a type of mediate state administration.*
–DERIVATIVES **me·di·ate·ly** /ˈmēdēətlē/ **adv.**
–ORIGIN late Middle English (as an adjective in the sense 'interposed'): from late Latin *mediatus* 'placed in the middle,' past participle of the verb *mediare*, from Latin *medius* 'middle.'

me·di·a·tion /ˌmēdēˈāSHən/ ▶ **n.** intervention in a dispute in order to resolve it; arbitration: *the parties have sought mediation and it has failed.* ■ intervention in a process or relationship; intercession: *they are offering sacrifice and mediation between God and man.*
–DERIVATIVES **me·di·a·tion·al adj.**

me·di·a·tor /ˈmēdēˌātər/ ▶ **n.** a person who attempts to make people involved in a conflict come to an agreement; a go-between.
–DERIVATIVES **me·di·a·to·ry** /ˈmēdēəˌtôrē/ **adj.**

med·ic[1] /ˈmedik/ ▶ **n.** informal a medical practitioner or student. ■ Military a medical corpsman who dispenses first aid at combat sites.
–ORIGIN mid 17th cent.: from Latin *medicus* 'physician,' from *mederi* 'heal.'

med·ic[2] ▶ **n.** variant spelling of MEDICK.

med·i·ca·ble /ˈmedikəbəl/ ▶ **adj.** rare able to be treated or cured medically.
–ORIGIN late 16th cent. (in the sense 'possessing medicinal properties'): from Latin *medicabilis*, from *medicari* 'administer remedies to' (see MEDICATE).

Med·i·caid /ˈmediˌkād/ a federal system of health insurance for those requiring financial assistance.
–ORIGIN 1960s: from MEDICAL + AID.

med·i·cal /ˈmedikəl/ ▶ **adj.** of or relating to the science of medicine, or to the treatment of illness and injuries: *a medical center | the medical profession.* ■ of or relating to conditions requiring medical but not surgical treatment: *he was transferred for further treatment to a medical ward.*
–DERIVATIVES **med·i·cal·ly adv.**
–ORIGIN mid 17th cent.: via French from medieval Latin *medicalis*, from Latin *medicus* 'physician.'

med·i·cal ex·am·in·er ▶ **n.** a medically qualified public officer whose duty is to investigate deaths occurring under unusual or suspicious circumstances, to perform postmortems, and to initiate inquests.

med·i·cal·ize /ˈmedikəˌlīz/ ▶ **v.** [with obj.] view (something) in medical terms; treat as a medical problem, esp. unwarrantedly: *doctors tend to medicalize manifestations of distress, prescribing drugs such as sleeping tablets.*
–DERIVATIVES **med·i·cal·i·za·tion** /ˌmedikələˈzāSHən/ **n.**
–ORIGIN 1970s: from MEDICAL + -IZE.

med·i·cal ju·ris·pru·dence ▶ **n.** the branch of law relating to medicine. ■ forensic medicine.

med·i·cal of·fi·cer ▶ **n.** a doctor serving in the armed forces, in a prison, or in a public health service.

med·i·cal prac·ti·tion·er ▶ **n.** a physician or surgeon.

me·dic·a·ment /məˈdikəmənt, ˈmedikəˌment/ ▶ **n.** a substance used for medical treatment.
–ORIGIN late Middle English: via French from Latin *medicamentum*, from *medicari* (see MEDICATE).

Med·i·care /ˈmediˌke(ə)r/ a federal system of health insurance for people over 65 years of age and for certain younger people with disabilities.
–ORIGIN 1960s: from MEDICAL + CARE.

med·i·cate /ˈmediˌkāt/ ▶ **v.** [with obj.] administer medicine or a drug to (someone): *both infants were heavily medicated to alleviate their seizures.* ■ treat (a condition) using medicine or a drug. ■ add a medicinal substance to (a dressing or product): (as adj. **medicated**) *medicated shampoo.*
–DERIVATIVES **med·i·ca·tive** /-ˌkātiv/ **adj.**
–ORIGIN early 17th cent.: from Latin *medicat-* 'treated,' from the verb *medicari* 'administer remedies to,' from *medicus* (see MEDIC[1]).

med·i·ca·tion /ˌmedəˈkāSHən/ ▶ **n.** a substance used for medical treatment, esp. a medicine or drug: *he'd been taking medication for depression | certain medications can cause dizziness.* ■ treatment using drugs: *chronic gastrointestinal symptoms which may require prolonged medication.*

Med·i·ce·an /ˌmediˈCHēən/ ▶ **adj.** of or relating to the Medici family.

Med·i·ci /ˈmediCHē/ (also **de' Medici** /də/) a powerful Italian family of bankers and merchants whose members effectively ruled Florence for much of the 15th century and from 1569 were grand dukes of Tuscany. **Cosimo** and **Lorenzo de' Medici** were notable rulers and patrons of the arts in Florence; the family also provided four popes (including **Leo X**) and two queens of France (**Catherine de' Medici** and **Marie de Médicis**).

me·dic·i·nal /məˈdisənl/ ▶ **adj.** (of a substance or plant) having healing properties: *medicinal herbs |* humorous *a large medicinal Scotch.* ■ relating to or involving medicines or drugs.
▶ **n.** a medicinal substance.
–DERIVATIVES **me·dic·i·nal·ly adv.**
–ORIGIN late Middle English: from Latin *medicinalis*, from *medicina* (see MEDICINE).

me·dic·i·nal leech ▶ **n.** a large European leech, introduced to North America, used in medicine for bloodletting. After biting, it secretes an anticoagulant to ensure the flow of blood. ● *Hirudo medicinalis*, family Hirudidae.

med·i·cine /ˈmedisən/ ▶ **n.** **1** the science or practice of the diagnosis, treatment, and prevention of disease (in technical use often taken to exclude surgery).
2 a compound or preparation used for the treatment or prevention of disease, esp. a drug or drugs taken by mouth: *give her some medicine | your doctor will be able to prescribe medicines.* ■ such substances collectively: *an aid convoy loaded with food and medicine.*
3 (among North American Indians and some other peoples) a spell, charm, or fetish believed to have healing, protective, or other power: *Fleur was murdering him by use of* ***bad medicine***.
–PHRASES **give someone a dose** (or **taste**) **of their own medicine** give someone the same bad treatment that they have given to others: *tired of his humiliation of me, I decided to give him a taste of his own medicine.* **take one's medicine** submit to something disagreeable such as punishment.
–ORIGIN Middle English: via Old French from Latin *medicina*, from *medicus* 'physician.'

med·i·cine ball ▶ **n.** a large, heavy solid ball thrown and caught for exercise.

Med·i·cine Bow Moun·tains /ˈmedisin bō/ a range in the Rocky Mountains that extends the Front Range in Colorado into southern Wyoming.

med·i·cine cab·i·net (also **medicine chest**) ▶ **n.** a box containing medicines and first-aid items, esp. one attached to a bathroom wall.

Med·i·cine Hat a commercial and industrial city in southeastern Alberta in Canada, on the South Saskatchewan River; pop. 56,997 (2006).

med·i·cine man ▶ **n.** (among North American Indians and some other peoples) a person believed to have magical powers of healing and of seeing into the future; a shaman.

med·i·cine wheel ▶ **n.** a stone circle built by North American Indians, believed to have religious, astronomical, territorial, or calendrical significance.

Mé·di·cis, Marie de, see MARIE DE MÉDICIS.

med·ick /ˈmedik/ ▶ **n.** a plant of the pea family related to alfalfa, some kinds of which are grown for fodder or green manure and some kinds of which are troublesome weeds. ● Genus *Medicago*, family Leguminosae: several species, including the prostrate **black medick** (*M. lupulina*).
–ORIGIN late Middle English: from Latin *medica*, from Greek *Mēdikē (poa)* 'Median (grass).'

med·i·co /ˈmediˌkō/ ▶ **n.** (pl. **medicos**) informal a medical practitioner or student.
–ORIGIN late 17th cent.: via Italian from Latin *medicus* 'physician.'

medico- ▶ **comb. form** relating to the field of medicine: *medico-social.*
–ORIGIN from Latin *medicus* 'physician.'

me·di·e·val /ˌmed(ē)ˈēvəl, ˌmēd-, ˌmid-/ (also **mediaeval**) ▶ **adj.** of or relating to the Middle Ages: *a medieval castle.* ■ informal, derogatory very old-fashioned or primitive: *the guerrillas' medieval behavior has become an embarrassment to their supporters.*
–DERIVATIVES **me·di·e·val·ism** /-ˌizəm/ **n.**, **me·di·e·val·ist** /-ist/ **n.**, **me·di·e·val·ize** /-ˌīz/ **v.**, **me·di·e·val·ly adv.**
–ORIGIN early 19th cent.: from modern Latin *medium aevum* 'middle age' + -AL.

me·di·e·val Lat·in ▶ **n.** Latin of about AD 600–1500.

Me·di·na /məˈdēnə/ a city in western Saudi Arabia, around an oasis about 200 miles (320 km) north of Mecca; pop. 1,010,000 (est. 2007). It is Muhammad's burial place and the site of the first Islamic mosque, which is constructed around his tomb. It is considered by Muslims to be the second most holy city after Mecca, and a visit to the prophet's tomb at Medina often forms a sequel to the formal pilgrimage to Mecca. Arabic name AL-MADINAH.

me·di·na /məˈdēnə/ ▶ **n.** the old Arab or non-European quarter of a North African town.
–ORIGIN Arabic, literally 'town.'

me·di·oc·ra·cy /ˌmēdēˈäkrəsē/ ▶ **n.** (pl. **mediocracies**) a dominant class consisting of mediocre people, or a system in which mediocrity is rewarded.

me·di·o·cre /ˌmēdēˈōkər/ ▶ **adj.** of only moderate quality; not very good: *a mediocre actor.*
–DERIVATIVES **me·di·o·cre·ly adv.**
–ORIGIN late 16th cent.: from French *médiocre*, from Latin *mediocris* 'of middle height or degree,' literally 'somewhat rugged or mountainous,' from *medius* 'middle' + *ocris* 'rugged mountain.'

me·di·oc·ri·ty /ˌmēdēˈäkrətē/ ▶ **n.** (pl. **mediocrities**) the quality or state of being mediocre: *heroes rising above the mediocrity that surrounds them.* ■ a person of mediocre ability.

med·i·tate /ˈmedəˌtāt/ ▶ **v.** [no obj.] think deeply or focus one's mind for a period of time, in silence or with the aid of chanting, for religious or spiritual purposes or as a method of relaxation. ■ (**meditate on/upon**) think deeply or carefully about (something): *he went off to meditate on the new idea.* ■ [with obj.] plan mentally; consider: *they had suffered severely, and they began to meditate retreat.*
–DERIVATIVES **med·i·ta·tor** /-ˌtātər/ **n.**
–ORIGIN mid 16th cent.: from Latin *meditat-* 'contemplated,' from the verb *meditari*, from a base meaning 'measure'; related to METE[1].

med·i·ta·tion /ˌmedəˈtāSHən/ ▶ **n.** the action or practice of meditating: *a life of meditation.* ■ a written or spoken discourse expressing considered thoughts on a subject: *his later letters are intense meditations on man's exploitation of his fellows.*
–ORIGIN Middle English: from Old French, from Latin *meditatio(n-)*, from *meditari* (see MEDITATE).

med·i·ta·tive /ˈmedəˌtātiv/ ▶ **adj.** of, involving, or absorbed in meditation or considered thought: *meditative techniques.*
–DERIVATIVES **med·i·ta·tive·ly adv.**, **med·i·ta·tive·ness n.**
–ORIGIN early 17th cent.: from MEDITATE + -IVE, reinforced by French *méditatif, -ive*.

Med·i·ter·ra·ne·an /ˌmedətəˈrānēən/ ▶ **adj.** of or characteristic of the Mediterranean Sea, the countries bordering it, or their inhabitants: *a leisurely Mediterranean cruise | our temperatures are Mediterranean.* ■ (of a person's complexion) relatively dark, as is common in some Mediterranean countries.
▶ **n.** **1** the Mediterranean Sea or the countries bordering it.
2 a native of a country bordering on the Mediterranean.
–ORIGIN mid 16th cent.: from Latin *mediterraneus* 'inland' (from *medius* 'middle' + *terra* 'land') + -AN.

Med·i·ter·ra·ne·an cli·mate ▶ **n.** a climate distinguished by warm, wet winters under prevailing westerly winds and calm, hot, dry summers, as is characteristic of the Mediterranean region and parts of California, Chile, South Africa, and southwestern Australia.

Med·i·ter·ra·ne·an fruit fly ▶ **n.** a fruit fly whose larvae can be a serious pest of citrus and other fruits. Native to the Mediterranean region, it has spread to other regions including the US. Also called MEDFLY. ● *Ceratitis capitata*, family Tephritidae.

Med·i·ter·ra·ne·an Sea an almost landlocked sea between southern Europe, the northern coast of Africa, and southwestern Asia. It is connected to the Atlantic Ocean by the Strait of Gibraltar, with the Red Sea by the Suez Canal and with the Black Sea by the Dardanelles, the Sea of Marmara, and the Bosporus.

me·di·um /ˈmēdēəm/ ▶ **n.** (pl. **media** /-dēə/ or **mediums**) **1** an agency or means of doing something: *using the latest technology as a medium for job creation | their primitive valuables acted as a* ***medium of exchange.*** ■ a means by which something is communicated or expressed: *here the Welsh language is the medium of instruction.*
2 the intervening substance through which impressions are conveyed to the senses or a force acts on objects at a distance: *radio communication needs no physical medium between the two stations | the medium between the cylinders is a vacuum.* ■ the substance in which an organism lives or is cultured: *grow bacteria in a nutrient-rich medium.*
3 a particular form of storage for digitized information, such as magnetic tape or discs: *moving or copying backed-up data through a hierarchy of different mediums.*
4 a liquid (e.g., oil or water) with which pigments are mixed to make paint. ■ the material or form used by an artist, composer, or writer: *oil paint is the most popular medium for glazing.*
5 (pl. **mediums**) a person claiming to be in contact with the spirits of the dead and to communicate between the dead and the living.
6 the middle quality or state between two extremes; a reasonable balance: *you have to* ***strike a happy medium between*** *looking like royalty and looking like a housewife.*
▶ **adj.** about halfway between two extremes of size or another quality; average: *John is six feet tall, of medium build | medium-length hair.* ■ (of cooked meat) halfway between rare and well-done: *I wanted my burger to be medium.*
– DERIVATIVES **me·di·um·ism** /-ˌmizəm/ **n.** (sense 5 of the noun), **me·di·um·is·tic** /ˌmēdēəˈmistik/ **adj.** (sense 5 of the noun), **me·di·um·ship** /-ˌSHip/ **n.** (sense 5 of the noun).
– ORIGIN late 16th cent. (originally denoting something intermediate in nature or degree): from Latin, literally 'middle,' neuter of *medius.*

me·di·um fre·quen·cy ▶ **n.** a radio frequency between 300 kilohertz and 3 megahertz.

me·di·um-range ▶ **adj.** (of an aircraft or missile) able to travel or operate over a medium distance: *medium-range nuclear missiles.*

med·i·vac ▶ **n.** & **v.** variant spelling of MEDEVAC.

med·lar /ˈmedlər/ ▶ **n.** a small, bushy tree of the rose family that bears small, brown, applelike fruits. ● *Mespilus germanica*, family Rosaceae. ■ the fruit of this tree, which is edible only after it has begun to decay.
– ORIGIN late Middle English: from Old French *medler*, from *medle* 'medlar fruit,' from Latin *mespila*, from Greek *mespilē, mespilon.*

Med. Lat. ▶ **abbr.** Medieval Latin.

med·ley /ˈmedlē/ ▶ **n.** (pl. **medleys**) a varied mixture of people or things; a miscellany: *an interesting medley of flavors.* ■ a collection of songs or other musical items performed as a continuous piece: *a medley of Beatles songs.* ■ a swimming race in which contestants swim sections in different strokes, either individually or in relay teams.
▶ **adj.** archaic mixed; motley: *a medley range of vague and variable impressions.*
▶ **v.** (past and past participle **medleyed** or **medlied**) [with obj.] archaic make a medley of; intermix.
– ORIGIN Middle English (denoting hand-to-hand combat, also cloth made of variegated wool): from Old French *medlee*, variant of *meslee* 'melee,' based on medieval Latin *misculare* 'to mix'; compare with MEDDLE.

Mé·doc /māˈdôk, -ˈdäk/ ▶ **n.** (pl. **same**) a red wine produced in Médoc, the area along the left bank of the Gironde estuary in southwestern France.

me·dre·se /məˈdresə/ ▶ **n.** variant spelling of MADRASA.

me·dul·la /məˈdələ/ ▶ **n.** Anatomy the inner region of an organ or tissue, esp. when it is distinguishable from the outer region or cortex (as in a kidney, an adrenal gland, or hair). ■ short for MEDULLA OBLONGATA. ■ Botany the soft internal tissue or pith of a plant.
– DERIVATIVES **med·ul·lar·y** /ˈmedəˌlerē, ˈmejələˌrē/ **adj.**
– ORIGIN late Middle English (in the sense 'bone marrow'): from Latin, 'pith or marrow.'

me·dul·la ob·long·a·ta /äbˌlôNGˈgätə/ ▶ **n.** the continuation of the spinal cord within the skull, forming the lowest part of the brainstem and containing control centers for the heart and lungs.
– ORIGIN late 17th cent.: modern Latin, literally 'elongated medulla.'

Me·du·sa /məˈd(y)o͞osə, -zə/ Greek Mythology the only mortal Gorgon, whom Perseus killed by cutting off her head.

me·du·sa /məˈdo͞osə, -zə/ ▶ **n.** (pl. **medusae** /-sē, -sī, -zē, -zī/ or **medusas**) Zoology a free-swimming sexual form of a coelenterate such as a jellyfish, typically having an umbrella-shaped body with stinging tentacles around the edge. In some species, medusae are a phase in the life cycle that alternates with a polypoid phase. Compare with POLYP. ■ a jellyfish.
– ORIGIN mid 18th cent.: named by association with MEDUSA.

me·du·soid /məˈdo͞oˌsoid, -ˌzoid/ Zoology ▶ **adj.** of, relating to, or resembling a medusa or jellyfish. ■ of, relating to, or denoting the medusa phase in the life cycle of a coelenterate. Compare with POLYPOID (sense 1).
▶ **n.** a medusa or jellyfish. ■ a medusoid reproductive bud.

meed /mēd/ ▶ **n.** archaic a deserved share or reward: *he must extract from her some meed of approbation.*
– ORIGIN Old English *mēd*, of Germanic origin; from an Indo-European root shared by Greek *misthos* 'reward.'

meek /mēk/ ▶ **adj.** quiet, gentle, and easily imposed on; submissive: *I used to call her Miss Mouse because she was so meek and mild | the meek compliance of our politicians.*
– DERIVATIVES **meek·ly adv.**
– ORIGIN Middle English *me(o)c* (also in the sense 'courteous or indulgent'), from Old Norse *mjúkr* 'soft, gentle.'

meek·ness /ˈmēknis/ ▶ **n.** the fact or condition of being meek; submissiveness: *all his best friends make fun of him for his meekness.*

meer·kat /ˈmi(ə)rˌkat/ ▶ **n.** a small southern African mongoose, esp. the suricate. ● *Suricata* and other genera, family Herpestidae: three species.
– ORIGIN early 18th cent.: from South African Dutch, from Dutch, 'long-tailed monkey,' apparently from *meer* 'sea' + *kat* 'cat,' but perhaps originally an alteration of an South Asian word; compare with Hindi *markaṭ* 'ape.'

meer·schaum /ˈmi(ə)rˌSHôm, -SHəm/ ▶ **n.** a soft white claylike material consisting of hydrated magnesium silicate, found chiefly in Turkey. ■ (also **meerschaum pipe**) a tobacco pipe with the bowl made from this.
– ORIGIN late 18th cent.: from German, literally 'sea-foam,' from *Meer* 'sea' + *Schaum* 'foam,' translation of Persian *kef-i-daryā* (alluding to the frothy appearance of the silicate).

Mee·rut /ˈmi(ə)rət/ a city in northern India, in Uttar Pradesh, northeast of Delhi; pop. 1,365,100 (est. 2009). It was the scene in May 1857 of the first uprising against the British in the Indian Mutiny.

meet[1] /mēt/ ▶ **v.** (past and past participle **met** /met/) [with obj.] **1** come into the presence or company of (someone) by chance or arrangement: *a week later I met him in the street* | [no obj.] *we met for lunch | they arranged to* ***meet up*** *that afternoon.* ■ make the acquaintance of (someone) for the first time: *she took Paul to meet her parents* | [no obj.] *we met at an office party.* ■ [no obj.] (of a group of people) assemble for a particular purpose: *the committee meets once a week.* ■ [no obj.] (**meet with**) have a meeting with (someone): *he met with the president on September 16.* ■ go to a place and wait there for (a person or their means of transport) to arrive: *I offered to meet their train.* ■ play or oppose in a contest: *in the final match, the U.S. will meet Brazil* | [no obj.] *the Twins and Mariners will not meet again until September.* ■ touch; join: *Harry's lips met hers* | [no obj.] *the curtains failed to meet in the middle* | figurative *our eyes met across the table.* ■ encounter or be faced with (a particular fate, situation, attitude, or reaction): *he met his death in 1946* | [no obj.] *we met with a slight setback.* ■ (**meet something with**) have (a particular reaction) to: *the announcement was met with widespread protests.* ■ [no obj.] (**meet with**) receive (a particular reaction): *I'm sorry if it doesn't meet with your approval.*
2 fulfill or satisfy (a need, requirement, or condition): *this policy is doing nothing to meet the needs of women | they failed to meet the noon deadline.* ■ pay (a financial claim or obligation): *all your household expenses will still have to be met.*
▶ **n.** an organized event at which a number of races or other sporting contests are held: *a swim meet.*
– PHRASES **meet someone's eye** (or **eyes**) be visible: *the sight that met his eyes was truly amazing.* **meet someone's eye** (or **eyes** or **gaze**) look directly at someone: *for a moment, he refused to meet her eyes.* **meet someone halfway** make a compromise with someone: *I am prepared to meet him halfway by paying an additional $25,000.* **meet one's Maker** see MAKER. **meet one's match** see MATCH[1]. **there's more to someone/something than meets the eye** a person or situation is more complex or interesting than they appear.
– ORIGIN Old English *mētan* 'come upon, come across,' of Germanic origin; related to Dutch *moeten*, 'meet,' also to MOOT.

meet[2] ▶ **adj.** archaic suitable; fit; proper: *it is a theater meet for great events.*
– DERIVATIVES **meet·ly adv.**, **meet·ness n.**
– ORIGIN Middle English (in the sense 'made to fit'): shortening of Old English *gemǣte*, of Germanic origin; related to METE[1].

meet-and-greet ▶ **n.** an organized event during which a celebrity, politician, or other well-known figure meets and talks to the public.

meet·ing /ˈmētiNG/ ▶ **n. 1** an assembly of people, esp. the members of a society or committee, for discussion or entertainment: *the early-dismissal policy will be discussed at our next meeting.* ■ a gathering of people, esp. Quakers, for worship.
2 a coming together of two or more people, by chance or arrangement: *he intrigued her on their first meeting.*
– PHRASES **a meeting of (the) minds** an understanding or agreement between people.

meet·ing·house /ˈmētiNGˌhous/ (also **meeting house**) ▶ **n.** a Quaker place of worship. ■ historical a Protestant place of worship.

mef·lo·quine /ˈmefləˌkwēn, -ˌkwīn/ ▶ **n.** Medicine an antimalarial drug consisting of a fluorinated derivative of quinoline.
– ORIGIN 1970s: from *me(thyl)* + *fl(uor)o* + *quin(olin)e.*

meg /meg/ ▶ **n.** (pl. **same** or **megs**) short for MEGABYTE.

meg·a /ˈmegə/ informal ▶ **adj.** very large; huge: *a mega city.*
▶ **adv.** [as submodifier] extremely: *they are mega rich.*
– ORIGIN 1980s: independent usage of MEGA-.

mega- ▶ **comb. form 1** very large in size, extent, capacity, or amount: *megalith.*
2 (in units of measurement) denoting a factor of one million (10^6): *megahertz | megadeath.*
3 Computing denoting a factor of 2^{20}.
– ORIGIN from Greek *megas* 'great.'

meg·a·bit /ˈmegəˌbit/ ▶ **n.** Computing a unit of data size or (when expressed per second) network speed, equal to one million or (strictly) 1,048,576 bits.

meg·a·buck /ˈmegəˌbək/ ▶ **n.** (usu. **megabucks**) informal a million dollars. ■ a huge sum of money: *he has been earning megabucks for decades* | [as modifier] *megabuck salaries.*

meg·a·byte /ˈmegəˌbīt/ (abbr.: **Mb** or **MB**) ▶ **n.** Computing a unit of information equal to 2^{20} bytes or, loosely, one million bytes.

Meg·a·chi·rop·ter·a /ˌmegəˌkīˈräptərə/ Zoology a division of bats that comprises the fruit bats and flying foxes. ● Suborder Megachiroptera and family Pteropodidae, order Chiroptera.
– DERIVATIVES **meg·a·chi·rop·ter·an** /-tərən/ **n.** & **adj.**
– ORIGIN modern Latin (plural), from MEGA- 'large' + CHIROPTERA.

me·ga·church /ˈmegəCHərCH/ ▶ **n.** a church with an unusually large congregation, typically one preaching a conservative or evangelical form of Christianity.

meg·a·cit·y /ˈmegəsitē/ ▶ **n.** (pl. **megacities**) a very large city, typically one with a population of over ten million people.

meg·a·death /ˈmegəˌdeTH/ ▶ **n.** a unit used in quantifying the casualties of nuclear war, equal to the deaths of one million people.

meg·a·dose /ˈmegəˌdōs/ ▶ **n.** a dose many times larger than the usual, esp. of a vitamin or drug.

Me·gae·ra /məˈji(ə)rə/ Greek Mythology one of the Furies.

meg·a·fau·na /ˈmegəˌfônə/ ▶ **n.** Zoology the large mammals of a particular region, habitat, or geological period. ■ Ecology animals that are large enough to be seen with the naked eye.
– DERIVATIVES **meg·a·fau·nal** /ˌmegəˈfônl/ **adj.**

meg·a·flop[1] /ˈmegəˌfläp/ ▶ **n.** Computing a unit of computing speed equal to one million floating-point operations per second.
– ORIGIN 1970s: back-formation from *megaflops* (see MEGA-, -FLOP).

meg·a·flop[2] ▶ **n.** informal a thing that is a complete failure.
– ORIGIN late 20th cent.: a pun on MEGAFLOP[1].

meg·a·ga·mete /ˌmegəˈgamˌēt, ˌmegəgəˈmēt/ ▶ **n.** another term for MACROGAMETE.

meg·a·hertz /ˈmegəˌhərts/ (abbr.: **MHz**) ▶ **n.** (pl. **same**) one million hertz, esp. as a measure of the frequency of radio transmissions or the clock speed of a computer.

meg·a·lith /ˈmegəˌliTH/ ▶ **n.** Archaeology a large stone that forms a prehistoric monument (e.g., a menhir) or part of one (e.g., a stone circle or chamber tomb).
– ORIGIN mid 19th cent.: back-formation from MEGALITHIC.

meg·a·lith·ic /ˌmegəˈliTHik/ ▶ **adj.** Archaeology **1** of, relating to, or denoting prehistoric monuments made of or containing megaliths. ■ (often **Megalithic**) of, relating to, or denoting prehistoric cultures characterized by the erection of megalithic monuments.
2 (of an organization or system) massive or monolithic: *since June, the committee has become megalithic.*
– ORIGIN mid 19th cent.: from MEGA- 'large' + Greek *lithos* 'stone' + -IC.

megalo- ▶ **comb. form** abnormally large or great: *megaloblast | megalopolis.*
– ORIGIN from Greek *megas, megal-* 'great.'

meg·a·lo·blast /ˈmegələˌblast/ ▶ **n.** Medicine a large, abnormally developed red blood cell typical of certain forms of anemia, associated with a deficiency of folic acid or of vitamin B_{12}.
– DERIVATIVES **meg·a·lo·blas·tic** /ˌmegəlōˈblastik/ **adj.**

Meg·a·loc·er·os /ˌmegəˈläsərəs/ ▶ **n.** a very large extinct deer of the Pleistocene epoch, of which the Irish elk was the main example.
– ORIGIN modern Latin, from Greek *megas, megalo-* 'great' + *keras* 'horn.'

meg·a·lo·ma·ni·a /ˌmegəlōˈmānēə/ ▶ **n.** obsession with the exercise of power, esp. in the domination of others. ■ delusion about one's own power or importance (typically as a symptom of manic or paranoid disorder).
– DERIVATIVES **meg·a·lo·man·ic** /-ˈmanik/ **adj.**

meg·a·lo·ma·ni·ac /ˌmegəlōˈmānēˌak/ ▶ **n.** a person who is obsessed with their own power. ■ a person who suffers delusions of their own power or importance.
▶ **adj.** exhibiting megalomania.
– DERIVATIVES **meg·a·lo·ma·ni·a·cal** /-məˈnīəkəl/ **adj.**

meg·a·lop·o·lis /ˌmegəˈläpəlis/ ▶ **n.** a very large, heavily populated city or urban complex.
– ORIGIN mid 19th cent.: from MEGALO- 'great' + Greek *polis* 'city.'

meg·a·lo·pol·i·tan /ˌmegələˈpälətn/ ▶ **adj.** of or denoting a very large city: *megalopolitan traffic.*
▶ **n.** an inhabitant of a very large city.
– ORIGIN mid 17th cent.: from MEGALO- 'great' + Greek *politēs* 'citizen' + -AN.

meg·a·lo·saur /ˌmegələˈsôr/ (also **megalosaurus** /-ˈsôrəs/) ▶ **n.** a large carnivorous bipedal dinosaur of the mid Jurassic period, whose remains have been found only in England and France. ● Genus *Megalosaurus*, suborder Theropoda, order Saurischia; the first dinosaur to be described and named (1824).
– DERIVATIVES **meg·a·lo·sau·ri·an** /-ˈsôrēən/ **adj.**
– ORIGIN modern Latin, from MEGALO- 'great' + Greek *sauros* 'lizard.'

meg·a·mouth /ˈmegəˌmouTH/ (also **megamouth shark**) ▶ **n.** a shark with a very large wide mouth and tiny teeth, first captured in 1976 off the Hawaiian Islands. ● *Megachasma pelagios*, the only member of the family Megachasmidae.

Meg·an's Law /ˈmegənz, ˈmā-/ ▶ **n.** a law requiring authorities to notify communities of the whereabouts of convicted sex offenders. It was first enacted by New Jersey in 1995.
– ORIGIN named after *Megan Kanka*, a 7-year old New Jersey girl murdered by a neighbor who was a convicted sex offender.

meg·a·phone /ˈmegəˌfōn/ ▶ **n.** a large funnel-shaped device for amplifying and directing the voice.
▶ **v.** [with obj.] utter through, or as if through, a megaphone: *the director stood around megaphoning orders* | [no obj.] *it was only their guides megaphoning to them.*
– DERIVATIVES **meg·a·phon·ic** /ˌmegəˈfänik/ **adj.**

megaphone

meg·a·pix·el /ˈmegəˌpiksəl/ ▶ **n.** one million pixels, used as a measure of the resolution in digital cameras: [in combination] *a 3.2-megapixel camera.*

meg·a·pode /ˈmegəˌpōd/ ▶ **n.** a large ground-dwelling Australasian and Southeast Asian bird that builds a large mound of debris to incubate its eggs by the heat of decomposition. Also called MOUND BUILDER. ● Family Megapodiidae (the **megapode family**), which includes the brush turkeys and mallee fowl.
– ORIGIN mid 19th cent.: from modern Latin *Megapodius* (genus name), from MEGA- 'large' + Greek *pous, pod-* 'foot.'

meg·a·spore /ˈmegəˌspôr/ ▶ **n.** Botany the larger of the two kinds of spores produced by some ferns. Compare with MICROSPORE.

meg·a·star /ˈmegəˌstär/ ▶ **n.** informal a very famous person, esp. in the world of entertainment.
– DERIVATIVES **meg·a·star·dom** /ˌmegəˈstärdəm/ **n.**

meg·a·store /ˈmegəˌstôr/ ▶ **n.** a very large store, typically one specializing in a particular type of product: *a computer megastore.*

meg·a·struc·ture /ˈmegəˌstrəkCHər/ ▶ **n.** a massive construction or structure, esp. a complex of many buildings.

meg·a·the·ri·um /ˌmegəˈTHi(ə)rēəm/ ▶ **n.** (pl. **megatheriums** or **megatheria** /-ˈTHi(ə)rēə/) an extinct giant ground sloth of the Pliocene and Pleistocene epochs in America, reaching a height of 16 feet (5 m) when standing erect. ● Genus *Megatherium*, family Megatheriidae.
– ORIGIN modern Latin, from Greek *mega thērion* 'great animal.'

meg·a·ton /ˈmegəˌtən/ (abbr.: **MT**) ▶ **n.** a unit of explosive power chiefly used for nuclear weapons, equivalent to one million tons of TNT: *H-bombs of fifteen megatons each.*
– DERIVATIVES **meg·a·ton·nage** /ˌmegəˈtənij/ **n.**

meg·a·volt /ˈmegəˌvōlt/ (abbr.: **MV**) ▶ **n.** a unit of electromotive force equal to one million volts.

meg·a·watt /ˈmegəˌwät/ (abbr.: **MW**) ▶ **n.** a unit of power equal to one million watts, esp. as a measure of the output of a power station.

me gen·er·a·tion ▶ **n.** a generation of people that are concerned chiefly with themselves, esp. in being selfishly materialistic.

Me·gha·la·ya /ˌmāgəˈlāə/ a small state in northeastern India, on the northern border of Bangladesh; capital, Shillong. It was created in 1970 from part of Assam.

Me·gid·do /miˈgidō/ an ancient city in northwestern Palestine, southeast of Haifa in present-day Israel. Its commanding location made the city the scene of many early battles, and the word *Armageddon* ("hill of Megiddo") is derived from its name. It was the scene in 1918 of the defeat of Turkish forces by the British under General Allenby.

Me·gil·lah /məˈgilə/ one of five books of the Hebrew scriptures (the Song of Solomon, Ruth, Lamentations, Ecclesiastes, and Esther) that are appointed to be read on certain Jewish notable days, esp. the Book of Esther, read at the festival of Purim. ■ (as noun **the whole megillah**) informal something in its entirety, esp. a complicated set of arrangements or a long-winded story.
– ORIGIN from Hebrew *mĕgillāh*, literally 'scroll.'

me·gilp /məˈgilp/ ▶ **n.** a mixture of mastic resin and linseed oil added to oil paints, widely used in the 19th century.
– ORIGIN mid 18th cent.: of unknown origin.

meg·ohm /ˈmegˌōm/ ▶ **n.** a unit of electrical resistance equal to one million ohms.
– ORIGIN mid 19th cent.: from MEGA- (as a unit of measurement) + OHM.

me·grim /ˈmēgrim/ ▶ **n.** archaic **1** (**megrims**) depression; low spirits: *fresh air and exercise, she generally found, could banish most megrims.*
2 a whim or fancy.
3 old-fashioned term for MIGRAINE.
– ORIGIN late Middle English: variant of MIGRAINE.

meh /me/ informal ▶ **exclam.** expressing a lack of interest or enthusiasm: *Meh. I'm not impressed so far.*
▶ **adj.** uninspiring; unexceptional: *a lot of his movies are ... meh.* ■ unenthusiastic; apathetic: *everyone else I talked to was kind of meh.*
– ORIGIN 1990s: apparently popularized by the television series *The Simpsons.*

Meh·ta /ˈmātä/, Zubin (1936–), Indian symphony conductor. Often heading more than one orchestra at the same time, he has been music director of the Montreal Symphony Orchestra 1960–67, the Los Angeles Philharmonic 1962–78, the New York Philharmonic 1978–91, the Israel Philharmonic since 1977 (appointed for life), and the Bavarian State Opera 1998–2006.

Meighen /ˈmēən/, Arthur (1874–1960), Canadian Conservative statesman; prime minister 1920–21.

Mei·ji /ˈmājē/ ▶ **n.** [usu. as modifier] the period when Japan was ruled by the emperor Meiji Tenno, marked by the modernization and westernization of the country.
– ORIGIN Japanese, literally 'enlightened government.'

Mei·ji Ten·no /māˈjē ˈteˌnō/ (1852–1912), emperor of Japan 1868–1912; born *Mutsuhito*. He encouraged Japan's rapid modernization and political reform.

mei·o·fau·na /ˈmīəˌfônə/ ▶ **n.** Ecology minute interstitial animals living in soil and aquatic sediments.
– ORIGIN 1960s: from Greek *meiōn* 'less or smaller' + FAUNA.

mei·o·sis /mīˈōsəs/ ▶ **n.** (pl. **meioses** /-sēz/) **1** Biology a type of cell division that results in four daughter cells each with half the number of chromosomes of the parent cell, as in the production of gametes and plant spores. Compare with MITOSIS.
2 another term for LITOTES.
– DERIVATIVES **mei·ot·ic** /mīˈätik/ **adj.**, **mei·ot·i·cal·ly** /-ik(ə)lē/ **adv.**
– ORIGIN mid 16th cent. (sense 2): modern Latin, from Greek *meiōsis*, from *meioun* 'lessen,' from *meiōn* 'less.' Sense 1 dates from the early 20th cent.

Me·ir /māˈi(ə)r/, Golda (1898–1978), Israeli stateswoman, born in Ukraine; prime minister 1969–74; born *Goldie Mabovich*. She emigrated to the US in 1907 and to Palestine in 1921. Following Israel's independence, she served in cabinet posts from 1949 to 1966 before being elected prime minister.

Golda Meir

Meis·sen /ˈmīsən/ ▶ **n.** a fine hard-paste porcelain produced in Meissen since 1710. Often called DRESDEN[2].
– ORIGIN named after the city of *Meissen* in eastern Germany.

Meiss·ner ef·fect /ˈmīsnər/ ▶ **n.** Physics the expulsion of magnetic flux when a material becomes superconducting in a magnetic field. If the magnetic field is applied after the material has become superconducting, the flux cannot penetrate it.
– ORIGIN 1930s; named after Fritz W. *Meissner* (1882–1974), German physicist.

Meiss·ner's cor·pus·cle ▶ **n.** Anatomy a sensory nerve ending that is sensitive to mechanical stimuli, found in the dermis in various parts of the body.
– ORIGIN late 19th cent.: named after Georg *Meissner* (1829–1905), German anatomist.

-meister ▶ **comb. form** denoting a person regarded as skilled or prominent in a specified area of activity: *funk-meister | gag-meister.*
– ORIGIN from German *Meister* 'master.'

Mei·ster·sing·er /ˈmīstərˌsiNGər/ ▶ **n.** (pl. **same**) a member of one of the guilds of German lyric poets and musicians that flourished from the 12th to 17th century. Their technique was elaborate and they were subject to rigid regulations.
– ORIGIN German, from *Meister* 'master' + *Singer* 'singer.'

Meit·ner /ˈmītnər/, Lise (1878–1968), Austrian-born Swedish physicist. She worked in the field of radiochemistry with Otto Hahn, discovering the element protactinium with him in 1917. She also formulated the concept of nuclear fission with her nephew Otto Frisch.

meit·ner·i·um /mītˈni(ə)rēəm/ ▶ **n.** the chemical element of atomic number 109, a very unstable element made by high-energy atomic collisions. (Symbol: **Mt**)
– ORIGIN modern Latin, from the name of L. MEITNER.

Mek·nès /mekˈnes/ a city in northern Morocco, in the Middle Atlas Mountains, west of Fez; pop. 713,609 (2004).

m

Me·kong /'mā'kông, -'mē-/ a river in Southeast Asia that rises in Tibet and flows southeast and south for 2,600 miles (4,180 km) through southern China, Laos, Cambodia, and Vietnam to its extensive delta on the South China Sea. It forms the boundary between Laos, Burma (Myanmar), and Thailand.

me·la /'mālə/ ▶ n. Indian a fair or Hindu festival.
– ORIGIN from Sanskrit *melā* 'assembly.'

me·lae·na ▶ n. British spelling of MELENA.

Me·la·ka /mə'läkə/ (also **Malacca**) a state of Malaysia, on the southwestern coast of the Malay Peninsula, on the Strait of Malacca. ■ its capital and chief port; pop. 194,400 (est. 2009). Conquered by the Portuguese in 1511, it played an important role in the development of trade between Europe and the East, esp. China.

mel·a·leu·ca /,melə'lo͞okə/ ▶ n. an Australian shrub or tree that bears spikes of flowers. Some kinds are a source of timber or medicinal oil. ● Genus *Melaleuca*, family Myrtaceae: many species, including the Australian paperbarks.
– ORIGIN modern Latin: from Greek *melas* 'black' + *leukos* 'white' (because of the fire-blackened white bark of some Asian species).

mel·a·mine /'melə,mēn/ ▶ n. 1 Chemistry a white crystalline compound made by heating cyanamide and used in making plastics. ● A heterocyclic amine; chem. formula: $(CNH_2)_3N_3$.
2 (also **melamine resin**) a plastic used chiefly for laminated coatings, made by copolymerizing this compound with formaldehyde.
– ORIGIN mid 19th cent.: from German *melam* (an arbitrary formation), denoting an insoluble amorphous organic substance, + AMINE.

mel·an·cho·li·a /,melən'kōlēə/ ▶ n. deep sadness or gloom; melancholy: *rain slithered down the windows, encouraging a creeping melancholia.* ■ dated a mental condition marked by persistent depression and ill-founded fears.
– DERIVATIVES **mel·an·cho·li·ac** /-'kōlē-ak/ n. & adj.
– ORIGIN late Middle English (denoting black bile): from late Latin (see MELANCHOLY).

mel·an·chol·y /'melən,kälē/ ▶ n. a feeling of pensive sadness, typically with no obvious cause: *an air of melancholy surrounded him.* ■ another term for MELANCHOLIA (as a mental condition). ■ historical another term for BLACK BILE.
▶ adj. having a feeling of melancholy; sad and pensive: *she felt a little melancholy | the dog has a melancholy expression.* ■ causing or expressing sadness; depressing: *the study makes melancholy if instructive reading.*
– DERIVATIVES **mel·an·chol·ic** /,melən'kälik/ adj., **mel·an·chol·i·cal·ly** /,melən'kälək(ə)lē/ adv.
– ORIGIN Middle English: from Old French *melancolie*, via late Latin from Greek *melankholia*, from *melas, melan-* 'black' + *kholē* 'bile,' an excess of which was formerly believed to cause depression.

Me·lanch·thon /mə'laNGkTHən, mā'länKHtôn/, Philipp (1497–1560), German reformer; born *Philipp Schwarzerd.* He succeeded Luther as leader of the Reformation movement in Germany in 1521 and drew up the Augsburg Confession in 1530.

Mel·a·ne·sia /,melə'nēZHə/ a region in the western Pacific Ocean, south of Micronesia and west of Polynesia. Its area includes the Bismarck Archipelago, the Solomon Islands, Vanuatu, New Caledonia, and Fiji.
– ORIGIN from Greek *melas* 'black' + *nēsos* 'island.'

Mel·a·ne·sian /,melə'nēZHən/ ▶ adj. of or relating to Melanesia, its peoples, or their languages.
▶ n. 1 a native or inhabitant of any of the islands of Melanesia.
2 any of the languages of Melanesia, mostly Austronesian languages related to Malay but also including Neo-Melanesian (or Tok Pisin), an English-based pidgin.

mé·lange /mā'länj/ (also **melange**) ▶ n. a mixture; a medley: *a mélange of tender vegetables and herbs.*
– ORIGIN from French *mélange*, from *mêler* 'to mix.'

mel·a·nin /'melənin/ ▶ n. a dark brown to black pigment occurring in the hair, skin, and iris of the eye in people and animals. It is responsible for tanning of skin exposed to sunlight.
– ORIGIN mid 19th cent.: from Greek *melas, melan-* 'black' + -IN[1].

mel·a·nism /'melə,nizəm/ ▶ n. chiefly Zoology unusual darkening of body tissues caused by excessive production of melanin, esp. as a form of color variation in animals.
– DERIVATIVES **me·lan·ic** /mə'lanik/ adj., **mel·a·nis·tic** /,melə'nistik/ adj.

mel·a·nite /'melə,nīt/ ▶ n. a velvet-black variety of andradite (garnet).
– ORIGIN early 19th cent.: from Greek *melas, melan-* 'black' + -ITE[1].

me·lan·o·cyte /'melənə,sīt, mə'lanō-/ ▶ n. Physiology a mature melanin-forming cell, typically in the skin.

me·lan·o·cyte-stim·u·lat·ing hor·mone (abbr.: **MSH**) ▶ n. Physiology a hormone secreted by the pituitary gland that is involved in pigmentation changes in some animals.

mel·a·noid /'melə,noid/ ▶ adj. 1 resembling melanin.
2 resembling melanosis.

mel·a·no·ma /,melə'nōmə/ ▶ n. (pl. **melanomas** or **melanomata** /-'nōmətə/) Medicine a tumor of melanin-forming cells, typically a malignant tumor associated with skin cancer: *melanomas can appear anywhere on the body | the incidence of melanoma is rising steadily.*
– ORIGIN mid 19th cent.: from Greek *melas, melan-* 'black' + -OMA.

mel·a·no·sis /,melə'nōsəs/ ▶ n. Medicine a condition of abnormal or excessive production of melanin in the skin or other tissue.
– DERIVATIVES **mel·a·not·ic** /-'nätik/ adj.
– ORIGIN early 19th cent.: modern Latin, from Greek *melas, melan-* 'black' + -OSIS.

mel·a·to·nin /,melə'tōnin/ ▶ n. Biochemistry a hormone secreted by the pineal gland that inhibits melanin formation and is thought to be concerned with regulating the reproductive cycle.
– ORIGIN 1950s: from Greek *melas* 'black' + (*sero*) *tonin.*

Mel·ba /'melbə/, Dame Nellie (1861–1931), Australian opera singer; born *Helen Porter Mitchell.* Born near Melbourne, she took her professional name from that of the city.

Mel·ba sauce ▶ n. a sauce made from puréed raspberries thickened with powdered sugar.

Mel·ba toast ▶ n. very thin crisp toast.

Mel·bourne[1] /'melbərn/ 1 the capital of Victoria, in southeastern Australia, on the Bass Strait, opposite Tasmania; pop. 3,892,419 (2008). A major port and the country's second-largest city, it was the capital of Australia 1901–27.
2 a resort city in east central Florida, south of Cape Canaveral; pop. 77,351 (est. 2008).

Mel·bourne[2], William Lamb, 2nd Viscount (1779–1848), British statesman; prime minister 1834 and 1835–41. He became chief political adviser to Queen Victoria after her accession in 1837.

Mel·chi·or[1] /'melkē,ôr/ one of the three Magi, represented as a king of Nubia.

Mel·chi·or[2], Lauritz (Lebrecht Hommel) (1890–1973), US tenor; born in Denmark. Considered the outstanding heldentenor of his day, he sang with the Metropolitan Opera 1926–50.

Mel·chiz·e·dek /mel'kizə,dek/ (in the Bible) a priest and king of Salem (which is usually identified with Jerusalem). He was revered by Abraham, who paid tithes to him.

meld[1] /meld/ ▶ v. blend; combine: [with obj.] *Australia's winemakers have melded modern science with traditional art* | [no obj.] *the nylon bristles shrivel and meld together.*
▶ n. a thing formed by merging or blending: *a meld of many contributions.*
– ORIGIN 1930s: perhaps a blend of MELT and WELD[1].

meld[2] ▶ v. [with obj.] (in rummy, canasta, and other card games) lay down or declare (a combination of cards) in order to score points: *a player has melded four kings.*
▶ n. a completed set or run of cards in any of these games.
– ORIGIN late 19th cent. (originally US): from German *melden* 'announce.'

me·lee /'mā,lā, mā'lā/ (also **mêlée**) ▶ n. a confused fight, skirmish, or scuffle: *several people were hurt in the melee.* ■ a confused mass of people: *the melee of people that was always thronging the streets.*
– ORIGIN mid 17th cent.: from French *mêlée*, from an Old French variant of *meslee* (see MEDLEY).

me·le·na /mə'lēnə/ (Brit. **melaena**) ▶ n. Medicine dark sticky feces containing partly digested blood. ■ the production of such feces, following internal bleeding or the swallowing of blood.
– ORIGIN early 19th cent.: modern Latin, from Greek *melaina*, feminine of *melas* 'black.'

mel·ic /'melik/ ▶ adj. (of a poem, esp. an ancient Greek lyric) meant to be sung.
– ORIGIN late 17th cent.: via Latin from Greek *melikos*, from *melos* 'song.'

Me·lil·la /mə'lēə/ a Spanish enclave on the Mediterranean coast of Morocco; pop. 71,448 (2008). It was occupied by Spain in 1497, and with Ceuta forms a community of Spain.

mel·i·lot /'melə,lät/ ▶ n. a fragrant herbaceous plant of the pea family, native to Eurasia and north Africa, now widespread and sometimes grown as forage or green manure. Also called SWEET CLOVER. ● Genus *Melilotus*, family Leguminosae: several species, esp. the **white sweet clover** (*M. alba*).
– ORIGIN Middle English: from Old French, via Latin from Greek *melilōtos* 'honey lotus.'

mel·io·rate /'mēlēə,rāt/ ▶ v. formal another term for AMELIORATE.
– DERIVATIVES **mel·io·ra·tion** /,mēlēə'rāSHən/ n., **mel·io·ra·tive** /-,rātiv/ adj.
– ORIGIN mid 16th cent.: from late Latin *meliorat-* 'improved,' from the verb *meliorare*, based on *melior* 'better.'

mel·io·rism /'mēlēə,rizəm/ ▶ n. Philosophy the belief that the world can be made better by human effort.
– DERIVATIVES **mel·io·rist** n. & adj., **mel·io·ris·tic** /,mēlēə'ristik/ adj.
– ORIGIN late 19th cent.: from Latin *melior* 'better' + -ISM.

me·lis·ma /mə'lizmə/ ▶ n. (pl. **melismas** or **melismata** /-mətə/) Music a group of notes sung to one syllable of text.
– DERIVATIVES **mel·is·mat·ic** /,meliz'matik/ adj.
– ORIGIN late 19th cent.: from Greek, literally 'melody.'

Mel·kite /'mel,kīt/ ▶ n. an Orthodox or Uniate Christian belonging to the patriarchate of Antioch, Jerusalem, or Alexandria. ■ historical an Eastern Christian adhering to the Orthodox faith as defined by the councils of Ephesus (AD 431) and Chalcedon (AD 451) and as accepted by the Byzantine emperor.
– ORIGIN via ecclesiastical Latin from Byzantine Greek *Melkhitai*, representing Syriac *malkāyā* 'royalists' (i.e., expressing agreement with the Byzantine emperor), from *malkā* 'king.'

mel·lif·er·ous /mə'lifərəs/ ▶ adj. yielding or producing honey.
– ORIGIN mid 17th cent.: from Latin *mellifer* (from *mel* 'honey' + *-fer* 'bearing') + -OUS.

mel·lif·lu·ent /mə'liflo͞oənt/ ▶ adj. another term for MELLIFLUOUS.
– DERIVATIVES **mel·lif·lu·ence** /-lo͞oəns/ n.
– ORIGIN early 17th cent.: from late Latin *mellifluent-*, from Latin *mel, mell(i)-* 'honey' + *fluent-* 'flowing' (from the verb *fluere*).

mel·lif·lu·ous /mə'liflo͞oəs/ ▶ adj. (of a voice or words) sweet or musical; pleasant to hear: *the voice was mellifluous and smooth.*
– DERIVATIVES **mel·lif·lu·ous·ly** adv., **mel·lif·lu·ous·ness** n.
– ORIGIN late 15th cent.: from late Latin *mellifluus* (from *mel* 'honey' + *fluere* 'to flow') + -OUS.

Mel·lon /'melən/ the name of a family of US financiers and philanthropists, notably: ■ **Andrew (William)** (1855–1937), US secretary of the treasury 1923–32. He donated his art collection and made gifts to establish the National Gallery of Art in Washington, DC, in 1941. ■ **Paul** (1855–1937), son of Andrew. He served as president of the Board of Trustees for the National Gallery 1938–39, 1963–78 and donated many works of art to the gallery.

mel·lo·phone /'melə,fōn/ ▶ n. a brass instrument similar to the orchestral French horn, played mainly in military and concert bands.
– ORIGIN 1920s: from MELLOW + -PHONE.

mel·lo·tron /'melə,trän/ ▶ n. trademark an electronic keyboard instrument in which each key controls the playback of a single prerecorded musical sound.
– ORIGIN 1960s: from MELLOW + *-tron*, element of ELECTRONIC.

mel·low /'melō/ ▶ adj. 1 (esp. of sound, taste, and color) pleasantly smooth or soft; free from harshness: *she was hypnotized by the mellow tone of his voice | slow cooking gives the dish a sweet, mellow flavor.* ■ archaic (of fruit) ripe, soft, sweet, and juicy: *a dish of mellow apples.* ■ (of wine) well-matured and smooth: *delicious, mellow, ripe, fruity wines.*
2 (of a person's character) softened or matured by age or experience: *a more mellow personality.* ■ relaxed and good-humored: *Jean was feeling mellow.* ■ informal relaxed and cheerful through being slightly drunk: *everybody got very mellow and slept well.*
3 (of earth) rich and loamy.
▶ v. make or become mellow: [with obj.] *getting older does mellow the hard edges around the anger* | [no obj.] *fuller-flavored whiskeys mellow with wood maturation* | informal *I need to* **mellow out**, *I need to calm down.*
– DERIVATIVES **mel·low·ly** adv., **mel·low·ness** n.
– ORIGIN late Middle English (in the sense '(of fruit) ripe, soft, sweet, and juicy'): perhaps from attributive use of Old English *melu, melw-* (see MEAL[2]). The verb dates from the late 16th cent.

me·lo·de·on /mə'lōdēən/ (also **melodion**) ▶ n. 1 a small accordion of German origin, played esp. by folk musicians. [mid 19th cent.: probably from MELODY, on the pattern of *accordion.*]
2 a small organ popular in the 19th century, similar to the harmonium. [alteration of earlier *melodium.*]

m

me·lod·ic /mə'lädik/ ▶ **adj.** of, having, or producing melody: *melodic and rhythmic patterns.* ■ pleasant-sounding; melodious: *his voice was deep and melodic.*
– DERIVATIVES **me·lod·i·cal·ly** /-(ə)lē/ **adv.**, **me·lod·i·cism** **n.**
– ORIGIN early 19th cent.: from French *mélodique*, via late Latin from Greek *melōidikos*, from *melōidia* 'melody.'

me·lod·i·ca /mə'lädikə/ ▶ **n.** a wind instrument with a small keyboard controlling a row of reeds, and a mouthpiece at one end.
– ORIGIN 1960s: from **MELODY**, on the pattern of *harmonica*.

me·lod·ic mi·nor ▶ **n.** Music a minor scale with the sixth and seventh degrees raised when ascending and lowered when descending.

me·lo·di·ous /mə'lōdēəs/ ▶ **adj.** of, producing, or having a pleasant tune; tuneful: *the melodious chant of the monks.* ■ pleasant-sounding: *a melodious voice.*
– DERIVATIVES **me·lo·di·ous·ly** **adv.**, **me·lo·di·ous·ness** **n.**
– ORIGIN late Middle English: from Old French *melodieus*, from *melodie* (see **MELODY**).

mel·o·dist /'melədist/ ▶ **n.** a composer of melodies. ■ a singer.

mel·o·dize /'melə,dīz/ ▶ **v.** [no obj.] rare make or play music.

mel·o·dra·ma /'melə,drämə/ ▶ **n. 1** a sensational dramatic piece with exaggerated characters and exciting events intended to appeal to the emotions. ■ the genre of drama of this type. ■ language, behavior, or events that resemble drama of this kind: *what little is known of his early life is cloaked in melodrama.*
2 historical a play interspersed with songs and orchestral music accompanying the action.
– DERIVATIVES **mel·o·dram·a·tist** /,melə'drämətist/ **n.**, **mel·o·dram·a·tize** /,melə'drämə,tīz/ **v.**
– ORIGIN early 19th cent.: from French *mélodrame*, from Greek *melos* 'music' + French *drame* 'drama.'

mel·o·dra·mat·ic /,melədrə'matik/ ▶ **adj.** of or relating to melodrama. ■ characteristic of melodrama, esp. in being exaggerated, sensationalized, or overemotional: *he flung the door open with a melodramatic flourish.*
– DERIVATIVES **mel·o·dra·mat·i·cal·ly** /-ik(ə)lē/ **adv.**

mel·o·dra·mat·ics /,melədrə'matiks/ ▶ **plural n.** melodramatic behavior, action, or writing.

mel·o·dy /'melədē/ ▶ **n.** (pl. **melodies**) a sequence of single notes that is musically satisfying: *he picked out an intricate melody on his guitar.* ■ such sequences of notes collectively: *his great gift was for melody.* ■ the principal part in harmonized music: *we have the melody and bass of a song composed by Strozzi.*
– ORIGIN Middle English (also in the sense 'sweet music'): from Old French *melodie*, via late Latin from Greek *melōidia*, from *melos* 'song.'

mel·on /'melən/ ▶ **n. 1** the large round fruit of a plant of the gourd family, with sweet pulpy flesh and many seeds.
2 the Old World plant that yields this fruit. ● *Cucumis melo* subsp. *melo*, family Cucurbitaceae: many varieties.
3 Zoology a mass of waxy material in the head of dolphins and other toothed whales, thought to focus acoustic signals.
4 a large profit, esp. a stock dividend, to be divided among a number of people: *you can just see them sitting around the room cutting up the melon in advance.*
– ORIGIN late Middle English: via Old French from late Latin *melo*, *melon-*, contraction of Latin *melopepo*, from Greek *mēlopepōn*, from *mēlon* 'apple' + *pepōn* 'gourd.'

Me·los /'mē,läs/ a Greek island in the Aegean Sea, in the southwest of the Cyclades group. The center of a flourishing civilization during the Bronze Age, it is the site of the discovery in 1820 of a Hellenistic marble statue of Aphrodite, the **VENUS DE MILO**. Greek name **MÍLOS**.

Mel·pom·e·ne /mel'päm əne/ Greek & Roman Mythology the Muse of tragedy.
– ORIGIN Greek, literally 'singer.'

melt /melt/ ▶ **v. 1** make or become liquefied by heat: [no obj.] *place under the broiler until the cheese has melted* | [with obj.] *the hot metal melted the wax* | *the icebergs were melting away* | (as adj. **melted**) *asparagus with melted butter.* ■ [with obj.] (**melt something down**) melt something, esp. a metal article, so that the material it is made of can be used again: *beautiful objects are being melted down and sold for scrap.* ■ dissolve in liquid: *add a cup of sugar and boil until the sugar melts.*
2 make or become more tender or loving: [no obj.] *she was so beautiful that I melted* | [with obj.] *Richard gave her a smile that melted her heart.*
3 [no obj.] leave or disappear unobtrusively: *the compromise was accepted and the opposition melted away* | *the figure melted into thin air.* ■ (**melt into**) change or merge imperceptibly into (another form or state): *the cheers melted into gasps of admiration.*
▶ **n.** an act of melting: *the precipitation falls as snow and is released during the spring melt.* ■ metal or other material in a melted condition. ■ an amount melted at any one time. ■ [with modifier] a sandwich, hamburger, or other dish containing or topped with melted cheese: *a tuna melt.*
– PHRASES **melt in the** (or **your**) **mouth** (of food) be deliciously light or tender and need little or no chewing: *my shortbread melts in the mouth* | [as adj.] *melt-in-your-mouth chicken livers.*
– PHRASAL VERBS **melt down 1** collapse or break down disastrously: *many expected him to melt down at the first sign of trouble.* **2** (of a nuclear reactor) undergo a catastrophic failure as a result of the fuel overheating.
– DERIVATIVES **melt·a·ble** **adj.**, **melt·er** **n.**, **melt·ing·ly** **adv.**
– ORIGIN Old English *meltan*, *mieltan*, of Germanic origin; related to Old Norse *melta* 'to malt, digest,' from an Indo-European root shared by Greek *meldein* 'to melt,' Latin *mollis* 'soft,' also by **MALT**.

melt·down /'melt,doun/ ▶ **n. 1** a disastrous event, esp. a rapid fall in share prices: *the 1987 stock market meltdown.*
2 an accident in a nuclear reactor in which the fuel overheats and melts the reactor core or shielding.

> **WORD TRENDS** A meltdown was originally a catastrophic accident in a nuclear reactor, but this literal meaning has been swamped by the figurative sense of 'a disastrous collapse or breakdown.' This is a fairly recent coinage, first recorded in 1983, with the 'Black Monday' stock market crash of October 1987 labeled a *market meltdown*. The Oxford English Corpus shows a fairly steady use throughout the last decade, but in 2007 there was a massive leap in the number of examples. This reflects the beginning of the recession, with *financial, economic, global,* and *mortgage* becoming the word's most common collocates: *the global financial meltdown sent oil prices plummeting today.*

mel·te·mi /mel'temē/ (also **meltemi wind**) ▶ **n.** a dry northwesterly wind that blows during the summer in the eastern Mediterranean. Also called **ETESIAN WIND**.
– ORIGIN from modern Greek *meltémi*, Turkish *meltem*.

melt·ing point ▶ **n.** the temperature at which a given solid will melt.

melt·ing pot ▶ **n.** a pot in which metals or other materials are melted and mixed. ■ a place where different peoples, styles, theories, etc., are mixed together: *a melting pot of disparate rhythms and cultures.*

mel·ton /'meltən/ ▶ **n.** heavy woolen cloth with a close-cut nap, used for overcoats and jackets.
– ORIGIN early 19th cent.: named after *Melton Mowbray*, a town in central England, formerly a center of manufacturing.

melt·wa·ter /'melt,wôtər, -,wätər/ ▶ **n.** (also **meltwaters**) water formed by the melting of snow and ice, esp. from a glacier.

Mel·ville /'melvəl, -,vil/, Herman (1819–91), US novelist and short-story writer. His experiences on a whaling ship formed the basis of several novels, notably *Moby Dick* (1851). Other notable works: *White-Jacket* (1850), *The Confidence Man* (1857), and *Billy Budd* (first published in 1924).

mem. ▶ **abbr.** ■ member. ■ memoir. ■ memorandum. ■ memorial.

mem·an·tine /'memən,tēn/ ▶ **n.** a prescription drug for the treatment of Alzheimer's disease. It protects the brain's nerve cells against glutamate, which is released in excess by Alzheimer's-damaged brain cells. Also called **NAMENDA** (trademark).

mem·ber /'membər/ ▶ **n. 1** an individual, thing, or organization belonging to a group: *a member of the drama club* | *interest from members of the public* | *a member of the lily family* | [as modifier] *member countries of the Central African Customs Union.* ■ (also **Member**) a person formally elected to take part in the proceedings of certain organizations: *members of Congress* | *Member of Parliament.*
2 a constituent piece of a complex structure: *the main member that joins the front and rear axles.* ■ a part of a sentence, equation, group of figures, mathematical set, etc.
3 archaic a part or organ of the body, esp. a limb. ■ (also **male member**) the penis. Compare with **MEMBRUM VIRILE**.
– DERIVATIVES **mem·bered** **adj.** [in combination] (chiefly Chemistry) *a six-membered oxygen-containing ring.*
– ORIGIN Middle English: via Old French from Latin *membrum* 'limb.'

mem·ber·ship /'membər,SHip/ ▶ **n.** the fact of being a member of a group: *I was selected for membership in the National Honor Society* | [as modifier] *a membership card.* ■ [in sing.] the number or body of members in a group: *our membership has grown by 600,000 in the past 18 months.*

mem·brane /'mem,brān/ ▶ **n.** Anatomy & Zoology a pliable sheetlike structure acting as a boundary, lining, or partition in an organism. ■ a thin pliable sheet or skin of various kinds: *the concrete should include a membrane to prevent water seepage.* ■ Biology a microscopic double layer of lipids and proteins that bounds cells and organelles and forms structures within cells.
– DERIVATIVES **mem·bra·na·ceous** /,membrə'nāSHəs/ **adj.**, **mem·bra·ne·ous** /mem'brānēəs/ **adj.**, **mem·bra·nous** /'membrənəs, mem'brānəs/ **adj.**
– ORIGIN late Middle English: from Latin *membrana*, from *membrum* 'limb.'

mem·bra·nous lab·y·rinth /'membrənəs, mem'brānəs/ ▶ **n.** see **LABYRINTH**.

mem·brum vir·ile /'membrəm 'viralā, vi'rīlē/ ▶ **n.** archaic the penis.
– ORIGIN Latin, literally 'male member.'

meme /mēm/ ▶ **n.** an element of a culture or system of behavior that may be considered to be passed from one individual to another by nongenetic means, esp. imitation. ■ an image, video, phrase, etc. that is passed electronically from one Internet user to another.
– DERIVATIVES **me·met·ic** /mē'metik, mə-/ **adj.**
– ORIGIN 1970s: from Greek *mimēma* 'that which is imitated,' on the pattern of *gene*.

> **WORD TRENDS** When the British scientist Richard Dawkins coined the word **meme** in his 1976 book *The Selfish Gene*, he wanted a word like **gene** that conveyed the way in which ideas and behavior spread within society by nongenetic means. Since then, the word has been picked up to describe a piece of information spread by e-mail or via blogs and social networking sites. A **meme** can be almost anything—a joke, a video clip, a cartoon, a news story—and can also evolve as it spreads, with users editing the content or adding comments. Common collocates in the Oxford English Corpus are *spread, pass,* and *transmit*: as with the Internet sense of **VIRAL**, **meme** uses the metaphor of disease and infection.

Me·mel /'māməl/ **1** German name for **KLAIPEDA**. ■ a former district of East Prussia, centered on the city of Memel (Klaipeda).
2 the Neman River in its lower course (see **NEMAN**).

me·men·to /mə'men,tō/ ▶ **n.** (pl. **mementos** or **mementoes**) an object kept as a reminder or souvenir of a person or event: *you can purchase a memento of your visit.*
– ORIGIN late Middle English (denoting a prayer of commemoration): from Latin, literally 'remember!,' imperative of *meminisse*.

me·men·to mo·ri /mə'men,tō 'môrē/ ▶ **n.** (pl. **same**) an object serving as a warning or reminder of death, such as a skull.
– ORIGIN Latin, literally 'remember (that you have) to die.'

mem·o /'memō/ ▶ **n.** (pl. **memos**) informal a written message, esp. in business.
– ORIGIN early 18th cent.: abbreviation of **MEMORANDUM**.

mem·oir /'mem,wär, -,wôr/ ▶ **n. 1** a historical account or biography written from personal knowledge or special sources: *in 1924 she published a short memoir of her husband.* ■ (**memoirs**) an autobiography or a written account of one's memory of certain events or people.
2 an essay on a learned subject: *an important memoir on Carboniferous crustacea.* ■ (**memoirs**) the proceedings or transactions of a learned society: *Memoirs of the Horticultural Society.*
– DERIVATIVES **mem·oir·ist** /-ist/ **n.**
– ORIGIN late 15th cent. (denoting a memorandum or record): from French *mémoire* (masculine), a special use of *mémoire* (feminine) 'memory.'

mem·o·ra·bil·i·a /,mem(ə)rə'bilēə/ ▶ **plural n.** [treated as sing. or pl.] objects kept or collected because of their historical interest, esp. those associated with memorable people or events: *World Series memorabilia.* ■ archaic memorable or noteworthy things.

m

– ORIGIN late 18th cent.: from Latin, neuter plural of *memorabilis* 'memorable.'

mem·o·ra·ble /ˈmem(ə)rəbəl/ ▶ **adj.** worth remembering or easily remembered, esp. because of being special or unusual: *this victory was one of the most memorable of his career.*
– DERIVATIVES **mem·o·ra·bil·i·ty** /ˌmem(ə)rəˈbilətē/ **n.**, **mem·o·ra·bly** /-blē/ **adv.**
– ORIGIN late 15th cent.: from Latin *memorabilis*, from *memorare* 'bring to mind,' from *memor* 'mindful.'

mem·o·ran·dum /ˌmeməˈrandəm/ ▶ **n.** (pl. **memoranda** /-də/ or **memorandums**) a note or record made for future use: *the two countries signed a memorandum of understanding on economic cooperation.* ■ a written message, esp. in business or diplomacy: *he told them of his decision in a memorandum.* ■ Law a document recording the terms of a contract or other legal details.
– ORIGIN late Middle English: from Latin, literally 'something to be brought to mind,' gerundive of *memorare*. The original use was as an adjective, placed at the head of a note of something to be remembered or of a record made for future reference.

me·mo·ri·al /məˈmôrēəl/ ▶ **n.** **1** something, esp. a structure, established to remind people of a person or event: *a monument built as a memorial to those who fell in the Civil War.* ■ [as modifier] intended to commemorate someone or something: *a memorial service in the dead man's honor.*
2 chiefly historical a statement of facts, esp. as the basis of a petition: *the council sent a strongly worded memorial to the chancellor.* ■ a record or chronicle: *Mrs. Carlyle's Letters and Memorials.* ■ an informal diplomatic paper.
– ORIGIN late Middle English: from late Latin *memoriale* 'record, memory, monument,' from Latin *memorialis* 'serving as a reminder,' from *memoria* 'memory.'

Me·mo·ri·al Day ▶ **n.** a day on which those who died in active military service are remembered, traditionally observed on May 30 but now officially observed on the last Monday in May. Also called (esp. formerly) **Decoration Day**. ■ (also **Confederate Memorial Day**) (in the southern states) any of various days (esp. the fourth Monday in April) on which similar remembrances are observed.

m

me·mo·ri·al·ist /məˈmôrēəlist/ ▶ **n.** a person who writes a memorial or memoir.

me·mo·ri·al·ize /məˈmôrēəˌlīz/ ▶ **v.** [with obj.] preserve the memory of; commemorate: *the novel memorialized their childhood summers.*
– DERIVATIVES **me·mo·ri·al·i·za·tion** /məˌmôrēələˈzāsʜən/ **n.**, **me·mo·ri·al·iz·er n.**

me·mo·ri·al park ▶ **n.** a cemetery: *Pine View Memorial Park.* ■ a park designed for contemplation or recreation, commemorating the death of an individual or of many people through a natural or other disaster, or through military action: *Fort Griswold Memorial Park | Martin Luther King, Jr., Memorial Park.*

mem·o·rize /ˈmeməˌrīz/ ▶ **v.** [with obj.] commit to memory; learn by heart: *he memorized thousands of verses.*
– DERIVATIVES **mem·o·riz·a·ble** /-ˌrīzəbəl/ **adj.**, **mem·o·ri·za·tion** /ˌmemərəˈzāsʜən/ **n.**, **mem·o·riz·er n.**

mem·o·ry /ˈmem(ə)rē/ ▶ **n.** (pl. **memories**) **1** the faculty by which the mind stores and remembers information: *I've a great memory for faces | my grandmother is losing her memory | the brain regions responsible for memory.* ■ the mind regarded as a store of things remembered: *he searched his memory frantically for an answer.*
2 something remembered from the past; a recollection: *one of my earliest memories is of sitting on his knee | the mind can bury all memory of traumatic abuse.* ■ the remembering or recollection of a dead person, esp. one who was popular or respected: *clubs devoted to the memory of Sherlock Holmes.* ■ the length of time over which people continue to remember a person or event: *the worst slump in recent memory.*
3 the part of a computer in which data or program instructions can be stored for retrieval. ■ capacity for storing information in this way: *the module provides 16Mb of memory.*
– PHRASES **from memory** without reading or referring to notes: *each child was required to recite a verse from memory.* **in memory of** intended to remind people of, esp. to honor a dead person. **take a trip** (or **walk**) **down memory lane** deliberately recall pleasant or sentimental memories.
– ORIGIN Middle English: from Old French *memorie*, from Latin *memoria*, from *memor* 'mindful, remembering.'

mem·o·ry bank ▶ **n.** the memory device of a computer or other device.

mem·o·ry board ▶ **n.** Computing a detachable board containing memory chips, which can be connected to a computer.

mem·o·ry book ▶ **n.** a scrapbook.

mem·o·ry card ▶ **n.** a small, flat flash drive used esp. in digital cameras and cell phones.

mem·o·ry cell ▶ **n.** Physiology a long-lived lymphocyte capable of responding to a particular antigen on its reintroduction, long after the exposure that prompted its production.

mem·o·ry hole ▶ **n.** an imaginary place where inconvenient or unpleasant information is put and quickly forgotten.
– ORIGIN from George Orwell's *Nineteen Eighty-Four*, which described a slot where historical documents could be disposed of to allow for manipulation of memories of the past.

mem·o·ry leak ▶ **n.** Computing a failure in a program to release discarded memory, causing impaired performance or failure.

mem·o·ry map·ping ▶ **n.** a technique in which a computer treats peripheral devices as if they were located in the main memory.

Mem·o·ry Stick ▶ **n.** trademark a type of memory card.

mem·o·ry trace ▶ **n.** a hypothetical permanent change in the nervous system brought about by memorizing something; an engram.

Mem·phis /ˈmemfəs/ **1** an ancient city in Egypt, whose ruins are situated on the Nile River about 10 miles (15 km) south of Cairo. It is the site of the pyramids of Saqqara and Giza and the Sphinx.
2 a river port on the Mississippi River in extreme southwestern Tennessee; pop. 669,651 (est. 2008). Founded in 1819, it was the home of blues music in the late 19th century and the scene of the assassination of Martin Luther King in 1968. It is also the childhood home and burial place of Elvis Presley.
– DERIVATIVES **Mem·phi·an n. & adj.**

MEMS ▶ **abbr.** microelectromechanical systems.

mem·sa·hib /ˈmemˌsä(h)ib, -ˌsäb/ ▶ **n.** Indian dated a married white or upper-class woman (often used as a respectful form of address by nonwhites).
– ORIGIN from *mem* (representing an Indian pronunciation of **ma'am**) + **sahib**.

men /men/ plural form of **man**.

men·ace /ˈmenəs/ ▶ **n.** a person or thing that is likely to cause harm; a threat or danger: *a new initiative aimed at beating the menace of drugs | the snakes are a menace to farm animals.* ■ a threatening quality, tone, or atmosphere: *he spoke the words with a hint of menace.* ■ often humorous a person or thing that causes trouble or annoyance: *his kid sister, that chatty little menace, had become the knockout of the neighborhood.*
▶ **v.** [with obj.] threaten, esp. in a malignant or hostile manner: *Africa's elephants are still menaced by poaching.*
– DERIVATIVES **men·ac·er n.**
– ORIGIN Middle English: via Old French from late Latin *minacia*, from Latin *minax, minac-* 'threatening,' from *minae* 'threats.'

men·ac·ing /ˈmenəsiɴɢ/ ▶ **adj.** suggesting the presence of danger; threatening: *a menacing tone of voice.*
– DERIVATIVES **men·ac·ing·ly adv.**

men·a·di·one /ˌmenəˈdīˌōn/ ▶ **n.** Medicine a synthetic yellow compound related to menaquinone, used to treat hemorrhage. Also called **vitamin K3** (see **vitamin K**). ● Alternative name: **2-methyl-1,4-naphthoquinone**; chem. formula: $C_{11}H_8O_2$.
– ORIGIN 1940s: from *me(thyl)* + *na(phthalene)* + the suffix *-dione*, used in names of compounds containing two carbonyl groups.

mé·nage /māˈnäzʜ, mə-/ ▶ **n.** the members of a household: *crisis had recently unsettled the Clelland ménage.* ■ the management of a household: *they were forced to conduct their ménage on a humbler scale than heretofore.*
– ORIGIN Middle English: from Old French *menage*, from *mainer* 'to stay,' influenced by Old French *mesnie* 'household,' both ultimately based on Latin *manere* 'remain.'

mé·nage à trois /māˈnäzʜ ä ˈt(r)wä, mə-/ ▶ **n.** (pl. **ménages à trois** pronunc. **same**) an arrangement in which three people share a sexual relationship, typically a domestic situation involving a married couple and the lover of one of them.
– ORIGIN French, 'household of three.'

me·nag·er·ie /məˈnajərē, -ˈnazʜ-/ ▶ **n.** a collection of wild animals kept in captivity for exhibition. ■ a strange or diverse collection of people or things: *some other specimen in the television menagerie.*
– ORIGIN late 17th cent.: from French *ménagerie*, from *ménage* (see **ménage**).

Men·ai Strait /ˈmeˌnī/ a channel that separates Anglesey from the mainland of northwestern Wales.

Me·nan·der /məˈnandər/ (*c.*342–292 BC), Greek playwright. His comic plays deal with domestic situations and capture colloquial speech patterns. The sole complete extant play is *Dyskolos*.

Men·ap·i·an /məˈnapēən/ ▶ **adj.** Geology of, relating to, or denoting a Middle Pleistocene glaciation in northern Europe, possibly corresponding to the Günz of the Alps. ■ (as noun **the Menapian**) the Menapian glaciation or the system of deposits laid down during it.
– ORIGIN 1950s: from Latin *Menapii*, a people of northern Gaul in Roman times, + **-ian**.

men·a·qui·none /ˌmenəˈkwinˌōn, -ˈkwīˌnōn/ ▶ **n.** Biochemistry one of the K vitamins, a compound produced by bacteria in the large intestine and essential for the blood-clotting process. It is an isoprenoid derivative of menadione. Also called **vitamin K2** (see **vitamin K**).
– ORIGIN 1940s: from the chemical name *me(thyl)-na(phtho)quinone*.

men·ar·che /ˈmenˌärkē/ ▶ **n.** the first occurrence of menstruation.
– DERIVATIVES **men·ar·che·al** /menˈärkēəl/ (or **menarchial**) **adj.**
– ORIGIN late 19th cent.: modern Latin, from Greek *mēn* 'month' + *arkhē* 'beginning.'

Men·ci·us /ˈmencʜēəs/ (*c.*371–*c.*289 BC), Chinese philosopher; Latinized name of *Meng-tzu* or *Mengzi* ("Meng the Master"). Known as a developer of Confucianism, he believed that rulers should provide for the welfare of the people and that human nature is intrinsically good. ■ one of the Four Books of Confucianism, containing the teachings of Mencius.

Menck·en /ˈmeɴɢkən/, H. L. (1880–1956), US journalist and literary and social critic; full name *Henry Louis Mencken*. From 1908, he attacked the political and literary Establishment. In *The American Language* (1919) he opposed the dominance of European culture in the US, arguing for and establishing the study of American English in its own right.

mend /mend/ ▶ **v.** [with obj.] repair (something that is broken or damaged): *workmen were mending faulty cabling | a patch was used to mend the garment.* ■ [no obj.] return to health; heal: *foot injuries can take months to mend.* ■ improve (an unpleasant situation, esp. a disagreement): *quarrels could be mended by talking.*
▶ **n.** a repair in a material: *the mends were so perfect you could not even tell the board had been damaged.*
– PHRASES **mend (one's) fences** make peace with a person: *is it too late to mend fences with your ex-wife?* **mend one's ways** improve one's habits or behavior. **on the mend** improving in health or condition; recovering: *on the mend after a stomach operation | the economy is on the mend.*
– DERIVATIVES **mend·a·ble adj.**, **mend·er n.**
– ORIGIN Middle English: shortening of **amend**.

men·da·cious /menˈdāsʜəs/ ▶ **adj.** not telling the truth; lying: *mendacious propaganda.*
– DERIVATIVES **men·da·cious·ly adv.**, **men·da·cious·ness n.**
– ORIGIN early 17th cent.: from Latin *mendax, mendac-* 'lying' (related to *mendum* 'fault') + **-ious**.

men·dac·i·ty /menˈdasitē/ ▶ **n.** untruthfulness: *people publicly castigated for past mendacity.*
– ORIGIN mid 17th cent.: from ecclesiastical Latin *mendacitas*, from *mendax, mendac-* 'lying' (see **mendacious**).

Men·de /ˈmendē/ ▶ **n.** (pl. **same** or **Mendes**) **1** a member of a people inhabiting Sierra Leone in West Africa.
2 the Mende language of this people.
▶ **adj.** relating to or denoting this people or their language.
– ORIGIN the name in Mende.

Men·del /ˈmendl/, Gregor Johann (1822–84), Moravian monk; the father of genetics. From systematically breeding peas, he demonstrated the transmission of characteristics in a predictable way by factors (genes) that remain intact and independent between generations and do not blend, although they may mask one another's effects.

Men·de·le·ev /ˌmendəˈläəf, myindiˈleyef/, Dmitri (Ivanovich) (1834–1907), Russian chemist. He developed the periodic table.

men·de·le·vi·um /ˌmendəˈlēvēəm, -ˈlā-/ ▶ **n.** the chemical element of atomic number 101, a radioactive metal of the actinide series. It does not occur naturally and was first made in 1955

by bombarding einsteinium with helium ions. (Symbol: **Md**)
– ORIGIN modern Latin, from the name of D. MENDELEEV.

Men·de·li·an /menˈdēlēən/ ▶ **adj.** Biology of or relating to Mendel's theory of heredity: *Mendelian genetics.*
▶ **n.** a person who accepts or advocates Mendel's theory of heredity.

Men·del·ism /ˈmendlˌizəm/ ▶ **n.** Biology the theory of heredity as formulated by Mendel.

Men·dels·sohn /ˈmendl-sən/, Felix (1809–47), German composer and pianist; full name *Jakob Ludwig Felix Mendelssohn-Bartholdy.* His romantic music is elegant, light, and melodically inventive. Notable works: *Fingal's Cave* (1830–32), *Elijah* (1846), and eight volumes of *Lieder ohne Worte* (*Songs Without Words*) for piano.

Men·de·res /ˌmendəˈres/ a river in southwestern Turkey. It rises in the Anatolian plateau and flows for about 240 miles (384 km) to the Aegean Sea south of the Greek island of Samos. Known in ancient times as the Maeander—and noted for its winding course—it gave its name to the verb *meander.*

men·di·cant /ˈmendikənt/ ▶ **adj.** given to begging. ■ of or denoting one of the religious orders that originally relied solely on alms: *a mendicant friar.*
▶ **n.** a beggar. ■ a member of a mendicant order.
– DERIVATIVES **men·di·can·cy** /-kənsē/ **n.**
– ORIGIN late Middle English: from Latin *mendicant-* 'begging,' from the verb *mendicare,* from *mendicus* 'beggar,' from *mendum* 'fault.'

men·dic·i·ty /menˈdisitē/ ▶ **n.** the condition or activities of a beggar.
– ORIGIN late Middle English: from Old French *mendicite,* from Latin *mendicitas,* from *mendicus* 'beggar.'

mend·ing /ˈmendiNG/ ▶ **n.** things to be repaired by sewing or darning: *a muddle of books and mending.*

Men·do·ci·no /ˌmendəˈsēnō/ a resort community in northwestern California, on the Pacific coast. *Cape Mendocino,* the most western point in the state, is farther to the north.

Men·do·za[1] /menˈdōzə/ a city in western Argentina, located in the foothills of the Andes at the center of a wine-producing region; pop. 112,900 (est. 2008).

Men·do·za[2], Antonio de (*c.*1490–1552), Spanish colonial administrator; first viceroy of New Spain (1535–50).

Men·e·la·us /ˌmenəˈlāəs/ Greek Mythology king of Sparta, husband of Helen and brother of Agamemnon. Helen was stolen from him by Paris, an event that provoked the Trojan War.

Me·nes /ˈmēnēz/, Egyptian pharaoh; reigned *c.*3100 BC. He founded the first dynasty that ruled Egypt.

men·folk /ˈmenˌfōk/ (also **menfolks**) ▶ **plural n.** a group of men considered collectively, esp. the men of a particular family or community: *the menfolk of the village watch the goings-on.*

Meng-tzu /ˌmeNG ˈtsōō, dzə/ (also **Mengzi** /-ˈzē/) Chinese name for MENCIUS.

men·ha·den /menˈhādn, mən-/ ▶ **n.** a large deep-bodied fish of the herring family that occurs along the east coast of North America. The oil-rich flesh is used to make fish meal and fertilizer. ● Genus *Brevoortia,* family Clupeidae: several species, in particular *B. tyrannus.*
– ORIGIN late 18th cent.: from Algonquian.

men·hir /ˈmenˌhi(ə)r/ ▶ **n.** Archaeology a tall upright stone of a kind erected in prehistoric times in western Europe.
– ORIGIN mid 19th cent.: from Breton *men* 'stone' + *hir* 'long.'

me·ni·al /ˈmēnēəl/ ▶ **adj.** (of work) not requiring much skill and lacking prestige: *menial factory jobs.* ■ [attrib.] dated (of a servant) domestic.
▶ **n.** a person with a menial job. ■ dated a domestic servant.
– DERIVATIVES **me·ni·al·ly** **adv.**
– ORIGIN late Middle English (in the sense 'domestic'): from Old French, from *mesnee* 'household.'

Mé·nière's dis·ease /mānˈye(ə)rz/ (also **Ménière's syndrome**) ▶ **n.** a disease of unknown cause affecting the membranous labyrinth of the ear, causing progressive deafness and attacks of tinnitus and vertigo.
– ORIGIN late 19th cent.: named after Prosper *Ménière* (1799–1862), French physician.

me·nin·ges /məˈninjēz/ ▶ **plural n.** (sing. **meninx** /ˈmēniNGks, ˈmeniNGks/) Anatomy the three membranes (the dura mater, arachnoid, and pia mater) that line the skull and vertebral canal and enclose the brain and spinal cord.
– DERIVATIVES **me·nin·ge·al** /məˈninjēəl/ **adj.**
– ORIGIN modern Latin, from Greek *mēninx, mēning-* 'membrane.'

me·nin·gi·o·ma /məˌninjēˈōmə/ ▶ **n.** (pl. **meningiomas** or **meningiomata** /-ˈōmətə/) Medicine a tumor, usually benign, arising from meningeal tissue of the brain.

men·in·gi·tis /ˌmenənˈjītis/ ▶ **n.** inflammation of the meninges caused by viral or bacterial infection and marked by intense headache and fever, sensitivity to light, and muscular rigidity, leading (in severe cases) to convulsions, delirium, and death.
– DERIVATIVES **men·in·git·ic** /-ˈjitik/ **adj.**

me·nin·go·cele /məˌniNGgōˈsēl/ ▶ **n.** Medicine a protrusion of the meninges through a gap in the spine due to a congenital defect.

me·nin·go·coc·cus /məˌniNGgōˈkäkəs/ ▶ **n.** (pl. **meningococci** /-ˈkäksī, -ˈkäksē/) a bacterium involved in some forms of meningitis and cerebrospinal infection. ● *Neisseria meningitidis,* a nonmotile spherical Gram-negative bacterium.
– DERIVATIVES **me·nin·go·coc·cal** /-ˈkäkəl/ **adj.**
– ORIGIN late 19th cent.: from MENINGES + COCCUS.

me·nin·go·en·ceph·a·li·tis /məˌniNGgōinˌsefəˈlītis/ ▶ **n.** Medicine inflammation of the membranes of the brain and the adjoining cerebral tissue.

me·ninx /ˈmēniNGks, ˈmen-/ singular form of MENINGES.

men·is·cec·to·my ▶ **n.** surgical removal of a meniscus, esp. that of the knee.

me·nis·cus /məˈniskəs/ ▶ **n.** (pl. **menisci** /-kē, -kī/ or **meniscuses**) Physics the curved upper surface of a liquid in a tube. ■ [usu. as modifier] Optics a lens that is convex on one side and concave on the other. ■ Anatomy a thin fibrous cartilage between the surfaces of some joints, e.g., the knee.
– ORIGIN late 17th cent.: modern Latin, from Greek *mēniskos* 'crescent,' diminutive of *mēnē* 'moon.'

Men·lo Park a historic community in central New Jersey, in the township of Edison, northeast of New Brunswick, the site of the laboratory of Thomas Edison.

Men·nin·ger /ˈmenənjər/, Karl Augustus (1893–1990), US psychiatrist. He cofounded the Menninger Clinic 1920, where psychiatrists received training in psychoanalysis. In 1941, the Menninger Foundation, which he headed until 1990, was established.

Men·non·ite /ˈmenəˌnīt/ ▶ **n.** (chiefly in the US and Canada) a member of a Protestant sect originating in Friesland in the 16th century, emphasizing adult baptism and rejecting church organization, military service, and public office.
– DERIVATIVES **Men·no·nit·ism** /-izəm/ **n.**
– ORIGIN from the name of its founder, *Menno* Simons (1496–1561), + -ITE.

me·no /ˈmenō/ ▶ **adv.** Music (in directions) less.
– ORIGIN Italian.

meno- ▶ **comb. form** relating to menstruation: *menopause.*
– ORIGIN from Greek *mēn* 'month.'

me·nol·o·gy /məˈnäləjē/ ▶ **n.** (pl. **menologies**) an ecclesiastical calendar of the months, esp. a calendar of the Greek Orthodox Church containing biographies of the saints in the order of the dates on which they are commemorated.
– ORIGIN early 17th cent.: via modern Latin from ecclesiastical Greek *mēnologion,* from *mēn* 'month' + *logos* 'account.'

Me·nom·i·nee /məˈnämənē/ (also **Menomini**) ▶ **n.** (pl. **same** or **Menominees** or **Menominis**)
1 a member of an American Indian people of northeastern Wisconsin.
2 the Algonquian language of this people.
▶ **adj.** relating to or denoting this people or their language.
– ORIGIN from Ojibwa *manōminī,* literally 'wild-rice person.'

me·no mos·so /ˈmenō ˈmäsō/ ▶ **adv. & adj.** Music (esp. as a direction) less quickly.
– ORIGIN Italian.

men·o·pause /ˈmenəˌpôz/ ▶ **n.** the ceasing of menstruation. ■ the period in a woman's life (typically between 45 and 50 years of age) when this occurs.
– DERIVATIVES **men·o·pau·sal** /ˌmenəˈpôzəl/ **adj.**
– ORIGIN late 19th cent.: from modern Latin *menopausis* (see MENO-, PAUSE).

me·nor·ah /məˈnôrə/ ▶ **n.** (**the Menorah**) a sacred candelabrum with seven branches used in the Temple in Jerusalem, originally that made by the craftsman Bezalel and placed in the sanctuary of the Tabernacle (Exod. 37:17–24). ■ a candelabrum used in Jewish worship, esp. one with eight branches and a central socket used at Hanukkah.
– ORIGIN Hebrew.

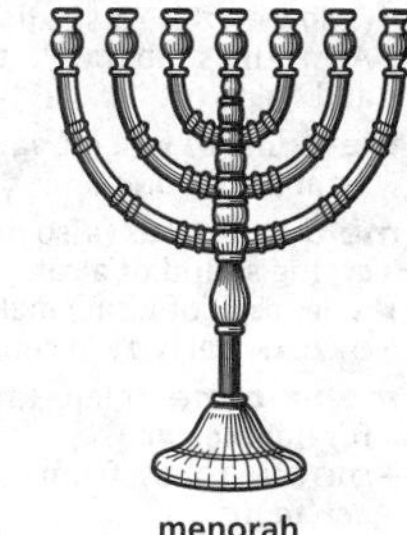
menorah

men·or·rha·gi·a /ˌmenəˈrāj(ē)ə/ ▶ **n.** Medicine abnormally heavy bleeding at menstruation.
– ORIGIN late 18th cent.: modern Latin, from MENO- 'of menstruation' + *-rrhag-,* stem of Greek *rhēgnunai* 'to burst.'

men·or·rhe·a /ˌmenəˈrēə/ (also chiefly Brit. **menorrhoea**) ▶ **n.** Medicine the flow of blood at menstruation.
– ORIGIN mid 19th cent.: back-formation from AMENORRHEA.

Me·not·ti /məˈnätē/, Gian (1911–2007), US composer; born in Italy. He wrote the operas *The Old Maid and the Thief* (1939), *The Consul* (1950), and *Amahl and the Night Visitors* (1951).

Men·sa[1] /ˈmensə/ Astronomy a small, faint southern constellation (the Table or Table Mountain), lying between Dorado and the south celestial pole. It contains part of the Large Magellanic Cloud. ■ (as genitive **Mensae** /ˈmensē/) used with a preceding letter or numeral to designate a star in this constellation: *the star Alpha Mensae.*
– ORIGIN Latin.

Men·sa[2] /ˈmensə/ an international organization founded in England in 1945 whose members must achieve very high scores in IQ tests to be admitted.
– ORIGIN Latin, 'table,' with allusion to a round table at which all members have equal status.

mensch /menCH/ ▶ **n.** (pl. **menschen** /ˈmenCHən/ or **mensches**) informal a person of integrity and honor.
– ORIGIN 1930s: Yiddish *mensh,* from German *Mensch,* literally 'person.'

men·ses /ˈmenˌsēz/ ▶ **plural n.** blood and other matter discharged from the uterus at menstruation. ■ [treated as sing.] the time of menstruation: *a late menses.*
– ORIGIN late 16th cent.: from Latin, plural of *mensis* 'month.'

Men·she·vik /ˈmenCHəˌvik/ ▶ **n.** (pl. **Mensheviks** /ˈmenCHəˌviks/ or **Mensheviki** /ˌmenCHəˈvikē/) historical a member of the non-Leninist wing of the Russian Social Democratic Workers' Party, opposed to the Bolsheviks and defeated by them after the overthrow of the tsar in 1917.
▶ **adj.** of, relating to, or characteristic of Mensheviks or Menshevism.
– DERIVATIVES **Men·she·vism** /-ˌvizəm/ **n.**, **Men·she·vist** /-vist/ **n.**
– ORIGIN from Russian *Men'shevik* 'a member of the minority,' from *men'she* 'less.' Lenin coined the name at a time when the party was (untypically) in the minority for a brief period.

men's move·ment ▶ **n.** a movement aimed at liberating men from traditional views about their character and role in society.

mens re·a /menz ˈrēə/ ▶ **n.** Law the intention or knowledge of wrongdoing that constitutes part of a crime, as opposed to the action or conduct of the accused. Compare with ACTUS REUS.
– ORIGIN mid 19th cent.: Latin, literally 'guilty mind.'

men's room ▶ **n.** a restroom for men in a public or institutional building.

men·stru·al /ˈmenstr(ōō)əl/ ▶ **adj.** of or relating to the menses or menstruation: *menstrual blood.*
– ORIGIN late Middle English: from Latin *menstrualis,* from *menstruum* 'menses,' from *mensis* 'month.'

men·stru·al cy·cle ▶ **n.** the process of ovulation and menstruation in women and other female primates.

men·stru·al per·i·od ▶ **n.** see PERIOD (sense 4 of the noun).

men·stru·ate /ˈmenstrəˌwāt, ˈmenˌstrāt/ ▶ **v.** [no obj.] (of a woman) discharge blood and other material from the lining of the uterus as part of the menstrual cycle.
– ORIGIN mid 17th cent.: from late Latin *menstruat-* 'menstruated,' from the verb *menstruare,* from Latin *menstrua* 'menses.'

men·stru·a·tion /ˌmenstrōōˈāSHən, menˈstrā-/ ▶ **n.** the process in a woman of discharging blood and other materials from the lining of the uterus at intervals of about one lunar month from puberty until menopause, except during pregnancy.

men·stru·ous /ˈmenstr(ōō)əs/ ▶ **adj.** of, relating to, or in the process of menstruation.

–ORIGIN late Middle English: from Old French *menstrueus*, from late Latin *menstruosus*, from *menstrua* 'menses.'

men·stru·um /ˈmenstr(o͞o)əm/ ▶ **n.** (pl. **menstrua** /-str(o͞o)ə/) **1** menses.
2 (pl. also **menstruums**) archaic a solvent.
–ORIGIN late Middle English (sense 1): from Latin, neuter of *menstruus* 'monthly,' from *mensis* 'month.' Sense 2.

men·sur·a·ble /ˈmenCHərəbəl, ˈmensər-/ ▶ **adj.** able to be measured; having fixed limits. ■ Music another term for MENSURAL.
–DERIVATIVES **men·sur·a·bil·i·ty** /ˌmenCHərəˈbilətē, ˌmensər-/ **n.**
–ORIGIN late Middle English (in the sense 'moderate'): from late Latin *mensurabilis*, from *mensurare* 'to measure,' from Latin *mensura* 'measure.'

men·su·ral /ˈmenCHərəl, ˈmensərəl/ ▶ **adj.** of or involving measuring: *mensural investigations*. ■ Music involving notes of definite duration and usually a regular meter.
–ORIGIN late 16th cent.: from Latin *mensuralis*, from *mensura* 'measure.'

men·su·ra·tion /ˌmenCHəˈrāSHən, ˌmensə-/ ▶ **n.** measuring. ■ Mathematics the measuring of geometric magnitudes, lengths, areas, and volumes.
–ORIGIN late 16th cent. (denoting measurement in general): from late Latin *mensuratio(n-)*, from *mensurare* 'to measure.'

mens·wear /ˈmenzˌwe(ə)r/ (also **men's wear**) ▶ **n.** clothes for men.

-ment /mənt/ ▶ **suffix 1** forming nouns expressing the means or result of an action: *curtailment* | *excitement* | *treatment*.
2 forming nouns from adjectives (such as *merriment* from *merry*).
–ORIGIN from French, or from Latin *-mentum*.

men·tal /ˈmentl/ ▶ **adj. 1** of or relating to the mind: *mental faculties* | *mental phenomena*. ■ carried out by or taking place in the mind: *a quick mental calculation* | *I started my mental journey*.
2 of, relating to, or suffering from disorders or illnesses of the mind: *a mental hospital*. ■ [predic.] informal insane; crazy: *every time I'm five minutes late, they go mental*.
–ORIGIN late Middle English: from late Latin *mentalis*, from Latin *mens, ment-* 'mind.'

m

> **USAGE** The use of **mental** in compounds such as **mental hospital** and **mental patient** is first recorded at the end of the 19th century and was the normal accepted term in the first half of the 20th century. It is still current and standard even though the term **psychiatric** has more recently come to be used in both general and official use.

men·tal age ▶ **n.** a person's mental ability expressed as the age at which an average person reaches the same ability: *she was 65 but had a mental age of 2*.

men·tal a·rith·me·tic ▶ **n.** arithmetical calculations performed in the mind, without writing figures down or using a calculator.

men·tal block ▶ **n.** an inability to recall some specific thing or perform some mental action.

men·tal cru·el·ty ▶ **n.** conduct that makes another person suffer but does not involve physical assault.

men·tal·ism /ˈmentlˌizəm/ ▶ **n.** Philosophy the theory that physical and psychological phenomena are ultimately explicable only in terms of a creative and interpretative mind.

men·tal·ist[1] /ˈmentlˌist/ ▶ **n. 1** a magician who performs feats that apparently demonstrate extraordinary mental powers, such as mind-reading.
2 Brit. informal an eccentric or mad person.

men·tal·ist[2] Philosophy /ˈmentlˌist/ ▶ **n.** an adherent of mentalism.
▶ **adj.** relating to mentalists or mentalism.
–DERIVATIVES **men·tal·is·tic** /ˌmentlˈistik/ **adj.**

men·tal·i·ty /menˈtalitē/ ▶ **n.** (pl. **mentalities**)
1 often derogatory the characteristic attitude of mind or way of thinking of a person or group: *the yuppie mentality of the eighties*.
2 the capacity for intelligent thought.
–ORIGIN late 17th cent. (in the sense 'mental process'): from the adjective MENTAL + -ITY. Current senses date from the mid 19th cent.

men·tal·ly /ˈment(ə)lē/ ▶ **adv.** in a manner relating to the mind: *soldiers become physically and mentally exhausted*.

men·tal·ly hand·i·capped /ˈmen(t)lē ˈhandēˌkapt/ ▶ **adj.** (of a person) having very limited intellectual functions.

men·ta·tion /menˈtāSHən/ ▶ **n.** technical mental activity.

–ORIGIN mid 19th cent.: from Latin *mens, ment-* 'mind' + -ATION.

men·tee /menˈtē/ ▶ **n.** a person who is advised, trained, or counseled by a mentor.

men·thol /ˈmenˌTHôl, -ˌTHäl/ ▶ **n.** a crystalline compound with a cooling minty taste and odor, found in peppermint and other natural oils. It is used as a flavoring and in decongestants and analgesics. ● An alcohol, **2-isopropyl-5-methylcyclohexanol**; chem. formula: $C_{10}H_{19}OH$.
–ORIGIN late 19th cent.: from German, from Latin *mentha* 'mint' + -OL.

men·tho·lat·ed /ˈmenTHəˌlātid/ ▶ **adj.** treated with or containing menthol: *mentholated shaving creams*.

men·tion /ˈmenCHən/ ▶ **v.** [with obj.] refer to something briefly and without going into detail: *I haven't* **mentioned** *it to William yet* | [with clause] *I mentioned that my father was meeting me later*. ■ [with obj.] make a reference to (someone) as being noteworthy, esp. as a potential candidate for a post: *he is still regularly* **mentioned as** *a possible secretary of state*.
▶ **n.** a reference to someone or something: *their eyes light up at a mention of Sartre* | *she* **made no mention of** *her disastrous trip to Paris*. ■ a formal acknowledgment of something outstanding or noteworthy: *he received a special mention and a prize of $100* | *two other points are worthy of mention*. See also HONORABLE MENTION.
–PHRASES **don't mention it** a polite expression used to indicate that an apology or an expression of thanks is not necessary. **mention someone in one's will** leave a legacy to someone. **not to mention** used to introduce an additional fact or point that reinforces the point being made: *I'm amazed you find the time, not to mention the energy, to do any work at all*.
–DERIVATIVES **men·tion·a·ble** **adj.**
–ORIGIN Middle English (originally in *make mention of*): via Old French from Latin *mentio(n-)*; related to MIND.

men·to /ˈmentō/ ▶ **n.** (pl. **mentos**) a style of Jamaican folk music based on a traditional dance rhythm in duple time.
–ORIGIN early 20th cent.: of unknown origin.

men·tor /ˈmenˌtôr, -tər/ ▶ **n.** an experienced and trusted adviser: *he was her friend and mentor until his death in 1915*. ■ an experienced person in a company, college, or school who trains and counsels new employees or students.
▶ **v.** [with obj.] advise or train (someone, esp. a younger colleague).
–DERIVATIVES **men·tor·ship** /-ˌSHip/ **n.**
–ORIGIN mid 18th cent.: via French and Latin from Greek *Mentōr*, the name of the adviser of the young Telemachus in Homer's *Odyssey*.

men·tum /ˈmentəm/ ▶ **n.** Entomology a part of the base of the labium in some insects.
–ORIGIN early 19th cent.: from Latin, literally 'chin.'

men·u /ˈmenyo͞o/ ▶ **n.** (pl. **menus**) a list of dishes available in a restaurant: *the waiter handed her a menu* | figurative *politics and sport are* **on the menu** *tonight*. ■ the food available or to be served in a restaurant or at a meal: *a no-fuss dinner-party menu*. ■ Computing a list of commands or options, esp. one displayed on screen.
–ORIGIN mid 19th cent.: from French, 'detailed list' (noun use of *menu* 'small, detailed'), from Latin *minutus* 'very small.'

men·u bar ▶ **n.** Computing a horizontal bar, typically located at the top of the screen below the title bar, containing drop-down menus.

me·nu·do /məˈno͞odō/ ▶ **n.** (pl. **menudos**) a spicy Mexican soup made from tripe.
–ORIGIN noun use of a Mexican Spanish adjective meaning 'small.'

men·u-driv·en ▶ **adj.** (of a program or computer) used by making selections from menus.

Men·u·hin /ˈmenyo͞oin/, Sir Yehudi (1916–99), British violinist; born in the US In 1962, he founded a school of music, which is named after him, in Surrey, England.

Men·zies /ˈmenzēz/, Sir Robert Gordon (1894–1978), Australian statesman and founder of Australia's Liberal Party; prime minister 1939–41 and 1949–66.

Me·o /mēˈō/ ▶ **n.** (pl. **same** or **Meos**) **& adj.** another term for HMONG.

me·ow /mēˈou/ (also **miaow**) ▶ **n.** the characteristic crying sound of a cat.
▶ **v.** [no obj.] (of a cat) make such a sound.
–ORIGIN early 17th cent.: imitative.

mep·a·crine /ˈmepəˌkrin, -ˌkrēn/ ▶ **n.** another term for QUINACRINE.
–ORIGIN 1940s: from *me(thoxy-)* + *p(entane)* + *acr(id)ine*.

me·per·i·dine /məˈperəˌdēn, -ˌdin/ ▶ **n.** Medicine a synthetic compound used as a painkilling drug, esp. for women in labor.
–ORIGIN 1940s: blend of METHYL and PIPERIDINE.

Meph·i·stoph·e·les /ˌmefəˈstäfəˌlēz/ (also **Mephisto** /məˈfistō/) ▶ **n.** an evil spirit to whom Faust, in the German legend, sold his soul.
–DERIVATIVES **Meph·is·to·phe·le·an** /məˌfistəˈfēlēən, ˌmefəstə-/ (also **Mephistophelian**) **adj.**

me·phit·ic /məˈfitik/ ▶ **adj.** (esp. of a gas or vapor) foul-smelling; noxious.
–ORIGIN early 17th cent.: from late Latin *mephiticus*, from *mephitis* 'noxious exhalation.'

me·phi·tis /məˈfītis/ ▶ **n.** a noxious gas emanating from something, esp. from the earth. ■ a foul or poisonous stench.
–ORIGIN early 18th cent.: from Latin.

me·pro·ba·mate /məˈprōbəˌmāt, ˌmeprōˈba-/ ▶ **n.** a bitter-tasting addictive carbamate used, esp. before the 1970s, as a mild tranquilizer. ● Chem. formula: $CH_3CH_2CH_2C(CH_2OCONH_2)_2CH_3$.
–ORIGIN mid 20th cent.: from *me(thyl)* + *pro(pyl)* + *(car)bamate*.

mer. ▶ **abbr.** meridian.

-mer ▶ **comb. form** denoting polymers and related kinds of molecule: *elastomer*.
–ORIGIN from Greek *meros* 'part.'

mer·bro·min /ˌmərˈbrōmən/ ▶ **n.** a greenish iridescent crystalline compound that dissolves in water to give a red solution used as an antiseptic. It is a fluorescein derivative containing bromine and mercury.
–ORIGIN 1940s: from MERCURIC + BROMO- + -IN[1].

mer·ca·do /mərˈkädō/ ▶ **n.** (pl. **mercados**) (in Spanish-speaking regions) a market.
–ORIGIN Spanish, from Latin *mercatus* 'market.'

Mer·cal·li scale /mərˈkalē/ a twelve-point scale for expressing the local intensity of an earthquake, ranging from I (virtually imperceptible) to XII (total destruction).
–ORIGIN 1920s: named after Giuseppe *Mercalli* (1850–1914), Italian geologist.

mer·can·tile /ˈmərkənˌtēl, -ˌtīl/ ▶ **adj.** of or relating to trade or commerce; commercial: *the shift of wealth to the mercantile classes*.
▶ **n.** dated a general store: *we walked to the local mercantile*.
–ORIGIN mid 17th cent.: from French, from Italian, from *mercante* 'merchant.'

mer·can·til·ism /ˈmərkəntiˌlizəm, -ˌtē-, -ˌtī-/ ▶ **n.** belief in the benefits of profitable trading; commercialism. ■ chiefly historical the economic theory that trade generates wealth and is stimulated by the accumulation of profitable balances, which a government should encourage by means of protectionism.
–DERIVATIVES **mer·can·til·ist** **n. & adj.**, **mer·can·til·is·tic** /ˌmərkəntiˈlistik, -ˌtē-, -ˌtī-/ **adj.**

mer·cap·tan /mərˈkapˌtan/ ▶ **n.** Chemistry another term for THIOL.
–ORIGIN mid 19th cent.: from modern Latin *mer(curium) captan(s)*, literally 'capturing mercury.'

Mer·ca·tor /mərˈkātər/, Gerardus (1512–94), Flemish geographer and cartographer, a resident in Germany from 1552; Latinized name of *Gerhard Kremer*. He invented the system of map projection that is named after him.

Mer·ca·tor pro·jec·tion /mərˈkātər/ (also **Mercator's projection**) ▶ **n.** a projection of a map of the world onto a cylinder in such a way that all the parallels of latitude have the same length as the equator, used esp. for marine charts and certain climatological maps.

Mer·ced /mərˈsed/ a city in central California, in the San Joaquin Valley; pop. 77,160 (est. 2008).

mer·ce·nar·y /ˈmərsəˌnerē/ ▶ **adj.** derogatory (of a person or their behavior) primarily concerned with making money at the expense of ethics: *she's nothing but a mercenary little gold digger*.
▶ **n.** (pl. **mercenaries**) a professional soldier hired to serve in a foreign army. ■ a person primarily concerned with material reward at the expense of ethics: *the sport's most infamous mercenary*.
–DERIVATIVES **mer·ce·nar·i·ness** **n.**
–ORIGIN late Middle English (as a noun): from Latin *mercenarius* 'hireling,' from *merces, merced-* 'reward.'

Mer·cer /ˈmərsər/, Johnny (1909–76), US songwriter; full name *John Herndon Mercer*. He wrote lyrics for hundreds of popular songs, including "Moon River" (1961) and "Days of Wine and Roses" (1962). His Broadway musicals include *Top Banana* (1951) and *Saratoga* (1959).

mer·cer /ˈmərsər/ ▶ **n.** Brit. chiefly historical a dealer in textile fabrics, esp. silks, velvets, and other fine materials.
– DERIVATIVES **mer·cer·y n.**
– ORIGIN Middle English: from Old French *mercier*, based on Latin *merx, merc-* 'goods.'

mer·cer·ize /ˈmərsəˌrīz/ ▶ **v.** [with obj.] (often as adj. **mercerized**) treat (cotton fabric or thread) under tension with caustic alkali to increase its strength and give it a shiny, silky appearance.
– ORIGIN mid 19th cent.: from the name of John *Mercer* (died 1866), said to have invented the process, + **-IZE**.

mer·chan·dise ▶ **n.** /ˈmərCHənˌdīz, -ˌdīs/ goods to be bought and sold: *stores that offered an astonishing range of merchandise.* ■ products used to promote a particular movie, popular music group, etc., or linked to a particular fictional character; merchandising.
▶ **v.** /ˈmərCHənˌdīz/ (also **merchandize**) [with obj.] promote the sale of (goods), esp. by their presentation in retail outlets: *a new breakfast food can easily be merchandised.* ■ advertise or publicize (an idea or person): *they are merchandising "niceness" to children.* ■ archaic trade or traffic in (something), esp. inappropriately. ■ [no obj.] archaic engage in the business of a merchant.
– DERIVATIVES **mer·chan·dis·a·ble** /-ˌdīzəbəl/ **adj.**, **mer·chan·dis·er** /-ˌdīzər/ **n.**
– ORIGIN late Middle English: from Old French *marchandise*, from *marchand* 'merchant.'

mer·chan·dis·ing /ˈmərCHənˌdīziNG/ ▶ **n.** the activity of promoting the sale of goods, esp. by their presentation in retail outlets: *problems rooted in overexpansion and poor merchandising.* ■ products used to promote a particular movie, popular music group, etc., or linked to a particular fictional character: *the characters are still popular and found on a wide variety of merchandising.*

Mer·chant /ˈmərCHənt/, Ismail (1936–2005), Indian movie producer. In 1961, he partnered with James Ivory to form Merchant Ivory Productions. Together, they produced movies such as *The Bostonians* (1984), *Howard's End* (1992), and *The White Countess* (2005).

mer·chant /ˈmərCHənt/ ▶ **n. 1** a person or company involved in wholesale trade, esp. one dealing with foreign countries or supplying merchandise to a particular trade: *the area's leading timber merchant | a tea merchant.* ■ a retail trader; a store owner: *the credit cards are accepted by 10 million merchants worldwide.* ■ (esp. in historical contexts) a person involved in trade or commerce: *prosperous merchants and clothiers had established a middle class.*
2 [usu. with modifier] informal, chiefly derogatory a person with a partiality or aptitude for a particular activity or viewpoint: *his driver was no speed merchant | a merchant of death.*
▶ **adj.** [attrib.] of or relating to merchants, trade, or commerce: *the growth of the merchant classes.* ■ (of ships, sailors, or shipping activity) involved with commerce rather than military activity: *a merchant seaman.*
– ORIGIN Middle English: from Old French *marchant*, based on Latin *mercari* 'to trade,' from *merx, merc-* 'merchandise.'

mer·chant·a·ble /ˈmərCHəntəbəl/ ▶ **adj.** suitable for purchase or sale; marketable: *goods must be of merchantable quality.*
– ORIGIN late 15th cent.: from the verb *merchant* 'haggle, trade as a merchant,' from Old French *marchander*, from *marchand* 'merchant.'

mer·chant ac·count ▶ **n.** a bank account that enables the holder to accept credit cards for payment.

mer·chant bank ▶ **n.** a bank dealing in commercial loans and investment.
– DERIVATIVES **mer·chant bank·er n.**, **mer·chant bank·ing n.**

mer·chant·man /ˈmərCHəntmən/ ▶ **n.** (pl. **merchantmen**) a ship used in commerce; a vessel of the merchant marine.

mer·chant ma·rine ▶ **n.** (often **the merchant marine**) a country's shipping that is involved in commerce and trade, as opposed to military activity.

mer·chant prince ▶ **n.** a person involved in trade whose wealth is sufficient to confer political influence.

Mer·ci·a /ˈmərSH(ē)ə/ a former kingdom in central England. It was established by invading Angles in the 6th century in the border areas between the new Anglo-Saxon settlements in the east and the Celtic regions in the west.
– DERIVATIVES **Mer·ci·an adj. & n.**

mer·ci·ful /ˈmərsifəl/ ▶ **adj.** showing or exercising mercy: *it was the will of a merciful God that all should be saved.* ■ (of an event) coming as a mercy; bringing someone relief from something unpleasant: *her death was a merciful release.*
– DERIVATIVES **mer·ci·ful·ness n.**

mer·ci·ful·ly /ˈmərsif(ə)lē/ ▶ **adv. 1** in a merciful manner.
2 to one's great relief; fortunately: [sentence adverb] *mercifully, I was able to complete all I had to do within a few days.*

mer·ci·less /ˈmərsiləs/ ▶ **adj.** showing no mercy or pity: *a merciless attack with a blunt instrument |* figurative *the merciless summer heat.*
– DERIVATIVES **mer·ci·less·ly adv.**, **mer·ci·less·ness n.**

Merckx /mərks/, Eddy (1945–), Belgian cyclist; full name *Edouard Louis Joseph Merckx, Baron Merckx.* During his professional career he won the Tour de France five times (1969–72 and 1974).

Mer·cou·ri /mərˈko͝orē/, Melina (1925–94), Greek actress and politician; born *Anna Amalia Mercouri.* Her movies include *Never on Sunday* (1960) and *Phaedra* (1962). Exiled for opposing the military junta that took power in Greece in 1967, she was elected to Parliament in 1978 and became minister of culture in 1985.

mer·cu·ri·al /mərˌkyo͝orēəl/ ▶ **adj. 1** (of a person) subject to sudden or unpredictable changes of mood or mind: *his mercurial temperament.* ■ (of a person) sprightly; lively.
2 of or containing the element mercury.
3 (**Mercurial**) of the planet Mercury.
▶ **n.** (usu. **mercurials**) a drug or other compound containing mercury.
– DERIVATIVES **mer·cu·ri·al·i·ty** /-ˌkyo͝orēˈalitē/ **n.**, **mer·cu·ri·al·ly adv.**
– ORIGIN late Middle English (sense 3 of the adjective): from Latin *mercurialis* 'relating to the god Mercury,' from *Mercurius* 'Mercury.' Sense 1 of the adjective dates from the mid 17th cent.

mer·cu·ric /mərˌkyo͝orik/ ▶ **adj.** Chemistry of mercury with a valence of two; of mercury(II). Compare with **MERCUROUS**.

mer·cu·ric chlo·ride ▶ **n.** a toxic white crystalline compound, used as a fungicide and antiseptic. ● Chem. formula: $HgCl_2$.

Mer·cu·ro·chrome /mə(r)ˈkyo͝orəˌkrōm/ (also **mercurochrome**) ▶ **n.** trademark for **MERBROMIN**.
– ORIGIN early 20th cent.: from **MERCURY**[1] + Greek *khrōma* 'color.'

mer·cu·rous /ˈmərkyərəs/ ▶ **adj.** Chemistry of mercury with a valence of one; of mercury(I). Compare with **MERCURIC**.

mer·cu·rous chlor·ide ▶ **n.** another term for **CALOMEL**.

Mer·cu·ry /ˈmərkyərē/ **1** Roman Mythology the Roman god of eloquence, skill, trading, and thieving, herald and messenger of the gods, who was identified with Hermes. [from Latin *Mercurius*, from *merx, merc-* 'merchandise.'] ■ used in names of newspapers and journals: *the San Jose Mercury News.*
2 Astronomy a small planet that is the closest to the sun in the solar system, sometimes visible to the naked eye just after sunset.

> Mercury orbits within the orbit of Venus at an average distance of 36 million miles (57.9 million km) from the sun. With a diameter of 3,031 miles (4,878 km), it is only a third larger than earth's moon, which it resembles in having a heavily cratered surface. Its 'day' (equivalent to 58.65 Earth days) is precisely two thirds the length of its 'year' (87.97 Earth days). Daytime temperatures average 338°F (170°C). There is no atmosphere and the planet has no satellites.

3 a series of space missions, launched by the US from 1958 to 1963, that achieved the first US manned space flights.
– DERIVATIVES **Mer·cu·ri·an** /mərˈkyo͝orēən/ **adj.**

mer·cu·ry[1] /ˈmərkyərē/ ▶ **n.** the chemical element of atomic number 80, a heavy silvery-white metal that is liquid at ordinary temperatures. (Symbol: **Hg**) Also called **QUICKSILVER**. ■ the column of such metal in a thermometer or barometer, or its height as indicating atmospheric temperature or pressure: *the mercury rises, the skies steam, and the nights swelter.* ■ historical this metal or one of its compounds used medicinally, esp. to treat syphilis.
– ORIGIN Middle English: from Latin *Mercurius* (see **MERCURY** (sense 1)).

mer·cu·ry[2] ▶ **n.** a plant of the spurge family. ● Genera *Mercurialis* and *Acalypha*, family Euphorbiaceae: several species, in particular the poisonous **dog's mercury** (*M. perennis*) of Eurasia and the **three-seeded mercury** (*A. virginica*) of North America.
– ORIGIN mid 16th cent.: from Latin *mercurialis* 'of the god Mercury.'

mer·cu·ry switch ▶ **n.** an electric switch in which the circuit is made by mercury flowing into a gap when the device tilts.

mer·cu·ry va·por lamp ▶ **n.** a lamp in which light is produced by an electrical discharge through mercury vapor.

mer·cy /ˈmərsē/ ▶ **n.** (pl. **mercies**) compassion or forgiveness shown toward someone whom it is within one's power to punish or harm: *the boy was screaming and begging for mercy | the mercies of God.* ■ an event to be grateful for, esp. because its occurrence prevents something unpleasant or provides relief from suffering: *his death was in a way a mercy.* ■ [as modifier] (esp. of a journey or mission) performed out of a desire to relieve suffering; motivated by compassion: *mercy missions to refugees caught up in the fighting.*
▶ **exclam.** archaic used in expressions of surprise or fear: *"Mercy me!" uttered Mrs. Garfield.*
– PHRASES **at the mercy of** completely in the power or under the control of: *consumers were at the mercy of every rogue in the marketplace.* **be thankful** (or **grateful**) **for small mercies** be relieved that an unpleasant situation is alleviated by minor advantages. **have mercy on** (or **upon**) show compassion or forgiveness to: *may the Lord have mercy on her soul.* **leave someone/something to the mercy of** expose someone or something to a situation of probable danger or harm: *the forest is left to the mercy of the loggers.* **throw oneself on someone's mercy** intentionally place oneself in someone's hands in the expectation that they will behave mercifully toward one.
– ORIGIN Middle English: from Old French *merci* 'pity' or 'thanks,' from Latin *merces, merced-* 'reward,' in Christian Latin 'pity, favor, heavenly reward.'

mer·cy kill·ing ▶ **n.** the killing of a patient suffering from an incurable and painful disease, typically by the administration of large doses of painkilling drugs. See also **EUTHANASIA**.

merde /me(ə)rd/ ▶ **exclam.** a French word for "shit," used as a mild, generally humorous exclamation in English: *Merde! What had she done!*

mere[1] /mi(ə)r/ ▶ **adj.** [attrib.] that is solely or no more or better than what is specified: *it happened a mere decade ago | questions that cannot be answered by mere mortals.* ■ (**the merest**) the smallest or slightest: *the merest hint of makeup.*
– ORIGIN late Middle English (in the senses 'pure' and 'sheer, downright'): from Latin *merus* 'undiluted.'

mere[2] ▶ **n.** chiefly literary a lake, pond, or arm of the sea.
– ORIGIN Old English, of Germanic origin; related to Dutch *meer* 'lake' and German *Meer* 'sea,' from an Indo-European root shared by Russian *more* and Latin *mare.*

Mer·e·dith /ˈmerədiTH/, James Howard (1933–), US civil rights activist. In 1962, he became the first African American to attend the University of Mississippi after 3,000 troops quelled riots. He wrote *Three Years in Mississippi* (1966) and *Mississippi: A Volume of Eleven Books* (1995).

mere·ly /ˈmi(ə)rlē/ ▶ **adv.** just; only: *she seemed to him not merely an intelligent woman, but a kind of soul mate.*

me·ren·gue /məˈreNGgā/ ▶ **n.** a Caribbean style of dance music typically in duple and triple time, chiefly associated with Dominica and Haiti. ■ a style of dancing associated with such music, with alternating long and short stiff-legged steps.
– ORIGIN late 19th cent.: probably American Spanish; compare perhaps with the sense 'upheaval, disorder,' attested in Argentina, Paraguay, and Uruguay.

mer·e·tri·cious /merəˈtriSHəs/ ▶ **adj. 1** apparently attractive but having in reality no value or integrity: *meretricious souvenirs for the tourist trade.*
2 archaic of, relating to, or characteristic of a prostitute.
– DERIVATIVES **mer·e·tri·cious·ly adv.**, **mer·e·tri·cious·ness n.**
– ORIGIN early 17th cent.: from Latin *meretricius* (adjective from *meretrix, meretric-* 'prostitute,' from *mereri* 'be hired') + **-OUS**.

mer·gan·ser /mərˈgansər/ ▶ **n.** a fish-eating diving duck with a long, thin serrated and hooked bill. Also called **SAWBILL**. ● Genus *Mergus*, subfamily Merginae, family Anatidae: six species, including the conspicuously crested **red-breasted merganser** (*M. serrator*); **common merganser** (*M. merganser*), the male of which has a white body and dark green head; and smew.

m

–ORIGIN mid 17th cent.: modern Latin, from Latin *mergus* 'diver' (from *mergere* 'to dive') + *anser* 'goose.'

merge /mərj/ ▶ **v.** combine or cause to combine to form a single entity: [no obj.] *the utility companies are cutting costs and* **merging with** *other companies* | [with obj.] *the company plans to* **merge** *its U.S. oil production operations* **with** *those of a London-based organization* | *the files were merged using the patient identification code as the common variable.* ■ [no obj.] blend or fade gradually into something else so as to become indistinguishable from it: *he crouched low and endeavored to merge into the darkness of the forest.* ■ [with obj.] cause to blend or fade into something else in such a way.
–ORIGIN mid 17th cent. (in the sense 'immerse (oneself)'): from Latin *mergere* 'to dip, plunge.' The use in legal contexts is from Anglo-Norman French *merger.*

merg·er /'mərjər/ ▶ **n.** a combination of two things, esp. companies, into one: **a merger between** *two supermarket chains* | *local companies ripe for merger or acquisition.*
–ORIGIN early 18th cent.: from Anglo-Norman French *merger* (verb used as a noun): see MERGE.

mer·guez /mər'gez/ (also **merguez sausage**) ▶ **n.** (pl. **same**) a spicy beef and lamb sausage colored with red peppers, originally made in parts of North Africa.
–ORIGIN French, from Arabic *mirkās, mirqās.*

Me·riç /mə'rēCH/ Turkish name for MARITSA.

Mé·ri·da /'meridə, 'mārē,dä/ a city in southeastern Mexico, capital of the state of Yucatán; pop. 734,153 (2005).

Mer·i·den /'merid(ə)n/ an industrial city in south central Connecticut; pop. 59,186 (est. 2008).

Me·rid·i·an /mə'ridēən/ **1** a city in southwestern Idaho, west of Boise; pop. 66,916 (est. 2008).
2 a city in eastern Mississippi; pop. 38,232 (est. 2008).

me·rid·i·an /mə'ridēən/ ▶ **n. 1** a circle of constant longitude passing through a given place on the earth's surface and the terrestrial poles. ■ (also **celestial meridian**) Astronomy a circle passing through the celestial poles and the zenith of a given place on the earth's surface.
2 (in acupuncture and Chinese medicine) each of a set of pathways in the body along which vital energy is said to flow. There are twelve such pathways associated with specific organs.
▶ **adj.** [attrib.] relating to or situated at a meridian: *the meridian moon.* ■ literary of noon. ■ literary of the period of greatest splendor, vigor, etc.
–ORIGIN late Middle English: from Old French *meridien,* from Latin *meridianum* (neuter, used as a noun) 'noon,' from *medius* 'middle' + *dies* 'day.' The use in astronomy is due to the fact that the sun crosses a meridian at noon.

me·rid·i·an cir·cle ▶ **n.** Astronomy a telescope mounted so as to move only on a north–south line, for observing the transit of celestial objects across the meridian.

me·rid·i·o·nal /mə'ridēənəl/ ▶ **adj. 1** of or in the south; southern: *the meridional leg of the journey.* ■ relating to or characteristic of the inhabitants of southern Europe, esp. the south of France: *she was meridional in temperament.*
2 of or relating to a meridian: *the meridional line of demarcation.* ■ Meteorology (chiefly of winds and air flow) aligned with lines of longitude.
▶ **n.** a native or inhabitant of the south, esp. the south of France.
–ORIGIN late Middle English: via Old French from late Latin *meridionalis,* formed irregularly from Latin *meridies* 'midday, south.'

me·ringue /mə'raNG/ ▶ **n.** an item of sweet food made from a mixture of well-beaten egg whites and sugar, baked until crisp and typically used as a topping for desserts, esp. pies. Individual meringues are often filled with fruit or whipped cream.
–ORIGIN from French, of unknown origin.

me·ri·no /mə'rēnō/ ▶ **n.** (pl. **merinos**) (also **merino sheep**) a sheep of a breed with long, fine wool. ■ a soft woolen or wool-and-cotton material resembling cashmere, originally of merino wool. ■ a fine woolen yarn.
–ORIGIN late 18th cent.: from Spanish, of unknown origin.

mer·i·stem /'merə,stem/ ▶ **n.** Botany a region of plant tissue, found chiefly at the growing tips of roots and shoots and in the cambium, consisting of actively dividing cells forming new tissue.
–DERIVATIVES **mer·i·ste·mat·ic** /merəstə'matik/ **adj.**
–ORIGIN late 19th cent.: formed irregularly from Greek *meristos* 'divisible,' from *merizein* 'divide into parts,' from *meros* 'part.' The suffix *-em* is on the pattern of words such as *xylem.*

mer·it /'merit/ ▶ **n.** the quality of being particularly good or worthy, esp. so as to deserve praise or reward: *composers of outstanding merit.* ■ a feature or fact that deserves praise or reward: *the relative merits of both approaches have to be considered.* ■ Brit. a pass grade in an examination denoting above-average performance: *if you expect to pass, why not go for a merit or a distinction?* Compare with DISTINCTION. ■ (**merits**) chiefly Law the intrinsic rights and wrongs of a case, outside of any other considerations: *a plaintiff who has a good arguable case* **on the merits**. ■ (**merits**) Theology good deeds regarded as entitling someone to a future reward from God.
▶ **v.** (**merits, meriting, merited**) [with obj.] deserve or be worthy of (something, esp. reward, punishment, or attention): *the results have been encouraging enough to merit further investigation.*
–PHRASES **judge** (or **consider**) **something on its merits** assess something solely with regard to its intrinsic quality rather than other external factors.
–ORIGIN Middle English (originally in the sense 'deserved reward or punishment'): via Old French from Latin *meritum* 'due reward,' from *mereri* 'earn, deserve.'

mer·i·toc·ra·cy /,meri'täkrəsē/ ▶ **n.** (pl. **meritocracies**) government or the holding of power by people selected on the basis of their ability. ■ a society governed by such people or in which such people hold power. ■ a ruling or influential class of educated or skilled people.
–DERIVATIVES **mer·i·to·crat·ic** /,meritə'kratik/ **adj.**

mer·i·to·ri·ous /,meri,tôrēəs/ ▶ **adj.** deserving reward or praise: *a medal for meritorious conduct.* ■ Law (of an action or claim) likely to succeed on the merits of the case.
–DERIVATIVES **mer·i·to·ri·ous·ly adv.**, **mer·i·to·ri·ous·ness n.**
–ORIGIN late Middle English (in the sense 'entitling a person to reward'): from late Latin *meritorius* (from *merit-* 'earned,' from the verb *mereri*) + -OUS.

Mer·kel /'markəl/, Angela (Dorothea) (1954–), German stateswoman, chancellor of Germany since 2005.

mer·kin /'markən/ ▶ **n.** an artificial covering of hair for the pubic area.
–ORIGIN early 17th cent.: apparently a variant of dialect *malkin,* diminutive of *Malde* (early form of the given name *Maud*).

merle /'mərl/ (also **merl**) ▶ **n.** Scottish or archaic a blackbird.
–ORIGIN late Middle English: via Old French from Latin *merula.*

Mer·lin /'mərlən/ (in Arthurian legend) a magician who aided and supported King Arthur.

mer·lin ▶ **n.** a small dark falcon that hunts small birds, found throughout most of Eurasia and much of North America. Also called PIGEON HAWK. ● *Falco columbarius,* family Falconidae.
–ORIGIN late Middle English: from Anglo-Norman French *merilun,* from Old French *esmerillon,* augmentative of *esmeril,* of Germanic origin; related to German *Schmerl.*

mer·lon /'mərlən/ ▶ **n.** the solid part of an embattled parapet between two embrasures.
–ORIGIN early 18th cent.: from French, from Italian *merlone,* from *merlo* 'battlement.'

Mer·lot /mər'lō/ (also **merlot**) ▶ **n.** a variety of black wine grape originally from the Bordeaux region of France. ■ a red wine made from this grape.
–ORIGIN French.

mer·maid /'mər,mād/ ▶ **n.** a fictitious or mythical half-human sea creature with the head and trunk of a woman and the tail of a fish, conventionally depicted as beautiful and with long flowing golden hair.
–ORIGIN Middle English: from MERE[2] (in the obsolete sense 'sea') + MAID.

mer·maid's purse ▶ **n.** the horny egg case of a skate, ray, or small shark.

Mer·man /'mərmən/, Ethel (1908–1984), US singer and actress; born *Ethel Zimmerman.* The "queen of Broadway" for three decades, she performed in many plays and musicals, including *Annie Get Your Gun* (1946), *Call Me Madam* (1950), *Gypsy* (1959), and *Hello, Dolly!* (1970).

mer·man /'mər,man, -mən/ ▶ **n.** (pl. **mermen**) the male equivalent of a mermaid.

mero- ▶ **comb. form** partly; partial: *meronym.* Often contrasted with HOMO-.
–ORIGIN from Greek *meros* 'part.'

Mer·oe /'merō,ē/ an ancient city on the Nile River, in present-day Sudan northeast of Khartoum. Founded in *c.*750 BC, it was the capital of the ancient kingdom of Cush from *c.*590 BC until it fell to the invading Aksumites in the early 4th century AD.
–DERIVATIVES **Mer·o·it·ic** /,merō'itik/ **adj. & n.**

mer·o·nym /'merə,nim/ ▶ **n.** Linguistics a term that denotes part of something but which is used to refer to the whole of it, e.g., *faces* when used to mean *people* in *I see several familiar faces present.*
–DERIVATIVES **meronymy** /mə'ränəmē/ **n.**
–ORIGIN from Greek *meros* 'part' + *onuma* 'name.'

-merous ▶ **comb. form** Biology having a specified number of parts: *pentamerous.*
–ORIGIN on the pattern of words such as *(di)merous* (see also -MER).

Mer·o·vin·gi·an /'merə,vinj(ē)ən/ ▶ **adj.** of or relating to the Frankish dynasty founded by Clovis and reigning in Gaul and Germany *c.*500–750.
▶ **n.** a member of this dynasty.
–ORIGIN from French *mérovingien,* from medieval Latin *Merovingi* 'descendants of Merovich' (Clovis' grandfather, semilegendary 5th-cent. Frankish leader).

mer·ri·ly /'merəlē/ ▶ **adv. 1** in a cheerful way. ■ in a brisk and lively way: *a fire burned merrily in the hearth.*
2 without consideration of possible problems or future implications: *no candidate can denounce high public spending while merrily buying local votes with the taxpayers' money.*

Mer·ri·mack /'merə,mak/ a town in southern New Hampshire; pop. 26,457 (est. 2008).

Mer·ri·mack Riv·er a river that flows for 110 miles (180 km) from New Hampshire through eastern Massachusetts to the Atlantic Ocean.

mer·ri·ment /'merēmənt/ ▶ **n.** gaiety and fun: *her eyes sparkled with merriment.*

mer·ry /'merē/ ▶ **adj.** (**merrier, merriest**) cheerful and lively: *the narrow streets were dense with merry throngs of students* | *a merry grin.* ■ (of an occasion or season) characterized by festivity and rejoicing: *he wished me a merry Christmas.* ■ [predic.] Brit. informal slightly and good-humoredly drunk: *after the third bottle of beer he began to feel quite merry.*
–PHRASES **go on one's merry way** informal carry on with a course of action regardless of the consequences. **make merry** enjoy oneself with others, esp. by dancing and drinking. **the more the merrier** the more people or things there are, the better or more enjoyable a situation will be.
–DERIVATIVES **mer·ri·ness n.**
–ORIGIN Old English *myrige* 'pleasing, delightful,' of Germanic origin; related to MIRTH.

mer·ry an·drew /,merē 'andrōō/ ▶ **n.** archaic a person who entertains others by means of comic antics; a clown.

mer·ry-go-round ▶ **n.** a revolving machine with model horses or other animals on which people ride for amusement. ■ a large revolving device in a playground, for children to ride on. ■ a continuous cycle of activities or events, esp. when perceived as having no purpose or producing no result: *the football management merry-go-round.*

mer·ry·mak·ing /'merē,mākiNG/ ▶ **n.** the process of enjoying oneself with others, esp. by dancing and drinking.
–DERIVATIVES **mer·ry·mak·er** /-,mākər/ **n.**

mer·ry·thought /'merē,THôt/ ▶ **n.** dated, chiefly Brit. the wishbone of a bird.

Mer·sa Ma·truh /'mərsə mə'trōō/ a town on the Mediterranean coast of Egypt, 156 miles (250 km) west of Alexandria; pop. 120,500 (est. 2006).

Mer·senne num·ber /mər'sen/ ▶ **n.** Mathematics a number of the form $2n-1$, where n is a prime number. Such a number which is itself prime is also called a **Mersenne prime**.
–ORIGIN late 19th cent.: named after Marin *Mersenne* (1588–1648), French mathematician.

Mer·sey /'mərzē/ a river in northwestern England that rises in the county of Derbyshire and flows 70 miles (112 km) to the Irish Sea near Liverpool.

Mer·sin /mer'sēn/ an industrial port in southern Turkey, on the Mediterranean Sea, southwest of Adana; pop. 623,900 (est. 2007).

Mer·ton /'mərtn/, Thomas (James) (1915–68), US Roman Catholic monk and writer; born in France. He was ordained 1949 as Father Louis in the Trappist order. His works include *The Seven Storey Mountain* (1948).

Me·sa /'māsə/ a city in south central Arizona, east of Phoenix; pop. 463,552 (est. 2008).

me·sa /'māsə/ ▶ **n.** an isolated flat-topped hill with steep sides, found in landscapes with horizontal strata.
–ORIGIN mid 18th cent.: Spanish, literally 'table,' from Latin *mensa.*

Me·sa·bi Range /mə'säbē/ low hills in northeastern Minnesota, site of one of the largest iron sources in the world.

mé·sal·li·ance /ˌmāzəˈlīəns, ˌmā,zalˈyäNs/ ▶ **n.** a marriage with a person thought to be unsuitable or of a lower social position.
– ORIGIN French, from *més-* 'wrong, misdirected' + *alliance* (see ALLIANCE).

Me·sa Ver·de /ˈmāsə ˈvərdē/ a high plateau in southern Colorado, with the remains of many prehistoric Pueblo Indian dwellings.
– ORIGIN Spanish, literally 'green table(land).'

mes·cal /meˈskal, mə-/ ▶ **n. 1** another term for MAGUEY. ■ an intoxicating liquor distilled from the sap of an agave. Compare with TEQUILA, PULQUE.
2 another term for PEYOTE.
– ORIGIN early 18th cent.: from Spanish *mezcal*, from Nahuatl *mexcalli*.

mes·cal but·tons ▶ **plural n.** another term for PEYOTE BUTTONS.

Mes·ca·le·ro /ˌmeskəˈle(ə)rō/ ▶ **n.** (pl. **same** or **Mescaleros**) **1** a member of an American Indian people of New Mexico.
2 the Athabaskan (Apache) language of this people.
▶ **adj.** of or relating to this people or their language.
– ORIGIN Spanish, literally 'people of the mescal,' with reference to their traditional use of the flesh of the mescal plant as part of their staple diet.

mes·ca·line /ˈmeskəlin, -ˌlēn/ ▶ **n.** a hallucinogenic and intoxicating compound present in mescal buttons from the peyote cactus. ● Alternative name: **3,4,5-trimethoxyphenethylamine**; chem. formula: $(CH_3O)_3C_6H_2CH_2CH_2NH_2$.

mes·clun /ˈmesklən/ (also **mesclun salad**) ▶ **n.** a salad made from a selection of lettuces with other edible leaves such as dandelion greens, mustard greens, and radicchio.
– ORIGIN Provençal, literally 'mixture,' from *mesclar* 'mix thoroughly.'

Mes·dames /māˈdäm/ ▶ **plural n. 1** plural form of MADAME.
2 formal used as a title to refer to more than one woman simultaneously: *prizes were won by Mesdames Carter, Roseby, and Barrington.*

Mes·de·moi·selles /ˈmādəm(w)əˌzel, ˈmādˌmwäˌzel/ plural form of MADEMOISELLE.

me·sem·bry·an·the·mum /məˌzembrēˈanTHəməm/ ▶ **n.** a fleshy succulent plant of the carpetweed family, often with showy flowers. Several varieties are grown as ornamentals. ● *Mesembryanthemum* and related genera (esp. *Carpobrotus*), family Aizoaceae.
– ORIGIN modern Latin, based on Greek *mesēmbria* 'noon' + *anthemon* 'flower.'

mes·en·ceph·a·lon /ˌmezˌenˈsefəˌlän, ˌmes-, -lən/ ▶ **n.** Anatomy another term for MIDBRAIN.
– DERIVATIVES **mes·en·ce·phal·ic** /-ˌensəˈfalik/ **adj.**
– ORIGIN mid 19th cent.: from Greek *mesos* 'middle' + ENCEPHALON.

mes·en·chyme /ˈmezənˌkīm, ˈmes-/ ▶ **n.** Embryology a loosely organized, mainly mesodermal embryonic tissue that develops into connective and skeletal tissues, including blood and lymph.
– DERIVATIVES **mes·en·chy·mal** /ˌmezˌenˈkīməl, ˌmes-/ **adj.**
– ORIGIN late 19th cent.: from Greek *mesos* 'middle' + *enkhuma* 'infusion.'

mes·en·ter·on /məˈzentəˌrän, məˈsent-/ ▶ **n.** Zoology the middle section of the intestine, esp. in an embryo or in an arthropod.
– DERIVATIVES **mes·en·ter·on·ic** /-ˌzentəˈränik, -ˌsent-/ **adj.**
– ORIGIN late 19th cent.: from Greek *mesos* 'middle' + *enteron* 'intestine.'

mes·en·ter·y /ˈmezənˌterē, ˈmes-/ ▶ **n.** (pl. **mesenteries**) Anatomy a fold of the peritoneum that attaches the stomach, small intestine, pancreas, spleen, and other organs to the posterior wall of the abdomen.
– DERIVATIVES **mes·en·ter·ic** /ˌmezənˈterik, ˌmes-/ **adj.**
– ORIGIN late Middle English: via medieval Latin from Greek *mesenterion*, from *mesos* 'middle' + *enteron* 'intestine.'

mesh /mesH/ ▶ **n. 1** material made of a network of wire or thread: *mesh for fishing nets | finer wire meshes are used for smaller particles.* ■ the spacing of the strands of such material: *if the mesh is too big, small rabbits can squeeze through.*
2 an interlaced structure: *cell fragments that agglutinate and form intricate meshes.* ■ [in sing.] used with reference to a complex or constricting situation: *the raveled mesh of events and her own emotions.* ■ Computing a set of finite elements used to represent a geometric object for modeling or analysis. ■ Computing a computer network in which each computer or processor is connected to a number of others, esp. as an n-dimensional lattice.
▶ **v. 1** [no obj.] (of the teeth of a gearwheel) lock together or be engaged with another gearwheel: *one gear meshes with the input gear.* ■ make or become entangled or entwined: [no obj.] *their fingers meshed* | [with obj.] *I don't want to get meshed in the weeds.* ■ be in or bring into harmony: [no obj.] *her memory of events doesn't mesh with the world around her.*
2 [with obj.] represent (a geometric object) as a set of finite elements for computational analysis or modeling.
– PHRASES **in mesh** (of the teeth of gearwheels) engaged.
– DERIVATIVES **meshed adj.**, **mesh·y adj.**
– ORIGIN late Middle English: probably from an unrecorded Old English word related to (and perhaps reinforced in Middle English by) Middle Dutch *maesche*, of Germanic origin.

Me·shed variant of MASHHAD.

me·shu·ga /məˈsHŏŏgə/ (also **meshugga** or **meshugah**) ▶ **adj.** informal (of a person) crazy; idiotic: *either a miracle is taking place, or we're all meshuga.*
– ORIGIN late 19th cent.: from Yiddish *meshuge*, from Hebrew.

me·shu·gaas /məsHŏŏgˈäs/ ▶ **n.** informal mad or idiotic ideas or behavior: *there's method in this man's meshugaas.*
– ORIGIN early 20th cent.: Yiddish, noun from MESHUGA.

me·shug·ga·na /məˈsHŏŏgənə/ (also **meshuggener** or **meshugenah**) ▶ **n.** informal a mad or idiotic person.
– ORIGIN early 20th cent.: variant of MESHUGA.

me·si·al /ˈmezēəl/ ▶ **adj.** Anatomy of, in, or directed toward the middle line of a body.
– DERIVATIVES **me·si·al·ly adv.**
– ORIGIN early 19th cent.: formed irregularly from Greek *mesos* 'middle' + -IAL.

mes·ic[1] /ˈmezik, ˈmē-/ ▶ **adj.** Ecology (of an environment or habitat) containing a moderate amount of moisture. Compare with HYDRIC and XERIC.
– ORIGIN 1920s: from Greek *mesos* 'middle' + -IC.

mes·ic[2] ▶ **adj.** Physics of or relating to a meson. ■ denoting a system analogous to an atom in which a meson takes the place of either an orbital electron or the nucleus.

Mes·mer /ˈmesmər, ˈmez-/, Franz Anton (1734–1815), Austrian physician. He is noted for introducing a therapeutic technique involving hypnotism.

mes·mer·ic /mezˈmerik/ ▶ **adj.** causing a person to become completely transfixed and unaware of anything else around them: *she found herself staring into his mesmeric gaze.* ■ archaic of, relating to, or produced by mesmerism.
– DERIVATIVES **mes·mer·i·cal·ly adv.**

mes·mer·ism /ˈmezməˌrizəm/ ▶ **n.** historical the therapeutic system of F. A. Mesmer. ■ (in general use) hypnotism.
– DERIVATIVES **mes·mer·ist** /-ist/ **n.**
– ORIGIN late 18th cent.: named after F. A. MESMER.

mes·mer·ize /ˈmezməˌrīz/ ▶ **v.** [with obj.] hold the attention of (someone) to the exclusion of all else or so as to transfix them: *she was mesmerized by the blue eyes that stared so intently into her own* | (as adj. **mesmerizing**) *a mesmerizing stare.* ■ archaic hypnotize (someone).
– DERIVATIVES **mes·mer·i·za·tion** /ˌmezmərəˈzāsHən/ **n.**, **mes·mer·iz·er n.**, **mes·mer·iz·ing·ly adv.**

mesne /mēn/ ▶ **adj.** Law intermediate.
– ORIGIN late Middle English (as adverb and noun): from legal French, variant of Anglo-Norman French *meen* 'middle' (see MEAN[3]).

mesne prof·its ▶ **plural n.** Law the profits of an estate received by a tenant in wrongful possession and recoverable by the landlord.

meso- ▶ **comb. form** middle; intermediate: *mesomorph.*
– ORIGIN from Greek *mesos* 'middle.'

Mes·o·A·mer·i·ca /ˈmezō, ˈmesō/ the central region of America, from central Mexico to Nicaragua, esp. as a region of ancient civilizations and native cultures before the arrival of the Spanish.
– DERIVATIVES **Mes·o·A·mer·i·can adj. & n.**

mes·o·blast /ˈmezəˌblast, ˈmē-/ ▶ **n.** Embryology the mesoderm of an embryo in its earliest stages.
– DERIVATIVES **mes·o·blas·tic** /ˌmezəˈblastik, ˌmē-/ **adj.**

mes·o·carp /ˈmezəˌkärp, ˈmē-/ ▶ **n.** Botany the middle layer of the pericarp of a fruit, between the endocarp and the exocarp.

mes·o·ce·phal·ic /ˈmezəsəˈfalik, ˌmē-/ ▶ **adj.** Anatomy having a head of medium proportions, not markedly brachycephalic or dolichocephalic.
– DERIVATIVES **mes·o·ceph·al·y** /-ˈsefəlē/ **n.**

mes·o·cy·clone /ˌmezəˈsīklōn, ˌmesə-, ˌmēzə-, ˌmēsə-/ ▶ **n.** Meteorology a cyclonic air mass associated with a supercell; its presence is a condition for a tornado warning.
– ORIGIN late 20th cent.

mes·o·derm /ˈmezəˌdərm, ˈmē-/ ▶ **n.** Embryology the middle layer of an embryo in early development, between the endoderm and ectoderm.
– DERIVATIVES **mes·o·der·mal** /ˌmezəˈdəməl, mē-/ **adj.**, **mes·o·der·mic** /-ˈdərmik/ **adj.**
– ORIGIN late 19th cent.: from MESO- 'middle' + Greek *derma* 'skin.'

mes·o·gas·tri·um /ˌmezəˈgastrēəm, ˌmē-/ ▶ **n.** (pl. **mesogastria** /-trēə/) Anatomy the middle region of the abdomen between the epigastrium and the hypogastrium.
– DERIVATIVES **mes·o·gas·tric** /-trik/ **adj.**
– ORIGIN mid 19th cent.: modern Latin, from MESO- 'middle' + Greek *gastēr, gastr-* 'stomach.'

mes·o·kur·tic /ˌmezəˈkərtik, ˌmē-/ ▶ **adj.** Statistics (of a frequency distribution or its graphical representation) having the same kurtosis as the normal distribution. Compare with LEPTOKURTIC, PLATYKURTIC.
– DERIVATIVES **mes·o·kur·to·sis** /ˌmezəkərˈtōsis, ˌmē-/ **n.**
– ORIGIN early 20th cent.: from MESO- 'middle' + Greek *kurtos* 'bulging' + -IC.

mes·o·lect /ˈmezəˌlekt, ˈmesə-, ˈmēzə-, ˈmēsə-/ ▶ **n.** (relative to the acrolect and the basilect) an intermediate dialect or variety of a particular language (used esp. in the study of Creoles).
– DERIVATIVES **mes·o·lec·tal** /ˌmezəˈlektəl, ˌmesə-, ˌmēzə-, ˌmēsə-/ **adj.**

Mes·o·lith·ic /ˌmezəˈliTHik, ˌmē-/ ▶ **adj.** Archaeology of, relating to, or denoting the middle part of the Stone Age, between the Paleolithic and Neolithic. ■ (as noun **the Mesolithic**) the Mesolithic period. Also called MIDDLE STONE AGE.

> In Europe, the Mesolithic falls between the end of the last glacial period (c.8500 BC) and the beginnings of agriculture. Mesolithic people lived by hunting, gathering, and fishing, and the period is characterized by the use of microliths and the first domestication of an animal (the dog).

– ORIGIN mid 19th cent.: from MESO- 'middle' + Greek *lithos* 'stone' + -IC.

m

me·som·er·ism /məˈsäməˌrizəm, -ˈzä-/ ▶ **n.** Chemistry old-fashioned term for RESONANCE.
– DERIVATIVES **mes·o·mer·ic** /ˌmezəˈmerik, ˌmes-/ **adj.**

mes·o·morph /ˈmezəˌmôrf, ˈmē-/ ▶ **n.** Physiology a person with a compact and muscular body build. Compare with ECTOMORPH and ENDOMORPH.
– DERIVATIVES **mes·o·mor·phic** /ˌmezəˈmôrfik, ˌmē-/ **adj.**
– ORIGIN 1920s: *meso-* from *mesodermal* (being the layer of the embryo giving rise to physical characteristics that predominate) + -MORPH.

me·son /ˈmezˌän, ˈmāˌzän, ˈmēˌzän/ ▶ **n.** Physics a subatomic particle that is intermediate in mass between an electron and a proton and transmits the strong interaction that binds nucleons together in the atomic nucleus.
– DERIVATIVES **me·son·ic** /meˈzänik, mā-, mē-/ **adj.**
– ORIGIN 1930s: from MESO- 'intermediate' + -ON.

mes·o·pause /ˈmezəˌpôz, ˈmē-/ ▶ **n.** the boundary in the earth's atmosphere between the mesosphere and the thermosphere, at which the temperature stops decreasing with increasing height and begins to increase.

mes·o·pe·lag·ic /ˌmezəpəˈlajik, ˌmē-/ ▶ **adj.** Biology (of fish and other organisms) inhabiting the intermediate depths of the sea, approximately 650–3,300 feet (200–1,000 m) below the surface.

mes·o·phyll /ˈmezəˌfil, ˈmē-/ ▶ **n.** Botany the inner tissue (parenchyma) of a leaf, containing many chloroplasts.
– DERIVATIVES **mes·o·phyl·lic** /ˌmezəˈfilik, ˌmē-/ **adj.**, **mes·o·phyl·lous** /ˌmezəˈfiləs, ˌmē-/ **adj.**
– ORIGIN mid 19th cent.: from MESO- 'middle' + Greek *phullon* 'leaf.'

mes·o·phyte /ˈmezəˌfit, ˈmē-/ ▶ **n.** Botany a plant needing only a moderate amount of water.
– DERIVATIVES **mes·o·phyt·ic** /ˌmezəˈfitik, ˌmē-/ **adj.**

Mes·o·po·ta·mi·a /ˌmesəpəˈtāmēə/ an ancient region of southwestern Asia in present-day Iraq, lying between the Tigris and Euphrates rivers. Its alluvial plains were the site of the civilizations of Akkad, Sumer, Babylonia, and Assyria.
– DERIVATIVES **Mes·o·po·ta·mi·an adj. & n.**
– ORIGIN from Greek *mesos* 'middle' + *potamos* 'river.'

mes·o·saur /ˈmezəˌsôr, ˈmē-/ (also **mesosaurus** /ˌmezəˈsôrəs/) ▶ **n.** an extinct small aquatic reptile of the early Permian period, with an elongated body, flattened tail, and a long narrow snout with numerous needlelike teeth. ● Genus *Mesosaurus*, order Mesosauria, subclass Anapsida.
– DERIVATIVES **mes·o·sau·ri·an adj.**
– ORIGIN 1950s: modern Latin, from Greek *mesos* 'middle' + *sauros* 'lizard.'

mes·o·scale /ˈmezəˌskāl, ˈmē-/ ▶ **n.** chiefly Meteorology an intermediate scale, esp. that between the scales of weather systems and of microclimates, on which storms and other phenomena occur.

mes·o·sphere /ˈmezəˌsfi(ə)r, ˈmē-/ ▶ **n.** the region of the earth's atmosphere above the stratosphere and below the thermosphere, between about 30 and 50 miles (50 and 80 km) in altitude.
– DERIVATIVES **mes·o·spher·ic** /ˌmezəˈsfi(ə)rik, ˌmē-/ **adj.**

mes·o·the·li·o·ma /ˈmezəˌTHēlēˈōmə, ˌmē-/ ▶ **n.** (pl. **mesotheliomas** or **mesotheliomata**) Medicine a cancer of mesothelial tissue, associated esp. with exposure to asbestos.

mes·o·the·li·um /ˌmezəˈTHēlēəm, ˌmē-/ ▶ **n.** (pl. **mesothelia** /-ˈTHēlēə/) Anatomy the epithelium that lines the pleurae, peritoneum, and pericardium. ■ Embryology the surface layer of the embryonic mesoderm, from which this is derived.
– DERIVATIVES **mes·o·the·li·al** /-ˈTHēlēəl/ **adj.**
– ORIGIN late 19th cent.: from **MESO-** 'middle' + a shortened form of **EPITHELIUM**.

mes·o·ther·a·py /ˌmezəˈTHerəpi, ˌmēsə-/ ▶ **n.** (in cosmetic surgery) a procedure in which multiple tiny injections of pharmaceuticals, vitamins, etc., are delivered into the mesodermal layer of tissue under the skin, to promote the loss of fat or cellulite.

mes·o·tho·rax /ˌmezəˈTHôrˌaks/ ▶ **n.** (pl. **mesothoraxes** or **mesothoraces** /-ˈTHôrəˌsēz/) Entomology the middle segment of the thorax of an insect, bearing the forewings or elytra.
– DERIVATIVES **mes·o·tho·rac·ic** /-THəˈrasik/ **adj.**

mes·o·zo·an /ˌmezəˈzōən, ˌmē-/ ▶ **n.** Zoology a minute worm that is an internal parasite of marine invertebrates. It lacks any internal organs other than reproductive cells, and dissolved nutrients are absorbed directly from the host's tissues. ● Phyla Orthonectida and Rhombozoa; formerly placed together in the phylum Mesozoa, which was thought to be intermediate between protozoans and metazoans.
– ORIGIN early 20th cent.: from modern Latin *Mesozoa* (from *mesos* 'intermediate' + *zōion* 'animal') + **-AN**.

Mes·o·zo·ic /ˈmezəˈzōik, ˌmē-/ ▶ **adj.** Geology of, relating to, or denoting the era between the Paleozoic and Cenozoic eras, comprising the Triassic, Jurassic, and Cretaceous periods. ■ (as noun **the Mesozoic**) the Mesozoic era or the system of rocks deposited during it.

> The Mesozoic lasted from about 245 million to 65 million years ago. Large reptiles were dominant on land and sea throughout this time; vegetation had become abundant, and the first mammals, birds, and flowering plants appeared.

– ORIGIN mid 19th cent.: from **MESO-** 'intermediate' + Greek *zōion* 'animal' (referring to the appearance of the first mammals) + **-IC**.

Mes·quite /məˈskēt/ a city in northeastern Texas, east of Dallas; pop. 132,123 (est. 2008).

mes·quite /meˈskēt/ ▶ **n.** a spiny tree or shrub of the pea family, native to arid regions of southwestern US and Mexico. It yields useful timber, tanbark, medicinal products, and edible pods. The timber is used for fencing and flooring, and burned in barbecues as flavoring. ● Genus *Prosopis*, family Leguminosae: several species, in particular *P. glandulosa*.
– ORIGIN mid 18th cent.: from Mexican Spanish *mezquite*.

mes·quite bean ▶ **n.** an edible pod from the mesquite that can be eaten whole, used to produce flour, or fed to animals.

mess /mes/ ▶ **n.** [usu. in sing.] **1** a dirty or untidy state of things or of a place: *she made a mess of the kitchen | my hair was a mess.* ■ a thing or collection of things causing such a state: *she replaced the jug and mopped up the mess.* ■ a person who is dirty or untidy: *I look a mess.* ■ a portion of semisolid or pulpy food, esp. one that looks unappetizing: *a mess of mashed black beans and rice.* ■ [with modifier] used euphemistically to refer to the excrement of a domestic animal: *dog mess.*
2 a situation or state of affairs that is confused or full of difficulties: *the economy is still in a terrible mess.* ■ a person whose life or affairs are confused or troubled: *he needs treatment of some kind—he's a real mess.*
3 a building or room in which members of the armed forces take their meals; mess hall: *the sergeants' mess.* ■ a meal taken there.
▶ **v. 1** [with obj.] make untidy or dirty: *you've messed up my beautiful carpet.* ■ [no obj.] (of a domestic animal) defecate: *they had some problems with dogs messing in the store.* ■ make dirty by defecating: *he feared he would mess the bed.*
2 [no obj.] take one's meals in a particular place or with a particular person, esp. in an armed forces' mess: *I messed at first with Harry, who was to become a lifelong friend | they messed together.*
– PHRASES **mess with someone's head** informal cause someone to feel frustrated, anxious, or upset.
– PHRASAL VERBS **mess around/about** behave in a silly or playful way, esp. so as to cause irritation. ■ spend time doing something in a pleasantly desultory way, with no definite purpose or serious intent: *messing about in boats.* **mess around/about with** interfere with: *we don't want outsiders messing around with our schools.* ■ informal engage in a sexual relationship with (someone, esp. the partner of another person). **mess up** informal mishandle a situation: *he singled out the health care fiasco as an example of how the government has messed up.* **mess someone up** informal cause someone emotional or psychological problems: *I was unhappy and really messed up.* ■ inflict violence or injury on someone: *the wreck messed him up so much that he can't walk.* **mess something up** informal cause something to be spoiled by inept handling: *an error like that could easily mess up an entire day's work.* **mess with** informal meddle or interfere with so as to spoil or cause trouble: *stop messing with things you don't understand.*
– ORIGIN Middle English: from Old French *mes* 'portion of food,' from late Latin *missum* 'something put on the table,' past participle of *mittere* 'send, put.' The original sense was 'a serving of food,' also 'a serving of liquid or pulpy food,' later 'liquid food for an animal'; this gave rise (early 19th cent.) to the senses 'unappetizing concoction' and 'predicament,' on which sense 1 is based. In late Middle English the term also denoted any of the small groups into which the company at a banquet was divided (who were served from the same dishes); hence, 'a group of people who regularly eat together' (recorded in military use from the mid 16th cent).

mes·sage /ˈmesij/ ▶ **n. 1** a verbal, written, or recorded communication sent to or left for a recipient who cannot be contacted directly: *if I'm not there, leave a message on the voice mail.* ■ an official or formal communication, esp. a speech delivered by a head of state to a legislative assembly or the public: *the president's message to Congress.* ■ an e-mail or similar electronic communication. ■ an electronic communication generated automatically by a computer program and displayed on a screen: *an error message.* ■ a significant point or central theme, esp. one that has political, social, or moral importance: *a campaign to get the message about home security across.* ■ a divinely inspired communication from a prophet or preacher. ■ a television or radio commercial: *we will return after these messages.*
2 chiefly Brit. an errand: *all she did was make the tea and run messages.*
– PHRASES **get the message** informal infer an implication from a remark or action. **send a message** make a significant statement, either implicitly or by one's actions: *the elections sent a message to political quarters that the party was riding a wave of popularity.*
– ORIGIN Middle English: from Old French, based on Latin *missus*, past participle of *mittere* 'send.'

mes·sage board ▶ **n.** Computing an Internet site where people can post and read messages, usually on a specific topic or area of interest. Compare with **BULLETIN BOARD**.

mes·sage box ▶ **n.** Computing a small box that appears on a computer screen to inform the user of something, such as the occurrence of an error.

mes·sage switch·ing ▶ **n.** Computing & Telecommunications a mode of data transmission in which a message is sent as a complete unit and routed via a number of intermediate nodes at which it is stored and then forwarded.

mes·sag·ing /ˈmesijiNG/ ▶ **n.** the sending and processing of e-mail by computer.

Mes·sei·gneurs /ˌmāsānˈyər(z)/ plural form of **MONSEIGNEUR**.

mes·sen·ger /ˈmesənjər/ ▶ **n. 1** a person who carries a message or is employed to carry messages. ■ Biochemistry a substance that conveys information or a stimulus within the body.
2 Nautical (also **messenger line**) an endless rope, cable, or chain used with a capstan to haul an anchor cable or to drive a powered winch. ■ a light line used to haul or support a larger cable.
▶ **v.** [with obj.] send (a document or package) by messenger: *could you have it messengered over to me?*
– PHRASES **shoot** (or **kill**) **the messenger** treat the bearer of bad news as if they were to blame for it.
– ORIGIN Middle English: from Old Northern French *messanger*, variant of Old French *messager*, from Latin *missus* (see **MESSAGE**).

mes·sen·ger bag ▶ **n.** a large bag with a long strap, worn across the body.

mes·sen·ger RNA (abbr.: **mRNA**) ▶ **n.** the form of RNA in which genetic information transcribed from DNA as a sequence of bases is transferred to a ribosome.

Mes·ser·schmidt /ˈmesərˌSHmit/, Willy (1898–1978), German aircraft designer and industrialist; full name *Wilhelm Emil Messerschmidt*. The Messerschmidt 109 became the standard fighter of the Luftwaffe during World War II.

mess hall ▶ **n.** a room or building where groups of people, esp. soldiers, eat together.

Mes·siaen /mesˈyäN/, Olivier (Eugène Prosper Charles) (1908–92), French composer. His music was influenced by Greek and Hindu rhythms, birdsong, Stravinsky, Debussy, and his Roman Catholic faith.

mes·si·ah /məˈsīə/ ▶ **n. 1** (**the Messiah**) the promised deliverer of the Jewish nation prophesied in the Hebrew Bible. ■ Jesus regarded by Christians as the Messiah of the Hebrew prophecies and the savior of humankind.
2 a leader or savior of a particular group or cause: *he was regarded as a messiah by liberal and conservatives alike.*
– DERIVATIVES **mes·si·ah·ship** /-ˌSHip/ **n.**
– ORIGIN Old English *Messias*: via late Latin and Greek from Hebrew *māšīaḥ* 'anointed.'

mes·si·an·ic /ˌmesēˈanik/ ▶ **adj.** (also **Messianic**) of or relating to the Messiah: *the messianic role of Jesus.* ■ inspired by hope or belief in a messiah: *the messianic expectations of that time.* ■ fervent or passionate: *an admirable messianic zeal.*
– DERIVATIVES **mes·si·a·nism** /ˈmesēəˌnizəm, məˈsīə-/ **n.**
– ORIGIN mid 19th cent.: from French *messianique*, from *Messie* (see **MESSIAH**), on the pattern of *rabbinique* 'rabbinical.'

Mes·si·dor /ˌmesiˈdôr/ ▶ **n.** the tenth month of the French Republican calendar (1793–1805), originally running from June 19 to July 18.
– ORIGIN French, from Latin *messis* 'harvest' + Greek *dōron* 'gift.'

Mes·sier /ˈmesēˌā, mesˈyā/, Charles (1730–1817), French astronomer. He discovered a number of nebulae, galaxies, and star clusters, which he designated by M numbers.

Mes·sieurs /məsˈyœ(r)(z), mās-, məˈsi(ə)r(z)/ plural form of **MONSIEUR**.

Mes·si·na /məˈsēnə/ a city in northeastern Sicily, on the Strait of Messina; pop. 243,381 (2008).

Mes·si·na, Strait of a channel that separates the island of Sicily from the "toe" of Italy. It forms a link between the Tyrrhenian and Ionian seas. The strait, which is 20 miles (32 km) long, is noted for the strength of its currents.

mess jacket ▶ **n.** a short jacket worn by a military officer on formal occasions.

mess kit ▶ **n.** a set of cooking and eating utensils, as used esp. by soldiers, scouts, or campers.

mess·mate /ˈmesˌmāt/ ▶ **n.** a person with whom one takes meals, esp. in the armed forces.

Messrs. ▶ **plural n.** dated or chiefly Brit. used as a title to refer formally to more than one man simultaneously, or in names of companies: *Messrs. Sotheby.*
– ORIGIN late 18th cent.: abbreviation of **MESSIEURS**.

mes·suage /ˈmeswij/ ▶ **n.** Law a dwelling house with outbuildings and land assigned to its use.
– ORIGIN late Middle English: from Anglo-Norman French, based on Latin *manere* 'dwell.'

mess·y /ˈmesē/ ▶ **adj.** (**messier, messiest**) **1** untidy or dirty: *his messy hair.* ■ generating or involving mess or untidiness: *stripping wallpaper can be a messy job.*
2 (of a situation) confused and difficult to deal with: *a messy divorce.*
– DERIVATIVES **mess·i·ly** /ˈmesəlē/ **adv.**, **mess·i·ness n.**

mes·ti·za /məˈstēzə/ ▶ **n.** (in Latin America) a woman of mixed race, esp. the offspring of a Spaniard and an American Indian.
– ORIGIN Spanish, feminine of *mestizo* (see **MESTIZO**).

mes·ti·zo /me'stēzō/ ▸ **n.** (pl. **mestizos**) (in Latin America) a man of mixed race, esp. the offspring of a Spaniard and an American Indian.
– ORIGIN Spanish, 'mixed,' based on Latin *mixtus*.

Met /met/ ▸ **abbr.** (**the Met**) informal ■ the Metropolitan Opera House in New York City. ■ the Metropolitan Museum of Art in New York City.

met /met/ past and past participle of MEET[1].

met. ▸ **abbr.** ■ metaphor. ■ metaphysics. ■ meteorology. ■ metropolitan.

met- ▸ **comb. form** variant spelling of META- shortened before a vowel or *h* (as in *metonym*).

met·a /'metə/ ▸ **n.** short for META KEY.
▸ **adj.** (of a creative work) referring to itself or to the conventions of its genre; self-referential.
– ORIGIN 1980s: from *meta-* in the sense 'beyond.'

meta- (also **met-** before a vowel or h) ▸ **comb. form**
1 denoting a change of position or condition: *metamorphosis* | *metathesis*.
2 denoting position behind, after, or beyond: *metacarpus*.
3 denoting something of a higher or second-order kind: *metalanguage* | *metonym*.
4 Chemistry denoting substitution at two carbon atoms separated by one other in a benzene ring, e.g., in 1,3 positions: *metadichlorobenzene*. Compare with ORTHO- and PARA-[1].
5 Chemistry denoting a compound formed by dehydration: *metaphosphoric acid*.
– ORIGIN from Greek *meta* 'with, across, after.'

met·a·bol·ic path·way /'metə'bälik/ ▸ **n.** see PATHWAY.

me·tab·o·lism /mə'tabə,lizəm/ ▸ **n.** the chemical processes that occur within a living organism in order to maintain life.

> Two kinds of metabolism are often distinguished: **constructive metabolism**, the synthesis of the proteins, carbohydrates, and fats that form tissue and store energy, and **destructive metabolism**, the breakdown of complex substances and the consequent production of energy and waste matter.

– DERIVATIVES **met·a·bol·ic** /'metə'bälik/ **adj.**, **met·a·bol·i·cal·ly** /,metə'bälik(ə)lē/ **adv.**
– ORIGIN late 19th cent.: from Greek *metabolē* 'change' (from *metaballein* 'to change') + -ISM.

me·tab·o·lite /mə'tabə,līt/ ▸ **n.** Biochemistry a substance formed in or necessary for metabolism.

me·tab·o·lize /mə'tabə,līz/ ▸ **v.** [with obj.] (of a body or organ) process (a substance) by metabolism. ■ [no obj.] (of a substance) undergo processing by metabolism: *the refined foods soon metabolize*.
– DERIVATIVES **me·tab·o·liz·a·ble adj.**, **me·tab·o·liz·er n.**

met·a·car·pal /'metə'kärpəl/ ▸ **n.** any of the five bones of the hand. ■ any of the equivalent bones in an animal's forelimb.
▸ **adj.** of or relating to these bones.

met·a·car·pus /'metə,kärpəs/ ▸ **n.** (pl. **metacarpi** /-pē, -,pī/) the group of five bones of the hand between the wrist (carpus) and the fingers.
– ORIGIN late Middle English: modern Latin, alteration of Greek *metakarpion*.

met·a·cen·ter /'metə,sentər/ (Brit. **metacentre**) ▸ **n.** the point of intersection between a vertical line through the center of buoyancy of a floating body such as a ship and a vertical line through the new center of buoyancy when the body is tilted, which must be above the center of gravity to ensure stability.
– DERIVATIVES **met·a·cen·tric** /,metə'sentrik/ **adj.**
– ORIGIN late 18th cent.: from French *métacentre* (see META-, CENTER).

met·a·chro·ma·sia /,metəkrō'māzh(ē)ə/ (also **metachromasy** /-'krōməsē/) ▸ **n.** Biology the property of certain biological materials of staining a different color from that of the stain used. ■ the property of certain stains of changing color in the presence of certain biological materials.
– DERIVATIVES **met·a·chro·mat·ic** /-krō'matik/ **adj.**
– ORIGIN early 20th cent.: modern Latin, from META- (expressing change) + Greek *khrōma* 'color.'

met·a·cog·ni·tion /,metə,käg'nishən/ ▸ **n.** Psychology awareness and understanding of one's own thought processes.
– DERIVATIVES **met·a·cog·ni·tive** /-'kägnətiv/ **adj.**

Met·a·com·et /,metə'kämit/ see PHILIP[4].

met·a·da·ta /'metə,datə, -,dātə/ ▸ **n.** a set of data that describes and gives information about other data.

met·a·fic·tion /'metə,fikshən/ ▸ **n.** fiction in which the author self-consciously alludes to the artificiality or literariness of a work by parodying or departing from novelistic conventions (esp. naturalism) and traditional narrative techniques.
– DERIVATIVES **met·a·fic·tion·al** /,metə'fikshənl/ **adj.**

met·a·file /'metə,fīl/ ▸ **n.** Computing a piece of graphical information stored in a format that can be exchanged between different systems or software.

met·age /'metij/ ▸ **n.** the official weighing of loads of coal, grain, or other material. ■ the duty paid for this.
– ORIGIN early 16th cent.: from METE[1] + -AGE.

met·a·gen·e·sis /,metə'jenəsis/ ▸ **n.** Biology the alternation of generations between sexual and asexual reproduction.
– ORIGIN late 19th cent.: modern Latin.

Met·air·ie /'metərē/ a community in southeastern Louisiana, northwest of New Orleans; pop. 146,136 (2000).

met·a key ▸ **n.** Computing a function key on a keyboard that is activated by simultaneously holding down a control key.

met·al /'metl/ ▸ **n. 1** a solid material that is typically hard, shiny, malleable, fusible, and ductile, with good electrical and thermal conductivity (e.g., iron, gold, silver, copper, and aluminum, and alloys such as brass and steel): *vessels made of ceramics or metal* | *being a metal, aluminum readily conducts heat*. ■ Heraldry gold and silver (as tinctures in blazoning).
2 Brit. (also **road metal**) broken stone for use in making roads.
3 molten glass before it is blown or cast.
4 heavy metal or similar rock music.
▸ **v.** (**metals, metaling, metaled**; chiefly Brit. **metals, metalling, metalled**) [with obj.] (usu. as adj. **metaled**)
1 make out of or coat with metal: *metaled key rings*.
2 Brit. make or mend (a road) with road metal: *follow the metalled road for about 200 yards*.
– ORIGIN Middle English: from Old French *metal* or Latin *metallum*, from Greek *metallon* 'mine, quarry, or metal.'

metal. (also **metall.**) ▸ **abbr.** metallurgical or metallurgy.

met·a·lan·guage /'metə,laNG(g)wij/ ▸ **n.** a form of language or set of terms used for the description or analysis of another language. Compare with OBJECT LANGUAGE (sense 1). ■ Logic a system of propositions about propositions.

met·al de·tec·tor ▸ **n.** an electronic device that gives an audible or other signal when it is close to metal, used for example to search for buried objects or to detect hidden weapons.

met·al·flake /'metl,flāk/ ▸ **n.** [usu. as modifier] a metalized film added to paint to increase protection against rust.
– ORIGIN 1950s: from *Metalflake*, a trademark.

met·al·head /'metl,hed/ ▸ **n.** informal another term for HEADBANGER.

met·a·lin·guis·tics /,metə,liNG'gwistiks/ ▸ **plural n.** [treated as sing.] the branch of linguistics that deals with metalanguages, self-reference in language, and the philosophy of science as it applies to linguistics.
– DERIVATIVES **met·a·lin·guis·tic adj.**

met·al·ize /'metl,īz/ (also **metallize**) ▸ **v.** [with obj.] coat with a thin layer of metal. ■ make metallic in form or appearance.
– DERIVATIVES **met·al·i·za·tion** /,metlə'zāshən/ **n.**

metall. ▸ **abbr.** variant spelling of METAL.

me·tal·lic /mə'talik/ ▸ **adj.** of, relating to, or resembling metal or metals: *metallic alloys* | *a curious metallic taste*. ■ (of sound) resembling that produced by metal objects striking each other; sharp and ringing: *the terrifying, metallic clamor of the fire-engine bell*. ■ (of a person's voice); emanating or as if emanating via an electronic medium: *a metallic voice rasped tinnily from a concealed speaker*. ■ having the sheen or luster of metal: *a metallic green sports car*.
▸ **n.** a paint, fiber, fabric, or color with a metallic sheen: *dresses that shine with sequins and metallics*.
– DERIVATIVES **me·tal·li·cal·ly** /-ik(ə)lē/ **adv.**
– ORIGIN late Middle English: via Latin from Greek *metallikos*, from *metallon* (see METAL).

met·al·lic·i·ty /,metl'isətē/ ▸ **n.** (pl. **metallicities**) the property of being metallic. ■ Astronomy the proportion of the material of a star or other celestial object that is in elements other than hydrogen or helium.

met·al·lif·er·ous /,metl'ifərəs/ ▸ **adj.** (chiefly of deposits of minerals) containing or producing metal.
– ORIGIN mid 17th cent.: from Latin *metallifer* 'metal-bearing' + -OUS.

met·al·line /'metl,īn/ ▸ **adj.** rare metallic.

me·tal·lo·gen·ic /mə,talə'jenik/ ▸ **adj.** Geology of or relating to the formation or occurrence of deposits of metals or their ores.

met·al·log·ra·phy /,metl'ägrəfē/ ▸ **n.** the descriptive science of the structure and properties of metals.
– DERIVATIVES **met·al·log·ra·pher** /-fər/ **n.**, **me·tal·lo·graph·ic** /'metl-ə'grafik/ **adj.**, **me·tal·lo·graph·i·cal** /,metl-ə'grafikəl/ **adj.**, **me·tal·lo·graph·i·cal·ly** /,metl-ə'grafik(ə)lē/ **adv.**

met·al·loid /'metl,oid/ ▸ **n.** Chemistry an element (e.g., germanium or silicon) whose properties are intermediate between those of metals and solid nonmetals. They are electrical semiconductors.

met·al·lur·gy /'metl,ərjē/ ▸ **n.** the branch of science and technology concerned with the properties of metals and their production and purification.
– DERIVATIVES **met·al·lur·gic** /,metl'ərjik/ **adj.**, **met·al·lur·gi·cal adj.**, **met·al·lur·gi·cal·ly adv.**, **met·al·lur·gist n.**
– ORIGIN early 18th cent.: from Greek *metallon* 'metal' + *-ourgia* 'working.'

met·al·mark /'metl,märk/ ▸ **n.** a butterfly with brilliant metallic markings on the wings, found chiefly in tropical America. ● Family Riodinidae: several genera.

met·al·ware /'metl,we(ə)r/ ▸ **n.** utensils or other articles made of metal.

met·al·work /'metl,wərk/ ▸ **n.** the art of making things out of metal. ■ metal objects collectively: *a wealth of fine metalwork, including a sword*. ■ the metal part of a construction: *engineers spotted cracks in the metalwork*.
– DERIVATIVES **met·al·work·er n.**, **met·al·work·ing n.**

met·a·math·e·mat·ics /,metə,math(ə)'matiks/ ▸ **plural n.** [usu. treated as sing.] the field of study that deals with the structure and formal properties of mathematics and similar formal systems.
– DERIVATIVES **met·a·math·e·mat·i·cal** /-'matikəl/ **adj.**, **met·a·math·e·ma·ti·cian** /-mə'tishən/ **n.**

met·a·mere /'metəmi(ə)r/ ▸ **n.** Zoology another term for SOMITE.
– ORIGIN late 19th cent.: from META- 'together with' + Greek *meros* 'part.'

met·a·mer·ic /,metə'merik/ ▸ **adj. 1** Zoology of, relating to, or consisting of several similar segments or somites.
2 Chemistry, dated having the same proportional composition and molecular weight, but different functional groups and chemical properties; isomeric.
– DERIVATIVES **met·a·mer** /'metəmər/ **n.**, **me·tam·er·ism** /mə'tamə,rizəm/ **n.**

met·a·mes·sage /'metə,mesij/ ▸ **n.** an underlying meaning or implicit message, esp. in advertising.

met·a·mor·phic /'metə'môrfik/ ▸ **adj. 1** Geology denoting rock that has undergone transformation by heat, pressure, or other natural agencies, e.g., in the folding of strata or the nearby intrusion of igneous rocks.
2 of or marked by metamorphosis: *the shift from dead stillness to hurricane-force winds was as metamorphic as Jekyll to Hyde*.
– ORIGIN early 19th cent.: from META- (denoting a change of condition) + Greek *morphē* 'form' + -IC.

met·a·mor·phism /'metə'môr,fizəm/ ▸ **n.** Geology alteration of the composition or structure of a rock by heat, pressure, or other natural agency.

met·a·mor·phose /,metə'môr,fōz, -,fōs/ ▸ **v.** [no obj.] (of an insect or amphibian) undergo metamorphosis, esp. into the adult form: *feed the larvae to your fish before they metamorphose into adults*. ■ change or cause to change completely in form or nature: *a father seeing his daughter metamorphosing from girl into woman*. ■ [with obj.] Geology subject (rock) to metamorphism: (as adj. **metamorphosed**) *a metamorphosed sandstone*.
– ORIGIN late 16th cent.: from French *métamorphoser*, from *métamorphose* (see METAMORPHOSIS).

met·a·mor·pho·sis /,metə'môrfəsəs/ ▸ **n.** (pl. **metamorphoses** /-fə,sēz/) Zoology (in an insect or amphibian) the process of transformation from an immature form to an adult form in two or more distinct stages. ■ a change of the form or nature of a thing or person into a completely different one, by natural or supernatural means: *his metamorphosis from presidential candidate to talk-show host*.
– ORIGIN late Middle English: via Latin from Greek *metamorphōsis*, from *metamorphoun* 'transform, change shape.'

met·a·noi·a /,metə'noiə/ ▸ **n.** change in one's way of life resulting from penitence or spiritual conversion.
– ORIGIN late 19th cent.: from Greek, from *metanoein* 'change one's mind.'

met·a·phase /'metə,fāz/ ▸ **n.** Biology the second stage of cell division, between prophase and anaphase,

m

during which the chromosomes become attached to the spindle fibers.

met·a·phor /ˈmetəˌfôr, -fər/ ▶ **n.** a figure of speech in which a word or phrase is applied to an object or action to which it is not literally applicable: *"I had fallen through a trapdoor of depression," said Mark, who was fond of theatrical metaphors | her poetry depends on suggestion and metaphor.* ■ a thing regarded as representative or symbolic of something else, esp. something abstract: *the amounts of money being lost by the company were enough to make it a metaphor for an industry that was teetering.*
– DERIVATIVES **met·a·phor·ic** /ˌmetəˈfôrik/ **adj.**
– ORIGIN late 15th cent.: from French *métaphore*, via Latin from Greek *metaphora*, from *metapherein* 'to transfer.'

met·a·phor·i·cal /ˌmetəˈfôrikəl/ ▶ **adj.** characteristic of or relating to metaphor; figurative: *many of our metaphorical expressions develop from our perceptions of the body.*
– DERIVATIVES **met·a·phor·i·cal·ly** /ˌmetəˈfôrik(ə)lē/ **adv.**

met·a·phos·phor·ic ac·id /ˌmetəˌfäsˈfôrik/ ▶ **n.** Chemistry a glassy deliquescent solid obtained by heating orthophosphoric acid. ● A polymer; chem. formula $(HPO_3)_n$.
– DERIVATIVES **met·a·phos·phate** /-ˈfäsˌfāt/ **n.**

met·a·phrase /ˈmetəˌfrāz/ ▶ **n.** a literal, word-for-word translation, as opposed to a paraphrase.
▶ **v.** [with obj.] alter the phrasing or language of.
– DERIVATIVES **met·a·phras·tic** /ˌmetəˈfrastik/ **adj.**
– ORIGIN early 17th cent. (denoting a metrical translation): from Greek *metaphrazein*, literally 'word differently.'

met·a·phys·ic /ˌmetəˈfizik/ ▶ **n.** a system of metaphysics.

met·a·phys·i·cal /ˌmetəˈfizikəl/ ▶ **adj.** **1** of or relating to metaphysics: *the essentially metaphysical question of the nature of the mind.* ■ based on abstract (typically, excessively abstract) reasoning: *an empiricist rather than a metaphysical view of law.* ■ transcending physical matter or the laws of nature: *Good and Evil are inextricably linked in a metaphysical battle across space and time.*
2 of or characteristic of the metaphysical poets.
▶ **n.** (**the Metaphysicals**) the metaphysical poets.
– DERIVATIVES **met·a·phys·i·cal·ly** /-ik(ə)lē/ **adv.**

m

met·a·phys·i·cal po·ets a group of 17th-century poets whose work is characterized by the use of complex and elaborate images or conceits, typically using an intellectual form of argumentation to express emotional states. Members of the group include John Donne, George Herbert, Henry Vaughan, and Andrew Marvell.

met·a·phys·ics /ˌmetəˈfiziks/ ▶ **plural n.** [usu. treated as sing.] the branch of philosophy that deals with the first principles of things, including abstract concepts such as being, knowing, substance, cause, identity, time, and space. ■ abstract theory or talk with no basis in reality: *his concept of society as an organic entity is, for market liberals, simply metaphysics.*

> Metaphysics has two main strands: that which holds that what exists lies beyond experience (as argued by Plato), and that which holds that objects of experience constitute the only reality (as argued by Kant, the logical positivists, and Hume). Metaphysics has also concerned itself with a discussion of whether what exists is made of one substance or many, and whether what exists is inevitable or driven by chance.

– DERIVATIVES **met·a·phy·si·cian** /-fəˈzisHən/ **n.**
– ORIGIN mid 16th cent.: representing medieval Latin *metaphysica* (neuter plural), based on Greek *ta meta ta phusika* 'the things after the Physics,' referring to the sequence of Aristotle's works: the title came to denote the branch of study treated in the books, later interpreted as meaning 'the science of things transcending what is physical or natural.'

met·a·pla·sia /ˌmetəˈplāzH(ē)ə/ ▶ **n.** Physiology abnormal change in the nature of a tissue.
– DERIVATIVES **met·a·plas·tic** /-ˈplastik/ **adj.**
– ORIGIN late 19th cent.: modern Latin, from German *Metaplase*, based on Greek *metaplassein* 'mold into a new form.'

met·a·psy·chol·o·gy /ˈmetəˌsīˈkäləjē/ ▶ **n.** speculation concerning mental processes and the mind–body relationship, beyond what can be studied experimentally.
– DERIVATIVES **met·a·psy·cho·log·i·cal** /-ˌsīkəˈläjikəl/ **adj.**

Me·ta Riv·er /ˈmātə/ a river that flows northeast for 650 miles (1,050 km) from central Colombia into the Orinoco River and that forms part of the Colombia-Venezuela boundary.

met·a·rule /ˈmetəˌrool/ ▶ **n.** a rule governing the content, form, or application of other rules: *three particular metarules of international law provide especially weak support.*

met·a·se·quoi·a /ˌmetəsiˈkwoiə/ ▶ **n.** another term for **DAWN REDWOOD**.

met·a·so·ma·tism /ˌmetəˈsōməˌtizəm/ ▶ **n.** Geology change in the composition of a rock as a result of the introduction or removal of chemical constituents.
– DERIVATIVES **met·a·so·mat·ic** /-səˈmatik/ **adj.**, **met·a·so·ma·tize** /-ˈsōməˌtīz/ **v.**
– ORIGIN late 19th cent.: from **META-** (expressing change) + Greek *sōma, somat-* 'body' + **-ISM**.

met·a·sta·ble /ˈmetəˌstābəl, ˌmetəˈstābəl/ ▶ **adj.** Physics (of a state of equilibrium) stable provided it is subjected to no more than small disturbances. ■ (of a substance or particle) theoretically unstable but so long-lived as to be stable for practical purposes.
– DERIVATIVES **met·a·sta·bil·i·ty** /-stəˈbilətē/ **n.**

me·tas·ta·sis /məˈtastəsəs/ ▶ **n.** (pl. **metastases** /-ˌsēz/) Medicine the development of secondary malignant growths at a distance from a primary site of cancer. ■ a growth of this type.
– DERIVATIVES **met·a·stat·ic** /ˌmetəˈstatik/ **adj.**
– ORIGIN late 16th cent. (as a rhetorical term, meaning 'rapid transition from one point to another'): from Greek, literally 'removal or change,' from *methistanai* 'to change.'

me·tas·ta·size /məˈtastəˌsīz/ ▶ **v.** [no obj.] Medicine (of a cancer) spread to other sites in the body by metastasis: *cancers that metastasize to the brain.*

met·a·tar·sal /ˌmetəˈtärsəl/ ▶ **n.** any of the bones of the foot (metatarsus). ■ any of the equivalent bones in an animal's hind limb.

met·a·tar·sus /ˌmetəˈtärsəs/ ▶ **n.** (pl. **metatarsi** /-sē, -ˌsī/) the group of bones in the foot, between the ankle and the toes. ■ this part of the foot.
– ORIGIN late Middle English: modern Latin (see **META-**, **TARSUS**).

me·ta·te /məˈtätā/ (also **metate stone**) ▶ **n.** (in Central America) a flat or slightly hollowed oblong stone on which materials such as grain and cocoa are ground using a smaller stone.
– ORIGIN from American Spanish, from Nahuatl *métatl*.

Met·a·the·ri·a /ˌmetəˈTHi(ə)rēə/ Zoology a group of mammals that comprises the marsupials. Compare with **EUTHERIA**. ● Infraclass Metatheria, subclass Theria.
– ORIGIN modern Latin (plural), from **META-** (expressing change) + Greek *thēria*, plural of *thērion* 'wild animal.'

met·a·the·ri·an /ˌmetəˈTHi(ə)rēən/ Zoology ▶ **n.** a mammal of the group Metatheria; a marsupial.
▶ **adj.** relating to or denoting metatherians.

me·tath·e·sis /məˈtaTHəsəs/ ▶ **n.** (pl. **metatheses** /-ˌsēz/) **1** Grammar the transposition of sounds or letters in a word.
2 (also **metathesis reaction**) Chemistry a reaction in which two compounds exchange ions, typically with precipitation of an insoluble product. Also called **DOUBLE DECOMPOSITION**.
– DERIVATIVES **met·a·thet·ic** /ˌmetəˈTHetik/ **adj.**, **met·a·thet·i·cal** /ˌmetəˈTHetikəl/ **adj.**
– ORIGIN late 16th cent.: from Greek, from *metatithenai* 'transpose, change the position of.'

met·a·tho·rax /ˌmetəˈTHôrˌaks/ ▶ **n.** (pl. **metathoraxes** or **metathoraces** /-ˈTHôrəˌsēz/) Entomology the posterior segment of the thorax of an insect, bearing the hind wings.
– DERIVATIVES **met·a·tho·rac·ic** /-THəˈrasik/ **adj.**

met·a·verse /ˈmetəˌvərs/ ▶ **n.** Computing a virtual-reality space in which users can interact with a computer-generated environment and other users.
– ORIGIN 1990s: blend of **META-** (sense 3) and **UNIVERSE**.

Met·a·zo·a /ˌmetəˈzōə/ Zoology a major division of the animal kingdom that comprises all animals other than protozoans and sponges. They are multicellular animals with differentiated tissues. ● Subkingdom Metazoa, kingdom Animalia. ■ (as plural noun **metazoa**) animals of this division.
– ORIGIN modern Latin (plural), from **META-** (expressing change) + *zōia* (plural of *zōion* 'animal').

met·a·zo·an /ˌmetəˈzōən/ Zoology ▶ **n.** an animal of the Metazoa division.
▶ **adj.** relating to or denoting metazoans.

mete[1] /mēt/ ▶ **v.** [with obj.] (**mete something out**) dispense or allot justice, a punishment, or harsh treatment: *he denounced the maltreatment meted out to minorities.* ■ (in biblical use) measure out: *with what measure ye mete, it shall be measured to you again.*
– ORIGIN Old English *metan* 'measure, determine the quantity of,' of Germanic origin; related to Dutch *meten* and German *messen* 'to measure,' from an Indo-European root shared by Latin *meditari* 'meditate,' Greek *medesthai* 'care for,' also by **MEET**[2].

mete[2] ▶ **n.** (usu. **metes and bounds**) chiefly historical a boundary or boundary stone.
– ORIGIN late Middle English: from Old French, from Latin *meta* 'boundary, goal.'

me·tem·psy·cho·sis /ˌmetəmˌsīˈkōsəs, məˌtemsīˈkōsəs/ ▶ **n.** (pl. **metempsychoses** /-sēz/) the supposed transmigration at death of the soul of a human being or animal into a new body of the same or a different species.
– DERIVATIVES **me·tem·psy·chot·ic** /-ˈkätik/ **adj.**, **me·tem·psy·chot·i·cal·ly** /-ˈkätik(ə)lē/ **adv.**, **me·tem·psy·cho·sist** /-ˈkōsist/ **n.**
– ORIGIN late 16th cent.: via late Latin from Greek *metempsukhōsis*, from *meta-* (expressing change) + *en* 'in' + *psukhē* 'soul.'

me·te·or /ˈmētēər, -ēˌôr/ ▶ **n.** a small body of matter from outer space that enters the earth's atmosphere, becoming incandescent as a result of friction and appearing as a streak of light.
– ORIGIN mid 16th cent. (denoting any atmospheric phenomenon): from modern Latin *meteorum*, from Greek *meteōron*, neuter (used as a noun) of *meteōros* 'lofty.'

meteor. ▶ **abbr.** ■ meteorological. ■ meteorology.

me·te·or·ic /ˌmētēˈôrik/ ▶ **adj.** **1** of or relating to meteors or meteorites: *meteoric iron.* ■ (of the development of something, esp. a person's career) very rapid: *her meteoric rise to the top of her profession.*
2 chiefly Geology relating to or denoting water derived from the atmosphere by precipitation or condensation.
– DERIVATIVES **me·te·or·i·cal·ly** /-ik(ə)lē/ **adv.**

me·te·or·ite /ˈmētēəˌrīt/ ▶ **n.** a meteor that survives its passage through the earth's atmosphere such that part of it strikes the ground. More than 90 percent of meteorites are of rock, while the remainder consist wholly or partly of iron and nickel.
– DERIVATIVES **me·te·or·it·ic** /ˈˌmētēəˈritik/ **adj.**

me·te·or·o·graph /ˌmētēˈôrəˌgraf/ ▶ **n.** archaic an apparatus that records several meteorological phenomena at the same time.
– ORIGIN late 18th cent.: from French *météorographe* (see **METEOR**, **-GRAPH**).

me·te·or·oid /ˈmētēəˌroid/ ▶ **n.** Astronomy a small body moving in the solar system that would become a meteor if it entered the earth's atmosphere.
– DERIVATIVES **me·te·o·roid·al** /ˌmētēəˈroidl/ **adj.**

me·te·or·ol·o·gist /ˌmētēəˈräləjist/ ▶ **n.** an expert in or student of meteorology; a weather forecaster: *meteorologists predict rain for the rest of the week.*

me·te·or·ol·o·gy /ˌmētēəˈräləjē/ ▶ **n.** the branch of science concerned with the processes and phenomena of the atmosphere, esp. as a means of forecasting the weather. ■ the climate and weather of a region.
– DERIVATIVES **me·te·or·o·log·i·cal** /-rəˈläjikəl/ **adj.**, **me·te·or·o·log·i·cal·ly** /-rəˈläjik(ə)lē/ **adv.**
– ORIGIN early 17th cent.: from Greek *meteōrologia*, from *meteōron* 'of the atmosphere' (see **METEOR**).

me·te·or show·er ▶ **n.** Astronomy a number of meteors that appear to radiate from one point in the sky at a particular date each year, due to the earth's regularly passing through a field of particles at that position in its orbit. Meteor showers are named after the constellation in which the radiant is situated, e.g., the Perseids.

me·ter[1] /ˈmētər/ (Brit. **metre**) ▶ **n.** the fundamental unit of length in the metric system, equal to 100 centimeters or approximately 39.37 inches. ■ (**— meters**) a race over a specified number of meters: *he placed third in the 1,000 meters.*
– DERIVATIVES **me·ter·age** /-ij/ **n.**
– ORIGIN late 18th cent.: from French *mètre*, from Greek *metron* 'measure.'

me·ter[2] (Brit. **metre**) ▶ **n.** the rhythm of a piece of poetry, determined by the number and length of feet in a line: *the Horatian ode has an intricate governing meter | unexpected changes of stress and meter.* ■ the basic pulse and rhythm of a piece of music.
– ORIGIN Old English, reinforced in Middle English by Old French *metre*, from Latin *metrum*, from Greek *metron* 'measure.'

me·ter[3] ▶ **n.** a device that measures and records the quantity, degree, or rate of something, esp. the amount of electricity, gas, or water used: *they read the meters once a month.* ■ Philately an imprint or label of specified value produced under government permit for the prepayment of postage.
▶ **v.** [with obj.] (often as adj. **metered**) measure by means of a meter: *a metered supply of water.*
– ORIGIN Middle English (in the sense 'person who measures'): from **METE**[1] + **-ER**[1]. The current sense dates from the 19th cent.

-meter ▶ comb. form **1** in names of measuring instruments: *thermometer*.
2 Prosody in nouns denoting lines of poetry with a specified number of feet or measures: *hexameter*.
– ORIGIN from Greek *metron* 'measure.'

me·ter-kil·o·gram-sec·ond (abbr.: **mks**) ▶ adj. denoting a system of measure using the meter, kilogram, and second as the basic units of length, mass, and time.

meth /meTH/ ▶ n. informal **1** (also **crystal meth**) the drug methamphetamine.
2 short for METHADONE.

meth·a·cryl·ic ac·id /ˌmeTHəˈkrilik/ ▶ n. Chemistry a colorless, low-melting solid that polymerizes when distilled and is used in the manufacture of synthetic resins. ● Alternative name: **1-methylacrylic acid**; chem. formula: $CH_2 \colon C(CH_3)COOH$.
– DERIVATIVES **meth·ac·ry·late** /meTHˈakrəˌlāt/ n.

meth·a·done /ˈmeTHəˌdōn/ ▶ n. a synthetic analgesic drug that is similar to morphine in its effects but longer acting, used as a substitute drug in the treatment of morphine and heroin addiction.
– ORIGIN 1940s: from its chemical name, *(6-di) meth(yl)a(mino-4,4-)d(iphenyl-3-heptan)one*.

meth·am·phet·a·mine /ˌmeTHəmˈfetəˌmēn, -min/ ▶ n. a synthetic drug with more rapid and lasting effects than amphetamine, used illegally as a stimulant and as a prescription drug to treat narcolepsy and maintain blood pressure. ● A methyl derivative of amphetamine; chem. formula $C_6H_5CH_2CH(CH_3)NH(CH_3)$.

meth·a·nal /ˈmeTHəˌnal/ ▶ n. systematic chemical name for FORMALDEHYDE.
– ORIGIN late 19th cent.: blend of METHANE and ALDEHYDE.

meth·ane /ˈmeTHˌān/ ▶ n. Chemistry a colorless, odorless flammable gas that is the main constituent of natural gas. It is the simplest member of the alkane series of hydrocarbons. ● Chem. formula: CH_4.
– ORIGIN mid 19th cent.: from METHYL + -ANE².

meth·an·o·gen /ˈmeTHənəjən/ ▶ n. Biology a methane-producing bacterium, esp. an archaean that reduces carbon dioxide to methane.
– DERIVATIVES **meth·an·o·gen·ic** /ˌmeTHənəˈjenik/ adj.

meth·a·no·ic ac·id /ˌmeTHəˈnōik/ ▶ n. systematic chemical name for FORMIC ACID.
– ORIGIN late 19th cent.: *methanoic*, from METHANE + *-oic* (perhaps on the pattern of *benzoic*).

meth·a·nol /ˈmeTHəˌnôl, -ˌnōl/ ▶ n. Chemistry a toxic, colorless, volatile flammable liquid alcohol, originally made by distillation from wood and now chiefly by oxidizing methane. Also called METHYL ALCOHOL. ● Chem. formula: CH_3OH.
– ORIGIN late 19th cent.: from METHANE + -OL.

me·thaq·ua·lone /məˈTHakwəˌlōn/ ▶ n. a sedative and sleep-inducing drug. Also called QUAALUDE (trademark).
– ORIGIN 1960s: from elements of its chemical name *meth-* + *-a-* + *qu(inine)* + *a(zo-* + *-o)l* + *-one*.

meth·e·drine /ˈmeTHəˌdrēn, -drin/ (also **Methedrine**) ▶ n. trademark another term for METHAMPHETAMINE.
– ORIGIN 1930s: blend of METHYL and BENZEDRINE.

me·theg·lin /məˈTHeglən/ ▶ n. historical a spiced or medicated variety of mead, associated particularly with Wales.
– ORIGIN mid 16th cent.: from Welsh *meddyglyn*, from *meddyg* 'medicinal' (from Latin *medicus*) + *llyn* 'liquor.'

meth·e·mo·glo·bin /metˈhēməˌglōbən/ (Brit. **methaemoglobin**) ▶ n. Biochemistry a stable oxidized form of hemoglobin that is unable to release oxygen to the tissues, produced in some inherited abnormalities and by oxidizing drugs.

met·he·mo·glo·bi·ne·mi·a /ˌmetˌhēməˌglōbəˈnēmēə/ (Brit. **methaemoglobinaemia**) ▶ n. Medicine the presence of methemoglobin in the blood.

meth·i·cil·lin /ˌmeTHəˈsilən/ ▶ n. Medicine a semisynthetic form of penicillin used against staphylococci that produce penicillinase.
– ORIGIN 1960s: from *meth(yl)* and *(pen)icillin*.

me·thinks /miˈTHiNGks/ ▶ v. (past **methought** /miˈTHôt/) [no obj.] archaic or humorous it seems to me: *life has been rather hard on her, methinks* | [with clause] *methought you knew all about it*.
– ORIGIN Old English *mē thyncth*, from *mē* 'to me' + *thyncth* 'it seems' (from *thyncan* 'seem,' related to, but distinct from, THINK).

me·thi·o·nine /məˈTHīəˌnēn/ ▶ n. Biochemistry a sulfur-containing amino acid that is a constituent of most proteins. It is an essential nutrient in the diet of vertebrates. ● Chem. formula: $CH_3S(CH_2)_2CH(NH_2)COOH$.
– ORIGIN 1920s: from METHYL + Greek *theion* 'sulfur.'

meth·od /ˈmeTHəd/ ▶ n. (often **method for/of**) a particular form of procedure for accomplishing or approaching something, esp. a systematic or established one: *a method for software maintenance* | *labor-intensive production methods*. ■ orderliness of thought or behavior; systematic planning or action: *historical study is the rigorous combination of knowledge and method*. ■ (often **Method**) short for METHOD ACTING.
– PHRASES **there is method in one's madness** there is a sensible foundation for what appears to be foolish or strange behavior. [from Shakespeare's *Hamlet* (II. ii. 211).]
– ORIGIN late Middle English (in the sense 'prescribed medical treatment for a disease'): via Latin from Greek *methodos* 'pursuit of knowledge,' from *meta-* (expressing development) + *hodos* 'way.'

meth·od act·ing ▶ n. a technique of acting in which an actor aspires to complete emotional identification with a part, based on the system evolved by Stanislavsky and brought into prominence in the US in the 1930s. Method acting was developed in institutions such as the Actors' Studio in New York City, notably by Elia Kazan and Lee Strasberg, and is particularly associated with actors such as Marlon Brando and Dustin Hoffman.
– DERIVATIVES **meth·od ac·tor** n.

mé·thode cham·pen·oise /māˈtōd ˌSHänpənˈwäz/ ▶ n. [often as modifier] a method of making sparkling wine by allowing the last stage of fermentation to take place in the bottle. ■ sparkling wine made in this way, esp. a kind not made in the Champagne region of France.
– ORIGIN French, literally 'champagne method.'

me·thod·i·cal /məˈTHädikəl/ ▶ adj. done according to a systematic or established form of procedure: *a methodical approach to the evaluation of computer systems*. ■ (of a person) orderly or systematic in thought or behavior.
– DERIVATIVES **me·thod·ic** adj., **me·thod·i·cal·ly** /-ik(ə)lē/ adv.
– ORIGIN late 16th cent.: via late Latin from Greek *methodikos* (from *methodos*: see METHOD) + -AL.

Meth·od·ist /ˈmeTHədəst/ ▶ n. a member of a Christian Protestant denomination originating in the 18th-century evangelistic movement of Charles and John Wesley and George Whitefield.

> The Methodist Church grew out of a religious society established within the Church of England, from which it formally separated in 1791. It is particularly strong in the US and now constitutes one of the largest Protestant denominations worldwide, with more than 30 million members. Methodism has a strong tradition of missionary work and concern with social welfare, and emphasizes the believer's personal relationship with God.

▶ adj. of or relating to Methodists or Methodism: *a Methodist chapel*.
– DERIVATIVES **Meth·od·ism** /-ˌdizəm/ n., **Meth·od·is·tic** /ˌmeTHəˈdistik/ adj., **Meth·od·is·ti·cal** /ˌmeTHəˈdistikəl/ adj.
– ORIGIN probably from the notion of following a specified "method" of Bible study.

Me·tho·di·us, St. /məˈTHōdēəs/ the brother of St. Cyril (see CYRIL, ST.).

meth·od·ize /ˈmeTHəˌdīz/ ▶ v. [with obj.] rare arrange in an orderly or systematic manner.
– DERIVATIVES **meth·od·iz·er** n.

meth·od·ol·o·gy /ˌmeTHəˈdäləjē/ ▶ n. (pl. **methodologies**) a system of methods used in a particular area of study or activity: *a methodology for investigating the concept of focal points* | *courses in research methodology and practice*.
– DERIVATIVES **meth·od·o·log·i·cal** /-dəˈläjikəl/ adj., **meth·od·o·log·i·cal·ly** /dəˈläjik(ə)lē/ adv., **meth·od·ol·o·gist** /-ˈdäləjist/ n.
– ORIGIN early 19th cent.: from modern Latin *methodologia* or French *méthodologie*.

meth·o·trex·ate /ˌmeTHəˈtrekˌsāt/ ▶ n. Medicine a synthetic compound that interferes with cell growth and is used to treat leukemia and other forms of cancer. ● Alternative name: **4-amino-10-methylfolic acid**; chem. formula: $C_{20}H_{22}N_8O_5$.
– ORIGIN 1950s: from *meth-* (denoting a substance containing methyl groups) + elements of unknown origin.

me·thought /miˈTHôt/ past of METHINKS.

Me·thu·se·lah /məˈTH(y)o͞oz(ə)lə/ (in the Bible) a patriarch, the grandfather of Noah, who is said to have lived for 969 years. ■ used to refer to a very old person: *I'm feeling older than Methuselah*.

me·thu·se·lah ▶ n. a wine bottle of eight times the standard size.
– ORIGIN 1930s: from METHUSELAH.

meth·yl /ˈmeTHəl/ ▶ n. [as modifier] Chemistry of or denoting the alkyl radical $-CH_3$, derived from methane and present in many organic compounds: *methyl bromide*.
– ORIGIN mid 19th cent.: from German *Methyl* or French *méthyle*, back-formations from German *Methylen* and French *méthylène* (see METHYLENE).

meth·yl al·co·hol ▶ n. another term for METHANOL.

meth·yl·ate /ˈmeTHəˌlāt/ ▶ v. [with obj.] (often as adj. **methylated**) mix or impregnate with methanol or methylated spirit. ■ Chemistry introduce a methyl group into (a molecule or compound).
– DERIVATIVES **meth·yl·a·tion** /ˌmeTHəˈlāSHən/ n.

meth·yl·at·ed spir·it (also **methylated spirits**) ▶ n. alcohol for general use that has been made unfit for drinking by the addition of about 10 percent methanol and typically also some pyridine and a violet dye.

meth·yl·ben·zene /ˌmeTHəlˈbenˌzēn/ ▶ n. systematic chemical name for TOLUENE.

meth·yl cy·a·nide ▶ n. another term for ACETONITRILE.

meth·yl·ene /ˈmeTHəˌlēn/ ▶ n. [as modifier] Chemistry the divalent radical or group $-CH_2-$, derived from methane by loss of two hydrogen atoms: *methylene chloride*.
– ORIGIN mid 19th cent.: from French *méthylène* (formed irregularly from Greek *methu* 'wine' + *hulē* 'wood') + -ENE.

meth·yl·phen·i·date /ˌmeTHəlˈfenəˌdāt/ ▶ n. Medicine a synthetic drug that stimulates the sympathetic and central nervous systems and is used to improve mental activity in attention deficit disorder and other conditions.

met·ic /ˈmetik/ ▶ n. a foreigner living in an ancient Greek city who had some of the privileges of citizenship.
– ORIGIN early 19th cent.: formed irregularly from Greek *metoikos*, from *meta-* (expressing change) + *oikos* 'dwelling.'

me·ti·cal /ˈmetikəl/ ▶ n. (pl. **meticais** /metiˈkīSH/) the basic monetary unit of Mozambique, equal to 100 centavos.
– ORIGIN Portuguese, based on Arabic *miṯkāl*, from *ṯakala* 'to weigh.'

me·tic·u·lous /məˈtikyələs/ ▶ adj. showing great attention to detail; very careful and precise: *he had always been so meticulous about his appearance*.
– DERIVATIVES **me·tic·u·lous·ly** adv., **me·tic·u·lous·ness** n.
– ORIGIN mid 16th cent. (in the sense 'fearful or timid'): from Latin *meticulosus*, from *metus* 'fear.' The word came to mean 'overcareful about detail,' hence the current sense (early 19th cent).

mé·tier /meˈtyā, ˈmeˌtyā/ ▶ n. a trade, profession, or occupation: *those who work honestly at their métier*. ■ an occupation or activity that one is good at: *she decided that her real métier was grand opera*. ■ an outstanding or advantageous characteristic: *subtlety is not his métier*.
– ORIGIN late 18th cent.: French, based on Latin *ministerium* 'service.'

Mé·tis /māˈtēs/ (also **Metis**) ▶ n. (pl. **same**) (esp. in western Canada) a person of mixed American Indian and Euro-American ancestry, in particular one of a group of such people who in the 19th century constituted the so-called **Métis nation** in the areas around the Red and Saskatchewan rivers.
▶ adj. denoting or relating to such people.
– ORIGIN from French, from Late Latin *mixticius*, from Latin *mixtus* 'mixed' (see also MESTIZO).

Me·tol /ˈmeˌtôl, -ˌtōl/ ▶ n. trademark a soluble white compound used as a photographic developer. ● A sulfate of 4-methylaminophenol (chem. formula: $CH_3NHC_6H_4OH$).
– ORIGIN late 19th cent.: from German, arbitrarily named by the inventor.

Me·ton·ic cy·cle /meˈtänik/ ▶ n. a period of 19 years (235 lunar months), after which the new and full moons return to the same days of the year. It was the basis of the ancient Greek calendar and is still used for calculating movable feasts such as Easter.
– ORIGIN named after *Metōn*, an Athenian astronomer of the 5th cent. BC.

met·o·nym /ˈmetəˌnim/ ▶ n. a word, name, or expression used as a substitute for something else with which it is closely associated. For example, *Washington* is a metonym for the federal government of the US.

m

PRONUNCIATION KEY ə *ago, up*; ər *over, fur*; a *hat*; ā *ate*; ä *car*; e *let*; ē *see*; i *fit*; ī *by*; NG *sing*; ō *go*; ô *law, for*; oi *toy*; o͝o *good*; o͞o *goo*; ou *out*; TH *thin*; T͟H *then*; ZH *vision*

– ORIGIN mid 19th cent.: back-formation from METONYMY.

me·ton·y·my /mə'tänəmē/ ▶ n. (pl. **metonymies**) the substitution of the name of an attribute or adjunct for that of the thing meant, for example *suit* for *business executive*, or *the track* for *horse racing*.
– DERIVATIVES **met·o·nym·ic** /ˌmetə'nimik/ **adj.**, **met·o·nym·i·cal** /ˌmetə'nimikəl/ **adj.**, **met·o·nym·i·cal·ly** /ˌmetə'nimik(ə)lē/ **adv.**
– ORIGIN mid 16th cent.: via Latin from Greek *metōnumia*, literally 'change of name.'

me-too ▶ **adj.** informal relating to the adoption or imitation of another person's views or policies, often for political advantage: *he has been a me-too liberal on many of the issues that matter most.* ■ (of a product) designed to emulate or rival another that has already been successful: *me-too drugs.*

met·o·pe /'metəpē/ ▶ **n.** Architecture a square space between triglyphs in a Doric frieze.
– ORIGIN mid 16th cent.: via Latin from Greek *metopē*, from *meta* 'between' + *opē* 'hole for a beam-end.'

me·to·pro·lol /mə'täprəˌlôl, -ˌläl/ ▶ **n.** Medicine a beta-blocking drug related to propranolol, used to treat hypertension and angina.
– ORIGIN 1970s: from *met-* (from METHYL) + *pro(prano)lol*.

me·tre ▶ **n.** British spelling of METER[1], METER[2].

met·ric[1] /'metrik/ ▶ **adj.** **1** of or based on the meter as a unit of length; relating to the metric system: *all measurements are given in metric form.* ■ using the metric system: *we should have **gone metric** years ago.* **2** Mathematics & Physics relating to or denoting a metric.
▶ **n.** **1** technical a system or standard of measurement. ■ Mathematics & Physics a binary function of a topological space that gives, for any two points of the space, a value equal to the distance between them, or to a value treated as analogous to distance for the purpose of analysis.
2 informal metric units, or the metric system: *it's easier to work in metric.*
– ORIGIN mid 19th cent. (as an adjective relating to length): from French *métrique*, from *mètre* (see METER[1]).

met·ric[2] ▶ **adj.** relating to or composed in a poetic meter.
▶ **n.** (**metrics**) [treated as sing.] the meter of a poem.
– ORIGIN late 15th cent. (denoting the branch of study dealing with meter): via Latin from Greek *metrikos*, from *metron* (see METER[2]).

-metric ▶ **comb. form** in adjectives corresponding to nouns ending in *-meter* (such as *geometric* corresponding to *geometer* and *geometry*).
– ORIGIN from French *-métrique*, from Latin (see METRIC[1]).

met·ri·cal /'metrikəl/ ▶ **adj.** **1** of, relating to, or composed in poetic meter: *metrical translations of the Psalms.*
2 of or involving measurement: *a metrical analysis of male and female scapulae.*
– DERIVATIVES **met·ri·cal·ly** /-ik(ə)lē/ **adv.**
– ORIGIN late Middle English: via Latin from Greek *metrikos* (from *metron*: see METER[2]) + -AL.

-metrical ▶ **comb. form** equivalent to -METRIC.

-metrically ▶ **comb. form** in adverbs corresponding to adjectives ending in *-meter* (such as *geometrically* corresponding to *geometric*).

met·ri·cate /'metriˌkāt/ ▶ **v.** [with obj.] change or adapt to a metric system of measurement.
– DERIVATIVES **met·ri·ca·tion** /ˌmetri'kāsHən/ **n.**

met·ric hun·dred·weight ▶ **n.** see HUNDREDWEIGHT.

met·ric mile ▶ **n.** a distance of 1,500 meters, or a race over this distance.

met·rics /'metriks/ ▶ **n.** [treated as sing. or pl.] **1** the use or study of poetic meters; prosody.
2 a method of measuring something, or the results obtained from this: *the report provides various metrics at the class and method level.*

-met·rics ▶ **comb. form** denoting the science of measuring as applied to a specific field of study: *econometrics.*

met·ric sys·tem ▶ **n.** the decimal measuring system based on the meter, liter, and gram as units of length, capacity, and weight or mass. The system was first proposed by the French astronomer and mathematician Gabriel Mouton (1618–94) in 1670 and was standardized in France under the Republican government in the 1790s.

met·ric ton (also **tonne**) ▶ **n.** a unit of weight equal to 1,000 kilograms (2,205 lb).

me·tri·tis /mi'trītəs/ ▶ **n.** Medicine inflammation of the uterus.
– ORIGIN mid 19th cent.: from Greek *mētra* 'womb' + -ITIS.

met·ro /'metrō/ ▶ **n.** (pl. **metros**) (also **Metro**) a subway system in a city, esp. Paris. ■ a subway train, esp. in Paris.
▶ **adj.** [attrib.] metropolitan: *the Detroit metro area.*
– ORIGIN early 20th cent.: from French *métro*, abbreviation of *métropolitain* (from *Chemin de Fer Métropolitain* 'Metropolitan Railroad').

me·trol·o·gy /me'träləjē/ ▶ **n.** the scientific study of measurement.
– DERIVATIVES **met·ro·log·i·cal** /ˌmetrə'läjikəl/ **adj.**, **me·trol·o·gist** /-jist/ **n.**
– ORIGIN early 19th cent.: from Greek *metron* 'measure' + -LOGY.

met·ro·ni·da·zole /ˌmetrə'nīdəˌzōl/ ▶ **n.** Medicine a synthetic drug used to treat trichomoniasis and some similar infections. ● A nitro-derivative of imidazole; chem. formula: $C_6H_9N_3O_3$.
– ORIGIN mid 20th cent.: from *me(thyl)* + *ni)tro-* + *((im) idazole.*

met·ro·nome /'metrəˌnōm/ ▶ **n.** a device used by musicians that marks time at a selected rate by giving a regular tick.
– DERIVATIVES **met·ro·nom·ic** /ˌmetrə'nämik/ **adj.**, **met·ro·nom·i·cal·ly** /ˌmetrə'nämik(ə)lē/ **adv.**
– ORIGIN early 19th cent.: from Greek *metron* 'measure' + *nomos* 'law.'

metronome

me·tro·nym·ic /ˌmetrə'nimik/ ▶ **adj.** & **n.** variant spelling of MATRONYMIC.

met·ro·plex /'metrəˌpleks/ ▶ **n.** a very large metropolitan area, esp. one that is an aggregation of two or more cities.
– ORIGIN 1960s: blend of METROPOLITAN and COMPLEX.

met·ro·pole /'metrəˌpōl/ ▶ **n.** the parent state of a colony.
– ORIGIN late 15th cent.: from Old French *metropole*, based on Greek *mētēr, mētr-* 'mother' + *polis* 'city' (see METROPOLIS).

me·trop·o·lis /mə'träp(ə)ləs/ ▶ **n.** the capital or chief city of a country or region. ■ a very large and densely populated industrial and commercial city.
– ORIGIN late Middle English (denoting the see of a metropolitan bishop): via late Latin from Greek *mētropolis* 'mother state,' from *mētēr, mētr-* 'mother' + *polis* 'city.'

met·ro·pol·i·tan /ˌmetrə'pälitn/ ▶ **adj.** **1** of, relating to, or denoting a metropolis, often inclusive of its surrounding areas: *the Boston metropolitan area.*
2 of, relating to, or denoting the parent state of a colony or dependency: *metropolitan Spain.*
3 Christian Church of, relating to, or denoting a metropolitan or his see: *a metropolitan bishop.*
▶ **n.** **1** Christian Church a bishop having authority over the bishops of a province, in particular (in many Orthodox Churches) one ranking above archbishop and below patriarch.
2 an inhabitant of a metropolis: *the sophisticated metropolitan.*
– DERIVATIVES **met·ro·pol·i·tan·ate** /-'pälitnˌāt/ **n.** (sense 1 of the noun), **met·ro·pol·i·tan·ism** /-ˌpälətnˌizəm/ **n.**
– ORIGIN late Middle English (in the ecclesiastical sense): from late Latin *metropolitanus*, from Greek *mētropolitēs* 'citizen of a mother state,' from *mētropolis* (see METROPOLIS).

Met·ro·pol·i·tan Mu·se·um of Art a major museum of art and archaeology in New York City, founded in 1870.

me·tror·rha·gi·a /ˌmētrə'rāj(ē)ə, ˌmetrə-/ ▶ **n.** abnormal bleeding from the uterus.
– ORIGIN mid 19th cent.: modern Latin, from Greek *mētra* 'womb' + *-rrhag-*, stem of *rhēgnunai* 'to burst.'

met·ro·sex·ual /ˌmetrō'sekSHo͞oəl/ ▶ **n.** a young, urban, heterosexual male with liberal political views, an interest in fashion, and a refined sense of taste.
– DERIVATIVES **met·ro·sex·u·al·i·ty** /-ˌsekSHo͞o'alitē/ **n.**
– ORIGIN from *metro-* + *(homo)sexual.*

-metry ▶ **comb. form** in nouns denoting procedures and systems corresponding to names of instruments ending in *-meter* (such as *calorimetry* corresponding to *calorimeter*).
– ORIGIN from Greek *-metria*, from *-metrēs* 'measurer.'

Met·ter·nich /'metərˌnik, -ˌniKH/, Klemens Wenzel Nepomuk Lothar, Prince of Metternich-Winneburg-Beilstein (1773–1859), Austrian statesman. As foreign minister (1809–48), he was one of the organizers of the Congress of Vienna (1814–15), which determined the settlement of Europe after the Napoleonic Wars.

met·tle /'metl/ ▶ **n.** a person's ability to cope well with difficulties or to face a demanding situation in a spirited and resilient way: *the team showed their true mettle in the second half.*
– PHRASES **be on one's mettle** be ready or forced to prove one's ability to cope well with a demanding situation. **put someone on their mettle** (of a demanding situation) test someone's ability to face difficulties.
– ORIGIN mid 16th cent.: specialized spelling (used for figurative senses) of METAL.

met·tle·some /'metlsəm/ ▶ **adj.** literary (of a person or animal) full of spirit and courage: *their horses were beasts of burden, not mettlesome chargers.*

Metz /mets/ a city in Lorraine, in northeastern France, on the Moselle River; pop. 126,706 (2006).

meu·nière /mœn'yer/ ▶ **adj.** [usu. postpositive] (esp. of fish) cooked or served in lightly browned butter with lemon juice and parsley: *sole meunière.*
– ORIGIN from French *(à la) meunière* '(in the manner of) a miller's wife.'

Meur·sault /mər'sō, mœr-/ ▶ **n.** (pl. **same**) a burgundy wine, typically white, produced near Beaune in eastern France.
– ORIGIN named after a commune in the Côte d'Or region of France.

Meuse /myo͞oz, mo͞oz, mœz/ a river in western Europe that rises in northeastern France and flows 594 miles (950 km) through Belgium and the Netherlands to the North Sea south of Dordrecht. Flemish and Dutch name MAAS.

MeV ▶ **abbr.** mega-electronvolt(s).

mew[1] /myo͞o/ ▶ **v.** [no obj.] (of a cat or some kinds of bird) make a characteristic high-pitched crying noise: *a throng of cats and kittens mewing to be fed* | (as noun **mewing**) *the mewing of gulls.*
▶ **n.** the high-pitched crying noise made by a cat or bird: *a kitten's mew.*
– ORIGIN Middle English: imitative.

mew[2] Falconry ▶ **n.** (usu. **mews**) a cage or building for trained hawks, esp. while they are molting.
▶ **v.** **1** [no obj.] (esp. of a trained hawk) molt.
2 [with obj.] confine (a trained hawk) to a cage or building at the time of molting.
– ORIGIN late Middle English: from Old French *mue*, from *muer* 'to molt,' from Latin *mutare* 'to change.'

mew gull ▶ **n.** a migratory gull with greenish-gray legs, found locally in northern and eastern Eurasia and northwestern North America. ● *Larus canus*, family Laridae.
– ORIGIN mid 19th cent.: *mew* (in Old English *meau* 'mew gull'), of Germanic origin; related to Dutch *meeuw* and German *Möwe*.

mewl /myo͞ol/ ▶ **v.** [no obj.] (often as adj. **mewling**) (esp. of a baby) cry feebly or querulously; whimper: *dozens of mewling babies.* ■ (of a cat or bird) mew: *the mewling cry of a hawk.*
– ORIGIN late Middle English: imitative.

mews /myo͞oz/ ▶ **n.** (pl. **same**) chiefly Brit. a row or street of houses or apartments that have been converted from stables or built to look like former stables. ■ a group of stables, typically with rooms above, built around a yard or along an alley.
– ORIGIN late Middle English: plural of MEW[2], originally referring to the royal stables on the site of the hawk mews at Charing Cross, London. The sense 'converted dwellings' dates from the early 19th cent.

Mex ▶ **adj.** & **n.** informal Mexican.

Mex·i·cal·i /ˌmeksə'kalē/ the capital of the state of Baja California, in northwestern Mexico; pop. 653,046 (2005).

Mex·i·can bam·boo ▶ **n.** another term for JAPANESE KNOTWEED.

Mex·i·can hair·less ▶ **n.** a small dog of a breed lacking hair except for tufts on the head and tail.

Mex·i·can jump·ing bean ▶ **n.** see JUMPING BEAN.

Mex·i·ca·no /ˌmeksi'känō, ˌmāhē-/ ▶ **n.** & **adj.** (pl. **Mexicanos**) informal Mexican or a Mexican.
– ORIGIN Spanish.

Mex·i·co /'meksiˌkō/ a country in southwestern North America, with extensive coastlines on the Gulf of Mexico and the Pacific Ocean, bordered by the US on the north; pop. 111,211,800 (est. 2009); capital, Mexico City; language, Spanish (official). ■ a state in central Mexico, west of Mexico City; capital, Toluca de Lerdo.

The center of both Mayan and Aztec civilizations, Mexico was conquered and colonized by the Spanish in the early 16th century. It remained under Spanish rule until independence was achieved in 1821; a republic was established three years later. Texas rebelled and broke away in 1836, while all the remaining territory north of the Rio Grande was lost to the US in the Mexican War of 1846–48.

– DERIVATIVES **Mex·i·can** /ˈmeksəkən/ adj. & n.

Mex·i·co, Gulf of a large extension of the western Atlantic Ocean. Bounded in a sweeping curve by the US on the north, by Mexico on the west and south, and by Cuba on the southeast, it is linked to the Atlantic Ocean by the Straits of Florida and to the Caribbean Sea by the Yucatán Channel.

Mex·i·co Cit·y the capital of Mexico; pop. 8,720,916 (2005). Founded about 1300 as the Aztec capital Tenochtitlán, it was destroyed in 1521 by the Spanish conquistador Cortés, who rebuilt it as the capital of New Spain.

Mey·er·beer /ˈmāərbi(ə)r, ˈmīərˌbe(ə)r/, Giacomo (1791–1864), German composer; born *Jakob Liebmann Beer*. After settling in Paris, he established himself as a leading exponent of French grand opera.

Mey·er·hof /ˈmīərˌhôf/, Otto Fritz (1884–1951), US biochemist, born in Germany. He worked on the biochemical processes involved in muscle action and provided the basis for understanding the process by which glucose is broken down to produce energy. He shared the 1922 Nobel Prize for Physiology or Medicine with Archibald Hill (1886–1977).

me·ze /meˈze/ (also **mezze**) ▸ **n.** (pl. **mezedes** /meˈzeᴛʜəs/) in the Mediterranean, an appetizer.
– ORIGIN Turkish and modern Greek.

me·ze·re·on /məˈzi(ə)rēən/ (also **mezereum** /-əm/) ▸ **n.** a Eurasian shrub with fragrant purplish-red flowers and poisonous red berries, found chiefly in calcareous woodlands. ● *Daphne mezereum*, family Thymelaeaceae.
– ORIGIN late 15th cent.: from medieval Latin, from Arabic *māzaryūn*.

me·zu·zah /məˈzo͝ozə/ (also **mezuza**) ▸ **n.** (pl. **mezuzahs** or **mezuzas** or **mezuzot** or **mezuzoth** /məˈzo͝ozōt/) a parchment inscribed with religious texts and attached in a case to the doorpost of a Jewish house as a sign of faith.
– ORIGIN mid 17th cent.: from Hebrew *mĕzūzāh* 'doorpost.'

mez·za·lu·na /ˌmetsəˈlo͞onə/ ▸ **n.** a utensil for chopping herbs, vegetables, etc., with a semicircular blade and a handle at each end.
– ORIGIN 1950s: from Italian, literally 'half moon.'

mez·za·nine /ˈmezəˌnēn, ˌmezəˈnēn/ ▸ **n.** a low story between two others in a building, typically between the ground and first floors. ■ the lowest balcony of a theater, stadium, etc., or the front rows of the balcony.
▸ **adj.** [attrib.] Finance relating to or denoting unsecured, higher-yielding loans that are subordinate to bank loans and secured loans but rank above equity.
– ORIGIN early 18th cent.: from French, from Italian *mezzanino*, diminutive of *mezzano* 'middle,' from Latin *medianus* 'median.'

mez·za vo·ce /ˌmetsä ˈvōᴄʜä, ˌmedzä/ Music ▸ **adv. & adj.** (esp. as a direction) using about half the singer's vocal power.
▸ **n.** singing performed in this way.
– ORIGIN Italian, literally 'half voice.'

mez·zo /ˈmetsō, ˈmedzō/ ▸ **n.** (pl. **mezzos**) (also **mezzo-soprano**) a female singer with a voice pitched between soprano and contralto. ■ a singing voice of this type, or a part written for one.
▸ **adv.** half, moderately.
– ORIGIN mid 18th cent.: Italian, from Latin *medius* 'middle.'

mez·zo for·te /ˌmetsō ˈfôrtā, ˌmedzō/ Music ▸ **adv. & adj.** (esp. as a direction) moderately loud.
▸ **n.** a moderately high volume of sound.

Mez·zo·gior·no /ˌmetsōˈjôrnō/ the southern part of Italy, including Sicily and Sardinia.
– ORIGIN Italian, literally 'midday'; compare with **MIDI**.

mez·zo pi·a·no /ˌmetsō ˈpyänō, ˌmedzō/ Music ▸ **adv. & adj.** (esp. as a direction) moderately soft.
▸ **n.** a moderately low volume of sound.

mez·zo·tint /ˈmetsōˌtint, ˈmedzō-/ ▸ **n.** a print made from an engraved copper or steel plate on which the surface has been partially roughened, for shading, and partially scraped smooth, giving light areas. The technique was much used in the 17th, 18th, and early 19th centuries for the reproduction of paintings. ■ the technique or process of making pictures in this way.
▸ **v.** [with obj.] engrave (a picture) in mezzotint.
– DERIVATIVES **mez·zo·tint·er** n.
– ORIGIN from Italian *mezzotinto*, from *mezzo* 'half' + *tinto* 'tint.'

MF ▸ **abbr.** medium frequency.

mf ▸ **abbr.** mezzo forte.

MFA ▸ **abbr.** Master of Fine Arts.

mfd. ▸ **abbr.** ■ manufactured. ■ microfarad.

mfg. ▸ **abbr.** manufacturing.

MFH ▸ **abbr.** Master of Foxhounds.

MFN ▸ **abbr.** most favored nation.

MFP ▸ **abbr.** Physics mean free path.

mfr. ▸ **abbr.** ■ manufacture. ■ (pl. **mfrs.**) manufacturer.

MG ▸ **abbr.** ■ machine gun. ■ historical Morris Garages.

Mg ▸ **symbol** the chemical element magnesium.

mg ▸ **abbr.** milligram(s): *100 mg acetaminophen.*

m.g.d. ▸ **abbr.** millions of gallons per day.

MGM Metro-Goldwyn-Mayer, a movie company formed in 1924 by Samuel Goldwyn and Louis B. Mayer. The company released both *The Wizard of Oz* and *Gone With the Wind* in 1939, and also produced many famous musicals, including *Meet Me in St. Louis* (1944) and *An American in Paris* (1951).

mgmt. ▸ **abbr.** management.

MGR ▸ **abbr.** Brit. merry-go-round (train).

Mgr ▸ **abbr.** ■ (**mgr**) manager. ■ Monseigneur. ■ Monsignor: *Mgr O'Flaherty.*

mgt. ▸ **abbr.** management.

MGySgt ▸ **abbr.** master gunnery sergeant.

MH ▸ **abbr.** Medal of Honor.

mh (also **mH**) ▸ **abbr.** millihenry or millihenries.

MHC ▸ **abbr.** major histocompatibility complex.

MHD ▸ **abbr.** Physics magnetohydrodynamics.

MHL ▸ **abbr.** Master of Hebrew Literature.

mho /mō/ ▸ **n.** (pl. **mhos**) the reciprocal of an ohm, a former unit of electrical conductance.
– ORIGIN late 19th cent.: the word **OHM** reversed.

MHR ▸ **abbr.** (in the US and Australia) Member of the House of Representatives.

MHW (also **m.h.w.** or **M.H.W.**) ▸ **abbr.** mean high water.

MHz ▸ **abbr.** megahertz.

MI ▸ **abbr.** ■ Michigan (in official postal use). ■ Brit. historical Military Intelligence: *MI5.*

mi /mē/ ▸ **n.** Music (in solmization) the third note of a major scale. ■ the note E in the fixed-do system.
– ORIGIN late Middle English *mi*, representing (as an arbitrary name for the note) the first syllable of *mira*, taken from a Latin hymn (see **SOLMIZATION**).

mi. ▸ **abbr.** mile(s): *10 km/6 mi.*

MI5 (in the UK) the governmental agency responsible for dealing with internal security and counter-intelligence on British territory. Formed in 1909, the agency was officially named the Security Service in 1964, but the name MI5 remains in popular use.
– ORIGIN from *Military Intelligence section 5.*

MI6 (in the UK) the governmental agency responsible for dealing with matters of internal security and counter-intelligence overseas. Formed in 1912, the agency was officially named the Secret Intelligence Service in 1964, but the name MI6 remains in popular use.

MIA ▸ **abbr.** ■ missing in action. ■ [as noun] a member of the armed forces who is missing in action.

Mi·am·i[1] /mīˈamē/ a city and port in southeastern Florida; pop. 413,201 (est. 2008). Its subtropical climate and miles of beaches make this and the resort island of Miami Beach, separated from the mainland by Biscayne Bay, a year-round holiday resort.

Mi·am·i[2] ▸ **n.** (pl. **same** or **Miamis**) **1** a member of an American Indian people formerly living mainly in Illinois, Indiana, and Wisconsin and more recently inhabiting areas of Ohio, Kansas, and Oklahoma. **2** the dialect of Illinois (an Algonquian language) of this people.
▸ **adj.** of or relating to this people or their language.
– ORIGIN French, from Illinois (an Algonquian language).

Mi·ami Beach a city in southeastern Florida, on the Atlantic Ocean, across Biscayne Bay from Miami; pop. 84,633 (est. 2008).

Mi·ao /mēˈou/ ▸ **n.** (pl. **same**) **& adj.** another term for **HMONG**.
– ORIGIN from Chinese *Miáo*, literally 'tribes.'

mi·aow ▸ **n. & v.** variant spelling of **MEOW**.

mi·asm /ˈmīˌazəm, ˈmē-/ ▸ **n.** (in homeopathy) any of the three underlying chronic diseases that afflict humankind: sycosis, syphilis, and psora.
– ORIGIN 19th cent.: from Greek *miasma*, 'stain.'

mi·as·ma /mīˈazmə, mē-/ ▸ **n.** (pl. **miasmas** or **miasmata** /-mətə/) literary a highly unpleasant or unhealthy smell or vapor: ***a miasma of stale alcohol hung around him like marsh gas.*** ■ an oppressive or unpleasant atmosphere that surrounds or emanates from something: ***a miasma of despair rose from the black workshops.***
– DERIVATIVES **mi·as·mal** adj., **mi·as·mat·ic** /ˌmīəzˈmatik/ adj.
– ORIGIN mid 17th cent.: from Greek, literally 'defilement,' from *miainein* 'pollute.'

mi·as·mic /mīˈazmik, mē-/ ▸ **adj.** literary producing an unpleasant smell; noxious. ■ characterized by an oppressive and unpleasant atmosphere: *we know the territory, its long and miasmic history.*
– DERIVATIVES **miasmically** /mik(ə)lē/ adv.

mic ▸ **n.** short for **MICROPHONE**.

Mic. ▸ **abbr.** Bible Micah.

mi·ca /ˈmīkə/ ▸ **n.** a shiny silicate mineral with a layered structure, found as minute scales in granite and other rocks, or as crystals. It is used as a thermal or electrical insulator.
– DERIVATIVES **mi·ca·ceous** /mīˈkāsʜəs/ adj.
– ORIGIN early 18th cent.: from Latin, literally 'crumb.'

Mi·cah /ˈmīkə/ (in the Bible) a Hebrew minor prophet. ■ a book of the Bible bearing his name, foretelling the destruction of Samaria and of Jerusalem.

mi·ca schist ▸ **n.** a metamorphic rock that contains quartz and mica and resembles slate in being easily split.

mice /mīs/ plural form of **MOUSE**.

mi·celle /mīˈsel/ ▸ **n.** Chemistry an aggregate of molecules in a colloidal solution, such as those formed by detergents.
– DERIVATIVES **mi·cel·lar** /mīˈselər/ adj.
– ORIGIN late 19th cent.: coined as a diminutive of Latin *mica* 'crumb.'

Mich. ▸ **abbr.** Michigan.

Mi·chae·lis con·stant /məˈkālis/ ▸ **n.** Biochemistry the concentration of a given enzyme that catalyzes the associated reaction at half the maximum rate.
– ORIGIN 1930s: named after Leonor *Michaelis* (1875–1949), German-born American chemist.

Mich·ael·mas /ˈmikəlməs/ ▸ **n.** the feast of St. Michael, September 29.
– ORIGIN Old English *Sanct Michaeles mæsse* 'Saint Michael's Mass,' referring to the Archangel.

Mich·ael·mas dai·sy ▸ **n.** chiefly Brit. an aster, esp. *Aster novae-belgii*, a North American aster with numerous pinkish-lilac daisylike flowers that bloom around Michaelmas.

Mi·chel·an·ge·lo /ˌmikəlˈanjəlō, ˌmīkəl-, ˌmēkeˈlänjəlō/ (1475–1564), Italian sculptor, painter, architect, and poet; full name *Michelangelo Buonarroti*. A leading figure of the High Renaissance, Michelangelo established his reputation with sculptures such as the *Pietà* (*c.*1497–1500) and *David* (1501–04). Under papal patronage he decorated the ceiling of the Sistine Chapel in Rome (1508–12) and painted the fresco *The Last Judgment* (1536–41), both important mannerist works. His architectural achievements include the completion of St. Peter's cathedral in Rome (1546–64).

Michelangelo

Mi·che·lin /ˈmisʜələn/, André (1853–1931) and Édouard (1859–1940), French industrialists. They founded the Michelin Tire Company in 1888 and pioneered the use of pneumatic tires on automobiles.

Mich·el·in man ▸ **n.** informal a fat person.
– ORIGIN 1990s: from the name of an advertising icon with a body and limbs made up of stacked white tires.

PRONUNCIATION KEY ə *ago, up*; ər *over, fur*; a *hat*; ā *ate*; ä *car*; e *let*; ē *see*; i *fit*; ī *by*; ɴɢ *sing*; ō *go*; ô *law, for*; oi *toy*; o͝o *good*; o͞o *goo*; ou *out*; ᴛʜ *thin*; T̲H̲ *then*; ᴢʜ *vision*

m

Mi·che·loz·zo /ˌmēkeˈlôtsō/ (1396–1472), Italian architect and sculptor; full name *Michelozzo di Bartolommeo*. In partnership with Ghiberti and Donatello, he led a revival of interest in Roman architecture.

Mi·chel·son /ˈmīkəlsən/, Albert Abraham (1852–1931), US physicist. He specialized in precision measurement in experimental physics. Nobel Prize for Physics (1907).

Mi·chel·son–Mor·ley ex·per·i·ment /ˌmīkəlsən ˈmôrlē/ Physics an experiment performed in 1887 that attempted to measure the relative motion of the earth and the ether by measuring the speed of light in directions parallel and perpendicular to the earth's motion. The result disproved the existence of the ether, which contradicted Newtonian physics but was explained by Einstein's special theory of relativity.
– ORIGIN named after A. A. MICHELSON and E. W. MORLEY.

Miche·ner /ˈmiCH(ə)nər/, James (Albert) (1907–97), US writer. He wrote *Tales of the South Pacific* (1947), which was made into the Broadway musical *South Pacific* (1949). He was also known for other fictionalized histories that included *Hawaii* (1959), *Chesapeake* (1978), *Texas* (1985), *Alaska* (1988), and *A Miracle in Seville* (1995).

Mich·i·gan /ˈmisHigən/ a state in the northern US, bordered on the west, north, and east by lakes Michigan, Superior, Huron, and Erie; pop. 10,003,422 (est. 2008); capital, Lansing; statehood, Jan. 26, 1837 (26). It was acquired from Britain by the US in 1783.

Mich·i·gan, Lake one of the five Great Lakes. Bordered by Michigan, Wisconsin, Illinois, and Indiana, it is the only one of the Great Lakes to lie wholly within the US. The cities of Milwaukee and Chicago are on its shores.

Mich·i·gan·der /ˌmisHiˈgandər/ ▶ **n.** a native or inhabitant of Michigan.

Mi·cho·a·cán /ˌmēCHō-əˈkän/ a state of western Mexico, on the Pacific coast; capital, Morelia.

Mick /mik/ ▶ **n.** informal, offensive an Irishman.
– ORIGIN mid 19th cent.: nickname for the given name *Michael*.

mick·ey /ˈmikē/ ▶ **n.** informal **1** short for **MICKEY FINN**: *I bet some guy **slipped me a mickey**.*
2 (in phrase **take the mickey**) chiefly Brit. tease or ridicule someone.
– ORIGIN 1930s: of unknown origin.

Mick·ey Finn /ˈmikē ˈfin/ ▶ **n.** informal a surreptitiously drugged or doctored drink given to someone so as to make them drunk or insensible. ■ the substance used to adulterate such a drink.
– ORIGIN 1920s: of unknown origin; sometimes said to be the name of a notorious Chicago saloonkeeper (*c.*1896–1906).

Mick·ey Mouse /ˌmikē ˈmous/ a Walt Disney cartoon character who first appeared as Mortimer Mouse in 1927, becoming Mickey in 1928. During the 1930s, he became established as the central Disney character. ■ [as adj.] (also **mickey mouse**) informal trivial or of inferior quality.

mick·le /ˈmikəl/ (also **muckle** /ˈməkəl/) archaic or Scottish & N. English ▶ **n.** a large amount.
▶ **adj.** very large: *she had a great big elephant ... that's one of those mickle beasts from Africa.*
▶ **determiner & pron.** much; a large amount.
– PHRASES **many a little makes a mickle** (also **many a mickle makes a muckle**) proverb many small amounts accumulate to make a large amount.
– ORIGIN Old English *micel* 'great, numerous, much,' of Germanic origin; from an Indo-European root shared by Greek *megas, megal-*.

Mic·mac /ˈmikˌmak/ (also **Mi'kmaq**) ▶ **n.** (pl. **same** or **Micmacs**) **1** a member of an American Indian people inhabiting the Maritime Provinces of Canada.
2 the Algonquian language of this people.
▶ **adj.** of or relating to this people or their language.
– ORIGIN via French from the Micmac self-designation *mīkəmaw*.

mi·crite /ˈmikˌrīt, ˈmīˌkrīt/ ▶ **n.** Geology microcrystalline calcite present in some types of limestone. ■ limestone consisting chiefly of this.
– DERIVATIVES **mi·crit·ic** /miˈkritik, mī-/ **adj.**
– ORIGIN 1950s: from *micr(ocrystalline)* + **-ITE**¹.

mi·cro /ˈmīkrō/ ▶ **n.** (pl. **micros**) **1** short for **MICROCOMPUTER**.
2 short for **MICROPROCESSOR**.
▶ **adj.** [attrib.] extremely small: *a micro dining area.* ■ small-scale: CO_2 *emissions cannot be dealt with at the micro level.* Often contrasted with **MACRO**.

micro- ▶ **comb. form 1** small: *microcar.* ■ of reduced or restricted size: *microdot* | *microprocessor.*
2 (used commonly in units of measurement) denoting a factor of one millionth (10^{-6}): *microfarad.*
– ORIGIN from Greek *mikros* 'small.'

mi·cro·a·nal·y·sis /ˌmīkrōəˈnaləsəs/ ▶ **n.** the quantitative analysis of chemical compounds using a sample of a few milligrams.
– DERIVATIVES **mi·cro·an·a·lyt·ic** /-ˌanlˈitik/ **adj.**, **mi·cro·an·a·lyt·i·cal** /-ˌanlˈitikəl/ **adj.**

mi·cro·an·a·lyz·er /ˌmīkrōˈanlˌīzər/ ▶ **n.** another term for **MICROPROBE**.

mi·cro·ar·ray /ˈmīkrō-əˌrā/ ▶ **n.** a grid of DNA segments of known sequence that is used to test and map DNA fragments, antibodies, or proteins.

mi·cro·bal·ance /ˌmīkrōˈbaləns/ ▶ **n.** a balance for weighing masses of a fraction of a gram.

mi·crobe /ˈmīˌkrōb/ ▶ **n.** a microorganism, esp. a bacterium causing disease or fermentation.
– DERIVATIVES **mi·cro·bi·al** /mīˈkrōbēəl/ **adj.**, **mi·cro·bic** /mīˈkrōbik/ **adj.**
– ORIGIN late 19th cent.: from French, from Greek *mikros* 'small' + *bios* 'life.'

mi·cro·bi·ol·o·gy /ˌmīkrōˌbīˈäləjē/ ▶ **n.** the branch of science that deals with microorganisms.
– DERIVATIVES **mi·cro·bi·o·log·ic** /-ˌbīəˈläjik/ **adj.**, **mi·cro·bi·o·log·i·cal** /-ˌbīəˈläjikəl/ **adj.**, **mi·cro·bi·o·log·i·cal·ly** /-ˌbīəˈläjik(ə)lē/ **adv.**, **mi·cro·bi·ol·o·gist** /-jist/ **n.**

mi·cro·bi·o·ta /ˌmīkrōˌbīˈōtə/ ▶ **n.** the microorganisms of a particular site, habitat, or geological period.

mi·cro·blog·ging /ˈmīkrōˌbläɡiNG/ ▶ **n.** the posting of very short entries or updates on a blog or social networking site, typically via a cellular phone.
– DERIVATIVES **mi·cro·blog n.**

mi·cro·brew /ˈmīkrəˌbrōō/ ▶ **n.** a type of beer produced in a microbrewery.
▶ **v.** [with obj.] produce (beer) in a microbrewery: *the beer is microbrewed in Racine* | (as adj. **microbrewed**) *microbrewed beer.*
– DERIVATIVES **mi·cro·brew·er n.**

mi·cro·brew·er·y /ˌmīkrəˈbrōōərē/ ▶ **n.** (pl. **microbreweries**) a limited-production brewery, typically producing specialty beers and often selling its products only locally.

mi·cro·brows·er /ˈmīkrōˌbrouzər/ ▶ **n.** Computing a small Internet browser for use with cellular phones and other handheld devices.

mi·cro·burst /ˈmīkrōˌbərst/ ▶ **n.** a sudden, powerful, localized air current, esp. a downdraft.

mi·cro·cap·sule /ˌmīkrōˈkapsəl, -sōōl/ ▶ **n.** a small capsule used to contain drugs, dyes, or other substances and render them temporarily inactive.

mi·cro·car /ˈmīkrōˌkär/ ▶ **n.** a small and fuel-efficient car.

mi·cro·cel·lu·lar /ˌmīkrōˈselyələr/ ▶ **adj.** containing or made up of minute cells. ■ (of a mobile telephone system) having small cells, typically with a radius of less than half a mile.

mi·cro·ceph·a·ly /ˌmīkrōˈsefəlē/ ▶ **n.** Medicine abnormal smallness of the head, a congenital condition associated with incomplete brain development.
– DERIVATIVES **mi·cro·ce·phal·ic** /-səˈfalik/ **adj. & n.**, **mi·cro·ceph·a·lous** /-ˈsefələs/ **adj.**

mi·cro·chem·is·try /ˌmīkrōˈkeməstrē/ ▶ **n.** the branch of chemistry concerned with the reactions and properties of substances in minute quantities, e.g., in living tissue.

mi·cro·chip /ˈmīkrōˌCHip/ ▶ **n.** a tiny wafer of semiconducting material used to make an integrated circuit.
▶ **v.** (**microchips, microchipping, microchipped**) [with obj.] implant a microchip under the skin of (a domestic animal) as a means of identification.

Mi·cro·chi·rop·ter·a /ˌmīkrōkəˈräptərə/ Zoology a major division of bats that comprises all but the fruit bats. ● Suborder Microchiroptera, order Chiroptera: many families.
– DERIVATIVES **mi·cro·chi·rop·ter·an n. & adj.**
– ORIGIN modern Latin (plural), from **MICRO-** 'small' + Greek *kheir* 'hand' + *pteron* 'wing.'

mi·cro·cir·cuit /ˈmīkrōˌsərkət/ ▶ **n.** a minute electric circuit, esp. an integrated circuit.
– DERIVATIVES **mi·cro·cir·cuit·ry** /ˌmīkrōˈsərkətrē/ **n.**

mi·cro·cir·cu·la·tion /ˌmīkrōˌsərkyəˈlāsHən/ ▶ **n.** circulation of the blood in the smallest blood vessels.
– DERIVATIVES **mi·cro·cir·cu·la·to·ry** /-ˈsərkyələˌtôrē/ **adj.**

mi·cro·cli·mate /ˈmīkrōˌklīmət/ ▶ **n.** the climate of a very small or restricted area, esp. when this differs from the climate of the surrounding area.
– DERIVATIVES **mi·cro·cli·mat·ic** /ˌmīkrōˌklīˈmatik/ **adj.**, **mi·cro·cli·mat·i·cal·ly** /ˌmīkrōˌklīˈmatik(ə)lē/ **adv.**

mi·cro·cline /ˈmīkrōˌklīn/ ▶ **n.** a green, pink, or brown crystalline mineral consisting of potassium-rich feldspar, characteristic of granite and pegmatites.
– ORIGIN mid 19th cent.: from German *Mikroklin*, from Greek *mikros* 'small' + *klinein* 'to lean' (because its angle of cleavage differs only slightly from 90 degrees).

mi·cro·coc·cus /ˌmīkrōˈkäkəs/ ▶ **n.** (pl. **micrococci** /-ˈkäkˌ(s)ī, -ˈkäk(s)ē/) a spherical bacterium that is typically found on dead or decaying organic matter. Nonpathogenic forms are found on human and animal skin. ● Family Micrococcaceae of Gram-positive nonmotile bacteria, in particular the genera *Micrococcus* and *Staphylococcus*.
– DERIVATIVES **mi·cro·coc·cal adj.**

mi·cro·code /ˈmīkrəˌkōd/ ▶ **n.** Computing a very low-level instruction set that is stored permanently in a computer or peripheral controller and controls the operation of the device.

mi·cro·com·pu·ter /ˈmīkrōkəmˌpyōōtər/ ▶ **n.** a small computer that contains a microprocessor as its central processor.

mi·cro·con·ti·nent /ˌmīkrōˈkäntn-ənt/ ▶ **n.** Geology an isolated fragment of continental crust forming part of a small crust plate.

mi·cro·cop·y /ˈmīkrōˌkäpē/ ▶ **n.** (pl. **microcopies**) a copy of printed matter that has been reduced in size by microphotography.
▶ **v.** (**microcopies, microcopying, microcopied**) [with obj.] make a microcopy of.

mi·cro·cosm /ˈmīkrəˌkäzəm/ (also **microcosmos** /ˌmīkrəˈkäzməs, -mōs/) ▶ **n.** a community, place, or situation regarded as encapsulating in miniature the characteristic qualities or features of something much larger: *Berlin is a microcosm of Germany, in unity as in division.* ■ humankind regarded as the epitome of the universe.
– PHRASES **in microcosm** in miniature.
– DERIVATIVES **mi·cro·cos·mic** /ˌmīkrəˈkäzmik/ **adj.**, **mi·cro·cos·mi·cal·ly** /-ˈkäzmik(ə)lē/ **adv.**
– ORIGIN Middle English: from Old French *microcosme* or medieval Latin *microcosmus*, from Greek *mikros kosmos* 'little world.'

mi·cro·cos·mic salt /ˌmīkrəˈkäzmik/ ▶ **n.** Chemistry a white crystalline salt obtained from human urine. ● Hydrated sodium ammonium hydrogen phosphate; chem. formula: $HNaNH_4PO_4 4H_2O$.
– ORIGIN late 18th cent.: translating Latin *sal microcosmicus*.

mi·cro·cred·it /ˈmīkrōˌkredit/ ▶ **n.** the lending of small amounts of money at low interest to new businesses in the developing world. ■ such a loan considered individually: *microcredits should not be considered a substitute for long-term investment in infrastructure.*

mi·cro·crys·tal·line /ˌmīkrōˈkristəlin, -ˌlīn, -ˌlēn/ ▶ **adj.** (of a material) formed of microscopic crystals.

mi·cro·cyte /ˈmīkrəˌsīt/ ▶ **n.** Medicine an unusually small red blood cell, associated with certain anemias.
– DERIVATIVES **mi·cro·cyt·ic** /ˌmīkrəˈsitik/ **adj.**

mi·cro·den·si·tom·e·ter /ˌmīkrōˌdensəˈtämətər/ ▶ **n.** a densitometer for measuring the density of very small areas of a photographic image.

mi·cro·derm·a·bra·sion /ˌmīkrōˌdərməˈbrāZHən/ ▶ **n.** a cosmetic treatment in which the face is sprayed with exfoliant crystals to remove dead epidermal cells.

mi·cro·dose /ˈmīkrōˌdōs/ ▶ **n.** a dose of as little as one milligram of a drug that is intended to produce a beneficial result while avoiding undesirable side effects.

mi·cro·dot /ˈmīkrəˌdät/ ▶ **n. 1** a microphotograph, esp. of a printed or written document, that is only about 0.04 inch (1 mm) across. ■ [usu. as modifier] denoting a pattern of very small dots.
2 a tiny tablet or capsule (of LSD): *more than 1,000 microdots of LSD.*

mi·cro·ec·o·nom·ics /ˌmīkrōˌekəˈnämiks, -ˌēkə-/ ▶ **plural n.** [treated as sing.] the part of economics concerned with single factors and the effects of individual decisions.
– DERIVATIVES **mi·cro·ec·o·nom·ic adj.**

mi·cro·e·lec·tro·me·chan·i·cal /ˌmīkrō-iˌlektrōməˈkanikəl/ ▶ **adj.** denoting systems or components relating to microscopic electronic machines that are typically built on computer chips: *optical true-time delay devices with microelectromechanical mirror arrays.*
– DERIVATIVES **mi·cro·e·lec·tro·me·chan·ics n.**

mi·cro·e·lec·tron·ics /ˌmīkrōiˌlekˈträniks/ ▶ **plural n.** [usu. treated as sing.] the design, manufacture, and use of microchips and microcircuits.
– DERIVATIVES **mi·cro·e·lec·tron·ic adj.**

mi·cro·en·ter·prise /ˌmīkrōˈentərprīz/ ▶ **n.** a business operating on a very small scale, esp. one with a sole proprietor and fewer than six employees.

mi·cro·en·vi·ron·ment /ˌmīkrōinˈvīrə(n)mənt, -ˈvī(ə)r(n)mənt/ ▶ **n.** Biology the immediate small-scale environment of an organism or a part of an organism, esp. as a distinct part of a larger environment.
– DERIVATIVES **mi·cro·en·vi·ron·men·tal** /-ˌvīrə(n)ˈmentl, -ˌvī(ə)r(n)-/ **adj.**

mi·cro·ev·o·lu·tion /ˌmīkrō-evəˈlo͞osHən, -ˌēvə-/ ▶ **n.** Biology evolutionary change within a species or small group of organisms, esp. over a short period.
– DERIVATIVES **mi·cro·ev·o·lu·tion·ar·y** /-ˈlo͞osHəˌnerē/ **adj.**

mi·cro·far·ad /ˈmīkrōˌfarəd, -ad/ ▶ **n.** one millionth of a farad. Symbol μF.

mi·cro·fau·na /ˌmīkrōˈfônə, -ˈfänə/ ▶ **n.** (pl. **microfaunas** or **microfaunae** /-ˈfônē, -ˈfänē/) Biology microscopic animals.
– DERIVATIVES **mi·cro·fau·nal adj.**

mi·cro·fi·ber /ˈmīkrōˌfībər/ ▶ **n.** a very fine synthetic yarn.

mi·cro·fi·bril /ˌmīkrōˈfībrəl, -ˈfibrəl/ ▶ **n.** Biology a small fibril in the cytoplasm or wall of a cell, visible only under an electron microscope, and typically aggregated into coarser fibrils or structures.

mi·cro·fiche /ˈmīkrəˌfēsH/ ▶ **n.** (pl. **same** or **microfiches**) a flat piece of film containing microphotographs of the pages of a newspaper, catalog, or other document: *this new journal is available as a microfiche | the index will be made available on microfiche.*
▶ **v.** [with obj.] make a microfiche of (a newspaper, catalog, or other document).

mi·cro·fil·a·ment /ˌmīkrōˈfiləmənt/ ▶ **n.** Biology a small rodlike structure, about 4–7 nanometers in diameter, present in numbers in the cytoplasm of many eukaryotic cells.

mi·cro·fi·lar·i·a /ˌmīkrōfəˈle(ə)rēə/ ▶ **n.** (pl. **microfilariae** /-fəˈle(ə)rēˌē, -ēˌī/) Zoology the minute larva of a filaria.

mi·cro·film /ˈmīkrəˌfilm/ ▶ **n.** a length of film containing microphotographs of a newspaper, catalog, or other document: *all those forms go on microfilm | his vast hoard of microfilms.*
▶ **v.** [with obj.] make a microfilm of (a newspaper, catalog, or other document).

mi·cro·fi·nance /ˌmīkrōˈfīnans/ ▶ **n.** another term for MICROCREDIT.

mi·cro·flo·ra /ˌmīkrōˈflôrə/ ▶ **n.** (pl. **microfloras** or **microflorae** /-ˈflôrē/) Biology bacteria and microscopic algae and fungi, esp. those living in a particular site or habitat.
– DERIVATIVES **mi·cro·flo·ral adj.**

mi·cro·form /ˈmīkrəˌfôrm/ ▶ **n.** microphotographic reproduction on film or paper of a manuscript, map, or other document.

mi·cro·fos·sil /ˈmīkrōˌfäsəl/ ▶ **n.** a fossil or fossil fragment that can be seen only with a microscope.

mi·cro·fun·gus /ˌmīkrōˈfəNGgəs/ ▶ **n.** (pl. **microfungi** /-ˈfənˌjī, -ˌgī, -ˌjē, -ˌgē/) Biology a fungus in which no sexual process has been observed or in which the reproductive organs are microscopic.

mi·cro·gam·ete /ˌmīkrōˈgamˌēt, -gəˈmēt/ ▶ **n.** Biology (esp. in protozoans) the smaller of a pair of conjugating gametes, usually regarded as male.

mi·crog·li·a /ˌmīkrəˈglēə, ˈglīə/ ▶ **plural n.** Anatomy glial cells derived from mesoderm that function as macrophages (scavengers) in the central nervous system and form part of the reticuloendothelial system.
– DERIVATIVES **mi·crog·li·al adj.**

mi·cro·gram /ˈmīkrəˌgram/ (abbr.: **mcg**) ▶ **n.** one millionth of a gram. (Symbol: μg)

mi·cro·graph /ˈmīkrəˌgraf/ ▶ **n.** a photograph taken by means of a microscope.
– DERIVATIVES **mi·cro·graph·ic** /ˌmīkrəˈgrafik/ **adj.**, **mi·cro·graph·ics** /ˌmīkrəˈgrafiks/ **n.**, **mi·crog·ra·phy** /mīˈkrägrəfē/ **n.**

mi·cro·grav·i·ty /ˌmīkrōˈgravətē/ ▶ **n.** very weak gravity, as in an orbiting spacecraft.

mi·cro·greens /ˈmīkrōˌgrēnz/ ▶ **plural n.** the shoots of salad vegetables such as arugula, Swiss chard, mustard, beetroot, etc., picked just after the first leaves have developed.

mi·cro·groove /ˈmīkrəˌgro͞ov/ ▶ **n.** the very narrow groove on a long-playing phonograph record.

mi·cro·hab·i·tat /ˌmīkrōˈhabəˌtat/ ▶ **n.** Ecology a habitat that is of small or limited extent and which differs in character from some surrounding more extensive habitat.

mi·cro·in·ject /ˌmīkrō-inˈjekt/ ▶ **v.** [with obj.] Biology inject (something) into a microscopic object.
– DERIVATIVES **mi·cro·in·jec·tion** /-ˈjeksHən/ **n.**

mi·cro·in·struc·tion /ˌmīkrō-inˈstrəksHən/ ▶ **n.** Computing a single instruction in microcode.

mi·cro·in·va·sive /ˌmīkrōinˈvāsiv/ ▶ **adj.** **1** Pathology (of a cancerous growth) invasive at a microscopic level.
2 Surgery denoting or relating to techniques and procedures that minimize the extent of surgical intervention.

mi·cro·ker·nel /ˈmīkrōˌkərnl/ ▶ **n.** Computing a small modular part of an operating system kernel that implements its basic features.

mi·cro·lend·ing /ˈmīkrōˌlendiNG/ ▶ **n.** another term for MICROCREDIT.
– DERIVATIVES **mi·cro·lend·er n.**

mi·cro·lep·i·dop·ter·a /ˌmīkrōˌlepəˈdäptərə/ ▶ **plural n.** Entomology the numerous small moths. Compare with MACROLEPIDOPTERA.
– ORIGIN modern Latin (plural), from MICRO- 'small' + LEPIDOPTERA.

mi·cro·li·ter /ˌmīkrōˈlētər/ (Brit. also **microlitre**) ▶ **n.** one millionth of a liter. (Symbol: μl)

mi·cro·lith /ˈmīkrəˌliTH/ ▶ **n.** Archaeology a minute shaped flint, typically part of a composite tool such as a spear.
– DERIVATIVES **mi·cro·lith·ic** /ˌmikrəˈliTHik/ **adj.**

mi·cro·man·age /ˌmīkrōˈmanij/ ▶ **v.** [with obj.] control every part, however small, of (an enterprise or activity).
– DERIVATIVES **mi·cro·man·age·ment** /ˈmanijmənt/ **n.**, **mi·cro·man·ag·er n.**

mi·cro·me·te·or·ite /ˌmīkrōˈmētēəˌrīt/ ▶ **n.** a micrometeoroid that has entered the earth's atmosphere.

mi·cro·me·te·or·oid /ˌmīkrōˈmētēəˌroid/ ▶ **n.** a microscopic particle in space or of extraterrestrial origin that is small enough so that if it enters the earth's atmosphere, it will not burn up but drift to the earth's surface instead.

mi·cro·me·te·or·ol·o·gy /ˌmīkrōˌmētēəˈräləjē/ ▶ **n.** the branch of meteorology concerned with small areas and with small-scale meteorological phenomena.
– DERIVATIVES **mi·cro·me·te·or·o·log·i·cal** /-ˌmētēərəˈläjikəl/ **adj.**

mi·crom·e·ter[1] /mīˈkrämətər/ (also **micrometer caliper**) ▶ **n.** a gauge that measures small distances or thicknesses between its two faces, one of which can be moved away from or toward the other by turning a screw with a fine thread.
– DERIVATIVES **mi·crom·e·try** /-ətrē/ **n.**

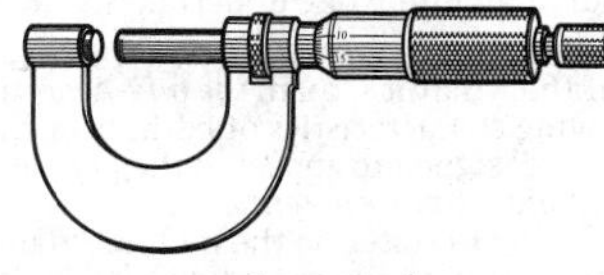

micrometer[1]

mi·cro·me·ter[2] /ˈmīkrōˈmētər/ (abbr.: **μm**) ▶ **n.** one millionth of a meter.

mi·crom·e·tre ▶ **n.** British spelling of MICROMETER[2].

mi·cro·min·i·a·tur·i·za·tion /ˌmīkrōˌminēəCHəriˈzāsHən, -ˌminiCHər-/ ▶ **n.** the manufacture of extremely small versions of electronic devices.
– DERIVATIVES **mi·cro·min·i·a·tur·ize** /-ˈminēəCHəˌrīz, -ˌminiCHə-/ **v.**

mi·cron /ˈmīˌkrän/ ▶ **n.** a unit of length equal to one millionth of a meter, used in many technological and scientific fields.
– ORIGIN late 19th cent.: from Greek *mikron*, neuter of *mikros* 'small.'

Mi·cro·ne·sia /ˌmīkrəˈnēZHə/ **1** a region of the western Pacific Ocean, north of Melanesia and north and west of Polynesia. It includes the Mariana, Caroline, and Marshall island groups and Kiribati.
2 a country in the western Pacific Ocean, north of the equator, composed of hundreds of islands in the Caroline Islands group; pop. 107,400 (est. 2009); capital, Palikir; languages, English (official) and Austronesian languages. Full name FEDERATED STATES OF MICRONESIA.

> The group was administered by the US as part of the Pacific Islands Trust Territory from 1947 and entered into free association with the US as an independent state in 1986.

– ORIGIN from Greek *mikros* 'small' + *nēsos* 'island.'

Mi·cro·ne·sian /ˌmīkrəˈnēZHən/ ▶ **adj.** of or relating to Micronesia, its people, or their languages.
▶ **n.** **1** a native of Micronesia.
2 the group of Austronesian languages spoken in Micronesia.

mi·cron·ize /ˈmīkrəˌnīz/ ▶ **v.** [with obj.] break (a substance) into very fine particles.
– DERIVATIVES **mi·cron·i·za·tion** /ˌmīkrənəˈzāsHən/ **n.**, **mi·cron·iz·er n.**

mi·cro·nu·tri·ent /ˌmīkrōˈn(y)o͞otrēənt/ ▶ **n.** a chemical element or substance required in trace amounts for the normal growth and development of living organisms.

mi·cro·or·gan·ism /ˌmīkrōˈôrgəˌnizəm/ ▶ **n.** a microscopic organism, esp. a bacterium, virus, or fungus.

mi·cro·pay·ment /ˈmīkrōˌpāmənt/ ▶ **n.** a very small payment made each time a user accesses an Internet page or service.

mi·cro·phage /ˈmīkrōˌfāj/ ▶ **n.** Physiology a small phagocytic blood cell, in particular a polymorphonuclear leukocyte.

mi·croph·a·gous /mīˈkräfəgəs/ ▶ **adj.** Zoology (of an invertebrate) feeding on minute particles or microorganisms.
– DERIVATIVES **mi·cro·phag·ic** /ˌmīkrəˈfājik, -ˈfajik/ **adj.**

mi·cro·phone /ˈmīkrəˌfōn/ ▶ **n.** an instrument for converting sound waves into electrical energy variations, which may then be amplified, transmitted, or recorded.
– DERIVATIVES **mi·cro·phon·ic** /ˌmīkrəˈfänik/ **adj.**

mi·cro·pho·to·graph /ˌmīkrəˈfōtəˌgraf/ ▶ **n.** a photograph reduced to a very small size. ■ another term for PHOTOMICROGRAPH.
– DERIVATIVES **mi·cro·pho·to·graph·ic** /-ˌfōtəˈgrafik/ **adj.**, **mi·cro·pho·tog·ra·phy** /-fəˈtägrəfē/ **n.**

mi·cro·phys·ics /ˌmīkrōˈfiziks/ ▶ **plural n.** [treated as sing.] the branch of physics that deals with bodies and phenomena on a microscopic or smaller scale, esp. with molecules, atoms, and subatomic particles.
– DERIVATIVES **mi·cro·phys·i·cal** /-ˈfizikəl/ **adj.**

mi·cro·pi·pette /ˌmīkrōˌpīˈpet/ (also **micropipet**) ▶ **n.** a very fine pipette for measuring, transferring, or injecting very small quantities of liquid.

mi·cro·pol·i·tan /ˌmīkrōˈpälətn/ ▶ **adj.** relating to an urban area with a population of at least 10,000 but less than 50,000.

mi·cro·pore /ˈmīkrəˌpôr/ ▶ **n.** a very narrow pore, esp. in a material.
– DERIVATIVES **mi·cro·po·ros·i·ty** /ˌmīkrōpəˈräsətē, -pôrˈäsətē/ **n.**, **mi·cro·po·rous** /ˌmīkrəˈpôrəs/ **adj.**

mi·cro·pow·er /ˈmīkrōˌpou(ə)r/ ▶ **n.** [often as modifier] electrical power that is generated or utilized in relatively small quantities: *micropower technologies.*

mi·cro·print /ˈmīkrəˌprint/ ▶ **n.** printed text reduced by microphotography.
– DERIVATIVES **mic·ro·print·ing n.**

mi·cro·probe /ˈmīkrəˌprōb/ ▶ **n.** Chemistry an instrument in which a beam of electrons or other radiation is focused onto a minute area of a sample and the resulting secondary radiation (usually X-ray fluorescence) is analyzed to yield chemical information.

mi·cro·proc·es·sor /ˌmīkrəˈpräsesər, -ˈprōˌsesər/ ▶ **n.** an integrated circuit that contains all the functions of a central processing unit of a computer.
– DERIVATIVES **mi·cro·proc·ess·ing n.**

mi·cro·pro·gram /ˈmīkrəˌprōgrəm, -gram/ ▶ **n.** a microinstruction program that controls the functions of a central processing unit or peripheral controller of a computer.
▶ **v.** [with obj.] use microprogramming with (a computer); bring about by means of a microprogram: *by 1980 virtually all computers were microprogrammed.*
– DERIVATIVES **mi·cro·pro·gram·ma·ble adj.**, **mi·cro·pro·gram·mer n.**

mi·cro·pro·gram·ming /ˈmīkrəˌprōgrəmiNG, ˈmīkrəˌprōgramiNG/ ▶ **n.** the technique of making machine instructions generate sequences of microinstructions in accordance with a microprogram rather than initiate the desired operations directly.

mi·cro·prop·a·ga·tion /ˌmīkrōˌpräpəˈgāsHən/ ▶ **n.** Botany the propagation of plants by growing plantlets in tissue culture and then planting them out.

mi·crop·si·a /mīˈkräpsēə/ ▶ **n.** a condition of the eyes in which objects appear smaller than normal.
– ORIGIN mid 19th cent.: from MICRO- 'small' + Greek *-opsia* 'seeing.'

PRONUNCIATION KEY ə *ago, up*; ər *over, fur*; a *hat*; ā *ate*; ä *car*; e *let*; ē *see*; i *fit*; ī *by*; NG *sing*; ō *go*; ô *law, for*; oi *toy*; o͝o *good*; o͞o *goo*; ou *out*; TH *thin*; T͟H *then*; ZH *vision*

m

mi·cro·pyle /ˈmīkrəˌpīl/ ▶ **n.** Botany a small opening in the surface of an ovule, through which the pollen tube penetrates, often visible as a small pore in the ripe seed. ■ a small opening in the egg of a fish, insect, etc., through which spermatozoa can enter.
– DERIVATIVES **mi·cro·py·lar** /ˌmīkrəˈpīlər/ **adj.**
– ORIGIN early 19th cent.: from **MICRO-** 'small' + Greek *pulē* 'gate.'

mi·cro·RNA /ˈmīkrōˌärenˈā/ ▶ **n.** Genetics a cellular RNA fragment that prevents the production of a particular protein by binding to and destroying the messenger RNA that would have produced the protein.

mi·cro·scope /ˈmīkrəˌskōp/ ▶ **n.** an optical instrument used for viewing very small objects, such as mineral samples or animal or plant cells, typically magnified several hundred times.
– PHRASES **under the microscope** under critical examination.
– ORIGIN mid 17th cent.: from modern Latin *microscopium* (see **MICRO-**, **-SCOPE**).

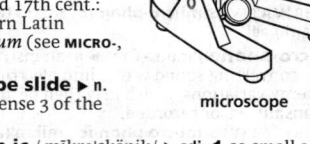

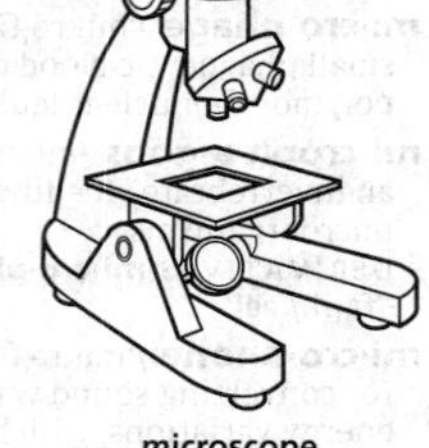
microscope

mi·cro·scope slide ▶ **n.** see **SLIDE** (sense 3 of the noun).

mi·cro·scop·ic /ˌmīkrəˈskäpik/ ▶ **adj. 1** so small as to be visible only with a microscope: *microscopic algae.* ■ informal extremely small: *a microscopic skirt.* ■ concerned with minute detail: *such a vision is as microscopic as his is panoramic.*
2 of or relating to a microscope: *microscopic analysis of the soil.*
– DERIVATIVES **mi·cro·scop·i·cal adj.** (sense 2), **mi·cro·scop·i·cal·ly** /-ik(ə)lē/ **adv.**

Mi·cro·sco·pi·um /ˌmīkrəˈskōpēəm/ Astronomy a small and inconspicuous southern constellation (the Microscope), between Piscis Austrinus and Sagittarius. ■ (as genitive **Microscopii** /ˌmīkrəˈskōpē-ē, -pēˌī/) used with a preceding letter or numeral to designate a star in this constellation: *the star Gamma Microscopii.*
– ORIGIN modern Latin.

mi·cros·co·py /mīˈkräskəpē/ ▶ **n.** the use of the microscope.
– DERIVATIVES **mi·cros·co·pist** /-pist/ **n.**

mi·cro·sec·ond /ˈmīkrōˌsekənd/ (abbr.: μs) ▶ **n.** one millionth of a second.

mi·cro·seism /ˈmīkrōˌsīzəm/ ▶ **n.** Geology a very small earthquake, less than 2 on the Richter scale.
– DERIVATIVES **mi·cro·seis·mic** /ˌmīkrōˈsīzmik/ **adj.**

mi·cro·site /ˈmīkrəˌsīt/ ▶ **n. 1** an auxiliary website with independent links and address that is accessed mainly from a larger site.
2 a small part of an ecosystem that differs markedly from its immediate surroundings.

mi·cro·some /ˈmīkrəˌsōm/ ▶ **n.** Biology a fragment of endoplasmic reticulum and attached ribosomes obtained by the centrifugation of homogenized cells.
– DERIVATIVES **mi·cro·so·mal** /ˌmīkrəˈsōməl/ **adj.**

mi·cro·sphere /ˈmīkrōˌsfir/ ▶ **n.** a microscopic hollow sphere, esp. of a protein or synthetic polymer.

mi·cro·spo·ran·gi·um /ˌmīkrōspəˈranj(ē)əm/ ▶ **n.** (pl. **microsporangia** /-j(ē)ə/) Botany a sporangium containing microspores.

mi·cro·spore /ˈmīkrəˌspôr/ ▶ **n.** Botany the smaller of the two kinds of spore produced by some ferns. See also **MEGASPORE**.

mi·cro·struc·ture /ˌmīkrəˈstrəkCHər/ ▶ **n.** the fine structure (in a metal or other material) that can be made visible and examined with a microscope.

mi·cro·suede /ˈmīkrəˌswād/ ▶ **n.** a polyester microfiber fabric with a suedelike, water-repellent finished surface.

mi·cro·sur·ger·y /ˌmīkrōˈsərjərē/ ▶ **n.** intricate surgery performed using miniaturized instruments and a microscope.
– DERIVATIVES **mi·cro·sur·geon** /-ˈsərjən/ **n.**, **mi·cro·sur·gi·cal** /-ˈsərjikəl/ **adj.**

mi·cro·switch /ˈmīkrəˌswiCH/ ▶ **n.** an electric switch that can be operated rapidly by a small movement.

mi·cro·tech·nol·o·gy /ˌmīkrōtekˈnäləjē/ ▶ **n.** technology that uses microelectronics.
– DERIVATIVES **mi·cro·tech·no·log·i·cal** /-nəˈläjikəl/ **adj.**

mi·cro·tome /ˈmīkrəˌtōm/ ▶ **n.** chiefly Biology an instrument for cutting extremely thin sections of material for examination under a microscope.

mi·cro·tone /ˈmīkrəˌtōn/ ▶ **n.** Music an interval smaller than a semitone.
– DERIVATIVES **mi·cro·ton·al** /ˌmīkrəˈtōnl/ **adj.**, **mi·cro·to·nal·i·ty** /ˌmīkrətōˈnalətē/ **n.**, **mi·cro·ton·al·ly** /ˌmīkrəˈtōnl-e/ **adv.**

mi·cro·tu·bule /ˌmīkrəˈt(y)o͞obyo͞ol/ ▶ **n.** Biology a microscopic tubular structure present in numbers in the cytoplasm of cells, sometimes aggregating to form more complex structures.

mi·cro·vas·cu·lar /ˌmīkrōˈvaskyələr/ ▶ **n.** of or relating to the smallest blood vessels.

mi·cro·vil·lus /ˌmīkrōˈviləs/ ▶ **n.** (pl. **microvilli** /-ˈvilˌī, -ˈvilē/) Biology each of a large number of minute projections from the surface of some cells.
– DERIVATIVES **mi·cro·vil·lar** /-ˈvilər/ **adj.**, **mi·cro·vil·lous** /-ˈviləs/ **adj.**

mi·cro·wave /ˈmīkrəˌwāv/ ▶ **n.** an electromagnetic wave with a wavelength in the range 0.001–0.3 m, shorter than that of a normal radio wave but longer than those of infrared radiation. Microwaves are used in radar, in communications, and for heating in microwave ovens and in various industrial processes. ■ short for **MICROWAVE OVEN**.
▶ **v.** [with obj.] cook (food) in a microwave oven.
– DERIVATIVES **mi·cro·wave·a·ble** (also **microwavable**) **adj.**

mi·cro·wave back·ground ▶ **n.** Astronomy weak uniform microwave radiation that is detectable in nearly every direction of the sky. It is believed to be evidence of the Big Bang.

mi·cro·wave ov·en ▶ **n.** an oven that uses microwaves to cook or heat food.

mic·tu·rate /ˈmikCHəˌrāt/ ▶ **v.** [no obj.] formal urinate.
– DERIVATIVES **mic·tu·ri·tion** /ˌmikCHəˈrisHən/ **n.**
– ORIGIN mid 19th cent.: back-formation from *micturition*, from Latin *micturit-* 'urinated,' from the verb *micturire*.

mid[1] /mid/ ▶ **adj.** [attrib.] of or in the middle part or position of a range: *the mid 17th century* | *in mid air.* ■ Phonetics (of a vowel) pronounced with the tongue neither high nor low: *a mid-central vowel.*

mid[2] ▶ **prep.** literary in the middle of. ■ in the course of.
– ORIGIN Shortening of **AMID**.

mid- ▶ **comb. form** denoting the middle of: *midsection* | *mid-sentence.* ■ in the middle; medium; half: *midway.*
– ORIGIN Old English *midd*, of Germanic origin; from an Indo-European root shared by Latin *medius* and Greek *mesos*.

mid·air /ˈmidˈe(ə)r/ ▶ **n.** a part or section of the air above ground level or above another surface: *he caught Murray's keys in midair* | [as modifier] *a midair collision.*

Mi·das /ˈmīdəs/ Greek Mythology a king of Phrygia, who, according to one story, was given by Dionysus the power of turning everything he touched into gold.
– PHRASES **the Midas touch** the ability to make money out of anything one undertakes.

mid-At·lan·tic ▶ **adj. 1** situated or occurring in the middle of the Atlantic Ocean: *the mid-Atlantic fault line.* ■ having characteristics of both Britain and America, or designed to appeal to the people of both countries: *mid-Atlantic accents.*
2 of or relating to states on the middle Atlantic coast of the US, typically including New York, Pennsylvannia, New Jersey, West Virginia, Delaware, and Maryland.

Mid-At·lan·tic Ridge a submarine ridge system that extends the length of the Atlantic Ocean from the Arctic to the Antarctic. It is seismically and (in places) volcanically active; the islands of Iceland, the Azores, Ascension, St. Helena, and Tristan da Cunha are located on it.

Mid-At·lan·tic States term for the US states between New England and the South that are on or near the Atlantic coast, usually including New York, New Jersey, and Pennsylvania, and sometimes also Delaware and Maryland.

mid·brain /ˈmidˌbrān/ ▶ **n.** Anatomy a small central part of the brainstem, developing from the middle of the primitive or embryonic brain. Also called **MESENCEPHALON**.

mid·day /ˈmidˈdā/ ▶ **n.** the middle of the day; noon: *he awoke* ***at midday*** | [as modifier] *the midday sun.*
– ORIGIN Old English *middæg* (see **MID-**, **DAY**).

mid·den /ˈmidn/ ▶ **n.** a dunghill or refuse heap. ■ short for **KITCHEN MIDDEN**.
– ORIGIN late Middle English *myddyng*, of Scandinavian origin; compare with Danish *mødding* 'dunghill.'

mid·dle /ˈmidl/ ▶ **adj.** [attrib.] **1** at an equal distance from the extremities of something; central: *the early and middle part of life* | *middle and eastern Europe.* ■ (of a member of a group, series, or sequence) so placed as to have the same number of members on each side: *the woman was in her middle forties.* ■ intermediate in rank, quality, or ability: *there is a dearth of talent at the middle level.* ■ (of a language) of the period between the old and modern forms: *Middle High German.*
2 Grammar denoting a voice of verbs in some languages, such as Greek, that expresses reciprocal or reflexive action. ■ denoting a transitive or intransitive verb in English with a passive sense, e.g., *cuts* in *this meat cuts well.*
▶ **n. 1** [usu. in sing.] the point or position at an equal distance from the sides, edges, or ends of something: *she stood alone in the middle of the street.* ■ the point at or around the center of a process or activity, period of time, etc.: *we were married in the middle of December.* ■ informal a person's waist or waist and stomach: *he had a towel around his middle.*
2 Grammar the form or voice of a verb expressing reflexive or reciprocal action, or a passive sense for a transitive or intransitive verb.
3 short for **MIDDLE TERM**.
– PHRASES **down the middle** divided or dividing something equally into two parts. **in the middle of** engaged in or in the process of doing something. ■ involved in something, typically something unpleasant or dangerous: *he was caught in the middle of the emotional triangle.* **the middle of nowhere** informal a place that is remote and isolated. **steer** (or **take**) **a middle course** adopt a policy that avoids extremes.
– ORIGIN Old English *middel*; related to Dutch *middel* and German *Mittel*, also to **MID**[1].

mid·dle age ▶ **n.** the period between early adulthood and old age, usually considered as the years from about 45 to 65.
– DERIVATIVES **mid·dle-aged** (also **middle-age**) **adj.**

Mid·dle Ag·es ▶ **plural n.** the period of European history from the fall of the Roman Empire in the West (5th century) to the fall of Constantinople (1453), or, more narrowly, from *c.*1100 to 1453.

> The earlier part of the period (*c.*500–*c.*1100) or *early Middle Ages* is sometimes distinguished as the Dark Ages, while the later part (*c.*1100–1453) or *high* or *late Middle Ages* is often thought of as the Middle Ages proper. The whole period is characterized by the emergence of separate kingdoms, the growth of trade and urban life, and the growth in power of monarchies and the Church. The growth of interest in classical models within art and scholarship in the 15th century is seen as marking the transition to the Renaissance period and the end of the Middle Ages.

mid·dle-age spread ▶ **n.** the fat that may accumulate around the areas of the abdomen and buttocks during one's middle age.

Mid·dle A·mer·i·ca ▶ **n. 1** the middle class in the US, esp. when regarded as a conservative political force. ■ the Midwest of the US.
2 the North American region that includes Mexico and Central America, and often the West Indies.
– DERIVATIVES **Mid·dle A·mer·i·can n.**, **Mid·dle-A·mer·i·can adj.**

Mid·dle At·lan·tic the region of the US that generally includes New Jersey, Pennsylvania, and Delaware, and often also New York and Maryland.

mid·dle·brow /ˈmidlˈbrou/ often derogatory ▶ **adj.** (of art or literature or a system of thought) demanding or involving only a moderate degree of intellectual application, typically as a result of not deviating from convention: *middlebrow fiction.*
▶ **n.** a person who is capable of or enjoys only a moderate degree of intellectual effort.

mid·dle C ▶ **n.** Music the C near the middle of the piano keyboard, written on the first ledger line below the treble staff or the first ledger line above the bass staff.

mid·dle class ▶ **n.** [treated as sing. or pl.] the social group between the upper and working classes, including professional and business workers and their families.
▶ **adj.** (**middle-class**) of, relating to, or characteristic of this section of society: *a middle-class suburb.* ■ attaching too much importance to convention, security, and material comfort: *the sterile goals of middle-class life.*
– DERIVATIVES **mid·dle-class·ness n.**

mid·dle dis·tance ▶ **n. 1** (**the middle distance**) the part of a real or painted landscape between the foreground and the background.
2 [usu. as modifier] Track & Field a race distance of between 800 and 5,000 meters: *middle-distance runners.*

Mid·dle Dutch ▶ **n.** the Dutch language from *c.*1100 to 1500.

mid·dle ear ▶ **n.** the air-filled central cavity of the ear, behind the eardrum.

Mid·dle East an extensive area of southwestern Asia and northern Africa, stretching from the Mediterranean Sea to Pakistan and including the Arabian peninsula.
– DERIVATIVES **Mid·dle East·ern adj.**

mid·dle eight ▶ n. a short section (typically of eight bars) in the middle of a conventionally structured popular song, generally of a different character from the other parts of the song.

Mid·dle Eng·lish ▶ n. the English language from c.1150 to c.1470.

mid·dle fin·ger ▶ n. the finger between the forefinger and the ring finger.

mid·dle game ▶ n. the phase of a chess game after the opening, when all or most of the pieces and pawns remain on the board.

mid·dle ground ▶ n. (usu. **the middle ground**) **1** an area of compromise or possible agreement between two extreme positions, esp. political ones: *each party wants to capture the votes of those perceived as occupying the middle ground.* **2** the middle distance of a painting or photograph.

Mid·dle High Ger·man ▶ n. the language of southern Germany from c.1200 to 1500.

Mid·dle King·dom 1 a period of ancient Egyptian history (c.2040–1640 BC, 11th–14th dynasty). **2** historical China or its eighteen inner provinces.

Mid·dle Low Ger·man ▶ n. the Low German language (spoken in northern Germany) from c.1200 to 1500.

mid·dle·man /ˈmidlˌman/ ▶ n. (pl. **middlemen**) a person who buys goods from producers and sells them to retailers or consumers: *we aim to maintain value for money by cutting out the middleman and selling direct.* ■ a person who arranges business or political deals between other people.

mid·dle man·age·ment ▶ n. the level in an organization just below that of senior administrators. ■ the managers at this level regarded collectively.
– DERIVATIVES **mid·dle man·ag·er** n.

mid·dle name ▶ n. a person's name (typically a personal name) placed after the first name and before the surname. ■ a quality for which a person is notable: *optimism is my middle name.*

mid·dle-of-the-road ▶ adj. avoiding extremes; moderate: *the paper reflected the views of its middle-of-the-road readers.* ■ (of music) tuneful but somewhat bland and unadventurous.
– DERIVATIVES **mid·dle-of-the-road·er** n.

mid·dle pas·sage ▶ n. historical the sea journey undertaken by slave ships from West Africa to the West Indies.

Mid·dle Per·sian ▶ n. the Persian language from c.300 BC to AD 800. See also **Pahlavi**[2].

Mid·dles·brough /ˈmidlzbrə/ a port in northeastern England, on the estuary of the Tees River; pop. 140,200 (est. 2009).

mid·dl·es·cent /ˌmidlˈesənt/ ▶ adj. middle-aged, but typically still maintaining the interests and activities of younger people.
– DERIVATIVES **mid·dl·es·cence** /ˌmidlˈesəns/ n.
– ORIGIN 1960s: blend of *middle* + *adolescent*.

mid·dle school ▶ n. a school intermediate between an elementary school and a high school, typically for children in the sixth, seventh, and eighth grades.

mid·dle-sized ▶ adj. of medium size: *a middle-sized farm.*

Mid·dle Stone Age the Mesolithic period.

mid·dle term ▶ n. Logic the term common to both premises of a syllogism.

Mid·dle·ton /ˈmidltən/, Thomas (c.1570–1627), English playwright. Notable works: *The Changeling* (1622), written with playwright **William Rowley**, and *Women Beware Women* (1620–27).

Mid·dle·town /ˈmidlˌtoun/ **1** a commercial and industrial city in central Connecticut, on the Connecticut River, south of Hartford, home to Wesleyan University; pop. 48,030 (est. 2008). **2** an industrial city in southwestern Ohio, between Cincinnati and Dayton; pop. 51,422 (est. 2008).

mid·dle·ware /ˈmidlˌwe(ə)r/ ▶ n. Computing software that acts as a bridge between an operating system or database and applications, esp. on a network.

mid·dle watch ▶ n. the period from midnight to 4 a.m. on board a ship.

mid·dle way ▶ n. **1** a policy or course of action that avoids extremes: *there is no middle way between central planning and capitalism.* **2** (**the Middle Way**) the eightfold path of Buddhism between indulgence and asceticism.

mid·dle·weight /ˈmidlˌwāt/ ▶ n. a weight in boxing and other sports intermediate between welterweight and light heavyweight. ■ a boxer or other competitor of this weight.

Middle West another term for **Midwest**.
– DERIVATIVES **Mid·dle Wes·tern·er** n.

mid·dling /ˈmidliNG, ˈmidlin/ ▶ adj. moderate or average in size, amount, or rank: *the village contained no poor households but a lot of middling ones.* ■ neither very good nor very bad: *he had had a fair to middling season.* ■ [predic.] informal (of a person) in reasonably good but not perfect health.
▶ n. (**middlings**) bulk goods of medium grade, esp. flour of medium fineness.
▶ adv. [as submodifier] informal, dated fairly or moderately: *middling rich.*
– DERIVATIVES **mid·dling·ly** adv.
– ORIGIN late Middle English (originally Scots): probably from **mid-** + the adverbial suffix *-ling*.

mid·dy /ˈmidē/ ▶ n. (pl. **middies**) **1** informal a midshipman. **2** (also **middy blouse**) chiefly historical a woman's or child's loose blouse with a collar that is cut deep and square at the back and tapering to the front, resembling that worn by a sailor.

Mid·east US term for **Middle East**.

mid-en·gine (also **mid-engined**) ▶ adj. (of a car) having the engine located centrally between the front and rear axles.

mid·field /ˈmidˌfēld, midˈfēld/ ▶ n. (in football, soccer, etc.) the central part of the field. ■ Soccer the players on a team who play in a central position between attack and defense.
– DERIVATIVES **mid·field·er** n.

Mid·gard /ˈmidˌgärd/ Scandinavian Mythology the region, encircled by the sea, in which human beings live; the earth.

midge /mij/ ▶ n. **1** a small two-winged fly that is often seen in swarms near water or marshy areas where it breeds. ● The families Chironomidae (the **nonbiting midges**), and Ceratopogonidae (see **biting midge**): numerous species. ■ [with modifier] any of a number of small flies whose larvae can be pests of plants, typically producing galls or damaging leaves. **2** informal a small person.
– ORIGIN Old English *mycg(e)*, of Germanic origin; related to Dutch *mug* and German *Mücke*, from an Indo-European root shared by Latin *musca* and Greek *muia* 'fly.'

mid·get /ˈmijit/ ▶ n. often offensive an extremely or unusually small person.
▶ adj. [attrib.] very small: *a midget submarine.*
– ORIGIN mid 19th cent.: from **midge** + **-et**[1].

mid·gut /ˈmidˌgət/ ▶ n. Zoology the middle part of the alimentary canal, including (in vertebrates) the small intestine.

mid·heav·en /ˈmidˌhevən/ ▶ n. Astrology (on an astrological chart) the point where the ecliptic intersects the meridian.

MIDI /ˈmidē/ ▶ n. [usu. as modifier] a widely used standard for interconnecting electronic musical instruments and computers: *a MIDI controller.*
– ORIGIN 1980s: acronym from *musical instrument digital interface*.

Mi·di /mēˈdē/ the south of France.
– ORIGIN French, literally 'midday'; compare with **Mezzogiorno**.

mid·i /ˈmidē/ ▶ n. (pl. **midis** /ˈmidēz/) short for **midiskirt**, a skirt that ends at the middle of the calf.
– ORIGIN 1960s: from **mid**[1], on the pattern of *maxi* and *mini*.

mid·i·nette /ˌmidnˈet, ˌmēdēˈnet/ ▶ n. a seamstress or assistant in a Parisian fashion house.
– ORIGIN French, from *midi* 'midday' + *dînette* 'light dinner' (because only a short break was taken at lunchtime).

Mi·di-Py·ré·nées /mēˌdē ˌpirəˈnā/ a region in southern France, between the Pyrenees and the Massif Central, centered on Toulouse.

mid·i·ron /ˈmidˌī(ə)rn/ ▶ n. Golf an iron with a medium degree of loft, such as a four-, five-, or six-iron.

Mid·land /ˈmidlənd/ **1** a city in central Michigan; pop. 40,917 (est. 2008). **2** a city in western Texas, an oil industry center in the Permian Basin; pop. 106,561 (est. 2008).

mid·land /ˈmidlənd, -ˌland/ ▶ n. the middle part of a country. ■ (**the Midlands**) the inland counties of central England. ■ (**Midland**) a part of the central US, roughly bounded by Illinois, South Carolina, and Delaware.
▶ adj. of or in the middle part of a country. ■ (**Midland**) of or in the English Midlands. ■ (**Midland**) of or in the Midland of the US.
– DERIVATIVES **mid·land·er** n.

mid·lat·i·tudes ▶ plural n. areas lying between 35 and 55 (or more broadly, between 30 and 60) degrees north or south of the equator: *mesoscaleconvective systems in the tropics and midlatitudes.*
– DERIVATIVES **mid·lat·i·tude** adj.

mid·life /midˈlīf/ ▶ n. the central period of a person's life, generally considered as the years from about 45 to 55: *a woman in midlife* | [as modifier] *your midlife financial review.*

mid·life cri·sis ▶ n. an emotional crisis of identity and self-confidence that can occur in early middle age.

mid·line /ˈmidˌlīn/ ▶ n. [often as modifier] a median line or plane of bilateral symmetry, esp. that of the body: *the abdomen was opened by a midline incision.*

mid·most /ˈmidˌmōst/ ▶ adj. & adv. literary in the very middle or nearest the middle.

Midn. ▶ abbr. Midshipman.

mid·night /ˈmidˌnīt/ ▶ n. twelve o'clock at night: *I left at midnight* | [as modifier] *a midnight deadline.* ■ [often as modifier] the middle period of the night: *the midnight hours.*
– ORIGIN Old English *midniht* (see **mid-**, **night**).

mid·night blue ▶ n. a very dark blue.

mid·night sun ▶ n. the sun when seen at midnight during the summer in either the Arctic or Antarctic Circle.

mid·o·cean ridge /midˈōSHən/ ▶ n. Geology a long, seismically active submarine ridge system situated in the middle of an ocean basin and marking the site of the upwelling of magma associated with seafloor spreading. An example is the Mid-Atlantic Ridge.

mid·point /ˈmidˌpoint/ ▶ n. the exact middle point: *the midpoint of the line segment.* ■ a point somewhere in the middle: *he would have been at the midpoint in his career.*

mid·range /ˈmidˈrānj/ ▶ n. **1** Statistics the arithmetic mean of the largest and the smallest values in a sample or other group. **2** the middle part of the range of audible frequencies.
▶ adj. (of a product) in the middle of a range of products with regard to size, quality, or price.

Mid·rash /ˈmidˌräSH/ (also **midrash**) ▶ n. (pl. **Midrashim** /midˈräSHim/) an ancient commentary on part of the Hebrew scriptures, attached to the biblical text. The earliest Midrashim come from the 2nd century AD, although much of their content is older.
– DERIVATIVES **Mid·rash·ic** /midˈräSHik/ adj.
– ORIGIN from Hebrew *miḏrāš* 'commentary,' from *dāraš* 'expound.'

mid·rib /ˈmidˌrib/ ▶ n. a large strengthened vein along the midline of a leaf.

mid·riff /ˈmidˌrif/ ▶ n. the region of the front of the body between the chest and the waist. ■ Anatomy, dated the diaphragm.
– ORIGIN Old English *midhrif*, from **mid**[1] + *hrif* 'belly.'

mid·sec·tion /ˈmidˌsekSHən/ ▶ n. the middle part of something. ■ the midriff.

mid·ses·sion /ˈmidˌseSHən, ˌmidˈseSH-/ ▶ n. the middle of a session, particularly. ■ a period of active trading on a securities exchange: *the Mexico peso regained some lost ground to the U.S. dollar toward midsession Friday.* ■ a period of instruction: *both students and instructors can be called away in midsession to cope with emergencies.* ■ a legislative session.

mid·ship /ˈmidˌSHip/ ▶ n. [usu. as modifier] the middle part of a ship or boat: *its powerful midship section.*

mid·ship·man /ˈmidˌSHipmən, midˈSHip-/ ▶ n. (pl. **midshipmen**) **1** a naval cadet in the US Navy. ■ an officer in the Royal Navy ranking below sublieutenant. [early 17th cent.: so named because the officer was stationed amidships; he was, however, allowed to walk the quarterdeck, to which he aspired in promotion.] **2** an American toadfish with dorsal and anal fins that run most of the length of the body and rows of light organs on the underside. ● Genus *Porichthys*, family *Batrachoididae*: two or three species.

mid·ships /ˈmidˌSHips/ ▶ adv. & adj. another term for **amidships**.

mid·size /ˈmidsīz/ (also **midsized**) ▶ adj. of an average size; intermediate in size between large and small: *a midsize pickup.*

mid·sole /ˈmidˌsōl/ ▶ n. a layer of material between the inner and outer soles of a shoe, for absorbing shock.

midst /midst, mitst/ ▶ prep. archaic or literary in the middle of.
▶ n. archaic the middle point or part.
– PHRASES **in the midst of** in the middle of: *we were in the midst of a losing streak.* **in our** (or **your**, **their**, etc.) **midst** among us (or you or them).

PRONUNCIATION KEY ə *ago, up*; ər *over, fur*; a *hat*; ā *ate*; ä *car*; e *let*; ē *see*; i *fit*; ī *by*; NG *sing*; ō *go*; ô *law, for*; oi *toy*; o͝o *good*; o͞o *goo*; ou *out*; TH *thin*; T͟H *then*; ZH *vision*

m

– ORIGIN late Middle English: from *in middes* 'in the middle.'

mid·stream /ˈmidˈstrēm/ ▶ **n.** the middle of a stream or river: *the ferry was moving out into midstream.*
▶ **adj.** Medicine (of urine) passed in the middle part of an act of urinating.
– PHRASES **in midstream** (of an activity or process, esp. one that is interrupted) partway through its course: *our conversation was interrupted in midstream.*

mid·sum·mer /ˈmidˈsəmər/ ▶ **n.** [often as modifier] the middle part of summer: *the midsummer heat.* ■ another term for SUMMER SOLSTICE.
– ORIGIN Old English *midsumor* (see MID-, SUMMER[1]).

Mid·sum·mer Day (also **Midsummer's Day**) ▶ **n.** (in England, Wales, and Ireland) June 24, originally coinciding with the summer solstice and in some countries marked by a summer festival.

mid·term /ˈmid,tərm/ ▶ **n.** the middle of a period of office, an academic term, or a pregnancy: *Nixon resigned in midterm* | [as modifier] *midterm elections.* ■ an exam in the middle of an academic term.

mid·town /ˈmid,toun/ ▶ **n.** [usu. as modifier] the central part of a city between the downtown and uptown areas: *a huge midtown apartment.*

mid-Vic·to·ri·an ▶ **adj.** of or relating to the middle of the Victorian era.

mid·wa·ter /ˈmid,wôtər, -,wätər/ ▶ **n.** the part of a body of water near neither the bottom nor the surface: *whales and seals feed in midwater or on the seabed* | [as modifier] *midwater fish.*

mid·way /ˈmid,wā, -ˈwā/ ▶ **adv. & adj.** in or toward the middle of something: [as adv.] *Father Peter came to a halt midway down the street* | [as adj.] *midway profits roared from $130 million to $160 million.* ■ having some of the characteristics of one thing and some of another: [as adj.] *a midway path is chosen between the diverging aspirations of the two factions* | [as adv.] *the leaves have a unique smell midway between eucalyptus and mint.*
▶ **n.** an area of sideshows, games of chance or skill, or other amusements at a fair or exhibition: *the kids head straight for the midway.*

Mid·way Is·lands two small islands, in the central Pacific Ocean, in the western part of the Hawaiian chain, surrounded by a coral atoll. The islands were annexed by the US in 1867 and remain a US territory and naval base. They were the scene of the decisive Battle of Midway in 1942, in which Japanese expansion in the Pacific Ocean was ended.

mid·week /ˈmid,wēk/ ▶ **n.** the middle of the week, usually regarded as being from Tuesday to Thursday: *by midweek the strike could affect subways and buses.*
▶ **adj. & adv.** in the middle of the week: [as adj.] *a special midweek reduction* | [as adv.] *we have opportunities to fish midweek.*

Mid·west /ˈmidˈwest/ the region of northern states of the US from Ohio west to the Rocky Mountains. Formerly called FAR WEST.
– DERIVATIVES **Mid·west·ern** /,midˈwestərn/ **adj.**

Mid·west Cit·y /ˈmid,west/ a city in central Oklahoma, east of Oklahoma City; pop. 56,394 (est. 2008).

mid·wife /ˈmid,wīf/ ▶ **n.** (pl. **midwives**) a person (typically a woman) trained to assist women in childbirth. ■ a person or thing that helps to bring something into being or assists its development: *he survived to be one of the midwives of the Reformation.*
▶ **v.** [with obj.] assist (a woman) during childbirth. ■ bring into being: *revolutions midwifed by new technologies of communication.*
– DERIVATIVES **mid·wif·e·ry** /midˈwif(ə)rē, -ˈwīf(ə)rē/ **n.**
– ORIGIN Middle English: probably from the obsolete preposition *mid* 'with' + WIFE (in the archaic sense 'woman'), expressing the sense 'a woman who is with (the mother).'

mid·wife toad ▶ **n.** a European toad, the male of which has a distinctive piping call in spring and carries the developing eggs wrapped around his hind legs. ● *Alytes obstetricans*, family Discoglossidae.

mid·win·ter /ˈmidˈwintər/ ▶ **n.** the middle part of winter: *in midwinter the track became a muddy morass* | [as modifier] *the midwinter full moon.* ■ another term for WINTER SOLSTICE.
– ORIGIN Old English (see MID-, WINTER).

mien /mēn/ ▶ **n.** literary a person's look or manner, esp. one of a particular kind indicating their character or mood: *he has a cautious, academic mien.*
– ORIGIN early 16th cent.: probably from French *mine* 'expression,' influenced by obsolete *demean* 'bearing, demeanor' (from DEMEAN[2]).

Mies van der Ro·he /ˈmēz van dər ˈrōə, ˈmēs vän/, Ludwig (1886–1969), German architect and designer. He designed the German pavilion at the 1929 International Exhibition at Barcelona and the Seagram Building in New York 1954–58 and was noted for his tubular steel furniture. Before emigrating to the US in 1937, he served as director of the Bauhaus 1930–33.
– DERIVATIVES **Mies·i·an** /ˈmēzēən/ **adj.**

mi·fep·ri·stone /,mifəˈpris,tōn/ ▶ **n.** Medicine a synthetic steroid that inhibits the action of progesterone, given orally in early pregnancy to induce abortion. Also called RU-486 (trademark).
– ORIGIN 1980s: probably from Dutch *mifepriston*, from *mife-* (representing *aminophenol*) + *-pr-* (representing *propyl*) + *-ist-* (representing ESTRADIOL) + -ONE.

miff /mif/ ▶ **v.** [with obj.] (usu. **be miffed**) informal annoy: *she was slightly miffed at not being invited.*
▶ **n.** archaic a petty quarrel or fit of pique.
– ORIGIN early 17th cent.: perhaps imitative; compare with early modern German *muff*, an exclamation of disgust.

MiG /mig/ (also **Mig** or **MIG**) ▶ **n.** a type of Russian fighter aircraft.
– ORIGIN 1940s: from the initial letters of the surnames of A. I. Mikoyan and M. I. Gurevich, linked by Russian *i* 'and.'

might[1] /mīt/ ▶ **modal v.** (3rd sing. present **might**) **1** past of MAY[1], used esp. ■ in reported speech, expressing possibility or permission: *he said he might be late.* ■ expressing a possibility based on a condition not fulfilled: *we might have won if we'd played better.* ■ expressing annoyance about something that someone has not done: *you might have told me!* ■ expressing purpose: *he avoided social engagements so that he might work.*
2 used in questions and requests. ■ tentatively asking permission: *might I ask one question?* ■ expressing a polite request: *you might just call me Jane, if you don't mind.* ■ asking for information, esp. condescendingly: *and who might you be?*
3 used to express possibility or make a suggestion: *this might be true* | *you might try nonprescription pain relievers.*
– PHRASES **might as well 1** used to make an unenthusiastic suggestion: *I might as well begin.* **2** used to indicate that a situation is the same as if the hypothetical thing stated were true: *for readers seeking illumination, this book might as well have been written in Serbo-Croatian.* **might have known** (or **guessed**) used to express one's lack of surprise about something: *I might have known it was you.*

> **USAGE** On the difference in use between **might** and **may**, see usage at MAY[1].

might[2] ▶ **n.** great and impressive power or strength, esp. of a nation, large organization, or natural force: *a convincing display of military might.*
– PHRASES **might is right** those who are powerful can do what they wish unchallenged, even if their action is in fact unjustified. **with all one's might** using all one's power or strength. **with might and main** with all one's strength or power.
– ORIGIN Old English *miht, mieht*, of Germanic origin; related to MAY[1].

might-have-been ▶ **n.** informal a past possibility that no longer applies: *fretting about might-have-beens won't get us anywhere.*

might·i·ly /ˈmītl-ē/ ▶ **adv. 1** with a lot of force; fiercely: *Holly struggled mightily with her mother over doing her homework.*
2 to a great or impressive extent; enormously: *this little town has contributed mightily to the life of the nation* | [as submodifier] *I am mightily relieved that it is all over.*

might·n't /ˈmītnt/ ▶ **contraction** might not: *you mightn't believe it, but I saw him stop a fight.*

might·y /ˈmītē/ ▶ **adj.** (**mightier, mightiest**) possessing great and impressive power or strength, esp on account of size: *three mighty industrial countries* | *mighty beasts.* ■ (of an action) performed with or requiring great strength: *a mighty heave* | figurative *a mighty blow against racism.* ■ informal very large: *she gave a mighty hiccup.*
▶ **adv.** [as submodifier] informal extremely: *this is mighty early to be planning a presidential campaign.*
– DERIVATIVES **might·i·ness n.**
– ORIGIN Old English *mihtig* (see MIGHT[2], -Y[1]).

mig·ma·tite /ˈmigmə,tīt/ ▶ **n.** Geology a rock composed of two intermingled but distinguishable components, typically a granitic rock within a metamorphic host rock.
– ORIGIN early 20th cent.: from Greek *migma, migmat-* 'mixture' + -ITE[1].

mi·gnon·ette /,minyəˈnet/ ▶ **n.** a herbaceous plant with spikes of small fragrant greenish flowers. ● Genus *Reseda*, family Resedaceae: several species, in particular the North African *R. odorata*, which is cultivated as an ornamental and for its essential oil, and the widespread **wild mignonette** (*R. alba*), originally a Mediterranean plant.
– ORIGIN early 18th cent.: from French *mignonnette*, diminutive of *mignon* 'small and sweet.'

mi·graine /ˈmī,grān/ (also **migraine headache**) ▶ **n.** a recurrent throbbing headache that typically affects one side of the head and is often accompanied by nausea and disturbed vision.
– DERIVATIVES **mi·grain·ous** /-,grānəs/ **adj.**
– ORIGIN late Middle English: from French, via late Latin from Greek *hēmikrania*, from *hēmi-* 'half' + *kranion* 'skull.'

mi·grain·eur /,mēgrəˈnər, ,mīgrā-/ ▶ **n.** someone who suffers from migraine headaches.

mi·grant /ˈmīgrənt/ ▶ **n.** an animal that migrates. ■ (also **migrant worker**) a worker who moves from place to place to do seasonal work.
▶ **adj.** [attrib.] tending to migrate or having migrated: *migrant birds.*

mi·grate /ˈmī,grāt/ ▶ **v.** [no obj.] (of an animal, typically a bird or fish) move from one region or habitat to another, esp. regularly according to the seasons: *as autumn arrives, the birds migrate south.* ■ (of a person) move from one area or country to settle in another, esp. in search of work: *rural populations have migrated to urban areas.* ■ move from one specific part of something to another: *cells that can form pigment migrate beneath the skin.* ■ Computing change or cause to change from using one system to another. ■ [with obj.] Computing transfer (programs or hardware) from one system to another.
– DERIVATIVES **mi·gra·tor** /-,grātər/ **n.**
– ORIGIN early 17th cent. (in the general sense 'move from one place to another'): from Latin *migrat-* 'moved, shifted,' from the verb *migrare.*

mi·gra·tion /mīˈgrāsʜən/ ▶ **n. 1** seasonal movement of animals from one region to another: *this butterfly's annual migration across North America.* ■ movement of people to a new area or country in order to find work or better living conditions.
2 movement from one part of something to another: *there is virtually no cell migration in plants.*
– DERIVATIVES **mi·gra·tion·al** /mīˈgrāsʜənl/ **adj.**

mi·gra·to·ry /ˈmīgrə,tôrē/ ▶ **adj.** denoting an animal that migrates: *migratory birds.* ■ relating to animal migration: *the migratory route for whale sharks.*

mih·rab /ˈmi(ə)rəb/ ▶ **n.** a niche in the wall of a mosque, at the point nearest to Mecca, toward which the congregation faces to pray.
– ORIGIN from Arabic *miḥrāb* 'place for prayer.'

mi·ka·do /miˈkädō/ ▶ **n.** historical a title given to the emperor of Japan.
– ORIGIN Japanese, from *mi* 'august' + *kado* 'gate'; the title is a transferred use of "gate (to the Imperial palace)," an ancient place of audience. Compare with PORTE.

mike[1] /mīk/ ▶ **n.** a code word representing the letter M, used in radio communication.

mike[2] informal ▶ **n.** a microphone.
▶ **v.** [with obj.] place a microphone close to (someone or something) or in (a place).
– ORIGIN 1920s: abbreviation.

Mi·ki·ta /miˈkētə/, Stanley (1940–), Canadian hockey player; born *Stanislav Gvoth*; born in Czechoslovakia. He played for the Chicago Blackhawks 1958–80 and led the National Hockey League in scoring four times 1964, 1965, 1967, 1968. Hockey Hall of Fame (1983).

Mi'k·maq /ˈmik,mak/ ▶ **n. & adj.** variant spelling of MICMAC.

Mí·ko·nos /ˈmēkə,nôs/ Greek name for MYKONOS.

mik·veh /ˈmikvə/ (also **mikva** or **mikvah**) ▶ **n.** (pl. **mikvehs** or **mikvahs** or **mikvoth** /mēkˈvōt/ or **mikvot** /mēkˈvōt/ or **mikvos** /mēkˈvəz, -ˈvōs/) a bath in which certain Jewish ritual purifications are performed. ■ the action of taking such a bath.
– ORIGIN mid 19th cent.: from Yiddish *mikve*, from Hebrew *miqweh*, literally 'collection (usually of water).'

mil[1] /mil/ informal ▶ **abbr.** ■ millimeters. ■ milliliters. ■ (used in sums of money) millions: *the insurance company coughed up five mil.*

mil[2] ▶ **n.** one thousandth of an inch.
– ORIGIN late 17th cent.: from Latin *millesimum* 'thousandth,' from *mille* 'thousand.'

mil. ▶ **abbr.** ■ military. ■ militia.

mi·la·dy /məˈlādē, mī-/ ▶ **n.** (pl. **miladies**) historical or humorous used to address or refer to an English noblewoman or great lady: *I went off to milady's boudoir.*
– ORIGIN late 18th cent.: via French from English *my lady*; compare with MILORD.

mil·age ▶ n. variant spelling of MILEAGE.

Mi·lan /mə'län, mə'lan/ an industrial city in northwestern Italy, the capital of Lombardy region; pop. 1,295,705 (2008). A powerful city, particularly from the 13th to the 15th centuries, Milan is today a leading financial and commercial center. Italian name **Milano**.
– DERIVATIVES **Mil·a·nese** /,milə'nēz, -'nēs/ adj. & n.

milch /milk, milCH/ ▶ adj. denoting a cow or other domestic mammal giving or kept for milk.
– ORIGIN Middle English: from Old English *-milce*, only in *thrimilce* 'May' (when cows could be milked three times a day), from the Germanic base of MILK.

mild /mīld/ ▶ adj. gentle and not easily provoked: *she was implacable, despite her mild exterior.* ■ (of a rule or punishment) of only moderate severity: *he received a mild sentence.* ■ not keenly felt or seriously intended: *she looked at him in mild surprise.* ■ (of an illness or pain) not serious or dangerous. ■ (of weather) moderately warm, esp. less cold than expected: *it is still mild enough to work outdoors.* ■ (of a medicine or cosmetic) acting gently and without causing harm. ■ (of food, drink, or tobacco) not sharp or strong in flavor: *a mild Italian cheese.*
– DERIVATIVES **mild·ish** adj.
– ORIGIN Old English *milde* (originally in the sense 'gracious, not severe in command'), of Germanic origin; related to Dutch and German *mild*, from an Indo-European root shared by Latin *mollis* and Greek *malthakos* 'soft.'

mil·dew /'mil,d(y)o͞o/ ▶ n. a thin whitish coating consisting of minute fungal hyphae, growing on plants or damp organic material such as paper or leather.
▶ v. affect or be affected with mildew.
– ORIGIN Old English *mildēaw* 'honeydew,' of Germanic origin. The first element is related to Latin *mel* and Greek *meli* 'honey.'

mil·dew·y /'mil,d(y)o͞oē/ ▶ adj. affected by mildew; moldy: *the first room had a mildewy smell to it.*

mild·ly /'mīldlē/ ▶ adv. in a mild manner, in particular without anger or severity. ■ not seriously or dangerously: *he had suffered mildly from the illness since he was 23.* ■ [as submodifier] to a slight extent: *he kept his voice mildly curious.*
– PHRASES **to put it mildly** (or **putting it mildly**) used to imply that the reality is more extreme, usually worse: *the proposals were, to put it mildly, unpopular.*

mild-man·nered ▶ adj. (of a person) gentle and not given to extremes of emotion.

mild·ness /'mīldnis/ ▶ n. **1** lack of intensity: *the tomatoes were sweet, compensating for the mildness of the cheese.*
2 lack of severity: *the mildness of her disease.* ■ relative warmth of weather.
3 a person's lack of aggressiveness: *the mildness of his manner and his desire to please everyone.*

mild steel ▶ n. steel containing a small percentage of carbon, strong and tough but not readily tempered.

mile /mīl/ ▶ n. (also **statute mile**) a unit of linear measure equal to 5,280 feet, or 1,760 yards (approximately 1.609 kilometers). ■ historical (also **Roman mile**) a Roman measure of 1,000 paces (approximately 1,620 yards). ■ (usu. **miles**) informal a very long way or a very great amount: *vistas that stretch for miles.* ■ a race extending over a mile.
▶ adv. (as submodifier **miles**) informal by a great amount or a long way: *the second tape is miles better.*
– PHRASES **be miles away** informal be lost in thought and consequently unaware of what is happening around one. **go the extra mile** be especially assiduous in one's attempt to achieve something. **a mile a minute** informal very quickly: *he talks a mile a minute.* **miles from anywhere** informal in a very isolated place. **see** (or **tell** or **spot**) **something a mile off** informal recognize something very easily: *the first-year campers can be spotted a mile off.* **stand** (or **stick**) **out a mile** informal be very obvious or incongruous.
– ORIGIN Old English *mīl*, based on Latin *mil(l)ia*, plural of *mille* 'thousand' (the original Roman unit of distance was *mille passus* 'a thousand paces').

mile·age /'mīlij/ ▶ n. **1** [usu. in sing.] a number of miles traveled or covered: *the car is in good condition, considering its mileage.* ■ [usu. as modifier] traveling expenses paid according to the number of miles traveled: *the mileage rate will be 34 cents per mile.*
2 informal actual or potential benefit from something: *he was getting a lot of mileage out of the mix-up.*
– PHRASES **your mileage may vary** informal your experience may be different: *as with all holistic treatments, you have to keep doing them, and your mileage may vary.*

mile-a-min·ute weed ▶ n. an invasive and noxious vine, native to Asia, that has downward-pointing barbs on the stem and the underside of leaves. It is considered an ecological threat in the eastern US. ● *Polygonum perfoliatum*, family Polygonaceae.

mile·post /'mīl,pōst/ ▶ n. a marker set up to indicate how distant a particular place is. ■ another term for MILESTONE. ■ a post one mile from the finishing post of a race.

mil·er /'mīlər/ ▶ n. informal a person or horse trained specially to run a mile.
– DERIVATIVES **mil·ing** /'mīliNG/ n.

mi·les glo·ri·o·sus /'mē,lās ,glôrē'ōəs/ ▶ n. (pl. **milites gloriosi** /'mēlə,tās ,glôrē'ōsē/) (in literature) a boastful soldier as a stock figure.
– ORIGIN Latin, from the title of a comedy by Plautus.

Mi·le·sian /mə'lēZHən, mī-/ ▶ n. a native or inhabitant of ancient Miletus.
▶ adj. of or relating to Miletus or its inhabitants.
– ORIGIN mid 16th cent.: via Latin from Greek *Milēsios* + -AN.

mile·stone /'mīl,stōn/ ▶ n. **1** a stone set up beside a road to mark the distance in miles to a particular place.
2 an action or event marking a significant change or stage in development: *the speech is being hailed as a milestone in race relations.*

Mi·le·tus /mī'lētəs, mə-/ an ancient city of the Ionian Greeks in southwestern Asia Minor. In the 7th and 6th centuries BC it was a powerful port, from which more than 60 colonies were founded on the shores of the Black Sea and in Italy and Egypt.

MILF /'milf/ ▶ n. (pl. **MILFs**) vulgar slang a sexually attractive older woman, typically one who has children.
– ORIGIN 1990s: acronym from *mom I'd like to fuck.*

mil·foil /'mil,foil/ ▶ n. **1** the common Eurasian yarrow.
2 (also **water milfoil**) a widely distributed and highly invasive aquatic plant with whorls of fine submerged leaves and wind-pollinated flowers. ● Genus *Myriophyllum*, family Haloragaceae.
– ORIGIN Middle English: via Old French from Latin *millefolium*, from *mille* 'thousand' + *folium* 'leaf.'

Mil·ford /,milfərd/ a city in southwestern Connecticut, west of New Haven; pop. 54,136 (est. 2008).

Mi·lhaud /mē'(y)ō/, Darius (1892–1974), French composer. A member of the group Les Six, he composed the music to Cocteau's ballet *Le Boeuf sur le toit* (1919). Much of his music was polytonal and influenced by jazz.

mil·i·a /'milēə/ plural form of MILIUM.

mil·i·ar·i·a /,milē'e(ə)rēə/ ▶ n. medical term for PRICKLY HEAT.
– ORIGIN early 19th cent.: modern Latin, from Latin *miliarius* (see MILIARY).

mil·i·ar·y /'milē,erē/ ▶ adj. (of a disease) accompanied by a rash with lesions resembling millet seed: *miliary tuberculosis.*
– ORIGIN late 17th cent.: from Latin *miliarius*, from *milium* 'millet.'

mi·lieu /mil'yo͞o, -'yə(r)/ ▶ n. (pl. **milieux** pronunc. same, or **milieus**) a person's social environment: *he grew up in a military milieu.*
– ORIGIN mid 19th cent.: French, from *mi* 'mid' + *lieu* 'place.'

Mi·li·la·ni Town /,mēlē'länē/ a planned community in Hawaii, on central Oahu Island, northwest of Honolulu; pop. 28,608 (2000).

mil·i·tant /'milətənt/ ▶ adj. combative and aggressive in support of a political or social cause, and typically favoring extreme, violent, or confrontational methods: *a militant nationalist.*
▶ n. a person who is active in this way.
– DERIVATIVES **mil·i·tance** /-təns/ n., **mil·i·tan·cy** /-tənsē/ n., **mil·i·tant·ly** adv.
– ORIGIN late Middle English (in the sense 'engaged in warfare'): from Old French, or from Latin *militant-* 'serving as a soldier,' from the verb *militare* (see MILITATE). The current sense dates from the early 20th cent.

WORD TRENDS See FIGHTER.

mil·i·tar·i·a /,mili'te(ə)rēə/ ▶ plural n. military articles of historical interest, such as weapons, uniforms, and equipment.
– ORIGIN 1960s: from MILITARY + -IA[2].

mil·i·ta·rism /'milətə,rizəm/ ▶ n. chiefly derogatory the belief or desire of a government or people that a country should maintain a strong military capability and be prepared to use it aggressively to defend or promote national interests.
– DERIVATIVES **mil·i·ta·rist** n. & adj.
– ORIGIN mid 19th cent.: from French *militarisme*, from *militaire* (see MILITARY).

mil·i·ta·ris·tic /,milətə'ristik/ ▶ adj. advocating or pursuing an aggressive military policy; hawkish: *the president and his militaristic administration.*

mil·i·ta·rize /'milətə,rīz/ ▶ v. [with obj.] (often as adj. **militarized**) give (something, esp. an organization) a military character or style: *militarized police forces.* ■ equip or supply (a place) with soldiers and other military resources: *a militarized security zone.*
– DERIVATIVES **mil·i·ta·ri·za·tion** /,milətərə'zāSHən/ n.

mil·i·tar·y /'milə,terē/ ▶ adj. of, relating to, or characteristic of soldiers or armed forces: *both leaders condemned the buildup of military activity.*
▶ n. (**the military**) the armed forces of a country.
– DERIVATIVES **mil·i·tar·i·ly** /,milə'te(ə)rəlē/ adv.
– ORIGIN late Middle English: from French *militaire* or Latin *militaris*, from *miles, milit-* 'soldier.'

mil·i·tar·y at·ta·ché ▶ n. an army officer serving with an embassy or attached as an observer to a foreign army.

mil·i·tar·y band ▶ n. a group of musicians playing brass, woodwind, and percussion instruments, typically while marching.

mil·i·tar·y hon·ors ▶ plural n. ceremonies performed by troops as a mark of respect at the burial of a member of the armed forces: *he was buried with full military honors.*

mil·i·tar·y-in·dus·tri·al com·plex ▶ n. a country's military establishment and those industries producing arms or other military materials, regarded as a powerful vested interest.

mil·i·tar·y law ▶ n. the law governing the armed forces.

mil·i·tar·y po·lice ▶ n. [treated as pl.] the corps responsible for police and disciplinary duties in an army.
– DERIVATIVES **mil·i·tar·y po·lice·man** n., **mil·i·tar·y po·lice·wom·an** n.

mil·i·ta·ry sci·ence ▶ n. the study of the causes and tactical principles of warfare.

mil·i·tar·y trib·une ▶ n. see TRIBUNE[1].

mil·i·tate /'milə,tāt/ ▶ v. [no obj.] (**militate against**) (of a fact or circumstance) be a powerful or conclusive factor in preventing: *these fundamental differences will militate against the two communities coming together.*
– ORIGIN late 16th cent.: from Latin *militat-* 'served as a soldier,' from the verb *militare*, from *miles, milit-* 'soldier.'

USAGE The verbs militate and mitigate are sometimes confused. See usage at MITIGATE.

mi·li·tes glo·ri·o·si /'mēlə,tās ,glôrē'ōsē/ plural form of MILES GLORIOSUS.

mi·li·tia /mə'lisHə/ ▶ n. a military force that is raised from the civil population to supplement a regular army in an emergency. ■ a military force that engages in rebel or terrorist activities, typically in opposition to a regular army. ■ all able-bodied civilians eligible by law for military service.
– ORIGIN late 16th cent.: from Latin, literally 'military service,' from *miles, milit-* 'soldier.'

mi·li·tia·man /mə'lisHəmən/ ▶ n. (pl. **militiamen**) a member of a militia.

mil·i·um /'milēəm/ ▶ n. (pl. **milia** /'milēə/) Medicine a small, hard, pale keratinous nodule formed on the skin, typically by a blocked sebaceous gland.
– ORIGIN mid 19th cent.: from Latin, literally 'millet' (because of a resemblance to a millet seed).

milk /milk/ ▶ n. an opaque white fluid rich in fat and protein, secreted by female mammals for the nourishment of their young. ■ the milk of cows (or occasionally goats or ewes) as food for humans: *a glass of milk.* ■ the white juice of certain plants: *coconut milk.* ■ a creamy-textured liquid with a particular ingredient or use: *cleansing milk.*
▶ v. [with obj.] **1** draw milk from (a cow or other animal), either by hand or mechanically. ■ [no obj.] (of an animal, esp. a cow) produce or yield milk: *the breed does seem to milk better in harder conditions.* ■ extract sap, venom, or other substances from.
2 exploit or defraud (someone), typically by taking regular small amounts of money over a period of time: [with complement] *he had milked his grandmother dry of all her money.* ■ get all possible advantage from (a situation): *the newspapers were milking the story for every possible drop of drama.* ■ elicit a favorable reaction from (an audience) and prolong

it for as long as possible: *he milked the crowd for every last drop of applause.*
– PHRASES **in milk** (of an animal, esp. a cow) producing milk. **it's no use crying over spilt** (or **spilled**) **milk** proverb there is no point in regretting something that has already happened and cannot be changed or reversed. **milk and honey** prosperity and abundance. [with biblical allusion to the prosperity of the Promised Land (Exod. 3:8).] **milk of human kindness** care and compassion for others. [with allusion to Shakespeare's *Macbeth*.]
– ORIGIN Old English *milc, milcian*, of Germanic origin; related to Dutch *melk* and German *Milch*, from an Indo-European root shared by Latin *mulgere* and Greek *amelgein* 'to milk.'

milk-and-wa·ter ▶ **adj.** [attrib.] lacking the will or ability to act effectively: *a milk-and-water rebel.*

milk bar ▶ **n.** Brit. a snack bar that sells milk drinks and other refreshments.

milk choc·o·late ▶ **n.** solid chocolate made with the addition of milk.

milk·er /ˈmilkər/ ▶ **n. 1** a cow or other animal that is kept for milk, esp. one of a specified productivity: *the cows were no more than fair milkers.*
2 a person or device that milks cows.

milk fe·ver ▶ **n. 1** an acute illness in female cows, goats, etc., that have just produced young, caused by calcium deficiency.
2 a fever in women caused by infection after childbirth, formerly supposed to be due to the swelling of the breasts with milk.

milk·fish /ˈmilkˌfisʜ/ ▶ **n.** (pl. **same** or **milkfishes**) a large active silvery fish of the Indo-Pacific region, farmed for food in Southeast Asia and the Philippines. ● *Chanos chanos*, the only member of the family Chanidae.

milk glass ▶ **n.** semitranslucent glass, whitened by the addition of various ingredients: [as modifier] *milk-glass jars.* Also called OPALINE.

milk·ing par·lor ▶ **n.** see PARLOR (sense 3 of the noun).

milk·ing stool ▶ **n.** a short three-legged stool, of a kind traditionally used while milking cows.

milk leg ▶ **n.** painful swelling of the leg after giving birth, caused by thrombophlebitis in the femoral vein.

milk·maid /ˈmilkˌmād/ ▶ **n.** chiefly archaic a girl or woman who milks cows or does other work in a dairy.

milk·man /ˈmilkmən, -ˌman/ ▶ **n.** (pl. **milkmen**) a person who delivers and sells milk.

milk of mag·ne·sia ▶ **n.** a white suspension of hydrated magnesium carbonate in water, used as an antacid or laxative.
– ORIGIN from the trademark.

Milk Riv·er a river that flows for 625 miles (1,000 km) through northwestern Montana and southern Alberta, into the Missouri River. It is the most northwestern part of the Missouri-Mississippi river system.

milk run ▶ **n.** a routine, uneventful journey, esp. by plane.

milk shake (also **milkshake**) ▶ **n.** a cold drink made of milk, a sweet flavoring such as fruit or chocolate, and typically ice cream, whisked until it is frothy.

milk sick·ness ▶ **n.** a condition of cattle and sheep in the western US, caused by eating white snakeroot, which contains a toxic alcohol. It sometimes occurs in humans who have eaten meat or dairy products from affected animals.

milk snake ▶ **n.** a harmless North American constrictor that is typically strongly marked with red and black on yellow or white. It was formerly supposed to suck milk from sleeping cows. ● Genus *Lampropeltis*, family Colubridae: several species, in particular *L. triangulum*. Compare with KING SNAKE.

milk·sop /ˈmilkˌsäp/ ▶ **n.** a person who is indecisive and lacks courage.

milk sug·ar ▶ **n.** another term for LACTOSE.

milk this·tle ▶ **n.** a European thistle with a solitary purple flower and glossy marbled leaves, naturalized in North America and used in herbal medicine. ● *Silybum marianum*, family Compositae. ■ another term for SOW THISTLE.

milk tooth ▶ **n.** any of a set of early, temporary (deciduous) teeth in children or young mammals that fall out as the permanent teeth erupt (in children, between the ages of about 6 and 12).

milk vetch ▶ **n.** a plant of the pea family found throughout the temperate zone of the northern hemisphere, grown in several regions as a fodder plant. ● Genus *Astragalus*, family Leguminosae: numerous species, including the widespread *A. canadensis*.

milk·weed /ˈmilkˌwēd/ ▶ **n.**
1 a herbaceous American plant with milky sap. Some kinds attract butterflies, some yield a variety of useful products, and some are grown as ornamentals. ● Genus *Asclepias*, family Asclepiadaceae: several species, in particular the **common milkweed** (A. syriaca).
2 (also **milkweed butterfly**) another term for MONARCH BUTTERFLY.

common milkweed

milk-white ▶ **adj.** of the opaque white color of milk: *she had milk-white skin.*

milk·wort /ˈmilkˌwərt, -ˌwôrt/ ▶ **n.** a small plant that was formerly believed to increase the milk yield of cows and nursing mothers. Its tiny flowers, which may be white, pink, yellow-orange, blue, or greenish, usually appear in cloverlike heads. ● Genus *Polygala*, family Polygalaceae: several species, including the **cross-leaved milkwort** (*P. cruciata*) and the **yellow milkwort** (*P. lutea*).

milk·y /ˈmilkē/ ▶ **adj.** (**milkier, milkiest**)
1 containing or mixed with a large amount of milk: *a cup of sweet milky coffee.* ■ (of a cow) producing a lot of milk. ■ resembling milk, esp. in color: *not a blemish marred her milky skin.* ■ (of something that is usually clear) cloudy: *the old man's milky, uncomprehending eyes.*
2 informal, dated weak and compliant: *they just talk that way to make you turn milky.*
– DERIVATIVES **milk·i·ly** /-əlē/ **adv.**, **milk·i·ness n.**

milk·y spore ▶ **n.** a bacterial disease of beetle larvae, including the Japanese beetle; the bacterium has been isolated and used in a commercial pesticide sold under the same name. ● *Bacillus popilliae*, family Bacillaceae.

Milk·y Way a faint band of light crossing the sky, made up of vast numbers of faint stars. It corresponds to the plane of our Galaxy, in which most of its stars are located. ■ the galaxy in which our sun is located.

Mill /mil/, John Stuart (1806–73), English philosopher and economist. He is best known for his political and moral works, esp. *On Liberty* (1859), which argued for the importance of individuality, and *Utilitarianism* (1861), which extensively developed Bentham's theory.
– DERIVATIVES **Mill·i·an** /ˈmilēən/ **adj.**

mill[1] /mil/ ▶ **n. 1** a building equipped with machinery for grinding grain into flour. ■ a piece of machinery of this type. ■ a domestic device for grinding a solid substance to powder or pulp: *a coffee mill.* ■ a building fitted with machinery for a manufacturing process: *a steel mill* | [as modifier] *a mill town.* ■ a piece of manufacturing machinery. ■ a place that processes things or people in a mechanical way: *a correspondence school that was just a diploma mill.*
2 informal an engine.
3 informal, dated a boxing match or a fistfight.
▶ **v. 1** [with obj.] grind or crush (something) in a mill: *hard wheats are easily milled into white flour* | (as adj., with submodifier **milled**) *freshly milled black pepper.* ■ cut or shape (metal) with a rotating tool: (as adj. **milling**) *lathes and milling machines.* ■ (usu. as adj. **milled**) produce regular ribbed markings on the edge of (a coin) as a protection against illegal clipping.
2 [no obj.] (**mill about/around**) (of people or animals) move around in a confused mass: *people milled about the room, shaking hands* | (as adj. **milling**) *the milling crowds of guests.*
3 [with obj.] thicken (wool or another animal fiber) by fulling it.
– PHRASES **go** (or **put someone**) **through the mill** undergo (or cause someone to undergo) an unpleasant experience.
– DERIVATIVES **mill·a·ble adj.**
– ORIGIN Old English *mylen*, based on late Latin *molinum*, from Latin *mola* 'grindstone, mill,' from *molere* 'to grind.'

mill[2] ▶ **n.** a monetary unit used only in calculations, worth one thousandth of a dollar.
– ORIGIN late 18th cent.: from Latin *millesimum* 'thousandth part'; compare with CENT.

Mil·lais /məˈlā/, Sir John Everett (1829–96), English painter. A founding member of the Pre-Raphaelite Brotherhood, he produced lavishly painted portraits and landscapes.

Mil·lay /məˈlā/, Edna St. Vincent (1892–1950), US poet and writer; pen name **Nancy Boyd**. Much of her poetry is collected in *Renascence and Other Poems* (1917), *Collected Sonnets* (1941), and *Collected Lyrics* (1943).

mill·board /ˈmilˌbôrd/ ▶ **n.** stiff gray pasteboard, used for the covers of books.

Mill·creek /ˈmilˌkrēk/ a township in northwestern Pennsylvania; pop. 51,799 (est. 2008).

mill·dam /ˈmilˌdam/ ▶ **n.** a dam built across a stream to raise the level of the water so that it will turn the wheel of a water mill.

Mille, Cecil B. de, see DE MILLE.

mille-feuille /ˌmēl ˈfœy(ə), fəˈwē/ ▶ **n.** a rich dessert consisting of many very thin layers of puff pastry and such fillings as whipped cream, custard, fruit, etc.
– ORIGIN French, literally 'thousand-leaf.'

mil·le·fi·o·ri /ˌmiləfēˈôrē/ ▶ **n.** a kind of ornamental glass in which a number of glass rods of different sizes and colors are fused together and cut into sections that form various patterns, typically embedded in colorless transparent glass to make items such as paperweights.
– ORIGIN mid 19th cent.: from Italian *millefiore*, literally 'a thousand flowers.'

mille·fleurs /mēlˈflər, -ˈflo͝or/ ▶ **n.** a pattern of flowers and leaves used in tapestry, on porcelain, or in other decorative items.
– ORIGIN mid 19th cent.: French, literally 'a thousand flowers.'

mil·le·nar·i·an /ˌmiləˈne(ə)rēən/ ▶ **adj.** relating to or believing in Christian millenarianism.
▶ **n.** a person who believes in the doctrine of the millennium.
– ORIGIN mid 17th cent.: from late Latin *millenarius* (see MILLENARY) + -AN.

mil·le·nar·i·an·ism /ˌmiləˈne(ə)rēəˌnizəm/ ▶ **n.** the doctrine of or belief in a future (and typically imminent) thousand-year age of blessedness, beginning with or culminating in the Second Coming of Christ. It is central to the teaching of groups such as Plymouth Brethren, Adventists, Mormons, and Jehovah's Witnesses. ■ belief in a future golden age of peace, justice, and prosperity.
– DERIVATIVES **mil·le·nar·i·an·ist n. & adj.**

mil·le·nar·y /ˈmiləˌnerē/ ▶ **n.** (pl. **millenaries**) a period of a thousand years. Compare with MILLENNIUM. ■ a thousandth anniversary.
▶ **adj.** consisting of a thousand people, years, etc.
– ORIGIN mid 16th cent.: from late Latin *millenarius* 'containing a thousand,' based on Latin *mille* 'thousand.'

Mil·len·nial /miˈlenēəl/ ▶ **n.** informal another term for GEN-YER.

mil·len·ni·al·ism /məˈlenēəˌlizəm/ ▶ **n.** another term for MILLENARIANISM.
– DERIVATIVES **mil·len·ni·al·ist n. & adj.**

mil·len·ni·um /məˈlenēəm/ ▶ **n.** (pl. **millennia** /-ˈlenēə/ or **millenniums**) **1** a period of a thousand years, esp. when calculated from the traditional date of the birth of Christ. ■ (**the millennium**) Christian Theology the prophesied thousand-year reign of Christ at the end of the age (Rev. 20:1–5). ■ (**the millennium**) a utopian period of good government, great happiness, and prosperity.
2 an anniversary of a thousand years: *the millennium of the Russian Orthodox Church.* ■ (**the millennium**) the point at which one period of a thousand years ends and another begins.
– DERIVATIVES **mil·len·ni·al** /-ēəl/ **adj.**
– ORIGIN mid 17th cent.: modern Latin, from Latin *mille* 'thousand,' on the pattern of *biennium*.

> **USAGE** The spelling of **millennium** is less difficult if one remembers that it comes ultimately from two Latin words containing double letters: *mille*, 'thousand,' and *annum*, 'year.'

mil·le·pede /ˈmiləˌpēd/ ▶ **n.** variant spelling of MILLIPEDE.

mil·le·pore /ˈmiləˌpôr/ ▶ **n.** Zoology a fire coral.
– ORIGIN mid 18th cent.: from French *millépore* or modern Latin *millepora*, from Latin *mille* 'thousand' + *porus* 'pore.'

Mill·er[1] /ˈmilər/, Arthur (1915–2005), US playwright. He achieved success with *Death of a Salesman* (1949). *The Crucible* (1953) used the Salem witch trials of 1692 as an allegory for McCarthyism. He was married to Marilyn Monroe 1955–1961. Other notable works: *All My Sons* (1947), *After the Fall* (1964), and *The Ryan Interview* (1995).

Mill·er[2], Glenn (1904–44), US jazz trombonist and bandleader; full name *Alton Glenn Miller*. From 1938, he led his celebrated big band, with which he recorded his signature tune "Moonlight Serenade." He died when his airplane disappeared on a routine flight across the English Channel.

Mill·er[3], Henry (Valentine) (1891–1980), US novelist. His autobiographical novels *Tropic of Cancer* (1934) and *Tropic of Capricorn* (1939) were banned in the US until the 1960s because of frank depictions of sex and the use of obscenities.

Mil·ler[4], Samuel Freeman (1816–90), US Supreme Court associate justice 1862–90. A strong advocate of individual rights, he was appointed to the Court by President Lincoln.

mill·er /ˈmilər/ ▶ **n.** a person who owns or works in a grain mill.

mill·er·ite /ˈmiləˌrīt/ ▶ **n.** a mineral consisting of nickel sulfide and typically occurring as slender needle-shaped bronze crystals.
– ORIGIN mid 19th cent.: named after William H. *Miller* (1801–80), English scientist, + -ITE[1].

mill·er's thumb ▶ **n.** a small European freshwater fish of the sculpin family, having a broad flattened head and most active at night. Also called BULLHEAD. ● *Cottus gobio*, family Cottidae.

mil·les·i·mal /məˈlesəməl/ ▶ **adj.** consisting of thousandth parts; thousandth.
▶ **n.** a thousandth part.
– DERIVATIVES **mil·les·i·mal·ly** adv.
– ORIGIN early 18th cent.: from Latin *millesimus* (from *mille* 'thousand') + -AL.

Mil·let /mēˈye, -ˈlā/, Jean (François) (1814–75), French painter. He was noted for the dignity he brought to the treatment of peasant subjects.

mil·let /ˈmilit/ ▶ **n.** a fast-growing cereal plant that is widely grown in warm countries and regions with poor soils. The numerous small seeds are used to make flour or alcoholic drinks. ● Several species in the family Gramineae, in particular **common millet** (*Panicum miliaceum*), of temperate regions, the tropical **finger millet** (*Eleusine caracana*), which is a staple in parts of Africa and India, and PEARL MILLET.
– ORIGIN late Middle English: from French, diminutive of dialect *mil*, from Latin *milium*.

Mil·lett /ˈmilit/, Kate (1934–), US feminist; full name *Katherine Murray Millett*. She became involved in the civil rights movement of the 1960s and advocated a radical feminism in *Sexual Politics* (1970).

mill·hand /ˈmilˌhand/ ▶ **n.** a worker in a mill or factory.

milli- ▶ **comb. form** (used commonly in units of measurement) a thousand, chiefly denoting a factor of one thousandth: *milligram* | *millipede*.
– ORIGIN from Latin *mille* 'thousand.'

mil·li·am·me·ter /ˌmilēˈa(m)ˌmētər/ ▶ **n.** an instrument for measuring electric current in milliamperes.

mil·li·amp /ˈmilēˌamp/ ▶ **n.** short for MILLIAMPERE.

mil·li·am·pere /ˌmilēˈamˌpi(ə)r/ ▶ **n.** one thousandth of an ampere, a measure for small electric currents.

mil·liard /ˈmilˌyärd, -yərd/ ▶ **n.** Brit. one thousand million (a term now largely superseded by billion).
– ORIGIN late 18th cent.: French, from *mille* 'thousand.'

mil·li·bar /ˈmiləˌbär/ ▶ **n.** one thousandth of a bar, the cgs unit of atmospheric pressure equivalent to 100 pascals.

mil·lieme /mē(l)ˈyem/ ▶ **n.** a monetary unit of Egypt, equal to one thousandth of a pound.
– ORIGIN from French *millième* 'thousandth.'

mil·li·gram /ˈmiləˌgram/ (Brit. also **milligramme**) (abbr.: **mg**) ▶ **n.** one thousandth of a gram.

Mil·li·kan /ˈmilikən/, Robert Andrews (1868–1953), US physicist. He was the first to give an accurate figure for the electric charge on an electron. Nobel Prize for Physics (1923).

mil·li·li·ter /ˈmiləˌlētər/ (Brit. **millilitre**) (abbr.: **ml**) ▶ **n.** one thousandth of a liter (0.002 pint).

mil·li·me·ter /ˈmiləˌmētər/ (Brit. **millimetre**) (abbr.: **mm**) ▶ **n.** one thousandth of a meter (0.039 in.).

mil·li·ner /ˈmilənər/ ▶ **n.** a person who makes or sells women's hats.
– ORIGIN late Middle English (originally in the sense 'native of Milan,' later 'a vendor of fancy goods from Milan'): from MILAN + -ER[1].

mil·li·ner·y /ˈmiləˌnerē/ ▶ **n.** (pl. **millineries**) women's hats. ■ the trade or business of a milliner.

mil·lion /ˈmilyən/ ▶ **cardinal number** (pl. **millions** or (with numeral or quantifying word) **same**) (**a/one million**) the number equivalent to the product of a thousand and a thousand; 1,000,000 or 10^6: *a million people will benefit* | *a population of half a million* | *a cost of more than $20 million.* ■ (**millions**) the numbers from a million to a billion. ■ (**millions**) several million things or people: *millions of TV viewers.* ■ informal an unspecified but very large number or amount of something: *I've got millions of beer bottles in my cellar* | *you're one in a million.* ■ (**the millions**) the bulk of the population: *movies for the millions.* ■ a million dollars: *the author is set to make millions.*
– PHRASES **look** (or **feel**) (**like**) **a million dollars** informal (of a person) look or feel extremely good.
– DERIVATIVES **mil·lion·fold** /-ˌfōld/ adj. & adv., **mil·lionth** /-yənTH/ ordinal number.
– ORIGIN late Middle English: from Old French, probably from Italian *milione*, from *mille* 'thousand' + the augmentative suffix *-one*.

mil·lion·aire /ˌmilyəˈne(ə)r, ˈmilyəˌne(ə)r/ ▶ **n.** a person whose assets are worth one million dollars or more.
– ORIGIN early 19th cent.: from French *millionnaire*, from *million* (see MILLION).

mil·lion·air·ess /ˌmilyəˈne(ə)rəs/ ▶ **n.** a female millionaire.

mil·li·pede /ˈmiləˌpēd/ (also **millepede**) ▶ **n.** a myriapod invertebrate with an elongated body composed of many segments, most of which bear two pairs of legs. Most kinds are herbivorous and shun light, living in the soil or under stones and logs. ● Class Diplopoda: several orders.
– ORIGIN early 17th cent.: from Latin *millepeda* 'wood louse,' from *mille* 'thousand' + *pes, ped-* 'foot.'

mil·li·sec·ond /ˈmiləˌsekənd/ ▶ **n.** one thousandth of a second.

mil·li·volt /ˈmiləˌvôlt/ ▶ **n.** one thousandth of a volt.

mill·pond /ˈmilˌpänd/ (also **mill pond**) ▶ **n.** the pool that is created by a milldam and provides the head of water that powers a water mill.

mill·race /ˈmilˌrās/ ▶ **n.** the channel carrying the swift current of water that drives a mill wheel.

mill·stone /ˈmilˌstōn/ ▶ **n. 1** each of two circular stones used for grinding grain.
2 a heavy and inescapable responsibility: *she threatened to become a millstone around his neck.*

mill·stream /ˈmilˌstrēm/ ▶ **n.** the current of water in a millrace. ■ another term for MILLRACE.

mill wheel ▶ **n.** a wheel used to drive a water mill.

mill·work·er /ˈmilˌwərkər/ ▶ **n.** a worker in a mill or factory.

mill·wright /ˈmilˌrīt/ ▶ **n.** a person who designs or builds mills or who maintains mill machinery.

Milne /miln/, A. A. (1882–1956), English writer of stories and poems for children; full name *Alan Alexander Milne*. He created the character Winnie the Pooh for his son **Christopher Robin** (1920–1996). Notable works: *Winnie-the-Pooh* (1926) and *When We Were Very Young* (verse collection, 1924).

mi·lo /ˈmīlō/ ▶ **n.** sorghum of a drought-resistant variety that is an important grain in the central US, Africa, and Asia.
– ORIGIN late 19th cent.: from Sesotho *maili*.

mi·lord /məˈlôrd, mī-/ ▶ **n.** historical or humorous used to address or refer to an English nobleman, esp. one traveling in Europe.
– ORIGIN early 17th cent.: via French from English *my lord*; compare with MILADY.

Mí·los /ˈmēˌläs, -ˌlôs/ Greek name for **MELOS**.

Mi·lo·se·vic /miˈläsəvitsH/, Slobodan (1941–2006), Serbian politician, president of Serbia 1989–97 and of Yugoslavia 1997–2000. His nationalist policies accelerated the breakup of Yugoslavia and led to war in Bosnia and Herzegovina, Croatia, and Kosovo. He was extradited to face war crimes charges at a UN tribunal in The Hague, but died before the trial ended.

Mi·losz /ˈmēlôsH/, Czeslaw (1911–2004), US poet and writer; born in Lithuania. He wrote the political essay *The Captive Mind* (1953). His novels include *The Seizure of Power* (1953), and his poetry is collected in volumes such as *Bells in Winter* (1978) and *The Collected Poems, 1931–1987* (1988). Nobel Prize for Literature (1980).

milque·toast /ˈmilkˌtōst/ (also **Milquetoast**) ▶ **n.** a person who is timid or submissive: [as modifier] *a soppy, milquetoast composer.*
– ORIGIN 1930s: from the name of a cartoon character, Caspar *Milquetoast*, created by H. T. Webster in 1924.

mil·reis /milˈrāsH, -ˈrās/ ▶ **n.** (pl. **same**) a former monetary unit of Portugal and Brazil, equal to one thousand reis.
– ORIGIN Portuguese, from *mil* 'thousand' + *reis*, plural of *real* (see REAL[2]).

milt /milt/ ▶ **n.** the semen of a male fish. ■ a sperm-filled reproductive gland of a male fish.
– ORIGIN Old English *milte* 'spleen,' of Germanic origin; perhaps related to MELT. The current sense dates from the late 15th cent.

Mil·ton /ˈmiltn/, John (1608–74), English poet. His three major works, *Paradise Lost* (1667; revised, 1674), *Paradise Regained* (1671), and *Samson Agonistes* (1671), which were completed after he had gone blind in 1652, show his mastery of blank verse.
– DERIVATIVES **Mil·to·ni·an** /milˈtōnēən/ adj., **Mil·ton·ic** /milˈtänik/ adj.

Mil·ton Keynes /ˌmiltn ˈkēnz/ a town in south central England; pop. 235,280 (est. 2009).

Mil·wau·kee /milˈwôkē/ an industrial port and city in southeastern Wisconsin, on the western shore of Lake Michigan; pop. 604,477 (est. 2008). It is noted for its brewing industry and is an important port on the St. Lawrence Seaway.

mim /mim/ ▶ **adj.** Scottish affectedly modest or demure.
– ORIGIN late 16th cent.: imitative of pursing the lips.

Mi·mas /ˈmīməs, ˈmē-/ Astronomy a satellite of Saturn, the seventh closest to the planet, discovered by W. Herschel in 1789. It has a diameter of 242 miles (390 km) and has many craters, one of which has a diameter of 80 miles (130 km), a third of the diameter of Mimas.
– ORIGIN named after a giant in Greek mythology, killed by Ares.

mim·bar /ˈmimˌbär/ ▶ **n.** variant spelling of MINBAR.

MIME /mīm, ˈem ˈī ˈem ˈē/ ▶ **n.** Computing a standard for formatting files of different types, such as text, graphics, or audio, so they can be sent over the Internet and seen or played by a Web browser or e-mail application.
– ORIGIN late 20th cent.: an acronym for *multipurpose Internet mail extensions.*

mime /mīm/ ▶ **n. 1** the theatrical technique of suggesting action, character, or emotion without words, using only gesture, expression, and movement. ■ a theatrical performance or part of a performance using such a technique. ■ an action or set of actions intended to convey the idea of another action or an idea or feeling: *he performed a brief mime of someone fencing.* ■ a practitioner of mime or a performer in a mime.
2 (in ancient Greece and Rome) a simple farcical drama including mimicry.
▶ **v.** [with obj.] use gesture and movement without words in the acting of (a play or role). ■ convey an impression of (an idea or feeling) by gesture and movement, without using words; mimic (an action or set of actions) in this way: *he stands up and mimes throwing a spear.*
– DERIVATIVES **mim·er** n.
– ORIGIN early 17th cent. (also in the sense 'mimic or jester'): from Latin *mimus*, from Greek *mimos*.

mim·e·o /ˈmimēˌō/ ▶ **n.** short for MIMEOGRAPH.

mim·e·o·graph /ˈmimēəˌgraf/ ▶ **n.** a duplicating machine that produces copies from a stencil, now superseded by the photocopier. ■ a copy produced on such a machine.
▶ **v.** [with obj.] make a copy of (a document) with such a machine.
– ORIGIN late 19th cent.: formed irregularly from Greek *mimeomai* 'I imitate' + -GRAPH.

mi·me·sis /məˈmēsis, mī-/ ▶ **n.** formal or technical imitation, in particular: ■ representation or imitation of the real world in art and literature. ■ the deliberate imitation of the behavior of one group of people by another as a factor in social change. ■ Zoology another term for MIMICRY.
– ORIGIN mid 16th cent.: from Greek *mimēsis*, from *mimeisthai* 'to imitate.'

mi·met·ic /məˈmetik/ ▶ **adj.** formal or technical relating to, constituting, or habitually practicing mimesis: *mimetic patterns in butterflies.*
– DERIVATIVES **mi·met·i·cal·ly** /-ik(ə)lē/ adv.
– ORIGIN mid 17th cent.: from Greek *mimētikos* 'imitation,' from *mimeisthai* 'to imitate.'

mim·e·tite /ˈmiməˌtīt, ˈmī-/ ▶ **n.** a yellow or brown mineral consisting of a chloride and arsenate of lead, typically found as a crust or needlelike crystals in lead deposits.
– ORIGIN mid 19th cent.: from Greek *mimētēs* 'imitator' + -ITE[1].

mim·ic /ˈmimik/ ▶ **v.** (**mimics, mimicking, mimicked**) [with obj.] imitate (someone or their actions or words), typically in order to entertain or ridicule: *she mimicked Eileen's voice.* ■ (of an animal or plant) resemble or imitate (another animal or plant), esp. to deter predators or for camouflage. ■ (of a drug) replicate the physiological effects of (another substance). ■ (of a disease) exhibit symptoms that bear a deceptive resemblance to those of (another disease).
▶ **n.** a person skilled in imitating the voice, mannerisms, or movements of others in an

m

entertaining way. ■ an animal or plant that exhibits mimicry.
▶ **adj.** [attrib.] imitative of something, esp. for amusement: *they were waging mimic war.*
– DERIVATIVES **mim·ick·er** n.
– ORIGIN late 16th cent. (as noun and adjective): via Latin from Greek *mimikos*, from *mimos* 'mime.'

mim·ic·ry /'mimәkrē/ ▶ **n.** (pl. **mimicries**) the action or art of imitating someone or something, typically in order to entertain or ridicule: *the word was spoken with gently teasing mimicry | a playful mimicry of the techniques of realist writers.* ■ Biology the close external resemblance of an animal or plant (or part of one) to another animal, plant, or inanimate object. See also BATESIAN MIMICRY, MÜLLERIAN MIMICRY.

mi·mo·sa /mi'mōsә, mī-, -zә/ ▶ **n. 1** an Australian acacia tree with delicate fernlike leaves and yellow flowers that are used by florists. ● *Acacia dealbata*, family Leguminosae.
2 another name for the SILK TREE.
3 a plant of a genus that includes the sensitive plant. ● Genus *Mimosa*, family Leguminosae.
4 a drink of champagne and orange juice.
– ORIGIN modern Latin, apparently from Latin *mimus* 'mime' (because the plant seemingly mimics the sensitivity of an animal) + the feminine suffix *-osa*.

Min /min/ ▶ **n.** a dialect of Chinese spoken by more than 50 million people, mainly in Fujian province, Hainan, and Taiwan.
– ORIGIN Chinese.

min. ▶ **abbr.** ■ minim (fluid measure). ■ minimum. ■ minute(s).

mi·na·cious /mә'nāSHәs/ ▶ **adj.** rare menacing; threatening.
– ORIGIN mid 17th cent.: from Latin *minax, minac-* 'threatening' (from *minari* 'threaten') + **-ous**.

Min·a·ma·ta dis·ease /,mēnә'mätә/ ▶ **n.** chronic poisoning by alkyl mercury compounds from industrial waste, characterized by (usually permanent) impairment of brain functions such as speech, sight, and muscular coordination.
– ORIGIN 1950s: named after *Minamata*, a town in Japan.

m

Mi·nang·ka·bau /,mē,naNGkә'bou/ ▶ **n.** an Indonesian language spoken by more than 6 million people in Sumatra and elsewhere.
– ORIGIN Malay and Indonesian.

min·a·ret /,minә'ret/ ▶ **n.** a tall slender tower, typically part of a mosque, with a balcony from which a muezzin calls Muslims to prayer.
– DERIVATIVES **min·a·ret·ed** adj.
– ORIGIN late 17th cent.: from French, or from Spanish *minarete*, Italian *minaretto*, via Turkish from Arabic *manār(a)* 'lighthouse, minaret,' based on *nār* 'fire or light.'

minaret

min·a·to·ry /'minә,tôrē, 'mī-/ ▶ **adj.** formal expressing or conveying a threat: *he is unlikely to be deterred by minatory finger-wagging.*
– ORIGIN mid 16th cent.: from late Latin *minatorius*, from *minat-* 'threatened,' from the verb *minari*.

min·au·dière /,mēnōd'yer/ ▶ **n.** a small, decorative handbag without handles or a strap.
– ORIGIN French, literally 'coquettish woman,' from *minauder* 'simper.'

min·bar /'min,bär/ (also **mimbar** /'mim-/) ▶ **n.** a short flight of steps used as a platform by a preacher in a mosque.
– ORIGIN from Arabic *minbar*.

mince /mins/ ▶ **v.** [with obj.] **1** (often as adj. **minced**) cut up or grind (food, esp. meat) into very small pieces, typically in a machine with revolving blades: *minced beef.*
2 [no obj.] walk with an affected delicacy or fastidiousness, typically with short quick steps: *there were plenty of secretaries mincing about.*
▶ **n.** something minced, esp. mincemeat: *put the mince on a dish.*
– PHRASES **not mince words** (or **one's words**) speak candidly and directly, esp. when criticizing someone or something: *a gruff surgeon who does not mince words.*
– DERIVATIVES **minc·er** n.
– ORIGIN late Middle English: from Old French *mincier*, based on Latin *minutia* 'smallness.'

mince·meat /'mins,mēt/ ▶ **n. 1** a mixture of currants, raisins, sugar, apples, candied citrus peel, spices, and suet, typically baked in a pie.
2 minced meat.
– PHRASES **make mincemeat of someone** informal defeat someone decisively or easily in a fight, contest, or argument.

mince pie ▶ **n.** a small, round pie or tart containing sweet mincemeat, typically eaten at Christmas.

Minch /minCH/ (**the Minch** or **the Minches**) a channel in the Atlantic Ocean, between the mainland of Scotland and the Outer Hebrides. The northern stretch is called the **North Minch**; the southern stretch, northwest of Skye, is called the **Little Minch**.

minc·ing /'minsiNG/ ▶ **adj.** (of a man) affectedly dainty in manner or gait: *he followed her with quick, mincing steps.*
– DERIVATIVES **minc·ing·ly** adv.

mind /mīnd/ ▶ **n. 1** the element of a person that enables them to be aware of the world and their experiences, to think, and to feel; the faculty of consciousness and thought: *as the thoughts ran through his mind, he came to a conclusion | people have the price they are prepared to pay settled in their minds.* ■ a person's mental processes contrasted with physical action: *I wrote a letter in my mind.*
2 a person's intellect: *his keen mind.* ■ a person's memory: *the company's name **slips my mind**.* ■ a person identified with their intellectual faculties: *he was one of the greatest minds of his time.*
3 a person's attention: *I expect my employees to keep their minds on the job.* ■ the will or determination to achieve something: *anyone can lose weight if they set their mind to it.*
▶ **v.** [with obj.] **1** [often with negative] be distressed, annoyed, or worried by: *I don't mind the rain.* ■ have an objection to: *what does that mean, if you don't mind my asking?* | [with clause] *do you mind if I have a cigarette?* ■ [with negative or in questions] (**mind doing something**) be reluctant to do something (often used in polite requests): *I don't mind admitting I was worried.* ■ (**would not mind something**) informal used to express one's strong enthusiasm for something: *I wouldn't mind some coaching from him!*
2 regard as important; feel concern about: *never mind the opinion polls* | [no obj.] *why should she mind about a few snubs from people she didn't care for?* ■ [with clause in imperative] dated used to urge someone to remember or take care to bring about something: *mind you look after the children.* ■ [no obj.] (also **mind you**) used to introduce a qualification to a previous statement: *we've got some decorations up—not a lot, mind you.* ■ [no obj.] informal used to make a command more insistent or to draw attention to a statement: *be early to bed tonight, mind.* ■ be obedient to: *you think about how much Cal does for you, and you mind her, you hear?* ■ Scottish remember: *I mind the time when he lost his false teeth.*
3 take care of temporarily: *we left our husbands to mind the children while we went out.* ■ [in imperative] used to warn someone to avoid injury or damage from a hazard: *mind your head on that cupboard!* ■ [in imperative] be careful about the quality or nature of: *mind your manners!*
4 [with infinitive] (**be minded**) chiefly formal be inclined or disposed to do a particular thing: *he was minded to reject the application | the Board was given leave to object if it was so minded.*
– PHRASES **be of two minds** be unable to decide between alternatives. **be of one** (or **a different**) **mind** share the same (or hold a different) opinion. **bear** (or **keep**) **in mind** remember and take into account: [with clause] *you need to bear in mind that the figures vary from place to place.* **close one's mind to** refuse to consider or acknowledge. **come** (or **spring**) **to mind** (of a thought or idea) occur to someone. **don't mind if I do** informal used to accept an invitation. **give someone a piece of one's mind** tell someone what one thinks of them, esp. in anger. **have a** (or **a good** or **half a**) **mind to do something** be very much inclined to do something: *I've a good mind to write to the manager to complain.* **have someone or something in mind** be thinking of. ■ intend: *I had it in mind to ask you to work for me.* **have a mind of one's own** be capable of independent opinion or action. ■ (of an inanimate object) seem capable of thought and intention, esp. by behaving contrary to the will of the person using it: *the shopping cart had a mind of its own.* **in one's mind's eye** in one's imagination or mental view. **mind over matter** the use of willpower to overcome physical problems. **mind one's own business** refrain from prying or interfering. **mind one's Ps & Qs** be careful to behave well and avoid giving offense. [of unknown origin; said by some to refer to the care a young student must take in differentiating the tailed letters *p* and *q*.] **mind the store** informal have charge of something temporarily. **never mind 1** used to urge someone not to feel anxiety or distress: *never mind—it's all right now.* ■ used to suggest that a problem or objection is not important: *that's getting off the subject, but never mind.* **2** (also **never you mind**) used in refusing to answer a question: *never mind where I'm going.* **3** used to indicate that what has been said of one thing applies even more to another: *he was so tired that he found it hard to think, never mind talk.* **not pay someone any mind** not pay someone any attention. **on someone's mind** preoccupying someone, esp. in a disquieting way: *new parents have many worries on their minds.* **an open mind** the readiness to consider something without prejudice. **open one's mind to** be receptive to: *he opened his mind to the ways of the rest of the world.* **out of one's mind** having lost control of one's mental faculties. ■ informal suffering from a particular condition to a very high degree: *she was bored out of her mind.* **put someone in mind of** resemble and so cause someone to think of or remember: *he was a small, well-dressed man who put her in mind of a jockey.* **put** (or **set**) **one's mind to** direct all one's attention to (achieving something): *she'd have made an excellent dancer, if she'd have put her mind to it.* **put someone/something out of one's mind** deliberately forget someone or something. **to my mind** in my opinion: *this story is, to my mind, a masterpiece.*
– ORIGIN Old English *gemynd* 'memory, thought,' of Germanic origin, from an Indo-European root meaning 'revolve in the mind, think,' shared by Sanskrit *manas* and Latin *mens* 'mind.'

mind-al·ter·ing ▶ **adj.** (of a hallucinogenic drug) producing mood changes or giving a sense of heightened awareness.

Min·da·na·o /,mindә'nä,ō, -'nou/ an island in southeastern Philippines, the country's second largest island. Its chief town is Davao.

mind-bend·ing ▶ **adj.** informal (chiefly of a hallucinogenic drug) influencing or altering one's state of mind.
– DERIVATIVES **mind-bend·er** n., **mind-bend·ing·ly** adv.

mind-blow·ing ▶ **adj.** informal overwhelmingly impressive: *for a kid, Chicago was really mind-blowing.* ■ (of a drug) inducing hallucinations.
– DERIVATIVES **mind-blow·ing·ly** adv.

mind-bog·gling ▶ **adj.** informal overwhelming; startling: *a chip that processes data at mind-boggling speed.*
– DERIVATIVES **mind-bog·gling·ly** adv.

mind·ed /'mīndid/ ▶ **adj.** [in combination or with submodifier] inclined to think in a particular way: *liberal-minded scholars | I'm not scientifically minded.* ■ [in combination] interested in or enthusiastic about the thing specified: *conservation-minded citizens.*

Min·del /'mindәl/ ▶ **n.** [usu. as modifier] Geology a Pleistocene glaciation in the Alps preceding the Riss, possibly corresponding to the Elsterian of northern Europe. ■ the system of deposits laid down at this time.
– ORIGIN early 20th cent.: from the name of a river in southern Germany.

mind·er /'mīndәr/ ▶ **n.** chiefly Brit. a person whose job it is to look after someone or something: [in combination] *their baby-minder is getting married.* ■ informal a bodyguard employed to protect a celebrity or criminal: *he was accompanied by his personal minder.*

mind-ex·pand·ing ▶ **adj.** (esp. of a hallucinogenic drug) giving a sense of heightened or broader awareness.

mind·ful /'mīndfәl/ ▶ **adj.** [predic.] conscious or aware of something: *we can be more **mindful of** the energy we use to heat our homes.*
– DERIVATIVES **mind·ful·ly** adv.

mind·ful·ness /'mīndfәlnәs/ ▶ **n. 1** the quality or state of being conscious or aware of something: *their mindfulness of the wider cinematic tradition.*
2 a mental state achieved by focusing one's awareness on the present moment, while calmly acknowledging and accepting one's feelings, thoughts, and bodily sensations, used as a therapeutic technique.

mind game ▶ **n.** a series of deliberate actions or responses planned for psychological effect on another, typically for amusement or competitive advantage.

mind·less /'mīn(d)lis/ ▶ **adj.** acting or done without justification or concern for the consequences: *a generation of mindless vandals | mindless violence.* ■ [predic.] (**mindless of**) not thinking of or concerned about: *mindless of the fact she was in her nightgown, she rushed to the door.* ■ (of an activity) so simple or repetitive as to be performed automatically without thought or skill: *the monotony of housework turns it into a mindless task.*
– DERIVATIVES **mind·less·ly** adv., **mind·less·ness** n.

mind-numb·ing ▶ **adj.** so extreme or intense as to prevent normal thought: *the jury sat through hours of mind-numbing testimony.*
– DERIVATIVES **mind-numb·ing·ly adv.**

Min·do·ro /min'dôrō/ an island in the Philippines, southwest of Luzon.

mind read·er ▶ **n.** a person who can supposedly discern what another person is thinking.
– DERIVATIVES **mind-read** /'mīnd,red/ **v.**, **mind-read·ing n.**

mindset /'mīnd,set/ ▶ **n.** [usu. in sing.] the established set of attitudes held by someone: *the region seems stuck in a medieval mindset.*

mind·share /'mīnd,sHe(ə)r/ ▶ **n.** relative public awareness of a phenomenon: *the need to compete for mindshare from an audience with a short attention span.*

mine[1] /mīn/ ▶ **possessive pron.** used to refer to a thing or things belonging to or associated with the speaker: *you go your way and I'll go mine* | *some friends of mine.*
▶ **possessive determiner** archaic (used before a vowel) my: *tears did fill mine eyes.*
– ORIGIN Old English *mīn*, of Germanic origin; related to **ME** and to Dutch *mijn* and German *mein.*

mine[2] ▶ **n. 1** an excavation in the earth for extracting coal or other minerals: *a copper mine.* ■ [in sing.] an abundant source of something: *the book contains a mine of information.*
2 a type of bomb placed on or just below the surface of the ground or in the water that detonates when disturbed by a person, vehicle, or ship. ■ historical a subterranean passage under the wall of a besieged fortress, esp. one in which explosives are put to blow up fortifications.
▶ **v.** [with obj.] **1** obtain (coal or other minerals) from a mine. ■ dig in (the earth) for coal or other minerals: *the hills were* **mined for** *copper oxide* | [no obj.] *many financiers managed to obtain concessions to* **mine for** *silver.* ■ dig or burrow in (the earth). ■ delve into (an abundant source) to extract something of value, esp. information or skill: *how do they manage to mine such a rich vein of talent?*
2 lay explosive mines on or just below the surface of (the ground or water): *the area was heavily mined.* ■ destroy by means of an explosive mine.
– DERIVATIVES **mine·a·ble** /'mīnəbəl/ (also **minable**) **adj.**
– ORIGIN late Middle English: from Old French *mine* (noun), *miner* (verb), perhaps of Celtic origin; compare with Welsh *mwyn* 'ore,' earlier 'mine.'

mine de·tec·tor ▶ **n.** an instrument used for detecting explosive mines.

mine·field /'mīn,fēld/ (also **mine field**) ▶ **n.** an area planted with explosive mines. ■ a subject or situation presenting unseen hazards: *a minefield of technical regulations.*

mine·lay·er /'mīn,lāər/ ▶ **n.** a warship, aircraft, or land vehicle from which explosive mines are laid.
– DERIVATIVES **mine·lay·ing** /-,lāiNG/ **n.**

min·er /'mīnər/ ▶ **n. 1** a person who works in a mine. ■ historical a person who digs tunnels in order to destroy an enemy position with explosives.
2 an Australian bird of the honeyeater family, having a loud call and typically nesting colonially. ● Genus *Manorina*, family Meliphagidae: five species, including the **bell miner** or bellbird (*M. melanophrys*), with greenish plumage and a bell-like call.
3 a small South American bird of the ovenbird family that excavates a long burrow for breeding. ● Genus *Geositta*, family Furnariidae: several species.
4 short for **LEAF MINER.**
– ORIGIN Middle English: from Old French *minour*, from *miner* 'to mine' (see **MINE**[2]).

min·er·al /'min(ə)rəl/ ▶ **n. 1** a solid inorganic substance of natural occurrence. ■ a substance obtained by mining. ■ an inorganic substance needed by the human body for good health.
2 (**minerals**) Brit. (in commercial use) effervescent soft drinks.
▶ **adj.** of or denoting a mineral: *mineral ingredients such as zinc oxide.*
– ORIGIN late Middle English: from medieval Latin *minerale*, neuter (used as a noun) of *mineralis*, from *minera* 'ore.'

min·er·al·ize /'min(ə)rə,līz/ ▶ **v.** [with obj.] convert (organic matter) wholly or partly into a mineral or inorganic material or structure. ■ impregnate (water or another liquid) with a mineral substance.
– DERIVATIVES **min·er·al·i·za·tion** /,min(ə)rələ'zāsHən/ **n.**

min·er·al·o·cor·ti·coid /,min(ə)rə,lō'kôrti,koid/ ▶ **n.** Biochemistry a corticosteroid, such as aldosterone, that is involved with maintaining the salt balance in the body.

min·er·al·o·gy /,minə'räləjē, -'ral-/ ▶ **n.** the scientific study of minerals.
– DERIVATIVES **min·er·al·og·i·cal** /,min(ə)rə'läjikəl/ **adj.**, **min·er·al·og·i·cal·ly** /,min(ə)rə'läjik(ə)lē/ **adv.**, **min·er·al·o·gist** /-jist/ **n.**

min·er·al oil ▶ **n.** a distillation product of petroleum, esp. one used as a lubricant, moisturizer, or laxative.

min·er·al spir·its ▶ **n.** a volatile, colorless liquid distilled from petroleum, used as a paint thinner and solvent.

min·er·al wa·ter ▶ **n.** water found in nature with some dissolved salts present. ■ chiefly Brit. an artificial imitation of this, esp. soda water.

min·er·al wool ▶ **n.** a substance resembling matted wool and made from inorganic mineral material, used chiefly for packing or insulation.

Mi·ner·va /mə'nərvə/ Roman Mythology the goddess of handicrafts, widely worshiped and regularly identified with the Greek goddess Athena, which led to her being regarded also as the goddess of war.

mine shaft (also **mineshaft**) ▶ **n.** a deep narrow vertical hole, or sometimes a horizontal tunnel, that gives access to a mine.

min·e·stro·ne /,minə'strōnē/ ▶ **n.** a thick soup containing vegetables and pasta.
– ORIGIN Italian.

mine·sweep·er /'mīn,swēpər/ ▶ **n.** a ship or aircraft equipped for detecting and removing or destroying tethered explosive mines.
– DERIVATIVES **mine·sweep·ing** /-,swēpiNG/ **n. & adj.**

mine·work·er /'mīn,wərkər/ ▶ **n.** a person who works in a mine, esp. a coal mine.

Ming /miNG/ ▶ **n.** the dynasty ruling China 1368–1644 founded by **Zhu Yuanzhang** (1328–98). ■ [usu. as modifier] Chinese porcelain made during the rule of the Ming dynasty, characterized by elaborate designs and vivid colors: *a priceless Ming vase.*
– ORIGIN Chinese, literally 'clear or bright.'

ming·er /'miNGər/ ▶ **n.** Brit. informal an unattractive or unpleasant person or thing: *Why can't anyone see that Spencer is a complete minger?*
– ORIGIN 1990s: from **MINGING.**

ming·ing /'miNGiNG/ ▶ **adj.** Brit. informal foul-smelling. ■ very bad or unpleasant: *I'd really like to burn that minging beige jacket he has glued to him all the time.*
– ORIGIN 1970s: perhaps from Scots dialect *ming* 'excrement.'

min·gle /'miNGgəl/ ▶ **v.** mix or cause to mix together: [no obj.] *the sound of voices mingled with a scraping of chairs* | [with obj.] *an expression that mingled compassion and bewilderment.* ■ [no obj.] move freely around a place or at a social function, associating with others: *over aperitifs, there was a chance to* **mingle with** *friends old and new.*
– ORIGIN late Middle English: frequentative of obsolete *meng* 'mix or blend' (related to **AMONG**), perhaps influenced by Middle Dutch *mengelen.*

Min·gus /'miNGgəs/, Charles (1922–79), US jazz bassist and composer. A leading figure of the 1940s jazz scene, he experimented with atonality and was influenced by gospel and blues.

min·gy /'minjē/ ▶ **adj.** (**mingier, mingiest**) informal mean and stingy: *you've been too mingy with the sunscreen.* ■ unexpectedly or undesirably small: *a mingy kitchenette tucked in the corner.*
– DERIVATIVES **ming·i·ly** /'minjəlē/ **adv.**
– ORIGIN early 20th cent.: perhaps a blend of **MEAN**[2] and **STINGY.**

Mi·nho /'mēnyoo/ Portuguese name for **MIÑO.**

min·i /'minē/ ▶ **adj.** [attrib.] denoting a miniature version of something: *a bouquet of mini carnations.*
▶ **n.** (pl. **minis**) **1** short for **MINISKIRT.**
2 short for **MINICOMPUTER.**
– ORIGIN 1960s: abbreviation.

mini- ▶ **comb. form** very small or minor of its kind; miniature: *minicab* | *minicomputer.*
– ORIGIN from **MINIATURE**, reinforced by **MINIMUM.**

min·i·a·ture /'min(ē)əCHər, -,CHoor/ ▶ **adj.** [attrib.] (esp. of a replica of something) of a much smaller size than normal; very small: *children dressed as miniature adults.*
▶ **n.** a thing that is much smaller than normal, esp. a small replica or model. ■ a plant or animal that is a smaller version of an existing variety or breed. ■ a very small and highly detailed portrait or other painting. ■ a picture or decorated letter in an illuminated manuscript.
▶ **v.** [with obj.] rare represent on a smaller scale; reduce to miniature dimensions.
– PHRASES **in miniature** on a small scale, but otherwise a replica: *a place that is Greece in miniature.*
– ORIGIN early 18th cent.: from Italian *miniatura*, via medieval Latin from Latin *miniare* 'rubricate, illuminate,' from *minium* 'red lead, vermilion' (used to mark particular words in manuscripts).

min·i·a·ture golf ▶ **n.** an informal version of golf played on a series of short constructed obstacle courses.

min·i·a·tur·ist /'min(ē)ə,CHoorist, -CHərist/ ▶ **n.** a painter of miniatures or an illuminator of manuscripts.

min·i·a·tur·ize /'min(ē)əCHə,rīz/ ▶ **v.** [with obj.] (usu. as adj. **miniaturized**) make on a smaller or miniature scale: *miniaturized computers.*
– DERIVATIVES **min·i·a·tur·i·za·tion** /,min(ē)əCHərə'zāsHən/ **n.**

min·i·bar /'minē,bär/ ▶ **n.** a refrigerator in a hotel room containing a selection of refreshments that are charged for on the bill if used by the occupant.

min·i·bus /'minē,bəs/ ▶ **n.** a small bus for about ten to fifteen passengers.

min·i·cab /'minē,kab/ ▶ **n.** Brit. a car that is used as a taxi but that must be ordered in advance because it is not licensed to pick up passengers who hail it in the street.

min·i·cam /'minē,kam/ ▶ **n.** a handheld video camera.

min·i·camp /'minē,kamp/ ▶ **n.** a session run by a professional sports team to train particular players, or to test potential new players, before the main preseason training.

min·i·car /'minē,kär/ ▶ **n.** a very small car, esp. a subcompact.

min·i·com·pu·ter /'minēkəm,pyootər/ ▶ **n.** a computer of medium power, more than a microcomputer but less than a mainframe.

Min·i·coy Is·lands /'minə,koi/ one of the groups of islands forming the Indian Union Territory of Lakshadweep in the Indian Ocean.

min·i·disc /'minē,disk/ ▶ **n.** a disc having a format similar to a small CD but able to record sound or data as well as play it back.

min·i·dress /'minē,dres/ ▶ **n.** a very short dress.

mini-golf ▶ **n.** short for **MINIATURE GOLF.**

min·i·kin /'minikin/ ▶ **adj.** chiefly archaic small; insignificant: *capable men devoting their lives to such minikin pursuits.*

min·im /'minim/ ▶ **n. 1** one sixtieth of a fluid dram, about one drop of liquid.
2 Music British term for **HALF NOTE.**
3 (in calligraphy) a short vertical stroke, as in the letters *i, m, n, u.*
– ORIGIN late Middle English: from Latin *minima*, from *minimus* 'smallest.'

min·i·ma /'minəmə/ plural form of **MINIMUM.**

min·i·mal /'minəməl/ ▶ **adj. 1** of a minimum amount, quantity, or degree; negligible: *a minimal amount of information* | *production costs are minimal.*
2 Art characterized by the use of simple or primary forms or structures, esp. geometric or massive ones. ■ characterized by simplicity and lack of adornment or decoration: *minimal, simple evening dresses in luxurious fabrics.*
3 Music characterized by the repetition and gradual alteration of short phrases.
4 Linguistics (of a pair of forms) distinguished by only one feature: *"p" and "b" are a minimal pair, distinguished by the feature of voicing.*
– DERIVATIVES **min·i·mal·ly adv.**
– ORIGIN mid 17th cent.: from Latin *minimus* 'smallest' + **-AL.**

min·i·mal·ism /'minəmə,lizəm/ ▶ **n. 1** a trend in sculpture and painting that arose in the 1950s and used simple, typically massive, forms.
2 an avant-garde movement in music characterized by the repetition of very short phrases that change gradually, producing a hypnotic effect.

min·i·mal·ist /'minəməlist/ ▶ **n. 1** a person advocating minor or moderate reform in politics.
2 a person who advocates or practices minimalism in art or music.
▶ **adj.** (also **minimalistic**) **1** advocating moderate political policies.
2 of or relating to minimalism in art or music.
– ORIGIN early 20th cent.: first used with reference to the Russian Mensheviks. Usage in art and music dates from the 1960s.

min·i·mall ▶ **n.** a shopping mall containing a relatively small number of retail outlets and with access to each shop from the outside rather than from an interior hallway.

min·i·mart /ˈminēˌmärt/ ▶ **n.** a convenience store.

min·i·max /ˈminēˌmaks/ ▶ **n.** Mathematics the lowest of a set of maximum values. Compare with MAXIMIN. ■ [as modifier] denoting a method or strategy in game theory that minimizes the greatest risk to a participant in a game or other situation of conflict. ■ [as modifier] denoting the theory that in a game with two players, a player's smallest possible maximum loss is equal to the same player's greatest possible minimum gain.
– ORIGIN 1940s: blend of MINIMUM and MAXIMUM.

mi·ni-me /ˈminēˌmē/ ▶ **n.** informal a person closely resembling a smaller or younger version of another: *so far, Eminem's mini-me has failed to get himself a moneymaking deal.*
– ORIGIN the name of a small cloned character in the movie *Austin Powers: The Spy Who Shagged Me* (1999).

min·i·mize /ˈminəˌmīz/ ▶ **v.** [with obj.] reduce (something, esp. something unwanted or unpleasant) to the smallest possible amount or degree: *the aim is to minimize costs.* ■ represent or estimate at less than the true value or importance: *they may minimize, or even overlook, the importance of such beliefs.*
– DERIVATIVES **min·i·mi·za·tion** /ˌminəməˈzāSHən/ **n.**, **min·i·miz·er n.**

min·i·mum /ˈminəməm/ ▶ **n.** (pl. **minima** /-mə/ or **minimums**) [usu. in sing.] the least or smallest amount or quantity possible, attainable, or required: *technical difficulties have been **kept to a minimum** | they checked passports with **the minimum of fuss**.* ■ the lowest or smallest amount of a varying quantity (e.g., temperature) allowed, attained, or recorded: *clients with a minimum of $500,000 to invest | winter minima of –40°C have been recorded.* ■ Mathematics a point at which a continuously varying quantity ceases to decrease and begins to increase; the value of a quantity at such a point.
▶ **adj.** [attrib.] smallest or lowest: *this can be done with the minimum amount of effort.*
– PHRASES **at a** (or **the**) **minimum** at the very least: *we zipped along at a minimum of 55 mph.*
– ORIGIN mid 17th cent.: from Latin, neuter of *minimus* 'least.'

min·i·mum wage ▶ **n.** the lowest wage permitted by law or by a special agreement (such as one with a labor union).

m

min·ing /ˈmīniNG/ ▶ **n.** the process or industry of obtaining coal or other minerals from a mine.

min·ion /ˈminyən/ ▶ **n.** a follower or underling of a powerful person, esp. a servile or unimportant one.
– ORIGIN late 15th cent.: from French *mignon, mignonne.*

min·i-pill ▶ **n.** a contraceptive pill containing progestin and not estrogen.

min·is·cule ▶ **adj.** see MINUSCULE.

min·i·se·ries /ˈminēˌsi(ə)rēz/ ▶ **n.** (pl. **same**) a television drama shown in a number of episodes.

min·i·skirt /ˈminēˌskərt/ ▶ **n.** a very short skirt.

min·is·ter /ˈminəstər/ ▶ **n. 1** (also **minister of religion**) a member of the clergy, esp. in Protestant churches. ■ (also **minister general**) the superior of some religious orders.
2 (in certain countries) a head of a government department: *Britain's defense minister.* ■ a diplomatic agent, usually ranking below an ambassador, representing a state or sovereign in a foreign country.
3 archaic a person or thing used to achieve or convey something: *the Angels are ministers of the Divine Will.*
▶ **v.** [no obj.] **1** (**minister to**) attend to the needs of (someone): *her doctor was busy ministering to the injured.* ■ [with obj.] archaic provide (something necessary or helpful): *the story was able to minister true consolation.*
2 act as a minister of religion. ■ [with obj.] administer (a sacrament).
– DERIVATIVES **min·is·ter·ship** /-ˌSHip/ **n.**
– ORIGIN Middle English (sense 1 of the noun and sense 3 of the noun): from Old French *ministre* (noun), *ministrer* (verb), from Latin *minister* 'servant,' from *minus* 'less.'

min·is·te·ri·al /ˌminəˈsti(ə)rēəl/ ▶ **adj. 1** of or relating to a minister of religion.
2 of or relating to a government minister or ministers: *ministerial officials.*
3 archaic acting as an agent, instrument, or means in achieving a purpose: *those uses of conversation which are ministerial to intellectual culture.*
– DERIVATIVES **min·is·te·ri·al·ly adv.**
– ORIGIN mid 16th cent.: from French *ministériel* or late Latin *ministerialis*, from Latin *ministerium* 'ministry.'

min·is·tra·tion /ˌminəˈstrāSHən/ ▶ **n.** (usu. **ministrations**) chiefly formal or humorous the provision of assistance or care: *a kitchen made spotless by the **ministrations** of a cleaning lady.* ■ the services of a minister of religion or of a religious institution. ■ the action of administering the sacrament.
– DERIVATIVES **min·is·trant** /ˈminəstrənt/ **n.**
– ORIGIN late Middle English: from Latin *ministratio(n-)*, from *ministrare* 'wait upon,' from *minister* (see MINISTER).

min·i·stroke /ˈminēˌstrōk/ ▶ **n.** a temporary blockage of the blood supply to the brain, lasting only a few minutes and leaving no noticeable symptoms or deficits. Also called TRANSIENT ISCHEMIC ATTACK.

min·is·try /ˈminəstrē/ ▶ **n.** (pl. **ministries**) **1** [usu. in sing.] the work or vocation of a minister of religion: *he is training for the ministry.* ■ the period of tenure of a minister of religion. ■ the spiritual work or service of any Christian or a group of Christians, esp. evangelism: *a ministry of Christian healing.*
2 (in certain countries) a government department headed by a minister of state: *the Ministry of Agriculture.*
3 (in certain countries) a period of government under one prime minister: *Gladstone's first ministry was outstanding.*
4 rare the action of ministering to someone: *the soldiers were no less in need of his ministry.*
– ORIGIN Middle English (sense 1): from Latin *ministerium*, from *minister* (see MINISTER).

min·i·tow·er /ˈminēˌtou-ər/ ▶ **n.** a small vertical case for a computer, or a computer mounted in such a case: *the desk has a compartment for a minitower* | [as modifier] *the minitower case is sturdy.*

min·i·van /ˈminēˌvan/ ▶ **n.** a small van, typically one fitted with seats in the back for passengers.

min·i·ver /ˈminəvər/ ▶ **n.** plain white fur used for lining or trimming clothes.
– ORIGIN Middle English: from Old French *menu vair* 'little vair,' from *menu* 'little' + *vair* 'squirrel fur' (see VAIR).

mink /miNGk/ ▶ **n.** (pl. **same** or **minks**) a small, semiaquatic, stoatlike carnivore native to North America and Eurasia. The American mink is widely farmed for its fur, resulting in its becoming naturalized in many parts of Europe. ● Genus *Mustela*, family Mustelidae: the **American mink** (*M. vison*) and the smaller **European mink** (*M. lutreola*). ■ the thick brown fur of the mink. ■ a coat made of this.
– ORIGIN late Middle English (denoting the animal's fur): from Swedish.

min·ke /ˈmiNGkē/ (also **minke whale**) ▶ **n.** a small rorqual whale with a dark gray back, white underparts, and pale markings on the fins and behind the head. ● *Balaenoptera acutorostrata*, family Balaenopteridae.
– ORIGIN 1930s: probably from *Meincke*, the name of a Norwegian whaler.

Minn. ▶ **abbr.** Minnesota.

Min·ne·ap·o·lis /ˌminēˈapəlis/ an industrial city and port on the Mississippi River in southeastern Minnesota; pop. 382,605 (est. 2008) It is a major agricultural center for the upper Midwest.

Min·nel·li /miˈnelē/, Vincente (1910–86), US movie director. His movies include *The Clock* (1945), *Kismet* (1955), and *Gigi* (1958). His daughter with wife Judy Garland, **Liza Minnelli** (1946–), has starred in such movies as *The Sterile Cuckoo* (1969), *Cabaret* (1972), *Arthur* (1981), and *Stepping Out* (1991).

min·ne·o·la /ˌminēˈōlə/ ▶ **n.** a deep reddish tangelo of a thin-skinned variety.
– ORIGIN mid 20th cent.: named after a town in Florida.

min·ne·sing·er /ˈminiˌsiNGər, -əˌziNGər/ ▶ **n.** a German lyric poet and singer of the 12th–14th centuries who performed songs of courtly love.
– ORIGIN early 19th cent.: from German *Minnesinger* 'love-singer.'

Min·ne·so·ta /ˌminəˈsōtə/ a state in the northern central US, on the Canadian border; pop. 5,220,393 (est. 2008); capital, St. Paul; statehood, May 11, 1858 (32). Part of it was ceded to Britain by the French in 1763 and then acquired by the US in 1783. The remainder formed part of the Louisiana Purchase in 1803.
– DERIVATIVES **Min·ne·so·tan n. & adj.**

Min·ne·so·ta Mul·ti·pha·sic Per·son·al·i·ty In·ven·to·ry (abbr.: **MMPI**) ▶ **n.** a test consisting of hundreds of true-false questions, used as a diagnostic tool by psychologists.

Min·ne·so·ta Riv·er a river that flows for 320 miles (530 km) through Minnesota to join the Mississippi River just south of the Twin Cities of Minneapolis and St. Paul.

Min·ne·ton·ka /ˌminəˈtäNGkə/ a city in southeastern Minnesota, west of Minneapolis; pop. 50,081 (est. 2008).

min·now /ˈminō/ ▶ **n. 1** a small freshwater Eurasian cyprinoid fish that typically forms large shoals. ● *Phoxinus phoxinus*, family Cyprinidae. ■ any fish of the family Cyprinidae, the largest family of fishes, which includes carps, shiners, spinefins, squawfishes, chubs, daces, and stonerollers. ■ used in names of similar small freshwater fishes, e.g., **mudminnow, topminnow.** ■ Fishing an artificial lure imitating a minnow.
2 a person or organization of relatively small size, power, or influence.
– ORIGIN late Middle English: probably related to Dutch *meun* and German *Münne*, influenced by Anglo-Norman French *menu* 'small, minnow.'

Mi·ño /ˈmēnyō/ a river that rises in northwestern Spain and flows south to the Portuguese border, which it follows before entering the Atlantic Ocean north of Viana do Castelo. Portuguese name **MINHO**.

Mi·no·an /məˈnōən, mī-/ ▶ **adj.** of, relating to, or denoting a Bronze Age civilization centered on Crete (*c.*3000–1050 BC), its people, or its language.
▶ **n. 1** an inhabitant of Minoan Crete or member of the Minoan people.
2 the language or scripts associated with the Minoans.

> The Minoan civilization had reached its zenith by the beginning of the late Bronze Age; impressive remains reveal the existence of large urban centers dominated by palaces. The civilization is also noted for its script (see **LINEAR A**) and distinctive art and architecture.

– ORIGIN named after the legendary Cretan king **MINOS**, to whom a palace excavated at Knossos was attributed.

mi·nor /ˈmīnər/ ▶ **adj. 1** lesser in importance, seriousness, or significance: *minor alterations.*
2 Music (of a scale) having intervals of a semitone between the second and third degrees, and (usually) the fifth and sixth, and the seventh and eighth. Contrasted with MAJOR. ■ (of an interval) characteristic of a minor scale and less by a semitone than the equivalent major interval. Compare with DIMINISHED. ■ [usu. postpositive] (of a key or mode) based on a minor scale, tending to produce a sad or pensive effect: *Concerto in A minor.*
3 Logic (of a term) occurring as the subject of the conclusion of a categorical syllogism. ■ (of a premise) containing the minor term in a categorical syllogism.
▶ **n. 1** a person under the age of full legal responsibility.
2 Music a minor key, interval, or scale. ■ (**Minor**) Bell-ringing a system of change-ringing using six bells.
3 (**the minors**) the minor leagues in a particular professional sport, esp. baseball: *he's been pitching in the minors for six years.*
4 a college student's subsidiary subject or area of concentration: *a minor in American Indian studies.*
5 Logic a minor term or premise.
6 Bridge short for MINOR SUIT.
– PHRASES **in a minor key** (esp. of a literary work) understated.
– PHRASAL VERBS **minor in** study or qualify in as a subsidiary subject at college or university.
– ORIGIN Middle English: from Latin, 'smaller, less'; related to *minuere* 'lessen.' The term originally denoted a Franciscan friar, suggested by the Latin name *Fratres Minores* ('Lesser Brethren'), chosen by St. Francis for the order.

mi·nor ar·ca·na ▶ **n.** see ARCANA.

mi·nor ax·is ▶ **n.** Geometry the shorter axis of an ellipse that is perpendicular to its major axis.

Mi·nor·ca /məˈnôrkə/ the most easterly and second largest of the Balearic Islands of Spain, in the western Mediterranean Sea; pop. 92,434 (2008); capital, Mahón. Spanish name **Menorca**.
– DERIVATIVES **Mi·nor·can adj. & n.**

Mi·nor·ite /ˈmīnəˌrīt/ a Franciscan friar, or Friar Minor.

mi·nor·i·ty /məˈnôrətē/ ▶ **n.** (pl. **minorities**) **1** the smaller number or part, esp. a number that is less than half the whole number: *harsher measures for the minority of really serious offenders* | [as modifier] *a minority party.* ■ the number of votes cast for or by the smaller party in a legislative assembly: *a blocking minority of 23 votes.* ■ a relatively small group of people, esp. one commonly discriminated against in a community, society, or nation, differing from others in race, religion, language, or political persuasion: *representatives of ethnic minorities* | [as modifier] *minority rights.*
2 the state or period of being under the age of full legal responsibility.
– PHRASES **be** (or **find oneself**) **in a minority of one** often humorous be the sole person to be in favor of or against something. **in the minority** belonging to or constituting the smaller group or number: *those*

who acknowledge his influence are certainly in the minority.
– ORIGIN late 15th cent. (denoting the state of being a minor): from French *minorité* or medieval Latin *minoritas*, from Latin *minor* 'smaller' (see MINOR).

mi·nor·i·ty gov·ern·ment ▶ n. a government in which the governing party has most seats but still less than half the total.

mi·nor·i·ty lead·er ▶ n. the head of the minority party in a legislative body, esp. the US Senate or House of Representatives.

mi·nor·i·ty re·port ▶ n. a separate report presented by members of a committee or other group who disagree with the majority.

mi·nor league ▶ n. a league below the level of the major league in a particular professional sport, esp. baseball: *he hit a lot of home runs in the minor leagues* | [as modifier] *a minor-league outfielder.* ■ [as modifier] of lesser power or significance: *a minor-league villain.*
– DERIVATIVES **mi·nor-lea·guer** n.

mi·nor or·ders ▶ plural n. chiefly historical the formal grades of Catholic or Orthodox clergy below the rank of deacon (most now discontinued).

mi·nor piece ▶ n. Chess a bishop or knight.
– ORIGIN early 19th cent.: named in contrast to the rook or queen.

mi·nor plan·et ▶ n. an asteroid. Often contrasted with MAJOR PLANET.

mi·nor proph·et ▶ n. any of the twelve prophets after whom the shorter prophetic books of the Bible, from Hosea to Malachi, are named.

mi·nor suit ▶ n. Bridge diamonds or clubs.
– ORIGIN early 20th cent.: so named because of their lower scoring value.

mi·nor tran·quil·iz·er ▶ n. a tranquilizer of the kind used to treat anxiety states, esp. a benzodiazepine; an anxiolytic.

Mi·nos /ˈmīˌnäs, -nôs/ Greek Mythology a legendary king of Crete, son of Zeus and Europa. His wife Pasiphaë gave birth to the Minotaur; Minos later exacted tribute from Athens in the form of young people to be devoured by the monster.

Mi·not /ˈmīnät/ a commercial and industrial city in north central North Dakota; pop. 35,419 (est. 2008).

Min·o·taur /ˈminəˌtôr, ˈmī-/ Greek Mythology a creature who was half man and half bull, the offspring of Pasiphaë and a bull with which she fell in love. Confined in Crete in a labyrinth made by Daedalus and fed on human flesh, it was eventually slain by Theseus.
– ORIGIN from Old French, via Latin from Greek *Minōtauros*, from *Minōs* (see MINOS) + *tauros* 'bull.'

min·ox·i·dil /məˈnäksəˌdil/ ▶ n. Medicine a synthetic drug that is used as a vasodilator in the treatment of hypertension, and is also used in lotions to promote hair growth.
– ORIGIN 1970s: from AMINO + OXIDE + *-dil* (perhaps representing DILATE).

Minsk /minsk/ the capital of Belarus, an industrial city in the central region of the country; pop. 1,829,100 (est. 2009).

min·ster /ˈminstər/ ▶ n. a large or important church, typically one of cathedral status in the north of England that was built as part of a monastery: *York Minster.*
– ORIGIN Old English *mynster*, via ecclesiastical Latin from Greek *monastērion* (see MONASTERY).

min·strel /ˈminstrəl/ ▶ n. a medieval singer or musician, esp. one who sang or recited lyric or heroic poetry to a musical accompaniment for the nobility. ■ chiefly historical a member of a band of entertainers with blackened faces who performed songs and music ostensibly of black American origin.
– ORIGIN Middle English: from Old French *menestral* 'entertainer, servant,' via Provençal from late Latin *ministerialis* 'servant' (see MINISTERIAL).

min·strel show ▶ n. a popular stage entertainment featuring songs, dances, and comic dialogue in highly conventionalized patterns, usually performed by white actors in blackface. It developed in the US in the early and mid 19th century.

min·strel·sy /ˈminstrəlsē/ ▶ n. the practice of performing as a minstrel: *a long tradition of minstrelsy.*
– ORIGIN Middle English: from Old French *menestralsie*, from *menestrel* (see MINSTREL).

mint[1] /mint/ ▶ n. **1** an aromatic plant native to temperate regions of the Old World, several kinds of which are used as culinary herbs. ● Genus *Mentha*, family Labiatae (or Lamiaceae; the **mint family**): several species and hybrids, in particular the widely cultivated **common mint** or **spearmint** (*M. spicata*) and **peppermint** (*M.* × piperita). The mint family, the members of which have distinctive two-lobed flowers and square stems, includes numerous aromatic herbs, such as lavender, rosemary, sage, and thyme. ■ the flavor of mint, esp. peppermint.
2 a peppermint candy.
– DERIVATIVES **mint·y** adj. (**mintier, mintiest**).
– ORIGIN Old English *minte*; related to German *Minze*, ultimately via Latin from Greek *minthē*.

mint[2] ▶ n. a place where money is coined, esp. under state authority. ■ (**a mint**) informal a vast sum of money: *the car doesn't cost a mint.*
▶ adj. (of an object) in pristine condition; as new: *a pair of speakers including stands, mint, $160.* [elliptically from *in mint condition.*]
▶ v. [with obj.] make (a coin) by stamping metal. ■ (usu. as adj., with submodifier **minted**) produce for the first time: *an example of newly minted technology.*
– PHRASES **in mint condition** (of an object) new or as if new.
– DERIVATIVES **mint·er** n.
– ORIGIN Old English *mynet* 'coin'; related to Dutch *munt* and German *Münze*, from Latin *moneta* 'money.'

mint·age /ˈmintij/ ▶ n. the minting of coins. ■ the number of copies issued of a particular coin: *an estimated mintage of about 800.*

mint·ed /ˈmintid/ ▶ adj. flavored or seasoned with mint: *grilled lamb chops with minted potatoes.*

mint ju·lep ▶ n. a drink consisting of bourbon, crushed ice, sugar, and fresh mint, typically served in a tall frosted glass and associated chiefly with the southern US.

mint·mark /ˈmintˌmärk/ (also **mint mark**) ▶ n. a mark on a coin indicating the mint at which it was struck.

Min·ton /ˈmintn/, Sherman (1890–1965), US Supreme Court associate justice 1949–56. A former US senator 1935–41 and a US circuit court of appeals judge 1941–49, he was appointed to the Court by President Truman.

mint par (also **mint parity**) ▶ n. Finance the ratio between the gold equivalents of currency in two countries. ■ their rate of exchange based on such a ratio.

min·u·end /ˈminyəˌwend/ ▶ n. Mathematics a quantity or number from which another is to be subtracted.
– ORIGIN early 18th cent.: from Latin *minuendus*, gerundive of *minuere* 'diminish.'

min·u·et /ˌminyo͞oˈet/ ▶ n. a slow, stately ballroom dance for two in triple time, popular esp. in the 18th century. ■ a piece of music in triple time in the style of such a dance, typically as a movement in a suite, sonata, or symphony and frequently coupled with a trio.
▶ v. (**minuets, minueting, minueted**) [no obj.] dance a minuet.
– ORIGIN late 17th cent.: from French *menuet*, 'fine, delicate,' diminutive (used as a noun) of *menu* 'small.'

Min·u·it /ˈminyo͞oit/, Peter (1580–1638), Dutch colonial administrator. He was the first director general of the North American Dutch colony of New Netherland 1626–31. He purchased Manhattan Island from the Algonquin Indians in 1626 for 60 guilders ($24).

mi·nus /ˈmīnəs/ ▶ prep. **1** with the subtraction of: *what's ninety-three minus seven?* ■ informal lacking; deprived of: *he was minus a finger on each hand.*
2 (of temperature) below zero: *minus 10° Fahrenheit.*
▶ adj. **1** (before a number) below zero; negative: *minus five.*
2 (after a grade) slightly worse than: *my lowest grade was a B minus.*
3 having a negative electric charge.
▶ n. **1** short for MINUS SIGN. ■ a mathematical operation of subtraction.
2 a disadvantage: *for every plus with this equipment there can be a minus.*
– ORIGIN late 15th cent.: from Latin, neuter of *minor* 'less.'

mi·nus·cule /ˈminəˌskyo͞ol, minˈəsˌkyo͞ol/ (also **miniscule**) ▶ adj. **1** extremely small; tiny: *a minuscule fragment of DNA.* ■ informal so small as to be negligible or insufficient: *he believed the risk of infection was minuscule.*
2 of or in lowercase letters, as distinct from capitals or uncials. ■ of or in a small cursive script of the Roman alphabet, with ascenders and descenders, developed in the 7th century AD.
▶ n. minuscule script. ■ a small or lowercase letter.
– DERIVATIVES **mi·nus·cu·lar** /məˈnəskyələr/ adj.
– ORIGIN early 18th cent.: from French, from Latin *minuscula (littera)* 'somewhat smaller (letter).'

> **USAGE** The standard spelling is **minuscule** rather than **miniscule**. The latter form is a very common one (accounting for almost half of citations for the term in the Oxford English Corpus), and has been recorded since the late 19th century. It arose by analogy with other words beginning with **mini-**, where the meaning is similarly 'very small.' It is now so widely used that it can be considered as an acceptable variant, although it should be avoided in formal contexts.

mi·nus sign ▶ n. the symbol −, indicating subtraction or a negative value.

mi·nute[1] /ˈminit/ ▶ n. **1** a period of time equal to sixty seconds or a sixtieth of an hour: *he stood in the shower for twenty minutes* | *in ten minutes' time he could be on his way.* ■ the distance covered in this length of time by someone driving or walking: *the hotel is situated just ten minutes from the center of the resort.* ■ informal a very short time: *come and sit down for a minute.* ■ an instant or a point of time: *she had been laughing one minute and crying the next.*
2 (also **arc minute** or **minute of arc**) a sixtieth of a degree of angular measurement (symbol: ′).
– PHRASES **any minute** (or **at any minute**) very soon. **by the minute** (esp. of the progress of a change) very rapidly: *matters grew worse by the minute.* **just** (or **wait**) **a minute 1** used as a request to delay an action, departure, or decision for a short time, usually to allow the speaker to do something: *wait a minute—I have to put my makeup on.* **2** as a prelude to a challenge, query, or objection: *just a minute—where do you think you're going?* **the minute** (or **the minute that**) as soon as: *let me know the minute he returns.* **not for a minute** not at all: *don't think for a minute that our pricing has affected our quality standards.* **this minute** (or **this very minute**) informal at once; immediately: *pull yourself together this minute.*
– ORIGIN late Middle English: via Old French from late Latin *minuta*, feminine (used as a noun) of *minutus* 'made small.' The senses 'period of sixty seconds' and 'sixtieth of a degree' derive from medieval Latin *pars minuta prima* 'first minute part.'

mi·nute[2] /mīˈn(y)o͞ot, mə-/ ▶ adj. (**minutest**) extremely small: *a minute fraction of an inch.* ■ so small as to verge on insignificance: *he will have no more than a minute chance of exercising significant influence.* ■ (of an inquiry or investigation, or an account of one) taking the smallest points into consideration; precise and meticulous: *a minute examination of the islands.*
– DERIVATIVES **mi·nute·ness** n.
– ORIGIN late Middle English (in the sense 'lesser,' with reference to a tithe or tax): from Latin *minutus* 'lessened,' past participle of *minuere.*

mi·nute[3] /ˈminit/ ▶ n. (**minutes**) a summarized record of the proceedings at a meeting. ■ an official memorandum authorizing or recommending a course of action.
▶ v. [with obj.] record or note (the proceedings of a meeting or a specified item among such proceedings): *the Secretary shall minute the proceedings of each meeting.*
– ORIGIN late Middle English (in the singular in the sense 'note or memorandum'): from French *minute*, from the notion of a rough copy in "small writing" (Latin *scriptura minuta*) as distinct from the fair copy in book hand. The verb dates from the mid 16th cent.

mi·nute gun ▶ n. a gun fired at intervals of a minute, esp. at a funeral.

min·ute hand ▶ n. the hand on a watch or clock that indicates minutes.

mi·nute·ly /mīˈn(y)o͞otlē, mə-/ ▶ adv. with great attention to detail; meticulously: *systems of politics are examined minutely by academics* | [as submodifier] *minutely detailed descriptions covering every angle.*

min·ute·man /ˈminətˌman/ ▶ n. (pl. **minutemen**) historical (in the period preceding and during the American Revolution) a member of a class of American militiamen who volunteered to be ready for service at a minute's notice. ■ (**Minuteman**) a type of three-stage intercontinental ballistic missile.

mi·nu·ti·ae /məˈn(y)o͞oshēˌē, -shēˌī/ (also **minutia** /-shēˌə, -shə/) ▶ plural n. the small, precise, or trivial details of something: *the minutiae of everyday life.*
– ORIGIN mid 18th cent.: Latin, literally 'trifles,' from *minutia* 'smallness,' from *minutus* (see MINUTE[2]).

minx /miNGks/ ▶ n. humorous or derogatory an impudent, cunning, or boldly flirtatious girl or young woman.
– DERIVATIVES **minx·ish** adj.
– ORIGIN mid 16th cent. (denoting a pet dog): of unknown origin.

m

min·yan /ˈminyən/ ▶ **n.** (pl. **minyanim** /ˌminyəˈnēm/) a quorum of ten men (or in some synagogues, men and women) over the age of 13 required for traditional Jewish public worship. ■ a meeting of Jews for public worship.
– ORIGIN mid 18th cent.: from Hebrew *minyān*, literally 'reckoning.'

Mi·o·cene /ˈmīəˌsēn/ ▶ **adj.** Geology of, relating to, or denoting the fourth epoch of the Tertiary period, between the Oligocene and Pliocene epochs. ■ (as noun **the Miocene**) the Miocene epoch or the system of rocks deposited during it.

> The Miocene epoch lasted from 23.3 million to 5.2 million years ago. During this time, the Alps and Himalayas were being formed and there was diversification of the primates, including the first apes.

– ORIGIN mid 19th cent.: formed irregularly from Greek *meiōn* 'less' + *kainos* 'new.'

mi·o·sis /mīˈōsəs/ (also **myosis**) ▶ **n.** excessive constriction of the pupil of the eye.
– DERIVATIVES **mi·ot·ic** /mīˈätik/ **adj.**
– ORIGIN early 19th cent.: from Greek *muein* 'shut the eyes' + -OSIS.

MIP ▶ **abbr.** monthly investment plan.

MIPS /mips/ ▶ **n.** a unit of computing speed equivalent to a million instructions per second.
– ORIGIN 1970s: acronym.

Mique·lon /mēˈklôn/ see ST. PIERRE AND MIQUELON.

Mir /ˈmi(ə)r/ a Soviet space station, launched in 1986 and designed to be permanently manned.

> Owing largely to its financial demands on an impoverished Russian government, the Mir program was terminated in March 2001, when the space station made its fiery re-entry into the earth's atmosphere, splashing down in the South Pacific. During its 14 years in space, Mir (which means 'world' and 'peace' in Russian) housed a total of 104 astronauts from various nations.

Mi·ra /ˈmīrə/ Astronomy a star in the constellation Cetus, regarded as the prototype of long-period variable stars.
– ORIGIN Latin, literally 'wonderful.'

m

Mi·ra·beau /ˌmi(ə)rəˈbō/, Honoré Gabriel Riqueti, Comte de (1749–91), French revolutionary politician. Prominent in the early days of the French Revolution, he pressed for a form of constitutional monarchy.

mir·a·belle /ˈmirəˌbel/ ▶ **n.** a sweet yellow plumlike fruit that is a variety of the greengage. ■ the tree that bears such fruit. ■ a liqueur distilled from such fruit.
– ORIGIN early 18th cent.: from French.

mi·ra·bi·le dic·tu /məˈräbəˌlā ˈdiktōō, məˈrabəlē/ ▶ **adv.** wonderful to relate: *and for once, mirabile dictu, they all seem to be getting along.*
– ORIGIN Latin.

mi·ra·cid·i·um /ˌmīrəˈsidēəm/ ▶ **n.** (pl. **miracidia** /-sidēə/) Zoology a free-swimming ciliated larval stage in which a parasitic fluke passes from the egg to its first host, typically a snail.
– ORIGIN late 19th cent.: from Greek *meirakidion*, diminutive of *meirakion* 'boy, stripling.'

mir·a·cle /ˈmirikəl/ ▶ **n.** a surprising and welcome event that is not explicable by natural or scientific laws and is therefore considered to be the work of a divine agency: *the miracle of rising from the grave.* ■ a highly improbable or extraordinary event, development, or accomplishment that brings very welcome consequences: *it was a miracle that more people hadn't been killed or injured.* ■ an amazing product or achievement, or an outstanding example of something: *a machine which was a miracle of design* | [as modifier] *a miracle drug.*
– ORIGIN Middle English: via Old French from Latin *miraculum* 'object of wonder,' from *mirari* 'to wonder,' from *mirus* 'wonderful.'

mir·a·cle play ▶ **n.** a mystery play.

mi·rac·u·lous /məˈrakyələs/ ▶ **adj.** occurring through divine or supernatural intervention, or manifesting such power: *a miraculous cure.* ■ highly improbable and extraordinary and bringing very welcome consequences: *I felt amazed and grateful for our miraculous escape.*
– DERIVATIVES **mi·rac·u·lous·ly** **adv.**, **mi·rac·u·lous·ness** **n.**
– ORIGIN late Middle English: from French *miraculeux* or medieval Latin *miraculosus*, from Latin *miraculum* (see MIRACLE).

mir·a·dor /ˈmirəˌdôr, ˌmirəˈdôr/ ▶ **n.** a turret or tower attached to a building and providing an extensive view.
– ORIGIN late 17th cent.: from Spanish, from *mirar* 'to look.'

mi·rage /məˈräzh/ ▶ **n.** an optical illusion caused by atmospheric conditions, esp. the appearance of a sheet of water in a desert or on a hot road caused by the refraction of light from the sky by heated air. ■ something that appears real or possible but is not in fact so: *the notion that the public is pro-business is a mirage.*
– ORIGIN early 19th cent.: from French, from *se mirer* 'be reflected,' from Latin *mirare* 'look at.'

Mir·a·mar /ˈmirəˌmär/ a city in south Florida; pop. 108,484 (est. 2008).

Mi·ran·da[1] /məˈrandə/ Astronomy a satellite of Uranus, the eleventh closest to the planet, with a diameter of 301 miles (485 km). Discovered in 1948, it is the innermost and smallest of the five major Uranian satellites and has a complex terrain of cratered areas and tracts of grooves and ridges.
– ORIGIN named after the daughter of Prospero in Shakespeare's *The Tempest*.

Mi·ran·da[2] ▶ **adj.** Law denoting or relating to the duty of the police to inform a person taken into custody of their right to legal counsel and the right to remain silent under questioning: *the patrolman read Lee his Miranda rights.*
– ORIGIN mid 20th cent.: from *Miranda v. Arizona* (1966), the case that led to this ruling by the US Supreme Court.

Mi·ran·dize /miˈrandīz/ ▶ **v.** [with obj.] inform (a person who has been arrested) of their legal rights, in accordance with the Miranda decision.
– ORIGIN 1970s: from MIRANDA[2].

mire /mīr/ ▶ **n.** **1** a stretch of swampy or boggy ground. ■ soft and slushy mud or dirt. ■ Ecology a wetland area or ecosystem based on peat.
2 a situation or state of difficulty, distress, or embarrassment from which it is hard to extricate oneself: *he has been left to squirm in a mire of new allegations.*
▶ **v.** [with obj.] cause to become stuck in mud: *sometimes a heavy truck gets **mired down**.* ■ cover or spatter with mud. ■ (**mire someone/something in**) involve someone or something in (a difficulti situation): *the economy is mired in its longest recession since World War II.*
– ORIGIN Middle English: from Old Norse *mýrr*, of Germanic origin; related to MOSS.

mire·poix /mi(ə)rˈpwä/ ▶ **n.** a mixture of sautéed chopped vegetables used in various sauces.
– ORIGIN French, named after the Duc de *Mirepoix* (1699–1757), French general.

mi·rex /ˈmīˌreks/ ▶ **n.** a synthetic insecticide of the organochlorine type used chiefly against ants.
– ORIGIN 1960s: of unknown origin.

Mir·i·am /ˈmirēəm/ (in the Bible) sister of Moses and Aaron and a leader of Hebrew women during the Exodus.

mi·rid /ˈmīrid, ˈmi(ə)r-/ ▶ **n.** an active plant bug of a large family that includes numerous plant pests. Formerly called CAPSID[1]. ● Family Miridae (formerly Capsidae), suborder Heteroptera.
– ORIGIN 1940s: from modern Latin *Miridae*, from *mirus* 'wonderful.'

mirk ▶ **n. & adj.** archaic spelling of MURK.

mirk·y ▶ **adj.** archaic spelling of MURKY.

mir·li·ton /ˈmərləˌtän/ ▶ **n.** **1** a musical instrument with a nasal tone produced by a vibrating membrane, typically a toy instrument resembling a kazoo.
2 another term for CHAYOTE (sense 1).
– ORIGIN early 19th cent.: from French, 'reed pipe,' of imitative origin.

Mi·ró /miˈrō/, Joan (1893–1983), Spanish painter. A prominent figure of surrealism, he painted a brightly colored fantasy world of variously spiky and amebic calligraphic forms against plain backgrounds.

mir·ror /ˈmirər/ ▶ **n.** a reflective surface, now typically of glass coated with a metal amalgam, that reflects a clear image. ■ something regarded as accurately representing something else: *the stage is supposed to be the mirror of life.* ■ (also **mirror site**) Computing a site on a network that stores some or all of the contents from another site.
▶ **v.** [with obj.] (of a reflective surface) show a reflection of: *the clear water mirrored the sky.* ■ correspond to: *gradations of educational attainment that mirror differences in social background.* ■ Computing keep a copy of some or all of the contents of (a network site) at another site, typically in order to improve accessibility. ■ (usu. as noun **mirroring**) Computing store copies of data on (two or more hard disks) as a method of protecting it.
– DERIVATIVES **mir·rored** **adj.**
– ORIGIN Middle English: from Old French *mirour*, based on Latin *mirare* 'look at.' Early senses also included 'a crystal used in magic' and 'a person deserving imitation.'

mir·ror ball (also **mirrorball**) ▶ **n.** a revolving ball covered with small mirrored facets, used to provide lighting effects at discos or dances.

mir·ror carp ▶ **n.** a common carp of an ornamental variety that has a row of large shiny platelike scales along each side. It has been naturalized in North America, Britain, and elsewhere.

mir·ror fin·ish ▶ **n.** a very smooth reflective finish produced on the surface of a metal.

mir·ror glass ▶ **n.** glass with a reflective metallic coating, as used for mirrors.

mir·ror im·age ▶ **n.** an image or object that is identical in form to another, but with the structure reversed, as in a mirror. ■ a person or thing that closely resembles another: *the city was the mirror image of Algiers.*

mir·ror sym·me·try ▶ **n.** symmetry about a plane, like that between an object and its reflection.

mir·ror writ·ing ▶ **n.** reversed writing resembling ordinary writing reflected in a mirror.

mirth /mərth/ ▶ **n.** amusement, esp. as expressed in laughter: *his six-foot frame shook with mirth.*
– ORIGIN Old English *myrgth*, of Germanic origin; related to MERRY.

mirth·ful /ˈmərthfəl/ ▶ **adj.** full of mirth; merry or amusing: *mirthful laughter.*
– DERIVATIVES **mirth·ful·ly** /-fəlē/ **adv.**

mirth·less /ˈmərthləs/ ▶ **adj.** (of a smile or laugh) lacking real amusement and typically expressing irony: *he gave a short, mirthless laugh.*
– DERIVATIVES **mirth·less·ly** **adv.**, **mirth·less·ness** **n.**

MIRV /mərv/ ▶ **n.** a type of intercontinental nuclear missile carrying several independent warheads.
– ORIGIN 1960s: acronym from *Multiple Independently targeted Re-entry Vehicle.*

mir·y /ˈmīrē/ ▶ **adj.** very muddy or boggy: *the roads were miry in winter.*

MIS ▶ **abbr.** Computing management information system.

mis-[1] ▶ **prefix** (added to verbs and their derivatives) wrongly: *misapply.* ■ badly: *mismanage.* ■ unsuitably: *misname.*
– ORIGIN Old English, of Germanic origin.

mis-[2] ▶ **prefix** occurring in a few words adopted from French expressing a sense with negative force: *misadventure* | *mischief.*
– ORIGIN from Old French *mes-* (based on Latin *minus*), assimilated to MIS-[1].

mis·ad·ven·ture /ˌmisədˈvenchər/ ▶ **n.** an unfortunate incident; a mishap: *an expensive misadventure in financial services.*
– ORIGIN Middle English: from Old French *mesaventure*, from *mesavenir* 'turn out badly.'

mis·a·ligned /ˌmisəˈlīnd/ ▶ **adj.** having an incorrect position or alignment: *misaligned headlights.*

mis·a·lign·ment /ˌmisəˈlīnmənt/ ▶ **n.** the incorrect arrangement or position of something in relation to something else.

mis·al·li·ance /ˌmisəˈlīəns/ ▶ **n.** an unsuitable, unhappy, or unworkable alliance or marriage.
– ORIGIN mid 18th cent.: from MIS-[1] 'awry' + ALLIANCE, on the pattern of French *mésalliance.*

mis·an·dry /misˈandrē/ ▶ **n.** the hatred of men by women: *her brand of feminism is just poorly disguised misandry.*
– DERIVATIVES **mis·an·drist** **n.**
– ORIGIN 1940s: from Greek *miso-* 'hating' + *anēr*, *andr-* 'man,' on the pattern of *misogyny.*

mis·an·thrope /ˈmisənˌthrōp, ˈmiz/ (also **misanthropist** /misˈanthrəpist/) ▶ **n.** a person who dislikes humankind and avoids human society.
– ORIGIN mid 16th cent.: from Greek *misanthrōpos*, from *misein* 'to hate' + *anthrōpos* 'man.'

mis·an·throp·ic /ˌmisənˈthräpik/ ▶ **adj.** disliking humankind and avoiding human society: *a misanthropic drunken loner.*
– DERIVATIVES **mis·an·throp·i·cal** /ˌmisənˈthräpikəl/ **adj.**, **mis·an·throp·i·cal·ly** /ˌmisənˈthräpik(ə)lē/ **adv.**

mis·an·thro·py /misˈsanthrəpē/ ▶ **n.** a dislike of humankind.
– ORIGIN mid 17th cent.: from Greek *misanthrōpia*, from *miso-* 'hating' + *anthrōpos* 'man.'

mis·ap·ply /ˌmisəˈplī/ ▶ **v.** (**misapplies, misapplying, misapplied**) [with obj.] (usu. **be misapplied**) use (something) for the wrong purpose or in the wrong way: *once new technology is adopted, it is often underused or misapplied.*
– DERIVATIVES **mis·ap·pli·ca·tion** /-ˌapləˈkāshən/ **n.**

mis·ap·pre·hend /ˌmisˌapriˈhend/ ▶ **v.** [with obj.] misunderstand (words, a person, a situation, etc.).

mis·ap·pre·hen·sion /ˌmisˌapriˈhenshən/ ▶ **n.** a mistaken belief about or interpretation of something: *she must have been laboring **under the misapprehension** that you are nice.*

– DERIVATIVES **mis·ap·pre·hen·sive** /-'hensiv/ **adj.**

mis·ap·pro·pri·ate /ˌmisə'prōprēˌāt/ ▶ **v.** [with obj.] (of a person) dishonestly or unfairly take (something, esp. money, belonging to another) for one's own use: *department officials had misappropriated funds.*

mis·ap·pro·pri·a·tion /ˌmisəˌprōprē'āsHən/ ▶ **n.** the action of misappropriating something; embezzlement: *an alleged misappropriation of funds.*

mis·be·got·ten /ˌmisbə'gätn/ ▶ **adj.** badly conceived, designed, or planned: *a misbegotten journey to Indianapolis.* ■ contemptible (used as a term of abuse): *you misbegotten hound!* ■ archaic (of a child) illegitimate.

mis·be·have /ˌmisbi'hāv/ ▶ **v.** [no obj.] (of a person, esp. a child) fail to conduct oneself in a way that is acceptable to others; behave badly. ■ (of a machine) fail to function correctly: *her regularly serviced car was misbehaving.*

mis·be·hav·ior /ˌmisbi'hāvyər/ (Brit. **misbehaviour**) ▶ **n.** the action of misbehaving; bad behavior: *he had denied all sexual misbehavior.*

mis·be·lief /ˌmisbə'lēf/ ▶ **n.** a wrong or false belief or opinion: *the misbelief that alcohol problems require a specialist response.* ■ less common term for **DISBELIEF**.

– DERIVATIVES **mis·be·liev·er** /-bəlēvər, -bē-/ **n.**

misc. ▶ **abbr.** miscellaneous.

mis·cal·cu·late /mis'kalkyəˌlāt/ ▶ **v.** [with obj.] calculate (an amount, distance, or measurement) wrongly. ■ assess (a situation) wrongly: *the government has seriously miscalculated the effect of privatization* | [no obj.] *you miscalculated if you imagined I'd fallen for your little scheme.*

mis·cal·cu·la·tion /ˌmisˌkalkyə'lāsHən/ ▶ **n.** an act of miscalculating; an error or misjudgment: *miscalculations were made in counting properties* | *it was a fatal miscalculation.*

mis·call /mis'kôl/ ▶ **v.** [with obj. and complement] **1** call (something) by a wrong or inappropriate name: *the motile bacteria have been miscalled zoospores.* **2** wrongly predict the result of (a future event, esp. an election or a vote).

mis·car·riage /mis'karij, 'misˌkarij/ ▶ **n. 1** the expulsion of a fetus from the womb before it is able to survive independently, esp. spontaneously or as the result of accident: *his wife had a miscarriage* | *some pregnancies result in miscarriage.* **2** an unsuccessful outcome of something planned: *the miscarriage of the project.*

mis·car·riage of jus·tice ▶ **n.** a failure of a court or judicial system to attain the ends of justice, esp. one that results in the conviction of an innocent person.

mis·car·ry /mis'karē, 'misˌkarē/ ▶ **v.** (**miscarries, miscarrying, miscarried**) [no obj.] **1** also (of a pregnant woman) have a miscarriage: *Wendy conceived, but she miscarried after five weeks* | [with obj.] *an ultrasound scan showed that she had miscarried her baby.* **2** (of something planned) fail to attain an intended or expected outcome: *such a rash crime, and one so very likely to miscarry!* ■ dated (of a letter) fail to reach its intended destination.

mis·cast /mis'kast/ ▶ **v.** (past and past participle **miscast**) [with obj.] (usu. **be miscast**) allot an unsuitable role to (a particular actor): *he is badly miscast in the romantic lead.* ■ allot the roles in (a play, movie, television show, etc.) to unsuitable actors.

mis·ceg·e·na·tion /miˌsejə'nāsHən, ˌmisəjə-/ ▶ **n.** the interbreeding of people considered to be of different racial types.

– ORIGIN mid 19th cent.: formed irregularly from Latin *miscere* 'to mix' + *genus* 'race' + **-ATION**.

mis·cel·la·ne·a /ˌmisə'lānēə/ ▶ **plural n.** miscellaneous items, esp. literary compositions, that have been collected together.

– ORIGIN late 16th cent.: from Latin, neuter plural of *miscellaneus* (see **MISCELLANEOUS**).

mis·cel·la·ne·ous /ˌmisə'lānēəs/ ▶ **adj.** (of items or people gathered or considered together) of various types or from different sources: *he picked up the miscellaneous papers.* ■ (of a collection or group) composed of members or elements of different kinds: *a miscellaneous collection of well-known ne'er-do-wells.*

– DERIVATIVES **mis·cel·la·ne·ous·ly adv.**, **mis·cel·la·ne·ous·ness n.**

– ORIGIN early 17th cent.: from Latin *miscellaneus* (from *miscellus* 'mixed,' from *miscere* 'to mix') + **-OUS**. In earlier use the word also described a person as 'having various qualities.'

mis·cel·la·ny /'misəˌlānē, mi'selənē/ ▶ **n.** (pl. **miscellanies**) a group or collection of different items; a mixture: *Talkeetna was a random miscellany of log cabins.* ■ a book containing a collection of pieces of writing by different authors.

– ORIGIN late 16th cent.: from French *miscellanées* (feminine plural), from Latin *miscellanea* (see **MISCELLANEA**).

mis·chance /mis'cHans/ ▶ **n.** bad luck: *by pure mischance, the secret was revealed.* ■ an unlucky occurrence: *innumerable mischances might ruin the enterprise.*

– ORIGIN Middle English: from Old French *mescheance*, from the verb *mescheoir*, from *mes-* 'adversely' + *cheoir* 'befall.'

mis·chief /'miscHif/ ▶ **n.** playful misbehavior or troublemaking, esp. in children: *she'll make sure Danny doesn't get into mischief.* ■ playfulness that is intended to tease, mock, or create trouble: *her eyes twinkled with irrepressible mischief.* ■ harm or trouble caused by someone or something: *she was bent on making mischief.* ■ archaic a person responsible for harm or annoyance.

– ORIGIN late Middle English (denoting misfortune or distress): from Old French *meschief*, from the verb *meschever*, from *mes-* 'adversely' + *chever* 'come to an end' (from *chef* 'head').

mis·chief-mak·er ▶ **n.** a person who deliberately creates trouble for others.

– DERIVATIVES **mis·chief-mak·ing n.**

mis·chie·vous /'miscHivəs/ ▶ **adj.** (of a person, animal, or their behavior) causing or showing a fondness for causing trouble in a playful way: *two mischievous kittens had decorated the bed with shredded newspaper.* ■ (of an action or thing) causing or intended to cause harm or trouble: *a mischievous allegation for which there is not a shred of evidence.*

– DERIVATIVES **mis·chie·vous·ly adv.**, **mis·chie·vous·ness n.**

– ORIGIN Middle English: from Anglo-Norman French *meschevous*, from Old French *meschever* 'come to an unfortunate end' (see **MISCHIEF**). The early sense was 'unfortunate or calamitous,' later 'having harmful effects'; the sense 'playfully troublesome' dates from the late 17th cent.

> **USAGE** Mischievous is a three-syllable word. Take care not to use this incorrect four-syllable pronunciation: /mis'cHēvēəs/.

misch met·al /misH/ ▶ **n.** an alloy of cerium, lanthanum, and other rare earth metals, used as an additive in various alloys, e.g., in flints for cigarette lighters.

– ORIGIN 1920s: from German *Mischmetall*, from *mischen* 'to mix' + *Metall* 'metal.'

mis·ci·ble /'misəbəl/ ▶ **adj.** (of liquids) forming a homogeneous mixture when added together: *sorbitol is miscible with glycerol.*

– DERIVATIVES **mis·ci·bil·i·ty** /ˌmisə'bilətē/ **n.**

– ORIGIN late 16th cent.: from medieval Latin *miscibilis*, from Latin *miscere* 'to mix.'

mis·com·mu·ni·ca·tion /ˌmiskəˌmyo͞onə'kāsHən/ ▶ **n.** failure to communicate adequately.

mis·con·ceive /ˌmiskən'sēv/ ▶ **v.** [with obj.] fail to understand correctly: *she was frustrated by professors who consistently misconceived her essays.* ■ (usu. **be misconceived**) judge or plan badly, typically on the basis of faulty understanding: *criticism of the trade surplus in Washington is misconceived* | (as adj. **misconceived**) *misconceived notions about gypsies.*

– DERIVATIVES **mis·con·ceiv·er n.**

mis·con·cep·tion /ˌmiskən'sepsHən/ ▶ **n.** a view or opinion that is incorrect because it is based on faulty thinking or understanding: *public misconceptions about AIDS remain high.*

mis·con·duct ▶ **n.** /mis'känˌdəkt/ **1** unacceptable or improper behavior, esp. by an employee or professional person: *she was found guilty of professional misconduct by a disciplinary tribunal.* ■ Ice Hockey a penalty assessed against a player for unsportsmanlike conduct. **2** mismanagement, esp. culpable neglect of duties.

▶ **v.** /ˌmiskən'dəkt/ **1** (**misconduct oneself**) behave in an improper or unprofessional manner. **2** [with obj.] mismanage (duties or a project).

mis·con·fig·ure /ˌmiskən'figyər/ ▶ **v.** [with obj.] (often as adj. **misconfigured**) Computing configure (a system or part of it) incorrectly: *misconfigured Windows systems.*

– DERIVATIVES **mis·con·fig·u·ra·tion** /ˌmiskənˌfigyə'rāsHən/ **n.**

mis·con·struct /ˌmiskən'strəkt/ ▶ **v.** [with obj.] rare misconstrue (something).

mis·con·struc·tion /ˌmiskən'strəksHən/ ▶ **n.** the action of misconstruing words or actions; misinterpretation: *I used a phrase that may be open to misconstruction.*

mis·con·strue /ˌmiskən'stro͞o/ ▶ **v.** (**misconstrues, misconstruing, misconstrued**) [with obj.] interpret (something, esp. a person's words or actions) wrongly: *my advice was deliberately misconstrued.*

mis·count ▶ **v.** /mis'kount/ [with obj.] count (something) incorrectly.

▶ **n.** /'misˌkount/ an incorrect reckoning of the total number of something: *a miscount necessitates a recount.*

mis·cre·ant /'miskrēənt/ ▶ **n.** a person who behaves badly or in a way that breaks the law. ■ archaic a heretic.

▶ **adj.** (of a person) behaving badly or in a way that breaks a law or rule: *her miscreant husband.* ■ archaic heretical.

– ORIGIN Middle English (as an adjective in the sense 'disbelieving'): from Old French *mescreant*, present participle of *mescreire* 'disbelieve,' from *mes-* 'mis-' + *creire* 'believe' (from Latin *credere*).

mis·cue[1] /mis'kyo͞o/ ▶ **n.** (in billiards) a shot in which the player fails to strike the ball properly with the cue. ■ (in other sports) a faulty strike, kick, or catch. ■ a miscalculated action; a mistake: *political miscues that led to resignations.*

▶ **v.** (**miscues, miscueing** or **miscuing, miscued**) [with obj.] (in billiards and other games) fail to strike (the ball or a shot) properly.

mis·cue[2] ▶ **n.** Linguistics an error in reading, esp. one caused by failure to respond correctly to a phonetic or contextual cue in the text.

▶ **v.** [no obj.] (of a performer, esp. an actor on stage) miss one's cue, or answer to another's cue. ■ [with obj.] give (a performer) the wrong cue.

mis·date /mis'dāt/ ▶ **v.** [with obj.] assign an incorrect date to (a document, event, or work of art).

mis·deal /mis'dēl/ ▶ **v.** (past and past participle **misdealt**) [no obj.] make a mistake when dealing cards.

▶ **n.** a hand dealt wrongly.

mis·deed /mis'dēd/ ▶ **n.** a wicked or illegal act.

– ORIGIN Old English *misdǣd* (see **MIS-[1]**, **DEED**).

mis·de·mean·ant /ˌmisdə'mēnənt/ ▶ **n.** formal a person convicted of a misdemeanor or guilty of misconduct.

– ORIGIN early 19th cent.: from archaic *misdemean* 'misbehave' + **-ANT**.

mis·de·mean·or /'misdiˌmēnər/ (Brit. **misdemeanour**) ▶ **n.** a minor wrongdoing: *the player can expect a lengthy suspension for his latest misdemeanor.* ■ Law a nonindictable offense, regarded in the US (and formerly in the UK) as less serious than a felony.

mis·de·scribe /ˌmisdi'skrīb/ ▶ **v.** [with obj.] describe inaccurately or misleadingly: *he misdescribed the play as a tragedy.*

– DERIVATIVES **mis·de·scrip·tion** /-'skripsHən/ **n.**

mis·di·ag·nose /mis'dīigˌnōs, -ˌnōz/ ▶ **v.** [with obj.] make an incorrect diagnosis of (a particular illness). ■ make an incorrect diagnosis of the illness from which (someone) is suffering: *the consultant misdiagnosed her as having cancer.*

– DERIVATIVES **mis·di·ag·no·sis** /ˌmisˌdīig'nōsəs/ **n.**

mis·di·al /ˌmis'dī(ə)l/ ▶ **v.** (**misdials, misdialing, misdialed**; Brit. **misdials, misdialling, misdialled**) [no obj.] dial a telephone number incorrectly.

▶ **n.** an act of dialing a number incorrectly.

mis·di·rect /ˌmisdə'rekt, -dī-/ ▶ **v.** [with obj.] send (someone or something) to the wrong place or in the wrong direction: *voters were misdirected to the wrong polling place.* ■ aim (something) in the wrong direction: *he misdirected a shot.* ■ (of a judge) instruct wrongly: *the appeals court was satisfied that the trial judge had misdirected the jury.* ■ use or apply (something) wrongly or inappropriately: *their efforts have been largely misdirected.*

– DERIVATIVES **mis·di·rec·tion** /-'reksHən/ **n.**

mis·do·ing /mis'do͞oiNG/ ▶ **n.** a misdeed.

mis·doubt /mis'dout/ ▶ **v.** [with obj.] chiefly archaic have doubts about the truth, reality, or existence of: *he was diffident and always misdoubted his own ability.* ■ fear or be suspicious about: *for I fear my father, and I misdoubt his hindrances.*

mis·ed·u·cate /mis'ejəˌkāt/ ▶ **v.** [with obj.] educate, teach, or inform wrongly.

– DERIVATIVES **mis·ed·u·ca·tion** /ˌmisˌejə'kāsHən/ **n.**, **mis·ed·u·ca·tive** /-'ejəˌkātiv/ **adj.**

mise en scène /ˌmēz ˌän 'sen/ ▶ **n.** [usu. in sing.] the arrangement of scenery and stage properties in a play. ■ the setting or surroundings of an event or action.

– ORIGIN French, literally 'putting on stage.'

PRONUNCIATION KEY ə *ago, up*; ər *over, fur*; a *hat*; ā *ate*; ä *car*; e *let*; ē *see*; i *fit*; ī *by*; NG *sing*; ō *go*; ô *law, for*; oi *toy*; o͝o *good*; o͞o *goo*; ou *out*; TH *thin*; T͟H *then*; ZH *vision*

m

mis·em·ploy /ˌmisˌimˈploi/ ▶ **v.** [with obj.] employ or use (something) wrongly or improperly.
– DERIVATIVES **mis·em·ploy·ment** **n.**

mi·ser /ˈmīzər/ ▶ **n.** a person who hoards wealth and spends as little money as possible.
– ORIGIN late 15th cent. (as an adjective in the sense 'miserly'): from Latin, literally 'wretched.'

mis·er·a·bi·lism /ˈmiz(ə)rəbəˌlizəm/ ▶ **n.** gloomy pessimism or negativity: *the duo spent much of the eighties exploring the lonely outer reaches of miserabilism.*
– DERIVATIVES **mis·er·a·bi·list** **n. & adj.**

mis·er·a·ble /ˈmiz(ə)rəbəl/ ▶ **adj. 1** (of a person) wretchedly unhappy or uncomfortable: *their happiness made Anne feel even more miserable.* ■ (of a situation or environment) causing someone to feel wretchedly unhappy or uncomfortable: *horribly wet and miserable conditions.* ■ (of a person) habitually morose: *a miserable man in his late sixties.*
2 pitiably small or inadequate: *all they pay me is a miserable $10,000 a year.* ■ [attrib.] contemptible (used as a term of abuse or for emphasis): *you miserable old creep!*
– DERIVATIVES **mis·er·a·ble·ness** **n.**, **mis·er·a·bly** /-blē/ **adv.**
– ORIGIN late Middle English: from French *misérable*, from Latin *miserabilis* 'pitiable,' from *miserari* 'to pity,' from *miser* 'wretched.'

mis·e·re·re /ˌmizəˈre(ə)rē, -ˈri(ə)rē/ ▶ **n. 1** (also **Miserere**) a psalm in which mercy is sought, esp. Psalm 51 or the music written for it.
2 another term for **MISERICORD** (sense 1).
– ORIGIN Middle English: from Latin, 'have mercy!,' imperative of *misereri*, from *miser* 'wretched.'

mis·er·i·cord /məˈzeriˌkôrd/ ▶ **n. 1** a ledge projecting from the underside of a hinged seat in a choir stall that, when the seat is turned up, gives support to someone standing.
2 historical an apartment in a monastery in which some relaxations of the monastic rule are permitted.
3 historical a small dagger used to deliver a death stroke to a wounded enemy.
– ORIGIN Middle English (denoting pity): from Old French *misericorde*, from Latin *misericordia*, from *misericors* 'compassionate,' from the stem of *misereri* 'to pity' + *cor, cord-* 'heart.'

m

mi·ser·li·ness /ˈmīzərlēnis/ ▶ **n.** excessive desire to save money; extreme meanness: *the party earned a damaging reputation for miserliness by cutting pensions.* ■ the quality of being small or inadequate; meagerness: *the relative miserliness of the prizes involved.*

mi·ser·ly /ˈmīzərlē/ ▶ **adj.** of, relating to, or characteristic of a miser: *his miserly great-uncle proved to be worth nearly $1 million.* ■ (of a quantity) pitiably small or inadequate: *last year's miserly growth in sales.*

mis·er·y /ˈmiz(ə)rē/ ▶ **n.** (pl. **miseries**) a state or feeling of great distress or discomfort of mind or body: *she went upstairs and cried in misery | he wrote endlessly about his frustrations and miseries.* ■ (usu. **miseries**) a cause or source of great distress or discomfort: *the miseries of war.*
– PHRASES **make someone's life a misery** (or **make life a misery for someone**) cause someone severe distress by continued unpleasantness or harassment. **put someone/something out of their misery** end the suffering of a person or animal in pain by killing them. ■ informal release someone from suspense or anxiety by telling them something they are anxious to know.
– ORIGIN late Middle English: from Old French *miserie*, from Latin *miseria*, from *miser* 'wretched.'

mis·fea·sance /misˈfēzəns/ ▶ **n.** Law a transgression, esp. the wrongful exercise of lawful authority.
– ORIGIN early 17th cent.: from Old French *mesfaisance*, from *mesfaire*, from *mes-* 'wrongly' + *faire* 'do' (from Latin *facere*). Compare with **MALFEASANCE**.

mis·feed /misˈfēd, ˈmisˌfēd/ ▶ **n.** an instance of faulty feeding of something (typically paper) through a machine.

mis·field /misˈfēld/ ▶ **v.** [with obj.] (in cricket and rugby) field (a ball) badly or clumsily.

mis·file /misˈfīl/ ▶ **v.** [with obj.] file wrongly.

mis·fire ▶ **v.** /misˈfīr/ [no obj.] (of a gun or missile) fail to discharge or fire properly. ■ (of an internal combustion engine) undergo failure of the fuel to ignite correctly or at all: *the car would misfire occasionally from the cold.* ■ (esp. of a plan) fail to produce the intended result: *the killer didn't know that his plan had misfired.* ■ (of a nerve cell) fail to transmit an electrical impulse at an appropriate moment.
▶ **n.** /ˈmisˌfīr/ a failure of a gun or missile to fire correctly or of fuel in an internal combustion engine to ignite.

mis·fit /ˈmisˌfit/ ▶ **n.** a person whose behavior or attitude sets them apart from others in an uncomfortably conspicuous way: *a motley collection of social misfits.* ■ archaic something that does not fit or that fits badly.

mis·for·tune /misˈfôrCHən/ ▶ **n.** bad luck: *the project was dogged by misfortune.* ■ an unfortunate condition or event: *never laugh at other people's misfortunes.*

mis·give /misˈgiv/ ▶ **v.** (past **misgave**; past participle **misgiven**) [with obj.] literary (of a person's mind or heart) fill (that person) with doubt, apprehension, or foreboding: *my heart misgave me when I saw him.*

mis·giv·ing /misˈgiviNG/ ▶ **n.** (usu. **misgivings**) a feeling of doubt or apprehension about the outcome or consequences of something: *we have* ***misgivings about*** *the way the campaign is being run | I felt a sense of misgiving at the prospect of retirement.*

mis·gov·ern /misˈgəvərn/ ▶ **v.** [with obj.] govern (a state or country) unfairly or inefficiently.
– DERIVATIVES **mis·gov·ern·ment** /-ˈgəvər(n)mənt/ **n.**

mis·guide /misˈgīd/ ▶ **v.** [with obj.] rare mislead: *a long survey that can only baffle and misguide the general reader.*
– DERIVATIVES **mis·guid·ance** /-gīdns/ **n.**

mis·guid·ed /misˈgīdid/ ▶ **adj.** having or showing faulty judgment or reasoning: *misguided attempts to promote political correctness.*
– DERIVATIVES **mis·guid·ed·ly** **adv.**, **mis·guid·ed·ness** **n.**

mis·han·dle /misˈhandəl/ ▶ **v.** [with obj.] **1** manage or deal with (something) wrongly or ineffectively: *the officer had mishandled the situation.*
2 manipulate roughly or carelessly: *the equipment could be dangerous if mishandled.*

mis·hap /ˈmisˌhap/ ▶ **n.** an unlucky accident: *although there were a few minor mishaps, none of the pancakes stuck to the ceiling | the event passed without mishap.*

Mi·sha·wa·ka /ˌmisHəˈwäkə, -ˈwôkə/ an industrial city in northeastern Indiana, east of South Bend; pop. 50,026 (est. 2008).

mis·hear /misˈhi(ə)r/ ▶ **v.** (past and past participle **misheard**) [with obj.] fail to hear (a person or their words) correctly.

Mi·shi·ma /miˈsHēmə, ˈmēsHēˌmä/, Yukio (1925–70), Japanese writer; pseudonym of *Hiraoka Kimitake*. His books include the *The Sea of Fertility* (1965–70), which looks at reincarnation and the sterility of modern life. An avowed imperialist, he committed hara-kiri after failing to incite soldiers against the postwar regime.

mis·hit /ˌmisˈhit/ ▶ **v.** (**mishits, mishitting**; past and past participle **mishit**) [with obj.] (in various sports) hit or kick (a ball) badly or in the wrong direction.
▶ **n.** an instance of hitting or kicking a ball in such a way.

mish·mash /ˈmisHˌmasH, -ˌmäsH/ ▶ **n.** [in sing.] a confused mixture: *a mishmash of outmoded ideas.*
– ORIGIN late 15th cent.: reduplication of **MASH**.

Mish·nah /ˈmisHnə/ ▶ **n.** (**the Mishnah**) an authoritative collection of exegetical material embodying the oral tradition of Jewish law and forming the first part of the Talmud.
– DERIVATIVES **Mish·na·ic** /misHˈnāik/ **adj.**
– ORIGIN from Hebrew *mišnāh* '(teaching by) repetition.'

mi·shu·gas /məsHo͝oˈgäs/ ▶ **n.** variant spelling of **MESHUGAAS**.

mis·i·den·ti·fy /ˌmisīˈdentəˌfī/ ▶ **v.** (**misidentifies, misidentifying, misidentified**) [with obj.] identify (something or someone) incorrectly.
– DERIVATIVES **mis·i·den·ti·fi·ca·tion** /-īˌdentəfəˈkāsHən/ **n.**

mis·in·form /ˌmisinˈfôrm/ ▶ **v.** [with obj.] give (someone) false or inaccurate information.

mis·in·for·ma·tion /ˌmisinfərˈmāsHən/ ▶ **n.** false or inaccurate information, esp. that which is deliberately intended to deceive: *nuclear matters are often entangled in a web of secrecy and misinformation.*

mis·in·ter·pret /ˌmisinˈtərprət/ ▶ **v.** (**misinterprets, misinterpreting, misinterpreted**) [with obj.] interpret (something or someone) wrongly.
– DERIVATIVES **mis·in·ter·pre·ta·tion** /-inˌtərprəˈtāsHən/ **n.**, **mis·in·ter·pret·er** **n.**

mis·judge /ˌmisˈjəj/ ▶ **v.** [with obj.] form a wrong opinion or conclusion about: *he felt that he had completely misjudged the man.* ■ make an incorrect estimation or assessment of: *the horse misjudged the fence and Mrs. Weaver was thrown off.*
– DERIVATIVES **mis·judg·ment** (also **misjudgement**) **n.**

mis·key /misˈkē/ ▶ **v.** (**miskeys, miskeying, miskeyed**) [with obj.] key (a word or piece of data) into a computer or other machine incorrectly.

Mis·ki·to /məˈskētō/ (also **Mosquito**) ▶ **n.** (pl. **same** or **Miskitos**) **1** a member of an American Indian people of the Atlantic coast of Nicaragua and Honduras.
2 the language of this people, possibly related to Chibchan.
▶ **adj.** of or relating to the Miskito or their language.
– ORIGIN the name in Miskito.

Mis·kolc /ˈmisHˌkōlts/ a city in northeastern Hungary; pop. 170,234 (2009).

mis·la·bel /misˈlābəl/ ▶ **v.** (**mislabels, mislabeling, mislabeled**; Brit. **mislabels, mislabelling, mislabelled**) [with obj.] label wrongly.

mis·lay /misˈlā/ ▶ **v.** (past and past participle **mislaid**) [with obj.] unintentionally put (an object) where it cannot readily be found and so lose it temporarily: *I seem to have mislaid my car keys.*

mis·lead /misˈlēd/ ▶ **v.** (past and past participle **misled**) [with obj.] cause (someone) to have a wrong idea or impression about someone or something: *the government misled the public about the road's environmental impact.*
– DERIVATIVES **mis·lead·er** **n.**

mis·lead·ing /misˈlēdiNG/ ▶ **adj.** giving the wrong idea or impression: *your article contains a number of misleading statements.*
– DERIVATIVES **mis·lead·ing·ly** **adv.**, **mis·lead·ing·ness** **n.**

mis·like /misˈlīk/ archaic ▶ **v.** [with obj.] consider to be unpleasant; dislike: *the pony snorted, misliking the smell of blood.*
▶ **n.** distaste; dislike.
– ORIGIN Old English *mislīcian* (see **MIS-**[1], **LIKE**[2]).

mis·man·age /misˈmanij/ ▶ **v.** [with obj.] manage (something) badly or wrongly.
– DERIVATIVES **mis·man·age·ment** **n.**

mis·match ▶ **n.** /ˈmisˌmaCH/ a failure to correspond or match; a discrepancy: *a huge* ***mismatch between*** *supply and demand.*
▶ **v.** /ˌmisˈmaCH/ [with obj.] (usu. as adj. **mismatched**) match (people or things) unsuitably or incorrectly: *funky mismatched chairs and tables.*

mis·mat·ed /ˌmisˈmātid/ ▶ **adj.** badly matched or not matching.

mis·name /misˈnām/ ▶ **v.** [with obj.] give (something) a wrong or inappropriate name: *summer peas—misnamed, because they are beans—thrive in hot weather.*

mis·no·mer /misˈnōmər/ ▶ **n.** a wrong or inaccurate name or designation: *"king crab" is a misnomer—these creatures are not crustaceans at all.* ■ a wrong or inaccurate use of a name or term: *to call this "neighborhood policing" would be a misnomer.*
– ORIGIN late Middle English: from Anglo-Norman French, from the Old French verb *mesnommer*, from *mes-* 'wrongly' + *nommer* 'to name' (based on Latin *nomen* 'name').

mi·so /ˈmēsō/ ▶ **n.** paste made from fermented soybeans and barley or rice malt, used in Japanese cooking.
– ORIGIN Japanese.

mi·sog·a·my /məˈsägəmē/ ▶ **n.** rare the hatred of marriage.
– DERIVATIVES **mi·sog·a·mist** /-mist/ **n.**
– ORIGIN mid 17th cent.: from Greek *misos* 'hatred' + *gamos* 'marriage.'

mi·sog·y·nist /məˈsäjənist/ ▶ **n.** a man who hates women.
▶ **adj.** reflecting or inspired by a hatred of women: *a misogynist attitude.*
– DERIVATIVES **mi·sog·y·nis·tic** /məˌsäjəˈnistik/ **adj.**

mi·sog·y·ny /məˈsäjənē/ ▶ **n.** the hatred of women by men: *she felt she was struggling against thinly disguised misogyny.*
– DERIVATIVES **mi·sog·y·nous** /-nəs/ **adj.**
– ORIGIN mid 17th cent.: from Greek *misos* 'hatred' + *gunē* 'woman.'

mis·pick·el /ˈmisˌpikəl/ ▶ **n.** another term for **ARSENOPYRITE**.
– ORIGIN late 17th cent.: from German.

mis·place /misˈplās/ ▶ **v.** [with obj.] (usu. **be misplaced**) put in the wrong place and lose temporarily because of this; mislay: *I'm sure the jewelry has just been misplaced, and not stolen.*
– DERIVATIVES **mis·place·ment** **n.**

mis·placed /misˈplāst/ ▶ **adj. 1** incorrectly positioned: *a million dollars had been lost because of a misplaced comma.* ■ not appropriate or correct in the circumstances: *a telling sign of misplaced priorities.* ■ (of an emotion) directed unwisely or to an inappropriate object: *he began to wonder if his sympathy were misplaced.*
2 [attrib.] temporarily lost: *her misplaced keys.*

mis·placed mod·i·fi·er ▶ **n.** Grammar a phrase or clause placed awkwardly in a sentence so that it appears to modify or refer to an unintended word.

mis·play ▶ **v.** /misˈplā/ [with obj.] play (a ball or card) wrongly, badly, or in contravention of the rules.
▶ **n.** /ˈmisˌplā/ an instance of playing a ball or card in such a way.

mis·print ▶ **n.** /ˈmisprint/ an error in printed text: *Galway might be a misprint for Galloway.*
▶ **v.** /misˈprint/ [with obj.] print (something) incorrectly.

mis·pri·sion[1] /misˈprizHən/ (also **misprision of treason** or **felony**) ▶ **n.** Law, chiefly historical the deliberate concealment of one's knowledge of a treasonable act or a felony.
– ORIGIN late Middle English: from Old French *mesprision* 'error,' from *mesprendre*, from *mes-* 'wrongly' + *prendre* 'to take.'

mis·pri·sion[2] ▶ **n.** rare erroneous judgment, esp. of the value or identity of something: *he despised himself for his misprision.*
– ORIGIN late 16th cent.: from MISPRIZE, influenced by MISPRISION[1].

mis·prize /misˈprīz/ ▶ **v.** [with obj.] rare fail to appreciate the value of (something); undervalue.
– ORIGIN late 15th cent.: from Old French *mesprisier*, from *mes-* 'wrongly' + *prisier* 'estimate the value of.'

mis·pro·nounce /ˌmisprəˈnouns/ ▶ **v.** [with obj.] pronounce (a word) incorrectly: *she mispronounced my name.*
– DERIVATIVES **mis·pro·nun·ci·a·tion** /-prəˌnənsēˈāsHən/ **n.**

mis·quote /misˈkwōt/ ▶ **v.** [with obj.] quote (a person or a piece of written or spoken text) inaccurately: *the foreign secretary had misquoted Qian.*
▶ **n.** a passage or remark quoted inaccurately: *a misquote from a poem by Robert Burns.*
– DERIVATIVES **mis·quo·ta·tion** /ˌmiskwōˈtāsHən/ **n.**

mis·read /misˈrēd/ ▶ **v.** (past and past participle **misread** /-ˈred/) [with obj.] read (a piece of text) wrongly. ■ judge or interpret (a situation or a person's manner or behavior) incorrectly: *had she been completely misreading his intentions?*

mis·re·mem·ber /ˌmisriˈmembər/ ▶ **v.** [with obj.] remember imperfectly or incorrectly.

mis·re·port /ˌmisriˈpôrt/ ▶ **v.** [with obj.] give a false or inaccurate account of (something): *the press exaggerated and misreported the response to the book.*
▶ **n.** a false or incorrect report.

mis·rep·re·sent /ˌmisrepriˈzent/ ▶ **v.** [with obj.] give a false or misleading account of the nature of: *you are misrepresenting the views of the government.*
– DERIVATIVES **mis·rep·re·sen·ta·tive** /-ˈzentətiv/ **adj.**

mis·rep·re·sen·ta·tion /ˌmisreprizenˈtāsHn/ ▶ **n.** the action or offence of giving a false or misleading account of the nature of something: *she is seeking damages on allegations of misrepresentation | this is a gross misrepresentation of the situation.*

mis·route /misˈro͞ot, -ˈrout/ ▶ **v.** [with obj.] divert or direct to the wrong place or by the wrong route.

mis·rule /misˈro͞ol/ ▶ **n.** the unfair or inefficient conduct of the affairs of a country or state: *forty years of misrule by local elites.* ■ the disruption of peace; disorder: *there was a tradition of misrule before, during, and after games.*
▶ **v.** [with obj.] govern (a country or state) badly.

miss[1] /mis/ ▶ **v.** [with obj.] **1** fail to hit, reach, or come into contact with (something aimed at): *a laser-guided bomb had missed its target* | [no obj.] *he was given two free throws, but missed both times.* ■ pass by without touching; chance not to hit: *a piece of shrapnel missed him by inches.* ■ fail to catch (something thrown or dropped). ■ be too late to catch (a passenger vehicle, etc.): *we'll miss the train if he doesn't hurry.* ■ fail to notice, hear, or understand: *the villa is impossible to miss—it's right by the road.* ■ fail to attend, participate in, or watch (something one is expected to do or habitually does): *teachers were supposed to report those students who missed class that day.* ■ fail to see or have a meeting with (someone): *"Potter's been here this morning?" "You've just missed him."* ■ not be able to experience or fail to take advantage of (an opportunity or chance): *don't miss the chance to visit the breathtaking Dolomites* | [no obj.] *he failed to recover from a leg injury and* ***missed out on*** *a trip to Barcelona.* ■ avoid; escape: *smart Christmas shoppers go out early to miss the crowds.* ■ fail to include (someone or something); omit: *if we miss a few things in the first draft, we can add them later.* ■ (of a woman) fail to have (a monthly period). ■ [no obj.] (of an engine or motor vehicle) undergo failure of ignition in one or more cylinders.
2 notice the loss or absence of: *he's rich—he won't miss the money | she slipped away when she thought she wouldn't be missed.* ■ feel regret or sadness at no longer being able to enjoy the presence of: *she misses all her old friends.* ■ feel regret or sadness at no longer being able to go to, do, or have: *I still miss France and I wish I could go back.*
▶ **n.** a failure to hit, catch, or reach something: *Elster's stunning catch in the third inning made up for his dreadful miss in the first.* ■ a failure, esp. an unsuccessful movie, television show, recording, etc.: *audiences will decide whether Brando's latest flick is a hit or a miss.*
– PHRASES **give something a miss** Brit. informal decide not to do or have something: *we decided to give the popcorn a miss.* **miss a beat 1** (of the heart) temporarily fail or appear to fail to beat. **2** [usu. with negative] informal hesitate or falter, esp. in demanding circumstances or when making a transition from one activity to another: *his speech segued from child-care subsidies to nuclear disarmament, without missing a beat.* **miss the boat** (or **bus**) informal be too slow to take advantage of an opportunity: *the company missed the boat with its first attempt at a computer line five years ago.* **a miss is as good as a mile** proverb the fact of failure or escape is not affected by the narrowness of the margin. **not miss a trick** informal never fail to take advantage of a situation.
– DERIVATIVES **miss·a·ble** /ˈmisəbəl/ **adj.**
– ORIGIN Old English *missan*, of Germanic origin; related to Dutch and German *missen*.

miss[2] ▶ **n. 1** (**Miss**) a title prefixed to the name of an unmarried woman or girl, or to that of a married woman retaining her maiden name for professional purposes: *Miss Hazel Armstrong.* ■ used in the title of the winner in a beauty contest: *Miss World.* ■ used as a polite form of address to a young woman or to a waitress, etc.: *where will you be staying in England, miss?* ■ chiefly Brit. used by children in addressing a female teacher: *please, Miss, can I be excused?*
2 often derogatory or humorous a girl or young woman, esp. one regarded as silly or headstrong: *there was none of the country bumpkin about this young miss.*
3 (**misses**) a range of standard sizes, usually 8 to 20, in women's clothing.
– ORIGIN mid 17th cent.: abbreviation of MISTRESS.

Miss. ▶ **abbr.** Mississippi.

mis·sal /ˈmisəl/ ▶ **n.** a book containing the texts used in the Catholic Mass throughout the year.
– ORIGIN Middle English: from medieval Latin *missale*, neuter of ecclesiastical Latin *missalis* 'relating to the Mass,' from *missa* 'Mass.'

mis·sel thrush ▶ **n.** variant spelling of MISTLE THRUSH.

mis·shape /misˈsHāp/ ▶ **v.** [with obj.] give a bad or ugly shape or form to; deform.

mis·shap·en /misˈsHāpən/ ▶ **adj.** not having the normal or natural shape or form: *misshapen fruit.*
– DERIVATIVES **mis·shap·en·ly adv.**, **mis·shap·en·ness n.**

mis·sile /ˈmisəl/ ▶ **n.** an object that is forcibly propelled at a target, either by hand or from a mechanical weapon. ■ a weapon that is self-propelled or directed by remote control, carrying a conventional or nuclear explosive.
– ORIGIN early 17th cent. (as an adjective in the sense 'suitable for throwing (at a target)'): from Latin *missile*, neuter (used as a noun) of *missilis*, from *miss-* 'sent,' from the verb *mittere*.

mis·sile·ry /ˈmisəlrē/ ▶ **n. 1** the study of the use and characteristics of missiles.
2 missiles collectively.

miss·ing /ˈmisiNG/ ▶ **adj.** (of a thing) not able to be found because it is not in its expected place: *a quantity of cash has* ***gone missing.*** ■ not present or included when expected or supposed to be: *passion was an element that had been* ***missing from*** *her life for too long | you can fill in the missing details later.* ■ (of a person) absent from a place, esp. home, and of unknown whereabouts: *she alerted police that her son was missing.* ■ (of a person) not yet traced or confirmed as alive, but not known to be dead, after an accident or during wartime: *servicemen listed as* ***missing in action.***

miss·ing link ▶ **n.** a thing that is needed in order to complete a series, provide continuity, or gain complete knowledge: *she is the missing link between the European ballad tradition and Anglo-American white soul.* ■ a hypothetical fossil form intermediate between two living forms, esp. between humans and apes.

mis·si·ol·o·gy /ˌmisēˈäləjē/ ▶ **n.** the study of religious (typically Christian) missions and their methods and purposes.
– DERIVATIVES **mis·sio·log·i·cal** /ˌmisēəˈläjikəl/ **adj.**
– ORIGIN 1930s: formed irregularly from MISSION + -LOGY.

mis·sion /ˈmisHən/ ▶ **n. 1** an important assignment carried out for political, religious, or commercial purposes, typically involving travel: *a trade mission to Mexico.* ■ [treated as sing. or pl.] a group of people taking part in such an assignment: *by then, the mission had journeyed more than 3,500 miles.* ■ [in sing.] an organization or institution involved in a long-term assignment in a foreign country: *the head of the West German mission.* ■ an operation carried out by military aircraft: *he was shot down on a supply mission.* ■ an expedition into space.
2 the vocation or calling of a religious organization, esp. a Christian one, to go out into the world and spread its faith: *the Christian mission | Gandhi's attitude to mission and conversion.* ■ a building or group of buildings used by a Christian mission.
3 a strongly felt aim, ambition, or calling: *his main mission in life has been to cut unemployment.*
– ORIGIN mid 16th cent. (denoting the sending of the Holy Spirit into the world): from Latin *missio(n-)*, from *mittere* 'send.'

mis·sion·ar·y /ˈmisHəˌnerē/ ▶ **n.** (pl. **missionaries**) a person sent on a religious mission, esp. one sent to promote Christianity in a foreign country.
▶ **adj.** of, relating to, or characteristic of a missionary or a religious mission: *missionary work | they have lost the missionary zeal they once had.*
– ORIGIN mid 17th cent.: from modern Latin *missionarius*, from Latin *missio* (see MISSION).

mis·sion·ar·y po·si·tion ▶ **n.** informal a position for sexual intercourse in which a couple lies face to face with the woman underneath the man.
– ORIGIN said to be so named because early missionaries advocated the position as "proper" to primitive peoples, to whom the practice was unknown.

Mis·sion·ary Ridge /ˈmisHəˌnerē/ a historic site southeast of Chattanooga in Tennessee, on the Georgia border, scene of a November 1863 Civil War battle that followed that at nearby Lookout Mountain.

mis·sion creep ▶ **n.** a gradual shift in objectives during the course of a military campaign, often resulting in an unplanned long-term commitment.

mis·sion-crit·i·cal ▶ **adj.** Computing (of hardware or software) vital to the functioning of an organization.

mis·sion·er /ˈmisHənər/ ▶ **n. 1** a person in charge of a religious or charitable mission.
2 a missionary.

mis·sion state·ment ▶ **n.** a formal summary of the aims and values of a company, organization, or individual.

mis·sis ▶ **n.** variant spelling of MISSUS.

miss·ish /ˈmisisH/ ▶ **adj.** affectedly demure, squeamish, or sentimental.

Mis·sis·sau·ga /ˌmisəˈsôgə/ a town in southern Ontario, on the western shores of Lake Ontario, a southern suburb of Toronto; pop. 668,549 (2006).

Mis·sis·sip·pi /ˌmisəˈsipē/ **1** a major river in North America that rises in Minnesota near the Canadian border and flows south to a delta on the Gulf of Mexico. With its chief tributary, the Missouri River, it is 3,710 miles (5,970 km) long. In the second half of the 17th century it provided a route south through the center of the continent for French explorers from Canada. From the 1830s, it was noted for the sternwheeler steamboats that plied between New Orleans and St. Louis and other northern cities.
2 a state in the southern US, on the Gulf of Mexico, bounded on the west by the lower Mississippi River; pop. 2,938,618 (est. 2008); capital, Jackson; statehood, Dec. 10, 1817 (20). A French colony in the first half of the 18th century, it was ceded to Britain in 1763 and to the US in 1783.

Mis·sis·sip·pi·an /ˌmisiˈsipēən/ ▶ **adj. 1** of or relating to the state of Mississippi.
2 Geology of, relating to, or denoting the early part of the Carboniferous period in North America from about 363 to 323 million years ago, following the Devonian and preceding the Pennsylvanian. ■ Archaeology of, relating to, or denoting a settled culture of the southeastern US, dated to about AD 800–1300.
▶ **n. 1** a native or inhabitant of Mississippi.
2 (**the Mississippian**) Geology the Mississippian period or the system of rocks deposited during it. ■ Archaeology the Mississippian culture or period.

Mis·sis·sip·pi Del·ta see DELTA[2], YAZOO RIVER.

Mis·sis·sip·pi mud pie ▶ **n.** a type of rich, mousselike chocolate cake or pie.

mis·sive /ˈmisiv/ ▶ **n.** a letter, esp. a long or official one: *he hastily banged out electronic missives.*
– ORIGIN late Middle English (as an adjective, originally in the phrase LETTER MISSIVE): from

m

medieval Latin *missivus*, from Latin *mittere* 'send.' The current sense dates from the early 16th cent.

Mis·sou·la /məˈzo͞olə/ a commercial city in western Montana, on the Clark Fork River; pop. 68,202 (est. 2008).

Mis·sou·ri /məˈzo͞orē, -ˈzo͞orə/ **1** a major river in North America, one of the main tributaries of the Mississippi River. It rises in the Rocky Mountains in Montana and flows 2,315 miles (3,736 km) to meet the Mississippi River just north of St. Louis.
2 a state in the central part of the US, bounded on the east by the Mississippi River; pop. 5,911,605 (est. 2008); capital, Jefferson City; statehood, Aug. 10, 1821 (24). It was acquired as part of the Louisiana Purchase in 1803 and admitted as a state as part of the Missouri Compromise.
– DERIVATIVES **Mis·sour·i·an** /-ēən/ **n. & adj.**

mis·speak /misˈspēk/ ▶ **v.** (past **misspoke**; past participle **misspoken**) [no obj.] express oneself insufficiently clearly or accurately.

mis·spell /misˈspel/ ▶ **v.** (past and past participle **misspelt** or **misspelled**) [with obj.] spell (a word) incorrectly.

mis·spend /misˈspend/ ▶ **v.** (past and past participle **misspent**) [with obj.] (usu. as adj. **misspent**) spend (one's time or money) foolishly, wrongly, or wastefully: *perhaps I am atoning for my misspent youth.*

mis·state /misˈstāt/ ▶ **v.** [with obj.] make wrong or inaccurate statements about.
– DERIVATIVES **mis·state·ment n.**

mis·step /misˈstep, ˈmis,step/ ▶ **n.** a clumsy or badly judged step: *for a mountain goat, one misstep could be fatal.* ■ a mistake or blunder.

mis·sus /ˈmisəz, -əs/ (also **missis**) ▶ **n.** [in sing.] informal or humorous a man's wife: *I promised* ***the missus*** *I'd be home by eleven.* ■ informal used as a form of address to a woman whose name is not known: *sit down, missus.*

miss·y /ˈmisē/ ▶ **n.** (pl. **missies**) used as an affectionate or disparaging form of address to a young girl: *"Don't tell lies, missy," he said sternly.*
▶ **adj.** of or relating to the misses range of garment sizes: *available in missy and petite sizes.*

mist /mist/ ▶ **n.** a cloud of tiny water droplets suspended in the atmosphere at or near the earth's surface limiting visibility, but to a lesser extent than fog; strictly, with visibility remaining above 1.5 miles (1 km): *the peaks were shrouded in mist* | [in sing.] *a mist rose out of the river.* ■ [in sing.] a condensed vapor settling in fine droplets on a surface: *a breeze cooled the mist of perspiration that had dampened her temples.* ■ [in sing.] a haze or film over the eyes, esp. caused by tears, and resulting in blurred vision: *Ruth saw most of the scene through a mist of tears.* ■ used in reference to something that blurs one's perceptions or memory: *Sardinia's origins are* ***lost in the mists of time.***
▶ **v.** cover or become covered with mist: [with obj.] *the windows were* ***misted up*** *with condensation* | [no obj.] *the glass was beginning to* ***mist up.*** ■ [no obj.] (of a person's eyes) become covered with a film of tears causing blurred vision: *her eyes misted at this heroic image.* ■ [with obj.] spray (something, esp. a plant) with a fine cloud of water droplets.
– ORIGIN Old English, of Germanic origin; from an Indo-European root shared by Greek *omikhlē* 'mist, fog.'

mis·take /məˈstāk/ ▶ **n.** an action or judgment that is misguided or wrong: *coming here was a mistake* | *she* ***made the mistake of*** *thinking they were important.* ■ something, esp. a word, figure, or fact, that is not correct; an inaccuracy: *a couple of spelling mistakes.*
▶ **v.** (past **mistook**; past participle **mistaken**) [with obj.] be wrong about: *because I was inexperienced, I mistook the nature of our relationship.* ■ (**mistake someone/something for**) wrongly identify someone or something as: *she thought he'd mistaken her for someone else.*
– PHRASES **and no mistake** informal, dated without any doubt: *it's a bad business and no mistake.* **by mistake** accidentally; in error: *she'd left her purse at home by mistake.* **make no mistake (about it)** informal do not be deceived into thinking otherwise. **there is no mistaking someone or something** it is impossible not to recognize someone or something: *there was no mistaking her sincerity.*
– DERIVATIVES **mis·tak·a·ble adj.**, **mis·tak·a·bly** /-əblē/ **adv.**
– ORIGIN late Middle English (as a verb): from Old Norse *mistaka* 'take in error,' probably influenced in sense by Old French *mesprendre*.

mis·tak·en /məˈstākən/ ▶ **adj.** [predic.] wrong in one's opinion or judgment: *she wondered whether she'd been mistaken about his intentions.* ■ [attrib.] (esp. of a belief) based on or resulting from a misunderstanding or faulty judgment: *don't buy a hard bed in the mistaken belief that it is good for you* | *an unfortunate case of mistaken identity.*
– DERIVATIVES **mis·tak·en·ness n.**

mis·tak·en·ly /məˈstākənlē/ ▶ **adv.** in a mistaken way; wrongly: *they mistakenly believed her to be pregnant.* ■ by accident or oversight; accidentally: *warplanes mistakenly bombed a village.*

mis·ter¹ /ˈmistər/ ▶ **n.** variant form of **Mr.**, often used humorously or with offensive emphasis: *don't back-talk me, mister!* ■ informal used as a form of address to a man whose name is not known: *thanks, mister.*
– ORIGIN mid 16th cent.: weakened form of **master¹** in unstressed use before a name.

mis·ter² ▶ **n.** a device, such as a bottle, with a nozzle for spraying a mist of water, esp. on houseplants.

mis·time /misˈtīm/ ▶ **v.** [with obj.] choose a bad or inappropriate moment to do or say (something): *he lost $800 million by mistimimg his withdrawal from the market.*
– ORIGIN Old English *mistīmian* 'happen unfortunately' (see **mis-¹**, **time**).

mis·timed /misˈtīmd/ ▶ **adj.** done at an inappropriate moment; badly timed: *her mistimed resignation from the government.*

mis·tle thrush /ˈmisəl ,THrəsH/ (also **missel thrush**) ▶ **n.** a large Eurasian thrush with a spotted breast and harsh rattling call, with a fondness for mistletoe berries. ● *Turdus viscivorus*, subfamily Turdinae, family Muscicapidae.
– ORIGIN early 17th cent.: *mistle* from Old English *mistel* (see **mistletoe**).

mis·tle·toe /ˈmisəl,tō/ ▶ **n.** a leathery-leaved parasitic plant that grows on apple, oak, and other broadleaf trees and bears white glutinous berries in winter. ● Several species in the family Viscaceae, in particular the Eurasian *Viscum album*, and in the family Loranthaceae, in particular the American *Phoradendron serotinum*.
– ORIGIN Old English *misteltān*, from *mistel* 'mistletoe' (of Germanic origin, related to Dutch *mistel* and German *Mistel*) + *tān* 'twig.'

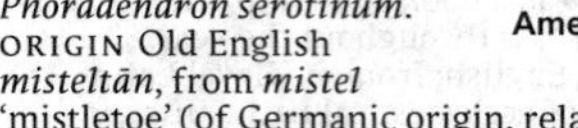
American mistletoe

mis·took /məˈsto͝ok/ past of **mistake**.

mis·tral /ˈmistrəl, miˈsträl/ ▶ **n.** a strong, cold northwesterly wind that blows through the Rhône valley and southern France into the Mediterranean, mainly in winter.
– ORIGIN early 17th cent.: French, from Provençal, from Latin *magistralis (ventus)*, literally 'master wind.'

mis·trans·late /,mis,tranzˈlāt, -,transˈlāt/ ▶ **v.** [with obj.] translate (something) incorrectly.
– DERIVATIVES **mis·trans·la·tion** /-ˈlāsHən/ **n.**

mis·treat /misˈtrēt/ ▶ **v.** [with obj.] treat (a person or animal) badly, cruelly, or unfairly.

mis·treat·ment /misˈtrētmənt/ ▶ **n.** the action of mistreating or fact of being mistreated; ill-treatment: *the alleged mistreatment of the animals that perform in those shows.*

mis·tress /ˈmistris/ ▶ **n.** **1** a woman in a position of authority or control: *she is always* ***mistress of the situation****, coolly self-possessed* | figurative *work is an unforgiving, implacable mistress.* ■ a woman who is skilled in a particular subject or activity: *a mistress of the sound bite, she is famed for the acidity of her tongue.* ■ the female owner of a dog, cat, or other domesticated animal. ■ [with modifier] chiefly Brit. a female schoolteacher who teaches a particular subject: *a Geography mistress.* ■ archaic a female head of a household: *he asked for the mistress of the house.* ■ (esp. formerly) a female employer of domestic staff.
2 a woman having an extramarital sexual relationship, esp. with a married man: *Elsie knew her husband had a mistress tucked away somewhere.* ■ archaic or literary a woman loved and courted by a man.
3 (**Mistress**) archaic or dialect used as a title prefixed to the name of a married woman; Mrs.
– ORIGIN Middle English: from Old French *maistresse*, from *maistre* 'master.'

mis·tri·al /ˈmis,trī(ə)l/ ▶ **n.** a trial rendered invalid through an error in the proceedings. ■ an inconclusive trial, such as one in which the jury cannot agree on a verdict.

mis·trust /misˈtrəst/ ▶ **v.** [with obj.] be suspicious of; have no confidence in: *she had no cause to mistrust him.*
▶ **n.** lack of trust: suspicion: *the public mistrust of government.*

mis·trust·ful /misˈtrəstfəl/ ▶ **adj.** lacking in trust; suspicious: *he wondered if he had been unduly mistrustful of her.*
– DERIVATIVES **mis·trust·ful·ly adv.**, **mis·trust·ful·ness n.**

mist·y /ˈmistē/ ▶ **adj.** (**mistier**, **mistiest**) full of, covered with, or accompanied by mist: *the evening was cold and misty* | *the misty air above the frozen river.* ■ (of a person's eyes) full of tears so as to blur the vision. ■ indistinct or dim in outline: *a misty out-of-focus silhouette* | figurative *a few misty memories.* ■ (of a color) not bright; soft: *a misty pink.*
– DERIVATIVES **mist·i·ly** /ˈmistəlē/ **adv.**, **mist·i·ness n.**
– ORIGIN Old English *mistig* (see **mist**).

mis·type /misˈtīp/ ▶ **v.** [with obj.] **1** make a mistake in typing (a word or letter).
2 assign (someone or something) to an incorrect category: *I mistyped you—I didn't think you looked the hunting type.*

mis·un·der·stand /,mis,əndərˈstand/ ▶ **v.** (past and past participle **misunderstood**) [with obj.] fail to interpret or understand (something) correctly: *he had misunderstood the policeman's hand signals* | [no obj.] *I must have misunderstood—I thought you were anxious to leave.* ■ fail to interpret or understand the words or actions of (someone) correctly: *don't misunderstand me—I'm not implying she should be working* | (as adj. **misunderstood**) *he is one of football's most misunderstood men.*

mis·un·der·stand·ing /,mis,əndərˈstandiNG/ ▶ **n.** a failure to understand something correctly: *a misunderstanding of the facts and the law* | *there must have been some kind of misunderstanding.* ■ a disagreement or quarrel: *he left the army after a slight misunderstanding with his commanding officer.*

mis·us·age /misˈyo͞osij/ ▶ **n.** archaic unjust treatment: *they were determined to defend themselves from misusage.*

mis·use ▶ **v.** /misˈyo͞oz, ˈmis,yo͞oz/ [with obj.] use (something) in the wrong way or for the wrong purpose: *he was found guilty of misusing public funds.* ■ treat (someone or something) badly or unfairly.
▶ **n.** /,misˈyo͞os, ˈmis,yo͞os/ the wrong or improper use of something: *drugs of such potency that their misuse can have dire consequences* | *a misuse of power.*
– DERIVATIVES **mis·us·er** /-ˈyo͞ozər/ **n.**

MIT ▶ **abbr.** Massachusetts Institute of Technology.

Mi·tan·ni /məˈtanē/ an ancient kingdom which flourished in northern Mesopotamia in the 15th–14th centuries BC.
– DERIVATIVES **Mi·tan·ni·an** /məˈtanēən/ **adj. & n.**

Mitch·ell¹ /ˈmicHəl/, Billy (1879–1936), US army officer; full name *William Mitchell*; born in France. An outspoken advocate of air power, he was court-martialed in 1925 for his criticism of the war and navy departments. As a civilian, he continued to preach the importance of air power in warfare.

Mitch·ell², John (Newton) (1913–88), US lawyer. He served as US attorney general 1969–72 under President Nixon and was convicted in 1975 of conspiracy in the Watergate break-in and cover-up.

Mitch·ell³, Joni (1943–), Canadian singer and songwriter; born *Roberta Joan Anderson*. She started to record in 1968 and gradually moved from folk to a fusion of folk, jazz, and rock. Notable albums: *Blue* (1971), *Hejira* (1976), and *Dog Eat Dog* (1986).

Mitch·ell⁴, Margaret (1900–49), US novelist. she wrote the best-selling and Pulitzer Prize–winning novel *Gone with the Wind* (1936; movie, 1939), set during the US Civil War.

Mitch·ell⁵, Maria (1818–89), US astronomer. She established the orbit of a newly discovered comet in 1847 and became the first woman elected 1848 to the American Academy of Arts and Sciences. She taught astronomy at Vassar College 1865–88.

Mitch·um /ˈmicHəm/, Robert (1917–97), US actor. He was a professional boxer before rising to stardom in movies such as *Out of the Past* (1947), *Night of the Hunter* (1955), *The Sundowners* (1960), and *Farewell My Lovely* (1975).

mite¹ /mīt/ ▶ **n.** a minute arachnid that has four pairs of legs when adult, related to the ticks. Many kinds live in the soil and a number are parasitic on plants or animals. ● Order (or subclass) Acari: numerous families.
– ORIGIN Old English *mīte*, of Germanic origin.

mite² ▶ **n.** **1** a small child or animal, esp. when regarded as an object of sympathy: ***the poor little mite*** *looks half-starved.*
2 a very small amount: *his teacher thought he needed a mite of discipline.* ■ historical a small coin, in particular a small Flemish copper coin of very low face value. See also **widow's mite**.

▶ **adv.** (**a mite**) informal a little; slightly: *all evening he's seemed a mite awkward.*
– ORIGIN late Middle English (denoting a small Flemish copper coin): from Middle Dutch *mīte*; probably from the same Germanic word as MITE[1].

mi·ter /ˈmītər/ (Brit. **mitre**) ▶ **n. 1** a tall headdress worn by bishops and senior abbots as a symbol of office, tapering to a point at front and back with a deep cleft between. ■ historical a headdress worn by a Jewish high priest. ■ historical a headband worn by women in ancient Greece.
2 (also **miter joint**) a joint made between two pieces of wood or other material at an angle of 90°, such that the line of junction bisects this angle. ■ a diagonal seam of two pieces of fabric that meet at a corner joining.
3 (also **miter shell**) a mollusk of warm seas that has a sharply pointed shell with a narrow aperture, supposedly resembling a bishop's miter. ● Family Mitridae, class Gastropoda: *Mitra* and other genera.

miter 1

miter joint

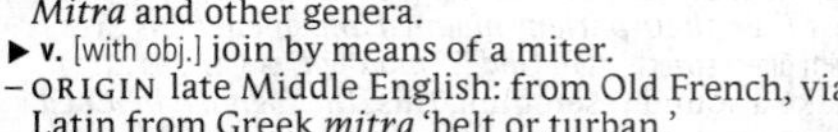

▶ **v.** [with obj.] join by means of a miter.
– ORIGIN late Middle English: from Old French, via Latin from Greek *mitra* 'belt or turban.'

mi·ter box ▶ **n.** a guide to enable a saw to cut miter joints at the desired angle.

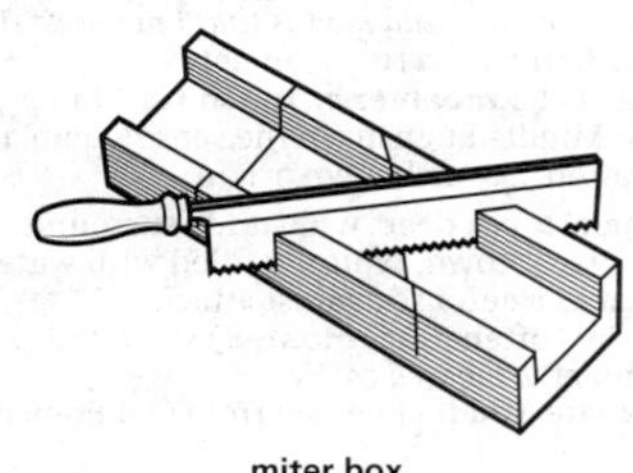

miter box

mi·tered /ˈmītərd/ ▶ **adj. 1** joined with a miter joint or seam: *complete the sides with mitered corners.* **2** bearing, wearing, or entitled to wear a miter: *the mitered bishop.*

Mit·ford /ˈmitfərd/, Nancy (Freeman) (1904–73) and her sister Jessica (Lucy) (1917–96), English writers. Nancy wrote comic novels, including *Love in a Cold Climate* (1949). Jessica became a US citizen in 1944 and is best known for her works on American culture, notably *The American Way of Death* (1963).

Mith·ra·ism /ˈmiᴛʜrəˌizəm/ ▶ **n.** the cult of the god Mithras, which became popular among Roman soldiers of the later empire, and was the main rival to Christianity in the first three centuries AD.
– DERIVATIVES **Mith·ra·ic** /miˈᴛʜrā-ik/ **adj.**, **Mith·ra·ist** /miˈᴛʜrā-ist/ **n.**

Mith·ras /ˈmiᴛʜˌräs/ Mythology a god of light, truth, and honor, the central figure of the cult of Mithraism but probably of Persian origin. He was also associated with merchants and the protection of warriors.

Mith·ri·da·tes VI /ˌmiᴛʜrəˈdātēz/ (also **Mithradates VI**) (c.132–63 BC), king of Pontus 120–163; known as **Mithridates the Great**. His expansionist policies led to three wars with Rome (88–85, 83–82, and 74–66). He was finally defeated by Pompey.

mith·ri·da·tize /ˌmiᴛʜrəˈdātīz/ ▶ **v.** [with obj.] rare render immune against a poison by administering gradually increasing doses of the poison.
– ORIGIN mid 19th cent.: from the name of *Mithridates* (see MITHRIDATES VI), who reputedly made himself immune to poisons by constantly taking antidotes, + -IZE.

mit·i·gate /ˈmitəˌgāt/ ▶ **v.** [with obj.] make less severe, serious, or painful: *he wanted to mitigate misery in the world.* ■ lessen the gravity of (an offense or mistake): (as adj. **mitigating**) *he would have faced a prison sentence but for **mitigating** circumstances.*
– DERIVATIVES **mit·i·ga·ble** /-gibəl/ **adj.**, **mit·i·ga·tor** /-ˌgātər/ **n.**, **mit·i·ga·to·ry** /-gəˌtôrē/ **adj.**
– ORIGIN late Middle English: from Latin *mitigat-* 'softened, alleviated,' from the verb *mitigare*, from *mitis* 'mild.'

USAGE The verbs **mitigate** and **militate** have a similarity in form but are quite different in meaning. **Mitigate** means 'make (something bad) less severe,' (*he wanted to mitigate misery in the world*), while **militate** is nearly always used in constructions with *against* to mean 'be a powerful factor in preventing' (*laws that **militate against** personal freedoms*).

mit·i·ga·tion /ˌmitəˈgāsʜən/ ▶ **n.** the action of reducing the severity, seriousness, or painfulness of something: *the emphasis is on the identification and mitigation of pollution.*
– PHRASES **in mitigation** so as to make something, esp. a crime, appear less serious and thus be punished more leniently: *in mitigation she said her client had been deeply depressed.*
– ORIGIN late Middle English: from Old French, or from Latin *mitigatio(n-)*, from the verb *mitigare* 'alleviate' (see MITIGATE).

mi·to·chon·dri·on /ˌmītəˈkändrēən/ ▶ **n.** (pl. **mitochondria** /-drēə/) Biology an organelle found in large numbers in most cells, in which the biochemical processes of respiration and energy production occur. It has a double membrane, the inner layer being folded inward to form layers (cristae).
– DERIVATIVES **mi·to·chon·dri·al** /-drēəl/ **adj.**
– ORIGIN early 20th cent.: modern Latin, from Greek *mitos* 'thread' + *khondrion* (diminutive of *khondros* 'granule').

mi·to·gen /ˈmītəjən/ ▶ **n.** Physiology a substance that induces or stimulates mitosis.
– DERIVATIVES **mi·to·gen·ic** /ˌmītəˈjenik/ **adj.**
– ORIGIN 1960s: from MITOSIS + -GEN.

mi·to·sis /mīˈtōsəs/ ▶ **n.** (pl. **mitoses** /-sēz/) Biology a type of cell division that results in two daughter cells each having the same number and kind of chromosomes as the parent nucleus, typical of ordinary tissue growth. Compare with MEIOSIS.
– DERIVATIVES **mi·tot·ic** /mīˈtätik/ **adj.**
– ORIGIN late 19th cent.: modern Latin, from Greek *mitos* 'thread.'

mi·tral /ˈmītrəl/ ▶ **adj.** denoting or relating to the mitral valve.
– ORIGIN early 17th cent.: from modern Latin *mitralis*, from Latin *mitra* 'belt or turban.'

mi·tral valve ▶ **n.** Anatomy the valve between the left atrium and the left ventricle of the heart, consisting of two tapered cusps.

mi·tre ▶ **n. & v.** British spelling of MITER.

mitt /mit/ ▶ **n.** (usu. **mitts**) a mitten: *oven mitts.* ■ Baseball a mittenlike glove, worn by the catcher and first baseman. ■ a glove leaving the fingers and thumb-tip exposed. ■ informal a person's hand.
– PHRASES **keep one's mitts off** informal keep one's hands away from; not touch: *keep your mitts off the fan control!*
– ORIGIN mid 18th cent.: abbreviation of MITTEN.

Mit·tel·land Ca·nal /ˈmitlˌländ/ a canal in northwestern Germany, part of an inland waterway network linking the Rhine and Elbe rivers, which was constructed between 1905 and 1930.

mit·ten /ˈmitn/ ▶ **n.** (usu. **mittens**) a glove with two sections, one for the thumb and the other for all four fingers. ■ (**mittens**) informal boxing gloves.
– DERIVATIVES **mit·tened** **adj.**
– ORIGIN Middle English: from Old French *mitaine*, perhaps from *mite*, pet name for a cat (because mittens were often made of fur).

Mit·ter·rand /ˈmitərän(d), mētˈräɴ/, François (Maurice Marie) (1916–96), French statesman; president 1981–95. As president, he initially moved to raise basic wages, increase social benefits, nationalize key industries, and decentralize government. When the Socialist Party lost its majority vote in the 1986 general election and right-wing Jacques Chirac became the prime minister, there was a reversal of some policies.

Mit·ty /ˈmitē/ see WALTER MITTY.

mitz·vah /ˈmitsvə/ ▶ **n.** (pl. **mitzvoth** /ˈmitsˌvōt, -ˌvōs/) Judaism a precept or commandment. ■ a good deed done from religious duty.
– ORIGIN mid 17th cent.: from Hebrew *miṣwāh* 'commandment.'

mix /miks/ ▶ **v.** [with obj.] combine or put together to form one substance or mass: *peppercorns are sometimes **mixed with** other spices for a table condiment | these two chemicals, when **mixed together**, literally explode.* ■ [no obj., often with negative] (of different substances) be able to be combined in this way: *oil and water don't mix.* ■ make or prepare by combining various ingredients: *mixing concrete is hard physical work.* ■ (esp. in sound recording) combine (two or more signals or soundtracks) into one: *up to eight tracks can be mixed simultaneously.* ■ produce (a sound signal or recording) by combining a number of separate signals or recorded soundtracks: *it took two years to mix his album.* ■ juxtapose or put together to form a whole whose constituent parts are still distinct: *he continues to mix an offhand sense of humor with a sharp insight.* ■ [no obj.] (of a person) associate with others socially: *the people he **mixed with** were nothing to do with show business.* ■ (**mix it** or **mix it up**) informal be belligerent verbally or physically, esp. with one's fists.
▶ **n.** [usu. in sing.] two or more different qualities, things, or people placed, combined, or considered together: *the decor is a mix of antique and modern.* ■ a group of people of different types within a particular society or community: *the school has a good social mix.* ■ [often with modifier] a commercially prepared mixture of ingredients for making a particular type of food or a product such as concrete: *cake mixes have made cooking easier.* ■ the proportion of different people or other constituents that make up a mixture: *arriving at the correct mix of full-time to part-time staff | pants made from a cotton and polyester mix.* ■ [often with modifier] a version of a recording in which the component tracks are mixed in a different way from the original: *a dance mix version of "This Charming Man."* ■ an image or sound produced by the combination of two separate images or sounds.
– PHRASES **be** (or **get**) **mixed up in** be (or become) involved in (something regarded as dubious or dishonest): *Steve was mixed up in an insurance swindle.* **be** (or **get**) **mixed up with** be (or become) associated with (someone unsuitable or unreliable). **mix and match** select and combine different but complementary items, such as clothing or pieces of equipment, to form a coordinated set: *mix and match this season's colors for a combination that says winter* | [as adj.] *a mix-and-match menu.* **mix one's drinks** drink different kinds of alcohol in close succession.
– PHRASAL VERBS **mix something up** spoil the order or arrangement of a collection of things: *disconnect all the cables, mix them up, then try to reconnect them.* **mix someone/something up** ■ confuse someone or something with another person or thing: *I'd got her **mixed up with** her sister.*
– DERIVATIVES **mix·a·ble** **adj.**
– ORIGIN late Middle English: back-formation from MIXED (taken as a past participle).

Mix·co /ˈmēsʜkō/ a city in south central Guatemala, west of Guatemala City; pop. 688,100 (est. 2009).

mixed /mikst/ ▶ **adj.** consisting of different qualities or elements: *a varied, mixed diet | beaches with mixed sand and shingle.* ■ (of an assessment of, reaction to, or feeling about something) containing a mixture of both favorable and negative elements: *the movie opened last Friday to mixed reviews | I had **mixed feelings** about seeing Laura again.* ■ composed of different varieties of the same thing: *crab on a bed of mixed greens.* ■ involving or showing a mixture of races or social classes: *people of mixed race.* ■ (esp. of an educational establishment or a sports team or competition) of or for members of both sexes: *the college's mixed hockey team.*
– ORIGIN late Middle English *mixt*: from Old French *mixte*, from Latin *mixtus*, past participle of *miscere* 'to mix.'

mixed bag ▶ **n.** [in sing.] a diverse assortment of things or people: *a mixed bag of applause and catcalls.*

mixed bless·ing ▶ **n.** a situation or thing that has disadvantages as well as advantages: *having children so early in their marriage was a mixed blessing.*

mixed com·pa·ny ▶ **n.** a group of people consisting of members of both sexes: *such questions were not asked in mixed company.*

mixed dou·bles ▶ **plural n.** [treated as sing.] (esp. in tennis and badminton) a game or competition involving teams, each consisting of a man and a woman.

mixed drink ▶ **n.** an alcoholic drink consisting of liquor combined with fruit juice or other ingredients, usually shaken or stirred before serving.

mixed e·con·o·my ▶ **n.** an economic system combining private and public enterprise.

mixed grill ▶ **n.** a dish consisting of various items of grilled food, typically meats, tomatoes, and mushrooms.

mixed mar·riage ▶ **n.** a marriage between people of different races or religions.

mixed me·di·a ▶ **n.** the use of a variety of media in an entertainment or work of art.
▶ **adj.** (**mixed-media**) another term for MULTIMEDIA.

mixed met·a·phor ▶ **n.** a combination of two or more incompatible metaphors, which produces a

m

ridiculous effect (e.g., *this tower of strength will forge ahead*).

mixed num·ber ▶ n. a number consisting of an integer and a proper fraction.

mixed-race ▶ adj. denoting or relating to people whose parents or ancestors are from different ethnic backgrounds: *mixed-race children* | *a mixed-race neighborhood.*

mixed-up ▶ adj. informal (of a person) suffering from psychological or emotional problems: *a lonely, mixed-up teenager.*

mix·er /ˈmiksər/ ▶ n. **1** [often with modifier] a machine or device for mixing things, esp. an electrical appliance for mixing foods: *a food mixer.*
2 [with adj.] a person considered in terms of their ability to mix socially with others: *media people need to be good mixers.*
3 a social gathering where people can make new acquaintances.
4 a soft drink that can be mixed with alcohol.
5 (in sound recording and cinematography) a device for merging input signals to produce a combined output in the form of sound or pictures. ■ [often with modifier] a person who operates such a device: *a sound mixer.*

Mix·mas·ter /ˈmiks,mastər/ ▶ n. trademark a type of electric food processor: figurative *he put together proposals, ideas, and advice in a kind of cerebral Mixmaster.* ■ (also **mixmaster**) informal a sound-recording engineer or disc jockey who is an accomplished mixer of music.

mix·ol·o·gist /mikˈsäləjist/ ▶ n. informal a person who is skilled at mixing cocktails and other drinks.
– DERIVATIVES **mix·ol·o·gy** /-əjē/ n.

Mix·o·lyd·i·an mode /ˌmiksəˈlidēən/ ▶ n. Music the mode represented by the natural diatonic scale G–G (containing a minor 7th).
– ORIGIN late 16th cent.: *Mixolydian* from Greek *mixo-ludios* 'half-Lydian' + -AN.

mixt /mikst/ ▶ v. archaic past and past participle of MIX.

mix·tape /ˈmikstāp/ ▶ n. a compilation of favorite pieces of music, typically by different artists, recorded onto a cassette tape or other medium by an individual.

m

Mix·tec /ˈmēstek/ ▶ n. (pl. **same** or **Mixtecs**) **1** a member of an American Indian people of southern Mexico, noted for their skill in pottery and metallurgy.
2 the Otomanguean language of this people.
▶ adj. of or relating to the Mixtec or their language.
– ORIGIN Spanish, from Nahuatl *mixtecah* 'person from a cloudy place.'

mix·ture /ˈmiksCHər/ ▶ n. a substance made by mixing other substances together: *form the mixture into a manageable dough* | *shandy is **a mixture of** beer and lemonade.* ■ the process of mixing or being mixed. ■ (**a mixture of**) a combination of different qualities, things, or emotions in which the component elements are individually distinct: *she thumped the pillow with a mixture of anger and frustration* | *the old town is a mixture of narrow medieval streets and 18th-century architecture.* ■ a person regarded as a combination of qualities and attributes: *he was a curious mixture, an unpredictable man.* ■ Chemistry the product of the random distribution of one substance through another without any chemical reaction, as distinct from a compound. ■ the charge of gas or vapor mixed with air that is admitted to the cylinder of an internal combustion engine, esp. as regards the ratio of fuel to air: *newer pilots often leave their mixture rich during an entire flight.* ■ (also **mixture stop**) an organ stop in which each key sounds a group of small pipes of different pitches, giving a very bright tone.
– ORIGIN late Middle English: from French *mixture* or Latin *mixtura* (see MIXED).

mix-up (also **mixup**) ▶ n. informal a confusion of one thing with another, or a misunderstanding or mistake that results in confusion: *there's been a mix-up over the tickets.* ■ a combination of different things, esp. one whose effect is inharmonious: *a ghastly mix-up of furniture styles.*

Mi·zo /ˈmēzō/ ▶ n. (pl. **same** or **Mizos**) **1** a member of a people inhabiting Mizoram.
2 the Tibeto-Burman language of this people. Also called LUSHAI.
▶ adj. of or relating to this people or their language.
– ORIGIN the name in Mizo, literally 'highlander,' from *mi-* 'person' + *zo* 'hill.'

Mi·zo·ram /məˈzôrəm/ a state in northeastern India that lies between Bangladesh and Burma (Myanmar); capital, Aizawl. Separated from Assam in 1972, it was administered as a Union Territory in India until 1986, when it became a state.

mi·zu·na /məˈzo͞onə/ (also **mizuna greens**) ▶ n. an oriental rape of a variety with finely cut leaves that are eaten as a salad vegetable. ● *Brassica rapa* var. *nipposinica*, family Brassicaceae.
– ORIGIN 1990s: from Japanese.

miz·zen /ˈmizən/ (also **mizen**) ▶ n. **1** (also **mizzenmast**) the mast aft of a ship's mainmast.
2 (also **mizzensail**) the lowest sail on a mizzenmast.
– ORIGIN late Middle English: from Italian *mezzana* 'mizzensail,' feminine (used as a noun) of *mezzano* 'middle,' from Latin *medianus* (see MEDIAN).

miz·zle /ˈmizəl/ chiefly dialect ▶ n. light rain; drizzle.
▶ v. [no obj.] (**it mizzles, it is mizzling**, etc.) rain lightly: *it was mizzling steadily.*
– DERIVATIVES **miz·zly** /ˈmizlē/ adj.
– ORIGIN late Middle English (as a verb): probably a frequentative from the base of MIST; compare with Low German *miseln* and Dutch dialect *miezelen.*

Mk ▶ abbr. ■ the German mark. ■ the Gospel of Mark (in biblical references). ■ (followed by a numeral) Mark, used to denote a design or model of car, aircraft, or other machine: *a VW Golf Mk III.*

mk. ▶ abbr. ■ (pl. **mks.**) MARK[2] (sense 1). ■ markka.

mks ▶ abbr. meter-kilogram-second.

mksA (also **MKSA** or **mksa**) ▶ abbr. meter-kilogram-second-ampere.

mkt. ▶ abbr. market.

mktg. ▶ abbr. marketing.

ml ▶ abbr. ■ mile(s). ■ milliliter(s).

MLA ▶ abbr. ■ Member of the Legislative Assembly. ■ Modern Language Association (of America).

MLB ▶ abbr. major league baseball.

MLC ▶ abbr. Member of the Legislative Council.

MLD ▶ abbr. ■ minimum lethal dose. ■ moderate learning difficulties: [as adj.] *a school for MLD pupils.*

MLF ▶ abbr. multilateral nuclear force.

MLitt ▶ abbr. Master of Letters: *Susan Williams, MLitt.*
– ORIGIN from Latin *Magister Litterarum.*

Mlle ▶ abbr. (pl. **Mlles**) Mademoiselle.

MLR ▶ abbr. Finance minimum lending rate, influenced by the overnight rate established by the Federal Reserve.

MLS ▶ abbr. ■ Master of Library Science. ■ Multiple Listing Service, an organization that holds computerized listings of US real estate offered for sale. ■ Major League Soccer.

MLW ▶ abbr. (of the tide) mean low water.

MM ▶ abbr. Messieurs.

mm ▶ abbr. millimeter(s).

Mme ▶ abbr. (pl. **Mmes**) Madame.

m.m.f. ▶ abbr. magnetomotive force.

MMPI ▶ abbr. Minnesota Multiphasic Personality Inventory.

MMR ▶ abbr. measles, mumps, and rubella, a vaccination given to small children.

MMS ▶ abbr. Multimedia Messaging Service, a system that enables cellular phones to send and receive pictures and sound clips as well as text messages.

MMus ▶ abbr. Master of Music.

MN ▶ abbr. Minnesota (in official postal use).

Mn ▶ symbol the chemical element manganese.

MNA ▶ abbr. (in Canada) Member of the National Assembly (of Quebec).

mne·mon·ic /nəˈmänik/ ▶ n. a device such as a pattern of letters, ideas, or associations that assists in remembering something.
▶ adj. aiding or designed to aid the memory. ■ of or relating to the power of memory.
– DERIVATIVES **mne·mon·i·cal·ly** /-ik(ə)lē/ adv.
– ORIGIN mid 18th cent. (as an adjective): via medieval Latin from Greek *mnēmonikos*, from *mnēmōn* 'mindful.'

mne·mon·ics /nəˈmäniks/ ▶ plural n. [usu. treated as sing.] the study and development of systems for improving and assisting the memory.

Mne·mos·y·ne /nəˈmäsənē, -ˈmäz-/ Greek Mythology the Greek goddess of memory, and the mother of the Muses by Zeus.
– ORIGIN from Greek *mnēmosunē*, literally 'memory.'

mngr. ▶ abbr. manager.

MO ▶ abbr. ■ Computing (of a disk or disk drive) magneto-optical. ■ Medical Officer. ■ Missouri (in official postal use). ■ modus operandi. ■ money order.

Mo ▶ symbol the chemical element molybdenum.

mo /mō/ ▶ n. [in sing.] informal, chiefly Brit. a short period of time: *hang on a mo!*
– ORIGIN late 19th cent.: abbreviation of MOMENT.

mo. ▶ abbr. month.

-mo ▶ suffix forming nouns denoting a book size by the number of leaves into which a sheet of paper has been folded: *twelvemo.*
– ORIGIN from the final syllable of Latin ordinal numbers such as *duodecimo* (masculine ablative singular).

mo·a /ˈmōə/ ▶ n. a large, extinct, flightless bird resembling the emu, formerly found in New Zealand. ● Family Dinornithidae: several genera and species; *Dinornis maximus* was the tallest known bird, with a height of about 10 feet (3 m), but *Megalapteryx didinus*, which may have survived until the early 19th century, was much smaller.
– ORIGIN mid 19th cent.: from Maori.

Mo·ab /ˈmō,ab/ the ancient kingdom of the Moabites, east of the Dead Sea.

Mo·ab·ite /ˈmōə,bīt/ ▶ n. a member of a Semitic people living in Moab in biblical times, traditionally descended from Lot.
▶ adj. of or relating to Moab or its people.

moan /mōn/ ▶ n. a long, low sound made by a person expressing physical or mental suffering or sexual pleasure: *she gave a low moan of despair.* ■ a sound resembling this, esp. one made by the wind: *the moan of the wind in the chimneys.* ■ informal a complaint that is perceived as trivial and not taken seriously by others: *there were moans about the car's feeble ventilation.*
▶ v. [no obj.] make a long, low sound expressing physical or mental suffering or sexual pleasure: *just then their patient moaned and opened his eyes* | [with direct speech] *"Oh God," I moaned.* ■ (of a thing) make a sound resembling this: *the foghorn moaned at intervals.* ■ [reporting verb] informal complain or grumble, typically about something trivial: [no obj.] *he joked and moaned about members of his family* | [with clause] *my husband moans that I'm not as slim as when we first met.* ■ literary lament.
– DERIVATIVES **moan·er** n., **moan·ful** /-fəl/ adj.
– ORIGIN Middle English (in the sense 'complaint or lamentation'): of unknown origin.

moat /mōt/ ▶ n. a deep, wide ditch surrounding a castle, fort, or town, typically filled with water and intended as a defense against attack.
▶ v. [with obj.] (often as adj. **moated**) surround (a place) with a moat: *a moated castle.*
– ORIGIN late Middle English: from Old French *mote* 'mound.'

mob /mäb/ ▶ n. a large crowd of people, esp. one that is disorderly and intent on causing trouble or violence: *a mob of protesters.* ■ (usu. **the Mob**) the Mafia or a similar criminal organization. ■ (**the mob**) the ordinary people: *the age-old fear that the mob may organize to destroy the last vestiges of civilized life.*
▶ v. (**mobs, mobbing, mobbed**) [with obj.] crowd around (someone) in an unruly and excitable way in order to admire or attack them: *he was mobbed by autograph hunters.* ■ (of a group of birds or mammals) surround and attack (a predator or other source of threat) in order to drive it off. ■ crowd into (a building or place): *an unruly crowd mobbed the White House during an inaugural reception.*
– DERIVATIVES **mob·ber** n.
– ORIGIN late 17th cent.: abbreviation of archaic *mobile*, short for Latin *mobile vulgus* 'excitable crowd.'

mob·cap /ˈmäb,kap/ ▶ n. a large soft hat covering all of the hair and typically having a decorative frill, worn indoors by women in the 18th and early 19th centuries.
– ORIGIN mid 18th cent.: *mob*, variant of obsolete *mab* 'slut.' The word *mob* was first used in the sense 'prostitute' (mid to late 17th cent.), later denoting a negligee (mid 17th cent. to mid 18th cent).

Mo·bile /mōˈbēl, ˈmō,bēl/ an industrial city and port on the coast of southern Alabama; pop. 191,022 (est. 2008). It is situated at the head of Mobile Bay, an inlet of the Gulf of Mexico.

mo·bile ▶ adj. /ˈmōbəl, -,bīl/ **1** able to move or be moved freely or easily: *he has a major weight problem and is not very mobile* | *highly mobile international capital.* ■ (of the face or its features) indicating feelings with fluid and expressive movements: *her mobile features working overtime to register shock and disapproval.* ■ (of a store, library, or other service) accommodated in a vehicle so as to travel around and serve various places. ■ (of a military or police unit) equipped and prepared to move quickly to any place it is needed: *mobile army combat units.*
2 of or relating to cellular phones, handheld computers, and similar technology: *the next generation of mobile networks* | *a mobile device.*
3 able or willing to move easily or freely between occupations, places of residence, or social classes: *an increasingly mobile and polarized society.*

▸ **n.** /ˈmōˌbēl/ a decorative structure that is suspended so as to turn freely in the air.
– ORIGIN late 15th cent.: via French from Latin *mobilis*, from *movere* 'to move.' The noun dates from the 1940s.

> **WORD TRENDS** People used to worry about being *upwardly* or *downwardly mobile*, but in the supposedly classless 21st century, **mobile** primarily refers to cellular phones and other forms of technology that let us communicate and use the Internet on the move. In the Oxford English Corpus, most of the words modified by **mobile** relate to technology, with *phone* followed by *operator, device, service*, and *network*—only the humble *mobile home* reminds us of a simpler low-tech world. Although *cell phone* is used in the US rather than *mobile phone*, **mobile** is still the adjective associated with it.

mo·bile home ▸ **n.** a large house trailer that is parked in one particular place and used as a permanent living accommodation.

mo·bile phone (also **mobile telephone**) ▸ **n.** another term for CELLULAR PHONE.

mo·bile sculp·ture ▸ **n.** a sculpture with moving parts.

mo·bil·i·ty /mōˈbilətē/ ▸ **n.** the ability to move or be moved freely and easily: *this exercise helps retain mobility in the damaged joints.* ■ the ability to move between different levels in society or employment: *industrialization would open up increasing chances of social mobility.*

mo·bi·lize /ˈmōbəˌlīz/ ▸ **v.** [with obj.] **1** (of a country or its government) prepare and organize (troops) for active service: *the government mobilized regular forces, reservists, and militia* | [no obj.] *Russia is in no position to mobilize any time soon.* ■ organize and encourage (people) to act in a concerted way in order to bring about a particular political objective: *he used the press to mobilize support for his party.* ■ bring (resources) into use in order to achieve a particular goal: *at sea we will mobilize any amount of resources to undertake a rescue.*
2 make (something) movable or capable of movement: *doing yoga stretches to mobilize compacted joints.* ■ make (a substance) able to be transported by or as a liquid: *acid rain mobilizes the aluminum in forest soils.*
– DERIVATIVES **mo·bi·liz·a·ble** adj., **mo·bi·li·za·tion** /ˌmōbələˈzāSHən/ n., **mo·bi·liz·er** n.
– ORIGIN mid 19th cent.: from French *mobiliser*, from *mobile* (see MOBILE).

Mö·bi·us strip /ˈmōbēəs/ ▸ **n.** a surface with one continuous side formed by joining the ends of a rectangular strip after twisting one end through 180°.
– ORIGIN early 20th cent.: named after August F. *Möbius* (1790–1868), German mathematician.

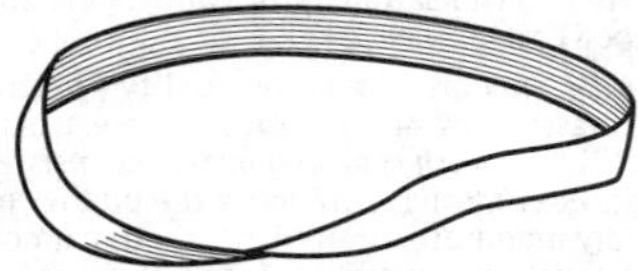
Möbius strip

mo·blog /ˈmōˌbläg/ ▸ **n.** a weblog whose content originates from mobile phones and other portable wireless devices.
– DERIVATIVES **mo·blog·ger** n., **mo·blog·ging** n.
– ORIGIN early 21st cent.: blend of MOBILE and WEBLOG.

mob·oc·ra·cy /mäbˈäkrəsē/ ▸ **n.** (pl. **mobocracies**) rule or domination by the masses.

mob rule ▸ **n.** control of a political situation by those outside the conventional or lawful realm, typically involving violence and intimidation.

mob·ster /ˈmäbstər/ ▸ **n.** informal a member of a group of violent criminals; a gangster.

Mo·bu·tu /mōˈbo͞oto͞o/, Sese Seko (1930–97), Zairean statesman; president 1965–97; born *Joseph-Désiré Mobutu*. Seizing power in a military coup in 1965, he retained control despite opposition until 1997, when he was finally forced to stand down.

Mobutu Se·se Se·ko, Lake Zairean name for Lake Albert (see ALBERT, LAKE).

moc /mäk/ ▸ **n.** informal short for MOCCASIN.

mo·cap /ˈmōˌkăp/ ▸ **n.** motion capture.

moc·ca·sin /ˈmäkəsən/ ▸ **n. 1** a soft leather slipper or shoe, strictly one without a separate heel, having the sole turned up on all sides and sewn to the upper in a simple gathered seam, in a style originating among North American Indians.
2 a venomous American pit viper. ● Genus *Agkistrodon*, family Viperidae: several species, in particular the **water moccasin** (see COTTONMOUTH) and the **highland moccasin** (see COPPERHEAD.).
– ORIGIN early 17th cent.: from Virginia Algonquian *mockasin*. The word is also found in other American Indian languages.

moc·ca·sin flow·er ▸ **n.** another term for PINK LADY'S-SLIPPER (see LADY'S-SLIPPER).

moc·ca·sin tel·e·graph ▸ **n.** Canadian term for BUSH TELEGRAPH.

mo·cha /ˈmōkə/ ▸ **n. 1** a fine-quality coffee. ■ a drink or flavoring made with or in imitation of this, typically with chocolate added. ■ a dark brown color.
2 a soft kind of leather made from sheepskin.
– ORIGIN late 18th cent.: named after *Mocha*, a port on the Red Sea, from where the coffee and leather were first shipped.

mo·chac·ci·no /ˌmōkəˈCHēnō/ ▸ **n.** (pl. **mochaccinos**) a cappuccino containing chocolate flavoring.
– ORIGIN 1990s: blend of *mocha* and *cappucino*.

Mo·che /ˈmōCHā/ ▸ **n.** Archaeology a pre-Inca culture that flourished on the coast of Peru in the 1st to 7th centuries AD.
– ORIGIN from the name of an archaeological site on the northwest coast of Peru.

mo·chi /ˈmōCHē/ ▸ **n.** a short-grained, sweet, glutinous rice with a high starch content, used in Japanese cooking.
– ORIGIN Japanese.

Mo·chi·ca /mōˈCHēkə/ ▸ **n.** (pl. **same**) **1** a member of the Moche people.
2 the language of this people.
▸ **adj.** of or relating to this people or their language.
– ORIGIN Spanish; compare with MOCHE.

mock /mäk/ ▸ **v.** [with obj.] tease or laugh at in a scornful or contemptuous manner: *he mocks them as Washington insiders.* ■ make (something) seem laughably unreal or impossible: *at Christmas, arguments and friction mock our pretense of peace.* ■ mimic (someone or something) scornfully or contemptuously.
▸ **adj.** [attrib.] not authentic or real, but without the intention to deceive: *a mock-Georgian red brick house* | *Jim threw up his hands in mock horror.* ■ (of an examination, battle, etc.) arranged for training or practice, or performed as a demonstration: *Dukakis will have a mock debate with Barnett.*
▸ **n.** dated an object of derision: *he has become the mock of all his contemporaries.*
– DERIVATIVES **mock·a·ble** adj., **mock·er** n.
– ORIGIN late Middle English: from Old French *mocquer* 'deride.'

mock·er·y /ˈmäk(ə)rē/ ▸ **n.** (pl. **mockeries**) derision; ridicule: *stung by her mockery, Frankie hung his head.* ■ [in sing.] an absurd misrepresentation or imitation of something: *after a mockery of a trial in London, he was executed.* ■ archaic ludicrously futile action: *in her bitterness she felt that all rejoicing was mockery.*
– PHRASES **make a mockery of** make (something) seem foolish or absurd: *new technology is making a mockery of our outdated laws.*
– ORIGIN late Middle English: from Old French *moquerie*, from *mocquer* 'to deride.'

mock-he·ro·ic ▸ **adj.** (of a literary work or its style) imitating the style of heroic literature in order to satirize an unheroic subject.
▸ **n.** (often as **mock heroics**) a burlesque imitation of the heroic character or literary style.

mock·ing /ˈmäkiNG/ ▸ **adj.** making fun of someone or something in a cruel way; derisive: *the mocking hostility in his voice made her wince.*
– DERIVATIVES **mock·ing·ly** adv.

mock·ing·bird /ˈmäkiNGˌbərd/ ▸ **n.** a long-tailed thrushlike songbird with grayish plumage, found mainly in tropical America and noted for its mimicry of the calls and songs of other birds.
● Family Mimidae (the **mockingbird family**): three genera and several species, esp. the **northern mockingbird** (*Mimus polyglottos*) of North America. The mockingbird family also includes the catbirds, thrashers, and tremblers.

northern mockingbird

mock moon ▸ **n.** informal term for PARASELENE.

mock or·ange ▸ **n.** a bushy shrub of north temperate regions that is cultivated for its strongly scented white flowers whose perfume resembles orange blossom. ● Genus *Philadelphus*, family Hydrangeaceae (formerly Philadelphaceae): several species and hybrids, in particular *P. coronarius*.

mock sun ▸ **n.** informal term for PARHELION.

mock·tail /ˈmäkˌtāl/ ▸ **n.** a nonalcoholic drink consisting of a mixture of fruit juices or other soft drinks.
– ORIGIN 1930s: blend of MOCK (adjective) and COCKTAIL.

mock tur·tle·neck ▸ **n.** a neck for a knit garment similar to a funnel neck but shorter and typically not as loose.

mock tur·tle soup ▸ **n.** imitation turtle soup made from a calf's head.

mock·u·men·ta·ry (also **mocumentary**) /ˌmäkyəˈment(ə)rē/) ▸ **n.** (pl. **mockumentaries**) a motion picture or television program that takes the form of a serious documentary in order to satirize its subject.
– DERIVATIVES **mock·u·men·tar·i·an** /ˌmäkyəmenˈte(ə)rēən/ n.
– ORIGIN 1960s: blend of *mock* and (*doc*)*umentary*.

mock-up (also **mockup**) ▸ **n.** a model or replica of a machine or structure, used for instructional or experimental purposes. ■ an arrangement of text and pictures to be printed: *a mock-up of the following day's front page.*

mod[1] /mäd/ ▸ **adj.** informal modern.
▸ **n.** Brit. (esp. in the early 1960s) a young person of a subculture characterized by stylish dress, the riding of motor scooters, and a liking for soul music.
– ORIGIN abbreviation of MODERN or MODERNIST.

mod[2] ▸ **prep.** Mathematics another term for MODULO.

mod[3] ▸ informal **n.** a modification: *a couple of minor mods to the wheels will ease the installation of the tires.*
▸ **v.** (**mods, modding, modded**) [with obj.] make modifications to; modify: *both the single-player and multiplayer games can be modded.*
– DERIVATIVES **mod·der** /ˈmädər/ n.

mod. ▸ **abbr.** ■ moderate. ■ Music moderato. ■ modern.

mod·a·cryl·ic /ˌmädəˈkrilik/ ▸ **adj.** of or denoting a synthetic textile fiber made from a polymer containing a high proportion of units derived from acrylonitrile.
▸ **n.** a textile fiber of this kind.
– ORIGIN 1950s: from *modified* (past participle of MODIFY) + ACRYLIC.

mod·al /ˈmōdl/ ▸ **adj. 1** of or relating to mode or form as opposed to substance.
2 Grammar of or denoting the mood of a verb. ■ relating to a modal verb.
3 Statistics of or relating to a mode; occurring most frequently in a sample or population.
4 Music of or denoting music using melodies or harmonies based on modes other than the ordinary major and minor scales.
5 Logic (of a proposition) in which the predicate is affirmed of the subject with some qualification, or which involves the affirmation of possibility, impossibility, necessity, or contingency.
▸ **n.** Grammar a modal word or construction.
– DERIVATIVES **mod·al·ly** /ˈmōdl-ē/ adv.
– ORIGIN mid 16th cent. (sense 5 of the adjective): from medieval Latin *modalis*, from Latin *modus* (see MODE).

mod·al·ism /ˈmodlˌizəm/ ▸ **n. 1** Theology the doctrine that the persons of the Trinity represent only three modes or aspects of the divine revelation, not distinct and coexisting persons in the divine nature.
2 Music the use of modal melodies and harmonies.
– DERIVATIVES **mod·al·ist** n. & adj.

mo·dal·i·ty /mōˈdalitē/ ▸ **n.** (pl. **modalities**) **1** modal quality: *the harmony had a touch of modality.*
2 a particular mode in which something exists or is experienced or expressed. ■ a particular method or procedure: *traditional modalities of representing time and space.* ■ a particular form of sensory perception: *the visual and auditory modalities.* ■ (in medicine, particularly homeopathy) a symptom or pattern that aids in diagnosis: *The modality of "worse with activity" is associated with Rhus Tox.*
– ORIGIN early 17th cent.: from medieval Latin *modalitas*, from *modalis* (see MODAL).

mod·al verb ▸ **n.** Grammar an auxiliary verb that expresses necessity or possibility. English modal verbs include *must, shall, will, should, would, can, could, may*, and *might*. See also AUXILIARY VERB.

mode /mōd/ ▸ **n. 1** a way or manner in which something occurs or is experienced, expressed, or done: *his preferred mode of travel was a kayak* | *differences between language modes, namely speech and writing.* ■ an option allowing a change in the method of operation of a device, esp. a camera: *a camcorder in automatic mode.* ■ Computing a way

PRONUNCIATION KEY ə *ago, up*; ər *over, fur*; a *hat*; ā *ate*; ä *car*; e *let*; ē *see*; i *fit*; ī *by*; NG *sing*; ō *go*; ô *law, for*; oi *toy*; o͝o *good*; o͞o *goo*; ou *out*; TH *thin*; T͟H *then*; ZH *vision*

of operating or using a system: *some computers provide several so-called processor modes.* ■ Physics any of the distinct kinds or patterns of vibration of an oscillating system. ■ Logic the character of a modal proposition (whether necessary, contingent, possible, or impossible). ■ Logic & Grammar another term for **MOOD**[2].
2 a fashion or style in clothes, art, literature, etc.: *in the Seventies, the mode for activewear took hold.*
3 Statistics the value that occurs most frequently in a given set of data.
4 Music a set of musical notes forming a scale and from which melodies and harmonies are constructed.

> The modes of plainsong and later Western music (including the usual major and minor scales) correspond to the diatonic scales played on the white notes of a piano. They are named arbitrarily after ancient Greek modes: Ionian (or major), Dorian, Phrygian, Lydian, Mixolydian, Aeolian, and Locrian.

– ORIGIN late Middle English (in the musical and grammatical senses): from Latin *modus* 'measure,' from an Indo-European root shared by **METE**[1]; compare with **MOOD**[2].

mod·el /'mädl/ ▶ **n. 1** a three-dimensional representation of a person or thing or of a proposed structure, typically on a smaller scale than the original: *a model of St. Paul's Cathedral* | [as modifier] *a model airplane.* ■ (in sculpture) a figure or object made in clay or wax, to be reproduced in another more durable material.
2 a system or thing used as an example to follow or imitate: *the law became a model for dozens of laws banning nondegradable plastic products* | [as modifier] *a model farm.* ■ a simplified description, esp. a mathematical one, of a system or process, to assist calculations and predictions: *a statistical model used for predicting the survival rates of endangered species.* ■ (**model of**) a person or thing regarded as an excellent example of a specified quality: *as she grew older, she became a model of self-control* | [as modifier] *he was a model husband and father.* ■ (**model for**) an actual person or place on which a specified fictional character or location is based: *the author denied that Marilyn was the model for his tragic heroine.*
3 a person, typically a woman, employed to display clothes by wearing them: *a fashion model.* ■ a person employed to pose for an artist, photographer, or sculptor.
4 a particular design or version of a product: *trading your car in for a newer model.*
▶ **v.** (**models, modeling, modeled**; Brit. **models, modelling, modelled**) [with obj.] **1** fashion or shape (a three-dimensional figure or object) in a malleable material such as clay or wax: *use the icing to model a house.* ■ (in drawing or painting) represent so as to appear three-dimensional: *the body of the woman to the right is modeled in softer, riper forms.* ■ (**model something on/after**) use (esp. a system or procedure) as an example to follow or imitate: *the research method will be modeled on previous work.* ■ (**model oneself on**) take (someone admired or respected) as an example to copy: *he models himself on rock legend Elvis Presley.* ■ devise a representation, esp. a mathematical one, of (a phenomenon or system): *a computer program that can model how smoke behaves.*
2 display (clothes) by wearing them. ■ [no obj.] work as a model by displaying clothes or posing for an artist, photographer, or sculptor.
– DERIVATIVES **mod·el·er** /'mädl-ər/ **n.**
– ORIGIN late 16th cent. (denoting a set of plans of a building): from French *modelle*, from Italian *modello*, from an alteration of Latin *modulus* (see **MODULUS**).

mod·el home ▶ **n.** a house in a newly built development that is furnished and decorated to be shown to prospective buyers.

mod·el·ing /'mädl-iNG/ (Brit. **modelling**) ▶ **n. 1** the work of a fashion model.
2 the art or activity of making three-dimensional models. ■ [often with adj.] the devising or use of abstract or mathematical models: *macroeconomic modeling and policy analysis.*

mo·dem /'mōdəm, 'mō,dem/ ▶ **n.** a combined device for modulation and demodulation, for example, between the digital data of a computer and the analog signal of a telephone line.
▶ **v.** [with obj.] send (data) by modem.
– ORIGIN mid 20th cent.: blend of *modulator* and *demodulator*.

Mo·de·na /'môdn,ä, 'môdinə/ a city in northern Italy, northwest of Bologna; pop. 181,807 (2008).

mod·er·ate ▶ **adj.** /'mäd(ə)rət/ average in amount, intensity, quality, or degree: *we walked at a moderate pace.* ■ (of a person, party, or policy); not radical or excessively right- or left-wing: *a moderate reform program.*
▶ **n.** /'mäd(ə)rət/ a person who holds moderate views, esp. in politics.
▶ **v.** /'mädə,rāt/ **1** make or become less extreme, intense, rigorous, or violent: [with obj.] *I shall not moderate my criticism* | (as adj. **moderating**) *his moderating influence in the army was now needed more than ever* | [no obj.] *the weather has moderated considerably.*
2 [with obj.] (in academic and ecclesiastical contexts) preside over (a deliberative body) or at (a debate): *a panel moderated by a Harvard University law professor.* ■ [no obj.] preside; act as a moderator.
3 [with obj.] monitor (an Internet message board or chat room) for inappropriate or offensive content.
4 [with obj.] Physics retard (neutrons) with a moderator.
– DERIVATIVES **mod·er·at·ism** /-,tizəm/ **n.**
– ORIGIN late Middle English: from Latin *moderat-* 'reduced, controlled,' from the verb *moderare*; related to **MODEST**.

mod·er·ate breeze ▶ **n.** a wind of force 4 on the Beaufort scale (13–18 miles per hour, or 11–16 knots).

mod·er·ate gale ▶ **n.** a wind of force 7 on the Beaufort scale (32–38 miles per hour, or 28–33 knots).

mod·er·ate·ly /'mäd(ə)rətlē/ ▶ **adv.** [as submodifier] to a certain extent; quite; fairly: *these events were moderately successful* | *he answered all the questions moderately well.* ■ in a moderate manner: *growth continues moderately.* ■ within reasonable limits: *both hotels are moderately priced.*

mod·er·a·tion /,mädə'rāsHən/ ▶ **n. 1** the avoidance of excess or extremes, esp. in one's behavior or political opinions: *he urged the police to show moderation.* ■ the action of making something less extreme, intense, or violent: *the union's approach was based on increased dialogue and the* **moderation** *of demands.*
2 Physics the retardation of neutrons by a moderator.
– PHRASES **in moderation** within reasonable limits; not to excess: *nuts can be eaten in moderation.*
– ORIGIN late Middle English: via Old French from Latin *moderatio(n-)*, from the verb *moderare* 'to control' (see **MODERATE**).

mod·e·ra·to /,mädə'rätō/ Music ▶ **adv. & adj.** (esp. as a direction after a tempo marking) at a moderate pace: *allegro moderato.*
▶ **n.** (pl. **moderatos**) a passage marked to be performed in such a way.
– ORIGIN Italian, literally 'moderate.'

mod·er·a·tor /'mädə,rātər/ ▶ **n. 1** an arbitrator or mediator: *Egypt managed to assert its role as a regional moderator.* ■ a presiding officer, esp. a chairman of a debate. ■ a Presbyterian minister presiding over an ecclesiastical body.
2 a person who moderates an Internet message board or chat room.
3 Physics a substance used in a nuclear reactor to retard neutrons.
– DERIVATIVES **mod·er·a·tor·ship** /-,sHip/ **n.**

mod·ern /'mädərn/ ▶ **adj.** of or relating to the present or recent times as opposed to the remote past: *the pace of modern life* | *modern U.S. history.* ■ characterized by or using the most up-to-date techniques, ideas, or equipment: *they do not have modern weapons.* ■ [attrib.] denoting the form of a language that is currently used, as opposed to any earlier form: *modern German.* ■ [attrib.] denoting a current or recent style or trend in art, architecture, or other cultural activity marked by a significant departure from traditional styles and values: *Matisse's contribution to modern art.*
▶ **n.** (usu. **moderns**) a person who advocates or practices a departure from traditional styles or values.
– DERIVATIVES **mod·ern·ly adv.**, **mod·ern·ness n.**
– ORIGIN late Middle English: from late Latin *modernus*, from Latin *modo* 'just now.'

mod·ern dance ▶ **n.** a free, expressive style of dancing started in the early 20th century as a reaction to classical ballet. In recent years it has included elements not usually associated with dance, such as speech and film.

mo·derne /mä'dern, mə-/ ▶ **adj.** of or relating to a popularization of the art deco style marked by bright colors and geometric shapes. ■ often derogatory denoting an ultramodern style.
– ORIGIN mid 20th cent.: French, 'modern.'

mod·ern Eng·lish ▶ **n.** the English language as it has been since about 1500.

Mod·ern Greats ▶ **plural n.** (at Oxford University) the school of philosophy, politics, and economics.

mod·ern his·to·ry ▶ **n.** history up to the present day, from some arbitrary point taken to represent the end of the Middle Ages. In some contexts it may be contrasted with "ancient" rather than "medieval" history, and start, e.g., from the fall of the Western Roman Empire.

mod·ern·ism /'mädər,nizəm/ ▶ **n.** modern character or quality of thought, expression, or technique: *when he waxes philosophical, he comes across as a strange mix of nostalgia and modernism.* ■ a style or movement in the arts that aims to break with classical and traditional forms. ■ a movement toward modifying traditional beliefs in accordance with modern ideas, esp. in the Roman Catholic Church in the late 19th and early 20th centuries.

mod·ern·ist /'mädərnist/ ▶ **n.** a believer in or supporter of modernism, esp. in the arts.
▶ **adj.** of or associated with modernism, esp. in the arts.
– DERIVATIVES **mod·ern·is·tic** /,mädər'nistik/ **adj.**

mo·der·ni·ty /mä'dərnitē, mə-, -'der-/ ▶ **n.** the quality or condition of being modern: *an aura of technological modernity.* ■ a modern way of thinking, working, etc.; contemporariness: *Hobbes was the genius of modernity.*

mod·ern·ize /'mädər,nīz/ ▶ **v.** [with obj.] adapt (something) to modern needs or habits, typically by installing modern equipment or adopting modern ideas or methods: *a five-year plan to modernize Algerian agriculture.*
– DERIVATIVES **mod·ern·i·za·tion** /,mädərnə'zāsHən/ **n.**, **mod·ern·iz·er n.**

mod·ern jazz ▶ **n.** jazz as developed in the 1940s and 1950s, esp. bebop and the related music that followed it.

mod·ern lan·guages ▶ **plural n.** European languages (esp. French and German) as a subject of study, as contrasted with classical Latin and Greek.

mod·ern Lat·in ▶ **n.** Latin as developed since 1500, used esp. in scientific terminology.

mod·ern pen·tath·lon ▶ **n.** see **PENTATHLON**.

mod·est /'mädəst/ ▶ **adj. 1** unassuming or moderate in the estimation of one's abilities or achievements: *he was a very modest man, refusing to take any credit for the enterprise.*
2 (of an amount, rate, or level of something) relatively moderate, limited, or small: *drink modest amounts of alcohol* | *employment growth was relatively modest.* ■ (of a place in which one lives, eats, or stays) not excessively large, elaborate, or expensive: *we had bought a modest house.*
3 (of a woman) dressing or behaving so as to avoid impropriety or indecency, esp. to avoid attracting sexual attention. ■ (of clothing) not revealing or emphasizing the figure: *modest dress means that hemlines must be below the knee.*
– DERIVATIVES **mod·est·ly adv.**
– ORIGIN mid 16th cent.: from French *modeste*, from Latin *modestus* 'keeping due measure,' related to *modus* 'measure.'

Mo·des·to /mə'destō/ a city in north central California, in the San Joaquin Valley; pop. 202,967 (est. 2008).

mod·es·ty /'mädəstē/ ▶ **n.** the quality or state of being unassuming or moderate in the estimation of one's abilities: *with typical modesty he insisted on sharing the credit with others.* ■ the quality of being relatively moderate, limited, or small in amount, rate, or level: *the modesty of his political aspirations.* ■ behavior, manner, or appearance intended to avoid impropriety or indecency: *modesty forbade her to undress in front of so many people.*

mod·i·cum /'mädikəm, 'mōd-/ ▶ **n.** [in sing.] a small quantity of a particular thing, esp. something considered desirable or valuable: *his statement had more than a modicum of truth.*
– ORIGIN late 15th cent.: from Latin, neuter of *modicus* 'moderate,' from *modus* 'measure.'

mod·i·fi·ca·tion /,mädəfə'kāsHən/ ▶ **n.** the action of modifying something: *the parts supplied should fit with little or no modification.* ■ a change made: *there will be a number of modifications to the engines.*
– ORIGIN late 15th cent. (in Scots law, denoting the assessment of a payment): from French, or from Latin *modificatio(n-)*, from *modificare* (see **MODIFY**).

mod·i·fi·er /'mädə,fīər/ ▶ **n.** a person or thing that makes partial or minor changes to something. ■ Grammar a word, esp. an adjective or noun used attributively, that restricts or adds to the sense of a head noun (e.g., *good* and *family* in *a good family house*). ■ Genetics a gene that modifies the phenotypic expression of a gene at another locus.

mod·i·fy /'mädə,fī/ ▶ **v.** (**modifies, modifying, modified**) [with obj.] make partial or minor changes to (something), typically so as to improve it or to make it less extreme: *she may be prepared to modify her views* | (as adj. **modified**) *a modified version of the aircraft.* ■ Biology transform (a structure) from its original anatomical form during development or evolution. ■ Grammar (esp. of an adjective) restrict or add to the sense of (a noun): *the target noun is*

modified by a "direction" word. ■ Phonetics pronounce (a speech sound) in a way that is different from the norm for that sound.
– DERIVATIVES **mod·i·fi·a·ble** adj., **mod·i·fi·ca·to·ry** /'mädəfəkəˌtôrē, ˌmädə'fikəˌtôrē/ adj.
– ORIGIN late Middle English: from Old French *modifier*, from Latin *modificare*, from *modus* (see **MODE**).

Mo·di·glia·ni /ˌmōdēl'yänē/, Amedeo (1884–1920), Italian painter and sculptor, resident in France from 1906. His portraits and nudes are noted for their elongated forms, linear qualities, and earthy colors.

mo·dil·lion /mō'dilyən/ ▶ n. Architecture a projecting bracket under the corona of a cornice in the Corinthian and other orders.
– ORIGIN mid 16th cent.: from French *modillon*, from Italian *modiglione*, based on Latin *mutulus* 'mutule.'

mo·di·o·lus /mə'dīələs/ ▶ n. (pl. **modioli** /-ˌlī, -ˌlē/) Anatomy the conical central axis of the cochlea of the ear.
– ORIGIN early 19th cent.: from Latin, literally 'nave of a wheel.'

mod·ish /'mōdisH/ ▶ adj. often derogatory conforming to or following what is currently popular and fashionable: *it seems sad that such a scholar should feel compelled to use this modish jargon.*
– DERIVATIVES **mod·ish·ly** adv., **mod·ish·ness** n.

mo·diste /mō'dēst/ ▶ n. dated a fashionable milliner or dressmaker.
– ORIGIN mid 19th cent.: French, from *mode* 'fashion.'

mod·u·lar /'mäjələr/ ▶ adj. employing or involving a module or modules as the basis of design or construction: *modular housing units.* ■ Mathematics of or relating to a modulus.
– DERIVATIVES **mod·u·lar·i·ty** /ˌmäjə'le(ə)ritē/ n.
– ORIGIN late 18th cent.: from modern Latin *modularis*, from Latin *modulus* (see **MODULUS**).

mod·u·late /'mäjəˌlāt/ ▶ v. [with obj.] exert a modifying or controlling influence on: *the state attempts to modulate private business's cash flow.* ■ vary the strength, tone, or pitch of (one's voice): *we all modulate our voice by hearing it.* ■ alter the amplitude or frequency of (an electromagnetic wave or other oscillation) in accordance with the variations of a second signal, typically one of a lower frequency: *radio waves are modulated to carry the analog information of the voice.* ■ [no obj.] Music change from one key to another: *the first half of the melody, modulating from E minor to G.* ■ [no obj.] (**modulate into**) change from one form or condition into (another): *ideals and opinions are not modulated into authoritative journalese.*
– DERIVATIVES **mod·u·la·tion** /ˌmäjə'lāsHən/ n., **mod·u·la·tor** /-ˌlātər/ n.
– ORIGIN mid 16th cent. (in the sense 'intone [a song]'): from Latin *modulat-* 'measured, made melody,' from the verb *modulari*, from *modulus* 'measure' (see **MODULUS**).

mod·ule /'mäjo͞ol/ ▶ n. each of a set of standardized parts or independent units that can be used to construct a more complex structure, such as an item of furniture or a building. ■ [usu. with adj.] an independent self-contained unit of a spacecraft. ■ Computing any of a number of distinct but interrelated units from which a program may be built up or into which a complex activity may be analyzed.
– ORIGIN late 16th cent. (in the senses 'allotted scale' and 'plan, model'): from French, or from Latin *modulus* (see **MODULUS**). Current senses date from the 1950s.

mod·u·lo /'mäjəˌlō/ ▶ prep. Mathematics (in number theory) with respect to or using a modulus of a specified number. Two numbers are congruent modulo a given number if they give the same remainder when divided by that number: *19 and 64 are congruent modulo 5.* ■ [as adj.] using moduli: *modulo operations.*
– ORIGIN late 19th cent.: from Latin, ablative of *modulus* (see **MODULUS**).

mod·u·lus /'mäjələs/ Mathematics ▶ n. (pl. **moduli** /-ˌlī, -ˌlē/) **1** another term for **ABSOLUTE VALUE**. ■ the positive square root of the sum of the squares of the real and imaginary parts of a complex number.
2 a constant factor or ratio. ■ a constant indicating the relation between a physical effect and the force producing it.
3 a number used as a divisor for considering numbers in sets, numbers being considered congruent when giving the same remainder when divided by a particular modulus.
– ORIGIN mid 16th cent. (denoting an architectural unit of length): from Latin, literally 'measure,' diminutive of *modus*.

mo·dus op·e·ran·di /'mōdəs ˌäpə'randē, -ˌdī/ ▶ n. (pl. **modi operandi** /'mōdē, 'mōdī/) [usu. in sing.] a particular way or method of doing something, esp. one that is characteristic or well-established: *the volunteers were instructed to buy specific systems using our usual modus operandi—anonymously and with cash.* ■ the way something operates or works.
– ORIGIN Latin, literally 'way of operating.'

mo·dus po·nens /'mōdəs 'pōˌnenz/ ▶ n. the rule of logic stating that if a conditional statement ("if *p* then *q*") is accepted, and the antecedent (*p*) holds, then the consequent (*q*) may be inferred. ■ an argument using this rule.
– ORIGIN Latin, literally 'mood that affirms.'

mo·dus tol·lens /'mōdəs 'tälˌenz/ ▶ n. the rule of logic stating that if a conditional statement ("if *p* then *q*") is accepted, and the consequent does not hold (*not-q*), then the negation of the antecedent (*not-p*) can be inferred. ■ an argument using this rule.
– ORIGIN Latin, literally 'mood that denies.'

mo·dus vi·ven·di /'mōdəs və'vendē, -ˌdī/ ▶ n. (pl. **modi vivendi** /'mōdē, 'mōdī/) [usu. in sing.] an arrangement or agreement allowing conflicting parties to coexist peacefully, either indefinitely or until a final settlement is reached. ■ a way of living.
– ORIGIN Latin, literally 'way of living.'

moe·ri·the·ri·um /ˌmirə'THi(ə)rēəm/ ▶ n. (pl. **moeritheria** /-rēə/) a medium-sized mammal of the late Eocene and Oligocene epochs with a long snout and short legs, related to modern elephants. ● *Moeritherium trigodon.*
– ORIGIN modern Latin, from the name of Lake *Moeris* in Egypt, where the first fossils were found + Greek *thērion* 'wild beast.'

mo·fette /mō'fet/ ▶ n. archaic term for **FUMAROLE**.
– ORIGIN early 19th cent.: from French, from Neapolitan Italian *mofetta.*

mo·fo /'mōˌfō/ ▶ n. (pl. **mofos**) vulgar slang short for **MOTHERFUCKER**.

Mo·ga·di·shu /ˌmôgə'disHo͞o, ˌmägə-, -'dēsHo͞o/ the capital of Somalia, a port on the Indian Ocean; pop. 1,100,000 (est. 2007). Italian name **Mogadiscio**. Also called **MUQDISHO**.

Mo·gi·lyov /ˌməgil'yôf/ (also **Mogilev**) Russian name for **MAHILYOW**.

Mo·gul /'mōgəl/ (also **Moghul** or **Mughal**) ▶ n. a member of the Muslim dynasty of Mongol origin founded by the successors of Tamerlane, which ruled much of India from the 16th to the 19th century: [as modifier] *Mogul architecture.* ■ (often **the Great Mogul**) historical the Mogul emperor of Delhi.
– ORIGIN from Persian *muġul* 'Mongol.'

mo·gul[1] /'mōgəl/ ▶ n. **1** informal an important or powerful person, esp. in the motion picture or media industry.
2 (**Mogul**) a steam locomotive with three pairs of driving wheels and one pair of smaller wheels in the front.
– ORIGIN late 17th cent.: figurative use of **MOGUL**.

mo·gul[2] ▶ n. a bump on a ski slope formed by the repeated turns of skiers over the same path: [as modifier] *a mogul field.*
– ORIGIN 1960s: probably from southern German dialect *Mugel, Mugl.*

MOH ▶ abbr. ■ Medical Officer of Health (chief health executive of a local authority). ■ Ministry of Health.

mo·hair /'mōˌhe(ə)r/ ▶ n. the long, silky hair of the angora goat. ■ a yarn or fabric made from this, typically mixed with wool: [as modifier] *a mohair sweater.*
– ORIGIN late 16th cent.: from Arabic *mukayyar* 'cloth made of goat's hair' (literally 'choice, select'). The change in ending was due to association with **HAIR**.

Mo·ham·med ▶ n. variant spelling of **MUHAMMAD**[1].

Mo·ham·me·dan /mo͝o'hamid(ə)n, mo-/ ▶ n. variant spelling of **MUHAMMADAN**.

Mo·ham·me·rah /mə'hämərə/ former name (until 1924) for **KHORRAMSHAHR**.

Mo·ha·ve Des·ert variant spelling of **MOJAVE DESERT**.

Mo·hawk /'mōˌhôk/ ▶ n. (pl. **same** or **Mohawks**) **1** a member of an American Indian people, one of the Five Nations, originally inhabiting parts of eastern New York.
2 the Iroquoian language of this people.
3 a hairstyle with the head shaved except for a strip of hair from the middle of the forehead to the back of the neck, typically stiffened to stand erect or in spikes. [erroneously associated with the Mohawk people (see **HURON**).]
4 Figure Skating a step from either edge of the skate to the same edge on the other foot in the opposite direction.
▶ adj. of or relating to the Mohawks or their language.
– ORIGIN from Narragansett *mohowawog*, literally 'man-eaters.'

Mo·hawk Riv·er a river that flows across central New York for 140 miles (230 km) to join the Hudson River above Albany. The Mohawk Valley is the site of much of the Erie Canal.

Mo·he·gan /mō'hēgən/ (also **Mohican** /-'hēkən/) ▶ n. (pl. **same** or **Mohegans**) **1** a member of an American Indian people formerly inhabiting eastern Connecticut. Compare with **MAHICAN**.
2 the Algonquian language of this people, closely related to Pequot.
▶ adj. of or relating to the Mohegans or their language.
– ORIGIN from Mohegan, literally 'people of the tidal waters.'

mo·hel /moil, 'mō(h)el/ ▶ n. a person who performs the Jewish rite of circumcision.
– ORIGIN mid 17th cent.: from Hebrew *mōhēl.*

Mo·hen·jo-Da·ro /mō'henjō 'därō/ an ancient city of the civilization of the Indus valley (c.2600–1700 BC), now a major archaeological site in Pakistan, southwest of Sukkur.

Mo·hi·can /mō'hēkən/ ▶ adj. & n. old-fashioned variant spelling of **MAHICAN** or **MOHEGAN**.

Mo·ho /'mōˌhō/ ▶ n. Geology short for **MOHOROVIČIC DISCONTINUITY**.

Mo·holy-Nagy /məˌhōlē 'näj, ˌmôholi 'nädyə/, László (1895–1946), US painter, sculptor, and photographer; born in Hungary. He pioneered the experimental use of plastic materials, light, photography, and film.

Mo·ho·ro·vi·čić dis·con·ti·nu·i·ty /ˌmōhə'rōviˌCHiCH/ ▶ n. Geology the boundary surface between the earth's crust and the mantle, lying at a depth of about 6–7 miles (10–12 km) under the ocean bed and about 24–30 miles (40–50 km) under the continents.
– ORIGIN 1930s: named after Andrija *Mohorovičić* (1857–1936), Yugoslav seismologist.

Mohs' scale /mōz, mōs, 'mōsəz/ ▶ n. a scale of hardness used in classifying minerals. It runs from 1 to 10 using a series of reference minerals, and a position on the scale depends on the ability to scratch minerals rated lower.
– ORIGIN late 19th cent.: named after Friedrich *Mohs* (1773–1839), German mineralogist.

moi /mwä/ ▶ exclam. (usu. **moi?**) humorous me? (used esp. when accused of something that one knows one is guilty of): *sarcastic, moi?*
– ORIGIN French, 'me.'

moi·dore /'moiˌdôr/ ▶ n. a Portuguese gold coin, current in England in the early 18th century and then worth about 27 shillings.
– ORIGIN from Portuguese *moeda d'ouro* 'money of gold.'

moi·e·ty /'moiətē/ ▶ n. (pl. **moieties**) formal or technical each of two parts into which a thing is or can be divided. ■ Anthropology each of two social or ritual groups into which a people is divided, esp. among Australian Aborigines and some American Indians. ■ a part or portion, esp. a lesser share. ■ Chemistry a distinct part of a large molecule: *the enzyme removes the sulfate moiety.*
– ORIGIN late Middle English: from Old French *moite*, from Latin *medietas* 'middle,' from *medius* 'mid, middle.'

moil /moil/ ▶ v. [no obj.] work hard: *men who moiled for gold.* ■ [with adverbial] move around in confusion or agitation: *a crowd of men and women moiled in the smoky haze.*
▶ n. hard work; drudgery. ■ turmoil; confusion: *the moil of his intimate thoughts.*
– ORIGIN late Middle English (in the sense 'moisten or bedaub'): from Old French *moillier* 'paddle in mud, moisten,' based on Latin *mollis* 'soft.' The sense 'work' dates from the mid 16th cent., often in the phrase *toil and moil.*

Moi·rai /'moiˌrī/ Greek Mythology the Fates.

moi·re /mô'rā, mwä-, mwär/ (also **moiré** /mwä'rā, mô-/) ▶ n. silk fabric that has been subjected to heat and pressure rollers after weaving to give it a rippled appearance.
▶ adj. (of silk) having a rippled, lustrous finish. ■ denoting or showing a pattern of irregular wavy lines like that of such silk, produced by the superposition at a slight angle of two sets of closely spaced lines.
– ORIGIN mid 17th cent.: French *moire* 'mohair' (the original fabric); the variant *moiré* 'given a watered appearance' (past participle of *moirer*, from *moire*).

Mois·san /mwä'sän/, Ferdinand Frédéric Henri (1852–1907), French chemist. In 1886 he succeeded

m

in isolating the element fluorine. In 1892, he invented the electric-arc furnace that bears his name. Nobel Prize for Chemistry (1906).

moist /moist/ ▶ **adj.** slightly wet; damp or humid: *the air was moist and heavy.* ■ (of the eyes) wet with tears: *her brother's eyes became moist.* ■ (of a climate) rainy. ■ Medicine marked by a fluid discharge.
– DERIVATIVES **moist·ly adv., moist·ness n.**
– ORIGIN late Middle English: from Old French *moiste*, based on Latin *mucidus* 'moldy' (influenced by *musteus* 'fresh,' from *mustum*: see MUST[2]).

mois·ten /ˈmoisən/ ▶ **v.** [with obj.] wet slightly: *she moistened her lips with the tip of her tongue.* ■ [no obj.] (of the eyes) fill with tears: *her eyes moistened.*

mois·ture /ˈmoisCHər/ ▶ **n.** water or other liquid diffused in a small quantity as vapor, within a solid, or condensed on a surface.
– DERIVATIVES **mois·ture·less adj.**
– ORIGIN late Middle English (denoting moistness): from Old French *moistour*, from *moiste* (see MOIST).

mois·tur·ize /ˈmoisCHəˌrīz/ ▶ **v.** [with obj.] make (something, esp. the skin) less dry.

mois·tur·iz·er /ˈmoisCHəˌrīzər/ ▶ **n.** a lotion or cream used to prevent dryness in the skin.

mo·jar·ra /mōˈhärə/ ▶ **n.** a small, typically silvery fish with a very protrusible mouth. It is particularly abundant in shallow coastal and brackish waters of tropical America. ● Family Gerreidae: several genera and numerous species.
– ORIGIN mid 19th cent.: from American Spanish.

Mo·ja·ve Des·ert /mōˈhävē/ (also **Mohave**) a desert in southern California, southeast of the Sierra Nevada and north and east of Los Angeles.

mo·ji·to /mōˈhētō/ ▶ **n.** (pl. **mojitos**) a cocktail consisting of white rum, lime or lemon juice, sugar, mint, ice, and sparkling water or club soda.
– ORIGIN 1930s: Cuban Spanish, from MOJO[2] + diminutive suffix *-ito*.

mo·jo[1] /ˈmōˌjō/ ▶ **n.** (pl. **mojos**) a magic charm, talisman, or spell: *someone must have their mojo working over at the record company.* ■ magic power.
– ORIGIN early 20th cent.: probably of African origin; compare with Gullah *moco* 'witchcraft.'

mo·jo[2] /ˈmōˌjō, -ˌhō/ ▶ **n.** a Cuban sauce or marinade containing garlic, olive oil, and sour oranges.
– ORIGIN probably from Spanish *mojo* 'wet' from *mojar* 'make wet.'

moke /mōk/ ▶ **n.** Brit. informal a donkey. ■ Austral./NZ a horse, typically one of inferior quality.
– ORIGIN mid 19th cent.: of unknown origin.

mo·ksha /ˈmōkSHə/ ▶ **n.** (in Hinduism and Jainism) release from the cycle of rebirth impelled by the law of karma. ■ the transcendent state attained by this liberation.
– ORIGIN from Sanskrit *mokṣa*.

MOL ▶ **abbr.** Manned Orbital Laboratory.

mol /mōl/ ▶ **abbr.** Chemistry see MOLE[4].

mo·la /ˈmōlə/ ▶ **n.** (pl. **same** or **molas**) another term for SUNFISH (sense 1).
– ORIGIN late 16th cent.: from Latin, literally 'millstone,' with reference to the shape.

mo·lal /ˈmōləl/ ▶ **adj.** Chemistry (of a solution) containing one mole of solute per kilogram of solvent.
– DERIVATIVES **mo·lal·i·ty** /mōˈlalitē/ **n.**

mo·lar[1] /ˈmōlər/ ▶ **n.** a grinding tooth at the back of a mammal's mouth.
– ORIGIN late Middle English: from Latin *molaris*, from *mola* 'millstone.'

mo·lar[2] ▶ **adj.** of or relating to mass; acting on or by means of large masses or units.
– ORIGIN mid 19th cent.: from Latin *moles* 'mass' + -AR[1].

mo·lar[3] ▶ **adj.** Chemistry of or relating to one mole of a substance. ■ (of a solution) containing one mole of solute per liter of solution.
– DERIVATIVES **mo·lar·i·ty** /mōˈle(ə)ritē/ **n.**

mo·las·ses /məˈlasəz/ ▶ **n.** thick, dark brown juice obtained from raw sugar during the refining process. ■ a paler, sweeter version of this used as a table syrup and in baking.
– ORIGIN mid 16th cent.: from Portuguese *melaço*, from late Latin *mellacium* 'must,' based on *mel* 'honey.'

mold[1] /mōld/ (Brit. **mould**) ▶ **n. 1** a hollow container used to give shape to molten or hot liquid material (such as wax or metal) when it cools and hardens. ■ something made in this way, esp. a gelatin dessert or a mousse: *lobster mold with a sauce of carrots and port.*
2 [in sing.] a distinctive and typical style, form, or character: *he planned to conquer the world as a roving reporter* **in the mold of** *his hero | the latest policy document is still stuck in the old mold.* ■ archaic the form or shape of something, esp. the features or physique of a person or the build of an animal.
3 a frame or template for producing moldings.
▶ **v.** [with obj.] form (an object with a particular shape) out of easily manipulated material: *a Connecticut inventor molded a catamaran out of polystyrene foam.* ■ give a shape to (a malleable substance): *take the marzipan and* **mold** *it* **into** *a cone shape.* ■ influence the formation or development of: *the professionals who were helping to mold US policy.* ■ (often as adj. **molded**) shape (a column, ceiling, or other part of a building) to a particular design, esp. a decorative molding: *a corridor with a molded cornice.*
– PHRASES **break the mold** put an end to a restrictive pattern of events or behavior by doing things in a markedly different way: *his work did much to break the mold of the old urban sociology.*
– DERIVATIVES **mold·a·ble adj.**
– ORIGIN Middle English: apparently from Old French *modle*, from Latin *modulus* (see MODULUS).

mold[2] (Brit. **mould**) ▶ **n.** a furry growth of minute fungal hyphae occurring typically in moist warm conditions, esp. on food or other organic matter. ● The fungi belong to the subdivision Deuteromycotina (or Ascomycotina).
– ORIGIN late Middle English: probably from obsolete *mould*, past participle of *moul* 'grow moldy,' of Scandinavian origin; compare with Old Norse *mygla* 'grow moldy.'

mold[3] (Brit. **mould**) ▶ **n.** soft loose earth. See also LEAF MOLD. ■ the upper soil of cultivated land, esp. when rich in organic matter.
– ORIGIN Old English *molde*, from a Germanic base meaning 'pulverize or grind'; related to MEAL[2].

Mol·dau /ˈmôlˌdou/ German name for VLTAVA.

Mol·da·vi·a /mälˈdāvēə, môl-, -vyə/ **1** a former principality of southeastern Europe. Formerly a part of the Roman province of Dacia, it came under Turkish rule in the 16th century. In 1861, Moldavia united with Wallachia to form Romania.
2 another name for MOLDOVA.

Mol·da·vi·an /mälˈdāvēən, mô-/ ▶ **n. 1** a native or inhabitant of Moldavia.
2 the Romanian language as spoken and written (in the Cyrillic alphabet) in Moldavia.
▶ **adj.** of or relating to Moldavia, its inhabitants, or their language.

mold·board /ˈmōldˌbôrd/ ▶ **n.** a curved metal blade in a plow that turns the earth over: [as modifier] *moldboard plows.* ■ a similar device on the front of a snowplow or bulldozer, used for pushing snow or loose earth.

mold·er[1] /ˈmōldər/ (Brit. **moulder**) ▶ **v.** [no obj.] (often as adj. **moldering**) slowly decay or disintegrate, esp. because of neglect: *there was a mushroomy smell of disuse and moldering books* | figurative *I couldn't permit someone of your abilities to molder away in a backwater.*
– ORIGIN mid 16th cent.: perhaps from MOLD[3], but compare with Norwegian dialect *muldra* 'crumble.'

mold·er[2] /ˈmōldər/ (Brit. **moulder**) ▶ **n.** a person or thing that molds something: *a molder of public opinion.*

mold·ing /ˈmōldiNG/ (Brit. **moulding**) ▶ **n.** an ornamentally shaped outline as an architectural feature, esp. in a cornice. ■ material such as wood, plastic, or stone shaped for use as a decorative or architectural feature.

Mol·do·va /məlˈdōvə/ a landlocked country in southeastern Europe, between Romania and Ukraine; pop. 4,320,700 (est. 2009); capital, Chişinău; languages, Moldavian (official) and Russian;. Also called MOLDAVIA.

> A constituent republic of the former Soviet Union, Moldova was formed from territory ceded by Romania in 1940. It became independent as a member of the Commonwealth of Independent States in 1991.

– DERIVATIVES **Mol·do·van adj. & n.**

mold·y /ˈmōldē/ (Brit. **mouldy**) ▶ **adj.** (**moldier, moldiest**) covered with a fungal growth that causes decay, due to age or damp conditions: *moldy bread.* ■ tediously old-fashioned: *moldy conventions.* ■ informal, chiefly Brit. dull or depressing: *evenings filled with moldy old shows.*
– DERIVATIVES **mold·i·ness n.**

mole[1] /mōl/ ▶ **n. 1** a small burrowing insectivorous mammal with dark velvety fur, a long muzzle, and very small eyes. ● Family Talpidae: several genera and species, including the **eastern mole** (*Scalopus aquaticus*) of North America.
2 a spy who achieves over a long period an important position within the security defenses of a country. ■ someone within an organization who anonymously betrays confidential information.
– ORIGIN late Middle English: from the Germanic base of Middle Dutch and Middle Low German *mol*.

eastern mole

mole[2] /mōl/ ▶ **n.** a small, often slightly raised blemish on the skin made dark by a high concentration of melanin.
– ORIGIN Old English *māl* 'discolored spot,' of Germanic origin.

mole[3] /mōl/ ▶ **n.** a large solid structure on a shore serving as a pier, breakwater, or causeway. ■ a harbor formed or protected by such a structure.
– ORIGIN mid 16th cent.: from French *môle*, from Latin *moles* 'mass.'

mole[4] /mōl/ (abbrev. **mol**) ▶ **n.** Chemistry the SI unit of amount of substance, equal to the quantity containing as many elementary units as there are atoms in 0.012 kg of carbon-12.
– ORIGIN early 20th cent.: from German *Mol*, from *Molekul*, from Latin (see MOLECULE).

mole[5] /mōl/ ▶ **n.** Medicine an abnormal mass of tissue in the uterus. See also HYDATIDIFORM MOLE.
– ORIGIN late Middle English: from French *môle*, from Latin *mola* in the sense 'false conception.'

mo·le[6] /ˈmōlā/ ▶ **n.** a highly spiced Mexican sauce made chiefly from chili peppers and chocolate, served with meat.
– ORIGIN Mexican Spanish, from Nahuatl *molli* 'sauce, stew.'

mole crick·et ▶ **n.** a large burrowing nocturnal cricket with broad forelegs, the female of which lays her eggs in an underground nest and guards the young. ● Family Gryllotalpidae, subfamily Gryllotalpinae: several genera.

mo·lec·u·lar /məˈlekyələr/ ▶ **adj.** of, relating to, or consisting of molecules: *interactions between polymer and solvent at the molecular level | ozone is produced by dissociation of molecular oxygen.*
– DERIVATIVES **mo·lec·u·lar·i·ty** /məˌlekyəˈle(ə)ritē/ **n., mo·lec·u·lar·ly adv.**

mo·lec·u·lar bi·ol·o·gy ▶ **n.** the branch of biology that deals with the structure and function of the macromolecules (e.g., proteins and nucleic acids) essential to life.

mo·lec·u·lar clock ▶ **n.** Genetics the average rate at which a species' genome accumulates mutations, used to measure their evolutionary divergence and in other calculations.

mo·lec·u·lar e·lec·tron·ics ▶ **plural n.** [treated as singular] a branch of electronics in which individual molecules perform the same function as microelectronic devices such as diodes.
– DERIVATIVES **mo·lec·u·lar e·lec·tron·ic adj.** *molecular electronic materials and inorganic particles.*

mo·lec·u·lar for·mu·la ▶ **n.** Chemistry a formula giving the number of atoms of each of the elements present in one molecule of a specific compound. Compare with EMPIRICAL FORMULA, STRUCTURAL FORMULA.

mo·lec·u·lar sieve ▶ **n.** a crystalline substance (esp. a zeolite) with pores of molecular dimensions that permit the passage of molecules below a certain size.

mo·lec·u·lar weight ▶ **n.** Chemistry the ratio of the average mass of one molecule of an element or compound to one twelfth of the mass of an atom of carbon-12.

mol·e·cule /ˈmäləˌkyo͞ol/ ▶ **n.** Chemistry a group of atoms bonded together, representing the smallest fundamental unit of a chemical compound that can take part in a chemical reaction.
– ORIGIN late 18th cent.: from French *molécule*, from modern Latin *molecula*, diminutive of Latin *moles* 'mass.'

mole·hill /ˈmōlˌhil/ ▶ **n.** a small mound of earth thrown up by a mole burrowing near the surface.
– PHRASES **make a mountain out of a molehill** exaggerate the importance of something trivial.

mole rat ▶ **n.** a herbivorous, short-legged, ratlike rodent that typically lives permanently underground, with long incisors that protrude from the mouth and are used in digging. ● Family Bathyergidae (African mole rats): several genera;

also two subfamilies and three genera in the family Muridae (Eurasian blind mole rats and Asiatic mole rats).

mole sal·a·man·der ▶ **n.** a stocky, broad-headed North American salamander that spends much of its life underground. ● Family Ambystomatidae: several genera, in particular *Ambystoma*, and numerous species, including *A. talpoideum*.

mole·skin /ˈmōlˌskin/ ▶ **n. 1** the skin of a mole used as fur.
2 a thick, strong cotton fabric with a shaved pile surface: [as modifier] *a moleskin coat.* ■ (**moleskins**) clothes, esp. trousers, made of such a fabric. ■ a soft fabric with adhesive backing used as a foot bandage.

mo·lest /məˈlest/ ▶ **v.** [with obj.] pester or harass (someone), typically in an aggressive or persistent manner: *the crowd was shouting abuse and molesting the two police officers.* ■ assault or abuse (a person, esp. a woman or child) sexually.
– DERIVATIVES **mo·les·ta·tion** /ˌmōˌleˌ-, ˌmōləˈstāsHən/ **n.**, **mo·lest·er n.**
– ORIGIN late Middle English (in the sense 'cause trouble to, vex'): from Old French *molester* or Latin *molestare* 'annoy,' from *molestus* 'troublesome.'

mol·et·ron·ics /ˌmäliˈträniks/ ▶ **plural n.** [treated as singular] short for **MOLECULAR ELECTRONICS**.
– DERIVATIVES **mol·et·ron·ic adj.**

Mo·lière /mōlˈye(ə)r, môlˈyer/ (1622–73), French playwright; pseudonym of *Jean-Baptiste Poquelin*. He wrote more than 20 comic plays about contemporary France, developing stock characters from Italian *commedia dell'arte*. Notable works: *Tartuffe* (1664), *Le Misanthrope* (1666), and *Le Bourgeois gentilhomme* (1670).

Mo·line /mōˈlēn/ a city on the Rock and Mississippi rivers in northwestern Illinois, one of the Quad Cities; pop. 43,088 (est. 2008).

mo·line /məˈlēn, -ˈlīn/ ▶ **adj.** [postpositive] Heraldry (of a cross) having each extremity broadened, split, and curved back.
– ORIGIN mid 16th cent.: probably from Anglo-Norman French *moliné*, from *molin* 'mill,' because of a resemblance to the iron support of a millstone.

moll /mäl/ ▶ **n.** informal **1** (also **gun moll**) a gangster's female companion.
2 a prostitute.
– ORIGIN early 17th cent.: nickname for the given name *Mary*.

mol·li·fy /ˈmäləˌfī/ ▶ **v.** (**mollifies, mollifying, mollified**) [with obj.] appease the anger or anxiety of (someone): *nature reserves were set up around the power stations to mollify local conservationists.* ■ rare reduce the severity of (something); soften.
– DERIVATIVES **mol·li·fi·ca·tion** /ˌmäləfəˈkāsHən/ **n.**, **mol·li·fi·er n.**
– ORIGIN late Middle English (also in the sense 'make soft or supple'): from French *mollifier* or Latin *mollificare*, from *mollis* 'soft.'

mol·li·sol /ˈmäləˌsäl, -ˌsôl/ ▶ **n.** Soil Science a soil of an order comprising temperate grassland soils with a dark, humus-rich surface layer containing high concentrations of calcium and magnesium.
– ORIGIN mid 20th cent.: from Latin *mollis* 'soft' + *solum* 'ground, soil.'

mol·lus·cum con·ta·gi·o·sum /mälˈəskəm kənˌtājēˈōsəm/ ▶ **n.** Medicine a chronic viral disorder of the skin characterized by groups of small, smooth, painless pinkish nodules with a central depression, that yield a milky fluid when squeezed.
– ORIGIN early 19th cent.: from Latin *molluscum* (as a noun denoting a kind of fungus), neuter of *molluscus* + *contagiosum* (neuter of *contagiosus* 'contagious').

mol·lusk /ˈmäləsk/ (chiefly Brit. also **mollusc**) ▶ **n.** an invertebrate of a large phylum that includes snails, slugs, mussels, and octopuses. They have a soft, unsegmented body and live in aquatic or damp habitats, and most kinds have an external calcareous shell. ● Phylum Mollusca: several classes, in particular Gastropoda, Bivalvia, and Cephalopoda.
– DERIVATIVES **mol·lus·kan** /məˈləsˌkən/ (or **molluscan**) **adj.**
– ORIGIN late 18th cent.: from modern Latin *mollusca*, neuter plural of Latin *molluscus*, from *mollis* 'soft.'

Moll·wei·de pro·jec·tion /ˈmôlˌvīdə, -ˌwīdə/ ▶ **n.** a projection of a map of the world onto an ellipse, with lines of latitude represented by straight lines (spaced more closely toward the poles) and meridians represented by equally spaced elliptical curves. This projection distorts shape but preserves relative area.
– ORIGIN early 20th cent.: named after Karl B. *Mollweide* (died 1825), German mathematician and astronomer.

mol·ly /ˈmälē/ (also **mollie**) ▶ **n.** a small, livebearing freshwater fish that is popular in aquariums and has been bred in many colors, esp. black. ● Genus *Poecilia*, family Poeciliidae: several species, in particular *P. sphenops*. See also **SAILFIN MOLLY**.
– ORIGIN 1930s: from modern Latin *Mollienisia* (former genus name), from the name of Count *Mollien* (1758–1850), French statesman.

mol·ly·cod·dle /ˈmälēˌkädl/ ▶ **v.** [with obj.] treat (someone) very indulgently or protectively.
▶ **n.** an effeminate or ineffectual man or boy; a milksop.
– ORIGIN mid 19th cent.: from *molly* 'girl or prostitute' (see **MOLL**) + **CODDLE**.

Mo·loch /ˈmäləkˌ ˈmōˌläk/ a Canaanite idol to whom children were sacrificed. ■ (as noun **a Moloch**) a tyrannical object of sacrifices.
– ORIGIN via late Latin from Greek *Molokh*, from Hebrew *mōlek*.

mo·loch /ˈmäləkˌ ˈmōˌläk/ ▶ **n.** a harmless spiny lizard of grotesque appearance that feeds chiefly on ants and is found in arid inland Australia. ● *Moloch horridus*, family Agamidae.

Mo·lo·kai /ˌmäləˈkī, ˌmō-/ an island in Hawaii, east of Oahu Island, site of numerous resorts.

Mo·lo·tov[1] /ˈmäləˌtôf, -ˌtôv, ˈmōlə-/ former name (1940–57) for **PERM**.

Mo·lo·tov[2] /ˈmäləˌtôf, -ˌtäf, ˈmō-/, Vyacheslav (Mikhailovich) (1890–1986), Soviet statesman; born *Vyacheslav Mikhailovich Skryabin*. As commissar (later minister) for foreign affairs 1939–49 and 1953–56, he negotiated the nonaggression pact with Nazi Germany in 1939 and after 1945 represented the former Soviet Union at the United Nations.

Mo·lo·tov cock·tail ▶ **n.** a crude incendiary device typically consisting of a bottle filled with flammable liquid and with a means of ignition. The production of similar grenades was organized by Vyacheslav Molotov during World War II.

molt /mōlt/ (Brit. **moult**) ▶ **v.** [no obj.] (of an animal) shed old feathers, hair, or skin, or an old shell, to make way for a new growth: *the adult birds were already molting into their winter shades of gray* | [with obj.] *the snake molts its skin.* ■ (of hair or feathers) fall out to make way for new growth: *the last of his juvenile plumage had molted.*
▶ **n.** a loss of plumage, skin, or hair, esp. as a regular feature of an animal's life cycle.
– ORIGIN Middle English *moute*, from an Old English verb based on Latin *mutare* 'to change.' For the intrusive *-l-*, compare with words such as *fault*.

mol·ten /ˈmōltn/ ▶ **adj.** (esp. of materials with a high melting point, such as metal and glass) liquefied by heat.
– ORIGIN Middle English: archaic past participle of **MELT**.

mol·to /ˈmōlˌtō, ˈmôl-/ ▶ **adv.** Music (in directions) very: *molto maestoso* | *allegro molto*.
– ORIGIN Italian, from Latin *multus* 'much.'

Mo·luc·ca Is·lands /məˈləkə/ an island group in Indonesia, between Sulawesi and New Guinea; capital, Amboina. Settled by the Portuguese in the early 16th century, the islands were captured a century later by the Dutch. They were formerly known as the Spice Islands. Indonesian name **MALUKU**.
– DERIVATIVES **Mo·luc·can n. & adj.**

mol·vi /ˈmôlvē/ ▶ **n.** variant spelling of **MOULVI**.

mol. wt. ▶ **abbr.** molecular weight.

mo·ly[1] /ˈmōlē/ ▶ **n.** (pl. **molies**) **1** a southern European plant related to the onions, with small yellow flowers. ● *Allium moly*, family Liliaceae (or Alliaceae).
2 a mythical herb with white flowers and black roots, endowed with magic properties.
– ORIGIN mid 16th cent. (sense 2): via Latin from Greek *mōlu*.

mol·y[2] ▶ **n.** short for **MOLYBDENUM**. See also **CHROME-MOLY**.

mo·lyb·date /məˈlibˌdāt/ ▶ **n.** Chemistry a salt in which the anion contains both molybdenum and oxygen, esp. one of the anion MoO_4^{2-}.
– ORIGIN late 18th cent.: from *molybdic* (*acid*), a parent acid of molybdates, + **-ATE**[1].

mo·lyb·de·nite /məˈlibdəˌnīt/ ▶ **n.** a blue-gray mineral, typically occurring as hexagonal crystals. It consists of molybdenum disulfide and is the most common ore of molybdenum.

mo·lyb·de·num /məˈlibdənəm/ ▶ **n.** the chemical element of atomic number 42, a brittle silver-gray metal of the transition series, used in some alloy steels. (Symbol: **Mo**)
– ORIGIN early 19th cent.: modern Latin, earlier *molybdena* (originally denoting a salt of lead), from Greek *molubdaina* 'plummet,' from *molubdos* 'lead.'

mom /mäm/ ▶ **n.** informal one's mother.
– ORIGIN late 19th cent.: abbreviation of **MOMMA**.

mom-and-pop ▶ **adj.** informal denoting a small store or business of a type often run by a married couple: *most of the town relies on a local mom-and-pop ISP for their e-mail.*

Mom·ba·sa /mämˈbäsə/ a seaport and industrial city in southeastern Kenya, on the Indian Ocean; pop. 862,100 (est. 2006). It is the country's leading port and second largest city.

mo·ment /ˈmōmənt/ ▶ **n. 1** a very brief period of time: *she was silent* ***for a moment*** *before replying* | *a few moments later he returned to the office.* ■ an exact point in time: *she would always remember the moment they met.* ■ an appropriate time for doing something; an opportunity: *I was waiting for the* ***right moment.*** ■ a particular stage in something's development or in a course of events: *one of the great moments in aviation history.*
2 formal importance: *the issues were* ***of little moment*** *to the electorate.*
3 Physics a turning effect produced by a force acting at a distance on an object. ■ the magnitude of such an effect, expressed as the product of the force and the distance from its line of action to a given point.
4 Statistics a quantity that expresses the average or expected value of the first, second, third, or fourth power of the deviation of each component of a frequency distribution from some given value, typically mean or zero. The **first moment** is the mean, the **second moment** the variance, the **third moment** the skew, and the **fourth moment** the kurtosis.
– PHRASES **any moment** (or **at any moment**) very soon. **at the** (or **this**) **moment** at the present time; now. **for the moment** for now. **have one's** (or **its**) **moments** have short periods that are better or more impressive than others: *thanks to his gently comic performance, the film has its moments.* **in a moment 1** very soon: *I'll be back in a moment.* **2** instantly: *the fugitive was captured in a moment.* **live for the moment** live or act without worrying about the future. **the moment —— as soon as ——:** *the heavens opened the moment we left the house.* **moment of truth** a time when a person or thing is tested, a decision has to be made, or a crisis has to be faced. [with allusion to the final sword-thrust in a bullfight.] **not a moment too soon** almost too late. **not for a** (or **one**) **moment** not at all; never. **of the moment** currently popular, famous, or important: *the buzzword of the moment.* **one moment** (or **just a moment**) a request for someone to wait for a short period of time, esp. to allow the speaker to do or say something. **share a moment** informal experience a joint sensation of heightened emotion: *Alan and Barbara shared a moment yesterday after the memorial service.*
– ORIGIN late Middle English: from Latin *momentum* (see **MOMENTUM**).

mo·men·ta /mōˈmentə, mə-/ plural form of **MOMENTUM**.

mo·men·tar·i·ly /ˌmōmənˈte(ə)rəlē/ ▶ **adv. 1** for a very short time: *as he passed Jenny's door, he paused momentarily.*
2 at any moment; very soon: *my husband will be here to pick me up momentarily.*

mo·men·tar·y /ˈmōmənˌterē/ ▶ **adj.** lasting for a very short time; brief: *a momentary lapse of concentration.*
– DERIVATIVES **mo·men·tar·i·ness n.**
– ORIGIN late Middle English: from Latin *momentarius*, from *momentum* (see **MOMENT**).

mo·ment·ly /ˈmōməntlē/ ▶ **adv.** archaic or literary
1 from moment to moment; continually.
2 at any moment.
3 for a moment; briefly.

mo·ment of in·er·tia ▶ **n.** Physics a quantity expressing a body's tendency to resist angular acceleration. It is the sum of the products of the mass of each particle in the body with the square of its distance from the axis of rotation.

mo·men·tous /mōˈmen(t)əs, məˈ-/ ▶ **adj.** (of a decision, event, or change) of great importance or significance, esp. in its bearing on the future: *a period of momentous changes in East-West relations.*
– DERIVATIVES **mo·men·tous·ly adv.**, **mo·men·tous·ness n.**

mo·men·tum /mōˈmentəm, mə-/ ▶ **n.** (pl. **momenta** /-tə/ or **momentums**) **1** Physics the quantity of motion of a moving body, measured as a product of its mass and velocity.

m

2 the impetus gained by a moving object: *the vehicle gained momentum as the road dipped.* ■ the impetus and driving force gained by the development of a process or course of events: *the investigation gathered momentum in the spring.*
– ORIGIN late 17th cent.: from Latin, from *movimentum*, from *movere* 'to move.'

mom·ism /ˈmäm,izəm/ ▶ n. informal excessive attachment to or domination by one's mother.

mom·ma ▶ n. variant spelling of **MAMA**.

mom·my /ˈmämē/ ▶ n. (pl. **mommies**) informal one's mother (chiefly as a child's term).
– ORIGIN early 20th cent.: from **MOMMA** + **-Y**[2].

mom·my track ▶ n. informal a career path for women who opt to sacrifice promotions and pay raises in order to devote more time to raising their children.
– DERIVATIVES **mom·my track·er** n., **mom·my track·ing** n.

Mon /mōn/ ▶ n. (pl. **same** or **Mons**) **1** a member of a people now inhabiting parts of southeastern Burma (Myanmar) and western Thailand but having their ancient capital at Pegu in southern Burma. **2** the language of this people, related to Khmer (Cambodian).
▶ adj. of or relating to this people or their language. See also **MON-KHMER**.
– ORIGIN the name in Mon.

Mon. ▶ abbr. Monday.

mon- ▶ comb. form variant spelling of **MONO-** shortened before a vowel (as in *monamine*).

Mon·a·co /ˈmänəkō/ a principality that forms an enclave within French territory, on the Mediterranean coast near the Italian frontier; pop. 33,000 (est. 2009); language, French (official).

The smallest sovereign state in the world apart from the Vatican, Monaco was ruled by the Genoese from medieval times and by the Grimaldi family from 1297. It became a constitutional monarchy in 1911. Monaco includes the resort of Monte Carlo.

mon·ad /ˈmō,nad/ ▶ n. technical a single unit; the number one. ■ Philosophy (in the philosophy of Leibniz) an indivisible and hence ultimately simple entity, such as an atom or a person. ■ Biology, dated a single-celled organism, esp. a flagellate protozoan, or a single cell.
– DERIVATIVES **mo·nad·ic** /mōˈnadik, mə-/ adj., **mon·ad·ism** /-,izəm/ n. (Philosophy).
– ORIGIN early 17th cent.: via late Latin from Greek *monas, monad-* 'unit,' from *monos* 'alone.'

mon·a·del·phous /,mänəˈdelfəs/ ▶ adj. Botany (of stamens) united by their filaments so as to form one group.
– ORIGIN early 19th cent.: from Greek *monos* 'one' + *adelphos* 'brother' + **-OUS**.

mo·nad·nock /məˈnad,näk/ ▶ n. an isolated hill or ridge or erosion-resistant rock rising above a peneplain.
– ORIGIN late 19th cent.: named after Mount *Monadnock* in New Hampshire.

Mo·nad·nock, Mount /məˈnad,näk/ an isolated peak in southwestern New Hampshire whose name stands for any mountain of its type.

Mon·a·ghan /ˈmänə,han, -hən/ a county of the Republic of Ireland, part of the old province of Ulster. ■ its county town; pop. 6,221 (2006).

Mo·na Li·sa /ˈmōnə ˈlēsə, ˈlēzə/ a painting (now in the Louvre in Paris) executed 1503–06 by Leonardo da Vinci. The sitter was the wife of **Francesco del Giocondo**; her enigmatic smile has become one of the most famous images in Western art. Also called **LA GIOCONDA**.

mon·amine /ˈmänə,mēn/ ▶ n. variant spelling of **MONOAMINE**.

mo·na mon·key /ˈmōnə/ ▶ n. a West African guenon that has a bluish-gray face with a pink muzzle. The female has a distinctive moaning call. ● *Cercopithecus mona*, family Cercopithecidae.
– ORIGIN late 18th cent.: *mona* from Spanish and Portuguese *mona, mono*, Italian *monna*.

mo·nan·dry /ˈmän,andrē, məˈnan/ ▶ n. **1** the custom of having only one husband at a time. **2** Botany the state of having a single stamen.
– DERIVATIVES **mo·nan·drous** /məˈnandrəs/ adj.
– ORIGIN mid 19th cent.: from **MONO-** 'single,' on the pattern of words such as *polyandry*.

mon·arch /ˈmänərk, ˈmän,ärk/ ▶ n. **1** a sovereign head of state, esp. a king, queen, or emperor. **2** see **MONARCH BUTTERFLY**.
– DERIVATIVES **mo·nar·chal** /məˈnärkəl/ adj., **mo·nar·chi·al** /məˈnärkēəl/ adj., **mo·nar·chic** /məˈnärkik/ adj., **mo·nar·chi·cal** /məˈnärkikəl/ adj., **mo·nar·chi·cal·ly** /məˈnärkik(ə)lē/ adv.
– ORIGIN late Middle English: from late Latin *monarcha*, from Greek *monarkhēs*, from *monos* 'alone' + *arkhein* 'to rule.'

monarch butterfly

mon·arch but·ter·fly (also **monarch**) ▶ n. a large migratory orange and black butterfly that occurs mainly in North America. The caterpillar feeds on milkweed, using the toxins in the plant to render both itself and the adult unpalatable to predators. ● *Danaus plexippus*, subfamily Danainae, family Nymphalidae.

Mo·nar·chi·an /məˈnärkēən, mä-/ ▶ n. a Christian heretic of the 2nd or 3rd century who denied the doctrine of the Trinity.
▶ adj. of or relating to the Monarchians or their beliefs.
– ORIGIN from late Latin *monarchiani* (plural), from *monarchia* (see **MONARCHY**).

mon·ar·chism /ˈmänər,kizəm, ˈmän,är-/ ▶ n. support for the principle of having monarchs.
– DERIVATIVES **mon·ar·chist** n. & adj.
– ORIGIN mid 19th cent.: from French *monarchisme*.

mon·ar·chy /ˈmänərkē, ˈmän,är-/ ▶ n. (pl. **monarchies**) a form of government with a monarch at the head. ■ a state that has a monarch. ■ (**the monarchy**) the monarch and royal family of a country: *the monarchy is the focus of loyalty and service.*
– ORIGIN late Middle English: from Old French *monarchie*, via late Latin from Greek *monarkhia* 'the rule of one.'

mon·as·ter·y /ˈmänə,sterē/ ▶ n. (pl. **monasteries**) a building or buildings occupied by a community of monks living under religious vows.
– ORIGIN late Middle English: via ecclesiastical Latin from ecclesiastical Greek *monastērion*, from *monazein* 'live alone,' from *monos* 'alone.'

mo·nas·tic /məˈnastik/ ▶ adj. of or relating to monks, nuns, or others living under religious vows, or the buildings in which they live: *a monastic order.* ■ resembling or suggestive of monks or their way of life, esp. in being austere, solitary, or celibate: *a monastic student bedroom.*
▶ n. a monk or other follower of a monastic rule.
– DERIVATIVES **mo·nas·ti·cal·ly** /-ik(ə)lē/ adv., **mo·nas·ti·cism** /-tə,sizəm/ n.
– ORIGIN late Middle English (in the sense 'anchoritic'): from late Latin *monasticus*, from Greek *monastikos*, from *monazein* 'live alone.'

mon·a·tom·ic /,mänəˈtämik/ (also **monoatomic** /,mōnəˈtämik/) ▶ adj. Chemistry consisting of one atom.

mon·au·ral /,mänˈôrəl/ ▶ adj. of or involving one ear. ■ another term for **MONOPHONIC** (sense 1).
– DERIVATIVES **mon·au·ral·ly** adv.

mon·a·zite /ˈmänə,zīt/ ▶ n. a brown crystalline mineral consisting of a phosphate of cerium, lanthanum, other rare earth elements, and thorium.
– ORIGIN mid 19th cent.: from German *Monazit*, from Greek *monazein* 'live alone' (because of its rare occurrence).

Mön·chen·glad·bach /,mōōnkənˈglädˌbäk, ,mœnkHənˈglät,bäkH/ a city in northwestern Germany; pop. 261,000 (est. 2006). It is the site of NATO headquarters for northern Europe.

Monck /məNGk/, George, 1st Duke of Albemarle (1608–70), English general. Concerned at the growing unrest following Cromwell's death (1658), he negotiated the return of Charles II in 1660.

Mon·day /ˈməndā, -dē/ ▶ n. the day of the week before Tuesday and following Sunday: *I saw him on Monday* | *the Monday before last* | [as modifier] *Monday morning.*
▶ adv. on Monday: *I'll call you Monday.* ■ (**Mondays**) on Mondays; each Monday: *the restaurant is closed Mondays.*
– ORIGIN Old English *Mōnandæg* 'day of the moon,' translation of late Latin *lunae dies*; compare with Dutch *maandag* and German *Montag*.

Mon·day morn·ing quar·ter·back ▶ n. informal a person who passes judgment on and criticizes something after the event.

mon·de·green /ˈmändəgrēn/ ▶ n. a misunderstood or misinterpreted word or phrase resulting from a mishearing of the lyrics of a song.
– ORIGIN 1950s: from *Lady Mondegreen*, a misinterpretation of the phrase *laid him on the green*, from the traditional ballad "The Bonny Earl of Murray."

mon·do /ˈmändō/ ▶ adv. & adj. informal used in reference to something very striking or remarkable of its kind (often in conjunction with a pseudo-Italian noun or adjective): [as adv.] *I think it's going to be mondo weirdo this year, Andy.*
– ORIGIN from Italian *Mondo Cane*, literally 'dog's world,' the title of a film (1961) depicting bizarre behavior.

Mon·dri·an /ˈmôndrē,än/, Piet (1872–1944), Dutch painter; born *Pieter Cornelis Mondriaan*. He was a cofounder of the De Stijl movement and the originator of neo-plasticism, one of the earliest and strictest forms of geometric abstract painting.

Mon·é·gasque /,mänəˈgäsk, -ˈgask/ ▶ n. a native or inhabitant of Monaco.
▶ adj. of or relating to Monaco or its inhabitants.
– ORIGIN French.

Mo·nel /mōˈnel/ (also **Monel metal**) ▶ n. trademark a nickel-copper alloy with high tensile strength and resistance to corrosion.
– ORIGIN early 20th cent.: named after Ambrose *Monell* (died 1921), US businessman.

Mo·net /mōˈnā/, Claude (1840–1926), French painter. A founding member of the Impressionists (his painting *Impression: Sunrise* [1872] gave the movement its name), his fascination with the play of light on objects led him to produce series of single subjects painted at different times of day and under different weather conditions, such as the *Haystacks* series (1890–91) and *Rouen Cathedral* (1892–95). Among his most famous paintings are the *Waterlilies* series, which he began in 1899 and which occupied him for the rest of his life.

mon·e·ta·rism /ˈmänitə,rizəm, ˈmən-/ ▶ n. the theory or practice of controlling the supply of money as the chief method of stabilizing the economy.
– DERIVATIVES **mon·e·ta·rist** n. & adj.

mon·e·tar·y /ˈmänə,terē, ˈmən-/ ▶ adj. of or relating to money or currency: *documents with little or no monetary value.*
– DERIVATIVES **mon·e·tar·i·ly** /-,te(ə)rəlē/ adv.
– ORIGIN early 19th cent.: from French *monétaire* or late Latin *monetarius*, from Latin *moneta* 'money.'

mon·e·tar·y u·nit ▶ n. a standard unit of value of a country's coinage.

mon·e·tize /ˈmänə,tīz/ ▶ v. [with obj.] convert into or express in the form of currency. ■ (usu. as adj. **monetized**) adapt (a society) to the use of money: *a fully monetized society.*
– DERIVATIVES **mon·e·ti·za·tion** /,mänətəˈzāsHən, ,mänə,tīˈzāsHən/ n.
– ORIGIN late 19th cent.: from French *monétiser*, from Latin *moneta* 'money.'

mon·ey /ˈmənē/ ▶ n. a current medium of exchange in the form of coins and banknotes; coins and banknotes collectively: *I counted the money before putting it in my wallet* | *he borrowed money to modernize the store.* ■ (**moneys** or **monies**) formal sums of money: *a statement of all moneys paid into and out of the account.* ■ the assets, property, and resources owned by someone or something; wealth: *the college is very short of money.* ■ financial gain: *the main aim of a commercial organization is to make money.* ■ payment for work; wages: *she accepted the job at the public school since the money was better.* ■ a wealthy person or group: *her aunt had married money.*
– PHRASES **be in the money** informal have or win a lot of money. **be money in the bank** be a guaranteed success, esp. in the sports or entertainment industry: *Roy was money in the bank come playoff time* | *The film that should prove to be money in the bank.* **for my money** in my opinion or judgment: *for my money, they're one of the best bands around.* (**the love of**) **money is the root of all evil** proverb greed gives rise to selfish or wicked actions. **money talks** proverb wealth gives power and influence to those who possess it. **one's money's worth** good value for one's money. **on the money** accurate; correct: *every criticism she made was right on the money.* **put money** (or **put one's money**) **on 1** place a bet on. **2** used to express one's confidence in the truth or success of something: *she won't have him back—I'd put money on it.* **put one's money where one's mouth is** informal take action to support one's statements or opinions. **see the color of someone's money** receive some proof that someone has enough money to pay for something. **throw one's money around** spend one's money extravagantly or carelessly. **throw money at something** try to solve a problem by recklessly spending money on it, without due consideration of what is required.
– DERIVATIVES **mon·ey·less** adj.

–ORIGIN Middle English: from Old French *moneie*, from Latin *moneta* 'mint, money,' originally a title of the goddess Juno, in whose temple in Rome money was minted.

mon·ey-back ▶ **adj.** denoting an agreement or guarantee that provides for the customer's money to be refunded if not satisfied.

mon·ey·bags /ˈmənēˌbagz/ ▶ **plural n.** [usu. treated as sing.] informal a wealthy person.

mon·ey·chang·er ▶ **n.** a person whose business is the exchanging of one currency for another.
–DERIVATIVES **mon·ey·chang·ing** (or **money-changing** or **money changing**) **n.**

mon·eyed /ˈmənēd/ ▶ **adj.** having much money; affluent: *the industrial revolution created a new moneyed class.* ■ characterized by affluence: *a moneyed lifestyle.*

mon·ey·er /ˈmənēər/ ▶ **n.** archaic a person who mints money.

mon·ey grab ▶ **n.** informal an undignified or unprincipled acquisition of a large sum of money with little effort.

mon·ey-grub·bing ▶ **adj.** informal overeager to make money; grasping: *money-grubbing speculators.*
–DERIVATIVES **mon·ey-grub·ber** /-ˌgrəbər/ **n.**

mon·ey·lend·er /ˈmənēˌlendər/ ▶ **n.** a person whose business is lending money to others who pay interest.
–DERIVATIVES **mon·ey·lend·ing** /-ˌlendiNG/ (or **money-lending**) **n. & adj.**

mon·ey·mak·er /ˈmənēˌmākər/ ▶ **n.** a person or thing that earns a lot of money: *the movie became one of the year's top moneymakers.*

mon·ey·mak·ing /ˈmənēˌmākiNG/ ▶ **adj.** producing a profit, esp. with little effort; profitable: *he hit on an unusual moneymaking scheme.*
▶ **n.** the action of earning a lot of money: *this cynical exercise in moneymaking.*

mon·ey mar·ket ▶ **n.** the trade in short-term loans between banks and other financial institutions.

mon·ey of ac·count ▶ **n.** a denomination of money used in reckoning, but not issued as actual coins or paper money.

mon·ey or·der ▶ **n.** a printed order for payment of a specified sum, issued by a bank or post office.

mon·ey plant ▶ **n.** another term for HONESTY.

mon·ey shot ▶ **n.** informal the scene in a pornographic movie in which the male ejaculates. ■ a scene in a movie or moment in a performance viewed as the most provocative, sensational, or profitable.

mon·ey-spin·ner ▶ **n.** chiefly Brit. a thing that brings in a profit.
–DERIVATIVES **mon·ey-spin·ning** /-ˌspiniNG/ **adj.**

mon·ey sup·ply ▶ **n.** the total amount of money in circulation or in existence in a country.

mon·ey tree ▶ **n.** a source of easily obtained or unlimited money: *I knew how to **shake the money tree**.* ■ a real or artificial tree to which people attach paper money, esp. as a gift or donation.

mon·ey wag·es ▶ **plural n.** income expressed in terms of its monetary value, with no account taken of its purchasing power.

mon·ey·wort /ˈmənēˌwərt, -ˌwôrt/ ▶ **n.** a trailing evergreen plant with round glossy leaves and yellow flowers, growing in damp places and by water. Native to Europe, it is also common throughout the northeastern and north central US. Also called CREEPING CHARLIE, CREEPING JENNY. ● *Lysimachia nummularia*, family Primulaceae.

-monger ▶ **comb. form** denoting a dealer or trader in a specified commodity: *fishmonger* | *cheesemonger.* ■ a person who promotes a specified activity, situation, or feeling, esp. one that is undesirable or discreditable: *rumormonger* | *warmonger.*
–ORIGIN Old English *mangere*, from *mangian* 'to traffic,' of Germanic origin, based on Latin *mango* 'dealer.'

mon·go /ˈmäNGgō/ ▶ **n.** (pl. **same** or **mongos**) a monetary unit of Mongolia, equal to one hundredth of a tugrik.
–ORIGIN from Mongolian *möngö* 'silver.'

Mon·gol /ˈmäNGgəl/ ▶ **adj. 1** of or relating to the people of Mongolia or their language.
2 (**mongol**) offensive affected with Down syndrome.
▶ **n. 1** a native or inhabitant of Mongolia; a Mongolian.
2 the language of this people; Mongolian.
3 (**mongol**) offensive a person affected with Down syndrome.

> In the 13th century AD, the Mongol empire under Genghis Khan extended across central Asia from Manchuria in the east to European Russia in the west. Under Kublai Khan, China was conquered and the Mongol capital moved to Khanbaliq (modern Beijing). The Mongol empire collapsed after a series of defeats culminating in the destruction of the Golden Horde by the Muscovites in 1380.

–ORIGIN Mongolian, perhaps from *mong* 'brave.'

> **USAGE** See usage at MONGOLOID.

Mon·go·li·a /mäNGˈgōlēə/ a large and sparsely populated country in eastern Asia that includes the Gobi Desert, bordered by Siberia in Russia on the north and by China on the south; pop. 3,041,100 (est. 2009); capital, Ulaanbaatar (Ulan Bator); language, Mongolian (official).

> The center of the medieval Mongol empire, Mongolia subsequently became a Chinese province and achieved de facto independence in 1911. In 1924, it became a communist state patterned on the Soviet model; a new democratic constitution was introduced in 1992. It was formerly known as Outer Mongolia to distinguish it from Inner Mongolia, which remains a province of China.

Mon·go·li·an /mänˈgōlēən, mäNG-/ ▶ **adj.** of or relating to Mongolia, its people, or their language.
▶ **n. 1** a native or inhabitant of Mongolia.
2 the Altaic language of Mongolia, written in an unusual vertical cursive script; related forms are spoken in northern China.

mon·gol·ism /ˈmäNGgəˌlizəm/ ▶ **n.** offensive another term for DOWN SYNDROME.

> **USAGE** See usage at MONGOLOID.

Mon·gol·oid /ˈmäNGgəˌloid/ ▶ **adj. 1** often offensive of or relating to the broad division of humankind including the indigenous peoples of eastern Asia, Southeast Asia, and the Arctic region of North America.
2 (**mongoloid**) offensive affected with Down syndrome.
▶ **n. 1** often offensive a person of a Mongoloid physical type.
2 offensive a person with Down syndrome.

> **USAGE 1** The terms **Mongoloid**, **Negroid**, **Caucasoid**, and **Australoid** were introduced by 19th-century anthropologists attempting to classify human racial types, but today they are recognized as having very limited validity as scientific categories. Although occasionally used when making broad generalizations about the world's populations, in most modern contexts they are potentially offensive, especially when used of individuals. Instead, the names of specific peoples or nationalities should be used wherever possible. **2** The term **mongol**, or **Mongoloid**, was adopted in the late 19th century to refer to a person with **Down syndrome**, owing to the similarity of some of the physical symptoms of the disorder with the normal facial characteristics of eastern Asian people. The syndrome itself was thus called **mongolism**. In modern English, this use of **mongol** (and related forms) is unacceptable and is considered offensive. In scientific, as well as in most general contexts, **mongolism** has been replaced by the term **Down syndrome** (first recorded in the early 1960s).

mon·goose /ˈmänˌgo͞os, ˈmäNG-/ ▶ **n.** (pl. **mongooses**) a small carnivorous mammal with a long body and tail and a grizzled or banded coat, native to Africa and Asia. ● Family Herpestidae (or Viverridae): several genera, in particular *Herpestes* and *Mungos*, and many species, including the **banded mongoose** (*M. mungo*).
–ORIGIN late 17th cent.: from Marathi *mangūs*.

banded mongoose

mon·grel /ˈmäNGgrəl, ˈməNG-/ ▶ **n.** a dog of no definable type or breed: [as modifier] *a lovable mongrel puppy.* ■ any other animal resulting from the crossing of different breeds or types. ■ offensive a person of mixed descent.
–DERIVATIVES **mon·grel·ism** /-grəˌlizəm/ **n.**
–ORIGIN late Middle English: of Germanic origin, apparently from a base meaning 'mix,' and related to MINGLE and AMONG.

mon·grel·ize /ˈmäNGgrəˌlīz, ˈməNG-/ ▶ **v.** [with obj.] cause to become mixed in race, composition, or character: (as adj. **mongrelized**) *a patois of mongrelized French.*
–DERIVATIVES **mon·grel·i·za·tion** /ˌmäNGgrələˈzāSHən, ˌməNG-/ **n.**

'mongst /ˈməNGst/ ▶ **prep.** literary short for AMONGST (see AMONG).

mon·ic /ˈmänik/ ▶ **adj.** Mathematics (of a polynomial) having the coefficient of the term of highest degree equal to one.

Mon·i·ca, St. /ˈmänikə/ (332–*c.*387), mother of St. Augustine of Hippo; often regarded as the model of Christian mothers for her patience with her son's spiritual crises. Feast day, August 27 (formerly May 4).

mon·ies /ˈmənēz/ plural form of MONEY, as used in financial contexts.

mon·i·ker /ˈmänikər/ (also **monicker**) ▶ **n.** informal a name.
–DERIVATIVES **mon·i·kered adj.**
–ORIGIN mid 19th cent.: of unknown origin.

mo·nil·i·a /məˈnilēə/ ▶ **n.** (pl. usu. **same** or **moniliae** /-ˈnilēˌē, -ēˌī/) former term for CANDIDA.
–ORIGIN modern Latin, from Latin *monile* 'necklace' (with reference to the chains of spores).

mo·nil·i·form /məˈniləˌfôrm/ ▶ **adj.** Zoology & Botany resembling a string of beads.
–ORIGIN early 19th cent.: from French *moniliforme* or modern Latin *moniliformis*, from Latin *monile* 'necklace' + -IFORM.

mon·ism /ˈmänˌizəm, ˈmōˌnizəm/ ▶ **n.** Philosophy & Theology a theory or doctrine that denies the existence of a distinction or duality in some sphere, such as that between matter and mind, or God and the world. ■ the doctrine that only one supreme being exists. Compare with PLURALISM.
–DERIVATIVES **mon·ist n. & adj.**, **mo·nis·tic** /mänˈistik, mōˈnistik/ **adj.**
–ORIGIN mid 19th cent.: from modern Latin *monismus*, from Greek *monos* 'single.'

mo·ni·tion /məˈniSHən/ ▶ **n.** rare a warning of impending danger. ■ a formal notice from a bishop or ecclesiastical court admonishing a person not to do something specified.
–ORIGIN late Middle English: via Old French from Latin *monitio(n-)*, from *monere* 'warn.'

mon·i·tor /ˈmänətər/ ▶ **n. 1** an instrument or device used for observing, checking, or keeping a continuous record of a process or quantity: *a heart monitor.* ■ a person operating such an instrument or device. ■ a person who observes a process or activity to check that it is carried out fairly or correctly, esp. in an official capacity: *the independent judicial monitor.* ■ a person who listens to and reports on foreign radio broadcasts and signals. ■ a raised section of roof running down the center of a railroad car, building, etc., providing light or ventilation; a clerestory.
2 a student with disciplinary or other special duties during school hours: *show the hall monitor your pass.*
3 a television receiver used in a studio to select or verify the picture being broadcast from a particular camera. ■ a screen that displays an image generated by a computer. ■ a loudspeaker, esp. one used by performers on stage to hear themselves or in the studio to hear what has been recorded.
4 (also **monitor lizard**) a large tropical Old World lizard with a long neck, narrow head, forked tongue, strong claws, and a short body. Monitors were formerly believed to give warning of crocodiles. ● Family Varanidae and genus *Varanus*: many species. See also KOMODO DRAGON.
5 historical a shallow-draft armored warship mounting one or two heavy guns for bombardment.
▶ **v.** [with obj.] observe and check the progress or quality of (something) over a period of time; keep under systematic review: *equipment was installed to monitor air quality.* ■ maintain regular surveillance over: *it was easy for the enemy to monitor his movements.* ■ listen to and report on (a foreign radio broadcast or a telephone conversation). ■ check or regulate the technical quality of (a radio transmission or television signal).
–DERIVATIVES **mon·i·to·ri·al** /ˌmänəˈtôrēəl/ **adj.**, **mon·i·tor·ship** /-ˌSHip/ **n.**
–ORIGIN early 16th cent. (sense 2 of the noun): from Latin, from *monit-* 'warned,' from the verb *monere*. Sense 1 of the noun dates from the 1930s.

PRONUNCIATION KEY ə *ago, up*; ər *over, fur*; a *hat*; ā *ate*; ä *car*; e *let*; ē *see*; i *fit*; ī *by*; NG *sing*; ō *go*; ô *law, for*; oi *toy*; o͝o *good*; o͞o *goo*; ou *out*; TH *thin*; T͟H *then*; ZH *vision*

mon·i·to·ry /ˈmänəˌtôrē/ ▶ **adj.** rare giving or serving as a warning: *the monitory wail of an air-raid siren.* ▶ **n.** (pl. **monitories**) (in church use) a letter of admonition from the pope or a bishop.

Monk /məNGk/, Thelonious (Sphere) (1917–82), US jazz pianist and composer; a founder of the bebop style in the early 1940s. Notable compositions: "Round Midnight," "Straight, No Chaser," and "Well, You Needn't."

monk /məNGk/ ▶ **n.** a member of a religious community of men typically living under vows of poverty, chastity, and obedience.
– DERIVATIVES **monk·ish adj.**, **monk·ish·ly adv.**, **monk·ish·ness n.**
– ORIGIN Old English *munuc*, based on Greek *monakhos* 'solitary,' from *monos* 'alone.'

monk·er·y /ˈməNGkərē/ ▶ **n.** derogatory monasticism. ■ a monastery.

mon·key /ˈməNGkē/ ▶ **n.** (pl. **monkeys**) **1** a small to medium-sized primate that typically has a long tail, most kinds of which live in trees in tropical countries. ● Families Cebidae and Callitrichidae (or Callithricidae) (**New World monkeys**, with prehensile tails), and Cercopithecidae (**Old World monkeys**, without prehensile tails). ■ (in general use) any primate. ■ a mischievous person, esp. a child: *where have you been, you little monkey!* ■ a person who is dominated or controlled by another (with reference to the monkey traditionally kept by an organ grinder).
2 a pile-driving machine consisting of a heavy hammer or ram working vertically in a groove.
▶ **v.** (**monkeys, monkeying, monkeyed**) [no obj.] (**monkey around/about**) behave in a silly or playful way. ■ (**monkey with**) tamper with: *don't monkey with that lock!* ■ [with obj.] archaic ape; mimic.
– PHRASES **make a monkey of** (or **out of**) **someone** humiliate someone by making them appear ridiculous. **a monkey on one's back** informal a burdensome problem. ■ a dependence on drugs.
– DERIVATIVES **mon·key·ish adj.**
– ORIGIN mid 16th cent.: of unknown origin, perhaps from Low German.

mon·key bars ▶ **plural n.** a piece of playground equipment consisting of a horizontally mounted overhead ladder, from which children may swing.

m

mon·key bread ▶ **n.** the baobab tree or its fruit.

mon·key busi·ness ▶ **n.** informal mischievous or deceitful behavior.

mon·key flow·er ▶ **n.** a plant of boggy ground, having yellow or red tubular, often spotted flowers. ● Genus *Mimulus*, family Scrophulariaceae: several species, in particular *M. guttatus*.

mon·key jack·et ▶ **n.** a short, close-fitting jacket worn by sailors or waiters or by officers in their mess.

mon·key·pox /ˈməNGkēˌpäks/ ▶ **n.** a viral disease of African origin, related to smallpox and transmitted to humans through fluid exchange by rodents and primates.

mon·key puz·zle (also **monkey puzzle tree**) ▶ **n.** an evergreen coniferous tree with branches covered in spirals of tough, spiny, leaflike scales, native to Chile. ● *Araucaria araucana*, family Araucariaceae.
– ORIGIN mid 19th cent.: said to be so named in response to a remark that an attempt to climb the tree would puzzle a monkey.

mon·key·shines /ˈməNGkēˌSHīnz/ ▶ **plural n.** informal mischievous behavior.

mon·key suit ▶ **n.** informal a man's evening dress or formal suit.

mon·key wrench ▶ **n.** an adjustable wrench with large jaws that has its adjusting screw contained in the handle.
▶ **v.** (**monkeywrench**) [with obj.] informal sabotage (something), esp. as a form of protest: (as noun **monkeywrenching**) *the five defendants who received jail sentences for monkeywrenching.*
– PHRASES **a monkey wrench in the works** (or **schedule, plan,** etc.) a person or thing that prevents the successful implementation of a plan: *even he couldn't throw a monkey wrench into the works | a cancellation can throw a real monkey wrench into the schedule.*
– DERIVATIVES **mon·key·wrench·er n.**

monk·fish /ˈməNGkˌfiSH/ ▶ **n.** (pl. **same** or **monkfishes**) a bottom-dwelling anglerfish of European waters. ● *Lophius piscatorius*, family Lophiidae. ■ this fish as food. ■ another term for **GOOSEFISH**, esp. when referring to the fish as food.

Mon-Khmer /ˌmōn kəˈme(ə)r, kme(ə)r/ ▶ **n.** a family of languages spoken throughout Southeast Asia, of which the most important are Mon and Khmer. They are distantly related to Munda, with which they form the Austro-Asiatic phylum.
▶ **adj.** relating to or denoting this group of languages.

monk seal ▶ **n.** a seal with a dark back and pale underside, occurring in warm waters of the northern hemisphere. ● Genus *Monachus*, family Phocidae: two or three species, including *M. tropicalis* of the Caribbean and the endangered *M. monachus* of the Mediterranean and adjacent seas.

monks·hood /ˈməNGksˌho͝od/ ▶ **n.** an aconite with blue or purple flowers. The upper sepal of the flower covers the topmost petals, giving a hoodlike appearance. ● Genus *Aconitum*, family Ranunculaceae: several species, including the North American *A. uncinatum* and the European *A. napellus*.

Mon·mouth /ˈmänməTH/, James Scott, Duke of (1649–85), English claimant to the throne of England. The illegitimate son of Charles II, he became the focus for Whig supporters of a Protestant succession. In 1685, he led a rebellion against the Catholic James II, but was defeated at the Battle of Sedgemoor and executed.

mon·o /ˈmänō/ ▶ **adj. 1** monophonic.
2 monochrome.
▶ **n.** (pl. **monos**) **1** a monophonic recording. ■ monophonic reproduction.
2 a monochrome picture. ■ monochrome reproduction.
3 short for **INFECTIOUS MONONUCLEOSIS**.
4 short for **MONOFILAMENT**.

mono- (also **mon-** before a vowel) ▶ **comb. form**
1 one; alone; single: *monorail.* ■ with an extreme, singular character to the point of dominance or exclusion: *monolithic | monomania | monopoly.*
2 Chemistry (forming names of compounds) containing one atom or group of a specified kind: *monoamine.*
– ORIGIN from Greek *monos* 'alone.'

mon·o·a·mine /ˌmänōəˈmēn, ˌmänōˈamēn/ (also **monamine** /ˈmänəˌmēn/) ▶ **n.** Chemistry a compound having a single amine group in its molecule, esp. one that is a neurotransmitter (e.g., serotonin, norepinephrine).

mon·o·a·mine ox·i·dase (abbr.: **MAO**) ▶ **n.** Biochemistry an enzyme (present in most tissues) that catalyzes the oxidation and inactivation of monoamine neurotransmitters.

mon·o·a·mine ox·i·dase in·hib·i·tor ▶ **n.** Medicine any of a group of antidepressant drugs that inhibit the activity of monoamine oxidase (so allowing accumulation of serotonin and norepinephrine in the brain).

mon·o·a·tom·ic ▶ **n.** variant spelling of **MONATOMIC**.

mon·o·brow /ˈmänəˌbrou/ ▶ **n.** informal another term for **UNIBROW**.
– DERIVATIVES **mon·o·browed adj.**

mon·o·car·pic /ˌmänōˈkärpik/ (also **monocarpous** /-pəs/) ▶ **adj.** Botany (of a plant) flowering only once and then dying.
– ORIGIN mid 19th cent.: from **MONO-** 'single' + Greek *karpos* 'fruit' + **-IC**.

mon·o·caus·al /ˌmänōˈkôzəl/ ▶ **adj.** in terms of a sole cause: *the pitfalls of monocausal explanations.*

Mo·noc·er·os /məˈnäsərəs/ Astronomy an inconspicuous constellation (the Unicorn), lying on the celestial equator in the Milky Way between Canis Major and Canis Minor. ■ (as genitive **Monocerotis** /məˌnäsəˈrōtis, ˌmänəsə-/) used with a preceding letter or numeral to designate a star in this constellation: *the star Alpha Monocerotis.*
– ORIGIN via Latin from Greek.

mon·o·cha·si·um /ˌmänōˈkaZH(ē)əm/ ▶ **n.** (pl. **monochasia** /-ZH(ē)ə/) Botany a cyme in which each flowering branch gives rise to one lateral branch, so that the inflorescence is helicoid or asymmetrical.
– ORIGIN late 19th cent.: modern Latin, from **MONO-** 'one' + Greek *khasis* 'separation.'

mon·o·chord /ˈmänəˌkôrd/ ▶ **n.** an instrument for comparing musical pitches mathematically, using a taut wire whose vibrating length can be adjusted with a movable bridge.
– ORIGIN late Middle English: from Old French *monacorde*, via late Latin from Greek *monokhordon*, neuter (used as a noun) of *monokhordos* 'having a single string.'

mon·o·chro·mat·ic /ˌmänəkrōˈmatik/ ▶ **adj.** containing or using only one color: *monochromatic light.* ■ Physics (of light or other radiation) of a single wavelength or frequency.
– DERIVATIVES **mon·o·chro·mat·i·cal·ly** /-ik(ə)lē/ **adv.**

mon·o·chro·ma·tism /ˌmänəˈkrōməˌtizəm/ ▶ **n.** complete color-blindness in which all colors appear as shades of one color.

mon·o·chrome /ˈmänəˌkrōm/ ▶ **n.** a photograph or picture developed or executed in black and white or in varying tones of only one color. ■ representation or reproduction in black and white or in varying tones of only one color.
▶ **adj.** (of a photograph or picture, or a television screen) consisting of or displaying images in black and white or in varying tones of only one color.
– DERIVATIVES **mon·o·chro·mic** /ˌmänəˈkrōmik/ **adj.**
– ORIGIN mid 17th cent.: based on Greek *monokhrōmatos* 'of a single color.'

mon·o·cle /ˈmänikəl/ ▶ **n.** a single eyeglass, kept in position by the muscles around the eye.
– DERIVATIVES **mon·o·cled** /-kəld/ **adj.**
– ORIGIN mid 19th cent.: from French (earlier in the sense 'one-eyed'), from late Latin *monoculus* 'one-eyed.'

mon·o·cline /ˈmänəˌklīn/ ▶ **n.** Geology a bend in rock strata that are otherwise uniformly dipping or horizontal.
– DERIVATIVES **mon·o·cli·nal** /ˌmänəˈklīnl/ **adj.**
– ORIGIN late 19th cent.: from **MONO-** 'single' + Greek *klinein* 'to lean.'

mon·o·clin·ic /ˌmänəˈklinik/ ▶ **adj.** of or denoting a crystal system or three-dimensional geometric arrangement having three unequal axes of which one is at right angles to the other two.

mon·o·clo·nal /ˌmänəˈklōnl/ ▶ **adj.** Biology forming a clone that is derived asexually from a single individual or cell.

mon·o·clo·nal an·ti·bod·y ▶ **n.** an antibody produced by a single clone of cells or cell line and consisting of identical antibody molecules.

mon·o·coque /ˈmänəˌkōk, -ˌkäk/ ▶ **n.** an aircraft or vehicle structure in which the chassis is integral with the body.
– ORIGIN early 20th cent.: from French, from *mono-* 'single' + *coque* 'shell.'

mon·o·cot /ˈmänəˌkät/ ▶ **n.** Botany short for **MONOCOTYLEDON**.

mon·o·cot·y·le·don /ˌmänəˌkätlˈēdn/ ▶ **n.** Botany a flowering plant with an embryo that bears a single cotyledon (seed leaf). Monocotyledons constitute the smaller of the two great divisions of flowering plants, and typically have elongated stalkless leaves with parallel veins (e.g., grasses, lilies, palms). Compare with **DICOTYLEDON**. ● Class Monocotyledoneae (or -donae, -dones; sometimes Liliopsida), subdivision Angiospermae.
– DERIVATIVES **mon·o·cot·y·le·don·ous** /-ˈēdn-əs/ **adj.**

mo·noc·ra·cy /məˈnäkrəsē, mä-/ ▶ **n.** (pl. **monocracies**) a system of government by only one person.
– DERIVATIVES **mon·o·crat** /ˈmänəˌkrat/ **n.**, **mon·o·crat·ic** /ˌmänəˈkratik/ **adj.**

mon·o·crop /ˈmänəˌkräp/ ▶ **n.** a cultivated crop that does not rotate with other crops in a particular field or area: [as modifier] *bananas grown in a monocrop system for commercial production.*

mo·noc·u·lar /məˈnäkyələr, mä-/ ▶ **adj.** with, for, or in one eye: *he had only monocular vision.*
▶ **n.** an optical instrument for viewing distant objects with one eye, like one half of a pair of binoculars.
– DERIVATIVES **mo·noc·u·lar·ly adv.**
– ORIGIN mid 17th cent.: from late Latin *monoculus* 'having one eye' + **-AR**[1].

mon·o·cul·ture /ˈmänəˌkəlCHər/ ▶ **n.** the cultivation of a single crop in a given area.
– DERIVATIVES **mon·o·cul·tur·al** /ˌmänəˈkəlCHərəl/ **adj.**

mon·o·cy·cle /ˈmänəˌsīkəl/ ▶ **n.** another term for **UNICYCLE**.

mon·o·cy·clic /ˌmänōˈsīklik, -ˈsik-/ ▶ **adj. 1** Chemistry having one ring of atoms in its molecule.
2 of or relating to a single cycle of activity.

mon·o·cyte /ˈmänəˌsīt/ ▶ **n.** Physiology a large phagocytic white blood cell with a simple oval nucleus and clear, grayish cytoplasm.

Mo·nod /môˈnō/, Jacques Lucien (1910–76), French biochemist. Together with fellow French biochemist François Jacob (1920–), he formulated a theory to explain how genes are activated, and, in 1961, he proposed the existence of messenger RNA. Nobel Prize for Physiology or Medicine (1965), shared with Jacob and André Lwoff (1902–94).

mon·o·dra·ma /ˈmänəˌdrämə, -ˌdramə/ ▶ **n.** a dramatic piece for one performer.

mon·o·dy /ˈmänədē/ ▶ **n.** (pl. **monodies**) **1** an ode sung by a single actor in a Greek tragedy.
2 a poem lamenting a person's death.
3 music with only one melodic line, esp. an early Baroque style with one singer and continuo accompaniment.

–DERIVATIVES **mo·nod·ic** /mə'nädik/ **adj.**, **mon·o·dist** /-dist/ **n.**
–ORIGIN early 17th cent.: via late Latin from Greek *monōdia*, from *monōdos* 'singing alone.'

mo·noe·cious /mə'nēsHəs/ ▶ **adj.** Biology (of a plant or invertebrate animal) having both the male and female reproductive organs in the same individual; hermaphrodite. Compare with **DIOECIOUS**.
–DERIVATIVES **mo·noe·cy** /'män,ēsē, 'mō-/ **n.**
–ORIGIN mid 18th cent.: from modern Latin *Monoecia* (denoting a class of such plants in Linnaeus's system), from Greek *monos* 'single' + *oikos* 'house.'

mon·o·fil·a·ment /,mänə'filəmənt/ (also **monofil** /'mänə,fil/) ▶ **n.** a single strand of man-made fiber. ■ a type of fishing line using such a strand.

mo·nog·a·my /mə'nägəmē/ ▶ **n.** the practice or state of being married to one person at a time. ■ the practice or state of having a sexual relationship with only one partner. ■ Zoology the habit of having only one mate at a time.
–DERIVATIVES **mo·nog·a·mist** /-mist/ **n.**, **mo·nog·a·mous** /-məs/ **adj.**, **mo·nog·a·mous·ly** /-məslē/ **adv.**
–ORIGIN early 17th cent.: from French *monogamie*, via ecclesiastical Latin from Greek *monogamia*, from *monos* 'single' + *gamos* 'marriage.'

mon·o·ge·ne·an /,mänə'jēnēən/ Zoology ▶ **adj.** of or relating to a group of flukes that are chiefly external or gill parasites of fish and only require a single host. Compare with **DIGENEAN**.
▶ **n.** a monogenean fluke. ● Class Monogenea, phylum Platyhelminthes; sometimes treated as a subclass of the class Trematoda.
–ORIGIN 1960s: from modern Latin *Monogenea* (from Greek *monos* 'single' + *genea* 'generation') + **-AN**.

mon·o·gen·e·sis /,mänə'jenəsəs/ ▶ **n.** the theory that humans are all descended from a single pair of ancestors. Also called **MONOGENY**. ■ Linguistics the hypothetical origination of language or of a surname from a single source at a particular place and time.
–DERIVATIVES **mon·o·ge·net·ic** /-jə'netik/ **adj.**

mon·o·gen·ic /,mänə'jenik/ ▶ **adj.** Genetics involving or controlled by a single gene.
–DERIVATIVES **mon·o·gen·i·cal·ly** /-ik(ə)lē/ **adv.**

mo·nog·e·ny /mə'näjənē/ ▶ **n.** another term for **MONOGENESIS**.
–DERIVATIVES **mo·nog·e·nism** /-,nizəm/ **n.**, **mo·nog·e·nist** /-jənist/ **n.**

mon·o·glot /'mänə,glät/ ▶ **adj.** using or speaking only one language: *the moment when the monoglot heroine suddenly finds she can understand French.*
▶ **n.** a person who speaks only one language.
–ORIGIN mid 19th cent.: from Greek *monoglōttos*, from *monos* 'single' + *glōtta* 'tongue.'

mon·o·gram /'mänə,gram/ ▶ **n.** a motif of two or more letters, typically a person's initials, usually interwoven or otherwise combined in a decorative design, used as a logo or to identify a personal possession.
▶ **v.** [with obj.] decorate with a monogram: (as adj. **monogrammed**) *monogrammed sheets.*
–DERIVATIVES **mon·o·gram·mat·ic** /,mänəgrə'matik/ **adj.**
–ORIGIN late 17th cent.: from French *monogramme*, from late Latin *monogramma*, from Greek.

mon·o·graph /'mänə,graf/ ▶ **n.** a detailed written study of a single specialized subject or an aspect of it: *a series of monographs on music in late medieval and Renaissance cities.*
▶ **v.** [with obj.] write a monograph on; treat in a monograph.
–DERIVATIVES **mo·nog·ra·pher** /mə'nägrəfər/ **n.**, **mo·nog·ra·phist** /mə'nägrəfist/ **n.**
–ORIGIN early 19th cent. (earlier *monography*): from modern Latin *monographia*, from *monographus* 'writer on a single genus or species.'

mon·o·graph·ic /,mänə'grafik/ ▶ **adj.** of or relating to a monograph. ■ (of an art gallery or exhibition) showing the works of a single artist.

mon·o·gyne /'mänə,jin/ ▶ **adj.** Entomology (of a social insect) having only one egg-laying queen in each colony.
–ORIGIN from **MONO-** 'one' + Greek *gunē* 'woman, wife.'

mo·nog·y·nous /mə'näjənəs/ ▶ **adj.** Botany having only one pistil.

mo·nog·y·ny /mə'näjənē/ ▶ **n.** the custom of having only one wife at a time.
–ORIGIN late 19th cent.: from **MONO-** 'one' + Greek *gunē* 'woman, wife.'

mon·o·hull /'mänō,həl/ ▶ **n.** a boat with only one hull, as opposed to a catamaran or multihull.

mon·o·hy·brid /,mänə'hībrid/ ▶ **n.** Genetics a hybrid that is heterozygous with respect to a specified gene.

mon·o·hy·drate /,mänō'hī,drāt/ ▶ **n.** Chemistry a hydrate containing one mole of water per mole of the compound.

mon·o·hy·dric /,mänō'hīdrik/ ▶ **adj.** Chemistry (of an alcohol) containing one hydroxyl group.

mon·o·ki·ni /'mänə,kinē/ ▶ **n.** a woman's one-piece beach garment equivalent to the lower half of a bikini.
–ORIGIN 1960s: from **MONO-** 'one' + a shortened form of **BIKINI** (the first syllable misinterpreted as *bi-* 'two').

Mo·no Lake /'mōnō/ a salt lake in east central California, near the Nevada border, noted for its rock exposed formations that occurred when local waters were diverted to the Los Angeles area.

mo·nol·a·try /mə'nälətrē/ ▶ **n.** the worship of one god without denial of the existence of other gods.
–DERIVATIVES **mo·nol·a·ter** /-tər/ **n.**, **mo·nol·a·trist** /-trist/ **n.**, **mo·nol·a·trous** /-trəs/ **adj.**

mon·o·lay·er /'mänə,lāər/ ▶ **n.** Chemistry a layer one molecule thick. ■ Biology & Medicine a cell culture in a layer one cell thick.

mon·o·line /'mänə,lin/ ▶ **n.** a company specializing in a single type of financial service, such as consumer credit, home mortgages, or a sole class of insurance.

mon·o·lin·gual /,mänə'liNGg(yə)wəl/ ▶ **adj.** (of a person or society) speaking only one language: *monolingual families.* ■ (of a text, conversation, etc.) written or conducted in only one language: *monolingual and bilingual editions.*
▶ **n.** a person who speaks only one language.
–DERIVATIVES **mon·o·lin·gual·ism** /-,lizəm/ **n.**

mon·o·lith /'mänl-iTH/ ▶ **n. 1** a large single upright block of stone, esp. one shaped into or serving as a pillar or monument. ■ a very large and characterless building: *the 72-story monolith overlooking the waterfront.* ■ a large block of concrete sunk in water, e.g., in the building of a dock.
2 a large and impersonal political, corporate, or social structure regarded as intractably indivisible and uniform: *the U.S.–E.U. trade rules-dictating monolith is no more.*
–ORIGIN mid 19th cent.: from French *monolithe*, from Greek *monolithos*, from *monos* 'single' + *lithos* 'stone.'

mon·o·lith·ic /,mänə'liTHik/ ▶ **adj. 1** formed of a single large block of stone. ■ (of a building) very large and characterless.
2 (of an organization or system) large, powerful, and intractably indivisible and uniform: *rejecting any move toward a monolithic European superstate.*
3 Electronics (of a solid-state circuit) composed of active and passive components formed in a single chip.

mon·o·logue /'mänl,ôg, -,äg/ ▶ **n.** a long speech by one actor in a play or movie, or as part of a theatrical or broadcast program. ■ a long and typically tedious speech by one person during a conversation: *Fred carried on with his monologue as if I hadn't spoken.*
–DERIVATIVES **mon·o·log·ic** /,mänl'äjik/ **adj.**, **mon·o·log·i·cal** /,mänl'äjikəl/ **adj.**, **mon·o·log·ist** /mə'näləjist/ (also **-loguist**) **n.**, **mon·o·log·ize** /mə'nälə,jiz/ **v.**
–ORIGIN mid 17th cent.: from French, from Greek *monologos* 'speaking alone.'

mon·o·ma·ni·a /,mänə'mānēə/ ▶ **n.** exaggerated or obsessive enthusiasm for or preoccupation with one thing.
–DERIVATIVES **mon·o·ma·ni·ac** /-'mānē,ak/ **n. & adj.**, **mon·o·ma·ni·a·cal** /-mə'nīəkəl/ **adj.**

mon·o·mer /'mänəmər/ ▶ **n.** Chemistry a molecule that can be bonded to other identical molecules to form a polymer.
–DERIVATIVES **mon·o·mer·ic** /,mänə'merik/ **adj.**

mon·o·me·tal·lic /,mänōmə'talik/ ▶ **adj.** consisting of one metal only. ■ of, involving, or using a standard of currency based on one metal.
–DERIVATIVES **mon·o·met·al·lism** /-'metl,izəm/ **n.**, **mon·o·met·al·list** /-metlist/ **n. & adj.**

mo·no·mi·al /mə'nōmēəl, mä-/ Mathematics ▶ **adj.** (of an algebraic expression) consisting of one term.
▶ **n.** an algebraic expression of this type.
–ORIGIN early 18th cent.: from **MONO-** 'one,' on the pattern of *binomial*.

mon·o·mo·lec·u·lar /,mänōmə'lekyələr/ ▶ **adj.** Chemistry (of a layer) one molecule thick. ■ consisting of or involving one molecule.

mon·o·mor·phic /,mänə'môrfik/ ▶ **adj.** chiefly Biology having or existing in only one form, in particular: ■ (of a species or population) showing little or no variation in morphology or phenotype. ■ (of an animal species) having sexes that are similar in size and appearance.
–DERIVATIVES **mon·o·mor·phism** /-,fizəm/ **n.**, **mon·o·mor·phous** /-fəs/ **adj.**
–ORIGIN late 19th cent.: from **MONO-** 'single' + Greek *morphē* 'form.'

Mo·non·ga·he·la Riv·er /mə,näNGgə'hēlə/ a river that flows for 128 miles (206 km) from West Virginia into western Pennsylvania to Pittsburgh where it joins the Allegheny River to form the Ohio River.

mon·o·nu·cle·ar /,mänō'n(y)ōōklēər/ ▶ **adj.** Biology (of a cell) having one nucleus.

mon·o·nu·cle·o·sis /,mänə,n(y)ōōklē'ōsəs/ ▶ **n.** Medicine an abnormally high proportion of monocytes in the blood. ■ short for **INFECTIOUS MONONUCLEOSIS**. Also called **MONO**.

mo·noph·a·gous /mə'näfəgəs/ ▶ **adj.** Zoology (of an animal) eating only one kind of food.

mon·o·phon·ic /,mänə'fänik/ ▶ **adj. 1** Music consisting of a single musical line, without accompaniment: *the style of monophonic singing known as Gregorian chant.*
2 (of sound reproduction) using only one channel of transmission. Compare with **STEREOPHONIC**.
–DERIVATIVES **mon·o·phon·i·cal·ly** /-ik(ə)lē/ **adv.**, **mo·noph·o·ny** /mə'näfənē/ **n.**
–ORIGIN early 19th cent.: from **MONO-** 'one' + Greek *phonē* 'sound' + **-IC**.

mon·oph·thong /'mänə(f),THôNG/ ▶ **n.** Phonetics a vowel that has a single perceived auditory quality. Contrasted with **DIPHTHONG, TRIPHTHONG**.
–DERIVATIVES **mon·oph·thon·gal** /,mänə(f)'THôNG(g)əl/ **adj.**
–ORIGIN early 17th cent.: from Greek *monophthongos*, from *monos* 'single' + *phthongos* 'sound.'

mon·o·phy·let·ic /,mänōfī'letik/ ▶ **adj.** Biology (of a group of organisms) descended from a common evolutionary ancestor or ancestral group, esp. one not shared with any other group.

Mo·noph·y·site /mə'näfə,sīt/ ▶ **n.** Christian Theology a person who holds that in the person of Jesus Christ there is only one nature (wholly divine or only subordinately human), not two.
–DERIVATIVES **Mo·noph·y·sit·ism** /-,sīt,izəm/ **n.**
–ORIGIN late 17th cent.: via ecclesiastical Latin from ecclesiastical Greek *monophusitēs*, from *monos* 'single' + *phusis* 'nature.'

mon·o·plane /'mänə,plān/ ▶ **n.** an airplane with one pair of wings. Often contrasted with **BIPLANE, TRIPLANE**.

mon·o·ple·gi·a /,mänō'plēj(ē)ə/ ▶ **n.** paralysis restricted to one limb or region of the body. Compare with **PARAPLEGIA**.
–DERIVATIVES **mon·o·ple·gic** /-'plējik/ **adj.**

mon·o·ploid /'mänə,ploid/ ▶ **adj.** less common term for **HAPLOID**.

mon·o·pod /'mänə,päd/ ▶ **n.** a one-legged support for a camera or fishing rod.
–ORIGIN early 19th cent.: via Latin from Greek *monopodion*, from *monos* 'single' + *pous, pod-* 'foot.'

mon·o·po·di·um /,mänə'pōdēəm/ ▶ **n.** (pl. **monopodia** /-'pōdēə/) Botany a single continuous growth axis that extends at its apex and produces successive lateral shoots. Compare with **SYMPODIUM**.
–DERIVATIVES **mon·o·po·di·al** /-dēəl/ **adj.**

mon·o·pole /'mänə,pōl/ ▶ **n. 1** Physics a single electric charge or magnetic pole, esp. a hypothetical isolated magnetic pole.
2 a radio antenna or pylon consisting of a single pole or rod.
–DERIVATIVES **mon·o·po·lar adj.**

mo·nop·o·list /mə'näpəlist/ ▶ **n.** a person or business that has a monopoly.
–DERIVATIVES **mo·nop·o·lis·tic** /mə,näpə'listik/ **adj.**, **mo·nop·o·lis·ti·cal·ly** /mə,näpə'listik(ə)lē/ **adv.**

mo·nop·o·lize /mə'näpə,līz/ ▶ **v.** [with obj.] (of an organization or group) obtain exclusive possession or control of (a trade, commodity, or service). ■ have or take the greatest share of: *the bigger teams monopolize the most profitable sponsorships and TV deals.* ■ get or keep exclusively to oneself: *Sophie monopolized the guest of honor for most of the evening.*
–DERIVATIVES **mo·nop·o·li·za·tion** /mə,näpələ'zāsHən/ **n.**, **mo·nop·o·liz·er n.**

m

mo·nop·o·ly /mə'näpəlē/ ▶ **n.** (pl. **monopolies**) **1** the exclusive possession or control of the supply or trade in a commodity or service: *his likely motive was to protect his regional* ***monopoly on furs.*** ■ [usu. with negative] the exclusive possession, control, or exercise of something: *men don't have a* ***monopoly on*** *unrequited love.* ■ a company or group having exclusive control over a commodity or service: *areas where cable companies operate as monopolies.* ■ a commodity or service controlled in this way: *electricity, gas, and water were considered to be natural monopolies.*
2 (**Monopoly**) trademark a board game in which players engage in simulated property and financial dealings using imitation money. It was invented in the US and the name was coined by **Charles Darrow** *c.*1935.
– ORIGIN mid 16th cent.: via Latin from Greek *monopōlion*, from *monos* 'single' + *pōlein* 'sell.'

mo·nop·o·ly cap·i·tal·ism ▶ **n.** Economics a capitalist system typified by trade monopolies in the hands of a few people.

Mo·nop·o·ly mon·ey ▶ **n.** informal money regarded as having no real existence or value.
– ORIGIN from the imitation money used in the game of *Monopoly* (see **MONOPOLY** (sense 2).

mon·o·pro·pel·lant /ˌmänōprə'pelənt/ ▶ **n.** a substance used as rocket fuel without an additional oxidizing agent.
▶ **adj.** using such a substance.

mo·nop·so·ny /mə'näpsənē/ ▶ **n.** (pl. **monopsonies**) Economics a market situation in which there is only one buyer.
– ORIGIN 1930s: from **MONO-** 'one' + Greek *opsōnein* 'buy provisions' + **-Y**[3].

mon·o·pulse /'mänəˌpəls/ ▶ **adj.** denoting a system of radar in which the angular location of a target is determined by comparison of two or more simultaneously received signals.
▶ **n.** a monopulse radar system or installation.
– ORIGIN late 1950s: from *mono*, 'one' + *pulse*.

mon·o·rail /'mänəˌrāl/ ▶ **n.** a railroad in which the track consists of a single rail, typically elevated, with the trains suspended from it or balancing on it.

m

mon·or·chid /mä'nôrkid/ ▶ **adj.** (of a person or animal) having only one testicle.
▶ **n.** such a person or animal.
– DERIVATIVES **mon·or·chid·ism** /mä'nôrkiˌdizəm/ **n.**
– ORIGIN early 19th cent.: from modern Latin *monorchis, monorchid-*, from Greek *monos* 'single' + *orkhis* 'testicle.'

mon·o·sac·cha·ride /ˌmänə'sakəˌrīd/ ▶ **n.** Chemistry any of the class of sugars (e.g., glucose) that cannot be hydrolyzed to give a simpler sugar.

mon·o·se·my /'mänəˌsēmē/ ▶ **n.** Linguistics the property of having only one meaning.
– DERIVATIVES **mon·o·se·mous** /ˌmänə'sēməs/ **adj.**
– ORIGIN 1950s: from **MONO-** 'one' + Greek *sēma* 'sign' + **-Y**[3].

mon·o·ski /'mänəˌskē/ ▶ **n.** a single broad ski attached to both feet.
– DERIVATIVES **mon·o·ski·er** /-ˌskēər/ **n.**, **mon·o·ski·ing** /-ˌskē-iNG/ **n.**

mon·o·so·di·um glu·ta·mate /ˌmänəˌsōdēəm 'glo͞otəˌmāt/ (abbr.: **MSG**) ▶ **n.** a compound that occurs naturally as a breakdown product of proteins and is used as a flavor enhancer in food (although itself tasteless). A traditional ingredient in Asian cooking, it was originally obtained from seaweed but is now mainly made from bean and cereal protein. ● Chem. formula: $HOOC(CH_2)_2(NH_2)COONa$.

mon·o·some /'mänəˌsōm/ ▶ **n.** Biology an unpaired (usually X) chromosome in a diploid chromosome complement.

mon·o·so·my /'mänəˌsōmē/ ▶ **n.** Biology the condition of having a diploid chromosome complement in which one (usually the X) chromosome lacks its homologous partner.
– DERIVATIVES **mon·o·so·mic** /ˌmänə'sōmik/ **adj.**

mon·o·spe·cif·ic /ˌmänōspə'sifik/ ▶ **adj.** Biology relating to or consisting of only one species. ■ (of an antibody) specific to one antigen.

mon·o·stroph·ic /ˌmänə'sträfik, -'strōfik/ ▶ **adj.** Prosody consisting of repetitions of the same strophic arrangement.

mon·o·syl·lab·ic /ˌmänəsə'labik/ ▶ **adj.** (of a word or utterance) consisting of one syllable. ■ (of a person) using brief words to signify reluctance to engage in conversation: *the nearer they came to Rome, the more quiet and monosyllabic Paul seemed to become.*
– DERIVATIVES **mon·o·syl·lab·i·cal·ly** /-ik(ə)lē/ **adv.**

mon·o·syl·la·ble /ˌmänə'siləbəl, 'mänəˌsil-/ ▶ **n.** a word consisting of only one syllable. ■ (**monosyllables**) brief words, signifying reluctance to engage in conversation: *if she spoke at all it was* ***in monosyllables.***

mon·o·syn·ap·tic /ˌmänōsə'naptik/ ▶ **adj.** Physiology (of a reflex pathway) involving a single synapse.

mon·o·the·ism /'mänəˌTHēˌizəm/ ▶ **n.** the doctrine or belief that there is only one God.
– DERIVATIVES **mon·o·the·ist** **n. & adj.**, **mon·o·the·is·tic** /ˌmänəTHē'istik/ **adj.**, **mon·o·the·is·ti·cal·ly** /ˌmänəTHē'istik(ə)lē/ **adv.**
– ORIGIN mid 17th cent.: from **MONO-** 'one' + Greek *theos* 'god' + **-ISM**.

Mo·noth·e·lite /mə'näTHəˌlīt/ (also **Monothelete** /-ˌlēt/) ▶ **n.** Christian Theology an adherent of the doctrine that Jesus had only one will, proposed in the 7th century to reconcile Monophysite and orthodox parties in the Byzantine Empire but condemned as heresy.
– ORIGIN late Middle English: via ecclesiastical Latin from ecclesiastical Greek *monothelētēs*, from *monos* 'single' + *thelētēs* 'one that wills' (from *thelein* 'to will').

mon·o·tint /'mänəˌtint/ ▶ **n.** archaic term for **MONOCHROME**.

mon·o·tone /'mänəˌtōn/ ▶ **n.** [usu. in sing.] a continuing sound, esp. of someone's voice, that is unchanging in pitch and without intonation: *he sat and answered the questions* ***in a monotone.***
▶ **adj.** (of a voice or other sound) unchanging in pitch; without intonation or expressiveness: *his monotone reading of the two-hour report.* ■ without vividness or variety; dull: *the monotone housing developments of the big cities.*
– ORIGIN mid 17th cent.: from modern Latin *monotonus*, from late Greek *monotonos*.

mon·o·ton·ic /ˌmänə'tänik/ ▶ **adj.** **1** Mathematics (of a function or quantity) varying in such a way that it either never decreases or never increases.
2 speaking or uttered with an unchanging pitch or tone: *her dour, monotonic husband.*
– DERIVATIVES **mon·o·ton·i·cal·ly** /-ik(ə)lē/ **adv.**, **mon·o·to·nic·i·ty** /ˌmänətn'isətē/ **n.**

mo·not·o·nous /mə'nätn-əs/ ▶ **adj.** dull, tedious, and repetitious; lacking in variety and interest: *the statistics that he quotes with monotonous regularity.* ■ (of a sound or utterance) lacking in variation in tone or pitch: *soon we heard a low, monotonous wailing of many voices.*
– DERIVATIVES **mo·not·o·nous·ly** **adv.**

mo·not·o·ny /mə'nätn-ē/ ▶ **n.** lack of variety and interest; tedious repetition and routine: *you can become resigned to the* ***monotony of*** *captivity.* ■ sameness of pitch or tone in a sound or utterance: *depression flattens the voice almost to monotony.*

mon·o·treme /'mänəˌtrēm/ ▶ **n.** Zoology a primitive mammal that lays large yolky eggs and has a common opening for the urogenital and digestive systems. Monotremes are now restricted to Australia and New Guinea, and comprise the platypus and the echidnas. ● Order Monotremata and subclass Prototheria: two families.
– ORIGIN mid 19th cent.: from **MONO-** 'single' + Greek *trēma* 'hole.'

mon·o·type /'mänəˌtīp/ ▶ **n.** **1** (**Monotype**) [usu. as modifier] Printing, trademark a typesetting machine, now little used, that casts type in metal, one character at a time.
2 a single print taken from a design created in oil paint or printing ink on glass or metal.

mon·o·typ·ic /ˌmänə'tipik/ ▶ **adj.** chiefly Biology having only one type or representative, esp. (of a genus) containing only one species.

mon·o·un·sat·u·rat·ed /ˌmänōˌən'saCHəˌrātid/ ▶ **adj.** Chemistry (of an organic compound, esp. a fat) saturated except for one multiple bond.

mon·o·va·lent /ˌmänə'vālənt/ ▶ **adj.** Chemistry having a valence of one.

mon·ox·ide /mə'näkˌsīd/ ▶ **n.** Chemistry an oxide containing one atom of oxygen in its molecule or empirical formula.

mon·o·zy·got·ic /ˌmänōˌzī'gätik/ (also **monozygous** /ˌmänə'zīgəs/) ▶ **adj.** (of twins) derived from a single ovum, and so identical.
– DERIVATIVES **mon·o·zy·gos·i·ty** /-'gäsitē/ **n.**
– ORIGIN early 20th cent.: from **MONO-** 'single' + **ZYGOTE** + **-IC**.

Mon·roe[1] /mən'rō/ an industrial and commercial city in north central Louisiana, in a natural gas producing area; pop. 51,215 (est. 2008).

Mon·roe[2], James (1758–1831), 5th president of the US 1817–25. In 1803, while minister to France under President Jefferson, he negotiated and ratified the Louisiana Purchase. During his presidency, the Adams-Onis Treaty 1819, which allowed the US to acquire Florida from Spain, was negotiated. A Democratic-Republican, he is chiefly remembered as the originator of the Monroe Doctrine.

James Monroe

Mon·roe[3], Marilyn (1926–62), US actress; born *Norma Jean Mortenson*; later *Norma Jean Baker*. Her movie roles, largely in comedies, made her the definitive Hollywood sex symbol. Notable movies: *Gentlemen Prefer Blondes* (1953), *Some Like it Hot* (1959), and *The Misfits* (1961).

Marilyn Monroe

Mon·roe Doc·trine /mən'rō/ a principle of US policy, originated by President James Monroe in 1823, that any intervention by external powers in the politics of the Americas is a potentially hostile act against the US.

Mon·ro·vi·a /mən'rōvēə/ the capital and chief port of Liberia; pop. 1,010,970 (2008). Founded in 1822 for resettled US slaves, it was later named for President James Monroe.

mons /mänz/ ▶ **n.** short for **MONS PUBIS**.

Mon·sei·gneur /ˌmôNsān'yər/ ▶ **n.** (pl. **Messeigneurs** /ˌmāsān'yər(z)/) a title or form of address used of or to a French-speaking prince, cardinal, archbishop, or bishop.
– ORIGIN French, from *mon* 'my' + *seigneur* 'lord.'

Mon·sieur /mə'syœ(r), mə'syər/ ▶ **n.** (pl. **Messieurs** /mə'syœ(r)(z), mā-, mə'syər(z)/) a title or form of address used of or to a French-speaking man, corresponding to *Mr.* or *sir*: *Monsieur Hulot | you are right, Monsieur.*
– ORIGIN French, from *mon* 'my' + *sieur* 'lord.'

Mon·si·gnor /män'sēnyər, mən-/ ▶ **n.** (pl. **Monsignors** or **Monsignori** /ˌmänsēn'yôrē/) the title of various senior Roman Catholic positions, such as a prelate or an officer of the papal court.
– ORIGIN Italian, on the pattern of French *Monseigneur*.

mon·soon /män'so͞on, 'mänˌso͞on/ ▶ **n.** a seasonal prevailing wind in the region of South and Southeast Asia, blowing from the southwest between May and September and bringing rain (the **wet monsoon**), or from the northeast between October and April (the **dry monsoon**). ■ the rainy season accompanying the wet monsoon.
– DERIVATIVES **mon·soon·al** /män'so͞onl/ **adj.**
– ORIGIN late 16th cent.: from Portuguese *monção*, from Arabic *mawsim* 'season,' from *wasama* 'to mark, brand.'

mons pu·bis /'mänz 'pyo͞obis/ ▶ **n.** (pl. **montes pubis** /'mäntēz/) the rounded mass of fatty tissue lying over the joint of the pubic bones, in women typically more prominent and also called the **mons veneris**.
– ORIGIN late 19th cent.: Latin, 'mount of the pubes.'

mon·ster /'mänstər/ ▶ **n.** an imaginary creature that is typically large, ugly, and frightening. ■ an

inhumanly cruel or wicked person: *he was an unfeeling, treacherous monster.* ■ often humorous a person, typically a child, who is rude or badly behaved: *Christopher is only a year old, but already he is a little monster.* ■ a thing or animal that is excessively or dauntingly large: *this is a monster of a book, almost 2,000 pages* | [as modifier] *a monster 120-mm gun.* ■ a congenitally malformed or mutant animal or plant.
▶ v. [with obj.] informal, chiefly Brit. criticize or reprimand severely: *my mother used to monster me for coming home so late.*
– ORIGIN late Middle English: from Old French *monstre*, from Latin *monstrum* 'portent or monster,' from *monere* 'warn.'

mon·ster·a /'mänstərə/ ▶ n. a large tropical American climbing plant of the arum family that typically has divided or perforated leaves and corky aerial roots. Several kinds are cultivated as indoor plants when young. ● Genus *Monstera*, family Araceae: several species.
– ORIGIN modern Latin, perhaps from Latin *monstrum* 'monster' (because of the unusual appearance of the leaves in some species).

mon·ster truck ▶ n. an extremely large pickup truck, typically with greatly oversized tires. They are often raced across rough terrain or featured in exhibitions in which they drive over and demolish smaller automobiles.

mon·strance /'mänstrəns/ ▶ n. (in the Roman Catholic Church) an open or transparent receptacle in which the consecrated Host is exposed for veneration.
– ORIGIN late Middle English (also in the sense 'demonstration or proof'): from medieval Latin *monstrantia*, from Latin *monstrare* 'to show.'

mon·stros·i·ty /män'sträsətē/ ▶ n. (pl. **monstrosities**) **1** something, esp. a building, that is very large and is considered unsightly: *the shopping center, a multistory monstrosity of raw concrete.* ■ something that is outrageously or offensively wrong: *how could anyone be capable of such monstrosities?* ■ a grossly malformed animal, plant, or person.
2 the state or fact of being monstrous.
– ORIGIN mid 16th cent. (denoting an abnormality of growth): from late Latin *monstrositas*, from Latin *monstrosus* (see MONSTROUS).

mon·strous /'mänstrəs/ ▶ adj. having the ugly or frightening appearance of a monster: *monstrous, bug-eyed fish.* ■ (of a person or an action) inhumanly or outrageously evil or wrong: *he wasn't lovable, he was monstrous and violent* | *it is a monstrous waste of money.* ■ extremely and dauntingly large: *the monstrous tidal wave swamped the surrounding countryside.*
– DERIVATIVES **mon·strous·ly** adv., **mon·strous·ness** n.
– ORIGIN late Middle English (in the sense 'strange or unnatural'): from Old French *monstreux* or Latin *monstrosus*, from *monstrum* (see MONSTER). Current senses date from the 16th cent.

mons ve·ne·ris /'mänz 'venərəs/ ▶ n. (pl. **montes veneris** /'mäntēz/) (in women) the mons pubis.
– ORIGIN late 17th cent.: Latin, 'mount of Venus.'

Mont. ▶ abbr. Montana.

mon·tage /män'täZH, mōn-, mōN-/ ▶ n. the process or technique of selecting, editing, and piecing together separate sections of film to form a continuous whole. ■ a sequence of film resulting from this: *a dazzling montage of the movie's central banquet scene.* ■ the technique of producing a new composite whole from fragments of pictures, text, or music: *the play often verged on montage.*
– ORIGIN early 20th cent.: French, from *monter* 'to mount.'

Mon·ta·gnais /,mäntən'yā/ ▶ n. (pl. **same**) **1** a member of an American Indian people living in a vast area of Canada from north of the Gulf of St. Lawrence to the southern shores of Hudson Bay.
2 the Algonquian language of this people, closely related to Cree.
▶ adj. of or relating to this people or their language.
– ORIGIN from French, literally 'of the mountains.'

Mon·ta·gnard /,mäntən'yärd/ ▶ n. a member of any of various hill-dwelling people of Southeast Asia, esp. those inhabiting the highlands of Vietnam.
▶ adj. of or relating to this people or their language.
– ORIGIN French, from *montagne* 'mountain.'

Mon·taigne /män'tān, môn'tenyə/, Michel (Eyquem) de (1533–92), French essayist. Widely regarded as the originator of the modern essay, he wrote about prominent personalities and ideas of his age in his skeptical *Essays* (1580 and 1588).

Mon·tan·a[1] /män'tanə/ a state in the western US, on the Canadian border, east of the Rocky Mountains; pop. 967,440 (est. 2008); capital, Helena; statehood, Nov. 8, 1889 (41). Acquired from France as part of the Louisiana Purchase in 1803, it was explored by Lewis and Clark in 1805–06.
– DERIVATIVES **Mon·tan·an** adj. & n.

Mon·tan·a[2] /män'tanə/, Joe (1956–), US football player. He joined the San Francisco 49ers as quarterback in 1980 and played in four winning Super Bowls (1982, 1985, 1989, 1990). He retired in 1995 after two seasons with the Kansas City Chiefs. Football Hall of Fame (2000).

mon·tane /män'tān, 'män,tān/ ▶ adj. [attrib.] of or inhabiting mountainous country: *montane grasslands.*
– ORIGIN mid 19th cent.: from Latin *montanus*, from *mons, mont-* 'mountain.'

Mon·ta·nism /'mäntə,nizəm/ ▶ n. the tenets of a heretical millenarian and ascetic Christian sect that set great store by prophecy, founded in Phrygia by the priest Montanus in the middle of the 2nd century.
– DERIVATIVES **Mon·ta·nist** n.

Mont Blanc /,môN 'bläNGk/ a mountain in the Alps on the border between France and Italy that is 15,771 feet (4,807 m) high. It is the highest peak in the Alps and in western Europe.

mont·bre·tia /mänt'brēSH(ē)ə/ ▶ n. a plant of the iris family with bright orange-yellow trumpet-shaped flowers. ● *Crocosmia* × crocosmiflora, family Iridaceae.
– ORIGIN late 19th cent.: modern Latin, named after A. F. E. Coquebert de *Montbret* (1780–1801), French botanist.

Mont·calm /,mänt'käm/, Louis Joseph de Montcalm-Gozon, Marquis de (1712–59), French general. He defended Quebec against British troops, but was defeated and fatally wounded in the battle on the Plains of Abraham.

Mont Cer·vin /,môN sər'ven/ French name for MATTERHORN.

mon·te /'mäntē/ ▶ n. **1** short for THREE-CARD MONTE.
2 a Spanish game of chance, played with forty-five cards.
– ORIGIN early 19th cent.: Spanish, literally 'mountain,' also 'heap of cards left after dealing' (from an earlier game of chance played with forty-five cards).

Mon·te Al·bán /'môntā äl'bän/ an ancient city, now in ruins, in Oaxaca, southern Mexico. Occupied from the 8th century BC, it was a center of the Zapotec culture from about the 1st century BC to the 8th century AD.

Mon·te Car·lo /,mäntē 'kärlō/ a resort in Monaco that forms one of the four communes of the principality; pop. 14,600 (est. 2008). It is famous as a gambling resort and as the terminus of the annual Monte Carlo automobile rally.

Mon·te Car·lo meth·od ▶ n. Statistics a technique in which a large quantity of randomly generated numbers are studied using a probabilistic model to find an approximate solution to a numerical problem that would be difficult to solve by other methods.
– ORIGIN 1940s: named after *Monte Carlo* (see MONTE CARLO), a resort famous for its gambling casino.

Mon·te Cas·si·no /,mäntē kə'sēnō/ a hill in central Italy near the town of Cassino, the site of the principal monastery of the Benedictines, founded by St. Benedict *c.*529. The monastery and the town were destroyed in 1944 during bitter fighting between Allied and German forces, but have since been restored.

Mon·te Cer·vi·no /,môntā CHər'vēnō/ Italian name for MATTERHORN.

Mon·te·go Bay /mən'tēgō/ a free port and tourist resort on the northern coast of Jamaica; pop. 80,400 (est. 2009).

Mon·te·ne·gro /,mäntə'negrō/ a mountainous, landlocked republic in the Balkans, formerly part of Yugoslavia; pop. 672,200 (est. 2009); capital, Podgorica. Joined with Serbia before the Turkish conquest of 1355, Montenegro became independent in 1851. In 1918, it became part of the federation of Yugoslavia. On the breakup of Yugoslavia in 1992, it formed a federation with Serbia, but voted in 2006 to become independent.
– DERIVATIVES **Mon·te·ne·grin** /-'negrən/ adj. & n.

Mon·te·rey /,mäntə'rā, 'mäntə,rā/ a city and fishing port on the coast of California, founded by the Spanish in the 18th century; pop. 27,763 (est. 2008).

Mon·te·rey cy·press ▶ n. a cypress tree with a large spreading crown of horizontal branches and leaves that smell of lemon when crushed, native to a small area of California and widely planted in temperate climates worldwide. Also called MACROCARPA. ● *Cupressus macrocarpa*, family Cupressaceae.

Mon·te·rey Jack (also **Monterey cheese** or **Jack cheese**) ▶ n. a kind of cheese resembling cheddar.
– ORIGIN from the name of *Monterey* County, California, where it was first made; the origin of *Jack* is unknown.

Mon·ter·rey /,mäntə'rā/ an industrial city in northeastern Mexico, capital of the state of Nuevo León; pop. 1,133,070 (2005).

Mon·tes·pan /'mäntə,span, môNtes'päN/, Françoise-Athénaïs de Rochechouart, Marquise de (1641–1707), French noblewoman. The mistress of Louis XIV from 1667 to 1679, she had seven children by him. She was replaced in the king's affections by Madame de Maintenon, the children's governess.

Mon·tes·quieu /,mänti'skyoo, môNtes'kyœ/, Charles Louis de Secondat, Baron de La Brède et de (1689–1755), French political philosopher. He is best known for *L'Esprit des lois* (1748), a comparative study of political systems in which he championed the separation of judicial, legislative, and executive powers as being most conducive to individual liberty.

Mon·tes·so·ri[1] /,mäntə'sôrē/, Maria (1870–1952), Italian educator. In her book, *The Montessori Method* (1909), she advocated a child-centered approach to education, developed from her success with mentally handicapped children.

Mon·tes·so·ri[2] ▶ n. [usu. as modifier] a system of education for young children that seeks to develop natural interests and activities rather than use formal teaching methods: *a Montessori school.*
– ORIGIN early 20th cent.: named after M. *Montessori* (see MONTESSORI[1]).

Mon·te·ver·di /,mäntə'verdē, ,mônte-/, Claudio (1567–1643), Italian composer. He is noted for the use of harmonic dissonance in his madrigals. He wrote the opera *Orfeo* (1607) and *Vespers* (1610).

Mon·te·vi·de·o /,mäntəvi'dāō/ the capital and chief port of Uruguay, on the Plate River; pop. 1,513,000 (est. 2007).

Mon·tez /'mäntez, män'tez/, Lola (1818–61), Irish dancer; born *Marie Dolores Eliza Rosanna Gilbert*. She became the mistress of Ludwig I of Bavaria in 1846 and exercised great influence over him until she was banished the following year.

Mon·te·zu·ma II /,mänti'zoomə/ (1466–1520), Aztec emperor 1502–20. The last ruler of the Aztec empire in Mexico, he was defeated and imprisoned by the Spanish under Cortés in 1519.

Mon·te·zu·ma's re·venge ▶ n. informal diarrhea suffered by travelers, esp. visitors to Mexico.

Mont·fort[1] /'mäntfərt, môN'fôr/, Simon de (*c.*1165–1218), French soldier; father of Simon de Montfort, Earl of Leicester. From 1209, he led the Albigensian Crusade against the Cathars in southern France.

Mont·fort[2], Simon de, Earl of Leicester (*c.*1208–65), English soldier, born in Normandy. The son of Simon de Montfort, he led the baronial opposition to Henry III, defeating the king at Lewes in 1264 and summoning a Parliament in 1265.

Mont·gol·fi·er /mänt'gälfēər, môNgôl'fyā/, Joseph Michel (1740–1810) and Jacques Étienne (1745–99), French inventors and pioneers in hot-air ballooning.

Mont·gom·er·y[1] /mənt'gəm(ə)rē/ the state capital of Alabama; pop. 202,696 (est. 2008). It served as the capital of the Confederate States of America from February until July during 1861.

Mont·gom·er·y[2], Bernard Law, 1st Viscount Montgomery of Alamein (1887–1976), British field marshal; known as **Monty**. His victory at El Alamein in 1942 was the first significant Allied success in World War II. He commanded the Allied ground forces in the invasion of Normandy in 1944 and accepted the German surrender on May 7, 1945.

Mont·gom·er·y[3], L. M. (1874–1942), Canadian novelist; full name *Lucy Maud Montgomery*. She is noted for *Anne of Green Gables* (1908) and its sequels, set on Prince Edward Island.

Mont·gom·ery Coun·ty a county in central Maryland that contains many suburbs north of Washington, DC; pop. 950,680 (est. 2008).

month /mənTH/ ▶ n. (also **calendar month**) each of the twelve named periods into which a year is divided: *the first six months of 1992* | *it was the end of the month.* ■ a period of time between the same dates in successive calendar months: *the president's rule was extended for six more months from March 3.* ■ a period of 28 days or four weeks: *the fourth month of pregnancy.*

– PHRASES **a month of Sundays** informal a very long, seemingly endless period of time: *no one will find them in a month of Sundays.*
– ORIGIN Old English *mōnath*, of Germanic origin; related to Dutch *maand* and German *Monat*, also to MOON.

month-long (also **monthlong**) ▶ **adj.** [attrib.] of a month's duration: *a month-long fishing trip.*

month·ly /ˈmənTHlē/ ▶ **adj.** [attrib.] done, produced, or occurring once a month: *the council held monthly meetings.*
▶ **adv.** once a month; every month; from month to month: *most of us get paid monthly.*
▶ **n.** (pl. **monthlies**) **1** a magazine that is published once a month.
2 (**monthlies**) informal a menstrual period.

Mon·ti·cel·lo /ˌmäntəˈselō/ a historic estate southeast of Charlottesville, in central Virginia, the home of Thomas Jefferson.

Monticello

mon·ti·cule /ˈmäntiˌkyo͞ol/ ▶ **n.** a small hill. ■ a small mound caused by a volcanic eruption.
– ORIGIN late 18th cent.: from French, from late Latin *monticulus*, diminutive of *mons*, *mont-* 'mountain.'

Mont·mar·tre /môNˈmärtrə/ a district in northern Paris, on a hill above the Seine River, much frequented by artists in the late 19th and early 20th centuries when it was a separate village.

mont·mo·ril·lon·ite /ˌmäntməˈrilәˌnīt/ ▶ **n.** an aluminum-rich clay mineral of the smectite group, containing some sodium and magnesium.
– ORIGIN mid 19th cent.: from *Montmorillon*, the name of a town in France, + -ITE[1].

Mont·par·nasse /ˌmôNpärˈnäs/ a district of Paris, on the left bank of the Seine River. Frequented in the late 19th century by writers and artists, it is traditionally associated with Parisian cultural life.

Mont·pe·lier /mäntˈpēlyər/ the capital of Vermont, in the north central part of the state, on the Winooski River; pop. 7,760 (est. 2008).

Mont·pel·lier /ˌmôNpelˈyā/ a city in southern France, near the Mediterranean coast, capital of Languedoc-Roussillon; pop. 254,974 (2006). A medical school and university, world famous in medieval times, was founded here in 1221.

Mon·tra·chet /ˌmôNträˈSHe/ ▶ **n.** a white wine produced in the Montrachet region of France.

Mont·re·al /ˌmäntrēˈôl/ a port on the St. Lawrence River in Quebec, southeastern Canada; pop. 1,162,693 (2006). Founded in 1642, it was under French rule until 1763; almost two thirds of its present-day population are French-speaking. French name **Montréal**.

Mont St. Mi·chel /ˈmôN saN mēˈsHel/, a rocky islet off the coast of Normandy, northwestern France. An island only at high tide, it is surrounded by sandbanks and linked to the mainland by a causeway. It is home to a medieval Benedictine abbey-fortress.

Mont·ser·rat /ˌmäntsəˈrät/ an island in the Caribbean, one of the Leeward Islands; pop. 5,100 (est. 2009); capital, Plymouth. It was visited by Columbus in 1493 and named after a Benedictine monastery on the mountain of Montserrat in Catalonia, northeastern Spain. Colonized by Irish settlers in 1632 and now a British overseas territory, it has been severely affected by the ongoing eruption of the Soufrière Hills volcano since 1995.
– DERIVATIVES **Mont·ser·ra·ti·an** /-ˈrātēən/ **adj. & n.**
– ORIGIN visited by Columbus in 1493, the island was named after a Benedictine monastery on the mountain of *Montserrat* in Catalonia in northeastern Spain.

mon·tu·no /mänˈto͞onō/ ▶ **n.** (pl. **montunos**) an improvised passage in a rumba.
– ORIGIN mid 20th cent.: American Spanish, 'native to mountains, wild.'

mon·ty /ˈmäntē/ ▶ **n.** (in phrase **the full monty**) Brit. informal the full amount expected, desired, or possible: *they'll do the full monty for a few thousand each.*
– ORIGIN of unknown origin; the phrase is only recorded recently. Among various (unsubstantiated) theories, one cites the phrase *the full Montague Burton*, apparently meaning 'Sunday-best three-piece suit' (from the name of a tailor of made-to-measure clothing in the early 20th cent.); another recounts the possibility of a military usage, *the full monty* being 'the full cooked English breakfast' insisted upon by Field Marshal *Montgomery*.

mon·u·ment /ˈmänyəmənt/ ▶ **n.** a statue, building, or other structure erected to commemorate a famous or notable person or event. ■ a statue or other structure placed by or over a grave in memory of the dead. ■ a building, structure, or site that is of historical importance or interest: *the amphitheater is one of the many Greek monuments in Sicily.* ■ an outstanding, enduring, and memorable example of something: *recordings that are a* ***monument to*** *the art of playing the piano.*
– ORIGIN Middle English (denoting a burial place): via French from Latin *monumentum*, from *monere* 'remind.'

mon·u·men·tal /ˌmänyəˈmentl/ ▶ **adj.** great in importance, extent, or size: *it's been a monumental effort* | *the ballet came across as one of MacMillan's most monumental works.* ■ of or serving as a monument: *additional details are found in monumental inscriptions.*
– DERIVATIVES **mon·u·men·tal·ism** **n.**, **mon·u·men·tal·i·ty** /ˌmänyəˌmenˈtalətē/ **n.**, **mon·u·men·tal·ly** /-ˈmentl-ē/ **adv.**

mon·u·men·tal·ize /ˌmänyəˈmentlˌīz/ ▶ **v.** [with obj.] make a permanent record of (something) by or as if by creating a monument: *a culture that too eagerly monumentalizes what it values.*

Mon·u·ment Val·ley a region in northeastern Arizona and southern Utah, west of the Four Corners, whose scenery has been the backdrop for many movies.

-mony ▶ **suffix** forming nouns often denoting an action, state, or quality: *ceremony* | *harmony.*
– ORIGIN from Latin *-monia*, *-monium*.

mon·zo·nite /ˈmänzəˌnīt/ ▶ **n.** Geology a granular igneous rock with a composition intermediate between syenite and diorite, containing approximately equal amounts of orthoclase and plagioclase.
– DERIVATIVES **mon·zo·nit·ic** /ˌmänzəˈnitik/ **adj.**
– ORIGIN late 19th cent.: named after Mount *Monzoni* in the Tyrol, Italy, + -ITE[1].

moo /mo͞o/ ▶ **v.** (**moos, mooing, mooed**) [no obj.] make the characteristic deep vocal sound of a cow.
▶ **n.** (pl. **moos**) a sound of this kind.
– ORIGIN mid 16th cent.: imitative.

mooch /mo͞oCH/ ▶ **v.** informal **1** [with obj.] ask for or obtain (something) without paying for it: *a bunch of your friends will show up, mooching food* | [no obj.] *I'm mooching off you all the time.*
2 [no obj.] (**mooch around/about**) loiter in a bored or listless manner: *he didn't want them mooching around all day.*
▶ **n.** (also **moocher**) a beggar or scrounger: *the mooch who got everything from his dad.*
– ORIGIN late Middle English (in the sense 'to hoard'): probably from Anglo-Norman French *muscher* 'hide, skulk.' A dialect sense 'play truant' dates from the early 16th cent.; current senses date from the mid 19th cent.

moo-cow ▶ **n.** a child's name for a cow.

mood[1] /mo͞od/ ▶ **n.** a temporary state of mind or feeling: *he appeared to be in a very good mood about something.* ■ an angry, irritable, or sullen state of mind: *he was obviously* ***in a mood.*** ■ the atmosphere or pervading tone of something, esp. a work of art: *Monet's "Mornings on the Seine" series, with their hushed and delicate mood.*
▶ **adj.** [attrib.] (esp. of music) inducing or suggestive of a particular feeling or state of mind: *mood music* | *a Chekhov mood piece.*
– PHRASES **in the mood for** (or **to do**) **something** feeling like doing or experiencing something: *if you're in the mood for an extra thrill, you can go paragliding.* **in no mood for** (or **to do**) **something** not wanting to do or experience something: *she was in no mood for sightseeing.*
– ORIGIN Old English *mōd* (also in the senses 'mind' and 'fierce courage'), of Germanic origin; related to Dutch *moed* and German *Mut*.

mood[2] ▶ **n. 1** Grammar a category or form that indicates whether a verb expresses fact (indicative mood), command (imperative mood), question (interrogative mood), wish (optative mood), or conditionality (subjunctive mood).
2 Logic any of the valid forms into which each of the figures of a categorical syllogism may occur.
– ORIGIN mid 16th cent.: variant of MODE, influenced by MOOD[1].

mood-al·ter·ing ▶ **adj.** (of a drug) capable of inducing changes of mood.

mood swing ▶ **n.** an abrupt and apparently unaccountable change of mood.

Moo·dy /ˈmo͞odē/, William Henry (1853–1917), US Supreme Court associate justice 1906–10. He was the US attorney general 1904–06 before he was appointed to the Court by President Theodore Roosevelt.

mood·y /ˈmo͞odē/ ▶ **adj.** (**moodier, moodiest**) (of a person) given to unpredictable changes of mood, esp. sudden bouts of gloominess or sullenness: *she met his moody adolescent brother.* ■ giving an impression of melancholy or mystery: *grainy film that gives a soft, moody effect.*
– DERIVATIVES **mood·i·ly** /ˈmo͞odl-ē/ **adv.**, **mood·i·ness** **n.**
– ORIGIN Old English *mōdig* 'brave or willful' (see MOOD[1], -Y[1]).

mook /mo͝ok/ ▶ **n.** informal a stupid or incompetent person.
– ORIGIN 1930s: of uncertain origin.

moo·la /ˈmo͞oˌlä/ (also **moolah**) ▶ **n.** informal money.

Moon /mo͞on/, Sun Myung (1920–), Korean industrialist and religious leader. In 1954, he founded the Holy Spirit Association for the Unification of World Christianity, which became known as the Unification Church. Disciples are called "Moonies."

moon /mo͞on/ ▶ **n.** (also **Moon**) the natural satellite of the earth, visible (chiefly at night) by reflected light from the sun. ■ a natural satellite of any planet. ■ literary or humorous a month: *many moons had passed since he brought a prospective investor home.* ■ (**the moon**) anything that one could desire: *you must know he'd give any of us the moon.*

> The earth's moon orbits the earth in a period of 29.5 days, going through a series of phases from new moon to full moon and back again during that time. Its average distance from the earth is some 239,000 miles (384,000 km) and it is 2,160 miles (3,476 km) in diameter. The bright and dark features that outline the face of "the man in the moon" are highland and lowland regions, the high regions being heavily pockmarked by craters due to the impact of meteorites. The moon has no atmosphere, and the same side is always presented to the earth.

▶ **v. 1** [no obj.] behave or move in a listless and aimless manner: *lying in bed eating candy, mooning around.* ■ act in a dreamily infatuated manner: *Timothy's* ***mooning over*** *her like a schoolboy.*
2 [with obj.] informal expose one's buttocks to (someone) in order to insult or amuse them: *Dan had whipped around, bent over, and mooned the crowd.*
– PHRASES **many moons ago** informal a long time ago. **over the moon** informal extremely happy; delighted. [from *the cow jumped over the moon*, a line from a nursery rhyme.]
– DERIVATIVES **moon·less** **adj.**, **moon·like** /-ˌlīk/ **adj.**
– ORIGIN Old English *mōna*, of Germanic origin; related to Dutch *maan* and German *Mond*, also to MONTH, from an Indo-European root shared by Latin *mensis* and Greek *mēn* 'month,' and also Latin *metiri* 'to measure' (the moon being used to measure time).

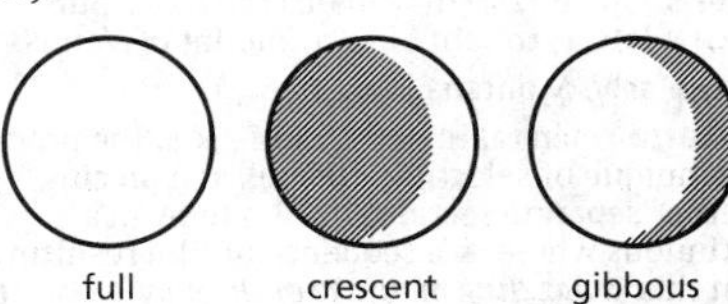
full crescent gibbous
phases of the moon

moon·beam /ˈmo͞onˌbēm/ ▶ **n.** a ray of moonlight.

moon blind·ness ▶ **n.** (in horses) a recurrent inflammatory disease of the eyes, causing intermittent blindness.
– DERIVATIVES **moon-blind** **adj.**

moon boot ▶ **n.** a warm, thickly padded boot with an outer surface of fabric or plastic.

moon bug·gy ▶ **n.** informal term for LUNAR ROVING VEHICLE.

moon·calf /ˈmo͞onˌkaf/ ▶ **n.** (pl. **mooncalves**) a foolish person.
– ORIGIN mid 16th cent.: from MOON + CALF[1], perhaps on the pattern of German *Mondkalb*. Originally in the sense 'shapeless mass in the womb,' thought to be produced by the influence of the moon.

moon child ▶ **n.** a person born under the astrological sign of Cancer.

moon dog (also **moondog**) ▶ **n.** informal term for PARASELENE.

moon·eye /ˈmo͞onˌī/ ▶ **n.** a herringlike freshwater fish with large eyes, found exclusively in central and eastern North America. ● Genus *Hiodon*, family Hiodontidae: two species, the **goldeye** (*H. alosoides*) and the larger-eyed **mooneye** (*H. tergisus*).

moon-faced ▶ **adj.** having a round face.

Moon Fes·ti·val ▶ **n.** a Chinese festival held in the middle of the autumn.

moon·fish /ˈmo͞onˌfisн/ ▶ **n.** (pl. **same** or **moonfishes**) a deep-bodied laterally compressed marine fish, in particular: ● a silvery fish of the jack family (Carangidae), including *Selene setapinnis* of the Atlantic. ● an opah.

moon·flow·er /ˈmo͞onˌflou(-ə)r/ ▶ **n.** a tropical American climbing plant of the morning glory family, with large, sweet-smelling white flowers that open at dusk and close at midday. ● *Ipomoea alba*, family Convolvulaceae.

moon gate (also **moongate**) ▶ **n.** (in China) a circular gateway in a wall.

Moon·ie /ˈmo͞onē/ ▶ **n.** often offensive a member of the Unification Church.
– ORIGIN 1970s: from the name of its founder, Sun Myung *Moon*.

moon·let /ˈmo͞onlət/ ▶ **n.** a small moon. ■ an artificial satellite.

moon·light /ˈmo͞onˌlīt/ ▶ **n.** the light of the moon: *I wanted you to see the courtyard by moonlight* | [as modifier] *a moonlight stroll.*
▶ **v.** (past and past participle **moonlighted**) [no obj.] informal have a second job in addition to one's regular employment: *many instructors moonlight as professional consultants.*
– DERIVATIVES **moon·light·er n.**

moon·lit /ˈmo͞onˌlit/ ▶ **adj.** lit by the moon.

moon pool ▶ **n.** a shaft through the bottom of a drilling ship, oil rig, etc., for lowering and raising equipment into or from the water.

moon·quake /ˈmo͞onˌkwāk/ ▶ **n.** a tremor of the moon's surface.

moon·rat /ˈmo͞onˌrat/ ▶ **n.** a shy insectivorous mammal of the hedgehog family, with a long snout and ratlike appearance, native to Southeast Asia and China. Also called **GYMNURE**. ● Subfamily Galericinae, family Erinaceidae: several genera and species, in particular *Echinosorex gymnurus.*

moon·rise /ˈmo͞onˌrīz/ ▶ **n.** [in sing.] the rising of the moon above the horizon. ■ the time of this: *it was actually about an hour after moonrise.*

moon·roof /ˈmo͞onˌro͞of, -ˌro͝of/ ▶ **n.** a transparent section of the roof of an automobile, typically tinted and able to be opened.

moon·scape /ˈmo͞onˌskāp/ ▶ **n.** a landscape having features characteristic of the surface of the moon, esp. in being rocky and barren: *regrowth on the once-barren moonscape around Mount St. Helens.*

moon·seed /ˈmo͞onˌsēd/ ▶ **n.** a North American climbing plant with crescent-shaped seeds. ● Genus *Menispermum*, family Menispermaceae: several species, in particular **Canada moonseed** (*M. canadense*).

moon·set /ˈmo͞onˌset/ ▶ **n.** [in sing.] the setting of the moon below the horizon: *I'm greeted with a spectacular moonset.* ■ the time of this: *we left before moonset in the morning.*

moon-shaped ▶ **adj.** **1** crescent-shaped: *blood cells that instead of being round are moon-shaped.* **2** round: *her moon-shaped face.*

moon·shine /ˈmo͞onˌsнīn/ ▶ **n.** **1** informal illicitly distilled or smuggled liquor.
2 foolish talk or ideas: *whatever I said, it was moonshine.*
3 another term for **MOONLIGHT**.

moon·shin·er /ˈmo͞onˌsнīnər/ ▶ **n.** informal an illicit distiller or smuggler of liquor.

moon shot (also **moonshot**) ▶ **n.** the launching of a spacecraft to the moon.

moon snail (also **moon shell**) ▶ **n.** a marine mollusk with a shiny, almost spherical, shell and a large foot. ● Family Naticidae, class Gastropoda: *Natica* and other genera.

moon·stone /ˈmo͞onˌstōn/ ▶ **n.** a pearly white semiprecious stone consisting of alkali feldspar.

moon·struck /ˈmo͞onˌstrək/ ▶ **adj.** unable to think or act normally, esp. because of being in love.
– ORIGIN late 17th cent.: from **MOON** + *struck*, past participle of **STRIKE**; because it was believed that the moon could affect the mind.

moon·walk /ˈmo͞onˌwôk/ ▶ **n.** **1** an act of walking on the surface of the moon.
2 a dance with a gliding motion, in which the dancer appears to be moving forward but in fact is moving backwards.
▶ **v.** [no obj.] **1** walk on the surface of the moon.
2 dance a moonwalk.
– DERIVATIVES **moon·walk·er n.**

moon·wort /ˈmo͞onˌwərt, -ˌwôrt/ ▶ **n.** a widely distributed fern with a single small frond of fan-shaped lobes and a separate spike bearing the spore-producing organs, growing typically in grassy uplands and old meadows. ● Genus *Botrychium*, family Ophioglossaceae: several species, in particular the rare *B. lunaria.*

moon·y /ˈmo͞onē/ ▶ **adj.** (**moonier, mooniest**) dreamy and unaware of one's surroundings, for example because one is in love: *she's not drunk, but still smiling in the same moony way* | *little girls go moony over horses.*

Moor /mo͝or/ ▶ **n.** a member of a northwestern African Muslim people of mixed Berber and Arab descent. In the 8th century they conquered the Iberian peninsula, but were finally driven out of their last stronghold in Granada at the end of the 15th century.
– DERIVATIVES **Moor·ish adj.**
– ORIGIN from Old French *More*, via Latin from Greek *Mauros* 'inhabitant of Mauretania.'

moor[1] /mo͝or/ ▶ **n.** a tract of open uncultivated upland; a heath. ■ a tract of such land preserved for shooting: *a grouse moor.* ■ a fen.
– DERIVATIVES **moor·ish adj., moor·y adj.**
– ORIGIN Old English *mōr*, of Germanic origin.

moor[2] ▶ **v.** [with obj.] make fast (a vessel) to the shore or to an anchor: *twenty or so fishing boats were moored to the pier.* ■ [no obj.] (of a boat) be made fast somewhere in this way: *we moored alongside a jetty.*
– DERIVATIVES **moor·age** /ˈmo͝orij/ **n.**
– ORIGIN late 15th cent.: probably from the Germanic base of Dutch *meren*.

moor·cock /ˈmo͝orˌkäk/ ▶ **n.** Brit. a male red grouse.

Moore[1] /mo͝or/ a city in central Oklahoma, a southern suburb of Oklahoma City; pop. 52,615 (est. 2008).

Moore[2], Alfred (1755–1810), US Supreme Court associate justice 1799–1804. A native of North Carolina, he was appointed to the Court by President John Adams.

Moore[3], Clement (Clarke) (1779–1863), US writer. He is best known for his poem "A Visit from St. Nicholas" (1822), which was published anonymously.

Moore[4], G. E. (1873–1958), English moral philosopher and member of the Bloomsbury Group; full name *George Edward Moore.*

Moore[5], Henry (Spencer) (1898–1986), English sculptor and draftsman. His work is characterized by semiabstract reclining forms, large upright figures, and family groups, which Moore intended to be viewed in the open air.

Moore[6], Marianne (Craig) (1887–1972), US poet. Her work is collected in *The Complete Poems of Marianne Moore* (1967).

Moore[7], Thomas (1779–1852), Irish poet and musician. He wrote patriotic and nostalgic songs set to Irish tunes.

moor·fowl /ˈmo͝orˌfoul/ ▶ **n.** (pl. **same**) Brit. another term for **RED GROUSE**.

Moor·head /ˈmo͝orˌhed/ a commercial city in western Minnesota, a transportation hub across the Red River of the North from Fargo in North Dakota; pop. 36,012 (est. 2008).

moor·hen /ˈmo͝orˌhen/ ▶ **n.** **1** a small aquatic rail with mainly blackish plumage. ● Family Rallidae: two genera and four species, in particular the widespread common gallinule (*Gallinula chloropus*), with a red and yellow bill.
2 Brit. a female red grouse.

moor·ing /ˈmo͝oriNG/ ▶ **n.** (often **moorings**) a place where a boat or ship is moored: *the boat had been at its usual moorings immediately prior to the storm.* ■ the ropes, chains, or anchors by or to which a boat, ship, or buoy is moored: *the great ship slipped its moorings and slid out into the Atlantic* | figurative *the little ways in which those who grieve regain their moorings.*

moor·land /ˈmo͝o(ə)rlənd, -ˌland/ ▶ **n.** (also **moorlands**) an extensive area of moor.

moose /mo͞os/ ▶ **n.** (pl. **same**) a large deer with palmate antlers, a sloping back, and a growth of skin hanging from the neck. It is native to northern Eurasia and northern North America. Also called **ELK** in Britain. ● *Alces alces*, family Cervidae.
– ORIGIN early 17th cent.: from an Eastern Algonquian language; compare Narragansett *moòs.*

moose

moose·burg·er /ˈmo͞osˌbərgər/ ▶ **n.** a burger containing moose meat. ■ ground moose meat for use in burgers or other dishes.

Moose·head Lake /ˈmo͞osˌhed/ the largest lake in Maine, in the west central part of the state.

moose milk ▶ **n.** Canadian an alcoholic drink consisting typically of rum, milk, and other ingredients such as eggs. ■ homemade liquor.

moose pas·ture ▶ **n.** Canadian land of no value.

moose·wood /ˈmo͞osˌwo͝od/ ▶ **n.** another term for **STRIPED MAPLE**.

moot /mo͞ot/ ▶ **adj.** subject to debate, dispute, or uncertainty, and typically not admitting of a final decision: *whether the temperature rise was mainly due to the greenhouse effect was **a moot point**.* ■ having no practical significance, typically because the subject is too uncertain to allow a decision: *it is moot whether this phrase should be treated as metaphor or not.*
▶ **v.** [with obj.] (usu. **be mooted**) raise (a question or topic) for discussion; suggest (an idea or possibility): *Sylvia needed a vacation, and a trip to Ireland had been mooted.*
▶ **n.** **1** Brit. an assembly held for debate, esp. in Anglo-Saxon and medieval times. ■ a regular gathering of people having a common interest.
2 Law a mock trial set up to examine a hypothetical case as an academic exercise.
– ORIGIN Old English *mōt* 'assembly or meeting' and *mōtian* 'to converse,' of Germanic origin; related to **MEET**[1]. The adjective (originally an attributive noun use: see **MOOT COURT**) dates from the mid 16th cent.; the current verb sense dates from the mid 17th cent.

> **USAGE** Note that a question subject to debate or dispute is a **moot point**, not a **mute point.** As **moot** is a relatively uncommon word, people sometimes mistakenly interpret it as the more familar word **mute.**

moot court ▶ **n.** a mock court at which law students argue imaginary cases for practice.

mop /mäp/ ▶ **n.** an implement consisting of a sponge or a bundle of thick loose strings attached to a handle, used for wiping floors or other surfaces. ■ a thick mass of disordered hair: *her tousled mop of blonde hair.* ■ [in sing.] an act of wiping something clean, esp. a floor: *the kitchen needed a quick mop.*
▶ **v.** (**mops, mopping, mopped**) [with obj.] clean or soak up (something) by wiping: *he was mopping his plate with a piece of bread.* ■ wipe (something) away from a surface: *a barmaid rushed forward to **mop up** the spilled beer.* ■ wipe sweat or tears from (one's face or eyes): *he pulled a handkerchief from his pocket to **mop his brow**.*
– PHRASAL VERBS **mop something up** (also **mop up**) complete the military conquest of an area by capturing or killing remaining enemy troops: *troops mopped up the last pockets of resistance.*
– DERIVATIVES **mop·py adj.**
– ORIGIN late 15th cent.: perhaps ultimately related to Latin *mappa* 'napkin.'

mop·board /ˈmäpˌbôrd/ ▶ **n.** another term for **BASEBOARD**.

mope /mōp/ ▶ **v.** [no obj.] be dejected and apathetic: *no use moping—things could be worse.* ■ (**mope around/about**) wander around listlessly and aimlessly because of unhappiness or boredom: *moping around at home won't get you anywhere.*
▶ **n.** a person given to prolonged spells of low spirits: *they're just a bunch of mopes.* ■ (**mopes**) dated low spirits; depression.
– DERIVATIVES **mop·er n., mop·ey** (also **mopy**) **adj., mop·i·ly** /ˈmōpəlē/ **adv., mop·i·ness** /ˈmōpēnis/ **n., mop·ish adj.**
– ORIGIN mid 16th cent. (the early noun sense being 'fool or simpleton'): perhaps of Scandinavian origin; compare with Swedish dialect *mopa* 'to sulk.'

mo·ped /ˈmōˌped/ ▶ **n.** a low-power, lightweight motorized bicycle.
– ORIGIN 1950s: from Swedish, from (*trampcykel med*) *mo*(*tor och*) *ped*(*aler*) 'pedal cycle with motor and pedals.'

mop·er·y /ˈmōpərē/ ▶ **n.** **1** informal the action of committing a minor or petty offense such as loitering: *we got guys doing stretches for passing bad checks and aggravated mopery.*
2 feelings of apathy and dejection.

mop·pet /ˈmäpət/ ▶ **n.** informal a small endearingly sweet child.
– ORIGIN early 17th cent.: from obsolete *moppe* 'baby or rag doll' + **-ET**[1].

PRONUNCIATION KEY ə *ago, up;* ər *over, fur;* a *hat;* ā *ate;* ä *car;* e *let;* ē *see;* i *fit;* ī *by;* NG *sing;* ō *go;* ô *law, for;* oi *toy;* o͝o *good;* o͞o *goo;* ou *out;* TH *thin;* T̲H̲ *then;* ZH *vision*

mo·quette /mō'ket/ ▶ **n.** a thick pile fabric used for carpets and upholstery.
– ORIGIN 1930s: from French, perhaps from obsolete Italian *mocaiardo* 'mohair.'

MOR ▶ **abbr.** (of music) middle-of-the-road: *their music is too MOR for college radio.*

mor /môr/ ▶ **n.** Soil Science humus formed under acid conditions.
– ORIGIN 1930s: from Danish.

Mo·rad·a·bad /mə'rädəbäd/ a city and railroad junction in northern India, in Uttar Pradesh; pop. 806,700 (est. 2009).

mo·raine /mə'rān/ ▶ **n.** Geology a mass of rocks and sediment carried down and deposited by a glacier, typically as ridges at its edges or extremity.
– DERIVATIVES **mo·rain·al** /-'rānl/ **adj.**, **mo·rain·ic** /-'rānik/ **adj.**
– ORIGIN late 18th cent.: from French, from Italian dialect *morena*, from French dialect *morre* 'snout'; related to **MORION**¹.

mor·al /'môrəl, 'mär-/ ▶ **adj.** **1** concerned with the principles of right and wrong behavior and the goodness or badness of human character: *the moral dimensions of medical intervention | a moral judgment.* ■ concerned with or derived from the code of interpersonal behavior that is considered right or acceptable in a particular society: *an individual's ambitions may get out of step with the general moral code | the moral obligation of society to do something about the inner city's problems.* ■ [attrib.] examining the nature of ethics and the foundations of good and bad character and conduct: *moral philosophers.*
2 holding or manifesting high principles for proper conduct: *he prides himself on being a highly moral and ethical person.*
▶ **n.** **1** a lesson, esp. one concerning what is right or prudent, that can be derived from a story, a piece of information, or an experience: ***the moral of this story** was that one must see the beauty in what one has.*
2 (**morals**) a person's standards of behavior or beliefs concerning what is and is not acceptable for them to do: *the corruption of public morals | they believe addicts have no morals and cannot be trusted.*
– DERIVATIVES **mor·al·ly adv.** *theories that assert that all inequality is morally wrong.*
– ORIGIN late Middle English: from Latin *moralis*, from *mos, mor-* 'custom,' (plural) *mores* 'morals.' As a noun the word was first used to translate Latin *Moralia*, the title of St. Gregory the Great's moral exposition of the Book of Job, and was subsequently applied to the works of various classical writers.

m

mor·al cer·tain·ty ▶ **n.** probability so great as to allow no reasonable doubt: *it enjoys moral certainty and consequently has a normative role.*

mo·rale /mə'ral/ ▶ **n.** the confidence, enthusiasm, and discipline of a person or group at a particular time: *their morale was high.*
– ORIGIN mid 18th cent.: from French *moral*, respelled to preserve the final stress in pronunciation.

mor·al haz·ard ▶ **n.** Economics lack of incentive to guard against risk where one is protected from its consequences, e.g., by insurance.

mor·al·ism /'môrə,lizəm, 'mär-/ ▶ **n.** the practice of moralizing, esp. showing a tendency to make judgments about others' morality: *the patriotic moralism of many political leaders.*

mor·al·ist /'môrəlist/ ▶ **n.** a person who teaches or promotes morality. ■ a person given to moralizing. ■ a person who behaves in a morally commendable way.
– DERIVATIVES **mor·al·is·tic** /,môrə'listik/ **adj.**, **mor·al·is·ti·cal·ly** /,môrə'listik(ə)lē/ **adv.**

mo·ral·i·ty /mə'ralətē, mô-/ ▶ **n.** (pl. **moralities**) principles concerning the distinction between right and wrong or good and bad behavior. ■ a particular system of values and principles of conduct, esp. one held by a specified person or society: *a bourgeois morality.* ■ the extent to which an action is right or wrong: *behind all the arguments lies the issue of the morality of the possession of nuclear weapons.*
– ORIGIN late Middle English: from Old French *moralite* or late Latin *moralitas*, from Latin *moralis* (see **MORAL**).

mo·ral·i·ty play ▶ **n.** a kind of drama with personified abstract qualities as the main characters and presenting a lesson about good conduct and character, popular in the 15th and early 16th centuries.

mor·al·ize /'môrə,līz, 'mär-/ ▶ **v.** [no obj.] (often as noun **moralizing**) comment on issues of right and wrong, typically with an unfounded air of superiority: *the self-righteous moralizing of his aunt was ringing in his ears.* ■ [with obj.] interpret or explain as giving lessons on good and bad character and conduct: *mythographers normally moralize Narcissus as the man who wastes himself in pursuing worldly goods.* ■ [with obj.] reform the character and conduct of: *he endeavored to moralize an immoral society.*
– DERIVATIVES **mor·al·i·za·tion** /,môrələ'zāsHən, ,mär-/ **n.**, **mor·al·iz·er n.**, **mor·al·iz·ing·ly adv.**
– ORIGIN late Middle English (in the sense 'explain the moral meaning of'): from French *moraliser* or medieval Latin *moralizare*, from late Latin *moralis* (see **MORAL**).

mor·al law ▶ **n.** (in some systems of ethics) an absolute principle defining the criteria of right action (whether conceived as a divine ordinance or a truth of reason).

Mor·al Ma·jor·i·ty ▶ **n.** a political action group formed in the 1970s to further a conservative and religious agenda, including the allowance of prayer in schools and strict laws against abortion. ■ (**moral majority**) [treated as pl.] the majority of people, regarded as favoring firm moral standards: *smokers are often made to feel like social outcasts by the moral majority.*

mor·al phi·los·o·phy ▶ **n.** the branch of philosophy concerned with ethics.

Mor·al Re·ar·ma·ment an organization founded by the American Lutheran evangelist Frank Buchman (1878–1961) and first popularized in Oxford, England, in the 1920s (hence until about 1938 called the **Oxford Group Movement**). It emphasizes personal integrity and confession of faults, cooperation, and mutual respect, esp. as a basis for social transformation.

mor·al sci·ence ▶ **n.** dated social sciences and/or philosophy.

mor·al sense ▶ **n.** the ability to distinguish between right and wrong.

mor·al sup·port ▶ **n.** support or help, the effect of which is psychological rather than physical.

mor·al vic·to·ry ▶ **n.** a defeat that can be interpreted as a victory on moral terms, for example because the defeated party defended their principles.

Mor·ar, Loch /'môrər, läk/ a lake in western Scotland. At 1,017 feet (310 m), it is Scotland's deepest lake.

mo·rass /mə'ras, mô-/ ▶ **n.** **1** an area of muddy or boggy ground.
2 a complicated or confused situation: *she would become lost in **a morass of** lies and explanations.*
– ORIGIN late 15th cent.: from Dutch *moeras*, alteration (by assimilation to *moer* 'moor') of Middle Dutch *marasch*, from Old French *marais* 'marsh,' from medieval Latin *mariscus.*

mor·a·to·ri·um /,môrə'tôrēəm, ,mär-/ ▶ **n.** (pl. **moratoriums** or **moratoria** /-'tôrēə/) a temporary prohibition of an activity: *an indefinite **moratorium on** the use of drift nets.* ■ Law a legal authorization to debtors to postpone payment.
– ORIGIN late 19th cent.: modern Latin, neuter (used as a noun) of late Latin *moratorius* 'delaying,' from Latin *morat-* 'delayed,' from the verb *morari*, from *mora* 'delay.'

Mo·ra·vi·a /mə'rāvēə/ a region of the Czech Republic, located between Bohemia on the west and the Carpathians on the east; chief town, Brno. A province of Bohemia from the 11th century, it was made an Austrian province in 1848 and became a part of Czechoslovakia in 1918.

Mo·ra·vi·an /mə'rāvēən/ ▶ **n.** a native of Moravia. ■ a member of a Protestant Church founded in Saxony by emigrants from Moravia holding views derived from the Hussites and accepting the Bible as the only source of faith.
▶ **adj.** of or relating to Moravia or its people. ■ of or relating to the Moravian Church.

mo·ray /'môr,ā, mə'rā/ (also **moray eel**) ▶ **n.** a mainly nocturnal eellike predatory fish of warm seas that typically hides in crevices with just the head protruding. ● Family Muraenidae: several genera and numerous species, including the **spotted moray** (*Gymnothorax moringa*) of the Gulf of Mexico and the southeastern US Atlantic coast, and *Muraena helena* of the eastern Atlantic and Mediterranean.
– ORIGIN early 17th cent.: from Portuguese *moréia*, via Latin from Greek *muraina.*

Mor·ay Firth a deep inlet of the North Sea on the northeastern coast of Scotland.

mor·bid /'môrbəd/ ▶ **adj.** **1** characterized by or appealing to an abnormal and unhealthy interest in disturbing and unpleasant subjects, esp. death and disease: *he had long held a morbid fascination with the horrors of contemporary warfare.*
2 Medicine of the nature of or indicative of disease: *the treatment of morbid obesity.*
– DERIVATIVES **mor·bid·i·ty** /môr'bidətē/ **n.**, **mor·bid·ly adv.**, **mor·bid·ness n.**
– ORIGIN mid 17th cent. (in the medical sense): from Latin *morbidus*, from *morbus* 'disease.'

mor·bid a·nat·o·my ▶ **n.** the anatomy of diseased organs and tissues.

mor·bif·ic /môr'bifik/ ▶ **adj.** dated causing disease: *in cholera the morbific matter is taken into the alimentary canal.*
– ORIGIN mid 17th cent.: from French *morbifique* or modern Latin *morbificus*, from Latin *morbus* 'disease.'

mor·bil·li /môr'bil,ī/ ▶ **plural n.** technical term for **MEASLES.**
– ORIGIN mid 16th cent.: Latin, plural of *morbillus* 'pustule,' from *morbus* 'disease.'

mor·bil·li·vi·rus /môr'bilə,vīrəs/ ▶ **n.** Medicine any of a group of paramyxoviruses that cause measles, rinderpest, and canine distemper.
– ORIGIN 1970s: from Latin *morbilli* (plural of *morbillus* 'pustule,' from *morbus* 'disease') + **VIRUS.**

mor·ceau /môr'sō/ ▶ **n.** (pl. **morceaux** /-'sō(z)/) a short literary or musical composition.
– ORIGIN mid 18th cent.: French, literally 'morsel, piece.'

mor·da·cious /môr'dāsHəs/ ▶ **adj.** formal **1** denoting or using biting sarcasm or invective.
2 (of a person or animal) given to biting.
– ORIGIN mid 17th cent.: from Latin *mordax, mordac-* 'biting' + **-IOUS.**

mor·dant /'môrdnt/ ▶ **adj.** (esp. of humor) having or showing a sharp or critical quality; biting: *a mordant sense of humor.*
▶ **n.** a substance, typically an inorganic oxide, that combines with a dye or stain and thereby fixes it in a material. ■ an adhesive compound for fixing gold leaf. ■ a corrosive liquid used to etch the lines on a printing plate.
▶ **v.** [with obj.] impregnate or treat (a fabric) with a mordant.
– DERIVATIVES **mor·dan·cy** /-dnsē/ **n.**, **mor·dant·ly adv.**
– ORIGIN late 15th cent.: from French, present participle of *mordre* 'to bite,' from Latin *mordere.*

mor·dent /'môrdnt/ ▶ **n.** Music a rapid alternation of a note with the note immediately below or above it in the scale (sometimes further distinguished as **lower mordent** and **upper mordent**). The term **inverted mordent** usually refers to the **upper mordent.**
– ORIGIN early 19th cent.: via German from Italian *mordente*, present participle of *mordere* 'to bite.'

Mor·dred /'môrdrəd/ (in Arthurian legend) the nephew of King Arthur who abducted Guinevere and raised a rebellion against Arthur.

Mord·vin·i·a /môrd'vinēə/ an autonomous republic in Russia, southeast of Nizhni Novgorod; pop. 835,400 (est. 2009); capital, Saransk. Also called **Mordvinian Autonomous Republic.**

More /môr/, Sir Thomas (1478–1535), English scholar and statesman; lord chancellor 1529–32; canonized as **St. Thomas More.** His *Utopia* (1516), which described an ideal city state, established him as a leading humanist of the Renaissance. He was imprisoned in 1534 after opposing Henry's marriage to Anne Boleyn and was beheaded for opposing the Act of Supremacy. Feast day, June 22.

more /môr/ ▶ **determiner & pron.** **1** comparative of **MANY, MUCH.**
2 a greater or additional amount or degree: [as determiner] *I poured myself more coffee* | [as pronoun] *tell me more | they proved **more of** a hindrance than a help.*
▶ **adv.** **1** comparative of **MUCH.**
2 forming the comparative of adjectives and adverbs, esp. those of more than one syllable: *for them, enthusiasm is more important than talent.*
3 to a greater extent: *I like chicken **more than** turkey.* ■ (**more than**) extremely (used before an adjective conveying a positive feeling or attitude): *she is more than happy to oblige.*
4 again: *repeat once more.*
5 moreover: *he was rich, and more, he was handsome.*
– PHRASES **more and more** at a continually increasing rate: *vacancies were becoming more and more rare.* **more like it** see **LIKE**¹. **more or less** speaking imprecisely; to a certain extent: *they are more or less a waste of time.* ■ approximately: *more or less symmetrical.* **more so** of the same kind to a greater degree: *the waiter found me delightful and my little sister even more so.* **no more 1** nothing further: *there was no more to be said about it.* **2** no further: *you must have some soup, but no more wine.* **3** (**be no more**) exist no longer. **4** never again: *mention his name no more to me.* **5** neither: *I had no complaints and no more did Tom.*
– ORIGIN Old English *māra*, of Germanic origin; related to Dutch *meer* and German *mehr.*

mo·reen /mô'rēn, mə-/ ▶ **n.** a strong, ribbed cotton or wool fabric, used chiefly for curtains and upholstery.
– ORIGIN mid 17th cent.: perhaps a fanciful formation from **MOIRE**.

mo·rel /mə'rel, mô-/ ▶ **n.** a widely distributed edible fungus that has a brown oval or pointed fruiting body with an irregular honeycombed surface bearing the spores. ● Genus *Morchella*, family Morchellaceae, subdivision Ascomycotina: several species, in particular the common *M. esculenta*.
– ORIGIN late 17th cent.: from French *morille*, from Dutch *morilje*; related to German *Morchel* 'fungus.'

Mo·re·li·a /mə'rālyə/ a city in central Mexico, capital of the state of Michoacán; pop. 608,049 (2005). Founded in 1541, it was known as Valladolid until 1828.
– ORIGIN renamed in honor of J. M. *Morelos* y Pavón (1765–1815), a key figure in Mexico's independence movement.

mo·rel·lo /mə'relō/ ▶ **n.** (pl. **morellos**) a dark cherry of a sour kind used in cooking: [as modifier] *morello cherries*.
– ORIGIN mid 17th cent.: from Italian *morello* 'blackish,' from medieval Latin *morellus*, diminutive of Latin *Maurus* 'Moor.'

Mo·re·los /mə'rāləs/ a state in central Mexico, west of Mexico City; capital, Cuernavaca.

Mo·re·no Val·ley /mə'rānō/ a city in southwestern California, east of Riverside; pop. 190,871 (est. 2008).

more·o·ver /môr'ōvər/ ▶ **adv.** as a further matter; besides: *moreover, glass is electrically insulating*.

mo·res /'môr,āz/ ▶ **plural n.** the essential or characteristic customs and conventions of a community: *an offense against social mores*.
– ORIGIN late 19th cent.: from Latin, plural of *mos*, *mor-* 'custom.'

Mo·resque /mə'resk/ ▶ **adj.** (of art or architecture) Moorish in style or design.
– ORIGIN late Middle English (as a noun denoting arabesque ornament): from French, from Italian *moresco*, from *Moro* 'Moor.'

Mor·gan[1] /'môrgən/, J. P. (1837–1913), US financier, philanthropist, and art collector; full name *John Pierpont Morgan*. He created General Electric in 1891 and the US Steel Corporation in 1901. He bequeathed his large art collection to the Museum of Modern Art in New York City.

Mor·gan[2], Thomas Hunt (1866–1945), US zoologist. His studies on inheritance using the fruit fly *Drosophila* showed that the genetic information is carried by genes arranged along the length of the chromosomes. Nobel Prize for Physiology or Medicine (1933).

Mor·gan[3] ▶ **n.** a horse of a light thickset breed developed in New England.
– ORIGIN mid 19th cent.: named after Justin *Morgan* (1747–98), US teacher and owner of the original sire of the breed.

mor·ga·nat·ic /,môrgə'natik/ ▶ **adj.** of or denoting a marriage in which neither the spouse of lower rank nor any children have any claim to the possessions or title of the spouse of higher rank.
– DERIVATIVES **mor·ga·nat·i·cal·ly** /-ik(ə)lē/ **adv.**
– ORIGIN early 18th cent.: from modern Latin *morganaticus*, from medieval Latin *matrimonium ad morganaticam* 'marriage with a morning gift' (because a morning gift, given by a husband to his wife on the morning after the marriage, was the wife's sole entitlement in a marriage of this kind).

mor·gan·ite /'môrgə,nīt/ ▶ **n.** a pink transparent variety of beryl, used as a gemstone.
– ORIGIN early 20th cent.: from the name of J. P. *Morgan* (see **MORGAN**[1]) + **-ITE**[1].

Mor·gan le Fay /'môrgən lə 'fā/ (in Arthurian legend) an enchantress, sister of King Arthur.

mor·gen /'môrgən/ ▶ **n.** a measure of land, in particular: ■ (in the Netherlands, South Africa, and parts of the US) a measure of land equal to about 0.8 hectare or two acres. ■ (in Norway, Denmark, and Germany) a measure of land now equal to about 0.3 hectare or two thirds of an acre.
– ORIGIN early 17th cent.: from Dutch, or from German *Morgen* 'morning,' apparently from the notion of "an area of land that can be plowed in a morning."

morgue /môrg/ ▶ **n. 1** a place where bodies are kept, esp. to be identified or claimed: *the cadavers were bagged and removed to the city morgue*. ■ used metaphorically to refer to a place that is quiet, gloomy, or cold: *she put us in that drafty morgue of a sitting room*.
2 informal in a newspaper office, a collection of old cuttings, photographs, and information: *conducting research in either a news morgue or a library*.
– ORIGIN early 19th cent.: from French, originally the name of a building in Paris where bodies were kept until identified.

mor·i·bund /'môrə,bənd, 'mär-/ ▶ **adj.** (of a person) at the point of death. ■ (of a thing) in terminal decline; lacking vitality or vigor: *the moribund commercial property market*.
– DERIVATIVES **mor·i·bun·di·ty** /,môrə'bəndətē, ,mär-/ **n.**
– ORIGIN early 18th cent.: from Latin *moribundus*, from *mori* 'to die.'

mo·ri·on[1] /'môrēən/ ▶ **n.** a kind of helmet without beaver or visor, worn by soldiers in the 16th and 17th centuries.
– ORIGIN French, from Spanish *morrión*, from *morro* 'round object.'

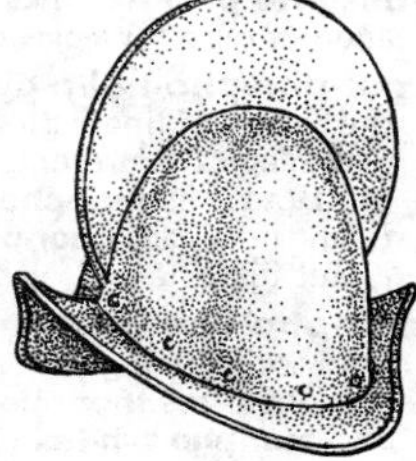
morion[1]

mo·ri·on[2] ▶ **n.** a brown or black variety of quartz.
– ORIGIN mid 18th cent.: from French, from Latin *morion*, a misreading (in Pliny) for *mormorion*.

Mo·ris·co /mə'riskō/ ▶ **n.** (pl. **Moriscos** or **Moriscoes**) historical a Moor in Spain, esp. one who had accepted Christian baptism.
– ORIGIN Spanish, from *Moro* 'Moor.'

Mor·i·son /'môrəsən, 'mär-/, Samuel Eliot (1887–1976), US historian and naval officer. He wrote *Oxford History of the United States* (1927), *Admiral of the Ocean Sea: A Life of Christopher Columbus* (1942), and *John Paul Jones* (1959).

Mo·ri·sot /môrē'sō, -'zō/, Berthe (Marie Pauline) (1841–95), French painter; the first woman to join the Impressionists. Her works typically depicted women and children and waterside scenes.

Mor·ley /'môrlē/, Edward Williams (1838–1923), US chemist. In 1887, he collaborated with Albert Michelson in an experiment to determine the speed of light, the result of which disproved the existence of the ether. See also **MICHELSON–MORLEY EXPERIMENT**.

Mor·mon /'môrmən/ ▶ **n.** a member of the Church of Jesus Christ of Latter-Day Saints, a religion founded in the US in 1830 by Joseph Smith, Jr.

> Smith claimed to have found and translated *The Book of Mormon* by divine revelation. It tells the story of a group of Hebrews who migrated to America c.600 BC and is taken as scriptural alongside the Bible. The Mormons came into conflict with the US government over their practice of polygamy (officially abandoned in 1890) and moved their headquarters from Illinois to Salt Lake City, Utah, in 1847 under Smith's successor, Brigham Young. Mormon doctrine emphasizes tithing, missionary work, and the Second Coming of Christ.

▶ **adj.** of or relating to the Church of Jesus Christ of Latter-Day Saints: *the leader of a Mormon congregation*.
– DERIVATIVES **Mor·mon·ism** /-,nizəm/ **n.**
– ORIGIN the name of a prophet to whom Smith attributed *The Book of Mormon*.

morn /môrn/ ▶ **n.** literary term for **MORNING**.
– ORIGIN Old English *morgen*, of Germanic origin.

mor·nay /môr'nā/ (also **Mornay**) ▶ **adj.** denoting or served in a cheese-flavored white sauce: *mornay sauce* | [postpositive] *cauliflower mornay*.
– ORIGIN named after *Mornay*, the French cook and eldest son of Joseph Voiron, chef of the restaurant Durand at the end of the 19th cent. and inventor of the sauce.

morn·ing /'môrniNG/ ▶ **n.** the period of time between midnight and noon, esp. from sunrise to noon: *I toiled in the fields from morning till night* | *it was a little after eight **in the morning*** | *it was a beautiful sunny morning*. ■ sunrise: *a hint of steely light showed that morning was on its way*.
▶ **adv.** (**mornings**) informal every morning: *mornings, she'd sleep late*.
▶ **exclam.** informal short for **GOOD MORNING**.
– PHRASES **morning, noon, and night** all the time.
– ORIGIN Middle English: from **MORN**, on the pattern of *evening*.

morn·ing af·ter ▶ **n.** informal a morning on which a person has a hangover. ■ a hangover. ■ an unpleasant aftermath of imprudent behavior: *his first year of college was one long party—eventually he would have to face the morning after*.

morn·ing-af·ter pill ▶ **n.** a contraceptive pill that is effective up to about seventy-two hours after intercourse.

morn·ing coat ▶ **n.** a man's formal coat with a cutaway.

morn·ing dress ▶ **n.** a man's cutaway coat and striped pants, worn on formal occasions such as weddings, typically with a top hat.

morn·ing glo·ry ▶ **n.** a climbing plant often cultivated for its showy trumpet-shaped flowers, which typically open in the early morning and wither by midday. ● Genus *Ipomoea*, family Convolvulaceae: several species, in particular the **common morning glory** *I. purpurea*.

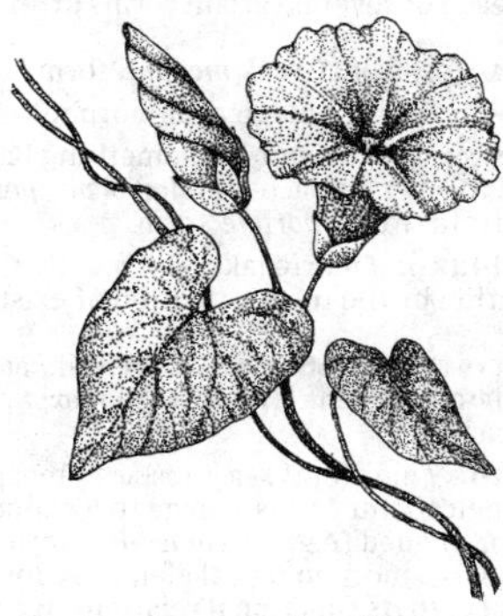
common morning glory

morn·ing prayer ▶ **n.** (usu. **morning prayers**) a formal act of worship held in the morning, esp. regularly or by a group assembled for this purpose. ■ [in sing.] (in the Anglican Church) the service of matins.

morn·ing sick·ness ▶ **n.** nausea in pregnancy, typically occurring in the first few months. Despite its name, the nausea can affect pregnant women at any time of day.

morn·ing star ▶ **n. 1** (**the morning star**) a bright planet, esp. Venus, when visible in the east before sunrise.
2 historical a club with a heavy spiked head, sometimes attached to the handle by a chain. [translating German *Morgenstern*, comparing the weapon's spikes to rays of the star.]

morn·ing watch ▶ **n.** the period from 4 to 8 a.m. on board a ship.

Mo·ro /'môrō/ ▶ **n.** (pl. **Moros**) a Muslim inhabitant of the Philippines.
– ORIGIN Spanish, literally 'Moor.'

Mo·roc·co /mə'räkō/ a country in northwestern Africa, with coastlines on the Mediterranean Sea and Atlantic Ocean; pop. 31,285,200 (est. 2009); capital, Rabat; languages, Arabic (official) and Berber.

> Conquered by the Arabs in the 7th century, Morocco later fell under French and Spanish influence as each country established protectorates in the early 20th century. It became an independent monarchy after the withdrawal of the colonial powers in 1956 and the sultan became king. A bicameral legislature was established in 1997.

– DERIVATIVES **Mo·roc·can** /-'räkən/ **adj. & n.**

mo·roc·co /mə'räkō/ ▶ **n.** (pl. **moroccos**) fine flexible leather made (originally in Morocco) from goatskin tanned with sumac, used esp. for book covers and shoes: *a volume bound in red morocco* | [as modifier] *morocco leather*.

mo·ron /'môr,än/ ▶ **n.** informal a stupid person.
– ORIGIN early 20th cent. (as a medical term denoting an adult with a mental age of about 8–12): from Greek *mōron*, neuter of *mōros* 'foolish.'

Mo·rón /mə'rōn/ a city in eastern Argentina, southwest of Buenos Aires; pop. 327,600 (est. 2008).

Mo·ro·ni /mə'rōnē, mô-/ the capital of Comoros, on the island of Grande Comore; pop. 46,000 (est. 2007).

mo·ron·ic /mə'ränik, mô-/ ▶ **adj.** informal very foolish or stupid: *a truly moronic movie*.
– DERIVATIVES **mo·ron·i·cal·ly** /mə'ränik(ə)lē, mô-/ **adv.**

mo·rose /mə'rōs, mô-/ ▶ **adj.** sullen and ill-tempered.
– DERIVATIVES **mo·rose·ly adv.**, **mo·rose·ness n.**
– ORIGIN mid 16th cent.: from Latin *morosus* 'peevish,' from *mos*, *mor-* 'manner.'

morph[1] /môrf/ ▶ **v.** change smoothly from one image to another by small gradual steps using computer animation techniques: [with obj.] *3-D objects can be morphed into other objects*. ■ undergo or cause to

m

undergo a gradual process of transformation: [no obj.] *the cute moppet has morphed into the moody moll of the indie world.*
▶ **n.** an image that has been morphed by computer animation. ■ an instance of morphing an image.
– ORIGIN 1990s: element from **METAMORPHOSIS**.

morph[2] ▶ **n. 1** Linguistics an actual linguistic form: *the present participle in English is always the morph "-ing."*
2 Biology each of several variant forms of an animal or plant.
– ORIGIN 1940s: from Greek *morphē* 'form.'

morph. ▶ **abbr.** morphological or morphology.

-morph ▶ **comb. form** denoting something having a specified form or character: *endomorph* | *polymorph*.
– ORIGIN from Greek *morphē* 'form.'

mor·phal·lax·is /ˌmôrfəˈlaksəs/ ▶ **n.** Zoology regeneration by the transformation of existing body tissues.
– DERIVATIVES **mor·phal·lac·tic** /-ˈlaktik/ **adj.**
– ORIGIN late 19th cent.: from Greek *morphē* 'form' + *allaxis* 'exchange.'

mor·pheme /ˈmôrˌfēm/ ▶ **n.** Linguistics a meaningful morphological unit of a language that cannot be further divided (e.g., *in*, *come*, *-ing*, forming *incoming*). ■ a morphological element considered with respect to its functional relations in a linguistic system.
– DERIVATIVES **mor·phe·mic** /môrˈfēmik/ **adj.**, **mor·phe·mi·cal·ly** /môrˈfēmik(ə)lē/ **adv.**
– ORIGIN late 19th cent.: from French *morphème*, from Greek *morphē* 'form,' on the pattern of French *phonème* 'phoneme.'

mor·phe·mics /môrˈfēmiks/ ▶ **plural n.** [treated as sing.] Linguistics the study of word structure in terms of minimal meaningful units.

Mor·phe·us /ˈmôrfēəs/ Roman Mythology the son of Somnus (god of sleep), the god of dreams and, in later writings, also god of sleep.

mor·phi·a /ˈmôrfēə/ ▶ **n.** old-fashioned term for **MORPHINE**.

mor·phic res·o·nance /ˈmôrfik/ ▶ **n.** (according to the theory developed by Rupert Sheldrake, British biologist 1942–) a paranormal influence by which a pattern of events or behavior can facilitate subsequent occurrences of similar patterns.

mor·phine /ˈmôrˌfēn/ ▶ **n.** an analgesic and narcotic drug obtained from opium and used medicinally to relieve pain. ● An alkaloid; chem. formula: $C_{17}H_{19}NO_3$. Compare with **HEROIN**.
– ORIGIN early 19th cent.: from German *Morphin*, from the name of the Roman god *Morpheus* (see **MORPHEUS**).

mor·phin·ism /ˈmôrfəˌnizəm/ ▶ **n.** Medicine dependence on or addiction to morphine.

mor·pho /ˈmôrfō/ ▶ **n.** (pl. **morphos**) a large tropical butterfly, the male of which has bright blue iridescent wings. Native to the Central and South American rain forests, they are caught in large numbers each year for use in the jewelry trade. ● Genus *Morpho*, subfamily Morphinae, family Nymphalidae.
– ORIGIN modern Latin, from Greek *Morphō*, an epithet of Aphrodite.

mor·pho·gen /ˈmôrfəjən/ ▶ **n.** Biology a chemical agent able to cause or determine morphogenesis.

mor·pho·gen·e·sis /ˌmôrfəˈjenəsəs/ ▶ **n. 1** Biology the origin and development of morphological characteristics.
2 Geology the formation of landforms or other structures.
– DERIVATIVES **mor·pho·ge·net·ic** /-jəˈnetik/ **adj.**, **mor·pho·gen·ic** /-ˈjenik/ **adj.**
– ORIGIN late 19th cent.: modern Latin, from Greek *morphē* 'form' + **GENESIS**.

mor·pho·line /ˈmôrfəˌlēn/ ▶ **n.** Chemistry a synthetic compound used as a solvent for resins and dyes and (in the form of salts) as an ingredient of emulsifying soaps used in floor polishes. ● A cyclic amine; chem. formula: C_4H_9NO.
– ORIGIN late 19th cent.: from **MORPHINE**, with the insertion of the syllable *-ol-* (see **-OL**).

mor·phol·o·gy /môrˈfäləjē/ ▶ **n.** (pl. **morphologies**) the study of the forms of things, in particular: ■ Biology the branch of biology that deals with the form of living organisms, and with relationships between their structures. ■ Linguistics the study of the forms of words.
– DERIVATIVES **mor·pho·log·ic** /ˌmôrfəˈläjik/ **adj.**, **mor·pho·log·i·cal** /ˌmôrfəˈläjikəl/ **adj.**, **mor·pho·log·i·cal·ly** /ˌmôrfəˈläjik(ə)lē/ **adv.**, **mor·phol·o·gist** /-jist/ **n.**
– ORIGIN mid 19th cent.: from Greek *morphē* 'form' + **-LOGY**.

mor·pho·met·rics /ˌmôrfəˈmetriks/ ▶ **plural n.** [usu. treated as sing.] chiefly Biology morphometry, esp. of living organisms.

mor·phom·e·try /môrˈfämətrē/ ▶ **n.** the process of measuring the external shape and dimensions of landforms, living organisms, or other objects.
– DERIVATIVES **mor·pho·met·ric** /ˌmôrfəˈmetrik/ **adj.**, **mor·pho·met·ri·cal·ly** /ˌmôrfəˈmetrik(ə)lē/ **adv.**

mor·pho·pho·neme /ˌmôrfəˈfōˌnēm/ ▶ **n.** Phonetics any of the variant forms of a phoneme as determined by the context in which it is used.
– DERIVATIVES **mor·pho·pho·ne·mic** /ˌmôrfōfəˈnēmik/ **adj.**

mor·pho·pho·ne·mics /ˌmôrfōfəˈnēmiks/ ▶ **n.** another term for **MORPHOPHONOLOGY**.

mor·pho·pho·nol·o·gy /ˌmôrfōfəˈnäləjē/ ▶ **n.** the branch of linguistics that deals with the phonological representation of morphemes.
– DERIVATIVES **mor·pho·phon·o·log·i·cal** /-ˌfänlˈäjikəl/ **adj.**, **mor·pho·phon·o·log·i·cal·ly** /-ˌfänlˈäjik(ə)lē/ **adv.**

mor·pho·syn·tac·tic /ˌmôrfōsinˈtaktik/ ▶ **adj.** Linguistics involving both morphology and syntax.
– DERIVATIVES **mor·pho·syn·tac·ti·cal·ly** /-ik(ə)lē/ **adv.**, **mor·pho·syn·tax** /-ˈsinˌtaks/ **n.**

Mor·ris[1] /ˈmôris, ˈmär-/, Desmond John (1928–), British zoologist and writer. He studied animal behavior and the implications for the human condition. He put forth his findings in works such as *The Naked Ape* (1967) and *Animal-Watching* (1990).

Mor·ris[2], Gouverneur (1752–1816), US politician. An active proponent of American independence, he represented New York as a member of the Continental Congress 1777–79, at the Constitutional Convention 1787, and in the US Senate 1800–1803. It was while serving as Robert Morris's assistant superintendent of finance 1781–85 that he proposed the adoption of a decimal monetary system based on dollars and cents.

Mor·ris[3], Robert (1734–1806), US politician and financier. He represented Pennsylvania at the Continental Congress 1775–78 and signed the Declaration of Independence in 1776. He provided extensive financial support for the colonial war effort and was later appointed superintendent of finance 1781–84 by the Continental Congress. After serving in the US Senate 1789–95, he lost all his money in western land speculations and spent his final years in poverty.

Mor·ris[4], William (1834–96), English designer, craftsman, poet, and writer. He was a leading figure in the Arts and Crafts Movement.

Mor·ris[5], William Richard, see **NUFFIELD**.

Mor·ris chair /ˈmôrəs, ˈmärəs/ ▶ **n.** a type of armchair with open padded arms and an adjustable back.
– ORIGIN late 19th cent.: named after William *Morris* (see **MORRIS**[4]).

mor·ris dance ▶ **n.** a lively traditional English dance performed outdoors by groups known as "sides." Dancers wear distinctive costumes that are mainly black and white and have small bells attached, and often carry handkerchiefs or sticks.
– DERIVATIVES **mor·ris danc·er n.**, **mor·ris danc·ing n.**
– ORIGIN late Middle English: *morris* from *morys*, variant of *Moorish* (see **MOOR**); the association with the Moors remains unexplained.

Mor·ri·son, Toni (1931–), US novelist; full name *Chloe Anthony Morrison*. Her novels depict the black American experience and heritage, often focusing on rural life in the South, as in *The Bluest Eye* (1970). Notable works: *Beloved* (1987), *Sula* (1973), *Tar Baby* (1981), and *Paradise* (1998). Nobel Prize for Literature (1993).

Toni Morrison

mor·row /ˈmôrō, ˈmärō/ ▶ **n.** (**the morrow**) archaic or literary the following day: *on the morrow, they attacked the city.* ■ the time following an event: *in the morrow of great victory, will they show some equanimity?* ■ the near future: *we have the religious enthusiast who takes no thought for the morrow.*
– ORIGIN Middle English *morwe*, from Old English *morgen* (see **MORN**).

Morse code /ˈmôrs/ ▶ **n.** an alphabet or code in which letters are represented by combinations of long and short signals of light or sound.
▶ **v.** [with obj.] signal (something) using Morse code.
– ORIGIN mid 19th cent.: named after Samuel F. B. *Morse* (1791–1872), US inventor.

mor·sel /ˈmôrsəl/ ▶ **n.** a small piece or amount of food; a mouthful: *Julie pushed a last **morsel** of toast into her mouth* | figurative *real estate agents think the mansion will be a very tasty morsel for an international company.* ■ a small piece or amount: *reporters do their best to ferret out every morsel of information.*
– ORIGIN Middle English: from Old French, diminutive of *mors* 'a bite,' from Latin *mors-* 'bitten,' from the verb *mordere*.

mort /môrt/ ▶ **n.** Hunting, archaic the note sounded on a horn when the quarry is killed.
– ORIGIN Middle English: via Old French from Latin *mors*, *mort-* 'death.'

mor·ta·del·la /ˌmôrtəˈdelə/ ▶ **n.** a type of light pink, smooth-textured Italian sausage containing pieces of fat, typically served in slices.
– ORIGIN Italian diminutive, formed irregularly from Latin *murtatum* '(sausage) seasoned with myrtle berries.'

mor·tal /ˈmôrtl/ ▶ **adj. 1** (of a living human being, often in contrast to a divine being) subject to death: *all men are mortal.* ■ of or relating to humanity as subject to death: *the coffin held the mortal remains of her uncle.* ■ informal conceivable or imaginable: *punishment out of all mortal proportion to the offense.*
2 [attrib.] causing or liable to cause death; fatal: *a mortal disease* | figurative *the scandal appeared to have struck **a mortal blow** to the government.* ■ (of a battle) fought to the death: *from the outbuildings came the screams of men in **mortal combat**.* ■ (of an enemy or a state of hostility) admitting or allowing no reconciliation until death. ■ Christian Theology denoting a grave sin that is regarded as depriving the soul of divine grace. Often contrasted with **VENIAL**. ■ (of a feeling, esp. fear) very intense: *parents live in mortal fear of children's diseases.* ■ informal very great: *he was in a mortal hurry.* ■ informal, dated long and tedious: *for three mortal days it rained.*
▶ **n.** a human being subject to death, often contrasted with a divine being. ■ humorous a person contrasted with others regarded as being of higher status or ability: *an ambassador had to live in a style that was not expected of **lesser mortals**.*
– ORIGIN late Middle English: from Old French, or from Latin *mortalis*, from *mors*, *mort-* 'death.'

mor·tal·i·ty /môrˈtalətē/ ▶ **n.** (pl. **mortalities**) **1** the state of being subject to death: *the work is increasingly haunted by thoughts of mortality.*
2 death, esp. on a large scale: *the causes of mortality among infants and young children.* ■ (also **mortality rate**) the number of deaths in a given area or period, or from a particular cause: *postoperative mortality was 90 percent for some operations.*
– ORIGIN late Middle English: via Old French from Latin *mortalitas*, from *mortalis* (see **MORTAL**).

mor·tal·ly /ˈmôrtl-ē/ ▶ **adv.** in such a manner as to cause death: *the gunner was mortally wounded.* ■ very intensely or seriously: *I expected him to be mortally offended.*

mor·tar[1] /ˈmôrtər/ ▶ **n.**
1 a cup-shaped receptacle made of hard material, in which ingredients are crushed or ground, used esp. in cooking or pharmacy: *a mortar and pestle.*
2 a short, smoothbore gun for firing shells (technically called bombs) at high angles. ■ a similar device used for firing a lifeline or firework.

mortar and pestle

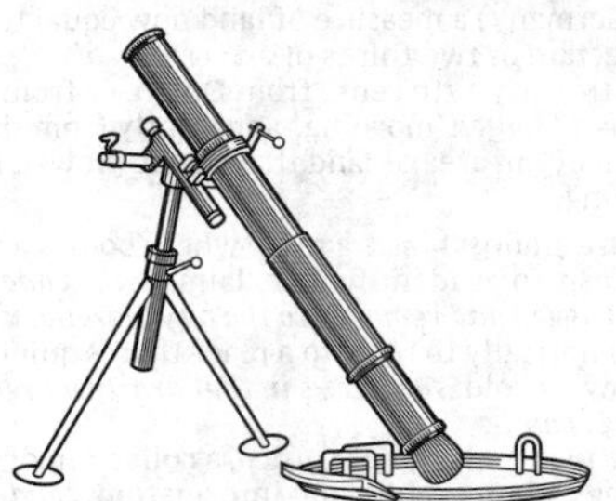
mortar[1] 2

▶ **v.** [with obj.] attack or bombard with shells fired from a mortar.
– ORIGIN late Old English (sense 2 of the noun), from Old French *mortier*, from Latin *mortarium* (to which the English spelling was later assimilated).

mor·tar² ▶ **n.** a mixture of lime with cement, sand, and water, used in building to bond bricks or stones.
▶ **v.** [with obj.] fix or join using mortar: *the pipe can be mortared in place.*
– DERIVATIVES **mor·tar·less** adj., **mor·tar·y** adj.
– ORIGIN Middle English: from Old French *mortier*, from Latin *mortarium*, probably a transferred sense of the word denoting a container (see MORTAR¹).

mor·tar·board /ˈmôrtərˌbôrd/ ▶ **n. 1** an academic cap with a stiff, flat, square top and a tassel.
2 a small square board with a handle on the underside, used by bricklayers for holding mortar.

mortarboard 1

mort·gage /ˈmôrgij/ ▶ **n.** the charging of real (or personal) property by a debtor to a creditor as security for a debt (esp. one incurred by the purchase of the property), on the condition that it shall be returned on payment of the debt within a certain period. ■ a deed effecting such a transaction. ■ a loan obtained through the conveyance of property as security: *I put down a hundred thousand in cash and took out a mortgage for the rest.*
▶ **v.** [with obj.] convey (a property) to a creditor as security on a loan: *the estate was mortgaged up to the hilt.* ■ expose to future risk or constraint for the sake of immediate advantage: *some people worry that selling off federal assets mortgages the country's future.*
– DERIVATIVES **mort·gage·a·ble** adj.
– ORIGIN late Middle English: from Old French, literally 'dead pledge,' from *mort* (from Latin *mortuus* 'dead') + *gage* 'pledge.'

mort·ga·gee /ˌmôrgəˈjē/ ▶ **n.** the lender in a mortgage, typically a bank.

mort·gage rate ▶ **n.** the rate of interest charged by a mortgage lender.

mort·ga·gor /ˌmôrgiˈjôr, ˈmôrgijər/ ▶ **n.** the borrower in a mortgage, typically a homeowner.

mor·tice /ˈmôrtəs/ ▶ **n. & v.** variant spelling of MORTISE.

mor·ti·cian /môrˈtisHən/ ▶ **n.** an undertaker.
– ORIGIN late 19th cent.: from Latin *mors, mort-* 'death' + -ICIAN.

mor·ti·fi·ca·tion /ˌmôrtəfəˈkāsHən/ ▶ **n. 1** great embarrassment and shame: *they mistook my mortification for an admission of guilt.*
2 the action of subduing one's bodily desires: *mortification of the flesh has a long tradition in some religions.*

mor·ti·fy /ˈmôrtəˌfī/ ▶ **v.** (**mortifies, mortifying, mortified**) [with obj.] **1** cause (someone) to feel embarrassed, ashamed, or humiliated: [with obj.] *she was mortified to see her wrinkles in the mirror* | (as adj. **mortifying**) *she refused to accept this mortifying disgrace.*
2 subdue (the body or its needs and desires) by self-denial or discipline: *return to heaven by mortifying the flesh.*
3 [no obj.] archaic (of flesh) be affected by gangrene or necrosis: *the cut in Henry's arm had mortified.*
– DERIVATIVES **mor·ti·fy·ing·ly** adv.
– ORIGIN late Middle English (in the senses 'put to death,' 'deaden,' and 'subdue by self-denial'): from Old French *mortifier*, from ecclesiastical Latin *mortificare* 'kill, subdue,' from *mors, mort-* 'death.'

Mor·ti·mer /ˈmôrtəmər/, Roger de, 8th Baron of Wigmore and 1st Earl of March (*c.*1287–1330), English noble. In 1326, he invaded England with his lover Isabella of France and replaced her husband Edward II with her son, the future Edward III. When Edward III assumed power in 1330, he had Mortimer executed.

mor·tise /ˈmôrtis/ (also **mortice**) ▶ **n.** a hole or recess cut into a part, designed to receive a corresponding projection (a tenon) on another part so as to join or lock the parts together.
▶ **v.** [with obj.] join securely by using a mortise and tenon. ■ [with obj.] (often as adj. **mortised**) cut a mortise in or through: *the mortised ports.*
– DERIVATIVES **mor·tis·er** n.
– ORIGIN late Middle English: from Old French *mortaise*.

mor·tise lock ▶ **n.** a lock that is set within the body of a door in a recess or mortise, as opposed to one attached to the door surface.

mort·main /ˈmôrtˌmān/ ▶ **n.** Law the status of lands or tenements held inalienably by an ecclesiastical or other corporation.
– ORIGIN late Middle English: from Anglo-Norman French and Old French *mortemain*, from medieval Latin *mortua manus* 'dead hand' (probably alluding to impersonal ownership).

Mor·ton¹ /ˈmôrtn/, Jelly Roll (1885–1941), US jazz pianist, composer, and bandleader; born *Ferdinand Joseph La Menthe Morton*. He was one of the principal links between ragtime and New Orleans jazz. He formed his band, the Red Hot Peppers, in 1926.

Mor·ton², John (*c.*1420–1500), English prelate and statesman. He was appointed archbishop of Canterbury in 1486 and chancellor under Henry VII a year later.

mor·tu·ar·y /ˈmôrCHo͞oˌerē/ ▶ **n.** (pl. **mortuaries**) a funeral home or morgue.
▶ **adj.** [attrib.] of or relating to burial or tombs: *mortuary rituals* | *a mortuary temple.*
– ORIGIN late Middle English (denoting a gift claimed by a parish priest from a deceased person's estate): from Latin *mortuarius*, from *mortuus* 'dead.' The current noun sense dates from the mid 19th cent.

mor·u·la /ˈmôrələ, ˈmär-/ ▶ **n.** (pl. **morulae** /-lē/) Embryology a solid ball of cells resulting from division of a fertilized ovum, and from which a blastula is formed.
– ORIGIN mid 19th cent.: modern Latin, diminutive of Latin *morum* 'mulberry.'

MOS ▶ **abbr.** Electronics metal oxide semiconductor.

mos. ▶ **abbr.** months.

Mo·sa·ic /mōˈzā-ik/ ▶ **adj.** of or associated with Moses.
– ORIGIN mid 17th cent.: from French *mosaïque* or modern Latin *Mosaicus*.

mo·sa·ic /mōˈzā-ik/ ▶ **n. 1** a picture or pattern produced by arranging together small colored pieces of hard material, such as stone, tile, or glass: *the mosaic shows the baptism of Christ* | *the walls and vaults are decorated by marble and mosaic* | [as modifier] *a mosaic floor.* ■ a colorful and variegated pattern: *the bird's plumage was a* **mosaic of** *slate-gray, blue, and brown.* ■ a combination of diverse elements forming a more or less coherent whole: *an incompetently constructed* **mosaic of** *competing interests.* ■ an arrangement of photosensitive elements in a television camera.
2 Biology an individual (esp. an animal) composed of cells of two genetically different types.
3 (also **mosaic disease**) a viral disease that results in leaf variegation in tobacco, corn, sugar cane, and other plants.
▶ **v.** (**mosaics, mosaicking, mosaicked**) [with obj.] decorate with a mosaic: (as adj. **mosaicked**) *the mosaicked swimming pool.* ■ combine (distinct or disparate elements) to form a picture or pattern: *the digital data were combined, or mosaicked, to delineate counties.*
– DERIVATIVES **mo·sa·i·cist** /mōˈzāəsist/ n.
– ORIGIN late Middle English: from French *mosaïque*, based on Latin *musi(v)um* decoration with small square stones, perhaps ultimately from Greek *mousa* 'a muse.'

mo·sa·ic gold ▶ **n.** an imitation gold pigment consisting of tin disulfide.

mo·sa·i·cism /mōˈzāəˌsizəm/ ▶ **n.** Biology the property or state of being composed of cells of two genetically different types.

Mo·sa·ic Law ▶ **n.** another term for THE LAW OF MOSES (see LAW (sense 3)).

Mo·san·der /mōˈsändər/, Carl Gustaf (1797–1858), Swedish chemist. He discovered the elements lanthanum, erbium, and terbium, and the supposed element didymium.

mo·sa·saur /ˈmōsəˌsôr/ (also **mosasaurus** /ˌmōsəˈsôrəs/) ▶ **n.** a large extinct marine reptile of the late Cretaceous period, with large toothed jaws, paddlelike limbs, and a long flattened tail, related to the monitor lizards. ● Family Mosasauridae, suborder Lacertilia: several genera, including *Mosasaurus*.
– DERIVATIVES **mo·sa·sau·ri·an** adj.
– ORIGIN mid 19th cent.: from modern Latin *Mosasaurus*, from Latin *Mosa* 'Meuse' (a river in western Europe, near which it was first discovered) + Greek *sauros* 'lizard.'

mos·ca·to /masˈkätō/ ▶ **n.** a sweet Italian dessert wine.
– ORIGIN Italian; related to MUSCAT.

Mos·cow /ˈmäsˌkou, -kō/ the capital of Russia, located at the center of European Russia, on the Moskva River; pop. 10,470,300 (est. 2008). It became the capital when Ivan the Terrible proclaimed himself the first tsar in the 16th century. Peter the Great moved his capital to St. Petersburg in 1712, but, after the Bolshevik Revolution of 1917, Moscow was made the capital of the new Soviet government, with its center in the Kremlin. Russian name MOSKVA.

Mo·sel /mōˈzel/ (also **Moselle**) a river of western Europe that rises in the Vosges mountains of northeastern France and flows northeast for 346 miles (550 km) through Luxembourg and Germany to meet the Rhine River at Koblenz.

Mose·ley /ˈmōzlē/, Henry Gwyn Jeffreys (1887–1915), English physicist. He determined the atomic numbers of elements from their X-ray spectra, demonstrated that an element's chemical properties are determined by this number, and showed that there are only 92 naturally occurring elements.

Mo·selle /mōˈzel/ (also **Mosel**) ▶ **n.** a light medium-dry white wine produced in the valley of the Moselle River (see MOSEL).

Mo·ses¹ /ˈmōzis, -zəz/ (*fl.* *c.*14th–13th centuries BC), Hebrew prophet and lawgiver; brother of Aaron. According to the biblical account, he was born in Egypt and led the Israelites across the desert toward the Promised Land. During the journey he was inspired by God on Mount Sinai to write down the Ten Commandments on tablets of stone (Exod. 20).

Mo·ses², Grandma (1860–1961), US painter; full name *Anna Mary Robertson Moses*. She took up painting as a hobby when widowed in 1927 and produced more than a thousand paintings in a primitive style, mostly of rural life.

Grandma Moses

Mo·ses³, Edwin (Corley) (1955–), US track athlete. He won Olympic gold medals for the 400-meter hurdles in 1976 and 1984. He also set successive world records in the event throughout these years.

mo·sey /ˈmōzē/ informal ▶ **v.** (**moseys, moseying, moseyed**) [no obj.] walk or move in a leisurely manner: *we decided to mosey on up to Montgomery.*
▶ **n.** chiefly Brit. a leisurely walk or drive.
– ORIGIN early 19th cent.: of unknown origin. The original sense was 'go away quickly.'

MOSFET /ˈmäsˌfet/ ▶ **n.** Electronics a field-effect transistor that has a thin layer of silicon oxide between the gate and the channel.
– ORIGIN 1960s: acronym from *metal oxide semiconductor field-effect transistor*.

mosh /mäsH/ ▶ **v.** [no obj.] dance to rock music in a violent manner involving jumping up and down and deliberately colliding with other dancers.
– ORIGIN 1980s: perhaps from MASH or MUSH¹.

mo·shav /mōˈsHäv/ ▶ **n.** (pl. **moshavim** /ˌmōsHəˈvēm/) in Israel, a cooperative community of farmers.
– ORIGIN from Hebrew *mōšāb*, literally 'dwelling.'

mosh pit ▶ **n.** an area where moshing occurs, esp. in front of the stage at a rock concert.

Mos·kva /ˈmäskvä, ˈməsk-/ Russian name for MOSCOW.

Mos·lem /ˈmäzləm, ˈmäs-/ ▶ **n. & adj.** variant spelling of MUSLIM.

USAGE See usage at MUSLIM.

Mo·so·tho /məˈso͞oto͞o/ singular form of BASOTHO.

mosque /mäsk/ ▶ **n.** a Muslim place of worship.

Mosques consist of an area reserved for communal prayers, frequently in a domed building with a minaret, and with a niche (mihrab) or other structure indicating the direction of Mecca. There may also be a platform for preaching (minbar), and an adjacent courtyard in which water is provided for the obligatory ablutions before prayer.

– ORIGIN late Middle English: from French *mosquée*, via Italian and Spanish from Egyptian Arabic *masgid*.

Mos·qui·to ▶ n. (pl. **Mosquitos**) & adj. variant spelling of **MISKITO**.

mos·qui·to /mə'skētō/ ▶ n. (pl. **mosquitoes** or **mosquitos**) a slender long-legged fly with aquatic larvae. The bite of the bloodsucking female can transmit a number of serious diseases including malaria and encephalitis. ● *Culex, Anopheles*, and other genera, family Culicidae.
– ORIGIN late 16th cent.: from Spanish and Portuguese, diminutive of *mosca*, from Latin *musca* 'fly.'

Mos·qui·to Coast /mə'skētō 'kōst/ a sparsely populated coastal strip of swamp, lagoon, and tropical forest along the Caribbean coast of Nicaragua and northeastern Honduras, occupied by the Miskito people after whom it is named.

mos·qui·to coil ▶ n. a spiral typically made from a dried paste of pyrethrum powder, which when lit burns slowly to produce a mosquito-repellent smoke.

mos·qui·to·fish /mə'skētō,fisн/ (also **mosquito fish**) ▶ n. a small livebearing fish found chiefly in vegetated ponds and lakes and brackish waters of the US and northern Mexico. Also called **GAMBUSIA**. ● Genus *Gambusia*, family Poeciliidae: several species, in particular *G. affinis*, widely introduced for mosquito control. Its introduction has often resulted in the depletion of other fish populations.

mos·qui·to hawk ▶ n. **1** a nighthawk.
2 a dragonfly.

mos·qui·to net·ting (also **mosquito net**) ▶ n. a fine net hung across a door or window or around a bed to keep mosquitoes away.

moss /môs/ ▶ n. **1** a small flowerless green plant that lacks true roots, growing in low carpets or rounded cushions in damp habitats and reproducing by means of spores released from stalked capsules: *the trees are overgrown with vines and moss* | *the bog is home to rare mosses*. ● Class Musci, division Bryophyta. ■ used in names of algae, lichens, and higher plants resembling moss, e.g., **reindeer moss**, **Ceylon moss**, **Spanish moss**.
2 Scottish & N. English a bog, esp. a peat bog.
▶ v. (usu. as adj. **mossed**) cover with moss.
– DERIVATIVES **moss·like** /-,līk/ adj.
– ORIGIN Old English *mos* 'bog or moss,' of Germanic origin; related to Dutch *mos* and German *Moos*.

Mos·sad /mä'säd, mə-/ **1** the Supreme Institution for Intelligence and Special Assignments, the principal secret intelligence service of the state of Israel, founded in 1951.
2 the Institution for the Second Immigration, an earlier organization formed in 1938 for the purpose of bringing Jews from Europe to Palestine.
– ORIGIN from Hebrew *mōsād* 'institution.'

moss ag·ate ▶ n. agate with mosslike dendritic inclusions.

moss an·i·mal ▶ n. a sedentary colonial aquatic animal found chiefly in the sea, either encrusting rocks, seaweeds, or other surfaces, or forming stalked fronds. Each minute zooid filter-feeds by means of a crown of ciliated tentacles (lophophore). ● Phylum Bryozoa (or Polyzoa, Ectoprocta).

moss·back /'môs,bak/ ▶ n. informal an old-fashioned or extremely conservative person.
– DERIVATIVES **moss·backed** adj.

Möss·bau·er ef·fect /'məs,bouər/ ▶ n. Chemistry an effect in which certain atomic nuclei bound in a crystal emit gamma rays of sharply defined frequency, which can be used as a probe of energy levels in other nuclei.
– ORIGIN 1960s: named after Rudolf L. *Mössbauer* (1929–), German physicist.

moss cam·pi·on ▶ n. an almost stemless campion with pink flowers, found on mountains and in arctic areas of both Eurasia and North America. ● *Silene acaulis*, family Caryophyllaceae.

moss green ▶ n. a bright green color like that of moss.

moss-grown ▶ adj. **1** overgrown with moss.
2 old; antiquated: *the mystery of its moss-grown, cobwebby past*.

Mos·si /'mäsē/ ▶ n. (pl. **same** or **Mossis**) a member of a people of Burkina Faso in West Africa.
▶ adj. of or relating to this people.
– ORIGIN the name in More.

moss·troop·er /'môs,troopər/ ▶ n. historical a person who lived by plundering property in the border region between England and Scotland during the 17th century.

moss·y /'môsē/ ▶ adj. (**mossier**, **mossiest**) covered in or resembling moss: *mossy tree trunks*. ■ informal old-fashioned or extremely conservative.
– DERIVATIVES **moss·i·ness** n.

moss·y·cup oak /'môsē,kəp/ ▶ n. another term for **BUR OAK**.

moss·y rose gall ▶ n. a reddish mosslike growth on rose bushes that forms in response to the developing larvae of a gall wasp. Also called **BEDEGUAR**. ● The wasp is *Diplolepis rosae*, family Cynipidae.

most /mōst/ ▶ determiner & pron. **1** superlative of **MANY**, **MUCH**.
2 greatest in amount or degree: [as determiner] *they've had the most success* | [as pronoun] *they had the most to lose*. ■ the majority of; nearly all of: [as determiner] *most oranges are sweeter than these* | [as pronoun] *I spent most of the winter on the coast*.
▶ adv. **1** superlative of **MUCH**.
2 to the greatest extent: *the things he most enjoyed* | *what she wanted most of all*. ■ forming the superlative of adjectives and adverbs, esp. those of more than one syllable: *the most important event of my life* | *sandy plains where fire tends to spread most quickly*.
3 extremely; very: *it was most kind of you* | *that is most probably correct*.
4 informal almost: *most everyone understood*.
– PHRASES **at (the) most** not more than: *the walk took four minutes at the most*. **be the most** informal be the best of all; be the ultimate. **for the most part** in most cases; usually: *the older members, for the most part, shun him*. **make the most of** use to the best advantage: *he was eager to make the most of his visit*. ■ represent at its best: *how to make the most of your features*.
– ORIGIN Old English *māst*, of Germanic origin; related to Dutch *meest* and German *meist*.

-most ▶ suffix forming superlative adjectives and adverbs from prepositions and other words indicating relative position: *innermost* | *uppermost*.
– ORIGIN Old English *-mest*, assimilated to **MOST**.

Mo·star /'mōstär/ a city in southern Bosnia and Herzegovina, southwest of Sarajevo, the chief town of Herzegovina; pop. 111,116 (2008). Its chief landmark, an old Turkish bridge across the Neretva River, was destroyed during the siege of the city by Serbian forces in 1993. The majority of Mostar's inhabitants are Muslim.

most·est /'mōstəst/ ▶ pron. humorous most: *the winner is the person who can get there quickest with the mostest*.

most fa·vored na·tion ▶ n. a country that has been granted the most favorable trading terms available by another country.

Most High (**the Most High**) God.

most·ly /'mōstlē/ ▶ adv. as regards the greater part or number: *I grow mostly annuals*. ■ usually; generally: *the weekends were spent mostly alone*.

Most Rev·er·end ▶ n. the title of an Anglican archbishop or an Irish Roman Catholic bishop.

most sig·nif·i·cant bit (abbr.: **MSB**) ▶ n. Computing the bit in a binary number that is of the greatest numerical value.

Mo·sul /mə'sōōl, 'mō,sōōl/ a city in northern Iraq, on the Tigris River, opposite the ruins of Nineveh; pop. 1,316,000 (est. 2007).

mot /mō/ ▶ n. (pl. **mots** /mō(z)/) short for **BON MOT**.

mote /mōt/ ▶ n. a tiny piece of a substance: *the tiniest mote of dust*.
– PHRASES **a mote in someone's eye** a fault in a person that is less serious than one in someone else who is being critical. [with biblical allusion to Matt. 7:3.]
– ORIGIN Old English *mot*, related to Dutch *mot* 'dust, sawdust.'

mo·tel /mō'tel/ ▶ n. a roadside hotel designed primarily for motorists, typically having the rooms arranged in a low building with parking directly outside.
– ORIGIN 1920s: blend of **MOTOR** and **HOTEL**.

mo·tet /mō'tet/ ▶ n. a short piece of sacred choral music, typically polyphonic and unaccompanied.
– ORIGIN late Middle English: from Old French, diminutive of *mot* 'word.'

moth /môTH/ ▶ n. (pl. **moths** /môTHz, môTHs/) a chiefly nocturnal insect related to the butterflies. It lacks the clubbed antennae of butterflies and typically has a stout body, drab coloration, and wings that fold flat when resting. ● Most superfamilies of the order Lepidoptera. Formerly placed in a grouping known as the Heterocera. ■ informal short for **CLOTHES MOTH**.
– PHRASES **like a moth to the flame** with an irresistible attraction for someone or something: *wealthy amateurs who have been attracted like moths to the glittering flames of showbiz*.
– ORIGIN Old English *moththe*, of Germanic origin; related to Dutch *mot* and German *Motte*.

moth·ball /'môTH,bôl/ ▶ n. (usu. **mothballs**) a small pellet of a pungent substance, typically naphthalene, put among stored clothes to keep away moths.
▶ v. [with obj.] store (clothes) among or in mothballs. ■ stop using (a piece of equipment or a building) but keep it in good condition so that it can readily be used again. ■ cancel or postpone work on (a plan or project): *plans to invest in four superstores have been mothballed*.
– PHRASES **in mothballs** unused but kept in good condition for future use.

moth-eat·en /'môTH ,ētn/ ▶ adj. damaged or destroyed by moths. ■ old-fashioned and no longer appropriate or useful.

moth·er /'məTHər/ ▶ n. **1** a woman in relation to a child or children to whom she has given birth. ■ a female animal in relation to its offspring: [as modifier] *a mother penguin*. ■ archaic (esp. as a form of address) an elderly woman. ■ (**Mother**, **Mother Superior**, or **Reverend Mother**) (esp. as a title or form of address) the head of a female religious community. ■ [as modifier] denoting an institution or organization from which more recently founded institutions of the same type derive: *the mother church*. ■ informal an extreme example or very large specimen of something: *I got stuck in the mother of all traffic jams*.
2 vulgar slang short for **MOTHERFUCKER**.
▶ v. [with obj.] **1** (often as noun **mothering**) bring up (a child) with care and affection: *the art of mothering*. ■ look after kindly and protectively, sometimes excessively so: *she felt mothered by her older sister*.
2 dated give birth to.
– DERIVATIVES **moth·er·hood** /-,hŏŏd/ n., **moth·er·less** adj., **moth·er·less·ness** n., **moth·er·like** /-,līk/ adj. & adv.
– ORIGIN Old English *mōdor*, of Germanic origin; related to Dutch *moeder* and German *Mutter*, from an Indo-European root shared by Latin *mater* and Greek *mētēr*.

Moth·er Ann see **LEE**[1].

moth·er·board /'məTHər,bôrd/ ▶ n. Computing a printed circuit board containing the principal components of a computer or other device, with connectors into which other circuit boards can be slotted.

Moth·er Car·ey's chick·en /'ke(ə)rēz/ ▶ n. old-fashioned term for **STORM PETREL**.
– ORIGIN mid 18th cent.: of unknown origin.

moth·er coun·try ▶ n. (often **the mother country**) a country in relation to its colonies: *the bicentennial of our separation from the mother country*.

moth·er·craft /'məTHər,kraft/ ▶ n. archaic skill in or knowledge of looking after children as a mother.

Moth·er Earth ▶ n. the earth considered as the source of all its living beings and inanimate things.

moth·er fig·ure ▶ n. a woman who is regarded as a source of nurture and support: *a housekeeper named Evelyn became a mother figure to him*.

moth·er·fuck·er /'məTHər,fəkər/ ▶ n. vulgar slang a despicable or very unpleasant person or thing.
– DERIVATIVES **moth·er·fuck·ing** /-,fəkiNG/ adj.

moth·er god·dess ▶ n. a mother-figure deity, a central figure of many early nature cults in which maintenance of fertility was of prime religious importance. Examples of such goddesses include Isis, Astarte, Cybele, and Demeter. Also called **GREAT MOTHER**.

Moth·er Goose ▶ n. the fictitious creator of a collection of nursery rhymes that was first published in London in the 1760s.

moth·er hen ▶ n. a person who sees to the needs of others, esp. in a fussy or interfering way.

moth·er·house /'məTHər,hous/ ▶ n. the founding house of a religious order.

Moth·er Hub·bard /'həbərd/ ▶ n. a long, loose-fitting, shapeless woman's dress or undergarment. ■ a kind of cloak.
– ORIGIN so named from early illustrations of the nursery rhyme.

moth·er-in-law ▶ n. (pl. **mothers-in-law**) the mother of one's husband or wife.

moth·er-in-law's tongue ▶ n. a West African plant of the agave family, having long slender leaves with yellow marginal stripes, often grown as a houseplant. ● *Sansevieria trifasciata*, family Agavaceae.

moth·er·land /'məTHər,land/ ▶ n. (often **the motherland**) one's native country.

moth·er lode ▶ **n.** Mining a principal vein of an ore or mineral. ■ a rich source of something: *your portfolio holds a mother lode of opportunities.*

moth·er·ly /ˈməT͟Hərlē/ ▶ **adj.** of, resembling, or characteristic of a mother, esp. in being caring, protective, and kind: *she held both her arms wide in a gesture of motherly love.*
– DERIVATIVES **moth·er·li·ness n.**
– ORIGIN Old English *mōdorlic* (see MOTHER, -LY[1]).

moth·er·na·ked ▶ **adj.** [predic.] wearing no clothes at all: *Dan was lying mother-naked.*

Moth·er Na·ture nature personified as a creative and controlling force: *Mother Nature has 80 percent control in putting out fires like this.*

Moth·er of God Christian Church a name given to the Virgin Mary (as mother of the divine Christ).

moth·er-of-pearl ▶ **n.** a smooth shining iridescent substance forming the inner layer of the shell of some mollusks, esp. oysters and abalones, used in ornamentation.

Moth·er of Pres·i·dents a nickname for the state of VIRGINIA[1].

Moth·er of States a nickname for the state of VIRGINIA[1].

Moth·er of the West a nickname for the state of MISSOURI.

Moth·er's Day ▶ **n.** a day of the year (in the US, the second Sunday in May) on which mothers are honored by their children.

moth·er's help·er ▶ **n.** a person who helps a mother, mainly by looking after her children.

moth·er ship (also **mothership**) ▶ **n.** a large spacecraft or ship from which smaller craft are launched or maintained. ■ a place regarded as a base, source, or headquarters: *the gallery quickly became Modernism's mother ship in jazz-age New York.*

moth·er's milk ▶ **n.** something regarded as absolutely necessary or appropriate: *the early work of Sturtevant and Morgan was mother's milk to geneticists.*

moth·er's son ▶ **n.** informal a man: ***every mother's son** personally knew his friendly local CIA agent.*

Moth·er Su·pe·ri·or (also **mother superior**) ▶ **n.** the head of a female religious community.

Moth·er Te·re·sa see TERESA, MOTHER.

moth·er-to-be ▶ **n.** (pl. **mothers-to-be**) a woman who is expecting a baby.

moth·er tongue ▶ **n.** the language that a person has grown up speaking from early childhood.

Moth·er·well /ˈməT͟Hərˌwel/, Robert (1915–91), US artist. He was a founder and leading exponent of the New York school of abstract expressionism. Many of his works, such as *Elegies to the Spanish Republic* (1948–68) were done in black and white oil paints.

moth·er wit ▶ **n.** natural ability to cope with everyday matters; common sense.

moth·er·wort /ˈməT͟Hərˌwərt, -ˌwôrt/ ▶ **n.** a tall strong-smelling plant of the mint family, with purplish-pink lipped flowers clustering close to the axils. It is used in herbal medicine, esp. in the treatment of gynecological disorders. ● *Leonurus cardiaca*, family Labiatae.

moth·proof /ˈmôTHˌpro͞of/ ▶ **adj.** (of clothes or fabrics) treated with a substance that repels moths.
▶ **v.** [with obj.] treat with a substance that repels moths.

moth·y /ˈmôTHē/ ▶ **adj.** (**mothier, mothiest**) infested with or damaged by moths: *tattered mothy curtains.*

mo·tif /mōˈtēf/ ▶ **n.** a decorative design or pattern: *T-shirts featuring spiral motifs.* ■ a distinctive feature or dominant idea in an artistic or literary composition: *the nautical motif of his latest novel.* ■ Music a short succession of notes producing a single impression; a brief melodic or rhythmic formula out of which longer passages are developed: *the motif in the second violin is submerged by the first violin's countermelody.* ■ an ornament of lace, braid, etc., sewn separately on a garment. ■ Biochemistry a distinctive sequence on a protein or DNA, having a three-dimensional structure that allows binding interactions to occur.
– ORIGIN mid 19th cent.: from French.

mo·tile /ˈmōtl, ˈmōˌtīl/ ▶ **adj. 1** Zoology & Botany (of cells, gametes, and single-celled organisms) capable of motion.
2 Psychology of, relating to, or characterized by responses that involve muscular rather than audiovisual sensations.
– DERIVATIVES **mo·til·i·ty** /mōˈtilətē/ **n.**
– ORIGIN mid 19th cent.: from Latin *motus* 'motion,' on the pattern of *mobile*.

mo·tion /ˈmōSHən/ ▶ **n. 1** the action or process of moving or being moved: *the laws of planetary motion* | *a cushioned shoe that doesn't restrict motion.* ■ a gesture: *she made a motion with her free hand.* ■ a piece of moving mechanism.
2 a formal proposal put to a legislature or committee: *the head of our commission **made a motion** that we rewrite the constitution.* ■ Law an application for a rule or order of court.
▶ **v.** [with obj.] **1** direct or command (someone) with a movement of the hand or head: *he motioned Dennis to a plush chair* | [with obj. and infinitive] *he motioned the young officer to sit down* | [no obj.] *he **motioned for** a time out.*
2 [no obj.] make a proposal in a deliberative or legislative body: [with clause] *she recognized the majority leader, who motioned that the body adjourn.*
– PHRASES **go through the motions** do something perfunctorily, without any enthusiasm or commitment. ■ simulate an action: *a child goes through the motions of washing up.* **in motion** moving: *flowing blonde hair that was constantly in motion.* **set something in motion** start something moving or working. ■ start or trigger a process or series of events: *plunging oil prices set in motion an economic collapse.*
– DERIVATIVES **mo·tion·al** /-SHənl/ **adj.**
– ORIGIN late Middle English: via Old French from Latin *motio(n-)*, from *movere* 'to move.'

mo·tion cap·ture (also **mocap**) ▶ **n.** a filmmaking technique in which actors wear special suits that allow computers to track their movements, to use as a basis for lifelike animated characters.

mo·tion·less /ˈmōSHənlis/ ▶ **adj.** not moving; stationary: *an eagle hung almost motionless close to the ground.*
– DERIVATIVES **mo·tion·less·ly adv.**

mo·tion pic·ture ▶ **n.** another term for MOVIE: [as modifier] *the motion-picture industry.*

mo·tion sick·ness ▶ **n.** nausea caused by motion, esp. by traveling in a vehicle.

mo·ti·vate /ˈmōtəˌvāt/ ▶ **v.** [with obj.] provide (someone) with a motive for doing something: *he was primarily motivated by the desire for profit.* ■ stimulate (someone's) interest in or enthusiasm for doing something: *I'm going to motivate kids to study civics.*
– DERIVATIVES **mo·ti·va·tor** /-ˌvātər/ **n.**

mo·ti·va·tion /ˌmōtəˈvāSHən/ ▶ **n.** the reason or reasons one has for acting or behaving in a particular way: *escape can be a strong motivation for travel.* ■ the general desire or willingness of someone to do something: *keep staff up to date and maintain interest and motivation.*
– DERIVATIVES **mo·ti·va·tion·al** /-SHənl/ **adj.**, **mo·ti·va·tion·al·ly** /-SHənl-ē/ **adv.**
– ORIGIN late 19th cent.: from MOTIVE, reinforced by MOTIVATE.

mo·ti·va·tion re·search ▶ **n.** the psychological or sociological investigation of motives, esp. those influencing the decisions of consumers.

mo·tive /ˈmōtiv/ ▶ **n. 1** a reason for doing something, esp. one that is hidden or not obvious: *a motive for his murder.*
2 (in art, literature, or music) a motif: *the entire work grows organically from the opening horn motive.*
▶ **adj.** [attrib.] **1** producing physical or mechanical motion: *the charge of gas is the motive force for every piston stroke.*
2 causing or being the reason for something: *the motive principle of a writer's work.*
– DERIVATIVES **mo·tive·less adj.**, **mo·tive·less·ly adv.**, **mo·tive·less·ness n.**
– ORIGIN late Middle English: from Old French *motif* (adjective used as a noun), from late Latin *motivus*, from *movere* 'to move.'

mo·tive pow·er ▶ **n.** the energy (in the form of steam, electricity, etc.) used to drive machinery. ■ the locomotive engines of a railroad system collectively.

mo·ti·vic /ˈmōtəvik/ ▶ **adj.** Music of or relating to a motif or motifs.

mot juste /ˌmō ˈZHYst/ ▶ **n.** (pl. **mots justes** pronunc. **same**) the exact, appropriate word.
– ORIGIN French.

Mot·lan·the /motˈlantā/, Kgalema (1949–), South African statesman, president 2008–09.

mot·ley /ˈmätlē/ ▶ **adj.** (**motlier, motliest**) incongruously varied in appearance or character; disparate: ***a motley crew** of discontents and zealots.*
▶ **n. 1** [usu. in sing.] an incongruous mixture: ***a motley of** interacting interest groups.*
2 historical the particolored costume of a jester: *life-size mannequins **in full motley**.*
– ORIGIN late Middle English: of unknown origin; perhaps ultimately related to MOTE.

mot·mot /ˈmätˌmät/ ▶ **n.** a tree-dwelling tropical American bird with colorful plumage, typically having two long racketlike tail feathers. ● Family Momotidae: several genera and species, in particular the widespread **blue-crowned motmot** (*Momotus momota*).
– ORIGIN mid 19th cent.: from Latin American Spanish, of imitative origin.

mo·to·cross /ˈmōtōˌkrôs, -ˌkräs/ ▶ **n.** cross-country racing on motorcycles.
– DERIVATIVES **mo·to·cross·er n.**
– ORIGIN late 20th cent.: abbreviation of MOTOR + CROSS.

mo·to·neu·ron /ˌmōtəˈn(y)o͞orˌän/ ▶ **n.** another term for MOTOR NEURON.

mo·to per·pet·u·o /ˈmōtō pərˈpeto͞oˌō/ ▶ **n.** (pl. **moto perpetui** /pərˈpetoo͞ˌē/) Music another term for PERPETUUM MOBILE.
– ORIGIN Italian, literally 'perpetual motion.'

mo·tor /ˈmōtər/ ▶ **n.** a machine, esp. one powered by electricity or internal combustion, that supplies motive power for a vehicle or for some other device with moving parts. ■ a source of power, energy, or motive force: *hormones are the motor of the sexual functions.*
▶ **adj.** [attrib.] **1** giving, imparting, or producing motion or action: *demand is the principle motor force governing economic activity.* ■ Physiology relating to muscular movement or the nerves activating it: *the motor functions of each hand.*
2 chiefly Brit. driven by a motor. ■ of or relating to motor vehicles: *a dominant figure in the world of motor sports.*
▶ **v.** [no obj.] informal travel in a motor vehicle, typically a car or a boat: *we motored along a narrow road* | *we motored out of Breton Bay to begin our return trip down the Potomac.* ■ informal run or move as fast as possible: *he had motored along to second base on a passed ball.* ■ [with obj.] chiefly Brit. convey (someone) somewhere in a motor vehicle: *he hired someone to motor him back.*
– ORIGIN late Middle English (denoting a person who imparts motion): from Latin, literally 'mover,' based on *movere* 'to move.' The current sense of the noun dates from the mid 19th cent.

mo·tor ar·e·a ▶ **n.** Anatomy a part of the central nervous system concerned with muscular action, esp. the motor cortex.

mo·tor·bike /ˈmōtərˌbīk/ ▶ **n.** a lightweight motorcycle.

mo·tor·boat /ˈmōtərˌbōt/ ▶ **n.** a boat powered by a motor, esp. a recreational boat.

mo·tor·bus /ˈmōtərˌbəs/ ▶ **n.** old-fashioned term for BUS (sense 1 of the noun).

mo·tor·cade /ˈmōtərˌkād/ ▶ **n.** a procession of motor vehicles, typically carrying and escorting a prominent person.
– ORIGIN early 20th cent.: from MOTOR, on the pattern of *cavalcade*.

mo·tor·car /ˈmōtərˌkär/ ▶ **n. 1** dated or Brit. an automobile.
2 a self-propelled railroad vehicle used to carry railroad workers.

mo·tor coach ▶ **n.** another term for COACH[1] (sense 3 of the noun).

mo·tor cor·tex ▶ **n.** Anatomy the part of the cerebral cortex in the brain where the nerve impulses originate that initiate voluntary muscular activity.

mo·tor·cy·cle /ˈmōtərˌsīkəl/ ▶ **n.** a two-wheeled vehicle that is powered by a motor and has no pedals.
– DERIVATIVES **mo·tor·cy·cling** /-ˌsīk(ə)liNG/ **n.**, **mo·tor·cy·clist** /-ˌsīk(ə)list/ **n.**

motorcycle

mo·tor drive ▶ **n.** a mechanical system that includes an electric motor and drives a machine. ■ a battery-driven motor in a camera used to wind the film rapidly between exposures.

mo·tor gen·er·a·tor ▶ **n.** a device consisting of a mechanically coupled electric motor and generator that may be used to control the voltage, frequency, or phase of an electrical supply.

mo·tor home ▶ n. a motor vehicle equipped like a trailer for living in, with kitchen facilities, beds, etc.

mo·tor·ic /ˈmōtərik/ ▶ adj. **1** Physiology relating to muscular movement: *the infants' motoric and linguistic capabilities*.
2 (usu. **motorik**) (of music) marked by a repetitive beat suggestive of mechanized action or movement.
– ORIGIN late 19th cent.: from MOTOR + -IC, after German *Motorik* 'motor functions.'

mo·tor inn (also **motor hotel** or **motor lodge**) ▶ n. a motel.

mo·tor·ist /ˈmōtərist/ ▶ n. the driver of an automobile.

mo·tor·ize /ˈmōtəˌrīz/ ▶ v. [with obj.] (usu. as adj. **motorized**) equip (a vehicle or device) with a motor to operate or propel it: *a motorized wheelchair*. ■ equip (troops) with motor transportation: *three motorized divisions*.
– DERIVATIVES **mo·tor·i·za·tion** /ˌmōtərəˈzāshən/ n.

mo·tor launch ▶ n. see LAUNCH².

mo·tor·man /ˈmōtərˌmən/ ▶ n. (pl. **motormen**) the driver of an electric vehicle, esp. a streetcar or subway train.

mo·tor·mouth /ˈmōtərˌmouTH/ ▶ n. informal a person who talks quickly and incessantly.
– DERIVATIVES **mo·tor·mouthed** /-ˌmouT͟Hd, -ˌmouTHt/ (or **motor-mouthed**) adj.

mo·tor nerve ▶ n. a nerve carrying impulses from the brain or spinal cord to a muscle or gland.

mo·tor neu·ron ▶ n. a nerve cell forming part of a pathway along which impulses pass from the brain or spinal cord to a muscle or gland.

mo·tor·sail·er /ˈmōtərˌsālər/ ▶ n. a boat equipped with both sails and an engine.

mo·tor scoot·er ▶ n. see SCOOTER.

mo·tor·sport /ˈmōtərˌspôrt/ ▶ n. a sport involving the racing of motor vehicles, esp. cars and motorcycles: *they claim drag racing is the most exciting motorsport* | (as modifier **motorsports**) *a first-rate motorsports facility*.

mo·tor ve·hi·cle ▶ n. a road vehicle powered by an internal combustion engine; an automobile.

mo·tor vo·ter law ▶ n. another name for the National Voter Registration Act of 1993, designed to reverse declining voter registration by allowing voters to register at motor vehicle departments.

mo·tor·way /ˈmōtərˌwā/ ▶ n. Brit. an expressway. ■ informal a wide, fast, easy ski run.

Mo·town /ˈmōˌtoun/ ▶ n. **1** (also trademark **Tamla Motown**) music released on or reminiscent of the US record label Tamla Motown. The first black-owned record company in the US, Tamla Motown was founded in Detroit in 1959 by Berry Gordy, and was important in popularizing soul music, producing artists such as the Supremes, Stevie Wonder, and Marvin Gaye.
2 informal name for DETROIT.
– ORIGIN 1960s: shortening of *Motor Town*, by association with the car manufacturing industry of Detroit.

Mott /mät/, Lucretia (Coffin) (1793–1880), US social reformer. A progressive Quaker minister, she was a highly motivated activist in the cause of abolition, women's rights, and freedom of religion. She wrote *Discourse on Women* (1850) and helped to form the Free Religious Association 1867.

motte /mät/ ▶ n. **1** (also **mott**) a stand of trees, esp. in the southwestern US; a grove.
2 historical a mound forming the site of a castle or camp.
– ORIGIN late 19th cent.: from French, 'mound,' from Old French *mote* (see MOAT).

mot·tle /ˈmätl/ ▶ v. [with obj.] (usu. **be mottled**) mark with spots or smears of color: *the cow's coat was light red mottled with white* | (as adj. **mottled**) *a bird with mottled brown plumage*.
▶ n. an irregular arrangement of spots or patches of color: *the ship was a mottle of khaki and black*. ■ (also **mottling**) a spot or patch forming part of such an arrangement: *the mottles on a trout* | *white marble with mottlings of black and gray*.
– ORIGIN late 18th cent.: probably a back-formation from MOTLEY.

mot·to /ˈmätō/ ▶ n. (pl. **mottoes** or **mottos**) a short sentence or phrase chosen as encapsulating the beliefs or ideals guiding an individual, family, or institution: *the school motto, "Serve and obey"* | *he soon adopted the motto "work hard and play hard."* ■ Music a phrase that recurs throughout a musical work and has some symbolic significance.
– ORIGIN late 16th cent.: from Italian, 'word.'

mo·tu pro·pri·o /ˈmōtoo ˈprōprēˌō/ ▶ n. (pl. **motu proprios**) an edict issued by the pope personally to the Roman Catholic Church or to a part of it.
– ORIGIN Latin, literally 'of one's own volition.'

moue /moo/ ▶ n. a pouting expression used to convey annoyance or distaste.
– ORIGIN mid 19th cent.: French, earlier having the sense 'lip.'

mouf·lon /ˈmoofˌlôN/ (also **moufflon**) ▶ n. a small wild sheep with chestnut-brown wool, found in mountainous country from Iran to Asia Minor. It is the ancestor of the domestic sheep. ● *Ovis orientalis*, family Bovidae.
– ORIGIN late 18th cent.: from French, from Italian *muflone*.

mouil·lé /mooˈyā/ ▶ adj. Phonetics (of a consonant) palatalized.
– ORIGIN French, 'wetted.'

mou·jik /mooˈZHēk, -ˈZHik/ ▶ n. variant spelling of MUZHIK.

mould /mōld/ ▶ n. & v. British spelling of MOLD¹, MOLD², and MOLD³.

mould·er /ˈmōldər/ ▶ v. & n. British spelling of MOLDER¹.

mould·ing /ˈmōldiNG/ ▶ n. British spelling of MOLDING.

mould·y /ˈmōldē/ ▶ adj. British spelling of MOLDY.

mou·lin /mooˈlan/ ▶ n. a vertical or nearly vertical shaft in a glacier, formed by surface water percolating through a crack in the ice.
– ORIGIN mid 19th cent.: French, literally 'mill.'

Mou·lin Rouge /mooˈlan ˈroozh/ a cabaret in Montmartre, Paris, a favorite resort of poets and artists around the end of the 19th century. Toulouse-Lautrec immortalized its dancers in his posters.
– ORIGIN French, literally 'red windmill.'

Moul·mein /ˌmoolˈmān, ˌmōlˈmīn/ a port in southeastern Burma (Myanmar); pop. 405,800 (est. 2004).

moult /mōlt/ ▶ v. & n. British spelling of MOLT.

moul·vi /ˈmoolvē, ˈmôl-/ (also **maulvi**, **molvi**) ▶ n. (pl. **moulvis**) a Muslim doctor of law; an imam.
– ORIGIN from Urdu *maulvī*, from Arabic *mawlawī* 'judicial' (adjective used as a noun), from *mawlā* 'mullah.'

mound¹ /mound/ ▶ n. a rounded mass projecting above a surface. ■ a raised mass of earth, stones, or other compacted material, sometimes created artificially for purposes of defense or burial. ■ a small hill. ■ (**a mound of/mounds of**) a large pile or quantity of something: *burying potential problems under mounds of cash*. ■ Baseball (in full **pitcher's mound**) the elevated area from which the pitcher delivers the ball.
▶ v. [with obj.] heap up into a rounded pile: *mound the pie filling slightly in the center*. ■ archaic enclose, bound, or fortify with an embankment: *hills that mound the sea*.
– PHRASES **take the mound** Baseball (of a pitcher) have a turn at pitching: *Morris will take the mound Tuesday*.
– ORIGIN early 16th cent. (as a verb in the sense 'enclose with a fence or hedge'): of obscure origin. An early sense of the noun was 'boundary hedge or fence.'

mound² ▶ n. archaic a ball representing the earth, used as part of royal regalia, e.g., on top of a crown, typically of gold and surmounted by a cross.
– ORIGIN Middle English (denoting the world): from Old French *monde*, from Latin *mundus* 'world.'

mound build·er ▶ n. another term for MEGAPODE.

mounds·man /ˈmoun(d)zmən/ ▶ n. (pl. **moundsmen**) Baseball a pitcher.

mount¹ /mount/ ▶ v. [with obj.] **1** climb up (stairs, a hill, or other rising surface): *he mounted the steps to the front door*. ■ climb or move up onto (a raised surface): *the master of ceremonies mounted the platform*. ■ get up on (an animal or bicycle) in order to ride it. ■ set (someone) on horseback; provide with a horse: *she was mounted on a white horse*. ■ (of a male mammal or bird) get on (a female) for the purpose of copulation. ■ [no obj.] (of the blood or its color) rise into the cheeks: *feeling the blush mount in her cheeks, she looked down quickly*.
2 organize and initiate (a campaign or other significant course of action): *the company had successfully mounted takeover bids*. ■ establish; set up: *security forces mounted checkpoints at every key road*. ■ produce (a play, exhibition, or other artistic event); present for public view or display.
3 [no obj.] grow larger or more numerous: *the costs mount up when you buy a home*. ■ (of a feeling) become stronger or more intense: *his anxiety mounted as messages were left unanswered*.
4 place or fix (an object) in its operating position: *fluorescent lights are mounted on the ceiling* | *the engine is mounted behind the rear seats*. ■ set in or attach to a backing or setting: *the photographs will be mounted and framed*. ■ fix (an object for viewing) on a microscope slide. ■ Computing make (a disk or disk drive) available for use.
▶ n. **1** a backing or setting on which a photograph, gem, or work of art is set for display. ■ a glass microscope slide for securing a specimen to be viewed. ■ Philately a clear plastic or paper sleeve used to display a postage stamp.
2 a support for a gun, camera, or similar piece of equipment.
3 a horse being ridden or that is available for riding: *he hung onto his mount's bridle*. ■ an opportunity to ride a horse, esp. as a jockey: *the jockey's injuries forced him to give up the coveted mount on Cool Ground*.
– PHRASES **mount guard** keep watch, esp. for protection or to prevent escape.
– DERIVATIVES **mount·a·ble** adj., **mount·er** n.
– ORIGIN Middle English: from Old French *munter*, based on Latin *mons, mont-* 'mountain.'

mount² ▶ n. a mountain or hill (archaic except in place names): *Mount Everest*. ■ any of several fleshy prominences on the palm of the hand regarded in palmistry as signifying the degree of influence of a particular planet: *mount of Mars*.
– ORIGIN Old English *munt*, from Latin *mons, mont-* 'mountain,' reinforced in Middle English by Old French *mont*.

moun·tain /ˈmountn/ ▶ n. a large natural elevation of the earth's surface rising abruptly from the surrounding level; a large steep hill: *the village is backed by awe-inspiring mountains* | *we set off down the mountain* | [as modifier] *the ice and snow of a mountain peak*. ■ (**mountains**) a region where there are many such features, characterized by remoteness and inaccessibility: *they sought refuge in the mountains* | (as adj. **mountain**) *his attempt to picture the mountain folk in ridiculous attire*. ■ (**a mountain/mountains of**) a large pile or quantity of something: *a mountain of paperwork*. ■ [usu. with modifier] a large surplus stock of a commodity: *this farming produced huge food mountains*.
– PHRASES **make a mountain out of a molehill** see MOLEHILL. **move mountains 1** achieve spectacular and apparently impossible results. **2** make every possible effort: *his fans move mountains to catch as many of his performances as possible*.
– DERIVATIVES **moun·tain·y** adj.
– ORIGIN Middle English: from Old French *montaigne*, based on Latin *mons, mont-* 'mountain.'

moun·tain ash ▶ n. **1** a small deciduous tree of the rose family, with compound leaves, white flowers, and red berries. Also called ROWAN. ● Genus *Sorbus*, family Rosaceae: several species, in particular the North American *S. americana*.
2 Austral. a eucalyptus tree that is widely used for timber. ● Genus *Eucalyptus*, family Myrtaceae: several species, in particular the very tall *E. regnans*.

moun·tain av·ens ▶ n. a creeping arctic-alpine plant with white flowers and glossy leaves. See also DRYAS. ● *Dryas octopetala*, family Rosaceae.

moun·tain bea·ver ▶ n. a burrowing forest-dwelling rodent occurring only in western North America, from British Columbia to California. Also called SEWELLEL. ● *Aplodontia rufa*, the only member of the family Aplodontidae.

moun·tain bike ▶ n. a bicycle with a light sturdy frame, broad deep-treaded tires, and multiple gears, originally designed for riding on mountainous terrain.
– DERIVATIVES **moun·tain bik·er** n., **moun·tain bik·ing** n.

moun·tain·board·ing /ˈmountnˌbôrdiNG/ ▶ n. the sport or recreational activity of riding a dirtboard down hills and mountains.
– DERIVATIVES **moun·tain·board** n.

moun·tain chain ▶ n. a connected series of mountains.

moun·tain cran·ber·ry ▶ n. (pl. **mountain cranberries**) a low-growing evergreen dwarf shrub of the heath family that bears dark red berries and grows in upland habitats in the north. Also called COWBERRY, LINGONBERRY. ● *Vaccinium vitis-idaea*, family Ericaceae. ■ the edible acid berry of this plant, which may be used as a cranberry substitute.

moun·tain dew ▶ n. informal illicitly distilled liquor, esp. whiskey or rum; moonshine.

moun·tain dul·ci·mer ▶ n. see DULCIMER.

moun·tain·eer /ˌmountnˈi(ə)r/ ▶ n. a person who takes part in mountaineering. ■ rare a person living in a mountainous area.

moun·tain·eer·ing /ˌmountnˈi(ə)riNG/ ▶ n. the sport or activity of climbing mountains.

moun·tain gem ▶ n. a green hummingbird found in the upland forests of Central America. ● Genus *Lampornis*, family Trochilidae: several species.

moun·tain goat ▶ n. **1** (also **Rocky Mountain goat**) a goat-antelope with shaggy white hair and backward curving horns, living in the Rocky Mountains. ● *Oreamnos americanus*, family Bovidae.
2 any goat that lives on mountains, proverbial for agility.

mountain goat

moun·tain lau·rel ▶ n. a North American kalmia that bears clusters of white or pink flowers. ● *Kalmia latifolia*, family Ericaceae.

moun·tain li·on ▶ n. another term for COUGAR.

moun·tain·ous /'mountn-əs/ ▶ adj. (of a region) having many mountains. ■ huge: *struggling under mountainous debts.*

moun·tain range ▶ n. a line of mountains connected by high ground.

moun·tain sheep ▶ n. another term for BIGHORN. ■ any sheep that lives on mountains.

moun·tain sick·ness ▶ n. another term for ALTITUDE SICKNESS.

moun·tain·side /'mountn,sīd/ ▶ n. the sloping surface of a mountain.

Moun·tain State a nickname for the state of WEST VIRGINIA.

Moun·tain States the region of the US that includes states that contain part of the Rocky Mountains. New Mexico, Colorado, Wyoming, Utah, Idaho, and Montana are generally considered Mountain States.

Moun·tain time the standard time in a zone including parts of the US and Canada in or near the Rocky Mountains, specifically. ● (**Mountain Standard Time** abbrev.: **MST**) standard time based on the mean solar time at the meridian 105° W., seven hours behind GMT. ● (**Mountain Daylight Time** abbrev.: **MDT**) Mountain time during daylight saving time, six hours behind GMT.

moun·tain·top /'mountəntäp/ ▶ n. the summit or top part of a mountain.

Moun·tain View a city in north central California, near the southern end of San Francisco Bay, part of the Silicon Valley complex; pop. 71,348 (est. 2008).

Mount Ar·a·rat, Mount Car·mel, etc. see ARARAT, MOUNT; CARMEL, MOUNT, etc.

Mount·bat·ten /,moun(t)'batn/, Louis (Francis Albert Victor Nicholas), 1st Earl Mountbatten of Burma (1900–79), British admiral and administrator; his nephew was Britain's Prince Philip. He was supreme Allied commander in Southeast Asia 1943–45; after the war, he was the last viceroy 1947 and first governor general of India 1947–48. He was killed by an IRA bomb while on his yacht.

Mount Des·ert Is·land an island in the Atlantic Ocean, in southeastern Maine, site of Bar Harbor and other resorts. Most of the island is in Acadia National Park.

moun·te·bank /'mounti,baNGk/ ▶ n. a person who deceives others, esp. in order to trick them out of their money; a charlatan. ■ historical a person who sold patent medicines in public places.
– DERIVATIVES **moun·te·bank·er·y** /-,baNGkərē/ n.
– ORIGIN late 16th cent.: from Italian *montambanco*, from the imperative phrase *monta in banco!* 'climb on the bench!' (with allusion to the raised platform used to attract an audience).

mount·ed /'mountid/ ▶ adj. [attrib.] riding an animal, typically a horse, esp. for military or other duty: *mounted police controlled the crowd.*

Moun·tie /'mountē/ ▶ n. informal a member of the Royal Canadian Mounted Police.

mount·ing /'mountiNG/ ▶ n. **1** a backing, setting, or support for something: *he pulled the curtain rod from its mounting.*
2 the action of mounting something: *the mounting of rapid-fire guns.*

Mount of Ol·ives the highest point in the range of hills to the east of Jerusalem. It is a holy place for both Judaism and Christianity and is frequently mentioned in the Bible. The Garden of Gethsemane is located nearby.

Mount Pleas·ant a town in southeastern South Carolina, a resort on the Atlantic Ocean, east of Charleston; pop. 65,472 (est. 2008).

Mount Ver·non /'vərnən/ **1** a city in southeastern New York, north of the Bronx in New York City; pop. 68,653 (est. 2008).
2 an estate in northeastern Virginia, about 15 miles (24 km) from Washington, DC, on a site overlooking the Potomac River. Built in 1743, it was the home of George Washington 1747–99.

mourn /môrn/ ▶ v. [with obj.] feel or show deep sorrow or regret for (someone or their death), typically by following conventions such as the wearing of black clothes: *Isabel mourned her husband* | [no obj.] *she had to mourn for her friends who died in the accident.* ■ feel regret or sadness about (the loss or disappearance of something): *publishers mourned declining sales of hardback fiction.*
– ORIGIN Old English *murnan*, of Germanic origin.

mourn·er /'môrnər/ ▶ n. **1** a person who attends a funeral as a relative or friend of the dead person. ■ chiefly historical a person hired to attend a funeral.
2 any of a number of drab-colored South American tyrant flycatchers and related birds. ● Families Tyrannidae, Pipridae, and Cotingidae: four genera and several species; the classification is uncertain.

mourn·ful /'môrnfəl/ ▶ adj. feeling, expressing, or inducing sadness, regret, or grief: *the third boy stared fixedly at me with mournful, basset-hound eyes* | *his voice on one track, mournful piano on another.*
– DERIVATIVES **mourn·ful·ly** adv., **mourn·ful·ness** n.

mourn·ing /'môrniNG/ ▶ n. the expression of deep sorrow for someone who has died, typically involving following certain conventions such as wearing black clothes: *she's still in mourning after the death of her husband.* ■ black clothes worn as an expression of grief when someone dies.

mourn·ing band ▶ n. a strip of black material that is worn around a person's sleeve as a mark of respect for someone who has recently died.

mourn·ing cloak ▶ n. a migratory butterfly with deep purple yellow-bordered wings. ● *Nymphalis antiopa*, subfamily Nymphalinae, family Nymphalidae.

mourning cloak

mourn·ing dove ▶ n. a North and Central American dove with a long tail, a gray-brown back, and a plaintive call. ● *Zenaida macroura*, family Columbidae.

mourn·ing ring ▶ n. historical a ring worn to remind the wearer of someone who has died.

mouse ▶ n. /mous/ (pl. **mice** /mīs/) **1** a small rodent that typically has a pointed snout, relatively large ears and eyes, and a long tail. ● Family Muridae: many genera and numerous species. Also, some species in the families Heteromyidae, Zapodidae, and Muscardinidae. ■ (in general use) any similar small mammal, such as a shrew or vole. ■ a shy, timid, and quiet person.
2 a dull light brown color reminiscent of a mouse's fur: *her blonde hair dulled to mouse.*
3 (pl. also **mouses**) a small handheld device that is dragged across a flat surface to move the cursor on a computer screen, typically having buttons that are pressed to control functions.
4 informal a lump or bruise, esp. one on or near the eye.
▶ v. /mouz/ [no obj.] **1** (of a cat or owl) hunt for or catch mice. ■ [with adverbial] prowl around as if searching: *he was mousing among the books of the old library.*
2 [with adverbial of direction] use a mouse to move a cursor on a computer screen: *mouse over to the window and click on it.*
– DERIVATIVES **mouse·like** adj.
– ORIGIN Old English *mūs*, (plural) *mȳs*, of Germanic origin; related to Dutch *muis* and German *Maus*, from an Indo-European root shared by Latin and Greek *mus*.

> **USAGE** Is the plural of **mouse** in the computing sense **mice** or **mouses**? People often feel that this sense needs its own distinctive plural, but in fact the ordinary plural **mice** is more common, and the first recorded use of the term in the plural (1984) is **mice**.

mouse·bird /'mous,bərd/ ▶ n. a small gregarious African bird with mainly drab plumage, a crest, and a long tail. ● Genera *Colius* and *Urocolius*, family Coliidae: six species.

mouse deer ▶ n. another term for CHEVROTAIN.

mouse-ear chickweed ▶ n. see CHICKWEED.

mouse-eared bat ▶ n. another term for MYOTIS.

mouse le·mur ▶ n. a small nocturnal Madagascan lemur with large ears, close-set eyes, and a long tail. ● Genus *Microcebus*, family Cheirogaleidae: three species. See also DWARF LEMUR.

mouse mat (also **mousemat**) ▶ n. British term for MOUSE PAD.

mouse o·pos·sum ▶ n. a mouselike opossum with large ears and no marsupial pouch, native to Central and South America. ● Genus *Marmosa*, family Didelphidae: several species.

mouse pad (also **mousepad**) ▶ n. a piece of rigid or slightly resilient material on which a computer mouse is moved.

mous·er /'mousər, -zər/ ▶ n. an animal that catches mice, esp. a cat.

mouse-tailed bat ▶ n. an insectivorous bat with a long mouselike tail, native to Africa and Asia and often found in man-made structures. ● Family Rhinopomatidae and genus *Rhinopoma*: three species.

mouse·trap /'mous,trap/ ▶ n. a trap for catching and usually killing mice, esp. one with a spring bar that snaps down onto the mouse when it touches a piece of cheese or other bait attached to the mechanism.
▶ v. (**mousetraps, mousetrapping, mousetrapped**) [with obj.] informal induce (someone) to do something by means of a trick: *the editor mousetrapped her into giving him an article.* ■ block (a user's) efforts to exit from a website, usually one to which they have been redirected.
– PHRASES **a better mousetrap** an improved version of a well-known item. [from 'If a man ... make a better mouse-trap than his neighbour ... the world will make a beaten path to his door,' attributed to Ralph Waldo Emerson.]

mous·ey ▶ adj. variant spelling of MOUSY.

mous·sa·ka /mo͞o'säkə, ,mo͞osə'kä/ ▶ n. a Greek dish made of ground lamb, eggplant, and tomatoes, with cheese on top.
– ORIGIN from Turkish *musakka*, based on Arabic.

mousse /mo͞os/ ▶ n. a sweet or savory dish made as a smooth light mass with whipped cream and beaten egg white, flavored with chocolate, fish, etc., and typically served chilled: *roulade of sole with a lobster mousse* | *dark chocolate mousse.* ■ a soft, light, or aerated gel such as a soap preparation: *fragrant shower mousse.* ■ a frothy preparation that is applied to the hair, enabling it to be styled more easily. ■ (also **chocolate mousse**) a brown frothy emulsion of oil and seawater formed by weathering of an oil slick.
▶ v. [with obj.] style (hair) using mousse.
– ORIGIN mid 19th cent.: from French, 'moss or froth.'

mousse·line /,mo͞osə'lēn, -'slēn/ ▶ n. **1** a fine, semiopaque fabric similar to muslin, typically made of silk, wool, or cotton.
2 a soft, light mousse.
3 (also **sauce mousseline**) hollandaise sauce that has been made frothy with whipped cream or egg white, served mainly with fish or asparagus.
– ORIGIN late 17th cent.: from French (see MUSLIN).

mousse·ron /,mo͞os(ə)'rôN/ ▶ n. an edible mushroom with a flattish white cap, pink gills, and a mealy smell. ● *Clitopilus prunulus*, family Agaricaceae, class Hymenomycetes.

mous·seux /mo͞o'sœ/ ▶ adj. (of wine) sparkling: *vin mousseux.*
▶ n. (pl. **same**) sparkling wine.
– ORIGIN from French, from *mousse* 'froth.'

mous·tache ▶ n. variant spelling of MUSTACHE.

Mous·te·ri·an /mo͞o'sti(ə)rēən/ ▶ adj. Archaeology of, relating to, or denoting the main culture of the Middle Paleolithic period in Europe, between the Acheulian and Aurignacian periods (chiefly 80,000–35,000 years ago), and associated with Neanderthal peoples. ■ (as noun **the Mousterian**) the Mousterian culture or period.
– ORIGIN late 19th cent.: from French *moustérien*, from *Le Moustier*, a cave in southwestern France where objects from this culture were found.

m

mous·y /ˈmousē, -zē/ (also **mousey**) ▶ **adj.** (**mousier**, **mousiest**) of or like a mouse. ■ (of hair) of a dull light brown color. ■ (of a person) nervous, shy, or timid; lacking in presence or charisma: *his mousy sister had become a dynamic journalist.*
– DERIVATIVES **mous·i·ness** **n.**

Mou·tan /ˈmo͞oˌtan/ (also **Moutan peony**) ▶ **n.** a tall shrubby peony with pink or white mottled flowers, native to China and Tibet and the parent of many garden varieties. ● *Paeonia suffruticosa*, family Paeoniaceae.
– ORIGIN early 19th cent.: from Chinese *mudan.*

mouth ▶ **n.** /mouTH/ (pl. **mouths** /mouT͟Hz, mouTHs/) **1** the opening in the lower part of the human face, surrounded by the lips, through which food is taken in and from which speech and other sounds are emitted. ■ the corresponding opening through which an animal takes in food (at the front of the head in vertebrates and many other creatures), or the cavity behind this. ■ [usu. with adj.] a horse's readiness to feel and obey the pressure of the bit in its mouth: *the horse had a* **hard mouth**. ■ the character or quality of a wine as judged by its feel or flavor in the mouth (rather than its aroma). ■ informal talkativeness; impudence: *you've got more mouth on you than anyone I've ever known.*
2 an opening or entrance to a structure that is hollow, concave, or almost completely enclosed: *standing before the mouth of a cave.* ■ the opening for filling or emptying something used as a container: *the mouth of the bottle.* ■ the muzzle of a gun. ■ the opening or entrance to a harbor or bay: *walking to the mouth of the bay to absorb the view.* ■ the place where a river enters the sea.
▶ **v.** /mouT͟H, mouTH/ [with obj.] **1** say (something dull or unoriginal), esp. in a pompous or affected way: *this clergyman mouths platitudes in breathy, soothing tones.* ■ utter very clearly and distinctly: *she would carefully mouth the right pronunciation.* ■ move the lips as if saying (something) or in a grimace: *she mouthed a silent farewell* | [with direct speech] *"Come on," he mouthed.*
2 take in or touch with the mouth: *puppies may mouth each other's collars during play.* ■ train the mouth of (a horse) so that it responds to a bit.
– PHRASES **a mouth to feed** a person, typically a child, who has to be looked after and fed: *how can they afford another mouth to feed?* **be all mouth** informal tend to talk boastfully without any intention of acting on one's words. **keep one's mouth shut** informal not say anything, esp. not reveal a secret: *would he keep his mouth shut under interrogation?* **open one's mouth** informal say something: *sorry, I'll never open my mouth about you again.* **watch one's mouth** informal be careful about what one says.
– PHRASAL VERBS **mouth off** informal talk in an unpleasantly loud and boastful or opinionated way: *he was mouthing off about society in general.* ■ (**mouth off at**) loudly criticize or abuse.
– DERIVATIVES **mouthed** /mouT͟Hd, mouTHt/ **adj.** [in combination] *wide-mouthed*, **mouth·er** /ˈmouT͟Hər/ **n.**, **mouth·less** /ˈmouTHləs/ **adj.**
– ORIGIN Old English *mūth*, of Germanic origin; related to Dutch *mond* and German *Mund*, from an Indo-European root shared by Latin *mentum* 'chin.'

mouth-breath·er ▶ **n.** informal a stupid person.

mouth·brood·er /ˈmouTHˌbro͞odər/ ▶ **n.** a freshwater cichlid fish that protects its eggs (and in some cases its young) by carrying them in its mouth. ● *Sarotherodon* and other genera, family Cichlidae.

mouth·feel /ˈmouTHˌfēl/ ▶ **n.** the physical sensations in the mouth produced by a particular food: *this Cabernet has a dense, tightly woven mouthfeel, with complex, chewy, and velvety tannins.*

mouth·ful /ˈmouTHˌfo͝ol/ ▶ **n.** (pl. **mouthfuls**) **1** a quantity of food or drink that fills or can be put into the mouth: *he took* **a mouthful of** *beer* | *savor the flavor of each mouthful.*
2 a long or complicated word or phrase that is difficult to say: *"Galinsoga" was too much of a mouthful for most nonbotanists.*
– PHRASES **give someone a mouthful** informal talk to or shout at someone in an angry, abusive, or severely critical way. **say a mouthful** informal say something noteworthy.

mouth·guard /ˈmouTHˌgärd/ ▶ **n.** a plastic shield held in the mouth by an athlete to protect the teeth and gums.

mouth or·gan ▶ **n.** another term for HARMONICA.

mouth·part /ˈmouTHˌpärt/ ▶ **n.** (usu. **mouthparts**) Zoology any of the appendages, typically found in pairs, surrounding the mouth of an insect or other arthropod and adapted for feeding.

mouth·piece /ˈmouTHˌpēs/ ▶ **n.** **1** a thing designed to be put in or against the mouth: *the snorkel's mouthpiece.* ■ a part of a musical instrument placed between or against the lips. ■ the part of a telephone for speaking into. ■ the part of a tobacco pipe placed between the lips. ■ a mouthguard.
2 chiefly derogatory a person or organization that speaks on behalf of another person or organization: *they become nothing more than a mouthpiece for the company.* ■ informal a lawyer.

mouth-to-mouth ▶ **adj.** denoting a method of artificial respiration in which a person breathes into an unconscious patient's lungs through the mouth: *mouth-to-mouth resuscitation.*
▶ **n.** respiration of this kind.

mouth·wash /ˈmouTHˌwôsH, -ˌwäsH/ ▶ **n.** a liquid used for rinsing the mouth or gargling with, typically containing an antiseptic.

mouth·wa·ter·ing /ˈmouTHˌwôtəriNG/ ▶ **adj.** smelling, looking, or sounding delicious: *a small but mouthwatering collection of recipes.* ■ highly attractive or tempting: *investors expected the new boss to tie up some mouthwatering deals.*

mouth·y /ˈmouT͟Hē, ˈmouTHē/ ▶ **adj.** (**mouthier**, **mouthiest**) informal inclined to talk a lot, esp. in an impudent way.

mou·ton /ˈmo͞oˌtän, mo͞oˈtän/ ▶ **n.** sheepskin cut and dyed to resemble beaver fur or sealskin.
– ORIGIN mid 20th cent.: from French, literally 'sheep.'

mov·a·ble /ˈmo͞ovəbəl/ (also **moveable**) ▶ **adj.**
1 capable of being moved: *they stripped the town of all movable objects and fled.* ■ (of a feast or festival) variable in date from year to year. See also MOVABLE FEAST.
2 Law (of property) of the nature of a chattel, as distinct from land or buildings. Compare with HERITABLE.
▶ **n.** (usu. **movables**) property or possessions not including land or buildings. ■ an article of furniture that may be removed from a house, as distinct from a fixture.
– DERIVATIVES **mov·a·bil·i·ty** /ˌmo͞ovəˈbilətē/ **n.**, **mov·a·bly** /-blē/ **adv.**
– ORIGIN late Middle English: from Old French, from *moveir* 'to move.'

mov·a·ble-do /dō/ (Brit. **movable-doh**) ▶ **adj.** [attrib.] Music denoting a system of solmization (such as tonic sol-fa) in which do is the keynote of any major scale. Compare with FIXED-DO.

mov·a·ble feast ▶ **n.** a religious feast day that does not occur on the same calendar date each year. The term refers most often to Easter and other Christian holy days whose dates are related to it.

mov·ant /ˈmo͞ovənt/ ▶ **n.** Law a person who applies to or petitions a court or judge for a ruling in his or her favor.
– ORIGIN late 19th cent.: from MOVE + -ANT.

move /mo͞ov/ ▶ **v.** **1** [no obj.] go in a specified direction or manner; change position: *she stood up and moved to the door* | *he let his eyes move across the rows of faces.* ■ [with obj.] change the place or position of: *she moved the tray to a side table.* ■ change one's place of residence or work: *his family moved to London when he was a child.* ■ (of a player) change the position of a piece in a board game: *White has forced his opponent to move* | [with obj.] *if Black moves his bishop, he loses a pawn.*
2 change or cause to change from one state, opinion, sphere, or activity to another: [no obj.] *the school moved over to the new course in 1987* | [with obj.] *she deftly moved the conversation to safer territory.* ■ [with obj.] influence or prompt (someone) to do something: *his deep love of music moved him to take lessons with Dr. Hill.* ■ [no obj.] take action: *hard-liners may yet* **move against** *him, but their success might be limited.* ■ [with obj.] provoke a strong feeling, esp. of sorrow or sympathy, in: *he was* **moved to tears** *by a get-well message from the president.* ■ [with obj.] archaic stir up (an emotion) in someone: *he justly moves one's derision.*
3 [no obj.] make progress; develop in a particular manner or direction: *aircraft design had moved forward a long way* | *legislators are anxious to get things moving as soon as possible.* ■ informal depart; start off: *let's move—it's time we started shopping.* ■ [in imperative] (**move it**) informal used to urge or command someone to hurry up: *come on—move it!* ■ informal go quickly: *Kenny was really moving when he made contact with a tire at the hairpin and flipped over.* ■ (with reference to merchandise) sell or be sold: [no obj.] *despite the high prices, goods are moving* | [with obj.] *She moves more pickups than her male counterparts.*
4 [no obj.] (**move in/within**) spend one's time or be socially active in (a particular sphere) or among (a particular group of people): *they moved in different circles of friends.*
5 [with obj.] propose for discussion and resolution at a meeting or legislative assembly: *she intends to move an amendment to the bill* | [with clause] *I beg to move that this House deplores the current economic policies.* ■ make a formal request or application to (a court or assembly) for something: *his family moved the court for adequate "maintenance expenses" to run the household.*
6 [with obj.] empty (one's bowels).
▶ **n.** a change of place, position, or state: *she made a sudden move toward me* | *his eyes followed her every move* | *the country's move to independence* | *a career move.* ■ a change of house or business premises. ■ an action that initiates or advances a process or plan: *my next move is to talk to Matthew.* ■ a maneuver in a sport or game. ■ a change of position of a piece in a board game: *that move will put your king in check.* ■ a player's turn to make such a change: *it's your move.*
– PHRASES **get a move on** [often in imperative] informal hurry up. **get moving** [often in imperative] informal make a prompt start (on a journey or an undertaking): *you're here to work, so get moving.* **make a move** take action: *each army was waiting for the other side to make a move.* ■ Brit. set off; leave somewhere: *I think I'd better be making a move.* **make a move on** (or **put the moves on**) informal make a proposition to (someone), esp. of a sexual nature. **move the goalposts** see GOALPOST. **move heaven and earth** see HEAVEN. **move mountains** see MOUNTAIN. **move with the times** keep abreast of current thinking or developments. **not move a muscle** see MUSCLE. **on the move** in the process of moving from one place or job to another: *it's difficult to contact her because she's always on the move.* ■ making progress: *the economy appeared to be on the move.*
– PHRASAL VERBS **move along** [often in imperative] change to a new position, esp. to avoid causing an obstruction: *"Move along, move along," said the cop.* **move aside** see MOVE OVER below. **move in 1** take possession of a new house or business premises. ■ (**move in with**) start to share accommodations with (an existing resident). **2** intervene, esp. so as to take control of a situation: *this riot could have been avoided had the police moved in earlier.* **move in on** approach, esp. so as to take action: *the police moved in on him.* ■ become involved with so as to take control of or put pressure on: *the bank did not usually move in on doubtful institutions until they were almost bankrupt.* **move on** (or **move someone on**) go or cause to leave somewhere, esp. because one is causing an obstruction: *the Mounties briskly ordered them to move on.* ■ (**move on**) progress: *ballet has moved on, leaving Russia behind.* **move out** (or **move someone out**) leave or cause to leave one's place of residence or work. **move over** (or **aside**) adjust one's position to make room for someone else: *Jo motioned to the girls on the couch to move over.* ■ relinquish a job or leading position, typically because of being superseded by someone or something more competent or important: *it's time for the film establishment to move aside and make way for a new generation.* **move up** adjust one's position, either to be nearer or make room for someone else: *there'd be room for me if you'd just move up a bit.*
– ORIGIN Middle English: from Old French *moveir*, from Latin *movere.*

move·a·ble /ˈmo͞ovəbəl/ ▶ **adj.** & **n.** variant spelling of MOVABLE.

move·less /ˈmo͞ovləs/ ▶ **adj.** chiefly literary not moving or capable of moving or being moved.

move·ment /ˈmo͞ovmənt/ ▶ **n.** **1** an act of changing physical location or position or of having this changed: *a slight movement of the upper body* | *the principle of the free movement of goods between member states.* ■ an arrival or departure of an aircraft. ■ (also **bowel movement**) an act of defecation. ■ (**movements**) the activities and whereabouts of someone, esp. during a particular period of time: *your movements and telephone conversations are recorded.* ■ the general activity or bustle of people or things in a particular place: *the scene was almost devoid of movement.* ■ the progressive development of a poem or story: *the novel shows minimal concern for narrative movement.* ■ a change or development in something: *movements in the underlying financial markets.*
2 [often with modifier] a group of people working together to advance their shared political, social, or artistic ideas: *the labor movement.* ■ [usu. in sing.] a campaign undertaken by such a group: *a movement to declare war on poverty.*
3 Music a principal division of a longer musical work, self-sufficient in terms of key, tempo, and structure: *the slow movement of his violin concerto.*
4 the moving parts of a mechanism, esp. a clock or watch.
– ORIGIN late Middle English: via Old French from medieval Latin *movimentum*, from Latin *movere* 'to move.'

mov·er /ˈmo͞ovər/ ▶ **n.** **1** a person or thing in motion, esp. an animal: *this horse is a lovely mover and jumper.* ■ a person whose job is to remove and transport furniture from one building, esp. a house,

to another: *he watched movers load the remaining boxes.*
2 a person who makes a formal proposal at a meeting or in an assembly: *movers and seconders rise and give speeches.* ■ a person who instigates or organizes something: *she was a key mover in making this successful conference happen.*
– PHRASES **mover and shaker** a powerful person who initiates events and influences people. [from *movers and shakers*, a phrase from O'Shaughnessy's *Music & Moonlight* (1874).]

mov·ie /'mo͞ovē/ ▶ **n.** a story or event recorded by a camera as a set of moving images and shown in a theater or on television; a motion picture. ■ (**the movies**) a movie theater: *we decided to go to the movies.* ■ motion pictures generally or the motion-picture industry: *a lifelong love of the movies.*

mov·ie·go·er /'mo͞ovē,gōər/ ▶ **n.** a person who goes to the movies, esp. regularly.
– DERIVATIVES **mov·ie·go·ing** /-,gō-iNG/ **n. & adj.**

mov·ie·mak·er /'mo͞ovē,mākər/ ▶ **n.** a person who makes motion pictures; a filmmaker.
– DERIVATIVES **mov·ie·mak·ing** /-,mākiNG/ **n.**

mov·ie star ▶ **n.** an actor or actress who is famous for playing leading roles in movies.

mov·ie the·a·ter (also **movie house**) ▶ **n.** a theater where movies are shown for public entertainment.

mov·ing /'mo͞oviNG/ ▶ **adj. 1** [often with submodifier] in motion: *a fast-moving river.*
2 producing strong emotion, esp. sadness or sympathy: *an unforgettable and moving book.*
3 relating to the process of changing one's residence: *moving expenses.*
4 [attrib.] involving a moving vehicle: *tickets for moving violations.*
– DERIVATIVES **mov·ing·ly adv.** (sense 2).

mov·ing av·er·age ▶ **n.** Statistics a succession of averages derived from successive segments (typically of constant size and overlapping) of a series of values.

mov·ing-coil ▶ **adj.** [attrib.] (of an electrical device such as a voltmeter or microphone) containing a wire coil suspended in a magnetic field, so that the coil either moves in response to a current or produces a current when it is made to move.

mov·ing pic·ture ▶ **n.** dated a movie.

mov·ing side·walk (Brit. **moving pavement**) ▶ **n.** a mechanism resembling a conveyor belt for pedestrians in a place such as an airport.

mov·ing stair·way ▶ **n.** another term for **ESCALATOR**.

mov·ing van ▶ **n.** a large truck used to transport the contents of one house (or business establishment) to another.

mov·i·o·la /,mo͞ovē'ōlə/ (also **Moviola** or **movieola**) ▶ **n.** trademark a device that reproduces the picture and sound of a movie on a small scale, to allow checking and editing.
– ORIGIN 1920s: from **MOVIE** + *-ola* (probably from **PIANOLA**).

mow[1] /mō/ ▶ **v.** (past participle **mowed** or **mown** /mōn/) [with obj.] cut down (an area of grass) with a machine: *Roger mowed the lawn* | (as adj. **mown**) *the smell of newly mown grass.* ■ chiefly historical cut down (grass or a cereal crop) with a scythe or a sickle.
– PHRASAL VERBS **mow someone down** kill someone with a fusillade of bullets or other missiles. ■ recklessly knock someone down with a car or other vehicle.
– DERIVATIVES **mow·er n.**
– ORIGIN Old English *māwan*, of Germanic origin; related to Dutch *maaien*, German *mähen* 'mow,' also to **MEAD**[2].

mow[2] /mou/ ▶ **n.** [often with modifier] a stack of hay, grain, or other similar crop: *the hay mow.* ■ a place in a barn where such a stack is put.
– ORIGIN Old English *mūga*; of unknown ultimate origin; compare with Swedish and Norwegian *muga* 'heap.'

mow·ing /'mō-iNG/ ▶ **n.** (**mowings**) loose pieces of grass resulting from mowing. ■ a field of grass grown for hay.

MOX /mäks/ ▶ **n.** a type of nuclear fuel designed for use in breeder reactors, consisting of a blend of uranium and plutonium oxides.
– ORIGIN from *m(ixed) ox(ides)*.

mox·a /'mäksə/ ▶ **n.** a downy substance obtained from the dried leaves of an Asian plant related to mugwort. It is burned on or near the skin in Eastern medicine as a counterirritant. ● The plant is *Crossostephium artemisioides*, family Compositae.
– ORIGIN late 17th cent.: from Japanese *mogusa*, from *moe kusa* 'burning herb.'

mox·i·bus·tion /,mäksə'bəsCHən/ ▶ **n.** (in Eastern medicine) the burning of moxa on or near a person's skin as a counterirritant.

mox·ie /'mäksē/ ▶ **n.** informal force of character, determination, or nerve: *when you've got moxie, you need the clothes to match.*
– ORIGIN mid 20th cent.: from *Moxie*, the proprietary name of a soft drink.

Moy·ga·shel /'moigəSHəl/ ▶ **n.** trademark a type of Irish linen.
– ORIGIN 1930s: named after a village in County Tyrone, Northern Ireland.

Moy·ni·han /'moi-nə,han/, Daniel Patrick (1927–2003), US politician and educator. He taught at various colleges before serving in the US senate 1977–2001 as a Democrat from New York. He wrote *The Negro Family: The Case for National Action* (1965).

Mo·zam·bique /,mōzam'bēk/ a country on the eastern coast of southern Africa; pop. 21,669,300 (est. 2009); capital, Maputo; languages, Portuguese (official) and Bantu languages.

> First visited by Vasco da Gama, Mozambique was colonized by the Portuguese in the early 16th century and became a center of the slave trade in the 17th and 18th centuries. It became an independent republic in 1975, after a ten-year armed struggle by the Frelimo liberation movement; civil war between the Frelimo government and the Renamo opposition followed until a peace agreement was signed in 1992.

– DERIVATIVES **Mo·zam·bi·can** /-'bēkən/ **adj. & n.**

Mo·zam·bique Chan·nel an arm of the Indian Ocean that separates the eastern coast of mainland Africa from the island of Madagascar.

Moz·ar·a·bic /mō'zarəbik/ ▶ **adj.** historical of or relating to the Christian inhabitants of Spain under the Muslim Moorish kings.
– DERIVATIVES **Moz·ar·ab n.**
– ORIGIN late 17th cent.: from Spanish *mozárabe* (from Arabic *musta'rib*, literally 'making oneself an Arab') + **-IC**.

Mo·zart /'mō,tsärt/, Wolfgang Amadeus (1756–91), Austrian composer; full name *Johann Chrysostom Wolfgang Amadeus Mozart*. A child prodigy, he came to epitomize classical music in its purity of form and melody. He wrote many symphonies, piano concertos, and string quartets, as well as operas, including *The Marriage of Figaro* (1786), *Don Giovanni* (1787), *Così fan tutte* (1790), and *The Magic Flute* (1791).
– DERIVATIVES **Mo·zar·ti·an** /mō'tsärtēən/ **adj. & n.**

mo·zo /'mōsō, -zō/ ▶ **n.** (pl. **mozos**) (in Spanish-speaking regions) a male servant or attendant.
– ORIGIN Spanish, literally 'boy.'

moz·za·rel·la /,mätsə'relə/ ▶ **n.** a mild, semisoft white Italian cheese, often used in Italian cooking as a melted topping, esp. on pizzas.
– ORIGIN Italian, diminutive of *mozza*, denoting a kind of cheese, from *mozzare* 'cut off.'

moz·zet·ta /mōt'setə, mō'zetə/ (also **mozetta**) ▶ **n.** (pl. **mozzettas** or **mozzette** /-'setā, -'zetā/) a short cape with a hood, worn by the pope, cardinals, and some other ecclesiastics in the Roman Catholic Church.
– ORIGIN late 18th cent.: Italian, shortened form of *almozzetta*, from medieval Latin *almucia* 'amice' + the diminutive suffix *-etta*.

MP ▶ **n.** (pl. **MPs**) a Member of Parliament: *less than one percent of Quebec's MPs will be voting against the bill.*
▶ **abbr.** ■ military police. ■ military policeman.

mp ▶ **abbr.** mezzo piano.

m.p. ▶ **abbr.** melting point.

MP3 ▶ **n.** a means of compressing a sound sequence into a very small file, to enable digital storage and transmission. ■ a file in this format: [as modifier] *an MP3 player.*
– ORIGIN 1990s: from **MPEG** + *Audio Layer-3*.

MPA ▶ **abbr.** ■ Master of Public Administration. ■ Master of Public Accounting.

MPC ▶ **abbr.** multimedia personal computer.

MPD ▶ **abbr.** multiple personality disorder.

MPE ▶ **abbr.** Master of Public Education.

MPEG ▶ **n.** Computing an international standard for encoding and compressing video images.
– ORIGIN late 20th cent.: from *Motion Pictures Experts Group*.

mpg ▶ **abbr.** miles per gallon (a measurement of a vehicle's rate of fuel consumption).

MPH ▶ **abbr.** Master of Public Health.

mph ▶ **abbr.** miles per hour.

MPhil ▶ **abbr.** Master of Philosophy.

MPLA the Popular Movement for the Liberation of Angola, a Marxist organization founded in the 1950s that emerged as the ruling party in Angola after independence from Portugal in 1975. Once in power, the MPLA fought UNITA and other rival groups for many years.
– ORIGIN abbreviation of Portuguese *Movimento Popular de Libertação de Angola*.

MPV ▶ **abbr.** multipurpose vehicle, a large vanlike car.

Mr. /'mistər/ ▶ **n.** a title used before a surname or full name to address or refer to a man without a higher or honorific or professional title: *Mr. Robert Smith.* ■ used before the name of an office to address a man who holds it: *yes, Mr. President.* ■ humorous used before an invented surname to imply that someone has a particular characteristic: *Mr. Big-Shot.* ■ (often as **Mister**) used in the armed forces to address a senior warrant officer, officer cadet, or junior naval officer.
– ORIGIN late Middle English: originally an abbreviation of **MASTER**[1]; compare with **MISTER**[1].

MRA ▶ **abbr.** Moral Rearmament.

MRBM ▶ **abbr.** medium-range ballistic missile.

Mr. Clean ▶ **n.** informal a man, esp. a public figure, who has an impeccable image, record, or reputation. Sometimes used with **Miss**, **Mrs.**, or **Ms.** when referring to a woman: *he comes up Mr. Clean on the sheets—not even a parking ticket.*
– ORIGIN from the trademark *Mr. Clean*, a brand of household cleaner.

MRE ▶ **abbr.** meal ready to eat (a precooked and prepackaged meal used by military personnel).

MRI ▶ **abbr.** magnetic resonance imaging.

MRIA ▶ **abbr.** Member of the Royal Irish Academy.

mri·dan·gam /mri'däNGgəm/ ▶ **n.** a barrel-shaped double-headed drum with one head larger than the other, used in southern Indian music.
– ORIGIN late 19th cent.: Tamil alteration of Sanskrit *mṛdaṅga*.

mRNA ▶ **abbr.** Biology messenger RNA.

Mr. Right ▶ **n.** informal the ideal future husband: *I expect you're waiting for Mr. Right.*

Mrs. /'misəz, 'miz-, -əs/ ▶ **n.** a title used before a surname or full name to address or refer to a married woman, or a woman who has been married, without a higher or honorific or professional title: *Mrs. Sally Jones.*
– ORIGIN early 17th cent.: abbreviation of **MISTRESS**; compare with **MISSUS**.

MRSA /'mərsə/ ▶ **abbr.** methicillin-resistant *Staphylococcus aureus*, a bacterium with antibiotic resistance.

Mrs. Grun·dy /'grəndē/ ▶ **n.** (pl. **Mrs. Grundys**) a person with conventional standards of propriety.
– ORIGIN early 19th cent.: a person repeatedly mentioned in T. Morton's comedy *Speed the Plough* (1798), often in the phrase "What will Mrs. Grundy say?," which became a popular catchphrase.

MS ▶ **abbr.** ■ (also **ms**) manuscript. ■ Master of Surgery. ■ Master of Science. ■ Mississippi (in official postal use). ■ motor ship. ■ multiple sclerosis.

Ms. /miz/ ▶ **n.** a title used before the surname or full name of any woman regardless of her marital status (a neutral alternative to **Mrs.** or **Miss**): *Ms. Sarah Brown.* ■ humorous used before an invented surname to imply that someone has a particular characteristic: *Ms. Do-Right.*
– ORIGIN 1950s: combination of **MRS.** and **MISS**[2].

MSB ▶ **abbr.** most significant bit.

MSc ▶ **abbr.** Master of Science.

MS-DOS ▶ **abbr.** Computing, trademark Microsoft disk operating system.

msec. ▶ **abbr.** millisecond or milliseconds.

Mses. ▶ **abbr.** plural form of **Ms.**

MSG ▶ **abbr.** monosodium glutamate.

msg. ▶ **abbr.** message.

Msgr ▶ **abbr.** ■ Monseigneur. ■ Monsignor.

MSgt (also **MSGT**) ▶ **abbr.** master sergeant.

MSH ▶ **abbr.** melanocyte-stimulating hormone.

MS in LS ▶ **abbr.** Master of Science in Library Science.

m.s.l. (also **MSL**) ▶ **abbr.** mean sea level.

MSM ▶ **abbr.** mainstream media (as opposed to the blogosphere).

MSN ▶ **abbr.** ■ trademark Microsoft Network. ■ Master of Science in Nursing.

MSRP ▶ **abbr.** manufacturer's suggested retail price.

MSS (also **mss**) ▶ **abbr.** manuscripts.

m

MST ▶ **abbr.** Mountain Standard Time (see **Mountain time**).

MSTS ▶ **abbr.** Military Sea Transportation Service.

MSW ▶ **abbr.** ■ Master of Social Welfare. ■ Master of Social Work.

MSY ▶ **abbr.** maximum sustainable yield.

MT ▶ **abbr.** ■ machine translation. ■ megaton. ■ (also **m.t.**) metric ton. ■ Montana (in official postal use).

Mt ▶ **abbr.** ■ the Gospel of Matthew (in biblical references). ■ (**Mt.**) (in place names) Mount: *Mt. Everest.* ▶ **symbol** the chemical element meitnerium.

MTB ▶ **abbr.** mountain bike.

MTBF ▶ **abbr.** mean time between failures, a measure of the reliability of a device or system.

mtg. ▶ **abbr.** ■ meeting. ■ mortgage.

mtge. ▶ **abbr.** mortgage.

mtn. ▶ **abbr.** mountain.

M2M ▶ **abbr.** ■ machine-to-machine. ■ machine-to-mobile. ■ mobile-to-machine.

mts. (also **Mts.**) ▶ **abbr.** mountains.

MTV trademark a cable and satellite television channel that broadcasts popular music and promotional music videos.
– ORIGIN late 20th cent.: abbreviation of *music television.*

mu /m(y)o͞o/ ▶ **n.** the twelfth letter of the Greek alphabet (M, μ), transliterated as 'm.' ■ (**Mu**) [followed by Latin genitive] Astronomy the twelfth star in a constellation: *Mu Cassiopeiae.* ■ [as modifier] Physics relating to muons: *mu particle.* ▶ **symbol** ■ (μ) micron. ■ (μ) [in combination] "micro-" in symbols for units: *the recommended daily amount is 750μg.* ■ (μ) permeability.

Mu·ba·rak /mo͞o'bärək/, Hosni (1928–), Egyptian statesman; president 1981– ; full name *Muhammad Hosni Said Mubarak.* He did much to establish closer links among Egypt and other Arab nations, while opposing militant Islamic fundamentalism in Egypt.

much /məCH/ ▶ **determiner & pron.** (**more, most**) [often with negative or in questions] a large amount: [as determiner] *I did not get much sleep* | *I did* **so much** *shopping* | [as pronoun] *he does not eat much* | *they must bear much of the blame.* ■ [as pronoun with negative] used to refer disparagingly to someone or something as being a poor specimen: *I'm* **not much of a** *gardener.*
▶ **adv.** to a great extent; a great deal: *did it hurt much?* | *thanks* **very much** | *they did not mind, much to my surprise* | [with comparative] *they look much better* | [with superlative] *Nicolai's English was much the worst.* ■ [usu. with negative or in questions] for a large part of one's time; often: *I'm not there much.*
– PHRASES **as much** the same: *I am sure she would do as much for me.* **a bit much** informal somewhat excessive or unreasonable: *his earnestness can be a bit much.* **how much** used to ask what a particular amount or cost is. **make much of** give or ascribe a significant amount of attention or importance to: *the island can make much of its history as a trading post between Europe and the Arab world.* (**as**) **much as** even though: *much as I had enjoyed my adventure, it was good to be back.* **much less** see **less**. **so much the better** (or **worse**) that is even better (or worse): *we want to hear what you have to say, but if you can make it short, so much the better.* **this much** the fact about to be stated: *I know this much, you would defy the world to get what you wanted.* **too much** an intolerable, impossible, or exhausting situation or experience: *the effort proved* **too much** *for her.*
– DERIVATIVES **much·ly adv.** (humorous).
– ORIGIN Middle English: shortened from *muchel*, from Old English *micel* (see **mickle**).

mu·cha·cha /mo͞o'CHäCHə/ ▶ **n.** (in Spanish-speaking regions) a young woman.
– ORIGIN Spanish, feminine of *muchacho* (see **muchacho**).

mu·cha·cho /mo͞o'CHäCHō/ ▶ **n.** (pl. **muchachos**) (in Spanish-speaking regions) a young man.
– ORIGIN Spanish.

much·ness /'məCHnəs/ ▶ **n.** [in sing.] greatness in quantity or degree: *this romantic muchness can be overlooked in a story that has a good deal to say.*
– PHRASES (**much**) **of a muchness** informal very similar: *to the untrained eye, anything to do with railroad memorabilia seems much of a muchness.*

mu·cho /'mo͞oCHō/ informal, humorous ▶ **determiner** much or many: *that caused me mucho problems.*
▶ **adv.** [usu. as submodifier] very: *he was being mucho macho.*
– ORIGIN Spanish.

mu·ci·lage /'myo͞os(ə)lij/ ▶ **n.** a viscous secretion or bodily fluid. ■ a polysaccharide substance extracted as a viscous or gelatinous solution from plant roots, seeds, etc., and used in medicines and adhesives. ■ an adhesive solution; gum or glue.
– DERIVATIVES **mu·ci·lag·i·nous** /ˌmyo͞osə'lajənəs/ **adj.**
– ORIGIN late Middle English: via French from late Latin *mucilago* 'musty juice,' from Latin *mucus* (see **mucus**).

mu·cin /'myo͞osən/ ▶ **n.** Biochemistry a glycoprotein constituent of mucus.
– ORIGIN mid 19th cent.: from **mucus** + **-in**[1].

mu·ci·nous /'myo͞osənəs/ ▶ **adj.** of, relating to, or covered with mucus.

muck /mək/ ▶ **n.** dirt, rubbish, or waste matter: *I'll just clean the muck off the windshield.* ■ farmyard manure, widely used as fertilizer. ■ informal something regarded as worthless, sordid, or corrupt: *the muck that passes for music in the pop charts.*
▶ **v.** [with obj.] **1** (**muck up**) informal mishandle (a job or situation); spoil (something): *she had mucked up her first few weeks at college.*
2 (**muck out**) chiefly Brit. remove (manure and other dirt) from a horse's stable or other animal's dwelling.
3 rare spread manure on (land).
– PHRASES **as common as muck** Brit. informal of low social status. **make a muck of** informal, chiefly Brit. handle incompetently: *it's useless now that they've made a muck of it.*
– PHRASAL VERBS **muck about/around** informal, chiefly Brit. behave in a silly or aimless way, esp. by wasting time when serious activity is expected: *he spent his summers mucking about in boats.* ■ (**muck about/around with**) spoil (something) by interfering with it: *they did not want designers mucking about with their newspapers.*
– ORIGIN Middle English *muk*, probably of Scandinavian origin: compare with Old Norse *myki* 'dung,' from a Germanic base meaning 'soft,' shared by **meek**.

muck·er /'məkər/ ▶ **n. 1** informal or dated a rough or coarse person. [late 19th cent.: probably from German *Mucker* 'sulky person.']
2 a person who removes dirt and waste, esp. from stables. [Middle English: from **muck** + **-er**[1].]

muck·et·y-muck /'məkətē ˌmək/ (also **mucky-muck** /'məkē ˌmək/ or **muck-a-muck** /'mək ə ˌmək/) ▶ **n.** informal a person of great importance or self-importance: *a big Hollywood muckety-muck.*
– ORIGIN mid 19th cent.: from Chinook Jargon, shortening of **high muck-a-muck**.

muck·le /'məkəl/ ▶ **n., adj., determiner, & pron.** variant form of **mickle**.

muck·rak·ing /'mək,rākiNG/ ▶ **n.** the action of searching out and publicizing scandalous information about famous people in an underhanded way: *candidacy was threatened by her opponent's muckraking* | [as modifier] *a muckraking journalist.*
– DERIVATIVES **muck·rake** /-ˌrāk/ **v.**, **muck·rak·er** /-ˌrākər/ **n.**
– ORIGIN coined by President T. Roosevelt in a speech (1906) alluding to Bunyan's *Pilgrim's Progress* and the man with the *muck rake.*

muck sweat ▶ **n.** informal a state of perspiring profusely: *I arrived in a muck sweat.*

muck·y /'məkē/ ▶ **adj.** (**muckier, muckiest**) covered with or consisting of dirt or filth: *guests carried their food on trays to mucky tables.*
– DERIVATIVES **muck·i·ness n.**

muco- /'myo͞okō/ ▶ **comb. form** Biochemistry representing **mucus**.

mu·coid /'myo͞oˌkoid/ ▶ **adj.** of, involving, resembling, or of the nature of mucus.

mu·co·pol·y·sac·cha·ride /ˌmyo͞okōˌpälē'sakəˌrīd/ ▶ **n.** Biochemistry former term for **glycosaminoglycan**.

mu·co·sa /myo͞o'kōzə/ ▶ **n.** (pl. **mucosae** /-zē, -ˌzī/) a mucous membrane: *the intestinal mucosa.*
– DERIVATIVES **mu·co·sal adj.**
– ORIGIN late 19th cent.: modern Latin, feminine of *mucosus* (see **mucous**).

mu·cous /'myo͞okəs/ ▶ **adj.** relating to, producing, covered with, or of the nature of mucus.
– DERIVATIVES **mu·cos·i·ty** /ˌmyo͞o'käsətē/ **n.**
– ORIGIN mid 17th cent.: from Latin *mucosus* (see **mucus**).

mu·cous mem·brane ▶ **n.** an epithelial tissue that secretes mucus and that lines many body cavities and tubular organs including the gut and respiratory passages.

mu·cro /'myo͞okrō/ ▶ **n.** (pl. **mucros**) Botany & Zoology a short sharp point at the end of a part or organ.
– ORIGIN mid 17th cent.: from Latin, 'sharp point.'

mu·cro·nate /'myo͞okrəˌnāt/ ▶ **adj.** Botany & Zoology ending abruptly in a short sharp point or mucro.
– ORIGIN late 18th cent.: from Latin *mucronatus*, from *mucro, mucron-* 'point.'

mu·cus /'myo͞okəs/ ▶ **n.** a slimy substance, typically not miscible with water, secreted by mucous membranes and glands for lubrication, protection, etc. ■ a gummy substance found in plants; mucilage.
– ORIGIN mid 17th cent.: from Latin.

MUD /məd/ ▶ **n.** a computer-based text or virtual reality game that several players play at the same time, interacting with each other as well as with characters controlled by the computer.
– ORIGIN 1980s: from *multiuser dungeon* or *multiuser dimension.*

mud /məd/ ▶ **n. 1** soft, sticky matter resulting from the mixing of earth and water.
2 information or allegations regarded as damaging, typically concerned with corruption: *they are trying* **to sling mud** *at me to cover up their defeat.*
– PHRASES **as clear as mud** informal not at all easy to understand. **drag someone through the mud** slander or denigrate someone publicly. **here's mud in your eye!** informal, chiefly Brit. used to express friendly feelings toward one's companions before drinking. **one's name is mud** informal one is in disgrace or unpopular: *if you forget their birthdays, your name is mud.*
– ORIGIN late Middle English: probably from Middle Low German *mudde.*

Mu·dan·jiang /'mo͞o'dän'jyäNG/ a city in Heilongjiang province, in northeastern China, on the Mudan River, southeast of Harbin; pop. 649,200 (est. 2006).

mud·bank /'mədˌbaNGk/ ▶ **n.** a bank of mud on the bed of a river or the bottom of the sea.

mud bath ▶ **n.** a bath in the mud of mineral springs, taken esp. for therapeutic purposes, such as to relieve rheumatic ailments, or as part of a beauty treatment. ■ a muddy place.

mud brick ▶ **n.** a brick made from baked mud: [as modifier] *mud-brick houses.*

mud·bug /'mədˌbəg/ ▶ **n.** informal a freshwater crayfish.

mud daub·er ▶ **n.** a solitary wasp that builds a mud nest typically consisting of a series of tubelike cells on an exposed surface. ● Several genera in the family Sphecidae.

blue mud dauber

mud·der /'mədər/ ▶ **n.** a horse that runs well in wet or muddy conditions.

mud·dle /'mədl/ ▶ **v.** [with obj.] bring into a disordered or confusing state: *they were muddling up the cards.* ■ confuse (a person or their thoughts): *I do not wish to muddle him by making him read more books.* ■ [no obj.] busy oneself in a confused and ineffective way: *he was muddling about in the kitchen.* ■ mix (a drink) or stir (an ingredient) into a drink.
▶ **n.** [usu. in sing.] an untidy and disorganized state or collection: *a muddle of French, English, Ojibwa, and a dash of Gaelic* | *the finances were* **in a muddle** | *an admirable chairman, she cut through the confusion and muddle.* ■ a mistake arising from or resulting in confusion: *a bureaucratic muddle.*
– PHRASAL VERBS **muddle through** cope more or less satisfactorily despite lack of expertise, planning, or equipment: *we don't have an ultimate ambition; we just muddle through.* **muddle something up** confuse two or more things with each other: *at the time, archaeology was commonly muddled up with paleontology.*
– DERIVATIVES **mud·dling·ly** /'mədliNGlē, 'mədl-iNGlē/ **adv.**, **mud·dly** /'mədlē, 'mədl-ē/ **adj.**
– ORIGIN late Middle English (in the sense 'wallow in mud'): perhaps from Middle Dutch *moddelen*, frequentative of *modden* 'dabble in mud'; compare with **mud**. The sense 'confuse' was initially associated with alcoholic drink (late 17th cent.), giving rise to 'busy oneself in a confused way' and 'jumble up' (mid 19th cent).

mud·dled /'mədld/ ▶ **adj.** in a state of bewildered or bewildering confusion or disorder: *misplaced suggestions and muddled thinking.*

mud·dle-head·ed (also **muddleheaded**) ▶ **adj.** mentally disorganized or confused: *a muddle-headed idealist with utopian views.*
– DERIVATIVES **mud·dle-head·ed·ness** (or **muddleheadedness**) **n.**

mud·dler /'mədlər, 'mədl-ər/ ▶ **n. 1** a person who creates muddles, esp. because of a disorganized method of thinking or working.
2 (also **muddler minnow**) a type of fly used in trout fishing.
3 a stick used to stir mixed drinks.

mud·dy /'mədē/ ▶ **adj.** (**muddier, muddiest**) covered in or full of mud: *they changed their muddy boots | it was very muddy underfoot.* ■ (of a color) dull and dirty-looking: *the original colors were blurred into muddy pink and yellow.* ■ (of a sound, esp. in music) not clearly defined: *an awful muddy sound that renders his vocal incoherent.* ■ confused, vague, or illogical: *some sentences are so muddy that their meaning can only be guessed.*
▶ **v.** (**muddies, muddying, muddied**) [with obj.] cause to become covered in or full of mud: *the linoleum floor was muddied* | (as adj. **muddied**) *cold, muddied feet.* ■ make (something) hard to perceive or understand: *the first year's results muddy rather than clarify the situation.*
– PHRASES **muddy the waters** make an issue or a situation more confusing by introducing complications.
– DERIVATIVES **mud·di·ly** /'mədl-ē/ **adv.**, **mud·di·ness n.**

Mu·dé·jar /mo͞o'THe,här/ ▶ **adj.** of or denoting a partly Gothic, partly Islamic style of architecture and art prevalent in Spain in the 12th to 15th centuries. ■ of or relating to Muslim subjects of Christian monarchs during the reconquest of the Iberian peninsula from the Moors (11th–15th centuries).
▶ **n.** (pl. **Mudéjares** /-häräs/) a subject Muslim during the Christian reconquest of the Iberian peninsula from the Moors who, until 1492, was allowed to retain Islamic laws and religion in return for loyalty to a Christian monarch.
– ORIGIN via Spanish from Arabic *mudajjan* 'allowed to stay.'

mud·fish /'məd,fisH/ ▶ **n.** (pl. **same** or **mudfishes**) **1** any of a number of elongated fish that are able to survive long periods of drought by burrowing in the mud. ● a New Zealand fish (genus *Neochanna*, family Galaxiidae). ● an African lungfish (*Protopterus annectens*, family Protopteridae).
2 another term for BOWFIN.

mud flap (also **mudflap**) ▶ **n.** a flap that hangs behind the wheel of a vehicle and is designed to prevent water, mud, and stones thrown up from the road from hitting the bodywork of the vehicle or any following vehicles.

mud·flat /'məd,flat/ (also **mud flat**) ▶ **n.** (usu. **mudflats**) a stretch of muddy land left uncovered at low tide.

mud·flow /'məd,flō/ ▶ **n.** a fluid or hardened stream or avalanche of mud.

mud·guard /'məd,gärd/ ▶ **n.** a curved strip or cover over a wheel of a vehicle, esp. a bicycle or motorcycle, designed to the protect the vehicle and rider from water and dirt thrown up from the road.

mud·lark /'məd,lärk/ (also **mudlarker**) ▶ **n.** a person who scavenges in river mud for objects of value. ■ historical a street urchin.

mud·min·now /'məd,minō/ ▶ **n.** a small stout-bodied freshwater fish of both Eurasia and North America, able to survive low concentrations of oxygen and very low temperatures. ● Genus *Umbra*, family Umbridae: several species.

mud·pack /'məd,pak/ ▶ **n.** a paste of fuller's earth or a similar substance, applied thickly to the face to improve the condition of the skin.

mud pie (also **mudpie**) ▶ **n. 1** mud made into a pie shape by a child.
2 short for MISSISSIPPI MUD PIE. ■ any of a variety of similar desserts, typically with a chocolate cookie crust, an ice cream filling and a chocolate sauce topping.

mud·pup·py ▶ **n.** a large aquatic salamander of the eastern US, reaching sexual maturity while retaining an immature body form with feathery external gills. ● *Necturus maculosus*, family Proteidae. Compare with WATERDOG.

mu·dra /mə'drä/ ▶ **n.** a symbolic hand gesture used in Hindu and Buddhist ceremonies and statuary, and in Indian dance. ■ a movement or pose in yoga.
– ORIGIN from Sanskrit *mudrā* 'sign or token.'

mud·skip·per /'məd,skipər/ ▶ **n.** a goby (fish) with its eyes on raised bumps on top of the head, found in mangrove swamps from East Africa to Australia. It moves around on land with great agility, often basking on mud or mangrove roots. ● *Periopthalmodon* and related genera, family Gobiidae: several species, including the common and widespread *P. schlosseri* (or *barbarus*).

mud·slide /'məd,slīd/ ▶ **n.** a mass of mud and other earthy material that is falling or has fallen down a hillside or other slope.

mud·sling·ing /'məd,sliNGiNG/ ▶ **n.** informal the use of insults and accusations, esp. unjust ones, with the aim of damaging the reputation of an opponent.
– DERIVATIVES **mud·sling** (also **mud-sling**) **v.**, **mud·sling·er** /-,sliNGər/ (also **mud-slinger**) **n.**

mud·stone /'məd,stōn/ ▶ **n.** a dark sedimentary rock formed from consolidated mud and lacking the laminations of shale.

mud tur·tle ▶ **n.** any of a number of drab-colored freshwater turtles that often crawl onto mudbanks, in particular: ● an American turtle with scent glands that produce an unpleasant odor (genus *Kinosternon*, family Kinosternidae). ● an African side-necked turtle (genus *Pelusios*, family Pelomedusidae). ● an Asian soft-shell (genera *Lissemys* and *Pelochelys*, family Trionychidae).

Mud·ville /'mədvil/ ▶ **n.** informal used allusively to designate the world of baseball, often with reference to a particular team and the disappointment felt after an unexpected loss: *the Astros aren't exactly the Yankees, and the unbridled joy here in Mudville South was short-lived.*
– ORIGIN from the fictional locality in the 1888 poem *Casey at the Bat*, written by Ernest L. Thayer (1863–1940).

mud vol·ca·no ▶ **n.** a small vent or fissure in the ground discharging hot mud.

Muen·ster /'mənstər, 'mo͝on-/ (also **muenster, Munster**, or **munster**) ▶ **n.** a mild, semisoft cheese made from whole milk.
– ORIGIN for *Munster*, a town in the Alsace region of France.

mues·li /'m(y)o͞ozlē/ ▶ **n.** (pl. **mueslis**) a mixture of cereals (esp. rolled oats), dried fruit, and nuts, typically eaten with milk at breakfast.
– ORIGIN Swiss German.

mu·ez·zin /m(y)o͞o'ezən, 'mo͞oəzən/ ▶ **n.** a man who calls Muslims to prayer from the minaret of a mosque.
– ORIGIN late 16th cent.: dialect variant of Arabic *mu'addin*, active participle of *'addana* 'proclaim.'

muff[1] /məf/ ▶ **n. 1** a tube made of fur or other warm material into which the hands are placed for warmth. ■ a warm or protective covering for other parts of the body.
2 vulgar slang a woman's genitals.
– ORIGIN mid 16th cent.: from Dutch *mof*, Middle Dutch *muffel*, from medieval Latin *muff(u)la*, of unknown ultimate origin.

muff[2] informal ▶ **v.** [with obj.] handle (a situation, task, or opportunity) clumsily or badly: *the administration muffed several of its biggest projects | the catcher muffed a perfect throw home.*
▶ **n.** a mistake or failure, esp. a failure to catch or receive a ball cleanly. ■ dated, chiefly Brit. a person who is awkward or stupid, esp. in relation to a sport or manual skill.
– ORIGIN early 19th cent.: of unknown origin.

muff div·er ▶ **n.** vulgar slang a person who performs cunnilingus.
– DERIVATIVES **muff-div·ing n.**

muf·fin /'məfən/ ▶ **n.** a small domed cake or quick bread made from batter or dough: *blueberry muffins.* ■ short for ENGLISH MUFFIN.
– ORIGIN early 18th cent.: of unknown origin.

muf·fin pan ▶ **n.** a pan with cylindrical indentations used for baking cupcakes or muffins.

muf·fin top ▶ **n.** informal a roll of fat visible above the top of a pair of women's tight-fitting low-waisted pants.

muf·fle /'məfəl/ ▶ **v.** [with obj.] wrap or cover for warmth: *on a chair by the far wall, muffled in an absurd overcoat.* ■ cover or wrap up (a source of sound) to reduce its loudness: (as adj. **muffled**) *the soft beat of a muffled drum.* ■ make (a sound) quieter or less distinct: *his voice was muffled.* ■ restrain or conceal (someone) with wrappings: *the boy was bound and muffled.*
▶ **n.** [usu. as modifier] a receptacle in a furnace or kiln in which things can be heated without contact with combustion products.
– ORIGIN late Middle English (as a verb): perhaps a shortening of Old French *enmoufler*; the noun (mid 17th cent.) from Old French *moufle* 'thick glove.'

muf·fled /'məfəld/ ▶ **adj.** (of a sound) not loud because of being obstructed in some way; muted: *they heard the sounds of muffled voices.*

muf·fler /'məf(ə)lər/ ▶ **n. 1** a scarf or wrap worn around the neck and face for warmth.
2 a part of a motor vehicle's exhaust system, serving to muffle the sound of the vehicle. ■ a device used to deaden the sound of a drum, bell, piano, or other instrument.

muf·ti[1] /'məftē/ ▶ **n.** (pl. **muftis**) a Muslim legal expert who is empowered to give rulings on religious matters.
– ORIGIN late 16th cent.: from Arabic *muftī*, active participle of *'aftā* 'decide a point of law.'

muf·ti[2] ▶ **n.** plain clothes worn by a person who wears a uniform for their job, such as a soldier or police officer: *I was a flying officer in mufti.*
– ORIGIN early 19th cent.: perhaps humorously from MUFTI[1].

mug[1] /məg/ ▶ **n. 1** a large cup, typically cylindrical and with a handle and used without a saucer. ■ the contents of such a cup: *a large **mug of** tea vanished in a single gulp.*
2 informal a person's face.
3 informal a hoodlum or thug.
4 Brit. informal a stupid or gullible person.
▶ **v.** (**mugs, mugged, mugging**) informal **1** [with obj.] attack and rob (someone) in a public place: *he was mugged by three men who stole his bike* | (as noun **mugging**) *a brutal mugging.* ■ dated fight or hit (someone).
2 [no obj.] make faces, esp. silly or exaggerated ones, before an audience or a camera: *he mugged for the camera.*
– PHRASES **a mug's game** informal an activity in which it is foolish to engage because it is likely to be unsuccessful or dangerous: *playing with drugs is a mug's game.*
– DERIVATIVES **mug·ful** /'məg,fo͝ol/ **n.** (pl. **mugfuls**).
– ORIGIN early 16th cent. (originally Scots and northern English, denoting an earthenware bowl): probably of Scandinavian origin; compare with Norwegian *mugge*, Swedish *mugg* 'pitcher with a handle.'

mug[2] ▶ **v.** (**mugs, mugging, mugged**) [with obj.] (**mug something up**) Brit. informal learn or review a subject as much as possible in a short time; cram: *I'm constantly having to mug up things ahead of teaching them* | [no obj.] *we had **mugged up on** all things Venetian before the start of the course.*
– ORIGIN mid 19th cent.: of unknown origin.

Mu·ga·be /mo͞o'gäbē/, Robert (Gabriel) (1924–), Zimbabwean statesman; prime minister 1980–87 and president 1987–.

Mu·gan·da /mo͞o'gändə/ ▶ **n.** singular form of BAGANDA.

mug·ger[1] /'məgər/ ▶ **n.** a person who attacks and robs another in a public place.

mug·ger[2] ▶ **n.** a large short-snouted Indian crocodile, venerated by many Hindus. ● *Crocodylus palustris*, family Crocodylidae.
– ORIGIN mid 19th cent.: from Hindi *magar*.

mug·gins /'məginz/ ▶ **n.** (pl. **same** or **mugginses**) Brit. informal humorous a foolish and gullible person (often used humorously to refer to oneself): *muggins has volunteered to do the catering.*
– ORIGIN mid 19th cent.: perhaps a use of the surname *Muggins*, with allusion to MUG[1].

mug·gle /'məgəl/ ▶ **n.** informal a person who is not conversant with a particular activity or skill: *this video game won't appeal to muggles.*
– ORIGIN 1990s: from MUG[1] + -LE[2]; used in the *Harry Potter* books by J. K. Rowling to mean 'a person without magical powers.'

Mug·gle·to·nian /,məgəl'tōnēən/ ▶ **n.** a member of a small Christian sect founded in England *c.*1651 by Lodowicke Muggleton (1609–98) and John Reeve (1608–58), who claimed to be the two witnesses mentioned in the book of Revelation (Rev. 11:3–6). Despite many eccentric doctrines, the sect survived into the late 19th century.
▶ **adj.** of or relating to this sect.

mug·gy /'məgē/ ▶ **adj.** (**muggier, muggiest**) (of the weather) unpleasantly warm and humid.
– DERIVATIVES **mug·gi·ness n.**
– ORIGIN mid 18th cent.: from dialect *mug* 'mist, drizzle,' from Old Norse *mugga*.

Mu·ghal /'mo͞ogəl/ variant spelling of MOGUL.

mug shot (also **mugshot**) ▶ **n.** informal a photograph of a person's face made for an official purpose, esp. police records. ■ humorous any photograph of a person's face.

mug·wort /'məgwərt, -,wôrt/ ▶ **n.** a plant of the daisy family, with aromatic divided leaves that are dark green above and whitish below, native to north temperate regions. ● Genus *Artemisia*, family Compositae: several species, in particular the common *A. vulgaris*, which has long been connected with magic and superstition.
– ORIGIN Old English *mucgwyrt* (see MIDGE, WORT).

mug·wump /'məg,wəmp/ ▶ **n.** a person who remains aloof or independent, esp. from party politics.
– ORIGIN mid 19th cent.: from Algonquian *mugquomp* 'great chief.'

Mu·ham·mad[1] /mo͞o'hämad, -'ham-, -'KHäm-, mō-/ (also **Mohammed**) (*c.*570–632), Arab prophet and founder of Islam. In *c.*610, in Mecca, he received the first of a series of revelations that, as the Koran, became the doctrinal and legislative basis of Islam.

PRONUNCIATION KEY ə *ago, up*; ər *over, fur*; a *hat*; ā *ate*; ä *car*; e *let*; ē *see*; i *fit*; ī *by*; NG *sing*; ō *go*; ô *law, for*; oi *toy*; o͝o *good*; o͞o *goo*; ou *out*; TH *thin*; TH *then*; ZH *vision*

In the face of opposition to his preaching, he and his small group of supporters were forced to flee to Medina in 622 (the Hegira). Muhammad led his followers into a series of battles against the Meccans. In 630, Mecca capitulated and by his death Muhammad had united most of Arabia.

Mu·ham·mad² /məˈhäməd/, Elijah (1897–1975), US activist; born *Elijah Poole*. He directed the growth of the Black Muslim movement from 1934 and advocated black separatism.

Mu·ham·mad Ah·mad /ˈaməd, ˈäm-/ see **Mahdi**.

Mu·ham·mad A·li¹ /mōˈhäməd äˈlē, -ˈham-/ (1769–1849), Ottoman viceroy and pasha of Egypt 1805–49. He modernized Egypt's infrastructure, making it a leading power and established a dynasty that survived until 1952.

Mu·ham·mad A·li² see **Ali²**.

Mu·ham·mad·an /mōˈhämədən, mə-, ˈham-/ (also **Mohammedan**) ▶ **n. & adj.** archaic term for **Muslim** (not favored by Muslims).
– DERIVATIVES **Mu·ham·mad·an·ism** /-ˌizəm/ **n.**
– ORIGIN late 17th cent.: from the name of the prophet *Muhammad* (see **Muhammad¹**), + **-an**.

USAGE See usage at **Muslim**.

Mu·har·ram /mo͞oˈhärəm/ ▶ **n.** the first month of the year in the Islamic calendar. ■ an annual celebration in this month commemorating the death of Husayn, grandson of Muhammad, and his retinue.
– ORIGIN from Arabic *muḥarram* 'inviolable.'

Muir /myo͝or/, John (1838–1914), US naturalist, born in Scotland. An early advocate of wilderness preservation, he founded the Sierra Club in 1892.

mu·ja·hi·deen /ˌmo͞ojəhiˈdēn/ (also **mujahedin**, **mujahidin**) ▶ **plural n.** guerrilla fighters in Islamic countries, esp. those who are fighting against non-Muslim forces.
– ORIGIN from Persian and Arabic *mujāhidīn*, colloquial plural of *mujāhid*, denoting a person who fights a jihad.

Mu·ji·bur Rah·man /ˈmo͞oji͝boor ˈräkHmən, ˈräkH͟ˌmän/ (1920–75), Bangladeshi statesman; first prime minister of independent Bangladesh 1972–75 and president 1975; known as **Sheikh Mujib**. After failing to establish parliamentary democracy as prime minister, he assumed dictatorial powers in 1975. He and his family were assassinated in a military coup.

muj·ta·hid /mo͞ojˈtähid/ ▶ **n.** (pl. **mujtahids** or **mujtahidūn** /-ˈtähiˌdo͞on/) Islam a person accepted as an original authority in Islamic law. Such authorities continue to be recognized in the Shia tradition, but Sunni Muslims accord this status only to the great lawmakers of early Islam.
– ORIGIN Persian, from Arabic, active participle of *ijtahada* 'strive.'

Mu·kal·la /mo͞oˈkalə/ a port on the southern coast of Yemen, in the Gulf of Aden; pop. 182,500 (est. 2004).

Muk·den /ˈmo͝okdən/ former name for **Shenyang**.

mukh·tar /mo͝okˈtär/ ▶ **n.** (in Turkey and some Arab countries) the head of local government of a town or village.
– ORIGIN from Arabic *muktār*, passive participle of *iktāra* 'choose.'

muk·luk /ˈməkˌlək/ ▶ **n.** a high, soft boot that is worn in the American Arctic and is traditionally made from sealskin.
– ORIGIN mid 19th cent.: from Yupik *maklak* 'bearded seal.'

muk·tuk /ˈməkˌtək/ ▶ **n.** the skin and blubber of a whale, typically the narwhal or the beluga, used as food by the Inuit.
– ORIGIN from Inuit *maktak*.

mu·lat·to /m(y)o͞oˈlätō, -ˈlatō/ dated ▶ **n.** (pl. **mulattoes** or **mulattos**) a person of mixed white and black ancestry, esp. a person with one white and one black parent.
– ORIGIN late 16th cent.: from Spanish *mulato*, from Arabic *muwallad* 'person of mixed race.'

mul·ber·ry /ˈməlˌberē/ ▶ **n.** (pl. **mulberries**) **1** (also **mulberry tree** or **bush**) a small deciduous tree with broad leaves, native to East Asia and long cultivated elsewhere. ● Genus *Morus*, family Moraceae, in particular the **white mulberry** (*M. alba*), originally grown for feeding silkworms, and the **black** (or **common**) **mulberry** (*M. nigra*), grown for its fruit. See also **paper mulberry**. ■ the dark red or white loganberrylike fruit of this tree.
2 a dark red or purple color: [as modifier] *a mulberry carpet*.
– ORIGIN Old English *mōrberie*, from Latin *morum* + **berry**; related to Dutch *moerbezie* and German *Maulbeere*.

mulch /məlCH/ ▶ **n.** a material (such as decaying leaves, bark, or compost) spread around or over a plant to enrich or insulate the soil. ■ an application of such a material: *regular mulches keep down annual weeds*.
▶ **v.** treat or cover with mulch.
– ORIGIN mid 17th cent.: probably from dialect *mulch* 'soft' used as a noun, from Old English *melsc*, *mylsc*.

mulct /məlkt/ formal ▶ **v.** [with obj.] extract money from (someone) by fine or taxation: *no government dared propose to mulct the taxpayer for such a purpose*. ■ (**mulct someone of**) deprive someone of (money or possessions) by fraudulent means: *he mulcted Shelly of $75,000*.
▶ **n.** a fine or compulsory payment.
– ORIGIN late 15th cent.: from Latin *mulctare*, *multare*, from *mulcta* 'a fine.'

mule¹ /myo͞ol/ ▶ **n.** **1** the offspring of a donkey and a horse (strictly, a male donkey and a female horse), typically sterile and used as a beast of burden. Compare with **hinny**. ■ a person compared to a mule, esp. in being stubborn or obstinate. ■ informal a courier for illegal drugs. ■ a small tractor or locomotive, typically one that is electrically powered.
2 a hybrid plant or animal, esp. a sterile one. ■ any of several standard crossbred varieties of sheep.
3 (also **spinning mule**) a kind of spinning machine producing yarn on spindles, invented by Samuel Crompton (1753–1827) in 1779.
4 a coin with the obverse and reverse of designs not originally intended to be used together.
– ORIGIN Old English *mūl*, probably of Germanic origin, from Latin *mulus*, *mula*; reinforced in Middle English by Old French *mule*.

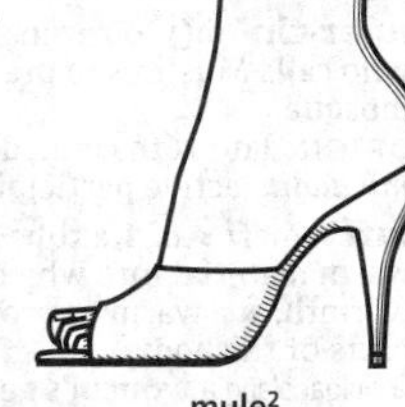
mule²

mule² ▶ **n.** a slipper or light shoe without a back.
– ORIGIN mid 16th cent.: from French, 'slipper.'

mule deer ▶ **n.** a western North American deer with large ears. The mule deer of the Rocky Mountains has a black tipped tail; the subspecies of the northwest Pacific coast (**blacktail deer**.) has a tail with a blackish upper side. ● *Odocoileus hemionus*, family Cervidae.

mule ears ▶ **plural n.** [usu. treated as sing.] a sunflowerlike composite plant of the western US, with large oval leaves. ● Genus *Wyethia*, family Compositae: several species, including the yellow-flowered **gray mule ears** (*W. helenioides*), with gray-haired leaves and very large bracts, and the white-flowered **white mule ears** (*W. helianthoides*).

gray mule ears

mu·le·ta /myo͞oˈlātə/ ▶ **n.** a small red cape fixed to a stick, employed by a matador to guide the bull during a bullfight.
– ORIGIN Spanish.

mu·le·teer /ˌmyo͞oləˈtir/ ▶ **n.** a person who drives mules.
– ORIGIN mid 16th cent.: from French *muletier*, from *mulet*, diminutive of Old French *mul* 'mule.'

mul·ey¹ /ˈmyo͞olē/ ▶ **adj.** (of cattle) hornless.
– ORIGIN late 16th cent. (as noun): perhaps from Irish *maol* or Welsh *moel*, literally 'bald,' used in the sense 'hornless cow.' The adjective dates from the mid 19th cent.

mul·ey² (also **mulie**) ▶ **n.** (pl. **muleys** or **mulies**) informal a mule deer.

mul·ga /ˈməlgə/ ▶ **n.** (also **mulga tree** or **bush**) a small Australian acacia tree or shrub with grayish foliage, forming dense scrubby growth and yielding brown and yellow timber. ● *Acacia aneura*, family Leguminosae. ■ an area of scrub or bush dominated by this plant. ■ (**the mulga**) Austral. informal the outback.
– ORIGIN mid 19th cent.: from Yuwaalaraay (an Aboriginal language of New South Wales).

Mül·hau·sen /ˈmyo͞olˌhouzən, ˈmʏl-/ German name for **Mulhouse**.

Mül·heim /ˈmyo͞olˌhīm, ˈmʏl-/ an industrial city in western Germany, in North Rhine–Westphalia, southwest of Essen; pop. 169,400 (est. 2006). Full name **Mülheim an der Ruhr**.

Mul·house /məˈlo͞oz, mʏ-/ an industrial city in northeastern France, in Alsace; pop. 112,260 (2006). It was a free imperial city until it joined the French Republic in 1798. In 1871, after the Franco-Prussian War, the city became part of the German Empire until it was reunited with France in 1918. German name **Mülhausen**.

mu·li·eb·ri·ty /ˌmyo͞olēˈebrətē/ ▶ **n.** literary womanly qualities; womanhood.
– ORIGIN late 16th cent.: from late Latin *muliebritas*, from Latin *mulier* 'woman.'

mul·ish /ˈmyo͞olisH/ ▶ **adj.** resembling or likened to a mule in being stubborn: *Belinda's face took on a mulish expression*.
– DERIVATIVES **mul·ish·ly adv.**, **mul·ish·ness n.**

Mull /məl/ a large island of the Inner Hebrides; chief town, Tobermory.

mull¹ /məl/ ▶ **v.** [with obj.] think about (a fact, proposal, or request) deeply and at length: *she began to mull over the various possibilities*.
– ORIGIN mid 19th cent.: of uncertain origin.

mull² ▶ **v.** [with obj.] (usu. as adj. **mulled**) warm (a beverage, esp. wine, beer, or cider) and add spices and sweetening to it: *a tankard of mulled ale*.
– ORIGIN early 17th cent.: of unknown origin.

mull³ ▶ **n.** Soil Science humus formed under nonacid conditions.
– ORIGIN 1920s: from Danish *muld* 'soil.'

mull⁴ ▶ **n.** thin, soft, plain muslin, used in bookbinding for joining the spine of a book to its cover.
– ORIGIN late 17th cent.: abbreviation, from Hindi *malmal*.

mul·lah /ˈmo͝olə, ˈmo͞olə/ (also **mulla**) ▶ **n.** a Muslim learned in Islamic theology and sacred law.
– ORIGIN early 17th cent.: from Persian, Turkish, and Urdu *mullā*, from Arabic *mawlā*.

mul·lein /ˈmələn/ ▶ **n.** a herbaceous plant of the figwort family with woolly leaves and tall spikes of yellow flowers, native to Eurasia but now widely and commonly distributed. ● Genus *Verbascum*, family Scrophulariaceae: several species, in particular the widespread **common** (or **great**) **mullein** (*V. thapsus*).
– ORIGIN late Middle English: from Old French *moleine*, of Celtic origin; compare with the Breton *melen*, Cornish and Welsh *melyn* 'yellow.'

common mullein

Mul·ler /ˈmələr, ˈmyo͞o-/, Hermann Joseph (1890–1967), US geneticist. He discovered that X-rays induce mutations in the genetic material of the fruit fly *Drosophila* and thus recognized the danger of X-radiation to living things. Nobel Prize for Physiology or Medicine (1946).

mull·er /ˈmələr/ ▶ **n.** a stone or other heavy weight used for grinding artists' pigments or other material on a slab.
– ORIGIN late Middle English: perhaps from Anglo-Norman French *moldre* 'to grind.'

Mül·ler¹ /ˈm(y)o͞olər/, Johannes Peter (1801–58), German anatomist and zoologist. He was a pioneer of comparative and microscopical methods in biology. His investigations included the physiology of respiration, the nervous and sensory systems, and the glandular system, as well as a method for the classification of marine animals.

Mül·ler², Paul Hermann (1899–1965), Swiss chemist. He synthesized DDT in 1939 and patented it as an insecticide. It was immediately successful, but was withdrawn by most countries in the 1970s when its environmental persistence and toxicity in higher animals was realized. Nobel Prize for Physiology and Medicine (1948).

Mül·le·ri·an mim·ic·ry /myo͞oˈli(ə)rēən, milˈi(ə)r-/ ▶ **n.** Zoology a form of mimicry in which two or more noxious animals develop similar appearances as a shared protective device, the theory being that if a predator learns to avoid one of the noxious species, it will avoid the mimic species as well. Compare with **Batesian mimicry**.
– ORIGIN late 19th cent.: named after Johann F. T. *Müller* (1821–97), German zoologist.

mul·let[1] /ˈmələt/ ▶ **n. 1** a chiefly marine fish that is widely caught for food. ● Families Mullidae (see **RED MULLET**) and Mugilidae (see **GRAY MULLET**).
2 a hairstyle in which the hair is cut short at the front and sides and left long in back.
– ORIGIN late Middle English: from Old French *mulet*, diminutive of Latin *mullus* 'red mullet,' from Greek *mullos*. The origin of sense two is unknown but may be related to the fish.

mul·let[2] ▶ **n.** Heraldry a star with five (or more) straight-edged points or rays, as a charge or a mark of cadency for a third son.
– ORIGIN late Middle English: from Old French *molette* 'rowel,' diminutive of *meule* 'millstone,' from Latin *mola* 'grindstone.'

Mul·li·gan /ˈməligən/, Gerry (1927–96), US jazz baritone saxophonist and songwriter; full name *Gerald Joseph Mulligan*. He is most often identified with cool jazz.

mul·li·gan /ˈməligən/ ▶ **n.** informal **1** (also **mulligan stew**) a stew made from odds and ends of food.
2 (in informal golf) an extra stroke allowed after a poor shot, not counted on the scorecard.
– ORIGIN early 20th cent.: apparently from the surname *Mulligan*.

mul·li·ga·taw·ny /ˌməligəˈtônē, -ˈtänē/ (also **mulligatawny soup**) ▶ **n.** a spicy meat or chicken soup originally made in India.
– ORIGIN from Tamil *miḷaku-taṇṇi* 'pepper-water.'

mul·lion /ˈməlyən/ ▶ **n.** a vertical bar between the panes of glass in a window. Compare with **TRANSOM**.
– DERIVATIVES **mul·lioned** adj.
– ORIGIN mid 16th cent.

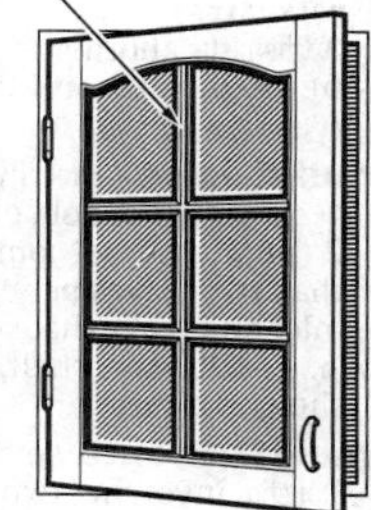
mullion

mul·lo·way /ˈmələˌwā/ ▶ **n.** a large edible fast-swimming predatory fish of Australian coastal waters, popular with anglers. Also called **JEWFISH**. ● *Johnius antarcticus*, family Sciaenidae.
– ORIGIN mid 19th cent.: from Yaralde (an Aboriginal language of South Australia).

Mul·ro·ney /məlˈrōōnē/, Brian (1939–), Canadian Progressive Conservative statesman; prime minister 1984–93; full name *Martin Brian Mulroney*.

Mul·tan /mōōlˈtän/ a commercial city in Punjab province, in east central Pakistan; pop. 1,566,900 (est. 2009).

mul·tan·gu·lar /ˌməlˈtaNGgyələr/ ▶ **adj.** rare (of a polygon) having many angles.
– ORIGIN late 17th cent.: from medieval Latin *multangularis*.

multi- ▶ **comb. form** more than one; many, esp. variegated: *multicolor* | *multicultural*.
– ORIGIN from Latin *multus* 'much, many.'

mul·ti·ac·cess /ˌməltēˈakˌses, ˌməltī-/ ▶ **adj.** (of a computer system) allowing the simultaneous connection of a number of terminals.

mul·ti·a·gen·cy /ˌməltēˈājənsē, ˌməltī-/ ▶ **adj.** involving cooperation among several organizations, esp. in crime prevention, social welfare programs, or research: *a multiagency team has been working to nurture community support*.

mul·ti·bil·lion /ˈməltēˌbilyən, ˈməltī-/ ▶ **adj.** denoting something costing or valued at several billions of a currency: [in combination] *a multibillion-dollar industry*.

mul·ti·cast /ˈməltiˌkast, ˌməltiˈkast/ ▶ **v.** (past and past participle **multicast**) [with obj.] send (data) across a computer network to several users at the same time.
▶ **n.** a set of data sent across a computer network to many users at the same time.

mul·ti·cel·lu·lar /ˌməltiˈselyələr, ˌməltī-/ ▶ **adj.** Biology (of an organism or part) having or consisting of many cells.
– DERIVATIVES **mul·ti·cel·lu·lar·i·ty** /-ˌselyəˈleratē/ **n.**

mul·ti·chan·nel /ˈməltiˌCHanl, ˈməltī-/ ▶ **adj.** employing or possessing many television or communications channels.

mul·ti·col·ored /ˌməltiˈkələrd, ˌməltī-/ (also **multicolor**) ▶ **adj.** having many colors.

mul·ti·cul·ti /ˌməltēˈkəltē, ˌməltī-/ informal ▶ **adj.** informal multicultural: *the author's multiculti persona comes through, or it may just be sloppy editing*.
▶ **n. 1** popular music incorporating ethnically disparate elements.
2 one who is literate or comfortable in more than one culture: *the multiculti*.
– ORIGIN 1990s: rhyming alteration of *multicultural*.

mul·ti·cul·tur·al /ˌməltēˈkəlCH(ə)rəl, ˌməltī-/ ▶ **adj.** of, relating to, or constituting several cultural or ethnic groups within a society: *multicultural education*.
– DERIVATIVES **mul·ti·cul·tur·al·ism n., mul·ti·cul·tur·al·ist n. & adj., mul·ti·cul·tur·al·ly adv.**

mul·ti·di·men·sion·al /ˌməltidəˈmenCHənl, ˌməltī-/ ▶ **adj.** of or involving several dimensions or aspects: *multidimensional space* | *a novel that lends itself to multidimensional readings*.
– DERIVATIVES **mul·ti·di·men·sion·al·i·ty** /-dəˌmenCHəˈnalətē/ **n., mul·ti·di·men·sion·al·ly** /-dəˈmenCHənl-ē/ **adv.**

mul·ti·di·rec·tion·al /ˌməltidəˈrekSHənl/ ▶ **adj.** of, involving, or operating in several directions: *a multidirectional antenna*.

mul·ti·dis·ci·pli·nar·y /ˌməltiˈdisəpliˌnerē, ˌməltī-/ ▶ **adj.** combining or involving several academic disciplines or professional specializations in an approach to a topic or problem.

mul·ti·eth·nic /ˌməltēˈeTHnik, ˌməltī-/ ▶ **adj.** of, relating to, or constituting several ethnic groups: *she teaches science in a multiethnic secondary school*.

mul·ti·fac·et·ed /ˌməltiˈfasətəd, ˌməltī-/ ▶ **adj.** having many facets: *the play of light on the diamond's multifaceted surface* | figurative *this is a multifaceted subject*.

mul·ti·fac·to·ri·al /ˌməltiˌfakˈtôrēəl, ˌməltī-/ ▶ **adj.** involving or dependent on a number of factors or causes.

mul·ti·far·i·ous /ˌməlt(ə)ˈfe(ə)rēəs/ ▶ **adj.** many and of various types: *multifarious activities*. ■ having many varied parts or aspects: *a vast multifarious organization*.
– DERIVATIVES **mul·ti·far·i·ous·ly adv., mul·ti·far·i·ous·ness n.**
– ORIGIN late 16th cent.: from Latin *multifarius* + **-OUS**.

mul·ti·fe·tal /ˌməltēˈfētl, ˌməltī-/ ▶ **adj.** involving two or more fetuses: *multifetal pregnancy*.

mul·ti·fid /ˈməltiˌfid, ˈməltə-, ˈməltī-/ ▶ **adj.** Botany & Zoology divided into several or many parts by deep clefts or notches.
– ORIGIN mid 18th cent.: from Latin *multifidus*, from *multus* 'much, many' + *-fid* from *fidus* 'cleft, split.'

mul·ti·fil·a·ment /ˌməltiˈfiləmənt, ˌməltī-/ ▶ **adj.** denoting a cord or yarn composed of a number of strands or filaments wound together.

mul·ti·flo·ra /ˈməltiˌflôrə/ (also **multiflora rose**) ▶ **n.** an eastern Asian shrubby or climbing rose that bears clusters of small single pink or white flowers. ● *Rosa multiflora*, family Rosaceae.
– ORIGIN early 19th cent.: from late Latin, feminine of *multiflorus* 'multiflorous.'

mul·ti·fo·cal /ˌməltiˈfōkəl, ˌməltī-/ ▶ **adj.** chiefly Medicine & Optics having more than one focus.

mul·ti·fold /ˈməltiˌfōld/ ▶ **adj.** manifold.

mul·ti·form /ˈməltiˌfôrm/ ▶ **adj.** existing in many forms or kinds: *a complex, multiform illness like cancer*.
– DERIVATIVES **mul·ti·for·mi·ty** /-ˈfôrmətē/ **n.**

mul·ti·func·tion·al /ˌməltiˈfəNGkSHənl, ˌməltī-/ (also **multifunction** /-SHən/) ▶ **adj.** having or fulfilling several functions: *a multifunctional analog meter*.

mul·ti·gen·er·a·tion·al /ˌməltiˌjenəˈrāSHənl, ˌməltī-/ ▶ **adj.** of or relating to several generations: *multigenerational families*.

mul·ti·grade /ˈməltiˌgrād, ˈməltə-, ˈməltī-/ ▶ **n. 1** an engine oil meeting the requirements of several standard grades.
2 (**Multigrade**) trademark a kind of photographic paper made with two emulsions of different sensitivities, from which prints with different levels of contrast can be made using color filters: [as modifier] *Multigrade paper*.

mul·ti·grain /ˈməltiˌgrān, ˈməltī-/ ▶ **adj.** (of bread) made from more than one kind of grain.

mul·ti·grav·i·da /ˌməltiˈgravədə/ ▶ **n.** (pl. **multigravidae** /-ˈgravəˌdē, -ˌdī/) Medicine & Zoology a woman (or female animal) who is or has been pregnant for at least a second time.
– ORIGIN late 19th cent.: from **MULTI-** 'many,' on the pattern of *primigravida*.

mul·ti·hull /ˈməltihəl, ˈməltī-/ ▶ **n.** a boat with two or more hulls, esp. three.

mul·ti·lat·er·al /ˌməltiˈlatərəl/ ▶ **adj.** agreed upon or participated in by three or more parties, esp. the governments of different countries: *multilateral negotiations* | *multilateral nuclear disarmament*. ■ having members or contributors from several groups, esp. several different countries: *multilateral aid agencies*.
– DERIVATIVES **mul·ti·lat·er·al·ism** /-ˌlizəm/ **n., mul·ti·lat·er·al·ist** /-list/ **adj. & n., mul·ti·lat·er·al·ly adv.**

mul·ti·lay·er /ˈməltiˈlāər, ˈməltī-/ chiefly technical ▶ **adj.** relating to or consisting of several or many layers: *a multilayer circuit board*.
▶ **n.** a coating or deposit consisting of several or many layers.

mul·ti·lay·ered /ˈməltiˈlāərd, ˈməltī-/ ▶ **adj.** having or involving several or many layers.

mul·ti·lev·el /ˈməltēˈlevəl, ˈˌməltī-/ ▶ **adj.** of, relating to, or involving many levels.

mul·ti·lin·gual /ˌməltēˈliNGg(yə)wəl, ˌməltī-/ ▶ **adj.** in or using several languages: *a multilingual dictionary*.
– DERIVATIVES **mul·ti·lin·gual·ism** /-ˌlizəm/ **n., mul·ti·lin·gual·ly adv.**

mul·ti·me·di·a /ˈməltiˈmēdēə, ˈməltī-/ ▶ **adj.** (of art, education, etc.) using more than one medium of expression or communication: *a multimedia art form*. ■ (of computer applications) incorporating audio and video, esp. interactively.
▶ **n.** the use of a variety of artistic or communicative media. ■ an extension of hypertext allowing the provision of audio and video material cross-referenced to a computer text.

mul·tim·e·ter /ˈməltiˌmētər, ˌməlˈtimətər/ ▶ **n.** an instrument designed to measure electric current, voltage, and usually resistance, typically over several ranges of value.

mul·ti·mil·lion /ˈməltiˈmilyən, ˈməltī-/ ▶ **adj.** [attrib.] costing or involving several million units of a currency: [in combination] *a multimillion-dollar advertising campaign*.

mul·ti·mil·lion·aire /ˌməltiˌmilyəˈner, ˌməltī-/ ▶ **n.** a person with assets worth several million dollars.

mul·ti·mod·al /ˈməltiˌmōd, ˈməltī-/ (also **multimode**) ▶ **adj.** characterized by several different modes of activity or occurrence. ■ Statistics (of a frequency curve or distribution) having several modes or maxima. ■ Statistics (of a property) occurring with such a distribution.

mul·ti·na·tion·al /ˌməltiˈnasHənl, ˌməltī-/ ▶ **adj.** including or involving several countries or individuals of several nationalities: *1,500 troops were sent to join the multinational force*. ■ (of a business organization) operating in several countries: *multinational corporations*.
▶ **n.** a company operating in several countries.
– DERIVATIVES **mul·ti·na·tion·al·ly adv.**

mul·ti·no·mi·al /ˌməltiˈnōmēəl, ˌməltī-/ ▶ **adj. & n.** Mathematics, rare another term for **POLYNOMIAL**.
– ORIGIN early 17th cent.: from **MULTI-** 'many,' on the pattern of *binomial*.

mul·ti·pack /ˈməltiˌpak, ˈməltī-/ ▶ **n.** a package containing a number of similar or identical products sold at a discount compared to the price when bought separately.

mul·tip·a·ra /məlˈtipərə/ ▶ **n.** (pl. **multiparae** /-ˌrē, -ˌrī/) Medicine & Zoology a woman (or female animal) who has had more than one pregnancy resulting in viable offspring.
– ORIGIN mid 19th cent.: modern Latin, feminine of *multiparus* 'multiparous.'

mul·tip·a·rous /ˌməlˈtipərəs/ ▶ **adj.** Medicine (of a woman) having borne more than one child. ■ chiefly Zoology producing more than one young at a birth.

mul·ti·par·tite /ˌməltiˈpärˌtīt/ ▶ **adj.** having several or many parts or divisions. ■ Biology (of a virus) existing as two or more separate but incomplete particles. ■ another term for **MULTIPARTY**.

mul·ti·par·ty /ˈməltiˈpärtē, ˈməltī-/ ▶ **adj.** of or involving several political parties: *multiparty elections*.

mul·ti·phase /ˈməltēˌfāz/ ▶ **adj.** in, of, or relating to more than one phase. ■ (of an electrical device or circuit) polyphase.

mul·ti·plat·i·num /ˈməltēˌplatn-əm, ˈməltī-/ ▶ **adj.** denoting or relating to a musical recording that has sold more than two million copies.

mul·ti·play /ˈməltiˌplā, ˈməltī-/ ▶ **adj.** denoting a compact disc player that can be stacked with a number of discs before needing to be reloaded.

mul·ti·play·er /ˈməltiˌplāər, ˈməltī-/ ▶ **n.** a multimedia computer and home entertainment system that integrates a number of conventional and interactive audio and video functions with those of a computer.
▶ **adj.** denoting a computer game designed for or involving several players.

mul·ti·ple /ˈməltəpəl/ ▶ **adj.** having or involving several parts, elements, or members: *multiple occupancy* | *a multiple birth*. ■ numerous and often

PRONUNCIATION KEY ə *ago, up*; ər *over, fur*; a *hat*; ā *ate*; ä *car*; e *let*; ē *see*; i *fit*; ī *by*; NG *sing*; ō *go*; ô *law, for*; oi *toy*; ŏŏ *good*; ōō *goo*; ou *out*; TH *thin*; T͟H *then*; ZH *vision*

varied: *words with multiple meanings.* ■ (of a disease, injury, or disability) complex in its nature or effects, or affecting several parts of the body: *a multiple fracture of the femur.* ■ of or designating an electrical circuit that has several points at which connection can occur.
▶ **n. 1** a number that can be divided by another number without a remainder: *15, 20, or any other multiple of five.*
2 an arrangement of terminals that allows connection with an electrical circuit at any one of several points.
– ORIGIN mid 17th cent.: from French, from late Latin *multiplus*, alteration of Latin *multiplex* (see MULTIPLEX).

mul·ti·ple-choice ▶ **adj.** (of a question on a test) accompanied by several possible answers from which the candidate must try to choose the correct one.

mul·ti·ple fruit ▶ **n.** Botany a fruit formed from carpels derived from several flowers, such as a pineapple.

mul·ti·ple per·son·al·i·ty ▶ **n.** [often as modifier] Psychology a rare dissociative disorder in which two or more personalities with distinct memories and behavior patterns apparently exist in one individual: *multiple-personality disorder.*

mul·ti·ple scle·ro·sis ▶ **n.** a chronic, typically progressive disease involving damage to the sheaths of nerve cells in the brain and spinal cord, whose symptoms may include numbness, impairment of speech and of muscular coordination, blurred vision, and severe fatigue.

mul·ti·ple star ▶ **n.** a group of stars very close together as seen from the earth, esp. one whose members are in fact close together and rotate around a common center.

mul·ti·plet /ˈməltəplit/ ▶ **n.** Physics a group of closely associated things, esp. closely spaced spectral lines or atomic energy levels, or subatomic particles differing only in a single property (e.g., charge or strangeness).
– ORIGIN 1920s: from MULTIPLE, on the pattern of words such as *doublet* and *triplet.*

mul·ti·plex /ˈməltiˌpleks/ ▶ **adj.** consisting of many elements in a complex relationship: *multiplex ties of work and friendship.* ■ involving simultaneous transmission of several messages along a single channel of communication. ■ (of a movie theater) having several separate screens within one building.
▶ **n. 1** a system or signal involving simultaneous transmission of several messages along a single channel of communication. Compare with DUPLEX, SIMPLEX.
2 a movie theater with several separate screens.
▶ **v.** [with obj.] incorporate into a multiplex signal or system.
– DERIVATIVES **mul·ti·plex·er** (also **multiplexor**) **n.**
– ORIGIN late Middle English in the mathematical sense 'multiple': from Latin.

mul·ti·pli·a·ble /ˈməltəˌplīəbəl, ˈməltē-/ (also **multiplicable** /ˌməltəˈplikəbəl, ˌməltēˈplikəbəl/) ▶ **adj.** able to be multiplied.

mul·ti·pli·cand /ˌməltəpliˈkand/ ▶ **n.** a quantity that is to be multiplied by another (the multiplier).
– ORIGIN late 16th cent.: from medieval Latin *multiplicandus* 'to be multiplied,' gerundive of Latin *multiplicare* (see MULTIPLY[1]).

mul·ti·pli·ca·tion /ˌməltəpliˈkāsHən/ ▶ **n.** the process or skill of multiplying: *we need to use both multiplication and division to find the answers | the rapid multiplication of abnormal white blood cells.* ■ Mathematics the process of combining matrices, vectors, or other quantities under specific rules to obtain their product.
– ORIGIN late Middle English: from Old French, or from Latin *multiplicatio(n-)*, from *multiplicare* (see MULTIPLY[1]).

mul·ti·pli·ca·tion sign ▶ **n.** a sign, esp. ×, used to indicate that one quantity is to be multiplied by another, as in 2×3=6.

mul·ti·pli·ca·tion ta·ble ▶ **n.** a table of the products of two factors, esp. the integers 1 to 12.

mul·ti·pli·ca·tive /ˌməltəˈplikətiv, ˈməltəpləˌkātiv/ ▶ **n.** subject to or of the nature of multiplication: *coronary risk factors are multiplicative.*

mul·ti·plic·i·ty /ˌməltəˈplisətē/ ▶ **n.** (pl. **multiplicities**) a large number: *his climbing record lists a multiplicity of ascents.* ■ a large variety: *the rain forests and the multiplicity of species that they harbor.*
– ORIGIN late Middle English: from late Latin *multiplicitas*, from Latin *multiplex* (see MULTIPLEX).

mul·ti·pli·er /ˈməltəˌplīər/ ▶ **n.** a person or thing that multiplies. ■ a quantity by which a given number (the multiplicand) is to be multiplied. ■ Economics a factor by which an increment of income exceeds the resulting increment of savings or investment. ■ a device for increasing by repetition the intensity of an electric current, force, etc., to a measurable level.

mul·ti·ply[1] /ˈməltəˌplī/ ▶ **v.** (**multiplies, multiplying, multiplied**) [with obj.] obtain from (a number) another that contains the first number a specified number of times: *I asked you to* **multiply** *fourteen* **by** *nineteen* | [no obj.] *we all know how to multiply by ten.* ■ increase or cause to increase greatly in number or quantity: [no obj.] *ever since I became a landlord my troubles have multiplied tenfold* | [with obj.] *cigarette smoking combines with other factors to multiply the risks of atherosclerosis.* ■ [no obj.] (of an animal or other organism) increase in number by reproducing. ■ propagate (plants).
– ORIGIN Middle English: from Old French *multiplier*, from Latin *multiplicare.*

mul·ti·ply[2] /ˈməltəplē/ ▶ **adv.** [often as submodifier] in several different ways or respects: *multiply injured patients.*

mul·ti·po·lar /ˌməltiˈpōlər, ˌməltī-/ ▶ **adj. 1** having many poles or extremities.
2 polarized in several ways or directions.
– DERIVATIVES **mul·ti·po·lar·i·ty** /-pōˈlaritē, -pə-/ **n.**, **mul·ti·pole** /ˈməltiˌpōl, ˈməltī-/ **n.**

mul·ti·proc·ess·ing /ˌməltiˈpräsesiNG, ˌməltī-, -ˈpräsəsiNG/ (also **multiprogramming**) ▶ **n.** Computing the running of two or more programs or sequences of instructions simultaneously by a computer with more than one central processor.

mul·ti·proc·es·sor /ˌməltiˈpräsesər, -ˈpräsəsər/ ▶ **n.** a computer with more than one central processor.

mul·ti·pur·pose /ˌməltēˈpərpəs, ˌməltī-/ ▶ **adj.** having several purposes or functions: *a seven-acre multipurpose civic center.*

mul·ti·ra·cial /ˌməltiˈrāsHəl, ˌməlˌtī-/ ▶ **adj.** made up of or relating to people of several or many races: *multiracial education.*
– DERIVATIVES **mul·ti·ra·cial·ism** /-ˌlizəm/ **n.**, **mul·ti·ra·cial·ist** /-list/ **adj. & n.**, **mul·ti·ra·cial·ly adv.**

mul·ti·role /ˈməltiˌrōl, ˈməltī-/ ▶ **adj.** [attrib.] (chiefly of an aircraft) capable of performing several roles.

mul·ti·ses·sion /ˈməltiˌsesHən, ˈməltī-/ ▶ **adj.** Computing denoting a format for recording digital information onto a CD-ROM disc over two or more separate sessions.

mul·ti·spec·tral /ˌməltiˈspektrəl, ˌməltī-/ ▶ **adj.** operating in or involving several regions of the electromagnetic spectrum: *multispectral images from satellites.*

mul·ti·stage /ˈməltiˈstāj, ˌməltī-/ ▶ **adj.** [attrib.] consisting of or relating to several stages or processes: *a multistage decision-making process.* ■ (of a rocket) having at least two sections, each of which contains its own motor and is jettisoned as its fuel runs out. ■ (of a pump, turbine, or similar device) having more than one rotor.

mul·ti·sto·ry /ˈməltiˌstôrē, ˈməltī-/ (also **multistoried**) ▶ **adj.** (of a building) having several stories.

mul·ti·tal·ent·ed /ˌməltiˈtaləntəd, ˌməlti -/ ▶ **adj.** having many skills or talents: *a multitalented musician and songwriter.*

mul·ti·task·ing /ˌməltiˈtaskiNG, ˌməltī-/ ▶ **n.** Computing the simultaneous execution of more than one program or task by a single computer processor. ■ the handling of more than one task at the same time by a single person.
– DERIVATIVES **mul·ti·task** /ˈməltiˌtask, ˈməltī-/ **v.**

mul·ti·thread·ing /ˈməltiˈTHrediNG, ˈməltī-/ ▶ **n.** Computing a technique by which a single set of code can be used by several processors at different stages of execution.
– DERIVATIVES **mul·ti·thread·ed** /-ˈTHredəd/ **adj.**

mul·ti·track /ˈməltiˌtrak, ˈməltī-/ ▶ **adj.** relating to or made by the mixing of several separately recorded tracks of sound: *a digital multitrack recorder.*
▶ **n.** a recording made from the mixing of several separately recorded tracks.
▶ **v.** [with obj.] record using multitrack recording: (as adj. **multitracked**) *multitracked vocals.*

mul·ti·tu·ber·cu·late /ˌməltit(y)əˈbərkyələt/ ▶ **n.** a small primitive extinct mammal of a mainly Cretaceous and Paleocene order, distinguished by having molar teeth with several cusps arranged in two or three rows. ● Order Multituberculata, subclass Allotheria.
– ORIGIN late 19th cent.: from modern Latin *Multituberculata*, from MULTI- 'many' + Latin *tuberculum* 'tubercle.'

mul·ti·tude /ˈməltəˌt(y)o͞od/ ▶ **n.** a large number: ***a multitude of*** *medical conditions are due to being overweight.* ■ (**the multitudes**) large numbers of people: *the multitudes using the roads.* ■ (**the multitude**) a large gathering of people: *Father Peter addressed the multitude.* ■ (**the multitude**) the mass of ordinary people without power or influence: *placing ultimate political power in the hands of the multitude.* ■ archaic the state of being numerous: *they would swarm over the river in their multitude.*
– PHRASES **cover a multitude of sins** see COVER.
– ORIGIN Middle English: via Old French from Latin *multitudo*, from *multus* 'many.'

mul·ti·tu·di·nous /ˌməltəˈt(y)o͞odn-əs/ ▶ **adj.** very numerous: *the tinkling of multitudinous bells from the herd.* ■ consisting of or containing many individuals or elements: *the multitudinous array of chemical substances that exist in the natural world.* ■ literary (of a body of water) vast.
– DERIVATIVES **mul·ti·tu·di·nous·ly adv.**, **mul·ti·tu·di·nous·ness n.**
– ORIGIN early 17th cent.: from Latin *multitudo* (see MULTITUDE) + -OUS.

mul·ti·us·er /ˈməltēˈyo͞ozər, ˈməltī-/ ▶ **adj.** [attrib.] (of a computer system) able to be used by a number of people simultaneously. ■ denoting a computer game in which several players interact simultaneously using the Internet or other communications.

mul·ti·va·lent /ˌməltiˈvālənt, ˌməltī-/ ▶ **adj. 1** having or susceptible to many applications, interpretations, meanings, or values: *visually complex and multivalent work.*
2 Medicine (of an antigen or antibody) having several sites at which attachment to an antibody or antigen can occur: *a multivalent antiserum.* Compare with POLYVALENT.
3 Chemistry another term for POLYVALENT.
– DERIVATIVES **mul·ti·va·lence n.**, **mul·ti·va·len·cy n.** (Brit.).

mul·ti·valve /ˌməltiˈvalv, ˌməltī-/ ▶ **adj.** [attrib.] **1** Zoology (of a shell, etc.) having several valves.
2 (of an internal combustion engine) having more than two valves per cylinder, typically four (two inlet and two exhaust).
▶ **n.** a multivalve shell, or an animal having such a shell, as a chiton.

mul·ti·var·i·ate /ˌməltiˈve(ə)rēət, ˌməltī-/ ▶ **adj.** Statistics involving two or more variable quantities.

mul·ti·ven·dor /məltiˈvendər/ ▶ **adj.** [attrib.] denoting or relating to computer hardware or software products or network services from more than one supplier.

mul·ti·verse /ˈməltiˌvərs/ ▶ **n.** an infinite realm of being or potential being of which the universe is regarded as a part or instance.

mul·ti·ver·si·ty /ˌməltiˈvərsətē/ ▶ **n.** (pl. **multiversities**) a large university with many different departments.
– ORIGIN mid 20th cent.: from MULTI- + a shortened form of UNIVERSITY.

mul·ti·vi·bra·tor /ˌməltiˈvīˌbrātər/ ▶ **n.** Electronics a device consisting of two amplifying transistors or valves, each with its output connected to the input of the other, producing an oscillatory signal.

mul·ti·vi·ta·min /ˌməltiˈvītəmən/ ▶ **adj.** [attrib.] containing a combination of vitamins: *a daily multivitamin supplement.*
▶ **n.** a pill containing a combination of vitamins.

mul·ti·way /ˈməltiˌwā, ˈməltī-/ ▶ **adj.** having several paths, routes, or channels: *a multiway switch.*

mul·tum in par·vo /ˈmo͝oltəm in ˈpärvō, -ˈpärwō/ ▶ **n.** a great deal in a small space.
– ORIGIN Latin, literally 'much in little.'

mul·ture /ˈməlCHər/ ▶ **n.** historical a toll of grain or flour due to a miller in return for grinding grain. ■ the right to collect this.
– ORIGIN Middle English: from Old French *moulture*, from medieval Latin *molitura*, from *molit-* 'ground,' from the verb *molere.*

mum[1] /məm/ ▶ **adj.** silent.
– PHRASES **keep mum** informal remain silent, esp. so as not to reveal a secret: *he was keeping mum about a possible move to Canada.* **mum's the word** informal (as a request or warning) say nothing; don't reveal a secret.
– ORIGIN late Middle English: imitative of a sound made with closed lips.

mum[2] ▶ **v.** (**mums, mumming, mummed**) [no obj.] act in a traditional masked mime or a mummers' play.
– ORIGIN late Middle English: compare with MUM[1] and Middle Low German *mummen.*

mum[3] ▶ **n.** informal a cultivated chrysanthemum.
– ORIGIN late 19th cent.: abbreviation.

mum[4] ▶ **n.** British term for MOM.
– ORIGIN mid 17th cent.: abbreviation of MUMMY[2].

Mum·bai /ˈməmˌbī/ a city and port on the western coast of India, capital of the state of Maharashtra; pop. 13,922,100 (est. 2009). Former name (until 1995) **BOMBAY.**
– DERIVATIVES **Mum·bai·kar** /ˌməmbīˈkär/ **n. & adj.**

mum·ble /'məmbəl/ ▶ **v. 1** [reporting verb] say something indistinctly and quietly, making it difficult for others to hear: [with obj.] *he mumbled something she didn't catch* | [with direct speech] *"Sorry," she mumbled.*
2 [with obj.] bite or chew with toothless gums or eat without making much use of the teeth.
▶ **n.** [usu. in sing.] a quiet and indistinct utterance: *Rosie had replied in a mumble.*
– DERIVATIVES **mum·bler** /'məmb(ə)lər/ **n.**, **mum·bling·ly** /'məmb(ə)liNGlē/ **adv.**
– ORIGIN Middle English: frequentative of MUM[1].

mum·ble·ty-peg /'məmbəltē ˌpeg/ (also **mumbletypeg**) ▶ **n.** a game in which each player in turn throws a knife or pointed stick from a series of positions, continuing until it fails to stick in the ground.
– ORIGIN early 17th cent.: also in the form *mumble the peg,* from *mumble* in the late 16th-cent. sense 'bite as if with toothless gums,' from the requirement of the game that an unsuccessful player withdraw a peg from the ground using the mouth.

mum·bo jum·bo /'məmbō 'jəmbō/ ▶ **n.** informal language or ritual causing or intended to cause confusion or bewilderment: *a maze of legal mumbo jumbo.*
– ORIGIN mid 18th cent. (as *Mumbo Jumbo,* denoting a supposed African idol): of unknown origin; the current sense dates from the late 19th cent.

mu me·son /myo͞o/ ▶ **n.** another term for MUON.

Mum·ford /'məmfərd/, Lewis (1895–1990), US social philosopher. He was an expert on regional and city planning and wrote *The Renewal of Life* in four volumes (1934–51), *The Culture of Cities* (1938), *The City in History* (1961), and *The Myth of the Machine* (1967).

mum·mer /'məmər/ ▶ **n.** an actor in a traditional masked mime, esp. of a type associated with Christmas and popular in England in the 18th and early 19th centuries. ■ a pantomimist. ■ archaic or derogatory an actor in the theater.
– ORIGIN late Middle English: from Old French *momeur,* from *momer* 'act in a mime'; perhaps of Germanic origin.

mum·mer·y /'məmərē/ ▶ **n.** (pl. **mummeries**) a performance by mummers. ■ ridiculous ceremonial, esp. of a religious nature: *that's all it is, mere mummery.*
– ORIGIN mid 16th cent.: from Old French *momerie,* from *momer* (see MUMMER).

mum·mi·chog /'məmiˌCHôg, -ˌCHäg/ ▶ **n.** a small marine killifish that lives along the sheltered shores and estuaries of eastern North America. It is widely kept in aquariums and is also used as bait and for biological research. ● *Fundulus heteroclitus,* family Fundulidae (or Cyprinodontidae).
– ORIGIN late 18th cent.: from Narragansett *moamitteaug.*

mum·mi·fy /'məməˌfī/ ▶ **v.** (**mummifies, mummifying, mummified**) [with obj.] (usu. as adj. **mummified**) (esp. in ancient Egypt) preserve (a body) by embalming it and wrapping it in cloth: *the mummified bodies entombed in the pyramids of Egypt.* See also MUMMY[1]. ■ shrivel or dry up (a body or a thing), thus preserving it: *the wind must have dehydrated and mummified the body.*
– DERIVATIVES **mum·mi·fi·ca·tion** /ˌməməfi'kāSHən/ **n.**

mum·my[1] /'məmē/ ▶ **n.** (pl. **mummies**) (esp. in ancient Egypt) a body of a human being or animal that has been ceremonially preserved by removal of the internal organs, treatment with natron and resin, and wrapping in bandages.
– ORIGIN late Middle English (denoting a substance taken from embalmed bodies and used in medicines): from French *momie,* from medieval Latin *mumia* and Arabic *mūmiyā* 'embalmed body,' perhaps from Persian *mūm* 'wax.'

mum·my[2] ▶ **n.** (pl. **mummies**) British term for MOMMY.
– ORIGIN late 18th cent.: perhaps an alteration of earlier MAMMY.

mump·ish /'məmpiSH/ ▶ **adj.** informal, dated sullen or sulky.
– ORIGIN early 18th cent.: from obsolete *mump* 'grimace, have a miserable expression' + -ISH[1].

mumps /məmps/ ▶ **plural n.** [treated as sing.] a contagious and infectious viral disease causing swelling of the parotid salivary glands in the face, and a risk of sterility in adult males.
– ORIGIN late 16th cent.: from obsolete *mump* 'grimace, have a miserable expression.'

mump·si·mus /'məmpsiməs/ ▶ **n.** (pl. **mumpsimuses**) a traditional custom or notion adhered to although shown to be unreasonable. ■ a person who obstinately adheres to such a custom or notion.
– ORIGIN mid 16th cent.: erroneously for Latin *sumpsimus* in *quod in ore sumpsimus* 'which we have taken into the mouth' (Eucharist), in a story of an illiterate priest who, when corrected, replied "I will not change my old mumpsimus for your new sumpsimus."

Munch /məNGk, mo͝oNGk/, Edvard (1863–1944), Norwegian painter and engraver. He infused his subjects with an intense emotionalism, exploring the use of vivid color and linear distortion to express feelings about life and death. His works include the painting *The Scream* (1893).

munch /mənCH/ ▶ **v.** [with obj.] eat (something) with a continuous and often audible action of the jaws: *he munched a chicken wing* | [no obj.] *popcorn to* **munch on** *while watching the movie.*
– DERIVATIVES **munch·er n.**
– ORIGIN late Middle English: imitative; compare with CRUNCH.

Mun·chau·sen, Ba·ron /'mo͝onˌCHouzən, 'mən-/ the hero of a book of fantastic travelers' tales (1785) written in English by a German, **Rudolph Erich Raspe**. The original Baron Munchausen is said to have lived 1720–97, to have served in the Russian army against the Turks, and to have related extravagant tales of his prowess.

Mun·chau·sen's syn·drome ▶ **n.** Psychiatry a mental disorder in which a person repeatedly feigns severe illness so as to obtain hospital treatment. ■ (**Munchausen's syndrome by proxy**) a mental disorder in which a person seeks attention by inducing or feigning illness in another person, typically a child.

Mün·chen /'minCHən, 'mYnKHən/ German name for MUNICH.

munch·ie /'mənCHē/ ▶ **n.** (pl. **munchies**) (usu. **munchies**) informal a snack or small item of food. ■ (**the munchies**) a sudden strong desire for food: *these camping trips always give me the munchies.*

munch·kin /'mənCHkin/ ▶ **n.** informal a child or short person.
– ORIGIN from the *Munchkins,* depicted as a race of small childlike creatures, in L. Frank Baum's *The Wonderful Wizard of Oz* (1900).

Mun·cie /'mənsē/ an industrial city in east central Indiana, noted as the 'Middletown' of sociological literature; pop. 64,975 (est. 2008).

Mun·da /'mo͝ondə/ ▶ **n.** (pl. **same** or **Mundas**) **1** a member of a group of indigenous peoples living scattered in a region from east central India to Nepal and Bangladesh.
2 a family of languages spoken by these peoples, distantly related to the Mon-Khmer family, with which they are sometimes classified as Austro-Asiatic. ■ any language of this family.
▶ **adj.** relating to or denoting the Munda or their languages.
– ORIGIN the name in Munda.

mun·dane /ˌmən'dān/ ▶ **adj. 1** lacking interest or excitement; dull: *seeking a way out of his mundane, humdrum existence.*
2 of this earthly world rather than a heavenly or spiritual one: *the boundaries of the mundane world.* ■ of, relating to, or denoting the branch of astrology that deals with political, social, economic, and geophysical events and processes.
– DERIVATIVES **mun·dane·ly adv.**, **mun·dane·ness n.**, **mun·dan·i·ty** /-'dānətē/ **n.** (pl. **mundanities**).
– ORIGIN late Middle English (sense 2): from Old French *mondain,* from late Latin *mundanus,* from Latin *mundus* 'world.' Sense 1 dates from the late 19th cent.

mung /məNG/ (also **mung bean**) ▶ **n. 1** a small round green bean.
2 the tropical Old World plant that yields these beans, commonly grown as a source of bean sprouts. ● *Vigna radiata* (or *Phaseolus aureus*), family Leguminosae.
– ORIGIN early 19th cent.: from Hindi *mūng.*

mun·go /'məNGgō/ ▶ **n.** cloth made from recycled woven or felted material.
– ORIGIN mid 19th cent.: of unknown origin.

mu·ni[1] /'myo͞onē/ ▶ **n.** (pl. **munis**) short for MUNICIPAL BOND.

mu·ni[2] /'mo͞onē/ ▶ **n.** (pl. **munis**) (in India) an inspired holy person; an ascetic, hermit, or sage.
– ORIGIN from Sanskrit, literally 'silent,' from *man* 'think.'

Mu·nich /'myo͞onik, -niKH/ a city in southeastern Germany, capital of Bavaria; pop. 1,294,600 (est. 2006). German name MÜNCHEN.

Mu·nich Pact (also **Munich Agreement**) an agreement between Britain, France, Germany, and Italy, signed at Munich on September 29, 1938, under which the Sudetenland was ceded to Nazi Germany, often cited as an example of misjudged or dishonorable appeasement.

mu·nic·i·pal /myo͞o'nisəpəl, myə-/ ▶ **adj.** of or relating to a city or town or its governing body: *national and municipal elections* | *municipal offices.*
– DERIVATIVES **mu·nic·i·pal·ly adv.**
– ORIGIN mid 16th cent. (originally relating to the internal affairs of a state as distinct from its foreign relations): from Latin *municipalis,* from *municipium* 'free city,' from *municeps, municip-* 'citizen with privileges,' from *munia* 'civic offices' + *capere* 'take.'

mu·nic·i·pal bond ▶ **n.** a security issued by or on behalf of a local authority.

mu·nic·i·pal·i·ty /myo͞oˌnisə'palətē, myə-/ ▶ **n.** (pl. **municipalities**) a city or town that has corporate status and local government. ■ the governing body of such an area.
– ORIGIN late 18th cent.: from French *municipalité,* from *municipal* (see MUNICIPAL).

mu·nic·i·pal·ize /myo͞o'nisəpəˌlīz, myə-/ ▶ **v.** [with obj.] bring under the control or ownership of the authorities of a city or town: *an expensive commitment to municipalize rented housing.*
– DERIVATIVES **mu·nic·i·pal·i·za·tion** /-ˌnisəpələ'zāSHən/ **n.**

mu·nif·i·cence /myo͞o'nifəsəns, myə-/ ▶ **n.** the quality or action of being lavishly generous; great generosity: *we must be thankful for his munificence.*

mu·nif·i·cent /myo͞o'nifəsənt, myə-/ ▶ **adj.** (of a gift or sum of money) larger or more generous than is usual or necessary: *a munificent gesture.* ■ (of a person) very generous.
– DERIVATIVES **mu·nif·i·cent·ly adv.**
– ORIGIN late 16th cent.: from Latin *munificent-,* stem of *munificentior,* comparative of *munificus* 'bountiful,' from *munus* 'gift.'

mu·ni·ment /'myo͞onəmənt/ ▶ **n.** (usu. **muniments**) a document or record, esp. one kept in an archive.
– ORIGIN late Middle English: via Old French from Latin *munimentum* 'defense' (in medieval Latin 'title deed'), from *munire* 'fortify.'

mu·ni·tion /myo͞o'niSHən, myə-/ ▶ **plural n.** (**munitions**) military weapons, ammunition, equipment, and stores: *reserves of nuclear, chemical, and conventional munitions* | [as modifier] *a munitions expert* | *munition factories.*
▶ **v.** [with obj.] supply with munitions.
– DERIVATIVES **mu·ni·tion·er n.** (rare).
– ORIGIN late Middle English (denoting a granted right or privilege): from French, from Latin *munitio(n-)* 'fortification,' from *munire* 'fortify or secure.'

Mun·ro[1] /mən'rō/, Alice (1931–), Canadian writer. Many of her short stories are collected in *Dance of the Happy Shades* (1968), *The Progress of Love* (1987), *Open Secrets* (1995), and *The Love of a Good Woman* (1998). Her novels include *Lives of Girls and Women* (1971).

Mun·ro[2], H. H., see SAKI.

Mun·si /'mo͝onsē/ ▶ **n.** see DELAWARE[2] (sense 2 of the noun).
– ORIGIN the name in Munsi.

Mun·ster /'mənstər/ a province of the Republic of Ireland, in the southwestern part of the country.

Mün·ster /'minstər, 'mYn-/ a city in northwestern Germany; pop. 272,100 (est. 2006). It was formerly the capital of Westphalia; the Treaty of Westphalia, which ended the Thirty Years War, was signed simultaneously here and at Osnabrück in 1648.

mun·tin /'məntn/ ▶ **n.** a bar or rigid supporting strip between adjacent panes of glass.
– DERIVATIVES **mun·tined** /'məntnd/ **adj.**
– ORIGIN early 17th cent.: variant of obsolete *montant* (from French, literally 'rising').

munt·jac /'məntˌjak/ ▶ **n.** a small Southeast Asian deer, the male of which has tusks, small antlers, and a doglike bark. Also called BARKING DEER. ● Genus *Muntiacus,* family Cervidae: several species, including the **Chinese muntjac** (*M. reevesi*), which is naturalized in England and France.
– ORIGIN late 18th cent.: from Sundanese *minchek.*

mu·on /'myo͞oˌän/ ▶ **n.** Physics an unstable subatomic particle of the same class as an electron (a lepton), but with a mass around 200 times greater. Muons make up much of the cosmic radiation reaching the earth's surface.
– DERIVATIVES **mu·on·ic** /myo͞o'änik/ **adj.**
– ORIGIN 1950s: contraction of MU MESON; the particle, however, is no longer regarded as a meson.

Muq·di·sho /mo͝ok'diSHō/ another name for MOGADISHU.

PRONUNCIATION KEY ə *ago, up;* ər *over, fur;* a *hat;* ā *ate;* ä *car;* e *let;* ē *see;* i *fit;* ī *by;* NG *sing;* ō *go;* ô *law, for;* oi *toy;* o͝o *good;* o͞o *goo;* ou *out;* TH *thin;* T͟H *then;* ZH *vision*

m

mu·ral /ˈmyo͝orəl/ ▶ **n.** a painting or other work of art executed directly on a wall.
▶ **adj.** [attrib.] of, like, or relating to a wall: *a mural escarpment.* ■ Medicine of, relating to, or occurring in the wall of a body cavity or blood vessel: *mural thrombosis.*
– DERIVATIVES **mu·ral·ist n.**
– ORIGIN late Middle English: from French, from Latin *muralis*, from *murus* 'wall.' The adjective was first used in MURAL CROWN; later (mid 16th cent.) the sense 'placed or executed on a wall' arose, reflected in the current noun use (dating from the early 20th cent).

mu·ral crown ▶ **n. 1** Heraldry a representation of a city wall in the form of a crown, borne above the shield in the arms of distinguished soldiers and of some civic authorities.
2 (in ancient Roman times) a crown or garland given to the soldier who was first to scale the wall of a besieged town.

Mu·ra·no glass /myo͞oˈränō/ ▶ **n.** another term for VENETIAN GLASS.

Mu·rat /m(y)o͞oˈrä(t), mʏˈrä/, Joachim (*c.*1767–1815), French general, king of Naples 1808–15. A cavalry commander in Napoleon's Italian campaign 1800, he was made king of Naples. His attempt to become king of all Italy in 1815 failed, and he was captured in Calabria and executed.

Mur·chi·son Falls /ˈmərCHəsən/ former name for KABALEGA FALLS.

Mur·cia /ˈmərSH(ē)ə, ˈmo͝orsēə/ an autonomous region in southeastern Spain. In the Middle Ages, along with Albacete, it formed an ancient Moorish kingdom. ■ its capital city; pop. 430,571 (2008).

mur·der /ˈmərdər/ ▶ **n.** the unlawful premeditated killing of one human being by another: *the stabbing murder of an off-Broadway producer | he was put on trial for attempted murder.* ■ informal a very difficult or unpleasant task or experience: *my first job at the steel mill was murder.*
▶ **v.** [with obj.] kill (someone) unlawfully and with premeditation: *somebody tried to murder Joe.* ■ informal punish severely or be very angry with: *my father will murder me if I'm home late.* ■ informal conclusively defeat (an opponent) in a game or sport. ■ spoil by lack of skill or knowledge: *the only thing he had murdered was the English language.*
– PHRASES **get away with murder** informal succeed in doing whatever one chooses without being punished or suffering any disadvantage. **murder one** (or **two**) informal first-degree (or second-degree) murder. **murder will out** murder cannot remain undetected. **scream** (or **yell**) **bloody** (or Brit. **blue**) **murder** informal scream loudly due to pain or fright; make an extravagant and noisy protest: *she had tripped and was screaming bloody murder.*
– ORIGIN Old English *morthor*, of Germanic origin; related to Dutch *moord* and German *Mord*, from an Indo-European root shared by Sanskrit *mará* 'death' and Latin *mors*; reinforced in Middle English by Old French *murdre*.

mur·der·er /ˈmərdərər/ ▶ **n.** a person who commits murder; a killer: *convicted murderers.*

mur·der·ess /ˈmərdərəs/ ▶ **n.** a female murderer.

mur·der·ous /ˈmərdərəs/ ▶ **adj.** capable of or intending to murder; dangerously violent: *a brutal and murderous despot | her estranged husband was seized with murderous jealousy.* ■ (of an action, event, or plan) involving murder or extreme violence: *murderous acts of terrorism.* ■ informal extremely arduous or unpleasant: *the team had a murderous schedule of four games in ten days.*
– DERIVATIVES **mur·der·ous·ly adv.**, **mur·der·ous·ness n.**

Mur·doch[1] /ˈmərdäk, -dək/, Iris (1919–99), British novelist and philosopher, born in Ireland; full name *Dame Jean Iris Murdoch*. She is primarily known for her novels, many of which explore complex sexual relationships and spiritual life. Notable novels: *The Sandcastle* (1957), *The Sea, The Sea* (1978), and *The Philosopher's Pupil* (1983).

Mur·doch[2], (Keith) Rupert (1931–), US publisher and media entrepreneur, born in Australia; full name *Keith Rupert Murdoch*. As the founder and head of the News International Communications empire, he owned major newspapers in Australia, Britain, and the US, together with movie and television companies and HarperCollins, a publisher.

mure /ˈmyo͝or/ ▶ **v.** [with obj.] archaic shut up in an enclosed space; immure.
– ORIGIN late Middle English: from Old French *murer*, from Latin *murare*, from *murus* 'wall.'

mu·rex /ˈmyo͝orˌeks/ ▶ **n.** (pl. **murices** /-rəˌsēz/ or **murexes**) a predatory tropical marine mollusk, the shell of which bears spines and forms a long narrow canal extending downward from the aperture. ● Genus *Murex*, family Muricidae, class Gastropoda.
– ORIGIN late 16th cent.: from Latin; perhaps related to Greek *muax* 'sea mussel.'

Mur·frees·boro /ˈmərfrēzˌbərō, -ˌbərə/ a commercial city in central Tennessee, southeast of Nashville; pop. 101,753 (est. 2008). A Civil War battle fought near here in January 1863 is also called the Battle of Stones River.

mu·ri·at·ic ac·id /ˌmyo͝orēˈatik/ ▶ **n.** archaic term for HYDROCHLORIC ACID.
– DERIVATIVES **mu·ri·ate** /ˈmyo͝orēˌāt/ **n.**
– ORIGIN late 17th cent.: *muriatic* from Latin *muriaticus*, from *muria* 'brine.'

mu·ri·cate /ˈmyo͝oriˌkāt, -kit/ (also **muricated**) ▶ **adj.** Botany & Zoology studded with short rough points.
– ORIGIN mid 17th cent.: from Latin *muricatus* 'shaped like a murex.'

mu·rid[1] /ˈmyo͝orid/ ▶ **n.** Zoology a rodent of a very large family (Muridae) that includes most kinds of rats, mice, and voles.
– ORIGIN early 20th cent.: from modern Latin *Muridae* (plural), based on Latin *mus, mur-* 'mouse.'

mu·rid[2] ▶ **n.** a follower of a Muslim holy man, esp. a Sufi disciple. ■ (**Murid**) a member of any of several Muslim movements, esp. one that advocated rebellion against the Russians in the Caucasus in the late 19th century.
– ORIGIN from Arabic *murīd*, literally 'he who desires.'

Mu·ril·lo /m(y)o͞oˈrilō, mo͞oˈrē(y)ō/, Bartolomé Esteban (*c.*1618–82), Spanish painter. He is noted for his genre scenes of urchins and peasants and for his devotional pictures.

mu·rine /ˈmyo͝orˌīn/ ▶ **adj.** Zoology of, relating to, or affecting mice or related rodents. ● Murine rodents belong to the family Muridae, in particular the subfamily Murinae of the Old World.
– ORIGIN early 17th cent.: from Latin *murinus*, from *mus, mur-* 'mouse.'

murk /mərk/ ▶ **n.** darkness or thick mist that makes it difficult to see: *my eyes were straining to see through the murk of the rainy evening.*
▶ **adj.** archaic murky; gloomy.
– ORIGIN Old English *mirce*, of Germanic origin; reinforced in Middle English by Old Norse *myrkr*.

murk·y /ˈmərkē/ ▶ **adj.** (**murkier**, **murkiest**) dark and gloomy, esp. due to thick mist: *the sky was murky and a thin drizzle was falling.* ■ (of liquid) dark and dirty; not clear: *the murky silt of a muddy pond.* ■ not fully explained or understood, esp. with concealed dishonesty or immorality: *the murky world of espionage.*
– DERIVATIVES **murk·i·ly adv.**, **murk·i·ness n.**

Mur·mansk /mo͝orˈmansk, -ˈmänsk/ a port in northwestern Russia, on the northern coast of the Kola Peninsula, in the Barents Sea; pop. 314,700 (est. 2008). It is the largest city located north of the Arctic Circle. Its port is ice-free throughout the year.

mur·mur /ˈmərmər/ ▶ **n.** a soft, indistinct sound made by a person or group of people speaking quietly or at a distance: *his voice was little more than a murmur.* ■ a softly spoken or almost inaudible utterance: *she accepted his offer with a quiet murmur of thanks.* ■ the quiet or subdued expression of a particular feeling by a group of people: *there was a murmur of approval from the crowd.* ■ a rumor: *he had heard hints only, murmurs.* ■ a low continuous sound: *the murmur of bees in the rhododendrons.* ■ Medicine a recurring sound heard in the heart through a stethoscope that is usually a sign of disease or damage. ■ informal a condition in which the heart produces or is apt to produce such a sound: *she had been born with a heart murmur.*
▶ **v.** [reporting verb] say something in a low, soft, or indistinct voice: [with obj.] *Nina murmured an excuse and hurried away* | [with direct speech] *"How interesting," he murmured quietly.* ■ [no obj.] make a low continuous sound: *the wind was murmuring through the trees.* ■ say something cautiously and discreetly: [no obj.] *they began to murmur of an uprising.* ■ [no obj.] (**murmur against**) archaic express one's discontent about (someone or something) in a subdued manner.
– PHRASES **without a murmur** without complaining.
– DERIVATIVES **mur·mur·er n.**, **mur·mur·ous** /-mərəs/ **adj.**
– ORIGIN late Middle English: from Old French *murmure*, from *murmurer* 'to murmur,' from Latin *murmurare*, from *murmur* 'a murmur.'

mur·mur·a·tion /ˌmərməˈrāSHən/ ▶ **n.** literary **1** the action of murmuring: *the murmuration of a flock of warblers.*
2 rare a flock of starlings.
– ORIGIN late Middle English: from French, from Latin *murmuratio(n-)*, from *murmurare* 'to murmur.' The usage as a collective noun dates from the late 15th cent.

mur·mur·ing /ˈmərməriNG/ ▶ **n.** a soft, low, or indistinct sound produced by a person or group of people speaking quietly or at a distance. ■ (usu. **murmurings**) a subdued or private expression of discontent or dissatisfaction: *murmurings of discontent from the fans.* ■ (usu. **murmurings**) an insinuation: *his father's life had been ruined by the murmurings and innuendoes of lesser men.* ■ a low continuous sound: *the murmuring of the wind.*
– DERIVATIVES **mur·mur·ing·ly adv.**

Mur·phy[1] /ˈmərfē/, Audie (Leon) (1924–71), US soldier and actor. The most decorated combat soldier of World War II, he appeared in war adventure movies such as *Beyond Glory* (1948) and *To Hell and Back* (1955), the latter being a movie version of his autobiography.

Mur·phy[2], Frank (1890–1949), US Supreme Court associate justice 1940–49. Governor-general of the Philippines 1933–35 and the governor of Michigan 1937–38, he was appointed to the Court by President Franklin D. Roosevelt.

mur·phy /ˈmərfē/ ▶ **n.** (pl. **murphies**) informal a potato.
– ORIGIN early 19th cent.: from *Murphy*, an Irish surname.

Mur·phy's Law /ˈmərfēz/ a supposed law of nature, expressed in various humorous popular sayings, to the effect that anything that can go wrong will go wrong.

mur·rain /ˈmərən/ ▶ **n. 1** an infectious disease, esp. babesiosis, affecting cattle or other animals.
2 archaic or humorous a plague, epidemic, or crop blight.
– ORIGIN late Middle English: from Old French *morine*, based on Latin *mori* 'to die.'

Mur·ray[1] /ˈmərē, mə-rē/ a city in northern Utah, a southern suburb of Salt Lake City; pop. 46,201 (est. 2008).

Mur·ray[2], Gilbert (1866–1957), British classical scholar, born in Australia; full name *George Gilbert Aimé*. His translations of Greek dramatists helped to revive interest in Greek drama. He was also a founder of the League of Nations and later a joint president of the United Nations.

Mur·ray[3], Sir James (Augustus Henry) (1837–1915), Scottish lexicographer. He was chief editor of the *Oxford English Dictionary*, but did not live to see the work completed.

Mur·ray Riv·er the principal river of Australia. It rises in the Great Dividing Range in New South Wales and flows 1,610 miles (2,590 km) generally northwest, forming part of the border between the states of Victoria and New South Wales, before turning south in South Australia to empty into the Indian Ocean southeast of Adelaide.

murre /mər/ ▶ **n.** a white-breasted North American auk (seabird). ● Genus *Uria*, family Alcidae: two species, the **thick-billed** (or **Brunnich's**) **murre** (*U. lomvia*) and the **thin-billed** (or **common**) **murre** (*U. aalge*).
– ORIGIN late 16th cent.: of unknown origin.

murre·let /ˈmərlit/ ▶ **n.** a small North Pacific auk (seabird), typically having a gray back and white underparts. ● Genera *Brachyramphus* and *Synthliboramphus*, family Alcidae: six species.

mur·rey /ˈmərē/ ▶ **n.** archaic a deep purple-red cloth. ■ the deep purple-red color of a mulberry. ■ Heraldry another term for SANGUINE.
– ORIGIN late Middle English: via Old French from medieval Latin *moratus*, from *morum* 'mulberry.'

Mur·row /ˈmərō, ˈmə-rō/, Edward R. (1908–65), US journalist; born *Egbert Roscoe Murrow*. He broadcast from bomb-ridden London during World War II, ending each program with "Good night, and good luck." He produced and narrated the radio series *Hear It Now* (1950–51) and the television series *See It Now* (1951–58). He was also well known for his television series *Person to Person* (1953–59).

Edward R. Murrow

Mur·rum·bidg·ee /ˌmərəmˈbijē/ a river in southeastern Australia, in New South Wales. Rising in the Great Dividing Range, it flows west for 1,099 miles (1,759 km) to join the Murray River, of which it is a major tributary.

mur·ther /ˈmər<u>TH</u>ər/ ▶ **n. & v.** archaic spelling of MURDER.

mus. ▶ **abbr.** ▪ museum. ▪ music or musical or musician.

MusB (also **Mus Bac**) ▶ **abbr.** Bachelor of Music.
– ORIGIN from Latin *Musicae Baccalaureus.*

Mus·ca /ˈməskə/ Astronomy a small southern constellation (the Fly), lying in the Milky Way between the Southern Cross and the south celestial pole. ▪ (as genitive **Muscae** /ˈməskē/) used with a preceding letter or numeral to designate a star in this constellation: *the star Beta Muscae.*
– ORIGIN Latin.

mus·ca·del /ˌməskəˈdel/ ▶ **n.** variant spelling of MUSCATEL.

Mus·ca·det /ˌməskəˈdā, -ˈde/ ▶ **n.** a dry white wine from the part of the Loire region in France nearest the west coast.
– ORIGIN French, from *muscade* 'nutmeg,' from *musc* 'musk.'

mus·ca·dine /ˈməskəˌdīn/ ▶ **n.** any of a group of species and varieties of wine grape native to Mexico and the southeastern US, typically having thick skins and a musky flavor. ● Genus *Vitis* (section Muscadinia): several species, in particular *V. rotundifolia.*
– ORIGIN probably an alteration of MUSCATEL.

mus·cae vol·i·tan·tes /ˈməskē ˌväləˈtanˌtēz/ ▶ **plural n.** Medicine dark specks appearing to float before the eyes, generally caused by particles in the vitreous humor of the eye.
– ORIGIN mid 18th cent.: Latin, literally 'flying flies.'

mus·ca·rine /ˈməskəˌrēn/ ▶ **n.** Chemistry a poisonous compound present in certain fungi, including the fly agaric. ● An alkaloid; chem. formula: $C_9H_{21}NO_3$.
– ORIGIN late 19th cent.: based on Latin *musca* 'fly.'

Mus·cat /ˈməˌskät/ the capital of Oman, a port in the northeastern part of the country on the southeastern coast of the Arabian peninsula; pop. 620,000 (est. 2007).

mus·cat /ˈməsˌkat, -kət/ ▶ **n.** [often as modifier] a variety of white, red, or black grape with a musky scent, grown in warm climates for wine or raisins or as table grapes. ▪ a wine made from a muscat grape, esp. a sweet or fortified white wine.
– ORIGIN French, from Provençal, from *musc* 'musk.'

Mus·cat and O·man former name (until 1970) for OMAN.

mus·ca·tel /ˌməskəˈtel/ (also **muscadel** /-ˈdel/) ▶ **n.** a muscat grape, esp. as grown for drying to make raisins. ▪ a raisin made from such a grape. ▪ a wine made from such a grape.
– ORIGIN via Old French from Provençal, diminutive of *muscat* (see MUSCAT).

Mu·schel·kalk /ˈmo͞oSHəlˌkälk/ ▶ **n.** Geology a limestone or chalk deposit from the Middle Triassic in Europe, esp. in Germany.
– ORIGIN mid 19th cent.: from German, literally 'mussel chalk.'

mus·cid /ˈməsid/ ▶ **n.** Entomology an insect of the housefly family (Muscidae).
– ORIGIN late 19th cent.: from modern Latin *Muscidae* (plural), from Latin *musca* 'fly.'

mus·cle /ˈməsəl/ ▶ **n. 1** a band or bundle of fibrous tissue in a human or animal body that has the ability to contract, producing movement in or maintaining the position of parts of the body: *the calf muscle | the sheet of muscle between the abdomen and chest.* ▪ such a band or bundle of tissue when well developed or prominently visible under the skin: *showing off our muscles to prove how strong we were.*

> Muscles are formed of bands, sheets, or columns of elongated cells (or fibers) containing interlocking parallel arrays of the proteins actin and myosin. Projections on the myosin molecules respond to chemical signals by forming and reforming chemical bonds to the actin, so that the filaments move past each other and interlock more deeply. This converts chemical energy into the mechanical force of contraction, and also generates heat.

2 physical power; strength: *he had muscle but no brains.* ▪ informal a person or people exhibiting such power or strength: *an ex-marine of enormous proportions who'd been brought along as muscle.* ▪ power or influence, esp. in a commercial or political context: *he had enough muscle and resources to hold his position on the council.*
▶ **v.** [with obj.] informal move (an object) in a particular direction by using one's physical strength: *they were muscling baggage into the hold of the plane.* ▪ informal coerce by violence or by economic or political pressure: *he was eventually muscled out of business.*
– PHRASES **flex one's muscles** give a show of strength or power. **not move a muscle** be completely motionless.
– PHRASAL VERBS **muscle in/into** informal force one's way into (something), typically in order to gain an advantage: ***muscling his way into meetings and important conferences*** *|* ***he was determined to muscle in on the union's affairs.*** **muscle up** informal build up one's muscles.
– DERIVATIVES **mus·cled** /ˈməsəld/ **adj.** [in combination] *hard-muscled*, **mus·cle·less adj.**
– ORIGIN late Middle English: from French, from Latin *musculus*, diminutive of *mus* 'mouse' (some muscles being thought to be mouselike in form).

mus·cle-bound ▶ **adj.** having well-developed or overdeveloped muscles: *the muscle-bound bartender.*

mus·cle dys·mor·phi·a ▶ **n.** a psychological disorder marked by a negative body image and an obsessive desire to have a muscular physique.

mus·cle·man /ˈməsəlˌman/ ▶ **n.** (pl. **musclemen**) a large, strong man, esp. one employed to protect someone or to intimidate people.

mus·cle tone ▶ **n.** see TONE (sense 6 of the noun).

mus·cly /ˈməs(ə)lē/ ▶ **adj.** muscular: *his muscly forearms.*

mus·co·va·do /ˌməskəˈvādō, -ˈvädō/ (also **muscovado sugar**) ▶ **n.** unrefined sugar made from the juice of sugar cane by evaporating it and draining off the molasses.
– ORIGIN early 17th cent.: from Portuguese *mascabado (açúcar)* '(sugar) of the lowest quality.'

Mus·co·vite /ˈməskəˌvīt/ ▶ **n.** a native or citizen of Moscow. ▪ archaic a Russian.
▶ **adj.** of or relating to Moscow. ▪ archaic of or relating to Russia.
– ORIGIN from modern Latin *Muscovita*, from *Muscovia* (see MUSCOVY).

mus·co·vite /ˈməskəˌvīt/ ▶ **n.** a silver-gray form of mica occurring in many igneous and metamorphic rocks.
– ORIGIN mid 19th cent.: from obsolete *Muscovy glass* (in the same sense) + -ITE¹.

Mus·co·vy /ˈməskəvē/ a medieval principality in west central Russia, centered around Moscow, that formed the nucleus of modern Russia. As Muscovy expanded, princes of Muscovy became the rulers of Russia; in 1472 Ivan III, grand duke of Muscovy, completed the unification of the country, and in 1547 Ivan the Terrible became the first tsar of Russia. ▪ archaic name for Russia.
– ORIGIN from obsolete French *Muscovie*, from modern Latin *Moscovia*, from Russian *Moskva* 'Moscow.'

Mus·co·vy duck /ˈməskəvē, -ˌkōvē/ ▶ **n.** a large tropical American tree-nesting duck, having glossy greenish-black plumage in the wild but bred in a variety of colors as a domestic bird. ● *Cairina moschata*, family Anatidae.

mus·cu·lar /ˈməskyələr/ ▶ **adj.** of or affecting the muscles: *energy is needed for muscular activity | muscular tension.* ▪ having well-developed muscles: *her legs were strong and muscular.* ▪ vigorously robust: *a muscular economy.*
– DERIVATIVES **mus·cu·lar·i·ty** /ˌməskyəˈle(ə)ritē/ **n.**, **mus·cu·lar·ly adv.**
– ORIGIN late 17th cent.: alteration of earlier *musculous*, in the same sense.

mus·cu·lar Chris·ti·an·i·ty ▶ **n.** a Christian life of brave and cheerful physical activity, esp. as popularly associated with the writings of Charles Kingsley and with boys' prep schools of the Victorian British Empire.

mus·cu·lar dys·tro·phy ▶ **n.** a hereditary condition marked by progressive weakening and wasting of the muscles.

mus·cu·la·ture /ˈməskyələCHər, -ˌCHo͝or/ ▶ **n.** the system or arrangement of muscles in a body, a part of the body, or an organ.
– ORIGIN late 19th cent.: from French, from Latin *musculus* (see MUSCLE).

mus·cu·lo·skel·e·tal /ˌməskyəlōˈskelətl/ ▶ **adj.** relating to or denoting the musculature and skeleton together.

MusD (also **Mus Doc**) ▶ **abbr.** Doctor of Music.
– ORIGIN from Latin *Musicae Doctor.*

Mus.Dr. (also **Mus.D.** or **Mus.Doc.**) ▶ **abbr.** Doctor of Music.
– ORIGIN from modern Latin *Mūsicae Doctor.*

Muse /myo͞oz/ ▶ **n.** (in Greek and Roman mythology) each of nine goddesses, the daughters of Zeus and Mnemosyne, who preside over the arts and sciences. ▪ (**muse**) a woman, or a force personified as a woman, who is the source of inspiration for a creative artist.

> The Muses are generally listed as Calliope (epic poetry), Clio (history), Euterpe (flute playing and lyric poetry), Terpsichore (choral dancing and song), Erato (lyre playing and lyric poetry), Melpomene (tragedy), Thalia (comedy and light verse), Polyhymnia (hymns, and later mime), and Urania (astronomy).

– ORIGIN late Middle English: from Old French, or from Latin *musa*, from Greek *mousa.*

muse /myo͞oz/ ▶ **v.** [no obj.] be absorbed in thought: *he was* ***musing on*** *the problems he faced.* ▪ say to oneself in a thoughtful manner: *"I think I've seen him somewhere before," mused Rachel.* ▪ (**muse on**) gaze thoughtfully at.
▶ **n.** dated an instance or period of reflection.
– ORIGIN Middle English: from Old French *muser* 'meditate, waste time,' perhaps from medieval Latin *musum* 'muzzle.'

muse·og·ra·phy /ˌmyo͞ozēˈägrəfē/ ▶ **n.** another term for MUSEOLOGY. ▪ rare the systematic description of objects in museums.
– DERIVATIVES **museographic** /ˌmyo͞ozēəˈgrafik/ **adj.**, **museographical** /ˌmyo͞ozēəˈgrafikəl/ **adj.**

mu·se·ol·o·gy /ˌmyo͞ozēˈäləjē/ ▶ **n.** the science or practice of organizing, arranging, and managing museums.
– DERIVATIVES **mu·se·o·log·i·cal** /-zēəˈläjikəl/ **adj.**, **mu·se·ol·o·gist** /-jist/ **n.**

mu·sette /myo͞oˈzet/ ▶ **n. 1** a kind of small bagpipe played with bellows, common in the French court in the 17th–18th centuries and in later folk music. ▪ a tune or piece of music imitating the sound of this, typically with a drone. ▪ a dance to such a tune, esp. in the 18th-century French court. ▪ a small simple variety of oboe, used chiefly in 19th-century France.
2 (also **musette bag**) a small knapsack.
– ORIGIN late Middle English: from Old French, diminutive of *muse* 'bagpipe.'

mu·se·um /myo͞oˈzēəm/ ▶ **n.** a building in which objects of historical, scientific, artistic, or cultural interest are stored and exhibited.
– ORIGIN early 17th cent. (denoting a university building, specifically one erected at Alexandria by Ptolemy Soter): via Latin from Greek *mouseion* 'seat of the Muses,' based on *mousa* 'muse.'

mu·se·um piece ▶ **n.** an object that is worthy of display in a museum. ▪ a person or object regarded as old-fashioned, irrelevant, or useless: *we're nothing but museum pieces—machines can do everything that we can do.*

Mu·se·ve·ni /ˌmo͞osəˈvānē/, Yoweri (Kaguta) (1944–), Ugandan statesman; president 1986– . After ousting Milton Obote, he brought some stability to a country that had suffered under the dictatorial Obote and Idi Amin.

mush[1] /məSH/ ▶ **n. 1** a soft, wet, pulpy mass: *red lentils cook quickly and soon turn to mush.* ▪ thick porridge, esp. made of cornmeal.
2 feeble or cloying sentimentality: *the film's not just romantic mush.*
▶ **v.** [with obj.] (usu. as adj. **mushed**) reduce (a substance) to a soft, wet, pulpy mass: *simmer until the apples and potatoes are tender but not mushed.*
– ORIGIN late 17th cent. (sense 2 of the noun): apparently a variant of MASH.

mush[2] ▶ **v.** [no obj.] go on a journey across snow with a dogsled: *by the end of winter he will have snowshoed up to 700 miles and mushed about the same.* ▪ [with obj.] urge on (the dogs) during such a journey.
▶ **exclam.** a command urging on dogs during such a journey.
▶ **n.** a journey across snow with a dogsled: *a twelve-day mush.*
– ORIGIN mid 19th cent.: probably an alteration of French *marchez!* or *marchons!*, imperatives of *marcher* 'to advance.'

Mu·shar·raf /mo͞oˈSHärəf/, Pervez (1943–), Pakistani general and statesman; president of Pakistan 2001–08. He became head of state in 1999 following a bloodless coup d'état.

mush·er /ˈməSHər/ ▶ **n.** the driver of a dogsled.

mush·rat /ˈməSHˌrat/ ▶ **n.** another term for MUSKRAT.

mush·room /ˈməSHˌro͞om, -ˌro͝om/ ▶ **n. 1** a fungal growth that typically takes the form of a domed cap on a stalk, often with gills on the underside of the cap. ▪ a thing resembling a mushroom in shape: *a mushroom of smoke and flames.*

m

common morel
Morchella esculenta

false morel
Gyromitra esculenta

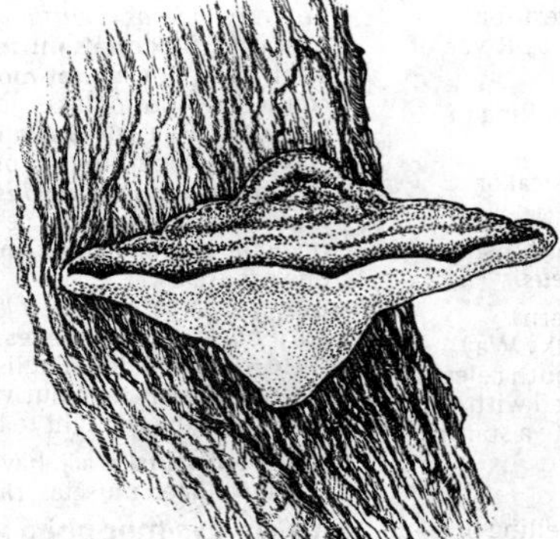

artist's fungus
Ganoderma applanatum

turkey tail
Coriolus versicolor

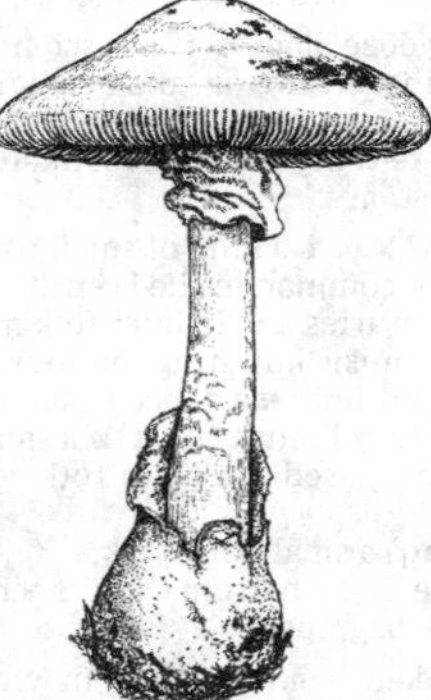

destroying angel
Amanita bisporigera

honey mushroom
Armillaria mellea

puffball
Lycoperdon perlatum

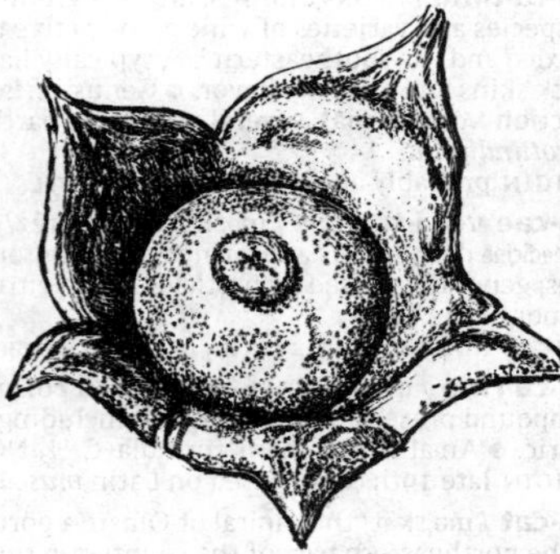

earthstar
Geastrum saccatum

common chanterelle
Cantharellus cibarius

golden coral
Ramaria largentii

king bolete
Boletus edulis

fly agaric
Amanita muscaria

mushrooms and related fungi

> Mushrooms are fruiting bodies that produce spores, growing from the hyphae of fungi concealed in soil or wood. They are proverbial for rapid growth. Toadstools are often called mushrooms, esp. when they are considered to be edible. Numerous varieties are poisonous.

2 a pale pinkish-brown color: [as modifier] ***a mushroom** leather bag.*
▶ **v.** [no obj.] **1** increase, spread, or develop rapidly: *environmental concern mushroomed in the 1960s.* **2** (of the smoke, fire, or flames produced by an explosion) spread into the air in a shape resembling that of a mushroom: *the grenade mushroomed into red fire as it hit the hillside.* ■ (of a bullet) expand and flatten on reaching its target. **3** (usu. as noun **mushrooming**) (of a person) gather mushrooms.
– DERIVATIVES **mush·room·y** adj.
– ORIGIN late Middle English (originally denoting any fungus having a fleshy fruiting body): from Old French *mousseron*, from late Latin *mussirio(n-)*.

mush·room an·chor ▶ **n.** an anchor whose shape resembles that of a mushroom.

mush·room cloud ▶ **n.** a mushroom-shaped cloud of dust and debris formed after a nuclear explosion.

mush·y /ˈməSHē/ ▶ **adj.** (**mushier, mushiest**) **1** soft and pulpy: *cook until the fruit is mushy | mushy vegetables.* **2** excessively sentimental: *he gets as mushy as a Hallmark valentine.*
– DERIVATIVES **mush·i·ly** /ˈməSHəlē/ **adv.**, **mush·i·ness n.**

Mu·si·al /ˈmyo͞ozēəl/, Stan (1920–), US baseball player; full name *Stanley Frank Musial*; known as **Stan the Man**. A first baseman and an outfielder, he played for the St. Louis Cardinals 1941–63 and led the National League in batting seven times. Baseball Hall of Fame (1969).

mu·sic /ˈmyo͞ozik/ ▶ **n. 1** the art or science of combining vocal or instrumental sounds (or both) to produce beauty of form, harmony, and expression of emotion: *he devoted his life to music.* ■ the vocal or instrumental sound produced in this way: *couples were dancing to the music | baroque music.* ■ a sound perceived as pleasingly harmonious: *the background music of softly lapping water.* **2** the written or printed signs representing such sound: *Tony learned to read music.* ■ the score or scores of a musical composition or compositions: *the music was open on a stand.*
– PHRASES **face the music** see FACE. **music of the spheres** see SPHERE. **music to one's ears** something that is pleasant or gratifying to hear or discover: *the commission's report was music to the ears of the administration.*
– ORIGIN Middle English: from Old French *musique*, via Latin from Greek *mousikē (tekhnē)* '(art) of the Muses,' from *mousa* 'muse.'

mu·si·ca fic·ta /ˈmyo͞ozikə ˈfiktə/ ▶ **n.** Music (in early contrapuntal music) the introduction by a performer of sharps, flats, or other accidentals to avoid unacceptable intervals.
– ORIGIN early 19th cent.: Latin, literally 'feigned music.'

mu·si·cal /ˈmyo͞ozikəl/ ▶ **adj. 1** of or relating to music: *they shared similar musical tastes.* ■ set to or accompanied by music: *an evening of musical entertainment.* ■ fond of or skilled in music: *Henry was very musical, but his wife was tone-deaf.* **2** having a pleasant sound; melodious; tuneful: *they burst out into rich, musical laughter.*

▶ **n.** a play or movie in which singing and dancing play an essential part. Musicals developed from light opera in the early 20th century.
– DERIVATIVES **mu·si·cal·ly** /-ik(ə)lē/ **adv.**
– ORIGIN late Middle English: from Old French, from medieval Latin *musicalis*, from Latin *musica* (see **MUSIC**).

mu·si·cal chairs ▶ **n.** a party game in which players compete for a decreasing number of chairs, the losers in successive rounds being those unable to find a chair to sit on when the accompanying music is abruptly stopped. ■ a series of changes or exchanges of position, esp. in a political or commercial organization: *the appointment of the chief executive comes after a prolonged period of musical chairs involving top management.*

mu·si·cal com·e·dy ▶ **n.** a light play or movie with songs, dialogue, and dancing, connected by a plot.

mu·si·cal di·rec·tor ▶ **n.** the person responsible for the musical aspects of a performance, production, or organization, typically the conductor or leader of a music group: *in 1991 the New York Philharmonic hired a new musical director.*

mu·si·cale /ˌmyo͞oziˈkal/ ▶ **n.** a musical gathering or concert, typically small and informal.
– ORIGIN late 19th cent.: French, from *soirée musicale* 'evening of music.'

mu·si·cal glass·es ▶ **plural n.** a series of drinking glasses or bowls filled with varying amounts of water and played as a musical instrument by rubbing the rims with the fingers. See also **GLASS HARMONICA**.

mu·si·cal in·stru·ment ▶ **n.** see **INSTRUMENT** (sense 3 of the noun).

mu·si·cal·i·ty /ˌmyo͞oziˈkalətē/ ▶ **n.** tastefulness and accomplishment in music: *she sings with unfailing musicality.* ■ the quality of being melodious and tuneful: *his speaking voice hinted at musicality.* ■ awareness of music and rhythm, esp. in dance: *the audition panel was looking for coordination, musicality, and flexibility.*

mu·si·cal·ize /ˈmyo͞ozikəˌlīz/ ▶ **v.** [with obj.] set (a text or play) to music: *a problem inherent in any attempt to musicalize science fiction.*

mu·si·cal saw ▶ **n.** a saw used as a musical instrument, typically held between the knees and played with a bow like a cello, the note varying with the degree of bending of the blade.

mu·sic box ▶ **n.** a small box that plays a tune, typically when the lid is opened. A traditional music box contains a cylinder, turned by clockwork, with projecting teeth that pluck a row of tuned metal strips as it revolves.

mu·sic dra·ma ▶ **n.** an opera whose structure is governed by considerations of dramatic effectiveness, rather than by the convention of having a series of formal arias.

mu·sic hall ▶ **n.** a theater where musical events are staged. ■ a form of variety entertainment popular in Britain from *c.*1850, consisting of singing, dancing, comedy, acrobatics, and novelty acts. Its popularity declined after World War I with the rise of the movie industry.

mu·si·cian /myo͞oˈzisHən/ ▶ **n.** a person who plays a musical instrument, esp. as a profession, or is musically talented: *your father was a fine musician* | *aspiring rock and pop musicians.*
– DERIVATIVES **mu·si·cian·ly adj.**, **mu·si·cian·ship** /-ˌsHip/ **n.**
– ORIGIN late Middle English: from Old French *musicien*, from Latin *musica* (see **MUSIC**).

mu·si·col·o·gy /ˌmyo͞oziˈkäləjē/ ▶ **n.** the study of music as an academic subject, as distinct from training in performance or composition; scholarly research into music.
– DERIVATIVES **mu·si·co·log·i·cal** /-kəˈläjikəl/ **adj.**, **mu·si·col·o·gist** /-jist/ **n.**
– ORIGIN early 20th cent.: from French *musicologie*.

mu·sic stand ▶ **n.** a rack or light frame on which written or printed music is supported.

mu·sic the·a·ter ▶ **n.** a combination of music and drama in modern form distinct from traditional opera, typically for a small group of performers.

mus·ing /ˈmyo͞oziNG/ ▶ **n.** (usu. **musings**) a period of reflection or thought: *his musings were interrupted by the sound of the telephone.*
▶ **adj.** characterized by reflection or deep thought: *the sad musing gaze.*
– DERIVATIVES **mus·ing·ly adv.**

mu·sique con·crète /m(y)o͞oˈzēk kōNˈkret/ ▶ **n.** music constructed by mixing recorded sounds, first developed by experimental composers in the 1940s.
– ORIGIN French, literally 'concrete music.'

musk /məsk/ ▶ **n. 1** a strong-smelling reddish-brown substance that is secreted by the male musk deer for scent-marking and is an important ingredient in perfumery. ■ a similar secretion of another animal: *civets habitually deposit tiny amounts of musk.*
2 (also **musk plant** or **musk flower**) a relative of the monkey flower that was formerly cultivated for its musky perfume, which has been lost in the development of modern varieties. ● Genus *Mimulus*, family Scrophulariaceae: several species, in particular *M. moschatus*.
– ORIGIN late Middle English: from late Latin *muscus*, from Persian *mušk*, perhaps from Sanskrit *muṣka* 'scrotum' (because of the similarity in shape of a musk deer's musk bag).

musk deer ▶ **n.** a small solitary deerlike eastern Asian mammal without antlers, the male having long protruding upper canine teeth. Musk is produced in a sac on the abdomen of the male. ● Family Moschidae and genus *Moschus*: several species.

musk duck ▶ **n.** an Australian stiff-tailed duck with dark gray plumage and a musky smell, the male having a large black lobe of skin hanging below the bill. ● *Biziura lobata*, family Anatidae.

mus·keg /ˈməsˌkeg/ ▶ **n.** a North American swamp or bog consisting of a mixture of water and partly dead vegetation, frequently covered by a layer of sphagnum or other mosses.
– ORIGIN early 19th cent.: from Cree.

Mus·ke·gon /məsˈkēgən/ an industrial port in western Michigan, on Lake Michigan; pop. 39,401 (est. 2008).

mus·kel·lunge /ˈməskəˌlənj/ ▶ **n.** a large pike that occurs only in the Great Lakes region. Also called **MASKINONGE** or **LUNGE**[3]. ● *Esox masquinongy*, family Esocidae.
– ORIGIN late 18th cent.: from Canadian French *maskinongé*, from Ojibwa *māskinōšē*.

mus·ket /ˈməskit/ ▶ **n.** historical an infantryman's light gun with a long barrel, typically smooth-bored, muzzleloading, and fired from the shoulder.
– ORIGIN late 16th cent.: from French *mousquet*, from Italian *moschetto* 'crossbow bolt,' from *mosca* 'a fly.'

mus·ket·eer /ˌməskəˈtir/ ▶ **n.** historical a soldier armed with a musket.

mus·ket·ry /ˈməskətrē/ ▶ **n.** musket fire: *a terrible explosion of musketry.* ■ soldiers armed with muskets: *the Prussian musketry.* ■ the art or technique of handling a musket.

musk·mel·on /ˈməskˌmelən/ ▶ **n.** an edible melon of a type that has a raised network of markings on the skin. Its many varieties include those with orange, yellow, green, or white juicy flesh.

Mus·ko·ge·an /məˈskōgēən/ ▶ **n.** a family of American Indian languages spoken in southeastern North America, including Chikasaw, Choctaw, Creek, and Seminole.
▶ **adj.** of or relating to this language family.
– ORIGIN from **MUSKOGEE**[2] + **-AN**.

Mus·ko·gee[1] /ˌməˈskōgē/ a commercial city in east central Oklahoma, on the Arkansas River; pop. 40,099 (est. 2008).

Mus·ko·gee[2] ▶ **n.** (pl. **same** or **Muskogees**) **1** a member of an American Indian people of the southeastern US, who led the Creek Indian confederacy.
2 the Muskogean language of this people.
▶ **adj.** of or relating to the Muskogees or their language.
– ORIGIN from Creek *ma:skó:ki*.

musk·ox /ˈməskˌäks/ (also **musk ox**) ▶ **n.** (pl. **muskoxen**) a large heavily built goat-antelope with a thick shaggy coat and large curved horns, native to the tundra of North America and Greenland. ● *Ovibos moschatus*, family Bovidae.

musk·rat /ˈməˌskrat/ ▶ **n.** a large semiaquatic North American rodent with a musky smell, valued for its fur. ● *Ondatra zibethicus*, family Muridae. ■ the fur of the muskrat.

musk rose ▶ **n.** a rambling rose with large white musk-scented flowers. ● *Rosa moschata*, family Rosaceae.

musk tur·tle ▶ **n.** a small drab-colored American freshwater turtle that has scent glands that produce an unpleasant musky odor when the turtle is disturbed. Also called **STINKPOT**. ● Genus *Sternotherus*, family Kinosternidae: several species, including the **common musk turtle** (*S. odoratus*).

musk·y /ˈməskē/ ▶ **adj.** (**muskier**, **muskiest**) of or having a smell or taste of musk, or suggestive of musk.
– DERIVATIVES **musk·i·ness n.**

Mus·lim /ˈməzləm, ˈmo͝oz-, ˈmäz-/ (also **Moslem**) ▶ **n.** a follower of the religion of Islam.
▶ **adj.** of or relating to the Muslims or their religion.
– ORIGIN early 17th cent.: from Arabic, active participle of *'aslama* (see **ISLAM**).

> **USAGE** **Muslim** is the preferred term for 'follower of Islam,' although **Moslem** is also widely used. The archaic term **Muhammadan** (or **Mohammedan**) should be avoided.

Mus·lim Broth·er·hood an Islamic religious and political organization dedicated to the establishment of a nation based on Islamic principles. Founded in Egypt in 1928, it has become a radical underground force in Egypt and other Sunni countries, promoting strict moral discipline and opposing Western influence, often by violence.

mus·lin /ˈməzlən/ ▶ **n.** lightweight cotton cloth in a plain weave: [as modifier] *a white muslin dress.*
– DERIVATIVES **mus·lined** /ˈməzlənd/ **adj.**
– ORIGIN early 17th cent.: from French *mousseline*, from Italian *mussolina*, from *Mussolo* 'Mosul' (the name of the place of manufacture in Iraq).

Mus.M. ▶ **abbr.** Master of Music.
– ORIGIN from modern Latin *Mūsicae Magister*.

mu·so /ˈmyo͞ozō/ ▶ **n.** (pl. **musos**) Brit. informal a musician, esp. one overly concerned with technique. ■ an avid music fan, esp. one who has expensive stereo equipment.
– ORIGIN 1960s: abbreviation.

mus·quash /ˈməˌskwäsH, ˈməˌskwôsH/ ▶ **n.** archaic term for **MUSKRAT**. ■ Brit. the fur of the muskrat.
– ORIGIN early 17th cent.: from Abnaki *mòskwas*.

muss /məs/ informal ▶ **v.** [with obj.] make (someone's hair or clothes) untidy or messy: *she sat down carefully so she wouldn't muss her clothes.*
▶ **n.** [usu. in sing.] a state of disorder.
– DERIVATIVES **muss·y** /ˈməsē/ **adj.** (dated).
– ORIGIN mid 19th cent. (also as a noun in the sense 'disturbance or row'): apparently a variant of **MESS**.

mus·sel /ˈməsəl/ ▶ **n.** any of a number of bivalve mollusks with a brown or purplish-black shell. ● a marine bivalve that uses byssus threads to anchor to a firm surface (family Mytilidae, order Mytiloidea), including the **edible mussel** (*Mytilus edulis*). ● a freshwater bivalve that typically lies on the bed of a river, some species forming small pearls (family Unionidae, order Unionoida).
– ORIGIN Old English *mus(c)le*, superseded by forms from Middle Low German *mussel*, Middle Dutch *mosscele*; ultimately from late Latin *muscula*, from Latin *musculus* (see **MUSCLE**).

m

Mus·so·li·ni /ˌmo͞osəˈlēnē/, Benito (Amilcaro Andrea) (1883–1945), Italian statesman; prime minister 1922–43; known as **Il Duce** ('the leader'). He founded the Italian Fascist Party in 1919, annexed Abyssinia in 1936, and entered World War II on Germany's side in 1940. He was captured and executed by Italian communist partisans a few weeks before the end of the war.

Benito Mussolini

Mus·sorg·sky /məˈsôrgskē, -ˈzôrg-/ (also **Moussorgsky**), Modest (Petrovich) (1839–81), Russian composer. He wrote the opera *Boris Godunov* (1874) and *Songs and Dances of Death* (1875–77).

Mus·sul·man /ˈməsəlmən/ ▶ **n.** (pl. **Mussulmans** or **Mussulmen**) & **adj.** archaic term for **MUSLIM**.
– ORIGIN late 16th cent.: from Persian *musulmān* (originally an adjective), from *muslim* (see **MUSLIM**).

must[1] /məst/ ▶ **modal v.** (past **had to** or in reported speech **must**) **1** be obliged to; should (expressing necessity): *you must show your ID card* | *it must not be over 2,000 words* | *she said she must be going.* ■ expressing insistence: *you must try some of this fish* | *if you must smoke, you could at least go in the living room.* ■ used in ironic questions expressing irritation: *must you look so utterly suburban?*
2 expressing an opinion about something that is logically very likely: *there must be something wrong* | *you must be tired.*

PRONUNCIATION KEY ə *ago, up*; ər *over, fur*; a *hat*; ā *ate*; ä *car*; e *let*; ē *see*; i *fit*; ī *by*; NG *sing*; ō *go*; ô *law, for*; oi *toy*; o͝o *good*; o͞o *goo*; ou *out*; TH *thin*; T͟H *then*; ZH *vision*

▶ n. informal something that should not be overlooked or missed: *this video is a must for parents.*
– PHRASES **I must say** see SAY. **must needs do something** see NEEDS.
– ORIGIN Old English *mōste*, past tense of *mōt* 'may,' of Germanic origin; related to Dutch *moeten* and German *müssen.*

must[2] ▶ n. grape juice before or during fermentation.
– ORIGIN Old English, from Latin *mustum*, neuter (used as a noun) of *mustus* 'new.'

must[3] ▶ n. mustiness, dampness, or mold: *a pervasive smell of must.*
– ORIGIN early 17th cent.: back-formation from MUSTY.

must[4] (also **musth**) ▶ n. the frenzied state of certain male animals, esp. elephants or camels, that is associated with the rutting season: *a big old bull elephant in must.*
▶ adj. (of a male elephant or camel) in such a state.
– ORIGIN late 19th cent.: via Urdu from Persian *mast* 'intoxicated.'

must- ▶ comb. form used to form adjectives and nouns denoting things that are essential or highly recommended: *a must-visit destination | the new material on this disc makes it a must-buy.*

mus·tache /ˈməs,taSH, məˈstaSH/ (also **moustache**) ▶ n. a strip of hair left to grow above the upper lip. ■ (**mustaches**) a long mustache. ■ a similar growth, or a marking that resembles it, around the mouth of some animals.
– DERIVATIVES **mus·tached** adj.
– ORIGIN late 16th cent.: from French, from Italian *mostaccio*, from Greek *mustax, mustak-*.

mus·tache cup ▶ n. a cup with a partial cover that protects the mustache of the person drinking from it.

mus·ta·chios /məˈstasHē,ōz/ ▶ plural n. a long or elaborate mustache.
– DERIVATIVES **mus·ta·chioed** /-,ōd/ adj.
– ORIGIN mid 16th cent.: from Spanish *mostacho* (singular), from Italian *mostaccio* (see MUSTACHE).

mus·tang /ˈməs,taNG/ ▶ n. an American feral horse, typically small and lightly built.
– ORIGIN early 19th cent.: from a blend of Spanish *mestengo* (from *mesta* 'company of graziers') and *mostrenco*, both meaning 'wild or masterless cattle.'

m

mus·tard /ˈməstərd/ ▶ n. **1** a pungent-tasting yellow or brown paste made from the crushed seeds of certain plants, typically eaten with meat or used as a cooking ingredient.
2 the yellow-flowered Eurasian plant of the cabbage family whose seeds are used to make this paste. ● Genera *Brassica* and *Sinapis*, family Brassicaceae: several species, in particular **black mustard** (*B. nigra*) and **white mustard** (*S. alba*). ■ used in names of related plants, only some of which are used to produce mustard for the table, e.g., **hedge mustard**.
3 a dark yellow color.
– PHRASES **cut the mustard** see CUT.
– DERIVATIVES **mus·tard·y** adj.
– ORIGIN Middle English: from Old French *moustarde*, from Latin *mustum* 'must' (the condiment being originally prepared with 'must').

mus·tard gas ▶ n. a colorless oily liquid whose vapor is a powerful irritant and vesicant, used in chemical weapons. ● Chem. formula: $(ClCH_2CH_2)_2S$.

mus·tard greens ▶ plural n. the leaves of the mustard plant used in salads.

mus·tard plas·ter ▶ n. a poultice made with mustard.

mus·te·lid /ˈməstəlid/ ▶ n. Zoology a mammal of the weasel family (Mustelidae), distinguished by having a long body, short legs, and musky scent glands under the tail.
– ORIGIN early 20th cent.: from modern Latin *Mustelidae* (plural), from Latin *mustela* 'weasel.'

mus·ter /ˈməstər/ ▶ v. [with obj.] **1** assemble (troops), esp. for inspection or in preparation for battle. ■ [no obj.] (of troops) come together in this way: *the cavalrymen mustered beside the other regiments.* ■ [no obj.] (of a group of people) gather together: *reporters mustered outside her house.*
2 collect or assemble (a number or amount): *he could fail to muster a majority.* ■ summon up (a particular feeling, attitude, or response): *he replied with as much dignity as he could muster.*
▶ n. a formal gathering of troops, esp. for inspection, display, or exercise. ■ short for MUSTER ROLL.
– PHRASES **pass muster** be accepted as adequate or satisfactory: *a treaty that might pass muster with the voters.*
– PHRASAL VERBS **muster someone in** (or **out**) enroll someone into (or discharge someone from) military service.
– ORIGIN late Middle English: from Old French *moustrer* (verb), *moustre* (noun), from Latin *monstrare* 'to show.'

mus·ter roll ▶ n. an official list of officers and men in a military unit or ship's company.

musth /ˈməst/ ▶ n. variant spelling of MUST[4].

must-have ▶ adj. essential or highly desirable: *the must-have blouse of the season.*
▶ n. an essential or highly desirable item: *this classic volume is a must-have for any collector.*

must·n't /ˈməsənt/ ▶ contraction must not.

must-read /rēd/ ▶ adj. denoting a piece of writing that should or must be read: *his must-read article in the NY Times.*
▶ n. a compelling or particularly useful piece of writing: *it's a must-read for anyone interested in movies.*

must-see ▶ adj. highly recommended as worth seeing: *one of the must-see pieces at the exhibition.*
▶ n. a place, event, or entertainment that is highly recommended as worth seeing: *this sassy and superior suspense thriller is a must-see.*

mus·ty /ˈməstē/ ▶ adj. (**mustier, mustiest**) having a stale, moldy, or damp smell: *a dark musty library filled with old books.* ■ having a stale taste: *the beer tasted sour, thin, and musty.* ■ lacking originality or vitality: *when I read it again, the play seemed musty.*
– DERIVATIVES **mus·ti·ly** /-təlē/ adv., **mus·ti·ness** n.
– ORIGIN early 16th cent.: perhaps an alteration of *moisty* 'moist,' influenced by MUST[2].

Mut /mo͞ot/ Egyptian Mythology a goddess who was the wife of Amun and mother of Khonsu.

mu·ta·ble /ˈmyo͞otəbəl/ ▶ adj. liable to change: *the mutable nature of fashion.* ■ literary inconstant in one's affections: *youth is said to be fickle and mutable.*
– DERIVATIVES **mu·ta·bil·i·ty** /,myo͞otəˈbilətē/ n.
– ORIGIN late Middle English: from Latin *mutabilis*, from *mutare* 'to change.'

mu·ta·gen /ˈmyo͞otəjən/ ▶ n. an agent, such as radiation or a chemical substance, that causes genetic mutation.
– DERIVATIVES **mu·ta·gen·e·sis** /,myo͞otəˈjenəsəs/ n., **mu·ta·gen·ic** /,myo͞otəˈjenik/ adj., **mu·ta·ge·nic·i·ty** /-ˈnisiti/ n.
– ORIGIN 1940s: from MUTATION + -GEN.

mu·ta·gen·ize /ˈmyo͞otəjə,nīz/ ▶ v. [with obj.] (usu. as adj. **mutagenized**) Biology treat (a cell, organism, etc.) with mutagenic agents: *mutagenized DNA.*

mu·tant /ˈmyo͞otnt/ ▶ adj. resulting from or showing the effect of mutation: *a mutant gene.*
▶ n. a mutant form.
– ORIGIN early 20th cent.: from Latin *mutant-* 'changing,' from the verb *mutare.*

Mu·ta·re /mo͞oˈtärā/ an industrial town in the eastern highlands of Zimbabwe; pop. 183,500 (est. 2009). Former name (until 1982) **UMTALI**.

mu·tate /ˈmyo͞o,tāt/ ▶ v. change or cause to change in form or nature: [no obj.] *technology continues to mutate at an alarming rate* | [with obj.] *the quick-dry solution really worked, even if it did mutate the skin on her fingers to reptilian scales.* ■ Biology (with reference to a cell, DNA molecule, etc.) undergo or cause to undergo change in a gene or genes: [no obj.] *the virus is able to* **mutate into** *new forms that are immune to the vaccine* | [with obj.] *certain nucleotides were mutated.*
– DERIVATIVES **mu·ta·tor** /-,tātər/ n.
– ORIGIN early 19th cent.: back-formation from MUTATION.

mu·ta·tion /myo͞oˈtāsHən/ ▶ n. **1** the action or process of mutating: *the mutation of ethnic politics into nationalist politics | his first novel went through several mutations.*
2 the changing of the structure of a gene, resulting in a variant form that may be transmitted to subsequent generations, caused by the alteration of single base units in DNA, or the deletion, insertion, or rearrangement of larger sections of genes or chromosomes. ■ a distinct form resulting from such a change.
3 Linguistics regular change of a sound when it occurs adjacent to another, in particular: ■ (in Germanic languages) the process by which the quality of a vowel was altered in certain phonetic contexts; umlaut. ■ (in Celtic languages) change of an initial consonant in a word caused (historically) by the preceding word. See also LENITION.
– DERIVATIVES **mu·ta·tion·al** /-sHənl/ adj., **mu·ta·tion·al·ly** /-sHənl-ē/ adv., **mu·ta·tive** /ˈmyo͞otətiv/ adj.
– ORIGIN late Middle English: from Latin *mutatio(n-)*, from *mutare* 'to change.'

mu·ta·tis mu·tan·dis /m(y)o͞oˈtätəs m(y)o͞oˈtändəs, -ˈtātəs, -ˈtandəs/ ▶ adv. (used when comparing two or more cases or situations) making necessary alterations while not affecting the main point at issue: *what is true of undergraduate teaching in England is equally true, mutatis mutandis, of American graduate schools.*
– ORIGIN Latin, literally 'things being changed that have to be changed.'

mutch·kin /ˈməCHkin/ ▶ n. a Scottish unit of capacity equal to a little less than a pint, or roughly three quarters of an imperial pint (0.43 liters).
– ORIGIN late Middle English: from early modern Dutch *mudsekin*, diminutive of *mud* 'hectoliter.'

mute /myo͞ot/ ▶ adj. **1** refraining from speech or temporarily speechless: *Irene, the talkative one, was now mute.* ■ not expressed in speech: *she gazed at him in mute appeal.* ■ characterized by an absence of sound; quiet: *the great church was mute and dark.* ■ dated, usu. offensive (of a person) without the power of speech.
2 (of a letter) not pronounced: *mute e is generally dropped before suffixes beginning with a vowel.*
▶ n. **1** a person without the power of speech. ■ historical (in some Asian countries) a servant who was deprived of the power of speech. ■ historical an actor in a dumbshow. ■ historical a professional attendant or mourner at a funeral.
2 a clamp placed over the bridge of a stringed instrument to deaden the resonance without affecting the vibration of the strings. ■ a pad or cone placed in the opening of a brass or other wind instrument.
3 a device on a television, telephone, or other appliance that temporarily turns off the sound: *she put the remote on mute.*
▶ v. [with obj.] deaden, muffle, or soften the sound of: *her footsteps were muted by the thick carpet | he turns the set on, mutes the sound, but flicks through the channels.* ■ muffle the sound of (a musical instrument), esp. by the use of a mute. ■ reduce the strength or intensity of: *his professional contentment was muted by personal sadness.*
– DERIVATIVES **mute·ly** adv., **mute·ness** n.
– ORIGIN Middle English: from Old French *muet*, diminutive of *mu*, from Latin *mutus.*

> **USAGE** 1 To describe a person without the power of speech as **mute** (especially as in **deaf-mute**) is today likely to cause offense and is often regarded as outdated. Nevertheless, there is no directly equivalent term for **mute** in general use, apart from **speech-impaired**. The term **profoundly deaf** may be used to imply that a person has not developed any spoken language skills. See also usage at DEAF-MUTE. 2 Is it **mute point** or **moot point**? See usage at MOOT.

mute but·ton ▶ n. a button that can be pressed to temporarily halt the sound on a television, telephone, remote, or other apparatus.

mut·ed /ˈmyo͞otid/ ▶ adj. (of a sound or voice) quiet and soft: *they discussed the accident in muted voices.* ■ (of a musical instrument) having a muffled sound as a result of being fitted with a mute. ■ not expressed strongly or openly: *muted anger.* ■ (of color or lighting) not bright; subdued: *a dress in muted tones of powder blue and dusty pink.*

mute swan ▶ n. the most common Eurasian swan, having white plumage and an orange-red bill with a black knob at the base. Introduced to the northeastern US, its range is expanding along the Atlantic coast and the Great Lakes region. ● *Cygnus olor*, family Anatidae.

mute swan

muth·a /ˈməT͟Hə/ ▶ n. variant spelling of MOTHER (sense 2 of the noun).

mu·ti·late /ˈmyo͞otl,āt/ ▶ v. [with obj.] (usu. **be mutilated**) inflict a violent and disfiguring injury on: *the leg was badly mutilated* | (as adj. **mutilated**) *mutilated bodies.* ■ inflict serious damage on: *the 14th-century church had been partly mutilated in the 18th century.*
– DERIVATIVES **mu·ti·la·tor** /-,ātər/ n.
– ORIGIN early 16th cent.: from Latin *mutilat-* 'maimed, mutilated, lopped off,' from the verb *mutilare*, from *mutilus* 'maimed.'

mu·ti·la·tion /,myo͞otlˈāsHən/ ▶ n. the action of mutilating or being mutilated: *a culture which found any mutilation of the body abhorrent* | [count noun] *there were fatalities and appalling mutilations.* ■ the infliction of serious damage on something: *the mutilation of the English language.*

mu·ti·neer /ˌmyo͞otnˈi(ə)r/ ▶ **n.** a person, esp. a soldier or sailor, who rebels or refuses to obey the orders of a person in authority.
– ORIGIN early 17th cent.: from French *mutinier*, from *mutin* 'rebellious,' from *muete* 'movement,' based on Latin *movere* 'to move.'

mu·ti·nous /ˈmyo͞otn-əs/ ▶ **adj.** (of a soldier or sailor) refusing to obey the orders of a person in authority. ■ willful or disobedient: *Antoinette looked mutinous, but she obeyed.*
– DERIVATIVES **mu·ti·nous·ly** adv.
– ORIGIN late 16th cent.: from obsolete *mutine* 'rebellion' (see MUTINY) + -OUS.

mu·ti·ny /ˈmyo͞otn-ē/ ▶ **n.** (pl. **mutinies**) an open rebellion against the proper authorities, esp. by soldiers or sailors against their officers: *a mutiny by those manning the weapons could trigger a global war | mutiny at sea.*
▶ **v.** (**mutinies, mutinying, mutinied**) [no obj.] refuse to obey the orders of a person in authority.
– ORIGIN mid 16th cent.: from obsolete *mutine* 'rebellion,' from French *mutin* 'mutineer,' based on Latin *movere* 'to move.'

mut·ism /ˈmyo͞otˌizəm/ ▶ **n.** inability to speak, typically as a result of congenital deafness or brain damage. ■ (in full **elective mutism**) unwillingness or refusal to speak, arising from psychological causes such as depression or trauma.
– ORIGIN early 19th cent.: from French *mutisme*, from Latin *mutus* 'mute.'

mu·ton /ˈmyo͞oˌtän, ˈmyo͞otn/ ▶ **n.** Biology the smallest element of genetic material capable of undergoing a distinct mutation, usually identified as a single pair of nucleotides.

Mu·tsu·hi·to /ˌmo͞otso͝oˈhētō/ see MEIJI TENNO.

mutt /mət/ ▶ **n.** informal **1** humorous or derogatory a dog, esp. a mongrel: *a long-haired mutt of doubtful pedigree.*
2 a person regarded as stupid or incompetent: *"Do not give me orders, mutt."*
– ORIGIN late 19th cent.: abbreviation of MUTTONHEAD.

mut·ter /ˈmətər/ ▶ **v.** [reporting verb] say something in a low or barely audible voice, esp. in dissatisfaction or irritation: [with obj.] *he muttered something under his breath* | [with direct speech] *"I knew she was a troublemaker," Rebecca muttered* | [no obj.] *she muttered in annoyance as the keys slid from her fingers.* ■ [no obj.] speak privately or unofficially about someone or something; spread rumors: *when he disappeared, people began to mutter.*
▶ **n.** a barely audible utterance, esp. a dissatisfied or irritated one: *a little mutter of disgust.*
– DERIVATIVES **mut·ter·er** n., **mut·ter·ing·ly** adv.
– ORIGIN late Middle English: imitative; compare with German dialect *muttern*.

mut·ton /ˈmətn/ ▶ **n.** the flesh of sheep, esp. mature sheep, used as food: *roast mutton.*
– DERIVATIVES **mut·ton·y** adj.
– ORIGIN Middle English: from Old French *moton*, from medieval Latin *multo(n-)*, probably of Celtic origin; compare with Scottish Gaelic *mult*, Welsh *mollt*, and Breton *maout*.

muttonchops

mut·ton·chops /ˈmətnˌCHäps/ (also **muttonchop whiskers**) ▶ **n.** the whiskers on a man's cheek when shaped like a meat chop, narrow at the top and broad and rounded at the bottom.

mut·ton·head /ˈmətnˌhed/ ▶ **n.** informal or dated a dull or stupid person (often used as a general term of abuse).
– DERIVATIVES **mut·ton·head·ed** adj.

mu·tu·al /ˈmyo͞oCHo͞oəl/ ▶ **adj.** **1** (of a feeling or action) experienced or done by each of two or more parties toward the other or others: *a partnership based on mutual respect and understanding | my father hated him from the start, and the feeling was mutual.* ■ (of two or more people) having the same specified relationship to each other: *they were mutual beneficiaries of the settlement.*
2 held in common by two or more parties: *we were introduced by a mutual friend.* ■ denoting an insurance company or other corporate organization owned by its members and dividing some or all of its profits between them.
– ORIGIN late 15th cent.: from Old French *mutuel*, from Latin *mutuus* 'mutual, borrowed'; related to *mutare* 'to change.'

USAGE Some traditionalists consider using **mutual** to mean 'common to two or more people' (*a mutual friend; a mutual interest*) to be incorrect, holding that a sense of reciprocity is necessary (*mutual respect; mutual need*). The use they object to has a long and respectable history, however, being first recorded in Shakespeare and appearing in the writing of Sir Walter Scott, George Eliot, and, most famously, as the title of Dickens's novel *Our Mutual Friend*. It is now generally accepted as part of standard English.

mu·tu·al fund ▶ **n.** an investment program funded by shareholders that trades in diversified holdings and is professionally managed.

mu·tu·al in·duct·ance ▶ **n.** Physics a measure or coefficient of mutual induction, usually expressed in henries. ■ the property of a circuit that permits mutual induction.

mu·tu·al in·duc·tion ▶ **n.** Physics the production of an electromotive force in a circuit by a change in the current in an adjacent circuit that is linked to the first by the flux lines of a magnetic field.

mu·tu·al in·sur·ance ▶ **n.** insurance in which some or all of the profits are divided among the policyholders.

mu·tu·al·ism /ˈmyo͞oCHo͞oəˌlizəm/ ▶ **n.** the doctrine that mutual dependence is necessary to social well-being. ■ Biology symbiosis that is beneficial to both organisms involved.
– DERIVATIVES **mu·tu·al·ist** n. & adj., **mu·tu·al·is·tic** /ˌmyo͞oCHo͞oəˈlistik/ adj., **mu·tu·al·is·ti·cal·ly** /ˌmyo͞oCHo͞oəˈlistik(ə)lē/ adv.

mu·tu·al·i·ty /ˌmyo͞oCHo͞oˈalitē/ ▶ **n.** mutual character, quality, or activity: *a high degree of mutuality of respect for each other's expertise.*

mu·tu·al·ize /ˈmyo͞oCHo͞oəˌlīz/ ▶ **v.** [with obj.] organize (a company or business) on mutual principles. ■ divide (something, esp. insurance losses) between involved parties.

mu·tu·al·ly /ˈmyo͞oCHo͞oəlē/ ▶ **adv.** with mutual action; in a mutual relationship: [as submodifier] *adoption and fostering are not necessarily mutually exclusive alternatives.*

mu·tu·el /ˈmyo͞oCHo͞oəl/ ▶ **n.** (in betting) a pari-mutuel.
– ORIGIN early 20th cent.: shortening of PARI-MUTUEL.

mu·tule /ˈmyo͞oˌCHo͞ol/ ▶ **n.** Architecture a stone block projecting under a cornice in the Doric order.
– ORIGIN mid 17th cent.: from French, from Latin *mutulus*.

muu·muu /ˈmo͞oˌmo͞o/ ▶ **n.** a woman's loose, brightly colored dress, esp. one traditionally worn in Hawaii.
– ORIGIN early 20th cent.: from Hawaiian *mu'u mu'u*, literally 'cut off.'

mux /məks/ ▶ **n.** a multiplexer.
▶ **v.** short for MULTIPLEX.

Mu·zak /ˈmyo͞oˌzak/ ▶ **n.** trademark recorded light background music played through speakers in public places.
– ORIGIN 1930s: alteration of MUSIC.

mu·zhik /mo͞oˈZHēk, -ˈZHik/ (also **moujik**) ▶ **n.** historical a Russian peasant.
– ORIGIN Russian.

Muz·tag /mo͞osˈtäg/ a mountain in western China, on the northern Tibetan border close to the Karamiran Shankou pass. Rising to 25,338 feet (7,723 m), it is the highest peak in the Kunlun Shan range.

muzz /məz/ ▶ **n.** informal a muddle or blur: *in the echoey hall, every other word is lost in the muzz.*
– ORIGIN mid 18th cent. (as a verb in the sense 'study intently'): of unknown origin; based partly perhaps on an alteration of MUSE.

muz·zle /ˈməzəl/ ▶ **n.** **1** the projecting part of the face, including the nose and mouth, of an animal such as a dog or horse. ■ a guard, typically made of straps or wire, fitted over this part of an animal's face to stop it from biting or feeding. ■ informal the part of a person's face including the nose, mouth, and chin.
2 the open end of the barrel of a firearm.
▶ **v.** [with obj.] put a muzzle on (an animal). ■ prevent (a person or group) from expressing their opinions freely: *the politicians want to muzzle us and control what we write.*
– ORIGIN late Middle English: from Old French *musel*, diminutive of medieval Latin *musum*, of unknown ultimate origin.

muz·zle·load·er /ˈməzəlˌlōdər/ ▶ **n.** historical a gun that is loaded through its muzzle.
– DERIVATIVES **muz·zle·load·ing** /-ˌlōdiNG/ (also **muzzle-loading**) adj.

muz·zle ve·loc·i·ty ▶ **n.** the velocity with which a bullet or shell leaves the muzzle of a gun.

muz·zy /ˈməzē/ ▶ **adj.** (**muzzier, muzziest**) **1** unable to think clearly; confused: *she was shivering and her head felt muzzy from sleep.* ■ not thought out clearly; vague: *society's muzzy notion of tolerance.*
2 blurred; indistinct: *a slightly muzzy picture | the bass and drums are, even on CD, appallingly muzzy.*
– DERIVATIVES **muz·zi·ly** /ˈməzəlē/ adv., **muz·zi·ness** n.
– ORIGIN early 18th cent.: of unknown origin.

MV ▶ **abbr.** ■ megavolt(s). ■ motor vessel: *on board the MV Alcinous.* ■ muzzle velocity.

MVD the Ministry of Internal Affairs in the former Soviet Union and now in Russia.
– ORIGIN abbreviation of Russian *Ministerstvo vnutrennikh del.*

MVP ▶ **abbr.** most valuable player (an award given in various sports to the best player on a team or in a league): *Bill Walton was named NBA MVP in 1978* | [as adj.] *he earned MVP honors in the All-Star Game.*

MW ▶ **abbr.** megawatt(s).

mW ▶ **abbr.** milliwatt(s).

MX ▶ **abbr.** missile experimental (a US intercontinental ten-warhead ballistic missile).

Mx ▶ **abbr.** maxwell(s).

mxd. ▶ **abbr.** mixed.

my /mī/ ▶ **possessive determiner** **1** belonging to or associated with the speaker: *my name is John | my friend.* ■ informal used with a name to refer to a member of the speaker's family: *my Francine won top honors in the science fair.* ■ used with forms of address in affectionate, sympathetic, humorous, or patronizing contexts: *my dear boy | my poor baby.*
2 used in various expressions of surprise: *my goodness! | oh my!*
– PHRASES **My Lady** (or **Lord**) a polite form of address to certain titled people.
– ORIGIN Middle English *mi* (originally before words beginning with any consonant except *h-*), reduced from *min*, from Old English *mīn* (see MINE[1]).

m.y. ▶ **abbr.** million years.

my- ▶ **comb. form** variant spelling of MYO- shortened before a vowel (as in *myalgia*).

my·al·gi·a /mīˈalj(ē)ə/ ▶ **n.** pain in a muscle or group of muscles.
– DERIVATIVES **my·al·gic** /-jik/ adj.
– ORIGIN mid 19th cent.: modern Latin, from Greek *mus* 'muscle' + -ALGIA.

my·al·gic en·ceph·a·li·tis (also **myalgic encephalopathy**) ▶ **n.** clinical term for CHRONIC FATIGUE SYNDROME.

My·an·mar /myänˈmär, ˌmīˌänˈmär/ see BURMA.

my·as·the·ni·a /ˌmīəsˈTHēnēə/ ▶ **n.** a condition causing abnormal weakness of certain muscles. ■ (in full **myasthenia gravis** /ˈgravis/) a rare chronic autoimmune disease marked by muscular weakness without atrophy, and caused by a defect in the action of acetylcholine at neuromuscular junctions.
– ORIGIN mid 19th cent.: modern Latin, from Greek *mus* 'muscle' + ASTHENIA.

my·ce·li·um /mīˈsēlēəm/ ▶ **n.** (pl. **mycelia** /-lēə/) Botany the vegetative part of a fungus, consisting of a network of fine white filaments (hyphae).
– DERIVATIVES **my·ce·li·al** /-lēəl/ adj.
– ORIGIN mid 19th cent.: modern Latin, from Greek *mukēs* 'fungus,' on the pattern of *epithelium*.

My·ce·nae /mīˈsēnē/ an ancient city in Greece, situated near the coast in the northeastern Peloponnese, the center of the late Bronze Age Mycenaean civilization. The capital of King Agamemnon, it was at its most prosperous *c.*1400–1200 BC; systematic excavation of the site began in 1840.

My·ce·nae·an /mīsēˈnēən/ (also **Mycenean**) Archaeology ▶ **adj.** of, relating to, or denoting a late Bronze Age civilization in Greece represented by finds at Mycenae and other ancient cities of Peloponnesus.
▶ **n.** an inhabitant of Mycenae or member of the Mycenaean people.

The Mycenaeans controlled the Aegean after the fall of the Minoan civilization c.1400 BC, and built fortified citadels and impressive palaces. They spoke a form of Greek, written in a distinctive script (see LINEAR B), and their culture is identified with that portrayed in the Homeric poems. Their power declined during widespread upheavals at the end of the Mediterranean Bronze Age, around 1100 BC.

my·ce·to·ma /ˌmīsəˈtōmə/ ▶ **n.** Medicine chronic inflammation of the tissues caused by infection with a fungus or with certain bacteria.
– ORIGIN late 19th cent.: modern Latin, from Greek *mukēs, mukēt-* 'fungus' + -OMA.

-mycin ▶ **comb. form** in names of antibiotic compounds derived from fungi: *streptomycin*.
– ORIGIN based on **MYCO-**.

myco- ▶ **comb. form** relating to fungi: *mycoprotein*.
– ORIGIN formed irregularly from Greek *mukēs* 'fungus, mushroom.'

my·co·bac·te·ri·um /ˌmīkōbakˈti(ə)rēəm/ ▶ **n.** (pl. **mycobacteria** /-ˈti(ə)rēə/) a bacterium of a group that includes the causative agents of leprosy and tuberculosis. ● Genus *Mycobacterium*, family Mycobacteriaceae.
– DERIVATIVES **my·co·bac·te·ri·al** /-ˈti(ə)rēəl/ **adj.**

mycol. ▶ **abbr.** mycological or mycology.

my·col·o·gy /mīˈkäləjē/ ▶ **n.** the scientific study of fungi.
– DERIVATIVES **my·co·log·i·cal** /ˌmīkəˈläjikəl/ **adj.**, **my·co·log·i·cal·ly** /ˌmīkəˈläjik(ə)lē/ **adv.**, **my·col·o·gist** /-jist/ **n.**

my·co·plas·ma /ˌmīkōˈplazmə/ ▶ **n.** (pl. **mycoplasmas** or **mycoplasmata** /-mətə/) any of a group of small typically parasitic bacteria that lack cell walls and sometimes cause diseases. ● Class Mollicutes and order Mycoplasmatales.

my·co·plas·ma pneu·mo·nia ▶ **n.** technical term for **WALKING PNEUMONIA**.

my·cor·rhi·za /ˌmīkəˈrīzə/ ▶ **n.** (pl. **mycorrhizae** /-ˈrīzē/) Botany a fungus that grows in association with the roots of a plant in a symbiotic or mildly pathogenic relationship.
– DERIVATIVES **my·cor·rhi·zal adj.**
– ORIGIN late 19th cent.: modern Latin, from **MYCO-** 'of fungi' + Greek *rhiza* 'root.'

my·co·sis /mīˈkōsəs/ ▶ **n.** (pl. **mycoses** /-sēz/) a disease caused by infection with a fungus, such as ringworm or thrush.
– DERIVATIVES **my·cot·ic** /-ˈkätik/ **adj.**

my·co·tox·in /ˌmīkəˈtäksən/ ▶ **n.** any toxic substance produced by a fungus.

my·co·troph·ic /ˌmīkəˈträfik/ ▶ **adj.** Botany (of a plant) living in association with a mycorrhiza or another fungus that appears to improve the uptake of nutrients.
– DERIVATIVES **my·cot·ro·phy** /mīˈkätrəfē/ **n.**
– ORIGIN 1920s: from **MYCO-** 'of fungi' + Greek *trophē* 'nourishment.'

my·dri·a·sis /məˈdrīəsəs/ ▶ **n.** Medicine dilation of the pupil of the eye.
– ORIGIN early 19th cent.: via Latin from Greek *mudriasis*.

my·e·lin /ˈmīələn/ ▶ **n.** Anatomy & Physiology a mixture of proteins and phospholipids forming a whitish insulating sheath around many nerve fibers, increasing the speed at which impulses are conducted.
– DERIVATIVES **my·e·li·nat·ed** /-ləˌnātəd/ **adj.**, **my·e·li·na·tion** /ˌmīələˈnāsHən/ **n.**
– ORIGIN late 19th cent.: from Greek *muelos* 'marrow' + **-IN**¹.

my·e·li·tis /ˌmīəˈlītəs/ ▶ **n.** Medicine inflammation of the spinal cord.
– ORIGIN mid 19th cent.: modern Latin, from Greek *muelos* 'marrow' + **-ITIS**.

my·e·loid /ˈmīəˌloid/ ▶ **adj.** **1** of or relating to bone marrow. ■ (of leukemia) characterized by the proliferation of cells originating in the bone marrow.
2 of or relating to the spinal cord.
– ORIGIN mid 19th cent.: from Greek *muelos* 'marrow' + **-OID**.

my·e·lo·ma /ˌmīəˈlōmə/ ▶ **n.** (pl. **myelomas** or **myelomata** /-mətə/) Medicine a malignant tumor of the bone marrow.
– ORIGIN mid 19th cent.: modern Latin, from Greek *muelos* 'marrow' + **-OMA**.

my·e·lop·a·thy /ˌmīəˈläpəTHē/ ▶ **n.** Medicine disease of the spinal cord.

my·en·ter·ic /ˌmīenˈterik/ ▶ **adj.** Anatomy relating to or denoting a plexus of nerves of the sympathetic and parasympathetic systems situated between and supplying the two layers of muscle in the small intestine.

myg·a·lo·morph /ˈmigələˌmôrf/ ▶ **n.** Zoology a large spider of a group that includes the tarantulas and funnel-web spiders. Mygalomorphs have several primitive features, including fangs that stab downward rather than toward one another. ● Suborder Mygalomorphae, order Araneae.
– ORIGIN 1920s: from modern Latin *Mygalomorphae*, from Greek *mugalē* 'shrew' + *morphē* 'form.'

My·ko·la·yiv /ˌmēkəˈlīəf/ an industrial city in southern Ukraine, on the Southern Bug River near the northern tip of the Black Sea; pop. 504,300 (est. 2009). Russian name **NIKOLAEV**.

Myk·o·nos /ˈmēkəˌnôs, ˈmikəˌnäs/ a Greek island in the Aegean Sea, one of the Cyclades. Greek name **MÍKONOS**.

My Lai /ˈmēˈlī/ a village in Son My district, in central Vietnam, south of Quang Ngai, site of a 1968 massacre of Vietnamese civilians by US troops during the Vietnam War.

My·lar /ˈmīˌlär/ ▶ **n.** trademark a form of polyester resin used to make heat-resistant plastic films and sheets.
– ORIGIN 1950s: an arbitrary formation.

my·lo·don /ˈmīləˌdän/ ▶ **n.** an extinct giant ground sloth found in deposits formed during the ice age of the Pleistocene epoch in South America. It died out only 11,000 years ago. ● Genus *Glossotherium* (formerly *Mylodon*), family Mylodontidae.
– ORIGIN mid 19th cent.: modern Latin, from Greek *mulē* 'mill, molar' + *odous, odont-* 'tooth.'

my·lo·nite /ˈmīləˌnīt, ˈmil-/ ▶ **n.** Geology a fine-grained metamorphic rock, typically banded, resulting from the grinding or crushing of other rocks.
– ORIGIN late 19th cent.: from Greek *mulōn* 'mill' + **-ITE**¹.

My·men·singh /ˈmīmənˌsiNG/ a port on the Brahmaputra River in central Bangladesh; pop. 388,600 (est. 2009).

my·nah /ˈmīnə/ (also **myna** or **mynah bird**) ▶ **n.** an Asian and Australasian starling that typically has dark plumage, gregarious behavior, and a loud call. ● Family Sturnidae: several genera and species, in particular the **hill mynah** (*Gracula religiosa*), which is popular as a pet bird because of its ability to mimic the human voice.
– ORIGIN mid 18th cent.: from Hindi *mainā*.

hill mynah

myo- (also **my-** before a vowel) ▶ **comb. form** of muscle; relating to muscles: *myocardium* | *myometrium*.
– ORIGIN from Greek *mus, mu-* 'mouse or muscle.'

my·o·car·di·al in·farc·tion /ˌmīəˈkärdēəl/ ▶ **n.** another term for **HEART ATTACK**.

my·o·car·di·tis /ˌmīəˌkärˈdītəs/ ▶ **n.** Medicine inflammation of the heart muscle.

my·o·car·di·um /ˌmīəˈkärdēəm/ ▶ **n.** Anatomy the muscular tissue of the heart.
– DERIVATIVES **my·o·car·di·al** /-dēəl/ **adj.**
– ORIGIN late 19th cent.: modern Latin, from **MYO-** 'muscle' + Greek *kardia* 'heart.'

my·oc·lo·nus /mīˈäklənəs/ ▶ **n.** Medicine spasmodic jerky contraction of groups of muscles.
– DERIVATIVES **my·o·clon·ic** /ˌmīəˈklänik/ **adj.**

my·o·fi·bril /ˌmīōˈfībrəl, -ˈfib-/ ▶ **n.** any of the elongated contractile threads found in striated muscle cells.

my·o·gen·ic /ˌmīəˈjenik/ ▶ **adj.** Physiology originating in muscle tissue (rather than from nerve impulses).

my·o·glo·bin /ˌmīəˈglōbən, ˈmīəˌglōbən/ ▶ **n.** Biochemistry a red protein containing heme that carries and stores oxygen in muscle cells. It is structurally similar to a subunit of hemoglobin.

my·ol·o·gy /mīˈäləjē/ ▶ **n.** the study of the structure, arrangement, and action of muscles.
– DERIVATIVES **my·o·log·i·cal** /ˌmīəˈläjikəl/ **adj.**, **my·ol·o·gist** /-jist/ **n.**

my·o·mere /ˈmīəˌmir/ ▶ **n.** another term for **MYOTOME**.

my·o·me·tri·um /ˌmīəˈmētrēəm/ ▶ **n.** Anatomy the smooth muscle tissue of the uterus.
– ORIGIN early 20th cent.: modern Latin, from **MYO-** 'muscle' + Greek *mētra* 'womb.'

My·o·mor·pha /ˌmīəˈmôrfə/ Zoology a major division of the rodents that includes the rats, mice, voles, hamsters, and their relatives. ● Suborder Myomorpha, order Rodentia.
– DERIVATIVES **my·o·morph** /ˈmīəˌmôrf/ **n. & adj.**
– ORIGIN modern Latin (plural), from Greek *mus, mu-* 'mouse' + *morphē* 'form.'

my·op·a·thy /mīˈäpəTHē/ ▶ **n.** (pl. **myopathies**) Medicine a disease of muscle tissue.
– DERIVATIVES **my·o·path·ic** /ˌmīəˈpaTHik/ **adj.**

my·ope /ˈmīˌōp/ ▶ **n.** a nearsighted person.
– ORIGIN early 18th cent.: from French, via late Latin from Greek *muōps*, from *muein* 'to shut' + *ōps* 'eye.'

my·o·pi·a /mīˈōpēə/ ▶ **n.** nearsightedness. ■ lack of imagination, foresight, or intellectual insight: *historians have been censured for their myopia in treating modern science as a western phenomenon.*
– ORIGIN early 18th cent.: modern Latin, from late Greek *muōpia*, from Greek *muōps* (see **MYOPE**).

my·op·ic /mīˈäpik/ ▶ **adj.** nearsighted. ■ lacking imagination, foresight, or intellectual insight: *the government still has a myopic attitude to public spending.*
– DERIVATIVES **my·op·i·cal·ly** /mīˈäpik(ə)lē/ **adv.**

my·o·sin /ˈmīəsən/ ▶ **n.** Biochemistry a fibrous protein that forms (together with actin) the contractile filaments of muscle cells and is also involved in motion in other types of cells.

my·o·sis /mīˈōsəs/ ▶ **n.** variant spelling of **MIOSIS**.

my·o·si·tis /mīōˈsītəs/ ▶ **n.** Medicine inflammation and degeneration of muscle tissue.
– ORIGIN early 19th cent.: formed irregularly from Greek *mus, mu-* 'muscle' + **-ITIS**.

my·o·so·tis /ˌmīəˈsōtəs/ ▶ **n.** a plant of a genus that includes the forget-me-nots. ● Genus *Myosotis*, family Boraginaceae.
– ORIGIN modern Latin, from Greek *muosōtis*, from *mus, mu-* 'mouse' + *ous, ōt-* 'ear.'

my·o·tis /mīˈōtəs/ ▶ **n.** an insectivorous bat with mouselike ears, a slender muzzle, and a flight membrane that extends between the hind legs and the tip of the tail. Also called **MOUSE-EARED BAT**. ● Genus *Myotis*, family Vespertilionidae: numerous species, including the **little brown myotis** (*M. lucifugus*), one of the most common and widespread bats in the US and Canada.
– ORIGIN modern Latin, based on Greek *mus, mu-* 'mouse.'

my·o·tome /ˈmīəˌtōm/ ▶ **n.** Embryology the dorsal part of each somite in a vertebrate embryo, giving rise to the skeletal musculature. Compare with **DERMATOME**, **SCLEROTOME**. ■ each of the muscle blocks along either side of the spine in vertebrates (esp. fish and amphibians). Also called **MYOMERE**.

my·o·to·ni·a /ˌmīəˈtōnēə/ ▶ **n.** inability to relax voluntary muscle after vigorous effort.
– DERIVATIVES **my·o·ton·ic** /-ˈtänik/ **adj.**
– ORIGIN late 19th cent.: from **MYO-** 'muscle' + Greek *tonos* 'tone.'

my·o·ton·ic dys·tro·phy /ˌmīəˈtänik/ ▶ **n.** Medicine a form of muscular dystrophy accompanied by myotonia.

Myr·dal¹ /ˈmi(ə)rˌdäl/, Alva (Reimer) (1902–86), Swedish diplomat and peace activist; wife of Gunnar Myrdal. She served the United Nations as director of social welfare 1949–50 and was Swedish ambassador to India 1955–61. An advocate of disarmament, she wrote *The Game of Disarmament* (1976). Nobel Peace Prize (1982), shared with Alfonso Garcia Robles (1911–91).

Myr·dal² Gunnar (1898–1987), Swedish economist and writer; full name *Karl Gunnar Myrdal*; husband of Alva Myrdal. His works include *An American Dilemma* (1944) and *The Challenge of Affluence* (1963). Nobel Prize for Economics (1974), shared with Friedrich Hayek.

myr·i·ad /ˈmirēəd/ literary ▶ **n.** **1** a countless or extremely great number: *networks connecting a myriad of computers.*
2 (chiefly in classical history) a unit of ten thousand.
▶ **adj.** countless or extremely great in number: *the myriad lights of the city.* ■ having countless or very many elements or aspects: *the myriad political scene.*
– ORIGIN mid 16th cent. (sense 2 of the noun): via late Latin from Greek *murias, muriad-*, from *murioi* '10,000.'

> **USAGE** **Myriad** is derived from a Greek noun and adjective meaning 'ten thousand.' It was first used in English as a noun in reference to a great but indefinite number. The adjectival sense of 'countless, innumerable' appeared much later. In modern English, use of **myriad** as a noun and adjective are equally standard and correct, despite the fact that some traditionalists consider the adjective as the only acceptable use of the word.

myr·i·a·pod /ˈmirēəˌpäd/ ▶ **n.** Zoology an arthropod of a group that includes the centipedes, millipedes, and related animals. Myriapods have elongated bodies with numerous leg-bearing segments. ● Classes Chilopoda, Diplopoda, Pauropoda, and Symphyla; formerly placed together in the class Myriapoda.
▶ **adj.** (also **myriapodous**) of or belonging to the myriapods.
– ORIGIN early 19th cent.: from modern Latin *Myriapoda*, from Greek *murias* (see **MYRIAD**) + *pous, pod-* 'foot.'

myr·in·got·o·my /ˌmirənˈgätəmē/ ▶ **n.** surgical incision into the eardrum, to relieve pressure or drain fluid.
– ORIGIN late 19th cent.: from modern Latin *myringa* 'eardrum' + **-TOMY**.

myr·me·col·o·gy /ˌmərməˈkäləjē/ ▶ **n.** the branch of entomology that deals with ants.
– DERIVATIVES **myr·me·co·log·i·cal** /-kəˈläjikəl/ **adj.**, **myr·me·col·o·gist** /-jist/ **n.**
– ORIGIN late 19th cent.: from Greek *murmēx*, *murmēk-* 'ant' + **-LOGY**.

myr·me·co·phile /ˈmərmikōˌfīl/ ▶ **n.** Biology an invertebrate or plant that has a symbiotic relationship with ants, such as being tended and protected by ants or living inside an ants' nest.
– DERIVATIVES **myr·me·coph·i·lous** /ˌmərməˈkäfələs/ **adj.**, **myr·me·coph·i·ly** /ˌmərməˈkäfəlē/ **n.**
– ORIGIN late 19th cent.: from Greek *murmēx*, *murmēk-* 'ant' + **-PHILE**.

Myr·mi·don /ˈmərməˌdän, -mədən/ ▶ **n.** a member of a warlike Thessalian people led by Achilles at the siege of Troy. ■ (usu. **myrmidon**) a hired ruffian or unscrupulous subordinate: *he and his myrmidons were ensconced in a bunker.*
– ORIGIN late Middle English: from Latin *Myrmidones* (plural), from Greek *Murmidones*.

my·rob·a·lan /mīˈräbələn, mə-/ ▶ **n. 1** (also **myrobalan plum**) another term for **PURPLE-LEAF PLUM**.
2 a tropical tree of a characteristic pagoda shape that yields a number of useful items including dye, timber, and medicinal products. ● Genus *Terminalia*, family Combretaceae: several species, in particular *T. chebula*. ■ (also **myrobalan nut**) the fruit of this tree, used esp. for tanning leather.
– ORIGIN late Middle English: from French *myrobolan* or Latin *myrobalanum*, from Greek *murobalanos*, from *muron* 'unguent' + *balanos* 'acorn.'

myrrh[1] /mər/ ▶ **n.** a fragrant gum resin obtained from certain trees and used, esp. in the Near East, in perfumery, medicines, and incense. ● The trees belong to the genus *Commiphora*, family Burseraceae, in particular *C. myrrha*.
– DERIVATIVES **myrrh·y** **adj.**
– ORIGIN Old English *myrra*, *myrre*, via Latin from Greek *murra*, of Semitic origin; compare with Arabic *murr* 'bitter.'

myrrh[2] ▶ **n.** another term for **CICELY**.
– ORIGIN late 16th cent.: from Latin *myrris*, from Greek *murris*.

myr·tle /ˈmərtl/ ▶ **n. 1** an evergreen shrub that has glossy aromatic foliage and white flowers followed by purple-black oval berries. ● *Myrtus communis*, family Myrtaceae (the **myrtle family**). This family also includes several aromatic plants (clove, allspice) and many characteristic Australian plants (eucalyptus trees, bottlebrushes).
2 the lesser periwinkle. ● *Vinca minor*, family Apocynaceae. See **PERIWINKLE**[1].
– ORIGIN late Middle English: from medieval Latin *myrtilla*, *myrtillus*, diminutive of Latin *myrta*, *myrtus*, from Greek *murtos*.

Myr·tle Beach /ˈmərtl/ a resort city in northeastern South Carolina, the hub of the part of the Atlantic coast that is called the Grand Strand; pop. 30,596 (est. 2008).

my·self /mīˈself, mə-/ ▶ **pron.** [first person singular]
1 [reflexive] used by a speaker to refer to himself or herself as the object of a verb or preposition when he or she is the subject of the clause: *I hurt myself by accident* | *I strolled around, muttering to myself.*
2 [emphatic] I or me personally (used to emphasize the speaker): *I myself am unsure how this problem should be handled* | *I wrote it myself.*
3 literary term for **I**[2]: *myself presented to him a bronze sword.*
– PHRASES **(not) be myself** see **BE ONESELF, NOT BE ONESELF** at **BE**. **by myself** see **MYSELF** at **BY**.
– ORIGIN Old English *me self*, from **ME** + **SELF** (used adjectivally); the change of *me* to *my* occurred in Middle English.

My·sia /ˈmisHēə/ an ancient region in northwestern Asia Minor, on the Mediterranean coast south of the Sea of Marmara.
– DERIVATIVES **My·si·an** **adj. & n.**

my·sid /ˈmīsid/ ▶ **n.** Zoology a crustacean of an order that comprises the opossum shrimps. ● Order Mysidacea, class Malacostraca.
– ORIGIN mid 20th cent.: from modern Latin *Mysis* (genus name) + **-ID**[3].

My·sore /mīˈsôr/ **1** a city in the Indian state of Karnataka; pop. 480,000.
2 former name (until 1973) for **KARNATAKA**.

mys·ta·gogue /ˈmistəˌgäg/ ▶ **n.** a teacher or propounder of mystical doctrines.
– DERIVATIVES **mys·ta·go·gy** /-ˌgōjē/ **n.**
– ORIGIN mid 16th cent.: from French, or via Latin from Greek *mustagōgos*, from *mustēs* 'initiated person' + *agōgos* 'leading.'

mys·te·ri·ous /məˈsti(ə)rēəs/ ▶ **adj. 1** difficult or impossible to understand, explain, or identify: *his colleague had vanished in mysterious circumstances* | *a mysterious benefactor provided the money.* ■ (of a location) having an atmosphere of strangeness or secrecy: *a dark, mysterious, windowless building.*
2 (of a person) deliberately enigmatic: *she was mysterious about herself but said plenty about her husband.*
– DERIVATIVES **mys·te·ri·ous·ly** **adv.**, **mys·te·ri·ous·ness** **n.**
– ORIGIN late 16th cent.: from French *mystérieux*, from *mystère* 'mystery.'

mys·ter·y[1] /ˈmist(ə)rē/ ▶ **n.** (pl. **mysteries**)
1 something that is difficult or impossible to understand or explain: *the mysteries of outer space* | *hoping that the inquest would solve the mystery.* ■ the condition or quality of being secret, strange, or difficult to explain: *much of her past is shrouded in mystery.* ■ a person or thing whose identity or nature is puzzling or unknown: *"He's a bit of a mystery," said Nina* | [as modifier] *a mystery guest.*
2 a novel, play, or movie dealing with a puzzling crime, esp. a murder.
3 (**mysteries**) the secret rites of Greek and Roman pagan religion, or of any ancient or tribal religion, to which only initiates are admitted. ■ the practices, skills, or lore peculiar to a particular trade or activity and regarded as baffling to those without specialized knowledge: *the mysteries of analytical psychology.* ■ the Christian Eucharist.
4 chiefly Christian Theology a religious belief based on divine revelation, esp. one regarded as beyond human understanding: *the mystery of Christ.* ■ an incident in the life of Jesus or of a saint as a focus of devotion in the Roman Catholic Church, esp. each of those commemorated during recitation of successive decades of the rosary.
– ORIGIN Middle English (in the sense 'mystic presence, hidden religious symbolism'): from Old French *mistere* or Latin *mysterium*, from Greek *mustērion*; related to **MYSTIC**.

mys·ter·y[2] ▶ **n.** (pl. **mysteries**) archaic a handicraft or trade.
– ORIGIN late Middle English: from medieval Latin *misterium*, contraction of *ministerium* 'ministry,' by association with *mysterium* (see **MYSTERY**[1]).

mys·ter·y play ▶ **n.** a popular medieval play based on biblical stories or the lives of the saints. Also called **MIRACLE PLAY**.

> Mystery plays were performed by members of trade guilds in Europe from the 13th century, in churches or later on wagons or temporary stages along a route, frequently introducing apocryphal and satirical elements. Several cycles of plays survive in association with particular English cities and towns.

mys·ter·y re·li·gion ▶ **n.** a religion centered on secret or mystical rites for initiates, esp. any of a number of cults popular during the late Roman Empire.

mys·ter·y shop·per ▶ **n.** another term for **SECRET SHOPPER**.

mys·tic /ˈmistik/ ▶ **n.** a person who seeks by contemplation and self-surrender to obtain unity with or absorption into the Deity or the absolute, or who believes in the spiritual apprehension of truths that are beyond the intellect.
▶ **adj.** another term for **MYSTICAL**.
– ORIGIN Middle English (in the sense 'mystical meaning'): from Old French *mystique*, or via Latin from Greek *mustikos*, from *mustēs* 'initiated person,' from *muein* 'close the eyes or lips,' also 'initiate.' The current sense of the noun dates from the late 17th cent.

mys·ti·cal /ˈmistikəl/ ▶ **adj. 1** of or relating to mystics or religious mysticism: *the mystical experience.* ■ spiritually allegorical or symbolic; transcending human understanding: *the mystical body of Christ.* ■ of or relating to ancient religious mysteries or other occult or esoteric rites: *the mystical practices of the Pythagoreans.* ■ of hidden or esoteric meaning: *a geometric figure of mystical significance.*
2 inspiring a sense of spiritual mystery, awe, and fascination: *the mystical forces of nature.* ■ concerned with the soul or the spirit, rather than with material things: *the beliefs of a more mystical age.*
– DERIVATIVES **mys·ti·cal·ly** /-ik(ə)lē/ **adv.**

Mys·ti·ce·ti /ˌmistəˈsēˌtī/ Zoology a division of the whales that comprises the baleen whales. ● Suborder Mysticeti, order Cetacea.
– DERIVATIVES **mys·ti·cete** /ˈmistəˌsēt/ **n. & adj.**
– ORIGIN modern Latin (plural), from Greek *mustikētos* representing (in old editions of Aristotle) the phrase *ho mus to kētos* 'the mouse, the whale so called.'

mys·ti·cism /ˈmistəˌsizəm/ ▶ **n. 1** belief that union with or absorption into the Deity or the absolute, or the spiritual apprehension of knowledge inaccessible to the intellect, may be attained through contemplation and self-surrender.
2 belief characterized by self-delusion or dreamy confusion of thought, esp. when based on the assumption of occult qualities or mysterious agencies.

mys·ti·fy /ˈmistəˌfī/ ▶ **v.** (**mystifies, mystifying, mystified**) [with obj.] utterly bewilder or perplex (someone): *maladies that have mystified and alarmed researchers for over a decade* | (as adj. **mystifying**) *a mystifying phenomenon.* ■ make obscure or mysterious: *lawyers who mystify the legal system so that laymen find it unintelligible.*
– DERIVATIVES **mys·ti·fi·ca·tion** /ˌmistəfiˈkāsHən/ **n.**, **mys·ti·fi·er** **n.**, **mys·ti·fy·ing·ly** **adv.**
– ORIGIN early 19th cent.: from French *mystifier*, formed irregularly from *mystique* 'mystic' or from *mystère* 'mystery.'

mys·tique /misˈtēk/ ▶ **n.** a fascinating aura of mystery, awe, and power surrounding someone or something: *the West is lately rethinking its cowboy mystique* | *the tiger has a mystique that man has always respected and revered.* ■ an air of secrecy surrounding a particular activity or subject that makes it impressive or baffling to those without specialized knowledge: *eliminating the mystique normally associated with computers.*
– ORIGIN late 19th cent.: from French, from Old French (see **MYSTIC**).

myth /miTH/ ▶ **n. 1** a traditional story, esp. one concerning the early history of a people or explaining some natural or social phenomenon, and typically involving supernatural beings or events. ■ such stories collectively: *the heroes of Greek myth.*
2 a widely held but false belief or idea: *he wants to dispel the myth that sea kayaking is too risky or too strenuous* | *there is a popular myth that corporations are big people with lots of money.* ■ a misrepresentation of the truth: *attacking the party's irresponsible myths about privatization.* ■ a fictitious or imaginary person or thing. ■ an exaggerated or idealized conception of a person or thing: *the book is a scholarly study of the Churchill myth.*
– ORIGIN mid 19th cent.: from modern Latin *mythus*, via late Latin from Greek *muthos*.

myth. ▶ **abbr.** mythological or mythology.

myth·ic /ˈmiTHik/ ▶ **adj.** of, relating to, or resembling myth: *we explain spiritual forces in mythic language.* ■ exaggerated or idealized: *he was a national hero of mythic proportions.* ■ fictitious: *a mythic land of plenty.*
– ORIGIN mid 17th cent.: via late Latin from Greek *muthikos*, from *muthos* 'myth.'

myth·i·cal /ˈmiTHikəl/ ▶ **adj.** occurring in or characteristic of myths or folk tales: *one of Denmark's greatest mythical heroes.* ■ idealized, esp. with reference to the past: *a mythical age of contentment and social order.* ■ fictitious: *a mythical customer whose name appears in brochures.*
– DERIVATIVES **myth·i·cal·ly** /-ik(ə)lē/ **adv.**

myth·i·cize /ˈmiTHəˌsīz/ ▶ **v.** [with obj.] turn into myth; interpret mythically.
– DERIVATIVES **myth·i·cism** /-ˌsizəm/ **n.**, **myth·i·cist** /-sist/ **n.**

myth·i·fy /ˈmiTHəˌfī/ ▶ **v.** (**mythifies, mythifying, mythified**) [with obj.] mythicize: *as success mythified their reputation, the stormtroopers grew in distinctiveness.*
– DERIVATIVES **myth·i·fi·ca·tion** /ˌmiTHəfiˈkāsHən/ **n.**
– ORIGIN early 20th cent.: from *myth* + *-fy*.

mytho- ▶ **comb. form** of or relating to myth: *mythography.*
– ORIGIN from Greek *muthos*, or from **MYTH**.

my·thog·ra·pher /məˈTHägrəfər/ ▶ **n.** a writer or collector of myths.

my·thog·ra·phy /məˈTHägrəfē/ ▶ **n. 1** the representation of myths, esp. in the plastic arts.
2 the creation or collection of myths.

myth·o·log·i·cal /ˌmiTHəˈläjikəl/ ▶ **adj.** relating to, based on, or appearing in myths or mythology: *the tree of life is one of the oldest of all mythological symbols.*
– DERIVATIVES **myth·o·log·ic** /ˌmiTHəˈläjik/ **adj.**, **myth·o·log·i·cal·ly** /ˌmiTHəˈläjik(ə)lē/ **adv.**

my·thol·o·gize /məˈTHäləˌjīz/ ▶ **v.** [with obj.] convert into myth or mythology; make the subject of a myth: *there is a grave danger of mythologizing the past.* ■ create or promote an exaggerated or idealized image of: *much of his life was devoted to mythologizing his own career.*
– DERIVATIVES **my·thol·o·giz·er** **n.**

m

my·thol·o·gy /mə'THäləjē/ ▶ **n.** (pl. **mythologies**) **1** a collection of myths, esp. one belonging to a particular religious or cultural tradition: *Ganesa was the god of wisdom and success in Hindu mythology | a book discussing Jewish and Christian mythologies.* ■ a set of stories or beliefs about a particular person, institution, or situation, esp. when exaggerated or fictitious: *in popular mythology, truckers are kings of the road.* **2** the study of myths.
– DERIVATIVES **my·thol·o·ger** /-jər/ **n.**, **my·thol·o·gist** /-jist/ **n.**
– ORIGIN late Middle English: from French *mythologie*, or via late Latin from Greek *muthologia*, from *muthos* 'myth' + *-logia* (see **-LOGY**).

myth·o·ma·ni·a /,miTHə'mānēə/ ▶ **n.** an abnormal or pathological tendency to exaggerate or tell lies.
– DERIVATIVES **myth·o·ma·ni·ac** /-'mānē,ak/ **n. & adj.**

myth·o·poe·ia /,miTHə'pēə/ ▶ **n.** the making of a myth or myths.
– DERIVATIVES **myth·o·poe·ic** /-'pēik/ **adj.**
– ORIGIN 1950s: from Greek *muthopoiia*, from *muthos* 'myth' + *poiein* 'make.'

myth·o·po·et·ic /,miTHəpō'etik/ ▶ **adj.** of or relating to the making of a myth or myths. ■ relating to or denoting a movement for men that uses activities such as storytelling and poetry reading as a means of self-understanding.

myth·os /'miTHōs, -äs/ ▶ **n.** (pl. **mythoi** /'miTHoi/) chiefly technical a myth or mythology. ■ (in literature) a traditional or recurrent narrative theme or plot structure. ■ a set of beliefs or assumptions about something: *the rhetoric and mythos of science create the comforting image of linear progression toward truth.*
– ORIGIN mid 18th cent.: from Greek.

myx·e·de·ma /,miksə'dēmə/ (Brit. **myxoedema**) ▶ **n.** Medicine swelling of the skin and underlying tissues giving a waxy consistency, typical of patients with underactive thyroid glands. ■ the more general condition associated with hypothyroidism, including weight gain, mental dullness, and sensitivity to cold.

myxo- (also **myx-**) ▶ **comb. form** relating to mucus: *myxovirus | myxedema.*
– ORIGIN from Greek *muxa* 'slime, mucus.'

myx·o·ma /mik'sōmə/ ▶ **n.** (pl. **myxomas** or **myxomata** /-mətə/) Medicine a benign tumor of connective tissue containing mucous or gelatinous material.
– DERIVATIVES **myx·om·a·tous** /-mətəs/ **adj.**

myx·o·ma·to·sis /mik,sōmə'tōsəs/ ▶ **n.** a highly infectious and usually fatal viral disease of rabbits, causing swelling of the mucous membranes and inflammation and discharge around the eyes.

myx·o·my·cete /,miksə'mī,sēt/ ▶ **n.** Biology a slime mold, esp. an acellular one whose vegetative stage is a multinucleate plasmodium. ● Division Myxomycota, kingdom Fungi, in particular the class Myxomycetes; also treated as protozoan (phylum Gymnomyxa, kingdom Protista).
– ORIGIN late 19th cent.: from modern Latin *Myxomycetes*, from **MYXO-** 'slime' + Greek *mukētes* 'fungi.'

myx·o·vi·rus /'miksə,vīrəs/ ▶ **n.** any of a group of RNA viruses, including the influenza virus.

Nn

N¹ /en/ (also **n**) ▶ **n.** (pl. **Ns** or **N's**) the fourteenth letter of the alphabet. See also **EN**. ■ denoting the next after M in a set of items, categories, etc.

N² ▶ **abbr.** ■ (used in recording moves in chess) knight: *17.Na4?* [N represents *knight*, since the initial letter *k-* represents 'king.'] ■ Nationalist. ■ (on a gear lever) neutral. ■ (chiefly in place names) New: *N Zealand.* ■ Physics newton(s). ■ Noon. ■ Chemistry (with reference to solutions) normal: *the pH was adjusted to 7.0 with 1 N HCl.* ■ Norse. ■ North or Northern: *78° N | N Ireland.* ■ Finance note. ■ nuclear: *the N bomb.* ▶ **symbol** the chemical element nitrogen.

n ▶ **abbr.** ■ name. ■ [in combination] (in units of measurement) nano- (10^{-9}): *the plates were coated with 500 ng of protein in sodium carbonate buffer.* ■ born. [from Latin *nātus.*] ■ nephew. ■ net. ■ Grammar neuter. ■ new. ■ nominative. ■ noon. ■ (*n-*) [in combination] Chemistry normal (denoting straight-chain hydrocarbons): *n-hexane.* ■ north or northern. ■ note (used in a book's index to refer to a footnote): *450n.* ■ Finance note. ■ Grammar noun. ■ number. ▶ **symbol** an unspecified or variable number: *at the limit where n equals infinity.* See also **NTH**.

'n' /ən/ ▶ **contraction** and (conventionally used in informal contexts to coordinate two closely connected elements): *rock 'n' roll.*

-n¹ ▶ **suffix** variant spelling of **-EN²**.

-n² ▶ **suffix** variant spelling of **-EN³**.

NA ▶ **abbr.** ■ National Army. ■ North America. ■ not applicable. ■ numerical aperture.

Na ▶ **symbol** the chemical element sodium.
– ORIGIN from modern Latin *natrium.*

na /nə/ ▶ **adv.** Scottish form of **NOT**, used after an auxiliary verb: *I couldna sleep nights.*

n/a ▶ **abbr.** ■ not applicable. ■ not available.

NAACP /'en dəbəl ā sē 'pē/ ▶ **abbr.** National Association for the Advancement of Colored People.

naan ▶ **n.** variant spelling of **NAN**.

NAB ▶ **abbr.** ■ National Association of Broadcasters. ■ New American Bible.

nab /nab/ ▶ **v.** (**nabs, nabbing, nabbed**) [with obj.] informal catch (someone) doing something wrong: *Olympic drug tests nabbed another athlete yesterday.* ■ take, grab, or steal (something): *Dan nabbed the seat next to mine.*
– ORIGIN late 17th cent. (also as *napp*; compare with **KIDNAP**): of unknown origin.

Nab·a·tae·an /ˌnabə'tēən/ (also **Nabatean**) ▶ **n. 1** a member of an ancient Arabian people who from 312 BC formed an independent kingdom with its capital at Petra (now in Jordan).
2 the Aramaic dialect of this people, strongly influenced by Arabic.
▶ **adj.** of or relating to the Nabataeans or their language.
– ORIGIN from Latin *Nabat(h)aeus*, Greek *Nabat(h)aios* (compare with the Arabic adjective *Nabaṭī* 'relating to the Nabataeans') + **-AN**.

nabe /nāb/ ▶ **n.** informal a neighborhood. ■ a local movie theater. ■ a neighbor.

Na·bi Group /'näbē/ a group of late 19th-century French painters, largely symbolist in their approach and heavily indebted to Gauguin. Members of the group included Maurice Denis, Pierre Bonnard, and Edouard Vuillard.
– ORIGIN *Nabi* from Hebrew *nāḇī'* 'prophet.'

Nab·lus /'näbləs, 'na-/ a town in the West Bank; pop. 190,600 (est. 2009).

na·bob /'nābäb/ ▶ **n.** historical a Muslim official or governor under the Mogul empire. ■ a person of conspicuous wealth or high status. ■ chiefly historical a person who returned from India to Europe with a fortune.
– ORIGIN from Portuguese *nababo* or Spanish *nabab*, from Urdu; see also **NAWAB**.

Na·bo·kov /'näbəˌkôf, nə'bôˌkôf/, Vladimir (Vladimirovich) (1899–1977), US novelist and poet, born in Russia. His most notable novel is *Lolita* (1955), about a middle-aged man's obsession with a 12-year-old girl. Other notable works: *The Real Life of Sebastian Knight* (1941), *Pale Fire* (1962), and *Ada: A Family Chronicle* (1969).

Nacala /nə'kälə/ a deep-water port on the eastern coast of Mozambique; pop. 104,828 (2007). It is linked by rail with landlocked Malawi.

na·celle /nə'sel/ ▶ **n.** a streamlined housing or tank for something on the outside of an aircraft or motor vehicle. ■ the outer casing of an aircraft engine. ■ chiefly historical the car of an airship.
– ORIGIN early 20th cent. (originally denoting the car of an airship): from French, from late Latin *navicella*, diminutive of Latin *navis* 'ship.'

nach·es /'näkHəs/ (also **nachas**) ▶ **n.** pride or gratification, esp. at the achievements of one's children. ■ congratulations: *naches to Miriam Goldstein on her acceptance into rabbinic school.*
– ORIGIN early 20th cent.: from Yiddish *nakhes*, from Hebrew *naḥaṯ* 'contentment.'

na·cho /'näcHō/ ▶ **n.** (pl. **nachos**) a small crisp piece of a tortilla, typically topped with melted cheese and spices.
– ORIGIN perhaps from Mexican Spanish *Nacho*, nickname for *Ignacio*, given name of the chef credited with creation of the dish. An alternative derivation is from Spanish *nacho* 'flat-nosed.'

Nac·og·do·ches /ˌnakə'dōcHəz/ a historic city in eastern Texas, on the Angelina River; pop. 32,205 (est. 2008).

na·cre /'nākər/ ▶ **n.** mother-of-pearl.
– DERIVATIVES **na·cre·ous** /-krēəs/ **adj.**
– ORIGIN late 16th cent.: from French, of unknown origin.

NACU ▶ **abbr.** National Association of Colleges and Universities.

NAD ▶ **abbr.** Biochemistry nicotinamide adenine dinucleotide, a coenzyme important in many biological oxidation reactions.

na·da /'nädə/ ▶ **pron.** informal nothing.
– ORIGIN Spanish.

Na-De·ne /ˌnä dā'nā, nä 'dānē/ ▶ **adj.** denoting or belonging to a postulated phylum of North American Indian languages including the Athabaskan family, Tlingit, and (in some classifications) Haida.
▶ **n.** this language group.
– ORIGIN early 20th cent.: from Tlingit *naa* 'tribe' (related to Haida *náa* 'dwell') + North Athabaskan *dene* 'tribe.'

Na·der /'nādər/, Ralph (1934–), US consumer-rights advocate and lawyer. He has campaigned on behalf of public safety and given impetus to the consumer rights movement from the 1960s. He prompted legislation concerning car design, radiation hazards, food packaging, and insecticides. He made unsuccessful bids for the presidency in 1996 and 2000 as a Green Party candidate and in 2004 and 2008 as an Independent.

Ralph Nader

NADH ▶ **abbr.** nicotinamide adenine dinucleotide.

na·dir /'nādər, 'nādi(ə)r/ ▶ **n.** [in sing.] the lowest point in the fortunes of a person or organization: *they had reached the nadir of their sufferings.* ■ Astronomy the point on the celestial sphere directly below an observer. The opposite of **ZENITH**.
– ORIGIN late Middle English (in the astronomical sense): via French from Arabic *naẓīr (as-samt)* 'opposite (to the zenith).'

NADP ▶ **abbr.** nicotinamide adenine dinucleotide phosphate.

NADPH ▶ **abbr.** nicotinamide adenine dinucleotide phosphate.

nae /nā/ ▶ **determiner, exclam., adv. & n.** Scottish form of **NO**.
▶ **adv. & n.** Scottish form of **NOT**.

nae·vus ▶ **n.** (pl. **naevi**) British spelling of **NEVUS**.

naff¹ /naf/ ▶ **v.** [no obj.] (**naff off**) Brit. informal go away: *she told press photographers to naff off.*
– ORIGIN 1950s: euphemism for **FUCK**; compare with **EFF**.

naff² ▶ **adj.** Brit. informal lacking taste or style.
– DERIVATIVES **naff·ness** **n.**
– ORIGIN 1960s: of unknown origin.

NAFTA /'naftə/ (also **Nafta**) ▶ **abbr.** North American Free Trade Agreement.

nag¹ /nag/ ▶ **v.** (**nags, nagging, nagged**) [with obj.] annoy or irritate (a person) with persistent fault-finding or continuous urging: *she constantly nags her daughter* **about** *getting married* | [with infinitive] *she nagged him to do the housework* | [no obj.] *he's always* **nagging at** *her for staying out late.* ■ be persistently painful, troublesome, or worrying to: [no obj.] *something nagged at the back of his mind.*
▶ **n.** a person who nags someone. ■ a persistent feeling of anxiety: *he felt once again that little nag of doubt.*
– DERIVATIVES **nag·ger** **n.**, **nag·gy** **adj.**
– ORIGIN early 19th cent. (originally dialect in the sense 'gnaw'): perhaps of Scandinavian or Low German origin; compare with Norwegian and Swedish *nagga* 'gnaw, irritate' and Low German *(g)naggen* 'provoke.'

nag² ▶ **n.** informal, often derogatory a horse, esp. one that is old or in poor health. ■ archaic a horse suitable for riding as opposed to a draft animal.
– ORIGIN Middle English: of unknown origin.

Na·ga /ˈnägə/ ▶ **n. 1** a member of a group of peoples living in or near the Naga Hills of Burma (Myanmar) and northeastern India.
2 any of the Tibeto-Burman languages of these peoples.
▶ **adj.** of or relating to the Nagas or their language.
– ORIGIN perhaps from Sanskrit *nagna* 'naked' or *naga* 'mountain.'

na·ga /ˈnägə/ ▶ **n.** (in Indian mythology) a member of a semidivine race, part human and part cobra in form, associated with water and sometimes with mystical initiation.
– ORIGIN from Sanskrit *nāga* 'serpent.'

Na·ga·land /ˈnägəˌland, nəˈgälənd/ a state in northeast India, on the border with Burma (Myanmar); capital, Kohima. It was created in 1962 from parts of Assam.

na·ga·na /nəˈgänə/ ▶ **n.** a disease of cattle, antelope, and other livestock in southern Africa, characterized by fever, lethargy, and edema, and caused by trypanosome parasites transmitted by the tsetse fly.
– ORIGIN late 19th cent.: from Zulu *nakane*.

Na·ga·no /näˈgänō, ˈnägänō/ a commercial and industrial city in central Japan, on central Honshu Island, site of a major Buddhist shrine and of the 1998 Winter Olympic games; pop. 378,163 (2008).

Na·ga·sa·ki /ˌnägəˈsäkē/ a city and port in southwestern Japan, on the western coast of Kyushu island; pop. 452,064 (2007). On August 9, 1945, it became the target of the second atom bomb dropped by the US.

nage /näZH/ ▶ **n.** an aromatic court bouillon or stock, used for cooking shellfish.
– ORIGIN from French.

nag·ging /ˈnaɡiNG/ ▶ **adj. 1** (of a person) constantly harassing someone to do something: *their overprotective and nagging parents*.
2 persistently painful or worrying: *a nagging pain | only a handful of nagging doubts remained*.
– DERIVATIVES **nag·ging·ly** adv.

Na·gor·no-Ka·ra·bakh /nəˈgôrnō ˌkarəˈbäk, -ˈbäKH/ a region of Azerbaijan in the southern foothills of the Caucasus; pop. 134,900 (est. 2005); capital, Xankändi. Fighting between Azerbaijan and Armenia began in 1985, with the majority of the Armenian population desiring to be separated from Muslim Azerbaijan and united with Armenia; the region declared unilateral independence in 1991. A ceasefire was signed in 1994.

Na·go·ya /nəˈgoiə, ˈnägōyä/ a city in central Japan, on the southern coast of the island of Honshu; pop. 2,154,287 (2007).

Nag·pur /ˈnägˌpo͝or/ a city in central India, in the state of Maharashtra; pop. 2,403,200 (est. 2009).

Nags Head /ˈnags/ a resort town in eastern North Carolina, in the Outer Banks; pop. 3,016 (est. 2008).

nag·ware /ˈnagˌwe(ə)r/ ▶ **n.** informal computer software that is free for a trial period during which the user is frequently reminded on screen to register and pay for the program in order to continue using it when the trial period is over.

Nagy /näj, ˈnädyə/, Imre (1896–1958), Hungarian communist statesman, prime minister 1953–55 and 1956. In 1956, seeking neutral status for his country, he withdrew Hungary from the Warsaw Pact. He was executed after the Red Army crushed the uprising.

nah /nä/ ▶ **exclam.** variant spelling of **NO**, used to answer a question: *"Want a lift?" "Nah, that's okay."*

Nah. ▶ **abbr.** Bible Nahum.

Na·ha /ˈnähä/ a port in southern Japan, capital of Okinawa island; pop. 312,938 (2007).

Na·hua·tl /ˈnäˌwätl/ ▶ **n.** (pl. **same**) **1** a member of a group of peoples native to southern Mexico and Central America, including the Aztecs.
2 the Uto-Aztecan language of these peoples.
▶ **adj.** of or relating to these peoples or their language.
– ORIGIN via Spanish from Nahuatl *náhuatl* 'what pleases the ear.'

Na·hum /ˈnāhəm/ (in the Bible) a Hebrew minor prophet. ■ a book of the Bible containing his prophecy of the fall of Nineveh (early 7th century BC).

NAIA ▶ **abbr.** National Association of Intercollegiate Athletics.

nai·ad /ˈnāad, -əd, nī-/ ▶ **n.** (pl. **naiads** or **naiades** /-əˌdēz/) **1** (also **Naiad**) (in classical mythology) a water nymph said to inhabit a river, spring, or waterfall.
2 the aquatic larva or nymph of a dragonfly, mayfly, or stonefly.
3 a submerged aquatic plant with narrow leaves and minute flowers. ● Genus *Najas*, family Najadaceae.
– ORIGIN via Latin from Greek *Naias*, *Naiad-*, from *naein* 'to flow.' Use as a term in entomology and botany dates from the early 20th cent.

na·iant /ˈnāənt/ ▶ **adj.** [postpositive] Heraldry (of a fish or marine creature) swimming horizontally.
– ORIGIN mid 16th cent.: from Anglo-Norman French, variant of Old French *noiant* 'swimming,' present participle of *noier*, from Latin *natare* 'to swim.'

na·if /nīˈēf/ (also **naïf**) ▶ **adj.** naive or ingenuous.
▶ **n.** a naive or ingenuous person.
– ORIGIN from French (see **NAIVE**).

nail /nāl/ ▶ **n. 1** a small metal spike with a broadened flat head, driven typically into wood with a hammer to join things together or to serve as a peg or hook.
2 a horny covering on the upper surface of the tip of the finger and toe in humans and other primates. ■ an animal's claw. ■ a hard growth on the upper mandible of some soft-billed birds.
3 historical a medieval unit of measurement. ■ a measure of length for cloth, equal to $2^1/_4$ inches. ■ a measure of wool, beef, or other commodity, roughly equal to 7 or 8 pounds.
▶ **v.** [with obj.] **1** fasten to a surface or to something else with a nail or nails: *nail the edge framing to the wall | the teacher was nailing up the lists*.
2 informal expose (someone) as deceitful or criminal; catch or arrest: *have you nailed the killer?* ■ expose (a lie or other instance of deception).
3 Football, informal tackle the quarterback or ballcarrier, esp. at or behind the line of scrimmage. ■ Baseball (of a fielder) put (a runner) out by throwing to a base: *he dropped a perfect throw home that should have nailed Joe by yards*. ■ (of a player) defeat or outwit (an opponent): *Navratilova tried to nail her on the backhand side*. ■ (of a player) secure (esp. a victory) conclusively: *there's no doubt I had chances to nail it in the last set*.
4 vulgar slang (of a man) have sexual intercourse with (someone).
– PHRASES **fight tooth and nail** see **TOOTH**. **hard as nails** (of a person) very tough; completely callous or unfeeling. **a nail in the coffin** an action or event regarded as likely to have a detrimental or destructive effect on a situation, enterprise, or person: *this was going to put the final nail in the coffin of his career*. **on the nail** Brit. (of payment) without delay.
– PHRASAL VERBS **nail someone down** elicit a firm promise or commitment from someone: *I can't nail her down to a specific date*. **nail something down 1** fasten something securely with nails. **2** identify something precisely: *something seems unexpected—I can't nail it down, but it makes me uneasy*. **3** secure something, esp. an agreement: *the company has finally nailed down the agreement with its distributors*.
– DERIVATIVES **nailed** adj. [in combination] *dirty-nailed fingers*, **nail·less** adj.
– ORIGIN Old English *nægel* (noun), *næglan* (verb), of Germanic origin; related to Dutch *nagel* and German *Nagel*, from an Indo-European root shared by Latin *unguis* and Greek *onux*.

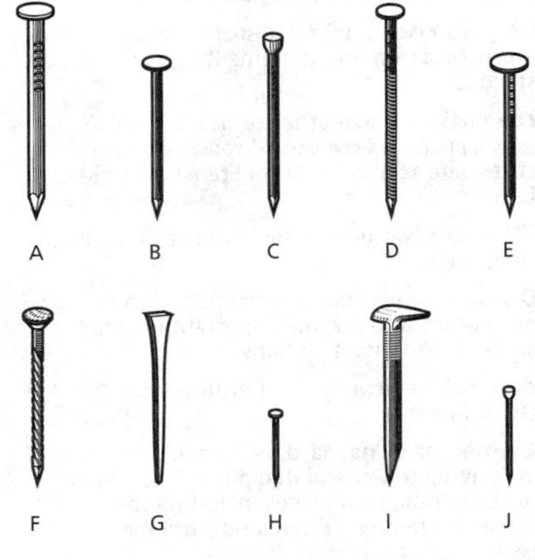

A common nail
B box nail
C finish *or* finishing nail
D ring *or* anchor nail
E roofing nail
F screw nail
G cut *or* flooring nail
H wire nail
I wrought nail
J brad

nails

nail bed ▶ **n.** the formative layer of cells underlying the fingernail or toenail.

nail-bit·er (also **nail biter**) ▶ **n.** a situation causing great anxiety or tension: *a nail-biter of a victory*.
– DERIVATIVES **nail-bit·ing** adj.

nail brush ▶ **n.** a small brush designed for cleaning the fingernails and toenails.

nail e·nam·el ▶ **n.** nail polish.

nail·er /ˈnālər/ ▶ **n. 1** chiefly historical a maker of nails.
2 a power tool for inserting nails.
– DERIVATIVES **nail·er·y n.**

nail file ▶ **n.** a strip of roughened metal or an emery board used for smoothing and shaping the fingernails and toenails.

nail gall ▶ **n.** a small, conical, nail-shaped gall that forms on the leaves of lime trees in response to the presence of mites. ● The mite is *Eriophyes tiliae*, family Eriophyidae.

nail·head /ˈnālˌhed/ ▶ **n.** the rounded head of a nail. ■ an ornament like the head of a nail, used chiefly in architecture and on clothing.

nail pol·ish ▶ **n.** varnish applied to the fingernails or toenails to color them or make them shiny.

nail scis·sors ▶ **plural n.** small scissors with curved blades for cutting the fingernails or toenails.

nail set (also **nail punch**) ▶ **n.** a tool hit with a hammer to sink the head of a nail below a surface.

nail sick·ness ▶ **n.** the condition of a structure that is held together with corroded nails.

nail var·nish ▶ **n.** Brit. nail polish.

nail wrap ▶ **n.** a type of beauty treatment, in which a nail strengthener, usu. containing fibers, is either brushed on or applied with adhesive.

nain·sook /ˈnānˌso͝ok/ ▶ **n.** a fine, soft cotton fabric, originally from South Asia.
– ORIGIN late 18th cent.: from Hindi *nainsukh*, from *nain* 'eye' + *sukh* 'pleasure.'

Nai·paul /ˈnīpôl, nīˈpôl/, V. S. (1932–), Trinidadian writer, resident in Britain from 1950; full name *Sir Vidiadhar Surajprasad Naipaul*. He is best known for his satirical novels, such as *A House for Mr. Biswas* (1961) and *In a Free State* (1971). Other notable works: *A Way in the World* (1994) and *Beyond Belief: Islamic Excursions among the Converted People* (1998). Nobel Prize for Literature (2001).

nai·ra /ˈnīrə/ ▶ **n.** the basic monetary unit of Nigeria, equal to 100 kobo.
– ORIGIN contraction of **NIGERIA**.

Nai·ro·bi /nīˈrōbē/ the capital of Kenya; pop. 3,010,000 (est. 2007). It is situated on the central Kenyan plateau at an altitude of 5,500 feet (1,680 m).

Nai·smith /ˈnāˌsmiTH/, James (1861–1939), Canadian-American physical education teacher. He invented the game of basketball in 1891, while teaching at the International YMCA Training School in Springfield, Massachusetts. Basketball Hall of Fame (1959).

nais·sant /ˈnāsənt/ ▶ **adj.** Heraldry (of a charge, esp. an animal) issuing from the middle of an ordinary, esp. a fess.
– ORIGIN late 16th cent.: from French, literally 'being born,' present participle of *naître*, from Latin *nasci* 'be born.'

na·ive /nīˈēv/ (also **naïve**) ▶ **adj.** (of a person or action) showing a lack of experience, wisdom, or judgment: *the rather naive young man had been totally misled*. ■ (of a person) natural and unaffected; innocent: *Andy had a sweet, naive look when he smiled*. ■ of or denoting art produced in a straightforward style that deliberately rejects sophisticated artistic techniques and has a bold directness resembling a child's work, typically in bright colors with little or no perspective.
– DERIVATIVES **na·ive·ly** adv., **na·ive·ness** n.
– ORIGIN mid 17th cent.: from French *naïve*, feminine of *naïf*, from Latin *nativus* 'native, natural.'

na·ive·té /ˌnīˌēv(ə)ˈtā, nīˈēv(ə)ˌtā/ (also **naïveté**, Brit. **naivety**) ▶ **n.** lack of experience, wisdom, or judgment: *the administration's naiveté and inexperience in foreign policy*. ■ innocence or unsophistication: *they took advantage of his naiveté and deep pockets*.
– ORIGIN late 17th cent.: from French *naïveté*, from *naïf*, *-ive* (see **NAIVE**).

Na·jaf /ˈnäjəf/ (also **an-Najaf** /än ˈnäjəf/) a city in southern Iraq, on the Euphrates River; pop. 500,000 (est. 2003). It contains the shrine of **Ali**, the prophet Muhammad's son-in-law, and is a holy city for the Shiite Muslims.

na·ked /ˈnākid/ ▶ **adj. 1** (of a person or part of the body) without clothes: *he'd never seen a naked woman before | he was stripped naked*. ■ (of an object) without the usual covering or protection: *her room was lit by a single naked bulb*. ■ (of a tree, plant, or animal) without leaves, hairs, scales, shell,

etc.: *the twisted trunks and naked branches of the trees.* ■ exposed to harm; unprotected or vulnerable: *John looked naked and defenseless without his glasses.* **2** [attrib.] (of something such as feelings or behavior) undisguised; blatant: *naked, unprovoked aggression | the naked truth.*
– DERIVATIVES **na·ked·ly** adv.
– ORIGIN Old English *nacod*, of Germanic origin; related to Dutch *naakt* and German *nackt*, from an Indo-European root shared by Latin *nudus* and Sanskrit *nagna*.

na·ked eye ▶ **n.** (usu. **the naked eye**) unassisted vision, without a telescope, microscope, or other device: *threadworm eggs are so small that they cannot be seen with the naked eye.*

na·ked mole rat ▶ **n.** a blind and hairless mole rat living in large underground colonies in eastern Africa. The colony structure is similar to that of social insects, with only one pair breeding and most other individuals acting as workers. ● *Heterocephalus glaber*, family Bathyergidae.

na·ked·ness /ˈnākidnis/ ▶ **n.** the state or fact of being naked: *he made no attempt to conceal his nakedness.*

na·ker /ˈnākər/ ▶ **n.** historical a kettledrum.
– ORIGIN late Middle English: from Old French *nacaire*, from Arabic *naķķāra* 'drum.'

nak·fa /ˈnäkfə/ ▶ **n.** (pl. **same** or **nakfas**) the basic monetary unit of Eritrea, equal to 100 cents.
– ORIGIN 1990s: from *Nakfa*, the name of the town where the country's armed struggle against the Ethiopian regime was launched.

Na·khi·che·van /ˌnäkicHəˈvän/ Russian name for **NAXÇIVAN**.

Na·ku·ru /nəˈko͝oro͞o/ an industrial city in western Kenya; pop. 275,700 (est. 2009). Nearby is Lake Nakuru, noted for its spectacular flocks of flamingos.

Nal·chik /ˈnälcHik/ a city in the Caucasus, in southwestern Russia, capital of the republic of Kabardino-Balkaria; pop. 269,600 (est. 2008).

na·li·dix·ic ac·id /ˌnāliˈdiksik/ ▶ **n.** Medicine a synthetic compound that inhibits the multiplication of bacteria, used chiefly to treat urinary infections. ● A heterocyclic compound; chem. formula: $C_{12}H_{12}N_2O_3$.
– ORIGIN 1960s: *nalidixic* by rearrangement of elements from **NAPHTHALENE**, *carboxylic*, and **DI-**[1] (forming the systematic name).

nal·ox·one /nəˈläksōn/ ▶ **n.** Medicine a synthetic drug, similar to morphine, that blocks opiate receptors in the nervous system.
– ORIGIN 1960s: contraction of *N-allylnoroxymorphone*.

nal·trex·one /nalˈtreksōn/ ▶ **n.** Medicine a synthetic drug, similar to morphine, that blocks opiate receptors in the nervous system and is used chiefly in the treatment of heroin addiction.
– ORIGIN 1970s: from a contraction of *N-al(lylnoroxymorph)one* (see **NALOXONE**), with the insertion of the arbitrary element *-trex-*.

NAM ▶ abbr. National Association of Manufacturers.

Nam /näm, nam/ (also **'Nam**) informal name for **VIETNAM** in the context of the Vietnam War.

Na·ma /ˈnämä/ ▶ **n.** (pl. **same** or **Namas**) **1** a member of one of the Khoikhoi peoples of South Africa and southwestern Namibia.
2 the Khoisan language of this people.
▶ **adj.** of or relating to this people or their language.
– ORIGIN the name in Nama.

Na·man·gan /ˌnämənGˈgän/ a city in eastern Uzbekistan, near the border with Kyrgyzstan; pop. 446,200 (est. 2007).

Na·ma·qua·land /nəˈmäkwəˌland/ a region of southwestern Africa, the homeland of the Nama people. **Little Namaqualand** lies immediately to the south of the Orange River in South Africa, while **Great Namaqualand** lies to the north of the river in Namibia.

nam·as·kar /ˌnäməsˈkär/ ▶ **n.** a traditional Indian greeting or gesture of respect, made by bringing the palms together before the face or chest and bowing.
– ORIGIN via Hindi from Sanskrit *namaskāra*, from *namas* 'bowing' + *kāra* 'action.'

na·ma·ste /ˈnäməˌstā/ ▶ **exclam.** a respectful greeting said when giving a namaskar.
▶ **n.** another term for **NAMASKAR**.
– ORIGIN via Hindi from Sanskrit *namas* 'bowing' + *te* 'to you.'

Na·math /ˈnāməTH/, Joe (1943–), US football player; full name *Joseph William Namath*; nickname **Broadway Joe**. A quarterback with the New York Jets 1965–76, he led them to a 1969 Super Bowl title. He also played for the Los Angeles Rams 1977–78. Football Hall of Fame (1985).

nam·by-pam·by /ˌnambē ˈpambē/ ▶ **adj.** derogatory lacking energy, strength, or courage; feeble or effeminate in behavior or expression: *these weren't namby-pamby fights, but brutal affairs where heads hit the sidewalk.*
▶ **n.** (pl. **namby-pambies**) a feeble or effeminate person.
– ORIGIN mid 18th cent.: fanciful formation based on the given name of *Ambrose* Philips (died 1749), an English writer whose pastorals were ridiculed by the writers Henry Carey (1687?–1743) and Alexander Pope (1688–1744).

name /nām/ ▶ **n. 1** a word or set of words by which a person, animal, place, or thing is known, addressed, or referred to: *my name is Parsons, John Parsons | Köln is the German* **name for** *Cologne.*
2 a famous person: *as usual, the big race will lure the top names.* ■ [in sing.] a reputation, esp. a good one: *he set up a school that gained a name for excellence.*
▶ **v.** [with obj.] **1** give a name to: *hundreds of diseases had not yet been isolated or named* | [with obj. and complement] *she named the child Edward.* ■ identify by name; give the correct name for: *the dead man has been* **named as** *John Mackintosh.* ■ give a particular title or epithet to: *she was named "Artist of the Decade."* ■ mention or cite by name: *the sea is as crystal clear as any spot in the Caribbean you might care to name.* ■ appoint (someone) to a particular position or task: *he was named to head a joint UN–OAS diplomatic effort.*
2 specify (an amount, time, or place) as something desired, suggested, or decided on: *he showed them the picture and named a price.*
▶ **adj.** [attrib.] (of a person or commercial product) having a name that is widely known: *countless specialized* **name brands** *geared to niche markets.*
– PHRASES **by name** using the name of someone or something: *ask for the street by name.* **by the name of** called: *a woman by the name of Smith.* **call someone names** insult someone verbally. **give one's name to** invent, discover, found, or be closely associated with something that then becomes known by one's name: *Lou Gehrig gave his name to the disease that claimed his life.* **something has someone's name on it** a person is destined or particularly suited to receive or experience a specified thing: *he feared the next bullet would have his name on it.* **have to one's name** [often with negative] have in one's possession: *I had a child on the way and hardly a penny to my name.* **in all but name** existing in a particular state but not formally recognized as such: *these new punks are hippies in all but name.* **in someone's name 1** formally registered as belonging to or reserved for someone: *the house was in her name.* **2** on behalf of someone: *he began to question what had been done in his name.* **in the name of** bearing or using the name of a specified person or organization: *a driver's license in the name of William Sanders.* ■ for the sake of: *he withdrew his candidacy in the name of party unity.* ■ by the authority of: *crimes committed in the name of religion.* ■ **(in the name of Christ/God/heaven**, etc.) used for emphasis: *what in the name of God do you think you're doing?* **in name only** by description but not in reality: *a college in name only.* **make a name for oneself** become well known: *by the time he was thirty-five, he had made a name for himself as a contractor.* **name the day** arrange a date for a specific occasion, esp. a wedding. **one's name is mud** see **MUD**. **name names** mention specific names, esp. of people involved in something wrong or illegal: *if you're convinced my staff is part of this operation, then name names.* **the name of the game** informal the main purpose or most important aspect of a situation: *the name of the game is short-term gain.* **put down** (or **enter**) **one's** (or **someone's**) **name** apply to enter an educational institution, course, competition, etc.: *I put my name down for the course.* **put a name to** remember or report what someone or something is called: *viewers were asked if they could put a name to the voice of the kidnapper.* **take someone's name in vain** see **VAIN**. **to name** (**but**) **a few** giving only these as examples, even though more could be cited: *the ingredients used are drawn from nature—avocado, lemongrass, and chamomile to name a few.* **what's in a name?** names are arbitrary labels: *What's in a name? If you know her by Elizabeth or Lizzie, she's still the same person.* **you name it** informal whatever you can think of (used to express the extent or variety of something): *easy-to-assemble kits of trains, cars, trucks, ships ... you name it.*
– PHRASAL VERBS **name someone/something after** (also **for**) call someone or something by the same name as: *Nathaniel* **was named after** *his maternal grandfather | Ricksburg, Idaho,* **named for** *one Thomas Ricks.*
– DERIVATIVES **name·a·ble** /ˈnāməbəl/ adj., **nam·er** n.
– ORIGIN Old English*nama, noma* (noun), *(ge) namian* (verb), of Germanic origin; related to Dutch *naam* and German *Name*, from a root shared by Latin *nomen* and Greek *onoma*.

name-call·ing ▶ **n.** abusive language or insults.
– DERIVATIVES **name-call·er** n.

name·check /ˈnām,cHek/ ▶ **n.** a public mention or listing of the name of a person or thing such as a product, esp. in acknowledgment or for publicity purposes.
▶ **v.** [with obj.] publicly mention or list the name of: *he namechecks a legion of producers and DJs.*

name day ▶ **n.** the feast day of a saint after whom a person is named.

name-drop·ping ▶ **n.** the practice of casually mentioning the names of famous people one knows or claims to know in order to impress others.
– DERIVATIVES **name-drop** v., **name-drop·per** n.

name·less /ˈnāmlis/ ▶ **adj. 1** having no name or no known name. ■ deliberately not identified; anonymous: *the director of a voluntary organization which shall remain nameless.* ■ archaic (of a child) illegitimate.
2 (esp. of an emotion) not easy to describe; indefinable: *a nameless yearning for transcendence.* ■ too loathsome or horrific to be described: *the myths talk about nameless horrors infesting our universe.*
– DERIVATIVES **name·less·ly** adv., **name·less·ness** n.

name·ly /ˈnāmlē/ ▶ **adv.** that is to say; to be specific (used to introduce detailed information or a specific example): *to me there is only one kind of rock, namely, loud rock.*

Na·men /ˈnämən/ Flemish name for **NAMUR**.

Na·men·da /nəˈmendə/ ▶ **n.** trademark for **MEMANTINE**.

name·plate /ˈnām,plāt/ ▶ **n.** a plate or sign, typically made of metal, displaying the name of someone, such as the person working in a building or the builder of a ship. ■ a brand of a product, esp. a maker of automobiles: *Honda is busiest among the import nameplates, with three new cars and a sport utility vehicle.*

name·sake /ˈnām,sāk/ ▶ **n.** a person or thing that has the same name as another: *Hugh Capet paved the way for his son and namesake to be crowned king of France.*
– ORIGIN mid 17th cent.: from the phrase *for the name's sake*.

name·tape /ˈnām,tāp/ ▶ **n.** a piece of cloth tape bearing the name of a person, fixed to a garment of theirs to identify it.

Na·mib Des·ert /ˈnämib/ a desert in southwestern Africa. It extends for 1,200 miles (1,900 km) along the Atlantic coast from the Curoca River in southwestern Angola through Namibia to the border between Namibia and South Africa.

Na·mib·i·a /nəˈmibēə/ a country in southwestern Africa, largely desert, with a coastline on the Atlantic Ocean; pop. 2,108,700 (est. 2009); capital, Windhoek; languages, English (official), Afrikaans, and various Bantu and Khoisan languages.

> Namibia was made the protectorate of German South West Africa in 1884. In 1920, it was mandated to South Africa by the League of Nations and became known as South West Africa. Despite international pressure, South Africa continued to administer the country after the ending of the UN mandate in 1964 and agreed to withdraw only after several years of fighting by SWAPO guerrillas. Namibia became fully independent in 1990.

– DERIVATIVES **Na·mib·i·an** adj. & n.

Nam·pa /ˈnampə/ a city in southwestern Idaho, southwest of Boise; pop. 80,362 (est. 2008).

nam pla /ˌnäm ˈplä/ ▶ **n.** Thai term for **FISH SAUCE**.

Nam·po /ˈnämˈpō/ (also **Chinnampo**) an industrial city in western North Korea, southwest of Pyongyang, for which it is the port; pop. 471,100 (est. 2009).

Na·mur /nəˈmo͝or/ a province in central Belgium. It was the scene of the last German offensive in the Ardennes in 1945. Flemish name **NAMEN**. ■ the capital of this province, at the junction of the Meuse and Sambre rivers; pop. 107,939 (2008).

nan /nän/ (also **naan**) ▶ **n.** (in Indian cooking) a type of leavened bread, typically of teardrop shape and traditionally cooked in a clay oven.
– ORIGIN from Urdu and Persian *nān*.

nan·a /ˈnanə/ ▶ **n.** informal one's grandmother.
– ORIGIN mid 19th cent.: child's pronunciation of **NANNY** or **GRAN**.

Na·nai·mo bar /nə'nīmō/ ▶ n. Canadian a dessert consisting of a crust of chocolate and cookie crumbs, typically covered with vanilla buttercream icing and a chocolate glaze.
– ORIGIN from *Nanaimo*, the name of a city in the Canadian province of British Columbia.

Na·nak /'nänək/ (1469–1539), Indian religious leader and founder of Sikhism; known as **Guru Nanak**. He preached that spiritual liberation could be achieved through meditating on the name of God. His teachings are contained in a number of hymns that form part of the Adi Granth.

nance /nans/ ▶ n. another term for NANCY.

Nan·chang /'nän'CHäNG/ a city in southeastern China, capital of Jiangxi province; pop. 1,613,200 (est. 2006).

Nan·cy /nän'sē/ a city in northeastern France, chief town of Lorraine; pop. 107,434 (2006).

nan·cy /'nansē/ ▶ n. (pl. **nancies**) (also **nancy boy**) derogatory, chiefly Brit. an effeminate or homosexual man.
▶ adj. effeminate.
– ORIGIN early 20th cent.: nickname for the given name *Ann*.

NAND /nand/ ▶ n. Electronics a Boolean operator that gives the value zero if and only if all the operands have a value of one, and otherwise has a value of one (equivalent to NOT AND). ■ (also **NAND gate**) a circuit that produces an output signal until there are signals on all of its inputs.

Nan·di /'nändē/ Hinduism a bull that serves as the mount of Shiva and symbolizes fertility.
– ORIGIN Sanskrit.

nan·di·na /nan'dēnə/ ▶ n. an evergreen eastern Asian shrub that resembles bamboo and is cultivated for its foliage, which turns red or bronze in autumn. Also called CELESTIAL BAMBOO. ● *Nandina domestica*, family Berberidaceae.
– ORIGIN mid 19th cent.: modern Latin (genus name), adapted from Japanese *nanten*.

nan·dro·lone /'nandrə,lōn/ ▶ n. an anabolic steroid with tissue-building properties, used unlawfully to enhance performance in sports.
– ORIGIN 1950s: shortened form of its chemical name *norandrostenolone*.

Nan·ga Par·bat /,nəNGgə 'pərbət/ a mountain in northern Pakistan, in the western Himalayas. It is 26,660 feet (8,126 m) high.

Nan·jing /'nän'jiNG/ (also **Nanking** /'nan'kiNG/) a city in eastern China, on the Yangtze River, capital of Jiangsu province; pop. 4,105,400 (est. 2006).

nan·keen /nan'kēn/ ▶ n. a yellowish cotton cloth. ■ (**nankeens**) historical pants made of this cloth. ■ the characteristic yellowish-buff color of this cloth.
▶ adj. of this color.
– ORIGIN mid 18th cent.: from the name of the city of *Nanking* (see NANJING), where it was first made.

Nan·ning /'nä'niNG/ the capital of Guangxi Zhuang, an autonomous region in southern China; pop. 1,277,300 (est. 2006).

nan·no·fos·sil /,nanə'fäsəl/ (also **nanofossil**) ▶ n. the fossil of a minute planktonic organism, esp. a calcareous unicellular alga.
– ORIGIN 1960s: *nanno-* from *nannoplankton* (variant of NANOPLANKTON) + FOSSIL.

nan·ny /'nanē/ ▶ n. (pl. **nannies**) **1** a person, typically a woman, employed to care for a child in its own home. ■ a person or institution regarded as interfering and overprotective.
2 (in full **nanny goat**) a female goat.
▶ v. (**nannies, nannying, nannied**) [with obj.] (usu. as noun **nannying**) be overprotective toward: *his well-intentioned nannying.*
– DERIVATIVES **nannyish** adj.
– ORIGIN early 18th cent. (as a noun): nickname for the given name *Ann*. The verb dates from the 1950s.

nan·ny·gai /'nanē,gī/ ▶ n. (pl. **nannygais**) the redfish of Australia (*Centroberyx affinis*).
– ORIGIN late 19th cent.: from a New South Wales Aboriginal language.

nan·ny state ▶ n. chiefly Brit. the government regarded as overprotective or as interfering unduly with personal choice.

na·no /'nanō/ ▶ n. informal short for NANOTECHNOLOGY.

nano- ▶ comb. form denoting a factor of 10^{-9} (used commonly in units of measurement): *nanosecond.* ■ denoting a very small item: *nanoplankton.*
– ORIGIN via Latin from Greek *nanos* 'dwarf.'

nan·o·bac·te·ri·um /,nanōbak'ti(ə)rēəm, ,nā-/ ▶ n. (pl. **nanobacteria** /-'ti(ə)rēə/) a microorganism about a tenth the size of the smallest normal bacteria, claimed to have been discovered in living tissue and in rock.

nan·obe /'nan,ōb, 'nā,nōb/ another term for NANOBACTERIUM.
– ORIGIN by shortening and alteration.

nan·o·bot /'nanə,bät/ ▶ n. a hypothetical, very small, self-propelled machine, esp. one that has some degree of autonomy and can reproduce.

nan·o·com·pos·ite /,nanō'kämpəzit/ ▶ adj. denoting a composite material that has a grain size measured in nanometers.
▶ n. a nanocomposite material.

nan·o·gram /'nanō,gram/ (abbr.: **ng**) ▶ n. one billionth of a gram.

nan·o·ma·te·ri·al /'nanōmə,ti(ə)rēəl/ ▶ n. a material having particles or constituents of nanoscale dimensions, or one that is produced by nanotechnology.

nan·o·me·ter /'nanə,mētər/ (Brit. **nanometre**) (abbr.: **nm**) ▶ n. one billionth of a meter.

nan·o·par·ti·cle /'nanō,pärtikəl/ ▶ n. a nanoscale particle.

nan·o·plank·ton /,nanə'plaNGktən/ ▶ n. Biology very small unicellular plankton, at the limits of resolution of light microscopy.
– ORIGIN early 20th cent.: from German, from Greek *nanos* 'dwarf' + PLANKTON.

nan·o·ro·bot /'nanə,rōbät, -bət, 'nā-/ ▶ n. a machine made from individual atoms or molecules that is designed to perform a small and specific job.

nan·o·scale /'nanə,skāl, 'nā-/ ▶ adj. of a size measurable in nanometers or microns: *the use of viruses as nanoscale building tools.*

nan·o·scop·ic /,nanə'skäpik/ ▶ adj. another term for NANOSCALE. ■ extremely small: *his comment contains a nanoscopic grain of truth.*

nan·o·sec·ond /'nanə,sekənd/ (abbr.: **ns**) ▶ n. one billionth of a second. ■ informal a very short time; a moment: *he replied without a nanosecond's hesitation.*

nan·o·struc·ture /'nanə,strəkCHər, 'nā-/ ▶ n. a structure, esp. a semiconductor device, that has dimensions of only a few nanometers.

nan·o·tech /'nanōtek/ ▶ n. short for NANOTECHNOLOGY.

nan·o·tech·nol·o·gy /,nanə,tek'näləjē, ,nanō-/ ▶ n. the branch of technology that deals with dimensions and tolerances of less than 100 nanometers, esp. the manipulation of individual atoms and molecules.
– DERIVATIVES **nan·o·tech·no·log·i·cal** /,teknə'läjikəl/ adj., **nan·o·tech·nol·o·gist** /-jist/ n.

nan·o·tube /'nanə,t(y)o͞ob/ ▶ n. Chemistry a cylindrical molecule of a fullerene.

nan·o·wire /'nanə,wī(ə)r, 'nā-/ ▶ n. a nanoscale rod made of semiconducting material, used in miniature transistors and some laser applications.

Nan·sen /'nansən, 'nän-/, Fridtjof (1861–1930), Norwegian Arctic explorer. In 1888, he led the first expedition to cross the Greenland ice fields, and, five years later, on board the *Fram*, he sailed from Siberia for the North Pole, which he failed to reach. He later organized relief work among the victims of famine in Russia. Nobel Peace Prize (1922).

Nan·sen pass·port ▶ n. historical a document of identification issued to stateless people after World War I.

Nantes /näNt/ a city in western France, on the Loire River; pop. 290,871 (2006).

Nantes, E·dict of an edict of 1598 signed by Henry IV of France granting toleration to Protestants and ending the French Wars of Religion. It was revoked by Louis XIV in 1685.

Nan·tuck·et /nan'təkit/ an island off the coast of Massachusetts, south of Cape Cod and east of Martha's Vineyard. Now a popular resort, it was an important whaling center during the 18th and 19th centuries.

nap¹ /nap/ ▶ v. (**naps, napping, napped**) [no obj.] sleep lightly or briefly, esp. during the day.
▶ n. a short sleep, esp. during the day: *excuse me, I'll just take a little nap.*
– PHRASES **catch someone napping** informal (of a person, action, or event) find someone off guard and unprepared to respond: *he caught the runner napping off second base and tagged him out.*
– ORIGIN Old English *hnappian*, probably of Germanic origin.

nap² ▶ n. [in sing.] the raised hairs, threads, or similar small projections on the surface of fabric or suede (used esp. with reference to the direction in which they naturally lie): *carefully machine the seam, following the direction of the nap.*
– DERIVATIVES **nap·less** adj.
– ORIGIN late Middle English *noppe*, from Middle Dutch and Middle Low German *noppe* 'nap,' *noppen* 'trim the nap from.'

nap³ ▶ n. a card game resembling whist in which players declare the number of tricks they expect to take, up to five.
– ORIGIN early 19th cent.: abbreviation of NAPOLEON, the original name of the card game.

nap⁴ ▶ v. (**naps, napping, napped**) [no obj.] (of a horse) refuse, esp. habitually, to go on at the rider's instruction; jib.
– ORIGIN 1950s: back-formation from *nappy*, an adjective first used to describe heady beer (late Middle English), later used in the sense 'intoxicated by drink' (early 18th cent.), and since the 1920s used to describe a disobedient horse.

NAPA ▶ abbr. National Association of Performing Artists.

Na·pa /'napə/ a commercial city in north central California, hub of the wine-making Napa Valley; pop. 74,547 (est. 2008).

na·pa ▶ n. variant spelling of NAPPA.

na·pa cab·bage /'napə, 'nä-/ ▶ n. a cabbagelike Chinese plant whose long, white leaves are used in salads and cooking.
– ORIGIN *napa*, of unknown origin.

na·palm /'nā,pä(l)m/ ▶ n. a highly flammable sticky jelly used in incendiary bombs and flamethrowers, consisting of gasoline thickened with special soaps.
▶ v. [with obj.] attack with bombs containing napalm.
– ORIGIN 1940s: from *na(phthenic)* and *palm(itic acid)*.

nape /nāp/ ▶ n. (also **nape of the neck**) the back of a person's neck.
– ORIGIN Middle English: of unknown origin.

Na·per·ville /'nāpər,vil/ a city in northeastern Illinois, west of Chicago; pop. 143,117 (est. 2008).

na·per·y /'nāpərē/ ▶ n. household linen, esp. tablecloths and napkins.
– ORIGIN Middle English: from Old French *naperie*, from *nape* 'tablecloth.'

Naph·ta·li /'naftə,lī/ (in the Bible) a Hebrew patriarch, second son of Jacob and Bilhah. ■ the tribe of Israel traditionally descended from him.

naph·tha /'nafTHə, 'nap-/ ▶ n. Chemistry a flammable oil containing various hydrocarbons, obtained by the dry distillation of organic substances such as coal, shale, or petroleum.
– ORIGIN late Middle English *napte*, from Latin *naphtha*, from Greek, of Asian origin; the Latin spelling was introduced in the late 16th cent.

naph·tha·lene /'nafTHə,lēn, 'nap-/ ▶ n. Chemistry a volatile white crystalline compound produced by the distillation of coal tar, used in mothballs and as a raw material for chemical manufacture. ● A bicyclic aromatic hydrocarbon; chem. formula: $C_{10}H_8$.
– DERIVATIVES **naph·thal·ic** /naf'THalik, nap-/ adj.
– ORIGIN early 19th cent.: from NAPHTHA + -ENE, with the insertion of *-l-* for ease of pronunciation.

naph·thene /'nafTHēn, nap-/ ▶ n. Chemistry any of a group of cyclic aliphatic hydrocarbons (e.g., cyclohexane) obtained from petroleum.
– DERIVATIVES **naph·the·nic** /naf'THēnik, nap-, -THenik/ adj.

naph·thol /'nafTHôl, 'nap-, -THäl/ ▶ n. Chemistry a crystalline solid derived from naphthalene, used to make antiseptics and dyes. ● Chem. formula: $C_{10}H_7OH$; two isomers, esp. naphthalen-2-ol (**β-naphthol**).

Na·pi·er /'nāpēər, nə'pi(ə)r/, John (1550–1617), Scottish mathematician. He invented the logarithm.

na·pi·er grass /'nāpēər/ ▶ n. another term for ELEPHANT GRASS.

Na·pier·i·an log·a·rithm /nā'pi(ə)rēən, nə-/ ▶ n. another term for NATURAL LOGARITHM.
– ORIGIN early 19th cent.: named after J. NAPIER.

Na·pier's bones ▶ plural n. Mathematics slips of ivory or other material divided into sections marked with digits, devised by John Napier and formerly used to facilitate multiplication and division.

nap·kin /'napkin/ ▶ n. **1** (also **table napkin**) a square piece of cloth or paper used at a meal to wipe the fingers or lips and to protect garments, or to serve food on.
2 another term for SANITARY NAPKIN.
3 Brit. dated a baby's diaper.
– ORIGIN late Middle English: from Old French *nappe* 'tablecloth' (from Latin *mappa*: see MAP) + -KIN.

nap·kin ring ▶ n. a ring used to hold (and distinguish) a person's table napkin when not in use.

Na·ples /'nāpəlz/ **1** a city and port on the western coast of Italy; pop. 963,661 (2008). It was formerly the capital of the kingdom of Naples and Sicily (1816–60). Italian name NAPOLI.
2 a resort city in southwestern Florida, on the Gulf of Mexico; pop. 21,532 (est. 2008).
– ORIGIN from Latin *Neapolis*, from Greek *neos* 'new' + *polis* 'city.'

Na·ples yel·low ▶ **n.** a pale yellow pigment containing lead and antimony oxides. ■ the pale yellow color of this pigment, now commonly produced using cadmium, zinc, or iron-based substitutes.
– ORIGIN mid 18th cent.: named after **NAPLES**, the city where such a pigment was originally made.

Na·po·le·on /nə'pōlēən, -yən/ the name of three rulers of France. ■ **Napoleon I** (1769–1821), emperor 1804–14 and 1815; full name *Napoleon Bonaparte*; known as **Napoleon**. In 1799, he joined a conspiracy that overthrew the Directory, becoming the supreme ruler of France. He declared himself emperor in 1804 and established an empire stretching from Spain to Poland. After defeats at Trafalgar in 1805 and in Russia in 1812, he abdicated and was exiled to the island of Elba in 1814. He returned to power in 1815, but was defeated at Waterloo and was exiled to the island of St. Helena. ■ **Napoleon II** (1811–32), son of Napoleon I and Empress Marie-Louise; full name *Napoleon François Charles Joseph Bonaparte*. ■ **Napoleon III** (1808–73), emperor 1852–70; full name *Charles Louis Napoleon Bonaparte*; known as **Louis-Napoleon**. A nephew of Napoleon I, Napoleon III was elected president of the Second Republic in 1848 and staged a coup in 1851.

na·po·le·on /nə'pōlēən, -yən/ ▶ **n. 1** a flaky rectangular pastry with a sweet filling.
2 historical a gold twenty-franc French coin minted during the reign of Napoleon I.
3 (also **napoleon boot**) historical a 19th-century man's boot reaching above the knee in front and with a piece cut out behind, originally worn by cavalrymen.

Na·po·le·on·ic Wars /nə,pōlē'änik/ a series of campaigns (1800–15) of French armies under Napoleon against Austria, Russia, Great Britain, Portugal, Prussia, and other European powers. They ended with Napoleon's defeat at the Battle of Waterloo.

Na·po·li /'näpəlē/ Italian name for **NAPLES**.

nap·pa /'napə/ (also **napa**) ▶ **n.** a soft leather made by a special tawing process from the skin of sheep or goats.
– ORIGIN late 19th cent.: from *Napa*, the name of a valley in California.

nappe /nap/ ▶ **n.** Geology a sheet of rock that has moved sideways over neighboring strata as a result of an overthrust or folding.
– ORIGIN late 19th cent.: from French *nappe* 'tablecloth.'

napped[1] /napt/ ▶ **adj.** [usu. in combination] (of a textile) having a nap, usually of a specified kind: *a long-napped paint roller.*

napped[2] ▶ **adj.** (of food) served in a sauce or other liquid: *mushrooms napped with melted butter.*
– ORIGIN 1970s: from French *napper* 'coat with (a sauce),' from *nappe* 'cloth,' figuratively 'pool of liquid,' + **-ED**[2].

nap·py[1] /'napē/ ▶ **n.** (pl. **nappies**) Brit. a baby's diaper.
– ORIGIN early 20th cent.: abbreviation of **NAPKIN**.

nap·py[2] ▶ **adj.** informal (of a black person's hair) frizzy.
– ORIGIN late 15th cent. (in the sense 'shaggy'): from Middle Dutch *noppigh*, Middle Low German *noppich*, from *noppe* (see **NAP**[2]). The current sense dates from the early 20th cent.

na·prox·en /nə'präksən/ ▶ **n.** Medicine a synthetic compound used as an anti-inflammatory drug, esp. in the treatment of headache and arthritis. ● Chem. formula: $C_{14}H_{14}O_3$.
– ORIGIN 1970s: from *na(phthyl)* + *pr(opionic)* + *ox(y-)*, + *-en* on the pattern of words such as *tamoxifen*.

Na·ra /'närä/ a city in central Japan, on the island of Honshu; pop. 367,902 (2007). It was the first capital of Japan (710–784) and an important center of Japanese Buddhism.

Na·ra·yan /nə'rīən/, R. K. (1906–2001), Indian novelist and short-story writer; full name *Rasipuram Krishnaswamy Narayan*. Many of his novels are set in Malgudi, an imaginary small Indian town. Notable works: *Swami and Friends* (1935), *The Man-Eater of Malgudi* (1961), and *The Painter of Signs* (1977).

Na·ra·yan·ganj /nə'räyəNG,gənj/ a river port in Bangladesh, on the Ganges delta southeast of Dhaka; pop. 286,699 (2006).

narc /närk/ (also **nark**) ▶ **n.** informal a federal agent or police officer who enforces the laws regarding illicit sale or use of drugs and narcotics.
– ORIGIN 1960s: abbreviation of **NARCOTIC**.

nar·cis·sism /'närsə,sizəm/ ▶ **n.** excessive or erotic interest in oneself and one's physical appearance. ■ Psychology extreme selfishness, with a grandiose view of one's own talents and a craving for admiration, as characterizing a personality type. ■ Psychoanalysis self-centeredness arising from failure to distinguish the self from external objects, either in very young babies or as a feature of mental disorder.
– DERIVATIVES **nar·cis·sist** /'närsəsəst/ **n.**
– ORIGIN early 19th cent.: via Latin from the Greek name *Narkissos* (see **NARCISSUS**) + **-ISM**.

nar·cis·sis·tic /,närsə'sistik/ ▶ **adj.** having an excessive or erotic interest in oneself and one's physical appearance: *a narcissistic actress.* ■ relating to narcissism: *narcissistic personality disorder.*
– DERIVATIVES **nar·cis·sis·ti·cal·ly** /,närsə'sistik(ə)lē/ **adv.**

Nar·cis·sus /när'sisəs/ Greek Mythology a beautiful youth who rejected the nymph Echo and fell in love with his own reflection in a pool. He pined away and was changed into the flower that bears his name.

nar·cis·sus /när'sisəs/ ▶ **n.** (pl. **same**, **narcissi** /-'sisī, -sē/, or **narcissuses**) a bulbous Eurasian plant of a genus that includes the daffodil, esp. (in gardening) one with flowers that have white or pale outer petals and a shallow orange or yellow cup in the center. ● Genus *Narcissus*, family Liliaceae (or Amaryllidaceae): many species and varieties, in particular *N. poeticus*.
– ORIGIN via Latin from Greek *narkissos*, perhaps from *narkē* 'numbness,' with reference to its narcotic effects.

nar·co /'närkō/ ▶ **n.** (pl. **narcos**) informal short for **NARCOTIC**. ■ a dealer in drugs. ■ a narcotics officer.

narco- ▶ **comb. form** relating to a state of insensibility: *narcolepsy.* ■ relating to narcotic drugs or their use: *narcoterrorism.*
– ORIGIN from Greek *narkē* 'numbness.'

nar·co·lep·sy /'närkə,lepsē/ ▶ **n.** Medicine a condition characterized by an extreme tendency to fall asleep whenever in relaxing surroundings.
– DERIVATIVES **nar·co·lep·tic** /,närkə'leptik/ **adj. & n.**
– ORIGIN late 19th cent.: from Greek *narkē* 'numbness,' on the pattern of *epilepsy*.

nar·co·sis /när'kōsis/ ▶ **n.** Medicine a state of stupor, drowsiness, or unconsciousness produced by drugs. See also **NITROGEN NARCOSIS**.
– ORIGIN late 17th cent.: from Greek *narkōsis*, from *narkoun* 'make numb.'

nar·co·ter·ror·ism /,närkō'terə,rizəm/ ▶ **n.** terrorism associated with trade in illicit drugs.
– DERIVATIVES **nar·co·ter·ror·ist n.**
– ORIGIN 1980s: from **NARCO-** 'relating to illegal narcotics' + *terrorism* (see **TERRORIST**).

nar·cot·ic /när'kätik/ ▶ **n.** a drug or other substance affecting mood or behavior and sold for nonmedical purposes, esp. an illegal one. ■ Medicine a drug that relieves pain and induces drowsiness, stupor, or insensibility.
▶ **adj.** relating to or denoting narcotics or their effects or use: *the substance has a mild narcotic effect.*
– DERIVATIVES **nar·cot·i·cal·ly** /-tik(ə)lē/ **adv.**, **nar·co·tism** /'närkə,tizəm/ **n.**
– ORIGIN late Middle English: from Old French *narcotique*, via medieval Latin from Greek *narkōtikos*, from *narkoun* 'make numb.'

nar·co·tize /'närkə,tīz/ ▶ **v.** [with obj.] stupefy with or as if with a drug. ■ make (something) have a soporific or narcotic effect: *the essence of apple blossom narcotizes the air.*
– DERIVATIVES **nar·co·ti·za·tion** /,närkəti'zāsHən/ **n.**

nard /närd/ ▶ **n.** the Himalayan spikenard.
– ORIGIN late Old English, via Latin from Greek *nardos*; related to Sanskrit *nalada*, *narada*.

nar·es /'ne(ə)rēz/ ▶ **plural n.** (sing. **naris** /'ne(ə)ris/) Anatomy & Zoology the nostrils.
– DERIVATIVES **nar·i·al** /-ēəl/ **adj.**
– ORIGIN late 17th cent.: plural of Latin *naris* 'nostril, nose.'

nar·ghi·le /'närgəlē/ (also **nargileh**) ▶ **n.** an oriental tobacco pipe with a long tube that draws the smoke through water; a hookah.
– ORIGIN mid 18th cent.: from Persian *nārgīl* 'coconut, hookah,' from Sanskrit *nārikela* 'coconut.'

nar·is /'ne(ə)ris/ singular form of **NARES**.

nark /närk/ informal ▶ **n. 1** variant spelling of **NARC**.
2 Brit. a police informer.
3 Austral./NZ an annoying person or thing.
▶ **v.** [with obj.] Brit. annoy or exasperate: *I was narked at being pushed around.*
– PHRASES **nark it!** Brit. stop that!
– ORIGIN mid 19th cent.: from Romany *nāk* 'nose.'

Nar·ma·da /nər'mədə/ a river that rises in Madhya Pradesh, central India, and flows west for 778 miles (1,245 km) to the Gulf of Cambay. Hindus consider it a sacred river.

Nar·ra·gan·sett /,narə'gansit/ (also **Narraganset**) ▶ **n.** (pl. **same** or **Narragansetts**) **1** a member of an American Indian people originally of Rhode Island. They came into conflict with the New England colonists in the 17th century, and few now remain.
2 the Algonquian language of this people.
– ORIGIN the name in Narragansett, literally 'people of the promontory.'

Nar·ra·gan·sett Bay an inlet of the Atlantic Ocean in southeastern Rhode Island.

nar·rate /'nar,āt/ ▶ **v.** [with obj.] give a spoken or written account of: *the voyages, festivities, and intrigues are narrated with unflagging gusto | the tough-but-sensitive former bouncer narrates much of the story.* ■ provide a spoken commentary to accompany (a movie, broadcast, piece of music, etc.).
– DERIVATIVES **nar·rat·a·ble adj.**
– ORIGIN mid 17th cent.: from Latin *narrat-* 'related, told,' from the verb *narrare* (from *gnarus* 'knowing').

nar·ra·tion /na'rāsHən/ ▶ **n.** the action or process of narrating a story: *the style of narration in the novel.* ■ a commentary delivered to accompany a movie, broadcast, etc.: *Moore's narration is often sarcastic.*

nar·ra·tive /'narətiv/ ▶ **n.** a spoken or written account of connected events; a story: *the hero of his modest narrative.* ■ the narrated part or parts of a literary work, as distinct from dialogue. ■ the practice or art of narration: *traditions of oral narrative.*
▶ **adj.** in the form of or concerned with narration: *a narrative poem | narrative technique.*
– DERIVATIVES **nar·ra·tive·ly adv.**
– ORIGIN late Middle English (as an adjective): from French *narratif, -ive*, from late Latin *narrativus* 'telling a story,' from the verb *narrare* (see **NARRATE**).

nar·ra·tiv·i·ty /,narə'tivətē/ ▶ **n.** the quality or condition of presenting a narrative: *music has developed a narrativity that lends it the character of language.*
– ORIGIN 1970s: from French *narrativité*.

nar·ra·tiv·ize /'narəti,vīz/ ▶ **v.** [with obj.] present or interpret (something such as experience or theory) in the form of a story or narrative.

nar·ra·tol·o·gy /,narə'täləjē/ ▶ **n.** the branch of knowledge or literary criticism that deals with the structure and function of narrative and its themes, conventions, and symbols.
– DERIVATIVES **nar·ra·to·log·i·cal** /,narətl'äjikəl/ **adj.**, **nar·ra·tol·o·gist** /-jist/ **n.**

nar·ra·tor /'narātər/ ▶ **n.** a person who narrates something, esp. a character who recounts the events of a novel or narrative poem. ■ a person who delivers a commentary accompanying a movie, broadcast, piece of music, etc.
– DERIVATIVES **nar·ra·to·ri·al** /,narə'tôrēəl/ **adj.**

nar·row /'narō/ ▶ **adj.** (**narrower**, **narrowest**)
1 (esp. of something that is considerably longer or higher than it is wide) of small width: *he made his way down the narrow road.*
2 limited in extent, amount, or scope; restricted: *his ability to get good results within narrow constraints of money and manpower.* ■ (of a person's attitude or beliefs) limited in range and lacking willingness or ability to appreciate alternative views: *companies fail through their narrow view of what contributes to profit.* ■ precise or strict in meaning: *some of the narrower definitions of democracy.* ■ (of a phonetic transcription) showing fine details of accent.
■ Phonetics denoting a vowel pronounced with the root of the tongue drawn back so as to narrow the pharynx.
3 (esp. of a victory, defeat, or escape) with only a small margin; barely achieved.
▶ **v. 1** become or make less wide: [no obj.] *the road narrowed and crossed an old bridge* | [with obj.] *the embankment was built to narrow the river.* ■ almost close (one's eyes) so as to focus on something or someone, or to indicate anger, suspicion, or other emotion: [with obj.] *she narrowed her eyes at him suspiciously* | [no obj.] *Jake's eyes had narrowed to pinpoints.*
2 become or make more limited or restricted in extent or scope: [no obj.] *their trade surplus narrowed to $70 million in January* | [with obj.] *New England had narrowed Denver's lead from 13 points to 4.*
▶ **n.** (**narrows**) a narrow channel connecting two larger areas of water: *a basaltic fang rising from the narrows of the Upper Missouri.*
– PHRASES **narrow circumstances** poverty.
– PHRASAL VERBS **narrow something down** reduce the number of possibilities or options of something: *the company has narrowed down the candidates for the job to two.*
– DERIVATIVES **nar·row·ish adj.**, **nar·row·ness n.**

–ORIGIN Old English *nearu*, of Germanic origin; related to Dutch *naar* 'dismal, unpleasant' and German *Narbe* 'scar.' Early senses in English included 'constricted' and 'miserly.'

nar·row·band /'narō,band/ ▶ **adj.** of or involving signals over a narrow range of frequencies.

nar·row·boat /'narō,bōt/ ▶ **n.** Brit. a canal boat less than 7 feet (2.1 m) wide with a maximum length of 70 feet (21.3 m) and steered with a tiller rather than a wheel.

nar·row·cast /'narō,kast/ ▶ **v.** (past and past participle **narrowcast** or **narrowcasted**) [no obj.] transmit a television program, esp. by cable, or otherwise disseminate information, to a comparatively small audience defined by special interest or geographical location: *the channel is licensed to narrowcast only to nondomestic outlets* | (as noun **narrowcasting**) *one journal has avoided the narrowcasting that seems to enslave so many mainstream magazines.*
▶ **n.** transmission or dissemination in this way: *Colorado women's volleyball narrowcasts* | [as modifier] *narrowcast specialty channels.*
–DERIVATIVES **nar·row·cast·er** **n.**
–ORIGIN 1930s: back-formation from *narrowcasting*, on the pattern of *broadcasting*.

nar·row gauge ▶ **n.** a railroad gauge that is narrower than the standard gauge of 56.5 inches (143.5 cm).

nar·row·ly /'nerōlē/ ▶ **adv.** **1** by only a small margin; barely: *he narrowly defeated Anderson to win a 12th term in office.*
2 closely or carefully: *he was looking at her narrowly.*
3 in a limited or restricted way: *narrowly defined tasks.*

nar·row-mind·ed ▶ **adj.** not willing to listen to or tolerate other people's views; prejudiced.
–DERIVATIVES **nar·row-mind·ed·ly** **adv.**, **nar·row-mind·ed·ness** **n.**

nar·row mon·ey ▶ **n.** Economics money in forms that can be used as a medium of exchange, generally banknotes, coins, and certain balances held by banks.

Nar·rows /'narōz/ (**the Narrows**) a strait about 2 miles (3.2 km) long connecting upper and lower New York Bay, between Staten Island and Brooklyn.

nar·thex /'närTHeks/ ▶ **n.** an antechamber, porch, or distinct area at the western entrance of some early Christian churches, separated off by a railing and used by catechumens, penitents, etc. ■ an antechamber or large porch in a modern church.
–ORIGIN late 17th cent.: via Latin from Greek *narthēx*.

nar·whal /'närwəl/ ▶ **n.** a small Arctic whale, the male of which has a long forward-pointing spirally twisted tusk developed from one of its teeth. ● *Monodon monoceros*, family Monodontidae.
–ORIGIN mid 17th cent.: from Dutch *narwal*, Danish *narhval*, based on Old Norse *nár* 'corpse,' with reference to skin color.

nar·y /'ne(ə)rē/ ▶ **adj.** informal or dialect form of NOT: *nary a murmur or complaint.*
–ORIGIN mid 18th cent.: from the phrase *ne'er a.*

NASA /'nasə/ ▶ **abbr.** National Aeronautics and Space Administration.

na·sal /'nāzəl/ ▶ **adj.** **1** of, for, or relating to the nose: *the nasal passages* | *a nasal spray.*
2 (of a speech sound) pronounced by the voice resonating in the nose, e.g., *m, n, ng.* Compare with ORAL (sense 2 of the adjective). ■ (of the voice or speech) produced or characterized by resonating in the nose as well as the mouth.
▶ **n.** **1** a nasal speech sound.
2 historical a nosepiece on a helmet.
–DERIVATIVES **na·sal·i·ty** /nā'zalitē/ **n.**, **na·sal·ly** **adv.**
–ORIGIN Middle English (sense 2 of the noun): from medieval Latin *nasalis*, from Latin *nasus* 'nose.'

na·sal con·cha ▶ **n.** see CONCHA.

na·sal·ize /'nāzə,līz/ ▶ **v.** [with obj.] pronounce or utter (a speech sound) with the breath resonating in the nose: (as adj. **nasalized**) *a nasalized vowel.*
–DERIVATIVES **na·sal·i·za·tion** /,nāzəli'zāSHən/ **n.**

NASCAR /'nas,kär/ ▶ **abbr.** National Association for Stock Car Auto Racing.

NAS·CAR Dad (also **Nascar Dad**) ▶ **n.** informal a representative of a demographic category: a blue-collar, high school-educated father with relatively conservative values but without predictable political affiliation.
–ORIGIN early 21st cent.: from the popularity of stock car racing with white, working-class men.

nas·cent /'nāsənt, 'nasənt/ ▶ **adj.** (esp. of a process or organization) just coming into existence and beginning to display signs of future potential: *the nascent space industry.* ■ Chemistry (chiefly of hydrogen) freshly generated in a reactive form.
–DERIVATIVES **nas·cence** **n.**, **nas·cen·cy** **n.**
–ORIGIN early 17th cent.: from Latin *nascent-* 'being born,' from the verb *nasci.*

NASD ▶ **abbr.** National Association of Securities Dealers.

NASDAQ /'nazdak/ ▶ **abbr.** National Association of Securities Dealers Automated Quotations, a computerized system for trading in securities.

Nase·by, Bat·tle of /'nāzbē/ a major battle of the English Civil War that took place in 1645 near the village of Naseby in Northamptonshire. The Royalist army of Prince Rupert and King Charles I was decisively defeated by the New Model Army under General Thomas Fairfax (1612–71) and Oliver Cromwell.

Nash[1] /naSH/, Ogden (1902–71), US poet; full name *Frederic Ogden Nash.* His sophisticated light verse comprised puns, epigrams, and other verbal eccentricities and appeared in many collections from 1931.

Nash[2], John (1752–1835), English town planner and architect. He planned the layout of Regent's Park 1811–25 and Trafalgar Square 1826–*c.*1835, and designed the Marble Arch.

Nashe /naSH/, Thomas (1567–1601), English pamphleteer, prose writer, and playwright.

Nash e·qui·lib·ri·um ▶ **n.** (in economics and game theory) a stable state of a system involving the interaction of different participants, in which no participant can gain by a unilateral change of strategy if the strategies of the others remain unchanged.

na·shi /'näSHē/ (also **nashi pear**) ▶ **n.** another term for ASIAN PEAR.
–ORIGIN 1960s: from Japanese, literally 'pear.'

Na·shik /'näsik/ (also **Nasik**) a city in western India, in Maharashtra, on the Godavari River, northeast of Mumbai (Bombay); pop. 1,521,700 (est. 2009).

Nash·ua /'naSHōōə/ an industrial city on the Merrimack River in southern New Hampshire; pop. 86,576 (est. 2008).

Nash·ville /'naSH,vil, -vəl/ the capital of Tennessee, in the north central part of the state, on the Cumberland River; pop. 626,144 (est. 2008). It is noted for its music industry and for the Country Music Hall of Fame.

naso- ▶ **comb. form** relating to the nose: *nasogastric.*
–ORIGIN from Latin *nasus* 'nose.'

na·so·gas·tric /,nāzō'gastrik/ ▶ **adj.** reaching or supplying the stomach via the nose: *she had to be fed by a nasogastric tube.*

na·so·phar·ynx /,nāzō'fariNGks/ ▶ **n.** Anatomy the upper part of the pharynx, connecting with the nasal cavity above the soft palate.
–DERIVATIVES **na·so·pha·ryn·ge·al** /-fə'rinj(ē)əl, -,farin'jēəl/ **adj.**

Nass /näs, nas/ ▶ **n.** another name for NISHGA.
–ORIGIN from the name of a river in British Colombia, Canada.

Nas·sau[1] /'na,sô/ **1** a former duchy of western Germany from which the House of Orange arose.
2 a port on the island of New Providence, capital of the Bahamas; pop. 240,000 (est. 2007).

Nas·sau[2] ▶ **n.** Golf an eighteen-hole match in which the players bet on the first nine holes, the second nine holes, and the entire round.

Nas·sau Coun·ty /'nas,ô/ a county in central Long Island in New York, immediately east of Queens and home to many New York suburbs; pop. 1,351,625 (est. 2008).

Nas·ser /'nasər, 'nä-/, Gamal Abdel (1918–70), Egyptian colonel and statesman; prime minister 1954–56 and president 1956–70. He deposed King Farouk in 1952 and President Muhammad Neguib in 1954. His nationalization of the Suez Canal brought war with Britain, France, and Israel in 1956; he also waged two unsuccessful wars against Israel (1956 and 1967).

Nas·ser, Lake a lake in southeastern Egypt that was created in the 1960s by building two dams on the Nile River at Aswan.

Nast /nast/, Thomas (1840–1902), US political cartoonist; born in Germany. He was a staff artist at *Harper's Weekly* 1861–86 and creator of the Republican elephant and the Democratic donkey symbols, as well as of the US image of Santa Claus.

nas·tic /'nastik/ ▶ **adj.** Botany (of the movement of plant parts) caused by an external stimulus but unaffected in direction by it.
–ORIGIN early 20th cent.: from Greek *nastos* 'squeezed together' (from *nassein* 'to press') + -IC.

nas·ti·ness /'nastēnis/ ▶ **n.** the state or quality of being nasty: *the nastiness of the campaign.*

nas·tur·tium /nə'stərSHəm, na-/ ▶ **n.** a South American trailing plant with round leaves and bright orange, yellow, or red edible flowers that is widely grown as an ornamental. ● *Tropaeolum majus*, family Tropaeolaceae.
–ORIGIN Old English, from Latin, apparently from *naris* 'nose' + *torquere* 'to twist.'

nas·ty /'nastē/ ▶ **adj.** (**nastier**, **nastiest**) **1** highly unpleasant, esp. to the senses; physically nauseating: *plastic bags burn with a nasty, acrid smell.* ■ (of the weather) unpleasantly cold or wet: *a cold, nasty day.* ■ repugnant to the mind; morally bad: *her stories are very nasty, full of murder and violence.*
2 (of a person or animal) behaving in an unpleasant or spiteful way: *Harry was a nasty, foul-mouthed old devil* | *when she confronted him, he turned nasty.* ■ annoying or unwelcome: *life has a nasty habit of repeating itself.*
3 physically or mentally damaging or harmful: *a nasty, vicious-looking hatchet.*
▶ **n.** (pl. **nasties**) (often **nasties**) informal an unpleasant or harmful person or thing: *bacteria and other nasties.* ■ chiefly Brit. a horror video or movie.
–DERIVATIVES **nas·ti·ly** /-təlē/ **adv.**
–ORIGIN late Middle English: of unknown origin.

nat. ▶ **abbr.** ■ national. ■ nationalist. ■ native. ■ natural.

Na·tal /nə'täl/ **1** a province on the eastern coast of South Africa that was renamed KwaZulu-Natal in 1994.
2 a port on the Atlantic coast of northeastern Brazil; pop. 774,230 (2007).

na·tal[1] /'nātl/ ▶ **adj.** of or relating to the place or time of one's birth: *her natal home.*
–ORIGIN late Middle English: from Latin *natalis*, from *nat-* 'born,' from the verb *nasci.*

na·tal[2] ▶ **adj.** Anatomy of or relating to the buttocks: *the natal cleft.*
–ORIGIN late 19th cent.: from NATES + -AL.

na·tal·i·ty /nā'talitē, nə-/ ▶ **n.** the ratio of the number of births to the size of the population; birth rate: *in spite of falling natality, the population as a whole went up.*
–ORIGIN late 19th cent.: from French *natalité*, from *nat-* 'born,' from the verb *nasci.*

na·tant /'nātnt/ ▶ **adj.** formal, rare swimming or floating.
–ORIGIN mid 18th cent.: from Latin *natant-* 'swimming,' from the verb *natare.*

na·ta·tion /nā'tāSHən, na-/ ▶ **n.** technical or literary swimming.
–DERIVATIVES **na·ta·to·ri·al** /,nātə'tôrēəl, ,na-/ **adj.**, **na·ta·to·ry** /'nātə,tôrē, 'na-/ **adj.**
–ORIGIN mid 16th cent.: from Latin *natatio(n-)*, from *natare* 'to swim.'

na·ta·to·ri·um /,nātə'tôrēəm, ,na-/ ▶ **n.** a swimming pool, esp. one that is indoors.
–ORIGIN late 19th cent.: from late Latin, neuter (used as a noun) of *natatorius* 'relating to a swimmer,' from *natare* 'to swim.'

natch /naCH/ ▶ **adv.** informal term for NATURALLY.

Natch·ez /'naCHiz/ a historic port city on the Mississippi River in southwestern Mississippi; pop. 16,413 (est. 2008). The ***Natchez Trace***, which leads from here to Nashville in Tennessee, was a 19th-century route for riverboatmen returning north from trips to New Orleans.

NATE ▶ **abbr.** National Association of Teachers of English.

na·tes /'nā,tēz/ ▶ **plural n.** Anatomy the buttocks.
–ORIGIN late 17th cent.: Latin, plural of *natis* 'buttock, rump.'

nathe·less /'nāTHlis, 'na-/ (also **nathless**) ▶ **adv.** archaic nevertheless.
–ORIGIN Old English.

Na·tion /'nāSHən/, Carrie Amelia (Moore) (1846–1911), US temperance reformer. Her Prohibitionist activism was characterized by scenes of hatchet-wielding saloon smashing, primarily in Kansas.

na·tion /'nāSHən/ ▶ **n.** a large aggregate of people united by common descent, history, culture, or language, inhabiting a particular country or territory: *leading industrialized nations.* ■ a North American Indian people or confederation of peoples.
–DERIVATIVES **na·tion·hood** /-,hŏŏd/ **n.**
–ORIGIN Middle English: via Old French from Latin *natio(n-)*, from *nat-* 'born,' from the verb *nasci.*

na·tion·al /'naSHənl/ ▶ **adj.** of or relating to a nation; common to or characteristic of a whole nation: *this policy may have been in the national interest* | *a national newspaper.* ■ owned, controlled, or financially supported by the federal government: *plans for a national art library.*
▶ **n.** **1** a citizen of a particular country, typically entitled to hold that country's passport: *a German national* | *the new law on foreign nationals.*

2 (usu. **nationals**) a nationwide competition or tournament: *she finished 16th at the nationals that year.*
– DERIVATIVES **na·tion·al·ly** adv. [sentence adverb] *nationally, there has been a 2.5% drop in car crime.*
– ORIGIN late 16th cent.: from French, from Latin *natio(n-)* 'birth, race of people' (see NATION).

na·tion·al an·them ▶ n. see ANTHEM (sense 1).

Na·tion·al As·sem·bly ▶ n. an elected legislature in various countries. ■ historical the elected legislature in France during the first part of the French Revolution, 1789–91.

Na·tion·al As·so·ci·a·tion for the Ad·vance·ment of Col·ored Peo·ple (abbr.: **NAACP**) a US civil rights organization set up in 1909 to oppose racial segregation and discrimination by nonviolent means.

na·tion·al bank ▶ n. another term for CENTRAL BANK. ■ a commercial bank that is chartered under the federal government and is a member of the Federal Reserve System.

Na·tion·al Cap·i·tal Ter·ri·to·ry of Del·hi a territory in north central India containing the old city of Delhi and the capital New Delhi.

Na·tion·al Cit·y a city in southwestern California, south of San Diego, site of numerous naval facilities; pop. 58,680 (est. 2008).

na·tion·al con·ven·tion ▶ n. a convention of a major political party, esp. one that nominates a candidate for the presidency.

na·tion·al debt ▶ n. the total amount of money that a country's government has borrowed, by various means.

Na·tion·al Foot·ball League (abbr. **NFL**) ▶ n. the major professional football league in the US, consisting of the National and American football conferences and totaling thirty-one teams.

na·tion·al for·est ▶ n. a large expanse of forest that is owned, maintained, and preserved by the federal government.

Na·tion·al Guard ▶ n. **1** (in the US) the primary reserve military force, partly maintained by the states but also available for federal use. ■ the primary military force of some other countries. **2** an armed force existing in France at various times between 1789 and 1871, first commanded by the Marquis de Lafayette. ■ a member of this force.
– DERIVATIVES **Na·tion·al Guards·man** n.

na·tion·al in·come ▶ n. the total amount of money earned within a country.

na·tion·al·ism /ˈnasHənəˌlizəm/ ▶ n. patriotic feeling, principles, or efforts. ■ an extreme form of this, esp. marked by a feeling of superiority over other countries. ■ advocacy of political independence for a particular country.

na·tion·al·ist /ˈnasHənəlist/ ▶ n. a person who advocates political independence for a country: *a Scottish nationalist.* ■ a person with strong patriotic feelings, esp. one who believes in the superiority of their country over others.
▶ adj. of or relating to nationalists or nationalism: *a nationalist movement.*

na·tion·al·is·tic /ˌnasHənəˈlistik/ ▶ adj. having strong patriotic feelings, esp. a belief in the superiority of one's own country over others: *a nationalistic awareness in politics and literature.*
– DERIVATIVES **na·tion·al·is·ti·cal·ly** /ˌnasHənəˈlistik(ə)lē/ adv.

na·tion·al·i·ty /ˌnasHəˈnalitē/ ▶ n. (pl. **nationalities**) **1** the status of belonging to a particular nation: *they changed their nationality and became Lebanese.* ■ distinctive national or ethnic character: *the change of a name does not discard nationality.* **2** an ethnic group forming a part of one or more political nations: *all the main nationalities of Ethiopia.*

na·tion·al·ize /ˈnasHənəˌlīz/ ▶ v. [with obj.] **1** transfer (a major branch of industry or commerce) from private to state ownership or control. **2** make distinctively national; give a national character to: *in the 13th and 14th centuries church designs were further nationalized.* **3** (usu. as adj. **nationalized**) naturalize (a foreigner): *he is now a nationalized Frenchman.*
– DERIVATIVES **na·tion·al·i·za·tion** /ˌnasHənəliˈzāsHən/ n., **na·tion·al·iz·er** n.

Na·tion·al League ▶ n. one of the two major leagues in American professional baseball.

na·tion·al mon·u·ment ▶ n. a historic site or geographical area set aside by a national government and maintained for public use.

na·tion·al park ▶ n. a scenic or historically important area of countryside protected by the federal government for the enjoyment of the general public or the preservation of wildlife.

Na·tio·nal Ri·fle As·so·ci·a·tion (abbr. **NRA**) ▶ n. a national organization founded in 1871 that promotes the legal use of guns and gun safety in the US and defends a US citizen's constitutional right to own and bear arms.

Na·tion·al Road a historic highway that in the early 19th century led from Maryland through the Appalachian Mountains to St. Louis in Missouri. It was once the major route for western expansion.

na·tion·al sea·shore ▶ n. an expanse of sea coast protected and maintained by the federal government for the study of wildlife and for recreational use by the public.

Na·tion·al Se·cu·ri·ty A·gen·cy (abbr.: **NSA**) a secret body established in the US after World War II to gather intelligence, deal with coded communications from around the world, and safeguard US transmissions.

Na·tion·al Se·cu·ri·ty Coun·cil (abbr.: **NSC**) a body created in the US by Congress after World War II to advise the president (who chairs it) on issues relating to national security in domestic, foreign, and military policy.

na·tion·al serv·ice ▶ n. a period of compulsory service in the armed forces of some countries during peacetime. ■ a federal program that enables young people to pay back government loans through community work.

Na·tion·al So·cial·ism ▶ n. historical the political doctrine of the Nazi Party of Germany. See NAZI.
– DERIVATIVES **Na·tion·al So·cial·ist** n.

na·tion·al trea·sure ▶ n. an artifact, institution, or public figure regarded as being emblematic of a nation's cultural heritage or identity.

Na·tion·al Trust a trust for the preservation of places of historic interest or natural beauty in Britain.

Na·tion of Is·lam an exclusively black Islamic sect proposing a separate black nation, founded in Detroit *c.*1930. It was led from 1934 by **Elijah Muhammad** (1897–1975) and came to prominence under the influence of Malcolm X. Its current leader is Louis Farrakhan.

na·tion-state ▶ n. a sovereign state whose citizens or subjects are relatively homogeneous in factors such as language or common descent.

na·tion·wide /ˈnāsHənˈwīd/ ▶ adj. extending or reaching throughout the whole nation: *a nationwide hunt.*
▶ adv. throughout a whole nation: *it employs 6,000 people nationwide.*

na·tive /ˈnātiv/ ▶ n. a person born in a specified place or associated with a place by birth, whether subsequently resident there or not: *a **native of** Montreal | an eighteen-year-old Brooklyn native.* ■ a local inhabitant: *New York in the summer was too hot even for the natives.* ■ dated, often offensive one of the original inhabitants of a country, esp. a nonwhite as regarded by European colonists or travelers. ■ an animal or plant indigenous to a place: *the marigold **is a native of** southern Europe.*
▶ adj. **1** associated with the country, region, or circumstances of a person's birth: *he's a native New Yorker | her native country.* ■ of the indigenous inhabitants of a place: *a ceremonial native dance from Fiji.* **2** (of a plant or animal) of indigenous origin or growth: *these plants are **native to** North America | America's native black bear.* **3** (of a quality) belonging to a person's character from birth rather than acquired; innate: *some last vestige of native wit prompted Guy to say nothing | a jealousy and rage **native to** him.* ■ Computing designed for or built into a given system, esp. denoting the language associated with a given processor, computer, or compiler, and programs written in it. **4** (of a metal or other mineral) found in a pure or uncombined state.
– PHRASES **go native** humorous or derogatory (of a person living away from their own country or region) abandon one's own culture, customs, or way of life and adopt those of the country or region one is living in.
– DERIVATIVES **na·tive·ly** adv., **na·tive·ness** n.
– ORIGIN late Middle English: from Latin *nativus*, from *nat-* 'born,' from the verb *nasci*.

> **USAGE** In contexts such as *a **native** of Boston* or *New York in the summer was too hot even for the **natives***, the noun **native** is quite acceptable. But when it is used to mean 'a nonwhite original inhabitant of a country,' as in *this dance is a favorite with the **natives***, it is more problematic. This meaning has an old-fashioned feel and, because of its associations with a colonial European outlook, it may cause offense.

Na·tive A·mer·i·can ▶ n. a member of any of the indigenous peoples of the Americas.
▶ adj. of or relating to these peoples.

> **USAGE** Native American is now an accepted term in many contexts. The term **American Indian** is also used widely and acceptably. See also usage at AMERICAN INDIAN.

na·tive bear Austral. another name for KOALA.

na·tive speak·er ▶ n. a person who has spoken the language in question from earliest childhood: *native speakers of English.*

na·tiv·ism /ˈnātiˌvizəm/ ▶ n. **1** the policy of protecting the interests of native-born or established inhabitants against those of immigrants: *a deep vein of xenophobia and nativism.* **2** a return to or emphasis on traditional or local customs, in opposition to outside influences. **3** the theory or doctrine that concepts, mental capacities, and mental structures are innate rather than acquired or learned.
– DERIVATIVES **na·tiv·ist** n. & adj., **na·tiv·is·tic** /ˌnātiˈvistik/ adj.

na·tiv·i·ty /nəˈtivitē, nā-/ ▶ n. (pl. **nativities**) the occasion of a person's birth: *the place of my nativity.* ■ (usu. **the Nativity**) the birth of Jesus Christ. ■ a picture, carving, or model representing Jesus Christ's birth. ■ a nativity play. ■ the Christian festival of Christ's birth; Christmas. ■ Astrology, dated a horoscope relating to the time of birth; a birth chart.
– ORIGIN Middle English: from Old French *nativite*, from late Latin *nativitas*, from Latin *nativus* 'arisen by birth' (see NATIVE).

na·tiv·i·ty play ▶ n. a play, typically performed by children at Christmas, based on the events surrounding the birth of Jesus Christ.

na·tiv·i·ty scene ▶ n. another term for CRÈCHE (sense 1).

natl. ▶ abbr. national.

NATO /ˈnātō/ ▶ abbr. North Atlantic Treaty Organization.

na·tri·u·re·sis /ˌnātrəyo͝oˈrēsis/ ▶ n. Physiology excretion of sodium in the urine.
– DERIVATIVES **na·tri·u·ret·ic** /-ˈretik/ adj.
– ORIGIN 1950s: from NATRON + Greek *ourēsis* 'urination.'

na·tron /ˈnāträn, -trən/ ▶ n. a mineral salt found in dried lake beds, consisting of hydrated sodium carbonate.
– ORIGIN late 17th cent.: from French, from Spanish *natrón*, via Arabic from Greek *nitron* (see NITER).

Na·tron, Lake /ˈnātrən/ a lake in northern Tanzania, on the border with Kenya, containing large deposits of salt and soda.

nat·ter /ˈnatər/ informal ▶ v. [no obj.] talk casually, esp. about unimportant matters; chatter: *they **nattered** away for hours.*
▶ n. [in sing.] a casual and leisurely conversation: *I could do with a drink and a natter.*
– DERIVATIVES **nat·ter·er** n.
– ORIGIN early 19th cent. (in the dialect sense 'grumble, fret'): imitative.

nat·ter·jack /ˈnatərˌjak/ (also **natterjack toad**) ▶ n. a small European toad that has a bright yellow stripe down its back and runs in short bursts. ● *Bufo calamita*, family Bufonidae.
– ORIGIN mid 18th cent.: perhaps from NATTER (because of its loud croak) + JACK[1].

nat·ty[1] /ˈnatē/ ▶ adj. (**nattier, nattiest**) informal (esp. of a person or an article of clothing) smart and fashionable: *a natty blue blazer and designer jeans.*
– DERIVATIVES **nat·ti·ly** /-təlē/ adv., **nat·ti·ness** n.
– ORIGIN late 18th cent. (originally slang): perhaps related to NEAT[1].

nat·ty[2] ▶ adj. [attrib.] (among Rastafarians) denoting hair that is unstraightened, uncombed, or matted, as in dreadlocks.
– ORIGIN variant of KNOTTY.

Na·tu·fi·an /nəˈto͞ofēən/ ▶ adj. Archaeology of, relating to, or denoting a late Mesolithic culture of the Middle East, dated to about 12,500–10,000 years ago. It provides evidence for the first settled villages. ■ (as noun **the Natufian**) the Natufian culture or period.
– ORIGIN 1930s: from Wadi *an-Natuf*, the type site (a cave northwest of Jerusalem), + -IAN.

nat·u·ral /ˈnacHərəl/ ▶ adj. **1** existing in or caused by nature; not made or caused by humankind: *carrots contain a natural antiseptic that fights bacteria | natural disasters such as earthquakes.* ■ (of fabric) having a color characteristic of the unbleached and undyed state; off-white.

PRONUNCIATION KEY ə *ago, up*; ər *over, fur*; a *hat*; ā *ate*; ä *car*; e *let*; ē *see*; i *fit*; ī *by*; NG *sing*; ō *go*; ô *law, for*; oi *toy*; o͝o *good*; o͞o *goo*; ou *out*; TH *thin*; T͟H *then*; ZH *vision*

2 of or in agreement with the character or makeup of, or circumstances surrounding, someone or something: *sharks have no natural enemies.* ■ [attrib.] (of a person) born with a particular skill, quality, or ability: *he was a natural entertainer.* ■ (of a skill, quality, or ability) coming instinctively to a person; innate: *writing appears to demand muscular movements that are not **natural to** children.* ■ (of a person or their behavior) relaxed and unaffected; spontaneous: *he replied with too much nonchalance to sound natural.* ■ occurring as a matter of course and without debate; inevitable: *Ken was a natural choice for coach.* ■ [attrib.] (of law or justice) based on innate moral sense; instinctively felt to be right and fair. See also NATURAL LAW. ■ Bridge (of a bid) straightforwardly reflecting one's holding of cards. Often contrasted with CONVENTIONAL or ARTIFICIAL.
3 [attrib.] (of a parent or child) related by blood: *such adopted children always knew who their natural parents were.* ■ chiefly archaic illegitimate: *the Baron left a natural son by his mistress.*
4 Music (of a note) not sharped or flatted: [postpositive, in combination] *the bassoon plays G-natural instead of A-flat.* ■ (of a brass instrument) having no valves and able to play only the notes of the harmonic series above a fundamental note. ■ of or relating to the notes and intervals of the harmonic series.
5 Christian Theology relating to earthly or unredeemed human or physical nature as distinct from the spiritual or supernatural realm.
▶ **n. 1** a person regarded as having an innate gift or talent for a particular task or activity: *she was **a natural for** the sort of television work required of her.* ■ a thing that is particularly suited for something: *perky musical accompaniment would seem **a natural for** this series.*
2 Music a sign (♮) denoting a natural note when a previous sign or the key signature would otherwise demand a sharp or a flat. ■ a natural note. ■ any of the longer keys on a keyboard instrument that are normally white.
3 a creamy beige color.
4 a hand of cards, throw of dice, or other result that wins immediately, in particular: ■ a hand of two cards making 21 in the first deal in blackjack and similar games. ■ a first throw of 7 or 11 at craps.
5 Fishing an insect or other small creature used as bait, rather than an artificial imitation.
6 archaic a person born with a learning disability.
▶ **adv.** informal or dialect naturally: *keep walking—just act natural.*
–ORIGIN Middle English (in the sense 'having a certain status by birth'): from Old French, from Latin *naturalis*, from *natura* 'birth, nature, quality' (see NATURE).

n

nat·u·ral-born ▶ **adj.** having a specified innate characteristic or ability: *Glen was a natural-born sailor.* ■ archaic having a position by birth.

nat·u·ral child·birth ▶ **n.** childbirth with minimal medical or technological intervention, usually involving special breathing and relaxation techniques.

nat·u·ral clas·si·fi·ca·tion ▶ **n.** a scientific classification according to features that are held to be objectively significant, rather than being selected for convenience.

nat·u·ral fam·i·ly plan·ning ▶ **n.** another term for RHYTHM METHOD.

nat·u·ral food ▶ **n.** food that has undergone a minimum of processing or treatment with preservatives.

nat·u·ral fre·quen·cy ▶ **n.** Physics the frequency at which a system oscillates when not subjected to a continuous or repeated external force.

nat·u·ral gas ▶ **n.** flammable gas, consisting largely of methane and other hydrocarbons, occurring naturally underground (often in association with petroleum) and used as fuel.

nat·u·ral his·to·ry ▶ **n. 1** the scientific study of animals or plants, esp. as concerned with observation rather than experiment, and presented in popular rather than academic form. ■ the study of the whole natural world, including mineralogy and paleontology.
2 Medicine the usual course of development of a disease or condition, esp. in the absence of treatment: *the natural history of cancerous tumors.*
–DERIVATIVES **nat·u·ral his·to·ri·an** n.

nat·u·ral·ism /ˈnaCHərəˌlizəm/ ▶ **n. 1** (in art and literature) a style and theory of representation based on the accurate depiction of detail.

> The name "Naturalism" was given to a 19th-century artistic and literary movement, influenced by contemporary ideas of science and society, that rejected the idealization of experience and adopted an objective and often uncompromisingly realistic approach to art. Notable figures include the novelist Zola and the painter Théodore Rousseau.

2 a philosophical viewpoint according to which everything arises from natural properties and causes, and supernatural or spiritual explanations are excluded or discounted. [translating French *naturalisme*.] ■ (in moral philosophy) the theory that ethical statements can be derived from nonethical ones. ■ another term for NATURAL RELIGION.

nat·u·ral·ist /ˈnaCHərəlist/ ▶ **n. 1** an expert in or student of natural history.
2 a person who practices naturalism in art or literature. ■ a person who adopts philosophical naturalism.
▶ **adj.** another term for NATURALISTIC.

nat·u·ral·is·tic /ˌnaCHərəˈlistik/ ▶ **adj. 1** derived from real life or nature, or imitating it very closely: *verbatim records of children's speech in naturalistic settings.*
2 based on the theory of naturalism in art or literature: *naturalistic paintings of the city.* ■ of or according to the philosophy of naturalism: *phenomena once considered supernatural have yielded to naturalistic explanation.*
–DERIVATIVES **nat·u·ral·is·ti·cal·ly** adv.

nat·u·ral·ize /ˈnaCHərəˌlīz/ ▶ **v.** [with obj.] **1** (often **be/become naturalized**) admit (a foreigner) to the citizenship of a country: *he was born in a foreign country and had never been naturalized* | (as adj. **naturalized**) *a naturalized U.S. citizen born in Germany.* ■ [no obj.] (of a foreigner) be admitted to the citizenship of a country: *the opportunity to naturalize as American.* ■ alter (an adopted foreign word) so that it conforms more closely to the phonology or orthography of the adopting language: *the stoccafisso of Liguria was naturalized in Nice as stocofícada.*
2 (usu. as adj. **naturalized**) Biology establish (a plant or animal) so that it lives wild in a region where it is not indigenous: *native and naturalized species* | *black mustard has become naturalized in America.* ■ (with reference to a cultivated plant) establish or become established in a natural situation: [with obj.] *this species of crocus **naturalizes itself** very easily.*
3 regard as or cause to appear natural: *although women do more child care than men, feminists should beware of naturalizing that fact.* ■ explain (a phenomenon) in a naturalistic way.
–DERIVATIVES **nat·u·ral·i·za·tion** /ˌnaCHərələˈzāSHən/ n.
–ORIGIN mid 16th cent.: from French *naturaliser*, from Old French *natural* (see NATURAL).

nat·u·ral kill·er cell ▶ **n.** Medicine a lymphocyte able to bind to certain tumor cells and virus-infected cells without the stimulation of antigens, and kill them by the insertion of granules containing perforin.

nat·u·ral lan·guage ▶ **n.** a language that has developed naturally in use (as contrasted with an artificial language or computer code).

nat·u·ral law ▶ **n. 1** a body of unchanging moral principles regarded as a basis for all human conduct.
2 an observable law relating to natural phenomena: *the natural laws of perspective.* ■ such laws collectively.

nat·u·ral life ▶ **n.** the expected span of a person's life or a thing's existence under normal circumstances: *a man sentenced to spend the rest of his natural life in prison.*

nat·u·ral log·a·rithm (abbr.: **ln** or **log$_e$**) ▶ **n.** Mathematics a logarithm to the base *e* (2.71828...).

nat·u·ral·ly /ˈnaCHərəlē/ ▶ **adv. 1** in a natural manner, in particular: ■ in a normal manner; without distortion or exaggeration: *act naturally.* ■ as a natural result: *one leads naturally into the other.* ■ without special help or intervention: *naturally curly hair.*
2 [sentence adverb] as may be expected; of course: *naturally, I hoped for the best.*

nat·u·ral mag·ic ▶ **n.** (in the Middle Ages) magic practiced for beneficial purposes, involving the making of images, healing, and the use of herbs.

nat·u·ral·ness /ˈnaCHərəlnis/ ▶ **n.** the quality or state of being natural.

nat·u·ral num·bers ▶ **plural n.** the positive integers (whole numbers) 1, 2, 3, etc., and sometimes zero as well.

nat·u·ral phi·los·o·phy ▶ **n.** archaic natural science, esp. physical science.
–DERIVATIVES **nat·u·ral phi·los·o·pher** n.

nat·u·ral re·li·gion ▶ **n.** religion, esp. deism, based on reason rather than divine revelation.

nat·u·ral re·sources ▶ **plural n.** materials or substances such as minerals, forests, water, and fertile land that occur in nature and can be used for economic gain.

nat·u·ral sci·ence ▶ **n.** (usu. **natural sciences**) a branch of science that deals with the physical world, e.g., physics, chemistry, geology, and biology. ■ the branch of knowledge that deals with the study of the physical world.
–DERIVATIVES **nat·u·ral sci·en·tist** n.

nat·u·ral se·lec·tion ▶ **n.** Biology the process whereby organisms better adapted to their environment tend to survive and produce more offspring. The theory of its action was first fully expounded by Charles Darwin and is now believed to be the main process that brings about evolution. Compare with SURVIVAL OF THE FITTEST (see SURVIVAL).

nat·u·ral the·ol·o·gy ▶ **n.** theology or knowledge of God based on observed facts and experience apart from divine revelation.

nat·u·ral vir·tue ▶ **n.** any of the traditional chief moral virtues, esp. the cardinal virtues.

na·ture /ˈnāCHər/ ▶ **n. 1** the phenomena of the physical world collectively, including plants, animals, the landscape, and other features and products of the earth, as opposed to humans or human creations: *the breathtaking beauty of nature.* ■ the physical force regarded as causing and regulating these phenomena: *it is impossible to change the laws of nature.* See also MOTHER NATURE.
2 [in sing.] the basic or inherent features of something, esp. when seen as characteristic of it: *helping them to realize the nature of their problems* | *there are a lot of other documents **of that nature**.* ■ the innate or essential qualities or character of a person or animal: *it's not in her nature to listen to advice* | *I'm not violent **by nature**.* See also HUMAN NATURE. ■ inborn or hereditary characteristics as an influence on or determinant of personality. Often contrasted with NURTURE. ■ [with adj.] archaic a person of a specified character: *Emerson was so much more luminous a nature.*
–PHRASES **against nature** unnatural or immoral. **someone's better nature** the good side of a person's character; their capacity for tolerance, generosity, or sympathy: *Charlotte planned to appeal to his better nature.* **call of nature** used euphemistically to refer to a need to urinate or defecate. **from nature** (in art) using natural scenes or objects as models: *I wanted to paint landscape directly from nature.* **get** (or **go**) **back to nature** return to the type of life (regarded as being more in tune with nature) that existed before the development of complex industrial societies. **in the nature of** similar in type to or having the characteristics of: *the promise was in the nature of a check that bounced.* **in the nature of things 1** inevitable: *it is in the nature of things that the majority of music prizes get set up for performers rather than composers.* **2** inevitably: *in the nature of things, old people spend much more time indoors.* **in a state of nature 1** in an uncivilized or uncultivated state. **2** totally naked. **3** Christian Theology in a morally unregenerate condition, unredeemed by divine grace. **the nature of the beast** informal the inherent or essential quality or character of something, which cannot be changed.
–ORIGIN Middle English (denoting the physical power of a person): from Old French, from Latin *natura* 'birth, nature, quality,' from *nat-* 'born,' from the verb *nasci*.

na·tured /ˈnāCHərd/ ▶ **adj.** [in combination] having a nature or disposition of a specified kind: *a good-natured man.*

na·ture print·ing ▶ **n.** a method of producing a print of a natural object (such as a leaf) or a textile (such as lace) by making an impression of it directly onto a soft metal printing plate under great pressure and then taking an inked impression on paper.

na·ture re·serve (also **nature preserve**) ▶ **n.** a tract of land managed so as to preserve its flora, fauna, and physical features.

na·ture stud·y ▶ **n.** the practical study of plants, animals, and natural phenomena, esp. as a school subject.

na·ture trail ▶ **n.** a path through a forest or countryside designed to draw attention to natural features.

na·tur·ism /ˈnāCHəˌrizəm/ ▶ **n. 1** the practice of wearing no clothes in a vacation camp or for other leisure activities; nudism.
2 the worship of nature or natural objects.

na·tur·ist /ˈnāCHəˌrist/ ▶ **n. 1** a person who goes naked in designated areas; a nudist.
2 a person who worships nature or natural objects.

na·tur·op·a·thy /ˌnāCHəˈräpəTHē, ˌna-/ ▶ **n.** a system of alternative medicine based on the theory that diseases can be successfully treated or prevented without the use of drugs, by techniques such as control of diet, exercise, and massage.

– DERIVATIVES **na·tur·o·path** /ˈnāCHərə,paTH, ˈna-/ **n.**, **na·tur·o·path·ic** /ˌnāCHərəˈpaTHik, ˌna-/ **adj.**

Nau·cal·pan de Jua·rez /nouˈkälpän dā ˈhwäres/ an industrial city in central Mexico, northwest of Mexico City; pop. 763,351 (2005).

Nau·ga·hyde /ˈnôgə,hīd/ ▸ **n.** trademark an artificial material designed to resemble leather, made from fabric coated with rubber or vinyl resin.
– ORIGIN mid 20th cent.: from *Nauga(tuck)*, the name of a town in Connecticut, where rubber is manufactured, + *-hyde* (alteration of **HIDE²**).

naught /nôt/ ▸ **n.** the digit 0; zero.
▸ **pron.** archaic nothing: *he's naught but a worthless fool.*
– PHRASES **bring to naught** archaic ruin; foil. **come to naught** be ruined or foiled. **set at naught** archaic disregard; despise.
– ORIGIN Old English *nāwiht, -wuht*, from *nā* 'no' + *wiht* 'thing' (see **WIGHT**).

naugh·ty /ˈnôtē/ ▸ **adj.** (**naughtier**, **naughtiest**)
1 (esp. of children) disobedient; badly behaved: *you've been a really naughty boy.*
2 informal mildly rude or indecent, typically because related to sex: *naughty drawings | naughty goings-on.*
3 archaic wicked.
– DERIVATIVES **naugh·ti·ly** /-təlē/ **adv.**, **naugh·ti·ness n.**
– ORIGIN late Middle English: from **NAUGHT** + **-Y¹**. The earliest recorded sense was 'possessing nothing'; the sense 'wicked' also dates from late Middle English, and gave rise to the current senses.

naugh·ty bits ▸ **plural n.** Brit. informal, humorous the parts of a person's body connected with sexual activity or attraction, esp. the genitals.

nau·pli·us /ˈnôplēəs/ ▸ **n.** (pl. **nauplii** /-plē,ī/) Zoology the first larval stage of many crustaceans, having an unsegmented body and a single eye.
– ORIGIN mid 19th cent.: from Latin, denoting a kind of shellfish, or from the Greek name *Nauplios*, the son of Poseidon.

Na·u·ru /näˈo͞oro͞o/ an island country in the southwestern Pacific Ocean, near the equator; pop. 14,000 (est. 2009); no official capital but government is in Yaren District; official languages, Nauruan (an Austronesian language) and English.

> Since 1968 it has been an independent republic with a limited form of membership of the Commonwealth of Nations. The world's smallest independent republic, Nauru joined the United Nations in 1999. It has the world's richest deposits of phosphates.

– DERIVATIVES **Na·u·ru·an** /-ro͞owən/ **adj. & n.**

nau·se·a /ˈnôzēə, -ZHə/ ▸ **n.** a feeling of sickness with an inclination to vomit. ■ loathing; revulsion: *intended to induce a feeling of nostalgia, it only induces in me a feeling of nausea.*
– ORIGIN late Middle English: via Latin from Greek *nausia*, from *naus* 'ship.'

nau·se·ate /ˈnôzē,āt, - ZHē,āt/ ▸ **v.** [with obj.] make (someone) feel sick; affect with nausea: *the thought of food nauseated her.* ■ fill (someone) with revulsion; disgust: *I was nauseated by the vicious comment.*
– ORIGIN mid 17th cent.: from Latin *nauseat-* 'made to feel sick,' from the verb *nauseare*, from *nausea* (see **NAUSEA**).

> **USAGE** A distinction has traditionally been drawn between **nauseated**, meaning 'affected with nausea,' and **nauseous**, meaning 'causing nausea.' Today, however, the use of **nauseous** to mean 'affected with nausea' is so common that it is generally considered to be standard.

nau·se·at·ing /ˈnôzē,āting/ ▸ **adj.** causing or liable to cause a feeling of nausea or disgust; disgusting: *the stench became nauseating | some nauseating, sentimental ditty.*
– DERIVATIVES **nau·se·at·ing·ly adv.**

nau·seous /ˈnôSHəs, -ZHəs, -ēəs/ ▸ **adj. 1** affected with nausea; inclined to vomit: *a rancid, cloying odor that made him nauseous.*
2 causing nausea; offensive to the taste or smell: *the smell was nauseous.* ■ disgusting, repellent, or offensive: *this nauseous account of a court case.*
– DERIVATIVES **nau·seous·ly adv.**, **nau·seous·ness n.**
– ORIGIN early 17th cent.: from Latin *nauseosus* (from *nausea* 'seasickness').

> **USAGE** See usage at **NAUSEATE**.

naut. ▸ **abbr.** nautical.

nautch /nôCH/ ▸ **n.** (in South Asia) a traditional dance performed by professional dancing girls.
– ORIGIN from Hindi *nāc*, from Prakrit *nachcha*, from Sanskrit *nṛtya* 'dancing.'

nau·ti·cal /ˈnôtikəl/ ▸ **adj.** of or concerning sailors or navigation; maritime: *nautical charts.*
– DERIVATIVES **nau·ti·cal·ly** /-ik(ə)lē/ **adv.**
– ORIGIN mid 16th cent.: from French *nautique*, or via Latin from Greek *nautikos*, from *nautēs* 'sailor,' from *naus* 'ship.'

nau·ti·cal al·ma·nac ▸ **n.** a yearbook containing astronomical and sometimes also tidal and other information for navigators.

nau·ti·cal mile ▸ **n.** a unit used in measuring distances at sea, equal to approximately 2,025 yards (1,852 m). Compare with **SEA MILE**.

nau·ti·loid /ˈnôtl,oid/ ▸ **n.** Zoology a mollusk of a group of mainly extinct marine mollusks that includes the pearly nautilus. ● Subclass Nautiloidea, class Cephalopoda: *Nautilus* is the only surviving genus.
– ORIGIN mid 19th cent.: from the modern Latin genus name *Nautilus* (from Greek *nautilos* 'sailor') + **-OID**.

Nau·ti·lus /ˈnôtl-əs/ the first nuclear-powered submarine, launched in 1954. This US Navy vessel made a historic journey (August 1–5, 1958) under the ice of the North Pole. ■ trademark an exercise machine that matches resistance with output of force.
– ORIGIN a name previously given to Robert Fulton's "diving boat" (1800), also to the fictitious submarine in Jules Verne's *Twenty Thousand Leagues under the Sea.*

nau·ti·lus /ˈnôtl-əs/ ▸ **n.** (pl. **nautiluses** or **nautili** /ˈnôtl-ī/) **1** a cephalopod mollusk with a light external spiral shell and numerous short tentacles around the mouth. Nautiluses swim with the buoyant gas-filled shell upright and descend to greater depths during the day. ● Genus *Nautilus*, the only surviving genus of the subclass Nautiloidea: several species, in particular the common **chambered nautilus** (*Nautilus pompilius*) of the Indo-Pacific, with a shell that is white with brownish bands on the outside and lined with mother-of-pearl on the inside.
2 (also **paper nautilus**) another term for **ARGONAUT**.
– ORIGIN modern Latin, from Latin, from Greek *nautilos*, literally 'sailor.'

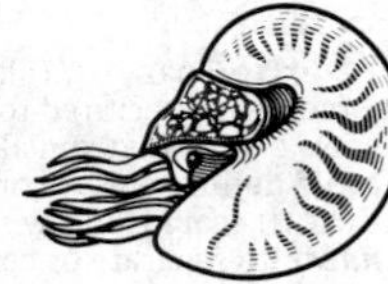

chambered nautilus

NAV ▸ **abbr.** net asset value.

nav /nav/ ▸ **n.** informal short for **NAVIGATION**. ■ short for **NAVIGATOR**.

nav·aid /ˈnav,ād/ ▸ **n.** a navigational device in an aircraft, ship, or other vehicle.
– ORIGIN 1950s: from *navigational aid*.

Nav·a·jo /ˈnavə,hō, ˈnä-/ (also **Navaho**) ▸ **n.** (pl. **same** or **Navajos**) **1** a member of an American Indian people of New Mexico and Arizona.
2 the Athabaskan language of this people.
▸ **adj.** of or relating to this people or their language.
– ORIGIN from Spanish (*Apaches de*) *Navajó* '(Apaches from) Navajo,' from Tewa *navahu:* 'fields adjoining an arroyo.'

na·val /ˈnāvəl/ ▸ **adj.** of, in, or relating to a navy or navies: *a naval officer | naval operations.*
– ORIGIN late Middle English: from Latin *navalis*, from *navis* 'ship.'

na·val a·cad·e·my ▸ **n.** a college where naval officers are trained.

na·val ar·chi·tec·ture ▸ **n.** the designing of ships.
– DERIVATIVES **na·val ar·chi·tect n.**

na·val stores ▸ **plural n.** articles or materials used in shipping.

Na·va·ra·tri /ˌnəvəˈrätrē/ (also **Navaratra** /-trə/) ▸ **n.** a Hindu autumn festival extending over nine nights. It is associated with many local observances, esp. the Bengali festival of Durga.
– ORIGIN Sanskrit, literally 'nine nights.'

na·va·rin /ˈnavərin/ ▸ **n.** a stew of lamb or mutton with vegetables.
– ORIGIN French.

Nav·a·ri·no, Bat·tle of /ˌnavəˈrēnō/ a decisive naval battle in the Greek struggle for independence from the Ottoman Empire, fought in 1827 in the Bay of Navarino off Pylos in Peloponnesus. Britain, Russia, and France sent a combined fleet that destroyed the Egyptian and Turkish fleet.

Na·varre /nəˈvär/ an autonomous region of northern Spain, on the border with France; capital, Pamplona. It represents the southern part of the former kingdom of Navarre. Spanish name **Navarra**.

nave¹ /nāv/ ▸ **n.** the central part of a church building, intended to accommodate most of the congregation. In traditional Western churches it is rectangular, separated from the chancel by a step or rail, and from adjacent aisles by pillars.
– ORIGIN late 17th cent.: from Latin *navis* 'ship.'

nave² ▸ **n.** the hub of a wheel.
– ORIGIN Old English *nafu, nafa*, of Germanic origin; related to Dutch *naaf* and German *Nabe*, from an Indo-European root shared by Sanskrit *nābhis* 'nave, navel.' Compare with **NAVEL**.

na·vel /ˈnāvəl/ ▸ **n.** a rounded, knotty depression in the center of a person's belly caused by the detachment of the umbilical cord after birth; the umbilicus. ■ the central point of a place: *the Incas saw Cuzco as the navel of the world.*
– PHRASES **contemplate one's navel** spend time complacently considering oneself or one's own interests; concentrate on one issue at the expense of a wider view.
– ORIGIN Old English *nafela*, of Germanic origin; related to Dutch *navel* and German *Nabel*, from an Indo-European root shared by Latin *umbo* 'boss of a shield,' *umbilicus* 'navel,' and Greek *omphalos* 'boss, navel.' Compare with **NAVE²**.

na·vel-gaz·ing ▸ **n.** complacent self-absorption; concentration on a single issue at the expense of a wider view.

na·vel or·ange ▸ **n.** a large, seedless orange that has a navellike depression at the top and contains a small secondary fruit underneath it.

na·vel·wort /ˈnāvəl,wərt, -,wôrt/ ▸ **n.** a low plant of the borage family that resembles the forget-me-not and is cultivated for ground cover and rock gardens. ● Genus *Omphalodes*, family Boraginaceae: several species, including *O. cappadocica*, widely introduced from Turkey.

na·vic·u·lar /nəˈvikyələr/ ▸ **adj.** chiefly archaic boat-shaped.
▸ **n. 1** (also **navicular bone**) a boat-shaped bone in the ankle or wrist, esp. that in the ankle between the talus and the cuneiform bones.
2 (also **navicular disease** or **navicular syndrome**) a chronic disorder of the navicular bone in horses, causing lameness in the front feet.
– ORIGIN late Middle English: from French *naviculaire* or late Latin *navicularis*, from Latin *navicula* 'little ship,' diminutive of *navis*.

nav·i·ga·ble /ˈnavigəbəl/ ▸ **adj.** (of a waterway or sea) able to be sailed on by ships or boats. ■ (of a track or road) suitable for transportation; passable: *those minor roads would be navigable in emergencies.* ■ (esp. of a website) easy to get around in; maneuverable: *a navigable Web browser.*
– DERIVATIVES **nav·i·ga·bil·i·ty** /ˌnavəgəˈbilitē/ **n.**
– ORIGIN early 16th cent.: from French *navigable* or Latin *navigabilis*, from the verb *navigare* 'to sail' (see **NAVIGATE**).

nav·i·gate /ˈnavi,gāt/ ▸ **v. 1** [no obj.] plan and direct the route or course of a ship, aircraft, or other form of transportation, esp. by using instruments or maps: *they navigated by the stars.* ■ [no obj., with adverbial of direction] travel on a desired course after planning a route: *he taught them how to navigate across the oceans.* ■ (of an animal or bird) find its way, esp. over a long distance: *whales use their own inbuilt sonar system to navigate.* ■ (of a passenger in a vehicle) assist the driver by reading the map and planning a route: *we'll go in my car—you can navigate.* ■ (of a ship or boat) sail; proceed: [with adverbial of direction] *we sailed out surrounded by loose ice while navigating around larger grounded icebergs.*
2 [with obj.] sail or travel over (a stretch of water or terrain), esp. carefully or with difficulty: *ships had been lost while navigating the narrows | the drivers skillfully navigated a twisting and muddy course.* ■ guide (a vessel or vehicle) over a specified route or terrain: *she navigated the car safely through the traffic.* ■ [no obj.] Computing move from one accessible page, section, or view of a file or website to another: *the new layout makes it easier to navigate through their atlas of world maps.*
– ORIGIN late 16th cent. (in the sense 'travel in a ship'): from Latin *navigat-* 'sailed,' from the verb *navigare*, from *navis* 'ship' + *agere* 'drive.'

nav·i·ga·tion /ˌnaviˈgāSHən/ ▸ **n. 1** the process or activity of accurately ascertaining one's position and planning and following a route.
2 the passage of ships: *bridges to span rivers without hindering navigation.*
– DERIVATIVES **nav·i·ga·tion·al** /-nəl/ **adj.**
– ORIGIN early 16th cent. (denoting the action of traveling on water): from French, or from Latin *navigatio(n-)*, from the verb *navigare* (see **NAVIGATE**).

nav·i·ga·tion lights ▸ **plural n.** a set of lights shown by a ship or aircraft at night to indicate its position and orientation, esp. with respect to other vessels or aircraft.

nav·i·ga·tor /ˈnaviˌgātər/ ▶ **n.** a person who directs the route or course of a ship, aircraft, or other form of transportation, esp. by using instruments and maps. ■ an instrument or device that assists in directing the course of a vessel or aircraft. ■ Computing a browser program for retrieving data on the World Wide Web or another information system. ■ historical a person who explores by sea.

Nav·ra·ti·lo·va /ˌnavrətəˈlōvə, ˌnäv-/, Martina (1956–), US tennis player, born in Czechoslovakia. During 1978–90, she won the women's singles title at nine Wimbledon, three Australian Open, two French Open, and four US Open tournaments.

NAVSTAR ▶ **abbr.** Navigation Satellite Timing and Ranging.

nav·vy /ˈnavē/ ▶ **n.** (pl. **navvies**) Brit. dated a laborer employed in the excavation and construction of a road, railroad, or canal.
– ORIGIN early 19th cent.: abbreviation of NAVIGATOR.

na·vy /ˈnāvē/ ▶ **n.** (pl. **navies**) **1** (often **the navy** or **the Navy**) the branch of a nation's armed services that conducts military operations at sea. ■ the ships of a navy: *a 600-ship navy* | *we built their navy.* ■ literary a fleet of ships.
2 (also **navy blue**) a dark blue color: [as modifier] *a navy-blue suit.*
– ORIGIN late Middle English (in the sense 'ships collectively, fleet'): from Old French *navie* 'ship, fleet,' from popular Latin *navia* 'ship,' from Latin *navis* 'ship.'

na·vy bean ▶ **n.** a small white type of kidney bean.

Na·vy Cross ▶ **n.** a decoration bestowed by the US Navy upon individuals who have shown exceptional heroism, esp. in enemy combat.

na·vy yard ▶ **n.** a shipyard for the construction, repair, and equipping of naval vessels.

naw /nô/ ▶ **exclam.** informal variant spelling of NO, used to answer a question: *"Want some toast?" "Naw."*

na·wab /nəˈwäb/ ▶ **n.** Indian historical a native governor during the time of the Mogul empire: [as title] *Nawab Haider Beg.* ■ a Muslim nobleman or person of high status.
– ORIGIN from Urdu *nawwāb*, variant of Arabic *nuwwāb*, plural (used as singular) of *nā'ib* 'deputy'; compare with NABOB.

Naw·lins /ˈnôlənz/ (also **N'awlins**) informal New Orleans.

Nax·al·ite /ˈnaksəlīt/ ▶ **n.** (in South Asia) a member of an armed revolutionary group advocating Maoist communism.
– ORIGIN 1960s: from *Naxal(bari)*, a place name in West Bengal, India, + -ITE¹.

Nax·çi·van /ˌnəkēCHiˈvän/ an Azerbaijani autonomous republic, predominantly Muslim, that is located on the borders of Turkey and northern Iran and is separated from the rest of Azerbaijan by a narrow strip of Armenia; pop. 71,200 (est. 2008). In 1990, it was the first Soviet territory to declare unilateral independence. It has a predominantly Azerbaijani population and, along with Nagorno-Karabakh, is a point of conflict between Armenia and Azerbaijan. Russian name NAKHICHEVAN. ■ the capital city of this republic; pop. 51,000.

Nax·os /ˈnäkˌsôs, ˈnaksəs/ a Greek island in the southern Aegean Sea, the largest of the Cyclades.

nay /nā/ ▶ **adv. 1** or rather; and more than that (used to emphasize a more appropriate word than one just used): *it will take months, nay years.*
2 archaic or dialect no: *nay, I must not think thus.*
▶ **n.** a negative answer or vote: *the final yea or nay.*
– ORIGIN Middle English (sense 2 of the adverb): from Old Norse *nei*, from *ne* 'not' + *ei* 'ever' (compare with AYE²).

Na·ya·rit /näyäˈrēt/ a state in western Mexico, on the Pacific coast; capital, Tepic.

Nay·pyi·daw /ˈnāpyēˌdô/ (also **Nay Pyi Taw**) the capital of Burma (Myanmar); pop. 925,000 (est. 2007). Situated in a previously undeveloped area of relative isolation, the city was founded in 2005 for the express purpose of replacing Rangoon as the nation's administrative capital.

nay·say /ˈnāˌsā/ ▶ **v.** (past and past participle **naysaid**) [with obj.] say no to; deny or oppose: *I'm not going to naysay anything he does.*
– DERIVATIVES **nay·say·er n.**

Naz·a·rene /ˈnazəˌrēn/ ▶ **n. 1** a native or inhabitant of Nazareth. ■ (**the Nazarene**) Jesus Christ. ■ (chiefly in Jewish or Muslim use) a Christian. ■ a member of an early sect or faction of Jewish Christians, esp. one in 4th-century Syria using an Aramaic version of the Gospels and observing much of the Jewish law. ■ a member of the Church of the Nazarene, a Christian Protestant denomination originating in the American holiness movement.
2 a member of a group of German painters working mainly in Rome who from 1809 sought to revive the art and techniques of medieval Germany and early Renaissance Italy.
▶ **adj.** of or relating to Nazareth or Nazarenes.
– ORIGIN via late Latin from Greek *Nazarēnos*, from *Nazaret* 'Nazareth.'

Naz·a·reth /ˈnaz(ə)rəTH/ a historic town in lower Galilee, in present-day northern Israel; pop. 66,400 (est. 2008). Mentioned in the Gospels as the home of Mary and Joseph, it is closely associated with the childhood of Jesus Christ and is a center of Christian pilgrimage.

Na·zi /ˈnätsē/ ▶ **n.** (pl. **Nazis**) historical a member of the National Socialist German Workers' Party. ■ a member of an organization with similar ideology. ■ derogatory a person who holds and acts brutally in accordance with extreme racist or authoritarian views.

> The Nazi Party was formed in Munich after World War I. It advocated right-wing authoritarian nationalist government and developed a racist ideology based on anti-Semitism and a belief in the superiority of "Aryan" Germans. Its charismatic leader, Adolf Hitler, who was elected Chancellor in 1933, established a totalitarian dictatorship, rearmed Germany in support of expansionist foreign policies in central Europe, and thus precipitated World War II. The Nazi Party collapsed at the end of the war and was outlawed in Germany.

▶ **adj.** of or concerning the Nazis or Nazism.
– DERIVATIVES **Na·zi·dom** /-dəm/ **n.**, **Na·zi·fy** /ˈnätsiˌfī/ **v.** (**Nazifies, Nazifying, Nazified**), **Na·zi·ism** /-ˌizəm/ **n.**, **Na·zism** /ˈnätˌsizəm/ **n.**
– ORIGIN German, abbreviation representing the pronunciation of *Nati-* in *Nationalsozialist* 'national socialist.'

Naz·i·rite /ˈnazəˌrīt/ (also **Nazarite**) ▶ **n.** historical an Israelite consecrated to the service of God, under vows to abstain from alcohol, let the hair grow, and avoid defilement by contact with corpses (Num. 6).
– ORIGIN from Hebrew *nāzîr* 'consecrated one,' from *nāzar* 'to separate or consecrate oneself,' + -ITE¹.

Na·zi sa·lute ▶ **n.** a gesture or salute in which the right arm is straightened and inclined upward, with the hand open and palm down.

NB ▶ **abbr.** ■ New Brunswick (in official postal use). ■ nota bene; take special note (used to precede a written note). [Latin.]

Nb ▶ **symbol** the chemical element niobium.

NBA ▶ **abbr.** ■ (in North America) National Basketball Association. ■ (in the US) National Boxing Association.

NBC ▶ **abbr.** ■ (in the US) National Broadcasting Company. ■ (of weapons or warfare) nuclear, biological, and chemical.

NbE ▶ **abbr.** north by east.

NbW ▶ **abbr.** north by west.

NC ▶ **abbr.** ■ network computer; a computer with reduced functionality intended to be used to access services on a network. ■ North Carolina (in official postal use).

NC-17 ▶ **symbol** no one 17 and under admitted, a rating in the Voluntary Movie Rating System forbidding admission to children 17 years old and under.
– ORIGIN representing *no children (under) 17.*

NCAA ▶ **abbr.** National Collegiate Athletic Association.

NCLB ▶ **abbr.** No Child Left Behind (Act), a 2001 federal law that revised and upgraded standards for public elementary education.

NCO ▶ **abbr.** noncommissioned officer.

NCTE ▶ **abbr.** National Council of Teachers of English.

NCTM ▶ **abbr.** National Council of Teachers of Mathematics.

ND ▶ **abbr.** North Dakota (in official postal use).

Nd ▶ **symbol** the chemical element neodymium.

n.d. ▶ **abbr.** no date (used esp. in bibliographies).

-nd ▶ **suffix** variant spelling of -AND, -END.

N.Dak. ▶ **abbr.** North Dakota.

NDEA ▶ **abbr.** National Defense Education Act.

Nde·be·le /ˌəndəˈbelā, -ˈbēlē/ ▶ **n.** (pl. **same** or **Ndebeles**) **1** a member of a Bantu people of Zimbabwe and northeastern South Africa. See also MATABELE.
2 the Nguni language of this people.
▶ **adj.** of or relating to this people or their language.
– ORIGIN the name in the Nguni languages.

N'Dja·me·na /ənjəˈmā/ the capital of Chad; pop. 989,000 (est. 2007). Former name (1900–73) FORT LAMY.

Ndo·la /ənˈdōlə/ a city in central Zambia; pop. 482,300 (est. 2009).

NE ▶ **abbr.** ■ Nebraska (in official postal use). ■ New England. ■ northeast or northeastern.

Ne ▶ **symbol** the chemical element neon.

né /nā/ ▶ **adj.** originally called; born (used before the name by which a man was originally known): *Al Kelly, né Kabish.*
– ORIGIN 1930s: French, literally 'born,' masculine past participle of *naître*; compare with NÉE.

NEA ▶ **abbr.** ■ National Education Association. ■ National Endowment for the Arts. ■ Nuclear Energy Agency.

Neagh, Lough /nā/ a shallow lake in Northern Ireland, the largest freshwater lake in the British Isles.

Ne·an·der·thal /nēˈandərˌTHôl/ ▶ **n.** (also **Neanderthal man**) an extinct species of human that was widely distributed in ice-age Europe between *c.*120,000–35,000 years ago, with a receding forehead and prominent brow ridges. The Neanderthals were associated with the Mousterian flint industry of the Middle Paleolithic. ● *Homo neanderthalensis*; now usually regarded as a separate species from *H. sapiens* and probably at the end of a different evolutionary line. ■ an uncivilized, unintelligent, or uncouth person, esp. a man: *the stereotype of the mechanic as a macho Neanderthal.*
▶ **adj.** of or relating to this extinct human species. ■ (esp. of a man) uncivilized, unintelligent, or uncouth: *your attitude to women is Neanderthal.*
– ORIGIN mid 19th cent.: from *Neanderthal*, the name of a region in Germany (now *Neandertal*), where remains of Neanderthal man were found.

neap /nēp/ ▶ **n.** (usu. **neap tide**) a tide just after the first or third quarters of the moon when there is the least difference between high and low water.
▶ **v.** (**be neaped**) (of a boat) be kept aground or in harbor by a neap tide. ■ [no obj.] archaic (of a tide) tend toward or reach the highest point of a neap tide.
– ORIGIN late Middle English, originally an adjective from Old English *nēp*, first element of *nēpflōd* 'neap flood,' of unknown origin.

Ne·a·pol·i·tan /ˌnēəˈpälitn/ ▶ **n.** a native or citizen of Naples.
▶ **adj.** of or relating to Naples.
– ORIGIN from Latin *Neapolitanus*, from Latin *Neapolis* 'Naples,' from Greek *neos* 'new' + *polis* 'city.'

Ne·a·pol·i·tan ice cream ▶ **n.** ice cream made in layers of different colors, typically including chocolate, vanilla, and strawberry.

near /ni(ə)r/ ▶ **adv. 1** at or to a short distance away; nearby: *a bomb exploding somewhere near* | [comparative] *she took a step nearer.*
2 a short time away in the future: *the time for his retirement was drawing near.*
3 [as submodifier] almost: *a near perfect fit.*
4 archaic or dialect almost: *I near fell out of the chair.*
▶ **prep.** (also **near to**) **1** at or to a short distance away from (a place): *the parking lot near the sawmill* | *do you live near here?* | [superlative] *the table nearest the door.*
2 a short period of time from: *near the end of the war* | [comparative] *details will be given nearer the date.*
3 close to (a state); verging on: *she gave a tiny smile, brave but near tears* | *she was near death.* ■ (used before an amount) a small amount below (something); approaching: *temperatures near 2 million degrees K.*
4 similar to: *a shape near to the original.*
▶ **adj. 1** located a short distance away: *a big house in the near distance* | [superlative] *I was fifteen miles from the nearest town.*
2 only a short time ahead: *the conflict is unlikely to be resolved in the near future.*
3 similar: [superlative] *walking in these shoes is the nearest thing to floating on air.* ■ [attrib.] close to being (the thing mentioned): *his state of near despair* | *a near disaster.* ■ [attrib.] having a close family connection: *the loss of a child or other near relative.*
4 [attrib.] located on the side of a vehicle that is normally closest to the curb: *the near right-hand end window of the trailer.* Compare with OFF (sense 3 of the adjective).
5 archaic (of a person) stingy; miserly.
▶ **v.** [with obj.] come near to (someone or something); approach: *soon the cab would be nearing State Street* | [no obj.] *lunchtime neared.*
– PHRASES **near at hand** close in distance or time: *an all-electric future was near at hand.* **near enough** sufficiently close to being the case for all practical purposes: *this price was near enough the going rate for rent.* **one's nearest and dearest** one's close friends and relatives. **so near and yet so far** a rueful comment on someone's narrow failure to achieve an aim.
– DERIVATIVES **near·ish adj.**
– ORIGIN Middle English: from Old Norse *nær* 'nearer,' comparative of *ná*, corresponding to Old English *nēah* 'nigh.'

near·by ▶ **adj.** /ˈni(ə)rˌbī/ close at hand; not far away: *he slung his jacket over a nearby chair.*
▶ **adv.** /ˌni(ə)rˈbī/ (Brit. also **near by**) close by; very near: *his four sisters live nearby.*

Ne·arc·tic /nēˈärktik, -ˈärtik/ ▶ **adj.** Zoology of, relating to, or denoting a zoogeographical region comprising North America as far south as northern Mexico, together with Greenland. The fauna is closely related to that of the Palearctic region. Compare with **HOLARCTIC.** ■ (as noun **the Nearctic**) the Nearctic region.
– ORIGIN mid 19th cent.: from **NEO-** 'new' + **ARCTIC.**

near-death ex·pe·ri·ence ▶ **n.** an unusual experience taking place on the brink of death and recounted by a person after recovery, typically an out-of-body experience or a vision of a tunnel of light.

Near East (**the Near East**) a term originally applied to the Balkan states of southeastern Europe, but now generally applied to the countries of southwestern Asia between the Mediterranean Sea and India (including the Middle East), esp. in historical contexts.
– DERIVATIVES **Near East·ern adj.**

near gale ▶ **n.** another term for **MODERATE GALE.**

near-in·fra·red ▶ **adj.** pertaining to or being in the infrared spectrum that is closest to visible light; it is used for studying red dwarfs, red giants, and other celestial objects.

Near Is·lands an island group at the western end of the Aleutian Islands, in southwestern Alaska. Attu is one of the Near Islands.

near·ly /ˈni(ə)rlē/ ▶ **adv. 1** very close to; almost: *David was nearly asleep | a rise of nearly 25 percent.*
2 closely: *in the absence of anyone more nearly related, I had been designated next of kin.*
– PHRASES **not nearly** nothing like; far from: *you're not nearly as clever as you think you are.*

near miss ▶ **n. 1** a narrowly avoided collision or other accident.
2 a bomb or shot that just misses its target.
■ something almost achieved: *a victory in Houston and a near miss in the semifinals of the French Open.*

near mon·ey ▶ **n.** Finance assets that can readily be converted into cash, such as government bonds.

near·ness /ˈni(ə)rnis/ ▶ **n.** the condition of being near; proximity: *the park's nearness to Washington, DC.*

near rhyme ▶ **n.** rhyming in which the words sound the same but do not rhyme perfectly. Also called **OFF RHYME.**

near·shore /ˈni(ə)rˌSHôr/ ▶ **adj.** [attrib.] relating to or denoting the region of the sea or seabed relatively close to a shore.

near·sight·ed /ˈnirˌsītid/ ▶ **adj.** unable to see things clearly unless they are relatively close to the eyes, owing to the focusing of rays of light by the eye at a point in front of the retina; myopic.
– DERIVATIVES **near·sight·ed·ly adv.**, **near·sight·ed·ness n.**

near-term ▶ **adj.** short-term. ■ (of a pregnant female or a fetus) close to the time of birth: *near-term sheep fetuses.*

neat[1] /nēt/ ▶ **adj. 1** (of a place or thing) arranged in an orderly, tidy way: *the books had been stacked up in neat piles.* ■ (of a person) habitually tidy, well groomed, or well organized: *her daughter was always neat and clean.* ■ having a pleasing shape or appearance; well formed or regular: *Alan noted down the orders in his neat, precise script.* ■ informal very good or pleasant; excellent: *I've been taking lessons in tracking from this really neat Indian guide.*
2 done with or demonstrating skill or efficiency: *Howard's neat, precise tackling.* ■ tending to disregard specifics for the sake of convenience; slick or facile: *this neat division does not take into account a host of associated factors.*
3 (of liquid, esp. liquor) not diluted or mixed with anything else: *he drank neat Scotch.*
– ORIGIN late 15th cent. (in the sense 'clean, free from impurities'): from French *net*, from Latin *nitidus* 'shining,' from *nitere* 'to shine'; related to **NET**[2]. The sense 'bright' (now obsolete) was recorded in English in the late 16th cent.

neat[2] ▶ **n.** archaic a bovine animal. ■ cattle.
– ORIGIN Old English, of Germanic origin; related to Dutch *noot*, also to the base of dialect *nait* meaning 'companion.'

neat·en /ˈnētn/ ▶ **v.** [with obj.] make neat; arrange in an orderly, tidy way: *she made an attempt to neaten her hair.*

'neath /nēTH/ (also **neath**) ▶ **prep.** chiefly literary beneath: *'neath the trees.*

neat·ly /ˈnētlē/ ▶ **adv.** in a neat way: *neatly folded shirts | she neatly sidestepped the question.*

neat·ness /ˈnētnis/ ▶ **n.** the quality or condition of being neat: *his obsessive neatness.*

neat's-foot oil ▶ **n.** oil obtained by boiling the feet of cattle, used to dress leather.

NEB ▶ **abbr.** ■ (in the UK) National Enterprise Board. ■ New English Bible.

neb /neb/ ▶ **n.** Scottish & N. English a projecting part of something, in particular: ■ a nose or snout. ■ a bird's beak or bill. ■ the brim of a cap.
– ORIGIN Old English *nebb*, of Germanic origin; related to Dutch *neb(be)*; compare with **NIB.**

Neb. ▶ **abbr.** Nebraska.

Neb·bi·o·lo /ˌnebēˈōlō/ ▶ **n.** a variety of black wine grape grown in Piedmont in northern Italy. ■ a red wine made from this.
– ORIGIN Italian, from *nebbia* 'mist' (because the grape ripens in the autumn).

neb·bish /ˈnebiSH/ ▶ **n.** informal a person, esp. a man, who is regarded as pitifully ineffectual, timid, or submissive.
– DERIVATIVES **neb·bish·y adj.**
– ORIGIN late 19th cent.: from Yiddish *nebekh* 'poor thing.'

NEbE ▶ **abbr.** northeast by east.

NEbN ▶ **abbr.** northeast by north.

Nebr. ▶ **abbr.** Nebraska.

Ne·bras·ka /nəˈbraskə/ a state in the central US, west of the Missouri River; pop. 1,783,432 (est. 2008); capital, Lincoln; statehood, Mar. 1, 1867 (37). It was acquired as part of the Louisiana Purchase in 1803.
– DERIVATIVES **Ne·bras·kan adj. & n.**

neb·u·chad·nez·zar /ˌneb(y)əkə(d)ˈnezər/ ▶ **n.** a very large wine bottle, equivalent in capacity to about twenty regular bottles.
– ORIGIN early 20th cent.: from *Nebuchadnezzar* (see **NEBUCHADNEZZAR II**).

Neb·u·chad·nez·zar II /ˌneb(y)əkədˈnezər/ (*c.*630–562 BC), king of Babylon 605–562 BC. He rebuilt the city with massive walls, a huge temple, and a ziggurat, and extended his rule over neighboring countries. In 586 BC, he captured and destroyed Jerusalem and deported many Israelites in what is known as the Babylonian Captivity.

neb·u·la /ˈnebyələ/ ▶ **n.** (pl. **nebulae** /-lē/ or **nebulas**) **1** Astronomy a cloud of gas and dust in outer space, visible in the night sky either as an indistinct bright patch or as a dark silhouette against other luminous matter. ■ (in general use) any indistinct bright area in the night sky, for example, a distant galaxy.
2 Medicine a clouded spot on the cornea causing defective vision.
– ORIGIN mid 17th cent. (as a medical term): from Latin, literally 'mist.'

neb·u·lar /ˈnebyələr/ ▶ **adj.** of, relating to, or denoting a nebula or nebulae: *a vast nebular cloud.*

neb·u·lar hy·poth·e·sis (also **nebular theory**) ▶ **n.** the theory that the solar and stellar systems were developed from a primeval nebula.

ne·bu·li·um /nəˈbyo͞olēəm/ ▶ **n.** Chemistry, historical a hypothetical chemical element proposed in the 1860s to explain certain lines in the spectra of nebulae, later discovered to arise from forbidden transitions in oxygen and nitrogen ions.

neb·u·liz·er /ˈnebyəˌlīzər/ ▶ **n.** a device for producing a fine spray of liquid, used for example for inhaling a medicinal drug.
– DERIVATIVES **neb·u·lize v.**
– ORIGIN late 19th cent.: from Latin *nebula* 'mist' + -*izer* (see **-IZE**).

neb·u·lous /ˈnebyələs/ ▶ **adj.** in the form of a cloud or haze; hazy: *a giant nebulous glow.* ■ (of a concept or idea) unclear, vague, or ill-defined: *nebulous concepts like quality of life.* ■ another term for **NEBULAR.**
– DERIVATIVES **neb·u·los·i·ty** /ˌnebyəˈläsitē/ **n.**, **neb·u·lous·ly adv.**, **neb·u·lous·ness n.**
– ORIGIN late Middle English (in the sense 'cloudy'): from French *nébuleux* or Latin *nebulosus*, from *nebula* 'mist.' The sense 'cloudlike, vague' dates from the early 19th cent.

neb·u·lous star ▶ **n.** Astronomy a small cluster of indistinct stars, or a star in a luminous haze.

neb·u·ly /ˈnebyəlē/ ▶ **adj.** Heraldry divided or edged with a line formed of deeply interlocking curves.
– ORIGIN mid 16th cent.: from French *nébulé*, from medieval Latin *nebulatus* 'clouded' (the curves being thought of as representing clouds), from Latin *nebula* 'mist.'

NEC ▶ **abbr.** ■ National Executive Committee. ■ (in the UK) National Exhibition Centre.

nec·es·sar·i·an /ˌnesəˈse(ə)rēən/ ▶ **n. & adj.** Philosophy another term for **DETERMINIST** (see **DETERMINISM**).
– DERIVATIVES **nec·es·sar·i·an·ism** /-ˌnizəm/ **n.**

nec·es·sar·i·ly /ˌnesəˈse(ə)rəlē/ ▶ **adv.** as a necessary result; inevitably: *the prognosis can necessarily be only an educated guess.*
– PHRASES **not necessarily** (as a response) what has been said or suggested may not be true or unavoidable.

nec·es·sar·y /ˈnesəˌserē/ ▶ **adj. 1** required to be done, achieved, or present; needed; essential: *members are admitted only after they have gained the necessary experience | it's not* **necessary for** *you to be here.*
2 determined, existing, or happening by natural laws or predestination; inevitable: *a necessary consequence.* ■ Philosophy (of a concept, statement, judgment, etc.) inevitably resulting from or produced by the nature of things, so that the contrary is impossible. ■ Philosophy (of an agent) having no independent volition.
▶ **n.** (usu. **necessaries**) (also **necessaries of life**) the basic requirements of life, such as food and warmth. ■ small items required for a particular journey or purpose: *I hastily threw a few necessaries into a kit bag.*
– PHRASES **a necessary evil** something that is undesirable but must be accepted.
– ORIGIN late Middle English: from Latin *necessarius*, from *necesse* 'needful.'

ne·ces·si·tar·i·an /nəˌsesəˈte(ə)rēən/ ▶ **n. & adj.** Philosophy another term for **DETERMINIST** (see **DETERMINISM**).
– DERIVATIVES **ne·ces·si·tar·i·an·ism** /-ˌnizəm/ **n.**

ne·ces·si·tate /nəˈsesəˌtāt/ ▶ **v.** [with obj.] make (something) necessary as a result or consequence: *the severe arthritis eventually necessitated a total hip replacement.* ■ [with obj.] force or compel (someone) to do something: *the late arrival had necessitated her getting out of bed.*
– ORIGIN early 17th cent.: from medieval Latin *necessitat-* 'compelled,' from the verb *necessitare*, based on Latin *necesse* 'needful.'

ne·ces·si·tous /nəˈsesitəs/ ▶ **adj.** (of a person) lacking the necessities of life; needy.
– ORIGIN early 17th cent.: from French *nécessiteux*, or from **NECESSITY** + **-OUS.**

ne·ces·si·ty /nəˈsesətē/ ▶ **n.** (pl. **necessities**) **1** the fact of being required or indispensable: *the* **necessity** *of providing parental guidance should be apparent | the* **necessity for** *law and order.* ■ unavoidability: *the* **necessity of** *growing old.* ■ a state of things or circumstances enforcing a certain course: *created more by necessity than design.*
2 an indispensable thing: *a good book is a necessity when traveling.*
3 Philosophy the principle according to which something must be so, by virtue either of logic or of natural law. ■ a condition that cannot be otherwise, or a statement asserting this.
– PHRASES **necessity is the mother of invention** proverb when the need for something becomes imperative, you are forced to find ways of getting or achieving it. **of necessity** unavoidably: *to alleviate labor shortages employers will, of necessity, offer better deals for part-timers.*
– ORIGIN late Middle English: from Old French *necessite*, from Latin *necessitas*, from *necesse* 'needful.'

neck /nek/ ▶ **n. 1** the part of a person's or animal's body connecting the head to the rest of the body: *she is wearing a silk scarf around her neck |* [as modifier] *the neck muscles.* ■ the part of a shirt, dress, or other garment that is around or close to the neck: *her dress had three buttons at the neck undone | a polo neck.* ■ meat from an animal's neck: *neck of lamb made an excellent stew.* ■ a person's neck regarded as bearing a burden of responsibility or guilt for something: *he'll be stuck with a loan* **around his neck.**
2 a narrow part of something, resembling a neck in shape or position. ■ the part of a bottle or other container near the mouth. ■ a narrow piece of terrain or sea, such as an isthmus, channel, or pass. ■ Anatomy a narrow part near one end of an organ such as the uterus. ■ the part of a violin, guitar, or other similar instrument that bears the fingerboard. ■ Architecture another term for **NECKING.** ■ (often **volcanic neck**) Geology a column of solidified lava or igneous rock formed in a volcanic vent, esp. when exposed by erosion. ■ Botany a narrow supporting part in a plant, esp. the terminal part of the fruiting body in a fern, bryophyte, or fungus.
3 the length of a horse's head and neck as a measure of its lead in a race: *the colt won the 122nd running of the Midsummer Derby by a neck.*
▶ **v. 1** [no obj.] informal (of two people) kiss and caress amorously: *we started necking on the sofa.*

PRONUNCIATION KEY ə *ago, up*; ər *over, fur*; a *hat*; ā *ate*; ä *car*; e *let*; ē *see*; i *fit*; ī *by*; NG *sing*; ō *go*; ô *law, for*; oi *toy*; o͝o *good*; o͞o *goo*; ou *out*; TH *thin*; T͟H *then*; ZH *vision*

n

2 [no obj.] form a narrowed part at a particular point when subjected to tension: *the nylon filament necks down to a fraction of its original diameter.*
3 [with obj.] Brit. informal swallow (something, esp. a drink): *after necking some beers, we left the bar.*
– PHRASES **break one's neck 1** dislocate or seriously damage a vertebra or the spinal cord in one's neck. **2** (**break one's neck to do something**) informal exert oneself to the utmost to achieve something. **get** (or **catch**) **it in the neck** informal be severely criticized or punished. **neck and neck** even in a race, competition, or comparison: *we have six contestants who are neck and neck.* **neck of the woods** informal a particular area or locality: *imagine seeing her in this neck of the woods.* **save someone's neck** see SAVE[1]. **up to one's neck in** informal heavily burdened by or busily involved in: *they were up to their necks in debt* | *I'm up to my neck in rearranging the tournament.*
– DERIVATIVES **necked** adj. [in combination] *an open-necked shirt*, **neck·er** n., **neck·less** adj.
– ORIGIN Old English *hnecca* 'back of the neck,' of Germanic origin; related to Dutch *nek* 'neck' and German *Nacken* 'nape.'

Neck·ar /ˈnekər/ a river in western Germany that rises in the Black Forest and flows 228 miles (367 km) north and then west through Stuttgart to meet the Rhine River at Mannheim.

neck·band /ˈnekˌband/ ▶ n. a strip of material around the neck of a garment.

neck·cloth /ˈnekˌklôTH/ ▶ n. a cravat.

Neck·er /ˈnekər, neˈker/, Jacques (1732–1804), Swiss-born banker and director general of French finances (1777–81; 1788–89). In 1789 he recommended summoning the States General and was dismissed, this being one of the factors that resulted in the storming of the Bastille.

neck·er·chief /ˈnekərˌCHif, -ˌCHēf/ ▶ n. a square of cloth worn around the neck.

Neck·er cube ▶ n. a line drawing of a transparent cube in which the lines of opposite sides are drawn parallel, so that the perspective is ambiguous and the orientation of the cube appears to alternate.
– ORIGIN early 20th cent.: named after L. A. *Necker* (1786–1861), Swiss naturalist.

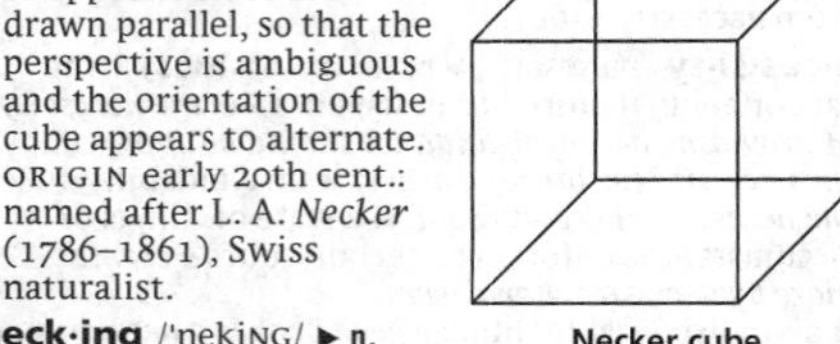
Necker cube

n

neck·ing /ˈnekiNG/ ▶ n. Architecture a short, plain, concave section between the capital and the shaft of a classical Doric or Tuscan column.

neck·lace /ˈneklis/ ▶ n. **1** an ornamental chain or string of beads, jewels, or links worn around the neck.
2 (chiefly in South Africa) a tire doused or filled with gasoline, placed around a victim's neck, and set on fire.
▶ v. [with obj.] (chiefly in South Africa) kill (someone) with a tire necklace.

neck·let /ˈneklit/ ▶ n. a fairly close-fitting and typically rigid ornament worn around the neck.

neck·line /ˈnekˌlīn/ ▶ n. the edge of a woman's garment at or below the neck, used with reference to its height or shape: *a sundress with a square neckline.*

neck·tie /ˈnekˌtī/ ▶ n. another term for TIE (sense 4 of the noun).

neck·tie par·ty ▶ n. informal a lynching or hanging.

neck·wear /ˈnekˌwe(ə)r/ ▶ n. items worn around the neck, such as ties or scarves, collectively.

necro- ▶ comb. form relating to a corpse or death: *necromancy.*
– ORIGIN from Greek *nekros* 'corpse.'

nec·ro·bi·o·sis /ˌnekrōbīˈōsis/ ▶ n. Medicine gradual degeneration and death of cells in the body tissues.
– DERIVATIVES **nec·ro·bi·ot·ic** /-ˌbīˈätik/ adj.

ne·crol·o·gist /neˈkräləjist/ ▶ n. the author of an obituary notice.

ne·crol·o·gy /neˈkräləjē/ ▶ n. (pl. **necrologies**) formal
1 an obituary notice.
2 a list of deaths.
– DERIVATIVES **ne·cro·log·i·cal** /ˌnekrəˈläjikəl/ adj.

nec·ro·man·cer /ˈnekrəˌmansər/ ▶ n. a person who practices necromancy; a wizard or magician.

nec·ro·man·cy /ˈnekrəˌmansē/ ▶ n. the supposed practice of communicating with the dead, esp. in order to predict the future. ■ witchcraft, sorcery, or black magic in general.
– DERIVATIVES **nec·ro·man·tic** /ˌnekrəˈmantik/ adj.
– ORIGIN Middle English *nigromancie*, via Old French from medieval Latin *nigromantia*, changed (by association with Latin *niger, nigr-* 'black') from late Latin *necromantia*, from Greek (see NECRO-, -MANCY). The spelling was changed in the 16th cent. to conform with the late Latin form.

nec·ro·phil·i·a /ˌnekrəˈfilēə/ ▶ n. sexual intercourse with or attraction toward corpses.
– DERIVATIVES **nec·ro·phile** /ˈnekrəˌfil/ n., **nec·ro·phil·i·ac** /-ˈfilēˌak/ n., **nec·ro·phil·ic** /-ˈfilik/ adj., **ne·croph·i·lism** /neˈkräfəˌlizəm/ n., **ne·croph·i·list** /neˈkräfəlist/ n.

nec·ro·pho·bi·a /ˌnekrəˈfōbēə/ ▶ n. extreme or irrational fear of death or dead bodies.

ne·crop·o·lis /neˈkräpəlis/ ▶ n. a cemetery, esp. a large one belonging to an ancient city.
– ORIGIN early 19th cent.: from Greek, from *nekros* 'dead person' + *polis* 'city.'

nec·rop·sy /ˈnekräpsē/ ▶ n. (pl. **necropsies**) another term for AUTOPSY.

ne·cro·sis /neˈkrōsis/ ▶ n. Medicine the death of most or all of the cells in an organ or tissue due to disease, injury, or failure of the blood supply.
– DERIVATIVES **ne·crot·ic** /-ˈkrätik/ adj.
– ORIGIN mid 17th cent.: modern Latin, from Greek *nekrōsis* (see NECRO-, -OSIS).

nec·ro·tiz·ing /ˈnekrəˌtīziNG/ ▶ adj. [attrib.] causing or accompanied by necrosis.
– DERIVATIVES **nec·ro·tized** /-ˌtīzd/ adj.

nec·ro·tiz·ing fas·ci·i·tis /ˌfaSHēˈītis/ ▶ n. Medicine an acute disease in which inflammation of the fasciae of muscles or other organs results in rapid destruction of overlying tissues. ● This disease is caused by the bacterium *Streptococcus pyogenes.*

nec·tar /ˈnektər/ ▶ n. **1** a sugary fluid secreted by plants, esp. within flowers to encourage pollination by insects and other animals. It is collected by bees to make into honey.
2 (in Greek and Roman mythology) the drink of the gods. ■ a delicious drink: *the cold beer at the pub was nectar.* ■ a thick fruit juice: *peach nectar.*
– DERIVATIVES **nec·tar·e·an** /nekˈte(ə)rēən/ adj., **nec·tar·e·ous** /nekˈte(ə)rēəs/ adj., **nec·tar·ous** /-əs/ adj.
– ORIGIN mid 16th cent. (sense 2): via Latin from Greek *nektar.*

nec·tar·if·er·ous /ˌnektəˈrifərəs/ ▶ adj. Botany (of a flower) producing nectar.

nec·tar·ine /ˌnektəˈrēn/ ▶ n. a peach of a variety with smooth, thin, brightly colored skin and rich firm flesh. ■ the tree bearing this fruit.
– ORIGIN early 17th cent. (also used as an adjective meaning 'nectarlike'): from NECTAR + -INE[4].

nec·tar·iv·o·rous /ˌnektəˈrivərəs/ ▶ adj. Zoology (of an animal) feeding on nectar.

nec·ta·ry /ˈnektərē/ ▶ n. (pl. **nectaries**) Botany a nectar-secreting glandular organ in a flower (floral) or on a leaf or stem (extrafloral).
– ORIGIN mid 18th cent.: from modern Latin *nectarium*, from *nectar* (see NECTAR).

Ne·der·land /ˈnādərˌlänt/ Dutch name for NETHERLANDS.

née /nā/ ▶ adj. originally called; born (used esp. in adding a woman's maiden name after her married name): *Mary Toogood, née Johnson.*
– ORIGIN mid 18th cent.: French, literally 'born,' feminine past participle of *naître*; compare with NÉ.

need /nēd/ ▶ v. [with obj.] **1** require (something) because it is essential or very important: *I need help now* | [with present participle] *this shirt needs washing* | [with infinitive] *they need to win tomorrow.* ■ (**not need something**) not want to be subjected to something: *I don't need your sarcasm.*
2 [as modal verb with negative or in questions] expressing necessity or obligation: *need I say more?* | *I need not have worried.*
3 [no obj.] archaic be necessary: *lest you, even more than needs, embitter our parting.*
▶ n. **1** circumstances in which something is necessary, or that require some course of action; necessity: *the basic human need for food* | [with infinitive] *there's no need to cry.*
2 (often **needs**) a thing that is wanted or required: *his day-to-day needs.*
3 the state of requiring help, or of lacking basic necessities such as food: *help us in our hour of need* | *children in need.*
– PHRASES **at need** archaic when needed; in an emergency: *men whose experience could be called upon at need.* **had need** archaic ought to: *you had need hire men to chip it all over artistically.* **have need of** formal need: *Alida had need of company.* **if need be** if necessary. **in need of** requiring or needing (something): *he was in desperate need of medical care.*
– ORIGIN Old English *nēodian* (verb), *nēod, nēd* (noun), of Germanic origin; related to Dutch *nood* and German *Not* 'danger.'

need-blind /ˈnēd ˌblīnd/ ▶ adj. of or denoting a college admissions policy in which applicants are judged solely on their merits, irrespective of their ability to pay for tuition.

need·ful /ˈnēdfəl/ ▶ adj. **1** formal necessary; requisite: *a further word was needful.*
2 needy: *she gave her money away to needful people.*
– DERIVATIVES **need·ful·ly** adv., **need·ful·ness** n.

nee·dle /ˈnēdl/ ▶ n. **1** a very fine slender piece of metal with a point at one end and a hole or eye for thread at the other, used in sewing.
2 something resembling a sewing needle in use, shape, or appearance, esp.: ■ an instrument used in crafts such as crochet, knitting, and lacemaking. ■ the pointed hollow end of a hypodermic syringe. ■ a very fine metal spike used in acupuncture. ■ a thin pointer on a dial, compass, or other instrument. ■ an etching tool. ■ the sharp, stiff, slender leaf of a fir or pine tree. ■ a pointed rock or peak. ■ a stylus used to play phonograph records. ■ an obelisk: *Cleopatra's Needle.* ■ a steel pin that explodes the cartridge of a breech-loading gun. ■ Building a beam used as a temporary support during underpinning.
▶ v. [with obj.] **1** prick or pierce (something) with or as if with a needle: *dust needled his eyes.*
2 informal provoke or annoy (someone), esp. by continual criticism or questioning: *I just said that to Charlie to needle him.*
– PHRASES **the eye of a needle** a tiny aperture or opening through which it would seem impossible to pass (esp. with reference to Matt. 19:24). **give someone the needle** informal provoke or annoy someone: *Lady gives him the needle because she knows it isn't true.* **a needle in a haystack** something that is almost impossible to find because it is hidden among so many other things.
– ORIGIN Old English *nǣdl*, of Germanic origin; related to Dutch *naald* and German *Nadel*, from an Indo-European root shared by Latin *nere* 'to spin' and Greek *nēma* 'thread.'

nee·dle·cord /ˈnēdlˌkôrd/ ▶ n. British term for PINWALE.

nee·dle·craft /ˈnēdlˌkraft/ ▶ n. needlework.

nee·dle·fish /ˈnēdlˌfiSH/ ▶ n. (pl. **same** or **needlefishes**) another term for GARFISH.

nee·dle·lace /ˈnēdlˌlās/ ▶ n. another term for NEEDLEPOINT (sense 2 of the noun).

nee·dle·point /ˈnēdlˌpoint/ ▶ n. **1** embroidery worked over canvas, typically in a diagonal stitch covering the entire surface of the fabric.
2 (also **needlepoint lace**) lace made by hand using a needle rather than bobbins.
▶ v. [with obj.] embroider in needlepoint.

nee·dler /ˈnēdl-ər, -lər/ ▶ n. **1** a person who annoys or antagonizes another.
2 (in science fiction) a weapon that fires needlelike projectiles.

need·less /ˈnēdlis/ ▶ adj. (of something bad) unnecessary; avoidable: *I deplore needless waste.*
– PHRASES **needless to say** of course.
– DERIVATIVES **need·less·ly** adv., **need·less·ness** n.

nee·dle valve ▶ n. a valve closed by a thin tapering part.

nee·dle·wom·an /ˈnēdlˌwŏŏmən/ ▶ n. (pl. **needlewomen**) a woman or girl who has particular sewing skills or who sews for a living.

nee·dle·work /ˈnēdlˌwərk/ ▶ n. the art or practice of sewing or embroidery: *Mrs. Zurndorfer specializes in needlework.* ■ sewn or embroidered items collectively: *exhibits include European and Eastern needlework.*
– DERIVATIVES **nee·dle·work·er** n.

need·n't /ˈnēdnt/ ▶ contraction need not.

needs /nēdz/ ▶ adv. (in phrase **must needs** (or **needs must**) **do something**) archaic cannot avoid or help doing something: *they must needs depart.*
– ORIGIN Old English *nēdes* (see NEED, -S[3]).

need·y /ˈnēdē/ ▶ adj. (**needier, neediest**) (of a person) lacking the necessities of life; very poor: *needy and elderly people.* ■ (of circumstances) characterized by poverty: *those from needy backgrounds.*
– DERIVATIVES **need·i·ness** n.

neem /nēm/ ▶ n. a tropical Old World tree that yields mahoganylike timber, oil, medicinal products, and insecticide. Also called MARGOSA. ● *Azadirachta indica*, family Meliaceae.
– ORIGIN early 19th cent.: via Hindi from Sanskrit *nimba.*

neep /nēp/ ▶ n. Scottish & N. English a turnip.
– ORIGIN Old English *nǣp*, from Latin *napus.*

ne'er /ne(ə)r/ ▶ contraction literary or dialect never.

ne'er-do-well /ˈne(ə)r dŏŏ ˌwel/ ▶ n. a person who is lazy and irresponsible.
▶ adj. [attrib.] lazy and irresponsible.

nef /nef/ ▶ **n.** an elaborate table decoration in the shape of a ship for holding such things as table napkins and condiments.
– ORIGIN mid 19th cent.: from French, literally 'ship' (see **NAVE**[1]).

ne·far·i·ous /ni'fe(ə)rēəs/ ▶ **adj.** (typically of an action or activity) wicked or criminal: *the nefarious activities of the organized-crime syndicates.*
– DERIVATIVES **ne·far·i·ous·ly** adv., **ne·far·i·ous·ness** n.
– ORIGIN early 17th cent.: from Latin *nefarius*, from *nefas, nefar-* 'wrong' (from *ne-* 'not' + *fas* 'divine law') + **-OUS**.

Nef·er·ti·ti /ˌnefər'tētē/ (also **Nofretete** /ˌnäfri'tētē/) (*fl.* 14th century BC), Egyptian queen; wife of Akhenaten and half-sister of Tutankhamen.

Nefertiti

neg /neg/ ▶ **n.** informal a photographic negative.
– ORIGIN late 19th cent.: abbreviation.

neg. ▶ **abbr.** negative: *HIV neg.*

nega- ▶ **comb. form** denoting the negative counterpart of a unit of measurement, in particular a unit of energy saved as a result of conservation measures.
– ORIGIN abbreviation of **NEGATIVE**.

ne·gate /nə'gāt/ ▶ **v.** [with obj.] **1** nullify; make ineffective: *alcohol negates the effects of the drug.*
2 . Logic & Grammar make (a clause, sentence, or proposition) negative in meaning.
3 deny the existence of (something): *negating the political nature of education.*
– ORIGIN early 17th cent. (sense 1 and sense 3): from Latin *negat-* 'denied,' from the verb *negare.*

ne·ga·tion /nə'gāsHən/ ▶ **n. 1** the contradiction or denial of something: *there should be confirmation—or negation—of the findings.* ■ Grammar denial of the truth of a clause or sentence, typically involving the use of a negative word (e.g., *not, no, never*) or a word or affix with negative force (e.g., *nothing, non-*). ■ Logic a proposition whose assertion specifically denies the truth of another proposition: *the negation of A is, briefly, "not A."* ■ Mathematics inversion: *these formulae and their negations.*
2 the absence or opposite of something actual or positive: *evil is not merely the negation of goodness.*
– DERIVATIVES **neg·a·to·ry** /'negəˌtôrē/ adj.
– ORIGIN late Middle English: from Latin *negatio(n-)*, from the verb *negare* 'deny' (see **NEGATE**).

neg·a·tive /'negətiv/ ▶ **adj. 1** consisting in or characterized by the absence rather than the presence of distinguishing features. ■ (of a statement or decision) expressing or implying denial, disagreement, or refusal: *that, I take it, was a negative answer.* ■ (of the results of a test or experiment) indicating that a certain substance is not present or a certain condition does not exist: *so far all the patients have tested negative for TB.* ■ [in combination] (of a person or their blood) not having a specified substance or condition: *HIV-negative.* ■ informal denoting a complete lack of something: *they were described as having negative vulnerability to water entry.* ■ Grammar & Logic (of a word, clause, or proposition) expressing denial, negation, or refutation; stating or asserting that something is not the case. Contrasted with **AFFIRMATIVE** and **INTERROGATIVE**.
2 (of a person, attitude, or situation) not desirable or optimistic: *the new tax was having a very negative effect on car sales | I don't want to be negative, but I don't see how we could do it.*
3 (of a quantity) less than zero; to be subtracted from others or from zero. ■ denoting a direction of decrease or reversal: *the industry suffered negative growth in 1992.*
4 of, containing, producing, or denoting the kind of electric charge carried by electrons.
5 (of a photographic image) showing light and shade or colors reversed from those of the original.
6 Astrology relating to or denoting any of the earth or water signs, considered passive in nature.
▶ **n. 1** a word or statement that expresses denial, disagreement, or refusal: *she replied in the negative.* ■ (often **the negative**) a bad, unwelcome, or unpleasant quality, characteristic, or aspect of a situation or person: *confidence will not be instilled by harping solely on the negative | the bus trip and the positive media have not had time to turn his significant negatives around.* ■ Grammar a word, affix, or phrase expressing negation. ■ Logic another term for **NEGATION**.
2 a photographic image made on film or specially prepared glass that shows the light and shade or color values reversed from the original, and from which positive prints can be made.
3 a result of a test or experiment indicating that a certain substance is not present or a certain condition does not exist: *the percentage of false negatives generated by a cancer test was of great concern.*
4 the part of an electric circuit that is at a lower electrical potential than another part designated as having zero electrical potential.
5 a number less than zero.
▶ **exclam.** no (usually used in a military context): *"Any snags, Captain?" "Negative, she's running like clockwork."*
▶ **v.** [with obj.] **1** reject; refuse to accept; veto: *the bill was negatived by 130 votes to 129.* ■ disprove; contradict: *the insurer's main arguments were negatived by Lawrence.*
2 render ineffective; neutralize: *should criminal law allow consent to negative what would otherwise be a crime?*
– DERIVATIVES **neg·a·tive·ly** adv., **neg·a·tive·ness** n.
– ORIGIN late Middle English: from late Latin *negativus*, from *negare* 'deny' (see **NEGATE**).

neg·a·tive eq·ui·ty ▶ **n.** Brit. potential indebtedness arising when the market value of a property falls below the outstanding amount of a mortgage secured on it.

neg·a·tive ev·i·dence ▶ **n.** evidence for a theory provided by the nonoccurrence or absence of something.

neg·a·tive feed·back ▶ **n.** chiefly Biology the diminution or counteraction of an effect by its own influence on the process giving rise to it, as when a high level of a particular hormone in the blood may inhibit further secretion of that hormone, or where the result of a certain action may inhibit further performance of that action. ■ Electronics the return of part of an output signal to the input, which is out of phase with it, so that amplifier gain is reduced and the output is improved.

neg·a·tive in·come tax ▶ **n.** money credited as allowances to a taxed income, and paid as a benefit when it exceeds debited tax.

neg·a·tive in·stance ▶ **n.** a piece of negative evidence.

neg·a·tive pole ▶ **n.** the south-seeking pole of a magnet. ■ a cathode.

neg·a·tive sign ▶ **n.** another term for **MINUS SIGN**.

neg·a·tiv·ism /'negətivˌizəm/ ▶ **n.** the practice of being or tendency to be negative or skeptical in attitude while failing to offer positive suggestions or views.
– DERIVATIVES **neg·a·tiv·ist** n. & adj., **neg·a·tiv·is·tic** /ˌnegətiv'istik/ adj.

neg·a·tiv·i·ty /ˌnegə'tivitē/ ▶ **n.** the expression of criticism of or pessimism about something: *he was taken aback by the negativity of the press.*

ne·ga·tor /nə'gātər/ ▶ **n.** Grammar a word expressing negation, esp. (in English) the word *not.*

neg·en·trop·ic /ˌnegən'träpik/ ▶ **adj.** Physics of or characterized by a reduction in entropy (and corresponding increase in order).
– DERIVATIVES **neg·en·tro·py** /neg'entrəpē/ n.
– ORIGIN mid 20th cent.: from **NEGATIVE** + *entropic* (see **ENTROPY**).

Neg·ev /'neˌgev/ (**the Negev**) an arid region that forms most of southern Israel, between Beersheba and the Gulf of Aqaba, on the Egyptian border. Large areas are irrigated for agriculture and many Israeli communities have been established here.

ne·glect /ni'glekt/ ▶ **v.** [with obj.] fail to care for properly: *the old churchyard has been sadly neglected.* ■ not pay proper attention to; disregard: *you neglect our advice at your peril.* ■ [with infinitive] fail to do something: *he neglected to write to her.*
▶ **n.** the state or fact of being uncared for: *animals dying through disease or neglect.* ■ the action of not taking proper care of someone or something: *she was accused of child neglect.* ■ failure to do something: *he was reported for* ***neglect of duty.***
– ORIGIN early 16th cent.: from Latin *neglect-* 'disregarded,' from the verb *neglegere*, from *neg-* 'not' + *legere* 'choose, pick up.'

ne·glect·ed /ni'glektid/ ▶ **adj.** suffering a lack of proper care: *some severely neglected children.* ■ not receiving proper attention; disregarded: *a neglected area of research.*

ne·glect·ful /ni'glektfəl/ ▶ **adj.** not giving proper care or attention to someone or something: *you are being* ***neglectful of*** *our guests | born to wealthy but neglectful parents.*
– DERIVATIVES **ne·glect·ful·ly** /-fəlē/ adv., **ne·glect·ful·ness** /-fəlnəs/ n.

neg·li·gee /ˌneglə'zHā/ ▶ **n.** a woman's light dressing gown, typically made of a filmy, soft fabric.
– ORIGIN mid 18th cent. (denoting a kind of loose gown worn by women in the 18th cent.): from French, literally 'given little thought or attention,' feminine past participle of *négliger* 'to neglect.'

neg·li·gence /'negləjəns/ ▶ **n.** failure to take proper care in doing something: *some of these accidents are due to negligence.* ■ Law failure to use reasonable care, resulting in damage or injury to another.

neg·li·gent /'negləjənt/ ▶ **adj.** failing to take proper care in doing something: *directors have been negligent in the performance of their duties.*
– DERIVATIVES **neg·li·gent·ly** adv.
– ORIGIN late Middle English: from Old French, or from Latin *negligent-* 'disregarding,' from the verb *negligere* (variant of *neglegere* 'disregard, slight': see **NEGLECT**).

neg·li·gi·ble /'neglijəbəl/ ▶ **adj.** so small or unimportant as to be not worth considering; insignificant: *sound could at last be recorded with incredible ease and at negligible cost.*
– DERIVATIVES **neg·li·gi·bil·i·ty** /ˌnegləjə'bilitē/ n., **neg·li·gi·bly** /-blē/ adv.
– ORIGIN early 19th cent.: from obsolete French, from *négliger* 'to neglect.'

ne·go·ti·a·ble /nə'gōsHəbəl/ ▶ **adj.** open to discussion or modification: *the price was not negotiable.* ■ (of a document) able to be transferred or assigned to the legal ownership of another person. ■ (of an obstacle or pathway) able to be traversed; passable: *such walkways must be accessible and negotiable for all users.*
– DERIVATIVES **ne·go·ti·a·bil·i·ty** /nəˌgōsHə'bilitē/ n.

ne·go·ti·ate /nə'gōsHēˌāt/ ▶ **v. 1** [no obj.] try to reach an agreement or compromise by discussion with others: *his government's willingness to negotiate.* ■ [with obj.] obtain or bring about by negotiating: *he negotiated a new contract with the sellers.*
2 [with obj.] find a way over or through (an obstacle or difficult path): *there was a puddle to be negotiated.*
3 [with obj.] transfer (a check, bill, or other document) to the legal ownership of another person. ■ convert (a check) into cash.
– DERIVATIVES **ne·go·ti·ant** /-sH(ē)ənt/ n. (archaic).
– ORIGIN early 17th cent.: from Latin *negotiat-* 'done in the course of business,' from the verb *negotiari*, from *negotium* 'business,' from *neg-* 'not' + *otium* 'leisure.'

ne·go·ti·a·tion /nəˌgōsHē'āsHən/ ▶ **n.** (also **negotiations**) discussion aimed at reaching an agreement: *a worldwide ban is currently* ***under negotiation*** | ***negotiations between unions and employers.*** ■ the action or process of negotiating: *negotiation of the deals.* ■ the action or process of transferring ownership of a document.
– ORIGIN late 15th cent. (denoting an act of dealing with another person): from Latin *negotiatio(n-)*, from the verb *negotiari* (see **NEGOTIATE**).

ne·go·ti·a·tor /nə'gōsHēˌātər/ ▶ **n.** a person who conducts negotiations: *US trade negotiators | a hostage negotiator.*

Ne·gress /'nēgris/ ▶ **n.** dated, often offensive a woman or girl of black African origin.
– ORIGIN late 18th cent.: from French *négresse*, feminine of *nègre* 'negro.'

USAGE See usage at **NEGRO**.

Ne·gril·lo /nə'grilō/ ▶ **n.** (pl. **Negrillos**) a member of a black people of short stature native to central and southern Africa.
– ORIGIN Spanish, diminutive of *negro* 'black' (see **NEGRO**); compare with **NEGRITO**.

Ne·gri·to /nə'grētō/ ▶ **n.** (pl. **Negritos**) a member of a black people of short stature native to the Austronesian region.
– ORIGIN Spanish, diminutive of *negro* 'black' (see **NEGRO**); compare with **NEGRILLO**.

ne·gri·tude /'negriˌt(y)o͞od, 'nē-/ (also **Negritude**) ▶ **n.** the quality or fact of being of black African origin. ■ the affirmation or consciousness of the value of black or African culture, heritage, and

identity: *Negritude helped to guide Senegal into independence with pride.*
– ORIGIN 1950s: from French *négritude* 'blackness.'

Ne·gro /ˈnēgrō/ dated, often offensive ▶ **n.** (pl. **Negroes**) a member of a dark-skinned group of peoples originally native to Africa south of the Sahara.
▶ **adj.** of or relating to such people.
– ORIGIN via Spanish and Portuguese from Latin *niger, nigr-* 'black.'

USAGE The word **Negro** was adopted from Spanish and Portuguese and first recorded from the mid 16th century. It remained the standard term throughout the 17th–19th centuries and was used by such prominent black American campaigners as W.E.B. DuBois and Booker T. Washington in the early 20th century. Since the Black Power movement of the 1960s, however, when the term **black** was favored as the term to express racial pride, **Negro** has dropped out of favor and now seems out of date or even offensive in both US and British English. The 2010 US Census questionnaire was criticized when it retained the racial designation **Negro** as an option (along with **Black** and **African Am.**). The Census Bureau defended its decision, citing the 2000 Census forms, on which more than 56,000 individuals handwrote "Negro" (even though it was already on the form). Apparently, **Negro** continues to be the identity strongly preferred by some Americans. See also usage at **BLACK**.

Ne·groid /ˈnēgroid/ ▶ **adj.** often offensive of or relating to the division of humankind represented by the indigenous peoples of central and southern Africa.

USAGE The term **Negroid** belongs to a set of terms introduced by 19th-century anthropologists attempting to categorize human races. Such terms are associated with outdated notions of racial types, and so are now potentially offensive and best avoided. See also usage at **MONGOLOID**.

Ne·gro Leagues ▶ **n.** associations of professional baseball teams made up of African-American players, esp. active from the 1920s through the 1940s.

ne·gro·ni /nəˈgrōnē/ (also **Negroni**) ▶ **n.** a cocktail made from gin, vermouth, and Campari.
– ORIGIN Italian.

Ne·gro·pho·bi·a /ˌnēgrəˈfōbēə/ ▶ **n.** intense or irrational dislike or fear of black people.
– DERIVATIVES **Ne·gro·phobe** /ˈnēgrəˌfōb/ **n.**

Ne·gros /ˈnāgrōs, ˈne-/ the fourth largest of the Philippine islands; pop. 3,602,200 (est. 2007); chief city, Bacolod.

n

Ne·gro spir·it·u·al ▶ **n.** see **SPIRITUAL**.

Ne·gus /ˈnēgəs/ ▶ **n.** historical a ruler, or the supreme ruler, of Ethiopia.
– ORIGIN from Amharic *n'gus* 'king.'

ne·gus /ˈnēgəs/ ▶ **n.** historical a hot drink of port, sugar, lemon, and spices.
– ORIGIN named after Colonel Francis *Negus* (died 1732), who created it.

Neh. ▶ **abbr.** Bible Nehemiah.

Ne·he·mi·ah /ˌnēəˈmīə/ (5th century BC) a Hebrew leader who supervised the rebuilding of the walls of Jerusalem (*c.*444) and introduced moral and religious reforms (*c.*432). ■ a book of the Bible telling of this rebuilding and of the reforms.

Neh·ru /ˈnāˌrōō, ˈne(ə)rˌōō/, Jawaharlal (1889–1964), Indian statesman; prime minister 1947–64; known as **Pandit Nehru**; father of Indira Gandhi. Nehru was elected leader of the Indian National Congress in 1929. Imprisoned nine times by the British for his nationalist campaigns, he went on to become the first prime minister of independent India.

Jawaharlal Nehru

neigh /nā/ ▶ **n.** a characteristic high-pitched sound uttered by a horse.
▶ **v.** [no obj.] (of a horse) make such a sound; utter a neigh. ■ (of a person) make a similar sound: *they neighed dutifully at jokes they did not understand.*
– ORIGIN Old English *hnǣgan* (verb), of imitative origin; compare with Dutch dialect *neijen*.

neigh·bor /ˈnābər/ (Brit. **neighbour**) ▶ **n.** a person living near or next door to the speaker or person referred to: *our garden was the envy of the neighbors.* ■ a person or place in relation to others near or next to it: *I chatted with my neighbor on the flight to New York | matching our investment levels with those of our North American neighbors.* ■ any person in need of one's help or kindness (after biblical use): *love thy neighbor as thyself.*
▶ **v.** [with obj.] (of a place or thing) be situated next to or very near (another): *the square neighbors the old quarter of the town.*
– DERIVATIVES **neigh·bor·less** **adj.**
– ORIGIN Old English *nēahgebūr*, from *nēah* 'nigh, near' + *gebūr* 'inhabitant, peasant, farmer' (compare with **BOOR**).

neigh·bor·hood /ˈnābərˌhŏŏd/ (Brit. **neighbourhood**) ▶ **n.** a district, esp. one forming a community within a town or city: *she lived in a wealthy neighborhood of Boston | the party disturbed the whole neighborhood.* ■ neighborly feeling or conduct: *the importance of neighborhood to old people.* ■ the area surrounding a particular place, person, or object: *he was reluctant to leave the neighborhood of Butte.* ■ Mathematics the set of points whose distance from a given point is less than (or less than or equal to) some value.
– PHRASES **in the neighborhood of** approximately; about: *the cost would be in the neighborhood of three billion.*

neigh·bor·hood watch ▶ **n.** a program of systematic local vigilance by residents of a neighborhood to discourage crime, esp. burglary.

neigh·bor·ing /ˈnābəriNG/ (Brit. **neighbouring**) ▶ **adj.** next to or very near another place; adjacent: *a couple at a neighboring table | neighboring countries.*

neigh·bor·ly /ˈnābərlē/ (Brit. **neighbourly**) ▶ **adj.** characteristic of a good neighbor, esp. helpful, friendly, or kind.
– DERIVATIVES **neigh·bor·li·ness** **n.**

Neis·se /ˈnīsə/ **1** a river in central Europe that rises in the north of the Czech Republic and flows over 140 miles (225 km) north, forming the southern part of the border between Germany and Poland (the Oder–Neisse Line) and joining the Oder River northeast of Cottbus. German name **LAUSITZER NEISSE**; Polish name **NYSA**.
2 a river in southern Poland that rises near the border with the Czech Republic and flows 120 miles (195 km) northeast, through the town of Nysa, and joins the Oder River southeast of Wrocław. German name **GLATZER NEISSE**.

nei·ther /ˈnēT͟Hər, ˈnī-/ ▶ **determiner & pron.** not the one nor the other of two people or things; not either: [as determiner] *neither side of the brain is dominant over the other* | [as pronoun] ***neither of us** believes it.*
▶ **adv. 1** used before the first of two (or occasionally more) alternatives that are being specified (the others being introduced by "nor") to indicate that they are each untrue or each do not happen: *I am neither a liberal nor a conservative.*
2 used to introduce a further negative statement: *he didn't remember, and neither did I.*
– PHRASES **neither here nor there** see **HERE**.
– ORIGIN Middle English: alteration (by association with **EITHER**) of Old English *nawther*, contraction of *nāhwæther* (from *nā* 'no' + *hwæther* 'whether').

USAGE 1 The use of **neither** with another negative, as in *I **don't** like him **neither*** or *not much good at reading **neither*** is recorded from the 16th century onward, but is not thought to be good English. This is because it is an example of a **double negative**, which, though standard in some other languages such as Spanish and found in many dialects of English, is not acceptable in standard English. In the sentences above, **either** should be used instead. For more information, see usage at **DOUBLE NEGATIVE**. **2** When **neither** is followed by **nor**, it is important in good English style that the two halves of the structure mirror each other: *she saw herself as **neither** wife **nor** mother* rather than *she **neither** saw herself as wife **nor** mother.* For more details, see usage at **EITHER**.

Nejd /nejd/ an arid plateau region in central Saudi Arabia, north of the Rub' al-Khali desert, at an altitude of about 5,000 feet (1,500 m).

nek·ton /ˈnektən, -ˌtän/ ▶ **n.** Zoology aquatic animals that are able to swim and move independently of water currents. Often contrasted with **PLANKTON**.
– DERIVATIVES **nek·ton·ic** /nekˈtänik/ **adj.**
– ORIGIN late 19th cent.: via German from Greek *nēkton*, neuter of *nēktos* 'swimming,' from *nēkhein* 'to swim.'

Nel·lore /nəˈlôr/ a city and river port in southeastern India, in Andhra Pradesh, on the Penner River; pop. 427,400 (est. 2009).

nel·ly /ˈnelē/ ▶ **n.** (pl. **nellies**) informal **1** a silly person. **2** offensive an effeminate homosexual man.
– PHRASES **not on your nelly** Brit. certainly not. [originally as *not on your Nelly Duff*, rhyming slang for 'puff' (i.e., breath of life); modeled on the phrase *not on your life*.]
– ORIGIN mid 20th cent.: from the given name *Nelly*.

Nel·son¹ /ˈnelsən/, Byron (1912–2006), US golfer; full name *John Byron Nelson, Jr.* He set the all-time PGA stroke average with 68.33 strokes per round over 120 rounds in 1945. PGA Hall of Fame (1953).

Nel·son², Horatio, Viscount Nelson, Duke of Bronte (1758–1805), British admiral. He became a national hero as a result of his victories at sea in the Napoleonic Wars, esp. at the Battle of Trafalgar, in which he was mortally wounded.

Nel·son³, Samuel (1792–1873), US Supreme Court associate justice 1845–72. Chief justice of New York state 1837–45, he was appointed to the US Supreme Court by President Tyler.

nel·son /ˈnelsən/ ▶ **n.** a wrestling hold in which one arm is passed under the opponent's arm from behind and the hand is applied to the neck (**half nelson**), or both arms and hands are applied (**full nelson**).
– ORIGIN late 19th cent.: apparently from the surname *Nelson*, but the reference is unknown.

Nel·son Riv·er /ˈnelsən/ a river that flows for 400 miles (640 km) across eastern Manitoba, to Hudson Bay, once a fur trade route.

ne·lum·bo /nəˈləmbō/ ▶ **n.** (pl. **nelumbos**) a lotus with huge leaves and solitary large flowers that grow on stalks that can extend 6 feet (2 m) above the surface of the water. ● Genus *Nelumbo*, family Nelumbonaceae: two species, the **American lotus** and the **sacred lotus** (see **LOTUS**).
– ORIGIN modern Latin, from Sinhalese *nelumba*.

Ne·man /ˈnemən/ a river in eastern Europe that rises south of Minsk in Belarus and flows 597 miles (955 km) west and then north to the Baltic Sea. Its lower course, which forms the boundary between Lithuania and the Russian enclave of Kaliningrad, is called the Memel. Lithuanian name **Nemunas**. Belorussian name **NYOMAN**.

ne·mat·ic /niˈmatik/ ▶ **adj.** relating to or denoting a state of a liquid crystal in which the molecules are oriented in parallel but not arranged in well-defined planes. Compare with **SMECTIC**.
▶ **n.** a nematic substance.
– ORIGIN early 20th cent.: from Greek *nēma, nēmat-* 'thread' + **-IC**.

nemato- (also **nemat-** before a vowel) ▶ **comb. form** denoting something threadlike in shape: *nematocyst.* ■ relating to Nematoda: *nematocide.*
– ORIGIN from Greek *nēma, nēmat-* 'thread.'

nem·a·to·cide /niˈmatəˌsīd, ˈnemətə-/ (also **nematicide**) ▶ **n.** a substance used to kill nematode worms.
– DERIVATIVES **nem·a·to·cid·al** /ˌnematəˈsīdl/ **adj.**
– ORIGIN late 19th cent.: from **NEMATO-** 'of nematode worms' + **-CIDE**.

nem·a·to·cyst /ˈnemətəˌsist, niˈmatə-/ ▶ **n.** Zoology a specialized cell in the tentacles of a jellyfish or other coelenterate, containing a barbed or venomous coiled thread that can be projected in self-defense or to capture prey.
– ORIGIN late 19th cent.: from **NEMATO-** 'of threadlike shape' + **CYST**.

Nem·a·to·da /ˌnēməˈtōdə/ Zoology a large phylum of worms with slender, unsegmented, cylindrical bodies, including the roundworms, threadworms, and eelworms. They are found abundantly in soil and water, and many are parasites.
– ORIGIN modern Latin (plural), from Greek *nēma, nēmat-* 'thread.'

nem·a·tode /ˈnēməˌtōd/ ▶ **n.** Zoology a worm of the large phylum Nematoda, such as a roundworm or threadworm.

nem·a·tol·o·gy /ˌneməˈtäləjē/ ▶ **n.** the scientific study of nematode worms.
– DERIVATIVES **nem·a·tol·o·gist** /-jist/ **n.**

Nem·a·to·mor·pha /ˌnemətəˈmôrfə, nəˌmatə-/ Zoology a small phylum that comprises the horsehair worms.
– DERIVATIVES **nem·a·to·morph** /ˈnemətəˌmôrf, nəˈmatə-/ **n.**
– ORIGIN modern Latin (plural), from Greek *nēma, nēmat-* 'thread' + *morphē* 'form.'

Nem·bu·tal /ˈnembyəˌtäl/ ▶ **n.** trademark the drug pentobarbital sodium (see **PENTOBARBITAL**).
– ORIGIN mid 20th cent.: from *N(a)* (symbol for sodium) + *e(thyl), m(ethyl), but(yl)*, elements of the systematic name, + **-AL**.

nem. con. ▶ **abbr.** nemine contradicente, with no one dissenting; unanimously: *the motions were carried nem. con.*
– ORIGIN Latin.

Ne·mer·te·a /niˈmərtēə/ Zoology a small phylum that comprises the ribbon worms.

–ORIGIN modern Latin (plural), from Greek *Nēmertēs*, the name of a sea nymph.

ne·mer·te·an /ni'mərtēən/ (also **nemertine** /'nemər,tēn/) Zoology ▶ **n.** a member of the small phylum Nemertea; a ribbon worm.
▶ **adj.** relating to or denoting nemerteans.

ne·me·sia /nə'mēzhə/ ▶ **n.** a plant related to the snapdragon that is cultivated for its colorful, obliquely funnel-shaped flowers. ● Genus *Nemesia*, family Scrophulariaceae: several species, in particular *N. strumosa* and its hybrids.
–ORIGIN modern Latin, from Greek *nemesion*, denoting various similar plants.

Nem·e·sis /'neməsis/ Greek Mythology a goddess usually portrayed as the agent of divine punishment for wrongdoing or presumption (hubris).

nem·e·sis /'neməsis/ ▶ **n.** (pl. **nemeses** /-,sēz/) the inescapable agent of someone's or something's downfall: *the balance beam was the team's nemesis, as two gymnasts fell from the apparatus.* ■ a long-standing rival; an archenemy: *will Harry Potter finally defeat his nemesis, Voldemort?* ■ a downfall caused by an inescapable agent: *one risks nemesis by uttering such words.* ■ (often **Nemesis**) retributive justice: *nemesis is notoriously slow.*
–ORIGIN late 16th cent.: Greek, literally 'retribution,' from *nemein* 'give what is due.'

ne·mo dat /'nāmō 'dat, 'nēmō, 'dät/ (in full **nemo dat quod non habet**) ▶ **n.** Law the basic principle that a person who does not own property, esp. a thief, cannot confer it on another except with the true owner's authority.
–ORIGIN Latin, literally 'no one gives (what he or she does not have).'

ne·ne /'nānā/ (also **ne-ne**) ▶ **n.** (pl. **same** or **nenes**) a rare goose native to Hawaii, now breeding chiefly in captivity. Also called **HAWAIIAN GOOSE**. ● *Branta sandvicensis*, family Anatidae.
–ORIGIN early 20th cent.: from Hawaiian.

Nen·ets /'nenets/ ▶ **n.** (pl. **same** or **Nentsy** /'nentsē/ or **Nentsi** /'nentsē/) **1** a member of a nomadic people of Siberia, whose main traditional occupation is reindeer herding.
2 the Samoyedic language of this people.
–ORIGIN the name in Russian.

neo- ▶ **comb. form 1** new: *neonate*.
2 a new or revived form of: *neo-Georgian*.
–ORIGIN from Greek *neos* 'new.'

ne·o·clas·si·cal /,nēō'klasikəl/ (also **neoclassic** /-'klasik/) ▶ **adj.** of or relating to neoclassicism.

ne·o·clas·si·cism /,nēō'klasi,sizəm/ ▶ **n.** the revival of a classical style or treatment in art, literature, architecture, or music.

> As an aesthetic and artistic style this originated in Rome in the mid 18th century, combining a reaction against the late baroque and rococo with a new interest in antiquity. In music, the term refers to a return by composers of the early 20th century to the forms and styles of the 17th and 18th centuries, as a reaction against 19th-century romanticism.

–DERIVATIVES **ne·o·clas·si·cist n. & adj.**

ne·o·co·lo·ni·al·ism /,nēōkə'lōnēə,lizəm/ ▶ **n.** the use of economic, political, cultural, or other pressures to control or influence other countries, esp. former dependencies.
–DERIVATIVES **ne·o·co·lo·ni·al adj., ne·o·co·lo·ni·al·ist n. & adj.**

ne·o·con /,nēō'kän/ ▶ **adj.** (in politics) a person with neoconservative views.
▶ **n.** a neoconservative.

ne·o-Con·fu·cian·ism /,nēōkən'fyōōshənizəm/ ▶ **n.** a movement in religious philosophy derived from Confucianism in China around AD 1000 in response to the ideas of Taoism and Buddhism.
–DERIVATIVES **ne·o-Con·fu·cian adj.**

ne·o·con·serv·a·tive /,nēōkən'sərvətiv/ ▶ **adj.** relating to or denoting a return to a modified form of a traditional viewpoint, in particular a political ideology characterized by an emphasis on free-market capitalism and an interventionist foreign policy.
▶ **n.** a person with neoconservative views.
–DERIVATIVES **ne·o·con·serv·a·tism** /-tizəm/ **n.**

ne·o·cor·tex /,nēō'kôrteks/ ▶ **n.** (pl. **neocortices** /-'kôrti,sēz/) Anatomy a part of the cerebral cortex concerned with sight and hearing in mammals, regarded as the most recently evolved part of the cortex.
–DERIVATIVES **ne·o·cor·ti·cal** /-'kôrtikəl/ **adj.**

ne·o-Dar·win·i·an /,nēōdär'winēən/ ▶ **adj.** Biology of or relating to the modern version of Darwin's theory of evolution by natural selection, incorporating the findings of genetics.
–DERIVATIVES **ne·o-Dar·win·ism** /'därwinizəm/ **n.**, **ne·o-Dar·win·ist** /'därwinist/ **n.**

ne·o·dym·i·um /,nēō'dimēəm/ ▶ **n.** the chemical element of atomic number 60, a silvery-white metal of the lanthanide series. Neodymium is a component of misch metal and some other alloys, and its compounds are used in coloring glass and ceramics. (Symbol: **Nd**)
–ORIGIN late 19th cent.: from **NEO-** 'new' + a shortened form of **DIDYMIUM**.

ne·o·fas·cist /,nēō'fashist/ (also **neo-Fascist**) ▶ **n.** a member of an organization similar to the Italian Fascist movement of the early 20th century.
▶ **adj.** of or relating to neofascists or neofascism.
–DERIVATIVES **ne·o·fas·cism n.**

Ne·o·gae·a /,nēə'jēə/ (also **Neogea**) Zoology a zoogeographical area comprising the Neotropical region.
–DERIVATIVES **Ne·o·gae·an adj.**
–ORIGIN modern Latin, from Greek *neos* 'new' + *gaia* 'earth.'

Ne·o·gene /'nēə,jēn/ ▶ **adj.** Geology of, relating to, or denoting the later division of the Tertiary period, comprising the Miocene and Pliocene epochs. ■ (as noun **the Neogene**) the Neogene subperiod or the system of rocks deposited during it.

> The Neogene lasted from about 23 million to 1.6 million years ago. The mammals continued to evolve during this time, developing into the forms that are familiar today.

–ORIGIN late 19th cent.: from **NEO-** 'new' + Greek *-genēs* 'born, of a specified kind' (see **-GEN**).

ne·o-Geor·gian ▶ **adj.** of, relating to, or imitative of a revival of a Georgian style in architecture.

ne·o-Goth·ic ▶ **adj.** of or in an artistic style that originated in the 19th century, characterized by the revival of Gothic and other medieval forms. In architecture it is manifested in pointed arches, vaulted ceilings, and mock fortifications.
▶ **n.** the neo-Gothic style.

Ne·o·gram·mar·i·an /,nēōgrə'merēən/ ▶ **n.** any of a group of 19th-century German scholars who, having noticed that sound changes in language are regular and that therefore lost word forms can be reconstructed, postulated the forms of entire lost languages such as Proto-Indo-European by the comparison of related forms in existing languages. They also believed that phonetic laws had no exceptions.
–ORIGIN translation of German *Junggrammatiker*.

ne·o-Im·pres·sion·ism (also **Neo-Impressionism**) ▶ **n.** a late 19th-century movement in French painting that sought to improve on Impressionism through a systematic approach to form and color, particularly using pointillist technique. The movement's leading figures included Georges Seurat, Paul Signac, and Camille Pissarro.
–DERIVATIVES **ne·o-Im·pres·sion·ist adj. & n.**

ne·o-Lat·in ▶ **n.** another term for **MODERN LATIN**.

ne·o·lib·er·al /,nēō'libərəl/ ▶ **adj.** relating to or denoting a modified form of liberalism tending to favor free-market capitalism.
▶ **n.** a person holding such views.
–DERIVATIVES **ne·o·lib·er·al·ism** /-,lizəm/ **n.**

ne·o·lith /'nēə,lith/ ▶ **n.** a stone implement used during the Neolithic Period.

Ne·o·lith·ic /,nēə'lithik/ ▶ **adj.** Archaeology of, relating to, or denoting the later part of the Stone Age, when ground or polished stone weapons and implements prevailed. ■ (as noun **the Neolithic**) the Neolithic period. Also called **NEW STONE AGE**.

> In the Neolithic period farm animals were first domesticated, and agriculture was introduced. It began in the Near East by the 8th millennium BC and spread to northern Europe by the 4th millennium BC. Neolithic societies in northwestern Europe left such monuments as henges, long barrows, chamber tombs, and settlements inside concentric ditches spanned by causeways.

–ORIGIN mid 19th cent.: from **NEO-** 'new' + Greek *lithos* 'stone' + **-IC**.

ne·ol·o·gism /nē'älə,jizəm/ ▶ **n.** a newly coined word or expression. ■ the coining or use of new words.
–DERIVATIVES **ne·ol·o·gist** /-jist/ **n.**, **ne·ol·o·gize** /-,jīz/ **v.**
–ORIGIN early 19th cent.: from French *néologisme*.

ne·o-Mal·thu·sian·ism /,nēōmal'thōōzhə,nizəm/ ▶ **n.** the view that the rate of increase of a population should be controlled.
–DERIVATIVES **ne·o-Mal·thu·sian adj. & n.**

ne·o-Marx·ist /,nēō'märksist/ ▶ **adj.** of or relating to forms of political philosophy that arise from the adaptation of Marxist thought to accommodate or confront modern issues such as the global economy, the capitalist welfare state, and the stability of liberal democracies.
▶ **n.** a person with neo-Marxist views.
–DERIVATIVES **ne·o-Marx·ism** /-,izəm/ **n.**

Ne·o-Mel·a·ne·sian /,nēō,melə'nēzhən/ ▶ **n.** another term for **TOK PISIN**.

ne·o·my·cin /,nēō'mīsin/ ▶ **n.** Medicine an antibiotic related to streptomycin, active against a wide variety of bacterial infections. ● This antibiotic is obtained from the bacterium *Streptomyces fradiae*.

ne·on /'nēän/ ▶ **n.** the chemical element of atomic number 10, an inert gaseous element of the noble gas group. It is obtained by the distillation of liquid air and is used in fluorescent lamps and advertising signs. (Symbol: **Ne**) ■ fluorescent lighting or signs (whether containing neon or some other gas): *the lobby of the hotel was bright with neon.* ■ a small lamp containing neon. ■ short for **NEON TETRA**. ■ a very bright or fluorescent color: *a denim cap outlined in neon* | [as modifier] *we bought ourselves neon bandannas*.
–ORIGIN late 19th cent.: from Greek, literally 'something new,' neuter of the adjective *neos*.

ne·o·na·tal /,nēō'nātl/ ▶ **adj.** of or relating to newborn children (or mammals).
–DERIVATIVES **ne·o·na·tol·o·gist** /-nā'täləjist/ **n.**, **ne·o·na·tol·o·gy** /-nā'täləjē/ **n.**

ne·o·nate /'nēə,nāt/ ▶ **n.** a newborn child or mammal. ■ Medicine an infant less than four weeks old.
–ORIGIN 1930s: from modern Latin *neonatus*, from Greek *neos* 'new' + Latin *nat-* 'born' (from the verb *nasci*).

ne·o-Na·zi ▶ **n.** (pl. **neo-Nazis**) a member of an organization similar to the German Nazi Party. ■ a person of extreme racist or nationalist views.
▶ **adj.** of or relating to neo-Nazis or neo-Nazism.
–DERIVATIVES **ne·o-Na·zism n.**

ne·on tet·ra ▶ **n.** a small Amazonian characin (fish) with a shining blue-green stripe along each side and a red band near the tail, popular in aquariums. ● *Paracheirodon innesi*, family Characidae.

ne·on·tol·o·gy /,nēän'täləjē/ ▶ **n.** the branch of zoology dealing with living forms as distinct from fossils. Often contrasted with **PALEONTOLOGY**.
–DERIVATIVES **ne·on·to·log·i·cal** /-tə'läjikəl/ **adj.**
–ORIGIN late 19th cent.: from **NEO-** 'new,' on the pattern of *paleontology*.

ne·o·pa·gan·ism /,nēō'pāgi,nizəm, -gə-/ ▶ **n.** a modern religious movement that seeks to incorporate beliefs or ritual practices from traditions outside the main world religions, esp. those of pre-Christian Europe and North America.

> Neopaganism is a highly varied mixture of ancient and modern elements, in which nature worship (influenced by modern environmentalism) often plays a major role. Other influences include shamanism, magical and occult traditions, and radical feminist critiques of Christianity.

–DERIVATIVES **ne·o·pa·gan n. & adj.**

ne·o·pho·bi·a /,nēō'fōbēə/ ▶ **n.** extreme or irrational fear or dislike of anything new, novel, or unfamiliar.
–DERIVATIVES **ne·o·pho·bic** /-bik/ **adj.**

ne·o·phyte /'nēə,fīt/ ▶ **n.** a person who is new to a subject, skill, or belief: *four-day cooking classes are offered to neophytes and experts.* ■ a new convert to a religion. ■ a novice in a religious order, or a newly ordained priest.
–ORIGIN late Middle English: via ecclesiastical Latin from Greek *neophutos*, literally 'newly planted' but first used in the sense 'new convert' by St. Paul (1 Tim. 3:6), from *neos* 'new' + *phuton* 'plant.'

ne·o·pla·sia /,nēō'plāzhə/ ▶ **n.** Medicine the formation or presence of a new, abnormal growth of tissue.

ne·o·plasm /'nēə,plazəm/ ▶ **n.** a new and abnormal growth of tissue in some part of the body, esp. as a characteristic of cancer.
–ORIGIN mid 19th cent.: from **NEO-** 'new' + Greek *plasma* 'formation' (see **PLASMA**).

ne·o·plas·tic[1] /,nēə'plastik/ ▶ **adj.** Medicine of or relating to a neoplasm or neoplasia.

ne·o·plas·tic[2] ▶ **adj.** Art of or relating to neoplasticism.
–ORIGIN 1930s: back-formation from **NEOPLASTICISM**.

ne·o·plas·ti·cism /,nēō'plasti,sizəm/ ▶ **n.** a style of abstract painting developed by Piet Mondrian, using only vertical and horizontal lines and rectangular shapes in black, white, gray, and primary colors.
–ORIGIN 1920s: coined by Piet Mondrian.

n

Ne·o·pla·to·nism /ˌnēōˈplātnˌizəm/ a philosophical and religious system developed by the followers of Plotinus in the 3rd century AD.

Neoplatonism combined ideas from Plato, Aristotle, Pythagoras, and the Stoics with oriental mysticism. Predominant in pagan Europe until the early 6th century, it was a major influence on early Christian writers, on later medieval and Renaissance thought, and on Islamic philosophy. It envisages the human soul rising above the imperfect material world through virtue and contemplation toward knowledge of the transcendent One.

– DERIVATIVES **Ne·o·pla·ton·ic** /-pləˈtänik/ **adj.**, **Ne·o·pla·to·nist n.**

ne·o·prene /ˈnēəˌprēn/ ▶ **n.** a synthetic polymer resembling rubber, resistant to oil, heat, and weathering.
– ORIGIN 1930s: from **NEO-** 'new' + *prene* (perhaps from **PROPYL** + **-ENE**), on the pattern of words such as *chloroprene*.

Ne·op·tol·e·mus /ˌnēäpˈtäləməs/ Greek Mythology the son of Achilles and killer of Priam after the fall of Troy.

ne·o·re·al·ism /ˌnēōˈrēlizəm/ ▶ **n.** a movement or school in art or philosophy representing a modified form of realism. ■ a naturalistic movement in Italian literature and cinema that emerged in the 1940s. Important exponents include the writer Italo Calvino and the film director Federico Fellini.
– DERIVATIVES **ne·o·re·al·ist n. & adj.**

Ne·o·sho Riv·er /nēˈōsHō, -sHə/ (also **Grand River**) a river that flows for 460 miles (740 km) from central Kansas through northeastern Oklahoma, into the Arkansas River.

ne·o·stig·mine /ˌnēōˈstigmēn/ ▶ **n.** Medicine a synthetic compound that inhibits cholinesterase and is used to treat ileus, glaucoma, and myasthenia gravis.
– ORIGIN 1940s: from **NEO-** 'new,' on the pattern of *physostigmine*.

ne·ot·e·ny /nēˈätn-ē/ ▶ **n.** Zoology the retention of juvenile features in the adult animal. Also called **PEDOMORPHOSIS**. ■ the sexual maturity of an animal while it is still in a mainly larval state, as in the axolotl. Also called **PEDOGENESIS**.
– DERIVATIVES **ne·o·te·nic** /ˌnēōˈtenik, -ˈtēnik/ **adj.**, **ne·o·te·nous** /nēˈätn-əs/ **adj.**
– ORIGIN late 19th cent.: coined in German as *Neotenie*, from Greek *neos* 'new' (in the sense 'juvenile') + *teinein* 'extend.'

n

ne·o·ter·ic /ˌnēəˈterik/ ▶ **adj.** recent; new; modern: *another effort by the White House to display its neoteric wizardry went awry*.
▶ **n.** a modern person; a person who advocates new ideas.
– ORIGIN late 16th cent.: via late Latin from Greek *neōterikos*, from *neōteros* 'newer,' comparative of *neos*.

Ne·o·trop·i·cal /ˌnēōˈträpikəl/ (also **neotropical**) ▶ **adj.** Zoology of, relating to, or denoting a zoogeographical region comprising Central and South America, including the tropical southern part of Mexico and the Caribbean. Distinctive animals include edentates, opossums, marmosets, and tamarins. Compare with **NEOGAEA**. ■ Botany of, relating to, or denoting a phytogeographical kingdom comprising Central and South America but excluding the southern parts of Chile and Argentina.
– DERIVATIVES **Ne·o·trop·ics** /-piks/ **plural n.**

NEP ▶ **abbr.** ■ New Economic Policy, a program instituted by Lenin in 1921 in the Soviet Union. ■ non-English proficient.

Ne·pal /nəˈpäl, -ˈpôl/ a mountainous landlocked country in southern Asia, in the Himalayas (including Mount Everest); pop. 28,563,400 (est. 2009); capital, Kathmandu; language, Nepali (official).

Conquered by the Gurkhas in the 18th century, Nepal maintained its independence despite border defeats by the British in the 19th century. It was for long an absolute monarchy, but in 1990 democratic elections were held under a new constitutional monarchy. In 2001 the crown prince killed ten members of the royal family and took his own life.

– DERIVATIVES **Nep·a·lese** /ˌnepəˈlēz, -ˈlēs/ **adj. & n.**

Ne·pal·i /nəˈpôlē, -ˈpälē/ ▶ **n.** (pl. **same** or **Nepalis**) a native or inhabitant of Nepal. ■ the Indic language that is the official language of Nepal; also used in the Indian state of Sikkim.
▶ **adj.** of or relating to Nepal or its language or people.

ne·pen·thes /nəˈpenTHēz/ ▶ **n. 1** (also **nepenthe**) /-THē/ literary a drug described in Homer's *Odyssey* as banishing grief or trouble from a person's mind. ■ any drug or potion bringing welcome forgetfulness. [via Latin from Greek *nēpenthēs* 'dispelling pain,' from *nē-* 'not' + *penthos* 'grief.']
2 a plant of a genus that comprises the Old World pitcher plants. [modern Latin.] ● Genus *Nepenthes* and family Nepenthaceae.

ne·per /ˈnēpər, ˈnā-/ ▶ **n.** Physics a unit used in comparing voltages, currents, and power levels, esp. in communications circuits. The difference between two values in nepers is equal to the natural logarithm of their ratio for voltages and currents or to half of this for power differences.
– ORIGIN early 20th cent.: from *Neperus*, Latinized form of *Napier* (see **NAPIER**).

nep·e·ta /nəˈpētə/ ▶ **n.** a plant of a genus that includes catnip and several kinds cultivated for their spikes of blue or violet flowers. ● Genus *Nepeta*, family Labiatae.
– ORIGIN modern Latin, from Latin *nepeta* 'calamint' (formerly in this genus).

neph·e·line /ˈnefəlin/ ▶ **n.** a colorless, greenish, or brownish mineral consisting of an aluminosilicate of sodium (often with potassium) and occurring as crystals and grains in igneous rocks.
– ORIGIN early 19th cent.: from French *néphéline*, from Greek *nephelē* 'cloud' (because its fragments are made cloudy on immersion in nitric acid) + **-INE**[2].

neph·e·line-sy·e·nite ▶ **n.** Geology a plutonic rock resembling syenite but containing nepheline and lacking quartz.

neph·e·lin·ite /ˈnefələˌnit/ ▶ **n.** Geology a fine-grained basaltic rock containing nepheline in place of plagioclase feldspar.

neph·e·lom·e·ter /ˌnefəˈlämitər/ ▶ **n.** an instrument for measuring the size and concentration of particles suspended in a liquid or gas, esp. by means of the light they scatter.
– ORIGIN late 19th cent.: from Greek *nephelē* 'cloud' + **-METER**.

neph·ew /ˈnefyo͞o/ ▶ **n.** a son of one's brother or sister, or of one's brother-in-law or sister-in-law.
– ORIGIN Middle English: from Old French *neveu*, from Latin *nepos* 'grandson, nephew,' from an Indo-European root shared by Dutch *neef* and German *Neffe*.

ne·phol·o·gy /nəˈfäləjē/ ▶ **n.** the study or contemplation of clouds.
– ORIGIN late 19th cent.: from Greek *nephos* 'cloud' + **-LOGY**.

nephr- ▶ **comb. form** variant spelling of **NEPHRO-** shortened before a vowel (as in *nephrectomy*).

ne·phrec·to·my /nəˈfrektəmē/ ▶ **n.** (pl. **nephrectomies**) surgical removal of one or both of the kidneys.

ne·phrid·io·pore /nəˈfridēəˌpôr/ ▶ **n.** Zoology the external opening of a nephridium.

ne·phrid·i·um /nəˈfridēəm/ ▶ **n.** (pl. **nephridia** /-ˈfridēə/) Zoology (in many invertebrate animals) a tubule open to the exterior that acts as an organ of excretion or osmoregulation. It typically has ciliated or flagellated cells and absorptive walls.
– DERIVATIVES **ne·phrid·i·al** /-ēəl/ **adj.**
– ORIGIN late 19th cent.: modern Latin, from Greek *nephrion* (diminutive of *nephros* 'kidney') + the diminutive ending *-idium*.

neph·rite /ˈnefrīt/ ▶ **n.** a hard pale green or white mineral that is one of the forms of jade. It is a silicate of calcium and magnesium.
– ORIGIN late 18th cent.: from German *Nephrit*, from Greek *nephros* 'kidney' (with reference to its supposed efficacy in treating kidney disease).

ne·phrit·ic /nəˈfritik/ ▶ **adj.** of or in the kidneys; renal. ■ of or relating to nephritis.
– ORIGIN early 19th cent.: via late Latin from Greek *nephritikos* 'of the kidneys' (see **NEPHRITIS**).

ne·phri·tis /nəˈfrītis/ ▶ **n.** Medicine inflammation of the kidneys. Also called **BRIGHT'S DISEASE**.
– ORIGIN late 16th cent.: via late Latin from Greek, from *nephros* 'kidney.'

nephro- (also **nephr-** before a vowel) ▶ **comb. form** of a kidney; relating to the kidneys: *nephrotoxic*.
– ORIGIN from Greek *nephros* 'kidney.'

ne·phrol·o·gy /nəˈfräləjē/ ▶ **n.** the branch of medicine that deals with the physiology and diseases of the kidneys.
– DERIVATIVES **neph·ro·log·i·cal** /ˌnefrəˈläjikəl/ **adj.**, **ne·phrol·o·gist** /-jist/ **n.**

neph·ron /ˈnefrän/ ▶ **n.** Anatomy each of the functional units in the kidney, consisting of a glomerulus and its associated tubule, through which the glomerular filtrate passes before emerging as urine.
– ORIGIN 1930s: via German from Greek *nephros* 'kidney.'

ne·phro·sis /nəˈfrōsis/ ▶ **n.** kidney disease, esp. when characterized by edema and the loss of protein from the plasma into the urine due to increased glomerular permeability. Also called **nephrotic syndrome**.
– DERIVATIVES **ne·phrot·ic** /nəˈfrätik/ **adj.**

neph·ro·tox·ic /ˌnefrəˈtäksik/ ▶ **adj.** damaging or destructive to the kidneys.
– DERIVATIVES **neph·ro·tox·ic·i·ty** /-täkˈsisitē/ **n.**, **neph·ro·tox·in** /-sin/ **n.**

ne plus ul·tra /ˈnē ˌpləs ˈəltrə, ˈnā ˌplo͞os ˈo͞oltrə/ ▶ **n.** the perfect or most extreme example of its kind; the ultimate: *he became the ne plus ultra of bebop trombonists*.
– ORIGIN Latin, literally 'not further beyond,' the supposed inscription on the Pillars of Hercules prohibiting passage by ships.

nep·o·tism /ˈnepəˌtizəm/ ▶ **n.** the practice among those with power or influence of favoring relatives or friends, esp. by giving them jobs.
– DERIVATIVES **nep·o·tist n.**, **nep·o·tis·tic** /ˌnepəˈtistik/ **adj.**
– ORIGIN mid 17th cent.: from French *népotisme*, from Italian *nepotismo*, from *nipote* 'nephew' (with reference to privileges bestowed on the "nephews" of popes, who were in many cases their illegitimate sons).

Nep·tune /ˈnept(y)o͞on/ **1** Roman Mythology the god of water and of the sea. Greek equivalent **POSEIDON**. [from Latin *Neptunus*.]
2 Astronomy a distant planet of the solar system, eighth in order from the sun, discovered in 1846.

Neptune orbits between Uranus and Pluto at an average distance of 2,794 million miles (4,497 million km) from the sun (but temporarily outside the orbit of Pluto 1979–99). It is the fourth largest planet, with an equatorial diameter of 30,200 miles (48,600 km), and the most remote of the gas giants. The planet is predominantly blue, with an upper atmosphere mainly of hydrogen and helium with some methane. It has at least eight satellites, the largest of which is Triton, and a faint ring system.

Nep·tu·ni·an /nepˈt(y)o͞onēən/ ▶ **adj. 1** of or relating to the Roman sea god Neptune or to the sea. **2** of or relating to the planet Neptune. **3** Geology, historical advocating Neptunism.

nep·tu·ni·an dike ▶ **n.** Geology a deposit of sand cutting through sedimentary strata in the manner of an igneous dike, formed by the filling of an underwater fissure.

Nep·tun·ism /ˈnept(y)o͞oˌnizəm/ ▶ **n.** Geology, historical the erroneous theory that rocks such as granite were formed by crystallization from the waters of a primeval ocean. The chief advocate of this theory was Abraham Gottlob Werner (1749–1817). Compare with **PLUTONISM**.
– DERIVATIVES **Nep·tun·ist n. & adj.**

nep·tu·ni·um /nepˈt(y)o͞onēəm/ ▶ **n.** the chemical element of atomic number 93, a radioactive metal of the actinide series. Neptunium was discovered as a product of the bombardment of uranium with neutrons, and occurs only in trace amounts in nature. (Symbol: **Np**)
– ORIGIN late 19th cent.: from **NEPTUNE**, on the pattern of *uranium* (Neptune being the next planet beyond Uranus).

nerd /nərd/ ▶ **n.** informal a foolish or contemptible person who lacks social skills or is boringly studious: *one of those nerds who never asked a girl to dance*. ■ a single-minded expert in a particular technical field: *a computer nerd*.
– DERIVATIVES **nerd·i·ness n.**, **nerd·ish adj.**, **nerd·y adj.**
– ORIGIN 1950s: of unknown origin.

WORD TRENDS See **GEEK**.

Ne·re·id /ˈni(ə)rēid/ **1** (also **nereid**) Greek Mythology any of the sea nymphs, daughters of Nereus. They include Thetis, mother of Achilles.
2 Astronomy a satellite of Neptune, the farthest from the planet, discovered in 1949. It has an irregular shape, a diameter of 211 miles (340 km), and an eccentric orbit.

ne·re·id /ˈni(ə)rēid/ ▶ **n.** Zoology a bristle worm of the polychaete family (Nereidae).
– ORIGIN mid 19th cent.: from modern Latin *Nereidae*, from the Greek name *Nēreus* (see **NEREID**).

Ne·re·us /ˈni(ə)rēəs/ Greek Mythology an old sea god, the father of the Nereids. Like Proteus, he had the power of assuming various forms.

ne·ri·ne /nəˈrīnē/ ▶ **n.** a bulbous South African plant with narrow, strap-shaped petals that are typically crimped and twisted and appear when there are no leaves. ● Genus *Nerine*, family Liliaceae (or Amaryllidaceae).
– ORIGIN modern Latin, derivative of Greek *Nērēis*, the name of a water nymph.

ner·ite /ˈni(ə)rˌīt/ ▶ **n.** a chiefly tropical mollusk with a somewhat globe-shaped and brightly marked shell, typically found in water. ● Superfamily Neritacea, class Gastropoda: several genera and species, including the European freshwater snail *Theodoxus fluviatilis*.
– ORIGIN early 18th cent.: from Latin *nerita*, from Greek *nēritēs* 'sea mussel,' from the name of the sea god **NEREUS**.

ne·rit·ic /nəˈritik/ ▶ **adj.** Biology & Geology of, relating to, or denoting the shallow part of the sea near a coast and overlying the continental shelf.
– ORIGIN late 19th cent.: from **NERITE** + **-IC**.

Nernst /nərnst, nernst/, Hermann Walther (1864–1941), German physical chemist. He is noted for his discovery of the third law of thermodynamics (also known as **Nernst's heat theorem**). Nobel Prize for Chemistry (1920).

Ne·ro /ˈni(ə)rō/ (AD 37–68), Roman emperor 54–68; full name *Nero Claudius Caesar Augustus Germanicus*. Infamous for his cruelty, he ordered the murder of his mother Agrippina in 59 and wantonly executed leading Romans. His reign witnessed a fire that destroyed half of Rome in 64. A wave of uprisings in 68 led to his flight from Rome and his eventual suicide.

ner·o·li /ˈnerəlē/ (also **neroli oil**) ▶ **n.** an essential oil distilled from the flowers of the Seville orange, used in perfumery.
– ORIGIN late 17th cent.: via French from Italian *neroli*, said to be from the name of an Italian princess.

Ne·ru·da /nəˈro͞odə, neˈro͞odä/, Pablo (1904–73), Chilean poet and diplomat; born *Ricardo Eliezer Neftalí Reyes*. His *Canto General*, which he completed in 1950, is an epic covering the history of the Americas. Nobel Prize for Literature (1971).

Ner·va /ˈnərvə/, Marcus Cocceius (*c.* AD 30–98), Roman emperor 96–98. He returned to a liberal and constitutional form of rule after the autocracy of his predecessor, Domitian.

ner·va·tion /ˌnərˈvāsHən/ ▶ **n.** Botany the arrangement of nerves in a leaf.
– ORIGIN early 18th cent.: from French, based on *nerf* 'nerve.'

nerve /nərv/ ▶ **n. 1** (in the body) a whitish fiber or bundle of fibers that transmits impulses of sensation to the brain or spinal cord, and impulses from these to the muscles and organs: *the optic nerve*.
2 (**nerves**) a person's mental state, in particular the extent to which they are agitated or worried: *an amazing journey that tested her nerves to the full*. ■ nervousness or anxiety: *his first-night nerves soon disappeared*.
3 (often **one's nerve**) a person's steadiness, courage, and sense of purpose when facing a demanding situation: *the army's commanders were beginning to lose their nerve | I got up the nerve to ask Miss Kinnian to have dinner with me*. ■ informal impudence or audacity: *he had the nerve to insult my cooking | she's got nerve wearing that short skirt with those legs*.
4 Botany a prominent unbranched rib in a leaf, esp. in the midrib of the leaf of a moss.
▶ **v.** (**nerve oneself**) brace oneself mentally to face a demanding situation: *she nerved herself to enter the room*.
– PHRASES **a bundle of nerves** see **BUNDLE**. **get on someone's nerves** informal irritate or annoy someone. **have nerves of steel** not be easily upset or frightened. **strain every nerve** make every possible effort. [from the earlier sense of *nerve* as 'tendon, sinew.'] **touch** (or **hit** or **strike**) **a nerve** (or **a raw nerve**) provoke a reaction by referring to a sensitive topic: *there are signs that some comments strike a raw nerve*. **war of nerves** a struggle in which opponents try to wear each other down by psychological means.
– DERIVATIVES **nerved adj.** [usu. in combination] *she was still raw-nerved from reliving the past*.
– ORIGIN late Middle English (also in the sense 'tendon, sinew'): from Latin *nervus*; related to Greek *neuron* 'nerve' (see **NEURON**).

nerve block ▶ **n.** Medicine the production of insensibility in a part of the body by injecting an anesthetic close to the nerves that supply it.

nerve cell ▶ **n.** a neuron.

nerve cen·ter ▶ **n.** a group of closely connected nerve cells that perform a particular function in the body; a ganglion. ■ the control center of an organization or operation: *Frankfurt is the economic nerve center of Germany*.

nerve cord ▶ **n.** Zoology the major cord of nerve fibers running the length of an animal's body, esp. a ventral cord in invertebrates that connects segmental nerve ganglia.

nerve fi·ber ▶ **n.** the axon of a neuron. A nerve is formed of a bundle of many such fibers, with their sheaths.

nerve gas ▶ **n.** a poisonous vapor that rapidly disables or kills by disrupting the transmission of nerve impulses.

nerve im·pulse ▶ **n.** a signal transmitted along a nerve fiber. It consists of a wave of electrical depolarization that reverses the potential difference across the nerve cell membranes.

nerve·less /ˈnərvlis/ ▶ **adj. 1** inert; lacking vigor or feeling: *the knife dropped from Grant's nerveless fingers*. ■ (of literary or artistic style) diffuse or insipid: *Wilde and his art are described as "nerveless and effeminate."*
2 confident; not nervous: *with nerveless panache*.
3 Anatomy & Biology lacking nerves or nervures.
– DERIVATIVES **nerve·less·ly adv.**, **nerve·less·ness n.**

nerve net ▶ **n.** Zoology (in invertebrates such as coelenterates and flatworms) a diffuse network of neurons that conducts impulses in all directions from a point of stimulus.

nerve-rack·ing (also **nerve-wracking**) ▶ **adj.** causing stress or anxiety: *his driving test was a nerve-racking ordeal*.

nerve trunk ▶ **n.** Anatomy the main stem of a nerve.

Ner·vi /ˈnərvē, ˈner-/, Pier Luigi (1891–1979), Italian engineer and architect. A pioneer of reinforced concrete, he helped to design the UNESCO building in Paris (1953) and designed the Pirelli skyscraper in Milan (1958) and Saint Mary's Cathedral in San Francisco (1970).

nerv·ine /ˈnərvēn/ ▶ **adj.** (of a medicine) used to calm the nerves.
▶ **n.** a medicine of this kind.
– ORIGIN mid 17th cent.: from medieval Latin *nervinus* 'of the nerves or sinews,' or suggested by French *nervin*.

nerv·ous /ˈnərvəs/ ▶ **adj. 1** easily agitated or alarmed; tending to be anxious; highly strung: *a sensitive, nervous person | these quick, nervous birds*. ■ anxious or apprehensive: *staying in the house on her own made her nervous | I was nervous about my new job*. ■ (of a feeling or reaction) resulting from anxiety or anticipation: *nervous energy*.
2 relating to or affecting the nerves: *a nervous disorder*.
– DERIVATIVES **ner·vous·ly adv.**
– ORIGIN late Middle English (in the senses 'containing nerves' and 'relating to the nerves'): from Latin *nervosus* 'sinewy, vigorous,' from *nervus* 'sinew' (see **NERVE**). Sense 1 dates from the mid 18th cent.

nerv·ous break·down ▶ **n.** a period of mental illness resulting from severe depression, stress, or anxiety.

ner·vous·ness /ˈnərvəsnis/ ▶ **n.** the quality or state of being nervous: *there was a trace of nervousness in his voice*.

nerv·ous sys·tem ▶ **n.** the network of nerve cells and fibers that transmits nerve impulses between parts of the body. See also **AUTONOMIC NERVOUS SYSTEM, CENTRAL NERVOUS SYSTEM, PERIPHERAL NERVOUS SYSTEM**.

nerv·ous wreck ▶ **n.** informal a person suffering from stress or emotional exhaustion: *by the end of the day I was a nervous wreck*.

ner·vure /ˈnərvyo͝or/ ▶ **n.** Entomology each of the hollow veins that form the framework of an insect's wing. ■ Botany the principal vein of a leaf.
– ORIGIN early 19th cent.: from French, from *nerf* 'nerve.'

nerv·y /ˈnərvē/ ▶ **adj.** (**nervier, nerviest**) **1** informal bold or impudent: *it was kind of nervy for Billy to be telling him how to play*.
2 chiefly Brit. easily agitated or alarmed; nervous: *he was nervy and on edge*. ■ characterized or produced by apprehension or uncertainty: *they made a nervy start*.
3 archaic or literary sinewy or strong.
– DERIVATIVES **nerv·i·ly** /ˈnərvəlē/ **adv.**, **nerv·i·ness n.**

n.e.s. (also **N.E.S.**) ▶ **abbr.** not elsewhere specified.

Nes·bit /ˈnezbit/, E. (1858–1924), English novelist; full name *Edith Nesbit*. Noted for her children's books, which include *Five Children and It* (1902) and *The Railway Children* (1906).

nes·cient /ˈnesH(ē)ənt/ ▶ **adj.** literary lacking knowledge; ignorant: *I ventured into the new Korean restaurant with some equally nescient companions*.
– DERIVATIVES **nesc·ience n.**
– ORIGIN late Middle English: from Latin *nescient-* 'not knowing,' from the verb *nescire*, from *ne-* 'not' + *scire* 'know.'

ness /nes/ ▶ **n.** (usu. in place names) a headland or promontory: *Orford Ness*.
– ORIGIN Old English *næs*, perhaps reinforced in Middle English by Old Norse *nes*; related to Old English *nasu* 'nose.'

-ness /nəs, nis/ ▶ **suffix** forming nouns chiefly from adjectives: **1** denoting a state or condition: *liveliness | sadness*. ■ an instance of this: *a kindness*.
2 something in a certain state: *wilderness*.
– ORIGIN Old English *-nes, -ness*, of Germanic origin.

Ness, Loch see **LOCH NESS**.

Nes·sus /ˈnesəs/ Greek & Roman Mythology a centaur who was killed by Hercules, but whose blood soaked Hercules's tunic and consumed him in fire.
– PHRASES **Nessus shirt** (or **shirt of Nessus**) used to refer to a destructive or expurgatory force or influence: *after the lost election of 1979 he found himself wearing this shirt of Nessus*.

nest /nest/ ▶ **n. 1** a structure or place made or chosen by a bird for laying eggs and sheltering its young. ■ a place where an animal or insect breeds or shelters: *an ants' nest*. ■ a person's snug or secluded retreat or shelter. ■ a bowl-shaped object likened to a bird's nest: *arrange in nests of lettuce leaves*. ■ a place filled with or frequented by undesirable people or things: *a nest of spies*.
2 a set of similar objects of graduated sizes, made so that each smaller one fits into the next in size for storage: *a nest of tables*.
▶ **v. 1** [no obj.] (of a bird or other animal) use or build a nest: *the owls often nest in barns* | (as adj. **nesting**) *do not disturb nesting birds*.
2 [with obj.] fit (an object or objects) inside a larger one: *the town is nested inside a large crater on the flanks of a volcano*. ■ [no obj.] (of a set of objects) fit inside one another: *Russian dolls that nest inside one another*. ■ (esp. in computing and linguistics) place (an object or element) in a hierarchical arrangement, typically in a subordinate position: (as adj. **nested**) *organisms classified in a series of nested sets*.
– DERIVATIVES **nest·ful** /-ˌfo͝ol/ **n.** (pl. **nestfuls**), **nest·like** /-ˌlīk/ **adj.**
– ORIGIN Old English *nest*, of Germanic origin; related to Latin *nidus*, from the Indo-European bases of **NETHER** (meaning 'down') and **SIT**.

nest box (also **nesting box**) ▶ **n.** a box provided for a bird to make its nest in.

nest egg ▶ **n. 1** a sum of money saved for the future: *I worked hard to build up a nice little nest egg*.
2 a real or artificial egg left in a nest to induce hens to lay eggs there.

nest·er /ˈnestər/ ▶ **n. 1** a bird that nests in a specified manner or place: *redstarts are nesters here | hole-nesters*. See also **EMPTY NESTER**.
2 a squatter who occupies rangeland in the US West.

nes·tle /ˈnesəl/ ▶ **v.** [no obj.] settle or lie comfortably within or against something: *the baby deer nestled in her arms* | [with obj.] *she nestled her head against his shoulder*. ■ (of a place) lie or be situated in a half-hidden or obscured position: *picturesque villages nestle in the wooded hills* | (**be nestled**) *the hotel is nestled between two headlands*.
– ORIGIN Old English *nestlian*, from **NEST**; compare with Dutch *nestelen*.

nest·ling /ˈnes(t)liNG/ ▶ **n.** a bird that is too young to leave its nest.

Nes·tor /ˈnestər/ Greek Mythology a king of Pylos in Peloponnesus, who in old age led his subjects to the Trojan War. His wisdom and eloquence were proverbial.

Nes·to·ri·an·ism /nesˈtôrēəˌnizəm/ ▶ **n.** Theology the doctrine that there were two separate persons, one human and one divine, in the incarnate Christ. It is named after **Nestorius**, patriarch of Constantinople (428–31), and was maintained by some ancient churches of the Middle East. A small Nestorian Church still exists in Iraq.
– DERIVATIVES **Nes·to·ri·an adj. & n.**

net[1] /net/ ▶ **n. 1** a length of open-meshed material made of twine, cord, rope, or something similar, used typically for catching fish or other animals. ■ a piece of such material supported by a frame at the end of a handle, used typically for catching fish or other aquatic animals or insects. ■ a length of such material supported on a frame and forming part of the goal in various games such as soccer and hockey: *he turned Wilson's cross into the net*. ■ a length of such material supported on a cord between two posts to divide the playing area in various games such as tennis, badminton, and volleyball. ■ a safety net: *he felt like a tightrope-walker without a net*.
2 a fine fabric with a very open weave: [as modifier] *net curtains*.

PRONUNCIATION KEY ə *ago, up*; ər *over, fur*; a *hat*; ā *ate*; ä *car*; e *let*; ē *see*; i *fit*; ī *by*; NG *sing*; ō *go*; ô *law, for*; oi *toy*; o͝o *good*; o͞o *goo*; ou *out*; TH *thin*; T̲H̲ *then*; ZH *vision*

n

3 a system or procedure for catching or entrapping someone; a trap: *the search was delayed, allowing the murderers to escape the net.* ■ a system or procedure for selecting or recruiting someone: *he spread his net far and wide in his search for success.*
4 a network, in particular: ■ a communications or broadcasting network: *the radio net was brought to life with a mayday.* ■ a network of interconnected computers: *a computer news net.* ■ **(the Net)** the Internet.
▶ v. **(nets, netted, netting)** [with obj.] **1** catch or land (a fish or other animal) with a net. ■ fish with nets in (a river): *he has netted the creeks and found them clogged with fish.* ■ acquire or obtain as if with a net: *customs officials have netted large caches of drugs.*
2 (in sports) hit or kick (a ball or puck) into the net; score (a goal): *in six years Wright has netted 177 goals* | [no obj.] *Aldridge netted twice.*
3 cover with a net: *we fenced off a rabbit-proof area for vegetables and netted the top.*
– DERIVATIVES **net·ful** /-ˌfo͝ol/ n. (pl. **netfuls**), **net·like** /-ˌlīk/ adj.
– ORIGIN Old English *net, nett*, of Germanic origin; related to Dutch *net* and German *Netz*.

net[2] ▶ adj. **1** (of an amount, value, or price) remaining after a deduction, such as tax or a discount, has been made: *net earnings per share rose* | *the net worth of the business.* Often contrasted with GROSS (sense 2 of the adjective). ■ (of a price) to be paid in full; not reducible. ■ (of a weight) excluding that of the packaging or container. ■ (of a score in golf) adjusted to take account of a player's handicap.
2 (of an effect or result) final or overall: *the net result is the same.*
▶ v. **(nets, netting, netted)** [with obj.] acquire or obtain (a sum of money) as clear profit: *they sold their 20% stake, netting a huge profit in the process.* ■ [with two objs.] return (profit or income) for (someone): *the land netted its owner a turnover of $800,000.* ■ **(net something down/off/out)** exclude a non-net amount, such as tax, when making a calculation, in order to reduce the amount left to a net sum.
– ORIGIN Middle English (in the senses 'clean' and 'smart'): from French *net* 'neat'; see NEAT[1]. The sense 'free from deductions' is first recorded in late Middle English commercial documents.

Net·an·ya·hu /ˌnetän'yäho͞o/, Benjamin (1949–), Israeli statesman; prime minister 1996–99 and since 2009. As leader of the center-right Likud party, he formed a coalition government following the 2009 elections.

n

net as·set val·ue ▶ n. the value of a mutual fund that is reached by deducting the fund's liabilities from the market value of all of its shares and then dividing by the number of issued shares.

net·ball /'netˌbôl/ ▶ n. chiefly Brit. a game with seven players on a side, similar to basketball except that a player receiving the ball must stand still until they have passed it to another player. ■ the ball used in this game.

net·book /'netbo͝ok/ ▶ n. a small laptop computer designed primarily for accessing Internet-based applications.
– ORIGIN early 21st cent.: blend of INTERNET and NOTEBOOK.

net book val·ue ▶ n. Finance the value of an asset as recorded in the accounts of its owner.

neth·er /'neT͟Hər/ ▶ adj. lower in position: *the ballast is suspended from its nether end.*
– DERIVATIVES **neth·er·most** /-ˌmōst/ adj.
– ORIGIN Old English *nithera, neothera*, of Germanic origin; related to Dutch *neder-* (found in compounds), *neer*, and German *nieder*, from an Indo-European root meaning 'down.'

Neth·er·lands /'neT͟Hərlən(d)z/ a country in western Europe, on the North Sea; pop. 16,716,000 (est. 2009); capital, Amsterdam; seat of government, The Hague; language, Dutch. Dutch name NEDERLAND. Also called HOLLAND. ■ historical the Low Countries.

> Following a struggle against the Spanish Habsburg empire, the northern (Dutch) part of the Low Countries won full independence in 1648 and became a leading imperial power. In 1814, north and south were united under a monarchy, but the south revolted in 1830 and, by 1839, had become the independent kingdom of Belgium. In 1948, the Netherlands formed the Benelux Customs Union with Belgium and Luxembourg. It became a founding member of the EEC in 1957. The name **Holland** strictly refers to the western coastal provinces of the country.

– DERIVATIVES **Neth·er·land·er** /-ˌlandər/ n., **Neth·er·land·ish** /-ˌlandisH/ adj.

Neth·er·lands An·til·les two widely separated groups of Dutch islands in the Caribbean Sea, in the Lesser Antilles; capital, Willemstad, on Curaçao; pop. 227,000 (est. 2009). The southernmost group, situated just off the north coast of Venezuela, consists of the islands of Bonaire and Curaçao. The northern group comprises the islands of St. Eustatius, St. Martin, and Saba. In 1954, the islands were granted self-government and became an autonomous region of the Netherlands.

Neth·er·lands Re·formed Church the largest Protestant church in the Netherlands, established in 1816 as the successor to the Dutch Reformed Church.

neth·er re·gions ▶ plural n. the lowest or furthest parts of a place, esp. with allusion to hell or the underworld: *rumors of strange creatures haunting the lake's bottomless nether regions.* ■ **(one's nether regions)** used euphemistically to refer to a person's genitals and buttocks.

neth·er·world /'neT͟Hərˌwərld/ ▶ n. **(the netherworld)** the underworld of the dead; hell. ■ a hidden underworld or ill-defined area: *the narcotic netherworld thriving in postwar America.*

net·i·quette /'netəkit, -ˌket/ ▶ n. the correct or acceptable way of communicating on the Internet.
– ORIGIN 1990s: blend of NET[1] and ETIQUETTE.

net·i·zen /'netəzən/ ▶ n. a user of the Internet, esp. a habitual or avid one.
– ORIGIN 1990s: blend of NET[1] (sense 4 of the noun) and CITIZEN.

net·keep·er /'netˌkēpər/ ▶ n. another term for GOALKEEPER.

net me·ter·ing ▶ n. a system in which solar panels or other renewable energy generators are connected to a public-utility power grid and surplus power is transferred onto the grid, allowing customers to offset the cost of power drawn from the utility.
– ORIGIN surplus energy, measured by an electric meter, is netted from the amount passing from the utility to the customer.

net na·tion·al prod·uct (abbr.: **NNP**) ▶ n. the total value of goods produced and services provided in a country during one year, after depreciation of capital goods has been allowed for.

net pres·ent val·ue ▶ n. see PRESENT VALUE.

net prof·it ▶ n. the actual profit after working expenses not included in the calculation of gross profit have been paid.

net·roots /'netro͞ots/ ▶ plural n. political activists and campaigners who communicate their message over the Internet, esp. via blogs: *in the last election, the netroots exerted their influence through prodigious fundraising.*
– ORIGIN early 21st cent.: blend of INTERNET and GRASS ROOTS.

ne·tsu·ke /'netsəkē/ ▶ n. (pl. **same** or **netsukes** /-kēz/) a carved buttonlike ornament, esp. of ivory or wood, formerly worn in Japan to suspend articles from the sash of a kimono.
– ORIGIN late 19th cent.: from Japanese.

net·ter /'netər/ ▶ n. **1** a fisherman who uses nets to catch fish: *because of the ban on gill nets, Louisianans fear an influx of jobless Florida netters.* ■ [usu. in combination] someone who uses a net of a specified type: *drift-netters.*
2 (also **Netter**) a person who uses the Internet.

net·ting /'netiNG/ ▶ n. open-meshed material made by knotting together twine, wire, rope, or thread.

net·tle /'netl/ ▶ n. a herbaceous plant that has jagged leaves covered with stinging hairs. ● Genus *Urtica*, family Urticaceae: several species, in particular the Eurasian **stinging nettle** (*U. dioica*). ■ used in names of other plants of a similar appearance or properties, e.g., **dead-nettle**.
▶ v. [with obj.] **1** irritate or annoy (someone): *I was nettled by Alene's tone of superiority.*
2 archaic beat or sting (someone) with nettles.
– ORIGIN Old English *netle, netele*, of Germanic origin; related to Dutch *netel* and German *Nessel*. The verb dates from late Middle English.

net·tle·rash /'netlˌrasH/ ▶ n. another term for URTICARIA (from its resemblance to the sting of a nettle).

net·tle·some /'netlsəm/ ▶ adj. causing annoyance or difficulty: *complicated and nettlesome regional disputes.*

net·tle tree ▶ n. an Old World tree related to the hackberries, with a straight, silvery-gray trunk and rough, toothed, nettlelike leaves. ● Genus *Celtis*, family Ulmaceae: several species, in particular *C. australis*, which is a popular street and shade tree in Mediterranean countries.

net ton /tən/ ▶ n. another term for TON[1] (sense 1).

net·work /'netˌwərk/ ▶ n. **1** an arrangement of intersecting horizontal and vertical lines. ■ a complex system of roads, railroads, or other transportation routes: *a network of railroads.*
2 a group or system of interconnected people or things: *a trade network.* ■ a group of people who exchange information, contacts, and experience for professional or social purposes: *a support network.* ■ a group of broadcasting stations that connect for the simultaneous broadcast of a program: *the introduction of a second TV network* | [as modifier] *network television.* ■ a number of interconnected computers, machines, or operations: *specialized computers that manage multiple outside connections to a network* | *a local cellular phone network.* ■ a system of connected electrical conductors.
▶ v. [with obj.] connect as or operate with a network: *the stock exchanges have proven to be resourceful in networking these deals.* ■ link (machines, esp. computers) to operate interactively: (as adj. **networked**) *networked workstations.* ■ [no obj.] (often as noun **networking**) interact with other people to exchange information and develop contacts, esp. to further one's career: *the skills of networking, bargaining, and negotiation.*
– DERIVATIVES **net·work·a·ble** adj.

net·work a·nal·y·sis ▶ n. the mathematical analysis of complex working procedures in terms of a network of related activities. ■ calculation of the electric currents flowing in the various meshes of a network, often carried out by a device used to model the network.

net·work ap·pli·ance ▶ n. a relatively low-cost computer designed chiefly to provide Internet access without the full capabilities of a standard computer.

net·work·er /'netˌwərkər/ ▶ n. **1** Computing a person who works from home or from an external office via a computer network.
2 a person who interacts or exchanges information with others working in a similar field, esp. to further their career.

Neu·châ·tel, Lake /ˌno͞osHä'tel, nœ-/ the largest lake that lies wholly within Switzerland, located at the foot of the Jura Mountains in western Switzerland.

Neue Sach·lich·keit /'noiə 'zäKHlisHkīt/ a movement in the visual arts, music, and literature that developed in Germany during the 1920s and was characterized by realism and a deliberate rejection of romantic attitudes.
– ORIGIN German, literally 'new objectivity.'

Neuf·châ·tel /ˌno͞osHə'tel, ˌnœsHä-/ ▶ n. a creamy white cheese made from whole or partly skimmed milk in Neufchâtel, France.

Neu·mann /'n(y)o͞omən, 'noimän/, John von (1903–57), US mathematician and computer pioneer, born in Hungary. He pioneered game theory and the design and operation of electronic computers.

neume /n(y)o͞om/ ▶ n. Music (in plainsong) a note or group of notes to be sung to a single syllable. ■ a sign indicating this.
– ORIGIN late Middle English: from Old French *neume*, from medieval Latin *neu(p)ma*, from Greek *pneuma* 'breath.'

neur. ▶ abbr. neurological or neurology.

neu·ral /'n(y)o͝orəl/ ▶ adj. of or relating to a nerve or the nervous system: *patterns of neural activity.*
– DERIVATIVES **neu·ral·ly** adv.
– ORIGIN mid 19th cent.: from Greek *neuron* in the sense 'nerve' + -AL.

neu·ral arch ▶ n. Anatomy the curved rear (dorsal) section of a vertebra, enclosing the canal through which the spinal cord passes.

neu·ral com·pu·ter ▶ n. a computer that uses neural networks based on the human brain. Also called NEUROCOMPUTER.
– DERIVATIVES **neu·ral com·put·ing** n.

neu·ral·gia /n(y)o͝o'raljə/ ▶ n. intense, typically intermittent pain along the course of a nerve, esp. in the head or face.
– DERIVATIVES **neu·ral·gic** /-jik/ adj.

neu·ral net·work (also **neural net**) ▶ n. a computer system modeled on the human brain and nervous system.

neu·ral tube ▶ n. Zoology & Medicine (in an embryo) a hollow structure from which the brain and spinal cord form. Defects in its development can result in congenital abnormalities such as spina bifida.

neu·ra·min·ic ac·id /ˌn(y)o͝orə'minik/ ▶ n. Biochemistry a crystalline compound of which derivatives occur in many animal substances, chiefly as sialic acids. ● A sugar with amino and acid groups; chem. formula: $C_9H_{17}NO_8$.
– ORIGIN mid 20th cent.: *neuraminic* from NEURO- (because it was originally isolated from brain tissue) + AMINE + -IC.

neu·ra·min·i·dase /ˌn(y)o͝orə'minəˌdās/ ▶ n. Biochemistry an enzyme, present in many pathogenic or symbiotic microorganisms, that catalyzes the breakdown of glycosides containing neuraminic acid.

neur·as·the·ni·a /ˌn(y)o͝orəsˈTHēnēə/ ▶ **n.** chiefly dated an ill-defined medical condition characterized by lassitude, fatigue, headache, and irritability, associated chiefly with emotional disturbance.
– DERIVATIVES **neur·as·then·ic** /-ˈTHenik/ **adj. & n.**

neu·rec·to·my /n(y)o͝oˈrektəmē/ ▶ **n.** Medicine surgical removal of all or part of a nerve.

neu·ri·lem·ma /ˌn(y)o͝orəˈlemə/ ▶ **n.** (pl. **neurilemmas** or **neurilemmata** /-liˈmätə/) Anatomy the thin sheath around a nerve axon (including myelin where this is present).
– DERIVATIVES **neu·ri·lem·mal** **adj.**

neu·ri·tis /n(y)o͝oˈrītis/ ▶ **n.** Medicine inflammation of a peripheral nerve or nerves, usually causing pain and loss of function. ■ (in general use) neuropathy.
– DERIVATIVES **neu·rit·ic** /-ˈritik/ **adj.**

neuro- ▶ **comb. form** relating to nerves or the nervous system: *neuroanatomy* | *neurohormone.*
– ORIGIN from Greek *neuron* 'nerve, sinew, tendon.'

neu·ro·a·nat·o·my /ˌn(y)o͝oröəˈnatəmē/ ▶ **n.** the anatomy of the nervous system.
– DERIVATIVES **neu·ro·an·a·tom·i·cal** /-ˌanəˈtämikəl/ **adj.**, **neu·ro·a·nat·o·mist** /-mist/ **n.**

neu·ro·bics /n(y)o͝oˈrōbiks/ ▶ **n.** mental exercises designed to create new neural pathways in the brain by using the senses in unconventional ways.

neu·ro·bi·ol·o·gy /ˌn(y)o͝orōbīˈäləjē/ ▶ **n.** the biology of the nervous system.
– DERIVATIVES **neu·ro·bi·o·log·i·cal** /-bīəˈläjikəl/ **adj.**, **neu·ro·bi·ol·o·gist** /-jist/ **n.**

neu·ro·blast /ˈn(y)o͝orəˌblast/ ▶ **n.** Embryology an embryonic cell from which nerve fibers originate.

neu·ro·blas·to·ma /ˌn(y)o͝orōblaˈstōmə/ ▶ **n.** Medicine a malignant tumor composed of neuroblasts, most commonly in the adrenal gland.

neu·ro·com·pu·ter /ˈn(y)o͝orōkəmˌpyo͞otər/ another term for **NEURAL COMPUTER.**

neu·ro·de·gen·er·a·tive /ˌno͝orōdəˈjenərətiv/ ▶ **adj.** resulting in or characterized by degeneration of the nervous system, esp. the neurons in the brain.

neu·ro·e·co·nom·ics /ˌno͝orōˌekəˈnämiks, -ˌēkə-/ ▶ **plural n.** [treated as sing.] the combination of economics, neuroscience, and psychology used to determine how individuals make economic decisions.

neu·ro·en·do·crine /ˌn(y)o͝orōˈendəkrin/ ▶ **adj.** Physiology relating to or involving both nervous stimulation and endocrine secretion.
– DERIVATIVES **neu·ro·en·do·cri·nol·o·gy** /-ˌendōkrəˈnäləjē/ **n.**

neu·ro·ep·i·the·li·um /ˌn(y)o͝orōˌepiˈTHēlēəm/ ▶ **n.** Anatomy **1** a type of epithelium containing sensory nerve endings and found in certain sense organs (e.g., the retina, the inner ear, the nasal membranes, and the taste buds).
2 (in embryology) ectoderm that develops into nerve tissue.
– DERIVATIVES **neu·ro·ep·i·the·li·al** /-lēəl/ **adj.**

neu·ro·fi·bril /ˌn(y)o͝orəˈfībrəl, -ˈfib-/ ▶ **n.** Anatomy a fibril in the cytoplasm of a nerve cell, visible by light microscopy.
– DERIVATIVES **neu·ro·fi·bril·lar·y** /-ˈfibrəˌlerē/ **adj.**

neu·ro·fi·bro·ma /ˌn(y)o͝orōfīˈbrōmə/ ▶ **n.** (pl. **neurofibromas** or **neurofibromata** /-mətə/) Medicine a tumor formed on a nerve cell sheath, frequently symptomless but occasionally malignant.

neu·ro·fi·bro·ma·to·sis /ˌn(y)o͝orōˌfībrəməˈtōsis/ ▶ **n.** Medicine a disease in which neurofibromas form throughout the body. Also called **VON RECKLINGHAUSEN'S DISEASE.**

neu·ro·gen·e·sis /ˌn(y)o͝orəˈjenəsis/ ▶ **n.** Physiology the growth and development of nervous tissue.

neu·ro·gen·ic /ˌn(y)o͝orəˈjenik/ ▶ **adj.** Physiology caused by, controlled by, or arising in the nervous system.

neu·rog·li·a /n(y)o͝oˈräglēə/ ▶ **n.** another term for **GLIA.**
– ORIGIN mid 19th cent.: from **NEURO-** 'of nerves' + Greek *glia* 'glue.'

neu·ro·hor·mone /ˌn(y)o͝orōˈhôrˌmōn/ ▶ **n.** Physiology a hormone (such as vasopressin or norepinephrine) produced by nerve cells and secreted into the circulation.
– DERIVATIVES **neu·ro·hor·mo·nal** /-hôrˈmōnəl/ **adj.**

neu·ro·hy·poph·y·sis /ˌn(y)o͝orōhīˈpäfəsis/ ▶ **n.** (pl. **neurohypophyses** /-ˌsēz/) Anatomy the posterior lobe of the hypophysis (pituitary gland), which stores and releases oxytocin and vasopressin produced in the hypothalamus.
– DERIVATIVES **neu·ro·hy·po·phys·e·al** /-ˌpäfəˈsēəl/ **adj.**

neu·ro·lep·tic /ˌn(y)o͝orəˈleptik/ Medicine ▶ **adj.** (chiefly of a drug) tending to reduce nervous tension by depressing nerve functions.
▶ **n.** a drug of this kind; a major tranquilizer.
– ORIGIN mid 20th cent.: from **NEURO-** 'relating to nerves,' on the pattern of *psycholeptic.*

neu·ro·lin·guis·tic pro·gram·ming /ˌn(y)o͝orōˌliNGˈgwistik/ (abbr.: **NLP**) ▶ **n.** a system of alternative therapy intended to educate people in self-awareness and effective communication, and to model and change their patterns of mental and emotional behavior.

neu·ro·lin·guis·tics /ˌn(y)o͝orōˌliNGˈgwistiks/ ▶ **plural n.** [treated as sing.] the branch of linguistics dealing with the relationship between language and the structure and functioning of the brain.
– DERIVATIVES **neu·ro·lin·guis·tic** **adj.**

neu·rol·o·gy /n(y)o͝oˈräləjē/ ▶ **n.** the branch of medicine or biology that deals with the anatomy, functions, and organic disorders of nerves and the nervous system.
– DERIVATIVES **neu·rolog·i·cal** /-rəˈläjikəl/ **adj.**, **neu·ro·log·i·cal·ly** **adv.**, **neu·rol·o·gist** **n.**
– ORIGIN late 17th cent.: from modern Latin *neurologia*, from **NEURO-** + **-LOGY.**

neu·ro·ma /n(y)o͝oˈrōmə/ ▶ **n.** (pl. **neuromas** or **neuromata** /-mətə/) another term for **NEUROFIBROMA.**

neu·ro·mast /ˈn(y)o͝orəˌmast/ ▶ **n.** Zoology a sensory organ of fishes and larval or aquatic amphibians, typically forming part of the lateral line system.
– ORIGIN early 20th cent.: from **NEURO-** 'of nerves' + Greek *mastos* 'breast.'

neu·ro·mus·cu·lar /ˌn(y)o͝orōˈməskyələr/ ▶ **adj.** of or relating to nerves and muscles.

neu·ron /ˈn(y)o͝orän/ (chiefly Brit. also **neurone** /-rōn/) ▶ **n.** a specialized cell transmitting nerve impulses; a nerve cell.
– DERIVATIVES **neu·ron·al** /ˈn(y)o͝orənl, n(y)o͝oˈrōnl/ **adj.**, **neu·ron·ic** /n(y)o͝oˈränik/ **adj.**
– ORIGIN late 19th cent.: from Greek *neuron*, special use of the literal sense 'sinew, tendon.' See **NERVE.**

neu·ro·path /ˈn(y)o͝orəˌpaTH/ ▶ **n.** dated a person affected by nervous disease, or with an abnormally sensitive nervous system.

neu·ro·pa·thol·o·gy /ˌn(y)o͝orōpəˈTHäləjē/ ▶ **n.** the branch of medicine concerned with diseases of the nervous system.
– DERIVATIVES **neu·ro·path·o·log·i·cal** /-ˌpaTHəˈläjikəl/ **adj.**, **neu·ro·pa·thol·o·gist** **n.**

neu·rop·a·thy /n(y)o͝oˈräpəTHē/ ▶ **n.** Medicine disease or dysfunction of one or more peripheral nerves, typically causing numbness or weakness.
– DERIVATIVES **neu·ro·path·ic** /ˌn(y)o͝orəˈpaTHik/ **adj.**

neu·ro·pep·tide /ˌn(y)o͝orōˈpeptīd/ ▶ **n.** Biochemistry any of a group of compounds that act as neurotransmitters and are short-chain polypeptides.

neu·ro·phar·ma·col·o·gy /ˌn(y)o͝orōˌfärməˈkäləjē/ ▶ **n.** the branch of pharmacology that deals with the action of drugs on the nervous system.
– DERIVATIVES **neu·ro·phar·ma·co·log·ic** /-kəˈläjik/ **adj.**, **neu·ro·phar·ma·co·log·i·cal** **adj.**, **neu·ro·phar·ma·col·o·gist** **n.**

neu·ro·phys·i·ol·o·gy /ˌn(y)o͝orōˌfizēˈäləjē/ ▶ **n.** the physiology of the nervous system.
– DERIVATIVES **neu·ro·phys·i·o·log·i·cal** /-ˌfizēəˈläjikəl/ **adj.**, **neu·ro·phys·i·ol·o·gist** **n.**

neu·ro·pil /ˈn(y)o͝orəˌpil/ ▶ **n.** Anatomy & Zoology a dense network of interwoven nerve fibers and their branches and synapses, together with glial filaments.
– ORIGIN late 19th cent.: probably an abbreviation of obsolete *neuropilema*, from Greek *neuron* 'nerve' + *pilēma* 'felt.'

neu·ro·psy·chi·a·try /ˌn(y)o͝orōsəˈkīətrē, -sīˈkī-/ ▶ **n.** psychiatry relating mental or emotional disturbance to disordered brain function.
– DERIVATIVES **neu·ro·psy·chi·at·ric** /-ˌsīkēˈatrik/ **adj.**, **neu·ro·psy·chi·a·trist** **n.**

neu·ro·psy·chol·o·gy /ˌn(y)o͝orōsīˈkäləjē/ ▶ **n.** the study of the relationship between behavior, emotion, and cognition on the one hand, and brain function on the other.
– DERIVATIVES **neu·ro·psy·cho·log·i·cal** /-ˌsīkəˈläjikəl/ **adj.**, **neu·ro·psy·chol·o·gist** **n.**

Neu·rop·ter·a /n(y)o͝oˈräptərə/ Entomology an order of predatory flying insects that includes the lacewings, snake flies, and ant lions. They have four finely veined membranous wings. ■ (**neuroptera**) [as plural noun] insects of this order.
– ORIGIN modern Latin (plural), from **NEURO-** in the sense 'veined' + Greek *pteron* 'wing.'

neu·rop·ter·an /n(y)o͝oˈräptərən/ Entomology ▶ **n.** a predatory flying insect of the order Neuroptera, such as a lacewing or alderfly.
▶ **adj.** relating to or denoting neuropterans.
– DERIVATIVES **neu·rop·ter·ous** /-rəs/ **adj.**

neu·ro·sci·ence /ˌn(y)o͝orōˈsīəns/ ▶ **n.** any of the sciences that deal with the structure or function of the nervous system and brain. ■ such sciences collectively.
– DERIVATIVES **neu·ro·sci·en·tist** /-ˈsīəntist/ **n.**

neu·ro·sis /n(y)o͝oˈrōsis/ ▶ **n.** (pl. **neuroses** /-ˌsēz/) Medicine a relatively mild mental illness that is not caused by organic disease, involving symptoms of stress (depression, anxiety, obsessive behavior, hypochondria) but not a radical loss of touch with reality. Compare with **PSYCHOSIS.** ■ (in nontechnical use) excessive and irrational anxiety or obsession: *apprehension over mounting debt has created a collective neurosis in the business world.*
– ORIGIN mid 18th cent.: modern Latin, from **NEURO-** 'of nerves' + **-OSIS.**

neu·ro·sur·ger·y /ˌn(y)o͝orōˈsərjərē/ ▶ **n.** surgery performed on the nervous system, esp. the brain and spinal cord.
– DERIVATIVES **neu·ro·sur·geon** /ˈn(y)o͝orōˌsərjən/ **n.**, **neu·ro·sur·gi·cal** /-jikəl/ **adj.**

neu·ro·syph·i·lis /ˌn(y)o͝orōˈsifəlis/ ▶ **n.** syphilis that involves the central nervous system.
– DERIVATIVES **neu·ro·syph·i·lit·ic** /-sifəˈlitik/ **adj. & n.**

neu·rot·ic /n(y)o͝oˈrätik/ ▶ **adj.** Medicine suffering from, caused by, or relating to neurosis.
■ abnormally sensitive, obsessive, or tense and anxious: *everyone was neurotic about burglars* | *a neurotic obsession with neat handwriting.*
▶ **n.** a neurotic person.
– DERIVATIVES **neu·rot·i·cal·ly** **adv.**, **neu·rot·i·cism** /-ˈrätəˌsizəm/ **n.**

neu·rot·o·my /n(y)o͝oˈrätəmē/ ▶ **n.** the surgical cutting of a nerve to produce sensory loss and relief of pain or to suppress involuntary movements.

neu·ro·tox·in /ˈn(y)o͝orōˌtäksin/ ▶ **n.** a poison that acts on the nervous system.
– DERIVATIVES **neu·ro·tox·ic** /ˌn(y)o͝orōˈtäksik/ **adj.**, **neu·ro·tox·ic·i·ty** /ˌn(y)o͝orōtäkˈsisitē/ **n.**, **neu·ro·tox·i·col·o·gy** /ˌn(y)o͝orōˌtäksiˈkäləjē/ **n.**

neu·ro·trans·mit·ter /ˌn(y)o͝orōˈtranzmitər/ ▶ **n.** Physiology a chemical substance that is released at the end of a nerve fiber by the arrival of a nerve impulse and, by diffusing across the synapse or junction, causes the transfer of the impulse to another nerve fiber, a muscle fiber, or some other structure.
– DERIVATIVES **neu·ro·trans·mis·sion** /-ˌtranzˈmiSHən/ **n.**

neu·ro·troph·ic /ˌn(y)o͝orəˈträfik, -ˈtrō-/ ▶ **adj.** Physiology of or relating to the growth of nervous tissue.

neu·ro·trop·ic /ˌn(y)o͝orəˈträpik, -ˈtrō-/ ▶ **adj.** Medicine (of a virus, toxin, or chemical) tending to attack or affect the nervous system preferentially.
– DERIVATIVES **neu·rot·ro·pism** /n(y)o͝oˈrätrəˌpizəm/ **n.**

neus·ton /ˈn(y)o͞ostän/ ▶ **n.** Biology small aquatic organisms inhabiting the surface layer or moving on the surface film of water.
– DERIVATIVES **neus·ton·ic** /n(y)o͞oˈstänik/ **adj.**
– ORIGIN early 20th cent.: via German from Greek, neuter of *neustos* 'swimming,' on the pattern of *plankton.*

neut. ▶ **abbr.** ■ neuter. ■ neutral.

neu·ter /ˈn(y)o͞otər/ ▶ **adj. 1** of or denoting a gender of nouns in some languages, typically contrasting with masculine and feminine or common: *it is a neuter word in Greek.*
2 (of an animal) lacking developed sexual organs, or having had them removed. ■ (of a plant or flower) having neither functional pistils nor functional stamens. ■ (of a person) apparently having no sexual characteristics; asexual.
▶ **n. 1** Grammar a neuter word. ■ (**the neuter**) the neuter gender.
2 a nonfertile caste of social insect, esp. a worker bee or ant. ■ a castrated or spayed domestic animal. ■ a person who appears to lack sexual characteristics.
▶ **v.** [with obj.] castrate or spay (a domestic animal): (as adj. **neutered**) *a neutered tomcat.* ■ render ineffective; deprive of vigor or force: *disarmament negotiations that will neuter their military power.*
– ORIGIN late Middle English: via Old French from Latin *neuter* 'neither,' from *ne-* 'not' + *uter* 'either.'

neu·tral /ˈn(y)o͞otrəl/ ▶ **adj. 1** not helping or supporting either side in a conflict, disagreement, etc.; impartial: *during the Second World War, Portugal was neutral.* ■ belonging to an impartial party, country, or group: *on neutral ground.*
2 having no strongly marked or positive characteristics or features: *the tone was neutral,*

PRONUNCIATION KEY ə *ago, up*; ər *over, fur*; a *hat*; ā *ate*; ä *car*; e *let*; ē *see*; i *fit*; ī *by*; NG *sing*; ō *go*; ô *law, for*; oi *toy*; o͝o *good*; o͞o *goo*; ou *out*; TH *thin*; T̲H̲ *then*; ZH *vision*

n

devoid of sentiment | a fairly neutral background will make any small splash of color stand out. ■ Chemistry neither acid nor alkaline; having a pH of about 7. ■ electrically neither positive nor negative.
▶ **n. 1** an impartial or unbiased country or person: *he acted as a neutral between the parties | Sweden and its fellow neutrals.*
2 a neutral color or shade, esp. light gray or beige.
3 a disengaged position of gears in which the engine is disconnected from the driven parts: *she slipped the gear into neutral.*
4 an electrically neutral point, terminal, conductor, or wire.
– DERIVATIVES **neu·tral·ly adv.**
– ORIGIN late Middle English (as a noun): from Latin *neutralis* 'of neuter gender,' from *neuter* (see NEUTER).

neu·tral ax·is ▶ n. Engineering a line or plane through a beam or plate connecting points at which no extension or compression occurs when the beam or plate is bent.

neu·tral cor·ner ▶ n. Boxing either of the two corners of a boxing ring not used by the boxers and their handlers between rounds.

neu·tral den·si·ty fil·ter ▶ n. a photographic or optical filter that absorbs light of all wavelengths to the same extent, causing overall dimming but no change in color.

neu·tral·ism /ˈn(y)o͞otrəˌlizəm/ **▶ n.** a policy of political neutrality.
– DERIVATIVES **neu·tral·ist n. & adj.**

neu·tral·i·ty /n(y)o͞oˈtralitē/ **▶ n. 1** the state of not supporting or helping either side in a conflict, disagreement, etc.; impartiality: *during the war, Switzerland maintained its neutrality.*
2 absence of decided views, expression, or strong feeling: *the clinical neutrality of the description.*
3 the condition of being chemically or electrically neutral.

neu·tral·ize /ˈn(y)o͞otrəˌlīz/ **▶ v.** [with obj.] render (something) ineffective or harmless by applying an opposite force or effect: *impatience at his frailty began to neutralize her fear.* ■ make (an acidic or alkaline substance) chemically neutral. ■ disarm (a bomb or similar weapon). ■ a euphemistic way of saying kill or destroy, esp. in a covert or military operation.
– DERIVATIVES **neu·tral·i·za·tion** /ˌn(y)o͞otrəliˈzāSHən/ **n.**, **neu·tral·iz·er n.**
– ORIGIN mid 17th cent.: from French *neutraliser*, from medieval Latin *neutralizare*, from Latin *neutralis* (see NEUTRAL).

n

neu·tral zone ▶ n. 1 the central area of a hockey rink, lying between the two blue lines.
2 Football (before the start of a play) the imaginary zone running sideline to sideline from the front to the back point of the football.

neu·tri·no /n(y)o͞oˈtrēnō/ **▶ n.** (pl. **neutrinos**) a neutral subatomic particle with a mass close to zero and half-integral spin, rarely reacting with normal matter. Three kinds of neutrinos are known, associated with the electron, muon, and tau particle.
– ORIGIN mid 20th cent.: from Italian, diminutive of *neutro* 'neutral.'

neu·tron /ˈn(y)o͞oträn/ **▶ n.** a subatomic particle of about the same mass as a proton but without an electric charge, present in all atomic nuclei except those of ordinary hydrogen.
– ORIGIN early 20th cent.: from NEUTRAL + -ON.

neu·tron bomb ▶ n. a nuclear weapon that produces large numbers of neutrons rather than heat or blast like conventional nuclear weapons.

neu·tron star ▶ n. Astronomy a celestial object of very small radius (typically 18 miles/30 km) and very high density, composed predominantly of closely packed neutrons. Neutron stars are thought to form by the gravitational collapse of the remnant of a massive star after a supernova explosion, provided that the star is insufficiently massive to produce a black hole.

neu·tro·pe·ni·a /ˌn(y)o͞otrəˈpēnēə/ **▶ n.** Medicine the presence of abnormally few neutrophils in the blood, leading to increased susceptibility to infection. It is an undesirable side effect of some cancer treatments.
– DERIVATIVES **neu·tro·pe·nic** /ˌn(y)o͞otrəˈpēnik, -ˈpenik/ **adj.**
– ORIGIN 1930s: from *neutral*+ Greek, *penia* 'poverty, lack.'

neu·tro·phil /ˈn(y)o͞otrəfil/ **▶ n.** Physiology a neutrophilic white blood cell.

neu·tro·phil·ic /ˌn(y)o͞otrəˈfilik/ **▶ adj.** Physiology (of a cell or its contents) readily stained only by neutral dyes.
– ORIGIN late 19th cent.: from NEUTRAL + *-philic* (see -PHILIA).

Nev. ▶ abbr. Nevada.

Ne·va /ˈnēvə, ˈnā-/ a river in northwestern Russia that flows 46 miles (74 km) west from Lake Ladoga to the Gulf of Finland, passing through St. Petersburg.

Ne·va·da /nəˈvadə, -ˈvädə/ a state in the western US, on an arid plateau, almost totally in the Great Basin area; pop. 2,600,167 (est. 2008); capital, Carson City; statehood, Oct. 31, 1864 (36). It was acquired from Mexico in 1848. An abundance of gold and silver ore (called the Comstock Lode) was discovered in 1859 near Virginia City.
– DERIVATIVES **Ne·vad·an adj. & n.**

né·vé /nāˈvā/ **▶ n.** another term for FIRN.
– ORIGIN mid 19th cent.: from Swiss French, literally 'glacier,' based on Latin *nix, niv-* 'snow.'

nev·er /ˈnevər/ **▶ adv. 1** at no time in the past or future; on no occasion; not ever: *they had never been camping in their lives | I will never ever forget it.*
2 not at all: *he never turned up.*
– PHRASES **never fear** see FEAR. **never mind** see MIND. **never say die** see DIE¹. **well I never!** informal expressing great surprise or indignation: *Well I never—that's not like you!*
– ORIGIN Old English *nǣfre*, from *ne* 'not' + *ǣfre* 'ever.'

nev·er-end·ing ▶ adj. (esp. of something unpleasant) having or seeming to have no end.

nev·er·more /ˌnevərˈmôr/ **▶ adv.** literary at no future time; never again: *I order you gone, nevermore to return.*

nev·er-nev·er land ▶ n. an imaginary utopian place or situation: *a never-never land of unreal prices and easy bank loans.*
– ORIGIN often with allusion to the ideal country in J. M. Barrie's *Peter Pan*.

nev·er·the·less /ˌnevərT͟Həˈles/ **▶ adv.** in spite of that; notwithstanding; all the same: *statements which, although literally true, are nevertheless misleading.*

Nev·ille /ˈnevəl/, Richard, see WARWICK².

Ne·vis /ˈnēvəs/ one of the Leeward Islands in the Caribbean Sea, part of St. Kitts and Nevis; capital, Charlestown.
– DERIVATIVES **Nevisian** /ˌnevəˈsēən/ **n. & adj.**

Nev·sky, Alexander, see ALEXANDER NEVSKY, ST.

ne·vus /ˈnēvəs/ (Brit. **naevus**) **▶ n.** (pl. **nevi** /-ˌvī/) a birthmark or a mole on the skin, esp. a birthmark in the form of a raised red patch.
– ORIGIN mid 19th cent.: from Latin.

new /n(y)o͞o/ **▶ adj. 1** not existing before; made, introduced, or discovered recently or now for the first time: *new crop varieties | this tendency is not new* | (as noun **the new**) *a fascinating mix of the old and the new.* ■ not previously used or owned: *a secondhand bus cost a fraction of a new one.* ■ of recent origin or arrival: *a new baby.* ■ (of food or drink) freshly or recently produced. ■ (of vegetables) dug or harvested early in the season: *new potatoes.*
2 already existing but seen, experienced, or acquired recently or now for the first time: *her new bike.* ■ [predic.] (**new to**) unfamiliar or strange to (someone): *a way of living that was new to me.* ■ [predic.] (**new to/at**) (of a person) inexperienced at or unaccustomed to doing (something): *I'm quite new to gardening.* ■ different from a recent previous one: *I have a new assistant | this would be her new home.* ■ in addition to another or others already existing: *recruiting new pilots overseas.* ■ (in place names) discovered or founded later than and named after: *New York.*
3 just beginning or beginning anew and regarded as better than what went before: *starting a new life | the new South Africa.* ■ (of a person) reinvigorated or restored: *a bottle of pills would make him a new man.* ■ superseding another or others of the same kind, and advanced in method or theory: *the new architecture.* ■ reviving another or others of the same kind: *the New Bohemians.*
▶ **adv.** [usu. in combination] newly; recently: *new-mown hay | new-fallen snow.*
– PHRASES **a new one** informal an account, idea, or joke not previously encountered by someone: *I've heard of lazy, but somebody being too lazy to talk—that's* **a new one on me**. **what's new? 1** (said on greeting someone) what's going on? how are you? **2** (also **what else is new?**) that is the usual situation: *she and I squabbled—so what's new? | men like to see women's legs. So what else is new?*
– DERIVATIVES **new·ish adj.**, **new·ness n.**
– ORIGIN Old English *nīwe, nēowe*, of Germanic origin; related to Dutch *nieuw* and German *neu*, from an Indo-European root shared by Sanskrit *nava*, Latin *novus*, and Greek *neos* 'new.'

New Age ▶ n. a broad movement characterized by alternative approaches to traditional Western culture, with an interest in spirituality, mysticism, holism, and environmentalism: [as modifier] *the New Age movement.*
– DERIVATIVES **New Ag·er n.**, **New Age·y adj.**

New Age mus·ic ▶ n. a style of chiefly instrumental music characterized by light melodic harmonies, improvisation, and sounds reproduced from the natural world, intended to promote serenity.

New Am·ster·dam former name for the city of NEW YORK.

New·ark 1 /ˈn(y)o͞oˌärk/ a city in northwestern Delaware, home to the University of Delaware; pop. 29,886 (est. 2008).
2 /ˈn(y)o͞oərk/ an industrial city in New Jersey; pop. 278,980 (est. 2008).
3 /ˈn(y)o͞oərk/ an industrial and commercial city in central Ohio; pop. 47,236 (est. 2008).

New Bed·ford an industrial port city in southeastern Massachusetts, on Buzzards Bay, a noted 19th-century whaling center; pop. 91,365 (est. 2008).

New Bern a historic commercial city in eastern North Carolina; pop. 28,586 (est. 2008).

new·bie /ˈn(y)o͞obē/ **▶ n.** (pl. **newbies**) an inexperienced newcomer to a particular activity.

new·born /ˈn(y)o͞oˌbôrn/ **▶ adj.** (of a child or animal) recently or just born: *newborn babies* | figurative *a newborn star.*
▶ **n.** a recently born child or animal.

New Braun·fels /ˈbrounfəlz/ a city in south central Texas; pop. 53,547 (est. 2008).

New Brit·ain 1 a mountainous island in the South Pacific Ocean, part of Papua New Guinea, that lies off the northeastern coast of New Guinea; pop. 404,600 (est. 2008); capital, Rabaul.
2 an industrial city in central Connecticut, noted for its hardware manufacturing; pop. 70,486 (est. 2008).

New Bruns·wick 1 a maritime province on the southeastern coast of Canada; pop. 729,997 (2006); capital, Fredericton. It was first settled by the French and was ceded to Britain in 1713. It became one of the original four provinces in the Dominion of Canada in 1867.
2 a city in central New Jersey, on the Raritan River; pop. 51,149 (est. 2008).

New·burgh /ˈn(y)o͞oˌbərg/ a historic industrial city in southeastern New York, on the Hudson River; pop. 28,101 (est. 2008).

New·bury·port /ˈn(y)o͞obərēˌpôrt, -ˌberē-/ a historic port city, now chiefly residential, in northeastern Massachusetts, at the mouth of the Merrimack River; pop. 17,542 (est. 2008).

New Cal·e·do·ni·a /ˌkaləˈdōnēə/ an island in the South Pacific, east of Australia; pop. 227,400 (est. 2009); capital, Nouméa. Since 1946 it has formed, with its dependencies, a French overseas territory. French name NOUVELLE-CALÉDONIE.
– DERIVATIVES **New Cal·e·do·ni·an n. & adj.**
– ORIGIN named, by Captain Cook in 1774, after the Roman name *Caledonia* 'Scotland.'

New·cas·tle¹ /ˈn(y)o͞oˌkasəl/ **1** an industrial city in northeastern England, a port on the Tyne River; pop. 170,200 (est. 2009). Full name **Newcastle-upon-Tyne**.
2 an industrial town in west central England, southwest of Stoke-on-Trent; pop. 77,500 (est. 2009). Full name **Newcastle-under-Lyme**.
3 an industrial port on the southeastern coast of Australia, in New South Wales; pop. 152,659 (2008).

New·cas·tle², Thomas Pelham-Holles, 1st Duke of (1693–1768), British statesman; prime minister 1754–56 and 1757–62. During his second term in office, he headed a coalition with William Pitt the Elder until 1761.

New·cas·tle dis·ease ▶ n. an acute infectious viral fever affecting birds, esp. poultry. Also called FOWL PEST.
– ORIGIN 1920s: so named because it was first recorded near Newcastle upon Tyne, England, in 1927.

New·combe /ˈn(y)o͞okəm/, John (1944–), Australian tennis player. During 1967–75, he won the men's singles title at three Wimbledon, two US Open, and two Australian Open tournaments.

New·com·en /n(y)o͞oˈkəmən/, Thomas (1663–1729), English engineer; developer of the first practical steam engine—an engine that operated a pump for the removal of water from mines—in 1712.

new·com·er /ˈn(y)o͞oˌkəmər/ **▶ n.** a person or thing that has recently arrived in a place or joined a group. ■ a novice in a particular activity or situation.

New Crit·i·cism an influential movement in literary criticism in the mid 20th century that stressed the importance of focusing on the text itself rather than being concerned with external biographical or social considerations. Associated with the movement were

John Crowe Ransom (who first used the term in 1941), I. A. Richards, and Cleanth Brooks.

New Deal the economic measures introduced by President Franklin D. Roosevelt in 1933 to counteract the effects of the Great Depression. It involved a massive public works program, complemented by the large-scale granting of loans, and succeeded in reducing unemployment by between 7 and 10 million.
– DERIVATIVES **New Deal·er** n.

New Del·hi the capital of India, a city in north central India built 1912–29 to replace Calcutta (now Kolkata) as the capital of British India. With Delhi, it is part of the National Capital Territory of Delhi. Pop. (with Delhi) 12,259,200 (est. 2009).

new e·con·o·my ▶ n. new industries, such as biotechnology or the Internet, that are characterized by cutting-edge technology and high growth.

new·el /'n(y)o͞owəl/ ▶ n. the central supporting pillar of a spiral or winding staircase. ■ (also **newel post**) a post at the head or foot of a flight of stairs, supporting a handrail.
– ORIGIN late Middle English: from Old French *nouel* 'knob,' from medieval Latin *nodellus*, diminutive of Latin *nodus* 'knot.'

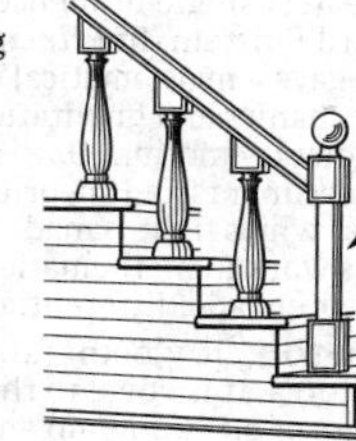
newel post

New Eng·land an area on the northeastern coast of the US that consists of the states of Maine, New Hampshire, Vermont, Massachusetts, Rhode Island, and Connecticut.
– DERIVATIVES **New Eng·land·er** n.

New Eng·land boiled din·ner ▶ n. a dish of meat (often corned beef), cabbage or other vegetables, and potatoes, prepared by simmering in water.

New Eng·land clam chow·der ▶ n. a thick chowder made with clams, onions, potatoes, salt pork, and milk or cream.

New Eng·lish Bi·ble (abbr.: **NEB**) ▶ n. a modern English translation of the Bible, published in the UK in 1961–70 and revised (as the **Revised English Bible**) in 1989.

new·fan·gled /'n(y)o͞o'faNGgəld, -,faNG-/ ▶ adj. derogatory different from what one is used to; objectionably new: *I've no time for such newfangled nonsense.*
– ORIGIN Middle English: from *newfangle* (now dialect) 'liking what is new,' from the adverb NEW + a second element related to an Old English word meaning 'to take.'

new-fash·ioned ▶ adj. of a new type or style; up to date: *selling your product the new-fashioned way.*

New·fie /'n(y)o͞ofē/ informal ▶ n. (pl. **Newfies**) a Newfoundlander.
▶ adj. coming from or associated with Newfoundland.

new·found /'n(y)o͞o,found/ ▶ adj. recently found or discovered: *armed with this newfound political consciousness, he sells his condo and quits his job.*

New·found·land[1] /,n(y)o͞ofənd'land, 'n(y)o͞ofəndlənd, -,land/ a large island off the eastern coast of Canada, at the mouth of the St. Lawrence River. It was united with Labrador (as Newfoundland and Labrador) in 1949 to form a province of Canada.
– DERIVATIVES **New·found·land·er** n.

New·found·land[2] (in full **Newfoundland dog**) ▶ n. a dog of a very large breed with a thick, coarse coat.

Newfoundland²

New·found·land and Lab·ra·dor a province of Canada that consists of the island of Newfoundland and the Labrador coast of eastern Canada; pop. 505,469 (2006); capital, St. John's. It joined the confederation of Canada in 1949.

New France the former colonies and possessions of France (until 1763) in North America, including Quebec, Acadia, and Louisiana.

New·gate /'n(y)o͞o,gāt/ a former London prison whose unsanitary conditions became notorious in the 18th century before the building was burned down in 1780.

New Geor·gia a volcanic island group in the west central Solomon Islands, northwest of Guadalcanal. *New Georgia Sound*, along the north side, was called "the Slot" by Americans during World War II, when the area saw heavy fighting with Japanese forces. ■ the largest of these islands.

New Guin·ea an island in the western South Pacific Ocean, off the northern coast of Australia, the world's second largest island. It is divided into two parts; the western half comprises the Indonesian provinces of Papua and West Papua; the eastern half forms part of Papua New Guinea.
– DERIVATIVES **New Guin·e·an** /'ginēən/ n. & adj.

New Hamp·shire /'hampsHər/ a state in the northeastern US, with a short border on the Atlantic coast, one of the six New England states; pop. 1,315,809 (est. 2008); capital, Concord; statehood, June 21, 1788 (9). It was the first colony to declare independence from Britain in 1776 and then became one of the original thirteen states.

New Ha·ven /,n(y)o͞o 'hāvən/ an industrial city in south central Connecticut, on Long Island Sound, home to Yale University; pop. 123,669 (est. 2008).

New Heb·ri·des former name (until 1980) for VANUATU.

New Hope a borough in southeastern Pennsylvania, on the Delaware River, a well-known tourist destination and artists' colony; pop. 2,278 (est. 2008).

New·house /'n(y)o͞o,hous/ Samuel Irving, Sr. (1895–1979), US publisher; born *Solomon Neuhaus*. He founded Advance Publications, now the largest privately held media company, the holdings of which are controlled by his sons, **Si** (1927–; full name *Samuel Irving Newhouse, Jr.*) and **Donald E.** (1930–).

Ne Win /,ne 'win/ (1911–2002), Burmese general and socialist statesman; prime minister 1958–60; head of state 1962–74; president 1974–81. After a military coup in 1962, he established a military dictatorship and formed a one-party state.

New In·ter·na·tion·al Ver·sion (abbr.: **NIV**) ▶ n. a modern English translation of the Bible published in 1973–78.

New Ire·land an island in the South Pacific Ocean, part of Papua New Guinea, that lies north of New Britain; pop. 145,700 (est. 2009); capital, Kavieng.

New Jer·sey a state in the northeastern US, on the Atlantic coast; pop. 8,682,661 (est. 2008); capital, Trenton; statehood, Dec. 18, 1787 (3). Colonized by Dutch settlers and ceded to Britain in 1664, it became one of the original thirteen states.
– DERIVATIVES **New Jer·sey·an** /-zēən/ n. & adj.

New Je·ru·sa·lem Theology the abode of the blessed in heaven (with reference to Rev. 21:2). ■ (as noun a **New Jerusalem**) an ideal place or situation.

New Je·ru·sa·lem Church a Christian sect instituted by followers of Emanuel Swedenborg. It was founded in London in 1787.

New Lat·in ▶ n. another term for MODERN LATIN.

New Lon·don an industrial port city in southeastern Connecticut, across the Thames River from Groton, on Long Island Sound; pop. 25,891 (est. 2008).

New Look a style of women's clothing introduced in 1947 by Christian Dior, featuring calf-length full skirts and a generous use of material in contrast to wartime austerity.

new·ly /'n(y)o͞olē/ ▶ adv. **1** recently: *a newly acquired skill.*
2 again; afresh: *social confidence for the newly single.* ■ in a new or different manner: *we have to make ourselves newly aware of each text.*

new·ly·wed /'n(y)o͞olē,wed/ ▶ n. (usu. **newlyweds**) a recently married person.

New·man[1] /'n(y)o͞omən/, Barnett (1905–70), US painter. A seminal figure in color-field painting, he juxtaposed large blocks of uniform color with narrow marginal strips of contrasting colors, such as in *Who's Afraid of Red, Yellow, and Blue III* (1966–67).

New·man[2], John Henry (1801–90), English prelate and theologian; a founder of the Oxford Movement. He turned to Roman Catholicism in 1845 and became a cardinal in 1879.

New·man[3], Paul (1925–2008), US actor and movie director. Notable movies: *Cat on a Hot Tin Roof* (1958), *The Hustler* (1961), *Hud* (1963), *Butch Cassidy and the Sundance Kid* (1969), *The Sting* (1973), *The Color of Money* (1987), and *Message in a Bottle* (1999). He was also known for his philanthropic activities.

Paul Newman

new man ▶ n. a man who rejects sexist attitudes and the traditional male role, esp. in the context of domestic responsibilities and child care.

New·man–Keuls test /'n(y)o͞omən kəlz/ ▶ n. Statistics a test for assessing the significance of differences between all possible pairs of different sets of observations, with a fixed error rate for the whole set of comparisons.
– ORIGIN mid 20th cent.: named after D. *Newman* (*fl.* 1939), English statistician, and M. *Keuls* (*fl.* 1952), Dutch horticulturalist.

New·mar·ket /'n(y)o͞o,märkət/ ▶ n. **1** a card game in which the players put down cards in sequence, hoping to be the first to play all their cards and also to play certain special cards on which bets have been placed.
2 (also **Newmarket coat**) a close-fitting overcoat of a style originally worn for riding.

new math (Brit. **new maths**) ▶ n. a system of teaching mathematics to younger children, with emphasis on investigation and discovery and on set theory.

New Mex·i·co a state in the southwestern US, on the border with Mexico; pop. 1,984,356 (est. 2008); capital, Santa Fe; statehood, Jan. 6, 1912 (47). It was obtained from Mexico in 1845 (annexation of Texas), 1848 (Treaty of Guadalupe Hidalgo that ended the Mexican-American War), and 1853 (Gadsden Purchase).
– DERIVATIVES **New Mex·i·can** /-kən/ adj. & n.

new mon·ey ▶ n. a fortune recently acquired; funds recently raised. ■ those whose wealth is recently acquired rather than inherited; the nouveau riche.

new moon ▶ n. the phase of the moon when it is in conjunction with the sun and invisible from earth, or shortly thereafter when it appears as a slender crescent. ■ the time when this occurs.

new or·der ▶ n. a new system, regime, or government: *a new economic order.* ■ (**New Order**) Hitler's planned reorganization of Europe under Nazi rule.

New Or·le·ans /'ôrlinz, ôr'lēnz/ a city and port in southeastern Louisiana, on the Mississippi River; pop. 311,853 (est. 2008). Founded by the French in 1718, it was named after the Duc d'Orléans, regent of France. It is known for its annual Mardi Gras celebrations and for its association with the development of blues and jazz. It 2005, Hurricanes Katrina and Rita caused extensive devastation and loss of life when the levees failed, leaving floodwaters to engulf the city.

New·port /'n(y)o͞o,pôrt/ **1** an industrial town and port in southern Wales, on the Bristol Channel; pop. 119,600 (est. 2009). Welsh name CASNEWYDD.
2 a historic port city in southern Rhode Island, on the island of Rhode Island. Home to naval facilities, it became known in the 19th century as a fashionable resort where the wealthy built opulent "cottages"; pop. 23,523 (est. 2008).

New·port Beach a resort, residential, and industrial city in southwestern California, southeast of Los Angeles; pop. 79,661 (est. 2008).

New·port News a city in southeastern Virginia, at the mouth of the James River on the Hampton Roads estuary; pop. 179,614 (est. 2008).

New Prov·i·dence an island in the central Bahamas, home to most of the people in the Bahamas and to the capital (Nassau); pop. 242,000 (est. 2009).

PRONUNCIATION KEY ə *ago, up*; ər *over, fur*; a *hat*; ā *ate*; ä *car*; e *let*; ē *see*; i *fit*; ī *by*; NG *sing*; ō *go*; ô *law, for*; oi *toy*; o͝o *good*; o͞o *goo*; ou *out*; TH *thin*; T͟H *then*; ZH *vision*

n

New Red Sand·stone ▶ **n.** Geology a series of sedimentary rocks, chiefly soft red sandstones, belonging to the Permo-Triassic system of northwestern Europe.

New Re·vised Stand·ard Ver·sion (abbr.: **NRSV**) ▶ **n.** a modern English translation of the Bible, based on the Revised Standard Version and published in 1990.

New River a river that flows for 320 miles (515 km) from North Carolina through Virginia and into West Virginia, where it enters the Kanawha River.

New Ro·chelle /rəˈsHel, rō-/ a city in southeastern New York, northeast of New York City, on Long Island Sound; pop. 74,115 (est. 2008).

New Ro·man·tic ▶ **adj.** denoting a style of popular music and fashion popular in Britain in the early 1980s in which both men and women wore makeup and dressed in flamboyant clothes.
▶ **n.** a performer or enthusiast of New Romantic music.

news /n(y)o͞oz/ ▶ **n.** newly received or noteworthy information, esp. about recent or important events: *I've got some good news for you.* ■ (**the news**) a broadcast or published report of news: *he was back in the news again.* ■ (**news to**) informal information not previously known to someone: *this was hardly news to her.* ■ a person or thing considered interesting enough to be reported in the news: *Chanel became the hottest news in fashion.*
– PHRASES **make news** become a story in the news: *stolen babies make news.* **no news is good news** proverb without information to the contrary you can assume that all is well.
– ORIGIN late Middle English: plural of **NEW**, translating Old French *noveles* or medieval Latin *nova* 'new things.'

news a·gen·cy ▶ **n.** an organization that collects news items and distributes them to newspapers or broadcasters.

news·a·gent /ˈn(y)o͞oz,ājənt/ ▶ **n.** Brit. a person or a shop selling newspapers and magazines.

news·boy /ˈn(y)o͞oz,boi/ ▶ **n.** a boy who sells or delivers newspapers.

news brief ▶ **n.** a brief item of print or broadcast news.

news bul·le·tin ▶ **n.** Brit. a short radio or television broadcast of news reports.

news·cast /ˈn(y)o͞oz,kast/ ▶ **n.** a radio or television broadcast of news reports.

news·cast·er /ˈn(y)o͞oz,kastər/ ▶ **n.** a person who reads broadcast news stories.

news con·fer·ence ▶ **n.** a press conference.

news crawl ▶ **n.** another term for **NEWS TICKER**.

news desk ▶ **n.** the department of a broadcasting organization or newspaper responsible for collecting and reporting the news.

news·feed /ˈn(y)o͞oz,fēd/ ▶ **n.** an electronic transmission of news, as from a broadcaster or an Internet newsgroup.

news flash ▶ **n.** a single item of important news that is broadcast separately and often interrupts other programs.

newsgath·er·ing /ˈn(y)o͞oz,gaTHəriNG/ ▶ **n.** the process of researching news items, esp. those for broadcast or publication.
– DERIVATIVES **news·gath·er·er** /-(ə)rər/ **n.**

news·group /ˈn(y)o͞oz,gro͞op/ ▶ **n.** a forum on the Usenet service for the discussion of a particular topic.

news·hound /ˈn(y)o͞oz,hound/ ▶ **n.** informal a newspaper reporter.

news·ie /ˈn(y)o͞ozē/ ▶ **n.** (also **newsy**) (pl. **newsies**) informal a reporter. ■ informal a person who sells or delivers newspapers.

news·let·ter /ˈn(y)o͞oz,letər/ ▶ **n.** a bulletin issued periodically to the members of a society, business, or organization.

news·mag·a·zine /ˈn(y)o͞oz,magə,zēn/ ▶ **n.** a periodical, usually published weekly, that reports and comments on current events. ■ a regularly scheduled television news program consisting of short segments on a variety of subjects and featuring a varied format combining interviews, commentary, and entertainment.

news·mak·er /ˈno͞oz,mākər/ ▶ **n.** a newsworthy person or event.

news·man /ˈn(y)o͞oz,man/ ▶ **n.** (pl. **newsmen**) a reporter or journalist.

news·mon·ger /ˈn(y)o͞oz,mäNGgər/ ▶ **n.** a gossip.

New South Wales a state of southeastern Australia; pop. 6,984,172 (2008); capital, Sydney. First colonized by Britain in 1788, it was federated with the other states of Australia in 1901.

New Spain a former Spanish viceroyalty established in Central and North America in 1535 that was centered around present-day Mexico City. It was comprised of all the land under Spanish control north of the Isthmus of Panama and included parts of the southern US. It also came to include the Spanish possessions in the Caribbean and the Philippines. The viceroyalty was abolished in 1821, when Mexico achieved independence.

news·pa·per /ˈn(y)o͞oz,pāpər/ ▶ **n.** a printed publication (usually issued daily or weekly) consisting of folded unstapled sheets and containing news, feature articles, advertisements, and correspondence. ■ the organization responsible for producing a particular newspaper. ■ another term for **NEWSPRINT**.

news·pa·per·man /ˈn(y)o͞oz,pāpər,man, -mən/ ▶ **n.** (pl. **newspapermen**) a male newspaper journalist.

news·pa·per·wom·an /ˈn(y)o͞oz,pāpər,wo͝omən/ ▶ **n.** (pl. **newspaperwomen**) a female newspaper journalist.

new·speak /ˈn(y)o͞o,spēk/ ▶ **n.** ambiguous euphemistic language used chiefly in political propaganda.
– ORIGIN 1949: the name of an artificial official language in George Orwell's *Nineteen Eighty-Four*.

news peg ▶ **n.** an aspect or angle of a story that makes it newsworthy: *Talese further expanded traditional journalistic practice by delaying a story's news peg until as late in a story as he could manage.*

news·peo·ple /ˈn(y)o͞oz,pēpəl/ ▶ **plural n.** professional reporters or journalists: *there's nothing wrong with docudrama so long as newspeople don't do it.*

news·print /ˈn(y)o͞oz,print/ ▶ **n.** cheap, low-quality, absorbent printing paper made from coarse wood pulp and used chiefly for newspapers.

news·read·er /ˈn(y)o͞oz,rēdər/ ▶ **n. 1** a computer program for reading messages posted to newsgroups.
2 Brit. a newscaster.

news·reel /ˈn(y)o͞oz,rēl/ ▶ **n.** a short film of news and current affairs, formerly made for showing as part of the program in a movie theater.

news·room /ˈn(y)o͞oz,ro͞om, -,ro͝om/ ▶ **n.** the area in a newspaper or broadcasting office where news is written and edited.

news·serv·er /n(y)o͞oz,sərvər/ ▶ **n.** a server that receives and disseminates messages for a newsgroup.

news·sheet ▶ **n.** a simple form of newspaper; a newsletter.

news·stand /ˈn(y)o͞oz,stand/ ▶ **n.** a stand or stall for the sale of newspapers.

new star ▶ **n.** a nova.

news tick·er ▶ **n.** a scrolling electronic display of news headlines on a building or along the lower portion of a television or computer screen. Also called **NEWS CRAWL**.

New Stone Age another name for **THE NEOLITHIC** (see **NEOLITHIC**).

New Style (abbr.: **NS**) ▶ **n.** the method of calculating dates using the Gregorian calendar. It superseded the use of the Julian calendar in Scotland in England in 1752.

new-style ▶ **adj.** [attrib.] having a new style; different from and usually better than a previous version: *a new-style retail and entertainment mix.*

news·week·ly /ˈn(y)o͞oz,wēklē/ ▶ **n.** (pl. **newsweeklies**) a newspaper or newsmagazine published on a weekly basis.

news wire ▶ **n.** an electronically transmitted service providing up-to-the-minute news stories, financial market updates, and other information.

news·wor·thy /ˈn(y)o͞oz,wərT͟Hē/ ▶ **adj.** noteworthy as news; topical: *you had to cover a lot of ground to find anything newsworthy.*
– DERIVATIVES **news·wor·thi·ness** **n.**

news·y ▶ **adj.** (**newsier**, **newsiest**) informal full of news, esp. of a personal kind: *short, newsy letters.*
▶ **n.** variant spelling of **NEWSIE**.

newt /n(y)o͞ot/ ▶ **n.** a small, slender-bodied amphibian with lungs and a well-developed tail, typically spending its adult life on land and returning to water to breed. ● *Notophthalmus*, *Taricha*, and other genera, family Salamandridae: numerous species, including the **red-spotted newt** (*N. viridescens viridescens*) of eastern North America and the **rough-skinned newt** (*T. granulosa*) of the Pacific coast from southern Alaska to northern California.
– ORIGIN late Middle English: from *an ewt* (*ewt* from Old English *efeta*: see **EFT**), interpreted (by wrong division) as *a newt*.

rough-skinned newt

New Ter·ri·to·ries the part of Hong Kong on the southern coast of mainland China that lies north of the Kowloon peninsula and includes the islands of Lantau, Tsing Yi, and Lamma.

New Tes·ta·ment ▶ **n.** the second part of the Christian Bible, written originally in Greek and recording the life and teachings of Jesus and his earliest followers. It includes the four Gospels, the Acts of the Apostles, twenty-one epistles by St. Paul and others, and the book of Revelation.

New·ton[1] /ˈn(y)o͞otn/ a city in eastern Massachusetts, on the Charles River, west of Boston; pop. 82,139 (est. 2008).

New·ton[2], Sir Isaac (1642–1727), English mathematician and physicist, considered the greatest single influence on theoretical physics until Einstein. In *Principia Mathematica* (1687), he gave a mathematical description of the laws of mechanics and gravitation and applied these to planetary motion. *Opticks* (1704) records his optical experiments and theories, including the discovery that white light is made up of a mixture of colors. His work in mathematics included the binomial theorem and differential calculus.

new·ton /ˈn(y)o͞otn/ (abbr.: **N**) ▶ **n.** Physics the SI unit of force. It is equal to the force that would give a mass of one kilogram an acceleration of one meter per second per second, and is equivalent to 100,000 dynes.
– ORIGIN early 20th cent.: named after Sir Isaac **NEWTON**[2].

New·to·ni·an /n(y)o͞oˈtōnēən/ ▶ **adj.** relating to or arising from the work of Sir Isaac Newton. ■ formulated or behaving according to the principles of classical physics.

New·to·ni·an me·chan·ics ▶ **plural n.** [usu. treated as sing.] the system of mechanics that relies on Newton's laws of motion concerning the relations between forces acting and motions occurring.

New·to·ni·an tel·e·scope ▶ **n.** Astronomy a reflecting telescope in which the light from the main mirror is deflected by a small, flat secondary mirror set at 45°, sending it to a magnifying eyepiece in the side of the telescope.

New·ton's laws of mo·tion Physics three fundamental laws of classical physics. The first states that a body continues in a state of rest or uniform motion in a straight line unless it is acted on by an external force. The second states that the rate of change of momentum of a moving body is proportional to the force acting to produce the change. The third states that if one body exerts a force on another, there is an equal and opposite force (or reaction) exerted by the second body on the first.

New·ton's rings ▶ **plural n.** Optics a set of concentric circular fringes seen around the point of contact when a convex lens is placed on a plane surface or on another lens, caused by interference between light reflected from the upper and lower surfaces.

new town ▶ **n.** a planned urban center created in an undeveloped or rural area, esp. with government sponsorship.

new wave ▶ **n. 1** another term for **NOUVELLE VAGUE**.
2 a style of rock music popular in the 1970s and 1980s, deriving from punk but generally more pop in sound and less aggressive in performance.

New World North and South America regarded collectively in relation to Europe, esp. after the early voyages of European explorers.

new year ▶ **n.** the calendar year just begun or about to begin: *we're looking ahead to a profitable start to the new year* | *Happy New Year!* ■ the first few days or weeks of a year: *interest rates may climb in the new year.* ■ (usu. **New Year**) the period immediately before and after December 31: *the facilities are closed over Christmas and New Year.*
– PHRASES **New Year's** informal New Year's Eve or New Year's Day. **ring in** (or **out**) **the new year** see **RING**[2].

New Year's Day ▶ **n.** the first day of the year; in the modern Western calendar, January 1.

New Year's Eve ▶ **n.** the last day of the year; in the modern Western calendar, December 31. ■ the evening of this day, typically marked with a celebration.

New·yor·i·can /n(y)o͞oˈyôrikən/ ▶ **n.** another term for **NUYORICAN**.

New York 1 a state in the northeastern US, on the Canadian border and Lake Ontario in the northwest, as well as on the Atlantic coast in the southeast; pop. 19,490,297 (est. 2008); capital, Albany; statehood, July 26, 1788 (11). Originally settled by the Dutch,

it was surrendered to the British in 1664. New York was one of the original thirteen states.
2 a major city and port in southeastern New York, situated on the Atlantic coast at the mouth of the Hudson River; pop. 8,363,710 (est. 2008). It is situated mainly on islands, linked by bridges, and consists of five boroughs: Manhattan, Brooklyn, the Bronx, Queens, and Staten Island. Manhattan is the economic and cultural heart of the city, containing the stock exchange on Wall Street and the headquarters of the United Nations. Former name (until 1664) **New Amsterdam**.
– DERIVATIVES **New York·er n.**

New York min·ute ▶ **n.** informal a very short time; a moment: *you mention that price and she'll be out of here in a New York minute.*
– ORIGIN with reference to the hectic pace of life in New York City.

New Zea·land /ˈzēlənd/ an island country in the South Pacific Ocean about 1,200 miles (1,900 km) east of Australia; pop. 4,213,400 (est. 2009); capital, Wellington; languages, English (official) and Maori. Maori name **Aotearoa**.

New Zealand consists of two major islands (North and South Islands), separated by Cook Strait, and several smaller ones. The first European to sight New Zealand was Dutch navigator Abel Tasman in 1642; the islands were circumnavigated by Captain James Cook in 1769–70 and came under British sovereignty in 1840. Full dominion status was granted in 1907, and independence within the Commonwealth of Nations came in 1931.

– DERIVATIVES **New Zea·land·er n.**

NEX ▶ **abbr.** Navy exchange.

NEXRAD /ˈneksˌrad/ ▶ **n.** a system of Doppler radars across the US that is used to track the location and movement of storm systems.
– ORIGIN 1990s: acronym from *NEXt generation weather RADar.*

next /nekst/ ▶ **adj. 1** (of a time or season) coming immediately after the time of writing or speaking: *we'll go next year | next week's parade.* ■ (of a day of the week) nearest (or the nearest but one) after the present: *not this Wednesday, next Wednesday |* [postpositive] *on Monday next.* ■ (of an event or occasion) occurring directly in time after the present or most recent one, without anything of the same kind intervening: *the next election | next time I'll bring a hat.*
2 coming immediately after the present one in order, rank, or space: *the woman in the next room | the next chapter | building materials were next in importance.*
▶ **adv.** on the first or soonest occasion after the present; immediately afterward: *wondering what would happen next | next, I heard the sound of voices.* ■ [with superlative] following in the specified order: *Joe was the next oldest after Martin.*
▶ **n.** the next person or thing: *one moment he wasn't there, the next he was | the week* ***after next.***
▶ **prep.** archaic next to: *he plodded along next him.*
– PHRASES **next in line** immediately below the present holder of a position in order of succession: *he is* ***next in line*** *to the throne.* **next to 1** in or into a position immediately to one side of; beside: *we sat next to each other.* **2** following in order or importance: *next to buying a whole new wardrobe, nothing lifts the spirits quite like a new hairdo!* **3** almost: *Charles knew* ***next to nothing*** *about farming.* **4** in comparison with: *next to her I felt like a fraud.* **the next world** (according to some religious beliefs) the place where one goes after death. **what next** an expression of surprise or amazement.
– ORIGIN Old English *nēhsta* 'nearest,' superlative of *nēah* 'nigh'; compare with Dutch *naast* and German *nächste.*

next best ▶ **adj.** [attrib.] second in order of preference; to be preferred if one's first choice is not available: ***the next best thing*** *to flying is gliding.*

next door ▶ **adv.** in or to the next house or room: *the caretaker lives next door.*
▶ **adj.** (**next-door**) living or situated next door: *next-door neighbors.*
▶ **n.** the building, room, or people next door: *a bleary-eyed man emerged from next door.*
– PHRASES **the boy** (or **girl**) **next door** a person or type of person perceived as familiar, approachable, and dependable, typically in the context of a romantic partnership. **next door to** in the next house or room to: *the Old Executive Office Building next door to the White House.* ■ nearly; almost; near to: *it is next door to impossible.*

next of kin ▶ **n.** [treated as sing. or pl.] a person's closest living relative or relatives.

nex·us /ˈneksəs/ ▶ **n.** (pl. **same** or **nexuses**) a connection or series of connections linking two or more things: *the nexus between industry and political power.* ■ a connected group or series: *a nexus of ideas.* ■ the central and most important point or place: *the nexus of all this activity was the disco.*
– ORIGIN mid 17th cent.: from Latin, 'a binding together,' from *nex-* 'bound,' from the verb *nectere.*

Nez Per·cé /ˌnez ˈpərz, pərˈsā/ ▶ **n.** (pl. **same** or **Nez Percés**) **1** a member of an American Indian people of central Idaho, northeastern Oregon, and southeastern Washington.
2 the Sahaptian language of this people.
▶ **adj.** of or relating to this people or their language.
– ORIGIN French, literally 'pierced nose.'

NF ▶ **abbr.** Newfoundland (in official postal use).

n/f (also **N/F**) ▶ **abbr.** no funds.

NFC ▶ **abbr.** ■ National Finance Center. ■ National Football Conference.

NFL ▶ **abbr.** National Football League.

Nfld ▶ **abbr.** Newfoundland.

NFZ ▶ **abbr.** no-fly zone.

NG ▶ **abbr.** ■ National Guard. ■ natural gas. ■ newsgroup. ■ no good. ■ Football nose guard.

ng ▶ **abbr.** nanogram(s).

Nga·li·e·ma, Mount /əNGˌgālēˈāmə/ Zairean name for Mount Stanley (see **Stanley, Mount**).

NGF ▶ **abbr.** ■ National Golf Foundation. ■ nerve growth factor.

NGO ▶ **abbr.** nongovernmental organization.

ngo·ma /əNGˈgōmə/ ▶ **n.** (in East Africa) a dance; a night of dancing and music.
– ORIGIN Kiswahili, literally 'drum, dance, music.'

Ngo·ni /əNGˈgōnē/ ▶ **n.** (pl. **same** or **Ngonis**) **1** a member of a people now living chiefly in Malawi.
2 (**ngoni**) a kind of traditional African drum.
▶ **adj.** of or relating to the Ngoni.
– ORIGIN a local name.

Ngo·ron·go·ro /əNGˌgôrôNGˈgôrō/ an extinct volcanic crater in the Great Rift Valley in northeastern Tanzania, 126 sq. mi. (326 sq. km.) in area.

NGU ▶ **abbr.** nongonococcal urethritis.

ngul·trum /əNGˈgəltrəm/ ▶ **n.** (pl. **same**) the basic monetary unit of Bhutan, equal to 100 chetrum.
– ORIGIN Dzongkha.

Ngu·ni /əNGˈgo͞onē/ ▶ **n.** (pl. **same**) **1** a member of a group of peoples living mainly in southern Africa.
2 the group of closely related Bantu languages, including Ndebele, Swazi, Xhosa, and Zulu, spoken by these peoples.
▶ **adj.** of or relating to this group of peoples or their languages.
– ORIGIN from Zulu.

ngwee /əNGˈgwē/ ▶ **n.** (pl. **same**) a monetary unit of Zambia, equal to one hundredth of a kwacha.
– ORIGIN a local word.

NH ▶ **abbr.** New Hampshire (in official postal use).

NHL ▶ **abbr.** National Hockey League.

Ni ▶ **symbol** the chemical element nickel.

ni·a·cin /ˈnīəsin/ ▶ **n.** another term for **nicotinic acid.**

Ni·ag·a·ra Falls /nīˈag(ə)rə/ waterfalls on the Niagara River that consist of two principal parts separated by Goat Island: the Horseshoe Falls adjoin the western (Canadian) bank and fall 158 feet (47 m); the American Falls adjoin the eastern (US) bank and fall 167 feet (50 m). ■ a city in upper New York located on the right bank of the Niagara River beside Niagara Falls; pop. 51,345 (est. 2008). ■ a city in Canada, in southern Ontario, situated on the left bank of the Niagara River beside Niagara Falls, opposite the city of Niagara Falls, US, to which it is linked by bridges; pop. 82,184 (2006).

Niagara Falls

Ni·ag·a·ra Riv·er a river in North America that flows north for 35 miles (56 km) from Lake Erie to Lake Ontario and forms part of the border between Canada and the US.

Nia·mey /nēˈämā/ the capital of Niger, a port on the Niger River; pop. 915,000 (est. 2007).

nib /nib/ ▶ **n. 1** the pointed end part of a pen, which distributes the ink on the writing surface. ■ a pointed or projecting part of an object.
2 (**nibs**) shelled and crushed coffee or cocoa beans. ■ small pieces of caramel, licorice, or other sweets.
– ORIGIN late 16th cent. (in the sense 'beak, nose'): probably from Middle Dutch *nib* or Middle Low German *nibbe*, variant of *nebbe* 'beak' (see **neb**).

nib·ble /ˈnibəl/ ▶ **v. 1** take small bites out of: [with obj.] *he sat nibbling a cookie |* [no obj.] *she* ***nibbled at*** *her food.* ■ [no obj.] eat in small amounts, esp. between meals. ■ gently bite at (a part of the body), esp. amorously or nervously: [with obj.] *Tamar nibbled her bottom lip |* [no obj.] *he* ***nibbled at*** *her earlobe.* ■ gradually erode or eat away: [no obj.] *inflation was* ***nibbling away at*** *spending power.*
2 [no obj.] show cautious interest in a project or proposal: *there's a New York agent nibbling.*
▶ **n.** [in sing.] **1** an instance of nibbling something. ■ a small piece of food bitten off. ■ (**nibbles**) informal small savory snacks, typically eaten before a meal or with drinks.
2 an expression of cautious interest in a project or proposal: *now and then she gets a nibble, but no one will commit to an interview.*
– ORIGIN late 15th cent.: probably of Low German or Dutch origin; compare with Low German *nibbeln* 'gnaw.'

nib·bler /ˈnib(ə)lər/ ▶ **n. 1** a person who habitually nibbles at food.
2 a cutting tool in which a rapidly reciprocating punch knocks out a line of overlapping small holes from a metal sheet.

Ni·be·lung /ˈnēbəˌlo͝oNG/ ▶ **n.** (pl. **Nibelungs** or **Nibelungen** /-ˌlo͝oNGgen/) Germanic Mythology **1** a member of a Scandinavian race of dwarfs, owners of a hoard of gold and magic treasures, who were ruled by Nibelung, king of Nibelheim (land of mist).
2 (in the *Nibelungenlied*) a supporter of Siegfried or one of the Burgundians who stole the hoard from him.
– ORIGIN from Old High German, from *nibel* 'mist' + the patronymic ending *-ung.*

Ni·be·lung·en·lied /ˌnēbəˈlo͝oNGgənˌlēd/ a 13th-century German poem, embodying a story found in the (Poetic) Edda, telling of the life and death of Siegfried, a prince of the Netherlands. There have been many adaptations of the story, including Wagner's epic music drama *Der Ring des Nibelungen* (1847–74).
– ORIGIN German, from the name **Nibelung** + *Lied* 'song.'

nib·let /ˈniblit/ ▶ **n.** a small piece of food.
– ORIGIN late 19th cent.: from **nibble** + **-let.**

n

nib·lick /ˈniblik/ ▶ **n.** Golf, dated an iron with a heavy, lofted head, such as a nine-iron, used esp. for playing out of bunkers.
– ORIGIN mid 19th cent.: of unknown origin.

nibs /nibz/ ▶ **n.** (**his nibs**) informal a mock title used to refer to a self-important man, esp. one in authority.
– ORIGIN early 19th cent.: of unknown origin; compare with earlier *nabs*, used similarly with a possessive adjective as in *his nabs*, on the pattern of references to the aristocracy such as *his lordship.*

NIC ▶ **abbr.** newly industrialized country.

Ni·Cad /ˈnīˌkad/ (also trademark **Nicad**) ▶ **n.** a battery or cell with a nickel anode, a cadmium cathode, and a potassium hydroxide electrolyte. NiCads are used chiefly as a rechargeable power source for portable equipment.
– ORIGIN 1950s: blend of **nickel** and **cadmium.**

Ni·cae·a /nīˈsēə/ an ancient city in Asia Minor, on the site of modern Iznik in Turkey. Two ecumenical councils of the early Christian Church were held here in 325 and 787 .See also **Nicene Creed.**

Nic·a·ra·gua /nikəˈrägwə/ a country, the largest, in Central America, with a coastline on both the Atlantic and the Pacific oceans; pop. 5,891,200 (est. 2009); capital, Managua; official language, Spanish.

Colonized by the Spaniards, Nicaragua broke away from Spain in 1821 and became an independent republic in 1838. In 1979, the dictator Anastasio Somoza was overthrown by a popular revolution; the new left-wing Sandinista regime then faced a counterrevolutionary guerrilla campaign by the US-backed Contras. The Sandinistas lost power to an opposition coalition in the 1990 election and were defeated again in 1996 and 2001.

– DERIVATIVES **Nic·a·ra·guan adj. & n.**

Nic·a·ra·gua, Lake a lake near the western coast of Nicaragua, the largest lake in Central America.

Nice /nēs/ a resort city on the French Riviera, near the border with Italy; pop. 348,721 (2007).

nice /nīs/ ▶ **adj. 1** pleasant; agreeable; satisfactory: *we had a nice time | that wasn't very nice of him | Jeremy had been very nice to her.* ■ (of a person) pleasant in manner; good-natured; kind: *he's a really nice guy.*
2 fine or subtle: *a nice distinction.* ■ requiring careful thought or attention: *a nice point.*
3 archaic fastidious; scrupulous.
– PHRASES **make nice** (or **nice-nice**) informal be pleasant or polite to someone, typically in a hypocritical way: *the seat next to him was empty, so he wasn't required to make nice with a stranger.* **nice and ——** satisfactorily or adequately in terms of the quality described: *it's nice and warm in here.* **nice one** informal expressing approval or commendation. ■ used sarcastically to comment on an inept act: *oh, nice one, she put her finger up to her eye and tugged at the skin.* **nice to meet you** a polite formula used on being introduced to someone. **nice work** informal expressing approval of a task well done. **nice work if you can get it** informal used to express envy of what is perceived to be another person's more favorable situation, esp. if they seem to have reached it with little effort.
– ORIGIN Middle English (in the sense 'stupid'): from Old French, from Latin *nescius* 'ignorant,' from *nescire* 'not know.' Other early senses included 'coy, reserved,' giving rise to 'fastidious, scrupulous': this led both to the sense 'fine, subtle' (regarded by some as the "correct" sense), and to the main current senses.

> **USAGE** Nice originally had a number of meanings, including 'fine, subtle, discriminating' (*they are not very nice in regard to the company they keep*); 'refined in taste, hard to please, fastidious' (*for company so nice, the finest caterers would be engaged*); and 'precise, strict' (*she has a nice sense of decorum*). The overuse of **nice** to mean 'pleasant, agreeable, satisfactory' has rendered the word rather trite: *we had a very nice time | this is a nice room | he's a nice boy.*

nice·ly /ˈnīslē/ ▶ **adv.** in a pleasant, agreeable, or attractive manner: *nicely dressed in flowered cotton.* ■ satisfactorily; perfectly well: *we're doing very nicely now.*

Ni·cene Creed /ˈnīsēn, nīˈsēn/ a formal statement of Christian belief that is widely used in Christian liturgies, based on that adopted at the first Council of Nicaea in 325.

nice·ness /ˈnīsnis/ ▶ **n.** the quality of being nice; pleasantness: *her sheer niceness won her many friends.*

ni·ce·ty /ˈnīsitē/ ▶ **n.** (pl. **niceties**) (usu. **niceties**) a fine detail or distinction, esp. one regarded as intricate and fussy: *she was never interested in the niceties of Greek and Latin.* ■ accuracy or precision: *she prided herself on her nicety of pronunciation.* ■ a minor aspect of polite social behavior; a detail of etiquette: *we were brought up to observe the niceties.*
– PHRASES **to a nicety** precisely.
– ORIGIN Middle English (in the sense 'folly, foolish conduct'): from Old French *nicete,* based on Latin *nescius* 'ignorant' (see **NICE**).

niche /nicH/ ▶ **n.** a shallow recess, esp. one in a wall to display a statue or other ornament. ■ (**one's niche**) a comfortable or suitable position in life or employment: *he is now a partner at a leading law firm and feels he has found his niche.* ■ a specialized but profitable corner of the market: [as modifier] *important new niche markets.* ■ Ecology a position or role taken by a kind of organism within its community. Such a position may be occupied by different organisms in different localities, e.g., antelopes in Africa and kangaroos in Australia.
▶ **v.** [with obj.] place or position (something) in a niche.
– ORIGIN early 17th cent.: from French, literally 'recess,' from *nicher* 'make a nest,' based on Latin *nidus* 'nest.'

Ni·chi·ren /ˈnicHərən/ (also **Nichiren Buddhism**) ▶ **n.** a Japanese Buddhist sect founded by the religious teacher Nichiren (1222–82) with the Lotus Sutra as its central scripture. See also **SOKA GAKKAI**.

Nich·o·las /ˈnik(ə)ləs/ the name of two tsars of Russia. ■ **Nicholas I** (1796–1855), brother of Alexander I; reigned 1825–55. At home he pursued rigidly conservative policies, while his expansionism in the Near East led to the Crimean War. ■ **Nicholas II** (1868–1918), son of Alexander III; reigned 1894–1917. Forced to abdicate after the Russian Revolution in 1917, he was shot along with his family a year later.

Nich·o·las, St. (4th century), Christian prelate. Said to have been bishop of Myra in Lycia, he is the patron saint of children, sailors, Greece, and Russia. The cult of Santa Claus (a corruption of his name) comes from the Dutch custom of giving gifts to children on his feast day. Feast day December 6.

Nich·ols /ˈnikəlz/, Mike (1931–), US director; born in Germany; born *Michael Igor Peschowsky.* He directed *Barefoot in the Park* (1963), *The Odd Couple* (1965), and *Annie* (1977) on Broadway. Movies he directed include *Who's Afraid of Virginia Woolf?* (1966), *The Graduate* (1967), *The Birdcage* (1996), and *Charlie Wilson's War* (2007).

Nich·ol·son[1] /ˈnikəlsən/, Ben (1894–1982), English painter; full name *Benjamin Lauder Nicholson.* A pioneer of British abstract art, he was noted for his painted reliefs with circular and rectangular motifs.

Nich·ol·son[2], Jack (1937–), US actor; full name *John Joseph Nicholson.* Notable movies: *Easy Rider* (1969), *One Flew Over the Cuckoo's Nest* (1975), *Terms of Endearment* (1983), *As Good as It Gets* (1997), *About Schmidt* (2002), and *The Departed* (2006).

Jack Nicholson

ni·chrome /ˈnīˌkrōm/ (also **Nichrome**) ▶ **n.** trademark an alloy of nickel with chromium (10 to 20 percent) and sometimes iron (up to 25 percent), used chiefly in high-temperature applications such as electrical heating elements.
– ORIGIN early 20th cent.: blend of **NICKEL** and **CHROME**.

nick /nik/ ▶ **n. 1** a small cut or notch.
2 (**the nick**) Brit. informal prison. ■ a police station.
3 the junction between the floor and sidewalls in a court for playing tennis or squash.
▶ **v.** [with obj.] **1** make a nick or nicks in: *he had nicked himself while shaving.*
2 (**nick someone for**) informal cheat someone of (something, typically a sum of money): *he nicked me for fifteen hundred dollars.*
3 Brit. informal steal: *he'd had his car nicked by joyriders.* ■ arrest or apprehend (someone): *I got nicked for burglary.*
– PHRASES **in the nick of time** only just in time.
– ORIGIN late Middle English: of unknown origin.

nick·el /ˈnikəl/ ▶ **n. 1** a silvery-white metal, the chemical element of atomic number 28. (Symbol: **Ni**)

> Nickel occurs naturally in various minerals, and the earth's core is believed to consist largely of metallic iron and nickel. The chief use of nickel is in alloys, esp. with iron, to which it imparts strength and resistance to corrosion, and with copper for coinage.

2 informal a five-cent coin; five cents.
▶ **v.** (**nickels, nickeling, nickeled**; Brit. **nickels, nickelling, nickelled**) [with obj.] coat with nickel.
– ORIGIN mid 18th cent.: shortening of German *Kupfernickel,* the copper-colored ore from which nickel was first obtained, from *Kupfer* 'copper' + *Nickel* 'demon' (with reference to the ore's failure to yield copper).

nick·el-and-dime ▶ **v.** [with obj.] put a financial strain on (someone) by charging small amounts for many minor services: *we don't nickel-and-dime our customers like some vendors that charge extra for every little utility.*
▶ **adj.** [attrib.] of little importance; petty: *the only games this weekend are nickel-and-dime stuff.*
– ORIGIN 1970s: originally designating a store selling articles costing five or ten cents.

nick·el brass ▶ **n.** an alloy of copper, zinc, and a small amount of nickel.

nick·el-cad·mi·um bat·ter·y ▶ **n.** a storage battery with a negative electrode made of cadmium, a positive electrode of nickel oxide, and a solution of potassium hydroxide as the electrolyte. Nickel-cadmium batteries have the advantage of an airtight battery container, which prevents the corrosive electrolyte from leaking.

nick·el·o·de·on /ˌnikəˈlōdēən/ ▶ **n. 1** informal, dated a jukebox, originally one operated by the insertion of a nickel coin.
2 historical a movie theater with an admission fee of one nickel.
– ORIGIN early 20th cent.: from **NICKEL** in the sense 'five-cent coin' + a shortened form of **MELODEON**.

nick·el sil·ver ▶ **n.** another term for **GERMAN SILVER**.

nick·el steel ▶ **n.** a type of stainless steel containing chromium and nickel.

nick·er[1] /ˈnikər/ ▶ **v.** [no obj.] (of a horse) give a soft, low whinny.
▶ **n.** a sound of this kind.
– ORIGIN late 16th cent.: imitative.

nick·er[2] ▶ **n.** (pl. **same**) Brit. informal a pound sterling.
– ORIGIN early 20th cent.: of unknown origin.

Nick·laus /ˈnikləs/, Jack William (1940–), US golfer. He won more than 80 tournaments during his professional career, including the Masters (1963, 1965, 1966, 1972, 1975, 1986), the PGA (1963, 1971, 1973, 1975, 1980), the US Open (1962, 1967, 1972, 1980), and the British Open (1966, 1970, 1978).

nick·nack /ˈnikˌnak/ ▶ **n.** variant spelling of **KNICKKNACK**.

nick·name /ˈnikˌnām/ ▶ **n.** a familiar or humorous name given to a person or thing instead of or as well as the real name.
▶ **v.** [with obj. and complement] give a nickname to; call by a nickname: *his fraternity brothers nicknamed him "The Bird" because of his skydiving skills.*
– ORIGIN late Middle English: from *an eke-name* (*eke* meaning 'addition': see **EKE**[2]), misinterpreted, by wrong division, as *a neke name.*

Nic·o·bar·ese /ˌnikəbäˈrēz, -ˈrēs/ ▶ **n.** (pl. **same**) **1** a native or inhabitant of the Nicobar Islands.
2 an ancient language spoken in the Nicobar Islands, distantly related to the Mon-Khmer and Munda families.
▶ **adj.** of or relating to the Nicobar Islands, their inhabitants, or their language.

Nic·o·bar Is·lands /ˈnikəˌbär/ see **ANDAMAN AND NICOBAR ISLANDS**.

Ni·çois /nēˈswä/ ▶ **n.** (fem. **Niçoise** /nēˈswäz/) a native or inhabitant of the city of Nice, France.
▶ **adj.** of, relating to, or characteristic of Nice or its inhabitants: *the Niçois dialect.* ■ [postpositive] denoting food that is characteristic of Nice or the surrounding region, typically garnished with tomatoes, capers, and anchovies: *salade Niçoise.*
– ORIGIN French.

Ni·col·let /ˌnikəˈlet/, Joseph Nicolas (1786–1843), US explorer; born in France. With John Frémont as his assistant, he led a government surveying expedition that mapped the region between the upper Mississippi and Missouri rivers 1838–39.

Nic·ol prism /ˈnikəl/ ▶ **n.** a device for producing plane-polarized light, consisting of two pieces of optically clear calcite or Iceland spar cemented together with Canada balsam in the shape of a prism.
– ORIGIN mid 19th cent.: named after William *Nicol* (died 1851), the Scottish physicist who invented it.

Nic·o·sia /ˌnikəˈsēə/ the capital of Cyprus; pop. 233,000 (est. 2007). Since 1974 it has been divided into Greek and Turkish sectors.

ni·co·ti·a·na /niˌkōsHēˈänə, -ˈanə/ ▶ **n.** an ornamental plant related to tobacco, with tubular flowers that are particularly fragrant at night. Also called **TOBACCO PLANT**. ● Genus *Nicotiana,* family Solanaceae: several species, in particular *N. alata.*
– ORIGIN from modern Latin *nicotiana* (*herba*) 'tobacco (plant),' named after Jean *Nicot,* a 16th-cent. French diplomat who introduced tobacco to France in 1560.

nic·o·tin·a·mide /ˌnikəˈtinəˌmīd, -ˈtēn-/ ▶ **n.** Biochemistry a compound that is the form in which nicotinic acid often occurs in nature. ● The amide of nicotinic acid; chem. formula: $(C_5H_4N)CONH_2$.

nic·o·tin·a·mide ad·e·nine di·nu·cle·o·tide /ˈadn-in dīˈn(y)o͞oklēəˌtīd/ ▶ **n.** see **NAD**.

nic·o·tine /ˈnikəˌtēn/ ▶ **n.** a toxic colorless or yellowish oily liquid that is the chief active constituent of tobacco. It acts as a stimulant in small doses, but in larger amounts blocks the action of autonomic nerve and skeletal muscle cells. Nicotine is also used in insecticides. ● An alkaloid; chem. formula: $C_{10}H_{14}N_2$.
– ORIGIN early 19th cent.: from French, from **NICOTIANA** + **-INE**[4].

nic·o·tine patch ▶ **n.** a patch impregnated with nicotine and worn on the skin by a person trying to give up smoking. Nicotine is gradually absorbed into the bloodstream, helping reduce the craving for cigarettes.

nic·o·tin·ic ac·id /ˌnikəˈtinik, -ˈtēnik/ ▶ **n.** Biochemistry a vitamin of the B complex that is widely distributed in foods such as milk, wheat germ, and meat, and can be synthesized in the body from tryptophan. Its deficiency causes pellagra. ● Alternative name: **3-pyridinecarboxylic acid**; chem. formula: $(C_5H_4N)COOH$.

– DERIVATIVES **nic·o·tin·ate** /-ˈtēˌnāt/ **n.**

nic·tate /ˈnikˌtāt/ (also **nictitate** /ˈniktiˌtāt/) ▶ **v.** [no obj.] technical (esp. of the eyelid) blink.
– ORIGIN late 17th cent.: from Latin *nictat-* 'blinked,' from the verb *nictare*. The variant *nictitate* is from the medieval Latin frequentative of *nictare*.

nic·ta·tion /nikˈtāSHən/ ▶ **n.** technical the action or process of blinking.
– ORIGIN late 18th cent.: from Latin *nictatio(n-)*, from the verb *nictare* 'to blink.'

nic·ti·tat·ing mem·brane /ˈniktiˌtātiNG/ ▶ **n.** Zoology a whitish or translucent membrane that forms an inner eyelid in birds, reptiles, and some mammals. It can be drawn across the eye to protect it from dust and keep it moist. Also called **THIRD EYELID**.
– ORIGIN early 18th cent.: *nictitating* based on medieval Latin *nictitat-* 'blinked,' frequentative of *nictare*.

ni·da·tion /nīˈdāSHən/ ▶ **n.** another term for **IMPLANTATION**.
– ORIGIN late 19th cent.: from Latin *nidus* 'nest' + **-ATION**.

nide /nīd/ ▶ **n.** archaic a brood or nest of pheasants.
– ORIGIN late 17th cent.: from French *nid* or Latin *nidus* 'nest.'

ni·dic·o·lous /nīˈdikələs/ ▶ **adj.** another term for **ALTRICIAL**.
– ORIGIN early 20th cent.: from Latin *nidus* 'nest' + *-colus* 'inhabiting' (from the verb *colere* 'live in, cultivate').

nid·i·fi·ca·tion /ˌnidəfiˈkāSHən/ ▶ **n.** Zoology nest-building.
– ORIGIN mid 17th cent.: from Latin *nidificat-* 'made into a nest' (from the verb *nidificare*, from *nidus* 'nest') + **-ATION**.

ni·dif·u·gous /nīˈdifyəgəs/ ▶ **adj.** another term for **PRECOCIAL**.
– ORIGIN early 20th cent.: from Latin *nidus* 'nest' + *fugere* 'flee' + **-OUS**.

ni·dus /ˈnīdəs/ ▶ **n.** (pl. **nidi** /-ˌdī/ or **niduses**) a place in which something is formed or deposited; a site of origin. ■ Medicine a place in which bacteria have multiplied or may multiply; a focus of infection.
– ORIGIN early 18th cent. (in the medical sense 'focus of infection'): from Latin, literally 'nest.'

Nie·buhr /ˈnēˌbo͝or/, Reinhold (1892–1971), US theologian and political activist. Professor of Christian ethics at Union Theological Seminary 1928–60, he wrote *Moral Man and Immoral Society* (1932) and *The Irony of American History* (1952).

niece /nēs/ ▶ **n.** a daughter of one's brother or sister, or of one's brother-in-law or sister-in-law.
– ORIGIN Middle English: from Old French, based on Latin *neptis* 'granddaughter,' feminine of *nepos* 'nephew, grandson' (see **NEPHEW**), from an Indo-European root shared by Dutch *nicht*, German *Nichte*.

Nie·der·sach·sen /ˈnēdərˌsäksən/ German name for **LOWER SAXONY**.

ni·el·lo /nēˈelō/ ▶ **n.** a black compound of sulfur with silver, lead, or copper, used for filling in engraved designs in silver or other metals. ■ objects decorated with this.
– DERIVATIVES **ni·el·loed** **adj.**
– ORIGIN early 19th cent.: from Italian, from Latin *nigellus*, diminutive of *niger* 'black.'

niels·bohr·i·um /ˌnēlzˈbôrēəm/ ▶ **n.** a name proposed by the American Chemical Society for the chemical element of atomic number 107, now called **bohrium**.
– ORIGIN modern Latin, from the name of the scientist *Niels Bohr* (see **BOHR**). The term was originally proposed (*c.*1971) by Soviet scientists for element 105 (hahnium).

Niel·sen /ˈnēlsən/, Carl August (1865–1931), Danish composer. He is best known for his six symphonies (1890–1925).

Nie·mey·er /ˈnēˌmīər/, Oscar (1907–), Brazilian architect. An early exponent of modernist architecture in Latin America, he designed the main public buildings of Brasilia (1950–60) and in 1996 created the Niterói Contemporary Art Museum in Rio de Janeiro.

ni·en·te /nēˈentā/ ▶ **adv. & adj.** Music (esp. as a direction) with a soft sound or tone gradually fading to nothing.
– ORIGIN Italian, literally 'nothing.'

Nier·stein·er /ˈni(ə)rˌstīnər, -ˌSHtīn-/ ▶ **n.** a white Rhine wine produced in the region around Nierstein, a town in Germany.

Nietz·sche /ˈnēCHə/, Friedrich Wilhelm (1844–1900), German philosopher. He is known for repudiating Christianity's compassion for the weak, exalting the "will to power," and formulating the idea of the *Übermensch* (superman), who can rise above the restrictions of ordinary morality.
– DERIVATIVES **Nietzs·che·an** /ˈnēCHēən/ **adj. & n.**, **Nietzs·che·an·ism** /ˈnēCHēəˌnizəm/ **n.**

ni·fed·i·pine /nīˈfedəpēn/ ▶ **n.** Medicine a synthetic compound that acts as a calcium antagonist and is used as a coronary vasodilator in the treatment of cardiac and circulatory disorders.
– ORIGIN 1970s: from *ni(tro-)* + *fe* (alteration of **PHENYL**) + **DI-**¹ + *p(yrid)ine*, elements of the systematic name.

Ni·fl·heim /ˈnivəlˌhām/ Scandinavian Mythology an underworld of eternal cold, darkness, and mist inhabited by those who died of old age or illness.
– ORIGIN from Old Norse *Niflheimr*, literally 'world of mist.'

nif·ty /ˈniftē/ ▶ **adj.** (**niftier**, **niftiest**) informal particularly good, skillful, or effective: *nifty footwork*. ■ fashionable; stylish: *a nifty black shirt*.
– DERIVATIVES **nif·ti·ly** /-təlē/ **adv.**, **nif·ti·ness** **n.**
– ORIGIN mid 19th cent.: of unknown origin.

ni·gel·la /nīˈjelə/ ▶ **n.** a plant of a genus that includes love-in-a-mist. ● Genus *Nigella*, family Ranunculaceae.
– ORIGIN modern Latin, feminine of Latin *nigellus*, diminutive of *niger* 'black.'

Ni·ger 1 /ˈnījər/ a river in northwestern Africa that rises on the northeastern border of Sierra Leone and flows northeast and then southeast in a great arc for 2,550 miles (4,100 km) to Mali and through western Niger and Nigeria before turning south into the Gulf of Guinea.
2 /nēˈZHe(ə)r/ a landlocked country in West Africa, on the southern edge of the Sahara Desert; pop. 15,306,300 (est. 2009); capital, Niamey; languages, French (official), Hausa, and other West African languages.
– DERIVATIVES **Ni·ger·i·en** /nēˈZHe(ə)riən/ **adj. & n.**

> Part of French West Africa from 1922, it became an autonomous republic within the French Community in 1958 and fully independent in 1960. Niger's first free elections were held in 1993.

Ni·ger–Con·go ▶ **adj.** denoting or belonging to a large phylum of languages in Africa, named after the rivers Niger and Congo. It comprises most of the languages spoken by the indigenous peoples of Africa south of the Sahara and includes the Bantu, Mande, Gur, and Kwa families.

Ni·ge·ri·a /nīˈji(ə)rēə/ a country on the coast of West Africa, bordered by the Niger River on the north; pop. 149,229,100 (est. 2009); capital, Abuja; languages, English (official), Hausa, Ibo, Yoruba, and others.

> The site of highly developed kingdoms in the Middle Ages, the area came under British influence during the 19th century and was consolidated into a single colony in 1914. Independence came in 1960, and it became a federal republic in 1963, while remaining a member of the Commonwealth of Nations. Oil was discovered in the 1960s and 1970s; since then, Nigeria has emerged as one of the world's major exporters.

– DERIVATIVES **Ni·ge·ri·an** **adj. & n.**

Ni·ge·ri·an let·ter ▶ **n.** an e-mail whose sender promises to greatly enrich the recipient in exchange for personal information, such as bank account details.
– ORIGIN early 2000s: from the fact that many such e-mails originally came from Nigerians.

nig·gard /ˈnigərd/ ▶ **n.** a stingy or ungenerous person.
▶ **adj.** archaic term for **NIGGARDLY**.
– ORIGIN late Middle English: alteration of earlier *nigon*.

> **USAGE** The words **niggard** and **niggardly** have no connection with the highly offensive term **nigger**, but because of the similarity of sound and its negative meaning of 'mean, ungenerous,' many people are uncomfortable with using it for fear of causing offense, and in the US it is now widely avoided.

nig·gard·ly /ˈnigərdlē/ ▶ **adj.** not generous; stingy: *serving out the rations with a niggardly hand*. ■ meager; scanty: *their share is a niggardly 2.7 percent*.
▶ **adv.** archaic in a stingy or meager manner.
– DERIVATIVES **nig·gard·li·ness** **n.**

> **USAGE** See usage at **NIGGARD**.

nig·ger /ˈnigər/ ▶ **n.** offensive a contemptuous term for a black or dark-skinned person.
– ORIGIN late 17th cent. (as an adjective): from earlier *neger*, from French *nègre*, from Spanish *negro* 'black' (see **NEGRO**).

> **USAGE** The word **nigger** was used as an adjective denoting a black person as early as the 17th century and has long had strong offensive connotations. Today it remains one of the most racially offensive words in the language. Also referred to as 'the n-word,' **nigger** is sometimes used by black people in reference to other black people in a jocular or disparaging manner, or some variant in between (in somewhat the same way that *queer* has been adopted by some gay and lesbian people as a term of self-reference, acceptable only when used by those within the community).

nig·gle /ˈnigəl/ ▶ **v.** [no obj.] cause slight but persistent annoyance, discomfort, or anxiety: *a suspicion niggled at the back of her mind* | (as adj. **niggling**) *niggling aches and pains*. ■ [with obj.] find fault with (someone) in a petty way: *colleagues say he loved to niggle and criticize people*.
▶ **n.** a trifling complaint, dispute, or criticism.
– DERIVATIVES **nig·gling·ly** **adv.**
– ORIGIN early 17th cent. (in the sense 'do something in a fiddling or ineffectual way'): apparently of Scandinavian origin; compare with Norwegian *nigla*. Current senses date from the late 18th cent.

nigh /nī/ ▶ **adv., prep., & adj.** near: [as adj.] *departure time was drawing nigh* | [as adv.] *they drew nigh unto the city*. ■ almost: [as adv.] *a car weighing nigh on two tons* | *recovery will be well nigh impossible*.
– ORIGIN Old English *nēh*, *nēah*, of Germanic origin; related to Dutch *na*, German *nah*. Compare with **NEAR**.

night /nīt/ ▶ **n.** **1** the period of darkness in each twenty-four hours; the time from sunset to sunrise: *a moonless night* | *the office door is always locked at night*. ■ this as the interval between two days: *a two-bedroom cabin costs $90 per night* | *somebody put him up for the night*. ■ the darkness of night: *a line of watchfires stretched away into the night*. ■ literary nightfall.
2 the period of time between afternoon and bedtime; an evening: *he was not allowed to go out on weekday nights*. ■ an evening appointed for some activity, or spent or regarded in a certain way: *wasn't it a great night out?*
▶ **exclam.** informal short for **GOOD NIGHT**.
– PHRASES **night and day** all the time; constantly: *she studied night and day*.
– DERIVATIVES **night·less** **adj.**
– ORIGIN Old English *neaht*, *niht*, of Germanic origin; related to Dutch *nacht* and German *Nacht*, from an Indo-European root shared by Latin *nox* and Greek *nux*.

night ad·der ▶ **n.** a venomous nocturnal African viper. ● Genus *Causus*, family Viperidae: several species, in particular the gray and black *C. rhombeatus*, common in southern Africa.

night·bird /ˈnītˌbərd/ ▶ **n.** another term for **NIGHT OWL**.

night blind·ness ▶ **n.** less technical term for **NYCTALOPIA**.

night-bloom·ing ce·re·us ▶ **n.** a tropical climbing cactus with aerial roots and heavily scented flowers that open only at night and are typically pollinated by bats. ● Genera *Hylocereus* and *Selenicereus*, family Cactaceae: several species, in particular *H. undatus*.

night·cap /ˈnītˌkap/ ▶ **n.** **1** historical a cap worn in bed.
2 an alcoholic or hot drink taken at the end of the day or before going to bed.
3 Baseball the second game of a doubleheader: *he pitched a four-hit shutout in the nightcap*.

night·clothes /ˈnītˌklō(TH)z/ ▶ **plural n.** clothes worn to bed.

night·club /ˈnītˌkləb/ ▶ **n.** an establishment for nighttime entertainment, typically serving drinks and offering music, dancing, etc.
– DERIVATIVES **night·club·ber** **n.**, **night·club·bing** **n.**

night court ▶ **n.** a criminal court that holds sessions at night for granting bail and quickly disposing of charges.

night crawl·er (also **nightcrawler**) ▶ **n.** an earthworm, in particular one that comes to the surface at night and is collected for use as fishing bait. ■ informal a person who is socially active at night: *the bar and nightclub are hot items with chic night crawlers*.

night·dress /ˈnītˌdres/ ▶ **n.** another term for **NIGHTGOWN**.

night·fall /ˈnītˌfôl/ ▶ **n.** the onset of night; dusk.

night·gown /ˈnītˌgoun/ ▶ **n.** **1** a light, loose garment worn by a woman or child in bed.
2 historical a dressing gown.

night·hawk /ˈnītˌhôk/ ▶ **n.** **1** an American nightjar with sharply pointed wings. ● Family Caprimulgidae: four genera and several species, in particular the **common nighthawk** (*Chordeiles minor*).
2 another term for **NIGHT OWL**.

night her·on ▶ **n.** a small short-necked heron that is active mainly at night. ● Genus *Nycticorax*, family Ardeidae: several species.

night·ie /ˈnītē/ ▶ **n.** informal a nightgown.

Night·in·gale /ˈnītnˌgāl, ˈnītiNG-/, Florence (1820–1910), English nurse and medical reformer. In 1854, during the Crimean War, she improved sanitation and medical procedures at the army hospital at Scutari, achieving a dramatic reduction in the mortality rate. She became known as the "Lady of the Lamp" for her nightly rounds.

night·in·gale /ˈnītnˌgāl, ˈnītiNG-/ ▶ **n.** a small European thrush with drab brownish plumage, noted for the rich melodious song of the male, heard esp. at night in breeding season. ● *Luscinia megarhynchos*, subfamily Turdinae, family Muscicapidae.
– ORIGIN Old English *nihtegala*, of Germanic origin; related to Dutch *nachtegaal* and German *Nachtigall*, from the base of **NIGHT** and a base meaning 'sing.'

nightingale

night·jar /ˈnītˌjär/ ▶ **n.** a nocturnal insectivorous bird with gray-brown camouflaged plumage, large eyes and gape, and a distinctive call. Also called **GOATSUCKER**. ● Family Caprimulgidae (the **nightjar family**): several genera, esp. *Caprimulgus*, and many species, including the **European nightjar** (*C. europaeus*), which has a chirring call. The nightjar family also includes the nighthawks, pauraques, poor-wills, whippoorwills, and chuck-will's-widow.

Night Jour·ney (in Muslim tradition) the journey through the air made by Muhammad, guided by the archangel Gabriel. They flew first to Jerusalem, where Muhammad prayed with earlier prophets, including Abraham, Moses, and Jesus, before entering the presence of Allah in heaven.

night·life /ˈnītˌlīf/ ▶ **n.** social activities or entertainment available at night in a town or city.

night·light /ˈnīt ˌlīt/ ▶ **n.** a small lamp, typically attached directly to an electrical outlet, providing a dim light during the night.

night liz·ard ▶ **n.** a small dull-colored nocturnal lizard with large scales or bony plates on the head, occurring from the southwestern US to Central America. ● Family Xantusiidae: several genera and species, including the **desert night lizard** (*Xantusia vigilis*).

night·long /ˈnītˌlôNG/ ▶ **adj.** lasting throughout the night: *a nightlong blizzard*.

night·ly /ˈnītlē/ ▶ **adj.** **1** happening or done every night: *his prime-time, nightly TV talk show*.
2 happening, done, or existing in the night.
▶ **adv.** every night: *the hotel features live music nightly*.

night·mare /ˈnītˌme(ə)r/ ▶ **n.** a frightening or unpleasant dream: *I had nightmares after watching the horror movie*. ■ a terrifying or very unpleasant experience or prospect: *the nightmare of racial hatred | an astronaut's worst nightmare is getting detached during an extravehicle activity*. ■ a person, thing, or situation that is very difficult to deal with: *buying wine can be a nightmare if you don't know enough about it*.
– ORIGIN Middle English (denoting a female evil spirit thought to lie upon and suffocate sleepers): from **NIGHT** + Old English *mære* 'incubus.'

night·mar·ish /ˈnītˌme(ə)riSH/ ▶ **adj.** of the nature of a nightmare; very frightening or unpleasant: *a nightmarish vision of the future | a nightmarish eight-hour journey*.
– DERIVATIVES **night·mar·ish·ly** **adv.**

night mon·key ▶ **n.** another term for **DOUROUCOULI**.

night owl ▶ **n.** informal a person who is habitually active or wakeful at night.

night·rid·er /ˈnītˌrīdər/ ▶ **n.** a member of a secret band of mounted men who committed nocturnal acts of violence and intimidation against blacks in the southern US during Reconstruction.

nights /nīts/ ▶ **adv.** informal during the night; at night: *investments that won't keep us awake nights with worry*.

night school ▶ **n.** an institution providing evening classes for those working during the day.

night·shade /ˈnītˌSHād/ ▶ **n.** a plant related to the potato, typically having poisonous black or red berries. Several kinds of nightshade have been used in the production of herbal medicines. ● *Solanum* and other genera, family Solanaceae (the **nightshade family**): several species, including the European **woody nightshade** (*S. dulcamara*), a climber with purple flowers and red berries. The nightshade family includes many commercially important plants (potato, tomato, capsicum peppers, tobacco) as well as a number of highly poisonous ones (henbane, jimson weed). See also **DEADLY NIGHTSHADE**.
– ORIGIN Old English *nihtscada*, apparently from **NIGHT** + **SHADE**, probably with reference to the dark color and poisonous properties of the berries. Compare with German *Nachtschatten*.

night shift ▶ **n.** the period of time scheduled for work at night, as in a factory or other institution. ■ the group of people working during this period.

night·shirt /ˈnītˌSHərt/ ▶ **n.** a long, loose shirt worn to bed.

night·side /ˈnītˌsīd/ ▶ **n.** **1** Astronomy the side of a planet or moon that is facing away from the sun and is therefore in darkness.
2 the world at night; activities that take place during the night: *nightside was the province of the professional criminals*.

night soil ▶ **n.** human excrement collected at night from buckets, cesspools, and outhouses and sometimes used as manure.

night·spot /ˈnītˌspät/ ▶ **n.** informal a nightclub.

night·stand /ˈnītˌstand/ (also **night table**) ▶ **n.** a small low bedside table, typically having drawers.

night·stick /ˈnītˌstik/ ▶ **n.** a police officer's club or billy.

night ter·rors ▶ **plural n.** feelings of great fear experienced on suddenly waking in the night.

night·time /ˈnītˌtīm/ ▶ **n.** the time between evening and morning; the time of darkness: *slipping away over the river in the nighttime* | [as modifier] *the government imposed a nighttime curfew*.

night vi·sion ▶ **n.** the faculty of seeing in very low light, esp. after the eyes have become adapted.
▶ **adj.** (**night-vision**) denoting devices that enhance nighttime vision: *night-vision goggles*.

night watch·man ▶ **n.** (pl. **night watchmen**) a person whose job is to guard a building at night.

night·wear /ˈnītˌwe(ə)r/ ▶ **n.** clothing suitable for wearing to bed.

ni·gi·ri zu·shi /ˌnigərē ˈzo͞oSHē/ ▶ **n.** sushi consisting of a small ball of rice, smeared with wasabi sauce and topped with raw fish or other seafood.
– ORIGIN 1990s: Japanese, from *nigiri-* (combining form of *nigiru*, 'clasp, clench, roll in the hands') + *zushi* 'sushi.'

ni·gres·cent /nīˈgresənt/ ▶ **adj.** rare blackish.
– DERIVATIVES **ni·gres·cence** **n.**
– ORIGIN mid 18th cent.: from Latin *nigrescent-* 'growing black,' from the verb *nigrescere*, from *niger, nigr-* 'black.'

nig·ri·tude /ˈnigriˌt(y)o͞od/ ▶ **n.** rare blackness.
– ORIGIN mid 17th cent.: from Latin *nigritudo* 'blackness,' from *niger, nigr-* 'black.'

NIH ▶ **abbr.** National Institutes of Health.

ni·hil·ism /ˈnīəˌlizəm, ˈnē-/ ▶ **n.** the rejection of all religious and moral principles, often in the belief that life is meaningless. ■ Philosophy extreme skepticism maintaining that nothing in the world has a real existence. ■ historical the doctrine of an extreme Russian revolutionary party *c.*1900, which found nothing to approve of in the established social order.
– DERIVATIVES **ni·hil·ist** **n.**
– ORIGIN early 19th cent.: from Latin *nihil* 'nothing' + **-ISM**.

ni·hil·is·tic /ˌnīəˈlistik, ˌnēə-/ ▶ **adj.** rejecting all religious and moral principles in the belief that life is meaningless: *an embittered, nihilistic teenager*.

ni·hil·i·ty /nīˈhilitē, ˈnē-/ ▶ **n.** rare nonexistence; nothingness.
– ORIGIN late 17th cent.: from medieval Latin *nihilitas*, from Latin *nihil* 'nothing.'

ni·hil ob·stat /ˈnīhil ˈäbstat/ ▶ **n.** (in the Roman Catholic Church) a certification by an official censor that a book is not objectionable on doctrinal or moral grounds.
– ORIGIN Latin, literally 'nothing hinders.'

Ni·i·ga·ta /ˌnē-ēˈgätə/ an industrial port in central Japan, on the northwestern coast of Honshu; pop. 803,791 (2007).

Ni·i·hau /ˈnē-ēˌhou/ an island in Hawaii, southwest of Kauai. Its residents are all native Hawaiians.

Ni·jin·sky /nəˈZHinskē, -ˈjin-, nyi-/, Vaslav (Fomich) (1890–1950), Russian ballet dancer and choreographer. The leading dancer with Diaghilev's Ballets Russes from 1909, he also choreographed Debussy's *L'Après-midi d'un faune* (1912) and Stravinsky's *The Rite of Spring* (1913).

Nij·me·gen /ˈnīˌmāgən/ an industrial town in the eastern Netherlands, south of Arnhem; pop. 161,251 (2008).

-nik ▶ **suffix** (forming nouns) denoting a person associated with a specified thing or quality: *beatnik | refusenik*.
– ORIGIN from Russian (on the pattern of *(sput)nik*) and Yiddish.

ni·kah /niˈkä/ ▶ **n.** a Muslim marriage ceremony.
– ORIGIN Urdu and Arabic.

Ni·ke /ˈnīkē/ Greek Mythology the goddess of victory.
– ORIGIN Greek, literally 'victory.'

Nik·kei in·dex /ˈnēkā/ a figure indicating the relative price of representative shares on the Tokyo Stock Exchange. Also called **Nikkei average**.
– ORIGIN 1970s: *Nikkei*, abbreviation of *Ni(hon) Kei(zai Shimbun)* 'Japanese Economic Journal.'

Ni·ko·la·ev /ˌnēkəˈlīəf/ Russian name for **MYKOLAYIV**.

nil /nil/ ▶ **n.** zero, esp. as a score in certain games: *they beat us three-nil*.
▶ **adj.** nonexistent: *his chances for survival were slim, almost nil*.
– ORIGIN mid 19th cent.: from Latin, contraction of *nihil* 'nothing.'

nil de·spe·ran·dum /ˈnil ˌdespəˈrändəm/ ▶ **exclam.** do not despair; never despair.
– ORIGIN from Latin *nil desperandum Teucro duce* 'no need to despair with Teucer as your leader,' from Horace's *Odes* 1.vii.27.

Nile /nīl/ a river in eastern Africa, the longest river in the world, that rises in east central Africa near Lake Victoria and flows 4,160 miles (6,695 km) north through Uganda, Sudan, and Egypt to empty through a large delta into the Mediterranean Sea. See also **BLUE NILE, ALBERT NILE, VICTORIA NILE, WHITE NILE**.

Nile blue ▶ **n.** a pale greenish blue.
– ORIGIN late 19th cent.: suggested by French *eau de Nil*.

Nile croc·o·dile ▶ **n.** a large crocodile with a long narrow head, native to Africa and Madagascar. ● *Crocodilus niloticus*, family Crocodylidae.

Nile green ▶ **n.** a pale bluish green.

Nile mon·i·tor ▶ **n.** a large heavily built African lizard that has grayish-olive skin with yellow markings and is semiaquatic. ● *Varanus niloticus*, family Varanidae.

Nile perch ▶ **n.** a large predatory fish found in lakes and rivers in northeastern and central Africa, widely caught for food or sport. ● *Lates niloticus*, family Centropomidae.

nil·gai /ˈnilgī/ ▶ **n.** a large Indian antelope, the male of which has a blue-gray coat and short horns, and the female a tawny coat and no horns. ● *Boselaphus tragocamelus*, family Bovidae.
– ORIGIN late 18th cent.: from Hindi *nīlgāī*, from *nīl* 'blue' + *gāī* 'cow.'

Nil·gi·ri Hills /ˈnilgərē/ a range of hills in southern India, in western Tamil Nadu. They are a branch of the Western Ghats.

Ni·lom·e·ter /nīˈlämətər/ ▶ **n.** a graduated pillar or other vertical surface, serving to indicate the height to which the Nile rises during its annual floods.
– DERIVATIVES **Ni·lo·met·ric** /ˌnīləˈmetrik/ **adj.**

Ni·lo-Sa·har·an /ˌnīlōsəˈharən, -ˈhär-/ ▶ **adj.** denoting or belonging to a phylum of languages that includes the Nilotic family together with certain other languages of northern and eastern Africa.
▶ **n.** this phylum of languages.

Ni·lot·ic /nīˈlätik/ ▶ **adj.** **1** of or relating to the Nile River or to the Nile region of Africa.
2 denoting or belonging to a subgroup of Nilo-Saharan languages spoken in Egypt, Sudan, Kenya, and Tanzania. The western group includes Luo and Dinka; the eastern group includes Masai and Turkana.
– ORIGIN via Latin from Greek *Neilōtikos*, from *Neilos* 'Nile.'

nil·po·tent /nilˈpōtnt/ ▶ **adj.** Mathematics equal to zero when raised to a positive integral power.
– ORIGIN late 19th cent.: from **NIL** + Latin *potens, potent-* 'power.'

Nils·son /ˈnilsən/, Birgit (1918–2005), Swedish opera singer; full name *Märta Birgit Nilsson*. A soprano, she gained international success in the 1950s, being particularly noted for her interpretation of Wagnerian roles.

nim /nim/ ▶ **n.** a game in which two players alternately take one or more objects from one of a number of heaps, each trying to take, or to compel the other to take, the last remaining object.
– ORIGIN early 20th cent.: apparently from archaic *nim* 'to take' or from German *nimm!* 'take!,' imperative of *nehmen*.

nim·ble /'nimbəl/ ▶ **adj.** (**nimbler, nimblest**) quick and light in movement or action; agile: *with a deft motion of her nimble fingers*. ■ (of the mind) quick to comprehend: *she is well-read and intellectually nimble*.
– ORIGIN Old English *næmel* 'quick to seize or comprehend,' related to *niman* 'take,' of Germanic origin. The *-b-* was added for ease of pronunciation.

nim·ble·ness /'nimbəlnis/ ▶ **n.** the quality of being nimble.

nim·bly /'nimblē/ ▶ **adv.** in a nimble way: *the monkey leapt nimbly from rock to rock*.

nim·bo·stra·tus /ˌnimbō'stratəs, -'strā-/ ▶ **n.** a type of cloud forming a thick uniform gray layer at low altitude, from which rain or snow often falls (without any lightning or thunder).
– ORIGIN late 19th cent.: modern Latin, from NIMBUS + STRATUS.

nim·bus /'nimbəs/ ▶ **n.** (pl. **nimbi** /-ˌbī/ or **nimbuses**) **1** a luminous cloud or a halo surrounding a supernatural being or a saint. ■ a light, color, etc., that surrounds someone or something.
2 a large gray rain cloud: [as modifier] *nimbus clouds*.
– ORIGIN early 17th cent.: from Latin, literally 'cloud, aureole.'

Nimby /'nimbē/ ▶ **n.** (pl. **Nimbys** or **Nimbies**) a person who objects to the siting of something perceived as unpleasant or potentially dangerous in their own neighborhood, such as a landfill or hazardous waste facility, esp. while raising no such objections to similar developments elsewhere.
– DERIVATIVES **Nim·by·ism** /-izəm/ **n.**
– ORIGIN 1980s: acronym from *not in my back yard*.

Nîmes /nēm/ a city in southern France; pop. 147,114 (2006). It is noted for its well-preserved Roman remains.

nim·i·ny-pim·i·ny /'nimənē 'pimənē/ ▶ **adj.** affectedly prim or refined: *she had a niminy-piminy ladylike air*.
– ORIGIN late 18th cent.: fanciful coinage; compare with NAMBY-PAMBY.

Nimitz /'nimits/, Chester William (1885–1966), US naval officer. Chief of the Bureau of Navigation (1939–41), he became commander in chief of the Pacific Fleet after the Japanese attack on Pearl Harbor in 1941. A noted strategist, he introduced the practice of island hopping, which contributed to many victories. Nimitz accepted the Japanese surrender for the US in 1945 aboard his flagship, the USS *Missouri*, and after World War II served as chief of naval operations 1945–47.

nim·rod /'nimräd/ ▶ **n. 1** literary a skillful hunter.
2 informal an inept person.
– ORIGIN late 16th cent.: from Hebrew *Nimrōd*, the name of the great-grandson of Noah, reputed for his skill as a hunter (see Gen. 10:8-9).

Nim·rud /'nimˌro͝od/ modern name of an ancient Mesopotamian city on the east bank of the Tigris south of Nineveh, near the modern city of Mosul. It was the capital of Assyria 879–722 BC. The city was known in biblical times as Calah (Gen. 10:11); the modern name arose through association in Islamic mythology with the biblical figure of Nimrod.

Nin /nin, nēn/, Anaïs (1903–77), US writer, born in France. She published her first novel *House of Incest* in 1936 and went on to produce collections of short stories, essays, diaries, and erotica. She is noted for her introspective *Diaries* (1966–81).

Ni·ña, La ▶ **n.** see LA NIÑA.

nin·com·poop /'ninkəmˌpo͞op, 'niNG-/ ▶ **n.** a foolish or stupid person.
– ORIGIN late 17th cent.: perhaps from the given name *Nicholas* or from *Nicodemus* (by association with the Pharisee of this name, and his naive questioning of Jesus Christ; compare with French *nicodème* 'simpleton').

nine /nīn/ ▶ **cardinal number** equivalent to the product of three and three; one more than eight, or one less than ten; 9: *all nine justices agreed that the law could not stand | nine of the twelve members*. (Roman numeral: **ix** or **IX**) ■ a group or unit of nine individuals. ■ nine years old: *I was only nine*. ■ nine o'clock: *it's ten to nine*. ■ a size of garment or other merchandise denoted by nine. ■ a playing card with nine pips. ■ (**the Nine**) Greek Mythology the nine Muses.
– PHRASES **dressed to the nines** see DRESS. **nine times out of ten** on nearly every occasion; almost always.
– ORIGIN Old English *nigon*, of Germanic origin; related to Dutch *negen* and German *neun*, from an Indo-European root shared by Sanskrit *nava*, Latin *novem*, and Greek *ennea*.

Nine-e·lev·en (also **9/11**) see SEPTEMBER 11.

nine·fold /'nīnˌfōld/ ▶ **adj.** nine times as great or as numerous: *a ninefold increase in the amount of traffic*. ■ having nine parts or elements.
▶ **adv.** by nine times; to nine times the number or amount: *consumption increased ninefold*.

nine·pins /'nīnˌpinz/ ▶ **plural n.** [usu. treated as sing.] a British game similar to bowling, using nine wooden pins and played in an alley; the traditional form of skittles. ■ [treated as pl.] the pins used in this game.
– PHRASES **go down** (or **drop** or **fall**) **like ninepins** Brit. succumb in large numbers or without much opposition.

nine·teen /nīn'tēn, 'nīnˌtēn/ ▶ **cardinal number** one more than eighteen; nine more than ten; 19: *nineteen of the interviewees had never worked*. (Roman numeral: **xix** or **XIX**) ■ nineteen years old: *she married at nineteen*.
– DERIVATIVES **nine·teenth** /nīn'tēnTH, 'nīnˌtēnTH/ **ordinal number**.
– ORIGIN Old English *nigontȳne*.

nine·teenth hole ▶ **n.** informal the bar in a golf clubhouse, as reached after a standard round of eighteen holes.

nine-to-five ▶ **adj.** used in reference to typical hours of work in an office, often to express an idea of routine or predictability: *a nine-to-five job*.
▶ **n.** an occupation involving such hours.
– DERIVATIVES **nine-to-fiv·er n.**

nine·ty /'nīntē/ ▶ **n.** (pl. **nineties**) equivalent to the product of nine and ten; ten less than one hundred; 90: *ninety acres of soybeans will be harvested*. (Roman numeral: **xc** or **XC**) ■ (**nineties**) the numbers from 90 to 99, esp. the years of a century or of a person's life: *art in the nineties*. ■ ninety years old: *she is nearly ninety*. ■ ninety miles an hour: *we passed the junction doing about ninety*.
– DERIVATIVES **nine·ti·eth** /-tēiTH/ **ordinal number**, **nine·ty·fold** /-ˌfōld/ **adj. & adv.**
– ORIGIN Old English *nigontig*.

Nin·e·veh /'ninəvə/ an ancient city located on the eastern bank of the Tigris River, opposite the modern city of Mosul. It was the oldest city of the ancient Assyrian empire and its capital until it was destroyed by a coalition of Babylonians and Medes in 612 BC.

Ning·xia /'niNG'SHä/ (also **Ningsia**) an autonomous region of north central China; capital, Yinchuan.

nin·hy·drin /nin'hīdrin/ ▶ **n.** Chemistry a synthetic crystalline compound that forms deeply colored products with primary amines and is used in analytical tests for amino acids. ● A ketone derivative of indene; chem. formula: $C_9H_6O_4$.
– ORIGIN early 20th cent.: from *nin-* (of unknown origin) + HYDRO- + -IN[1].

nin·ja /'ninjə/ ▶ **n.** a person skilled in ninjutsu.
– ORIGIN Japanese, literally 'spy.'

nin·jut·su /nin'jo͞otso͞o/ ▶ **n.** The traditional Japanese art of stealth, camouflage, and sabotage, developed in feudal times for espionage and now practiced as a martial art.
– ORIGIN Japanese, from *nin* 'stealth' + *jutsu* 'art, science.'

nin·ny /'ninē/ ▶ **n.** (pl. **ninnies**) informal a foolish person.
– ORIGIN late 16th cent.: perhaps from INNOCENT.

Ni·ño, El ▶ **n.** see EL NIÑO.

ni·non /'nēnän/ ▶ **n.** a lightweight sheer or silk fabric used for curtains and women's garments.
– ORIGIN early 20th cent.: from French.

ninth /nīnTH/ ▶ **ordinal number** constituting number nine in a sequence; 9th: *the ninth century | the ninth of March*. ■ (**a ninth/one ninth**) each of nine equal parts into which something is or may be divided. ■ the ninth finisher or position in a race or competition: *he came in ninth*. ■ the ninth and final inning of a regulation baseball game: *he was rocked for five runs in the ninth*. ■ Music an interval spanning nine consecutive notes in a diatonic scale. ■ Music the note that is higher by this interval than the tonic of a diatonic scale or root of a chord. ■ Music a chord in which the ninth note above the root forms an important component.
– DERIVATIVES **ninth·ly adv.**

Ni·o·be /'nīəbē/ Greek Mythology the daughter of Tantalus. Apollo and Artemis, enraged because Niobe boasted herself superior to their mother Leto, slew her children and turned her into a stone.

ni·o·bi·um /nī'ōbēəm/ ▶ **n.** the chemical element of atomic number 41, a silver-gray metal of the transition series, used in superconducting alloys. (Symbol: **Nb**)
– ORIGIN mid 19th cent.: modern Latin, from NIOBE, by association with her father Tantalus (so named because the element was first found in TANTALITE).

Nip /nip/ ▶ **n.** informal, offensive a Japanese person.
– ORIGIN mid 20th cent.: abbreviation of the synonym *Nipponese*, from *Nippon* (see NIPPON).

nip[1] /nip/ ▶ **v.** (**nips, nipping, nipped**) **1** [with obj.] pinch, squeeze, or bite sharply: *the dog nipped him on the leg*. ■ (of the cold or frost) cause sharp pain or harm to: *the vegetable garden, nipped now by frost*. ■ (**nip something off**) remove something by pinching or squeezing sharply.
2 informal defeat by a narrow margin.
3 [with obj.] informal steal or snatch (something): *if I nipped a five-dollar bill I could slip it back the next day*.
▶ **n.** a sharp pinch, squeeze, or bite. ■ a feeling of biting cold: *there was a real winter nip in the air*.
– PHRASES **nip something in the bud** suppress or destroy something, esp. at an early stage: *the idea has been nipped in the bud at the local level*.
– ORIGIN late Middle English: probably of Low German or Dutch origin.

nip[2] ▶ **n.** a small quantity or sip of liquor.
▶ **v.** (**nips, nipping, nipped**) [no obj.] take a sip or sips of liquor: *the men nipped from the bottle*.
– ORIGIN late 18th cent. (originally denoting a half-pint of ale): probably an abbreviation of the rare term *nipperkin* 'small measure'; compare with Low German and Dutch *nippen* 'to sip.'

ni·pa /'nēpə/ (also **nipa palm**) ▶ **n.** a palm tree with creeping roots, characteristic of mangrove swamps in India and the Pacific islands. ● *Nypa fruticans*, family Palmae.
– ORIGIN late 16th cent. (denoting an alcoholic drink made from the sap of the tree): via Spanish or Portuguese from Malay *nīpah*.

nip and tuck ▶ **adv. & adj.** neck and neck; closely contested: [as adv.] *it was nip and tuck until the Tigers took the lead*.
▶ **n.** informal a cosmetic surgical operation.

nip·per /'nipər/ ▶ **n. 1** informal a child, esp. a small boy.
2 (**nippers**) pliers, pincers, forceps, or a similar tool for gripping or cutting.
3 an insect or other creature that nips or bites. ■ (usu. **nippers**) the grasping claw of a crab or lobster.

nip·ple /'nipəl/ ▶ **n. 1** the small projection in which the mammary ducts of female mammals terminate and from which milk can be secreted. ■ the corresponding vestigial structure in a male. ■ the flexible tip of a baby's pacifier or feeding bottle.
2 a small projection on a device or machine, esp. one from which oil, grease, or other fluid is dispensed in small amounts. ■ a short section of pipe with a screw thread at each end for coupling.
▶ **v.** [with obj.] (usu. **be nippled**) provide (something) with a projection like a nipple: *rocks nippled with limpets*.
– ORIGIN mid 16th cent. (also as *neble, nible*): perhaps a diminutive of NEB.

nip·ple·wort /'nipəlˌwərt, -ˌwôrt/ ▶ **n.** a yellow-flowered plant of the daisy family, growing in woods and empty lots. ● *Lapsana communis*, family Compositae.

Nip·pon /ni'pän/ Japanese name for JAPAN.
– ORIGIN literally 'land where the sun rises or originates.'

Nip·pon·ese /ˌnipə'nēz, -'nēs/ ▶ **n. & adj.** another term for JAPANESE.

nip·py /'nipē/ ▶ **adj.** (**nippier, nippiest**) informal **1** (of the weather) rather cold; chilly: *it's a bit nippy this morning*.
2 inclined to nip or bite: *macaws can sometimes be nippy and unpredictable*.
3 chiefly Brit. quick; nimble.
– DERIVATIVES **nip·pi·ly** /'nipəlē/ **adv.**

ni·qab /ni'käb/ ▶ **n.** a veil worn by some Muslim women in public, covering all of the face apart from the eyes.
– ORIGIN Arabic *niqāb*.

Ni·ro, Robert De, see DE NIRO.

nir·va·na /nər'vänə, nir-/ ▶ **n.** (in Buddhism) a transcendent state in which there is neither suffering, desire, nor sense of self, and the subject is released from the effects of karma and the cycle of death and rebirth. It represents the final goal of Buddhism. ■ another term for MOKSHA.

■ a state of perfect happiness; an ideal or idyllic place: *Hollywood's dearest dream of small-town nirvana.*
– ORIGIN from Sanskrit *nirvāṇa*, from *nirvā* 'be extinguished,' from *nis* 'out' + *vā-* 'to blow.'

Niš /nēsh/ (also **Nish**) a historically dominant industrial city in southeastern Serbia, on the Nišava River near its confluence with the Morava River; pop. 172,900 (est. 2008).

Ni·san /'nisən, nē'sän/ ▶ **n.** (in the Jewish calendar) the seventh month of the civil and first of the religious year, usually coinciding with parts of March and April.
– ORIGIN from Hebrew *nīsān*.

ni·sei /nē'sā, 'nēsā/ (also **Nisei**) ▶ **n.** (pl. **same** or **niseis**) a person born in the US or Canada whose parents were immigrants from Japan. Compare with ISSEI and SANSEI.
– ORIGIN 1940s: from Japanese, literally 'second generation.'

Nish·ga /'nishgə/ (also **Niska** /'niskə/) ▶ **n.** (pl. **same**) **1** a member of a branch of the Tsimshian people of British Columbia inhabiting the Nass river basin. **2** the dialect of Tsimshian spoken by this people.
▶ **adj.** of or relating to this people or their language.
– ORIGIN the name in Nishga *nisqá'a*.

ni·si /'nīsī/ ▶ **adj.** [postpositive] Law (of a decree, order, or rule) taking effect or having validity only after certain specified conditions are met.
– ORIGIN mid 19th cent.: from Latin, literally 'unless.'

ni·sin /'nīsin/ ▶ **n.** an antibiotic substance that is a mixture of related polypeptides and is used in some countries as a food preservative. ● This substance is produced by the bacterium *Streptococcus lactis*.
– ORIGIN 1940s: from *(Group) N i(nhibitory) s(ubstance)* + -IN¹.

Nis·sen hut /'nisən/ ▶ **n.** chiefly Brit. a hut made of corrugated iron with a concrete floor, similar to a Quonset hut.
– ORIGIN early 20th cent.: named after Peter N. *Nissen* (1871–1930), the British engineer who invented it.

nit /nit/ ▶ **n.** the egg or young form of a louse or other parasitic insect, esp. the egg of a head louse attached to a human hair.
– PHRASES **pick nits** look for and criticize small or insignificant faults or errors; nitpick.
– DERIVATIVES **nit·ty** adj.
– ORIGIN Old English *hnitu*; related to Dutch *neet* and German *Nisse*.

n

nite /nīt/ ▶ **n.** informal simplified spelling of NIGHT: *grist for a million late-nite TV jokes.*

ni·ter /'nītər/ (Brit. **nitre**) ▶ **n.** another term for POTASSIUM NITRATE.
– ORIGIN late Middle English: from Old French, from Latin *nitrum*, from Greek *nitron*.

Ni·te·rói /,nētə'roi/ an industrial port on the coast of southeastern Brazil, on Guanabara Bay opposite Rio de Janeiro; pop. 474,002 (2007).

nit·er·y /'nītərē/ ▶ **n.** informal (pl. **niteries**) a nightclub.

ni·ti·nol /'nitn-äl, -ôl/ ▶ **n.** an alloy of nickel and titanium.
– ORIGIN 1960s: from the chemical symbols NI and TI + the initial letters of *Naval Ordnance Laboratory* (in Silver Spring, Maryland, where it was first produced).

nit·pick·ing /'nit,piking/ informal ▶ **adj.** looking for small or unimportant errors or faults, esp. in order to criticize unnecessarily: *a nitpicking legalistic exercise.*
▶ **n.** such fault-finding: *nitpicking over tiny details.*
– DERIVATIVES **nit·pick** v., **nit·pick·er** /-,pikər/ n., **nit·pick·y** adj.

ni·trate /'nīträt/ ▶ **n.** Chemistry a salt or ester of nitric acid, containing the anion NO_3^- or the group $-NO_3$. ■ sodium nitrate, potassium nitrate, or ammonium nitrate, used as fertilizer: *the fertilizer is usually a basic nitrate.*
▶ **v.** [with obj.] treat (a substance) with nitric acid (typically a concentrated mixture of nitric and sulfuric acids), esp. so as to introduce nitro groups.
– DERIVATIVES **ni·tra·tion** /nī'träshən/ n.
– ORIGIN late 18th cent.: from French (see NITER, -ATE¹).

ni·traz·e·pam /nī'trazə,pam/ ▶ **n.** Medicine a short-acting hypnotic drug of the benzodiazepine group, used to treat insomnia, myoclonic seizures, and infantile spasms.
– ORIGIN 1960s: from *nitr(o)* + *az(o-)* + *ep(ine)* + *am(ide)*.

ni·tre ▶ **n.** British spelling of NITER.

ni·tric /'nītrik/ ▶ **adj.** Chemistry of or containing nitrogen with a higher valence, often five. Compare with NITROUS.
– ORIGIN late 18th cent.: from French *(acide) nitrique* (see NITER, -IC).

ni·tric ac·id ▶ **n.** Chemistry a colorless or pale yellow liquid acid that is corrosive and poisonous and has strong oxidizing properties, made in the laboratory by distilling nitrates with sulfuric acid. ● Chem. formula: HNO_3.
– ORIGIN late 18th cent.: from French *acide nitrique*.

ni·tric ox·ide ▶ **n.** Chemistry a colorless toxic gas formed in many reactions in which nitric acid is reduced, as in reaction with copper. It reacts immediately with oxygen to form nitrogen dioxide. ● Chem. formula: NO. Also called NITROGEN MONOXIDE.

ni·tride /'nītrīd/ ▶ **n.** Chemistry a binary compound of nitrogen with a more electropositive element.
▶ **v.** [with obj.] (usu. as noun **nitriding**) Metallurgy heat steel in the presence of ammonia or other nitrogenous material so as to increase hardness and corrosion resistance.
– ORIGIN mid 19th cent.: from *nitr-* (from NITER) + -IDE.

ni·tri·fy /'nītrə,fī/ ▶ **v.** (**nitrifies, nitrifying, nitrified**) [with obj.] Chemistry **1** convert (ammonia or another nitrogen compound) into nitrites or nitrates. **2** impregnate with nitrogen or nitrogen compounds.
– DERIVATIVES **ni·tri·fi·ca·tion** /,nītrəfi'kāshən/ n.
– ORIGIN early 19th cent.: from French *nitrifier*.

ni·trile /'nītril, -trīl/ ▶ **n.** Chemistry an organic compound containing a cyanide group −CN bound to an alkyl group.
– ORIGIN mid 19th cent.: from *nitr-* (from NITER) + *-ile* (alteration of -YL).

ni·trite /'nītrīt/ ▶ **n.** Chemistry a salt or ester of nitrous acid, containing the anion NO_2^- or the group $-NO_2$.
– ORIGIN early 19th cent.: from *nitr-* (from NITER) + -ITE¹.

ni·tro /'nītrō/ ▶ **n.** short for NITROGLYCERIN.
▶ **adj.** Chemistry containing the NITRO GROUP.

nitro- ▶ **comb. form** of or containing nitric acid, nitrates, or nitrogen: *nitrogenous.* ■ Chemistry containing a nitro group: *nitromethane.*
– ORIGIN from NITER or NITROGEN.

ni·tro·ben·zene /,nītrō'benzēn/ ▶ **n.** Chemistry a yellow oily liquid made by nitrating benzene, used in chemical synthesis. ● Chem. formula: $C_6H_5NO_2$.

ni·tro·blue tet·ra·zo·li·um /'nītrō,bloo/ ▶ **n.** see TETRAZOLIUM.

ni·tro·cel·lu·lose /,nītrō'selyə,lōs/ ▶ **n.** Chemistry a highly flammable material made by treating cellulose with concentrated nitric acid, used to make explosives and celluloid. Also called CELLULOSE NITRATE.

ni·tro·fur·an·to·in /,nītrō,fyoo'rantōin/ ▶ **n.** Medicine a synthetic compound with antibacterial properties, used to treat infections of the urinary tract. ● A bicyclic furan derivative; chem. formula: $C_8H_6N_4O_5$.

ni·tro·gen /'nītrəjən/ ▶ **n.** the chemical element of atomic number 7, a colorless, odorless unreactive gas that forms about 78 percent of the earth's atmosphere. Liquid nitrogen (made by distilling liquid air) boils at 77.4 kelvins (−195.8°C) and is used as a coolant. (Symbol: **N**)
– ORIGIN late 18th cent.: from French *nitrogène* (see NITRO-, -GEN).

ni·tro·gen cy·cle ▶ **n.** Ecology the series of processes by which nitrogen and its compounds are interconverted in the environment and in living organisms, including nitrogen fixation and decomposition.

ni·tro·gen di·ox·ide ▶ **n.** Chemistry a reddish-brown poisonous gas used in the manufacture of nitric acid. It is also an air pollutant, a constituent of untreated automobile exhaust. ● Chem. formula: NO_2. It usually exists in equilibrium with **dinitrogen tetroxide**, N_2O_4.

ni·tro·gen fix·a·tion ▶ **n.** Biology the chemical processes by which atmospheric nitrogen is assimilated into organic compounds, esp. by certain microorganisms as part of the nitrogen cycle.

ni·tro·gen mon·ox·ide ▶ **n.** another term for NITRIC OXIDE.

ni·tro·gen mus·tard ▶ **n.** Chemistry any of a group of organic compounds containing the group $-N(CH_2CH_2Cl)_2$. They are powerful cytotoxic alkylating agents and some are used in chemotherapy to treat cancer.
– ORIGIN 1940s: *mustard* denoting a substance chemically similar to MUSTARD GAS.

ni·tro·gen nar·co·sis ▶ **n.** Medicine a drowsy state induced by breathing air under higher than atmospheric pressure, for example, in deep-sea diving.

ni·trog·e·nous /nī'träjənəs/ ▶ **adj.** containing nitrogen in chemical combination.

ni·tro·glyc·er·in /,nītrō'glisərin/ (also **nitroglycerine**) ▶ **n.** Chemistry an explosive yellow liquid made by nitrating glycerol, used in explosives such as dynamite. It is also used in medicine as a vasodilator in the treatment of angina pectoris. ● Alternative name: **glyceryl trinitrate**; chem. formula: $CH_2(NO_3)CH(NO_3)CH_2(NO_3)$.

ni·tro group ▶ **n.** Chemistry a group, $-NO_2$, attached to an organic group in a molecule.

ni·tro·meth·ane /,nītrō'methän/ ▶ **n.** Chemistry an oily liquid used as a solvent and as a rocket fuel. ● Chem. formula: CH_3NO_2.

ni·troph·i·lous /nī'träfələs/ ▶ **adj.** Botany (of a plant) preferring soils rich in nitrogen.

ni·tros·a·mine /nī'trōsəmēn/ ▶ **n.** Chemistry a compound containing the group ·NNO attached to two organic groups. Compounds of this kind are generally carcinogenic.
– ORIGIN late 19th cent.: from *nitroso-* (relating to nitric oxide in combination) + AMINE.

ni·trous /'nītrəs/ ▶ **adj. 1** Chemistry of or containing nitrogen with a lower valence, often three. Compare with NITRIC. **2** of nitrogen; nitrogenous: *the effect of nitrous emissions on acid rain.*
– ORIGIN early 17th cent.: from Latin *nitrosus* 'nitrous.'

ni·trous ac·id ▶ **n.** Chemistry an unstable and weak acid, existing only in solution and in the gas phase, made by the action of acids on nitrites. ● Chem. formula: HNO_2.

ni·trous ox·ide ▶ **n.** Chemistry a colorless gas with a sweetish odor, prepared by heating ammonium nitrate. It produces exhilaration or anesthesia when inhaled and is used as an anesthetic and as an aerosol propellant. Also called LAUGHING GAS. ● Chem. formula: N_2O.

nit·ty-grit·ty /,nitē 'gritē/ ▶ **n.** (**the nitty-gritty**) informal the most important aspects or practical details of a subject or situation: *let's get down to the nitty-gritty of finding a job* | [as modifier] *the nitty-gritty details.*
– ORIGIN 1960s: of unknown origin.

nit·wit /'nit,wit/ ▶ **n.** informal a silly or foolish person (often as a general term of abuse).
– DERIVATIVES **nit·wit·ted** adj., **nit·wit·ted·ness** n.
– ORIGIN early 20th cent.: apparently from NIT + WIT¹.

Ni·ue /nē'oo/ an island territory in the South Pacific Ocean east of Tonga; pop. 1,400 (est. 2009); capital, Alofi. Annexed by New Zealand in 1901, the island achieved self-government in free association with New Zealand in 1974. Niue is the world's largest coral island.

NIV ▶ **abbr.** New International Version (of the Bible).

ni·val /'nīvəl/ ▶ **adj.** of, relating to, or characteristic of a region of perpetual snow.
– ORIGIN mid 17th cent.: from Latin *nivalis*, from *nix, niv-* 'snow.'

ni·va·tion /nī'vāshən/ ▶ **n.** Geography erosion of the ground beneath and at the sides of a snow bank, mainly as a result of alternate freezing and thawing.
– ORIGIN early 20th cent.: from Latin *nix, niv-* 'snow' + -ATION.

niv·e·ous /'nivēəs/ ▶ **adj.** literary snowy or resembling snow.
– ORIGIN early 17th cent.: from Latin *niveus* (from *nix, niv-* 'snow') + -OUS.

Ni·vose /nē'vōz/ (also **Nivôse**) ▶ **n.** the fourth month of the French Republican calendar (1793–1805), originally running from December 21 to January 19.
– ORIGIN French *Nivôse*, from Latin *nivosus* 'snowy,' from *nix, niv-* 'snow.'

nix[1] /niks/ informal ▶ **n.** nothing: *apart from that, nix.*
▶ **exclam.** expressing denial or refusal: *"I owe you some money." "Nix, nix."*
▶ **v.** [with obj.] put an end to; cancel: *he nixed the deal just before it was to be signed.*
– ORIGIN late 18th cent. (as a noun): from German, colloquial variant of *nichts* 'nothing.'

nix[2] ▶ **n.** (fem. **nixie** /'niksē/) (in Germanic mythology) a water sprite.
– ORIGIN mid 19th cent.: from German; related to the archaic English word *nicker*, denoting a water demon believed to live in the sea.

Nix·on /'niksən/, Richard Milhous (1913–94), 37th president of the US 1969–74. His period of office was overshadowed by the Vietnam War. A Republican, he restored Sino-American diplomatic relations by his visit to China in 1972 and successfully ended the Vietnam War when peace negotiations were concluded by his secretary of state, Henry Kissinger, in 1973. Although he was re-elected in 1972, he became the first president to resign from office, owing to his involvement in the Watergate scandal.

Richard M. Nixon

Ni·zam /ni'zäm, -'zam/ ▶ **n.** historical **1** the title of the hereditary ruler of Hyderabad. [abbreviation of Urdu *nizām-al-mulk* 'administrator of the realm.'] **2** (**the nizam**) the Turkish regular army. [abbreviation of Turkish *nizām askeri* 'regular soldier.']

Ni·za·ri /ni'zärē/ ▶ **n.** a member of a Muslim sect that split from the Ismaili branch in 1094 over disagreement about the succession to the caliphate. The majority of Nizaris now live in South Asia; their leader is the Aga Khan.

Nizh·ni Nov·go·rod /'nizHnē 'nôvgərəd/ a river port in western Russia on the Volga River; pop. 1,274,700 (est. 2008). From 1932 to 1991, it was named Gorky after writer Maxim Gorky, who was born there.

Nizh·ni Ta·gil /'nizHnē tə'gil/ an industrial and metal-mining city in central Russia, in the Ural Mountains north of Yekaterinburg; pop. 375,700 (est. 2008).

NJ ▶ **abbr.** New Jersey (in official postal use).

NK cell ▶ **abbr.** natural killer cell.

Nko·mo /(ə)NG'kōmō/, Joshua (Mqabuko Nyongolo) (1917–99), Zimbabwean statesman; leader of the Zimbabwe African People's Union (ZAPU).

Nkru·mah /(ə)NG'kroomə/, Kwame (1909–72), Ghanaian statesman; prime minister 1957–60; president 1960–66. The first prime minister after independence, he became increasingly dictatorial and was finally overthrown in a military coup.

NKVD the secret police agency in the former Soviet Union that absorbed the functions of the former OGPU in 1934. It merged with the MVD in 1946.
– ORIGIN abbreviation of Russian *Narodnyĭ komissariat vnutrennikh del* 'People's Commissariat of Internal Affairs.'

NL ▶ **abbr.** Baseball National League.

NLF ▶ **abbr.** National Liberation Front.

NLP ▶ **abbr.** ■ natural language processing. ■ neurolinguistic programming.

NLRB ▶ **abbr.** National Labor Relations Board.

NLT ▶ **abbr.** night letter.

NM ▶ **abbr.** New Mexico (in official postal use).

nm ▶ **abbr.** ■ nanometer. ■ nautical mile.

n.m. ▶ **abbr.** nautical mile.

N.Mex. ▶ **abbr.** New Mexico.

NMI ▶ **abbr.** no middle initial.

NMR ▶ **abbr.** Physics nuclear magnetic resonance.

NNE ▶ **abbr.** north-northeast.

NNP ▶ **abbr.** net national product.

NNW ▶ **abbr.** north-northwest.

No[1] ▶ **symbol** the chemical element nobelium.

No[2] ▶ **n.** variant spelling of **NOH**.

no /nō/ ▶ **determiner 1** not any: *there is no excuse | no two plants are alike.*
2 used to indicate that something is quite the opposite of what is being specified: *it was no easy task persuading her | Toby is no fool.*
3 hardly any: *you'll be back in no time.*
4 used in notices or slogans forbidding or rejecting something specified: *"No Smoking" signs | no nukes.*
▶ **exclam.** used to give a negative response: *"Is anything wrong?" "No."* ■ expressing disagreement or contradiction: *"This is boring." "No, it's not!"* ■ expressing agreement with or affirmation of a negative statement: *they would never cause a fuss, oh no.* ■ expressing shock or disappointment at something one has heard or discovered: *oh no, look at this!*
▶ **adv.** [with comparative] not at all; to no extent: *they were no more able to perform the task than I was.*
▶ **n.** (pl. **noes**) a negative answer or decision, as in voting: *he was unable to change his automatic yes to a no.*
– PHRASES **no can do** informal I am unable to do it. **the noes have it** the negative votes are in the majority. **no less** see **LESS**. **no longer** not now as formerly: *they no longer live here.* **no more** see **MORE**. **no place** nowhere. **no sooner —— than** see **SOON**. **not take no for an answer** persist in spite of refusals. **no two ways about it** used to convey that there can be no doubt about something. **no way** informal under no circumstances; not at all: *You think she's alone? No way.* **or no** or not: *she'd have ridden there, winter or no.* **—— or no ——** regardless of the specified thing: *recession or no recession there is always going to be a shortage of good people.*
– ORIGIN Old English *nō, nā* (adverb), from *ne* 'not' + *ō, ā* 'ever' The determiner arose in Middle English (originally before words beginning with any consonant except *h*-), reduced from *non*, from Old English *nān* (see **NONE**[1]).

No. ▶ **abbr.** ■ North. ■ (also **no.**) number: *No. 27.* [from Latin *numero*, ablative of *numerus* 'number.']

NOAA ▶ **abbr.** National Oceanic and Atmospheric Administration.

no-ac·count informal ▶ **adj.** of little or no importance, value, or use; worthless: *a series of no-account boyfriends.*
▶ **n.** such a person: *I do not intend to let some no-account get his hands on my money.*

No·a·chi·an /nō'ākēən/ ▶ **adj. 1** of or relating to the biblical patriarch Noah or his time.
2 Astronomy of, relating to, or denoting an early geological period on the planet Mars.

No·ah /'nōə/ (in the Bible) a patriarch represented as tenth in descent from Adam. According to a story in Genesis, he made the ark that saved his family and specimens of every animal from the Flood.

No·ah's ark ▶ **n. 1** the ship in which Noah, his family, and the animals were saved from the Flood, according to the biblical account (Genesis 6–8).
2 a small bivalve mollusk with a boat-shaped shell, found in the Mediterranean and off the Atlantic coasts of Africa and southern Europe. ● *Arca noae*, family Arcidae. See also **ARK SHELL** at **ARK**.

nob[1] /näb/ ▶ **n.** Brit. informal a person of wealth or high social position.
– DERIVATIVES **nob·by adj.**
– ORIGIN late 17th cent. (originally Scots as *knab*): of unknown origin.

nob[2] ▶ **n.** informal a person's head.
– PHRASES **one for his nob** Cribbage a bonus point scored for holding the jack of the same suit as the card turned up by the dealer.
– ORIGIN late 17th cent.: apparently a variant of **KNOB**.

nob·ble /'näbəl/ ▶ **v.** [with obj.] Brit. informal **1** try to influence or thwart (someone or something) by underhanded or unfair methods: *an attempt to nobble the jury.* ■ accost (someone), esp. in order to persuade them to do something: *people always tried to nobble her at parties.* ■ tamper with (a racehorse or greyhound) to prevent it from winning a race, esp. by giving it a drug.
2 obtain dishonestly; steal: *he intended to nobble Rose's money.* ■ seize: *they nobbled him and threw him onto the train.*
– DERIVATIVES **nob·bler n.**
– ORIGIN mid 19th cent.: probably a variant of dialect *knobble, knubble* 'knock, strike with the knuckles.'

No·bel /nō'bel/, Alfred Bernhard (1833–96), Swedish chemist, engineer, and philanthropist. He invented dynamite in 1866, making a large fortune that enabled him to endow the prizes that bear his name.

No·bel·ist /nō'belist/ ▶ **n.** a winner of a Nobel Prize.

no·bel·i·um /nō'belēəm/ ▶ **n.** the chemical element of atomic number 102, a radioactive metal of the actinide series. Nobelium does not occur naturally and was first produced by bombarding curium with carbon nuclei. (Symbol: **No**)
– ORIGIN 1950s: modern Latin, from the name **NOBEL** + **-IUM**.

No·bel Prize /'nōbel/ ▶ **n.** any of six international prizes awarded annually for outstanding work in physics, chemistry, physiology or medicine, literature, economics (since 1969), and the promotion of peace. The Nobel Prizes, first awarded in 1901, were established by the will of Alfred Nobel and are traditionally awarded on December 10, the anniversary of his death. The awards are decided by boards of deputies appointed by Swedish learned societies and, in the case of the peace prize, by the Norwegian Parliament.
– DERIVATIVES **No·bel Prize win·ner n.**

Nob Hill /näb/ a commercial district of northern San Francisco in California, long noted for the homes of the wealthy ("nobs").

no·bil·i·ar·y /nō'bilē,erē, -'bilyərē/ ▶ **adj.** rare of or relating to the nobility.
– ORIGIN mid 18th cent.: from French *nobiliaire*, based on Latin *nobilis* (see **NOBLE**).

no·bil·i·ty /nō'bilitē/ ▶ **n.** (pl. **nobilities**) **1** the quality of being noble in character, mind, birth, or rank.
2 (usu. **the nobility**) the group of people belonging to the noble class in a country, esp. those with a hereditary or honorary title: *a member of the English nobility.*
– ORIGIN late Middle English: from Old French *nobilite* or Latin *nobilitas*, from *nobilis* 'noted, highborn' (see **NOBLE**).

no·ble /'nōbəl/ ▶ **adj.** (**nobler, noblest**) **1** belonging to a hereditary class with high social or political status; aristocratic: *the Duchess of Kent and other noble ladies.*
2 having or showing fine personal qualities or high moral principles and ideals: *the promotion of human rights was a noble aspiration.* ■ of imposing or magnificent size or appearance: *entering the building with its noble arches and massive granite columns.* ■ of excellent or superior quality.
▶ **n. 1** (esp. in former times) a person of noble rank or birth.
2 historical a former English gold coin.
– DERIVATIVES **no·ble·ness n., no·bly** /-blē/ **adv.**
– ORIGIN Middle English: from Old French, from Latin *(g)nobilis* 'noted, highborn,' from an Indo-European root shared by **KNOW**.

no·ble gas ▶ **n.** Chemistry any of the gaseous elements helium, neon, argon, krypton, xenon, and radon, occupying Group 0 (18) of the periodic table. They were long believed to be totally unreactive but compounds of xenon, krypton, and radon are now known.

no·ble·man /'nōbəlmən/ ▶ **n.** (pl. **noblemen**) a man who belongs to the noble class.

no·ble met·al ▶ **n.** Chemistry a metal (e.g., gold, silver, or platinum) that resists chemical action, does not corrode, and is not easily attacked by acids.

no·ble rot ▶ **n.** a gray mold that is deliberately cultivated on grapes to enhance the making of certain sweet wines. ● The fungus is *Botrytis cinerea*, subdivision Deuteromycotina.
– ORIGIN 1930s: translation of French *pourriture noble*.

no·ble sav·age ▶ **n.** (usu. **the noble savage**) a representative of primitive humankind as idealized in Romantic literature, symbolizing the innate goodness of humanity when free from the corrupting influence of civilization.

no·blesse /nō'bles/ ▶ **n.** the nobility.
– PHRASES **noblesse oblige** /nō'bles ō'blēzH/ the inferred responsibility of privileged people to act with generosity and nobility toward those less privileged: *there was to being a celebrity a certain element of noblesse oblige.*
– ORIGIN French, literally 'nobility.'

no·ble·wom·an /'nōbəl,woomən/ ▶ **n.** (pl. **noblewomen**) a woman who belongs to the noble class.

no·bod·y /'nō,bädē, -bədē/ ▶ **pron.** no person; no one: *nobody was at home | nobody could predict how it might end.*
▶ **n.** (pl. **nobodies**) a person of no importance or authority: *they went from nobodies to superstars.*
– PHRASES **be nobody's fool** see **FOOL**[1]. **like nobody's business** see **BUSINESS**.
– ORIGIN Middle English: originally as *no body*.

no-brain·er ▶ **n.** informal something that requires or involves little or no mental effort.

no·ce·bo /nə'sēbō/ ▶ **n.** (pl. **nocebos**) a detrimental effect on health produced by psychological or psychosomatic factors such as negative expectations of treatment or prognosis.
– ORIGIN 1960s: from Latin, literally 'I shall cause harm,' from *nocere*, 'to harm,' on the pattern of *placebo*.

no·ci·cep·tive /,nōsi'septiv/ ▶ **adj.** Physiology of, relating to, or denoting pain arising from the stimulation of nerve cells (often as distinct from that arising from damage or disease in the nerves themselves).
– ORIGIN early 20th cent.: from Latin *nocere* 'to harm' + **RECEPTIVE**.

no·ci·cep·tor /,nōsi'septər/ ▶ **n.** Physiology a sensory receptor for painful stimuli.
– ORIGIN early 20th cent.: from Latin *nocere* 'to harm' + **RECEPTOR**.

PRONUNCIATION KEY ə *ago, up*; ər *over, fur*; a *hat*; ā *ate*; ä *car*; e *let*; ē *see*; i *fit*; ī *by*; NG *sing*; ō *go*; ô *law, for*; oi *toy*; oo *good*; oo *goo*; ou *out*; TH *thin*; TH *then*; ZH *vision*

n

nock /näk/ ▶ **n.** Archery a notch at either end of a bow for holding the string. ■ a notch at the back end of an arrow into which the bowstring fits.
▶ **v.** [with obj.] fit (an arrow) to the bowstring to ready it for shooting.
– ORIGIN late Middle English: perhaps from Middle Dutch *nocke* 'point, tip.'

no-'count (also **no-count**) ▶ **adj.** informal term for NO-ACCOUNT.

noc·tam·bu·list /näk'tambyəlist/ ▶ **n.** rare a sleepwalker.
– DERIVATIVES **noc·tam·bu·lism** /-ˌlizəm/ **n.**
– ORIGIN mid 18th cent.: from Latin *nox, noct-* 'night' + *ambulare* 'walk' + -IST.

noc·ti·lu·ca /ˌnäktə'lo͞okə/ ▶ **n.** (pl. **noctilucae** /-'lo͞oˌsē/) a roughly spherical marine dinoflagellate that is strongly phosphorescent, esp. when disturbed. ● Genus *Noctiluca*, division (or phylum) Dinophyta.
– ORIGIN modern Latin, from Latin, literally 'night light, lantern.'

noc·ti·lu·cent cloud /ˌnäktə'lo͞osənt/ ▶ **n.** a high-altitude cloud that is luminous at night, esp. in summer in high latitudes.
– ORIGIN late 19th cent.: from Latin *nox, noct-* 'night' + *lucere* 'to shine' + -ENT.

noc·tu·id /'näkCHo͞owid/ ▶ **n.** Entomology a moth of a large family (Noctuidae) whose members typically have dull forewings and pale or colorful hind wings. Also called OWLET.
– ORIGIN late 19th cent.: from modern Latin *Noctuidae* (plural), based on Latin *noctua* 'owl.'

noc·tule /'näkCHo͞ol/ ▶ **n.** a large golden-brown bat native to Eurasia and North Africa with long slender wings, rounded ears, and a short muzzle. ● *Nyctalus noctula*, family Vespertilionidae.
– ORIGIN late 18th cent.: from French, from Italian *nottola* 'bat,' literally 'small night creature.'

noc·turn /'näktərn/ ▶ **n.** (in the Roman Catholic Church) a part of matins originally said at night.
– ORIGIN Middle English: from Old French *nocturne* or ecclesiastical Latin *nocturnum*, neuter of Latin *nocturnus* 'of the night.'

noc·tur·nal /näk'tərnl/ ▶ **adj.** done, occurring, or active at night: *most owls are nocturnal.*
– DERIVATIVES **noc·tur·nal·ly adv.**
– ORIGIN late 15th cent.: from late Latin *nocturnalis*, from Latin *nocturnus* 'of the night,' from *nox, noct-* 'night.'

noc·tur·nal e·mis·sion ▶ **n.** an involuntary ejaculation of semen during sleep.

noc·turne /'näkˌtərn/ ▶ **n. 1** Music a short composition of a romantic or dreamy character suggestive of night, typically for piano.
2 Art a picture of a night scene.
– ORIGIN mid 19th cent.: French, from Latin *nocturnus* 'of the night.'

noc·u·ous /'näkyo͞owəs/ ▶ **adj.** literary noxious, harmful, or poisonous.
– ORIGIN mid 17th cent.: from Latin *nocuus* (from *nocere* 'to hurt') + -OUS.

nod /näd/ ▶ **v.** (**nods, nodding, nodded**) **1** [no obj.] lower and raise one's head slightly and briefly, esp. in greeting, assent, or understanding, or to give someone a signal: *he nodded to Monica to unlock the door* | [with obj.] *she nodded her head in agreement.* ■ [with obj.] signify or express (greeting, assent, or understanding) in this way: *he nodded his consent.* ■ draw or direct attention to someone or something by moving one's head: *he nodded toward the corner of the room.* ■ move one's head up and down repeatedly: *he shut his eyes, nodding to the beat* | figurative *foxgloves nodding by the path.*
2 [no obj.] have one's head fall forward when drowsy or asleep: *Anna nodded over her book.*
▶ **n.** an act of nodding the head: *at a nod from his father, he left the room.* ■ a gesture of acknowledgment or concession: *a feel-good musical with a nod to pantomime.*
– PHRASES **a nodding acquaintance** a slight acquaintance with a person or cursory knowledge of a subject: *students will need* ***a nodding acquaintance*** *with three other languages.* **even Homer nods** proverb even the best person sometimes makes a mistake due to a momentary lack of alertness or attention. [with allusion to Latin *dormitat Homerus* (Horace *Ars Poetica* 359).] **get the nod 1** be selected or approved. **2** receive a signal or information. **give someone/something the nod 1** select or approve someone or something: *they banned one book but gave the other the nod.* **2** give someone a signal. **on the nod** informal **1** Brit. by general agreement and without discussion: *parliamentary approval of the treaty went through on the nod.* **2** dated on credit. **3** alternating between wakefulness and sleepiness on account of heroin use.
– PHRASAL VERBS **nod off** informal fall asleep, esp. briefly or unintentionally: *some of the congregation nodded off during the sermon.* **nod out** informal fall asleep, esp. from the effects of a drug: *they go to a coffee shop, get stoned, go to a club at 11, and nod out at midnight.*
– ORIGIN late Middle English (as a verb): perhaps of Low German origin; compare with Middle High German *notten* 'move around, shake.' The noun dates from the mid 16th cent.

nod·dle /'nädl/ ▶ **n.** informal, dated a person's head.
– ORIGIN late Middle English (denoting the back of the head): of unknown origin.

nod·dy /'nädē/ ▶ **n.** (pl. **noddies**) **1** dated a silly or foolish person (esp. as a general term of abuse). [perhaps from the verb NOD + -Y[1].]
2 a tropical tern with mainly dark-colored plumage. [perhaps from the nodding behavior of the birds during courtship.] ● Genera *Anous* and *Procelsterna*, family Sternidae (or Laridae): four species.

node /nōd/ ▶ **n. 1** a point at which lines or pathways intersect or branch; a central or connecting point. ■ Computing a piece of equipment, such as a PC or peripheral, attached to a network. ■ Mathematics a point at which a curve intersects itself. ■ Astronomy either of the two points at which a planet's orbit intersects the plane of the ecliptic or the celestial equator. ■ (in generative grammar) a vertex or endpoint in a tree diagram.
2 Botany the part of a plant stem from which one or more leaves emerge, often forming a slight swelling or knob.
3 Anatomy a lymph node or other structure consisting of a small mass of differentiated tissue.
4 Physics & Mathematics a point at which the amplitude of vibration in a standing wave system is zero. ■ a point at which a harmonic function has the value zero, esp. a point of zero electron density in an orbital. ■ a point of zero current or voltage.
– DERIVATIVES **nod·al** /'nōdl/ **adj.**
– ORIGIN late Middle English (denoting a knotty swelling or a protuberance): from Latin *nodus* 'knot.'

node of Ran·vier /'ränvyā/ (also **Ranvier's node**) ▶ **n.** Anatomy a gap in the myelin sheath of a nerve, between adjacent Schwann cells.
– ORIGIN late 19th cent.: named after Louis Antoine *Ranvier* (1835–1922), French histologist.

nod·i·cal /'nōdikəl, 'nä-/ ▶ **adj.** Astronomy of or relating to a node or the nodes of an orbit.

no·dose /'nōdōs/ ▶ **adj.** technical having or characterized by hard or tight lumps; knotty.
– DERIVATIVES **no·dos·i·ty** /nō'däsitē/ **n.**
– ORIGIN early 18th cent.: from Latin *nodosus*, from *nodus* 'knot.'

nod·ule /'näjo͞ol/ ▶ **n. 1** a small swelling or aggregation of cells in the body, esp. an abnormal one. ■ (usu. **root nodule**) a swelling on a root of a leguminous plant, containing nitrogen-fixing bacteria.
2 a small rounded lump of matter distinct from its surroundings, for example, of flint in chalk, carbon in cast iron, or a mineral on the seabed.
– DERIVATIVES **nod·u·lar** /-jələr/ **adj.**, **nod·u·lat·ed** /-jəˌlātid/ **adj.**, **nod·u·la·tion** /ˌnäjə'lāSHən/ **n.**, **nod·u·lose** /-jəlōs/ **adj.**, **nod·u·lous** /-jələs/ **adj.**
– ORIGIN late Middle English: from Latin *nodulus*, diminutive of *nodus* 'knot.'

no·dus /'nōdəs/ ▶ **n.** (pl. **nodi** /-dī/) rare a problem, difficulty, or complication.
– ORIGIN late Middle English (denoting a knotty swelling): from Latin, literally 'knot.'

NOED ▶ **abbr.** *New Oxford English Dictionary.*

No·el /nō'el/ ▶ **n.** Christmas, esp. as a refrain in carols and on Christmas cards.
– ORIGIN early 19th cent.: French *Noël* 'Christmas.'

no·et·ic /nō'etik/ ▶ **adj.** of or relating to mental activity or the intellect.
– ORIGIN mid 17th cent.: from Greek *noētikos*, from *noētos* 'intellectual,' from *noein* 'perceive.'

no-fault ▶ **adj.** [attrib.] not assigning fault or blame, in particular: ■ denoting an insurance policy that is valid regardless of whether the policyholder was at fault: *no-fault automobile insurance.* ■ denoting an insurance or compensation plan (esp. one covering medical or industrial accidents) whereby a claimant need not legally prove negligence against any party. ■ of or denoting a form of divorce granted without requiring one party to prove that the other is to blame for the breakdown of the marriage.

no-fly ▶ **adj.** designating a list, person, or category of people prevented from flying for security reasons.

no-fly zone ▶ **n.** a designated area over which aircraft may not fly without risk of interception, esp. during a conflict.

no-frills ▶ **adj.** [attrib.] without unnecessary extras, esp. ones for decoration or additional comfort: *cheap fast food in no-frills surroundings.*

nog[1] /näg/ ▶ **n.** archaic a small block or peg of wood.
– ORIGIN early 17th cent.: of unknown origin.

nog[2] ▶ **n.** short for EGGNOG.
– ORIGIN late 17th cent.: of unknown origin.

No·gal·es /nō'galəs, -'gäles/ a commercial city in northwestern Mexico, in Sonora state, on the US border across from Nogales in Arizona; pop. 186,901 (2005).

nog·gin /'nägin/ ▶ **n.** informal **1** a person's head.
2 a small quantity of liquor, typically a quarter of a pint.
– ORIGIN mid 17th cent. (in the sense 'small drinking cup'): of unknown origin.

nog·ging /'nägiNG/ ▶ **n.** Building brickwork that fills the spaces between studs or framing members. ■ a horizontal piece of wood fixed to a framework to strengthen it.
– ORIGIN early 19th cent.: from NOG[1] + -ING[1].

no-go ▶ **adj.** informal not ready or not functioning properly. ■ impossible, hopeless, or forbidden: *no-go zones for cars.*
▶ **n.** a negative response; no.

no-go ar·e·a ▶ **n.** an area that is dangerous or impossible to enter or to which entry is restricted or forbidden.

no-good ▶ **adj.** [attrib.] informal (of a person) contemptible; worthless: *a no-good layabout.*
▶ **n.** a worthless or contemptible person.

No·gu·chi /nō'go͞oCHē/, Isamu (1904–88), US sculptor and designer. He created two bridges for Peace Park in Hiroshima, Japan, in 1951, as well as the Billy Rose Sculpture Garden at the Israeli Museum in Jerusalem between 1960 and 1965 and a sculpture called "Red Cube" at the Marine Midland building in New York City in 1968.

Noh /nō/ (also **No** or **Nō**) ▶ **n.** traditional Japanese masked drama with dance and song, evolved from Shinto rites.

> Noh dates from the 14th and 15th centuries, and its subject matter is taken mainly from Japan's classical literature. Traditionally the players were all male, with the chorus playing a passive narrative role.

– ORIGIN Japanese.

no-hit·ter ▶ **n.** Baseball a complete game in which a pitcher yields no hits to the opposing team.

no-hop·er ▶ **n.** informal a person who is not expected to be successful.

no·how /'nōˌhou/ ▶ **adv. 1** used, esp. in jocular or dialectal speech, to emphasize a negative: *the records simply don't exist—never, nowhere, and nohow.*
2 archaic not attractive, well, or in good order.

noil /noil/ ▶ **n.** (usu. **noils**) short strands and knots combed out of wool fiber before spinning.
– ORIGIN early 17th cent.: probably from Old French *noel*, from medieval Latin *nodellus*, diminutive of Latin *nodus* 'knot.'

no-i·ron ▶ **adj.** (of clothes or fabric) wrinkle-resistant, and so not needing to be ironed after washing.

noise /noiz/ ▶ **n. 1** a sound, esp. one that is loud or unpleasant or that causes disturbance: *making a noise like a pig in a trough* | *what's that rustling noise outside the door?* ■ a series or combination of loud, confused sounds, esp. when causing disturbance: *dazed with the heat and noise* | *vibration and noise from traffic.* ■ (**noises**) conventional remarks or other sounds that suggest some emotion or quality: *Clarissa made encouraging noises.*
2 technical irregular fluctuations that accompany a transmitted electrical signal but are not part of it and tend to obscure it. ■ random fluctuations that obscure or do not contain meaningful data or other information: *over half the magnitude of the differences came from noise in the data.*
▶ **v.** [with obj.] (usu. **be noised about**) dated talk about or make known publicly: *you've discovered something that should not be noised about.* ■ [no obj.] literary make much noise.
– ORIGIN Middle English (also in the sense 'quarreling'): from Old French, from Latin *nausea* 'seasickness' (see NAUSEA).

noise·core /'noizˌkôr/ ▶ **n.** a type of rock music derived from hardcore punk, characterized by the use of loud distorted guitar and feedback.

noise·less /'noizlis/ ▶ **adj.** silent; quiet: *the bicycle is a benign form of transportation, being noiseless and nonpolluting.* ■ technical accompanied by or introducing no random fluctuations that would obscure the real signal or data.
– DERIVATIVES **noise·less·ly adv.**, **noise·less·ness n.**

noise·mak·er /'noizˌmākər/ ▶ **n.** a device for making a loud noise, as at a party or sporting event.
– DERIVATIVES **noise·mak·ing n. & adj.**

noise pol·lu·tion ▶ **n.** harmful or annoying levels of noise, as from airplanes, industry, etc.

nois·es off ▶ **plural n.** sounds made offstage to be heard by the audience of a play. ■ distracting or intrusive background noise.

noi·sette /nwäˈzet/ ▶ **n. 1** a small round piece of lean meat, esp. lamb. [French, diminutive of *noix* 'nut.']
2 a chocolate made with hazelnuts. [French, in the sense 'hazelnut.']

noi·some /ˈnoisəm/ ▶ **adj.** literary having an extremely offensive smell: *noisome vapors from the smoldering waste.* ■ disagreeable; unpleasant: *noisome scandals.*
– DERIVATIVES **noi·some·ness n.**
– ORIGIN late Middle English: from obsolete *noy* (shortened form of **ANNOY**) + **-SOME**¹.

USAGE Noisome means 'bad-smelling.' It has no relation to the word *noise;* it is related to the word *annoy.*

nois·y /ˈnoizē/ ▶ **adj.** (**noisier, noisiest**) **1** making or given to making a lot of noise: *a noisy, giggling group of children* | *diesel cars can be very noisy.* ■ full of or characterized by noise: *noisy scenes outside the court building* | *the bar was crowded and noisy.* ■ (of a person or group of people) stridently seeking to attract attention to their views.
2 technical accompanied by or introducing random fluctuations that obscure the real signal or data.
– DERIVATIVES **nois·i·ly** /-əlē/ **adv.**, **nois·i·ness n.**

no-kill (also **no kill**) ▶ **n.** a policy or an animal shelter in which abandoned, neglected, or lost animals are not put to sleep even if no home can be found for them: *there are thousands of no-kills that rescue pets.*
▶ **adj.** opposed to or not killing animals that live in shelters: *find out if the organization has a no-kill policy.*

no-knock ▶ **adj.** denoting or relating to a search or raid by the police made without warning or identification: *during a no-knock raid.*

No·lan /ˈnōlən/, Sir Sidney Robert (1917–93), Australian painter. He was known for his paintings of famous characters and events from Australian history.

no·lens vo·lens /ˈnōlənz ˈvōlənz/ ▶ **adv.** formal whether a person wants or likes something or not.
– ORIGIN Latin, from *nolens* 'not willing' and *volens* 'willing.'

no·li me tan·ge·re /ˈnōlē ˌmā ˈtäNGgəˌrā/ ▶ **n.**
1 a warning or prohibition against meddling or interference. ■ a painting representing the appearance of Jesus to Mary Magdalen at the sepulcher (John 20:17).
2 another term for **TOUCH-ME-NOT**.
– ORIGIN Latin, literally 'do not touch me.'

nol·le pros /ˌnôl ˈpräs/ (also **nol-pros**) (abbr.: **nol. pros.**) ▶ **v.** (**nolle pross, prossing, prossed**) [with obj.] Law abandon or dismiss (a suit) by issuing a nolle prosequi.

nol·le pros·e·qui /ˌnälē ˈpräsiˌkwē/ ▶ **n.** Law a formal notice of abandonment by a plaintiff or prosecutor of all or part of a suit or action. ■ the entry of this in a court record.
– ORIGIN late 17th cent.: Latin, literally 'be unwilling to pursue.'

nol·lie /ˈnäli/ ▶ **n.** (in skateboarding and snowboarding) a jump performed without the aid of a takeoff ramp, executed by pressing the foot down on the nose of the board.
– ORIGIN 1990s: probably short for *nose ollie*: see **OLLIE**.

no-load ▶ **adj.** (of shares in a mutual fund) sold without a commission being charged at the time of sale.

no·lo con·ten·de·re /ˌnōlō kənˈtendərē/ ▶ **n.** (also **nolo**) Law a plea by which a defendant in a criminal prosecution accepts conviction as though a guilty plea had been entered but does not admit guilt.
– ORIGIN Latin, literally 'I do not wish to contend.'

nom. ▶ **abbr.** nominal.

no·mad /ˈnōˌmad/ ▶ **n.** a member of a people having no permanent abode, and who travel from place to place to find fresh pasture for their livestock. ■ a person who does not stay long in the same place; a wanderer.
– DERIVATIVES **no·mad·ic** /nōˈmadik/ **adj.**, **no·mad·i·cal·ly** /nōˈmadiklē/ **adv.**, **no·mad·ism** /ˈnōmaˌdizəm/ **n.**
– ORIGIN late 16th cent.: from French *nomade*, via Latin from Greek *nomas, nomad-* 'roaming in search of pasture,' from the base of *nemein* 'to pasture.'

no man's land ▶ **n.** disputed ground, as between the front lines or trenches of two opposing armies: *enemy soldiers facing you across no man's land* | figurative *an unmapped no man's land between the traditional command economy and the market.* ■ land or area that is unowned, uninhabited, or undesirable.
– ORIGIN Middle English: originally the name of a plot of ground lying outside the north wall of the city of London, the site of a place of execution.

nom·ar·chy /ˈnämärkē/ ▶ **n.** (pl. **nomarchies**) formerly a province, now a smaller administrative division, of modern Greece.
– ORIGIN mid 17th cent.: from Greek *nomarkhia*, from *nomos* 'nome' + *arkhē* 'government.'

nom·bril /ˈnämbrəl/ ▶ **n.** Heraldry the point halfway between fess point and the base of the shield.
– ORIGIN mid 16th cent.: from French, literally 'navel.'

nom de guerre /ˌnäm də ˈger/ ▶ **n.** (pl. **noms de guerre** pronunc. **same**) an assumed name under which a person engages in combat or some other activity or enterprise.
– ORIGIN French, literally 'war name.'

nom de plume /ˌnäm də ˈplo͞om/ ▶ **n.** (pl. **noms de plume** pronunc. **same**) a pen name.
– ORIGIN early 19th cent.: formed in English from French words, to render the sense 'pen name,' on the pattern of *nom de guerre.*

Nome /nōm/ a city in western Alaska, on the southern coast of the Seward Peninsula; pop. 3,576 (est. 2008). Founded in 1896 as a gold-mining camp, it became a center of the Alaskan gold rush several years later.

nome /nōm/ ▶ **n. 1** one of the thirty-six territorial divisions of ancient Egypt.
2 an administrative division of modern Greece.
– ORIGIN early 18th cent.: from Greek *nomos* 'division,' from *nemein* 'to divide.'

no·men /ˈnōmen/ ▶ **n.** Roman History the second personal name of a citizen of ancient Rome, indicating the gens to which he belonged, for example, Marcus *Tullius* Cicero.
– ORIGIN Latin, literally 'name.'

no·men·cla·ture /ˈnōmənˌklāCHər/ ▶ **n.** the devising or choosing of names for things, esp. in a science or other discipline. ■ the body or system of such names in a particular field: *the nomenclature of chemical compounds.* ■ formal the term or terms applied to someone or something: *"customers" was preferred to the original nomenclature "passengers."*
– DERIVATIVES **no·men·cla·tor n.**, **no·men·cla·tur·al** /ˌnōmənˈklāCHərəl/ **adj.**
– ORIGIN early 17th cent.: from French, from Latin *nomenclatura*, from *nomen* 'name' + *clatura* 'calling, summoning' (from *calare* 'to call').

no·men·kla·tu·ra /ˌnōmənkləˈt(y)o͝orə/ ▶ **n.** (in the former Soviet Union) a list of influential posts in government and industry to be filled by Communist Party appointees. ■ the holders of such posts collectively.
– ORIGIN Russian, from Latin *nomenclatura* (see **NOMENCLATURE**).

nom·i·nal /ˈnämənl/ ▶ **adj. 1** (of a role or status) existing in name only: *Thailand retained nominal independence under Japanese military occupation.* ■ of, relating to, or consisting of names. ■ Grammar relating to, headed by, or having the function of a noun.
2 (of a price or amount of money) very small; far below the real value or cost: *some firms charge only a nominal fee for the service.*
3 (of a quantity or dimension, esp. of manufactured articles) stated or expressed but not necessarily corresponding exactly to the real value: *legislation allowed variation around the nominal weight (that printed on each packet).* ■ Economics (of a rate or other figure) expressed in terms of a certain amount, without making allowance for changes in real value over time: *the nominal exchange rate.*
4 informal (chiefly in the context of space travel) functioning normally or acceptably.
– DERIVATIVES **nom·i·nal·ly adv.**
– ORIGIN late 15th cent. (as a term in grammar): from Latin *nominalis*, from *nomen, nomin-* 'name.'

nom·i·nal ac·count ▶ **n.** Finance an account recording the financial transactions of a business in a particular category, rather than with a person or other organization.

nom·i·nal def·i·ni·tion ▶ **n.** Logic a definition that describes something in terms of its properties, in order to distinguish it from other things, but without describing its underlying structure or essence.

nom·i·nal·ism /ˈnäminəˌlizəm/ ▶ **n.** Philosophy the doctrine that universals or general ideas are mere names without any corresponding reality, and that only particular objects exist; properties, numbers, and sets are thought of as merely features of the way of considering the things that exist. Important in medieval scholastic thought, nominalism is associated particularly with William of Occam. Often contrasted with **REALISM** (sense 3).
– DERIVATIVES **nom·i·nal·ist n.**, **nom·i·nal·is·tic** /ˌnämənəˈlistik/ **adj.**
– ORIGIN mid 19th cent.: from French *nominalisme*, from *nominal* 'relating to names' (see **NOMINAL**).

nom·i·nal·ize /ˈnäminəˌlīz/ ▶ **v.** [with obj.] Grammar convert (a word or phrase, as a verb or adjective) into a noun, for example, *output* from *put out*; *the poor* from *poor.*
– DERIVATIVES **nom·i·nal·i·za·tion** /ˌnäminəlˈzāSHən/ **n.**

nom·i·nal ledg·er ▶ **n.** Finance a ledger containing nominal accounts, or one containing both nominal and real accounts.

nom·i·nal val·ue ▶ **n.** Economics the value that is stated on currency; face value. ■ the price of a share, bond, or security when it was issued, rather than its current market value.

nom·i·nate ▶ **v.** /ˈnäməˌnāt/ [with obj.] **1** propose or formally enter as a candidate for election or for an honor or award: *the film was nominated for several Oscars.* ■ appoint to a job or position: *the company nominated her as a delegate to the convention.*
2 specify (something) formally, typically the date or place for an event: *a day was nominated for the exchange of contracts.*
▶ **adj.** /-nit/ Zoology & Botany denoting a race or subspecies that is given the same epithet as the species to which it belongs, for example, *Homo sapiens sapiens.*
– DERIVATIVES **nom·i·na·tor** /-ˌnātər/ **n.**
– ORIGIN late Middle English (as an adjective in the sense 'named'): from Latin *nominat-* 'named,' from the verb *nominare*, from *nomen, nomin-* 'a name.' The verb senses are first found in English in the 16th cent.

nom·i·na·tion /ˌnäməˈnāSHən/ ▶ **n.** the action of nominating or state of being nominated: *women's groups opposed the nomination of the judge* | *the film received five nominations.* ■ a person or thing nominated: *send your nominations in by November 30th.*

nom·i·na·tive /ˈnämənətiv/ ▶ **adj. 1** Grammar relating to or denoting a case of nouns, pronouns, and adjectives (as in Latin and other inflected languages) used for the subject of a verb.
2 /-ˌnātiv/ of or appointed by nomination as distinct from election.
▶ **n.** Grammar a word in the nominative case. ■ (**the nominative**) the nominative case.
– ORIGIN late Middle English: from Latin *nominativus* 'relating to naming,' translation of Greek *onomastikē (ptōsis)* 'naming (case).'

nom·i·nee /ˌnäməˈnē/ ▶ **n. 1** a person who is proposed or formally entered as a candidate for an office or as the recipient of a grant or award: *the party's presidential nominee* | *an Oscar nominee.*
2 a person or company whose name is given as having title to a stock, real estate, etc., but who is not the actual owner.
– ORIGIN mid 17th cent.: from **NOMINATE** + **-EE**.

nom·o·gram /ˈnäməˌgram/ (also **nomograph** /-ˌgraf/) ▶ **n.** a diagram representing the relations between three or more variable quantities by means of a number of scales, so arranged that the value of one variable can be found by a simple geometric construction, for example, by drawing a straight line intersecting the other scales at the appropriate values.
– DERIVATIVES **nom·o·graph·ic** /ˌnäməˈgrafik, ˌnō-/ **adj.**, **nom·o·graph·i·cal·ly** /ˌnäməˈgrafik(ə)lē, ˌnō-/ **adv.**, **no·mog·ra·phy** /nəˈmägrəfē/ **n.**
– ORIGIN early 20th cent.: from Greek *nomos* 'law' + **-GRAM**¹.

nom·o·log·i·cal /ˌnäməˈläjikəl/ ▶ **adj.** relating to or denoting certain principles, such as laws of nature, that are neither logically necessary nor theoretically explicable, but are simply taken as true. ■ another term for **NOMOTHETIC**.
– DERIVATIVES **nom·o·log·i·cal·ly** /-ik(ə)lē/ **adv.**
– ORIGIN mid 19th cent.: from Greek *nomos* 'law' + *-logical* (see **-LOGY**).

nom·o·thet·ic /ˌnäməˈTHetik/ ▶ **adj.** of or relating to the study or discovery of general scientific laws. Often contrasted with **IDIOGRAPHIC**.
– ORIGIN mid 17th cent.: from obsolete *nomothete* 'legislator' (from Greek *nomothetēs*) + **-IC**.

-nomy ▶ **comb. form** denoting a specified area of knowledge or the laws governing it: *astronomy* | *gastronomy.*
– ORIGIN from Greek *-nomia*; related to *nomos* 'law' and *nemein* 'distribute.'

non- ▶ **prefix 1** not doing; not involved with: *nonaggression* | *nonrecognition.*

2 not of the kind or class described: *nonbeliever* | *nonconformist*. ■ also forming nouns used attributively (such as *nonunion* in *nonunion miners*).
3 not of the importance implied: *nonissue*.
4 a lack of: *nonsense*.
5 (added to adverbs). not in the way described: *nonuniformly*.
6 (added to verbs to form adjectives) not causing or requiring: *nonskid* | *noniron*.
7 expressing a neutral negative sense when a corresponding form beginning with *in-* or *un-* has a special connotation (such as *nonhuman* compared with *inhuman*).
– ORIGIN from Latin *non* 'not.'

> **USAGE** The prefixes **non-** and **un-** both have the meaning 'not,' but tend to be used with a difference of emphasis. See usage at **UN-**[1].

nona- ▶ **comb. form** nine; having nine: *nonagon*.
– ORIGIN from Latin *nonus* 'ninth.'

non·a·bra·sive /ˌnänəˈbrāsiv/ ▶ **adj.** containing no abrasive substances or elements: *nonabrasive cleaners*.

non·a·bu·sive /ˌnänəˈbyo͞osiv/ ▶ **adj.** not constituting abuse: *nonabusive forms of maltreatment*. ■ not practicing abuse: *nonabusive mothers*.

non·ac·cep·tance /ˌnänakˈseptəns/ ▶ **n.** refusal to accept, receive, or agree to something: *they endured hatred, resentment, and nonacceptance*.

non·ac·tive /nänˈaktiv/ ▶ **adj.** not participating or active: *nonactive trustees*.

non·ad·dic·tive /ˌnänəˈdiktiv/ ▶ **adj.** (of a drug or other substance) not causing addiction.

non·ad·just·a·ble /ˌnänəˈjəstəbəl/ ▶ **adj.** not subject to adjustment or modification: *nonadjustable legs*.

non·af·fec·tive /ˌnänəˈfektiv/ ▶ **adj.** Psychology denoting or relating to mental disorders that are not characterized by disturbance of mood.

non·age /ˈnänij, ˈnō-/ ▶ **n.** [in sing.] formal the period of immaturity or youth.
– ORIGIN late Middle English: from Old French *nonage*, from *non-* 'non-' + *age* 'age.'

non·a·ge·nar·i·an /ˌnänəjəˈne(ə)rēən, ˌnōnə-/ ▶ **n.** a person who is from 90 to 99 years old.
– ORIGIN early 19th cent.: from Latin *nonagenarius* (based on *nonaginta* 'ninety') + **-AN**.

n

non·ag·gres·sion /ˌnänəˈgresHən/ ▶ **n.** absence of the desire or intention to be aggressive, esp. on the part of nations or governments: *a treaty of nonaggression and friendship* | [as modifier] *a nonaggression pact*.

non·a·gon /ˈnänəˌgän/ ▶ **n.** a plane figure with nine straight sides and nine angles.
– DERIVATIVES **non·ag·o·nal** /nänˈagənəl/ **adj.**
– ORIGIN mid 17th cent.: formed irregularly from Latin *nonus* 'ninth,' on the pattern of words such as *hexagon*.

non·al·co·hol·ic /ˌnänˌalkəˈhôlik, -ˈhälik/ ▶ **adj.** (of a drink) not containing alcohol.

non·a·ligned /ˌnänəˈlīnd/ ▶ **adj.** not aligned with something else. ■ (of countries) not aligned with a major power, esp. the former Soviet Union or the US.
– DERIVATIVES **non·a·lign·ment** /-ˈlīnmənt/ **n.**

non·al·ler·gen·ic /ˌnänaləˈjenik/ ▶ **adj.** not causing an allergic reaction.

non·al·ler·gic /ˌnänəˈlərjik/ ▶ **adj.** not having an allergy: *get a nonallergic person to do this job*. ■ not caused by an allergy: *nonallergic skin rashes*.

no-name ▶ **adj.** (of a product) having no brand name: *cheap, no-name cigarettes*. ■ (of a person) unknown, esp. in a particular profession: *no-name, no-frills chefs*.
▶ **n.** such a person.

non-A·mer·i·can ▶ **adj.** not American: *a major non-American news source*.
▶ **n.** a person who is not American: *the first non-American to win the International Blues Challenge*.

no·nane /ˈnōnān/ ▶ **n.** Chemistry a colorless liquid hydrocarbon of the alkane series, present in petroleum spirit. ● Chem. formula: C_9H_{20}; many isomers, esp. the straight-chain isomer (*n*-**nonane**).
– ORIGIN mid 19th cent.: from **NONA-** (denoting nine carbon atoms) + **-ANE**[2].

non·ap·pear·ance /ˌnänəˈpi(ə)rəns/ ▶ **n.** failure to appear or be present, esp. at a gathering or engagement. ■ Law failure to appear or be present in a court of law, esp. as a witness, defendant, or plaintiff.

non·art /ˈnänˈärt/ ▶ **n.** something that is not art or that rejects the conventional forms or methods of art.

no·na·ry /ˈnōnərē/ ▶ **adj.** rare relating to or based on the number nine.
– ORIGIN mid 17th cent. (as a noun): from Latin *nonus* 'ninth,' on the pattern of words such as *denary*.

non-Ar·y·an ▶ **n.** dated a person who is not Aryan nor of Aryan descent. ■ (esp. in Nazi ideology) a person who is not of Caucasian race, esp. one of Jewish descent.
▶ **adj.** (of a person or language) not Aryan or of Aryan descent.

non·as·so·ci·a·tive /ˌnänəˈsōsēˌātiv, -sHē-, -sēətiv, -sHətiv/ ▶ **adj. 1** not characterized by association, esp. of ideas.
2 Mathematics involving the condition that a group of quantities connected by operations gives a result dependent upon the order in which the operations are performed.

non·at·ten·dance /ˌnänəˈtendəns/ ▶ **n.** failure to attend or be present at a place where you are expected to be: *students' nonattendance at school*.

non·at·trib·ut·a·ble /nonəˈtribyətəbəl/ ▶ **adj.** not able to be attributed to a particular source or cause.

non·a·vail·a·bil·i·ty /ˌnänəˌvāləˈbilitē/ ▶ **n.** the state of not being available, free, or able to be used.

non·bank /ˈnänˈbaNGk/ ▶ **adj.** [attrib.] not relating to, connected with, or transacted by a bank.
▶ **n.** a financial institution that is not a bank.

non·be·ing /nänˈbēiNG/ ▶ **n.** the state of not being; nonexistence.

non·be·liev·er /ˌnänbəˈlēvər/ ▶ **n.** a person who does not believe in something, esp. one who has no religious faith.

non·bel·lig·er·ent /ˌnänbəˈlijərənt/ ▶ **adj.** not aggressive or engaged in a war or conflict.
▶ **n.** a nation or person that is not engaged in a war or conflict.
– DERIVATIVES **non·bel·lig·er·ence n.**, **non·bel·lig·er·en·cy n.**

non·bi·o·log·i·cal /ˌnänbīəˈläjikəl/ ▶ **adj.** not involving, relating to, or derived from biology or living organisms. ■ (of a detergent) not containing enzymes.

non·black ▶ **adj.** (of a person) not black. ■ of or relating to people who are not black.
▶ **n.** a person who is not black.

non·call·a·ble /nänˈkôləbəl/ ▶ **adj.** (of stocks and bonds) not subject to redemption before a certain date or until maturity.

non·can·cer·ous /nonˈkansərəs/ ▶ **adj.** not malignant; without evidence of cancer: *noncancerous growths*.

non·cap·i·tal /nänˈkapitl/ ▶ **adj.** Law (of an offense) not punishable by death.

non-Cath·o·lic ▶ **adj.** not Roman Catholic.
▶ **n.** a person who is not a Roman Catholic.

nonce[1] /näns/ ▶ **adj.** (of a word or expression) coined for or used on one occasion: *a nonce usage*.
– PHRASES **for the nonce** for the present; temporarily: *the room had been converted for the nonce into a nursery*.
– ORIGIN Middle English: from *then anes* 'the one (purpose)' (from *then*, obsolete oblique form of **THE** + *ane* 'one' + **-S**[3]), altered by misdivision; compare with **NEWT** and **NICKNAME**.

nonce[2] ▶ **n.** Brit. informal a person convicted of a sexual offense, esp. child molesting.
– ORIGIN 1970s: of unknown origin.

non·cha·lance /ˌnänsHəˈläns/ ▶ **n.** the state of being nonchalant: *an air of nonchalance*.

non·cha·lant /ˌnänsHəˈlänt/ ▶ **adj.** (of a person or manner) feeling or appearing casually calm and relaxed; not displaying anxiety, interest, or enthusiasm: *she gave a nonchalant shrug*.
– DERIVATIVES **non·cha·lant·ly adv.**
– ORIGIN mid 18th cent.: from French, literally 'not being concerned,' from the verb *nonchaloir*.

non-Chris·tian ▶ **adj.** relating to people or beliefs that are not Christian: *forms of non-Christian religious observance*.
▶ **n.** a person who is not a Christian.

non·cit·i·zen /nänˈsitizən/ ▶ **n.** a person who is not an inhabitant or national of a particular country or town.

non·clas·si·fied /nänˈklasəfīd/ ▶ **adj.** (of information or documents) not designated as officially secret; freely available (tending to be less forceful in meaning than **unclassified**).

non·cler·i·cal /ˌnänˈklerikəl/ ▶ **adj. 1** not doing or involving routine clerical work in an office.
2 not relating to or belonging to the clergy.

non·clin·i·cal /ˌnänˈklinikəl/ ▶ **adj.** not clinical: *the word 'depression' is used in a nonclinical sense*. ■ not accompanied by directly observable symptoms.

non·cod·ing /nänˈkōdiNG/ ▶ **adj.** Biology (of a section of a nucleic acid molecule) not directing the production of a peptide sequence.

non·com /ˈnänˌkäm/ ▶ **n.** Military, informal a noncommissioned officer.

non·com·bat·ant /ˌnänkəmˈbatnt/ ▶ **n.** a person who is not engaged in fighting during a war, esp. a civilian, chaplain, or medical practitioner.

non·com·bus·ti·ble /ˌnänkəmˈbəstəbəl/ ▶ **adj.** not flammable.

non·com·e·do·gen·ic /ˌnänˌkämədōˈjenik/ ▶ **adj.** denoting a skin-care product or cosmetic that is specially formulated so as not to cause blocked pores.

non·com·mer·cial /ˌnänkəˈmərsHl/ ▶ **adj.** not having a commercial objective; not intended to make a profit: *a noncommercial radio station*.

non·com·mis·sioned /ˌnankəˈmisHənd/ ▶ **adj.** Military (of an officer in the armed forces) ranking below warrant officer, as sergeant or petty officer.

non·com·mit·tal /ˌnänkəˈmitl/ ▶ **adj.** (of a person or a person's behavior or manner) not expressing or revealing commitment to a definite opinion or course of action: *her tone was noncommittal, and her face gave nothing away*.
– DERIVATIVES **non·com·mit·tal·ly adv.**

non·com·mu·ni·cant /ˌnänkəˈmyo͞onikənt/ ▶ **n.** (in church use) a person who does not receive Holy Communion, esp. regularly or at a particular service.

non·com·mu·ni·cat·ing /ˌnänkəˈmyo͞onəˌkātiNG/ ▶ **adj.** lacking a means of communication.

non·com·mu·nist (also **non-Communist**) /ˌnänˈkämyənist/ ▶ **adj.** not advocating or practicing communism.
▶ **n.** a person who is not a communist.

non·com·pete ▶ **adj.** denoting or relating to a clause, provision, or agreement by which parties are bound not to compete: *he didn't have a non-compete agreement with his former employer*.

non·com·pet·i·tive /ˌnänkəmˈpetətiv/ ▶ **adj.** not involving competition; not competitive: *they joined in noncompetitive activities like friendship week*. ■ not subject to competition: *noncompetitive eligibility*.

non·com·pli·ance /ˌnänkəmˈplīəns/ ▶ **n.** failure to act in accordance with a wish or command. ■ failure to conform to rules or standards.
– DERIVATIVES **non·com·pli·ant adj.**

non com·pos men·tis /ˌnän ˈkämpəs ˈmentis/ (also **non compos**) ▶ **adj.** not sane or in one's right mind.
– ORIGIN Latin, literally 'not having control of one's mind.'

non·con·duc·tor /ˌnänkənˈdəktər/ ▶ **n.** a substance that does not conduct heat or electricity.
– DERIVATIVES **non·con·duct·ing** /-ˈdəktiNG/ **adj.**

non·con·fi·den·tial /ˌnänˌkänfəˈdencHəl/ ▶ **adj.** (of a subject or information) not secret or confidential.
– DERIVATIVES **non·con·fi·den·tial·ly adv.**

non·con·form·ist /ˌnänkənˈfôrmist/ ▶ **n. 1** a person whose behavior or views do not conform to prevailing ideas or practices.
2 (**Nonconformist**) a member of a Protestant church in England that dissents from the established Anglican Church.
▶ **adj. 1** of or characterized by behavior or views that do not conform to prevailing ideas or practices.
2 (**Nonconformist**) of or relating to Nonconformists or their principles and practices.
– DERIVATIVES **non·con·form·ism** /-ˌmizəm/ **n.**

non·con·form·i·ty /ˌnänkənˈfôrmitē/ ▶ **n. 1** failure or refusal to conform to a prevailing rule or practice. ■ lack of similarity in form or type.
2 (**Nonconformity**) Nonconformists as a body, esp. Protestants in England dissenting from the Anglican Church. ■ the principles or practice of Nonconformists, esp. Protestant dissent.

non·con·fron·ta·tion·al /ˌnänkänfrənˈtāsHənl/ ▶ **adj.** tending to deal with situations calmly and diplomatically; not aggressive or hostile: *a nonconfrontational approach to matrimonial disputes*.
– DERIVATIVES **non·con·fron·ta·tion·al·ly adv.**

non·con·sec·u·tive /ˌnänkənˈsekyətiv/ ▶ **adj.** not in order or following continuously: *the only president to serve two nonconsecutive terms*.
– DERIVATIVES **non·con·sec·u·tive·ly adv.**

non·con·ten·tious /ˌnänkənˈtencHəs/ ▶ **adj. 1** not causing or likely to cause an argument.
2 Law not involving differences between contending parties.

non·con·tra·dic·tion /ˌnänkäntrəˈdiksHən/ ▶ **n.** a lack or absence of contradiction, esp. as a principle of logic that a proposition and its opposite cannot both be true.
– DERIVATIVES **non·con·tra·dic·to·ry** /-ˈdiktərē/ **adj.**

non·con·trib·u·to·ry /ˌnänkənˈtribyəˌtôrē/ ▶ **adj.** **1** not playing a part in bringing something about. **2** (of a pension or pension plan) funded by regular payments by the employer, not the employee.

non·con·tro·ver·sial /ˌnänˌkäntrəˈvərsHəl/ ▶ **adj.** not giving rise to disagreement; not controversial (tending to be less forceful in meaning than **uncontroversial**).

non·co·op·er·a·tion /ˌnänkōˌäpəˈrāsHən/ ▶ **n.** failure or refusal to cooperate, esp. as a form of protest.

non·core /ˈnonˌkôr/ ▶ **adj.** not considered to be essential; expendable: *substantial expenditure cuts in noncore service areas.*

non·count /ˈnänˌkount/ ▶ **adj.** Grammar (of a noun) not countable.

non·cus·to·di·al /ˌnänˌkəˈstōdēəl/ ▶ **adj.** Law not having custody of one's children after a divorce: *the relationship between the children and their noncustodial father was virtually destroyed.*

non·dair·y /nänˈde(ə)rē/ ▶ **adj.** containing no milk or milk products: *a nondairy creamer.*

non·de·duct·i·ble /ˌnändiˈdəktəbəl/ ▶ **adj.** not allowable as a deduction from income for the calculation of taxes.

non·de·grad·a·ble /ˌnändiˈgrādəbəl/ ▶ **adj.** not biodegradable or subject to decomposition: *nondegradable waste that ends up in the water.*

non·de·liv·er·y /ˌnändəˈlivərē/ ▶ **n.** chiefly Law failure to provide or deliver goods.

non·de·nom·i·na·tion·al /ˌnändəˌnäməˈnāsHənəl/ ▶ **adj.** open or acceptable to people of any Christian denomination.

non·de·script /ˌnändəˈskript/ ▶ **adj.** lacking distinctive or interesting features or characteristics: *she lived in a nondescript suburban apartment block.* ▶ **n.** a nondescript person or thing.

– DERIVATIVES **non·de·script·ly** adv., **non·de·script·ness** /-ˈskrip(t)nis/ n.

– ORIGIN late 17th cent. (in the sense 'not previously described or identified scientifically'): from **NON-** + obsolete *descript* 'described, engraved' (from Latin *descriptus*).

non·de·struc·tive /ˌnändəˈstrəktiv/ ▶ **adj.** technical not involving damage or destruction, esp. of an object or material that is being tested: *instruments subjected to nondestructive analysis by X-ray fluorescence.*

non·dig·i·tal /nänˈdijitl/ ▶ **adj.** **1** not represented by numbers, esp. binary codes; not digitized: *nondigital items have only their location information (catalog records) in the digital library, as it happens in a traditional automated library situation.* **2** not using the Internet or computers: *nondigital submissions will be accepted only until February 1st.*

non·di·rec·tion·al /ˌnändəˈreksHənəl/ ▶ **adj.** lacking directional properties. ■ (of sound, light, radio waves, etc.) equally sensitive, intense, etc., in every direction.

non·dis·clo·sure /ˌnändisˈklōzHər/ ▶ **n.** failure to reveal or disclose information, or an instance of this: *security requirements are used to justify the nondisclosure of basic information.*

non·dis·junc·tion /ˌnändisˈjəNGksHən/ ▶ **n.** Genetics the failure of one or more pairs of homologous chromosomes or sister chromatids to separate normally during nuclear division, usually resulting in an abnormal distribution of chromosomes in the daughter nuclei.

non·drink·er /nänˈdriNGkər/ ▶ **n.** a person who does not drink alcohol.

non·drip /ˌnänˈdrip/ ▶ **adj.** (of paint) specially formulated so that it does not drip or run when wet.

non·driv·er /ˈnänˈdrīvər/ ▶ **n.** a person who does not or cannot drive a motor vehicle.

non·dry·ing /ˌnänˈdrī-iNG/ ▶ **adj.** **1** not causing dryness: *wash your complexion with a nondrying cleanser.* **2** (of an oil) that does not harden when exposed to air.

none[1] /nən/ ▶ **pron.** not any: *none of you want to work | don't use any more water, or there'll be none left for me.* ■ no person; no one: *none could match her looks.* ▶ **adv.** **(none the)** [with comparative] by no amount; not at all: *it is made none the easier by the differences in approach.*

– PHRASES **none the less** see **NONETHELESS**. **none other than** used to emphasize the surprising identity of a person or thing: *her first customer was none other than Henry du Pont.* **be none the wiser** see **WISE[1]**. **none the worse for** see **WORSE**. **none too** see **TOO**. **want** (or **will have**) **none of** (esp. with reference to behavior) refuse to accept (something): *Danny offered to wait below, but Peter would have none of it.*

– ORIGIN Old English *nān*, from *ne* 'not' + *ān* 'one,' of Germanic origin; compare with German *nein* 'no!'

> **USAGE** It is sometimes held that **none** can take only a singular verb, never a plural verb: *none of them is coming tonight*, rather than *none of them are coming tonight*. There is little justification, historical or grammatical, for this view. **None** is descended from Old English **nān**, meaning 'not one,' and has been used for around a thousand years with both a singular and a plural verb, depending on the context and the emphasis needed.

none[2] (also **nones**) ▶ **n.** a service forming part of the Divine Office of the Western Christian Church, traditionally said (or chanted) at the ninth hour of the day (3 p.m.).

– ORIGIN mid 19th cent.: from French, from Latin *nona*, feminine singular of *nonus* 'ninth.' Compare with **NOON**.

non·emp·ty /ˌnänˈem(p)tē/ ▶ **adj.** Mathematics & Logic (of a set or class) not empty; having at least one element or member.

non·en·ti·ty /nänˈentitē/ ▶ **n.** (pl. **nonentities**) **1** a person or thing with no special or interesting qualities; an unimportant person or thing: *a political nonentity.* **2** nonexistence: *asserting the nonentity of evil.*

– ORIGIN late 16th cent.: from medieval Latin *nonentitas* 'nonexistence.'

nones /nōnz/ ▶ **plural n.** **1** in the ancient Roman calendar, the ninth day before the ides by inclusive reckoning, that is, the 7th day of March, May, July, and October, or the 5th of other months. **2** another term for **NONE[2]**.

– ORIGIN via Old French from Latin *nonas*, feminine accusative plural of *nonus* 'ninth.'

non·es·sen·tial /ˌnänəˈsenCHəl/ ▶ **adj.** not absolutely necessary: *during the strike nonessential hospital services were halted.* ▶ **n.** (usu. **nonessentials**) a nonessential thing.

non est fac·tum /ˌnōn ˌest ˈfaktəm/ ▶ **n.** Law a plea that a written agreement is invalid because the defendant was mistaken about its character when signing it.

– ORIGIN Latin, literally 'it was not done.'

none·such /ˈnənˌsəCH/ (also **nonsuch**) ▶ **n.** **1** a person or thing that is regarded as perfect or excellent. **2** another term for **BLACK MEDICK** (see **MEDICK**).

– ORIGIN early 17th cent.: coined on the pattern of *nonpareil.*

no·net /nōˈnet/ ▶ **n.** a group of nine people or things, esp. musicians. ■ a musical composition for nine voices or instruments.

– ORIGIN mid 19th cent.: from Italian *nonetto*, from *nono* 'ninth,' from Latin *nonus*.

none·the·less /ˌnənT͟Həˈles/ (also **none the less**) ▶ **adv.** in spite of that; nevertheless: *it was the barest of welcomes, but it was a welcome nonetheless.*

non-Eu·clid·e·an /ˌnän yo͞oˈklidēən/ ▶ **adj.** Geometry denying or going beyond Euclidean principles in geometry, esp. in contravening the postulate that only one line through a given point can be parallel to a given line.

non-Eu·ro·pe·an ▶ **adj.** not European: *a wide range of non-European cultures.* ▶ **n.** a person who is not European: *the art and music of non-Europeans.*

non·e·vent /ˌnäneˈvent/ ▶ **n.** a disappointing or insignificant event or occasion, esp. one that was expected or intended to be exciting or interesting. ■ a scheduled event that did not happen.

non·ex·ec·u·tive /ˌnänigˈzekyətiv/ ▶ **adj.** not having an executive function: *a nonexecutive director.* ▶ **n.** a person without executive responsibilities.

non·ex·ist·ent /ˌnänigˈzistənt/ ▶ **adj.** not existing, or not real or present: *she pretended to tie a nonexistent shoelace.*

– DERIVATIVES **non·ex·ist·ence** n.

non·ex·plo·sive /ˌnänikˈsplōsiv/ ▶ **adj.** not able or likely to explode or to cause an explosion.

non·fac·tive /nänˈfaktiv/ ▶ **adj.** Linguistics denoting a verb that takes a clausal object that may or may not designate a true fact, for example, *believe* as opposed to *know*. Contrasted with **CONTRAFACTIVE**, **FACTIVE**.

non·fat /ˈnänˈfat/ ▶ **adj.** (of a food) containing no fat; with all fat solids removed: *nonfat buttermilk.*

non·fea·sance /nänˈfēzəns/ ▶ **n.** Law failure to perform an act that is required by law.

non·fer·rous /nänˈferəs/ ▶ **adj.** relating to or denoting a metal other than iron or steel.

non·fic·tion /nänˈfiksHən/ ▶ **n.** prose writing that is based on facts, real events, and real people, such as biography or history.

– DERIVATIVES **non·fic·tion·al** /-nəl/ **adj.**

non·fig·ur·a·tive ▶ **adj.** not figurative. ■ (of an artist or work of art) abstract.

non·fi·nite /nänˈfīnīt/ ▶ **adj.** not finite. ■ Grammar (of a verb form) not limited by tense, person, or number. Contrasted with **FINITE**.

non·flam·ma·ble /nänˈflaməbəl/ ▶ **adj.** not catching fire easily; not flammable.

> **USAGE** See usage at **INFLAMMABLE**.

non·ful·fill·ment /ˌnänfo͝olˈfilmənt/ ▶ **n.** failure to fulfill or carry out something desired, planned, or promised.

non·func·tion·al /nänˈfəNGksHənəl/ ▶ **adj.** not having any particular purpose or function. ■ not operating or in working order.

non·gov·ern·men·tal /ˌnängəvər(n)ˈmentl/ ▶ **adj.** (esp. of an organization) not belonging to or associated with any government.

non·he·red·i·tar·y /ˌnänhəˈrediˌterē/ ▶ **adj.** not acquired or acquirable by inheritance: *nonhereditary forms of breast cancer.*

non·his·tor·i·cal /ˌnänhiˈstôrikəl, -ˈstär-/ ▶ **adj.** not based on or drawn from history: *nonhistorical data.* ■ without regard for history: *pontificating from a nonhistorical perspective.*

non-Hodg·kin's lym·pho·ma ▶ **n.** Medicine a form of malignant lymphoma distinguished from Hodgkin's disease only by the absence of binucleate giant cells.

non·hu·man /nänˈ(h)yo͞omən/ ▶ **adj.** of, relating to, or characteristic of a creature or thing that is not a human being: *ascribing human characteristics to nonhuman animals.* ▶ **n.** a creature that is not a human being.

no·ni /ˈnōnē/ ▶ **n.** any of various evergreen trees or shrubs of the madder family (Genus *Morinda*) native to the South Pacific. Various medicinal preparations are made from their leaves, roots, and fruit.

– ORIGIN Tahitian.

non·in·clu·sive /ˌnäninˈklo͞osiv/ ▶ **adj.** not including all possible elements; not exhaustive: *a noninclusive list.* ■ excluding some parties, interests, or concerns: *the book is further hampered by noninclusive language.*

non·in·fec·tious /ˌnäninˈfeksHəs/ ▶ **adj.** (of a disease or disease-causing organism) not liable to be transmitted through the environment. ■ not liable to spread infection.

non·in·flam·ma·ble /ˌnäninˈflaməbəl/ ▶ **adj.** not catching fire easily; not flammable.

> **USAGE** Technically, there is no difference between **nonflammable** and **noninflammable**, but the preferred, less confusing choice is **nonflammable**. See also usage at **INFLAMMABLE**.

non·in·flam·ma·to·ry /ˌnäninˈflaməˌtôrē/ ▶ **adj.** Medicine not accompanied by or associated with inflammation: *noninflammatory acne.* ■ not controversial or contentious: *a noninflammatory report.*

non·in·her·ent /ˌnäninˈherənt/ ▶ **adj.** (of an adjective) having the relevant meaning only when used attributively with reference to a particular individual; for example, *poor* and *old* in *the poor old fellow*, which is not equivalent to *the fellow was poor and old*. Contrasted with **INHERENT**.

non·in·su·lin-de·pend·ent ▶ **adj.** Medicine relating to or denoting a type of diabetes in which there is some insulin secretion. Such diabetes typically develops in adulthood and can frequently be managed by diet and hypoglycemic agents.

non·in·ter·fer·ence /ˌnänˌintərˈfi(ə)rəns/ ▶ **n.** failure or refusal to intervene without invitation or necessity, esp. in political matters.

non·in·ter·ven·tion /ˌnänintərˈvenCHən/ ▶ **n.** the principle or practice of not becoming involved in the affairs of others. ■ such a policy adopted by a country in its international relations.

– DERIVATIVES **non·in·ter·ven·tion·ism** /-ˌnizəm/ **n.**, **non·in·ter·ven·tion·ist** /-nist/ **adj. & n.**

non·in·va·sive /ˌnäninˈvāsiv/ ▶ **adj.** **1** (of medical procedures) not requiring the introduction of instruments into the body: *noninvasive techniques such as ultrasound.* **2** (of a cancerous disease) not tending to spread. ■ (of plants) not tending to spread undesirably.

non·i·on·ic /ˌnänīˈänik/ ▶ **adj.** Chemistry not ionic. ■ (of a detergent) not dissociating into ions in aqueous solution.

non·ism /ˈnänizəm/ ▶ **n.** general abstention from activities and substances regarded as damaging to one's health or well-being.

non·is·sue /ˈnänˈisHo͞o/ ▶ **n.** a topic of little or no importance.

non·judg·men·tal /ˌnänjəjˈmentl/ (also **nonjudgemental**) ▶ **adj.** not judgmental; avoiding moral judgments.

non·ju·di·cial /ˌnänjo͞oˈdisHəl/ ▶ **adj. 1** not resulting from a court ruling or judgment: *nonjudicial punishment.*
2 not involving courts or judges: *nonjudicial appointments.*

Non·ju·ror /nänˈjo͝orər/ ▶ **n.** a member of the English clergy who refused to take the oath of allegiance to William and Mary in 1689.

non·ju·ry /nänˈjo͝orē/ ▶ **adj.** Law denoting a trial or legal action not having or requiring a jury.

non·league /nänˈlēg/ ▶ **adj.** denoting or relating to a team, game, or match that is not affiliated with a country's main professional leagues: *the Wildcats were cocky in the preseason but were humbled by some nonleague losses.*

non li·cet /ˈnän ˈlīsit/ ▶ **adj.** not allowed; unlawful.
– ORIGIN Latin.

non·lin·e·ar /nänˈlinēər/ ▶ **adj. 1** not denoting, involving, or arranged in a straight line. ■ Mathematics designating or involving an equation whose terms are not of the first degree. ■ Physics involving a lack of linearity between two related qualities such as input and output. ■ Mathematics involving measurement in more than one dimension. ■ not linear, sequential, or straightforward; random: *Joyce's stream-of-consciousness, nonlinear narrative.*
2 of or denoting digital editing whereby a sequence of edits is stored on computer as opposed to videotape, thus facilitating further editing.
– PHRASES **go nonlinear** informal become excited or angry, esp. about a particular obsession.
– DERIVATIVES **non·lin·e·ar·i·ty** /ˌnänlinēˈaritē/ **n.**, **non·lin·e·ar·ly adv.**

non·li·quid /ˌnänˈlikwid/ ▶ **adj. 1** having a form other than liquid: *nonliquid hydrocarbons.*
2 not readily convertible to cash: *nonliquid assets.*

non·liv·ing /ˌnänˈliviNG/ ▶ **adj. 1** inanimate; inorganic: *materials that come from nonliving sources.*
2 no longer alive: *a kidney from a nonliving donor.*

non·log·i·cal /nänˈläjikəl/ ▶ **adj.** not derived from or according to the rules of logic or formal argument (less forceful in meaning than **illogical**).
– DERIVATIVES **non·log·i·cal·ly** /-ik(ə)lē/ **adv.**

non·mem·ber /ˈnänˌmembər/ ▶ **n.** a person, body, or country that is not a member of a particular organization.
– DERIVATIVES **non·mem·ber·ship** /nänˈmembərˌSHip/ **n.**

non·met·al /ˌnänˈmetl/ ▶ **n.** an element or substance that is not a metal.
– DERIVATIVES **non·me·tal·lic** /ˌnänməˈtalik/ **adj.**

non·mil·i·tar·y /ˌnänˈmiləˌterē/ ▶ **adj.** not belonging to, characteristic of, or involving the armed forces; civilian: *the widespread destruction of nonmilitary targets.*

non·min·is·te·ri·al /ˌnänˌminəˈsti(ə)rēəl/ ▶ **adj. 1** not involving religious ministry; lay: *nonministerial staff at the church.*
2 not relating to the role of a government minister.

non·mor·al /nänˈmôrəl/ ▶ **adj.** not holding or manifesting moral principles: *nonmoral value judgments.*

non·na·tive /ˈnänˌnātiv/ ▶ **adj.** (of a person, plant, or animal) not indigenous or native to a particular place. ■ (of a speaker) not having spoken the language in question from earliest childhood.

non·nat·u·ral /nänˈnacHərəl/ ▶ **adj.** not involving or manifesting natural means or processes. ■ Philosophy existing but not part of the natural world (a term used by G. E. Moore of ethical properties).

non·neg·a·tive /nänˈnegətiv/ ▶ **adj.** not negative. ■ Mathematics either positive or equal to zero.

non·ne·go·ti·a·ble /ˌnä(n)nəˈgōsHəbəl/ ▶ **adj.** not open to discussion or modification. ■ (of a document) not able to be transferred or assigned to the legal ownership of another person.

non-net /nänˈnet/ ▶ **adj.** (of an amount) including tax and other sums in addition to the net amount.

non·nu·cle·ar /nänˈn(y)o͞oklēər/ ▶ **adj. 1** not involving or relating to nuclear energy or nuclear weapons. ■ (of a country) not possessing nuclear weapons.
2 Physics not involving, relating to, or forming part of a nucleus or nuclei.

no-no ▶ **n.** (pl. **no-nos**) informal a thing that is not possible or acceptable: *perming highlighted hair used to be a definite no-no, but it's now possible.*

non·ob·jec·tive /ˌnänəbˈjektiv/ ▶ **adj. 1** (of a person or their judgment) influenced by personal feeling or opinions in considering and representing facts.
2 of or relating to abstract art.

non·ob·serv·ance /ˌnänəbˈzərvəns/ ▶ **n.** failure to fulfill or comply with an obligation, rule, or custom.

non·of·fi·cial /ˌnänəˈfisHəl/ ▶ **adj.** not sanctioned or controlled by an authority: *mission personnel will limit nonofficial travel.*

no-non·sense ▶ **adj.** simple and straightforward; sensible.

non·op·er·a·tion·al /ˌnänˌäpəˈrāsHənl/ ▶ **adj.** not working or in use: *nonoperational equipment.* ■ not engaged in or involving active duties. ■ not derived from or involving normal business operations.

non·or·gan·ic /ˌnänôrˈganik/ ▶ **adj.** not organic, in particular: ■ not relating to or derived from living matter: *nonorganic archaeological finds.* ■ (esp. of food or farming methods) not involving or relating to production by organic methods: *nonorganic hens' eggs | nonorganic pesticides.*

non·pa·ra·met·ric /ˌnänparəˈmetrik/ ▶ **adj.** Statistics not involving any assumptions as to the form or parameters of a frequency distribution.

non·pa·reil /ˌnänpəˈrel/ ▶ **adj.** having no match or equal; unrivaled: *he is a nonpareil storyteller* | [postpositive] *a film critic nonpareil.*
▶ **n. 1** an unrivaled or matchless person or thing.
2 a flat round candy made of chocolate covered with white sugar sprinkles.
3 Printing an old type size equal to six points (larger than ruby or agate, smaller than emerald or minion).
– ORIGIN late Middle English: from French, from *non-* 'not' + *pareil* 'equal' (from popular Latin *pariculus*, diminutive of Latin *par* 'equal').

non·par·tic·i·pat·ing /ˌnänpərˈtisəˌpātiNG/ ▶ **adj.**
1 not involved or taking part in an activity.
2 (of an insurance policy) not allowing the holder a share of the profits, typically in the form of a bonus, made by the company.

non·par·ti·san /nänˈpärtizən/ ▶ **adj.** not biased or partisan, esp. toward any particular political group.

non·par·ty ▶ **adj.** independent of any political party.

non·past /ˈnänˌpast/ ▶ **n.** Grammar a tense not expressing a past action or state.

non·pay·ment ▶ **n.** failure to pay an amount of money that is owed: *homes repossessed for nonpayment of mortgages.*

non·pen·e·tra·tive ▶ **adj.** (of sexual activity) in which penetration by the penis does not take place.

non·per·for·mance /ˌnänpərˈfôrməns/ ▶ **n.** failure or refusal to perform or fulfill a condition, promise, etc.: *the vendor will be sued by the customer for nonperformance.* ■ the state of not being performed: *plays developed in nonperformance workshops.*

non·per·son /ˌnänˈpərsən/ ▶ **n.** a person regarded as nonexistent or unimportant, or as having no rights; an ignored or forgotten person: *these players were famous within their own communities, but nonpersons outside them.* Compare with **UNPERSON**.

non·phys·i·cal /ˌnänˈfizikəl/ ▶ **adj. 1** not relating to or concerning the body: *both physical and nonphysical ill-treatment.*
2 not tangible or concrete: *nonphysical digital money.*

non pla·cet /ˌnän ˈplāsit/ ▶ **n.** a negative vote in a church or college assembly.
– ORIGIN Latin, literally 'it does not please.'

non·plus /nänˈpləs/ ▶ **v.** (**nonpluses** or **nonplusses**, **nonplussing**, **nonplussed**) [with obj.] surprise and confuse (someone) so much that they are unsure how to react: *Diane was nonplussed by such an odd question.*
▶ **n.** a state of being surprised and confused in this way.
– ORIGIN late 16th cent.: from Latin *non plus* 'not more.' The noun originally meant 'a state in which no more can be said or done.'

non·plussed /nänˈpləst/ (also **nonplused**) ▶ **adj.**
1 (of a person) surprised and confused so much that they are unsure how to react: *he would be completely nonplussed and embarrassed at the idea.*
2 informal (of a person) not disconcerted; unperturbed.

> **USAGE** In standard use, **nonplussed** means 'surprised and confused': *the hostility of the new neighbor's refusal left Mrs. Walker nonplussed.* In North American English, a new use has developed in recent years, meaning 'unperturbed'—more or less the opposite of its traditional meaning: *hoping to disguise his confusion, he tried to appear* ***nonplussed***. This new use probably arose on the assumption that **non-** was the normal negative prefix and must therefore have a negative meaning. It is not considered part of standard English.

non·point source /nänˈpoint/ ▶ **n.** a source of pollution that issues from widely distributed or pervasive environmental elements. Compare with **POINT SOURCE**: *cattle are the leading nonpoint source of pollution in Canada today.*

non·po·lit·i·cal /ˌnänpəˈlitikəl/ ▶ **adj.** not relating to or motivated by politics: *nonpolitical speeches.*

non·pol·lut·ing /ˌnänpəˈlo͞otiNG/ ▶ **adj.** not releasing pollutants, esp. carbon dioxide, into the atmosphere: *wind power is a nonpolluting alternative to fossil fuels.*

non pos·su·mus /ˌnän ˈpäs(y)əməs/ ▶ **n.** used as a statement expressing inability to act in a matter.
– ORIGIN Latin, literally 'we cannot.'

non·prac·tic·ing /nänˈpraktisiNG/ ▶ **adj.**
1 not currently practicing one's profession: *a nonpracticing lawyer.*
2 not observant of or practicing one's religion: *nonpracticing Jews.*

non·pre·scrip·tion /ˌnänprəˈskripsHən/ ▶ **adj.** (of a medicine) available for sale without a prescription. ■ denoting such sale or purchase.

non·pro·duc·tive /ˌnänprəˈdəktiv/ ▶ **adj.** not producing or able to produce goods, crops, or economic benefit (tending to be less forceful in meaning than **unproductive**). ■ achieving little.
– DERIVATIVES **non·pro·duc·tive·ly adv.**

non·pro·fes·sion·al /ˌnänprəˈfesHənəl/ ▶ **adj.** relating to or engaged in a paid occupation that does not require advanced education or training: *nonprofessional grades of staff.* ■ relating to or engaged in an activity (esp. an interest or hobby) that is not a person's main paid occupation: *nonprofessional actors.*
▶ **n.** a nonprofessional person.

non·prof·it /ˈnänˈpräfit/ ▶ **adj.** [attrib.] not making or conducted primarily to make a profit: *charities and other nonprofit organizations.*
▶ **n.** a nonprofit organization: *I spent the next six years working for small nonprofits.*

non·pro·lif·er·a·tion /ˌnänprəˌlifəˈrāsHən/ ▶ **n.** the prevention of an increase or spread of something, esp. the number of countries possessing nuclear weapons: [as modifier] *a nuclear nonproliferation treaty.*

non·pro·pri·e·tar·y /ˌnänprəˈprīəˌterē/ ▶ **adj.** (esp. of computer hardware or software) conforming to standards that are in the public domain or are widely licensed, and so not restricted to one manufacturer. ■ not registered or protected as a trademark or brand name; generic.

non-pros (abbr.: **non pros.** /nänˈpräs/) ▶ **v.** [with obj.] Law adjudge (a plaintiff) in default.

non·pub·lic /ˌnänˈpəblik/ ▶ **adj. 1** not open or available to the public: *the museum's nonpublic spaces.*
2 not publicly owned or controlled; private: *nonpublic schools.*
3 not taking place in public: *nonpublic behavior.*

non·ra·cial /nänˈrāsHəl/ ▶ **adj.** not involving racial factors or racial discrimination.

non·ran·dom /ˌnänˈrandəm/ ▶ **adj.** determined by or resulting from factors other than chance: *a nonrandom distribution pattern.*
– DERIVATIVES **non·ran·dom·ly adv.**

non·read·er /ˈnänˈrēdər/ ▶ **n.** a person who cannot or does not read.

non·re·cur·ring /nänriˈkəriNG/ ▶ **adj. 1** (of costs, charges, taxes, etc.) occurring one time only: *nonrecurring grants to officers.*
2 not returning or recurring: *a nonrecurring illness.*

non·re·fill·a·ble /ˌnänrēˈfiləbəl/ ▶ **adj. 1** (of a container) not allowed to be refilled and resold.
2 (of a medical prescription) to be dispensed only once.

non·re·new·a·ble /ˌnänriˈn(y)o͞oəbəl/ ▶ **adj. 1** (of a fuel or energy source) existing in finite quantity.
2 (of a contract, agreement, etc.) not allowed to be renewed: *nonrenewable licenses.*
▶ **n.** a nonrenewable energy source.

non·res·i·dent /nänˈrezidənt/ ▶ **adj.** not living in a particular place, esp. a country or a place of work: *the building had a nonresident, part-time caretaker.* ■ (of a job or program of study) not requiring the holder or participant to reside at the place of work or instruction. ■ Computing (of software) not kept permanently in memory but available to be loaded

from secondary storage or external device: *if you want to use a nonresident font, you can manually download it.*
▶ **n.** a person not living in a particular place: *parking permits are available for Richmond residents and nonresidents.*
– DERIVATIVES **non·res·i·dence** **n.**

non·res·i·den·tial /ˌnänrezəˈdenCHəl/ ▶ **adj.** not requiring or providing facilities for people to live on the premises: *two-day nonresidential workshops.* ■ (of property or land) containing or suitable for commercial premises rather than private houses.

non·re·sis·tance /ˌnänriˈzistəns/ ▶ **n.** the practice or principle of not resisting authority, even when it is unjustly exercised.

non·re·sis·tant /ˌnänriˈzistənt/ ▶ **adj.** **1** (of an organism) vulnerable to particular diseases or pathogens: *nonresistant rice plants.*
2 not mounting resistance to authority: *nonresistant pacifism.*

non·re·stric·tive /ˌnänriˈstriktiv/ ▶ **adj.** **1** not involving restrictions or limitations.
2 Grammar (of a relative clause or descriptive phrase) giving additional information about a noun phrase whose particular reference has already been specified.

> **USAGE** On the use of **restrictive** and **nonrestrictive** relative clauses, see usage at **RESTRICTIVE, THAT,** and **WHICH.**

non·re·turn /ˌnänriˈtərn/ ▶ **adj.** Brit. permitting the flow of air or liquid in one direction only: *a nonreturn valve.*

non·re·turn·a·ble /ˌnänriˈtərnəbəl/ ▶ **adj.** (esp. of a deposit paid) not repayable in any circumstances. ■ (of bottles or other containers) not intended to be returned empty to the suppliers.

non·rho·tic /nänˈrōtik/ ▶ **n.** Phonetics relating to or denoting a dialect of English in which *r* is pronounced in prevocalic position only, common in eastern New England, New York City, and Britain.

non·rig·id /nänˈrijid/ ▶ **adj.** (esp. of materials) not rigid. ■ denoting an airship whose shape is maintained solely by the pressure of the gas inside.

non·scene /nänˈsēn/ ▶ **adj.** informal, chiefly Brit. (of a homosexual) not inclined to participate in the social environment frequented predominantly by other homosexuals.

non·sched·uled /ˈnänˈskejəld, -jo͞old/ ▶ **adj.** denoting or relating to an airline that operates without fixed or published flying schedules: *measures for nonscheduled sites are being considered.*

non·sci·en·tif·ic /ˌnänˌsīənˈtifik/ ▶ **adj.** not involving or relating to science or scientific methods.
– DERIVATIVES **non·sci·en·tist** **n.**

non·sec·tar·i·an /ˌnänsekˈte(ə)rēən/ ▶ **adj.** not involving or relating to a specific religious sect or political group.

non·sense /ˈnänˌsens/ ▶ **n.** **1** spoken or written words that have no meaning or make no sense: *he was talking absolute nonsense.* ■ [as exclamation] used to show strong disagreement: *"Nonsense! No one can do that."* ■ [as modifier] denoting verse or other writing intended to be amusing by virtue of its absurd or whimsical language: *nonsense poetry.*
2 foolish or unacceptable behavior: *put a stop to that nonsense, will you?*

non·sense mu·ta·tion ▶ **n.** Genetics a mutation in which a sense codon that corresponds to one of the twenty amino acids specified by the genetic code is changed to a chain-terminating codon.

non·sense word ▶ **n.** a word having no conventionally accepted meaning.

non·sen·si·cal /nänˈsensikəl/ ▶ **n.** **1** having no meaning; making no sense: *a nonsensical argument | he dismissed the claim as nonsensical.*
2 ridiculously impractical or ill-advised: *a tax that everyone recognizes was nonsensical.*
– DERIVATIVES **non·sen·si·cal·i·ty** /ˌnänsensəˈkalitē/ **n.**, **non·sen·si·cal·ly** /nänˈsensik(ə)lē/ **adv.**

non se·qui·tur /ˌnän ˈsekwitər/ ▶ **n.** a conclusion or statement that does not logically follow from the previous argument or statement.
– ORIGIN Latin, literally 'it does not follow.'

non·sex·u·al /ˌnänˈseksHo͞oəl/ ▶ **adj.** not involving or relating to sex or sexual reproduction.
– DERIVATIVES **non·sex·u·al·ly** **adv.**

non·skid /ˌnänˈskid/ ▶ **adj.** designed to prevent sliding or skidding: *nonskid tires.*

non·slip ▶ **adj.** designed to prevent slipping: *a nonslip bath mat.*

non·smok·er /ˌnänˈsmōkər/ ▶ **n.** a person who does not smoke tobacco.
– DERIVATIVES **non·smok·ing** **adj.**

non·so·lid col·or /nänˈsälid/ ▶ **n.** Computing a color simulated by a pattern of dots of other colors, extending the range of colors available.

non·speak·ing /ˌnänˈspēkiNG/ ▶ **adj.** (of a role or part) not requiring the actor to speak. ■ unable or unwilling to speak: *the equipment will make an amazing difference to nonspeaking children at the school.*

non·spe·cial·ist /ˌnänˈspesHəlist/ ▶ **n.** a person who is not an expert or specialist in a particular subject.
▶ **adj.** not having or requiring specialist knowledge.

non·spe·cif·ic /ˌnänspəˈsifik/ ▶ **adj.** not detailed or exact; general. ■ Medicine not assignable to a particular cause, condition, or category.

non·spe·cif·ic u·re·thri·tis /ˌyo͝orəˈTHrītis/ (abbr.: **NSU**) ▶ **n.** Medicine inflammation of the urethra due to infection by chlamydiae or other organisms (other than gonococci).

non·stain·ing /ˌnänˈstāniNG/ ▶ **adj.** not causing a stain: *nonstaining modeling clay.* ■ not responding to the application of a stain or dye: *nonstaining cells.*

non·stand·ard /ˈnänˈstandərd/ ▶ **adj.** not average, normal, or usual: *people working nonstandard hours.* ■ (of language) not of the form that is accepted as standard.

non·start·er /ˈnänˈstärtər/ ▶ **n.** a person or animal that fails to take part in a race. ■ informal a person, plan, or idea that has no chance of succeeding or being effective.

non·state ac·tor ▶ **n.** an individual or organization that has significant political influence but is not allied to any particular country or state.

non·stick /ˈnänˈstik/ ▶ **adj.** (of a pan or surface) covered with a substance that prevents food from sticking to it during cooking: *a nonstick frying pan.*

non·stop /ˈnänˈstäp/ ▶ **adj.** continuing without stopping or pausing: *we had two days of almost nonstop rain.* ■ (of a passenger vehicle or journey) not having or making stops at intermediate places on the way to its destination: *a nonstop flight to Los Angeles.* ■ oppressively constant; relentless: *the show was axed after nonstop criticism.*
▶ **adv.** without stopping or pausing: *Stephen had been working nonstop.*
▶ **n.** a nonstop flight or train: *seven nonstops to New York every business day.*

non·struck /nänˈstrək/ ▶ **adj.** **1** not having been the subject of a labor strike: *nonstruck Association members.*
2 not having been stricken: *occupants of the nonstruck side of the vehicle.*
3 not having been eliminated: *nonstruck jurors.*

non·such ▶ **n.** variant spelling of **NONESUCH.**

non·suit /nänˈso͞ot/ Law ▶ **v.** [with obj.] (of a judge or court) subject (a plaintiff) to the stoppage of their suit on the grounds of failure to make a legal case or bring sufficient evidence.
▶ **n.** the stoppage of a suit on such grounds.
– ORIGIN late Middle English (as a noun): from Anglo-Norman French, literally 'not pursuing' (see **NON-, SUIT**).

non·sup·port /ˌnänsəˈpôrt/ ▶ **n.** Law failure to provide for the maintenance of a child, spouse, or other dependent as required by law.

non·swim·mer /ˈnänˌswimər/ ▶ **n.** a person who cannot or does not swim.

non·tech·ni·cal /nänˈteknikəl/ ▶ **adj.** not relating to or involving science or technology: *a simple, nontechnical procedure.* ■ without specialized or technical knowledge: *a nontechnical background.* ■ not using technical terms or requiring specialized knowledge.

non·tox·ic /nänˈtäksik/ ▶ **adj.** not poisonous or toxic: *nontoxic waste.*

non·tra·di·tion·al /ˌnäntrəˈdisHənl/ ▶ **adj.** new and different from an established norm, custom, or method: *moves to encourage women into nontraditional occupations.*

non·triv·i·al /nänˈtrivēəl/ ▶ **adj.** not trivial; significant. ■ Mathematics having some variables or terms that are not equal to zero or an identity.

non·trop·i·cal sprue /nänˈträpikəl ˈspro͞o/ ▶ **n.** see **SPRUE[2]**.

non-U /nänˈyo͞o/ ▶ **adj.** informal, chiefly Brit. (of language or social behavior) not characteristic of the upper social classes; not socially acceptable to certain people.
– ORIGIN 1950s: from **NON-** + **U[3]**.

non·u·ni·form /ˌnänˈyo͞onəˌfôrm/ ▶ **adj.** not uniform, regular, or constant; varying.
– DERIVATIVES **non·u·ni·form·i·ty** **n.**, **non·u·ni·form·ly** **adv.**

non·un·ion /nänˈyo͞onyən/ ▶ **adj.** not belonging or relating to a labor union: *nonunion farm workers | nonunion agreements.* ■ (of a company) not having labor union members: *a high proportion of newly established firms are nonunion.* ■ not done or produced by members of a labor union: *he sells nonunion doughnuts.*

non·un·ion·ized /ˌnänˈyo͞onyənīzd/ ▶ **n.** not belonging to or recognizing a labor union: *a nonunionized workforce.*

non·use /ˌnänˈyo͞os/ (also **nonusage**) ▶ **n.** the refusal or failure to use something.
– DERIVATIVES **non·us·er** **n.**

non·ver·bal /nänˈvərbəl/ ▶ **adj.** not involving or using words or speech: *forms of nonverbal communication.*
– DERIVATIVES **non·ver·bal·ly** **adv.**

non·vi·a·ble /ˌnänˈvīəbəl/ ▶ **adj.** **1** not able to develop, grow, or survive: *nonviable embryos.*
2 not practical or workable.
– DERIVATIVES **non·vi·a·bil·i·ty** **n.**

non·vin·tage /nänˈvintij/ ▶ **adj.** denoting a wine that is not made from the crop of a single identified district in a good year.

non·vi·o·lence /nänˈvīələns/ ▶ **n.** the use of peaceful means, not force, to bring about political or social change.

non·vi·o·lent /ˌnänˈvīələnt/ ▶ **adj.** (esp. of political action or resistance) characterized by nonviolence. ■ (esp. of a person) not using violence.
– DERIVATIVES **non·vi·o·lent·ly** **adv.**

non·vol·a·tile /nänˈvälətl/ ▶ **adj.** not volatile. ■ Computing (of a computer's memory) retaining data even if there is a break in the power supply.

non·vot·ing /nänˈvōtiNG/ ▶ **adj.** not having or using a vote: *a nonvoting delegate | nonvoting stock.*
– DERIVATIVES **non·vot·er** **n.**

non·white /ˌnänˈ(h)wīt/ ▶ **adj.** denoting or relating to a person whose origin is not predominantly European.
▶ **n.** a person whose origin is not predominantly European.

> **USAGE** The term **nonwhite** has been objected to as politically incorrect on the grounds that it assumes that the norm is white. However, although alternatives such as **person of color** have been put forward in recent years, they have not yet become widespread, or at least not appropriate in all contexts. **Nonwhite** continues to be broadly accepted where a collective term is required to show a distinction, as in statistical or demographic categories. See also **PERSON OF COLOR.**

non·word /ˈnänˈwərd/ ▶ **n.** a group of letters or speech sounds that looks or sounds like a word but is not accepted as such by native speakers.

non·work·ing /ˌnänˈwərkiNG/ ▶ **adj.** not earning an income: *a nonworking spouse.* ■ not requiring or involving work for money: *nonworking days.* ■ not functional or operational: *responsible disposal of nonworking products.*
– DERIVATIVES **non·work** **n.**, **non·work·er** **n.**

non·yl /ˈnänil, ˈnō-/ ▶ **n.** [as modifier] Chemistry of or denoting an alkyl radical $-C_9H_{19}$, derived from nonane.

non·ze·ro /nänˈzērō/ ▶ **adj.** having a positive or negative value; not equal to zero.

noo·dle[1] /ˈno͞odl/ ▶ **n.** (usu. **noodles**) a strip, ring, or tube of pasta or a similar dough, typically made with egg and usually eaten with a sauce or in a soup.
– ORIGIN late 18th cent.: from German *Nudel*, of unknown origin.

noo·dle[2] ▶ **n.** informal a stupid or silly person. ■ a person's head.
– ORIGIN mid 18th cent.: of unknown origin. The sense 'head' dates from the early 20th cent.

noo·dle[3] /ˈno͞odl/ ▶ **v.** [no obj.] informal improvise or play casually on a musical instrument: *tapes of him noodling on his guitar* | (as noun **noodling**) *ambient synthesizer noodling.*
– ORIGIN mid 19th cent.: of unknown origin.

noog·ie /ˈno͝ogē/ ▶ **n.** a hard poke or grind with the knuckles, esp. on a person's head.
– ORIGIN 1970s: perhaps a diminutive of **KNUCKLE.**

nook /no͝ok/ ▶ **n.** a corner or recess, esp. one offering seclusion or security: *the nook beside the fire.*
– PHRASES **every nook and cranny** every part or aspect of something: *the party reached into every nook and cranny of people's lives.*
– ORIGIN Middle English (denoting a corner or fragment): of unknown origin.

n

nook·y /ˈnŏŏkē/ (also **nookie**) ▶ **n.** vulgar slang sexual activity or intercourse.
– ORIGIN early 20th cent.: perhaps from **NOOK**.

noon /nōōn/ ▶ **n.** twelve o'clock in the day; midday: *his classes let out at noon | the service starts at **twelve noon**.*
– ORIGIN Old English *nōn* 'the ninth hour from sunrise, i.e., approximately 3 p.m.,' from Latin *nona (hora)* 'ninth hour'; compare with **NONE²**.

noon·day /ˈnōōn,dā/ ▶ **n.** the middle of the day: [as modifier] *the blinds were lowered to keep out the noonday sun.*

no one ▶ **pron.** no person; not a single person: *no one came | she told no one she was going.*

noon·er /ˈnōōnər/ ▶ **n.** informal an event that occurs in the middle of the day, esp. an act of sexual intercourse.

noon·ing /ˈnōōniNG/ ▶ **n.** dialect a rest or meal at midday.

noon·tide /ˈnōōn,tīd/ (also **noontime** /-,tīm/) ▶ **n.** literary noon.

noose /nōōs/ ▶ **n.** a loop with a running knot, tightening as the rope or wire is pulled and typically used to hang people or trap animals. ■ (**the noose**) death by hanging. ■ (**the noose**) a difficult situation regarded as a restraint or bond: *the West is exploring ways to **tighten the economic noose**.*
▶ **v.** [with obj.] put a noose on (someone): *she was noosed and hooded, then strangled by the executioner.* ■ catch (an animal) with a noose. ■ form (a rope) into a noose.
– PHRASES **put one's head in a noose** bring about one's own downfall.
– ORIGIN late Middle English: probably via Old French *no(u)s* from Latin *nodus* 'knot.'

no·o·sphere /ˈnōə,sfi(ə)r/ ▶ **n.** a postulated sphere or stage of evolutionary development dominated by consciousness, the mind, and interpersonal relationships (frequently with reference to the writings of Teilhard de Chardin).
– ORIGIN 1940s: from French *noösphere*, based on Greek *noos* 'mind.'

Noot·ka /ˈnōōtkə, ˈnŏŏt-/ ▶ **n.** (pl. **same** or **Nootkas**)
1 a member of an American Indian people of Vancouver Island, Canada.
2 the Wakashan language of this people.
▶ **adj.** of or relating to this people or their language.
– ORIGIN named after *Nootka* Sound, an inlet on the coast of Vancouver Island.

n

Noot·ka cy·press ▶ **n.** a conical cypress whose foliage has a turpentine smell when crushed. Native to western North America and typically growing at high altitudes, it is one of the parent species of the Leyland cypress. Also called **ALASKA CEDAR**. ● *Chamaecyparis nootkatensis*, family Cupressaceae.

no·o·trop·ic /,nōəˈträpik/ ▶ **adj.** (of a drug) used to enhance memory or other cognitive functions.
▶ **n.** a drug of this kind.
– ORIGIN 1970s: from French *nootrope* (from Greek *noos* 'mind' + *tropē* 'turning') + **-IC**.

n.o.p. (also **NOP**) ▶ **abbr.** not our publication.

no·pal /ˈnōpəl, nōˈpäl/ ▶ **n.** (pl. **nopales** /-ˈpäles/) a cactus that is a major food plant of the bugs from which cochineal is obtained. ● Genus *Nopalea*, family Cactaceae: several species, in particular *N. cochinellifera*. ■ (**nopales**) the edible fleshy pads of this cactus, used as a staple in Mexican cuisine. ■ the prickly pear cactus, when used in food supplements and herbal preparations.
– ORIGIN mid 18th cent.: via French and Spanish from Nahuatl *nopalli* 'cactus.'

no·pal·es /nōˈpäles/ ▶ **n.** the fleshy leaves of a prickly pear cactus, used as an ingredient in Mexican cuisine.

nope /nōp/ ▶ **exclam.** informal variant of **NO**.

nor /nôr/ ▶ **conj. & adv. 1** used before the second or further of two or more alternatives (the first being introduced by a negative such as "neither" or "not") to indicate that they are each untrue or each do not happen: *they were neither cheap nor convenient | the sheets were never washed, nor the towels, nor his shirts.* ■ [as adv.] literary term for **NEITHER**: *nor God nor demon can undo the done.*
2 used to introduce a further negative statement: *the struggle did not end, nor was it any less diminished.*
3 [conjunction or prep.] archaic or dialect than: *she thinks she knows better nor me.*
▶ **n.** (usu. **NOR**) Electronics a Boolean operator that gives the value one if and only if all operands have a value of zero and otherwise has a value of zero. ■ (also **NOR gate**) a circuit that produces an output signal only when there are no signals on any of the input connections.
– ORIGIN Middle English: contraction of Old English *nother* 'neither.'

USAGE On the use of **neither ... nor**, see usage at **NEITHER**.

nor' /nôr/ ▶ **abbr.** (esp. in compounds) north: *seek shelter from a raging nor'easter.*

nor- ▶ **prefix** Chemistry denoting an organic compound derived from another, in particular by the shortening of a chain or ring by the removal of one methylene group or by the replacement of one or more methyl side chains by hydrogen atoms: *norepinephrine.*
– ORIGIN from *nor(mal)*.

NORAD /ˈnôr,ad/ ▶ **abbr.** North American Aerospace Defense Command.

nor·a·dren·a·line /,nôrəˈdrenəlin/ (also **noradrenalin**) ▶ **n.** another term for **NOREPINEPHRINE**.
– ORIGIN 1930s: from **NOR-** + **ADRENALINE**.

Nor·dic /ˈnôrdik/ ▶ **adj.** of or relating to Scandinavia, Finland, Iceland, and the Faroe Islands. ■ relating to or denoting a physical type of northern European peoples characterized by tall stature, a bony frame, light coloring, and a dolichocephalic head. ■ Skiing relating to or denoting the disciplines of cross-country skiing or ski jumping. Often contrasted with **ALPINE**.
▶ **n.** a native of Scandinavia, Finland, or Iceland.
– ORIGIN from French *nordique*, from *nord* 'north.'

Nord·ic walk·ing ▶ **n.** a sport or activity that involves walking across country with the aid of long poles resembling ski poles.

Nord·kapp /ˈnŏŏr,käp/ Norwegian name for **NORTH CAPE**.

Nord·kyn /ˈnŏŏrkin, -,kYn/ a promontory on the northern coast of Norway, to the east of North Cape, the northernmost point on the European mainland.

Nord-Pas-de-Ca·lais /nôr ,pä də käˈlā/ a region of northern France, on the border with Belgium.

Nord·rhein-West·fa·len /ˈnôrt,rīn vestˈfälən/ German name for **NORTH RHINE–WESTPHALIA**.

nor·ep·i·neph·rine /,nôrepəˈnefrin/ ▶ **n.** Biochemistry a hormone that is released by the adrenal medulla and by the sympathetic nerves and functions as a neurotransmitter. It is also used as a drug to raise blood pressure. Also called **NORADRENALINE**. ● Chem. formula: $(HO)_2C_6H_3CHOHCH_2NH_2$.
– ORIGIN 1940s: from **NOR-** + **EPINEPHRINE**.

Nor·folk /ˈnôrfək/ **1** a county on the eastern coast of England, east of an inlet of the North Sea called the Wash; county town, Norwich.
2 an industrial and naval port city in southeastern Virginia, on Hampton Roads; pop. 234,220 (est. 2008).

Nor·folk Is·land an island in the Pacific Ocean, off the eastern coast of Australia, administered since 1913 as an external territory of Australia; pop. 2,100 (est. 2009).

Nor·folk Is·land pine (also **Norfolk pine**) ▶ **n.** an evergreen tree having horizontal branches with upswept shoots bearing small scalelike leaves. Native to Norfolk Island, it is widely grown as a houseplant. ● *Araucaria heterophylla*, family Araucariaceae.

Nor·folk jack·et ▶ **n.** a loose belted jacket with box pleats, typically made of tweed.

Nor·folk ter·ri·er ▶ **n.** a small thickset terrier of a breed with a rough red or black-and-tan coat and drop ears.

Nor·ge /ˈnôrgə/ Norwegian name for **NORWAY**.

no·ri /ˈnôrē/ ▶ **n.** an edible seaweed, eaten either fresh or dried in sheets, esp. by the Japanese.
– ORIGIN Japanese.

no·ri·a /ˈnôrēə/ ▶ **n.** a device for raising water from a stream or river, consisting of a chain of pots or buckets revolving around a wheel driven by the water current.
– ORIGIN via Spanish from Arabic *nāʻūra*.

No·ri·e·ga /,nôrēˈägə/, Manuel (Antonio Morena) (1940–), Panamanian statesman and general; head of state 1983–89. Charged with drug trafficking by a US grand jury in 1988, he eventually surrendered to US troops sent into Panama to capture him; he was brought to trial and convicted in 1992.

nor·ite /ˈnôrīt/ ▶ **n.** Geology a coarse-grained plutonic rock similar to gabbro but containing hypersthene.
– ORIGIN late 19th cent.: from **NORWAY** + **-ITE¹**.

norm /nôrm/ ▶ **n. 1** (**the norm**) something that is usual, typical, or standard: *this system has been the norm in Germany for decades.* ■ (usu. **norms**) a standard or pattern, esp. of social behavior, that is typical or expected of a group: *the norms of good behavior in the civil service.* ■ a required standard; a level to be complied with or reached: [with modifier] *the 7% pay norm had been breached again.*
2 Mathematics the product of a complex number and its conjugate, equal to the sum of the squares of its real and imaginary components, or the positive square root of this sum. ■ an analogous quantity used to represent the magnitude of a vector.
– ORIGIN early 19th cent.: from Latin *norma* 'precept, rule, carpenter's square.'

norm. ▶ **abbr.** normal.

Nor·ma /ˈnôrmə/ Astronomy a small and inconspicuous southern constellation (the Rule), lying partly in the Milky Way between Lupus and Ara. ■ (as genitive **Normae** /ˈnôrmē/) used with a preceding letter or numeral to designate a star in this constellation: *the star Gamma Normae.*
– ORIGIN Latin, 'carpenter's square.'

Nor·mal /ˈnôrməl/ a town in central Illinois, home to Illinois State University (originally a *normal*, or teachers, school); pop. 52,056 (est. 2008).

nor·mal /ˈnôrməl/ ▶ **adj. 1** conforming to a standard; usual, typical, or expected: *it's quite **normal** for puppies to bolt their food | normal working hours.* ■ (of a person) free from physical or mental disorders.
2 technical (of a line, ray, or other linear feature) intersecting a given line or surface at right angles.
3 Medicine (of a salt solution) containing the same salt concentration as the blood. ■ Chemistry, dated (of a solution) containing one gram-equivalent of solute per liter.
4 Geology denoting a fault or faulting in which a relative downward movement occurred in the strata situated on the upper side of the fault plane.
▶ **n. 1** the usual, average, or typical state or condition: *her temperature was **above normal** | the service will be **back to normal** next week.* ■ informal a person who is conventional or healthy .
2 technical a line at right angles to a given line or surface.
– ORIGIN mid 17th cent. (in the sense 'right-angled'): from Latin *normalis*, from *norma* 'carpenter's square' (see **NORM**). Current senses date from the early 19th cent.

nor·mal dis·tri·bu·tion ▶ **n.** Statistics a function that represents the distribution of many random variables as a symmetrical bell-shaped graph.

nor·mal form ▶ **n. 1** Computing a defined standard structure for relational databases in which a relation may not be nested within another relation.
2 Philosophy a standard structure or format in which all propositions in a (usually symbolic) language can be expressed.

nor·mal·i·ty /nôrˈmalitē/ (also **normalcy** /ˈnôrməlsē/) ▶ **n.** the condition of being normal; the state of being usual, typical, or expected: *let's try to get some normality back in our lives.*

USAGE **Normalcy** has been criticized as an uneducated alternative to **normality**, but actually is a common American usage and can be taken as standard: *we are anticipating a return to normalcy.*

nor·mal·ize /ˈnôrmə,līz/ ▶ **v. 1** [with obj.] bring or return to a normal condition or state: *he wants to begin negotiations to normalize relations* | [no obj.] *the situation had normalized.*
2 [with obj.] Mathematics multiply (a series, function, or item of data) by a factor that makes the norm or some associated quantity such as an integral equal to a desired value (usually 1). ■ Computing (in floating-point representation) express (a number) in the standard form with regard to the position of the radix point, usually immediately following the first nonzero digit.
– DERIVATIVES **nor·mal·i·za·tion** /,nôrmələˈzāSHən/ **n.**, **nor·mal·iz·er n.**

nor·mal·ly /ˈnôrməlē/ ▶ **adv. 1** [sentence adverb] under normal or usual conditions; as a rule: *normally, it takes three or four years to complete the training.*
2 in a normal manner; in the usual way: *try to breathe normally.*
3 technical at right angles to a given line or surface.

nor·mal·ly as·pi·rat·ed ▶ **adj.** (of an engine) not turbocharged or supercharged.

nor·mal school ▶ **n.** formerly, a school or college for the training of teachers.

Nor·man¹ /ˈnôrmən/ a city in central Oklahoma, south of Oklahoma City, home to the University of Oklahoma; pop. 106,957 (est. 2008).

Nor·man² ▶ **n. 1** a member of a people of mixed Frankish and Scandinavian origin who settled in Normandy from about AD 912 and became a dominant military power in western Europe and the Mediterranean in the 11th century. ■ in particular, any of the Normans who conquered England in 1066 or their descendants. ■ a native or inhabitant of modern Normandy. ■ any of the English kings from William I to Stephen.
2 the form of French spoken by the Normans.
▶ **adj.** of, relating to, or denoting the Normans. ■ denoting, relating to, or built in the style of

Romanesque architecture used in Britain under the Normans. ■ of or relating to modern Normandy.
– DERIVATIVES **Nor·man·esque** /ˌnôrməˈnesk/ **adj.**, **Nor·man·ism** /-ˌnizəm/ **n.**, **Nor·man·ize** /-ˌnīz/ **v.**
– ORIGIN Middle English: from Old French *Normans*, plural of *Normant*, from Old Norse *Northmathr* 'Northman.'

Nor·man³, Greg (1955–), Australian golfer; full name *Gregory John Norman*; called ***Great White Shark***. He won the Australian Open in 1980, 1985, 1987, and 1995 and the British Open in 1986 and 1993.

Nor·man⁴, Jessye (1945–), US opera singer. She is noted for her interpretations of the works of Wagner, Schubert, and Mahler.

Nor·man Con·quest the conquest of England by William of Normandy (William the Conqueror) after the Battle of Hastings in 1066.

Nor·man·dy /ˈnôrməndē/ a former province of northwestern France with a coastline on the English Channel, now divided into the two regions of Lower Normandy (Basse-Normandie) and Upper Normandy (Haute-Normandie); chief town, Rouen.

Nor·man French ▶ **n.** the northern form of Old French spoken by the Normans. ■ the variety of this used in English law courts from the 11th to 13th centuries; Anglo-Norman French. ■ the French dialect of modern Normandy.

nor·ma·tive /ˈnôrmətiv/ ▶ **adj.** formal establishing, relating to, or deriving from a standard or norm, esp. of behavior: *negative sanctions to enforce normative behavior.*
– DERIVATIVES **nor·ma·tive·ly adv.**, **nor·ma·tive·ness n.**, **nor·ma·tiv·i·ty n.**
– ORIGIN late 19th cent.: from French *normatif, -ive*, from Latin *norma* 'carpenter's square' (see NORM).

nor·mo·gly·ce·mi·a /ˌnôrmōˌglīˈsēmēə/ (Brit. **normoglycaemia**) ▶ **n.** Medicine a normal concentration of sugar in the blood (as contrasted with hyper- or hypoglycemia).
– DERIVATIVES **nor·mo·gly·ce·mic** /-ˈsēmik/ **adj.**

nor·mo·ten·sive /ˌnôrmōˈtensiv/ ▶ **adj.** Medicine having or denoting a normal blood pressure.

Norn /nôrn/ ▶ **n.** a form of Norse formerly spoken in the Orkney and Shetland Islands and some other parts of northern Scotland but largely extinct by the 19th century.
▶ **adj.** of or relating to this language.
– ORIGIN from Old Norse *norrœn* 'Norn, northern,' from *northr* 'north.'

Norns /nôrnz/ Scandinavian Mythology the three virgin goddesses of destiny (Urd or Urdar, Verdandi, and Skuld), who sit by the well of fate at the base of the ash tree Yggdrasil and spin the web of fate.
– ORIGIN from Old Norse, of unknown origin.

no·ro·vi·rus /ˈnôrəˌvīrəs/ ▶ **n.** Medicine any of various single-stranded RNA viruses comprising the Norwalk virus, which can cause acute gastroenteritis in humans. ● Genus *Norovirus*, family Caliciviridae.
– ORIGIN early 21st century: from *nor-* in *Norwalk*, Ohio (where an outbreak of gastroenteritis occurred from which the virus was isolated) + *-o-* + VIRUS.

Nor·plant /ˈnôrˌplant/ ▶ **n.** trademark a contraceptive for women consisting of small rods implanted under the skin that gradually release the hormone levonorgestrel over a number of years.
– ORIGIN 1980s: from *(levo)nor(gestrel) (im)plant.*

Nor·ris /ˈnôris/, Frank (1870–1902), US journalist and writer; full name *Benjamin Franklin Norris, Jr.* His fiction includes *McTeague: A Story of San Francisco* (1899) and *The Octopus* (1901). His unfinished trilogy *Epic of Wheat* documents the history of muckraking.

Norr·kö·ping /ˈnôrˌSHəpiNG, -ˌSHœ-/ an industrial city and port on an inlet of the Baltic Sea in southeastern Sweden; pop. 128,060 (2008).

Norse /nôrs/ ▶ **n.** **1** the Norwegian language, esp. in its medieval form. ■ the Scandinavian language group.
2 [treated as pl.] Norwegians or Scandinavians, esp. in medieval times.
▶ **adj.** of or relating to medieval Norway or Scandinavia, or their inhabitants or language.
– DERIVATIVES **Norse·man** /ˈnôrsmən/ **n.** (pl. **Norsemen**).
– ORIGIN from Dutch *noor(d)sch*, from *noord* 'north'; compare with Swedish, Danish, and Norwegian *Norsk*.

nor·te·ño /nôrˈtānyō/ ▶ **n. 1** (pl. **norteños**) an inhabitant or native of northern Mexico.
2 (also **norteña** /nôrˈtānyə/) a style of folk music, associated particularly with northern Mexico and Texas, typically featuring an accordion and using polkas and other rhythms found in the music of central European immigrants.
– ORIGIN Spanish, literally 'northerner.'

North /nôrTH/, Frederick, Lord (1732–92), British statesman; prime minister 1770–82. He sought to avoid the American Revolution but was regarded as responsible for the loss of the American colonies.

north /nôrTH/ ▶ **n.** (usu. **the north**) **1** the direction in which a compass needle normally points, toward the horizon on the left side of a person facing east, or the part of the horizon lying in this direction: *a bitter wind blew from the north | Mount Kenya is to the north of Nairobi.* ■ the compass point corresponding to this. ■ a direction in space parallel to the earth's axis of rotation and toward the point on the celestial sphere around which the stars appear to turn counterclockwise.
2 the northern part of the world or of a specified country, region, or town: *cuisine from the north of Spain | limber pine in the central Rockies, and whitebark pine and alpine larch in the north.* ■ (usu. **the North**) the northern part of the US, esp. the northeastern states that fought to preserve the Union during the Civil War: *delegates from Virginia voted to join the North.*
3 (**North**) [as name] Bridge the player occupying a designated position at the table, sitting opposite and partnering South.
▶ **adj.** [attrib.] **1** lying toward, near, or facing the north: *the north bank of the river | the north door.* ■ (of a wind) blowing from the north.
2 of or denoting the northern part of a specified area, city, or country or its inhabitants: *North African.*
▶ **adv. 1** to or toward the north: *the landscape became more dramatic as we drove north | a north-facing wall.*
2 (**north of**) above (a particular amount, cost, etc.): *they expect to spend north of $6 million for this latest campaign.*
– PHRASES **north by east** (or **west**) between north and north-northeast (or north-northwest). **up north** informal to or in the north of a country: *he's taken a teaching job up north.*
– ORIGIN Old English, of Germanic origin; related to Dutch *noord* and German *nord*.

North Af·ri·ca the northern part of the African continent, esp. the countries bordering the Mediterranean and the Red Sea.

North A·mer·i·ca a continent comprising the northern half of the American landmass, connected to South America by the Isthmus of Panama. It contains Canada, the US, Mexico, the countries of Central America, and usually Greenland.

North A·mer·i·can ▶ **adj.** of or relating to North America.
▶ **n.** a native or inhabitant of North America, esp. a citizen of the US or Canada.

North A·mer·i·can Free Trade A·gree·ment (abbr.: **NAFTA**) an agreement that came into effect in January 1994 between the US, Canada, and Mexico to remove barriers to trade between the three countries over a ten-year period.

North·amp·ton /nôrˈTHamptən/ **1** a town in southeast central England, on the Nene River; pop. 185,600 (est. 2009).
2 an industrial and commercial city in west central Massachusetts, home to Smith College; pop. 28,379 (est. 2008).

North At·lan·tic Drift a continuation of the Gulf Stream across the Atlantic Ocean and along the coast of northwestern Europe, where it has a significant warming effect on the climate.

North At·lan·tic O·cean see ATLANTIC OCEAN.

North At·lan·tic Trea·ty Or·gan·i·za·tion (abbr.: **NATO**) an association of European and North American countries, formed in 1949 for the defense of Europe and the North Atlantic against the perceived threat of Soviet aggression. By 2005, the alliance consisted of 26 countries, including several eastern European nations. NATO's purpose is to safeguard member countries by political and military means.

north·bound /ˈnôrTHˌbound/ ▶ **adj.** traveling or leading toward the north: *they slowly drove back along the shoulder of the northbound lane | northbound traffic.*

North Ca·na·di·an Riv·er (also **Beaver River**) a river that flows for 800 miles (1,300 km) from northeastern New Mexico, through Texas and Oklahoma, to the Canadian River.

North Cape a promontory on Magerøya, an island off the northern coast of Norway. North Cape is the northernmost point of the world accessible by road. Norwegian name **NORDKAPP**.

North Car·o·li·na a state in the eastern central US, on the Atlantic coast; pop. 9,222,414 (est. 2008); capital, Raleigh; statehood, Nov. 21, 1789 (12). First settled by the English in the late 1600s, it was one of the original thirteen states.
– DERIVATIVES **North Car·o·lin·i·an n. & adj.**
– ORIGIN *Carolina* from *Carolus*, the Latin name for Charles I and Charles II.

North Chan·nel the stretch of sea that separates southwestern Scotland from Northern Ireland and connects the Irish Sea to the Atlantic Ocean.

North Charles·ton a city in southeastern South Carolina, a residential suburb with naval facilities; pop. 94,407 (est. 2008).

North Chi·ca·go an industrial city in northeastern Illinois, on Lake Michigan, south of Waukegan; pop. 32,608 (est. 2008).

North Coun·try in New York state, areas north of the Mohawk and Hudson rivers that extend to the St. Lawrence Valley and Lake Ontario.

North Da·ko·ta an agricultural state in the northern central US, on the border with Canada; pop. 641,481 (est. 2008); capital, Bismarck; statehood, Nov. 2, 1889 (39). Its territory was acquired partly by the Louisiana Purchase in 1803 and partly from Britain by a treaty in 1818. The geographical center of North America lies within its boundaries.
– DERIVATIVES **North Da·ko·tan n. & adj.**

North·east /ˌnôrTHˈēst/ a region of the US, usually thought to include the six New England states, New Jersey, and the eastern portions of New York state and Pennsylvania.

north·east /ˌnôrTHˈēst/ ▶ **n. 1** (usu. **the northeast**) the point of the horizon midway between north and east: *I pointed to the northeast.* ■ the compass point corresponding to this. ■ the direction in which this lies: *the entrance was through a small door to the northeast.*
2 the northeastern part of a country, region, or town: *people from the predominantly Russian towns in the northeast | the northeast of Brazil.*
▶ **adj. 1** lying toward, near, or facing the northeast. ■ (of a wind) coming from the northeast: *there was a strong northeast wind.*
2 of or denoting the northeastern part of a specified country, region, or town, or its inhabitants: *northeast Baltimore.*
▶ **adv.** to or toward the northeast: *the ship sailed northeast | the northeast-facing slopes.*
– DERIVATIVES **north·east·ern** /-ˈēstərn/ **adj.**

north·east·er /ˌnôrTHˈēstər/ (also **nor'easter** /ˌnôrˈēstər/) ▶ **n.** a storm or wind blowing from the northeast, esp. in New England.

north·east·er·ly /ˌnôrTHˈēstərlē/ ▶ **adj. & adv.** another term for NORTHEAST.
▶ **n.** another term for NORTHEASTER.

North·east King·dom a nickname for the region that includes the three northernmost counties of Vermont.

Northeast Pas·sage a passage for ships along the northern coast of Europe and Asia, from the Atlantic Ocean to the Pacific Ocean via the Arctic Ocean, sought for many years as a possible trade route to the East. It was first navigated in 1878–79 by Swedish Arctic explorer *Baron Nordenskjöld* (1832–1901).

north·east·ward /ˌnôrTHˈēstwərd/ ▶ **adv.** toward the northeast; in a northeast direction.
▶ **adj.** situated in, directed toward, or facing the northeast.

North E·qua·to·ri·al Cur·rent an ocean current that flows west across the Pacific Ocean just north of the equator.

north·er /ˈnôrT͟Hər/ ▶ **n.** a strong cold north wind blowing in autumn and winter over Texas, Florida, and the Gulf of Mexico.

north·er·ly /ˈnôrT͟Hərlē/ ▶ **adj. & adv.** in a northward position or direction: [as adj.] *he set off in a northerly direction.* ■ (of wind) blowing from the north: [as adj.] *it will feel cold in the fresh northerly wind* | [as adv.] *the wind was gusting northerly.*
▶ **n.** (often **northerlies**) a wind blowing from the north.

north·ern /ˈnôrT͟Hərn/ ▶ **adj. 1** [attrib.] situated in the north, or directed toward or facing the north: *the northern slopes | northern Europe.* ■ (of a wind) blowing from the north.
2 living in or originating from the north: *northern breeds of cattle.* ■ of, relating to, or characteristic of the north or its inhabitants: *an unmistakable northern accent.*
– DERIVATIVES **north·ern·most** /-ˌmōst/ **adj.**
– ORIGIN Old English *northerne* (see NORTH, -ERN).

North·ern blot ▶ **n.** Biology an adaptation of the Southern blot procedure used to detect specific sequences of RNA by hybridization with complementary DNA.

north·ern·er /ˈnôrTHərnər/ (also **Northerner**) ▶ **n.** a native or inhabitant of the north, esp. of the northern US.

north·ern har·ri·er ▶ **n.** a widespread harrier of open country, the male of which is mainly pale gray and the female brown. Also called MARSH HAWK. ● *Circus cyaneus*, family Accipitridae.

north·ern hem·i·sphere the half of the earth that is north of the equator.

North·ern Ire·land a province of the United Kingdom that occupies the northeastern part of Ireland, comprised of six counties of Ulster; pop. 1,775,000 (est. 2008); capital, Belfast.

> Northern Ireland was established as a self-governing province in 1920, after refusing to be part of the Irish Free State. Domination by the Protestant majority and discrimination against the Roman Catholic minority led to violent conflicts and, from 1969, British army units were present in an attempt to keep the peace. Terrorism and sectarian violence by the Provisional IRA and other paramilitary groups, both Republican and Loyalist, resulted in the imposition of direct rule from London in 1972. Multiparty talks begun in 1996 led to an agreement between most political parties in 1998. In 1999, a devolved parliament was inaugurated, with representation from both Nationalist and Unionist groups. British troops left the province in 2007.

North·ern Lights another name for the aurora borealis. See AURORA.

North·ern Mar·i·an·a Is·lands /ˌme(ə)rēˈanə, ˌmar-, -ˈänə/ a self-governing territory in the western Pacific, comprising the Mariana Islands with the exception of Guam; pop. 51,500 (est. 2009); capital, Chalan Kanoa (on Saipan). The Northern Mariana Islands are constituted as a self-governing commonwealth in union with the US.

North·ern Neck a region in eastern Virginia between the Potomac and Rappahannock rivers, a tidewater peninsula.

North·ern Rho·de·sia /rōˈdēZHə/ former name (until 1964) of ZAMBIA.

north·ern snake·head ▶ **n.** an Asian food fish of the carp family that is also a voracious predator. It is able to survive adverse conditions and has been inadvertently released into the wild in the US. ● *Channa argus*, family Channidae.

North·ern Ter·ri·to·ry a state in northern central Australia; pop. 219,818 (2008); capital town, Darwin. The territory was annexed by the state of South Australia in 1863 and administered by the Commonwealth of Australia from 1911. It became a self-governing territory in 1978.

North Fri·sian Is·lands see FRISIAN ISLANDS.

North Ger·man·ic ▶ **n.** the northern branch of the Germanic languages, descended from Old Norse and comprising Danish, Norwegian, Swedish, Icelandic, and Faroese.
▶ **adj.** of or relating to North Germanic.

north·ing /ˈnôrTHiNG, -T͟HiNG/ ▶ **n.** distance traveled or measured northward, esp. at sea: *we should have to make 300 miles of northing.* ■ a figure or line representing northward distance on a map (expressed by convention as the second part of a grid reference, after easting).

North Is·land the most northern of the two main islands of New Zealand, separated from South Island by Cook Strait.

North Kings·town /ˈkiNGstən, ˈkiNGzˌtoun/ a town in south central Rhode Island, on the western banks of Narragansett Bay; pop. 26,539 (est. 2008).

North Ko·re·a a country in East Asia that occupies the northern part of the peninsula of Korea; pop. 22,665,300 (est. 2009); capital, Pyongyang; official language, Korean. Official name KOREA, DEMOCRATIC PEOPLE'S REPUBLIC OF.

> North Korea was formed in 1948 when Korea was partitioned along the 38th parallel. In 1950, North Korean forces invaded the south, but in the war that followed were forced back to more or less the previous border (see KOREAN WAR). A communist state, which was dominated by its leader Kim Il-sung from 1948 until 1994, North Korea has always sought Korean reunification.

– DERIVATIVES **North Ko·re·an** adj. & n.

north·land /ˈnôrTHlənd, -ˌland/ ▶ **n.** (also **northlands**) literary the northern part of a country or region.
– ORIGIN Old English (see NORTH, LAND).

North Las Ve·gas a city in southeastern Nevada, a northeastern suburb of Las Vegas; pop. 217,253 (est. 2008).

north light ▶ **n.** good natural light without direct sun, esp. as desired by artists.

North Lit·tle Rock a city in central Arkansas, an industrial center across the Arkansas River from Little Rock; pop. 59,430 (est. 2008).

North·man /ˈnôrTHmən/ ▶ **n.** (pl. **Northmen**) archaic a native or inhabitant of Scandinavia, esp. of Norway.
– ORIGIN Old English (see NORTH, MAN).

North Minch see MINCH.

north-north·east ▶ **n.** the compass point or direction midway between north and northeast.

north-north·west ▶ **n.** the compass point or direction midway between north and northwest.

North Os·se·ti·a an autonomous republic of Russia, in the Caucasus, on the border with Georgia; pop. 699,400 (est. 2009); capital, Vladikavkaz. Since 1994 it has been called Alania. See also OSSETIA.

North Platte /plat/ a city in central Nebraska, where the North and South Platte rivers meet; pop. 24,107 (est. 2008).

North Platte Riv·er a river that flows for 620 miles (960 km) from northern Colorado, across Wyoming and Nebraska, to the Platte River. Its valley was part of the Oregon Trail.

North Pole ▶ **n.** see POLE².

North Rhine–West·pha·lia a state in west central Germany; capital, Düsseldorf. German name NORDRHEIN-WESTFALEN.

North Sea an arm of the Atlantic Ocean that lies between the mainland of Europe and the coast of Britain, important for its oil and gas deposits.

North Slope a name for regions of Alaska that lie north of the Brooks Range and extend to the Arctic Ocean. Sparsely populated, it is a site of much oil exploration and extraction.

North Star Astronomy another term for POLARIS.

North Star State a nickname for the state of MINNESOTA.

North Ton·a·wan·da /ˌtänəˈwändə/ an industrial city in western New York, on the Niagara River, north of Buffalo, at the western end of the historic Erie Canal; pop. 31,222 (est. 2008).

North Uist see UIST.

Northumb. ▶ **abbr.** Northumberland.

North·um·ber·land /nôrˈTHəmbərlənd/ a county in northeastern England, on the Scottish border.

North·um·ber·land Strait /nôrˈTHəmbərlənd/ an ocean passage in the Gulf of St. Lawrence that separates Prince Edward Island from New Brunswick and Nova Scotia.

North·um·bri·a /nôrˈTHəmbrēə/ an area of northeastern England. ■ an ancient Anglo-Saxon kingdom in northeastern England that extends from the Humber Estuary to the Forth River.
– DERIVATIVES **North·um·bri·an** adj. & n.
– ORIGIN from obsolete *Northumber*, denoting a person living beyond the Humber.

North Vi·et·nam a former communist republic in Southeast Asia, in the northern part of Vietnam, created in 1954 when Vietnam was partitioned. After defeating noncommunist South Vietnam in the Vietnam War, it declared a reunited, socialist republic (1976).

north·ward /ˈnôrTHwərd/ ▶ **adj.** in a northerly direction.
▶ **adv.** (also **northwards**) toward the north.
▶ **n.** (**the northward**) the direction or region to the north.
– DERIVATIVES **north·ward·ly** adj. & adv.

north·west /ˌnôrTHˈwest/ ▶ **n.** (usu. **the northwest**) **1** the point of the horizon midway between north and west: *he pointed to the northwest.* ■ the compass point corresponding to this. ■ the direction in which this lies.
2 the northwestern part of a country, region, or town: *they had originally come from someplace in the northwest of Mexico.*
▶ **adj. 1** lying toward, near, or facing the northwest: *the northwest corner of the square.* ■ (of a wind) blowing from the northwest.
2 of or denoting the northwestern part of a country, region, or town, or its inhabitants: *northwest Europe.*
▶ **adv.** to or toward the northwest: *he turned onto the highway and headed northwest.*
– DERIVATIVES **north·west·ern** /-ˈwestərn/ adj.

North·west An·gle a forested region in northern Minnesota that is separated from the rest of the state and the US by Lake of the Woods. It is the most northern part of the contiguous US.

north·west·er /ˌnôrTHˈwestər/ ▶ **n.** a wind or storm blowing from the northwest.

north·west·er·ly /ˌnôrTHˈwestərlē/ ▶ **adj. & adv.** another term for NORTHWEST.
▶ **n.** another term for NORTHWESTER.

North-West Fron·tier Prov·ince a province of northwestern Pakistan, on the border with Afghanistan; capital, Peshawar.

Northwest Pas·sage a sea passage along the northern coast of the North American continent, through the Canadian Arctic from the Atlantic Ocean to the Pacific Ocean. It was sought for many years as a possible trade route by explorers that included Sebastian Cabot, Sir Francis Drake, and Martin Frobisher; it was first navigated 1903-06 by Roald Amundsen.

North·west Ter·ri·to·ries a territory of northern Canada, between Yukon Territory and Nunavut; capital: Yellowknife. Much of it consists of sparsely inhabited forests and tundra. The Northwest Territories, then including the land that is now Nunavut, was ceded by Britain to Canada in 1870. Nunavut became a separate territory in 1999.

North·west Ter·ri·to·ry a region and former territory of the US that lies between the Mississippi and Ohio rivers and the Great Lakes. It was acquired in 1783 after the American Revolution and now forms the states of Indiana, Ohio, Michigan, Illinois, and Wisconsin.

north·west·ward /ˌnôrTHˈwestwərd/ ▶ **adv.** (also **northwestwards**) toward the northwest; in a northwest direction.
▶ **adj.** situated in, directed toward, or facing the northwest.

Nor·walk /ˈnôrˌwôk/ **1** a city in southwestern California, southeast of Los Angeles; pop. 102,982 (est. 2008).
2 an industrial city in southwestern Connecticut, on Long Island Sound; pop. 83,185 (est. 2008).

Nor·walk vi·rus ▶ **n.** a virus that can cause epidemics of severe gastroenteritis. It has been subsumed under the genus *Norovirus*.
– ORIGIN 1970s: from *Norwalk*, a town in Ohio where an outbreak of gastroenteritis occurred from which the virus was isolated.

Nor·way /ˈnôrˌwā/ a mountainous European country on the northern and western coastline of Scandinavia, on the Norwegian Sea and the Arctic Ocean; pop. 4,660,500 (est. 2009); capital, Oslo; language, Norwegian (official). Norwegian name NORGE.

> Norway was united with Denmark and Sweden by the Union of Kalmar in 1397, but after Sweden's withdrawal in 1523 became subject to Denmark. Ceded to Sweden in 1814, Norway emerged as an independent kingdom in 1905. An invitation to join the EC was rejected after a referendum in 1972; an application to join the European Union twenty years later was accepted by the European Parliament but failed to win approval in a 1994 referendum.

Nor·way lob·ster ▶ **n.** another term for LANGOUSTINE.

Nor·way ma·ple ▶ **n.** a large Eurasian maple with yellow flowers that appear before the lobed leaves, widely planted as an ornamental shade tree. ● *Acer platanoides*, family Aceraceae.

Nor·way rat ▶ **n.** another term for BROWN RAT.

Nor·way spruce ▶ **n.** a long-coned European spruce that is widely grown as an ornamental and for timber and pulp. ● *Picea abies*, family Pinaceae.

Nor·we·gian /nôrˈwējən/ ▶ **adj.** of or relating to Norway or its people or language.
▶ **n. 1** a native or inhabitant of Norway, or a person of Norwegian descent.
2 the North Germanic language of Norway.

> Norwegian today exists in two forms, *Bokmål*, the more widely used, a modified form of Danish, and *Nynorsk* ('new Norwegian'), a 19th-century literary form devised from the country dialects most closely descended from Old Norse and considered to be a purer form of the language than *Bokmål*.

– ORIGIN from medieval Latin *Norvegia* 'Norway' (from Old Norse *Norvegr*, literally 'north way') + -AN.

Nor·we·gian Sea a sea that lies between Iceland and Norway and links the Arctic Ocean with the northeastern Atlantic Ocean.

Nor·wich /ˈnôr(w)iCH, ˈnôrij, ˈnär-/ a city in eastern England, the county town of Norfolk; pop. 171,500 (est. 2009).

Nor·wich ter·ri·er ▶ **n.** a small thickset terrier of a breed with a rough red or black-and-tan coat and pricked ears.

nos ▶ **abbr.** numbers.
– ORIGIN plural of **No**.

n.o.s. ▶ **abbr.** not otherwise specified.

nose /nōz/ ▶ **n.** **1** the part projecting above the mouth on the face of a person or animal, containing the nostrils and used for breathing and smelling. ■ [in sing.] the sense of smell, esp. a dog's ability to track something by its scent: *a dog with a keen nose.* ■ [in sing.] an instinctive talent for detecting something: *he has **a nose for** a good script.* ■ the aroma of a particular substance, esp. wine.
2 the front end of an aircraft, car, or other vehicle. ■ a projecting part of something: *the nose of the saddle.*
3 [in sing.] a look, esp. out of curiosity: *she wanted a good **nose around** the house.* ■ informal a police informer.
▶ **v.** **1** [no obj.] (of an animal) thrust its nose against or into something, esp. in order to smell it: *the pony nosed at the straw.* ■ [with obj.] smell or sniff (something).
2 [no obj.] investigate or pry into something: *I was anxious to get inside and **nose around** her house | she's always **nosing into** my business.* ■ [with obj.] detect in such a way.
3 [no obj.] (of a vehicle or its driver) make one's way cautiously forward: *he turned left and nosed into an empty parking space.* ■ (of a competitor) manage to achieve a winning or leading position, esp. by a small margin: *they nosed ahead by one point.*
– PHRASES **by a nose** (of a victory) by a very narrow margin. **count noses** count people, typically in order to determine the numbers in a vote. **cut off one's nose to spite one's face** hurt oneself in the course of trying to hurt another. **give someone a bloody nose** inflict a resounding defeat on someone. **have one's nose in a book** be reading studiously or intently. **keep one's nose clean** informal stay out of trouble. **keep one's nose out of** refrain from interfering in (someone else's affairs). **keep one's nose to the grindstone** see GRINDSTONE. **nose to tail** (of vehicles) moving or standing close behind one another, esp. in heavy traffic. **not see further than one's** (or **the end of one's**) **nose** be unwilling or fail to consider different possibilities or to foresee the consequences of one's actions. **on the nose 1** to a person's sense of smell: *the wine is pungently smoky and peppery on the nose.* **2** informal precisely: *at ten on the nose the van pulled up.* **3** informal (of betting) on a horse to win (as opposed to being placed). **put someone's nose out of joint** informal upset or annoy someone. **speak through one's nose** pronounce words with a nasal twang. **turn one's nose up at something** informal show distaste or contempt for something: *he turned his nose up at the job.* **under someone's nose** informal directly in front of someone: *he thrust the paper under the inspector's nose.* ■ (of an action) committed openly and boldly, but without someone noticing or noticing in time to prevent it. **with one's nose in the air** haughtily: *she walked past the cars with her nose in the air.*
– DERIVATIVES **nosed adj.** [in combination] *snub-nosed*, **nose·less adj.**
– ORIGIN Old English *nosu*; related to Dutch *neus*, and more remotely to German *Nase*, Latin *nasus*, and Sanskrit *nāsā*; also to NESS.

nose·bag /ˈnōzˌbag/ ▶ **n.** another term for FEEDBAG.

nose·band /ˈnōzˌband/ ▶ **n.** the strap of a bridle or halter that passes over the horse's nose and under its chin.

nose·bleed /ˈnōzˌblēd/ ▶ **n.** an instance of bleeding from the nose. ■ [as modifier] informal denoting cheap seating located in an extremely high position in a sports stadium, large theater, or concert hall: *he declined an offer of $2,200 for his game ticket in the **nosebleed section**.*

nose can·dy ▶ **n.** informal an illegal drug that is inhaled, esp. cocaine.

nose cone ▶ **n.** the cone-shaped nose of a rocket or aircraft.

nose·dive /ˈnōzˌdīv/ ▶ **n.** a steep downward plunge by an aircraft. ■ a sudden dramatic deterioration: *the player's fortunes **took a nosedive**.*
▶ **v.** [no obj.] (of an aircraft) make a nosedive. ■ deteriorate suddenly and dramatically: *massive strikes caused the economy to nosedive.*

no-see-um /nō ˈsē ˌəm/ ▶ **n.** a minute bloodsucking insect, esp. a biting midge.

nose flute ▶ **n.** a musical instrument of the flute type played by blowing through the nose rather than the mouth, associated esp. with Southeast Asia and the Pacific islands.

nose·gay /ˈnōzˌgā/ ▶ **n.** a small bunch of flowers, typically one that is sweet-scented.
– ORIGIN late Middle English: from NOSE + GAY in the obsolete sense 'ornament.'

nose guard ▶ **n.** another term for NOSE TACKLE.

nose job ▶ **n.** informal an operation involving rhinoplasty or cosmetic surgery on a person's nose.

nose leaf ▶ **n.** a fleshy leaf-shaped structure on the nose of many bats, used for echolocation.

no·se·ma /nōˈsēmə/ ▶ **n.** a spore-forming parasitic protozoan that chiefly affects insects. ● Genus *Nosema*, phylum Microspora, kingdom Protista: several species, in particular *N. apis*, which causes infectious dysentery (**nosema disease**) in honeybees.
– ORIGIN modern Latin, from Greek *nosēma* 'disease.'

nose·piece /ˈnōzˌpēs/ ▶ **n.** **1** the part of a helmet or headdress that protects a person's nose. ■ another term for NOSEBAND. ■ the central part of a pair of glasses that fits over the bridge of the nose.
2 the part of a microscope to which the objective lenses are attached.

nose ring ▶ **n.** a ring fixed in the nose of an animal, typically a bull, for leading it. ■ a ring worn in a person's nose as a piece of jewelry.

nose tack·le ▶ **n.** Football a defensive lineman positioned opposite the center.

nose wheel ▶ **n.** a landing wheel under the nose of an aircraft.

nos·ey /ˈnōzē/ ▶ **adj. & v.** variant spelling of NOSY.

nos·ey Par·ker ▶ **n.** variant spelling of NOSY PARKER.

nosh /näsн/ informal ▶ **n.** food: *filling the freezer with all kinds of nosh.* ■ a snack or small item of food: *have plenty of noshes and nibbles conveniently placed.*
▶ **v.** [no obj.] eat food enthusiastically or greedily: *there are several restaurants, so you can nosh to your heart's content* | [with obj.] *there I sat, noshing my favorite food.* ■ eat between meals: *today's grazing is different from what we used to call noshing or snacking.*
– ORIGIN early 20th cent. (denoting a snack bar): Yiddish.

nosh·er·y /ˈnäsнərē/ ▶ **n.** (pl. **nosheries**) informal a restaurant or snack bar.

no-show ▶ **n.** a person who has made a reservation, booking, or appointment but neither keeps nor cancels it.

nos·ing /ˈnōzinɢ/ ▶ **n.** a rounded edge of a step or molding. ■ a metal shield for such an edge.

nos·o·co·mi·al /ˌnäsəˈkōmēəl/ ▶ **adj.** Medicine (of a disease) originating in a hospital.
– ORIGIN mid 19th cent.: from Greek *nosokomos* 'person who tends the sick' + -IAL.

nos·ode /ˈnäsˌōd/ ▶ **n.** (in homeopathy) a preparation of substances secreted in the course of a disease, used in the treatment of that disease.
– ORIGIN late 19th cent.: from Greek *nosos* 'disease' + -ODE[1].

no·sog·ra·phy /nōˈsägrəfē/ ▶ **n.** the systematic description of diseases.
– DERIVATIVES **no·so·graph·ic** /ˌnōsəˈgrafik, ˌnä-/ **adj.**
– ORIGIN mid 17th cent.: from Greek *nosos* 'disease' + -GRAPHY.

no·sol·o·gy /nōˈsäləjē/ ▶ **n.** the branch of medical science dealing with the classification of diseases.
– DERIVATIVES **nos·o·log·i·cal** /ˌnäsəˈläjikəl/ **adj.**, **no·sol·o·gist** /-jist/ **n.**
– ORIGIN early 18th cent.: from Greek *nosos* 'disease' + -LOGY.

nos·tal·gia /näˈstaljə, nə-/ ▶ **n.** a sentimental longing or wistful affection for the past, typically for a period or place with happy personal associations: *I was overcome with acute nostalgia for my days in college.* ■ the evocation of these feelings or tendencies, esp. in commercialized form: *an evening of TV nostalgia.*
– DERIVATIVES **nos·tal·gist** /-jist/ **n.**
– ORIGIN late 18th cent. (in the sense 'acute homesickness'): modern Latin (translating German *Heimweh* 'homesickness'), from Greek *nostos* 'return home' + *algos* 'pain.'

nos·tal·gic /näˈstaljik, nə-/ ▶ **adj.** characterized by or exhibiting feelings of nostalgia.
▶ **n.** a nostalgic person: *to see classmates' E-mail addresses, nostalgics pay $36 a year.*
– DERIVATIVES **nos·tal·gi·cal·ly** /näˈstaljik(ə)lē, nə-/ **adv.**

nos·tal·gie de la boue /ˌnôstälˈzнēd lä ˈbo͞o/ ▶ **n.** a desire for degradation and depravity.
– ORIGIN French, literally 'nostalgia for mud.'

nos·toc /ˈnästäk/ ▶ **n.** Biology a microorganism composed of beaded filaments that aggregate to form a gelatinous mass, growing in water and damp places and able to fix nitrogen from the atmosphere. ● Genus *Nostoc*, division Cyanobacteria.
– ORIGIN name invented by Paracelsus.

nos·tos /ˈnästōs/ ▶ **n.** (pl. **nostoi** /-ˌtoi/) literary a homecoming.
– ORIGIN Greek.

Nos·tra·da·mus /ˌnôstrəˈdāməs, ˌnästrəˈdāməs/ (1503–66), French astrologer and physician; Latinized name of *Michel de Nostredame*. His cryptic and apocalyptic predictions in rhyming quatrains appeared in two collections, in 1555 and 1558, and their interpretation continues to be the subject of controversy.

Nos·trat·ic /näˈstratik/ ▶ **n.** a hypothetical phylum of languages of which the principal members are the Indo-European, Semitic, Altaic, and Dravidian families.
▶ **adj.** of or relating to this language phylum.
– ORIGIN 1960s: from German *nostratisch*, based on Latin *nostras, nostrat-* 'of our country.'

nos·tril /ˈnästrəl/ ▶ **n.** either of two external openings of the nasal cavity in vertebrates that admit air to the lungs and smells to the olfactory nerves.
– DERIVATIVES **nos·trilled adj.** [in combination].
– ORIGIN Old English *nosterl, nosthyrl*, from *nosu* 'nose' + *thȳr(e)l* 'hole.'

nos·trum /ˈnästrəm/ ▶ **n.** a medicine, esp. one that is not considered effective, prepared by an unqualified person. ■ a pet scheme or favorite remedy, esp. one for bringing about some social or political reform or improvement.
– ORIGIN early 17th cent.: from Latin, used in the sense '(something) of our own making,' neuter of *noster* 'our.'

nos·y /ˈnōzē/ (also **nosey**) informal ▶ **adj.** (**nosier**, **nosiest**) (of a person or their behavior) showing too much curiosity about other people's affairs: *he had to whisper to avoid being overheard by their nosy neighbors.*
▶ **v.** [no obj.] pry into something: *they don't nosy into your business like some people.*
– DERIVATIVES **nos·i·ly** /-zəlē/ **adv.**, **nos·i·ness n.**

nos·y par·ker (also **Nosy Parker**) ▶ **n.** informal an overly inquisitive person.
– ORIGIN early 20th cent.: from the picture postcard caption, "The adventures of Nosey Parker," referring to a peeping Tom in Hyde Park, London.

not /nät/ ▶ **adv.** **1** (also **n't** joined to a preceding verb) used with an auxiliary verb or "be" to form the negative: *he would not say | she isn't there | didn't you tell me?* ■ used in some constructions with other verbs: [with infinitive] *he has been warned not to touch | the pain of not knowing | she **not only** wrote the text **but also** researched the photographs.*
2 used as a short substitute for a negative clause: *maybe I'll regret it, but I hope not | "Don't you keep in touch?" "I'm afraid not." | they wouldn't know if I was telling the truth **or not**.*
3 used to express the negative of other words: *not a single attempt was made | treating the symptoms and not the cause | "How was it?" "Not so bad."* ■ used with a quantifier to exclude a person or part of a group: *not all the poems are serious.* ■ less than (used to indicate a surprisingly small quantity): *the brakes went on not ten feet from him.*
4 used in understatements to suggest that the opposite of a following word or phrase is true: *the not too distant future | not a million miles away.* ■ informal, humorous following and emphatically negating a statement: *that sounds like quality entertainment—not.* [a usage popularized by the film *Wayne's World*.]
▶ **n.** (often **NOT**) Electronics a Boolean operator with only one variable that has the value one when the variable is zero and vice versa. ■ (also **not gate**) a circuit that produces an output signal only when there is not a signal on its input.
▶ **adj.** (often **Not**) Art (of paper) not hot-pressed, and having a slightly textured surface.
– PHRASES **not at all 1** used as a polite response to thanks. **2** definitely not: *"You don't mind?" "Not at all."* **not but what** archaic nevertheless: *not but what the picture has its darker side.* **not half** see HALF. **not least** see LEAST. **not quite** see QUITE. **not that** it is not to be inferred that: *I'll never be allowed back—not that I'd want to go back.* **not a thing** nothing at all. **not very** see VERY.
– ORIGIN Middle English: contraction of the adverb NOUGHT.

no·ta be·ne /ˈnōtə ˈbenē/ (abbr.: **n.b.** or **N.B.**) ▶ **v.** [in imperative] formal observe carefully or take special notice (used in written text to draw attention to what follows).
– ORIGIN Latin, literally 'note well!'

no·ta·bil·i·ty /ˌnōtəˈbilitē/ ▶ **n.** (pl. **notabilities**) a famous or important person: *I have met a number of new notabilities including Henry Moore, the sculptor.*

no·ta·ble /ˈnōtəbəl/ ▶ **adj.** worthy of attention or notice; remarkable: *the gardens are **notable for** their collection of magnolias and camellias | the results, with one notable exception, have been superb.*

PRONUNCIATION KEY ə *ago, up*; ər *over, fur*; a *hat*; ā *ate*; ä *car*; e *let*; ē *see*; i *fit*; ī *by*; nɢ *sing*; ō *go*; ô *law, for*; oi *toy*; o͝o *good*; o͞o *goo*; ou *out*; th *thin*; t͟h *then*; zн *vision*

n

▶ n. (usu. **notables**) a famous or important person: *businessmen and local notables.*
– ORIGIN Middle English: from Old French, from Latin *notabilis* 'worthy of note,' from the verb *notare* 'to note, mark.'

no·ta·bly /ˈnōtəblē/ ▶ adv. especially; in particular: *a diet low in animal fat protects against potentially fatal diseases, notably diabetes.* ■ in a way that is striking or remarkable: [as submodifier] *such a statement is notably absent from the administration's proposals.*

no·tam /ˈnōtəm/ (also **Notam**) ▶ n. a written notification issued to pilots before a flight, advising them of circumstances relating to the state of flying.
– ORIGIN 1940s: from *no(tice) t(o) a(ir)m(en).*

no·taph·i·ly /nōˈtafəlē/ ▶ n. the collecting of banknotes as a hobby.
– DERIVATIVES **no·ta·phil·ic** /ˌnōtəˈfilik/ adj., **no·taph·i·list** /-list/ n.

no·ta·rize /ˈnōtəˌrīz/ ▶ v. [with obj.] have (a document) legalized by a notary.

no·ta·ry /ˈnōtərē/ (in full **notary public**) ▶ n. (pl. **notaries**) a person authorized to perform certain legal formalities, esp. to draw up or certify contracts, deeds, and other documents for use in other jurisdictions.
– DERIVATIVES **no·tar·i·al** /nōˈterēəl/ adj.
– ORIGIN Middle English (in the sense 'clerk or secretary'): from Latin *notarius* 'secretary,' from *nota* 'mark.'

no·tate /ˈnōˌtāt/ ▶ v. [with obj.] write (something, typically music) in notation.
– DERIVATIVES **no·ta·tor** /-ˌtātər/ n.
– ORIGIN early 20th cent.: back-formation from NOTATION.

no·ta·tion /nōˈtāSHən/ ▶ n. **1** a series or system of written symbols used to represent numbers, amounts, or elements in something such as music or mathematics: *algebraic notation.*
2 a note or annotation: *he noticed the notations in the margin.*
3 short for SCALE OF NOTATION (see SCALE[3] (sense 2 of the noun)).
– DERIVATIVES **no·ta·tion·al** /-nəl/ adj.
– ORIGIN late 16th cent.: from Latin *notatio(n-)*, from the verb *notare*, from *nota* 'mark.'

not-be·ing ▶ n. nonexistence.

notch /näCH/ ▶ n. **1** an indentation or incision on an edge or surface: *there was a notch in the end of the arrow for the bowstring.* ■ each of a series of holes for the tongue of a buckle: *he tightened his belt an extra notch.* ■ a nick made on something in order to keep a score or record: *he had a six-gun with four notches in it for guys he had killed.* ■ a point or degree in a scale: *her opinion of Nicole dropped a few notches.*
2 a deep, narrow mountain pass.
▶ v. [with obj.] **1** make notches in: (as adj. **notched**) *notched bamboo sticks.* ■ secure or insert by means of notches: *she notched her belt tighter.*
2 score or achieve (something): *she notched her second major championship.*
– DERIVATIVES **notch·er** n.
– ORIGIN mid 16th cent.: probably from Anglo-Norman French *noche*, variant of Old French *osche*, of unknown origin.

notch·back /ˈnäCHˌbak/ ▶ n. a car with a back that extends approximately horizontally from the bottom of the rear window so as to make a distinct angle with it.

notch fil·ter ▶ n. Electronics a filter that attenuates signals within a very narrow band of frequencies.

notch·y /ˈnäCHē/ ▶ adj. (**notchier, notchiest**) Brit. (of a manual gear-changing mechanism) difficult to use because the lever has to be moved accurately (as if into a narrow notch).

note /nōt/ ▶ n. **1** a brief record of facts, topics, or thoughts, written down as an aid to memory: *I'll make a note in my diary | Robyn arranged her notes on the lectern.* ■ a short comment on or explanation of a word or passage in a book or article; an annotation: *see note iv above.*
2 a short informal letter or written message: *I left her a note explaining where I was going.* ■ an official letter sent from the representative of one government to another. ■ [usu. with modifier] a short official document that certifies a particular thing: *you need a sick note from your doctor.*
3 Brit. a banknote: *a ten-pound note.*
4 a single tone of definite pitch made by a musical instrument or the human voice: *the last notes of the symphony died away.* ■ a written sign representing the pitch and duration of such a sound. ■ a key of a piano or similar instrument: *black notes | white notes.* ■ a bird's song or call, or a single tone in this: *the tawny owl has a harsh flight note.*
5 [in sing.] a particular quality or tone that reflects or expresses a mood or attitude: *there was a note of scorn in her voice | the decade could have ended on an optimistic note.* ■ any of the basic components of fragrance or flavor: *the fresh note of bergamot.*
▶ v. [with obj.] **1** notice or pay particular attention to (something): *noting his mother's unusual gaiety |* [with clause] *please note that you will not receive a reminder that final payment is due.* ■ remark upon (something), typically in order to draw someone's attention to it: *we noted earlier the difficulties inherent in this strategy.*
2 record (something) in writing: *he **noted down** her address on a piece of paper.*
– PHRASES **hit** (or **strike**) **the right** (or **wrong**) **note** say or do something in a way that is very suitable (or unsuitable) for a particular audience or occasion. **of note 1** worth paying attention to: *many of his comments are worthy of note.* **2** important; distinguished: *Roman historians of note include Livy, Tacitus, and Sallust.* **strike a false note** appear insincere or inappropriate: *she greeted him gushingly, and that struck a false note.* **strike** (or **sound**) **a note of** express (a particular feeling or view) about something: *he sounded a note of caution about the trend toward health foods.* **take note** pay attention: *investors should **take note of** the company's resilience.*
– ORIGIN Middle English (sense 4 of the noun and sense 1 of the verb): from Old French *note* (noun), *noter* (verb), from Latin *nota* 'a mark,' *notare* 'to mark.'

note·book /ˈnōtˌbo͝ok/ ▶ n. a small book with blank or ruled pages for writing notes in. ■ a laptop computer, esp. a small, slim one.

note·card /ˈnōtˌkärd/ (also **note card**) ▶ n. a decorative card with a blank space for a short message.

note·case /ˈnōtˌkās/ ▶ n. Brit. dated a small billfold or wallet.

note clus·ter ▶ n. Music a chord containing a number of closely adjacent notes. Also called TONE CLUSTER.

not·ed /ˈnōtid/ ▶ adj. well known; famous: *the restaurant **is noted for** its high standards of cuisine | a noted patron of the arts.*

note·pad /ˈnōtˌpad/ ▶ n. a pad of blank or ruled pages for writing notes on. ■ (also **notepad computer**) a pocket-sized computer that has a stylus with which the user writes on the screen to input text.

note·pa·per /ˈnōtˌpāpər/ ▶ n. paper for writing letters on.

note-per·fect ▶ adj. (of music) performed with technical perfection: *they sounded like the other time I saw them: not incredibly exciting, but note-perfect.*

note·wor·thy /ˈnōtˌwərT͟Hē/ ▶ adj. interesting, significant, or unusual: [with clause] *it is noteworthy that no one at the bank has accepted responsibility for the failure.*
– DERIVATIVES **note·wor·thi·ness** n.

not-for-prof·it ▶ adj. another term for NONPROFIT.

'noth·er /ˈnəT͟Hər/ ▶ adj. & pron. informal nonstandard spelling of ANOTHER, used to represent informal speech:*'nother thing just occurred to me.*

noth·ing /ˈnəTHiNG/ ▶ pron. not anything; no single thing: *I said nothing | there's nothing you can do | they found nothing wrong.* ■ something of no importance or concern: *"What are you laughing at?" "Oh, nothing, sir." | they are nothing to him |* [as noun] *no longer could we be treated as nothings.* ■ (in calculations) no amount; zero.
▶ adj. [attrib.] informal having no prospect of progress; of no value: *he had a series of nothing jobs.*
▶ adv. not at all: *she cares nothing for others | he looks nothing like the others.* ■ [postpositive] informal used to contradict something emphatically: *"This is a surprise." "Surprise nothing."*
– PHRASES **be nothing to do with** see DO[1]. **for nothing 1** at no cost; without payment: *working for nothing.* **2** to no purpose: *he died anyway; so it had all been for nothing.* **have nothing on someone** see HAVE. **have nothing to do with** see DO[1]. **no nothing** informal (concluding a list of negatives) nothing at all: *how could you solve it with no clues, no witnesses, no nothing?* **not for nothing** for a very good reason: *not for nothing have I got a brother-in-law who cooks professionally.* **nothing but** only: *nothing but the best will do.* **nothing daunted** see DAUNT. **nothing doing** informal **1** there is no prospect of success or agreement: *He wants to marry her. Nothing doing!* **2** nothing is happening: *there's nothing doing, and I've been waiting for weeks.* **nothing** (or **nothing else**) **for it** Brit. no alternative: *there was nothing for it but to follow.* **nothing less than** used to emphasize how extreme something is: *it was nothing less than sexual harassment.* **nothing loath** quite willing. **nothing much** not a great amount; nothing of importance. **there is nothing to it** there is no difficulty involved. **stop at nothing** see STOP. **sweet nothings** words of affection exchanged by lovers: *whispering sweet nothings in her ear.* **think nothing of it** do not apologize or feel bound to show gratitude (used as a polite response). **you ain't seen nothing yet** informal used to indicate that although something may be considered extreme or impressive, there is something even more extreme or impressive in store: *if you think that was muddy, you ain't seen nothing yet.*
– ORIGIN Old English *nān thing* (see NO, THING).

noth·ing·ness /ˈnəTHiNGnis/ ▶ n. the absence or cessation of life or existence: *the fear of the total nothingness of death.* ■ worthlessness; insignificance; unimportance: *the nothingness of it all overwhelmed him.*

noth·o·saur /ˈnōTHəˌsôr/ (also **nothosaurus** /ˌnōTHəˈsôrəs/) ▶ n. an extinct semiaquatic carnivorous reptile of the Triassic period, having a slender body and long neck, related to the plesiosaurs. ● Infraorder Nothosauria, superorder Sauropterygia.
– DERIVATIVES **noth·o·sau·ri·an** adj.
– ORIGIN 1930s: from modern Latin *Nothosauria*, from Greek *nothos* 'false' + *sauros* 'lizard.'

no·tice /ˈnōtis/ ▶ n. **1** attention; observation: *their silence did not escape my notice | it has **come to our notice** that you have been missing school.*
2 notification or warning of something, esp. to allow preparations to be made: *interest rates are subject to fluctuation without notice.* ■ a formal declaration of one's intention to end an agreement, typically one concerning employment or tenancy, at a specified time: *she handed in her notice.*
3 a displayed sheet or placard giving news or information: *the jobs were advertised in a notice posted in the common room.* ■ a small advertisement or announcement in a newspaper or magazine: *an obituary notice.* ■ (usu. **notices**) a short published review or comment about a new film, play, or book: *she had good notices in her first film.*
▶ v. [with obj.] become aware of: *he noticed the youths behaving suspiciously |* [with clause] *I noticed that she was looking tired |* [no obj.] *they were too drunk to notice.* ■ (usu. **be noticed**) treat (someone) with some degree of attention or recognition: *it was only last year that the singer really began to be noticed.* ■ archaic remark upon: *she looked so much better that Sir Charles noticed it to Lady Harriet.*
– PHRASES **at short** (or **a moment's**) **notice** with little warning or time for preparation: *tours may be canceled at short notice.* **put someone on notice** (or **serve notice**) warn someone of something about or likely to occur, esp. in a formal or threatening manner: *we're going to put foreign governments on notice that we want a change of trade policy.* **take no notice** pay no attention to someone or something. **take notice** pay attention; show signs of interest.
– ORIGIN late Middle English (sense 2 of the noun): from Old French, from Latin *notitia* 'being known,' from *notus* 'known' (see NOTION).

no·tice·a·ble /ˈnōtisəbəl/ ▶ adj. easily seen or noticed; clear or apparent: *a noticeable increase in staff motivation.* ■ noteworthy: *a noticeable new phenomenon.*
– DERIVATIVES **no·tice·a·bly** /-blē/ adv.

no·ti·fi·a·ble /ˌnōtəˈfīəbəl/ ▶ adj. denoting something, typically a serious infectious disease, that must be reported to the appropriate authorities.

no·ti·fi·ca·tion /ˌnōtəfiˈkāSHən/ ▶ n. the action of notifying someone or something: *we have yet to receive formal notification of the announcement.*

no·ti·fy /ˈnōtəˌfī/ ▶ v. (**notifies, notifying, notified**) [with obj.] inform (someone) of something, typically in a formal or official manner: *you will **be notified of** our decision as soon as possible |* [with obj. and clause] *they were notified that John had been taken prisoner.* ■ chiefly Brit. give notice of or report (something) formally or officially: *if he does not notify the occurrences, he may be guilty of nondisclosure.*
– ORIGIN late Middle English: from Old French *notifier*, from Latin *notificare* 'make known,' from *notus* 'known' (see NOTION) + *facere* 'make.'

no-till·age (also **no-till**) ▶ adj. designating a method of planting in which soil is not tilled but instead is planted by insertion of seeds in small slits, weeds being controlled by other means: *a no-tillage tomato production system using hairy vetch and subterranean clover mulches.*

no·tion /ˈnōSHən/ ▶ n. **1** a conception of or belief about something: *children have different notions about the roles of their parents | I had no notion of what her words meant.*
2 an impulse or desire, esp. one of a whimsical kind: *she had a notion to call her friend at work.*
3 (**notions**) items used in sewing, such as buttons, pins, and hooks.
– ORIGIN late Middle English: from Latin *notio(n-)* 'idea,' from *notus* 'known,' past participle of *noscere.*

no·tion·al /ˈnōsHənəl/ ▶ **adj. 1** existing only in theory or as a suggestion or idea: *notional budgets for hospital and community health services.* ■ existing only in the imagination: *Lizzie seemed to vanish into thin air, as if her presence were merely notional.*
2 Linguistics denoting or relating to an approach to grammar that is dependent on the definition of terminology (e.g., "a verb is an action word") as opposed to identification of structures and processes.
3 (in language teaching) denoting or relating to a syllabus that aims to develop communicative competence.
– DERIVATIVES **no·tion·al·ly adv.**
– ORIGIN late Middle English (in the Latin sense): from obsolete French, or from medieval Latin *notionalis* 'relating to an idea,' from *notion-* 'idea' (see **NOTION**).

no·to·chord /ˈnōtəˌkôrd/ ▶ **n.** Zoology a cartilaginous skeletal rod supporting the body in all embryonic and some adult chordate animals.
– ORIGIN mid 19th cent.: from Greek *nōton* 'back' + **CHORD²**.

No·to·gae·a /ˌnōtəˈjēə/ (also **Notogea**) Zoology a zoogeographical area comprising the Australian region.
– DERIVATIVES **No·to·gae·an adj.**
– ORIGIN mid 19th cent.: modern Latin, from Greek *notos* 'south wind' + *gaia* 'earth.'

no·to·ri·e·ty /ˌnōtəˈrīətē/ ▶ **n.** the state of being famous or well known for some bad quality or deed: *the song has gained some notoriety in the press | she has a certain notoriety.*

no·to·ri·ous /nəˈtôrēəs, nō-/ ▶ **adj.** famous or well known, typically for some bad quality or deed: *Los Angeles is* ***notorious for*** *its smog | he was a notorious drinker and womanizer.*
– DERIVATIVES **no·to·ri·ous·ly adv.**
– ORIGIN late 15th cent. (in the sense 'generally known'): from medieval Latin *notorius* (from Latin *notus* 'known') + **-OUS**.

no·tor·nis /nōˈtôrnis/ ▶ **n.** another term for **TAKAHE**.
– ORIGIN mid 19th cent.: from Greek *notos* 'south' + *ornis* 'bird.'

no·to·un·gu·late /ˌnōtōˈəNGgyəlit/ ▶ **n.** an extinct hoofed mammal of a large and varied group that lived in South America throughout the Tertiary period, finally dying out in the Pleistocene. ● Order Notoungulata: many families.
– ORIGIN late 20th cent.: from modern Latin *Notoungulata*, from Greek *notos* 'south' + Latin *ungula* 'nail.'

not-out Cricket ▶ **adj.** denoting a batsman who is not out when the team's innings ends, or a score or innings made by such a batsman.
▶ **n.** a not-out score or innings.

No·tre Dame /ˌnōtrə ˈdäm/ a Gothic cathedral in Paris, dedicated to the Virgin Mary, on the Île de la Cité (an island in the Seine). It was built between 1163 and 1250 and is noted for its innovative flying buttresses and sculptured facade.
– ORIGIN French, literally 'our lady.'

Notre Dame

no-trump ▶ **n.** Bridge a situation in which no suit is designated as trump: *she reached three no-trump after her partner had opened with a weak two bid |* [as modifier] *a no-trump contract.*

Not·ting·ham /ˈnätiNGəm/ a city in east central England, the county town of Nottinghamshire; pop. 237,600 (est. 2009).

Not·ting·ham lace /ˈnätiNGəm, -ˌham/ ▶ **n.** a type of machine-made flat lace.

Not·ting·ham·shire /ˈnätiNGəmSHər, -ˌSHi(ə)r/ a county in central England; county town, Nottingham.

Notts. ▶ **abbr.** Nottinghamshire.

no·tum /ˈnōtəm/ ▶ **n.** (pl. **nota** /-tə/) Entomology the dorsal exoskeleton of the thorax of an insect.
– DERIVATIVES **no·tal** /ˈnōtl/ **adj.**
– ORIGIN late 19th cent.: from Greek *nōton* 'back.'

not·with·stand·ing /ˌnätwiTHˈstandiNG, -wiT͟H-/ ▶ **prep.** in spite of: *notwithstanding the evidence, the consensus is that the jury will not reach a verdict |* [postpositive] *this small contretemps notwithstanding, they both had a good time.*
▶ **adv.** nevertheless; in spite of this: *she tells us she is an intellectual; notwithstanding, she faces the future as unprovided for as a beauty queen.*
▶ **conj.** although; in spite of the fact that: ***notwithstanding that*** *the hall was packed with bullies, our champion played on steadily and patiently.*
– ORIGIN late Middle English: from **NOT** + *withstanding*, present participle of **WITHSTAND**, on the pattern of Old French *non obstant* 'not providing an obstacle to.'

Nouak·chott /nəˈwäkˌSHät/ the capital of Mauritania, situated on the Atlantic coast; pop. 673,000 (est. 2007).

nou·gat /ˈno͞ogit/ ▶ **n.** a candy made from sugar or honey, nuts, and egg white.
– ORIGIN early 19th cent.: from French, from Provençal *nogat*, from *noga* 'nut.'

nou·ga·tine /ˌno͞ogəˈtēn/ ▶ **n.** nougat covered with chocolate.
– ORIGIN late 19th cent.: from **NOUGAT** + *-ine* 'resembling' (see **-INE¹**).

nought ▶ **n. & pron.** variant spelling of **NAUGHT**.

nought·ies /ˈnôtēz/ ▶ **plural n.** chiefly Brit. the decade from 2000 to 2009.
– ORIGIN 1990s: from *nought* 'zero,' on the pattern of *twenties, thirties*, etc.

noughts and cross·es ▶ **plural n.** [treated as sing.] British term for **TIC-TAC-TOE**.

Nou·mé·a /no͞oˈmāə/ the capital of the island of New Caledonia; pop. 91,386 (2004). Former name **PORT DE FRANCE**.

nou·me·non /ˈno͞oməˌnän/ ▶ **n.** (pl. **noumenona** /-nə/) (in Kantian philosophy) a thing as it is in itself, as distinct from a thing as it is knowable by the senses through phenomenal attributes.
– DERIVATIVES **nou·me·nal** /-nəl/ **adj.**
– ORIGIN late 18th cent.: via German from Greek, literally '(something) conceived,' from *noien* 'conceive, apprehend.'

noun /noun/ ▶ **n.** Grammar a word (other than a pronoun) used to identify any of a class of people, places, or things (**common noun**), or to name a particular one of these (**proper noun**).
– DERIVATIVES **noun·al** /ˈnounəl/ **adj.**
– ORIGIN late Middle English: from Anglo-Norman French, from Latin *nomen* 'name.'

noun phrase ▶ **n.** Grammar a word or group of words that functions in a sentence as subject, object, or prepositional object.

nour·ish /ˈnəriSH, ˈnə-riSH/ ▶ **v.** [with obj.] **1** provide with the food or other substances necessary for growth, health, and good condition: *I was doing everything I could to nourish and protect the baby |* figurative *spiritual resources that nourished her in her darkest hours.* ■ enhance the fertility of (soil): *a clay base nourished with plant detritus.*
2 keep (a feeling or belief) in one's mind, typically for a long time: *he has long nourished an ambition to bring the show to Broadway.*
– DERIVATIVES **nour·ish·er n.**
– ORIGIN Middle English: from Old French *noriss-*, lengthened stem of *norir*, from Latin *nutrire* 'feed, cherish.'

nour·ish·ing /ˈnəriSHiNG, ˈnə-ri-/ ▶ **adj.** (of food) containing substances necessary for growth, health, and good condition: *a simple but nourishing meal.*
– DERIVATIVES **nour·ish·ing·ly adv.**

nour·ish·ment /ˈnəriSHmənt, ˈnə-riSH-/ ▶ **n.** the food or other substances necessary for growth, health, and good condition: *tubers from which plants obtain nourishment.* ■ the action of nourishing someone or something: *they suck out the sap and eliminate from it a sweet liquid for the nourishment of their young.*

nous /no͞os, nous/ ▶ **n. 1** Philosophy the mind or intellect.
2 informal, chiefly Brit. common sense; practical intelligence: *if he had any nous at all, he'd sell the movie rights.*
– ORIGIN late 17th cent. (sense 1): from Greek, 'mind, intelligence, intuitive apprehension.'

nou·veau /ˈno͞ovō, no͞oˈvō/ ▶ **adj.** informal **1** short for **NOUVEAU RICHE**.
2 modern; up to date.

nou·veau riche /ˈno͞ovō ˈrēSH/ ▶ **n.** (treated as pl., usu. **the nouveau riche**) people who have recently acquired wealth, typically those perceived as ostentatious or lacking in good taste.
▶ **adj.** of, relating to, or characteristic of such people: *nouveau-riche social climbers.*
– ORIGIN French, literally 'new rich.'

nou·veau ro·man /ˌno͞ovō rōˈmän/ ▶ **n.** a style of avant-garde French novel that came to prominence in the 1950s. It rejected the plot, characters, and omniscient narrator central to the traditional novel in an attempt to reflect more faithfully the sometimes random nature of experience.
– ORIGIN French, literally 'new novel.'

nou·velle /no͞oˈvəl/ ▶ **adj.** of, relating to, or specializing in nouvelle cuisine: *nouvelle bistros.*

Nou·velle-Ca·lé·do·nie /no͞oˈvel ˌkälədôˈnē/ French name for **NEW CALEDONIA**.

nou·velle cui·sine /no͞oˈvel kwiˈzēn/ ▶ **n.** a modern style of cooking that avoids rich, heavy foods and emphasizes the freshness of the ingredients and the presentation of the dishes.
– ORIGIN French, literally 'new cooking.'

nou·velle vague /no͞oˈvel ˌväg/ ▶ **n.** a grouping of French movie directors in the late 1950s and 1960s who reacted against established French cinema and sought to make more individualistic and stylistically innovative films. Exponents included Claude Chabrol, Jean-Luc Godard, Alain Resnais, and François Truffaut.
– ORIGIN French, literally 'new wave.'

Nov. ▶ **abbr.** November.

no·va /ˈnōvə/ ▶ **n.** (pl. **novae** /-vē, -ˌvī/ or **novas**) Astronomy a star showing a sudden large increase in brightness and then slowly returning to its original state over a few months. See also **SUPERNOVA**.
– ORIGIN late 19th cent.: from Latin, feminine of *novus* 'new' (because such stars were thought to be newly formed).

no·vac·u·lite /nōˈvakyəˌlīt/ ▶ **n.** Geology a hard, dense, fine-grained siliceous rock resembling chert, with a high content of microcrystalline quartz.
– ORIGIN late 18th cent.: from Latin *novacula* 'razor' + **-ITE¹**.

No·va Lis·bo·a /ˈnōvə lēZHˈbōə, ˌnôvə lēZHˈvōə/ former name (until 1978) for **HUAMBO**.

No·va Sco·tia /ˈnōvə ˈskōSHə/ **1** a peninsula on the southeastern coast of Canada that projects into the Atlantic Ocean and separates the Bay of Fundy from the Gulf of St. Lawrence.
2 a province in eastern Canada that consists of the Nova Scotia peninsula and adjoining Cape Breton Island; pop. 913,462 (2006); capital, Halifax. Settled as Acadia by the French in the early 18th century, it changed hands several times before being awarded to Britain in 1713. It became one of the original four provinces in the Dominion of Canada in 1867.
– DERIVATIVES **No·va Sco·tian adj. & n.**

n

no·va·tion /nōˈvāSHən/ ▶ **n.** Law the substitution of a new contract in place of an old one.
– DERIVATIVES **no·vate** /ˈnōvāt, nōˈvāt/ **v.**
– ORIGIN early 16th cent.: from late Latin *novatio(n-)*, from the verb *novare* 'make new.'

No·va·to /nəˈvätō/ a city in northwestern California, north of San Francisco; pop. 52,785 (est. 2008).

No·va·ya Zem·lya /ˈnōvəyə ˌzemlēˈä, zimlēˈä/ two large uninhabited islands in the Arctic Ocean off the northern coast of Siberian Russia. The name means "new land."

nov·el¹ /ˈnävəl/ ▶ **n.** a fictitious prose narrative of book length, typically representing character and action with some degree of realism: *the novels of Jane Austen | she was reading a paperback novel.* ■ (**the novel**) the literary genre represented or exemplified by such works: *the novel is the most adaptable of all literary forms.*
– ORIGIN mid 16th cent.: from Italian *novella (storia)* 'new (story),' feminine of *novello* 'new,' from Latin *novellus*, from *novus* 'new.' The word is also found from late Middle English until the 18th cent. in the sense 'a novelty, a piece of news,' from Old French *novelle* (see **NOVEL²**).

nov·el² ▶ **adj.** new or unusual in an interesting way: *he hit on a novel idea to solve his financial problems.*
– DERIVATIVES **nov·el·ly adv.**
– ORIGIN late Middle English (in the sense 'recent'): from Old French, from Latin *novellus*, from *novus* 'new.'

no·vel·a /nōˈvelə/ ▶ **n.** another term for **TELENOVELA**.

nov·el·ette /ˌnävəˈlet/ ▶ **n.** chiefly derogatory a short novel, typically one that is light and romantic or sentimental in character.
– DERIVATIVES **nov·el·et·tish adj.**

nov·el·ist /ˈnävəlist/ ▶ **n.** a writer of novels.

nov·el·is·tic /ˌnävəˈlistik/ ▶ **adj.** characteristic of or used in novels: *the novelistic detail of his film.*

nov·el·ize /ˈnävəˌlīz/ ▶ **v.** [with obj.] (usu. as adj. **novelized**) convert (a story, typically one in the form of a movie or screenplay) into a novel.
– DERIVATIVES **nov·el·i·za·tion** /ˌnävəliˈzāsHən/ **n.**

no·vel·la /nōˈvelə/ ▶ **n.** a short novel or long short story.
– ORIGIN early 20th cent.: from Italian, 'novel.'

nov·el·ty /ˈnävəltē/ ▶ **n.** (pl. **novelties**) **1** the quality of being new, original, or unusual: *the novelty of being a married woman wore off.* ■ a new or unfamiliar thing or experience: *in 1914 air travel was still a novelty.* ■ [as modifier] denoting something intended to be amusing as a result of its new or unusual quality: *a novelty teapot.*
2 a small and inexpensive toy or ornament: *he bought chocolate novelties to decorate the Christmas tree.*
– ORIGIN late Middle English: from Old French *novelte,* from *novel* 'new, fresh' (see NOVEL[2]).

No·vem·ber /nōˈvembər, nə-/ ▶ **n. 1** the eleventh month of the year, in the northern hemisphere usually considered the last month of autumn: *the store opened in November* | [as modifier] *November days.*
2 a code word representing the letter N, used in radio communication.
– ORIGIN Old English, from Latin, from *novem* 'nine' (being originally the ninth month of the Roman year).

no·ve·na /nōˈvēnə/ ▶ **n.** (in the Roman Catholic Church) a form of worship consisting of special prayers or services on nine successive days.
– ORIGIN mid 19th cent.: from medieval Latin, from Latin *novem* 'nine.'

no·ven·ni·al /ˌnōˈveniəl/ ▶ **adj.** recurring every nine years. ■ lasting for or relating to a period of nine years.
– ORIGIN mid 17th cent.: from late Latin *novennis* 'nine years old' (from Latin *novem* 'nine') + -AL.

No·verre /nōˈver/, Jean-Georges (1727–1810), French choreographer and dance theorist. He stressed the importance of dramatic motivation, as opposed to technical virtuosity, in ballet.

Nov·go·rod /ˈnôvgərət, ˈnävgəˌräd/ a city in northwestern Russia, on the Volkhov River at the northern tip of Lake Ilmen; pop. 214,400 (est. 2009). Russia's oldest city, it was settled by Varangian chief Rurik in 862 and ruled by Alexander Nevsky 1238–63, when it was an important center of medieval eastern Europe.

nov·ice /ˈnävəs/ ▶ **n.** a person new to or inexperienced in a field or situation: *he was a complete novice in foreign affairs.* ■ a person who has entered a religious order and is under probation, before taking vows. ■ an animal, esp. a racehorse, that has not yet won a major prize or reached a level of performance to qualify for important events.
– ORIGIN Middle English: from Old French, from late Latin *novicius,* from *novus* 'new.'

No·vi Sad /ˌnôvē ˈsäd/ an industrial city in Serbia, on the Danube River, capital of the autonomous province of Vojvodina; pop. 197,900 (est. 2008).

no·vi·ti·ate /nōˈvisH(ē)ət, nə-/ (also **noviciate**) ▶ **n.** the period or state of being a novice, esp. in a religious order. ■ a place housing religious novices. ■ a novice, esp. in a religious order.
– ORIGIN early 17th cent.: from ecclesiastical Latin *noviciatus,* from Latin *novicius* 'new' (see NOVICE).

no·vo·caine /ˈnōvəˌkān/ (also trademark **Novocain**) ▶ **n.** another term for PROCAINE.
– ORIGIN early 20th cent.: from Latin *novus* 'new' + *-caine* (from COCAINE).

No·vo·kuz·netsk /ˌnōvəko͝oz'n(y)etsk/ an industrial city in Russia, in central Siberia, in the Kuznets Basin; pop. 562,200 (est. 2008).

No·vo·si·birsk /ˌnōvəsiˈbirsk/ a city in Russia, in central Siberia, west of the Kuznets Basin, on the Ob River; pop. 1,390,500 (est. 2008).

No·vot·ný /ˈnôvôtˌnē/, Antonín (1904–75), Czech statesman; president 1957–68. A founding member of the Czechoslovak Communist Party in 1921, he played a major part in the communist seizure of power in 1948. He was ousted by the reform movement in 1968.

NOW ▶ **abbr.** National Organization for Women.

now /nou/ ▶ **adv. 1** at the present time or moment: *where are you living now?* | *it's the most popular style of jazz* ***right now*** | *not now, I'm late* | [after prep.] *they should be* ***back by now.*** ■ at the time directly following the present moment; immediately: *if we leave now, we can be home by ten* | *I'd rather do it now than leave it till later.* ■ under the present circumstances; as a result of something that has recently happened: *it is now clear that we should not pursue this policy* | *I didn't receive the letter, but it hardly matters now.* ■ on this further occasion, typically as the latest in a series of annoying situations or events: *what do you want now?* ■ used to emphasize a particular length of time: *they've been married four years now.* ■ (in a narrative or account of past events) at the time spoken of or referred to: *it had happened three times now* | *she was nineteen now, and she was alone.*
2 used, esp. in conversation, to draw attention to a particular statement or point in a narrative: *now, my first impulse was to run away* | *I don't like Scotch. Now, if it had been Irish Whiskey you'd offered me.*
3 used in or as a request, instruction, or question, typically to give a slight emphasis to one's words: *now, if you'll excuse me?* | *we can hardly send her back, now can we?* | *run along now.* ■ used when pausing or considering one's next words: *let me see now; oh yes, I remember.*
4 used at the end of an ironic question echoing a previous statement: *"Mom says for you to give me some of your stamps." "Does she now?"*
▶ **conj.** as a consequence of the fact: *they spent a lot of time together* ***now that*** *he had retired* | ***now that*** *you mention it, I haven't seen her around for ages.*
▶ **adj.** informal fashionable; up to date: *seventies disco dancing—very now.*
– PHRASES **for now** until a later time: *that's all the news there is for now.* **now and again** (or **then**) from time to time. **now now** used as an expression of mild remonstrance: *now now, that's not the way to behave.* **now ——, now ——** at one moment ——, at the next ——: *a wind whipped about the house, now this way, now that.* **now or never** used to convey urgency: ***it was now or never****—I had to move fast.* **now then 1** used to get someone's attention or to invite a response: *now then, who's for a coffee?* **2** used as an expression of mild remonstrance or warning: *now then, Emily, I think Sarah has suffered enough.* **now you're talking** used to express one's enthusiastic agreement with or approval of a statement or suggestion: *The Beatles! Now you're talking.*
– DERIVATIVES **now·ness n.**
– ORIGIN Old English *nū,* of Germanic origin; related to Dutch *nu,* German *nun,* from an Indo-European root shared by Latin *nunc* and Greek *nun.*

now·a·days /ˈnouəˌdāz/ ▶ **adv.** at the present time, in contrast with the past: *the sort of clothes worn by almost all young people nowadays* | [sentence adverb] *nowadays, many people condemn hunting.*

no·way /ˈnōˌwā/ (also **noways**) ▶ **adv.** another term for NOWISE. See also NO WAY at NO.

now·cast /ˈnouˌkast/ ▶ **n.** a description of present weather conditions and forecast of those immediately expected.
– DERIVATIVES **now·cast·er n., now·cast·ing n.**

nowed /noud/ ▶ **adj.** [often postpositive] Heraldry knotted; (of a snake) depicted interlaced in a knot.
– ORIGIN late 16th cent.: from French *noué* 'knotted.'

no·where /ˈnōˌ(h)we(ə)r/ ▶ **adv.** not in or to any place; not anywhere: *plants and animals found nowhere else in the world* | *Andrea is nowhere to be found.*
▶ **pron. 1** no place: *there was nowhere for her to sit* | *there's nowhere better to experience the wonders of the Rockies.*
2 a place that is remote, uninteresting, or nondescript: *a stretch of road between nowhere and nowhere* | [as noun] *the town is a particularly American nowhere.*
▶ **adj.** [attrib.] informal having no prospect of progress or success: *she's involved in a nowhere affair with a married executive.*
– PHRASES **from** (or **out of**) **nowhere** appearing or happening suddenly and unexpectedly: *he materialized a taxi out of nowhere.* **get** (or **go**) **nowhere** make no progress: *I'm getting nowhere—maybe I should give up* | *the project was* ***going nowhere fast.*** **get someone nowhere** be of no use or benefit to someone: *being angry would get her nowhere.* **nowhere near** not nearly: *he's* ***nowhere near*** *as popular as he used to be.* **a road to nowhere** a situation or course of action offering no prospects of progress or advancement.
– ORIGIN Old English *nāhwǣr* (see NO, WHERE).

no·wheres /ˈnōˌ(h)werz/ informal ▶ **adv.** nowhere: *that boat was going nowheres.*

no·wheres·ville /ˈnō(h)werzˌvil/ ▶ **n.** informal a place or situation of no significance, promise, or interest: *some American village that might justifiably lay claim to the title "Nowheresville."*

no-win ▶ **adj.** of or denoting a situation in which success or a favorable outcome is impossible.

no·wise /ˈnōˌwīz/ ▶ **adv.** archaic in no way or manner; not at all: *I can nowise accept the accusation.*

nowt /nout/ ▶ **pron. & adv.** N. English nothing: *it's nowt to do with me.*

NOx ▶ **n.** oxides of nitrogen, esp. as atmospheric pollutants.

nox·ious /ˈnäksHəs/ ▶ **adj.** harmful, poisonous, or very unpleasant: *they were overcome by the noxious fumes.*
– DERIVATIVES **nox·ious·ly adv., nox·ious·ness n.**
– ORIGIN late 15th cent.: from Latin *noxius* (from *noxa* 'harm') + -OUS.

nox·ious weed ▶ **n.** a plant considered harmful to animals or the environment.

no·yade /nwäˈyäd/ ▶ **n.** historical an execution carried out by drowning.
– ORIGIN early 19th cent. (referring esp. to a mass execution by drowning, carried out in France in 1794): from French, literally 'drowning,' from the verb *noyer,* from Latin *necare* 'kill without use of a weapon,' later 'drown.'

no·yau /nwäˈyō, ˈnwäˌyō/ ▶ **n.** (pl. **noyaux** /-ˈyō(z), -ˌyō(z)/) a liqueur made of brandy flavored with fruit kernels.
– ORIGIN French, literally 'kernel,' based on Latin *nux, nuc-* 'nut.'

noz·zle /ˈnäzəl/ ▶ **n.** a cylindrical or round spout at the end of a pipe, hose, or tube, used to control a jet of gas or liquid.
– ORIGIN early 17th cent.: from NOSE + -LE[2].

NP ▶ **abbr.** notary public.

Np ▶ **symbol** the chemical element neptunium.

n.p. ▶ **abbr.** ■ new paragraph. ■ no place of publication (used esp. in book classification).

NPN ▶ **adj.** Electronics denoting a semiconductor device in which a *p*-type region is sandwiched between two *n*-type regions.

NPR ▶ **abbr.** National Public Radio.

NPV ▶ **abbr.** net present value. See PRESENT VALUE.

nr ▶ **abbr.** near.

NRA ▶ **abbr.** National Rifle Association.

NRC ▶ **abbr.** ■ National Research Council. ■ National Response Center. ■ Nuclear Regulatory Commission.

NRSV ▶ **abbr.** New Revised Standard Version (of the Bible).

NS ▶ **abbr.** ■ New Style. ■ Nova Scotia (in official postal use).

ns ▶ **abbr.** nanosecond.

n/s ▶ **abbr.** nonsmoker; nonsmoking (used in personal advertisements).

NSA ▶ **abbr.** National Security Agency.

NSAID /ˈenˌsed/ ▶ **abbr.** nonsteroidal anti-inflammatory drug, of which aspirin is the archetype.

NSC ▶ **abbr.** National Security Council.

NSE ▶ **abbr.** National Stock Exchange.

nsec ▶ **abbr.** nanosecond.

NSF ▶ **abbr.** National Science Foundation.

n.s.f. ▶ **abbr.** not sufficient funds.

NSPCA ▶ **abbr.** National Society for the Prevention of Cruelty to Animals.

NSU ▶ **abbr.** Medicine nonspecific urethritis.

NSW ▶ **abbr.** New South Wales.

NT ▶ **abbr.** ■ New Testament. ■ Northern Territory. ■ Northwest Territories (in official postal use). ■ Bridge no-trump.

n't ▶ **contraction** not, used with auxiliary verbs (e.g., *can't, won't, didn't,* and *isn't*).

Nth ▶ **abbr.** North.

nth /enTH/ ▶ **adj.** Mathematics denoting an unspecified member of a series of numbers or enumerated items: *systematic sampling by taking every nth name from the list.* ■ (in general use) denoting an unspecified item or instance in a series, typically the last or latest in a long series: *for the nth time that day they were forced to relate the whole story.*
– PHRASES **to the nth degree** to the utmost: *the gullibility of the electorate was tested to the nth degree by such promises.*

NTP ▶ **abbr.** Chemistry normal temperature and pressure.

NTSB ▶ **abbr.** National Transportation Safety Board.

NTSC ▶ **n.** the television broadcasting system used in North America and Japan.
– ORIGIN 1950s: acronym from *National Television Standards Committee.*

n-tu·ple ▶ **n.** Mathematics an ordered set with *n* elements.

nt. wt. ▶ **abbr.** net weight.

n-type ▶ **adj.** Electronics denoting a region in a semiconductor in which electrical conduction is due chiefly to the movement of electrons. Often contrasted with P-TYPE.

NU ▶ **abbr.** Nunavut (in official postal use).

nu /n(y)o͞o/ ▶ **n.** the thirteenth letter of the Greek alphabet (Ν, ν), transliterated as 'n.' ■ (**Nu**) [followed by Latin genitive] Astronomy the thirteenth star in a constellation: *Nu Draconis*. ▶ **symbol** (ν) frequency.

nu- /n(y)o͞o/ ▶ **comb. form** informal respelling of 'new,' used esp. in names of new or revived genres of popular music: *nu-metal bands* | *nu-disco*.

nu·ance /ˈn(y)o͞oˌäns/ ▶ **n.** a subtle difference in or shade of meaning, expression, or sound: *the nuances of facial expression and body language*.
▶ **v.** [with obj.] (usu. **be nuanced**) give nuances to: *the effect of the music is nuanced by the social situation of listeners*.
– ORIGIN late 18th cent.: from French, 'shade, subtlety,' from *nuer* 'to shade,' based on Latin *nubes* 'cloud.'

nub /nəb/ ▶ **n. 1** (**the nub**) the crux or central point of a matter: *the nub of the problem lies elsewhere*. **2** a small lump or protuberance: *he pressed down on the two nubs on top of the phone*. ■ a small chunk or nugget of metal or rock: *a nub of gold*.
– ORIGIN late 17th cent.: apparently a variant of dialect *knub* 'protuberance,' from Middle Low German *knubbe, knobbe* 'knob.'

Nu·ba /ˈno͞obə/ ▶ **n.** (pl. **same** or **Nubas**) a member of a Nilotic people inhabiting southern Kordofan, a region in Sudan.
▶ **adj.** of or relating to this people.
– ORIGIN from Latin *Nubae* 'Nubians.'

nub·bin /ˈnəbən/ ▶ **n.** a small lump or residual part: *nubbins of bone or cartilage*.
– ORIGIN late 17th cent.: diminutive of **NUB**.

nub·by /ˈnəbē/ (also **nubbly** /ˈnəblē/) ▶ **adj.** (of fabric) coarse or knobbly in texture: *upholstered in nubby blue cotton*. ■ stubby; lumpy: *the nubby points of the new leaves*.
– ORIGIN early 19th cent. (as *nubbly*): derivative of *nubble* 'small lump.'

Nu·bi·a /ˈn(y)o͞obēə/ an ancient region of southern Egypt and northern Sudan, including the Nile valley between Aswan and Khartoum and the surrounding area. Much of Nubia is now drowned by the waters of Lake Nasser, formed by the building of the two dams at Aswan. Nubians constitute an ethnic minority group in Egypt.

Nu·bi·an /ˈn(y)o͞obēən/ ▶ **adj.** of or relating to Nubia, its people, or their language.
▶ **n. 1** a native or inhabitant of Nubia. **2** the Nilo-Saharan language of the Nubians. **3** a goat of a short-haired breed with long pendant ears and long legs, originally from Africa.
– ORIGIN from medieval Latin *Nubianus*, from *Nubia* 'Nubia,' from Latin *Nubae* 'Nubians.'

nu·bile /ˈn(y)o͞oˌbīl, -bəl/ ▶ **adj.** (of a girl or young woman) sexually mature; suitable for marriage. ■ (of a girl or young woman) sexually attractive: *he employed a procession of nubile young secretaries*.
– DERIVATIVES **nu·bil·i·ty** /n(y)o͞oˈbilitē/ **n.**
– ORIGIN mid 17th cent.: from Latin *nubilis* 'marriageable,' from *nubere* 'cover or veil oneself for a bridegroom' (from *nubes* 'cloud').

nu·buck /ˈn(y)o͞oˌbək/ ▶ **n.** cowhide leather that has been rubbed on the flesh side to give it a feel like that of suede.
– ORIGIN early 20th cent.: origin obscure, perhaps a respelling of **NEW** + **BUCK**[1].

nu·cel·lus /n(y)o͞oˈseləs/ ▶ **n.** (pl. **nucelli** /-ˈselˌī, -ˈselē/) Botany the central part of an ovule, containing the embryo sac.
– DERIVATIVES **nu·cel·lar** /-ˈselər/ **adj.**
– ORIGIN late 19th cent.: modern Latin, apparently an irregular diminutive of **NUCLEUS**.

nu·chal /ˈn(y)o͞okəl/ ▶ **adj.** Anatomy of or relating to the nape of the neck.
– ORIGIN mid 19th cent.: from obsolete *nucha* 'nape' (from medieval Latin *nucha* 'medulla oblongata,' from Arabic *nukā*ʿ 'spinal marrow') + **-AL**.

nuci- ▶ **comb. form** of a nut or nuts.
– ORIGIN from Latin *nux, nuc-* 'nut.'

nu·cle·ar /ˈn(y)o͞oklēər, -kli(ə)r/ ▶ **adj. 1** of or relating to the nucleus of an atom. ■ denoting, relating to, or powered by the energy released in nuclear fission or fusion: *nuclear energy* | *nuclear submarines*. ■ denoting, possessing, or involving weapons using this energy: *a nuclear bomb* | *nuclear nations*. **2** Biology of or relating to the nucleus of a cell: *nuclear DNA*.
– ORIGIN mid 19th cent.: from **NUCLEUS** + **-AR**[1].

nu·cle·ar age ▶ **n.** the period in history usu. considered to have begun with the first use of the atomic bomb (1945). It is characterized by nuclear energy as a military, industrial, and sociopolitical factor. Also called **ATOMIC AGE**.

nu·cle·ar club ▶ **n.** the nations possessing nuclear weapons.

nu·cle·ar en·er·gy ▶ **n.** the energy released during nuclear fission or fusion, esp. when used to generate electricity.

nu·cle·ar fam·i·ly ▶ **n.** a couple and their dependent children, regarded as a basic social unit.

nu·cle·ar fis·sion ▶ **n.** a nuclear reaction in which a heavy nucleus splits spontaneously or on impact with another particle, with the release of energy.

nu·cle·ar force ▶ **n.** Physics a strong attractive force between nucleons in the atomic nucleus that holds the nucleus together.

nu·cle·ar-free ▶ **adj.** (of a country or region) not having or allowing any nuclear weapons, materials, or power: *a nuclear-free zone*.

nu·cle·ar fu·el ▶ **n.** a substance that will sustain a fission chain reaction so that it can be used as a source of nuclear energy.

nu·cle·ar fu·sion ▶ **n.** a nuclear reaction in which atomic nuclei of low atomic number fuse to form a heavier nucleus with the release of energy.

nu·cle·ar mag·net·ic res·o·nance (abbr.: **NMR**) ▶ **n.** the absorption of electromagnetic radiation by a nucleus having a magnetic moment when in an external magnetic field, used mainly as an analytical technique and in diagnostic body imaging.

nu·cle·ar med·i·cine ▶ **n.** the branch of medicine that deals with the use of radioactive substances in research, diagnosis, and treatment.

nu·cle·ar op·tion ▶ **n.** the most drastic or extreme response possible to a particular situation.

nu·cle·ar phys·ics ▶ **plural n.** [treated as sing.] the physics of atomic nuclei and their interactions, esp. in the generation of nuclear energy.

nu·cle·ar pow·er ▶ **n. 1** electric or motive power generated by a nuclear reactor. **2** a country that has nuclear weapons.
– DERIVATIVES **nu·cle·ar-pow·ered adj.**

nu·cle·ar re·ac·tion ▶ **n.** Physics a change in the identity or characteristics of an atomic nucleus that results when it is bombarded with an energetic particle, as in fission, fusion, or radioactive decay.

nu·cle·ar re·ac·tor ▶ **n.** see **REACTOR**.

nu·cle·ar thresh·old ▶ **n.** a point in a conflict at which nuclear weapons are or would be brought into use.

nu·cle·ar um·brel·la ▶ **n.** the supposed protection gained from an alliance with a country possessing nuclear weapons.

nu·cle·ar war ▶ **n.** a war in which nuclear weapons are used.

nu·cle·ar waste ▶ **n.** radioactive waste material, for example from the use or reprocessing of nuclear fuel.

nu·cle·ar win·ter ▶ **n.** a period of abnormal cold and darkness predicted to follow a nuclear war, caused by a layer of smoke and dust in the atmosphere blocking the sun's rays.

nu·cle·ase /ˈn(y)o͞okléˌās, -ˌāz/ ▶ **n.** Biochemistry an enzyme that cleaves the chains of nucleotides in nucleic acids into smaller units.

nu·cle·ate ▶ **adj.** /ˈn(y)o͞oklēət, -ˌāt/ chiefly Biology having a nucleus.
▶ **v.** /ˈn(y)o͞oklēˌāt/ [no obj.] (usu. as adj. **nucleated**) form a nucleus. ■ form around a central area: *a nucleated village*.
– DERIVATIVES **nu·cle·a·tion** /ˌn(y)o͞oklēˈāsHən/ **n.**

nu·cle·i /ˈn(y)o͞okléˌī/ plural form of **NUCLEUS**.

nu·cle·ic ac·id /n(y)o͞oˈklē-ik/ ▶ **n.** Biochemistry a complex organic substance present in living cells, esp. DNA or RNA, whose molecules consist of many nucleotides linked in a long chain.

nucleo- ▶ **comb. form** representing **NUCLEUS**, **NUCLEAR**, or **NUCLEIC ACID**.

nu·cle·o·cap·sid /ˌn(y)o͞oklē-ōˈkapsid/ ▶ **n.** Biology the capsid of a virus with the enclosed nucleic acid.

nu·cle·o·lus /n(y)o͞oˈklēələs/ ▶ **n.** (pl. **nucleoli** /-ˌlī, -ˌlē/) Biology a small dense spherical structure in the nucleus of a cell during interphase.
– DERIVATIVES **nu·cle·o·lar** /-lər/ **adj.**
– ORIGIN mid 19th cent.: from late Latin, diminutive of Latin *nucleus* 'inner part, kernel' (see **NUCLEUS**).

nu·cle·on /ˈn(y)o͞okléˌän/ ▶ **n.** Physics a proton or neutron.

nu·cle·on·ics /ˌn(y)o͞okléˈäniks/ ▶ **plural n.** [treated as sing.] the branch of science and technology concerned with atomic nuclei and nucleons, esp. the exploitation of nuclear power.
– DERIVATIVES **nu·cle·on·ic adj.**
– ORIGIN 1940s: from **NUCLEAR**, on the pattern of *electronics*.

nu·cle·o·phil·ic /ˌn(y)o͞oklē-ōˈfilik/ ▶ **adj.** Chemistry (of a molecule or group) having a tendency to donate electrons or react at electron-poor sites such as protons. Often contrasted with **ELECTROPHILIC**.
– DERIVATIVES **nu·cle·o·phile** /ˈn(y)o͞oklēəˌfīl/ **n.**

nu·cle·o·plasm /ˈn(y)o͞oklēəˌplazəm/ ▶ **n.** Biology the substance of a cell nucleus, esp. that not forming part of a nucleolus.

nu·cle·o·pro·tein /ˌn(y)o͞oklē-ōˈprōˌtēn/ ▶ **n.** Biochemistry a complex consisting of a nucleic acid bonded to a protein.

nu·cle·o·side /ˈn(y)o͞oklēəˌsīd/ ▶ **n.** Biochemistry a compound (e.g., adenosine or cytidine) commonly found in DNA or RNA, consisting of a purine or pyrimidine base linked to a sugar.

nu·cle·o·some /ˈn(y)o͞oklēəˌsōm/ ▶ **n.** Biology a structural unit of a eukaryotic chromosome, consisting of a length of DNA coiled around a core of histones.
– DERIVATIVES **nu·cle·o·so·mal** /ˌn(y)o͞oklēəˈsōməl/ **adj.**

nu·cle·o·syn·the·sis /ˌn(y)o͞oklē-ōˈsinTHəsis/ ▶ **n.** Astronomy the cosmic formation of atoms more complex than the hydrogen atom.
– DERIVATIVES **nu·cle·o·syn·thet·ic** /-sinˈT͟Hetik/ **adj.**

nu·cle·o·tide /ˈn(y)o͞oklēəˌtīd/ ▶ **n.** Biochemistry a compound consisting of a nucleoside linked to a phosphate group. Nucleotides form the basic structural unit of nucleic acids such as DNA.

nu·cle·us /ˈn(y)o͞oklēəs/ ▶ **n.** (pl. **nuclei** /-kléˌī/) the central and most important part of an object, movement, or group, forming the basis for its activity and growth: *the nucleus of a film-producing industry*. ■ Physics the positively charged central core of an atom, containing most of its mass. ■ Biology a dense organelle present in most eukaryotic cells, typically a single rounded structure bounded by a double membrane, containing the genetic material. ■ Astronomy the solid part of the head of a comet. ■ Anatomy a discrete mass of gray matter in the central nervous system.
– ORIGIN early 18th cent.: from Latin, literally 'kernel, inner part,' diminutive of *nux, nuc-* 'nut.'

nu·clide /ˈn(y)o͞oˌklīd/ ▶ **n.** Physics a distinct kind of atom or nucleus characterized by a specific number of protons and neutrons.
– DERIVATIVES **nu·clid·ic** /n(y)o͞oˈklidik/ **adj.**
– ORIGIN 1940s: from **NUCLEUS** + *-ide* (from Greek *eidos* 'form').

nude /n(y)o͞od/ ▶ **adj.** wearing no clothes; naked: *a painting of a nude model*. ■ [attrib.] depicting or performed by naked people: *he was asked to act in a frank nude scene*. ■ (esp. of hosiery) flesh-colored: *black shoes with beige or nude stockings*.
▶ **n.** a naked human figure, typically as the subject of a painting, sculpture, or photograph: *a study of a kneeling nude*. ■ flesh color.
– PHRASES **in the nude** in an unclothed state: *I like to swim in the nude*.
– ORIGIN late Middle English (in the sense 'plain, explicit'): from Latin *nudus*. The current sense is first found in noun use in the early 18th cent.

nudge /nəj/ ▶ **v.** [with obj.] prod (someone) gently, typically with one's elbow, in order to draw their attention to something: *people were nudging each other and pointing at me*. ■ touch or push (something) gently or gradually: *the canoe nudged a bank of reeds*. ■ coax or gently encourage (someone) to do something: *we have to nudge the politicians in the right direction*. ■ approach (an age, figure, or level) very closely: *both men were nudging fifty*.
▶ **n.** a light touch or push: *he gave her shoulder a nudge* | figurative *she appreciated the nudge to her memory*.
– PHRASES **nudge nudge** (**wink wink**) used to draw attention to a sexual innuendo in the previous statement: *haven't seen much of the beach—we've been catching up on our sleep* (*nudge nudge*). [a catch phrase from *Monty Python's Flying Circus*, a British television comedy program.]
– DERIVATIVES **nudg·er n.**
– ORIGIN late 17th cent. (as a verb): of unknown origin; compare with Norwegian dialect *nugga, nyggja* 'to push, rub.'

nu·di·branch /ˈn(y)o͞odəˌbraNGk/ ▶ **n.** Zoology a shell-less marine mollusk of the order Nudibranchia; a sea slug.

Nu·di·bran·chi·a /ˌn(y)o͞odəˈbraNGkēə/ Zoology an order of shell-less marine mollusks that comprises the sea slugs. ● Order Nudibranchia, class Gastropoda.
– ORIGIN modern Latin (plural), from Latin *nudus* 'nude' + **BRANCHIA**.

nud·ie /ˈn(y)o͞odē/ ▶ **n.** (pl. **nudies**) informal a publication, entertainment, or venue featuring nude performers or models: *the magazine says the editor was fired, and for reasons unrelated to nudies of the star*.

PRONUNCIATION KEY ə *ago, up*; ər *over, fur*; a *hat*; ā *ate*; ä *car*; e *let*; ē *see*; i *fit*; ī *by*; NG *sing*; ō *go*; ô *law, for*; oi *toy*; o͝o *good*; o͞o *goo*; ou *out*; TH *thin*; T͟H *then*; ZH *vision*

▶ **adj.** portraying, featuring, or including people in the nude: *a nudie bar.*

nud·ist /ˈn(y)o͞odist/ ▶ **n.** a person who engages in the practice of going naked wherever possible: *a mission to encourage more public places to allow nudists* | [as modifier] *a nudist beach.*
– DERIVATIVES **nud·ism** /-ˌdizəm/ **n.**

nu·di·ty /ˈn(y)o͞odətē/ ▶ **n.** the state or fact of being naked: *scenes of full frontal nudity.*

nud·nik /ˈno͝odˌnik/ (also **nudnick**) ▶ **n.** informal a pestering, nagging, or irritating person; a bore.
– ORIGIN mid 20th cent.: Yiddish, from Russian *nudnyĭ* 'tedious.'

Nu·e·ces Riv·er /n(y)o͞oˈāsəs/ a river that flows for 315 miles (515 km) from central Texas, past Corpus Christi, into the Gulf of Mexico at Nueces Bay.

nu·ée ar·dente /n(y)o͞oˈā ärˈdänt/ ▶ **n.** Geology an incandescent cloud of gas, ash, and lava fragments ejected from a volcano, typically as part of a pyroclastic flow.
– ORIGIN French, literally 'burning cloud.'

Nu·er /ˈno͞oər/ ▶ **n.** (pl. **same** or **Nuers**) **1** a member of an African people of southeastern Sudan and Ethiopia, traditionally rearers of cattle.
2 the Nilotic language of this people.
▶ **adj.** of or relating to this people or their language.
– ORIGIN the name in Dinka.

Nue·vo La·re·do /ˈnwāvō ləˈrādō/ a commercial city in eastern Mexico, in Tamaulipas state, across the Rio Grande from Laredo in Texas; pop. 338,363 (2005).

Nue·vo Le·ón /ˌnwāvō lāˈōn, lēˈōn/ a state in northeastern Mexico, on the border with the US; capital, Monterrey.

nue·vo sol /ˌnwāvō ˈsōl/ ▶ **n.** another term for SOL³.
– ORIGIN Spanish, 'new sol.'

nuff /nəf/ (also **'nuff**) ▶ **determiner, pron., & adv.** nonstandard spelling of ENOUGH, representing informal speech: *The pen is mightier than the sword. Nuff said.* ■ [as determiner] black English much: *nuff respect goes out to Galliano.*

nu·gac·i·ty /n(y)o͞oˈgasitē/ ▶ **n.** (pl. **nugacities**) rare triviality; frivolity. ■ a trivial or frivolous thing or idea.
– ORIGIN late 16th cent.: from late Latin *nugacitas*, from Latin *nugax, nugac-* 'trifling, frivolous.'

nu·ga·to·ry /ˈn(y)o͞ogəˌtôrē/ ▶ **adj.** of no value or importance: *a nugatory and pointless observation.* ■ useless; futile: *the teacher shortages will render nugatory the hopes of implementing the new curriculum.*
– ORIGIN early 17th cent.: from Latin *nugatorius*, from *nugari* 'to trifle,' from *nugae* 'jests.'

nug·get /ˈnəgət/ ▶ **n.** a small lump of gold or other precious metal found ready-formed in the earth. ■ a small chunk or lump of another substance: *tiny nuggets of chicken and shrimp.* ■ a valuable idea or fact: *nuggets of information.*
– DERIVATIVES **nug·get·y adj.**
– ORIGIN mid 19th cent.: apparently from dialect *nug* 'lump,' of unknown origin.

nui·sance /ˈn(y)o͞osəns/ ▶ **n.** a person, thing, or circumstance causing inconvenience or annoyance: *an unreasonable landlord could become a nuisance* | *I hope you're not going to make a nuisance of yourself.* ■ (also **private nuisance**) Law an unlawful interference with the use and enjoyment of a person's land. ■ Law see PUBLIC NUISANCE.
– ORIGIN late Middle English (in the sense 'injury, hurt'): from Old French, 'hurt,' from the verb *nuire*, from Latin *nocere* 'to harm.'

nui·sance val·ue ▶ **n.** the significance of a person or thing arising from their capacity to cause inconvenience or annoyance.

nuit blanche /ˌnwē ˈbläNSH/ ▶ **n.** (pl. **nuits blanches** pronunc. **same**) a sleepless night.
– ORIGIN French, literally 'white night.'

Nu·jol /ˈn(y)o͞oˌjôl, -ˌjäl/ ▶ **n.** trademark a paraffin oil used as an emulsifying agent in pharmacy and for making mulls in infrared spectroscopy.
– ORIGIN early 20th cent.: perhaps from *New J(ersey)*, site of the original manufacturing company, + Latin *oleum* 'oil.'

nuke /n(y)o͞ok/ informal ▶ **n.** a nuclear weapon. ■ a nuclear power station. ■ a nuclear-powered vessel.
▶ **v.** [with obj.] attack or destroy with nuclear weapons. ■ destroy; get rid of: *I fertilized the lawn and nuked the weeds.* ■ cook or heat up (food) in a microwave oven: *I nuked a quick burger.*
– ORIGIN 1950s: abbreviation of NUCLEAR.

Nu·ku·'a·lo·fa /ˌno͞oko͞oˈlōfə/ the capital of Tonga, situated on the island of Tongatapu; pop. 25,000 (est. 2007).

null /nəl/ ▶ **adj. 1** [predic.] having no legal or binding force; invalid: *the establishment of a new interim government was declared null and void.*
2 having or associated with the value zero. ■ Mathematics (of a set or matrix) having no elements, or only zeros as elements. ■ lacking distinctive qualities; having no positive substance or content: *his curiously null life.*
▶ **n.** literary a zero. ■ a dummy letter in a cipher. ■ Electronics a condition of no signal. ■ a direction in which no electromagnetic radiation is detected or emitted.
▶ **v.** [with obj.] Electronics combine (a signal) with another in order to create a null; cancel out.
– ORIGIN late Middle English: from French *nul, nulle*, from Latin *nullus* 'none,' from *ne* 'not' + *ullus* 'any.'

nul·lah /ˈnələ/ ▶ **n.** Indian a dry riverbed or ravine.
– ORIGIN late 18th cent.: from Hindi *nālā*.

null char·ac·ter ▶ **n.** Computing a character denoting nothing, usually represented by a binary zero.

null hy·poth·e·sis ▶ **n.** (in a statistical test) the hypothesis that there is no significant difference between specified populations, any observed difference being due to sampling or experimental error.

nul·li·fid·i·an /ˌnələˈfidēən/ rare ▶ **n.** a person having no faith or religious belief.
▶ **adj.** having no faith or religious belief.
– ORIGIN mid 16th cent.: from medieval Latin *nullifidius* (from *nullus* 'no, none' + *fides* 'faith') + -AN.

nul·li·fy /ˈnələˌfī/ ▶ **v.** (**nullifies, nullifying, nullified**) [with obj.] make legally null and void; invalidate: *judges were unwilling to nullify government decisions.* ■ make of no use or value; cancel out: *insulin can block the release of the hormone and thereby nullify the effects of training.*
– DERIVATIVES **nul·li·fi·ca·tion** /ˌnələfəˈkāSHən/ **n.**, **nul·li·fi·er n.**

nul·lip·a·ra /ˌnəˈlipərə/ ▶ **n.** (pl. **nulliparae** /-ˌrē/) Medicine & Zoology a woman or female animal that has never given birth. Compare with PRIMIPARA.
– DERIVATIVES **nul·lip·a·rous** /-ˈlip(ə)rəs/ **adj.**
– ORIGIN late 19th cent.: modern Latin, from Latin *nullus* 'none' + *-para* (feminine of *-parus*), from *parere* 'bear children.'

nul·li·ty /ˈnəlitē/ ▶ **n.** (pl. **nullities**) **1** Law an act or thing that is legally void. ■ the state of being legally void; invalidity, esp. of a marriage.
2 a thing of no importance or worth. ■ nothingness.
– ORIGIN mid 16th cent.: from French *nullité*, from medieval Latin *nullitas*, from Latin *nullus* 'none.'

null link ▶ **n.** Computing a reference incorporated into the last item in a list to indicate that there are no further items in the list.

Num. ▶ **abbr.** Bible Numbers.

Nu·ma Pom·pil·i·us /ˈn(y)o͞omə pämˈpilēəs/ the legendary second king of Rome, successor to Romulus, revered by the ancient Romans as the founder of nearly all their religious institutions.

numb /nəm/ ▶ **adj.** deprived of the power of sensation: *my feet were numb with cold.* ■ unable to think, feel, or respond normally: *the tragic events left us shocked and numb.*
▶ **v.** [with obj.] deprive of feeling or responsiveness: *the cold had numbed her senses.* ■ cause (a sensation) to be felt less intensely; deaden: *vodka might numb the pain in my hand.*
– DERIVATIVES **numb·ly adv.**
– ORIGIN late Middle English *nome(n)*, past participle of obsolete *nim* 'take.'

num·bat /ˈnəmˌbat/ ▶ **n.** a small termite-eating Australian marsupial with a black and white striped back and a bushy tail. ● *Myrmecobius fasciatus*, family Myrmecobiidae.
– ORIGIN early 20th cent.: from Nyungar.

num·ber /ˈnəmbər/ ▶ **n. 1** an arithmetical value, expressed by a word, symbol, or figure, representing a particular quantity and used in counting and making calculations and for showing order in a series or for identification: *she dialed the number carefully* | *an even number.* ■ (**numbers**) dated arithmetic: *the boy was adept at numbers.*
2 a quantity or amount: *the company is seeking to increase the number of women on its staff* | *the exhibition attracted vast numbers of visitors.* ■ (**a number of**) several: *we have discussed the matter on a number of occasions.* ■ a group or company of people: *there were some distinguished names among our number.* ■ (**numbers**) a large quantity or amount, often in contrast to a smaller one; numerical preponderance: *the weight of numbers turned the battle against them.*
3 a single issue of a magazine: *the October number of "Travel."* ■ a song, dance, piece of music, etc., esp. one of several in a performance: *they go from one melodious number to another.* ■ [usu. with adj.] informal a thing, typically an item of clothing, of a particular type, regarded with approval or admiration: *Yvonne was wearing a little black number.*
4 Grammar a distinction of word form denoting reference to one person or thing or to more than one. See also SINGULAR (sense 2 of the adjective), PLURAL, COUNT NOUN, and MASS NOUN.
▶ **v.** [with obj.] **1** amount to (a specified figure or quantity); comprise: *the demonstrators numbered more than 5,000.* ■ include or classify as a member of a group: *the orchestra* **numbers** *Brahms* **among** *its past conductors.*
2 mark with a number or assign a number to, typically to indicate position in a series: *each document was numbered consecutively.* ■ count: *strategies like ours can be numbered on the fingers of one hand.*
– PHRASES **any number of** any particular whole quantity of: *the game can involve any number of players.* ■ a large and unlimited quantity or amount of: *the results can be read any number of ways.* **by numbers** following simple instructions identified or as if identified by numbers: *painting by numbers.* **by the numbers** following standard operating procedure. ■ all together with a shouted-out count. **someone's/something's days are numbered** someone or something will not survive or remain in a position of power or advantage for much longer: *my days as director were numbered.* **do a number on** informal treat someone badly, typically by deceiving, humiliating, or criticizing them in a calculated and thorough way. **have someone's number** informal understand a person's real motives or character and thereby gain some advantage. **have someone's number on it** informal (of a bomb, bullet, or other missile) destined to find a specified person as its target. **someone's number is up** informal the time has come when someone is doomed to die or suffer some other disaster or setback. [with reference to a lottery number or a number by which one may be identified.] **without number** too many to count: *they forgot the message times without number.*
– ORIGIN Middle English: from Old French *nombre* (noun), *nombrer* (verb), from Latin *numerus*.

> **USAGE** The construction **the number of** + plural noun is used with a singular verb (as in ***the number of people affected remains small***). Thus it is the noun **number** rather than the noun **people** that is taken to agree with the verb (and is therefore functioning as the **head noun**). By contrast, the apparently similar construction **a number of** + plural noun is used with a plural verb (as in ***a number of people remain to be contacted***). In this case, it is the noun **people** that acts as the head noun and with which the verb agrees. In the latter case, **a number of** works as if it were a single word, such as **some** or **several**. See also usage at COLLECTIVE NOUN and LOT.

num·ber crunch·er ▶ **n.** informal **1** a computer or software capable of performing rapid calculations with large amounts of data.
2 often derogatory a statistician, accountant, or other person whose job involves dealing with large amounts of numerical data.
– DERIVATIVES **num·ber crunch·ing n.**

num·bered ac·count ▶ **n.** a bank account, esp. in a Swiss bank, identified only by a number and not bearing the owner's name.

num·ber·less /ˈnəmbərləs/ ▶ **adj.** too many to be counted; innumerable.

num·ber line ▶ **n.** Mathematics a line on which numbers are marked at intervals, used to illustrate simple numerical operations.

num·ber one informal ▶ **n. 1** oneself: *you must look after number one.*
2 a person or thing that is the best or the most important in an activity or area: *businesses that were number one in their markets.* ■ a best-selling record or book: *an album featuring seventeen top movie themes and six number ones.*
3 used euphemistically to refer to urine, esp. in reference to children.
4 a lieutenant junior grade in the navy or the coast guard.
5 (or **number two, etc.**) the shortest (or next shortest, etc.) men's haircut produced with electric hair clippers.
▶ **adj.** most important or prevalent: *a number-one priority.* ■ best-selling: *a number-one album.*

num·ber op·er·a ▶ **n.** an opera in which arias and other sections are clearly separable.

num·ber plate ▶ **n.** British term for LICENSE PLATE.

Num·bers /ˈnəmbərz/ the fourth book of the Bible, relating the experiences of the Israelites in the wilderness after Moses led them out of Egypt.
– ORIGIN named in English from the book's accounts of a census; the title in Hebrew means 'in the wilderness.'

num·bers game ▶ **n.** often derogatory the use or manipulation of statistics or figures, esp. in support of an argument: *legislators were today playing the* *numbers game as the vote drew closer.* ■ (also **the numbers** or **numbers racket**) an illegal lottery based on the occurrence of unpredictable numbers in the results of races, etc.

num·ber sign ▶ **n.** the sign #, used to introduce a number (as in *question #2*).

num·ber the·o·ry ▶ **n.** the branch of mathematics that deals with the properties and relationships of numbers, esp. the positive integers.

num·ber two ▶ **n.** informal **1** a second in command: *my conscientious number two in the task force.* ■ a person or thing ranked second in ability or size. **2** used euphemistically to refer to feces, esp. in reference to children.

numb·fish /ˈnəm,fisн/ ▶ **n.** (pl. **same** or **numbfishes**) an electric ray, esp. a heavy-bodied Australian ray that lies partly buried on sand flats and estuaries and can give a severe electric shock. ● Family Torpedinidae: many species, in particular *Hypnos monopterygium*.

numb·ing /ˈnəmiNG/ ▶ **adj.** depriving one of feeling or responsiveness: *the numbing effect of alcohol | a numbing defeat.*
– DERIVATIVES **numb·ing·ly adv.**

num·bles /ˈnəmbəlz/ (also **umbles**) ▶ **plural n.** Brit. archaic the entrails of an animal, esp. a deer, used for food.
– ORIGIN Middle English (denoting the back and loins of a deer): from Old French, from Latin *lumbulus*, diminutive of *lumbus* 'loin.'

numb·ness /ˈnəmnis/ ▶ **n.** the state of being numb: *tingling and numbness in the left arm.*

numb·skull /ˈnəm,skəl/ (also **numskull**) ▶ **n.** informal a stupid or foolish person.

num·dah /ˈnəmdə/ ▶ **n.** (in South Asia and the Middle East) an embroidered rug or carpet made of felt or coarse woolen cloth. ■ cloth of this type.
– ORIGIN from Urdu *namdā*, from Persian *namad* 'carpet.'

nu·men /ˈn(y)o͞omən/ ▶ **n.** (pl. **numina** /-mənə/) the spirit or divine power presiding over a thing or place.
– ORIGIN early 17th cent.: from Latin.

nu·mer·a·ble /ˈn(y)o͞om(ə)rəbəl/ ▶ **adj.** able to be counted.
– ORIGIN mid 16th cent.: from Latin *numerabilis*, from *numerare* 'to number.'

nu·mer·a·cy /ˈn(y)o͞om(ə)rəsē/ ▶ **n.** the ability to understand and work with numbers.

nu·me·raire /ˈn(y)o͞omə,rer, ,n(y)o͞oməˈre(ə)r/ ▶ **n.** Economics an item or commodity acting as a measure of value or as a standard for currency exchange.
– ORIGIN 1960s: from French *numéraire*, from late Latin *numerarius*, from Latin *numerus* 'a number.'

nu·mer·al /ˈn(y)o͞om(ə)rəl/ ▶ **n.** a figure, symbol, or group of these denoting a number. ■ a word expressing a number.
▶ **adj.** of or denoting a number.
– ORIGIN late Middle English (as an adjective): from late Latin *numeralis*, adjective from Latin *numerus* 'a number' (see **NUMBER**).

nu·mer·ate /ˈn(y)o͞om(ə)rət/ ▶ **adj.** having a good basic knowledge of arithmetic; able to understand and work with numbers.
– ORIGIN 1950s: from Latin *numerus* 'a number,' on the pattern of *literate*.

nu·mer·a·tion /,n(y)o͞oməˈrāsнən/ ▶ **n.** the action or process of calculating or assigning a number to something. ■ a method or process of numbering, counting, or computing.
- ORIGIN late Middle English: from Latin *numeratio(n-)* 'payment' (in late Latin 'numbering'), from the verb *numerare* 'to number.'

nu·mer·a·tor /ˈn(y)o͞omə,rātər/ ▶ **n.** the number above the line in a common fraction showing how many of the parts indicated by the denominator are taken, for example, 2 in $^2/_3$.

nu·mer·i·cal /n(y)o͞oˈmerikəl/ ▶ **adj.** of, relating to, or expressed as a number or numbers: *the lists are in numerical order.*
– DERIVATIVES **nu·mer·ic adj.**, **nu·mer·i·cal·ly adv.**
– ORIGIN early 17th cent.: from medieval Latin *numericus* (from Latin *numerus* 'a number') + **-AL**.

nu·mer·i·cal a·nal·y·sis ▶ **n.** the branch of mathematics that deals with the development and use of numerical methods for solving problems.

nu·mer·i·cal con·trol ▶ **n.** Engineering computer control of machine tools, where operations are directed by numerical data.

nu·mer·ol·o·gy /,n(y)o͞oməˈräləjē/ ▶ **n.** the branch of knowledge that deals with the occult significance of numbers.
– DERIVATIVES **nu·mer·o·log·i·cal** /-rəˈläjikəl/ **adj.**, **nu·mer·ol·o·gist** /-jist/ **n.**
– ORIGIN early 20th cent.: from Latin *numerus* 'a number' + **-LOGY**.

nu·me·ro u·no /ˈn(y)o͞omərō ˈo͞onō/ ▶ **n.** (pl. **unos**) informal the best or most important person or thing.
– ORIGIN Italian, literally 'number one.'

nu·mer·ous /ˈn(y)o͞om(ə)rəs/ ▶ **adj.** great in number; many: *he has attended numerous meetings and social events.* ■ consisting of many members: *the orchestra and chorus were numerous.*
– DERIVATIVES **nu·mer·ous·ly adv.**, **nu·mer·ous·ness n.**
– ORIGIN late Middle English: from Latin *numerosus*, from *numerus* 'a number.'

nu·me·rus clau·sus /ˈnyo͞omərəs ˈklousəs/ ▶ **n.** a fixed maximum number of entrants admissible to an academic institution.
– ORIGIN Latin, literally 'closed number.'

Nu·mid·i·a /n(y)o͞oˈmidēə/ an ancient kingdom, later a Roman province, which was located in North Africa, north of the Sahara, corresponding roughly to present-day Algeria.
– DERIVATIVES **Nu·mid·i·an adj. & n.**

nu·mi·na /ˈn(y)o͞omənə/ plural form of **NUMEN**.

nu·mi·nous /ˈn(y)o͞omənəs/ ▶ **adj.** having a strong religious or spiritual quality; indicating or suggesting the presence of a divinity: *the strange, numinous beauty of this ancient landmark.*
– ORIGIN mid 17th cent.: from Latin *numen, numin-* 'divine power' + **-OUS**.

numis. ▶ **abbr.** numismatic; numismatics.

nu·mis·mat·ic /,n(y)o͞oməzˈmatik, -məs-/ ▶ **adj.** of, relating to, or consisting of coins, paper currency, and medals.
– DERIVATIVES **nu·mis·mat·i·cal·ly** /-ik(ə)lē/ **adv.**
– ORIGIN late 18th cent.: from French *numismatique*, via Latin from Greek *nomisma, nomismat-* 'current coin,' from *nomizein* 'use currently.'

nu·mis·mat·ics /,n(y)o͞oməzˈmatiks, -məs-/ ▶ **plural n.** [usu. treated as sing.] the study or collection of coins, paper currency, and medals.
– DERIVATIVES **nu·mis·ma·tist** /n(y)o͞oˈmizmətist, -ˈmis-/ **n.**

num·mu·lar /ˈnəmyələr/ ▶ **adj.** resembling a coin or coins.
– ORIGIN mid 18th cent.: from Latin *nummulus* (diminutive of *nummus* 'coin') + **-AR**¹.

num·mu·lite /ˈnəmyə,līt/ ▶ **n.** Paleontology the flat disk-shaped calcareous shell of a foraminifer, found commonly as a fossil up to 8 cm across in marine Tertiary deposits. ● Family Nummulitidae, order Foraminiferida: several genera, including *Nummulites*.
– ORIGIN early 19th cent.: from Latin *nummulus* (diminutive of *nummus* 'coin') + **-ITE**¹.

num·my /ˈnəmē/ ▶ **adj.** informal (of food) delicious.
– ORIGIN early 20th cent.: variant of **YUMMY**.

num·nah /ˈnəmnə/ ▶ **n.** chiefly Brit. a pad, typically made of sheepskin or foam, that is placed under a saddle.
– ORIGIN mid 19th cent.: from Urdu *namdā*.

num·skull ▶ **n.** variant spelling of **NUMBSKULL**.

nun /nən/ ▶ **n.** a member of a religious community of women, esp. a cloistered one, living under vows of poverty, chastity, and obedience. ■ any of a number of birds whose plumage resembles a nun's habit, esp. an Asian mannikin. ■ a pigeon of a breed with a crest on its neck.
– DERIVATIVES **nun·like** /-,līk/ **adj.**, **nun·nish adj.**
– ORIGIN Old English *nonne*, from ecclesiastical Latin *nonna*, feminine of *nonnus* 'monk,' reinforced by Old French *nonne*.

nun·a·tak /ˈnənə,tak/ ▶ **n.** an isolated peak of rock projecting above a surface of inland ice or snow.
– ORIGIN late 19th cent.: from Eskimo *nunataq*.

Nu·na·vut /ˈno͞oˈnä,vo͞ot, ˈno͞onə-, ,vo͞ot/ a territory in northern Canada that includes the eastern part of the original Northwest Territories and most of the islands of the Arctic Archipelago; capital Iqaluit. It is the homeland of the Inuit people.

nun buoy ▶ **n.** a buoy that is circular in the middle and tapering to each end.
– ORIGIN early 18th cent.: from obsolete *nun* 'child's top' and **BUOY**.

Nunc Di·mit·tis /ˈnəNGk dəˈmitis, ˈno͞oNGk/ ▶ **n.** the Song of Simeon (Luke 2:29–32) used as a canticle in Christian liturgy, esp. at compline and evensong.
– ORIGIN Latin, the opening words of the canticle, '(Lord) now you let (your servant) depart.'

nun·cha·ku /,nənˈCHäko͞o/ (also **nunchuk** /ˈnən,CHək/) ▶ **n.** (pl. **same** or **nunchakus**) a Japanese martial arts weapon consisting of two hardwood sticks joined together by a chain, rope, or thong.
– ORIGIN Japanese, from Okinawa dialect.

nun·ci·a·ture /ˈnənsēə,CHər, ˈno͞on-, -,CHo͝or/ ▶ **n.** the office or tenure of a nuncio in the Roman Catholic Church.
– ORIGIN early 17th cent.: from Italian *nunziatura*, from *nunzio* 'message-bearer' (see **NUNCIO**).

nun·ci·o /ˈnənsē,ō, ˈno͞on-/ ▶ **n.** (pl. **nuncios**) (in the Roman Catholic Church) a papal ambassador to a foreign court or government.
– ORIGIN early 16th cent.: from Italian, from Latin *nuntius* 'messenger.'

nun·cle /ˈnəNGkəl/ ▶ **n.** archaic or dialect a person's uncle.
– ORIGIN late 16th cent.: by misdivision of *mine uncle*.

nun·cu·pa·tive /ˈnəNGkyə,pātiv/ ▶ **adj.** Law (of a will or testament) declared orally as opposed to in writing, esp. by a mortally wounded soldier or sailor.
– ORIGIN mid 16th cent.: from late Latin *nuncupativus*, from Latin *nuncupat-* 'named, declared,' from the verb *nuncupare*.

nun·ner·y /ˈnən(ə)rē/ ▶ **n.** (pl. **nunneries**) a building or group of buildings in which nuns live as a religious community; a convent.

nu·oc cham /nəˈwäk ˈCHäm/ ▶ **n.** a dipping sauce made from nuoc mam, chilies, garlic, sugar, lime juice, and rice vinegar.
– ORIGIN Vietnamese.

nuoc mam /nəˈwäk ˈmäm/ ▶ **n.** a spicy Vietnamese fish sauce.
– ORIGIN Vietnamese.

nup·tial /ˈnəpsнəl, -CHəl/ ▶ **adj.** of or relating to marriage or weddings: *moments of nuptial bliss.* ■ Zoology denoting the characteristic breeding behavior, coloration, or structures of some animals: *nuptial plumage.*
▶ **n.** (usu. **nuptials**) a wedding: *the forthcoming nuptials between Richard and Jocelyn.*
– ORIGIN late 15th cent.: from Old French, or from Latin *nuptialis*, from *nuptiae* 'wedding,' from *nubere* 'to wed'; related to **NUBILE**.

nup·tial mass ▶ **n.** (in the Roman Catholic Church) a mass celebrated as part of a wedding ceremony.

nup·tial pad ▶ **n.** Zoology a pigmented swelling on the inner side of the hand in some male frogs and toads, assisting grip during copulation.

Nu·rem·berg /ˈn(y)o͝orəm,bərg/ a city in southern Germany, in Bavaria; pop. 500,900 (est. 2006). During the 1930s, Nazi Party congresses and annual rallies were held here, and in 1945–46 it was the site of the Nuremberg war trials, in which Nazi war criminals were tried by an international military tribunal. German name **NÜRNBERG**.

Nu·re·yev /ˈno͝orə,yef, -,yev, no͝oˈrāəf/, Rudolf (1939–93), Austrian ballet dancer and choreographer, born in Russia. He defected to the West in 1961 and joined the Royal Ballet in London, where he began his noted partnership with Margot Fonteyn.

Nürn·berg /ˈno͝orn,berk, ˈnYrn-/ German name for **NUREMBERG**.

nurse /nərs/ ▶ **n.** a person trained to care for the sick or infirm, esp. in a hospital. ■ dated a person employed or trained to take charge of young children: *her mother's old nurse.* ■ archaic a wet nurse. ■ [often as modifier] Forestry a tree or crop planted as a shelter to others. ■ Entomology a worker bee, ant, or other social insect, caring for a young brood.
▶ **v.** [with obj.] **1** give medical and other attention to (a sick person): *she nursed the girl through a dangerous illness.* ■ [no obj.] care for the sick and infirm, esp. as a profession: *she nursed at the hospital for thirty years.* ■ try to cure or alleviate (an injury, injured part, or illness) by treating it carefully and protectively: *he has been nursing a cold* | figurative *he nursed his hurt pride.* ■ hold closely and carefully or caressingly: *he nursed his small case on his lap.* ■ hold (a cup or glass) in one's hands, drinking from it occasionally: *I nursed a double brandy.* ■ harbor (a belief or feeling), esp. for a long time: *I still nurse anger and resentment.* ■ take special care of, esp. to promote development or well-being: *our political unity needs to be protected and nursed.* ■ Billiards try to play strokes that keep (the balls) close together. **2** feed (a baby) at the breast: *lionesses who were nursing their own cubs* | (as adj. **nursing**) *nursing mothers.* ■ [no obj.] be fed at the breast: *the baby snuffled as he nursed.* ■ (**be nursed in**) dated be brought up in (a specified condition): *he was nursed in the lap of plenty.*

– ORIGIN late Middle English: contraction of earlier *nourice*, from Old French, from late Latin *nutricia*, feminine of Latin *nutricius* '(person) that nourishes,' from *nutrix*, *nutric-* 'nurse,' from *nutrire* 'nourish.' The verb was originally a contraction of NOURISH, altered under the influence of the noun.

nurse·ling ▶ n. archaic spelling of NURSLING.

nurse·maid /ˈnərs,mād/ ▶ n. a woman or girl employed to look after a young child or children. ▶ v. [with obj.] look after or be overprotective toward: *I haven't got time to nursemaid you through these blips.*

nurse prac·ti·tion·er ▶ n. a nurse who is qualified to treat certain medical conditions without the direct supervision of a doctor.

nurs·er·y /ˈnərs(ə)rē/ ▶ n. (pl. **nurseries**) a room in a house for the special use of young children. ■ a place where young children are cared for during the working day; a nursery school. ■ a place where young plants and trees are grown for sale or for planting elsewhere. ■ a place or natural habitat that breeds or supports animals: *this estuary provides a vast nursery for fish.* ■ an institution or environment in which certain types of people or qualities are fostered or bred: *that nursery of traitors.*
– ORIGIN late Middle English: from Old French *nourice* 'nurse' (see NURSE) + -ERY.

nurs·er·y·man /ˈnərs(ə)rēmən/ ▶ n. (pl. **nurserymen**) a worker in or owner of a plant or tree nursery.

nurs·er·y rhyme ▶ n. a simple traditional song or poem for children.

nurs·er·y school ▶ n. a school for young children, mainly between the ages of three and five.

nurse's aide ▶ n. (pl. **nurses' aides**) a person who assists professional nurses in a hospital or other medical facility by performing routine tasks, such a making beds and serving meals, that require little or no formal training.

nurse shark ▶ n. a shark with barbels on the snout. ● Three species in the family Orectolobidae (or Ginglymostomatidae), in particular *Ginglymostoma cirratum*, a slow-swimming brownish shark of warm Atlantic waters.
– ORIGIN mid 19th cent.: *nurse* 'dogfish shark,' alteration of Middle English *nusse*, perhaps derived (by wrong division) from *an huss* (see HUSS).

nurs·ing /ˈnərsiNG/ ▶ n. the profession or practice of providing care for the sick and infirm.

nurs·ing home ▶ n. a private institution providing residential accommodations with health care, esp. for elderly people.

nurs·ling /ˈnərsliNG/ ▶ n. a baby that is being breastfed.

nur·tur·ance /ˈnərCHərəns/ ▶ n. emotional and physical nourishment and care given to someone. ■ the ability to provide such care.
– DERIVATIVES **nur·tur·ant** /-rənt/ adj.

nur·ture /ˈnərCHər/ ▶ v. [with obj.] care for and encourage the growth or development of: *Jarrett was nurtured by his parents in a close-knit family.* ■ help or encourage the development of: *my father nurtured my love of art.* ■ cherish (a hope, belief, or ambition): *for a long time she had nurtured the dream of buying a shop.*
▶ n. the process of caring for and encouraging the growth or development of someone or something: *the nurture of ethics and integrity.* ■ upbringing, education, and environment, contrasted with inborn characteristics as an influence on or determinant of personality. Often contrasted with NATURE.
– DERIVATIVES **nur·tur·er** n.
– ORIGIN Middle English: from Old French *noureture* 'nourishment,' based on Latin *nutrire* 'feed, cherish.'

Nus·selt num·ber /ˈno͞osəlt/ ▶ n. Physics a dimensionless parameter used in calculations of heat transfer between a moving fluid and a solid body. ● It is equal to hD/k, where h is the rate of heat loss per unit area per degree difference in temperature between the body and its surroundings, D is a characteristic length of the body, and k is the thermal conductivity of the fluid.
– ORIGIN mid 20th cent.: named after Ernst K. W. *Nusselt* (1882–1957), German engineer.

Nut /no͞ot/ Egyptian Mythology the sky goddess, thought to swallow the sun at night and give birth to it in the morning.

nut /nət/ ▶ n. **1** a fruit consisting of a hard or tough shell around an edible kernel. ■ the hard kernel of such a fruit. ■ informal a person's head. ■ (usu. **nuts**) vulgar slang testicles.
2 a small flat piece of metal or other material, typically square or hexagonal, with a threaded hole through it for screwing onto a bolt as a fastener. ■ Music the part at the lower end of the bow of a violin or similar instrument, with a screw for adjusting the tension of the hair.
3 informal a crazy or eccentric person. ■ [with modifier] a person who is excessively interested in or enthusiastic about a specified thing: *a football nut.*
4 the fixed ridge on the neck of a stringed instrument over which the strings pass.
▶ v. (**nuts, nutting, nutted**) **1** [no obj.] (usu. as noun **nutting**) archaic gather nuts.
2 [with obj.] Brit. informal butt (someone) with one's head.
– PHRASES **do one's nut** Brit. informal be extremely angry or agitated. **nuts and bolts** informal the basic practical details: *the nuts and bolts of public policy.* **off one's nut** informal out of one's mind; crazy. **a tough** (or **hard**) **nut** informal someone who is difficult to deal with; a formidable person. **a tough** (or **hard**) **nut to crack** informal a difficult problem or an opponent hard to beat.
– DERIVATIVES **nut·like** /-,līk/ adj.
– ORIGIN Old English *hnutu*, of Germanic origin; related to Dutch *noot* and German *Nuss*.

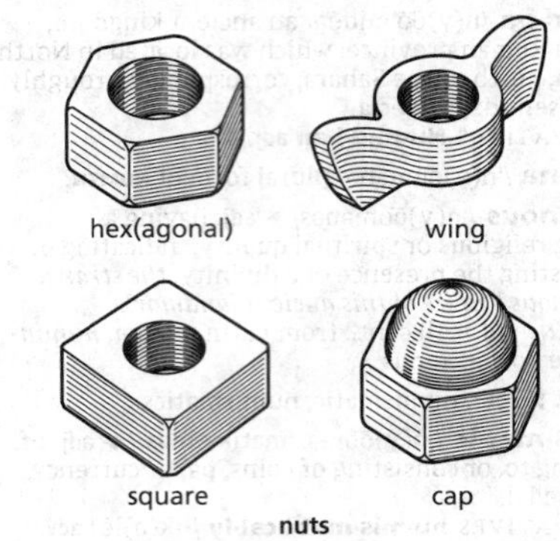

nuts

nu·ta·tion /n(y)o͞oˈtāSHən/ ▶ n. a periodic variation in the inclination of the axis of a rotating object. ■ Astronomy a periodic oscillation of the earth's axis that causes the precession of the poles to follow a wavy rather than a circular path. ■ Botany the circular swaying movement of the tip of a growing shoot.
– ORIGIN early 17th cent. (denoting nodding of the head): from Latin *nutatio(n-)*, from *nutare* 'to nod.'

nut-brown ▶ adj. of a rich dark brown color: *a nut-brown face.*

nut·case /ˈnətkās/ (also **nut case**) ▶ n. informal a crazy or foolish person.

nut·crack·er /ˈnət,krakər/ ▶ n. **1** a device for cracking nuts.
2 a crow that feeds on the seeds of conifers, found widely in Eurasia and in western North America. ● Genus *Nucifraga*, family Corvidae: the Eurasian **spotted nutcracker** (*N. caryocatactes*), with white-spotted brown plumage, and the North American **Clark's nutcracker** (*N. columbiana*), with pale gray and black plumage.

Nut·crack·er Man /ˈnət,krakər/ ▶ n. the nickname of a fossil hominid with massive jaws and molar teeth, esp. the original specimen found near Olduvai Gorge in 1959. ● *Australopithecus* (or *Zinjanthropus*) *boisei*, family Hominidae. See AUSTRALOPITHECUS, PARANTHROPUS.

nut·gall /ˈnət,gôl/ ▶ n. **1** another term for ALEPPO GALL.
2 a gall that forms in response to the presence of mites, esp. one that forms inside the buds of hazel bushes, causing the buds to enlarge greatly. ● The mite is *Phytoptus avellanae*, family Eriophyidae.

nut·grass /ˈnət,gras/ ▶ n. another term for NUTSEDGE.

nut·hatch /ˈnət,haCH/ ▶ n. a small songbird with a long strong bill, a stiffened square-cut tail, and the habit of climbing down tree trunks head first. ● Family Sittidae and genus *Sitta*: numerous species, including the North American **white-breasted nuthatch** (*S. carolinensis*), with a gray back, black cap (male), black eyes, and white face and underparts.
– ORIGIN Middle English: from NUT + obsolete *hatch* (related to HACK¹), from the bird's habit of hacking with the beak at nuts wedged in a crevice.

white-breasted nuthatch

nuth·in /ˈnəTHin/ (also **nuthin'**) ▶ pron. adj. & adv. informal nonstandard spelling of NOTHING, used to represent informal speech.

nut·house /ˈnət,hous/ ▶ n. informal, offensive a home or hospital for people with mental illnesses.

nut·job /ˈnətjäb/ (also **nut job**) ▶ n. informal a crazy or foolish person.

nut·let /ˈnətlət/ ▶ n. Botany a small nut, esp. an achene.

nut loaf ▶ n. a baked vegetarian dish made from ground or chopped nuts, vegetables, and herbs.

nut meat (also **nutmeat**) ▶ n. the kernel of a nut, typically edible.

nut·meg /ˈnət,meg/ ▶ n. **1** the hard, aromatic, almost spherical seed of a tropical tree. ■ this seed grated and used as a spice.
2 the evergreen tree that bears these seeds, native to the Moluccas. ● *Myristica fragrans*, family Myristicaceae.
– ORIGIN late Middle English *notemuge*, partial translation of Old French *nois muguede*, based on Latin *nux* 'nut' + late Latin *muscus* 'musk.'

Nut·meg State a nickname for the state of CONNECTICUT.

nut·pick /ˈnət,pik/ (also **nut pick**) ▶ n. a thin, sharp-pointed table implement used to dig out the edible meat from nuts.

nu·tra·ceu·ti·cal /,n(y)o͞otrəˈso͞otikəl/ ▶ n. a food containing health-giving additives and having medicinal benefit.
– ORIGIN 1990s: from Latin *nutrire* 'nourish' + PHARMACEUTICAL.

nu·tri·a /ˈn(y)o͞otrēə/ ▶ n. a large semiaquatic beaverlike rodent, native to South America. It is kept in captivity for its fur and has become naturalized in many other areas. ● *Myocastor coypus*, the only member of the family Myocastoridae. ■ the pelt of this animal.
– ORIGIN early 19th cent.: from Spanish, literally 'otter.'

nu·tri·ent /ˈn(y)o͞otrēənt/ ▶ n. a substance that provides nourishment essential for growth and the maintenance of life: *fish is a source of many important nutrients, including protein, vitamins, and minerals.*
– ORIGIN mid 17th cent.: from Latin *nutrient-* 'nourishing,' from the verb *nutrire*.

nu·tri·ge·no·mics /,n(y)o͞otrijēˈnōmiks, -ˈnäm-/ ▶ plural n. [treated as singular] the scientific study of the interaction of nutrition and genes, esp. the role of diet in causing disease: *nutrigenomics holds great promise in fighting obesity and cancer.*
– ORIGIN blend of *nutrition* and *genomics* 'analysis of an organism's complete set of genes.'.

nu·tri·ment /ˈn(y)o͞otrəmənt/ ▶ n. rare nourishment; sustenance.
– DERIVATIVES **nu·tri·men·tal** /,n(y)o͞otrəˈmentl/ adj.
– ORIGIN late Middle English: from Latin *nutrimentum*, from *nutrire* 'feed, nourish.'

nu·tri·tion /n(y)o͞oˈtriSHən/ ▶ n. the process of providing or obtaining the food necessary for health and growth: *a guide to good nutrition.* ■ food; nourishment: *a feeding tube gives her nutrition and water.* ■ the branch of science that deals with nutrients and nutrition, particularly in humans: *she took a short course in nutrition* | [as modifier] *nutrition experts.*
– DERIVATIVES **nu·tri·tion·al** /-SHənl/ adj., **nu·tri·tion·al·ly** /-SHənl-ē/ adv.
– ORIGIN late Middle English: from late Latin *nutritio(n-)*, from *nutrire* 'feed, nourish.'

nu·tri·tion·ist /n(y)o͞oˈtriSH(ə)nist/ ▶ n. a person who studies or is an expert in nutrition.

nu·tri·tious /n(y)o͞oˈtriSHəs/ ▶ adj. nourishing; efficient as food: *like all spinach, it is very nutritious and best when young.*
– DERIVATIVES **nu·tri·tious·ly** adv., **nu·tri·tious·ness** n.
– ORIGIN mid 17th cent.: from Latin *nutritius* 'that nourishes' (from *nutrex* 'a nurse') + -OUS.

nu·tri·tive /ˈn(y)o͞otrətiv/ ▶ adj. of or relating to nutrition: *the food was low in nutritive value.* ■ providing nourishment; nutritious: *nutritive food.*
– ORIGIN late Middle English: from medieval Latin *nutritivus*, from *nutrire* 'feed, nourish.'

nuts /nəts/ ▶ adj. [predic.] informal insane: *the way he turns on the television as soon as he walks in drives me nuts.*
▶ exclam. informal an expression of contempt or derision: *keep up the good work, and nuts to everyone who doesn't like it.*
– PHRASES **be nuts about** (or Brit. **on**) informal like very much: *I was nuts about him.*

nut·sedge /ˈnət,sej/ ▶ n. an invasive sedge with small edible nutlike tubers. Also called NUTGRASS. ● Genus *Cyperus*, family Cyperaceae: two species, **purple nutsedge** (*C. rotundus*) and **yellow nutsedge** (*C. esculentus*). See also CHUFA.

nut·shell /ˈnət,SHel/ ▶ **n.** the hard woody covering around the kernel of a nut.
– PHRASES **in a nutshell** in the fewest possible words: *she put the matter in a nutshell.*

nut·so /ˈnətsō/ informal ▶ **adj.** insane: *his nutso neighbors.*
▶ **n.** (pl. **nutsos**) an insane or eccentric person.

nut·sy /ˈnətsē/ ▶ **adj.** (**nutsier, nutsiest**) informal insane.

nut·ter /ˈnətər/ ▶ **n.** Brit. informal a crazy or eccentric person.

nut tree ▶ **n.** a tree that bears nuts, esp. the hazel.

nut·ty /ˈnətē/ ▶ **adj.** (**nuttier, nuttiest**) **1** tasting like nuts: *wild rice has a very nutty flavor.* ■ containing a lot of nuts: *a nutty vegetable bake.*
2 informal peculiar; insane: *he came up with a few nutty proposals.*
– PHRASES **be nutty about** informal like very much: *he is nutty about boats.* (**as**) **nutty as a fruitcake** informal completely insane.
– DERIVATIVES **nut·ti·ness n.**

Nuuk /nŏŏk/ the capital of Greenland, a port on the Davis Strait; pop. 15,000 (est. 2007). It was known by the Danish name Godthåb until 1979.

nux vom·i·ca /ˈnəks ˈvämikə/ ▶ **n.** a spiny southern Asian tree with berrylike fruit and toxic seeds that are a commercial source of strychnine. ● *Strychnos nux-vomica*, family Loganiaceae. ■ a homeopathic preparation of this plant used esp. for the treatment of symptoms of overeating and overdrinking.
– ORIGIN late Middle English: from medieval Latin, from Latin *nux* 'nut' + *vomica* 'causing vomiting' (from *vomere* 'to vomit').

Nu·yor·i·can /n(y)o͞oˈyôrikən/ (also **Newyorican**) ▶ **n.** a Puerto Rican living in the US, esp. in New York City.

nuz·zle /ˈnəzəl/ ▶ **v.** [with obj.] rub or push against gently with the nose and mouth: *he nuzzled her hair* | [no obj.] *the foal nuzzled at its mother.* ■ [no obj.] (**nuzzle up to/against**) lean or snuggle against: *the dog nuzzled up against me.*
– ORIGIN late Middle English (in the sense 'grovel'): frequentative from **NOSE**, reinforced by Dutch *neuzelen* 'poke with the nose.'

NV ▶ **abbr.** Nevada (in official postal use).

nvCJD ▶ **abbr.** see **vCJD**.

NVI ▶ **abbr.** no value indicated, a postage stamp that does not bear a monetary value on it but instead shows which postal service it is valid for.

NW ▶ **abbr.** ■ northwest. ■ northwestern.

NWbN ▶ **abbr.** northwest by north.

NWbW ▶ **abbr.** northwest by west.

N-word ▶ **n.** informal used instead of or in reference to the word "nigger" because of its taboo nature: *I can't believe he used the N-word in front of her.*

NWT ▶ **abbr.** Northwest Territories (in Canada).

n.wt. ▶ **abbr.** net weight.

NY ▶ **abbr.** New York (in official postal use).

nyah /nya, nyä/ ▶ **exclam.** used to express the speaker's feeling of superiority or contempt for another: *I won the gold and she didn't. Nyah, nyah, nyah.*
– ORIGIN early 20th cent.: imitative of a child's reduplicated phrase used in taunting.

nya·la /ˈnyälə/ ▶ **n.** (pl. **same**) a southern African antelope, with a conspicuous crest on the neck and back and lyre-shaped horns. ● *Tragelaphus angasi*, family Bovidae.
– ORIGIN late 19th cent.: from Zulu.

Nyan·ja /ˈnyänjə, ˈnyan-/ ▶ **n.** (pl. **same** or **Nyanjas**)
1 a member of a people of Malawi and eastern and central Zambia.
2 the Bantu language of this people.
▶ **adj.** of or relating to this people or their language.
– ORIGIN a local name, literally 'lake.'

Ny·as·a, Lake /ˈnyäsə, ˈnīasə/ a lake in east central Africa, Africa's third largest. About 350 miles (580 km) long, it forms most of the eastern border of Malawi with Mozambique and Tanzania. Also called **MALAWI, LAKE**.
– ORIGIN *Nyasa*, literally 'lake.'

Ny·as·a·land /ˈnyäsə,land, nīˈas-/ former name (until 1966) for **MALAWI**.

NYC ▶ **abbr.** New York City.

nyc·ta·lo·pi·a /,niktəˈlōpēə/ ▶ **n.** Medicine the inability to see in dim light or at night. Also called **NIGHT BLINDNESS**.
– ORIGIN late 17th cent.: via late Latin from Greek *nuktalōps*, from *nux, nukt-* 'night' + *alaos* 'blind' + *ōps* 'eye.'

nyc·ti·nas·tic /,niktəˈnastik/ ▶ **adj.** Botany (of the periodic movement of flowers or leaves) caused by nightly changes in light intensity or temperature.
– DERIVATIVES **nyc·ti·nas·ty** /ˈniktə,nastē/ **n.**
– ORIGIN early 20th cent.: from Greek *nux, nukt-* 'night' + *nastos* 'pressed' + **-IC**.

nyc·tog·e·nous /nikˈtäjənəs/ ▶ **adj.** (of symptoms or behavior) occurring or demonstrated only in the night or in darkness: *nyctogenous bouts of anxiety.*
– ORIGIN early 20th cent.: from Greek *nux, nukt-* 'night' + **-GENOUS**.

nyc·to·pho·bi·a /,niktəˈfōbēə/ ▶ **n.** extreme or irrational fear of the night or of darkness.
– ORIGIN early 20th cent.: from Greek *nux, nukt-* 'night' + **PHOBIA**.

ny·lon /ˈnī,län/ ▶ **n.** a tough, lightweight, elastic synthetic polymer with a proteinlike chemical structure, able to be produced as filaments, sheets, or molded objects. ■ fabric or yarn made from nylon fibers. ■ (**nylons**) stockings or hose made of nylon.
– ORIGIN 1930s: an invented word, on the pattern of *cotton* and *rayon.*

nymph /nimf/ ▶ **n.** **1** a mythological spirit of nature imagined as a beautiful maiden inhabiting rivers, woods, or other locations. ■ chiefly literary a beautiful young woman.
2 an immature form of an insect that does not change greatly as it grows, e.g., a dragonfly, mayfly, or locust. Compare with **LARVA**. ■ an artificial fly made to resemble the aquatic nymph of an insect, used in fishing.
3 a mainly brown butterfly that frequents woods and forest glades. ● Several genera in the subfamily Satyrinae, family Nymphalidae. See also **WOOD NYMPH**.
– DERIVATIVES **nymph·al** /ˈnimfəl/ **adj.**, **nym·phe·an** /ˈnimfēən/ **adj.**, **nymph·like** /-līk/ **adj.**
– ORIGIN late Middle English: from Old French *nimphe*, from Latin *nympha*, from Greek *numphē* 'nymph, bride'; related to Latin *nubere* 'be the wife of.'

nym·phae·um /nimˈfēəm/ ▶ **n.** (pl. **nymphaea** /-ˈfēə/) a grotto or shrine dedicated to a nymph or nymphs.
– ORIGIN via Latin from Greek.

nym·pha·lid /nimˈfaləd, ˈnimfəlid/ ▶ **n.** Entomology an insect of a large family of strikingly marked butterflies that have small forelegs not used for walking, including many familiar butterflies of temperate regions, such as the monarch and viceroy. ● Family Nymphalidae (sometimes restricted to those that are now usually placed in the subfamily Nymphalinae).
– ORIGIN late 19th cent.: from modern Latin *Nymphalidae*, from Latin *nympha* 'nymph.'

nymph·et /nimˈfet, ˈnimfit/ ▶ **n.** an attractive and sexually mature young girl.
– ORIGIN 1950s: from **NYMPH** + **-ET**¹.

nym·pho /ˈnimˈfō/ ▶ **n.** (pl. **nymphos**) informal a nymphomaniac.

nym·pho·lep·sy /ˈnimfə,lepsē/ ▶ **n.** literary passion aroused in men by beautiful young girls. ■ wild frenzy caused by desire for an unattainable ideal.
– ORIGIN late 18th cent.: from **NYMPHOLEPT**, on the pattern of *epilepsy.*

nym·pho·lept /ˈnimfə,lept/ ▶ **n.** a person affected by nympholepsy.
– DERIVATIVES **nym·pho·lep·tic** /,nimfəˈleptik/ **adj.**
– ORIGIN early 19th cent.: from Greek *numpholēptos* 'caught by nymphs,' from *numphē* 'nymph' + *lambanein* 'take.'

nym·pho·ma·ni·a /,nimfəˈmānēə/ ▶ **n.** uncontrollable or excessive sexual desire in a woman. Compare with **SATYRIASIS**.
– DERIVATIVES **nym·pho·ma·ni·ac** /-ˈmānē,ak/ **n.** & **adj.**, **nym·pho·ma·ni·a·cal** /-məˈnīəkəl/ **adj.**
– ORIGIN late 18th cent.: modern Latin, from Latin *nympha* (see **NYMPH**) + **-MANIA**.

Ny·norsk /ˈno͞o,nôrsk, ,no͞oˈnôrsk/ ▶ **n.** a literary form of Norwegian, based on country dialects and constructed in the 19th century to serve as a national language more clearly distinct from Danish than Bokmål. See **NORWEGIAN** (sense 2 of the noun).
– ORIGIN Norwegian, from *ny* 'new' + *Norsk* 'Norwegian.'

Nyo·man /ˈnyō,män/ Belorussian name for **NEMAN**.

NYP ▶ **abbr.** not yet published.

Ny·quist cri·te·ri·on /ˈnīkwist/ ▶ **n.** Electronics a criterion for determining the stability or instability of a feedback system.
– ORIGIN 1930s: named after Harry *Nyquist* (1889–1976), Swedish-born American engineer.

Ny·quist di·a·gram (also **Nyquist plot**) ▶ **n.** Electronics a representation of the vector response of a feedback system (esp. an amplifier) as a complex graphical plot showing the relationship between feedback and gain.
– ORIGIN 1930s: see **NYQUIST CRITERION**.

Ny·quist fre·quen·cy (also **Nyquist rate**) ▶ **n.** Electronics the minimum rate at which a signal can be sampled without introducing errors, which is twice the highest frequency present in the signal.
– ORIGIN 1930s: see **NYQUIST CRITERION**.

Ny·sa /ˈnisə/ Polish name for **NEISSE**.

NYSE ▶ **abbr.** New York Stock Exchange.

nys·tag·mus /nəˈstagməs/ ▶ **n.** rapid involuntary movements of the eyes.
– DERIVATIVES **nys·tag·mic** /-mik/ **adj.**
– ORIGIN early 19th cent.: from Greek *nustagmos* 'nodding, drowsiness,' from *nustazein* 'nod, be sleepy.'

nys·ta·tin /ˈnistətin, ˈnī-/ ▶ **n.** an antibiotic used chiefly to treat fungal infections. ● This antibiotic is obtained from the bacterium *Streptomyces noursei.*
– ORIGIN 1950s: from *N(ew) Y(ork) Stat(e)* (where it was developed) + **-IN**¹.

Nyx /niks/ Greek Mythology the female personification of the night, daughter of Chaos.

NZ ▶ **abbr.** New Zealand.

n

Oo

O[1] /ō/ (also **o**) ▶ **n.** (pl. **Os** or **O's** /ōz/) **1** the fifteenth letter of the alphabet. ■ denoting the next after N in a set of items, categories, etc. ■ a human blood type (in the ABO system) lacking both the A and B antigens. In blood transfusion, a person with blood of this group is a potential universal donor.
2 (also **oh**) zero (in a sequence of numerals, esp. when spoken).
3 a shape like that of a capital O; a circle.

O[2] ▶ **abbr.** ■ Ocean. ■ (in prescriptions) a pint. [from Latin *octarius*.] ■ octavo. ■ October. ■ Ohio. ■ old. ■ Ontario. ■ Oregon. ▶ **symbol** the chemical element oxygen.

O[3] ▶ **exclam. 1** archaic spelling of **OH**[1].
2 archaic used before a name in direct address, as in prayers and poetry: *give peace in our time, O Lord.*
– ORIGIN natural exclamation: first recorded in Middle English.

o ▶ **abbr.** ■ pint. [from Latin *octarius*.] ■ octavo. ■ off. ■ old. ■ only. ■ order. ■ Baseball out; outs.

O' ▶ **prefix** in Irish patronymic names such as *O'Neill.*
– ORIGIN mid 18th cent.: from Irish *ó, ua* 'descendant.'

o' /ə, ō/ ▶ **prep.** short for **OF**, used to represent an informal pronunciation: *a cup o' coffee.*

o- ▶ **abbr.** [used in combination] Chemistry ortho-: *o-xylene.*

-o ▶ **suffix** forming chiefly informal or slang variants or derivatives such as *righto, wino.*
– ORIGIN perhaps from **OH**[1], reinforced by abbreviated forms such as *hippo, photo.*

-o- ▶ **suffix** used as the terminal vowel of combining forms: *chemico-* | *Gallo-.*
– ORIGIN from Greek.

o/a ▶ **abbr.** on or about.

oaf /ōf/ ▶ **n.** a stupid, uncultured, or clumsy person.
– ORIGIN early 17th cent.: variant of obsolete *auf,* from Old Norse *álfr* 'elf.' The original meaning was 'elf's child, changeling,' later 'idiot child' and 'halfwit,' generalized in the current sense.

oaf·ish /'ōfisH/ ▶ **adj.** stupid, uncultured, or clumsy: *oafish behavior.*
– DERIVATIVES **oaf·ish·ly adv., oaf·ish·ness n.**

Oahe, Lake /ō'āhē/ a reservoir northwest of Pierre in South Dakota, in the Missouri River, created since 1963 by the huge Oahe Dam.

O·a·hu /ō'wähōō/ the third largest of the Hawaiian islands; pop. 905,000 (est. 2008). Its principal town, Honolulu, is the capital of Hawaii. It is the site of Pearl Harbor, a US naval base.

oak /ōk/ ▶ **n.** (also **oak tree**) a tree that bears acorns as fruit, and typically has lobed deciduous leaves. Oaks are common in many north temperate forests and are an important source of hard and durable wood used chiefly in construction, furniture, and (formerly) shipbuilding. ● Genus *Quercus,* family Fagaceae: many species, including the deciduous **Eastern white oak** (*Q. alba*) and **Eastern black oak** (*Q. velutina*) and the evergreen **live oak** (*Q. virginiana*). ■ a smoky flavor or aroma characteristic of wine aged in barrels made from this wood.
– PHRASES **mighty** (or **great**) **oaks from little acorns grow** proverb something of small or modest dimensions may grow into something very large or impressive.
– DERIVATIVES **oak·en** /'ōkən/ **adj., oak·y adj.**
– ORIGIN Old English *āc,* of Germanic origin; related to Dutch *eik* and German *Eiche.*

oak ap·ple ▶ **n.** a spongy spherical gall that forms on oak trees in response to the developing larvae of a gall wasp. ● The wasp is *Biorhiza pallida* (in Europe) or *Amphibolips confluenta* (in America), family Cynipidae.

oak fern ▶ **n.** a delicate fern of woods and damp places in the uplands of northern Eurasia and North America. ● Genus *Gymnocarpium* (formerly *Thelypteris*), family Woodsiaceae: two species, in particular *G. dryopteris.*

oak ker·mes ▶ **n.** see **KERMES** (sense 2).

Oak·land /'ōklənd/ an industrial port in California, on the eastern side of San Francisco Bay; pop. 404,155 (est. 2008).

oak leaf clus·ter ▶ **n.** an attachment to a military decoration depicting a twig with oak leaves and acorns, indicating distinguished action or a subsequent award of the same decoration.

oak·leaf let·tuce /'ōk,lēf/ (also **oak leaf lettuce**) ▶ **n.** a red or green variety of lettuce that has leaves with serrated edges and a slightly bitter taste.

Oak·ley /'ōklē/, Annie (1860–1926), US markswoman; full name *Phoebe Anne Oakley Mozee.* In 1885, she joined Buffalo Bill's Wild West Show and was the star attraction for the next seventeen years.

Annie Oakley

Oak Park a village in northeastern Illinois, west of Chicago; pop. 49,557 (est. 2008).

Oak Ridge a city in eastern Tennessee, on the Clinch River, established in 1942 as part of US nuclear development; pop. 27,677 (est. 2008).

oak·tag /'ōk,tag/ (also **oak tag**) ▶ **n.** another term for **TAGBOARD**.

oa·kum /'ōkəm/ ▶ **n.** chiefly historical loose fiber obtained by untwisting old rope, used esp. in caulking wooden ships.
– ORIGIN Old English *ācumbe,* literally 'off-combings' The current sense dates from Middle English.

oak wilt ▶ **n.** a fungal disease of oaks and other trees that makes the foliage wilt and eventually kills the tree. ● The fungus is *Ceratocystis fagacearum,* subdivision Ascomycotina.

O & M ▶ **abbr.** ■ operations and maintenance. ■ organization and methods.

OAPEC /ō,pek/ ▶ **abbr.** Organization of Arab Petroleum Exporting Countries.

oar /ôr/ ▶ **n.** a pole with a flat blade, pivoting in an oar lock, used to row or steer a boat through the water. ■ a rower.
▶ **v.** [with obj.] row; propel with or as with oars: *oaring the sea like madmen* | [no obj.] *oaring through the weeds.*
– PHRASES **put in one's oar** informal give an opinion without being asked. **rest on one's oars** relax one's efforts.
– DERIVATIVES **oar·less adj.**
– ORIGIN Old English *ār,* of Germanic origin; related to Danish and Norwegian *åre.*

oar·fish /'ôr,fisH/ ▶ **n.** (pl. **same** or **oarfishes**) a very long, narrow, silvery marine fish of deep water, with a deep red dorsal fin running the length of the body. Also called **RIBBONFISH**. ● *Regalecus glesne,* family Regalecidae.

oar·lock /'ôr,läk/ ▶ **n.** a fitting on the gunwale of a boat that serves as a fulcrum for an oar and keeps it in place.

oarlock

oars·man /'ôrzmən/ ▶ **n.** (pl. **oarsmen**) a rower, esp. as a member of a racing team.
– DERIVATIVES **oars·man·ship** /'ôrzmən,SHip/ **n.**

oars·wom·an /'ôrz,wŏŏmən/ ▶ **n.** (pl. **oarswomen**) a female rower, esp. as a member of a racing team.

oar·weed /'ôr,wēd/ ▶ **n.** a large brown kelp with a long hard stalk and a large oar-shaped frond divided into ribbonlike strips, growing on rocky shores. Also called **TANGLE**[2]. ● Genus *Laminaria,* class Phaeophyceae, in particular *L. digitata.*

OAS ▶ **abbr. ORGANIZATION OF AMERICAN STATES.**

o·a·sis /ō'āsis/ ▶ **n.** (pl. **oases** /ō'āsēz/) **1** a fertile spot in a desert where water is found. ■ a pleasant or peaceful area or period in the midst of a difficult, troubled, or hectic place or situation: *an oasis of calm in the center of the city.*
2 (**Oasis**) trademark a type of rigid foam into which the stems of flowers can be secured in flower arranging.
– ORIGIN early 17th cent.: via late Latin from Greek, apparently of Egyptian origin.

oast /ōst/ ▶ **n.** a kiln used for drying hops.
– ORIGIN Old English *āst* (originally denoting any kiln), of Germanic origin; related to Dutch *eest,* from an Indo-European root meaning 'burn.'

oat /ōt/ ▶ **n.** a cereal plant cultivated chiefly in cool climates and widely used for animal feed as well as human consumption. ● *Avena sativa,* family Gramineae. ■ (**oats**) the grain yielded by this, used as food. ■ used in names of wild grasses related to the cultivated oat, e.g., **wild oat**.
– PHRASES **feel one's oats** informal feel lively and energetic. **sow one's wild oats** go through a period of wild or promiscuous behavior while young.
– DERIVATIVES **oat·en** /'ōtn/ **adj.** (archaic), **oat·y adj.**
– ORIGIN Old English *āte,* plural *ātan,* of unknown origin. Unlike other names of cereals (such as *wheat, barley,* etc.), *oat* is not a mass noun and may originally have denoted the individual grain, which may imply that oats were eaten in grains and not as meal.

oat·cake /'ōt,kāk/ ▶ **n.** a thin, unleavened cake made of oatmeal.

oat·er /'ōtər/ ▶ **n.** informal a western movie or television show.
– ORIGIN 1950s: derivative of **OAT**, with allusion to horse feed; compare with the synonym **HORSE OPERA**.

Oates[1] /ōts/, Joyce Carol (1938–) US writer. Her works include *Bellefleur* (1980), *You Must*

Remember This (1988), *Zombie* (1995), *Man Crazy* (1997), *Blonde* (2000), and *My Sister, My Love* (2008).

Oates², Titus (1649–1705), English clergyman and conspirator. He is known as the fabricator of the Popish Plot in 1678.

oat grass ▶ **n.** a wild grass that resembles the oat. ● *Avenula* and other genera, family Gramineae.

oath /ōTH/ ▶ **n.** (pl. **oaths** /ōTHS, ōT͟HZ/) **1** a solemn promise, often invoking a divine witness, regarding one's future action or behavior: *they took an oath of allegiance to the king.* ■ a sworn declaration that one will tell the truth, esp. in a court of law.
2 a profane or offensive expression used to express anger or other strong emotions.
– PHRASES **under oath** having sworn to tell the truth, esp. in a court of law.
– ORIGIN Old English *āth*, of Germanic origin; related to Dutch *eed* and German *Eid*.

oat·meal /ˈōtˌmēl/ ▶ **n. 1** meal made from ground oats, used in breakfast cereals or other food.
2 a grayish-beige color flecked with brown: [as modifier] *an oatmeal jacket.*

OAU ▶ **abbr.** Organization of African Unity.

Oa·xa·ca /wäˈhäkə, -ˈKHäkä/ a state in southern Mexico. ■ its capital city; pop. 265,006 (2005). Full name **Oaxaca de Juárez**.

Ob /äb, ôb/ the principal river of the western Siberian lowlands and one of the largest rivers in Russia. Rising in the Altai Mountains, it flows north and west for 3,481 miles (5,410 km) before entering the Gulf of Ob (or Ob Bay), an inlet of the Kara Sea, a part of the Arctic Ocean.

ob. ▶ **abbr.** he or she died: *ob. 1867.*
– ORIGIN from Latin *obiit*.

ob- ▶ **prefix 1** denoting exposure or openness: *obverse.* ■ expressing meeting or facing: *observe.*
2 denoting opposition, hostility, or resistance: *obstacle.* ■ denoting hindrance, blocking, or concealment: *obliterate* | *obviate.*
3 denoting extensiveness, finality, or completeness: *obdurate* | *obsolete.*
4 (in modern technical words) inversely; in a direction or manner contrary to the usual: *obconical.*
– ORIGIN from Latin *ob* 'toward, against, in the way of.'

Obad. ▶ **abbr.** Bible Obadiah.

O·ba·di·ah /ˌōbəˈdīə/ (in the Bible) a Hebrew minor prophet. ■ the shortest book of the Bible, bearing his name.

O·ba·ma /ōˈbämə/, Barack (1961–), 44th president of the US, since 2009; full name *Barack Hussein Obama*. A Democrat, he is the first African American to be elected to the presidency. Nobel Peace Prize (2009).

Barack Obama

ob·bli·ga·to /ˌäbləˈgätō/ (also **obligato**) ▶ **n.** (pl. **obbligatos** or **obbligati** /-ˈgätē/) [usu. with or as modifier] an instrumental part, typically distinctive in effect, that is integral to a piece of music and should not be omitted in performance.
– ORIGIN Italian, literally 'obligatory,' from Latin *obligatus*, past participle of *obligare* (see **OBLIGE**).

ob·con·i·cal /äbˈkänikəl/ (also **obconic** /-ˈkänik/) ▶ **adj.** Botany in the form of an inverted cone.

ob·cor·date /äbˈkôrˌdāt/ ▶ **adj.** Botany (of a leaf) in the shape of a heart with the pointed end at the base.

ob·du·rate /ˈäbd(y)ərit/ ▶ **adj.** stubbornly refusing to change one's opinion or course of action.
– DERIVATIVES **ob·du·ra·cy** /-rəsē/ **n.**, **ob·du·rate·ly adv.**, **ob·du·rate·ness n.**
– ORIGIN late Middle English (originally in the sense 'hardened in sin, impenitent'): from Latin *obduratus*, past participle of *obdurare*, from *ob-* 'in opposition' + *durare* 'harden' (from *durus* 'hard').

o·beah /ˈōbēə/ (also **obi** /ˈōbē/) ▶ **n.** a kind of sorcery practiced esp. in the Caribbean.
– ORIGIN Twi, from *bayi* 'sorcery.'

o·be·che /ōˈbēCHē/ ▶ **n.** a tropical tree native to West and central Africa, used for its pale timber that is used for plywood and veneers. ● *Triplochiton scleroxylon*, family Sterculiaceae.
– ORIGIN early 20th cent.: a term used in Nigeria.

o·be·di·ence /ōˈbēdēəns/ ▶ **n.** compliance with an order, request, or law or submission to another's authority: *children were taught to show their parents obedience* | *obedience to moral standards.* ■ observance of a monastic rule: *vows of poverty, chastity, and obedience.*
– PHRASES **in obedience to** in accordance with: *he was acting in obedience to his conscience.*
– ORIGIN Middle English: via Old French from Latin *oboedientia*, from the verb *oboedire* (see **OBEY**).

o·be·di·ent /ōˈbēdēənt/ ▶ **adj.** complying or willing to comply with orders or requests; submissive to another's will: *she was totally obedient to him.*
– PHRASES **your obedient servant** dated a formula used to end a letter.
– DERIVATIVES **o·be·di·ent·ly adv.**
– ORIGIN Middle English: via Old French from Latin *oboedient-* 'obeying,' from the verb *oboedire* (see **OBEY**).

o·bei·sance /ōˈbāsəns, ōˈbē-/ ▶ **n.** deferential respect: *they paid obeisance to the prince.* ■ a gesture expressing deferential respect, such as a bow or curtsy: *she made a deep obeisance.*
– DERIVATIVES **o·bei·sant** /ōˈbāsənt/ **adj.**
– ORIGIN late Middle English (in the sense 'obedience'): from Old French *obeissance*, from *obeissant* 'obeying,' present participle of *obeir*.

ob·e·li /ˈäbəˌlī/ plural form of **OBELUS**.

o·be·lia /ōˈbēlyə, -ˈbēlēə/ ▶ **n.** Zoology a genus of marine animals that bear polyps and produce medusae, and that form colonies that attach to rocks or the ocean bottom. ● Genus *Obelia*, class Hydrozoa.
– ORIGIN modern Latin, from Greek *obelos* 'tapering column.'

ob·e·lisk /ˈäbəˌlisk/ ▶ **n.**
1 a stone pillar, typically having a square or rectangular cross section and a pyramidal top, set up as a monument or landmark. ■ a mountain, tree, or other natural object of similar shape.
2 another term for **OBELUS**.
– ORIGIN mid 16th cent.: via Latin from Greek *obeliskos*, diminutive of *obelos* 'pointed pillar.'

obelisk 1

ob·e·lize /ˈäbəˌlīz/ ▶ **v.** [with obj.] mark (a word or passage) with an obelus to show that it is spurious, corrupt, or doubtful.
– ORIGIN mid 17th cent.: from Greek *obelizein*, in the same sense.

ob·e·lus /ˈäbələs/ ▶ **n.** (pl. **obeli** /-ˌlī/) **1** a symbol (†) used as a reference mark in printed matter, or to indicate that a person is deceased. Also called **DAGGER**.
2 a mark (– or ÷) used in ancient texts to mark a word or passage as spurious, corrupt, or doubtful.
– ORIGIN late Middle English: via Latin from Greek *obelos* 'pointed pillar,' also 'critical mark.'

O·ber·am·mer·gau /ˌōbərˈämərgou/ a village in the Bavarian Alps of southwestern Germany; pop. 5,400 (est. 2006). It is the site of one of the few surviving passion plays, which has been performed by the villagers every tenth year (with few exceptions) from 1634 as a result of a vow made during an epidemic of plague.

O·ber·hau·sen /ˈōbərˌhouzən/ an industrial city in western Germany, in the Ruhr valley of North Rhine–Westphalia; pop. 218,200 (est. 2006).

O·ber·on /ˈōbəˌrän/ Astronomy a satellite of Uranus, the furthest from the planet, discovered by W. Herschel in 1787. It has a heavily cratered surface and a diameter of 963 miles (1,550 km).
– ORIGIN from the name of the king of the fairies in Shakespeare's *A Midsummer Night's Dream*.

o·bese /ōˈbēs/ ▶ **adj.** grossly fat or overweight.
– ORIGIN mid 17th cent.: from Latin *obesus* 'having eaten until fat,' from *ob-* 'away, completely' + *esus* (past participle of *edere* 'eat').

o·be·si·ty /ōˈbēsitē/ ▶ **n.** the condition of being grossly fat or overweight: *the problem of obesity among children.*

o·bey /ōˈbā/ ▶ **v.** [with obj.] comply with the command, direction, or request of (a person or a law); submit to the authority of: *I always obey my father.* ■ carry out (a command or instruction): *the officer was convicted for refusing to obey orders* | [no obj.] *when the order was repeated, he refused to obey.* ■ behave in accordance with (a general principle, natural law, etc.): *the universe was complex but it obeyed certain rules.*
– DERIVATIVES **o·bey·er n.**
– ORIGIN Middle English: from Old French *obeir*, from Latin *oboedire*, from *ob-* 'in the direction of' + *audire* 'hear.'

ob·fus·cate /ˈäbfəˌskāt/ ▶ **v.** [with obj.] render obscure, unclear, or unintelligible: *the spelling changes will deform some familiar words and obfuscate their etymological origins.* ■ bewilder (someone): *it is more likely to obfuscate people than enlighten them.*
– DERIVATIVES **ob·fus·ca·tion** /ˌäbfəˈskāSHən/ **n.**, **ob·fus·ca·to·ry** /äbˈfəskəˌtôrē/ **adj.**
– ORIGIN late Middle English: from Latin *obfuscat-* 'darkened,' from the verb *obfuscare*, based on Latin *fuscus* 'dark.'

ob-gyn ▶ **abbr.** obstetrics and gynecology.

o·bi¹ /ˈōbē/ ▶ **n.** (pl. **obis**) a broad sash worn around the waist of a Japanese kimono.
– ORIGIN Japanese, literally 'belt.'

o·bi² ▶ **n.** variant form of **OBEAH**.

o·bit /ˈōbit, ōˈbit/ ▶ **n.** informal an obituary.
– ORIGIN late Middle English: now regarded as an abbreviation of **OBITUARY**, but originally also used in the senses 'death' and 'funeral service,' from Latin *obitus* 'going down, death.'

ob·i·ter dic·tum /ˈōbitər ˈdiktəm/ ▶ **n.** (pl. **dicta** /ˈdiktə/) Law a judge's incidental expression of opinion, not essential to the decision and not establishing precedent. ■ an incidental remark.
– ORIGIN Latin *obiter* 'in passing' + *dictum* 'something that is said.'

o·bit·u·ar·y /ōˈbiCHo͞oˌerē/ ▶ **n.** (pl. **obituaries**) a notice of a death, esp. in a newspaper, typically including a brief biography of the deceased person: *the obituary of a friend* | [as modifier] *an obituary notice.*
– DERIVATIVES **o·bit·u·ar·ist** /-ərist/ **n.**
– ORIGIN early 18th cent.: from medieval Latin *obituarius*, from Latin *obitus* 'death,' from *obit-* 'perished,' from the verb *obire*.

obj. ▶ **abbr.** ■ object. ■ objection. ■ objective.

ob·ject ▶ **n.** /ˈäbjəkt/ **1** a material thing that can be seen and touched: *he was dragging a large object* | *small objects such as shells.* ■ Philosophy a thing external to the thinking mind or subject.
2 a person or thing to which a specified action or feeling is directed: *disease became the object of investigation.* ■ a goal or purpose: *the institute was opened with the object of promoting scientific study.* ■ Grammar a noun or noun phrase governed by an active transitive verb or by a preposition. ■ Computing a data construct that provides a description of something that may be used by a computer (such as a processor, a peripheral, a document, or a data set) and defines its status, its method of operation, and how it interacts with other objects.
▶ **v.** /əbˈjekt/ [reporting verb] say something to express one's disapproval of or disagreement with something: [no obj.] *residents object to the volume of traffic* | [with clause] *the boy's father objected that the police had arrested him unlawfully.* ■ [with obj.] archaic adduce as a reason against something: *Bryant objects this very circumstance to the authenticity of the Iliad.*
– PHRASES **no object** not influencing or restricting choices or decisions: *a tycoon for whom money is no object.*
– DERIVATIVES **ob·ject·less** /ˈäbjəktləs/ **adj.**, **ob·jec·tor** /əbˈjektər/ **n.**
– ORIGIN late Middle English: from medieval Latin *objectum* 'thing presented to the mind,' neuter past participle (used as a noun) of Latin *obicere*, from *ob-* 'in the way of' + *jacere* 'to throw'; the verb may also partly represent the Latin frequentative *objectare*.

ob·ject ball ▶ **n.** Billiards any ball other than the cue ball.

ob·ject choice ▶ **n.** Psychoanalysis a person or thing external to the ego, chosen as a focus of desire or sexual activity.

ob·ject code ▶ **n.** Computing code produced by a compiler or assembler.

ob·ject glass ▶ **n.** another term for **OBJECTIVE** (sense 3 of the noun).

ob·jec·ti·fy /əbˈjektəˌfī/ ▶ **v.** (**objectifies, objectifying, objectified**) [with obj.] express (something abstract) in a concrete form: *good poetry objectifies feeling.* ■ degrade to the status of a mere object: *a deeply sexist attitude that objectifies women.*

PRONUNCIATION KEY ə *ago, up*; ər *over, fur*; a *hat*; ā *ate*; ä *car*; e *let*; ē *see*; i *fit*; ī *by*; NG *sing*; ō *go*; ô *law, for*; oi *toy*; o͝o *good*; o͞o *goo*; ou *out*; TH *thin*; T͟H *then*; ZH *vision*

– DERIVATIVES **ob·jec·ti·fi·ca·tion** /əbˌjektəfiˈkāSHən/ **n.**

ob·jec·tion /əbˈjekSHən/ ▶ **n.** an expression or feeling of disapproval or opposition; a reason for disagreeing: *they have raised no objections to the latest plans.* ■ the action of challenging or disagreeing with something: *his view is open to objection.*
– ORIGIN late Middle English: from Old French, or from late Latin *objectio(n-)*, from the verb *obicere* (see OBJECT).

ob·jec·tion·a·ble /əbˈjekSHənəbəl/ ▶ **adj.** arousing distaste or opposition; unpleasant or offensive: *I find his theory objectionable in its racist undertones.*
– DERIVATIVES **ob·jec·tion·a·ble·ness n., ob·jec·tion·a·bly** /-blē/ **adv.**

ob·jec·tive /əbˈjektiv/ ▶ **adj. 1** (of a person or their judgment) not influenced by personal feelings or opinions in considering and representing facts: *historians try to be objective and impartial.* Contrasted with SUBJECTIVE. ■ not dependent on the mind for existence; actual: *a matter of objective fact.*
2 [attrib.] Grammar of, relating to, or denoting a case of nouns and pronouns used as the object of a transitive verb or a preposition.
▶ **n. 1** a thing aimed at or sought; a goal: *the system has achieved its objective.*
2 (**the objective**) Grammar the objective case.
3 (also **objective lens**) the lens in a telescope or microscope nearest to the object observed.
– DERIVATIVES **ob·jec·tive·ly adv., ob·jec·tive·ness n., ob·jec·ti·vi·za·tion** /əbˌjektəviˈzāSHən/ **n., ob·jec·tiv·ize** /-ˌvīz/ **v.**
– ORIGIN early 17th cent.: from medieval Latin *objectivus*, from *objectum* (see OBJECT).

ob·jec·tive cor·rel·a·tive ▶ **n.** the artistic and literary technique of representing or evoking a particular emotion by means of symbols that objectify that emotion and are associated with it.

ob·jec·tive func·tion ▶ **n.** Mathematics (in linear programming) the function that it is desired to maximize or minimize.

ob·jec·tiv·ism /əbˈjektəˌvizəm/ ▶ **n. 1** the tendency to lay stress on what is external to or independent of the mind.
2 Philosophy the belief that certain things, esp. moral truths, exist independently of human knowledge or perception of them.
– DERIVATIVES **ob·jec·tiv·ist n. & adj., ob·jec·ti·vis·tic** /əbˌjektəˈvistik/ **adj.**

ob·jec·tiv·i·ty /ˌäbjekˈtivitē/ ▶ **n.** the quality of being objective: *the piece lacked any objectivity.*

ob·ject lan·guage ▶ **n. 1** a language described by means of another language. Compare with METALANGUAGE, TARGET LANGUAGE.
2 Computing a language into which a program is translated by means of a compiler or assembler.

ob·ject les·son ▶ **n.** a striking practical example of some principle or ideal: *they responded to emergencies in a way that was an object lesson to us all.*

ob·ject-o·ri·ent·ed ▶ **adj.** Computing (of a programming language) using a methodology that enables a system to be modeled as a set of objects that can be controlled and manipulated in a modular manner.
– DERIVATIVES **ob·ject o·ri·en·ta·tion n.**

ob·ject pro·gram ▶ **n.** Computing a program into which some other program is translated by an assembler or compiler.
– DERIVATIVES **ob·ject pro·gram·ming n.**

ob·ject re·la·tions ▶ **n.** Psychoanalysis a theory describing the relationship felt or the emotional energy directed by the self or ego toward a chosen object.

ob·ject world ▶ **n.** the world external to the self, apprehended through the objects in it.

ob·jet d'art /ˌôbZHä ˈdär/ ▶ **n.** (pl. **objets d'art** pronunc. **same**) a small decorative or artistic object, typically when regarded as a collectible item.
– ORIGIN French, literally 'object of art.'

ob·jet trou·vé /ôbˌZHä trōōˈvā/ ▶ **n.** (pl. **objets trouvés** pronunc. **same**) an object found or picked up at random and considered aesthetically pleasing.
– ORIGIN French, literally 'found object.'

ob·jur·gate /ˈäbjərˌgāt/ ▶ **v.** [with obj.] rebuke severely; scold.
– DERIVATIVES **ob·jur·ga·tion** /ˌäbjərˈgāSHən/ **n., ob·jur·ga·tor** /-gātər/ **n., ob·jur·ga·to·ry** /əbˈjərgəˌtôrē/ **adj.**
– ORIGIN early 17th cent.: from Latin *objurgat-* 'chided, rebuked,' from the verb *objurgare*, based on *jurgium* 'strife.'

obl. ▶ **abbr.** ■ oblique. ■ oblong.

ob·lan·ce·o·late /äbˈlansēəˌlāt/ ▶ **adj.** technical (esp. of leaves) lanceolate, with the more pointed end at the base.

o·blast /ˈôbləst, ˈäblast/ ▶ **n.** an administrative division or region in Russia and the former Soviet Union, and in some of its former constituent republics.
– ORIGIN Russian.

ob·late[1] /ˈäbˌlāt, ˌōˈblāt/ ▶ **adj.** Geometry (of a spheroid) flattened at the poles. Often contrasted with PROLATE.
– ORIGIN early 18th cent.: from modern Latin *oblatus* (from *ob-* 'inversely' + *-latus* 'carried'), on the pattern of Latin *prolatus* 'prolonged.'

ob·late[2] ▶ **n.** a person dedicated to a religious life, but typically having not taken full monastic vows.
– ORIGIN late 17th cent.: from French, from medieval Latin *oblatus*, past participle (used as a noun) of Latin *offerre* 'to offer.'

ob·la·tion /əˈblāSHən/ ▶ **n.** a thing presented or offered to God or a god. ■ Christian Church the presentation of bread and wine to God in the Eucharist.
– DERIVATIVES **ob·la·tion·al** /-SHənl, -SHənəl/ **adj., ob·la·to·ry** /ˈäbləˌtôrē/ **adj.**
– ORIGIN late Middle English: from Old French, or from late Latin *oblatio(n-)*, from Latin *offerre* 'to offer.'

ob·li·gate ▶ **v.** /ˈäbliˌgāt/ **1** bind or compel (someone), esp. legally or morally: *the medical establishment is obligated to take action in the best interest of the public.*
2 [with obj.] commit (assets) as security: *the money must be obligated within thirty days.*
▶ **adj.** /ˈäbligit/ [attrib.] Biology restricted to a particular function or mode of life: *an obligate intracellular parasite.* Often contrasted with FACULTATIVE.
– DERIVATIVES **ob·li·ga·tor** /-ˌgātər/ **n.**
– ORIGIN late Middle English (as an adjective in the sense 'bound by law'): from Latin *obligatus*, past participle of *obligare* (see OBLIGE). The current adjectival use dates from the late 19th cent.

ob·li·ga·tion /ˌäbliˈgāSHən/ ▶ **n.** an act or course of action to which a person is morally or legally bound; a duty or commitment: *he has enough cash to meet his present obligations* | [with infinitive] *I have an obligation to look after her.* ■ the condition of being morally or legally bound to do something: *they are* ***under no obligation*** *to stick to the scheme.* ■ a debt of gratitude for a service or favor: *she didn't want to be under an obligation to him.* ■ Law a binding agreement committing a person to a payment or other action.
– DERIVATIVES **ob·li·ga·tion·al** /-SHənl, -SHənəl/ **adj.**
– ORIGIN Middle English (in the sense 'formal promise'): via Old French from Latin *obligatio(n-)*, from the verb *obligare* (see OBLIGE).

ob·li·ga·to /ˌäbliˈgätō/ ▶ **n.** variant spelling of OBBLIGATO.

o·blig·a·to·ry /əˈbligəˌtôrē/ ▶ **adj.** required by a legal, moral, or other rule; compulsory: *use of seat belts in cars is now obligatory.* ■ so customary or routine as to be expected of everyone or on every occasion: *after the obligatory preamble on the weather he got down to business.* ■ (of a ruling) having binding force: *a sovereign whose laws are obligatory.*
– DERIVATIVES **ob·lig·a·to·ri·ly** /-ˌtôrəlē/ **adv.**
– ORIGIN late Middle English: from late Latin *obligatorius*, from Latin *obligat-* 'obliged,' from the verb *obligare* (see OBLIGE).

o·blige /əˈblīj/ ▶ **v.** [with obj. and infinitive] make (someone) legally or morally bound to an action or course of action: *doctors are obliged by law to keep patients alive while there is a chance of recovery.* ■ [with obj.] do as (someone) asks or desires in order to help or please them: ***oblige me by*** *not being sorry for yourself* | [no obj.] *tell me what you want to know and I'll see if I can oblige.* ■ (**be obliged**) be indebted or grateful: *if you can give me a few minutes of your time I'll be much obliged.* ■ [with obj.] archaic bind (someone) by an oath, promise, or contract.
– DERIVATIVES **o·blig·er n.**
– ORIGIN Middle English (in the sense 'bind by oath'): from Old French *obliger*, from Latin *obligare*, from *ob-* 'toward' + *ligare* 'to bind.'

ob·li·gee /ˌäbliˈjē/ ▶ **n.** Law a person to whom another is bound by contract or other legal procedure. Compare with OBLIGOR.

o·blig·ing /əˈblījiNG/ ▶ **adj.** willing to do a service or kindness; helpful.
– DERIVATIVES **o·blig·ing·ly adv., o·blig·ing·ness n.**

ob·li·gor /ˌäbliˈgôr/ ▶ **n.** Law a person who is bound to another by contract or other legal procedure. Compare with OBLIGEE.

o·blique /əˈblēk, ōˈblēk/ ▶ **adj. 1** neither parallel nor at a right angle to a specified or implied line; slanting: *we sat on the settee oblique to the fireplace.* ■ not explicit or direct in addressing a point: *he issued an oblique attack on the president.* ■ Geometry (of a line, plane figure, or surface) inclined at other than a right angle. ■ Geometry (of an angle) acute or obtuse. ■ Geometry (of a cone, cylinder, etc.) with an axis not perpendicular to the plane of its base. ■ Anatomy (esp. of a muscle) neither parallel nor perpendicular to the long axis of a body or limb.
2 Grammar denoting any case other than the nominative or vocative.
▶ **n. 1** a muscle neither parallel nor perpendicular to the long axis of a body or limb.
2 Brit. another term for SLASH[1] (sense 2 of the noun).
– DERIVATIVES **o·blique·ness n., o·bliq·ui·ty** /əˈblikwətē/ **n.**
– ORIGIN late Middle English: from Latin *obliquus*.

o·blique·ly /əˈblēklē, ōˈblēklē/ ▶ **adv. 1** not in a direct way; indirectly: *he referred only obliquely to current events.*
2 in an oblique direction; slantwise: *these markings cross the wing obliquely.*

ob·lit·er·ate /əˈblitəˌrāt/ ▶ **v.** [with obj.] destroy utterly; wipe out: figurative *the memory was so painful that he obliterated it from his mind.* ■ cause to become invisible or indistinct; blot out: *clouds were darkening, obliterating the sun.*
– DERIVATIVES **ob·lit·er·a·tive** /-ˌrātiv/ **adj., o·blit·er·a·tor** /-ˌrātər/ **n.**
– ORIGIN mid 16th cent.: from Latin *obliterat-* 'struck out, erased,' from the verb *obliterare*, based on *littera* 'letter, something written.'

ob·lit·er·a·tion /əˌblitəˈrāSHən/ ▶ **n.** the action or fact of obliterating or being obliterated; total destruction: *the obliteration of vast green spaces.*

ob·liv·i·on /əˈblivēən/ ▶ **n. 1** the state of being unaware or unconscious of what is happening: *they drank themselves into oblivion.* ■ the state of being forgotten, esp. by the public: *his name will fade into oblivion.* ■ extinction: *only our armed forces stood between us and oblivion.*
2 Law, historical amnesty or pardon.
– ORIGIN late Middle English: via Old French from Latin *oblivio(n-)*, from *oblivisci* 'forget.'

ob·liv·i·ous /əˈblivēəs/ ▶ **adj.** not aware of or not concerned about what is happening around one: *she became absorbed,* ***oblivious to*** *the passage of time* | *the women were oblivious of his presence.*
– DERIVATIVES **ob·liv·i·ous·ly adv., ob·liv·i·ous·ness n.**
– ORIGIN late Middle English: from Latin *obliviosus*, from *oblivio(n-)* (see OBLIVION).

ob·long /ˈäbˌlôNG, -ˌläNG/ ▶ **adj.** having an elongated shape, as a rectangle or an oval.
▶ **n.** an object or flat figure in this shape.
– ORIGIN late Middle English: from Latin *oblongus* 'longish.'

ob·lo·quy /ˈäbləkwē/ ▶ **n.** strong public criticism or verbal abuse: *he endured years of contempt and obloquy.* ■ disgrace, esp. that brought about by public abuse: *conduct to which no more obloquy could reasonably attach.*
– DERIVATIVES **ob·lo·qui·al** /äbˈlōkwēəl/ **adj., ob·lo·qui·ous** /äbˈlōkwēəs/ **adj.**
– ORIGIN late Middle English: from late Latin *obloquium* 'contradiction,' from Latin *obloqui*, from *ob-* 'against' + *loqui* 'speak.'

ob·nox·ious /əbˈnäkSHəs/ ▶ **adj.** extremely unpleasant.
– DERIVATIVES **ob·nox·ious·ly adv., ob·nox·ious·ness n.**
– ORIGIN late 16th cent. (in the sense 'vulnerable [to harm]'): from Latin *obnoxiosus*, from *obnoxius* 'exposed to harm,' from *ob-* 'toward' + *noxa* 'harm.' The current sense, influenced by NOXIOUS, dates from the late 17th cent.

ob·nu·bi·late /äbˈn(y)ōōbəˌlāt/ ▶ **v.** [with obj.] literary darken, dim, or cover with or as if with a cloud; obscure.
– DERIVATIVES **ob·nu·bi·la·tion** /äbˌn(y)ōōbəˈlāSHən/ **n.**
– ORIGIN late 16th cent.: from Latin *obnubilat-* 'covered with clouds or fog,' from the verb *obnubilare*.

obo (also **o.b.o.**) ▶ **abbr.** or best offer (used in advertisements): *$2,700 obo.*

o·boe /ˈōbō/ ▶ **n.** a woodwind instrument with a double-reed mouthpiece, a slender tubular body, and holes stopped by keys. ■ an organ stop resembling an oboe in tone.
– DERIVATIVES **o·bo·ist** /-wist/ **n.**
– ORIGIN early 18th cent.: from Italian, or from French *hautbois*, from *haut* 'high' + *bois* 'wood.'

oboe

o·boe d'a·mo·re /ˈōbō däˈmôrā/ ▶ **n.** a type of oboe with a bulbous bell, sounding a minor third lower

than the ordinary oboe. It has a soft tone and is used in baroque music.
– ORIGIN late 19th cent.: from Italian, literally 'oboe of love.'

ob·ol /ˈäbəl/ ▶ n. an ancient Greek coin worth one sixth of a drachma.
– ORIGIN via Latin from Greek *obolos*, variant of *obelos* (see OBELUS).

O-Bon /ō ˈbôn/ ▶ n. another name for **Bon**.

O·bo·te /ōˈbōtā/, Milton (1924–2005), Ugandan statesman; prime minister 1962–66; president 1966–71 and 1980–85; full name *Apollo Milton Obote*. Overthrown by Idi Amin in 1971, he was re-elected president in 1980, but was removed in a second military coup in 1985.

ob·o·vate /äˈbō,vāt/ ▶ adj. Botany (of a leaf) ovate with the narrower end at the base.

O'Bri·en[1] /ōˈbrīən/, Edna (1932–), Irish novelist and short-story writer. Her works include the novels *The Country Girls* (1960) and *In the Forest* (2002), the collection *A Fanatic Heart: Selected Stories* (1984), and the biography *Byron in Love* (2009).

O'Bri·en[2], Flann (1911–66), Irish novelist and journalist; pseudonym of *Brian O'Nolan*. Writing under the name of Myles na Gopaleen, he contributed a satirical column to the *Irish Times* for nearly twenty years. Notable novels: *At Swim-Two-Birds* (1939); *The Third Policeman* (1967).

obs. (also **Obs.**) ▶ abbr. ■ observation. ■ observatory. ■ obsolete.

ob·scene /əbˈsēn/ ▶ adj. (of the portrayal or description of sexual matters) offensive or disgusting by accepted standards of morality and decency: *obscene jokes | obscene literature*. ■ offensive to moral principles; repugnant: *using animals' skins for fur coats is obscene*.
– DERIVATIVES **ob·scene·ly** adv.
– ORIGIN late 16th cent.: from French *obscène* or Latin *obscaenus* 'ill-omened or abominable.'

ob·scen·i·ty /əbˈsenitē/ ▶ n. (pl. **obscenities**) the state or quality of being obscene; obscene behavior, language, or images: *the book was banned for obscenity*. ■ an extremely offensive word or expression: *the men scowled and muttered obscenities*.
– ORIGIN late 16th cent.: from French *obscénité* or Latin *obscaenitas*, from *obscaenus* (see OBSCENE).

ob·scu·rant·ism /əbˈskyo͝orən,tizəm, äb-, ,äbskyəˈran-/ ▶ n. the practice of deliberately preventing the facts or full details of something from becoming known.
– DERIVATIVES **ob·scu·rant** /ˈäbskyərənt/ n. & adj., **ob·scu·rant·ist** n. & adj.
– ORIGIN mid 19th cent.: from earlier *obscurant*, denoting a person who obscures something, via German from Latin *obscurant-* 'making dark,' from the verb *obscurare*.

ob·scure /əbˈskyo͝or/ ▶ adj. (**obscurer, obscurest**) not discovered or known about; uncertain: *his origins and parentage are obscure*. ■ not clearly expressed or easily understood: *obscure references to Proust*. ■ not important or well known: *an obscure religious sect*. ■ hard to make out or define; vague: figurative *I feel an obscure resentment*. ■ (of a color) not sharply defined; dim or dingy.
▶ v. [with obj.] keep from being seen; conceal: *gray clouds obscure the sun*. ■ make unclear and difficult to understand: *the debate has become obscured by conflicting ideological perspectives*. ■ overshadow: *none of this should obscure the skill, experience, and perseverance of the workers*.
– DERIVATIVES **ob·scu·ra·tion** /,äbskyəˈrāsʜən/ n., **ob·scure·ly** adv.
– ORIGIN late Middle English: from Old French *obscur*, from Latin *obscurus* 'dark,' from an Indo-European root meaning 'cover.'

ob·scure vow·el ▶ n. another term for INDETERMINATE VOWEL.

ob·scu·ri·ty /əbˈskyo͝oritē/ ▶ n. (pl. **obscurities**) the state of being unknown, inconspicuous, or unimportant: *he is too good a player to slide into obscurity*. ■ the quality of being difficult to understand: *poems of impenetrable obscurity*. ■ a thing that is unclear or difficult to understand: *the obscurities in his poems and plays*.
– ORIGIN late Middle English: from Old French *obscurite*, from Latin *obscuritas*, from *obscurus* 'dark.'

obsd. ▶ abbr. (esp. in medical and scientific abstracts) observed.

ob·se·cra·tion /,äbsəˈkrāsʜən/ ▶ n. rare earnest pleading or supplication.
– ORIGIN late Middle English: from Latin *obsecratio(n-)*, from *obsecrare* 'entreat,' based on *sacer, sacr-* 'sacred.'

ob·se·quies /ˈäbsəkwēz/ ▶ plural n. funeral rites.
– ORIGIN late Middle English: plural of obsolete *obsequy*, from Anglo-Norman French *obsequie*, from the medieval Latin plural *obsequiae* (from Latin *exsequiae* 'funeral rites,' influenced by *obsequium* 'dutiful service').

ob·se·qui·ous /əbˈsēkwēəs/ ▶ adj. obedient or attentive to an excessive or servile degree: *they were served by obsequious waiters*.
– DERIVATIVES **ob·se·qui·ous·ly** adv., **ob·se·qui·ous·ness** n.
– ORIGIN late 15th cent. (not depreciatory in sense in early use): from Latin *obsequiosus*, from *obsequium* 'compliance,' from *obsequi* 'follow, comply with.'

ob·serv·a·ble /əbˈzərvəbəl/ ▶ adj. able to be noticed or perceived; discernible: *observable differences*.
– DERIVATIVES **ob·serv·a·bil·i·ty** n., **ob·serv·a·bly** /-blē/ adv.

ob·serv·ance /əbˈzərvəns/ ▶ n. **1** the action or practice of fulfilling or respecting the requirements of law, morality, or ritual: *strict **observance of the rules** | the decline in religious observance*. ■ (usu. **observances**) an act performed for religious or ceremonial reasons: *official anniversary observances*. ■ a rule to be followed by a religious order: *he drew up a body of monastic observances*. ■ archaic respect; deference.
2 the action of watching or noticing something: *the baby's motionless observance of me*.
– ORIGIN Middle English: via Old French from Latin *observantia*, from *observant-* 'watching, paying attention to,' from the verb *observare* (see OBSERVE).

ob·serv·ant /əbˈzərvənt/ ▶ adj. **1** quick to notice things: *her observant eye took in every detail*.
2 adhering strictly to the rules of a particular religion, esp. Judaism.
▶ n. (**Observant**) historical a member of a branch of the Franciscan order that followed a strict rule.
– ORIGIN late Middle English (as a noun): from French, literally 'watching,' present participle of *observer* (see OBSERVE).

ob·ser·va·tion /,äbzərˈvāsʜən/ ▶ n. **1** the action or process of observing something or someone carefully or in order to gain information: *she was brought into the hospital for observation | detailed observations were carried out on the students' behavior*. ■ the ability to notice things, esp. significant details: *his powers of observation*. ■ the taking of the altitude of the sun or another celestial body for navigational purposes.
2 a remark, statement, or comment based on something one has seen, heard, or noticed: *he made a telling observation about Hugh*.
– PHRASES **under observation** (esp. of a patient or a suspected criminal) being closely and constantly watched or monitored: *he spent two nights in the hospital under observation*.
– DERIVATIVES **ob·ser·va·tion·al** /-sʜənl/ adj., **ob·ser·va·tion·al·ly** /-sʜənl-ē/ adv.
– ORIGIN late Middle English (in the sense 'respectful adherence to the requirements of [rules, a ritual, etc.]'): from Latin *observatio(n-)*, from the verb *observare* (see OBSERVE).

ob·ser·va·tion car ▶ n. a railroad car with large windows designed to provide a good view of passing scenery.

ob·ser·va·tion post ▶ n. Military a post for watching the movement of enemy forces or the effect of artillery fire.

ob·serv·a·to·ry /əbˈzərvə,tôrē/ ▶ n. (pl. **observatories**) a room or building housing an astronomical telescope or other scientific equipment for the study of natural phenomena. ■ a position or building that gives an extensive view.
– ORIGIN late 17th cent.; from modern Latin *observatorium*, from Latin *observat-* 'watched,' from the verb *observare* (see OBSERVE).

ob·serve /əbˈzərv/ ▶ v. [with obj.] **1** notice or perceive (something) and register it as being significant: [with clause] *young people observe that decisions are made by others*. ■ watch (someone or something) carefully and attentively: *Rob stood in the hallway, where he could observe the happenings on the street*. ■ take note of or detect (something) in the course of a scientific study: *the behavior observed in groups of chimpanzees*. ■ [reporting verb] make a remark or comment: [with direct speech] *"It's chilly," she observed* | [with clause] *a stockbroker once observed that dealers live and work in hell*.
2 fulfill or comply with (a social, legal, ethical, or religious obligation): *a tribunal must observe the principles of natural justice*. ■ maintain (silence) in compliance with a rule or custom, or temporarily as a mark of respect: *a minute's silence will be observed*. ■ perform or take part in (a rite or ceremony): *relations gather to observe the funeral rites*. ■ celebrate or acknowledge (an anniversary): *many observed the one-year anniversary of the flood*.
– ORIGIN late Middle English (sense 2): from Old French *observer*, from Latin *observare* 'to watch,' from *ob-* 'toward' + *servare* 'attend to, look at.'

ob·serv·er /əbˈzərvər/ ▶ n. a person who watches or notices something: *to a casual observer, he was at peace*. ■ a person who follows events, esp. political ones, closely and comments publicly on them: *some observers expect interest rates to rise*. ■ a person posted to an area in an official capacity to monitor political or military events: *elections scrutinized by international observers*. ■ a person who attends a conference, inquiry, etc., to note the proceedings without participating in them.

ob·sess /əbˈses/ ▶ v. [with obj.] preoccupy or fill the mind of (someone) continually, intrusively, and to a troubling extent: *he was obsessed with the theme of death* | (as adj. **obsessed**) *he became completely obsessed about germs*. ■ [no obj.] (of a person) be preoccupied in this way: *her husband, who is **obsessing about** the wrong she has done him*.
– ORIGIN late Middle English (in the sense 'haunt, possess,' referring to an evil spirit): from Latin *obsess-* 'besieged,' from the verb *obsidere*, from *ob-* 'opposite' + *sedere* 'sit.' The current sense dates from the late 19th cent.

ob·ses·sion /əbˈsesʜən/ ▶ n. the state of being obsessed with someone or something: *she cared for him with a devotion bordering on obsession*. ■ an idea or thought that continually preoccupies or intrudes on a person's mind: *he was in the grip of an obsession he was powerless to resist*.
– DERIVATIVES **ob·ses·sion·al** /-sʜənl/ adj., **ob·ses·sion·al·ly** /-sʜənl-ē/ adv.
– ORIGIN early 16th cent. (in the sense 'siege'): from Latin *obsessio(n-)*, from the verb *obsidere* (see OBSESS).

ob·ses·sive /əbˈsesiv/ ▶ adj. of the nature of an obsession: *people dogged by obsessive jealousy*. ■ affected by an obsession: *she became obsessive about her schoolwork*.
▶ n. a person who is affected by an obsession: *an online store for garage-rock obsessives*.
– DERIVATIVES **ob·ses·sive·ly** /-ˈsesivlē/ adv., **ob·ses·sive·ness** /-ˈsesivnis/ n.

ob·ses·sive–com·pul·sive ▶ adj. Psychiatry denoting or relating to a disorder in which a person feels compelled to perform certain meaningless actions repeatedly in order to alleviate obsessive fears or intrusive thoughts, typically resulting in severe disruption of daily life.
▶ n. a person characterized by such obsessive behavior.

ob·sid·i·an /əbˈsidēən, äb-/ ▶ n. a hard, dark, glasslike volcanic rock formed by the rapid solidification of lava without crystallization.
– ORIGIN mid 17th cent.: from Latin *obsidianus*, error for *obsianus*, from *Obsius*, the name (in Pliny) of the discoverer of a similar stone.

ob·so·les·cent /,äbsəˈlesənt/ ▶ adj. becoming obsolete: *the custom is now obsolescent*.
– DERIVATIVES **ob·so·lesce** v. *existing systems begin to obsolesce*, **ob·so·les·cence** n.
– ORIGIN mid 18th cent.: from Latin *obsolescent-* 'falling into disuse,' from the verb *obsolescere*.

ob·so·lete /,äbsəˈlēt/ ▶ adj. **1** no longer produced or used; out of date: *the disposal of old and obsolete machinery | the phrase was obsolete after 1625*.
2 Biology (of a part or characteristic of an organism) less developed than formerly or in a related species; rudimentary; vestigial.
▶ v. [with obj.] cause (a product or idea) to be or become obsolete by replacing it with something new: *we're trying to stimulate the business by obsoleting last year's designs*.
– DERIVATIVES **ob·so·lete·ly** adv., **ob·so·lete·ness** n., **ob·so·let·ism** /-ˈlē,tizəm/ n.
– ORIGIN late 16th cent.: from Latin *obsoletus* 'grown old, worn out,' past participle of *obsolescere* 'fall into disuse.'

ob·sta·cle /ˈäbstəkəl/ ▶ n. a thing that blocks one's way or prevents or hinders progress: *the major **obstacle to** achieving that goal is money*.
– ORIGIN Middle English: via Old French from Latin *obstaculum*, from *obstare* 'impede,' from *ob-* 'against' + *stare* 'stand.'

ob·sta·cle course ▶ n. a course over which participants negotiate obstacles to be climbed, crawled under, crossed on suspended ropes, etc., as used for training soldiers. ■ a series of difficulties that have to be negotiated in order to achieve a particular aim.

ob·stet·ri·cal /əbˈstetrikəl, äb-/ ▶ adj. of or relating to childbirth and the processes associated with it.

PRONUNCIATION KEY ə ago, up; ər over, fur; a hat; ā ate; ä car; e let; ē see; i fit; ī by; NG sing; ō go; ô law, for; oi toy; o͝o good; o͞o goo; ou out; TH thin; T͟H then; ZH vision

O

– DERIVATIVES **ob·stet·ric** adj., **ob·stet·ri·cal·ly** /-ik(ə)lē/ adv.
– ORIGIN mid 18th cent.: from modern Latin *obstetricus* for Latin *obstetricius* (based on *obstetrix* 'midwife'), from *obstare* 'be present.'

ob·ste·tri·cian /ˌäbstəˈtrisHən/ ▶ n. a physician or surgeon qualified to practice in obstetrics.

ob·stet·rics /əbˈstetriks, äb-/ ▶ plural n. [usu. treated as sing.] the branch of medicine and surgery concerned with childbirth and the care of women giving birth.

ob·sti·na·cy /ˈäbstənəsē/ ▶ n. the quality or condition of being obstinate; stubbornness: *his reputation for obstinacy.*

ob·sti·nate /ˈäbstənit/ ▶ adj. stubbornly refusing to change one's opinion or chosen course of action, despite attempts to persuade one to do so. ■ (of an unwelcome phenomenon or situation) very difficult to change or overcome: *the obstinate problem of unemployment.*
– DERIVATIVES **ob·sti·nate·ly** adv.
– ORIGIN Middle English: from Latin *obstinatus*, past participle of *obstinare* 'persist.'

ob·sti·pa·tion /ˌäbstəˈpāsHən/ ▶ n. Medicine severe or complete constipation.
– ORIGIN late 16th cent.: alteration of CONSTIPATION, by substitution of the prefix OB- for *con-*.

ob·strep·er·ous /əbˈstrepərəs, äb-/ ▶ adj. noisy and difficult to control: *the boy is cocky and obstreperous.*
– DERIVATIVES **ob·strep·er·ous·ly** adv., **ob·strep·er·ous·ness** n.
– ORIGIN late 16th cent. (in the sense 'clamorous, vociferous'): from Latin *obstreperus* (from *obstrepere*, from *ob-* 'against' + *strepere* 'make a noise') + -OUS.

ob·struct /əbˈstrəkt, äb-/ ▶ v. [with obj.] block (an opening, path, road, etc.); be or get in the way of: *she was obstructing the entrance.* ■ prevent or hinder (movement or someone or something in motion): *they had to alter the course of the stream and obstruct the natural flow of the water.* ■ deliberately make (something) difficult: *fears that the regime would obstruct the distribution of food.* ■ Law commit the offense of intentionally hindering (a legal process). ■ (in various sports) impede (a player on the opposing team) in a manner that constitutes an offense.
– DERIVATIVES **ob·struc·tor** /-tər/ n.
– ORIGIN late 16th cent.: from Latin *obstruct-* 'blocked up,' from the verb *obstruere*, from *ob-* 'against' + *struere* 'build, pile up.'

ob·struc·tion /əbˈstrəksHən, äb-/ ▶ n. the action of obstructing or the state of being obstructed: *they faced obstruction in carrying out their research* | *walkers could proceed with the minimum of obstruction.* ■ a thing that impedes or prevents passage or progress; an obstacle or blockage: *the tractor hit an obstruction.* ■ (in various sports) the action of unlawfully obstructing a player on the opposing team. ■ Medicine blockage of a bodily passageway, as the intestines. ■ Law the action of deliberately hindering a legal process.
– ORIGIN mid 16th cent.: from Latin *obstructio(n-)*, from the verb *obstruere* (see OBSTRUCT).

ob·struc·tion·ism /əbˈstrəksHəˌnizəm, äb-/ ▶ n. the practice of deliberately impeding or delaying the course of legal, legislative, or other procedures.
– DERIVATIVES **ob·struc·tion·ist** n. & adj.

ob·struc·tive /əbˈstrəktiv, äb-/ ▶ adj. **1** causing a blockage or obstruction: *all tubing should be cleared of obstructive algae and detritus.* ■ of or relating to obstruction of a passage in the body, esp. the intestines or the bronchi: *the child developed severe obstructive symptoms.*
2 causing or tending to cause deliberate difficulties and delays: *instead of being helpful, she had been a shade obstructive.*
– DERIVATIVES **ob·struc·tive·ly** adv., **ob·struc·tive·ness** n.

ob·stru·ent /ˈäbstrōōənt/ ▶ n. **1** Phonetics a fricative or plosive speech sound.
2 Medicine a medicine or substance that closes the natural passages or pores of the body.
– ORIGIN mid 17th cent.: from Latin *obstruent-* 'blocking up,' from the verb *obstruere*.

ob·tain /əbˈtān, äb-/ ▶ v. **1** [with obj.] get, acquire, or secure (something): *an opportunity to obtain advanced degrees.*
2 [no obj.] formal be prevalent, customary, or established: *the price of silver fell to that obtaining elsewhere in the ancient world.*
– DERIVATIVES **ob·tain·er** n., **ob·tain·ment** n.
– ORIGIN late Middle English: from Old French *obtenir*, from Latin *obtinere* 'obtain, gain.'

ob·tain·a·ble /əbˈtānəbəl, äb-/ ▶ adj. able to be obtained: *customers' financial details are easily obtainable.*
– DERIVATIVES **ob·tain·a·bil·i·ty** /-nəˈbilətē/ n.

ob·tect /əbˈtekt/ (also **obtected** /-ˈtektid/) ▶ adj. Entomology (of an insect pupa or chrysalis) covered in a hard case with the legs and wings attached immovably against the body.
– ORIGIN late 19th cent.: from Latin *obtectus*, past participle of *obtegere* 'cover over.'

ob·ten·tion /əbˈtencHən, äb-/ ▶ n. the action of obtaining something: *their protests serve no purpose and will only make their obtention of a diploma almost impossible.*
– ORIGIN early 17th cent.: French, or from late Latin, *obtentio(n-)*, from *obtinere*, 'obtain, gain.'

ob·trude /əbˈtrōōd/ ▶ v. [no obj.] become noticeable in an unwelcome or intrusive way: *a sound from the reception hall obtruded into his thoughts.* ■ [with obj.] impose or force (something) on someone in such a way: *I felt unable to obtrude my private sorrow upon anyone.*
– DERIVATIVES **ob·trud·er** n., **ob·tru·sion** /-ˈtrōōzHən/ n.
– ORIGIN mid 16th cent.: from Latin *obtrudere*, from *ob-* 'toward' + *trudere* 'to push.'

ob·tru·sive /əbˈtrōōsiv, äb-/ ▶ adj. noticeable or prominent in an unwelcome or intrusive way: *high-powered satellites can reach smaller and less obtrusive antennas.*
– DERIVATIVES **ob·tru·sive·ly** adv., **ob·tru·sive·ness** n.
– ORIGIN mid 17th cent.: from Latin *obtrus-* 'thrust forward,' from the verb *obtrudere* (see OBTRUDE).

ob·tund /äbˈtənd/ ▶ v. [with obj.] dated, chiefly Medicine dull the sensitivity of; blunt; deaden.
– ORIGIN late Middle English: from Latin *obtundere*, from *ob-* 'against' + *tundere* 'to beat.'

ob·tu·rate /ˈäbt(y)əˌrāt/ ▶ v. [with obj.] formal or technical block up; obstruct.
– DERIVATIVES **ob·tu·ra·tion** /-ˈrāsHən/ n.
– ORIGIN mid 17th cent.: from Latin *obturat-* 'stopped up,' from the verb *obturare*.

ob·tu·ra·tor /ˈäbt(y)əˌrātər/ ▶ n. Anatomy either of two muscles covering the outer front part of the pelvis on each side and involved in movements of the thigh and hip. ■ [as modifier] relating to this muscle or to the obturator foramen.
– ORIGIN early 18th cent.: from medieval Latin, literally 'obstructor,' from *obturare* 'stop up.'

ob·tu·ra·tor fo·ra·men ▶ n. Anatomy a large opening in the hipbone between the pubis and the ischium.

ob·tuse /əbˈt(y)ōōs, äb-/ ▶ adj. **1** annoyingly insensitive or slow to understand: *he wondered if the doctor was being deliberately obtuse.* ■ difficult to understand: *some of the lyrics are a bit obtuse.*
2 (of an angle) more than 90° and less than 180°. ■ not sharp-pointed or sharp-edged; blunt.
– DERIVATIVES **ob·tuse·ly** adv., **ob·tuse·ness** n., **ob·tu·si·ty** /-sitē/ n.
– ORIGIN late Middle English (in the sense 'blunt'): from Latin *obtusus*, past participle of *obtundere* 'beat against' (see OBTUND).

Ob-U·gric /äbˈ(y)ōōgrik, ôb/ (also **Ob-Ugrian** /ˈ(y)ōōgrēən/) ▶ adj. of or denoting a branch of the Finno-Ugric language family containing two languages of western Siberia related to Hungarian. ▶ n. this group of languages.
– ORIGIN 1930s: from *Ob*, the name of a Siberian river, + UGRIC.

ob·verse ▶ n. /ˈäbˌvərs/ [usu. in sing.] **1** the side of a coin or medal bearing the head or principal design. ■ the design or inscription on this side.
2 the opposite or counterpart of a fact or truth: *true solitude is the obverse of true society.*
▶ adj. /əbˈvərs, äb-/ [attrib.] **1** of or denoting the obverse of a coin or medal.
2 corresponding to something else as its opposite or counterpart.
3 Biology narrower at the base or point of attachment than at the apex or top: *an obverse leaf.*
– DERIVATIVES **ob·verse·ly** /əbˈvərslē, äb-/ adv.
– ORIGIN mid 17th cent. (in the sense 'turned toward the observer'): from Latin *obversus*, past participle of *obvertere* 'turn toward' (see OBVERT).

ob·vert /əbˈvərt, äb-/ ▶ v. [with obj.] Logic alter (a proposition) so as to infer another proposition with a contradictory predicate, e.g., *"no men are immortal"* to *"all men are mortal."*
– DERIVATIVES **ob·ver·sion** /əbˈvərzHən, äb-/ n.
– ORIGIN early 17th cent. (in the sense 'turn something until it is facing'): from Latin *obvertere*, from *ob-* 'toward' + *vertere* 'to turn.'

ob·vi·ate /ˈäbvēˌāt/ ▶ v. [with obj.] remove (a need or difficulty): *the Venetian blinds obviated the need for curtains.* ■ avoid; prevent: *a parachute can be used to obviate disaster.*
– DERIVATIVES **ob·vi·a·tion** /äbvēˈāsHən/ n., **ob·vi·a·tor** /-ˌātər/ n.
– ORIGIN late 16th cent.: from late Latin *obviat-* 'prevented,' from the verb *obviare*, based on Latin *via* 'way.'

ob·vi·ous /ˈäbvēəs/ ▶ adj. easily perceived or understood; clear, self-evident, or apparent: *unemployment has been the most obvious cost of the recession* | [with clause] *it was obvious a storm was coming in.* ■ derogatory predictable and lacking in subtlety: *it was an obvious remark to make.*
– DERIVATIVES **ob·vi·ous·ness** n.
– ORIGIN late 16th cent. (in the sense 'frequently encountered'): from Latin *obvius* (from the phrase *ob viam* 'in the way') + -OUS.

ob·vi·ous·ly /ˈäbvēəslē/ ▶ adv. in a way that is easily perceived or understood; clearly: *she was obviously sick* | [sentence adverb] *obviously, everyone has to do what they think is right.*

ob·vo·lute /ˈäbvəˌlōōt/ ▶ adj. Botany (of a leaf) having a margin that alternately overlaps and is overlapped by that of an opposing leaf.
– DERIVATIVES **ob·vo·lu·tion** /ˌäbvəˈlōōsHən/ n.
– ORIGIN mid 18th cent.: from Latin *obvolutus*, past participle of *obvolvere* 'wrap around.'

oc. (also **Oc.**) ▶ abbr. ocean.

o.c. ▶ abbr. Architecture on center. ■ in the work cited. [from Latin *opere citato*.]

oc- ▶ prefix variant spelling of OB-. assimilated before *c* (as in *occasion, occlude*).

o/c ▶ abbr. overcharge.

o·ca /ˈōkə/ ▶ n. a South American plant related to wood sorrel, long cultivated in Peru for its edible tubers. ● *Oxalis tuberosa*, family Oxalidaceae.
– ORIGIN early 17th cent.: from American Spanish, from Quechua *ócca*.

O·cal·a /ōˈkälə/ an industrial and resort city in north central Florida; pop. 54,801 (est. 2008).

oc·a·ri·na /ˌäkəˈrēnə/ ▶ n. a small egg-shaped wind instrument with a mouthpiece and holes for the fingers. Also called SWEET POTATO.
– ORIGIN late 19th cent.: from Italian, from *oca* 'goose' (from its shape).

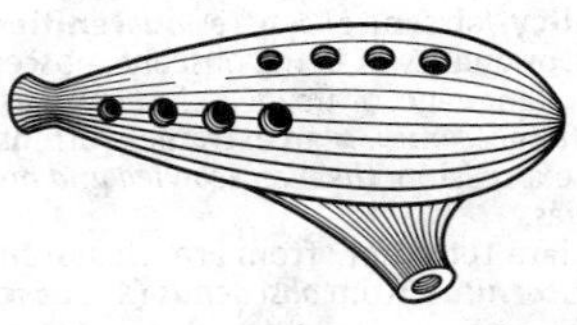

ocarina

OCAS ▶ abbr. Organization of Central American States.

O'Ca·sey /ōˈkāsē/, Sean (1880–1964), Irish playwright. His plays, such as *The Shadow of a Gunman* (1923) and *Juno and the Paycock* (1924), deal with the Irish poor before and during the civil war that followed the establishment of the Irish Free State in 1922.

occ. ▶ abbr. ■ occasional; occasionally. ■ Occident; occidental. ■ occupation.

Oc·cam, William of see WILLIAM OF OCCAM.

Oc·cam's ra·zor /ˈäkəmz/ (also **Ockham's razor**) the principle (attributed to William of Occam) that in explaining a thing, no more assumptions should be made than are necessary. The principle is often invoked to defend reductionism or nominalism. Compare with PRINCIPLE OF PARSIMONY at PARSIMONY.

occas. ▶ abbr. occasional; occasionally.

oc·ca·sion /əˈkāzHən/ ▶ n. **1** a particular time or instance of an event: *on one occasion I stayed up until two in the morning.* ■ a special or noteworthy event, ceremony, or celebration: *she was presented with a gold watch to mark the occasion.* ■ a suitable or opportune time for doing something: *elections are an occasion for registering protest votes.*
2 formal reason; cause: [with infinitive] *it's the first time that I've had occasion to complain.*
▶ v. [with obj.] formal cause (something): *something vital must have occasioned this visit* | [with two objs.] *his death occasioned her much grief.*
– PHRASES **on occasion** (or chiefly Brit. **occasions**) occasionally; from time to time: *on occasion, the state was asked to intervene.* **rise to the occasion** perform very well in response to a special situation or event. **take occasion** archaic make use of an opportunity to do something.
– ORIGIN late Middle English: from Latin *occasio(n-)* 'juncture, reason,' from *occidere* 'go down, set,' from *ob-* 'toward' + *cadere* 'to fall.'

oc·ca·sion·al /əˈkāzHənl/ ▶ adj. occurring, appearing, or done infrequently and irregularly: *the occasional car went by but no taxis.* ■ (of furniture) made or adapted for use on a particular occasion or for irregular use: *an occasional table.* ■ (of a literary composition, speech, religious service, etc.) produced on or intended for a special occasion: *he* *wrote occasional verse for patrons.* ■ dated employed for a particular occasion or on an irregular basis: *occasional freelancer seeks full-time position.*

oc·ca·sion·al·ism /əˈkāZHənlˌizəm/ ▶ **n.** Philosophy the doctrine ascribing the connection between mental and bodily events to the continuing intervention of God.

oc·ca·sion·al·ly /əˈkāZHənl-ē/ ▶ **adv.** at infrequent or irregular intervals; now and then: *he met her occasionally for coffee | very occasionally the condition can result in death.*

oc·ca·sion·al ta·ble ▶ **n.** a small table for infrequent and varied use.

Oc·ci·dent /ˈäksidənt, -ˌdent/ ▶ **n.** (**the Occident**) formal or literary the countries of the West, esp. Europe and the Americas (contrasted with **ORIENT**).
– ORIGIN late Middle English: via Old French from Latin *occident-* 'going down, setting' (in reference to the sun), from the verb *occidere.*

oc·ci·den·tal /ˌäksəˈdentl/ ▶ **adj.** of or relating to the countries of the Occident: *an Asian challenge to occidental dominance.*
▶ **n.** (**Occidental**) a native or inhabitant of the Occident.
– DERIVATIVES **oc·ci·den·tal·ism** /-ˌizəm/ **n.**, **oc·ci·den·tal·ize** /-ˌīz/ **v.**
– ORIGIN late Middle English: from Old French, or from Latin *occidentalis,* from *occident-* 'going down' (see **OCCIDENT**).

oc·cip·i·tal bone /äkˈsipitl/ ▶ **n.** Anatomy the bone that forms the back and base of the skull, and through which the spinal cord passes.

oc·cip·i·tal con·dyle ▶ **n.** Anatomy each of two rounded knobs on the occipital bone that form a joint with the first cervical vertebra.

oc·cip·i·tal lobe ▶ **n.** Anatomy the rearmost lobe in each cerebral hemisphere of the brain.

occipito- ▶ **comb. form** relating to the occipital lobe or the occipital bone: *occipitotemporal.*
– ORIGIN from medieval Latin *occipitalis,* from Latin *caput, capit-* 'head.'

oc·ci·put /ˈäksəpət/ ▶ **n.** (pl. **occiputs** or **occipita** /äkˈsipitə/) Anatomy the back of the head or skull.
– DERIVATIVES **oc·cip·i·tal** /äkˈsipitl/ **adj.**
– ORIGIN late Middle English: from Latin *occiput,* from *ob-* 'against' + *caput* 'head.'

Oc·ci·tan /ˈäksiˌtan/ ▶ **n.** the medieval or modern language of Languedoc, including literary Provençal of the12th–14th centuries.
▶ **adj.** of or relating to this language.
– DERIVATIVES **Oc·ci·ta·ni·an** /ˌäksəˈtānēən/ **n. & adj.**
– ORIGIN French (see also **LANGUE D'OC**).

oc·clude /əˈklo͞od/ ▶ **v.** formal or technical **1** [with obj.] stop, close up, or obstruct (an opening, orifice, or passage): *thick makeup can occlude the pores.* ■ shut (something) in: *they were occluding the waterfront with a wall of buildings.* ■ technical cover (an eye) to prevent its use: *it is placed at eye level with one eye occluded.* ■ Chemistry (of a solid) absorb and retain (a gas or impurity).
2 [no obj.] (of a tooth) close on or come into contact with another tooth in the opposite jaw.
– ORIGIN late 16th cent.: from Latin *occludere* 'shut up.'

oc·clud·ed front ▶ **n.** Meteorology a composite front produced by occlusion.

oc·clu·sal /əˈklo͞osəl/ ▶ **adj.** Dentistry of, relating to, or involved in the occlusion of teeth. ■ denoting a portion of a tooth that comes into contact with a tooth in the other jaw.

oc·clu·sion /əˈklo͞oZHən/ ▶ **n.** **1** Medicine the blockage or closing of a blood vessel or hollow organ. ■ Phonetics the momentary closure of the passage of breath during the articulation of a consonant.
2 Meteorology a process in which the cold front of a rotating low-pressure system overtakes the warm front, forcing the warm air upward above a wedge of cold air. ■ an occluded front.
3 Dentistry the position of the teeth when the jaws are closed.
– DERIVATIVES **oc·clu·sive** /-siv/ **adj.**
– ORIGIN mid 17th cent.: from Latin *occlus-* 'shut up' (from the verb *occludere*) + **-ION**.

oc·cult /əˈkəlt/ ▶ **n.** (**the occult**) supernatural, mystical, or magical beliefs, practices, or phenomena: *a secret society to study alchemy and the occult.*
▶ **adj.** **1** of, involving, or relating to supernatural, mystical, or magical powers or phenomena: *a follower of occult practices similar to voodoo.* ■ beyond the range of ordinary knowledge or experience; mysterious: *a weird occult sensation of having experienced the identical situation before.* ■ communicated only to the initiated; esoteric: *the typically occult language of the time.*
2 Medicine (of a disease or process) not accompanied by readily discernible signs or symptoms. ■ (of blood) abnormally present, e.g., in feces, but detectable only chemically or microscopically.
▶ **v.** [with obj.] cut off from view by interposing something: *a wooden screen designed to occult the competitors.* ■ Astronomy (of a celestial body) conceal (an apparently smaller body) from view by passing or being in front of it.
– DERIVATIVES **oc·cul·ta·tion** /ˌäkəlˈtāSHən/ **n.**, **oc·cult·ism** /-ˌtizəm/ **n.**, **oc·cult·ist** /-tist/ **n.**, **oc·cult·ly adv.**, **oc·cult·ness n.**
– ORIGIN late 15th cent. (as a verb): from Latin *occultare* 'secrete,' frequentative of *occulere* 'conceal,' based on *celare* 'to hide'; the adjective and noun from *occult-* 'covered over,' from the verb *occulere.*

oc·cult·ing light ▶ **n.** a light in a lighthouse or buoy that is cut off briefly at regular intervals.

oc·cu·pan·cy /ˈäkyəpənsē/ ▶ **n.** the action or fact of occupying a place: *the house is finally ready for occupancy.* ■ the proportion of accommodations occupied or in use, typically in a hotel: *the 70-percent occupancy needed to give a profit.*

oc·cu·pant /ˈäkyəpənt/ ▶ **n.** a person who resides or is present in a house, vehicle, seat, place, etc., at a given time. ■ the holder of a position or office: *the first occupant of the Oval Office.* ■ Law a person holding property, esp. land, in actual possession.
– ORIGIN late 16th cent. (in the legal sense 'person who establishes a title'): from French, or from Latin *occupant-* 'seizing,' from the verb *occupare.*

oc·cu·pa·tion /ˌäkyəˈpāSHən/ ▶ **n.** **1** a job or profession: *his prime occupation was as editor.* ■ a way of spending time: *a game of cards is a pretty harmless occupation.*
2 the action, state, or period of occupying or being occupied by military force: *the Roman occupation of Britain | the Nazi occupation.* ■ the action of entering and taking control of a building: *the workers remained in occupation until October 16.*
3 the action or fact of living in or using a building or other place: *a property suitable for occupation by older people.*
– ORIGIN Middle English: via Old French from Latin *occupatio(n-),* from the verb *occupare* (see **OCCUPY**). Sense 2 dates from the mid 16th cent.

oc·cu·pa·tion·al /ˌäkyəˈpāSHənl/ ▶ **adj.** of or relating to a job or profession: *hepatitis B may be an occupational disease for some health-care workers.*
– DERIVATIVES **oc·cu·pa·tion·al·ly adv.**

oc·cu·pa·tion·al haz·ard ▶ **n.** a risk accepted as a consequence of a particular occupation.

oc·cu·pa·tion·al med·i·cine ▶ **n.** the branch of medicine dealing with the prevention and treatment of job-related injuries and illnesses.

oc·cu·pa·tion·al ther·a·py ▶ **n.** a form of therapy for those recuperating from physical or mental illness that encourages rehabilitation through the performance of activities required in daily life.
– DERIVATIVES **oc·cu·pa·tion·al ther·a·pist n.**

oc·cu·pied /ˈäkyəˌpīd/ ▶ **adj.** **1** (of a building, seat, etc.) being used by someone: *only the first floor is fully occupied.*
2 busy and active: *tasks that kept her occupied for the remainder of the afternoon.*
3 (of a place, esp. a country) taken control of by military conquest or settlement: *the occupied territories.*

oc·cu·py /ˈäkyəˌpī/ ▶ **v.** (**occupies, occupying, occupied**) [with obj.] **1** reside or have one's place of business in (a building): *the apartment she occupies in Manhattan.* ■ fill or take up (a space or time): *two long windows occupied almost the whole wall.* ■ be situated in or at (a place or position in a system or hierarchy): *on the corporate ladder, they occupy the lowest rungs.* ■ hold (a position or job).
2 (often **be occupied with/in**) fill or preoccupy (the mind or thoughts): *her mind was occupied with alarming questions.* ■ keep (someone) busy and active: *Sarah* ***occupied herself*** *taking the coffee cups over to the sink.*
3 take control of (a place, esp. a country) by military conquest or settlement: *the region was occupied by Britain during World War I.* ■ enter, take control of, and stay in (a building) illegally and often forcibly, esp. as a form of protest: *the workers occupied the factory.*
– DERIVATIVES **oc·cu·pi·er** /-ˌpīər/ **n.**
– ORIGIN Middle English: formed irregularly from Old French *occuper,* from Latin *occupare* 'seize.' A now obsolete vulgar sense 'have sexual relations with' seems to have led to the general avoidance of the word in the 17th and most of the 18th cent.

oc·cur /əˈkər/ ▶ **v.** (**occurs, occurring, occurred**) [no obj.] happen; take place: *the accident occurred at about 3:30 p.m.* ■ exist or be found to be present in a place or under a particular set of conditions: *radon occurs naturally in rocks such as granite.* ■ (**occur to**) (of a thought or idea) come into the mind of (someone): [with clause] *it occurred to him that he hadn't eaten.*
– ORIGIN late 15th cent.: from Latin *occurrere* 'go to meet, present itself,' from *ob-* 'against' + *currere* 'to run.'

oc·cur·rence /əˈkərəns/ ▶ **n.** an incident or event: *vandalism used to be a rare occurrence.* ■ the fact or frequency of something happening: *the occurrence of cancer increases with age.* ■ the fact of something existing or being found in a place or under a particular set of conditions: *the occurrence of natural gas fields.*
– ORIGIN mid 16th cent.: probably from the plural of archaic *occurrent,* in the same sense, via French from Latin *occurrent-* 'befalling,' from the verb *occurrere* (see **OCCUR**).

oc·cur·rent /əˈkərənt/ ▶ **adj.** actually occurring or observable, not potential or hypothetical.
– ORIGIN late 15th cent.: from French, or from Latin *occurrent-* 'befalling,' from the verb *occurrere.*

OCD ▶ **abbr.** obsessive-compulsive disorder.

o·cean /ˈōSHən/ ▶ **n.** a very large expanse of sea, in particular, each of the main areas into which the sea is divided geographically: *the Atlantic Ocean.* ■ (usu. **the ocean**) the sea: [as modifier] *the ocean floor.* ■ (**an ocean of/oceans of**) informal a very large expanse or quantity: *she had oceans of energy.*
– DERIVATIVES **o·cean·ward** /-wərd/ (also **-wards**) **adv. & adj.**
– ORIGIN Middle English: from Old French *occean,* via Latin from Greek *ōkeanos* 'great stream encircling the earth's disk.' "The ocean" originally denoted the whole body of water regarded as encompassing the earth's single land mass.

o·cea·nar·i·um /ˌōSHəˈne(ə)rēəm/ ▶ **n.** (pl. **oceanariums** or **oceanaria** /-ˈne(ə)rēə/) a large seawater aquarium in which marine animals are kept for study and public exhibit.
– ORIGIN 1940s: from **OCEAN**, on the pattern of *aquarium.*

o·cean bo·ni·to ▶ **n.** another term for **SKIPJACK** (sense 1).

o·cean·front /ˈōSHənˌfrənt/ ▶ **n.** the land that borders an ocean.

o·cean·go·ing /ˈōSHənˌgō-iNG/ ▶ **adj.** (of a ship) designed to cross oceans.

O·ce·an·i·a /ˌōSHēˈanēə, -ˈänēə/ an area that encompasses the islands of the Pacific Ocean and adjacent seas.
– DERIVATIVES **O·ce·an·i·an adj. & n.**
– ORIGIN modern Latin, from French *Océanie.*

o·ce·an·ic /ˌōSHēˈanik/ ▶ **adj.** **1** of or relating to the ocean: *oceanic atolls.* ■ of or inhabiting the part of the ocean beyond the edge of a continental shelf: *stocks of oceanic fish.* ■ (of a climate) governed by the proximity of the ocean. ■ of enormous size or extent; huge; vast: *an oceanic failure.*
2 (**Oceanic**) of or relating to Oceania: *a gallery specializing in Oceanic art.*

o·ce·an·ic crust ▶ **n.** Geology the relatively thin part of the earth's crust that underlies the ocean basins. It is geologically young compared with the continental crust and consists of basaltic rock overlain by sediments.

O·ce·a·nid /ōˈsēənid/ ▶ **n.** (pl. **Oceanids** or **Oceanides** /ˌōsēˈanidēz/) Greek Mythology a sea nymph; one of the daughters of Oceanus.
– ORIGIN from French *Océanide,* from Greek *ōkeanis, ōkeanid-.*

O·cean Is·land another name for **BANABA**.

o·cean lin·er ▶ **n.** see **LINER**[1] (sense 1).

o·cea·nog·ra·phy /ˌōSHəˈnägrəfē/ ▶ **n.** the branch of science that deals with the physical and biological properties and phenomena of the sea.
– DERIVATIVES **o·cea·nog·ra·pher** /-fər/ **n.**, **o·cea·no·graph·ic** /-nəˈgrafik/ **adj.**, **o·cea·no·graph·i·cal** /-nəˈgrafəkəl/ **adj.**

o·cea·nol·o·gy /ˌōSHəˈnäləjē/ ▶ **n.** another term for **OCEANOGRAPHY**. ■ the branch of technology and economics dealing with human use of the sea.
– DERIVATIVES **o·cea·no·log·i·cal** /-nəˈläjikəl/ **adj.**, **o·cea·nol·o·gist** /-jist/ **n.**

O·cean·side /ˈōSHənˌsīd/ a residential and commercial city in southwestern California, north of San Diego; pop. 169,684 (est. 2008).

o·cean·side /ˈōSHənˌsīd/ ▶ **n.** a place or area of land by the sea: [as modifier] *an oceanside resort.*

O·cean State a nickname for the state of **RHODE ISLAND**.

O·ce·a·nus /ōˈsēənəs/ Greek Mythology the son of Uranus (Heaven) and Gaia (Earth), the personification of the great river believed to encircle the whole world.

o·cel·lat·ed /ˈäsəˌlātid/ ▶ **adj.** (of an animal, or its plumage or body surface) having one or more ocelli, or eyelike markings.

o·cel·lus /ōˈseləs/ ▶ **n.** (pl. **ocelli** /ōˈselī, ōˈselē/) Zoology **1** another term for SIMPLE EYE. **2** another term for EYESPOT (sense 1) and.
– DERIVATIVES **o·cel·lar** /ōˈselər/ **adj.**
– ORIGIN early 19th cent.: from Latin, diminutive of *oculus* 'eye.'

oc·e·lot /ˈäsəˌlät, ˈōsə-/ ▶ **n.** a medium-sized wild cat that has a tawny yellow coat marked with black blotches and spots, and ranges from southern Texas through South America. ● *Felis pardalis*, family Felidae. ■ the fur of the ocelot.
– ORIGIN late 18th cent.: from French, from Nahuatl *tlatlocelotl*, literally 'field tiger.'

o·cher /ˈōkər/ (chiefly Brit. also **ochre**) ▶ **n.** an earthy pigment containing ferric oxide, typically with clay, varying from light yellow to brown or red. ■ a pale brownish yellow color.
– DERIVATIVES **o·cher·ish** /ˈōk(ə)risH/ **adj.**, **o·cher·oid** /ˈōk(ə)roid/ **adj.**, **o·cher·ous** /ˈōk(ə)rəs/ **adj.**, **o·cher·y** **adj.**
– ORIGIN Middle English: from Old French *ocre*, via Latin from Greek *ōkhra* 'yellow ocher.'

och·loc·ra·cy /äkˈläkrəsē/ ▶ **n.** government by a mob; mob rule.
– DERIVATIVES **och·lo·crat** /ˈäkləˌkrat/ **n.**, **och·lo·crat·ic** /ˌäkləˈkratik/ **adj.**
– ORIGIN late 16th cent.: via French from Greek *okhlokratia*, from *okhlos* 'mob' + *-kratia* 'power.'

och·lo·pho·bi·a /ˌäkləˈfōbēə/ ▶ **n.** extreme or irrational fear of or aversion to crowds.

o·chre ▶ **n.** chiefly Brit. variant spelling of OCHER.

Ochs /ōks/, Adolph Simon (1858–1935), US publisher. He acquired *The New York Times* in 1896 and made it one of the nation's preeminent newspapers.

-ock ▶ **suffix** forming nouns originally with diminutive sense: *haddock* | *pollock*. ■ also occasionally forming words from other sources: *bannock* | *hassock*.
– ORIGIN Old English *-uc*, *-oc*.

ock·er /ˈäkər/ informal ▶ **n.** Austral. a boorish or aggressive person, esp. an Australian man. ▶ **adj.** denoting or characteristic of such a person: *an ocker sports writer*.
– ORIGIN alteration of *Oscar*, popularized by the name of a character in an Australian television series (1965–68).

O

Ock·ham, William of see WILLIAM OF OCCAM.

Ock·ham's ra·zor ▶ **n.** variant spelling of OCCAM'S RAZOR.

o'clock /əˈkläk/ ▶ **adv.** used to specify the hour in telling time: *the gates will open at eight o'clock*. ■ used following a numeral to indicate direction or bearing with reference to an imaginary clock face, 12 o'clock being thought of as directly in front or overhead.

O'Con·nell /ōˈkänl/, Daniel (1775–1847), Irish nationalist leader and social reformer; known as **the Liberator**. His election to Parliament in 1828 forced the British government to grant emancipation to Catholics in order to enable him to take his seat in the House of Commons.

O'Con·nor[1], Flannery (1925–64), US novelist and short-story writer; full name *Mary Flannery O'Connor*. Her short stories are notable for their dark humor and grotesque characters and are published in collections such as *A Good Man Is Hard to Find, and Other Stories* (1955). Notable novels: *Wise Blood* (1952) and *The Violent Bear It Away* (1960).

O'Con·nor[2], Sandra Day (1930–), US Supreme Court associate justice 1981–2006. Appointed by President Reagan, she was the first woman to sit on the Court.

o·co·til·lo /ˌōkəˈtē(y)ō/ ▶ **n.** (pl. **ocotillos**) a spiny, scarlet-flowered desert shrub of the southwestern US and Mexico, sometimes planted as a hedge. ● *Fouquieria splendens*, family Fouquieriaceae.
– ORIGIN mid 19th cent.: via American Spanish (diminutive form) from Nahuatl *ocotl* 'torch.'

OCR ▶ **abbr.** ■ optical character reader. ■ optical character recognition.

O·cra·coke Is·land /ˈōkrəˌkōk/ a barrier island in eastern North Carolina, part of the Outer Banks.

oc·re·a /ˈäkrēə, ˈōkrēə/ (also **ochrea**) ▶ **n.** (pl. **ocreae** /ˈäkrē-ē, ˈōkrē-ē/ or **ocreas**) Botany a sheath around a stem formed by the cohesion of two or more stipules, characteristic of the dock family.
– ORIGIN mid 19th cent.: from Latin, literally 'protective legging.'

OCS ▶ **abbr.** ■ Military officer candidate school. ■ Old Church Slavonic. ■ outer continental shelf.

Oct. ▶ **abbr.** October.

oct. ▶ **abbr.** octavo.

oct- ▶ **comb. form** variant spelling of OCTA- and OCTO- assimilated before a vowel (as in *octennial*).

octa- (also **oct-** before a vowel) ▶ **comb. form** eight; having eight: *octahedron*.
– ORIGIN from Greek *oktō* 'eight.'

oc·tad /ˈäktad/ ▶ **n.** technical a group or set of eight.
– ORIGIN mid 19th cent.: via late Latin from Greek *oktas*, *oktad-*, from *oktō* 'eight.'

oc·ta·gon /ˈäktəˌgän, -gən/ ▶ **n.** a plane figure with eight straight sides and eight angles. ■ an object or building with a plan or cross section of this shape.
– DERIVATIVES **oc·tag·o·nal** /äkˈtagənl/ **adj.**
– ORIGIN late 16th cent.: via Latin from Greek *octagōnos* 'eight-angled.'

oc·ta·he·drite /ˌäktəˈhēdrit/ ▶ **n. 1** another term for ANATASE. **2** an iron meteorite containing plates of kamacite and taenite in an octahedral orientation.
– ORIGIN early 19th cent.: from OCTAHEDRON + -ITE[1].

oc·ta·he·dron /ˌäktəˈhēdrən/ ▶ **n.** (pl. **octahedrons** or **octahedra** /-drə/) a three-dimensional shape having eight plane faces, esp. a regular solid figure with eight equal triangular faces. ■ a body, esp. a crystal, in the form of a regular octahedron.
– DERIVATIVES **oc·ta·he·dral** /-drəl/ **adj.**
– ORIGIN late 16th cent.: from Greek *oktaedron*, neuter (used as a noun) of *oktaedros* 'eight-faced.'

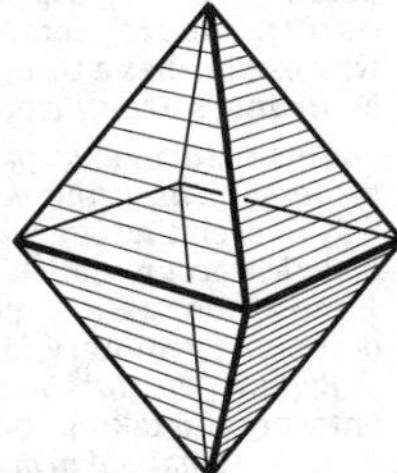
octahedron

oc·tal /ˈäktl/ ▶ **adj.** relating to or using a system of numerical notation that has 8 rather than 10 as a base. ▶ **n.** the octal system; octal notation.

oc·tam·er·ous /äkˈtamərəs/ ▶ **adj.** Botany & Zoology having parts arranged in groups of eight. ■ consisting of eight joints or parts.

oc·tam·e·ter /äkˈtamitər/ ▶ **n.** Prosody a line of verse consisting of eight metrical feet.

oc·tane /ˈäktān/ ▶ **n.** Chemistry a colorless flammable hydrocarbon of the alkane series, obtained in petroleum refining. ● Chem. formula: C_8H_{18}; many isomers, esp. the straight-chain isomer (*n*-**octane**). See also ISOOCTANE.
– ORIGIN late 19th cent.: from OCTO- 'eight' (denoting eight carbon atoms) + -ANE[2].

oc·tane num·ber (also **octane rating**) ▶ **n.** a figure indicating the antiknock properties of a fuel, based on a comparison with a mixture of isooctane and heptane.

oc·tan·gu·lar /äkˈtaNGgyələr/ ▶ **adj.** having eight angles.

Oc·tans /ˈäktanz/ Astronomy a faint southern constellation (the Octant), containing the south celestial pole. ■ (as genitive **Octantis** /äkˈtantis/) used with a preceding letter or numeral to designate a star in this constellation: *the star Delta Octantis*.
– ORIGIN Latin.

oc·tant /ˈäktənt/ ▶ **n.** an arc of a circle equal to one eighth of its circumference, or the area enclosed by such an arc with two radii of the circle. ■ each of eight parts into which a space or solid body is divided by three planes that intersect (esp. at right angles) at a single point. ■ an obsolete instrument in the form of a graduated eighth of a circle, used in astronomy and navigation.
– ORIGIN late 17th cent.: from Latin *octans*, *octant-* 'half-quadrant,' from *octo* 'eight.'

oc·tave /ˈäktəv, ˈäkˌtāv/ ▶ **n. 1** Music a series of eight notes occupying the interval between (and including) two notes, one having twice or half the frequency of vibration of the other. ■ the interval between these two notes. ■ each of the two notes at the extremes of this interval. ■ these two notes sounding together. **2** a poem or stanza of eight lines; an octet. **3** the eighth day after a church festival, inclusive of the day of the festival. ■ a period of eight days beginning with the day of such a festival. **4** Fencing the last of eight standard parrying positions.
– ORIGIN Middle English (sense 3): via Old French from Latin *octava dies* 'eighth day.'

Oc·ta·vi·an /äkˈtāvēən/ see AUGUSTUS.

oc·ta·vo /äkˈtävō/ (abbr.: **8vo**) ▶ **n.** (pl. **octavos**) a size of book page that results from the folding of each printed sheet into eight leaves (sixteen pages). ■ a book of this size.
– ORIGIN late 16th cent.: from Latin *in octavo* 'in an eighth,' from *octavus* 'eighth.'

oc·ten·ni·al /äkˈtenēəl/ ▶ **adj.** rare recurring every eight years. ■ lasting for or relating to a period of eight years.
– ORIGIN mid 17th cent.: from late Latin *octennium* 'period of eight years' + -AL.

oc·tet /äkˈtet/ (also **octette**) ▶ **n.** a group of eight people or things, in particular: ■ a group of eight musicians. ■ a musical composition for eight voices or instruments. ■ the first eight lines of a sonnet. ■ Chemistry a stable group of eight electrons occupying a single shell in an atom.
– ORIGIN mid 19th cent.: from Italian *ottetto* or German *Oktett*, on the pattern of *duet* and *quartet*.

octo- (also **oct-** before a vowel) ▶ **comb. form** eight; having eight: *octosyllabic*.
– ORIGIN from Latin *octo* or Greek *oktō* 'eight.'

Oc·to·ber /äkˈtōbər/ ▶ **n.** the tenth month of the year, in the northern hemisphere usually considered the second month of autumn: *the project started in October* | [as modifier] *on an October night*.
– ORIGIN late Old English, from Latin, from *octo* 'eight' (being originally the eighth month of the Roman year).

Oc·to·ber Rev·o·lu·tion ▶ **n.** see RUSSIAN REVOLUTION.

Oc·to·ber sur·prise ▶ **n.** any political event orchestrated (or apparently orchestrated) in the month before an election, in the hopes of affecting the outcome: *even the much-vaunted October surprise might fail to move the race in one direction or another*.

Oc·to·ber War Arab name for YOM KIPPUR WAR.

Oc·to·brist /äkˈtōbrist/ ▶ **n.** historical a member of the moderate party in the Russian Duma that supported Tsar Nicholas II's reforming manifesto of October 30, 1905.
– ORIGIN suggested by Russian *oktyabrist*.

oc·to·cen·ten·ar·y /ˌäktōsenˈtenərē/ ▶ **n.** (pl. **octocentenaries**) the eight-hundredth anniversary of a significant event.

oc·to·dec·i·mo /ˌäktōˈdesəˌmō/ ▶ **n.** (pl. **octodecimos**) a size of book page that results from the folding of each printed sheet into eighteen leaves (36 pages). ■ a book of this size.
– ORIGIN mid 19th cent.: from Latin *in octodecimo* 'in an eighteenth,' from *octodecimus* 'eighteenth.'

oc·to·ge·nar·i·an /ˌäktəjəˈne(ə)rēən/ ▶ **n.** a person who is from 80 to 89 years old: [as modifier] *his octogenarian mother-in-law*.
– ORIGIN early 19th cent.: from Latin *octogenarius* (based on *octoginta* 'eighty') + -AN.

oc·to·nar·y /ˈäktəˌnerē/ ▶ **adj.** rare relating to or based on the number eight.

oc·to·pa·mine /äkˈtōpəˌmēn/ ▶ **n.** Biochemistry a compound that can accumulate in nerves as a result of the use of monoamine oxidase inhibitors and cause a rise in blood pressure. ● An amine related to norepinephrine; chem. formula: $HOC_6H_4CHOHCH_2NH_2$.
– ORIGIN 1940s: from OCTOPUS (from which it was first extracted) + AMINE.

oc·to·pod /ˈäktəˌpäd/ ▶ **n.** Zoology a cephalopod mollusk of the order Octopoda; an octopus.

Oc·top·o·da /äkˈtäpədə/ Zoology an order of cephalopod mollusks that comprises the octopuses.
– ORIGIN modern Latin (plural), from Greek *oktōpous*, *oktōpod-*, from *oktō* 'eight' + *pous*, *pod-* 'foot.'

oc·to·pus /ˈäktəpəs/ ▶ **n.** (pl. **octopuses**) a cephalopod mollusk with eight sucker-bearing arms, a soft saclike body, strong beaklike jaws, and no internal shell. ● Order Octopoda, class Cephalopoda: *Octopus* and other genera.
– DERIVATIVES **oc·to·poid** /-ˌpoid/ **adj.**
– ORIGIN mid 18th cent.: modern Latin, from Greek *oktōpous* (see also OCTOPODA).

> **USAGE** The standard plural in English of **octopus** is **octopuses**. However, the word **octopus** comes from Greek, and the Greek plural form **octopodes** is still occasionally used. The plural form **octopi** is mistakenly formed according to rules for Latin plurals, and is therefore incorrect.

oc·to·roon /ˌäktəˈro͞on/ ▶ **n.** historical a person whose parents are a quadroon and a white person and who is therefore one-eighth black by descent.
– ORIGIN mid 19th cent.: from OCTO- 'eight,' on the pattern of *quadroon*.

oc·to·syl·la·bic /ˌäktəsəˈlabik, ˌäktō-/ ▶ **adj.** having or written in lines that have eight syllables.

oc·to·syl·la·ble /'äktə'siləbəl/ ▶ **n.** a word or line of verse with eight syllables.
▶ **adj.** having eight syllables.

oc·to·thorp /'äktə,THôrp/ (also **octothorpe**) ▶ **n.** another term for the pound sign (#).
– ORIGIN 1970s: of uncertain origin; probably from **OCTO-** (referring to the eight points on the symbol) + the surname *Thorpe*.

oc·troi /'äktroi, äk'trwä/ ▶ **n.** a tax levied in some countries on various goods entering a town or city.
– ORIGIN late 16th cent. (in the sense 'concession,' esp. one giving an exclusive right of trade): from French *octroyer* 'to grant,' based on medieval Latin *auctorizare* (see **AUTHORIZE**). The current senses dates from the early 18th cent.

oc·tu·ple /äk'təpəl, -'t(y)o͞opəl/ ▶ **adj.** [attrib.] consisting of eight parts or things. ■ eight times as many or as much.
▶ **v.** make or become eight times as numerous or as large.
– ORIGIN early 17th cent.: from French *octuple* or Latin *octuplus* (both adjectives), from *octo* 'eight' + *-plus* (as in *duplus* 'double').

oc·tup·let /äk'təplit, -'t(y)o͞o-/ ▶ **n.** (usu. in pl. **octuplets**) each of eight children born at one birth.

oc·tyl /'äktl/ ▶ **n.** [as modifier] Chemistry of or denoting an alkyl radical – C_8H_{17}, derived from octane.

oc·u·lar /'äkyələr/ ▶ **adj.** [attrib.] Medicine of or connected with the eyes or vision: *ocular trauma.*
▶ **n.** another term for **EYEPIECE**.
– DERIVATIVES **oc·u·lar·ly adv.**
– ORIGIN late 16th cent.: from late Latin *ocularis*, from Latin *oculus* 'eye.'

oc·u·lar dom·i·nance ▶ **n.** the priority of one eye over the other as regards preference of use or acuity of vision.

oc·u·lar·ist /'äkyələrist/ ▶ **n.** a person who makes artificial eyes.
– ORIGIN mid 19th cent.: from French *oculariste*, from late Latin *ocularis* (see **OCULAR**).

oc·u·list /'äkyəlist/ ▶ **n.** dated a person who specializes in the medical treatment of diseases or defects of the eye; an ophthalmologist. ■ an optometrist.
– ORIGIN late 16th cent.: from French *oculiste*, from Latin *oculus* 'eye.'

oculo- ▶ **comb. form** relating to the eye or the sense of vision: *oculomotor*.
– ORIGIN from Latin *oculus* 'eye.'

oc·u·lo·mo·tor /,äkyəlō'mōtər/ ▶ **adj.** of or relating to the motion of the eye.

oc·u·lo·mo·tor nerve ▶ **n.** Anatomy each of the third pair of cranial nerves, supplying most of the muscles around and within the eyeballs.

oc·u·lus /'äkyələs/ ▶ **n.** (pl. **oculi** /-,lī, -,lē/) Architecture a round or eyelike opening or design, in particular: ■ a circular window. ■ the central boss of a volute. ■ an opening at the apex of a dome.
– ORIGIN mid 19th cent.: from Latin, literally 'eye.'

OD[1] ▶ **abbr.** ordnance datum.

OD[2] informal ▶ **v.** (**OD's, OD'ing, OD'd**) [no obj.] take an overdose of a drug: *Spike had OD'd on barbiturates.* ■ humorous have too much of something: *I almost OD'd on mushroom salad.*
▶ **n.** an overdose of a narcotic drug.

Od /äd/ ▶ **n.** an archaic euphemism for God, used in exclamations: *Od damn it all!*

od /äd/ ▶ **n.** historical a hypothetical power once thought to pervade nature and account for various phenomena, such as magnetism.
– ORIGIN mid 19th cent.: arbitrary term coined in German by Baron von Reichenbach (1788–1869), German scientist.

o.d. ▶ **abbr.** outer diameter.

o·da·lisque /'ōdl,isk/ (also **odalisk**) ▶ **n.** historical a female slave or concubine in a harem, esp. one in the seraglio of the sultan of Turkey.
– ORIGIN late 17th cent.: from French, from Turkish *odalik*, from *oda* 'chamber' + *lik* 'function.'

odd /äd/ ▶ **adj. 1** different from what is usual or expected; strange: *the neighbors thought him very odd* | [with clause] *it's odd that she didn't recognize me.* **2** (of whole numbers such as 3 and 5) having one left over as a remainder when divided by two. ■ (of things numbered consecutively) represented or indicated by such a number: *he has come to us every odd year since 1981.* ■ [postpositive in combination] in the region of or somewhat more than a particular number or quantity: *she looked younger than her fifty-odd years.*
3 [attrib.] happening or occurring infrequently and irregularly; occasional: *neither did she want a secret affair, snatching odd moments together.* ■ spare; unoccupied: *when you've got an odd five minutes, could I have a word?*
4 separated from a usual pair or set and therefore out of place or mismatched: *he's wearing odd socks.*
– DERIVATIVES **odd·ish adj.** (sense 1), **odd·ly adv.** (sense 1): [sentence adverb] *oddly enough, I didn't feel nervous* | [as submodifier] *she felt oddly guilty*, **odd·ness n.**
– ORIGIN Middle English (sense 2): from Old Norse *odda-*, found in combinations such as *odda-mathr* 'third or odd man,' from *oddi* 'angle.'

odd·ball /'äd,bôl/ informal ▶ **n.** a strange or eccentric person.
▶ **adj.** strange; bizarre: *oddball training methods.*

Odd Fel·low (also **Oddfellow**) ▶ **n.** a member of the Independent Order of Odd Fellows, a fraternal and benevolent society.
– DERIVATIVES **Odd·fel·low·ship n.**

odd·i·ty /'äditē/ ▶ **n.** (pl. **oddities**) a strange or peculiar person, thing, or trait: *she was regarded as a bit of an oddity.* ■ the quality of being strange or peculiar: *realizing the* **oddity of** *the remark, he retracted it.*

odd job ▶ **n.** (usu. **odd jobs**) a casual or isolated piece of work, esp. one of a routine domestic or manual nature.
– DERIVATIVES **odd-job·ber n., odd-job·bing n.**

odd lot ▶ **n.** an incomplete set or random mixture of things. ■ Stock Exchange a transaction involving less than the usual round number of shares.

odd man out /',äd ,man 'out/ ▶ **n.** a person differing from all other members of a particular group or set in some way.

odd·ment /'ädmənt/ ▶ **n.** (usu. **oddments**) a remnant or part of something, typically left over from a larger piece or set: *a quilt made from oddments of silk.*

odd-pin·nate ▶ **adj.** Botany (of a leaf) pinnate with an odd terminal leaflet.

odds /ädz/ ▶ **plural n.** the ratio between the amounts staked by the parties to a bet, based on the expected probability either way: *the bookies are offering* **odds** *of 8-1* | *it is possible for the race to be won* **at very long odds.** ■ (usu. **the odds**) the chances or likelihood of something happening or being the case: ***the odds are that*** *he is no longer alive* | ***the odds against*** *this ever happening are high.* ■ (usu. **the odds**) superiority in strength, power, or resources; advantage: *she clung to the lead* ***against all the odds*** | ***the odds were*** *overwhelmingly* ***in favor of*** *the banks rather than the customer.*
– PHRASES **at odds** in conflict or at variance: *his behavior is* **at odds with** *the interests of the company.* **by all odds** certainly; by far. **lay** (or **give**) **odds** offer a bet with odds favorable to the other bettor. ■ be very sure about something: *I'd lay odds that the person responsible is an insider.* **take odds** offer a bet with odds unfavorable to the other bettor.
– ORIGIN early 16th cent.: apparently the plural of the obsolete noun *odd* 'odd number or odd person.'

odds and ends ▶ **plural n.** miscellaneous articles or remnants.

odds·mak·er /'ädz,mākər/ ▶ **n.** a person who calculates or predicts the outcome of a contest, such as a horse race or an election, and sets betting odds.

odds-on ▶ **adj.** (esp. of a horse) rated as most likely to win: *the odds-on favorite.*

odd-toed un·gu·late ▶ **n.** a hoofed mammal of an order that includes horses, rhinoceroses, and tapirs. Mammals of this group have either one or three toes on each foot. Compare with **EVEN-TOED UNGULATE**.
● Order Perissodactyla: three families.

ode /ōd/ ▶ **n.** a lyric poem in the form of an address to a particular subject, often elevated in style or manner and written in varied or irregular meter. ■ historical a poem meant to be sung.
– DERIVATIVES **od·ic** /'ōdik/ **adj.**
– ORIGIN late 16th cent.: from French, from late Latin *oda*, from Greek *ōidē*, Attic form of *aoidē* 'song,' from *aeidein* 'sing.'

-ode[1] ▶ **comb. form** of the nature of a specified thing: *geode.*
– ORIGIN from Greek adjectival ending *-ōdēs*.

-ode[2] ▶ **comb. form** in names of electrodes, or devices having them: *diode.*
– ORIGIN from Greek *hodos* 'way.'

O·den·se /'ōdn-sə, 'ōōd-/ a port in eastern Denmark, on the island of Fyn; pop. 158,678 (2009).

O·der /'ōdər/ a river of central Europe that rises in the mountains in western Czech Republic, flows north through western Poland to meet the Neisse River, and then continues north to form the northern part of the border between Poland and Germany before flowing into the Baltic Sea. Czech and Polish name **ODRA**.

O·des·sa /ō'desə/ **1** a city and port on the southern coast of Ukraine, on the Black Sea; pop. 1,008,600 (est. 2009). Ukrainian name **Odesa**.
2 a city in southwestern Texas, an oil industry center (with its neighbor Midland) in the Permian Basin; pop. 98,801 (est. 2008).

O·dets /ō'dets/, Clifford (1906–63), US playwright. He was a founding member in 1931 of the avant-garde Group Theater, which staged his well-known play, *Waiting for Lefty* (1935).

o·de·um /'ōdēəm/ ▶ **n.** (pl. **odeums** or **odea** /'ōdēə/) (esp. in ancient Greece or Rome) a building used for musical performances.
– ORIGIN from French *odéum* or Latin *odeum*, from Greek *ōideion* (see **ODE**).

o·dif·er·ous /ō'difərəs/ ▶ **adj.** variant spelling of **ODORIFEROUS**.

O·din /'ōdin/ (also **Woden** or **Wotan**) Scandinavian Mythology the supreme god and creator, god of victory and the dead. Wednesday is named after him.

o·di·ous /'ōdēəs/ ▶ **adj.** extremely unpleasant; repulsive.
– DERIVATIVES **o·di·ous·ly adv., o·di·ous·ness n.**
– ORIGIN late Middle English: from Old French *odieus*, from Latin *odiosus*, from *odium* 'hatred.'

o·di·um /'ōdēəm/ ▶ **n.** general or widespread hatred or disgust directed toward someone as a result of their actions: ***his job had made him the target of public hostility and odium.***
– ORIGIN early 17th cent.: from Latin, 'hatred,' from the verb stem *od-* 'hate.'

o·dom·e·ter /ō'dämitər/ ▶ **n.** an instrument for measuring the distance traveled by a vehicle.
– ORIGIN late 18th cent.: from French *odomètre*, from Greek *hodos* 'way' + **-METER**.

O·do·na·ta /,ōdn'ätə, ō'dänə-/ Entomology an order of predatory insects that comprises the dragonflies and damselflies. They have long slender bodies, two pairs of membranous wings, large compound eyes, and aquatic larvae. ■ (as plural noun **odonata**) insects of this order; dragonflies and damselflies.
– ORIGIN modern Latin (plural), formed irregularly from Greek *odōn* (variant of *odous*) 'tooth,' with reference to the insect's mandibles.

o·do·nate /'ōdnət, -,āt/ Entomology ▶ **n.** a predatory insect of the order Odonata; a dragonfly or damselfly.
▶ **adj.** relating to or denoting odonates.

odonto- ▶ **comb. form** relating to a tooth or teeth: *odontology* | *odontophore.*
– ORIGIN from Greek *odous, odont-* 'tooth.'

o·don·to·blast /ō'däntə,blast/ ▶ **n.** Anatomy a cell in the pulp of a tooth that produces dentin.

O·don·to·ce·ti /ō,däntə'sētē/ Zoology the taxonomic division that comprises the toothed whales.
● Suborder Odontoceti, order Cetacea.
– DERIVATIVES **o·don·to·cete** /ō'dän(t)ə,sēt/ **n. & adj.**
– ORIGIN modern Latin (plural), from Greek *odous, odont-* 'tooth' + *ceti* 'of a whale' (genitive of *cetus*, from Greek *kētos* 'whale').

o·don·toid /ō'däntoid/ (also **odontoid process**) ▶ **n.** Anatomy a toothlike projection from the second cervical vertebra on which the first vertebra pivots.
– ORIGIN early 19th cent.: from Greek *odontoeidēs*, from *odous, odont-* 'tooth' + *eidos* 'form.'

o·don·tol·o·gy /,ōdän'täləjē/ ▶ **n.** the scientific study of the structure and diseases of teeth.
– DERIVATIVES **o·don·to·log·i·cal** /ō,däntl'äjəkəl/ **adj., o·don·tol·o·gist** /-jist/ **n.**

o·don·to·phore /ō'däntə,fôr/ ▶ **n.** Zoology a projection in the mouth of most mollusks that supports the radula.
– DERIVATIVES **o·don·toph·o·ral** /,ōdän'täfərəl/ **adj.**

o·dor /'ōdər/ (Brit. **odour**) ▶ **n. 1** a distinctive smell, esp. an unpleasant one: *the odor of cigarette smoke.* **2** a lingering quality, impression, or feeling attaching to something: *an odor of suspicion.* ■ [with adj.] the state of being held in a specified regard: *a decade of bad odor between Britain and the European Community.*
– PHRASES **be in good** (or **bad**) **odor with someone** be in or out of favor with someone: *the players were in bad odor with the fans.*
– ORIGIN Middle English: from Anglo-Norman French, from Latin *odor* 'smell, scent.'

o·dor·ant /'ōdərənt/ ▶ **n.** a substance giving off a smell, esp. one used to give a particular scent or odor to a product.
– ORIGIN late Middle English (as an adjective in the sense 'odorous'): from Old French, present participle of *odorer*, from Latin *odorare* 'give an odor to.' The current sense dates from the 1940s.

PRONUNCIATION KEY ə *ago, up*; ər *over, fur*; a *hat*; ā *ate*; ä *car*; e *let*; ē *see*; i *fit*; ī *by*; NG *sing*; ō *go*; ô *law, for*; oi *toy*; o͝o *good*; o͞o *goo*; ou *out*; TH *thin*; TH *then*; ZH *vision*

o·dor·if·er·ous /ˌōdəˈrifərəs/ ▶ **adj.** having or giving off a smell, esp. an unpleasant or distinctive one: *spicily concocted with odoriferous herbs | an odoriferous pile of fish remains.*
– DERIVATIVES **o·dor·if·er·ous·ly adv.**
– ORIGIN late Middle English: from Latin *odorifer* 'odor-bearing' + **-OUS**.

o·dor·ize /ˈōdəˌrīz/ ▶ **v.** [with obj.] give an odor or scent to.
– DERIVATIVES **o·dor·iz·er n.**
– ORIGIN late 19th cent.: from Latin *odor* 'odor' + **-IZE**.

o·dor·less /ˈōdərlis/ ▶ **adj.** having no odor: *an odorless gas.*

o·dor·ous /ˈōdərəs/ ▶ **adj.** having or giving off a smell.
– ORIGIN late Middle English: from Latin *odorus* 'fragrant' (from *odor* 'odor') + **-OUS**.

o·dour ▶ **n.** British spelling of **ODOR**.

O·dra /ˈôdrä/ Polish name for **ODER**.

O·dys·se·us /ōˈdisēəs, ōˈdisyo͞os/ Greek Mythology the king of Ithaca and central figure of the *Odyssey*, renowned for his cunning and resourcefulness. Roman name **ULYSSES**.

Od·ys·sey /ˈädəsē/ a Greek epic poem traditionally ascribed to Homer, describing the travels of Odysseus during his ten years of wandering after the fall of Troy. He eventually returned home to Ithaca and killed the suitors who had plagued his wife Penelope during his absence. ■ (**odyssey**) a long and eventful or adventurous journey or experience: *his odyssey from military man to politician.*
– DERIVATIVES **Od·ys·se·an** /əˈdisēən/ **adj.**

OE ▶ **abbr.** Old English.

Oe ▶ **abbr.** oersted(s).

Oe·a /ˈēə/ ancient name for **TRIPOLI** (sense 1).

OECD ▶ **abbr.** Organization for Economic Cooperation and Development.

OED ▶ **abbr.** Oxford English Dictionary.

oe·de·ma ▶ **n.** variant British spelling of **EDEMA**.

Oed·i·pus /ˈedəpəs, ˈēdə-/ Greek Mythology the son of Jocasta and of Laius, king of Thebes.

> Left to die on a mountain by Laius, who had been told by an oracle that he would be killed by his own son, the infant Oedipus was saved by a shepherd. Returning eventually to Thebes, Oedipus solved the riddle of the sphinx, but unwittingly killed his father and married Jocasta. On discovering what he had done, he put out his own eyes in a fit of madness, and Jocasta hanged herself.

O

Oed·i·pus com·plex ▶ **n.** Psychoanalysis (in Freudian theory) the complex of emotions aroused in a young child, typically around the age of four, by an unconscious sexual desire for the parent of the opposite sex and a wish to exclude the parent of the same sex. (The term was originally applied to boys, the equivalent in girls being called the **Electra complex**.).
– DERIVATIVES **Oed·i·pal** /-pəl/ **adj.**
– ORIGIN early 20th cent.: by association with **OEDIPUS**.

oeil-de-boeuf /ˈoi də ˈbœf/ ▶ **n.** (pl. **oeils-de-boeuf** pronunc. **same**) Architecture a small round window.
– ORIGIN mid 18th cent.: French, literally 'ox-eye.'

OEM ▶ **abbr.** original equipment manufacturer (an organization that makes devices from component parts bought from other organizations).

oe·nol·o·gy ▶ **n.** variant spelling of **ENOLOGY**.

Oe·no·ne /ēˈnōnē/ Greek Mythology a nymph of Mount Ida and lover of Paris, who deserted her for Helen.

oe·no·phile /ˈēnəˌfīl/ (also **enophile**) ▶ **n.** a connoisseur of wines.
– DERIVATIVES **oe·noph·i·list** /ēˈnäfəlist/ **n.**
– ORIGIN 1930s: from Greek *oinos* 'wine' + **-PHILE**.

OEO ▶ **abbr.** Office of Economic Opportunity.

o'er /ôr/ ▶ **adv. & prep.** archaic or poetic/literary contraction for **OVER**.

Oer·sted /ˈərsted, ˈœrstiTH/, Hans Christian (1777–1851), Danish physicist. He discovered the magnetic effect of an electric current.

oer·sted /ˈərˌsted/ (abbr.: **Oe**) ▶ **n.** Physics a unit of magnetic field strength equivalent to 79.58 amperes per meter.
– ORIGIN late 19th cent.: named after H. C. **OERSTED**.

Oer·ter /ˈôrtər/, Al (1936–2007), US track and field athlete; full name *Alfred Adolf Oerter, Jr.* He held an Olympic record for consecutive medals, winning the discus throw in four Olympic games (1956, 1960, 1964, 1968).

oe·soph·a·gus, etc. ▶ **n.** British spelling of **ESOPHAGUS**, etc.

oes·tra·di·ol ▶ **n.** British spelling of **ESTRADIOL**.

oes·tri·ol ▶ **n.** British spelling of **ESTRIOL**.

oes·tro·gen ▶ **n.** British spelling of **ESTROGEN**.

oes·trone ▶ **n.** British spelling of **ESTRONE**.

oes·trus ▶ **n.** chiefly Brit. variant spelling of **ESTRUS**.

oeu·vre /ˈœvrə/ ▶ **n.** the works of a painter, composer, or author regarded collectively: *the complete oeuvre of Mozart.* ■ a work of art, music, or literature: *an early oeuvre.*
– ORIGIN late 19th cent.: French, literally 'work.'

OF ▶ **abbr.** Old French.

of /əv/ ▶ **prep. 1** expressing the relationship between a part and a whole: *the sleeve of his coat | in the back of the car | the days of the week | a series of programs | a piece of cake | a lot of money.*
2 expressing the relationship between a scale or measure and a value: *an increase of 5 percent | a height of 10 feet.* ■ expressing an age: *a boy of fifteen.*
3 indicating an association between two entities, typically one of belonging: *the son of a friend | the government of India | a photograph of the bride* | [with a possessive] *a former colleague of John's.* ■ expressing the relationship between an author, artist, or composer and their works collectively: *the plays of Shakespeare | the paintings of Rembrandt.*
4 expressing the relationship between a direction and a point of reference: *north of Chicago | on the left of the picture.*
5 expressing the relationship between a general category and the thing being specified which belongs to such a category: *the city of Prague | the idea of a just society | the set of all genes.* ■ governed by a noun expressing the fact that a category is vague: *this type of book | the general kind of answer that would satisfy me.*
6 indicating the relationship between a verb and an indirect object. ■ with a verb expressing a mental state: *they must be persuaded of the severity of the problem | I don't know of anything that would be suitable.* ■ expressing a cause: *he died of cancer.*
7 indicating the material or substance constituting something: *the house was built of bricks | walls of stone.*
8 expressing time in relation to the following hour: *it would be just a quarter of three in New York.*
– PHRASES **be of** possess intrinsically; give rise to: *this work is of great interest and value.* **of all** denoting the least likely or expected example: *Jordan, of all people, committed a flagrant foul.* **of all the nerve** (or Brit. **cheek**) an expression of indignation. **of an evening** (or **morning**, etc.) informal **1** on most evenings (or mornings, etc.). **2** at some time in the evenings (or mornings, etc.).
– ORIGIN Old English, of Germanic origin; related to Dutch *af* and German *ab*, from an Indo-European root shared by Latin *ab* and Greek *apo*.

> **USAGE** It is a mistake to use **of** instead of **have** in constructions such as *you should **have** asked* (not *you should **of** asked*). For more information, see usage at **HAVE**.

of- ▶ **prefix** variant spelling of **OB-** assimilated before *f* (as in *offend*).

O'Fal·lon /ōˈfalən/ a city in eastern Missouri, northwest of St. Louis; pop. 76,819 (est. 2008).

o·fay /ˈōˌfā/ ▶ **n.** informal, offensive an offensive term for a white person, used by black people.
– ORIGIN 1920s: of unknown origin.

off /ôf, äf/ ▶ **adv. 1** away from the place in question; to or at a distance: *the man ran off | she dashed off to her room | we must be off now.* ■ away from the main route: *turning off for Ripon.*
2 so as to be removed or separated: *he whipped off his coat | a section of the runway had been cordoned off.* ■ absent; away from work: *take a day off | he is off on sick leave.*
3 starting a journey or race; leaving: *the gunmen made off on foot | they're off!*
4 so as to bring to an end or be discontinued: *the Christmas party rounded off a hugely successful year | she broke off her reading to look at her husband.* ■ canceled: *tell them the wedding's off.* ■ Brit. informal (of a menu item) temporarily unavailable: *strawberries are off.*
5 (of an electrical appliance or power supply) not functioning or so as to cease to function: *switch the TV off | the electricity was off for four days.*
6 chiefly Brit. having access to or possession of material goods or wealth to the extent specified: *we'd been rather **badly off** for books | how are you off for money?*
▶ **prep. 1** moving away and often down from: *he rolled off the bed | the coat slipped off his arms | trying to get us off the stage.*
2 situated or leading in a direction away from (a main route or intersection): *single wires leading off the main lines | a backstreet off Olympic Boulevard.* ■ out at sea from (a place on the coast): *anchoring off Blue Bay | six miles off Dunkirk.*
3 so as to be removed or separated from: *threatening to tear it off its hinges | they are knocking $2,000 off the price* | figurative *it's a huge burden off my shoulders.* ■ absent from: *I took a couple of days off work.* ■ informal abstaining from: *he managed to stay off alcohol.*
▶ **adj. 1** [attrib.] characterized by someone performing or feeling worse than usual; unsatisfactory or inadequate: *even the greatest athletes have off days.*
2 [predic.] (of food) no longer fresh: *the fish was a bit off.*
3 [attrib.] located on the side of a vehicle that is normally furthest from the curb; offside. Compare with **NEAR** (sense 4 of the adjective).
4 [predic.] Brit. informal annoying or unfair: *His boss deducted the money from his pay. That was a bit off.*
5 [predic.] Brit. informal unwell: *I felt decidedly off.*
▶ **n.** (also **off side**) Cricket the half of the field (as divided lengthways through the pitch) toward which the batsman's feet are pointed when standing to receive the ball. The opposite of **LEG**.
▶ **v.** [with obj.] informal kill; murder: *she might off a cop, but she wouldn't shoot her boyfriend.*
– PHRASES **off and on** intermittently; now and then.
– ORIGIN Old English, originally a variant of **OF** (which combined the senses of 'of' and 'off').

> **USAGE** **Off of** is often used in place of the preposition **off** in contexts such as *she picked it up off of the floor* (compared with *she picked it up off the floor*). Although **off of** is recorded from the 16th century (it was used by Shakespeare) and is logically parallel to the standard **out of**, it is regarded as incorrect in standard modern English.

Off. ▶ **abbr.** ■ Office. ■ Officer.

Of·fa /ˈôfə, ˈäfə/ (died 796), king of Mercia 757–796. He organized the construction of Offa's Dyke, a series of earthworks marking the traditional boundary between England and Wales.

of·fa ▶ **prep.** informal off of; off from: *get offa your horse!*

off-air ▶ **adj. & adv. 1** not being broadcast: [as adv.] *he is exactly the same off-air as he is on.*
2 of or relating to the reception of programs not broadcast by cable or satellite: *an area where off-air reception is poor.*

of·fal /ˈôfəl, ˈäfəl/ ▶ **n.** the entrails and internal organs of an animal used as food. ■ refuse or waste material. ■ decomposing animal flesh.
– ORIGIN late Middle English (in the sense 'refuse from a process'): probably suggested by Middle Dutch *afval*, from *af* 'off' + *vallen* 'to fall.'

Of·fa·ly /ˈôfəlē, ˈäf-/ a county in the central part of the Republic of Ireland, in the province of Leinster; county town, Tullamore.

off·beat /ˈôfˌbēt, ˈäf-/ ▶ **adj. 1** Music not coinciding with the beat.
2 informal unconventional; unusual: *she's a little offbeat, but she's a wonderful actress.*
▶ **n.** Music any of the normally unaccented beats in a bar.

off-brand ▶ **n.** [usu. as modifier] an unknown, unpopular, or inferior brand of retail product: *you bought me off-brand sneakers instead of Keds.*

off-Broad·way (also **Off-Broadway** or **off Broadway** or **Off Broadway**) ▶ **adj. & adv.** (of a theater, play, or performer) located in, appearing in, or associated with an area of New York City other than the Broadway theater district, typically with reference to experimental and less commercial productions.
▶ **n.** such theaters and productions collectively.

off-cam·pus ▶ **adj. & adv.** away from a university or college campus: *asked to live in an off-campus residence.*

off-cen·ter ▶ **adj. & adv.** not quite in the center of something. ■ [as adj.] strange or eccentric: *people say she's off-center.*

off-col·or (also **off color**) ▶ **adj. 1** somewhat indecent or in poor taste: *off-color jokes.*
2 of the wrong or an inferior color: *the new paint doesn't match, it's off-color.* ■ (of a diamond) neither white nor any definite color.
3 chiefly Brit. slightly unwell: *I'm feeling a bit off-color.*

off-dry ▶ **adj.** (of wine) having a nearly dry flavor, with just a trace of sweetness.

Of·fen·bach /ˈôfənˌbäk, ˈäf-/, Jacques (1819–80), German composer, a resident of France from 1833; born *Jacob Offenbach*. He contributed to the rise of the operetta with such works as *Orpheus in the Underworld* (1858) and *The Tales of Hoffmann* (1881).

of·fence ▶ **n.** British spelling of **OFFENSE**.

of·fend /əˈfend/ ▶ **v. 1** [with obj.] cause to feel upset, annoyed, or resentful: *viewers said they had been offended by bad language.* ■ be displeasing to: *he didn't smoke and the smell of ash offended him* | (as

adj. **offending**) *they must redesign the offending section of road.*
2 [no obj.] commit an illegal act: *a small hard core of young criminals who offended again and again.* ■ break a commonly accepted rule or principle: *those activities which **offend against** public order and decency.*
– ORIGIN late Middle English: from Old French *offendre*, from Latin *offendere* 'strike against.'

of·fend·ed /ə'fendid/ ▶ **adj.** resentful or annoyed, typically as a result of a perceived insult: *she sounded slightly offended.*
– DERIVATIVES **of·fend·ed·ly adv.**

of·fend·er /ə'fendər/ ▶ **n. 1** a person who commits an illegal act: *an institution for juvenile offenders.*
2 a person or thing that offends, does something wrong, or causes problems: *of atmospheric pollutants, the worst offender is sulfur dioxide | he himself may be an offender of the very issues he is discussing.*

of·fense /ə'fens/ (Brit. **offence**) ▶ **n. 1** a breach of a law or rule; an illegal act: *neither offense violates any federal law.* ■ a thing that constitutes a violation of what is judged to be right or natural: *the outcome is an offense to basic justice.*
2 annoyance or resentment brought about by a perceived insult to or disregard for oneself or one's standards or principles: *he went out, making it clear he'd **taken offense** | I didn't intend to give offense.*
3 /'ôfens, 'äf-/ the action of attacking: [as modifier] *reductions in strategic offense arsenals.* ■ (in sports) the team or players who are attempting to score or advance the ball. ■ (in sports) the condition of possessing the ball or being on the team attempting to score.
– PHRASES **no offense** informal do not be offended.
– ORIGIN late Middle English: from Old French *offens* 'misdeed,' from Latin *offensus* 'annoyance,' reinforced by French *offense*, from Latin *offensa* 'a striking against, a hurt, or displeasure'; based on Latin *offendere* 'strike against.'

of·fen·sive ▶ **adj. 1** /ə'fensiv/ causing someone to feel deeply hurt, upset, or angry: *the allegations made are deeply offensive to us | offensive language.* ■ (of a sight or smell) disgusting; repulsive: *an offensive odor.*
2 /'äfensiv/ [attrib.] actively aggressive; attacking: *offensive operations against the insurgents.* ■ (of a weapon) meant for use in attack. ■ (in a game) of or relating to the team or player who is seeking to score.
▶ **n.** /ə'fensiv/ an attacking military campaign: *an impending military offensive against the guerrillas.* ■ an organized and forceful campaign to achieve something, typically a political or social end: *the need to **launch an offensive** against crime.*
– PHRASES **be on the offensive** act or be ready to act aggressively. **go on** (or **take**) **the offensive** take the initiative by beginning to attack or act aggressively: *security forces took the offensive ten days ago.*
– DERIVATIVES **of·fen·sive·ly adv.**, **of·fen·sive·ness n.**
– ORIGIN mid 16th cent.: from French *offensif, -ive* or medieval Latin *offensivus*, from Latin *offens-* 'struck against,' from the verb *offendere* (see **OFFEND**).

of·fer /'ôfər, 'äfər/ ▶ **v.** [with two objs.] present or proffer (something) for (someone) to accept or reject as so desired: *may I offer you a drink?* ■ [reporting verb] express readiness or the intention to do something for or on behalf of someone: [with infinitive] *he offered to fix the gate* | [with direct speech] *"Can I help you, dear?" a kindly voice offered.* ■ [with obj.] (usu. **be offered**) make available for sale: *the product is offered at a very competitive price.* ■ [with obj.] provide (access or an opportunity): *the highway offers easy access to the public beaches | a good understanding of what a particular career can offer.* ■ [with obj.] present (a prayer or sacrifice) to a deity: *villagers have gone to offer prayers for the souls of the sailors.* ■ [with obj.] make an attempt at or show one's readiness for (violence or resistance): *he had to offer some resistance to her tirade.* ■ [with obj.] archaic give an opportunity for (battle) to an enemy: *Darius was about to meet him and to offer battle.*
▶ **n.** an expression of readiness to do or give something if desired: [with infinitive] *he had accepted Mallory's offer to buy him a drink | a job offer.* ■ an amount of money that someone is willing to pay for something: *the prospective purchaser who made the highest offer.* ■ a specially reduced price or terms for something on sale: *the offer runs right up until Christmas Eve.* ■ a proposal of marriage.
– PHRASES **have something to offer** have something available to be used or appreciated. **offer one's hand** extend one's hand to be shaken as a sign of friendship. **on offer** available: *the number of permanent jobs on offer is relatively small.* **open to offers** willing to sell something or do a job for a reasonable price.
– DERIVATIVES **of·fer·er** (or **offeror**) **n.**
– ORIGIN Old English *offrian* 'sacrifice (something) to a deity,' of Germanic origin, from Latin *offerre* 'bestow, present' (in ecclesiastical Latin 'offer to God'), reinforced by French *offrir* (which continued to express the primary sense). The noun (late Middle English) is from French *offre.*

of·fer·ing /'ôf(ə)riNG, äf-/ ▶ **n.** a thing offered, esp. as a gift or contribution: *animals as sacrificial offerings.* ■ a thing produced or manufactured for entertainment or sale: *Hollywood's latest offerings for the European market.* ■ a contribution, esp. of money, to a church. ■ a thing offered as a religious sacrifice or token of devotion.

of·fer·ing price ▶ **n.** the price at which a dealer or institution is prepared to sell securities or other assets. Compare with **BID PRICE**.

of·fer·to·ry /'ôfər,tôrē, 'äfər-/ ▶ **n.** (pl. **offertories**) Christian Church **1** the offering of the bread and wine at the Eucharist. ■ prayers or music accompanying this.
2 an offering or collection of money made at a religious service.
– ORIGIN late Middle English: from ecclesiastical Latin *offertorium* 'offering,' from late Latin *offert-* (which replaced Latin *oblat-*) 'offered,' from the verb *offerre* (see **OFFER**).

off-gas ▶ **n.** a gas that is given off, esp. one emitted as the byproduct of a chemical process.
▶ **v.** [no obj.] give off a chemical, esp. a harmful one, in the form of a gas.

off-glide ▶ **n.** Phonetics a glide produced just following the articulation of another speech sound. Compare with **ON-GLIDE**.

off·hand /'ôf'hand, 'äf-/ ▶ **adj.** (also **offhanded**) ungraciously or offensively nonchalant or cool in manner: *his offhand way of talking.*
▶ **adv.** without previous thought or consideration: *I can't think of a better answer offhand.*
– DERIVATIVES **off·hand·ed·ly adv.**, **off·hand·ed·ness n.**

off-hours ▶ **plural n.** the time when one is not at work; one's leisure time.

of·fice /'ôfis, 'äf-/ ▶ **n. 1** a room, set of rooms, or building used as a place for commercial, professional, or bureaucratic work: *computers first appeared in offices in the late 1970s* | [as modifier] *an office job.* ■ the local center of a large business: *a company that has four U.S. and four European offices.* ■ a room, department, or building used to provide a particular service: *a ticket office | a post office.* ■ the consulting room of a professional person.
2 a position of authority, trust, or service, typically one of a public nature: *the office of attorney general.* ■ tenure of an official position, esp. a government position: *a year ago, when the president **took office** | he was ejected from office in 1988.* ■ (**Office**) Brit. the quarters, staff, or collective authority of a particular government department or agency: *the Foreign Office.*
3 (usu. **offices**) a service or kindness done for another person or group of people. ■ dated a duty attaching to one's position; a task or function: *the offices of a nurse | rescued **through the good offices** of the Italian Ambassador, he was returned safely to England.*
4 (also **Divine Office**) Christian Church the series of services of prayers and psalms said (or chanted) daily by Roman Catholic priests, members of religious orders, and other clergy. ■ one of these services: *the noon office.*
– ORIGIN Middle English: via Old French from Latin *officium* 'performance of a task' (in medieval Latin also 'office, divine service'), based on *opus* 'work' + *facere* 'do.'

of·fice boy (also **office girl**) ▶ **n.** a young man (or woman) employed to do less important jobs in a business office.

of·fice·hold·er /'ôfis,hōldər/ ▶ **n.** a person who holds public office.

of·fice hours ▶ **plural n.** the hours during which business is normally conducted. ■ the hours set by a professional person for office consultation.

of·fice park ▶ **n.** an area where a number of office buildings are built together on landscaped grounds.

of·fi·cer /'ôfisər, 'äf-/ ▶ **n. 1** a person holding a position of command or authority in the armed services, in the merchant marine, or on a passenger ship. ■ a policeman or policewoman. ■ a bailiff.
2 a holder of a public, civil, or ecclesiastical office: *a probation officer | the chief medical officer.* ■ a holder of a post in a society, company, or other organization, esp. one who is involved at a senior level in its management: *a chief executive officer.*
3 a member of a certain grade in some honorary orders.
▶ **v.** [with obj.] provide with military officers: *the aristocracy continued to wield considerable political power, officering the army.* ■ act as the commander of (a unit): *foreign mercenaries were hired to officer new regiments.*
– ORIGIN Middle English: via Anglo-Norman French from medieval Latin *officiarius*, from Latin *officium* (see **OFFICE**).

of·fi·cer of arms ▶ **n.** Heraldry a heraldic official; a herald or pursuivant.

of·fi·cial /ə'fiSHəl/ ▶ **adj.** of or relating to an authority or public body and its duties, actions, and responsibilities: *the governor's official engagements.* ■ having the approval or authorization of such a body: *French is the official language of Quebec.* ■ employed by such a body in a position of authority or trust: *an official spokesman.* ■ emanating from or attributable to a person in office; properly authorized: *official statistics.* ■ often derogatory perceived as characteristic of officials and bureaucracy; officious: *he sat up straight and became official.*
▶ **n.** a person holding public office or having official duties, esp. as a representative of an organization or government department: *a union official.*
– DERIVATIVES **of·fi·cial·dom n.**, **of·fi·cial·ism n.**, **of·fi·cial·ize v.**
– ORIGIN Middle English (originally as a noun): via Old French from Latin *officialis*, from *officium* (see **OFFICE**).

of·fi·cial·ese /ə,fiSHə'lēz/ ▶ **n.** the formal and typically verbose style of writing considered to be characteristic of official documents, esp. when it is difficult to understand.

of·fi·cial·ly /ə'fiSHəlē/ ▶ **adv.** in a formal and public way: *next month the election campaign will officially begin.* ■ with the authority of the government or some other organization: *it was officially acknowledged that the economy was in recession.* ■ in public and for official purposes but not necessarily so in reality: [sentence adverb] *there is a possibility he was murdered—officially, he died in a car crash.*

of·fi·ci·ant /ə'fiSHēənt/ ▶ **n.** a person, typically a priest or minister, who performs a religious service or ceremony.
– ORIGIN mid 19th cent.: from medieval Latin *officiant-* 'performing divine service,' from the verb *officiare.*

of·fi·ci·ate /ə'fiSHē,āt/ ▶ **v.** act as an official in charge of something, as a sporting event: *the first woman to officiate a men's basketball game.* ■ perform a religious service or ceremony: *he baptized children and officiated at weddings.*
– DERIVATIVES **of·fi·ci·a·tion** /ə,fiSHē'āSHən/ **n.**, **of·fi·ci·a·tor** /-,ātər/ **n.**
– ORIGIN mid 17th cent.: from medieval Latin *officiare* 'perform divine service,' from *officium* (see **OFFICE**).

of·fic·i·nal /ə'fisənl/ ▶ **adj.** chiefly historical (of an herb or drug) standardly used in medicine.
– DERIVATIVES **of·fic·i·nal·ly adv.**
– ORIGIN late 17th cent. (as a noun denoting an officinal medicine): from medieval Latin *officinalis* 'storeroom for medicines,' from Latin *officina* 'workshop.'

of·fi·cious /ə'fiSHəs/ ▶ **adj.** assertive of authority in an annoyingly domineering way, esp. with regard to petty or trivial matters: *a policeman came to move them on, an officious, spiteful man.* ■ intrusively enthusiastic in offering help or advice; interfering: *an officious bystander.*
– DERIVATIVES **of·fi·cious·ly adv.**, **of·fi·cious·ness n.**
– ORIGIN late 15th cent.: from Latin *officiosus* 'obliging,' from *officium* (see **OFFICE**). The original sense was 'performing its function, efficacious,' whence 'ready to help or please' (mid 16th cent.), later becoming depreciatory (late 16th cent).

off·ing /'ôfiNG, 'äf-/ ▶ **n.** the more distant part of the sea in view.
– PHRASES **in the offing** likely to happen or appear soon: *there are several initiatives in the offing.*
– ORIGIN early 17th cent.: perhaps from **OFF** + **-ING**[1].

off·ish /'ôfiSH, 'äf-/ ▶ **adj.** informal aloof or distant in manner; not friendly: *he was being offish with her.*
– DERIVATIVES **off·ish·ly adv.**, **off·ish·ness n.**

off-is·land ▶ **adv.** away from an island.
▶ **n.** an island off the shore of a larger or central island.
▶ **adj.** located on or coming from such an island.
– DERIVATIVES **off-is·land·er n.**

off-key ▶ **adj. & adv.** (of music or singing) not having the correct tone or pitch; out of tune. ■ not in accordance with what is appropriate or correct in the circumstances: [as adv.] *some of the cinematic effects are distractingly off-key.*

O

off-kil·ter ▶ **adj. & adv. 1** not aligned or balanced. **2** [as adj.] unconventional or eccentric: *an off-kilter comedy about living in mud.*

off-la·bel ▶ **adj.** relating to the prescription of a drug for a condition other than that for which it has been officially approved: *the off-label use of potent antipsychotic medications* | [as adv.] *children with severe anxiety disorders are given antidepressants off label.*

off-li·cence ▶ **n.** Brit. a store selling alcoholic beverages for consumption elsewhere. ■ a license for this.

off·line /ˈôfˈlīn, ˈäf-/ Computing ▶ **adj.** not controlled by or directly connected to a computer or external network.
▶ **adv.** (also **off line**) while not directly controlled by or connected to a computer or external network. ■ with a delay between the production of data and its processing.

off·load /ˈôfˌlōd, ˈäf-/ ▶ **v.** [with obj.] unload (a cargo): *men were offloading bags of salt.* ■ rid oneself of (something) by selling or passing it on to someone else: *a dealer offloaded 5,000 of these shares on a client.* ■ relieve oneself of (a problem or worry) by talking to someone else: *it would be nice to have been able to offload your worries onto someone.* ■ Computing move (data or a task) from one processor to another in order to free the first processor for other tasks: *a system designed to offload the text on to a host computer.*

off-mes·sage ▶ **adj.** departing from an expected or regular theme or issue.

off-off-Broad·way (also **off-off Broadway** or **Off-Off-Broadway** or **Off-Off Broadway**) ▶ **adj. & adv.** denoting or relating to avant-garde, experimental theatrical productions in New York City taking place in small or informal venues.
▶ **n.** theatrical productions of this kind.

off-pat·ent /ôf ˈpatnt, äf/ ▶ **adj. & adv.** no longer subject to patent restrictions.

off-peak ▶ **adj. & adv.** at a time when demand is less: [as adj.] *off-peak travel.*

off-piste ▶ **adj. & adv.** Skiing away from prepared ski runs: [as adj.] *challenging expanses of off-piste skiing.*

off-price ▶ **n.** a method of retailing in which brand-name goods (esp. clothing) are sold for less than the usual retail price: [as modifier] *an off-price store.*
▶ **adv.** using this method: *selling goods off-price.*

off·print /ˈôfˌprint, ˈäf-/ ▶ **n.** a printed copy of an article that originally appeared as part of a larger publication.

off-put·ting ▶ **adj.** unpleasant, disconcerting, or repellent: *his scar is somewhat off-putting.*
– DERIVATIVES **off-put·ting·ly adv.**

off-ramp ▶ **n.** a one-way road leading off a main highway.

off rhyme ▶ **n.** another term for **NEAR RHYME.**

off-road ▶ **adv.** away from a smooth road; on rough terrain. ▶ **adj.** (of a vehicle or bicycle) designed for use over rough terrain.

off-road·ing ▶ **n.** the activity or sport of driving a motor vehicle over rough terrain.
– DERIVATIVES **off-road·er n.**

off·scour·ings /ˈôfˌskouriNGz, ˈäf-/ ▶ **plural n.** refuse, rubbish, or dregs.

off-screen (also **off screen** or **offscreen**) ▶ **adj.** not appearing on a movie or television screen: *he drawls to an off-screen interrogator.* ■ [attrib.] happening in real life rather than fictionally on-screen: *they were off-screen lovers.*
▶ **adv.** outside what can be seen on a movie or television screen: *the girl is looking off-screen to the right.* ■ in real life rather than fictionally in a movie or on television: *happy endings rarely happen off-screen.*

off-sea·son (also **offseason** or **off season**) ▶ **n.** a time of year when a particular activity, typically a sport, is not engaged in: *during baseball's winter off-season.* ■ a time of year when business in a particular sphere is slack: [as modifier] *off-season rates.*
▶ **adv.** in or during the off-season: *he never trains off-season.*

off·set ▶ **n.** /ˈôfˌset, ˈäf-/ **1** a consideration or amount that diminishes or balances the effect of a contrary one: *an offset against taxable profits.* **2** the amount or distance by which something is out of line: *these wheels have an offset of four inches.* ■ Surveying a short distance measured perpendicularly from the main line of measurement. ■ Electronics a small deviation or bias in a voltage or current. **3** a side shoot from a plant serving for propagation. ■ a spur in a mountain range. **4** Architecture a sloping ledge in a wall or other feature where the thickness of the part above is diminished. **5** a bend in a pipe to carry it past an obstacle. **6** [often as modifier] a method of printing in which ink is transferred from a plate or stone to a uniform rubber surface and from that to the paper.
▶ **v.** /ˌôfˈset, ˌäf-/ (**offsets, offsetting**; past and past participle **offset**) **1** [with obj.] counteract (something) by having an opposing force or effect: *the deficit has been more than offset by capital inflows.* **2** [with obj.] place out of line: *several places where the ridge was offset at right angles to its length.* **3** [no obj.] (of ink or a freshly printed page) transfer an impression to the next leaf or sheet.

off·shoot /ˈôfˌSHo͞ot, ˈäf-/ ▶ **n.** a side shoot or branch on a plant. ■ a thing that originated or developed from something else: *commercial offshoots of universities.*

off·shore /ˈôfˈSHôr, ˈäf-/ ▶ **adj. & adv. 1** situated at sea some distance from the shore: [as adj.] *this huge stretch of coastline is dominated by offshore barrier islands* | [as adv.] *we dropped anchor offshore.* ■ (of the wind) blowing toward the sea from the land. ■ of or relating to the business of extracting oil or gas from the seabed: *offshore drilling.* **2** made, situated, or conducting business abroad, esp. in order to take advantage of lower costs or less stringent regulation: [as adj.] *deposits in offshore accounts.* ■ of, relating to, or derived from a foreign country: [as adj.] *offshore politics.*
▶ **v.** [with obj.] relocate (a business or department) to a foreign country to take advantage of lower costs: *firms had offshored some activities by early 2004.*

off·shor·ing ▶ **n.** the practice of basing some of a company's processes or services overseas, so as to take advantage of lower costs.

off·side /ˈôfˈsīd, ˈäf-/ ▶ **adj. & adv.** (of a player in certain sports) occupying an illegal position on the field, in particular: ■ Ice Hockey moving into the attacking zone ahead of the puck. ■ (usu. **offsides**) Football over the scrimmage line or otherwise ahead of the ball before the play has begun. ■ Soccer in the attacking half ahead of the ball and having fewer than two defenders nearer the goal line at the moment the ball is played. ■ Field Hockey in the attacking half of the field when there are fewer than three defenders nearer the goal line at the moment the ball is played.
▶ **n.** the fact or an instance of being offside.

off·side trap ▶ **n.** Soccer a maneuver in which players on the defending team push upfield in order to put one or more opposing players into an offside position.

off-site ▶ **adj. & adv.** taking place or situated away from a particular site or premises.

off-speed ▶ **adj.** slower than expected.

off·spring /ˈôfˌspriNG, ˈäf-/ ▶ **n.** (pl. **same**) a person's child or children: *the offspring of middle-class parents.* ■ an animal's young. ■ the product or result of something: *German nationalism was the offspring of military ambition.*
– ORIGIN Old English *ofspring* (see **OFF, SPRING**).

off·stage /ˈôfˈstāj, ˈäf-/ ▶ **adj. & adv.** (in a theater) not on the stage and so not visible to the audience.

off-the-shoul·der ▶ **adj.** (esp. of a dress or blouse) not covering the shoulders.

off-top·ic ▶ **adj. & adv.** (esp. of posts on an Internet message board) not relevant to the subject in question: [as adj.] *his second comment is entirely off-topic* | [as adv.] *you're driftng off-topic.*

off-track ▶ **adj.** (of betting on a race) situated or taking place away from a racetrack.

off-white ▶ **n.** a white color with a gray or yellowish tinge: [as modifier] *a frilly off-white blouse.*

off-world ▶ **n.** in science fiction, any place away from the earth, or from that world that serves as the location of a given narrative or is regarded in a given context as the native world.
▶ **adj.** involving, located in, inhabiting, or coming from, a place outside the native world.
▶ **adv.** away from the native world.
– DERIVATIVES **off-world·er n.**

off year ▶ **n. 1** a year in which there is no major election, esp. one in which there is a congressional election but no presidential election: [as modifier] *November was an off-year election month.* **2** a year that is inferior or substandard compared to previous ones: *it's very difficult to make good wines in off years.*

Of·lag /ˈôfˌläg, ˈäf-/ ▶ **n.** historical a German prison camp for captured enemy officers. Compare with **STALAG.**
– ORIGIN German, contraction of *Offizier(s)lager* 'officers' camp.'

OFM ▶ **abbr.** Order of Friars Minor (Franciscans).
– ORIGIN Latin *Ordo Fratrum Minorum.*

oft /ôft, äft/ ▶ **adv.** archaic, poetic/literary, or jocular form of **OFTEN:** [in combination] *an oft-quoted tenet.*
– ORIGIN Old English, of Germanic origin; related to German *oft.*

of·ten /ˈôf(t)ən, ˈäf-/ ▶ **adv.** (**oftener, oftenest**) frequently; many times: *he often goes for long walks by himself* | *how often do you have your hair cut?* ■ in many instances: *vocabulary often reflects social standing.*
– PHRASES **as often as not** quite frequently or commonly: *I had two homes really, because as often as not I was down at her house.* **more often than not** usually: *food is scarce and more often than not they go hungry.*
– ORIGIN Middle English: extended form of **OFT,** probably influenced by *selden* 'seldom.' Early examples appear to be northern English; the word became general in the 16th cent.

of·ten·times /ˈôf(t)ənˌtīmz, ˈäf-/ ▶ **adv.** often.
– ORIGIN late Middle English: extended form of **OFTTIMES,** influenced by **OFTEN.**

oft·times /ˈôftˌtīmz, ˈäf(t)-/ ▶ **adv.** archaic or poetic/literary form of **OFTEN.**

OG ▶ **abbr.** officer of the guard.

O·ga·den /ˌôgəˈden, ˌägə-, ōˈgäden/ (**the Ogaden**) a desert region in southeastern Ethiopia, largely inhabited by Somali nomads. It has been claimed by successive governments of neighboring Somalia.

O·gal·la·la Aq·ui·fer /ˌōgəˈlälə/ a vast groundwater resource under eight US states, used esp. for crop irrigation, that stretches from southern South Dakota to western Texas and eastern New Mexico.

og·am /ˈägəm/ ▶ **n.** variant spelling of **OGHAM.**

Og·bo·mo·sho /ˌägbəˈmōSHō/ a city and agricultural market in southwestern Nigeria, north of Ibadan; pop. 951,000 (est. 2007).

Og·den /ˈägdən/ an industrial city in northern Utah, north of Salt Lake City, site of the US Air Force base; pop. 82,865 (est. 2008).

og·do·ad /ˈägdəˌwad/ ▶ **n.** rare a group or set of eight.
– ORIGIN early 17th cent.: via late Latin from Greek *ogdoas, ogdoad-,* from *ogdoos* 'eighth,' from *oktō* 'eight.'

o·gee /ōˈjē/ Architecture ▶ **adj.** having a double continuous S-shaped curve.
▶ **n.** an S-shaped line or molding.
– DERIVATIVES **o·geed adj.**
– ORIGIN late Middle English: apparently from **OGIVE** (with which it was originally synonymous). The current sense arose in the late 17th cent.

o·gee arch ▶ **n.** Architecture an arch with two ogee curves meeting at the apex.

og·ham /ˈägəm/ (also **ogam**) ▶ **n.** an ancient British and Irish alphabet, consisting of twenty characters formed by parallel strokes on either side of or across a continuous line. ■ an inscription in this alphabet. ■ each of its characters.
– ORIGIN early 18th cent.: from Irish *ogam,* connected with *Ogma,* the name of its mythical inventor.

o·give /ōˈjīv/ ▶ **n. 1** Architecture a pointed or Gothic arch. ■ one of the diagonal groins or ribs of a vault. ■ a thing having the profile of an ogive, esp. the head of a projectile or the nose cone of a rocket. **2** Statistics a cumulative frequency graph.
– DERIVATIVES **o·gi·val** /ōˈjīvəl/ **adj.**
– ORIGIN late Middle English: from French, of unknown origin.

Og·la·la /ōgˈlälə/ (also **Ogalala** /ˌōgəˈlälə/) ▶ **n.** (pl. **same** or **Oglalas** or **Oglalas**) a member of the chief division of the Lakota people.
▶ **adj.** of or relating to this people.
– ORIGIN the name in Lakota.

o·gle /ˈōgəl/ ▶ **v.** [with obj.] stare at in a lecherous manner: *he was ogling her breasts* | [no obj.] *men who had turned up to ogle.*
▶ **n.** a lecherous look.
– DERIVATIVES **o·gler** /ˈōg(ə)lər/ **n.**
– ORIGIN late 17th cent.: probably from Low German or Dutch; compare with Low German *oegeln,* frequentative of *oegen* 'look at.'

O·gle·thorpe /ˈōgəlˌTHôrp/, James Edward (1696–1785), British soldier and politician. A member of Parliament 1722–54, he received the charter for the colony of Georgia in 1732 and founded Savannah 1733. In 1742, he assured the survival of Georgia by defeating the Spanish at Bloody Marsh.

OGPU /ˈägˌpo͞o/ (also **Ogpu**) an organization for investigating and combating counterrevolutionary activities in the former Soviet Union, existing from 1922 (1922–23 as the GPU) to 1934 and replacing the Cheka. It was absorbed into the NKVD in 1934.
– ORIGIN acronym from Russian *Ob"edinënnoe gosudarstvennoe politicheskoe upravlenie* 'Unified State Political Directorate.'

o·gre /ˈōgər/ ▶ **n.** (in folklore) a man-eating giant. ■ a cruel or terrifying person.
– DERIVATIVES **o·gre·ish** /ˈōg(ə)riSH/ (also **ogrish**) **adj.**
– ORIGIN early 18th cent.: from French, first used by the French writer Perrault in 1697.

o·gress /ˈōgris/ ▶ **n.** a female ogre.

OH ▶ **abbr.** Ohio (in official postal use).

oh[1] /ō/ ▶ **exclam.** used to express a range of emotions including surprise, anger, disappointment, or joy, or when reacting to something that has just been said: *"Oh no," said Daisy, appalled | Me? Oh, I'm fine | oh, shut up.*
– PHRASES **oh boy** used to express surprise or excitement. **oh well** used to express resignation: *oh well, please yourself.* **oh yeah?** used to express disbelief. ■ used to express a threatening or taunting reaction.
– ORIGIN mid 16th cent.: variant of **O**[3].

oh[2] ▶ **n.** variant spelling of **O**[1] (sense 2).

O'Ha·ra[1] /ōˈhe(ə)rə, ōˈharə/, Frank (1926–66), US poet and art critic; full name *Francis Russell O'Hara.* His poetry reflects his close ties to the art world in New York City and is collected in volumes such as *A City in Winter* (1952), *Meditations in an Emergency* (1956), and *Lunch Poems* (1964).

O'Ha·ra[2], John (Henry) (1905–70), US writer. He wrote *Butterfield 8* (1935), *Pal Joey* (1940), *Ten North Frederick* (1955), and *Waiting for Winter* (1966).

OHC ▶ **abbr.** overhead camshaft.

O'Hig·gins /ōˈhiginz, ôˈēgēns/, Bernardo (*c.*1778–1842), Chilean revolutionary leader and statesman; head of state 1817–23. With the help of José de San Martín, he led the army that defeated Spanish forces in 1817 and paved the way for Chilean independence the following year.

O·hi·o /ōˈhī-ō/ a state in the northeastern US, bordering on Lake Erie; pop. 11,485,910 (est. 2008); capital, Columbus; statehood, Mar. 1, 1803 (17). It was acquired by Britain from France in 1763 and by the US in 1783 after the American Revolution.
– DERIVATIVES **O·hi·o·an adj. & n.**

O·hi·o Riv·er a river that flows for 980 miles (1,580 km) from Pittsburgh in Pennsylvania, where it is formed by the Allegheny and Monongahela rivers, through the eastern Midwest to join the Mississippi River at Cairo in Illinois.

Ohm /ōm/, Georg Simon (1789–1854), German physicist. The units ohm and mho are named after him, as is Ohm's law on electricity.

ohm /ōm/ ▶ **n.** the SI unit of electrical resistance, expressing the resistance in a circuit transmitting a current of one ampere when subjected to a potential difference of one volt. (Symbol: Ω)
– DERIVATIVES **ohm·ic** /ˈōmik/ **adj.**, **ohm·i·cal·ly** /ˈōmik(ə)lē/ **adv.**
– ORIGIN mid 19th cent.: named after G. S. **Ohm**.

ohm·me·ter /ˈō(m),mētər/ ▶ **n.** an instrument for measuring electrical resistance.

OHMS ▶ **abbr.** on Her (or His) Majesty's Service.

Ohm's law Physics a law stating that electric current is proportional to voltage and inversely proportional to resistance.

o·ho /ōˈhō/ ▶ **exclam.** used to express pleased surprise or recognition.
– ORIGIN Middle English: from **O**[3] + **HO**[2].

oh-oh ▶ **exclam.** another spelling for **UH-OH**.

-oholic ▶ **suffix** variant spelling of **-AHOLIC**.

oh-so ▶ **adv.** [as submodifier] informal extremely: *their oh-so-ordinary lives.*

OHV ▶ **abbr.** overhead valve.

oi /oi/ (also **oy**) ▶ **exclam.** Brit. informal used to attract someone's attention, esp. in a rough or angry way: *oi, don't lean out!*
▶ **n.** a type of harsh, aggressive punk music originally popular in the late 1970s and early 1980s.
– ORIGIN variant of **HOY**[1]: first recorded in the 1930s.

OIC ▶ **abbr.** Organization of the Islamic Conference, a permanent delegation to the United Nations representing the interests of Muslims in several dozen countries.

-oid ▶ **suffix** forming adjectives and nouns: **1** Zoology denoting an animal belonging to a higher taxon with a name ending in *-oidea*: *hominoid | percoid.* **2** denoting form or resemblance: *asteroid | rhomboid.*
– ORIGIN from modern Latin *-oides*, from Greek *-oeidēs*; related to *eidos* 'form.'

-oidal ▶ **suffix** forming adjectives corresponding to nouns ending in *-oid* (such as *anthropoidal* corresponding to *anthropoidal*).
– ORIGIN see **-OID**, **-AL**.

-oidally ▶ **suffix** forming adverbs corresponding to nouns adjectives *-oidal* (such as *adenoidally* corresponding to *adenoidal*).
– ORIGIN see **-OIDAL -LY**[2].

o·id·i·um /ōˈidēəm/ ▶ **n.** (pl. **oidia** /ōˈidēə/) **1** Botany a type of fungal spore (conidium) formed by the breaking up of fungal hyphae into cells, esp. as produced by powdery mildews. **2** a fungal disease affecting vines, caused by a powdery mildew. ● The fungus is *Uncinula necator* (formerly *Oidium tuckeri*), family Erysiphaceae, subdivision Ascomycotina.
– ORIGIN mid 19th cent.: modern Latin, from Greek *ōion* 'egg' + the diminutive suffix *-idion*.

oik /oik/ (also **oick**) ▶ **n.** informal, chiefly Brit. an uncouth or obnoxious person.
– ORIGIN 1930s: of unknown origin.

oil /oil/ ▶ **n. 1** a viscous liquid derived from petroleum, esp. for use as a fuel or lubricant. ■ petroleum. ■ [with modifier] any of various thick, viscous, typically flammable liquids that are insoluble in water but soluble in organic solvents and are obtained from animals or plants: *potatoes fried in vegetable oil.* ■ a liquid preparation used on the hair or skin as a cosmetic: *suntan oil.* ■ Chemistry any of a group of natural esters of glycerol and various fatty acids that are liquid at room temperature. Compare with **FAT**.
2 (often **oils**) oil paint: *a portrait in oils.*
▶ **v.** [with obj.] (often as adj. **oiled**) lubricate or coat (something) with oil: *a lightly oiled baking tray.* ■ impregnate or treat (something) with oil: *her hair was heavily oiled.*
– PHRASES **oil and water** used to refer to two elements, factors, or people that do not agree or blend together.
– DERIVATIVES **oil·less adj.**
– ORIGIN Middle English: from Old Northern French *olie*, Old French *oile*, from Latin *oleum* '(olive) oil'; compare with *olea* 'olive.'

oil bar·on ▶ **n.** derogatory a magnate in the oil industry.

oil bee·tle ▶ **n.** a slow-moving flightless beetle that releases a foul-smelling oily secretion when disturbed. The larvae develop as parasites in the nests of solitary bees. ● *Meloe* and other genera, family Meloidae.

oil·bird /ˈoil,bərd/ ▶ **n.** chiefly British term for **GUACHARO**. ● *Steatornis caripensis*, the only member of the family Steatornithidae.

oil burn·er ▶ **n.** a device, esp. a furnace, in which oil is vaporized and burned to produce heat.

oil cake ▶ **n.** a mass of compressed linseed or other plant material left after its oil has been extracted, used as fodder or fertilizer.

oil·can /ˈoil,kan/ ▶ **n.** a can containing lubricating oil, esp. one with a long nozzle.

oil·cloth /ˈoil,klôTH/ ▶ **n.** fabric treated on one side with oil to make it waterproof. ■ a canvas coated with linseed or other oil and used to cover a table or floor.

oil col·or ▶ **n.** another term for **OIL PAINT**.

oil drum ▶ **n.** a metal drum used for transporting oil.

oiled silk ▶ **n.** silk treated on one side with oil to make it waterproof.

oil·er /ˈoilər/ ▶ **n. 1** a thing that holds or supplies oil, in particular: ■ an oil tanker. ■ an oilcan. ■ a person who oils machinery. ■ informal an oil well.
2 (**oilers**) informal oilskin garments.

oil field (also **oilfield**) ▶ **n.** an area of land or seabed underlain by strata yielding petroleum, esp. in amounts that justify commercial exploitation.

oil-fired ▶ **adj.** (esp. of a heating system or power station) using oil as fuel.

oil·fish /ˈoil,fiSH/ ▶ **n.** (pl. **same** or **oilfishes**) a large violet or purple-brown escolar, the flesh of which is oily and unpalatable. ● *Ruvettus pretiosus*, family Gempylidae.

oil lamp ▶ **n.** a lamp using oil as fuel.

oil·man /ˈoil,man, -mən/ ▶ **n.** (pl. **oilmen**) an owner or employee of an oil company.

oil meal ▶ **n.** ground oil cake.

oil of cloves ▶ **n.** see **CLOVE**[1] (sense 1).

oil of tur·pen·tine ▶ **n.** see **TURPENTINE** (sense 1 of the noun).

oil of vit·ri·ol ▶ **n.** archaic term for **SULFURIC ACID**.

oil of win·ter·green ▶ **n.** see **WINTERGREEN** (sense 1).

oil paint ▶ **n.** a paste made with ground pigment and a drying oil such as linseed oil, used chiefly by artists.

oil paint·ing ▶ **n.** the art of painting with oil paints. ■ a picture painted with oil paints.

oil palm ▶ **n.** a widely cultivated tropical West African palm tree that is the chief source of palm oil. ● *Elaeis guineensis*, family Palmae: several cultivars.

oil pan ▶ **n.** the bottom section of the crankcase of an internal combustion engine, serving as the reservoir for its lubricating oil.

oil·pa·per /ˈoil,pāpər/ (also **oil paper**) ▶ **n.** paper made transparent or waterproof by treatment with oil.

oil plat·form ▶ **n.** a structure designed to stand on the seabed to provide a stable base above water for drilling and servicing oil wells.

oil press ▶ **n.** an apparatus for pressing oil from seeds, fruits, etc.

oil rig ▶ **n.** a structure with equipment for drilling and servicing an oil well.

oil sand ▶ **n.** (often **oil sands**) a deposit of loose sand or partially consolidated sandstone containing petroleum or other hydrocarbons.

oil·seed /ˈoil,sēd/ ▶ **n.** any of several seeds from cultivated crops yielding oil, e.g., rape, peanut, soybean, or cotton.

oil·seed rape ▶ **n.** see **RAPE**[2].

oil shale ▶ **n.** fine-grained sedimentary rock from which oil can be extracted.

oil·skin /ˈoil,skin/ ▶ **n.** heavy cotton cloth waterproofed with oil. ■ (also **oilskins**) a garment or set of garments made of such cloth.

oil slick ▶ **n.** a film or layer of oil floating on an expanse of water, esp. one that has leaked or been discharged from a ship.

oil spot ▶ **n.** an oily patch or mark. ■ a silvery marking on brown Chinese porcelain (esp. of the Sung period) caused by precipitation of iron in firing: [as modifier] *oil-spot glaze.*

oil·stone /ˈoil,stōn/ ▶ **n.** a fine-grained flat stone used with oil for sharpening cutting edges.

oil tank·er ▶ **n.** a ship designed to carry oil in bulk.

oil well ▶ **n.** a well or shaft drilled through rock, from which petroleum is drawn.

oil·y /ˈoilē/ ▶ **adj.** (**oilier, oiliest**) **1** containing oil: *oily fish such as mackerel and sardines.* ■ covered or soaked with oil: *an oily rag.* ■ resembling oil in appearance or behavior: *the oily swell of the river.*
2 (of a person or their behavior) unpleasantly smooth and ingratiating: *his oily smile.*
– DERIVATIVES **oil·i·ness n.**

oink /oiNGk/ ▶ **n.** the characteristic grunting sound of a pig.
▶ **v.** [no obj.] make such a sound.
– ORIGIN 1940s: imitative.

oint·ment /ˈointmənt/ ▶ **n.** a smooth oily preparation that is rubbed on the skin for medicinal purposes or as a cosmetic.
– ORIGIN Middle English: alteration of Old French *oignement*, from a popular Latin form of Latin *unguentum* (see **UNGUENT**); influenced by obsolete *oint* 'anoint' (from Old French, past participle of *oindre* 'anoint').

Oi·sin another name for **OSSIAN**.

OJ ▶ **n.** informal orange juice.
– ORIGIN 1940s: abbreviation.

O·jib·wa /ōˈjib,wā, -wə/ (also **Ojibway** /-,wā/) ▶ **n.** (pl. **same** or **Ojibwas** or **Ojibways**) **1** a member of a North American Indian people native to the region around Lake Superior. Also called **CHIPPEWA**.
2 the Algonquian language of this people.
▶ **adj.** of or relating to this people or their language.
– ORIGIN from Ojibwa *očipwē*, probably meaning 'puckered,' with reference to their style of moccasins.

OK[1] (also **okay** /ˈōˈkā/) informal ▶ **exclam.** used to express assent, agreement, or acceptance: *OK, I'll pass on your message | OK, OK, I give in.* ■ used to introduce an utterance: *"OK, let's go."*
▶ **adj.** [predic.] satisfactory but not exceptionally or especially good: *the flight was OK.* ■ (of a person) in a satisfactory physical or mental state: *are you OK, Ben?* ■ permissible; allowable: *I'm not sure if it's OK to say that to a teacher.*
▶ **adv.** in a satisfactory manner or to a satisfactory extent: *the computer continues to work OK.*
▶ **n.** [in sing.] an authorization or approval: *do you know how long it takes for those pen-pushers to give us the OK?*
▶ **v.** (**OK's, OK'ing, OK'd**) [with obj.] sanction or give approval to: *the governor recently OK'd the execution of a man who had committed murder.*
– ORIGIN mid 19th cent.: probably an abbreviation of *orl korrect*, humorous form of *all correct*, popularized as a slogan during President Van Buren's re-election campaign of 1840; his nickname *Old Kinderhook* (derived from his birthplace) provided the initials.

OK² ▶ abbr. Oklahoma (in official postal use).

o·ka /ˈōkə/ (also **oke**) ▶ n. **1** an Egyptian and former Turkish unit of weight, variable but now usually equal to approximately 1.3 kg (2³/₄ lb). **2** an Egyptian and former Turkish unit of capacity equal to approximately 0.2 liter (¹/₃ pint).
– ORIGIN early 17th cent.: via Italian and French *oque* from Turkish *okka*, from Arabic *ūḳiya*, based on Latin *uncia* 'ounce.'

o·ka·pi /ōˈkäpē/ ▶ n. (pl. **same** or **okapis**) a large browsing mammal of the giraffe family that lives in the rain forests of the northern Democratic Republic of the Congo (formerly Zaire). It has a dark chestnut coat with stripes on the hindquarters and upper legs. ● *Okapia johnstoni*, family Giraffidae.
– ORIGIN early 20th cent.: a local word.

O·ka·ra /ōˈkärə/ a commercial city in northeastern Pakistan, in Punjab province; pop. 232,400 (est. 2009).

O·ka·van·go /ˌōkəˈvänggō/ a river in southwestern Africa that rises in central Angola and flows 1,000 miles (1,600 km) south and then east to Namibia, where it turns east to form part of the border between Angola and Namibia before entering Botswana, where it drains into the extensive Okavango marshes. Also called **CUBANGO**.

o·kay /ˈōˈkā/ ▶ exclam. adj. adv. n. & v. variant spelling of **OK¹**.

O·ka·ya·ma /ˌōkäˈyämə/ an industrial city and major railroad junction in southwestern Japan, on the southwestern coast of the island of Honshu; pop. 683,258 (2007).

O.K. Cor·ral /ˈōˈkā kəˈral/ see **TOMBSTONE**, Arizona.

oke¹ ▶ n. variant spelling of **OKA**.

oke² /ōk/ ▶ exclam. adj. adv. n. & v. another term for **OKAY**.

O·kee·cho·bee, Lake /ˌōkiˈchōbē/ a lake in southern Florida, part of the Okeechobee Waterway that crosses the Florida peninsula from west to east and links the Gulf of Mexico with the Atlantic Ocean.

O'Keeffe /ōˈkēf/, Georgia (1887–1986), US painter. A pioneer of modernism in America, she first produced largely abstract work, adopting a more figurative style in the 1920s. Her best-known paintings depict enlarged studies, particularly of flowers, and are often regarded as being sexually symbolic. She married photographer Alfred Stieglitz in 1924.

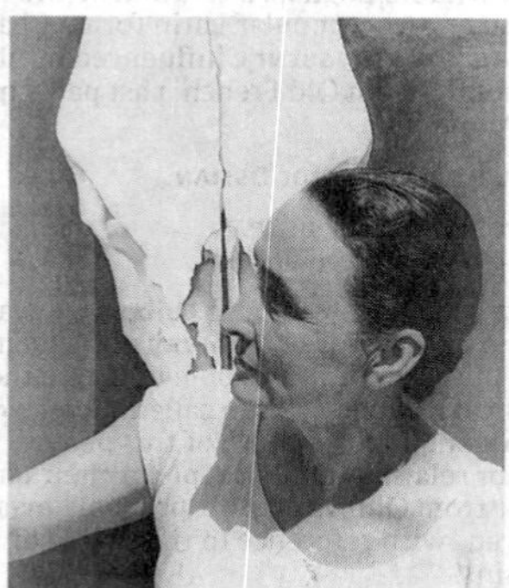

Georgia O'Keeffe

O·ke·fe·no·kee Swamp /ˌōkēfəˈnōkē/ an area of swampland in southeastern Georgia and northeastern Florida.

o·key-doke /ˌōkē ˈdōk/ (also **okey-dokey** /ˈdōkē/) ▶ exclam., adj., & adv. variant form of **OK¹**.

O·khotsk, Sea of /ōˈkätsk, əˈkhôtsk/ an inlet of the northern Pacific Ocean on the eastern coast of Russia, between the Kamchatka peninsula and the Kuril Islands.

O·kie /ˈōkē/ ▶ n. (pl. **Okies**) informal a native or inhabitant of Oklahoma. ■ historical, derogatory a migrant agricultural worker from Oklahoma who had been forced to leave during the Depression of the 1930s.

O·ki·na·wa /ˌōkəˈnäwə/ an island in southern Japan, the largest of the Ryukyu Islands; chief town, Naha. An important World War II battle here in 1945 allowed the victorious Allies to establish bases close to the Japanese mainland.

Okla. ▶ abbr. Oklahoma.

O·kla·ho·ma /ˌōkləˈhōmə/ a state in the southwestern central US, north of Texas; pop. 3,642,361 (est. 2008); capital, Oklahoma City; statehood, Nov. 16, 1907 (46). In 1803, most of it was acquired from the French as part of the Louisiana Purchase.
– DERIVATIVES **O·kla·ho·man** n. & adj.

O·kla·ho·ma Cit·y the capital of Oklahoma, in the central part of the state; pop. 551,789 (est. 2008). It expanded rapidly after the discovery of oil in 1928.

o·kou·me /ˌōkəˈmā/ ▶ n. another term for **GABOON**.

o·kra /ˈōkrə/ ▶ n. a plant of the mallow family with long ridged seedpods, native to the Old World tropics. ● *Abelmoschus esculentus*, family Malvaceae. ■ the immature seedpods of this plant eaten as a vegetable and also used to thicken soups and stews. Also called **GUMBO**.
– ORIGIN early 18th cent.: a West African word, perhaps from the root *nkru*; compare with *nkran*, the name of the town Europeanized as *Accra*.

Ok·to·ber·fest /äkˈtōbərˌfest/ ▶ n. a traditional autumn festival held in Munich, Germany, every October that features beer-drinking and merrymaking. ■ any similar autumn festival.

-ol ▶ suffix Chemistry forming names of organic compounds: **1** denoting alcohols and phenols: *glycerol* | *retinol*. **2** denoting oils and oil-derived compounds: *benzol*.
– ORIGIN Sense 1 from *(alcoh)ol*; sense 2 from Latin *oleum* 'oil.' See also **-OLE**.

O·laf /ˈōläf/ the name of five kings of Norway. ■ **Olaf I Tryggvason** (969–1000), reigned 995–1000. ■ **Olaf II Haraldsson** (*c.*995–1030), reigned 1016–30; canonized as **St. Olaf** for his attempts to spread Christianity in his kingdom. He is the patron saint of Norway. Feast day, July 29. ■ **Olaf III Haraldsson** (died 1093), reigned 1066–93. ■ **Olaf IV Haakonson** (1370–87), reigned 1380–87. ■ **Olaf V** (1903–91), reigned 1957–91; full name *Olaf Alexander Edmund Christian Frederik*.

Ö·land /ˈəˌländ, ˈœˌländ/ a narrow island in the Baltic Sea, off the southeastern coast of Sweden, separated from the mainland by Kalmar Sound.

O·la·the /ōˈlāthə/ an industrial city in northeastern Kansas, southwest of Kansas City; pop. 119,993 (est. 2008).

Ol·bers' par·a·dox /ˈōlbərz/ Astronomy the apparent paradox that if stars are distributed evenly throughout an infinite universe of infinite age, the night sky should display a uniform glow, since every line of sight would terminate at a star. But with an expanding universe of finite age, visible light from very distant stars has not reached the Earth.
– ORIGIN 1950s: named after Heinrich W. M. *Olbers* (1758–1840), the German astronomer who propounded it in 1826.

old /ōld/ ▶ adj. (**older, oldest**) See also **ELDER¹, ELDEST**. **1** having lived for a long time; no longer young: *the old man lay propped up on cushions.* ■ made or built long ago: *the old quarter of the town.* ■ possessed or used for a long time: *he gave his old clothes away.* ■ having the characteristics or showing the signs of age: *marble now so old that it has turned gray and chipped.* **2** [attrib.] belonging only or chiefly to the past; former or previous: *valuation under the old rating system was inexact.* ■ used to refer to the first of two or more similar things: *I was going to try to get my old job back.* ■ dating from far back; long-established or known: *we greet each other like old friends* | *I get sick of the same old routine.* ■ (of a form of a language) as used in former or earliest times. **3** [in combination] of a specified age: *he was fourteen years old* | *a seven-month-old baby.* ■ [as noun in combination] a person or animal of the age specified: *a nineteen-year-old.* **4** [attrib.] informal used to express affection, familiarity, or contempt: *it gets the old adrenaline going* | *"Good old Mom," she said.*
– PHRASES **any old** any item of a specified type (used to show that no particular or special individual is in question): *any old room would have done.* **any old way** in no particular order: *they've dropped things just any old way.* **as old as the hills** of very long standing or very great age (often used in exaggerated statements). **be old enough to be someone's father** (or **mother**) informal of a much greater age than someone (esp. used to suggest that a romantic or sexual relationship between the people concerned is inappropriate). **for old times' sake** see **SAKE¹**. **of old 1** in or belonging to the past: *he was more reticent than of old.* **2** starting long ago; for a long time: *they knew him of old.* **the old days** a period in the past, often seen as significantly different from the present, esp. noticeably better or worse: *it was easier in the old days* | *we are less confident than in the good old days* | *the bad old days of incoherence and irresponsibility.*
– DERIVATIVES **old·ish** adj., **old·ness** n.
– ORIGIN Old English *ald*; related to Dutch *oud* and German *alt*, from an Indo-European root meaning 'grown-up, adult,' shared by Latin *alere* 'nourish.'

> **USAGE** Where two, and no more, are involved, they may be **older** and **younger**: *the older of the twins, by ten minutes, is Sam; the younger is Pamela.* Where there are more than two, one may be the **oldest** or **youngest**: *I have four siblings, of whom Jane is the oldest.* See also **FORMER¹** and **LATTER**.

old age ▶ n. the later part of normal life: *loneliness affects many people in old age.* ■ the state of being old: *old age itself is not a disease.*

Old Bai·ley the central criminal court in London, England.

old bean ▶ n. see **BEAN**.

Old Be·liev·er ▶ n. a member of a Russian Orthodox group that refused to accept the liturgical reforms of the patriarch Nikon (1605–81).

old boy ▶ n. **1** Brit. a former male pupil of a school, college, or university. ■ a former male member of a sports team, company, or other organization. **2** informal an elderly man. ■ humorous an affectionate form of address to a boy or man.

old-boy net·work (also **old boy network**) ▶ n. an informal system of support and friendship through which men use their positions of influence to help others who went to the same school or college as they did or who share a similar social background.

Old Cath·o·lic ▶ n. a member of any of various religious groups that have separated from the Roman Catholic Church since the Reformation, esp. over the tenets of papal primacy and infallibility. ■ a member of an English family that has remained Roman Catholic since the Reformation.

Old Church Slav·ic (also **Old Church Slavonic**) ▶ n. the oldest recorded Slavic language, as used by the apostles Cyril and Methodius and surviving in texts from the 9th–12th centuries. It is related particularly to the South Slavic languages. See also **CHURCH SLAVIC**.

old coun·try ▶ n. (**the old country**) the native country of a person who has gone to live abroad.

Old Del·hi see **DELHI**.

olde ▶ adj. [attrib.] pseudoarchaic variant spelling of **OLD**, intended to be quaint: *Ye Olde Tea Shoppe.*

old·en /ˈōldən/ ▶ adj. [attrib.] archaic or humorous of or relating to former times: *the olden days.*

Ol·den·burg /ˈōldənˌbərg/, Claes (Thure) (1929–), US pop artist and sculptor; born in Sweden. During the 1960s, he conducted "happenings," participatory art events such as *Autobodys* (1964), in which he used actual cars and crowds of people. He later worked with soft materials and foam rubber to create soft sculptures of everyday objects.

Old Eng·lish ▶ n. the language of the Anglo-Saxons (up to about 1150), a highly inflected language with a largely Germanic vocabulary, very different from modern English. Also called **ANGLO-SAXON**.

Old Eng·lish sheep·dog ▶ n. a large sheepdog of a breed with a shaggy blue-gray and white coat.

Old English sheepdog

Old Faith·ful one of the best-known geysers in Yellowstone National Park. Its eruptions occur every 33 to 90 minutes and last about four minutes, sending up a column of hot water and steam that rises 116 to 175 feet (35.4 to 53.4 m).

old-fan·gled /ˈōldˈfanggəld/ ▶ adj. characterized by adherence to what is old; old-fashioned.

old-fash·ioned ▶ adj. in or according to styles or types no longer current or common; not modern: *an old-fashioned kitchen range.* ■ (of a person or their views) favoring traditional and usually restrictive styles, ideas, or customs: *she's stuffy and old-fashioned.*
▶ n. a cocktail consisting chiefly of whiskey, bitters, water, and sugar.
– DERIVATIVES **old-fash·ioned·ness** n.

Old French ▶ n. the French language up to *c.*1400.

Old Fri·sian ▶ n. the Frisian language up to *c.*1400, closely related to both Old English and Old Saxon.

old fus·tic ▶ n. see **FUSTIC** (sense 2).

Old Glo·ry an informal name for the US national flag.

old gold ▶ n. a dull brownish-gold color.

old-growth ▶ adj. (of a tree or forested area) never felled, harvested, or cleared; mature: *old-growth forests.*

old guard (also **Old Guard**) ▶ n. (usu. **the old guard**) the original or long-standing members of a group or party, esp. ones who are unwilling to accept change or new ideas: *the aging right-wing old guard.*
– DERIVATIVES **old guard·ism** n., **old guards·man** n. (pl. **old guardsmen**).

old hand ▶ n. a person with a lot of experience in something: *he was an old hand at red-tape cutting.*

old hat ▶ n. informal used to refer to something considered uninteresting, predictable, tritely familiar, or old-fashioned.

Old High Ger·man ▶ n. the language of southern Germany up to *c.*1200, from which modern standard German is derived. See GERMAN.

Old Ice·lan·dic ▶ n. the Icelandic language up to the 16th century, a form of Old Norse in which medieval sagas were composed.

old·ie /ˈōldē/ ▶ n. informal an old song, film, or television program that is still well known or popular.

Old I·rish ▶ n. the Irish Gaelic language up to *c.*1000, from which modern Irish and Scottish Gaelic are derived.

Old I·ron·sides nickname for the frigate *Constitution*, the oldest commissioned vessel in the US Navy. Launched in 1797, it defeated four British frigates in the War of 1812 and is permanently berthed at the Boston Navy Yard.
– ORIGIN early 19th cent.: conferred by her crew when, during her first battle with the British vessel *Guerrière*, the cannon balls glanced off her thick oak hull.

old la·dy ▶ n. informal a person's mother, wife, or girlfriend.

Old Lat·in ▶ n. Latin before about 100 BC.

old-line ▶ adj. **1** holding conservative views.
2 well established.
– DERIVATIVES **old-lin·er** n.

Old Line State a nickname for the state of MARYLAND.

Old Low Ger·man ▶ n. the language of northern Germany and the Netherlands up to *c.*1200, from which modern Dutch and modern Low German are derived.

old maid ▶ n. **1** derogatory a single woman regarded as too old for marriage. ■ a prim and fussy person: *he said James was an old maid.*
2 a card game in which players collect pairs and try not to be left with an odd penalty card, typically a black queen.
– DERIVATIVES **old-maid·ish** adj.

old man ▶ n. **1** informal a person's father, husband, or boyfriend. ■ (**the old man**) a man in authority over others, esp. an employer or commanding officer: *the old man wants a progress report.* ■ used with a surname instead of "Mr.": *old man Roberts.*
2 another term for SOUTHERNWOOD.

old man's beard ▶ n. **1** a wild clematis that has fluffy gray hairs around the seeds. ● Genus *Clematis*, family Ranunculaceae: several species, in particular traveler's joy and virgin's bower.
2 a large lichen that forms shaggy grayish beardlike growths on the branches of trees. ● *Usnea barbata* and related species, order Parmeliales.

Old Man Win·ter ▶ n. a personification of winter: *spring is just three days away, but Old Man Winter isn't going away quietly.*

old mas·ter ▶ n. a great artist of former times, esp. of the 13th–17th century in Europe. ■ a painting by such a painter: *he formed a large collection of old masters.*

old mon·ey ▶ n. established, inherited wealth. ■ those whose families have been wealthy for many generations: *the list of Canada's wealthiest people, once dominated by old money, is no longer so exclusive.*

old moon ▶ n. the moon in its last quarter, before the new moon.

Old Nick /nik/ an informal name for the Devil.
– ORIGIN mid 17th cent.: probably from a nickname for the given name *Nicholas.*

Old Norse ▶ n. the North Germanic (Scandinavian) language of medieval Norway, Iceland, Denmark, and Sweden up to the 14th century, from which the modern Scandinavian languages are derived. See also OLD ICELANDIC.

Old North Church an Episcopal church, still active, built in 1723 in the Georgian style in Boston's North End. On April 18, 1775, Robert Newman, the sexton of the church, hung two lanterns from the church steeple, warning Paul Revere that British regulars were moving up the Charles River toward Cambridge to begin their march on Lexington. Revere then rode from Charlestown to Lexington to alert the militia that the British were coming.

Old North State a nickname for the state of NORTH CAROLINA.

Ol·do·wan /ˈōldəwən, ˈôl-/ ▶ adj. Archaeology of, relating to, or denoting an early Lower Paleolithic culture of Africa, dated to about 2.0–1.5 million years ago. It is characterized by primitive stone tools that are associated chiefly with *Homo habilis.* ■ (as noun **the Oldowan**) the Oldowan culture or period.
– ORIGIN 1930s: from *Oldoway*, alteration of OLDUVAI GORGE, Tanzania, + -AN.

Old Per·sian ▶ n. the Persian language up to the 3rd century BC, used in the ancient Persian empire and written in cuneiform.

Old Pre·tend·er see STUART[2].

Old Prus·sian ▶ n. a Baltic language, related to Lithuanian, spoken in Prussia until the 17th century.

old re·li·gion ▶ n. a religion that has been supplanted by another, in particular: ■ paganism. ■ witchcraft. ■ Roman Catholicism.

old rose ▶ n. **1** a double-flowered rose of a variety or hybrid evolved before the development of the hybrid tea rose.
2 a shade of grayish or purplish pink.
▶ adj. (usu. **old-rose**) of this shade of pink.

Old Sax·on ▶ n. **1** a member of the Saxon peoples who remained in Germany, as opposed to an Anglo-Saxon.
2 the dialect of Old Low German spoken in Saxony up to *c.*1200.
▶ adj. of or relating to the Old Saxons or their language.

old school ▶ n. (often **of/from the old school**) used, usually approvingly, to refer to someone or something that is old-fashioned or traditional: *amenities that my parents, being of the old school, still take for granted.*

old school tie ▶ n. chiefly Brit. a necktie with a characteristic pattern worn by the former students of an exclusive English public school. ■ used to refer to the group loyalty, mutual assistance, social class, and traditional attitudes associated with people who attended such schools: *appointments based on social class and the old school tie.*

Old Slav·ic (also **Old Slavonic**) ▶ n. another name for CHURCH SLAVIC.

Old South ▶ n. (**the Old South**) the southern states of the US before the Civil War (1861–65).

old·squaw /ˈōld,skwô/ (also **old squaw** or **old squaw duck**) ▶ n. a marine diving duck that breeds in Arctic Eurasia and North America, the male having very long tail feathers and mainly white plumage in winter. ● *Clangula hyemalis*, family Anatidae.

old stag·er ▶ n. a person who is experienced at something or who has been in a place or position for a long time: *the changes aroused the suspicions of the old stagers.*

old·ster /ˈōl(d)stər/ ▶ n. informal an older person.
– ORIGIN early 19th cent.: from OLD, on the pattern of *youngster.*

Old Stone Age the Paleolithic period.

Old Style (abbr.: **OS**) ▶ n. [often as modifier] the method of calculating dates using the Julian calendar.

old style ▶ n. a style that is no longer current, common, or fashionable: *the old style of gabled manor.* ■ Printing an early style of type characterized by strokes of relatively equal thickness and the use of serifs, often slanted.
▶ adj. [attrib.] denoting or according to such a style: *old-style farmers | urban centers of old-style manufacturing.*

Old Tes·ta·ment ▶ n. the first part of the Christian Bible, comprising thirty-nine books and corresponding approximately to the Hebrew Bible. Most of the books were originally written in Hebrew, some in Aramaic, between about 1200 and 100 BC. They comprise the chief texts of the law, history, prophecy, and wisdom literature of the ancient people of Israel.

old-time ▶ adj. [attrib.] relating to or characteristic of the past; long-standing: *the charm of old-time steam engines.* ■ denoting traditional or folk styles of American popular music, such as gospel or bluegrass.
– PHRASES **for old times' sake** see SAKE[1].

old-tim·er ▶ n. informal a person who has had the same job, membership, or residence, etc., for a long time. ■ derogatory an old person.

Ol·du·vai Gorge /ˈôldə,vī, -,wä, -,vä/ a gorge in northern Tanzania, 30 miles (48 km) long and up to 300 feet (90 m) deep. The exposed strata contain numerous fossils (esp. hominids) spanning the full range of the Pleistocene period.

Old Vic /vik/ the popular name of the Royal Victoria Theatre in London. Under the management of Lilian Baylis from 1912, it gained an enduring reputation for its Shakespearean productions.

Old Welsh ▶ n. the Welsh language up to *c.*1150.

old·wife /ˈōld,wīf/ ▶ n. **1** any of a number of deep-bodied edible marine fishes, in particular: ● a brightly patterned tropical Atlantic triggerfish (*Balistes vetula*, family Balistidae). ● a small brightly patterned Australian fish (*Enoplosus armatus*, the only member of the family Enoplosidae). ● the black sea bream of European Atlantic waters (*Spondyliosoma cantharus*, family Sparidae).
2 another term for OLDSQUAW.

old wives' tale ▶ n. a superstition or traditional belief that is regarded as unscientific or incorrect.

old wom·an ▶ n. **1** informal a person's mother, wife, or girlfriend.
2 derogatory a fussy or timid person, esp. a man: *he's always telling me I'm an old woman about security.*
– DERIVATIVES **old-wom·an·ish** adj. (sense 2).

Old World Europe, Asia, and Africa, regarded collectively as the part of the world known before the discovery of the Americas. Compare with NEW WORLD.

old-world (also **old world**; **Old World**) ▶ adj. belonging to or associated with former times, esp. when considered quaint and attractive: *medieval towns that still retain old-world charm.*

OLE ▶ abbr. Computing object linking and embedding, denoting a set of techniques for transferring an object from one application to another.

ole /ōl/ ▶ adj. informal or humorous old: *that ole truck of my daddy's.*
– ORIGIN mid 19th cent.: representing a folk pronunciation.

o·lé /ōˈlā/ ▶ exclam. a cry of approval, joy, etc.
– ORIGIN Spanish, a cry used at bullfights.

-ole ▶ comb. form in names of organic compounds, esp. heterocyclic compounds: *thiazole.*
– ORIGIN from Latin *oleum* 'oil' (compare with -OL).

o·le·ag·i·nous /,ōlēˈajənəs/ ▶ adj. **1** rich in, covered with, or producing oil; oily or greasy.
2 exaggeratedly and distastefully complimentary; obsequious: *candidates made the usual oleaginous speeches in the debate.*
– ORIGIN late Middle English: from French *oléagineux*, from Latin *oleaginus* 'of the olive tree,' from *oleum* 'oil.'

o·le·an·der /ˈōlē,andər/ ▶ n. a poisonous evergreen Old World shrub that is widely grown in warm countries for its clusters of white, pink, or red flowers. ● *Nerium oleander*, family Apocynaceae.
– ORIGIN early 16th cent.: from medieval Latin, of unknown ultimate origin.

o·le·as·ter /,ōlēˈastər/ ▶ n. a Eurasian shrub or small tree that is often cultivated as an ornamental. ● Genus *Elaeagnus*, family Elaeagnaceae: several species, in particular *E. angustifolia*, commonly called **Russian olive**, which bears edible yellow olive-shaped fruit.
– ORIGIN late Middle English: from Latin, from *olea* 'olive tree.'

o·lec·ra·non /ōˈlekrə,nän, ,ōləˈkrā-/ ▶ n. Anatomy the bony prominence of the elbow, on the upper end of the ulna.
– ORIGIN early 18th cent.: from Greek *ōle(no)kranon*, from *ōlenē* 'elbow' + *kranion* 'head.'

o·le·fin /ˈōləfin/ (also **olefine**) ▶ n. Chemistry another term for ALKENE.
– DERIVATIVES **o·le·fin·ic** /,ōləˈfinik/ adj.
– ORIGIN mid 19th cent.: from French *oléfiant* 'oil-forming' (with reference to oily ethylene dichloride).

o·le·ic ac·id /ōˈlē-ik/ ▶ n. Chemistry an unsaturated fatty acid present in many fats and soaps. ● Chem. formula: $CH_3(CH_2)_7CH{=}CH(CH_2)_7COOH$.
– DERIVATIVES **o·le·ate** /ˈōlē,āt/ n.
– ORIGIN early 19th cent.: *oleic* from Latin *oleum* 'oil.'

o·le·if·er·ous /,ōlēˈifərəs/ ▶ adj. Botany (of seeds, glands, etc.) producing oil.

O

– ORIGIN early 19th cent.: from Latin *oleum* 'oil' + -FEROUS.

o·le·o /ˈōlēō/ ▶ n. another term for MARGARINE.

oleo- ▶ comb. form relating to or containing oil: *oleomargarine* | *oleoresin*.
– ORIGIN from Latin *oleum* 'oil.'

o·le·o·chem·i·cal /ˌōlēōˈkemikəl/ ▶ n. a chemical compound derived industrially from animal or vegetable oils or fats.

o·le·o·graph /ˈōlēəˌgraf/ ▶ n. a lithographic print textured to resemble an oil painting.
– DERIVATIVES **o·le·o·graph·ic** /ˌōlēəˈgrafik/ adj., **o·le·og·ra·phy** /ˌōlēˈägrəfē/ n.

o·le·o·mar·ga·rine /ˌōlēōˈmärj(ə)rən/ ▶ n. another term for MARGARINE.

o·le·o·res·in /ˌōlē-ōˈrezən/ ▶ n. a natural or artificial mixture of essential oils and a resin, e.g., balsam.
– DERIVATIVES **o·le·o·res·in·ous** /-nəs/ adj.

O·les·tra /ōˈlestrə/ (also **olestra**) ▶ n. trademark a synthetic cooking oil used as a calorie-free fat substitute in various foods.
– ORIGIN 1980s: from *(p)ol(y)est(e)r* + the suffix *-a*.

o·le·um /ˈōlēəm/ ▶ n. a dense, corrosive liquid consisting of concentrated sulfuric acid containing excess sulfur trioxide in solution.
– ORIGIN early 20th cent.: from Latin, literally 'oil.'

O lev·el ▶ n. historical (in the UK except Scotland) the lower of the two main levels of standardized examinations in secondary schools. Compare with A LEVEL.
– ORIGIN short for *ordinary level*.

ol·fac·tion /älˈfaksHən, ōl-/ ▶ n. technical the action or capacity of smelling; the sense of smell.
– DERIVATIVES **ol·fac·tive** /-tiv/ adj.
– ORIGIN mid 19th cent.: from Latin *olfactus* 'a smell' (from *olere* 'to smell' + *fact-* 'made,' from the verb *facere*) + -ION.

ol·fac·tom·e·ter /ˌälfakˈtämitər, ˌōl-/ ▶ n. an instrument for measuring the intensity of an odor or sensitivity to odor.
– DERIVATIVES **ol·fac·tom·e·try** /-ˈtämitrē/ n.

ol·fac·to·ry /älˈfakt(ə)rē, ōl-/ ▶ adj. of or relating to the sense of smell: *the olfactory organs*.
– ORIGIN mid 17th cent.: from Latin *olfactare* (frequentative of *olfacere* 'to smell') + -ORY[2].

ol·fac·to·ry nerve ▶ n. Anatomy each of the first pair of cranial nerves, transmitting impulses to the brain from the smell receptors in the mucous membrane of the nose.

o·lib·a·num /ōˈlibənəm/ ▶ n. another term for FRANKINCENSE.
– ORIGIN late Middle English: from medieval Latin, from late Latin *libanus*, from Greek *libanos* 'frankincense.'

ol·i·garch /ˈäliˌgärk, ˈōl-/ ▶ n. **1** a ruler in an oligarchy.
2 (esp. in Russia) a very rich businessman with a great deal of political influence.
– ORIGIN late 19th cent.: from Greek *oligarkhēs*, from *oligoi* 'few' + *arkhein* 'to rule.'

> **WORD TRENDS** If it's true that money is power, then **oligarch** is the perfect name for the new breed of ultrarich businessmen. Originally, an **oligarch** was one of a very small group of leaders of a country. Most of today's **oligarchs** gained their fortunes very quickly after the fall of the former Soviet republics, and although they do not have any official political power, their massive fortunes can mean they have great influence over governments and politicians. Not surprisingly, the word *oligarch* has acquired some negative associations, reflected in the examples seen in the Oxford English Corpus—*corrupt, exiled,* and *jailed* are all common collocates, as is *so-called*, a sign of anger at the assumption of political influence the name **oligarch** implies: *millions of citizens revile the so-called oligarchs*. See also TSAR.

ol·i·gar·chy /ˈäliˌgärkē, ˈōli-/ ▶ n. (pl. **oligarchies**) a small group of people having control of a country, organization, or institution: *the ruling oligarchy of military men around the president*. ■ a state governed by such a group: *the English aristocratic oligarchy of the 19th century*. ■ government by such a group.
– DERIVATIVES **ol·i·gar·chic** /ˌäliˈgärkik, ˌōli-/ adj., **ol·i·gar·chi·cal** /ˌäliˈgärkikəl, ˌōli-/ adj., **ol·i·gar·chi·cal·ly** /ˌäliˈgärkik(ə)lē, ˌōli-/ adv.
– ORIGIN late 15th cent.: from Greek *oligarkhia* (probably via medieval Latin).

> **USAGE** See usage at ARISTOCRACY.

ol·i·go /ˈäligō/ ▶ n. (pl. **oligos**) Biochemistry short for OLIGONUCLEOTIDE.

oligo- ▶ comb. form having few; containing a relatively small number of units: *oligopoly* | *oligosaccharide*.
– ORIGIN from Greek *oligos* 'small,' *oligoi* 'few.'

Ol·i·go·cene /ˈäligōˌsēn/ ▶ adj. Geology of, relating to, or denoting the third epoch of the Tertiary period, between the Eocene and Miocene epochs. ■ (as noun **the Oligocene**) the Oligocene epoch or the system of rocks deposited during it.

> The Oligocene epoch lasted from 35.4 million to 23.3 million years ago. It was a time of falling temperatures, with evidence of the first primates.

– ORIGIN mid 19th cent.: from OLIGO- 'few' + Greek *kainos* 'new.'

Ol·i·go·chae·ta /ˌäligōˈkētə/ Zoology a class of annelid worms that includes the earthworms. They have simple setae projecting from each segment and a small head lacking sensory appendages.
– ORIGIN modern Latin (plural), from OLIGO- 'few' + Greek *khaitē* 'long hair' (taken to mean 'bristle'), because they have fewer setae than polychaetes.

ol·i·go·chaete /ˈäligōˌkēt/ ▶ n. Zoology an annelid worm of the class Oligochaeta, such as an earthworm.

ol·i·go·clase /ˈäligōˌklās/ ▶ n. a feldspar mineral common in siliceous igneous rocks, consisting of a sodium-rich plagioclase (with more calcium than albite).
– ORIGIN mid 19th cent.: from OLIGO- 'relatively little' + Greek *klasis* 'breaking' (because thought to have a less perfect cleavage than albite).

ol·i·go·den·dro·cyte /ˌäligōˈdendrəˌsīt/ ▶ n. Anatomy a glial cell similar to an astrocyte but with fewer protuberances, concerned with the production of myelin in the central nervous system.
– ORIGIN 1930s: from OLIGODENDROGLIA + -CYTE.

ol·i·go·den·drog·li·a /ˌäligōdenˈdräglēə/ ▶ plural n. Anatomy oligodendrocytes collectively.
– DERIVATIVES **ol·i·go·den·drog·li·al** adj.
– ORIGIN 1920s: from OLIGO- 'few' + DENDRO- 'branching' + a shortened form of NEUROGLIA.

o·lig·o·mer /əˈligəmər/ ▶ n. Chemistry a polymer whose molecules consist of relatively few repeating units.
– DERIVATIVES **o·lig·o·mer·ic** /əˌligəˈmerik/ adj.

ol·i·go·nu·cle·o·tide /ˌäligōˈn(y)o͞oklēəˌtīd/ ▶ n. Biochemistry a polynucleotide whose molecules contain a relatively small number of nucleotides.

ol·i·go·pep·tide /ˌäligōˈpepˌtīd/ ▶ n. Biochemistry a peptide whose molecules contain a relatively small number of amino-acid residues.

ol·i·gop·o·ly /ˌäliˈgäpəlē/ ▶ n. (pl. **oligopolies**) a state of limited competition, in which a market is shared by a small number of producers or sellers.
– DERIVATIVES **ol·i·gop·o·list** /-list/ n., **ol·i·gop·o·lis·tic** /ˌäliˌgäpəˈlistik/ adj.
– ORIGIN late 19th cent.: from OLIGO- 'small number,' on the pattern of *monopoly*.

ol·i·gop·so·ny /ˌäliˈgäpsənē/ ▶ n. (pl. **oligopsonies**) a state of the market in which only a small number of buyers exists for a product.
– DERIVATIVES **ol·i·gop·so·nis·tic** /ˌäliˌgäpsəˈnistik/ adj.
– ORIGIN 1940s: from OLIGO- 'small number' + Greek *opsōnein* 'buy provisions,' on the pattern of *monopsony*.

ol·i·go·sac·cha·ride /ˌäligōˈsakəˌrīd/ ▶ n. Biochemistry a carbohydrate whose molecules are composed of a relatively small number of monosaccharide units.

ol·i·go·troph·ic /ˌäligōˈtrōfik, -ˈträfik/ ▶ adj. Ecology (esp. of a lake) relatively low in plant nutrients and containing abundant oxygen in the deeper parts. Compare with DYSTROPHIC, EUTROPHIC.
– DERIVATIVES **ol·i·got·ro·phy** /ˌäliˈgätrəfē/ n.

ol·i·gu·ri·a /ˌäliˈgyo͝orēə/ ▶ n. Medicine the production of abnormally small amounts of urine.
– DERIVATIVES **ol·igu·ric** /-rik/ adj.

o·lin·go /ōˈliNGgō/ ▶ n. (pl. **olingos**) a small nocturnal mammal related to the kinkajou and the raccoon, living in tropical Central and South American rain forests. ● Genus *Bassaricyon*, family Procyonidae: between one and five species.
– ORIGIN 1920s: via American Spanish from Mayan.

o·li·o /ˈōlēō/ ▶ n. (pl. **olios**) another term for OLLA PODRIDA. ■ a miscellaneous collection of things. ■ a variety act or show.
– ORIGIN mid 17th cent.: from Spanish *olla* 'stew,' from Latin *olla* 'cooking pot.'

ol·i·va·ceous /ˌäləˈvāsHəs/ ▶ adj. technical of a dusky yellowish green color; olive green.

ol·i·va·ry /ˈäləˌverē/ ▶ adj. Anatomy relating to or denoting each of the pair of oval bodies of nerve tissue on the medulla oblongata of the brain.
– ORIGIN late Middle English: from Latin *olivarius* 'relating to olives,' from *oliva* (see OLIVE).

ol·ive /ˈäliv/ ▶ n. **1** a small oval fruit with a hard pit and bitter flesh, green when unripe and brownish black when ripe, used as food and as a source of oil.
2 (also **olive tree**) the widely cultivated evergreen tree that yields this fruit, native to warm regions of the Old World. ● *Olea europaea*, family Oleaceae (the **olive family**). This family also includes the ash, lilac, jasmine, and privet. ■ used in names of other trees that are related to the olive, resemble it, or bear similar fruit, e.g., **Russian olive**.
3 (also **olive green**) a grayish-green color like that of an unripe olive.
4 a metal ring or fitting that is tightened under a threaded nut to form a seal, as in a compression joint.
5 (also **olive shell**) a marine mollusk with a smooth, roughly cylindrical shell that is typically brightly colored. ● Genus *Oliva*, family Olividae, class Gastropoda.
▶ adj. grayish-green, like an unripe olive: *a small figure in olive fatigues*. ■ (of the complexion) yellowish brown; sallow.
– ORIGIN Middle English: via Old French from Latin *oliva*, from Greek *elaia*, from *elaion* 'oil.'

ol·ive branch ▶ n. the branch of an olive tree, traditionally regarded as a symbol of peace (in allusion to the story of Noah in Gen. 8:1, in which a dove returns with an olive branch after the Flood). ■ an offer of reconciliation: *the government is holding out an olive branch to the demonstrators*.

ol·ive drab ▶ n. a dull olive-green color, used in some military uniforms.

ol·ive oil ▶ n. an oil pressed from ripe olives, used in cooking, medicines, soap, etc.

Ol·i·ver /ˈälәvәr/ the companion of Roland in the *Chanson de Roland* (see ROLAND).

O·liv·i·er /əˈlivēā, ōˈlivi-/, Laurence (Kerr), Baron Olivier of Brighton (1907–89), English actor and director. Following his professional debut in 1924, he performed all the major Shakespearean roles; he was also director of the National Theatre (1963–73). His movies include *Wuthering Heights* (1939), *Rebecca* (1940), *Pride and Prejudice* (1940), *Henry V* (1944), and *Hamlet* (1948).

ol·i·vine /ˈäləˌvēn/ ▶ n. an olive-green, gray-green, or brown mineral occurring widely in basalt, peridotite, and other basic igneous rocks. It is a silicate containing varying proportions of magnesium, iron, and other elements.
– ORIGIN late 18th cent.: from Latin *oliva* (see OLIVE) + -INE[4].

ol·la po·dri·da /ˌälə pəˈdrēdə, ˌô(l)yə/ ▶ n. a highly spiced Spanish-style stew containing a mixture of meat and vegetables. ■ any miscellaneous assortment or collection: *an olla podrida of romance, comedy, and tragedy*.
– ORIGIN Spanish, literally 'rotten pot,' from Latin *olla* 'jar' + *putridus* 'rotten.'

ol·lie /ˈälē/ ▶ n. (pl. **ollies**) (in skateboarding and snowboarding) a jump performed without the aid of a takeoff ramp, executed by pushing the back foot down on the tail of the board, bringing the board off the ground.
▶ v. (**ollies, ollieing, ollied**) [no obj.] perform such a jump.
– ORIGIN 1980s: of unknown origin.

Ol·mec /ˈälˌmek, ˈōl-/ ▶ n. (pl. **same** or **Olmecs**) **1** a member of a prehistoric people inhabiting the coast of Veracruz and western Tabasco on the Gulf of Mexico (*c.*1200–400 BC), who established what was probably the first Meso-American civilization.
2 a people living in the same general area during the 15th and 16th centuries.
– ORIGIN from Nahuatl *Olmecatl*, (plural) *Olmeca*, literally 'inhabitants of the rubber country.'

Olm·sted /ˈōmˌsted/, Frederick Law (1822–1903) US landscape architect. He designed Central Park in New York City, Fairmount Park in Philadelphia, and the Capitol grounds in Washington, DC.

ol·o·gy /ˈäləjē/ ▶ n. (pl. **ologies**) informal, humorous a subject of study; a branch of knowledge.
– DERIVATIVES **ol·o·gist** /-jist/ n.

-ology ▶ comb. form common form of -LOGY.

O·lo·mouc /ˈôlômōts/ an industrial city in the Czech Republic, on the Morava River, in northern Moravia; pop. 99,966 (2007).

o·lo·ro·so /ˌōləˈrōsō/ ▶ n. a dry or medium-dry Spanish sherry.
– ORIGIN Spanish, literally 'fragrant.'

Olsz·tyn /ˈôlsHtin/ a city in northern Poland, in the Masuria region; pop. 175,098 (2007). Founded in 1348 by the Teutonic Knights, it was part of Prussia from 1772 until 1945. German name ALLENSTEIN.

O·lym·pi·a /əˈlimpēə, ōˈlim-/ **1** a plain in Greece, in the western Peloponnese. In ancient Greece it was the site of the chief sanctuary of the god Zeus, the place where the original Olympic Games were held.

2 the capital of Washington, a port on Puget Sound; pop. 45,322 (est. 2008).

O·lym·pi·ad /ō'limpē,ad, ə'lim-/ ▶ **n.** a celebration of the ancient or modern Olympic Games. ■ a period of four years between Olympic Games, used by the ancient Greeks in dating events. ■ a major national or international contest in some activity, notably chess or bridge.
– ORIGIN via French or Latin from Greek *Olumpias, Olumpiad-*, from *Olumpios* (see also **OLYMPIAN** and **OLYMPIC**).

O·lym·pi·an /ə'limpēən, ō'lim-/ ▶ **adj. 1** associated with Mount Olympus in northeastern Greece, or with the Greek gods whose home was traditionally held to be there. ■ resembling or appropriate to a god, esp. in superiority and aloofness: *the court is capable of an Olympian detachment.*
2 [attrib.] relating to the ancient or modern Olympic Games.
▶ **n. 1** any of the twelve Greek gods regarded as living on Olympus. ■ a person of great attainments or exalted position.
2 a competitor in the Olympic Games.
– ORIGIN late 15th cent.: sense 1 of the adjective from Latin *Olympus* (see **OLYMPUS**) + **-IAN**; sense 2 of the adjective from *Olympia* (see **OLYMPIA**) + **-AN**.

O·lym·pic /ə'limpik, ō'lim-/ ▶ **adj.** [attrib.] of or relating to the ancient city of Olympia or the Olympic Games: *an Olympic champion.*
▶ **n.** (**the Olympics**) the Olympic Games.
– ORIGIN late 16th cent.: via Latin from Greek *Olumpikos* 'of Olympus or Olympia,' the latter (see **OLYMPIA**) being the site of games in honor of Zeus of *Olympus.*

O·lym·pic Games (also **the Olympics**) a modern sports festival held traditionally every four years in different venues, instigated by the Frenchman **Baron de Coubertin** (1863–1937) in 1896. Athletes representing more than 200 countries compete for gold, silver, and bronze medals in a great variety of sports. Since 1992, the Summer Games and Winter Games alternate every two years. ■ an ancient Greek festival with athletic, literary, and musical competitions, held at Olympia every four years traditionally from 776 BC until abolished by the Roman emperor Theodosius I in AD 393.

O·lym·pic Pe·nin·su·la a region in northwestern Washington, on the Pacific Ocean and Juan de Fuca Strait. The Olympic Mountains and Olympic National Park are here.

O·lym·pic-sized (also **Olympic-size**) ▶ **adj.** (of a swimming pool or other sports venue) of the dimensions prescribed for modern Olympic competitions.

O·lym·pus /ə'limpəs, ō'lim-/ Greek Mythology the home of the twelve principal gods, identified in later antiquity with Mount Olympus in northern Greece.

O·lym·pus, Mount 1 a mountain in northern Greece that rises to 9,570 feet (2,917 m), at the eastern end of the range dividing Thessaly from Macedonia.
2 a mountain in Cyprus that rises to 6,400 feet (1,951 m), in the Troodos range. It is the highest peak on the island.

OM ▶ **abbr.** (in the UK) Order of Merit.

om /ōm/ ▶ **n.** Hinduism & Tibetan Buddhism a mystic syllable, considered the most sacred mantra. It appears at the beginning and end of most Sanskrit recitations, prayers, and texts.
– ORIGIN Sanskrit, sometimes regarded as three sounds, *a-u-m*, symbolic of the three major Hindu deities.

-oma ▶ **suffix** (forming nouns) denoting tumors and other abnormal growths: *carcinoma.*
– ORIGIN modern Latin, from a Greek suffix denoting the result of verbal action.

O·ma·ha[1] /'ōmə,hô, -,hä/ a city in eastern Nebraska, on the Missouri River; pop. 438,646 (est. 2008).

O·ma·ha[2] ▶ **n.** (pl. **same** or **Omahas**) **1** a member of an American Indian people of northeastern Nebraska.
2 the Siouan language of this people.
▶ **adj.** of or relating to this people or their language.
– ORIGIN from Omaha *umāhā* 'upstream.'

O·ma·ha Beach the name used during the D-Day landing in June 1944 for one part of the Norman coast where US troops landed. It is at the mouth of the Vire River, at the village of Saint-Laurent-sur-Mer, northwest of Bayeux.

O·man /ō'män/ a country at the eastern corner of the Arabian peninsula; pop. 3,418,100 (est. 2009); capital, Muscat; language, Arabic (official).

> An independent sultanate known as Muscat and Oman until 1970, Oman was the most influential power in the region during the 19th century; it controlled Zanzibar and other territory. Since the late 19th century, it has had strong links with Britain. The economy is dependent on oil, discovered in 1964.

– DERIVATIVES **O·ma·ni** /ō'mänē/ **adj. & n.**

O·man, Gulf of an inlet of the Arabian Sea, connected by the Strait of Hormuz to the Persian Gulf.

O·mar I /'ōmär/ (*c.*581–644), Muslim caliph 634–44. He conquered Syria, Palestine, and Egypt.

O·mar Khay·yám /kī'äm, -'am/ (died 1123), Persian poet, mathematician, and astronomer. His *rubáiyát* (quatrains), found in *The Rubáiyát of Omar Khayyám* (translation published 1859), are meditations on the mysteries of existence and celebrations of worldly pleasures.

o·ma·sum /ō'māsəm/ ▶ **n.** (pl. **omasa** /-sə/) Zoology the muscular third stomach of a ruminant animal, between the reticulum and the abomasum. Also called **PSALTERIUM**.
– ORIGIN early 18th cent.: from Latin, literally 'bullock's tripe.'

O·may·yad /ō'mī(y)ad/ variant spelling of **UMAYYAD**.

OMB ▶ **abbr.** (in the federal government) Office of Management and Budget.

om·bre /'ämbər/ ▶ **n.** a trick-taking card game for three people using a pack of forty cards, popular in Europe in the 17th–18th centuries.
– ORIGIN from Spanish *hombre* 'man,' with reference to one player seeking to win the pool.

om·bré /'äm,brā/ ▶ **adj.** (of a fabric) having a dyed, printed, or woven design in which the color is graduated from light to dark.
– ORIGIN French, past participle of *ombrer* 'to shade.'

ombro- ▶ **comb. form** relating to rain: *ombrotrophic.*
– ORIGIN from Greek *ombros* 'rain shower.'

om·bro·troph·ic /,ämbrə'trōfik, -'träfik/ ▶ **adj.** Ecology (of a bog or its vegetation) dependent on atmospheric moisture for its nutrients.

om·buds·man /'ämbədzmən, -,bo͝odz-/ ▶ **n.** (pl. **ombudsmen**) an official appointed to investigate individuals' complaints against maladministration, esp. that of public authorities.
– ORIGIN 1950s: from Swedish, 'legal representative.'

om·buds·per·son /'ämbədz,pərsən, -bo͝odz-/ ▶ **n.** (pl. **ombudspersons**) a person acting as an ombudsman.

Om·dur·man /,ämdər'män/ a city in central Sudan, on the Nile River opposite Khartoum; pop. 3,151,600 (est. 2007).

-ome ▶ **suffix** chiefly Biology forming nouns denoting objects or parts having a specified nature: *rhizome* | *trichome.*
– ORIGIN variant form of **-OMA**.

o·me·ga /ō'māgə, ō'mē-/ ▶ **n.** the twenty-fourth, and last, letter of the Greek alphabet (Ω, ω), transliterated as 'o' or 'ō.' ■ the last of a series; the final development: [as modifier] *the omega point.* ■ (**Omega**) [followed by Latin genitive] Astronomy the twenty-fourth star in a constellation: *Omega Scorpii.*
▶ **symbol** (Ω) ohm(s): *a 100Ω resistor.*
– ORIGIN from Greek *ō mega* 'big O.'

o·me·ga-3 fat·ty ac·id ▶ **n.** an unsaturated fatty acid of a kind occurring chiefly in fish oils, with three double bonds at particular positions in the hydrocarbon chain.

om·e·let /'äm(ə)lit/ (also **omelette**) ▶ **n.** a dish of beaten eggs cooked in a frying pan until firm, often with a filling added while cooking, and usually served folded over.
– ORIGIN French *omelette*, earlier *amelette*, alteration of *alumette*, variant of *alumelle*, from *lemele* 'knife blade,' from Latin *lamella* (see **LAMELLA**). The association with 'knife blade' is probably because of the thin flat shape of an omelet.

o·men /'ōmən/ ▶ **n.** an event regarded as a portent of good or evil: *the ghost's appearance was an ill omen* | *a rise in imports might be an omen of recovery.* ■ prophetic significance: *the raven seemed a bird of evil omen.*
– ORIGIN late 16th cent.: from Latin.

o·men·tum /ō'mentəm/ ▶ **n.** (pl. **omenta** /-tə/) Anatomy a fold of peritoneum connecting the stomach with other abdominal organs.
– DERIVATIVES **o·men·tal** /ō'mentl/ **adj.**
– ORIGIN late Middle English: from Latin.

o·mer /'ōmər, 'ōmer/ ▶ **n. 1** an ancient Hebrew dry measure, the tenth part of an ephah.
2 (**Omer**) Judaism a sheaf of corn or omer of grain presented as an offering on the second day of Passover. ■ the period of 49 days between this day and Shavuoth (Pentecost).
– ORIGIN from Hebrew *'ōmer.*

o·mer·tà /ō'me(ə)rtə, ,ōmer'tä/ ▶ **n.** (as practiced by the Mafia) a code of silence about criminal activity and a refusal to give evidence to authorities.

-ometer ▶ **comb. form** forming nouns denoting an instrument for measuring something: *speedometer.* ■ informal forming nouns denoting a measure of a quality, emotion, etc.: *stress-ometer* | *drunkometer.*

OMG ▶ **abbr.** informal oh my God: *OMG! If my parents find out they will go crazy!*

om·i·cron /'ämi,krän, 'ōm-/ ▶ **n.** the fifteenth letter of the Greek alphabet (Ο, ο), transliterated as 'o.' ■ (**Omicron**) [followed by Latin genitive] Astronomy the fifteenth star in a constellation: *Omicron Piscium.*
– ORIGIN from Greek *o mikron* 'little O.'

o·mi·god /,ōmī'gäd/ ▶ **exclam.** informal used to express shock or disbelief: *omigod, omigod, I'm going to be famous!*
– ORIGIN 1960s: altered spelling of *oh my God.*

om·i·nous /'ämənəs/ ▶ **adj.** giving the impression that something bad or unpleasant is going to happen; threatening; inauspicious: *there were ominous dark clouds gathering overhead.*
– DERIVATIVES **om·i·nous·ly adv., om·i·nous·ness n.**
– ORIGIN late 16th cent.: from Latin *ominosus*, from *omen, omin-* 'omen.'

o·mis·sion /ō'misHən/ ▶ **n.** someone or something that has been left out or excluded: *there are glaring omissions in the report.* ■ the action of excluding or leaving out someone or something: *the omission of recent publications from his bibliography.* ■ a failure to do something, esp. something that one has a moral or legal obligation to do: *to pay compensation for a wrongful act or omission.*
– DERIVATIVES **o·mis·sive** /ō'misiv/ **adj.**
– ORIGIN late Middle English: from late Latin *omissio(n-)*, from the verb *omittere* (see **OMIT**).

o·mit /ō'mit/ ▶ **v.** (**omits, omitting, omitted**) [with obj.] leave out or exclude (someone or something), either intentionally or forgetfully: *a significant detail was omitted from your story.* ■ fail or neglect to do (something); leave undone: *the final rinse is omitted* | [with infinitive] *he modestly omits to mention that he was pole-vault champion.*
– DERIVATIVES **o·mis·si·ble** /ō'misəbəl/ **adj., o·mit·ta·ble adj.**
– ORIGIN late Middle English: from Latin *omittere*, from *ob-* 'down' + *mittere* 'let go.'

om·ma·tid·i·um /,ämə'tidēəm/ ▶ **n.** (pl. **ommatidia** /-'tidēə/) Entomology each of the optical units that make up a compound eye, as of an insect.
– DERIVATIVES **om·ma·tid·i·al** /-'tidēə/ **adj.**
– ORIGIN late 19th cent.: modern Latin, from Greek *ommatidion*, diminutive of *omma, ommat-* 'eye.'

om·mat·o·phore /ə'matə,fôr/ ▶ **n.** Zoology a part of an invertebrate animal, esp. a stalk or tentacle, that bears an eye.
– ORIGIN late 19th cent.: from Greek *omma, ommat-* 'eye' + **-PHORE**.

omni- ▶ **comb. form** all; of all things: *omniscient* | *omnifarious.* ■ in all ways or places: *omnicompetent* | *omnipresent.*
– ORIGIN from Latin *omnis* 'all.'

om·ni·bus /'ämnə,bəs/ ▶ **n. 1** a volume containing several novels or other items previously published separately: *an omnibus of her first trilogy.*
2 dated a bus.
▶ **adj.** comprising several items: *Congress passed an omnibus anticrime package.*
– ORIGIN early 19th cent.: via French from Latin, literally 'for all,' dative plural of *omnis.*

om·ni·di·rec·tion·al /,ämnidi'reksHənl/ ▶ **adj.** Telecommunications receiving signals from or transmitting in all directions.

om·ni·far·i·ous /,ämnə'fe(ə)rēəs/ ▶ **adj.** formal comprising or relating to all sorts or varieties.
– DERIVATIVES **om·ni·far·i·ous·ly adv., om·ni·far·i·ous·ness n.**
– ORIGIN mid 17th cent.: from late Latin *omnifarius* + **-OUS**; compare with **MULTIFARIOUS**.

om·nip·o·tence /äm'nipətəns/ ▶ **n.** the quality of having unlimited or very great power: *God's omnipotence.*

om·nip·o·tent /äm'nipətənt/ ▶ **adj.** (of a deity) having unlimited power; able to do anything. ■ having ultimate power and influence: *an omnipotent sovereign.*
▶ **n.** (**the Omnipotent**) God.
– DERIVATIVES **om·nip·o·tent·ly adv.**
– ORIGIN Middle English (as a divine attribute): via Old French from Latin *omnipotent-* 'all-powerful.'

om·ni·pres·ent /,ämnə'preznt/ ▶ **adj.** (of God) present everywhere at the same time. ■ widely or constantly encountered; common or widespread: *the omnipresent threat of natural disasters.*
– DERIVATIVES **om·ni·pres·ence n.**

PRONUNCIATION KEY ə *ago, up*; ər *over, fur*; a *hat*; ā *ate*; ä *car*; e *let*; ē *see*; i *fit*; ī *by*; NG *sing*; ō *go*; ô *law, for*; oi *toy*; o͝o *good*; o͞o *goo*; ou *out*; TH *thin*; TH *then*; ZH *vision*

– ORIGIN early 17th cent.: from medieval Latin *omnipraesent-*.

om·ni·range /ˈämniˌrānj/ ▶ n. a navigation system in which short-range omnidirectional VHF transmitters serve as radio beacons.

om·nis·cient /ämˈnisHənt/ ▶ adj. knowing everything: *the story is told by an omniscient narrator.*
– DERIVATIVES **om·nis·cience** n., **om·nis·cient·ly** adv.
– ORIGIN early 17th cent.: from medieval Latin *omniscient-* 'all-knowing,' based on *scire* 'to know.'

om·ni·sex·u·al /ˌämniˈseksHo͞oəl/ ▶ adj. involving, related to, or characterized by a diverse sexual propensity.
– DERIVATIVES **om·ni·sex·u·al·i·ty** /-ˌseksHo͞oˈalitē/ n.

om·ni·um gath·er·um /ˌämnēəm ˈgaTHərəm/ ▶ n. a collection of miscellaneous people or things.
– ORIGIN early 16th cent.: mock Latin, from Latin *omnium* 'of all' and GATHER + the Latin suffix *-um*.

om·ni·vore /ˈämnəˌvôr/ ▶ n. an animal or person that eats food of both plant and animal origin.
– ORIGIN late 19th cent.: from French, from Latin *omnivorus* 'omnivorous.'

om·niv·o·rous /ämˈniv(ə)rəs/ ▶ adj. (of an animal or person) feeding on food of both plant and animal origin. ■ taking in or using whatever is available: *an omnivorous reader.*
– DERIVATIVES **om·niv·o·rous·ly** adv., **om·niv·o·rous·ness** n.
– ORIGIN mid 17th cent.: from Latin *omnivorus* + -OUS.

o·moph·a·gy /ōˈmäfəjē/ (also **omophagia** /ˌōməˈfāj(ē)ə/) ▶ n. the eating of raw food, esp. raw meat.
– DERIVATIVES **o·mo·phag·ic** /ˌōməˈfajik/ adj., **o·moph·a·gist** /-jist/ n., **o·moph·a·gous** /-gəs/ adj.
– ORIGIN early 18th cent.: from Greek *ōmophagia*, from *ōmos* 'raw' + *-phagia* (from *phagein* 'eat').

O·mot·ic /ōˈmätik/ ▶ n. a subfamily of Afro-Asiatic languages spoken in Ethiopia, with over thirty members.
▶ adj. denoting or belonging to this subfamily.
– ORIGIN 1970s: from *Omo*, the name of a river in southwestern Ethiopia, + -OTIC.

omphalo- ▶ comb. form relating to the navel.
– ORIGIN from Greek *omphalos* 'navel.'

om·pha·los /ˈämfələs/ ▶ n. (pl. **omphaloi** /-loi/) literary the center or hub of something: *this was the omphalos of confusion and strife.* ■ a rounded stone (esp. that at Delphi) representing the navel of the earth in ancient Greek mythology.
– ORIGIN Greek, literally 'navel.'

O

Omsk /ômsk/ a city in south central Russia, on the Irtysh River; pop. 1,131,100 (est. 2008).

ON[1] ▶ abbr. Ontario (in official postal use).

ON[2] ▶ abbr. Old Norse.

on /än, ôn/ ▶ prep. **1** physically in contact with and supported by (a surface): *on the table was a water jug | she was lying on the floor | a sign on the front gate.* ■ located somewhere in the general surface area of (a place): *an internment camp on the island | the house on the corner.* ■ as a result of accidental physical contact with: *one of the children had cut a foot on some glass | he banged his head on a beam.* ■ supported by (a part of the body): *he was lying on his back.* ■ so as to be supported or held by: *put it on the table.* ■ in the possession of (the person referred to): *she only had a few dollars on her.*
2 forming a distinctive or marked part of (the surface of something): *a scratch on her arm | a smile on her face.*
3 having (the thing mentioned) as a topic: *a book on careers | essays on a wide range of issues.* ■ having (the thing mentioned) as a basis: *modeled on the Mayflower Compact | dependent on availability.*
4 as a member of (a committee, jury, or other body): *they would be allowed to serve on committees.*
5 having (the thing mentioned) as a target, aim, or focus: *five air raids on the city | thousands marching on Washington | her eyes were fixed on his dark profile.*
6 having (the thing mentioned) as a medium for transmitting or storing information: *put your ideas down on paper | stored on the client's own computer.* ■ being broadcast by (a radio or television channel): *a new TV series on Channel 4.*
7 in the course of (a journey): *he was on his way to see his mother.* ■ while traveling in (a public conveyance): *John got some sleep on the plane.* ■ onto (a public conveyance) with the intention of traveling in it: *we got on the train.*
8 indicating the day or part of a day during which an event takes place: *reported on September 26 | on a very hot evening in July.* ■ at the time of: *she was booed on arriving home.*
9 engaged in: *his attendant was out on errands.*
10 regularly taking (a drug or medicine): *he is on morphine to relieve the pain.*
11 paid for by: *the drinks are on me.*
12 added to: *a few cents on the electric bill is nothing compared with your security.*
▶ adv. **1** physically in contact with and supported by a surface: *make sure the lid is on.* ■ (of clothing) being worn by a person: *sitting with her coat on | get your shoes on.*
2 indicating continuation of a movement or action: *she burbled on | he drove on | and so on.* ■ further forward; in an advanced state: *later on | time's getting on.*
3 (of an entertainment or other event) taking place or being presented: *what's on at the festival | there's a good film on this afternoon.* ■ due to take place as planned: *the reorganization is still on.*
4 (of an electrical appliance or power supply) functioning: *they always left the lights on.* ■ (of a performer, etc.) broadcasting or acting. ■ (of an employee) working.
– PHRASES **be on about** Brit. informal talk about tediously and at length: *she's always on about doing one's duty.* **it's not on** informal, chiefly Brit. it's impractical or unacceptable. **on and off** intermittently: *it rained on and off most of the afternoon.* **on and on** continually; at tedious length: *he went on and on about his grandad's trombone.* **what are you on?** informal said to express incredulity at someone's behavior, with the implication that they must be under the influence of drugs. **you're on** informal said by way of accepting a challenge or bet.
– ORIGIN Old English *on, an*, of Germanic origin; related to Dutch *aan* and German *an*, from an Indo-European root shared by Greek *ana*.

-on ▶ suffix Physics, Biochemistry, & Chemistry forming nouns: **1** denoting subatomic particles or quanta: *neutron | photon.*
2 denoting molecular units: *codon.*
3 denoting substances: *interferon.*
– ORIGIN Sense 1 originally in *electron*, from ION, influenced (as in sense 2) by Greek *on* 'being'; sense 3 is on the pattern of words such as *cotton* or from German *-on*.

on·a·ger /ˈänəjər/ ▶ n. an animal of a race of the Asian wild ass native to northern Iran. ● *Equus hemionus onager*, family Equidae. Compare with KIANG.
– ORIGIN Middle English: via Latin from Greek *onagros*, from *onos* 'ass' + *agrios* 'wild.'

on-air ▶ adj. & adv. being broadcast on radio or television: [as adj.] *live, on-air interviews* | [as adv.] *he apologized on-air for the comment.*

o·nan·ism /ˈōnəˌnizəm/ ▶ n. formal **1** masturbation.
2 coitus interruptus.
– DERIVATIVES **o·nan·ist** n., **o·nan·is·tic** /ˌōnəˈnistik/ adj.
– ORIGIN early 18th cent.: from French *onanisme* or modern Latin *onanismus*, from the biblical story of Onan (Gen. 38:8).

O·nas·sis[1] /ōˈnasis/, Aristotle (Socrates) (1906–75), Greek shipping magnate and international businessman. He owned a substantial shipping empire and founded Olympic Airways, Greece's national airline, in 1957. In 1968, he married Jacqueline Bouvier Kennedy, the widow of John F. Kennedy.

O·nas·sis[2], Jacqueline Lee Bouvier Kennedy (1929–94), US first lady (1961–63). She worked as a photographer before she married John F. Kennedy in 1953. After he was assassinated, she married Aristotle Onassis in 1968 and, after his death, pursued a career in publishing.

Jacqueline Kennedy Onassis

on-board ▶ adj. [attrib.] **1** available or situated on a ship, aircraft, or other vehicle.
2 Computing denoting or controlled from a facility or feature incorporated into the main circuit board of a computer or computerized device.

once /wəns/ ▶ adv. **1** on one occasion or for one time only: *they deliver once a week.* ■ (usu. with negative or **if**) at all; on even one occasion (used for emphasis): *he never once complained | if she once got an idea in her head you'd never move it.*
2 at some time in the past; formerly: *He had once been an Army officer.*
▶ conj. as soon as; when: *once the grapes were pressed, the juice was put into barrels.*
– PHRASES **all at once 1** without warning; suddenly: *all at once the noise stopped.* **2** all at the same time: *scared and excited all at once.* **at once 1** immediately: *I fell asleep at once.* **2** simultaneously: *computers that can do many things at once.* **for once** (or **this once**) on this occasion only, as an exception: *He was glad that for once he had not listened.* **once a ——, always a ——** proverb a person cannot change their fundamental nature: *once a whiner, always a whiner.* **once again** (or **more**) one more time. **once and for all** (or **once for all**) now and for the last time; finally. **once and future** denoting someone or something that is eternal, enduring, or constant. [1950s: from T. H. White's *Once and Future King* (1958).] **once bitten, twice shy** see BITE. **once** (or **every once**) **in a while** from time to time; occasionally. **once or twice** a few times. **once upon a time** at some time in the past (used as a conventional opening of a story). ■ formerly: *once upon a time she would have been jealous, but no longer.*
– ORIGIN Middle English *ones*, genitive of ONE. The spelling change in the 16th cent. was in order to retain the unvoiced sound of the final consonant.

once-o·ver ▶ n. informal a rapid inspection or search: *some doctor came and gave us all a once-over.* ■ a piece of work that is done quickly: *a quick once-over with a broom.*

on-chip ▶ adj. Electronics denoting or relating to circuitry included in a single integrated circuit or in the same integrated circuit as a given device.

on·cho·cer·ci·a·sis /ˌäNGkōsərˈkīəsis/ ▶ n. technical term for RIVER BLINDNESS.
– ORIGIN early 20th cent.: from modern Latin *Onchocerca* (from Greek *onkos* 'barb' + *kerkos* 'tail') + -IASIS.

onco- ▶ comb. form of or relating to tumors: *oncology.*
– ORIGIN from Greek *onkos* 'mass.'

on·co·gene /ˈäNGkəˌjēn/ ▶ n. Medicine a gene that in certain circumstances can transform a cell into a tumor cell.

on·co·gen·ic /ˌäNGkəˈjenik/ ▶ adj. Medicine causing development of a tumor or tumors.
– DERIVATIVES **on·co·gen·e·sis** /-ˈjenisis/ n., **on·co·ge·nic·i·ty** /-jəˈnisitē/ n.

on·col·o·gy /änˈkäləjē, äNG-/ ▶ n. Medicine the study and treatment of tumors.
– DERIVATIVES **on·co·log·ic** /ˌänkəˈläjik, ˌäNG-/ adj., **on·co·log·i·cal** /-kəˈläjikəl/ adj., **on·col·o·gist** /-ˈkäləjist/ n.

on·com·ing /ˈänˌkəmiNG, ˈôn-/ ▶ adj. [attrib.] approaching; moving toward: *she walked into the path of an oncoming car.* ■ due to happen or occur in the near future: *the oncoming Antarctic winter.*
▶ n. the fact of being about to happen in the near future: *the oncoming of age.*

On·co·Mouse /ˈäNGkəˌmous/ (also **oncomouse**) ▶ n. trademark a transgenic mouse carrying an activated human cancer gene, used in laboratory experiments.
– ORIGIN from ONCO- + MOUSE.

on·co·pro·tein /ˌäNGkəˈprōtē(ə)n/ ▶ n. a protein encoded by an oncogene which can cause the transformation of a cell into a tumor cell if introduced into it.
– ORIGIN from ONCO- + PROTEIN.

OND ▶ abbr. historical (in the UK) Ordinary National Diploma (a qualification in technical subjects).

On·daat·je /änˈdäjə, änˈdätyə/, Michael (1943–), Canadian writer, born in Sri Lanka; full name *Philip Michael Ondaatje*. Notable works: *Running in the Family* (autobiography, 1982), *The English Patient* (novel, Booker Prize, 1992; film 1996), and *Anil's Ghost* (2000).

one /wən/ ▶ cardinal number the lowest cardinal number; half of two; 1: *there's only room for one person | two could live as cheaply as one | one hundred miles | World War One | a one-bedroom apartment.* (Roman numeral: **i, I**) ■ a single person or thing, viewed as taking the place of a group: *they would straggle home in ones and twos.* ■ single; just one as opposed to any more or to none at all (used for emphasis): *her one concern is to save her daughter.* ■ denoting a particular item of a pair or number of items: *electronics is one of his hobbies | he put one hand over her shoulder and one around her waist | a glass tube closed at one end.* ■ denoting a particular but unspecified occasion or period: *one afternoon in late October.* ■ used before a name to denote a person who is not familiar or has not been previously mentioned; a certain: *he worked as a clerk for one Mr. Ming.* ■ informal a noteworthy example of (used for emphasis): *the actor was one smart-mouthed troublemaker | he was* ***one hell of a*** *snappy dresser.* ■ identical; the same: *all types of training meet one common standard.* ■ one year old. ■ one o'clock: *it's half past one | I'll be there at one.* ■ informal a one-dollar bill. ■ informal an alcoholic drink: *a cool one after a day on the water.* ■ informal a joke or story: *the one about the chicken farmer and the spaceship.* ■ a size of garment or other merchandise denoted by one. ■ a domino or dice with one spot.

▶ **pron. 1** referring to a person or thing previously mentioned or easily identified: *her mood changed from one of moroseness to one of joy | her best apron, the white one | do you want one?*

2 a person of a specified kind: *you're the one who ruined her life | Eleanor was never one to be trifled with | my friends and* ***loved ones.*** ■ a person who is remarkable or extraordinary in some way: *you never saw* ***such a one*** *for figures.*

3 [third person singular] used to refer to the speaker, or any person, as representing people in general: *one must admire him for his willingness | one gets the impression that he is ahead.*

– PHRASES **at one** in agreement or harmony: *they were completely* ***at one with*** *their environment.* **for one** used to stress that the person named holds the specified view, even if no one else does: *I for one am getting a little sick of writing about it.* **one after another** (or **the other**) following one another in quick succession: *one after another, the buses drew up.* **one and all** everyone: *well done, one and all!* **one and only** unique; single (used for emphasis or as a designation of a celebrity): *the title of his one and only book | the one and only Muhammad Ali.* **one by one** separately and in succession; singly. **one day** at a particular but unspecified time in the past or future: *one day a boy started teasing Grady | he would one day be a great president.* **one-for-one** denoting or referring to a situation or arrangement in which one thing corresponds to or is exchanged for another: *donations would be matched on a one-for-one basis with public revenues.* **one of a kind** see KIND[1]. **one-on-one** (or **one-to-one**) denoting or referring to a situation in which two parties come into direct contact, opposition, or correspondence: *maybe we should talk to them one-on-one.* **one or another** (or **the other**) denoting or referring to a particular but unspecified one out of a set of items: *not all instances fall neatly into one or another of these categories.* **one or two** informal a few: *there are one or two signs worth watching for.* **one thing and another** informal used to cover various unspecified matters, events, or tasks: ***what with one thing and another*** *she hadn't had much sleep recently.*

– ORIGIN Old English *ān*, of Germanic origin; related to Dutch *een* and German *ein*, from an Indo-European root shared by Latin *unus*. The initial *w* sound developed before the 15th cent. and was occasionally represented in the spelling; it was not accepted into standard English until the late 17th cent.

> **USAGE** In modern English, the use of **one** as a pronoun to mean 'anyone' or 'me and people in general,' as in *one must try one's best*, is generally restricted to formal contexts, outside which it is likely to be regarded as rather pompous or old-fashioned. In informal and spoken contexts, the normal alternative is **you**, as in *you have to do what you can, don't you?*

-one ▶ **suffix** Chemistry forming nouns denoting various compounds, esp. ketones: *acetone | quinone.*

– ORIGIN from Greek patronymic *-ōnē*.

one-act·er ▶ **n.** a one-act play.

O'Neal /ōˈnēl/, Shaquille (1972–), US basketball player. During his career as a center since 1992, he has played for the Orlando Magic, Los Angeles Lakers, Miami Heat, Phoenix Suns, and Cleveland Cavaliers.

one an·oth·er ▶ **pron.** each other: *the children used to tease one another.*

one-armed ban·dit ▶ **n.** informal a slot machine operated by pulling a long handle at the side.

one-di·men·sion·al ▶ **adj.** having or relating to a single dimension: *one-dimensional curves.* ■ lacking depth; superficial: *the supporting roles are alarmingly one-dimensional creations.*

– DERIVATIVES **one-di·men·sion·al·i·ty n.**

one-down ▶ **adj.** informal at a psychological disadvantage in a game or a competitive situation.

O·ne·ga, Lake /ōˈnegə, əˈnyegə/ a lake in northwestern Russia, near the border with Finland, the second largest lake in Europe.

one-horse ▶ **adj.** drawn by or using a single horse. ■ informal small and insignificant: *a one-horse town.*

– PHRASES **one-horse race** a contest in which one candidate or competitor is clearly superior to all the others and seems certain to win.

O·nei·da /ōˈnīdə/ ▶ **n.** (pl. **same** or **Oneidas**) **1** a member of an American Indian people formerly inhabiting upper New York state, one of the Five Nations.

2 the Iroquoian language of this people.

▶ **adj.** of or relating to this people or their language.

– ORIGIN from Oneida *onęyóteʔ* 'erected stone,' referring to the large syenite boulder said to have appeared near the successive principal Oneida settlements.

O·nei·da Com·mu·ni·ty a utopian religious community, founded in New York state in 1848 and originally embracing primitive Christian beliefs and radical social and economic ideas, later relaxed. Successful in various commercial enterprises, it was formed into a joint-stock company in 1881.

O'Neill /ōˈnēl/, Eugene (Gladstone) (1888–1953), US playwright. He was awarded the Pulitzer Prize for his first full-length play, *Beyond the Horizon* (1920). Other notable works: *The Iceman Cometh* (1946) and *Long Day's Journey into Night* (1956, posthumously). Nobel Prize for Literature (1936).

o·nei·ric /ōˈnīrik/ ▶ **adj.** formal of or relating to dreams or dreaming.

– ORIGIN mid 19th cent.: from Greek *oneiros* 'dream' + -IC.

oneiro- ▶ **comb. form** relating to dreams or dreaming: *oneiromancy.*

– ORIGIN from Greek *oneiros* 'dream.'

o·nei·ro·man·cy /ōˈnīrəˌmansē/ ▶ **n.** the interpretation of dreams in order to foretell the future.

one-lin·er ▶ **n.** informal a short joke or witty remark.

one-lung·er /ˈləNGər/ ▶ **n.** informal a single-cylinder engine. ■ a vehicle or boat driven by such an engine.

one-man ▶ **adj.** [attrib.] involving, done, or operated by only one person: *a one-man show.*

one-man band ▶ **n.** a street entertainer who plays several instruments at the same time. ■ a person who runs a business alone.

one·ness /ˈwən(n)is/ ▶ **n. 1** the fact or state of being unified or whole, though comprised of two or more parts: *the oneness of man and nature.* ■ identity or harmony with someone or something: *a strong sense of oneness is felt with all things.*

2 the fact or state of being one in number: *belief in the oneness of God.*

one-night stand ▶ **n. 1** informal (also **one-nighter**) a sexual relationship lasting only one night. ■ a person with whom one has such a relationship.

2 a single performance of a play or show in a particular place.

one-off informal, chiefly Brit. ▶ **adj.** done, made, or happening only once and not repeated: *one-off tax deductible donations to charity.*

▶ **n.** something done, made, or happening only once, not as part of a regular sequence: *the meeting is a one-off.* ■ a person who is unusual or unique, esp. in an admirable way: *he's a one-off, no one else has his skills.*

one-on-one (also chiefly Brit. **one-to-one**) ▶ **n.** informal a face-to-face encounter.

one-piece ▶ **adj.** [attrib.] (esp. of an article of clothing) made or consisting of a single piece.

▶ **n.** an article of clothing made or consisting of a single piece: *I was wearing a tight black one-piece.*

on·er /ˈwənər/ ▶ **n.** informal, archaic, chiefly Brit. a remarkable person or thing.

on·er·ous /ˈōnərəs, ˈänərəs/ ▶ **adj.** (of a task, duty, or responsibility) involving an amount of effort and difficulty that is oppressively burdensome: *he found his duties increasingly onerous.* ■ Law involving heavy obligations: *an onerous lease.*

– DERIVATIVES **on·er·ous·ly adv.**, **on·er·ous·ness n.**

– ORIGIN late Middle English: from Old French *onereus*, from Latin *onerosus*, from *onus*, *oner-* 'burden.'

one·self /wənˈself/ (also **one's self**) ▶ **pron.** [third person singular] **1** [reflexive] a person's own self: *it is difficult to wrest oneself away | resolves that one makes to oneself.*

2 [emphatic] used to emphasize that one does something individually or unaided: *the idea of publishing a book oneself.*

3 in one's normal and individual state of body or mind; not influenced by others: *freedom to be oneself.*

– PHRASES **by oneself** see BY.

one-sid·ed ▶ **adj.** unfairly giving or dealing with only one side of a contentious issue or question; biased or partial: *the press was accused of being one-sided, of not giving a balanced picture.* ■ (of a contest or conflict) having a gross inequality of strength or ability between the opponents. ■ (of a relationship or conversation) having all the effort or activity coming from one participant. ■ having or occurring on one side of something only: *printing one-sided documents.*

– DERIVATIVES **one-sid·ed·ly adv.**, **one-sid·ed·ness n.**

one·sie /ˈwənzē/ ▶ **n.** trademark an infant's one-piece close-fitting lightweight garment, usually having sleeves but leaving the legs uncovered and fastening with snaps at the crotch.

one-star ▶ **adj.** (esp. of a hotel or restaurant) given one star in a grading system in which this denotes the lowest class or quality: *a good one-star hotel.* ■ (in the US armed forces) having or denoting the rank of brigadier general, distinguished by one star on the uniform: *a one-star general.*

one-step ▶ **n.** a vigorous kind of ballroom dance in duple time.

▶ **adj.** (of a process or procedure) consisting of only one stage; straightforward: *a one-step self-help program.*

one-stop ▶ **adj.** (of a store or other business) capable of supplying all a customer's needs within a particular range of goods or services: *one-stop shopping.*

one-tailed ▶ **adj.** Statistics denoting a test for deviation from the null hypothesis in one direction only.

one-time (also **onetime**) ▶ **adj. 1** former: *a one-time football player.*

2 of or relating to a single occasion: *a one-time charge.*

one-touch ▶ **adj.** [attrib.] (of an electrical device or facility) able to be operated simply at or as though at the touch of a button.

one-track mind ▶ **n.** used in reference to a person whose thoughts are preoccupied with one subject or interest.

one-trick po·ny ▶ **n.** informal a person or thing with only one special feature, talent, or area of expertise.

one-two ▶ **n.** a pair of punches in quick succession, esp. with alternate hands: [as modifier] *a one-two punch.*

one up informal ▶ **adj.** having a psychological advantage over someone: *you're always trying to be* ***one up on*** *whoever you're with.*

▶ **v.** [with obj.] (**one-up**) do better than (someone): *he deftly one-upped the interrogator.*

one-up·man·ship /wən ˈəpmənˌSHip/ ▶ **n.** informal the technique or practice of gaining a feeling of superiority over another person.

one-way ▶ **adj.** moving or allowing movement in one direction only: *a one-way valve.* ■ (of a road or system of roads) along which traffic may pass in one direction only. ■ (of a ticket) allowing a person to travel to a place but not back again. ■ (of glass or a mirror) seen as a mirror from one side but transparent from the other. ■ denoting a relationship in which all the action or contribution of a particular kind comes from only one member: *interaction between the organism and the environment is not a one-way process.*

one-wom·an ▶ **adj.** involving, done, or operated by only one woman.

one-world ▶ **adj.** of, relating to, or holding the view that the world's inhabitants are interdependent and should behave accordingly.

– DERIVATIVES **one-world·er n.**, **one-world·ism n.**

on-glide ▶ **n.** Phonetics a glide produced just before the articulation of another speech sound. Compare with OFF-GLIDE.

on·go·ing /ˈänˌgōiNG, ˈôn-/ ▶ **adj.** continuing; still in progress: *ongoing negotiations.*

– DERIVATIVES **on·go·ing·ness n.**

ONI ▶ **abbr.** Office of Naval Intelligence.

on·i·o·man·i·a /ˌōnēōˈmānēə/ ▶ **n.** an obsessive or uncontrollable urge to buy things: *Oniomania can affect either sex, but the vast majority of compulsive shoppers are adult females.*

– ORIGIN from Greek *ōnios* 'for sale,' from *ōnos* 'price, purchase': see -MANIA.

on·ion /ˈənyən/ ▶ **n. 1** an edible bulb with a pungent taste and smell, composed of several concentric layers, used in cooking.

2 the plant that produces this bulb, with long rolled or straplike leaves and spherical heads of greenish-white flowers. ● *Allium cepa*, family Liliaceae (or Alliaceae).

O

– PHRASES **know one's onions** informal be very knowledgeable about something.
– DERIVATIVES **on·ion·y** adj.
– ORIGIN Middle English: from Old French *oignon*, based on Latin *unio(n-)*, denoting a kind of onion.

on·ion bag ▶ n. Soccer, informal a goal net (used esp. in the context of scoring a goal).

on·ion dome ▶ n. a dome that bulges in the middle and rises to a point, used esp. in Russian church architecture.
– DERIVATIVES **on·ion-domed** adj.

on·ion set ▶ n. a small onion bulb planted instead of seed to yield a mature bulb.

on·ion·skin /ˈənyən,skin/ (also **onionskin paper**) ▶ n. very fine smooth translucent paper.

on·li·est /ˈōnlē-ist/ ▶ adj. dialect or humorous emphatic form of ONLY.

on·line /ˈänlīn, ˈôn-/ Computing ▶ adj. controlled by or connected to another computer or to a network. ■ connected to the Internet or World Wide Web: *the ease and convenience of online shopping.*
▶ adv. **1** while so connected or under computer control. ■ with processing of data carried out simultaneously with its production.
2 in or into operation or existence: *the town's new high-tech power plant is expected to go online this month.*

on·look·er /ˈän,lo͝okər, ˈôn-/ ▶ n. a nonparticipating observer; a spectator: *a crowd of fascinated onlookers.*
– DERIVATIVES **on·look·ing** /-,lo͝okiNG/ adj.

on·ly /ˈōnlē/ ▶ adv. **1** and no one or nothing more besides; solely or exclusively: *there are only a limited number of tickets available | only their faith sustained them.* ■ no more than (implying that more was hoped for or expected); merely: *deaths from heart disease have only declined by 10 percent | she was still only in her mid-thirties.* ■ no longer ago than: *genes that were discovered only last year.* ■ not until: *a final report reached him only on January 15.*
2 [with infinitive] with the negative or unfortunate result that: *she turned into the parking car, only to find her way blocked.* ■ [with modal] inevitably, although unfortunate or undesirable: *if banks canceled the debts, these countries **would only** borrow more | rebellion **will only** bring more unhappiness.*
▶ adj. [attrib.] alone of its or their kind; single or solitary: *the only medal we had ever won | he was an only child.* ■ alone deserving consideration: *it's simply the only place to be seen these days.*
▶ conj. informal except that; but for the fact that: *he is still a young man, only he seems older because of his careworn expression.*
– PHRASES **only just** by a very small margin; almost not: *the building survived the earthquake, but only just.* ■ very recently: *I'd only just arrived back from Paris.* **only too ——** used to emphasize that something is the case to an extreme or regrettable extent: *you should be only too glad to be rid of him | they found that the rumor was only too true.*
– ORIGIN Old English *ānlic* (adjective) (see ONE, -LY[1]).

> **USAGE** In normal, everyday English, the tendency is to place **only** as early as possible in the sentence, generally just before the verb, and the result is rarely ambiguous. Misunderstandings are possible, however, and grammarians have debated the matter for more than two hundred years. Advice varies, but in general, ambiguity is less likely if **only** is placed as close as is naturally possible to the word(s) to be modified or emphasized. *I saw her **only** once* stresses the single instance; *I **only** saw her once* leaves it unclear whether she was heard (or otherwise perceived) in addition to being seen.

on–off ▶ adj. **1** (of a switch) having two positions, "on" and "off."
2 (of a relationship) not continuous or steady.

on·o·ma·si·ol·o·gy /,änə,māsēˈäləjē, -,māzē-/ ▶ n. the branch of knowledge that deals with terminology, in particular contrasting terms for similar concepts. Compare with SEMASIOLOGY.
– DERIVATIVES **on·o·ma·si·o·log·i·cal** /-əˈläjikəl/ adj.
– ORIGIN early 20th cent.: from Greek *onomasia* 'term' + -LOGY.

on·o·mast /ˈänə,mast/ ▶ n. a person who studies proper names, esp. personal names.
– ORIGIN 1980s: back-formation from ONOMASTIC.

on·o·mas·tic /,änəˈmastik/ ▶ adj. of or relating to the study of the history and origin of proper names.
– ORIGIN late 16th cent. (as a noun in the sense 'alphabetical list of proper nouns,' later also 'lexicographer'): from Greek *onomastikos*, from *onoma* 'name.' The adjective dates from the early 18th cent.

on·o·mas·tics /,änəˈmastiks/ ▶ plural n. [usu. treated as sing.] the study of the history and origin of proper names, esp. personal names.

on·o·mat·o·poe·ia /,änə,matəˈpēə, -,mätə-/ ▶ n. the formation of a word from a sound associated with what is named (e.g., *cuckoo, sizzle*). ■ the use of such words for rhetorical effect.
– ORIGIN late 16th cent.: via late Latin from Greek *onomatopoiia* 'word-making,' from *onoma, onomat-* 'name' + *-poios* 'making' (from *poiein* 'to make').

on·o·mat·o·poe·ic /,änə,matəˈpē-ik, -,mätə-/ ▶ adj. using or relating to onomatopoeia: *onomatopoeic words like 'bang' and 'coo'*
– DERIVATIVES **on·o·mat·o·poe·i·cal·ly** /-ˈpē-ik(ə)lē/ adv., **on·o·mat·o·po·et·ic** /-pōˈetik/ adj.

On·on·da·ga /,änənˈdôgə, ,ōnən-, -ˈdāgə/ ▶ n. (pl. **same** or **Onondagas**) **1** a member of an Iroquois people, one of the Five Nations, formerly inhabiting an area near Syracuse, New York.
2 the Iroquoian language of this people.
▶ adj. of or relating to this people or their language.
– ORIGIN from the Onondaga name of their main settlement, literally 'on the hill.'

on-ramp ▶ n. a lane for traffic entering a turnpike or freeway.

on-road ▶ adj. denoting or relating to events or conditions on a road, esp. a vehicle's performance.

on·rush /ˈän,rəSH, ˈôn-/ ▶ n. a surging rush forward: *the mesmerizing onrush of the sea.*
▶ v. [no obj.] (usu. as adj. **onrushing**) move forward in a surging rush: *the walls of onrushing whitewater.*

on-screen (also **on screen** or **onscreen**) ▶ adj. & adv. shown or appearing in a movie or television program: [as adj.] *on-screen violence.* ■ making use of or performed with the aid of a video screen: [as adj.] *on-screen editing facilities.*

on·sen /ˈänsen/ ▶ n. (in Japan) a hot spring, or a resort that has developed around a hot spring.
– ORIGIN Japanese.

on·set /ˈän,set, ˈôn-/ ▶ n. the beginning of something, esp. something unpleasant: *the **onset** of winter.* ■ archaic a military attack.

on·shore /ˈänˈSHôr, ˈôn-/ ▶ adj. & adv. situated or occurring on land: [as adj.] *an onshore oil field.* ■ (esp. of the direction of the wind) from the sea toward the land.

on·side /ˈänˈsīd, ˈôn-/ ▶ adj. & adv. (of a player, esp. in soccer or hockey) occupying a position on the field where playing the ball or puck is allowed; not offside.

on·side kick (also **onsides kick**) ▶ n. Football an intentionally short kickoff that travels forward the required distance of 10 yards, which the kicking team can attempt to recover.

on-site ▶ adj. & adv. taking place or situated on a particular site or premises.

on·slaught /ˈän,slôt, ˈôn-/ ▶ n. a fierce or destructive attack: *a series of **onslaughts on** the citadel.* ■ a large quantity of people or things that is difficult to cope with: *an onslaught of electronic mail.*
– ORIGIN early 17th cent. (also in the form *anslaight*): from Middle Dutch *aenslag*, from *aen* 'on' + *slag* 'blow.' The change in the ending was due to association with (now obsolete) *slaught* 'slaughter.'

on·stage /ˈänˈstāj, ˈôn-/ ▶ adj. & adv. (in a theater) on the stage and so visible to the audience.

on-stream ▶ adv. & adj. in or into industrial production or useful operation.

Ont. ▶ abbr. Ontario.

-ont ▶ comb. form Biology denoting an individual or cell of a specified type: *schizont.*
– ORIGIN from Greek *ont-* 'being,' present participle of *einai* 'be.'

On·tar·i·o[1] /änˈte(ə)rē,ō/ a province in eastern Canada, between Hudson Bay and the Great Lakes; pop. 12,160,282 (2006); capital, Toronto. It was settled by the French and the English in the 1600s, ceded to Britain in 1763, and became one of the original four provinces in the Dominion of Canada in 1867.
– DERIVATIVES **On·tar·i·an** /-ēən/ adj. & n.

On·tar·i·o[2] a commercial city in southwestern California, east of Los Angeles; pop. 171,691 (est. 2008).

On·tar·i·o, Lake the smallest and most easterly of the Great Lakes. It lies on the US–Canadian border between Ontario and New York and is linked to Lake Erie by the Niagara River and to the Atlantic Ocean by the St. Lawrence Seaway.

on·tic /ˈäntik/ ▶ adj. Philosophy of or relating to entities and the facts about them; relating to real as opposed to phenomenal existence.
– ORIGIN 1940s: from Greek *ōn, ont-* 'being' + -IC.

on·to /ˈän,to͞o, ˈôn-/ ▶ prep. **1** moving to a location on (the surface of something): *they went up onto the ridge.*
2 moving aboard (a public conveyance) with the intention of traveling in it: *we got onto the train.*
– PHRASES **be onto someone** informal be close to discovering the truth about an illegal or undesirable activity that someone is engaging in. **be onto something** informal have an idea or information that is likely to lead to an important discovery.

> **USAGE** The preposition **onto** written as one word (instead of **on to**) is recorded from the early 18th century and has been widely used ever since. In US English, it is the regular form, although it is not wholly accepted in British English. Nevertheless, it is important to maintain a distinction between the preposition **onto** or **on to** and the use of the adverb **on** followed by the preposition **to**: *she climbed **onto** (sometimes **on to**) the roof*, but *let's go **on to** (never **onto**) the next chapter.*

on·to·gen·e·sis /,äntəˈjenəsis/ ▶ n. Biology the development of an individual organism or anatomical or behavioral feature from the earliest stage to maturity. Compare with PHYLOGENESIS.
– DERIVATIVES **on·to·ge·net·ic** /-jəˈnetik/ adj., **on·to·ge·net·i·cal·ly** /-jəˈnetik(ə)lē/ adv.
– ORIGIN late 19th cent.: from Greek *ōn, ont-* 'being' + *genesis* 'birth.'

on·tog·e·ny /änˈtäjənē/ ▶ n. the branch of biology that deals with ontogenesis. Compare with PHYLOGENY. ■ another term for ONTOGENESIS.
– DERIVATIVES **on·to·gen·ic** /,äntəˈjenik/ adj., **on·to·gen·i·cal·ly** /,äntəˈjenik(ə)lē/ adv.
– ORIGIN late 19th cent.: from Greek *ōn, ont-* 'being' + -GENY.

on·to·log·i·cal ar·gu·ment /,äntəˈläjikəl/ ▶ n. Philosophy the argument that God, being defined as most great or perfect, must exist, since a God who exists is greater than a God who does not. Compare with ARGUMENT FROM DESIGN, COSMOLOGICAL ARGUMENT, and TELEOLOGICAL ARGUMENT.

on·tol·o·gy /änˈtäləjē/ ▶ n. the branch of metaphysics dealing with the nature of being.
– DERIVATIVES **on·to·log·i·cal** /,äntəˈläjikəl/ adj., **on·to·log·i·cal·ly** /,äntəˈläjik(ə)lē/ adv., **on·tol·o·gist** /-jist/ n.
– ORIGIN early 18th cent.: from modern Latin *ontologia*, from Greek *ōn, ont-* 'being' + -LOGY.

on-top·ic ▶ adj. & adv. (esp. of posts on an Internet message board) relevant to the subject in question: [as adj.] *on-topic contributions to the discussion* | [as adv.] *I'll do my best to stay on-topic.*

o·nus /ˈōnəs/ ▶ n. (usu. as **the onus**) used to refer to something that is one's duty or responsibility: *the onus is on you to show that you have suffered loss.*
– ORIGIN mid 17th cent.: from Latin, literally 'load or burden.'

o·nus pro·ban·di /ˈōnəs prōˈbändē, -ˈban-/ ▶ n. Law the obligation to prove an assertion or allegation one makes; the burden of proof.
– ORIGIN Latin, 'the burden of proving.'

on·ward /ˈänwərd, ˈôn-/ ▶ adv. (also **onwards**) in a continuing forward direction; ahead: *she stumbled onward.* ■ forward in time: *the period **from** 1969 **onward**.* ■ so as to make progress or become more successful: *the business moved **onward and upward**.*
▶ adj. going further rather than coming to an end or halt; moving forward: *oil was pumped to a port for onward shipment* | figurative *the onward march of history.*

On·y·choph·o·ra /,äniˈkäfərə/ Zoology a small phylum of terrestrial invertebrates commonly known as velvet worms. They share characteristics with the arthropods and annelids, having a long soft segmented body with stubby legs (lobopods).
– ORIGIN modern Latin (plural), from Greek *onux, onukh-* 'nail, claw' + *-phoros* 'bearing.'

on·y·choph·o·ran /,äniˈkäfərən/ Zoology ▶ n. a terrestrial invertebrate of the small phylum Onychophora; a velvet worm.
▶ adj. relating to or denoting onychophorans.

-onym ▶ comb. form forming nouns: **1** denoting a type of name: *pseudonym.*
2 denoting a word having a specified relationship to another: *antonym.*
– ORIGIN from Greek *-ōnumon*, neuter of *-ōnumos*, combining form of *onoma* 'name.'

on·yx /ˈäniks/ ▶ n. a semiprecious variety of agate with different colors in layers.
– ORIGIN Middle English: from Old French *oniche, onix*, via Latin from Greek *onux* 'fingernail or onyx.'

on·yx mar·ble ▶ n. banded calcite or other stone used as a decorative material.

oo- ▶ comb. form Biology relating to or denoting an egg or ovum.
– ORIGIN from Greek *ōion* 'egg.'

o-o /ˈō,ō/ (also **oo**) ▶ n. (pl. **o-os**) a honeyeater (bird) found in Hawaii, now probably extinct, which had a thin curved bill and climbed about on tree trunks. ● Genus *Moho*, family Meliphagidae.

O

– ORIGIN late 19th cent.: from Hawaiian.

o·o·cyst /ˈōəˌsist/ ▶ **n.** Zoology a cyst containing a zygote formed by a parasitic protozoan such as the malaria parasite.

o·o·cyte /ˈōəˌsīt/ ▶ **n.** Biology a cell in an ovary that may undergo meiotic division to form an ovum.

OOD ▶ **abbr.** ■ officer of the deck. ■ officer of the day.

oo·dles /ˈo͞odlz/ ▶ **plural n.** informal a very great number or amount of something: *if only I had oodles of cash.*
– ORIGIN mid 19th cent. (originally US): of unknown origin.

oof /o͞of/ ▶ **exclam.** expressing discomfort, as from sudden exertion or a blow to one's body.
– ORIGIN natural exclamation: first recorded in English in the mid 19th cent.

o·og·a·mous /ōˈägəməs/ ▶ **adj.** Biology relating to or denoting reproduction by the union of mobile male and immobile female gametes.
– DERIVATIVES **o·og·a·mous·ly adv.**, **o·og·a·my** /-gəmē/ **n.**

o·o·gen·e·sis /ˌōəˈjenəsis/ ▶ **n.** Biology the production or development of an ovum.

o·o·go·ni·um /ˌōəˈgōnēəm/ ▶ **n.** (pl. **oogonia** /-nēə/) **1** Botany the female sex organ of certain algae and fungi, typically a rounded cell or sac containing one or more oospheres.
2 Biology an immature female reproductive cell that gives rise to primary oocytes by mitosis.
– DERIVATIVES **o·o·go·ni·al** /-nēəl/ **adj.**
– ORIGIN mid 19th cent.: from **oo-** 'of an egg' + Greek *gonos* 'generation' + **-IUM**.

ooh /o͞o/ ▶ **exclam.** used to express a range of emotions including surprise, delight, or pain: *ooh, this is fun | ooh, my feet!*
▶ **n.** an utterance of such an exclamation: *the oohs and aahs of the enthusiastic audience.*
▶ **v.** (**oohs, oohing, oohed**) [no obj.] utter such an exclamation: *visitors oohed and aahed at the Christmas tree.*
– ORIGIN natural exclamation: first recorded in English in the early 20th cent.

o·o·lite /ˈōəˌlīt/ ▶ **n.** Geology limestone consisting of a mass of rounded grains (ooliths) made up of concentric layers. ■ another term for **OOLITH**.
– DERIVATIVES **o·o·lit·ic** /ˌōəˈlitik/ **adj.**
– ORIGIN early 19th cent.: from French *oölithe*, modern Latin *oolites* (see **OO-**, **-LITE**).

o·o·lith /ˈōəˌliTH/ ▶ **n.** Geology any of the rounded grains making up oolite.

o·ol·o·gy /ōˈäləjē/ ▶ **n.** the study or collecting of birds' eggs.
– DERIVATIVES **o·o·log·i·cal** /ˌōəˈläjikəl/ **adj.**, **o·ol·o·gist** /-jist/ **n.**

oo·long /ˈo͞oˌlôNG, -ˌläNG/ ▶ **n.** a dark-colored China tea made by fermenting the withered leaves to about half the degree usual for black teas.
– ORIGIN mid 19th cent.: from Chinese *wūlóng*, literally 'black dragon.'

oo·mi·ak ▶ **n.** variant spelling of **UMIAK**.

oom·pah /ˈo͞omˌpä, ˈo͝om-/ (also **oompah-pah**) informal ▶ **n.** used to refer to the rhythmical sound of deep-toned brass instruments in a band.
▶ **v.** (**oompahs, oompahing, oompahed**) [no obj.] make such a sound.
– ORIGIN late 19th cent.: imitative.

oomph /o͝omf, o͞omf/ (also **umph**) ▶ **n.** informal the quality of being exciting, energetic, or sexually attractive: *he showed entrepreneurial oomph.*
– ORIGIN 1930s: perhaps imitative.

-oon ▶ **suffix** forming nouns, originally from French words having the final stressed syllable *-on*: *balloon | buffoon.*
– ORIGIN from Latin *-onis*, sometimes via Italian *-one*.

o·o·pho·rec·to·my /ˌōəfəˈrektəmē/ ▶ **n.** (pl. **oophorectomies**) surgical removal of one or both ovaries; ovariectomy.
– ORIGIN late 19th cent.: from modern Latin *oophoron* 'ovary' (from Greek *ōophoros* 'egg-bearing') + **-ECTOMY**.

o·o·pho·ri·tis /ˌōəfəˈrītis/ ▶ **n.** Medicine inflammation of an ovary; ovaritis.

oops /o͝ops, o͞ops/ ▶ **exclam.** informal used to show recognition of a mistake or minor accident, often as part of an apology: *"Oops! I'm sorry. I just made you miss your bus."*
– ORIGIN natural exclamation: first recorded in English in the 1930s.

oop·sy-dai·sy ▶ **exclam.** variant spelling of **UPSY-DAISY**.

Oort /ôrt/, Jan Hendrik (1900–92), Dutch astronomer. He proved that the galaxy rotates and determined the position and orbital period of the sun within it.

Oort cloud Astronomy a spherical cloud of small rocky and icy bodies postulated to orbit the sun beyond the orbit of Pluto and up to 1.5 light years from the sun, and to be the source of comets. Its existence was proposed by J. H. Oort.

o·o·sphere /ˈōəˌsfir/ ▶ **n.** Botany the female reproductive cell of certain algae or fungi, which is formed in the oogonium and when fertilized becomes the oospore.

o·o·spore /ˈōəˌspôr/ ▶ **n.** Botany the thick-walled zygote of certain algae and fungi, formed by fertilization of an oosphere. Compare with **ZYGOSPORE**.

Oost·en·de /ōˈstendə/ Flemish name for **OSTEND**.

o·o·the·ca /ˌōəˈTHēkə/ ▶ **n.** (pl. **oothecae** /-ˌsē, -ˌkē/) Entomology the egg case of cockroaches, mantises, and related insects.
– ORIGIN mid 19th cent.: from **oo-** 'of an egg' + Greek *thēkē* 'receptacle.'

o·o·tid /ˈōəˌtid/ ▶ **n.** Biology a haploid cell formed by the meiotic division of a secondary oocyte, esp. the ovum, as distinct from the polar bodies.
– ORIGIN early 20th cent.: from **oo-** 'egg,' on the pattern of *spermatid*.

ooze¹ /o͞oz/ ▶ **v. 1** [no obj.] (of a fluid) slowly trickle or seep out of something; flow in a very gradual way: *blood was oozing from a wound in his scalp | honey oozed out of the comb.* ■ slowly exude or discharge a viscous fluid: *her mosquito bites were oozing and itching like mad.*
2 [with obj.] give a powerful impression of (a quality): *he oozed charm and poise | the town oozes history.*
▶ **n. 1** the sluggish flow of a fluid.
2 an infusion of oak bark or other vegetable matter, used in tanning.
– DERIVATIVES **ooz·y** /ˈo͞ozē/ **adj.**
– ORIGIN Old English *wōs* 'juice or sap'; the verb dates from late Middle English.

ooze² ▶ **n.** wet mud or slime, esp. that found at the bottom of a river, lake, or sea. ■ Geology a deposit of white or gray calcareous matter largely composed of foraminiferan remains, covering extensive areas of the ocean floor.
– DERIVATIVES **ooz·y adj.**
– ORIGIN Old English *wāse*; related to Old Norse *veisa* 'stagnant pool.' In Middle English and the 16th cent. the spelling was *wose* (rhyming with *repose*), but beginning in 1550 spellings imply a change in pronunciation and influence by **OOZE**¹.

OP ▶ **abbr.** ■ observation post. ■ (in the theater) opposite prompt. ■ organophosphate(s). ■ (in the Roman Catholic Church) *Ordo Praedicatorum* Order of Preachers (Dominican).

op /äp/ ▶ **n.** informal a surgical or other operation. ■ (**ops**) military operations.

Op. (also **op.**) ▶ **abbr.** Music opus (before a number given to each work of a particular composer, usually indicating the order of publication).

o.p. ▶ **abbr.** ■ (of a book) out of print. ■ (of alcohol) overproof.

op- ▶ **suffix 1** variant spelling of **OB-**.
2 assimilated before *p* (as in *oppress, oppugn*).

o·pac·i·fy /ōˈpasəˌfī/ ▶ **v.** (**opacifies, opacifying, opacified**) technical make or become opaque.
– DERIVATIVES **o·pac·i·fi·ca·tion** /ōˌpasəfiˈkāSHən/ **n.**, **o·pac·i·fi·er n.**

o·pac·i·ty /ōˈpasitē/ ▶ **n.** the condition of lacking transparency or translucence; opaqueness: *thinner paints need black added to increase opacity.* ■ obscurity of meaning: *the difficulty and opacity in Barthes' texts.*
– ORIGIN mid 16th cent.: from French *opacité*, from Latin *opacitas*, from *opacus* 'darkened.'

o·pah /ˈōpə/ ▶ **n.** a large deep-bodied fish with a deep blue back, silvery belly, and crimson fins, living in deep oceanic waters. Also called **MOONFISH**. ● *Lampris guttatus*, family Lampridae.
– ORIGIN mid 18th cent.: a West African word.

o·pal /ˈōpəl/ ▶ **n.** a gemstone consisting of hydrated silica, typically semitransparent and showing varying colors against a pale or dark ground.
– ORIGIN late 16th cent.: from French *opale* or Latin *opalus*, probably based on Sanskrit *upala* 'precious stone' (having been first brought from India).

o·pal·es·cent /ˌōpəˈlesənt/ ▶ **adj.** showing varying colors as an opal does.
– DERIVATIVES **o·pal·es·cence n.**

o·pal glass ▶ **n.** a type of semitranslucent white glass.

o·pal·ine /ˈōpəˌlēn, -ˌlīn/ ▶ **adj.** another term for **OPALESCENT**.
▶ **n.** another term for **MILK GLASS**. ■ translucent glass of a color other than white.

op-amp /ˈäp ˌamp/ ▶ **abbr.** operational amplifier.

o·paque /ōˈpāk/ ▶ **adj.** (**opaquer, opaquest**) not able to be seen through; not transparent: *the windows were opaque with steam.* ■ (esp. of language) hard or impossible to understand; unfathomable: *technical jargon that was opaque to her.*
▶ **n.** an opaque thing or substance. ■ Photography a substance for producing opaque areas on negatives.
– DERIVATIVES **o·paque·ly adv.**, **o·paque·ness n.**
– ORIGIN late Middle English *opake*, from Latin *opacus* 'darkened.' The current spelling (rare before the 19th cent.) has been influenced by the French form.

op art (also **optical art**) ▶ **n.** a form of abstract art that gives the illusion of movement by the precise use of pattern and color, or in which conflicting patterns emerge and overlap. Bridget Riley and Victor Vasarely are its most famous exponents.
– ORIGIN 1960s: on the pattern of *pop art*.

op. cit. /ˈäp ˌsit/ ▶ **adv.** in the work already cited.
– ORIGIN from Latin *opere citato*.

ope /ōp/ ▶ **adj. & v.** literary or archaic form of **OPEN**.

OPEC /ˈōpek/ ▶ **abbr.** Organization of the Petroleum Exporting Countries.

op-ed (also **Op-Ed**) ▶ **adj.** denoting or printed on the page opposite the editorial page in a newspaper, devoted to commentary, feature articles, etc.
– ORIGIN 1940s: shortening of *op(posite the) ed(itorial page)*.

O·pel /ˈōpel/, Wilhelm von (1871–1948), German automobile manufacturer. His company was the first in Germany to introduce assembly-line production. Opel was sold to General Motors in 1929.

o·pen /ˈōpən/ ▶ **adj. 1** allowing access, passage, or a view through an empty space; not closed or blocked up: *it was a warm evening and the window was open | the door was* **wide open** *| the pass is kept open all year by snowplows.* ■ (of a container) not fastened or sealed: *the case burst open and its contents flew all over the place.* ■ (of the mouth or eyes) with lips or lids parted: *his eyes were open but he could see nothing.* ■ (of a garment or its fasteners) not buttoned or fastened: *his tie was knotted below the open collar of his shirt.* ■ Phonetics (of a vowel) produced with a relatively wide opening of the mouth and the tongue kept low. ■ Phonetics (of a syllable) ending in a vowel. ■ (of the bowels) not constipated. ■ (of a game or style of play) characterized by action that is spread out over the field.
2 [attrib.] exposed to the air or to view; not covered: *an open fire burned in the grate | days without food and water in an open boat.* ■ (of an area of land) not covered with buildings or trees: *increasing numbers of new houses in open countryside.* ■ (of a fabric) loosely knitted or woven. ■ (of a team member in a game) unguarded and therefore able to receive a pass: *the trick is spreading the defense so that at least one receiver gets open.* ■ (of a goal or other object of attack in a game) unprotected; vulnerable. ■ [predic.] (**open to**) likely to suffer from or be affected by; vulnerable or subject to: *the system is open to abuse.* ■ (of a town or city) officially declared to be undefended, and so immune under international law from bombardment. ■ with the outer edges or sides drawn away from each other; unfolded: *the trees had buds and a few open flowers.* ■ (of a book or file) with the covers parted or the contents in view, allowing it to be read: *she was copying verses from an open Bible.* ■ (of a hand) not clenched into a fist. ■ [as complement] damaged or injured by a deep cut in the surface: *he had his arm slashed open.*
3 [predic.] (of a store, place of entertainment, etc.) officially admitting customers or visitors; available for business: *the store stays open until 9 p.m.* ■ (of a bank account) available for transactions: *the minimum required to keep the account open.* ■ (of a telephone line) ready to take calls: *our free advice line is open from 8:30 to 5:30.* ■ (of a choice, offer, or opportunity) still available; such that people can take advantage of it: *the offer is open while supplies last | we need to consider what options are left open.*
4 (of a person) frank and communicative; not given to deception or concealment: *she was open and naive | I was quite open about my views.* ■ not concealed; manifest: *his eyes showed open admiration.* ■ [attrib.] (of conflict) fully developed and unconcealed: *the dispute erupted into open war.* ■ involving no concealment, restraint, or deception; welcoming discussion, criticism, and inquiry: *the conclusions were reached in open discussion.*
5 (of a question, case, or decision) not finally settled; still admitting of debate: *students' choice of major can be kept open until the second year.* ■ (of the mind) accessible to new ideas; unprejudiced: *I'm keeping an open mind about my future.* ■ [predic.]

(**open to**) receptive to: *the union was open to suggestions for improvements.* ■ [predic.] (**open to**) admitting of; making possible: *the message is open to different interpretations.* ■ freely available or accessible; offered without restriction: *the service is **open to** all students at the university.* ■ (also **Open**) with no restrictions on those allowed to attend or participate: *an open audition was announced | each horse had won two open races.* ■ (of a ticket) not restricted as to day of travel.
6 Music (of a string) allowed to vibrate along its whole length. ■ (of a pipe) unstopped at each end. ■ (of a note) sounded from an open string or pipe.
7 (of an electrical circuit) having a break in the conducting path.
8 Mathematics (of a set) not containing any of its limit points.
▶ **v.** [with obj.] **1** move or adjust (a door or window) so as to leave a space allowing access and view: *she opened the door and went in* | [no obj.] *"Open up!" he said.* ■ [no obj.] (of a door or window) be moved or adjusted to leave a space allowing access and view: *the door opened and a man came out.* ■ undo or remove the lid, cover, or fastening of (a container, package, letter, etc.) to get access to the contents: *he opened a bottle inexpertly, spilling some of the wine | can we open the presents now?* ■ part the lips or lids of (a mouth or eye): *she opened her mouth to argue.* ■ [no obj.] (of the mouth or eyes) have the lips or lids parted in this way: *her eyes slowly opened.* ■ [no obj.] come apart; lose or lack its protective covering: *old wounds opened and I bled a little bit.* ■ improve or make possible access to or passage through: *the president announced that his government would open the border.* ■ cause evacuation of (the bowels). ■ [no obj.] (**open onto/into**) (of a room, door, or window) give access to: *beautiful French doors that opened onto a balcony.* ■ [no obj.] (of a panorama) come into view; spread out before someone: *stop to marvel at the views that **open out** below.* ■ Nautical achieve a clear view of (a place) by sailing past a headland or other obstruction: *we shall open Simon's Bay at any minute now.*
2 unfold or be unfolded; spread out: [with obj.] *the eagle opened its wings and circled up into the air | the tail looks like a fan when it is **opened out** fully* | [no obj.] *the flowers never opened beyond narrow points.* ■ part the covers or display the contents of (a book or file) to read it: *she opened her book at the prologue.* ■ [no obj.] (**open out**) become wider or more spacious: *the path opened out into a glade.*
3 make available or more widely known: *the new plan proposed to **open up** opportunities to immigrants | the move may force the company to **open up** its plans for the future.* ■ [no obj.] (**open up**) become more communicative or confiding: *neither one of them had opened up to me about their troubles.* ■ make (one's mind or heart) more receptive or sympathetic: ***open your mind to** what is going on around you.* ■ (**open someone** (**up**) **to**) make someone vulnerable to: *the process is going to open them to a legal threat.*
4 establish (a new business, movement, or enterprise): *they have opened a new restaurant across the street.* ■ [no obj.] (of an enterprise, meeting, or event) begin or be formally established: *two new restaurants open this week.* ■ make or become officially ready for customers, visitors, or business: [with obj.] *one woman raised $731 by opening her home and selling coffee and tea* | [no obj.] *the mall didn't open until 10.* ■ take the action required to make ready for use: *they have the $10 necessary to open a savings account | click twice to open a file.* ■ [no obj.] (of a piece of writing or music) begin: *the chapter opens with a discussion of Anglo-American relations.* ■ (**open up**) [no obj.] (of a process) start to develop: *a new and dramatic phase was opening up.* ■ officially or ceremonially declare (a building, road, etc.) to be completed and ready for use: *we will have to wait until a new bypass is opened before we can tackle the problem of congestion.* ■ (of a counsel in a court of law) make a preliminary statement in (a case) before calling witnesses. ■ Bridge make (the first bid) in the auction.
5 break the conducting path of (an electrical circuit): *the switch opens the motor circuit.* ■ [no obj.] (of an electrical circuit or device) suffer a break in its conducting path.
▶ **n. 1** (**Open**) a championship or competition with no restrictions on who may qualify to compete: *the venue for the British Open.*
2 an accidental break in the conducting path for an electrical current.
– PHRASES **be open with** speak frankly to; conceal nothing from: *I had always been completely open with my mother.* **an open book** a person or thing that is easy to understand or about which everything is known: *her mind was an open book to him.* **in** (or **into**) **the open** out of doors; not under cover. ■ not subject to concealment or obfuscation; made public: *we have never let our dislike for him come into the open.* **in open court** in a court of law, before the judge and the public. **open-and-shut** (of a case or argument) admitting no doubt or dispute; straightforward. **open the door to** see DOOR. **open someone's eyes** see EYE. **open fire** begin to shoot a weapon. **an open mind** see MIND. **with one's eyes open** (or **with open eyes**) fully aware of the risks and other implications of an action or situation: *I went into the job with my eyes open.* **with open arms** see ARM[1].
– PHRASAL VERBS **open up** begin shooting: *the enemy artillery had opened up.* **open something up 1** accelerate a motor vehicle. **2** (of an athlete or team) create an advantage for one's side: *he opened up a lead of 14–8.*
– DERIVATIVES **o·pen·a·ble** adj., **o·pen·ness** n.
– ORIGIN Old English *open* (adjective), *openian* (verb), of Germanic origin; related to Dutch *open* and German *offen*, from the root of the adverb UP.

o·pen ac·cess ▶ n. availability to all: *open access to scientific and technological information.* ■ a system where users of a library have direct access to bookshelves.

o·pen air ▶ n. a free or unenclosed space outdoors: *getting out in the open air.*
▶ adj. (**open-air**) positioned or taking place out of doors: *an open-air swimming pool.*

o·pen bar ▶ n. a bar at a special function at which the drinks have been paid for by the host or are prepaid through an admission fee.

o·pen book ▶ n. a person or thing that is easily understood or interpreted: *my life's an open book.*

O·pen Breth·ren one of the two principal divisions of the Plymouth Brethren (the other is the Exclusive Brethren), formed in 1849 in Plymouth, England, as a result of doctrinal and other differences. The Open Brethren are less rigorous and less exclusive in matters such as conditions for membership and contact with outsiders than the Exclusive Brethren.

o·pen·cast /ˈōpənˌkast/ ▶ adj. British term for OPEN-PIT.

o·pen chain ▶ n. Chemistry a molecular structure consisting of a chain of atoms with no closed rings.

o·pen cir·cuit ▶ n. an electrical circuit that is not complete.
– DERIVATIVES **o·pen-cir·cuit·ed** adj.

o·pen cit·y ▶ n. a city declared to be unfortified and undefended and so, by international law, exempt from enemy attack.

o·pen class·room ▶ n. an approach to elementary education that emphasizes spacious classrooms where learning is informally structured, flexible, and individualized. ■ a spacious instructional area shared by several groups of elementary students that facilitates such an approach and the movement of students from one activity to another.

o·pen clus·ter ▶ n. Astronomy a relatively loose grouping of stars.

o·pen com·mun·ion ▶ n. Christian Church communion made available to any Christian believer.

o·pen date ▶ n. a future date for which no event has yet been arranged.

o·pen door ▶ n. [in sing.] free or unrestricted means of admission or access: [as modifier] *many companies encourage open-door management.* ■ the policy or practice by which a country does not restrict the admission of immigrants or foreign imports: [as modifier] *an open-door immigration policy.*

o·pen-end·ed (also **open-end**) ▶ adj. having no determined limit or boundary: *the return invitation was open-ended.* ■ (of a question) allowing the formulation of any answer, rather than a selection from a set of possible answers: *the interview includes both open-ended and multiple-choice questions.*
– DERIVATIVES **o·pen-end·ed·ness** n.

o·pen en·roll·ment ▶ n. **1** the unrestricted enrollment of students at schools, colleges, or universities of their choice.
2 a period during which a health insurance company or HMO is statutorily required to accept applicants without regard to health history. ■ such a period when employees can change insurance plans offered by their employer, without proof of insurability.

o·pen·er /ˈōp(ə)nər/ ▶ n. **1** [usu. with modifier] a device for opening something, esp. a container: *a bottle opener | a letter opener.*
2 the first of a series of games, cultural events, etc.: *the league opener is three weeks away.* ■ the first point or points scored in a sports event. ■ a remark used as an excuse to initiate a conversation: *we blurted out the obvious opener.* ■ (**openers**) Poker a hand of sufficient value to allow the opening of betting.
– PHRASES **for openers** informal to start with; first of all: *for openers, the car is roomier than the old model.*

o·pen-eyed ▶ adj. with the eyes open or wide open. ■ clear-sighted; perceptive; fully aware: *an open-eyed approach to political manipulation.*

o·pen-faced ▶ adj. **1** having a frank or ingenuous expression.
2 (of a watch) having no cover other than the glass. ■ (also **open-face**) (of a sandwich or pie) without an upper layer of bread or pastry.

o·pen-hand·ed /ˈōpənˈhandid/ ▶ adj. **1** (of a blow) delivered with the palm of the hand: *an openhanded slap to the side of the face.*
2 giving freely; generous: *openhanded philanthropy.*
– DERIVATIVES **o·pen·hand·ed·ly** adv., **o·pen·hand·ed·ness** n.

o·pen-heart·ed (also **openhearted**) ▶ adj. expressing or displaying one's warm and kindly feelings without concealment: *Betty's open-hearted goodwill.*
– DERIVATIVES **o·pen-heart·ed·ness** n.

o·pen-hearth ▶ adj. denoting a steelmaking process in which the charge is laid on a hearth in a shallow furnace and heated by burning gas.

o·pen-heart sur·ger·y ▶ n. surgery in which the heart is exposed and the blood made to bypass it.

o·pen house ▶ n. a place or situation in which all visitors are welcome: *they **kept open house**, entertaining a wide variety of artists and writers.* ■ a day when members of the public are invited to visit a place or institution, esp. one to which they do not normally have access: *the president spent all morning greeting thousands of visitors to a White House open house.* ■ an occasion when real estate offered for sale can be viewed by prospective buyers without an appointment.

o·pen·ing /ˈōp(ə)niNG/ ▶ n. **1** an aperture or gap, esp. one allowing access: *she peered through one of the smaller openings.*
2 a beginning; an initial part: *Maya started tapping out the opening of her story.* ■ the occasion of a play, exhibition, public building, etc. being declared open or ready for use, marked by a celebratory gathering or ceremony. ■ Chess a recognized sequence of moves at the beginning of a game. ■ an attorney's preliminary statement of a case in a court of law. ■ an open piece of ground in a wooded area; a clearing: *I reached an opening in the forest.*
3 an opportunity to achieve something: *they seem to have exploited fully the openings offered.* ■ an available job or position: *an opening for a professional engineer in the public works department.*
▶ adj. [attrib.] coming at the beginning of something; initial: *she stole the show with her opening remark.*

o·pen·ing night ▶ n. the first night of a theatrical play or other entertainment.

o·pen in·ter·est ▶ n. Finance the number of contracts or commitments outstanding in futures and options that are trading on an official exchange at any one time.

o·pen jaw ▶ adj. denoting or relating to a trip in which an airline passenger flies in to one destination and returns from another: *an open-jaw ticket for Washington-Chicago-Philly.*

o·pen let·ter ▶ n. a letter, often critical, addressed to a particular person or group of people but intended for publication.

o·pen line ▶ n. a means of easy access or communication: *to keep an open line to the White House.*
▶ adj. denoting a radio or television program in which the public can participate by telephone: *the open-line portion of his daily radio show.*

o·pen·ly /ˈōpənlē/ ▶ adv. without concealment, deception, or prevarication, esp. where these might be expected; frankly or honestly: *he could no longer speak openly of his problems.*
– ORIGIN Old English *openlīce* (see OPEN, -LY[2]).

o·pen mar·ket ▶ n. (often **the open market**) an unrestricted market with free access by and competition of buyers and sellers.

o·pen mar·riage (also **open relationship**) ▶ n. a marriage or relationship in which both partners agree that each may have sexual relations with others.

o·pen mike ▶ n. [often as modifier] a session in a club during which anyone is welcome to sing or perform stand-up comedy.

o·pen-mind·ed ▶ adj. willing to consider new ideas; unprejudiced.
– DERIVATIVES **o·pen-mind·ed·ly** adv., **o·pen-mind·ed·ness** n.

o·pen-mouthed ▶ adj. with the mouth open, as in surprise or excitement: *open-mouthed astonishment.*

o·pen-necked ▶ adj. (of a dress shirt) worn with the collar unbuttoned and without a tie.

o·pen out·cry ▶ n. a system of financial trading in which dealers shout their bids and contracts aloud.

o·pen-pit ▶ adj. denoting a method of mining in which coal or ore is extracted at or from a level near the earth's surface, rather than from underground workings.

o·pen-plan ▶ adj. (of a building or floor plan) having large open areas with few or no internal dividing walls: *an open-plan office.*

o·pen pri·ma·ry ▶ n. a primary election in which voters are not required to declare party affiliation.

o·pen ques·tion ▶ n. a matter on which differences of opinion are possible; a matter not yet decided.

o·pen range ▶ n. a large area of grazing land without fences or other barriers.

o·pen-reel ▶ adj. (of an audiotape recorder) having reels of tape requiring individual threading, as distinct from a cassette.

o·pen road ▶ n. a road or highway allowing easy travel, esp. one outside an urban area: *we hit the open road and raced along.*

o·pen sea ▶ n. (usu. **the open sea**) an expanse of sea away from land.

o·pen sea·son ▶ n. [in sing.] a period when restrictions on the hunting of certain types of wildlife are lifted. ■ a period when all restrictions on a particular activity or product are abandoned or ignored: *an hour before departure, it's open season on all remaining seats.*

o·pen se·cret ▶ n. a supposed secret that is in fact known to many people.

o·pen ses·a·me ▶ n. a free or unrestricted means of admission or access: *academic success is not an automatic open sesame to the job market.* [from the magic formula in the tale of Ali Baba and the Forty Thieves (see **Ali Baba**).]

o·pen shop ▶ n. a system whereby employees in a place of work are not required to join a labor union. Compare with **closed shop, union shop.** ■ a place of work following such a system.

o·pen so·ci·e·ty ▶ n. a society characterized by a flexible structure, freedom of belief, and wide dissemination of information.

o·pen-source ▶ adj. Computing denoting software for which the original source code is made freely available and may be redistributed and modified.

o·pen stock ▶ n. merchandise, esp. china, silverware, and glassware, that is sold in sets and kept in stock so that customers can purchase or replace individual pieces.

o·pen sys·tem ▶ n. **1** Computing a system in which the components and protocols conform to standards independent of a particular supplier.
2 Physics a material system in which mass or energy can be lost to or gained from the environment.

o·pen-toed ▶ adj. (of a shoe) having an upper that does not cover the toes.

o·pen ver·dict ▶ n. Law a verdict of a coroner's jury affirming the occurrence of a suspicious death but not specifying the cause.

o·pen·work /ˈōpənˌwərk/ ▶ n. [usu. as modifier] ornamental work in cloth, metal, leather, or other material with regular patterns of openings and holes.

o·pera¹ /ˈäp(ə)rə/ ▶ n. a dramatic work in one or more acts, set to music for singers and instrumentalists. ■ such works as a genre of classical music. ■ a building for the performance of opera.
– ORIGIN mid 17th cent.: from Italian, from Latin, literally 'labor, work.'

o·pe·ra² plural form of **opus**.

op·er·a·ble /ˈäp(ə)rəbəl/ ▶ adj. **1** able to be used: *the storm left only one operable voice channel.*
2 able to be treated by means of a surgical operation: *operable breast cancer.*
– DERIVATIVES **op·er·a·bil·i·ty** /ˌäp(ə)rəˈbilitē/ n.
– ORIGIN mid 17th cent.: from late Latin *operabilis*, from Latin *operari* 'expend labor on' (see **operate**).

o·pé·ra bouffe /ˈäp(ə)rə ˈbo͞of, ˌôpärä/ ▶ n. (pl. **opéras bouffes** pronunc. **same**) a French comic opera, with dialogue in recitative and characters drawn from everyday life. ■ such works as a genre.
– ORIGIN French, from Italian (see **opera buffa**).

o·pe·ra buf·fa /ˈäp(ə)rə ˈbo͞ofə, ˌôperä ˈbo͞ofä/ ▶ n. a comic opera, typically in Italian, esp. one with characters drawn from everyday life. ■ such works as a genre.
– ORIGIN Italian.

o·pe·ra cloak ▶ n. a cloak of rich material worn over evening clothes, esp. by women.

o·pé·ra co·mique /ˈäp(ə)rə käˈmēk, ˌôpärä kôˈmēk/ ▶ n. an opera on a lighthearted theme, typically in French and with spoken dialogue. ■ such works as a genre.

op·er·a glass·es (or **opera glass**) ▶ plural n. small binoculars for use at the opera or theater.

op·er·a·go·er /ˈäp(ə)rəˌgōər/ ▶ n. one who attends opera performances.

op·er·a hat ▶ n. a collapsible top hat.

op·er·a house ▶ n. a theater designed for the performance of opera.

op·er·and /ˈäpəˌrand/ ▶ n. Mathematics the quantity on which an operation is to be done.
– ORIGIN late 19th cent.: from Latin *operandum*, neuter gerundive of *operari* 'expend labor on' (see **operate**).

op·er·ant /ˈäpərənt/ Psychology ▶ adj. involving the modification of behavior by the reinforcing or inhibiting effect of its own consequences (instrumental conditioning).
▶ n. an item of behavior that is initially spontaneous, rather than a response to a prior stimulus, but whose consequences may reinforce or inhibit recurrence of that behavior.
– ORIGIN late Middle English: from Latin *operant-* 'being at work,' from the verb *operari*.

op·er·a queen ▶ n. informal a male homosexual who is fanatical about opera, esp. one characterized as being affectedly haughty and overrefined.

o·pe·ra se·ri·a /ˈäp(ə)rə ˈsi(ə)rēə, ˈôpeˌrä ˈserēˌä/ ▶ n. an opera, typically one of the 18th century in Italian, on a serious, usually classical or mythological theme. ■ such works as a genre.
– ORIGIN Italian, literally 'serious opera.'

op·er·ate /ˈäpəˌrāt/ ▶ v. **1** [with obj.] (of a person) control the functioning of (a machine, process, or system): *a shortage of workers to operate new machines.* ■ [no obj.] (of a machine, process, or system) function in a specified manner: *market forces were allowed to operate freely.* ■ [no obj.] be in effect: *there is a powerful law that operates in politics.* ■ (of a person or organization) manage and run (a business): *many foreign companies operate factories in the U.S.* ■ [no obj.] (of an organization) be managed and run in a specified way: *neither company had operated within the terms of its charter.* ■ [no obj.] (of an armed force) conduct military activities in a specified area or from a specified base: *the mountain bases from which the guerrillas were operating.*
2 [no obj.] perform a surgical operation: *the surgeons refused to operate | my brother had to be **operated on** last week.*
– ORIGIN early 17th cent.: from Latin *operat-* 'done by labor,' from the verb *operari*, from *opus, oper-* 'work.'

op·er·at·ic /ˌäpəˈratik/ ▶ adj. of, relating to, or characteristic of opera: *operatic arias.* ■ extravagantly theatrical; overly dramatic: *she wrung her hands in operatic despair.*
– DERIVATIVES **op·er·at·i·cal·ly** /-ik(ə)lē/ adv.
– ORIGIN mid 18th cent.: formed irregularly from **opera¹**, on the pattern of words such as *dramatic*.

op·er·at·ics /ˌäpəˈratiks/ ▶ plural n. [often treated as sing.] the production or performance of operas. ■ theatrically exaggerated or overemotional behavior.

op·er·at·ing prof·it ▶ n. profit from business operations (gross profit less operating expenses) before deduction of fixed costs.

op·er·at·ing room (abbr.: **OR**) (Brit. **operating theatre**) ▶ n. a room in a hospital specially equipped for surgical operations.

op·er·at·ing sys·tem ▶ n. the software that supports a computer's basic functions, such as scheduling tasks, executing applications, and controlling peripherals.

op·er·a·tion /ˌäpəˈrāsʜən/ ▶ n. **1** the fact or condition of functioning or being active: *the construction and operation of power stations | some of these ideas could be **put into operation**.* ■ an active process; a discharge of a function: *the operations of the mind.* ■ a business organization; a company: *he reopened his operation under a different name.* ■ an activity in which such an organization is involved: *the company is selling most of its commercial banking operations.*
2 an act of surgery performed on a patient.
3 [often with modifier] a piece of organized and concerted activity involving a number of people, esp. members of the armed forces or the police: *a rescue operation | military operations.* ■ (**Operation**) preceding a code name for such an activity: *Operation Desert Storm.*
4 Mathematics a process in which a number, quantity, expression, etc., is altered or manipulated according to formal rules, such as those of addition, multiplication, and differentiation.
– ORIGIN late Middle English: via Old French from Latin *operatio(n-)*, from the verb *operari* 'expend labor on' (see **operate**).

op·er·a·tion·al /ˌäpəˈrāsʜənl/ ▶ adj. in or ready for use: *the new laboratory is fully operational.* ■ of or relating to the routine functioning and activities of a business or organization: *the coffee bar's initial operational costs.* ■ engaged in or relating to active operations of the armed forces, police, or emergency services: *an operational fighter squadron.*
– DERIVATIVES **op·er·a·tion·al·ly** adv.

op·er·a·tion·al am·pli·fi·er (abbr.: **op-amp**) ▶ n. Electronics an amplifier with high gain and high input impedance (usually with external feedback), used esp. in circuits for performing mathematical operations on an input voltage.

op·er·a·tion·al·ism /äpəˈrāsʜənlˌizəm/ ▶ n. (also **operationism**) Philosophy a form of positivism that defines scientific concepts in terms of the operations used to determine or prove them.
– DERIVATIVES **op·er·a·tion·al·ist** n. & adj.

op·er·a·tion·al·ize /ˌäpəˈrāsʜənlˌīz/ ▶ v. [with obj.] **1** put into operation or use.
2 Philosophy express or define (something) in terms of the operations used to determine or prove it.

op·er·a·tions re·search ▶ n. the application of scientific principles to business management, providing a quantitative basis for complex decisions.

op·er·a·tive /ˈäp(ə)rətiv, ˈäpəˌrātiv/ ▶ adj. **1** functioning; having effect: *the transmitter is operative | the mining ban would remain operative.* ■ [attrib.] (of a word) having the most relevance or significance in a phrase or sentence: *a young man, and the operative word is young, should go into the armed services at around seventeen.*
2 [attrib.] of or relating to surgery: *they had wounds needing operative treatment.*
▶ n. a worker, esp. a skilled one in a manufacturing industry. ■ a private detective or secret agent.
– DERIVATIVES **op·er·a·tive·ly** adv., **op·er·a·tive·ness** n.
– ORIGIN late Middle English: from late Latin *operativus*, from Latin *operat-* 'done by labor,' from the verb *operari* (see **operate**).

op·er·a·tor /ˈäpəˌrātər/ ▶ n. **1** [often with modifier] a person who operates equipment or a machine: *a radio operator.* ■ (usu. **the operator**) a person who works for a telephone company assisting users, or who works at a telephone switchboard.
2 [usu. with modifier] a person or company that engages in or runs a business or enterprise: *a tour operator.*
3 [with adj.] informal a person who acts in a specified, esp. a manipulative, way: *her reputation as a cool, clever operator.*
4 Mathematics a symbol or function denoting an operation (e.g., ×, +).

op·er·a win·dow ▶ n. a small fixed window usually behind the rear side window of an automobile.

o·per·cu·lum /ōˈpərkyələm/ ▶ n. (pl. **opercula** /-lə/) Zoology & Botany a structure that closes or covers an aperture, in particular: ■ technical term for **gill cover**. ■ a secreted plate that serves to close the aperture of a gastropod mollusk's shell when the animal is retracted. ■ a lidlike structure of the spore-containing capsule of a moss.
– DERIVATIVES **o·per·cu·lar** /-lər/ adj., **o·per·cu·late** /-ˌlāt/ adj., **o·per·cu·li-** comb. form.
– ORIGIN early 18th cent.: from Latin, literally 'lid, covering,' from *operire* 'to cover.'

op·er·et·ta /ˌäpəˈretə/ ▶ n. a short opera, usually on a light or humorous theme and typically having spoken dialogue. Notable composers of operettas include Offenbach, Johann Strauss, Lehár, and Gilbert and Sullivan.
– ORIGIN late 18th cent.: from Italian, diminutive of *opera* (see **opera¹**).

op·er·on /ˈäpəˌrän/ ▶ n. Biology a unit made up of linked genes that is thought to regulate other genes responsible for protein synthesis.
– ORIGIN 1960s: from French *opérer* 'to effect, work' + **-on**.

op·er·ose /ˈäpəˌrōs/ ▶ adj. rare involving or displaying much industry or effort.
– ORIGIN late 17th cent.: from Latin *operosus*, from *opus* 'work.'

oph·i·cleide /ˈäfiˌklīd/ ▶ n. an obsolete bass brass instrument with keys, used in bands in the 19th century but superseded by the tuba.
– ORIGIN mid 19th cent.: from French *ophicléide*, from Greek *ophis* 'serpent' + *kleis, kleid-* 'key.'

O

O·phid·i·a /ōˈfidēə/ Zoology a group of reptiles that comprises the snakes. Also called **Serpentes**. ● Suborder Ophidia, order Squamata.
– ORIGIN modern Latin (plural), from Greek *ophis, ophid-* 'snake.'

o·phid·i·an /ōˈfidēən/ Zoology ▶ **n.** a reptile of the group Ophidia; a snake.
▶ **adj.** relating to or denoting snakes.

oph·i·o·lite /ˈäfēəˌlīt, ˈōfē-/ ▶ **n.** Geology an igneous rock consisting largely of serpentine, believed to have been formed from the submarine eruption of oceanic crustal and upper mantle material.
– DERIVATIVES **oph·i·o·lit·ic** /ˌäfēəˈlitik, ˌōfē-/ **adj.**
– ORIGIN mid 19th cent.: from Greek *ophis* 'snake' + **-LITE**.

oph·i·ol·o·gy /ˌäfēˈäləjē, ˌōfē-/ ▶ **n.** the branch of zoology that deals with snakes.
– DERIVATIVES **oph·i·ol·o·gist** /-jist/ **n.**
– ORIGIN early 19th cent.: from Greek *ophis* 'snake' + **-LOGY**.

O·phir /ˈōfər/ (in the Bible) an unidentified region, perhaps in southeastern Arabia, famous for its fine gold and precious stones.

oph·ite /ˈäfīt, ˈōfīt/ ▶ **n.** Geology a green rock with spots or markings like a snake that can be either eruptive or metamorphic; serpentine.
– ORIGIN mid 17th cent.: via Latin from Greek *ophitēs* 'serpentine stone,' from *ophis* 'snake,' + **-ITE**[1].

o·phit·ic /ōˈfitik/ ▶ **adj.** Geology relating to or denoting a poikilitic rock texture in which crystals of feldspar are interposed between plates of augite.
– ORIGIN late 19th cent.: via Latin from Greek *ophitēs* 'serpentine stone' (from *ophis* 'snake') + **-IC**.

Oph·i·u·chus /ˌäf(ē)ˈyo͞okəs, ˌōf(ē)-/ Astronomy a large constellation (the Serpent Bearer or Holder), said to represent a man in the coils of a snake. Both the celestial equator and the ecliptic pass through it, but it is not counted among the signs of the zodiac. ■ (as genitive **Ophiuchi** /ˌäf(ē)ˈyo͞okī, ˌōf(ē)-/) used with a preceding letter or numeral to designate a star in this constellation: *the star Eta Ophiuchi.*
– ORIGIN via Latin from Greek *Ophioukos.*

oph·i·ur·oid /ˌäfēˈyo͝oroid/ Zoology ▶ **n.** an echinoderm of the class Ophiuroidea, which comprises the brittlestars.
▶ **adj.** relating to or denoting ophiuroids.

Oph·i·u·roi·de·a /ˌäfēyo͝oroidēə, ˌōfē-/ Zoology a class of echinoderms that comprises the brittle stars.
– ORIGIN modern Latin (plural), based on the genus name *Ophiura*, from Greek *ophis* 'snake' + *oura* 'tail.'

oph·thal·mi·a /äfˈTHalmēə, äp-/ ▶ **n.** Medicine inflammation of the eye, esp. conjunctivitis.
– ORIGIN late Middle English: via late Latin from Greek, from *ophthalmos* 'eye.'

oph·thal·mic /äfˈTHalmik, äp-/ ▶ **adj.** [attrib.] of or relating to the eye and its diseases.
– ORIGIN early 17th cent.: via Latin from Greek *ophthalmikos*, from *ophthalmos* 'eye.'

oph·thal·mi·tis /ˌäfTHəlˈmīdis, ˌäp-/ ▶ **n.** Medicine inflammation of the eye.

ophthalmo- ▶ **comb. form** Medicine relating to the eyes: *ophthalmoscope.*
– ORIGIN from Greek *ophthalmos* 'eye.'

oph·thal·mol·o·gy /ˌäfTHə(l)ˈmäləjē, ˌäp-/ ▶ **n.** the branch of medicine concerned with the study and treatment of disorders and diseases of the eye.
– DERIVATIVES **oph·thal·mo·log·i·cal** /-məˈläjikəl/ **adj.**, **oph·thal·mol·o·gist** /-jist/ **n.**

oph·thal·mo·ple·gia /äfˌTHalməˈplēj(ē)ə/ ▶ **n.** Medicine paralysis of the muscles within or surrounding the eye.
– DERIVATIVES **oph·thal·mo·ple·gic** /-ˈplējik/ **adj.**

oph·thal·mo·scope /äfˈTHalməˌskōp, äp-/ ▶ **n.** an instrument for inspecting the retina and other parts of the eye.
– DERIVATIVES **oph·thal·mo·scop·ic** /ˌäfTHalməˈskäpik, ˌäp-/ **adj.**, **oph·thal·mos·co·py** /ˌäfTHəlˈmäskəpē, ˌäp-/ **n.**

-opia ▶ **comb. form** denoting a visual disorder: *myopia.*
– ORIGIN from Greek *ōps, ōp-* 'eye, face.'

o·pi·ate ▶ **adj.** /ˈōpē-it, -ˌāt/ relating to, resembling, or containing opium: *the use of opiate drugs.*
▶ **n.** /ˈōpē-it, -ˌāt/ a drug with morphinelike effects, derived from opium. ■ a thing that soothes or stupefies.
▶ **v.** /-ˌāt/ [with obj.] (often as adj. **opiated**) impregnate with opium.
– PHRASES **the opiate of the masses** (or **people**) something regarded as inducing a false and unrealistic sense of contentment among people. [translating the German phrase *Opium des Volks*, used by Karl Marx in reference to religion (1844).]
– ORIGIN late Middle English (as a noun): from medieval Latin *opiatus* (adjective), *opiatus* (noun), based on Latin *opium* (see **OPIUM**).

o·pine /ōˈpīn/ ▶ **v.** [reporting verb] formal hold and state as one's opinion: [with direct speech] *"The man is a genius," he opined* | [with clause] *the critic opined that the most exciting musical moment occurred when the orchestra struck up the national anthem.*
– ORIGIN late Middle English: from Latin *opinari* 'think, believe.'

o·pin·ion /əˈpinyən/ ▶ **n.** a view or judgment formed about something, not necessarily based on fact or knowledge: *I'm writing to voice my opinion on an issue of great importance* | *that, in my opinion, is dead right.* ■ the beliefs or views of a large number or majority of people about a particular thing: *the changing climate of opinion.* ■ (**opinion of**) an estimation of the quality or worth of someone or something: *I had a higher opinion of myself than I deserved.* ■ a formal statement of advice by an expert on a professional matter: *seeking a second opinion from a specialist.* ■ Law a formal statement of reasons for a judgment given. ■ Law a lawyer's advice on the merits of a case.
– PHRASES **be of the opinion that** believe or maintain that: *economists are of the opinion that the economy could contract.* **a matter of opinion** something not capable of being proven either way.
– ORIGIN Middle English: via Old French from Latin *opinio(n-)*, from the stem of *opinari* 'think, believe.'

o·pin·ion·at·ed /əˈpinyəˌnātid/ ▶ **adj.** conceitedly assertive and dogmatic in one's opinions: *an arrogant and opinionated man.*
– ORIGIN early 17th cent.: from the (rare) verb *opinionate* 'hold the opinion (that),' from **OPINION**.

o·pin·ion poll ▶ **n.** an assessment of public opinion obtained by questioning a representative sample.

o·pi·oid /ˈōpēˌoid/ Biochemistry ▶ **n.** an opiumlike compound that binds to one or more of the three opioid receptors of the body.
▶ **adj.** relating to or denoting such compounds.
– ORIGIN 1950s: from **OPIUM** + **-OID**.

opistho- ▶ **prefix** behind; to the rear: *opisthosoma.*
– ORIGIN from Greek *opisthen* 'behind.'

O·pis·tho·bran·chi·a /əˌpisTHəˈbraNGkēə/ Zoology a group of mollusks that includes the sea slugs and sea hares. They have a small or absent shell and are typically brightly colored with conspicuous external gills. ● Subclass Opisthobranchia, class Gastropoda.
– DERIVATIVES **o·pis·tho·branch** /əˈpisTHəˌbraNGk/ **n.**
– ORIGIN modern Latin (plural), from **OPISTHO-** 'to the rear' + *brankhia* 'gills.'

op·is·thog·na·thous /äpisˈTHägnəTHəs/ ▶ **adj.** Zoology (of an animal) having retreating jaws or teeth.

op·is·thot·o·nos /ˌäpisˈTHätnəs/ (also **opisthotonus**) ▶ **n.** Medicine spasm of the muscles causing backward arching of the head, neck, and spine, as in severe tetanus, some kinds of meningitis, and strychnine poisoning.
– ORIGIN mid 17th cent.: via late Latin from Greek *opisthotonos* 'drawn backward.'

o·pi·um /ˈōpēəm/ ▶ **n.** a reddish-brown heavy-scented addictive drug prepared from the juice of the opium poppy, used as a narcotic and in medicine as an analgesic.
– PHRASES **the opium of the people** (or **masses**) see **THE OPIATE OF THE MASSES** at **OPIATE**.
– ORIGIN late Middle English: via Latin from Greek *opion* 'poppy juice,' from *opos* 'juice,' from an Indo-European root meaning 'water.'

o·pi·um den ▶ **n.** a place where opium is sold and smoked.

o·pi·um pop·py ▶ **n.** a Eurasian poppy with ornamental white, red, pink, or purple flowers. Its immature capsules yield a latex from which opium is obtained. ● *Papaver somniferum*, family Papaveraceae.

O·pi·um Wars two wars involving Britain and China regarding the question of trading rights.

> That between Britain and China (1839–42) followed China's attempt to prohibit the illegal importation of opium from British India into China. The second, involving Britain and France against China (1856–60), followed Chinese restrictions on foreign trade. Defeat of the Chinese resulted in the ceding of Hong Kong to Britain and the opening of five "treaty ports" to traders.

OPM ▶ **abbr.** informal other people's money.

O·por·to /ōˈpôrtō/ the principal city and port of northern Portugal, near the mouth of the Douro River, known for port wine; pop. 221,800 (2007). Portuguese name **Porto**.

o·pos·sum /(ə)ˈpäsəm/ ▶ **n.** an American marsupial that has a ratlike prehensile tail and hind feet with an opposable thumb. ● Family Didelphidae: several genera and numerous species, in particular the cat-sized **common opossum** (*Didelphis marsupialis*) of North, Central, and South America, which in North America was formerly known as the **Virginia opossum** and was considered a distinct species (*D. virginiana*).
– ORIGIN early 17th cent.: from Virginia Algonquian *opassom*, from *op* 'white' + *assom* 'dog.'

common opossum

o·pos·sum shrimp ▶ **n.** a small shrimplike crustacean that has a long abdomen and conspicuous eyes, and that is typically transparent. ● Order Mysidacea: *Praunus* and other genera. See also **MYSID**.

opp. ▶ **abbr.** opposite.

Op·pen·heim·er /ˈäpənˌhīmər/, Julius Robert (1904–67), US theoretical physicist. He was director of the laboratory at Los Alamos, New Mexico, during the development of the first atom bomb, but opposed the development of the hydrogen bomb after World War II.

op·po·nens /əˈpōnənz/ ▶ **n.** Anatomy another term for **OPPONENT MUSCLE**.
– ORIGIN late 18th cent.: from Latin, literally 'setting against.'

op·po·nent /əˈpōnənt/ ▶ **n.** someone who competes against or fights another in a contest, game, or argument; a rival or adversary: *he beat his opponent by a landslide margin.* ■ a person who disagrees with or resists a proposal or practice: *an opponent of the economic reforms.*
– ORIGIN late 16th cent. (denoting a person opening an academic debate by proposing objections to a philosophical or religious thesis): from Latin *opponent-* 'setting against,' from the verb *opponere*, from *ob-* 'against' + *ponere* 'place.'

op·po·nent mus·cle ▶ **n.** Anatomy any of several muscles enabling the thumb to be moved toward a finger of the same hand.

op·por·tune /ˌäpərˈt(y)o͞on/ ▶ **adj.** (of a time) well-chosen or particularly favorable or appropriate: *he couldn't have arrived at a less opportune moment.* ■ done or occurring at a favorable or useful time; well-timed: *the opportune use of humor to lower tension.*
– DERIVATIVES **op·por·tune·ly adv.**, **op·por·tune·ness n.**
– ORIGIN late Middle English: from Old French *opportun(e)*, from Latin *opportunus*, from *ob-* 'in the direction of' + *portus* 'harbor,' originally describing the wind driving toward the harbor, hence 'seasonable.'

op·por·tun·ism /ˌäpərˈt(y)o͞onizəm/ ▶ **n.** the taking of opportunities as and when they arise, regardless of planning or principle: *he was accused of political opportunism.*

op·por·tun·ist /ˌäpərˈt(y)o͞onist/ ▶ **n.** a person who exploits circumstances to gain immediate advantage rather than being guided by consistent principles or plans: *most burglaries are committed by casual opportunists.*
▶ **adj.** opportunistic: *the calculating and opportunist politician.*
– ORIGIN late 19th cent.: from **OPPORTUNE** + **-IST**.

op·por·tun·is·tic /ˌäpərt(y)o͞oˈnistik/ ▶ **adj.** exploiting chances offered by immediate circumstances without reference to a general plan or moral principle: *the change was cynical and opportunistic.* ■ Ecology (of a plant or animal) able to spread quickly in a previously unexploited habitat. ■ Medicine (of a microorganism or an infection caused by it) rarely affecting patients except in unusual circumstances, typically when the immune system is depressed.
– DERIVATIVES **op·por·tun·is·ti·cal·ly** /-ik(ə)lē/ **adv.**

op·por·tu·ni·ty /ˌäpərˈt(y)o͞onitē/ ▶ **n.** (pl. **opportunities**) a set of circumstances that makes it possible to do something: *we may see increased opportunities for export* | *the collection gives students the opportunity of reading works by well-known authors.* ■ a chance for employment or promotion: *career opportunities in our New York headquarters.*
– PHRASES **opportunity knocks** a chance for success or advancement occurs.

– ORIGIN late Middle English: from Old French *opportunite*, from Latin *opportunitas*, from *opportunus* (see OPPORTUNE).

op·por·tu·ni·ty cost ▶ n. Economics the loss of potential gain from other alternatives when one alternative is chosen: *idle cash balances represent an opportunity cost in terms of lost interest.*

op·pos·a·ble /əˈpōzəbəl/ ▶ adj. Zoology (of the thumb of a primate) capable of moving toward and touching the other digits on the same hand.

op·pose /əˈpōz/ ▶ v. [with obj.] disapprove of and attempt to prevent, esp. by argument: *those of you who oppose capital punishment.* ■ actively resist or refuse to comply with (a person or a system): *off-roaders who adamantly opposed new trail restrictions.* ■ compete against (someone) in a contest: *a candidate to oppose the leader in the presidential contest.*
– DERIVATIVES **op·pos·er** n.
– ORIGIN late Middle English: from Old French *opposer*, from Latin *opponere* (see OPPONENT), but influenced by Latin *oppositus* 'set or placed against' and Old French *poser* 'to place.'

op·posed /əˈpōzd/ ▶ adj. **1** [predic.] (**opposed to**) eager to prevent or put an end to; disapproving of or disagreeing with: *opposed to the construction of nuclear power plants.* ■ in conflict or disagreement with; hostile to: *most critics were opposed to the work.*
2 (of two or more things) contrasting or conflicting with each other: *the agency is being asked to do two **diametrically opposed** things.*
– PHRASES **as opposed to** distinguished from or in contrast with: *an approach that is theoretical as opposed to practical.*

op·pos·ing /əˈpōziNG/ ▶ adj. [attrib.] in conflict or competition with a specified or implied subject: *the opposing team.* ■ (of two or more subjects) differing from or in conflict with each other: *the brothers fought on opposing sides in the war.* ■ facing; opposite: *on the opposing page there were two addresses.*

op·po·site /ˈäpəzit/ ▶ adj. **1** [attrib.] having a position on the other or further side of something; facing something, esp. something of the same type: *a crowd gathered on the opposite side of the street.* ■ [postpositive] facing the speaker or a specified person or thing: *he went into the store opposite.* ■ Botany (of leaves or shoots) arising in opposed pairs, one on each side of the stem.
2 diametrically different; of a contrary kind: *a word that is **opposite** in meaning **to** another | currents flowing in **opposite directions**.* ■ [attrib.] being the other of a contrasted pair: *the opposite ends of the price range.*
▶ n. a person or thing that is totally different from or the reverse of someone or something else: *we were **opposites** in temperament | the literal is **the opposite of** the figurative.*
▶ adv. in a position facing a specified or implied subject: *she was sitting almost opposite.*
▶ prep. **1** in a position on the other side of a specific area from; facing: *they sat opposite one another.*
2 (of a leading actor) in a complementary role to (another performer).
– DERIVATIVES **op·po·site·ly** adv., **op·po·site·ness** n.
– PHRASES **opposites attract** used to explain the phenomenon of dissimilar people taking a strong or romantic interest in each other: *Clearly, opposites attract, but fortunately, the film doesn't follow typical romantic movie conventions | would such opposites attract, or would these two conflicting musical spirits lock horns and fight it out?*
– ORIGIN late Middle English: via Old French from Latin *oppositus*, past participle of *opponere* 'set against.'

op·po·site num·ber ▶ n. (**someone's opposite number**) a person whose position or rank in another group, organization, or country is equivalent to that held by someone already mentioned.

op·po·site prompt ▶ n. Brit. the offstage area of a theater stage to the right of an actor facing the audience.

op·po·site sex ▶ n. women in relation to men or vice versa.

op·po·si·tion /ˌäpəˈzisHən/ ▶ n. resistance or dissent, expressed in action or argument: *there was considerable **opposition to** the proposal | the regime cracked down against the threat of opposition.* ■ (often **the opposition**) a group of adversaries or competitors, esp. a rival political party or athletic team. ■ (**the opposition**) the principal political party opposed to the one in office. ■ a contrast or antithesis: *a nature-culture opposition.* ■ Logic (of two propositions) the relation of having the same subject and predicate, but differing in quantity, quality, or both. ■ Astronomy & Astrology the apparent position of two celestial objects that are directly opposite each other in the sky, esp. when a superior planet is opposite the sun.
– PHRASES **in opposition** in contrast or conflict: *they found themselves **in opposition to** federal policy.*
– DERIVATIVES **op·po·si·tion·al** /-sHənl/ adj.
– ORIGIN late Middle English: from Latin *oppositio(n-)*, from *opponere* 'set against.'

op·press /əˈpres/ ▶ v. [with obj.] keep (someone) in subservience and hardship, esp. by the unjust exercise of authority: *a system that oppressed working people.* ■ cause (someone) to feel distressed, anxious, or uncomfortable: *he was oppressed by some secret worry.*
– ORIGIN late Middle English: from Old French *oppresser*, from medieval Latin *oppressare*, from Latin *oppress-* 'pressed against,' from the verb *opprimere*.

op·pressed /əˈprest/ ▶ adj. subject to harsh and authoritarian treatment: *oppressed racial minorities* | (as plural noun **the oppressed**) *his sympathies were with the oppressed.*

op·pres·sion /əˈpresHən/ ▶ n. prolonged cruel or unjust treatment or control: *a region shattered by oppression and killing.* ■ the state of being subject to such treatment or control. ■ mental pressure or distress: *her mood had initially been alarm and a sense of oppression.*
– ORIGIN Middle English: from Old French, from Latin *oppressio(n-)*, from the verb *opprimere* (see OPPRESS).

op·pres·sive /əˈpresiv/ ▶ adj. unjustly inflicting hardship and constraint, esp. on a minority or other subordinate group: *an oppressive dictatorship.* ■ weighing heavily on the mind or spirits; causing depression or discomfort: *a profound loneliness, an oppressive emptiness.* ■ (of weather) excessively hot and humid.
– DERIVATIVES **op·pres·sive·ly** adv., **op·pres·sive·ness** n.
– ORIGIN late 16th cent.: from medieval Latin *oppressivus*, from Latin *oppress-* 'pressed against,' from the verb *opprimere* (see OPPRESS).

op·pres·sor /əˈpresər/ ▶ n. a person or group that oppresses people: *they overthrew their colonial oppressors.*

op·pro·bri·ous /əˈprōbrēəs/ ▶ adj. (of language) expressing opprobrium.
– DERIVATIVES **op·pro·bri·ous·ly** adv.
– ORIGIN late Middle English: from late Latin *opprobriosus*, from *opprobrium* (see OPPROBRIUM).

op·pro·bri·um /əˈprōbrēəm/ ▶ n. harsh criticism or censure: *his films and the critical opprobrium they have generated.* ■ the public disgrace arising from someone's shameful conduct: *the opprobrium of being closely associated with thugs and gangsters.* ■ archaic an occasion or cause of reproach or disgrace.
– ORIGIN mid 17th cent.: from Latin, literally 'infamy,' from *opprobrum*, from *ob-* 'against' + *probrum* 'disgraceful act.'

op·pugn /əˈpyo͞on/ ▶ v. [with obj.] rare call into question the truth or validity of.
– DERIVATIVES **op·pugn·er** n.
– ORIGIN late Middle English (in the sense 'fight against'): from Latin *oppugnare* 'attack, besiege,' from *ob-* 'against' + *pugnare* 'to fight.'

op·pug·nant /əˈpəgnənt/ ▶ adj. rare opposing; antagonistic.
– DERIVATIVES **op·pug·nan·cy** /-nənsē/ n.
– ORIGIN early 16th cent.: from Latin *oppugnant-* 'fighting against,' from the verb *oppugnare* (see OPPUGN).

OP·SEC ▶ abbr. operations (or operational) security.

op·si·math /ˈäpsəˌmaTH/ ▶ n. a person who begins to learn or study only late in life.
– ORIGIN late 19th cent.: from Greek *opsimathēs*, from *opse* 'late' + the stem *math-* 'learn.'

op·sin /ˈäpsin/ ▶ n. Biochemistry a protein that forms part of the visual pigment rhodopsin and is released by the action of light.
– ORIGIN 1950s: shortening of RHODOPSIN.

op·so·nin /ˈäpsənin/ ▶ n. Biochemistry an antibody or other substance that binds to foreign microorganisms or cells, making them more susceptible to phagocytosis.
– DERIVATIVES **op·son·ic** /äpˈsänik/ adj.
– ORIGIN early 20th cent.: from Latin *opsonare* 'buy provisions' (from Greek *opsōnein*) + -IN¹.

op·so·nize /ˈäpsəˌnīz/ ▶ v. [with obj.] Medicine make (a foreign cell) more susceptible to phagocytosis.
– DERIVATIVES **op·so·ni·za·tion** /ˌäpsəˌniˈzāsHən/ n.

opt /äpt/ ▶ v. [no obj.] make a choice from a range of possibilities: *consumers will **opt for** low-priced goods* | [with infinitive] *students opting to continue with physics.*
– PHRASAL VERBS **opt out** choose not to participate in or carry on with something: *they had both opted out of the medical plan.*
– ORIGIN late 19th cent.: from French *opter*, from Latin *optare* 'choose, wish.'

opt. ▶ abbr. ■ optative. ■ optical. ■ optician. ■ optics. ■ optional.

op·ta·tive /ˈäptətiv/ Grammar ▶ adj. relating to or denoting a mood of verbs in Greek and other languages, expressing a wish, equivalent to English expressions *if only*.
▶ n. a verb in the optative mood. ■ (**the optative**) the optative mood.
– DERIVATIVES **op·ta·tive·ly** adv.
– ORIGIN mid 16th cent.: from French *optatif, -ive*, from late Latin *optativus*, from *optat-* 'chosen,' from the verb *optare* (see OPT).

op·tic /ˈäptik/ ▶ adj. of or relating to the eye or vision.
▶ n. **1** a lens or other optical component in an optical instrument.
2 archaic or humorous the eye.
– ORIGIN late Middle English: from French *optique* or medieval Latin *opticus*, from Greek *optikos*, from *optos* 'seen.'

op·ti·cal /ˈäptikəl/ ▶ adj. **1** of or relating to sight, esp. in relation to the physical action of light: *optical illusions.* ■ constructed to assist sight. ■ devised on the principles of optics.
2 Physics operating in or employing the visible part of the electromagnetic spectrum: *optical telescopes.* ■ Electronics (of a device) requiring electromagnetic radiation for its operation: *integrated optical circuits.*
– DERIVATIVES **op·ti·cal·ly** /-ik(ə)lē/ adv.

op·ti·cal ac·tiv·i·ty ▶ n. Chemistry the property (displayed by solutions of some compounds, notably many sugars) of rotating the plane of polarization of plane-polarized light.

op·ti·cal art ▶ n. another term for OP ART.

op·ti·cal ax·is ▶ n. Physics a line passing through the center of curvature of a lens or spherical mirror and parallel to the axis of symmetry. ■ Crystallography a direction in a doubly refracting crystal along which a light ray does not undergo double refraction.

op·ti·cal bench ▶ n. a straight rigid bar, typically marked with a scale, to which lenses, light sources, and other optical components can be attached.

op·ti·cal bright·en·er ▶ n. a fluorescent substance added to detergents in order to produce a whitening effect on laundry.

op·ti·cal char·ac·ter rec·og·ni·tion (abbr.: **OCR**) ▶ n. the identification of printed characters using photoelectric devices and computer software.

op·ti·cal den·si·ty ▶ n. Physics the degree to which a refractive medium retards transmitted rays of light.

op·ti·cal disk ▶ n. see DISK (sense 1 of the noun).

op·ti·cal dou·ble ▶ n. Astronomy two stars that are in the same line of sight as seen from the earth, but that may be at far different distances. See also DOUBLE STAR.

op·ti·cal fi·ber ▶ n. a thin glass fiber through which light can be transmitted.

op·ti·cal glass ▶ n. a very pure kind of glass used for lenses.

op·ti·cal il·lu·sion ▶ n. an experience of seeming to see something that does not exist or that is other than it appears. ■ something that deceives one's eyes and causes such an experience.

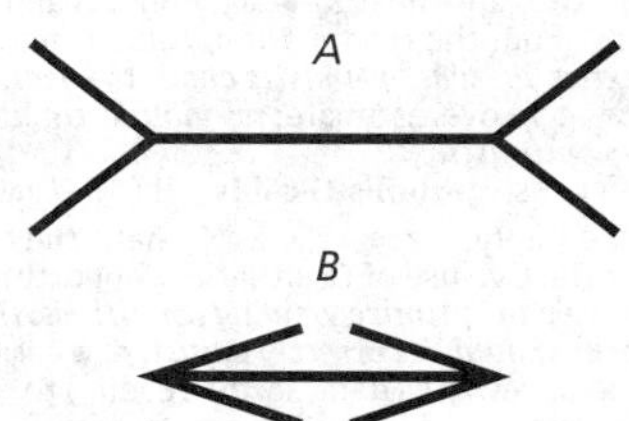

(horizontal line *A* appears to be longer than horizontal line *B*, but in fact, they are of equal length)

optical illusion

op·ti·cal i·so·mer ▶ n. Chemistry each of two or more forms of a compound that have the same structure but are mirror images of each other and typically differ in optical activity.
– DERIVATIVES **op·ti·cal i·som·er·ism** n.

PRONUNCIATION KEY ə *ago, up*; ər *over, fur*; a *hat*; ā *ate*; ä *car*; e *let*; ē *see*; i *fit*; ī *by*; NG *sing*; ō *go*; ô *law, for*; oi *toy*; o͝o *good*; o͞o *goo*; ou *out*; TH *thin*; T͟H *then*; ZH *vision*

O

op·ti·cal mi·cro·scope ▶ n. a microscope using visible light, typically viewed directly by the eye.

op·ti·cal path ▶ n. Physics the distance of the path that in a vacuum would contain the same number of wavelengths as the actual path taken by a ray of light traveling through a medium.

op·ti·cal ro·ta·tion ▶ n. Chemistry the rotation of the plane of polarization of plane-polarized light by an optically active substance.

op·ti·cal scan·ner ▶ n. Electronics a device that performs optical character recognition and produces coded signals corresponding to the characters identified.

op·ti·cal turn·stile ▶ n. an access control system without barriers in which those attempting to enter are evaluated by closed-circuit television or other visual means.

op·ti·cal tweez·ers ▶ plural n. a device that uses light from a low-wattage laser to manipulate individual molecules within cells. Also called **LASER TWEEZERS**.

op·tic ax·is ▶ n. another term for **OPTICAL AXIS**.

op·tic chi·as·ma ▶ n. (also **optic chiasm**) Anatomy the X-shaped structure formed at the point below the brain where the two optic nerves cross over each other.

op·tic cup ▶ n. Anatomy a cuplike outgrowth of the brain of an embryo that develops into the retina.

op·tic disk ▶ n. (also **optic disc**) Anatomy the raised disk on the retina at the point of entry of the optic nerve, lacking visual receptors and so creating a blind spot.

op·ti·cian /äp'tisHən/ ▶ n. a person qualified to make and supply eyeglasses and contact lenses for correction of vision. ■ rare a person who makes or sells optical instruments.
– ORIGIN late 17th cent.: from French *opticien*, from medieval Latin *optica* 'optics.'

op·tic lobe ▶ n. Anatomy a lobe in the midbrain from which the optic nerve partly arises.

op·tic nerve ▶ n. Anatomy each of the second pair of cranial nerves, transmitting impulses to the brain from the retina at the back of the eye.

op·tics /'äptiks/ ▶ plural n. [usu. treated as sing.] the scientific study of sight and the behavior of light, or the properties of transmission and deflection of other forms of radiation.

op·tic tract ▶ n. Anatomy the pathway between the optic chiasma and the brain.

op·ti·ma /'äptəmə/ plural form of **OPTIMUM**.

op·ti·mal /'äptəməl/ ▶ adj. best or most favorable; optimum: *seeking the optimal solution.*
– DERIVATIVES **op·ti·mal·i·ty** /,äptə'malitē/ n., **op·ti·mal·ly** /-(ə)lē/ adv.
– ORIGIN late 19th cent.: from Latin *optimus* 'best' + **-AL**.

O

op·ti·mism /'äptə,mizəm/ ▶ n. **1** hopefulness and confidence about the future or the successful outcome of something: *the talks had been amicable, and there were grounds for optimism.*
2 Philosophy the doctrine, esp. as set forth by Leibniz, that this world is the best of all possible worlds.
■ the belief that good must ultimately prevail over evil in the universe.
– DERIVATIVES **op·ti·mist** n.
– ORIGIN mid 18th cent.: from French *optimisme*, from Latin *optimum* 'best thing' (see **OPTIMUM**).

op·ti·mis·tic /,äptə'mistik/ ▶ adj. hopeful and confident about the future: *the optimistic mood of the sixties | he was optimistic about the deal.*
■ involving an overestimate: *previous estimates may be wildly optimistic.*
– DERIVATIVES **op·ti·mis·ti·cal·ly** /-ik(ə)lē/ adv.

op·ti·mize /'äptə,mīz/ ▶ v. [with obj.] make the best or most effective use of (a situation, opportunity, or resource): *to optimize viewing conditions, the microscope should be correctly adjusted.* ■ Computing rearrange or rewrite (data, software, etc.) to improve efficiency of retrieval or processing.
– DERIVATIVES **op·ti·mi·za·tion** /,äptə,mī'zāsHən/ n., **op·ti·miz·er** n.
– ORIGIN early 19th cent.: from Latin *optimus* 'best' + **-IZE**.

op·ti·mum /'äptəməm/ ▶ adj. most conducive to a favorable outcome; best: *the optimum childbearing age.*
▶ n. (pl. **optimuma** /-mə/ or **optimums**) the most favorable conditions or level for growth, reproduction, or success.
– ORIGIN late 19th cent.: from Latin, neuter (used as a noun) of *optimus* 'best.'

op·tion /'äpsHən/ ▶ n. **1** a thing that is or may be chosen: *choose the cheapest options for supplying energy.* ■ [in sing.] the freedom, power, or right to choose something: *she was given the option of resigning or being dismissed | he has* ***no option but to*** *pay up.* ■ a right to buy or sell a particular thing at a specified price within a set time: *Columbia Pictures has an option on the script* | [with infinitive] *an option to buy the land.*
2 Football an offensive play in which the ball carrier has the option to run, pass, hand off, or lateral.
▶ v. [with obj.] buy or sell an option on (something): *his second script will have been optioned by the time you read this.* ■ Sports transfer a player (to a minor league team) with an option to recall him.
– PHRASES **keep** (or **leave**) **one's options open** not commit oneself. **not be an option** not be feasible: *traveling by road is not an option here.*
– ORIGIN mid 16th cent.: from French, or from Latin *optio(n-)*, from the stem of *optare* 'choose.' The verb dates from the 1930s.

op·tion·aire /,äpsHə'ne(ə)r, 'äpsHə,ne(ə)r/ ▶ n. informal a person whose great wealth is based on owning or exercising employee stock options.
– ORIGIN late 1990s: on the pattern of *millionaire*.

op·tion·al /'äpsHənl/ ▶ adj. available to be chosen but not obligatory: *a wide range of optional excursions is offered.*
– DERIVATIVES **op·tion·al·i·ty** /,äpsHə'nalitē/ n., **op·tion·al·ly** adv.

op·to·cou·pler /'äptō,kəplər/ ▶ n. Electronics a device containing light-emitting and light-sensitive components, used to couple isolated circuits.

op·to·e·lec·tron·ics /'äptōəlek'träniks, -ē,lek-/ ▶ plural n. [treated as sing.] the branch of technology concerned with the combined use of electronics and light. ■ [treated as pl.] circuitry constructed using this technology.
– DERIVATIVES **op·to·e·lec·tron·ic** adj.

op·tom·e·ter /äp'tämitər/ ▶ n. an instrument for testing the refractive power of the eye.
– ORIGIN mid 18th cent.: from Greek *optos* 'seen' + **-METER**.

op·tom·e·trist /äp'tämitrist/ ▶ n. a person who practices optometry.

op·tom·e·try /äp'tämitrē/ ▶ n. the practice or profession of examining the eyes for visual defects and prescribing corrective lenses.
– DERIVATIVES **op·to·met·ric** /,äptə'metrik/ adj.

op·to·phone /'äptə,fōn/ ▶ n. an instrument that scans printed characters and converts them into sound, thus enabling blind people to read by ear.
– ORIGIN early 20th cent.: from Greek *optos* 'seen' + **-PHONE**.

opt-out ▶ n. an instance of choosing not to participate in something: *opt-outs from key parts of the treaty.*

op·tron·ics /äp'träniks/ ▶ plural n. [treated as sing.] short for **OPTOELECTRONICS**.
– DERIVATIVES **op·tron·ic** adj.

op·u·lence /'äpyələns/ ▶ n. great wealth or luxuriousness: *rooms of spectacular opulence.*

op·u·lent /'äpyələnt/ ▶ adj. ostentatiously rich and luxurious or lavish: *the opulent comfort of a limousine.* ■ wealthy: *his more opulent tenants.*
– DERIVATIVES **op·u·lent·ly** adv.
– ORIGIN mid 16th cent. (in the sense 'wealthy, affluent'): from Latin *opulent-* 'wealthy, splendid,' from *opes* 'wealth.'

o·pun·tia /ō'pənsH(ē)ə/ ▶ n. a cactus of a genus that comprises the prickly pears. ● Genus *Opuntia*, family Cactaceae.
– ORIGIN early 17th cent.: from Latin, a name given to a plant growing around *Opus* (stem *Opunt-*), a city in Locris in ancient Greece. The term was later used as a genus name.

o·pus /'ōpəs/ ▶ n. (pl. **opuses** or **opera** /'äp(ə)rə/) **1** Music a separate composition or set of compositions by a particular composer, usually ordered by date of publication: *The Gambler was Prokofiev's sixth opera, despite its early* ***opus number***. See also **Op.**
2 any artistic work, esp. one on a large scale: *he was writing an opus on Mexico.*
– ORIGIN early 18th cent.: from Latin, literally 'work.'

o·pus·cule /ō'pəskyo͞ol/ (also **opusculum** /ō'pəskyələm/) ▶ n. (pl. **opuscules** or **opuscula** /-kyələ/) rare a small or minor literary or musical work.
– ORIGIN mid 17th cent.: from French, from Latin *opusculum*, diminutive of *opus* 'work.'

O·pus De·i /,ōpəs 'dā-ē/ ▶ n. a Roman Catholic organization of laymen and priests founded in Spain in 1928 with the aim of re-establishing Christian ideals in society.
– ORIGIN late 19th cent.: from medieval Latin, literally 'work of God.'

OR ▶ abbr. ■ operational research. ■ Oregon (in official postal use). ■ Brit. Military other ranks (as opposed to commissioned officers).

or¹ /ôr/ ▶ conj. **1** used to link alternatives: *a cup of tea or coffee | are you coming* ***or not?*** *| she couldn't read or write | I* ***either*** *take taxis* ***or*** *walk everywhere | it doesn't matter* ***whether*** *the theory is right* ***or*** *wrong.*
2 introducing a synonym or explanation of a preceding word or phrase: *the espionage novel, or, as it is known in the trade, the thriller.*
3 otherwise (used to introduce the consequences of something not being done or not being the case): *hurry up, or you'll miss it all.*
4 introducing an afterthought, usually in the form of a question: *John's indifference—or was it?—left her unsettled.*
5 literary either: *to love is the one way to know* ***or*** *God or man.*
▶ n. (often **OR**) Electronics a Boolean operator that gives the value one if at least one operand (or input) has a value of one, and otherwise has a value of zero.
■ (also **OR gate**) a circuit that gives an output signal if there is a signal on any of its inputs.
– PHRASES **or else** see **ELSE**. **or so** (after a quantity) approximately: *a dozen or so people.*
– ORIGIN Middle English: a reduced form of the obsolete conjunction *other* (which superseded Old English *oththe* 'or'), of uncertain ultimate origin.

> **USAGE** **1** Where a verb follows a list separated by **or**, the traditional rule is that the verb should be singular, as long as the things in the list are individually singular, as in *a sandwich* ***or*** *other snack is included in the price* (rather than *a sandwich* ***or*** *other snack are included in the price*). The argument is that each of the elements agrees separately with the verb. The opposite rule applies when the elements are joined by **and**—here the verb should be plural: *a sandwich* ***and*** *a cup of coffee are included in the price.* These traditional rules are observed in good English writing style but are often disregarded in speech. **2** On the use of **either … or**, see usage at **EITHER**.

or² ▶ n. gold or yellow, as a heraldic tincture: [postpositive] *a bend or.*
– ORIGIN early 16th cent.: from French, from Latin *aurum* 'gold.'

-or¹ ▶ suffix (forming nouns) denoting a person or thing performing the action of a verb, or denoting another agent: *escalator | governor | resistor.*
– ORIGIN from Latin, sometimes via Anglo-Norman French *-eour* or Old French *-eor* (see also **-ATOR**).

-or² ▶ suffix forming nouns denoting a state or condition: *error | pallor | terror.*
– ORIGIN from Latin, sometimes via Old French *-or, -ur.*

-or³ ▶ suffix forming adjectives expressing a comparative sense: *minor | major.*
– ORIGIN via Anglo-Norman French from Latin.

o·ra /'ôrə/ plural form of **os²**.

or·ache /'ôrəcH, 'är-/ (also **orach**) ▶ n. a plant of the goosefoot family with leaves that are sometimes covered in a white mealy substance. Several kinds are edible and can be used as a substitute for spinach or sorrel. ● Genus *Atriplex*, family Chenopodiaceae: several species, in particular the **common orache** (*A. hortensis*), which is cultivated in some areas.
– ORIGIN Middle English *orage*, from Anglo-Norman French *arasche*, from Latin *atriplex*, from Greek *atraphaxus*.

or·a·cle /'ôrəkəl/ ▶ n. **1** a priest or priestess acting as a medium through whom advice or prophecy was sought from the gods in classical antiquity. ■ a place at which such advice or prophecy was sought. ■ a person or thing regarded as an infallible authority or guide on something: *casting the attorney general as the oracle for and guardian of the public interest is simply impossible.*
2 a response or message given by an oracle, typically one that is ambiguous or obscure.
– ORIGIN late Middle English: via Old French from Latin *oraculum*, from *orare* 'speak.'

o·rac·u·lar /ô'rakyələr/ ▶ adj. of or relating to an oracle: *the oracular shrine.* ■ (of an utterance, advice, etc.) hard to interpret; enigmatic: *an ambiguous, oracular remark.* ■ holding or claiming the authority of an oracle: *he holds forth in oracular fashion.*
– DERIVATIVES **o·rac·u·lar·i·ty** /ô,rakyə'laritē/ n., **o·rac·u·lar·ly** adv.
– ORIGIN mid 17th cent.: from Latin *oraculum* (see **ORACLE**) + **-AR¹**.

o·ra·cy /'ôrəsē/ ▶ n. the ability to express oneself fluently and grammatically in speech.
– ORIGIN 1960s: from Latin *os, or-* 'mouth,' on the pattern of *literacy*.

O·ra·dea /ô'rädyä/ an industrial city in western Romania, near the border with Hungary; pop. 205,956 (2006).

o·ral /'ôrəl/ ▶ adj. **1** by word of mouth; spoken rather than written: *they had reached an oral agreement.* ■ relating to the transmission of information or literature by word of mouth rather than in writing:

oral literature. ■ (of a society) not having reached the stage of literacy.
2 of or relating to the mouth: *oral hygiene.* ■ done or taken by the mouth: *oral contraceptives.* ■ Phonetics (of a speech sound) pronounced by the voice resonating in the mouth, as the vowels in English. Compare with **NASAL** (sense 2 of the adjective). ■ Psychoanalysis (in Freudian theory) relating to or denoting a stage of infantile psychosexual development in which the mouth is the main source of pleasure and the center of experience.
▶ **n.** (often **orals**) a spoken examination or test: *he was preparing for his orals | a French oral.*
– DERIVATIVES **o·ral·ly** adv.
– ORIGIN early 17th cent.: from late Latin *oralis,* from Latin *os, or-* 'mouth.'

> **USAGE** See usage at **VERBAL**.See also usage at **AURAL**.

o·ral-for·mu·la·ic ▶ **adj.** relating to or denoting poetry belonging to an early spoken tradition characterized by the use of poetic formulas, e.g., the Homeric poems.

o·ral his·to·ry ▶ **n.** the collection and study of historical information using sound recordings of interviews with people having personal knowledge of past events.

o·ral·ism /ˈôrəˌlizəm/ ▶ **n.** the system of teaching deaf people to communicate by the use of speech and lip-reading rather than sign language.

o·ral·ist /ˈôrəlist/ ▶ **adj.** relating to or advocating oralism.
▶ **n.** a deaf person who uses speech and lip-reading to communicate, rather than sign language.

o·ral·i·ty /ôˈralitē/ ▶ **n. 1** the quality of being spoken or verbally communicated. ■ preference for or tendency to use spoken forms of language.
2 Psychoanalysis the focusing of sexual energy and feeling on the mouth.

o·ral sex ▶ **n.** sexual activity in which the genitals of one partner are stimulated by the mouth of the other; fellatio or cunnilingus.

O·ran /ōˈrän/ a port on the Mediterranean coast of Algeria; pop. 679,900 (est. 2009).

o·rang /ōˈraNG/ ▶ **n.** short for **ORANGUTAN**.

Or·ange /ôˈränZH, ˈär-/ **1** a town in southern France, on the Rhône River, home of the ancestors of the Dutch royal house. See **ORANGE, HOUSE OF**.
2 a city in southwestern California, southeast of Los Angeles in an agricultural area; pop. 136,392 (est. 2008).

or·ange /ˈôrənj, ˈär-/ ▶ **n. 1** a round juicy citrus fruit with a tough bright reddish-yellow rind. ■ a drink made from or flavored with orange: *a vodka and orange.*
2 (also **orange tree**) the leathery-leaved evergreen tree that bears this fruit, native to warm regions of south and Southeast Asia. Oranges are a major commercial crop in many warm regions of the world. ● Genus *Citrus,* family Rutaceae: several species, in particular the **sweet orange** (*C. sinensis*) and the **Seville orange**. ■ used in names of other plants with similar fruit or flowers, e.g., **mock orange**.
3 a bright reddish-yellow color like that of the skin of a ripe orange.
▶ **adj.** reddish yellow, like a ripe orange in color: *an orange glow in the sky.*
– DERIVATIVES **or·ang·ey** (also **orangy**) **adj.**, **or·ang·ish** (also **orangeish**) **adj.**
– ORIGIN late Middle English: from Old French *orenge* (in the phrase *pomme d'orenge*), based on Arabic *nāranj,* from Persian *nārang.*

Or·ange, House of the Dutch royal house, originally a princely dynasty of the principality centered on the town of Orange in the 16th century.

> Members of the family held the position of stadtholder or magistrate from the mid-16th until the late 18th century. In 1689 William of Orange became King William III of Great Britain and Ireland, and the son of the last stadtholder became King William I of the United Netherlands in 1815.

Or·ange, William of William III of Great Britain and Ireland (see **WILLIAM**).

or·ange·ade /ˌôrənjˈād, ˌär-/ ▶ **n.** a drink made with orange juice, sweetener, and water, sometimes carbonated.

or·ange blos·som ▶ **n. 1** flowers from an orange tree, traditionally worn by the bride at a wedding.
2 a cocktail made of gin, sugar, and orange juice.

Or·ange Coun·ty a county in southwestern California, between Los Angeles and San Diego; pop. 3,010,759 (est. 2008).

or·ange flow·er wa·ter ▶ **n.** a solution of neroli in water, used in perfumery and as a food flavoring.

Or·ange Free State an area and former province in central South Africa, north of the Orange River. First settled by Boers after the Great Trek, the area became a province of the Union of South Africa in 1910 and in 1994 became one of the new provinces of South Africa. Province named **FREE STATE** in 1995.

Or·ange·man /ˈôrənjmən, ˈär-/ ▶ **n.** (pl. **Orangemen**) a member of the Orange Order, a Protestant political society in Northern Ireland.

or·ange pe·koe ▶ **n.** a type of black tea made from young leaves.

Or·ange Riv·er the longest river in South Africa, which rises in the Drakensberg Mountains in northeastern Lesotho and flows westward for 1,155 miles (1,859 km) to the Atlantic Ocean. It forms the border between Namibia and South Africa.

or·ange rough·y ▶ **n.** an edible roughy, much prized for its white flesh. Found in deep waters of temperate oceans worldwide, its reddish body turns orange after being exposed to air. ● *Hoplostethus atlanticus,* family Trachichthyidae. ■ the flesh of this fish as food.

or·ange·ry /ˈôrənjrē, ˈär-/ ▶ **n.** (pl. **orangeries**) a greenhouse where orange trees are grown.

or·ange stick ▶ **n.** a thin stick, pointed at one end and typically made of orange wood, used for manicuring the fingernails.

o·rang·u·tan /əˈraNG(g)əˌtan/ (also **orangutang**, **orang-utan**) ▶ **n.** a large mainly solitary arboreal ape with long reddish hair, long arms, and hooked hands and feet, native to Borneo and Sumatra. The mature male develops fleshy cheek pads and a throat pouch. ● *Pongo pygmaeus,* family Pongidae.
– ORIGIN late 17th cent.: from Malay *orang utan* 'forest person.'

orangutan

O·ran·je·stad /ôˈrändyəˌstät/ the capital of the Dutch island of Aruba in the Caribbean Sea; pop. 32,000 (est. 2007).

Or·a·şul Sta·lin /ôrˈäsHo͝ol ˈstälin/ former name for **BRAŞOV**.

o·rate /ôˈrāt, ˈôrˌāt/ ▶ **v.** [no obj.] make a speech, esp. pompously or at length.
– ORIGIN early 17th cent.: back-formation from **ORATION**.

o·ra·tion /ôˈrāsHən/ ▶ **n.** a formal speech, esp. one given on a ceremonial occasion. ■ the style or manner in which such a speech is given.
– ORIGIN late Middle English (denoting a prayer): from Latin *oratio(n-)* 'discourse, prayer,' from *orare* 'speak, pray.'

or·a·tor /ˈôrətər, ˈär-/ ▶ **n.** a public speaker, esp. one who is eloquent or skilled.
– DERIVATIVES **or·a·to·ri·al** /ˌôrəˈtôrēəl/ **adj.**
– ORIGIN late Middle English: from Anglo-Norman French *oratour,* from Latin *orator* 'speaker, pleader.'

or·a·tor·i·cal /ˌôrəˈtôrikəl/ ▶ **adj.** relating to the art or practice of public speaking: *oratorical skills.*

or·a·to·ri·o /ˌôrəˈtôrēˌō, ˌär-/ ▶ **n.** (pl. **oratorios**) a large-scale musical work for orchestra and voices, typically a narrative on a religious theme, performed without the use of costumes, scenery, or action. Well-known examples include Bach's *Christmas Oratorio,* Handel's *Messiah,* and Haydn's *The Creation.*
– ORIGIN Italian, from ecclesiastical Latin *oratorium* 'oratory,' from the musical services held in the Church of the Oratory of St. Philip Neri in Rome.

or·a·to·ry[1] /ˈôrəˌtôrē, ˈär-/ ▶ **n.** (pl. **oratories**)
1 a small chapel, esp. for private worship. [Middle English: from Anglo-Norman French *oratorie,* from ecclesiastical Latin *oratorium,* based on Latin *orare* 'pray, speak.']
2 (**Oratory**) (in the Roman Catholic Church) a religious society of secular priests founded in Rome in 1564 to provide plain preaching and popular services and established in various countries. [from *Congregation of the Fathers of the Oratory.*]
– DERIVATIVES **Or·a·to·ri·an** /ˌôəˈtôrēən, ˈär-/ **n. & adj.** (sense 2).

or·a·to·ry[2] ▶ **n.** the art or practice of formal speaking in public. ■ exaggerated, eloquent, or highly colored language: *learned discussions degenerated into pompous oratory.*
– ORIGIN early 16th cent.: from Latin *oratoria,* feminine (used as a noun) of *oratorius* 'relating to an orator.'

orb /ôrb/ ▶ **n.** a spherical body; a globe. ■ a golden globe surmounted by a cross, forming part of the regalia of a monarch. ■ literary a celestial body. ■ (usu. **orbs**) literary an eyeball; an eye. ■ Astrology a circle of up to 10° radius around the position of a celestial object: *within an orb of 1° of Mars.*
▶ **v.** [with obj.] literary encircle; enclose. ■ form (something) into an orb; make circular or globular.
– ORIGIN late Middle English (denoting a circle): from Latin *orbis* 'ring.'

or·bic·u·lar /ôrˈbikyələr/ ▶ **adj.** technical **1** having the shape of a flat ring or disk.
2 having a rounded convex or globular shape. ■ Geology (of a rock) containing spheroidal igneous inclusions.
– DERIVATIVES **or·bic·u·lar·i·ty** /ôrˌbikyeˈlaritē/ **n.**, **or·bic·u·lar·ly** **adv.**
– ORIGIN late Middle English: from late Latin *orbicularis,* from Latin *orbiculus,* diminutive of *orbis* 'ring.'

Or·bi·son /ˈôrbisən/, Roy (1936–88), US singer and composer. After writing country music songs for other artists, he established himself as a singer with the ballads "Only the Lonely" (1960) and "Oh, Pretty Woman" (1964).

or·bit /ˈôrbit/ ▶ **n. 1** the curved path of a celestial object or spacecraft around a star, planet, or moon, esp. a periodic elliptical revolution. ■ one complete circuit around an orbited body. ■ the state of being on or moving in such a course: *planets in orbit around the sun.* ■ the path of an electron around an atomic nucleus.
2 a sphere of activity, interest, or application: *a radical filmmaker outside the Hollywood orbit.*
3 Anatomy the cavity in the skull of a vertebrate that contains the eye; the eye socket. ■ the area around the eye of a bird or other animal.
▶ **v.** (**orbits, orbiting, orbited**) [with obj.] (of a celestial object or spacecraft) move in orbit around (a star, planet, or moon): *Mercury orbits the Sun.* ■ [no obj.] fly or move around in a circle: *the mobile's disks spun and orbited slowly.* ■ put (a satellite) into orbit.
– PHRASES **into orbit** informal into a state of heightened performance, activity, anger, or excitement: *his goal sent the fans into orbit.*
– ORIGIN mid 16th cent. (sense 3 of the noun): from Latin *orbita* 'course, track' (in medieval Latin 'eye socket'), feminine of *orbitus* 'circular,' from *orbis* 'ring.'

or·bit·al /ˈôrbitl/ ▶ **adj.** of or relating to an orbit or orbits. ■ Brit. (of a road) passing around the outside of a town.
▶ **n.** Physics each of the actual or potential patterns of electron density that may be formed in an atom or molecule by one or more electrons, and that can be represented as a wave function.
– ORIGIN mid 16th cent. (referring to the eye socket): probably from medieval Latin *orbitalis,* from Latin *orbita* (see **ORBIT**).

or·bit·al sand·er ▶ **n.** a sander in which the sanding surface moves in a very tight orbital motion, driven at high speed by an electric motor.

or·bit·er /ˈôrbitər/ ▶ **n.** a spacecraft designed to go into orbit, esp. one not intended to land. Compare with **LANDER**.

or·bit·o·fron·tal cor·tex /ˌôrbitəˌfrəntlˈkôrteks/ ▶ **n.** Anatomy the area of the cerebral cortex located at the base of the frontal lobes above the orbits (or eye sockets), involved esp. in social and emotional behavior.

or·bi·to·sphe·noid /ˌôrbitōˈsfēˌnoid/ (also **orbitosphenoid bone**) ▶ **n.** Anatomy & Zoology a bone in the floor of the mammalian cranium, in the region of the optic nerve. In the human skull it is represented by the lesser wings of the sphenoid bone.

orb web ▶ **n.** a generally circular, upright spider's web formed of threads radiating from a central point, crossed by radial links that spiral in from the edge.

orc /ôrk/ ▶ **n.** (in fantasy literature and games) a member of an imaginary race of humanlike creatures, characterized as ugly, warlike, and malevolent.
– DERIVATIVES **orc·ish** **adj.**

PRONUNCIATION KEY ə *ago, up;* ər *over, fur;* a *hat;* ā *ate;* ä *car;* e *let;* ē *see;* i *fit;* ī *by;* NG *sing;* ō *go;* ô *law, for;* oi *toy;* o͝o *good;* o͞o *goo;* ou *out;* TH *thin;* T̲H̲ *then;* ZH *vision*

O

– ORIGIN late 16th cent. (denoting an ogre): perhaps from Latin *orcus* 'hell' or Italian *orco* 'demon, monster,' influenced by obsolete *orc* 'ferocious sea creature' and by Old English *orcneas* 'monsters.' The current sense is due to the use of the word in Tolkien's fantasy adventures.

or·ca /'ôrkə/ ▶ **n.** a large toothed whale with distinctive black-and-white markings and a prominent dorsal fin. It lives in groups that cooperatively hunt fish, seals, and penguins. Also called **KILLER WHALE**. ● *Orcinus orca*, family Delphinidae.
– ORIGIN mid 19th cent.: from French *orque* or Latin *orca*, denoting a kind of whale.

or·ce·in /'ôrsēin/ ▶ **n.** Chemistry a red dye obtained from orchil, used as a stain in microscopic study.
– ORIGIN mid 19th cent.: alteration of *orcin*, another name for **ORCINOL**.

orch. ▶ **abbr.** ■ orchestra. ■ orchestrated by.

or·chard /'ôrCHərd/ ▶ **n.** a piece of land planted with fruit trees.
– DERIVATIVES **or·chard·ist** /-ist/ **n.**
– ORIGIN Old English *ortgeard*; the first element from Latin *hortus* 'garden,' the second representing **YARD**[2].

or·chard grass ▶ **n.** a pasture grass with broad leaves and green or purplish flowering spikes. ● *Dactylis glomerata*, family Gramineae.

or·ches·tra /'ôrkistrə, -ˌkestrə/ ▶ **n.** **1** a group of instrumentalists, esp. one combining string, woodwind, brass, and percussion sections and playing classical music.
2 (also **orchestra pit**) the part of a theater where the orchestra plays, typically in front of the stage and on a lower level than the audience. ■ the seats on the ground floor in a theater.
3 the semicircular space in front of an ancient Greek theater stage where the chorus danced and sang.
– ORIGIN early 17th cent.: via Latin from Greek *orkhēstra*, from *orkheisthai* 'to dance.'

or·ches·tral /ôr'kestrəl/ ▶ **adj.** written for an orchestra to play: *orchestral music*. ■ of or relating to an orchestra: *an orchestral conductor*.
– DERIVATIVES **or·ches·tral·ly adv.**

or·ches·trate /'ôrkiˌstrāt/ ▶ **v.** [with obj.] **1** arrange or score (music) for orchestral performance.
2 arrange or direct the elements of (a situation) to produce a desired effect, esp. surreptitiously: *the developers were able to orchestrate a favorable media campaign*.
– DERIVATIVES **or·ches·tra·tion** /ˌôrkə'strāSHən/ **n.**, **or·ches·tra·tor** /-ˌstrātər/ **n.**
– ORIGIN late 19th cent.: from **ORCHESTRA**, perhaps suggested by French *orchestrer*.

O

or·ches·tri·on /ôr'kestrēən/ (also **orchestrina** /ˌôrki'strēnə/) ▶ **n.** a large mechanical musical instrument designed to imitate the sound of an orchestra.
– ORIGIN mid 19th cent.: from **ORCHESTRA**, on the pattern of *accordion*.

or·chid /'ôrkid/ ▶ **n.** a plant with complex flowers that are typically showy or bizarrely shaped, having a large specialized lip (labellum) and frequently a spur. Orchids occur worldwide, esp. as epiphytes in tropical forests, and are valuable hothouse plants. ● Family Orchidaceae: numerous genera and species. ■ the flowering stem of a cultivated orchid.
– DERIVATIVES **or·chid·ist** /-ist/ **n.**
– ORIGIN mid 19th cent.: from modern Latin *Orchid(ac)eae*, formed irregularly from Latin *orchis* (see **ORCHIS**).

or·chi·da·ceous /ˌôrki'dāSHəs/ ▶ **adj.** Botany of, relating to, or denoting plants of the orchid family (Orchidaceae).
– ORIGIN mid 19th cent.: from modern Latin *Orchidaceae* (plural) + **-OUS**.

or·chi·ec·to·my /ˌôrkē'ektəmē/ (also **orchidectomy** /ˌôrki'dektəmē/) ▶ **n.** surgical removal of one or both testicles.
– ORIGIN late 19th cent.: from modern Latin *orchido-* (from a Latinized stem of Greek *orkhis* 'testicle') + **-ECTOMY**.

or·chil /'ôrkəl, -CHil/ ▶ **n.** **1** a red or violet dye obtained from certain lichens, used as a source of litmus, orcinol, and other pigments.
2 a lichen with flattened fronds from which such a dye can be obtained. ● *Roccella* (order Graphidiales) and other genera: several species, including the Mediterranean *R. tinctoria*, used for dyeing, and the Madagascan *R. montagnei*, used for litmus.
– ORIGIN late 15th cent.: from Old French *orcheil*, related to Spanish *urchilla*; of uncertain origin.

or·chis /'ôrkis/ ▶ **n.** an orchid of (or formerly of) a genus native to north temperate regions, characterized by a tuberous root and an erect fleshy stem bearing a spike of typically purple or pinkish flowers. ● Genus *Orchis* (or *Dactylorhiza*), family Orchidaceae. ■ dated any wild orchid occurring in temperate regions.
– ORIGIN modern Latin, based on Greek *orkhis*, literally 'testicle' (with reference to the shape of its tuber).

or·chi·tis /ôr'kītis/ ▶ **n.** Medicine inflammation of one or both of the testicles.
– ORIGIN late 18th cent.: modern Latin, from Greek *orkhis* 'testicle' + **-ITIS**.

or·ci·nol /'ôrsəˌnäl, -ˌnôl/ ▶ **n.** Chemistry a crystalline compound extracted from certain lichens and used to make dyes. ● Alternative name: **2-hydroxyphenylmethanol**; chem. formula: $C_7H_8O_2$.
– ORIGIN mid 19th cent.: from modern Latin *orcina*, from Italian *orcello* 'orchil.'

Or·czy /'ôrtsē/, Baroness Emmusca (1865–1947), British novelist, born in Hungary. She wrote *The Scarlet Pimpernel* (1905).

ord. ▶ **abbr.** ■ order. ■ ordinary.

or·dain /ôr'dān/ ▶ **v.** [with obj.] **1** make (someone) a priest or minister; confer holy orders on.
2 order or decree (something) officially: *equal punishment was ordained for the two crimes*. ■ (esp. of God or fate) prescribe; determine (something): *the path ordained by God*.
– DERIVATIVES **or·dain·er n.**, **or·dain·ment n.**
– ORIGIN Middle English (also in the sense 'put in order'): from Anglo-Norman French *ordeiner*, from Latin *ordinare*, from *ordo*, *ordin-* (see **ORDER**).

or·deal /ôr'dēl/ ▶ **n.** **1** a painful or horrific experience, esp. a protracted one: *the **ordeal of** having to give evidence*.
2 historical an ancient test of guilt or innocence by subjection of the accused to severe pain, survival of which was taken as divine proof of innocence.
– ORIGIN Old English *ordāl*, *ordēl*, of Germanic origin; related to German *urteilen* 'give judgment,' from a base meaning 'share out.' The word is not found in Middle English (except once in Chaucer's *Troylus*); modern use of sense 2 began in the late 16th cent., whence sense 1 (mid 17th cent).

or·der /'ôrdər/ ▶ **n.** **1** the arrangement or disposition of people or things in relation to each other according to a particular sequence, pattern, or method: *I filed the cards in alphabetical order*. ■ a state in which everything is in its correct or appropriate place: *she tried to put her shattered thoughts into some semblance of order*. ■ a state in which the laws and rules regulating the public behavior of members of a community are observed and authority is obeyed: *the army was deployed to keep order*. ■ [with adj.] the overall state or condition of something: *the house had just been vacated and was in good order*. ■ a particular social, political, or economic system: *if only the peasantry would rise up against the established order* | *the social order of Britain*. ■ the prescribed or established procedure followed by a meeting, legislative assembly, debate, or court of law: *the meeting was **called to order***. ■ a stated form of liturgical service, or of administration of a rite or ceremony, prescribed by ecclesiastical authority.
2 an authoritative command, direction, or instruction: *he was not going to take orders from a mere administrator* | [with infinitive] *the skipper gave the order to abandon ship*. ■ an oral or written request for something to be made, supplied, or served: *the company has won an order for six tankers*. ■ a thing made, supplied, or served as a result of such a request: *orders will be delivered the next business day*. ■ a written direction of a court or judge: *a judge's order forbidding the reporting of evidence*. ■ a written direction to pay money or deliver property.
3 (often **orders**) a social class: *the upper social orders*. ■ Biology a principal taxonomic category that ranks below class and above family. ■ a grade or rank in the Christian ministry, esp. that of bishop, priest, or deacon. ■ (**orders**) the rank or position of a member of the clergy or an ordained minister of a church: *he took priest's orders*. See also **HOLY ORDERS**. ■ Theology any of the nine grades of angelic beings in the celestial hierarchy.
4 (also **Order**) a society of monks, priests, nuns, etc., living according to certain religious and social regulations and discipline and at least some of whose members take solemn vows: *the Franciscan Order*. ■ historical a society of knights bound by a common rule of life and having a combined military and monastic character. ■ an institution founded by a monarch for the purpose of conferring an honor or honors for merit on those appointed to it. ■ the insignia worn by members of such an institution. ■ a Masonic or similar fraternal organization.
5 [in sing.] used to describe the quality, nature, or importance of something: *with musical talent of this order, von Karajan would have been a phenomenon in any age*.
6 any of the five classical styles of architecture (Doric, Ionic, Corinthian, Tuscan, and Composite) based on the proportions of columns, amount of decoration, etc. ■ any style or mode of architecture subject to uniform established proportions.
7 [with modifier] Military equipment or uniform for a specified purpose or of a specified type: *drill order*. ■ (**the order**) the position in which a rifle is held after ordering arms. See **ORDER ARMS** below.
8 Mathematics the degree of complexity of an equation, expression, etc., as denoted by an ordinal number. ■ the number of differentiations required to reach the highest derivative in a differential equation. ■ the number of elements in a finite group. ■ the number of rows or columns in a square matrix.
▶ **v.** **1** [reporting verb] give an authoritative direction or instruction to do something: [with obj. and infinitive] *she ordered me to leave* | [with direct speech] *"Stop frowning," he ordered* | [with clause] *the court ordered that the case should be heard at the end of August* | [with obj.] *her father ordered her back home* | *the judge ordered a retrial*. ■ [with obj.] (**order someone around/about**) continually tell someone in an overbearing way what to do. ■ [with obj. and complement] command (something) to be done or (someone) to be treated in a particular way: *he ordered the anchor dropped*.
2 [with obj.] request (something) to be made, supplied, or served: *my friend ordered the tickets last week* | [with two objs.] *I asked the security guard to order me a taxi* | [no obj.] *Are you ready to order, sir?*
3 [with obj.] arrange (something) in a methodical or appropriate way: *all entries are ordered by date* | [as adj. in combination] (**-ordered**) *her normally well-ordered life*.
– PHRASES **by order of** according to directions given by the proper authority: *he was released from prison by order of the court*. **in order 1** according to a particular sequence. **2** in the correct condition for operation or use. **3** in accordance with the rules of procedure at a meeting, legislative assembly, etc. ■ appropriate in the circumstances: *a little bit of flattery was now in order*. **in order for** so that: *employees must be committed to the change in order for it to succeed*. **in order that** with the intention; so that: *she used her mother's kitchen in order that the turkey might be properly cooked*. **in order to** as a means to: *he slouched into his seat in order to avoid drawing attention to himself*. **of the order of 1** approximately: *sales increases are of the order of 20%*. **2** Mathematics having the order of magnitude specified by. **on order** (of goods) requested but not yet received from the supplier or manufacturer. **on the order of 1** another term for **OF THE ORDER OF** above. **2** along the lines of; similar to: *singers on the order of Janis Joplin*. **Order!** a call for silence or the observance of prescribed procedures by someone in charge of a trial, legislative assembly, etc. **order arms** Military hold a rifle with its butt on the ground close to one's right side. **order of battle** the units, formations, and equipment of a military force. **orders are orders** commands must be obeyed, however much one may disagree with them. **out of order 1** (of an electrical or mechanical device) not working properly or at all. **2** not in the correct sequence. **3** not according to the rules of a meeting, legislative assembly, etc. ■ informal (of a person or their behavior) unacceptable or wrong: *he's getting away with things that are out of order*. **to order** according to a customer's specific request or requirements: *the sweaters are knitted to order*.
– DERIVATIVES **or·der·er n.**
– ORIGIN Middle English: from Old French *ordre*, from Latin *ordo*, *ordin-* 'row, series, rank.'

or·dered pair ▶ **n.** Mathematics a pair of elements a, b having the property that $(a, b) = (u, v)$ if and only if $a = u$, $b = v$.

or·der·ly /'ôrdərlē/ ▶ **adj.** neatly and methodically arranged: *an orderly arrangement of objects*. ■ (of a person or group) well behaved; disciplined.
▶ **n.** (pl. **orderlies**) **1** an attendant in a hospital responsible for the nonmedical care of patients and the maintenance of order and cleanliness.
2 a soldier who carries out orders or performs minor tasks for an officer.
– DERIVATIVES **or·der·li·ness n.**

or·der·ly room ▶ **n.** Military the room used for regimental or company business.

or·der of busi·ness ▶ **n.** (pl. **orders of business**) a task assigned or a matter to be addressed: *the first order of business is learning who the hitters are*.

or·der of mag·ni·tude ▶ **n.** a class in a system of classification determined by size, each class being a number of times (usually ten) greater or smaller than the one before: *values might be compared by order of magnitude, a staple in making ballpark estimates*. ■ relative size, quantity, quality, etc.: *the new problems were of a different order of magnitude*. ■ the arrangement of a number of items determined by their relative size: *the items are arranged in ascending order of magnitude*.

or·der of the day ▶ n. (**the order of the day**) **1** the prevailing state of things: *confusion would seem to be the order of the day.* **2** something that is required or recommended: *on Sundays, a black suit was the order of the day.* **3** a program or agenda.

Or·der of the Gar·ter the highest order of English knighthood, founded by Edward III *c.*1344. According to tradition, the garter was that of the Countess of Salisbury, which the king placed on his own leg after it fell off while she was dancing with him. The king's comment to those present, "Honi soit qui mal y pense" (shame be to him who thinks evil of it), was adopted as the motto of the order.

or·di·nal /ˈôrdn-əl/ ▶ n. **1** short for ORDINAL NUMBER. **2** Christian Church, chiefly historical a service book, esp. one with the forms of service used at ordinations. ▶ adj. of or relating to a thing's position in a series: *ordinal position of birth.* ■ of or relating to an ordinal number. ■ Biology of or relating to a taxonomic order.
– ORIGIN Middle English (sense 2 of the noun): the noun from medieval Latin *ordinale* (neuter); the adjective from late Latin *ordinalis* 'relating to order in a series,' from Latin *ordo, ordin-* (see ORDER).

or·di·nal num·ber ▶ n. a number defining a thing's position in a series, such as "first," "second," or "third." Ordinal numbers are used as adjectives, nouns, and pronouns. Compare with CARDINAL NUMBER.

or·di·nance /ˈôrdn-əns/ ▶ n. **1** a piece of legislation enacted by a municipal authority: *a city ordinance banned smoking in nearly all types of restaurants.* **2** an authoritative order; a decree. **3** a prescribed religious rite: *Talmudic ordinances.*
– ORIGIN Middle English (also in the sense 'arrangement in ranks'): from Old French *ordenance,* from medieval Latin *ordinantia,* from Latin *ordinare* 'put in order' (see ORDAIN).

or·di·nand /ˈôrdn,and/ ▶ n. a candidate for ordination.
– ORIGIN mid 19th cent.: from Latin *ordinandus,* gerundive of *ordinare* 'put in order' (see ORDAIN).

or·di·nar·i·ly /,ôrdn'e(ə)rəlē/ ▶ adv. **1** usually: *the fixings that would ordinarily appear at a grand turkey dinner* | [sentence adverb] *ordinarily, Linda was the handy one around the house.* **2** in a normal way: *an effort to behave ordinarily.*

or·di·nar·y /ˈôrdn,erē/ ▶ adj. **1** with no special or distinctive features; normal: *he sets out to depict ordinary people* | *it was just an ordinary evening.* ■ uninteresting; commonplace: *ordinary items of everyday wear.* **2** (esp. of a judge or bishop) exercising authority by virtue of office and not by delegation. ▶ n. (pl. **ordinaries**) **1** (**the ordinary**) what is commonplace or standard: *their clichés were vested with enough emotion to elevate them above the ordinary.* **2** Law Brit. a person, esp. a judge, exercising authority by virtue of office and not by delegation. ■ in some US states, a judge of probate. **3** (usu. **Ordinary**) those parts of a Roman Catholic service, esp. the Mass, that do not vary from day to day. ■ a rule or book giving the order for saying the Mass. **4** Heraldry any of the simplest principal charges used in coats of arms (esp. chief, pale, bend, fess, bar, chevron, and saltire). **5** Brit. archaic a meal provided at a fixed time and price at an inn. ■ an inn providing this. **6** historical another term for PENNY-FARTHING.
– PHRASES **out of the ordinary** unusual: *nothing out of the ordinary happened.*
– DERIVATIVES **or·di·nar·i·ness** n.
– ORIGIN late Middle English: the noun partly via Old French; the adjective from Latin *ordinarius* 'orderly' (reinforced by French *ordinaire*), from *ordo, ordin-* 'order.'

or·di·nar·y ray ▶ n. Optics (in double refraction) the ray that obeys the ordinary laws of refraction.

or·di·nar·y sea·man ▶ n. the lowest rank of merchant seaman, below able-bodied seaman.

or·di·nar·y share ▶ n. British term for COMMON STOCK.

or·di·nate /ˈôrdnit, -,āt/ ▶ n. Mathematics (in a system of coordinates) the *y*-coordinate, representing the distance from a point to the horizontal or *x*-axis measured parallel to the vertical or *y*-axis.
– ORIGIN late 17th cent.: from Latin *linea ordinata applicata* 'line applied parallel,' from *ordinare* 'put in order.'

or·di·na·tion /,ôrdnˈāsHən/ ▶ n. **1** the action of ordaining or conferring holy orders on someone. ■ a ceremony in which someone is ordained. **2** chiefly Ecology a statistical technique in which data from a large number of sites or populations are represented as points in a two- or three-dimensional coordinate frame.
– ORIGIN late Middle English (in the general sense 'arrangement in order'): from Latin *ordinatio(n-),* from *ordinare* 'put in order' (see ORDAIN).

ordn. ▶ abbr. ordnance.

ord·nance /ˈôrdnəns/ ▶ n. **1** mounted guns; artillery. ■ military weapons, ammunition, and equipment used in connection with them. **2** a branch of the armed forces dealing with the supply and storage of weapons, ammunition, and related equipment.
– ORIGIN late Middle English: variant of ORDINANCE.

or·don·nance /ˈôrdn-əns, ,ôdōˈnäns/ ▶ n. the systematic or orderly arrangement of parts, esp. in art and architecture.
– ORIGIN mid 17th cent.: from French, alteration of Old French *ordenance* (see ORDINANCE).

Or·do·vi·cian /,ôrdəˈvisHən/ ▶ adj. Geology of, relating to, or denoting the second period of the Paleozoic era, between the Cambrian and Silurian periods. ■ (as noun **the Ordovician**) the Ordovician period or the system of rocks deposited during it.

> The Ordovician lasted from about 510 million to 439 million years ago. It saw the diversification of many invertebrate groups and the appearance of the first vertebrates (jawless fish).

– ORIGIN late 19th cent.: from *Ordovices,* the Latin name of an ancient British tribe in North Wales, + -IAN.

or·dure /ˈôrjər/ ▶ n. excrement; dung. ■ something regarded as vile or abhorrent.
– ORIGIN Middle English: from Old French, from *ord* 'foul,' from Latin *horridus* (see HORRID).

Or·dzho·ni·kid·ze /,ôrjäniˈkidzə, ərjənyiˈkyēdzyə/ former name (1954–93) for VLADIKAVKAZ.

ore /ôr/ ▶ n. a naturally occurring solid material from which a metal or valuable mineral can be profitably extracted.
– ORIGIN Old English *ōra* 'unwrought metal'; influenced in form by Old English *ār* 'bronze' (related to Latin *aes* 'crude metal, bronze').

Ore. ▶ abbr. Oregon.

ø·re /ˈərə/ ▶ n. (pl. **same**) a monetary unit of Denmark and Norway, equal to one hundredth of a krone.
– ORIGIN Danish and Norwegian.

ö·re /ˈərə/ ▶ n. (pl. **same**) a monetary unit of Sweden, equal to one hundredth of a krona.

o·re·ad /ˈôrē,ad/ ▶ n. Greek & Roman Mythology a nymph believed to inhabit mountains.
– ORIGIN from Latin *Oreas, Oread-,* from Greek *Oreias,* from *oros* 'mountain.'

ore·bod·y /ˈôr,bädē/ ▶ n. a connected mass of ore in a mine or suitable for mining.

Ö·re·bro /,ərəˈbrō, ,œrə-/ an industrial city in southern central Sweden; pop. 132,277 (2008).

o·rec·chi·et·te /,ôriˈkyetē/ ▶ n. a small ear-shaped pasta.
– ORIGIN Italian, literally 'little ears.'

o·rec·tic /ôˈrektik/ ▶ adj. technical, rare of or concerning desire or appetite.
– ORIGIN late 17th cent. (as a noun in the sense 'stimulant for the appetite'): from Greek *orektikos,* from *oregein* 'stretch out, reach for.' The current sense dates from the late 18th cent.

Oreg. ▶ abbr. Oregon.

o·reg·a·no /əˈregə,nō/ ▶ n. an aromatic plant related to marjoram, with leaves that are used fresh or dried as a culinary herb. ● *Origanum vulgare,* family Labiatae.
– ORIGIN late 18th cent.: from Spanish, variant of ORIGANUM.

Or·e·gon /ˈôrigən, ˈär-, -,gän/ a state in the northwestern US, on the Pacific coast; pop. 3,790,060 (est. 2008); capital, Salem; statehood, Feb. 14, 1859 (33). Many Americans arrived via the Oregon Trail during the early 1840s; by 1846, Britain formally ceded the territory to the US.
– DERIVATIVES **Or·e·go·ni·an** /,ôriˈgōnēən/ adj. & n.

Or·e·gon fir ▶ n. (also **Oregon pine**) another term for DOUGLAS FIR.

Or·e·gon grape (also **Oregon grape holly**) ▶ n. an evergreen shrub of the western coastal US bearing yellow flowers and edible blue berries. ● *Mahonia aquifolium,* family Berberidaceae.

Or·e·gon Trail a route across the central and western US used esp. from 1840 until 1860 by settlers moving west. It extends about 2,000 miles (3,200 km) from Missouri to Oregon.

O·rel /ôˈrel, əˈryôl/ an industrial city in southwestern Russia; pop. 320,800 (est. 2008).

O·rem /ˈōrəm/ a city in north central Utah, northwest of Provo; pop. 93,250 (est. 2008).

Ore Moun·tains another name for the ERZGEBIRGE.

O·ren·burg /ˈôrənbərg, əryinˈbo͝ork/ a city in southern Russia, on the Ural River; pop. 526,400 (est. 2008). It was known as Chkalov from 1938 to 1957.

O·re·o /ˈôrē,ō/ ▶ n. (pl. **Oreos**) trademark a brand of chocolate sandwich cookie with a creamy white filling. ■ derogatory an African-American who is seen, esp. by other blacks, as wishing to be part of the white establishment.

O·res·tes /ôˈrestēz/ Greek Mythology the son of Agamemnon and Clytemnestra and the brother of Electra and Iphigenia. He killed his mother and her lover Aegisthus to avenge the murder of Agamemnon.

Ø·re·sund /ˈôrə,so͝ond, ˈœrə-/ a narrow channel between Sweden and the Danish island of Zealand. Also called THE SOUND (see SOUND).

o·rex·in /ôˈrexin/ ▶ n. either of two hormones (**orexin-A** or **orexin-B**) produced by the mammalian hypothalamus and functional in the regulation of appetite and sleep. Also called HYPOCRETIN.

org /ôrg/ ▶ abbr. organization (in Internet addresses).

org. ▶ abbr. ■ organic. ■ organization or organized.

or·gan /ˈôrgən/ ▶ n. **1** (also **pipe organ**) a large musical instrument having rows of tuned pipes sounded by compressed air, and played using one or more keyboards to produce a wide range of musical effects. The pipes are generally arranged in ranks of a particular type, each controlled by a stop, and often into larger sets linked to separate keyboards. ■ a smaller instrument without pipes, producing similar sounds electronically. See also REED ORGAN. **2** Biology a part of an organism that is typically self-contained and has a specific vital function, such as the heart or liver in humans. ■ a department or organization that performs a specified function: *the central organs of administration and business.* ■ a medium of communication, esp. a newspaper or periodical that serves a particular organization, political party, etc.: *an article in the official organ of the Salvation Army.* ■ (used euphemistically) the penis. ■ archaic a region of the brain formerly held to be the seat of a particular faculty.
– ORIGIN late Old English, via Latin from Greek *organon* 'tool, instrument, sense organ,' reinforced in Middle English by Old French *organe.*

or·gan·dy /ˈôrgəndē/ (also **organdie**) ▶ n. (pl. **organdies**) a fine translucent cotton or silk fabric that is usually stiffened and used for women's clothing.
– ORIGIN early 19th cent.: from French *organdi,* of unknown origin.

or·gan·elle /,ôrgəˈnel/ ▶ n. Biology any of a number of organized or specialized structures within a living cell.
– ORIGIN early 20th cent.: from modern Latin *organella,* diminutive of *organum* 'instrument, tool' (see ORGAN).

or·gan grind·er ▶ n. a street musician who plays a barrel organ.

or·gan·ic /ôrˈganik/ ▶ adj. **1** of, relating to, or derived from living matter: *organic soils.* ■ Chemistry of, relating to, or denoting compounds containing carbon (other than simple binary compounds and salts) and chiefly or ultimately of biological origin. Compare with INORGANIC. ■ (of food or farming methods) produced or involving production without the use of chemical fertilizers, pesticides, or other artificial agents. **2** Physiology of or relating to a bodily organ or organs. ■ Medicine (of a disease) affecting the structure of an organ. **3** denoting a relation between elements of something such that they fit together harmoniously as necessary parts of a whole: *the organic unity of the integral work of art.* ■ characterized by continuous or natural development: *companies expand as much by acquisition as by organic growth.*
– DERIVATIVES **or·gan·i·cal·ly** /-ik(ə)lē/ adv.
– ORIGIN late Middle English: via Latin from Greek *organikos* 'relating to an organ or instrument.'

or·gan·ic chem·is·try ▶ n. the chemistry of carbon compounds (other than simple salts such as carbonates, oxides, and carbides).

or·gan·i·cism /ôrˈgani,sizəm/ ▶ n. **1** the doctrine that everything in nature has an organic basis or is part of an organic whole. **2** the use or advocacy of literary or artistic forms in which the parts are connected or coordinated to the whole.

PRONUNCIATION KEY ə *ago, up;* ər *over, fur;* a *hat;* ā *ate;* ä *car;* e *let;* ē *see;* i *fit;* ī *by;* NG *sing;* ō *go;* ô *law, for;* oi *toy;* o͝o *good;* o͞o *goo;* ou *out;* TH *thin;* T͟H *then;* ZH *vision*

O

– DERIVATIVES **or·gan·i·cist** adj. & n., **or·gan·i·cis·tic** /ôrˌganiˈsistik/ adj.
– ORIGIN mid 19th cent.: from French *organicisme*.

or·gan·ism /ˈôrgəˌnizəm/ ▶ n. an individual animal, plant, or single-celled life form. ■ the material structure of such an individual: *the heart's contribution to the maintenance of the human organism.* ■ a whole with interdependent parts, likened to a living being: *the upper strata of the American social organism.*
– DERIVATIVES **or·gan·is·mal** /ˌôrgəˈnizməl/ adj., **or·gan·is·mic** /ˌôrgəˈnizmik/ adj.
– ORIGIN early 18th cent. (in the sense 'organization,' from ORGANIZE): current senses derive from French *organisme*.

or·gan·ist /ˈôrgənist/ ▶ n. a person who plays the organ.

or·gan·i·za·tion /ˌôrgəniˈzāSHən/ ▶ n. **1** an organized body of people with a particular purpose, esp. a business, society, association, etc.: *a research organization.*
2 the action of organizing something: *the organization of conferences and seminars.* ■ the structure or arrangement of related or connected items: *the spatial organization of the cells.* ■ an efficient and orderly approach to tasks: *apparent disorder and lack of organization.*
– DERIVATIVES **or·gan·i·za·tion·al** /-SHənl/ adj., **or·gan·i·za·tion·al·ly** /-SHən-lē/ adv.

or·gan·i·za·tion chart ▶ n. a graphic representation of the structure of an organization, showing the relationships of the positions or jobs within it.

or·gan·i·za·tion man ▶ n. derogatory a man who lets his individuality and personal life be dominated by the organization he works for.

Or·gan·i·za·tion of Af·ri·can U·ni·ty (abbr.: **OAU**) an association of African states founded in 1963 for mutual cooperation and the elimination of colonialism in Africa. It is based in Addis Ababa, Ethiopia.

Or·gan·i·za·tion of A·mer·i·can States (abbr.: **OAS**) an association including most of the countries of North and South America, chartered in 1948 by members of the former Pan American Union. It has aimed to work for peace and prosperity in the region and to uphold the sovereignty of member nations. Its headquarters are in Washington, DC.

Or·gan·i·za·tion of the Pe·tro·le·um Ex·port·ing Coun·tries (abbr.: **OPEC**) an association of twelve major oil-producing countries, founded in 1960 to coordinate policies and prices, with headquarters in Vienna. Members are Algeria, Angola, Indonesia, Iran, Iraq, Kuwait, Libya, Nigeria, Qatar, Saudi Arabia, the United Arab Emirates, and Venezuela.

or·gan·ize /ˈôrgəˌnīz/ ▶ v. [with obj.] **1** arrange into a structured whole; order: *organize lessons in a planned way.* ■ coordinate the activities of (a person or group of people) efficiently: *organize and lead a group of people.* ■ form (a number of people) into a labor union, political group, etc.: *an attempt to organize unskilled workers* | [no obj.] *campaigns brought women together to organize.* ■ form (a labor union, political group, etc.). ■ archaic arrange or form into a living being or tissue: *the soul doth organize the body.*
2 make arrangements or preparations for (an event or activity); coordinate: *the union organized a 24-hour general strike* | *social and cultural programs are organized by the committee.* ■ take responsibility for providing or arranging: *he is sometimes asked to stay behind, organizing transportation.*
– DERIVATIVES **or·gan·iz·a·ble** adj.
– ORIGIN late Middle English: from medieval Latin *organizare*, from Latin *organum* 'instrument, tool' (see ORGAN).

or·gan·ized /ˈôrgəˌnīzd/ ▶ adj. arranged in a systematic way, esp. on a large scale: *organized crime.* ■ having one's affairs in order so as to deal with them efficiently: *I am systematic and organized enough to save things.* ■ having formed a labor union, political group, etc.: *a repressive regime that crushed organized labor.*

or·gan·iz·er /ˈôrgəˌnīzər/ ▶ n. **1** a person who organizes: *the organizers of the demonstration* | *he worked as a union organizer all around the state of New Jersey.*
2 a thing used for organizing. See also ELECTRONIC ORGANIZER, PERSONAL ORGANIZER.

or·gan loft ▶ n. a balcony in a church or concert hall for an organ.

organo- ▶ comb. form **1** chiefly Biology relating to bodily organs: *organogenesis.*
2 Chemistry (forming names of classes of organic compounds containing a particular element or group) organic: *organochlorine* | *organophosphate.*
– ORIGIN from Greek *organon* 'organ'; sense 2 from ORGANIC.

or·ga·no·chlo·rine /ˌôrgənōˈklôrēn/ ▶ n. [often as modifier] any of a large group of pesticides and other synthetic organic compounds with chlorinated aromatic molecules.

or·gan of Cor·ti /ˈkôrtē/ ▶ n. Anatomy a structure in the cochlea of the inner ear that produces nerve impulses in response to sound vibrations.
– ORIGIN late 19th cent.: named after Alfonso *Corti* (1822–76), Italian anatomist.

or·ga·no·gen·e·sis /ˌôrgənōˈjenisis/ ▶ n. (also **organogeny** /ˌôrgəˈnäjənē/) Biology the production and development of the organs of an animal or plant.

or·ga·no·lep·tic /ˌôrgənōˈleptik/ ▶ adj. acting on or involving the use of the sense organs.
– ORIGIN mid 19th cent.: from French *organoleptique*, from Greek *organon* 'organ' + *lēptikos* 'disposed to take' (from *lambanein* 'take').

or·ga·no·me·tal·lic /ˌôrgənōməˈtalik/ ▶ adj. Chemistry (of a compound) containing a metal atom bonded to an organic group or groups.

or·ga·non /ˈôrgəˌnän/ ▶ n. an instrument of thought, esp. a means of reasoning or a system of logic.
– ORIGIN late 16th cent. (denoting a bodily organ): from Greek, literally 'instrument, organ.' *Organon* was the title of Aristotle's logical treatises.

or·ga·no·phos·phate /ˌôrganəˈfäsfāt, ˌôrganō-/ ▶ n. any organic compound whose molecule contains one or more phosphate ester groups, esp. a pesticide of this kind.

or·ga·no·phos·pho·rus /ˌôrgənəˈfäsf(ə)rəs, ôrˌganō-/ ▶ n. [as modifier] denoting synthetic organic compounds containing phosphorus, esp. pesticides and nerve gases of this kind.

or·ga·no·ther·a·py /ˌôrgənōˈTHerəpē, ôrˌganō-/ ▶ n. the treatment of disease with extracts from animal organs, esp. glands.
– DERIVATIVES **or·ga·no·ther·a·peu·tic** /-ˌTHerəˈpyo͞otik/ adj.

or·gan pipe cac·tus ▶ n. a large cactus native to the southwestern US, having columnar stems or branches and typically flowering at night.
● Several species in the family Cactaceae, including *Lemaireocereus marginatus* and *Cereus thurberi*.

or·gan pipe cor·al ▶ n. a tropical coral that forms narrow parallel calcareous tubes linked by transverse plates. ● Genus *Tubipora*, order Stolonifera.

or·gan-screen ▶ n. an ornamental screen above which the organ is placed in some cathedrals and large churches, typically between the choir and the nave.

or·gan stop ▶ n. a set of pipes of a similar tone in an organ. ■ the handle of the mechanism that brings such a set into action.

or·ga·num /ˈôrgənəm/ ▶ n. (pl. **organa** /-nə/) (in medieval music) a form of early polyphony based on an existing plainsong.
– ORIGIN Latin, from Greek *organon*, literally 'instrument, organ.'

or·gan·za /ôrˈganzə/ ▶ n. a thin, stiff, transparent fabric made of silk or a synthetic yarn.
– ORIGIN early 19th cent.: probably from French *organsin* (see ORGANZINE).

or·gan·zine /ˈôrgənˌzēn/ ▶ n. a silk thread made of strands twisted together in the contrary direction to that of each individual strand.
– ORIGIN late 17th cent.: from French *organsin*, from Italian *organzino*, of unknown ultimate origin.

or·gasm /ˈôrˌgazəm/ ▶ n. a climax of sexual excitement, characterized by feelings of pleasure centered in the genitals and (in men) experienced as an accompaniment to ejaculation.
▶ v. [no obj.] experience an orgasm.
– ORIGIN late 17th cent.: from French *orgasme*, or from modern Latin *orgasmus*, from Greek *orgasmos*, from *organ* 'swell or be excited.'

or·gas·mic /ôrˈgazmik/ ▶ adj. of or relating to orgasm. ■ (of a person) able to achieve orgasm. ■ informal very enjoyable or exciting: *the album is an orgasmic whirl of techno soundscapes.*
– DERIVATIVES **or·gas·mi·cal·ly** /-mik(ə)lē/ adv., **or·gas·tic** /-ˈgastik/ adj., **or·gas·ti·cal·ly** /-ˈgastik(ə)lē/ adv.

OR gate ▶ n. see OR¹.

or·geat /ˈôr,ZHät, -ˌZHä/ ▶ n. a cooling drink made from orangeflower water and either barley or almonds.
– ORIGIN French, from Provençal *orjat*, from *ordi* 'barley,' from Latin *hordeum* 'barley.'

or·gi·as·tic /ˌôrjēˈastik/ ▶ adj. of or resembling an orgy.
– DERIVATIVES **or·gi·as·ti·cal·ly** /-ik(ə)lē/ adv.
– ORIGIN late 17th cent.: from Greek *orgiastikos*, from *orgiastēs*, agent noun from *orgiazein* 'hold an orgy.'

or·gone /ˈôrgōn/ ▶ n. (in the theory of Wilhelm Reich) a supposed sexual energy or life force distributed throughout the universe that can be collected and stored (in an orgone box) for therapeutic use.
– ORIGIN 1940s: coined by Wilhelm Reich (1897–1957), Austrian-born psychoanalyst.

or·gu·lous /ˈôrg(y)ələs/ ▶ adj. literary haughty.
– ORIGIN Middle English: from Old French *orguillus*, from *orguill* 'pride.' The word was rare from the 16th cent. until used by Robert Southey and Sir Walter Scott as a historical archaism and affected by 19th-cent. journalists.

or·gy /ˈôrjē/ ▶ n. (pl. **orgies**) a wild party, esp. one involving excessive drinking and unrestrained sexual activity: *he had a reputation for drunken orgies.* ■ excessive indulgence in a specified activity: *an orgy of buying.* ■ (usu. **orgies**) historical secret rites used in the worship of Bacchus, Dionysus, and other Greek and Roman deities, celebrated with dancing, drunkenness, and singing.
– ORIGIN early 16th cent.: originally plural, from French *orgies*, via Latin from Greek *orgia* 'secret rites or revels.'

-orial ▶ suffix forming adjectives corresponding to nouns ending in *-ory* (such as *accusatorial* corresponding to *accusatory*).
– ORIGIN see -ORY², -AL.

or·i·bi /ˈôrəbē, ˈär-/ ▶ n. (pl. **same** or **oribis**) a small antelope of the African savanna, having a reddish-beige back, white underparts, and short vertical horns. ● *Ourebia ourebi*, family Bovidae.
– ORIGIN late 18th cent.: from Afrikaans, from Khoikhoi.

or·i·chal·cum /ˌôriˈkalkəm/ (also **orichalc** /ˈôriˌkalk/) ▶ n. a yellow metal prized in ancient times, probably a form of brass or a similar alloy.
– ORIGIN late Middle English: via Latin from Greek *oreikhalkon*, literally 'mountain copper.'

o·ri·el /ˈôrēəl/ ▶ n. a projection from the wall of a building, typically supported from the ground or by corbels. ■ (also **oriel window**) a window in such a structure.
– ORIGIN late Middle English: from Old French *oriol* 'gallery,' of unknown origin; compare with medieval Latin *oriolum* 'upper chamber.'

oriel

o·ri·ent /ˈôrēˌənt/ ▶ n. **1** (**the Orient**) literary the countries of Asia, esp. eastern Asia.
2 the special luster of a pearl of the finest quality. ■ a pearl with such a luster.
▶ adj. literary situated in or belonging to the east; oriental. ■ (of the sun, daylight, etc.) rising. ■ (esp. of precious stones) lustrous (with reference to fine pearls from the East).
▶ v. /ˈôrēˌent/ **1** [with obj.] align or position (something) relative to the points of a compass or other specified positions: *the fires are oriented in direct line with the midsummer sunset.* ■ adjust or tailor (something) to specified circumstances or needs: *magazines oriented to the business community* | [as adj., in combination] (**-oriented**) *market-oriented economic reforms.* ■ guide (someone) physically in a specified direction.
2 (**orient oneself**) find one's position in relation to new and strange surroundings: *there are no street names that would enable her to orient herself.*
– ORIGIN late Middle English: via Old French from Latin *orient-* 'rising or east,' from *oriri* 'to rise.'

o·ri·en·tal /ˌôrēˈentl/ (also **Oriental**) ▶ adj. **1** of, from, or characteristic of East Asia: *oriental rugs.* ■ (**Oriental**) Zoology of, relating to, or denoting a zoogeographical region comprising Asia south of the Himalayas and Indonesia west of Wallace's line. Distinctive animals include pandas, gibbons, tree shrews, tarsiers, and moonrats.
2 (of a pearl or other jewel) orient.
▶ n. (**Oriental**) dated, often offensive a person of East Asian descent.
– DERIVATIVES **o·ri·en·tal·ize** /-īz/ v., **o·ri·en·tal·ly** adv.
– ORIGIN late Middle English: from Old French, or from Latin *orientalis*, from *orient-* (see ORIENT).

> **USAGE** The term **Oriental**, denoting a person from East Asia, is regarded as offensive by many Asians, especially Asian Americans. It has many associations with European imperialism in Asia. Therefore, it has an out-of-date feel and tends to be associated with a rather offensive stereotype of the people and their customs as inscrutable and exotic. **Asian** and more specific terms such as **East Asian, Chinese**, and **Japanese** are preferred. See also usage at **ASIAN**.

O·ri·en·ta·li·a /ˌôrē-enˈtālēə/ ▶ **plural n.** books and other items relating to or characteristic of the Orient.
– ORIGIN early 20th cent.: from Latin, neuter plural of *orientalis* 'oriental.'

o·ri·en·tal·ism /ˌôrēˈen(t)lˌizəm/ ▶ **n.** style, artefacts, or traits considered characteristic of the peoples and cultures of Asia. ■ the representation of Asia, esp. the Middle East, in a stereotyped way that is regarded as embodying a colonialist attitude.
– DERIVATIVES **o·ri·en·tal·ist n. & adj.**

o·ri·en·tal pop·py ▶ **n.** a southwestern Asian poppy with coarse, deeply cut, hairy leaves and large scarlet flowers with a black mark at the base of each petal, widely grown as a garden perennial. ● *Papaver orientale*, family Papaveraceae.

o·ri·en·tate /ˈôrēənˌtāt/ ▶ **v.** another term for **ORIENT**.
– ORIGIN mid 19th cent.: probably a back-formation from **ORIENTATION**.

o·ri·en·ta·tion /ˌôrēənˈtāSHən/ ▶ **n.** the determination of the relative position of something or someone (esp. oneself): *the child's surroundings provide clues to help in orientation.* ■ the relative physical position or direction of something: *two complex shapes, presented in different orientations.* ■ Zoology an animal's change of position in response to an external stimulus, esp. with respect to compass directions. ■ familiarization with something: *their training and orientation comes out of magazine and newspaper distribution.* ■ a program of introduction for students new to a school or college: *she attended freshman orientation.* ■ the direction of someone's interest or attitude, esp. political or sexual: *a common age of consent regardless of gender or sexual orientation.*
– DERIVATIVES **o·ri·en·ta·tion·al adj.**
– ORIGIN mid 19th cent.: apparently from **ORIENT**.

o·ri·en·teer /ˌôrēənˈtir/ ▶ **n.** a person who takes part in orienteering.
▶ **v.** [no obj.] take part in orienteering.

o·ri·en·teer·ing /ˌôriənˈti(ə)riNG/ ▶ **n.** a competitive sport in which participants find their way to various checkpoints across rough country with the aid of a map and compass, the winner being the one with the lowest elapsed time.
– ORIGIN 1940s: from Swedish *orientering*.

O·ri·ent Ex·press a train that ran between Paris and Istanbul and other Balkan cities, via Vienna, from 1883 to 1961. Since 1961 the name has been used for various trains running in Europe, Asia, and Australia, some of which run over parts of the old route.

or·i·fice /ˈôrəfis/ ▶ **n.** an opening, as of a pipe or tube, or one in the body, such as a nostril or the anus.
– ORIGIN late Middle English: from French, from late Latin *orificium*, from *os, or-* 'mouth' + *facere* 'make.'

or·i·flamme /ˈôrəˌflam, ˈär-/ ▶ **n.** literary (in historical use) a scarlet banner or knight's standard. ■ a principle or ideal that serves as a rallying point in a struggle.
– ORIGIN late Middle English: from Old French, from Latin *aurum* 'gold' + *flamma* 'flame.'

orig. ▶ **abbr.** ■ origin. ■ original; originally.

o·ri·ga·mi /ˌôrəˈgämē/ ▶ **n.** the Japanese art of folding paper into decorative shapes and figures.
– ORIGIN Japanese, from *oru, -ori* 'fold' + *kami* 'paper.'

origami

o·ri·ga·num /əˈrigənəm/ ▶ **n.** an aromatic plant of a genus that includes marjoram and oregano. ● Genus *Origanum*, family Labiatae.
– ORIGIN Latin, from Greek *origanon*, perhaps from *oros* 'mountain' + *ganos* 'brightness.'

Or·i·gen /ˈôriˌjen, ˈär-/ (*c.*185–*c.*254), Christian scholar and theologian, probably born in Alexandria, Egypt. His most well-known work was the *Hexapla*, an edition of the Old Testament with six or more parallel versions.

or·i·gin /ˈôrəjən/ ▶ **n. 1** the point or place where something begins, arises, or is derived: *a novel theory about the origin of oil | the name is Norse in origin | the terminology has its origins in America.* ■ a person's social background or ancestry: *they will be asked about their ethnic origin | a voice that betrays his Southern origins.*
2 Anatomy the place or point where a muscle, nerve, or other body part arises, in particular: ■ the more fixed end or attachment of a muscle. ■ a place where a nerve or blood vessel begins or branches from a main nerve or blood vessel.
3 Mathematics a fixed point from which coordinates are measured, as where axes intersect.
– ORIGIN early 16th cent.: from French *origine*, from Latin *origo, origin-*, from *oriri* 'to rise.'

o·rig·i·nal /əˈrijənl/ ▶ **adj. 1** present or existing from the beginning; first or earliest: *the original owner of the house | the plasterwork is probably original.*
2 created directly and personally by a particular artist; not a copy or imitation: *original Rembrandts | playing original material.*
3 not dependent on other people's ideas; inventive and unusual: *a subtle and original thinker.*
▶ **n. 1** something serving as a model or basis for imitations or copies: *the portrait may be a copy of the original | one set of originals and four photocopies.* ■ (**the original**) the form or language in which something was first produced or created: *the study of Russian texts in the original.* ■ (**the original of**) a person or place on which a character or location in a literary work is based: *the paper where the original of the play's Walter Burns worked.* ■ a book or recording that has not been previously made available in a different form: *paperback originals.* ■ a garment made to order from a design specially prepared for a fashion collection.
2 an eccentric or unusual person: *he was one of the true originals.*
– ORIGIN Middle English (the earliest use being in the phrase *original sin*): from Old French, or from Latin *originalis*, from *origin-* (see **ORIGIN**).

o·rig·i·nal grav·i·ty ▶ **n.** the relative density of the wort before it is fermented to produce beer, being chiefly dependent on the quantity of fermentable sugars in solution. It is regarded as a guide to the alcoholic strength of the finished beer.

o·rig·i·nal in·stru·ment ▶ **n.** a musical instrument, or a copy of one, dating from the time the music played on it was composed.

o·rig·i·nal·ism /əˈrijinlizm/ ▶ **n.** the principle or belief that the original intent of an author should be adhered to in later interpretations of a work. ■ Law the judicial interpretation of the constitution that aims to follow closely the original intentions of those who drafted it.

o·rig·i·nal·i·ty /əˌrijəˈnalitē/ ▶ **n.** the ability to think independently and creatively: *a writer of great originality.* ■ the quality of being novel or unusual: *he congratulated her on the originality of her costume.*

o·rig·i·nal·ly /əˈrijənl-ē/ ▶ **adv. 1** from or in the beginning; at first: *potatoes originally came from South America.*
2 in a novel and inventive way: *suggestions so originally and persuasively outlined.*

o·rig·i·nal sin ▶ **n.** Christian Theology the tendency to sin innate in all human beings, held to be inherited from Adam in consequence of the Fall. The concept of original sin was developed in the writings of St. Augustine.

o·rig·i·nate /əˈrijəˌnāt/ ▶ **v.** [no obj.] have a specified beginning: *the word originated as a marketing term.* ■ [with obj.] create or initiate (something): *he is responsible for originating this particular cliché.*
– DERIVATIVES **o·rig·i·na·tion** /əˌrijəˈnāSHən/ **n.**, **o·rig·i·na·tive** /-ˌnātiv/ **adj.**
– ORIGIN mid 17th cent.: from medieval Latin *originat-* 'caused to begin,' from Latin *origo, origin-* 'source, origin.'

o·rig·i·na·tion fee /əˌrijəˈnāSHən/ ▶ **n.** Finance a fee charged by a lender on entering into a loan agreement to cover the cost of processing the loan.

o·rig·i·na·tor /əˈrijəˌnātər/ ▶ **n.** a person who creates or initiates something: *Wegener was the originator of the theory of continental drift.*

Or·i·mul·sion /äriˈməlSHən/ ▶ **n.** trademark a fuel consisting of an emulsion of bitumen in water.
– ORIGIN 1980s: blend of *Orinoco* (the name of an oil belt in Venezuela, where the bitumen was originally extracted) and **EMULSION**.

O-ring ▶ **n.** a gasket in the form of a ring with a circular cross section, typically made of pliable material, used to seal connections in pipes, tubes, etc.

Or·i·no·co /ˌôrəˈnōkō/ a river in northern South America that rises in southeastern Venezuela and flows 1,280 miles (2,060 km), entering the Atlantic Ocean through a vast delta. For part of its length it forms the border between Colombia and Venezuela.

o·ri·ole /ˈôrēˌōl/ ▶ **n. 1** an Old World bird related to the starlings that feeds on fruit and insects, the male typically having bright yellow and black plumage. ● Family Oriolidae and genus *Oriolus*: many species, including the **golden oriole** (*Oriolus oriolus*).
2 a New World bird of the American blackbird family, with black and orange or yellow plumage. ● Genus *Icterus*, family Icteridae (sometimes called the **American oriole family**): many species, including the **Baltimore oriole**.
– ORIGIN late 18th cent.: from medieval Latin *oriolus* (in Old French *oriol*), from Latin *aureolus*, diminutive of *aureus* 'golden,' from *aurum* 'gold.'

O·ri·on /əˈrīən/ **1** Greek Mythology a giant and hunter who was changed into a constellation at his death.
2 Astronomy a conspicuous constellation (the Hunter), said to represent a hunter holding a club and shield. It lies on the celestial equator and contains many bright stars, including Rigel, Betelgeuse, and a line of three that form **Orion's belt**. ■ (as genitive **Orionis** /ˌôrēˈōnis/) used with a preceding letter or numeral to designate a star in this constellation: *the multiple star Theta Orionis.*
– ORIGIN via Latin from Greek.

Or·i·sha /ˈôrəˌSHä/ ▶ **n.** (pl. **same**) (in southern Nigeria) any of several minor gods. The term is also used in various religious cults of South America and the Caribbean.
– ORIGIN Yoruba.

or·i·son /ˈôrisən, -zən, ˈär-/ ▶ **n.** archaic a prayer.
– ORIGIN Middle English: from Old French *oreison*, from Latin *oratio(n-)* 'speech' (see **ORATION**).

O·ris·sa /ôˈrisə/ a state in eastern India, on the Bay of Bengal; capital, Bhubaneswar.

-orium ▶ **suffix** forming nouns denoting a place for a particular function: *auditorium | sanatorium.*
– ORIGIN from Latin; compare with **-ORY**[1].

O·ri·ya /ôˈrēə/ ▶ **n.** (pl. **same** or **Oriyas**) **1** a native or inhabitant of Orissa.
2 the Indic language of this people, closely related to Bengali.
– ORIGIN from Hindi *Uṛiyā*.

Ork·ney Is·lands /ˈôrknē/ (also **Orkney** or **the Orkneys**) a group of more than 70 islands off the northeastern tip of Scotland, constituting an administrative region of Scotland; pop. 20,100 (est. 2009); chief town, Kirkwall. They came into Scottish possession in 1472, having previously been ruled by Norway and Denmark.

Or·lan·do /ôrˈlandō/ a city in central Florida; pop. 230,519 (est. 2008). It is a popular tourist resort.

orle /ôrl/ ▶ **n.** Heraldry a narrow border inset from the edge of a shield.
– ORIGIN late 16th cent.: from French *ourle*, from *ourler* 'to hem,' based on Latin *ora* 'edge.'

Or·le·an·ist /ˈôrlēənist/ ▶ **n.** historical a person supporting the claim to the French throne of the descendants of the Duke of Orleans (1640–1701), younger brother of Louis XIV, esp. Louis Philippe (King of France, 1830–48).
– ORIGIN from French *Orléaniste*, from *Orléans*.

Or·le·ans /ˈôrlē(ə)nz, ôrˈlē(ə)nz, ôrlāˈäN/ a city in central France, on the Loire River; pop. 116,256 (2006). In 1429, it was the scene of Joan of Arc's first victory over the English during the Hundred Years War. French name **Orléans**.

Or·lon /ˈôrˌlän/ ▶ **n.** trademark a synthetic acrylic fiber used for textiles and knitwear, or a fabric made from it.
– ORIGIN 1950s: invented word, on the pattern of *nylon*.

or·lop /ˈôrˌläp/ (also **orlop deck**) ▶ **n.** the lowest deck of a wooden sailing ship with three or more decks.
– ORIGIN late Middle English: from Dutch *overloop* 'covering,' from *overlopen* 'run over.'

Or·man·dy /ˈôrməndē/, Eugene (1899–1985), US conductor; born in Hungary; born *Jeno Blau*. He was conductor of the Philadelphia Orchestra from 1938 to 1980, the longest directorship of an orchestra in US history.

Or·mazd /ˈôrməzd/ (also **Ormuzd**) another name for **AHURA MAZDA**.

or·mo·lu /ˈôrməˌlo͞o/ ▶ **n.** a gold-colored alloy of copper, zinc, and sometimes tin, cast into desired shapes and often gilded, used esp. in the 18th century for decorating furniture and making ornaments.
– ORIGIN mid 18th cent.: from French *or moulu* 'powdered gold' (used in gilding).

or·na·ment ▶ **n.** /ˈôrnəmənt/ a thing used to make something look more attractive but usually having

O

PRONUNCIATION KEY ə *ago, up*; ər *over, fur*; a *hat*; ā *ate*; ä *car*; e *let*; ē *see*; i *fit*; ī *by*; NG *sing*; ō *go*; ô *law, for*; oi *toy*; o͝o *good*; o͞o *goo*; ou *out*; TH *thin*; T͟H *then*; ZH *vision*

no practical purpose, esp. a small object such as a figurine. ■ a quality or person adding grace, beauty, or honor to something: *the design would be a great ornament to the metropolis.* ■ decoration added to embellish something, esp. a building: *it served more for ornament than for protection.* ■ (**ornaments**) Music embellishments and decorations, such as trills or grace notes, added to a melody. ■ (usu. **ornaments**) Christian Church the accessories of worship, such as the altar, chalice, and sacred vessels.
▶ **v.** /ˈôrnə,ment/ [with obj.] make (something) look more attractive by adding decorative items: *the men and women in the Stone Age ornamented their caves.*
– ORIGIN Middle English (also in the sense 'accessory'): from Old French *ournement*, from Latin *ornamentum* 'equipment, ornament,' from *ornare* 'adorn.' The verb dates from the early 18th cent.

or·na·men·tal /,ôrnəˈmentl/ ▶ **adj.** serving or intended as an ornament; decorative: *an ornamental fountain.*
▶ **n.** a plant or tree grown for its attractive appearance.
– DERIVATIVES **or·na·men·tal·ism** /-,izəm/ **n.**, **or·na·men·tal·ist** /-ist/ **n.**, **or·na·men·tal·ly adv.**

or·na·men·ta·tion /,ôrnəmenˈtāSHən/ ▶ **n.** things added to something to provide decoration: *a baroque chandelier with plasterwork ornamentation.* ■ the action of decorating something or making it more elaborate: *the rhetorical ornamentation of text.*

or·nate /ôrˈnāt/ ▶ **adj.** made in an intricate shape or decorated with complex patterns: *an ornate wrought-iron railing.* ■ (of literary style) using unusual words and complex constructions: *peculiarly ornate and metaphorical language.* ■ (of musical composition or performance) using many ornaments such as grace notes and trills.
– DERIVATIVES **or·nate·ly adv.**, **or·nate·ness n.**
– ORIGIN late Middle English: from Latin *ornatus* 'adorned,' past participle of *ornare*.

or·ner·y /ˈôrn(ə)rē/ ▶ **adj.** informal bad-tempered and combative: *some hogs are just mean and ornery.* ■ stubborn: *taking the singer's ornery radicalism in a different direction.*
– DERIVATIVES **or·ner·i·ness n.**
– ORIGIN early 19th cent.: variant of **ORDINARY**, representing a dialect pronunciation.

ornith. ▶ **abbr.** ■ ornithological. ■ ornithology.

or·ni·thine /ˈôrnə,THēn/ ▶ **n.** Biochemistry an amino acid produced by the body that is important in protein metabolism. ● Chem. formula: $NH_2(CH_2)_3CH(NH_2)COOH$.
– ORIGIN late 19th cent.: from **ORNITHO-** (with reference to a constituent found in bird excrement) + **-INE**[4].

or·nith·is·chi·an /,ôrnəˈTHiskēən/ Paleontology ▶ **adj.** of, relating to, or denoting herbivorous dinosaurs of an order distinguished by having a pelvic structure resembling that of birds. Compare with **SAURISCHIAN.**
▶ **n.** an ornithischian dinosaur. ● Order Ornithischia, superorder Dinosauria; comprises the stegosaurs, ankylosaurs, ornithopods, pachycephalosaurs, and ceratopsians.
– ORIGIN early 20th cent.: from modern Latin *Ornithiscia*, from Greek *ornis, ornith-* 'bird' + *iskhion* 'hip joint.'

ornitho- ▶ **comb. form** relating to or resembling a bird or birds: *ornithology | ornithopod.*
– ORIGIN from Greek *ornis, ornith-* 'bird.'

or·ni·thol·o·gy /,ôrnəˈTHäləjē/ ▶ **n.** the scientific study of birds.
– DERIVATIVES **or·ni·tho·log·i·cal** /,ôrniTHəˈläjikəl/ **adj.**, **or·ni·tho·log·i·cal·ly** /,ôrniTHəˈläjik(ə)lē/ **adv.**, **or·ni·thol·o·gist** /-jist/ **n.**
– ORIGIN late 17th cent.: from modern Latin *ornithologia*, from Greek *ornithologos* 'treating of birds.'

or·nith·o·mi·mo·saur /,ôrnəTHōˈmimə,sôr/ ▶ **n.** technical term for **OSTRICH DINOSAUR.**
– ORIGIN 1980s: from modern Latin *Ornithomimosauria*, from Greek *ornis, ornith-* 'bird' + *mimos* 'mime' + *sauros* 'lizard.'

or·ni·tho·pod /ˈôrnəTHə,päd/ ▶ **n.** a mainly bipedal herbivorous dinosaur. ● Infraorder Ornithopoda, order Ornithischia; includes the hadrosaurs, iguanodon, hypsilophodont, etc.
– ORIGIN late 19th cent.: from modern Latin *Ornithopoda*, from Greek *ornis, ornith-* 'bird' + *pous, pod-* 'foot.'

or·ni·thop·ter /,ôrnəˈTHäptər/ ▶ **n.** chiefly historical a machine designed to achieve flight by means of flapping wings.
– ORIGIN early 20th cent.: coined in French as *ornithoptère*.

or·ni·tho·rhyn·chus /,ôrnəTHəˈriNGkəs/ ▶ **n.** another term for **PLATYPUS.**
– ORIGIN early 19th cent.: modern Latin, from **ORNITHO-** + Greek *rhunkhos* 'bill.'

or·ni·tho·sis /,ôrnəˈTHōsis/ ▶ **n.** another term for **PSITTACOSIS.**

oro- ▶ **comb. form** of or relating to mountains: *orogeny.*
– ORIGIN from Greek *oros* 'mountain.'

or·o·gen /ˈôrə,jen, -jən/ ▶ **n.** Geology a belt of the earth's crust involved in the formation of mountains.
– ORIGIN 1920s: from Greek *oros* 'mountain' + **-GEN.**

o·rog·e·ny /ôˈräjənē/ ▶ **n.** Geology a process in which a section of the earth's crust is folded and deformed by lateral compression to form a mountain range.
– DERIVATIVES **or·o·gen·e·sis** /,ôrōˈjenəsis/ **n.**, **or·o·gen·ic** /,ôrōˈjenik/ **adj.**

or·o·graph·ic /,ôrəˈgrafik/ ▶ **adj.** of or relating to mountains, esp. with regard to their position and form. ■ (of clouds or rainfall) resulting from the effects of mountains in forcing moist air to rise.
– DERIVATIVES **or·o·graph·i·cal adj.**

o·rog·ra·phy /ôˈrägrəfē/ ▶ **n.** the branch of physical geography dealing with mountains.

O·ro·mo /ôˈrōmō/ ▶ **n.** (pl. **same** or **Oromos**) **1** a member of the largest ethnic group in Ethiopia.
2 the Cushitic language of this people.
▶ **adj.** of or relating to this people or their language.
– ORIGIN the name in Oromo. An earlier term, *Galla*, remains in use but is not favored by the Oromo themselves.

O·ro·no /ˈôrə,nō/ a town in east central Maine, on the Penobscot River, north of Bangor, home to the University of Maine; pop. 9,670 (est. 2008).

O·ron·tes /ôˈräntēz/ a river in southwestern Asia that rises near Baalbek in northern Lebanon and flows 355 miles (571 km) through western and northern Syria before turning west through southern Turkey to enter the Mediterranean Sea. It is an important source of water for irrigation, esp. in Syria.

o·ro·pen·do·la /,ôrəˈpendl-ə/ ▶ **n.** a gregarious tropical American bird of the American blackbird family that constructs a pendulous nest and has brown or black plumage with yellow outer tail feathers. ● Genus *Psarocolius*, family Icteridae: several species.
– ORIGIN late 19th cent.: from Spanish, literally 'golden oriole.'

o·ro·phar·ynx /,ôrōˈfariNGks/ ▶ **n.** (pl. **oropharynges** /-fəˈrinjēz/ or **oropharynxes**) Anatomy the part of the pharynx that lies between the soft palate and the hyoid bone.
– DERIVATIVES **o·ro·pha·ryn·ge·al** /-fəˈrinj(ē)əl, -,farənˈjēəl/ **adj.**
– ORIGIN late 19th cent.: formed irregularly from Latin *os, -or* 'mouth' + **PHARYNX.**

o·ro·tund /ˈôrə,tənd/ ▶ **adj.** (of the voice or phrasing) full, round, and imposing. ■ (of writing, style, or expression) pompous; pretentious.
– DERIVATIVES **o·ro·tun·di·ty** /,ôrəˈtəndité/ **n.**
– ORIGIN late 18th cent.: from Latin *ore rotundo* 'with rounded mouth.'

or·phan /ˈôrfən/ ▶ **n. 1** a child whose parents are dead.
2 Printing the first line of a paragraph set as the last line of a page or column, considered undesirable.
▶ **v.** [with obj.] make (a person or animal) an orphan: *John was orphaned at 12.*
– DERIVATIVES **or·phan·hood** /-,ho͝od/ **n.**
– ORIGIN late Middle English: via late Latin from Greek *orphanos* 'bereaved.'

or·phan·age /ˈôrfənij/ ▶ **n.** a residential institution for the care and education of orphans. ■ archaic the state or condition of being an orphan.

or·phan drug ▶ **n.** a pharmaceutical that remains commercially undeveloped owing to limited potential for profitability.

Or·phe·us /ˈôrfēəs/ Greek Mythology a poet who could entrance wild beasts with the beauty of his singing and lyre playing. He went to the underworld after the death of his wife Eurydice and secured her release from the dead, but lost her because he failed to obey the condition that he must not look back at her until they had reached the world of the living.
– DERIVATIVES **Or·phe·an** /-fēən/ **adj.**

Or·phic /ˈôrfik/ ▶ **adj.** of or concerning Orpheus or Orphism.
– ORIGIN late 17th cent.: via Latin from Greek *Orphikos*, from *Orpheus* (see **ORPHEUS**).

Or·phism /ˈôr,fizəm/ ▶ **n. 1** a mystic religion of ancient Greece, originating in the 7th or 6th century BC and based on poems (now lost) attributed to Orpheus, emphasizing the necessity for individuals to rid themselves of the evil part of their nature by ritual and moral purification throughout a series of reincarnations.
2 a short-lived art movement (*c.*1912) within cubism, pioneered by a group of French painters (including Robert Delaunay, Sonia Delaunay-Terk, and Fernand Léger) and emphasizing the lyrical use of color rather than the austere intellectual cubism of Picasso, Braque, and Gris.

or·phrey /ˈôrfrē/ ▶ **n.** (pl. **orphreys**) an ornamental stripe or border, esp. one on an ecclesiastical vestment such as a chasuble.
– ORIGIN Middle English: from Old French *orfreis*, from a medieval Latin alteration of *auriphrygium*, from Latin *aurum* 'gold' + *Phrygius* 'Phrygian' (also used in the sense 'embroidered').

or·pi·ment /ˈôrpəmənt/ ▶ **n.** a bright yellow mineral consisting of arsenic trisulfide, formerly used as a dye and artist's pigment.
– ORIGIN late Middle English: via Old French from Latin *auripigmentum*, from *aurum* 'gold' + *pigmentum* 'pigment.'

or·pine /ˈôrpən/ (also **orpin**) ▶ **n.** a purple-flowered Eurasian plant of the stonecrop family, a naturalized weed of North America. ● *Sedum telephium*, family Crassulaceae.
– ORIGIN Middle English: from Old French *orpine*, probably an alteration of **ORPIMENT**, originally applied to a yellow-flowered sedum.

Or·ping·ton /ˈôrpiNGtən/ ▶ **n. 1** a full-bodied breed of chicken of buff, white, or black color.
2 a duck of a buff or white breed, kept for its meat.
– ORIGIN late 19th cent.: from *Orpington*, the name of a town in Kent, England.

Orr /ôr/, Bobby (1948–), US hockey player; born in Canada; full name *Robert Gordon Orr*. He signed with the Boston Bruins at the age of eighteen in 1966 and played for them until 1976. He played for the Chicago Blackhawks before retiring in 1978. Hockey Hall of Fame (1979).

or·rer·y /ˈôrərē/ ▶ **n.** (pl. **orreries**) a mechanical model of the solar system, or of just the sun, earth, and moon, used to represent their relative positions and motions.
– ORIGIN early 18th cent.: named after the fourth Earl of *Orrery*, for whom one was made.

or·ris /ˈôris/ (also **orrisroot**) ▶ **n.** a preparation of the fragrant rootstock of an iris, used in perfumery and formerly in medicine. ● The root is usually taken from *Iris* × *germanica* var. *Florentina*.
– ORIGIN mid 16th cent.: apparently an unexplained alteration of **IRIS.**

Orsk /ôrsk/ a city in southern Russia, in the Ural Mountains, on the Ural River, near the border with Kazakhstan; pop. 245,500 (est. 2008).

ort /ôrt/ ▶ **n.** (usu. **orts**) archaic or dialect a scrap or remainder of food from a meal.
– ORIGIN late Middle English: from Middle Low German *orte* 'food remains,' originally a compound of which the second element is related to **EAT.**

ort·a·nique /,ôrtəˈnēk/ ▶ **n.** a citrus fruit that is a cross between an orange and a tangerine, developed in Jamaica in the 1920s. ● *Citrus sinensis* × reticulata, family Rutaceae.
– ORIGIN blend of **ORANGE, TANGERINE,** and **UNIQUE.**

Or·te·ga /ôrˈtāgə/, Daniel (1945–), Nicaraguan statesman; president 1985–90 and from 2007; full name *Daniel Ortega Saavedra*. He became the leader of the Sandinista National Liberation Front (FSLN) in 1966 and president after the Sandinista election victory in 1984. He was re-elected president in 2007.

Or·te·ga y Gas·set /ē gäˈset/, José (1883–1955), Spanish philosopher. His works include *The Revolt of the Masses* (1930), in which he proposed leadership by an intellectual elite.

orth. ▶ **abbr.** orthopedic; orthopedics.

ortho- ▶ **comb. form 1** straight; rectangular; upright: *orthodontics.* ■ right; correct: *orthoepy.*
2 Chemistry denoting substitution at two adjacent carbon atoms in a benzene ring, e.g., in 1, 2 positions: *orthodichlorobenzene.* Compare with **META-** and **PARA-**[1].
3 Chemistry denoting a compound from which a *meta*-compound is formed by dehydration: *orthophosphoric acid.*
– ORIGIN from Greek *orthos* 'straight, right.'

or·tho·ce·phal·ic /,ôrTHōsəˈfalik/ ▶ **adj.** having a head with a medium ratio of breadth to height.

or·tho·chro·mat·ic /,ôrTHōkrəˈmatik/ ▶ **adj.** (of black-and-white photographic film) sensitive to all visible light except red. Orthochromatic film can therefore be handled in red light in the darkroom but does not produce black-and-white tones that correspond very closely to the colors seen by the eye. Often contrasted with **PANCHROMATIC.**

or·tho·clase /ˈôrTHə,klās, -,klāz/ ▶ **n.** a common rock-forming mineral occurring typically as white or pink crystals. It is a potassium-rich alkali feldspar and is used in ceramics and glassmaking.
– ORIGIN mid 19th cent.: from **ORTHO-** 'straight' + Greek *klasis* 'breaking' (because of the characteristic two cleavages at right angles).

O

or·tho·don·tics /ˌôrTHəˈdäntiks/ (also **orthodontia** /-ˈdänsH(ē)ə/) ▶ **plural n.** [treated as sing.] the treatment of irregularities in the teeth (esp. of alignment and occlusion) and jaws, including the use of braces.
– DERIVATIVES **or·tho·don·tic** adj., **or·tho·don·ti·cal·ly** /-tik(ə)lē/ adv., **or·tho·don·tist** /-tist/ n.
– ORIGIN early 20th cent.: from ORTHO- 'straight' + Greek *odous, odont-* 'tooth.'

or·tho·dox /ˈôrTHəˌdäks/ ▶ **adj. 1** (of a person or their views, esp. religious or political ones, or other beliefs or practices) conforming to what is generally or traditionally accepted as right or true; established and approved: *the orthodox economics of today | orthodox medical treatment | orthodox Hindus.* ■ (of a person) not independent-minded; conventional and unoriginal: *a relatively orthodox artist.*
2 (of a thing) of the ordinary or usual type; normal: *they avoided orthodox jazz venues.*
3 (usu. **Orthodox**) (of the Jews or Judaism) strictly keeping to traditional doctrine and ritual.
4 (usu. **Orthodox**) of or relating to the Orthodox Church.
– DERIVATIVES **or·tho·dox·ly** adv.
– ORIGIN late Middle English: from Greek *orthodoxos* (probably via ecclesiastical Latin), from *orthos* 'straight or right' + *doxa* 'opinion.'

Or·tho·dox Church a Christian church or federation of churches originating in the Greek-speaking church of the Byzantine Empire, not accepting the authority of the pope, and using ancient forms of service.

> The chief Orthodox churches (often known collectively as the **Eastern Orthodox Church**) include the national churches of Greece, Russia, Bulgaria, Romania, and Serbia. The term is also used by other ancient churches, mainly of African or Asian origin, e.g., the Coptic, Syrian, and Ethiopian churches.

Or·tho·dox Ju·da·ism a major branch within Judaism that teaches strict adherence to rabbinical interpretation of Jewish law and its traditional observances.

or·tho·dox·y /ˈôrTHəˌdäksē/ ▶ **n.** (pl. **orthodoxies**) **1** authorized or generally accepted theory, doctrine, or practice: *monetarist orthodoxy | he challenged many of the established orthodoxies.* ■ the quality of conforming to such theories, doctrines, or practices: *writings of unimpeachable orthodoxy.*
2 the whole community of Orthodox Jews or Orthodox Christians.
– ORIGIN mid 17th cent.: via late Latin from late Greek *orthodoxia* 'sound doctrine,' from *orthodoxos* (see ORTHODOX).

or·tho·drom·ic /ˌôrTHəˈdrämik/ ▶ **adj.** Physiology (of an impulse) traveling in the normal direction in a nerve fiber. The opposite of ANTIDROMIC.
– ORIGIN 1940s: from ORTHO- 'right, correct' + Greek *dromos* 'running' + -IC.

or·tho·e·py /ôrˈTHōəpē/ ▶ **n.** the correct or accepted pronunciation of words. ■ the study of correct or accepted pronunciation.
– DERIVATIVES **or·tho·ep·ic** /ˌôrTHōˈepik/ adj., **or·tho·e·pist** /-pist/ n.
– ORIGIN mid 17th cent.: from Greek *orthoepeia* 'correct speech,' from *orthos* 'right or straight' + *epos, epe-* 'word.'

or·tho·gen·e·sis /ˌôrTHōˈjenəsis/ ▶ **n.** Biology, chiefly historical a theory that variations in evolution follow a particular direction and are not merely sporadic and fortuitous.
– DERIVATIVES **or·tho·gen·e·sist** n., **or·tho·ge·net·ic** /-jəˈnetik/ adj., **or·tho·ge·net·i·cal·ly** /-jəˈnetik(ə)lē/ adv.

or·thog·na·thous /ôrˈTHägnəTHəs/ ▶ **adj.** Anatomy (esp. of a person) having a jaw that does not project or recede, so that the facial profile is nearly vertical.
– ORIGIN mid 19th cent.: from ORTHO- 'straight' + Greek *gnathos* 'jaw' + -OUS.

or·thog·o·nal /ôrˈTHägənl/ ▶ **adj. 1** of or involving right angles; at right angles.
2 Statistics (of variates) statistically independent. ■ (of an experiment) having variates that can be treated as statistically independent.
– DERIVATIVES **or·thog·o·nal·i·ty** /ôrˌTHägəˈnalitē/ n., **or·thog·o·nal·ly** adv.
– ORIGIN late 16th cent.: from French, based on Greek *orthogōnios* 'right-angled.'

or·thog·o·nal pro·jec·tion ▶ **n.** Engineering a system of making engineering drawings showing two or more views of an object at right angles to each other on a single drawing. ■ a drawing made using this method.

or·tho·graph·ic pro·jec·tion /ˌôrTHəˈgrafik/ ▶ **n.** a method of projection in which an object is depicted or a surface mapped using parallel lines to project its shape onto a plane. ■ a drawing or map made using this method.

or·thog·ra·phy /ôrˈTHägrəfē/ ▶ **n.** (pl. **orthographies**) **1** the conventional spelling system of a language. ■ the study of spelling and how letters combine to represent sounds and form words.
2 another term for ORTHOGRAPHIC PROJECTION.
– DERIVATIVES **or·thog·ra·pher** /-fər/ n. (sense 1), **or·tho·graph·ic** /ˌôrTHəˈgrafik/ adj., **or·tho·graph·i·cal** /ˌôrTHəˈgrafikəl/ adj., **or·tho·graph·i·cal·ly** /ˌôrTHəˈgrafik(ə)lē/ adv.
– ORIGIN late Middle English: via Old French and Latin from Greek *orthographia*, from *orthos* 'correct' + *-graphia* 'writing.'

or·tho·ker·a·tol·o·gy /ˌôrTHōˌkerəˈtäləjē/ ▶ **n.** the temporary reshaping of the cornea (usually overnight) with specially made rigid contact lenses, in order to correct myopia.

or·tho·mo·lec·u·lar /ˌôrTHōməˈlekyələr/ ▶ **adj.** pertaining to a theory that illness can be treated and health maximized by creating the optimal molecular environment for the cells of the body through the introduction of natural substances: *orthomolecular nutrition/psychiatry/oncology.*
– ORIGIN 1968: coined by Linus *Pauling.*

or·tho·mor·phic /ˌôrTHōˈmôrfik/ ▶ **adj.** see CONFORMAL.

Or·tho·nec·ti·da /ˌôrTHəˈnektidə/ Zoology a minor phylum of mesozoan worms that are internal parasites of a range of marine invertebrates.
– DERIVATIVES **or·tho·nec·tid** n. & adj.
– ORIGIN modern Latin (plural), from Greek *orthos* 'straight' + *nektos* 'swimming' (see NEKTON).

or·tho·nor·mal /ˌôrTHəˈnôrməl/ ▶ **adj.** Mathematics both orthogonal and normalized.
– DERIVATIVES **or·tho·nor·mal·i·ty** /-nôrˈmalitē/ n., **or·tho·nor·mal·i·za·tion** /-ˌnôrməliˈzāsHən/ n.

or·tho·pe·dics /ˌôrTHəˈpēdiks/ (Brit. **orthopaedics**) ▶ **plural n.** [treated as sing.] the branch of medicine dealing with the correction of deformities of bones or muscles. [originally relating specifically to children.]
– DERIVATIVES **or·tho·pe·dic** adj., **or·tho·pe·di·cal·ly** /-ik(ə)lē/ adv., **or·tho·pe·dist** /-dist/ n.
– ORIGIN mid 19th cent.: from French *orthopédie*, from Greek *orthos* 'right or straight' + *paideia* 'rearing of children.'

or·tho·phos·phor·ic ac·id /ˌôrTHōfäsˈfôrik, -ˈfär-/ ▶ **n.** another term for PHOSPHORIC ACID.
– DERIVATIVES **or·tho·phos·phate** /-ˈfäsfāt/ n.

or·tho·pox·vi·rus /ˈôrTHōˌpäksˌvīrəs/ ▶ **n.** any of a set of viruses pathological in humans and animals that includes the cowpox, smallpox, and monkeypox viruses. ● Genus *Orthopoxvirus*, family Poxviridae.

or·tho·psy·chi·a·try /ˌôrTHōˌsīˈkīətrē/ ▶ **n.** the branch of psychiatry concerned with the study and prevention of mental or behavioral disorders, with emphasis on child development and family life.
– DERIVATIVES **or·tho·psy·chi·at·ric** /-ˌsīkēˈatrik/ adj., **or·tho·psy·chi·a·trist** /-trist/ n.

or·thop·ter /ôrˈTHäptər/ ▶ **n.** another term for ORNITHOPTER.

Or·thop·ter·a /ôrˈTHäptərə/ Entomology an order of insects that comprises the grasshoppers, crickets, katydids, etc. They have a saddle-shaped thorax, hind legs that are typically long and modified for jumping, and a characteristic song that the male produces by stridulation. ■ (as plural noun **orthoptera**) insects of this order.
– ORIGIN modern Latin (plural), from ORTHO- 'straight' + Greek *pteros* 'wing.'

or·thop·ter·an /ôrˈTHäptərən/ Entomology ▶ **n.** an insect of the order Orthoptera, such as a grasshopper or cricket.
▶ **adj.** relating to or denoting orthopterans.
– DERIVATIVES **or·thop·ter·ous** /-tərəs/ adj.

or·thop·ter·oid /ôrˈTHäptəˌroid/ ▶ **adj.** Entomology of or relating to a group of insect orders that are related to the grasshoppers and crickets, including also the stoneflies, stick insects, earwigs, cockroaches, mantises, and termites.

or·thop·tics /ôrˈTHäptiks/ ▶ **plural n.** [treated as sing.] the study or treatment of disorders of vision, esp. of eye movements or eye alignment.
– DERIVATIVES **or·thop·tic** adj., **or·thop·tist** /-tist/ n.
– ORIGIN late 19th cent.: from ORTHO- 'correct' + Greek *optikos* (see OPTIC).

or·tho·py·rox·ene /ˌôrTHōpīˈräksēn/ ▶ **n.** a mineral of the pyroxene group crystallizing in the orthorhombic system.

or·tho·rex·i·a /ˌôrTHəˈreksēə/ ▶ **n.** an obsession with eating foods that one considers healthy. ■ (also **orthorexia nervosa** /nərˈvōsə/) a medical condition in which the sufferer systematically avoids specific foods in the belief that they are harmful.
– DERIVATIVES **or·tho·rex·ic** adj. & n.
– ORIGIN 1990s: from *ortho-* + Greek *orexia*, 'appetite,' after *anorexia.*

or·tho·rhom·bic /ˌôrTHəˈrämbik/ ▶ **adj.** of or denoting a crystal system or three-dimensional geometric arrangement having three unequal axes at right angles.

or·tho·sis /ôrˈTHōsis/ ▶ **n.** (pl. **orthoses** /-ˌsēz/) Medicine the correction of disorders of the limbs or spine by use of braces and other devices to correct alignment or provide support. ■ a brace or other such device; orthotic.
– ORIGIN 1950s: from Greek *orthōsis* 'making straight,' from *orthoun* 'set straight.'

or·tho·stat·ic /ˌôrTHəˈstatik/ ▶ **adj.** Medicine relating to or caused by an upright posture.

or·thos·ti·chy /ôrˈTHästikē/ ▶ **n.** (pl. **orthostichies**) Botany (in phyllotaxis) a vertical row of leaves arranged one directly above another. Contrasted with PARASTICHY.
– ORIGIN late 19th cent.: from ORTHO- 'upright, straight' + Greek *stikhos* 'row, rank.'

or·thot·ic /ôrˈTHätik/ ▶ **adj.** relating to orthotics.
▶ **n.** an artificial support or brace for the limbs or spine.

or·thot·ics /ôrˈTHätiks/ ▶ **plural n.** [treated as sing.] the branch of medicine that deals with the provision and use of artificial devices such as splints and braces.
– DERIVATIVES **or·thot·ist** n.

or·tho·trop·ic /ˌôrTHəˈtrōpik, -ˈträp-/ ▶ **adj. 1** Botany (of a shoot, stem, or axis) growing vertically.
2 Engineering (of a material) having elastic properties in two or three planes perpendicular to each other.

or·thot·ro·pous /ôrˈTHätrəpəs/ ▶ **adj.** Botany (of a plant ovule) having the nucleus straight, i.e., not inverted, so that the micropyle is at the end opposite the base.

or·to·lan /ˈôrtl-ən/ (also **ortolanbunting**) ▶ **n.** a small Eurasian songbird that was formerly eaten as a delicacy, the male having an olive-green head and yellow throat. ● *Emberizahortulana*, family Emberizidae (subfamily Emberizinae).
– ORIGIN early 16th cent.: from French, from Provençal, literally 'gardener,' based on a diminutive of Latin *hortus* 'garden.'

O·ru·ro /ôˈrŏŏrō/ a city in western Bolivia; pop. 216,714 (2009). It is the center of an important mining region, with rich deposits of tin, zinc, silver, copper, and gold.

ORV ▶ **abbr.** off-road vehicle.

Or·vie·to[1] /ôrˈvyetō/ a town in Umbria, in central Italy in the middle of a wine-producing area; pop. 21,059 (2008).

Or·vi·e·to[2] /ôrˈvyedō/ ▶ **n.** a white wine made near Orvieto.

Or·well /ˈôrwel/, George (1903–50), British novelist and essayist, born in India; pseudonym of *Eric Arthur Blair*. His work is characterized by his concern about social injustice. His best-known works are *Animal Farm* (1945) and *Nineteen Eighty-Four* (1949).
– DERIVATIVES **Or·well·i·an** /ôrˈwelēən/ adj.

-ory[1] ▶ **suffix** (forming nouns) denoting a place for a particular function: *dormitory | repository.*
– ORIGIN from Latin *-oria, -orium*, sometimes via Anglo-Norman French *-orie*, Old French *-oire.*

-ory[2] ▶ **suffix** forming adjectives (and occasionally nouns) relating to or involving a verbal action: *compulsory | directory | mandatory.*
– ORIGIN from Latin *-orius*, sometimes via Anglo-Norman French *-ori(e).*

o·ryx /ˈôriks/ ▶ **n.** any of several species of antelopes native to arid regions of Africa and Asia, having dark markings on the face and long, pointed horns. ● Genus *Oryx*, family Bovidae: several species, including the **Arabian oryx** (*O. leucoryx*). See also GEMSBOK, SCIMITAR ORYX.
– ORIGIN late Middle English: via Latin from Greek *orux* 'stonemason's pickax' (because of its pointed horns).

or·zo /ˈôrzō/ ▶ **n.** a variety of pasta shaped like grains of barley or rice.
– ORIGIN Italian, literally 'barley.'

OS ▶ **abbr.** ■ (in calculating dates) Old Style. ■ Computing operating system. ■ Ordinary Seaman. ■ (in the UK) Ordnance Survey. ■ (as a size of clothing) outsize. ■ out of stock. ■ overseas.

Os ▶ **symbol** the chemical element osmium.

os[1] /äs/ ▶ **n.** (pl. **ossa** /ˈäsə/) Anatomy a bone (used chiefly in Latin names of individual bones, e.g., *os trapezium*).
– ORIGIN Latin.

os[2] ▶ **n.** (pl. **ora** /ˈôrə/) Anatomy an opening or entrance to a passage, esp. one at either end of the cervix of the uterus.
– ORIGIN mid 18th cent.: from Latin *os* 'mouth.'

o.s. ▶ **abbr.** (in prescriptions) the left eye. [Latin, *oculus sinister.*]

OSA ▶ **abbr.** Order of St. Augustine (Augustinians).

O·sage /ˈōˌsāj/ ▶ **n.** (pl. **same** or **Osages**) **1** a member of an American Indian people formerly inhabiting the Osage River valley in Missouri.
2 the Siouan language of this people.
▶ **adj.** of or relating to this people or their language.
– ORIGIN via French, from Osage *wažaže*, the name of one of the three groups that compose this people.

O·sage or·ange ▶ **n.** a small spiny North American deciduous tree that bears inedible green orangelike fruit. Its durable yellowish-orange wood was formerly used by American Indians for bows and other weapons. Also called **BOWWOOD**. ● *Maclura pomifera*, family Moraceae.

O·sage Riv·er a river that flows for 360 miles (580 km) through Missouri to the Missouri River.

O·sa·ka /ōˈsäkə/ a port and commercial city in central Japan, on the island of Honshu; pop. 2,510,459 (2007).

OSB ▶ **abbr.** Order of St. Benedict (Benedictines).

Os·borne /ˈäzˌbôrn, -bərn/, John (James) (1929–94), English playwright. His first play, *Look Back in Anger* (1956), ushered in a new era of kitchen-sink drama. Its hero, Jimmy Porter, personified contemporary disillusioned youth, the so-called angry young man.

Os·can /ˈäskən/ ▶ **n.** an extinct Italic language of southern Italy, related to Umbrian and surviving in inscriptions mainly of the 4th to 1st centuries BC.
▶ **adj.** of or relating to this language.
– ORIGIN late 16th cent.: from Latin *Oscus* 'Oscan' + **-AN**.

Os·car[1] /ˈäskər/ ▶ **n.** trademark the nickname for one of the golden statuettes given as an Academy Award. [one of the several speculative stories of its origin claims that the statuette reminded Margaret Herrick, an executive director of the Academy of Motion Picture Arts and Sciences, of her uncle Oscar.] ■ **(the Oscars)** the annual presentation of the Academy Awards.

Os·car[2] ▶ **n.** a code word representing the letter O, used in radio communication.

O

os·car /ˈäskər/ (also **oscar cichlid**) ▶ **n.** a South American cichlid fish with velvety brown young and multicolored adults, popular in aquariums. ● *Astronotus ocellatus*, family Cichlidae. Alternative name: **velvet cichlid**.

Os·ce·o·la /ˌäsēˈōlə, ˌōsē-/ (c.1804–38), leader of the Seminole Indians. Resisting all government efforts to remove his people from their homeland in Florida, he led them in the Seminole Wars 1835–42. He was captured while bearing a flag of truce.

os·cil·late /ˈäsəˌlāt/ ▶ **v.** [no obj.] **1** move or swing back and forth at a regular speed: *a pendulum oscillates about its lowest point.* ■ [with adverbial] waver between extremes of opinion, action, or quality: *he was* ***oscillating between*** *fear and bravery.*
2 Physics vary in magnitude or position in a regular manner around a central point. ■ (of a circuit or device) cause the electric current or voltage running through it to behave in this way.
– DERIVATIVES **os·cil·la·to·ry** /əˈsiləˌtôrē/ **adj.**
– ORIGIN early 18th cent.: from Latin *oscillat-* 'swung,' from the verb *oscillare*.

os·cil·la·tion /ˌäsəˈlāsHən/ ▶ **n. 1** movement back and forth at a regular speed: *the natural oscillation of a spring | the oscillations of a pendulum.* ■ variation or fluctuation between two extremes of opinion, action, or quality: *the plot's oscillation between bleak and comic elements.*
2 Physics regular variation in magnitude or position around a central point.

os·cil·la·tor /ˈäsəˌlātər/ ▶ **n.** a device for generating oscillating electric currents or voltages by nonmechanical means.

oscillo- ▶ **comb. form** relating to oscillation, esp. of electric current: *oscilloscope*.

os·cil·lo·gram /əˈsiləˌgram/ ▶ **n.** a record produced by an oscillograph.

os·cil·lo·graph /əˈsiləˌgraf/ ▶ **n.** a device for recording oscillations, esp. those of an electric current.
– DERIVATIVES **os·cil·lo·graph·ic** /əˌsiləˈgrafik/ **adj.**, **os·cil·log·ra·phy** /ˌäsəˈlägrəfē/ **n.**

os·cil·lo·scope /əˈsiləˌskōp/ ▶ **n.** a device for viewing oscillations, as of electrical voltage or current, by a display on the screen of a cathode ray tube.
– DERIVATIVES **os·cil·lo·scop·ic** /əˌsiləˈskäpik/ **adj.**

os·cine /ˈäsin, ˈäˌsīn/ Ornithology ▶ **adj.** of, relating to, or denoting passerine birds of a large division that includes the songbirds. Compare with **SUBOSCINE**. ● Suborder Oscines, order Passeriformes.
▶ **n.** a bird of this division.
– ORIGIN late 19th cent.: from Latin *oscen, oscin-* 'songbird' + **-INE**[1].

Os·co-Um·bri·an /ˌäskō ˈəmbrēən/ ▶ **n. 1** a group of ancient Italic languages including Oscan and Umbrian, spoken in Italy in the 1st millennium BC.
2 a member of any of the peoples who spoke a language of this group.
▶ **adj.** of or relating to these peoples or their languages.

os·cu·la /ˈäskyələ/ plural form of **OSCULUM**.

os·cu·lar /ˈäskyələr/ ▶ **adj. 1** humorous of or relating to kissing.
2 Zoology of or relating to an osculum.
– ORIGIN early 19th cent.: from Latin *osculum* 'mouth, kiss' (diminutive of *os* 'mouth') + **-AR**[1].

os·cu·late /ˈäskyəˌlāt/ ▶ **v.** [with obj.] **1** Mathematics (of a curve or surface) touch (another curve or surface) so as to have a common tangent at the point of contact: (as adj. **osculating**) *the plots have been drawn using osculating orbital elements.*
2 formal or humorous kiss.
– DERIVATIVES **os·cu·lant** /-lənt/ **adj.**, **os·cu·la·tion** /ˌäskyəˈlāsHən/ **n.**, **os·cu·la·to·ry** /-ləˌtôrē/ **adj.**
– ORIGIN mid 17th cent.: from Latin *osculat-* 'kissed,' from the verb *osculari*, from *osculum* 'little mouth or kiss.'

os·cu·lum /ˈäskyələm/ ▶ **n.** (pl. **oscula** /-lə/) Zoology a large aperture in a sponge through which water is expelled.
– ORIGIN early 17th cent.: from Latin, 'little mouth.'

-ose[1] ▶ **suffix** (forming adjectives) having a specified quality: *bellicose | comatose | verbose.*
– ORIGIN from Latin *-osus*.

-ose[2] ▶ **suffix** Chemistry forming names of sugars and other carbohydrates: *cellulose | glucose.*
– ORIGIN on the pattern of (*gluc*)*ose*.

-osely ▶ **suffix** forming adverbs corresponding to adjectives ending in *-ose* (such as *bellicosely* corresponding to *bellicose*).
– ORIGIN see **-OSE**[1], **-LY**[2].

-oseness ▶ **suffix** forming nouns corresponding to adjectives ending in *-ose* (such as *bellicoseness* corresponding to *bellicose*). Compare with **-OSITY**.
– ORIGIN see **-OSE**[1], **-NESS**.

OSF ▶ **abbr.** Order of St. Francis (Franciscans).

Osh /ôsH/ a city in western Kyrgyzstan, near the border with Uzbekistan; pop. 300,000 (est. 2009). It was, until the 15th century, an important post on an ancient trade route to China and India.

OSHA /ˈōsHə/ ▶ **abbr.** (in the US) Occupational Safety and Health Administration.

Osh·a·wa /ˈäsHəwə/ a city in Ontario, Canada, on the northern shores of Lake Ontario, east of Toronto; pop. 141,590 (2006).

o·shi /ˈōsHē/ ▶ **n.** [pl.] **(same)** (in sumo wrestling) a move in which an opponent is pushed backward or down.
– ORIGIN Japanese.

Osh·kosh /ˈäsHkäsH/ an industrial city in east central Wisconsin, on Lake Winnebago; pop. 63,679 (est. 2008).

o·sier /ˈōZHər/ ▶ **n. 1** a small Eurasian willow that grows mostly in wet habitats and is a major source of the long flexible shoots (withies) used in basketwork. ● *Salix viminalis*, family Salicaceae. ■ a shoot of a willow. ■ dated any willow tree.
2 any of several North American dogwoods.
– ORIGIN late Middle English: from Old French; compare with medieval Latin *auseria* 'osier bed.'

O·si·jek /ˈōsēˌyek/ a city in eastern Croatia, on the Drava River; pop. 85,800 (est. 2009).

O·si·ris /ōˈsīris/ Egyptian Mythology a god originally connected with fertility, husband of Isis and father of Horus. He is known chiefly through the story of his death at the hands of his brother Seth and his subsequent restoration to a new life as ruler of the afterlife.
– DERIVATIVES **O·si·ri·an** /-rēən/ **adj.**

-osis ▶ **suffix** (pl. **-oses**) denoting a process or condition: *metamorphosis.* ■ denoting a pathological state: *neurosis | thrombosis.*
– ORIGIN via Latin from Greek *-ōsis*, verbal noun ending.

-osity ▶ **suffix** forming nouns from adjectives ending in *-ose* (such as *verbosity* from *verbose*) and from adjectives ending in *-ous* (such as *pomposity* from *pompous*).
– ORIGIN from French *-osité* or Latin *-ositas*.

Os·lo /ˈäzˌlō, ˈäs-/ the capital and chief port of Norway, on the southern coast at the head of Oslofjord; pop. 839,423 (2007). Founded in the 11th century, it was known as Christiania (or Kristiania) from 1624 until 1924 in honor of Christian IV of Norway and Denmark (1577–1648).

Os·man I /ˈäzmən, ˈäs-, äsˈmän/ (also **Othman** /ˈäTH-/) (1259–1326), Turkish conqueror. He founded the Ottoman (Osmanli) dynasty and empire and assumed the title of emir in 1299.

Os·man·li /äzˈmänlē, äs-/ ▶ **adj. & n.** (pl. **same** or **Osmanlis**) old-fashioned term for **OTTOMAN**.
– ORIGIN Turkish, from the name *Osman*, from Arabic *ʿuṯmān* (see **OTTOMAN**), + the adjectival suffix *-li*.

os·mic /ˈäzmik/ ▶ **adj.** relating to odors or the sense of smell.
– DERIVATIVES **os·mi·cal·ly** /-ik(ə)lē/ **adv.**
– ORIGIN mid 20th cent.: from Greek *osmē* 'smell, odor' + **-IC**.

os·mic ac·id ▶ **n.** Chemistry a solution of osmium tetroxide.
– ORIGIN mid 19th cent.: *osmic* from **OSMIUM** + **-IC**.

os·mi·um /ˈäzmēəm/ ▶ **n.** the chemical element of atomic number 76, a hard, dense silvery-white metal of the transition series. (Symbol: **Os**)
– ORIGIN early 19th cent.: modern Latin, from Greek *osmē* 'smell' (from the pungent smell of its tetroxide).

os·mi·um te·trox·ide ▶ **n.** a poisonous pale yellow solid with a distinctive pungent smell, used in solution as a biological stain (esp. for lipids) and fixative. ● Chem. formula: OsO_4.

osmo- ▶ **comb. form** representing **OSMOSIS**.

os·mo·lal·i·ty /ˌäzməˈlalitē/ ▶ **n.** Chemistry the concentration of a solution expressed as the total number of solute particles per kilogram.
– ORIGIN 1950s: blend of *osmotic* (see **OSMOSIS**) and **MOLAL**, + **-ITY**.

os·mo·lar·i·ty /ˌäzməˈlaritē/ ▶ **n.** Chemistry the concentration of a solution expressed as the total number of solute particles per liter.
– ORIGIN 1950s: blend of *osmotic* (see **OSMOSIS**) and **MOLAR**[3], + **-ITY**.

os·mom·e·ter /äzˈmämitər/ ▶ **n.** an instrument for demonstrating or measuring osmotic pressure.
– DERIVATIVES **os·mo·met·ric** /-məˈmetrik/ **adj.**, **os·mom·e·try** /-trē/ **n.**

os·mo·reg·u·la·tion /ˌäzmōˌregyəˈlāsHən/ ▶ **n.** Biology the maintenance of constant osmotic pressure in the fluids of an organism by the control of water and salt concentrations.
– DERIVATIVES **os·mo·reg·u·la·to·ry** /-ˈregyələˌtôrē/ **adj.**

os·mose /ˈäzmōs, ˈäs-/ ▶ **v.** [no obj.] rare pass by or as if by osmosis.
– ORIGIN mid 19th cent. (as a noun in the sense 'osmosis'): from the element common to *endosmose* and *exosmose*.

os·mo·sis /äzˈmōsis, äs-/ ▶ **n. 1** Biology & Chemistry a process by which molecules of a solvent tend to pass through a semipermeable membrane from a less concentrated solution into a more concentrated one, thus equalizing the concentrations on each side of the membrane.
2 the process of gradual or unconscious assimilation of ideas, knowledge, etc.: *what she knows of the blue-blood set she learned not through birthright, not even through wealth, but through osmosis.*
– DERIVATIVES **os·mot·ic** /-mätik/ **adj.**, **os·mot·i·cal·ly** /-ˈmädik(ə)lē/ **adv.**
– ORIGIN mid 19th cent.: Latinized form of earlier *osmose*, from Greek *ōsmos* 'a push.'

os·mot·ic pres·sure /äzˈmätik/ ▶ **n.** Chemistry the pressure that would have to be applied to a pure solvent to prevent it from passing into a given solution by osmosis, often used to express the concentration of the solution.

os·mun·da /äzˈməndə/ ▶ **n.** a plant of a genus that includes the royal and cinnamon ferns. ● Genus *Osmunda*, family Osmundaceae.
– ORIGIN Anglo-Latin, from Anglo-Norman French *osmunde*, of unknown origin.

Os·na·brück /ˈäsnəˌbrŏŏk, ˈôsnäˌbrʏk/ a city in northwestern Germany, in Lower Saxony; pop. 163,000 (est. 2006). In 1648, the Treaty of Westphalia, which ended the Thirty Years War, was signed here and in Münster.

os·na·burg /ˈäznəˌbərg/ ▶ **n.** a kind of coarse, heavy linen or cotton used for such items as furnishings and sacks.
– ORIGIN late Middle English: alteration of **OSNABRÜCK**, where the cloth was originally produced.

os pe·nis /äs ˈpēnis/ ▶ **n.** Zoology a bone in the penis of carnivores and some other mammals. Also called **BACULUM**.

os·prey /ˈäsprā, -prē/ ▶ **n.** (pl. **ospreys**) a large fish-eating bird of prey with long narrow wings and a white underside and crown, found throughout the world. Also called **FISH HAWK**. ● *Pandion haliaetus*, the only member of the family Pandionidae.
– ORIGIN late Middle English: from Old French *ospres*, apparently based on Latin *ossifraga* (mentioned by Pliny and identified with the lammergeier), from *os* 'bone' + *frangere* 'to break,' probably because of the lammergeier's habit of dropping bones from a height to break them and reach the marrow.

OSS ▶ **abbr.** Office of Strategic Services, a US intelligence organization during World War II.

os·sa /ˈäsə/ plural form of **OS**[1].

Os·sa, Mount /ˈäsə/ **1** a mountain in Thessaly, in northeastern Greece, south of Mount Olympus, that rises to a height of 6,489 feet (1,978 m). In Greek mythology, the giants were said to have piled Mount Olympus and Mount Ossa onto Mount Pelion in an attempt to reach heaven so that they could destroy the gods.
2 the highest mountain on the island of Tasmania. It rises to a height of 5,305 feet (1,617 m).

os·se·in /ˈäsē-in/ ▶ **n.** Biochemistry the collagen of bones, used for glues and gelatin, derived by dissolving the mineral content in an acid solution.
– ORIGIN mid 19th cent.: from Latin *osseus* 'bony' + **-IN**.

os·se·ous /ˈäsēəs/ ▶ **adj.** chiefly Zoology & Medicine consisting of or turned into bone; ossified.
– ORIGIN late Middle English: from Latin *osseus* 'bony' + **-OUS**.

Os·sete /ˈäsēt/ ▶ **n.** (also **Osset**) **1** a native or inhabitant of Ossetia.
2 another term for **OSSETIAN**.
▶ **adj.** of or relating to Ossetia or the Ossetes.
– DERIVATIVES **Os·set·ic** /äˈsetik/ **adj. & n.**
– ORIGIN from Russian *osetin*, from Georgian.

Os·se·ti·a /əˈsetēə, ôˈsēshə/ a region of the central Caucasus. It is divided by the boundary between Russia and Georgia into two parts: North Ossetia and South Ossetia. It was the scene of ethnic conflict 1989–92.

Os·se·ti·an /əˈsetēən, äˈsēshən/ ▶ **n. 1** the Iranian language of the Ossetes.
2 a native or inhabitant of Ossetia.
▶ **adj.** of or relating to the Ossetes or their language.

Os·si /ˈäsē, ˈôsē/ ▶ **n.** (pl. **Ossies** or **Ossis**) informal, often derogatory (in Germany) a citizen of the former German Democratic Republic. Compare with **WESSI**.
– ORIGIN German, probably an abbreviation of *Ostdeutsche* 'East German.'

Os·sian /ˈäsēən/ a legendary Irish warrior and bard, whose name became well known in 1760–63 when the Scottish poet **James Macpherson** (1736–96) published his own verse as an alleged translation of 3rd-century Gaelic tales. Irish name **OISIN**.
– DERIVATIVES **Os·si·an·ic** **adj.**

os·si·cle /ˈäsikəl/ ▶ **n.** Anatomy & Zoology a very small bone, esp. one of those in the middle ear. ■ Zoology a small piece of calcified material forming part of the skeleton of an invertebrate animal such as an echinoderm.
– ORIGIN late 16th cent.: from Latin *ossiculum*, diminutive of *os* 'bone.'

os·sif·er·ous /äˈsifərəs/ ▶ **adj.** Geology (of a cave or stratum) containing or yielding deposits of bone, esp. fossil bone.
– ORIGIN early 19th cent.: from Latin *os, oss-* 'bone' + **-FEROUS**.

os·si·fy /ˈäsəˌfī/ ▶ **v.** (**ossifies, ossifying, ossified**) [no obj.] **1** turn into bone or bony tissue: *these tracheal cartilages may ossify.*
2 (often as adj. **ossified**) cease developing; be stagnant or rigid: *ossified political institutions.*
– DERIVATIVES **os·si·fi·ca·tion** /ˌäsəfiˈkāshən/ **n.**
– ORIGIN early 18th cent.: from French *ossifier*, from Latin *os, oss-* 'bone.'

Os·si·ning /ˈäsəniNG/ a town in southeastern New York, on the Hudson River, noted as the home of Sing Sing prison; pop. 36,788 (est. 2008).

os·so bu·co /ˈäsō ˈbo͝okō/ ▶ **n.** an Italian dish made with veal shank containing marrowbone, stewed in wine with vegetables and seasonings.
– ORIGIN Italian, literally 'marrowbone.'

os·su·ar·y /ˈäsHo͞oˌerē, ˈäs(y)o͞o-/ ▶ **n.** (pl. **ossuaries**) a container or room into which the bones of dead people are placed.
– ORIGIN mid 17th cent.: from late Latin *ossuarium*, formed irregularly from Latin *os, oss-* 'bone.'

OST ▶ **abbr.** original soundtrack.

Os·te·ich·thy·es /ˌästēˈikTHē-ēz/ Zoology a class of fishes that includes those with a bony skeleton. Compare with **CHONDRICHTHYES**.
– ORIGIN modern Latin (plural), from Greek *osteon* 'bone' + *ikhthus* 'fish.'

os·te·i·tis /ˌästēˈītis/ ▶ **n.** Medicine inflammation of the substance of a bone. ■ (**osteitis fibrosa cystica**) another term for **VON RECKLINGHAUSEN'S DISEASE** (sense 2). ■ (**osteitis deformans**) another term for **PAGET'S DISEASE** (sense 1).
– ORIGIN mid 19th cent.: from Greek *osteon* 'bone' + **-ITIS**.

Ost·end /ˈästend, ˈästend/ a port on the North Sea coast of northwestern Belgium, in West Flanders; pop. 69,175 (2008). French name **Ostende**. Flemish name **OOSTENDE**.

os·ten·si·ble /äˈstensəbəl, əˈsten-/ ▶ **adj.** [attrib.] stated or appearing to be true, but not necessarily so: *the delay may have a deeper cause than the ostensible reason.*
– DERIVATIVES **os·ten·si·bil·i·ty** /-ˌstensəˈbilitē/ **n.**
– ORIGIN mid 18th cent.: from French, from medieval Latin *ostensibilis* from Latin *ostens-* 'stretched out to view,' from the verb *ostendere*, from *ob-* 'in view of' + *tendere* 'to stretch.'

os·ten·si·bly /äˈstensiblē, əˈsten-/ ▶ **adv.** [sentence adverb] apparently or purportedly, but perhaps not actually: *portrayed as a blue-collar type, ostensibly a carpenter.*

os·ten·sive /äˈstensiv/ ▶ **adj.** directly or clearly demonstrative. ■ Linguistics denoting a way of defining by direct demonstration, e.g., by pointing.
– DERIVATIVES **os·ten·sive·ly** **adv.**, **os·ten·sive·ness** **n.**
– ORIGIN mid 16th cent.: from late Latin *ostensivus*, from *ostens-* 'stretched out to view' (see **OSTENSIBLE**).

os·ten·ta·tion /ˌästənˈtāsHən/ ▶ **n.** pretentious and vulgar display, esp. of wealth and luxury, intended to impress or attract notice: *the office was spacious, but without any trace of ostentation.*
– ORIGIN late Middle English: via Old French from Latin *ostentatio(n-)*, from the verb *ostentare*, frequentative of *ostendere* 'stretch out to view.'

os·ten·ta·tious /ˌästənˈtāsHəs/ ▶ **adj.** characterized by vulgar or pretentious display; designed to impress or attract notice: *books that people buy and display ostentatiously but never actually finish.*
– DERIVATIVES **os·ten·ta·tious·ly** **adv.**, **os·ten·ta·tious·ness** **n.**

osteo- ▶ **comb. form** of or relating to the bones: *osteoporosis.*
– ORIGIN from Greek *osteon* 'bone.'

os·te·o·ar·thri·tis /ˌästēōärˈTHrītis/ ▶ **n.** Medicine degeneration of joint cartilage and the underlying bone, most common from middle age onward. It causes pain and stiffness, esp. in the hip, knee, and thumb joints. Compare with **RHEUMATOID ARTHRITIS**.
– DERIVATIVES **os·te·o·ar·thrit·ic** /-ˈTHritik/ **adj.**

os·te·o·blast /ˈästēəˌblast/ ▶ **n.** Physiology a cell that secretes the matrix for bone formation.
– DERIVATIVES **os·te·o·blas·tic** /ˌästēəˈblastik/ **adj.**

os·te·o·clast /ˈästēəˌklast/ ▶ **n.** Physiology a large multinucleate bone cell that absorbs bone tissue during growth and healing.
– DERIVATIVES **os·te·o·clas·tic** /ˌästēəˈklastik/ **adj.**
– ORIGIN late 19th cent.: from **OSTEO-** 'bone' + Greek *klastēs* 'breaker.'

os·te·o·cyte /ˈästēəˌsīt/ ▶ **n.** Physiology a bone cell, formed when an osteoblast becomes embedded in the matrix it has secreted.
– DERIVATIVES **os·te·o·cyt·ic** /ˌästēəˈsitik/ **adj.**

os·te·o·gen·e·sis /ˌästēōˈjenəsis/ ▶ **n.** the formation of bone.
– DERIVATIVES **os·te·o·ge·net·ic** /-jəˈnetik/ **adj.**, **os·te·o·gen·ic** /ˈjenik/ **adj.**

os·te·o·gen·e·sis im·per·fec·ta /ˌimpərˈfektə/ ▶ **n.** Medicine an inherited disorder characterized by extreme fragility of the bones.
– ORIGIN modern Latin, from **OSTEOGENESIS** + Latin *imperfecta* 'imperfect' (feminine of *imperfectus*).

os·te·oid /ˈästēˌoid/ ▶ **adj.** Physiology & Medicine resembling bone in appearance or structure.
▶ **n.** Physiology & Medicine the unmineralized organic component of bone.

os·te·ol·o·gy /ˌästēˈäləjē/ ▶ **n.** the study of the structure and function of the skeleton and bony structures.
– DERIVATIVES **os·te·o·log·i·cal** /ˌästēəˈläjikəl/ **adj.**, **os·te·o·log·i·cal·ly** /ˌästēəˈläjik(ə)lē/ **adv.**, **os·te·ol·o·gist** /-jist/ **n.**

os·te·ol·y·sis /ˌästēˈäləsis/ ▶ **n.** Medicine the pathological destruction or disappearance of bone tissue.
– DERIVATIVES **os·te·o·lyt·ic** /-əˈlitik/ **adj.**

os·te·o·ma·la·cia /ˌästē-ōməˈlāsH(ē)ə/ ▶ **n.** softening of the bones, typically through a deficiency of vitamin D or calcium.
– DERIVATIVES **os·te·o·ma·lac·ic** /-ˈlasik/ **adj.**
– ORIGIN early 19th cent.: modern Latin, from **OSTEO-** 'bone' + Greek *malakos* 'soft.'

os·te·o·my·e·li·tis /ˌästēōˌmīəˈlītis/ ▶ **n.** Medicine inflammation of bone or bone marrow, usually due to infection.

os·te·o·ne·cro·sis /ˌästēōniˈkrōsis/ ▶ **n.** Medicine the death of bone tissue.
– DERIVATIVES **os·te·o·ne·crot·ic** /-ˈkrätik/ **adj.**

os·te·op·a·thy /ˌästēˈäpəTHē/ ▶ **n.** a branch of medical practice that emphasizes the treatment of medical disorders through the manipulation and massage of the bones, joints, and muscles.
– DERIVATIVES **os·te·o·path** /ˈästēəˌpaTH/ **n.**, **os·te·o·path·ic** /ˌästēəˈpaTHik/ **adj.**, **os·te·o·path·i·cal·ly** /ˌästēəˈpaTHik(ə)lē/ **adv.**

os·te·o·pe·ni·a /ˌästēōˈpēnēə/ ▶ **n.** reduced bone mass of lesser severity than osteoporosis.

os·te·o·phyte /ˈästēəˌfīt/ ▶ **n.** Medicine a bony outgrowth associated with the degeneration of cartilage at joints.
– DERIVATIVES **os·te·o·phyt·ic** /ˌästēəˈfitik/ **adj.**

os·te·o·po·ro·sis /ˌästēōpəˈrōsis/ ▶ **n.** a medical condition in which the bones become brittle and fragile from loss of tissue, typically as a result of hormonal changes, or deficiency of calcium or vitamin D.
– DERIVATIVES **os·te·o·po·rot·ic** /-ˈrätik/ **adj.**
– ORIGIN mid 19th cent.: from **OSTEO-** 'bone' + Greek *poros* 'passage, pore' + **-OSIS**.

os·te·o·sar·co·ma /ˌästēōsärˈkōmə/ ▶ **n.** (pl. **osteosarcomas** or **osteosarcomata** /-mətə/) Medicine a malignant tumor of bone in which there is a proliferation of osteoblasts.

os·te·o·sper·mum /ˌästēōˈspərməm/ ▶ **n.** (pl. **osteosperma** /-mə/) a plant or shrub of the daisy family, native to Africa and the Middle East, some varieties of which are cultivated for their yellow or violet flowers. ● Genus *Osteospermum*, family *Compositae*.
– ORIGIN mid 19th cent.: modern Latin, from Greek, *osteo-*, 'bone' + Greek, *sperma*, 'seed.'

os·te·o·tome /ˈästēəˌtōm/ ▶ **n.** a surgical instrument for cutting bone, typically resembling a chisel.

os·te·ot·o·my /ˌästēˈätəmē/ ▶ **n.** (pl. **osteotomies**) the surgical cutting of a bone or removal of a piece of bone.

os·ter·i·a /ˌästəˈrēə/ ▶ **n.** an Italian restaurant, typically a simple or inexpensive one.
– ORIGIN Italian, 'inn, hotel.'

Os·tia /ˈästēə/ an ancient city and harbor that was situated on the western coast of Italy at the mouth of the Tiber River. It was the first colony founded by ancient Rome and was a major port and commercial center.

os·ti·na·to /ˌästiˈnätō/ ▶ **n.** (pl. **ostinatos** or **ostinati** /-tē/) a continually repeated musical phrase or rhythm.
– ORIGIN Italian, literally 'obstinate.'

os·ti·ole /ˈästēˌōl/ ▶ **n.** Botany (in some small algae and fungi) a small pore through which spores are discharged.
– DERIVATIVES **os·ti·o·lar** /-ələr/ **adj.**
– ORIGIN mid 19th cent.: from Latin *ostiolum*, diminutive of *ostium* 'opening.'

os·ti·um /ˈästēəm/ ▶ **n.** (pl. **ostia** /-tēə/) Anatomy & Zoology an opening into a vessel or cavity of the body. ■ Zoology each of a number of pores in the wall of a sponge, through which water is drawn in.
– ORIGIN early 17th cent.: from Latin, 'door, opening.'

ost·ler /ˈäslər/ ▶ **n.** variant spelling of **HOSTLER**.

Ost·mark /ˈästˌmärk/ ▶ **n.** historical the basic monetary unit of the former German Democratic Republic, equal to 100 pfennigs.
– ORIGIN German, literally 'east mark' (see **MARK**[2]).

os·to·my /ˈästəmi/ ▶ **n.** (pl. **ostomies**) Medicine an artificial opening in an organ of the body, created during an operation such as a colostomy, ileostomy, or gastrostomy; a stoma.
– ORIGIN 1950s: from **COLOSTOMY, ILEOSTOMY**, etc.

Ost·po·li·tik /ˈôstˌpäliˈtēk/ ▶ **n.** historical the foreign policy of détente of western European countries with reference to the former communist bloc, esp. the opening of relations with the Eastern bloc by the Federal Republic of Germany (West Germany) in the 1960s.
– ORIGIN German, from *Ost* 'east' + *Politik* 'politics.'

os·tra·cism /ˈästrəˌsizəm/ ▶ **n. 1** exclusion from a society or group: *the family suffered social ostracism.*
2 (in ancient Greece) temporary banishment from a city by popular vote.

os·tra·cize /ˈästrəˌsīz/ ▶ **v.** [with obj.] exclude (someone) from a society or group: *a group of people who have been ridiculed, ostracized, and persecuted for centuries.* ■ (in ancient Greece) banish (an unpopular or too powerful citizen) from a city for five or ten years by popular vote.

PRONUNCIATION KEY ə *ago, up*; ər *over, fur*; a *hat*; ā *ate*; ä *car*; e *let*; ē *see*; i *fit*; ī *by*; NG *sing*; ō *go*; ô *law, for*; oi *toy*; o͝o *good*; o͞o *goo*; ou *out*; TH *thin*; T͟H *then*; ZH *vision*

O

– ORIGIN mid 17th cent.: from Greek *ostrakizein*, from *ostrakon* 'shell or potsherd' (on which names were written, in voting to banish unpopular citizens).

os·tra·cod /ˈästrəˌkäd/ (also **ostracode**) ▶ **n.** Zoology a minute aquatic crustacean of the class Ostracoda.

Os·tra·co·da /ˌästrəˈkōdə/ Zoology a class of minute aquatic crustaceans that have a hinged shell from which the antennae protrude, and a reduced number of appendages.
– ORIGIN modern Latin (plural), from Greek *ostrakōdēs* 'testaceous,' from *ostrakon* 'shell.'

os·tra·co·derm /ˈästrəkōˌdərm/ ▶ **n.** an extinct jawless fish of the Cambrian to Devonian periods, having a heavily armored body. ● Class Agnatha: several orders.
– ORIGIN late 19th cent.: from modern Latin *Ostracodermi* (former taxonomic name), from Greek *ostrakon* 'shell' + *derma* 'skin.'

os·tra·con /ˈästrəˌkän/ (also **ostrakon**) ▶ **n.** (pl. **ostraca** /-kə/ or **ostracon**) a potsherd used as a writing surface.
– ORIGIN Greek, 'hard shell or potsherd.'

Os·tra·va /ˈästrəvə, ˈôsträvä/ an industrial city in northeastern Czech Republic, in the Moravian lowlands; pop. 308,832 (2007). It is located in the coal-mining region of Silesia.

os·trich /ˈästricн/ ▶ **n. 1** a flightless swift-running African bird with a long neck, long legs, and two toes on each foot. It is the largest living bird, with males reaching an average height of 8 feet (2.5 m). ● *Struthio camelus*, the only member of the family Struthionidae.
2 a person who refuses to face reality or accept facts. [from the popular belief that ostriches bury their heads in the sand if pursued.]

ostrich

– ORIGIN Middle English: from Old French *ostriche*, from Latin *avis* 'bird' + late Latin *struthio* (from Greek *strouthiōn* 'ostrich,' from *strouthos* 'sparrow or ostrich').

os·trich di·no·saur ▶ **n.** a lightly built toothless bipedal dinosaur of the late Cretaceous period, adapted for running and somewhat resembling an ostrich. Also called **ORNITHOMIMOSAUR**. ● Infraorder Ornithomimisauria, suborder Theropoda, order Saurischia: several genera, including *Gallimimus*, *Ornithomimus*, and *Struthiomimus*.

Os·tro·goth /ˈästrəˌgäтн/ ▶ **n.** a member of the eastern branch of the Goths, who conquered Italy in the 5th–6th centuries AD.
– DERIVATIVES **Os·tro·goth·ic** /ˌästrəˈgäтнik/ **adj.**
– ORIGIN from late Latin *Ostrogothi* (plural), from the Germanic base of **EAST** + late Latin *Gothi* 'Goths.'

Ost·wald /ˈäs(t)ˌwôld, ˈôstvält/, Friedrich Wilhelm (1853–1932), German physical chemist. He established physical chemistry as a separate discipline.

OSU ▶ **abbr.** Order of St. Ursula.

Os·wald /ˈäzˌwôld/, Lee Harvey (1939–63), US alleged assassin of President John F. Kennedy. In November 1963, he was charged with the murder of the president. He denied the charge but was murdered by Dallas nightclub owner Jack Ruby (1911–67) before he could be brought to trial.

Os·wald of York, St. (died 992), English prelate and Benedictine monk. As archbishop of York, he founded several monasteries. Feast day, February 28.

Os·we·go /äsˈwēgō/ an industrial port city in north central New York, on Lake Ontario and the Oswego River; pop. 17,351 (est. 2008).

Os·we·go tea /äsˈwēgō/ ▶ **n.** see **BERGAMOT** (sense 3).
– ORIGIN mid 18th cent.: named after a river and town in the northern part of the state of New York.

OT ▶ **abbr.** ■ occupational therapist. ■ occupational therapy. ■ Old Testament. ■ overnight telegram. ■ overtime.

-ot[1] ▶ **suffix** forming nouns that were originally diminutives: *ballot* | *parrot*.
– ORIGIN from French.

-ot[2] ▶ **suffix** (forming nouns) denoting a person of a particular type: *harlot* | *idiot*. ■ denoting a native of a place: *Cypriot*.
– ORIGIN via French and Latin from Greek *-ōtēs*.

o·ta·ku /ˈōtäkoo͞/ ▶ **n.** (pl. **same**) (in Japan) a young person who is obsessed with computers or particular aspects of popular culture to the detriment of their social skills.
– ORIGIN Japanese, literally 'your house,' alluding to the reluctance of such young people to leave the house.

o·tal·gi·a /ōˈtalj(ē)ə/ ▶ **n.** Medicine earache.
– ORIGIN mid 17th cent.: from Greek *ōtalgia*, from *ous*, *ōt-* 'ear' + *algos* 'pain.'

OTB ▶ **abbr.** off-track betting.

OTC ▶ **abbr.** ■ over the counter. ■ (in the UK) Officers' Training Corps.

oth·er /ˈəтнər/ ▶ **adj. & pron. 1** used to refer to a person or thing that is different or distinct from one already mentioned or known about: [as adj.] *stick the camera on a tripod or* ***some other*** *means of support* | *other people found her difficult* | [as pronoun] *a language unrelated to any other*. ■ the alternative of two: [as adj.] *the other side of the page* | [as pronoun] *flinging up first one arm and then the other* | ***one or the other*** *of them is bound to be a liar.* ■ those remaining in a group; those not already mentioned: [as adj.] *they took the other three away in an ambulance* | [as pronoun] *Fred set off and* ***the others*** *followed*.
2 further; additional: [as adj.] *one other word of advice* | [as pronoun] *reporting three stories and rewriting three others*.
3 (**the Other**) [pronoun] Philosophy & Sociology that which is distinct from, different from, or opposite to something or oneself.
▶ **v.** [with obj.] view or treat (a person or group of people) as intrinsically different from and alien to oneself: *a critique of the ways in which the elderly are othered by society*.
– PHRASES **no other** archaic nothing else: *we can do no other*. **other than** [with negative or in questions] apart from; except: *he claims not to own anything other than his home*. ■ differently or different from; otherwise than: *there is no suggestion that we are to take this other than literally*. **on the other hand** see **HAND**. **the other day** (or **night**, **week**, etc.) a few days (or nights, weeks, etc.) ago. **someone** (or **something** or **somehow**, etc.) **or other** some unspecified or unknown person, thing, manner, etc. (used to express vagueness or uncertainty): *they were protesting about something or other*.
– ORIGIN Old English *ōther*, of Germanic origin; related to Dutch and German *ander*, from an Indo-European root meaning 'different.'

oth·er-di·rect·ed ▶ **adj.** Psychology (of a person or their behavior) governed by external circumstances and trends.

oth·er half ▶ **n.** (**one's other half**) informal a person's wife, husband, or partner: *treat your other half to a romantic outing for two*.
– PHRASES **how the other half lives** used to allude to the way of life of a different group in society, esp. a wealthier one.

oth·er·ness /ˈəтнərnis/ ▶ **n.** the quality or fact of being different: *the developed world has been celebrating African music while altogether denying its otherness*.

oth·er·where /ˈəтнərˌ(h)we(ə)r/ ▶ **adv. & pron.** archaic or literary elsewhere.

oth·er·wise /ˈəтнərˌwīz/ ▶ **adv. 1** in circumstances different from those present or considered; or else: *the collection brings visitors who might not come to the college otherwise* | [as conjunctive adverb] *I'm not motivated by money, otherwise I would have quit*.
2 in other respects; apart from that: *an otherwise totally black cat with a single white whisker*.
3 in a different way: *he means mischief—it's no good pretending otherwise* | *pretending that they are* ***otherwise engaged***. ■ as an alternative: *pre-Renaissance mathematician Leonardo Pisano,* ***otherwise known as*** *Fibonacci*.
▶ **adj.** [predic.] in a different state or situation: *if it were otherwise, we would be unable to acquire knowledge*.
– PHRASES **or** (or **and**) **otherwise** indicating the opposite of or a contrast to something stated: *we don't want a president, elected or otherwise*.
– ORIGIN Old English *on ōthre wisan* (see **OTHER**, **WISE**[2]).

oth·er wom·an ▶ **n.** (**the other woman**) the lover of a married or similarly attached man.

oth·er world ▶ **n.** (**the other world**) the spiritual world or afterlife.

oth·er·world·ly /ˌəтнərˈwərldlē/ ▶ **adj.** of or relating to an imaginary or spiritual world: *music of an almost otherworldly beauty*. ■ unworldly: *celibate clerics with a very otherworldly outlook*.
– DERIVATIVES **oth·er·world·li·ness n.**

Oth·man /ˈäтнmən, äтнˈmän/ variant form of **OSMAN I**.

O·tho /ˈōтнō/, Marcus Salvius (AD 32–69), Roman emperor from January until April of 69. Proclaimed emperor after the death of Galba, he was defeated by Vitellius and his German legions and committed suicide.

o·tic /ˈōtik, ˈätik/ ▶ **adj.** Anatomy of or relating to the ear.
– ORIGIN mid 17th cent.: from Greek *ōtikos*, from *ous*, *ōt-* 'ear.'

-otic ▶ **suffix** forming adjectives and nouns corresponding to nouns ending in *-osis* (such as *neurotic* corresponding to *neurosis*).
– ORIGIN from French *-otique*, via Latin from the Greek adjectival ending *-ōtikos*.

-otically ▶ **suffix** forming adverbs corresponding to adjectives ending in *-otic* (such as *neurotically* corresponding to *neurotic*).
– ORIGIN see **-OTIC**, **-LY**[2].

o·ti·ose /ˈōsнēˌōs, ˈōtēˌōs/ ▶ **adj.** serving no practical purpose or result: *he did fuss, uttering otiose explanations*. ■ archaic indolent; idle.
– DERIVATIVES **o·ti·ose·ly adv.**
– ORIGIN late 18th cent.: from Latin *otiosus*, from *otium* 'leisure.'

O·tis[1] /ˈōtis/, Elisha Graves (1811–61), US inventor and manufacturer. In 1852, he produced the first efficient elevator with a safety device. Five years later he installed the first public elevator for passengers in a New York department store.

O·tis[2], James (1725–83), American statesman. He led the majority in the Massachusetts legislature 1766–69 and opposed various revenue acts imposed by the British.

o·ti·tis /ōˈtītis/ ▶ **n.** Medicine inflammation of the ear, usually distinguished as **otitis externa** (of the passage of the outer ear), **otitis media** (of the middle ear), and **otitis interna** (of the inner ear; labyrinthitis).
– ORIGIN late 18th cent.: modern Latin, from Greek *ous*, *ōt-* 'ear' + **-ITIS**.

oto- ▶ **comb. form** (used chiefly in medical terms) of or relating to the ears: *otoscope*.
– ORIGIN from Greek *ous*, *ōt-* 'ear.'

o·to·cyst /ˈōtəˌsist/ ▶ **n.** another term for **STATOCYST**.

o·to·lar·yn·gol·o·gy /ˌōtōˌlarəngˈgäləjē/ ▶ **n.** the study of diseases of the ear and throat.
– DERIVATIVES **o·to·la·ryn·go·log·i·cal** /-rəngGəˈläjikəl/ **adj.**, **o·to·lar·yn·gol·o·gist** /-jist/ **n.**

o·to·lith /ˈōtlˌiтн/ ▶ **n.** Zoology each of three small oval calcareous bodies in the inner ear of vertebrates, involved in sensing gravity and movement.
– DERIVATIVES **o·to·lith·ic** /ˌōtlˈiтнik/ **adj.**

o·tol·o·gy /ōˈtäləjē/ ▶ **n.** the study of the anatomy and diseases of the ear.
– DERIVATIVES **o·to·log·i·cal** /ˌōtəˈläjəkəl/ **adj.**, **o·tol·o·gist** /-jist/ **n.**

O·to·man·gue·an /ˌōtōˈmänGGēən, -ˈmanG-/ ▶ **adj.** of, relating to, or denoting a family of American Indian languages of central and southern Mexico, including Mixtec and Zapotec.
– ORIGIN 1940s: from **OTOMI** + *Mangue* (an extinct language of Costa Rica) + **-AN**.

O·to·mi /ˌōtəˈmē/ ▶ **n.** (pl. **same**) **1** a member of an American Indian people inhabiting parts of central Mexico.
2 the Otomanguean language of this people.
▶ **adj.** of or relating to this people or their language.
– ORIGIN via American Spanish from Nahuatl *otomih*, literally 'unknown.'

O'Toole /ōˈtoo͞l/, Peter (Seamus) (1932–), British actor, born in Ireland. He is noted for his portrayals of eccentric characters. Notable movies: *Lawrence of Arabia* (1962), *Becket* (1964), *Lion in Winter* (1968), *Goodbye, Mr. Chips* (1969), and *The Last Emperor* (1987). He received an honorary Academy Award in 2003.

o·to·plas·ty /ˈōtəˌplastē/ ▶ **n.** (pl. **otoplasties**) a surgical operation to restore or enhance the appearance of an ear or the ears.

o·to·rhi·no·lar·yn·gol·o·gy /ˌōtōˌrīnōˌlarənGˈgäləjē/ ▶ **n.** the study of diseases of the ear, nose, and throat.
– DERIVATIVES **o·to·rhi·no·lar·yn·gol·o·gist** /-jist/ **n.**

o·to·scle·ro·sis /ˌōtōskləˈrōsis/ ▶ **n.** Medicine a hereditary disorder causing progressive deafness due to overgrowth of bone in the inner ear.
– DERIVATIVES **o·to·scle·rot·ic** /-ˈrätik/ **adj.**

o·to·scope /ˈōtəˌskōp/ ▶ **n.** an instrument designed for visual examination of the eardrum and the passage of the outer ear, typically having a light and a set of lenses. Also called **AURISCOPE**.
– DERIVATIVES **o·to·scop·ic** /ˌōtəˈskäpik/ **adj.**, **o·to·scop·i·cal·ly** /ˌōtəˈskäpik(ə)lē/ **adv.**

o·to·tox·ic /ˌōtəˈtäksik/ ▶ **adj.** Medicine having a toxic effect on the ear or its nerve supply.
– DERIVATIVES **o·to·tox·ic·i·ty** /-täkˈsisitē/ **n.**

O·tran·to, Strait of /ōˈträntō, ˈôtrântō/ a channel that links the Adriatic Sea with the Ionian Sea and separates the "heel" of Italy from Albania.

OTS (also **O.T.S.**) ▶ **abbr.** Officers' Training School.

ot·ta·va ri·ma /ōˈtävə ˈrēmə/ ▶ **n.** a form of poetry consisting of stanzas of eight lines of ten or eleven syllables, rhyming *abababcc*.
– ORIGIN late 18th cent.: from Italian, literally 'eighth rhyme.'

Ot·ta·wa /ˈätəwə/ the federal capital of Canada, in southeastern Ontario, on the Ottawa River; pop. 812,129 (2006). From its founding in 1827 until 1854, it was named Bytown after **Colonel John By** (1779–1836).

ot·ter /ˈätər/ ▶ **n.** a semiaquatic fish-eating mammal of the weasel family, with an elongated body, dense fur, and webbed feet. ● *Lutra* and other genera, family Mustelidae: several species, including the **river otter** (*L. canadensis*). See also **SEA OTTER**.
– ORIGIN Old English *otr, ot(t)or*, of Germanic origin; related to Greek *hudros* 'water snake.'

river otter

ot·ter board ▶ **n.** either of a pair of boards or metal plates attached to each side of the mouth of a trawl net at an angle that keeps the net open as it is pulled through the water.

ot·ter·hound /ˈätərˌhound/ ▶ **n.** a large dog of a breed with a long rough coat, used in otter hunting.

ot·ter shrew ▶ **n.** a semiaquatic mammal of the tenrec family, with a sleek body and long tail, native to central and West Africa. ● Genera *Potamogale* and *Micropotamogale*, family Tenrecidae: three species, including the **giant otter shrew** (*P. velox*), which resembles an otter.

ot·ter trawl ▶ **n.** a trawl net fitted with an otter board.

Ot·to /ˈätō, ˈôtō/, Nikolaus August (1832–91), German engineer, whose name is given to **Otto cycle**, the four-stroke cycle on which most internal combustion engines work.

ot·to /ˈätō/ ▶ **n.** another term for **ATTAR**.

ot·to·cen·to /ˌôtōˈCHentō/ ▶ **adj.** of or relating to the 19th century in Italy.
– ORIGIN Italian, literally '800' (shortened from *milottocento* '1800'), used with reference to the years 1800–99.

Ot·to I (912–73), king of the Germans 936–973, Holy Roman Emperor 962–973; known as **Otto the Great**. As king of the Germans he carried out a policy of eastward expansion, and as Holy Roman Emperor he established a presence in Italy to rival that of the papacy.

Ot·to·man /ˈätəmən/ ▶ **adj.** historical **1** of or relating to the Turkish dynasty of Osman I (Othman I). ■ of or relating to the branch of the Turks to which he belonged. ■ of or relating to the Ottoman Empire ruled by his successors.
2 Turkish.
▶ **n.** (pl. **Ottomans**) a Turk, esp. of the period of the Ottoman Empire.
– ORIGIN based on Arabic *ʿuṯmānī* (adjective), from *ʿUṯmān* 'Othman.'

ot·to·man /ˈätəmən/ ▶ **n.** (pl. **ottomans**) **1** a low upholstered seat, or footstool, without a back or arms that typically serves also as a box, with the seat hinged to form a lid.
2 a heavy ribbed fabric made from silk and either cotton or wool, typically used for coats.
– ORIGIN early 19th cent.: from French *ottomane*, feminine of *ottoman* 'Ottoman.'

Ot·to·man Em·pire the Turkish empire, established in northern Anatolia by Osman I at the end of the 13th century and expanded by his successors to include all of Asia Minor and much of southeastern Europe. After setbacks caused by the invasion of the Mongol ruler Tamerlane in 1402, the Ottomans captured Constantinople in 1453, and the empire reached its zenith under Suleiman in the mid 16th century. It had greatly declined by the 19th century and collapsed after World War I.

ou /ˈōˌo͞o/ ▶ **n.** a fruit-eating Hawaiian honeycreeper with a stout bill and green and yellow plumage. Compare with **O-O**. ● *Psittirostra psittacea*, family Drepanididae.
– ORIGIN late 19th cent.: the name in Hawaiian.

oua·bain /ˈwäbēˌin, -ˈbä-/ ▶ **n.** Chemistry a toxic compound obtained from certain trees, used as a very rapid cardiac stimulant. It is a polycyclic glycoside.
– ORIGIN late 19th cent.: via French from Somali *wabayo*, denoting a tree that yields poison (used on arrow points) containing ouabain.

Ouach·i·ta Moun·tains /ˈwäSHiˌtô/ a low range in western Arkansas and eastern Oklahoma, south of the Ozark Plateau.

Ouach·i·ta Riv·er a river that flows for 600 miles (970 km) across western Arkansas and into northern Louisiana, where it is known in part as the Black River and empties into the Red River.

Oua·ga·dou·gou /ˌwägəˈdo͞ogo͞o/ the capital of Burkina Faso; pop. 1,149,000 (est. 2007).

oua·na·niche /ˌwänäˈnēsH/ ▶ **n.** (pl. **same**) Canadian a salmon of landlocked populations living in lakes in Labrador and Newfoundland.
– ORIGIN late 19th cent.: via Canadian French from Algonquian.

ou·bli·ette /ˌo͞oblēˈet/ ▶ **n.** a secret dungeon with access only through a trapdoor in its ceiling.
– ORIGIN late 18th cent.: from French, from *oublier* 'forget.'

ouch /ouCH/ ▶ **exclam.** used to express pain.
– ORIGIN natural exclamation: first recorded in English in the mid 17th cent.

oud /o͞od/ ▶ **n.** a form of lute or mandolin played principally in Arab countries.
– ORIGIN mid 18th cent.: from Arabic *al-ʿūd*.

Oudh /oud/ (also **Audh** or **Awadh**) a region of northern India. Joined with Agra in 1877, it formed the United Provinces of Agra and Oudh in 1902 and was renamed Uttar Pradesh in 1950.

ought[1] /ôt/ ▶ **modal v.** (3rd sing. present and past **ought**) [with infinitive] **1** used to indicate duty or correctness, typically when criticizing someone's actions: *they ought to respect the law | it ought not to be allowed.* ■ used to indicate a desirable or expected state: *he ought to be able to take the initiative.* ■ used to give or ask advice: *you ought to go.*
2 used to indicate something that is probable: *five minutes ought to be enough time.*
– ORIGIN Old English *āhte*, past tense of *āgan* 'owe' (see **OWE**).

> **USAGE** The verb **ought** is a modal verb, which means that, grammatically, it does not behave like ordinary verbs. In particular, the negative is formed with the word **not** by itself, without auxiliary verbs such as **do** or **have**. Thus the standard construction for the negative is *he **ought not** to go.* Note that the preposition to is required in both negative and positive statements: *we ought to accept her offer, or we ought not to accept her offer* (not *we ought accept or we ought not accept*). The alternative forms *he **didn't ought** to have gone* and *he **hadn't ought** to have gone*, formed as if **ought** were an ordinary verb rather than a modal verb, are not acceptable in formal English. Reserve **ought** for expressing obligation, duty, or necessity, and use **should** for expressing suitability or appropriateness.

ought[2] ▶ **n.** archaic term for **AUGHT**[2].
– ORIGIN mid 19th cent.: perhaps from *an ought*, by wrong division of *a nought*; compare with **ADDER**.

ought[3] ▶ **pron.** variant spelling of **AUGHT**[1].

ought·n't /ˈôtnt/ ▶ **contraction** ought not.

ou·gui·ya /o͞oˈgēə/ (also **ougiya**) ▶ **n.** the basic monetary unit of Mauritania, equal to five khoums.
– ORIGIN via French from Mauritanian Arabic, from Arabic *ʾūkiyya*, from Greek *ounkia*, from Latin *uncia* 'ounce.'

Oui·ja board /ˈwējə, -jē/ ▶ **n.** trademark a board printed with letters, numbers, and other signs, to which a planchette or movable indicator points, supposedly in answer to questions from people at a seance.
– ORIGIN late 19th cent.: *Ouija* from French *oui* 'yes' + German *ja* 'yes.'

ounce[1] /ouns/ ▶ **n. 1** (abbr.: **oz**) a unit of weight of one sixteenth of a pound avoirdupois (approximately 28 grams). ■ a unit of one twelfth of a pound troy or apothecaries' measure, equal to 480 grains (approximately 31 grams).
2 a very small amount of something: *Robin summoned up every ounce of strength.*
3 short for **FLUID OUNCE**.
– ORIGIN Middle English: from Old French *unce*, from Latin *uncia* 'twelfth part (of a pound or foot)'; compare with **INCH**[1].

ounce[2] ▶ **n.** another term for **SNOW LEOPARD**.
– ORIGIN Middle English: from Old French *once*, earlier *lonce* (the *l-* being misinterpreted as the definite article), based on Latin *lynx, lync-* (see **LYNX**).

our /ou(ə)r, är/ ▶ **possessive determiner 1** belonging to or associated with the speaker and one or more other people previously mentioned or easily identified: *Jo and I had our hair cut.* ■ belonging to or associated with people in general: *when we hear a sound, our brains identify the source quickly.*
2 used by a writer, editor, or monarch to refer to something belonging to or associated with himself or herself: *we want to know what you, our readers, think.*
– ORIGIN Old English *ūre*, of Germanic origin; related to **US** and German *unser*.

-our[1] ▶ **suffix** chiefly Brit. variant spelling of **-OR**[1] (as in *saviour*).

-our[2] ▶ **suffix** chiefly Brit. variant spelling of **-OR**[2] surviving in some nouns such as *ardour, colour*.

Our La·dy Christian Church used as a title for the Virgin Mary.

ou·ro·bo·ros ▶ **n.** variant spelling of **UROBOROS**.

ours /ˈou(ə)rz, ärz/ ▶ **possessive pron.** used to refer to a thing or things belonging to or associated with the speaker and one or more other people previously mentioned or easily identified: *ours was the ugliest house on the block | this chat of ours is strictly between us.*

our·self /ou(ə)rˈself, är-/ ▶ **pron.** [first person plural] **1** used instead of "ourselves," typically when "we" refers to people in general rather than a definite group of people: [reflexive] *we must choose which aspects of ourself to express to the world* | [emphatic] *this is our affair—we deal with it ourself.*
2 archaic used instead of "myself" by a sovereign or other person in authority.

> **USAGE** The standard reflexive form corresponding to **we** and **us** is **ourselves**, as in *we can blame only ourselves*. The singular form **ourself**, first recorded in the 15th century, is sometimes used in modern English, typically where **we** refers to people in general. This use, though logical, is uncommon and not widely accepted in standard English. See also usage at **THEMSELF** and **THEY**.

our·selves /ou(ə)rˈselvz, är-/ ▶ **pron.** [first person plural] **1** [reflexive] used as the object of a verb or preposition when this is the same as the subject of the clause and the subject is the speaker and one or more other people considered together: *for this we can only blame ourselves.*
2 [emphatic] we or us personally (used to emphasize the speaker and one or more other people considered together): *we invented it ourselves.*
– PHRASES **(not) be ourselves** see **BE ONESELF, NOT BE ONESELF** at **BE**. **by ourselves** see **OURSELVES** at **BY**.

-ous ▶ **suffix** forming adjectives: **1** characterized by; of the nature of: *dangerous | mountainous.*
2 Chemistry denoting an element in a lower valence: *ferrous | sulfurous.* Compare with **-IC**.
– ORIGIN from Anglo-Norman French, or Old French *-eus*, from Latin *-osus*.

Ouse /o͞oz/ **1** (also **Great Ouse**) a river in eastern England that rises in the county of Northamptonshire and flows east and then north for 160 miles (257 km) through East Anglia to the Wash near King's Lynn.
2 a river in northeastern England that forms at the confluence of the Ure and Swale rivers and flows southeast for 57 miles (92 km) through York to the Humber estuary.
3 a river in southeastern England that flows southeast for 30 miles (48 km) to the English Channel.
4 (also **Little Ouse**) a river in East Anglia that forms a tributary of the Great Ouse.

ou·sel /ˈo͞ozəl/ ▶ **n.** variant spelling of **OUZEL**.

-ously ▶ **suffix** forming adverbs corresponding to adjectives ending in *-ous* (such as *dangerously* corresponding to *dangerous*).
– ORIGIN see **-OUS, -LY**[2].

-ousness ▶ **suffix** forming nouns corresponding to adjectives ending in *-ous* (such as *dangerousness* corresponding to *dangerous*).
– ORIGIN see **-OUS -NESS**.

oust /oust/ ▶ **v.** [with obj.] drive out or expel (someone) from a position or place: *he ousted a long-term incumbent by only 500 votes.* ■ Law deprive (someone) of or exclude (someone) from possession of something.
– ORIGIN late Middle English (as a legal term): from Anglo-Norman French *ouster* 'take away,' from Latin *obstare* 'oppose, hinder.'

oust·er /ˈoustər/ ▶ **n. 1** dismissal or expulsion from a position: *a showdown that may lead to his ouster as leader of the party.*

PRONUNCIATION KEY ə *ago, up*; ər *over, fur*; a *hat*; ā *ate*; ä *car*; e *let*; ē *see*; i *fit*; ī *by*; NG *sing*; ō *go*; ô *law, for*; oi *toy*; o͝o *good*; o͞o *goo*; ou *out*; TH *thin*; T͟H *then*; ZH *vision*

2 Law ejection from a freehold or other possession; deprivation of an inheritance.

out /out/ ▶ **adv.** **1** moving or appearing to move away from a particular place, esp. one that is enclosed or hidden: *he walked out into the street* | *watch the stars come out.* ■ situated or operating in the open air, not in buildings: *the search-and-rescue team have been out looking for you.* ■ no longer detained in custody or in jail: *they would be out on bail in no time.* **2** situated far or at a particular distance from somewhere: *an old farmhouse right out in the middle of nowhere* | *they lived eight miles* **out of** *town* | *the team had put on a marvelous display out in Georgia.* ■ to sea, away from the land: *the fleet put out from Cyprus.* ■ (of the tide) falling or at its lowest level: *the tide was going out.* **3** away from home: *he's gone out.* ■ in a public place for purposes of pleasure or entertainment: *an evening out at a restaurant.* **4** indicating a specified distance away from the goal line or finishing line: *he scored from 70 meters out.* **5** so as to be revealed or known: *find out what you can.* ■ aloud; so as to be heard: *Miss Beard cried out in horror.* **6** at or to an end: *the romance fizzled out.* ■ so as to be finished or complete: *I'll leave them to fight it out* | *I typed out the poem.* ■ (in various other completive uses): *the crowd had thinned out* | *he crossed out a word.* **7** (of a light or fire) so as to be extinguished or no longer burning: *at ten o'clock the lights went out.* ■ (of a stain or mark) no longer visible; removed: *try to get the stain out.* **8** (of a party, politician, etc.) not in office. **9** (of a jury) considering its verdict in secrecy.
▶ **prep.** through to the outside: *he ran out the door.*
▶ **adj.** [predic.] **1** not at home or at one's place of work: *if he called, she'd pretend to be out.* **2** revealed or made public: *the secret was soon out.* ■ (of a flower) in bloom; open. ■ published: *the book should be out before the end of the month.* ■ informal in existence or in use: *it works as well as any system that's out.* ■ not concealing one's homosexuality: *I had been out since I was seventeen.* **3** no longer alight; extinguished: *the fire was nearly out.* **4** at an end: *school was out for the summer.* ■ informal no longer in fashion: *life in the fast lane is out.* **5** not possible or worth considering: *a trip to the seaside is out.* **6** in a state of unconsciousness. ■ Boxing unable to rise before the count of ten. **7** mistaken; in error: *he was slightly out in his calculations.* **8** (of the ball in tennis and similar games) outside the designated playing area. **9** Baseball & Cricket no longer batting or on base, having had one's turn ended by the team in the field: *the Yankees are out in the ninth* | *Johnson was out at second.*
▶ **n.** **1** informal a way of escaping from a problem or dilemma: *he was desperately looking for an out.* **2** Baseball an act of putting a player out. **3** (**the outs**) the political party or politicians not in office.
▶ **v.** **1** [no obj.] come or go out; emerge: *the truth will out.* **2** [with obj.] informal reveal the homosexuality of (a prominent person).
– PHRASES **on the outs** in disagreement or dispute: *on the outs with established political trends.* **out and about** (of a person, esp. after inactivity) engaging in normal activity. **out for** intent on having: *he was out for a good time.* **out of 1** indicating the source or derivation of something; from: *a bench fashioned out of a fallen tree trunk* | *you should not expect too much out of life.* ■ having (the thing mentioned) as a motivation: *she did it out of spite.* ■ indicating the dam of a pedigree animal, esp. a horse. **2** from among (a number): *nine times out of ten.* **3** not having (a particular thing): *they had run out of cash.* **out of it** informal **1** not included; rejected: *I hate feeling out of it.* **2** unaware of what is happening as a result of being uninformed. ■ unable to think or react properly as a result of being drowsy. **out to** keenly striving to: *they were out to impress.* **out with** an exhortation to expel or dismiss (an unwanted person or thing). **out with it** say what you are thinking.
– ORIGIN Old English *ūt* (adverb), *ūtian* (verb), of Germanic origin; related to Dutch *uit* and German *aus.*

> **USAGE** The use of **out** as a preposition (rather than the standard prepositional phrase **out of**), as in *he threw it out the window*, is common in informal contexts, and is standard in American, Australian, and New Zealand English. Traditionalists do not accept it as part of standard British English, however.

out- ▶ **prefix 1** to the point of surpassing or exceeding: *outfight* | *outperform.* **2** external; separate; from outside: *outbuildings* | *outpatient.* **3** away from; outward: *outbound* | *outpost.*

ou·ta /'outə/ ▶ **prep.** variant spelling of OUTTA.

out·act /ˌout'akt/ ▶ **v.** [with obj.] surpass (someone) in acting or performing something.

out·age /'outij/ ▶ **n.** a period when a power supply or other service is not available or when equipment is closed down.

out-and-out ▶ **adj.** [attrib.] in every respect; absolute; without question: *an out-and-out crook.*

out-and-out·er ▶ **n.** archaic, informal a person or thing that possesses a particular quality to an extreme degree.

out·a·sight /'outə'sīt/ ▶ **exclam.** informal variant spelling of OUT OF SIGHT (see SIGHT).

out·back /'outˌbak/ ▶ **n.** (**the outback**) the remote and usually uninhabited inland regions of Australia. ■ any remote or sparsely populated region.
– DERIVATIVES **out·back·er n.**

out·bal·ance /ˌout'baləns/ ▶ **v.** [with obj.] be more valuable, important, or influential than; make up for: *their high capacity outbalances this defect.*

out bas·ket ▶ **n.** an outbox.

out·bid /ˌout'bid/ ▶ **v.** (**outbids, outbidding**; past and past participle **outbid**) [with obj.] offer to pay a higher price for something (than another person): *residential builders could always outbid any farmer for the land.*

out·board /'outˌbô(ə)rd/ ▶ **adj. & adv.** on, toward, or near the outside, esp. of a ship or other vehicle: [as adj.] *the outboard rear seats* | [as adv.] *the chart table faces outboard.* ■ [as adj.] (of a motor) portable and usually mounted on the outside of the stern of a boat. ■ [as adj.] (of an electronic accessory) in a separate container from the device with which it is used.
▶ **n.** an outboard motor. ■ a boat with such a motor.
– PHRASES **outboard of** to the outside or on the far side of: *the controls are placed just outboard of the wheel.*

out·bound /'out'bound/ ▶ **adj. & adv.** traveling away from a particular place, esp. on the first leg of a round trip: [as adj.] *an outbound flight* | [as adv.] *flying outbound.*

out·box /'outˌbäks/ ▶ **n.** a box or tray on a person's desk for outgoing letters and documents that have been dealt with. ■ a folder in which e-mails written by an individual are held before being sent.
▶ **v.** [with obj.] Boxing defeat (an opponent) by superior boxing ability.

out·brave /ˌout'brāv/ ▶ **v.** [with obj.] face (something) with a show of brave defiance: *he sat outfacing his accusers, and outbraving their accusations.* ■ archaic outdo in bravery.

out·break /'outˌbrāk/ ▶ **n.** the sudden or violent start of something unwelcome, such as war, disease, etc.: *the outbreak of World War II.*

out·breed /ˌout'brēd/ ▶ **v.** (past and past participle **outbred**) [with obj.] (usu. as noun **outbreeding**) breed from parents not closely related: *many specific genetic factors are known that regulate the degree of outbreeding.*

out·build·ing /'outˌbildiNG/ ▶ **n.** a building, such as a shed, barn, or garage, on the same property but separate from a more important one, such as a house.

out·burst /'outˌbərst/ ▶ **n.** a sudden release of strong emotion: *"she screamed at him about it one day," said one source who witnessed the outburst.* ■ a sudden outbreak of a particular activity: *a wild outburst of applause.* ■ a volcanic eruption. ■ Physics a sudden emission of energy or particles: *a very dramatic outburst of neutrons.*

out·call /'outˌkôl/ ▶ **n.** a visit by an escort, prostitute, etc., to the address of the caller.

out·cast /'outˌkast/ ▶ **n.** a person who has been rejected by society or a social group.
▶ **adj.** rejected or cast out: *made to feel outcast and inadequate.*

out·caste ▶ **n.** /'outˌkast/ (in Hindu society) a person who has no caste or has been expelled from a caste.
▶ **v.** /ˌout'kast/ [with obj.] cause (someone) to lose one's caste: *he has deliberately elected to outcaste himself.*

out·class /ˌout'klas/ ▶ **v.** [with obj.] be far superior to: *they totally outclassed us in the first half.*

out·come /'outˌkəm/ ▶ **n.** the way a thing turns out; a consequence: *it is the outcome of the vote that counts.*

out·com·pete /ˌoutkəm'pēt/ ▶ **v.** [with obj.] surpass (someone) in competition: *they were outcompeted by their foreign rivals.* ■ Biology displace (another species) in the competition for space, food, or other resources.

out·crop /'outˌkräp/ ▶ **n.** a rock formation that is visible on the surface: *dramatic limestone outcrops.*
▶ **v.** (**outcrops, outcropping, outcropped**) (often as noun **outcropping**) [no obj.] appear as an outcrop.

out·cross ▶ **v.** /ˌout'krôs, -'kräs/ [with obj.] breed (an animal or plant) with one not closely related.
▶ **n.** /'outˌkrôs, -ˌkräs/ an animal or plant produced as the result of such crossbreeding.

out·cry /'outˌkrī/ ▶ **n.** (pl. **outcries**) an exclamation or shout: *an outcry of spontaneous passion.* ■ a strong expression of public disapproval or anger: *the public outcry over the bombing.*

out·dat·ed /ˌout'dātid/ ▶ **adj.** out of date; obsolete.
– DERIVATIVES **out·dat·ed·ness n.**

out·dis·tance /ˌout'distəns/ ▶ **v.** [with obj.] leave (a competitor or pursuer) far behind: *she could maintain a fast enough pace to outdistance any pursuers.*

out·do /ˌout'do͞o/ ▶ **v.** (**outdoes, outdoing**; past **outdid**; past participle **outdone**) [with obj.] be more successful than: *the men tried to outdo each other in their generosity* | **not to be outdone,** *Vicky and Laura reached the same standard.*

out·door /'out'dôr/ ▶ **adj.** [attrib.] done, situated, or used out of doors: *a huge outdoor concert.* ■ (of a person) fond of the open air or open-air activities: *a rugged, outdoor type.*

out·doors /ˌout'dôrz/ ▶ **adv.** in or into the open air; outside a building or shelter: *it was warm enough to eat outdoors.*
▶ **n.** (usu. **the outdoors**) any area outside buildings or shelter, typically far away from human habitation: *a lover of the great outdoors.*

out·doors·man /out'dôrzmən/ ▶ **n.** (pl. **outdoorsmen**; fem. **outdoorswoman** /-ˌwo͝omən/ pl. **outdoorsman**) a person who spends a lot of time outdoors or doing outdoor activities.

out·doors·y /ˌout'dôrzē/ ▶ **adj.** informal of, associated with, or fond of the outdoors: *the outdoorsy fragrance of pines.*

out·draw /ˌout'drô/ ▶ **v.** (past **outdrew**; past participle **outdrawn**) [with obj.] (of a person or event) attract a larger crowd than (another person or event): *the stores in Paris outdraw both the Louvre and the Eiffel Tower.*

out·drink /ˌout'driNGk/ ▶ **v.** (past **outdrank**; past participle **outdrunk**) [with obj.] drink more alcohol than (another person).

out·drive /ˌout'drīv/ ▶ **v.** (past **outdrove**; past participle **outdriven**) [with obj.] **1** drive a golf ball farther than (another player): *he outdrove his playing partners by as much as seventy-five yards.* **2** drive a vehicle better or faster than (someone else): *he knew he couldn't outdrive the police.*
▶ **n.** the portion of an inboard-outboard engine that is outside the hull, providing steering and propulsion.

out·er /'outər/ ▶ **adj.** [attrib.] outside; external: *the outer door.* ■ further from the center or inside: *the outer hall at the museum's main entrance.* ■ (esp. in place names) more remote: *Outer Mongolia.* ■ objective or physical; not subjective.
– ORIGIN late Middle English: from OUT + -ER[2], replacing earlier UTTER[1].

Out·er Banks a chain of barrier islands extending southward for 175 miles (282 km) along the coast of North Carolina, consisting largely of sand dunes and serving as a buffer against the Atlantic Ocean.

out·er·course /'outərˌkôrs/ ▶ **n.** sexual stimulation that excludes penile penetration.
– ORIGIN 1980s: blend of OUTER and INTERCOURSE.

Out·er Mon·go·li·a see MONGOLIA.

out·er·most /'outərˌmōst/ ▶ **adj.** [attrib.] farthest from the center: *the outermost layer of the earth.*
▶ **pron.** the one that is farthest from the center: *the orbit of the outermost of these eight planets.*

out·er plan·et ▶ **n.** a planet whose orbit lies outside the asteroid belt, i.e., Jupiter, Saturn, Uranus, or Neptune.

out·er space ▶ **n.** the physical universe beyond the earth's atmosphere.

out·er·wear /'outərˌwe(ə)r/ ▶ **n.** clothing worn over other clothes, esp. for the outdoors.

out·face /ˌout'fās/ ▶ **v.** [with obj.] disconcert or defeat (an opponent) by bold confrontation: *to outface twenty-five or thirty antagonistic men.*

out·fall /'outˌfôl/ ▶ **n.** the place where a river, drain, or sewer empties into the sea, a river, or a lake.

out·field /'outˌfēld/ ▶ **n.** **1** the outer part of the field of play in various sports, in particular: ■ Baseball the grassy area beyond the infield. ■ Cricket the part of the field furthest from the wicket. ■ [treated as sing. or pl.] the players stationed in the outfield, collectively. **2** the outlying land of a farm.

O

–DERIVATIVES **out·field·er** n.

out·fight /ˌoutˈfīt/ ▶ v. (past and past participle **outfought**) [with obj.] fight better than and beat (an opponent).

out·fit /ˈoutˌfit/ ▶ n. a set of clothes worn together, typically for a particular occasion or purpose: *a riding outfit.* ■ informal a group of people undertaking a particular activity together, as a group of musicians, a military unit, or a business concern: *Tom was the brains of the outfit.* ■ [with modifier] a complete set of equipment or articles needed for a particular purpose: *a repair outfit.*
▶ v. (**outfits, outfitting, outfitted**) [with obj.] provide (someone) with a set of clothes: *an auction of dolls outfitted by world-famous designers | he outfitted himself in the best gray suit he could afford.* ■ provide with equipment: *planes outfitted with sophisticated electronic gear.*

out·fit·ter /ˈoutˌfitər/ (also **outfitters**) ▶ n. an establishment that sells clothing, equipment, and services, esp. for outdoor activities: *an outfitter that provides professional guides.* ■ Brit. dated an establishment that sells men's clothing.

out·flank /ˌoutˈflaNGk/ ▶ v. [with obj.] move around the side of (an enemy) so as to outmaneuver them: *the Germans had sought to outflank them from the northeast.* ■ outwit: *an attempt to outflank the opposition.*

out·flow /ˈoutˌflō/ ▶ n. a large amount of money, liquid, or people that moves or is transferred out of a place: *an outflow of foreign currency.* ■ Meteorology the outward flow of air from a weather system, associated with wind shift and temperature drop.

out·fly /ˌoutˈflī/ ▶ v. (**outflies, outflying**; past **outflew**; past participle **outflown**) [with obj.] fly faster, farther, or with more agility than: *a high-powered combat aircraft that can outfly anything.*

out·fox /ˌoutˈfäks/ ▶ v. [with obj.] informal defeat or deceive (someone) by being more clever or cunning than they are; outwit.

out·gas /ˌoutˈgas/ ▶ v. (**outgases, outgassing, outgasing, outgassed**) [with obj.] release or give off (a substance) as a gas or vapor: *glue may outgas smelly volatile organic compounds* | [no obj.] *samples are heated and begin to outgas.*

out·gen·er·al /ˌoutˈjen(ə)rəl/ ▶ v. (**outgenerals, outgeneraling, outgeneraled**; Brit. **outgenerals, outgeneralling, outgeneralled**) [with obj.] get the better of by superior strategy or tactics.

out·go ▶ n. /ˈoutˌgō/ the outlay of money: *the secret of success lies in the relation of income to outgo.*
▶ v. /outˈgō/ (**outgoes, outgoing**; past **outwent**; past participle **outgone**) [with obj.] archaic go faster than: *he on horseback outgoes him on foot.*

out·go·ing /ˈoutˌgōiNG/ ▶ adj. **1** friendly and socially confident: *she's an extremely affable, jovial, outgoing type of person.*
2 [attrib.] leaving an office or position, esp. after an election defeat or completed term of office: *the outgoing governor.* ■ going out or away from a particular place: *incoming and outgoing calls.*
▶ n. Brit. (**outgoings**) a person's regular expenditure.

out·gross /ˈoutˈgrōs/ ▶ v. [with obj.] surpass in gross income or profit: *the film has outgrossed all other movie comedies.*

out-group ▶ n. **1** Sociology those people who do not belong to a specific in-group.
2 Biology a group of organisms not belonging to the group whose evolutionary relationships are being investigated.

out·grow /ˌoutˈgrō/ ▶ v. (past **outgrew**; past participle **outgrown**) [with obj.] grow too big for (something): *babies outgrow their first car seat at six to nine months.* ■ leave behind as one matures: *is it a permanent injury, or will the colt outgrow it?* ■ grow faster or taller than: *the more vigorous plants outgrow their weaker neighbors.*

out·growth /ˈoutˌgrōTH/ ▶ n. something that grows out of something else: *outgrowths at the base of the leaf.* ■ a natural development or result of something: *the book is an imaginative outgrowth of practical criticism.* ■ the process of growing out: *with further outgrowth the radius and ulna develop.*

out·guess /ˌoutˈges/ ▶ v. [with obj.] outwit (someone) by guessing correctly what they intend to do: *a brilliant military commander outguesses the enemy.*

out·gun /ˌoutˈgən/ ▶ v. (**outguns, outgunning, outgunned**) [with obj.] (often as adj. **outgunned**) have better or more weaponry than: *offensives that overwhelmed the outgunned and outmanned armies.* ■ surpass in power or strength: *the team were outgunned by the joint title favorites.*

out·haul /ˈoutˌhôl/ ▶ n. Sailing a rope used to haul out the clew of a boom sail or the tack of a jib.

out·hit /ˌoutˈhit/ ▶ v. (**outhits, outhitting**; past and past participle **outhit**) [with obj.] (in baseball and other sports played with a ball) surpass (a player or a team) in hitting the ball into fair territory: *we outscored them for the Series, 55–27, and outhit them, 91–60.*

out·house /ˈoutˌhous/ ▶ n. an outbuilding containing a toilet, typically with no plumbing. ■ any outbuilding.

out·ing /ˈoutiNG/ ▶ n. **1** a trip taken for pleasure, esp. one lasting a day or less: *they would go on family outings to the movies.* ■ a brief journey from home: *her daily outing to the stores.* ■ informal an appearance in something, as an athletic event or show: *her first screen outing in three years.*
2 the act or practice of revealing the homosexuality of a person.
–ORIGIN late Middle English (in the sense 'the action of going out or of expelling'): from the verb OUT + -ING[1].

out·ing flan·nel ▶ n. a type of flannelette with a short nap on both sides, used in infant clothing.

out is·land ▶ n. an island situated away from the mainland.

out·land /ˈoutˌland/ ▶ n. (often **outlands**) remote or distant territory: *barbarian chiefs from the outlands.*
▶ adj. remote; distant. ■ foreign: *in the charge of outland kings.*

out·land·er /ˈoutˌlandər/ ▶ n. a foreigner; a stranger.

out·land·ish /outˈlandisH/ ▶ adj. **1** looking or sounding bizarre or unfamiliar: *outlandish brightly colored clothes | the most outlandish ideas.*
2 archaic foreign; alien.
–DERIVATIVES **out·land·ish·ly** adv., **out·land·ish·ness** n.
–ORIGIN Old English *ūtlendisc* 'not native,' from *ūtland* 'foreign country.'

out·last /ˌoutˈlast/ ▶ v. [with obj.] live or last longer than: *the kind of beauty that will outlast youth.*

out·law /ˈoutˌlô/ ▶ n. a person who has broken the law, esp. one who remains at large or is a fugitive. ■ an intractable horse or other animal. ■ historical a person deprived of the benefit and protection of the law.
▶ v. [with obj.] ban; make illegal: *Maryland outlawed cheap small-caliber pistols* | (as adj. **outlawed**) *the outlawed guerrilla group.* ■ historical deprive (someone) of the benefit and protection of the law.
–DERIVATIVES **out·law·ry** /-ˌlôrē/ n.
–ORIGIN late Old English *ūtlaga* (noun), *ūtlagian* (verb), from Old Norse *útlagi*, noun from *útlagr* 'outlawed or banished.'

out·law coun·try ▶ n. a genre of country music that draws from an earlier raw honky-tonk style, largely as a response to the more clean-cut image of mainstream country music.

out·lay /ˈoutˌlā/ ▶ n. an amount of money spent on something.

out·let /ˈoutˌlet/ ▶ n. **1** a pipe or hole through which water or gas may escape. ■ the mouth of a river. ■ a point in an electrical circuit from which current may be drawn.
2 a place from which goods are sold or distributed: *a fast-food outlet.* ■ a market for goods: *the indoor markets in Moscow were an outlet for surplus collective-farm produce.* ■ a retail store offering discounted merchandise, esp. overstocked or irregular items.
3 a means of expressing one's talents, energy, or emotions: *writing became the main outlet for his energies.*
–ORIGIN Middle English: from OUT- + the verb LET[1].

out·let box ▶ n. a box for mounting wall outlets and connecting them to electrical wiring.

out·let pass ▶ n. Basketball a quick pass from a player who has just taken a rebound to a teammate who can initiate a fast break.

out·li·er /ˈoutˌlīər/ ▶ n. a person or thing situated away or detached from the main body or system: *less accessible islands and outliers.* ■ a person or thing excluded from a group; an outsider. ■ Geology a younger rock formation isolated among older rocks. ■ Statistics a data point on a graph or in a set of results that is very much bigger or smaller than the next nearest data point.

out·line /ˈoutˌlīn/ ▶ n. **1** a line or set of lines enclosing or indicating the shape of an object in a sketch or diagram: *fill in the outlines with color.* ■ a line or set of lines of this type, perceived as defining the contours or bounds of an object: *the outlines of her face.*
2 a general description or plan giving the essential features of something but not the detail: *an outline of the theory of evolution | a course outline.*
▶ v. [with obj.] **1** draw, trace, or define the outer edge or shape of (something): *her large eyes were darkly outlined with eyeliner.*
2 give a summary of (something): *she outlined the case briefly.*

out·lin·er /ˈoutˌlīnər/ ▶ n. a computer application that produces a hierarchically arranged outline of the logical structure of a text document.

out·live /ˌoutˈliv/ ▶ v. [with obj.] (of a person) live longer than (another person): *women generally outlive men.* ■ survive or last beyond (a specified period or expected lifespan): *the organization had largely* **outlived its usefulness**. ■ archaic live through (an experience): *the world has outlived much.*

out·look /ˈoutˌlo͝ok/ ▶ n. **1** a person's point of view or general attitude to life: *broaden your* **outlook on life**.
2 a view: *the pleasant outlook from the lodge window.* ■ a place from which a view is possible; a vantage point. ■ the prospect for the future: *the deteriorating economic outlook.*

out·ly·ing /ˈoutˌlī-iNG/ ▶ adj. [attrib.] situated far from a center; remote: *an outlying village.*

out·man /ˌoutˈman/ ▶ v. (**outmans, outmanning, outmanned**) [with obj.] (usu. as adj. **outmanned**) outnumber: *the rebels are outmanned and outmatched in armaments.* ■ overpower with skill or physical strength: *Mexico controlled the game and ran circles around the outmanned Guatemalan team.*

out·ma·neu·ver /ˌoutməˈno͞ovər/ (Brit. **outmanoeuvre**) ▶ v. [with obj.] evade (an opponent) by moving faster or with greater agility: *the YF-22 can outmaneuver any fighter flying today.* ■ use skill and cunning to secure an advantage over (someone): *he would be able to outmaneuver his critics.*

out·match /ˌoutˈmaCH/ ▶ v. [with obj.] be superior to (an opponent or rival).

out·meas·ure /ˌoutˈmezHər/ ▶ v. [with obj.] archaic exceed in quantity or extent.

out·mi·grant /ˈoutˌmīgrənt/ ▶ n. a person who has migrated from one place to another, esp. within a country.
–DERIVATIVES **out·mi·gra·tion** /-mīˌgrāSHən/ n.

out·mod·ed /ˌoutˈmōdid/ ▶ adj. old-fashioned.
–DERIVATIVES **out·mod·ed·ness** n.

out·most /ˈoutˌmōst/ ▶ adj. farthest away: *the outmost reaches of the empire.*
–ORIGIN Middle English: variant of *utmost* 'utmost.'

out·mus·cle /outˈməsəl/ ▶ v. [with obj.] dominate or defeat by virtue of superior strength or force.

out·num·ber /ˌoutˈnəmbər/ ▶ v. [with obj.] be more numerous than: *women outnumbered men by three to one.*

out-of-bod·y ex·pe·ri·ence ▶ n. a sensation of being outside one's own body, typically of floating and being able to observe oneself from a distance.

out-of-court ▶ adj. [attrib.] (of a settlement) made or done without a court decision.

out of date ▶ adj. old-fashioned: *everything in her wardrobe must be hopelessly out of date | an out-of-date kitchen.* ■ no longer valid or relevant: *your passport is out of date.*

out-of-the-way ▶ adj. (also **out of the way**) (of a place) remote; secluded: *an out-of-the-way rural district.* ■ dealt with or finished: *economic recovery will begin once the election is out of the way.* ■ (of a person) no longer an obstacle or hindrance to someone's plans: *why did Josie want her out of the way?* ■ unusual, exceptional, or remarkable: *something very out of the way had happened.*

out-of-town ▶ adj. situated, originating from, or taking place outside a given or implied city or town: *a reception for influential out-of-town guests.*
–DERIVATIVES **out-of-town·er** n.

out·pace /ˌoutˈpās/ ▶ v. [with obj.] go, rise, or improve faster than: *he took the pass and outpaced the defense to score in the corner | salsa sales now outpace those for ketchup.*

out·par·cel /ˈoutˌpärsəl/ ▶ n. a building lot separated or separable from a commercial development, the selling of which provides liquidity for the developer.

out·pa·tient /ˈoutˌpāSHənt/ ▶ n. a patient who receives medical treatment without being admitted to a hospital: *attending a clinic as an outpatient* | [as modifier] *treatment is done on an outpatient basis.*

out·per·form /ˌoutpərˈfôrm/ ▶ v. [with obj.] perform better than: *an experienced employee will outperform the novice.* ■ (of an investment) be more profitable than: *silver has outperformed the stock market.*
–DERIVATIVES **out·per·for·mance** /-ˈfôrməns/ n.

out·place·ment /ˈoutplāsmənt/ ▶ n. the provision of assistance to laid-off employees in finding new

O

employment, either as a benefit provided by the employer directly, or through a specialist service.

out·play /ˌoutˈplā/ ▶ **v.** [with obj.] play better than: *they outshot and in general just outplayed us.*

out·point /ˌoutˈpoint/ ▶ **v.** [with obj.] **1** defeat (an opponent) on points: *he retained his featherweight title by outpointing the Colombian in twelve rounds.* **2** Nautical sail closer to the wind than (another ship).

out·poll /ˌoutˈpōl/ ▶ **v.** [with obj.] receive more votes than (another party or candidate).

out·port /ˈoutˌpôrt/ ▶ **n.** a subsidiary port built near an existing one.

out·post /ˈoutˌpōst/ ▶ **n. 1** a small military camp or position at some distance from the main force, used esp. as a guard against surprise attack. **2** a remote part of a country or empire. ■ something regarded as an isolated or remote branch of something: *the community is the last outpost of civilization in the far north.*

out·pour·ing /ˈoutˌpôriNG/ ▶ **n.** something that streams out rapidly: *a massive outpouring of high-energy gamma rays.* ■ (often **outpourings**) an outburst of strong emotion: *spontaneous outpourings of affection and support | the unprecedented outpouring of tearful grief.*

out·psych /ˌoutˈsīk/ (also **outpsyche**) ▶ **v.** [with obj.] informal defeat by psychological influence or intimidation: *each country tries to outpsych the other.*

out·put /ˈoutˌpo͝ot/ ▶ **n. 1** the amount of something produced by a person, machine, or industry: *the diverse range of Liszt's output | efficiency can lead to higher outputs.* ■ the action or process of producing something: *the output of epinephrine.* ■ the power, energy, or other results supplied by a device or system: *the quality of the output from the printer is very good.* **2** Electronics a place where power or information leaves a system.
▶ **v.** (**outputs, outputting**; past and past participle **output** or **outputted**) [with obj.] produce, deliver, or supply (data) using a computer or other device: *you can output the image directly to a video recording system.*

out·race /ˌoutˈrās/ ▶ **v.** [with obj.] exceed in speed, amount, or extent: *demand for trained clergy is outracing the supply.*

out·rage /ˈoutˌrāj/ ▶ **n.** an extremely strong reaction of anger, shock, or indignation: *her voice trembled with outrage.* ■ an action or event causing such a reaction: *the decision was an outrage.*
▶ **v.** [with obj.] (usu. **be outraged**) arouse fierce anger, shock, or indignation in (someone): *he was outraged at this attempt to take his victory away from him.* ■ violate or infringe flagrantly (a principle, law, etc.): *their behavior outraged all civilized standards.*
– ORIGIN Middle English (in the senses 'lack of moderation' and 'violent behavior'): from Old French *ou(l)trage*, based on Latin *ultra* 'beyond.' Sense development has been affected by the belief that the word is a compound of OUT and RAGE.

out·ra·geous /outˈrājəs/ ▶ **adj. 1** shockingly bad or excessive: *an outrageous act of bribery.* ■ wildly exaggerated or improbable: *the outrageous claims made by the previous administration.* **2** very bold, unusual, and startling: *her outrageous leotards and sexy routines.*
– DERIVATIVES **out·ra·geous·ly** adv., **out·ra·geous·ness** n.
– ORIGIN late Middle English: from Old French *outrageus*, from *outrage* 'excess' (see OUTRAGE).

out·ran /ˌoutˈran/ past of OUTRUN.

out·range /ˌoutˈrānj/ ▶ **v.** (of a gun or its user) have a longer range than.

out·rank /ˌoutˈraNGk/ ▶ **v.** [with obj.] have a higher rank than (someone else): *a father figure to many of the junior officers theoretically outranking him.* ■ be better, more important, or more significant than: *fishing provided the chief employment, outranking both clothing and canning.*

ou·tré /o͞oˈtrā/ ▶ **adj.** unusual and startling: *in 1975 the suggestion was considered outré—today it is orthodox.*
– ORIGIN French, literally 'exceeded,' past participle of *outrer* (see OUTRAGE).

out·reach ▶ **n.** /ˈoutˌrēCH/ the extent or length of reaching out. ■ an organization's involvement with or activity in the community, esp. in the context of social welfare: *her goal is to increase educational outreach* | [as modifier] *Phoenix's outreach effort to educate renters and homebuyers about their rights.*
▶ **v.** /ˌoutˈrēCH/ [with obj.] reach further than. ■ [no obj.] literary stretch out one's arms.

Ou·tre·mer /ˌo͞otrəˈmâr/ a name applied to the medieval French crusader states, including Armenia, Antioch, Tripoli, and Jerusalem.
– ORIGIN from French *outremer* (adverb) 'overseas,' from *outre* 'beyond' + *mer* 'sea.'

out·ride /ˌoutˈrīd/ ▶ **v.** (past **outrode**; past participle **outridden**) [with obj.] ride better, faster, or farther than.

out·rid·er /ˈoutˌrīdər/ ▶ **n.** a person in a motor vehicle or on horseback who goes in front of or beside a vehicle as an escort or guard: *an escort of police outriders.* ■ a mounted official who escorts racehorses to the starting post. ■ a cowhand who prevents cattle from straying beyond a certain limit.
– DERIVATIVES **out·rid·ing** /ˈoutˌrīdiNG/ n.

out·rig·ger /ˈoutˌrigər/ ▶ **n.** a beam, spar, or framework projecting from or over the side of a ship or boat. ■ a float or secondary hull fixed parallel to a canoe or other boat to stabilize it. ■ a boat fitted with such a structure. ■ a similar projecting support in another structure or vehicle.
– DERIVATIVES **out·rigged** /-ˌrigd/ adj.
– ORIGIN mid 18th cent.: perhaps influenced by the obsolete nautical term *outligger*, in the same sense.

outrigger

out·right ▶ **adv.** /ˈoutˌrīt/ **1** altogether; completely: *logging has been banned outright.* ■ without reservation; openly: *she couldn't ask him outright.* **2** immediately: *the impact killed four horses outright.* ■ not by degrees or installments: *they decided to buy the company outright.*
▶ **adj.** [attrib.] open and direct; not concealed: *an outright refusal.* ■ total; complete: *the outright abolition of the death penalty.* ■ undisputed; clear: *an outright victory.*

ou·tro /ˈoutrō/ ▶ **n.** (pl. **outros**) informal the concluding section of a piece of music or a radio or television program: *the intros, outros, and bridges of various segments.*
– ORIGIN 1970s: from OUT, on the pattern of *intro*.

out·run /ˌoutˈrən/ ▶ **v.** (**outruns, outrunning**; past **outran**; past participle **outrun**) [with obj.] run or travel faster or farther than. ■ escape from: *it's harder than anyone imagines to outrun destiny.* ■ go beyond; exceed: *his courage outran his prudence.*

out·rush /ˌoutˈrəSH/ ▶ **n.** a rushing out of something; a sudden outpouring.
– DERIVATIVES **out·rush·ing** adj.

out·sell /ˌoutˈsel/ ▶ **v.** (past and past participle **outsold**) [with obj.] sell or be sold in greater quantities than: *his first foray into the thriller area could well outsell his other books.*

out·sert /ˈoutsərt/ ▶ **n.** a piece of promotional material that is placed on the outside of a package, publication, or other product.
– ORIGIN 1960s: from OUT + INSERT.

out·set /ˈoutˌset/ ▶ **n.** [in sing.] the start or beginning of something: *a field of which he had known nothing at the outset and learned on the job.*
– PHRASES **at** (or **from**) **the outset** at or from the beginning.

out·shine /ˌoutˈSHīn/ ▶ **v.** (past and past participle **outshone**) [with obj.] shine more brightly than. ■ be much better than (someone) in a particular area: *it is a shame when a mother outshines a daughter.*

out·shoot /ˌoutˈSHo͞ot/ ▶ **v.** (past and past participle **outshot**) [with obj.] shoot better than (someone else). ■ Sports make or take more shots than (another player or team).

out·shout /outˈSHout/ ▶ **v.** [with obj.] shout louder than: *each team tried to outshout the other.*

out·side /ˈoutˈsīd/ ▶ **n.** the external side or surface of something: *record the date on the outside of the file.* ■ the side of a bend or curve where the edge or surface is longer in extent. ■ the side of a racetrack further from the center, where the lanes are longer. ■ the external appearance of someone or something: *was he as straight as he appeared* **on the outside**? ■ (in basketball) the area beyond the perimeter of the defense: *he often set up the Lakers' plays from the outside.*
▶ **adj.** [attrib.] **1** situated on or near the exterior or external surface of something: *put the outside lights on.* ■ Baseball (of a pitch) passing home plate on the side of the plate away from the batter, not in the strike zone. ■ (in soccer and other sports) denoting positions nearer to the sides of the field. ■ (in basketball) taking place beyond the perimeter of the defense: *he needs work on his outside shot.* **2** not belonging to or coming from within a particular group: *I have some outside help.* ■ beyond one's own immediate personal concerns: *I was able to face the outside world again.* **3** highest possible; greatest; maximum: *new monthly charges that, according to outside estimates, may total $8 per line.*
▶ **prep. & adv. 1** situated or moving beyond the boundaries or confines of: [as prep.] *there was a boy outside the door* | [as adv.] *the dog was still barking outside | outside, the wind was as wild as ever.* ■ not being a member of (a particular group): [as prep.] *those of us outside the university.* ■ (in football, soccer, and other sports) closer to the side of the field than (another player): [as prep.] *Swift appeared outside him with Andrews on his left.* **2** [prep.] beyond the limits or scope of: *the high cost of shipping has put it outside their price range.*
– PHRASES **at the outside** (of an estimate) at the most: *every minute, or at the outside, every ninety seconds.* **on the outside** away from or not belonging to a particular circle or institution: *when you're on the outside, then you have a much better view of what they're doing.* **on the outside looking in** (of a person) excluded from a group or activity. **an outside chance** a remote possibility. **outside of** informal beyond the boundaries of: *a village 20 miles outside of New York.* ■ apart from: *outside of his family, nobody cares too much about him.*

> **USAGE** **Outside of** tends to be more commonly used in the US than in Britain, where **outside** usually suffices, but, like its cousin *off of*, it is colloquial and not recommended for formal writing. (See usage at OFF.) The adverb **outside** is not problematic when referring to physical space, position, etc. (*I'm going outside*), but the compound preposition **outside of** is often used as a colloquial (and often inferior) way of saying *except for, other than, apart from* (*outside of what I just mentioned, I can't think of any reason not to*). Besides possibly sounding more informal than desired, **outside of** may cause misunderstanding by suggesting physical space or location when that is not the point to be emphasized, or when no such sense is intended—consider the ambiguity in this sentence: *outside of China, he has few interests.* Does this mean that his primary interest is China? Or does it mean that whenever he is not in China, he has few interests?

out·side in·ter·est ▶ **n.** an interest or hobby not connected with one's work or studies.

out·side line ▶ **n.** a telephone connection to an external dial tone, for outgoing calls.

out·side mon·ey ▶ **n.** Economics money held in a form such as gold that is an asset for the holder and does not represent a corresponding liability for someone else.

out·sid·er /ˌoutˈsīdər/ ▶ **n. 1** a person who does not belong to a particular group. ■ a person who is not accepted by or who is isolated from society. **2** a competitor, applicant, etc., thought to have little chance of success: *he started as a rank outsider for the title.*

out·sid·er art ▶ **n.** art produced by self-taught artists who are not part of the artistic establishment.
– DERIVATIVES **out·sid·er art·ist** n.

out·size /ˌoutˈsīz/ ▶ **adj.** (also **outsized**) exceptionally large.
▶ **n.** an exceptionally large person or thing, esp. a garment made to measurements larger than the standard.

out·skirts /ˈoutˌskərts/ ▶ **plural n.** the outer parts of a town or city: *the park was built on the outskirts of New York in 1857.* ■ the fringes of something: *he likes to be on the outskirts of a discussion.*

out·smart /ˌoutˈsmärt/ ▶ **v.** [with obj.] informal defeat or get the better of (someone) by being clever or cunning: *content with the illusion that they can outsmart the market.*

out·sold /ˌoutˈsōld/ past and past participle of OUTSELL.

out·sole /ˈoutˌsōl/ ▶ **n.** the outermost layer of the sole of a boot or shoe, esp. an athletic shoe.

out·source /ˈoutˌsôrs/ ▶ **v.** [with obj.] obtain (goods or a service) from an outside or foreign supplier, esp. in place of an internal source: *outsourcing components* **from** *other countries* | (as noun **outsourcing**) *outsourcing can dramatically lower total costs.* ■ contract (work) out or abroad: *you may choose to outsource this function* **to** *another company or do it yourself.*

out·spo·ken /ˌoutˈspōkən/ ▶ **adj.** frank in stating one's opinions, esp. if they are critical or controversial: *he has been outspoken in his criticism.*
– DERIVATIVES **out·spok·en·ly** adv., **out·spok·en·ness** n.

out·spread /ˌoutˈspred/ ▶ **adj.** fully extended or expanded: *outspread arms.*

▶ v. (past and past participle **outspread**) [with obj.] literary spread out: *that eagle outspreading his wings for flight.*

out·stand·ing /ˌout'standiNG, 'out-/ ▶ adj. **1** exceptionally good: *the team's outstanding performance.* ■ clearly noticeable: *works of outstanding banality.* **2** remaining to be paid, done, or dealt with: *there was a small charge outstanding | how much work is still outstanding?*

out·stand·ing·ly /ˌout'standiNGlē/ ▶ adv. [usu. as submodifier] exceptionally: *outstandingly beautiful gardens.*

out·stare /ˌout'ste(ə)r/ ▶ v. [with obj.] stare at (someone) for longer than they can stare back, typically in order to intimidate or disconcert them.

out·sta·tion /'outˌstāSHən/ ▶ n. a branch of an organization situated at some distance from its headquarters.

out·stay /ˌout'stā/ ▶ v. [with obj.] stay beyond the limit of (one's expected or permitted time): *employees who had outstayed their coffee break.*
– PHRASES **outstay one's welcome** see WELCOME.

out·step /ˌout'step/ ▶ v. (**outsteps, outstepping, outstepped**) [with obj.] rare exceed.

out·stretch /ˌout'streCH/ ▶ v. [with obj.] (usu. as adj. **outstretched**) extend or stretch out (something, esp. a hand or arm): *I walked with my arms outstretched.* ■ go beyond the limit of: *their good intentions far outstretched their capacity to offer help.*

out·strip /ˌout'strip/ ▶ v. (**outstrips, outstripping, outstripped**) [with obj.] move faster than and overtake (someone else). ■ exceed: *supply far outstripped demand.*

out·ta /'outə/ (also **outa**) ▶ prep. an informal contraction of "out of," used in representing colloquial speech: *we'd better get outta here.*

out·take /'ouˌtāk/ ▶ n. a scene or sequence filmed or recorded for a movie or program but not included in the final version.

out-talk ▶ v. (also **outtalk**) [with obj.] outdo or overcome in talking or argumentation: *whether you get ten years or go free can depend on whether your counsel can out-talk the other man's.*

out·think /ˌout'THiNGk/ ▶ v. [with obj.] outdo in thinking; outwit: *machines that can outthink humans.*

out·thrust /'outˌTHrəst/ ▶ adj. extended outward: *with his outthrust foot he sent the man keeling over.* ▶ n. a thing that projects or is extended outward: *root hairs are outthrusts from the root surface.*

out·turn /'outˌtərn/ ▶ n. the amount of something produced, esp. money; output: *the financial outturn.*

out·vote /ˌout'vōt/ ▶ v. [with obj.] defeat by tallying a greater number of votes.

out·ward /'outwərd/ ▶ adj. [attrib.] **1** of, on, or from the outside: *the vehicle's outward and interior appearance.* ■ relating to the external appearance of something rather than its true nature or substance: *an outward display of friendliness.* ■ archaic outer: *the outward physical body.* **2** going out or away from a place: *the outward voyage.*
▶ adv. away from the center or a particular point; toward the outside: *a window that opens outward | the solar wind that rushes outward from the sun.*
– DERIVATIVES **out·ward·ness** n.
– ORIGIN Old English *ūtweard* (see OUT-, -WARD).

out·ward-bound ▶ adj. (of a ship or passenger) going away from home or point of origin: *an outward-bound crude oil carrier.*

out·ward·ly /'outwərdlē/ ▶ adv. [often as submodifier] on the surface: *an outwardly normal life | [sentence adverb] outwardly she seemed no different.* ■ on or from the outside: *outwardly featureless modern offices | [sentence adverb] outwardly it's not a bad-looking car.*

out·wards /'outwərdz/ ▶ adv. chiefly Brit. variant of OUTWARD.

out·wash /'outˌwôSH, -ˌwäSH/ ▶ n. material carried away from a glacier by meltwater and deposited beyond the moraine.

out·watch /ˌout'wäCH/ ▶ v. [with obj.] archaic watch (something) until it disappears. ■ keep awake beyond the end of: *they outwatched the night, ever hopeful of a rescue.*

out·wear /ˌout'we(ə)r/ ▶ v. (past **outwore**; past participle **outworn**) [with obj.] last longer than: *a material that will outwear any other waterproof sheeting.* ■ exhaust; wear out; wear away.

out·weigh /ˌout'wā/ ▶ v. [with obj.] be heavier than: *Bob outweighed him by more than twenty-five pounds.* ■ be greater or more significant than: *the advantages greatly outweigh the disadvantages.*

out·went /ˌout'went/ past of OUTGO.

out·wit /ˌout'wit/ ▶ v. (**outwits, outwitting, outwitted**) [with obj.] deceive or defeat by greater ingenuity: *Ray had outwitted many an opponent.*

out·work /'outˌwərk/ ▶ n. **1** a section of a fortification or system of defense that is in front of the main part. **2** Brit. work done outside the factory or office that provides it.
▶ v. /ˌout'wərk/ [with obj.] work harder, faster, or longer than: *Irwin simply outworks his opponent.*
– DERIVATIVES **out·work·er** n. (sense 2 of the noun).

out·world /'outˌwərld/ ▶ n. (in science fiction) an outlying or alien planet.
– DERIVATIVES **out·world·er** n.

out·worn /ˌout'wôrn/ past participle of OUTWEAR.
▶ adj. out of date: *outworn prejudices.* ■ no longer usable or serviceable: *outworn lead flashings.*

out·yield /ˌout'yēld/ ▶ v. [with obj.] produce or yield more than: *plantations outyield managed natural forest.*

ou·zel /'o͞ozəl/ (also **ousel**) ▶ n. a bird that resembles the blackbird, esp. the ring ouzel. See also WATER OUZEL.
– ORIGIN Old English *ōsle* 'blackbird,' of Germanic origin; related to German *Amsel* 'blackbird.'

ou·zo /'o͞ozō/ ▶ n. (pl. **ouzos**) a Greek anise-flavored liqueur.
– ORIGIN modern Greek.

o·va /'ōvə/ plural form of OVUM.

o·val /'ōvəl/ ▶ adj. having a rounded and slightly elongated outline or shape, like that of an egg: *her smooth oval face | the game with the oval ball.*
▶ n. a body, object, or design with such a shape or outline: *cut out two small ovals from the felt.* ■ an oval playing field or racing track.
– DERIVATIVES **o·val·i·ty** /ō'valitē/ n., **o·val·ness** n.
– ORIGIN mid 16th cent.: from French, or modern Latin *ovalis*, from Latin *ovum* 'egg.'

ov·al·bu·min /ˌävəl'byo͞omən, ˌōvəl-/ ▶ n. Biochemistry albumin derived from the white of eggs.
– ORIGIN mid 19th cent.: from Latin *ovi albumen* 'albumen of egg,' altered on the pattern of *albumin*.

O·val Of·fice the office of the president of the US, in the White House. ■ this office regarded as representing the power of the executive branch of the US government: *on orders from the Oval Office.*

o·val win·dow ▶ n. informal term for FENESTRA OVALIS (see FENESTRA).

Ov·am·bo /ō'vambō/ ▶ n. (pl. **same** or **Ovambos**) **1** a member of a people of northern Namibia. **2** the Bantu language of this people.
▶ adj. of or relating to the Ovambo or their language.
– ORIGIN a local name, from *ova-* (prefix denoting a plural) + *ambo* 'man of leisure.'

Ov·am·bo·land /ō'vämbōˌland/ a semiarid region of northern Namibia, the homeland of the Ovambo people.

o·var·i·an /ō've(ə)rēən/ ▶ adj. of or relating to an ovary or the ovaries: *an ovarian cyst.*

o·var·i·an fol·li·cle ▶ n. another term for GRAAFIAN FOLLICLE.

o·var·i·ec·to·my /ōˌve(ə)rē'ektəmē/ ▶ n. (pl. **ovariectomies**) surgical removal of one or both ovaries; oophorectomy.

o·var·i·ot·o·my /ōˌve(ə)rē'ätəmē/ ▶ n. **1** surgical incision into an ovary. **2** another term for OVARIECTOMY.

o·va·ri·tis /ˌōvə'rītis/ ▶ n. another term for OOPHORITIS.

o·va·ry /'ōv(ə)rē/ ▶ n. (pl. **ovaries**) a female reproductive organ in which ova or eggs are produced, present in humans and other vertebrates as a pair. ■ Botany the hollow base of the carpel of a flower, containing one or more ovules.
– ORIGIN mid 17th cent.: from modern Latin *ovarium*, from Latin *ovum* 'egg.'

o·vate /'ōˌvāt/ ▶ adj. chiefly Biology having an oval outline or ovoid shape, like an egg.
– ORIGIN mid 18th cent.: from Latin *ovatus* 'egg-shaped.'

o·va·tion /ō'vāSHən/ ▶ n. **1** a sustained and enthusiastic show of appreciation from an audience, esp. by means of applause: *the performance received a thundering ovation.* **2** Roman History a processional entrance into Rome by a victorious commander, of lesser honor than a triumph.
– ORIGIN early 16th cent. (sense 2): from Latin *ovatio(n-)*, from *ovare* 'exult.' The word had the sense 'exultation' from the mid 17th to early 19th cent.

ov·en /'əvən/ ▶ n. **1** an enclosed compartment, as in a kitchen range, for cooking and heating food: figurative *the house was like an oven when I came in.* ■ a small furnace or kiln. **2** a cremation chamber in a Nazi concentration camp.
– ORIGIN Old English *ofen*, of Germanic origin; related to Dutch *oven*, German *Ofen*, from an Indo-European root shared by Greek *ipnos*.

ov·en·bird /'əvənˌbərd/ ▶ n. **1** a small tropical American bird belonging to a diverse family, many members of which make domed, ovenlike nests of mud. ● Family Furnariidae (the **ovenbird family**): many genera and numerous species. The ovenbird family comprises the horneros, miners,and many others. **2** a migratory brown North American warbler that builds a domed, ovenlike nest on the ground. ● *Seiurus aurocapillus*, subfamily Parulinae, family Emberizidae.

ov·en·proof /'əvənˌpro͞of/ ▶ adj. (of cookware) suitable for use in an oven; heat-resistant.

ov·en-read·y ▶ adj. (of food) prepared before sale so as to be ready for cooking in an oven.

ov·en·ware /'əvənˌwer/ ▶ n. dishes that can be used for cooking food in an oven.

o·ver /'ōvər/ ▶ prep. **1** extending directly upward from: *I saw flames over Berlin.* ■ above so as to cover or protect: *an oxygen tent over the bed | ladle this sauce over fresh pasta.* ■ extending above (a general area) from a vantage point: *views over Hyde Park.* ■ at the other side of; beyond: *over the hill is a small village.* **2** expressing passage or trajectory across: *she trudged over the lawn.* ■ beyond and falling or hanging from: *it toppled over the cliff.* ■ expressing duration: *inventories have been refined over many years | she told me over coffee.* ■ by means of; by the medium of: *over the loudspeaker.* **3** at a higher level or layer than: *watching a television hanging over the bar.* ■ higher in grade or rank than: *over him is the financial director.* ■ expressing authority or control: *editorial control over what is included.* ■ expressing preference: *I'd choose the well-known brand over that one.* ■ expressing greater number: *there was a slight predominance of boys over girls.* ■ higher in volume or pitch than: *he shouted over the noise of the taxis.* **4** higher than or more than (a specified number or quantity): *over 40 degrees C | they have lived together for over a year.* **5** on the subject of: *a heated debate over unemployment.*
▶ adv. **1** expressing passage or trajectory across an area: *he leaned over and tapped me on the hand.* ■ beyond and falling or hanging from a point: *listing over at an acute angle.* **2** in or to the place mentioned or indicated: *over here | come over and cheer us up.* **3** used to express action and result: *the car flipped over | hand the money over.* ■ finished: *the match is over | message understood, over and out.* **4** used to express repetition of a process: *twice over | the sums will have to be done over again.*
▶ n. Cricket a sequence of six balls bowled by a bowler from one end of the pitch.
– PHRASES **be over** no longer be affected by: *we were over the worst.* **get something over with** do or undergo something unpleasant or difficult, so as to be rid of it. **over against** adjacent to: *over against the wall.* ■ in contrast with: *over against heaven is hell.* **over and above** in addition to: *exceptional service over and above what normally might be expected.* **over and done with** completely finished. **over and over** again and again.
– ORIGIN Old English *ofer*, of Germanic origin; related to Dutch *over* and German *über*, from an Indo-European word (originally a comparative of the element represented by *-ove* in *above*) which is also the base of Latin *super* and Greek *huper*.

over- ▶ prefix **1** excessively; to an unwanted degree: *overambitious | overcareful.* ■ completely; utterly: *overawe | overjoyed.* **2** upper; outer; extra: *overcoat | overtime.* ■ overhead; above: *overcast | overhang.*

o·ver·a·bun·dant /ˌōvərə'bəndənt/ ▶ adj. excessive in quantity: *overabundant microbial growth.*
– DERIVATIVES **o·ver·a·bun·dance** n., **o·ver·a·bun·dant·ly** adv.

o·ver·a·chieve /ˌōvərə'CHēv/ ▶ v. [no obj.] do better than is expected, esp. in academic work: *David continued to overachieve all through high school.* ■ (often as adj. **overachieving**) be excessively dedicated to achieving success in one's work: *overachieving geeks.*

PRONUNCIATION KEY ə *ago, up*; ər *over, fur*; a *hat*; ā *ate*; ä *car*; e *let*; ē *see*; i *fit*; ī *by*; NG *sing*; ō *go*; ô *law, for*; oi *toy*; o͝o *good*; o͞o *goo*; ou *out*; TH *thin*; T͟H *then*; ZH *vision*

O

– DERIVATIVES **o·ver·a·chieve·ment** n., **o·ver·a·chiev·er** n.

o·ver·act /ˌōvərˈakt/ ▶ v. [no obj.] (of an actor) act a role in an exaggerated manner: *a weepy actress with a strong tendency to overact* | (as noun **overacting**) *there was a certain amount of overacting.*

o·ver·ac·tive /ˌōvərˈaktiv/ ▶ adj. excessively active: *the product of an overactive imagination.*
– DERIVATIVES **o·ver·ac·tiv·i·ty** n.

o·ver·age[1] /ˈōv(ə)rij/ ▶ n. an excess or surplus, esp. the amount by which a sum of money is greater than a previous estimate.

o·ver·age[2] /ˌōvərˈāj/ ▶ adj. over a certain age limit: *a team of overage and underage ball players.*

o·ver·all ▶ adj. /ˈōvəˌrôl/ [attrib.] taking everything into account: *the overall effect is impressive.*
▶ adv. /ˈōvəˈrôl/ [sentence adverb] in all parts; taken as a whole: *overall, 10,000 jobs will go.*
▶ n. /ˈōvəˌrôl/ (**overalls**) a garment consisting of trousers with a front flap over the chest held up by straps over the shoulders, made of sturdy material and worn esp. as casual or working clothes. Also called **BIB OVERALLS**. ■ Brit. a loose-fitting garment such as a smock worn typically over ordinary clothes for protection against dirt or heavy wear.
– DERIVATIVES **o·ver·alled** /ˈōvəˌrôld/ adj.

o·ver·am·bi·tious /ˌōvəramˈbiSHəs/ ▶ adj. excessively ambitious.
– DERIVATIVES **o·ver·am·bi·tion** n., **o·ver·am·bi·tious·ly** adv.

o·ver·an·a·lyze /ˌōvərˈanəlīz/ ▶ v. [with obj.] analyze (something) in too much detail: *his movies have been overanalyzed* | [no obj.] *I do tend to overanalyze.*
– DERIVATIVES **o·ver·a·nal·y·sis** n.

o·ver·anx·ious /ˌōvərˈaNG(k)SHəs/ ▶ adj. excessively anxious.
– DERIVATIVES **o·ver·anx·i·e·ty** n., **o·ver·anx·ious·ly** adv.

o·ver·arch /ˌōvərˈärCH/ ▶ v. [with obj.] form an arch over: *an old dirt road, overarched by forest.*

o·ver·arch·ing /ˌōvərˈärCHiNG/ ▶ adj. [attrib.] forming an arch over something: *the overarching mangroves.* ■ comprehensive; all-embracing: *a single overarching principle.*
– DERIVATIVES **o·ver·arch·ing·ly** adv.

o·ver·arm /ˈōvərˌärm/ ▶ adj. & adv. done with the arm moving above the level of the shoulder.

o·ver·awe /ˌōvərˈô/ ▶ v. [with obj.] (usu. **be overawed**) impress (someone) so much that they become silent or inhibited: *he used firepower to overawe the hostile tribes.*

o·ver·bal·ance /ˌōvərˈbaləns/ ▶ v. [with obj.] outweigh: *I fault the university for many things, but all are overbalanced by its unparalleled resources.* ■ fall or cause to fall over from loss of balance: [no obj.] *the ladder overbalanced on top of her.*
▶ n. archaic excess of weight, value, or amount: *overbalance of propriety.*

o·ver·bear /ˌōvərˈber/ ▶ v. (past **overbore**; past participle **overborne**) [with obj.] overcome by emotional pressure or physical force: *his will had not been overborne by another's influence* | *he overbore the others who still favored a bold policy.*

o·ver·bear·ing /ˌōvərˈbe(ə)riNG/ ▶ adj. unpleasantly or arrogantly domineering: *his overbearing, sometimes ruthless desire to succeed.*
– DERIVATIVES **o·ver·bear·ing·ly** adv., **o·ver·bear·ing·ness** n.

o·ver·bid ▶ v. /ˌōvərˈbid/ (**overbids, overbidding**; past and past participle **overbid**) [no obj.] **1** (in an auction) make a higher bid than a previous bid.
2 (in competitive bidding, the auction in bridge, etc.) bid more than is warranted or manageable.
▶ n. /ˈōvərˌbid/ a bid that is higher than is justified.
– DERIVATIVES **o·ver·bid·der** n.

o·ver·bite /ˈōvərˌbīt/ ▶ n. Dentistry the overlapping of the lower teeth by the upper.

o·ver·blouse /ˈōvərˌblous, -blouz/ ▶ n. a blouse designed to be worn without being tucked in at the waist.

o·ver·blow·ing /ˌōvərˈblōiNG/ ▶ n. a technique for playing a wind instrument so as to produce overtones.

o·ver·blown /ˌōvərˈblōn/ ▶ adj. **1** excessively inflated or pretentious: *overblown dreams of glory and success.*
2 (of a flower) past its prime: *an overblown rose.*

o·ver·board /ˈōvərˌbôrd/ ▶ adv. from a ship into the water: *the severe storm washed a man overboard.*
– PHRASES **go overboard 1** be very enthusiastic: *Gary went overboard for you.* **2** react in an immoderate way: *Chris has a bit of a temper and can sometimes go overboard.* **throw something overboard** abandon or discard something.

o·ver·bold /ˌōvərbōld/ ▶ adj. excessively bold.
– DERIVATIVES **o·ver·bold·ly** adv., **o·ver·bold·ness** n.

o·ver·book /ˌōvərˈbo͝ok/ ▶ v. [with obj.] accept more reservations for (a flight, hotel, etc.) than there is room for: *airlines deliberately overbook some scheduled flights.*

o·ver·boot /ˈōvərˌbo͞ot/ ▶ n. a boot worn over another boot or shoe to protect it or to provide extra warmth.

o·ver·bore /ˌōvərˈbôr/ past of **OVERBEAR**.

o·ver·borne /ˌōvərˈbôrn/ past participle of **OVERBEAR**.

o·ver·bought /ˌōvərˈbôt/ past and past participle of **OVERBUY**.
▶ adj. Stock Market overvalued owing to excessive buying at unjustifiably high prices.

o·ver·breed /ˌōvərˈbrēd/ ▶ v. (past and past participle **overbred**) breed or cause to breed to excess: *the husband and wife were forcing the female dogs to overbreed, and litters grew up with several health problems.*

o·ver·brim·ming /ˌōvərˈbrimiNG/ ▶ adj. abundant, esp. excessively so: *overbrimming confidence.*

o·ver·build /ˌōvərˈbild/ ▶ v. (past and past participle **overbuilt**) [with obj.] **1** put up too many buildings in (an area): *investors overbuilt the Atlantic and Mediterranean coasts.* ■ build (something) elaborately or to a very high standard, esp. unnecessarily: *overbuilding something will always be safer than taking shortcuts.*
2 (often as noun **overbuilding**) build on top of: *the preservation of the medieval field pattern by direct overbuilding.*

o·ver·bur·den ▶ v. /ˌōvərˈbərdn/ [with obj.] load (someone) with too many things to carry: *they were overburdened with luggage.* ■ give (someone) more work or pressure than they can deal with: *the courts became overburdened with large numbers of relatively trivial offenses* | (as adj. **overburdened**) *overburdened teachers.*
▶ n. /ˈōvərˌbərdn/ rock or soil overlying a mineral deposit, archaeological site, or other underground feature. ■ an excessive burden: *an overburden of costs.*
– DERIVATIVES **o·ver·bur·den·some** /-səm/ adj.

o·ver·bus·y /ˌōvərˈbizē/ ▶ adj. excessively busy: *their overbusy lives.*

o·ver·buy /ˌōvərˈbī/ ▶ v. (past and past participle **overbought**) [with obj.] buy more of (something) than one needs: *the tendency to overbuy software.*

o·ver·call Bridge ▶ v. /ˌōvərˈkôl/ [no obj.] make a higher bid than an opponent's bid.
▶ n. /ˈōvərˌkôl/ an act or instance of making such a bid.

o·ver·came /ˌōvərˈkām/ past of **OVERCOME**.

o·ver·ca·pac·i·ty /ˌōvərkəˈpasitē/ ▶ n. the situation in which an industry or factory cannot sell as much as it can produce.

o·ver·cap·i·tal·ize /ˌōvərˈkapitlˌīz/ ▶ v. [with obj.] (usu. as adj. **overcapitalized**) provide (a company) with more capital than is advisable or necessary: *a bleak time for the overcapitalized firm.* ■ estimate or set the capital value of (a company) at too high an amount.
– DERIVATIVES **o·ver·cap·i·tal·i·za·tion** /ˈōvərˌkapitl-iˈzāSHən/ n.

o·ver·care·ful /ˌōvərˈke(ə)rfəl/ ▶ adj. excessively careful.
– DERIVATIVES **o·ver·care·ful·ly** adv.

o·ver·cast ▶ adj. /ˈōvərˌkast, ˌōvərˈkast/ **1** (of the sky or weather) marked by a covering of gray clouds; dull: *a chilly overcast day.*
2 (in sewing) edged with stitching to prevent fraying.
▶ n. /ˈōvərˌkast/ clouds covering a large part of the sky: *the sky was leaden with overcast.*
▶ v. /ˌōvərˈkast/ (past and past participle **overcast**) [with obj.] **1** cover with clouds or shade: *the pebbled beach, overcast with the shadows of the high cliffs.*
2 stitch over (an unfinished edge) to prevent fraying: *finish off the raw edge of the hem by overcasting it.*

o·ver·cau·tious /ˌōvərˈkôSHəs/ ▶ adj. excessively cautious.
– DERIVATIVES **o·ver·cau·tion** n., **o·ver·cau·tious·ly** adv., **o·ver·cau·tious·ness** n.

o·ver·charge ▶ v. /ˌōvərˈCHärj/ [with obj.] **1** charge (someone) too high a price for goods or a service: *that makes it easy for wheeler-dealers to overcharge customers.* ■ charge someone (a sum) beyond the correct amount: [with two objs.] *the company overcharged the government $3 million.*
2 put too much electric charge into (a battery).
■ put exaggerated or excessive detail into (a text or work of art): *the scenes are overcharged.*
▶ n. /ˈōvərˌCHärj/ an excessive charge for goods or a service.

o·ver·check[1] /ˈōvərˌCHek/ ▶ n. a check pattern superimposed on a color or design.

o·ver·check[2] ▶ n. a strap passing over a horse's head between the ears, to pull up on the bit and make breathing easier.

o·ver·class /ˈōvərˌklas/ ▶ n. a privileged, wealthy, or powerful subgroup in society.

o·ver·cloud /ˌōvərˈkloud/ ▶ v. [with obj.] mar, dim, or obscure.

o·ver·coat /ˈōvərˌkōt/ ▶ n. **1** a long warm coat worn over other clothing.
2 a top, final layer of paint or a similar covering.

o·ver·come /ˌōvərˈkəm/ ▶ v. (past **overcame**; past participle **overcome**) [with obj.] succeed in dealing with (a problem or difficulty): *she worked hard to overcome her paralyzing shyness.* ■ defeat (an opponent); prevail: *without firing a shot they overcame the guards* | [no obj.] *we shall overcome.*
■ (usu. **be overcome**) (of an emotion) overpower or overwhelm: *she was obviously overcome with excitement.*
– ORIGIN Old English *ofercuman* (see **OVER-**, **COME**).

o·ver·com·mit /ˌōvərkəˈmit/ ▶ v. (**overcommits, overcommitting, overcommitted**) [with obj.] oblige (oneself or others) to do more than one is capable of, as to repay a loan one cannot afford: *multiple borrowers who may be overcommitting themselves.*
■ allocate more (resources) to a purpose than can be provided: *they could easily overcommit their budgets.*
– DERIVATIVES **o·ver·com·mit·ment** n.

o·ver·com·pen·sate /ˌōvərˈkämpənˌsāt/ ▶ v. [no obj.] take excessive measures in attempting to correct or make amends for an error, weakness, or problem: *he was overcompensating for fears about the future.*
– DERIVATIVES **o·ver·com·pen·sat·ing·ly** /ˈōvərˌkämpənˈsātiNGlē/ adv., **o·ver·com·pen·sa·tion** /ˈōvərˌkämpənˈsāSHən/ n., **o·ver·com·pen·sa·to·ry** /ˈōvərkəmˈpensəˌtôrē/ adj.

o·ver·com·pli·cate /ˌōvərˈkämplikāt/ ▶ v. [with obj.] make (something) more complicated than necessary: *the basic idea is quite simple, but some people tend to overcomplicate it.*

o·ver·con·fi·dent /ˌōvərˈkänfidənt/ ▶ adj. excessively or unreasonably confident: *mistakes made through being overconfident.*
– DERIVATIVES **o·ver·con·fi·dence** n., **o·ver·con·fi·dent·ly** adv.

o·ver·con·sump·tion /ˌōvərkənˈsəmpSHən/ ▶ n. the action or fact of consuming something to excess: *the overconsumption of alcohol* | *the environmental cost of overconsumption.*

o·ver·cook /ˌōvərˈko͝ok/ ▶ v. cook too much or for too long: [with obj.] *don't overcook the vegetables* | [no obj.] *ensure that the food doesn't overcook during reheating.*

o·ver·crit·i·cal /ˌōvərˈkritikəl/ ▶ adj. inclined to find fault too readily.

o·ver·crop /ˌōvərˈkräp/ ▶ v. (**overcrops, overcropping, overcropped**) [with obj.] (usu. as noun **overcropping**) deplete (soil) by growing crops continuously on it.

o·ver·crowd /ˌōvərˈkroud/ ▶ v. [with obj.] fill (accommodations or a space) beyond what is usual or comfortable: (as adj. **overcrowded**) *overcrowded dormitories* | (as noun **overcrowding**) *trying to eliminate overcrowding in the downtown area.*
■ house (people or animals) in accommodations that are too confined.

o·ver·date /ˈōvərˌdāt/ ▶ n. a coin on which one date has been superimposed over another.
– DERIVATIVES **o·ver·dat·ing** n.

o·ver·de·pend·ence /ˌōvərdiˈpendəns/ ▶ n. dependence to an excessive degree: *overdependence on the tourism sector.*
– DERIVATIVES **o·ver·de·pend·ent** adj.

o·ver·de·ter·mine /ˌōvərdiˈtərmən/ ▶ v. [with obj.] technical determine, account for, or cause (something) in more than one way or with more conditions than are necessary: *every gesture is overdetermined by cultural form, personal biography, historical contingency, and so on.*
– DERIVATIVES **o·ver·de·ter·mi·na·tion** /ˈˌōvərdiˌtərməˈnāSHən/ n.

o·ver·de·vel·op /ˌōvərdəˈveləp/ ▶ v. (**overdevelops, overdeveloping, overdeveloped**) [with obj.] develop too much or to excess: *cycling may overdevelop the calf muscles* | (as adj. **overdeveloped**) *Majorca's overdeveloped coastline.* ■ Photography treat with developer for too long: *you can overdevelop the film to make up for underexposure.*
– DERIVATIVES **o·ver·de·vel·op·ment** n.

o·ver·do /ˌōvərˈdo͞o/ ▶ v. (**overdoes, overdoing**; past **overdid**; past participle **overdone**) [with obj.] do, use, or carry to excess; exaggerate: *dramatic yet never overdone* | *I'd overdone the garlic in the curry.*
■ (**overdo it/things**) exhaust oneself by overwork

O

or overexertion: *I'd simply overdone it in the gym.* ■ overcook (food).
– ORIGIN Old English *oferdōn* (see OVER-, DO¹).

o·ver·done /ˌōvərˈdən/ ▶ adj. **1** (of food) overcooked: *he sat there chewing his overdone steak.* **2** carried to excess; exaggerated: *an overdone show of camaraderie.*

o·ver·dose ▶ n. /ˈōvərˌdōs/ an excessive and dangerous dose of a drug: *she took an overdose the day her husband left.*
▶ v. /ˈōvərˌdōs, ˌōvərˈdōs/ [no obj.] take an overdose of a drug: *he was admitted to the hospital after* **overdosing on** *cocaine.* ■ [with obj.] give an overdose to.
– DERIVATIVES **o·ver·dos·age** /-ˈdōsij/ n.

o·ver·draft /ˈōvərˌdraft/ ▶ n. a deficit in a bank account caused by drawing more money than the account holds.

o·ver·dram·a·tize /ˌōvərˈdraməˌtīz, -ˈdrämə-/ ▶ v. [with obj.] react to or portray (something) in an excessively dramatic manner.
– DERIVATIVES **o·ver·dra·mat·ic** /-drəˈmatik/ adj.

o·ver·draw /ˌōvərˈdrô/ ▶ v. (past **overdrew**; past participle **overdrawn**) [with obj.] **1** (usu. **be overdrawn**) draw money from (one's bank account) in excess of what the account holds: *you only pay interest if your account is overdrawn.* ■ (**be overdrawn**) (of a person) have taken money out of an account in excess of what it holds: *I'm already overdrawn this month.*
2 exaggerate in describing or depicting (someone or something): *some of the characters were overdrawn.*
3 draw (a bow) too far.

o·ver·dress ▶ v. /ˌōvərˈdres/ [no obj.] (also **be overdressed**) dress with too much display or formality: *Eugenie did not wish to overdress | she felt wildly overdressed in her velvet suit.*
▶ n. /ˈōvərˌdres/ chiefly Brit. a dress worn over another dress or other clothing.

o·ver·drink /ˌōvərˈdriNGk/ ▶ v. (past **overdrank**; past participle **overdrunk**) [no obj.] (usu. as noun **overdrinking**) drink too much alcohol.

o·ver·drive /ˈōvərˌdrīv/ ▶ n. a gear in a motor vehicle providing a gear ratio higher than that of the drive gear or top gear, so that engine speed and fuel consumption are reduced in highway travel. ■ a state of high or excessive activity: *the city's worried public relations arm* **went into overdrive**. ■ a mechanism that permits a higher than normal operating level in a piece of equipment, such as the amplifier of an electric guitar.
▶ v. [with obj.] (usu. as adj. **overdriven**) drive or work to exhaustion: *the overdriven mothers of ten or eleven hungry children.*

o·ver·dub ▶ v. /ˌōvərˈdəb/ (**overdubs, overdubbing, overdubbed**) record (additional sounds) on an existing recording: [with obj.] *she'd overdub her parts for a whole album in a single session* | [no obj.] *a live tape that I overdubbed on.*
▶ n. /ˈōvərdəb/ an instance of overdubbing: *a guitar overdub.*

o·ver·due /ˌōvərˈd(y)o͞o/ ▶ adj. **1** not having arrived, happened, or been done by the expected time: *the rent was nearly three months overdue.* ■ (of a woman) having gone beyond the expected time for a menstrual period. ■ (of a baby) not having been born by the expected time: *our daughter was six days overdue.* ■ (of a library book) retained longer than the period allowed.
2 having been needed for some time: *reform is now overdue | critics say action is* **long overdue**. ■ having deserved or needed something for some time: *she was* **overdue for** *some leave.*

o·ver·ea·ger /ˌōvərˈēgər/ ▶ adj. excessively eager.
– DERIVATIVES **o·ver·ea·ger·ly** adv., **o·ver·ea·ger·ness** n.

o·ver eas·y ▶ adj. (of a fried egg) turned over when the white is nearly done and fried lightly on the other side, so that the yolk remains slightly liquid.

o·ver·eat /ˌōvərˈēt/ ▶ v. (past **overate**; past participle **overeaten**) [no obj.] (usu. as noun **overeating**) eat too much: *the effect of overeating is weight gain.*
– DERIVATIVES **o·ver·eat·er** n.

o·ver·ed·u·cat·ed /ˌōvərˈedyəkātəd/ ▶ adj. having been educated to a higher academic level than is necessary: *an overeducated music snob.*

o·ver·e·lab·o·rate /ˌōvəriˈlab(ə)rit/ ▶ adj. excessively elaborate.
▶ v. [with obj.] explain or treat in excessive detail: *if they don't overelaborate the story I don't question it.*
– DERIVATIVES **o·ver·e·lab·o·rate·ly** adv., **o·ver·e·lab·o·ra·tion** n.

o·ver·e·mo·tion·al /ˌōvəriˈmōSHənl/ ▶ adj. (of a person) having feelings that are too easily excited and displayed: *we're not an overemotional family.*
– DERIVATIVES **o·ver·e·mo·tion·al·ly** adv.

o·ver·em·pha·sis /ˌōvərˈemfəsis/ ▶ n. excessive emphasis.

o·ver·em·pha·size /ˌōvərˈemfəˌsīz/ ▶ v. [with obj.] (usu. **be overemphasized**) place excessive emphasis on: *the importance of adequate preparation cannot be overemphasized.*

o·ver·en·thu·si·asm ▶ n. excessive enthusiasm.
– DERIVATIVES **o·ver·en·thu·si·as·tic** adj., **o·ver·en·thu·si·as·ti·cal·ly** adv.

o·ver·es·ti·mate ▶ v. /ˌōvərˈestəˌmāt/ [with obj.] estimate (something) to be better, larger, or more important than it really is: *his influence cannot be overestimated.*
▶ n. /-mit/ an excessively high estimate.
– DERIVATIVES **o·ver·es·ti·ma·tion** /ˈōvərˌestəˈmāSHən/ n.

o·ver·ex·cite /ˌōvərikˈsīt/ ▶ v. [with obj.] (often as adj. **overexcited**) excite excessively: *playing an active game can overexcite children.*
– DERIVATIVES **o·ver·ex·cit·a·ble** adj., **o·ver·ex·cite·ment** n.

o·ver·ex·ert /ˌōvərigˈzərt/ ▶ v. (**overexert oneself**) engage in too much or too strenuous exertion.
– DERIVATIVES **o·ver·ex·er·tion** n.

o·ver·ex·pan·sion /ˌōvərikˈspanSHən/ ▶ n. rapid or uncontrolled expansion that produces undesirable effects: *the explosive overexpansion of the telecommunications industry.*

o·ver·ex·pose /ˌōvərikˈspōz/ ▶ v. [with obj.] expose too much, esp. to the public eye or to risk: *anybody in the public eye has situations that make them feel overexposed.* ■ Photography expose (film or a part of an image) for too long a time or for extra time: *the sunlit background is overexposed.*
– DERIVATIVES **o·ver·ex·po·sure** /-ikˈspōZHər/ n.

o·ver·ex·tend /ˌōvərikˈstend/ ▶ v. [with obj.] (usu. **be overextended**) **1** make too long: *at nine minutes plus the song is somewhat overextended.*
2 impose on (someone) an excessive burden of work or commitments: *he should not overextend himself on the mortgage.*
– DERIVATIVES **o·ver·ex·ten·sion** /-ˈstenSHən/ n.

o·ver·fall /ˈōvərˌfôl/ ▶ n. a turbulent stretch of open water caused by the wind blowing against a current, by a strong current or tide over an underwater ridge, or by a meeting of currents. ■ a place where surplus water overflows from a dam, pond, etc.

o·ver·fa·mil·iar /ˌōvərfəˈmilyər/ ▶ adj. too well known: *the overfamiliar teacher's voice.* ■ [predic.] (**overfamiliar with**) too well acquainted with: *the researcher is overfamiliar with the community.* ■ behaving or speaking in an inappropriately informal way: *her private detective was dismissed for being* **overfamiliar with** *her.*
– DERIVATIVES **o·ver·fa·mil·i·ar·i·ty** /-fəˌmilēˈaritē/ n.

o·ver·feed /ˌōvərˈfēd/ ▶ v. (past and past participle **overfed**) [with obj.] give too much food to: *the general view was that you cannot overfeed a baby.*

o·ver·fill /ˌōvərˈfil/ ▶ v. [with obj.] put more into (a container) than it either should or can contain.

o·ver·fine /ˌōvərˈfīn/ ▶ adj. excessively or extremely fine or particular: *the distinction may seem overfine to Westerners.*

o·ver·fish /ˌōvərˈfiSH/ ▶ v. [with obj.] deplete the stock of fish in (a body of water) by too much fishing: *this part of the Mediterranean is terribly overfished.* ■ deplete the stock of (a fish): *yellowfin tuna has been overfished.*

o·ver·flow ▶ v. /ˌōvərˈflō/ [no obj.] (esp. of a liquid) flow over the brim of a receptacle: *chemicals overflowed from a storage tank* | [with obj.] *the river overflowed its banks.* ■ (of a container) be so full that the contents go over or extend above the sides: *a bath had overflowed upstairs | boxes* **overflowing with** *bright flowers* | (as adj. **overflowing**) *an overflowing ashtray.* ■ (of a space) be so crowded that people cannot fit inside: *the waiting area was overflowing.* ■ [with obj.] flood or flow over (a surface or area): *her hair overflowed her shoulders.* ■ (**overflow with**) be very full of (an emotion or quality): *her heart overflowed with joy.*
▶ n. /ˈōvərˌflō/ **1** [in sing.] the excess or surplus not able to be accommodated by an available space: *to accommodate the overflow, five more offices have been built.* ■ the flowing over of a liquid: *there was some overflow after heavy rainfall | an overflow of sewage.*
2 (also **overflow pipe**) (in a bathtub or sink) an outlet for excess water.
3 Computing the generation of a number or some other data item that is too large for an assigned location or memory space.
– PHRASES **full to overflowing** completely full.
– ORIGIN Old English *oferflōwan* (see OVER-, FLOW).

o·ver·fly /ˌōvərˈflī/ ▶ v. (**overflies, overflying**; past **overflew**; past participle **overflown**) [with obj.] fly over (a place or territory): *the first airship to overfly the North Pole.* ■ fly beyond (a place or thing): *overfly the radio beacon by approximately fifteen seconds.*
– DERIVATIVES **o·ver·flight** /ˈōvərˌflīt/ n.

o·ver·fold /ˈōvərˌfōld/ ▶ n. a part of something that is folded over another part: *the tunic is belted over a long overfold.*

o·ver·fond /ˌōvərˈfänd/ ▶ adj. having too great an affection or liking for someone or something: *he's been getting overfond of this Pinot Grigio.*
– DERIVATIVES **o·ver·fond·ness** n.

o·ver·ful·fill /ˌōvərˌfo͝olˈfil/ (Brit. **overfulfil**) ▶ v. (**overfulfills, overfulfilling, overfulfilled**) [with obj.] fulfill (a contract or quota) earlier or in greater quantity than required: *he overfulfilled the quota by forty percent.*
– DERIVATIVES **o·ver·ful·fill·ment** n.

o·ver·full /ˌōvərˈfo͝ol/ ▶ adj. containing an excessive amount of something: *an overfull cup of tea | overfull employment that leads to inflation.*

o·ver·fund /ˌōvərˈfənd/ ▶ v. [with obj.] provide more funding for (something) than is necessary or permitted.

o·ver·gar·ment /ˈōvərˌgärmənt/ ▶ n. a garment that is worn over others.

o·ver·gen·er·al·ize /ˌōvərˈjen(ə)rəˌlīz/ ▶ v. [with obj.] draw a conclusion or make a statement about (something) that is more general than is justified by the available evidence.
– DERIVATIVES **o·ver·gen·er·al·i·za·tion** /-ˌjen(ə)rəliˈzāSHən/ n.

o·ver·gen·er·ous /ˌōvərˈjenərəs/ ▶ adj. excessively generous: *she was not* **overgenerous with** *praise.*
– DERIVATIVES **o·ver·gen·er·os·i·ty** n., **o·ver·gen·er·ous·ly** adv.

o·ver·glaze /ˌōvərˈglāz/ ▶ n. decoration or a second glaze applied to glazed ceramic ware.
▶ adj. (of painting, printing, or other decoration) done on a glazed surface: *overglaze enamel.*

o·ver·graze /ˌōvərˈgrāz/ ▶ v. [with obj.] graze (grassland) so heavily that the vegetation is damaged and the ground becomes liable to erosion: *their own pastures were overgrazed and arid* | (as noun **overgrazing**) *the failure of the rains led to overgrazing and deforestation.*

o·ver·ground /ˈōvərˌground/ ▶ adv. & adj. on or above the ground: [as adv.] *subway lines that go overground* | [as attrib. adj.] *a heating system pipes heat along overground tubes.* ■ [as attrib. adj.] legitimate; not underground: *overground political processes.*

o·ver·grow /ˌōvərˈgrō/ ▶ v. (past **overgrew**; past participle **overgrown**) [with obj.] grow or spread over (something), esp. so as to choke or stifle it: *the mussels overgrow and smother whatever is underneath.*

o·ver·grown /ˌōvərˈgrōn/ ▶ adj. **1** covered with plants that have been allowed to grow wild: *the garden was overgrown and deserted.*
2 grown too large or beyond its normal size: *the town is only an overgrown village.* ■ chiefly derogatory used to describe an adult behaving in a childish manner: *a pair of overgrown schoolboys.*

o·ver·growth /ˈōvərˌgrōTH/ ▶ n. excessive growth: *intestinal bacterial overgrowth.*

o·ver·hand /ˈōvərˌhand/ ▶ adj. & adv. (chiefly of a throw or a stroke with a racket) made with the hand or arm passing above the level of the shoulder: *pitch overhand | sidearm and overhand techniques.* ■ with the palm of the hand over what it grasps: [as adj.] *an overhand grip.* ■ Boxing (of a punch) passing over the other hand: *caught him with an overhand right.*

o·ver·hand knot ▶ n. a simple knot made by forming a loop and passing a free end around the standing part and through the loop.

o·ver·hang ▶ v. /ˌōvərˈhaNG/ (past and past participle **overhung**) [with obj.] hang or extend outward over: *a concrete path overhung by trees* | (as adj. **overhanging**) *overhanging branches.*
▶ n. /ˈōvərˌhaNG/ a part of something that sticks out or hangs over another thing: *he crouched beneath an overhang of bushes.*

o·ver·haul ▶ v. /ˌōvərˈhôl/ [with obj.] **1** take apart (a piece of machinery or equipment) in order to examine it and repair it if necessary: *a company that overhauls and repairs aircraft engines* | figurative *moves to overhaul the income tax system.*
2 Brit. overtake (someone), esp. in a sporting event.
▶ n. /ˈōvərˌhôl/ a thorough examination of machinery or a system, with repairs or changes made if necessary: *a major overhaul of environmental policies.*

–ORIGIN early 17th cent. (originally in nautical use in the sense 'release (rope tackle) by slackening'): from **OVER-** + **HAUL**.

o·ver·head ▶ **adv.** /ˌōvərˈhed/ above the level of the head; in the sky: *a helicopter buzzed overhead.*
▶ **adj.** /ˈōvərˌhed/ **1** situated above the level of the head: *the sun was directly overhead* | *overhead power cables.*
2 (of a driving mechanism) above the object driven: *an overhead cam four-cylinder engine.*
3 [attrib.] (of a cost or expense) incurred in the general upkeep or running of a plant, premises, or business, and not attributable to specific products or items.
▶ **n.** /ˈōvərˌhed/ **1** overhead cost or expense: *research conducted in space requires more overhead.*
2 a transparency designed for use with an overhead projector.
3 short for **OVERHEAD PROJECTOR**.
4 an overhead compartment: *the bag fits in most airline overheads.*

o·ver·head pro·jec·tor ▶ **n.** a device that projects an enlarged image of a transparency placed on it onto a wall or screen by means of an overhead mirror.

o·ver·hear /ˌōvərˈhir/ ▶ **v.** (past and past participle **overheard**) [with obj.] hear (someone or something) without meaning to or without the knowledge of the speaker: *I couldn't help overhearing your conversation.*

o·ver·heat /ˌōvərˈhēt/ ▶ **v. 1** make or become too hot: [no obj.] *her car started to overheat* | [with obj.] *it's vital not to overheat the liquid.* ■ make too excited: (as adj. **overheated**) *his overheated imagination.*
2 [no obj.] (of a country's economy) show marked inflation when increased demand results in rising prices rather than increased output: *lending rates could soar as the economy overheats.*

o·ver·hit /ˌōvərˈhit/ ▶ **v.** (**overhits**, **overhitting**; past and past participle **overhit**) (in tennis and other sports played with a ball) hit the ball too strongly or too far: *Glenders has overhit another ball* | [no obj.] *Marat Safinwas overhitting, mucking up volleys, but he won anyway.*

o·ver·hype ▶ **v.** /ˌōvərˈhīp/ [with obj.] make exaggerated claims about (a product, idea, or event); publicize or promote excessively: *it would appear that the organizers overhyped the crowd size.*
▶ **n.** /ˈōvərˌhīp/ excessive publicity or promotion: *were the media more rational about it, the unmistakable taste of overhype would not be so strong.*

O·ver·ijs·sel /ˌōvərˈīsəl/ a province of the east central Netherlands, north of the IJssel River, on the border with Germany; capital, Zwolle.

O

o·ver·in·dulge /ˌōvərənˈdəlj/ ▶ **v.** [no obj.] have too much of something enjoyable, esp. food or drink: *it is easy to overindulge in these kinds of foods.* ■ [with obj.] gratify the wishes of (someone) to an excessive extent: *his mother had overindulged him.*

o·ver·in·dul·gence /ˌōvərənˈdəljəns/ ▶ **n. 1** the action or fact of having too much of something enjoyable: *her alleged* **overindulgence in** *alcohol.*
2 excessive gratification of a person's wishes: *his overindulgence of her whims.*
–DERIVATIVES **o·ver·in·dul·gent** /-ˈdəljənt/ **adj.**

o·ver·in·flat·ed /ˌōvərinˈflātid/ ▶ **adj. 1** (of a price or value) excessive: *overinflated land values.* ■ exaggerated: *there have been so many overinflated claims and unfulfilled promises.*
2 filled with too much air: *an overinflated balloon.*
–DERIVATIVES **o·ver·in·fla·tion** /-ˈflāSHən/ **n.**

o·ver·in·sured /ˌōvərinˈSHŏŏrd/ ▶ **adj.** having insurance coverage beyond what is necessary.
–DERIVATIVES **o·ver·in·sur·ance** /-ˈSHŏŏrəns/ **n.**

o·ver·is·sue /ˌōvərˈiSHŏŏ/ ▶ **v.** (**overissues**, **overissuing**, **overissued**) [with obj.] issue (bonds, shares of stock, etc.) beyond the authorized amount or the issuer's ability to pay them on demand.
▶ **n.** the action of overissuing bonds, shares of stock, etc.

o·ver·joyed /ˌōvərˈjoid/ ▶ **adj.** extremely happy: *Joanna will be overjoyed to see you.*

o·ver·kill /ˈōvərˌkil/ ▶ **n.** the amount by which destruction or the capacity for destruction exceeds what is necessary: *the existing nuclear overkill.* ■ excessive use, treatment, or action; too much of something: *animators now face a dilemma of technology overkill.*

o·ver·lad·en /ˌōvərˈlādn/ ▶ **adj.** having too large or too heavy a load: *an overladen trolley* | figurative *the film is overladen with tear-jerking moments.*

o·ver·laid /ˌōvərˈlād/ past and past participle of **OVERLAY**[1].

o·ver·lain /ˌōvərˈlān/ past participle of **OVERLIE**.

o·ver·land /ˈōvərˌland/ ▶ **adj. & adv.** by land: [as adj.] *an overland trade route* | [as adv.] *she journeyed overland.*

O·ver·land Park /ˈōvərlənd/ a city in northeastern Kansas, southwest of Kansas City; pop. 171,231 (est. 2008).

o·ver·lap ▶ **v.** /ˌōvərˈlap/ (**overlaps**, **overlapping**, **overlapped**) [with obj.] extend over so as to cover partly: *the canopy overlaps the house roof at one end* | [no obj.] *the curtains overlap at the center when closed.* ■ [no obj.] cover part of the same area of interest, responsibility, etc.: *their duties sometimes overlapped.* ■ [no obj.] partly coincide in time: *two new series overlapped.*
▶ **n.** /ˈōvərˌlap/ a part or amount that overlaps: *an overlap of about half an inch.* ■ a common area of interest, responsibility, etc.: *there are many overlaps between the approaches* | *there is some overlap in requirements.* ■ a period of time in which two events or activities happen together.

o·ver·large /ˌōvərˈlärj/ ▶ **adj.** too large: *an overlarge meal.*

o·ver·lay[1] ▶ **v.** /ˌōvərˈlā/ (past and past participle **overlaid**) [with obj.] (often **be overlaid with**)
1 cover the surface of (a thing) with a coating: *their fingernails were overlaid with silver or gold.* ■ lie on top of: *a third screen which will overlay the others.*
2 (of a quality or feeling) become more prominent than (a previous quality or feeling): *his openness had been overlaid by his new self-confidence.*
▶ **n.** /ˈōvərˌlā/ **1** something laid as a covering over something else: *a durable, cost-effective floor overlay.* ■ a transparency placed over artwork or something such as a map, marked with additional information or detail. ■ a graphical computer display that can be superimposed on another.
2 Computing the process of transferring a block of program code or other data into internal memory, replacing what is already stored. ■ a block of code or other data transferred in such a way.

o·ver·lay[2] /ˌōvərˈlā/ past of **OVERLIE**.

o·ver·leaf /ˈōvərˌlēf/ ▶ **adv.** on the other side of the page: *an information sheet is printed overleaf.*

o·ver·leap /ˌōvərˈlēp/ ▶ **v.** (past and past participle **overleaped** or **overleapt**) [with obj.] archaic jump over or across: *a stream that any five-year-old child might overleap.* ■ omit; ignore: *whatever objection made by us, he finds too heavy to remove, he overleaps it.*
–ORIGIN Old English *oferhlēapan* (see **OVER**, **LEAP**).

o·ver·lev·er·aged /ˌōvərˈlevərəjd/ ▶ **adj.** Finance (of a company) having taken on too much debt.

o·ver·lie /ˌōvərˈlī/ ▶ **v.** (**overlies**, **overlying**; past **overlay**; past participle **overlain**) [with obj.] lie on top of: *soft clays overlie the basalt* | figurative *the national situation was overlain by sharp regional differences.*

o·ver·load ▶ **v.** /ˌōvərˈlōd/ [with obj.] load with too great a burden or cargo: (as adj. **overloaded**) *overloaded vehicles are dangerous.* ■ give too much of something, typically something undesirable, to (someone): *the staff is heavily overloaded with casework.* ■ put too great a demand on (an electrical system): *the wiring had been overloaded.*
▶ **n.** /ˈōvərˌlōd/ [in sing.] an excessive load or amount: *an overload of stress* | *momentary surges and overloads in the circuit.*

o·ver·lock /ˌōvərˈläk/ ▶ **v.** [with obj.] strengthen and prevent fraying of (an edge of cloth) by oversewing it.
–DERIVATIVES **o·ver·lock·er** /ˈōvərˌläkər/ **n.**

o·ver·long /ˈōvərˈlôNG, -ˈläNG/ ▶ **adj. & adv.** too long: [as adj.] *an overlong sermon* | [as adv.] *the pass was delayed overlong.*

o·ver·look ▶ **v.** /ˌōvərˈlŏŏk/ [with obj.] **1** fail to notice (something): *he seems to have overlooked one important fact.* ■ ignore or disregard (something, esp. a fault or offense): *she was more than ready to overlook his faults.* ■ pass over (someone) in favor of another: *he was overlooked by the Nobel committee.*
2 have a view of from above: *the chateau overlooks fields of corn and olive trees.*
3 archaic supervise; oversee.
4 archaic bewitch with the evil eye: *they told them they were overlooked by some unlucky Person.*
▶ **n.** /ˈōvərlŏŏk/ a commanding position or view: *he veered off the highway onto an overlook.*

o·ver·lord /ˈōvərˌlôrd/ ▶ **n.** a ruler, esp. a feudal lord. ■ a person of great power or authority: *the undisputed overlord of the crime family.*
–DERIVATIVES **o·ver·lord·ship** /-ˌSHip/ **n.**

o·ver·ly /ˈōvərlē/ ▶ **adv.** [as submodifier] excessively: *she was a jealous and overly possessive woman.*

o·ver·ly·ing /ˈōvərˈlī-iNG/ present participle of **OVERLIE**.

o·ver·man ▶ **v.** /ˌōvərˈman/ (**overmans**, **overmanning**, **overmanned**) [with obj.] provide with more people than necessary: *the company was vastly overmanned.*
▶ **n.** /ˈōvərmən, -ˌman/ (pl. **overmen**) **1** an overseer.
2 Philosophy another term for **SUPERMAN**. [translation of Nietzsche's *Übermensch*.]

o·ver·man·tel /ˈōvərˌmantl/ ▶ **n.** an ornamental structure over a mantelpiece, typically of plaster or carved wood and sometimes including a mirror.

o·ver·mas·ter /ˌōvərˈmastər/ ▶ **v.** [with obj.] literary overcome; conquer: *he was overmastered by events* | (as adj. **overmastering**) *his first grand and overmastering love.*

o·ver·match /ˌōvərˈmaCH/ ▶ **v.** [with obj.] (usu. as adj. **overmatched**) be stronger, better armed, or more skillful than: *the city's overmatched police.*

o·ver·meas·ure /ˌōvərˈmeZHər/ ▶ **n.** an amount beyond what is proper or sufficient.

o·ver·much /ˈōvərˈməCH/ ▶ **adv., determiner, & pron.** too much: [as adv.] *I would not worry myself overmuch* | [as determiner] *the police may have overmuch regard for public order considerations* | [as pronoun] *she was requiring overmuch from him.*

o·ver·nice /ˌōvərˈnīs/ ▶ **adj.** dated excessively fussy or fastidious: *Mildred was overnice in regard to their father.*

o·ver·night /ˈōvərˈnīt/ ▶ **adv.** for the duration of a night: *they refused to stay overnight.* ■ during the course of a night: *you can recharge the battery overnight.* ■ very quickly; suddenly: *attitudes will not change overnight.*
▶ **adj.** /ˈōvərˌnīt/ [attrib.] for use overnight: *an overnight bag.* ■ done or happening overnight: *an overnight stay.* ■ sudden, rapid, or instant: *Tom became an overnight celebrity.*
▶ **v.** /ˌōvərˈnīt/ [no obj.] stay for the night in a particular place: *I overnighted at the Beverly Wilshire.* ■ [with obj.] ship for delivery the next day: *Forster overnighted the sample to headquarters by courier.*
▶ **n.** /ˈōvərˌnīt/ a stop or stay lasting one night: *overnights can be arranged in Kathmandu.*

o·ver·night·er /ˌōvərˈnītər/ ▶ **n.** a person who stops at a place overnight. ■ an overnight bag. ■ an overnight trip or stay.

o·ver·op·ti·mis·tic /ˌōvərˌäptəˈmistik/ ▶ **adj.** unjustifiably optimistic.
–DERIVATIVES **o·ver·op·ti·mism n.**, **o·ver·op·ti·mis·ti·cal·ly adv.**

o·ver·pack /ˌōvərˈpak/ ▶ **v.** [with obj.] pack too many items into (a container).

o·ver·paint /ˌōvərˈpānt/ ▶ **v.** [with obj.] cover with a layer of paint.
▶ **n.** paint added as a covering layer.

o·ver·pass ▶ **n.** /ˈōvərˌpas/ a bridge by which a road or railroad passes over another.
▶ **v.** /ˌōvərˈpas/ [with obj.] pass over; traverse. ■ surpass: *a capacity to overpass old limits.*

o·ver·pay /ˌōvərˈpā/ ▶ **v.** (past and past participle **overpaid**) [with obj.] pay (someone) too highly: *many fans think our top players are overpaid.* ■ pay (money) in excess of what is due: *to overpay taxes.*
–DERIVATIVES **o·ver·pay·ment n.**

o·ver·play /ˌōvərˈplā/ ▶ **v.** [with obj.] give undue importance to; overemphasize: *he thinks the idea of a special relationship between sitter and artist is much overplayed.* ■ exaggerate the performance of (a dramatic role): *the uncontrollable urge of ham actors to overplay their parts.*
–PHRASES **overplay one's hand 1** (in a card game) play or bet on one's hand with a mistaken optimism. **2** spoil one's chance of success through excessive confidence in one's position.

o·ver·plus /ˈōvərˌpləs/ ▶ **n.** dated a surplus or excess: *an overplus of one ingredient.*
–ORIGIN late Middle English: partial translation of French *surplus* or medieval Latin *superplus*.

o·ver·pop·u·late /ˌōvərˈpäpyəˌlāt/ ▶ **v.** [with obj.] populate (an area) in too large numbers: *the country was overpopulated.* ■ [no obj.] (of an animal) breed too rapidly: *without natural predators, deer would overpopulate.*
–DERIVATIVES **o·ver·pop·u·la·tion** /ˈōvərˌpäpyəˈlāSHən/ **n.**

o·ver·pow·er /ˌōvərˈpou(-ə)r/ ▶ **v.** [with obj.] defeat or overcome with superior strength. ■ be too intense for; overwhelm: *they were overpowered by the fumes.*

o·ver·pow·er·ing /ˌōvərˈpou(-ə)riNG/ ▶ **adj.** extremely strong or intense; overwhelming: *a feeling of overpowering sadness.*
–DERIVATIVES **o·ver·pow·er·ing·ly adv.**

o·ver·praise /ˌōvərˈprāz/ ▶ **v.** [with obj.] praise more highly than is warranted: *the island's tourist publications tend to overpraise their restaurants.*

o·ver·pre·scribe /ˌōvərpriˈskrīb/ ▶ **v.** [with obj.] prescribe (a drug or treatment) in greater amounts or on more occasions than necessary: *doctors have been overprescribing antibiotics for decades.*
–DERIVATIVES **o·ver·pre·scrip·tion** /-ˈskripSHən/ **n.**

o·ver·price /ˌōvərˈprīs/ ▶ **v.** [with obj.] (often as adj. **overpriced**) charge too high a price for: *overpriced hotels.*

o·ver·print ▶ **v.** /ˌōvərˈprint/ [with obj.] **1** print additional matter on (a stamp or other surface already bearing print): *menus will be overprinted with company logos.*
2 print too many copies of.
3 Photography make (a print or other positive) darker than intended.
▶ **n.** /ˈōvərˌprint/ words or other matter printed onto something already bearing print. ■ an overprinted postage stamp.

o·ver·pro·duce /ˌōvərprəˈd(y)o͞os/ ▶ **v.** [with obj.] **1** produce more of (a product or commodity) than is wanted or needed: *our unplanned manufacturing system continually overproduces consumer products.*
2 (often as adj. **overproduced**) record or produce (a song or film) in an elaborate or overdone way: *a series of overproduced albums.*
– DERIVATIVES **o·ver·pro·duc·tion** /-ˈdəksHən/ **n.**

o·ver·proof /ˈōvərˈpro͞of/ ▶ **adj.** containing more alcohol than proof spirit does: *overproof rum.*

o·ver·pro·tec·tive /ˌōvərprəˈtektiv/ ▶ **adj.** having a tendency to protect someone, esp. a child, excessively.
– DERIVATIVES **o·ver·pro·tect v.**, **o·ver·pro·tec·tion** /-ˈteksHən/ **n.**, **o·ver·pro·tec·tive·ness n.**

o·ver·qual·i·fied /ˌōvərˈkwäləˌfīd/ ▶ **adj.** having qualifications that exceed the requirements of a particular job.

o·ver·ran /ˌōvərˈran/ past of **OVERRUN**.

o·ver·rate /ˌōvərˈrāt/ ▶ **v.** [with obj.] (often as adj. **overrated**) have a higher opinion of (someone or something) than is deserved: *dismissing the work as pompous and overrated.*

o·ver·reach /ˌōvərˈrēCH/ ▶ **v. 1** [no obj.] reach too far: *never lean sideways from a ladder or overreach.* ■ (**overreach oneself**) defeat one's own purpose by trying to do more than is possible: *he was an arrogant egotist who overreached himself.* ■ (of a horse, dog, or other quadruped) bring the hind feet so far forward that they fall alongside or strike the forefeet: *the horse overreached jumping the first hurdle.*
2 [with obj.] get the better of (someone) by cunning: *Faustus's lunacy in thinking he can overreach the devil.*
▶ **n.** an injury to a forefoot of a horse resulting from its having overreached.
– DERIVATIVES **o·ver·reach·er n.**

o·ver·re·act /ˌōvər-rēˈakt/ ▶ **v.** [no obj.] respond more emotionally or forcibly than is justified: *they are urging people not to overreact to the problem.*
– DERIVATIVES **o·ver·re·ac·tion** /-rēˈaksHən/ **n.**

o·ver·re·fine /ˌōvər-riˈfīn/ ▶ **v.** [with obj.] refine excessively, as with subtle distinctions or needless delicacy: *the sole French character is frivolous and overrefined.*
– DERIVATIVES **o·ver·re·fine·ment n.**

o·ver·re·port /ˌōvər-riˈpôrt/ ▶ **v.** [with obj.] report (an event or instance of something) with disproportionately great frequency or emphasis: *newspapers overreported sexual offenses.*

o·ver·rep·re·sent ▶ **v.** [with obj.] include a disproportionately large number of (a particular category or type of person), as in a statistical study. ■ (**be overrepresented**) form a disproportionately large percentage: *they are relatively overrepresented in semiskilled occupations.*
– DERIVATIVES **o·ver·rep·re·sen·ta·tion n.**

o·ver·ride ▶ **v.** /ˌōvərˈrīd/ (past **overrode**; past participle **overridden**) [with obj.] **1** use one's authority to reject or cancel (a decision, view, etc.): *the legislature's insistence on overriding his budget vetoes.* ■ interrupt the action of (an automatic device), typically in order to take manual control: *you can override the cutout by releasing the switch.* ■ be more important than: *this commitment should override all other considerations.*
2 technical extend over; overlap: *the external rendering should not override the vapor barrier.*
3 travel or move over (a place or thing): *part of the deposit was overridden and covered by the advancing ice.*
▶ **n.** /ˈōvərˌrīd/ **1** a device for suspending an automatic function on a machine.
2 an excess or increase on a budget, salary, or cost.
3 a cancellation of a decision by exertion of authority or winning of votes: *the House vote in favor of the bill was ten votes short of the requisite majority for an override.*

o·ver·rid·ing /ˌōvərˈrīdiNG/ ▶ **adj. 1** more important than any other considerations: *their overriding need will be for advice.*
2 technical extending or moving over something, esp. while remaining in close contact: *oceanic lithosphere beneath an overriding continental plate.*

o·ver·ripe /ˌōvərˈrīp/ ▶ **adj.** too ripe; past its best: *overripe tomatoes.* ■ (esp. of an artistic work) exaggerated or overblown: *an overripe melodrama.*

o·ver·ruff /ˌōvərˈrəf/ ▶ **v.** another term for **OVERTRUMP**.

o·ver·rule /ˌōvərˈro͞ol/ ▶ **v.** [with obj.] reject or disallow by exercising one's superior authority: *the Supreme Court overruled the lower court.* ■ reject the decision or argument of (someone): *he was overruled by his senior managers.*

o·ver·run ▶ **v.** /ˌōvərˈrən/ (**overruns, overrunning**; past **overran**; past participle **overrun**) [with obj.] **1** spread over or occupy (a place) in large numbers: *the Mediterranean has been overrun by tourists | the northern frontier was overrun by invaders.* ■ move or extend over or beyond: *let the text overrun the right-hand margin.* ■ run over or beyond (a thing or place): *she overran third base.* ■ rotate faster than (another part of a machine): (as adj. **overrunning**) *an overrunning clutch.*
2 continue beyond or above (an expected or allowed time or cost): *he mustn't overrun his budget.*
▶ **n.** /ˈōvərˌrən/ **1** an instance of something exceeding an expected or allowed time or cost: *an unexpectedly large cost overrun in the program.*
2 the movement or extension of something beyond an allotted or particular position or space: *the system acts as a brake to prevent cable overrun.* ■ a clear area beyond the end of an airport runway.
3 the movement of a vehicle at a speed greater than is imparted by the engine.
– ORIGIN Old English *oferyrnan* (see **OVER-**, **RUN**).

o·ver·sam·pling /ˈōvərˈsampliNG/ ▶ **n.** Electronics the technique of increasing the apparent sampling frequency of a digital signal by repeating each digit a number of times, in order to facilitate the subsequent filtering of unwanted noise.

o·ver·scan /ˈōvərˌskan/ ▶ **n.** the facility on some computer screens or televisions to adjust the picture size so that objects appear bigger but the edges of the picture are lost.

o·ver·seas /ˈōvərˈsēz/ (Brit. also **oversea**) ▶ **adv.** in or to a foreign country, esp. one across the sea: *he spent quite a lot of time working overseas.*
▶ **adj.** [attrib.] from, to, or relating to a foreign country, esp. one across the sea: *overseas trips.*
– PHRASES **from overseas** from abroad.

o·ver·see /ˌōvərˈsē/ ▶ **v.** (**oversees, overseeing**; past **oversaw**; past participle **overseen**) [with obj.] supervise (a person or work), esp. in an official capacity: *a trustee appointed to oversee Corrie's finances.*
– ORIGIN Old English *oferseōn* 'look at from above' (see **OVER-**, **SEE**[1]).

o·ver·se·er /ˈōvərˌsi(ə)r, -ˌsēər/ ▶ **n.** a person who supervises others, esp. workers.
– ORIGIN late Middle English (also denoting a person appointed by a testator to assist the executor of a will): from **OVERSEE**.

o·ver·sell /ˌōvərˈsel/ ▶ **v.** (past and past participle **oversold** /-ˈsōld/) [with obj.] sell more of (something) than exists or can be delivered: *a surge in airlines overselling flights.* ■ exaggerate the merits of: *computer-aided software engineering has been oversold.*

o·ver·sen·si·tive /ˌōvərˈsensitiv/ ▶ **adj.** (esp. of a person or an instrument) excessively sensitive: *Bentley was oversensitive to criticism.*
– DERIVATIVES **o·ver·sen·si·tive·ness n.**, **o·ver·sen·si·tiv·i·ty n.**

o·ver·set /ˌōvərˈset/ ▶ **v.** (**oversets, oversetting**; past and past participle **overset**) [with obj.] **1** upset emotionally: *the small kindness nearly overset her again.*
2 chiefly Brit. overturn: *he jumped up and overset the canoe.*

o·ver·sew /ˌōvərˈsō/ ▶ **v.** (past participle **oversewn** or **oversewed**) [with obj.] sew (the edges of something) with every stitch passing over the join: *oversew the two long edges together.* ■ join the sections of (a book) in such a way.

o·ver·sexed /ˌōvərˈsekst/ ▶ **adj.** having unusually strong sexual desires.

o·ver·shad·ow /ˌōvərˈSHadō/ ▶ **v.** [with obj.] **1** tower above and cast a shadow over: *an enormous oak tree stood overshadowing the cottage.* ■ cast a gloom over: *it is easy to let this feeling of tragedy overshadow his story.*
2 appear much more prominent or important than: *his competitive nature often overshadows the other qualities.* ■ be more impressive or successful than (another person): *he was always overshadowed by his brilliant elder brother.*
– ORIGIN Old English *ofersceadwian* (see **OVER-**, **SHADOW**).

o·ver·shoe /ˈōvərˌSHo͞o/ ▶ **n.** a shoe worn over a normal shoe, typically either of waterproof material to protect the normal shoe in wet weather or of fabric to protect a floor surface.

o·ver·shoot ▶ **v.** /ˌōvərˈSHo͞ot/ (past and past participle **overshot**) [with obj.] go past (a point) unintentionally, esp. through traveling too fast or being unable to stop: *they overshot their intended destination* | [no obj.] *he had overshot by fifty yards but backed up to the junction.* ■ (of an aircraft) fly beyond or taxi too far along (the runway) when landing or taking off: *he has overshot the landing strip again.* ■ exceed (a target or limit): *the department may overshoot its cash limit.*
▶ **n.** /ˈōvərSHo͞ot/ an act of going past or beyond a point, target, or limit.

o·ver·shot /ˈōvərˌSHät/ past and past participle of **OVERSHOOT**.
▶ **adj. 1** (of a waterwheel) turned by water falling onto it from an overhead channel.
2 denoting an upper jaw that projects beyond the lower jaw.

o·ver·sight /ˈōvərˌsīt/ ▶ **n. 1** an unintentional failure to notice or do something: *he said his failure to pay for the tickets was an oversight | was the mistake due to oversight?*
2 the action of overseeing something: *effective oversight of the financial reporting process.*

o·ver·sim·pli·fy /ˌōvərˈsimpləˌfī/ ▶ **v.** (**oversimplifies, oversimplifying, oversimplified**) [with obj.] (often as adj. **oversimplified**) simplify (something) so much that a distorted impression of it is given: *a false and oversimplified view of human personality.*
– DERIVATIVES **o·ver·sim·pli·fi·ca·tion** /ˈōvərˌsimpləfiˈkāsHən/ **n.**

o·ver·sized /ˈōvərˈsīzd/ (also **oversize** /-ˈsīz/) ▶ **adj.** bigger than the usual size: *an oversized T-shirt.*

o·ver·skirt /ˈōvərˌskərt/ ▶ **n.** an outer skirt worn over the skirt of a dress.

o·ver·slaugh /ˌōvərˈslô/ ▶ **v.** [with obj.] dated pass over (someone) in favor of another.
– ORIGIN mid 18th cent.: from Dutch *overslag* (noun), from *overslaan* 'pass over.'

o·ver·sleep /ˌōvərˈslēp/ ▶ **v.** (past and past participle **overslept**) [no obj.] sleep longer or later than one intended: *we talked until the early hours and consequently I overslept.*

o·ver·sold /ˌōvərˈsōld/ past and past participle of **OVERSELL**.
▶ **adj.** Stock Market sold to a price below its true value: *technology stocks remain oversold and are considered ripe for buying.*

o·ver·so·lic·i·tous /ˌōvərsəˈlisitəs/ ▶ **adj.** showing excessive concern for another person's welfare or interests.
– DERIVATIVES **o·ver·so·lic·i·tude** /-ˌt(y)o͞od/ **n.**

o·ver·soul /ˈōvərˌsōl/ ▶ **n.** [in sing.] a divine spirit supposed to pervade the universe and to encompass all human souls. The term is associated particularly with Transcendentalism.

o·ver·spe·cial·ize /ˌōvərˈspesHəˌlīz/ ▶ **v.** [no obj.] concentrate too much on one aspect or area of something: (as adj. **overspecialized**) *overspecialized sub-disciplines of history.*
– DERIVATIVES **o·ver·spe·cial·i·za·tion n.**

o·ver·spend /ˌōvərˈspend/ ▶ **v.** (past and past participle **overspent**) [no obj.] spend more than the expected or allotted amount: *she overspent on her husband's funeral* | [with obj.] *the department can see that it is going to overspend its budget.*

o·ver·spill /ˈōvərˌspil/ ▶ **n.** chiefly Brit. people or things that spill over or are in excess.

o·ver·spin /ˈōvərˌspin/ ▶ **n.** a rotating motion given to a ball when throwing or hitting it, used to give it extra speed or distance or to make it bounce awkwardly.

o·ver·spray /ˈōvərˌsprā/ ▶ **n.** excess paint or other liquid that spreads or blows beyond an area being sprayed.

o·ver·spread /ˌōvərˈspred/ ▶ **v.** (past and past participle **overspread**) [with obj.] cover the surface of; spread over: *a broad smile overspread his face.*
– ORIGIN Old English *oferspr̄ǣdan* (see **OVER-**, **SPREAD**).

o·ver·staff /ˌōvərˈstaf/ ▶ **v.** [with obj.] supply (an organization) with surplus staff: *government departments are always overstaffed.*
– DERIVATIVES **o·ver·staff·ing n.**

o·ver·state /ˌōvərˈstāt/ ▶ **v.** [with obj.] express or state too strongly; exaggerate: *I may have overstated my case to make my point.*

o·ver·state·ment /ˌōvərˈstātmənt/ ▶ **n.** the action of expressing or stating something too strongly; exaggeration: *a classic piece of overstatement* | *to describe the show as a success would be an overstatement.*

o·ver·stay /ˌōvərˈstā/ ▶ **v.** [with obj.] stay longer than the time, limits, or duration of: *he was arrested for overstaying his visa.*
– PHRASES **overstay one's welcome** see WELCOME.
– DERIVATIVES **o·ver·stay·er** /ˈōvərˌstāər/ **n.**

o·ver·steer ▶ **v.** /ˌōvərˈstir/ [no obj.] (of a motor vehicle) have a tendency to turn more sharply than was intended.
▶ **n.** /ˈōvərˌstir/ the tendency of a vehicle to turn in such a way.

o·ver·step /ˌōvərˈstep/ ▶ **v.** (**oversteps, overstepping, overstepped**) pass beyond or exceed (a limit or standard): *you must not overstep your borrowing limit* | *he has overstepped the bounds of acceptable discipline.*
– PHRASES **overstep the mark** behave in an unacceptable way.

o·ver·stim·u·late /ˌōvərˈstimyəˌlāt/ ▶ **v.** [with obj.] stimulate physiologically or mentally to an excessive degree: *caffeine produced by coffee trees overstimulates insects that munch their leaves.*
– DERIVATIVES **overstimulation** /ˈōvərˌstimyəˈlāsнən/ **n.**

o·ver·stitch /ˈōvərˌsticн/ ▶ **n.** a stitch made over an edge or over another stitch.
▶ **v.** /ˌōvərˈsticн/ [with obj.] sew with such a stitch.

o·ver·stock ▶ **v.** /ˌōvərˈstäk/ [with obj.] supply with more of something than is necessary or required: *do not overstock the kitchen with food.*
▶ **n.** /ˈōvərˌstäk/ (esp. in a manufacturing or retailing context) a supply or quantity in excess of demand or requirements: *factory overstock* | *publishers' overstocks and remainders.*

o·ver·stored /ˌōvərˈstôrd/ ▶ **adj. 1** stored for too long a period: *an overstored apple.*
2 supplied with more retail stores than the market demands: *just at a time when this area is already overstored.*

o·ver·strain /ˌōvərˈstrān/ ▶ **v.** [with obj.] subject to an excessive demand on strength, resources, or abilities: *there was a risk he might overstrain his heart.*
▶ **n.** the action or result of subjecting someone or something to such a demand.

o·ver·stress /ˌōvərˈstres/ ▶ **v.** [with obj.] subject to too much physical or mental stress: *they are prone to nervous breakdowns if overstressed.* ■ lay too much emphasis on: *the value of good legal assistance cannot be overstressed.*
▶ **n.** excessive stress.

o·ver·stretch /ˌōvərˈstrecн/ ▶ **v.** [with obj.] (often as adj. **overstretched**) **1** stretch too much: *the aches and pains of overstretched muscles.*
2 make excessive demands on: *classes are very large and facilities are overstretched.*

o·ver·strike /ˈōvərˌstrīk/ ▶ **n.** the superimposing of one printed character or one coin design on another. ■ a coin showing one design superimposed on another.
– DERIVATIVES **o·ver·strik·ing** /ˌōvərˈstrīkiNG/ **n.**

o·ver·strung /ˈōvərˈstrəNG/ ▶ **adj. 1** (of a piano) with strings in sets crossing each other obliquely.
2 dated (of a person) extremely nervous or tense.

o·ver·stud·y ▶ **n.** /ˈōvərˌstədē/ excessive study.
▶ **v.** /ˌōvərˈstədē/ study too long or too intensely: *if your child is a high achiever, but overstudies for fear of not receiving an A+,help her to gradually study a little less.*

o·ver·stuff /ˌōvərˈstəf/ ▶ **v.** [with obj.] (usu. as adj. **overstuffed**) **1** force too much into (a container): *an overstuffed briefcase.*
2 cover (furniture) completely with padded upholstery: *an overstuffed armchair.*

o·ver·sub·scribed /ˌōvərsəbˈskrībd/ ▶ **adj.** applied for in greater quantities than are available or expected: *those bonds were said to be twelve to fourteen times oversubscribed.* ■ (of a course, etc.) having more applications than available places.

o·ver·sub·tle /ˌōvərˈsətl/ ▶ **adj.** making excessively fine distinctions: *an oversubtle argument.*

o·ver·sup·ply ▶ **n.** (pl. **oversupplies**) /ˈōvərsəˌplī/ an excessive supply: *an oversupply of teachers* | *oversupply causes prices to fall.*
▶ **v.** /ˌōvərsəˈplī/ (**oversupplies, oversupplying, oversupplied**) [with obj.] supply with too much or too many: *the country was oversupplied with lawyers.*

o·vert /ōˈvərt, ˈōvərt/ ▶ **adj.** done or shown openly; plainly or readily apparent, not secret or hidden: *an overt act of aggression* | *in untreated cases, overt psychosis may occur.*
– DERIVATIVES **o·vert·ly adv.**, **o·vert·ness n.**
– ORIGIN Middle English: from Old French, past participle of *ovrir* 'to open,' from Latin *aperire.*

o·ver·take /ˌōvərˈtāk/ ▶ **v.** (past **overtook**; past participle **overtaken**) [with obj.] **1** catch up with and pass while traveling in the same direction: *the driver overtook a line of vehicles.* ■ become greater or more successful than: *Germany rapidly overtook Britain in industrial output.*
2 (esp. of misfortune) come suddenly or unexpectedly upon: *the pattern of economic ruin overtook them.* ■ (of a feeling) affect (someone) suddenly and powerfully: *weariness overtook him and he retired to bed.*

o·ver·task /ˌōvərˈtask/ ▶ **v.** [with obj.] impose too much work on: (as adj. **overtasked**) *an overtasked school system.*

o·ver·tax /ˌōvərˈtaks/ ▶ **v.** [with obj.] **1** require (a person or company) to pay too much tax: *if you're overtaxed, we want you in our party.*
2 make excessive demands on (a person's strength, abilities, etc.): *do athletes overtax their hearts?*
– DERIVATIVES **o·ver·tax·a·tion** /-takˈsāsнən/ **n.** (sense 1).

o·ver·think /ˌōvərˈTHiNGk/ ▶ **v.** [with obj.] think about (something) too much or for too long: *must you overthink every relationship?* | [no obj.] *he doesn't make snap decisions, but he doesn't overthink either.*

o·ver·throw ▶ **v.** /ˌōvərˈTHrō/ (past **overthrew**; past participle **overthrown**) [with obj.] **1** remove forcibly from power: *military coups which had attempted to overthrow the king.* ■ put an end to (something), typically by the use of force or violence: *their subversive activities are calculated to overthrow parliamentary democracy.* ■ archaic knock or throw to the ground: *one who is already prostrate cannot be overthrown.*
2 throw (a ball) further or harder than intended: *he grips the ball too tight and overthrows it.* ■ throw a ball beyond (a receiving player): *he overthrew a receiver in the end zone.*
▶ **n.** /ˈōvərˌTHrō/ **1** [in sing.] a removal from power; a defeat or downfall: *plotting the overthrow of the government.*
2 (in baseball and other games) a throw that sends a ball past its intended recipient or target.
3 a panel of decorated wrought-iron work above an arch or gateway.

o·ver·thrust /ˈōvərˌTHrəst/ Geology ▶ **n.** the thrust of one series of rock strata over another, esp. along a fault line at a shallow angle to the horizontal.
▶ **v.** (past and past participle **overthrust**) [with obj.] force (a body of rock) over another: (as noun **overthrusting**) *the increased overburden resulting from overthrusting.* ■ (of a body of rock) be forced over (another formation): *the shales are overthrust by Carboniferous rocks.*

o·ver·time /ˈōvərˌtīm/ ▶ **n.** time in addition to what is normal, as time worked beyond one's scheduled working hours: *fewer opportunities for overtime* | [as modifier] *an overtime ban.* ■ payment for such extra work. ■ extra time played at the end of a game that is tied at the end of the regulation time: *they lost in overtime.*
▶ **adv.** in addition to normal working hours: *they were working overtime to fulfill a big order* | figurative *his brain was working overtime.*

o·ver·tip /ˌōvərˈtip/ ▶ **v.** (**overtips, overtipping, overtipped**) [with obj.] give (someone) an excessively generous tip.

o·ver·tire /ˌōvərˈtīr/ ▶ **v.** [with obj.] exhaust (someone): *walk at a pace that does not overtire you.*

o·ver·tone /ˈōvərˌtōn/ ▶ **n. 1** a musical tone that is a part of the harmonic series above a fundamental note and may be heard with it. ■ Physics a component of any oscillation whose frequency is an integral multiple of the fundamental frequency.
2 (often **overtones**) a subtle or subsidiary quality, implication, or connotation: *the decision may have political overtones.*
– ORIGIN mid 19th cent.: from OVER- + TONE, suggested by German *Oberton.*

o·ver·top /ˌōvərˈtäp/ ▶ **v.** (**overtops, overtopping, overtopped**) [with obj.] exceed in height: *no building is allowed to overtop the cathedral.* ■ (esp. of water) rise over the top of (a barrier constructed to hold it back): *the old sea wall is regularly overtopped by high tides.* ■ be superior to: *none can overtop him in goodness.*

o·ver·trade /ˌōvərˈtrād/ ▶ **v.** [no obj.] engage in more business than can be supported by the market or by the funds or resources available.

o·ver·train /ˌōvərˈtrān/ ▶ **v.** (with reference to an athlete) train or cause to train too hard or for too long.

o·ver·trick /ˈōvərˌtrik/ ▶ **n.** Bridge a trick taken by the declarer in excess of the contract.

o·ver·trump /ˌōvərˈtrəmp/ ▶ **v.** [no obj.] (in bridge and similar card games) play a trump that is higher than one already played in the same trick.
▶ **n.** an act of overtrumping.

o·ver·ture /ˈōvərcнər, -ˌcнŏŏr/ ▶ **n. 1** an introduction to something more substantial: *the talks were no more than an overture to a long debate.* ■ (usu. **overtures**) an approach or proposal made to someone with the aim of opening negotiations or establishing a relationship: *Coleen listened to his overtures of love.*
2 Music an orchestral piece at the beginning of an opera, suite, play, oratorio, or other extended composition. ■ an independent orchestral composition in one movement.
– ORIGIN late Middle English (in the sense 'aperture'): from Old French, from Latin *apertura* 'aperture.'

o·ver·turn ▶ **v.** /ˌōvərˈtərn/ [with obj.] **1** tip (something) over so that it is on its side or upside down: *the crowd proceeded to overturn cars and set them on fire.* ■ [no obj.] turn over and come to rest upside down, typically as the result of an accident: *a large housetrailer overturned in the middle of the road.*
2 abolish, invalidate, or reverse (a previous system, decision, situation, etc.): *the results overturned previous findings* | *he fought for eight years to overturn a conviction for armed robbery.*
▶ **n.** /ˈōvərˌtərn/ rare an act of turning over or upsetting something; a revolution, subversion, or reversal. ■ Ecology the occasional (typically twice yearly) mixing of the water of a thermally stratified lake.

o·ver·type /ˈōvərˌtīp/ ▶ **v.** [with obj.] type over (another character): *overtype it with the correct number and press Return.*
▶ **n.** a facility or operating mode allowing overtyping.

o·ver·use ▶ **v.** /ˌōvərˈyo͞oz/ [with obj.] use too much: *young children sometimes overuse "and" in their writing.*
▶ **n.** /ˈōvərˈyo͞os/ excessive use: *overuse of natural resources.*
– DERIVATIVES **o·ver·used** /ˌōvərˈyo͞ozd/ **adj.**

o·ver·val·ue /ˌōvərˈvalyo͞o/ ▶ **v.** (**overvalues, overvaluing, overvalued**) [with obj.] overestimate the importance of: *intelligence can be overvalued.* ■ fix the value of (something, esp. a currency) at too high a level: *sterling was overvalued against the dollar.*
– DERIVATIVES **o·ver·val·u·a·tion** /ˈōvərəˌvalyo͞oˈāsнən/ **n.**

o·ver·view /ˈōvərˌvyo͞o/ ▶ **n.** a general review or summary of a subject: *a critical overview of the scientific issues of our time.*
▶ **v.** [with obj.] give a general review or summary of: *the report overviews the needs of the community.*

o·ver·wa·ter ▶ **v.** /ˌōvərˈwôtər, -ˈwätər/ [with obj.] water (a plant, a lawn, etc.) too much: *your cutting needs some water, but make sure you don't overwater it.*
▶ **adj.** /ˈōvərwôtər, -wätər/ situated or taking place above water: *the airline is to initiate long-haul overwater operations.*

o·ver·wear /ˈōvərˌwe(ə)r/ ▶ **n.** outer clothing.

o·ver·ween·ing /ˈōvərˈwēniNG/ ▶ **adj.** showing excessive confidence or pride: *overweening ambition.*
– DERIVATIVES **o·ver·ween·ing·ly adv.**

o·ver·weight ▶ **adj.** /ˈōvərˈwāt/ above a weight considered normal or desirable: *he's forty pounds overweight.* ■ above legal weight: *an overweight truck.*
▶ **n.** /ˈōvərˌwāt/ excessive or extra weight.
▶ **v.** /ˌōvərˈwāt/ [with obj.] (usu. as adj. **overweighted**) put too much weight on; overload. ■ Finance invest in (a market sector, industry, etc.) to a greater than normal degree: *we have overweighted the banking sector* | [as adj.] *we were overweighted in technology last year.*

o·ver·whelm /ˌōvərˈ(h)welm/ ▶ **v.** [with obj.] bury or drown beneath a huge mass: *the water flowed through to overwhelm the whole dam and the village beneath.* ■ defeat completely: *his teams overwhelmed their opponents.* ■ give too much of a thing to (someone); inundate: *they were overwhelmed by farewell messages.* ■ (usu. **be overwhelmed**) have a strong emotional effect on: *I was overwhelmed with guilt.* ■ be too strong for; overpower: *the wine doesn't overwhelm the flavor of the trout.*

o·ver·whelm·ing /ˌōvərˈ(h)welmiNG/ ▶ **adj.** very great in amount: *he was elected president by an overwhelming majority.* ■ (esp. of an emotion) very strong: *an overwhelming feeling of gratitude.*
– DERIVATIVES **o·ver·whelm·ing·ly adv.**, **o·ver·whelm·ing·ness n.**

o·ver·wind /ˌōvərˈwīnd/ ▶ **v.** (past and past participle **overwound**) [with obj.] wind (a mechanism, esp. a watch) beyond the proper stopping point.

O

o·ver·win·ter /ˈōvərˈwin(t)ər/ ▶ **v.** [no obj.] **1** [with adverbial of place] spend the winter: *many birds overwinter in equatorial regions.*
2 (of an insect, plant, etc.) live through the winter: *the germinated seeds will overwinter.*

o·ver·with·hold /ˌōvərwiTHˈhōld, -wiTH-/ ▶ **v.** [with obj.] deduct (an amount in withholding tax) in excess of what is owed.

o·ver·work /ōvərˈwərk/ ▶ **v.** [with obj.] exhaust with too much work: *executives who are overworked and worried* | (as adj. **overworked**) *tired, overworked, demoralized staff.* ■ [no obj.] (of a person) work too hard: *the doctor advised a complete rest because he had been overworking.* ■ (usu. as adj. **overworked**) make excessive use of: *the city's overworked sewer system.* ■ (usu. as adj. **overworked**) use (a word or idea) too much and so make it weaker in meaning or effect: *"Breathtaking" is an overworked brochure cliché.*
▶ **n.** excessive work: *his health broke down under the strain of overwork.*

o·ver·write /ˌōvərˈrīt/ ▶ **v.** (past **overwrote**; past participle **overwritten**) [with obj.] **1** write on top of (other writing): *many names had been scratched out or overwritten.* ■ Computing destroy (data) or the data in (a file) by entering new data in its place: *an entry stating who is allowed to overwrite the file.* ■ another term for **OVERTYPE**.
2 write too elaborately or ornately: *there is a tendency to overwrite their parts and fall into cliché.*

o·ver·wrought /ˈōvəˈrôt/ ▶ **adj. 1** in a state of nervous excitement or anxiety: *she was too overwrought to listen to reason.*
2 (of a piece of writing or a work of art) too elaborate or complicated in design or construction.
– ORIGIN late Middle English: archaic past participle of **OVERWORK**.

o·ver·zeal·ous /ˌōvərˈzeləs/ ▶ **adj.** too zealous in attitude or behavior: *he's been overzealous in handing out parking tickets.*
– DERIVATIVES **o·ver·zeal·ous·ly adv.**, **o·ver·zeal·ous·ness n.**

ovi- ▶ **comb. form** chiefly Zoology of or relating to eggs or ova: *oviparous.*
– ORIGIN from Latin *ovum* 'egg.'

Ov·id /ˈävid/ (43 BC–c. AD 17), Roman poet; full name *Publius Ovidius Naso.* He is noted for his elegiac love poems (such as the *Amores* and the *Ars Amatoria*) and for the *Metamorphoses*, a hexametric series of tales of mythological, legendary, and historical figures.
– DERIVATIVES **Ov·id·i·an adj.**

o·vi·duct /ˈōviˌdəkt/ ▶ **n.** Anatomy & Zoology the tube through which an ovum or egg passes from an ovary.
– DERIVATIVES **o·vi·du·cal** /ˌōvəˈdo͞okəl/ **adj.**, **o·vi·duc·tal** /ˌōvəˈdəktəl/ **adj.**

O·vie·do /ôˈvyedō/ a city in northwestern Spain, capital of the Asturias region; pop. 220,644 (2008).

o·vi·form /ˈōvəˌfôrm/ ▶ **adj.** egg-shaped.

O·vim·bun·du /ˌōvimˈbo͝ondo͞o/ see **MBUNDU**.

o·vine /ˈōˌvīn/ ▶ **adj.** of, relating to, or resembling sheep.
– ORIGIN early 19th cent.: from late Latin *ovinus*, from Latin *ovis* 'sheep.'

o·vip·a·rous /ōˈvipərəs/ ▶ **adj.** Zoology (of a bird, etc.) producing young by means of eggs that are hatched after they have been laid by the parent. Compare with **VIVIPAROUS** and **OVOVIVIPAROUS**.
– DERIVATIVES **o·vi·par·i·ty** /-ˈparitē/ **n.**

o·vi·pos·it /ˌōvəˈpäzit/ ▶ **v.** (**oviposits, ovipositing, oviposited**) [no obj.] Zoology (esp. of an insect) lay an egg or eggs.
– DERIVATIVES **o·vi·po·si·tion** /-pəˈziSHən/ **n.**
– ORIGIN early 19th cent.: from **OVI-** 'egg' + Latin *posit-* 'placed' (from the verb *ponere*).

o·vi·pos·i·tor /ˌōvəˈpäzitər/ ▶ **n.** Zoology a tubular organ through which a female insect or fish deposits eggs.

ovi·rap·tor /ˌōviˈraptər/ ▶ **n.** a bipedal dinosaur of the late Cretaceous period, having a toothless jaw and long forelimbs with clawed fingers. ● Genus *Oviraptor*, family Oviraptoridae, suborder Theropoda.
– ORIGIN 1920s: from **OVI-** (from Latin *ovum* 'egg') + **RAPTOR**, the original supposition being that it fed on the eggs of other dinosaurs.

o·void /ˈōˌvoid/ ▶ **adj.** (of a solid or a three-dimensional surface) egg-shaped. ■ (of a plane figure) oval, esp. with one end more pointed than the other.
▶ **n.** an ovoid body or surface.
– ORIGIN early 19th cent.: from French *ovoïde*, from modern Latin *ovoides*, from Latin *ovum* 'egg.'

o·vo·lo /ˈōvəlō/ ▶ **n.** (pl. **ovoli** /-ˌlī/) Architecture a rounded convex molding, in cross section a quarter of a circle or ellipse.
– ORIGIN mid 17th cent.: from Italian, diminutive of *ovo* 'egg,' from Latin *ovum*.

o·vo·tes·tis /ˌōvōˈtestis/ ▶ **n.** (pl. **ovotestes** /-ˈtestēz/) Zoology an organ producing both ova and spermatozoa, as in some gastropod mollusks.
– ORIGIN late 19th cent.: from **OVUM** + **TESTIS**.

o·vo·vi·vip·a·rous /ˌōˌvōvīˈvip(ə)rəs, -vəˈvip-/ ▶ **adj.** Zoology (of an animal) producing young by means of eggs that are hatched within the body of the parent, as in some snakes. Compare with **OVIPAROUS** and **VIVIPAROUS**.
– DERIVATIVES **o·vo·vi·vi·par·i·ty** /-ˌvīvəˈparitē/ **n.**

ov·u·late /ˈövyəˌlāt, ˈäv-/ ▶ **v.** [no obj.] discharge ova or ovules from the ovary.
– DERIVATIVES **ov·u·la·tion** /ˌōvyəˈlāSHən, -ˈlāSHən/ **n.**, **ov·u·la·to·ry** /-ləˌtôrē/ **adj.**
– ORIGIN late 19th cent.: back-formation from *ovulation*, or from medieval Latin *ovulum* 'little egg' (see **OVULE**) + **-ATE**[3].

ov·ule /ˈōvyo͞ol, ˈäv-/ ▶ **n.** a small or immature ovum. ■ Botany the part of the ovary of seed plants that contains the female germ cell and after fertilization becomes the seed.
– DERIVATIVES **ov·u·lar** /-lər/ **adj.**
– ORIGIN early 19th cent.: from French, from medieval Latin *ovulum*, diminutive of **OVUM**.

o·vum /ˈōvəm/ ▶ **n.** (pl. **ova** /ˈōvə/) Biology a mature female reproductive cell, esp. of a human or other animal, that can divide to give rise to an embryo usually only after fertilization by a male cell.
– ORIGIN early 18th cent.: from Latin, literally 'egg.'

OW ▶ **abbr.** Old Welsh.

ow /ou/ ▶ **exclam.** used to express sudden pain: *Ow! You're hurting me!*
– ORIGIN natural exclamation: first recorded in English in the mid 19th cent.

owe /ō/ ▶ **v.** [with obj.] have an obligation to pay or repay (something, esp. money) in return for something received: *they have denied they owe money to the company* | [with two objs.] *I owe you 25 cents.* ■ owe something, esp. money, to (someone): *I owe you for the taxi.* ■ be under a moral obligation to give someone (gratitude, respect, etc.): *I owe it to him to explain what's happened* | [with two objs.] *I owe you an apology.* ■ (**owe something to**) have something because of (someone or something): *he owed his success not to chance but to insight.* ■ be indebted to someone or something for (something): *I owe my life to you.*
– PHRASES **owe it to oneself** need to do something to protect one's own interests: *you owe it to yourself to take care of your body.* **owe someone one** informal feel indebted to someone for a favor done: *thanks, I owe you one for this.* **owes someone a living** used to express disapproval of someone who expects to receive financial support or other benefits without doing any work: *they think the world owes them a living.*
– ORIGIN Old English *āgan* 'own, have it as an obligation,' of Germanic origin; from an Indo-European root shared by Sanskrit *īś* 'possess, own.' Compare with **OUGHT**[1].

Ow·ens /ˈō(w)ənz/, Jesse (1913–80), US athlete; born *James Cleveland Owens.* In 1935, he equaled or broke six world records in forty-five minutes, and in 1936, he won four gold medals at the Olympic Games in Berlin. The success of Owens, a black man, in Berlin outraged Hitler.

Ow·ens·bor·o /ˈōwənzˌbərō, -ˌbə-rō/ an industrial port city in northwestern Kentucky, on the Ohio River; pop. 55,516 (est. 2008).

Ow·ens Val·ley /ˈōwənz/ the valley of the Owens River, in east central California, between the Sierra Nevada and the Inyo Mountains, the source since 1913 of much of the water supply for Los Angeles.

ow·ing /ˈō-iNG/ ▶ **adj.** [predic.] (of money) yet to be paid: *no rent was owing.*
– PHRASES **owing to** because of or on account of: *his reading was hesitant owing to a stammer.*

owl /oul/ ▶ **n.** a nocturnal bird of prey with large forward-facing eyes surrounded by facial disks, a hooked beak, and typically a loud call. ● Order Strigiformes: families Strigidae (**typical owls** such as tawny owls and eagle owls) and Tytonidae (**barn owls** and their relatives).
– DERIVATIVES **owl·like** /-ˌlīk/ **adj.**
– ORIGIN Old English *ūle*, of Germanic origin; related to Dutch *uil* and German *Eule*, from a base imitative of the bird's call.

owl but·ter·fly ▶ **n.** a very large South American butterfly that flies at dusk, with a large eyelike marking on the underside of each hind wing. ● Genus *Caligo*, subfamily Brassolinae, family Nymphalidae.

owl·et /ˈoulit/ ▶ **n. 1** a small owl found chiefly in Asia and Africa. ● Genus *Glaucidium* and *Athene*, family Strigidae: several species. ■ a young owl of any kind.
2 another term for **NOCTUID**.

owl·et-night·jar ▶ **n.** a nocturnal Australasian bird resembling a small nightjar, with an owllike face and a large gape. ● Family Aegothelidae and genus *Aegotheles*: several species.

owl-faced mon·key ▶ **n.** a guenon that has a black face with white and yellow markings and bright blue skin on the rump, living in the forests of central Africa. ● *Cercopithecus hamlyni*, family Cercopithecidae.

owl·ish /ˈouliSH/ ▶ **adj.** like an owl, esp. in acting or appearing wise or solemn: *he had an owlish and solemn air.* ■ (of eyeglasses) resembling the large round eyes of an owl.
– DERIVATIVES **owl·ish·ly adv.**, **owl·ish·ness n.**

owl mon·key ▶ **n.** another term for **DOUROUCOULI**.

owl par·rot ▶ **n.** another term for **KAKAPO**.

own /ōn/ ▶ **adj. & pron.** used with a possessive to emphasize that someone or something belongs or relates to the person mentioned: [as adj.] *they can't handle their own children* | *I was an outcast among my own kind* | [as pronoun] *the Church would look after its own.* ■ done or produced by and for the person specified: [as adj.] *I used to design all my own clothes* | [as pronoun] *they claimed the work as their own.* ■ particular to the person or thing mentioned; individual: [as adj.] *the style had its own charm* | [as pronoun] *the film had a quality all its own.*
▶ **v. 1** [with obj.] have (something) as one's own; possess: *his father owns a restaurant* | [as adj., in combination] (**-owned**) *state-owned property.*
2 [no obj.] formal admit or acknowledge that something is the case or that one feels a certain way: *she owned to a feeling of profound jealousy* | [with clause] *he was reluctant to own that he was indebted.* ■ [with obj.] take or acknowledge full responsibility for (something): *I emphasize the importance of owning our anger and finding ways to control it.* ■ [with obj.] archaic acknowledge paternity, authorship, or possession of: *he has published little, trivial things which he will not own.*
3 [with obj.] informal utterly defeat or humiliate: *yeah right, she totally owned you, man.*
– PHRASES **as if** (or **like**) **one owns the place** informal in an overbearing or self-important manner: *he would have walked in and taken charge as if he owned the place.* **be one's own man** (or **woman**) act independently and with confidence. ■ archaic be in full possession of one's faculties. **come into its** (or **one's**) **own** become fully effective, used, or recognized: *Mexico will come into its own as a vacation spot.* **get one's own back** informal take action in retaliation for a wrongdoing or insult. **hold one's own** retain a position of strength in a challenging situation: *I can hold my own in a fight.* **of one's own** belonging to oneself alone: *at last I've got a place of my own.* **on one's own** unaccompanied by others; alone or unaided: *I have to do things on my own.*
– PHRASAL VERBS **own up** admit or confess to having done something wrong or embarrassing: *he owns up to few mistakes.*
– ORIGIN Old English *āgen* (adjective and pronoun) 'owned, possessed,' past participle of *āgan* 'owe'; the verb (Old English *āgnian* 'possess,' also 'make own's own') was originally from the adjective, later probably reintroduced from **OWNER**.

own·er /ˈōnər/ ▶ **n.** a person who owns something: *the proud owner of a huge Dalmatian.*
– DERIVATIVES **own·er·less adj.**

own·er-oc·cu·pied ▶ **adj.** (of a house or apartment) used as a dwelling by the owner.

own·er·ship /ˈōnərˌSHip/ ▶ **n.** the act, state, or right of possessing something: *the ownership of land* | *the rise in car ownership.*

own goal ▶ **n.** (in soccer) a goal scored inadvertently when the ball is struck into the goal by a player on the defensive team.

ox /äks/ ▶ **n.** (pl. **oxen** /ˈäksən/) a domesticated bovine animal kept for milk or meat; a cow or bull. See **CATTLE** (sense 1). ■ a castrated male of this, formerly much used as a draft animal: [as modifier] *an ox cart.* ■ an animal of a group related to the domestic ox. See **CATTLE** (sense 2).
– ORIGIN Old English *oxa*, of Germanic origin; related to Dutch *os* and German *Ochse*, from an Indo-European root shared by Sanskrit *ukṣán* 'bull.'

ox- ▶ **comb. form** variant spelling of **OXY-**[2] reduced before a vowel (as in *oxazole*).

O

ox·a·cil·lin /ˌäksəˈsilin/ ▶ **n.** Medicine an antibiotic drug made by chemical modification of penicillin and used to treat bacterial infections.
– ORIGIN 1960s: blend of OXAZOLE and PENICILLIN.

ox·al·ic ac·id /äkˈsalik/ ▶ **n.** Chemistry a poisonous crystalline acid with a sour taste, present in rhubarb leaves, wood sorrel, and other plants. Its uses include bleaching and cleansing. ● Alternative name: **ethanedioic acid**; chem. formula: $(COOH)_2$.
– DERIVATIVES **ox·a·late** /ˈäksəˌlāt/ **n.**
– ORIGIN late 18th cent.: *oxalic* from French *oxalique*, via Latin from Greek *oxalis* 'wood sorrel.'

ox·a·lis /ˈäksəlis, äkˈsalis/ ▶ **n.** a plant of a genus that includes the wood sorrel, typically having three-lobed leaves and white, yellow, or pink flowers. ● Genus *Oxalis*, family Oxalidaceae.
– ORIGIN early 17th cent.: via Latin from Greek, from *oxus* 'sour' (because of its sharp-tasting leaves).

ox·a·zole /ˈäksəˌzōl/ ▶ **n.** Chemistry a volatile liquid with weakly basic properties, whose molecule contains a five-membered ring that serves as the basis of a number of medicinal drugs. ● A heterocyclic compound; chem. formula: C_3H_3NO.
– ORIGIN late 19th cent.: from OX- 'oxygen' + AZO- + -OLE.

ox·a·zo·lid·i·none /ˌäksəzōˈlidnˌōn/ ▶ **n.** any of a class of synthetic antibiotics that inhibit protein synthesis, used against Gram-positive bacteria.

ox·bow /ˈäksˌbō/ ▶ **n. 1** a U-shaped bend in the course of a river. ■ short for OXBOW LAKE.
2 a U-shaped collar of an ox yoke.

ox·bow lake ▶ **n.** a curved lake formed at a former oxbow where the main stream of the river has cut across the narrow end and no longer flows around the loop of the bend.

Ox·bridge /ˈäksˌbrij/ ▶ **n.** Oxford and Cambridge universities regarded together: [as modifier] *Oxbridge colleges*.
– ORIGIN mid 19th cent.: blend of OXFORD and CAMBRIDGE.

ox·en /ˈäksən/ plural form of OX.

ox·eye /ˈäksˌī/ ▶ **n.** a yellow-flowered North American plant of the daisy family. ● *Heliopsis helianthoides*, family Compositae.

ox·eye dai·sy ▶ **n.** an often-cultivated Eurasian daisy that has large white flowers with yellow centers. Also called MARGUERITE. ● *Leucanthemum vulgare*, family Compositae.

Oxf. ▶ **abbr.** Oxford.

Ox·ford /ˈäksfərd/ **1** a city in central England, on the Thames River; pop. 146,100 (est. 2009). Oxford University is located here.
2 a town in north central Mississippi, home to the University of Mississippi and associated with novelist William Faulkner; pop. 17,265 (est. 2008). See also YOKNAPATAWPHA COUNTY.

Merton College, Oxford

ox·ford /ˈäksfərd/ ▶ **n. 1** (also **oxford shoe**) a type of lace-up shoe with a low heel.
2 (also **oxford cloth**) a heavy cotton cloth chiefly used to make shirts.

Ox·ford com·ma ▶ **n.** another term for SERIAL COMMA.
– ORIGIN a characteristic of the house style of *Oxford* University Press.

Ox·ford Group a Christian movement popularized in Oxford in the late 1920s, advocating discussion of personal problems by groups. Later known as MORAL REARMAMENT.

Ox·ford Move·ment a Christian movement started in Oxford, England, in 1833, seeking to restore traditional Catholic teachings and ceremony within the Church of England. Its leaders were John Keble, Edward Pusey, and (until he became a Roman Catholic) John Henry Newman. It formed the basis of the present Anglo-Catholic (or High Church) tradition. Also called TRACTARIANISM.

ox·herd /ˈäksˌhərd/ ▶ **n.** archaic a cowherd.
– ORIGIN Old English, from OX + obsolete *herd* 'herdsman.'

ox·hide /ˈäksˌhīd/ ▶ **n.** leather made from the hide of an ox.

ox·ic /ˈäksik/ ▶ **adj.** designating a process or environment in which oxygen is involved or present.
– ORIGIN 1960s: from *ox(ide)* or *ox(ygen)* + -IC.

ox·i·dant /ˈäksidənt/ ▶ **n.** an oxidizing agent.
– ORIGIN late 19th cent.: from French (modern French *oxydant*), present participle of *oxider* 'oxidize.'

ox·i·dase /ˈäksiˌdās, -ˌdāz/ ▶ **n.** Biochemistry an enzyme that promotes the transfer of a hydrogen atom from a particular substrate to an oxygen molecule, forming water or hydrogen peroxide.
– ORIGIN late 19th cent.: from French *oxydase*, from *oxyde* 'oxide.'

ox·i·da·tion /ˌäksiˈdāsʜən/ ▶ **n.** Chemistry the process or result of oxidizing or being oxidized.
– DERIVATIVES **ox·i·da·tion·al** /-sʜənl/ **adj.**, **ox·i·da·tive** /ˈäksiˌdātiv/ **adj.**
– ORIGIN late 18th cent.: from French (modern French *oxydation*), from *oxider* 'oxidize.'

ox·i·da·tion num·ber (also **oxidation state**) ▶ **n.** Chemistry a number assigned to an element in chemical combination that represents the number of electrons lost (or gained, if the number is negative) by an atom of that element in the compound.

ox·ide /ˈäkˌsīd/ ▶ **n.** Chemistry a binary compound of oxygen with another element or group.
– ORIGIN late 18th cent.: from French, from *oxygène* 'oxygen' + *-ide* (as in *acide* 'acid').

ox·i·dize /ˈäksiˌdīz/ ▶ **v.** combine or become combined chemically with oxygen: [with obj.] *when coal is burned any sulfur is oxidized to sulfur dioxide* | [no obj.] *the fats in the food will oxidize, turning it rancid*. ■ Chemistry undergo or cause to undergo a reaction in which electrons are lost to another species. The opposite of REDUCE.
– DERIVATIVES **ox·i·diz·a·ble adj.**, **ox·i·di·za·tion** /ˌäksidiˈzāsʜən/ **n.**, **ox·i·diz·er n.**

ox·i·diz·ing a·gent /ˈäksiˌdīziɴɢ/ ▶ **n.** Chemistry a substance that tends to bring about oxidation by being reduced and gaining electrons.

ox·im·e·ter /äkˈsimitər/ ▶ **n.** an instrument for measuring the proportion of oxygenated hemoglobin in the blood.
– DERIVATIVES **ox·im·e·try** /-trē/ **n.**

ox·i·sol /ˈäksiˌsôl, -säl/ ▶ **n.** Soil Science a soil of an order comprising stable, highly weathered, tropical mineral soils with highly oxidized subsurface horizons.
– ORIGIN 1960s: from OXIC + -SOL.

ox·lip /ˈäksˌlip/ ▶ **n.** a woodland Eurasian primula with yellow flowers that hang down one side of the stem. ● *Primula elatior*, family Primulaceae. ■ (also **false oxlip**) a natural hybrid between a primrose and a cowslip.
– ORIGIN Old English *oxanslyppe*, from *oxa* 'ox' + *slyppe* 'slime'; compare with COWSLIP.

Ox·nard /ˈäksˌnärd/ a city in southwestern California, northwest of Los Angeles, on the Pacific coast; pop. 185,717 (est. 2008).

Ox·on /ˈäksˌän/ ▶ **abbr.** (esp. in degree titles) of Oxford University: *BA, Oxon.*
– ORIGIN from medieval Latin *Oxoniensis*, from *Oxonia* (see OXONIAN).

Ox·o·ni·an /äkˈsōnēən, -ˈsōnyən/ ▶ **adj.** of or relating to Oxford, England, or Oxford University.
▶ **n.** a native or inhabitant of Oxford, England. ■ someone who attends or has a degree from Oxford University.
– ORIGIN mid 16th cent.: from *Oxonia* (Latinized name of Oxford, from its old form *Oxenford*) + -AN.

ox·peck·er /ˈäksˌpekər/ ▶ **n.** a brown African bird related to the starlings, feeding on parasites that infest the skins of large grazing mammals. ● Genus *Buphagus*, family Sturnidae (or Buphagidae): two species.

ox·tail /ˈäksˌtāl/ ▶ **n.** the tail of a cow. ■ meat from this, used esp. for making soup.

ox·ter /ˈäkstər/ ▶ **n.** Scottish & N. English a person's armpit.
– ORIGIN Old English *ōhsta, ōxta*.

ox·tongue ▶ **n.** an Old World plant of the daisy family with yellow dandelionlike flowers and prickly hairs on the stem and leaves. ● Genus *Picris*, family Compositae: several species, including the **bristly ox-tongue** (*P. echioides*), introduced to and now common in California.

Ox·us /ˈäksəs/ ancient name for AMU DARYA.

oxy-[1] ▶ **comb. form** denoting sharpness: *oxytone*.
– ORIGIN from Greek *oxus* 'sharp.'

oxy-[2] (also **ox-**) ▶ **comb. form** Chemistry representing OXYGEN.

ox·y·a·cet·y·lene /ˌäksēəˈsetl-in, -ˌēn/ ▶ **adj.** [attrib.] of or denoting welding or cutting techniques using a very hot flame produced by mixing acetylene and oxygen.

ox·y·ac·id /ˌäksēˈasid/ ▶ **n.** Chemistry an inorganic acid whose molecules contain oxygen, such as sulfuric or nitric acid.

ox·y·an·i·on /ˌäksēˈanˌīən/ ▶ **n.** Chemistry an anion containing one or more oxygen atoms bonded to another element (as in the sulfate and carbonate ions).

Ox·y·Con·tin /ˌäksēˈkäntin/ ▶ **n.** trademark a synthetic analgesic drug that is similar to morphine in its effects and subject to abuse and addiction.

ox·y·gen /ˈäksəjən/ ▶ **n.** a colorless, odorless reactive gas, the chemical element of atomic number 8 and the life-supporting component of the air. Oxygen forms about 20 percent of the earth's atmosphere, and is the most abundant element in the earth's crust, mainly in the form of oxides, silicates, and carbonates. (Symbol: **O**)
– DERIVATIVES **ox·yg·e·nous** /äkˈsijənəs/ **adj.**
– ORIGIN late 18th cent.: from French (*principe*) *oxygène* 'acidifying constituent' (because at first it was held to be the essential component in the formation of acids).

ox·y·gen·ate /ˈäksəjəˌnāt/ ▶ **v.** [with obj.] supply, treat, charge, or enrich with oxygen: (as adj. **oxygenated**) *a good supply of oxygenated blood*.
– DERIVATIVES **ox·y·gen·a·tion** /ˌäksəjəˈnāsʜən/ **n.**
– ORIGIN late 18th cent.: from French *oxygéner* 'supply with oxygen' + -ATE[3].

ox·y·gen·a·tor /ˈäksəjəˌnātər/ ▶ **n.** Medicine an apparatus for oxygenating the blood. ■ an aquatic plant that enriches the surrounding water with oxygen, esp. in a pond or aquarium.

ox·y·gen bar ▶ **n.** an establishment where people pay to inhale pure oxygen for its reputedly therapeutic effects.

ox·y·gen·ize /ˈäksəjəˌnīz/ ▶ **v.** alternate term for OXYGENATE.

ox·y·gen mask ▶ **n.** a mask placed over the nose and mouth and connected to a supply of oxygen, used when the body is not able to gain enough oxygen by breathing air, for example, at high altitudes or because of a medical condition.

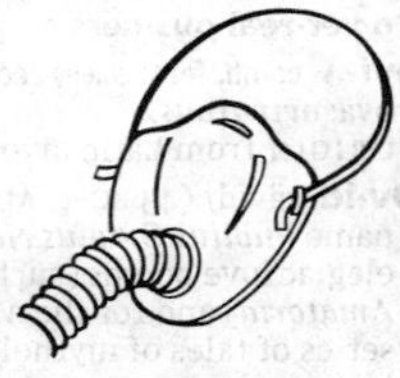

oxygen mask

ox·y·gen tent ▶ **n.** a tentlike enclosure within which the air supply can be enriched with oxygen to aid a patient's breathing.

ox·y·he·mo·glo·bin /ˌäksēˈhēməˌglōbən/ ▶ **n.** Biochemistry a bright red substance formed by the combination of hemoglobin with oxygen, present in oxygenated blood.

ox·y·mo·ron /ˌäksəˈmôrˌän/ ▶ **n.** a figure of speech in which apparently contradictory terms appear in conjunction (e.g., *faith unfaithful kept him falsely true*).
– DERIVATIVES **ox·y·mo·ron·ic** /-məˈränik/ **adj.**
– ORIGIN mid 17th cent.: from Greek *oxumōron*, neuter (used as a noun) of *oxumōros* 'pointedly foolish,' from *oxus* 'sharp' + *mōros* 'foolish.'

ox·yn·tic /äkˈsintik/ ▶ **adj.** of or denoting the secretory cells that produce hydrochloric acid in the main part of the stomach, or the glands that they compose.
– ORIGIN late 19th cent.: from Greek *oxunteos* (verbal noun from *oxunein* 'sharpen') + -IC.

ox·y·te·tra·cy·cline /ˌäksəˌtetrəˈsīklēn/ ▶ **n.** Medicine an antibiotic related to tetracycline, used to treat a variety of bacterial infections.

ox·y·to·cin /ˌäksəˈtōsən/ ▶ **n.** Biochemistry a hormone released by the pituitary gland that causes increased contraction of the uterus during labor and stimulates the ejection of milk into the ducts of the breasts.
– ORIGIN 1920s: from Greek *oxutokia* 'sudden delivery' (from *oxus* 'sharp' + *tokos* 'childbirth') + -IN[1].

ox·y·tone /ˈäksəˌtōn/ ▶ **adj.** (esp. in ancient Greek) having an acute accent on the last syllable.
▶ **n.** a word of this kind.
– ORIGIN mid 18th cent.: from Greek *oxutonos*, from *oxus* 'sharp' + *tonos* 'tone.'

oy /oi/ ▶ **exclam. 1** see OY VEY.
2 variant spelling of OI.

o·yer and ter·mi·ner /ˈoi-ər and ˈtərmənər/ ▶ **n.** historical a court authorized to hear certain criminal cases.
– ORIGIN late Middle English: from Anglo-Norman French *oyer et terminer* 'hear and determine.'

o·yez /ˈōˌyā, ˈōˌyez/ (also **oyes**) ▶ **exclam.** a call given by a court officer, or formerly by public criers, typically repeated two or three times to command silence and attention, as before court is in session.
– ORIGIN late Middle English: from Old French *oiez!*, *oyez!* 'hear!,' imperative plural of *oir*, from Latin *audire* 'hear.'

oys·ter /ˈoistər/ ▶ **n. 1** any of a number of bivalve mollusks with rough irregular shells. Several kinds are eaten (esp. raw) as a delicacy and may be farmed for food or pearls. ● a true oyster (family Ostreidae), in particular the edible **American oyster** (*Crassostrea virginica*). ● a similar bivalve of another family, in particular the **thorny oysters** (Spondylidae), **wing oysters** (Pteriidae), and **saddle oysters** (Anomiidae).
2 (also **oyster white**) a shade of grayish white.
3 an oyster-shaped morsel of meat on each side of the backbone in poultry.
▶ **v.** [no obj.] (usu. as noun **oystering**) raise, dredge, or gather oysters: *oystering is still the lifeblood of this town.*
– PHRASES **the world is your oyster** you are in a position to take the opportunities that life has to offer. [from Shakespeare's *Merry Wives of Windsor* (II. ii. 5).]
– ORIGIN Middle English: from Old French *oistre*, via Latin from Greek *ostreon*; related to *osteon* 'bone' and *ostrakon* 'shell or tile.'

oys·ter bar ▶ **n. 1** a hotel bar, small restaurant, or other place where oysters are served.
2 (esp. in the southeastern US) an oyster bed.

Oys·ter Bay a town in central Long Island in New York that includes the villages of Hicksville, Farmingdale, and Oyster Bay; pop. 301,474 (est. 2008).

oys·ter bed ▶ **n.** a part of the sea bottom where oysters breed or are bred.

oys·ter·catch·er /ˈoistərˌkacHər/ ▶ **n.** a coastal wading bird with black-and-white or all-black plumage and a strong orange-red bill, feeding chiefly on shellfish. ● Family Haematopodidae and genus *Haematopus*: several species, e.g., the black and white *H. ostralegus* of Eurasia.

oys·ter crab ▶ **n.** a minute, soft-bodied crab that lives inside the shell of a bivalve mollusk, where it filters food particles from the water drawn into the shell by its host. Also called **PEA CRAB**. ● Family Pinnotheridae: *Pinnotheres* and other genera.

oys·ter crack·er ▶ **n.** a small, round soda cracker served with soup, oysters, etc.

oys·ter farm ▶ **n.** an area of the seabed used for breeding oysters.

oys·ter·man /ˈoistərmən/ ▶ **n.** a person who gathers, cultivates, or sells oysters. ■ a boat equipped for harvesting oysters.

oys·ter mush·room ▶ **n.** a widely distributed edible fungus that has a grayish-brown, oyster-shaped cap and a very short or absent stem, growing on the wood of broadleaved trees and causing rot. ● *Pleurotus ostreatus*, family Pleurotaceae, class Hymenomycetes.

oys·ter plant ▶ **n.** another term for **SALSIFY**.

oys·ter sauce ▶ **n.** a sauce made with oysters and soy sauce, used esp. in oriental cooking.

oys·ters Rock·e·fel·ler ▶ **plural n.** oysters covered with a mixture of spinach, butter, seasonings, and bread crumbs and cooked on the half shell.

oys·ter white ▶ **n.** see **OYSTER** (sense 2 of the noun).

oy vey /oi ˈvā/ (also **oy**) ▶ **exclam.** indicating dismay or grief.
– ORIGIN late 19th cent.: Yiddish, literally 'oh woe.'

Oz /äz/ Austral. informal ▶ **adj.** Australian.
▶ **n.** Australia. ■ a person from Australia.
– ORIGIN 1940s: representing a pronunciation of an abbreviation of **AUSTRALIA**.

oz. ▶ **abbr.** ounce(s).
– ORIGIN from Italian *onza* 'ounce.'

Oz·a·lid /ˈäzəˌlid/ ▶ **n.** trademark a photocopy made by a process in which a diazonium salt and coupler are present in the paper coating, so that the image develops in the presence of ammonia.
– ORIGIN 1920s: by reversal of **DIAZO** and insertion of *-l*.

oz. ap. ▶ **abbr.** apothecaries' ounce.

O·zark Moun·tains /ˈōˌzärk/ (also **the Ozarks**) a heavily forested highland plateau dissected by rivers, valleys, and streams, lying between the Missouri and Arkansas rivers and within the states of Missouri, Arkansas, Oklahoma, Kansas, and Illinois.

oz. av. ▶ **abbr.** avoirdupois ounce.

O·za·wa /ōˈzäwə/, Seiji (1935–), Japanese conductor. He was conductor of the Toronto Symphony Orchestra 1965–70 and music director and conductor of the Boston Symphony Orchestra 1973–2002. In 2002 he became musical director of the Vienna State Opera.

O·zick /ˈōˌzik/, Cynthia (1928–), US writer and critic. Many of her works, such as *Bloodshed and Three Novellas* (1976) and *The Puttermesser Papers* (1997), examine being Jewish in contemporary life. Some of her essays are collected in *Fame and Folly* (1996).

o·zo·ce·rite /ōˈzōkəˌrīt, -səˌrīt, ˌōzōˈsirīt/ (also **ozokerite**) ▶ **n.** a brown or black paraffin wax occurring naturally in some shales and sandstones and formerly used in candles, polishes, and electrical insulation.
– ORIGIN mid 19th cent.: from German *Ozokerit*, from Greek *ozein* 'to smell' + *kēros* 'wax.'

o·zone /ˈōˌzōn/ ▶ **n.** a colorless unstable toxic gas with a pungent odor and powerful oxidizing properties, formed from oxygen by electrical discharges or ultraviolet light. It differs from normal oxygen (O_2) in having three atoms in its molecule (O_3). ■ short for **OZONE LAYER**. ■ informal fresh invigorating air, esp. that blowing onto the shore from the sea.
– DERIVATIVES **o·zon·ic** /ōˈzänik/ **adj.**
– ORIGIN mid 19th cent.: from German *Ozon*, from Greek *ozein* 'to smell.'

o·zone-friend·ly ▶ **adj.** (of manufactured products) not containing chemicals that are destructive to the ozone layer.

o·zone hole ▶ **n.** a region of marked thinning of the ozone layer in high latitudes, chiefly in winter, attributed to the chemical action of chlorofluorcarbons and other atmospheric pollutants. The resulting increase in ultraviolet light at ground level gives rise to an increased risk of skin cancer.

o·zone lay·er ▶ **n.** a layer in the earth's stratosphere at an altitude of about 6.2 miles (10 km) containing a high concentration of ozone, which absorbs most of the ultraviolet radiation reaching the earth from the sun.

o·zo·nide /ˈōzəˌnīd/ ▶ **n.** Chemistry any of a class of unstable cyclic compounds formed by the addition of ozone to a carbon–carbon double bond. ■ a salt of the anion O_3^-, derived from ozone.

o·zon·ize /ˈōzəˌnīz/ ▶ **v.** [with obj.] (often as adj. **ozonized**) convert (oxygen) into ozone. ■ enrich or treat with ozone: *ozonized air.*
– DERIVATIVES **o·zon·i·za·tion** /ˌōzəniˈzāsHən/ **n.**, **o·zon·iz·er n.**

o·zo·no·sphere /ōˈzōnəˌsfir/ ▶ **n.** technical term for **OZONE LAYER**.

oz. t. ▶ **abbr.** troy ounce.

Pp

P[1] /pē/ (also **p**) ▶ **n.** (pl. **Ps** or **P's** /pēz/) the sixteenth letter of the alphabet. ■ denoting the next after O (or N if O is omitted) in a set of items, categories, etc.
– PHRASES **mind one's Ps and Qs** see **MIND**.

P[2] ▶ **abbr.** ■ pastor. ■ father. [Latin *pater*.] ■ (in tables of sports results) games played. ■ (on an automatic gearshift) park. ■ (on road signs and street plans) parking. ■ peseta. ■ peso. ■ [in combination] (in units of measurement) peta- (10^{15}): *27 PBq of radioactive material*. ■ Physics poise (unit of viscosity). ■ post. ■ president. ■ pressure. ■ priest. ■ prince. ■ proprietary. ■ progressive. ▶ **symbol** the chemical element phosphorus.

p ▶ **abbr.** ■ page. ■ (*p*-) [in combination] Chemistry para-: *p-xylene*. ■ Brit. penny or pence. ■ Music piano (softly). ■ [in combination] (in units of measurement) pico- (10^{-12}): *a 220 pf capacitor*. ■ Chemistry denoting electrons and orbitals possessing one unit of angular momentum. [from *principal*, originally applied to lines in atomic spectra.] ▶ **symbol** ■ Physics pressure. ■ Statistics probability.

PA ▶ **abbr.** ■ Pennsylvania (in official postal use). ■ Press Association. ■ public address.

Pa ▶ **abbr.** ■ pascal; pascals. ■ Pennsylvania. ▶ **symbol** the chemical element protactinium.

pa /pä/ ▶ **n.** informal father: *my pa was no farmer* | [as name] *Pa is busy on the telephone*.
– ORIGIN early 19th cent.: abbreviation of **PAPA**.

p.a. ▶ **abbr.** per annum.

pa'an·ga /ˈpäNGgə, päˈäNGgə/ ▶ **n.** (pl. **same**) the basic monetary unit of Tonga, equal to 100 seniti.
– ORIGIN Tongan.

Paarl /pärl/ a town in southwestern South Africa, in the province of Western Cape, northeast of Cape Town; pop. 191,000 (est. 2009).

PABA /ˈpäbə, ˈpabə/ ▶ **abbr.** para-aminobenzoic acid.

pab·lum /ˈpabləm/ ▶ **n.** (also **pabulum** /ˈpabyələm/) bland or insipid intellectual fare, entertainment, etc.; pap.
– ORIGIN mid 17th cent. (in the sense 'food'): from Latin, from the stem of *pascere* 'to feed.'

PABX ▶ **abbr.** private automatic branch exchange, a private telephone switchboard.

PAC /pak/ ▶ **abbr.** ■ Pan-Africanist Congress. ■ political action committee.

pa·ca /ˈpäkə, ˈpakə/ ▶ **n.** a nocturnal South American rodent that has a reddish-brown coat patterned with rows of white spots. It is hunted for its edible flesh. Also called **SPOTTED CAVY**. ● Genus *Cuniculus*, family Dasyproctidae: two species, in particular *A. paca*.
– ORIGIN mid 17th cent.: via Spanish and Portuguese from Tupi.

paca

pace[1] /pās/ ▶ **n. 1** a single step taken when walking or running. ■ a unit of length representing the distance between two successive steps in walking. ■ a gait of a horse or other animal, esp. one of the recognized trained gaits of a horse. ■ literary a person's manner of walking or running: *I steal with quiet pace*.
2 consistent and continuous speed in walking, running, or moving: *most traffic moved at the pace of the riverboat* | [in sing.] *walking at a comfortably fast pace*. ■ the speed or rate at which something happens, changes, or develops: *the children work separately in the classroom at their own pace* | *the poor neighborhoods fester at an increasingly rapid pace*.
▶ **v.** [no obj.] walk at a steady and consistent speed, esp. back and forth and as an expression of one's anxiety or annoyance: *we paced up and down in exasperation* | [with obj.] *she had been pacing the room*. ■ [with obj.] measure (a distance) by walking it and counting the number of steps taken: *I paced out the dimensions of my new home*. ■ [with obj.] lead (another runner in a race) in order to establish a competitive speed: *Morales paced us for four miles*. ■ (**pace oneself**) do something at a slow and steady rate or speed in order to avoid overexerting oneself: *Frank was pacing himself for the long night and day ahead*. ■ [with obj.] move or develop (something) at a particular rate or speed: *the action is paced to the beat of a perky march* | [as adj. in combination] (**-paced**) *our fast-paced daily lives*. ■ (of a horse) move in a distinctive lateral gait in which both legs on the same side are lifted together, seen mostly in specially bred or trained horses.
– PHRASES **change of pace** a change from what one is used to: *the magenta is a change of pace from traditional red*. **keep pace with** move, develop, or progress at the same speed as: *fees have had to be raised a little to keep pace with inflation*. **off the pace** behind the leader or leading group in a race or contest. **put someone** (or **something**) **through their** (or **its**) **paces** make someone (or something) demonstrate their (or its) qualities or abilities: *the cars are examined by our safety experts and put through their paces by our drivers*. **set the pace** be the fastest runner in the early part of a race. ■ lead the way in doing or achieving something: *space movies have set the pace for the development of special effects*.
– ORIGIN Middle English: from Old French *pas*, from Latin *passus* 'stretch (of the leg),' from *pandere* 'to stretch.'

pace[2] /ˈpāˌsē, ˈpäˌCHā/ ▶ **prep.** with due respect to (someone or their opinion), used to express polite disagreement or contradiction: *narrative history, pace some theorists, is by no means dead*.
– ORIGIN Latin, literally 'in peace,' ablative of *pax*, as in *pace tua* 'by your leave.'

pace car ▶ **n.** Auto Racing a car that sets the pace and positions racers for a rolling start in a warm-up lap or laps before a race, or that returns to control the pace in temporarily hazardous conditions.

pace·mak·er /ˈpāsˌmākər/ ▶ **n. 1** an artificial device for stimulating the heart muscle and regulating its contractions. ■ the part of the heart muscle (the sinoatrial node) that normally performs this role. ■ the part of an organ or of the body that controls any other rhythmic physiological activity.
2 another term for **PACESETTER**.
– DERIVATIVES **pace·mak·ing** /-ˌmākiNG/ **adj. & n.**

pace notes ▶ **plural n.** (in rally driving) notes made before a rally by a competitor about the characteristics of a particular course, esp. with regard to advisable speeds for each section.

pac·er /ˈpāsər/ ▶ **n. 1** a pacesetter.
2 a horse bred or trained to have a distinctive lateral gait in which both legs on the same side are lifted together, used in some types of racing.

pace·set·ter /ˈpāsˌsetər/ ▶ **n.** a runner or competitor who sets the pace at the beginning of a race or competition, sometimes in order to help another runner break a record. ■ a person or organization viewed as taking the lead or setting standards of achievement for others: *Alaska is the pacesetter when it comes to salaries for teachers*.
– DERIVATIVES **pace·set·ting adj. & n.**

pa·cha ▶ **n.** variant spelling of **PASHA** (sense 1).

pa·chin·ko /pəˈCHiNGkō/ ▶ **n.** a Japanese form of pinball.
– ORIGIN Japanese.

pa·chi·si /pəˈCHēzē/ ▶ **n.** a four-person Indian board game in which cowrie shells are thrown to determine the movements of pieces around the board. ■ (also trademark **Parcheesi** /pärˈCHēzē/) a modern version of this game, using four marbles per player and dice.
– ORIGIN from Hindi *paccīsī*, literally '(throw) of 25' (the highest of the game).

Pa·chu·ca de So·to /päˈCHōōkə de ˈsōtō/ (also **Pachuca**) a city in Mexico, capital of the state of Hidalgo; pop. 267,751 (2005).

pa·chu·co /pəˈCHōōkō/ ▶ **n.** (pl. **pachucos**) dated a juvenile gang member of Mexican-American ethnic origin.
– ORIGIN Mexican Spanish, literally 'flashily dressed.'

pach·y·ceph·a·lo·saur /ˌpakiˈsefələˌsôr/ ▶ **n.** a bipedal herbivorous dinosaur of the late Cretaceous period with a thick domed skull. ● Infraorder Pachycephalosauria, order Ornithischia: several genera, including *Pachycephalosaurus*.
– ORIGIN from Greek *pakhus* 'thick' + *kephalē* 'head' + *sauros* 'lizard.'

pach·y·derm /ˈpakəˌdərm/ ▶ **n.** a very large mammal with thick skin, esp. an elephant, rhinoceros, or hippopotamus.
– DERIVATIVES **pach·y·der·mal** /ˌpakəˈdərməl/ **adj.**, **pach·y·der·ma·tous** /ˌpakəˈdərmətəs/ **adj.**, **pach·y·der·mic** /ˌpakəˈdərmik/ **adj.**
– ORIGIN mid 19th cent.: from French *pachyderme*, from Greek *pakhudermos*, from *pakhus* 'thick' + *derma* 'skin.'

pach·y·san·dra /ˌpakiˈsandrə/ ▶ **n.** an evergreen creeping shrubby plant of the box family. ● Genus *Pachysandra*, family Buxaceae: several species, in particular the Japanese *P. terminalis*.
– ORIGIN formed irregularly from Greek *pakhus* 'thick' + *anēr*, *andr-* 'male' (with reference to the thick stamens).

pach·y·tene /ˈpakəˌtēn/ ▶ **n.** Biology the third stage of the prophase of meiosis, following zygotene, during which the paired chromosomes shorten and thicken, the two chromatids of each separate, and exchange of segments between chromatids may occur.
– ORIGIN early 20th cent.: from Greek *pakhus* 'thick' + *tainia* 'band.'

pa·cif·ic /pəˈsifik/ ▶ **adj. 1** peaceful in character or intent: *a pacific gesture*.
2 (**Pacific**) of or relating to the Pacific Ocean: *the Pacific War*.
▶ **n.** (**Pacific**) **1** short for **PACIFIC OCEAN**.
2 a steam locomotive of 4-6-2 wheel arrangement.
– DERIVATIVES **pa·cif·i·cal·ly** /-(ə)lē/ **adv.**
– ORIGIN mid 16th cent.: from French *pacifique* or Latin *pacificus* 'peacemaking,' from *pax*, *pac-* 'peace.'

Pa·cif·ic Crest Trail a recreational trail that extends from the Mexican to the Canadian border, from California to Washington, and that follows mountain ridges for 2,600 miles (4,200 km).

Pa·cif·ic Is·land·er ▶ **n.** a native or inhabitant of any of the islands in the South Pacific, esp. an aboriginal native of Polynesia.

Pa·cif·ic Is·lands, Trust Ter·ri·to·ry of the a UN trusteeship established in 1947 under US administration and dissolved in 1994. It included the Caroline, Marshall, and Mariana islands, today all components of the Marshall Islands, the

Northern Mariana Islands, the Federated States of Micronesia, or Palau.

Pa·cif·ic O·cean /pəˈsifik/ the largest of the world's oceans. It lies between America on the east and Asia and Australasia on the west.

Pa·cif·ic Rim the countries and regions bordering the Pacific Ocean, esp. the small nations of eastern Asia.

Pa·cif·ic time the standard time in a zone including the Pacific coastal region of the US and Canada, specifically. ● (**Pacific Standard Time**, abbr.: **PST**) standard time based on the mean solar time at longitude 120° W, eight hours behind GMT. ● (**Pacific Daylight Time**, abbr.: **PDT**) Pacific time during daylight saving time, seven hours behind GMT.

pac·i·fi·er /ˈpasəˌfīər/ ▶ **n.** a person or thing that pacifies. ■ a rubber or plastic nipple for a baby to suck on.

pac·i·fism /ˈpasəˌfizəm/ ▶ **n.** the belief that any violence, including war, is unjustifiable under any circumstances, and that all disputes should be settled by peaceful means.
– ORIGIN early 20th cent.: from French *pacifisme*, from *pacifier* 'pacify.'

pac·i·fist /ˈpasəˌfist/ ▶ **n.** a person who believes that war and violence are unjustifiable: *she was a committed pacifist all her life.*
▶ **adj.** holding the belief that war and violence are unjustifiable.
– DERIVATIVES **pac·i·fis·tic** /ˌpasəˈfistik/ **adj.**

pac·i·fy /ˈpasəˌfī/ ▶ **v.** (**pacifies, pacifying, pacified**) [with obj.] quell the anger, agitation, or excitement of: *he had to pacify angry spectators.* ■ bring peace to (a country or warring factions), esp. by the use or threatened use of military force: *the general pacified northern Italy.*
– DERIVATIVES **pa·cif·i·ca·tion** /ˌpasifiˈkāsHən/ **n.**, **pa·cif·i·ca·to·ry** /pəˈsifikəˌtôrē/ **adj.**
– ORIGIN late 15th cent.: from Old French *pacefier*, from Latin *pacificare*, based on *pax, pac-* 'peace.'

Pa·cin·i·an cor·pus·cle /pəˈsinēən/ ▶ **n.** Anatomy an encapsulated ending of a sensory nerve that acts as a receptor for pressure and vibration.
– ORIGIN late 19th cent.: named after Filippo *Pacini* (1812–83), Italian anatomist.

Pa·ci·no /pəˈcHēnō/, Al (1940–), US movie actor; full name *Alfred James Pacino*. Notable movies: *The Godfather* (1972), *Serpico* (1973), *The Godfather Part II* (1974), *Scarface* (1983), *Scent of a Woman* (1992), *Carlito's Way* (1993), and *Ocean's Thirteen* (2007).

pack[1] /pak/ ▶ **n. 1** a small cardboard or paper container and the items contained within it: ***a pack of cigarettes.*** ■ a set of playing cards. ■ a knapsack or backpack. ■ a collection of related documents, esp. one kept in a folder: *an information pack.* ■ (often **the pack**) a quantity of fish, fruit, or other foods packed or canned in a particular season or year.
2 a group of wild animals, esp. wolves, living and hunting together. ■ a group of hounds kept and used for hunting, esp. fox hunting. ■ an organized group of Cub Scouts. ■ (**the pack**) the main body of competitors following the leader or leaders in a race or competition: figurative *the company was demonstrating the kind of innovations needed to keep it ahead of the pack.* ■ chiefly derogatory a group or set of similar things or people: *the reports were a pack of lies.* ■ short for PACK ICE. ■ Rugby a team's forwards considered as a group.
3 a hot or cold pad of absorbent material, esp. as used for treating an injury. ■ a cosmetic mask.
▶ **v.** [with obj.] fill (a suitcase or bag), esp. with clothes and other items needed when away from home: *I packed a bag with a few of my favorite clothes* | [no obj.] *she had packed and checked out of the hotel.* ■ place (something) in a container, esp. for transportation or storage: *I packed up my stuff and drove to Detroit.* ■ [no obj.] be capable of being folded up for transportation or storage: *these silver foil blankets pack into a small area.* ■ (**pack something in**) store something perishable in (a specified substance) in order to preserve it: *the organs were packed in ice.* ■ informal carry (a gun): *a sixteen-year-old can make a fortune selling drugs and pack a gun in the process.* ■ cram a large number of things into (a container or space): *it was a large room, packed with beds jammed side by side.* ■ (often as adj. **packed**) (of a large number of people) crowd into and fill (a room, building, or place): *the waiting room was packed.* ■ cover, surround, or fill (something): *he packed the wounds with healing malaguetta.* ■ [no obj.] Rugby (of players) form or take their places in a scrum: *we often packed down with only seven men.*
– PHRASES **pack heat** informal carry a gun. **pack it in** informal stop what one is doing. **pack a punch** be capable of hitting with skill or force: *Rosie could pack a hefty punch.* ■ have a powerful effect: *the Spanish wine packed quite a punch.* **packed out** Brit. informal (of a place) very crowded. **send someone packing** informal make someone leave in an abrupt or peremptory way.
– PHRASAL VERBS **pack something in** informal give up an activity or job. **pack someone off** informal send someone somewhere without much warning or notice: *they packed me off to the academy in Baltimore.* **pack something out** carry something away rather than leaving it behind (used esp. with respect to refuse at remote campsites): *pack out any garbage you have left.*
– DERIVATIVES **pack·a·ble adj.**
– ORIGIN Middle English: from Middle Dutch and Middle Low German *pak* (noun), *pakken* (verb). The verb appears early in Anglo-Latin and Anglo-Norman French in connection with the wool trade; trade in English wool was chiefly with the Low Countries.

pack[2] ▶ **v.** [with obj.] fill (a jury, committee, etc.) with people likely to support a particular verdict or decision: *his efforts to pack the Supreme Court with men who shared his ideology.*
– DERIVATIVES **packed adj.**
– ORIGIN early 16th cent. (in the sense 'enter into a private agreement'): probably from the obsolete verb *pact* 'enter into an agreement with,' the final *-t* being interpreted as an inflection of the past tense.

pack·age /ˈpakij/ ▶ **n.** an object or group of objects wrapped in paper or plastic, or packed in a box. ■ the box or bag in which things are packed. ■ (also **package deal**) a set of proposals or terms offered or agreed to as a whole: *a package of economic reforms.* ■ informal a package tour. ■ Computing a collection of programs or subroutines with related functionality.
▶ **v.** [with obj.] (usu. **be packaged**) put into a box or wrapping, esp. for sale: *choose products that are packaged in recyclable materials* | (as adj. **packaged**) *packaged foods.* ■ present (someone or something) in a particular way, esp. to make them more attractive: (as adj., with submodifier **packaged**) *everything became a carefully packaged photo opportunity.* ■ combine (various products) for sale as one unit: *films would be packaged with the pictures of a production company.* ■ commission and produce (a book, typically a highly illustrated one) to sell as a complete product to publishers: *it's a question of trying to package the book properly.*
– DERIVATIVES **pack·ag·er n.**
– ORIGIN mid 16th cent. (as a noun denoting the action or mode of packing goods): from the verb PACK[1] + -AGE; compare with Anglo-Latin *paccagium*. The verb dates from the 1920s.

pack·age store ▶ **n.** a store that sells alcoholic beverages in sealed containers for consumption elsewhere; a liquor store.

pack·age tour ▶ **n.** a vacation organized by a travel agent, with arrangements for transportation, accommodations, etc., made at an inclusive price.

pack·ag·ing /ˈpakijiNG/ ▶ **n.** materials used to wrap or protect goods. ■ the business or process of packing goods. ■ the presentation of a person, product, or action in a particular way: *diplomatic packaging of the key provisions will make a confrontation unlikely.*

pack an·i·mal ▶ **n. 1** an animal used to carry heavy loads.
2 an animal that lives and hunts in a pack.

pack·cloth /ˈpakˌklôTH/ ▶ **n.** a thick, coarse cloth used for packing.

pack drill ▶ **n.** a military punishment of marching back and forth carrying full equipment.
– PHRASES **no names, no pack drill** punishment will be prevented if names and details are not mentioned.

packed lunch ▶ **n.** Brit. a bag lunch.

pack·er /ˈpakər/ ▶ **n.** a person or machine that packs something, esp. someone who prepares and packs food for transportation and sale.

pack·et /ˈpakit/ ▶ **n. 1** a paper or cardboard container, typically one in which goods are packed to be sold: ***a packet of cigarettes.*** ■ the contents of such a container. ■ a block of data transmitted across a network.
2 (also **packet boat**) dated a ship traveling at regular intervals between two ports, originally for the conveyance of mail.
▶ **v.** (**packets, packeting, packeted**) [with obj.] make up into or wrap up in a packet: *packet a basket of take-out and head for Gooseberry Beach.*
– ORIGIN mid 16th cent.: diminutive of PACK[1], perhaps from Anglo-Norman French; compare with Anglo-Latin *paccettum*.

pack·e·tize /ˈpakəˌtīz/ ▶ **v.** [with obj.] Computing partition or separate (data) into units for transmission in a packet-switching network: *this layer packetizes and reassembles messages.*

pack·et net·work ▶ **n.** Computing a data transmission network using packet switching.

pack·et ra·di·o ▶ **n.** a method of broadcasting that makes use of radio signals carrying packets of data.

pack·et sniff·er ▶ **n.** Computing a sniffer program that targets packets of data transmitted over the Internet.

pack·et switch·ing ▶ **n.** Computing & Telecommunications a mode of data transmission in which a message is broken into a number of parts that are sent independently, over whatever route is optimum for each packet, and reassembled at the destination. Compare with MESSAGE SWITCHING.

pack·frame /ˈpakˌfrām/ ▶ **n.** a frame to which a backpack is attached to make it easier to carry.

pack·horse /ˈpakˌhôrs/ ▶ **n.** a horse used to carry loads.

pack ice ▶ **n.** an expanse of large pieces of floating ice driven together into a nearly continuous mass, as occurs in polar seas.

pack·ing /ˈpakiNG/ ▶ **n.** the action or process of packing something: *the handling, packing, and shipping of products.* ■ material used to protect fragile goods, esp. in transit: *polystyrene packing.* ■ material used to seal a joint or assist in lubricating an axle.

pack·ing case (also **packing box** or **packing crate**) ▶ **n.** a large strong box, typically a wooden one, in which goods are packed for transportation or storage.

pack·ing den·si·ty ▶ **n.** Computing the density of stored information in terms of bits per unit occupied of its storage medium.

pack·man /ˈpakmən/ ▶ **n.** (pl. **packmen**) archaic a peddler.

pack rat ▶ **n.** a ratlike rodent that accumulates a mound of sticks and debris in the nest hole, native to North and Central America. Also called WOOD RAT. ● *Neotoma* and other genera, family Muridae: many species. ■ a person who saves unnecessary objects or hoards things.

pack·sack /ˈpakˌsak/ ▶ **n.** a knapsack or backpack.

pack·sad·dle /ˈpakˌsadl/ ▶ **n.** a horse's saddle designed for supporting packs.

pack·thread /ˈpakˌTHred/ ▶ **n.** thick thread for sewing or tying up packages.

pact /pakt/ ▶ **n.** a formal agreement between individuals or parties.
– ORIGIN late Middle English: from Old French, from Latin *pactum* 'something agreed upon,' neuter past participle (used as a noun) of *paciscere* 'agree.'

pa·cu /ˈpako͞o, paˈko͞o/ ▶ **n.** (pl. **same**) a deep-bodied, herbivorous freshwater fish native to northern South America. ● *Colossoma nigripinnis*, family Characidae.
– ORIGIN early 19th cent.: from Tupi *pacú*.

pad[1] /pad/ ▶ **n. 1** a thick piece of soft material used to reduce friction or jarring, enlarge or change the shape of something, or hold or absorb liquid: *sterile gauze pads.* ■ short for INK PAD. ■ the fleshy underpart of an animal's foot or of a human finger. ■ a protective guard worn by a sports player to protect a part of the body from blows.
2 a number of sheets of blank paper fastened together at one edge, used for writing or drawing on.
3 a flat-topped structure or area used for helicopter takeoff and landing or for rocket launching. ■ Electronics a flat area on a track of a printed circuit or on the edge of an integrated circuit to which wires or component leads can be attached to make an electrical connection.
4 informal a person's home: *the police raided my pad.*
5 short for LILY PAD.
▶ **v.** (**pads, padding, padded**) [with obj.] (often as adj. **padded**) fill or cover (something) with a soft material in order to give it a particular shape, protect it or its contents, or make it more comfortable: *a padded envelope.* ■ add false items to (an expense report or bill) in order to receive unjustified payment: *faked repairs and padded expenses for government work reaped billions of dollars for the Mafia.*
– ORIGIN mid 16th cent. (in the sense 'bundle of straw to lie on'): the senses may not be of common origin; the meaning 'underpart of an animal's foot' is perhaps related to Low German *pad* 'sole of the foot'; the history remains obscure.

pad[2] ▶ **v.** (**pads, padding, padded**) [no obj.] walk with steady steps making a soft dull sound: *she padded*

P

along the corridor. ■ [with obj.] travel along (a road or route) on foot: *he was padding the streets*.
▶ n. [in sing.] the soft dull sound of steady steps: *he heard the pad of feet*.
– ORIGIN mid 16th cent.: from Low German *padden* 'to tread, go along a path,' partly imitative.

Pa·dang /pä'däng, 'pädäng/ a seaport in Indonesia, the largest city on the west coast of Sumatra; pop. 686,900 (est. 2005).

pa·dauk /pə'douk/ (also **padouk**) ▶ n. **1** timber from a tropical tree of the pea family, resembling rosewood.
2 the large hardwood tree of the Old World tropics that is widely grown for this timber. Some kinds yield a red dye that is used for religious and ritual purposes. ● Genus *Pterocarpus*, family Leguminosae: three species, in particular **African padauk** (*P. soyauxii*).
– ORIGIN mid 19th cent.: from Burmese.

pad·ded cell ▶ n. a room in a psychiatric hospital with padding on the walls to prevent violent patients from injuring themselves.

pad·ding /'padiNG/ ▶ n. soft material such as foam or cloth used to pad or stuff something. ■ superfluous material in a book, speech, etc., introduced in order to make it reach a desired length.

pad·dle[1] /'padl/ ▶ n. a short pole with a broad blade at one or both ends, used without an oarlock to move a small boat or canoe through the water. ■ an act of using a paddle in a boat: *a gentle paddle on sluggish water*. ■ a short-handled bat used in various ball games, esp. table tennis. ■ a paddle-shaped instrument used for mixing food or for stirring or mixing in industrial processes. ■ another term for **PEEL**[2]. ■ informal a paddle-shaped instrument used for administering corporal punishment. ■ each of the boards fitted around the circumference of a paddle wheel or mill wheel. ■ a flat array of solar cells projecting from a spacecraft. ■ the fin or flipper of an aquatic mammal or bird. ■ Medicine a plastic-covered electrode used in cardiac stimulation. ■ short for **BIDDING PADDLE**.
▶ v. **1** [no obj.] move through the water in a boat using a paddle or paddles: *he paddled along the coast*. ■ [with obj.] propel (a small boat or canoe) with a paddle or paddles: *he was teaching trainees to paddle canoes*. ■ [with obj.] travel along (a stretch of water) using such a method: *I had paddled the river through other hot July spells*. ■ (of a bird or other animal) swim with short fast strokes: *the swan paddled away*.
2 [with obj.] informal beat (someone) with a paddle as a punishment: *he was firm in his conviction that his children would never be paddled*.
– PHRASES **paddle one's own canoe** informal be independent and self-sufficient.
– DERIVATIVES **pad·dler** n.
– ORIGIN late Middle English (denoting a small spadelike implement): of unknown origin. Current senses date from the 17th cent.

pad·dle[2] ▶ v. [no obj.] walk with bare feet in shallow water: *the children paddled at the water's edge*. ■ dabble the feet or hands in water: *Peter paddled idly in the water with his fingers*.
▶ n. [in sing.] an act of walking with bare feet in shallow water.
– DERIVATIVES **pad·dler** n.
– ORIGIN mid 16th cent.: of obscure origin; compare with Low German *paddeln* 'tramp around'; the association with water remains unexplained.

pad·dle·ball /'padl,bôl/ ▶ n. a game played with a light ball and wooden bat in a four-walled handball court.

pad·dle·boat /'padl,bōt/ ▶ n. a small pleasure boat driven by pedals that in turn drive a paddle wheel.

pad·dle·fish /'padl,fisH/ ▶ n. (pl. **same** or **paddlefishes**) a large, mainly freshwater fish related to the sturgeon, with an elongated snout. ● The plankton-feeding *Polyodon spathula* of the Mississippi basin, and the fish-eating *Psephurus gladius* of the Yangtze River, the only surviving members of the family Polyodontidae.

pad·dle steam·er ▶ n. a boat powered by steam and propelled by paddle wheels.

pad·dle ten·nis ▶ n. a type of tennis played in a small court with a rubber ball and a wooden or plastic paddle.

pad·dle wheel ▶ n. a large steam-driven wheel with boards around its circumference, situated at the stern or side of a ship so as to propel the ship through the water by its rotation.

pad·dling pool /'padliNG/ ▶ n. British term for **WADING POOL**.

pad·dock /'padək/ ▶ n. a small field or enclosure where horses are kept or exercised. ■ an enclosure adjoining a racetrack where horses are gathered and displayed before a race.
▶ v. [with obj.] (usu. **be paddocked**) keep or enclose (a horse) in a paddock: *horses paddocked on a hillside*.
– ORIGIN early 17th cent.: apparently a variant of dialect *parrock*, of unknown ultimate origin.

Pad·dy /'padē/ ▶ n. (pl. **Paddies**) informal, usu. offensive an Irishman (often as a form of address).
– ORIGIN late 18th cent.: nickname for the Irish given name *Padraig*.

pad·dy /'padē/ ▶ n. (pl. **paddies**) (also **rice paddy**) a field where rice is grown. ■ rice before threshing or in the husk.
– ORIGIN early 17th cent.: from Malay *pādī*.

pad·dy·mel·on ▶ n. variant spelling of **PADEMELON**.

pad·dy wag·on ▶ n. informal a police van.
– ORIGIN 1930s: *paddy* from **PADDY**, perhaps because formerly many American police officers were of Irish descent.

pad·e·mel·on /'padē,melən/ (also **paddymelon**) ▶ n. a small wallaby inhabiting the coastal scrub of Australia and New Guinea. ● Genus *Thylogale*, family Macropodidae: three species.
– ORIGIN early 19th cent. (earlier as *paddymelon*): probably an alteration of Dharuk *badimalion*.

Pa·de·rew·ski /,padə'refskē, ,päd-/, Ignacy Jan (1860–1941), Polish pianist, composer, and statesman; prime minister 1919. He was the first prime minister of independent Poland, but resigned after only 10 months in office to resume his musical career.

pad eye ▶ n. a flat metal plate with a projecting loop or ring, made all in one piece.

pa·di·shah /,pädə'sHä/ ▶ n. historical a title formerly used for various rulers, including the shah of Iran and the sultan of Turkey.

pad·lock /'pad,läk/ ▶ n. a detachable lock hanging by a pivoted hook on the object fastened.
▶ v. [with obj.] (usu. as adj. **padlocked**) secure with such a lock: *a padlocked door*.
– ORIGIN late 15th cent.: from *pad-* (of unknown origin) + the noun **LOCK**[1].

Pad·ma /'padmə/ a river in southern Bangladesh, formed by the confluence of the Ganges and the Brahmaputra rivers near Rajbari.

pa·douk ▶ n. variant spelling of **PADAUK**.

Pa·do·va /'pädōvä/ Italian name for **PADUA**.

pa·dre /'pädrā/ ▶ n. the title of a priest or chaplain in some regions. ■ informal a chaplain (typically a Roman Catholic chaplain) in any of the armed services.
– ORIGIN late 16th cent.: from Italian, Spanish, and Portuguese, literally 'father, priest,' from Latin *pater, patr-* 'father.'

Pad·re Is·land /'pädrā/ a barrier island in southern Texas, on the Gulf of Mexico, 113 miles (183 km) long, noted for its resorts and its wildlife.

pa·dri·no /pə'drēnō/ ▶ n. (pl. **padrinos**) a godfather or patron. ■ a best man at a wedding.
– ORIGIN Spanish.

pa·dro·na /pə'drōnə/ ▶ n. (pl. **padronas**) a female boss or proprietress.
– ORIGIN Italian.

pa·dro·ne /pə'drōnā, pə'drōnē/ ▶ n. (pl. **padrones** /-'drōnāz, -'drōnz/) a patron or master, in particular: ■ a Mafia boss. ■ informal an employer, esp. one who exploits immigrant workers. ■ (in Italy) the proprietor of a hotel.
– ORIGIN Italian.

pad·saw /'pad,sô/ ▶ n. a small saw with a narrow blade, for cutting curves.

pad site ▶ n. a building lot adjacent to a shopping center or mall.

pad thai /,päd 'tī/ ▶ n. a Thai dish based on rice noodles.
– ORIGIN Thai.

Pad·u·a /'pajo͞oə/ a city in northeastern Italy; pop. 211,936 (2008). Italian name **PADOVA**.
– DERIVATIVES **Pad·u·an** adj.

pad·u·a·soy /'pajo͞oə,soi/ ▶ n. a heavy, rich corded or embossed silk fabric, popular in the 18th century.
– ORIGIN late 16th cent. (as *poudesoy*), from French *pou-de-soie*, of unknown origin; altered by association with *Padua say*, denoting a cloth resembling serge.

Pa·du·cah /pə'd(y)o͞okə/ a historic commercial city in western Kentucky, on the Ohio River, near the mouth of the Tennessee River; pop. 25,521 (est. 2008).

pae·an /'pēən/ ▶ n. a song of praise or triumph. ■ a thing that expresses enthusiastic praise: *his books are paeans to combat*.
– ORIGIN late 16th cent.: via Latin from Greek *paian* 'hymn of thanksgiving to Apollo' (invoked by the name *Paian*, originally the Homeric name for the physician of the gods).

pae·di·at·rics ▶ plural n. British spelling of **PEDIATRICS**.

paedo- ▶ comb. form British spelling of **PEDO-**[1].

pa·el·la /pä'äyä, pə'elə/ ▶ n. a Spanish dish of rice, saffron, chicken, seafood, etc., cooked and served in a large shallow pan.
– ORIGIN Catalan, from Old French *paele*, from Latin *patella* 'pan.'

pae·on /'pēən/ ▶ n. Prosody a metrical foot of one long syllable and three short syllables in any order.
– DERIVATIVES **pae·on·ic** /pē'änik/ adj.
– ORIGIN early 17th cent.: via Latin from Greek *paiōn*, the Attic form of *paian* 'hymn of thanksgiving to Apollo' (see **PAEAN**).

Pa·gan /pə'gän/ ruins in Burma (Myanmar), located on the Irrawaddy River southeast of Mandalay. It is the site of an ancient city that was the capital of a powerful Buddhist dynasty from the 11th to the 13th centuries.

pa·gan /'pāgən/ ▶ n. a person holding religious beliefs other than those of the main world religions. ■ dated, derogatory a non-Christian. ■ an adherent of neopaganism.
▶ adj. of or relating to such people or beliefs: *a pagan god*.
– DERIVATIVES **pa·gan·ish** adj., **pa·gan·ism** /-,nizəm/ n., **pa·gan·ize** /-,nīz/ v.
– ORIGIN late Middle English: from Latin *paganus* 'villager, rustic,' from *pagus* 'country district.' Latin *paganus* also meant 'civilian,' becoming, in Christian Latin, 'heathen' (i.e., one not enrolled in the army of Christ).

Pa·ga·ni·ni /,pagə'nēnē, ,pä-/, Niccolò (1782–1840), Italian violinist and composer. His virtuoso violin recitals, including widespread use of pizzicato and harmonics, established him as a major figure of the romantic movement.

Page /pāj/, Geraldine (Sue) (1924–87), US actress. Her Broadway credits include *Sweet Bird of Youth* (1959), *Strange Interlude* (1963), and *Agnes of God* (1982). Her movies include *Hondo* (1953), *Summer and Smoke* (1961), and *The Trip to Bountiful* (1985).

page[1] /pāj/ ▶ n. one side of a sheet of paper in a collection of sheets bound together, esp. as a book, magazine, or newspaper. ■ the material written or printed on such a sheet of paper: *she silently read several pages*. ■ [with modifier] a page of a newspaper or magazine set aside for a particular topic: *the editorial page*. ■ Printing the type set for the printing of a page. ■ Computing a section of stored data, esp. that which can be displayed on a screen at one time. ■ a significant episode or period considered as a part of a longer history: *the inconsistency of this transaction has no parallel on any page of our political history*.
▶ v. **1** [no obj.] (**page through**) leaf through (a book, magazine, or newspaper): *she was paging through an immense pile of Sunday newspapers*. ■ Computing move through and display (text) one page at a time.
2 [with obj.] (usu. as noun **paging**) Computing divide (a piece of software or data) into sections, keeping the most frequently accessed in main memory and storing the rest in virtual memory.
3 [with obj.] assign numbers to the pages in (a book or periodical); paginate.
– PHRASES **on the same page** (of two or more people) in agreement.
– DERIVATIVES **paged** adj. [in combination] *a many-paged volume*.
– ORIGIN late 16th cent.: from French, from Latin *pagina*, from *pangere* 'fasten.'

page[2] ▶ n. a young person, usually in uniform, employed in a hotel or other establishment to run errands, open doors, etc. ■ a young boy attending a bride at a wedding. ■ historical a boy in training for knighthood, ranking next below a squire in the personal service of a knight. ■ historical a man or boy employed as the personal attendant of a person of rank.
▶ v. [with obj.] summon (an individual) by name, typically over a public address system, so as to pass on a message: *no need to interrupt the background music just to page the concierge*. ■ (often as noun **paging**) contact (someone) by means of a pager: *many systems have paging as a standard feature*.
– ORIGIN Middle English (in the sense 'youth, male of uncouth manners'): from Old French, perhaps from Italian *paggio*, from Greek *paidion*, diminutive of *pais, paid-* 'boy.' Early use of the verb (mid 16th cent.) was in the sense 'follow as or like a page'; its current sense dates from the early 20th cent.

pag·eant /'pajənt/ ▶ n. a public entertainment consisting of a procession of people in elaborate, colorful costumes, or an outdoor performance of a historical scene. ■ (also **beauty pageant**) a beauty contest. ■ historical a scene erected on a fixed stage or moving vehicle as a public show.
– ORIGIN late Middle English *pagyn*, of unknown origin.

pag·eant·ry /ˈpajəntrē/ ▶ **n.** elaborate display or ceremony.

page·boy /ˈpāj,boi/ ▶ **n.**
1 a woman's hairstyle consisting of a shoulder-length bob with the ends rolled under.
2 a male page, esp. in a hotel or attending a bride at a wedding.

pageboy 1

page-one ▶ **adj.** worthy of being featured on the front page of a newspaper or magazine: *page-one news.*

page proof ▶ **n.** a printer's proof of a page to be published.

pag·er /ˈpājər/ ▶ **n.** an electronic device, usually worn on one's person, that receives messages and signals the user by beeping or vibrating.

Pag·et's dis·ease /ˈpajits/ ▶ **n. 1** a chronic disease of elderly people characterized by deterioration of bone tissue, esp. in the spine, skull, or pelvis, sometimes causing severe pain; osteitis deformans.
2 an inflammation of the nipple associated with breast cancer.
– ORIGIN late 19th cent.: named after Sir James *Paget* (1814–99), English surgeon.

page-turn·er ▶ **n.** informal an exciting book.

pag·i·nal /ˈpajənəl/ ▶ **adj.** of or relating to the pages of a book or periodical.
– ORIGIN mid 17th cent.: from late Latin *paginalis*, from *pagina* (see **PAGE**[1]).

pag·i·na·tion /,pajəˈnāsʜən/ ▶ **n.** the sequence of numbers assigned to pages in a book or periodical.
– DERIVATIVES **pag·i·nate** /ˈpajə,nāt/ **v.**
– ORIGIN mid 19th cent.: noun of action from *paginate*, from French *paginer*, based on Latin *pagina* 'a page' (see **PAGE**[1]).

Pa·gnol /pänˈyôl/, Marcel (1895–1974), French playwright, movie director, and writer. His novels include *La Gloire de mon père* (1957) and *Le Chateau de ma mère* (1958); the movies *Jean de Florette* and *Manon des Sources* (both 1986) were based on his *L'Eau des collines* (1963).

pa·go·da /pəˈgōdə/ ▶ **n.** a Hindu or Buddhist temple or sacred building, typically a many-tiered tower, in India and East Asia. ■ an ornamental imitation of this.
– ORIGIN late 16th cent.: from Portuguese *pagode*, perhaps based on Persian *butkada* 'temple of idols,' influenced by Prakrit *bhagodī* 'divine.'

pagoda

pa·go·da sleeve ▶ **n.** a funnel-shaped outer sleeve turned back to expose an inner sleeve and lining.

pa·go·da tree ▶ **n.** a Southeast Asian tree of the pea family that has hanging clusters of cream flowers and is cultivated as an ornamental. ● *Sophora japonica*, family Leguminosae.

Pa·go Pa·go /ˈpäɴɢ(g)ō ˈpäɴɢ(g)ō, ˈpägō ˈpägō/ the chief port of American Samoa, on Tutuila Island; pop. 4,600 (est. 2009). Fagatogo, the territorial capital, is just to the east.

PAH ▶ **abbr.** polycyclic aromatic hydrocarbon, any of a group of chemicals formed during the incomplete burning of organic substances.

pah /pä/ ▶ **exclam.** used to express disgust or contempt: *"Pah! They know nothing."*
– ORIGIN natural utterance: first recorded in English in the late 16th cent.

Pah·la·vi[1] /ˈpälə,vē/ the name of two shahs of Iran. ■ **Reza** (1878–1944), ruled 1925–41; born *Reza Khan*. An army officer, he took control of the Persian government after a coup in 1921. He was elected shah in 1925 but abdicated following the occupation of Iran by British and Soviet forces. ■ **Muhammad Reza** (1919–80), ruled 1941–79; son of Reza Pahlavi; also known as **Reza Shah**. Opposition to his regime culminated in the Islamic revolution of 1979 under Ayatollah Khomeini; Reza Shah was forced into exile and died in Egypt.

Pah·la·vi[2] (also **Pehlevi**) ▶ **n.** an Aramaic-based writing system used in Persia from the 2nd century BC to the advent of Islam in the 7th century AD. It was also used for the recording of ancient Avestan sacred texts. ■ the form of the Middle Persian language written in this script, used in the Sassanian empire.
– ORIGIN from Persian *pahlawī*, from *pahlav*, from *parthava* 'Parthia.'

pa·ho·e·ho·e /pəˈhōē,hōē/ ▶ **n.** Geology basaltic lava forming smooth undulating or ropy masses. Often contrasted with **AA**.
– ORIGIN mid 19th cent.: from Hawaiian.

paid /pād/ past and past participle of **PAY**[1].
▶ **adj.** (of work or leave) for or during which one receives pay: *a one-month paid vacation.* ■ [attrib.] (of a person in a specified occupation) in receipt of pay: *a paid, anonymous informer.*

pai·deia /pīˈdāə/ ▶ **n.** (in ancient Greece) education or upbringing. ■ the culture of a society.
– ORIGIN Greek.

paid-up ▶ **adj.** [attrib.] (of a member of an organization, esp. a labor union) having paid the necessary dues in full. ■ denoting the part of the subscribed capital of an undertaking that has actually been paid: *paid-up capital.* ■ denoting an endowment policy in which the policyholder has stopped paying premiums, resulting in the surrender value being used to purchase single-premium whole life insurance.

Paige /pāj/, Satchel (1906–82), US baseball player; born *Leroy Robert Paige*. A pitcher for the Negro leagues 1924–47 and the major leagues, he threw 55 career no-hitters. He pitched for the Cleveland Indians 1948–49, the St. Louis Browns 1951–53, and the Kansas City Athletics 1965. Baseball Hall of Fame (1971).

pail /pāl/ ▶ **n.** a bucket.
– DERIVATIVES **pail·ful** /-,fo͝ol/ **n.** (pl. **pailfuls**).
– ORIGIN Middle English: origin uncertain; compare with Old English *pægel* 'gill, small measure' and Old French *paelle* 'pan, liquid measure, brazier.'

Pai·lin /ˈpäˈlin/ a ruby-mining town in western Cambodia, close to the border with Thailand.

pail·lasse /,palˈyas, ˈpal,yas/ ▶ **n.** variant spelling of **PALLIASSE**.

pail·lette /pīˈyet, pä-, pəˈlet/ ▶ **n.** a piece of glittering material used to ornament clothing; a spangle. ■ a piece of bright metal used in enamel painting.
– ORIGIN mid 19th cent.: from French, diminutive of *paille*, from Latin *palea* 'straw, chaff.'

pain /pān/ ▶ **n. 1** physical suffering or discomfort caused by illness or injury: *she's in great pain | those who suffer from back pain | chest pains.* ■ mental suffering or distress: *the pain of loss.* ■ (also **pain in the neck** or vulgar slang **pain in the ass**) [in sing.] informal an annoying or tedious person or thing: *she's a pain.*
2 (**pains**) careful effort; great care or trouble: *she took pains to see that everyone ate well | he is at pains to point out that he isn't like that.*
▶ **v.** [with obj.] cause mental or physical pain to: *it pains me to say this | her legs had been paining her.* ■ [no obj.] (of a part of the body) hurt: *sometimes my right hand would pain.*
– PHRASES **for one's pains** informal as an unfairly bad return for efforts or trouble: *he was sued for his pains.* **no pain, no gain** suffering is necessary in order to achieve something. [originally used as a slogan in fitness classes.] **on** (or **under**) **pain of** the penalty for disobedience or shortcoming being: *all persons are commanded to keep silent on pain of imprisonment.*
– ORIGIN Middle English (in the sense 'suffering inflicted as punishment for an offense'): from Old French *peine*, from Latin *poena* 'penalty,' later 'pain.'

Paine /pān/, Thomas (1737–1809), English-American political writer. His pamphlet *Common Sense* (1776) called for American independence, and *The Rights of Man* (1791) defended the French Revolution. His radical views prompted the British government to indict him for treason, and he fled to France. He also wrote *The Age of Reason* (1794).

pained /pānd/ ▶ **adj.** affected with pain, esp. mental pain; hurt or troubled: *a pained expression came over his face | Susan looked pained.*

pain·ful /ˈpānfəl/ ▶ **adj.** (of a part of the body) affected with pain: *her ankle was very painful.* ■ causing physical pain: *a painful knock.* ■ causing distress or trouble: *a painful experience | change is inevitably slow and painful.*
– DERIVATIVES **pain·ful·ness n.**

pain·ful·ly /ˈpānfəlē/ ▶ **adv.** in a painful manner or to a painful degree: *she coughed painfully.* ■ [as submodifier] (with reference to something bad) exceedingly; acutely: *progress was painfully slow.*

pain·kil·ler /ˈpān,kilər/ ▶ **n.** a drug or medicine for relieving pain.
– DERIVATIVES **pain·kill·ing** /-,kiliɴɢ/ **adj.**

pain·less /ˈpānləs/ ▶ **adj.** not causing or suffering physical pain: *a painless death.* ■ involving little effort or stress: *a painless way to travel.*
– DERIVATIVES **pain·less·ly adv.**, **pain·less·ness n.**

pain per·du /ˈpän perˈdo͞o, paɴ perˈdʏ/ ▶ **n.** French term for **FRENCH TOAST**.
– ORIGIN French, literally 'lost bread.'

pains·tak·ing /ˈpānz,tākiɴɢ, ˈpān,stākiɴɢ/ ▶ **adj.** done with or employing great care and thoroughness: *painstaking attention to detail | he is a gentle, painstaking man.*
– DERIVATIVES **pains·tak·ing·ly adv.**, **pains·tak·ing·ness n.**

paint /pānt/ ▶ **n. 1** a colored substance that is spread over a surface and dries to leave a thin decorative or protective coating: *a can of paint | the paint has been applied to the surface with a palette knife.* ■ an act of covering something with paint: *it looked in need of a good paint.* ■ informal cosmetic makeup: *one has false curls, another too much paint.* ■ Basketball the rectangular area marked near the basket at each end of the court; the foul lane: *the two players jostled in the paint.* ■ Computing the function or capability of producing graphics, esp. those that mimic the effect of real paint: [as modifier] *a paint program.*
2 a piebald horse: [as modifier] *a paint mare.*
▶ **v.** [with obj.] **1** cover the surface of (something) with paint, as decoration or protection: *the walls hadn't been painted for years* | [with obj. and complement] *the ceiling was painted dark gray* | (as adj. with submodifier **painted**) *a brightly painted trailer.* ■ apply cosmetics to (the face or skin): *she couldn't have been more than fourteen but her face was thickly painted.* ■ apply (a liquid) to a surface with a brush. ■ (**paint something out**) efface something with paint: *the markings on the plane were hurriedly painted out.* ■ Computing create (a graphic or screen display) using a paint program. ■ display a mark representing (an aircraft or vehicle) on a radar screen.
2 depict (someone or something) or produce (a picture) with paint: *I painted a woman sitting next to a table lamp | Marr is a self-taught artist who paints portraits.* ■ give a description of (someone or something): *I'm painted as some nut case living in the woods.*
– PHRASES **like watching paint dry** (of an activity or experience) extremely boring. **paint a picture of** describe (someone or something) in a particular way: *the president painted a grim picture of life in the next century.* **paint oneself into a corner** leave oneself no means of escape or room to maneuver. **paint the town (red)** informal go out and enjoy oneself flamboyantly.
– DERIVATIVES **paint·a·ble adj.**, **paint·y adj.** (**paintier**, **paintiest**).
– ORIGIN Middle English: from *peint* 'painted,' past participle of Old French *peindre*, from Latin *pingere* 'to paint.'

paint·ball /ˈpānt,bôl/ ▶ **n.** a game in which participants simulate military combat using air guns to shoot capsules of paint at each other. ■ a capsule of paint used in this game.
– DERIVATIVES **paint·ball·er n.**

paint·box /ˈpānt,bäks/ ▶ **n.** a box holding dry paints for painting pictures. ■ (**Paintbox**) trademark an electronic system used to create video graphics by storing filmed material on disk and manipulating it using a graphics tablet.

paint·brush /ˈpānt,brəsʜ/ ▶ **n. 1** a brush for applying paint.
2 [with adj.] a North American plant that bears brightly colored flowering spikes with a brushlike appearance. See also **DEVIL'S PAINTBRUSH**. ● Genus *Castilleja*, family Scrophulariaceae: several species, including the **INDIAN PAINTBRUSH** (*C. coccinea*). Also called **PAINTED CUP**.

paint-by-num·ber ▶ **adj.** denoting a picture marked out in advance into sections that are numbered according to the color to be used. ■ denoting something mechanical or formulaic rather than imaginative, original, or natural: *a paint-by-number way to feel or act.*

paint chip ▶ **n.** a card showing a color or a range of related colors available in a type of paint.

paint·ed bunt·ing ▶ **n.** see **BUNTING**[1].

paint·ed cup ▶ **n.** see **PAINTBRUSH** (sense 2).

Paint·ed Des·ert a region in northeastern Arizona that is noted for its colorful eroded landscapes.

paint·ed la·dy ▶ **n. 1** a migratory butterfly with predominantly orange-brown wings and darker markings. ● Genus *Cynthia*, subfamily Nymphalinae, family Nymphalidae: the widely distributed *C. cardui*, with black and white markings, and the **American painted lady** (*C. virginiensis*), with markings resembling eyes on the undersides of the wings.

PRONUNCIATION KEY ə *ago, up*; ər *over, fur*; a *hat*; ā *ate*; ä *car*; e *let*; ē *see*; i *fit*; ī *by*; NG *sing*; ō *go*; ô *law, for*; oi *toy*; o͝o *good*; o͞o *goo*; ou *out*; TH *thin*; T͟H *then*; ZH *vision*

2 (also **Painted Lady**) a Victorian house, the exterior of which is painted in three or more colors, effectively highlighting the architecture.

painted lady 1

paint·ed snipe ▶ **n.** a small long-billed wading bird that has brown plumage with colorful markings. ● Family Rostratulidae: two species, in particular *Rostratula benghalensis* of the Old World.

paint·ed tur·tle ▶ **n.** a small American freshwater turtle with a smooth shell and colorful patterns of red, yellow, and black that appear along the border of the carapace and (in certain subspecies) on the plastron. ● *Chrysemys picta*, family Emydidae.

painted turtle

paint·er[1] /'pāntər/ ▶ **n. 1** an artist who paints pictures: *a German landscape painter.* **2** a person who paints buildings, walls, ceilings, and woodwork, esp. as a job.
– ORIGIN Middle English: from Anglo-Norman French *peintour*, based on Latin *pictor*, from the verb *pingere* 'to paint.'

paint·er[2] ▶ **n.** a rope attached to the bow of a boat for tying it to a quay.
– ORIGIN Middle English: of uncertain origin; compare with Old French *pentoir* 'something from which to hang things.'

paint·er[3] ▶ **n.** another term for **COUGAR**.

paint·er·ly /'pāntərlē/ ▶ **adj.** of or appropriate to a painter; artistic: *she has a painterly eye.* ■ (of a painting or its style) characterized by qualities of color, stroke, and texture rather than of line.
– DERIVATIVES **paint·er·li·ness** **n.**

paint gun ▶ **n.** an air gun firing capsules of paint, used in the game of paintball.

pain thresh·old ▶ **n.** the point beyond which a stimulus causes pain. ■ the upper limit of tolerance to pain.

paint·ing /'pāntiNG/ ▶ **n.** the process or art of using paint, in a picture, as a protective coating, or as decoration. ■ a painted picture: *an oil painting.*

paint job ▶ **n.** the decorative or finishing application of paint to an object. ■ derogatory a cosmetic treatment that does not address underlying problems: ***this administration will settle for a paint job to try to hide the fact that it lives in a La-La Land of its own construction.***

paint roll·er ▶ **n.** a roller covered in wool, sponge, synthetic fiber, or other absorbent material for applying paint to a surface, esp. in interior decorating.

paint shop ▶ **n.** the part of a factory where goods are painted, typically by spraying.

paint stick /pānt stik/ ▶ **n.** a stick of water-soluble paint used like a crayon.

paint·work /'pānt,wərk/ ▶ **n.** painted surfaces in a building or vehicle.

pair /pe(ə)r/ ▶ **n.** a set of two things used together or regarded as a unit: *a pair of gloves.* ■ an article or object consisting of two joined or corresponding parts not used separately: *a pair of jeans.* ■ two playing cards of the same denomination: *I have a pair of jacks.* ■ two people related in some way or considered together: *a company run by a pair of brothers | every naughty thing* ***the pair of them*** *did made their faces look worse | students work alone or* ***in pairs.*** ■ the second member of a pair in relation to the first: *each course member tries to persuade his pair of the merits of his model.* ■ a mated couple of animals: *nine breeding pairs of birds.* ■ two horses harnessed side by side. ■ either or both of two members of a legislative assembly on opposite sides who absent themselves from voting by mutual arrangement, leaving the relative position of the parties unaffected.
▶ **v.** [with obj.] join or connect to form a pair: *a cardigan* ***paired with*** *a matching skirt.* ■ [no obj.] (of animals) mate: *they bought a rooster to* ***pair with*** *the hen.* ■ [no obj.] (**pair off/up**) form a couple: *Rachel has* ***paired up with*** *Tommy.* ■ give (a member of a legislative assembly) another member as a pair, to allow both to absent themselves from a vote without affecting the result: *an absent member on one side is to be* ***paired with*** *an absentee on the other.*
– PHRASES **pair of hands** a person seen in terms of their participation in a task: *we can always do with an extra pair of hands.*
– DERIVATIVES **pair·wise** /-,wīz/ **adj. & adv.**
– ORIGIN Middle English: from Old French *paire*, from Latin *paria* 'equal things,' neuter plural of *par* 'equal.' Formerly phrases such as *a pair of gloves* were expressed without *of*, as in *a pair gloves* (compare with German *ein Paar Handschuhe*).

pair-bond ▶ **v.** [no obj.] (of an animal or person) form a close relationship through courtship and sexual activity with one other animal or person.
▶ **n.** (**pair bond**) a relationship so formed.

paired /pe(ə)rd/ ▶ **adj.** occurring in pairs or as a pair: *a characteristic arrangement of paired fins.*

pair·ing /'pe(ə)riNG/ ▶ **n.** an arrangement or match resulting from organizing or forming people or things into pairs: *the dancers made a fine pairing.* ■ the action of pairing things or people: *the pairing of food and wine | the step occurs very late in meiosis, well after the time of chromosome pairing.*

pair pro·duc·tion ▶ **n.** Physics the conversion of a radiation quantum into an electron and a positron.

pai·sa /'pīsä/ ▶ **n.** (pl. **paise** /-sä/) a monetary unit of Bangladesh, India, Pakistan, and Nepal, equal to one hundredth of a rupee.
– ORIGIN from Hindi *paisā*.

pai·san /pī'zän/ ▶ **n.** informal (among people of Italian or Spanish descent) a fellow countryman or friend (often as a term of address).
– ORIGIN from Italian *paisano* 'peasant, rustic.'

pai·sa·no /pī'zänō/ ▶ **n.** (pl. **paisanos**) a peasant of Spanish or Italian ethnic origin.
– ORIGIN Spanish.

pais·ley /'pāzlē/ ▶ **n.** [usu. as modifier] a distinctive intricate pattern of curved, feather-shaped figures based on a pine-cone design from India: *a paisley silk tie.*
– ORIGIN early 19th cent.: named after the town *Paisley*, Scotland, the original place of manufacture.

paisley

Pai·ute /'pī(y)o͞ot, pī'(y)o͞ot/ ▶ **n.** (pl. **same** or **Paiutes**) **1** a member of either of two culturally similar but geographically separate and linguistically distinct American Indian peoples, the **Southern Paiute** of the southwestern US and the **Northern Paiute** of Oregon and Nevada. **2** either of the Uto-Aztecan languages of these peoples.
▶ **adj.** of or relating to the Paiute or their languages.
– ORIGIN from Spanish *Payuchi*, *Payuta*, influenced by **UTE**.

pa·ja·mas /pə'jäməz, -'jaməz/ (Brit. **pyjamas**) ▶ **plural n.** a suit of loose pants and jacket or shirt for sleeping in: *a pair of pajamas* | (as modifier **pajama**) *pajama bottoms.* ■ [in sing.] (**pajama**) a pair of loose pants tied by a drawstring around the waist, worn by both sexes in some Asian countries.
– ORIGIN early 19th cent.: from Urdu and Persian, from *pāy* 'leg' + *jāma* 'clothing.'

pak choi /,päk 'CHoi/ ▶ **n.** another term for **BOK CHOY**.
– ORIGIN from Chinese (Cantonese dialect) *paâk ts'òi* 'white vegetable.'

Pa·ke·ha /'päki,hä, -kē,ä/ ▶ **n.** Austral./NZ a white New Zealander, as opposed to a Maori.
▶ **adj.** of or relating to white New Zealanders and their languages and culture.
– ORIGIN Maori.

Pakh·tun /pək'to͞on/ ▶ **n.** a form of **PATHAN**, used esp. in Asia.

Pak·i /'pakē/ ▶ **n.** (pl. **Pakis**) Brit. informal, offensive a person from Pakistan or South Asia by birth or descent, esp. one living in Britain.
– ORIGIN 1960s: abbreviation.

Pak·i·stan /'paki,stan, ,päki'stän/ a country in South Asia; pop. 174,578,600 (est. 2009); capital, Islamabad; languages, Urdu (official), English (official), Punjabi, Sindhi, and Pashto.

> Pakistan was created as a separate country in 1947, following Britain's withdrawal from India. It originally included two territories—one to the east and one to the west of India—in which the population was predominantly Muslim. Civil war in East Pakistan led to the establishment of the independent state of Bangladesh in 1972. Pakistan withdrew from the Commonwealth of Nations in 1972, but rejoined in 1989; it was suspended 1999–2004 following a military coup.

– DERIVATIVES **Pak·i·sta·ni** /,pakə'stanē, ,päki'stänē/ **adj. & n.**
– ORIGIN from *P*unjab, *A*fghan Frontier, *K*ashmir, Baluch*istan*, lands where Muslims predominated.

Pa·ki·stan Peo·ple's Par·ty (abbr.: **PPP**) one of the main political parties in Pakistan. It was founded in 1967 by Zulfikar Ali Bhutto, and was led 1984–2007 by his daughter Benazir Bhutto.

pa·ko·ra /pə'kôrə/ ▶ **n.** (in Indian cooking) a piece of vegetable or meat, coated in seasoned batter and deep-fried.
– ORIGIN from Hindi *pakorā*, denoting a dish of vegetables in gram flour.

pa kua /pä 'kwä/ ▶ **n.** variant spelling of **BA GUA**.

PAL /pal/ ▶ **n.** the television broadcasting system used in most of Europe.
– ORIGIN acronym from *Phase Alternate Line* (so named because the color information in alternate lines is inverted in phase).

pal /pal/ informal ▶ **n.** a friend: *we're best pals.* ■ used as a form of address, esp. to indicate anger or aggression: *back off, pal.*
▶ **v.** (**pals, palling, palled**) [no obj.] (**pal around**) spend time with a friend: *we got acquainted but we never really palled around.*
– ORIGIN late 17th cent.: from Romany, 'brother, mate,' based on Sanskrit *bhrātṛ* 'brother.'

pal·ace /'palis/ ▶ **n.** the official residence of a sovereign, archbishop, bishop, or other exalted person: *the royal palace.* ■ informal a large, splendid house.
– ORIGIN Middle English: from Old French *paleis*, from Latin *Palatium*, the name of the Palatine hill in Rome, where the house of the emperor was situated.

pal·ace car ▶ **n.** chiefly historical a luxurious railroad car.

pal·ace coup (also **palace revolution**) ▶ **n.** the nonviolent overthrow of a sovereign or government by senior officials within the ruling group.

pa·lac·sin·ta /,pälət'sintə/ ▶ **n.** (pl. **same** or **palacsintas**) (in Hungarian cuisine) a thin pancake eaten as a dessert, typically with a filling.
– ORIGIN Hungarian.

pal·a·din /'palədin/ ▶ **n.** historical any of the twelve peers of Charlemagne's court, of whom the count palatine was the chief. ■ a knight renowned for heroism and chivalry.
– ORIGIN late 16th cent.: from French *paladin*, from Italian *paladino*, from Latin *palatinus* '(officer) of the palace' (see **PALATINE**[1]).

Pa·lae·arc·tic ▶ **adj.** British spelling of **PALEARCTIC**.

palaeo- ▶ **comb. form** British spelling of **PALEO-**.

pa·laes·tra /pə'lestrə/ (also **palestra**) ▶ **n.** (in ancient Greece and Rome) a wrestling school or gymnasium.
– ORIGIN via Latin from Greek *palaistra*, from *palaiein* 'wrestle.'

Pa·lais de Jus·tice /pə'l ā də jə'stēs/ ▶ **n.** (pl. **same**) (in France and French-speaking countries) a court of law.
– ORIGIN French, literally 'palace of justice.'

pal·am·pore /'paləm,pôr/ ▶ **n.** Indian a type of chintz, used esp. for bedspreads. ■ a palampore bedspread.
– ORIGIN late 17th cent.: origin uncertain; perhaps from Portuguese, *palangapuz(es)* plural, from Urdu and Persian, *palangpoš*, 'bedcover,' or perhaps from *Pālanpur*, a town in Gujarat, India.

pal·an·quin /,palən'kēn/ (also **palankeen**) ▶ **n.** (in India and the East) a covered litter for one passenger, consisting of a large box carried on two horizontal poles by four or six bearers.
– ORIGIN late 16th cent.: from Portuguese *palanquim*, from Oriya *pālaṅki*, based on Sanskrit *palyanka* 'bed, couch.'

pa·la·pa /pə'läpə/ ▶ **n.** a traditional Mexican shelter roofed with palm leaves or branches. ■ a structure, esp. on a beach, of a similar kind.
– ORIGIN Mexican Spanish, denoting the palm *Orbignya cohune*.

pal·at·a·ble /ˈpalətəbəl/ ▶ **adj.** (of food or drink) pleasant to taste: *a very palatable local red wine.* ■ (of an action or proposal) acceptable or satisfactory: *a device that made increased taxation more palatable.*
– DERIVATIVES **pal·at·a·bil·i·ty** /ˌpalətəˈbilətē/ **n.**, **pal·at·a·bly** /-blē/ **adv.**

pal·a·tal /ˈpalətl/ ▶ **adj.** technical of or relating to the palate: *a palatal lesion.* ■ Phonetics (of a speech sound) made by placing the blade of the tongue against or near the hard palate (e.g., *y* in *yes*).
▶ **n.** Phonetics a palatal sound.
– DERIVATIVES **pal·a·tal·ly** **adv.**
– ORIGIN early 18th cent.: from French, from Latin *palatum* (see PALATE).

pal·a·tal·ize /ˈpalətlˌīz/ ▶ **v.** [with obj.] Phonetics make (a speech sound) palatal, esp. by changing a velar to a palatal by moving the point of contact between tongue and palate farther forward in the mouth. ■ [no obj.] (of a speech sound) become palatal.
– DERIVATIVES **pal·a·tal·i·za·tion** /ˌpalətl-iˈzāSHən/ **n.**

pal·ate /ˈpalit/ ▶ **n. 1** the roof of the mouth, separating the cavities of the nose and the mouth in vertebrates.
2 a person's appreciation of taste and flavor, esp. when sophisticated and discriminating: *a fine range of drink for sophisticated palates* | figurative *the suggestions may not suit everyone's palate.* ■ taste or flavor of wine or beer: *a wine with a zingy, peachy palate.*
– ORIGIN late Middle English: from Latin *palatum.*

pa·la·tial /pəˈlāSHəl/ ▶ **adj.** resembling a palace in being spacious and splendid: *her palatial apartment in Chicago.*
– DERIVATIVES **pa·la·tial·ly** **adv.**
– ORIGIN mid 18th cent.: from Latin *palatium* 'palace' (see PALACE) + -AL.

pa·lat·i·nate /pəˈlatnˌāt, -ˌit/ ▶ **n.** historical a territory under the jurisdiction of a count palatine. ■ (**the Palatinate**) the territory of the German Empire ruled by the count palatine of the Rhine.

Pal·a·tine /ˈpaləˌtīn/ a village in northeastern Illinois, northwest of Chicago; pop. 67,080 (est. 2008).

pal·a·tine¹ /ˈpaləˌtīn/ ▶ **adj.** [usu. postpositive] chiefly historical (of an official or feudal lord) having local authority that elsewhere belongs only to a sovereign. ■ (of a territory) subject to this authority.
– ORIGIN late Middle English: from French *palatin(e)*, from Latin *palatinus* 'of the palace.'

pal·a·tine² chiefly Anatomy ▶ **adj.** of or relating to the palate or esp. the palatine bone.
▶ **n.** (also **palatine bone**) each of two bones within the skull forming parts of the eye socket, the nasal cavity, and the hard palate.
– ORIGIN mid 17th cent.: from French *palatin(e)*, from Latin *palatum* 'palate.'

Pa·lau /pəˈlou/ (also **Belau** /bəˈlou/) a republic in the western Pacific Ocean, a group of about 100 of the Caroline Islands; pop. 20,800 (est. 2009); capital, Melekeok; languages, English, Palauan, Sonsorolese, Tobi, and Angaur.

> It became a part of the US Trust Territory of the Pacific Islands in 1947, began self-governing internally in 1980, and achieved independence in 1994.

pa·lav·er /pəˈlavər, -ˈläv-/ ▶ **n.** prolonged and idle discussion: *an hour of aimless palaver.* ■ dated a parley or improvised conference between two sides.
▶ **v.** [no obj.] talk unnecessarily at length: *it's too hot for palavering.*
– ORIGIN mid 18th cent. (in the sense 'a talk between tribespeople and traders'): from Portuguese *palavra* 'word,' from Latin *parabola* 'comparison' (see PARABLE).

Pa·la·wan /pəˈläwən, pä-/ a long, narrow island in the western Philippines that separates the Sulu Sea from the South China Sea.

pa·laz·zo /pəˈlätsō/ ▶ **n.** (pl. **palazzos** or **palazzi** /-ˈlätsē/) a palatial building, esp. in Italy.
– ORIGIN Italian, 'palace.'

pa·laz·zo pants ▶ **plural n.** a woman's loose, wide-legged pants.

pale¹ /pāl/ ▶ **adj. 1** light in color or having little color: *choose pale floral patterns for walls.* ■ (of a person's face or complexion) having less color than usual, typically as a result of shock, fear, or ill health: *she looked pale and drawn.*
2 feeble and unimpressive: *unconvincing rock that came across as a pale imitation of Bruce Springsteen.*
▶ **v.** [no obj.] **1** become pale in one's face from shock or fear: *I paled at the thought of what she might say.*
2 seem less impressive or important: *all else pales by comparison* | *his own problems paled into insignificance compared to the plight of this child.*
– DERIVATIVES **pale·ly** **adv.**, **pale·ness** **n.**, **pal·ish** **adj.**
– ORIGIN Middle English: from Old French *pale*, from Latin *pallidus*; the verb is from Old French *palir.*

pale² ▶ **n. 1** a wooden stake or post used as an upright along with others to form a fence. ■ a conceptual boundary: *bring these things back within the pale of decency.*
2 archaic or historical an area within determined bounds, or subject to a particular jurisdiction. ■ (**the Pale**) historical another term for ENGLISH PALE. ■ the areas of Russia to which Jewish residence was restricted.
3 Heraldry a broad vertical stripe down the middle of a shield.
– PHRASES **beyond the pale** outside the bounds of acceptable behavior: *the language my father used was beyond the pale.* **in pale** Heraldry arranged vertically. **per pale** Heraldry divided by a vertical line.
– ORIGIN Middle English: from Old French *pal*, from Latin *palus* 'stake.'

pa·le·a /ˈpālēə/ ▶ **n.** (pl. **paleae** /-lēˌē, -lēˌī/) Botany the upper bract of the floret of a grass. Compare with LEMMA².
– ORIGIN mid 18th cent.: from Latin, literally 'chaff.'

Pa·le·arc·tic /ˌpālēˈärktik, -ˈärtik/ (Brit. **Palaearctic**) ▶ **adj.** Zoology of, relating to, or denoting a zoogeographical region comprising Eurasia north of the Himalayas, together with North Africa and the temperate part of the Arabian peninsula. The fauna is closely related to that of the Nearctic region. Compare with HOLARCTIC. ■ (as noun **the Palearctic**) the Palearctic region.

pale·face /ˈpālˌfās/ ▶ **n.** a name supposedly used by North American Indians for a white person.

Pa·lekh /ˈpäˌlek, -ˌleKH/ ▶ **n.** [as modifier] denoting a type of Russian iconography or a style of miniature painting on boxes, trays, and other small items.
– ORIGIN from the name of a town northeast of Moscow renowned for this type of work.

Pa·lem·bang /päˈlemˌbäNG/ a city in Indonesia, in the southeastern part of Sumatra, a river port on the Musi River; pop. 1,323,200 (est. 2005).

paleo- (Brit. **palaeo-**) ▶ **comb. form** older or ancient, esp. relating to the geological past: *Paleolithic* | *paleomagnetism.*
– ORIGIN from Greek *palaios* 'ancient.'

pa·le·o·an·thro·pol·o·gy /ˌpālēōˌanTHrəˈpäləjē/ ▶ **n.** the branch of anthropology concerned with fossil hominids.
– DERIVATIVES **pa·le·o·an·thro·po·log·i·cal** /-pəˈläjikəl/ **adj.**, **pa·le·o·an·thro·pol·o·gist** /-jist/ **n.**

pa·le·o·bi·ol·o·gy /ˌpālēōbīˈäləjē/ ▶ **n.** the biology of fossil animals and plants.
– DERIVATIVES **pa·le·o·bi·o·log·i·cal** /-ˌbīəˈläjikəl/ **adj.**, **pa·le·o·bi·ol·o·gist** /-jist/ **n.**

pa·le·o·bot·a·ny /ˌpālēōˈbätn-ē/ ▶ **n.** the study of fossil plants.
– DERIVATIVES **pa·le·o·bo·tan·i·cal** /-bəˈtanikəl/ **adj.**, **pa·le·o·bot·a·nist** /-ˈbätn-ist/ **n.**

Pa·le·o·cene /ˈpālēəˌsēn/ ▶ **adj.** Geology of, relating to, or denoting the earliest epoch of the Tertiary period, between the Cretaceous period and the Eocene epoch. ■ (as noun **the Paleocene**) the Paleocene epoch or the system of rocks deposited during it.

> The Paleocene epoch lasted from 65 million to 56.5 million years ago. It was a time of sudden diversification among the mammals, probably as a result of the mass extinctions (notably of the dinosaurs) that occurred at the end of the Cretaceous period (see CRETACEOUS-TERTIARY BOUNDARY).

– ORIGIN late 19th cent.: from PALEO- (relating to prehistoric times) + Greek *kainos* 'new.'

pa·le·o·cli·mate /ˌpālēōˈklīmit/ ▶ **n.** a climate prevalent at a particular time in the geological past.
– DERIVATIVES **pa·le·o·cli·mat·ic** /-klīˈmatik/ **adj.**, **pa·le·o·cli·ma·tol·o·gist** /-ˌklīməˈtäləjist/ **n.**, **pa·le·o·cli·ma·tol·o·gy** /-ˌklīməˈtäləjē/ **n.**

pa·le·o·con /ˈpālēōˌkän/ ▶ **n.** informal short for PALEOCONSERVATIVE.

pa·le·o·con·serv·a·tive /ˌpālēōkənˈsərvətiv/ ▶ **n.** a person who advocates old or traditional forms of conservatism; an extremely right-wing conservative.

pa·le·o·cur·rent /ˌpālēōˈkərənt, -ˈkə-rənt/ ▶ **n.** a current that existed at some time in the geological past, as inferred from the features of sedimentary rocks.

pa·le·o·e·col·o·gy /ˌpālēōˌəˈkäləjē/ ▶ **n.** the ecology of fossil animals and plants.
– DERIVATIVES **pa·le·o·e·co·log·i·cal** /-ˌekəˈläjikəl, -ˌēkə-/ **adj.**, **pa·le·o·e·col·o·gist** /-ˌəˈkäləjist, -ˌēˈkäl-/ **n.**

pa·le·o·en·vi·ron·ment /ˌpālēōənˈvīrənmənt, -ˈvī(ə)rnmənt/ ▶ **n.** an environment prevailing at a particular time in the geological past.
– DERIVATIVES **pa·le·o·en·vi·ron·men·tal** /-ˌvīrənˈmentl, -ˌvī(ə)rn-/ **adj.**

Pa·le·o-Es·ki·mo ▶ **n.** a member of a prehistoric people inhabiting the Arctic from Greenland through North America to Siberia.
▶ **adj.** of or relating to this people.

pa·le·o·fe·ces /ˌpālēōˈfēˌsēz/ ▶ **plural n.** desiccated prehistoric fecal matter, esp. from humans: *sunflower-seed shells found in the paleofeces provide evidence that early American Indians in that region farmed the plants.* Compare with COPROLITE.
– DERIVATIVES **pa·le·o·fe·cal** /ˌpālēōˈfēkəl/ **adj.**

Pa·le·o·gene /ˈpālēəjēn/ ▶ **adj.** Geology of, relating to, or denoting the earlier division of the Tertiary period, comprising the Paleocene, Eocene, and Oligocene epochs. Compare with NEOGENE. ■ (as noun **the Paleogene**) the Paleogene subperiod or the system of rocks deposited during it.

> The Paleogene lasted from about 65 million to 23 million years ago. The mammals diversified following the demise of the dinosaurs, and many bizarre and gigantic forms appeared.

– ORIGIN late 19th cent.: from PALEO- (relating to prehistoric times) + Greek *genēs* 'of a specified kind' (see -GEN).

pa·le·o·ge·og·ra·phy /ˌpālēōjēˈägrəfē/ ▶ **n.** the study of geographical features at particular times in the geological past.
– DERIVATIVES **pa·le·o·ge·og·ra·pher** /-fər/ **n.**, **pa·le·o·ge·o·graph·i·cal** /-ˌjēəˈgrafikəl/ **adj.**

pa·le·og·ra·phy /ˌpālēˈägrəfē/ (Brit. **palaeography**) ▶ **n.** the study of ancient writing systems and the deciphering and dating of historical manuscripts.
– DERIVATIVES **pa·le·og·ra·pher** /-fər/ **n.**, **pa·le·o·graph·ic** /ˌpālēəˈgrafik/ **adj.**, **pa·le·o·graph·i·cal** /ˌpālēəˈgrafikəl/ **adj.**, **pa·le·o·graph·i·cal·ly** /ˌpālēəˈgrafik(ə)lē/ **adv.**

Pa·le·o-In·di·an ▶ **adj.** of, relating to, or denoting the earliest human inhabitants of the Americas, from as early as 40,000 years ago to *c.*5000 BC.
▶ **n. 1** (**the Paleo-Indian**) the Paleo-Indian culture or period.
2 a member of the Paleo-Indian peoples.

pa·le·o·lat·i·tude /ˌpālēōˈlatiˌt(y)o͞od/ ▶ **n.** the latitude of a place at some time in the past, measured relative to the earth's magnetic poles in the same period. Differences between this and the present latitude are caused by continental drift and movement of the earth's magnetic poles.

Pa·le·o·lith·ic /ˌpālēəˈliTHik/ ▶ **adj.** Archaeology of, relating to, or denoting the early phase of the Stone Age, lasting about 2.5 million years, when primitive stone implements were used. ■ (as noun **the Paleolithic**) the Paleolithic period. Also called OLD STONE AGE.

> The Paleolithic period extends from the first appearance of artifacts to the end of the last ice age (about 8,500 years ago). The period has been divided into the **Lower Paleolithic**, with the earliest forms of humankind and the emergence of hand-ax industries (ending about 120,000 years ago), the **Middle Paleolithic**, the era of Neanderthal humans (ending about 35,000 years ago), and the **Upper Paleolithic**, during which only modern *Homo sapiens* is known to have existed.

– ORIGIN mid 19th cent.: from PALEO- 'of prehistoric times' + Greek *lithos* 'stone' + -IC.

pa·le·o·mag·net·ism /ˌpālēōˈmagnəˌtizəm/ ▶ **n.** the branch of geophysics concerned with the magnetism in rocks that was induced by the earth's magnetic field at the time of their formation.
– DERIVATIVES **pa·le·o·mag·net·ic** /-magˈnetik/ **adj.**

pa·le·on·tol·o·gy /ˌpālēˌənˈtäləjē/ ▶ **n.** the branch of science concerned with fossil animals and plants.
– DERIVATIVES **pa·le·on·to·log·i·cal** /ˌpālēˌäntəˈläjikəl/ **adj.**, **pa·le·on·tol·o·gist** /-jist/ **n.**
– ORIGIN mid 19th cent.: from PALEO- 'of prehistoric times' + Greek *onta* 'beings' (neuter plural of *ōn*, present participle of *einai* 'be') + -LOGY.

pa·le·o·pal·li·um /ˌpālēōˈpalēəm/ (Brit. **palaeopallium**) ▶ **n.** (pl. **paleopallia** /-ˈpalēə/) Anatomy a phylogenetically older portion of the pallium of the brain, which comprises mainly the pyriform lobe.
– DERIVATIVES **pa·le·o·pal·li·al** /-ˈpalēəl/ **adj.**

pa·le·o·pa·thol·o·gy /ˌpālēōpəˈTHäləjē/ ▶ **n.** the branch of science concerned with the pathological conditions found in ancient human and animal remains.

– DERIVATIVES **pa·le·o·path·o·log·i·cal** /-ˌpaTHəˈläjikəl/ **adj.**, **pa·le·o·path·ol·o·gist** /-jist/ **n.**

pa·le·o·pole /ˈpālēəˌpōl/ ▶ **n.** a magnetic pole of the earth as it was situated at a particular time in the geological past.

pa·le·o·sol /ˈpālēəˌsôl, -ˌsäl/ ▶ **n.** Geology a stratum or soil horizon that was formed as a soil in a past geological period.

pa·le·o·tem·per·a·ture /ˌpālēōˈtemp(ə)rəCHər, -ˌCHo͝or/ ▶ **n.** Geology the temperature or mean temperature of a locality at a time in the geological past.

Pa·le·o·trop·i·cal /ˌpālēəˈträpikəl/ ▶ **adj.** Botany of, relating to, or denoting a phytogeographical kingdom comprising Africa, tropical Asia, New Guinea, and many Pacific islands (excluding Australia and New Zealand). ■ Zoology of, relating to, or denoting a zoogeographical region comprising the tropical parts of the Old World.

Pa·le·o·zo·ic /ˌpālēəˈzōik/ ▶ **adj.** Geology of, relating to, or denoting the era between the Precambrian eon and the Mesozoic era. Formerly called PRIMARY. ■ (as noun **the Paleozoic**) the Paleozoic era or the system of rocks deposited during it.

> The Paleozoic lasted from about 570 million to 245 million years ago, its end being marked by mass extinctions. The **Lower Paleozoic** sub-era comprises the Cambrian, Ordovician, and Silurian periods, and the **Upper Paleozoic** sub-era comprises the Devonian, Carboniferous, and Permian periods. The era began with the first invertebrates with hard external skeletons, notably trilobites, and ended with the rise to dominance of the reptiles.

– ORIGIN mid 19th cent.: from PALEO- 'of prehistoric times' + Greek *zōē* 'life' + -IC.

Pa·ler·mo /pəˈlərˌmō, -ˈle(ə)r-/ a port on the north coast of Sicily; pop. 734,000.

Pal·es·tine /ˈpaliˌstīn/ a territory in the Middle East on the eastern coast of the Mediterranean Sea.

> In biblical times Palestine comprised the kingdoms of Israel and Judah. The land was controlled at various times by the Egyptian, Assyrian, Persian, and Roman empires before being conquered by the Arabs in AD 634. It was part of the Ottoman Empire from 1516 to 1918. The name Palestine was used as the official political title for the land west of the Jordan mandated to Britain in 1920; in 1948, the state of Israel was established in what was traditionally Palestine, but the name continued to be used in the context of the struggle for territory and political rights of displaced Palestinian Arabs. In 1993, an agreement was signed between Israel and the Palestine Liberation Organization giving some autonomy to the Gaza Strip and the West Bank and setting up the Palestine National Authority and a police force, but this proved unsuccessful in bringing the conflict to a resolution.

P

– ORIGIN from Greek *Palaistinē* (used in early Christian writing), from Latin *(Syria) Palaestina* (the name of a Roman province), from *Philistia* 'land of the Philistines.'

Pal·es·tine Lib·er·a·tion Or·gan·i·za·tion (abbr.: **PLO**) a political and military organization formed in 1964 to unite various Palestinian Arab groups and ultimately to bring about an independent state of Palestine.

Pal·es·tin·i·an /ˌpaləˈstinēən/ ▶ **adj.** of or relating to Palestine or its peoples.
▶ **n.** a member of the native Arab population of the region of Palestine (including the modern state of Israel).

pa·les·tra ▶ **n.** variant spelling of PALAESTRA.

Pa·les·tri·na /ˌpaləˈstrēnə, ˌpäle-/, Giovanni Pierluigi da (*c.*1525–94), Italian composer. He is chiefly known for his sacred music.

pal·ette /ˈpalit/ ▶ **n.** a thin board or slab on which an artist lays and mixes colors. ■ the range of colors used by a particular artist or in a particular picture: *I choose a palette of natural, earthy colors.* ■ the range or variety of tonal or instrumental color in a musical piece: *he commands the sort of tonal palette that this music needs.* ■ (in computer graphics) the range of colors or shapes available to the user.
– ORIGIN late 18th cent.: from French, diminutive of *pale* 'shovel,' from Latin *pala* 'spade.'

pal·ette knife ▶ **n.** a thin steel blade with a handle for mixing colors or applying or removing paint.

pal·frey /ˈpôlfrē/ ▶ **n.** (pl. **palfreys**) archaic a docile horse used for ordinary riding, esp. by women.
– ORIGIN Middle English: from Old French *palefrei*, from medieval Latin *palefredus*, alteration of late Latin *paraveredus*, from Greek *para* 'beside, extra' + Latin *veredus* 'riding horse.'

Pa·li /ˈpālē/ ▶ **n.** an Indic language, closely related to Sanskrit, in which the sacred texts of Theravada Buddhism are written. Pali developed in northern India in the 5th–2nd centuries BC.
▶ **adj.** of or relating to this language.
– ORIGIN from Pali *pāli(-bhāsā)* 'canonical texts.'

pa·li /ˈpälē/ ▶ **n.** (pl. **same** or **palis**) (in Hawaii) a cliff.
– ORIGIN Hawaiian.

pali·la·lia /ˌpaləˈlālēə/ ▶ **n.** Medicine a speech disorder characterized by involuntary repetition of words, phrases, or sentences.
– ORIGIN early 20th cent.: from French *palilalie*, from Greek *palin* 'again' + *lalia* 'speech, chatter.'

pal·i·mo·ny /ˈpaləˌmōnē/ ▶ **n.** informal compensation made by one member of an unmarried couple to the other after separation.
– ORIGIN 1970s: from PAL + a shortened form of ALIMONY.

pal·imp·sest /ˈpalimpˌsest/ ▶ **n.** a manuscript or piece of writing material on which the original writing has been effaced to make room for later writing but of which traces remain. ■ something reused or altered but still bearing visible traces of its earlier form: *Sutton Place is a palimpsest of the taste of successive owners.*
– DERIVATIVES **pal·imp·ses·tic** /ˌpalimpˈsestik/ **adj.**
– ORIGIN mid 17th cent.: via Latin from Greek *palimpsēstos*, from *palin* 'again' + *psēstos* 'rubbed smooth.'

pal·in·drome /ˈpalinˌdrōm/ ▶ **n.** a word, phrase, or sequence that reads the same backward as forward, e.g., *madam* or *nurses run*.
– DERIVATIVES **pal·in·drom·ic** /ˌpalinˈdrämik/ **adj.**, **pa·lin·dro·mist** /pəˈlindrəmist/ **n.**
– ORIGIN early 17th cent.: from Greek *palindromos* 'running back again,' from *palin* 'again' + *drom-* (from *dramein* 'to run').

pal·ing /ˈpāliNG/ ▶ **n.** a fence made from pointed wooden or metal stakes. ■ a stake used in such a fence.

pal·in·gen·e·sis /ˌpalinˈjenəsis/ ▶ **n.** Biology the exact reproduction of ancestral characteristics in ontogenesis.
– DERIVATIVES **pal·in·ge·net·ic** /ˌpalinjəˈnetik/ **adj.**
– ORIGIN early 19th cent.: from Greek *palin* 'again' + *genesis* 'birth.'

pal·i·node /ˈpaləˌnōd/ ▶ **n.** a poem in which the poet retracts a view or sentiment expressed in a former poem.
– ORIGIN late 16th cent.: via Latin from Greek *palinōidia*, from *palin* 'again' + *ōidē* 'song.'

Pal·i·o /ˈpälēō/ (pl. **Palii** /ˈpälēˌē/) a traditional horse race held in Siena, Italy, twice a year, in July and August.
– ORIGIN Italian, from Latin *pallium* 'covering' (with reference to the cloth given as a prize).

pal·i·sade /ˌpaləˈsād/ ▶ **n.** a fence of wooden stakes or iron railings fixed in the ground, forming an enclosure or defense. ■ historical a strong pointed wooden stake fixed deeply in the ground with others in a close row, used as a defense. ■ (**palisades**) a line of high cliffs. ■ (**the Palisades**) a ridge of high basalt cliffs that line the western side of the Hudson River, in New Jersey and in New York, beginning across from New York City in New Jersey and extending north to Newburgh in New York.
▶ **v.** [with obj.] (usu. as adj. **palisaded**) enclose or provide (a building or place) with a palisade.
– ORIGIN early 17th cent.: from French *palissade*, from Provençal *palissada*, from *palissa* 'paling,' based on Latin *palus* 'stake.'

pal·i·sade lay·er ▶ **n.** Botany a layer of parallel elongated cells below the epidermis of a leaf.

Pal·i·sades /ˌpaləˈsādz/ (**the Palisades**) (also **Palisades of the Hudson**) cliffs that line the western side of the Hudson River, in New Jersey and in New York, beginning across from New York City in New Jersey and extending north to Newburgh in New York.

Palk Strait /pôk, pôlk/ an inlet of the Bay of Bengal that separates northern Sri Lanka from the coast of Tamil Nadu in India. It lies to the north of Adam's Bridge, which separates it from the Gulf of Mannar.

pall¹ /pôl/ ▶ **n. 1** a cloth spread over a coffin, hearse, or tomb.
2 a dark cloud or covering of smoke, dust, or similar matter: *a pall of black smoke hung over the quarry.* ■ something regarded as enveloping a situation with an air of gloom, heaviness, or fear: *torture and murder have cast a pall of terror over the villages.*
3 an ecclesiastical pallium. ■ Heraldry a Y-shaped charge representing the front of an ecclesiastical pallium.
– ORIGIN Old English *pæll* 'rich (purple) cloth,' 'cloth cover for a chalice,' from Latin *pallium* 'covering, cloak.'

pall² ▶ **v.** [no obj.] become less appealing or interesting through familiarity: *the novelty of the quiet life palled.*
– ORIGIN late Middle English: shortening of APPALL.

pal·la·di·a /pəˈlādēə/ plural form of PALLADIUM².

Pal·la·di·an /pəˈlādēən/ ▶ **adj.** Architecture of, relating to, or denoting the neoclassical style of Andrea Palladio, in particular with reference to the phase of English architecture from *c.*1715, when there was a revival of interest in Palladio and his English follower, Inigo Jones, and a reaction against the baroque.
– DERIVATIVES **Pal·la·di·an·ism** /-ˌnizəm/ **n.**

Pal·la·di·an win·dow ▶ **n.** a large window consisting of a central arched section flanked by two narrow rectangular sections.

Palladio, Andrea (1508–80), Italian architect. He led a revival of classical architecture, in particular promoting the Roman ideals of harmonic proportions and symmetrical planning. A notable example of his many villas, palaces, and churches is the church of San Giorgio Maggiore in Venice.

pal·la·di·um¹ /pəˈlādēəm/ ▶ **n.** the chemical element of atomic number 46, a rare silvery-white metal resembling platinum. (Symbol: **Pd**)
– ORIGIN early 19th cent.: modern Latin, from *Pallas*, the name given to an asteroid discovered (1802) just before the element.

pal·la·di·um² ▶ **n.** (pl. **palladia** /-dēə/) archaic a safeguard or source of protection.
– ORIGIN late Middle English (in the Greek sense): via Latin from Greek *palladion*, denoting an image of the goddess Pallas (Athena), on which the safety of Troy was believed to depend.

Pal·las /ˈpaləs/ **1** Greek Mythology (also **Pallas Athene**) one of the names (of unknown meaning) of ATHENA.
2 Astronomy asteroid 2, discovered in 1802. It is the second largest (diameter 523 km).

pal·las·ite /ˈpaləsīt/ ▶ **n.** a meteorite consisting of roughly equal proportions of iron and olivine.
– ORIGIN mid 19th cent.: from the name of Peter S. *Pallas* (1741–1811), German naturalist, + -ITE¹.

pall·bear·er /ˈpôlˌbe(ə)rər/ ▶ **n.** a person helping to carry or officially escorting a coffin at a funeral.

pal·let¹ /ˈpalit/ ▶ **n.** a straw mattress. ■ a crude or makeshift bed.
– ORIGIN Middle English: from Anglo-Norman French *paillete*, from *paille* 'straw,' from Latin *palea*.

pal·let² ▶ **n. 1** a portable platform on which goods can be moved, stacked, and stored, esp. with the aid of a forklift.
2 a flat wooden blade with a handle, used to shape clay or plaster.
3 an artist's palette.
4 a projection on a machine part, serving to change the mode of motion of a wheel. ■ (in a clock or watch) a projection transmitting motion from an escapement to a pendulum or balance wheel.
– ORIGIN late Middle English (sense 2): from French *palette* 'little blade,' from Latin *pala* 'spade'; compare with PALE².

pal·let³ ▶ **n.** Heraldry the diminutive of the pale, a narrow vertical strip, usually borne in groups of two or three.
– ORIGIN late 15th cent.: diminutive of the noun PALE².

pal·let·ize /ˈpaləˌtīz/ ▶ **v.** [with obj.] (usu. as adj. **palletized**) place, stack, or transport (goods) on a pallet or pallets: *a roller system for quick movement of palletized cargo.*

pal·li·a /ˈpalēə/ plural form of PALLIUM.

pal·liasse /ˌpalˈyas, ˈpalˌyas/ (also **paillasse**) ▶ **n.** a straw mattress.
– ORIGIN early 16th cent. (originally Scots): from French *paillasse*, based on Latin *palea* 'straw.'

pal·li·ate /ˈpalēˌāt/ ▶ **v.** [with obj.] make (a disease or its symptoms) less severe or unpleasant without removing the cause: *treatment works by palliating symptoms.* ■ allay or moderate (fears or suspicions): *this eliminated, or at least palliated, suspicions aroused by German unity.* ■ disguise the seriousness or gravity of (an offense): *there is no way to excuse or palliate his dirty deed.*
– DERIVATIVES **pal·li·a·tion** /ˌpalēˈāSHən/ **n.**, **pal·li·a·tor** /-ˌātər/ **n.**
– ORIGIN late Middle English: from late Latin *palliat-* 'cloaked,' from the verb *palliare*, from *pallium* 'cloak.'

pal·li·a·tive /ˈpalēˌātiv, ˈpalēətiv/ ▶ **adj.** (of a treatment or medicine) relieving pain or alleviating a problem without dealing with the underlying cause: *short-term, palliative measures had been taken.*
▶ **n.** a remedy, medicine, etc., of such a kind.
– DERIVATIVES **pal·li·a·tive·ly** **adv.**

– ORIGIN late Middle English (as an adjective): from French *palliatif, -ive* or medieval Latin *palliativus*, from the verb *palliare* 'to cloak' (see PALLIATE).

pal·lid /ˈpalid/ ▶ adj. (of a person's face) pale, typically because of poor health. ■ feeble or insipid: *an utterly pallid and charmless character*.
– DERIVATIVES **pal·lid·ly** adv., **pal·lid·ness** n.
– ORIGIN late 16th cent.: from Latin *pallidus* 'pale' (related to *pallere* 'be pale').

pal·li·um /ˈpalēəm/ ▶ n. (pl. **pallia** /ˈpalēə/ or **palliums**) **1** a woolen vestment conferred by the pope on an archbishop, consisting of a narrow, circular band placed around the shoulders with short lappets hanging from front and back.
2 historical a man's large rectangular cloak, esp. as worn by Greek philosophical and religious teachers.
3 Zoology the mantle of a mollusk or brachiopod.
4 Anatomy the outer wall of the mammalian cerebrum, corresponding to the cerebral cortex.
– DERIVATIVES **pal·li·al** /ˈpalēəl/ adj. (sense 3, sense 4).
– ORIGIN Middle English: from Latin, literally 'covering.'

pall-mall /ˌpel ˈmel, ˈpôl ˈmôl, ˈpal ˈmal/ ▶ n. historical a 16th- and 17th-century game in which a boxwood ball was driven through an iron ring suspended at the end of a long alley.
– ORIGIN from obsolete French *pallemaille*, from Italian *pallamaglio*, from *palla* 'ball' + *maglio* 'mallet.'

pal·lor /ˈpalər/ ▶ n. [in sing.] an unhealthy pale appearance.
– ORIGIN late Middle English: from Latin, from *pallere* 'be pale.'

pal·ly /ˈpalē/ ▶ adj. (**pallier, palliest**) [predic.] informal having a close, friendly relationship: *I see you're getting quite pally with Carlos*.

palm[1] /pä(l)m/ ▶ n. (also **palm tree**) an unbranched evergreen tree with a crown of long feathered or fan-shaped leaves, and typically having old leaf scars forming a regular pattern on the trunk. Palms grow in warm regions, esp. the tropics. ● Family Palmae (or Arecaceae): numerous genera and species, some of which are of great commercial importance, e.g., the **oil palm**, **date palm**, and coconut. ■ a leaf of such a tree awarded as a prize or viewed as a symbol of victory or triumph: *the consensus was that the palm should go to Doerner*.
– ORIGIN Old English *palm(a)*, of Germanic origin; related to Dutch *palm* and German *Palme*, from Latin *palma* 'palm (of a hand),' its leaf being likened to a spread hand.

palm[2] ▶ n. the inner surface of the hand between the wrist and fingers. ■ a part of a glove that covers this part of the hand. ■ a hard shield worn on the hand by sailmakers to protect the palm in sewing. ■ the palmate part of an antler.
▶ v. **1** [with obj.] conceal (a card or other small object) in the hand, esp. as part of a trick or theft: *he would spin wild tales while palming your wristwatch*.
2 [with obj.] hit (something) with the palm of the hand. ■ Basketball illegally grip (the ball) with the hand while dribbling.
– PHRASES **have** (or **hold**) **someone in the palm of one's hand** have someone under one's control or influence: *she had the audience in the palm of her hand*. **read someone's palm** tell someone's fortune by looking at the lines on their palm.
– PHRASAL VERBS **palm someone off** informal persuade someone to accept something by deception: *most sellers are palmed off with a fraction of what something is worth*. **palm something off** sell or dispose of something by misrepresentation or fraud: *they palmed off their shoddiest products on the Russians*.
– DERIVATIVES **pal·mar** /ˈpalmər, ˈpä(l)mər/ adj., **palmed** adj. [in combination] *sweaty-palmed*, **palm·ful** /-fəl/ n.
– ORIGIN Middle English: from Old French *paume*, from Latin *palma*. Current senses of the verb date from the late 17th cent.

Pal·ma /ˈpälmə/ an industrial port and resort on the island of Majorca in the Balearic Islands; pop. 396,570 (2008). Full name **Palma de Mallorca**.

pal·ma·ro·sa ▶ n. a fragrant tropical Indian grass related to citronella and lemongrass. It is cultivated for the essential oil it yields, which is used in perfumery and aromatherapy. ● *Cymbopogon martinii*, family Gramineae. ■ (also **palmarosa oil**) the essential oil obtained from this grass.

pal·mate /ˈpalˌmāt, ˈpä(l)-/ ▶ adj. **1** Botany (of a leaf) having several lobes (typically 5–7) whose midribs all radiate from one point.
2 Zoology (of an antler) in which the angles between the tines are partly filled in to form a broad flat surface, as in fallow deer and moose.
– DERIVATIVES **pal·mat·ed** adj.
– ORIGIN mid 18th cent.: from Latin *palmatus*, from *palma* 'palm' (see PALM[2]).

pal·mate newt ▶ n. a small, olive-brown, smooth-skinned newt native to western Europe, with partially webbed feet. ● *Triturus helveticus*, family Salamandridae.

palm ball (also **palmball**) ▶ n. Baseball an off-speed pitch in which the ball is released from the palm and thumb rather than the fingers.

Palm Bay a residential city in east central Florida, southwest of Melbourne; pop. 100,786 (est. 2008).

Palm Beach a resort town in southeastern Florida, located on an island just off the coast; pop. 9,535 (est. 2008).

palm civ·et ▶ n. a mainly arboreal civet that typically has powerful curved claws and pale spots or stripes on a dark coat, native to Africa and Asia. It is often a pest of banana plantations. ● *Paradoxurus* and other genera, family Viverridae: several species, including the **common palm civet** (*P. hermaphroditus*) of Asia.

palm·cord·er /ˈpä(l)mˌkôrdər/ ▶ n. a small, handheld camcorder.
– ORIGIN 1980s: blend of PALM[2] and RECORDER.

Palm·dale /ˈpämˌdāl/ a city in southwestern California, north of Los Angeles, near Edwards Air Force Base; pop. 143,197 (est. 2008).

Pal·me /ˈpälmə/, Olof (1927–86), Swedish statesman; full name *Sven Olof Joachim Palme*. He served as prime minister 1969–76 and 1982–86, until killed by an unknown assassin.

Pal·mer /ˈpä(l)mər/, Arnold (Daniel) (1929–), US golfer. His many championship victories include the Masters in 1958, 1960, 1962, and 1964; the US Open in 1960; and the British Open in 1961 and 1962. The huge galleries attracted by Palmer whenever he played were dubbed "Arnie's Army."

palm·er /ˈpä(l)mər/ ▶ n. **1** historical a pilgrim, esp. one who had returned from the Holy Land with a palm frond or leaf as a sign of having undertaken the pilgrimage. ■ historical an itinerant monk traveling from shrine to shrine under a vow of poverty.
2 a hairy artificial fly used in angling.
– ORIGIN Middle English: from Anglo-Norman French, from medieval Latin *palmarius* 'pilgrim,' from Latin *palma* 'palm.'

Pal·mer·ston /ˈpä(l)mərstən/, Henry John Temple, 3rd Viscount (1784–1865), British statesman; prime minister 1855–58 and 1859–65. He declared the second Opium War against China in 1856 and oversaw the successful conclusion of the Crimean War in 1856 and the suppression of the Indian Mutiny in 1858.

pal·mette /palˈmet/ ▶ n. Archaeology an ornament of radiating petals that resemble the leaflets of a palm.
– ORIGIN mid 19th cent.: from French, literally 'small palm,' diminutive of *palme*.

pal·met·to /pä(l)ˈmetō, pal-/ ▶ n. (pl. **palmettos**) a fan palm, esp. one of a number occurring from the southern US to northern South America. ● *Sabal* and other genera, family Palmae: several species, in particular the **cabbage palmetto** (*S. palmetto*), which is the state tree of Florida (where it is better known as the **sabal palm**) and South Carolina.
– ORIGIN mid 16th cent.: from Spanish *palmito*, literally 'small palm,' diminutive of *palma*, assimilated to Italian words ending in *-etto*.

cabbage palmetto

Pal·met·to State a nickname for the state of SOUTH CAROLINA.

palm·i·er /ˈpä(l)mēā/ ▶ n. (pl. or pronunc. **same**) a sweet, crisp pastry shaped like a palm leaf.
– ORIGIN French, literally 'palm tree.'

palm·ist /ˈpä(l)mist/ ▶ n. a person who practices palmistry; a palm-reader.

palm·is·try /ˈpä(l)məstrē/ ▶ n. the art or practice of supposedly interpreting a person's character or predicting their future by examining the lines and other features of the hand, esp. the palm and fingers.
– ORIGIN late Middle English: from PALM[2] + *-estry* (of unknown origin), later altered to *-istry*, perhaps on the pattern of *sophistry*.

pal·mit·ic ac·id /pä(l)ˈmitik/ ▶ n. Chemistry a solid saturated fatty acid obtained from palm oil and other vegetable and animal fats. ● Chem. formula: $CH_3(CH_2)_{14}COOH$.
– DERIVATIVES **pal·mi·tate** /ˈpä(l)miˌtāt/ n.
– ORIGIN mid 19th cent.: *palmitic* from French *palmitique*, from *palme* (see PALM[1]).

palm oil ▶ n. oil from the fruit of certain palms, esp. the West African oil palm.

Palm Pi·lot ▶ n. trademark a brand of handheld computer.

Palm Springs a resort city in the desert area of southern California, east of Los Angeles, noted for its hot mineral springs; pop. 47,952 (est. 2008).

palm squir·rel ▶ n. an Old World squirrel that frequents palm trees, esp. a tree squirrel with a striped back and a shrill, birdlike call. ● Genus *Funambulus* and other genera, family Sciuridae: several species, in particular the **five-striped northern palm squirrel** (*F. pennanti*), which is common in and around human habitation in northern India.

Palm Sun·day ▶ n. the Sunday before Easter, when the triumphal entry of Jesus into Jerusalem is celebrated in many Christian churches by processions in which palm fronds are carried.

palm·top /ˈpä(l)mˌtäp/ ▶ n. a computer small and lightweight enough to be held in one hand.

palm wine ▶ n. an alcoholic drink made from fermented palm sap.

palm·y /ˈpä(l)mē/ ▶ adj. (**palmier, palmiest**) **1** (esp. of a previous period of time) flourishing or successful: *the palmy days of the 1970s*.
2 covered with palms.

Pal·my·ra /palˈmīrə/ an ancient city in Syria, an oasis in the Syrian desert northeast of Damascus on the site of present-day Tadmur.
– ORIGIN Greek form of the city's modern and ancient pre-Semitic name Tadmur or Tadmor, meaning 'city of palms.'

pal·my·ra /palˈmīrə/ ▶ n. an Asian fan palm that yields a wide range of useful products, including timber, fiber, and fruit. ● *Borassus flabellifer*, family Palmae.
– ORIGIN late 17th cent.: from Portuguese *palmeira* 'palm tree.' The change in the ending was due to association with the name of the ancient city of PALMYRA.

Pal·o Al·to /ˈpalō ˈaltō/ a city in western California, south of San Francisco; pop. 59,395 (est. 2008). It is noted for electronics and computer technology and is the site of Stanford University.

pa·lo·lo worm /pəˈlōlō/ ▶ n. a marine bristle worm that swarms in response to changes in light intensity, particularly that of the moon. The worm's posterior segments detach themselves and swim to the surface where the reproductive cells are released into the sea. ● Several species in Eunicidae and other families, in particular the **Samoan palolo worm** (*Palola* (or *Eunice*) *viridis*), which occurs on South Pacific reefs.
– ORIGIN late 19th cent.: *palolo* from Samoan or Tongan.

Pal·o·mar, Mount /ˈpaləˌmär/ a mountain in southern California, northeast of San Diego, rising to a height of 6,126 feet (1,867 m). It is the site of an astronomical observatory.
– ORIGIN Spanish *Palomar*, literally 'place of the pigeon.'

pal·o·mi·no /ˌpaləˈmēnō/ ▶ n. **1** (pl. **palominos**) a pale golden or tan-colored horse or pony with a white mane and tail, originally bred in the southwestern US.
2 a variety of white grape, originally grown around Jerez in southern Spain, used esp. to make sherry and fortified wines.
– ORIGIN early 20th cent.: from Latin American Spanish, from Spanish *palomino* 'young pigeon,' from Latin *palumbinus* 'resembling a dove.'

pa·loo·ka /pəˈlo͝okə/ ▶ n. informal, dated an inferior or average prizefighter. ■ a stupid, uncouth person; a lout.
– ORIGIN 1920s: of unknown origin.

Pa·loo·ka·ville /pəˈlo͝okəˌvil/ ▶ n. informal **1** a state of obscurity: *a couple of bucks and a one-way ticket to Palookaville*.
2 an economically depressed, working-class community.

Pa·louse /pəˈlo͞os/ ▶ n. (pl. **same** or **Palouses**) a member of an American Indian people inhabiting the Palouse River valley in southeastern Washington.
▶ adj. of or relating to this people.
– ORIGIN from Sahaptin *palúus* 'which stands in the water,' referring to a large rock in the Snake River.

pal·o·ver·de /ˌpalōˈvərd(ē)/ ▶ n. a thorny, yellow-flowered tree or shrub that grows along

P

watercourses in the warm desert areas of America. ● Genus *Cercidium*, family Leguminosae.
– ORIGIN early 19th cent.: from Latin American Spanish, literally 'green tree.'

palp /palp/ ▶ n. another term for PALPUS.
– ORIGIN mid 19th cent.: from Latin *palpus*, literally 'feeler.'

pal·pa·ble /'palpəbəl/ ▶ adj. able to be touched or felt: *the palpable bump at the bridge of the nose.* ■ (esp. of a feeling or atmosphere) so intense as to be almost touched or felt: *a palpable sense of loss.* ■ clear to the mind or plain to see: *to talk of dawn raids in the circumstances is palpable nonsense.*
– DERIVATIVES **pal·pa·bil·i·ty** /ˌpalpə'bilitē/ n., **pal·pa·bly** /-blē/ adv.
– ORIGIN late Middle English: from late Latin *palpabilis*, from Latin *palpare* 'feel, touch gently.'

pal·pate /'palˌpāt/ ▶ v. [with obj.] examine (a part of the body) by touch, esp. for medical purposes.
– DERIVATIVES **pal·pa·tion** /pal'pāsHən/ n.
– ORIGIN mid 19th cent.: from Latin *palpat-* 'touched gently,' from the verb *palpare*.

pal·pe·bral /'palpəbrəl, pal'pē-/ ▶ adj. [attrib.] Anatomy of or relating to the eyelids.
– ORIGIN mid 19th cent.: from late Latin *palpebralis*, from Latin *palpebra* 'eyelid.'

pal·pi·tant /'palpitnt/ ▶ adj. rare palpitating.
– ORIGIN mid 19th cent.: from French, present participle of *palpiter*, from Latin *palpitare* 'continue to pat.'

pal·pi·tate /'palpiˌtāt/ ▶ v. [no obj.] (often as adj. **palpitating**) (of the heart) beat rapidly, strongly, or irregularly: *it wakened him in the night with a palpitating heart.* ■ shake; tremble: *she was palpitating with terror.*
– ORIGIN early 17th cent.: from Latin *palpitat-* 'patted,' from the verb *palpitare*, frequentative of *palpare* 'touch gently.'

pal·pi·ta·tion /ˌpalpi'tāsHən/ ▶ n. (usu. **palpitations**) a noticeably rapid, strong, or irregular heartbeat due to agitation, exertion, or illness.
– ORIGIN late Middle English: from Latin *palpitatio(n-)*, from the verb *palpitare* (see PALPITATE).

pal·pus /'palpəs/ (also **palp**) ▶ n. (pl. **palpi** /'palpī/ or **palps**) Zoology each of a pair of elongated segmented appendages near the mouth of an arthropod, usually concerned with the senses of touch and taste.
– DERIVATIVES **pal·pal** /-pəl/ adj.
– ORIGIN early 19th cent.: Latin, from *palpare* 'to feel.'

pals·grave /'pôlzˌgrāv, 'palz-/ ▶ n. historical a count palatine.
– ORIGIN mid 16th cent.: from early modern Dutch *paltsgrave*, from *palts* 'palatinate' + *grave* 'count.'

P

pal·sy /'pôlzē/ ▶ n. (pl. **palsies**) dated paralysis, esp. that which is accompanied by involuntary tremors: *a kind of palsy had seized him.* ■ archaic a condition of incapacity or helplessness.
▶ v. (**palsies, palsying, palsied**) [with obj.] affect with paralysis and involuntary tremors: *she feels as if the muscles on her face are palsied* | (as adj. **palsied**) figurative *the old-boy network laid its palsied hand upon the business of wealth creation.*
– ORIGIN Middle English: from Old French *paralisie*, from an alteration of Latin *paralysis* (see PARALYSIS).

pal·sy-wal·sy /ˌpalzē 'walzē/ ▶ adj. informal very friendly or intimate.
– ORIGIN 1930s (as a noun in the sense 'friend'): from the noun PAL + -SY, by reduplication.

pal·ter /'pôltər/ ▶ v. [no obj.] archaic **1** equivocate or prevaricate in action or speech.
2 (**palter with**) trifle with: *this great work should not be paltered with.*
– DERIVATIVES **pal·ter·er** n.
– ORIGIN mid 16th cent. (in the sense 'mumble or babble'): of unknown origin; no corresponding verb is known in any other language.

pal·try /'pôltrē/ ▶ adj. (**paltrier, paltriest**) (of an amount) small or meager: *she would earn a paltry $33 more each month.* ■ petty; trivial: *naval glory struck him as paltry.*
– DERIVATIVES **pal·tri·ness** n.
– ORIGIN mid 16th cent.: apparently based on dialect *pelt* 'trash, esp. rags'; compare with Low German *paltrig* 'ragged.'

pa·lu·dal /pə'lo͞odl, 'palyədl/ ▶ adj. Ecology (of a plant, animal, or soil) living or occurring in a marshy habitat.
– ORIGIN early 19th cent.: from Latin *palus, palud-* 'marsh' + -AL.

pal·y /'pālē/ ▶ adj. Heraldry divided into equal vertical stripes: *paly of six, argent and gules.*
– ORIGIN late Middle English: from Old French *pale* 'divided by stakes,' from *pal* 'pale, stake.'

pal·y·nol·o·gy /ˌpalə'näləjē/ ▶ n. the study of pollen grains and other spores, esp. as found in archaeological or geological deposits.
– DERIVATIVES **pal·y·no·log·i·cal** /-nə'läjikəl/ adj., **pal·y·nol·o·gist** /-jist/ n.
– ORIGIN 1940s: from Greek *palunein* 'sprinkle' + -LOGY.

pam. ▶ abbr. pamphlet.

Pa·mir Moun·tains /pə'mi(ə)r/ (also **the Pamirs**) a mountain system of central Asia that is centered in Tajikistan and extends into Kyrgyzstan, Afghanistan, Pakistan, and western China. The highest mountain is Ismail Samani Peak in Tajikistan.

Pam·li·co Sound /'pamliˌkō/ an inlet of the Atlantic Ocean in eastern North Carolina, inside the islands of the Outer Banks, south of Albemarle Sound.

pam·pas /'pampəz, -pəs/ ▶ n. [treated as sing. or pl.] extensive, treeless plains in South America.
– ORIGIN early 18th cent.: via Spanish from Quechua *pampa* 'plain.'

pam·pas grass /'pampəs/ ▶ n. a tall South American grass with silky flowering plumes, widely cultivated as an ornamental plant. ● *Cortaderia selloana*, family Gramineae.

pam·per /'pampər/ ▶ v. [with obj.] indulge with every attention, comfort, and kindness; spoil: *famous people just love being pampered.*
– ORIGIN late Middle English (in the sense 'cram with food'): probably of Low German or Dutch origin; compare with German dialect *pampfen* 'cram, gorge'; perhaps related to PAP[1].

pam·pe·ro /päm'perō/ ▶ n. (pl. **pamperos**) a strong, cold southwesterly wind in South America, blowing from the Andes across the pampas toward the Atlantic.
– ORIGIN late 18th cent.: from Spanish *pampas* 'plain' (see PAMPAS).

pam·phlet /'pamflit/ ▶ n. a small booklet or leaflet containing information or arguments about a single subject.
▶ v. (**pamphlets, pamphleting, pamphleted**) [with obj.] distribute pamphlets to.
– ORIGIN late Middle English: from *Pamphilet*, the familiar name of the 12th-cent. Latin love poem *Pamphilus, seu de Amore*.

pam·phlet·eer /ˌpamfli'ti(ə)r/ ▶ n. a writer of pamphlets, esp. ones of a political and controversial nature.
▶ v. [no obj.] (usu. as noun **pamphleteering**) write and issue such pamphlets.

Pam·phyl·i·a /pam'filēə/ an ancient coastal region of southern Asia Minor, between Lycia and Cilicia, to the east of the modern port of Antalya.
– DERIVATIVES **Pam·phyl·i·an** /pam'filēən/ adj. & n.

Pam·plo·na /pam'plōnə, päm-/ a city in northern Spain, capital of the former kingdom and modern region of Navarre; pop. 197,275 (2008). It is noted for the fiesta of San Fermin, held there in July, which is celebrated with the running of bulls through the streets of the city.

Pan /pan/ Greek Mythology a god of flocks and herds, typically represented with the horns, ears, and legs of a goat on a man's body. His sudden appearance was supposed to cause terror similar to that of a frightened and stampeding herd, and the word *panic* is derived from his name.
– ORIGIN probably originally in the sense 'the feeder' (i.e., herdsman), although the name was regularly associated with Greek *pas* or *pan* (= 'all'), giving rise to his identification as a god of nature or the universe.

pan[1] /pan/ ▶ n. **1** a container made of metal and used for cooking food in. ■ an amount of something contained in such a container: *a pan of hot water.* ■ a large container used in a technical or manufacturing process for subjecting a material to heat or a mechanical or chemical process. ■ a bowl fitted at either end of a balance, in which items to be weighed are set. ■ another term for STEEL DRUM. ■ a shallow bowl in which gold is separated from gravel and mud by agitation and washing. ■ a hollow in the ground in which water may collect or in which a deposit of salt remains after water has evaporated. ■ a part of the lock that held the priming in old types of guns.
2 informal a person's face.
3 a hard stratum of compacted soil.
▶ v. (**pans, panned, panning**) [with obj.] **1** informal criticize (someone or something) severely: *the movie was panned by the critics.*
2 wash gravel in a pan to separate out (gold): *the old-timers panned gold* | [no obj.] *prospectors panned for gold in the Yukon.* ■ (of gravel) yield gold.
– PHRASAL VERBS **pan out** turn out well: *Harold's idea had been a good one even if it hadn't panned out.* ■ end up; conclude: *he's happy with the way the deal panned out.*
– DERIVATIVES **pan·ful** /-ˌfo͝ol/ n. (pl. **panfuls**).
– ORIGIN Old English *panne*; related to Dutch *pan*, German *Pfanne*, perhaps based on Latin *patina* 'dish.'

pan[2] ▶ v. (**pans, panning, panned**) [with obj.] swing (a video or movie camera) in a horizontal or vertical plane, typically to give a panoramic effect or follow a subject. ■ [no obj.] (of a camera) be swung in such a way: *the camera panned to the dead dictator.*
▶ n. a panning movement: *that slow pan over Los Angeles.*
– PHRASES **pan and scan** a technique for narrowing the aspect ratio of a widescreen movie to fit the squarer shape of a television screen by continuously selecting the portion of the original picture with the most significance, rather than just the middle portion.
– ORIGIN early 20th cent.: abbreviation of PANORAMA.

pan- ▶ comb. form all-inclusive, esp. in relation to the whole of a continent, racial group, religion, etc.: *pan-African* | *pansexual.*
– ORIGIN from Greek *pan*, neuter of *pas* 'all.'

pan·a·ce·a /ˌpanə'sēə/ ▶ n. a solution or remedy for all difficulties or diseases: *the panacea for all corporate ills* | *the time-honored panacea, cod liver oil.*
– DERIVATIVES **pan·a·ce·an** /-'sēən/ adj.
– ORIGIN mid 16th cent.: via Latin from Greek *panakeia*, from *panakēs* 'all-healing,' from *pan* 'all' + *akos* 'remedy.'

pa·nache /pə'nasH, -'näsH/ ▶ n. **1** flamboyant confidence of style or manner: *he entertained Palm Springs society with great panache.*
2 historical a tuft or plume of feathers, esp. as a headdress or on a helmet.
– ORIGIN mid 16th cent.: from French, from Italian *pennacchio*, from late Latin *pinnaculum*, diminutive of *pinna* 'feather.'

pa·na·da /pə'nädə, -'nādə/ ▶ n. a dish consisting of bread boiled to a pulp and flavored.
– ORIGIN late 16th cent.: from Spanish and Portuguese, based on Latin *panis* 'bread.'

pan-Af·ri·can ▶ adj. of or relating to all people of African birth or descent.

pan-Af·ri·can·ism ▶ n. the principle or advocacy of the political union of all the indigenous inhabitants of Africa.
– DERIVATIVES **pan-Af·ri·can·ist** n.

Pan-Af·ri·can·ist Con·gress (in full **Pan-Africanist Congress of Azania**) (abbr.: **PAC**) a South African political movement formed in 1959 as a militant offshoot of the African National Congress. It was outlawed in 1960 after the Sharpeville massacre, but continued its armed opposition to the South African government until it was legalized in 1990.

Pan·a·ma /'panəˌmä, -ˌmô/ a country in Central America; pop. 3,360,500 (est. 2009); capital, Panama City; language, Spanish (official).

> Panama occupies the isthmus that connects North and South America. Colonized by Spain in the early 16th century, it was freed from imperial control in 1821 and became a Colombian province. It gained full independence in 1903, although the construction of the Panama Canal and the leasing of the zone around it to the US split the country in two. In 1989, US troops invaded Panama and arrested the country's president, Gen. Manuel Noriega, on charges of drug trafficking. According to an agreement signed in 1977, the Panama Canal and the surrounding zone were turned over to Panama at the end of 1999.

– DERIVATIVES **Pan·a·ma·ni·an** /ˌpanə'mānēən/ adj. & n.

pan·a·ma /'panəˌmä/ (also **panama hat**) ▶ n. a wide-brimmed hat of strawlike material, originally made from the leaves of a particular tropical palm tree, worn chiefly by men.
– ORIGIN mid 19th cent.: named after the country of PANAMA.

Pan·a·ma, Isth·mus of (formerly the ***Isthmus of Darien***) in the narrowest sense, the site of the Panama Canal. More broadly, all the territory of Panama, or the entire region that connects North and South America.

Pan·a·ma Ca·nal a canal about 50 miles (80 km) long, across the Isthmus of Panama, that connects the Atlantic and Pacific oceans. Its construction, begun by Ferdinand de Lesseps in 1881, was abandoned in 1889 and was completed by the US, 1904–14. Control of the canal remained with the US until 1999, when it was ceded to Panama.

Pan·a·ma Cit·y **1** the capital of Panama, situated on the Pacific coast close to the Panama Canal; pop. 425,600 (est. 2009).
2 a port city in northwestern Florida; pop. 36,644 (est. 2008).

Pan·a·ma dis·ease ▶ n. a fungal disease of bananas producing yellowing and wilting of the leaves. ● The fungus is a form of *Fusarium oxysporum*, subdivision Deuteromycotina.

Pan·a·ma Red ▶ n. a potent variety of marijuana from Panama that is reddish in color.

Pan·a·max /'panə,maks/ ▶ adj. denoting a ship having the maximum permissible dimensions (length, breadth, and draft) for transiting the Panama Canal, with a dead-weight capacity of about 75,000 tons.
– ORIGIN 1980s: blend of **PANAMA** and the adjective **MAXIMUM**.

pan-A·mer·i·can /,panə'merikən/ ▶ adj. of, relating to, representing, or involving all the countries of North and South America.

Pan-A·mer·i·can High·way a road system initiated in the 1920s to link nations of the western hemisphere from Alaska to Chile. Gaps remain in Panama and Colombia. The ***Inter-American Highway*** is the section from the Texas-Mexico border south to Panama City.

pan-A·mer·i·can·ism ▶ n. the principle or advocacy of political or commercial and cultural cooperation among all the countries of North and South America.

Pan·a·mint Range /'panəmint/ a mountain range in east central California, west of Death Valley, noted for its high walls and deep canyons.

pan-and-tilt ▶ adj. denoting a stand, tripod, or other item of mounting equipment that allows a camera to move in both horizontal and vertical planes.

pan-Ar·ab·ism ▶ n. the principle or advocacy of political alliance or union of all the Arab states.
– DERIVATIVES **pan-Ar·ab** adj.

pan·a·tel·a /,panə'telə/ ▶ n. a long thin cigar.
– ORIGIN mid 19th cent.: from Latin American Spanish *panatela*, denoting a long thin cookie, from Italian *panatello* 'small loaf,' diminutive of *panata*.

Pa·nay /pə'nī/ an island in the central Philippines; chief town, Iloilo.

pan·cake /'pan,kāk/ ▶ n. a thin, flat cake of batter, usually fried and turned in a pan. Pancakes are usually eaten with syrup or rolled up with a filling. ■ (also **pancake makeup**) makeup consisting of a flat solid layer of compressed powder, widely used in the theater.
▶ v. **1** with reference to an aircraft) make or cause to make a pancake landing. [with obj.] ***he pancaked it in about twenty meters.***
2 informal flatten or become flattened: [no obj.] ***the hotel had pancaked into a heap of concrete.***
– PHRASES **(as) flat as a pancake** completely flat.
– ORIGIN late Middle English: from **PAN¹** + **CAKE**.

pan·cake land·ing ▶ n. an emergency landing in which an aircraft levels out close to the ground and drops vertically with its undercarriage still retracted.

pan·cake race ▶ n. a race in which each competitor must toss a pancake in a pan as they run, traditionally held in some places on Shrove Tuesday.

Pan·cake Tues·day ▶ n. Shrove Tuesday, when pancakes are traditionally eaten.

pan·cet·ta /pan'CHetə/ ▶ n. Italian cured belly of pork.
– ORIGIN Italian, diminutive of *pancio* 'belly.'

pan·cha·kar·ma /,pənCHə'kärmə/ ▶ n. (in Ayurvedic medicine) a fivefold detoxification treatment involving massage, herbal therapy, and other procedures.
– ORIGIN 1980s: from Sanskrit, *panca*, 'five' + *karman*, 'action.'

pan·cha·yat /pan'CHīət/ ▶ n. Indian a village council.
– ORIGIN from Hindi (originally denoting a council consisting of five members), from Sanskrit *panca* 'five' + *āyatta* 'depending upon.'

Pan·chen La·ma /'pänCHen 'lämə/ ▶ n. a Tibetan lama ranking next after the Dalai Lama.
– ORIGIN Tibetan *panchen*, abbreviation of *pandi-tachen-po* 'great learned one'; compare with **PUNDIT**.

Pan·chiao /'pan'CHyou/ (also **Pan-ch'iao**) a city in northern Taiwan, southwest of Taipei; pop. 547,600 (est. 2007).

pan·chro·mat·ic /,pankrō'matik/ ▶ adj. Photography (of photographic film) sensitive to all visible colors of the spectrum. Often contrasted with **ORTHOCHROMATIC**.

pan·cre·as /'paNGkrēəs, 'pankrēəs/ ▶ n. (pl. **pancreases**) a large gland behind the stomach that secretes digestive enzymes into the duodenum. Embedded in the pancreas are the islets of Langerhans, which secrete into the blood the hormones insulin and glucagon.
– DERIVATIVES **pan·cre·at·ic** /-krē'atik/ adj.
– ORIGIN late 16th cent.: modern Latin, from Greek *pankreas*, from *pan* 'all' + *kreas* 'flesh.'

pan·cre·a·tec·to·my /,paNGkrēə'tektəmē, ,pan-/ ▶ n. (pl. **pancreatectomies**) surgical removal of the pancreas.

pan·cre·at·ic juice /,paNGkrē'atik, ,pan-/ ▶ n. the clear alkaline digestive fluid secreted by the pancreas.

pan·cre·a·tin /'paNGkrēətn, 'pan-, ,pan'krēətn/ ▶ n. a mixture of enzymes obtained from animal pancreases, given as a medicine to aid digestion.

pan·cre·a·ti·tis /,paNGkrēə'tītis, ,pan-/ ▶ n. Medicine inflammation of the pancreas.

pan·cre·o·zy·min /,paNGkrēə'zīmin, ,pan-/ ▶ n. Biochemistry a hormone that stimulates the production of enzymes by the pancreas.

pan·cy·to·pe·ni·a /,pansītə'pēnēə/ ▶ n. Medicine deficiency of all three cellular components of the blood (red cells, white cells, and platelets).
– ORIGIN mid 20th cent.: from **PAN-** 'all' + **CYTO-** 'cell' + Greek *penia* 'poverty, lack.'

pan·da /'pandə/ (also **giant panda**) ▶ n. a large bearlike mammal with characteristic black and white markings, native to certain mountain forests of central and western China. It feeds almost entirely on bamboo and has become increasingly rare. See also **RED PANDA**. ● *Ailuropoda melanoleuca*; it is now usually placed with the bears (family Ursidae), but was formerly thought to belong with the raccoons (family Procyonidae).
– ORIGIN mid 19th cent.: from Nepali.

panda

pan·da·nus /pan'dānəs, -'danəs/ (also **pandan** /'pandən/) ▶ n. a tropical tree or shrub that has a twisted and branched stem, stilt roots, spiral tufts of long, narrow, typically spiny leaves, and fibrous edible fruit. Also called **SCREW PINE**. ● Genus *Pandanus*, family Pandanaceae. ■ fiber from the leaves of this plant, or material woven from this fiber.
– ORIGIN modern Latin, from Malay *pandan*.

Pan·da·rus /'pandərəs/ Greek Mythology a Lycian who fought on the side of the Trojans, described in the *Iliad* as breaking the truce with the Greeks by wounding Menelaus with an arrow. The role as the lovers' go-between that he plays in Chaucer's (and later Shakespeare's) story of Troilus and Cressida originated with Boccaccio and is the origin of the word *pander*.

pan·dect /'pan,dekt/ ▶ n. chiefly historical a complete body of the laws of a country. ■ (usu. **the Pandects**) a compendium in 50 books of the Roman civil law made by order of Justinian in the 6th century.
– DERIVATIVES **pan·dect·ist** /pan'dektist/ n.
– ORIGIN mid 16th cent.: from French *pandecte*, from Latin *pandecta*, from Greek *pandektēs* 'all-receiver,' from *pan* 'all' + *dektēs* (from *dekhesthai* 'receive').

pan·dem·ic /pan'demik/ ▶ adj. (of a disease) prevalent over a whole country or the world.
▶ n. an outbreak of such a disease.
– ORIGIN mid 17th cent.: from Greek *pandēmos* (from *pan* 'all' + *dēmos* 'people') + **-IC**.

USAGE On the difference between **pandemic**, **endemic**, and **epidemic**, see usage at **EPIDEMIC**.

pan·de·mo·ni·um /,pandə'mōnēəm/ ▶ n. wild and noisy disorder or confusion; uproar: *pandemonium broke out.*
– ORIGIN mid 17th cent.: modern Latin (denoting the place of all demons, in Milton's *Paradise Lost*), from **PAN-** 'all' + Greek *daimōn* 'demon.'

pan·der /'pandər/ ▶ v. [no obj.] **(pander to)** gratify or indulge (an immoral or distasteful desire, need, or habit or a person with such a desire, etc.): *newspapers are pandering to people's baser instincts.*
▶ n. dated a pimp. ■ archaic a person who assists the baser urges or evil designs of others: ***the lowest panders of a venal press.***
– ORIGIN late Middle English (as a noun): from *Pandare*, the name of a character in Chaucer's *Troilus and Criseyde* (see **PANDARUS**). The verb dates from the early 17th cent.

Pan·dit /'pandit, 'pən-/, Vijaya (Lakshmi) (1900–90), Indian politician and diplomat, sister of Jawaharlal Nehru. Having been imprisoned three times by the British for nationalist activities, after independence she became the first woman to serve as president of the UN General Assembly (1953–54).

pan·dit /'pəndit, 'pan-/ (also **pundit**) ▶ n. a Hindu scholar learned in Sanskrit and Hindu philosophy and religion, typically also a practicing priest: [as title] *Pandit Misir.* ■ Indian a wise man or teacher. ■ Indian a talented musician (used as a respectful title or form of address).
– ORIGIN Of the same origin as **PUNDIT**.

P & L ▶ abbr. profit and loss account.

Pan·do·ra /pan'dôrə/ Greek Mythology the first mortal woman. In one story she was created by Zeus and sent to earth with a jar or box of evils in revenge for Prometheus' having brought the gift of fire back to the world. Pandora let out all the evils from the jar to infect the earth; hope alone remained to assuage the lot of humankind.
– ORIGIN from the Greek name *Pandōra* 'all-gifted' (from *pan* 'all' + *dōron* 'gift').

pan·do·ra /pan'dôrə/ (also **pandora shell** or **Pandora's box shell**) ▶ n. a burrowing bivalve mollusk with a fragile shell, the unequal valves of which form a "box" with a lid. ● Genus *Pandora*, family Pandoridae.
– ORIGIN modern Latin, from Greek *pandoura* 'three-stringed lute' (because of the shell's resemblance to the sound box of a stringed instrument).

Pan·do·ra's box ▶ n. a process that generates many complicated problems as the result of unwise interference in something.

pan·dow·dy /pan'doudē/ ▶ n. (pl. **pandowdies**) a kind of spiced apple pie baked in a deep dish.
– ORIGIN of unknown origin.

p. & p. ▶ abbr. Brit. postage and packing.

pane /pān/ ▶ n. a single sheet of glass in a window or door. ■ Computing a separate defined area within a window for the display of, or interaction with, a part of that window's application or output. ■ a sheet or page of postage stamps.
– ORIGIN late Middle English (originally denoting a section or piece of something, such as a fence or strip of cloth): from Old French *pan*, from Latin *pannus* 'piece of cloth.'

pan·e·gyr·ic /,panə'jirik/ ▶ n. a public speech or published text in praise of someone or something: *Vera's panegyric on friendship.*
– DERIVATIVES **pan·e·gyr·i·cal** /-'jirikəl/ adj., **pan·e·gyr·i·cal·ly** adv.
– ORIGIN early 17th cent.: from French *panégyrique*, via Latin from Greek *panēgurikos* 'of public assembly,' from *pan* 'all' + *aguris* 'agora, assembly.'

pan·e·gy·rize /'panəjə,rīz/ ▶ v. [with obj.] archaic speak or write in praise of; eulogize.
– DERIVATIVES **pan·e·gyr·ist** /,panə'jirist/ n.

pan·el /'panl/ ▶ n. **1** a thin, typically rectangular piece of wood or glass forming or set into the surface of a door, wall, or ceiling. ■ a thin piece of metal forming part of the outer shell of a vehicle: *body panels for the car business.* ■ a flat board on which instruments or controls are fixed: *a control panel.* ■ a decorated area within a larger design containing a separate subject: *the central panel depicts the Crucifixion.* ■ one of several drawings making up a comic strip. ■ a piece of material forming part of a garment.
2 a small group of people brought together to discuss, investigate, or decide on a particular matter, esp. in the context of business or government: *we assembled a panel of experts.* ■ a list of available jurors or a jury.
▶ v. **(panels, paneling, paneled**; Brit. **panels, panelling, panelled)** [with obj.] (usu. as adj. **paneled**) cover (a wall or other surface) with panels: *an elegant paneled dining room.*
– ORIGIN Middle English: from Old French, literally 'piece of cloth,' based on Latin *pannus* '(piece of) cloth.' The early sense 'piece of parchment' was extended to mean 'list,' whence the notion 'advisory group' sense 1 of the noun derives from the late Middle English sense 'distinct (usually framed) section of a surface.'

pan·el·ing /'panəliNG/ (Brit. **panelling**) ▶ n. panels collectively, when used to decorate a wall.

pan·el·ist /'panəlist/ (Brit. **panellist**) ▶ n. a member of a panel, esp. in a formal public discussion.

pan·el stud·y ▶ n. an investigation of attitude changes using a constant set of people and comparing each individual's opinions at different times.

pan·el truck ▶ n. a small enclosed delivery truck.

pan·en·the·ism /pa'nenTHē,izəm/ ▶ n. the belief or doctrine that God is greater than the universe and includes and interpenetrates it.

P

– DERIVATIVES **pan·en·the·is·tic** /ˌpanenTHēˈistik/ **adj.**

pan·et·to·ne /ˌpanəˈtōnē/ ▶ **n.** (pl. **panettoni** pronunc. **same**) a rich Italian bread made with eggs, fruit, and butter and typically eaten at Christmas.
– ORIGIN Italian, from *panetto* 'cake,' diminutive of *pane* 'bread' (from Latin *panis* 'bread').

pan·fish /ˈpanˌfiSH/ ▶ **n.** (pl. **same** or **panfishes**) a fish suitable for frying whole in a pan, esp. one caught by an angler rather than bought.
▶ **v.** [no obj.] (often as noun **panfishing**) catch, or try to catch, such fish: *panfishing picks up considerably during the fall and spring.*

pan·for·te /panˈfôrˌtā/ ▶ **n.** a hard, spicy Sienese cake containing nuts, candied citrus peel, and honey.
– ORIGIN Italian, from *pane* 'bread' + *forte* 'strong.'

pan-fry ▶ **v.** [with obj.] (often as adj. **pan-fried**) fry in a pan in a small amount of fat: *pan-fried trout.*

pang /paNG/ ▶ **n.** a sudden sharp pain or painful emotion: *Lindsey experienced a sharp pang of guilt* | *the snack bar will keep those hunger pangs at bay.*
– ORIGIN late 15th cent.: perhaps an alteration of **PRONG**.

pan·ga /ˈpäNGgə/ ▶ **n.** a bladed African tool like a machete.
– ORIGIN Kiswahili.

Pan·gae·a /panˈjēə/ (also **Pangea**) a supercontinent comprising all the continental crust of the earth, postulated to have existed in late Paleozoic and Mesozoic times before it broke into Gondwana and Laurasia.
– ORIGIN early 20th cent.: from **PAN-** 'all' + Greek *gaia* 'earth.'

pan-Ger·man ▶ **adj.** of, relating to, or advocating pan-Germanism. ■ of, relating to, or including both East and West Germany.
– DERIVATIVES **pan-Ger·man·ic adj.**

pan-Ger·man·ism ▶ **n.** the idea or principle of a political unification of all Europeans speaking German or a Germanic language.

Pan·gloss /ˈpanglôs, -gläs/ ▶ **n.** a person who is optimistic regardless of the circumstances.
– DERIVATIVES **Pan·gloss·i·an** /panˈglôsēən, -ˈgläs-/ **adj.**
– ORIGIN mid 19th cent.: from the name of the tutor and philosopher in Voltaire's *Candide* (1759).

pan·go·lin /ˈpaNGgəlin, paNGˈgōlin/ ▶ **n.** an African and Asian mammal that has a body covered with horny overlapping scales, a small head with elongated snout, a long sticky tongue for catching ants and termites, and a thick, tapering tail. Also called **SCALY ANTEATER**. ● Family Manidae and order Pholidota: genera *Manis* (three species in Asia) and *Phataginus* (four species in Africa).
– ORIGIN late 18th cent.: from Malay *peng-guling*, literally 'roller' (from its habit of rolling into a ball).

pan·gram /ˈpanˌgram/ ▶ **n.** a sentence or verse that contains all the letters of the alphabet.

pan·han·dle /ˈpanˌhandl/ ▶ **n.** (often in place names) a narrow strip of territory projecting from the main territory of one state into another state: *the Oklahoma Panhandle.*
▶ **v.** [no obj.] informal beg in the street: *she went back to the streets to panhandle for money.*
– DERIVATIVES **pan·han·dler n.**

Pan·han·dle State a nickname for the state of **WEST VIRGINIA**.

Pan·hel·len·ic /ˌpanhəˈlenik/ ▶ **adj.** of, concerning, or representing all people of Greek origin or ancestry. ■ relating to, advocating, or denoting the idea of a political union of all Greeks. ■ of, concerning, or representing all college fraternities and sororities.

pa·ni /ˈpänē/ ▶ **n.** a term used in India for **WATER**.
– ORIGIN from Hindi *pānī*.

pan·ic[1] /ˈpanik/ ▶ **n.** sudden uncontrollable fear or anxiety, often causing wildly unthinking behavior: *she hit him in panic* | [in sing.] *he ran to the library in a blind panic.* ■ widespread financial or commercial apprehension provoking hasty action: *he caused an economic panic by his sudden resignation* | [as modifier] *panic selling.* ■ informal a frenzied hurry to do something: *a workload of constant panics and rush jobs.*
▶ **v.** (**panics, panicking, panicked**) feel or cause to feel panic: [no obj.] *the crowd panicked and stampeded for the exit* | [with obj.] *talk of love panicked her.*
– DERIVATIVES **pan·ick·y adj.**
– ORIGIN early 17th cent.: from French *panique*, from modern Latin *panicus*, from Greek *panikos*, from the name of the god **PAN**, noted for causing terror, to whom woodland noises were attributed.

pan·ic[2] (also **panic grass**) ▶ **n.** any of a number of cereal and fodder grasses related to millet. ● *Panicum* and related genera, family Gramineae.
– ORIGIN late Middle English: from Latin *panicum*, from *panus* 'ear of millet' (literally 'thread wound on a bobbin'), based on Greek *pēnos* 'web,' *pēnion* 'bobbin.'

pan·ic at·tack ▶ **n.** a sudden feeling of acute and disabling anxiety.

pan·ic but·ton ▶ **n.** a button for summoning help in an emergency: *personal attack circuits are operated by panic buttons.*
– PHRASES **press** (or **push** or **hit**) **the panic button** informal respond to a situation by panicking or taking emergency measures.

pan·ic dis·or·der ▶ **n.** a psychiatric disorder in which debilitating anxiety and fear arise frequently and without reasonable cause.

pan·i·cle /ˈpanikəl/ ▶ **n.** Botany a loose, branching cluster of flowers, as in oats.
– DERIVATIVES **pan·i·cled adj.**
– ORIGIN late 16th cent.: from Latin *panicula*, diminutive of *panus* 'ear of millet' (see **PANIC**[2]).

pan·ic room ▶ **n.** another term for a **SAFE ROOM**.

pan·ic-strick·en (also **panic-struck**) ▶ **adj.** affected with panic; very frightened: *the panic-stricken victims rushed out of their blazing homes.*

pan-In·di·an ▶ **adj.** **1** of or relating to the whole of India, or to all its ethnic, religious, or linguistic groups.
2 denoting or relating to a cultural movement or religious practice participated in by many or all American Indian peoples.

Pa·ni·ni /ˈpäninē/, Indian grammarian. Sources vary as to when he lived, with dates ranging from the 4th to the 7th century BC. He is noted as the author of the *Eight Lectures*, a grammar of Sanskrit.

pa·ni·ni /pəˈnēnē/ (also **panino** /-nō/) ▶ **n.** (pl. **same** or **paninis**) a sandwich made with Italian bread, usually toasted.
– ORIGIN 1950s: from Italian, literally 'bread roll.'

pa·ni pu·ri /ˈpänē ˌpo͝orē/ ▶ **n.** (in Indian cooking) a puff-pastry ball filled with spiced mashed potato and tamarind juice and then fried.
– ORIGIN from Hindi *pānī* 'water' and *pūrī* from Sanskrit *pūrikā* 'small, fried wheaten cake.'

pa·nir /pəˈni(ə)r/ (also **paneer**) ▶ **n.** a type of curd cheese used in Indian, Iranian, and Afghan cooking.
– ORIGIN Hindi and Persian, 'cheese.'

Pan·ja·bi /pənˈjäbē/ ▶ **n.** (pl. **Panjabis**) & **adj.** variant spelling of **PUNJABI**.

pan·jan·drum /panˈjandrəm/ ▶ **n.** a person who has or claims to have a great deal of authority or influence.
– ORIGIN late 19th cent.: from *Grand Panjandrum*, an invented phrase in a nonsense verse (1755) by S. Foote.

Pank·hurst /ˈpaNGkˌhərst/ the name of a family of English suffragists, comprising **Mrs. Emmeline** (1858–1928) and her daughters, **Christabel** (1880–1958) and **(Estelle) Sylvia** (1882–1960). In 1903, they founded the Women's Social and Political Union. When Christabel was imprisoned in 1905, Emmeline initiated the militant suffrage campaign that continued until the outbreak of World War I.

pan·mix·i·a /panˈmiksēə/ ▶ **n.** Zoology random mating within a breeding population.
– DERIVATIVES **pan·mic·tic** /-ˈmiktik/ **adj.**
– ORIGIN late 19th cent.: modern Latin, from German *Panmixie*, from Greek *pan* 'all' + *mixis* 'mixing.'

Pan·mun·jom /ˈˌpanˈmo͝onˈjôm/ a village in the demilitarized zone between North and South Korea. It was here that the armistice ending the Korean War was signed on July 27, 1953.

pan·na cot·ta /ˌpanə ˈkotə/ ▶ **n.** a cold Italian custard, often served with fruit sauce or caramel syrup.
– ORIGIN Italian, literally 'cooked cream.'

pan·nage /ˈpanij/ ▶ **n.** chiefly historical the right or privilege of feeding pigs or other animals in a wood. ■ pasturage for pigs in woodland.
– ORIGIN late Middle English: from Old French *pasnage*, from medieval Latin *pastionaticum*, from *pastio(n-)* 'pasturing,' from the verb *pascere* 'to feed.'

panne /pan/ (also **panne velvet**) ▶ **n.** a lustrous fabric resembling velvet, made of silk or rayon and having a flattened pile.
– ORIGIN late 18th cent.: from French, of unknown origin.

pan·nier /ˈpanyər, ˈpanēər/ ▶ **n.** **1** a basket, esp. one of a pair carried by a beast of burden. ■ each of a pair of bags or boxes fitted on either side of the rear wheel of a bicycle or motorcycle.
2 historical part of a skirt looped up around the hips. ■ a frame supporting this.
– ORIGIN Middle English: from Old French *panier*, from Latin *panarium* 'breadbasket,' from *panis* 'bread.'

pan·ni·kin /ˈpanikin/ ▶ **n.** a small metal drinking cup.
– ORIGIN early 19th cent.: from **PAN**[1], on the pattern of *cannikin*.

pan·nist /ˈpanist/ ▶ **n.** W. Indian a person who plays a pan in a steel band. See **PAN**[1] (sense 1 of the noun).

Pan·no·ni·a /pəˈnōnēə/ an ancient country of southern Europe that was south and west of the Danube River, in present-day Austria, Hungary, Slovenia, and Croatia.

pan·nus /ˈpanəs/ ▶ **n.** Medicine a condition in which a layer of vascular fibrous tissue extends over the surface of an organ or other specialized anatomical structure, esp. the cornea.
– ORIGIN late Middle English: perhaps from Latin, literally 'cloth.'

pan·o·ply /ˈpanəplē/ ▶ **n.** a complete or impressive collection of things: *a deliciously inventive panoply of insults.* ■ a splendid display: *all the panoply of Western religious liturgy.* ■ historical or literary a complete set of arms or suit of armor.
– DERIVATIVES **pan·o·plied** /-plēd/ **adj.**
– ORIGIN late 16th cent. (in the sense 'complete protection for spiritual warfare,' often with biblical allusion to Eph. 6:11, 13): from French *panoplie* or modern Latin *panoplia* 'full armor,' from Greek, from *pan* 'all' + *hopla* 'arms.'

pan·op·tic /paˈnäptik/ ▶ **adj.** showing or seeing the whole at one view: *a panoptic aerial view.*
– ORIGIN early 19th cent.: from Greek *panoptos* 'seen by all,' from *panoptēs* 'all-seeing' + **-IC**.

pan·op·ti·con /paˈnäptiˌkän/ ▶ **n.** historical a circular prison with cells arranged around a central well, from which prisoners could at all times be observed.
– ORIGIN mid 18th cent.: from **PAN-** 'all' + Greek *optikon*, neuter of *optikos* 'optic.'

pan·o·ram·a /ˌpanəˈramə, -ˈrämə/ ▶ **n.** an unbroken view of the whole region surrounding an observer: *the tower offers a wonderful panorama of Prague.* ■ a picture or photograph containing a wide view. ■ a complete survey or presentation of a subject or sequence of events: *the galleries will offer a full panorama of 20th-century art.*
– ORIGIN late 18th cent.: from **PAN-** 'all' + Greek *horama* 'view' (from *horan* 'see').

pan·o·ram·ic /ˌpanəˈramik/ ▶ **adj.** (of a view or picture) with a wide view surrounding the observer; sweeping: *on a clear day there are panoramic views.* ■ including all aspects of a subject; wide-ranging: *his panoramic vision of post–World War I peace.*
– DERIVATIVES **pan·o·ram·i·cal·ly** /-ˈramik(ə)lē/ **adv.**

pan-pan /pan pan/ ▶ **n.** an international radio distress signal, of less urgency than a mayday signal.
– ORIGIN 1920s: *pan* from French *panne* 'breakdown.'

pan·pipes /ˈpanˌpīps/ ▶ **plural n.** a musical instrument made from a row of short pipes of varying length fixed together and played by blowing across the top.
– ORIGIN originally associated with the Greek rural god **PAN**.

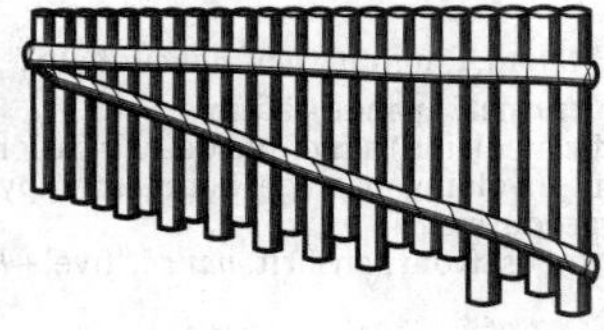

panpipes

pan·psy·chism /panˈsīˌkizəm/ ▶ **n.** the doctrine or belief that everything material, however small, has an element of individual consciousness.
– DERIVATIVES **pan·psy·chist adj. & n.**

pan·sex·u·al /panˈsekSHo͞oəl/ ▶ **adj.** not limited or inhibited in sexual choice with regard to gender or activity.
▶ **n.** a person who is sexually inclusive in this way.
– DERIVATIVES **pan·sex·u·al·i·ty** /-ˌsekSHo͞oˈalitē/ **n.**

pan-Slav·ism ▶ **n.** the principle or advocacy of the union of all Slavs or all Slavic peoples in one political organization.
– DERIVATIVES **pan-Slav·ist adj. & n.**

pan·sper·mi·a /panˈspərmēə/ ▶ **n.** the theory that life on the earth originated from microorganisms or chemical precursors of life present in outer space and able to initiate life on reaching a suitable environment.
– ORIGIN mid 19th cent.: from Greek, from *panspermos* 'containing all kinds of seed.'

pan·sy /ˈpanzē/ ▶ **n.** **1** a popular cultivated viola with flowers in rich colors, with both summer- and

winter-flowering varieties. ● Genus *Viola*, family Violaceae: several species and hybrids, in particular the commonly cultivated *V. cornuta*.
2 informal, offensive an effeminate or homosexual man.
– ORIGIN late Middle English: from French *pensée* 'thought; pansy,' from *penser* 'think,' from Latin *pensare*, frequentative of *pendere* 'weigh, consider.'

pansy 1

pant /pant/ ▶ **v.** [no obj.] breathe with short, quick breaths, typically from exertion or excitement: *he was panting when he reached the top.* ■ [with adverbial of direction] run or go in a specified direction while panting: *they panted up the stairs.* ■ [with direct speech] say something breathlessly: *"We'll never have time," she panted.* ■ long for, or long to do, something: *it makes you pant for more.* ■ literary (of the heart or chest) throb violently from strong emotions.
▶ **n.** a short, quick breath. ■ literary a throb or heave of a person's heart or chest.
– ORIGIN Middle English: related to Old French *pantaisier* 'be agitated, gasp,' based on Greek *phantasioun* 'cause to imagine,' from *phantasia* (see FANTASY).

Pan·ta·gru·el·i·an /ˌpantəgro͞o'elēən/ ▶ **adj.** rare enormous: *a Pantagruelian banquet*.
– ORIGIN late 17th cent.: from *Pantagruel* (the name of an enormous giant in Rabelais's *Gargantua and Pantagruel*) + -IAN.

pan·ta·lets /ˌpantl'ets/ (also **pantalettes**) ▶ **plural n.** long underpants with a frill at the bottom of each leg, worn by women and girls in the 19th century.

pan·ta·loon /ˌpantl'o͞on/ ▶ **n. 1** (**pantaloons**) women's baggy trousers gathered at the ankles. ■ historical men's close-fitting breeches fastened below the calf or at the foot. ■ informal pants.
2 (**Pantaloon**) a Venetian character in Italian commedia dell'arte represented as a foolish old man wearing pantaloons.
– ORIGIN late 16th cent. (sense 2): from French *pantalon*, from the Italian name *Pantalone* 'Pantaloon' (sense 2).

pan·tech·ni·con /pan'teknikən, -ˌkän/ ▶ **n.** Brit. dated a large van for transporting furniture.
– ORIGIN mid 19th cent.: from PAN- 'all' + *tekhnikon* 'piece of art,' originally the name of a bazaar in London for all kinds of artistic work, later converted into a furniture warehouse.

Pan·thal·as·sa /ˌpanTHə'lasə/ a universal sea or single ocean, such as would have surrounded Pangaea.
– ORIGIN late 19th cent.: from PAN- 'all' + Greek *thalassa* 'sea.'

pan·the·ism /'panTHēˌizəm/ ▶ **n. 1** a doctrine that identifies God with the universe, or regards the universe as a manifestation of God.
2 rare worship that admits or tolerates all gods.
– DERIVATIVES **pan·the·ist n.**, **pan·the·is·tic** /ˌpanTHē'istik/ **adj.**, **pan·the·is·ti·cal** /ˌpanTHē'istikəl/ **adj.**, **pan·the·is·ti·cal·ly** /ˌpanTHē'istik(ə)lē/ **adv.**
– ORIGIN mid 18th cent.: from PAN- 'all' + Greek *theos* 'god' + -ISM.

pan·the·on /'panTHēˌän, -THēən/ ▶ **n.** all the gods of a people or religion collectively: *the deities of the Hindu and Shinto pantheons.* ■ (also **Pantheon**) (esp. in ancient Greece and Rome) a temple dedicated to all the gods. ■ a building in which the illustrious dead of a nation are buried or honored. ■ a group of particularly respected, famous, or important people: *the pantheon of the all-time greats.*
– ORIGIN late Middle English (referring esp. to the circular temple built by Hadrian, Severus, and Caracalla in Rome): via Latin from Greek *pantheion*, from *pan* 'all' + *theion* 'holy' (from *theos* 'god').

Pantheon in Rome, Italy

pan·ther /'panTHər/ ▶ **n.** a leopard, esp. a black one. ■ a cougar.
– ORIGIN Middle English: from Old French *pantere*, from Latin *panthera*, from Greek *panthēr*. In Latin, *pardus* 'leopard' also existed; the two terms led to confusion: until the mid 19th cent. many taxonomists regarded the panther and the leopard as separate species.

pan·ther cap ▶ **n.** a poisonous toadstool that has a brownish-gray cap with fluffy white spots and white gills, found in woodlands in both Eurasia and North America. ● *Amanita pantherina*, family Amanitaceae, class Hymenomycetes.

pant·ies /'pantēz/ ▶ **plural n.** informal legless underpants worn by women and girls.

pan·tile /'panˌtīl/ ▶ **n.** a roof tile curved to form an S-shaped section, fitted to overlap its neighbor.
– DERIVATIVES **pan·tiled adj.**
– ORIGIN mid 17th cent.: from PAN[1] + TILE, probably suggested by Dutch *dakpan*, literally 'roof pan.'

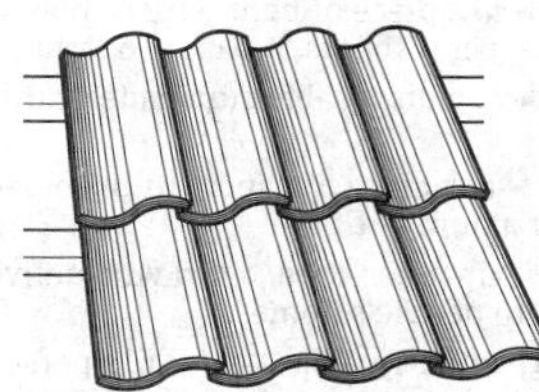

pantile

pant·ing /'pantiNG/ ▶ **adj.** breathing with short, quick breaths; out of breath: *a panting dog.*
– DERIVATIVES **pant·ing·ly adv.**

Pant·i·soc·ra·cy /ˌpanti'säkrəsē/ ▶ **n.** a form of utopian social organization in which all are equal in social position and responsibility.
– DERIVATIVES **Pant·i·so·cra·tic** /-sə'kratik/ **adj.**
– ORIGIN late 18th cent.: from PANTO- 'all' + Greek *isokratia* 'equality of power.'

pan·to /'panˌtō/ ▶ **n.** (pl. **pantos**) Brit. informal short for PANTOMIME (sense 1 of the noun).

panto- ▶ **comb. form** all; universal: *pantograph* | *pantomime.*
– ORIGIN from Greek *pas, pant-* 'all.'

Pan·toc·ra·tor /pan'täkrətər/ ▶ **n.** a title of Christ represented as the ruler of the universe, esp. in Byzantine church decoration.
– ORIGIN late 19th cent.: via Latin from Greek, 'ruler over all.'

pan·to·graph /'pantəˌgraf/ ▶ **n. 1** an instrument for copying a drawing or plan on a different scale by a system of hinged and jointed rods.
2 a jointed framework conveying a current to a train, streetcar, or other electric vehicle from overhead wires.
– DERIVATIVES **pan·to·graph·ic** /ˌpantə'grafik/ **adj.**
– ORIGIN early 18th cent.: from PANTO- 'all, universal' + Greek *-graphos* 'writing.'

pan·to·mime /'pantəˌmīm/ ▶ **n. 1** a dramatic entertainment, originating in Roman mime, in which performers express meaning through gestures accompanied by music. ■ an absurdly exaggerated piece of behavior: *he made a pantomime of checking his watch.* ■ informal a ridiculous or confused situation or event: *the drive to town was a pantomime.*
2 Brit. a theatrical entertainment, mainly for children, that involves music, topical jokes, and slapstick comedy and is based on a fairy tale or nursery story, usually produced around Christmas.
▶ **v.** [with obj.] express or represent (something) by extravagant and exaggerated mime: *the clown candidates pantomimed different emotions.*
– DERIVATIVES **pan·to·mim·ic** /ˌpantə'mimik/ **adj.**, **pan·to·mim·ist n.**
– ORIGIN late 16th cent. (first used in the Latin form and denoting an actor using mime): from French *pantomime* or Latin *pantomimus*, from Greek *pantomimos* 'imitator of all' (see PANTO-, MIME).

Pan·tone /'panˌtōn/ ▶ **n.** [usu. as modifier] trademark a system for matching colors, used in specifying printing inks: *Pantone colors.*

pan·to·then·ic ac·id /ˌpantə'THenik/ ▶ **n.** Biochemistry a vitamin of the B complex, found in rice, bran, and many other foods, and essential for the oxidation of fats and carbohydrates.
– DERIVATIVES **pan·to·then·ate** /pan'täTHənāt/ **n.**
– ORIGIN 1930s: *pantothenic* from Greek *pantothen* 'from every side' (with allusion to its widespread occurrence.).

pan·toum /pan'to͞om/ (also **pantun**) ▶ **n.** a Malay verse form, imitated in French and English, consisting of quotations with an *abab* rhyme scheme linked by repeated lines.
– ORIGIN late 18th cent.: Malay *pantun*.

pan·try /'pantrē/ ▶ **n.** (pl. **pantries**) a small room or closet in which food, dishes, and utensils are kept.
– ORIGIN Middle English: from Anglo-Norman French *panterie*, from *paneter* 'baker,' based on late Latin *panarius* 'bread seller,' from Latin *panis* 'bread.'

pan·try·man /'pantrēmən/ ▶ **n.** (pl. **pantrymen**) a butler or a butler's assistant.

pants /pants/ ▶ **plural n. 1** trousers: *baggy corduroy pants* | (as modifier **pant**) *his pant leg.*
2 Brit. underpants.
3 Brit. informal rubbish; nonsense: *he thought we were going to be absolute pants.*
– PHRASES **catch someone with their pants down** informal catch someone in an embarrassingly unprepared state. **fly** (or **drive**) **by the seat of one's pants** informal rely on instinct rather than logic or knowledge. **scare** (or **bore**, etc.) **the pants off someone** informal make someone extremely scared, bored, etc. **wear the pants** informal be the dominant partner in a relationship: *there's no doubt who'll wear the pants in that house.*
– ORIGIN mid 19th cent.: abbr. of *pantaloons* (see PANTALOON).

pant·suit /'pantˌso͞ot/ (also **pants suit**) ▶ **n.** a pair of pants and a matching jacket worn by women.

pan·tun /pan'to͞on/ ▶ **n.** variant spelling of PANTOUM.

pant·y gir·dle ▶ **n.** a woman's elasticized undergarment combining girdle and panties.

pant·y·hose /'pantēˌhōz/ ▶ **plural n.** women's thin nylon tights.

pant·y raid ▶ **n.** dated a visit by a group of male students to a women's dormitory with the object of stealing panties.

pant·y·waist /'pantēˌwāst/ informal ▶ **n.** a feeble or effeminate person.
▶ **adj.** [attrib.] effeminate or feeble.
– ORIGIN 1930s: extended use of the term's literal sense, 'child's garment consisting of panties attached to a bodice.'

pan·za·nel·la /ˌpanzə'nelə, ˌpansə-/ ▶ **n.** a type of Tuscan salad made with anchovies, chopped salad vegetables, and bread soaked in dressing.
– ORIGIN Italian, from *pane* 'bread' + *zanella* 'small basket.'

pan·zer /'panzər/ ▶ **n.** a German armored vehicle, esp. a tank used in World War II: [as modifier] *panzer divisions.*
– ORIGIN from German *Panzer*, literally 'coat of mail.'

pap[1] /pap/ ▶ **n.** often derogatory bland soft or semiliquid food such as that suitable for babies or invalids: *trying to eat a trayful of tasteless pap.* ■ derogatory reading matter or entertainment that is worthless or lacking in substance: *limitless channels serving up an undemanding diet of pap.*
– ORIGIN late Middle English: probably from Middle Low German and Middle Dutch *pappe*, probably based on Latin *pappare* 'eat.'

pap[2] ▶ **n.** archaic or dialect a woman's breast or nipple.
– ORIGIN Middle English: probably of Scandinavian origin, from a base imitative of the sound of sucking.

pap[3] informal ▶ **n.** a paparazzo.
▶ **v.** (**paps, papping, papped**) [with obj.] take a photograph of (a celebrity) without permission: *she can't go to the gym or anywhere without being papped.*

pa·pa /'päpə/ ▶ **n. 1** one's father: [as name] *Papa had taught her to ride a bicycle.*
2 a code word representing the letter P, used in radio communication.
– ORIGIN late 17th cent.: from French, via late Latin from Greek *papas*.

pa·pa·bi·le /pə'päbəˌlā/ ▶ **adj.** rare worthy of being or eligible to be pope.
– ORIGIN Italian, from Latin *papa* 'pope.'

pa·pa·cy /'pāpəsē/ ▶ **n.** (pl. **papacies**) (usu. **the papacy**) the office or authority of the pope. ■ the tenure of office of a pope: *during the papacy of Pope John.*
– ORIGIN late Middle English: from medieval Latin *papatia*, from *papa* 'pope.'

Papa Doc see DUVALIER.

Pap·a·go /'papəˌgō, 'pä-/ ▶ **n.** (pl. **same** or **Papagos**) **1** a member of an American Indian people of southern Arizona and northern Sonora.
2 a dialect of the Uto-Aztecan Pima-Papago language.
▶ **adj.** of or relating to this people or their language.
– ORIGIN via Spanish from an abbreviation of the Papago self-designation *bābāwĭ'-o'odham*.

pa·pa·in /pə'pā-in, -'pī-/ ▶ **n.** a protein-digesting enzyme obtained from unripe papaya fruit, used to tenderize meat and as a food supplement to aid digestion.
– ORIGIN late 19th cent.: from PAPAYA + -IN[1].

pa·pal /'pāpəl/ ▶ **adj.** of or relating to a pope or to the papacy.
– DERIVATIVES **pa·pal·ly adv.**

PRONUNCIATION KEY ə *ago, up*; ər *over, fur*; a *hat*; ā *ate*; ä *car*; e *let*; ē *see*; i *fit*; ī *by*; NG *sing*; ō *go*; ô *law, for*; oi *toy*; o͝o *good*; o͞o *goo*; ou *out*; TH *thin*; TH *then*; ZH *vision*

P

– ORIGIN late Middle English: from Old French, from medieval Latin *papalis*, from ecclesiastical Latin *papa* 'bishop (of Rome).'

pa·pal in·fal·li·bil·i·ty ▶ n. see INFALLIBILITY.

pa·pal·ist /ˈpāpəlist/ chiefly historical ▶ n. a supporter of the papacy, esp. an advocate of papal supremacy.

Pa·pal States historical the temporal dominions belonging to the pope, esp. in central Italy.

pa·pa·raz·zo /ˌpäpəˈrätsō/ ▶ n. (pl. **paparazzi** /-ˈrätsē/) (usu. **paparazzi**) a freelance photographer who pursues celebrities to get photographs of them.
– ORIGIN mid 20th cent.: from Italian, from the name of a character in Fellini's film *La Dolce Vita* (1960).

pa·pav·er·a·ceous /pəˌpavəˈrāsHəs/ ▶ adj. Botany of, relating to, or denoting plants of the poppy family (Papaveraceae).
– ORIGIN mid 19th cent.: from modern Latin *Papaveraceae* (plural), based on Latin *papaver* 'poppy,' + -OUS.

pa·pav·er·ine /pəˈpavəˌrēn, -rin/ ▶ n. Chemistry a compound present in opium used medicinally to alleviate muscle spasms and asthma. ● An alkaloid; chem. formula: $C_{20}H_{21}NO_4$.
– ORIGIN mid 19th cent.: from Latin *papaver* 'poppy' + -INE[4].

pa·paw /pəˈpô, ˈpôpô/ ▶ n. variant spelling of PAWPAW.

pa·pa·ya /pəˈpīə/ ▶ n. **1** a tropical fruit shaped like an elongated melon, with edible orange flesh and small black seeds. Also called PAPAW or PAWPAW.
2 (also **papaya tree**) the fast-growing tree that bears this fruit, native to warm regions of America. It is widely cultivated for its fruit, both for eating and for papain production. ● *Carica papaya*, family Caricaceae.
– ORIGIN late 16th cent.: from Spanish and Portuguese (see PAWPAW).

Pa·pe·e·te /pəˈpētē, ˌpäpēˈātā/ the capital of French Polynesia, located on the northwestern coast of Tahiti; pop. 26,000 (est. 2009).

pa·per /ˈpāpər/ ▶ n. **1** material manufactured in thin sheets from the pulp of wood or other fibrous substances, used for writing, drawing, or printing on, or as wrapping material: *a sheet of paper* | [as modifier] *a paper bag.* ■ a newspaper. ■ wallpaper. ■ (usu. **papers**) a piece or sheet of paper with something written or drawn on it: *he riffled through the papers on his desk.* ■ (**papers**) significant or important documents belonging to a person: *the personal papers of major political figures.* ■ [as modifier] denoting something that is officially documented but has no real existence or little merit or use: *a paper profit.* ■ a government report or policy document: *a recently leaked cabinet paper.* ■ (**papers**) documents attesting identity; credentials: *two men stopped us and asked us for our papers.* ■ short for COMMERCIAL PAPER. ■ short for CIGARETTE PAPER.
2 an essay or thesis, esp. one read at an academic lecture or seminar or published in an academic journal.
3 theatrical slang free passes of admission to a theater or other entertainment.
▶ v. [with obj.] **1** apply wallpaper to (a wall or room): *the walls were papered in a Regency stripe.* ■ [no obj.] (**paper something over**) cover a hole or blemish with wallpaper. ■ (**paper something over**) disguise an awkward problem instead of resolving it: *the ill feeling between her and Jenny must have been papered over.*
2 theatrical slang fill (a theater) by giving out free tickets.
– PHRASES **be not worth the paper it is written on** be of no value or validity whatsoever despite having been written down. **make the papers** be written about in newspapers and thus become famous or notorious. **on paper** in writing. ■ in theory rather than in reality: *the combatants were, on paper at least, evenly matched.*
– DERIVATIVES **pa·per·er** n., **pa·per·less** adj.
– ORIGIN Middle English: from Anglo-Norman French *papir*, from Latin *papyrus* 'paper-reed' (see PAPYRUS). The verb dates from the late 16th cent.

pa·per·back /ˈpāpərˌbak/ ▶ adj. (of a book) bound in stiff paper or flexible cardboard.
▶ n. a book bound in stiff paper or flexible cardboard.
– PHRASES **in paperback** in an edition bound in stiff paper or flexible cardboard: *now available in paperback.*

pa·per bag ▶ n. a small bag made of paper.
– PHRASES **be unable to punch** (or **sing**, **act**, etc.) **one's way out of a paper bag** informal be completely ineffectual or inept at the specified activity: *he couldn't act his way out of a paper bag.*

pa·per·bark /ˈpāpərˌbärk/ ▶ n. a cajuput tree. ■ used in names of other trees that have a peeling papery bark, e.g., **paperbark maple**, **paperbark birch**.

pa·per birch (also **paperbark birch**) ▶ n. a North American birch with peeling white bark. ● *Betula papyrifera*, family Betulaceae.

pa·per·board /ˈpāpərˌbôrd/ ▶ n. cardboard or pasteboard.

pa·per·boy /ˈpāpərˌboi/ ▶ n. a boy who delivers newspapers to people's homes.

pa·per chain ▶ n. a chain made of colored paper links and used for decorating a room, esp. at Christmas.

pa·per chase ▶ n. **1** informal the action of processing forms and other paperwork, esp. when considered excessive.
2 informal the attempt to gain academic qualifications, esp. a law degree.

pa·per clip ▶ n. a piece of bent wire or plastic used for holding several sheets of paper together.

pa·per cup ▶ n. a disposable cup made of thin cardboard.

pa·per doll ▶ n. a piece of paper cut or folded into the shape of a human figure.

pa·per·girl /ˈpāpərˌgərl/ ▶ n. a girl who delivers newspapers to people's homes.

pa·per·hang·er /ˈpāpərˌhaNGər/ ▶ n. a person who decorates with wallpaper, esp. professionally.

pa·per knife ▶ n. (pl. **paper knives**) a blunt knife used for cutting paper, such as when opening envelopes or slitting the uncut pages of books.

pa·per·mak·ing /ˈpāpərˌmākiNG/ ▶ n. the manufacture of paper.
– DERIVATIVES **pa·per·mak·er** n.

pa·per mill ▶ n. a mill in which paper is made.

pa·per mon·ey ▶ n. money in the form of banknotes.

pa·per mul·ber·ry ▶ n. a small tree of the mulberry family, the inner bark of which is used for making paper and tapa cloth, occurring from eastern Asia to Polynesia. ● *Broussonetia papyrifera*, family Moraceae.

pa·per nau·ti·lus ▶ n. another term for ARGONAUT.

pa·per plate ▶ n. a disposable plate made of cardboard.

pa·per-push·er ▶ n. informal a bureaucrat or menial clerical worker.
– DERIVATIVES **pa·per-push·ing** n. & adj.

pa·per route (Brit. **paper round**) ▶ n. a job of regularly delivering newspapers.

pa·per tape ▶ n. paper in the form of a long narrow strip. ■ such tape having holes punched in it, used in older computer systems for conveying data or instructions.

pa·per-thin ▶ adj. extremely thin or insubstantial: *paper-thin pancakes* | *her sophistication was paper-thin.*

pa·per ti·ger ▶ n. a person or thing that appears threatening but is ineffectual.

pa·per trail ▶ n. the written evidence of someone's activities: *the paper trail led the FBI to him in just six days.*

pa·per wasp ▶ n. a social wasp that forms a small, umbrella-shaped nest made from wood pulp. ● Genus *Polistes*, family Vespidae.

paper wasp

pa·per·weight /ˈpāpərˌwāt/ ▶ n. a small, heavy object for keeping loose papers in place.

pa·per·work /ˈpāpərˌwərk/ ▶ n. routine work involving written documents such as forms, records, or letters: *I need to catch up on some paperwork.* ■ such written documents.

pa·per·y /ˈpāpərē/ ▶ adj. thin and dry like paper.

Pa·pia·men·tu /ˌpäpyəˈmentōō/ (also **Papiamento** /-tō/) ▶ n. a Spanish Creole language with admixtures of Portuguese and Dutch, spoken on the Caribbean islands of Aruba, Bonaire, and Curaçao.
– ORIGIN from Spanish *Papiamento*.

pa·pier col·lé /päpˈyā kōˈlā/ ▶ n. (pl. **papiers collés** pronunc. **same**) the technique of using paper for collage. ■ a collage made from paper.
– ORIGIN French, literally 'glued paper.'

pa·pier mâ·ché /ˌpāpər məˈsHā, päˈp(y)ā/ ▶ n. a malleable mixture of paper and glue, or paper, flour, and water, that becomes hard when dry: *George was constructing a crocodile out of papier-mâché.*
– ORIGIN French, literally 'chewed paper.'

pa·pil·i·o·na·ceous /pəˌpilēəˈnāsHəs/ ▶ adj. Botany of, relating to, or denoting leguminous plants of a group (subfamily Papilionoideae or family Papilionaceae) with flowers that resemble a butterfly.
– ORIGIN mid 17th cent.: from modern Latin *Papilionaceae* (plural), based on Latin *papilio* 'butterfly,' + -OUS.

pa·pil·la /pəˈpilə/ ▶ n. (pl. **papillae** /-ˈpilˌē, -ˈpilˌī/) a small rounded protuberance on a part or organ of the body. ■ a small fleshy projection on a plant.
– DERIVATIVES **pap·il·lar·y** /ˈpapəˌlerē/ adj., **pap·il·late** /ˈpapəˌlāt, pəˈpilit/ adj., **pap·il·lose** /ˈpäpəˌlōs, -ˌlōz/ adj.
– ORIGIN late 17th cent.: from Latin, literally 'nipple,' diminutive of *papula* 'small protuberance.'

pap·il·lo·ma /ˌpapəˈlōmə/ ▶ n. (pl. **papillomas** or **papillomata** /-mətə/) Medicine a small wartlike growth on the skin or on a mucous membrane, derived from the epidermis and usually benign.
– ORIGIN mid 19th cent.: from PAPILLA + -OMA.

pap·il·lo·ma·vi·rus /ˌpapiˈlōməˌvīrəs/ ▶ n. Medicine any of a group of DNA viruses that cause the formation of papillomas or warts.

pap·il·lon /ˌpäpēˈyôn/ ▶ n. a dog of a toy breed with ears suggesting the form of a butterfly.
– ORIGIN early 20th cent.: from French, literally 'butterfly,' from Latin *papilio(n-)*.

pa·pist /ˈpāpist/ chiefly derogatory ▶ n. a Roman Catholic. ■ another term for PAPALIST.
▶ adj. of, relating to, or associated with the Roman Catholic Church.
– DERIVATIVES **pa·pism** /-ˌpizəm/ n., **pa·pis·ti·cal** /pəˈpistəkəl/ adj. (archaic), **pa·pist·ry** /-trē/ n.
– ORIGIN mid 16th cent.: from French *papiste* or modern Latin *papista*, from ecclesiastical Latin *papa* 'bishop (of Rome).'

pa·poose /paˈpōōs, pə-/ ▶ n. **1** a type of bag used to carry a child on one's back.
2 dated, offensive a young North American Indian child.
– ORIGIN mid 17th cent.: from Narragansett *papoos*.

Papp /pap/, Joseph (1921–91), US producer and director; born *Joseph Papirofsky*. He managed Hollywood's Actors Laboratory 1948–1950 and then founded the Shakespearean Theatre Workshop in 1954 that became the New York Shakespeare Festival. in 1960. He also founded the off-Broadway Public Theater in 1967 and directed the theaters at Lincoln Center from 1973 until 1978.

pap·pa·dam /ˈpäpäˌdəm/ ▶ n. a thin East Indian bread made with lentil flour.
– ORIGIN from Tamil.

pap·par·del·le /ˌpäpärˈdelā/ ▶ n. pasta in the form of broad flat ribbons, usually served with a meat sauce.
– ORIGIN Italian, from *pappare* 'eat hungrily.'

Pap·pus /ˈpapəs/ (*fl. c.* AD 300–350), Greek mathematician; known as **Pappus of Alexandria**. His *Collection* of six books (another two are missing) is the principal source of knowledge of the mathematics of his predecessors.

pap·pus /ˈpapəs/ ▶ n. (pl. **pappi** /ˈpaˌpī, -ˌpē/) Botany the tuft of hairs on each seed of thistles, dandelions, and similar plants that assists dispersal by the wind.
– DERIVATIVES **pap·pose** /ˈpaˌpōs, ˈpaˌpōz/ adj.
– ORIGIN early 18th cent.: via Latin from Greek *pappos*.

pap·py[1] /ˈpapē/ ▶ n. (pl. **pappies**) [usu. as name] a child's word for father: *Pappy was always busy.*
– ORIGIN mid 18th cent.: from PAPA + -Y[2].

pap·py[2] ▶ adj. of the nature of pap; soft and bland.

pap·ri·ka /pəˈprēkə, pa-/ ▶ n. a powdered spice with a deep orange-red color and a mildly pungent flavor, made from the dried and ground fruits of certain varieties of sweet pepper. ■ a deep orange-red color like that of paprika.
– ORIGIN late 19th cent.: from Hungarian.

Pap test /pap/ ▶ n. a test to detect cancer of the cervix or uterus, using a specimen of cellular material from the neck of the uterus spread on a microscope slide (**Pap smear**).
– ORIGIN 1960s: named after George N. *Papanicolaou* (1883–1962), Greek-born American scientist.

Pap·u·a /ˈpäpōōə, ˈpapyōōə/ **1** a province of Indonesia comprising most of the western part of the island of New Guinea, with some offshore islands; capital, Jayapura. Formerly called IRIAN JAYA, WEST IRIAN.
2 a name for the island of New Guinea. See also PAPUA NEW GUINEA.
– ORIGIN named by a Portuguese navigator who visited it 1526–27, from a Malay word meaning 'woolly-haired.'

Pap·u·an /ˈpäpōōən, ˈpapyōōən/ ▶ n. **1** a native or inhabitant of Papua, or of Papua New Guinea.
2 a heterogeneous group of around 750 languages spoken in Papua New Guinea and neighboring islands.

▶ **adj.** of or relating to Papua or its people or their languages.

Pap·u·a New Guin·ea a country in the western Pacific Ocean that includes the eastern half of the island of New Guinea as well as some neighboring islands; pop. 5,940,800 (est. 2009); capital, Port Moresby; languages, English (official), Tok Pisin, and several hundred native Austronesian and Papuan languages.

> Papua New Guinea was formed in 1949 from the administrative union of Papua, an Australian Territory since 1906, and the Trust Territory of New Guinea (Northeast New Guinea), which was formerly under German control and an Australian trusteeship since 1921. In 1975, it became an independent state within the Commonwealth of Nations.

– DERIVATIVES **Pap·u·a New Guin·e·an** **adj. & n.**

pap·ule /ˈpapˌyo͞ol/ (also **papula** /-yələ/) ▶ **n.** (pl. **papules** or **papulae** /-yəˌlē/) Medicine a small, raised, solid pimple or swelling, often forming part of a rash on the skin and typically inflamed but not producing pus.
– DERIVATIVES **pap·u·lar** /-yələr/ **adj.**, **pap·u·lose** /-yəlōs, -lōz/ **adj.**, **pap·u·lous** /-yələs/ **adj.**
– ORIGIN early 18th cent.: from Latin *papula*.

pap·y·rol·o·gy /ˌpapəˈräləjē/ ▶ **n.** the branch of study that deals with ancient papyri.
– DERIVATIVES **pa·py·ro·log·i·cal** /pəˌpīrəˈläjikəl, -pi(ə)rə-/ **adj.**, **pap·y·rol·o·gist** /ˌpapəˈräləjəst/ **n.**

pa·py·rus /pəˈpīrəs/ ▶ **n.** (pl. **papyri** /-ˈpīrī/ or **papyruses**) **1** a material prepared in ancient Egypt from the pithy stem of a water plant, used in sheets throughout the ancient Mediterranean world for writing or painting on and also for making rope, sandals, and boats. ■ a document written on papyrus.
2 the tall aquatic sedge from which this material is obtained, native to central Africa and the Nile valley. ● *Cyperus papyrus*, family Cyperaceae.
– ORIGIN late Middle English (sense 2): via Latin from Greek *papuros*. Sense 1 dates from the early 18th cent.

par¹ /pär/ ▶ **n. 1** Golf the number of strokes a first-class player should normally require for a particular hole or course: *the sixteenth is a par five* | *he had advanced from his overnight position of three under par*. ■ a score of this number of strokes at a hole: *a card that showed 16 pars, one eagle, and one birdie*.
2 Stock Market the face value of a stock or other security, as distinct from its market value. ■ (also **par of exchange**) the recognized value of one country's currency in terms of another's.
▶ **v.** (**pars, parring, parred**) [with obj.] Golf play (a hole) in par.
– PHRASES **above** (or **below** or **under**) **par** better (or worse) than is usual or expected: *poor nutrition can leave you feeling below par*. **on a par with** equal in importance or quality to; on an equal level with: *this home cooking is on a par with the best in the world*. **par for the course** what is normal or expected in any given circumstances: *given the high standards of the food, the prices seem par for the course*. **up to par** at an expected or usual level or quality.
– ORIGIN late 16th cent. (in the sense 'equality of value or standing'): from Latin, 'equal,' also 'equality.' The golf term dates from the late 19th cent.

par² /pär/ ▶ **n.** informal a paragraph.
– ORIGIN mid 19th cent.: abbreviation.

par. (also **para.**) ▶ **abbr.** paragraph.

par- ▶ **comb. form** variant spelling of PARA-¹ shortened before a vowel or *h* (as in *paraldehyde, parody, parhelion*).

par·a¹ /ˈparə/ informal ▶ **n. 1** a paratrooper.
2 a paragraph.

par·a² /ˈpärə/ ▶ **n.** (pl. **same** or **paras**) a monetary unit of Serbia, equal to one hundredth of a dinar.
– ORIGIN Turkish, from Persian *pāra* 'piece, portion.'

para-¹ (also **par-**) ▶ **prefix 1** beside; adjacent to: *parameter* | *parataxis* | *parathyroid*. ■ Medicine denoting a disordered function or faculty: *paresthesia*. ■ distinct from, but analogous to: *paramilitary* | *paraphrase* | *paratyphoid*. ■ beyond: *paradox* | *paranormal* | *parapsychology*. ■ subsidiary; assisting: *paramedic* | *paraprofessional*.
2 Chemistry denoting substitution at diametrically opposite carbon atoms in a benzene ring, e.g., in 1, 4 positions: *paradichlorobenzene*. Compare with META- and ORTHO-.
– ORIGIN from Greek *para* 'beside'; in combinations often meaning 'amiss, irregular' and denoting alteration or modification.

para-² ▶ **comb. form** denoting something that protects or wards off: *parachute* | *parasol*.
– ORIGIN from French, from the Italian imperative singular of *parare* 'defend, shield' (originally meaning 'prepare,' from Latin *parare*).

par·a·a·mi·no·ben·zo·ic ac·id /ˈparə əˌmēnōbenˈzōik/ (abbr.: **PABA**) ▶ **n.** Biochemistry a crystalline acid that is widely distributed in plant and animal tissue. It has been used to treat rickettsial infections and is widely used in suntan lotions and sunscreens to absorb ultraviolet light. ● Chem. formula: $NH_2C_6H_4COOH$.

Par·a·bel·lum /ˌparəˈbeləm/ ▶ **n.** trademark a make of automatic pistol or machine gun.
– ORIGIN early 20th cent.: from Latin *para bellum*, from *para!* 'prepare!' (imperative of *parare*) + *bellum* 'war.'

par·a·ben /ˈparəben/ ▶ **n.** Chemistry any of a group of compounds used as preservatives in pharmaceutical and cosmetic products and in the food industry.
– ORIGIN 1950s: from PARA-¹ + (*hydroxy*)*ben*(*zoic*).

par·a·bi·o·sis /ˌparəbīˈōsis/ ▶ **n.** Biology the anatomical joining of two individuals, esp. artificially in physiological research.
– DERIVATIVES **par·a·bi·ot·ic** /-ˈätik/ **adj.**
– ORIGIN early 20th cent.: modern Latin, from PARA-¹ 'beside, distinct from' + Greek *biōsis* 'mode of life' (from *bios* 'life').

par·a·ble /ˈparəbəl/ ▶ **n.** a simple story used to illustrate a moral or spiritual lesson, as told by Jesus in the Gospels.
– ORIGIN Middle English: from Old French *parabole*, from an ecclesiastical Latin sense 'discourse, allegory' of Latin *parabola* 'comparison,' from Greek *parabolē* (see PARABOLA).

pa·rab·o·la /pəˈrabələ/ ▶ **n.** (pl. **parabolas** or **parabolae** /-lē/) a symmetrical open plane curve formed by the intersection of a cone with a plane parallel to its side. The path of a projectile under the influence of gravity ideally follows a curve of this shape.
– ORIGIN late 16th cent.: modern Latin, from Greek *parabolē* 'placing side by side, application,' from *para-* 'beside' + *bolē* 'a throw' (from the verb *ballein*).

par·a·bol·ic /ˌparəˈbälik/ ▶ **adj. 1** of or like a parabola or part of one.
2 of or expressed in parables: *parabolic teaching*.
– DERIVATIVES **par·a·bol·i·cal** **adj.**, **par·a·bol·i·cal·ly** /-(ə)lē/ **adv.**
– ORIGIN late Middle English: via late Latin from Greek *parabolikos*, from *parabolē* 'application' (see PARABOLA).

pa·rab·o·loid /pəˈrabəˌloid/ ▶ **n. 1** (also **paraboloid of revolution**) a solid generated by the rotation of a parabola around its axis of symmetry.
2 a solid having two or more nonparallel parabolic cross sections.
– DERIVATIVES **pa·rab·o·loi·dal** /pəˌrabəˈloidl/ **adj.**

Pa·ra·cel Is·lands /ˌparəˈsel/ (also **the Paracels**) a group of about 130 small, barren coral islands and reefs in the South China Sea, southeast of Hainan. The islands are claimed by both China and Vietnam.

par·a·cel·lu·lar /ˌparəˈselyələr/ ▶ **adj.** Biology passing or situated beside or between cells.

Par·a·cel·sus /ˌparəˈselsəs/ (*c.*1493–1541), Swiss physician; born *Theophrastus Phillipus Aureolus Bombastus von Hohenheim*. He developed a new approach to medicine and philosophy based on observation and experience.

par·a·cen·te·sis /ˌparəsenˈtēsis/ ▶ **n.** (pl. **paracenteses** /-ˌsēz/) Medicine the perforation of a cavity of the body or of a cyst or similar outgrowth, esp. with a hollow needle to remove fluid or gas.
– ORIGIN late 16th cent.: via Latin from Greek *parakentēsis*, from *parakentein* 'pierce at the side.'

par·a·cen·tric in·ver·sion /ˌparəˈsentrik/ ▶ **n.** Genetics a reversal of the normal order of genes in a chromosome segment involving only the part of a chromosome at one side of the centromere.

par·a·ce·ta·mol /ˌparəˈsētəˌmäl, -ˌmôl/ ▶ **n.** (pl. **same** or **paracetamols**) British term for ACETAMINOPHEN.

pa·rach·ro·nism /pəˈrakrəˌnizəm/ ▶ **n.** an error in chronology, esp. by assigning too late a date.
– ORIGIN mid 17th cent.: from PARA-¹ 'beyond' + Greek *khronos* 'time' + -ISM, perhaps suggested by ANACHRONISM.

par·a·chute /ˈparəˌSHo͞ot/ ▶ **n.** a cloth canopy that fills with air and allows a person or heavy object attached to it to descend slowly when dropped from an aircraft, or that is released from the rear of an aircraft on landing to act as a brake.
▶ **v. 1** drop or cause to drop from an aircraft by parachute: [no obj.] *airborne units parachuted in to secure the airport* | [with obj.] *an air operation to parachute relief supplies into Bosnia*.
2 appoint or be appointed in an emergency or from outside the existing hierarchy: *an old crony of the CEO was controversially parachuted into the job*.
– ORIGIN late 18th cent.: from French *para-* 'protection against' + *chute* 'fall.'

parachute

par·a·chute flare ▶ **n.** a pyrotechnic signal flare that is carried up into the air by a rocket and floats suspended from a small parachute.

par·a·chut·ist /ˈparəˌSHo͞otist/ ▶ **n.** a person who uses a parachute.

Par·a·clete /ˈparəˌklēt/ ▶ **n.** (in Christian theology) the Holy Spirit as advocate or counselor (John 14:16, 26).
– ORIGIN via late Latin from Greek *paraklētos* 'called in aid,' from *para-* 'alongside' + *klētos* (from *kalein* 'to call').

par·a·crine /ˈparəkrin/ ▶ **adj.** Physiology of, relating to, or denoting a hormone that has effect only in the vicinity of the gland secreting it.
– ORIGIN 1970s: from PARA-¹ 'beside' + a shortened form of ENDOCRINE or EXOCRINE.

par·a·crys·tal /ˈparəˌkristəl/ ▶ **n.** Chemistry a piece of a substance that is not a true crystal but has some degree of order in its structure.
– DERIVATIVES **par·a·crys·tal·line** /ˌparəˈkristəlin/ **adj.**

pa·rade /pəˈrād/ ▶ **n. 1** a public procession, esp. one celebrating a special day or event and including marching bands and floats. ■ a formal march or gathering of troops for inspection or display. ■ a series of people or things appearing or being displayed one after the other: *the parade of Hollywood celebrities who troop onto his show*.
2 a parade ground. ■ Brit. a public square or promenade. ■ Brit. a row of stores: *a shopping parade*.
▶ **v.** walk or march in public in a formal procession or in an ostentatious or attention-seeking way: [no obj.] *officers will parade through the town center* | [with obj.] *carefree young men were parading the streets*. ■ [with obj.] display (someone or something) while marching or moving around a place: *revolutionary guards paraded him through the streets*. ■ [with obj.] display (something) publicly in order to impress or attract attention: *he paraded his knowledge*. ■ (**parade as**) appear falsely as; masquerade as: *these untruths parading as history*. ■ (of troops) assemble for a formal inspection or ceremonial occasion: *the recruits were due to parade that day*.
– PHRASES **on parade** taking part in a parade. ■ on public display: *politicians are always on parade*.
– DERIVATIVES **pa·rad·er** **n.**
– ORIGIN mid 17th cent.: from French, literally 'a showing,' from Spanish *parada* and Italian *parata*, based on Latin *parare* 'prepare, furnish.'

pa·rade ground ▶ **n.** a place where troops gather for parade.

par·a·did·dle /ˈparəˌdidl/ ▶ **n.** Music one of the basic patterns (rudiments) of drumming, consisting of four even strokes played in the order left-right-left-left or right-left-right-right.
– ORIGIN 1920s: imitative.

par·a·digm /ˈparəˌdīm/ ▶ **n. 1** technical a typical example or pattern of something; a model: *there is a new paradigm for public art in this country*. ■ a worldview underlying the theories and methodology of a particular scientific subject: *the discovery of universal gravitation became the paradigm of successful science*.
2 a set of linguistic items that form mutually exclusive choices in particular syntactic roles: *English determiners form a paradigm: we can say "a book" or "his book" but not "a his book."* Often contrasted with SYNTAGM. ■ (in the traditional grammar of Latin, Greek, and other inflected languages) a table of all the inflected forms of a particular verb, noun, or adjective, serving as a model for other words of the same conjugation or declension.
– ORIGIN late 15th cent.: via late Latin from Greek *paradeigma*, from *paradeiknunai* 'show side by side,' from *para-* 'beside' + *deiknunai* 'to show.'

par·a·dig·mat·ic /ˌparədigˈmatik/ ▶ **adj. 1** of the nature of a paradigm or model: *they offer this database as a paradigmatic example*.
2 of or denoting the relationship between a set of linguistic items that form mutually exclusive choices in particular syntactic roles. Contrasted with SYNTAGMATIC.
– DERIVATIVES **par·a·dig·mat·i·cal·ly** **adv.**

par·a·digm shift ▶ **n.** a fundamental change in approach or underlying assumptions.

PRONUNCIATION KEY ə *ago, up*; ər *over, fur*; a *hat*; ā *ate*; ä *car*; e *let*; ē *see*; i *fit*; ī *by*; NG *sing*; ō *go*; ô *law, for*; oi *toy*; o͝o *good*; o͞o *goo*; ou *out*; TH *thin*; T͟H *then*; ZH *vision*

– ORIGIN 1970s: term used in the writings of Thomas S. Kuhn (1922–96), philosopher of science.

par·a·dis·al /ˌparəˈdīsəl/ ▶ **adj.** (of a place or state) ideal or idyllic; heavenly: *she told me tales of her paradisal childhood.*

Par·a·dise /ˈparəˌdīs, ˈpe(ə)r-/ a community in southeastern Nevada, south of Las Vegas; pop. 186,070 (2000).

par·a·dise /ˈparəˌdīs/ ▶ **n.** (in some religions) heaven as the ultimate abode of the just. ■ (**Paradise**) the abode of Adam and Eve before the Fall in the biblical account of the Creation; the Garden of Eden. ■ an ideal or idyllic place or state: *the surrounding countryside is a walker's paradise | my idea of paradise is to relax on the seafront.*
– DERIVATIVES **par·a·di·si·a·cal** /ˌparədiˈsīəkəl/ (also **paradisaical** /ˌparədiˈsā-ikəl/ or **paradisical** /ˌparəˈdisikəl/) **adj.**
– ORIGIN Middle English: from Old French *paradis*, via ecclesiastical Latin from Greek *paradeisos* 'royal (enclosed) park,' from Avestan *pairidaēza* 'enclosure, park.'

par·a·dise fish ▶ **n.** a small colorful labyrinth fish that is native to Southeast Asia and popular in aquariums. ● Genus *Macropodus*, family Belontiidae: several species, including *M. opercularis.*

Par·a·dise of the Pa·cif·ic a nickname for the state of **HAWAII**.

pa·ra·dor /ˈparəˌdôr/ ▶ **n.** (pl. **paradors** or **paradores** /ˌparəˈdôres/) a hotel in Spain owned and administered by the Spanish government.
– ORIGIN Spanish, literally 'stopping place.'

par·a·dos /ˈparəˌdäs/ ▶ **n.** an elevation of earth behind a fortified place as a protection against attack from the rear, esp. a mound along the back of a trench.
– ORIGIN mid 19th cent.: from French, from *para-* 'protection against' + *dos* 'back' (from Latin *dorsum*).

par·a·dox /ˈparəˌdäks/ ▶ **n.** a statement or proposition that, despite sound (or apparently sound) reasoning from acceptable premises, leads to a conclusion that seems senseless, logically unacceptable, or self-contradictory: *a potentially serious conflict between quantum mechanics and the general theory of relativity known as the information paradox.* ■ a seemingly absurd or self-contradictory statement or proposition that when investigated or explained may prove to be well founded or true: *in a paradox, he has discovered that stepping back from his job has increased the rewards he gleans from it.* ■ a situation, person, or thing that combines contradictory features or qualities: *the mingling of deciduous trees with elements of desert flora forms a fascinating ecological paradox.*
– ORIGIN mid 16th cent. (originally denoting a statement contrary to accepted opinion): via late Latin from Greek *paradoxon* 'contrary (opinion),' neuter adjective used as a noun, from *para-* 'distinct from' + *doxa* 'opinion.'

par·a·dox·i·cal /ˌparəˈdäksikəl/ ▶ **adj.** seemingly absurd or self-contradictory: *by glorifying the acts of violence they achieve the paradoxical effect of making them trivial.*
– DERIVATIVES **par·a·dox·i·cal·ly** **adv.** [sentence adverb] *paradoxically, the more fuel a star starts off with, the sooner it runs out.*

par·a·drop /ˈparəˌdräp/ ▶ **n.** a descent or delivery by parachute.
▶ **v.** (**paradrops, paradropping, paradropped**) [with obj.] drop (someone or something) by parachute.
– DERIVATIVES **par·a·drop·per** **n.**

par·aes·the·sia ▶ **n.** British spelling of **PARESTHESIA**.

par·af·fin /ˈparəfin/ ▶ **n.** (also **paraffin wax**) a flammable, whitish, translucent, waxy solid consisting of a mixture of saturated hydrocarbons, obtained by distillation from petroleum or shale and used in candles, cosmetics, polishes, and sealing and waterproofing compounds. ■ (also **paraffin oil** or **liquid paraffin**) Brit. a colorless, flammable, oily liquid similarly obtained and used as fuel, esp. kerosene. ■ Chemistry old-fashioned term for **ALKANE**.
– ORIGIN mid 19th cent.: from German, from Latin *parum* 'little' + *affinis* 'related' (from its low reactivity).

par·a·gen·e·sis /ˌparəˈjenəsis/ ▶ **n.** (pl. **parageneses** /-ˌsēz/) Geology a set of minerals that were formed together, esp. in a rock, or with a specified mineral.
– DERIVATIVES **par·a·ge·net·ic** /-jəˈnetik/ **adj.**

par·a·glid·ing /ˈparəˌglīdiNG/ ▶ **n.** a sport in which a wide canopy resembling a parachute is attached to a person's body by a harness in order to allow them to glide through the air after jumping from or being lifted to a height.
– DERIVATIVES **par·a·glide** /-ˌglīd/ **v.**, **par·a·glid·er** /-ˌglīdər/ **n.**

par·a·gon /ˈparəˌgän, -gən/ ▶ **n.** a person or thing regarded as a perfect example of a particular quality: *it would have taken a paragon of virtue not to feel viciously jealous.* ■ a person or thing viewed as a model of excellence: *your cook is a paragon.* ■ a perfect diamond of 100 carats or more.
– ORIGIN mid 16th cent.: from obsolete French, from Italian *paragone* 'touchstone used to discriminate good (gold) from bad,' from medieval Greek *parakonē* 'whetstone.'

par·a·graph /ˈparəˌgraf/ ▶ **n.** a distinct section of a piece of writing, usually dealing with a single theme and indicated by a new line, indentation, or numbering.
▶ **v.** [with obj.] arrange (a piece of writing) in paragraphs.
– DERIVATIVES **par·a·graph·ic** /ˌparəˈgrafik/ **adj.**
– ORIGIN late 15th cent.: from French *paragraphe*, via medieval Latin from Greek *paragraphos* 'short stroke marking a break in sense,' from *para-* 'beside' + *graphein* 'write.'

par·a·graph mark (also **paragraph symbol**) ▶ **n.** a symbol (usually ¶) used in printed text to mark a new paragraph or as a reference mark.

Par·a·guay /ˈparəˌgwī, -ˌgwā/ a landlocked country in central South America; pop. 6,995,700 (est. 2009); capital, Asunción; languages, Spanish (official) and Guarani.

> The territory was occupied by seminomadic Guarani peoples before Spanish rule was established in the 16th century. Paraguay achieved independence in 1811. It lost more than half of its population in war, against Brazil, Argentina, and Uruguay 1865–70, but gained land in the Chaco War with Bolivia 1932–35. The country was ruled by military dictator Alfredo Stroessner (1912–2006) from 1954 until 1989.

– DERIVATIVES **Par·a·guay·an** /ˌparəˈgwīən, -ˈgwā-/ **adj. & n.**

Par·a·guay Riv·er a river that flows for 1,584 miles (2,549 km) from the Mato Grosso in western Brazil into Paraguay and into the Paraná River. It is navigable by larger vessels as far as Concepción.

par·a·in·flu·en·za /ˌparəˌinflo͞oˈenzə/ ▶ **n.** Medicine a disease caused by any of a group of viruses that resemble the influenza viruses.

par·a·keet /ˈparəˌkēt/ ▶ **n.** a small parrot with predominantly green plumage and a long tail. ● Family Psittacidae: five genera, e.g., *Psittacula* of Asia and Africa and *Cyanoramphus* of Australasia, and many species.
– ORIGIN mid 16th cent.: from Old French *paroquet*, Italian *parrocchetto*, and Spanish *periquito*; origin uncertain, perhaps (via Italian) based on a diminutive meaning 'little wig,' referring to head plumage, or (via Spanish) based on a diminutive of the given name *Pedro*.

par·a·lan·guage /ˈparəˌlaNGgwij/ ▶ **n.** the nonlexical component of communication by speech, for example intonation, pitch and speed of speaking, hesitation noises, gesture, and facial expression.

par·al·de·hyde /pəˈraldəˌhīd/ ▶ **n.** Chemistry a liquid made by treating acetaldehyde with acid, used medicinally as a sedative, hypnotic, and anticonvulsant. ● A cyclic trimer of acetaldehyde; chem. formula: $(CH_3CHO)_3$.

par·a·le·gal /ˌparəˈlēgəl/ ▶ **n.** a person trained in subsidiary legal matters but not fully qualified as a lawyer.
▶ **adj.** of or relating to auxiliary aspects of the law.

par·a·lin·guis·tic /ˌparəliNGˈgwistik/ ▶ **adj.** of, relating to, or denoting paralanguage or the nonlexical elements of communication by speech.

par·a·li·pom·e·na /ˌparəlīˈpämənə, -li-/ (also **paraleipomena**) ▶ **plural n.** (sing. **paralipomenon** /-ˈpäməˌnän/) formal things omitted from a work and added as a supplement. ■ (usu. **Paralipomenon**) archaic (in the Vulgate Bible and some other versions) the name of the books of Chronicles, regarded as supplementary to the books of Kings.
– ORIGIN late Middle English: via ecclesiastical Latin from Greek *paraleipomena*, from *paraleipein* 'omit,' from *para-* 'to one side' + *leipein* 'to leave.'

par·a·lip·sis /ˌparəˈlipsis/ ▶ **n.** Rhetoric the device of giving emphasis by professing to say little or nothing about a subject, as in *not to mention their unpaid debts of several million.*
– ORIGIN late 16th cent.: via late Latin from Greek *paraleipsis* 'passing over,' from *paraleipein* 'omit,' from *para-* 'aside' + *leipein* 'to leave.'

par·al·lax /ˈparəˌlaks/ ▶ **n.** the effect whereby the position or direction of an object appears to differ when viewed from different positions, e.g., through the viewfinder and the lens of a camera. ■ the angular amount of this in a particular case, esp. that of a star viewed from different points in the earth's orbit.
– DERIVATIVES **par·al·lac·tic** /ˌparəˈlaktik/ **adj.**
– ORIGIN late 16th cent. (also in the general sense 'fact of seeing wrongly'): from French *parallaxe*, from Greek *parallaxis* 'a change,' from *parallassein* 'to alternate,' based on *allassein* 'to exchange' (from *allos* 'other').

par·al·lel /ˈparəˌlel, -ləl/ ▶ **adj.** (of lines, planes, surfaces, or objects) side by side and having the same distance continuously between them: *parallel lines never meet | the road runs parallel to the Ottawa River.* ■ occurring or existing at the same time or in a similar way; corresponding: *a parallel universe | they shared an apartment in Dallas while establishing parallel careers.* ■ Computing involving the simultaneous performance of operations. ■ of or denoting electrical components or circuits connected to common points at each end, rather than one to another in sequence. The opposite of **SERIES**.
▶ **n.** **1** a person or thing that is similar or analogous to another: *a challenge that has no parallel in peacetime this century.* ■ a similarity or comparison: *he points to a parallel between biological evolution and cognitive development | he draws a parallel between personal destiny and social forces.*
2 (also **parallel of latitude**) each of the imaginary parallel circles of constant latitude on the earth's surface.
3 Printing two parallel lines (‖) as a reference mark.
▶ **v.** (**parallels, paralleling, paralleled**) [with obj.] (of something extending in a line) be side by side with (something extending in a line), always keeping the same distance: *a big concrete gutter that paralleled the road.* ■ be similar or corresponding to (something): *the lawlessness throughout officialdom was paralleled by an increase in lawlessness on the streets.*
– PHRASES **in parallel** occurring at the same time and having some connection. ■ (of electrical components or circuits) connected to common points at each end; not in series.
– ORIGIN mid 16th cent.: from French *parallèle*, via Latin from Greek *parallēlos*, from *para-* 'alongside' + *allēlos* 'one another.'

par·al·lel bars ▶ **plural n.** a pair of parallel rails mounted on posts, used in gymnastics.

par·al·lel cous·ins ▶ **plural n.** first cousins who are children of two brothers, or of two sisters. Compare with **CROSS COUSINS**.

par·al·lel dis·trib·ut·ed pro·cess·ing (abbr.: **PDP**) ▶ **n.** another term for **CONNECTIONISM**.

par·al·lel·e·pi·ped /ˌparəˌleləˈpīpid, -ˈpipid/ ▶ **n.** Geometry a solid body of which each face is a parallelogram.
– ORIGIN late 16th cent.: from Greek *parallēlepipedon*, from *parallēlos* 'beside another' + *epipedon* 'plane surface.'

par·al·lel·ism /ˈparəlelˌizəm/ ▶ **n.** the state of being parallel or of corresponding in some way. ■ the use of successive verbal constructions in poetry or prose that correspond in grammatical structure, sound, meter, meaning, etc. ■ the use of parallel processing in computer systems.
– DERIVATIVES **par·al·lel·is·tic** /ˌparəlelˈistik/ **adj.**

par·al·lel·ize /ˈparələlˌīz, -lelˌīz/ ▶ **v.** [with obj.] Computing adapt (a program) for running on a parallel processing system.
– DERIVATIVES **par·al·lel·i·za·tion** /ˌparəˌleləˈzāSHən/ **n.**

par·al·lel·o·gram /ˌparəˈleləˌgram/ ▶ **n.** a four-sided plane rectilinear figure with opposite sides parallel.
– PHRASES **parallelogram of forces** a parallelogram illustrating the theorem that if two forces acting at a point are represented in magnitude and direction by two sides of a parallelogram meeting at that point, their resultant is represented by the diagonal drawn from that point.
– ORIGIN late 16th cent.: from French *parallélogramme*, via late Latin from Greek *parallēlogrammon*, from *parallēlos* 'alongside another' + *grammē* 'line.'

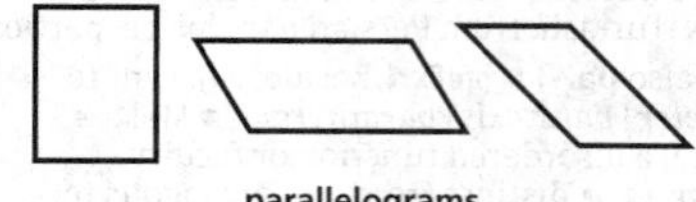

parallelograms

par·al·lel park·ing ▶ **n.** the parking of a vehicle or vehicles parallel to the roadside.
– DERIVATIVES **par·al·lel park** **v.**

par·al·lel port ▶ **n.** Computing a connector for a device that sends or receives several bits of data simultaneously by using more than one wire. Compare with **SERIAL PORT**.

par·al·lel pro·cess·ing ▶ **n.** a mode of computer operation in which a process is split into parts that execute simultaneously on different processors attached to the same computer.

par·al·lel rul·er ▶ **n.** an instrument for drawing parallel lines, consisting of two or more rulers connected by jointed crosspieces so as to be always parallel, at whatever distance they are set.

par·al·lel turn ▶ **n.** Skiing a turn with the skis kept parallel to each other.

par·a·log·i·cal /ˌparəˈläjikəl/ ▶ **adj.** of or relating to a form of reasoning that does not conform to the rules of logic.
– DERIVATIVES **par·a·log·i·cal·ly adv.**

pa·ral·o·gism /pəˈraləˌjizəm/ ▶ **n.** Logic a piece of illogical or fallacious reasoning, esp. one that appears superficially logical or that the reasoner believes to be logical.
– DERIVATIVES **pa·ral·o·gist n.**
– ORIGIN mid 16th cent.: from French *paralogisme*, via late Latin from Greek *paralogismos*, from *paralogizesthai* 'reason falsely.'

pa·ral·o·gous /pəˈraləgəs/ ▶ **adj.** Genetics of or relating to genes that are descended from the same ancestral gene by gene duplication in the course of evolution, esp. when present in different species that have diverged after the duplication.

pa·ral·o·gy /pəˈraləjē/ ▶ **n. 1** Genetics the state of being paralogous.
2 paralogical reasoning.

Par·a·lym·pi·an /ˌparəˈlimpiən/ ▶ **n.** a competitor in the Paralympic Games.

Par·a·lym·pic Games /ˌparəˈlimpik/ (also **the Paralympics**) ▶ **plural n.** an international athletic competition for disabled athletes, held every four years.
– DERIVATIVES **Par·a·lym·pic** /-pik/ **adj.**
– ORIGIN 1950s: blend of *paraplegic* (see **PARAPLEGIA**) and **OLYMPIC**.

pa·ral·y·sis /pəˈraləsis/ ▶ **n.** (pl. **paralyses** /-sēz/) the loss of the ability to move (and sometimes to feel anything) in part or most of the body, typically as a result of illness, poison, or injury. ■ inability to act or function in a person, organization, or place: *the paralysis gripping the country*.
– ORIGIN late Old English, via Latin from Greek *paralusis*, from *paraluesthai* 'be disabled at the side,' from *para* 'beside' + *luein* 'loosen.'

pa·ral·y·sis ag·i·tans /ˈajəˌtanz/ ▶ **n.** less common term for **PARKINSON'S DISEASE**.
– ORIGIN Latin, literally 'shaking paralysis.'

par·a·lyt·ic /ˌparəˈlitik/ ▶ **adj.** of or relating to paralysis: *the incidence of paralytic disease*.
▶ **n.** a person affected by paralysis.
– DERIVATIVES **par·a·lyt·i·cal·ly adv.**
– ORIGIN late Middle English: from Old French *paralytique*, via Latin from Greek *paralutikos* 'relating to paralysis' (see **PARALYSIS**).

par·a·lyze /ˈparəˌlīz/ (Brit. **paralyse**) ▶ **v.** [with obj.] cause (a person or part of the body) to become partly or wholly incapable of movement: *Mrs. Burrows had been paralyzed by a stroke*. ■ render (someone) unable to think or act normally, esp. through panic or fear: *some people are paralyzed by the thought of failure* | (as adj. **paralyzing**) *her paralyzing shyness*. ■ bring (a system, place, or organization) to a standstill by causing disruption or chaos: *the regional capital was paralyzed by a general strike*.
– DERIVATIVES **par·a·lyz·ing·ly** /-ˌlīziNGlē/ **adv.**
– ORIGIN early 19th cent.: from French *paralyser*, from *paralysie* 'paralysis.'

par·a·lyzed /ˈparəˌlīzd/ (Brit. **paralysed**) ▶ **adj.** (of a person or part of the body) partly or wholly incapable of movement: *he became partially paralyzed*.

par·a·mag·net·ic /ˌparəmagˈnetik/ ▶ **adj.** (of a substance or body) very weakly attracted by the poles of a magnet, but not retaining any permanent magnetism.
– DERIVATIVES **par·a·mag·net·ism** /-ˈmagnəˌtizəm/ **n.**

Par·a·mar·i·bo /ˌparəˈmarəˌbō, ˌperəˈmer-/ the capital of Suriname, a port on the Atlantic coast; pop. 252,000 (est. 2007).

par·a·mat·ta /ˌparəˈmatə/ (also **parramatta**) ▶ **n.** a fine-quality twill fabric with a weft of worsted and a warp of cotton or silk.
– ORIGIN early 19th cent.: named after *Parramatta*, a city in New South Wales, Australia, which was the site of a prison whose inmates manufactured the cloth for clothing supplied to the convict servants of settlers.

par·a·me·ci·um /ˌparəˈmēsH(ē)əm, -sēəm/ ▶ **n.** Zoology a single-celled freshwater animal that has a characteristic slipperlike shape and is covered with cilia. ● Genus *Paramecium*, phylum Ciliophora, kingdom Protista.
– ORIGIN mid 18th cent.: modern Latin, from Greek *paramēkēs* 'oval,' from *para-* 'against' + *mēkos* 'length.'

par·a·med·ic /ˌparəˈmedik/ ▶ **n.** a person who is trained to do medical work, esp. emergency first aid, but is not usually a fully qualified physician.

par·a·med·i·cal /ˌparəˈmedikəl/ ▶ **adj.** of or relating to services and professions that supplement and support medical work but do not require a fully qualified physician (such as nursing, radiography, emergency first aid, physical therapy, and dietetics).

pa·ram·e·ter /pəˈramitər/ ▶ **n.** technical a numerical or other measurable factor forming one of a set that defines a system or sets the conditions of its operation: *the transmission will not let you downshift unless your speed is within the lower gear's parameters*. ■ Mathematics a quantity whose value is selected for the particular circumstances and in relation to which other variable quantities may be expressed. ■ Statistics a numerical characteristic of a population, as distinct from a statistic of a sample. ■ (in general use) a limit or boundary that defines the scope of a particular process or activity: *they set the parameters of the debate*.
– ORIGIN mid 17th cent.: modern Latin, from Greek *para-* 'beside' + *metron* 'measure.'

> **USAGE** Until recently, use of the word **parameter** was confined to mathematics and related technical fields. Since around the mid 20th century, however, it has been used in nontechnical fields as a technical-sounding word for 'a limit or boundary,' as in *they set the* ***parameters*** *of the debate*. This use, probably influenced by the word **perimeter**, has been criticized for being a weakening of the technical sense. Careful writers will leave **parameter** to specialists in mathematics, computer science, and other technical disciplines. As a loose synonym for *limit, boundary, guideline, framework*, it is a vogue word that blurs more than it clarifies. **Perimeter** is a different word, meaning 'border, outer boundary, or the length of such a boundary.'

pa·ram·e·ter·ize /pəˈramitəˌrīz/ ▶ **v.** [with obj.] technical describe or represent in terms of a parameter or parameters.
– DERIVATIVES **pa·ram·e·ter·i·za·tion** /pəˌramitəriˈzāsHən/ **n.**

par·a·met·ric /ˌparəˈmetrik/ ▶ **adj.** of, relating to, or expressed in terms of a parameter or parameters. ■ Statistics assuming the value of a parameter for the purpose of analysis. ■ Electronics relating to or denoting a process in which amplification or frequency conversion is obtained using a device modulated by a pumping frequency, which enables power to be transferred from the pumping frequency to the signal.

par·a·met·ric e·qual·iz·er ▶ **n.** an electronic device or computer program that allows any specific part of the frequency range of a signal to be selected and altered in strength.

par·a·mil·i·tar·y /ˌparəˈmiliˌterē/ ▶ **adj.** (of an unofficial force) organized similarly to a military force: *soldiers and police have been killed in conflicts with the drug cartels and their paramilitary allies*.
▶ **n.** (pl. **paramilitaries**) a member of an unofficial paramilitary organization.

par·am·ne·sia /ˌparamˈnēzHə/ ▶ **n.** Psychiatry a condition or phenomenon involving distorted memory or confusions of fact and fantasy, such as confabulation or déjà vu.

pa·ra·mo /ˈpärəˌmō/ ▶ **n.** (pl. **paramos**) a high, treeless plateau in tropical South America.
– ORIGIN Spanish and Portuguese, from Latin *paramus*.

Par·a·mo·tor /ˈparəˌmōtər/ ▶ **n.** trademark a motorized steerable paraglider, powered by a motor and propeller harnessed to the pilot's back.
– DERIVATIVES **par·a·mo·tor·ing n.**

Par·a·mount /ˈparəˌmount/ a city in southwestern California, southeast of Los Angeles; pop. 55,236 (est. 2008).

par·a·mount /ˈparəˌmount/ ▶ **adj.** more important than anything else; supreme: *the interests of the child are of paramount importance*. ■ [attrib.] having supreme power: *a paramount chief*.
– DERIVATIVES **par·a·mount·cy** /-sē/ **n.**, **par·a·mount·ly adv.**
– ORIGIN mid 16th cent. (in the sense 'highest in jurisdiction' in the phrases *lord paramount* and *paramount chief*): from Anglo-Norman French *paramont*, from Old French *par* 'by' + *amont* 'above.'

par·a·mour /ˈparəˌmo͝or/ ▶ **n.** a lover, esp. the illicit partner of a married person.
– ORIGIN Middle English: from Old French *par amour* 'by love'; in English the phrase was written from an early date as one word and came to be treated as a noun.

par·a·myx·o·vi·rus /ˌparəˈmiksəˌvīrəs/ ▶ **n.** Medicine any of a group of RNA viruses similar to the myxoviruses but larger and hemolytic, including those causing mumps, measles, distemper, rinderpest, and various respiratory infections (parainfluenza).

Pa·ra·ná /ˌpärəˈnä/ **1** a river in South America that rises in southeastern Brazil and flows about 2,060 miles (3,300 km) south to the Plate River estuary in Argentina. For part of its length it forms the southeastern border of Paraguay.
2 a river port in eastern Argentina, on the Paraná River; pop. 249,500 (est. 2005).

pa·rang[1] /ˈpäräNG/ ▶ **n.** a Malayan machete.
– ORIGIN Malay.

pa·rang[2] /pəˈräNG/ ▶ **n.** a variety of Trinidadian folk music, traditionally played at Christmas by groups that travel from house to house.
– ORIGIN Spanish Creole, based on Spanish *parranda* 'spree, binge.'

par·a·noi·a /ˌparəˈnoiə/ ▶ **n.** a mental condition characterized by delusions of persecution, unwarranted jealousy, or exaggerated self-importance, typically elaborated into an organized system. It may be an aspect of chronic personality disorder, of drug abuse, or of a serious condition such as schizophrenia in which the person loses touch with reality. ■ suspicion and mistrust of people or their actions without evidence or justification: *the global paranoia about hackers and viruses*.
– DERIVATIVES **par·a·noi·ac** /-ˈnoi-ak, -ˈnoi-ik/ **adj. & n.**, **par·a·noi·a·cal·ly adv.**, **par·a·no·ic** /-ˈnoi-ik/ **adj.**, **par·a·no·i·cal·ly adv.**
– ORIGIN early 19th cent.: modern Latin, from Greek, from *paranoos* 'distracted,' from *para* 'irregular' + *noos* 'mind.'

par·a·noid /ˈparəˌnoid/ ▶ **adj.** of, characterized by, or suffering from the mental condition of paranoia: *paranoid schizophrenia*. ■ unreasonably or obsessively anxious, suspicious, or mistrustful: *you think I'm paranoid but I tell you there is something going on*.
▶ **n.** a person who is paranoid.

par·a·nor·mal /ˌparəˈnôrməl/ ▶ **adj.** denoting events or phenomena such as telekinesis or clairvoyance that are beyond the scope of normal scientific understanding: *a mystic who can prove he has paranormal powers* | (as noun **the paranormal**) *an investigator of the paranormal*.
– DERIVATIVES **par·a·nor·mal·ly adv.**

Par·an·thro·pus /pəˈranTHrəpəs/ ▶ **n.** a genus name often applied to robust fossil hominids first found in South Africa in 1938. ● *Australopithecus robustus* and *A.* (or *Zinjanthropus*) *boisei*, family Hominidae. See **AUSTRALOPITHECUS**.
– ORIGIN modern Latin, from Greek *para-* (expressing relationship) + *anthrōpos* 'man.'

par·a·pa·re·sis /ˌparəpəˈrēsis/ ▶ **n.** partial paralysis of the lower limbs.
– DERIVATIVES **paraparetic** /-ˈretik/ **adj.**

par·a·pente /ˈparəˌpänt/ ▶ **n.** the activity of gliding by means of an airfoil parachute launched from high ground. ■ the parachute used for this purpose.
▶ **v.** [no obj.] glide using an airfoil parachute.
– DERIVATIVES **par·a·pent·er n.**
– ORIGIN 1980s: from French, from *para(chute)* + *pente* 'slope.'

par·a·pet /ˈparəpit/ ▶ **n.** a low protective wall along the edge of a roof, bridge, or balcony. ■ a protective wall or earth defense along the top of a trench or other place of concealment for troops.
– DERIVATIVES **par·a·pet·ed adj.**
– ORIGIN late 16th cent.: from French, or from Italian *parapetto* 'breast-high wall,' from *para-* 'protecting' + *petto* 'breast' (from Latin *pectus*).

par·aph /ˈparəf, pəˈraf/ ▶ **n.** a flourish after a signature, originally as a precaution against forgery.
– ORIGIN late Middle English (denoting a paragraph): from French *paraphe*, from medieval Latin *paraphus* (contraction of *paragraphus* 'short horizontal stroke').

par·a·pha·sia /ˌparəˈfāzHə/ ▶ **n.** Psychology speech disturbance resulting from brain damage in which words are jumbled and sentences meaningless.
– DERIVATIVES **par·a·pha·sic** /-ˈfāzik/ **adj.**

par·a·pher·na·lia /ˌparəfə(r)ˈnālyə/ ▶ **n.** [treated as sing. or pl.] miscellaneous articles, esp. the equipment needed for a particular activity: *drills, saws, and other paraphernalia necessary for home improvements* | *drugs and drug paraphernalia that had been discovered on the premises*. ■ trappings associated with a particular institution or activity that are regarded as superfluous: *the rituals and paraphernalia of government*.

P

– ORIGIN mid 17th cent. (denoting property owned by a married woman): from medieval Latin, based on Greek *parapherna* 'property apart from a dowry,' from *para* 'distinct from' + *pherna* (from *phernē* 'dowry').

par·a·phil·i·a /ˌparəˈfilēə/ ▶ **n.** Psychiatry a condition characterized by abnormal sexual desires, typically involving extreme or dangerous activities.
– DERIVATIVES **par·a·phil·i·ac** /-ˈfilēˌak/ **adj. & n.**

par·a·phrase /ˈparəˌfrāz/ ▶ **v.** [with obj.] express the meaning of (the writer or speaker or something written or spoken) using different words, esp. to achieve greater clarity: *you can either quote or paraphrase literary texts.*
▶ **n.** a rewording of something written or spoken by someone else.
– DERIVATIVES **par·a·phras·a·ble adj.**, **par·a·phras·tic** /ˌparəˈfrastik/ **adj.**
– ORIGIN mid 16th cent. (as a noun): via Latin from Greek *paraphrasis*, from *paraphrazein*, from *para-* (expressing modification) + *phrazein* 'tell.'

par·a·phy·let·ic /ˌparəˌfīˈletik/ ▶ **adj.** Biology (of a group of organisms) descended from a common evolutionary ancestor or ancestral group, but not including all the descendant groups.

pa·raph·y·sis /pəˈrafəsəs/ ▶ **n.** (pl. **paraphyses** /-ˌsēz/) Botany a sterile hairlike filament present among the reproductive organs in many lower plants, esp. bryophytes, algae, and fungi.
– ORIGIN mid 19th cent.: modern Latin, from Greek *para-* 'beside, subsidiary' + *phusis* 'growth.'

Par·a·Plane /ˈparəˌplān/ (also **Paraplane**) ▶ **n.** trademark a motor-driven flying machine consisting of a parachute and a pair of fabric wings attached to a rigid framework.

par·a·ple·gi·a /ˌparəˈplēj(ē)ə/ ▶ **n.** paralysis of the legs and lower body, typically caused by spinal injury or disease.
– DERIVATIVES **par·a·ple·gic** /-jik/ **adj. & n.**
– ORIGIN mid 17th cent.: modern Latin, from Greek *paraplēgia*, from *paraplēssein* 'strike at the side,' from *para* 'beside' + *plēssein* 'to strike.'

par·a·po·di·um /ˌparəˈpōdēəm/ ▶ **n.** (pl. **parapodia** /-dēə/) Zoology (in a polychaete worm) each of a number of paired muscular bristle-bearing appendages used in locomotion, sensation, or respiration. ■ (in a sea slug or other mollusk) a lateral extension of the foot used as an undulating fin for swimming.
– DERIVATIVES **par·a·po·di·al** /-dēəl/ **adj.**
– ORIGIN late 19th cent.: modern Latin, from Greek *para-* 'subsidiary' + *pous, pod-* 'foot.'

par·a·pro·fes·sion·al /ˌparəprəˈfesHənl/ ▶ **n.** a person to whom a particular aspect of a professional task is delegated but who is not licensed to practice as a fully qualified professional.
▶ **adj.** of, relating to, or denoting such a person: *the union advocated paraprofessional help for nonteaching duties.*

P

par·a·pro·tein /ˌparəˈprōtē(ə)n/ ▶ **n.** Medicine a protein found in the blood only as a result of cancer or other disease.

par·a·psych·ic /ˌparəˈsikik/ ▶ **adj.** of, relating to, or denoting mental phenomena for which no adequate scientific explanation exists.

par·a·psy·chol·o·gy /ˌparəsīˈkäləjē/ ▶ **n.** the study of mental phenomena that are excluded from or inexplicable by orthodox scientific psychology (such as hypnosis, telepathy, etc.).
– DERIVATIVES **par·a·psy·cho·log·i·cal** /-ˌsīkəˈläjikəl/ **adj.**, **par·a·psy·chol·o·gist** /-jist/ **n.**

par·a·pto·sis /ˌparə(p)ˈtōsis/ ▶ **n.** a system of programmed cell death in which empty spaces form in the cell cytoplasm and the mitochondria swells, causing the cell to lose its vitality. It differs from apoptosis in that the cell does not fragment.
– DERIVATIVES **par·a·ptot·ic** /ˌparə(p)ˈtätik, -ˈtōtik/ **adj.**
– ORIGIN based on *para-* 'beside' + Greek *ptōsis* 'a falling.'

par·a·quat /ˈparəˌkwät/ ▶ **n.** a toxic, fast-acting herbicide that becomes deactivated in the soil.
– ORIGIN 1960s: from PARA-[1] (sense 2) + QUATERNARY (it is a quaternary ammonium salt containing pyridine rings linked at the para-position).

par·a·rhyme /ˈparəˌrīm/ ▶ **n.** partial rhyme between words with the same pattern of consonants but different vowels, such as *light* and *late*. See also IMPERFECT RHYME.

par·a·sag·it·tal /ˌparəˈsajitl/ ▶ **adj.** Anatomy relating to or situated in a plane adjacent or parallel to the plane that divides the body into right and left halves.
– DERIVATIVES **par·a·sag·it·tal·ly adv.**

par·a·sail /ˈparəˌsāl/ ▶ **v.** [no obj.] (often as noun **parasailing**) glide through the air wearing an open parachute while being towed by a motorboat.
▶ **n.** a parachute designed for parasailing.

par·a·se·le·ne /ˌparəsəˈlēnē/ ▶ **n.** (pl. **paraselenae** pronunc. **same**) a bright spot in the sky similar to a parhelion but formed by moonlight. Also called MOCK MOON, MOON DOG. Compare with PARHELION.
– ORIGIN mid 17th cent.: modern Latin, from Greek *para-* 'beside' + *selēnē* 'moon.'

par·a·site /ˈparəˌsīt/ ▶ **n.** an organism that lives in or on another organism (its host) and benefits by deriving nutrients at the host's expense. ■ derogatory a person who habitually relies on or exploits others and gives nothing in return.

> Parasites exist in huge variety, including animals, plants, and microorganisms. They may live as ectoparasites on the surface of the host (e.g., arthropods such as ticks, mites, lice, fleas, and many insects infesting plants) or as endoparasites in the gut or tissues (e.g., many kinds of worm), and cause varying degrees of damage or disease to the host.

– ORIGIN mid 16th cent.: via Latin from Greek *parasitos* '(person) eating at another's table,' from *para-* 'alongside' + *sitos* 'food.'

par·a·sit·e·mi·a /ˌparəsīˈtēmēə/ (Brit. **parasitaemia**) ▶ **n.** Medicine the demonstrable presence of parasites in the blood.

par·a·sit·ic /ˌparəˈsitik/ ▶ **adj.** (of an organism) living as a parasite: *mistletoe is parasitic on trees.* ■ resulting from infestation by a parasite: *mortality from parasitic diseases.* ■ derogatory habitually relying on or exploiting others: *attacks on the parasitic existence of Party functionaries.* ■ Phonetics (of a speech sound) inserted without etymological justification (e.g., the *b* in *thimble*); epenthetic.
– DERIVATIVES **par·a·sit·i·cal adj.**, **par·a·sit·i·cal·ly adv.**, **par·a·sit·ism** /ˈparəsiˌtizəm, -ˌsī-/ **n.**
– ORIGIN early 17th cent.: via Latin from Greek *parasitikos*, from *parasitos* '(person) eating at another's table.'

par·a·sit·i·cide /ˌparəˈsitəˌsīd/ ▶ **n.** a substance used in medicine and veterinary medicine to kill parasites (esp. those other than bacteria or fungi).

par·a·si·tize /ˈparəsiˌtīz, -sī-/ ▶ **v.** [with obj.] infest or exploit (an organism or part) as a parasite.
– DERIVATIVES **par·a·sit·i·za·tion** /ˌparəsiˌtīˈzāsHən, -sī-/ **n.**

par·a·sit·oid /ˈparəsiˌtoid, -ˌsī-/ Entomology ▶ **n.** an insect (e.g., the ichneumon wasp) whose larvae live as parasites that eventually kill their hosts (typically other insects).

par·a·si·tol·o·gy /ˌparəsiˈtäləjē, -sī-/ ▶ **n.** the branch of biology or medicine concerned with the study of parasitic organisms.
– DERIVATIVES **par·a·si·to·log·i·cal** /ˌparəˌsītlˈäjikəl, -ˌsitl-/ **adj.**, **par·a·si·tol·o·gist** /-jist/ **n.**

par·a·ski ▶ **v.** [no obj.] jump from an aircraft by parachute and ski from the landing place, as a sport or race: [as adj.] *he perennially competes in the intermediate class in the para-ski nationals.*
– DERIVATIVES **par·a·ski·ing n.**

par·a·sol /ˈparəˌsôl, -ˌsäl/ ▶ **n. 1** a light umbrella used to give shade from the sun.
2 (also **parasol mushroom**) a widely distributed large mushroom with a broad, scaly, grayish-brown cap and a tall, slender stalk, growing typically in grassy places. ● Genus *Lepiota*, family Lepiotaceae, class Hymenomycetes: numerous species, esp. the edible *L. procera*.
– ORIGIN early 17th cent.: from French, from Italian *parasole*, from *para-* 'protecting against' + *sole* 'sun' (from Latin *sol*).

par·a·stat·al /ˌparəˈstātl/ ▶ **adj.** (of an organization or industry) having some political authority and serving the state indirectly, esp. in some African countries.
▶ **n.** a parastatal organization.

par·a·state /ˈparəˌstāt/ ▶ **n.** a region that seeks or claims but does not have the status of a recognized independent state.

par·a·ster·nal /ˌparəˈstərnəl/ ▶ **adj.** Anatomy situated beside the sternum.

pa·ras·ti·chy /pəˈrastikē/ ▶ **n.** (pl. **parastichies**) Botany (in phyllotaxis) an oblique row of leaves arranged in a secondary spiral. Contrasted with ORTHOSTICHY.
– ORIGIN late 19th cent.: from PARA-[1] 'adjacent' + Greek *stikhos* 'row, rank.'

par·a·sym·pa·thet·ic /ˌparəˌsimpəˈTHetik/ ▶ **adj.** Physiology of or relating to the part of the automatic nervous system that counterbalances the action of the sympathetic nerves. It consists of nerves arising from the brain and the lower end of the spinal cord and supplying the internal organs, blood vessels, and glands.
– ORIGIN early 20th cent.: from PARA-[1] 'alongside' + SYMPATHETIC, because some of these nerves run alongside sympathetic nerves.

par·a·syn·the·sis /ˌparəˈsinTHəsis/ ▶ **n.** Linguistics a process by which a term is formed by adding a bound morpheme (e.g., *-ed*) to a combination of existing words (e.g., *black-eyed* from *black eye(s)* + *-ed*).
– DERIVATIVES **par·a·syn·thet·ic** /-sinˈTHetik/ **adj.**, **par·a·syn·thet·i·cal·ly adv.**
– ORIGIN mid 19th cent.: from Greek *parasunthesis*, from *para-* 'subsidiary' + SYNTHESIS.

par·a·tax·is /ˌparəˈtaksis/ ▶ **n.** Grammar the placing of clauses or phrases one after another, without words to indicate coordination or subordination, as in *Tell me, how are you?* Contrasted with HYPOTAXIS.
– DERIVATIVES **par·a·tac·tic** /-ˈtaktik/ **adj.**, **par·a·tac·ti·cal·ly** /-ˈtaktik(ə)lē/ **adv.**
– ORIGIN mid 19th cent.: from Greek *parataxis*, from *para-* 'beside' + *taxis* 'arrangement' (from *tassein* 'arrange').

pa·ra·tha /pəˈrätə/ ▶ **n.** (in Indian cooking) a flat, thick piece of unleavened bread fried on a griddle.
– ORIGIN from Hindi *parāṭhā*.

par·a·thi·on /ˌparəˈTHīˌän/ ▶ **n.** a highly toxic synthetic compound containing phosphorus and sulfur, used as an agricultural insecticide.
– ORIGIN 1940s: from PARA-[1] (sense 2) + THIO- + -ON.

par·a·thor·mone /ˌparəˈTHôrˌmōn/ ▶ **n.** Physiology parathyroid hormone.

par·a·thy·roid /ˌparəˈTHīˌroid/ ▶ **n.** Anatomy a gland next to the thyroid that secretes a hormone (**parathyroid hormone**) that regulates calcium levels in a person's body.

par·a·troop·er /ˈparəˌtro͞opər/ ▶ **n.** a member of a paratroop regiment or airborne unit.

par·a·troops /ˈparəˌtro͞ops/ ▶ **plural n.** troops equipped to be dropped by parachute from aircraft: (as modifier, usu. **paratroop**) *a paratroop regiment.*
– ORIGIN 1940s: from an abbreviation of PARACHUTE + *troops* (plural of TROOP).

par·a·ty·phoid /ˌparəˈtīˌfoid/ ▶ **n.** a fever resembling typhoid but caused by different (though related) bacteria. ● The bacteria are species of the genus *Salmonella*, in particular (in humans) *S. paratyphi*.

par·a·vane /ˈparəˌvān/ ▶ **n.** a device towed behind a boat at a depth regulated by its vanes or planes, so that the cable to which it is attached can cut the moorings of submerged mines.
– ORIGIN early 20th cent.: from PARA-[2] 'protecting' + VANE.

par·a·ven·tric·u·lar /ˌparəvenˈtrikyələr/ ▶ **adj.** Anatomy situated next to a ventricle of the brain.

par a·vion /ˌpär äˈvyôn/ ▶ **adv.** by airmail (written on a letter or parcel to indicate how it is to reach its destination).
– ORIGIN French, literally 'by airplane.'

par·a·wing /ˈparəˌwiNG/ ▶ **n.** a type of parachute or kite having a flattened shape like a wing, to give greater maneuverability.

par·ax·i·al /pəˈraksēəl/ ▶ **adj.** Anatomy & Zoology situated alongside, or on each side of, an axis, esp. the central axis of the body.

par·boil /ˈpärˌboil/ ▶ **v.** [with obj.] partly cook (food) by boiling.
– ORIGIN late Middle English: from Old French *parbouillir*, from late Latin *perbullire* 'boil thoroughly,' from Latin *per-* 'through, thoroughly' (later confused with PART) + *bullire* 'to boil.'

par·buck·le /ˈpärˌbəkəl/ ▶ **n.** a loop of rope arranged like a sling, used for raising or lowering casks and other cylindrical objects along an inclined plane.
▶ **v.** [with obj.] raise or lower with such a device.
– ORIGIN early 17th cent.: from earlier *parbunkle*, of unknown origin. The change in the ending was due to association with BUCKLE.

Par·cae /ˈpärsē/ Roman Mythology Roman name for THE FATES (see FATE).

par·cel /ˈpärsəl/ ▶ **n. 1** a thing or collection of things wrapped in paper in order to be carried or sent by mail.
2 a quantity or amount of something, esp. as dealt with in one commercial transaction: *a parcel of shares.* ■ a piece of land, esp. one considered as part of an estate. ■ technical a portion of a larger body of air or other fluid considered as a discrete element.
▶ **v.** (**parcels, parceling, parceled**; Brit. **parcels, parcelling, parcelled**) [with obj.] make (something) into a parcel by wrapping it: *he parceled up his only winter suit to take to the pawnbroker.* ■ (**parcel something out**) divide into portions and then distribute: *they will start parceling out radio frequencies for digital cordless telephones.* ■ Nautical wrap (rope) with strips of tarred canvas before binding it with yarn as part of a traditional technique to reduce chafing.

– PHRASES **be part and parcel of** see PART. **pass the parcel** chiefly Brit. a children's game in which a parcel is passed around to the accompaniment of music, the child holding the parcel when the music stops being allowed to unwrap a layer.
– ORIGIN late Middle English (chiefly in the sense 'small portion'): from Old French *parcelle*, from Latin *particula* 'small part.'

par·cel post ▶ **n.** mail consisting of parcels.

parch /pärCH/ ▶ **v.** make or become dry through intense heat: [with obj.] *a piece of grassland parched by the sun* | [no obj.] *his crops parched during the last two summers.* ■ [with obj.] roast (corn, peas, etc.) lightly.
– ORIGIN late Middle English: of unknown origin.

parched /pärCHt/ ▶ **adj.** dried out with heat: *the parched earth.* ■ [predic.] informal extremely thirsty: *I'm parched—I'll die without a drink.* ■ lightly roasted: *parched corn.*

par·chee·si /pär'CHēzē/ ▶ **n.** variant spelling of PACHISI.

parch·ment /'pärCHmənt/ ▶ **n.** a stiff, flat, thin material made from the prepared skin of an animal and used as a durable writing surface in ancient and medieval times. ■ a manuscript written on this material: *a large collection of ancient parchments.* ■ (also **parchment paper**) a type of stiff translucent paper treated to resemble parchment and used for lampshades, as a writing surface, and in baking. ■ informal a diploma or other formal document.
– ORIGIN Middle English: from Old French *parchemin*, from a blend of late Latin *pergamina* 'writing material from Pergamum' and *Parthica pellis* 'Parthian skin' (a kind of scarlet leather).

par·close /'pär,klōz/ ▶ **n.** a screen or railing in a church enclosing a tomb or altar or separating off a side chapel.
– ORIGIN Middle English: from Old French *parclos(e)* 'enclosed,' past participle of *parclore* (from Latin *per-* 'thoroughly' + *claudere* 'to close').

pard /pärd/ ▶ **n.** archaic or literary a leopard.
– ORIGIN late Middle English: from Old French, via Latin from Greek *pardos*.

par·da·lote /'pärdl,ōt/ ▶ **n.** a small, short-billed Australian songbird related to the flowerpeckers, typically having white spots or streaks on the dark wings and crown. ● Genus *Pardalotus*, family Dicaeidae (or Pardalotidae): several species.
– ORIGIN mid 19th cent.: from modern Latin *Pardalotus*, from Greek *pardalōtos* 'spotted like a leopard,' based on *pardos* (see PARD).

pard·ner /'pärdnər/ ▶ **n.** dated or humorous variant spelling of PARTNER, used to represent US dialect speech: *you and me, pardner, against the world.*

par·don /'pärdn/ ▶ **n.** the action of forgiving or being forgiven for an error or offense: *he obtained pardon for his sins.* ■ a remission of the legal consequences of an offense or conviction: *he offered a full pardon to five convicted men.* ■ Christian Church, historical an indulgence, as widely sold in medieval Europe.
▶ **v.** [with obj.] forgive or excuse (a person, error, or offense): *I know Catherine will pardon me.* ■ release (an offender) from the legal consequences of an offense or conviction, and often implicitly from blame: *he was pardoned for his treason.* ■ (**be pardoned**) used to indicate that the actions or thoughts of someone are justified or understandable given the circumstances: *one can be pardoned the suspicion that some of his errors were deliberate.*
▶ **exclam.** a request to a speaker to repeat something because one did not hear or understand it: *"Pardon?" I said, cupping a hand to my ear.*
– PHRASES **beg someone's pardon** express polite apology: *I beg your pardon for intruding.* **pardon me** (or **I beg your pardon**) used to indicate that one has not heard or understood something. ■ used to express one's anger or indignation at what someone has just said.
– ORIGIN Middle English: from Old French *pardun* (noun), *pardoner* (verb), from medieval Latin *perdonare* 'concede, remit,' from *per-* 'completely' + *donare* 'give.'

par·don·a·ble /'pärdn-əbəl/ ▶ **adj.** able to be forgiven; excusable: *no mistake, even a tiny one, is pardonable.*
– DERIVATIVES **par·don·a·bly** /-əblē/ **adv.**

par·don·er /'pärdn-ər/ ▶ **n.** historical a person licensed to sell papal pardons or indulgences.
– ORIGIN Middle English: from Anglo-Norman French.

pare /pe(ə)r/ ▶ **v.** [with obj.] trim (something) by cutting away its outer edges: *Carlo pared his thumbnails with his knife.* ■ cut off the outer skin of (something): *pare off the rind using a peeler.* ■ reduce (something) in size, extent, quantity, or number, usually in a number of small successive stages: *union leaders publicly pared down their demands* | *we pared costs by doing our own cleaning.*
– DERIVATIVES **par·er n.**
– ORIGIN Middle English: from Old French *parer* 'adorn, prepare,' also 'peel, trim,' from Latin *parare* 'prepare.'

par·e·gor·ic /,parə'gôrik/ ▶ **n.** a medicine consisting of opium flavored with camphor, aniseed, and benzoic acid, formerly used to treat diarrhea and coughing in children.
– ORIGIN late 17th cent.: via late Latin from Greek *parēgorikos* 'soothing,' from the verb *parēgorein*, literally 'speak in the assembly,' hence 'soothe, console.'

pa·ren /pə'ren/ ▶ **n.** (usu. **parens**) Printing a parenthesis.
– ORIGIN early 20th cent.: abbreviation of PARENTHESIS.

paren. ▶ **abbr.** parenthesis.

pa·ren·chy·ma /pə'reNGkəmə/ ▶ **n.** Anatomy the functional tissue of an organ as distinguished from the connective and supporting tissue. ■ Botany the cellular tissue, typically soft and succulent, found chiefly in the softer parts of leaves, pulp of fruits, bark and pith of stems, etc. ■ Zoology cellular tissue lying between the body wall and the organs of invertebrate animals lacking a coelom, such as flatworms.
– DERIVATIVES **pa·ren·chy·mal** /-məl/ **adj.** (chiefly Anatomy), **pa·ren·chym·a·tous** /,perəNG'kimətəs/ **adj.** (chiefly Botany).
– ORIGIN mid 17th cent.: from Greek *parenkhuma* 'something poured in beside,' from *para-* 'beside' + *enkhuma* 'infusion.'

pa·rens pa·tri·ae /'parənz 'patri-ē, 'patri-ī/ ▶ **n.** Law the government, or any other authority, regarded as the legal protector of citizens unable to protect themselves. ■ the principle that political authority carries with it the responsibility for such protection.
– ORIGIN modern Latin, literally 'parent of the country.'

par·ent /'pe(ə)rənt, 'par-/ ▶ **n.** a father or mother: *the parents of the bride* | *his adoptive parents.* ■ archaic a forefather or ancestor. ■ an animal or plant from which younger ones are derived. ■ a source or origin of a smaller or less important part. ■ [often as modifier] an organization or company that owns or controls a number of subsidiary organizations or companies: *policy considerations were determined largely by the parent institution.*
▶ **v.** [with obj.] (often as noun **parenting**) be or act as a mother or father to (someone): *the warmth and attention that are the hallmarks of good parenting.*
– DERIVATIVES **pa·ren·tal** /pə'rentl/ **adj.**, **pa·ren·tal·ly** /pə'rentl-ē/ **adv.**, **par·ent·less adj.**
– ORIGIN late Middle English: from Old French, from Latin *parent-* 'bringing forth,' from the verb *parere*. The verb dates from the mid 17th cent.

par·ent·age /'pe(ə)rəntij, 'par-/ ▶ **n.** the identity and origins of one's parents: *a boy of Jamaican parentage.* ■ the origin of something: *this ice cream boasts American parentage.*
– ORIGIN late 15th cent.: from Old French.

par·en·ter·al /pə'rentərəl/ ▶ **adj.** Medicine administered or occurring elsewhere in the body than the mouth and alimentary canal: *parenteral nutrition.* Often contrasted with ENTERAL.
– DERIVATIVES **par·en·ter·al·ly adv.**
– ORIGIN early 20th cent.: from PARA-[1] 'beside' + Greek *enteron* 'intestine' + -AL.

pa·ren·the·sis /pə'renTHəsis/ ▶ **n.** (pl. **parentheses** /-,sēz/) a word, clause, or sentence inserted as an explanation or afterthought into a passage that is grammatically complete without it, in writing usually marked off by curved brackets, dashes, or commas. ■ (usu. **parentheses**) one or both of a pair of marks () used to include such a word, clause, or sentence. ■ an interlude or interval: *the three months of coalition government were a lamentable political parenthesis.*
– PHRASES **in parenthesis** as a digression or afterthought.
– ORIGIN mid 16th cent.: via late Latin from Greek, from *parentithenai* 'put in beside.'

pa·ren·the·size /pə'renTHə,sīz/ ▶ **v.** [with obj.] (usu. as adj. **parenthesized**) put (a word, phrase, or clause) into parentheses: *parenthesized clauses.* ■ insert as a parenthesis; express or state in parenthesis.

par·en·thet·i·cal /,parən'THetikəl/ ▶ **adj.** of, relating to, or inserted as a parenthesis: *ignore the parenthetical remarks that pockmark every page.*
– DERIVATIVES **par·en·thet·ic** /-'THetik/ **adj.**, **par·en·thet·i·cal·ly adv.**
– ORIGIN late 18th cent.: from PARENTHESIS, on the pattern of pairs such as *synthesis, synthetic.*

par·ent·hood /'pe(ə)rənt,hŏŏd, 'par-/ ▶ **n.** the state of being a parent and the responsibilities involved: *high rates of single parenthood.*

par·ent–teach·er as·so·ci·a·tion (abbr.: **PTA**) ▶ **n.** a national organization devoted to furthering the safety and interests of children. ■ a local organization of parents and teachers for promoting closer relations and improving educational facilities at a school.

par·er·gon /pə'rər,gän/ ▶ **n.** (pl. **parerga** /-gə/) a piece of work that is supplementary to or a byproduct of a larger work. ■ archaic work that is subsidiary to one's ordinary employment: *he pursued astronomy as a parergon.*
– ORIGIN early 17th cent.: via Latin from Greek *parergon*, from *para-* 'beside, additional' + *ergon* 'work.'

pa·re·sis /pə'rēsis/ ▶ **n.** (pl. **pareses** /-sēz/) Medicine a condition of muscular weakness caused by nerve damage or disease; partial paralysis. ■ (also **general paresis**) inflammation of the brain in the later stages of syphilis, causing progressive dementia and paralysis.
– DERIVATIVES **pa·ret·ic** /-'retik/ **adj.**
– ORIGIN late 17th cent.: modern Latin, from Greek *parienai* 'let go,' from *para-* 'alongside' + *hienai* 'let go.'

par·es·the·si·a /,parəs'THēZH(ē)ə/ (Brit. **paraesthesia**) ▶ **n.** (pl. **paresthesiae** /-ZHē-ē/ or **paresthesias**) Medicine an abnormal sensation, typically tingling or pricking ("pins and needles"), caused chiefly by pressure on or damage to peripheral nerves.
– ORIGIN late 19th cent.: from PARA-[1] 'alongside, irregular' + Greek *aisthēsis* 'sensation' + -IA[1].

Pa·re·to /pə'retō/ ▶ **adj.** [attrib.] denoting or involving the theories and methods of the Italian economist and sociologist **Vilfredo Pareto** (1848–1923), esp. a formula used to express the income distribution of a society.

Pa·re·to-op·ti·mal ▶ **adj.** relating to or denoting a distribution of wealth such that any redistribution or other change beneficial to one individual is detrimental to one or more others.
– DERIVATIVES **Pa·re·to-op·ti·mal·i·ty n.**

pa·re·u /'pärä,o͞o/ ▶ **n.** a kind of sarong made of a single straight piece of printed cotton cloth, worn by Polynesians.
– ORIGIN Tahitian.

pa·re·ve /'pärəvə/ (also **parve**) ▶ **adj.** Judaism prepared without meat, milk, or their derivatives and therefore permissible to be eaten with both meat and dairy dishes according to dietary laws.
– ORIGIN Yiddish.

par ex·cel·lence /,pär ,eksə'läns/ ▶ **adj.** [postpositive] better or more than all others of the same kind: *he has won a reputation for being a designer par excellence.*
– ORIGIN French, literally 'by excellence.'

par·fait /pär'fā/ ▶ **n.** a dessert consisting of layers of ice cream, fruit, etc., served in a tall glass. ■ a rich cold dessert made with whipped cream, eggs, and often fruit.
– ORIGIN from the French adjective *parfait*, literally 'perfect.'

P

par·fleche /'pärfleSH, pär'fleSH/ ▶ **n.** (in American Indian culture) a hide, esp. a buffalo's hide, dried by being stretched on a frame after the hair has been removed. ■ an article, esp. a bag, made from this.
– ORIGIN from Canadian French *parflèche*, from French *parer* 'ward off' + *flèche* 'arrow.'

par·fum·er·ie /pär'fyo͞omərē/ ▶ **n.** (pl. **parfumeries**) a place where perfume is sold or made.
– ORIGIN French, from *parfum* PERFUME.

par·fum·i·er /pär'fo͞omyā/ ▶ **n.** a person who manufactures or retails perfume.
– ORIGIN French, from *parfum* PERFUME.

par·get /'pärjit/ (also **parge** /pärj/) ▶ **v.** (**pargets, pargeting, pargeted**) [with obj.] cover (a part of a building, esp. an external brick wall) with plaster or mortar that typically bears an ornamental pattern.
▶ **n.** another term for PARGETING.
– ORIGIN late Middle English: from Old French *parjeter*, from *par-* 'all over' + *jeter* 'to throw.'

par·get·ing /'pärjitiNG/ (also **parging** /'pärjiNG/) ▶ **n.** plaster or mortar applied in a layer over a part of a building, esp. ornamental plasterwork.

par·he·li·on /pär'hēlēən, -'hēlyən/ ▶ **n.** (pl. **parhelia** /-'hēlēə/) a bright spot in the sky appearing on either side of the sun, formed by refraction of sunlight through ice crystals high in the earth's atmosphere. Also called SUN DOG.
– ORIGIN mid 17th cent.: from Latin *parelion*, from Greek *para-* 'beside' + *hēlios* 'sun.'

pa·ri·ah /pə'rīə/ ▶ **n. 1** an outcast: *they were treated as social pariahs.*
2 historical a member of a low caste in southern India.

– ORIGIN early 17th cent.: from Tamil *paraiyar*, plural of *paraiyan* '(hereditary) drummer,' from *parai* 'a drum' (pariahs not being allowed to join in with a religious procession).

pa·ri·ah dog ▶ n. another term for PYE-DOG.

Par·i·an /ˈpe(ə)rēən, ˈpar-/ ▶ adj. of or relating to Paros or the fine white marble for which it is renowned. ■ denoting a form of fine white unglazed hard-paste porcelain likened to Parian marble.
▶ n. 1 a native or inhabitant of Paros.
2 Parian ware (porcelain).

pa·ri·e·tal /pəˈrīətəl/ ▶ adj. 1 Anatomy & Biology of, relating to, attached to, or denoting the wall of the body or of a body cavity or hollow structure. ■ of the parietal lobe: *the parietal cortex*.
2 relating to residence in a college or university dormitory and esp. to visits from members of the opposite sex: *parietal rules*.
3 Archaeology denoting prehistoric art found on rock walls.
▶ n. 1 Anatomy & Zoology a parietal structure. ■ short for PARIETAL BONE.
2 (**parietals**) informal dormitory rules governing visits from members of the opposite sex.
– ORIGIN late Middle English: from late Latin *parietalis*, from Latin *paries*, *pariet-* 'wall.'

pa·ri·e·tal bone ▶ n. a bone forming the central side and upper back part of each side of the skull.

pa·ri·e·tal cell ▶ n. an oxyntic (acid-secreting) cell of the stomach wall.

pa·ri·e·tal lobe ▶ n. either of the paired lobes of the brain at the top of the head, including areas concerned with the reception and correlation of sensory information.

par·i·mu·tu·el /ˌparə ˈmyo͞ocho͞oəl/ (also **parimutuel**) ▶ n. [often as modifier] a form of betting in which those backing the first three places divide the losers' stakes (less the operator's commission): *pari-mutuel betting*. ■ a booth for placing bets under such a system.
– ORIGIN French, literally 'mutual stake.'

par·ing knife ▶ n. a small knife used mainly for peeling fruits and vegetables.

par·ings /ˈpe(ə)riNGz/ ▶ plural n. thin strips that have been pared off from something: *fingernail parings*.

pa·ri pas·su /ˌpärē ˈpäˌso͞o/ ▶ adv. side by side; at the same rate or on an equal footing: *early opera developed pari passu with solo song*.
– ORIGIN Latin, literally 'with equal step.'

Par·is[1] /ˈparis/ the capital of France, on the Seine River; pop. 2,203,817 (2006). Paris was held by the Romans, who called it Lutetia, and by the Franks, and was established as the capital in 987 under Hugh Capet. It was organized into three parts—the Île de la Cité (an island in the Seine), the Right Bank, and the Left Bank—during the reign of Philippe-Auguste 1180–1223. The city's neoclassical architecture dates from the modernization of the Napoleonic era, which continued under Napoleon III, when the bridges and boulevards of the modern city were built.
– ORIGIN named after the *Parisii*, a Gallic people who settled on the Île de la Cité.

Par·is[2] Greek Mythology a Trojan prince, the son of Priam and Hecuba. Appointed by the gods to decide who among the three goddesses Hera, Athena, and Aphrodite should win a prize for beauty, he awarded it to Aphrodite, who promised him the most beautiful woman in the world—Helen, wife of King Menelaus of Sparta. He abducted Helen, bringing about the Trojan War, in which he killed Achilles but was later himself killed.

Par·is[3], Matthew, see MATTHEW PARIS.

Par·is, Trea·ty of 1 a treaty signed in 1763 by Great Britain, France, and Spain that ended the Seven Years War in Europe (1756–63) and the French and Indian War in North America.
2 a treaty signed in 1783 by the US and Great Britain that ended the American Revolution.
3 a treaty signed in 1898 by the US and Spain that ended the Spanish-American War.

Par·is club a group of the major creditor nations of the International Monetary Fund whose representatives meet informally in Paris to discuss the financial relations of the IMF member nations.

Par·is Com·mune ▶ n. see COMMUNE[1] (sense 3).

Par·is green ▶ n. a vivid green toxic crystalline salt of copper and arsenic, used as a preservative, pigment, and insecticide.

par·ish /ˈparish/ ▶ n. (in the Christian Church) a small administrative district typically having its own church and a priest or pastor: [as modifier] *a parish church*. ■ (in Louisiana) a territorial division corresponding to a county in other states.
– ORIGIN Middle English: from Anglo-Norman French and Old French *paroche*, from late Latin *parochia*, from Greek *paroikia* 'sojourning,' based on *para-* 'beside, subsidiary' + *oikos* 'dwelling.'

pa·ri·shad /ˈpə-riˌSHəd/ ▶ n. Indian a council or assembly.
– ORIGIN from Sanskrit, from *pari* 'around' + *sad-* 'sit.'

par·ish·ion·er /pəˈrisHənər/ ▶ n. an inhabitant of a parish, esp. one who belongs to or attends a particular church.

par·ish-pump ▶ adj. [attrib.] Brit. of local importance or interest only; parochial: *I looked down on parish-pump politics*.

Pa·ri·sian /pəˈrizHən, -ˈrē-, -ˈrizē-/ ▶ adj. of or relating to Paris.
▶ n. a native or inhabitant of Paris.
– ORIGIN late Middle English: from French *parisien*.

Pa·ri·si·enne /pəˌrēzēˈen/ ▶ n. a Parisian girl or woman.
▶ adj. (esp. of a girl or woman) Parisian.
– ORIGIN mid 17th cent.: French, feminine of *parisien* 'Parisian.'

par·i·son /ˈparəsən/ ▶ n. a rounded mass of molten glass formed by rolling the substance immediately after removal from the furnace.
– ORIGIN early 19th cent.: from French *paraison*, from *parer* 'prepare,' from Latin *parare*.

par·i·ty[1] /ˈparitē/ ▶ n. 1 the state or condition of being equal, esp. regarding status or pay: *parity of incomes between rural workers and those in industrial occupations*. ■ the value of one currency in terms of another at an established exchange rate. ■ a system of providing farmers with consistent purchasing power by regulating prices of farm products, usually with government price supports.
2 Mathematics (of a number) the fact of being even or odd. ■ Physics the property of a spatial wave equation that either remains the same (**even parity**) or changes sign (**odd parity**) under a given transformation. ■ Physics the value of a quantum number corresponding to this property. ■ Computing a function whose being even (or odd) provides a check on a set of binary values.
– ORIGIN late 16th cent.: from late Latin *paritas*, from *par* 'equal.'

par·i·ty[2] ▶ n. Medicine the fact or condition of having borne children. ■ the number of children previously borne: *very high parity (six children or more)*.
– ORIGIN late 19th cent.: from *parous* 'having borne offspring' (back-formation from adjectives ending in -PAROUS) + -ITY.

par·i·ty bit ▶ n. Computing a bit that acts as a check on a set of binary values, calculated in such a way that the number of 1s in the set plus the parity bit should always be even (or occasionally, should always be odd).

Park /pärk/, Mungo (1771–1806), Scottish explorer. He undertook a series of explorations in western Africa (1795–97), among them the navigation of the Niger.

park /pärk/ ▶ n. 1 a large public green area in a town, used for recreation: *a walk around the park*. ■ a large area of land kept in its natural state for public recreational use. ■ (also **wildlife park**) a large enclosed area of land used to accommodate wild animals in captivity. ■ a stadium or enclosed area used for sports. ■ a large enclosed piece of ground, typically with woodland and pasture, attached to a large country house: *the house is set in its own park*. ■ (in the western US) a broad, flat, mostly open area in a mountainous region.
2 [with adj. or noun modifier] an area devoted to a specified purpose: *an industrial park*. ■ chiefly Brit. a parking lot or garage: *a coach park*.
3 (in a car with automatic transmission) the position of the gear selector in which the gears are locked, preventing the vehicle's movement.
▶ v. [with obj.] bring (a vehicle that one is driving) to a halt and leave it temporarily, typically in a parking lot or by the side of the road: *he parked his car outside her house* | [no obj.] *he couldn't find anywhere to park*. ■ informal deposit and leave in a convenient place until required: *come on in, and park your bag by the door*. ■ (**park oneself in/on**) informal sit down on or in: *after dinner, we parked ourselves on a pair of couches*.
– PHRASES **a walk in the park** see WALK.
– ORIGIN Middle English: from Old French *parc*, from medieval Latin *parricus*, of Germanic origin; related to German *Pferch* 'pen, fold,' also to PADDOCK. The word was originally a legal term designating land held by royal grant for keeping game animals: this was enclosed and therefore distinct from a *forest* or *chase*, and (also unlike a *forest*) had no special laws or officers. A military sense 'space occupied by artillery, wagons, stores, etc., in an encampment' (late 17th cent.) is the origin of the verb sense (mid 19th cent.) and of sense 2 of the noun (early 20th cent).

par·ka /ˈpärkə/ ▶ n. a large windproof jacket with a hood, designed to be worn in cold weather. ■ a hooded jacket made of animal skin, worn by the Inuit.
– ORIGIN late 18th cent.: via Aleut from Russian.

par·kade /pärˈkād/ ▶ n. Canadian a multistory parking garage.
– ORIGIN 1950s: from PARK, on the pattern of *arcade*.

park-and-ride ▶ n. [often as modifier] a system for reducing urban traffic congestion, in which drivers leave their cars in parking lots on the outskirts of a city and travel to the city center on public transportation: *a new park-and-ride system in the town to cut traffic jams*.

Park Av·e·nue /ˈpärk/ a commercial and residential street in Manhattan in New York City, regarded as emblematic of worldly success.

Park Chung-hee /CHəNGˈhē/ (1917–79), South Korean statesman; president 1963–79. After staging a coup in 1961, he was elected president and by 1971 had assumed dictatorial powers. Under his presidency, South Korea emerged as a leading industrial nation.

Par·ker[1] /ˈpärkər/, Bonnie (1911–34), US bank robber and murderer. She and her partner, Clyde Barrow, were known for a criminal spree in which they shot and killed at least thirteen people before being stopped and shot to death at a Louisiana roadblock.

Par·ker[2], Charlie (1920–55), US saxophonist; full name *Charles Christopher Parker*; known as **Bird** or **Yardbird**. From 1944, he played with Thelonious Monk and Dizzy Gillespie and became one of the key figures of the bebop movement.

Par·ker[3], Dorothy (Rothschild) (1893–1967), US humorist, literary critic, and writer. From 1927, she wrote book reviews and short stories for *The New Yorker* magazine, becoming one of its legendary wits.

par·ker·iz·ing /ˈpärkərˌīziNG/ ▶ n. a process for rustproofing iron or steel by brief immersion in a hot acidic solution of a metal phosphate.
– DERIVATIVES **par·ker·ized** adj.
– ORIGIN 1920s: from *Parker* Rust-Proof Company of America (which introduced the process) + -IZE + -ING[1].

par·kin /ˈpärkin/ ▶ n. Brit. a kind of dark gingerbread, typically with a soft, dry texture, made with oatmeal and molasses.
– ORIGIN early 19th cent.: perhaps from the family name *Parkin*, diminutive of *Per* 'Peter.'

park·ing ga·rage ▶ n. a building, often of several stories, that provides parking space.

park·ing light ▶ n. [usu. in pl.] a small light on each side of a vehicle in the front and rear.

park·ing lot ▶ n. an area where cars or other vehicles may be left temporarily.

park·ing me·ter ▶ n. a machine next to a parking space in a street, into which the driver puts money so as to be authorized to park the vehicle for a particular length of time.

park·ing tick·et ▶ n. a notice telling a driver of a fine imposed for parking illegally, typically attached to a car windshield.

par·kin·son·ism /ˈpärkinsənˌizəm/ ▶ n. another term for PARKINSON'S DISEASE.

Par·kin·son's dis·ease /ˈpärkinsənz/ ▶ n. a progressive disease of the nervous system marked by tremor, muscular rigidity, and slow, imprecise movement, chiefly affecting middle-aged and elderly people. It is associated with degeneration of the basal ganglia of the brain and a deficiency of the neurotransmitter dopamine.
– ORIGIN late 19th cent.: named after James *Parkinson* (1755–1824), English surgeon.

Par·kin·son's law the notion that work expands to fill the time available for its completion.
– ORIGIN 1950s: named after Cyril Northcote *Parkinson* (1909–93), English writer.

park·land /ˈpärkˌland/ ▶ n. (also **parklands**) open land consisting of fields and scattered groups of trees. ■ land reserved for a public park.

Park·man /ˈpärkmən/, Francis (1823–93), US historian. He traveled the Oregon Trail in 1846 to improve his health and later wrote an account of his journey in *The California and Oregon Trail* (1849). He also wrote *The Discovery of the Great West* (1869) and *A Half-Century of Conflict* (1892).

par·kour /pärˈko͝or/ (also **parcour**) ▶ n. the activity or sport of running through an area, typically in an urban environment, using acrobatic techniques to negotiate obstacles.
– ORIGIN early 21st cent.: French, alteration of *parcours* 'route, course.'

P

Park Range a range of the Rocky Mountains in southern Wyoming and northern Colorado, west of the Front Range.

Parks[1] /pärks/, Gordon (Roger Alexander Buchanan) (1912–2006), US photographer, writer, movie director, and composer. He worked as a photographer for the Farm Security Administration 1941–44 before becoming a photojournalist for *Life* magazine 1949–70. He wrote *The Learning Tree* (1963), *Born Black* (1971), and *Shannon* (1981) and directed the movies *Shaft* (1971) and *The Super Cops* (1973).

Parks[2], Rosa (Louise McCauley) (1913–2005), US civil rights pioneer. On December 1, 1955, she refused to give up her bus seat to a white man in Montgomery, Alabama, an act that inspired the civil rights movement. After the ensuing boycott and NAACP protest, bus segregation was ruled unconstitutional. Congressional Gold Medal (1999).

Rosa Parks

park·way /ˈpärk,wā/ ▶ n. an open landscaped highway.

park·y /ˈpärkē/ ▶ adj. (**parkier, parkiest**) Brit. informal chilly.
– ORIGIN late 19th cent.: of unknown origin.

Parl. Brit. ▶ abbr. ■ Parliament. ■ Parliamentary.

par·lance /ˈpärləns/ ▶ n. a particular way of speaking or using words, esp. a way common to those with a particular job or interest: *dated terms that were once in common parlance* | *medical parlance.*
– ORIGIN late 16th cent. (denoting speech or debate): from Old French, from *parler* 'speak,' from Latin *parabola* 'comparison' (in late Latin 'speech').

par·lan·do /pärˈländō/ Music ▶ adv. & adj. (with reference to singing) expressive or declamatory in the manner of speech.
▶ n. composition or performance in this manner: *the high-lying parlando of Siegfried's narration.*
– ORIGIN Italian, literally 'speaking.'

par·lay /ˈpär,lā, -lē/ ▶ v. [with obj.] (**parlay something into**) turn an initial stake or winnings from a previous bet into (a greater amount) by gambling: *it involved parlaying a small bankroll into big winnings.* ■ informal transform into (something greater or more valuable): *a banker who parlayed a sizable inheritance into a financial empire* | *an excellent performance is quickly parlayed into lucrative contracts.*
▶ n. a cumulative series of bets in which winnings accruing from each transaction are used as a stake for a further bet.
– ORIGIN late 19th cent.: from French *paroli,* from Italian, from *paro* 'like,' from Latin *par* 'equal.'

par·ley /ˈpärlē/ ▶ n. (pl. **parleys**) a conference between opposing sides in a dispute, esp. a discussion of terms for an armistice.
▶ v. (**parleys, parleying, parleyed**) [no obj.] hold a conference with the opposing side to discuss terms: *they disagreed over whether to parley with the enemy.*
– ORIGIN late Middle English (denoting speech or debate): perhaps from Old French *parlee* 'spoken,' feminine past participle of the verb *parler.*

par·lia·ment /ˈpärləmənt/ ▶ n. (**Parliament**) (in the UK) the highest legislature, consisting of the sovereign, the House of Lords, and the House of Commons: *the Secretary of State will lay proposals before Parliament.* ■ the members of this legislature for a particular period, esp. between one dissolution and the next: *the act was passed by the last parliament of the reign.* ■ a similar legislature in other nations and states: *the Russian parliament.*
– ORIGIN Middle English: from Old French *parlement* 'speaking,' from the verb *parler.*

par·lia·men·tar·i·an /,pärləmenˈte(ə)rēən/ ▶ n. **1** a member of a parliament, esp. one well versed in parliamentary procedure and experienced in debate. **2** historical a supporter of Parliament in the English Civil War; a Roundhead.
▶ adj. **1** of or relating to Parliament or its members: *parliamentarian committees.* **2** historical of or relating to the Roundheads.
– DERIVATIVES **par·lia·men·tar·i·an·ism** /-,nizəm/ n.

par·lia·men·ta·ry /,pärləˈmentərē/ ▶ adj. relating to, enacted by, or suitable for a parliament: *parliamentary legislation.*

par·lia·men·ta·ry law ▶ n. the rules that govern the conduct of legislatures and other deliberative bodies.

par·lia·men·ta·ry pro·ce·dure ▶ n. **1** a rule that defines how a particular situation is to be handled, or a particular outcome achieved, in a legislature or deliberative body. **2** parliamentary law.

par·lor /ˈpärlər/ (Brit. **parlour**) ▶ n. **1** dated a sitting room in a private house. ■ a room in a public building for receiving guests: *the mayor's parlor.* ■ a room in a monastery or convent that is set aside for conversation. **2** [usu. with modifier] a shop or business providing specified goods or services: *an ice-cream parlor* | *a funeral parlor.* **3** (also **milking parlor**) a room or building equipped for milking cows.
▶ adj. [attrib.] dated, derogatory denoting a person who professes but does not actively give support to a specified (esp. radical) political view: *parlor libertarians.*
– ORIGIN Middle English: from Anglo-Norman French *parlur* 'place for speaking,' from Latin *parlare* 'speak.'

par·lor car ▶ n. a luxuriously fitted railroad car, typically with individually reserved seats.

par·lor game ▶ n. an indoor game, esp. a word game.

par·lor grand ▶ n. a grand piano intermediate in size between a concert grand and a baby grand.

par·lor·maid /ˈpärlər,mād/ ▶ n. historical a maid employed to serve at table.

par·lour ▶ n. British spelling of **PARLOR**.

par·lous /ˈpärləs/ ▶ adj. archaic or humorous full of danger or uncertainty; precarious: *the parlous state of the economy.*
▶ adv. archaic greatly or excessively: *she is parlous handsome.*
– DERIVATIVES **par·lous·ly** adv., **par·lous·ness** n.
– ORIGIN late Middle English: contraction of **PERILOUS**.

Par·ma /ˈpärmə/ **1** a city in northern Italy, southeast of Milan; pop. 182,389 (2008). Founded by the Romans in 183 BC, it became a bishopric in the 9th century AD and capital of the duchy of Parma and Piacenza in about 1547. **2** a city in northeastern Ohio, south of Cleveland; pop. 77,947 (est. 2008).

Par·ma ham ▶ n. a type of ham that is eaten uncooked.

Par·ma vi·o·let ▶ n. a sweet violet of a variety with a heavy scent and lavender-colored flowers that are often crystallized and used for food decoration.

par·ma wal·la·by ▶ n. a small dark brown Australian wallaby, restricted to the rain forests of New South Wales. ● *Macropus parma,* family Macropodidae.
– ORIGIN mid 19th cent.: *parma* (probably from a New South Wales Aboriginal language) was applied by George Robert Waterhouse (1810–88), English naturalist.

Par·men·i·des /pärˈmeni,dēz/ (*fl.* 5th century BC), Greek philosopher. He founded the Eleatic school of philosophers. In his work *On Nature,* he maintained that the apparent motion and changing forms of the universe are in fact manifestations of an unchanging and indivisible reality.

Par·men·tier /,pärmenˈtyā/ ▶ adj. [postpositive] cooked or served with potatoes: *soups such as potage Parmentier.*
– ORIGIN from the name of Antoine A. *Parmentier* (1737–1813), the French agriculturalist who popularized the potato in France.

Par·me·san /ˈpärmə,zän/ ▶ n. a hard, dry cheese used in grated form, esp. on Italian dishes.
– ORIGIN early 16th cent.: from French, from Italian *parmigiano* 'of Parma,' where it was originally made.

Par·mi·gia·na /,pärməˈZHänə/ ▶ adj. [postpositive] cooked or served with Parmesan cheese: *eggplant and veal Parmigiana.*
▶ n. a dish cooked in this way.
– ORIGIN Italian, feminine of *Parmigiano* 'of Parma.'

Par·nas·si·an /pärˈnasēən/ ▶ adj. **1** relating to poetry; poetic. **2** of or relating to a group of French poets of the late 19th century who emphasized strictness of form, named from the anthology *Le Parnasse contemporain* (1866).
▶ n. a member of this group of French poets.

Par·nas·sus, grass of /pärˈnasəs/ ▶ n. see **GRASS OF PARNASSUS**.

Par·nas·sus, Mount a mountain in central Greece, just north of Delphi, that rises to a height of 8,064 feet (2,457 m). Held to be sacred by the ancient Greeks, it was associated with Apollo and the Muses and was regarded as a symbol of poetry. Greek name **Parnassós**.

Par·nell /pärˈnel, ˈpärnl/, Charles Stewart (1846–91), Irish nationalist leader. He became leader of the Irish Home Rule faction in 1880 and raised the profile of Irish affairs through obstructive parliamentary tactics.
– DERIVATIVES **Par·nell·ite** /-ˈnelīt/ adj. & n.

pa·ro·chi·al /pəˈrōkēəl/ ▶ adj. of or relating to a church parish: *the parochial church council.* ■ having a limited or narrow outlook or scope: *this worldview seems incredibly naive and parochial.*
– DERIVATIVES **pa·ro·chi·al·i·ty** /-,rōkēˈalitē/ n., **pa·ro·chi·al·ly** adv.
– ORIGIN late Middle English: from Old French, from ecclesiastical Latin *parochialis* 'relating to an ecclesiastical district,' from *parochia* (see **PARISH**).

pa·ro·chi·al·ism /pəˈrōkēəl,izəm/ ▶ n. a limited or narrow outlook, esp. focused on a local area; narrow-mindedness: *accusations of parochialism.*

pa·ro·chi·al school ▶ n. a private school supported by a particular church or parish.

par·o·dy /ˈparədē/ ▶ n. (pl. **parodies**) an imitation of the style of a particular writer, artist, or genre with deliberate exaggeration for comic effect: *the movie is a parody of the horror genre* | *his provocative use of parody.* ■ an imitation or a version of something that falls far short of the real thing; a travesty: *he seems like a parody of an educated Englishman.*
▶ v. (**parodies, parodying, parodied**) [with obj.] produce a humorously exaggerated imitation of (a writer, artist, or genre): *his specialty was parodying schoolgirl fiction.* ■ mimic humorously: *he parodied his friend's voice.*
– DERIVATIVES **pa·rod·ic** /pəˈrädik/ adj., **par·o·dist** /-dist/ n.
– ORIGIN late 16th cent.: via late Latin from Greek *parōidia* 'burlesque poem,' from *para-* 'beside' (expressing alteration) + *ōidē* 'ode.'

par of ex·change ▶ n. see **PAR**[1] (sense 2 of the noun).

pa·rol /pəˈrōl, ˈparəl/ ▶ adj. Law given or expressed orally: *the parol evidence.* ■ (of a document) agreed orally, or in writing but not under seal: *there was a parol agreement.*
– PHRASES **by parol** by oral declaration.
– ORIGIN late 15th cent. (as a noun): from Old French *parole* 'word' (see **PAROLE**).

pa·role /pəˈrōl/ ▶ n. **1** the release of a prisoner temporarily (for a special purpose) or permanently before the completion of a sentence, on the promise of good behavior: *he committed a burglary while on parole.* ■ historical a promise or undertaking given by a prisoner of war not to escape or, if released, not to engage in hostilities, or to return to custody under stated conditions. **2** Linguistics the actual linguistic behavior or performance of individuals, in contrast to the linguistic system of a community. Contrasted with **LANGUE**.
▶ v. [with obj.] (usu. **be paroled**) release (a prisoner) on parole: *he was paroled after serving nine months of a two-year sentence.*
– DERIVATIVES **pa·rol·ee** /-,rōˈlē/ n.
– ORIGIN late 15th cent.: from Old French, literally 'word,' also 'formal promise,' from ecclesiastical Latin *parabola* 'speech'; compare with **PAROL**.

par·o·no·ma·sia /,parənōˈmāZH(ē)ə/ ▶ n. a play on words; a pun.
– ORIGIN late 16th cent.: via Latin from Greek *paronomasia,* from *para-* 'beside' (expressing alteration) + *onomasia* 'naming' (from *onomazein* 'to name,' from *onoma* 'a name').

par·o·nym /ˈparənim/ ▶ n. Linguistics a word that is a derivative of another and has a related meaning: *"wisdom" is a paronym of "wise."* ■ a word formed by adaptation of a foreign word: *"preface" is a paronym of Latin "prefatio."* Contrasted with **HETERONYM**.
– DERIVATIVES **par·o·nym·ic** /,parəˈnimik/ adj., **pa·ron·y·mous** /pəˈränəməs/ adj., **pa·ron·y·my** /pəˈränəmē/ n.
– ORIGIN mid 19th cent.: from Greek *parōnumon,* neuter (used as a noun) of *parōnumos* 'naming by modification,' from *para-* 'beside' + *onuma* 'name.'

PRONUNCIATION KEY ə ago, up; ər over, fur; a hat; ā ate; ä car; e let; ē see; i fit; ī by; NG sing; ō go; ô law, for; oi toy; o͝o good; o͞o goo; ou out; TH thin; T͟H then; ZH vision

Pa·ros /ˈparäs, ˈpe(ə)r-, ˈpärôs/ a Greek island in the southern Aegean Sea, in the Cyclades. It is noted for the translucent white Parian marble, quarried here since the 6th century BC.

pa·rot·id /pəˈrätid/ Anatomy ▶ **adj.** relating to, situated near, or affecting a parotid gland.
▶ **n.** short for PAROTID GLAND.
– ORIGIN late 17th cent.: via Latin from Greek *parōtis, parōtid-*, from *para-* 'beside' + *ous, ōt-* 'ear.'

pa·rot·id gland ▶ **n.** Anatomy either of a pair of large salivary glands situated just in front of each ear.

par·o·ti·tis /ˌparəˈtītis/ ▶ **n.** Medicine inflammation of a parotid gland, esp. (**infectious parotitis**) mumps.

-parous ▶ **comb. form** Biology bearing offspring of a specified number or reproducing in a specified manner: *multiparous | viviparous.*
– ORIGIN from Latin *-parus* '-bearing' (from *parere* 'bring forth, produce') + **-ous**.

Par·ou·si·a /pəˈro͞ozēə, ˌpäro͞oˈsēə/ ▶ **n.** Christian Theology another term for SECOND COMING.
– ORIGIN Greek, literally 'being present.'

par·ox·ysm /ˈparəkˌsizəm/ ▶ **n.** a sudden attack or violent expression of a particular emotion or activity: ***a paroxysm of weeping.*** ■ Medicine a sudden recurrence or attack of a disease; a sudden worsening of symptoms.
– DERIVATIVES **par·ox·ys·mal** /ˌparəkˈsizməl/ **adj.**
– ORIGIN late Middle English: from French *paroxysme*, via medieval Latin from Greek *paroxusmos*, from *paroxunein* 'exasperate,' from *para-* 'beyond' + *oxunein* 'sharpen' (from *oxus* 'sharp').

par·ox·y·tone /pəˈräksiˌtōn/ ▶ **adj.** (esp. in ancient Greek) having an acute accent on the penultimate syllable.
▶ **n.** a word with such an accent.
– ORIGIN mid 18th cent.: from modern Latin *paroxytonus*, from Greek *paroxutonos*, from *para-* 'alongside' + *oxutonos* 'sharp pitch.'

par·pen /ˈpärpən/ ▶ **n.** a stone passing through a wall from side to side, with two smooth vertical faces.
– ORIGIN Middle English: from Old French *parpain* 'length of a stone,' probably based on Latin *perpes* 'continuous.'

par·quet /pärˈkā/ ▶ **n. 1** (also **parquet flooring**) flooring composed of wooden blocks arranged in a geometric pattern.
2 the ground floor of a theater or auditorium.
3 (**the Parquet**) (in France and French-speaking countries) the branch of the administration of the law that deals with the prosecution of crime.
– ORIGIN late 17th cent. (as a verb, esp. as *parqueted*): from French, literally 'small park (i.e., delineated area).' The noun dates from the early 19th cent.

par·quet·ry /ˈpärkitrē/ ▶ **n.** inlaid work of blocks of various woods arranged in a geometric pattern, esp. for flooring or furniture.

Parr /pär/, Katherine (1512–48), English queen; sixth and last wife of Henry VIII. Having married the king in 1543, she influenced his decision to restore the succession to his daughters Mary and Elizabeth (later Mary I and Elizabeth I respectively).

parr /pär/ ▶ **n.** (pl. **same**) a young salmon or trout between the stages of fry and smolt, distinguished by dark rounded patches evenly spaced along its sides.
– ORIGIN early 18th cent.: of unknown origin.

par·ra·keet ▶ **n.** variant spelling of PARAKEET.

par·ra·mat·ta ▶ **n.** variant spelling of PARAMATTA.

par·ri·cide /ˈparəˌsīd/ ▶ **n.** the killing of a parent or other near relative. ■ a person who commits parricide.
– DERIVATIVES **par·ri·cid·al** /ˌparəˈsīdl/ **adj.**
– ORIGIN late 16th cent.: from French, from Latin *parricidium* 'murder of a parent,' with first element of unknown origin, but long associated with Latin *pater* 'father' and *parens* 'parent.'

par·rot /ˈparət/ ▶ **n.** a bird, often vividly colored, with a short down-curved hooked bill, grasping feet, and a raucous voice, found esp. in the tropics and feeding on fruits and seeds. Many are popular as cage birds, and some are able to mimic the human voice. ● Order Psittaciformes: numerous species, sometimes all placed in the family Psittacidae. The order also contains the cockatoos, lories, lovebirds, macaws, conures, and budgerigars.

parrot

▶ **v.** (**parrots, parroting, parroted**) [with obj.] repeat mechanically: *encouraging students to parrot back information.*
– ORIGIN early 16th cent.: probably from dialect French *perrot*, diminutive of the male given name *Pierre* 'Peter.' Compare with PARAKEET.

par·rot·bill /ˈparətˌbil/ ▶ **n.** a titlike Asian songbird with brown and gray plumage and a short arched bill. ● Family Panuridae (or Paradoxornithidae): two genera and several species.

par·rot fe·ver ▶ **n.** less formal term for PSITTACOSIS.

par·rot·fish /ˈparətˌfish/ ▶ **n.** (pl. **same** or **parrotfishes**) **1** any of a number of brightly colored marine fish with a parrotlike beak, which they use to scrape food from coral and other hard surfaces. ● a widespread fish of warm seas that may secrete a mucous cocoon to deter predators (family Scaridae: *Scarus* and other genera). ● an edible fish of the southern Indian ocean (*Oplegnathus conwayi*, family Oplegnathidae).
2 Austral. a brightly colored marine fish, esp. one of the wrasse family. ● Several species in the family Labridae.

par·rot·let /ˈparətlit/ ▶ **n.** a tiny tropical American parrot with mainly green plumage and a short tail. ● Family Psittacidae: three genera, in particular *Forpus* and *Touit*, and several species.

par·rot tu·lip ▶ **n.** a cultivated tulip of a variety that has irregularly fringed or wavy petals, typically of two colors.

par·ry /ˈparē/ ▶ **v.** (**parries, parrying, parried**) [with obj.] ward off (a weapon or attack), esp. with a countermove: *he parried the blow by holding his sword vertically.* ■ answer (a question or accusation) evasively: *he parried questions from reporters outside the building.*
▶ **n.** (pl. **parries**) an act of parrying: *her question met with a polite parry.*
– ORIGIN late 17th cent.: probably representing French *parez!* 'ward off!,' imperative of *parer*, from Italian *parare* 'ward off.'

parse /pärs/ ▶ **v.** [with obj.] analyze (a sentence) into its parts and describe their syntactic roles. ■ Computing analyze (a string or text) into logical syntactic components, typically in order to test conformability to a logical grammar. ■ examine or analyze minutely: *he has always been quick to parse his own problems in public.*
▶ **n.** Computing an act of or the result obtained by parsing a string or a text.
– ORIGIN mid 16th cent.: perhaps from Middle English *pars* 'parts of speech,' from Old French *pars* 'parts' (influenced by Latin *pars* 'part').

par·sec /ˈpärˌsek/ (abbr.: **pc**) ▶ **n.** a unit of distance used in astronomy, equal to about 3.25 light years (3.08×10^{16} meters). One parsec corresponds to the distance at which the mean radius of the earth's orbit subtends an angle of one second of arc.
– ORIGIN early 20th cent.: blend of PARALLAX and SECOND[2].

Par·see /ˈpärˈsē, ˈpärsē/ (also **Parsi**) ▶ **n.** an adherent of Zoroastrianism, esp. a descendant of those Zoroastrians who fled to India from Muslim persecution in Persia during the 7th–8th centuries.
– ORIGIN from Persian *pārsī* 'Persian,' from *pārs* 'Persia.'

pars·er /ˈpärsər/ ▶ **n.** Computing a program for parsing.

Par·si·fal /ˈpärsəfəl, -ˌfäl/ another name for PERCEVAL[1].

par·si·mo·ni·ous /ˌpärsəˈmōnēəs/ ▶ **adj.** unwilling to spend money or use resources; stingy or frugal: *parsimonious New Hampshire voters, who have a phobia about taxes.*
– DERIVATIVES **par·si·mo·ni·ous·ly adv.**, **par·si·mo·ni·ous·ness n.**

par·si·mo·ny /ˈpärsəˌmōnē/ ▶ **n.** extreme unwillingness to spend money or use resources: *a great tradition of public design has been shattered by government parsimony.*
– PHRASES **principle** (or **law**) **of parsimony** the scientific principle that things are usually connected or behave in the simplest or most economical way, esp. with reference to alternative evolutionary pathways. Compare with OCCAM'S RAZOR.
– ORIGIN late Middle English: from Latin *parsimonia, parcimonia*, from *parcere* 'be sparing.'

Par·sip·pa·ny–Troy Hills /pärˈsipənē troi/ a commercial and residential township in northern New Jersey; pop. 50,431 (est. 2008).

pars·ley /ˈpärslē/ ▶ **n.** a biennial plant with white flowers and aromatic leaves that are either crinkly or flat and used as a culinary herb and for garnishing food. ● *Petroselinum crispum*, family Umbelliferae (or Apiaceae; the **parsley family**). Members of this family have their flowers arranged in umbels and are known as umbellifers; typical members include hogweed and hemlock as well as many food plants and herbs (carrot, parsnip, celery, fennel, anise).
– ORIGIN Old English *petersilie*, via late Latin based on Greek *petroselinon*, from *petra* 'rock' + *selinon* 'parsley,' influenced in Middle English by Old French *peresil*, of the same origin.

pars·nip /ˈpärsnip/ ▶ **n. 1** a long tapering cream-colored root with a sweet flavor.
2 the widely cultivated Eurasian plant of the parsley family that yields this root. ● *Pastinaca sativa*, family Umbelliferae.
– ORIGIN late Middle English: from Old French *pasnaie*, from Latin *pastinaca* (related to *pastinare* 'dig and trench the ground'). The change in the ending was due to association with NEEP.

par·son /ˈpärsən/ ▶ **n.** a beneficed member of the clergy; a rector or a vicar. ■ informal any member of the clergy, esp. a Protestant one.
– DERIVATIVES **par·son·ic** /pärˈsänik/ **adj.**, **par·son·i·cal** /pärˈsänikəl/ **adj.**
– ORIGIN Middle English: from Old French *persone*, from Latin *persona* 'person' (in medieval Latin 'rector').

par·son·age /ˈpärsənij/ ▶ **n.** a church house provided for a member of the clergy.

pars pro to·to /pärz prō ˈtōtō/ ▶ **n.** formal a part or aspect of something taken as representative of the whole.
– ORIGIN Latin, literally 'part for the whole.'

part /pärt/ ▶ **n. 1** a piece or segment of something such as an object, activity, or period of time, which combined with other pieces makes up the whole: *divide the circle into three equal parts | the early part of 1989.* ■ an element or constituent that belongs to something and is essential to its nature: *I was part of the family.* ■ a component of a machine: *the production of aircraft parts.* ■ a measure allowing comparison between the amounts of different ingredients used in a mixture: *repot plants in a mixture of three parts soil, one part sand.* ■ a specified fraction of a whole: *they paid a twentieth part of the cost.* ■ a division of a book treated as a unit in which a particular topic is discussed. ■ (**parts**) informal short for PRIVATE PARTS.
2 some but not all of something: *the painting tells only part of the story.* ■ a point on or area of something: *hold the farthest part of your leg that you can reach.* ■ (**parts**) informal a region, esp. one not clearly specified or delimited: *they wanted to know why he was loitering in these parts.*
3 a character as represented in a play or movie; a role played by an actor or actress: *she played a lot of leading parts | he took the part of Prospero.* ■ the words and directions to be learned and performed by an actor in such a role: *she was memorizing a part.* ■ Music a melody or other constituent of harmony assigned to a particular voice or instrument in a musical work: *he coped well with the percussion part.* ■ the contribution made by someone or something to an action or situation: *he played a key part in ending the revolt | he may be jailed for his part in the robbery.* ■ the behavior appropriate to or expected of a person in a particular role or situation; a person's duty: *in such a place his part is to make good.*
4 (**parts**) archaic abilities.
5 a line of scalp revealed in a person's hair by combing the hair away in opposite directions on either side.
▶ **v.** [no obj.] (of two things) move away from each other: *his lips parted in a smile.* ■ divide to leave a central space: [no obj.] *at that moment the mist parted* | [with obj.] *she parted the ferns and looked between them.* ■ leave someone's company: *there was a good deal of kissing and more congratulations before we parted.* ■ (**be parted**) leave the company of someone: *she can't bear to be parted from her daughter again.* ■ (**part with**) give up possession of; hand over: *even quite small companies parted with large sums.* ■ [with obj.] separate (the hair of the head on either side of the part) with a comb.
▶ **adv.** to some extent; partly (often used to contrast different parts of something): *the city is now part slum, part consumer paradise.*
– PHRASES **act the part** behave in a way appropriate to the particular role or situation that one is in. **be part and parcel of** be an essential feature or element of: *it's best to accept that some inconveniences are part and parcel of travel.* **for my** (or **his**, **her**, etc.) **part** used to focus attention on one person or group and distinguish them from others involved in a situation: *for my part I was glad when the end of September came.* **in part** to some extent though not entirely: *the cause of the illness is at least in part psychological.* **look the part** have an appearance or style of dress appropriate to a particular role or situation. **a man of** (**many**) **parts** a man showing great ability in many different areas. **on the part of** (or **on my**, **their**, etc., **part**) used to ascribe responsibility for something to someone: *there was a series of errors on my part.* **part company** (of two or more people) cease to be together; go in different directions: *they parted*

company outside the Red Lion. ■ (of two or more parties) cease to associate with each other, esp. as the result of a disagreement: *the chairman has **parted company** with the club.* **take part** join in an activity; be involved: *we have come here to **take part** in a major game | they ran away and took no part in the battle.* **take the part of** give support and encouragement to (someone) in a dispute.
– ORIGIN Old English (denoting a part of speech), from Latin *pars, part-*. The verb (originally in Middle English in the sense 'divide into parts') is from Old French *partir*, from Latin *partire, partiri* 'divide, share.'

par·take /pär'tāk/ ▶ **v.** (past **partook** /-'to͝ok/; past participle **partaken** /-'tākən/) [no obj.] (**partake in**) formal join in (an activity): *visitors can partake in golfing or clay pigeon shooting.* ■ (**partake of**) be characterized by (a quality): *the birth of twins became an event that partook of the mythic.* ■ (**partake of**) eat or drink (something): *she had partaken of a cheese sandwich and a cup of coffee.*
– DERIVATIVES **par·tak·er** n.
– ORIGIN mid 16th cent.: back-formation from earlier *partaker* 'person who takes a part.'

part·er /'pärtər/ ▶ **n.** [in combination] a broadcast or published work with a specified number of parts: *the first in a six-parter.*

par·terre /pär'te(ə)r/ ▶ **n. 1** a level space in a garden or yard occupied by an ornamental arrangement of flower beds.
2 the part of the ground floor of an auditorium in the rear and on the sides, esp. the part beneath the balcony.
– ORIGIN early 17th cent.: from French, from *par terre* 'on the ground.'

par·the·no·car·py /'pärTHənō,kärpē/ ▶ **n.** Botany the development of a fruit without prior fertilization.
– DERIVATIVES **par·the·no·car·pic** /,pärTHənō'kärpik/ **adj.**
– ORIGIN early 20th cent.: from German *Parthenocarpie*, from Greek *parthenos* 'virgin' + *karpos* 'fruit.'

par·the·no·gen·e·sis /,pärTHənō'jenəsis/ ▶ **n.** Biology reproduction from an ovum without fertilization, esp. as a normal process in some invertebrates and lower plants.
– DERIVATIVES **par·the·no·ge·net·ic** /-jə'netik/ **adj.**, **par·the·no·ge·net·i·cal·ly** /-jə'netik(ə)lē/ **adv.**
– ORIGIN mid 19th cent.: modern Latin, from Greek *parthenos* 'virgin' + *genesis* 'creation.'

Par·the·non /'pärTHə,nän/ the temple of Athena Parthenos, built on the Acropolis in 447–432 BC by Pericles to honor Athens' patron goddess and to commemorate the recent Greek victory over the Persians. It was designed by Ictinus and Callicrates with sculptures by Phidias.
– ORIGIN from Greek *parthenos* 'virgin.'

Parthenon

par·the·note /'pärTHənōt/ ▶ **n.** Biology an organism produced from an unfertilized ovum, which is incapable of developing beyond the early embryonic stages.
– ORIGIN 1930s: from PARTHENOGENESIS and ZYGOTE.

Par·thi·a /'pärTHēə/ an ancient kingdom that lay southeast of the Caspian Sea in present-day Iran. From *c.*250 BC to *c.* AD 230 the Parthians ruled an empire stretching from the Euphrates to the Indus.
– DERIVATIVES **Par·thi·an** /-THēən/ **n. & adj.**

Par·thi·an shot ▶ **n.** another term for PARTING SHOT.
– ORIGIN late 19th cent.: so named because of the trick used by Parthians of shooting arrows backward while in real or pretended flight.

par·tial /'pärSHəl/ ▶ **adj. 1** existing only in part; incomplete: *a question to which we have only partial answers.*
2 favoring one side in a dispute above the other; biased: *the paper gave a distorted and very partial view of the situation.* ■ [predic.] (**partial to**) having a liking for: *you know I'm partial to bacon and eggs.*
▶ **n.** Music a component of a musical sound; an overtone or harmonic: *the upper partials of the string.*
– DERIVATIVES **par·tial·ness** n.
– ORIGIN late Middle English (in the sense 'inclined to favor one party in a cause'): from Old French *parcial* (sense 2 of the adjective), French *partiel* (sense 1 of the adjective), from late Latin *partialis*, from *pars, part-* 'part.'

par·tial-birth a·bor·tion ▶ **n.** a late-term abortion of a fetus that has already died, or is killed before being completely removed from the mother.

par·tial de·riv·a·tive ▶ **n.** Mathematics a derivative of a function of two or more variables with respect to one variable, the other(s) being treated as constant.

par·tial dif·fer·en·tial e·qua·tion ▶ **n.** Mathematics an equation containing one or more partial derivatives.

par·tial e·clipse ▶ **n.** an eclipse of a celestial body in which only part of the luminary is obscured or darkened.

par·tial frac·tion ▶ **n.** Mathematics each of two or more fractions into which a more complex fraction can be decomposed as a sum.

par·ti·al·i·ty /,pärSHē'alitē/ ▶ **n.** unfair bias in favor of one thing or person compared with another; favoritism: *an attack on the partiality of judges.* ■ a particular liking or fondness for something: *she spoke openly, not concealing her **partiality for** him.*
– ORIGIN late Middle English: from Old French *parcialite*, from medieval Latin *partialitas*, based on Latin *pars, part-* 'part.'

par·tial·ly /'pärSHəlē/ ▶ **adv.** only in part; to a limited extent: *the work partially fulfills the function of a historical memoir* | [as submodifier] *a partially open door.*

par·tial or·der (also **partial ordering**) ▶ **n.** Mathematics a transitive antisymmetric relation among the elements of a set, which does not necessarily apply to each pair of elements.

par·tial pres·sure ▶ **n.** Chemistry the pressure that would be exerted by one of the gases in a mixture if it occupied the same volume on its own.

par·tial prod·uct ▶ **n.** Mathematics the product of one term of a multiplicand and one term of its multiplier. ■ the product of the first *n* terms of a large or infinite series, where *n* is a finite integer (including 1).

par·ti·ble /'pärtəbəl/ ▶ **adj.** involving or denoting a system of inheritance in which a deceased person's estate is divided equally among the heirs.
– DERIVATIVES **par·ti·bil·i·ty** /,pärtə'bilətē/ **n.**
– ORIGIN late Middle English (in the sense 'able to be parted'): from late Latin *partibilis*, from Latin *partiri* 'divide into parts.'

par·tic·i·pant /pär'tisəpənt/ ▶ **n.** a person who takes part in something: *eager students would become firsthand **participants in** an archaeological exploration.*
– ORIGIN late Middle English: from Latin *participant-*, literally 'sharing in,' from the verb *participare* (see PARTICIPATE).

par·tic·i·pate /pär'tisə,pāt/ ▶ **v.** [no obj.] **1** take part: *thousands **participated in** a nationwide strike.*
2 (**participate of**) archaic have or possess (a particular quality): *both members participate of harmony.*
– DERIVATIVES **par·tic·i·pa·tive** /-,pātiv, -pətiv/ **adj.**, **par·tic·i·pa·tor** /-,pātər/ **n.**, **par·tic·i·pa·to·ry** /-pə,tôrē/ **adj.**
– ORIGIN early 16th cent.: from Latin *participat-* 'shared in,' from the verb *participare*, based on *pars, part-* 'part' + *capere* 'take.'

par·tic·i·pa·tion /pär,tisə'pāSHən/ ▶ **n.** the action of taking part in something: ***participation in** church activities | the scheme is based on employer participation.*

par·ti·cip·i·al ad·jec·tive /,pärtə'sipēəl/ ▶ **n.** Grammar an adjective that is a participle in origin and form, such as *burned, cutting, engaged.*

par·ti·ci·ple /'pärtə,sipəl/ ▶ **n.** Grammar a word formed from a verb (e.g., *going, gone, being, been*) and used as an adjective (e.g., *working woman, burned toast*) or a noun (e.g., *good breeding*). In English, participles are also used to make compound verb forms (e.g., *is going, has been*). Compare with GERUND.
– DERIVATIVES **par·ti·cip·i·al** /,pärtə'sipēəl/ **adj.**, **par·ti·cip·i·al·ly** /,pärtə'sipēəlē/ **adv.**
– ORIGIN late Middle English: from Old French, by-form of *participe*, from Latin *participium* '(verbal form) sharing (the functions of a noun),' from *participare* 'share in.'

par·ti·cle /'pärtikəl/ ▶ **n. 1** a minute portion of matter: *tiny **particles of** dust.* ■ [with negative] the least possible amount: *he agrees without hearing the least particle of evidence.* ■ Physics another term for ELEMENTARY PARTICLE. ■ Physics another term for SUBATOMIC PARTICLE. ■ Mathematics a hypothetical object having mass but no physical size.
2 Grammar a minor function word that has comparatively little meaning and does not inflect, in particular: ■ (in English) any of the class of words such as *in, up, off, over*, used with verbs to make phrasal verbs. ■ (in ancient Greek) any of the class of words such as *de* and *ge*, used for contrast and emphasis.
– ORIGIN late Middle English: from Latin *particula* 'little part,' diminutive of *pars, part-*.

par·ti·cle ac·cel·er·a·tor ▶ **n.** an apparatus for accelerating subatomic particles to high velocities by means of electric or electromagnetic fields. The accelerated particles are generally made to collide with other particles, either as a research technique or for the generation of high-energy X-rays and gamma rays.

par·ti·cle beam ▶ **n. 1** a concentrated stream of subatomic particles, generated in order to cause collisions between particles that will shed new light on their nature and structure.
2 such a stream used in an antimissile defense weapon.

par·ti·cle·board /'pärtikəl,bôrd/ ▶ **n.** material made in rigid sheets or panels from compressed wood chips and resin, often coated or veneered, and used in furniture, buildings, etc., where a stronger material is not required.

par·ti·cle phys·ics ▶ **plural n.** [treated as sing.] the branch of physics that deals with the properties, relationships, and interactions of subatomic particles.

par·ti-col·ored /'pärtē ,kələrd/ (also **particolored**) ▶ **adj.** having or consisting of two or more different colors: *their wonderful parti-colored light effects.*
– ORIGIN early 16th cent.: from the adjective PARTY[2] + COLORED.

par·tic·u·lar /pə(r)'tikyələr/ ▶ **adj. 1** [attrib.] used to single out an individual member of a specified group or class: *the action seems to discriminate against a particular group of companies.* ■ Logic denoting a proposition in which something is asserted of some but not all of a class. Contrasted with UNIVERSAL.
2 [attrib.] especially great or intense: *when handling or checking cash the cashier should exercise particular care.*
3 insisting that something should be correct or suitable in every detail; fastidious: *she is very **particular about** cleanliness.*
▶ **n. 1** Philosophy an individual item, as contrasted with a universal quality.
2 a detail: *he is wrong **in every particular**.*
■ (**particulars**) detailed information about someone or something: *a clerk took the woman's particulars.*
– PHRASES **in particular** especially (used to show that a statement applies to one person or thing more than any other): *he socialized with the other young people, one boy in particular.*
– ORIGIN late Middle English: from Old French *particuler*, from Latin *particularis* 'concerning a small part,' from *particula* 'small part.'

Par·tic·u·lar Bap·tist ▶ **n.** a member of a Baptist denomination holding the doctrine of the election and redemption of some but not all people.

par·tic·u·lar in·te·gral ▶ **n.** Mathematics another term for PARTICULAR SOLUTION.

par·tic·u·lar·ism /pə(r)'tikyələ,rizəm/ ▶ **n.** exclusive attachment to one's own group, party, or nation.
■ the principle of leaving each state in an empire or federation free to govern itself and promote its own interests, without reference to those of the whole.
■ Theology the doctrine that some but not all people are elected and redeemed.
– DERIVATIVES **par·tic·u·lar·ist** n. & adj., **par·tic·u·lar·is·tic** /-,tikyələ'ristik/ **adj.**
– ORIGIN early 19th cent.: from French *particularisme*, modern Latin *particularismus*, and German *Partikularismus*, based on Latin *particularis* 'concerning a small part.'

par·tic·u·lar·i·ty /pə(r),tikyə'laritē/ ▶ **n.** (pl. **particularities**) the quality of being individual: *the central figures of his novels are stripped of their particularity.* ■ fullness or minuteness of detail in the treatment of something: *parties must present their case with some degree of accuracy and particularity.* ■ (**particularities**) small details: *the tedious particularities of daily life | he wanted to disregard the particularities and establish general laws.* ■ Christian Theology God's incarnation as Jesus as a particular person at a particular time and place.
– ORIGIN early 16th cent. (as *particularities* 'details'): from Old French *particularite* or late Latin *particularitas*, from Latin *particularis* 'concerning a small part.'

par·tic·u·lar·ize /pə(r)'tikyələ,rīz/ ▶ **v.** [with obj.] formal mention or describe particularly; treat individually

or in detail: *he was unable to particularize what amounts he had paid and when.*
– DERIVATIVES **par·tic·u·lar·i·za·tion** /-ˌtikyələri'zāsʜən, pə(r)ˌtikyələˌrī'zāsʜən/ **n.**

par·tic·u·lar·ly /pə(r)'tikyələrlē/ ▶ **adv. 1** to a higher degree than is usual or average: *I don't particularly want to be reminded of that time* | [as submodifier] *particularly able students.* ■ used to single out a subject to which a statement is especially applicable: *the team's defense is excellent, particularly their two center backs.*
2 so as to give special emphasis to a point; specifically: *he particularly asked that I should help you.*

par·tic·u·lar so·lu·tion ▶ **n.** Mathematics the most general form of the solution of a differential equation, containing arbitrary constants.

par·tic·u·late /pär'tikyəlit, -ˌlāt/ ▶ **adj.** of, relating to, or in the form of minute separate particles: *particulate pollution.*
▶ **n.** (**particulates**) matter in such a form.
– ORIGIN late 19th cent.: from Latin *particula* 'particle' + -ATE².

part·ing /'pärtiɴɢ/ ▶ **n. 1** the action of leaving or being separated from someone: *they exchanged a few words on parting* | *her parting from Stephen.*
2 the action of dividing something into parts: *the parting of the Red Sea.* ■ Brit. a part in the hair.
– PHRASES a (or **the**) **parting of the ways** a point at which two people must separate or at which a decision must be taken: *the best course is to seek an amicable parting of the ways.*

part·ing shot ▶ **n.** a final remark, typically a cutting one, made by someone at the moment of departure: *as her parting shot she told me never to phone her again.*

par·ti pris /ˌpärtē 'prē/ ▶ **n.** (pl. **partis pris** pronunc. **same**) a preconceived view; a bias.
▶ **adj.** prejudiced; biased.
– ORIGIN French, literally 'side taken.'

par·ti·san /'pärtəzən/ ▶ **n. 1** a strong supporter of a party, cause, or person.
2 a member of an armed group formed to fight secretly against an occupying force, in particular one operating in enemy-occupied Yugoslavia, Italy, and parts of eastern Europe in World War II.
▶ **adj.** prejudiced in favor of a particular cause: *newspapers have become increasingly partisan.*
– ORIGIN mid 16th cent.: from French, via Italian dialect from Italian *partigiano*, from *parte* 'part' (from Latin *pars, part-*).

par·ti·san·ship /'pärtəzənˌsʜip/ ▶ **n.** prejudice in favor of a particular cause; bias: *an act of blatant political partisanship.*

par·ti·ta /pär'tētə/ ▶ **n.** (pl. **partitas** or **partite** /-'tētā/) Music a suite, typically for a solo instrument or chamber ensemble.
– ORIGIN late 19th cent.: from Italian, literally 'divided off,' feminine past participle of *partire.*

P

par·tite /'pärˌtīt/ ▶ **adj.** [usu. in combination] divided into parts. ■ Botany & Zoology (esp. of a leaf or an insect's wing) divided to or nearly to the base.
– ORIGIN late 16th cent.: from Latin *partitus* 'divided up,' past participle of *partiri.*

par·ti·tion /pär'tisʜən, pər-/ ▶ **n.** (esp. with reference to a country with separate areas of government) the action or state of dividing or being divided into parts: *the country's partition into separate states.* ■ a structure dividing a space into two parts, esp. a light interior wall. ■ Chemistry the distribution of a solute between two immiscible or slightly miscible solvents in contact with one another, in accordance with its differing solubility in each. ■ Computing each of a number of portions into which some operating systems divide memory or storage.
▶ **v.** [with obj.] divide into parts: *an agreement was reached to partition the country.* ■ divide (a room) into smaller rooms or areas by erecting partitions: *the hall was partitioned to contain the noise of the computers.* ■ (**partition something off**) separate a part of a room from the rest by erecting a partition: *partition off part of a large bedroom to create a small bathroom.*
– DERIVATIVES **par·ti·tion·er n.**, **par·ti·tion·ist** /-ist/ **n.**
– ORIGIN late Middle English: from Latin *partitio(n-)*, from *partiri* 'divide into parts.'

par·ti·tion co·ef·fi·cient ▶ **n.** Chemistry the ratio of the concentrations of a solute in two immiscible or slightly miscible liquids, or in two solids, when it is in equilibrium across the interface between them.

par·ti·tive /'pärtitiv/ Grammar ▶ **adj.** (of a grammatical construction or case) referring to only a part of a whole, for example *a slice of bacon, a series of accidents, some of the children.*
▶ **n.** such a construction. ■ a noun or pronoun used as the first term in such a construction.
– DERIVATIVES **par·ti·tive·ly adv.**

par·ti·tive gen·i·tive ▶ **n.** Grammar a genitive used to indicate a whole divided into or regarded in parts, expressed in English by *of* as in *most of us.*

par·ti·zan /'pärtəzən/ ▶ **n. & adj.** old-fashioned spelling of PARTISAN.

part·ly /'pärtlē/ ▶ **adv.** to some extent; not completely: *the result is partly a matter of skill and partly of chance* | *you're only partly right.*

part·ner /'pärtnər/ ▶ **n. 1** a person who takes part in an undertaking with another or others, esp. in a business or company with shared risks and profits. ■ either of two people dancing together or playing a game or sport on the same side. ■ either member of a married couple or of an established unmarried couple: *she lived with her partner.* ■ a person with whom one has sex; a lover. ■ dated or dialect a friendly form of address by one man to another: *how you doing, partner?*
2 (**partners**) Nautical a timber framework secured to and strengthening the deck of a wooden ship around a hole for a mast.
▶ **v.** [with obj.] be the partner of: *young farmers who partnered Isabel to the village dance.* ■ [no obj.] associate as partners: *I never expected to partner with a man like you.*
– DERIVATIVES **part·ner·less adj.**
– ORIGIN Middle English: alteration of *parcener* 'partner, joint heir,' from Anglo-Norman French *parcener*, based on Latin *partitio(n-)* 'partition.' The change in the first syllable was due to association with PART.

part·ners' desk (also **partnership desk**) ▶ **n.** a large flat-topped desk with space for two people to sit opposite each other.

part·ner·ship /'pärtnərˌsʜip/ ▶ **n.** the state of being a partner or partners: *we should go on working together in partnership.* ■ an association of two or more people as partners: *an increase in partnerships with housing associations.* ■ a business or firm owned and run by two or more partners. ■ a position as one of the partners in a business or firm.

part of speech ▶ **n.** a category to which a word is assigned in accordance with its syntactic functions. In English the main parts of speech are noun, pronoun, adjective, determiner, verb, adverb, preposition, conjunction, and interjection.

Par·ton /'pärtn/, Dolly Rebecca (1946–), US country singer and songwriter. She also made a number of movies, including *Nine to Five* (1980) and *Steel Magnolias* (1989), and she founded Dollywood, a theme park in Tennessee.

par·took /pär'to͝ok/ past of PARTAKE.

par·tridge /'pärtrij/ ▶ **n.** (pl. **same** or **partridges**) a short-tailed game bird with mainly brown plumage, native to Eurasia. ● Family Phasianidae: several genera and many species, in particular the **gray partridge** (*Perdix perdix*), introduced into the northern US, and the **red-legged partridge** (*Alectoris rufa*), introduced into Colorado.
– ORIGIN Middle English *partrich*, from Old French *pertriz, perdriz*, from Latin *perdix.*

red-legged partridge

par·tridge·ber·ry /'pärtrijˌberē/ ▶ **n.** (pl. **partridgeberries**) a creeping North American plant of the madder family with red berries that are a favored food of game birds. ● *Mitchella repens*, family Rubiaceae. ■ the fruit of this plant.

par·tridge pea ▶ **n.** a yellow-flowered leguminous plant with sensitive leaves. ● *Cassia fasciculata*, family Leguminosae.

part song ▶ **n.** an unaccompanied secular song with three or more voice parts, typically homophonic rather than contrapuntal in style.

part-time ▶ **adj. & adv.** for only part of the usual working day or week: [as adj.] *part-time jobs* | *a part-time teacher* | [as adv.] *he only worked part-time.*
– DERIVATIVES **part-tim·er n.**

par·tu·ri·ent /pär't(y)o͝orēənt/ ▶ **adj.** technical (of a woman or female mammal) about to give birth; in labor.
▶ **n.** a parturient woman.
– ORIGIN late 16th cent.: from Latin *parturient-* 'being in labor,' from the verb *parturire*, inceptive of *parere* 'bring forth.'

par·tu·ri·tion /ˌpärcʜo͝o'risʜən/ ▶ **n.** formal or technical the action of giving birth to young; childbirth: *the weeks following parturition.*
– ORIGIN mid 17th cent.: from late Latin *parturitio(n-)*, from *parturire* 'be in labor' (see PARTURIENT).

part·way /'pärtˌwā, 'pärt'wā/ ▶ **adv.** part of the way: *partway along the corridor he stopped.*

par·ty¹ /'pärtē/ ▶ **n.** (pl. **parties**) **1** a social gathering of invited guests, typically involving eating, drinking, and entertainment: *an engagement party.*
2 a formally constituted political group, typically operating on a national basis, that contests elections and attempts to form or take part in a government: *the party's conservative mainstream.* ■ a group of people taking part in a particular activity or trip, esp. one for which they have been chosen: *the fishing party.*
3 a person or people forming one side in an agreement or dispute: *a contract between two parties.* ■ informal a person, esp. one with specified characteristics: *will you help the party on line 2?*
▶ **v.** (**parties, partied**) [no obj.] informal enjoy oneself at a party or other lively gathering, typically with drinking and music: *put on your glad rags and party!*
– PHRASES **be (a) party to** be involved in: *I felt a wave of revulsion at the manipulations I'd been party to.*
– DERIVATIVES **par·ti·er n.** (informal).
– ORIGIN Middle English (denoting a body of people united in opposition to others, also in sense 2 of the noun): from Old French *partie*, based on Latin *partiri* 'divide into parts.' Sense 1 of the noun dates from the early 18th cent.

par·ty² ▶ **adj.** Heraldry divided into parts of different tinctures: *party per fess, or, and azure.*
– ORIGIN Middle English (in the sense 'particolored'): from Old French *parti* 'parted,' based on Latin *partitus* 'divided into parts' (from the verb *partiri*).

par·ty boat ▶ **n.** a boat available for renting by a group of people who want to go fishing.

par·ty fa·vor ▶ **n.** a gift, usually small and inexpensive, given to guests at a party.

par·ty·go·er /'pärtēˌgōər/ ▶ **n.** a person attending a party.

par·ty line ▶ **n. 1** a policy, or the policies collectively, officially adopted by a political party: *they rarely fail to toe the party line* | [as modifier] *a party-line voter.*
2 dated a telephone line or circuit shared by two or more subscribers.

par·ty list ▶ **n.** a voting system used with proportional representation, in which people vote for a party rather than a candidate. Each party is assigned a number of seats that reflects its share of the vote.

par·ty po·lit·i·cal broad·cast ▶ **n.** a television or radio program on which a representative of a political party presents material intended to foster support for it.

par·ty pol·i·tics ▶ **plural n.** [also treated as sing.] politics that relate to political parties rather than to the good of the general public.

par·ty poop·er ▶ **n.** informal a person who throws gloom over social enjoyment: *I hate to be a party pooper, but I've got to catch the last train.*
– DERIVATIVES **par·ty-poop·ing n.**

par·ty wall ▶ **n.** a wall common to two adjoining buildings or rooms.

pa·rure /pə'ro͝or/ ▶ **n.** a set of jewels intended to be worn together.
– ORIGIN early 19th cent.: from French, from *parer* 'adorn.'

par val·ue ▶ **n.** the nominal value of a bond, share of stock, or a coupon as indicated in writing on the document or specified by charter.

Par·va·ti /'pärvətē/ Hinduism a benevolent goddess, wife of Shiva, mother of Ganesh and Skanda, often identified in her malevolent aspect with Durga and Kali.
– ORIGIN from Sanskrit *Pārvatī*, literally 'daughter of the mountain.'

par·ve /'pärvə/ ▶ **n.** variant spelling of PAREVE.

par·ve·nu /'pärvəˌn(y)o͞o/ often derogatory ▶ **n.** a person of obscure origin who has gained wealth, influence, or celebrity: *the political inexperience of a parvenu* | [as modifier] *he concealed the details of his parvenu lifestyle.*
– ORIGIN early 19th cent.: from French, literally 'arrived,' past participle of *parvenir*, from Latin *pervenire* 'come to, reach.'

par·vis /'pärvis/ ▶ **n.** an enclosed area in front of a cathedral or church, typically one that is surrounded with colonnades or porticoes.
– ORIGIN late Middle English: from Old French, based on late Latin *paradisus* 'paradise,' in the Middle Ages denoting a court in front of St. Peter's, Rome.

par·vo·vi·rus /'pärvōˌvīrəs/ ▶ **n.** Medicine any of a class of very small viruses chiefly affecting animals, esp. one (**canine parvovirus**) that causes contagious disease in dogs.
– ORIGIN 1960s: from Latin *parvus* 'small' + VIRUS.

PAS ▶ **abbr.** power-assisted steering.

pas /pä/ ▶ **n.** (pl. **same**) a step in dancing, esp. in classical ballet.
– ORIGIN French.

Pas·a·de·na /ˌpasəˈdēnə/ **1** a city in California, in the San Gabriel Mountains, northeast of Los Angeles; pop. 143,080 (est. 2008). It is the site of the Rose Bowl stadium.
2 an industrial port city in southeastern Texas, on the eastern side of Houston; pop. 146,439 (est. 2008).

Pas·ca·gou·la /ˌpaskəˈgo͞olə/ an industrial port city in southeastern Mississippi, on the Gulf of Mexico; pop. 23,609 (est. 2008).

Pas·cal[1] /paˈskal, päˈskäl/, Blaise (1623–62), French mathematician, physicist, and religious philosopher. He founded the theory of probabilities, but is best known for deriving the principle that the pressure of a fluid at rest is transmitted equally in all directions.

Pas·cal[2] (also **PASCAL**) ▶ **n.** a high-level structured computer programming language used for teaching and general programming.

pas·cal /päˈskäl/ ▶ **n.** the SI unit of pressure, equal to one newton per square meter (approximately 0.000145 pounds per square inch, or 9.9×10^{-6} atmospheres).
– ORIGIN 1950s: named after B. *Pascal* (see PASCAL[1]).

Pas·cal's tri·an·gle ▶ **n.** Mathematics a triangular array of numbers in which those at the ends of the rows are 1 and each of the others is the sum of the nearest two numbers in the row above (the apex, 1, being at the top).

Pas·cal's wa·ger ▶ **n.** [in sing.] Philosophy the argument that it is in one's own best interest to behave as if God exists, since the possibility of eternal punishment in hell outweighs any advantage of believing otherwise.

pas·chal /ˈpaskəl/ ▶ **adj.** formal **1** of or relating to Easter.
2 of or relating to the Jewish Passover.
– ORIGIN late Middle English: from Old French, from ecclesiastical Latin *paschalis*, from *pascha* 'feast of Passover,' via Greek and Aramaic from Hebrew *Pesah* 'Passover.'

pas·chal can·dle ▶ **n.** Christian Church a large candle blessed and lit on Holy Saturday and placed by the altar until Pentecost.

pas·chal lamb ▶ **n. 1** a lamb sacrificed at Passover. **2** Christ.

Pa·schen se·ries /ˈpäsHən/ Physics a series of lines in the infrared spectrum of atomic hydrogen, between 1.88 and 0.82 micrometers.
– ORIGIN 1920s: named after L. C. H. Friedrich *Paschen* (1865–1947), German physicist.

pas de basque /ˌpä də ˈbäsk/ ▶ **n.** (pl. **same**) a ballet step in three beats, with a circular movement of the front leg on the second beat. ■ (esp. in jigs and reels) a step in three beats with one long and two short movements, transferring weight from one foot to the other.
– ORIGIN French, literally 'step of a Basque.'

pas de bour·rée /ˌpä də bo͞oˈrā/ ▶ **n.** Ballet a sideways step in which one foot crosses behind or in front of the other.
– ORIGIN French, literally 'bourrée step.'

pas de chat /ˌpä də ˈsHä/ ▶ **n.** (pl. **same**) Ballet a jump in which each foot in turn is raised to the opposite knee.
– ORIGIN French, literally 'step of a cat.'

pas de deux /ˌpä də ˈdo͞o/ ▶ **n.** (pl. **same**) a dance for two people, typically a man and a woman.
– ORIGIN French, literally 'step of two.'

pas de qua·tre /ˌpä də ˈkatrə/ ▶ **n.** (pl. **same**) a dance for four people.
– ORIGIN French, literally 'step of four.'

pas de trois /ˌpä də ˈtwä/ ▶ **n.** (pl. **same**) a dance for three people.
– ORIGIN French, literally 'step of three.'

pa·se /päˈsā/ ▶ **n.** a maneuver with the cape in bullfighting, the purpose of which is to get the bull's attention.
– ORIGIN Spanish, literally 'let him pass.'

pa·se·o /pəˈsāō/ ▶ **n.** (pl. **paseos**) a leisurely walk or stroll, esp. one taken in the evening; a promenade (used with reference to the tradition of taking such a walk in Spain or Spanish-speaking communities). ■ (also **paseo de cuadrillas** /dā kwäˈdrēlyäs, -ˈdrēäs/) a parade of bullfighters into the arena at the beginning of a bullfight. ■ a plaza or walkway for strolling.
– ORIGIN Spanish, literally 'step.'

pash /pasH/ ▶ **n.** informal, dated a brief infatuation: *Kath's got a pash on him.*
– ORIGIN early 20th cent.: abbreviation of PASSION.

pa·sha /ˈpäsHə, ˈpasHə, pəˈsHä/ ▶ **n. 1** (also **pacha**) historical the title of a Turkish officer of high rank. **2** (**two-tailed pasha**) a large orange-brown butterfly with two tails on each hind wing and complex patterns on the underwings, occurring around the Mediterranean and in Africa. ● *Charaxes jasius*, subfamily Nymphalinae, family Nymphalidae.
– ORIGIN mid 17th cent.: from Turkish *paşa*, from Pahlavi *pati* 'lord' + *šāh* 'shah.'

pashm /ˈpəsHəm/ ▶ **n.** the soft underfur of some Tibetan and Indian goats, of which cashmere represents a particularly fine and soft type.
– ORIGIN late 19th cent.: from Persian *pašm* 'wool.'

pash·mi·na /pəsHˈmēnə/ ▶ **n.** fine-quality material made from goat's wool.
– ORIGIN Persian, from *pašm* 'wool, down.'

Pash·to /ˈpəsHtō/ ▶ **n.** the Iranian language of the Pathans, also spoken in northern areas of Pakistan, that is an official language of Afghanistan.
▶ **adj.** of or relating to this language.
– ORIGIN the name in Pashto.

Pash·tun /pəsHˈto͞on/ ▶ **n.** variant spelling of PATHAN.

Pa·siph·a·ë /pəˈsifəˌē/ Greek Mythology the wife of Minos and mother of the Minotaur.

pas·kha /ˈpäskə/ (also **pashka** /ˈpäsHkə/) ▶ **n.** a rich Russian dessert made with soft cheese, dried fruit, nuts, and spices, and traditionally eaten at Easter.
– ORIGIN Russian, literally 'Easter.'

pa·so do·ble /ˌpäsō ˈdōblā/ ▶ **n.** (pl. **paso dobles**) a fast-paced ballroom dance based on a Latin American style of marching. ■ a piece of music for this dance, typically in duple time.
– ORIGIN 1920s: from Spanish, literally 'double step.'

Pa·so·li·ni /ˌpasəˈlēnē, ˌpä-/, Pier Paolo (1922–75), Italian movie director and novelist. A Marxist, he drew on his experiences in the slums of Rome for his work, but became recognized for his controversial, bawdy literary adaptations, such as *The Gospel According to St. Matthew* (1964) and *The Canterbury Tales* (1973).

pas·pa·lum /ˈpaspələm/ ▶ **n.** a grass of warm and tropical regions that is grown for fodder, erosion control, and as a pasture grass. ● Genus *Paspalum*, family Gramineae.
– ORIGIN modern Latin, from Greek *paspalos*, denoting a kind of millet.

pasque·flow·er /ˈpaskˌflou(-ə)r/ ▶ **n.** a spring-flowering plant of the buttercup family, with purple or white flowers. ● Genera *Anemone* and *Pulsatilla*, family Ranunculaceae: several species, in particular the North American *A. patens* and the Eurasian *P. vulgaris*.
– ORIGIN late 16th cent. (as *passeflower*): from French *passe-fleur*. The change in spelling of the first word was due to association with archaic *pasque* 'Easter' (because of the plant's early flowering).

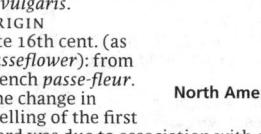

North American pasqueflower

pas·quin·ade /ˌpaskwəˈnād/ ▶ **n.** a satire or lampoon, originally one displayed or delivered publicly in a public place.
– ORIGIN late 16th cent.: from Italian *pasquinata*, from *Pasquino*, the name of a statue in Rome on which abusive Latin verses were posted annually.

pass[1] /pas/ ▶ **v. 1** move or cause to move in a specified direction: [no obj.] *he passed through towns and villages* | *the shells from the Allied guns were passing very low overhead* | [with obj.] *he passed a weary hand across his forehead* | *pass an electric current through it.* ■ change from one state or condition to another: *homes that have passed from public to private ownership.* ■ die (used euphemistically): *his father had passed to the afterlife* | *she **passed away** peacefully in her sleep* | *a good and decent man has **passed on**.*
2 [with obj.] go past or across; leave behind or on one side in proceeding: *she passed a rest area with a pay phone* | *the two vehicles had no room to pass each other* | [no obj.] *we will not let you pass.* ■ go beyond the limits of; surpass; exceed: *this item has passed its sell-by date.* ■ Tennis hit a winning shot past (an opponent).
3 [no obj.] (of time or a point in time) elapse; go by: *the day and night passed slowly* | *the moment had passed.* ■ happen; be done or said: *not another word **passed between** them* | [with complement] *this fact has passed almost unnoticed.* ■ [with obj.] spend or use up (a period of time): *this was how they passed the time.* ■ come to an end: *the danger had passed.*
4 [with obj.] transfer (something) to someone, esp. by handing or bequeathing it to the next person in a series: *your letter has been passed to Mr. Rich for action* | *please pass the fish* | [with two objs.] *he passed her a cup.* ■ [no obj.] be transferred from one person or place to another, esp. by inheritance: *infections can pass from mother to child at birth* | *if Ann remarried the estate would **pass to** her new husband.* ■ (in football, soccer, hockey, and other games) throw, kick, or hit (the ball or puck) to another player on one's own team. ■ put (something, esp. money) into circulation: *persons who have passed bad checks.* ■ [no obj.] (esp. of money) circulate; be current: *cash was passing briskly.*
5 [with obj.] (of a candidate) be successful in (an examination, test, or course): *she passed her driving test.* ■ judge the performance or standard of (someone or something) to be satisfactory: [with obj. and complement] *he was passed fit by army doctors.* ■ [no obj.] be accepted as adequate; go uncensured: *she couldn't agree, but **let it pass*** | *her rather revealing dress passed without comment.* ■ [no obj.] (**pass as/for**) be accepted as or taken for: *he could pass for a native of Sweden.*
6 [with obj.] (of a legislative or other official body) approve or put into effect (a proposal or law) by voting on it: *the bill was passed despite fierce opposition.* ■ [no obj.] (of a proposal or law) be examined and approved by (a legislative body or process): *the bill passed by 164 votes to 107.*
7 [with obj.] pronounce (a judgment or judicial sentence): ***passing judgment on** these crucial issues* | *it is now my duty to **pass** sentence **upon** you.* ■ utter (something, esp. criticism): *she would pass remarks about the Paxtons in their own house.* ■ [no obj.] (**pass on/upon**) archaic adjudicate or give a judgment on: *a jury could not be trusted to pass upon the question of Endicott's good faith.*
8 [with obj.] discharge (something, esp. urine or feces) from the body: *frequency of passing urine.*
9 [no obj.] forgo one's turn in a game or an offered opportunity: *we **pass on** dessert and have coffee.* ■ [as exclamation] said when one does not know the answer to a question, for example in a quizzing game: *to the enigmatic question we answered "Pass."* ■ [with obj.] (of a company) not declare or pay (a dividend). ■ Bridge make no bid when it is one's turn during an auction. ■ [with obj.] Bridge make no bid in response to (one's partner's bid): *East had passed his partner's opening bid of one club.*
▶ **n. 1** an act or instance of moving past or through something: *repeated passes with the swipe card* | *an unmarked plane had been making passes over his house.* ■ informal an amorous or sexual advance made to someone: *she **made a pass at** Stephen.* ■ an act of passing the hands over anything, as in conjuring or hypnotism. ■ a thrust in fencing. ■ a juggling trick. ■ Bridge an act of refraining from bidding during the auction. ■ Computing a single scan through a set of data or a program.
2 a successful completion of an examination or course: [as modifier] *a 100 percent pass rate.* ■ the grade indicating this. ■ Brit. an achievement of a university degree without honors: [as modifier] *a pass degree.*
3 a card, ticket, or permit giving authorization for the holder to enter or have access to a place, form of transportation, or event.
4 (in football, soccer, hockey, and other games) an act of throwing, kicking, or hitting the ball or puck to another player on the same team.
5 a state or situation of a specified, usually bad or difficult, nature: *this is a sad pass for a fixture that used to crackle with excitement.*
– PHRASES **come to a pretty pass** reach a bad or regrettable state of affairs. **pass the baton** see BATON. **pass the buck** see BUCK[3]. **pass one's eye over** read (a document) cursorily. **pass the hat** see HAT. **pass one's lips** see LIP. **pass muster** see MUSTER. **pass the parcel** see PARCEL. **pass the time of day** see TIME. **pass water** urinate.
– PHRASAL VERBS **pass someone by** happen without being noticed or fully experienced by someone: *sometimes I feel that life is passing me by.* **pass off** (of proceedings) happen or be carried through in a specified, usually satisfactory, way: *the weekend had passed off entirely without incident.* **pass something off 1** evade or lightly dismiss an awkward remark: *he made a light joke and passed it off.* **2** Basketball throw the ball to a teammate who is unguarded: *he scored eight times and passed off six assists.* **pass someone/something off as** falsely represent a person or thing as (something else): *the drink was packaged in champagne bottles and was*

P

being passed off as the real stuff. **pass out 1** become unconscious: *he consumed enough alcohol to make him pass out.* **2** Brit. complete one's initial training in the armed forces. **3** (of bridge players) not play a hand because all players have passed. **pass someone over** ignore the claims of someone to promotion or advancement: *he was passed over for a cabinet job.* **pass something over** avoid mentioning or considering something: *I shall pass over the matter of the transitional period.* **pass something up** refrain from taking up an opportunity: *he passed up a career in pro baseball.*

– DERIVATIVES **pass·er** n. *he's a good passer of the ball.*

– ORIGIN Middle English: from Old French *passer*, based on Latin *passus* 'pace.'

pass² ▶ n. a route over or through mountains: *the pass over the mountain was open again after the snows* | [in place names] *the Khyber Pass.* ■ a passage for fish over or past a weir or dam. ■ a navigable channel, esp. at the mouth of a river: *Sabine Pass.*

– PHRASES **head** (or **cut**) **someone/something off at the pass** forestall someone or something: *the doctor's aim to head the infection off at the pass.*

– ORIGIN Middle English (in the sense 'division of a text, passage through'): variant of PACE¹, influenced by PASS¹ and French *pas.*

pass. ▶ abbr. ■ passenger. ■ passim. ■ passive.

pass·a·ble /ˈpasəbəl/ ▶ adj. **1** just good enough to be acceptable; satisfactory: *he spoke passable English.* **2** (of a route or road) clear of obstacles and able to be traveled along or on: *the road was passable with care.*

– ORIGIN late Middle English: from Old French, from *passer* 'to pass.'

pass·a·bly /ˈpasəblē/ ▶ adv. in a way that is just good enough: [as submodifier] *he was passably attractive.*

pas·sa·ca·glia /ˌpäsəˈkälyə/ ▶ n. Music a composition similar to a chaconne, typically in slow triple time with variations over a ground bass.

– ORIGIN Italian, from Spanish *pasacalle*, from *pasar* 'to pass' + *calle* 'street' (because originally it was a dance often played in the streets).

pas·sade /pəˈsäd/ ▶ n. a movement performed in advanced dressage and classical riding, in which the horse performs a 180° turn, with its forelegs describing a large circle and its hind legs a smaller one.

– ORIGIN mid 17th cent.: French, from Italian *passata* or Provençal *passada*, from medieval Latin *passare* 'to pass.'

pas·sage¹ /ˈpasij/ ▶ n. **1** the act or process of moving through, under, over, or past something on the way from one place to another: *there were moorings for boats wanting passage through the lock.* ■ the act or process of moving forward: *despite the passage of time she still loved him.* ■ the right to pass through somewhere: *we obtained a permit for safe passage from the embassy.* ■ a journey or ticket for a journey by sea or air: *he then* **booked passage** *home aboard a Spanish warship.* ■ Ornithology (of a migrating bird) the action of passing through a place en route to its final destination: *the species occurs regularly on passage* | [as modifier] *a passage migrant.* ■ Medicine & Biology the process of propagating microorganisms or cells in a series of host organisms or culture media, so as to maintain them or modify their virulence. **2** a narrow way, typically having walls on either side, allowing access between buildings or to different rooms within a building; a passageway. ■ a duct, vessel, or other channel in the body. **3** the process of transition from one state to another: *an allegory on the theme of the passage from ignorance to knowledge.* ■ the passing of a bill into law: *a catalyst for the unrest was the passage of a privatization law.* **4** a short extract from a book or other printed material: *he picked up the newspaper and read the passage again.* ■ a section of a piece of music: *nothing obscures the outlines of an orchestral passage more than a drumroll on an unrelated note.* ■ an episode in a longer activity such as a sporting event: *a neat passage of midfield play.*

▶ v. [with obj.] Medicine & Biology subject (a strain of microorganisms or cells) to a passage: *each recombinant virus was passaged nine times successively.*

– PHRASES **passage of** (or **at**) **arms** a fight or dispute. **work one's passage** work in return for a free place on a voyage: *he worked his passage home as a steward.*

– ORIGIN Middle English: from Old French, based on Latin *passus* 'pace.'

pas·sage² ▶ n. a movement performed in advanced dressage and classical riding, in which the horse executes a slow elevated trot, giving the impression of dancing.

– ORIGIN early 18th cent.: from French *passage*, from an alteration of Italian *passeggiare* 'to walk, pace,' based on Latin *passus* 'pace.'

pas·sage hawk ▶ n. a hawk caught for training while on migration, esp. as an immature bird of less than twelve months. Compare with HAGGARD.

pas·sage·way /ˈpasijˌwā/ ▶ n. a long, narrow way, typically having walls on either side, that allows access between buildings or to different rooms within a building.

pas·sage·work /ˈpasijˌwərk/ ▶ n. music notable chiefly for the scope it affords for virtuoso playing: *some of the passagework in early Beethoven is very awkward.*

Pas·sa·ic /pəˈsāik/ an industrial city in northeastern New Jersey, on the Passaic River; pop. 66,884 (est. 2008).

Pas·sa·ma·quod·dy /ˌpasəməˈkwädē/ ▶ n. (pl. **same** or **Passamaquoddies**) **1** a member of a North American Indian people inhabiting parts of eastern Maine and, formerly, southwestern New Brunswick. **2** the Algonquian language of this people.

▶ adj. of or relating to this people or their language.

– ORIGIN from Passamaquoddy *pestəmokhatiyək*, 'place where pollack are plentiful,' referring to Passamaquoddy Bay.

Pas·sa·ma·quod·dy Bay /ˌpasəməˈkwädē/ (also **Quoddy Bay**) an inlet of the Bay of Fundy, at the border of Maine and New Brunswick, noted for its powerful tides.

pas·sant /ˈpasənt/ ▶ adj. [usu. postpositive] Heraldry (of an animal) represented as walking, with the right front foot raised. The animal is depicted in profile facing the dexter (left) side with the tail raised, unless otherwise specified (e.g., as "passant guardant").

– ORIGIN late Middle English: from Old French, literally 'proceeding,' present participle of *passer.*

pas·sa·ta /pəˈsätə/ ▶ n. a thick paste made from strained tomatoes and used esp. in Italian cooking.

– ORIGIN Italian.

pass·band /ˈpasˌband/ ▶ n. a frequency band within which signals are transmitted by a filter without attenuation.

pass·book /ˈpasˌbo͝ok/ ▶ n. a booklet issued by a bank to an account holder for recording sums deposited and withdrawn.

Pass·chen·daele, Battle of /ˈpasHənˌdāl/ (also **Passendale**) a prolonged episode of trench warfare involving appalling loss of life during World War I in 1917, near the village of Passchendaele in western Belgium. It is also known as the third Battle of Ypres.

pass door ▶ n. a door in a theater connecting the backstage area and the auditorium.

pas·sé /paˈsā/ ▶ adj. [predic.] no longer fashionable; out of date: *miniskirts are passé—the best skirts are knee-length.* ■ archaic (esp. of a woman) past one's prime.

– ORIGIN French, literally 'gone by,' past participle of *passer.*

passed ball ▶ n. Baseball a pitch that the catcher fails to stop or control, enabling a base runner to advance.

passed pawn ▶ n. Chess a pawn that no enemy pawn can stop from queening.

pas·seg·gia·ta /ˌpasəˈjätə/ ▶ n. (pl. **passeggiate** /-ˈjätā/) a leisurely walk or stroll, esp. one taken in the evening; a promenade (used with reference to the tradition of taking such a walk in Italy or Italian-speaking communities).

– ORIGIN Italian.

pas·sel /ˈpasəl/ ▶ n. informal a large group of people or things of indeterminate number; a pack: *a passel of journalists.*

– ORIGIN mid 19th cent.: representing a pronunciation of PARCEL.

passe·men·terie /pasˈmentrē/ ▶ n. decorative textile trimming consisting of gold or silver lace, gimp, or braid.

– ORIGIN early 17th cent.: from French, from *passement* 'gold lace.'

Pas·sen·dale, Battle of /ˈpasənˌdāl/ variant spelling of PASSCHENDAELE, BATTLE OF.

pas·sen·ger /ˈpasinjər/ ▶ n. a traveler on a public or private conveyance other than the driver, pilot, or crew.

– ORIGIN Middle English: from the Old French adjective *passager* 'passing, transitory,' used as a noun, from *passage* (see PASSAGE¹).

pas·sen·ger mile ▶ n. one mile traveled by one passenger, as a unit of traffic.

pas·sen·ger pi·geon ▶ n. an extinct long-tailed North American pigeon, noted for its long migrations in huge flocks. It was relentlessly hunted, the last individual dying in captivity in 1914. ● *Ectopistes migratorius*, family Columbidae.

passe-par·tout /ˌpas pärˈto͞o/ ▶ n. **1** a picture or photograph simply mounted between a piece of glass and a sheet of cardboard (or two pieces of glass) stuck together at the edges with adhesive tape. ■ adhesive tape or paper used in making such a frame. **2** archaic a master key.

– ORIGIN late 17th cent.: from French, literally 'passes everywhere.'

passe·pied /päsˈpyā/ ▶ n. a dance like a quick minuet, popular in the 17th and 18th centuries.

– ORIGIN French, from *passer* 'to pass' + *pied* 'foot.'

pass·er·by /ˈpasərˌbī/ ▶ n. (pl. **passersby**) a person who happens to be going past something, esp. on foot.

pas·ser·ine /ˈpasərin, -ˌrīn/ Ornithology ▶ adj. of, relating to, or denoting birds of a large order distinguished by feet that are adapted for perching, including all songbirds.

▶ n. a passerine bird; a perching bird.

> The order Passeriformes comprises more than half of all bird species, the remainder being known informally as the **nonpasserines**. All passerines in Europe belong to the suborder Oscines (the **oscine passerines**), so that the term is effectively synonymous with 'songbird' there (see SONGBIRD). Those of the suborder Deutero-Oscines (the **suboscine passerines**) are found mainly in America.

– ORIGIN late 18th cent.: from Latin *passer* 'sparrow' + -INE¹.

pas seul /ˌpä ˈsəl/ ▶ n. a dance for one person.

– ORIGIN French, literally 'single step.'

pass-fail ▶ adj. denoting a class, course, or system of grading in which the only two grades given are "pass" and "fail."

pas·si·ble /ˈpasəbəl/ ▶ adj. Christian Theology capable of feeling or suffering; susceptible to sensation or emotion: *only the humanity of Jesus is regarded as passible.*

– DERIVATIVES **pas·si·bil·i·ty** /ˌpasəˈbilitē/ n.

– ORIGIN late Middle English: from Old French, from late Latin *passibilis*, from Latin *pass-* 'suffered,' from the verb *pati.*

pas·sim /ˈpasim/ ▶ adv. (of allusions or references in a published work) to be found at various places throughout the text.

– ORIGIN Latin, from *passus* 'scattered,' from the verb *pandere.*

pass·ing /ˈpasiNG/ ▶ adj. [attrib.] **1** going past: *passing cars.* **2** (of a period of time) going by: *she detested him more with every passing second.* ■ carried out quickly and lightly: *a passing glance.* **3** meeting or surpassing the requirements of a course or examination: *a passing grade.*

▶ n. [in sing.] **1** the passage of something, esp. time: *with the passing of the years she had become a little eccentric.* ■ the action of throwing, kicking, or hitting a ball or puck to another team member during a sports match: *his play showed good passing and good control* | [as modifier] *a good passing movement.* **2** used euphemistically to refer to a person's death: *her passing will be felt deeply by many people.* ■ the end of something: *the passing of the Cold War and the rise of a new Europe.*

– PHRASES **in passing** briefly and casually: *the research was mentioned only in passing.*

– DERIVATIVES **pass·ing·ly** adv.

pass·ing bell ▶ n. chiefly historical a bell rung immediately after a death as a signal for prayers.

pass·ing note (also **passing tone**) ▶ n. Music a note not belonging to the harmony but interposed to secure a smooth transition from one chord to another.

pass·ing shot ▶ n. Tennis a winning shot beyond and out of reach of one's opponent.

pas·sion /ˈpasHən/ ▶ n. **1** strong and barely controllable emotion: *a man of impetuous passion.* ■ a state or outburst of such emotion: *oratory in which he gradually works himself up into a passion.* ■ intense sexual love: *their all-consuming passion for each other* | *she nurses a passion for Thomas.* ■ an intense desire or enthusiasm for something: *the English have a passion for gardens.* ■ a thing arousing enthusiasm: *modern furniture is a particular passion of Bill's.* **2** (**the Passion**) the suffering and death of Jesus: *meditations on the Passion of Christ.* ■ a narrative of this from any of the Gospels. ■ a musical setting of any of these narratives: *an aria from Bach's St. Matthew Passion.*

–ORIGIN Middle English: from Old French, from late Latin *passio(n-)* (chiefly a term in Christian theology), from Latin *pati* 'suffer.'

pas·sion·al /'pasHənl/ ▶ **adj.** rare of, relating to, or marked by passion: *a current of passional electric energy.*
▶ **n.** Christian Church a book about the sufferings of saints and martyrs, for reading on their feast days.

pas·sion·ate /'pasHənit/ ▶ **adj.** showing or caused by strong feelings or a strong belief: *passionate pleas for help | he's* ***passionate about*** *football.* ■ showing or caused by intense feelings of sexual love: *a passionate kiss.*
–DERIVATIVES **pas·sion·ate·ly** **adv.**, **pas·sion·ate·ness** **n.**
–ORIGIN late Middle English (also in the senses 'easily moved to passion' and 'enraged'): from medieval Latin *passionatus* 'full of passion,' from *passio* (see PASSION).

pas·sion·flow·er /'pasHən,flou(-ə)r/ (also **passion flower**) ▶ **n.** an evergreen climbing plant of warm regions that bears distinctive flowers with parts that supposedly resemble instruments of the Crucifixion. ● Genus *Passiflora*, family Passifloraceae.

pas·sion fruit (also **passionfruit**) ▶ **n.** the edible purple fruit of a kind of passionflower that is grown commercially, esp. in tropical America. Also called GRANADILLA. ● This fruit is obtained from *Passiflora edulis*, family Passifloraceae.

pas·sion·less /'pasHənlis/ ▶ **adj.** lacking strong emotion; unemotional: *the voice is passionless, monotone.*

Pas·sion play ▶ **n.** a dramatic performance representing Christ's Passion from the Last Supper to the Crucifixion.

Pas·sion Sun·day ▶ **n.** the fifth Sunday in Lent.

Pas·sion·tide /'pasHən,tīd/ ▶ **n.** the last two weeks of Lent.

Pas·sion Week ▶ **n.** **1** the week between Passion Sunday and Palm Sunday.
2 older name for HOLY WEEK.

pas·si·vate /'pasə,vāt/ ▶ **v.** [with obj.] (usu. as adj. **passivated**) make (a metal or other substance) unreactive by altering the surface layer or coating the surface with a thin inert layer: *components are made from passivated and anodized aluminum.* ■ Electronics coat (a semiconductor) with inert material to protect it from contamination.
–DERIVATIVES **pas·si·va·tion** /,pasə'vāsHən/ **n.**

pas·sive /'pasiv/ ▶ **adj.** **1** accepting or allowing what happens or what others do, without active response or resistance: *the women were portrayed as passive victims.* ■ Chemistry (of a metal) made unreactive by a thin inert surface layer of oxide. ■ (of a circuit or device) containing no source of electromotive force. ■ (of radar or a satellite) receiving or reflecting radiation from a transmitter or target rather than generating its own signal. ■ relating to or denoting heating systems that make use of incident sunlight as an energy source.
2 Grammar denoting or relating to a voice of verbs in which the subject undergoes the action of the verb (e.g., *they were killed* as opposed to *he killed them*). The opposite of ACTIVE.
▶ **n.** Grammar a passive form of a verb. ■ (**the passive**) the passive voice.
–DERIVATIVES **pas·sive·ly** **adv.**, **pas·sive·ness** **n.**, **pas·siv·i·ty** /pa'sivitē/ **n.**
–ORIGIN late Middle English (in sense 2 of the adjective, also in the sense '(exposed to) suffering, acted on by an external agency'): from Latin *passivus*, from *pass-* 'suffered,' from the verb *pati*.

pas·sive-ag·gres·sive ▶ **adj.** of or denoting a type of behavior or personality characterized by indirect resistance to the demands of others and an avoidance of direct confrontation, as in procrastinating, pouting, or misplacing important materials.

pas·sive im·mu·ni·ty ▶ **n.** Physiology the short-term immunity that results from the introduction of antibodies from another person or animal. Compare with ACTIVE IMMUNITY.

pas·sive ma·trix ▶ **n.** Electronics a display system in which individual pixels are selected using two control voltages for the row and column.

pas·sive re·sist·ance ▶ **n.** nonviolent opposition to authority, esp. a refusal to cooperate with legal requirements: *they called for protest in the form of passive resistance.*

pas·sive res·traint ▶ **n.** a car safety device that is activated by the force of a collision or other sudden stop and that aims to prevent injury to a passenger.

pas·sive smok·ing ▶ **n.** the involuntary inhaling of smoke from other people's cigarettes, cigars, or pipes: *children are more susceptible to the effects of passive smoking.*

pas·siv·ize /'pasə,vīz/ ▶ **v.** [with obj.] Grammar convert (a verb or clause) into the passive form: *a sentence that has been passivized.* ■ [no obj.] (of a verb or clause) be convertible in this way: *transitive verbs in idiomatic expressions frequently will not passivize.*
–DERIVATIVES **pas·siv·iz·a·ble** /-əbəl/ **adj.**, **pas·siv·i·za·tion** /,pasəvə'zāsHən/ **n.**

pass·key /'pas,kē/ ▶ **n.** **1** a key to the door of a restricted area, given only to those who are officially allowed access.
2 a master key.

Pas·sos, John Dos, see DOS PASSOS.

Pass·o·ver /'pas,ōvər/ ▶ **n.** the major Jewish spring festival that commemorates the liberation of the Israelites from Egyptian slavery, lasting seven or eight days from the 15th day of Nisan.
–ORIGIN from *pass over* 'pass without touching,' with reference to the exemption of the Israelites from the death of their firstborn (Exod. 12).

pass·port /'pas,pôrt/ ▶ **n.** an official document issued by a government, certifying the holder's identity and citizenship and entitling them to travel under its protection to and from foreign countries. ■ [in sing.] a thing that ensures admission to or the achievement of something: *the sport utility vehicle seemed like a* ***a passport to*** *new adventures.*
–ORIGIN late 15th cent. (denoting authorization to enter or depart from a port): from French *passeport*, from *passer* 'to pass' + *port* 'seaport.'

pas·sus /'pasəs/ ▶ **n.** (pl. **same**) a section, division, or canto of a story or poem, esp. a medieval one.
–ORIGIN late 16th cent.: from Latin, literally 'step, pace,' in medieval Latin 'passage of a book.'

pass·word /'pas,wərd/ ▶ **n.** a secret word or phrase that must be used to gain admission to something. ■ a string of characters that allows access to a computer, interface, or system.

past /past/ ▶ **adj.** gone by in time and no longer existing: *the danger is now past.* ■ [attrib.] belonging to a former time: *they made a study of the reasons why past attempts had failed | he is a past chairman of the society.* ■ [attrib.] (of a specified period of time) occurring before and leading up to the time of speaking or writing: *the band has changed over the past twelve months.* ■ Grammar (of a tense) expressing an action that has happened or a state that previously existed.
▶ **n.** **1** (usu. **the past**) the time or a period of time before the moment of speaking or writing: *she found it hard to make ends meet in the past | the war-damaged church is preserved as a reminder of the past.* ■ the history of a person, country, or institution: *the monuments act as guidelines through the country's colorful past.* ■ informal a part of a person's history that is considered to be shameful: *the heroine was a lady with a past.*
2 Grammar a past tense or form of a verb: *a simple past of the first conjugation.*
▶ **prep.** to or on the farther side of: *he rode on past the crossroads.* ■ in front of or from one side to the other of: *he began to drive slowly past the houses.* ■ beyond in time; later than: *by this time it was past 3:30.* ■ no longer capable of: *he is past giving the best advice.* ■ beyond the scope of: *my hair was past praying for.*
▶ **adv.** so as to pass from one side of something to the other: *large angelfish swim slowly past.* ■ used to indicate the lapse of time: *a week went past and nothing changed.*
–PHRASES **not put it past someone** believe someone to be capable of doing something wrong or rash: *I wouldn't put it past him to slip something into the drinks.*
–DERIVATIVES **past·ness** **n.**
–ORIGIN Middle English: variant of *passed*, past participle of PASS[1].

pas·ta /'pastə, 'pästə/ ▶ **n.** a dish originally from Italy consisting of dough made from durum wheat and water, extruded or stamped into various shapes and typically cooked in boiling water.
–ORIGIN late 19th cent.: from Italian, literally 'paste.'

paste /pāst/ ▶ **n.** a thick, soft, moist substance, usually produced by mixing dry ingredients with a liquid: *blend onions, sugar, and oil to a paste.* ■ a substance such as this that is used as an adhesive, esp. for sticking paper and other light materials: *wallpaper paste.* ■ a mixture consisting mainly of clay and water that is used in making ceramic ware, esp. a mixture of low plasticity based on kaolin for making porcelain. ■ a hard vitreous composition used in making imitation gems: [as modifier] *paste brooches.*
▶ **v.** [with obj.] **1** coat with paste: *when coating walls with fabric, paste the wall, not the fabric.* ■ [with obj. and adverbial of place] fasten or stick (something) onto something with paste: *ads are pasted on the walls.* ■ Computing insert (a piece of text or other data copied from elsewhere).
2 informal beat or defeat severely: *he pasted the guy and tied his ankles together.*
–ORIGIN late Middle English: from Old French, from late Latin *pasta* 'medicinal preparation in the shape of a small square,' probably from Greek *pastē*, (plural) *pasta* 'barley porridge,' from *pastos* 'sprinkled.'

paste·board /'pās(t),bôrd/ ▶ **n.** a type of thin board made by pasting together sheets of paper.

paste·down /'pās(t),doun/ ▶ **n.** (in bookbinding) the part of an endpaper that is pasted to the inside of the cover.

pas·tel /pa'stel/ ▶ **n.** **1** a crayon made of powdered pigments bound with gum or resin. ■ a work of art created using such crayons: *a pastel entitled "Girl Braiding Her Hair."*
2 a soft and delicate shade of a color: *the subtlest of pastels and creams.*
▶ **adj.** of a soft and delicate shade or color: *pastel blue curtains.*
–DERIVATIVES **pas·tel·ist** /-ist/ (also **pastellist**) **n.**
–ORIGIN mid 17th cent.: via French from Italian *pastello*, diminutive of *pasta* 'paste.'

pas·tern /'pastərn/ ▶ **n.** the sloping part of a horse's foot between the fetlock and the hoof. ■ a corresponding part in some other domestic animals.
–ORIGIN Middle English: from Old French *pasturon*, from *pasture* 'strap for hobbling a horse,' transferred in sense to the joint of the foot.

Pas·ter·nak /'pastər,nak/, Boris (Leonidovich) (1890–1960), Russian poet, novelist, and translator. His best-known novel, *Doctor Zhivago* (1957), describes the experience of the Russian intelligentsia during the Russian Revolution; it was banned in the former Soviet Union. He was forced by Soviet authorities to turn down the Nobel Prize for Literature in 1958.

paste-up ▶ **n.** a document prepared for copying or printing by combining and pasting various sections on a backing.

Pas·teur /pas'tər, pä'stœr/, Louis (1822–95), French chemist and bacteriologist. He introduced pasteurization and made pioneering studies in vaccination techniques.

pas·teu·rel·lo·sis /,pastərə'lōsis/ ▶ **n.** a bacterial infection commonly affecting animals and sometimes transferred to humans through bites and scratches. ● The causative bacteria are Gram-negative rods of the genus *Pasteurella*, in particular *P. multocida*.
–ORIGIN early 20th cent.: from French *pasteurellose* (from the name PASTEUR) + -OSIS.

pas·teur·ize /'pasCHə,rīz/ ▶ **v.** [with obj.] (often as adj. **pasteurized**) subject (milk, wine, or other products) to a process of partial sterilization, esp. one involving heat treatment or irradiation, thus making the product safe for consumption and improving its keeping quality: *pasteurized milk.*
–DERIVATIVES **pas·teur·i·za·tion** /,pasCHəri'zāsHən/ **n.**, **pas·teur·iz·er** **n.**
–ORIGIN late 19th cent.: from the name of L. PASTEUR + -IZE.

Pas·teur pi·pette ▶ **n.** a simple glass pipette drawn into a capillary tube at one end, used with a rubber nipple fitted to the other.

pas·tic·cio /pä'stēCHō/ ▶ **n.** (pl. **pasticcios**) another term for PASTICHE.
–ORIGIN Italian.

pas·tiche /pa'stēsH, pä-/ ▶ **n.** an artistic work in a style that imitates that of another work, artist, or period: *the operetta is* ***a pastiche of*** *18th century styles | the songs amount to much more than blatant pastiche.* ■ an artistic work consisting of a medley of pieces taken from various sources.
▶ **v.** [with obj.] imitate the style of (an artist or work): *Gauguin took himself to a Pacific island and pastiched the primitive art he found there.*
–ORIGIN late 19th cent.: from French, from Italian *pasticcio*, based on late Latin *pasta* 'paste.'

pas·ti·cheur /pas'tēsHər/ ▶ **n.** an artist who creates a pastiche: *he was unrivaled as a parodist and pasticheur.*

past·ie ▶ **n.** (pl. **pasties**) **1** /'pāstē/ (usu. **pasties**) informal a decorative covering for the nipple worn by a stripper.
2 /'pastē/ variant spelling of PASTY[1].

pas·til·la /pa'stilə/ ▶ **n.** a type of Moroccan meat pie, typically filled with spiced pigeon meat and apricots and having a sugared crust.
–ORIGIN Spanish, or Moroccan Arabic *bes̩tila*, from Spanish *pastel* pie.

PRONUNCIATION KEY ə *ago, up*; ər *over, fur*; a *hat*; ā *ate*; ä *car*; e *let*; ē *see*; i *fit*; ī *by*; NG *sing*; ō *go*; ô *law, for*; oi *toy*; o͝o *good*; o͞o *goo*; ou *out*; TH *thin*; T̲H̲ *then*; ZH *vision*

P

anelli

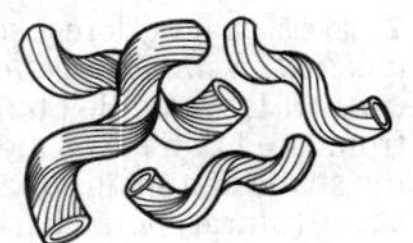

cavatappi

conchiglie

farfalle

funghetti

fusilli

garganelli

gemelli

gnocchi

lumache

orzo

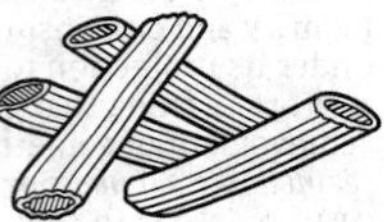

penne

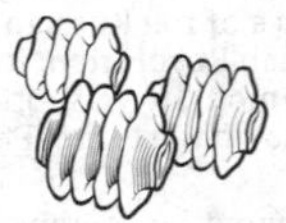

radiatori

ravioli

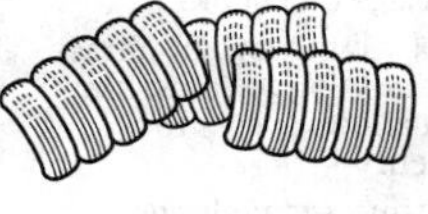

riccioli

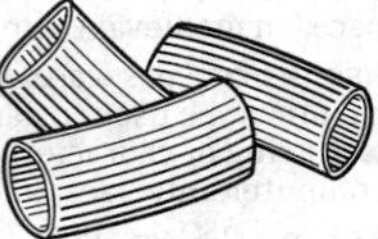

rigatoni

rotelle

stelline

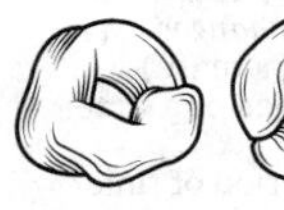

tortellini

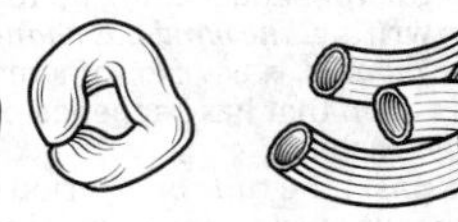

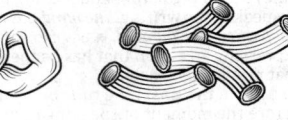

ziti

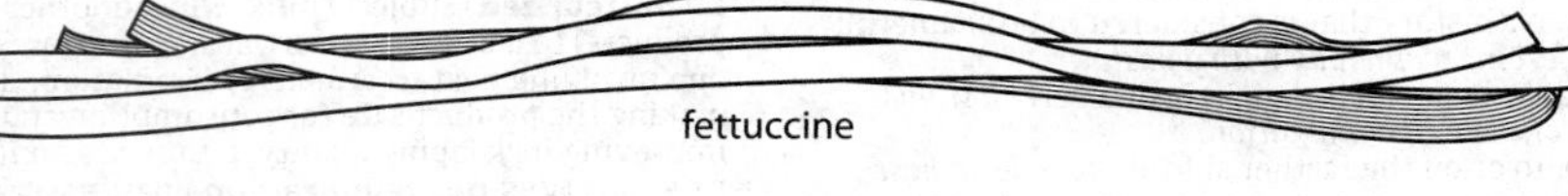

fettuccine

fusilli lunghi

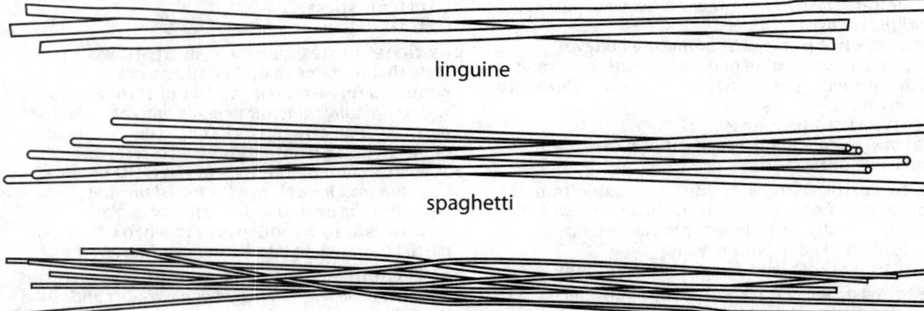

linguine

spaghetti

vermicelli

pasta shapes

pas·tille /paˈstēl/ ▶ **n.** a small candy or lozenge. ■ a small pellet of aromatic paste burned as a perfume or deodorizer.
– ORIGIN mid 17th cent.: from French, from Latin *pastillus* 'little loaf, lozenge,' from *panis* 'loaf.'

pas·time /ˈpasˌtīm/ ▶ **n.** an activity that someone does regularly for enjoyment rather than work; a hobby: *his favorite pastimes were shooting and golf.*
– ORIGIN late 15th cent.: from the verb **PASS**¹ + **TIME**, translating French *passe-temps.*

past·ing /ˈpāstiNG/ ▶ **n.** informal a severe beating or defeat: *an effort to raise party turnout at the polls and avoid a pasting.*

pas·tis /päˈstēs/ ▶ **n.** (pl. **same**) an aniseed-flavored aperitif.
– ORIGIN French.

pas·tit·sio /päˈstētsyō/ ▶ **n.** a Greek dish consisting of macaroni, ground lamb, grated cheese, and tomatoes topped with a béchamel sauce.
– ORIGIN from modern Greek, literally 'hodgepodge.'

past mas·ter ▶ **n. 1** a person who is particularly skilled at a specified activity or art: *he's a past master at keeping his whereabouts secret.*
2 a person who has held the position of master in an organization.

pas·tor /ˈpastər/ ▶ **n.** a minister in charge of a Christian church or congregation.
▶ **v.** [with obj.] be pastor of (a church or a congregation): *he pastored Peninsula Bible Church in Palo Alto* | [no obj.] *he continued to study law while pastoring in Chicago.*
– DERIVATIVES **pas·tor·ship** /-ˌSHip/ **n.**
– ORIGIN late Middle English: from Anglo-Norman French *pastour*, from Latin *pastor* 'shepherd,' from *past-* 'fed, grazed,' from the verb *pascere.*

pas·to·ral /ˈpastərəl, pasˈtôrəl/ ▶ **adj. 1** (esp. of land or a farm) used for or related to the keeping or grazing of sheep or cattle: *scattered pastoral farms.* ■ associated with country life: *the view was pastoral, with rolling fields and grazing sheep.* ■ (of a work of art) portraying or evoking country life, typically in a romanticized or idealized form.
2 (in the Christian Church) concerning or appropriate to the giving of spiritual guidance: *pastoral and doctrinal issues* | *clergy doing pastoral work.*
▶ **n.** a work of literature portraying an idealized version of country life: *the story, though a pastoral, has an actual connection with the life of agricultural labor.*
– DERIVATIVES **pas·to·ral·ism** /ˈpastərəˌlizəm/ **n.**, **pas·to·ral·ly adv.**
– ORIGIN late Middle English: from Latin *pastoralis* 'relating to a shepherd,' from *pastor* 'shepherd' (see **PASTOR**).

pas·to·rale /ˌpastəˈräl, -ˈral/ ▶ **n.** (pl. **pastorales** or **pastorali** /-ˈrälē/) **1** a slow instrumental composition in compound time, usually with drone notes in the bass.
2 a simple musical play with a rural subject.
– ORIGIN early 18th cent.: from Italian, literally 'pastoral' (adjective used as a noun).

Pas·to·ral E·pis·tles the books of the New Testament comprising the two letters of Paul to Timothy and the one to Titus.

pas·to·ral·ist /ˈpastərəlist/ ▶ **n. 1** a sheep or cattle farmer.
2 archaic a writer of pastorals.

pas·to·ral let·ter ▶ **n.** an official letter from a bishop to all the clergy or members of his or her diocese.

pas·to·ral staff ▶ **n.** a bishop's crozier.

pas·to·ral the·ol·o·gy ▶ **n.** Christian theology that considers religious truth in relation to spiritual needs.

pas·tor·ate /ˈpastərit/ ▶ **n.** the office or period of office of a pastor: *I left the pastorate in 1974.* ■ pastors collectively.

past par·ti·ci·ple ▶ **n.** Grammar the form of a verb, typically ending in *-ed* in English, that is used in forming perfect and passive tenses and sometimes as an adjective, e.g., *looked* in *have you looked?* and *lost* in *lost property.*

past per·fect ▶ **adj.** Grammar (of a tense) denoting an action completed prior to some past point of time specified or implied, formed in English by *had* and the past participle, as in *he had gone by then.*
▶ **n.** the past perfect tense.

pas·tra·mi /pəˈsträmē/ ▶ **n.** highly seasoned smoked beef, typically served in thin slices.
– ORIGIN Yiddish.

pas·try /ˈpāstrē/ ▶ **n.** (pl. **pastries**) a dough of flour, shortening, and water, used as a base and covering in baked dishes such as pies. ■ an item of food consisting of sweet pastry with a cream, jam, or fruit filling.
– ORIGIN late Middle English (as a collective term): from **PASTE**, influenced by Old French *pastaierie.*

pas·try chef ▶ **n.** a professional cook who specializes in making desserts, esp. cakes and pastries.

pas·try cream ▶ **n.** a thick, creamy custard used as a filling for cakes or flans.

pas·tur·age /ˈpasCHərij/ ▶ **n.** land used for pasture. ■ the occupation or process of pasturing cattle, sheep, or other grazing animals: *the human species has only engaged in pasturage for 12,000 to 15,000 years.*
– ORIGIN early 16th cent.: from Old French, from *pasture* (see **PASTURE**).

pas·ture /ˈpasCHər/ ▶ **n. 1** land covered with grass and other low plants suitable for grazing animals, esp. cattle or sheep.
2 (**pastures**) used to refer to a person's situation in life: *he has departed for the greener pastures of a corner office.*

p

▶ v. [with obj.] put (animals) in a pasture to graze: *they pastured their cows in the water meadow.* ■ [no obj.] (of animals) graze: *the livestock pastured and the crops grew.*
– PHRASES **put someone out to pasture** force someone to retire.
– ORIGIN Middle English: from Old French, from late Latin *pastura* 'grazing,' from *past-* 'grazed,' from the verb *pascere*.

pas·ture·land /ˈpasCHər,land/ ▶ n. land used as pasture.

pas·ture rose ▶ n. a wild rose of the eastern US with deep pink flowers and straight, thin thorns. Also called CAROLINA ROSE. ● *Rosa carolina*, family Rosaceae.

pasture rose

past·y[1] /ˈpastē/ (also **pastie**) ▶ n. (pl. **pasties**) chiefly Brit. a folded pastry case filled with seasoned meat and vegetables.
– ORIGIN Middle English: from Old French *paste(e)*, based on late Latin *pasta* 'paste.'

past·y[2] /ˈpāstē/ ▶ adj. (**pastier**, **pastiest**) **1** (of a person's face) unhealthily pale: *a pasty complexion.*
2 of or like paste: *a pasty mixture.*
– DERIVATIVES **past·i·ness** /-stēnis/ n.

pat[1] /pat/ ▶ v. (**pats**, **patting**, **patted**) [with obj.] touch quickly and gently with the flat of the hand: *he patted him consolingly on the shoulder* | [with obj. and complement] *a nurse washed her all over and patted her dry.* ■ draw attention to (something) by tapping it gently: *he patted the bench beside him and I sat down.* ■ mold into shape or put in position with gentle taps: *she patted down the earth in each pot.*
▶ n. **1** a light stroke with the hand: *giving him a friendly pat on the arm, she went off to join the others.*
2 a compact mass of soft material: *a pat of butter.*
– PHRASES **a pat on the back** an expression of approval or congratulation: *they deserve a pat on the back for a job well done.* **pat someone on the back** express approval of or admiration for someone: *she needs her own claque to applaud and pat her on the back.*
– ORIGIN late Middle English (as a noun denoting a blow with something flat): probably imitative. The verb dates from the mid 16th cent.

pat[2] ▶ adj. simple and somewhat glib or unconvincing: *instead of enlightened minds I found prejudice and pat answers.*
▶ adv. at exactly the right moment or in the right way; conveniently or opportunely: *the happy ending came rather pat.*
– PHRASES **down pat** see DOWN[1]. **stand pat** stick stubbornly to one's opinion or decision: *many ranchers stood pat with the old strains of cattle.* ■ (in poker and blackjack) retain one's hand as dealt, without drawing other cards.
– DERIVATIVES **pat·ly** adv., **pat·ness** n.
– ORIGIN late 16th cent.: related to PAT[1]; apparently originally symbolic: a frequently found early use was *hit pat* (i.e., hit as if with a flat blow).

Pat. ▶ abbr. Patent.

pa·ta·gi·um /pəˈtājēəm/ ▶ n. (pl. **patagia** /-jēə/) Zoology a membrane or fold of skin between the forelimbs and hind limbs on each side of a bat or gliding mammal. ■ Entomology a lobe that covers the wing joint in many moths.
– ORIGIN early 19th cent.: from Latin, denoting gold edging on the edge of a Roman lady's tunic, from Greek *patageion*.

Pat·a·go·ni·a /,patəˈgōnēə/ a region in South America, in southern Argentina and Chile. Mostly a dry, barren plateau, it extends from the Colorado River in central Argentina to the Strait of Magellan and from the Andes to the Atlantic coast.
– DERIVATIVES **Pat·a·go·ni·an** adj. & n.
– ORIGIN from obsolete *Patagon*, denoting a member of a native people alleged by travelers of the 17th and 18th cents. to be the tallest known.

Pat·a·go·ni·an tooth·fish /ˈto͞oTH,fiSH/ ▶ n. a demersal food fish of Antarctic waters, marketed as Chilean sea bass and recently overfished. ● *Dissostichus eleginoides*, family Nototheniidae.

Pa·ta·li·pu·tra /,pätäləˈpo͝otrə/ ancient name for PATNA.

pa·ta·phys·ics /,pätəˈfiziks/ ▶ plural n. [usu. treated as sing.] the branch of philosophy that deals with an imaginary realm additional to metaphysics.
– ORIGIN 1940s: from Greek *ta epi ta metaphusika*, literally 'the (works) imposed on the Metaphysics.' The concept was introduced by Alfred Jarry (1873–1907), French writer of the Absurd.

pa·tas mon·key /pəˈtä/ ▶ n. a central African guenon with reddish-brown fur, a black face, and a white mustache. ● *Erythrocebus patas*, family Cercopithecidae.
– ORIGIN mid 18th cent.: *patas* from Senegalese French, from Wolof *pata*.

Pa·tau's syn·drome /päˈtouz/ ▶ n. Medicine a congenital disorder in which there are three copies of chromosome 13, 14, or 15 instead of the usual two. This results in brain, heart, and kidney defects that are usually fatal soon after birth.
– ORIGIN 1960s: named after Klaus *Patau*, 20th-cent. German physician.

Pa·ta·vi·um /pəˈtāvēəm/ Latin name for PADUA.

patch /paCH/ ▶ n. **1** a piece of cloth or other material used to mend or strengthen a torn or weak point. ■ a pad or shield worn over a sightless or injured eye or an eye socket. ■ a piece of cloth sewn onto clothing as a badge or distinguishing mark. ■ Computing a small piece of code inserted into a program to improve its functioning or to correct an error. ■ an adhesive piece of drug-impregnated material worn on the skin so that the drug can be absorbed gradually over a period of time. ■ a part of something marked out from the rest by a particular characteristic: *his hair was combed forward to hide a growing bald patch.* ■ a small area or amount of something: *patches of bluebells in the grass.* ■ historical a small disk of black silk attached to the face, esp. as worn by women in the 17th and 18th centuries for adornment.
2 a small piece of ground, esp. one used for gardening: *they spent Sundays digging their vegetable patch.* ■ Brit. informal an area for which someone is responsible or in which they operate: *we didn't want any secret organizations on our patch.*
3 informal a period of time seen as a distinct unit with a characteristic quality: ***he may have been going through a bad patch.***
4 a temporary electrical or telephone connection. ■ a preset configuration or sound-data file in an electronic musical instrument, esp. a synthesizer.
▶ v. [with obj.] **1** mend or strengthen (fabric or an item of clothing) by putting a piece of material over a hole or weak point in it: *her jeans were neatly patched.* ■ Medicine place a patch over (a good eye) in order to encourage a lazy eye to work. ■ Computing correct, enhance, or modify (a routine or program) by inserting a patch. ■ (usu. **be patched**) cover small areas of (a surface) with something different, causing it to appear variegated: *the grass was patched with sandy stretches.* ■ (**patch someone/something up**) informal treat someone's injuries or repair the damage to something, esp. hastily: *they did their best to patch up the gaping wounds.* ■ (**patch something together**) construct something hastily from unsuitable components: *lean-tos patched together from aluminum siding and planks* | figurative *they were trying to patch together an arrangement for cooperation.* ■ (**patch something up**) informal restore peaceful or friendly relations after a quarrel or dispute: *any ill feeling could be patched up with a phone call* | *they sent him home to patch things up with his wife.*
2 connect by a temporary electrical, radio, or telephonic connection: *Ralph had **patched** her **through** to the meeting by walkie-talkie.* ■ [no obj.] become connected in this way: *stay on the open line and we'll patch in on you.*
– PHRASES **not a patch on** Brit. informal greatly inferior to: *he no longer looked so handsome—he wasn't a patch on Peter.*
– DERIVATIVES **patch·er** n.
– ORIGIN late Middle English: perhaps from a variant of Old French *pieche*, dialect variant of *piece* 'piece.'

patch·board /ˈpaCH,bôrd/ ▶ n. another term for PATCH PANEL.

patch box ▶ n. historical a decorated box for holding black silk patches for the face, used esp. by women in the 17th and 18th centuries.

patch cord ▶ n. an insulated cord with a plug at each end, for use with a patch panel.

patch·ou·li /pəˈCHo͞olē/ ▶ n. **1** an aromatic oil obtained from a Southeast Asian shrub and used in perfumery, insecticides, and medicine.
2 the strongly scented shrub of the mint family from which this oil is obtained. ● *Pogostemon cablin*, family Labiatae.
– ORIGIN mid 19th cent.: from Tamil.

patch pan·el (also **patchboard**) ▶ n. a board in a switchboard, computer, or other device with a number of electric sockets that can be connected in various combinations.

patch pock·et ▶ n. a pocket made of a separate piece of cloth sewn onto the outside of a garment.

patch reef ▶ n. a small, isolated platform of coral.

patch test ▶ n. a test to discover whether a person is allergic to any of several substances that are applied to the skin in light scratches or under a patch.

patch·work /ˈpaCH,wərk/ ▶ n. needlework in which small pieces of cloth in different designs, colors, or textures are sewn together: *a quilt of patchwork* | [as modifier] *patchwork bell-bottoms.* ■ the craft of sewing in this way: ***specialists in quilting and patchwork.*** ■ a thing composed of many different elements so as to appear variegated: *a patchwork of stone walls and green fields.*

patch·y /ˈpaCHē/ ▶ adj. (**patchier**, **patchiest**) existing or happening in small, isolated areas: *patchy fog.* ■ not of the same quality throughout; inconsistent: *your coursework was patchy* | *my knowledge of Egyptology is patchy.*
– DERIVATIVES **patch·i·ly** /ˈpaCHəlē/ adv., **patch·i·ness** /ˈpaCHēnis/ n.

patd. ▶ abbr. patented.

pate /pāt/ ▶ n. archaic or humorous a person's head: *he scratched his balding pate.*
– ORIGIN Middle English: of unknown origin.

pâte /pät/ ▶ n. the paste of which porcelain is made.
– ORIGIN mid 19th cent.: French, literally 'paste.'

pâ·té /päˈtā/ ▶ n. a rich, savory paste made from finely minced or mashed ingredients, typically seasoned meat or fish.
– ORIGIN French, from Old French *paste* 'pie of seasoned meat.'

pâ·té de cam·pag·ne /päˈtā də kämˈpänyə/ ▶ n. coarse pork and liver pâté.
– ORIGIN French, literally 'country pâté.'

pâ·té de foie gras /päˈtā də ,fwä ˈgrä/ ▶ n. a smooth rich paste made from fattened goose or duck liver.
– ORIGIN French.

pa·tel·la /pəˈtelə/ ▶ n. (pl. **patellae** /-lē/) Anatomy the kneecap.
– DERIVATIVES **pa·tel·lar** /-ˈtelər/ adj., **pa·tel·late** /-ˈtelit, -,lāt/ adj.
– ORIGIN late 16th cent.: from Latin, diminutive of *patina* 'shallow dish.'

pat·en /ˈpatn/ ▶ n. a plate, typically made of gold or silver, used for holding the bread during the Eucharist and sometimes as a cover for the chalice. ■ a shallow metal plate or dish.
– ORIGIN Middle English: from Old French *patene*, from Latin *patina* 'shallow dish,' from Greek *patanē* 'a plate.'

pa·ten·cy /ˈpatn-sē, ˈpātn-/ ▶ n. Medicine the condition of being open, expanded, or unobstructed. ■ the condition of showing detectable parasite infection.

pat·ent ▶ n. /ˈpatnt/ **1** a government authority or license conferring a right or title for a set period, especially the sole right to exclude others from making, using, or selling an invention: ***he took out a patent for an improved steam hammer.*** [Compare with LETTERS PATENT.]
2 short for PATENT LEATHER.
▶ adj. **1** /ˈpātnt, ˈpat-/ easily recognizable; obvious: *she was smiling with patent insincerity.*
2 Medicine /ˈpātnt, ˈpat-/ (of a vessel, duct, or aperture) open and unobstructed; failing to close. ■ (of a parasitic infection) showing detectable parasites in the tissues or feces.
3 /ˈpatnt/ [attrib.] made and marketed under a patent; proprietary: *patent milk powder.*
▶ v. /ˈpatnt/ [with obj.] obtain a patent for (an invention): *an invention is not your own until it is patented.*
– DERIVATIVES **pat·ent·a·bil·i·ty** n., **pat·ent·a·ble** adj.
– ORIGIN late Middle English: from Old French, from Latin *patent-* 'lying open,' from the verb *patere*.

pat·ent·ee /,patnˈtē/ ▶ n. a person or organization that obtains or holds a patent for something.

pat·ent leath·er ▶ n. leather with a glossy varnished surface, used chiefly for shoes, belts, and purses.

pat·ent log ▶ n. a mechanical device used to measure the speed and distance traveled through the water of a ship or boat.

pat·ent·ly /ˈpatntlē/ ▶ adv. [usu. as submodifier] clearly; without doubt: *these claims were patently false.*

pat·ent med·i·cine ▶ n. a proprietary medicine made and marketed under a patent and available without prescription.

pat·ent of·fice ▶ n. an office from which patents are issued.

pat·ent right ▶ n. the exclusive right conferred by a patent: *one of the collaborators has agreed to waive its patent rights to the cowpea gene.*

PRONUNCIATION KEY ə *ago, up*; ər *over, fur*; a *hat*; ā *ate*; ä *car*; e *let*; ē *see*; i *fit*; ī *by*; NG *sing*; ō *go*; ô *law, for*; oi *toy*; o͝o *good*; o͞o *goo*; ou *out*; TH *thin*; T̲H̲ *then*; ZH *vision*

P

pa·ter /ˈpātər, ˈpä-, ˈpa-/ ▶ **n. 1** Brit. informal, dated father: *the pater gives her fifty pounds a year as a dress allowance.*
2 Anthropology a person's legal father. Often contrasted with **GENITOR**.
– ORIGIN Latin.

pat·er·a /ˈpatərə/ ▶ **n.** (pl. **paterae** /-ərē/) **1** a broad shallow dish used in ancient Rome for pouring libations. ■ Architecture a flat, round ornament resembling a shallow dish.
2 a broad, shallow bowl-shaped feature on a planet's surface.
– ORIGIN Latin, from *patere* 'be or lie open.'

pa·ter·fa·mil·i·as /ˌpātərfəˈmilēəs, ˌpä-/ ▶ **n.** (pl. **patresfamilias** /ˌpātrēzfə-, ˌpä-/) the male head of a family or household. Compare with **MATERFAMILIAS**.
– ORIGIN Latin, literally 'father of the family.'

pa·ter·nal /pəˈtərnl/ ▶ **adj.** of or appropriate to a father: *he reasserted his paternal authority.* ■ showing a kindness and care associated with a father; fatherly: *my elders in the newsroom kept a paternal eye on me.* ■ [attrib.] related through the father: *his father and paternal grandfather were porcelain painters.*
– DERIVATIVES **pa·ter·nal·ly** adv.
– ORIGIN late Middle English: from late Latin *paternalis*, from Latin *paternus* 'fatherly, belonging to a father,' from *pater* 'father.'

pa·ter·nal·ism /pəˈtərnlˌizəm/ ▶ **n.** the policy or practice on the part of people in positions of authority of restricting the freedom and responsibilities of those subordinate to them in the subordinates' supposed best interest: *the arrogance and paternalism that underlies cradle-to-grave employment contracts.*
– DERIVATIVES **pa·ter·nal·ist** n. & adj., **pa·ter·nal·is·tic** /-ˌtərnlˈistik/ adj., **pa·ter·nal·is·ti·cal·ly** /-ˌtərnlˈistik(ə)lē/ adv.

pa·ter·ni·ty /pəˈtərnitē/ ▶ **n. 1** (esp. in legal contexts) the state of being someone's father: *he refused to admit paternity of the child.*
2 paternal origin: *his enemies made great play of the supposed dubiety of his paternity.*
– ORIGIN late Middle English: from Old French *paternité*, from late Latin *paternitas*, from *paternus* 'relating to a father.'

pa·ter·ni·ty suit ▶ **n.** a court case held to establish formally the identity of a child's father, typically in order to require the man to support the child financially.

pa·ter·ni·ty test ▶ **n.** a medical test, typically a blood test, to determine whether a man may be the father of a particular child.

pa·ter·nos·ter /ˈpātərˌnästər, ˈpatər-/ ▶ **n. 1** (in the Roman Catholic Church) the Lord's Prayer, esp. in Latin. ■ any of a number of special beads occurring at regular intervals in a rosary, indicating that the Lord's Prayer is to be recited.
2 (also **paternoster lift**) an elevator consisting of a series of linked doorless compartments moving continuously on an endless belt.
– ORIGIN Old English, from Latin *pater noster* 'our father,' the first words of the Lord's Prayer.

Pat·er·son[1] /ˈpatərsən/ a historic industrial city in northeastern New Jersey, on the Passaic River; pop. 145,643 (est. 2008).

Pat·er·son[2], William (1745–1806), US Supreme Court associate justice 1793–1806. A US senator 1789–90 and governor of New Jersey 1790–93, he was appointed to the Court by President Washington.

path /paTH/ ▶ **n.** (pl. **paths** /paT͟Hz, paTHs/) a way or track laid down for walking or made by continual treading. ■ the course or direction in which a person or thing is moving: *the missile traced a fiery path in the sky* | figurative *a chosen career path.* ■ a course of action or conduct: *an ordered, gradual path toward economic liberalization.* ■ a schedule available for allocation to an individual railroad train over a given route. ■ Computing a definition of the order in which an operating system or program searches for a file or executable program.
▶ **v.** [no obj.] (usu. as noun **pathing**) (esp. in computing and railroad contexts) allocate a path.
– PHRASES **the path of least resistance** see **RESISTANCE**.
– DERIVATIVES **path·less** adj.
– ORIGIN Old English *pæth*; related to Dutch *pad*, German *Pfad*, of unknown ultimate origin.

path. ▶ **abbr.** ■ pathological. ■ pathology.

-path ▶ **comb. form 1** denoting a practitioner of curative treatment: *homeopath.*
2 denoting a person who suffers from a disease: *psychopath.*
– ORIGIN back-formation from **-PATHY**, or from Greek *-pathēs* '-sufferer.'

Pa·than /pəˈtän/ (also **Pashtun** /pəSHˈto͞on/) ▶ **n.** a member of a Pashto-speaking people inhabiting northwestern Pakistan and southeastern Afghanistan.
– ORIGIN from Hindi *Paṭhān*.

path·break·ing /ˈpaTHˌbrākiNG/ ▶ **adj.** pioneering; innovative: *their pathbreaking work opened up a new era in cancer research.*
– DERIVATIVES **path·break·er** n.

Pa·thé /päˈtā/, Charles (1863–1957), French movie pioneer. In 1896 he and his brothers founded a company that eventually dominated the production and distribution of movies.

pa·thet·ic /pəˈTHetik/ ▶ **adj. 1** arousing pity, esp. through vulnerability or sadness: *she looked so pathetic that I bent down to comfort her.* ■ informal miserably inadequate: *his test scores in Chemistry were pathetic.*
2 archaic relating to the emotions.
– DERIVATIVES **pa·thet·i·cal·ly** /-(ə)lē/ adv.
– ORIGIN late 16th cent. (in the sense 'affecting the emotions'): via late Latin from Greek *pathētikos* 'sensitive,' based on *pathos* 'suffering.'

pa·thet·ic fal·la·cy ▶ **n.** the attribution of human feelings and responses to inanimate things or animals, esp. in art and literature.

Path·find·er /ˈpaTHˌfīndər/ (in full **Mars Pathfinder**) an unmanned American spacecraft that landed on Mars in 1997, deploying a small robotic rover (*Sojourner*) to explore the surface and examine the rocks.

path·find·er /ˈpaTHˌfīndər/ ▶ **n.** a person who goes ahead and discovers or shows others a path or way. ■ an aircraft or its pilot sent ahead to locate and mark the target area for bombing. ■ [usu. as modifier] an experimental plan or forecast: *a pathfinder prospectus.*

path length ▶ **n.** Physics the overall length of the path followed by a light ray or sound wave.

path·name /ˈpaTHˌnām/ (also **path name**) ▶ **n.** Computing a statement of the location of a file or other item in a hierarchy of directories.

patho- ▶ **comb. form** relating to disease: *pathogenesis* | *pathology.*
– ORIGIN from Greek *pathos* 'suffering, disease.'

path·o·gen /ˈpaTHəjən, -ˌjen/ ▶ **n.** Medicine a bacterium, virus, or other microorganism that can cause disease.
– DERIVATIVES **path·o·gen·ic** /ˌpaTHəˈjenik/ adj., **path·o·ge·nic·i·ty** /ˌpaTHəjəˌnisitē/ n., **pa·thog·e·nous** /pəˈTHäjənəs/ adj.

path·o·gen·e·sis /ˌpaTHəˈjenəsis/ ▶ **n.** Medicine the manner of development of a disease.
– DERIVATIVES **path·o·ge·net·ic** /-jəˈnetik/ adj.

pa·thog·no·mon·ic /pəˌTHägnəˈmänik, ˌpaTHəgnə-/ ▶ **adj.** Medicine (of a sign or symptom) specifically characteristic or indicative of a particular disease or condition.
– ORIGIN early 17th cent.: from Greek *pathognōmonikos* 'skilled in diagnosis,' from *pathos* 'suffering' + *gnōmōn* 'judge.'

pa·thog·ra·phy /pəˈTHägrəfē/ ▶ **n.** (pl. **pathographies**) a study of the life of an individual or the history of a community with regard to the influence of a particular disease or psychological disorder.

path·o·log·i·cal /ˌpaTHəˈläjikəl/ (also **pathologic**) ▶ **adj.** of or relating to pathology: *the interpretation of pathological studies.* ■ involving, caused by, or of the nature of a physical or mental disease: *pathological changes associated with senile dementia.* ■ informal compulsive; obsessive: *a pathological gambler.*
– DERIVATIVES **path·o·log·i·cal·ly** adv.

pa·thol·o·gize /pəˈTHäləˌjīz/ ▶ **v.** [with obj.] regard or treat (someone or something) as psychologically abnormal or unhealthy.
– DERIVATIVES **pa·thol·o·gi·za·tion** /pəˌTHäləjəˈzāSHən/ n.

pa·thol·o·gy /pəˈTHäləjē/ ▶ **n.** the science of the causes and effects of diseases, esp. the branch of medicine that deals with the laboratory examination of samples of body tissue for diagnostic or forensic purposes. ■ Medicine pathological features considered collectively; the typical behavior of a disease: *the pathology of Huntington's disease.* ■ Medicine a pathological condition: *the dominant pathology is multiple sclerosis.* ■ mental, social, or linguistic abnormality or malfunction: *the city's inability to cope with the pathology of a burgeoning underclass.*
– DERIVATIVES **pa·thol·o·gist** /-jist/ n.
– ORIGIN early 17th cent.: from modern or medieval Latin *pathologia* (see **PATHO-**, **-LOGY**).

path·o·phys·i·ol·o·gy /ˌpaTHəˌfizēˈäləjē/ ▶ **n.** Medicine the disordered physiological processes associated with disease or injury: *intracranial hypertension contributes to the pathophysiology of this condition.*
– DERIVATIVES **path·o·phys·i·o·log·ic** /-ˌfizēəˈläjik/ adj., **path·o·phys·i·o·log·i·cal** /-ˌfizēəˈläjikəl/ adj., **path·o·phys·i·o·log·i·cal·ly** /ˌfizēəˈläjik(ə)lē/ adv., **path·o·phys·i·ol·o·gist** /-jist/ n.

pa·thos /ˈpāˌTHäs, -ˌTHôs/ ▶ **n.** a quality that evokes pity or sadness: *the actor injects his customary humor and pathos into the role.*
– ORIGIN mid 17th cent.: from Greek *pathos* 'suffering'; related to *paskhein* 'suffer' and *penthos* 'grief.'

path·way /ˈpaTHˌwā/ ▶ **n.** a way that constitutes or serves as a path. ■ Physiology a route, formed by a chain of nerve cells, along which impulses of a particular kind usually travel. ■ (also **metabolic pathway**) Biochemistry a sequence of chemical reactions undergone by a compound or class of compounds in a living organism.

-pathy ▶ **comb. form 1** denoting feelings: *telepathy.*
2 denoting disorder in a particular part of the body: *neuropathy.*
3 relating to curative treatment of a specified kind: *hydropathy.*
– ORIGIN from Greek *patheia* 'suffering, feeling.'

pa·tience /ˈpāSHəns/ ▶ **n. 1** the capacity to accept or tolerate delay, trouble, or suffering without getting angry or upset: *you can find bargains if you have the patience to sift through the dross.*
2 chiefly British term for **SOLITAIRE** (sense 1).
– PHRASES **lose patience** (or **lose one's patience**) become unable to keep one's temper: *even Lawrence finally lost patience with him.*
– ORIGIN Middle English: from Old French, from Latin *patientia*, from *patient-* 'suffering,' from the verb *pati.*

pa·tient /ˈpāSHənt/ ▶ **adj.** able to accept or tolerate delays, problems, or suffering without becoming annoyed or anxious: *be patient, your time will come.*
▶ **n. 1** a person receiving or registered to receive medical treatment.
2 Linguistics the semantic role of a noun phrase denoting something that is affected or acted upon by the action of a verb.
– DERIVATIVES **pa·tient·ly** adv.
– ORIGIN Middle English: from Old French, from Latin *patient-* 'suffering,' from the verb *pati.*

pa·tient Lu·cy /ˈlo͞osē/ ▶ **n.** chiefly British term for **IMPATIENS**.

pa·ti·na /pəˈtēnə/ ▶ **n.** a green or brown film on the surface of bronze or similar metals, produced by oxidation over a long period. ■ a gloss or sheen on wooden furniture produced by age and polishing. ■ an impression or appearance of something: *he carries the patina of old money and good breeding.*
– DERIVATIVES **pat·i·nat·ed** /ˈpatnˌātid/ adj., **pat·i·na·tion** /ˌpatnˈāSHən/ n.
– ORIGIN mid 18th cent.: from Italian, from Latin *patina* 'shallow dish.'

pat·i·o /ˈpatēˌō/ ▶ **n.** (pl. **patios**) a paved outdoor area adjoining a house. ■ a roofless inner courtyard in a Spanish or Spanish-American house.
– ORIGIN early 19th cent.: from Spanish, denoting an inner courtyard.

pat·i·o rose ▶ **n.** a miniature floribunda rose.

pa·tis·se·rie /pəˈtisərē/ ▶ **n.** a shop where French pastries and cakes are sold. ■ French pastries and cakes collectively.
– ORIGIN late 16th cent.: from French *pâtisserie*, from medieval Latin *pasticium* 'pastry,' from *pasta* 'paste.'

pa·tis·sier /pätisˈyā/ ▶ **n.** (pl. pronunc. **same**) a maker or seller of pastries and cakes.
– ORIGIN mid 19th cent.: French.

pat·ka /ˈpətkä/ ▶ **n.** a man's head covering consisting of a small piece of cloth wrapped around the head, worn esp. by Sikh boys or young men.
– ORIGIN Punjabi *paṭkā* from Sanskrit *paṭṭikā* 'turban cloth.'

Pat·mos /ˈpatməs, -məs, ˈpatmôs/ a Greek island in the Aegean Sea, one of the Dodecanese group. It is believed that St. John was living here in exile (from AD 95) when he had the visions described in Revelation.

Pat·na /ˈpatnə, ˈpət-/ a city in northeastern India, on the Ganges River, capital of the state of Bihar; pop. 1,814,000 (est. 2009). An important city in ancient times, it was deserted by the 7th century but was refounded in 1541 by the Moguls and became a viceregal capital. Former name **PATALIPUTRA**.

pat·ois /ˈpaˌtwä, ˈpä-/ ▶ **n.** (pl. **same**) the dialect of the common people of a region, differing in various respects from the standard language of the rest of the country: *the nurse talked to me in a patois that even Italians would have had difficulty in understanding.* ■ the jargon or informal speech used by a particular social group: *the raunchy patois of inner-city kids.*

–ORIGIN mid 17th cent.: French, literally 'rough speech,' perhaps from Old French *patoier* 'treat roughly,' from *patte* 'paw.'

Pa·ton /'pātn/, Alan (Stewart) (1903–88), South African writer and politician. He is best known for his novel *Cry, the Beloved Country* (1948), a passionate indictment of the apartheid system.

pa·tonce /pə'täns/ ▶ **adj.** [postpositive] Heraldry (of a cross) with limbs that broaden from the center and end in three pointed lobes: *a cross patonce.*
–ORIGIN mid 16th cent.: probably related to French *potencé*, a heraldic term denoting T-shaped endings to each limb of a cross, based on medieval Latin *potentia* 'crutch.'

pa·too·tie /pə'to͞otē/ ▶ **n.** (pl. **patooties**) informal
1 dated a girlfriend or a pretty girl.
2 derogatory a person's or animal's buttocks.
–ORIGIN 1920s: perhaps an alteration of **POTATO**.

Pa·tras /pə'tras, 'patrəs/ an industrial port in the northwestern Peloponnese, on the Gulf of Patras; pop. 167,400 (est. 2009). It was the site in 1821 of the outbreak of the Greek war of independence. Greek name **Pátrai**.

pa·tres·fa·mil·i·as /ˌpatrēzfə'milēəs, ˌpä-/ plural form of **PATERFAMILIAS**.

pa·tri·a /'pātrēə, 'pa-, 'pä-/ ▶ **n.** one's native country or homeland: *they remained faithful to their patria, Spain.* ■ archaic heaven, regarded as the true home from which the soul is exiled while on earth.
–ORIGIN Latin.

pa·tri·arch /'pātrēˌärk/ ▶ **n. 1** the male head of a family or tribe. ■ a man who is the oldest or most venerable of a group: *Hollywood's reigning patriarch rose to speak.* ■ a person or thing that is regarded as the founder of something: *the patriarch of all spin doctors.*
2 any of those biblical figures regarded as fathers of the human race, esp. Abraham, Isaac, and Jacob, their forefathers, or the sons of Jacob.
3 the title of a most senior Orthodox or Catholic bishop, in particular: ■ a bishop of one of the most ancient Christian sees (Alexandria, Antioch, Constantinople, Jerusalem, and formerly Rome). ■ the head of an autocephalous or independent Orthodox church. ■ a Roman Catholic bishop ranking above primates and metropolitans and immediately below the pope, often the head of a Uniate community.
–ORIGIN Middle English: from Old French *patriarche*, via ecclesiastical Latin from Greek *patriarkhēs*, from *patria* 'family' + *arkhēs* 'ruling.'

pa·tri·ar·chal /ˌpātrē'ärkəl/ ▶ **adj. 1** of, relating to, or characteristic of a patriarch.
2 of, relating to, or characteristic of a system of society or government controlled by men: *patriarchal values.*
–DERIVATIVES **pa·tri·ar·chal·ly** **adv.**

pa·tri·ar·chal cross ▶ **n.** a Christian cross with a smaller crossbar above the main one. In heraldry it denotes the rank of bishop or archbishop.

pa·tri·arch·ate /'pātrēˌärkit/ ▶ **n.** the office, see, or residence of an ecclesiastical patriarch.

pa·tri·arch·y /'pātrēˌärkē/ ▶ **n.** (pl. **patriarchies**) a system of society or government in which the father or eldest male is head of the family and descent is traced through the male line. ■ a system of society or government in which men hold the power and women are largely excluded from it. ■ a society or community organized in this way.
–ORIGIN mid 17th cent.: via medieval Latin from Greek *patriarkhia*, from *patriarkhēs* 'ruling father' (see **PATRIARCH**).

pa·tri·ate /'pātrēˌāt/ ▶ **v.** [with obj.] transfer control over (a constitution) from a mother country to its former dependency: *the Canadian government moved to patriate the constitution from Great Britain.*

pa·tri·cian /pə'trisHən/ ▶ **n.** an aristocrat or nobleman. ■ a member of a long-established wealthy family. ■ a member of a noble family or class in ancient Rome.
▶ **adj.** belonging to or characteristic of the aristocracy: *a proud, patrician face.* ■ belonging to or characteristic of a long-established and wealthy family. ■ belonging to the nobility of ancient Rome.
–ORIGIN late Middle English: from Old French *patricien*, from Latin *patricius* 'having a noble father,' from *pater, patr-* 'father.'

pa·tri·ci·ate /pə'trisHē-it, -ˌāt/ ▶ **n.** a noble order or class: *the Venetian merchants became a great hereditary patriciate.* ■ the position or rank of patrician in ancient Rome.

pat·ri·cide /'patrəˌsīd/ ▶ **n.** the killing of one's father. ■ a person who kills their father.
–DERIVATIVES **pat·ri·cid·al** /ˌpatrə'sīdl/ **adj.**
–ORIGIN early 17th cent.: from late Latin *patricidium*, alteration of Latin *parricidium* (see **PARRICIDE**).

Pat·rick, St. /'patrik/ (5th century), apostle and patron saint of Ireland. Of Romano-British parentage, he was taken as a slave to Ireland, where he experienced a religious conversion. Feast day, March 17.

pat·ri·lin·e·al /ˌpatrə'linēəl/ ▶ **adj.** of, relating to, or based on relationship to the father or descent through the male line: *in Polynesia inheritance of land was predominantly patrilineal.*
–ORIGIN early 20th cent.: from Latin *pater, patr-* 'father' + **LINEAL**.

pat·ri·lo·cal /ˌpatrə'lōkəl/ ▶ **adj.** of or relating to a pattern of marriage in which the couple settles in the husband's home or community: *women moved more often than men because patterns of settlement after marriage tended to be patrilocal.*
–DERIVATIVES **pat·ri·lo·cal·i·ty** /-lō'kalətē/ **n.**
–ORIGIN early 20th cent.: from Latin *pater, patr-* 'father' + **LOCAL**.

pat·ri·mo·ny /'patrəˌmōnē/ ▶ **n.** (pl. **patrimonies**) property inherited from one's father or male ancestor. ■ heritage: *an organization that saves the world's cultural patrimony by restoring historic buildings.* ■ chiefly historical the estate or property belonging by ancient endowment or right to a church or other institution.
–DERIVATIVES **pat·ri·mo·ni·al** /ˌpatrə'mōnēəl/ **adj.**
–ORIGIN Middle English: from Old French *patrimoine*, from Latin *patrimonium*, from *pater, patr-* 'father.'

pa·tri·ot /'pātrēət/ ▶ **n. 1** a person who vigorously supports their country and is prepared to defend it against enemies or detractors.
2 (**Patriot**) trademark an automated surface-to-air missile designed for preemptive strikes.
–DERIVATIVES **pa·tri·ot·ism** /-ˌtizəm/ **n.**
–ORIGIN late 16th cent. (in the late Latin sense): from French *patriote*, from late Latin *patriota* 'fellow countryman,' from Greek *patriōtēs*, from *patrios* 'of one's fathers,' from *patris* 'fatherland.'

pa·tri·ot·ic /ˌpātrē'ätik/ ▶ **adj.** having or expressing devotion to and vigorous support for one's country: *today's game will be played before a fiercely patriotic crowd.*
–DERIVATIVES **pa·tri·ot·i·cal·ly** /-(ə)lē/ **adv.**
–ORIGIN mid 17th cent.: via late Latin from Greek *patriōtikos* 'relating to a fellow countryman' (see **PATRIOT**).

pa·tri·ot·ic front ▶ **n.** a militant nationalist political organization.

pa·tris·tic /pə'tristik/ ▶ **adj.** of or relating to the early Christian theologians or to patristics.
–ORIGIN mid 19th cent.: from German *patristisch*, from Latin *pater, patr-* 'father.'

pa·tris·tics /pə'tristiks/ ▶ **plural n.** [treated as sing.] the branch of Christian theology that deals with the lives, writings, and doctrines of the early Christian theologians.

Pa·tro·clus /pə'trōkləs/ Greek Mythology a Greek hero of the Trojan War, the close friend of Achilles.

pa·trol /pə'trōl/ ▶ **n.** a person or group of people sent to keep watch over an area, esp. a detachment of guards or police: *a police patrol stopped the man and searched him.* ■ the action of keeping watch over an area by walking or driving around it at regular intervals: *the policemen were* **on patrol** *when they were ordered to investigate the incident.* ■ an expedition to carry out reconnaissance: *we were ordered to investigate on a night patrol.* ■ a routine operational voyage of a ship or aircraft: *a submarine patrol.* ■ a unit of six to eight Girl Scouts or Boy Scouts forming part of a troop.
▶ **v.** (**patrols, patrolling, patrolled**) [with obj.] keep watch over (an area) by regularly walking or traveling around or through it: *the garrison had to patrol the streets to maintain order* | [no obj.] *pairs of men were patrolling on each side of the thoroughfare.*
–DERIVATIVES **pa·trol·ler** **n.**
–ORIGIN mid 17th cent. (as a noun): from German *Patrolle*, from French *patrouille*, from *patrouiller* 'paddle in mud,' from *patte* 'paw' + dialect (*gad*) *rouille* 'dirty water.'

pa·trol car ▶ **n.** a police car used used for patrolling the streets.

pa·trol·man /pə'trōlmən/ ▶ **n.** (pl. **patrolmen**) a patrolling police officer.

pa·trol·o·gy /pə'träləjē/ ▶ **n.** another term for **PATRISTICS**.
–DERIVATIVES **pa·trol·o·gist** /-jist/ **n.**
–ORIGIN early 17th cent.: from Greek *patēr, patr-* 'father' + **-LOGY**.

pa·trol wag·on ▶ **n.** a police van for transporting prisoners.

pa·tron /'pātrən/ ▶ **n. 1** a person who gives financial or other support to a person, organization, cause, or activity: *Charles became a patron of Rubens and van Dyck* | *a celebrated patron of the arts.*
2 a customer, esp. a regular one, of a store, restaurant, or theater: *we surveyed the plushness of the hotel and its sleek, well-dressed patrons.*
3 short for **PATRON SAINT**.
4 (in ancient Rome) a patrician in relation to a client. See also **CLIENT** (sense 3). ■ (in ancient Rome) the former owner and (frequently) protector of a freed slave.
5 Brit. chiefly historical a person or institution with the right to grant a benefice to a member of the clergy.
–ORIGIN Middle English: from Old French, from Latin *patronus* 'protector of clients, defender,' from *pater, patr-* 'father.'

pa·tron·age /'patrənij, 'pā-/ ▶ **n. 1** the support given by a patron: *the arts could no longer depend on private patronage.*
2 the power to control appointments to office or the right to privileges: *recruits are selected on merit, not through political patronage.*
3 a patronizing or condescending manner: *a twang of self-satisfaction—even patronage—about him.*
4 the regular business given to a store, restaurant, or public service by a person or group: *the direct train link was ending because of poor patronage.*
5 (in ancient Rome) the rights and duties or the position of a patron.
–ORIGIN late Middle English: from Old French, from *patron* 'protector, advocate' (see **PATRON**).

pa·tron·al /'pātrənl/ ▶ **adj.** of or relating to a patron saint: *the patronal festival of the parish church of St. Peter.*

pa·tron·ess /'pātrənis/ ▶ **n.** a female patron.

pa·tron·ize /'pātrəˌnīz, 'pa-/ ▶ **v.** [with obj.] **1** (often as adj. **patronizing**) treat with an apparent kindness that betrays a feeling of superiority: *"She's a good-hearted girl," he said in a patronizing voice* | *she was determined not to be put down or patronized.*
2 frequent (a store, theater, restaurant, or other establishment) as a customer: *restaurants remaining open in the evening were well patronized.* ■ give encouragement and financial support to (a person, esp. an artist, or a cause): *local churches and voluntary organizations were patronized by the family.*
–DERIVATIVES **pa·tron·i·za·tion** /ˌpātrəni'zāsHən, ˌpa-/ **n.**, **pa·tron·iz·er** **n.**, **pa·tron·iz·ing·ly** /-ˌnīziNGlē/ **adv.**

pa·tron saint ▶ **n.** the protecting or guiding saint of a person or place.

Pa·trons of Hus·band·ry ▶ **n.** see **GRANGE** (sense 2).

pat·ro·nym·ic /ˌpatrə'nimik/ ▶ **n.** a name derived from the name of a father or ancestor, typically by the addition of a prefix or suffix, e.g., *Johnson, O'Brien, Ivanovich.*
–ORIGIN early 17th cent.: via late Latin from Greek *patrōnumikos*, from *patrōnumos*, from *patēr, patr-* 'father' + *onuma* 'name.'

pa·troon /pə'tro͞on/ ▶ **n.** historical a person given land and granted certain manorial privileges under the former Dutch governments of New York and New Jersey.
–ORIGIN mid 17th cent.: from Dutch.

pat·sy /'patsē/ ▶ **n.** (pl. **patsies**) informal a person who is easily taken advantage of, esp. by being cheated or blamed for something.
–ORIGIN early 20th cent.: of unknown origin.

pat·tée /pə'tā/ ▶ **adj.** [postpositive] (of a cross) having almost triangular arms, narrow at the center and broadening to squared ends: *a cross pattée.*
–ORIGIN late 15th cent.: from French, from *patte* 'paw.'

pat·ten /'patn/ ▶ **n.** historical a shoe or clog with a raised sole or set on an iron ring, worn to raise one's feet above wet or muddy ground when walking outdoors.
–ORIGIN late Middle English: from Old French *patin*, perhaps from *patte* 'paw.'

pat·ter[1] /'patər/ ▶ **v.** [no obj.] make a repeated light tapping sound: *a flurry of rain pattered against the window.* ■ run with quick light steps: *plovers pattered at the edge of the marsh.*
▶ **n.** [in sing.] a repeated light tapping: *the rain had stopped its vibrating patter above him.*
–ORIGIN early 17th cent.: frequentative of **PAT**[1].

pat·ter[2] ▶ **n.** rapid or smooth-flowing continuous talk, such as that used by a comedian or salesman: *slick black hair, flashy clothes, and a New York line*

P

of patter. ■ rapid speech included in a song, esp. for comic effect: [as modifier] *a patter song of invective.* ■ the special language or jargon of a profession or other group: *he picked up the patter from watching his dad.*
▶ v. [no obj.] talk at length without saying anything significant: *she pattered on incessantly.*
– ORIGIN late Middle English (as a verb in the sense 'recite (a prayer, charm, etc.) rapidly'): from PATERNOSTER. The noun dates from the mid 18th cent.

pat·tern /'patərn/ ▶ n. **1** a repeated decorative design: *a neat blue herringbone pattern.* ■ an arrangement or sequence regularly found in comparable objects or events: *the house had been built on the usual pattern.* ■ a regular and intelligible form or sequence discernible in certain actions or situations: *a complicating factor is the change in working patterns.*
2 a model or design used as a guide in needlework and other crafts. ■ a set of instructions to be followed in making a sewn or knitted item. ■ a wooden or metal model from which a mold is made for a casting. ■ an example for others to follow: *he set the pattern for subsequent study.* ■ a sample of cloth or wallpaper.
▶ v. [with obj.] **1** (usu. as adj. **patterned**) decorate with a recurring design: *rosebud patterned wallpapers | violet-tinged flowers patterned the grassy banks.*
2 give a regular or intelligible form to: *the brain not only receives information, but interprets and patterns it.* ■ (**pattern something on/after**) give something a form based on that of (something else): *the clothing is patterned on athletes' wear.*
– ORIGIN Middle English *patron* 'something serving as a model,' from Old French (see PATRON). The change in sense is from the idea of a patron giving an example to be copied. Metathesis in the second syllable occurred in the 16th cent. By 1700 *patron* ceased to be used of things, and the two forms became differentiated in sense.

pat·tern bald·ness ▶ n. genetically determined baldness in which hair is gradually lost according to a characteristic pattern.

pat·tern bomb·ing ▶ n. the bombing of a target from a number of aircraft according to a prescribed pattern intended to produce the maximum effect.

pat·tern book ▶ n. a book containing samples of patterns and designs of cloth or wallpaper.

pat·tern drill ▶ n. another term for PATTERN PRACTICE.

pat·terned ground ▶ n. Geology ground showing a pattern of stones, fissures, and vegetation, typically forming polygons, rings, or stripes caused by repeated freezing and thawing.

pat·tern·less /'patərnləs/ ▶ adj. having no pattern; plain and undecorated: *smooth, patternless paper for covering poor or uneven walls.* ■ forming no discernible pattern: *phenomena that are completely patternless and disorganized.*

P

pat·tern prac·tice ▶ n. the intensive repetition of the distinctive constructions and patterns of a foreign language as a means of learning.

pat·ter of ti·ny feet ▶ n. humorous used in reference to the presence or imminent birth of a child: *I had long ago given up hope of ever **hearing the patter of tiny feet**.*

Pat·ter·son /'patərsən/, Floyd (1935–2006), US boxer. An Olympic middleweight champion 1952, he was also the world heavyweight champion 1956–59, 1960–62, becoming the first heavyweight to regain the title.

Pat·ton /'patn/, George Smith, Jr. (1885–1945), US army general. During World War II, he commanded the ground forces in the Allied invasion of northwest Africa 1942–43, the US Seventh Army in the Allied invasion of Sicily 1943, and the US Third Army in the drive through France 1944. His story was told in the movie *Patton* (1971).

pat·ty /'patē/ ▶ n. (pl. **patties**) a small flat cake of minced or finely chopped food, esp. meat. ■ a small, round, flat chocolate-covered peppermint candy. ■ chiefly Brit. a small pie or turnover.
– ORIGIN mid 17th cent.: alteration of French *pâté*, by association with PASTY[1].

pat·ty-cake (also **pat-a-cake**) ▶ n. a children's game in which participants gently clap each other's hands and their own in time to the words of a rhyme.

pat·ty·pan /'patē,pan/ (also **pattypan squash**) ▶ n. a squash of a saucer-shaped variety with a scalloped rim and creamy white flesh.
– ORIGIN so named from the resemblance in shape to a pan for baking a patty.

pat·ty shell ▶ n. a shell of puff pastry with a cooked meat or vegetable filling.

pat·u·lous /'pacHələs/ ▶ adj. rare (esp. of the branches of a tree) spreading.
– ORIGIN early 17th cent.: from Latin *patulus* (from *patere* 'be or lie open') + -OUS.

pat·zer /'pätsər, 'pat-/ ▶ n. a poor chess player.
– ORIGIN 1940s: perhaps related to German *patzen* 'to bungle.'

PAU ▶ abbr. Pan American Union.

pau·a /'pouə/ ▶ n. NZ a large edible abalone (mollusk). ■ the ornamental shell of this.
– ORIGIN mid 19th cent.: from Maori.

pau·ci·ty /'pôsitē/ ▶ n. [in sing.] the presence of something only in small or insufficient quantities or amounts; scarcity: *a **paucity of** information.*
– ORIGIN late Middle English: from Old French *paucite* or Latin *paucitas*, from *paucus* 'few.'

Paul /pôl/, Les (1915–2009), US jazz guitarist and guitar designer; born *Lester Polfus*. In the 1940s he pioneered the development of the solid-body electric guitar.

Paul III (1468–1549), Italian pope 1534–49; born *Alessandro Farnese*. He excommunicated Henry VIII of England in 1538, instituted the order of the Jesuits in 1540, and initiated the Council of Trent in 1545.

Paul, St. (died *c.*64), missionary; known as **Paul the Apostle**, **Saul of Tarsus**, or **the Apostle of the Gentiles**. He first opposed the followers of Jesus, but after a vision became one of the first major Christian missionaries and theologians. His epistles form part of the New Testament. Feast day, June 29.

Paul–Bun·nell test /'bənəl/ ▶ n. Medicine a test in which an antibody reaction to sheep red blood cells confirms a diagnosis of infectious mononucleosis.
– ORIGIN 1930s: named after John R. *Paul* (1893–1936) and Walls W. *Bunnell* (1902–1965), American physicians.

Pau·li /'pôlē, 'pou-/, Wolfgang (1900–58), US physicist, born in Austria. He made a major contribution to quantum theory with his **exclusion principle**, according to which only two electrons in an atom could occupy the same quantum level, provided they had opposite spins. Nobel Prize for Physics (1945).

Pau·li·cian /,pô'lisHən/ ▶ n. a member of a religious sect that arose in Armenia in the 7th century AD, professing a modified form of Manichaeism.
– DERIVATIVES **Pau·li·cian·ism** /-izəm/ n.
– ORIGIN from medieval Latin *Pauliciani*, Greek *Paulikianoi*, of unknown origin.

Pau·li ex·clu·sion prin·ci·ple (also **Pauli's exclusion principle**) Physics the assertion that no two fermions can have the same quantum number.
– ORIGIN 1920s: named after W. PAULI.

Pau·line /'pô,līn, -,lēn/ ▶ adj. Christian Theology of, relating to, or characteristic of St. Paul, his writings, or his doctrines. ■ (in the Roman Catholic Church) of or relating to Pope Paul VI, or the liturgical and doctrinal reforms pursued during his pontificate (1963–78) as a result of the Second Vatican Council.

Paul·ing /'pôliNG/, Linus Carl (1901–94), US chemist. He is renowned for his study of molecular structure and chemical bonding. His suggestion of a helical structure for proteins formed the foundation for the elucidation of the structure of DNA. Nobel Prize for Chemistry (1954).

Paul Jones ▶ n. a ballroom dance in which the dancers change partners after circling in concentric rings of men and women.
– ORIGIN 1920s: named after John *Paul Jones* (1747–92), Scottish-born American admiral.

pau·low·ni·a /pô'lōnēə/ ▶ n. a small Southeast Asian tree with heart-shaped leaves and fragrant lilac flowers. ● Genus *Paulownia*, family Scrophulariaceae.
– ORIGIN modern Latin, named after Anna *Pavlovna* (1795–1865), a Russian princess.

Paul Pry ▶ n. dated an inquisitive person.
– ORIGIN from the name of a character in a US song of 1820.

paunch /pôncH, päncH/ ▶ n. **1** a large or protruding abdomen or stomach.
2 Nautical, archaic a thick strong mat used to give protection from chafing on a mast or other spar.
– DERIVATIVES **paunch·i·ness** /'pôncHēnis/ n., **paunch·y** adj.
– ORIGIN late Middle English: from Anglo-Norman French *pa(u)nche*, based on Latin *pantex, pantic-*, usually in the plural in the sense 'intestines.'

pau·per /'pôpər/ ▶ n. a very poor person. ■ historical a recipient of government relief or public charity.
– DERIVATIVES **pau·per·dom** /-dəm/ n., **pau·per·ism** /-,rizəm/ n., **pau·per·i·za·tion** /,pôpəri'zāsHən/ n., **pau·per·ize** /-,rīz/ v.
– ORIGIN late 15th cent.: from Latin, literally 'poor.' The word's use in English originated in the Latin legal phrase *in forma pauperis*, literally 'in the form of a poor person' (allowing nonpayment of costs).

pau·piette /pō'pyet/ ▶ n. a long, thin slice of fish or meat, rolled and stuffed with a filling.
– ORIGIN French, probably from Italian *polpetta*, from Latin *pulpa* 'pulp.'

pau·ra·que /pou'räkā/ ▶ n. a long-tailed nightjar found in southern Texas, Mexico, and Central and South America. ● Family Caprimulgidae: two genera and species, in particular the **common pauraque** (*Nyctidromus albicollis*).
– ORIGIN probably a Hispanicized form of a local word.

Pau·rop·o·da /,pôrə'pädə/ Zoology a small class of myriapod invertebrates that resemble the centipedes. They are small, soft-bodied animals with one pair of legs per segment, living chiefly in forest litter.
– DERIVATIVES **pau·ro·pod** /'pôrə,päd/ n., **pau·rop·o·dan** n. & adj.
– ORIGIN modern Latin (plural), from Greek *pauros* 'small' + *pous, pod-* 'foot.'

Pau·sa·ni·as /pô'sānēəs/ (2nd century), Greek geographer and historian. His *Description of Greece* (also called the *Itinerary of Greece*) is a guide to the topography and remains of ancient Greece and is still considered an invaluable source of information.

pause /pôz/ ▶ n. a temporary stop in action or speech: *she dropped me outside during a brief pause in the rain | the admiral chattered away without pause.* ■ Music a mark over a note or rest that is to be lengthened by an unspecified amount; fermata. ■ (also **pause button**) a control allowing the temporary interruption of an electronic (or mechanical) process, esp. video or audio recording or reproduction.
▶ v. [no obj.] interrupt action or speech briefly: *she paused, at a loss for words.* ■ [with obj.] temporarily interrupt the operation of (a videotape, audiotape, or computer program): *she had paused a tape on the VCR.*
– PHRASES **give someone pause** cause someone to think carefully or hesitate before doing something: *public outrage has given him pause.*
– ORIGIN late Middle English: from Old French, from Latin *pausa*, from Greek *pausis*, from *pausein* 'to stop.'

pa·vane /pə'vän/ (also **pavan**) ▶ n. a stately dance in slow duple time, popular in the 16th and 17th centuries and performed in elaborate clothing. ■ a piece of music for this dance.
– ORIGIN mid 16th cent.: from French *pavane*, from Italian *pavana*, feminine adjective from *Pavo*, dialect name of Padua.

Pa·va·rot·ti /,pävə'rätē, -vä'rôtē/, Luciano (1935–2007), Italian opera singer. A tenor, he gained international acclaim and popularity for his bel canto singing. He was one of the Three Tenors, along with José Carreras and Placido Domingo.

pave /pāv/ ▶ v. [with obj.] cover (a piece of ground) with concrete, asphalt, stones, or bricks; lay paving over: *the yard at the front **was paved with** flagstones |* (as adj. **paved**) *chrysanthemums provide a cheerful border for the paved area.*
– PHRASES **pave the way for** create the circumstances to enable (something) to happen or be done: *the proposals will pave the way for a speedy resolution to the problem.* **the streets are paved with gold** used to suggest that it is easy to become rich and successful in a particular place: *few people now imagine that the streets of New York, Paris, or London are paved with gold.*
– ORIGIN Middle English: from Old French *paver* 'pave.'

pa·vé /pə'vā, pa-/ ▶ n. **1** a setting of precious stones placed so closely together that no metal shows: *a solid diamond pavé.*
2 archaic a paved street, road, or path.
– ORIGIN French, literally 'paved,' past participle of *paver*.

pave·ment /'pāvmənt/ ▶ n. any paved area or surface. ■ the hard surface of a road or street. ■ Brit. a sidewalk. ■ Geology a more or less horizontal expanse of bare rock.
– PHRASES **pound the pavement** see POUND[2].
– ORIGIN Middle English: from Old French, from Latin *pavimentum* 'trodden-down floor,' from *pavire* 'beat, tread down.'

pav·er /'pāvər/ ▶ n. **1** a paving stone.
2 a person who lays pavement or paving stones.

pa·vil·ion /pə'vilyən/ ▶ n. **1** a building or similar structure used for a specific purpose, in particular: ■ a summerhouse or other decorative building used as a shelter in a park or large garden. ■ in the names of buildings used for theatrical or other entertainments: *the second concert at the White Rock Pavilion.* ■ a detached or semidetached block at a hospital or other building complex. ■ a large tent with a peak and crenellated decorations, used esp. at a show or fair. ■ a temporary building, stand, or

other structure in which items are displayed by a dealer or exhibitor at a trade exhibition.
2 a usually highly decorated projecting subdivision of a building.
3 the part of a cut gemstone below the girdle.
– ORIGIN Middle English (denoting a large decorated tent): from Old French *pavillon*, from Latin *papilio(n-)* 'butterfly; tent.'

pav·ing /'pāviNG/ ▸ **n.** pavement. ■ the materials used for a pavement.

pav·ing stone ▸ **n.** a large, flat piece of stone or similar material, used in paving.

pav·ior /'pāvyər/ (also Brit. **paviour**) ▸ **n.** a paving stone. ■ a person who lays paving stones.
– ORIGIN Middle English: from Old French *paveur*, from *paver* 'pave.'

Pa·vlov /'pav,läv, -lôf, -ləf/, Ivan (Petrovich) (1849–1936), Russian physiologist. He is best known for his studies on the conditioned reflex. He showed by experimenting with dogs how the secretion of saliva can be stimulated not only by food but also by the sound of a bell associated with food. Nobel Prize for Physiology or Medicine (1904).

Pav·lo·va /päv'lōvə, 'pävləvə/ Anna (Pavlovna) (1881–1931), Russian dancer, resident in Britain from 1912. Her highly acclaimed solo dance *The Dying Swan* was created for her by Michel Fokine in 1905. On settling in Britain she formed her own company.

pa·vlo·va /päv'lōvə, 'pavləvə/ ▸ **n.** a dessert consisting of a meringue base or shell filled with whipped cream and fruit.
– ORIGIN named after A. PAVLOVA.

Pav·lov·i·an /pav'lōvēən, -'läv-/ ▸ **adj.** of or relating to classical conditioning as described by I. P. Pavlov.

Pa·vo /'pāvō/ Astronomy a southern constellation (the Peacock), between Grus and Triangulum Australe. Its brightest star is itself sometimes called "the Peacock." ■ (as genitive **Pavonis** /pə'vōnis/) used with a preceding letter or numeral to designate a star in this constellation: *the star Beta Pavonis*.
– ORIGIN Latin.

pav·o·nine /'pavə,nīn, -nin/ ▸ **adj.** literary, rare of or like a peacock.
– ORIGIN mid 17th cent.: from Latin *pavoninus*, from *pavo, pavon-* 'peacock.'

paw /pô/ ▸ **n.** an animal's foot having claws and pads. ■ chiefly derogatory a person's hand: *touch her with your filthy paws and I'll ram my fist into your face.*
▸ **v.** [with obj.] (of an animal) feel or scrape with a paw or hoof: *the horse rose on its strong haunches, its forelegs pawing the air* | [no obj.] *young dogs may paw at the floor and whine.* ■ informal (of a person) touch or handle clumsily or lasciviously: *some overweight, ugly Casanova had tried to paw her.*
– ORIGIN Middle English: from Old French *poue*, probably of Germanic origin and related to Dutch *poot*.

pawk·y /'pôkē/ ▸ **adj.** (**pawkier**, **pawkiest**) chiefly Brit. 1 having or showing a sly sense of humor: *a gentle man with a pawky wit.* ■ shrewd: *she shakes her head with a look of pawky, knowing skepticism.*
– DERIVATIVES **pawk·i·ly** /-kəlē/ **adv.**, **pawk·i·ness** /-kēnis/ **n.**
– ORIGIN mid 17th cent.: from Scots and northern English *pawk* 'trick,' of unknown origin.

pawl /pôl/ ▸ **n.** a pivoted curved bar or lever whose free end engages with the teeth of a cogwheel or ratchet so that the wheel or ratchet can only turn or move one way. ■ each of a set of short stout bars that engage with the whelps and prevent a capstan, windlass, or winch from recoiling.
– ORIGIN early 17th cent.: perhaps from Low German and Dutch *pal* (related to *pal* 'fixed').

pawn[1] /pôn/ ▸ **n.** a chess piece of the smallest size and value. A pawn moves one square forward along its file if unobstructed (or two on the first move), or one square diagonally forward when making a capture. Each player begins with eight pawns on the second rank, and can promote a pawn to become any other piece (typically a queen) if it reaches the opponent's end of the board. ■ a person used by others for their own purposes: *they had allowed themselves to be used as pawns within the Cold War.*
– ORIGIN late Middle English: from Anglo-Norman French *poun*, from medieval Latin *pedo, pedon-* 'foot soldier,' from Latin *pes, ped-* 'foot.' Compare with PEON.

pawn[2] ▸ **v.** [with obj.] deposit (an object) with a pawnbroker as security for money lent: *I pawned the necklace to cover the loan.*
▸ **n.** archaic an object left as security for money lent.
– PHRASES **in pawn** (of an object) held as security by a pawnbroker: *all our money was gone and everything was in pawn.*
– PHRASAL VERBS **pawn someone/something off** pass off someone or something unwanted: *newly industrialized economies are racing to **pawn off** old processes **on** poorer countries.*
– ORIGIN late 15th cent. (as a noun): from Old French *pan* 'pledge, security,' of West Germanic origin; related to Dutch *pand* and German *Pfand*.

pawn·brok·er /'pôn,brōkər/ ▸ **n.** a person who lends money at interest on the security of an article pawned.
– DERIVATIVES **pawn·brok·ing** /-kiNG/ **n.**

Paw·nee /pô'nē/ ▸ **n.** (pl. **same** or **Pawnees**) **1** a member of an American Indian confederacy formerly in Nebraska, and now mainly in Oklahoma.
2 the Caddoan language of these peoples.
▸ **adj.** of or relating to these people or their language.
– ORIGIN from Canadian French *Pani*, from a Siouan name.

pawn·shop /'pôn,SHäp/ ▸ **n.** a pawnbroker's shop, esp. one where unredeemed items are sold to the public.

pawn tick·et ▸ **n.** a ticket issued by a pawnbroker in exchange for an article pawned, bearing particulars of the loan.

paw·paw /'pôpô/ (also **papaw** /pə'pô, 'pôpô/) ▸ **n.**
1 another term for PAPAYA.
2 (also **pawpaw tree**) a North American tree of the custard apple family, with purple flowers and edible oblong yellow fruit with sweet pulp. ● *Asimina triloba*, family Annonaceae. ■ the fruit of this tree.
– ORIGIN early 17th cent.: from Spanish and Portuguese *papaya*, of Carib origin. The change in spelling is unexplained.

Paw·tuck·et /pə'təkət, pô-/ an industrial city in northeastern Rhode Island, on the Blackstone River, northeast of Providence, site of pioneering metal and textile plants; pop. 71,765 (est. 2008).

Pax /paks, päks/ Roman Mythology the goddess of peace. Greek equivalent EIRENE.

pax[1] /paks, päks/ ▸ **n.** chiefly historical (in the Christian Church) the kissing of a tablet by all the participants at a mass depicting the Crucifixion or other sacred object; the kiss of peace.
– ORIGIN Latin, literally 'peace.'

pax[2] /paks/ ▸ **n.** (pl. **same**) (chiefly in commercial use) a person or persons: *the buffet costs $53 per pax* | *two pilots and four pax on board.*
– ORIGIN 1970s: apparently an alteration of *pass-* (from PASSENGER).

Pax Amer·i·ca·na /,paks əmeri'känə/ (or **Pax Britannica** /brɪ'tanɪkə/) ▸ **n.** a state of relative international peace regarded as overseen by the US (or the UK).
– ORIGIN late 19th cent.: Latin, literally 'American peace,' after PAX ROMANA.

Pax Ro·ma·na /'päks rō'mänə/ ▸ **n.** the peace that existed between nationalities within the Roman Empire.
– ORIGIN Latin, literally 'Roman peace.'

Pax·ton /'pakstən/, Sir Joseph (1801–65), English gardener and architect. He designed the Crystal Palace in London in 1851.

pay[1] /pā/ ▸ **v.** (past and past participle **paid**) **1** [with obj.] give (someone) money that is due for work done, goods received, or a debt incurred: [with obj. and infinitive] *he paid the locals to pick his coffee beans* | [no obj.] *TV licenses can be **paid for** by direct debit.* ■ give (a sum of money) in exchange for goods or work done or in discharge of a debt: *he paid $1,000 to have it built in 1977* | [with two objs.] *a museum paid him a four-figure sum for it.* ■ hand over or transfer the amount due of (a debt, wages, etc.) to someone: *bonuses were paid to savers whose policies completed their full term.* ■ (of work, an investment, etc.) yield or provide someone with (a specified sum of money): *jobs that pay $5 or $6 an hour.* ■ [no obj.] (of a business or undertaking, or an attitude) be profitable or advantageous to someone: *crime doesn't pay* | [with infinitive] *it pays to choose varieties carefully.*
2 [no obj.] suffer a loss or other misfortune as a consequence of an action: *the destroyer responsible for these atrocities would have to pay with his life.* ■ [with obj.] give what is due or deserved to (someone); reward or punish.
3 [with two objs.] give or bestow (attention, respect, or a compliment) on (someone): *no one paid them any attention.* ■ make (a visit or a call) to (someone): *she has been prevailed upon to pay us a visit.*
▸ **n.** the money paid to someone for regular work: *those working on contract may receive higher rates of pay* | *showing up and collecting your pay.*
– PHRASES **in the pay of** employed by. **pay one's compliments** see COMPLIMENT. **pay court to** see COURT. **pay dearly** obtain something at a high cost or great effort: *his master must have paid dearly for such a magnificent beast.* ■ suffer for an error or failure: *they paid dearly for wasting goalscoring opportunities.* **pay one's dues** see DUE. **pay for itself** (of an object or system) earn or save enough money to cover the cost of its purchase: *the best insulation will pay for itself in less than a year.* **pay its** (or **one's**) **way** (of an enterprise or person) earn enough to cover its (or one's) costs: *some students are paying their way through college.* **pay one's last respects** show respect toward a dead person by attending their funeral. **pay one's respects** make a polite visit to someone: *we went to pay our respects to the head lama.* **pay through the nose** informal pay much more than a fair price.
– PHRASAL VERBS **pay someone back** repay a loan to someone: *a regular amount was deducted from my wages to pay her back.* ■ take revenge on someone: *would you like to **pay him back for** hitting you like that?* ■ reward someone for something done earlier: *I took Aunt Shirley a cake to **pay her back for** solving a problem my grandmother had.* **pay something back** repay a loan to someone: *the money should be paid back with interest* | [with two objs.] *they did pay me back the money.* **pay something in** pay money into a bank account. **pay off** informal (of a course of action) yield good results; succeed: *all the hard work I had done over the summer paid off.* **pay someone off** dismiss someone with a final payment: *when directors are fired, they should not be lavishly paid off.* **pay something off** pay a debt in full: *you may have saved up enough to pay off your second mortgage.* **pay something out** (or **pay out**) **1** pay a large sum of money from funds under one's control: *insurers can refuse to pay out.* **2** let out (a rope) by slackening it: *I began paying out the nylon line.* **pay up** (or **pay something up**) pay a debt in full: *you've got ninety days to pay up the principal.*
– DERIVATIVES **pay·er** **n.**
– ORIGIN Middle English (in the sense 'pacify'): from Old French *paie* (noun), *payer* (verb), from Latin *pacare* 'appease,' from *pax, pac-* 'peace.' The notion of 'payment' arose from the sense of 'pacifying' a creditor.

pay[2] ▸ **v.** (past and past participle **payed**) [with obj.] Nautical seal (the deck or hull seams of a wooden ship) with pitch or tar to prevent leakage.
– ORIGIN early 17th cent.: from Old Northern French *peier*, from Latin *picare*, from *pix, pic-* 'pitch.'

pay·a·ble /'pāəbəl/ ▸ **adj.** [predic.] **1** (of money) required to be paid; due: *interest is payable on the money owing* | *send a check, payable to the ASPCA.*
2 able to be paid: *it costs just $195, payable in five monthly installments.*
▸ **n.** (**payables**) debts owed by a business; liabilities.

pay-as-you-go ▸ **adj.** relating to a system of paying debts or meeting costs as they arise.

pay·back /'pā,bak/ ▸ **n.** **1** financial return or reward, esp. profit equal to the initial outlay of an investment: *a long time lag between investment and payback.*
2 an act of revenge or retaliation: *the drive-by shootings are mainly paybacks.*

pay·back pe·ri·od ▸ **n.** the length of time required for an investment to recover its initial outlay in terms of profits or savings.

pay ca·ble ▸ **n.** a cable television service available on a subscription basis.

pay·check /'pā,CHek/ ▸ **n.** a check for salary or wages made out to an employee. ■ a salary or income: *socking away money for the time when he wouldn't have a steady paycheck.*

pay·day /'pā,dā/ ▸ **n.** a day on which someone is paid or expects to be paid their wages. ■ informal money or success won or earned: *his two seasons in Dallas helped him land his first huge payday in the NFL when he signed with the Cardinals.*

pay dirt ▸ **n.** Mining ground containing ore in sufficient quantity to be profitably extracted. ■ profit; reward: *the gig pays three hundred bucks a week—looks like I just **hit pay dirt**.*

pay·ee /pā'ē/ ▸ **n.** a person to whom money is paid or is to be paid, esp. the person to whom a check is made payable.

pay en·ve·lope ▸ **n.** an envelope containing an employee's wages. ■ a salary or income: *a company cutting pay envelopes.*

pay·ess /'pā-is/ ▸ **plural n.** uncut sideburns worn by male Orthodox Jews.
– ORIGIN mid 20th cent.: Yiddish, from Hebrew *pē'ōṯ* 'corners' (see Lev. 19:27).

pay·ing guest ▸ **n.** a person who lives in someone else's house and pays for food and accommodations; a lodger.

pay·load /'pā,lōd/ ▸ **n.** the part of a vehicle's load, esp. an aircraft's, from which revenue is derived; passengers and cargo. ■ an explosive warhead

p

carried by a missile. ■ equipment, personnel, or satellites carried by a spacecraft.

pay·mas·ter /ˈpāˌmastər/ ▶ **n.** an official who pays troops or workers.

pay·ment /ˈpāmənt/ ▶ **n. 1** the action or process of paying someone or something, or of being paid: *ask for a discount for payment by cash | three interest-free monthly payments.*
2 an amount paid or payable: *an interim compensation payment of $2500.* ■ something given as a reward or in recompense for something done: *a suit with a velvet collar that I got as payment for being in the show.*
– ORIGIN late Middle English: from Old French *paiement*, from *payer* 'to pay.'

Payne's gray /pānz/ ▶ **n.** Printing a composite pigment composed of blue, red, black, and white permanent pigments, used esp. for watercolors.
– ORIGIN mid 19th cent.: named after William *Payne* (*fl.* 1800), English artist.

pay·nim /ˈpānim/ ▶ **n.** archaic a non-Christian, esp. a Muslim.
– ORIGIN Middle English: from Old French *paienime*, from ecclesiastical Latin *paganismus* 'heathenism,' from *paganus* 'heathen' (see **PAGAN**).

pay·off /ˈpāˌôf/ ▶ **n.** informal a payment made to someone, esp. as a bribe or reward, or on leaving a job: *widespread rumors of payoffs and kickbacks in the party.* ■ the return on an investment or a bet. ■ a final outcome; a conclusion: *it gave them the idea for the payoff of last night's episode.*

pay·o·la /pāˈōlə/ ▶ **n.** the practice of bribing someone to use their influence or position to promote a particular product or interest: *if a record company spends enough money on payola, it can make any record a hit.*
– ORIGIN 1930s: from **PAY**[1] + *-ola* as in *Victrola*, the name of a make of gramophone.

pay·out /ˈpāˌout/ ▶ **n.** a large payment of money, esp. as compensation or a dividend: *an insurance payout.*

pay pack·et ▶ **n.** British term for **PAY ENVELOPE**.

pay-per-view ▶ **adj.** see **PPV**.

pay phone ▶ **n.** a public telephone that is operated by coins or by a credit or prepaid card.

pay·roll /ˈpāˌrōl/ ▶ **n.** a list of a company's employees and the amount of money they are to be paid: *there are just three employees **on the payroll**.* ■ the total amount of wages and salaries paid by a company to its employees: *small employers with a payroll of less than $45,000.*

pay·sage /pāˈzäZH, ˈpāsij/ ▶ **n.** a rural scene depicted in art. ■ landscape painting.
– DERIVATIVES **pay·sa·gist** /ˈpāsəjist/ **n.**
– ORIGIN French, literally 'countryside,' from *pays* 'country.'

pay·san /pāˈzän/ ▶ **n.** a peasant or countryman, esp. in France.
– ORIGIN French.

Pays Basque /ˈpā ˈbäsk/ French name for **BASQUE COUNTRY**.

pay·slip /ˈpāˌslip/ ▶ **n.** a note given to an employee when they have been paid, detailing the amount of pay given and the tax and insurance deducted.

pay sta·tion ▶ **n.** dated another term for **PAY PHONE**.

payt. ▶ **abbr.** payment.

Pay·ton /ˈpātn/, Walter (1954–99) US football player. A running back, he played for the Chicago Bears 1975–87 and held the NFL's career record for most yards rushed: 16,726. Football Hall of Fame (1993).

pay TV (also **pay television**) ▶ **n.** television broadcasting in which viewers pay by subscription to watch a particular channel.

pay·wall /ˈpāwôl/ ▶ **n.** (on a website) an arrangement whereby access is restricted to users who have paid to subscribe to the site.

Paz /päz, päs/, Octavio (1914–98), Mexican poet and essayist. His poems reflect his interest in Aztec mythology. Nobel Prize for Literature (1990).

PB ▶ **abbr.** ■ British Pharmacopoeia. [Latin *Pharmacopoeia Britannica.*] ■ Prayer Book. ■ petabyte.

Pb ▶ **symbol** the chemical element lead.
– ORIGIN from Latin *plumbum.*

pb ▶ **abbr.** paperback: *hb $18.99, pb $6.99.*

PBS ▶ **abbr.** Public Broadcasting Service.

PBX ▶ **abbr.** private branch exchange, a private telephone switchboard.

PC ▶ **abbr.** ■ Past Commander. ■ personal computer. ■ Brit. Police Constable. ■ (also **pc**) politically correct; political correctness: *PC language | the cult of PC.* ■ Post Commander. ■ Brit. Prince Consort. ■ Brit. Privy Council. ■ professional corporation.

pc ▶ **abbr.** parsec.

p.c. ▶ **abbr.** ■ percent. ■ postcard.

p/c (also **P/C**) ▶ **abbr.** ■ petty cash. ■ price current.

PCB ▶ **abbr.** ■ Electronics printed circuit board. ■ Chemistry polychlorinated biphenyl.

PC card ▶ **n.** Computing a printed circuit board, esp. one built to the PCMCIA standard.

P-Celt·ic /ˈkeltik/ ▶ **n. & adj.** another term for **BRYTHONIC**.
– ORIGIN *P*, from the development of the Indo-European *kw* sound into *p* in this group of languages.

PCI ▶ **n.** Computing a standard for connecting computers and their peripherals.
– ORIGIN late 20th cent.: abbreviation of *Peripheral Component Interconnect.*

PCM ▶ **abbr.** pulse code modulation.

PCMCIA ▶ **abbr.** Computing Personal Computer Memory Card International Association, denoting a standard specification for memory cards and interfaces in personal computers.

PC mod ▶ **n.** Computing another term for **MOD**[3].

PCN ▶ **abbr.** personal communications network, a digital mobile telephone system.

p-code ▶ **n.** another term for **PSEUDOCODE**.

PCP ▶ **abbr.** ■ pentachlorophenol. ■ phencyclidine. ■ pneumocystis carinii pneumonia. ■ primary care physician. ■ (in Canada) Progressive-Conservative Party.

PCS ▶ **abbr.** personal communications services, a digital mobile telephone system.

pct. ▶ **abbr.** percent.

PCV ▶ **abbr.** Brit. passenger-carrying vehicle.

PD ▶ **abbr.** ■ Police Department: *the Chicago PD.* ■ public domain: *PD software.*

Pd ▶ **symbol** the chemical element palladium.

pd ▶ **abbr.** paid.

p.d. ▶ **abbr.** ■ per diem. ■ potential difference.

PDA[1] ▶ **n.** a palmtop computer that functions as a personal organizer but also provides e-mail and Internet access.
– ORIGIN 1990s: abbreviation of *personal digital assistant.*

PDA[2] ▶ **abbr.** informal public display of affection.

Pd.B. ▶ **abbr.** Bachelor of Pedagogy.

PDC ▶ **abbr.** program delivery control, a system for broadcasting a coded signal at the beginning and end of a television program which can be recognized by a video recorder and used to begin and end recording.

Pd.D. ▶ **abbr.** Doctor of Pedagogy.

PDF ▶ **n.** Computing a file format that provides an electronic image of text or text and graphics that looks like a printed document and can be viewed, printed, and electronically transmitted.
– ORIGIN abbreviation of *Portable Document Format.*

Pd.M. ▶ **abbr.** Master of Pedagogy.

PDP ▶ **abbr.** parallel distributed processing.

p.d.q. ▶ **abbr.** informal pretty damn quick.

PDT ▶ **abbr.** Pacific Daylight Time (see **PACIFIC TIME**).

PE ▶ **abbr.** ■ physical education. ■ Prince Edward Island (in official postal use).

pea /pē/ ▶ **n. 1** a spherical green seed that is widely eaten as a vegetable. ■ [with modifier] used in names of edible spherical seeds of the pea family, e.g., **chickpea** and **black-eyed pea**.
2 the hardy Eurasian climbing plant that yields pods containing these seeds. ● *Pisum sativum*, family Leguminosae (or Fabaceae; the **pea family**). The members of this family (known as legumes) are sometimes divided among three smaller families: Papilionaceae (peas, beans, clovers, vetches, brooms, laburnums, etc.), Mimosaceae (mimosas, acacias), and Caesalpiniaceae (cassia, carob, and many tropical timber trees).
– PHRASES **like peas** (or **two peas**) **in a pod** so similar as to be indistinguishable or nearly so.
– ORIGIN mid 17th cent.: back-formation from **PEASE** (interpreted as plural).

pea bean ▶ **n.** a variety of kidney bean with small rounded seeds.

pea·ber·ry /ˈpēˌberē/ ▶ **n.** (pl. **peaberries**) a coffee berry containing one rounded seed instead of the usual two, through nonfertilization of one ovule or subsequent abortion. Such beans are esteemed for their fine, strong flavor.

Pea·body /ˈpēˌbädē, -bədē/ an industrial city in northeastern Massachusetts; pop. 51,331 (est. 2008).

pea·brain /ˈpēˌbrān/ ▶ **n.** informal a stupid person.

pea-brained ▶ **adj.** informal stupid; foolish.

peace /pēs/ ▶ **n. 1** freedom from disturbance; quiet and tranquility: *you can while away an hour or two in peace and seclusion.* ■ mental calm; serenity: *the peace of mind this insurance gives you.*
2 freedom from or the cessation of war or violence: *the Straits were to be open to warships in time of peace.* ■ [in sing.] a period of this: *the peace didn't last.* ■ [in sing.] a treaty agreeing to the cessation of war between warring states: *support for a negotiated peace.* ■ freedom from civil disorder: *police action to restore peace.* ■ freedom from dispute or dissension between individuals or groups: *the 8.8 percent offer that promises peace with the board.*
3 (**the peace**) a ceremonial handshake or kiss exchanged during a service in some churches (now usually only in the Eucharist), symbolizing Christian love and unity. See also **KISS OF PEACE** at **KISS**.
▶ **exclam. 1** used as a greeting.
2 used as an order to remain silent.
– PHRASES **at peace 1** free from anxiety or distress. ■ dead (used to suggest that someone has escaped from the difficulties of life). **2** in a state of friendliness: *a man at peace with the world.* **hold one's peace** remain silent about something. **keep the peace** refrain or prevent others from disturbing civil order: *the police must play a crucial role in keeping the peace.* **make peace** (or **one's peace**) re-establish friendly relations; become reconciled: *not every conservative has **made peace with** big government.* **no peace for the weary** see **NO REST FOR THE WEARY** at **WEARY**.
– ORIGIN Middle English: from Old French *pais*, from Latin *pax, pac-* 'peace.'

peace·a·ble /ˈpēsəbəl/ ▶ **adj.** inclined to avoid argument or violent conflict: *they were famed as an industrious, peaceable, practical people.* ■ free from argument or conflict; peaceful: *the mainly peaceable daily demonstrations for democratic reform.*
– DERIVATIVES **peace·a·ble·ness** **n.**, **peace·a·bly** /-blē/ **adv.**
– ORIGIN Middle English: from Old French *peisible*, alteration of *plaisible*, from late Latin *placibilis* 'pleasing,' from Latin *placere* 'to please.'

Peace Corps /ˈpēs ˌkôr/ an organization sponsored by the US government that sends young people to work as volunteers in developing countries.

peace div·i·dend ▶ **n.** a sum of public money that becomes available for other purposes when spending on defense is reduced.

peace·ful /ˈpēsfəl/ ▶ **adj. 1** free from disturbance; tranquil: *everything was so quiet and peaceful in the early morning.*
2 not involving war or violence: *a soldier was shot and seriously wounded at an otherwise peaceful demonstration.* ■ (of a person) inclined to avoid conflict; not aggressive: *Dad was a peaceful, law-abiding citizen.*
– DERIVATIVES **peace·ful·ness** **n.**

peace·ful·ly /ˈpēsfəlē/ ▶ **adv. 1** without disturbance; tranquilly: *the baby slept peacefully in its cradle.* ■ (of death) without pain: *she suffered a stroke and died peacefully in her sleep.*
2 without war or violence: *the siege ended peacefully.*

Peace Gar·den State a nickname for the state of **NORTH DAKOTA**.

peace·keep·ing /ˈpēsˌkēpiNG/ ▶ **n.** [usu. as modifier] the active maintenance of a truce between nations or communities, esp. by an international military force: *the 2,300-strong UN peacekeeping force.*
– DERIVATIVES **peace·keep·er** /-ˌkēpər/ **n.**

peace·mak·er /ˈpēsˌmākər/ ▶ **n.** a person who brings about peace, esp. by reconciling adversaries.
– DERIVATIVES **peace·mak·ing** /-ˌmākiNG/ **n. & adj.**

peace·nik /ˈpēsˌnik/ ▶ **n.** informal, often derogatory a member of a pacifist movement.
– ORIGIN coined during peace protests in the 1960s.

peace of·fer·ing ▶ **n. 1** a propitiatory or conciliatory gift: *he took the flowers to Jean as a peace offering.*
2 (in biblical use) an offering presented as a thanksgiving to God.

peace of·fi·cer ▶ **n.** a civil officer appointed to preserve law and order, such as a sheriff or police officer.

peace or·der ▶ **n.** a court order offering protection to certain classes of person who are not eligible to petition for a protective order.

peace pipe ▶ **n.** a tobacco pipe offered and smoked as a token of peace among North American Indians.

Peace Riv·er a river that flows for 1,194 miles (1,923 km) from northern British Columbia into Alberta to the Slave River.

peace sign ▶ **n. 1** a sign of peace made by holding

peace sign 2

P

up the hand with palm turned outward and the first two fingers extended in a V-shape.
2 a figure representing peace, in the form of a circle with one line bisecting it from top to bottom and two shorter lines radiating downward on either side.

peace talk ▶ **n.** (usu. **peace talks**) a discussion about peace or the ending of hostilities, esp. a conference or series of discussions aimed at achieving peace.

peace·time /ˈpēsˌtīm/ ▶ **n.** a period when a country is not at war.

peach[1] /pēCH/ ▶ **n. 1** a round stone fruit with juicy yellow flesh and downy pinkish-yellow skin. ■ a pinkish-yellow color like that of a peach. ■ informal an exceptionally good or attractive person or thing: *what a peach of a shot!*
2 (also **peach tree**) the Chinese tree that bears this fruit. ● *Prunus persica*, family Rosaceae: many cultivars, including the nectarine.
– PHRASES **peaches and cream** (of a person's complexion) of a cream color with downy pink cheeks.
– ORIGIN late Middle English: from Old French *pesche*, from medieval Latin *persica*, from Latin *persicum (malum)*, literally 'Persian apple.'

peach[2] ▶ **v.** [no obj.] (**peach on**) informal inform on: *the other members of the gang would not hesitate to peach on him if it would serve their purpose.*
– ORIGIN late Middle English: shortening of archaic *appeach*, from Old French *empechier* 'impede' (see IMPEACH).

peach-bloom ▶ **n.** a matte glaze of reddish pink, mottled with green and brown, used on fine Chinese porcelain since around 1700. ■ a delicate purplish-pink color.
– ORIGIN early 19th cent.: applied to the porcelain glaze from the 1880s.

peach-blow ▶ **n.** another term for PEACH-BLOOM. ■ a type of late 19th-century American colored glass.
– ORIGIN early 19th cent.: from PEACH[1] + the noun BLOW[3].

peach fuzz ▶ **n.** informal the down on the chin of an adolescent boy whose beard has not yet developed.

pea·chick /ˈpēˌCHik/ ▶ **n.** a young peafowl.

peach Mel·ba ▶ **n.** a dish of ice cream and peaches with liqueur or sauce.
– ORIGIN named after Dame Nellie *Melba* (see MELBA).

Peach State a nickname for the state of GEORGIA.

Peach·tree State /ˈpēCHˌtrē/ a nickname for the state of GEORGIA.

peach·y /ˈpēCHē/ ▶ **adj.** (**peachier**, **peachiest**) informal of the nature or appearance of a peach. ■ fine; excellent: *everything is just peachy.*
– DERIVATIVES **peach·i·ness** /-ēnis/ **n.**

peach·y-keen ▶ **adj.** informal attractive; outstanding: *I enjoy my life, but it's not that peachy-keen.*
– ORIGIN mid 20th cent.: from PEACHY in the sense 'excellent' + KEEN[1] in the sense 'wonderful.'

pea·coat /ˈpēˌkōt/ (also **pea coat**) ▶ **n.** another term for PEA JACKET.

pea·cock /ˈpēˌkäk/ ▶ **n.** a male peafowl, which has very long tail feathers that have eyelike markings and that can be erected and expanded in display like a fan. ■ an ostentatious strutting person: *these young men have always considered themselves the peacocks of Europe.*
▶ **v.** [no obj.] display oneself ostentatiously; strut like a peacock: *he peacocks in front of the full-length mirror.*
– ORIGIN Middle English: from Old English *pēa* (from Latin *pavo*) 'peacock' + COCK[1].

pea·cock blue ▶ **n.** a greenish-blue color like that of a peacock's neck.

pea·cock but·ter·fly ▶ **n.** a brightly colored Eurasian butterfly with conspicuous eyespots on its wings. ● *Inachis io*, subfamily Nymphalinae, family Nymphalidae.

pea·cock ore ▶ **n.** another term for BORNITE, so named for its iridescence.

pea crab ▶ **n.** another term for OYSTER CRAB.

pea flour ▶ **n.** flour made from dried split peas.

pea·fowl /ˈpēˌfoul/ ▶ **n.** a large crested pheasant native to Asia. See PEACOCK, PEAHEN. ● Two genera and three species in the family Phasianidae, in particular the widely introduced **common peafowl** (*Pavo cristatus*).

pea green ▶ **n.** a yellowish green color like that of pea soup.

pea·hen /ˈpēˌhen/ ▶ **n.** a female peafowl, having drabber colors and a shorter tail than the male.

pea jack·et (also **peacoat**) ▶ **n.** a short, double-breasted overcoat of coarse woolen cloth, formerly worn by sailors.
– ORIGIN early 18th cent.: probably from Dutch *pijjakker*, from *pij* 'coat of coarse cloth' + *jekker* 'jacket.' The change in the ending was due to association with JACKET.

pea jacket

peak[1] /pēk/ ▶ **n.** the pointed top of a mountain: *the snowy peaks rose against the blue of a cloudless sky.* ■ a mountain, esp. one with a pointed top: *the rocky outcrops of peaks such as the Cassongrat offer a challenge to rock climbers.* ■ a projecting pointed part or shape: *whisk 2 egg whites to stiff peaks.* ■ a point in a curve or on a graph, or a value of a physical quantity, higher than those around it: *a slight increase in velocity provides a second peak on the general velocity curve.* ■ the point of highest activity, quality, or achievement: *anyone who saw Jones **at his peak** looked upon genius.* ■ chiefly Brit. a stiff brim at the front of a cap. ■ the narrow part of a ship's hold at the bow or stern. ■ the upper, outer corner of a sail extended by a gaff.
▶ **v.** [no obj.] reach a highest point, either of a specified value or at a specified time: *its popularity peaked in the 1940s* | *the rate of increase peaked at 34 percent last autumn.*
▶ **adj.** [attrib.] greatest; maximum: *he did not expect to be anywhere near peak fitness until Christmas.* ■ characterized by maximum activity or demand: *at peak hours, traffic speeds are reduced considerably.*
– DERIVATIVES **peak·i·ness** /-kēnis/ **n.**
– ORIGIN mid 16th cent.: probably a back-formation from *peaked*, variant of dialect *picked* 'pointed.'

USAGE See usage at PEEK.

peak[2] ▶ **v.** [no obj.] archaic decline in health and spirits; waste away.
– ORIGIN early 17th cent.: of unknown origin. The phrase *peak and pine* derives its currency from Shakespeare.

peaked[1] /pēkt/ ▶ **adj.** having a peak: *a peaked cap.*

peak·ed[2] /ˈpēˌkid/ (also **pekid**) ▶ **adj.** [predic.] (of a person) gaunt and pale from illness or fatigue: *you do look a little peaked.*

peak flow me·ter ▶ **n.** Medicine a calibrated instrument used to measure lung capacity in monitoring breathing disorders such as asthma.

peak load ▶ **n.** the maximum of electrical power demand.

peak oil ▶ **n.** the point in time when the global production of oil will reach its maximum rate, after which production will gradually decline.

peal /pēl/ ▶ **n. 1** a loud ringing of a bell or bells. ■ Bell-ringing a series of unique changes (strictly, at least five thousand) rung on a set of bells. ■ a set of bells.
2 a loud repeated or reverberating sound of thunder or laughter: *Ross burst into **peals of laughter**.*
▶ **v.** [no obj.] (of a bell or bells) ring loudly or in a peal: *all the bells of the city began to peal.* ■ (of laughter or thunder) sound in a peal: *Aunt Edie's laughter pealed around the parlor.* ■ [with obj.] convey or give out by the ringing of bells: *the carillon **pealed out** the news to the waiting city.*
– ORIGIN late Middle English: shortening of APPEAL.

Peale[1] /pēl/, Charles Willson (1741–1827), US artist. He was known for his portraits of well-known Americans, including that of George Washington. His son **Rembrandt** (1778–1860) also painted portraits of well-known people, as well as historical scenes. Another son **Raphaelle** (1774–1825), also an artist, favored silhouettes and still-life paintings.

Peale[2], Norman Vincent (1898–1993), US clergyman. The pastor of the Marble Collegiate Reformed Church in New York City 1932–84, he preached "applied Christianity," which encouraged people to think positively. His books included *The Art of Living* (1937), *The Art of Loving* (1948), and *The Power of Positive Thinking* (1952).

pe·an /ˈpēən/ ▶ **n.** Heraldry fur resembling ermine but with gold spots on a black ground.
– ORIGIN mid 16th cent.: of unknown origin.

Pe·a·no ax·i·oms /pāˈänō ˈaksēəmz/ ▶ **plural n.** Mathematics a set of axioms from which the properties of the natural numbers can be deduced.
– ORIGIN early 20th cent.: named after Giuseppe *Peano* (1858–1932), Italian mathematician.

pea·nut /ˈpēnət/ ▶ **n. 1** the oval seed of a South American plant, widely roasted and salted and eaten as a snack. ■ (**peanuts**) informal a paltry thing or amount, esp. a very small amount of money: *he pays peanuts.* ■ a small person (often used as a term of endearment). ■ (**peanuts**) small pieces of Styrofoam used for packing material.
2 the plant of the pea family that bears these seeds, which develop in pods that ripen underground. It is widely cultivated, esp. in the southern US, and large quantities are used to make oil or animal feed. ● *Arachis hypogaea*, family Leguminosae.

pea·nut but·ter ▶ **n.** a paste of ground roasted peanuts, usually eaten spread on bread.

pea·nut gal·ler·y ▶ **n.** informal the top gallery in a theater, where the cheaper seats are located. ■ a group of people who criticize someone, often by focusing on insignificant details: *he might find that playing the sport he loves isn't worth the aggravation from the peanut gallery's probing of his privacy.*

pea·nut oil ▶ **n.** oil produced from peanuts and used mainly for culinary purposes, but also in some soaps and pharmaceuticals.

pea·nut worm ▶ **n.** an unsegmented burrowing marine worm with a stout body and a slender anterior part. The latter bears a terminal mouth surrounded by tentacles, and can be retracted into the trunk. ● Phylum Sipuncula.

pear /pe(ə)r/ ▶ **n. 1** a yellowish- or brownish-green edible fruit that is typically narrow at the stalk and wider toward the base, with sweet, slightly gritty flesh.
2 (also **pear tree**) the Eurasian tree that bears this fruit. ● Genus *Pyrus*, family Rosaceae: several species and hybrids, in particular *P. communis*.
– ORIGIN Old English *pere*, *peru*; related to Dutch *peer*, from Latin *pirum*.

pearl /pərl/ ▶ **n. 1** a hard, lustrous spherical mass, typically white or bluish-gray, formed within the shell of a pearl oyster or other bivalve mollusk and highly prized as a gem. ■ an artificial imitation of this. ■ (**pearls**) a necklace of pearls. ■ something resembling a pearl in appearance: *the sweat stood in pearls along his forehead.* ■ short for MOTHER-OF-PEARL. ■ a very pale bluish gray or white like the color of a pearl.
2 a precious thing; the finest example of something: *the nation's media were assembled to hear his **pearls of wisdom**.*
▶ **v.** [no obj.] **1** literary form pearllike drops: *the juice on the blade pearled into droplets.* ■ [with obj.] make bluish-gray like a pearl: *the peaked hills, blue and pearled with clouds.*
2 (usu. as noun **pearling**) dive or fish for pearl oysters.
– PHRASES **pearls before swine** valuable things offered or given to people who do not appreciate them. [with biblical allusion to Matt. 7:6.]
– DERIVATIVES **pearl·er n.**
– ORIGIN late Middle English: from Old French *perle*, perhaps based on Latin *perna* 'leg,' extended to denote a leg-of-mutton-shaped bivalve.

pearl ash ▶ **n.** archaic commercial potassium carbonate.

pearl bar·ley ▶ **n.** barley reduced to small round grains by grinding.

Pearl Cit·y a city in Hawaii, on southern Oahu Island, on Pearl Harbor; pop. 30,976 (2000).

pearl div·er ▶ **n.** a person who dives for pearl oysters.

pearled /pərld/ ▶ **adj. 1** literary adorned with pearls: *we saw her pearled like the queen.* ■ bluish-gray, like a pearl.
2 formed into pearllike drops or grains: *pearled barley.*

pearl·es·cent /pərˈlesənt/ ▶ **adj.** having a luster resembling that of mother-of-pearl: *pearlescent colors.*

pearl ev·er·last·ing ▶ **n.** variant of PEARLY EVERLASTING.

pearl·eye /ˈpərlˌī/ ▶ **n.** a long-bodied, active fish of open oceans, with tubular eyes that are directed upward and bear a glistening white spot that may be a light organ. ● Family Scopelarchidae: several genera and species.

Pearl Har·bor a harbor on the island of Oahu, in Hawaii, the site of a major US naval base, where a surprise attack on December 7, 1941, by Japanese carrier-borne aircraft inflicted heavy damage and brought the US into World War II.

pearl·ite /ˈpərˌlīt/ ▶ **n.** Metallurgy a finely laminated mixture of ferrite and cementite present in cast iron and steel, formed by the cooling of austenite.
– ORIGIN late 19th cent.: from PEARL + -ITE[1].

pearl·ized /ˈpərlīzd/ ▶ **adj.** made to have or give a luster like that of mother-of-pearl.

pearl mil·let ▶ **n.** a tall tropical grain with long cylindrical ears, comprising an important food crop in the driest areas of Africa and South Asia. ● *Pennisetum glaucum* (or *typhoides*), family Gramineae.

pearl mus·sel ▶ **n.** an elongated freshwater bivalve mollusk that occasionally produces small pearls, found in large rivers of the northern hemisphere. ● *Margaritifera margaritifera*, family Margaritiferidae.

pearl on·ion ▶ **n.** a very small onion used esp. for pickling.

pearl oys·ter ▶ **n.** a tropical marine bivalve mollusk that has a ridged scaly shell and produces pearls. ● Genus *Pinctada*, family Pteriidae: several species, in particular *P. margaritifera*, a major source of commercial pearls.

Pearl Riv·er 1 a river in southern China that flows from Guangzhou (Canton) south to the South China Sea and forms part of the delta of the Xi River. Its lower reaches widen to form the Pearl River estuary, an inlet between Hong Kong and Macao. **2** a river that flows for 485 miles (780 km) across central Mississippi, to form part of the border with Louisiana, into the Gulf of Mexico.

pearl tea ▶ **n.** another term for **BUBBLE TEA**.

pearl·ware /ˈpərlˌwe(ə)r/ ▶ **n.** fine glazed earthenware pottery, typically white, of a type introduced by Josiah Wedgwood in 1779.

pearl·wort /ˈpərlwərt, -ˌwôrt/ ▶ **n.** a small plant of the pink family, with inconspicuous white flowers, native to north temperate regions. ● Genus *Sagina*, family Caryophyllaceae.

pearl·y /ˈpərlē/ ▶ **adj.** (**pearlier, pearliest**) resembling a pearl in luster or color: *the pearly light of a clear, still dawn.* ■ containing or adorned with pearls or mother-of-pearl.
– PHRASES **pearly whites** informal a person's teeth.
– DERIVATIVES **pearl·i·ness** /-lēnis/ **n.**

pearl·y ev·er·last·ing ▶ **n.** an ornamental North American plant with gray-green foliage and pearly white flower heads, used in dry flower arrangements. ● *Anaphalis margaritacea*, family Compositae.

pearl·y eye ▶ **n.** a brown American butterfly with pearly markings and distinctive eyespots on the undersides of the wings. ● Genus *Lethe*, subfamily Satyrinae, family Nymphalidae.

Pearl·y Gates ▶ **plural n.** informal the gates of heaven: *I am getting less fond of poems about old age as I near the Pearly Gates.*

pearl·y nau·ti·lus ▶ **n.** another term for **CHAMBERED NAUTILUS** (see **NAUTILUS**).

Pear·main /ˈpe(ə)rˌmān/ ▶ **n.** a pear-shaped apple of a variety with firm white flesh.
– ORIGIN Middle English (denoting an old variety of baking pear): from Old French *parmain*, probably based on Latin *parmensis* 'of Parma.'

pear-shaped ▶ **adj.** shaped like a pear; tapering toward the top. ■ (of a person) having hips that are disproportionately wide in relation to the upper part of the body.

Pear·son[1] /ˈpi(ə)rsən/, Karl (1857–1936), English mathematician; the principal founder of 20th-century statistics. He defined the concept of standard deviation and devised the chi-square test.

Pear·son[2], Lester Bowles (1897–1972), Canadian diplomat and Liberal statesman; prime minister 1963–68. As secretary of state for external affairs 1948–57, he acted as a mediator in the resolution of the Suez crisis in 1956. Nobel Peace Prize (1957).

Pear·son's cor·re·la·tion co·ef·fi·cient (also **Pearson's product-moment correlation coefficient**) ▶ **n.** Statistics a statistic measuring the linear interdependence between two variables or two sets of data.
– ORIGIN early 20th cent.: named after K. *Pearson* (see **PEARSON**[1]).

peart /pərt/ ▶ **adj.** dialect lively; cheerful.
– ORIGIN late 15th cent.: variant of **PERT**.

Pea·ry /ˈpi(ə)rē/, Robert Edwin (1856–1920), US explorer of the Arctic. He is generally credited with being the first person to reach the North Pole, on April 6, 1909, although his achievement is now doubted.

Pea·ry Land a mountainous region on the Arctic coast of northern Greenland. It is named after Robert Peary, who explored it in 1892 and 1900.

peas·ant /ˈpezənt/ ▶ **n.** a poor farmer of low social status who owns or rents a small piece of land for cultivation (chiefly in historical use or with reference to subsistence farming in poorer countries). ■ informal an ignorant, rude, or unsophisticated person; a person of low social status.
– DERIVATIVES **peas·ant·ry** /-trē/ **n.**, **peas·ant·y adj.**
– ORIGIN late Middle English: from Old French *paisent* 'country dweller,' from *pais* 'country,' based on Latin *pagus* 'country district.'

peas·ant e·con·o·my ▶ **n.** an agricultural economy in which the family is the basic unit of production.

Peas·ants' Re·volt an uprising in 1381 among the peasant and artisan classes in England. The rebels marched on London, occupying the city and executing unpopular ministers, but after the death of their leader, Wat Tyler, they were persuaded to disperse by Richard II.

pease /pēz/ ▶ **plural n.** archaic peas.
– ORIGIN Old English *pise* 'pea,' (plural) *pisan*, via Latin from Greek *pison*. Compare with **PEA**.

pea·shoot·er /ˈpēˌshōōtər/ ▶ **n.** a toy weapon consisting of a small tube that is blown through in order to shoot out dried peas.

pea soup ▶ **n.** soup made from peas, esp. a thick, yellowish-green soup made from dried split peas.

peat /pēt/ ▶ **n.** a brown, soil-like material characteristic of boggy, acid ground, consisting of partly decomposed vegetable matter. It is widely cut and dried for use in gardening and as fuel: *cuttings are rooted in a homemade mixture of equal parts peat and sand* | [as modifier] *most of Lewis is acid peat bog.*
– DERIVATIVES **peat·y adj.**
– ORIGIN Middle English: from Anglo-Latin *peta*, perhaps of Celtic origin.

peat·land /ˈpētˌland/ ▶ **n.** (also **peatlands**) land consisting largely of peat or peat bogs.

peat moss ▶ **n. 1** a large absorbent moss that grows in dense masses on boggy ground, where the lower parts decay slowly to form peat deposits. Peat moss is widely used in horticulture, esp. for packing plants and (as peat) for compost. Also called **BOG MOSS**, **SPHAGNUM**. ● Genus *Sphagnum*, family Sphagnaceae: many species. **2** a lowland peat bog.

pea tree (also **pea shrub**) ▶ **n.** a shrub or small tree with yellow pealike flowers, native to Siberia and grown as an ornamental. ● *Caragana arborescens*, family Leguminosae.

peau de soie /ˈpō də ˈswä/ ▶ **n.** a smooth, finely ribbed satin fabric of silk or rayon.
– ORIGIN mid 19th cent.: French, literally 'skin of silk.'

peau d'or·ange /ˈpō dôˈränzh/ ▶ **n.** a pitted or dimpled appearance of the skin, esp. as characteristic of some cases of breast cancer or due to cellulite.
– ORIGIN French, literally 'orange skin.'

pea·vey /ˈpēvē/ (also **peavy**) ▶ **n.** (pl. **peaveys** or **peavies**) a lumberjack's cant hook with a spike at the end.
– ORIGIN late 19th cent.: from the surname of the inventor.

pea·vine /ˈpēˌvīn/ ▶ **n.** a North American meadow vetch. ● *Vicia americana*, family Leguminosae.

peb·ble /ˈpebəl/ ▶ **n.** a small stone made smooth and round by the action of water or sand.
▶ **adj.** [attrib.] informal (of an eyeglass lens) very thick and convex: *pebble glasses.*
– DERIVATIVES **peb·bled adj.**, **peb·bly** /-(ə)lē/ **adj.**
– ORIGIN late Old English, recorded as the first element of *papel-stān* 'pebble-stone,' *pyppelrīpig* 'pebble-stream,' of unknown origin. The word is recorded in place names from the early 12th cent. onward.

Peb·ble Beach a resort on the Monterey Peninsula in west central California, site of a famous golf course.

peb·ble-dash ▶ **n.** chiefly Brit. mortar with pebbles in it, used as a coating for exterior walls.
– DERIVATIVES **peb·ble-dashed adj.**

peb·ble-grained ▶ **adj.** (of leather) having a rough and indented surface as a result of treatment with a patterned roller.

pec /pek/ ▶ **n.** (usu. **pecs**) informal a pectoral muscle (esp. with reference to the development of these muscles in bodybuilding).

pe·can /pəˈkän, ˈpēˌkan/ ▶ **n.** a smooth brown nut with an edible kernel similar to a walnut. ● This nut is obtained from a hickory tree (*Carya illinoensis*, family Juglandaceae), native to the southern US.
– ORIGIN late 18th cent.: from French *pacane*, from Illinois (an American Indian language).

pec·ca·ble /ˈpekəbəl/ ▶ **adj.** archaic, formal capable of sinning: *we hold all mankind to be peccable.*
– DERIVATIVES **pec·ca·bil·i·ty** /ˌpekəˈbilitē/ **n.**
– ORIGIN early 17th cent.: from French, from medieval Latin *peccabilis*, from Latin *peccare* 'to sin.'

pec·ca·dil·lo /ˌpekəˈdilō/ ▶ **n.** (pl. **peccadilloes** or **peccadillos**) a small, relatively unimportant offense or sin.
– ORIGIN late 16th cent.: from Spanish *pecadillo*, diminutive of *pecado* 'sin,' from Latin *peccare* 'to sin.'

pec·cant /ˈpekənt/ ▶ **adj.** archaic **1** having committed a fault or sin; offending. **2** diseased or causing disease.
– DERIVATIVES **pec·can·cy** /ˈpekənsē/ **n.**
– ORIGIN late 16th cent. (sense 2): from Latin *peccant-* 'sinning,' from the verb *peccare*.

pec·ca·ry /ˈpekərē/ ▶ **n.** (pl. **peccaries**) a gregarious piglike mammal that is found from the southwestern US to Paraguay. ● Family Tayassuidae: two genera and three species, in particular the **collared peccary** (*Tayassu tajacu*).
– ORIGIN early 17th cent.: from Carib *pakira*.

collared peccary

pec·ca·vi /pəˈkävē, -ˈkāvī/ ▶ **exclam.** archaic used to express one's guilt.
– ORIGIN Latin, literally 'I have sinned.'

Pe·chen·ga /pəˈchengə, pyiˈchyengə/ a region of northwestern Russia that lies west of Murmansk on the border with Finland. Formerly part of Finland, it was ceded to the former Soviet Union in 1940. It was known by its Finnish name, Petsamo, from 1920 until 1944.

Pe·cho·ra /pəˈchôrə, pyiˈchyôrə/ a river in northern Russia that rises in the Ural Mountains and flows about 1,125 miles (1,800 km) north and then east to the Barents Sea.

Peck /pek/, Gregory (1916–2002), US actor; full name *Eldred Gregory Peck*. Notable movies: *Spellbound* (1945), *Gentleman's Agreement* (1947), *The Big Country* (1958), and *To Kill a Mockingbird* (1962).

peck[1] /pek/ ▶ **v.** (of a bird) strike or bite something with its beak. [no obj.] *two geese were* ***pecking at*** *some grain* | *vultures swooping down to* ***peck out*** *the calf's eyes* | [with obj.] *beaks may be cut off to stop the hens pecking each other.* ■ [with obj.] make (a hole) by striking with the beak: *robins are the worst culprits, pecking holes in every cherry.* ■ [with obj.] kiss (someone) lightly or perfunctorily: *she pecked him on the cheek.* ■ (**peck at**) informal (of a person) eat (food) listlessly or daintily: *don't peck at your food, eat a whole mouthful.* ■ (**peck at**) criticize or nag: *defects for a critic to peck at.* ■ [with obj.] type (something) slowly and laboriously: *his son Paul was* ***pecking out*** *letters with two fingers on his typewriter.* ■ informal (of a horse) pitch forward or stumble as a result of striking the ground with the front rather than the flat of the hoof: *her father's horse had pecked slightly on landing.* [variant of obsolete *pick* 'fix (something pointed) in the ground.'] ■ [with obj.] archaic strike with a pick or other tool: *part of a wall was pecked down and carted away.*
▶ **n. 1** a stroke or bite by a bird with its beak: *the bird managed to give its attacker a sharp peck.* ■ a light or perfunctory kiss: *a fatherly* ***peck on the cheek.*** **2** archaic food: *he wants a little more peck.*
– ORIGIN late Middle English: of unknown origin; compare with Middle Low German *pekken* 'peck (with the beak).'

peck[2] ▶ **n.** a measure of capacity for dry goods, equal to a quarter of a bushel (8 US quarts = 8.81 liters, or 2 imperial gallons = 9.092 liters). ■ archaic a large number or amount of something: *a peck of dirt.*
– ORIGIN Middle English (used esp. as a measure of oats for horses): from Anglo-Norman French *pek*, of unknown origin.

peck·er /ˈpekər/ ▶ **n.** vulgar slang a penis.
– PHRASES **keep your pecker up** Brit. informal remain cheerful. [*pecker* probably in the sense 'beak, bill.']

peck·er·head /ˈpekərˌhed/ ▶ **n.** vulgar slang an aggressive, objectionable person.

peck·er·wood /ˈpekərˌwŏŏd/ ▶ **n.** informal, often derogatory a white person, esp. a poor one.
– ORIGIN 1920s: from a reversal of the elements of *woodpecker*, originally a dialect word for the bird, used commonly in Mississippi and Tennessee.

Peck·ham /ˈpekəm/, Rufus Wheeler, Jr. (1838–1909), US Supreme Court associate justice 1895–1909. A judge in New York's court of appeals 1886–95, he was appointed to the Court by President Cleveland.

peck·ing or·der (also **peck order**) ▶ **n.** a hierarchy of status seen among members of a group of people or animals, originally as observed among hens: *the luxurious office accentuated the manager's position in the pecking order.*

peck·ish /ˈpekish/ ▶ **adj.** informal, chiefly Brit. hungry: *we were both feeling a bit peckish and there was nothing to eat.*

Peck·sniff·i·an /pekˈsnifēən/ ▶ **adj.** affecting benevolence or high moral principles.

–ORIGIN mid 19th cent.: from *Pecksniff*, the name of a character in Dickens's *Martin Chuzzlewit*, + -IAN.

Pe·con·ic Bay /piˈkänik/ an inlet of the Atlantic Ocean at the eastern end of Long Island in New York that separates the North Fork and the South Fork of the island.

pec·o·ri·no /pekəˈrēnō/ ▶ n. (pl. **pecorinos**) an Italian cheese made from ewes' milk.
–ORIGIN Italian, from *pecorino* 'of ewes,' from *pecora* 'sheep.'

Pe·cos Riv·er /ˈpā,kōs/ a river that flows for 925 miles (1,490 km) from northern New Mexico through western Texas to the Rio Grande.

Pécs /pācH/ an industrial city in southwestern Hungary; pop. 156,974 (2009).

pec·ten /ˈpektən/ ▶ n. (pl. **pectens** /ˈpektnz/ or **pectines** /ˈpektnēz/) Zoology **1** any of a number of comblike structures occurring in animal bodies, in particular: ■ a pigmented vascular projection from the choroid in the eye of a bird. ■ an appendage of an insect consisting of or bearing a row of bristles or chitinous teeth. ■ a sensory appendage on the underside of a scorpion.
2 a scallop. ● Genus *Pecten*, family Pectinidae.
–DERIVATIVES **pec·ti·nate** /ˈpektənit, -,nāt/ adj., **pec·ti·nat·ed** /-,nātid/ adj., **pec·ti·na·tion** /,pektəˈnāsHən/ n. (sense 1).
–ORIGIN late Middle English (denoting the metacarpus): from Latin *pecten, pectin-* 'a comb, rake.'

pec·tin /ˈpektin/ ▶ n. a soluble gelatinous polysaccharide that is present in ripe fruits and is extracted for use as a setting agent in jams and jellies.
–DERIVATIVES **pec·tic** /ˈpektik/ adj.
–ORIGIN mid 19th cent.: from Greek *pektos* 'congealed' (from *pēgnuein* 'make solid') + -IN[1].

pec·to·ral /ˈpektərəl/ ▶ adj. of or relating to the breast or chest: *pectoral development*. ■ worn on the chest: *a pectoral shield*.
▶ n. (usu. **pectorals**) a pectoral muscle. ■ a pectoral fin. ■ an ornamental breastplate, esp. one worn by a Jewish high priest.
–ORIGIN late Middle English (in the sense 'breastplate'): from Latin *pectorale* 'breastplate,' *pectoralis* 'of the breast,' from *pectus, pector-* 'breast, chest.'

pec·to·ral cross ▶ n. Christian Church a cross or crucifix worn on a long chain around the neck so that it rests on the chest, worn esp. by bishops, abbots, and priests.

pec·to·ral fin ▶ n. Zoology each of a pair of fins situated on either side just behind a fish's head, helping to control the direction of movement during locomotion. They correspond to the forelimbs of other vertebrates.

pec·to·ral gir·dle ▶ n. (in vertebrates) the skeletal framework that provides attachment for the forelimbs or pectoral fins, usually consisting of the scapulas and clavicles.

pec·to·ral mus·cle ▶ n. (usu. **pectoral muscles**) each of the four large paired muscles that cover the front of the rib cage and serve to draw the forelimbs toward the chest.

pec·to·ral sand·pip·er ▶ n. a migratory sandpiper with dark streaks on the breast and a white belly, breeding chiefly in Arctic Canada. ● *Calidris melanotos*, family Scolopacidae.

pec·u·late /ˈpekyə,lāt/ ▶ v. [with obj.] formal embezzle or steal (money, esp. public funds): *the people accused them of having peculated the public money*.
–DERIVATIVES **pec·u·la·tion** /,pekyəˈlāsHən/ n., **pec·u·la·tor** /-,lātər/ n.
–ORIGIN mid 18th cent.: from Latin *peculat-* 'embezzled,' from the verb *peculari* (related to *peculium* 'property').

pe·cu·liar /pəˈkyōōlyər/ ▶ adj. **1** strange or odd; unusual: *his accent was a peculiar mixture of Cockney and Irish*. ■ [predic.] informal slightly and indefinably unwell; faint or dizzy: *I felt a little peculiar for a while, but I'm absolutely fine now*.
2 [predic.] (**peculiar to**) belonging exclusively to: *the air hung with an antiseptic aroma peculiar to hospitals*. ■ formal particular; special: *any attempt to explicate the theme is bound to run into peculiar difficulties*.
▶ n. chiefly Brit. a parish or church exempt from the jurisdiction of the diocese in which it lies, through being subject to the jurisdiction of the monarch or an archbishop.
–ORIGIN late Middle English (in the sense 'particular, special'): from Latin *peculiaris* 'of private property,' from *peculium* 'property,' from *pecu* 'cattle' (cattle being private property). The sense 'odd' dates from the early 17th cent.

pe·cu·liar in·sti·tu·tion ▶ n. historical the system of black slavery in the southern states of the US.

pe·cu·li·ar·i·ty /pə,kyōōlēˈaritē/ ▶ n. (pl. **peculiarities**) an odd or unusual feature or habit: *for all his peculiarities, she finds his personality quite endearing*. ■ a characteristic or quality that is distinctive of a particular person or place: *his essays characterized decency as a British peculiarity*. ■ the quality or state of being peculiar: *the peculiarity of their upbringing*.

pe·cu·liar·ly /pəˈkyōōlyərlē/ ▶ adv. **1** [as submodifier] more than usually; especially: *some patients were peculiarly difficult to cure*.
2 oddly: *the town is peculiarly built*.
3 used to emphasize restriction to an individual or group: *a manner peculiarly his own*.

pe·cu·ni·ar·y /piˈkyōōnē,erē/ ▶ adj. formal of, relating to, or consisting of money: *he admitted obtaining a pecuniary advantage by deception*.
–DERIVATIVES **pe·cu·ni·ar·i·ly** /pə,kyōōnēˈe(ə)rəlē/ adv.
–ORIGIN early 16th cent.: from Latin *pecuniarius*, from *pecunia* 'money,' from *pecu* 'cattle, money.'

ped·a·gog·ic /,pedəˈgäjik/ ▶ adj. of or relating to teaching: *they show great pedagogic skills*. ■ rare of or characteristic of a pedagogue.
–DERIVATIVES **ped·a·gog·i·cal** adj., **ped·a·gog·i·cal·ly** /-(ə)lē/ adv.
–ORIGIN late 18th cent.: from French *pédagogique*, from Greek *paidagōgikos*.

ped·a·gogue /ˈpedə,gäg/ ▶ n. a teacher, esp. a strict or pedantic one.
–ORIGIN late Middle English: via Latin from Greek *paidagōgos*, denoting a slave who accompanied a child to school (from *pais, paid-* 'boy' + *agōgos* 'guide').

ped·a·go·gy /ˈpedə,gäjē, -,gōjē/ ▶ n. (pl. **pedagogies**) the method and practice of teaching, esp. as an academic subject or theoretical concept: *the relationship between applied linguistics and language pedagogy | subject-based pedagogies*.
–DERIVATIVES **ped·a·gog·ics** /,pedəˈgäjiks/ n.
–ORIGIN late 16th cent.: from French *pédagogie*, from Greek *paidagōgia* 'office of a pedagogue,' from *paidagōgos* (see PEDAGOGUE).

ped·al[1] /ˈpedl/ ▶ n. a foot-operated lever or control for a vehicle, musical instrument, or other mechanism, in particular: ■ each of a pair of cranks used for powering a bicycle or other vehicle propelled by leg power. ■ a foot-operated throttle, brake, or clutch control in a motor vehicle. ■ each of a set of two or three levers on a piano, particularly (also **sustaining pedal**) one that, when depressed by the foot, prevents the dampers from stopping the sound when the keys are released. The second is the **soft pedal**; a third, if present, produces either selective sustaining or complete muffling of the tone. ■ Music (usu. **pedals**) each key of an organ keyboard that is played with the feet. ■ Music short for PEDAL NOTE.
▶ v. (**pedals, pedaling, pedaled**; Brit. **pedals, pedalling, pedalled**) [no obj.] move by working the pedals of a bicycle: *they pedaled along the canal towpath*. ■ [with obj.] move (a bicycle) by working its pedals: *she was pedaling a bicycle around town*. ■ work the pedals of a bicycle: *he was coming down the path on his bike, pedaling hard*. ■ use the pedals of a piano, esp. in a particular style: (as noun **pedaling**) *Chopin gave no indications of pedaling in his manuscript*.
–PHRASES **with the pedal to the metal** informal with the accelerator of a car pressed to the floor.
–DERIVATIVES **ped·al·er** (Brit. **pedaller**) n.
–ORIGIN early 17th cent. (denoting a foot-operated lever of an organ): from French *pédale*, from Italian *pedale*, from Latin *pedalis* 'a foot in length,' from *pes, ped-* 'foot.'

> **USAGE** People often confuse the words **pedal** and **peddle**. **Pedal** is a noun referring to a foot-operated lever, as on a bicycle, and a verb chiefly meaning 'move by working the pedals of a bicycle' (*they pedaled along the road*). **Peddle**, on the other hand, is a verb meaning 'sell goods or promote an idea' (*he peddled printing materials around the country | she peddled a ludicrously utopian view of the past*). The related words **peddler** and **pedaler** are also confused. A **peddler** (also spelled **pedlar**, especially in Britain) is a person who goes from place to place selling goods, while a **pedaler** (or, in Britain, a **pedaller**) is someone who rides a bike.

ped·al[2] /ˈpēdl/ ▶ adj. chiefly Medicine & Zoology of or relating to the foot or feet.
–ORIGIN early 17th cent.: from Latin *pedalis*, from *pes, ped-* 'foot.'

ped·al·board /ˈpedl,bôrd/ ▶ n. the keyboard of pedals on an organ.

ped·al boat /ˈpedl/ ▶ n. another term for PADDLEBOAT.

ped·al note /ˈpedl/ ▶ n. (also **pedal tone**) Music **1** the lowest or fundamental note of a harmonic series in some brass and wind instruments.
2 (also **pedal point**) a note sustained in one part (usually the bass) through successive harmonies, some of which are independent of it.

ped·al pow·er /ˈpedl/ ▶ n. informal cycling as a means of transportation.

ped·al push·er /ˈpedl/ ▶ n. **1** (**pedal pushers**) women's calf-length pants.
2 informal a cyclist.

ped·al steel /ˈpedl/ (also **pedal steel guitar**) ▶ n. a musical instrument played like a Hawaiian guitar, but set on a stand with pedals to adjust the tension of the strings.

ped·ant /ˈpednt/ ▶ n. a person who is excessively concerned with minor details and rules or with displaying academic learning.
–ORIGIN late 16th cent.: from French *pédant*, from Italian *pedante*, perhaps from the first element of Latin *paedagogus* (see PEDAGOGUE).

pe·dan·tic /pəˈdantik/ ▶ adj. of or like a pedant: *many of the essays are long, dense, and too pedantic to hold great appeal*.
–DERIVATIVES **pe·dan·ti·cal·ly** /-tik(ə)lē/ adv.

ped·ant·ry /ˈpedntrē/ ▶ n. excessive concern with minor details and rules: *to object to this is not mere pedantry*.

ped·dle /ˈpedl/ ▶ v. [with obj.] try to sell (something, esp. small goods) by going from house to house or place to place: *he peddled art and printing materials around the country*. ■ sell (an illegal drug or stolen item): (as noun **peddling**) *certain youths who were involved in theft and drug peddling*. ■ derogatory promote (an idea or view) persistently or widely: *he criticized his fellow candidate for peddling risky ideas*.
–ORIGIN early 16th cent.: back-formation from PEDDLER.

> **USAGE** see usage at PEDAL[1].

ped·dler /ˈpedlər, ˈpedl-ər/ (also **pedlar**) ▶ n. a person who goes from place to place selling small goods. ■ a person who sells illegal drugs or stolen goods: *a drug peddler*. ■ a person who promotes an idea or view persistently or widely: *peddlers of dangerous utopianism*.
–ORIGIN Middle English: perhaps an alteration of synonymous dialect *pedder*, apparently from dialect *ped* 'basket.'

> **USAGE** see usage at PEDAL[1].

ped·er·ast /ˈpedə,rast/ ▶ n. a man who indulges in pederasty.
–ORIGIN mid 17th cent.: from Greek *paiderastēs*.

ped·er·as·ty /ˈpedə,rastē/ ▶ n. sexual activity involving a man and a boy.
–DERIVATIVES **ped·er·as·tic** /,pedəˈrastik/ adj.
–ORIGIN early 17th cent.: from modern Latin *paederastia*, from Greek *paiderastia*, from *pais, paid-* 'boy' + *erastēs* 'lover.'

pe·des /ˈpēdēz, ˈpedēz/ plural form of PES.

ped·es·tal /ˈpedəstl/ ▶ n. **1** the base or support on which a statue, obelisk, or column is mounted. ■ each of the two supports of a kneehole desk or table, typically containing drawers. ■ the supporting column or base of a washbasin or toilet bowl.
2 a position in which someone is greatly or uncritically admired: *It's as if I'm on a pedestal and he worships me – I hate that*.
–PHRASES **put** (or **place**) **someone on a pedestal** give someone uncritical respect or admiration; treat someone as an ideal rather than a real person: *If you idolize a girl and put her on a pedestal, she will sense it instantly*.
–ORIGIN mid 16th cent.: from French *piédestal*, from Italian *piedestallo*, from *piè* 'foot' (from Latin *pes, ped-*, which later influenced the spelling) + *di* 'of' + *stallo* 'stall.'

ped·es·tal ta·ble ▶ n. a table with a single central support.

pe·des·tri·an /pəˈdestrēən/ ▶ n. a person walking along a road or in a developed area.
▶ adj. lacking inspiration or excitement; dull: *disenchantment with their present, pedestrian lives*.
–DERIVATIVES **pe·des·tri·an·ly** adv.
–ORIGIN early 18th cent.: from French *pédestre* or Latin *pedester* 'going on foot,' also 'written in prose' + -IAN. Early use in English was in the description of writing as 'prosaic.'

pe·des·tri·an cross·ing ▶ n. British term for CROSSWALK.

pe·des·tri·an·ize /pəˈdestrēəˌnīz/ ▶ v. [with obj.] close (a street or area) to traffic, making it accessible only to pedestrians: *the ancient center of the town was pedestrianized.*
– DERIVATIVES **pe·des·tri·an·i·za·tion** /pəˌdestrēəniˈzāsʜən/ n.

pe·des·tri·an mall ▶ n. see MALL (sense 2).

pe·di·a·tri·cian /ˌpēdēəˈtrisʜən/ (Brit. **paediatrician**) ▶ n. a medical practitioner specializing in children and their diseases.

pe·di·at·rics /ˌpēdēˈatriks/ (Brit. **paediatrics**) ▶ plural n. [treated as sing.] the branch of medicine dealing with children and their diseases.
– DERIVATIVES **pe·di·at·ric** /-ˈatrik/ adj.
– ORIGIN late 19th cent.: from PEDO-[1] 'of children' + Greek *iatros* 'physician' + -ICS.

ped·i·cab /ˈpediˌkab/ ▶ n. a small pedal-operated vehicle, serving as a taxi in some countries.

ped·i·cel /ˈpediˌsel/ ▶ n. Botany a small stalk bearing an individual flower in an inflorescence. Compare with PEDUNCLE. ■ Anatomy & Zoology another term for PEDICLE.
– DERIVATIVES **ped·i·cel·late** /ˌpediˈselit, -ˈseˌlāt/ adj.
– ORIGIN late 17th cent.: from modern Latin *pedicellus* 'small foot,' diminutive of *pes, ped-* 'foot.'

ped·i·cel·lar·i·a /ˌpedisəˈle(ə)rēə/ ▶ n. (pl. **pedicellariae** /-ˈle(ə)rēˌē/) Zoology a defensive organ like a minute pincer present in large numbers on an echinoderm.
– ORIGIN late 19th cent.: modern Latin, from Latin *pediculus* 'small foot' (see PEDICEL).

ped·i·cle /ˈpedikəl/ ▶ n. Anatomy & Zoology a small stalklike structure connecting an organ or other part to the human or animal body. Compare with PEDICEL. ■ Medicine part of a graft, esp. a skin graft, left temporarily attached to its original site.
– ORIGIN early 17th cent.: from Latin *pediculus* 'small foot,' diminutive of *pes, ped-*.

pe·dic·u·li·cide /ˌpediˈkyo͞oləsīd/ ▶ n. a chemical used to kill lice.
– ORIGIN early 20th cent.: from Latin *pediculus* 'louse' + -CIDE.

pe·dic·u·lo·sis /pəˌdikyəˈlōsis/ ▶ n. Medicine infestation with lice.
– ORIGIN early 19th cent.: from Latin *pediculus* 'louse' + -OSIS.

ped·i·cure /ˈpediˌkyo͝or/ ▶ n. a cosmetic treatment of the feet and toenails.
▶ v. [with obj.] (usu. as adj. **pedicured**) give such a cosmetic treatment to (the feet).
– ORIGIN mid 19th cent.: from French *pédicure*, from Latin *pes, ped-* 'foot' + *curare* 'attend to.'

ped·i·gree /ˈpedəˌgrē/ ▶ n. **1** the record of descent of an animal, showing it to be purebred. ■ informal a purebred animal.
2 the recorded ancestry, esp. upper-class ancestry, of a person or family. ■ the background or history of a person or thing, esp. as conferring distinction or quality. ■ a genealogical table.
– DERIVATIVES **ped·i·greed** adj.
– ORIGIN late Middle English: from Anglo-Norman French *pé de grue* 'crane's foot,' a mark used to denote succession in pedigrees.

ped·i·ment /ˈpedəmənt/ ▶ n. the triangular upper part of the front of a building in classical style, typically surmounting a portico of columns. ■ a similar feature surmounting a door, window, front, or other part of a building in another style. ■ Geology a broad, gently sloping expanse of rock debris extending outward from the foot of a mountain slope, esp. in a desert.
– DERIVATIVES **ped·i·men·tal** /ˌpedəˈmentl/ adj., **ped·i·ment·ed** adj.
– ORIGIN late 16th cent. (as *periment*): perhaps an alteration of PYRAMID.

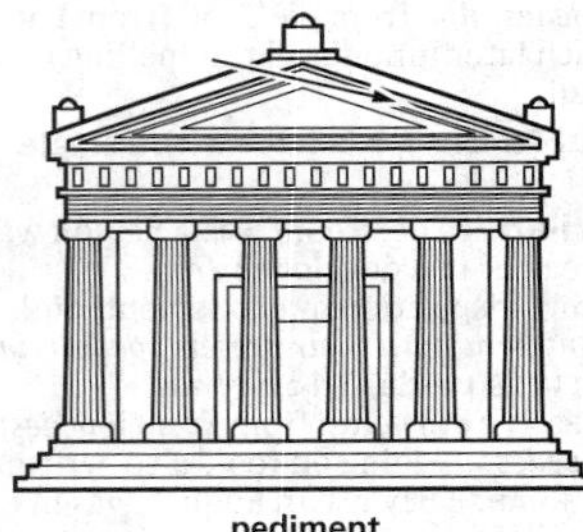

pediment

ped·i·palp /ˈpedəˌpalp/ ▶ n. Zoology each of the second pair of appendages attached to the cephalothorax of most arachnids. They are variously specialized as pincers in scorpions, sensory organs in spiders, and locomotory organs in horseshoe crabs.
– ORIGIN early 19th cent.: from modern Latin *pedipalpi* (plural), from Latin *pes, ped-* 'foot' + *palpus* 'palp.'

ped·i·plain /ˈpediˌplān/ ▶ n. Geology an extensive plain formed in a desert by the coalescence of neighboring pediments.
– ORIGIN 1930s: from PEDIMENT + PLAIN[1].

ped·i·pla·na·tion /ˌpediplәˈnāsʜən/ ▶ n. Geology the formation of pediplains by coalescence of pediments.

ped·lar ▶ n. variant spelling of PEDDLER.

pedo-[1] /ˈpedō/ (Brit. **paedo-**) ▶ comb. form of a child; relating to children: *pedophile*.
– ORIGIN from Greek *pais, paid-* 'child, boy.'

pedo-[2] ▶ comb. form relating to soil or soil types: *pedogenic*.
– ORIGIN from Greek *pedon* 'ground.'

pe·do·don·tics /ˌpēdəˈdäntiks/ (Brit. **paedodontics**) ▶ plural n. [treated as sing.] the branch of dentistry that deals with children's teeth.
– DERIVATIVES **pe·do·don·tic** /-tik/ adj., **pe·do·don·tist** /-ˈdäntist/ n.
– ORIGIN from PEDO-[1] + Greek *odous, odont-* 'tooth.'

ped·o·gen·e·sis /ˌpēdōˈjenəsəs/ ▶ n. Zoology see NEOTENY.
– DERIVATIVES **ped·o·ge·net·ic** adj.
– ORIGIN from PEDO-[1] + GENESIS.

pe·do·gen·ic /ˌpedəˈjenik/ ▶ adj. relating to or denoting processes occurring in soil or leading to the formation of soil.
– ORIGIN from PEDO-[2] + -GENIC.

pe·dol·o·gy /pəˈdäləjē/ ▶ n. another term for SOIL SCIENCE.
– DERIVATIVES **ped·o·log·i·cal** /ˌpedəˈläjikəl/ adj., **pe·dol·o·gist** /-jist/ n.
– ORIGIN from PEDO-[2] + -LOGY.

pe·dom·e·ter /pəˈdämitər/ ▶ n. an instrument for estimating the distance traveled on foot by recording the number of steps taken.
– ORIGIN early 18th cent.: from French *pédomètre*, from Latin *pes, ped-* 'foot.'

ped·o·mor·pho·sis /ˌpēdəˈmôrfəsəs/ ▶ n. Zoology see NEOTENY.
– DERIVATIVES **pe·do·mor·phic** /-fik/ adj.
– ORIGIN from PEDO-[1] + -MORPH + -OSIS.

pe·do·phile /ˈpedəˌfīl/ (Brit. **paedophile**) ▶ n. a person who is sexually attracted to children.
– ORIGIN from PEDO-[1] + -PHILE.

pe·do·phil·i·a /ˌpedəˈfilēə, ˌpēdə-/ (Brit. **paedophilia**) ▶ n. sexual feelings directed toward children.
– DERIVATIVES **pe·do·phil·i·ac** /-ˈfilēˌak/ n. & adj.
– ORIGIN from PEDO-[1] + -PHILIA.

Pe·dro Xi·me·nez /ˌpādrō hiˈmāniz/ (abbr.: **PX** or **px**) ▶ n. a variety of sweet white Spanish grape used in making sherry and sweet wine. ■ a sweet white wine made from this grape.
– ORIGIN from the name of the person who introduced the grape.

pe·dun·cle /ˈpēˌdəNGkəl, pəˈdəNGkəl/ ▶ n. Botany the stalk bearing a flower or fruit, or the main stalk of an inflorescence. Compare with PEDICEL. ■ Zoology a stalklike part by which an organ is attached to an animal's body, or by which a barnacle or other sedentary animal is attached to a substrate.
– DERIVATIVES **pe·dun·cu·lar** /pəˈdəNGkyələr/ adj.
– ORIGIN mid 18th cent.: from modern Latin *pedunculus*, from Latin *pes, ped-* 'foot.'

pe·dun·cu·late /pəˈdəNGkyəˌlāt, -lit/ ▶ adj. Botany & Zoology having a peduncle.

pe·dun·cu·late oak ▶ n. the common or English oak.

pee /pē/ informal ▶ v. (**pees, peeing, peed**) [no obj.] urinate: *the puppy was peeing on the carpet.* ■ [with obj.] (**pee in one's pants**) wet one's underpants by urinating involuntarily (often used to suggest the notion of losing control of oneself through fear or hilarity).
▶ n. [in sing.] an act of urinating: *I really need to take a pee.* ■ urine.
– ORIGIN late 18th cent. (as a verb): euphemistic use of the initial letter of PISS.

Pee Dee Riv·er /ˈpēˌdē/ a river that flows for 230 miles (370 km) through North Carolina and South Carolina to an inlet of the Atlantic Ocean south of the Grand Strand.

peek /pēk/ ▶ v. [no obj.] look quickly, typically in a furtive manner: *faces peeked from behind the curtains.* ■ protrude slightly so as to be just visible: *his socks were so full of holes his toes peeked through.*
▶ n. a quick and typically furtive look: *a peek through the window showed that the taxi had arrived.*
– ORIGIN late Middle English *pike, pyke*, of unknown origin.

USAGE The word meaning 'look quickly or furtively' and 'a quick or furtive look' is **peek**, not **peak**: *the sun peeks out only intermittently; a sneak peek at what's in store.* In some contexts, this error is very common: for example, almost a third of citations for the expression **a sneak peek** in the Oxford English Corpus are for the incorrect spelling (*a sneak peak*).

peek·a·boo /ˈpēkəˌbo͞o/ ▶ n. a game played with a young child, which involves hiding behind something and suddenly reappearing, saying "peekaboo."
▶ adj. [attrib.] (of a garment) revealing glimpses of the skin or body: *a black lace peekaboo dress.* ■ (of a hairstyle) concealing one eye with a fringe or wave of hair.
– ORIGIN late 16th cent. (as a noun): from the verb PEEK + BOO[1].

Peel /pēl/, Sir Robert (1788–1850), British statesman, prime minister 1834–35 and 1841–46. As home secretary 1828–30, he established the Metropolitan Police, whose members are called "bobbies" in his honor. His repeal of the Corn Laws in 1846 split the Conservatives and forced his resignation.

peel[1] /pēl/ ▶ v. **1** [with obj.] remove the outer covering or skin from (a fruit, vegetable, or shrimp): *she watched him peel an apple with deliberate care.* ■ remove (the outer covering or skin) from a fruit or vegetable: ***peel off** the skins and thickly slice the potatoes.* ■ [no obj.] (of a fruit or vegetable) have a skin that can be removed: *oranges that peel easily.* ■ (**peel something away/off**) remove or separate a thin covering or part from the outside or surface of something: *carefully peel away the wax paper.* ■ remove (an article of clothing): *Suzy peeled off her white pullover.*
2 [no obj.] (of a surface or object) lose parts of its outer layer or covering in small strips or pieces: *the walls are peeling.* ■ [with adverbial] (of an outer layer or covering) come off, esp. in strips or small pieces.
▶ n. the outer covering or rind of a fruit or vegetable.
– PHRASAL VERBS **peel off** (of a member of a formation, esp. a flying formation) leave the formation by veering away to one side: *the pace was much too hot for Beris, and he peeled off after five laps.* **peel out** informal leave quickly: *he peeled out down the street.*
– ORIGIN Middle English (in the sense 'to plunder'): variant of dialect *pill*, from Latin *pilare* 'to strip hair from,' from *pilus* 'hair.' The differentiation of *peel* and *pill* may have been by association with the French verbs *peler* 'to peel' and *piller* 'to pillage.'

peel[2] ▶ n. a flat, shovellike implement, esp. one used by baker for carrying loaves, pies, etc., into or out of an oven: *a wooden pizza peel.*
– ORIGIN late Middle English: from Old French *pele*, from Latin *pala*, from the base of *pangere* 'to fix, plant.'

peel[3] (also **pele** or **peel tower**) ▶ n. a small square defensive tower of a kind built in the 16th century in the border counties of England and Scotland.
– ORIGIN probably short for synonymous *peel-house*: *peel* from Anglo-Norman French *pel* 'stake, palisade,' from Latin *palus* 'stake.'

peel[4] ▶ v. [with obj.] Croquet send (another player's ball) through a wicket: *the better players are capable of peeling a ball through two or three wickets.*
– ORIGIN late 19th cent.: from the name of Walter H. Peel, founder of the All England Croquet Association, a leading exponent of the practice.

peel·er[1] /ˈpēlər/ ▶ n. [usu. with modifier] a device for removing the skin from fruit and vegetables: *a potato peeler.*

peel·er[2] ▶ n. Brit. informal, dated a police officer.
– ORIGIN early 19th cent. (originally denoting a member of the Irish constabulary): from the name of Sir Robert Peel (see PEEL).

peel·ings /ˈpēliNGz/ ▶ plural n. [usu. with modifier] strips of the outer skin of a vegetable or fruit: *potato peelings.*

peen /pēn/ ▶ n. the end of a hammer head opposite the face, typically wedge-shaped, curved, or spherical.
▶ v. [with obj.] strike with a hammer or the peen of a hammer. ■ another term for SHOT-PEEN.
– ORIGIN early 16th cent. (as a verb): probably of Scandinavian origin; compare with Swedish dialect *pena (ut)*, Danish dialect *pene (ud)* 'beat (out).'

Pee·ne·mun·de /ˌpēnəˈmo͝ondə, ˌpānəˈmʏndə/ a village in northeastern Germany, on a small island just off the Baltic coast. During World War II, it was the chief site of German rocket research and testing.

peep[1] /pēp/ ▶ v. [no obj.] look quickly and furtively at something, esp. through a narrow opening: *the door was ajar and she couldn't resist peeping in.* ■ (**peep out**) be just visible; appear slowly or partly or through a small opening: *a wad of money that was peeping out of his pocket | the sun began to peep out.*

▶ n. [usu. in sing.] a quick or furtive look: *Jonathan took a peep at his watch.* ■ a momentary or partial view of something: *black curls and a peep of gold earring.*
– ORIGIN late 15th cent.: symbolic; compare with PEEK.

peep[2] ▶ n. a high-pitched feeble sound made by a young bird or mammal. ■ [with negative] a slight sound, utterance, or complaint: *not a peep out of them since shortly after eight.* ■ (usu. **peeps**) informal a small sandpiper or similar wading bird.
▶ v. [no obj.] make a cheeping or beeping sound.
– ORIGIN late Middle English: imitative; compare with CHEEP.

pee-pee ▶ n. informal a child's word for an act of urinating. ■ urine. ■ a penis.

peep·er[1] /ˈpēpər/ ▶ n. a person who peeps at someone or something, esp. in a voyeuristic way. ■ (**peepers**) informal a person's eyes: *keep your peepers peeled for a familiar face.*

peep·er[2] (also **spring peeper**) ▶ n. a small North American tree frog that has brownish-gray skin with a dark cross on the back, the males of which sing in early spring. ● *Hyla crucifer*, family Hylidae.

peep·hole /ˈpēpˌhōl/ ▶ n. a small hole that may be looked through, esp. one in a door through which visitors may be identified before the door is opened.

peep·ing Tom ▶ n. a person who gets sexual pleasure from secretly watching people undressing or engaging in sexual activity.
– ORIGIN from the name of the person said to have watched Lady GODIVA ride naked through Coventry.

peep show ▶ n. a sequence of pictures viewed through a lens or hole set into a box, traditionally offered as a public entertainment. ■ an erotic or pornographic film or show viewed from a coin-operated booth.

peep sight ▶ n. a rear sight for rifles with a circular hole through which the front sight is brought into line with the object aimed at.

peep-toe ▶ adj. Brit. (of a shoe) having the tip cut away to leave the large toe partially exposed.
▶ n. a shoe of such a type.

pee·pul /ˈpēpəl/ (also **pipal**) ▶ n. another term for BO TREE.
– ORIGIN late 18th cent.: via Hindi from Sanskrit *pippala*.

peer[1] /pi(ə)r/ ▶ v. [no obj.] look keenly or with difficulty at someone or something: *Blake screwed up his eyes, trying to peer through the fog.* ■ be just visible: *the two towers peer over the roofs.* ■ archaic come into view; appear.
– ORIGIN late 16th cent.: perhaps a variant of dialect *pire*; perhaps partly from a shortening of APPEAR.

peer[2] ▶ n. **1** a member of the nobility in Britain or Ireland, comprising the ranks of duke, marquess, earl, viscount, and baron.

> In the British peerage, earldoms and baronies were the earliest to be conferred; dukes were created from 1337, marquesses from the end of the 14th century, and viscounts from 1440. Such peerages are hereditary, although since 1958 there have also been nonhereditary life peerages. Peers are entitled to a seat in the House of Lords and exemption from jury service; they are debarred from election to the House of Commons.

2 a person of the same age, status, or ability as another specified person: *he has incurred much criticism from his academic peers.*
▶ v. archaic make or become equal with or of the same rank.
– PHRASES **without peer** unequaled; unrivaled; peerless: *he is a goalkeeper without peer.*
– ORIGIN Middle English: from Old French *peer*, from Latin *par* 'equal.'

peer·age /ˈpi(ə)rij/ ▶ n. the title and rank of peer or peeress: *on his retirement as cabinet secretary, he was given a peerage.* ■ (**the peerage**) peers as a class; those holding a hereditary or honorary title: *he was elevated to the peerage two years ago.* ■ a book containing a list of peers and peeresses, with their genealogy and history.

peer·ess /ˈpi(ə)ris/ ▶ n. a woman holding the rank of a peer in her own right. ■ the wife or widow of a peer.

peer group ▶ n. a group of people of approximately the same age, status, and interests.

peer·less /ˈpi(ə)rlis/ ▶ adj. unequaled; unrivaled: *a peerless cartoonist.*

peer pres·sure ▶ n. influence from members of one's peer group: *his behavior was affected by drink and peer pressure.*

peer re·view ▶ n. evaluation of scientific, academic, or professional work by others working in the same field.
▶ v. [with obj.] (**peer-review**) subject (someone or something) to such evaluation.

peer-to-peer ▶ adj. [attrib.] denoting computer networks in which each computer can act as a server for the others, allowing shared access to files and peripherals without the need for a central server.

peeve /pēv/ informal ▶ v. [with obj.] (usu. **be peeved**) annoy; irritate: *he was peeved at being left out of the cabinet* | (as adj. **peeved**) *a somewhat peeved tone.*
▶ n. a cause of annoyance: *his pet peeve is not having answers for questions from players.*
– ORIGIN early 20th cent.: back-formation from PEEVISH.

peev·ish /ˈpēvisн/ ▶ adj. easily irritated, esp. by unimportant things: *all this makes Steve fretful and peevish.*
– DERIVATIVES **peev·ish·ly** adv., **peev·ish·ness** n.
– ORIGIN late Middle English (in the sense 'foolish, insane, spiteful'): of unknown origin.

pee·wee /ˈpēˌwē/ ▶ n. **1** [usu. as modifier] a level of amateur sports, involving children aged eight or nine: *a peewee baseball team.* ■ a player at such a level of amateur sport.
2 variant spelling of PEWEE.
3 a small marble.

pee·wit /ˈpēˌwit/ ▶ n. variant spelling of PEWIT.

PEG ▶ abbr. polyethylene glycol.

peg /peg/ ▶ n. **1** a short cylindrical piece of wood, metal, or plastic, typically tapered at one end, that is used for holding things together, hanging things on, or marking a position. ■ (also **tent peg**) such an object driven into the ground to hold one of the ropes or corners of a tent in position. ■ such an object in the neck of a stringed musical instrument around which the strings are wound, and which are turned to adjust their tension and so tune the instrument. ■ a bung for stoppering a cask. ■ informal a person's leg. ■ a point or limit on a scale, esp. of exchange rates.
2 chiefly Indian a measure of liquor: *have a peg of whiskey.*
3 informal a strong throw, esp. in baseball.
▶ v. (**pegs, pegging, pegged**) **1** [with obj.] fix or make fast with a peg or pegs: *drape individual plants with nets, pegging down the edges.*
2 [with obj.] fix (a price, rate, or amount) at a particular level. ■ informal form a fixed opinion of; categorize: *the officer probably has us pegged as anarchists.*
3 informal throw (a ball) hard and low, esp. in baseball: *the catcher pegs the ball to the first baseman.*
– PHRASES **a peg to hang a matter on** something used as a pretext or occasion for the discussion or treatment of a wider subject. **a square peg in a round hole** a person in a situation unsuited to their abilities or character. **take someone down a peg or two** make someone realize that they are less talented or important than they think are.
– PHRASAL VERBS **peg away** informal continue working hard at or trying to achieve something, esp. over a long period. **peg out 1** informal, chiefly Brit. die. **2** score the winning point at cribbage. **3** Croquet hit the peg with the ball as the final stroke in a game. **peg something out** mark the boundaries of an area of land: *I went out to peg out our assembly area.*
– ORIGIN late Middle English: probably of Low German origin; compare with Dutch dialect *peg* 'plug, peg.' The verb dates from the mid 16th cent.

Peg·a·sus /ˈpegəsəs/ **1** Greek Mythology a winged horse that sprang from the blood of Medusa when Perseus cut off her head.
2 Astronomy a large northern constellation, said to represent a winged horse. The three brightest stars, together with one star of Andromeda, form the prominent **Square of Pegasus**. ■ (as genitive **Pegasi** /ˈpegəsī/) used with a preceding letter or numeral to designate a star in this constellation: *the star Zeta Pegasi.*
– ORIGIN via Latin from Greek.

peg·board /ˈpegˌbôrd/ ▶ n. a board having a regular pattern of small holes for pegs, used chiefly for games or the display of information.

peg·box /ˈpegˌbäks/ ▶ n. a structure at the head of a stringed instrument where the strings are attached to the tuning pegs.

pegged /pegd/ ▶ adj. another term for PEGTOP.

peg·gy /ˈpegē/ ▶ n. (pl. **peggies**) Nautical slang a steward in a ship's mess (often used as a form of address).
– ORIGIN early 20th cent. (earlier denoting a man of feminine habits): alteration of *Meggy*, nickname for the given name *Margaret*.

peg leg ▶ n. informal an artificial leg, esp. a wooden one. ■ a person with such an artificial leg.

peg·ma·tite /ˈpegməˌtīt/ ▶ n. Geology a coarsely crystalline granite or other igneous rock with crystals several centimeters to several meters in length.
– ORIGIN early 19th cent.: from Greek *pēgma, pēgmat-* 'thing joined together' + -ITE[1].

peg·top /ˈpegˌtäp/ ▶ n. a pear-shaped spinning top with a metal pin or peg forming the point, spun by the rapid uncoiling of a string wound around it.
▶ adj. dated (of a garment) wide at the top and narrow at the bottom: *pegtop trousers were very wide in the hips.*

Pe·gu /peˈgo͞o/ a city and river port in southern Burma (Myanmar), on the Pegu River, northeast of Rangoon; pop. 200,900 (est. 2004). It is a center of Buddhist culture.

Peh·le·vi /ˈpāləˌvē/ ▶ n. variant spelling of PAHLAVI[2].

PEI ▶ abbr. Prince Edward Island.

Pei /pā/, I. M. (1917–), US architect, born in China; full name *Ieoh Ming Pei*. He designed monumental public buildings, including the east wing of the National Gallery of Art 1978 in Washington, DC, the John F. Kennedy Library 1979 in Boston, and the pyramid entrance to the Louvre 1983–89 in Paris.

Pei·gan /ˈpēgən/ ▶ n. (pl. **same** or **Peigans**) & adj. variant spelling of PIEGAN.

peign·oir /ˌpānˈwär/ ▶ n. a woman's light dressing gown or negligee.
– ORIGIN French, from *peigner* 'to comb' (because the garment was originally worn while combing the hair).

pein ▶ n. & v. variant spelling of PEEN.

Peirce /pi(ə)rs/, Charles Sanders (1839–1914), US philosopher and logician. A founder of pragmatism in the US, he argued that the meaning of a belief is to be understood by the actions and uses to which it gives rise.

Pei·sis·tra·tus variant spelling of PISISTRATUS.

pe·jo·ra·tive /pəˈjôrətiv, ˈpejəˌrātiv/ ▶ adj. expressing contempt or disapproval: *"permissiveness" is used almost universally as a pejorative term.*
▶ n. a word expressing contempt or disapproval.
– DERIVATIVES **pe·jo·ra·tive·ly** adv.
– ORIGIN late 19th cent.: from French *péjoratif, -ive*, from late Latin *pejorare* 'make worse,' from Latin *pejor* 'worse.'

pek·an /ˈpekən/ ▶ n. another term for FISHER (sense 2).
– ORIGIN mid 18th cent.: from Canadian French, from New England Algonquian.

peke /pēk/ ▶ n. informal a Pekingese dog.
– ORIGIN early 20th cent.: abbreviation.

pe·kid ▶ adj. variant spelling of PEAKED[2].

Pe·king /ˌpēˈkiNG, ˌpā-/ Another name for (esp. formerly) BEIJING.

Pe·king duck ▶ n. a Chinese dish consisting of strips of roast duck served with shredded vegetables and a sweet sauce.

Pe·king·ese (also **Pekinese**) ▶ n. /ˈpēkəˌnēz, -ˌnēs/ (pl. **same**) a lapdog of a short-legged breed with long hair and a snub nose, originally brought to Europe from the Summer Palace at Beijing (Peking) in 1860.
▶ adj. /ˌpēkiNGˈēz, -ˈēs/ of or relating to Beijing, its citizens, or their culture or cuisine.

Pekingese

Pe·king man ▶ n. a fossil hominid of the middle Pleistocene period, identified from remains found near Beijing in 1926. ● A late form of *Homo erectus* (formerly *Sinanthropus pekinensis*), family Hominidae.

Pe·king op·er·a ▶ n. a stylized Chinese form of opera dating from the late 18th century, in which speech, singing, mime, and acrobatics are performed to an instrumental accompaniment.

Pe·kin rob·in /ˈpēkin ˈräbin/ ▶ n. another term for LEIOTHRIX.

pe·koe /ˈpēˌkō/ ▶ n. a high-quality black tea made from young leaves.

– ORIGIN early 18th cent.: from Chinese dialect *pekho*, from *pek* 'white' + *ho* 'down' (the leaves being picked young when covered with down).

pel·age /'pelij/ ▶ **n.** Zoology the fur, hair, or wool of a mammal.
– ORIGIN early 19th cent.: from French, from Old French *pel* 'hair.'

pe·lag·ic /pə'lajik/ ▶ **adj.** technical of or relating to the open sea: *the kittiwakes return from their pelagic winter wanderings.* ■ (chiefly of fish) inhabiting the upper layers of the open sea. Often contrasted with **DEMERSAL**.
– ORIGIN mid 17th cent.: via Latin from Greek *pelagikos*, from *pelagios* 'of the sea' (from *pelagos* 'level surface of the sea').

Pe·la·gius /pə'lāj(ē)əs/ (*c.*360–*c.*420), British or Irish monk. He denied the doctrines of original sin and predestination, defending innate human goodness and free will. His beliefs were condemned as heretical by the Synod of Carthage in about 418.
– DERIVATIVES **Pe·la·gi·an** /-jēən/ **adj. & n.**, **Pe·la·gi·an·ism** /-ˌnizəm/ **n.**

pel·ar·go·ni·um /ˌpelär'gōnēəm/ ▶ **n.** a tender shrubby plant that is widely cultivated for its red, pink, or white flowers. Some kinds have fragrant leaves that yield an essential oil. See also **GERANIUM**. ● Genus *Pelargonium*, family Geraniaceae: many species and several hybrid groups, including the **zonal pelargoniums** (*P.* × hortorum), with rounded leaves bearing colored zones, and the trailing **ivy-leaved pelargoniums** (*P. peltatum*).
– ORIGIN modern Latin, from Greek *pelargos* 'stork,' apparently on the pattern of *geranium* (based on Greek *geranos* 'crane').

Pe·las·gi·an /pə'lazjēən/ ▶ **adj.** relating to or denoting an ancient people inhabiting the coasts and islands of the Aegean Sea and eastern Mediterranean before the arrival of Greek-speaking peoples in the Bronze Age.
▶ **n.** a member of this people.
– ORIGIN late 15th cent.: via Latin from Greek *Pelasgos* + **-IAN**.

pe·lau /pə'lou/ ▶ **n.** a spicy dish consisting of meat (typically chicken), rice, and pigeon peas.
– ORIGIN from French Creole *pêlao*.

pele ▶ **n.** variant spelling of **PEEL**[3].

Pe·lé /'pāˌlā/ (1940–), Brazilian soccer player; born *Edson Arantes do Nascimento*. Regarded as one of the greatest goal-scorers of all time, he played for the New York Cosmos 1975–77 and is credited with over 1,200 goals in first-class soccer.

pe·lec·y·pod /pə'lesəˌpäd/ ▶ **n.** another term for **BIVALVE**.
– ORIGIN late 19th cent.: from modern Latin *Pelecypoda* (alternative class name), from Greek *pelekus* 'hatchet' + *-podos* 'footed.'

Pe·lée, Mount /pə'lā/ a volcano on the island of Martinique, in the Caribbean Sea. Its eruption in 1902 killed about 30,000 people.

P

pel·er·ine /ˌpelə'rēn, 'pelərin/ ▶ **n.** historical a woman's cape of lace or silk with pointed ends at the center front, popular in the 19th century.
– ORIGIN mid 18th cent.: from French *pèlerine*, the sense being a transferred use of the feminine of *pèlerin* 'pilgrim.'

Pe·le's hair /'pelāz/ ▶ **n.** fine threads of volcanic glass, formed when a spray of lava droplets cools rapidly in the air.
– ORIGIN mid 19th cent.: translating Hawaiian *lauohu o Pele*, Pele being the goddess of volcanoes in Hawaiian mythology.

Pe·le·us /'pēlēəs/ Greek Mythology a king of Phthia in Thessaly, who was given as his wife the sea nymph Thetis; their child was Achilles.

pelf /pelf/ ▶ **n.** money, esp. when gained in a dishonest or dishonorable way.
– ORIGIN late Middle English (in the sense 'booty, pilfered property'): from a variant of Old French *pelfre* 'spoils,' of unknown origin. Compare with **PILFER**.

Pel·ham /'peləm/, Henry (1696–1754), British statesman; prime minister 1743–54.

pel·ham /'peləm/ ▶ **n.** a horse's bit that combines the action of a curb bit and a snaffle.
– ORIGIN mid 19th cent.: from the surname *Pelham*.

pel·i·can /'pelikən/ ▶ **n.** a large gregarious waterbird with a long bill, an extensible throat pouch for scooping up fish, and mainly white or gray plumage. ● Genus *Pelecanus*, family Pelecanidae: six species, including the **white pelican** (*P. erythrorhynchos*) of western and central North America, and the **brown pelican** (*P. occidentalis*) of northern and western South America and the southern US. ■ a heraldic or artistic representation of a pelican, typically depicted pecking its own breast as a symbol of Christ. [from an ancient legend that the pelican fed its young on its own blood.]
– ORIGIN late Old English *pellicane*, via late Latin from Greek *pelekan*, probably based on *pelekus* 'ax' (with reference to its bill).

white pelican

pel·i·can's-foot shell ▶ **n.** a burrowing European mollusk that has a heavily sculptured spiral shell with a flared lip that extends into several points. ● *Aporrhais pespelecani*, family Aporrhaidae, class Gastropoda.

Pel·i·can State a nickname for the state of **LOUISIANA**.

Pe·li·on /'pēlēən/ a wooded mountain in Greece, near the coast of southeastern Thessaly, that rises to 5,079 feet (1,548 m). In Greek mythology it was believed to be the home of the centaurs, and the giants were said to have piled Mounts Olympus and Ossa on its summit in their attempt to reach heaven and destroy the gods.
– PHRASES **pile** (or **heap**) **Pelion on Ossa** add a difficulty or task to something that is already difficult or onerous.

pe·lisse /pə'lēs/ ▶ **n.** historical a woman's cloak with armholes or sleeves, reaching to the ankles. ■ a fur-lined cloak, esp. as part of a hussar's uniform.
– ORIGIN early 18th cent.: from French, from medieval Latin *pellicia* (*vestis*) '(garment) of fur,' from *pellis* 'skin.'

pe·lite /'pēˌlīt/ ▶ **n.** Geology a very fine-grained sediment or sedimentary rock composed of clay or mud particles.
– ORIGIN late 19th cent.: from Greek *pēlos* 'clay, mud' + **-ITE**[1].

pel·la·gra /pə'lagrə, -'lāgrə, -'lägrə/ ▶ **n.** a deficiency disease caused by a lack of nicotinic acid or its precursor tryptophan in the diet. It is characterized by dermatitis, diarrhea, and mental disturbance, and is often linked to overdependence on corn as a staple food.
– DERIVATIVES **pel·la·grous** /-grəs/ **adj.**
– ORIGIN early 19th cent.: from Italian, from *pelle* 'skin,' on the pattern of *podagra*.

pel·let /'pelit/ ▶ **n.** a small, rounded, compressed mass of a substance: *fish food pellets.* ■ a piece of small shot or other lightweight bullet. ■ Ornithology a small mass of bones and feathers regurgitated by a bird of prey or other bird. ■ a small round piece of animal feces, esp. from a rabbit or rodent.
▶ **v.** (**pellets**, **pelleting**, **pelleted**) [with obj.] **1** form or shape (a substance, esp. animal food) into pellets.
2 hit with or as though with pellets: *the last drops of rain were pelleting the windshield.*
– ORIGIN late Middle English: from Old French *pelote* 'metal ball,' from a diminutive of Latin *pila* 'ball.'

pel·let·ize /'peliˌtīz/ ▶ **v.** [with obj.] form or shape (a substance) into pellets.

Pel·li /'pelē/, Cesar (1926–), US architect; born in Argentina. His designs incorporate the special characteristics of each project, such as the World Financial Center and its Winter Garden 1980–89 in New York City and Founders Hall 1987–92 in Charlotte, North Carolina.

pel·li·cle /'pelikəl/ ▶ **n.** technical a thin skin, cuticle, membrane, or film.
– DERIVATIVES **pel·lic·u·lar** /pə'likyələr/ **adj.**
– ORIGIN late Middle English: from French *pellicule*, from Latin *pellicula* 'small piece of skin,' diminutive of *pellis*.

pel·li·to·ry /'peliˌtôrē/ ▶ **n. 1** (in full **pellitory of Spain**) a plant of the daisy family, *Anacyclus pyrethrum*, with a pungent-flavored root, used as a local irritant, etc.
2 (also **pellitory of the wall**) a European plant of the nettle family with greenish flowers that grows on or at the foot of walls or in stony places. ● *Parietaria judaica*, family Urticaceae.
– ORIGIN late Middle English: alteration of obsolete *parietary*, from Old French *paritaire*, based on Latin *paries*, *pariet-* 'wall.'

pell-mell /ˌpel 'mel/ ▶ **adv.** in a confused, rushed, or disorderly manner: *the contents of the sacks were thrown pell-mell to the ground.*
▶ **adj.** recklessly hasty or disorganized; headlong: *steering the pell-mell development of Europe onto a new and more gradual course.*
▶ **n.** [in sing.] a state of affairs or collection of things characterized by haste or confusion: *the pell-mell of ascending gables and roof tiles.*
– ORIGIN late 16th cent.: from French *pêle-mêle*, from earlier *pesle mesle*, *mesle pesle*, reduplication from *mesler* 'to mix.'

pel·lu·cid /pə'lo͞osid/ ▶ **adj.** translucently clear: *mountains reflected in the pellucid waters.* ■ lucid in style or meaning; easily understood: *he writes, as always, in pellucid prose.* ■ (of music or other sound) clear and pure in tone: *a smooth legato and pellucid singing tone are his calling cards.*
– DERIVATIVES **pel·lu·cid·ly adv.**
– ORIGIN early 17th cent.: from Latin *pellucidus*, from *perlucere* 'shine through.'

Pel·man·ism /'pelmənˌizəm/ ▶ **n.** a system of memory training originally devised by the Pelman Institute for the Scientific Development of Mind, Memory, and Personality in London in the 1920s. ■ a game based on memorizing cards or other objects placed before the players.

pel·met /'pelmit/ ▶ **n.** a narrow border of cloth or wood, fitted across the top of a door or window to conceal the curtain fittings.
– ORIGIN early 20th cent.: probably an alteration of French *palmette*, literally 'small palm' (see **PALMETTE**).

Pel·o·pon·ne·sian War /ˌpeləpə'nēZHən/ the war of 431–404 BC fought between Athens and Sparta with their respective allies, occasioned largely by Spartan opposition to the Delian League. It ended in the total defeat of Athens and the transfer, for a brief period, of the leadership of Greece to Sparta.

Pel·o·pon·ne·sus /ˌpeləpə'nēsəs/ (also **the Peloponnese** /ˌpeləpə'nēz, -'nēs/) the mountainous southern peninsula of Greece, connected to central Greece by the Isthmus of Corinth. Greek name **Pelopónnisos**.
– ORIGIN from Greek, literally 'island of Pelops.'

Pel·ops /'pēˌläps/ Greek Mythology son of Tantalus, brother of Niobe, and father of Atreus. He was killed by his father and served up as food to the gods, but only one shoulder was eaten, and he was restored to life with an ivory shoulder replacing the one that was missing.

pe·lo·rus /pə'lôrəs/ ▶ **n.** a sighting device on a ship for taking the relative bearings of a distant object.
– ORIGIN mid 19th cent.: perhaps from *Pelorus*, said to be the name of Hannibal's pilot.

pe·lo·ta /pə'lōtə/ ▶ **n.** a Basque or Spanish game played in a walled court with a ball and basketlike rackets attached to the hand. ■ the ball used in such games as pelota and jai alai.
– ORIGIN Spanish, literally 'ball,' augmentative of *pella*, from Latin *pila* 'ball.'

pel·o·ton /'peləˌtän/ ▶ **n.** the main field or group of cyclists in a race.
– ORIGIN 1950s: from French, literally 'small ball' (because of the concentrated grouping of the pack).

pelt[1] /pelt/ ▶ **v.** [with obj.] attack (someone) by repeatedly hurling things at them: *two little boys pelted him with rotten apples.* ■ hurl (something) at someone or something in this way: *he spotted four boys aged about ten pelting stones at ducks.* ■ [no obj.] (**pelt down**) (of rain, hail, or snow) fall quickly and very heavily: *the rain was pelting down.* ■ [no obj.] informal run somewhere very quickly: *I pelted across the road.*
▶ **n.** archaic an act of hurling something at someone.
– ORIGIN late 15th cent.: of unknown origin.

pelt[2] ▶ **n.** the skin of an animal with the fur, wool, or hair still on it. ■ an animal's coat of fur or hair. ■ the raw skin of a sheep or goat, stripped and ready for tanning. ■ informal a person's hair.
– ORIGIN Middle English: either from obsolete *pellet* 'skin,' from an Old French diminutive of *pel* 'skin,' from Latin *pellis* 'skin,' or a back-formation from **PELTRY**.

pel·tate /'pelˌtāt/ ▶ **adj.** chiefly Botany shield-shaped. ■ (of a leaf) more or less circular, with the stalk attached at a point on the underside.

Pel·tier ef·fect /'peltēā/ ▶ **n.** Physics an effect whereby heat is emitted or absorbed when an electric current passes across a junction between two materials.
– ORIGIN mid 19th cent.: named after Jean C. A. *Peltier* (1785–1845), French amateur scientist.

pelt·ry /'peltrē/ ▶ **n.** (also **peltries**) animal pelts collectively.
– ORIGIN late Middle English: from Anglo-Norman French *pelterie*, based on Old French *pel* 'skin,' from Latin *pellis*.

pel·vic /'pelvik/ ▶ **adj.** of, relating to, or situated within the bony pelvis. ■ of or relating to the renal pelvis.

pel·vic fin ▶ **n.** Zoology each of a pair of fins on the underside of a fish's body, attached to the pelvic girdle and helping to control direction. Also called **VENTRAL FIN**.

pel·vic floor ▶ **n.** the muscular base of the abdomen, attached to the pelvis.

pel·vic gir·dle ▶ **n.** (in vertebrates) the enclosing structure formed by the pelvis, providing attachment for the hind limbs or pelvic fins.

pel·vic in·flam·ma·to·ry dis·ease (abbr.: **PID**) ▶ **n.** inflammation of the female genital tract, accompanied by fever and lower abdominal pain.

pel·vim·e·try /pel'vimətrē/ ▶ **n.** Medicine measurement of the dimensions of the pelvis, undertaken chiefly to help determine whether a woman can give birth normally or will require a Caesarean section.

pel·vis /'pelvis/ ▶ **n.** (pl. **pelvises** or **pelves** /-vēz/) **1** the large bony structure near the base of the spine to which the hind limbs or legs are attached in humans and many other vertebrates. ■ the part of the abdomen including or enclosed by the pelvis.

> In humans the pelvis, connected to the base of the spine, forms a basin-shaped hollow frame at the hips, partly supporting the internal organs and providing attachment for the bones and muscles of the legs.

2 (also **renal pelvis**) the broadened top part of the ureter into which the kidney tubules drain.
– ORIGIN early 17th cent.: from Latin, literally 'basin.'

pel·y·co·saur /'pelikəˌsôr/ ▶ **n.** a large extinct reptile of the late Carboniferous and Permian periods, typically having a line of long bony spines along the back supporting a sail-like crest. ● Order Pelycosauria, subclass Synapsida: several families and genera, including *Dimetrodon* and *Edaphosaurus*.
– ORIGIN mid 20th cent.: from Greek *pelux, peluk-* 'bowl' + *sauros* 'lizard.'

Pem·ba /'pembə/ **1** a seaport in northern Mozambique, on the Indian Ocean; pop. 141,316 (2007).
2 an island off the coast of Tanzania, in the western Indian Ocean, north of Zanzibar.

Pem·broke Pines /'pemˌbrōk/ a city in southeastern Florida, northwest of Miami; pop. 145,661 (est. 2008).

pem·mi·can /'pemikən/ ▶ **n.** a paste of dried and pounded meat mixed with melted fat and other ingredients, originally made by North American Indians and later adapted by Arctic explorers.
– ORIGIN from Cree *pimikan*, from *pime* 'fat.'

pem·phi·goid /'pemfiˌgoid/ ▶ **n.** Medicine a skin disease resembling pemphigus, chiefly affecting elderly people.

pem·phi·gus /'pemfigəs, pem'fīgəs/ ▶ **n.** Medicine a skin disease in which watery blisters form on the skin.
– ORIGIN late 18th cent.: modern Latin, from Greek *pemphix, pemphig-* 'bubble.'

PEN ▶ **abbr.** International Association of Poets, Playwrights, Editors, Essayists, and Novelists.

pen[1] /pen/ ▶ **n. 1** an instrument for writing or drawing with ink, typically consisting of a metal nib or ball, or a nylon tip, fitted into a metal or plastic holder. ■ (**the pen**) the occupation or practice of writing: *she was forced to support herself not only by the pen, but as a secret agent.* ■ an electronic penlike device used in conjunction with a writing surface to enter commands or data into a computer.
2 Zoology the tapering cartilaginous internal shell of a squid.
▶ **v.** (**pens, penning, penned**) [with obj.] write or compose: *he had not penned a line to Lizzie in three years.*
– PHRASES **the pen is mightier than the sword** proverb writing is more effective than military power or violence. **put** (or **set**) **pen to paper** write or begin to write something.
– ORIGIN Middle English (originally denoting a feather with a sharpened quill): from Old French *penne*, from Latin *penna* 'feather' (in late Latin 'pen').

pen[2] ▶ **n.** a small enclosure in which sheep, pigs, cattle, or other domestic animals are kept. ■ a number of animals in or sufficient to fill such an enclosure: *a pen of young horses.* ■ any small enclosure in which someone or something can be confined. ■ a covered dock for a submarine or other warship.
▶ **v.** (**pens, penning, penned**) [with obj.] put or keep (an animal) in a pen: *it was the practice to pen the sheep for clipping.* ■ (**pen someone up/in**) confine someone in a restricted space: *they had been penned up day and night in the house.*
– ORIGIN Old English *penn*, of unknown origin.

pen[3] ▶ **n.** a female swan.
– ORIGIN mid 16th cent.: of unknown origin.

pen[4] ▶ **n.** informal short for **PENITENTIARY** (sense 1).

Pen. ▶ **abbr.** Peninsula.

pe·nal /'pēnəl/ ▶ **adj.** relating to, used for, or prescribing the punishment of offenders under the legal system: *the campaign for penal reform.* ■ (of an act or offense) punishable by law.
– DERIVATIVES **pe·nal·ly adv.**
– ORIGIN late Middle English: from Old French *penal*, from Latin *poenalis*, from *poena* 'pain, penalty.'

pe·nal·ize /'penəlˌīz, 'pē-/ ▶ **v.** [with obj.] subject to some form of punishment: *you'll be penalized if you tap the account before age 59.* ■ (in various sports) punish (a player or team) for a breach of the rules by awarding an advantage to the opposition. ■ put in an unfavorable position or at an unfair disadvantage: *if the bill is not amended, genuine claimants will be penalized.* ■ Law make or declare (an act or offense) legally punishable: *section twenty penalizes possession of a firearm when trespassing.*
– DERIVATIVES **pe·nal·i·za·tion** /ˌpenəli'zāSHən, ˌpē-/ **n.**

pe·nal ser·vi·tude ▶ **n.** imprisonment with hard labor.

pen·al·ty /'penltē/ ▶ **n.** (pl. **penalties**) **1** a punishment imposed for breaking a law, rule, or contract: *the charge carries a maximum penalty of ten years' imprisonment.* ■ a disadvantage or unpleasant experience suffered as the result of an action or circumstance: *the cold never leaves my bones these days—one of the penalties of age.*
2 (in sports and games) a disadvantage or handicap imposed on a player or team, typically for infringement of rules. ■ a kick or shot awarded to a team because of a serious infringement of the rules by an opponent. ■ Bridge points won by the defenders when a declarer fails to make the contract.
– PHRASES **under** (or **on**) **penalty of** under the threat of: *he ordered enterprises to fulfill contracts under penalty of strict fines.*
– ORIGIN early 16th cent.: probably via Anglo-Norman French, from medieval Latin *poenalitas*, based on *poena* 'pain.'

pen·al·ty ar·e·a ▶ **n.** Soccer the rectangular area marked out in front of each goal, within which a foul by a defender involves the award of a penalty kick and outside which the goalkeeper is not allowed to handle the ball.

pen·al·ty box ▶ **n.** Ice Hockey an enclosure alongside the rink where players who have been assessed penalties must remain while they serve out their penalties.

pen·al·ty dou·ble ▶ **n.** Bridge another term for **BUSINESS DOUBLE**.

pen·al·ty kick ▶ **n. 1** Soccer a free kick at the goal from the penalty spot (which only the goalkeeper is allowed to defend), awarded to the attacking team after a foul within the penalty area by an opponent.
2 Rugby a placekick awarded to a team after an offense by an opponent.

pen·al·ty kill·er ▶ **n.** Hockey a player specializing in preventing the opposing side from scoring while that player's own team's strength is reduced through penalties.
– DERIVATIVES **pen·al·ty kill·ing n.**

pen·al·ty shoot-out ▶ **n.** see **SHOOT-OUT**.

pen·al·ty spot ▶ **n.** Soccer the point within the penalty area from which penalty kicks are taken.

pen·ance /'penəns/ ▶ **n. 1** voluntary self-punishment inflicted as an outward expression of repentance for having done wrong: *he had done public penance for those hasty words.*
2 a Christian sacrament in which a member of the Church confesses sins to a priest and is given absolution. In the Roman Catholic Church often called **SACRAMENT OF RECONCILIATION**. ■ a religious observance or other duty required of a person by a priest as part of this sacrament to indicate repentance.
▶ **v.** [with obj.] archaic impose a penance on: *a hair shirt to penance him for his folly in offending.*
– ORIGIN Middle English: from Old French, from Latin *paenitentia* 'repentance,' from the verb *paenitere* 'be sorry.'

Pe·nang /pə'naNG/ (also **Pinang**) an island in Malaysia, located off the western coast of the Malay Peninsula. ■ a state of Malaysia, consisting of this island and a coastal strip on the mainland; capital, George Town (on Penang island). ■ another name for **GEORGE TOWN** (sense 2).

pe·na·tes /pə'nātēz, -'nä-/ ▶ **plural n.** Roman History household gods worshiped in conjunction with Vesta and the lares by the ancient Romans.
– ORIGIN Latin, from *penus* 'provision of food'; related to *penes* 'within.'

pence /pens/ plural form of **PENNY**.

pen·chant /'penCHənt/ ▶ **n.** [usu. in sing.] a strong or habitual liking for something or tendency to do something: *he has a penchant for adopting stray dogs.*
– ORIGIN late 17th cent.: from French, 'leaning, inclining,' present participle of the verb *pencher*.

pen·cil /'pensəl/ ▶ **n.** an instrument for writing or drawing, consisting of a thin stick of graphite or a similar substance enclosed in a long thin piece of wood or fixed in a metal or plastic case. ■ graphite or a similar substance used in such a way as a medium for writing or drawing: *the words were scribbled in pencil.* ■ [usu. with modifier] a cosmetic in a long thin stick, designed to be applied to a particular part of the face: *an eyebrow pencil.* ■ something with the shape of a pencil: *a pencil of light* | [as modifier] *a long pencil beam.* ■ Physics & Geometry a set of light rays, lines, etc., converging to or diverging narrowly from a single point.
▶ **v.** (**pencils, penciling, penciled**; Brit. **pencils, pencilling, pencilled**) [with obj.] write, draw, or color (something) with a pencil: *a previous owner has penciled their name inside the cover* | (as adj. **penciled**) *a penciled note.*
– PHRASAL VERBS **pencil something in 1** fill in an area or shape with pencil strokes: *a lot of the outlines had been penciled in.* **2** arrange, forecast, or note down something provisionally or tentatively: *May 15 was penciled in as the date for the meeting.* ■ (**pencil someone in**) make a provisional or tentative arrangement with or for someone: *he was penciled in for surgery at the end of the month.*
– DERIVATIVES **pen·cil·er n.**
– ORIGIN Middle English (denoting a fine paintbrush): from Old French *pincel*, from a diminutive of Latin *peniculus* 'brush,' diminutive of *penis* 'tail.' The verb was originally (early 16th cent.) in the sense 'paint with a fine brush.'

pen·cil case ▶ **n.** a small container for pencils, pens, and other writing equipment.

pen·cil mus·tache ▶ **n.** a very thin mustache.

pen·cil push·er ▶ **n.** informal a person with a clerical job involving a lot of tedious and repetitive paperwork.

pen·cil sharp·en·er ▶ **n.** a device for sharpening a pencil by rotating a cutter around its point.

pend·ant /'pendənt/ ▶ **n. 1** a piece of jewelry that hangs from a chain worn around the neck. ■ a necklace with such a piece of jewelry. ■ a light designed to hang from the ceiling. ■ the part of a pocket watch by which it is suspended. ■ Nautical a short rope hanging from the head of a ship's mast, yardarm, or clew of a sail, used for attaching tackles.
2 an artistic, literary, or musical composition intended to match or complement another: *the triptych's pendant will occupy the corresponding wall in the south transept.*
▶ **adj.** hanging downward; pendent: *pendant flowers on frail stems.*
– ORIGIN Middle English (denoting an architectural decoration projecting downward): from Old French, literally 'hanging,' present participle of the verb *pendre*, from Latin *pendere*.

P

pend·ent /'pendənt/ ▶ **adj. 1** hanging down or overhanging: *pendent lichens.*
2 undecided; pending: *the use of jurisdiction to decide pendent claims.*
3 Grammar (esp. of a sentence) incomplete; not having a finite verb.
– DERIVATIVES **pen·den·cy n.**

pen·den·te li·te /pen'dentē 'lītē/ ▶ **adv.** Law during litigation.
– ORIGIN Latin, literally 'with the lawsuit pending.'

pen·den·tive /pen'dentiv/ ▶ **n.** Architecture a curved triangle of vaulting formed by the intersection of a dome with its supporting arches.
– ORIGIN early 18th cent.: from the French adjective *pendentif, -ive*, from Latin *pendent-* 'hanging down,' from the verb *pendere*.

Pen·de·rec·ki /ˌpendə'retskē/, Krzysztof (1933–), Polish composer. His music frequently features sounds drawn from extramusical sources and note clusters, as in his *Threnody for the Victims of Hiroshima* (1960) for fifty-two strings. Notable religious works: *Stabat Mater* (1962) and *Polish Requiem* (1980–84).

Pen·der·gast /'pendərˌgast/, Thomas (Joseph) (1872–1945), US politician. An early supporter of Harry Truman, he was the acknowledged Democratic boss of Kansas City, Missouri. He served time in prison for income tax evasion 1939–40.

pend·ing /'pendiNG/ ▶ **adj.** awaiting decision or settlement: *nine cases were still pending.* ■ about to happen; imminent: *with a presidential election*

pending, it would be wrong to force the changes through now | *the pending disaster.*
▶ **prep.** until (something) happens or takes place: *they were released on bail pending an appeal.*
– ORIGIN mid 17th cent.: anglicized spelling of French *pendant* 'hanging.'

Pen·drag·on /pen'dragən/ ▶ **n.** a title given to an ancient British or Welsh prince holding or claiming supreme power.
– ORIGIN Welsh, literally 'chief war-leader,' from *pen* 'head' + *dragon* 'standard.'

pen·du·lous /'penjələs, 'pendyə-/ ▶ **adj.** hanging down loosely: *pendulous branches.*
– DERIVATIVES **pen·du·lous·ly adv.**
– ORIGIN early 17th cent.: from Latin *pendulus* 'hanging down' (from *pendere* 'hang') + **-OUS**.

pen·du·lum /'penjələm, 'pendyə-/ ▶ **n.** a weight hung from a fixed point so that it can swing freely backward and forward, esp. a rod with a weight at the end that regulates the mechanism of a clock. ■ used to refer to the tendency of a situation to oscillate between one extreme and another: *the pendulum of fashion.*
– DERIVATIVES **pen·du·lar** /-lər/ **adj.**
– ORIGIN mid 17th cent.: from Latin, neuter (used as a noun) of *pendulus* 'hanging down.'

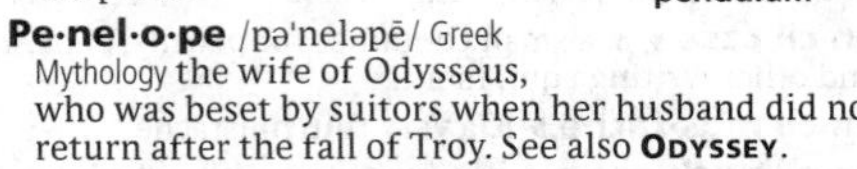

pendulum

pe·nec·to·my /pe'nektəmē/ ▶ **n.** surgical amputation of the penis.

Pe·nel·o·pe /pə'neləpē/ Greek Mythology the wife of Odysseus, who was beset by suitors when her husband did not return after the fall of Troy. See also **ODYSSEY**.

pe·ne·plain /'pēnə,plān/ (also **peneplane**) ▶ **n.** Geology a more or less level land surface produced by erosion over a long period, undisturbed by crustal movement.
– ORIGIN late 19th cent.: from Latin *paene* 'almost' + **PLAIN**[1].

pen·e·tra·ble /'penitrəbəl/ ▶ **adj. 1** allowing things to pass through; permeable: *the outer membrane is penetrable.*
2 possible to understand; understandable: *the translation makes the original text penetrable.*
– DERIVATIVES **pen·e·tra·bil·i·ty** /,penitrə'bilitē/ **n.**

pen·e·tra·li·a /,peni'trālēə/ ▶ **plural n.** the innermost parts of a building; a secret or hidden place.
– ORIGIN mid 17th cent.: from Latin, literally 'innermost things,' neuter plural of *penetralis* 'interior.'

pen·e·trance /'penətrəns/ ▶ **n.** Genetics the extent to which a particular gene or set of genes is expressed in the phenotypes of individuals carrying it, measured by the proportion of carriers showing the characteristic phenotype.
– ORIGIN 1930s: from German *Penetranz*.

pen·e·trant /'penətrənt/ ▶ **adj.** Genetics (of a gene or group of genes) producing characteristic effects in the phenotypes of individuals possessing it.
▶ **n.** a substance that can penetrate cracks, pores, and other surface defects.

pen·e·trate /'peni,trāt/ ▶ **v.** [with obj.] succeed in forcing a way into or through (a thing): *the shrapnel had penetrated his head and chest* | [no obj.] *tunnels that penetrate deep into the earth's core.* ■ (of a man) insert the penis into the vagina or anus of (a sexual partner). ■ infiltrate (an enemy group or rival organization) in order to spy on it: *they feared that their council had been penetrated by informers.* ■ (of a company) begin to sell its products in (a particular market or area): *Honda has succeeded in penetrating Western motorcycle markets.* ■ succeed in understanding or gaining insight into (something complex or mysterious): *a magician who seemed to have penetrated the mysteries of nature.* ■ [no obj.] be fully understood or realized by someone: *as his words penetrated, she saw a mental picture of him with Dawn.*
– ORIGIN mid 16th cent.: from Latin *penetrat-* 'placed or gone into,' from the verb *penetrare*; related to *penitus* 'inner.'

pen·e·trat·ing /'peni,trātiNG/ ▶ **adj.** able to make a way through or into something: *the problem of penetrating damp* | *the penetrating scents of pine and eucalyptus.* ■ (of a voice or sound) clearly heard through or above other sounds: *a single penetrating whistle.* ■ (of a person's eyes or expression) reflecting an apparent ability to see into the mind of the person being looked at; piercingly intense: *attempting to avoid her penetrating gaze.* ■ having or showing clear insight: *the students asked some penetrating questions.*
– DERIVATIVES **pen·e·trat·ing·ly adv.**

pen·e·tra·tion /,peni'trāSHən/ ▶ **n. 1** the action or process of making a way through or into something: *the plant grows in clear, still waters where there is strong sunlight penetration.* ■ the insertion by a man of his penis into the vagina or anus of a sexual partner. ■ the successful selling of a company's or country's products in a particular market or area: *Japanese import penetration.* ■ the extent to which a product is recognized and bought by customers in a particular market: *the software has attained a high degree of market penetration.*
2 the perceptive understanding of complex matters: *the survey shows subtlety and penetration.*
– ORIGIN late Middle English: from Latin *penetratio(n-)*, from the verb *penetrare* 'place within or enter.'

pen·e·tra·tive /'peni,trātiv/ ▶ **adj. 1** able to make a way into or through something: *the gunpowder weapons have extra penetrative power.* ■ (of sexual activity) in which a man inserts his penis into the vagina or anus of a sexual partner.
2 having or showing deep understanding and insight: *a remarkably thorough and penetrative survey of the organization's work.*

pen·e·tra·tor /'peni,trātər/ ▶ **n.** a person or thing that penetrates something. ■ a missile containing a hard alloy rod, designed to penetrate the armor of tanks or fortifications.

pen·e·trom·e·ter /,penə'trämitər/ ▶ **n.** an instrument for determining the consistency or hardness of a substance by measuring the depth or rate of penetration of a rod or needle driven into it by a known force.

pen·gö /'pengō/ ▶ **n.** (pl. **same** or **pengös**) the basic monetary unit of Hungary from 1927 until 1946, when it was replaced by the forint.
– ORIGIN Hungarian, literally 'ringing.'

pen·guin /'peNGgwin, 'pengwin/ ▶ **n.** a large flightless seabird of the southern hemisphere, with black upper parts and white underparts and wings developed into flippers for swimming under water. See also **ADÉLIE PENGUIN, EMPEROR PENGUIN, KING PENGUIN, MACARONI PENGUIN.** ● Family Spheniscidae: six genera and several species.
– ORIGIN late 16th cent. (originally denoting the great auk): of unknown origin.

pen·i·cil·late /,penə'silit, -'silāt/ ▶ **adj.** Biology having, forming, or resembling a small tuft or tufts of hair.
– ORIGIN early 19th cent.: from Latin *penicillus* 'paintbrush' + **-ATE**[2].

pen·i·cil·lin /,penə'silən/ ▶ **n. 1** an antibiotic or group of antibiotics produced naturally by certain blue molds, and now usually prepared synthetically.
2 a blue mold of a type that produces these antibiotics. ● Genus *Penicillium*, subdivision Deuteromycotina.
– ORIGIN from the modern Latin genus name *Penicillium* (from Latin *penicillus* 'paintbrush') + **-IN**[1].

pen·i·cil·lin·ase /,penə'silənās/ ▶ **n.** Biochemistry an enzyme that can inactivate penicillin, produced by certain bacteria.

pen·i·cil·li·um /,penə'silēəm/ ▶ **n.** (pl. **penicillia** /-'silēə/) a blue mold that is common on food, being added to some cheeses and used sometimes to produce penicillin.
– ORIGIN mid 19th cent.: modern Latin, from Latin *penicillus* 'paintbrush' (because of the brushlike fruiting bodies).

pe·nile /'pēnəl, -nīl/ ▶ **adj.** [attrib.] chiefly technical of, relating to, or affecting the penis.
– ORIGIN mid 19th cent.: from modern Latin *penilis*, from *penis* 'tail, penis.'

pen·in·su·la /pə'ninsələ/ ▶ **n.** a piece of land almost surrounded by water or projecting out into a body of water.
– DERIVATIVES **pen·in·su·lar** /-lər/ **adj.**
– ORIGIN mid 16th cent.: from Latin *paeninsula*, from *paene* 'almost' + *insula* 'island.'

> **USAGE** The spelling of the noun as **peninsular** instead of **peninsula** is a common mistake. The spelling **peninsula** should be used when a noun is intended (*the end of the Cape Peninsula*), whereas **peninsular** is the spelling of the adjective (*the peninsular part of Malaysia*).

pe·nis /'pēnis/ ▶ **n.** (pl. **penises** or **penes** /-nēz/) the male genital organ of higher vertebrates, carrying the duct for the transfer of sperm during copulation. In humans and most other mammals, it consists largely of erectile tissue and serves also for the elimination of urine. ■ Zoology a type of male copulatory organ present in some invertebrates, such as gastropod mollusks.
– ORIGIN late 17th cent.: from Latin, 'tail, penis.'

pe·nis en·vy ▶ **n.** Psychoanalysis supposed envy of the male's possession of a penis, postulated by Freud to account for some aspects of female behavior (notably the castration complex) but controversial among modern theorists.

pen·i·stone /'penistən/ ▶ **n.** a kind of coarse woolen cloth formerly used for making clothes.
– ORIGIN mid 16th cent.: from the name of a town in South Yorkshire, England, where the cloth was made.

pen·i·tence /'penitns/ ▶ **n.** the action of feeling or showing sorrow and regret for having done wrong; repentance: *a public display of penitence.*

pen·i·tent /'penitnt/ ▶ **adj.** feeling or showing sorrow and regret for having done wrong; repentant: *a penitent expression.*
▶ **n.** a person who repents their sins or wrongdoings and (in the Christian Church) seeks forgiveness from God. ■ (in the Roman Catholic Church) a person who confesses their sins to a priest and submits to the penance that he imposes.
– DERIVATIVES **pen·i·tent·ly adv.**
– ORIGIN Middle English: from Old French, from Latin *paenitent-* 'repenting,' from the verb *paenitere*.

pen·i·ten·tial /,penə'tenCHəl/ ▶ **adj.** relating to or expressing penitence or penance: *penitential tears.*
– DERIVATIVES **pen·i·ten·tial·ly adv.** (archaic).
– ORIGIN late 15th cent.: from late Latin *paenitentialis*, from Latin *paenitentia* 'repentance.'

Pen·i·ten·tial Psalms ▶ **plural n.** seven psalms (6, 32, 38, 51, 102, 130, 143) that express penitence.

pen·i·ten·tia·ry /,penə'tenSHərē/ ▶ **n.** (pl. **penitentiaries**) **1** a prison for people convicted of serious crimes.
2 (in the Roman Catholic Church) a priest charged with certain aspects of the administration of the sacrament of penance. ■ an office in the papal court forming a tribunal for deciding on questions relating to penance, dispensations, and absolution.
– ORIGIN late Middle English (as a term in ecclesiastical law): from medieval Latin *paenitentiarius*, from Latin *paenitentia* 'repentance.' Sense 1 dates from the early 19th cent.

pen·knife /'pen,nīf/ ▶ **n.** (pl. **penknives** /-,nīvz/) a small pocketknife with a blade that folds into the handle.
– ORIGIN so named because originally used for making and mending quill pens.

pen·light /'pen,līt/ ▶ **n.** a small flashlight shaped like a fountain pen.

pen·man /'pen,mən/ ▶ **n.** (pl. **penmen**) chiefly historical a person who was skilled or professionally engaged in writing by hand, typically, as a clerk, on behalf of others. ■ an author.

pen·man·ship /'penmən,SHip/ ▶ **n.** the art or skill of writing by hand. ■ a person's handwriting.

Penn /pen/, William (1644–1718), English Quaker, founder of Pennsylvania. Having been imprisoned in 1668 for his Quaker writings, he was granted a charter to land in North America by Charles II. He founded the colony of Pennsylvania as a sanctuary for Quakers and other nonconformists in 1682.

Penn. (also **Penna.**) ▶ **abbr.** Pennsylvania.

pen name ▶ **n.** an assumed name used by a writer instead of their real name.

pen·nant /'penənt/ ▶ **n. 1** a flag denoting a sports championship or other achievement.
2 a tapering flag on a ship, esp. one flown at the masthead of a vessel in commission. Also called **PENNON**. ■ a long triangular or swallow-tailed flag, esp. as a military ensign.
3 Nautical another term for **PENDANT**.
– ORIGIN early 17th cent.: blend of **PENDANT** and **PENNON**.

pen·nate /'penāt/ ▶ **adj.** Botany (of a diatom) bilaterally symmetrical. Compare with **CENTRIC**.
– ORIGIN mid 19th cent.: from Latin *pennatus* 'feathered, winged,' from *penna* 'feather.'

pen·ne /'penā/ ▶ **n.** pasta in the form of short wide tubes.
– ORIGIN Italian, plural of *penna* 'quill.'

Pen·ney /'penē/, James Cash (1875–1971), US businessman. He invested in a small store (called the Golden Rule Store) in 1902 and by 1913 had developed 34 stores, the beginning of the J. C. Penney department store chain. He was the company's president 1913–17 and chairman 1917–46.

pen·ni /'penē/ ▶ **n.** (pl. **penniä** /'penēə/) a monetary unit of Finland (until the introduction of the euro), equal to one hundredth of a markka.
– ORIGIN Finnish.

pen·ni·less /'penēlis/ ▶ **adj.** (of a person) having no money; very poor.
– DERIVATIVES **pen·ni·less·ness n.**

Pen·nine Hills /'penīn/ (also **Pennine Chain** or **the Pennines**) a range of hills in northern England that extends from the Scottish border south to the county of Derbyshire.

pen·non /ˈpenən/ ▶ **n.** another term for **PENNANT** (sense 2).
– DERIVATIVES **pen·noned adj.**
– ORIGIN late Middle English: from Old French, from a derivative of Latin *penna* 'feather.'

pen·n'orth /ˈpenərTH/ ▶ **n.** Brit. variant spelling of **PENNYWORTH.**

Penn·syl·va·nia /ˌpensəlˈvānyə/ a state in the northeastern US, with a short coastline along Lake Erie in the far northwest; pop. 12,448,279 (est. 2008); capital, Harrisburg; statehood, Dec. 12, 1787 (2). Founded in 1682 by William Penn, it became one of the original thirteen states.

Penn·syl·va·nia Av·e·nue a street in Washington, DC, along which the White House (at number 1600) and Capitol Hill are situated.

Penn·syl·va·nia Dutch (also **Pennsylvania German**) ▶ **n.** **1** a dialect of High German spoken in parts of Pennsylvania.
2 (as plural noun **the Pennsylvania Dutch** or **Germans**) the German-speaking inhabitants of Pennsylvania, descendants of 17th- and 18th-century Protestant immigrants from the Rhineland.
– ORIGIN *Dutch* from German *Deutsch* 'German.'

Penn·syl·va·nian /ˌpensəlˈvānyən, -ˈvānēən/ ▶ **adj.** **1** of or relating to the state of Pennsylvania.
2 Geology of, relating to, or denoting the later part of the Carboniferous period in North America, following the Mississippian and preceding the Permian, and corresponding to the Upper Carboniferous of Europe. This period lasted from about 323 to 290 million years ago.
▶ **n.** **1** a native or inhabitant of Pennsylvania.
2 (**the Pennsylvanian**) Geology the Pennsylvanian period or the system of rocks deposited during it.

pen·ny /ˈpenē/ ▶ **n.** **1** a one-cent coin equal to one hundredth of a dollar. ■ (pl. for separate coins **pennies**, for a sum of money **pence** /pens/) (abbr.: **p**) a British bronze coin and monetary unit equal to one hundredth of a pound. ■ (abbr.: **d**) a former British coin and monetary unit equal to one twelfth of a shilling and one 240th of a pound. ■ (**pennies**) a small sum of money: *in the current economic situation any chance to save a few pennies is welcome.* ■ (in biblical use) a denarius.
2 [with negative] (**a penny**) used for emphasis to denote no money at all: *we didn't get paid a penny.*
– PHRASES **be two** (or **ten**) **a penny** chiefly Brit. be plentiful or easily obtained and consequently of little value. **pinch** (or **count** or **watch**) (**one's**) **pennies** be careful about how much one spends: *he is pinching pennies to save for a movie | she's been watching her pennies.* **in for a penny, in for a pound** used to express someone's intention to complete an enterprise once it has been undertaken, however much time, effort, or money this entails. **look after the pennies and the pounds will look after themselves** proverb if you concentrate on saving small amounts of money, you'll soon amass a large amount. **pennies from heaven** unexpected benefits, esp. financial ones. **the penny dropped** informal, chiefly Brit. used to indicate that someone has finally realized or understood something. **a penny for your thoughts** used to ask someone what they are thinking about. **a pretty penny** a considerable amount of money: *old Sid charged a pretty penny for his services.* **spend a penny** see **SPEND.**
– ORIGIN Old English *penig, penning*, of Germanic origin; related to Dutch *penning*, German *Pfennig*, perhaps also to **PAWN**[2] and (with reference to shape) **PAN**[1].

pen·ny an·te ▶ **n.** poker played for very small stakes. ■ [as modifier] informal petty; contemptible: *a penny-ante scandal of little substance.*

pen·ny ar·cade ▶ **n.** historical an indoor area with coin-operated mechanical games, photography booths, picture shows, and other amusements.

pen·ny·cress /ˈpenēˌkres/ ▶ **n.** a weed of the cabbage family, similar to shepherd's purse but with deeply notched, flat round pods. Native to Europe, it has become well established in North America. ● *Thlaspi arvense*, family Brassicaceae.

pen·ny dread·ful ▶ **n.** a cheap, sensational comic or storybook.
– ORIGIN late 19th cent.: so named because the original cost was one penny.

pen·ny-far·thing ▶ **n.** historical an early type of bicycle with a very large front wheel and a small rear wheel. Also called **ORDINARY.**

pen·ny loaf·er ▶ **n.** a casual leather shoe with a decorative slotted leather strip over the upper, in which a coin may be placed.

pen·ny-pinch·ing ▶ **adj.** unwilling to spend or share money; miserly; mean.
▶ **n.** unwillingness to spend or share money.
– DERIVATIVES **pen·ny-pinch·er n.**

pen·ny·roy·al /ˈpenēˌroiəl/ ▶ **n.** either of two small-leaved plants of the mint family, used in herbal medicine. ● A creeping Eurasian plant (*Mentha pulegium*), and **American pennyroyal** (*Hedeoma pulegioides*), family Labiatae.
– ORIGIN mid 16th cent.: from Anglo-Norman French *puliol* (based on Latin *pulegium* 'thyme') + *real* 'royal.'

pen·ny stock ▶ **n.** a common stock valued at less than one dollar, and therefore highly speculative.

pen·ny·weight /ˈpenēˌwāt/ ▶ **n.** a unit of weight, 24 grains or one twentieth of an ounce troy.

pen·ny whis·tle ▶ **n.** another term for **TIN WHISTLE.**

pen·ny wise ▶ **adj.** extremely careful about the way one spends even small amounts of money.
– PHRASES **penny wise and pound foolish** careful and economical in small matters while being wasteful or extravagant in large ones.

pen·ny·wort /ˈpenēwərt, -ˌwôrt/ ▶ **n.** any of a number of plants with rounded leaves, in particular: ● a creeping perennial of the genus *Hydrocotyle*, family Umbelliferae: numerous species, including the North American **water pennywort** (*H. americana*).

pen·ny·worth /ˈpenēˌwərTH/ ▶ **n.** chiefly Brit. an amount of something that may be bought for a penny: ***a pennyworth of chips.*** ■ (**one's pennyworth**) a person's contribution to a discussion, esp. one that is unwelcome. ■ archaic value for one's money; a good bargain.

Pe·nob·scot /pəˈnäbskət, -ˌskät/ ▶ **n.** (pl. **same**) **1** a member of an American Indian people of the Penobscot River valley in Maine.
2 the Algonquian language of this people, a dialect of Eastern Abnaki.
▶ **adj.** of or relating to this people or their language.
– ORIGIN from an Abnaki place name *panáwahpskek* 'where the rocks open out.'

Pe·nob·scot Riv·er a river that flows for 350 miles (560 km) through central Maine into Penobscot Bay on the Atlantic Ocean.

pe·nol·o·gy /pēˈnäləjē/ ▶ **n.** the study of the punishment of crime and of prison management.
– DERIVATIVES **pe·no·log·i·cal** /ˌpēnəˈläjikəl/ **adj.**, **pe·nol·o·gist** /-jist/ **n.**
– ORIGIN mid 19th cent.: from Latin *poena* 'penalty' + **-LOGY.**

pen pal ▶ **n.** a person with whom one becomes friendly by exchanging letters, esp. someone in a foreign country whom one has never met.

pen-push·er ▶ **n.** another term for **PENCIL PUSHER.**

Pen·sa·cola /ˌpensəˈkōlə/ an industrial and port city in northwestern Florida, in the Panhandle, near the Alabama border, site of a naval installation; pop. 53,820 (est. 2008).

pen·sée /ˌpänˈsā/ ▶ **n.** a thought or reflection put into literary form; an aphorism.
– ORIGIN French.

pen shell ▶ **n.** a large, wedge-shaped, bivalve mollusk of warm seas that burrows into the seabed where it attaches itself by strong byssus threads. ● Family Pinnidae: *Pinna* and other genera.

pen·sile /ˈpenˌsīl, -sil/ ▶ **adj.** hanging down; pendulous: *pensile nests.*
– ORIGIN early 17th cent.: from Latin *pensilis*, from the verb *pendere* 'hang.'

pen·sion[1] /ˈpenSHən/ ▶ **n.** a regular payment made during a person's retirement from an investment fund to which that person or their employer has contributed during their working life. ■ a regular payment made by the government to people of or above the official retirement age and to some widows and disabled people. ■ chiefly historical a regular payment made to a royal favorite or to an artist or scholar to enable them to carry on work that is of public interest or value.
▶ **v.** [with obj.] (**pension someone off**) dismiss someone from employment, typically because of age or ill health, and pay them a pension: *he was pensioned off from the army at the end of the war.*
– DERIVATIVES **pen·sion·less adj.**
– ORIGIN late Middle English (in the sense 'payment, tax, regular sum paid to retain allegiance'): from Old French, from Latin *pensio(n-)* 'payment,' from *pendere* 'to pay.' The current verb sense dates from the mid 19th cent.

pen·sion[2] /pänsēˈōn/ ▶ **n.** a boarding house in France and other European countries, providing full or partial board at a fixed rate.
– ORIGIN French.

pen·sion·a·ble /ˈpenSHənəbəl/ ▶ **adj.** entitling to or qualifying for a pension: *single and widowed women over pensionable age.*
– DERIVATIVES **pen·sion·a·bil·i·ty** /ˌpenSHənəˈbilitē/ **n.**

pen·sion·ar·y /ˈpenSHəˌnerē/ ▶ **adj.** of or concerning a pension.
▶ **n.** (pl. **pensionaries**) **1** a pensioner.
2 a creature; a hireling.
– ORIGIN mid 16th cent.: from medieval Latin *pensionarius* 'receiver or payer of a pension.'

pen·si·o·ne /pänsēˈōnā/ ▶ **n.** (pl. **pensioni** /-ˈōnē/) a small hotel or boarding house in Italy.
– ORIGIN Italian.

pen·sion·er /ˈpenSHənər/ ▶ **n.** a person who receives a pension.

pen·sion fund ▶ **n.** a fund from which pensions are paid, accumulated from contributions from employers, employees, or both.

pen·sive /ˈpensiv/ ▶ **adj.** engaged in, involving, or reflecting deep or serious thought: *a pensive mood.*
– DERIVATIVES **pen·sive·ly adv.**, **pen·sive·ness n.**
– ORIGIN late Middle English: from Old French *pensif, -ive*, from *penser* 'think,' from Latin *pensare* 'ponder,' frequentative of *pendere* 'weigh.'

pen·ste·mon /penˈstēmən, ˈpenstəmən/ (also **pentstemon**) ▶ **n.** another term for **BEARDTONGUE.**
– ORIGIN modern Latin, formed irregularly from **PENTA-** 'five' + Greek *stēmōn* 'warp,' used to mean 'stamen.'

pen·stock /ˈpenˌstäk/ ▶ **n.** a sluice or floodgate for regulating the flow of a body of water. ■ a channel for conveying water to a waterwheel or turbine.
– ORIGIN early 17th cent.: from **PEN**[2] (in the sense 'milldam') + **STOCK.**

pent /pent/ ▶ **adj.** chiefly literary another term for **PENT-UP**: *with pent breath she waited out the meeting.*

penta- ▶ **comb. form** five; having five: *pentagram | pentadactyl.*
– ORIGIN from Greek *pente* 'five.'

pen·ta·chlo·ro·phe·nol /ˌpentəˌklôrəˈfēnäl/ ▶ **n.** Chemistry a colorless, crystalline, synthetic compound used in insecticides, fungicides, weed killers, and wood preservatives. ● Chem. formula: C_6Cl_5OH.

pen·ta·chord /ˈpentəˌkôrd/ ▶ **n.** a musical instrument with five strings. ■ a series of five musical notes.

pen·ta·cle /ˈpentəkəl/ ▶ **n.** a talisman or magical object, typically disk-shaped and inscribed with a pentagram or other figure, and used as a symbol of the element of earth. ■ another term for **PENTAGRAM.** ■ (**pentacles**) one of the suits in some tarot packs, corresponding to coins in others.
– ORIGIN late 16th cent.: from medieval Latin *pentaculum*, apparently based on Greek *penta-* 'five.'

pen·tad /ˈpenˌtad/ ▶ **n.** technical a group or set of five.
– ORIGIN mid 17th cent.: from Greek *pentas, pentad-*, from *pente* 'five.'

pen·ta·dac·tyl /ˌpentəˈdaktl/ ▶ **adj.** Zoology (of a vertebrate limb) having five toes or fingers, or derived from such a form, as characteristic of all tetrapods.
– DERIVATIVES **pen·ta·dac·tyl·y n.**
– ORIGIN early 19th cent.: from **PENTA-** 'five' + Greek *daktulos* 'finger.'

pen·ta·gas·trin /ˌpentəˈgastrin/ ▶ **n.** Biochemistry a synthetic peptide that has the same action as the hormone gastrin. It is used to promote gastric secretions prior to sampling them for tests.

pen·ta·gon /ˈpentəˌgän/ ▶ **n.** **1** a plane figure with five straight sides and five angles.
2 (**the Pentagon**) the pentagonal building serving as the headquarters of the US Department of Defense, near Washington, DC. ■ the US Department of Defense: *the Pentagon said 19 of its soldiers had been killed.*
– DERIVATIVES **pen·tag·o·nal** /penˈtagənəl/ **adj.**
– ORIGIN late 16th cent.: via Latin from Greek *pentagōnon*, neuter (used as a noun) of *pentagōnos* 'five-angled.'

the Pentagon

PRONUNCIATION KEY ə *ago, up*; ər *over, fur*; a *hat*; ā *ate*; ä *car*; e *let*; ē *see*; i *fit*; ī *by*; NG *sing*; ō *go*; ô *law, for*; oi *toy*; o͝o *good*; o͞o *goo*; ou *out*; TH *thin*; T̲H̲ *then*; ZH *vision*

Pen·ta·gon·ese /ˌpentəˌgänˈēz/ ▶ **n.** informal the euphemistic or cryptic language supposedly used among high-ranking US military personnel.
– ORIGIN 1950s: from PENTAGON (sense 2) + -ESE.

pen·ta·gram /ˈpentəˌgram/ ▶ **n.** a five-pointed star that is formed by drawing a continuous line in five straight segments, often used as a mystic and magical symbol. Compare with PENTACLE.
– ORIGIN mid 19th cent.: from Greek *pentagrammon* (see PENTA-, -GRAM[1]).

pentagram

pen·ta·he·dron /ˌpentəˈhēdrən/ ▶ **n.** (pl. **pentahedrons** or **pentahedra** /-drə/) a solid figure with five plane faces.
– DERIVATIVES **pen·ta·he·dral** /-drəl/ **adj.**
– ORIGIN late 18th cent.: from PENTA- 'five' + -HEDRON, on the pattern of words such as *polyhedron*.

pen·ta·mer /ˈpentəmər/ ▶ **n.** Chemistry a polymer comprising five monomer units.
– DERIVATIVES **pen·ta·mer·ic** /ˌpentəˈmerik/ **adj.**

pen·tam·er·al /penˈtamərəl/ ▶ **adj.** Zoology (of symmetry) fivefold, as typical of many echinoderms. Compare with PENTAMEROUS.
– DERIVATIVES **pen·tam·er·al·ly adv.**, **pen·tam·er·y** /-ˈtamərē/ **n.**

pen·tam·er·ous /penˈtamərəs/ ▶ **adj.** Botany & Zoology having parts arranged in groups of five. ■ consisting of five joints or parts. Compare with PENTAMERAL.

pen·tam·e·ter /penˈtamitər/ ▶ **n.** Prosody a line of verse consisting of five metrical feet, or (in Greek and Latin verse) of two halves each of two feet and a long syllable.
– ORIGIN early 16th cent.: via Latin from Greek *pentametros* (see PENTA-, -METER).

pen·tam·i·dine /penˈtamiˌdēn/ ▶ **n.** Medicine a synthetic antibiotic drug used chiefly in the treatment of pneumocystis carinii pneumonia (PCP) infection.
– ORIGIN 1940s: from PENTANE + AMIDE + -INE[4].

pen·tane /ˈpenˌtān/ ▶ **n.** Chemistry a volatile liquid hydrocarbon of the alkane series, present in petroleum-based solvents. ● Chem. formula: C_5H_{12}; three isomers, esp. the straight-chain isomer (*n*-**pentane**).
– ORIGIN late 19th cent.: from Greek *pente* 'five' (denoting five carbon atoms) + a shortened form of ALKANE.

pen·tan·gle /ˈpenˌtaNGgəl/ ▶ **n.** another term for PENTAGRAM.
– ORIGIN late Middle English: perhaps from medieval Latin *pentaculum* 'pentacle' (*-aculum* assimilated to Latin *angulus* 'an angle').

pen·ta·no·ic ac·id /ˌpentəˈnō-ik/ ▶ **n.** Chemistry a colorless liquid fatty acid present in various plant oils, used in making perfumes. ● Chem. formula: $CH_3(CH_2)_3COOH$.
– ORIGIN 1920s: *pentanoic* from PENTANE.

pen·ta·ploid /ˈpentəˌploid/ Genetics ▶ **adj.** (of a cell or nucleus) containing five homologous sets of chromosomes. ■ (of an organism or species) composed of pentaploid cells.
▶ **n.** a pentaploid organism, variety, or species.

pen·ta·prism /ˈpentəˌprizəm/ ▶ **n.** a five-sided prism with two silvered surfaces giving a constant deviation of all rays of light through 90°, used chiefly in the viewfinders of single-lens reflex cameras.

pen·ta·quark /ˈpentəˌkwärk, -ˌkwôrk/ ▶ **n.** a baryon consisting of four quarks and an antiquark.

Pen·ta·teuch /ˈpentəˌt(y)o͞ok/ the first five books of the Hebrew Bible (Genesis, Exodus, Leviticus, Numbers, and Deuteronomy). Traditionally ascribed to Moses, it is now held by scholars to be a compilation from texts of the 9th to 5th centuries BC. Jewish name TORAH.
– DERIVATIVES **Pen·ta·teuch·al** /-ˌt(y)o͞okəl/ **adj.**
– ORIGIN via ecclesiastical Latin from ecclesiastical Greek *pentateukhos*, from *penta-* 'five' + *teukhos* 'implement, book.'

pen·tath·lon /penˈtaTH(ə)ˌlän/ ▶ **n.** an athletic event comprising five different events for each competitor, in particular (also **modern pentathlon**) a men's event involving fencing, shooting, swimming, riding, and cross-country running.
– DERIVATIVES **pen·tath·lete** /-ˈtaTHlēt/ **n.**
– ORIGIN early 17th cent. (denoting the original five events of leaping, running, discus-throwing, spear-throwing, and wrestling): from Greek, from *pente* 'five' + *athlon* 'contest.'

pen·ta·thol ▶ **n.** variant spelling of PENTOTHAL, regarded as a misspelling in technical use.

pen·ta·ton·ic /ˌpentəˈtänik/ ▶ **adj.** Music relating to, based on, or denoting a scale of five notes, esp. one without semitones equivalent to an ordinary major scale with the fourth and seventh omitted.
– DERIVATIVES **pen·ta·ton·i·cism** /-ˈtänəsizəm/ **n.**

pen·ta·va·lent /ˌpentəˈvālənt/ ▶ **adj.** Chemistry having a valence of five.

pen·taz·o·cine /penˈtazəˌsēn/ ▶ **n.** Medicine a synthetic compound that is a potent, nonaddictive analgesic, often given during childbirth. ● A tricyclic compound; chem. formula: $C_{19}H_{27}NO$.
– ORIGIN 1960s: from PENTANE + AZO- + OCTA- + -INE[4].

Pen·te·cost /ˈpentəˌkôst, -ˌkäst/ ▶ **n. 1** the Christian festival celebrating the descent of the Holy Spirit on the disciples of Jesus after his Ascension, held on the seventh Sunday after Easter. ■ the day on which this festival is held. Also called WHITSUNDAY.
2 the Jewish festival of Shavuoth.
– ORIGIN Old English *pentecosten*, via ecclesiastical Latin from Greek *pentēkostē (hēmera)* 'fiftieth (day)' (because the Jewish festival is held on the fiftieth day after the second day of Passover).

Pen·te·cos·tal /ˌpentəˈkôstl, -ˈkästl/ ▶ **adj. 1** of or relating to Pentecost.
2 of, relating to, or denoting any of a number of Christian movement and individuals emphasizing baptism in the Holy Spirit, evidenced by speaking in tongues, prophecy, healing, and exorcism. [with reference to the baptism in the Holy Spirit at the first Pentecost (Acts 2: 9-11).]
▶ **n.** a member of a Pentecostal movement.
– DERIVATIVES **Pen·te·cos·tal·ism** /-ˌizəm/ **n.**, **Pen·te·cos·tal·ist** /-ist/ **adj. & n.**

pent·house /ˈpentˌhous/ ▶ **n. 1** an apartment on the top floor of a tall building, typically luxuriously fitted and offering fine views.
2 archaic an outhouse or shelter built onto the side of a building, having a sloping roof.
– ORIGIN Middle English *pentis* (sense 2), shortening of Old French *apentis*, based on late Latin *appendicium* 'appendage,' from Latin *appendere* 'hang on.' The change of form in the 16th cent. was by association with French *pente* 'slope' and HOUSE.

pen·ti·men·to /ˌpentəˈmentō/ ▶ **n.** (pl. **pentimenti** /-ˈmentē/) a visible trace of earlier painting beneath a layer or layers of paint on a canvas.
– ORIGIN early 20th cent.: from Italian, literally 'repentance.'

Pent·land Firth /ˈpentlənd/ a channel that separates the Orkney Islands from the northern tip of mainland Scotland. It links the North Sea with the Atlantic Ocean.

pent·land·ite /ˈpentlənˌdīt/ ▶ **n.** a bronze-yellow mineral that consists of a sulfide of iron and nickel and is the principal ore of nickel.
– ORIGIN mid 19th cent.: from the name of Joseph B. *Pentland* (1797–1873), Irish traveler, + -ITE[1].

pen·to·bar·bi·tal /ˌpentəˈbärbiˌtäl, -ˌtôl/ ▶ **n.** Medicine a narcotic and sedative barbiturate drug formerly used to relieve insomnia. ● Alternative name: **5-ethyl-5-(1-methylbutyl)-barbituric acid**; often used as the sodium salt (**sodium pentobarbitone**, Nembutal).
– ORIGIN 1930s: from PENTANE + BARBITAL (or BARBITONE).

pen·to·bar·bi·tone /ˌpentəˈbärbiˌtōn/ ▶ **n.** British term for PENTOBARBITAL.

pen·tode /ˈpentōd/ ▶ **n.** Electronics a thermionic tube having five electrodes.
– ORIGIN early 20th cent.: from Greek *pente* 'five' + *hodos* 'way.'

pen·tose /ˈpentōs/ ▶ **n.** Chemistry any of the class of simple sugars whose molecules contain five carbon atoms, such as ribose and xylose. They generally have the chemical formula $C_5H_{10}O_5$.
– ORIGIN late 19th cent.: from PENTA- 'five' + -OSE[2].

Pen·to·thal /ˈpentəˌTHôl, -ˌTHäl/ ▶ **n.** trademark for THIOPENTAL.

pent·ox·ide /pentˈäksīd/ ▶ **n.** Chemistry an oxide containing five atoms of oxygen in its molecule or empirical formula.

pent roof ▶ **n.** a roof consisting of a single sloping surface.
– ORIGIN mid 19th cent.: from PENTHOUSE + ROOF.

pent·ste·mon /pentˈstēmən, ˈpentstəmən/ ▶ **n.** variant spelling of PENSTEMON.

pent-up ▶ **adj.** closely confined or held back: *pent-up frustrations.*
– ORIGIN late 16th cent.: *pent*, obsolete past participle of PEN[2] (verb).

pen·tyl /ˈpentəl/ ▶ **n.** [as modifier] Chemistry of or denoting an alkyl radical $-C_5H_{11}$. Compare with AMYL.
– ORIGIN from PENTANE + ALKYL.

pe·nult /ˈpēˌnəlt, pəˈnəlt/ ▶ **n.** Linguistics the penultimate syllable of a word.
▶ **adj.** archaic term for PENULTIMATE.

pe·nul·ti·mate /pəˈnəltəmit/ ▶ **adj.** [attrib.] last but one in a series of things; second to the last: *the penultimate chapter of the book.*
– ORIGIN late 17th cent.: from Latin *paenultimus*, from *paene* 'almost' + *ultimus* 'last,' on the pattern of *ultimate*.

pe·num·bra /pəˈnəmbrə/ ▶ **n.** (pl. **penumbrae** /-brē, -brī/ or **penumbras**) the partially shaded outer region of the shadow cast by an opaque object. ■ Astronomy the shadow cast by the earth or moon over an area experiencing a partial eclipse. ■ Astronomy the less dark outer part of a sunspot, surrounding the dark core.
– DERIVATIVES **pe·num·bral** /-brəl/ **adj.**
– ORIGIN mid 17th cent.: modern Latin, from Latin *paene* 'almost' + *umbra* 'shadow.'

pe·nu·ri·ous /pəˈn(y)o͝orēəs/ ▶ **adj.** formal
1 extremely poor; poverty-stricken: *a penurious old tramp.* ■ characterized by poverty or need: *penurious years.*
2 parsimonious; mean: *he was generous and hospitable in contrast to his stingy and penurious wife.*
– DERIVATIVES **pe·nu·ri·ous·ly adv.**, **pe·nu·ri·ous·ness n.**
– ORIGIN late 16th cent.: from medieval Latin *penuriosus*, from Latin *penuria* 'need, scarcity' (see PENURY).

pen·u·ry /ˈpenyərē/ ▶ **n.** extreme poverty; destitution: *he died in a state of virtual penury.*
– ORIGIN late Middle English: from Latin *penuria* 'need, scarcity'; perhaps related to *paene* 'almost.'

Pe·nu·ti·an /pəˈno͞osHən, -ˈno͞otēən/ ▶ **n.** a proposed phylum of American Indian languages including Chinook, Klamath, and Nez Percé, most of which are now extinct or nearly so. Some scholars include certain living languages of Central and South America, principally Mayan and Mapuche, in this group.
▶ **adj.** of, relating to, or denoting these languages or any of the peoples speaking them.
– ORIGIN from *pen* and *uti*, words for 'two' in two groups of Penutian languages + -AN.

Pen·za /ˈpenzə, ˈpyen-/ a city in south central Russia; pop. 507,800 (est. 2008). Located on the Sura River, a tributary of the Volga River, it is an industrial and transportation center.

pe·on /ˈpēˌän, ˈpēən/ ▶ **n. 1** a Spanish-American day laborer or unskilled farm worker. ■ historical a debtor held in servitude by a creditor, esp. in the southern US and Mexico. ■ a person who does menial work; a drudge: *racing drivers aren't exactly normal nine-to-five peons.*
2 (in South and Southeast Asia) someone of low rank. ■ an attendant or messenger.
– DERIVATIVES **pe·on·age** /ˈpēənij/ **n.**
– ORIGIN from Portuguese *peão* and Spanish *peón*, from medieval Latin *pedo*, *pedon-* 'walker, foot soldier,' from Latin *pes*, *ped-* 'foot.' Compare with PAWN[1].

pe·o·ny /ˈpēənē/ ▶ **n.** a herbaceous or shrubby plant of north temperate regions, which has long been cultivated for its showy flowers. ● Genus *Paeonia*, family Paeoniaceae.
– ORIGIN Old English *peonie*, via Latin from Greek *paiōnia*, from *Paiōn*, the name of the physician of the gods.

peo·ple /ˈpēpəl/ ▶ **plural n. 1** human beings in general or considered collectively: *the earthquake killed 30,000 people.* ■ (**the people**) the citizens of a country, esp. when considered in relation to those who govern them: *his economic reforms no longer have the support of the people.* ■ (**the people**) those without special rank or position in society; the populace: *he is very much a man of the people.* ■ (**one's people**) a person's parents or relatives: *my people live in West Virginia.* ■ (**one's people**) the supporters or employees of a person in a position of power or authority: *I've had my people watching the house for some time now.* ■ (**the People**) the state prosecution in a trial: *pretrial statements made by the People's witnesses.*
2 (pl. **peoples**) [treated as sing. or pl.] the men, women, and children of a particular nation, community, or ethnic group: *the native peoples of Canada.*
▶ **v.** [with obj.] (usu. **be peopled**) (of a particular group of people) inhabit (an area or place): *an arid mountain region peopled by warring clans.* ■ fill or be present in (a place, environment, or domain): *the street is peopled with ragamuffin hippies.* ■ fill (an area or place) with a particular group of inhabitants: *it was his intention to people the town with English colonists.*
– DERIVATIVES **peo·ple·hood** /-ˌho͝od/ **n.** PEOPLE (sense 2 of the noun).
– ORIGIN Middle English: from Anglo-Norman French *poeple*, from Latin *populus* 'populace.'

USAGE See usage at PERSON.

peo·ple me·ter ▶ n. an electronic device used to record the television viewing habits of a household so that the information obtained can be used to compile ratings.

peo·ple mov·er ▶ n. informal a means of transportation, in particular any of a number of automated systems for carrying large numbers of people over short distances.

peo·ple per·son ▶ n. informal a person who enjoys or is particularly good at interacting with others.

peo·ple's court ▶ n. informal a small-claims court.

Peo·ple's Lib·er·a·tion Ar·my (abbr.: **PLA**) the armed forces of the People's Republic of China, including all its land, sea, and air forces. The PLA traces its origins to an unsuccessful uprising by Communist-led troops against pro-Nationalist forces in Jiangxi (Kiangsi) province on August 1, 1927, a date celebrated annually as its anniversary.

Peo·ple's par·ty ▶ n. another name for the Populist Party.

Peo·ple's Re·pub·lic ▶ n. used in the official title of several present or former communist or left-wing states. ■ (**the People's Republic**) short for **People's Republic of China**.

Peo·ple's Re·pub·lic of Chi·na official name (since 1949) of **China**.

Pe·or·i·a /pēˈôrēə/ **1** a river port and industrial city in central Illinois, on the Illinois River; pop. 114,114 (est. 2008). It developed around a fort built by the French in 1680.
2 a city in southwest central Arizona, a northwestern suburb of Phoenix; pop. 157,960 (est. 2008).
– ORIGIN named after the American Indians who occupied the area (in sense 1) when the French arrived.

PEP Brit. ▶ abbr. ■ personal equity plan. ■ Political and Economic Planning.

pep /pep/ informal ▶ n. energy and high spirits; liveliness: *he was an enthusiastic player, full of pep and fight.*
▶ v. (**peps, pepping, pepped**) [with obj.] (**pep someone/something up**) add liveliness or vigor to someone or something: *measures to pep up the economy.*
– ORIGIN early 20th cent.: abbreviation of **pepper**.

pep·er·o·mi·a /ˌpepəˈrōmēə/ ▶ n. a small, fleshy-leaved, tropical plant of the pepper family. Many are grown as houseplants, chiefly for their decorative foliage. ● Genus *Peperomia*, family Piperaceae.
– ORIGIN modern Latin, from Greek *peperi*.

pep·er·o·ni ▶ n. variant spelling of **pepperoni**.

Pe·pin III /ˈpepin/ (*c.* 714–768) king of the Franks 751–768; called **Pippin the Short**; father of Charlemagne. He founded the Carolingian dynasty in 751.

pe·pi·no /peˈpēnō/ ▶ n. (pl. **pepinos**) a spiny plant of the nightshade family, with edible, purple-streaked yellow fruit, native to the Andes. ● *Solanum muricatum*, family Solanaceae.
– ORIGIN mid 19th cent.: from Spanish, literally 'cucumber' (because of the elongated shape of the fruit).

pep·los /ˈpepləs, ˈpepˌläs/ (also **peplus**) ▶ n. a rich outer robe or shawl worn by women in ancient Greece, hanging in loose folds and sometimes drawn over the head.
– ORIGIN Greek.

pep·lum /ˈpepləm/ ▶ n. a short flared, gathered, or pleated strip of fabric attached at the waist of a woman's jacket, dress, or blouse to create a hanging frill or flounce. ■ (in ancient Greece) a woman's loose outer tunic or shawl. [via Latin from Greek *peplos*.]

pe·po /ˈpēpō/ ▶ n. (pl. **pepos**) any fleshy, watery fruit of the melon or cucumber type, with numerous seeds and a firm rind.
– ORIGIN mid 19th cent.: from Latin, literally 'pumpkin,' from Greek *pepōn* (from *pepōn sikuos* 'ripe gourd').

pep·per /ˈpepər/ ▶ n. **1** a pungent, hot-tasting powder prepared from dried and ground peppercorns, commonly used as a spice or condiment to flavor food. ■ a reddish and typically hot-tasting spice prepared from various forms of capsicum. See also **cayenne**. ■ a capsicum, esp. a sweet pepper.
2 a climbing vine with berries that are dried as black or white peppercorns. ● *Piper nigrum*, family Piperaceae. ■ used in names of other plants that are related to this, have hot-tasting leaves, or have fruits used as a pungent spice, e.g., **water pepper**.
3 Baseball a practice game in which fielders throw at close range to a batter who hits back to the fielders.
▶ v. [with obj.] sprinkle or season (food) with pepper: (as adj. **peppered**) *peppered beef.* ■ (usu. **be peppered with**) cover or fill with a liberal amount of scattered items: *the script is peppered with four-letter words.* ■ hit repeatedly with small missiles or gunshot: *another burst of enemy bullets peppered his defenseless body* | figurative *he peppered me with questions.* ■ archaic inflict severe punishment or suffering upon.
– ORIGIN Old English *piper, pipor*; related to Dutch *peper* and German *Pfeffer*; via Latin from Greek *peperi*, from Sanskrit *pippalī* 'berry, peppercorn.'

pep·per-and-salt ▶ adj. another way of saying **salt-and-pepper**.

pep·per·box /ˈpepərˌbäks/ ▶ n. **1** a gun or piece of artillery with a revolving set of barrels.
2 archaic a pepper shaker.

pep·per·corn /ˈpepərˌkôrn/ ▶ n. the dried berry of a climbing vine, used whole as a spice or crushed or ground to make pepper. See **pepper** (sense 2 of the noun).

pep·per·grass /ˈpepərˌgras/ ▶ n. a wild cress, particularly one with pungent leaves. ● Genus *Lepidium*, family Brassicaceae.

pep·per·idge /ˈpepərij/ ▶ n. another term for **sourgum**.
– ORIGIN late 17th cent.: alteration of dialect *pipperidge*, denoting the barberry and its fruit, of unknown origin.

pep·per mill ▶ n. a device for grinding peppercorns by hand to make pepper.

pep·per·mint /ˈpepərˌmint/ ▶ n. **1** the aromatic leaves of a plant of the mint family, or an essential oil obtained from them, used as a flavoring in food. ■ a candy flavored with such oil.
2 the cultivated Old World plant that yields these leaves or oil. ● *Mentha piperita*, family Labiatae.
3 Austral. any of a number of trees or shrubs with peppermint-scented foliage, in particular: ● a gum tree with leaves that yield an aromatic essential oil (genus *Eucalyptus*, family Myrtaceae). ● a myrtle grown as an ornamental tree or shrub (genus *Agonis*, family Myrtaceae).
– DERIVATIVES **pep·per·mint·y** adj.

pep·per·o·ni /ˌpepəˈrōnē/ (also **peperoni**) ▶ n. beef and pork sausage seasoned with pepper.
– ORIGIN from Italian *peperone* 'cayenne pepper plant.'

pep·per pot ▶ n. **1** British term for **pepper shaker**.
2 a West Indian dish consisting of stewed meat or fish with vegetables, typically flavored with cassareep.

pep·per shak·er ▶ n. a container with a perforated top for sprinkling pepper.

pep·per·shrike /ˈpepərˌSHrīk/ ▶ n. a tropical American songbird with mainly green and yellow plumage and a heavy bill like that of a shrike. ● Genus *Cyclarhis*, family Cyclarhidae (or merged with the vireo family, Vireonidae): two species, including the **rufous-browed peppershrike** (*C. gujanensis*) of Mexico.

pep·per spray ▶ n. an aerosol spray containing oils derived from cayenne pepper, irritating to the eyes and respiratory passages and used as a disabling weapon.

pep·per tree ▶ n. any of a number of shrubs or trees that have aromatic leaves or fruit with a pepperlike smell, in particular: ● an evergreen Peruvian tree of the cashew family, widely grown as a shade tree in hot countries (*Schinus molle*, family Anacardiaceae).

pep·per vine ▶ n. a bushy vine of the grape family, originally cultivated but now established in much of the southeastern US. It bears blackish fruits sought after by wildlife. ● *Ampelopsis arborea*, family Vitaceae.

pep·per·wort /ˈpepərˌwərt, -ˌwôrt/ ▶ n. another term for **peppergrass**.

pep·per·y /ˈpepərē/ ▶ adj. strongly flavored with pepper or other hot spices: *a hot, peppery dish.* ■ having a flavor or scent like that of pepper. ■ (of a person) irritable and sharp-tongued: *retired generals are expected to be peppery.*
– DERIVATIVES **pep·per·i·ness** /-rēnis/ n.

pep pill ▶ n. informal a pill containing a stimulant drug.

pep·py /ˈpepē/ ▶ adj. (**peppier, peppiest**) informal lively and high-spirited: *stickers bearing peppy slogans.*
– DERIVATIVES **pep·pi·ly** /ˈpepəlē/ adv., **pep·pi·ness** /-ēnis/ n.

pep ral·ly ▶ n. informal a meeting aimed at inspiring enthusiasm, esp. one held before a sporting event.

pep·sin /ˈpepsin/ ▶ n. Biochemistry the chief digestive enzyme in the stomach, which breaks down proteins into polypeptides.
– ORIGIN mid 19th cent.: from Greek *pepsis* 'digestion' + **-in**¹.

pep·sin·o·gen /pepˈsinəjen/ ▶ n. Biochemistry a substance that is secreted by the stomach wall and converted into the enzyme pepsin by gastric acid.

pep talk ▶ n. informal a talk intended to make someone feel more courageous or enthusiastic.

pep·tic /ˈpeptik/ ▶ adj. of or relating to digestion, esp. that in which pepsin is concerned.
– ORIGIN mid 17th cent.: from Greek *peptikos* 'able to digest.'

pep·tic gland ▶ n. Anatomy a gland that secretes the gastric juice containing pepsin.

pep·tic ul·cer ▶ n. a lesion in the lining (mucosa) of the digestive tract, typically in the stomach or duodenum, caused by the digestive action of pepsin and stomach acid.

pep·ti·dase /ˈneptiˌdās/ ▶ n. Biochemistry an enzyme that breaks down peptides into amino acids.

pep·tide /ˈpeptīd/ ▶ n. Biochemistry a compound consisting of two or more amino acids linked in a chain, the carboxyl group of each acid being joined to the amino group of the next by a bond of the type –OC–NH–.
– ORIGIN early 20th cent.: from German *Peptid*, back-formation from *Polypeptid* 'polypeptide.'

pep·ti·do·gly·can /ˌpeptidōˈglīˌkan/ ▶ n. Biochemistry a substance forming the cell walls of many bacteria, consisting of glycosaminoglycan chains interlinked with short peptides.

pep·tone /ˈpeptōn/ ▶ n. Biochemistry a soluble protein formed in the early stage of protein breakdown during digestion. ■ (also **peptone water**) a solution of this in saline, used as a liquid medium for growing bacteria.
– ORIGIN mid 19th cent.: from German *Pepton*, from Greek *pepton*, neuter of *peptos* 'cooked, digested.'

Pepys /pēps/, Samuel (1633–1703), English diarist and naval administrator. He is particularly remembered for his *Diary* (1660–69), which describes events such as the Great Plague and the Fire of London.

Pé·quiste /ˌpāˈkēst/ ▶ n. Canadian a member or supporter of the Parti Québecois, a political party originally advocating independent rule for Quebec.
– ORIGIN from the French pronunciation of the abbreviation *PQ* + the noun suffix *-iste*.

Pe·quot /ˈpēˌkwät/ ▶ n. (pl. **same** or **Pequots**) **1** a member of an American Indian people of southern New England.
2 the Algonquian language of this people, closely related to Mohegan.
▶ adj. of or relating to this people or their language.
– ORIGIN from Narragansett *pequttôog*, perhaps 'people of the shoals.'

per /pər/ ▶ prep. **1** for each (used with units to express a rate): *a gas station that charges $1.29 per gallon.*
2 archaic by means of: *send it per express.*
3 (**as per**) in accordance with: *made as per instructions.*
4 Heraldry divided by a line in the direction of: *per bend* | *per pale* | *per saltire.*
– PHRASES **as per usual** as usual.
– ORIGIN Latin, 'through, by means of'; partly via Old French.

per. ▶ abbr. ■ percentile. ■ period. ■ person.

per- ▶ prefix **1** through; all over: *percuss* | *perforation* | *pervade.* ■ completely; very: *perfect* | *perturb.* ■ to destruction; to ill effect: *perdition* | *pervert.*
2 Chemistry having the maximum proportion of some element in combination: *peroxide* | *perchloric* | *permanganate.*
– ORIGIN from Latin (see **per**).

per·ad·ven·ture /ˌpərədˈvenCHər, ˌpər-/ archaic humorous ▶ adv. archaic or humorous perhaps: *peradventure I'm not as wealthy as he is.*
▶ n. archaic or humorous uncertainty or doubt as to whether something is the case: *that shows* ***beyond peradventure*** *the strength of the economy.*
– ORIGIN Middle English: from Old French *per* (or *par*) *auenture* 'by chance.'

per·am·bu·late /pəˈrambyəˌlāt/ ▶ v. [no obj.] formal walk or travel through or around a place or area, esp. for pleasure and in a leisurely way: *he grew weary of perambulating over rough countryside in bad weather* | [with obj.] *she perambulated the square.* ■ [with obj.] Brit. historical walk around (a parish, forest, etc.) in order to officially assert and record its boundaries.
– DERIVATIVES **per·am·bu·la·tion** /pəˌrambyəˈlāSHən/ n., **per·am·bu·la·to·ry** /-ləˌtôrē/ adj.

PRONUNCIATION KEY ə *ago, up*; ər *over, fur*; a *hat*; ā *ate*; ä *car*; e *let*; ē *see*; i *fit*; ī *by*; NG *sing*; ō *go*; ô *law, for*; oi *toy*; o͝o *good*; o͞o *goo*; ou *out*; TH *thin*; T͟H *then*; ZH *vision*

p

– ORIGIN late Middle English: from Latin *perambulat-* 'walked around,' from the verb *perambulare*, from *per-* 'all over' + *ambulare* 'to walk.'

per·am·bu·la·tor /pəˈrambyəˌlātər/ ▶ **n.** **1** a machine, similar to an odometer, for measuring distances by means of a large wheel pushed along the ground by a long handle, with a mechanism for recording the revolutions.
2 Brit. a baby carriage; pram.
– ORIGIN early 17th cent.: see **PERAMBULATE**.

per an·num /pər ˈanəm/ ▶ **adv.** for each year (used in financial contexts): *an average growth rate of around 2 percent per annum.*
– ORIGIN early 17th cent.: Latin.

p/e ra·tio ▶ **abbr.** price-earnings ratio.

per·bo·rate /pərˈbôrˌāt/ ▶ **n.** Chemistry a salt that is an oxidized borate containing a peroxide linkage, esp. a sodium salt of this kind used as a bleach.

per·cale /pərˈkāl, -ˈkal/ ▶ **n.** a closely woven fine cotton or polyester fabric used esp. for sheets.
– ORIGIN early 17th cent.: from French, of unknown origin.

per cap·i·ta /pər ˈkapitə/ ▶ **adv. & adj.** for each person; in relation to people taken individually: [as adv.] *the state had fewer banks per capita than elsewhere* | [as adj.] *per capita spending.*
– ORIGIN late 17th cent.: Latin, literally 'by heads.'

per·ceive /pərˈsēv/ ▶ **v.** [with obj.] **1** become aware or conscious of (something); come to realize or understand: *his mouth fell open as he perceived the truth* | [with clause] *he was quick to perceive that there was little future in such arguments.* ■ become aware of (something) by the use of one of the senses, esp. that of sight: *he perceived the faintest of flushes creeping up her neck.*
2 interpret or look on (someone or something) in a particular way; regard as: *if Guy does not perceive himself as disabled, nobody else should* | [with obj. and infinitive] *some geographers perceive hydrology to be a separate field of scientific inquiry.*
– DERIVATIVES **per·ceiv·a·ble** adj., **per·ceiv·er** n.
– ORIGIN Middle English: from a variant of Old French *perçoivre*, from Latin *percipere* 'seize, understand,' from *per-* 'entirely' +*capere* 'take.'

per·cent /pərˈsent/ (also chiefly Brit. **per cent**) ▶ **adv.** by a specified amount in or for every hundred: *new car sales may be down nineteen percent* | *staff rejected a 1.8 percent increase.*
▶ **n.** one part in every hundred: *a reduction of half a percent or so in price.* ■ the rate, number, or amount in each hundred; percentage: *the percent of drug users who are infected.*
– ORIGIN mid 16th cent.: from **PER** + **CENT**, perhaps an abbreviation of pseudo-Latin *per centum.*

> **USAGE** Both spellings, **percent** and **per cent**, are acceptable, but consistency should be maintained. **Percent** is more common in US usage; **per cent** is more common in British usage.

per·cent·age /pərˈsentij/ ▶ **n.** a rate, number, or amount in each hundred: *the percentage of cesareans at the hospital was three percent higher than the national average* | [as modifier] *a large percentage increase in the population over 85.* ■ an amount, such as an allowance or commission, that is a proportion of a larger sum of money: *I hope to be on a percentage.* ■ any proportion or share in relation to a whole: *only a small percentage of black Americans have Caribbean roots.* ■ [in sing.] informal personal benefit or advantage: *you explain to me the percentage in looking like a hoodlum.*
– PHRASES **play the percentages** (or **the percentage game**) informal choose a safe and methodical course of action when calculating the odds in favor of success. [referring to the calculated percentage of success from statistics.]

per·cent·age point ▶ **n.** a unit of one percent: *interest rates rose by 1.75 percentage points.*

-percenter ▶ **comb. form 1** denoting a member of a group forming a specified and usually small percentage of the population: *he was a one-percenter, riding outside of the law.*
2 denoting a person who takes commission at a specified rate: *ten-percenters.*

per·cen·tile /pərˈsenˌtīl/ ▶ **n.** Statistics each of the 100 equal groups into which a population can be divided according to the distribution of values of a particular variable. ■ each of the 99 intermediate values of a random variable that divide a frequency distribution into 100 such groups: *the tenth percentile for weight.*

per·cept /ˈpərsept/ ▶ **n.** Philosophy an object of perception; something that is perceived. ■ a mental concept that is developed as a consequence of the process of perception.
– ORIGIN mid 19th cent.: from Latin *perceptum* 'something perceived,' neuter past participle of *percipere* 'seize, understand,' on the pattern of *concept.*

per·cep·ti·ble /pərˈseptəbəl/ ▶ **adj.** (esp. of a slight movement or change of state) able to be seen or noticed: *a perceptible decline in public confidence.*
– DERIVATIVES **per·cep·ti·bil·i·ty** /pərˌseptəˈbilitē/ **n.**, **per·cep·ti·bly** /-blē/ **adv.**
– ORIGIN late Middle English: from late Latin *perceptibilis*, from Latin *percipere* 'seize, understand' (see **PERCEIVE**).

per·cep·tion /pərˈsepSHən/ ▶ **n.** the ability to see, hear, or become aware of something through the senses: *the normal limits to human perception.* ■ the state of being or process of becoming aware of something in such a way: *the perception of pain.* ■ a way of regarding, understanding, or interpreting something; a mental impression: *Hollywood's perception of the tastes of the American public* | *we need to challenge many popular perceptions of old age.* ■ intuitive understanding and insight: *"He wouldn't have accepted," said my mother with unusual perception.* ■ Psychology & Zoology the neurophysiological processes, including memory, by which an organism becomes aware of and interprets external stimuli.
– DERIVATIVES **per·cep·tion·al** /-SHənl, -SHənəl/ **adj.**
– ORIGIN late Middle English: from Latin *perceptio(n-)*, from the verb *percipere* 'seize, understand' (see **PERCEIVE**).

per·cep·tive /pərˈseptiv/ ▶ **adj.** having or showing sensitive insight: *an extraordinarily perceptive account of their relationship.*
– DERIVATIVES **per·cep·tive·ly** adv., **per·cep·tive·ness** n., **per·cep·tiv·i·ty** /ˌpərsepˈtivitē/ **n.**

per·cep·tron /pərˈsepträn/ ▶ **n.** a computer model or computerized machine devised to represent or simulate the ability of the brain to recognize and discriminate.

per·cep·tu·al /pərˈsepCHo͞oəl/ ▶ **adj.** of or relating to the ability to interpret or become aware of something through the senses: *a patient with perceptual problems who cannot judge distances.*
– DERIVATIVES **per·cep·tu·al·ly** adv.

Per·ce·val¹ /ˈpərsəvəl/ a legendary figure dating back to ancient times, found in French, German, and English poetry from the late 12th century onward. He is the father of Lohengrin and the hero of a number of legends, some of which are associated with the Holy Grail. Also called **PARSIFAL**.

Per·ce·val², Spencer (1762–1812), British statesman; prime minister 1809–12. He was shot dead in the lobby of the House of Commons by a bankrupt merchant who blamed the government for his insolvency.

perch¹ /pərCH/ ▶ **n.** a thing on which a bird alights or roosts, typically a branch or a horizontal rod or bar in a birdcage. ■ a place where someone or something rests or sits, esp. a place that is high or precarious: *Marian looked down from her perch in a beech tree above the road.*
▶ **v.** [no obj.] (of a bird) alight or rest on something: *a herring gull perched on the mast.* ■ (of a person) sit somewhere, esp. on something high or narrow: *Eve perched on the side of the armchair.* ■ (**be perched**) (of a building) be situated above or on the edge of something: *the fortress is perched on a crag in the mountains.* ■ [with obj.] (**perch someone/something on**) set or balance someone or something on (something): *Peter perched a pair of gold-rimmed spectacles on his nose.*
– PHRASES **knock someone off their perch** informal cause someone to lose a position of superiority or preeminence: *will this knock London off its perch as Europe's leading financial center?*
– ORIGIN late Middle English: the noun from **PERCH³**; the verb from Old French *percher.*

perch² ▶ **n.** (pl. **same** or **perches**) an edible freshwater fish with a high spiny dorsal fin, dark vertical bars on the body, and orange lower fins. ● Genus *Perca*, family Percidae (the **perch family**): three species, in particular *P. fluviatilis* of Europe (also called **BASS²**), and the almost identical **yellow perch** (*P. flavescens*) of North America. The perch family also includes the pikeperches, ruffe, and darters. ■ used in names of other freshwater and marine fishes resembling or related to this, e.g., **climbing perch**, **sea perch**, **surfperch**.
– ORIGIN late Middle English: from Old French *perche*, via Latin from Greek *perkē.*

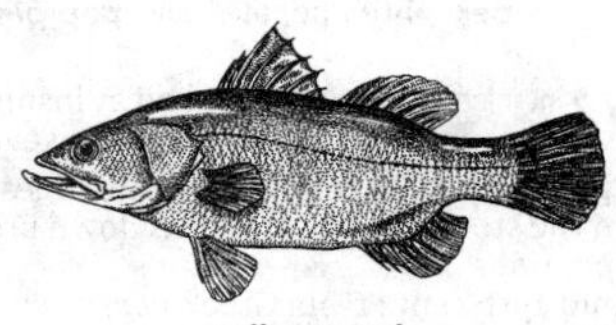
yellow perch

perch³ ▶ **n.** chiefly Brit. historical a linear or square rod (see **ROD** (sense 3)).
– ORIGIN Middle English (in the general sense 'pole, stick'): from Old French *perche*, from Latin *pertica* 'measuring rod, pole.'

per·chance /pərˈCHans/ ▶ **adv.** archaic or literary by some chance; perhaps: *we dare not go ashore lest perchance we should fall into some snare.*
– ORIGIN Middle English: from Old French *par cheance* 'by chance.'

Per·che·ron /ˈpərSHəˌrän, ˈpərCHə-/ ▶ **n.** a powerful draft horse of a gray or black breed, originally from France.
– ORIGIN late 19th cent.: from French, originally bred in le *Perche*, the name of a district of northern France.

per·chlo·ric ac·id /pərˈklôrik/ ▶ **n.** Chemistry a fuming toxic liquid with powerful oxidizing properties. ● Chem. formula: $HClO_4$.
– DERIVATIVES **per·chlo·rate** /-ˌrāt/ **n.**

per·cid /ˈpərsid/ ▶ **n.** Zoology a fish of the perch family (Percidae).
– ORIGIN late 19th cent.: from modern Latin *Percidae* (plural), from Latin *perca* 'perch.'

per·cip·i·ence /pərˈsipēəns/ ▶ **n.** good understanding of things; perceptiveness.

per·cip·i·ent /pərˈsipēənt/ ▶ **adj.** (of a person) having a good understanding of things; perceptive: *he is a percipient interpreter of the public mood.*
▶ **n.** (esp. in philosophy or with reference to psychic phenomena) a person who is able to perceive things.
– DERIVATIVES **per·cip·i·ent·ly** adv.
– ORIGIN mid 17th cent.: from Latin *percipient-* 'seizing, understanding,' from the verb *percipere.*

per·coid /ˈpərkoid/ Zoology ▶ **n.** a fish of a large group that includes the perches, basses, jacks, snappers, grunts, sea breams, and drums. ● Superfamily Percoidea: many families.
▶ **adj.** of or relating to fish of this group.
– ORIGIN mid 19th cent.: from modern Latin *Percoïdes* (plural), from Latin *perca* 'perch.'

per·co·late /ˈpərkəˌlāt/ ▶ **v. 1** [no obj.] (of a liquid or gas) filter gradually through a porous surface or substance: *the water percolating through the soil may leach out minerals.* ■ (of information or an idea or feeling) spread gradually through an area or group of people: *this issue has percolated into the public consciousness.*
2 [no obj.] (of coffee) be prepared in a percolator: *he put some coffee on to percolate.* ■ [with obj.] prepare (coffee) in a percolator: (as adj. **percolated**) *freshly percolated coffee.* ■ be or become full of lively activity or excitement: *the night was percolating with an expectant energy.*
– DERIVATIVES **per·co·la·tion** /ˌpərkəˈlāSHən/ **n.**
– ORIGIN early 17th cent.: from Latin *percolat-* 'strained through,' from the verb *percolare*, from *per-* 'through' + *colare* 'to strain' (from *colum* 'strainer').

per·co·la·tor /ˈpərkəˌlātər/ ▶ **n.** a machine for making coffee, consisting of a pot in which boiling water is circulated through a small chamber that holds the ground beans.

per con·tra /pər ˈkäntrə/ ▶ **adv.** formal on the other hand; on the contrary: *he had worked very hard on the place; she, per contra, had little to do.*
▶ **n.** the opposite side of an account or an assessment.
– ORIGIN mid 16th cent.: from Italian.

per cu·ri·am /pər ˈkyo͝orēəm/ Law ▶ **adv.** by decision of a judge, or of a court in unanimous agreement.
▶ **n.** such a decision: *in only a few cases did the panel publish a per curiam.*
– ORIGIN Latin, literally 'by a court.'

per·cuss /pərˈkəs/ ▶ **v.** [with obj.] Medicine gently tap (a part of the body) with a finger or an instrument as part of a diagnosis: *the bladder was percussed.*
– ORIGIN mid 16th cent. (in the general sense 'give a blow to'): from Latin *percuss-* 'struck forcibly,' from the verb *percutere*, from *per-* 'through' + *quatere* 'to shake, strike.'

per·cus·sion /pərˈkəSHən/ ▶ **n. 1** musical instruments played by striking with the hand or with a handheld or pedal-operated stick or beater, or by shaking, including drums, cymbals, xylophones, gongs, bells, and rattles: [as modifier] *percussion instruments* | *the percussion section.*
2 the striking of one solid object with or against another with some degree of force: *the clattering percussion of objects striking the walls and the shutters.* ■ Medicine the action of tapping a part of the body as part of a diagnosis: *the chest sounded dull on percussion.*
– DERIVATIVES **per·cus·sion·ist** /-ist/ **n.** (sense 1), **per·cus·sive** /-ˈkəsiv/ **adj.**, **per·cus·sive·ly** /-ˈkəsivlē/ **adv.**, **per·cus·sive·ness** /-ˈkəsivnis/ **n.**
– ORIGIN late Middle English: from Latin *percussio(n-)*, from the verb *percutere* 'to strike forcibly' (see **PERCUSS**).

per·cus·sion cap ▶ **n.** a small amount of explosive powder contained in metal or paper and exploded by striking. Percussion caps are used chiefly in toy guns and formerly in some firearms.

per·cu·ta·ne·ous /ˌpərkyo͞oˈtānēəs/ ▶ **adj.** Medicine made, done, or effected through the skin.
– DERIVATIVES **per·cu·ta·ne·ous·ly** adv.
– ORIGIN late 19th cent.: from Latin *per cutem* 'through the skin' + **-ANEOUS**.

Per·cy[1] /ˈpərsē/, Sir Henry (1364–1403), English soldier; known as **Hotspur** or **Harry Hotspur**. Son of the **1st Earl of Northumberland**, he was killed at the battle of Shrewsbury.

Per·cy[2], Walker (1916–90) US writer. His novels include *The Moviegoer* (1961), *Love in the Ruins* (1971), *The Second Coming* (1980), and *The Thanatos Syndrome* (1987).

per di·em /pər ˈdēəm/ ▶ **adv. & adj.** for each day (used in financial contexts): [as adv.] *he agreed to pay at certain specified rates per diem* | [as adj.] *they are now demanding a per diem rate.*
▶ **n.** an allowance or payment made for each day.
– ORIGIN early 16th cent.: Latin.

per·di·tion /pərˈdisHən/ ▶ **n.** (in Christian theology) a state of eternal punishment and damnation into which a sinful and unpenitent person passes after death.
– ORIGIN late Middle English: from Old French *perdiciun*, from ecclesiastical Latin *perditio(n-)*, from Latin *perdere* 'destroy,' from *per-* 'completely, to destruction' + the base of *dare* 'put.'

per·dur·a·ble /pərˈd(y)o͝orəbəl/ ▶ **adj.** formal enduring continuously; imperishable.
– DERIVATIVES **per·dur·a·bil·i·ty** /-ˌd(y)o͝orəˈbilitē/ **n.**, **per·dur·a·bly** adv.
– ORIGIN late Middle English: via Old French from late Latin *perdurabilis*, from Latin *perdurare* 'endure.'

per·dure /pərˈd(y)o͝or/ ▶ **v.** [no obj.] formal remain in existence throughout a substantial period of time; endure: *bell music has perdured in Venice throughout five centuries.*
– DERIVATIVES **per·dur·ance** /-ˈd(y)o͝orəns/ **n.**
– ORIGIN late 15th cent.: from Old French *perdurer*, from Latin *perdurare* 'endure,' from *per-* 'through' + *durare* 'to last.'

père /pe(ə)r/ ▶ **n.** used after a surname to distinguish a father from a son of the same name: *Alexandre Dumas père.* Compare with **FILS**[2].
– ORIGIN French, literally 'father.'

Père Da·vid's deer /ˌper ˈdāvidz/ ▶ **n.** a large deer with a red summer coat that turns dark gray in winter, and long antlers with backward pointing tines. Formerly a native of China, it is now found only in captivity. ● *Elaphurus davidianus*, family Cervidae.
– ORIGIN late 19th cent.: named after Father Armand *David* (1826–1900), French missionary and naturalist.

per·e·gri·nate /ˈperigrəˌnāt/ ▶ **v.** [no obj.] archaic or humorous travel or wander around from place to place.
– DERIVATIVES **per·e·gri·na·tion** /ˌperigrəˈnāsHən/ **n.**, **per·e·gri·na·tor** /-ˌnātər/ **n.**
– ORIGIN late 16th cent.: from Latin *peregrinat-* 'traveled abroad,' from the verb *peregrinari*, from *peregrinus* 'foreign, traveling.'

per·e·grine /ˈperəgrin/ ▶ **n.** (also **peregrine falcon**) a powerful falcon found on most continents, breeding chiefly on mountains and coastal cliffs and much used for falconry. [translating the modern Latin taxonomic name, literally 'pilgrim falcon,' because the bird was caught full-grown as a passage hawk, not taken from the nest.] ● *Falco peregrinus*, family Falconidae.

peregrine

▶ **adj.** archaic coming from another country; foreign or outlandish: *peregrine species of grass.*
– ORIGIN late Middle English: from Latin *peregrinus* 'foreign,' from *peregre* 'abroad,' from *per-* 'through' + *ager* 'field.'

pe·rei·o·pod /pəˈrīəˌpäd, -ˈrāə-/ ▶ **n.** Zoology each of the eight walking limbs of a crustacean such as a crab or lobster, growing from the thorax.
– ORIGIN late 19th cent.: from Greek *peraioōn* 'transporting' (present participle of *peraioun*) + *pous, pod-* 'foot.'

Per·el·man /ˈpərlmən, ˈperəl-/, S. J. (1904–79), US humorist and writer; full name *Sidney Joseph Perelman.* In the early 1930s he worked in Hollywood as a scriptwriter and from 1934 his name is linked with *The New Yorker* magazine, for which he wrote most of his short stories and sketches.

per·emp·to·ry /pəˈremptərē/ ▶ **adj.** (esp. of a person's manner or actions) insisting on immediate attention or obedience, esp. in a brusquely imperious way: *"Just do it!" came the peremptory reply.* ■ Law not open to appeal or challenge; final: *there has been no disobedience of a peremptory order of the court.*
– DERIVATIVES **per·emp·to·ri·ly** /-tərəlē/ **adv.**, **per·emp·to·ri·ness** /-rēnis/ **n.**
– ORIGIN late Middle English (as a legal term): via Anglo-Norman French from Latin *peremptorius* 'deadly, decisive,' from *perempt-* 'destroyed, cut off,' from the verb *perimere*, from *per-* 'completely' + *emere* 'take, buy.'

per·emp·to·ry chal·lenge ▶ **n.** Law a defendant's or lawyer's objection to a proposed juror, made without needing to give a reason.

per·en·nate /ˈperəˌnāt, pəˈrenāt/ ▶ **v.** [no obj.] (usu. as adj. **perennating**) Botany (of a plant or part of a plant) live through a number of years, usually with an annual quiescent period.
– DERIVATIVES **per·en·na·tion** /ˌperəˈnāsHən/ **n.**
– ORIGIN early 17th cent.: from Latin *perennat-* 'continued for many years' (from the verb *perennare*) + **-ATE**[3].

per·en·ni·al /pəˈrenēəl/ ▶ **adj.** lasting or existing for a long or apparently infinite time; enduring or continually recurring: *his perennial distrust of the media* | *perennial manifestations of urban crisis.* ■ (of a plant) living for several years: *tarragon is perennial.* Compare with **ANNUAL, BIENNIAL.** ■ [attrib.] (of a person) apparently permanently engaged in a specified role or way of life: *he's a perennial student.* ■ (of a stream or spring) flowing throughout the year.
▶ **n.** a perennial plant.
– DERIVATIVES **per·en·ni·al·ly** adv.
– ORIGIN mid 17th cent. (in the sense 'remaining leafy throughout the year, evergreen'): from Latin *perennis* 'lasting the year through' + **-IAL**.

Pe·res /ˈperez/, Shimon (1923–), Israeli statesman, born in Poland; prime minister 1984–86 and 1995–96; president since 2007; Polish name *Szymon Perski.* As foreign minister under Yitzhak Rabin, he played a major role in negotiating the PLO–Israeli peace accord of 1993. Nobel Peace Prize (1994), shared with Rabin and Yasser Arafat.

pe·re·stroi·ka /ˌperəˈstroikə/ ▶ **n.** (in the former Soviet Union) the policy or practice of restructuring or reforming the economic and political system. First proposed by Leonid Brezhnev in 1979 and actively promoted by Mikhail Gorbachev, perestroika originally referred to increased automation and labor efficiency, but came to entail greater awareness of economic markets and the ending of central planning. See also **GLASNOST**.
– ORIGIN Russian, literally 'restructuring.'

Pé·rez de Cué·llar /ˈpārās də ˈkwāyär/, Javier (1920–), Peruvian diplomat; secretary general of the United Nations 1982–91.

per·fect ▶ **adj.** /ˈpərfikt/ **1** having all the required or desirable elements, qualities, or characteristics; as good as it is possible to be: *she strove to be the perfect wife* | *life certainly isn't perfect at the moment.* ■ free from any flaw or defect in condition or quality; faultless: *the equipment was in perfect condition.* ■ precisely accurate; exact: *a perfect circle.* ■ highly suitable for someone or something; exactly right: *Gary was perfect for her—ten years older and with his own career.* ■ Printing denoting a way of binding books in which pages are glued to the spine rather than sewn together. ■ dated thoroughly trained in or conversant with: *she was perfect in French.*
2 [attrib.] absolute; complete (used for emphasis): *a perfect stranger* | *all that Joseph said made perfect sense to me.*
3 Mathematics (of a number) equal to the sum of its positive divisors, e.g., the number 6, whose divisors (1, 2, 3) also add up to 6.
4 Grammar (of a tense) denoting a completed action or a state or habitual action that began in the past. The perfect tense is formed in English with *have* or *has* and the past participle, as in *they have eaten* and *they have been eating (since dawn)* (**present perfect**), *they had eaten* (**past perfect**), and *they will have eaten* (**future perfect**).
5 Botany (of a flower) having both stamens and carpels present and functional. ■ Botany denoting the stage or state of a fungus in which the sexually produced spores are formed. ■ Entomology (of an insect) fully adult and (typically) winged.
▶ **v.** /pərˈfekt/ [with obj.] make (something) completely free from faults or defects, or as close to such a condition as possible: *he's busy perfecting his bowling technique.* ■ archaic bring to completion; finish. ■ complete (a printed sheet of paper) by printing the second side. ■ Law satisfy the necessary conditions or requirements for the transfer of (a gift, title, etc.): *equity will not perfect an imperfect gift.*
▶ **n.** /ˈpərfikt/ (**the perfect**) Grammar the perfect tense.
– DERIVATIVES **per·fect·er** /pərˈfektər/ **n.**, **per·fect·i·bil·i·ty** /pərˌfektəˈbilitē/ **n.**, **per·fect·i·ble** /pərˈfektəbəl/ **adj.**, **per·fect·ness** /ˈpərfək(t)nəs/ **n.**
– ORIGIN Middle English: from Old French *perfet*, from Latin *perfectus* 'completed,' from the verb *perficere*, from *per-* 'through, completely' + *facere* 'do.'

> **USAGE** In the literal sense, **perfect** and **unique** are absolute words and should not be modified, as they often are in such phrases as *most perfect, quite unique*, etc. See also usage at **UNIQUE**.

per·fec·ta /pərˈfektə/ ▶ **n.** another term for **EXACTA**.
– ORIGIN 1970s: from Latin American Spanish *quiniela perfecta* 'perfect quinella.'

per·fect bind·ing ▶ **n.** a form of bookbinding in which the leaves are bound by gluing, after the back folds have been cut off, rather than by sewing.

per·fect ca·dence ▶ **n.** Music a cadence in which the chord of the dominant immediately precedes that of the tonic.

per·fect com·pe·ti·tion ▶ **n.** the situation prevailing in a market in which buyers and sellers are so numerous and well informed that all elements of monopoly are absent and the market price of a commodity is beyond the control of individual buyers and sellers.

per·fect crime ▶ **n.** a crime so ingeniously contrived and carefully executed that it cannot be detected or solved.

per·fect fifth ▶ **n.** Music see **FIFTH**.

per·fect fourth ▶ **n.** Music see **FOURTH**.

per·fect game ▶ **n.** Baseball a game in which all the batters from one team are retired in order, with no one reaching base.

per·fect gas ▶ **n.** another term for **IDEAL GAS**.

per·fec·tion /pərˈfeksHən/ ▶ **n.** the condition, state, or quality of being free or as free as possible from all flaws or defects: *the satiny perfection of her skin* | *his pursuit of golfing perfection.* ■ a person or thing perceived as the embodiment of such a condition, state, or quality: *I am told that she is perfection itself.* ■ the action or process of improving something until it is faultless or as faultless as possible: *among the key tasks was the perfection of new mechanisms of economic management.*
– PHRASES **to perfection** in a manner or way that could not be better; perfectly: *a blue suit that showed off her blonde hair to perfection.*
– ORIGIN Middle English (in the sense 'completeness'): via Old French from Latin *perfectio(n-)*, from *perficere* 'to complete' (see **PERFECT**).

per·fec·tion·ism /pərˈfeksHəˌnizəm/ ▶ **n.** refusal to accept any standard short of perfection. ■ Philosophy a doctrine holding that religious, moral, social, or political perfection is attainable, esp. the theory that human moral or spiritual perfection should be or has been attained.

per·fec·tion·ist /pərˈfeksHəˌnist/ ▶ **n.** a person who refuses to accept any standard short of perfection: *he was a perfectionist who worked slowly.*
▶ **adj.** refusing to accept any standard short of perfection.
– DERIVATIVES **per·fec·tion·is·tic** /-ˌfeksHəˈnistik/ **adj.**

per·fec·tive /pərˈfektiv/ Grammar ▶ **adj.** denoting or relating to an aspect of verbs, esp. in Slavic languages that expresses completed action. The opposite of **IMPERFECTIVE**.
▶ **n.** a perfective form of a verb. ■ (**the perfective**) the perfective aspect.
– ORIGIN early 17th cent. (in the general sense 'tending to make complete'): from medieval Latin *perfectivus*, from Latin *perfectus* 'accomplished' (see **PERFECT**).

per·fect·ly /ˈpərfik(t)lē/ ▶ **adv.** in a manner or way that could not be better: *the ring fitted perfectly* | [as submodifier] *perfectly clean glass bottles.* ■ [as submodifier] used for emphasis, esp. in order to assert something that has been challenged or doubted: *you know perfectly well I can't stay.*

per·fec·to /pərˈfektō/ ▶ **n.** (pl. **perfectos**) a type of cigar that is thick in the center and tapered at each end.
– ORIGIN late 19th cent.: from Spanish, literally 'perfect.'

per·fect pitch ▶ **n.** the ability to recognize the pitch of a note or to produce any given note; a sense of absolute pitch.

P

per·fect rhyme ▶ **n. 1** the rhyme exemplified by homonyms, such as *bear/bare* or *wear/where.* **2** rhyme in which different consonants are followed by identical vowel and consonant sounds, such as in *moon* and *June.*

per·fect square ▶ **n.** the product of a rational number multiplied by itself. ■ the product of a polynomial multiplied by itself.

per·fect storm ▶ **n.** a particularly violent storm arising from a rare combination of adverse meteorological factors. ■ a particularly bad or critical state of affairs, arising from a number of negative and unpredictable factors: *the past two years have been a perfect storm for the travel industry.*

per·fer·vid /pər'fərvid/ ▶ **adj.** literary intense and impassioned: *perfervid nationalism.*
– DERIVATIVES **per·fer·vid·ly adv.**
– ORIGIN mid 19th cent.: from modern Latin *perfervidus,* from Latin *per-* 'utterly' + *fervidus* 'glowing hot, fiery.'

per·fid·i·ous /pər'fidēəs/ ▶ **adj.** literary deceitful and untrustworthy: *a perfidious lover.*
– DERIVATIVES **per·fid·i·ous·ly adv.**
– ORIGIN late 16th cent.: from Latin *perfidiosus,* from *perfidia* 'treachery.'

per·fi·dy /'pərfidē/ ▶ **n.** literary deceitfulness; untrustworthiness.
– ORIGIN late 16th cent.: via French from Latin *perfidia,* from *perfidus* 'treacherous,' based on *per-* 'to ill effect' + *fides* 'faith.'

perf·in /'pərfin/ ▶ **n.** Philately a postage stamp perforated with the initials or insignia of an organization, esp. to prevent misuse.
– ORIGIN 1950s: from *perf(orated) in(itials).*

per·fo·li·ate /pər'fōlē,āt, -it/ ▶ **adj.** Botany (of a stalkless leaf or bract) extended at the base to encircle the node, so that the stem apparently passes through it. ■ (of a plant) having such leaves.
– ORIGIN late 17th cent.: from modern Latin *perfoliatus,* from Latin *per-* 'through' + *foliatus* 'leaved.'

per·fo·rate ▶ **v.** /'pərfə,rāt/ [with obj.] pierce and make a hole or holes in: *the worms had perforated the pages of the book from cover to cover* | (as adj. **perforated**) *a perforated appendix.* ■ make a row of small holes in (paper) so that a part may be torn off easily.
▶ **adj.** /'pərfərit, -,rāt/ Biology & Medicine perforated: *a perforate shell.*
– DERIVATIVES **per·fo·ra·tor** /-,rātər/ **n.**
– ORIGIN late Middle English (as an adjective): from Latin *perforat-* 'pierced through,' from the verb *perforare,* from *per-* 'through' + *forare* 'pierce.'

per·fo·ra·tion /,pərfə'rāsHən/ ▶ **n.** a hole made by boring or piercing; an aperture passing through or into something: *the perforations allow water to enter the well.* ■ a small hole or row of small holes punched in a sheet of paper, e.g., of postage stamps, so that a part can be torn off easily. ■ the action or state of perforating or being perforated: *there was evidence of intestinal perforation.*
– ORIGIN late Middle English: from medieval Latin *perforatio(n-),* from the verb *perforare* (see **PERFORATE**).

per·force /pər'fôrs/ ▶ **adv.** formal used to express necessity or inevitability: *amateurs, perforce, have to settle for less expensive solutions.*
– ORIGIN Middle English: from Old French *par force* 'by force.'

per·fo·rin /'pərfərin/ ▶ **n.** Biochemistry a protein, released by killer cells of the immune system, that destroys targeted cells by creating lesions like pores in their membranes.
– ORIGIN 1980s: from the verb **PERFORATE** + **-IN**¹.

per·form /pər'fôrm/ ▶ **v.** [with obj.] **1** carry out, accomplish, or fulfill (an action, task, or function): *I have my duties to perform.* ■ [no obj.] work, function, or do something to a specified standard: *the car performs well at low speeds.* ■ [no obj.] informal have successful or satisfactory sexual intercourse with someone.
2 present (a form of entertainment) to an audience: *the cast of 14 perform the play superbly.* ■ [no obj.] entertain an audience, typically by acting, singing, or dancing on stage: *the band will be performing live in Hyde Park.*
– DERIVATIVES **per·form·a·bil·i·ty** /-,fôrmə'bilitē/ **n.**, **per·form·a·ble adj.**
– ORIGIN Middle English: from Anglo-Norman French *parfourmer,* alteration (by association with *forme* 'form') of Old French *parfournir,* from *par* 'through, to completion' + *fournir* 'furnish, provide.'

per·for·mance /pər'fôrməns/ ▶ **n. 1** an act of staging or presenting a play, concert, or other form of entertainment: *Don Giovanni had its first performance in 1787.* ■ a person's rendering of a dramatic role, song, or piece of music: *Bailey gives a sound performance as the doctor.* ■ [in sing.] informal a display of exaggerated behavior or a process involving a great deal of unnecessary time and effort; a fuss: *he stopped to tie his shoe and seemed to be making quite a performance of it.*
2 the action or process of carrying out or accomplishing an action, task, or function: *the continual performance of a single task reduces a man to the level of a machine.* ■ an action, task, or operation, seen in terms of how successfully it was performed: *pay increases are now being linked more closely to performance* | *a dynamic performance by Davis.* ■ the capabilities of a machine, vehicle, or product, esp. when observed under particular conditions: *the hardware is put through tests that assess the performance of the processor.* ■ the extent to which an investment is profitable, esp. in relation to other investments. ■ (also **linguistic performance**) Linguistics an individual's use of a language, i.e., what a speaker actually says, including hesitations, false starts, and errors. Often contrasted with **COMPETENCE**.

per·for·mance art ▶ **n.** an art form that combines visual art with dramatic performance.
– DERIVATIVES **per·for·mance art·ist n.**

per·for·mance bond ▶ **n.** a bond issued by a bank or other financial institution, guaranteeing the fulfillment of a particular contract.

per·for·mance cap·ture ▶ **n.** another term for **MOTION CAPTURE**.

per·for·mance po·et·ry ▶ **n.** a form of poetry intended to be performed as a dramatic monologue or exchange and frequently involving extemporization.
– DERIVATIVES **per·for·mance po·et n.**

per·for·mance test·ing ▶ **n.** the evaluation of a person's mental or manual ability. ■ the evaluation of the heritable characteristics of a bull or other breeding animal, or of a plant, as determined from the known characteristics of the offspring.

per·for·ma·tive /pər'fôrmətiv/ ▶ **adj.** Linguistics & Philosophy relating to or denoting an utterance by means of which the speaker performs a particular act (e.g., *I bet, I apologize, I promise*). Often contrasted with **CONSTATIVE**.
▶ **n.** Linguistics & Philosophy a performative verb, sentence, or utterance.

per·form·er /pər'fôrmər/ ▶ **n.** a person who entertains an audience: *a circus performer.*

per·form·ing arts ▶ **plural n.** forms of creative activity that are performed in front of an audience, such as drama, music, and dance.

per·fume /'pər,fyo͞om, ,pər'fyo͞om/ ▶ **n.** a fragrant liquid typically made from essential oils extracted from flowers and spices, used to impart a pleasant smell to one's body or clothes: *I caught a whiff of her fresh lemony perfume* | *musk-based perfumes.* ■ a pleasant smell: *the heady perfume of lilacs.*
▶ **v.** [with obj.] impart a pleasant smell to: *just one bloom of jasmine has the power to perfume a whole room.* ■ (usu. **be perfumed**) impregnate (something) with perfume or a sweet-smelling ingredient: *the cream is perfumed with rosemary and iris extracts.* ■ apply perfume to (someone or something): *her hair was oiled and perfumed.*
– DERIVATIVES **per·fum·y** /-mē/ **adj.**
– ORIGIN mid 16th cent. (originally denoting pleasant-smelling smoke from a burning substance, esp. one used in fumigation): from French *parfum* (noun), *parfumer* (verb), from obsolete Italian *parfumare,* literally 'to smoke through.'

per·fumed /,pər'fyo͞omd/ ▶ **adj.** naturally having or producing a sweet, pleasant smell: *the perfumed richness of the wine.* ■ impregnated or scented with a sweet-smelling substance: *perfumed soap.*

per·fum·er /pər'fyo͞omər/ ▶ **n.** a producer or seller of perfumes.

per·fum·er·y /pər'fyo͞omərē/ ▶ **n.** (pl. **perfumeries**) the action or business of producing or selling perfumes: *an oil used in perfumery.* ■ a store or store department that sells perfumes.

per·func·to·ry /pər'fəNGktərē/ ▶ **adj.** (of an action or gesture) carried out with a minimum of effort or reflection: *he gave a perfunctory nod.*
– DERIVATIVES **per·func·to·ri·ly** /-'fəNGktərəlē/ **adv.**, **per·func·to·ri·ness** /-rēnis/ **n.**
– ORIGIN late 16th cent.: from late Latin *perfunctorius* 'careless,' from Latin *perfunct-* 'done with, discharged,' from the verb *perfungi.*

per·fus·ate /pər'fyo͞o,zāt/ ▶ **n.** Medicine a fluid used in perfusion.

per·fuse /pər'fyo͞oz/ ▶ **v.** [with obj.] permeate or suffuse (something) with a liquid, color, quality, etc.: *Glaser perfused the yellow light with white* | figurative *such expression is perfused by rhetoric.* ■ Medicine supply (an organ, tissue, or body) with a fluid, typically treated blood or a blood substitute, by circulating it through blood vessels or other natural channels.
– DERIVATIVES **per·fu·sion** /-ZHən/ **n.**, **per·fu·sion·ist** /-ZHənist/ **n.**
– ORIGIN late Middle English (in the sense 'cause to flow through or away'): from Latin *perfus-* 'poured through,' from the verb *perfundere,* from *per-* 'through' + *fundere* 'pour.'

Per·ga·mum /'pərgəməm/ a city in ancient Mysia, in western Asia Minor, north of Izmir, capital in the 3rd and 2nd centuries BC of the Attalid dynasty. It was famed for its cultural institutions, esp. its library, which was second only to that at Alexandria.
– DERIVATIVES **Per·ga·mene** /-,mēn/ **adj. & n.**

per·go·la /'pərgələ/ ▶ **n.** an archway in a garden or park consisting of a framework covered with trained climbing or trailing plants.
– ORIGIN mid 17th cent.: from Italian, from Latin *pergula* 'projecting roof,' from *pergere* 'come or go forward.'

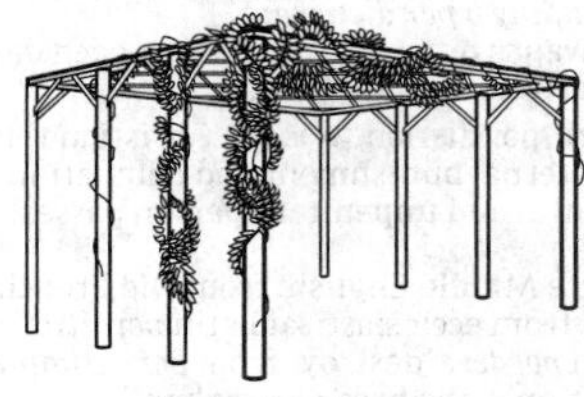
pergola

per·haps /pər'(h)aps/ ▶ **adv.** used to express uncertainty or possibility: *perhaps I should have been frank with him.* ■ used when one does not wish to be too definite or assertive in the expression of an opinion: *perhaps not surprisingly, he was cautious about committing himself.* ■ used when making a polite request, offer, or suggestion: *would you perhaps consent to act as our guide?*
– ORIGIN late 15th cent.: from **PER** + **HAP**.

pe·ri /'pi(ə)rē/ ▶ **n.** (pl. **peris**) (in Persian mythology) a mythical superhuman being, originally represented as evil but subsequently as a good or graceful genie or fairy.
– ORIGIN from Persian *perī.*

peri- ▶ **prefix 1** around; about: *pericardium* | *perimeter* | *peristyle.*
2 Astronomy denoting the point nearest to a specified celestial body: *perihelion* | *perilune.* Compare with **APO-**.
– ORIGIN from Greek *peri* 'about, around.'

pe·ri·a·nal /,perē'ānəl/ ▶ **adj.** Medicine situated in or affecting the area around the anus.

per·i·anth /'perē,anTH/ ▶ **n.** Botany the outer part of a flower, consisting of the calyx (sepals) and corolla (petals).
– ORIGIN early 18th cent.: from French *périanthe,* from modern Latin *perianthium,* from Greek *peri* 'around' + *anthos* 'flower.'

per·i·ap·sis /,perē'apsis/ ▶ **n.** (pl. **periapses** /-,sēz/) Astronomy the point in the path of an orbiting body at which it is nearest to the body that it orbits.

per·i·apt /'perē,apt/ ▶ **n.** archaic an item worn as a charm or amulet.
– ORIGIN late 16th cent.: from French *périapte,* from Greek *periapton,* from *peri* 'around' + *haptein* 'fasten.'

per·i·ar·tic·u·lar /,perē-är'tikyələr/ ▶ **adj.** Medicine situated or occurring around a joint of the body.

per·i·as·tron /,perē'astrən/ ▶ **n.** Astronomy the point nearest to a star in the path of a body orbiting that star.
– ORIGIN mid 19th cent.: from **PERI-** 'around' + Greek *astron* 'star,' on the pattern of *perigee* and *perihelion.*

per·i·car·di·tis /,perikär'dītis/ ▶ **n.** Medicine inflammation of the pericardium.

per·i·car·di·um /,peri'kärdēəm/ ▶ **n.** (pl. **pericardia** /-'kärdēə/) Anatomy the membrane enclosing the heart, consisting of an outer fibrous layer and an inner double layer of serous membrane.
– DERIVATIVES **per·i·car·di·al** /-'kärdēəl/ **adj.**
– ORIGIN late Middle English: modern Latin, from Greek *perikardion,* from *peri* 'around' + *kardia* 'heart.'

per·i·carp /'peri,kärp/ ▶ **n.** Botany the part of a fruit formed from the wall of the ripened ovary.
– ORIGIN late 17th cent.: from French *péricarpe,* from Greek *perikarpion* 'pod, shell,' from *peri-* 'around' + *karpos* 'fruit.'

per·i·chon·dri·um /,peri'kändrēəm/ ▶ **n.** Anatomy the connective tissue that envelops cartilage where it is not at a joint.
– ORIGIN mid 18th cent.: modern Latin, from **PERI-** 'around' + Greek *khondros* 'cartilage.'

per·i·clase /'peri,klās, -,klāz/ ▶ **n.** a colorless mineral consisting of magnesium oxide, occurring chiefly in marble and limestone.

– ORIGIN mid 19th cent.: from modern Latin *periclasia*, erroneously from Greek *peri* 'utterly' + *klasis* 'breaking' (because it cleaves perfectly).

Per·i·cles /ˈperiˌklēz/ (*c.*495–429 BC), Athenian statesman and general. A champion of Athenian democracy, he pursued an imperialist policy and masterminded Athenian strategy in the Peloponnesian War. He commissioned the building of the Parthenon in 447 and presided over the golden age of Athens.
– DERIVATIVES **Per·i·cle·an** adj.

per·i·cli·nal /ˌperiˈklīnl/ ▶ **adj.** Botany (of a cell wall) parallel to the surface of the meristem. ■ (of cell division) taking place by the formation of periclinal walls.
– DERIVATIVES **per·i·cli·nal·ly** adv.
– ORIGIN late 19th cent.: from Greek *periklinēs* 'sloping on all sides,' from *peri-* 'around' + *klinēs* 'sloping' (from the verb *klinein*).

pe·ric·o·pe /pəˈrikəpē/ ▶ **n.** an extract from a text, esp. a passage from the Bible.
– ORIGIN mid 17th cent.: via late Latin from Greek *perikopē* 'section,' from *peri-* 'around' + *kopē* 'cutting' (from *koptein* 'to cut').

per·i·cra·ni·um /ˌperiˈkrānēəm/ ▶ **n.** Anatomy the periosteum enveloping the skull.
– ORIGIN late Middle English: modern Latin, from Greek *peri-* 'around' + *kranion* 'skull.'

per·i·cy·cle /ˈperiˌsīkəl/ ▶ **n.** Botany a thin layer of plant tissue between the endodermis and the phloem.
– ORIGIN late 19th cent.: from Greek *perikuklos* 'spherical,' from *perikukloun* 'encircle.'

per·i·derm /ˈperiˌdərm/ ▶ **n.** Botany the corky outer layer of a plant stem formed in secondary thickening or as a response to injury or infection.
– DERIVATIVES **per·i·der·mal** /ˌperiˈdərməl/ adj.
– ORIGIN mid 19th cent.: from PERI- 'around' + Greek *derma* 'skin.'

pe·rid·i·um /pəˈridēəm/ ▶ **n.** (pl. **peridia** /-ˈridēə/) Botany the outer skin of a sporangium or other fruiting body of a fungus.
– ORIGIN early 19th cent.: from Greek *pēridion*, literally 'small wallet,' diminutive of *pēra*.

per·i·dot /ˈperiˌdät/ ▶ **n.** a green semiprecious variety of olivine.
– ORIGIN early 18th cent.: from French, from Old French *peritot*, of unknown origin.

per·i·do·tite /ˈperidəˌtīt, pəˈridəˌtīt/ ▶ **n.** Geology a dense, coarse-grained plutonic rock containing a large amount of olivine, believed to be the main constituent of the earth's mantle.
– DERIVATIVES **per·i·do·tit·ic** /ˌperidəˈtitik, pəˌridə-/ adj.

per·i·gee /ˈperəˌjē/ ▶ **n.** Astronomy the point in the orbit of the moon or a satellite at which it is nearest to the earth. The opposite of APOGEE.
– ORIGIN late 16th cent.: from French *périgée*, via modern Latin from Greek *perigeion* 'close around the earth,' from *peri-* 'around' + *gē* 'earth.'

per·i·gla·cial /ˌperəˈglāsHəl/ ▶ **adj.** Geology relating to or denoting an area adjacent to a glacier or ice sheet or otherwise subject to repeated freezing and thawing.

pe·rig·y·nous /pəˈrijənəs/ ▶ **adj.** Botany (of a plant or flower) having the stamens and other floral parts at the same level as the carpels. Compare with EPIGYNOUS, HYPOGYNOUS.
– DERIVATIVES **pe·rig·y·ny** /-ˈrijənē/ n.
– ORIGIN early 19th cent.: from modern Latin *perigynus* (from Greek *peri-* 'around' + *gunē* 'woman') + -OUS.

per·i·he·li·on /ˌperəˈhēlyən, -ˈhēlēən/ ▶ **n.** (pl. **perihelia** /-ˈhēlyə, -ˈhēlēə/ or **perihelions**) Astronomy the point in the orbit of a planet, asteroid, or comet at which it is closest to the sun. The opposite of APHELION.
– ORIGIN mid 17th cent.: alteration of modern Latin *perihelium* (by substitution of the Greek ending *-on*), from Greek *peri-* 'around' + *hēlios* 'sun.'

per·i·kar·y·on /periˈkarēˌän/ ▶ **n.** (pl. **perikarya** /-ˈkarēə/) Physiology the cell body of a neuron, containing the nucleus.
– DERIVATIVES **per·i·kar·y·al** /-ˈkarēəl/ adj.

per·il /ˈperəl/ ▶ **n.** serious and immediate danger: *his family was in peril* | *a setback to the state could present a peril to the regime.* ■ (**perils**) the dangers or difficulties that arise from a particular situation or activity: *she first witnessed the perils of pop stardom a decade ago.*
▶ **v.** (**perils, periling, periled**; Brit. **perils, perilling, perilled**) [with obj.] archaic expose to danger; threaten: *Jonathon periled his life for love of David.*
– PHRASES **at one's peril** at one's own risk (used esp. in warnings): *neglect our advice at your peril.* **in** (or **at**) **peril of** very likely to incur or to suffer from: *the movement is in peril of dying.* ■ at risk of losing or injuring: *anyone linked with the Republican cause would be in peril of their life.*
– ORIGIN Middle English: from Old French, from Latin *peric(u)lum* 'danger,' from the base of *experiri* 'to try.' The verb dates from the mid 16th cent.

pe·ril·la /pəˈrilə/ ▶ **n.** an Asian plant of the mint family with medicinal and culinary uses. It is regarded as an invasive weed in some areas. ● *Perilla frutescens*, family Labiatae.

per·il·ous /ˈperələs/ ▶ **adj.** full of danger or risk: *a perilous journey south.* ■ exposed to imminent risk of disaster or ruin: *the economy is in a perilous state.*
– DERIVATIVES **per·il·ous·ly** adv., **per·il·ous·ness** n.
– ORIGIN Middle English: from Old French *perillous*, from Latin *periculosus*, from *periculum* 'danger' (see PERIL).

per·i·lune /ˈperiˌlo͞on/ ▶ **n.** the point at which a spacecraft in lunar orbit is closest to the moon. The opposite of APOLUNE.
– ORIGIN 1960s: from PERI- 'around' + Latin *luna* 'moon,' on the pattern of *perigee*.

per·i·lymph /ˈperiˌlimf/ ▶ **n.** Anatomy the fluid between the membranous labyrinth of the ear and the bone that encloses it.
– DERIVATIVES **per·i·lym·phat·ic** /ˌperilimˈfatik/ adj.

pe·ri·men·o·pause /ˌperēˈmenəˌpôz/ ▶ **n.** the period of a woman's life shortly before the occurrence of the menopause.
– DERIVATIVES **per·i·men·o·pau·sal** adj.

pe·rim·e·ter /pəˈrimitər/ ▶ **n. 1** the continuous line forming the boundary of a closed geometric figure: *the perimeter of a rectangle.* ■ the outermost parts or boundary of an area or object: *the perimeter of the garden* | figurative *my presence on the perimeter of his life.* ■ a defended boundary of a military position or base. ■ Basketball an area away from the basket, beyond the reach of the defensive team: *he was very patient in working the ball around the perimeter.*
2 an instrument for measuring the extent and characteristics of a person's field of vision.
– DERIVATIVES **per·i·met·ric** /ˌperəˈmetrik/ adj.
– ORIGIN late Middle English: via Latin from Greek *perimetros*, based on *peri-* 'around' + *metron* 'measure.'

USAGE See usage at PARAMETER.

pe·rim·e·try /pəˈrimətrē/ ▶ **n.** measurement of a person's field of vision.

per·i·my·si·um /ˌperəˈmizēəm, -ˈmizH-/ ▶ **n.** Anatomy the sheath of connective tissue surrounding a bundle of muscle fibers.
– DERIVATIVES **per·i·my·si·al** /-ˈmizēəl, -ˈmizH-/ adj.
– ORIGIN mid 19th cent.: modern Latin, from Greek *peri-* 'around' + *mus* 'muscle.'

per·i·na·tal /ˌperəˈnātl/ ▶ **adj.** Medicine of or relating to the time, usually a number of weeks, immediately before and after birth.
– DERIVATIVES **per·i·na·tal·ly** adv.

per·i·na·tol·o·gy /ˌperināˈtäləjē/ ▶ **n.** Medicine the branch of obstetrics dealing with the period of time around childbirth.
– DERIVATIVES **per·i·na·tol·o·gist** /-jist/ n.

per·i·ne·um /ˌperəˈnēəm/ ▶ **n.** Anatomy the area between the anus and the scrotum or vulva.
– DERIVATIVES **per·i·ne·al** /-ˈnēəl/ adj.
– ORIGIN late Middle English: from late Latin, from Greek *perinaion*.

per·i·neu·ri·um /ˌperəˈn(y)o͝orēəm/ ▶ **n.** Anatomy the sheath of connective tissue surrounding a bundle (fascicle) of nerve fibers within a nerve.
– DERIVATIVES **per·i·neu·ral** /-ˈn(y)o͝orəl/ adj.
– ORIGIN mid 19th cent.: modern Latin, from Greek *peri-* 'around' + *neuron* 'sinew.'

pe·ri·od /ˈpi(ə)rēəd/ ▶ **n. 1** a length or portion of time: *he had long periods of depression* | *the ale will be available for a limited period* | *the period 1977–85* | *the training period is between 16 and 18 months.* ■ a portion of time in the life of a person, nation, or civilization characterized by the same prevalent features or conditions: *the early medieval period.* ■ one of the set divisions of the day in a school allocated to a lesson or other activity. ■ each of the intervals into which the playing time of a sporting event is divided. ■ a major division of geological time that is a subdivision of an era and is itself subdivided into epochs, corresponding to a system in chronostratigraphy.
2 a punctuation mark (.) used at the end of a sentence or an abbreviation. ■ informal added to the end of a statement to indicate that no further discussion is possible or desirable: *he is the sole owner of the trademark, period.*
3 Physics the interval of time between successive occurrences of the same state in an oscillatory or cyclic phenomenon, such as a mechanical vibration, an alternating current, a variable star, or an electromagnetic wave. ■ Astronomy the time taken by a celestial object to rotate around its axis, or to make one circuit of its orbit. ■ Mathematics the interval between successive equal values of a periodic function.
4 (also **menstrual period**) a flow of blood and other material from the lining of the uterus, lasting for several days and occurring in sexually mature women who are not pregnant at intervals of about one lunar month until the onset of menopause.
5 Chemistry a set of elements occupying an entire horizontal row in the periodic table.
6 Rhetoric a complex sentence, esp. one consisting of several clauses, constructed as part of a formal speech or oration. ■ Music a complete idea, typically consisting of two or four phrases.
▶ **adj.** [attrib.] belonging to or characteristic of a past historical time, esp. in style or design: *a splendid selection of period furniture.*
– ORIGIN late Middle English (denoting the time during which something, esp. a disease, runs its course): from Old French *periode*, via Latin from Greek *periodos* 'orbit, recurrence, course,' from *peri-* 'around' + *hodos* 'way, course.' The sense 'portion of time' dates from the early 17th cent.

pe·ri·od·ic /ˌpi(ə)rēˈädik/ ▶ **adj. 1** appearing or occurring at intervals: *the periodic visits she made to her father.*
2 Chemistry relating to the periodic table of the elements or the pattern of chemical properties that underlies it.
3 of or relating to a rhetorical period. See PERIOD (sense 6 of the noun).
– ORIGIN mid 17th cent.: from French *périodique*, or via Latin from Greek *periodikos* 'coming around at intervals,' from *periodos* (see PERIOD).

pe·ri·od·ic ac·id /ˌpəriˈädik/ ▶ **n.** Chemistry a hygroscopic solid acid with strong oxidizing properties. ● Chem. formula: H_5IO_6.
– DERIVATIVES **per·i·o·date** /pəˈrīəˌdāt/ n.
– ORIGIN mid 19th cent.: from PER- (sense 2) + IODIC ACID.

pe·ri·od·i·cal /ˌpi(ə)rēˈädikəl/ ▶ **n.** a magazine or newspaper published at regular intervals.
▶ **adj.** [attrib.] occurring or appearing at intervals; occasional: *she took periodical gulps of her tea.* ■ (of a magazine or newspaper) published at regular intervals: *a periodical newsletter.*
– DERIVATIVES **pe·ri·od·i·cal·ly** adv.

pe·ri·od·i·cal ci·ca·da ▶ **n.** an American cicada whose nymphs emerge from the soil in large numbers periodically. The mature nymphs of the northern species (**seventeen-year locust**) emerge every seventeen years; those of the southern species emerge every thirteen years. A cicada brood can be so abundant that the shrill sound emitted by the males can damage the human ear. ● Genus *Magicicada*, family Cicadidae, suborder Homoptera: six species.

pe·ri·od·ic func·tion /ˌpi(ə)rēˈädik/ ▶ **n.** Mathematics a function returning to the same value at regular intervals.

pe·ri·o·dic·i·ty /ˌpi(ə)rēəˈdisitē/ ▶ **n.** chiefly technical the quality or character of being periodic; the tendency to recur at intervals: *the periodicity of the sunspot cycle.*

pe·ri·od·ic law /ˌpi(ə)rēˈädik/ ▶ **n.** Chemistry a law stating that the elements, when listed in order of their atomic numbers (originally, atomic weights), fall into recurring groups, so that elements with similar properties occur at regular intervals.

pe·ri·od·ic ta·ble /ˌpi(ə)rēˈädik/ ▶ **n.** Chemistry a table of the chemical elements arranged in order of atomic number, usually in rows, so that elements with similar atomic structure (and hence similar chemical properties) appear in vertical columns.

pe·ri·od·ize /ˈpi(ə)rēəˌdīz/ ▶ **v.** [with obj.] formal divide (a portion of time) into periods.
– DERIVATIVES **pe·ri·od·i·za·tion** /ˌpi(ə)rēədəˈzāsHən/ n.

per·i·o·don·tics /ˌperēəˈdäntiks/ (also **periodontia** /ˈdänsHə/) ▶ **plural n.** [treated as sing.] the branch of dentistry concerned with the structures surrounding and supporting the teeth.
– DERIVATIVES **per·i·o·don·tal** /-ˈdäntl/ adj., **per·i·o·don·tist** /-ˈdäntist/ n.
– ORIGIN 1940s: from PERI- 'around' + Greek *odous, odont-* 'tooth' + -ICS.

per·i·o·don·ti·tis /ˌperēədänˈtītis/ ▶ **n.** Medicine inflammation of the tissue around the teeth, often causing shrinkage of the gums and loosening of the teeth.

per·i·o·don·tol·o·gy /ˌperēədänˈtäləjē/ ▶ **n.** another term for PERIODONTICS.

P

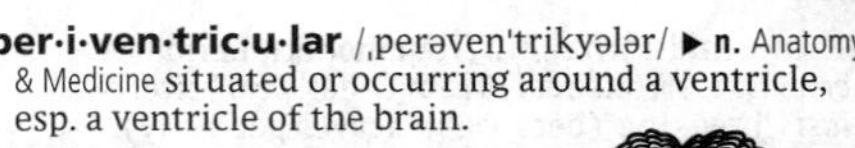

pe·ri·od piece ▶ **n.** an object or work that is set in or strongly reminiscent of an earlier historical period.

per·i·os·te·um /ˌperēˈästēəm/ ▶ **n.** (pl. **periostea** /-ˈästēə/) Anatomy a dense layer of vascular connective tissue enveloping the bones except at the surfaces of the joints.
– DERIVATIVES **per·i·os·te·al** /-ˈästēəl/ **adj.**
– ORIGIN late 16th cent.: modern Latin, from Greek *periosteon*, from *peri-* 'around' + *osteon* 'bone.'

per·i·os·ti·tis /ˌpereäˈstītis/ ▶ **n.** Medicine inflammation of the membrane enveloping a bone.

per·i·pa·tet·ic /ˌperipəˈtetik/ ▶ **adj. 1** traveling from place to place, esp. working or based in various places for relatively short periods: *the peripatetic nature of military life.*
2 (**Peripatetic**) Aristotelian. [with reference to Aristotle's practice of walking to and fro while teaching.]
▶ **n. 1** a person who travels from place to place.
2 (**Peripatetic**) an Aristotelian philosopher.
– DERIVATIVES **per·i·pa·tet·i·cal·ly** /-ik(ə)lē/ **adv.**, **per·i·pa·tet·i·cism** /-ˈtetəˌsizəm/ **n.**
– ORIGIN late Middle English (denoting an Aristotelian philosopher): from Old French *peripatetique*, via Latin from Greek *peripatētikos* 'walking up and down,' from the verb *peripatein*.

per·i·pe·tei·a /ˌperipəˈtēə, -ˈtīə/ ▶ **n.** formal a sudden reversal of fortune or change in circumstances, esp. in reference to fictional narrative.
– ORIGIN late 16th cent.: from Greek *peripeteia* 'sudden change,' from *peri-* 'around' + the stem of *piptein* 'to fall.'

pe·riph·er·al /pəˈrifərəl/ ▶ **adj.** of, relating to, or situated on the edge or periphery of something: *the peripheral areas of Europe.* ■ of secondary or minor importance; marginal: *she will see their problems as peripheral to her own.* ■ [attrib.] (of a device) able to be attached to and used with a computer, although not an integral part of it. ■ Anatomy near the surface of the body, with special reference to the circulation and nervous system: *lymphocytes from peripheral blood.*
▶ **n.** Computing a peripheral device.
– DERIVATIVES **pe·riph·er·al·i·ty** /-ˌrifəˈralitē/ **n.**, **pe·riph·er·al·i·za·tion** /pəˌrifərəliˈzāSHən/ **n.**, **pe·riph·er·al·ize** /-ˌīz/ **v.**, **pe·riph·er·al·ly** **adv.**

pe·riph·er·al nerv·ous sys·tem ▶ **n.** Anatomy the nervous system outside the brain and spinal cord.

pe·riph·er·al vi·sion ▶ **n.** side vision; what is seen on the side by the eye when looking straight ahead.

pe·riph·er·y /pəˈrifərē/ ▶ **n.** (pl. **peripheries**) the outer limits or edge of an area or object: *new buildings on the periphery of the hospital site.* ■ a marginal or secondary position in, or part or aspect of, a group, subject, or sphere of activity: *a shift in power from the center to the periphery.*
– ORIGIN late 16th cent. (denoting a line that forms the boundary of something): via late Latin from Greek *periphereia* 'circumference,' from *peripherēs* 'revolving around,' from *peri-* 'around' + *pherein* 'to bear.'

pe·riph·ra·sis /pəˈrifrəsis/ ▶ **n.** (pl. **periphrases** /-ˌsēz/) the use of indirect and circumlocutory speech or writing. ■ an indirect and circumlocutory phrase. ■ Grammar the use of separate words to express a grammatical relationship that is otherwise expressed by inflection, e.g., *did go* as opposed to *went* and *more intelligent* as opposed to *smarter*.
– ORIGIN mid 16th cent.: via Latin from Greek, from *periphrazein*, from *peri-* 'around' + *phrazein* 'declare.'

per·i·phras·tic /ˌperəˈfrastik/ ▶ **adj.** (of speech or writing) indirect and circumlocutory: *the periphrastic nature of legal syntax.* ■ Grammar (of a case or tense) formed by a combination of words rather than by inflection (such as *did go* and *of the people* rather than *went* and *the people's*).
– DERIVATIVES **per·i·phras·ti·cal·ly** /-(ə)lē/ **adv.**
– ORIGIN early 19th cent.: from Greek *periphrastikos*, from *periphrazein* 'declare in a roundabout way.'

pe·riph·y·ton /pəˈrifiˌtän/ ▶ **n.** Ecology freshwater organisms attached to or clinging to plants and other objects projecting above the bottom sediments.
– DERIVATIVES **per·i·phyt·ic** /ˌperəˈfitik/ **adj.**
– ORIGIN 1960s: from Greek *peri-* 'around' + *phuton* 'plant.'

pe·rip·ter·al /pəˈriptərəl/ ▶ **adj.** Architecture (of a building) having a single row of pillars on all sides in the style of the temples of ancient Greece.
– ORIGIN early 19th cent.: from Greek *peripteron* (from *peri-* 'around' + *pteron* 'wing') + **-AL**.

pe·rique /pəˈrēk/ ▶ **n.** a strong dark tobacco from Louisiana.
– ORIGIN late 19th cent.: Louisiana French, apparently from the nickname of Pierre Chenet, who first grew it.

per·i·scope /ˈperəˌskōp/ ▶ **n.** an apparatus consisting of a tube attached to a set of mirrors or prisms, by which an observer (typically in a submerged submarine or behind a high obstacle) can see things that are otherwise out of sight.

periscope

per·i·scop·ic /ˌperəˈskäpik/ ▶ **adj.** of or relating to a periscope. ■ (of a lens or an optical instrument) giving a wide field of view: *a periscopic sextant.*
– DERIVATIVES **per·i·scop·i·cal·ly** **adv.**

per·ish /ˈperiSH/ ▶ **v.** [no obj.] suffer death, typically in a violent, sudden, or untimely way: *a great part of his army perished of hunger and disease.* ■ suffer complete ruin or destruction: *the old regime had to perish.* ■ (of rubber, a foodstuff, or other organic substance) lose its normal qualities; rot or decay: *most domestic building was in wood and has perished.*
– PHRASES **perish the thought** informal used, often ironically, to show that one finds a suggestion or idea completely ridiculous or unwelcome: *he wasn't out to get drunk—perish the thought!*
– ORIGIN Middle English: from Old French *periss-*, lengthened stem of *perir*, from Latin *perire* 'pass away,' from *per-* 'through, completely' + *ire* 'go.'

per·ish·a·ble /ˈperiSHəbəl/ ▶ **adj.** (esp. of food) likely to decay or go bad quickly. ■ (of something abstract) having a brief life or significance; transitory: *ballet is the most perishable of arts.*
▶ **n.** (**perishables**) things, esp. foodstuffs, likely to decay or go bad quickly.
– DERIVATIVES **per·ish·a·bil·i·ty** /ˌperiSHəˈbilitē/ **n.**

pe·ris·so·dac·tyl /pəˌrisəˈdaktəl/ Zoology ▶ **n.** a mammal of the order Perissodactyla, such as a horse or rhinoceros.
▶ **adj.** relating to or denoting perissodactyls.

Pe·ris·so·dac·ty·la /pəˌrisəˈdaktələ/ Zoology an order of mammals that comprises the odd-toed ungulates. Compare with **ARTIODACTYLA**.
– ORIGIN modern Latin (plural), from Greek *perissos* 'uneven' + *daktulos* 'finger, toe.'

per·i·stal·sis /ˌperəˈstôlsis, -ˈstal-/ ▶ **n.** Physiology the involuntary constriction and relaxation of the muscles of the intestine or another canal, creating wavelike movements that push the contents of the canal forward.
– DERIVATIVES **per·i·stal·tic** /-ˈstôltik/ **adj.**, **per·i·stal·ti·cal·ly** **adv.**
– ORIGIN mid 19th cent.: modern Latin, from Greek *peristallein* 'wrap around,' from *peri-* 'around' + *stallein* 'to place.'

per·i·stome /ˈperəˌstōm/ ▶ **n.** Zoology the parts surrounding the mouth of various invertebrates. ■ Botany a fringe of small projections around the mouth of a capsule in mosses and certain fungi.
– ORIGIN late 18th cent.: from modern Latin *peristoma*, from Greek *peri-* 'around' + *stoma* 'mouth.'

per·i·style /ˈperəˌstīl/ ▶ **n.** Architecture a row of columns surrounding a space within a building such as a court or internal garden or edging a veranda or porch. ■ an architectural space such as a court or porch that is surrounded or edged by such columns.
– ORIGIN early 17th cent.: from French *péristyle*, from Latin *peristylum*, from Greek *peristulon*, from *peri-* 'around' + *stulos* 'pillar.'

per·i·the·ci·um /ˌperəˈTHēSH(ē)əm, -sēəm/ ▶ **n.** (pl. **perithecia** /-ˈTHēSH(ē)ə, -sēə/) Botany (in some fungi) a round or flask-shaped fruiting body with a pore through which the spores are discharged.
– ORIGIN mid 19th cent.: modern Latin, from **PERI-** 'around' + Greek *thēkē* 'case.'

per·i·to·ne·um /ˌperitnˈēəm/ ▶ **n.** (pl. **peritoneums** or **peritonea** /-ˈnēə/) Anatomy the serous membrane lining the cavity of the abdomen and covering the abdominal organs.
– DERIVATIVES **per·i·to·ne·al** /-ˈēəl/ **adj.**
– ORIGIN late Middle English: via late Latin from Greek *peritonaion*, from *peritonos* 'stretched around,' from *peri-* 'around' + *-tonos* 'stretched.'

per·i·to·ni·tis /ˌperitnˈītis/ ▶ **n.** Medicine inflammation of the peritoneum, typically caused by bacterial infection either via the blood or after rupture of an abdominal organ.

pe·ri·tus /pəˈrētōōs/ ▶ **n.** (pl. **periti** /-tē/) a theological adviser or consultant to a council of the Roman Catholic Church.
– ORIGIN 1960s: from Latin; related to *expertus* 'expert.'

per·i·vas·cu·lar /ˌperəˈvaskyələr/ ▶ **adj.** Medicine situated or occurring around a blood vessel.

per·i·ven·tric·u·lar /ˌperəvenˈtrikyələr/ ▶ **n.** Anatomy & Medicine situated or occurring around a ventricle, esp. a ventricle of the brain.

per·i·wig /ˈperiˌwig/ ▶ **n.** a highly styled wig worn formerly as a fashionable headdress by both women and men. ■ archaic term for **WIG**[1].
– DERIVATIVES **per·i·wigged** **adj.**
– ORIGIN early 16th cent.: alteration of **PERUKE**, with *-wi-* representing the French *-u-* sound.

periwig

per·i·win·kle[1] /ˈperiˌwiNGkəl/ ▶ **n.** an Old World plant with flat, five-petaled flowers and glossy leaves. Some kinds are grown as ornamentals, and some contain alkaloids used in medicine. ● Genera *Vinca* and *Catharanthus*, family Apocynaceae.
– ORIGIN late Old English *peruince*, from late Latin *pervinca*, reinforced in Middle English by Anglo-Norman French *pervenke*. The change of *-v-* to *-w-* and the addition of *-le* seem to have occurred before the appearance of **PERIWINKLE**[2].

per·i·win·kle[2] ▶ **n.** another term for **WINKLE**.
– ORIGIN mid 16th cent.: of unknown origin.

per·jure /ˈpərjər/ ▶ **v.** (**perjure oneself**) Law willfully tell an untruth when giving evidence to a court; commit perjury.
– DERIVATIVES **per·jur·er** **n.**
– ORIGIN late Middle English (as *perjured* in the sense 'guilty of perjury'): from Old French *parjurer*, from Latin *perjurare* 'swear falsely,' from *per-* 'to ill effect' + *jurare* 'swear.'

per·jured /ˈpərjərd/ ▶ **adj.** Law (of evidence) involving willfully told untruths. ■ (of a person) guilty of perjury: *a perjured witness.*

per·ju·ry /ˈpərjərē/ ▶ **n.** (pl. **perjuries**) Law the offense of willfully telling an untruth in a court after having taken an oath or affirmation.
– DERIVATIVES **per·ju·ri·ous** /pərˈjŏŏrēəs/ **adj.**
– ORIGIN late Middle English: from Anglo-Norman French *perjurie*, from Latin *perjurium* 'false oath,' from the verb *perjurare* (see **PERJURE**).

perk[1] /pərk/ ▶ **v.** [no obj.] (**perk up**) become more cheerful, lively, or interesting: *in the second half, the dance perked up | she'd been depressed, but she seemed to perk up last week.* ■ [with obj.] (**perk someone/something up**) make someone or something more cheerful, lively, or interesting: *the coffee had perked him up long enough to tackle the reviews.*
▶ **adj.** dialect perky; pert.
– ORIGIN late Middle English (in the senses 'perch' and 'be lively'): perhaps from an Old French dialect variant of *percher* 'to perch.'

perk[2] ▶ **n.** (usu. **perks**) informal money, goods, or other benefit to which one is entitled as an employee or as a shareholder of a company: *many agencies are helping to keep personnel at their jobs by providing perks.* ■ an advantage or benefit following from a job or situation: *they were busy discovering the perks of town life.*
– ORIGIN early 19th cent.: abbreviation of **PERQUISITE**.

perk[3] informal ▶ **v.** [no obj.] (of coffee) percolate: *while the coffee perks, head out for the morning paper.* ■ [with obj.] percolate (coffee).
– ORIGIN 1930s: abbreviation of **PERCOLATE**.

Per·kins[1] /ˈpərkinz/, Carl (1932–98), US singer and songwriter. A rockabilly artist, he wrote and recorded "Blue Suede Shoes" (1955), which became his first big hit. His albums include *Matchbox* (1977) and *Go, Cat, Go* (1993).

Per·kins[2], Frances (1882–1965), US public official; born *Fannie Coiralie Perkins*. As US secretary of labor 1933–45, she was the first woman to hold a federal cabinet post. She promoted the Social Security program and the minimum wage.

perk·y /ˈpərkē/ ▶ **adj.** (**perkier**, **perkiest**) cheerful and lively: *she certainly looked less than her usual perky self.*
– DERIVATIVES **perk·i·ly** /-kəlē/ **adv.**, **perk·i·ness** /-kēnis/ **n.**

Perl ▶ **n.** Computing a high-level general-purpose programming language used esp. for developing Web applications.
– ORIGIN 1980s: respelling of **PEARL**, arbitrarily chosen for its positive connotations.

per·lite /ˈpərlīt/ ▶ **n.** a form of obsidian characterized by spherulites formed by cracking of the volcanic glass during cooling, used as insulation or in plant growth media.
– ORIGIN mid 19th cent.: from French, from *perle* 'pearl.'

Perl·man /ˈpərlmən/, Itzhak (1945–) Israeli-American violinist and conductor. A preeminent virtuoso, he has appeared with most of the world's major orchestras.

per·lo·cu·tion /ˌpərləˈkyo͞oSHən/ ▶ **n.** Philosophy & Linguistics an act of speaking or writing that has an action as its aim but that in itself does not effect or constitute the action, for example persuading or convincing. Compare with ILLOCUTION.
– DERIVATIVES **per·lo·cu·tion·ar·y** /-ˌnerē/ **adj.**
– ORIGIN 1950s: from modern Latin *perlocutio(n-)*, from *per-* 'throughout' + *locutio(n-)* 'speaking.'

Perm /pərm, pyerm/ an industrial city in Russia, in the western foothills of the Ural Mountains; pop. 987,200 (est. 2008). Former name (1940–57) **MOLOTOV**[1].

perm /pərm/ ▶ **n.** (also **permanent wave**) a method of setting the hair in waves or curls and then treating it with chemicals so that the style lasts for several months.
▶ **v.** [with obj.] treat (the hair) in such a way: *her hair was permed and then set.*
– ORIGIN 1920s: abbreviation of PERMANENT.

perm. ▶ **abbr.** permanent.

per·ma·cul·ture /ˈpərməˌkəlCHər/ ▶ **n.** the development of agricultural ecosystems intended to be sustainable and self-sufficient.
– ORIGIN 1970s: blend of PERMANENT and AGRICULTURE.

per·ma·frost /ˈpərməˌfrôst, -ˌfräst/ ▶ **n.** a thick subsurface layer of soil that remains frozen throughout the year, occurring chiefly in polar regions.
– ORIGIN 1940s: from PERMANENT + FROST.

perm·al·loy /ˈpərməˌloi, ˌpərmˈaloi/ ▶ **n.** an alloy of nickel and iron that is easily magnetized and demagnetized, used in electrical equipment.
– ORIGIN 1920s: (originally as a trademark) from PERMEABLE + ALLOY. See PERMEABILITY (sense 2).

per·ma·nence /ˈpərmənəns/ ▶ **n.** the state or quality of lasting or remaining unchanged indefinitely: *the clarity and permanence of the dyes.*
– DERIVATIVES **per·ma·nen·cy** /-sē/ **n.**
– ORIGIN late Middle English: from medieval Latin *permanentia* (perhaps via French), from *permanent-* 'remaining to the end,' from the verb *permanere.*

per·ma·nent /ˈpərmənənt/ ▶ **adj.** lasting or intended to last or remain unchanged indefinitely: *a permanent ban on the dumping of radioactive waste at sea* | *damage was not thought to be permanent* | *some temporary workers did not want a permanent job.* ■ lasting or continuing without interruption: *he's in a permanent state of rage.*
▶ **n.** a perm for the hair.
– DERIVATIVES **per·ma·nent·ize** /-ˌtīz/ **v.** (rare).
– ORIGIN late Middle English: from Latin *permanent-* 'remaining to the end' (perhaps via Old French), from *per-* 'through' + *manere* 'remain.'

per·ma·nent·ly /ˈpərmənəntlē/ ▶ **adv.** in a way that lasts or remains unchanged indefinitely; for all time: *his lungs are permanently damaged.* ■ in a way that lasts or continues without interruption; continually: *we need to be permanently vigilant.*

per·ma·nent mag·net ▶ **n.** a magnet that retains its magnetic properties in the absence of an inducing field or current.

per·ma·nent rev·o·lu·tion ▶ **n.** the state or condition, envisaged by Leon Trotsky, of a country's continuing revolutionary progress being dependent on a continuing process of revolution in other countries.

per·ma·nent set ▶ **n.** an irreversible deformation that remains in a structure or material after it has been subjected to stress.

per·ma·nent tooth ▶ **n.** a tooth in a mammal that replaces a temporary milk tooth and lasts for most of the mammal's life.

per·ma·nent wave ▶ **n.** see PERM.

per·man·ga·nate /pərˈmaNGgəˌnāt/ ▶ **n.** Chemistry a salt containing the anion MnO_4^-, typically deep purplish-red and with strong oxidizing properties.

per·me·a·bil·i·ty /ˌpərmēəˈbilitē/ ▶ **n. 1** the state or quality of a material or membrane that causes it to allow liquids or gases to pass through it.
2 Physics a quantity measuring the influence of a substance on the magnetic flux in the region it occupies.

per·me·a·bil·ize /ˈpərmēəbəˌlīz/ ▶ **v.** [with obj.] (often as adj. **permeabilized**) technical make permeable.
– DERIVATIVES **per·me·a·bil·i·za·tion** /ˌpərmēəbəliˈzāSHən/ **n.**

per·me·a·ble /ˈpərmēəbəl/ ▶ **adj.** (of a material or membrane) allowing liquids or gases to pass through it: *a frog's skin is permeable to water.*
– ORIGIN late Middle English: from Latin *permeabilis*, from *permeare* 'pass through' (see PERMEATE).

per·me·ance /ˈpərmēəns/ ▶ **n.** Physics the property of allowing the passage of lines of magnetic flux.

per·me·ate /ˈpərmēˌāt/ ▶ **v.** [with obj.] spread throughout (something); pervade: *the aroma of soup permeated the air* | [no obj.] *his personality has begun to permeate through the whole organization.*
– DERIVATIVES **per·me·a·tion** /ˌpərmēˈāSHən/ **n.**
– ORIGIN mid 17th cent.: from Latin *permeat-* 'passed through,' from the verb *permeare*, from *per-* 'through' + *meare* 'pass, go.'

per·meth·rin /pərˈmēTHrin/ ▶ **n.** a synthetic insecticide of the pyrethroid class, used chiefly against disease-carrying insects.
– ORIGIN 1970s: from PER- (sense 2) + *(res)methrin*, denoting a synthetic pyrethroid.

Per·mi·an /ˈpərmēən/ ▶ **adj.** Geology of, relating to, or denoting the last period of the Paleozoic era, between the Carboniferous and Triassic periods. See also PERMO-TRIASSIC. ■ (as noun **the Permian**) the Permian period or the system of rocks deposited during it.

> The Permian lasted from about 290 million to 245 million years ago. The climate was hot and dry in many parts of the world during this period, which saw the extinction of many marine animals, including trilobites, and the proliferation of reptiles.

– ORIGIN late 16th cent.: from the name of the Russian province PERM, from the extensive development of such strata there.

Per·mi·an Ba·sin /ˈpərmēən/ a region in western Texas and the geologic structure underlying it, a major oil and gas reservoir. The cities of Midland and Odessa are production centers.

per mill (also **per mil**) ▶ **n.** one part in every thousand.
– ORIGIN late 17th cent.: Latin.

per·mis·si·ble /pərˈmisəbəl/ ▶ **adj.** permitted; allowed: *it is permissible to edit and rephrase the statement.*
– DERIVATIVES **per·mis·si·bil·i·ty** /-ˌmisəˈbilitē/ **n.**, **per·mis·si·bly** /-blē/ **adv.**
– ORIGIN late Middle English: from medieval Latin *permissibilis*, from *permiss-* 'allowed,' from the verb *permittere* (see PERMIT[1]).

per·mis·sion /pərˈmiSHən/ ▶ **n.** consent; authorization: *they had entered the country without permission* | [with infinitive] *he had received permission to go to Brussels.* ■ an official document giving authorization: *permissions to reproduce copyright material.*
– ORIGIN late Middle English: from Latin *permissio(n-)*, from the verb *permittere* 'allow' (see PERMIT[1]).

per·mis·sive /pərˈmisiv/ ▶ **adj. 1** allowing or characterized by great or excessive freedom of behavior: *I was not a permissive parent* | *the permissive society of the 60s and 70s.*
2 Law allowed but not obligatory; optional: *the Hague Convention was permissive, not mandatory.*
3 Biology allowing a biological or biochemical process to occur: *the mutants grow well at the permissive temperature.* ■ allowing the infection and replication of viruses.
– DERIVATIVES **per·mis·sive·ly** **adv.**, **per·mis·sive·ness** **n.**
– ORIGIN late 15th cent. (in the sense 'tolerated, allowed'): from Old French, or from medieval Latin *permissivus*, from *permiss-* 'allowed,' from the verb *permittere* (see PERMIT[1]).

per·mit[1] ▶ **v.** /pərˈmit/ (**permits, permitting, permitted**) give authorization or consent to (someone) to do something: [with obj. and infinitive] *the law permits councils to monitor any factory emitting smoke* | [with two objs.] *he would not permit anybody access to the library.* ■ [with obj.] authorize or give permission for (something): *the country is not ready to permit any rice imports.* ■ [with obj.] (of a thing, circumstance, or condition) provide an opportunity or scope for (something) to take place; make possible: *some properties are too small to permit mechanized farming* | [no obj.] *when weather permits, lunches are served outside.* ■ [no obj.] (**permit of**) dated allow for; admit of: *the camp permits of no really successful defense.*
▶ **n.** /ˈpərmit/ [often with modifier] an official document giving someone authorization to do something: *he is only in Britain on a work permit.*
– PHRASES **permit me** dated used for politeness before making a suggestion or expressing an intention: *permit me to correct you.* —— **permitting** if the specified thing does not prevent one from doing something: *weather permitting, guests can dine outside on the veranda.*
– DERIVATIVES **per·mit·tee** /ˌpərmiˈtē/ **n.**, **per·mit·ter** /pərˈmitər/ **n.**
– ORIGIN late Middle English (originally in the sense 'commit, hand over'): from Latin *permittere*, from *per-* 'through' + *mittere* 'send, let go.'

per·mit[2] /ˈpərmit/ ▶ **n.** a deep-bodied fish of the jack family, found in warm waters of the western Atlantic and Caribbean and caught for food and sport. ● *Trachinotus falcatus*, family Carangidae.
– ORIGIN alteration of Spanish *palometa* 'little dove.'

per·mit·tiv·i·ty /ˌpərmiˈtivitē/ ▶ **n.** Physics the ability of a substance to store electrical energy in an electric field.

Per·mo–Car·bon·if·er·ous /ˌpərmō ˌkärbəˈnifərəs/ ▶ **adj.** Geology of, relating to, or linking the Permian and Carboniferous periods or rock systems together.

Per·mo–Tri·as·sic /ˌpərmō ˌtrīˈasik/ ▶ **adj.** Geology of, relating to, or occurring at the boundary of the Permian and Triassic periods, about 245 million years ago. Mass extinctions occurred at this time, marking the end of the era. ■ of or relating to the Permian and Triassic periods or rock systems considered as a unit. ■ (as noun **the Permo–Triassic** or **Permo–Trias**) the Permian and Triassic periods together or the system of rocks deposited during them.

per·mu·tate /ˈpərmyo͝oˌtāt/ ▶ **v.** [with obj.] change the order or arrangement of: *statistics may be sorted and permutated according to requirements.*
– ORIGIN late 19th cent.: regarded as a back-formation from PERMUTATION.

per·mu·ta·tion /ˌpərmyo͝oˈtāSHən/ ▶ **n.** a way, esp. one of several possible variations, in which a set or number of things can be ordered or arranged: *his thoughts raced ahead to fifty different permutations of what he must do.* ■ Mathematics the action of changing the arrangement, esp. the linear order, of a set of items.
– DERIVATIVES **per·mu·ta·tion·al** /-ˈtāSHənəl/ **adj.**
– ORIGIN late Middle English (in the sense 'exchange, barter'): via Old French from Latin *permutatio(n-)*, from the verb *permutare* 'change completely' (see PERMUTE).

per·mute /pərˈmyo͞ot/ ▶ **v.** [with obj.] technical submit to a process of alteration, rearrangement, or permutation: *we wish to permute the order of the bytes.*
– ORIGIN late Middle English (also in the sense 'interchange'): from Latin *permutare* 'change completely,' from *per-* 'through, completely' + *mutare* 'to change.'

Per·nam·bu·co /ˌpərnəmˈb(y)o͞okō, ˌpernämˈ-/ a state of eastern Brazil, on the Atlantic coast; capital, Recife. ■ former name for RECIFE.

per·nam·bu·co /ˌpərnəmˈb(y)o͞okō/ (also **pernambuco wood**) ▶ **n.** the hard reddish timber of a Brazilian tree, used for making violin bows and as a source of red dye. ● The tree is *Caesalpinia echinata*, family Leguminosae.
– ORIGIN late 16th cent.: from the name of the Brazilian state PERNAMBUCO.

per·ni·cious /pərˈniSHəs/ ▶ **adj.** having a harmful effect, esp. in a gradual or subtle way: *the pernicious influences of the mass media.*
– DERIVATIVES **per·ni·cious·ly** **adv.**, **per·ni·cious·ness** **n.**
– ORIGIN late Middle English: from Latin *perniciosus* 'destructive,' from *pernicies* 'ruin,' based on *nex, nec-* 'death.'

per·ni·cious a·ne·mi·a ▶ **n.** a deficiency in the production of red blood cells through a lack of vitamin B_{12}.

per·nick·et·y /pərˈnikitē/ ▶ **adj.** British term for PERSNICKETY.

per·noc·tate /pərˈnäkˌtāt/ ▶ **v.** [no obj.] formal pass the night somewhere.
– DERIVATIVES **per·noc·ta·tion** /ˌpərnäkˈtāSHən/ **n.**
– ORIGIN early 17th cent.: from Latin *pernoctat-* 'spent the night,' from the verb *pernoctare*, from *per-* 'through' + *nox, noct-* 'night.'

Per·nod /perˈnō/ ▶ **n.** trademark an anise-flavored liqueur.
– ORIGIN named after the manufacturing firm *Pernod Fils.*

pe·ro·gi ▶ **n.** variant spelling of PIROGI.

Pe·rón[1] /peˈrōn/, Eva (1919–52), Argentine politician; second wife of Juan Perón; full name *María Eva Duarte de Perón*; known as **Evita**. A former actress, after her marriage in 1945 she became de facto minister of health and of labor until her death from cancer. Her social reforms earned her great popularity with the poor.

Pe·rón[2], Juan Domingo (1895–1974), Argentine soldier and statesman; president 1946–55 and 1973–74. The faltering economy and conflict with the Catholic Church led to his removal and exile. He returned to power in 1973, but died in office.

P

– DERIVATIVES **Pe·ro·nism** /-ˌnizəm/ n., **Pe·ro·nist** /-nist/ adj. & n.

per·o·ne·al /ˌperəˈnēəl/ ▶ adj. Anatomy relating to or situated in the outer side of the calf of the leg.
– ORIGIN mid 19th cent.: from modern Latin *peronaeus* 'peroneal muscle' (based on Greek *peronē* 'pin, fibula') + -AL.

per·o·rate /ˈperəˌrāt/ ▶ v. [no obj.] formal speak at length: *he reportedly would perorate against his colleague.* ■ archaic sum up and conclude a speech: *the following innocent conclusion with which she perorates.*
– ORIGIN early 17th cent.: from Latin *perorat-* 'spoken at length,' from the verb *perorare*, from *per-* 'through' + *orare* 'speak.'

per·o·ra·tion /ˌperəˈrāsHən/ ▶ n. the concluding part of a speech, typically intended to inspire enthusiasm in the audience.
– ORIGIN late Middle English: from Latin *peroratio(n-)*, from *perorare* 'speak at length' (see PERORATE).

pe·rovsk·ite /pəˈrävzkīt, -ˈräfs-/ ▶ n. a yellow, brown, or black mineral consisting largely of calcium titanate. ■ any of a group of related minerals and ceramics having the same crystal structure as this.
– ORIGIN mid 19th cent.: from the name of L. A. *Perovsky* (1792–1856), Russian mineralogist, + -ITE[1].

per·ox·i·dase /pəˈräksəˌdās/ ▶ n. Biochemistry an enzyme that catalyzes the oxidation of a particular substrate by hydrogen peroxide.

per·ox·ide /pəˈräksīd/ ▶ n. Chemistry a compound containing two oxygen atoms bonded together in its molecule or as the anion O_2^{2-}. ■ hydrogen peroxide, esp. as used as a bleach for the hair: [as modifier] *a peroxide blonde.*
▶ v. [with obj.] bleach (hair) with peroxide.
– ORIGIN early 19th cent.: from PER- (sense 2) + OXIDE.

per·ox·i·some /pəˈräksiˌsōm/ ▶ n. Biology a small organelle that is present in the cytoplasm of many cells and that contains the reducing enzyme catalase and usually some oxidases.
– DERIVATIVES **per·ox·i·so·mal** /-ˌräksiˈsōməl/ adj.
– ORIGIN 1960s: from PEROXIDE + -SOME[3].

perp /pərp/ ▶ n. informal the perpetrator of a crime.
– ORIGIN 1980s: abbreviation.

perp. ▶ abbr. perpendicular.

per·pend /pərˈpend/ ▶ n. a vertical layer of mortar between two bricks.

per·pen·dic·u·lar /ˌpərpənˈdikyələr/ ▶ adj. **1** at an angle of 90° to a given line, plane, or surface: *dormers and gables that extend* **perpendicular to** *the main roofline.* ■ at an angle of 90° to the ground; vertical: *the perpendicular cliff.* ■ (of something with a slope) so steep as to be almost vertical: *guest houses seem to cling by faith to the perpendicular hillside.*
2 (**Perpendicular**) denoting the latest stage of English Gothic church architecture, prevalent from the late 14th to mid 16th centuries and characterized by broad arches, elaborate fan vaulting, and large windows with vertical tracery: *the handsome Perpendicular church of St. Andrew.*
▶ n. a straight line at an angle of 90° to a given line, plane, or surface: *at each division, draw a perpendicular representing the surface line.* ■ (usu. **the perpendicular**) perpendicular position or direction: *the wall declines from the perpendicular a little inward.* ■ an instrument for indicating the vertical line from any point, as a spirit level or plumb line.
– DERIVATIVES **per·pen·dic·u·lar·i·ty** /-ˌdikyəˈlaritē/ n., **per·pen·dic·u·lar·ly** adv.
– ORIGIN late Middle English (as an adverb meaning 'at right angles'): via Old French from Latin *perpendicularis*, from *perpendiculum* 'plumb line,' from *per-* 'through' + *pendere* 'to hang.'

per·pe·trate /ˈpərpəˌtrāt/ ▶ v. [with obj.] carry out or commit (a harmful, illegal, or immoral action): *a crime has been perpetrated against a sovereign state.*
– DERIVATIVES **per·pe·tra·tion** /ˌpərpəˈtrāsHən/ n., **per·pe·tra·tor** /-ˌtrātər/ n.
– ORIGIN mid 16th cent.: from Latin *perpetrat-* 'performed,' from the verb *perpetrare*, from *per-* 'to completion' + *patrare* 'bring about.' In Latin the act perpetrated might be good or bad; in English the verb was first used in the statutes referring to crime, hence the negative association.

> **USAGE** To **perpetrate** something is to commit it: *the gang perpetrated outrages against several citizens.* To **perpetuate** something is to cause it to continue or to keep happening: *the stories only serve to perpetuate the legend that the house is haunted.*

per·pet·u·al /pərˈpecHo͞oəl/ ▶ adj. **1** never ending or changing: *deep caves in perpetual darkness.* ■ [attrib.] denoting a position, job, or trophy held for life rather than a limited period, or the person holding it: *a perpetual secretary of the society.* ■ (of an investment) having no fixed maturity date; irredeemable: *a perpetual bond.*
2 occurring repeatedly; so frequent as to seem endless and uninterrupted: *their perpetual money worries.* ■ (of a plant) blooming or fruiting several times in one season: *he grows perpetual carnations.*
– DERIVATIVES **per·pet·u·al·ly** adv.
– ORIGIN Middle English: from Old French *perpetuel*, from Latin *perpetualis*, from *perpetuus* 'continuing throughout,' from *perpes, perpet-* 'continuous.'

per·pet·u·al cal·en·dar ▶ n. a calendar that can be adjusted to show any combination of day, month, and year, and is therefore usable year after year. ■ a set of tables from which the day of the week can be reckoned for any date.

per·pet·u·al check ▶ n. Chess the situation of play when a draw is obtained by repeated checking of the king.

per·pet·u·al mo·tion ▶ n. a state in which movement or action is or appears to be continuous and unceasing. ■ the motion of a hypothetical machine that, once activated, would run forever unless subject to an external force or to wear.

per·pet·u·ate /pərˈpecHo͞oˌāt/ ▶ v. [with obj.] make (something, typically an undesirable situation or an unfounded belief) continue indefinitely: *the law perpetuated the interests of the ruling class.* ■ preserve (something valued) from oblivion or extinction: *how did these first humans survive to perpetuate the species?*
– DERIVATIVES **per·pet·u·ance** /-o͞oəns/ n., **per·pet·u·a·tion** /pərˌpecHo͞oˈāsHən/ n., **per·pet·u·a·tor** n.
– ORIGIN early 16th cent.: from Latin *perpetuat-* 'made permanent,' from the verb *perpetuare*, from *perpetuus* 'continuing throughout' (see PERPETUAL).

> **USAGE** See usage at PERPETRATE.

per·pe·tu·i·ty /ˌpərpiˈt(y)o͞oitē/ ▶ n. (pl. **perpetuities**) **1** a thing that lasts forever or for an indefinite period, in particular: ■ a bond or other security with no fixed maturity date. ■ Law a restriction making an estate inalienable perpetually or for a period beyond certain limits fixed by law. ■ Law an estate so restricted.
2 the state or quality of lasting forever: *he did not believe in the perpetuity of military rule.*
– PHRASES **in** (or **for**) **perpetuity** forever: *all the Bonapartes were banished from France in perpetuity.*
– ORIGIN late Middle English: from Old French *perpetuite*, from Latin *perpetuitas*, from *perpetuus* 'continuing throughout' (see PERPETUAL).

per·pet·u·um mo·bi·le /pərˈpecHo͞oəm ˈmōbəˌlā/ ▶ n. **1** Music a piece of fast-moving instrumental music consisting mainly of notes of equal length.
2 another term for PERPETUAL MOTION.
– ORIGIN Latin, literally 'continuously moving (thing),' on the pattern of *primum mobile.*

Per·pi·gnan /ˌperpēˈnyän/ a city in southern France, in the northeastern foothills of the Pyrenees, close to the border with Spain; pop. 117,500 (2006).

per·plex /pərˈpleks/ ▶ v. [with obj.] (of something complicated or unaccountable) cause (someone) to feel completely baffled: *she was perplexed by her husband's moodiness.* ■ dated complicate or confuse (a matter): *they were perplexing a subject plain in itself.*
– ORIGIN late 15th cent. (as the adjective *perplexed*): from the obsolete adjective *perplex* 'bewildered,' from Latin *perplexus* 'entangled,' based on *plexus* 'interwoven,' from the verb *plectere.*

per·plexed /pərˈplekst/ ▶ adj. completely baffled; very puzzled: *she gave him a perplexed look.*
– DERIVATIVES **per·plex·ed·ly** /-ˈpleksidlē/ adv.

per·plex·ing /pərˈpleksiNG/ ▶ adj. completely baffling; very puzzling: *a perplexing problem.*
– DERIVATIVES **per·plex·ing·ly** adv.

per·plex·i·ty /pərˈpleksitē/ ▶ n. (pl. **perplexities**) **1** inability to deal with or understand something complicated or unaccountable: *she paused in perplexity.* ■ (usu. **perplexities**) a complicated or baffling situation or thing: *the perplexities of international relations.*
2 archaic an entangled state: *the dense perplexity of dwarf palm, garlanded creepers, glossy undergrowth.*
– ORIGIN Middle English: from Old French *perplexite* or late Latin *perplexitas*, from Latin *perplexus* 'entangled, confused' (see PERPLEX).

per pro. /pər ˈprō/ ▶ abbr. per procurationem (used when signing a letter on behalf of someone else; now usually abbreviated to **pp**).
– ORIGIN Latin.

per·qui·site /ˈpərkwəzit/ ▶ n. formal another term for PERK[2]. ■ a thing regarded as a special right or privilege enjoyed as a result of one's position: *the wife of a president has all the perquisites of stardom.* ■ historical a thing that has served its primary use and is then given to a subordinate or employee as a customary right.
– ORIGIN late Middle English: from medieval Latin *perquisitum* 'acquisition,' from Latin *perquirere* 'search diligently for,' from *per-* 'thoroughly' + *quaerere* 'seek.'

> **USAGE** **Perquisite** and **prerequisite** are sometimes confused. **Perquisite** usually means 'an extra allowance or privilege': *he had all the perquisites of a movie star, including a stand-in.* **Prerequisite** means 'something required as a condition': *passing the examination was one of the prerequisites for a teaching position.*

Per·rault /pəˈrō/, Charles (1628–1703), French writer. He is noted for *Mother Goose Tales* (1697).

Per·ri·er /ˈperēˌyā/ (also **Perrier water**) ▶ n. trademark an effervescent natural mineral water sold as a drink.
– ORIGIN from the name of a spring at Vergèze, France, from which this water comes.

Per·rin /ˈperən, peˈraN/, Jean Baptiste (1870–1942), French physical chemist. He provided the definitive proof of the existence of atoms, proved that cathode rays are negatively charged, and investigated Brownian motion. Nobel Prize for Physics (1926).

per·ron /ˈperən, pəˈrōn/ ▶ n. Architecture an exterior set of steps and a platform at the main entrance to a large building such as a church or mansion.
– ORIGIN late Middle English: from Old French, literally 'large stone,' from Latin *petra* 'stone.'

Per·ry /ˈperē/, Fred (1909–95), US tennis player, born in Britain; full name *Frederick John Perry*. His record of winning three consecutive singles titles at Wimbledon (1934–36) was unequaled until 1979 when it was broken by Björn Borg.

per·ry /ˈperē/ ▶ n. (pl. **perries**) an alcoholic drink made from the fermented juice of pears.
– ORIGIN Middle English: from Old French *pere*, from an alteration of Latin *pirum* 'pear.'

pers. ▶ abbr. ■ person. ■ personal.

per se /pər ˈsā/ ▶ adv. by or in itself or themselves; intrinsically: *it is not these facts per se that are important.*
– ORIGIN Latin.

per·se·cute /ˈpərsəˌkyo͞ot/ ▶ v. [with obj.] subject (someone) to hostility and ill-treatment, esp. because of their race or political or religious beliefs: *his followers were persecuted by the authorities.* ■ harass or annoy (someone) persistently: *Hilda was persecuted by some of the other girls.*
– DERIVATIVES **per·se·cu·tor** /-ˌkyo͞otər/ n., **per·se·cu·to·ry** /-kyo͞oˌtôrē/ adj.
– ORIGIN late Middle English: from Old French *persecuter*, from Latin *persecut-* 'followed with hostility,' from the verb *persequi*, from *per-* 'through, utterly' + *sequi* 'follow, pursue.'

per·se·cu·tion /ˌpərsəˈkyo͞osHən/ ▶ n. hostility and ill-treatment, esp. because of race or political or religious beliefs: *her family fled religious persecution.* ■ persistent annoyance or harassment: *his persecution at the hands of other students.*

per·se·cu·tion com·plex ▶ n. an irrational and obsessive feeling or fear that one is the object of collective hostility or ill-treatment on the part of others.

Per·se·ids /ˈpərsēidz/ Astronomy an annual meteor shower radiating from a point in the constellation Perseus, reaching a peak about August 12.

Per·seph·o·ne /pərˈsefənē/ Greek Mythology a goddess, the daughter of Zeus and Demeter. Roman name PROSERPINA.

> She was carried off by Hades and made queen of the underworld. Demeter, vainly seeking her, refused to let the earth produce its fruits until her daughter was restored to her, but because Persephone had eaten some pomegranate seeds in the other world, she was obliged to spend part of every year there. Her story symbolizes the return of spring and the life and growth of grain.

Per·sep·o·lis /pərˈsepəlis/ a city in ancient Persia, northeast of Shiraz. It was founded in the late 6th century BC by Darius I as the ceremonial capital of Persia under the Achaemenid dynasty.

Per·se·us /ˈpərsēəs, -syo͞os/ **1** Greek Mythology the son of Zeus and Danae, a hero celebrated for many achievements. Riding the winged horse Pegasus, he cut off the head of the Gorgon Medusa and gave it to Athena; he also rescued and married Andromeda, and became king of Tiryns in Greece.
2 Astronomy a large northern constellation that includes a dense part of the Milky Way. It contains several star clusters and the variable star Algol. ■ (as genitive **Persei** /ˈpərsēˌī/) used with a preceding

letter or numeral to designate a star in this constellation: *the star Delta Persei.*

per·se·ver·ance /ˌpərsəˈvi(ə)rəns/ ▶ **n.** steadfastness in doing something despite difficulty or delay in achieving success: ***his perseverance** with the technique illustrates his single-mindedness | medicine is a field that requires dedication and perseverance.*
– ORIGIN Middle English: from Old French, from Latin *perseverantia*, from *perseverant-* 'abiding by strictly,' from the verb *perseverare* (see PERSEVERE).

per·sev·er·ate /pərˈsevəˌrāt/ ▶ **v.** [no obj.] Psychology repeat or prolong an action, thought, or utterance after the stimulus that prompted it has ceased.
– DERIVATIVES **per·sev·er·a·tion** /pərˌsevəˈrāSHən/ **n.**
– ORIGIN early 20th cent.: from Latin *perseverat-* 'strictly abided by,' from the verb *perseverare* (see PERSEVERE).

per·se·vere /ˌpərsəˈvi(ə)r/ ▶ **v.** [no obj.] continue in a course of action even in the face of difficulty or with little or no prospect of success: *his family **persevered with** his treatment.*
– DERIVATIVES **per·se·ver·ing·ly adv.**
– ORIGIN late Middle English: from Old French *perseverer*, from Latin *perseverare* 'abide by strictly,' from *perseverus* 'very strict,' from *per-* 'thoroughly' + *severus* 'severe.'

Per·shing[1] /ˈpərSHiNG, -ZHiNG/, John Joseph (1860–1948), US army officer; known as **Black Jack.** His early military years included active duty in Cuba 1889, the Philippines 1899–1903, and Mexico 1916–17 before he became commander in chief of the American Expeditionary Force 1917–19 in World War I. His Meuse-Argonne offensive 1918 led to the final collapse of the German Army. He served as US Army chief of staff 1921–24.

Per·shing[2] (also **Pershing missile**) ▶ **n.** a US short-range surface-to-surface ballistic missile, capable of carrying a nuclear or conventional warhead.
– ORIGIN 1950s: named after John J. *Pershing* (1860–1948), American general.

Per·sia /ˈpərZHə/ a former country in southwestern Asia, now called Iran. The ancient kingdom of Persia became the domain of the Achaemenid dynasty in the 6th century BC. Under Cyrus the Great, Persia became the center of a powerful empire that included western Asia, Egypt, and parts of eastern Europe; it was eventually overthrown by Alexander the Great in 330 BC. The country was conquered by Muslim Arabs between AD 633 and 651. It was renamed Iran in 1935.

Per·sian /ˈpərZHən/ ▶ **n. 1** a native or inhabitant of ancient or modern Persia (or Iran), or a person of Persian descent. ■ (also **Persian cat**) a long-haired domestic cat of a breed originating in Persia, having a broad round head, stocky body, and short thick legs.
2 the Iranian language of modern Iran, written in Arabic script. Also called FARSI. ■ an earlier form of this language spoken in ancient or medieval Persia.
▶ **adj.** of or relating to ancient Persia or modern Iran or its people or language.

> Persian (or Farsi) is spoken by more than 30 million people in Iran, by about 5 million in Afghanistan (as Dari), and by another 2.2 million in Tajikistan (as Tajik). Old Persian, written in cuneiform and attested from the 6th century BC, was the language of the Persian empire, which once extended from the Mediterranean to India. In the 2nd century BC, the Persians created their own alphabet (Pahlavi), which was used until the Islamic conquest in the 7th century.

– ORIGIN Middle English: from Old French *persien*, from Latin *Persia*, via Greek from Old Persian *pārsa* 'Persia' (modern Persian *pārs*, Arabic *fārs*).

Per·sian car·pet (also **Persian rug**) ▶ **n.** a carpet or rug woven in Iran in a traditional design incorporating stylized symbolic imagery, or made elsewhere in such a style.

Per·sian Gulf an arm of the Arabian Sea, to which it is connected by the Strait of Hormuz and the Gulf of Oman. It extends northwest between the Arabian peninsula and the coast of southwestern Iran. Also called ARABIAN GULF; informally THE GULF (see GULF).

Per·sian Gulf War ▶ **n.** another name for GULF WAR.

Per·sian lamb ▶ **n.** a silky, tightly curled fur made from or resembling the fleece of a young karakul, used to make clothing.

Per·sian Wars the wars fought between Greece and Persia in the 5th century BC, in which the Persians sought to extend their rule over the Greek world.

> The wars began in 490 BC when Darius I sent an expedition to punish the Greeks for having supported the Ionian cities in their unsuccessful revolt against Persian rule; the Persians were defeated by a small force of Athenians at Marathon. Ten years later, Darius's son Xerxes I attempted an invasion. He devastated Attica, but Persian forces were defeated on land at Plataea and in a sea battle at Salamis (480 BC), and retreated. Intermittent war continued until peace was signed in 449 BC.

per·si·flage /ˈpərsəˌfläZH/ ▶ **n.** formal light and slightly contemptuous mockery or banter.
– ORIGIN mid 18th cent.: from French *persifler* 'to banter,' based on *siffler* 'to whistle.'

per·sim·mon /pərˈsimən/ ▶ **n. 1** an edible fruit that resembles a large tomato and has very sweet flesh.
2 the tree that yields this fruit, related to ebony.
● Genus *Diospyros*, family Ebenaceae: the North American *D. virginiana*, an evergreen with dark red fruit, and the **Japanese persimmon** (*D. kaki*), cultivated for its orange fruit.
– ORIGIN early 17th cent.: alteration of Virginia Algonquian *pessemmins.*

per·sist /pərˈsist/ ▶ **v.** [no obj.] continue firmly or obstinately in an opinion or a course of action in spite of difficulty, opposition, or failure: *the minority of drivers who **persist in** drinking | we are **persisting with** policies that will create jobs for the future.* ■ continue to exist; be prolonged: *if the symptoms persist for more than a few days, contact your doctor.*
– ORIGIN mid 16th cent.: from Latin *persistere*, from *per-* 'through, steadfastly' + *sistere* 'to stand.'

per·sist·ence /pərˈsistəns/ ▶ **n.** firm or obstinate continuance in a course of action in spite of difficulty or opposition: *companies must have patience and persistence, but the rewards are there.* ■ the continued or prolonged existence of something: *the persistence of huge environmental problems.*
– DERIVATIVES **per·sist·en·cy** /-sē/ **n.**
– ORIGIN mid 16th cent.: from French *persistance*, from the verb *persister*; influenced in spelling by Latin *persistent-* 'continuing steadfastly.'

per·sist·ent /pərˈsistənt/ ▶ **adj. 1** continuing firmly or obstinately in a course of action in spite of difficulty or opposition: *one of the government's most persistent critics.*
2 continuing to exist or endure over a prolonged period: *persistent rain will affect many areas | persistent reports of human rights abuses by the military.* ■ (of a chemical or radioactivity) remaining within the environment for a long time after its introduction: *PCBs are persistent environmental contaminants.*
3 Botany & Zoology (of a part of an animal or plant, such as a horn, leaf, etc.) remaining attached instead of falling off in the normal manner.
– DERIVATIVES **per·sist·ent·ly adv.**

per·sis·tent or·gan·ic pol·lut·ant ▶ **n.** a hazardous organic chemical compound that is resistant to biodegradation and thus remains in the environment for a long time.

per·sist·ent veg·e·ta·tive state ▶ **n.** a condition in which a medical patient is completely unresponsive to psychological and physical stimuli and displays no sign of higher brain function, being kept alive only by medical intervention.

per·snick·et·y /pərˈsnikətē/ ▶ **adj.** informal placing too much emphasis on trivial or minor details; fussy: *persnickety gardeners | she's very **persnickety about** her food.* ■ requiring a particularly precise or careful approach: *it's hard to find a film more persnickety and difficult to use than black-and-white infrared.*
– ORIGIN early 19th cent. (originally Scots): of unknown origin.

per·son /ˈpərsən/ ▶ **n.** (pl. **people** /ˈpēpəl/ or **persons**) **1** a human being regarded as an individual: *the porter was the last person to see her | she is a person of astonishing energy.* ■ used in legal or formal contexts to refer to an unspecified individual: *the entrance fee is $10.00 per person.* ■ [in sing. with modifier] an individual characterized by a preference or liking for a specified thing: *she's not a cat person.* ■ an individual's body: *I have publicity photographs **on my person** at all times.* ■ a character in a play or story: *his previous roles in the person of a fallible cop.*
2 Grammar a category used in the classification of pronouns, possessive determiners, and verb forms, according to whether they indicate the speaker (**first person**), the addressee (**second person**), or a third party (**third person**).
3 Christian Theology each of the three modes of being of God, namely the Father, the Son, or the Holy Spirit, who together constitute the Trinity.
– PHRASES **be one's own person** do or be what one wishes or in accordance with one's own character rather than as influenced by others. **in person** with the personal presence or action of the individual specified: *he had to pick up his welfare check in person.* **in the person of** in the physical form of: *trouble arrived in the person of a short, mustached Berliner.*
– ORIGIN Middle English: from Old French *persone*, from Latin *persona* 'actor's mask, character in a play,' later 'human being.'

> **USAGE** The words **people** and **persons** can both be used as the plural of **person**, but they are not used in exactly the same way. **People** is by far the more common of the two words and is used in most ordinary contexts: *a group of **people**; there were only about ten **people**; several thousand **people** have been rehoused.* **Persons**, on the other hand, tends now to be restricted to official or formal contexts, as in *this vehicle is authorized to carry twenty **persons**; no **persons** admitted without a pass.* In some contexts, **persons**, by pointing to the individual, may sound less friendly than **people**: *the number should not be disclosed to any unauthorized persons.*

-person ▶ **comb. form** used as a neutral alternative to *-man* in nouns denoting professional status, a position of authority, etc.: *chairperson | salesperson | sportsperson.*

per·so·na /pərˈsōnə/ ▶ **n.** (pl. **personas** or **personae** /-ˈsōnē/) the aspect of someone's character that is presented to or perceived by others: *her public persona.* In psychology, often contrasted with ANIMA. ■ a role or character adopted by an author or an actor.
– ORIGIN early 20th cent.: Latin, literally 'mask, character played by an actor.'

per·son·a·ble /ˈpərsənəbəl/ ▶ **adj.** (of a person) having a pleasant appearance and manner.
– DERIVATIVES **per·son·a·ble·ness n.**, **per·son·a·bly** /-blē/ **adv.**

per·son·age /ˈpərsənij/ ▶ **n.** a person (often used to express their significance, importance, or elevated status): *it was no less a personage than the bishop.* ■ a character in a play or other work.
– ORIGIN late Middle English: from Old French, reinforced by medieval Latin *personagium* 'effigy.' In early use the word was qualified by words such as *honorable, eminent*, but since the 19th cent. the notion "significant, notable" has been implied in the word itself.

per·so·na gra·ta /pərˈsōnə ˈgrätə/ ▶ **n.** (pl. **personae gratae** /pərˈsōnē ˈgrätē/) a person, esp. a diplomat, acceptable to certain others: *I shall no longer be persona grata at the embassy.* Compare with PERSONA NON GRATA.
– ORIGIN Latin, from *persona* (see PERSONA) + *grata*, feminine of *gratus* 'pleasing.'

per·son·al /ˈpərsənəl/ ▶ **adj. 1** of, affecting, or belonging to a particular person rather than to anyone else: *her personal fortune was recently estimated at $37 million.* ■ done or made by a particular person; involving the actual presence or action of a particular individual: *the president and his wife made personal appearances for the re-election of the state governor.*
2 of or concerning one's private life, relationships, and emotions rather than matters connected with one's public or professional career: *the book describes his acting career and gives little information about his personal life.* ■ referring to an individual's character, appearance, or private life, esp. in a hostile or critical way: *his personal remarks about Mr. Mellor's work ethic were unprofessional | you look like a drowned rat—nothing personal.*
3 of or relating to a person's body: *personal hygiene.*
4 Grammar of or denoting one of the three persons. See PERSON (sense 2).
5 existing as a self-aware entity, not as an abstraction or an impersonal force: *he rejected the notion of a personal God.*
▶ **n.** an advertisement or message in the personal column of a newspaper; personal ad. ■ (**personals**) another term for PERSONAL COLUMN.
– ORIGIN late Middle English: from Old French, from Latin *personalis* 'of a person,' from *persona* (see PERSON).

per·son·al ad ▶ **n.** informal a private advertisement or message placed in a newspaper, esp. by someone searching for a romantic partner.

per·son·al as·sis·tant ▶ **n.** a secretary or administrative assistant working exclusively for one particular person.

per·son·al col·umn ▶ **n.** (usu. **personal columns**) a section of a newspaper devoted to personal ads.

PRONUNCIATION KEY ə *ago, up*; ər *over, fur*; a *hat*; ā *ate*; ä *car*; e *let*; ē *see*; i *fit*; ī *by*; NG *sing*; ō *go*; ô *law, for*; oi *toy*; o͝o *good*; o͞o *goo*; ou *out*; TH *thin*; T͟H *then*; ZH *vision*

P

per·son·al com·put·er ▶ n. a computer designed for use by one person at a time.

per·son·al es·tate ▶ n. Law another term for PERSONAL PROPERTY.

per·son·al foul ▶ n. Sports a rule violation involving illegal contact, as (in basketball) touching a player who is in the act of shooting.

per·son·al i·den·ti·fi·ca·tion num·ber (abbr.: **PIN**) ▶ n. a number allocated to an individual and used to validate electronic transactions.

per·son·al in·for·ma·tion man·ag·er (abbr.: **PIM**) ▶ n. a computer program functioning as an address book, organizer, calendar, etc.

per·son·al in·ju·ry ▶ n. Law physical injury inflicted on a person's body, as opposed to damage to property or reputation.

per·son·al·ism /ˈpərsənəlˌizəm/ ▶ n. the quality of being personal, esp. a theory or system based on subjective ideas or applications: *his sculpture investigating pure form from which all expressive personalism was eliminated.* ■ Philosophy a system of thought that maintains the primacy of the human or divine person on the basis that reality has meaning only through the conscious mind. ■ allegiance to a person, esp. a political leader, rather than to a party or ideology.
– DERIVATIVES **per·son·al·ist** n., **per·son·al·is·tic** /ˌpərsənəlˈistik/ adj.

per·son·al·i·ty /ˌpərsəˈnalitē/ ▶ n. (pl. **personalities**) **1** the combination of characteristics or qualities that form an individual's distinctive character: *she had a sunny personality that was very engaging* | figurative *each brand of gin has its own personality* | *she has triumphed by sheer force of personality.* ■ qualities that make someone interesting or popular: *she's always had loads of personality.*
2 a famous person, esp. in entertainment or sports: *an official opening by a famous personality.*
3 archaic the quality or fact of being a person as distinct from a thing or animal.
4 (**personalities**) archaic disparaging remarks about an individual.
– ORIGIN late Middle English (sense 3): from Old French *personalite*, from medieval Latin *personalitas*, from Latin *personalis* 'of a person' (see PERSONAL). Sense 1 dates from the late 18th cent.

per·son·al·i·ty cult ▶ n. excessive public admiration for or devotion to a famous person, esp. a political leader.

per·son·al·i·ty dis·or·der ▶ n. Psychiatry a deeply ingrained and maladaptive pattern of behavior of a specified kind, typically manifest by the time one reaches adolescence and causing long-term difficulties in personal relationships or in functioning in society.

per·son·al·i·ty in·ven·to·ry ▶ n. a type of questionnaire designed to reveal the respondent's personality traits.

per·son·al·i·ty type ▶ n. Psychology a collection of personality traits that are thought to occur together consistently, esp. as determined by a certain pattern of responses to a personality inventory.

per·son·al·ize /ˈpərsənəlˌīz/ ▶ v. [with obj.] **1** design or produce (something) to meet someone's individual requirements: *the wedding invitations will be personalized to your exact requirements.* ■ make (something) identifiable as belonging to a particular person, esp. by marking it with their name or initials: (as adj. **personalized**) *personalized license plates.*
2 cause (something, esp. an issue, argument, or debate) to become concerned with personalities or feelings rather than with general or abstract matters: *the mass media's tendency to personalize politics.*
3 (often **be personalized**) personify (something, esp. a deity or spirit): *evil spirits personalized in Satan.*
– DERIVATIVES **per·son·al·i·za·tion** /ˌpərsənəliˈzāSHən/ n.

per·son·al·ly /ˈpərsənəlē/ ▶ adv. **1** with the personal presence or action of the individual specified; in person: *she stayed to thank O'Brien personally.* ■ used to indicate that a specified person and no other is involved in something: *they had made conclusions without getting to know me personally* | [as submodifier] *he never forgave his father, holding him* ***personally responsible*** *for this betrayal.*
2 from someone's personal standpoint or according to their particular nature; in a subjective rather than an objective way: *he had spoken personally and emotionally* | [sentence adverb] *personally, I think he made a very sensible move.* ■ with regard to one's personal and private rather than public or professional capacity: *nothing had gone well personally or politically.*
– PHRASES **take something personally** interpret a remark or action as directed against oneself and be upset or offended by it, even if that was not the speaker's intention: *I took it personally when he yelled at the class.*

per·son·al or·gan·iz·er ▶ n. a loose-leaf notebook consisting of separate sections including a calendar and pages for recording addresses and telephone numbers. ■ a handheld computer serving the same purpose.

per·son·al pro·noun ▶ n. each of the pronouns in English (*I, you, he, she, it, we, they, me, him, her, us,* and *them*) comprising a set that shows contrasts of person, gender, number, and case.

> **USAGE** The correct use of personal pronouns is one of the most debated topics of English usage. **I, we, they, he,** and **she** are **subjective** personal pronouns, which means they are used as the subject of the sentence, often coming before the verb (***she*** *lives in Paris;* ***we*** *are leaving*). **Me, us, them, him,** and **her**, on the other hand, are **objective** personal pronouns, which means that they are used as the object (i.e., they receive the action) of a verb or preposition (*John likes* ***me****; his father left* ***him****; I did it for* ***her***). This explains why it is not correct to say *John and me went to the mall*: the personal pronoun is in subject position, so it must be **I**, not **me**. Using the pronoun alone makes the incorrect use obvious: ***me*** *went to the mall* is clearly not acceptable. This analysis also explains why it is not correct to say *he came with you and I*: the personal pronoun is governed by a preposition (*with*) and is therefore objective, so it must be **me**, not **I**. Again, a simple test for correctness is to use the pronoun alone: *he came with* ***I*** is clearly not acceptable. See also usage at BETWEEN.

per·son·al pro·per·ty ▶ n. Law movable property; belongings exclusive of land and buildings. Used in contrast to REAL PROPERTY.

per·son·al serv·ices ▶ n. used to refer collectively to commercial services, such as catering and cleaning, that supply the personal needs of customers.

per·son·al shop·per ▶ n. an individual who is paid to help another to purchase goods, either by accompanying them while shopping or by shopping on their behalf.

per·son·al space ▶ n. the physical space immediately surrounding someone, into which any encroachment feels threatening to or uncomfortable for them: *he was invading her personal space.*

per·son·al ster·e·o ▶ n. a small portable electronic device for playing music, used with lightweight headphones.

per·son·al touch ▶ n. an element or feature contributed by someone to make something less impersonal: *customers prefer to write the messages themselves for more of a personal touch.*

per·son·al·ty /ˈpərsənəltē/ ▶ n. Law personal, movable property. Used in contrast to REALTY.
– ORIGIN mid 16th cent. (in the legal phrase *in the personalty* 'for damages'): from Anglo-Norman French *personaltie*, from medieval Latin *personalitas* (see PERSONALITY).

per·son·al wa·ter·craft ▶ n. (abbr.: **PW** or **PWC**) a small, jet-powered craft, resembling a snowmobile in appearance and ridden astraddle, for individual use on water.

per·so·na non gra·ta /pərˈsōnə nän ˈgrätə/ ▶ n. (pl. **personae non gratae** /pərˈsōnē nän ˈgrätē/) an unacceptable or unwelcome person: *from now on, these yellow journalists can consider themselves personae non gratae.* Compare with PERSONA GRATA.
– ORIGIN Latin, from *persona* (see PERSONA) + *non* 'not' + *grata*, feminine of *gratus* 'pleasing.'

per·son·ate /ˈpərsəˌnāt/ ▶ v. [with obj.] formal play the part of (a character in a drama). ■ pretend to be (someone else), esp. for fraudulent purposes, such as casting a vote in another person's name.
– DERIVATIVES **per·son·a·tion** /ˌpərsəˈnāSHən/ n., **per·son·a·tor** /-ˌnātər/ n.
– ORIGIN late 16th cent.: from late Latin *personat-* 'represented by acting,' from Latin *persona* 'mask' (see PERSON).

per·son·hood /ˈpərsənˌho͝od/ ▶ n. the quality or condition of being an individual person.

per·son·i·fi·ca·tion /pərˌsänəfiˈkāSHən/ ▶ n. the attribution of a personal nature or human characteristics to something nonhuman, or the representation of an abstract quality in human form. ■ a figure intended to represent an abstract quality: *the design on the franc shows Marianne, the personification of the French republic.* ■ [in sing.] a person, animal, or object regarded as representing or embodying a quality, concept, or thing: *he was* ***the very personification of*** *British pluck and diplomacy.*

per·son·i·fy /pərˈsänəˌfī/ ▶ v. (**personifies, personifying, personified**) [with obj.] represent (a quality or concept) by a figure in human form: *public pageants and dramas in which virtues and vices were personified.* ■ (usu. **be personified**) attribute a personal nature or human characteristics to (something nonhuman): *in the poem, the oak trees are personified.* ■ represent or embody (a quality, concept, or thing) in a physical form: *he fairly personifies trustworthiness.*
– DERIVATIVES **per·son·i·fi·er** /-ˌfī(ə)r/ n.
– ORIGIN early 18th cent.: from French *personnifier*, from *personne* 'person.'

per·son·nel /ˌpərsəˈnel/ ▶ plural n. people employed in an organization or engaged in an organized undertaking such as military service compare with MATERIEL: *many of the personnel involved require training* | *sales personnel.* ■ short for PERSONNEL DEPARTMENT.
– ORIGIN early 19th cent.: from French (adjective used as a noun), contrasted with *matériel* 'equipment or materials used in an organization or undertaking.'

per·son·nel car·ri·er ▶ n. another term for ARMORED PERSONNEL CARRIER.

per·son·nel de·part·ment ▶ n. the part of an organization concerned with the hiring, training, and welfare of employees.

per·son of col·or (also **man of color, woman of color**) ▶ n. a person who is not white or of European parentage.

> **USAGE** The term **person of color** is first recorded at the end of the 18th century. It was revived in the 1990s as the recommended term to use in some official contexts, especially in US English, to refer to a person who is not white. In general use, however, it comes across as somewhat contrived, and even in official contexts it never quite took hold. The word **nonwhite**, for instance, which is one of the terms **person of color** was meant to replace, is often the preferred choice, especially in demographic descriptions. See also usage at BLACK, COLORED, and NONWHITE.

per·son-to-per·son ▶ adj. & adv. taking place directly between individuals: [as adj.] *person-to-person transmission of the disease* | [as adv.] (also **person to person**) *making contact with him person to person.* ■ denoting a phone call made through the operator to a specified person and paid for from the time that person answers the phone.

per·spec·tive /pərˈspektiv/ ▶ n. **1** the art of drawing solid objects on a two-dimensional surface so as to give the right impression of their height, width, depth, and position in relation to each other when viewed from a particular point: [as modifier] *a perspective drawing.* See also LINEAR PERSPECTIVE and AERIAL PERSPECTIVE. ■ a picture drawn in such a way, esp. one appearing to enlarge or extend the actual space, or to give the effect of distance. ■ a view or prospect. ■ Geometry the relation of two figures in the same plane, such that pairs of corresponding points lie on concurrent lines, and corresponding lines meet in collinear points.
2 a particular attitude toward or way of regarding something; a point of view: *most guidebook history is written from the editor's perspective.* ■ true understanding of the relative importance of things; a sense of proportion: *we must keep a sense of perspective about what he's done.*
3 an apparent spatial distribution in perceived sound.
– PHRASES **in** (or **out of**) **perspective** showing the right (or wrong) relationship between visible objects. ■ correctly (or incorrectly) regarded in terms of relative importance: *these expenses may seem high, but they need to be* ***put into perspective.***
– DERIVATIVES **per·spec·tiv·al** /-tivəl/ adj.
– ORIGIN late Middle English (in the sense 'optics'): from medieval Latin *perspectiva (ars)* 'science of optics,' from *perspect-* 'looked at closely,' from the verb *perspicere*, from *per-* 'through' + *specere* 'to look.'

per·spec·tiv·ism /pərˈspektiˌvizəm/ ▶ n. **1** Philosophy the theory that knowledge of a subject is inevitably partial and limited by the individual perspective from which it is viewed. See also RELATIVISM.
2 the practice of regarding and analyzing a situation or work of art from different points of view.
– DERIVATIVES **per·spec·tiv·ist** n.

Per·spex /ˈpərspeks/ ▶ n. trademark (often **perspex**) solid transparent plastic made of polymethyl methacrylate (the same material as plexiglas or lucite).
– ORIGIN 1930s: formed irregularly from Latin *perspicere* 'look through,' from *per-* 'through' + *specere* 'to look.'

per·spi·ca·cious /ˌpərspiˈkāsHəs/ ▶ **adj.** having a ready insight into and understanding of things: *it offers quite a few facts to the perspicacious reporter.*
– DERIVATIVES **per·spi·ca·cious·ly adv.**
– ORIGIN early 17th cent.: from Latin *perspicax, perspicac-* 'seeing clearly' + **-ACIOUS**.

per·spi·cac·i·ty /ˌpərspiˈkasitē/ ▶ **n.** the quality of having a ready insight into things; shrewdness: *the perspicacity of her remarks.*

per·spic·u·ous /pərˈspikyōōwəs/ ▶ **adj.** formal (of an account or representation) clearly expressed and easily understood; lucid: *it provides simpler and more perspicuous explanations than its rivals.* ■ (of a person) able to give an account or express an idea clearly.
– DERIVATIVES **per·spi·cu·i·ty** /ˌpərspiˈkyōōitē/ **n.**, **per·spic·u·ous·ly adv.**
– ORIGIN late 15th cent. (in the sense 'transparent'): from Latin *perspicuus* 'transparent, clear' (from the verb *perspicere* 'look at closely') + **-OUS**.

per·spi·ra·tion /ˌpərspəˈrāsHən/ ▶ **n.** the process of sweating: *it causes perspiration and a rapid heartbeat.* ■ sweat: *perspiration ran down his forehead.*
– DERIVATIVES **per·spir·a·to·ry** /pərˈspīrəˌtôrē/ **adj.**
– ORIGIN early 17th cent.: from French, from *perspirer* (see **PERSPIRE**).

per·spire /pərˈspīr/ ▶ **v.** [no obj.] give out sweat through the pores of the skin as the result of heat, physical exertion, or stress: *Will was perspiring heavily.*
– ORIGIN mid 17th cent.: from French *perspirer*, from Latin *perspirare*, from *per-* 'through' + *spirare* 'breathe.'

per·suad·a·ble /pərˈswādəbəl/ ▶ **adj.** easily persuaded; amenable: *they need to identify the most persuadable voters.*
– DERIVATIVES **per·suad·a·bil·i·ty** /-ˌswādəˈbilitē/ **n.**

per·suade /pərˈswād/ ▶ **v.** [with obj. and infinitive] cause (someone) to do something through reasoning or argument: *it wasn't easy, but I persuaded him to do the right thing.* ■ [with obj.] cause (someone) to believe something, esp. after a sustained effort; convince: *they must often be persuaded of the potential severity of their drinking problems* | [with obj. and clause] *he did everything he could to persuade the police that he was the robber.* ■ (of a situation or event) provide a sound reason for (someone) to do something: *the cost of the manor's restoration persuaded them to take in guests.*
– DERIVATIVES **per·sua·si·ble** /-ˈswāzəbəl/ **adj.**
– ORIGIN late 15th cent.: from Latin *persuadere*, from *per-* 'through, to completion' + *suadere* 'advise.'

> **USAGE** For a discussion of the difference between **persuade** and **convince**, see usage at **CONVINCE**.

per·suad·er /pərˈswādər/ ▶ **n.** a person who persuades someone to do something. ■ informal a thing used to compel submission or obedience, typically a gun or other weapon.

per·sua·sion /pərˈswāZHən/ ▶ **n. 1** the action or fact of persuading someone or of being persuaded to do or believe something: *Monica needed plenty of persuasion before she actually left.*
2 a belief or set of beliefs, esp. religious or political ones: *writers of all political persuasions.* ■ a group or sect holding a particular religious belief: *the village had two chapels for those of the Methodist persuasion.* ■ humorous any group or type of person or thing linked by a specified characteristic, quality, or attribute: *an ancient gas oven of the enamel persuasion.*
– ORIGIN late Middle English: from Latin *persuasio(n-)*, from the verb *persuadere* (see **PERSUADE**).

per·sua·sive /pərˈswāsiv, -ziv/ ▶ **adj.** good at persuading someone to do or believe something through reasoning or the use of temptation: *an informative and persuasive speech.*
– DERIVATIVES **per·sua·sive·ly adv.**, **per·sua·sive·ness n.**
– ORIGIN late 15th cent.: from French *persuasif, -ive* or medieval Latin *persuasivus*, from *persuas-* 'convinced by reasoning,' from the verb *persuadere* (see **PERSUADE**).

pert /pərt/ ▶ **adj. 1** (of a girl or young woman) attractively lively or cheeky: *a pert Belgian actress.* ■ (of a young person or their speech or behavior) impudent: *no need to be pert, miss.* ■ another term for **PEART**.
2 (of a bodily feature or garment) attractive because neat and jaunty: *she had a pert nose and deep blue eyes.*
– DERIVATIVES **pert·ly adv.**
– ORIGIN Middle English (in the sense 'manifest'): from Old French *apert*, from Latin *apertus* 'opened,' past participle of *aperire*, reinforced by Old French *aspert*, from Latin *expertus* (see **EXPERT**).

pert. ▶ **abbr.** pertaining.

per·tain /pərˈtān/ ▶ **v.** [no obj.] be appropriate, related, or applicable: *matters **pertaining to the organization** of government.* ■ chiefly Law belong to something as a part, appendage, or accessory: *the premises, stock, and all assets **pertaining to the business**.* ■ [with adverbial] be in effect or existence in a specified place or at a specified time: *their economic circumstances are vastly different from those which pertained in their land of origin.*
– ORIGIN late Middle English: from Old French *partenir*, from Latin *pertinere* 'extend to, have reference to,' from *per-* 'through' + *tenere* 'to hold.'

Perth /pərTH/ the capital of the state of Western Australia, in western Australia, on the Indian Ocean; pop. 1,602,559 (2008). Founded by the British in 1829, it developed rapidly after the discovery in 1890 of gold in the region and the opening in 1897 of the harbor at Fremantle.

Perth Am·boy /ˈpərTH ˈamˌboi/ a historic industrial city in northeastern New Jersey, on the Raritan River, across the Arthur Kill from Staten Island in New York; pop. 48,742 (est. 2008).

per·ti·na·cious /ˌpərtnˈāsHəs/ ▶ **adj.** formal holding firmly to an opinion or a course of action: *he worked with a pertinacious resistance to interruptions.*
– DERIVATIVES **per·ti·na·cious·ly adv.**, **per·ti·na·cious·ness n.**, **per·ti·nac·i·ty** /-ˈasitē/ **n.**
– ORIGIN early 17th cent.: from Latin *pertinax, pertinac-* 'holding fast' + **-OUS**.

per·ti·nent /ˈpərtn-ənt/ ▶ **adj.** relevant or applicable to a particular matter; apposite: *she asked me a lot of very pertinent questions* | *the unreleased section of tape was not **pertinent to** the investigation.*
– DERIVATIVES **per·ti·nence n.**, **per·ti·nen·cy n.**, **per·ti·nent·ly adv.**
– ORIGIN late Middle English: from Old French, or from Latin *pertinent-* 'having reference to,' from the verb *pertinere* (see **PERTAIN**).

pert·ness /ˈpərtnis/ ▶ **n. 1** the quality of being attractively neat and jaunty.
2 impudence; cheek.

per·turb /pərˈtərb/ ▶ **v.** [with obj.] **1** make (someone) anxious or unsettled: *they were perturbed by her capricious behavior* | [with obj. and clause] *they were perturbed that the bank had begun switching some of its problem loans.*
2 subject (a system, moving object, or process) to an influence tending to alter its normal or regular state or path: *nuclear weapons could be used to perturb the orbit of an asteroid.*
– DERIVATIVES **per·turb·a·ble adj.**, **per·tur·ba·tive** /ˈpərtərˌbātiv, pərˈtərbətiv/ **adj.** (sense 2), **per·turb·ing·ly adv.**
– ORIGIN late Middle English: from Old French *pertourber*, from Latin *perturbare*, from *per-* 'completely' + *turbare* 'disturb.'

per·tur·ba·tion /ˌpərtərˈbāsHən/ ▶ **n. 1** anxiety; mental uneasiness: *she sensed her friend's perturbation.* ■ a cause of such anxiety or uneasiness: *Frank's atheism was more than a perturbation to Michael.*
2 a deviation of a system, moving object, or process from its regular or normal state of path, caused by an outside influence: *some minor perturbation in his house's cash flow.* ■ Astronomy a minor deviation in the course of a celestial body, caused by the gravitational attraction of a neighboring body.
– ORIGIN late Middle English: from Latin *perturbatio(n-)*, from the verb *perturbare* 'disturb greatly' (see **PERTURB**).

per·turbed /pərˈtərbd/ ▶ **adj.** anxious or unsettled; upset: *she didn't seem perturbed about the noises around her.*

per·tus·sis /pərˈtəsis/ ▶ **n.** medical term for **WHOOPING COUGH**.
– ORIGIN late 18th cent.: modern Latin, from **PER-** 'away, extremely' + Latin *tussis* 'a cough.'

Pe·ru /pəˈrōō/ a country in South America on the Pacific coast, crossed throughout its length by the Andes; pop. 29,547,000 (est. 2009); capital, Lima; languages, Spanish and Quechua.

> The center of the Inca empire, Peru was conquered by the Spanish conquistador Pizarro in 1532. Liberated by Simón Bolívar and José de San Martín in 1820–24, a republic was established. It lost territory in the south in a war with Chile 1879–83 and also had border disputes with Colombia and Ecuador in the 1930s and 1940s. Peru was troubled by revolutionary guerrilla and terrorist activity in the 1980s and 1990s.

– DERIVATIVES **Pe·ru·vi·an** /-vēən/ **adj. & n.**

Pe·ru·gia /pəˈrōōj(ē)ə/ a city in central Italy, the capital of Umbria; pop. 165,207 (2008).

pe·ruke /pəˈrōōk/ ▶ **n.** archaic term for **PERIWIG**. ■ archaic term for **WIG**[1].
– ORIGIN mid 16th cent. (denoting a natural head of hair): from French *perruque*, from Italian *perrucca*, of unknown origin.

pe·rus·al /pəˈrōōzəl/ ▶ **n.** formal the action of reading or examining something: *I continued my perusal of the instructions* | *a quick perusal of the index to the book reveals an interesting fact.*

pe·ruse /pəˈrōōz/ ▶ **v.** [with obj.] formal read (something), typically in a thorough or careful way: *he has spent countless hours in libraries perusing art history books and catalogues.* ■ examine carefully or at length: *Laura perused a Caravaggio.*
– DERIVATIVES **pe·rus·er n.**
– ORIGIN late 15th cent. (in the sense 'use up, wear out'): perhaps from **PER-** 'thoroughly' + **USE**, but compare with Anglo-Norman French *peruser* 'examine.'

> **USAGE** Note that **peruse** means 'read,' typically with an implication of thoroughness and care. It does not mean 'read through quickly; glance over,' as in *documents will be **perused** rather than analyzed thoroughly.*

Pe·ru·vi·an bark /pəˈrōōvēən/ ▶ **n.** cinchona bark.

Pe·ru·vi·an Cur·rent a cold ocean current that moves north from the Antarctic Ocean along the Pacific coast of Chile and Peru before turning west into the South Equatorial Current.

perv /pərv/ informal ▶ **n.** (also **pervo** /ˈpərˌvō/) a sexual pervert.
– ORIGIN 1940s: abbreviation of the noun **PERVERT**.

per·vade /pərˈvād/ ▶ **v.** [with obj.] (esp. of a smell) spread through and be perceived in every part of: *a smell of stale cabbage pervaded the air.* ■ (of an influence, feeling, or quality) be present and apparent throughout: *the sense of crisis that pervaded Europe in the 1930s.*
– DERIVATIVES **per·va·sion** /pərˈvāZHən/ **n.**
– ORIGIN mid 17th cent. (also in the sense 'traverse'): from Latin *pervadere*, from *per-* 'throughout' + *vadere* 'go.'

per·va·sive /pərˈvāsiv/ ▶ **adj.** (esp. of an unwelcome influence or physical effect) spreading widely throughout an area or a group of people: *ageism is pervasive and entrenched in our society.*
– DERIVATIVES **per·va·sive·ly adv.**, **per·va·sive·ness n.**
– ORIGIN mid 18th cent.: from Latin *pervas-* 'passed through' (from the verb *pervadere*) + **-IVE**.

per·verse /pərˈvərs/ ▶ **adj.** (of a person or their actions) showing a deliberate and obstinate desire to behave in a way that is unreasonable or unacceptable, often in spite of the consequences: *Kate's perverse decision not to cooperate.* ■ contrary to the accepted or expected standard or practice: *in two general elections the outcome was quite perverse.* ■ Law (of a verdict) against the weight of evidence or the direction of the judge on a point of law. ■ sexually perverted.
– DERIVATIVES **per·verse·ly adv.** [sentence adverb] *perversely, she felt nearer to tears now than at any other moment in the conversation*, **per·verse·ness n.**
– ORIGIN late Middle English (in the sense 'turned away from what is right or good'): from Old French *pervers(e)*, from Latin *perversus* 'turned around,' from the verb *pervertere* (see **PERVERT**).

per·ver·sion /pərˈvərZHən/ ▶ **n.** the alteration of something from its original course, meaning, or state to a distortion or corruption of what was first intended: *all great evil is the perversion of a good* | *a scandalous perversion of the law.* ■ sexual behavior or desire that is considered abnormal or unacceptable.
– ORIGIN late Middle English: from Latin *perversio(n-)*, from the verb *pervertere* 'turn around' (see **PERVERT**).

per·ver·si·ty /pərˈvərsitē/ ▶ **n.** (pl. **perversities**) **1** a deliberate desire to behave in an unreasonable or unacceptable way; contrariness: *they responded with typical perversity.*
2 the quality of being contrary to accepted standards or practice: *the perversity of being able to carry a gun but not purchase a drink.*
3 the quality of being sexually perverted.

per·vert ▶ **v.** /pərˈvərt/ [with obj.] alter (something) from its original course, meaning, or state to a distortion or corruption of what was first intended: *he was charged with conspiring to pervert the course of justice.* ■ lead (someone) away from what is considered right, natural, or acceptable: *Hector is a man who is simply perverted by his time.*
▶ **n.** /ˈpərvərt/ a person whose sexual behavior is regarded as abnormal and unacceptable.

PRONUNCIATION KEY ə ago, up; ər over, fur; a hat; ā ate; ä car; e let; ē see; i fit; ī by; NG sing; ō go; ô law, for; oi toy; ŏŏ good; ōō goo; ou out; TH thin; TH then; ZH vision

P

– DERIVATIVES **per·vert·er** n.
– ORIGIN late Middle English (as a verb): from Old French *pervertir*, from Latin *pervertere*, from *per-* 'thoroughly, to ill effect' + *vertere* 'to turn.' The current noun sense dates from the late 19th cent.

per·vert·ed /pər'vərtid/ ▶ **adj.** (of a person or their actions) characterized by sexually abnormal and unacceptable practices or tendencies: *he whispered perverted obscenities.* ■ (of a thing) having been corrupted or distorted from its original course, meaning, or state: *this sudden surge of perverted patriotism.*
– DERIVATIVES **per·vert·ed·ly** adv.

per·vi·ous /'pərvēəs/ ▶ **adj.** (of a substance) allowing water to pass through; permeable: *pervious rocks.*
– DERIVATIVES **per·vi·ous·ness** n.
– ORIGIN early 17th cent.: from Latin *pervius* 'having a passage through' (based on *via* 'way') + **-ous**.

per·vo /'pərˌvō/ ▶ **n.** (pl. **pervos**) variant of PERV.

pes /pēs, pās/ ▶ **n.** (pl. **pedes** /'pēdēz, 'pedēz/) technical the human foot, or the corresponding terminal segment of the hind limb of a vertebrate animal.
– ORIGIN mid 19th cent.: from Latin, 'foot.'

Pe·sach /'pāˌsäk/ ▶ **n.** Jewish term for the Passover festival.
– ORIGIN from Hebrew *Pesaḥ*.

pes·ca·tar·i·an /ˌpeskə'te(ə)rēən/ (also **pescetarian**) ▶ **n.** a person who does not eat meat but does eat fish.
– ORIGIN 1990s: from Italian *pesce* 'fish,' on the pattern of *vegetarian*.

pe·se·ta /pə'sātə/ ▶ **n.** the basic monetary unit of Spain (until replaced by the euro), equal to 100 centimos. ■ historical a silver coin.
– ORIGIN Spanish, diminutive of *pesa* 'weight,' from Latin *pensa* 'things weighed,' from the verb *pendere* 'weigh.'

pe·se·wa /pā'sāwä/ ▶ **n.** a monetary unit of Ghana, equal to one hundredth of a cedi.
– ORIGIN Akan, literally 'penny.'

Pe·sha·war /pə'SHäwər/ the capital of North-West Frontier Province, in northwestern Pakistan; pop. 1,390,900 (est. 2009). Situated near the Khyber Pass on the border with Afghanistan, it is of strategic and military importance.

Pe·shit·ta /pə'SHētə/ (also **Peshito** /-tō/) ▶ **n.** the ancient Syriac version of the Bible, used in Syriac-speaking Christian countries from the early 5th century and still the official Bible of the Syrian Christian Churches.
– ORIGIN Syriac, literally 'simple, plain.'

pesh·mer·ga /pesH'mərgə/ ▶ **n.** (pl. **same** or **peshmergas**) a member of a Kurdish nationalist guerrilla organization.
– ORIGIN from Kurdish *pêshmerge*, from *pêsh* 'before' + *merg* 'death.'

P

pes·ky /'peskē/ ▶ **adj.** (**peskier, peskiest**) informal causing trouble; annoying: *pesky mosquitoes.*
– DERIVATIVES **pesk·i·ly** /-kəlē/ adv., **pesk·i·ness** /-kēnis/ n.
– ORIGIN late 18th cent.: perhaps related to PEST.

pe·so /'pāsō/ ▶ **n.** (pl. **pesos**) the basic monetary unit of Mexico, several other Latin American countries, and the Philippines, equal to 100 centésimos in Uruguay and 100 centavos elsewhere.
– ORIGIN Spanish, literally 'weight,' from Latin *pensum* 'something weighed,' from the verb *pendere* 'weigh.'

pes·sa·ry /'pesərē/ ▶ **n.** (pl. **pessaries**) a small soluble block that is inserted into the vagina to treat infection or as a contraceptive. ■ an elastic or rigid device that is inserted into the vagina to support the uterus.
– ORIGIN late Middle English: from late Latin *pessarium*, based on Greek *pessos* 'oval stone' (used in board games).

pes·si·mism /'pesəˌmizəm/ ▶ **n.** a tendency to see the worst aspect of things or believe that the worst will happen; a lack of hope or confidence in the future: *the dispute cast an air of deep pessimism over the future of the peace talks.* ■ Philosophy a belief that this world is as bad as it could be or that evil will ultimately prevail over good.
– DERIVATIVES **pes·si·mist** n.
– ORIGIN late 18th cent.: from Latin *pessimus* 'worst,' on the pattern of *optimism*.

pes·si·mis·tic /ˌpesə'mistik/ ▶ **adj.** tending to see the worst aspect of things or believe that the worst will happen: *he was pessimistic about the prospects.*
– DERIVATIVES **pes·si·mis·ti·cal·ly** adv.

pest /pest/ ▶ **n.** a destructive insect or other animal that attacks crops, food, livestock, etc. ■ informal an annoying person or thing; a nuisance. ■ (**the pest**) archaic bubonic plague.
– ORIGIN late 15th cent. (denoting the bubonic plague): from French *peste* or Latin *pestis* 'plague.'

pes·ter /'pestər/ ▶ **v.** [with obj.] trouble or annoy (someone) with frequent or persistent requests or interruptions: *she constantly pestered him with telephone calls.*
– DERIVATIVES **pes·ter·er** n.
– ORIGIN mid 16th cent. (in the senses 'overcrowd (a place)' and 'impede (a person)'): from French *empestrer* 'encumber,' influenced by PEST. The current sense is an extension of an earlier use, 'infest,' referring to vermin.

pes·ter pow·er ▶ **n.** informal the ability of children to nag adults, esp. to influence their parents to make certain purchases: *advertisers encourage the use of pester power, especially at Christmas.*

pest·house /'pestˌhous/ ▶ **n.** historical a hospital for people suffering from infectious diseases, esp. the plague.

pes·ti·cide /'pestəˌsīd/ ▶ **n.** a substance used for destroying insects or other organisms harmful to cultivated plants or to animals.
– DERIVATIVES **pes·ti·cid·al** /ˌpestə'sīdl/ adj.

pes·tif·er·ous /pe'stifərəs/ ▶ **adj.** literary harboring infection and disease: *the pestiferous area around the prison.* ■ humorous constituting a pest or nuisance; annoying: *that pestiferous nephew of yours.*
– ORIGIN late Middle English (in the sense 'morally corrupting'): from Latin *pestifer* 'bringing pestilence' + **-ous**.

pes·ti·lence /'pestələns/ ▶ **n.** archaic a fatal epidemic disease, esp. bubonic plague.
– ORIGIN Middle English (also denoting something morally corrupting): from Old French, from Latin *pestilentia*, based on *pestis* 'a plague.'

pes·ti·lent /'pestələnt/ ▶ **adj.** destructive to life; deadly: *pestilent diseases.* ■ informal, dated causing annoyance; troublesome: *he regarded journalists as a pestilent race.* ■ archaic harmful or dangerous to morals or public order; pernicious: *the pestilent sect of Luther.*
– DERIVATIVES **pes·ti·lent·ly** adv.
– ORIGIN late Middle English: from Latin *pestilens*, *pestilent-* 'unhealthy, destructive,' from *pestis* 'plague.'

pes·ti·len·tial /ˌpestə'lenCHəl/ ▶ **adj.** harmful or destructive to crops or livestock: *these pestilential lichens flourish only in unpolluted air.* ■ dated of, relating to, or tending to cause infectious diseases: *you shouldn't be out on a pestilential night like this.* ■ informal annoying: *what a pestilential man!*
– DERIVATIVES **pes·ti·len·tial·ly** adv.

pes·tle /'pestl, 'pesəl/ ▶ **n.** a heavy tool with a rounded end, used for crushing and grinding substances such as spices or drugs, usually in a mortar. ■ a mechanical device for grinding, pounding, or stamping something.
▶ **v.** [with obj.] crush or grind (a substance such as a spice or drug) with a pestle: *she measured seeds into the mortar and pestled them to powder.*
– ORIGIN Middle English: from Old French *pestel*, from Latin *pistillum*, from *pist-* 'pounded,' from the verb *pinsere*.

pes·to /'pestō/ ▶ **n.** a sauce of crushed basil leaves, pine nuts, garlic, Parmesan cheese, and olive oil, typically served with pasta.
– ORIGIN Italian, from *pestare* 'pound, crush.'

PET /pet/ ▶ **abbr.** ■ polyethylene terephthalate. ■ positron emission tomography, used esp. for brain scans.

pet[1] /pet/ ▶ **n.** a domestic or tamed animal or bird kept for companionship or pleasure and treated with care and affection: *the pony was a family pet* | [as modifier] *a pet cat.* ■ a person treated with special favor, esp. in a way that others regard as unfair: *Liz was teacher's pet* | [as modifier] *his pet performer was Hollander.* ■ used as an affectionate form of address: *don't cry, pet, it's all right.*
▶ **adj.** ■ denoting a thing that one devotes special attention to or feels particularly strongly about: *another of her pet projects was the arts center* | *my pet hate is bad telephone manners.*
▶ **v.** (**pets, petting, petted**) [with obj.] stroke or pat (an animal) affectionately: *the cats came to be petted.* ■ treat (someone) with affection or favoritism; pamper: *I was cosseted and petted and never shouted at.* ■ [no obj.] engage in sexually stimulating caressing and touching: *couples necking and petting in the cars.*
– DERIVATIVES **pet·ter** n.
– ORIGIN early 16th cent. (as a noun; originally Scots and northern English): of unknown origin.

pet[2] ▶ **n.** [in sing.] a fit of sulking or ill humor: *Mother's in a pet.*
– ORIGIN late 16th cent.: of unknown origin.

Pet. ▶ **abbr.** Bible Peter.

PETA /pētə/ ▶ **abbr.** People for the Ethical Treatment of Animals.

peta- ▶ **comb. form** (used in units of measurement) denoting a factor of 10^{15}: *petabytes.*
– ORIGIN from *pe(n)ta-* (see PENTA-), based on the supposed analogy of *tera-* and *tetra-*.

pe·ta·byte (abbr.: **PB**) ▶ **n.** 2^{50} bytes; 1024 terabytes, or a million gigabytes.

Pé·tain /pe'ten, pā'taN/, Philippe (1856–1951), French general and statesman; head of state 1940–44; full name *Henri Philippe Omer Pétain*. In 1940, he established the French government at Vichy (effectively a puppet regime for the Third Reich) until the German occupation in 1942. After the war, his death sentence for collaboration was commuted to life imprisonment.

pet·al /'petl/ ▶ **n.** each of the segments of the corolla of a flower, which are modified leaves and are typically colored.
– DERIVATIVES **pet·al·ine** /'petlˌīn, -in/ adj., **pet·aled** adj. [in combination] *pink-petaled trailing phlox*, **pet·al·like** /-ˌlīk/ adj., **pet·al·oid** /-ˌoid/ adj.
– ORIGIN early 18th cent.: from modern Latin *petalum* (in late Latin 'metal plate'), from Greek *petalon* 'leaf,' neuter (used as a noun) of *petalos* 'outspread.'

Pet·a·lu·ma /ˌpetl'ōōmə/ a city in northwestern California, north of San Francisco; pop. 54,666 (est. 2008).

pé·tanque /ˌpā'täNGk/ ▶ **n.** a lawn game similar to boules, played chiefly in Provence.
– ORIGIN French, from Provençal *pèd tanco*, literally 'foot fixed (to the ground),' describing the start position.

pe·tard /pi'tärd/ ▶ **n.** historical a small bomb made of a metal or wooden box filled with powder, used to blast down a door or to make a hole in a wall. ■ a kind of firework that explodes with a sharp report.
– PHRASES **hoist with** (or **by**) **one's own petard** have one's plans to cause trouble for others backfire on one. [from Shakespeare's *Hamlet* (III. iv. 207); *hoist* is in the sense 'lifted and removed,' past participle of dialect *hoise* (see HOIST).]
– ORIGIN mid 16th cent.: from French *pétard*, from *péter* 'break wind.'

pet·a·sus /'petəsəs/ (also **petasos**) ▶ **n.** a hat with a low crown and broad brim, worn in ancient Greece. ■ Greek Mythology a winged hat of such a type worn by the god Hermes.
– ORIGIN via Latin from Greek *petasos*.

pet·a·watt /'petəˌwät/ ▶ **n.** a quadrillion (10^{15}) watts: *each year warm-core eddies shed southward the equivalent of about 0.3 petawatt of power.*

pet·cock /'petˌkäk/ ▶ **n.** a small valve, esp. in the pipe of a steam boiler or cylinder of a steam engine for drainage or testing.

pe·te·chi·a /pə'tēkēə/ ▶ **n.** (pl. **petechiae** /-kēˌē/) Medicine a small red or purple spot caused by bleeding into the skin.
– DERIVATIVES **pe·te·chi·al** /-kēəl/ adj.
– ORIGIN late 18th cent.: modern Latin, from Italian *petecchia*, denoting a freckle or spot on the face, from Latin *petigo* 'scab, eruption.'

Pe·ter /'pētər/ ▶ **n.** either of two books of the New Testament, epistles ascribed to St. Peter.

pe·ter[1] /'pētər/ ▶ **v.** [no obj.] decrease or fade gradually before coming to an end: *the storm had petered out.*
– ORIGIN early 19th cent.: of unknown origin.

pe·ter[2] ▶ **n.** informal a man's penis.
– ORIGIN late Middle English: from the given name *Peter*, applied in many transferred uses. The current sense dates from the early 20th cent.

Pe·ter I (1672–1725), tsar of Russia 1682–1725; known as **Peter the Great**. Peter modernized his armed forces and expanded his territory in the Baltic. His extensive administrative reforms were instrumental in transforming Russia into a significant European power. In 1703, he made the new city of St. Petersburg his capital.

Pe·ter, St. an apostle; born *Simon*. Peter ("stone") is the name given him by Jesus, signifying the rock on which he would establish his church. He is regarded by Roman Catholics as the first bishop of the Church at Rome, where he is said to have been martyred *c.* AD 67 and is often represented as the keeper of the door of heaven. Feast day, June 29.

Pe·ter·bor·ough /'pētərˌbərō/ an industrial city in east central England; pop. 153,000 (est. 2009).

pe·ter·man /'pētərmən/ ▶ **n.** (pl. **petermen**) archaic a safecracker.
– ORIGIN early 20th cent.: from slang *peter* 'a safe' + MAN.

Pe·ter Pan /ˌpētər 'pan/ the hero of J. M. Barrie's play of the same name (1904), a boy with magical powers who never grew up. ■ (as noun **a Peter Pan**) a person, esp. a male who retains youthful features, or who is immature.

Pe·ter Pan col·lar ▶ **n.** a flat collar with rounded ends that meet at the front.

Pe·ter Prin·ci·ple the principle that members of a hierarchy are promoted until they reach the level at which they are no longer competent.
– ORIGIN 1960s: named after Laurence J. *Peter* (1919–90), the American educationalist who put forward the theory.

Pe·ters·burg /ˈpētərzˌbərg/ an industrial and commercial city in southeastern Virginia, south of Richmond, scene of heavy fighting during the Civil War; pop. 32,916 (est. 2008).

pe·ter·sham /ˈpētərˌsHam, -sHəm/ ▶ **n.** a corded tape used for stiffening, esp. in the making of belts and hatbands.
– ORIGIN early 19th cent.: named after Lord *Petersham* (1790–1851), English army officer.

Pe·ter·son[1] /ˈpētərsən/, Oscar (Emmanuel) (1925–2007), Canadian jazz pianist and composer. He often appeared with Ella Fitzgerald.

Pe·ter·son[2], Roger Tory (1908–96), US ornithologist and artist. Peterson produced his first book for identifying birds in the field in 1934, introducing the concept of illustrating similar birds in similar postures with their differences highlighted. The format of his work has become the standard in field guides.

Pe·ter's pence ▶ **plural n. 1** historical an annual tax of one penny from every English householder having land of a certain value, paid to the papal see at Rome from Anglo-Saxon times until it was discontinued in 1534 after Henry VIII's break with Rome.
2 a voluntary payment by Roman Catholics to the papal treasury, made since 1860.
– ORIGIN named after St. *Peter*, the first pope (see PETER, ST.).

Pe·ters pro·jec·tion a world map projection in which areas are shown in correct proportion at the expense of distorted shape, using a rectangular decimal grid to replace latitude and longitude. It was devised in 1973 to be a fairer representation of equatorial (i.e., mainly developing) countries, whose area is underrepresented by the usual projections such as Mercator's.
– ORIGIN named after Arno *Peters* (1916–2002), German historian.

Pe·ter the Her·mit (*c.*1050–1115), French monk. His preaching on the First Crusade rallied thousands of peasants throughout Europe to journey to the Holy Land.

pé·til·lant /ˌpātiˈyän/ ▶ **adj.** (of wine) slightly sparkling.
– ORIGIN French.

pet·i·ole /ˈpetēˌōl/ ▶ **n.** Botany the stalk that joins a leaf to a stem; leafstalk. ■ Zoology a slender stalk between two structures, esp. that between the abdomen and thorax of a wasp or ant.
– DERIVATIVES **pet·i·o·lar** /ˌpetēˈōlər/ **adj.**, **pet·i·o·late** /ˈpetēəˌlāt/ **adj.**
– ORIGIN mid 18th cent.: from French *pétiole*, from Latin *petiolus* 'little foot, stalk.'

Pe·ti·pa /ˈpetēˌpä, pətēˈpä/, Marius (Ivanovich) (1818–1910), French ballet dancer and choreographer, resident in Russia from 1847. He choreographed more than 50 ballets, working with Tchaikovsky on *Sleeping Beauty* (1890) and *The Nutcracker* (1892).

pet·it /ˈpetē/ ▶ **adj.** Law (of a crime) petty: *petit larceny*.
– ORIGIN late Middle English (in the sense 'small or insignificant'): from Old French, 'small'; the same word as PETTY, with retention of the French spelling.

pet·it batte·ment /pəˈtē ˌbatmä/ ▶ **n.** Ballet a movement in which one leg is extended and lightly moved forward and backward from the ankle of the supporting leg.

pet·it bour·geois /ˈpetē bo͝orˈzHwä, pəˈtē/ ▶ **adj.** of or characteristic of the lower middle class, esp. with reference to a perceived conventionalism and conservatism: *the frail facade of petit bourgeois respectability*.
▶ **n.** (pl. **petits bourgeois** pronunc. **same**) a member of the lower middle class, esp. when perceived as conventional and conservative.
– ORIGIN French, literally 'little citizen.'

pe·tite /pəˈtēt/ ▶ **adj.** (of a woman) having a small and attractively dainty build: *she was petite and vivacious*.
– ORIGIN late 18th cent.: French, feminine of *petit* 'small.'

pe·tite bour·geoi·sie /pəˈtēt ˌbo͝orzHwäˈzē/ (also **petit bourgeoisie**) ▶ **n.** (**the petite bourgeoisie**) [treated as sing. or pl.] the lower middle class.
– ORIGIN French, literally 'lesser citizenry.'

pe·tit four /ˈpetē ˈfôr/ ▶ **n.** (pl. **petits fours** /ˈpetē ˈfôrz/ or **petit fours** /ˈpetē ˈfôrz/) a very small fancy cake, cookie, or confection, typically made with marzipan and traditionally served after a meal.
– ORIGIN French, literally 'little oven.'

pe·ti·tion /pəˈtisHən/ ▶ **n.** a formal written request, typically one signed by many people, appealing to authority with respect to a particular cause: *she was asked to sign a petition against plans to build on the local playing fields*. ■ an appeal or request, esp. a solemn or humble one to a deity or a superior. ■ Law an application to a court for a writ, judicial action in a suit, etc.: *a divorce petition*.
▶ **v.** [with obj.] make or present a formal request to (an authority) with respect to a particular cause: *Americans who moved west **petitioned** Congress **for** admission to the Union as states* | [with obj. and infinitive] *leaders petitioned the government to hold free elections soon*. ■ make a solemn or humble appeal to (a figure of authority): *Russell **petitioned** her father **for** her hand in marriage*. ■ Law make a formal application to (a court) for a writ, judicial action in a suit, etc.: *the custodial parent **petitioned** the court **for** payment of the arrears* | [no obj.] *the process allows both spouses to jointly **petition for** divorce*.
– DERIVATIVES **pe·ti·tion·ar·y** /-ˌnerē/ **adj.**, **pe·ti·tion·er** **n.**
– ORIGIN Middle English: from Latin *petitio(n-)*, from *petit-* 'aimed at, sought, laid claim to,' from the verb *petere*.

pe·ti·ti·o prin·ci·pi·i /pəˈtisHēˌō prinˈsipēˌī/ ▶ **n.** Logic a fallacy in which a conclusion is taken for granted in the premises; begging the question.
– ORIGIN Latin, literally 'laying claim to a principle.'

pe·tit je·té /pəˈtē zHəˈtā/ ▶ **n.** Ballet a jump in which a dancer brushes one leg out to the side in the air then brings it back in again and lands on it with the other leg lifted and bent behind the body.

pe·tit mal /ˈpetē ˈmäl/ ▶ **n.** a mild form of epilepsy characterized by brief spells of unconsciousness without loss of posture. Compare with GRAND MAL. ■ an epileptic fit of this kind.
– ORIGIN late 19th cent.: from French, literally 'little sickness.'

pe·tit point /ˈpetē ˌpoint/ ▶ **n.** a type of embroidery on canvas, consisting of small, diagonal, adjacent stitches.
– ORIGIN late 19th cent.: from French, literally 'little stitch.'

pe·tits pois /peˈtē ˈpwä, pəˈtē ˈpwä/ ▶ **plural n.** young peas that are picked before they are grown to full size; small, fine peas.
– ORIGIN French, literally 'small peas.'

pet name ▶ **n.** a name that is used instead of someone's usual first name to express fondness or familiarity.

petr. ▶ **abbr.** petrology.

Pe·tra /ˈpetrə, ˈpē-/ an ancient city in southwestern Asia, in present-day Jordan. The city is accessible only through narrow gorges. Its extensive ruins include temples and tombs hewn from the rose-red sandstone cliffs.

Pe·trarch /ˈpēträrk, ˈpet-/ (1304–74), Italian poet; Italian name *Francesco Petrarca*. His reputation is chiefly based on the *Canzoniere* (*c.*1351–53), a sonnet sequence in praise of a woman he calls Laura. He was also an important figure in the rediscovery of Greek and Latin literature.

Pe·trar·chan /pəˈträrkən/ ▶ **adj.** denoting a sonnet of the kind used by the Italian poet Petrarch, with an octave rhyming *abbaabba*, and a sestet typically rhyming *cdcdcd* or *cdecde*.

pet·rel /ˈpetrəl/ ▶ **n.** a seabird related to the shearwaters, typically flying far from land. ● Order Procellariiformes, in particular the families Procellariidae (e.g., the **giant petrel** and **pintado petrel**) or Hydrobatidae (the **storm petrels**). See also DIVING PETREL.
– ORIGIN early 17th cent.: associated with St. Peter, from the bird's habit of flying low with legs dangling, giving the appearance of walking on the water (see Matt. 14:30).

pe·tri dish /ˈpētrē/ ▶ **n.** a shallow, circular, transparent dish with a flat lid, used for the culture of microorganisms.
– ORIGIN late 19th cent.: named after Julius R. *Petri* (1852–1922), German bacteriologist.

Pe·trie /ˈpetrē, ˈpētrē/, Sir Flinders (1853–1942), English archaeologist and Egyptologist; full name *William Matthew Flinders Petrie*. He began excavating the Great Pyramid in 1880. He established the system of sequence dating by which sites are excavated layer by layer and historical chronology is determined by the dating of artifacts found *in situ*.

pet·ri·fac·tion /ˌpetrəˈfaksHən/ ▶ **n.** another term for PETRIFICATION.

pet·ri·fi·ca·tion /ˌpetrəfiˈkāsHən/ ▶ **n.** the process by which organic matter exposed to minerals over a long period is turned into a stony substance. ■ a state of extreme fear, making someone unable to move: *his heavy footfalls served to spur Paul out of his petrification*. ■ an organic object that has been turned to stone.

pet·ri·fied /ˈpetrəˌfīd/ ▶ **adj. 1** so frightened that one is unable to move; terrified: *the petrified child clung to her mother*.
2 (of organic matter) changed into a stony substance; ossified: *petrified wood*.

Pet·ri·fied For·est a highland area in east central Arizona, noted for its agates and plant fossils, now a national park.

pet·ri·fy /ˈpetrəˌfī/ ▶ **v.** (**petrifies**, **petrifying**, **petrified**) [with obj.] **1** make (someone) so frightened that they are unable to move or think: *his icy controlled quietness petrified her*.
2 change (organic matter) into a stony concretion by encrusting or replacing its original substance with a calcareous, siliceous, or other mineral deposit.
– ORIGIN late Middle English: from French *pétrifier*, from medieval Latin *petrificare*, from Latin *petra* 'rock,' from Greek.

Pe·trine /ˈpēˌtrīn/ ▶ **adj. 1** Christian Theology of or relating to St. Peter or his writings or teachings. ■ of or relating to the authority of the pope over the Church, in his role as the successor of St. Peter.
2 of or relating to Peter I of Russia: *the Petrine reforms of the early 18th century*.

pet·riss·age /ˌpetriˈsäzH/ ▶ **n.** a massage technique that involves kneading the body.
– ORIGIN late 19th cent.: French *pétrissage*, from *pétrir* 'to knead.'

petro- ▶ **comb. form 1** of rock; relating to rocks: *petrography*.
2 relating to petroleum: *petrodollar*.
– ORIGIN Sense 1 from Greek *petros* 'stone,' *petra* 'rock'; sense 2 from PETROLEUM.

pet·ro·chem·i·cal /ˌpetrōˈkemikəl/ ▶ **adj.** relating to or denoting substances obtained by the refining and processing of petroleum or natural gas: *a huge petrochemical works producing plastics*. ■ of or relating to petrochemistry.
▶ **n.** (usu. **petrochemicals**) a chemical obtained from petroleum and natural gas.

pet·ro·chem·is·try /ˌpetrōˈkeməstrē/ ▶ **n.**
1 the branch of chemistry concerned with the composition and formation of rocks (as distinct from minerals and ore deposits).
2 the branch of chemistry concerned with petroleum and natural gas, and with their refining and processing.

pet·ro·dol·lar /ˈpetrōˌdälər/ ▶ **n.** a notional unit of currency earned by a country from the export of petroleum: *petrodollars were pouring into the kingdom*.

petrog. ▶ **abbr.** petrography.

pet·ro·glyph /ˈpetrəˌglif/ ▶ **n.** a rock carving, esp. a prehistoric one.
– ORIGIN late 19th cent.: from PETRO- 'rock' + Greek *gluphē* 'carving.'

Pet·ro·grad /ˈpetrəˌgrad, pyitrəˈgrät/ former name (1914–24) for **ST. PETERSBURG**.

pe·trog·ra·phy /pəˈträgrəfē/ ▶ **n.** the branch of science concerned with the description and classification of rocks, esp. by microscopic study. Compare with PETROLOGY.
– DERIVATIVES **pe·trog·ra·pher** **n.**, **pet·ro·graph·ic** /ˌpetrəˈgrafik/ **adj.**, **pet·ro·graph·i·cal** /ˌpetrəˈgrafikəl/ **adj.**

pet·rol /ˈpetrəl/ ▶ **n.** British term for GASOLINE.
– ORIGIN late 19th cent.: from French *pétrole*, from medieval Latin *petroleum* (see PETROLEUM).

petrol. ▶ **abbr.** petrology.

pet·ro·la·tum /ˌpetrəˈlātəm/ ▶ **n.** another term for PETROLEUM JELLY.
– ORIGIN late 19th cent.: modern Latin, from PETROL + the Latin suffix *-atum*.

pe·tro·le·um /pəˈtrōlēəm/ ▶ **n.** a liquid mixture of hydrocarbons that is present in certain rock strata and can be extracted and refined to produce fuels including gasoline, kerosene, and diesel oil; oil.
– ORIGIN late Middle English: from medieval Latin, from Latin *petra* 'rock' (from Greek) + Latin *oleum* 'oil.'

pe·tro·le·um jel·ly ▶ **n.** a translucent jelly consisting of a mixture of hydrocarbons, used as a lubricant or ointment.

pet·ro·lif·er·ous /ˌpetrəˈlifərəs/ ▶ **adj.** (of rock) yielding or containing petroleum.

pe·trol·o·gy /pəˈträləjē/ ▶ **n.** the branch of science concerned with the origin, small-scale structure,

PRONUNCIATION KEY ə *ago, up*; ər *over, fur*; a *hat*; ā *ate*; ä *car*; e *let*; ē *see*; i *fit*; ī *by*; NG *sing*; ō *go*; ô *law, for*; oi *toy*; o͝o *good*; o͞o *goo*; ou *out*; TH *thin*; T͟H *then*; ZH *vision*

and composition of rocks. Compare with **LITHOLOGY**, **PETROGRAPHY**.
– DERIVATIVES **pet·ro·log·ic** /ˌpetrəˈläjik/ **adj.**, **pet·ro·log·i·cal** /ˌpetrəˈläjikəl/ **adj.**, **pe·trol·o·gist** /-jist/ **n.**

Pet·ro·nas Tow·ers /peˈtrōnəs/ a building in Kuala Lumpur consisting of two twin towers linked by a bridge at the 41st floor. At 1,482 feet (452 m) in height it was the world's tallest building when it was completed in 1998. The building belongs to Petronas, the Malaysian national oil company.

Petronas Towers

Pe·tro·ni·us /piˈtrōnēəs/, Gaius (died AD 66), Roman writer; known as **Petronius Arbiter**. He is generally accepted as the author of the *Satyricon*, a work in prose and verse satirizing the excesses of Roman society.

Pet·ro·pav·lovsk /ˌpetrəˈpavlôfsk, pyitrəˈpävləfsk/ **1** (also **Petropavlovsk-Kamchatsky**) a Russian fishing port and naval base on the eastern coast of the Kamchatka peninsula in eastern Siberia; pop. 245,000.
2 (also **Petropavl** /ˌpetrəˈpävəl/) an industrial and commercial city in northern Kazakhstan, on the Trans-Siberian Railroad; pop. 190,100 (est. 2006).

pet·ro·phys·ics /ˌpetrōˈfiziks/ ▶ **plural n.** [treated as sing.] the branch of geology concerned with the physical properties and behavior of rocks.
– DERIVATIVES **pet·ro·phys·i·cal** /-ˈfizikəl/ **adj.**, **pet·ro·phys·i·cist** /-ˈfizəsist/ **n.**

pe·tro·sal /pəˈtrōsəl/ Anatomy ▶ **n.** the dense part of the temporal bone at the base of the skull, surrounding the inner ear.
▶ **adj.** relating to or denoting this part of the temporal bone, or the nerves that pass through it.
– ORIGIN mid 18th cent.: from Latin *petrosus* 'stony, rocky' (from *petra* 'rock') + **-AL**.

P

pet·rous /ˈpetrəs/ ▶ **adj.** Anatomy another term for **PETROSAL**.
– ORIGIN late Middle English: from Latin *petrosus* 'stony, rocky,' from *petra* 'rock,' from Greek.

Pet·ro·za·vodsk /ˌpetrəzəˈvätsk, pyitrəzəˈvôtsk/ a city in northwestern Russia, on Lake Onega, capital of the republic of Karelia; pop. 268,800 (est. 2008).

pe tsai /bä ˈtsī/ ▶ **n.** Chinese cabbage of a pale variety that resembles lettuce.
– ORIGIN late 18th cent.: from Chinese (Cantonese dialect) *báicài*, literally 'white vegetable.'

Pet·sa·mo /ˈpetsəˌmō/ former name (1920–44) for **PECHENGA**.

pet sit·ting (also **petsitting**) ▶ **n.** the activity of taking care of pets for absent owners: *an article on how to make money petsitting* | [as modifier] *a pet-sitting business.*
– DERIVATIVES **pet-sit v.** (**pet sits**, **pet sitting**, **pet sat**), **pet-sit·ter n.**

pet·ti·coat /ˈpetēˌkōt/ ▶ **n.** a woman's light, loose undergarment hanging from the shoulders or the waist, worn under a skirt or dress. ■ [as modifier] informal, often derogatory used to denote female control of something regarded as more commonly dominated by men: *he was in danger of succumbing to the petticoat government of Mary and Sarah.*
– DERIVATIVES **pet·ti·coat·ed adj.**
– ORIGIN late Middle English: from *petty coat*, literally 'small coat.'

pet·ti·fog /ˈpetēˌfôg, ˈpetēˌfäg/ ▶ **v.** (**pettifogs, pettifogging, pettifogged**) [no obj.] rare quibble about petty points. ■ archaic practice legal deception or trickery.
– DERIVATIVES **pet·ti·fog·ger·y** /ˌpetēˈfôgərē, -ˈfäg-/ **n.**
– ORIGIN early 17th cent.: back-formation from **PETTIFOGGER**.

pet·ti·fog·ger /ˈpetēˌfôgər, -ˌfäg-/ ▶ **n.** archaic an inferior legal practitioner, esp. one who deals with petty cases or employs dubious practices.
– ORIGIN mid 16th cent.: from **PETTY** + obsolete *fogger* 'underhanded dealer,' probably from *Fugger*, the name of a family of merchants in Augsburg, Germany, in the 15th and 16th centuries.

pet·ti·fog·ging /ˈpetēˌfôgiNG, -ˌfäg-/ ▶ **adj.** placing undue emphasis on petty details: *I'm working on the broad business vision here, not pettifogging little details* | *pettifogging attorneys were the bane of civil society.*

pet·ting zoo ▶ **n.** a zoo at which visitors, esp. children, may handle and feed the animals.

pet·tish /ˈpetisH/ ▶ **adj.** (of a person or their behavior) childishly bad-tempered and petulant: *he comes across in his journal entries as spoiled and pettish.*
– DERIVATIVES **pet·tish·ly adv.**, **pet·tish·ness n.**

Pet·ty /ˈpetē/, Richard (1937–), US race car driver 1960–92. The first stock car driver to achieve career winnings of $1 million, he has 200 career wins and was the first motor sportsman to receive the Medal of Freedom (1992). Motorsports Hall of Fame of America (1989).

pet·ty /ˈpetē/ ▶ **adj.** (**pettier, pettiest**) **1** of little importance; trivial: *the petty divisions of party politics.* ■ (of behavior) characterized by an undue concern for trivial matters, esp. in a small-minded or spiteful way: *he was prone to petty revenge on friends and family.*
2 [attrib.] of secondary or lesser importance, rank, or scale; minor: *a petty official.* ■ Law (of a crime) of lesser importance: *petty theft.* Compare with **GRAND**.
– DERIVATIVES **pet·ti·ly** /ˈpetəlē/ **adv.**, **pet·ti·ness** /ˈpetēnəs/ **n.**
– ORIGIN late Middle English (in the sense 'small in size'): from a phonetic spelling of the pronunciation of French *petit* 'small.' Compare with **PETIT**.

pet·ty bour·geois ▶ **n.** another term for **PETIT BOURGEOIS**.

pet·ty bour·geoi·sie ▶ **n.** another term for **PETITE BOURGEOISIE**.

pet·ty cash ▶ **n.** an accessible store of money kept by an organization for expenditure on small items.

pet·ty lar·ce·ny ▶ **n.** Law theft of personal property having a value less than a legally specified amount.

pet·ty of·fi·cer ▶ **n.** a noncommissioned officer in a navy, in particular an NCO in the US Navy or Coast Guard ranking above seaman and below chief petty officer.

pet·ty trea·son ▶ **n.** see **TREASON**.

pet·u·lance /ˈpecHələns/ ▶ **n.** the quality of being childishly sulky or bad-tempered: *a slight degree of petulance had crept into his voice.*

pet·u·lant /ˈpecHələnt/ ▶ **adj.** (of a person or their manner) childishly sulky or bad-tempered: *he was moody and petulant* | *a petulant shake of the head.*
– DERIVATIVES **pet·u·lant·ly adv.**
– ORIGIN late 16th cent. (in the sense 'immodest'): from French *pétulant*, from Latin *petulant-* 'impudent' (related to *petere* 'aim at, seek'). The current sense (mid 18th cent.) is influenced by **PETTISH**.

pe·tu·nia /pəˈt(y)o͞onyə/ ▶ **n.** a plant of the nightshade family with brightly colored funnel-shaped flowers. Native to tropical America, it has been widely developed as an ornamental hybrid, with numerous varieties. ● *Petunia* × hybrida, family Solanaceae.
– ORIGIN modern Latin, from French *petun*, from Guarani *petyn* 'tobacco' (to which these plants are related).

pe·tun·tse /pəˈto͝ontse/ ▶ **n.** a type of weathered volcanic tuff used to make Chinese porcelain.
– ORIGIN early 18th cent.: from Chinese (Mandarin dialect) *báidūnzi*, from *bái* 'white' + *dūn* 'stone' + the suffix *-zi*.

pew /pyo͞o/ ▶ **n.** a long bench with a back, placed in rows in the main part of some churches to seat the congregation. ■ an enclosure or compartment containing a number of seats, used in some churches to seat a particular worshiper or group of worshipers. ■ (**the pews**) the congregation of a church: *the pews settled down.*
– ORIGIN late Middle English (originally denoting a raised, enclosed place in a church, provided for particular worshipers): from Old French *puye* 'balcony,' from Latin *podia*, plural of *podium* 'elevated place.'

pe·wee /ˈpēˌwē/ (also **peewee**) ▶ **n.** a North American tyrant flycatcher with dark olive-gray plumage and a call that sounds like "pee-a-wee." ● Genus *Contopus*, family Tyrannidae: several species.
– ORIGIN late 18th cent.: imitative.

pe·wit /ˈpēwit, ˈpyo͞oit/ (also **peewit**) ▶ **n.** the northern lapwing (see **LAPWING**).
– ORIGIN early 16th cent.: imitative of the bird's call.

pew·ter /ˈpyo͞otər/ ▶ **n.** a gray alloy of tin with copper and antimony (formerly, tin and lead). ■ utensils made of this: *the kitchen pewter.* ■ a shade of bluish or silver gray: *looking back at that pewter sky.*
– DERIVATIVES **pew·ter·er n.**
– ORIGIN Middle English: from Old French *peutre*, of unknown origin.

Pey·er's patch·es /ˈpīərz/ ▶ **plural n.** Anatomy the numerous areas of lymphoid tissue in the wall of the small intestine that are involved in the development of immunity to antigens present there.
– ORIGIN mid 19th cent.: named after Johann K. *Peyer* (1653–1712), Swiss anatomist.

pe·yo·te /pāˈyōtē/ ▶ **n.** a small, soft, blue-green, spineless cactus, native to Mexico and the southern US. Also called **MESCAL**. ● *Lophophora williamsii*, family Cactaceae. ■ a hallucinogenic drug prepared from this cactus, containing mescaline.
– ORIGIN mid 19th cent.: from Latin American Spanish, from Nahuatl *peyotl*.

pe·yo·te but·tons ▶ **plural n.** the disk-shaped dried tops of the peyote cactus, eaten or chewed for their hallucinogenic effects. Also called **MESCAL BUTTONS**.

pf ▶ **abbr.** ■ perfect. ■ pfennig. ■ pianoforte; piano. ■ preferred (stock). ■ proof.

Pf. ▶ **abbr.** pfennig.

Pfc. ▶ **abbr.** Private First Class.

PFD ▶ **abbr.** personal flotation device, a life jacket or similar buoyancy aid.

pfd. ▶ **abbr.** preferred (stock).

pfen·nig /ˈfenig/ ▶ **n.** a monetary unit of Germany (until the introduction of the euro), equal to one hundredth of a mark.
– ORIGIN from German *Pfennig*; related to **PENNY**.

pfft /ft/ ▶ **exclam.** used to represent a dull abrupt sound as of a slight impact or explosion.
– PHRASES **go pfft** informal fail to work properly or at all.

pfg. ▶ **abbr.** pfennig.

pfu·i /ˈfo͞oē/ ▶ **exclam.** variant spelling of **PHOOEY**.
– ORIGIN mid 19th cent.: from German.

PG ▶ **abbr.** ■ parental guidance suggested, a rating in the Voluntary Movie Rating System indicating that some material may not be suitable for children. ■ paying guest.

pg. ▶ **abbr.** page.

PG-13 ▶ **symbol** parents strongly cautioned, a rating in the Voluntary Movie Rating System indicating that some material may be inappropriate for children under 13.

PGA ▶ **abbr.** Professional Golfers' Association (of America).

PH (also **P.H.**) ▶ **abbr.** ■ Public Health. ■ Purple Heart.

pH ▶ **n.** Chemistry a figure expressing the acidity or alkalinity of a solution on a logarithmic scale on which 7 is neutral, lower values are more acid, and higher values more alkaline. The pH is equal to $-\log_{10} c$, where *c* is the hydrogen ion concentration in moles per liter.
– ORIGIN early 20th cent.: from *p* representing German *Potenz* 'power' + H, the symbol for hydrogen.

ph. ▶ **abbr.** ■ phase. ■ phone.

PHA ▶ **abbr.** Public Housing Administration.

pha·ce·li·a /fəˈsēlēə/ ▶ **n.** a herbaceous American plant with clustered blue, violet, or white flowers. ● Genus *Phacelia*, family Hydrophyllaceae.
– ORIGIN modern Latin, from Greek *phakelos* 'cluster.'

Phae·a·cian /fēˈāsHən/ ▶ **n.** (in the *Odyssey*) an inhabitant of Scheria (Corfu), whose people were noted for their hedonism.
– ORIGIN from Latin *Phaeacia*, Greek *Phaiakia*, the name of the island of Scheria, + **-AN**.

Phae·dra /ˈfēdrə, ˈfedrə/ Greek Mythology the wife of Theseus. She fell in love with her stepson Hippolytus, who rejected her, whereupon she hanged herself, leaving behind a letter that accused him of raping her. Theseus would not believe his son's protestations of innocence and banished him.

Phae·o·phy·ce·ae /ˌfiəˈfisē/ Botany a class of lower plants that comprises the brown algae. ● Class Phaeophyceae, division Heterokontophyta (or phylum Heterokonta, kingdom Protista); formerly division Phaeophyta.
– ORIGIN modern Latin (plural), from Greek *phaios* 'dusky' + *phukos* 'seaweed.'

Pha·e·thon /ˈfāəTHən, -ˌTHän/ Greek Mythology the son of Helios the sun god. He asked to drive his father's solar chariot for a day, but could not control the immortal horses and the chariot plunged too near to the earth until Zeus killed Phaethon with a thunderbolt in order to save the earth from destruction.

pha·e·ton /ˈfā-itn/ ▶ **n.** historical a light, open, four-wheeled horse-drawn carriage. ■ a vintage touring car.
– ORIGIN mid 18th cent.: from French *phaéton*, via Latin from the Greek name *Phaethōn* (see PHAETHON).

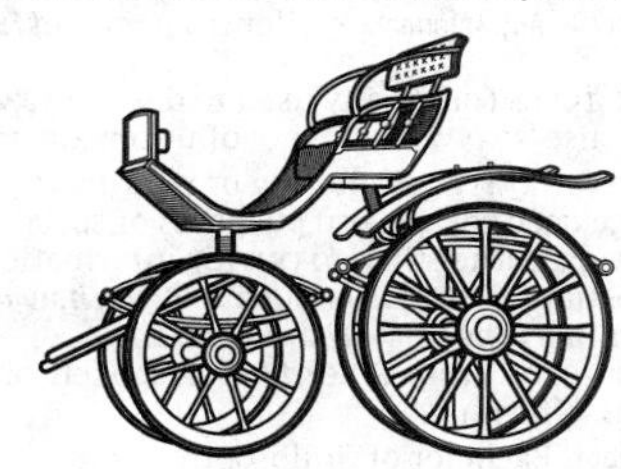
phaeton

phage /fāj/ ▶ **n.** short for BACTERIOPHAGE.

phage dis·play ▶ **n.** Biochemistry a technique for the production and screening of novel proteins and polypeptides by inserting a gene fragment into a gene responsible for the surface protein of a bacteriophage. The new protein appears in the surface coating of the phage, in which it can be manipulated and tested for biological activity.

phag·o·cyte /ˈfagəˌsīt/ ▶ **n.** Physiology a type of cell within the body capable of engulfing and absorbing bacteria and other small cells and particles.
– DERIVATIVES **phag·o·cyt·ic** /ˌfagəˈsitik/ **adj.**
– ORIGIN late 19th cent.: from Greek *phago-* 'eating' (from the verb *phagein*) + -CYTE.

phag·o·cy·to·sis /ˌfagəsīˈtōsis/ ▶ **n.** Biology the ingestion of bacteria or other material by phagocytes and ameboid protozoans.
– DERIVATIVES **phag·o·cyt·ize** /ˈfagəsiˌtīz/ **v.**, **phag·o·cy·tose** /ˈfagəˌsītōs, ˈfagəˌsītōz/ **v.**

phag·o·some /ˈfagəˌsōm/ ▶ **n.** Biology a vacuole in the cytoplasm of a cell, containing a phagocytosed particle enclosed within a part of the cell membrane.
– DERIVATIVES **phag·o·so·mal** /ˌfagəˈsōməl/ **adj.**

-phagous ▶ **comb. form** feeding or subsisting on a specified food: *coprophagous*.
– ORIGIN from Latin *-phagus*, Greek *-phagos* (from *phagein* 'eat') + -OUS.

-phagy ▶ **comb. form** denoting the practice of eating a specified food: *anthropophagy*.
– ORIGIN from Greek *-phagia*, from *phagein* 'eat.'

phal·ange /fəˈlanj, ˈfāˌlanj/ ▶ **n. 1** Anatomy another term for PHALANX (sense 2). [mid 19th cent.: back-formation from *phalanges*, plural of PHALANX.]
2 (**Phalange**) a right-wing Maronite party in Lebanon founded in 1936 by Pierre Gemayel. Compare with FALANGE. [mid 20th cent.: shortened from French *Phalanges Libanaises* 'Lebanese phalanxes.']
– DERIVATIVES **Phalangiste** /ˌfālanˈZHēst, fəˈlanjist/ **n. & adj.** (sense 2).

pha·lan·ge·al /fəˈlanjēəl/ ▶ **adj.** Anatomy of or relating to a phalanx or the phalanges.

pha·lan·ger /fəˈlanjər/ ▶ **n.** a lemurlike tree-dwelling marsupial native to Australia and New Guinea. ● Family Phalangeridae: several genera, in particular *Phalanger* and *Spilocuscus*, and including the cuscuses; the **common phalanger** is either the spotted cuscus or the gray cuscus. See also FLYING PHALANGER.
– ORIGIN late 18th cent.: from French, from Greek *phalangion* 'spider's web' (because of the webbed toes of their hind feet).

pha·lan·ges /fəˈlanjēz/ plural form of PHALANX (sense 2).

phal·an·ster·y /ˈfalənˌsterē/ ▶ **n.** (pl. **phalansteries**) a group of people living together in community, free of external regulation and holding property in common.
– ORIGIN mid 19th cent.: from French *phalanstère* (used by Fourier in his socialist scheme for the reorganization of society), blend of Latin *phalanx* 'band (of soldiers), group' and French *monastère* 'monastery.'

pha·lanx /ˈfālaNGks, ˈfal-/ ▶ **n. 1** (pl. **phalanxes**) a body of troops or police officers, standing or moving in close formation: *six hundred marchers set off, led by a phalanx of police*. ■ a group of people or things of a similar type forming a compact body: *he headed past the phalanx of waiting reporters to the line of limos*. ■ (in ancient Greece) a body of Macedonian infantry with long spears, drawn up in close order with shields overlapping.
2 (pl. **phalanges** /fəˈlanjēz, fāˈlanjēz/) Anatomy a bone of the finger or toe.
– ORIGIN mid 16th cent. (denoting a body of Macedonian infantry): via Latin from Greek.

phal·a·rope /ˈfaləˌrōp/ ▶ **n.** a small wading or swimming bird with a straight bill and lobed feet, unusual in that the female is more brightly colored than the male. ● Family Scolopacidae (subfamily Phalaropodinae): three species, **red phalarope** (*Phalaropus fulicarius*), **Wilson's phalarope** (*Steganopus tricolor*), and **northern phalarope** (*Lobipes lobatus*).
– ORIGIN late 18th cent.: from French, from modern Latin *Phalaropus*, formed irregularly from Greek *phalaris* 'coot' + *pous, pod-* 'foot.'

phal·li /ˈfalī/ plural form of PHALLUS.

phal·lic /ˈfalik/ ▶ **adj.** of, relating to, or resembling a phallus or erect penis: *a phallic symbol*. ■ Psychoanalysis of or denoting the genital phase of psychosexual development, esp. in males.
– DERIVATIVES **phal·li·cal·ly** /-(ə)lē/ **adv.**
– ORIGIN late 18th cent.: from French *phallique*, from Greek *phallikos*, from *phallos* (see PHALLUS).

phal·lo·cen·tric /ˌfalōˈsentrik/ ▶ **adj.** focused on or concerned with the phallus or penis as a symbol of male dominance: *the apartment block was an architectural monument to a phallocentric world*.
– DERIVATIVES **phal·lo·cen·tric·i·ty** /-senˈtrisitē/ **n.**, **phal·lo·cen·trism** /-sentrizəm/ **n.**

phal·loc·ra·cy /faˈläkrəsē/ ▶ **n.** (pl. **phallocracies**) a society or system that is dominated by men and in which the male sex is thought superior.
– DERIVATIVES **phal·lo·crat·ic** /ˌfaləˈkratik/ **adj.**
– ORIGIN 1970s: from Greek *phallos* 'phallus' + -CRACY.

phal·lo·plas·ty /ˈfaləˌplastē/ ▶ **n.** plastic surgery performed to construct, repair, or enlarge the penis.
– ORIGIN late 19th cent.: from Greek *phallos* 'phallus' + -PLASTY.

phal·lus /ˈfaləs/ ▶ **n.** (pl. **phalli** /ˈfalī/ or **phalluses**) a penis, esp. when erect (typically used with reference to male potency or dominance). ■ an image or representation of an erect penis, typically symbolizing fertility or potency.
– DERIVATIVES **phal·li·cism** /-ˌsizəm/ **n.**, **phal·lism** /ˈfalizəm/ **n.**
– ORIGIN early 17th cent.: via late Latin from Greek *phallos*.

phan·er·o·gam /ˈfanərəˌgam/ ▶ **n.** Botany old-fashioned term for SPERMATOPHYTE.
– DERIVATIVES **phan·er·o·gam·ic** /ˌfanərəˈgamik/ **adj.**, **phan·er·og·a·mous** /ˌfanəˈrägəməs/ **adj.**
– ORIGIN mid 19th cent.: from French *phanérogame*, from Greek *phaneros* 'visible' + *gamos* 'marriage.'

Phan·er·o·zo·ic /ˌfanərəˈzōik/ ▶ **adj.** Geology of, relating to, or denoting the eon covering the whole of time since the beginning of the Cambrian period, and comprising the Paleozoic, Mesozoic, and Cenozoic eras. Compare with CRYPTOZOIC. ■ (as noun **the Phanerozoic**) the Phanerozoic eon or the system of rocks deposited during it.

> The Phanerozoic began about 570 million years ago and covers the period in which rocks contain evidence of abundant life in the form of macroscopic mineralized fossils.

– ORIGIN late 19th cent.: from Greek *phaneros* 'visible, evident' + *zōion* 'animal' + -IC.

phan·ta·size ▶ **v.** variant spelling of FANTASIZE (restricted to archaic uses or, in modern use, to the fields of psychology and psychiatry).

phan·tasm /ˈfantazəm/ ▶ **n.** literary a figment of the imagination; an illusion or apparition: *the cart seemed to glide like a terrible phantasm*. ■ archaic an illusory likeness of something: *every phantasm of a hope was quickly nullified*.
– DERIVATIVES **phan·tas·mal** /fanˈtazməl/ **adj.**, **phan·tas·mic** /fanˈtazmik/ **adj.**
– ORIGIN Middle English (in the sense 'deceptive appearance'): from Old French *fantasme*, via Latin from Greek *phantasma*, from *phantazein* 'make visible,' from *phainein* 'to show.' The change from *f-* to *ph-* in the 16th cent. was influenced by the Latin spelling.

phan·tas·ma·go·ri·a /fanˌtazməˈgôrēə/ ▶ **n.** a sequence of real or imaginary images like those seen in a dream: *what happened next was a phantasmagoria of horror and mystery*.
– DERIVATIVES **phan·tas·ma·gor·ic** /-ˈgôrik/ **adj.**, **phan·tas·ma·gor·i·cal** /ˈgôrikəl/ **adj.**
– ORIGIN early 19th cent. (originally the name of a London exhibition (1802) of optical illusions produced chiefly by magic lantern): probably from French *fantasmagorie*, from *fantasme* 'phantasm' + a fanciful suffix.

phan·tast ▶ **n.** variant spelling of FANTAST.

phan·ta·sy ▶ **n.** variant spelling of FANTASY (restricted to archaic uses or, in modern use, to the fields of psychology and psychiatry).

phan·tom /ˈfantəm/ ▶ **n.** a ghost: *a phantom who haunts lonely roads* | figurative *the centrist and conservative parties were mere phantoms in 1943* | [as modifier] *a phantom ship*. ■ a figment of the imagination: *he tried to clear the phantoms from his head and grasp reality* | [as modifier] *the women suffered from phantom pain that no physician could ever find*. ■ [as modifier] denoting a financial arrangement or transaction that has been invented for fraudulent purposes but that does not really exist: *he diverted an estimated $1,500,000 into "phantom" bank accounts*.
– ORIGIN Middle English (also in the sense 'illusion, delusion'): from Old French *fantosme*, based on Greek *phantasma* (see PHANTASM).

phan·tom limb ▶ **n.** a sensation experienced by someone who has had a limb amputated that the limb is still there.

phar. (also **Phar.**) ▶ **abbr.** ■ pharmaceutical. ■ pharmacology. ■ pharmacopoeia. ■ pharmacy.

phar·aoh /ˈfarˌō, ˈfe(ə)rˌō, ˈfāˌrō/ ▶ **n.** a ruler in ancient Egypt.
– DERIVATIVES **phar·a·on·ic** /ˌfarāˈnik, ˌfe(ə)r-/ **adj.**
– ORIGIN Middle English: via ecclesiastical Latin from Greek *Pharaō*, from Hebrew *par'ōh*, from Egyptian *pr-'o* 'great house.'

phar·aoh ant (also **pharaoh's ant**) ▶ **n.** a small red or yellowish African ant that has established itself worldwide, living as a pest in heated buildings. ● *Monomorium pharaonis*, family Formicidae.
– ORIGIN so named because such ants were believed (erroneously) to be one of the plagues of ancient Egypt.

Phar·aoh hound ▶ **n.** a hunting dog of a short-coated tan-colored breed with large, pointed ears.
– ORIGIN 1960s: so named because the breed is said to have been first introduced to Malta and Gozo (a Maltese island) by Phoenician sailors.

Phar.B. ▶ **abbr.** Bachelor of Pharmacy.

Phar.D. ▶ **abbr.** Doctor of Pharmacy.

Phar·i·see /ˈfarəsē/ ▶ **n.** a member of an ancient Jewish sect, distinguished by strict observance of the traditional and written law, and commonly held to have pretensions to superior sanctity. ■ a self-righteous person; a hypocrite.

> The Pharisees are mentioned only by Josephus and in the New Testament. Unlike the Sadducees, who tried to apply Mosaic law strictly, the Pharisees allowed some freedom of interpretation. Although in the Gospels they are represented as the chief opponents of Jesus, they seem to have been less hostile than the Sadducees to the nascent Church, with which they shared belief in the Resurrection.

– DERIVATIVES **Phar·i·sa·ic** /ˌfarəˈsāik/ **adj.**, **Phar·i·sa·i·cal** /ˌfarəˈsāikəl/ **adj.**, **Phar·i·sa·ism** /-sāˌizəm/ **n.**
– ORIGIN Old English *fariseus*, via ecclesiastical Latin from Greek *Pharisaios*, from Aramaic *prišayyā* 'separated ones' (related to Hebrew *pārūš* 'separated').

pharm. ▶ **abbr.** ■ pharmaceutical. ■ pharmacology. ■ pharmacopoeia. ■ pharmacy.

P

Phar.M. ▶ **abbr.** Master of Pharmacy.

phar·ma /ˈfärmə/ ▶ **n. 1** (often in phrase **big pharma**) pharmaceutical companies collectively as a sector of industry.
2 a pharmaceutical company.

phar·ma·ceu·ti·cal /ˌfärməˈsōōtikəl/ ▶ **adj.** of or relating to medicinal drugs, or their preparation, use, or sale.
▶ **n.** (usu. **pharmaceuticals**) a compound manufactured for use as a medicinal drug. ■ (**pharmaceuticals**) companies manufacturing medicinal drugs.
– DERIVATIVES **phar·ma·ceu·ti·cal·ly** /-(ə)lē/ **adv.**, **phar·ma·ceu·tics** /-sōōtiks/ **n.**
– ORIGIN mid 17th cent.: via late Latin from Greek *pharmakeutikos* (from *pharmakeutēs* 'druggist,' from *pharmakon* 'drug') + -AL.

phar·ma·cist /ˈfärməsist/ ▶ **n.** a person who is professionally qualified to prepare and dispense medicinal drugs.

pharmaco- ▶ **comb. form** relating to drugs: *pharmacogenetics*.
– ORIGIN from Greek *pharmakon* 'drug, medicine.'

phar·ma·co·dy·nam·ics /ˌfärməkōdīˈnamiks/ ▶ **plural n.** [treated as sing.] the branch of pharmacology concerned with the effects of drugs and the mechanism of their action.
– DERIVATIVES **phar·ma·co·dy·nam·ic** /-mik/ **adj.**

phar·ma·co·ge·net·ics /ˌfärməkōjəˈnetiks/ ▶ **plural n.** [treated as sing.] the branch of pharmacology concerned with the effect of genetic factors on reactions to drugs.

PRONUNCIATION KEY ə *ago, up*; ər *over, fur*; a *hat*; ā *ate*; ä *car*; e *let*; ē *see*; i *fit*; ī *by*; NG *sing*; ō *go*; ô *law, for*; oi *toy*; ŏŏ *good*; ōō *goo*; ou *out*; TH *thin*; TH *then*; ZH *vision*

phar·ma·cog·no·sy /ˌfärməˈkägnəsē/ ▶ **n.** the branch of knowledge concerned with medicinal drugs obtained from plants or other natural sources.
– DERIVATIVES **phar·ma·cog·no·sist** /-sist/ **n.**
– ORIGIN mid 19th cent.: from PHARMACO- 'of drugs' + *gnōsis* 'knowledge.'

phar·ma·co·ki·net·ics /ˌfärməkōkiˈnetiks/ ▶ **plural n.** [treated as sing.] the branch of pharmacology concerned with the movement of drugs within the body.
– DERIVATIVES **phar·ma·co·ki·net·ic** /-tik/ **adj.**

phar·ma·col·o·gy /ˌfärməˈkäləjē/ ▶ **n.** the branch of medicine concerned with the uses, effects, and modes of action of drugs.
– DERIVATIVES **phar·ma·co·log·ic** /ˌfärməkəˈläjik/ **adj.**, **phar·ma·co·log·i·cal** /-ˈläjikəl/ **adj.**, **phar·ma·co·log·i·cal·ly adv.**, **phar·ma·col·o·gist** /-ˈkäləjist/ **n.**
– ORIGIN early 18th cent.: from modern Latin *pharmacologia*, from Greek *pharmakon* 'drug.'

phar·ma·co·pe·ia /ˌfärməkəˈpēə/ (also **pharmacopoeia**) ▶ **n.** a book, esp. an official publication, containing a list of medicinal drugs with their effects and directions for their use. ■ a stock of medicinal drugs.
– ORIGIN early 17th cent.: modern Latin, from Greek *pharmakopoiia* 'art of preparing drugs,' based on *pharmakon* 'drug' + *-poios* 'making.'

phar·ma·co·phore /ˈfärməkəˌfôr/ ▶ **n.** a part of a molecular structure that is responsible for a particular biological or pharmacological interaction that it undergoes.

phar·ma·co·ther·a·py /ˌfärməkōˈTHerəpē/ ▶ **n.** medical treatment by means of drugs.

phar·ma·cy /ˈfärməsē/ ▶ **n.** (pl. **pharmacies**) a store where medicinal drugs are dispensed and sold. ■ the science or practice of the preparation and dispensing of medicinal drugs.
– ORIGIN late Middle English (denoting the administration of drugs): from Old French *farmacie*, via medieval Latin from Greek *pharmakeia* 'practice of the druggist,' based on *pharmakon* 'drug.'

pharm·ing /ˈfärmiNG/ ▶ **n.** **1** the process of genetically modifying plants and animals so that they produce substances that may be used as pharmaceuticals.
2 the fraudulent practice of directing Internet users to a bogus website that mimics the appearance of a legitimate one, in order to obtain personal information such as passwords, account numbers, etc.
– ORIGIN 1990s: sense 1 from PHARMACEUTICAL, punningly after FARMING; sense 2 patterned on PHISHING.

Pha·ros /ˈfe(ə)rōs/ a lighthouse, often considered one of the Seven Wonders of the World, erected by **Ptolemy II** (308–246 BC) in *c.*280 BC on the island of Pharos, off the coast of Alexandria. ■ (as noun **pharos**) a lighthouse or a beacon to guide sailors.

Pharr /fär/ a city in southern Texas, in the Rio Grande valley; pop. 65,258 (est. 2008).

pha·ryn·ge·al /fəˈrinj(ē)əl, ˌfarinˈjēəl/ ▶ **adj.** of or relating to the pharynx. ■ Phonetics (of a speech sound) produced by articulating the root of the tongue with the pharynx, a feature of certain consonants in Arabic, for example.
▶ **n.** Phonetics a pharyngeal consonant.
– ORIGIN early 19th cent.: from modern Latin *pharyngeus* (from Greek *pharunx, pharung-* 'throat') + -AL.

pha·ryn·ge·al·ize /fəˈrinjēəˌlīz/ ▶ **v.** [with obj.] Phonetics articulate (a speech sound) with constriction of the pharynx.
– DERIVATIVES **pha·ryn·ge·al·i·za·tion** /fəˈrinjēəliˈzāSHən/ **n.**

phar·yn·gi·tis /ˌfarinˈjītis/ ▶ **n.** Medicine inflammation of the pharynx, causing a sore throat.

pharyngo- ▶ **comb. form** of or relating to the pharynx: *pharyngotomy*.
– ORIGIN from modern Latin *pharynx, pharyng-*.

phar·ynx /ˈfariNGks/ ▶ **n.** (pl. **pharynges** /fəˈrinjēz/ or **pharynxes**) Anatomy & Zoology the membrane-lined cavity behind the nose and mouth, connecting them to the esophagus. ■ Zoology the part of the alimentary canal immediately behind the mouth in invertebrates.
– ORIGIN late 17th cent.: modern Latin, from Greek *pharunx, pharung-*.

phase /fāz/ ▶ **n.** **1** a distinct period or stage in a process of change or forming part of something's development: *the final phases of the war* | [as modifier] *phase two of the development is in progress.* ■ a stage in a person's psychological development, esp. a period of temporary unhappiness or difficulty during adolescence or a particular stage during childhood: *you are not obsessed, but you are going through a phase.* ■ each of the aspects of the moon or a planet, according to the amount of its illumination, esp. the new moon, the first quarter, the full moon, and the last quarter. ■ Riding each of the separate events in an eventing competition.
2 Zoology a genetic or seasonal variety of an animal's coloration. ■ a stage in the life cycle or annual cycle of an animal.
3 Chemistry a distinct and homogeneous form of matter (i.e., a particular solid, liquid, or gas) separated by its surface from other forms.
4 Physics the relationship in time between the successive states or cycles of an oscillating or repeating system (such as an alternating electric current or a light or sound wave) and either a fixed reference point or the states or cycles of another system with which it may or may not be in synchrony.
▶ **v.** [with obj.] **1** carry out (something) in gradual stages: *the work is being phased over a number of years* | (as adj. **phased**) *a phased withdrawal of troops.* ■ (**phase something in/out**) introduce into (or withdraw from) use in gradual stages: *our armed forces policy was to be phased in over 10 years.*
2 Physics adjust the phase of (something), esp. so as to synchronize it with something else.
– PHRASES **in** (or **out of**) **phase** being or happening in (or out of) synchrony or harmony: *the cabling work should be carried out in phase with the building work.*
– ORIGIN early 19th cent. (denoting each aspect of the moon): from French *phase*, based on Greek *phasis* 'appearance,' from the base of *phainein* 'to show.'

USAGE See usage at FAZE.

phase an·gle ▶ **n.** Physics an angle representing a difference in phase, 360 degrees (2π radians) corresponding to one complete cycle. ■ Astronomy the angle between the lines joining a given planet to the sun and to the earth.

phase con·trast ▶ **n.** the technique in microscopy of introducing a phase difference between parts of the light supplied by the condenser so as to enhance the outlines of the sample, or the boundaries between parts differing in optical density.

phase di·a·gram ▶ **n.** Chemistry a diagram representing the limits of stability of the various phases in a chemical system at equilibrium, with respect to variables such as composition and temperature.

phase-lock ▶ **v.** [with obj.] Electronics fix the frequency of (an oscillator or a laser) relative to a stable oscillator of lower frequency by a method that utilizes a correction signal derived from the phase difference generated by any shift in the frequency.

phase mod·u·la·tion /ˌmäjəˈlāSHən/ ▶ **n.** Electronics variation of the phase of a radio or other wave as a means of carrying information such as an audio signal.

phase·out /ˈfāˌzout/ ▶ **n.** an act of discontinuing a process, project, or service in phases.

phas·er /ˈfāzər/ ▶ **n.** **1** an instrument that alters a sound signal by phasing it.
2 (in science fiction) a weapon that delivers a beam that can stun or annihilate.

phase rule ▶ **n.** Chemistry a rule relating the possible numbers of phases, constituents, and degrees of freedom in a chemical system.

phase shift ▶ **n.** Physics a change in the phase of a waveform.

phase space ▶ **n.** Physics a multidimensional space in which each axis corresponds to one of the coordinates required to specify the state of a physical system, all the coordinates being thus represented so that a point in the space corresponds to a state of the system.

pha·sic /ˈfāzik/ ▶ **adj.** of or relating to a phase or phases. ■ chiefly Physiology characterized by occurrence in phases rather than continuously: *phasic and tonic stretch reflexes.*

phas·ing /ˈfāziNG/ ▶ **n.** the relationship between the timing of two or more events, or the adjustment of this relationship: *graphical techniques were used to investigate the phasing of traffic lights.* ■ the modification of the sound signal from an electric guitar or other electronic instrument by introducing a phase shift into either of two copies of it and then recombining them. ■ the action of dividing a large task or process into several stages: *the phasing of the overall project.*

Phas·mi·da /ˈfazmidə/ **1** Entomology an order of insects that comprises the stick insects and leaf insects. They have very long bodies that resemble twigs or leaves.
2 Zoology a class of nematodes that includes the parasitic hookworms and roundworms. Also called SECERNENTEA.
– DERIVATIVES **phas·mid n. & adj.**
– ORIGIN modern Latin (plural), from Latin *phasma* 'apparition,' from Greek.

pha·sor /ˈfāzər/ ▶ **n.** Physics a line used to represent a complex electrical quantity as a vector.
– ORIGIN 1940s: from PHASE, on the pattern of *vector*.

phat /fat/ ▶ **adj.** informal excellent: *a phat and funky sound.*
– ORIGIN 1970s (originally used to describe a woman, in the sense 'sexy, attractive'): of uncertain origin.

phat·ic /ˈfatik/ ▶ **adj.** denoting or relating to language used for general purposes of social interaction, rather than to convey information or ask questions. Utterances such as *hello, how are you?* and *nice morning, isn't it?* are phatic.
– ORIGIN 1920s: from Greek *phatos* 'spoken' or *phatikos* 'affirming.'

Ph.B ▶ **abbr.** Bachelor of Philosophy.
– ORIGIN Latin *Philosophiae Baccalaureus.*

Ph.C. ▶ **abbr.** Pharmaceutical Chemist.

Ph.D. (also **PhD**) ▶ **abbr.** Doctor of Philosophy.
– ORIGIN from Latin *philosophiae doctor*.

pheas·ant /ˈfezənt/ ▶ **n.** a large long-tailed game bird native to Asia, the male of which typically has very showy plumage. ● Family Phasianidae: several genera and many species, in particular the **ring-necked pheasant** (*Phasianus colchicus*), which has been widely introduced for shooting.
– ORIGIN Middle English: from Old French *fesan*, via Latin from Greek *phasianos* '(bird) of *Phasis*,' the name of a river in the Caucasus, from which the bird is said to have spread westward.

ring-necked pheasant

Phei·dip·pi·des /fīˈdipiˌdēz/ (5th century BC), Athenian messenger. He was sent to Sparta to ask for help after the Persian landing at Marathon in 490 and is said to have covered the 150 miles (250 km) in two days on foot.

Phelps /felps/, Michael Fred (1985–) US swimmer. As of 2008, he had won fourteen Olympic gold medals, the most by any Olympian in any sport.

phen- ▶ **comb. form** variant spelling of PHENO- shortened before a vowel (as in *phenacetin*).

phe·nac·e·tin /fəˈnasitən/ ▶ **n.** Medicine a synthetic compound used as a painkilling and antipyretic drug.
– ORIGIN late 19th cent.: from PHENO- + *acet(yl)* + -IN[1].

phe·nan·threne /fəˈnanTHrēn/ ▶ **n.** Chemistry a crystalline hydrocarbon present in coal tar, used esp. in making dyes and synthetic drugs. ● A tricyclic compound: chem. formula: $C_{14}H_{10}$.

phen·cy·cli·dine /fenˈsīkliˌdēn, -ˈsik-/ (abbr.: **PCP**) ▶ **n.** a synthetic compound derived from piperidine, used as a veterinary anesthetic and in hallucinogenic drugs such as angel dust.
– ORIGIN 1950s: from PHENO- + CYCLO- + a shortened form of PIPERIDINE.

pheno- (also **phen-** before a vowel) ▶ **comb. form**
1 Chemistry derived from benzene: *phenobarbital.*
2 showing: *phenotype.*
– ORIGIN Sense 1 from French *phényle* 'phenyl,' from Greek *phaino-* 'shining'; both senses from Greek *phainein* 'to show.'

phe·no·bar·bi·tal /ˌfēnōˈbärbiˌtôl/ ▶ **n.** Medicine a narcotic and sedative barbiturate drug used chiefly to treat epilepsy.

phe·no·co·py /ˈfēnəˌkäpē/ ▶ **n.** (pl. **phenocopies**) Genetics an individual showing features characteristic of a genotype other than its own, but produced environmentally rather than genetically.

phe·no·cryst /ˈfēnəˌkrist/ ▶ **n.** Geology a large or conspicuous crystal in a porphyritic rock, distinct from the groundmass.
– ORIGIN late 19th cent.: from French *phénocryste*, from Greek *phainein* 'to show' + *krustallos* 'crystal.'

phe·nol /ˈfēˌnôl, -ˌnäl/ ▶ **n.** Chemistry a mildly acidic toxic white crystalline solid obtained from coal tar and used in chemical manufacture, and in dilute form (under the name **carbolic**) as a disinfectant. ● Chem. formula: C_6H_5OH. ■ any compound with a hydroxyl group linked directly to a benzene ring.
– DERIVATIVES **phe·no·lic** /fiˈnälik/ **adj.**
– ORIGIN mid 19th cent.: from French *phénole*, based on *phène* 'benzene.'

phe·nol·o·gy /fiˈnäləjē/ ▶ **n.** the study of cyclic and seasonal natural phenomena, esp. in relation to climate and plant and animal life.

– DERIVATIVES **phe·no·log·i·cal** /ˌfēnəˈläjikəl/ **adj.**
– ORIGIN late 19th cent.: from **PHENOMENON** + **-LOGY**.

phe·nol·phthal·ein /ˌfēnəlˈTHālē(i)n/ ▶ **n.** Chemistry a colorless crystalline solid (pink in alkaline solution) used as an acid–base indicator and medicinally as a laxative. ● Chem. formula: $C_{20}H_{14}O_4$.
– ORIGIN late 19th cent.: from **PHENOL** + *-phthal-* (from **NAPHTHALENE**) + **-IN**[1].

phe·nol red ▶ **n.** Chemistry a red dye that is used as a pH indicator and (in medicine) injected in testing kidney function.

phe·nom /ˈfēˌnäm, fiˈnäm/ ▶ **n.** informal a person who is outstandingly talented or admired, esp. an up-and-comer.
– ORIGIN late 19th cent.: abbreviation of **PHENOMENON**.

phe·nom·e·na /fəˈnämənə/ plural form of **PHENOMENON**.

phe·nom·e·nal /fəˈnämənəl/ ▶ **adj. 1** very remarkable; extraordinary: *the town expanded at a phenomenal rate.*
2 perceptible by the senses or through immediate experience: *the phenomenal world.*
– DERIVATIVES **phe·nom·e·nal·ize** /ˌīz/ **v.** (sense 2), **phe·nom·e·nal·ly** **adv.**

phe·nom·e·nal·ism /fəˈnämənəlˌizəm/ ▶ **n.** Philosophy the doctrine that human knowledge is confined to or founded on the realities or appearances presented to the senses.
– DERIVATIVES **phe·nom·e·nal·ist** **n. & adj.**, **phe·nom·e·nal·is·tic** /-ˌnämənəlˈistik/ **adj.**

phe·nom·e·nol·o·gy /fiˌnäməˈnäləjē/ ▶ **n.** Philosophy the science of phenomena as distinct from that of the nature of being. ■ an approach that concentrates on the study of consciousness and the objects of direct experience.
– DERIVATIVES **phe·nom·e·no·log·i·cal** /-ˌnämənəˈläjikəl/ **adj.**, **phe·nom·e·no·log·i·cal·ly** /-ˌnämənəˈläjik(ə)lē/ **adv.**, **phe·nom·e·nol·o·gist** /-ˈnäləjist/ **n.**

phe·nom·e·non /fəˈnäməˌnän, -nən/ ▶ **n.** (pl. **phenomenona** /-nə/) **1** a fact or situation that is observed to exist or happen, esp. one whose cause or explanation is in question: *glaciers are unique and interesting natural phenomena.* ■ a remarkable person, thing, or event.
2 Philosophy the object of a person's perception; what the senses or the mind notice.
– ORIGIN late 16th cent.: via late Latin from Greek *phainomenon* 'thing appearing to view,' based on *phainein* 'to show.'

> **USAGE** The word **phenomenon** comes from Greek, and its plural form is **phenomena**, as in *these **phenomena** are not fully understood.* It is a mistake to treat **phenomena** as if it were a singular form, as in *this is a strange **phenomena**.*

phe·no·thi·a·zine /fēnəˈTHīəˌzēn/ ▶ **n.** Chemistry a synthetic compound that is used in veterinary medicine to treat parasitic infestations of animals. ● A heterocyclic compound; chem. formula: $C_{12}H_9NS$. ■ Psychiatry any of a group of derivatives of this compound with tranquilizing properties, used as tranquilizers in the treatment of mental illness.

phe·no·type /ˈfēnəˌtīp/ ▶ **n.** Biology the set of observable characteristics of an individual resulting from the interaction of its genotype with the environment.
– DERIVATIVES **phe·no·typ·ic** /ˌfēnəˈtipik/ **adj.**, **phe·no·typ·i·cal** /ˌfēnəˈtipikəl/ **adj.**, **phe·no·typ·i·cal·ly** /ˌfēnəˈtipik(ə)lē/ **adv.**
– ORIGIN early 20th cent.: from German *Phaenotypus* (see **PHENO-**, **TYPE**).

phen·ter·mine /ˈfentərˌmēn/ ▶ **n.** Medicine a prescription appetite-suppressant drug that binds to receptors on the hypothalamus, and is one of the pair of drugs known as fen-phen. It is still prescribed independently for obesity, following the withdrawal of fenfluramine, the other component of fen-phen.

phen·tol·a·mine /fenˈtäləˌmēn/ ▶ **n.** Medicine a synthetic compound used as a vasodilator, esp. in certain cases of hypertension.
– ORIGIN 1950s: from **PHEN-** + *tol(yl)* (an isomeric cyclic radical derived from toluene) + **AMINE**.

phen·yl /ˈfenəl, ˈfē-/ ▶ **n.** [as modifier] Chemistry of or denoting the radical $-C_6H_5$, derived from benzene by removal of a hydrogen atom: *a phenyl group.*
– ORIGIN mid 19th cent.: from French *phényle*, from Greek *phaino-* 'shining' (because first used in names of compounds denoting byproducts of the manufacture of gas used for illumination).

phen·yl·al·a·nine /ˌfenəlˈaləˌnēn, ˌfēnəl-/ ▶ **n.** Biochemistry an amino acid widely distributed in plant proteins. It is an essential nutrient in the diet of vertebrates. ● Chem. formula: $C_6H_5CH_2CH(NH_2)COOH$.

phen·yl·bu·ta·zone /ˌfenəlˈbyo͞otəˌzōn, ˌfēnəl-/ ▶ **n.** a synthetic compound used as an analgesic drug, esp. in the treatment of horses.
– ORIGIN 1950s: from **PHENYL** + *but(yl)* + **AZO-** + **-ONE**.

phen·yl·eph·rine /ˌfēnəlˈefrin, ˌfenəl-/ ▶ **n.** Medicine a synthetic compound related to epinephrine, used as a vasoconstrictor and nasal decongestant.
– ORIGIN 1940s: from **PHENYL** + a contraction of **EPINEPHRINE**.

phen·yl·ke·to·nu·ri·a /ˌfenlˌkētōˈn(y)o͝orēə, ˌfēnl-/ (abbr.: **PKU**) ▶ **n.** Medicine an inherited inability to metabolize phenylalanine that causes brain and nerve damage if untreated.

phen·y·to·in /ˌfeniˈtō-in, fəˈnitō-in/ ▶ **n.** Medicine a synthetic compound related to hydantoin, used as an anticonvulsant in the treatment of epilepsy.
– ORIGIN 1940s: blend of **PHENYL** and **HYDANTOIN**.

phe·o·chro·mo·cy·to·ma /ˌfēōˌkrōməsīˈtōmə/ ▶ **n.** (pl. **pheochromocytomas** or **pheochromocytomata** /-ˈtōmətə/) Medicine a small vascular tumor of the adrenal medulla, causing irregular secretion of epinephrine and norepinephrine, leading to attacks of raised blood pressure, palpitations, and headache.
– ORIGIN 1920s: from *pheochrome*, another term for chromaffin (from Greek *phaios* 'dusky' + *khrōma* 'color'), + **-CYTE**.

pher·o·mone /ˈferəˌmōn/ ▶ **n.** Zoology a chemical substance produced and released into the environment by an animal, esp. a mammal or an insect, affecting the behavior or physiology of others of its species.
– DERIVATIVES **pher·o·mo·nal** /ferəˈmōnl/ **adj.**
– ORIGIN 1950s: from Greek *pherein* 'convey' + **HORMONE**.

phew /fyo͞o/ ▶ **exclam.** informal expressing a strong reaction of relief: *phew, what a year!*
– ORIGIN early 17th cent.: imitative of puffing.

Ph.G. ▶ **abbr.** Graduate in Pharmacy.

phi /fī/ ▶ **n.** the twenty-first letter of the Greek alphabet (Φ, φ), transliterated as 'ph.' ■ (**Phi**) [followed by Latin genitive] Astronomy the twenty-first star in a constellation: *Phi Eridani.* ▶ **symbol** ■ (φ) a plane angle. ■ (φ) a polar coordinate. Often coupled with **THETA**.

phi·al /ˈfīəl/ ▶ **n.** another term for **VIAL**.
– ORIGIN Middle English: from Old French *fiole*, via Latin from Greek *phialē*, denoting a broad flat container.

Phi Be·ta Kap·pa /ˈfī ˈbātə ˈkapə/ ▶ **n.** an honorary society of college and university undergraduates and some graduates to which members are elected on the basis of high academic achievement. ■ a member of this society.
– ORIGIN from the initial letters of a Greek motto *philosophia biou kubernētēs* 'philosophy is the guide to life.'

Phid·i·as /ˈfidēəs/ (5th century BC), Athenian sculptor. He is noted for the Elgin marbles and his colossal statue of Zeus at Olympia (*c.*430), which was one of the Seven Wonders of the Ancient World.

Phil. ▶ **abbr.** ■ Bible Philippians. ■ Bible Philemon. ■ Philadelphia. ■ Philharmonic. ■ Philippine.

phil- ▶ **comb. form** variant spelling of **PHILO-** shortened before a vowel or *h* (as in *philanthrope, philharmonic*).

-phil ▶ **comb. form** having a chemical affinity for a substance: *acidophil* | *neutrophil.*
– ORIGIN see **-PHILE**.

Phil·a·del·phi·a /ˌfiləˈdelfēə/ a city in Pennsylvania, on the Delaware River; pop. 1,447,395 (est. 2008). Established as a Quaker colony by William Penn and others in 1681, it was the site in 1776 of the signing of the Declaration of Independence and in 1787 of the adoption of the Constitution of the US.
– DERIVATIVES **Phil·a·del·phi·an** **n. & adj.**
– ORIGIN from Greek *philadelphia* 'brotherly love.'

Phil·a·del·phi·a cheese steak (also **Philly cheese steak**) ▶ **n.** see **CHEESESTEAK**.

Phil·a·del·phi·a chro·mo·some ▶ **n.** Genetics an abnormal small chromosome sometimes found in the leukocytes of leukemia patients.

Phil·a·del·phi·a law·yer ▶ **n.** a very shrewd lawyer who is expert in the exploitation of legal technicalities.
– ORIGIN with reference to Andrew Hamilton of Philadelphia, who successfully defended John Peter Zenger (1735), an American journalist and publisher, from libel charges.

phil·a·del·phus /ˌfiləˈdelfəs/ ▶ **n.** a mock orange.
– ORIGIN late 18th cent.: modern Latin (adopted by Linnaeus as a genus name), from Greek *philadelphos* 'loving one's brother.'

phi·lan·der /fəˈlandər/ ▶ **v.** [no obj.] (of a man) readily or frequently enter into casual sexual relationships with women: *they accepted that their husbands would philander with other women.*
– ORIGIN mid 18th cent.: from the earlier noun *philander* 'man, husband,' often used in literature as the given name of a lover, from Greek *philandros* 'fond of men,' from *philein* 'to love' + *anēr* 'man.'

phi·lan·der·er /fəˈlandərər/ ▶ **n.** a man who readily or frequently enters into casual sexual relationships with women; a womanizer: *he was known as a philanderer.*

phil·an·thrope /ˈfilənˌTHrōp/ ▶ **n.** archaic term for **PHILANTHROPIST**.
– ORIGIN mid 18th cent.: from Greek *philanthrōpos*, from *philein* 'to love' + *anthrōpos* 'human being.'

phil·an·throp·ic /ˌfilənˈTHräpik/ ▶ **adj.** (of a person or organization) seeking to promote the welfare of others, esp. by donating money to good causes; generous and benevolent: *they receive financial support from philanthropic bodies.*
– DERIVATIVES **phil·an·throp·i·cal·ly** /-(ə)lē/ **adv.**
– ORIGIN late 18th cent.: from French *philanthropique*, from Greek *philanthrōpos* 'man-loving' (see **PHILANTHROPE**).

phi·lan·thro·pist /fəˈlanTHrəpist/ ▶ **n.** a person who seeks to promote the welfare of others, esp. by the generous donation of money to good causes.

phi·lan·thro·py /fəˈlanTHrəpē/ ▶ **n.** the desire to promote the welfare of others, expressed esp. by the generous donation of money to good causes. ■ a philanthropic institution; a charity.
– DERIVATIVES **phi·lan·thro·pism** /-pizəm/ **n.**, **phi·lan·thro·pize** /-pīz/ **v.**
– ORIGIN early 17th cent.: via late Latin from Greek *philanthrōpia*, from *philanthrōpos* 'man-loving' (see **PHILANTHROPE**).

phi·lat·e·ly /fəˈlatl-ē/ ▶ **n.** the collection and study of postage stamps.
– DERIVATIVES **phil·a·tel·ic** /ˌfiləˈtelik/ **adj.**, **phil·a·tel·i·cal·ly** /ˌfiləˈtelik(ə)lē/ **adv.**, **phi·lat·e·list** /-ist/ **n.**
– ORIGIN mid 19th cent.: from French *philatélie*, from *philo-* 'loving' + Greek *ateleia* 'exemption from payment' (from *a-* 'not' + *telos* 'toll, tax'), used to mean a franking mark or postage stamp exempting the recipient from payment.

-phile ▶ **comb. form** denoting fondness for a specified thing: *bibliophile* | *Francophile.*
– ORIGIN from Greek *philos* 'loving.'

Philem. ▶ **abbr.** Bible Philemon.

Phi·le·mon[1] /fəˈlēmən, fī-/ Greek Mythology a good, old countryman living with his wife Baucis in Phrygia who offered hospitality to Zeus and Hermes when the two gods came to earth, without revealing their identities, to test people's piety. Philemon and Baucis were subsequently saved from a flood that covered the district.

Phi·le·mon[2] a book of the New Testament, an epistle of St. Paul to a well-to-do Christian living probably at Colossae in Phrygia.

phil·har·mon·ic /ˌfilərˈmänik, ˌfilhär-/ ▶ **adj.** devoted to music (chiefly used in the names of orchestras): *the Vienna Philharmonic Orchestra.*
– ORIGIN mid 18th cent.: from French *philharmonique*, from Italian *filarmonico* 'loving harmony' (see **PHIL-**, **HARMONIC**).

phil·hel·lene /filˈhelēn/ ▶ **n.** a lover of Greece and Greek culture: *a romantic philhellene.* ■ historical a supporter of Greek independence.
– DERIVATIVES **phil·hel·len·ic** /ˌfilheˈlenik/ **adj.**, **phil·hel·len·ism** /filˈheləˌnizəm/ **n.**
– ORIGIN early 19th cent.: from Greek *philellēn* 'loving the Greeks' (see **PHIL-**, **HELLENE**).

-philia ▶ **comb. form** denoting fondness, esp. an abnormal love for a specified thing: *pedophilia.* ■ denoting undue inclination: *spasmophilia.*
– ORIGIN from Greek *philia* 'fondness.'

-philiac ▶ **comb. form** in nouns and adjectives corresponding to nouns ending in *-philia* (such as *hemophiliac* corresponding to *hemophilia*).

phil·i·beg ▶ **n.** variant spelling of **FILIBEG**.

-philic ▶ **comb. form** in adjectives corresponding to nouns ending in *-philia* (such as *paraphilic* corresponding to *paraphilia*).

Phil·ip[1] /ˈfilip/ the name of five kings of ancient Macedonia, notably: ■ **Philip II** (382–336 BC), father of Alexander the Great; reigned 359–336; known as **Philip II of Macedon**. He unified and expanded ancient Macedonia. ■ **Philip V** (238–179 BC), reigned 221–179. His expansionist policies led to a series of confrontations with Rome, culminating in his defeat in 197 and his loss of control over Greece.

P

Phil·ip[2] the name of six kings of France. ■ **Philip I** (1052–1108), reigned 1059–1108. ■ **Philip II** (1165–1223), son of Louis VII; reigned 1180–1223; known as **Philip Augustus**. After mounting a series of campaigns against the English kings Henry II, Richard I, and John, Philip succeeded in regaining Normandy in 1204, Anjou in 1204, and most of Poitou in 1204–05. ■ **Philip III** (1245–85), reigned 1270–85; known as **Philip the Bold**. ■ **Philip IV** (1268–1314), son of Philip III; reigned 1285–1314; known as **Philip the Fair**. He continued to extend French dominions, waging wars with England from 1294 until 1303 and with Flanders 1302–05. ■ **Philip V** (1293–1322), reigned 1316–22; known as **Philip the Tall**. ■ **Philip VI** (1293–1350), reigned 1328–50; known as **Philip of Valois**. The founder of the Valois dynasty, Philip came to the throne on the death of **Charles IV**, whose only child was a girl and barred from ruling. His claim was challenged by Edward III of England; the dispute developed into the Hundred Years War.

Phil·ip[3] the name of five kings of Spain. ■ **Philip I** (1478–1506), reigned 1504–06; known as **Philip the Handsome**. Son of the Holy Roman Emperor **Maximilian I**, in 1496 Philip married the infanta **Joanna**, daughter of Ferdinand of Aragon and Isabella of Castile. After Isabella's death he ruled Castile jointly with Joanna, establishing the Habsburgs as the ruling dynasty in Spain. ■ **Philip II** (1527–98), son of Charles I (Holy Roman Emperor Charles V); reigned 1556–98. Philip came to the throne following his father's abdication. His reign was dominated by an anti-Protestant crusade that exhausted the Spanish economy. His Armada against England (1588) ended in defeat. ■ **Philip III** (1578–1621), reigned 1598–1621. ■ **Philip IV** (1605–65), reigned 1621–65. ■ **Philip V** (1683–1746), grandson of Louis XIV; reigned 1700–24 and 1724–46. The selection of Philip as successor to Charles II, and Louis XIV's insistence that Philip remain an heir to the French throne, gave rise to the War of the Spanish Succession (1701–14). In 1724, Philip abdicated in favor of his son **Louis I**, but returned to the throne following Louis's death.

Phil·ip[4], King (*c.*1639–76), chief of the Wampanoag Indians; Indian name *Metacomet*. From 1675, he waged King Philip's War on the New England colonists because they had taken some of his land and had killed three of his warriors. His defeat and death in battle ended Indian resistance in New England.

Phil·ip, Prince, Duke of Edinburgh (1921–), husband of Elizabeth II. The son of **Prince Andrew of Greece and Denmark**, he married Princess Elizabeth in 1947; on the eve of his marriage he was created Duke of Edinburgh.

Phil·ip, St.[1], an apostle. He is commemorated with St. James the Less on May 1.

Phil·ip, St.[2], deacon of the early Christian Church; known as **St. Philip the Evangelist**. He was one of seven deacons appointed to superintend the secular business of the Church at Jerusalem (Acts 6:5–6). Feast day, June 6.

Phil·ip II of Mac·e·don, Philip II of Macedonia (see **Philip**[1]).

Phil·ip Au·gus·tus, Philip II of France (see **Philip**[2]).

Phil·ip of Va·lois, Philip VI of France (see **Philip**[2]).

Phi·lip·pi /fəˈliˌpī, ˈfilə-/ a city in ancient Macedonia, close to the Aegean coast in northeastern Greece, near the port of Kavála (ancient Neapolis). It was the scene in 42 BC of two battles in which Mark Antony and Octavian defeated Brutus and Cassius. Greek name **Filippoi**.

Phi·lip·pi·ans /fəˈlipēənz/ a book of the New Testament, an epistle of St. Paul to the Church at Philippi in Macedonia.

phi·lip·pic /fəˈlipik/ ▶ **n.** literary a bitter attack or denunciation, esp. a verbal one.
– ORIGIN late 16th cent.: via Latin from Greek *philippikos*, the name given to Demosthenes' speeches against Philip II of Macedon, also to those of Cicero against Mark Antony.

Phil·ip·pine /ˈfiləˌpēn/ ▶ **adj.** of or relating to the Philippines. See also **Filipino**.

Phil·ip·pine ma·hog·a·ny ▶ **n. 1** reddish-brown timber from a tropical tree, used for paneling, cabinetry, and furniture. It resembles mahogany but is softer and less expensive.
2 the tree that produces this timber, harvested chiefly in Indonesia and the Philippines. Also called **lauan**. ● Genus *Shorea*, family Dipterocarpaceae: several species.

Phil·ip·pines /ˈfiləˌpēnz/ a country in Southeast Asia that consists of an archipelago of over 7,000 islands—the main ones being Luzon, Mindanao, Mindoro, Leyte, Samar, Negros, and Panay—that are separated from the Asian mainland by the South China Sea; pop. 97,976,600 (est. 2009); capital, Manila; languages, Filipino (based on Tagalog) and English.

> Conquered by Spain in 1565, the islands were ceded to the US in 1898, following the Spanish-American War. The Philippines achieved full independence as a republic in 1946. From 1965, the country was under the increasingly dictatorial rule of Ferdinand Marcos; he was driven from power in 1986 and replaced by Corazón Aquino, who was president until 1992. Economic improvements that emerged in the 1990s were undone by the East Asian financial crisis that closed the decade.

Phil·ip·pine Sea a section of the western Pacific on the east side of the Philippine Islands that extends north to Japan. During World War II, several major battles, including that at **Leyte Gulf**, were fought here.

Phil·ip·pop·o·lis /ˌfiləˈpäpəlis/ ancient Greek name for **Plovdiv**.

Phil·ip the Bold, Philip III of France (see **Philip**[2]).

Phil·ip the Fair, Philip IV of France (see **Philip**[2]).

Phil·ip the Hand·some, Philip I of Spain (see **Philip**[3]).

Phil·ip the Tall, Philip V of France (see **Philip**[2]).

Phil·is·tine /ˈfiləˌstēn, -ˌstīn/ ▶ **n. 1** a member of a non-Semitic (perhaps originally Anatolian) people of southern Palestine in ancient times, who came into conflict with the Israelites during the 12th and 11th centuries BC.

> According to the Bible, the Philistines, from whom the country of Palestine took its name, came from Crete and settled the southern coastal plain of Canaan in the 12th century BC.

2 (usu. **philistine**) a person who is hostile or indifferent to culture and the arts, or who has no understanding of them: [as modifier] *a philistine government*.
– DERIVATIVES **phil·is·tin·ism** /ˈfiləstēˌnizəm, fəˈlistə-/ **n.**
– ORIGIN from French *Philistin*, via late Latin from Greek *Philistinos*, from Hebrew *pĕlištī*. Sense 2 arose as a result of a confrontation between the townspeople and the students in Jena, Germany, in the late 17th cent.; a sermon on the conflict quoted: "the Philistines are upon you" (Judges 16), which led to an association between the townspeople and those hostile to culture. See **Palestine**.

Phil·lips /ˈfiləps/ ▶ **adj.** trademark denoting a screw with a cross-shaped slot for turning, the head of such a screw, or a corresponding screwdriver: *the screws have deeply cut Phillips heads | a Phillips screwdriver | a Phillips-head screwdriver.*
– ORIGIN 1930s: from the name of Henry F. *Phillips* (died 1958), the original American manufacturer.

Phil·lips curve ▶ **n.** Economics a supposed inverse relationship between the level of unemployment and the rate of inflation.
– ORIGIN 1960s: named after Alban W. H. *Phillips* (1914–75), New Zealand economist.

phil·lu·men·ist /fəˈlo͞omənist/ ▶ **n.** a collector of matchboxes or matchbooks.
– DERIVATIVES **phil·lu·men·y** /-mənē/ **n.**
– ORIGIN 1940s: from **phil-** 'loving' + Latin *lumen* 'light' + **-ist**.

Phil·ly /ˈfilē/ ▶ **n.** informal Philadelphia.

Phil·ly cheese·steak ▶ **n.** see **cheesesteak**.

philo- (also **phil-** before a vowel or *h*) ▶ **comb. form** denoting a liking for a specified thing: *philogynist | philopatric*.
– ORIGIN from Greek *philein* 'to love' or *philos* 'loving.'

phil·o·den·dron /ˌfiləˈdendrən/ ▶ **n.** (pl. **philodendrons** or **philodendra** /-drə/) a tropical American climbing plant that is widely grown as a greenhouse or indoor plant. ● Genus *Philodendron*, family Araceae.
– ORIGIN late 19th cent.: from **philo-** 'loving' + Greek *dendron* 'tree.'

phi·log·y·nist /fəˈläjənist/ ▶ **n.** formal a person who likes or admires women.
– DERIVATIVES **phi·log·y·ny** /-ˈläjənē/ **n.**
– ORIGIN mid 19th cent.: from **philo-** 'loving' + Greek *gunē* 'woman' + **-ist**.

phi·lol·o·gy /fəˈläləjē/ ▶ **n.** the branch of knowledge that deals with the structure, historical development, and relationships of a language or languages. ■ literary or classical scholarship.
– DERIVATIVES **phil·o·lo·gi·an** /ˌfiləˈlōjēən/ **n.**, **phil·o·log·i·cal** /ˌfiləˈläjikəl/ **adj.**, **phil·o·log·i·cal·ly** /ˌfiləˈläjik(ə)lē/ **adv.**, **phi·lol·o·gist** /-jist/ **n.**
– ORIGIN late Middle English (in the Greek sense): current usage (late 17th cent.) from French *philologie*, via Latin from Greek *philologia* 'love of learning' (see **philo-**, **-logy**).

Phil·o·me·la /ˌfiləˈmēlə/ (also **Philomel** /ˈfiləˌmel/) Greek Mythology the daughter of Pandion, king of Athens. She was turned into a swallow and her sister Procne into a nightingale (or, in Latin versions, into a nightingale with Procne the swallow) when they were being pursued by the cruel Tereus, who had married Procne and raped Philomela.
– ORIGIN earlier as *philomene*, from medieval Latin *philomena*, from Latin *philomela* 'nightingale,' from Greek *philomēla*.

phil·o·pat·ric /ˌfiləˈpatrik/ ▶ **adj.** Zoology (of an animal or species) tending to return to or remain near a particular site or area.
– DERIVATIVES **phil·op·a·try** /fəˈläpətrē/ **n.**
– ORIGIN 1940s: from **philo-** 'liking' + Greek *patra* 'fatherland' + **-ic**.

phil·o·pro·gen·i·tive /ˌfilōprōˈjenitiv/ ▶ **adj.** formal having many offspring: *the philoprogenitive senator*. ■ showing love toward one's offspring.
– DERIVATIVES **phil·o·pro·gen·i·tive·ness** **n.**

philos. ▶ **abbr.** ■ philosopher. ■ philosophical. ■ philosophy.

phi·los·o·pher /fəˈläsəfər/ ▶ **n.** a person engaged or learned in philosophy, esp. as an academic discipline.
– ORIGIN Middle English: from a variant of Old French *philosophe*, via Latin from Greek *philosophos* 'lover of wisdom,' from *philein* 'to love' + *sophos* 'wise.'

phi·los·o·pher kings ▶ **plural n.** (in the political theory of Plato) the elite whose knowledge enables them to rule justly.

phi·los·o·pher's stone ▶ **n.** (**the philosopher's stone**) a mythical substance supposed to change any metal into gold or silver and, according to some, to cure all diseases and prolong life indefinitely. Its discovery was the supreme object of alchemy.

phil·o·so·phi·a pe·ren·nis /fəˌläsəˈfēə pəˈrenis/ ▶ **n.** Philosophy a core of philosophical truths that is hypothesized to exist independently of and unaffected by time or place.
– ORIGIN mid 19th cent.: Latin, literally 'perennial philosophy.'

phil·o·soph·i·cal /ˌfiləˈsäfikəl/ ▶ **adj. 1** relating or devoted to the study of the fundamental nature of knowledge, reality, and existence: *philosophical discussions about free will | the American Philosophical Society*.
2 having or showing a calm attitude toward disappointments or difficulties: *he was* ***philosophical about*** *losing the contract*.
– DERIVATIVES **phil·o·soph·ic** /-ˈsäfik/ **adj.**, **phil·o·soph·i·cal·ly** /-ik(ə)lē/ **adv.**

phi·los·o·phize /fəˈläsəˌfīz/ ▶ **v.** [no obj.] speculate or theorize about fundamental or serious issues, esp. in a tedious or pompous way: *he paused for a while to philosophize on racial equality*. ■ [with obj.] explain or argue (a point or idea) in terms of one's philosophical theories.
– DERIVATIVES **phi·los·o·phiz·er** **n.**

phi·los·o·phy /fəˈläsəfē/ ▶ **n.** (pl. **philosophies**) the study of the fundamental nature of knowledge, reality, and existence, esp. when considered as an academic discipline. See also **natural philosophy**. ■ a set of views and theories of a particular philosopher concerning such study or an aspect of it: *Schopenhauer's philosophy*. ■ the study of the theoretical basis of a particular branch of knowledge or experience: ***the philosophy of science***. ■ a theory or attitude held by a person or organization that acts as a guiding principle for behavior: *don't expect anything and you won't be disappointed, that's my philosophy*.
– ORIGIN Middle English: from Old French *philosophie*, via Latin from Greek *philosophia* 'love of wisdom.'

-philous ▶ **comb. form** in adjectives corresponding to nouns ending in *-philia* (such as *coprophilous* corresponding to *coprophilia*).

phil·ter /ˈfiltər/ (Brit. **philtre**) ▶ **n.** a drink supposed to excite sexual love in the drinker.
– ORIGIN late 16th cent.: from French *philtre*, via Latin from Greek *philtron*, from *philein* 'to love.'

-phily ▶ **comb. form** equivalent to **-philia**.

phi·mo·sis /fīˈmōsis/ ▶ **n.** Medicine a congenital narrowing of the opening of the foreskin so that it cannot be retracted.
– DERIVATIVES **phi·mot·ic** /fīˈmätik/ **adj.**
– ORIGIN late 17th cent.: modern Latin, from Greek, literally 'muzzling.'

phish·ing /ˈfishing/ ▶ **n.** the activity of defrauding an online account holder of financial information by posing as a legitimate company: [as modifier] *phishing exercises in which criminals create replicas of commercial Web sites*.
– DERIVATIVES **phish** **v.**

– ORIGIN 1990s: inspired by *fishing*, on the pattern of *phreaking*.

phiz /fiz/ ▶ **n.** Brit. informal a person's face or expression.
– ORIGIN late 17th cent.: abbreviation of PHYSIOGNOMY.

phle·bi·tis /flə'bītis/ ▶ **n.** Medicine inflammation of the walls of a vein.
– DERIVATIVES **phle·bit·ic** /-'bitik/ **adj.**
– ORIGIN early 19th cent.: modern Latin, from Greek, from *phleps, phleb-* 'vein.'

phle·bog·ra·phy /flə'bägrəfē/ ▶ **n.** Medicine radiography of the veins carried out after injection of a radiopaque substance.
– DERIVATIVES **phleb·o·graph·ic** /ˌflebə'grafik/ **adj.**

phle·bot·o·my /flə'bätəmē/ ▶ **n.** (pl. **phlebotomies**) the surgical opening or puncture of a vein in order to withdraw blood or introduce a fluid, or (historically) as part of the procedure of letting blood.
– DERIVATIVES **phle·bot·o·mist** **n.**, **phle·bot·o·mize** /-'bätəˌmīz/ **v.** (archaic).
– ORIGIN late Middle English: via Old French from late Latin *phlebotomia*, from Greek, from *phleps, phleb-* 'vein' + *-tomia* 'cutting.'

phlegm /flem/ ▶ **n.** the thick viscous substance secreted by the mucous membranes of the respiratory passages, esp. when produced in excessive or abnormal quantities, e.g., when someone is suffering from a cold. ■ (in medieval science and medicine) one of the four bodily humors, believed to be associated with a calm, stolid, or apathetic temperament. ■ calmness of temperament: *phlegm and determination carried them through many difficult situations.*
– DERIVATIVES **phlegm·y** **adj.**
– ORIGIN Middle English *fleem, fleume*, from Old French *fleume*, from late Latin *phlegma* 'clammy moisture (of the body),' from Greek *phlegma* 'inflammation,' from *phlegein* 'to burn.' The spelling change in the 16th cent. was due to association with the Latin and Greek.

phleg·mat·ic /fleg'matik/ ▶ **adj.** (of a person) having an unemotional and stolidly calm disposition.
– DERIVATIVES **phleg·mat·i·cal·ly** /-ik(ə)lē/ **adv.**
– ORIGIN Middle English (in the sense 'relating to the humor phlegm'): from Old French *fleumatique*, via Latin from Greek *phlegmatikos*, from *phlegma* 'inflammation' (see PHLEGM).

phlo·em /'flōˌem/ ▶ **n.** Botany the vascular tissue in plants that conducts sugars and other metabolic products downward from the leaves.
– ORIGIN late 19th cent.: from Greek *phloos* 'bark' + the passive suffix *-ēma*.

phlo·gis·ton /flō'jistän, -tən/ ▶ **n.** a substance supposed by 18th-century chemists to exist in all combustible bodies, and to be released in combustion.
– ORIGIN mid 18th cent.: modern Latin, from Greek *phlogizein* 'set on fire,' from *phlox, phlog-* 'flame,' from the base of *phlegein* 'to burn.'

phlog·o·pite /'flägəˌpīt/ ▶ **n.** a brown micaceous mineral that occurs chiefly in metamorphosed limestone and magnesium-rich igneous rocks.
– ORIGIN mid 19th cent.: from Greek *phlogōpos* 'fiery' (from the base of *phlegein* 'to burn') + *ōps, ōp-* 'face' + -ITE[1].

phlox /fläks/ ▶ **n.** a North American plant that typically has dense clusters of colorful scented flowers, widely grown as a rock-garden or border plant. ● Genus *Phlox*, family Polemoniaceae.
– ORIGIN modern Latin, from Latin, denoting a flame-colored flower, from Greek, literally 'flame.'

Ph.M. ▶ **abbr.** Master of Philosophy.

Phnom Penh /(pə)ˌnäm 'pen/ the capital of Cambodia, a port at the junction of the Mekong and Tonlé Sap rivers; pop. 1,438,300 (est. 2009). Between 1975 and 1979, the Khmer Rouge forced a great many of its inhabitants (then 2.5 million) to leave the city and resettle in the country.

pho /fər/ ▶ **n.** a type of Vietnamese soup, typically made from beef stock and spices to which noodles and thinly sliced beef or chicken are added.
– ORIGIN Vietnamese, perhaps from French *feu* (in POT-AU-FEU).

-phobe ▶ **comb. form** denoting a person having a fear or dislike of what is specified: *homophobe* | *xenophobe*.
– ORIGIN from French, via Latin *-phobus* from Greek *-phobos* 'fearing,' from *phobos* 'fear.'

pho·bi·a /'fōbēə/ ▶ **n.** an extreme or irrational fear of or aversion to something: *he had a phobia about being under water* | *a phobia of germs* | *a snake phobia.*
– DERIVATIVES **pho·bic** /'fōbik/ **adj. & n.**
– ORIGIN late 18th cent.: independent usage of -PHOBIA.

-phobia ▶ **comb. form** extreme or irrational fear or dislike of a specified thing or group: *arachnophobia* | *Russophobia*.
– ORIGIN via Latin from Greek.

-phobic ▶ **comb. form** in adjectives corresponding to nouns ending in *-phobia* (such as *technophobic* corresponding to *technophobia*).

Pho·bos /'fōbəs, 'fōbäs/ Astronomy the inner, and larger, of the two satellites of Mars, discovered in 1877. Heavily cratered and shaped like a potato, it is 17 miles (28 km) long. Compare with DEIMOS.
– ORIGIN named after one of the sons of the Greek war god ARES. The name means literally 'fear.'

pho·cine /'fōsīn, 'fōsin/ ▶ **adj.** Zoology of, relating to, or affecting the true (earless) seals.
– ORIGIN mid 19th cent.: from modern Latin *Phocinae* (subfamily name), from Greek *phōkē* 'seal.'

pho·co·me·li·a /ˌfōkō'mēlyə, -'mēlēə/ ▶ **n.** Medicine a rare congenital deformity in which the hands or feet are attached close to the trunk, the limbs being grossly underdeveloped or absent. This condition was a side effect of the drug thalidomide taken during early pregnancy.
– ORIGIN late 19th cent.: modern Latin, from Greek *phōkē* 'seal' + *melos* 'limb.'

Phoe·be /'fēbē/ **1** Greek Mythology a Titaness, daughter of Uranus (Heaven) and Gaia (Earth). She became the mother of Leto and thus the grandmother of Apollo and Artemis. In the later Greek writers, her name was often used for Selene (Moon).
2 Astronomy a satellite of Saturn, the farthest from the planet and with an eccentric retrograde orbit, discovered in 1898. At a distance of 8 million miles (13 million km) from Saturn, it has a diameter of 137 miles (220 km).
– ORIGIN from Greek *Phoibē*, literally 'bright one.'

phoe·be /'fēbē/ ▶ **n.** an American tyrant flycatcher with mainly gray-brown or blackish plumage. ● Genus *Sayornis*, family Tyrannidae: three species, in particular the common **eastern phoebe** (*S. phoebe*).
– ORIGIN early 18th cent.: imitative; influenced by the name PHOEBE.

Phoe·bus /'fēbəs/ Greek Mythology an epithet of Apollo, used in contexts in which the god was identified with the sun.
– ORIGIN from Greek *Phoibos*, literally 'bright one.'

Phoe·ni·cia /fə'nisHə, -'nēsHə/ an ancient country on the shores of the eastern Mediterranean Sea, corresponding to modern Lebanon and the coastal plains of Syria. It consisted of a number of city states, including Tyre and Sidon, and was a flourishing center of Mediterranean trade and colonization during the early part of the 1st millennium BC.
– ORIGIN from Latin, from Greek *Phoinikē*.

Phoe·ni·cian /fə'nēsHən/ ▶ **n. 1** a member of a Semitic people inhabiting ancient Phoenicia and its colonies. The Phoenicians prospered from trade and manufacturing until the capital, Tyre, was sacked by Alexander the Great in 332 BC.
2 the Semitic language of this people, written in an alphabet that was the ancestor of the Greek and Roman alphabets.
▶ **adj.** of or relating to Phoenicia or its colonies, or its people, language, or alphabet.

Phoe·nix[1] /'fēniks/ Astronomy a southern constellation (the Phoenix), west of Grus. ■ (as genitive **Phoenicis** /fi'nēsis, -'nī-/) used with a preceding letter or numeral to designate a star in this constellation: *the star Delta Phoenicis.*
– ORIGIN Latin.

Phoe·nix[2] the capital of Arizona; pop. 1,567,924 (est. 2008). Its warm dry climate makes it a popular winter resort.

phoe·nix /'fēniks/ ▶ **n.** (in classical mythology) a unique bird that lived for five or six centuries in the Arabian desert, after this time burning itself on a funeral pyre and rising from the ashes with renewed youth to live through another cycle. ■ a person or thing regarded as uniquely remarkable in some respect.
– PHRASES **rise like a phoenix from the ashes** emerge renewed after apparent disaster or destruction.
– ORIGIN from Old French *fenix*, via Latin from Greek *phoinix* 'Phoenician, reddish purple, or phoenix.'

Phoe·nix Is·lands a group of eight islands that lie just south of the equator in the western Pacific Ocean. They form a part of Kiribati.

Phol·i·do·ta /ˌfäli'dōtə/ Zoology a small order of mammals that comprises the pangolins.
– ORIGIN modern Latin (plural), from Greek *pholidōtos* 'scaly,' from *pholis, pholid-* 'scale.'

phon /fän/ ▶ **n.** a unit of the perceived loudness of sounds.
– ORIGIN 1930s: from Greek *phōnē* 'sound.'

phon. ▶ **abbr.** phonetics.

pho·na·tion /fō'nāsHən/ ▶ **n.** Phonetics the production or utterance of speech sounds.
– DERIVATIVES **pho·nate** /'fōˌnāt/ **v.**, **pho·na·to·ry** /'fōnəˌtôrē/ **adj.**
– ORIGIN mid 19th cent.: from Greek *phōnē* 'sound, voice' + -ATION.

phone[1] /fōn/ ▶ **n. 1** a telephone: *a few seconds later the phone rang* | *a receptionist answered the phone* | [as modifier] *a phone number.*
2 (**phones**) informal headphones or earphones.
▶ **v.** call someone on the telephone.
– PHRASES **phone it in** informal work or perform in a desultory fashion.

phone[2] ▶ **n.** Phonetics a speech sound; the smallest discrete segment of sound in a stream of speech.
– ORIGIN mid 19th cent.: from Greek *phōnē* 'sound, voice.'

-phone ▶ **comb. form 1** denoting an instrument using or connected with sound: *megaphone.*
2 denoting a person who uses a specified language: *francophone.*
– ORIGIN from Greek *phōnē* 'sound, voice.'

phone bank ▶ **n.** a battery of telephones: *campaign volunteers have spent countless hours manning phone banks.*

phone book ▶ **n.** a telephone directory.

phone card ▶ **n.** another term for CALLING CARD (sense 2).

phone-in ▶ **n. & adj.** another term for CALL-IN.

pho·neme /'fōnēm/ ▶ **n.** Phonetics any of the perceptually distinct units of sound in a specified language that distinguish one word from another, for example *p, b, d,* and *t* in the English words *pad, pat, bad,* and *bat*. Compare with ALLOPHONE[1].
– DERIVATIVES **pho·ne·mic** /fə'nēmik, fō-/ **adj.**, **pho·ne·mics** /fə'nēmiks, fō-/ **n.**
– ORIGIN late 19th cent.: from French *phonème*, from Greek *phōnēma* 'sound, speech,' from *phōnein* 'speak.'

phone sex ▶ **n.** sexually explicit telephone conversation engaged in for the purposes of sexual gratification.

pho·net·ic /fə'netik/ ▶ **adj.** Phonetics of or relating to speech sounds: *detailed phonetic information.* ■ (of a system of writing) having a direct correspondence between symbols and sounds: *a phonetic alphabet.* ■ of or relating to phonetics: *the teachers should receive phonetic training.*
– DERIVATIVES **pho·net·i·cal·ly** /-ik(ə)lē/ **adv.**, **pho·net·i·cism** /-'netiˌsizəm/ **n.**, **pho·net·i·cist** /-'netisist/ **n.**
– ORIGIN early 19th cent.: from modern Latin *phoneticus*, from Greek *phōnētikos*, from *phōnein* 'speak.'

pho·net·ics /fə'netiks/ ▶ **plural n.** [treated as sing.] the study and classification of speech sounds.
– DERIVATIVES **pho·ne·ti·cian** /ˌfōnə'tisHən/ **n.**

phone tree ▶ **n. 1** a menu-driven system that routes callers to recordings, more menus, or a person, depending on their responses.
2 a system for contacting a large number of people quickly in which each person called then telephones a number of other designated people.

pho·ney ▶ **adj. & n.** variant spelling of PHONY.

phon·ic /'fänik/ ▶ **adj.** of or relating to speech sounds. ■ of or relating to phonics: *the English language presents difficulties if a purely phonic approach is attempted.*
– DERIVATIVES **phon·i·cal·ly** /ik(ə)lē/ **adv.**
– ORIGIN early 19th cent.: from Greek *phōnē* 'voice' + -IC.

phon·ics /'fäniks/ ▶ **plural n.** [treated as sing.] a method of teaching people to read by correlating sounds with letters or groups of letters in an alphabetic writing system.

pho·no /'fōnō/ ▶ **n.** short for PHONOGRAPH.
▶ **adj.** [attrib.] denoting a type of plug, and the corresponding socket, used with audio and video equipment, in which one conductor is cylindrical and the other is a central prong that extends beyond it.
– ORIGIN 1940s: abbreviation of PHONOGRAPH.

phono- ▶ **comb. form** relating to sound: *phonograph.*
– ORIGIN from Greek *phōnē* 'sound, voice.'

P

pho·no·car·di·o·gram /ˌfōnōˈkärdēəˌgram/ ▶ **n.** Medicine a chart or record of the sounds made by the heart.

pho·no·gram /ˈfōnəˌgram/ ▶ **n.** Phonetics a symbol representing a vocal sound.

pho·no·graph /ˈfōnəˌgraf/ ▶ **n.** a record player. ■ chiefly historical an early sound-reproducing machine that used cylinders to record as well as reproduce sound.
– DERIVATIVES **pho·no·graph·ic** /ˌfōnəˈgrafik/ **adj.**

pho·no·graph rec·ord ▶ **n.** fuller form of **RECORD** (sense 4 of the noun).

pho·no·lite /ˈfōnəˌlīt/ ▶ **n.** Geology a fine-grained volcanic rock composed of alkali feldspars and nepheline.
– ORIGIN early 19th cent.: from **PHONO-** 'relating to sound' (because of its resonance when struck) + **-LITE**.

pho·nol·o·gy /fəˈnäləjē, fō-/ ▶ **n.** the branch of linguistics that deals with systems of sounds (including or excluding phonetics), esp. in a particular language. ■ the system of relationships among the speech sounds that constitute the fundamental components of a language.
– DERIVATIVES **pho·no·log·i·cal** /ˌfōnəˈläjikəl/ **adj.**, **pho·no·log·i·cal·ly** /ˌfōnəˈläjik(ə)lē/ **adv.**, **pho·nol·o·gist** /-jist/ **n.**

pho·non /ˈfōnän/ ▶ **n.** Physics a quantum of energy or a quasiparticle associated with a compressional wave such as sound or a vibration of a crystal lattice.
– ORIGIN 1930s: from Greek *phōnē* 'sound,' on the pattern of *photon*.

pho·no·tac·tics /ˌfōnōˈtaktiks/ ▶ **plural n.** [treated as sing.] the study of the rules governing the possible phoneme sequences in a language.
– DERIVATIVES **pho·no·tac·tic** /–tik/ **adj.**

pho·ny /ˈfōnē/ (also **phoney**) informal ▶ **adj.** (**phonier, phoniest**) not genuine; fraudulent: *I thought your accent was a bit phony.*
▶ **n.** (pl. **phonies**) a fraudulent person or thing.
– DERIVATIVES **pho·ni·ly** /ˈfōnilē/ **adv.**, **pho·ni·ness n.**
– ORIGIN late 19th cent.: of unknown origin.

pho·ny war the period of comparative inaction at the beginning of World War II between the German invasion of Poland (September 1939) and that of Norway (April 1940).

phoo·ey /ˈfo͞oē/ informal ▶ **exclam.** (also **pfui**) used to express disdain or disbelief: *I say phooey to all their money and fine clothes.*
▶ **n.** nonsense: *those excuses are a lot of phooey.*
– ORIGIN 1920s: imitative.

-phore ▶ **comb. form** denoting an agent or bearer of a specified thing: *ionophore* | *semaphore.*
– ORIGIN from modern Latin *-phorus*, from Greek *-phoros, -phoron* 'bearing, bearer,' from *pherein* 'to bear.'

P

phor·e·sy /ˈfôrəsē/ ▶ **n.** Zoology an association between two organisms in which one (e.g., a mite) travels on the body of another, without being a parasite.
– DERIVATIVES **pho·ret·ic** /fəˈretik/ **adj.**
– ORIGIN 1920s: from French *phorésie*, from Greek *phorēsis* 'being carried.'

Pho·ron·i·da /fəˈränədə/ Zoology a small phylum of wormlike marine invertebrates.
– DERIVATIVES **pho·ro·nid** /fəˈrônid/ **n.**
– ORIGIN modern Latin (plural), from Latin *Phoronis, Phoronid-*, the name of a character in Greek mythology.

-phorous ▶ **comb. form** in adjectives corresponding to nouns ending in *-phore* (such as *ionophorous* corresponding to *ionophore*).

phos·gene /ˈfäsjēn/ ▶ **n.** Chemistry a colorless poisonous gas made by the reaction of chlorine and carbon monoxide. It was used as a poison gas, notably in World War I. ● Alternative name: **carbonyl chloride**; chem. formula: $COCl_2$.
– ORIGIN early 19th cent.: from Greek *phōs* 'light' + **-GEN**, with reference to its original production by the action of sunlight on chlorine and carbon monoxide.

phos·pha·tase /ˈfäsfəˌtās/ ▶ **n.** Biochemistry an enzyme that catalyzes the hydrolysis of organic phosphates in a specified (acid or alkaline) environment.

phos·phate /ˈfäsfāt/ ▶ **n. 1** Chemistry a salt or ester of phosphoric acid, containing PO_4^{3-} or a related anion or a group such as $-OPO(OH)_2$.
2 dated an effervescent soft drink containing phosphoric acid, soda water, and flavoring.
– ORIGIN late 18th cent.: from French, from *phosphore* 'phosphorus.'

phos·phat·ic /fäsˈfatik/ ▶ **adj.** (chiefly of rocks and fertilizer) containing or consisting of phosphates.

phos·pha·tide /ˈfäsfəˌtīd/ ▶ **n.** Biochemistry any of a class of compounds that are fatty acid esters of glycerol phosphate with a nitrogen base linked to the phosphate group.

phos·pha·ti·dyl·cho·line /ˌfäsfəˌtīdlˈkōlēn, fäsˌfatədl-/ ▶ **n.** Biochemistry another term for **LECITHIN**.

phos·phene /ˈfäsfēn/ ▶ **n.** a ring or spot of light produced by pressure on the eyeball or direct stimulation of the visual system other than by light.
– ORIGIN late 19th cent.: formed irregularly from Greek *phōs* 'light' + *phainein* 'to show.'

phos·phide /ˈfäsfīd/ ▶ **n.** Chemistry a binary compound of phosphorus with another element or group.

phos·phine /ˈfäsfēn/ ▶ **n.** Chemistry a colorless foul-smelling gaseous compound of phosphorus and hydrogen, analogous to ammonia, widely used as an insecticidal fumigant in agricultural products. ● Chem. formula: PH_3. It forms salts containing the **phosphonium** ion, PH_4^+.
– ORIGIN late 19th cent.: from **PHOSPHO-** 'relating to phosphorus' + **-INE**[4], on the pattern of *amine*.

phos·phite /ˈfäsfīt/ ▶ **n.** Chemistry old-fashioned term for **PHOSPHONATE** (see **PHOSPHONIC ACID**).

phospho- ▶ **comb. form** representing **PHOSPHORUS**.

phos·pho·cre·a·tine /ˌfäsfōˈkrēətin/ ▶ **n.** Biochemistry a phosphate ester of creatine found in vertebrate muscle, where it serves to store phosphates to provide energy for muscular contraction.

phos·pho·di·es·ter·ase /ˌfäsfōdīˈestərās/ ▶ **n.** Biochemistry an enzyme that breaks a phosphodiester bond in an oligonucleotide.

phos·pho·di·es·ter bond /ˌfäsfōdīˈestər/ ▶ **n.** Biochemistry a chemical bond of the kind joining successive sugar molecules in a polynucleotide.

phos·pho·li·pase /ˌfäsfōˈlīpās/ ▶ **n.** Biochemistry an enzyme that hydrolyzes lecithin or a similar phospholipid.

phos·pho·lip·id /ˌfäsfōˈlipid/ ▶ **n.** Biochemistry a lipid containing a phosphate group in its molecule, e.g., lecithin.

phos·phon·ic ac·id /fäsˈfänik/ ▶ **n.** Chemistry a crystalline acid obtained by the reaction of phosphorus trioxide with water. ● A dibasic acid; chem. formula: $HPO(OH)_2$.
– DERIVATIVES **phos·pho·nate** /ˈfäsfəˌnāt/ **n.**
– ORIGIN late 19th cent.: *phosphonic* from **PHOSPHO-** 'relating to phosphorus,' on the pattern of *sulfonic*.

phos·pho·ni·um /fäsˈfōnēəm/ ▶ **n.** see **PHOSPHINE**.
– ORIGIN late 19th cent.: blend of **PHOSPHORUS** and **AMMONIUM**.

phos·pho·pro·tein /ˌfäsfōˈprōtēn/ ▶ **n.** Biochemistry a protein that contains phosphorus (other than in an associated nucleic acid or phospholipid).

phos·phor /ˈfäsfər/ ▶ **n.** a synthetic fluorescent or phosphorescent substance, esp. any of those used to coat the screens of cathode ray tubes. ■ old-fashioned term for **PHOSPHORUS**.
– ORIGIN early 17th cent.: from Latin *phosphorus* (see **PHOSPHORUS**).

phos·pho·rat·ed /ˈfäsfəˌrātid/ ▶ **adj.** combined or impregnated with phosphorus.

phos·phor bronze ▶ **n.** a tough, hard form of bronze containing a small amount of phosphorus, used esp. for bearings.

phos·pho·resce /ˌfäsfəˈres/ ▶ **v.** [no obj.] emit light or radiation by phosphorescence.

phos·pho·res·cence /ˌfäsfəˈresəns/ ▶ **n.** light emitted by a substance without combustion or perceptible heat: *the stones overhead gleamed with phosphorescence.* ■ Physics the emission of radiation in a similar manner to fluorescence but on a longer timescale, so that emission continues after excitation ceases.
– DERIVATIVES **phos·pho·res·cent adj.**

phos·phor·ic /fäsˈfôrik/ ▶ **adj.** relating to or containing phosphorus. ■ Chemistry of phosphorus with a valence of five. Compare with **PHOSPHOROUS**.
– ORIGIN late 18th cent.: from French *phosphorique*, from *phosphore* 'phosphorus.'

phos·phor·ic ac·id ▶ **n.** Chemistry a crystalline acid obtained, e.g., by treating phosphates with sulfuric acid, and used in fertilizer and soap manufacture and in food processing. ● A tribasic acid; chem. formula: H_3PO_4.

phos·pho·rite /ˈfäsfəˌrīt/ ▶ **n.** a sedimentary rock containing a high proportion of calcium phosphate.
– ORIGIN late 18th cent.: from **PHOSPHORUS** + **-ITE**[1].

phos·pho·rous /ˈfäsfərəs, fäsˈfôrəs/ ▶ **adj.** relating to or containing phosphorus. Compare with **PHOSPHORIC**. ■ Chemistry of phosphorus with a valence of three. ■ phosphorescent.

USAGE The correct spelling for the noun denoting the chemical element is **phosphorus**, while the adjective meaning 'relating to or containing phosphorus' is spelled **phosphorous**. A common mistake is to use the spelling **phosphorous** for the noun as well as the adjective.

phos·pho·rous ac·id ▶ **n.** another term for **PHOSPHONIC ACID**.

phos·pho·rus /ˈfäsfərəs/ ▶ **n.** the chemical element of atomic number 15, a poisonous, combustible nonmetal that exists in two common allotropic forms, **white phosphorus**, a yellowish waxy solid that ignites spontaneously in air and glows in the dark, and **red phosphorus**, a less reactive form used in making matches. (Symbol: **P**)
– ORIGIN late 17th cent.: from Latin, from Greek *phōsphoros*, from *phōs* 'light' + *-phoros* '-bringing.'

USAGE See usage at **PHOSPHOROUS**.

phos·pho·ryl·ase /ˈfäsfərəˌlās, fäsˈfôrəˌlās/ ▶ **n.** Biochemistry an enzyme that introduces a phosphate group into an organic molecule, notably glucose.

phos·pho·ryl·ate /ˈfäsfərəˌlāt, fäsˈfôrə-/ ▶ **v.** [with obj.] chiefly Biochemistry introduce a phosphate group into (a molecule or compound).
– DERIVATIVES **phos·pho·ryl·a·tion** /ˈfäsfərəˈlāshən/ **n.**

phot /fōt/ ▶ **n.** a unit of illumination equal to one lumen per square centimeter.
– ORIGIN early 20th cent.: from Greek *phōs, phōt-* 'light.'

pho·tic /ˈfōtik/ ▶ **adj.** technical of or relating to light, esp. as an agent of chemical change or physiological response. ■ Ecology denoting the layers of the ocean reached by sufficient sunlight to allow plant growth: *an average depth for the photic zone is about 300 feet.*

pho·ti·no /fōˈtēnō/ ▶ **n.** (pl. **photinos**) Physics the hypothetical supersymmetric counterpart of the photon, with spin $-^1/_2$.
– ORIGIN 1970s: from **PHOTON** + *-ino* from **NEUTRINO**.

pho·to /ˈfōtō/ ▶ **n.** (pl. **photos**) a photograph. ■ informal a photo finish.
– ORIGIN mid 19th cent.: abbreviation.

photo- ▶ **comb. form 1** relating to light: *photochemical.*
2 relating to photography: *photocomposition.*
– ORIGIN Sense 1 from Greek *phōs, phōt-* 'light'; sense 2, abbreviation of **PHOTOGRAPHY**.

pho·to·ac·tive /ˌfōtōˈaktiv/ ▶ **adj.** (of a substance) capable of a chemical or physical change in response to illumination.

pho·to·bi·ol·o·gy /ˌfōtōbīˈäləjē/ ▶ **n.** the study of the effects of light on living organisms.

pho·to·bleach·ing /ˌfōtōˈblēchiNG/ ▶ **n.** Biochemistry loss of color by a pigment (such as chlorophyll or rhodopsin) when illuminated.

pho·to·ca·tal·y·sis /ˌfōtōkəˈtaləsis/ ▶ **n.** Chemistry the acceleration of a chemical reaction by light.
– DERIVATIVES **pho·to·cat·a·lyst** /-ˈkatl-ist/ **n.**, **pho·to·cat·a·lyt·ic** /-ˌkatəˈlitik/ **adj.**

pho·to·cath·ode /ˌfōtōˈkaTHōd/ ▶ **n.** a cathode that emits electrons when illuminated, causing an electric current.

pho·to CD ▶ **n.** a compact disc on which still photographs may be stored.

pho·to·cell /ˈfōtōˌsel/ ▶ **n.** short for **PHOTOELECTRIC CELL**.

pho·to·chem·i·cal /ˌfōtōˈkemikəl/ ▶ **adj.** of, relating to, or caused by the chemical action of light: *photochemical smog.* ■ of or relating to photochemistry.
– DERIVATIVES **pho·to·chem·i·cal·ly** /-ik(ə)lē/ **adv.**

pho·to·chem·is·try /ˌfōtōˈkeməstrē/ ▶ **n.** the branch of chemistry concerned with the chemical effects of light.

pho·to·chro·mic /ˌfōtəˈkrōmik/ ▶ **adj.** (of a substance) undergoing a reversible change in color or shade when exposed to light of a particular frequency or intensity: *photochromic sunglasses.*
– DERIVATIVES **pho·to·chro·mism** /-ˈkrōmizəm/ **n.**
– ORIGIN 1950s: from **PHOTO-** 'relating to light' + Greek *khrōma* 'color' + **-IC**.

pho·to·co·ag·u·la·tion /ˌfōtōkōˌagyəˈlāshən/ ▶ **n.** Medicine the use of a laser beam or other intense light source to coagulate and destroy or fuse small areas of tissue, esp. in the retina.

pho·to·com·po·si·tion /ˌfōtōˌkämpəˈzisHən/ ▶ **n.** Printing the setting of material to be printed by projecting it onto photographic film from which the printing surface is prepared.

pho·to·con·duc·tiv·i·ty /ˌfōtōˌkändəkˈtivitē/ ▶ **n.** increased electrical conductivity caused by the presence of light.
– DERIVATIVES **pho·to·con·duc·tive** /-kənˈdəktiv/ **adj.**, **pho·to·con·duc·tor** /-kənˈdəktər/ **n.**

pho·to·cop·i·er /ˈfōtəˌkäpēər/ ▶ **n.** a machine for making photocopies.

pho·to·cop·y /ˈfōtəˌkäpē/ ▶ n. (pl. **photocopies**) a photographic copy of printed or written material produced by a process involving the action of light on a specially prepared surface.
▶ v. (**photocopies, photocopying, photocopied**) [with obj.] make a photocopy of.
– DERIVATIVES **pho·to·cop·i·a·ble** /-ˌkäpēəbəl/ adj.

pho·to·cur·rent /ˌfōtōˈkərənt/ ▶ n. an electric current induced by the action of light.

pho·to·de·grad·a·ble /ˌfōtōdəˈgrādəbəl/ ▶ adj. capable of being decomposed by the action of light, esp. sunlight: *photodegradable plastic.*

pho·to·de·tec·tor /ˌfōtōdəˈtektər/ ▶ n. a device that detects or responds to incident light by using the electrical effect of individual photons.

pho·to·di·ode /ˈfōtōˌdīōd/ ▶ n. a semiconductor diode that, when exposed to light, generates a potential difference or changes its electrical resistance.

pho·to·dis·so·ci·a·tion /ˌfōtōdiˌsōsēˈāsʜən/ ▶ n. Chemistry dissociation of a chemical compound by the action of light.

pho·to·dy·nam·ic /ˌfōtōdīˈnamik/ ▶ adj. Medicine denoting treatment for cancer involving the injection of a cytotoxic compound that is relatively inactive until activated by a laser beam after collecting in the tumor.

pho·to·e·lec·tric /ˌfōtōiˈlektrik/ ▶ adj. characterized by or involving the emission of electrons from a surface by the action of light.
– DERIVATIVES **pho·to·e·lec·tric·i·ty** /ˌfōtōilekˈtrisitē/ n.

pho·to·e·lec·tric cell ▶ n. a device that generates an electric current or voltage dependent on the degree of illumination.

pho·to·e·lec·tron /ˌfōtōiˈlekˌträn/ ▶ n. an electron emitted from an atom by interaction with a photon, esp. an electron emitted from a solid surface by the action of light.
– DERIVATIVES **pho·to·e·lec·tron·ic** /-ilekˈtränik/ adj.

pho·to·e·mis·sion /ˌfōtōiˈmisʜən/ ▶ n. the emission of electrons from a surface caused by the action of light striking it.
– DERIVATIVES **pho·to·e·mis·sive** adj., **pho·to·e·mit·ter** /-iˈmitər/ n.

pho·to·es·say /ˌfōtōˈesā/ ▶ n. an essay or short article consisting of text and numerous photographs.

pho·to fin·ish ▶ n. a close finish of a race in which the winner is identifiable only from a photograph taken as the competitors cross the finish line.

pho·to·fin·ish·ing /ˌfōtōˈfinisʜiNG/ ▶ n. the commercial development and printing of film.

pho·to·fit /ˈfōtōfit/ ▶ n. Brit. a reconstructed picture of a person, esp. one wanted by the police, made from composite photographs of facial features.

pho·tog /fəˈtäg/ ▶ n. informal a photographer.

pho·to·gen·ic /ˌfōtəˈjenik/ ▶ adj. **1** (esp. of a person) looking attractive in photographs or on film: *a photogenic child.*
2 Biology (of an organism or tissue) producing or emitting light.
– DERIVATIVES **pho·to·gen·i·cal·ly** /-(ə)lē/ adv.

pho·to·ge·ol·o·gy /ˌfōtōjēˈäləjē/ ▶ n. the field of study concerned with the geological interpretation of aerial photographs.
– DERIVATIVES **pho·to·ge·o·log·i·cal** /-ˌjēəˈläjikəl/ adj., **pho·to·ge·ol·o·gist** /-jist/ n.

pho·to·gram /ˈfōtəˌgram/ ▶ n. a picture produced with photographic materials, such as light-sensitive paper, but without a camera. ■ archaic a photograph.

pho·to·gram·me·try /ˌfōtəˈgramitrē/ ▶ n. the use of photography in surveying and mapping to measure distances between objects.
– DERIVATIVES **pho·to·gram·met·ric** /-grəˈmetrik/ adj., **pho·to·gram·me·trist** /-trist/ n.

pho·to·graph /ˈfōtəˌgraf/ ▶ n. a picture made using a camera, in which an image is focused onto film or other light-sensitive material and then made visible and permanent by chemical treatment, or stored digitally.
▶ v. [with obj.] take a photograph of. ■ [no obj.] appear in a particular way when in a photograph: *that cityscape photographs well.*
– DERIVATIVES **pho·to·graph·a·ble** adj.

pho·tog·ra·pher /fəˈtägrəfər/ ▶ n. a person who takes photographs, esp. as a job: *a freelance press photographer.*

pho·to·graph·ic /ˌfōtəˈgrafik/ ▶ adj. relating to or resembling photographs: *high-tech digital photographic equipment.*
– DERIVATIVES **pho·to·graph·i·cal·ly** /ˌfōtəˈgrafik(ə)lē/ adv.

pho·to·graph·ic mem·o·ry /ˌfōtəˈgrafik/ ▶ n. the ability to remember information or visual images in great detail.

pho·tog·ra·phy /fəˈtägrəfē/ ▶ n. the art or practice of taking and processing photographs.

> Modern photography is based on the property of silver compounds decomposing to metallic silver when exposed to light. The light-sensitive salts are held in an emulsion (in color film, layers of emulsion) usually mounted on transparent roll film.

pho·to·gra·vure /ˌfōtəgrəˈvyo͝or/ ▶ n. an image produced from a photographic negative transferred to a metal plate and etched in. ■ the production of images in this way.
– ORIGIN late 19th cent.: from French, from *photo-* 'relating to light' + *gravure* 'engraving.'

pho·to·i·o·ni·za·tion /ˌfōtōˌīəniˈzāsʜən/ ▶ n. Physics ionization produced in a medium by the action of electromagnetic radiation.

pho·to·jour·nal·ism /ˌfōtōˈjərnəˌlizəm/ ▶ n. the art or practice of communicating news by photographs, esp. in magazines.
– DERIVATIVES **pho·to·jour·nal·ist** n.

pho·to·li·thog·ra·phy /ˌfōtōliˈᴛʜägrəfē/ ▶ n. lithography using plates made photographically.
– DERIVATIVES **pho·to·lith·o·graph·ic** /-ˌliᴛʜəˈgrafik/ adj., **pho·to·lith·o·graph·i·cal·ly** /-ˌliᴛʜəˈgrafik(ə)lē/ adv.

pho·tol·y·sis /fōˈtäləsis/ ▶ n. Chemistry the decomposition or separation of molecules by the action of light.
– DERIVATIVES **pho·to·lyze** /ˈfōtlˌīz/ v., **pho·to·lyt·ic** /ˌfōtlˈitik/ adj.

photom. ▶ abbr. photometry.

pho·to·map /ˈfōtōˌmap/ ▶ n. a map made from or drawn on photographs of the area concerned.

pho·to·mask /ˈfōtōˌmask/ ▶ n. Electronics a photographic pattern used in making microcircuits, ultraviolet light being shone through the mask onto a photoresist in order to transfer the pattern.

pho·to·me·chan·i·cal /ˌfōtōməˈkanikəl/ ▶ adj. relating to or denoting processes in which photography is involved in the making of a printing plate.
– DERIVATIVES **pho·to·me·chan·i·cal·ly** /-ik(ə)lē/ adv.

pho·tom·e·ter /fōˈtämitər/ ▶ n. an instrument for measuring the intensity of light.
– DERIVATIVES **pho·to·met·ric** /ˌfōtəˈmetrik/ adj., **pho·to·met·ri·cal·ly** /ˌfōtōˈmetrik(ə)lē/ adv., **pho·tom·e·try** /-ˈtämətrē/ n.

pho·to·mi·cro·graph /ˌfōtōˈmīkrōˌgraf/ ▶ n. a photograph of a microscopic object, taken with the aid of a microscope.
– DERIVATIVES **pho·to·mi·crog·ra·pher** /-mīˈkrägrəfər/ n., **pho·to·mi·crog·ra·phy** n.

pho·to·mon·tage /ˌfōtōmänˈtäzʜ/ ▶ n. a montage constructed from photographic images. ■ the technique of constructing such a montage.

pho·to·mor·pho·gen·e·sis /ˌfōtōˌmôrfəˈjenəsis/ ▶ n. Botany development of form and structure in plants that is affected by light, other than that occurring for photosynthesis.

pho·to·mo·sa·ic /ˌfōtōmōˈzāik/ ▶ n. a large-scale detailed picture or map built up by combining photographs of small areas.

pho·to·mul·ti·pli·er /ˌfōtōˈməltəplīər/ ▶ n. an instrument containing a photoelectric cell and a series of electrodes, used to detect and amplify the light from very faint sources.

pho·to·mu·ral /ˌfōtōˈmyo͝orəl/ ▶ n. a mural consisting of a single enlarged photograph or a collection of photographs covering a wall.

pho·ton /ˈfōtän/ ▶ n. Physics a particle representing a quantum of light or other electromagnetic radiation. A photon carries energy proportional to the radiation frequency but has zero rest mass.
– ORIGIN early 20th cent.: from Greek *phōs, phōt-* 'light,' on the pattern of *electron.*

pho·to·neg·a·tive /ˌfōtōˈnegətiv/ ▶ adj. **1** Biology (of an organism) tending to move away from light.
2 Physics (of a substance) exhibiting a decrease in electrical conductivity under illumination.

pho·ton·ic crys·tal /fōˈtänik/ ▶ n. a synthetic crystal that can manipulate or be sensitized to respond to specific wavelengths of light. Its development suggests the possibility of increased miniaturization and efficiency of computing components and other technologies.

pho·ton·ics /fōˈtäniks/ ▶ plural n. [treated as sing.] the branch of technology concerned with the properties and transmission of photons, for example in fiber optics.

pho·to·off·set ▶ n. offset printing using plates made photographically.

pho·to op /ˈfōtō äp/ ▶ n. informal term for **PHOTO OPPORTUNITY**.

pho·to op·por·tu·ni·ty ▶ n. an occasion on which famous people pose for photographers by arrangement.

pho·to·ox·i·da·tion /ˌfōtōˌäksiˈdāsʜən/ ▶ n. Chemistry oxidation caused by the action of light.

pho·to·pe·ri·od /ˈfōtōˌpi(ə)rēəd/ ▶ n. Botany & Zoology the period of time each day during which an organism receives illumination; day length.
– DERIVATIVES **pho·to·pe·ri·od·ic** /ˌfōtōˌpi(ə)rēˈädik/ adj.

pho·to·pe·ri·od·ism /ˌfōtōˈpi(ə)rēəˌdizəm/ (also **photoperiodicity** /-ˌpi(ə)rēəˈdisitē/) ▶ n. Botany & Zoology the response of an organism to seasonal changes in day length.

pho·to·pho·bi·a /ˌfōtəˈfōbēə/ ▶ n. extreme sensitivity to light.
– DERIVATIVES **pho·to·pho·bic** /ˌfōtəˈfōbik/ adj.

pho·to·phore /ˈfōtəˌfôr/ ▶ n. Zoology a light-producing organ in certain fishes and other animals.
– ORIGIN late 19th cent.: from Greek *phōtophoros* 'light-bearing.'

pho·top·ic /fōˈtäpik/ ▶ adj. Physiology relating to or denoting vision in daylight or other bright light, believed to involve chiefly the cones of the retina. Often contrasted with **SCOTOPIC**.
– ORIGIN early 20th cent.: from **PHOTO-** 'light' + **-OPIA** + **-IC**.

pho·to·pig·ment /ˌfōtōˈpigmənt/ ▶ n. a pigment whose chemical state depends on its degree of illumination, such as those in the retina of the eye.

pho·to·po·lar·im·e·ter /ˌfōtəˌpōləˈrimitər/ ▶ n. a telescopic apparatus for photographing stars, galaxies, etc., and measuring the polarization of light from them.

pho·to·pol·y·mer /ˌfōtōˈpäləmər/ ▶ n. a light-sensitive polymeric material, esp. one used in printing plates or microfilms.

pho·to·pos·i·tive /ˌfōtōˈpäzitiv/ ▶ adj. **1** Biology (of an organism) tending to move toward light.
2 Physics (of a substance) exhibiting an increase in electrical conductivity under illumination.

pho·to·prod·uct /ˈfōtōˌprädəkt/ ▶ n. a product of a photochemical reaction.

pho·to·pro·tein /ˌfōtōˈprōtēn/ ▶ n. Biochemistry a protein active in the emission of light by a living creature.

pho·to·re·al·ism /ˈfōtōˈrēəˌlizəm/ ▶ n. **1** detailed and unidealized representation in art, esp. of banal, mundane, or sordid aspects of life.
2 detailed visual representation, like that obtained in a photograph, in a nonphotographic medium such as animation or computer graphics.
– DERIVATIVES **pho·to·re·al·ist** n. & adj., **pho·to·re·al·is·tic** /ˌfōtōˌrēəˈlistik/ adj.

pho·to·re·cep·tor /ˌfōtōriˈseptər/ ▶ n. a structure in a living organism, esp. a sensory cell or sense organ, that responds to light falling on it.
– DERIVATIVES **pho·to·re·cep·tive** /ˈseptiv/ adj.

pho·to·re·con·nais·sance /ˌfōtōriˈkänəsəns/ ▶ n. military reconnaissance carried out by means of aerial photography.

pho·to·re·sist /ˌfōtōriˈzist/ ▶ n. a photosensitive resist that, when exposed to light, loses its resistance or its susceptibility to attack by an etchant or solvent. Such materials are used in making microcircuits.

pho·to·res·pi·ra·tion /ˌfōtōˌrespəˈrāsʜən/ ▶ n. Botany a respiratory process in many higher plants by which they take up oxygen in the light and give out some carbon dioxide, contrary to the general pattern of photosynthesis.

pho·to·re·sponse /ˌfōtōriˈspäns/ ▶ n. Biology a response of a plant or other organism to light, mediated otherwise than through photosynthesis.

pho·to·sen·si·tive /ˌfōtəˈsensitiv/ ▶ adj. having a chemical, electrical, or other response to light: *photosensitive cells | photosensitive drugs.*
– DERIVATIVES **pho·to·sen·si·tiv·i·ty** /-ˌsensəˈtivitē/ n.

pho·to ses·sion ▶ n. a prearranged session in which a photographer takes photographs of someone for publication.

pho·to shoot ▶ n. another term for **PHOTO SESSION**.

pho·to·shop /ˈfōtōˌsʜäp/ (also **Photoshop**) ▶ v. (**photoshops, photoshopping, photoshopped**)

PRONUNCIATION KEY ə *ago, up*; ər *over, fur*; a *hat*; ā *ate*; ä *car*; e *let*; ē *see*; i *fit*; ī *by*; NG *sing*; ō *go*; ô *law, for*; oi *toy*; o͝o *good*; o͞o *goo*; ou *out*; TH *thin*; TH *then*; ZH *vision*

P

[with obj.] alter (a photographic image) digitally using computer software: (as adj. **photoshopped**) *goofy photoshopped pictures of politicians.*
– ORIGIN 1990s: from *Adobe Photoshop*, the proprietary name of such a software package.

pho·to·sphere /ˈfōtəˌsfi(ə)r/ ▶ **n.** Astronomy the luminous envelope of a star from which its light and heat radiate.
– DERIVATIVES **pho·to·spher·ic** /ˌfōtəˈsfi(ə)rik, ˈsferik/ **adj.**

pho·to·stat /ˈfōtōˌstat/ (also **Photostat**) ▶ **n.** trademark a type of machine for making photocopies on special paper. ■ a copy made by this means.
▶ **v.** (**photostats, photostating, photostated**) [with obj.] make a copy of (a document) using a photostat machine.
– DERIVATIVES **pho·to·stat·ic** /ˌfōtōˈstatik/ **adj.**

pho·to·syn·thate /ˌfōtōˈsinTHāt/ ▶ **n.** Biochemistry a sugar or other substance made by photosynthesis.

pho·to·syn·the·sis /ˌfōtōˈsinTHəsis/ ▶ **n.** the process by which green plants and some other organisms use sunlight to synthesize foods from carbon dioxide and water. Photosynthesis in plants generally involves the green pigment chlorophyll and generates oxygen as a byproduct.
– DERIVATIVES **pho·to·syn·thet·ic** /-ˌsinˈTHetik/ **adj.**, **pho·to·syn·thet·i·cal·ly** /-ˌsinˈTHetik(ə)lē/ **adv.**

pho·to·syn·the·size /ˌfōtōˈsinTHəˌsīz/ ▶ **v.** [no obj.] (of a plant) synthesize sugars or other substances by means of photosynthesis.

pho·to·sys·tem /ˈfōtōˌsistəm/ ▶ **n.** a biochemical mechanism in plants by which chlorophyll absorbs light energy for photosynthesis. There are two such mechanisms (**photosystems I** and **II**) involving different chlorophyll-protein complexes.

pho·to·tax·is /ˌfōtōˈtaksis/ ▶ **n.** (pl. **phototaxes** /-ˈtaksēz/) Biology the bodily movement of a motile organism in response to light, either toward the source of light (**positive phototaxis**) or away from it (**negative phototaxis**). Compare with PHOTOTROPISM. ■ a movement of this kind.
– DERIVATIVES **pho·to·tac·tic** /-ˈtaktik/ **adj.**

pho·to·ther·a·py /ˌfōtōˈTHerəpē/ ▶ **n.** the use of light in the treatment of physical or mental illness.

pho·to·tran·sis·tor /ˌfōtōˌtranˈzistər/ ▶ **n.** a transistor that responds to light striking it by generating and amplifying an electric current.

pho·to·troph /ˈfōtəˌträf/ ▶ **n.** Biology a phototrophic organism.

pho·to·troph·ic /ˌfōtəˈträfik/ ▶ **adj.** Biology (of an organism) obtaining energy from sunlight to synthesize organic compounds for nutrition.

pho·tot·ro·pism /ˌfōtəˈtrōpizəm, fōˈtätrəˌpizəm/ ▶ **n.** Biology the orientation of a plant or other organism in response to light, either toward the source of light (**positive phototropism**) or away from it (**negative phototropism**). Compare with HELIOTROPISM, PHOTOTAXIS.
– DERIVATIVES **pho·to·trop·ic** /ˌfōtəˈtrōpik, -ˈträpik/ **adj.**

pho·to·tube /ˈfōtōˌt(y)o͞ob/ ▶ **n.** Electronics a photocell in the form of an electron tube with a photoemissive cathode.

pho·to·type·set·ter /ˌfōtōˈtīpˌsetər/ ▶ **n.** a machine for photocomposition.
– DERIVATIVES **pho·to·type·set** /-ˌset/ **adj.**, **pho·to·type·set·ting** /-ˌsetiNG/ **n.**

pho·to·vol·ta·ic /ˌfōtəvōlˈtāik, ˌfōtōvälˈ-/ ▶ **adj.** relating to the production of electric current at the junction of two substances exposed to light.

pho·to·vol·ta·ics /ˌfōtəvōlˈtāiks, ˌfōtōväl-/ ▶ **plural n.** [treated as sing.] the branch of technology concerned with the production of electric current at the junction of two substances. ■ [treated as pl.] devices having such a junction.

phr. ▶ **abbr.** phrase.

phrag·mi·tes /fragˈmītēz/ ▶ **n.** a common and invasive tall reed. ● Genus *Phragmites*, family Gramineae: several species, in particular the **common reed** (*P. communis*).
– ORIGIN modern Latin, from Greek *phragmitēs* 'growing in hedges,' from *phragma* 'hedge.'

phras·al /ˈfrāzəl/ ▶ **adj.** [attrib.] Grammar consisting of a phrase or phrases: *the text fragments itself into phrasal units.*
– DERIVATIVES **phras·al·ly** **adv.**

phras·al verb ▶ **n.** Grammar an idiomatic phrase consisting of a verb and another element, typically either an adverb, as in *break down*, or a preposition, for example *see to*, or a combination of both, such as *look down on*.

phrase /frāz/ ▶ **n.** a small group of words standing together as a conceptual unit, typically forming a component of a clause. ■ an idiomatic or short pithy expression: *his favorite phrase is "it's a pleasure."* ■ Music a group of notes forming a distinct unit within a longer passage. ■ Ballet a group of steps within a longer sequence or dance.
▶ **v.** [with obj.] put into a particular form of words: *it's important to phrase the question correctly.* ■ divide (music) into phrases in a particular way, esp. in performance: (as noun **phrasing**) *original phrasing brought out unexpected aspects of the music.*
– PHRASES **turn of phrase** a manner of expression: *an awkward turn of phrase.*
– ORIGIN mid 16th cent. (in the sense 'style or manner of expression'): via late Latin from Greek *phrasis*, from *phrazein* 'declare, tell.'

phrase book ▶ **n.** a book for people visiting a foreign country, listing useful expressions in the language of the country together with their equivalent in the visitor's own language.

phra·se·ol·o·gy /ˌfrāzēˈäləjē/ ▶ **n.** (pl. **phraseologies**) a mode of expression, esp. one characteristic of a particular speaker or writer: *legal phraseology.*
– DERIVATIVES **phra·se·o·log·i·cal** /-zēəˈläjikəl/ **adj.**
– ORIGIN mid 17th cent.: from modern Latin *phraseologia*, from Greek *phraseōn*, genitive plural of *phrasis* 'a phrase' + *-logia* (see -LOGY).

phra·try /ˈfrātrē/ ▶ **n.** (pl. **phratries**) Anthropology a descent group or kinship group in some tribal societies.
– ORIGIN mid 19th cent.: from Greek *phratria*, from *phratēr* 'clansman.'

phreak·ing /ˈfrēkiNG/ ▶ **n.** informal the action of hacking into telecommunications systems, esp. to obtain free calls.
– DERIVATIVES **phreak n.**, **phreak·er** /ˈfrēkər/ **n.**
– ORIGIN 1970s: alteration of *freaking* (see FREAK). The change from *f-* to *ph-* was due to association with PHONE[1].

phre·at·ic /frēˈatik/ ▶ **adj.** Geology relating to or denoting underground water in the zone of saturation (beneath the water table). Compare with VADOSE. ■ (of a volcanic eruption) caused by the heating and expansion of groundwater.
– ORIGIN late 19th cent.: from Greek *phrear, phreat-* 'a well' + -IC.

phre·at·o·mag·mat·ic /frēˌatəmagˈmatik/ ▶ **adj.** Geology (of a volcanic eruption) in which both magmatic gases and steam from groundwater are expelled.
– ORIGIN mid 20th cent.: from Greek *phrear, phreat-* 'a well' + *magmatic* (see MAGMA).

phre·at·o·phyte /frēˈatəˌfīt/ ▶ **n.** Botany a plant with a deep root system that draws its water supply from near the water table.
– DERIVATIVES **phre·at·o·phyt·ic** /-ˌatəˈfitik/ **adj.**
– ORIGIN 1920s: from Greek *phrear, phreat-* 'a well' + -PHYTE.

phren. ▶ **abbr.** ■ phrenological. ■ phrenology.

phren·ic /ˈfrenik/ ▶ **adj.** [attrib.] Anatomy of or relating to the diaphragm: *the phrenic nerves.*
– ORIGIN early 18th cent.: from French *phrénique*, from Greek *phrēn, phren-* 'diaphragm, mind' (because the mind was once thought to lie in the diaphragm).

phre·nol·o·gy /freˈnäləjē/ ▶ **n.** chiefly historical the detailed study of the shape and size of the cranium as a supposed indication of character and mental abilities.
– DERIVATIVES **phre·no·log·i·cal** /ˌfrenəˈläjikəl/ **adj.**, **phre·nol·o·gist** /-jist/ **n.**
– ORIGIN early 19th cent.: from Greek *phrēn, phren-* 'mind' + -LOGY.

Phryg·i·a /ˈfrijēə/ an ancient region in west central Asia Minor, to the south of Bithynia. It reached the peak of its power in the 8th century BC under King Midas. It was eventually absorbed into the kingdom of Lydia in the 6th century BC.

Phryg·i·an /ˈfrijēən/ ▶ **adj.** of or relating to Phrygia, its people, or their language.
▶ **n. 1** a native or inhabitant of ancient Phrygia.
2 the extinct Indo-European language of the ancient Phrygians, related to Greek and Armenian, of which only a few inscriptions survive.

Phryg·i·an cap ▶ **n.** a soft conical cap with the top bent forward, worn in ancient times and now identified with the liberty cap.

Phryg·i·an mode ▶ **n.** Music the mode represented by the natural diatonic scale E–E (containing a minor 2nd, 3rd, 6th, and 7th).

PHS ▶ **abbr.** Public Health Service.

phthal·ic ac·id /ˈTHalik/ ▶ **n.** Chemistry a crystalline acid derived from benzene, with two carboxylic acid groups attached to the benzene ring. ● Chem. formula: $C_6H_4(COOH)_2$; three isomers.
– DERIVATIVES **phthal·ate** /ˈTHalˌāt/ **n.**
– ORIGIN mid 19th cent.: *phthalic*, shortening of *naphthalic* (see NAPHTHALENE).

phthal·ic an·hy·dride ▶ **n.** Chemistry a crystalline compound made by oxidizing naphthalene, used as an intermediate in the manufacture of plastics, resins, and dyes. ● A bicyclic anhydride; chem. formula: $C_6H_4(CO)_2O$.
– ORIGIN mid 19th cent.: *phthalic*, shortening of *naphthalic* (see NAPHTHALENE).

phthal·o·cy·a·nine /ˌTHaləˈsīəˌnēn/ ▶ **n.** Chemistry a greenish-blue crystalline dye of the porphyrin group. ● Chem. formula: $C_{32}H_{18}N_8$. ■ any of a large class of green or blue pigments and dyes that are chelate complexes of this compound or one of its derivatives with a metal (in particular, copper).
– ORIGIN 1930s: from *phthalic* (see PHTHALIC ACID) + Greek *kuan(e)os* 'dark blue' + -INE[4].

Phthi·rap·ter·a /THīˈraptərə/ Entomology an order of insects comprising both the sucking lice and the biting lice.
– ORIGIN modern Latin (plural), from Greek *phtheir* 'louse' + *pteron* 'wing.'

phthi·sis /ˈTHīsis, ˈtī-/ ▶ **n.** Medicine, archaic pulmonary tuberculosis or a similar progressive systemic disease.
– DERIVATIVES **phthis·ic** /ˈtizik, ˈTHizik/ **adj.**, **phthis·i·cal** /ˈtizikəl, ˈTHiz-/ **adj.**
– ORIGIN mid 16th cent.: via Latin from Greek, from *phthinein* 'to decay.'

Phu·ket /ˌpo͞oˈket/ **1** an island in Thailand, located at the head of the Strait of Malacca off the western coast of the Malay Peninsula.
2 a port at the south end of Phuket Island, a major resort center and outlet to the Indian Ocean.

phut /fət/ ▶ **exclam.** British term for PFFT.
– ORIGIN late 19th cent.: perhaps from Hindi *phaṭnā* 'to burst.'

phyco- ▶ **comb. form** relating to seaweed: *phycology.*
– ORIGIN from Greek *phukos* 'seaweed.'

phy·co·bi·lin /ˌfīkōˈbilin, -ˈbilin/ ▶ **n.** Biochemistry any of a group of red or blue photosynthetic pigments present in some algae.

phy·co·cy·an·in /ˌfīkōˈsīənin/ ▶ **n.** Biochemistry any of a group of blue photosynthetic pigments present in cyanobacteria.

phy·co·e·ryth·rin /ˌfīkōˈerəTHrin, -iˈriTHrin/ ▶ **n.** Biochemistry any of a group of red photosynthetic pigments present in red algae and some cyanobacteria.

phy·col·o·gy /fīˈkäləjē/ ▶ **n.** the branch of botany concerned with seaweeds and other algae.
– DERIVATIVES **phy·co·log·i·cal** /ˌfīkəˈläjikəl/ **adj.**, **phy·col·o·gist** /-jist/ **n.**

phy·co·my·cete /ˌfīkōˈmīˌsēt, ˌfīkōmīˈsēt/ ▶ **n.** Botany any of the lower fungi, which typically form a nonseptate mycelium. ● Subdivisions Mastigomycotina and Zygomycotina; formerly placed in a class Phycomycetes.

phy·co·my·co·sis /ˌfīkōmīˈkōsis/ ▶ **n.** Medicine & Veterinary Medicine infection with a parasitic fungus that affects the sinuses and the tissues of the lungs, skin, and nerves. ● The fungus is typically a phycomycete, typically of the genus *Rhizopus*, *Absidia*, or *Mucor*.

Phyfe /fīf/, Duncan (1768–1854) US cabinetmaker; born in Scotland. Between 1792 and 1847, working mostly with mahogany, he made chairs, sofas, and tables noted for their graceful proportions and precisely carved simple ornaments.

phy·la /ˈfīlə/ plural form of PHYLUM.

phy·lac·ter·y /fīˈlaktərē/ ▶ **n.** (pl. **phylacteries**) a small leather box containing Hebrew texts on vellum, worn by Jewish men at morning prayer as a reminder to keep the law.
– ORIGIN late Middle English: via late Latin from Greek *phulaktērion* 'amulet,' from *phulassein* 'to guard.'

phylactery

phy·let·ic /fīˈletik/ ▶ **adj.** Biology relating to or denoting the evolutionary development of a species or other group.
– DERIVATIVES **phy·let·i·cal·ly** /-ik(ə)lē/ **adv.**
– ORIGIN late 19th cent.: from Greek *phuletikos*, from *phuletēs* 'tribesman,' from *phulē* 'tribe.'

phyl·lite /ˈfilīt/ ▶ **n.** Geology a fine-grained metamorphic rock with a well-developed laminar structure, intermediate between slate and schist in degree of metamorphism.
– ORIGIN late 19th cent.: from Greek *phullon* 'leaf' + -ITE[1].

phyl·lo /ˈfēlō/ (also **filo**) ▶ **n.** a kind of dough that can be stretched into thin sheets, used in layers to make pastries, esp. in eastern Mediterranean cooking: [as modifier] *phyllo pastry.*
– ORIGIN 1950s: from modern Greek *phullo* 'leaf.'

phyl·lo- ▶ comb. form of a leaf; relating to leaves: *phyllotaxis.*
– ORIGIN from Greek *phullon* 'leaf.'

phyl·lo·clade /ˈfiləˌklād/ ▶ n. Botany a flattened branch or stem-joint resembling and functioning as a leaf.
– ORIGIN mid 19th cent.: from modern Latin *phyllocladium*, from Greek *phullōdēs* 'leaflike,' from *phullon* 'leaf.'

phyl·lode /ˈfilōd/ ▶ n. Botany a winged leaf stalk that functions as a leaf.
– ORIGIN mid 19th cent.: from modern Latin *phyllodium*, from Greek *phullōdēs* 'leaflike,' from *phullon* 'leaf.'

phyl·lo·pod /ˈfiləˌpäd/ ▶ n. Zoology a branchiopod crustacean.
– ORIGIN from modern Latin *Phyllopoda* (former class name), from Greek *phullon* 'leaf' + *pous, pod-* 'foot.'

phyl·lo·qui·none /ˌfilōˈkwinōn, -kwiˈnōn/ ▶ n. Biochemistry one of the K vitamins, found in cabbage, spinach, and other leafy green vegetables, and essential for the blood-clotting process. Also called **VITAMIN K1** (see **VITAMIN K**).

phyl·lo·tax·is /ˌfiləˈtaksis/ (also **phyllotaxy** /ˈfiləˌtaksē/) ▶ n. Botany the arrangement of leaves on an axis or stem.
– DERIVATIVES **phyl·lo·tac·tic** /-ˈtaktik/ adj.

phyl·lox·e·ra /fiˈläksərə, ˌfiləkˈsi(ə)rə/ ▶ n. a plant louse that is a pest of vines. ● *Phylloxera vitifoliae*, family Phylloxeridae, suborder Homoptera.
– ORIGIN mid 19th cent.: modern Latin, from Greek *phullon* 'leaf' + *xēros* 'dry.'

phy·lo·gen·e·sis /ˌfiləˈjenəsis/ ▶ n. Biology the evolutionary development and diversification of a species or group of organisms, or of a particular feature of an organism. Compare with **ONTOGENESIS**.
– DERIVATIVES **phy·lo·ge·net·ic** /-jəˈnetik/ adj., **phy·lo·ge·net·i·cal·ly** /-jəˈnetik(ə)lē/ adv.
– ORIGIN late 19th cent.: from Greek *phulon, phulē* 'race, tribe' + **GENESIS**.

phy·log·e·ny /fīˈläjənē/ ▶ n. the branch of biology that deals with phylogenesis. Compare with **ONTOGENY**. ■ another term for **PHYLOGENESIS**.
– DERIVATIVES **phy·lo·gen·ic** /ˌfiləˈjenik/ adj., **phy·lo·gen·i·cal·ly** /ˌfiləˈjenik(ə)lē/ adv.
– ORIGIN late 19th cent.: from Greek *phulon, phulē* 'race, tribe' + **-GENY**.

phy·lum /ˈfīləm/ ▶ n. (pl. **phyla** /-lə/) Zoology a principal taxonomic category that ranks above class and below kingdom. ■ Linguistics a group of languages related to each other less closely than those forming a family, esp. one in which the relationships are disputed or unclear.
– ORIGIN late 19th cent.: modern Latin, from Greek *phulon* 'race.'

phys. ▶ abbr. ■ physical. ■ physician. ■ physics. ■ physiological. ■ physiology.

phy·sa·lis /ˈfisəlis, ˈfīs-/ ▶ n. a plant of a genus that includes the cape gooseberry and Chinese lantern, which have an inflated, lanternlike calyx. ● Genus *Physalis*, family Solanaceae: many species.
– ORIGIN modern Latin, from Greek *phusallis* 'bladder' (because of the inflated calyx).

phys ed /ˈfiz ˈed/ ▶ n. informal short for **PHYSICAL EDUCATION**.

phys·i·at·rics /ˌfizēˈatriks/ ▶ plural n. [treated as sing.] another term for **PHYSICAL THERAPY**.
– DERIVATIVES **phys·i·at·ric** adj., **phys·i·at·rist** /ˌfizēˈatrist, fiˈzīəˌtrist/ n.

phys·ic /ˈfizik/ archaic ▶ n. medicine, esp. a cathartic. ■ the art of healing.
▶ v. (**physics, physicking** /ˈfiziking/, **physicked** /ˈfizikt/) [with obj.] treat with a medicine.
– ORIGIN Middle English: from Old French *fisique* 'medicine,' from Latin *physica*, from Greek *phusikē* (*epistēmē*) '(knowledge) of nature.'

phys·i·cal /ˈfizikəl/ ▶ adj. **1** of or relating to the body as opposed to the mind: *a whole range of physical and mental challenges.* ■ involving bodily contact or activity: *verbal or physical abuse | football and other physical games.*
2 of or relating to things perceived through the senses as opposed to the mind; tangible or concrete: *pleasant physical environments | physical assets such as houses or cars.* ■ of or relating to physics or the operation of natural forces generally: *physical laws.*
▶ n. (also **physical examination**) a medical examination to determine a person's bodily fitness.
– PHRASES **get physical** informal become aggressive or violent. ■ become sexually intimate with someone.
– DERIVATIVES **phys·i·cal·i·ty** /ˌfiziˈkalitē/ n., **phys·i·cal·ly** /-ik(ə)lē/ adv., **phys·i·cal·ness** n.
– ORIGIN late Middle English (in the sense 'medicinal, relating to medicine'): from medieval Latin *physicalis*, from Latin *physica* 'things relating to nature' (see **PHYSIC**). Sense 2 dates from the late 16th cent. and sense 1 from the late 18th cent.

phys·i·cal an·thro·pol·o·gy ▶ n. see **ANTHROPOLOGY**.

phys·i·cal chem·is·try ▶ n. the branch of chemistry concerned with the application of the techniques and theories of physics to the study of chemical systems.

phys·i·cal ed·u·ca·tion ▶ n. instruction in physical exercise and games, esp. in schools.

phys·i·cal ge·og·ra·phy ▶ n. the branch of geography dealing with natural features and processes.

phys·i·cal·ism /ˈfizikəlˌizəm/ ▶ n. Philosophy the doctrine that the real world consists simply of the physical world.
– DERIVATIVES **phys·i·cal·ist** n. & adj., **phys·i·cal·is·tic** /ˌfizikəˈlistik/ adj.

phys·i·cal·ize /ˈfizikəlˌīz/ ▶ v. [with obj.] express or represent by physical means or in physical terms: *physicalizing your anger can help release tension.*
– DERIVATIVES **phys·i·cal·i·za·tion** /ˌfizikəliˈzāshən/ n.

phys·i·cal med·i·cine ▶ n. **1** the branch of medicine concerned with the treatment of disease by physical means such as manipulation, heat, electricity, or radiation, rather than by medication or surgery.
2 the branch of medicine that treats biomechanical disorders and injuries.

phys·i·cal sci·ences ▶ plural n. the sciences concerned with the study of inanimate natural objects, including physics, chemistry, astronomy, and related subjects. Often contrasted with **LIFE SCIENCES**.

phys·i·cal the·a·ter ▶ n. a form of theater that emphasizes the use of physical movement, as in dance and mime, for expression.

phys·i·cal ther·a·py ▶ n. the treatment of disease, injury, or deformity by physical methods such as massage, heat treatment, and exercise rather than by drugs or surgery.
– DERIVATIVES **phys·i·cal ther·a·pist** n.

phys·i·cal train·ing ▶ n. the systematic use of exercises to promote bodily fitness and strength.

phy·si·cian /fiˈzishən/ ▶ n. a person qualified to practice medicine. ■ a healer: *physicians of the soul.*
– PHRASES **physician, heal thyself** proverb before attempting to correct others, make sure that you aren't guilty of the same faults. [with biblical allusion to Luke 4:23.]
– ORIGIN Middle English: from Old French *fisicien*, based on Latin *physica* 'things relating to nature' (see **PHYSIC**).

phys·i·cian's as·sis·tant ▶ n. someone qualified to assist a physician and carry out routine clinical procedures under the supervision of a physician.

phys·i·cist /ˈfizəsist/ ▶ n. an expert in or student of physics.

physico- ▶ comb. form physical; physical and ...: *physico-mental.*
– ORIGIN from **PHYSICS**.

phys·i·co·chem·i·cal /ˌfizikōˈkemikəl/ ▶ adj. of or relating to physics and chemistry or to physical chemistry.

phys·ics /ˈfiziks/ ▶ plural n. [treated as sing.] the branch of science concerned with the nature and properties of matter and energy. The subject matter of physics, distinguished from that of chemistry and biology, includes mechanics, heat, light and other radiation, sound, electricity, magnetism, and the structure of atoms. ■ the physical properties and phenomena of something: *the physics of plasmas.*
– ORIGIN late 15th cent. (denoting natural science in general, esp. the Aristotelian system): plural of obsolete *physic* 'physical (thing),' suggested by Latin *physica*, Greek *phusika* 'natural things,' from *phusis* 'nature.'

physio- ▶ comb. form **1** relating to nature and natural phenomena: *physiography.*
2 representing **PHYSIOLOGY**.
– ORIGIN from Greek *phusis* 'nature.'

phys·i·o·chem·i·cal /ˌfizēōˈkemikəl/ ▶ adj. of or relating to physiological chemistry.

phys·i·o·crat /ˈfizēəˌkrat/ ▶ n. a member of an 18th-century group of French economists who believed that agriculture was the source of all wealth and that agricultural products should be highly priced. Advocating adherence to a supposed natural order of social institutions, they also stressed the necessity of free trade.
– DERIVATIVES **phys·i·oc·ra·cy** /ˌfizēˈäkrəsē/ n., **phys·i·o·crat·ic** /ˌfizēəˈkratik/ adj.
– ORIGIN late 18th cent.: from French *physiocrate*, from *physiocratie* 'physiocracy' (see **PHYSIO-**, **-CRACY**).

phys·i·og·no·mist /ˌfizēˈä(g)nəmist/ ▶ n. a person supposedly able to judge character (or, formerly, to predict the future) from facial characteristics.
– ORIGIN late 16th cent.: from Old French *physionomiste.*

phys·i·og·no·my /ˌfizēˈä(g)nəmē/ ▶ n. (pl. **physiognomies**) a person's facial features or expression, esp. when regarded as indicative of character or ethnic origin. ■ the supposed art of judging character from facial characteristics. ■ the general form or appearance of something: *the physiognomy of the landscape.*
– DERIVATIVES **phys·i·og·nom·ic** /ˌfizēəˈnämik/ adj., **phys·i·og·nom·i·cal** /ˌfizēəˈnämikəl/ adj., **phys·i·og·nom·i·cal·ly** /ˌfizēəˈnämik(ə)lē/ adv.
– ORIGIN late Middle English: from Old French *phisonomie*, via medieval Latin from Greek *phusiognōmonia* 'judging of a man's nature (by his features),' based on *gnōmōn* 'a judge, interpreter.'

phys·i·og·ra·phy /ˌfizēˈägrəfē/ ▶ n. another term for **PHYSICAL GEOGRAPHY**.
– DERIVATIVES **phys·i·og·ra·pher** /-fər/ n., **phys·i·o·graph·ic** /ˌfizēəˈgrafik/ adj., **phys·i·o·graph·i·cal** /ˌfizēəˈgrafikəl/ adj., **phys·i·o·graph·i·cal·ly** /ˌfizēəˈgrafik(ə)lē/ adv.
– ORIGIN early 19th cent.: from French *physiographie* (see **PHYSIO-**, **-GRAPHY**).

physiol. ▶ abbr. ■ physiological. ■ physiologist. ■ physiology.

phys·i·o·log·i·cal sa·line /ˌfizēəˈläjikəl/ ▶ n. a solution of salts that is isotonic with the body fluids.

phys·i·ol·o·gy /ˌfizēˈäləjē/ ▶ n. the branch of biology that deals with the normal functions of living organisms and their parts. ■ the way in which a living organism or bodily part functions: *the physiology of the brain.*
– DERIVATIVES **phys·i·o·log·ic** /ˌfizēəˈläjik/ adj., **phys·i·o·log·i·cal** /ˌfizēəˈläjikəl/ adj., **phys·i·o·log·i·cal·ly** /ˌfizēəˈläjik(ə)lē/ adv., **phys·i·ol·o·gist** /-jist/ n.
– ORIGIN early 17th cent.: from Latin *physiologia* (perhaps via French), from Greek *phusiologia* 'natural philosophy' (see **PHYSIO-**, **-LOGY**).

phys·i·o·ther·a·py /ˌfizēōˈtherəpē/ ▶ n. British term for **PHYSICAL THERAPY**.
– DERIVATIVES **phys·i·o·ther·a·pist** /-pist/ n.

phy·sique /fiˈzēk/ ▶ n. the form, size, and development of a person's body: *a sturdy, muscular physique | they were much alike in physique.*
– ORIGIN early 19th cent.: from French, literally 'physical' (used as a noun).

phy·so·stig·mine /ˌfīsōˈstigˌmēn/ ▶ n. Chemistry a compound that is the active ingredient of the Calabar bean and is used medicinally in eye drops because of its anticholinergic activity. ● A tricyclic alkaloid; chem. formula: $C_{15}H_{21}N_3O_2$.
– ORIGIN mid 19th cent.: from the modern Latin genus name *Physostigma* (to which the Calabar bean belongs) + **-INE**[4].

-phyte ▶ comb. form denoting a plant or plantlike organism: *epiphyte.*
– ORIGIN from Greek *phuton* 'a plant,' from *phuein* 'come into being.'

-phytic ▶ comb. form in adjectives corresponding to nouns ending in *-phyte* (such as *epiphytic* corresponding to *epiphyte*).

phyto- ▶ comb. form of a plant; relating to plants: *phytogeography.*
– ORIGIN from Greek *phuton* 'a plant,' from *phuein* 'come into being.'

phy·to·a·lex·in /ˌfītōəˈleksin/ ▶ n. Botany a substance that is produced by plant tissues in response to contact with a parasite and that specifically inhibits the growth of that parasite.
– ORIGIN 1940s: from **PHYTO-** 'of plants' + *alexin*, a name for a class of substances found in blood serum, able to destroy bacteria.

phy·to·chem·i·cal /ˌfītōˈkemikəl/ ▶ n. any of various biologically active compounds found in plants.
▶ adj. relating to phytochemistry or phytochemicals.

phy·to·chem·is·try /ˌfītōˈkeməstrē/ ▶ n. the branch of chemistry concerned with plants and plant products.
– DERIVATIVES **phy·to·chem·ist** /-ˈkemist/ n.

phy·to·chrome /ˈfītəˌkrōm/ ▶ n. Biochemistry a blue-green pigment found in many plants, in which it regulates various developmental processes.
– ORIGIN late 19th cent.: from **PHYTO-** 'relating to plants' + Greek *khrōma* 'color.'

phy·to·es·tro·gen /ˌfītō'estrəjən/ ▶ **n.** an estrogen occurring naturally in legumes, considered beneficial in some diets.

phy·to·ge·net·ic /ˌfītōjə'netik/ ▶ **adj.** Botany of or relating to the origin and evolution of plants.

phy·to·ge·o·graph·i·cal king·dom /ˌfītōˌjēə'grafikəl/ ▶ **n.** Botany each of a number of major areas of the earth distinguished on the basis of the characteristic plants present. They usually include the Boreal, Paleotropical, Neotropical, Australian, and Antarctic kingdoms.

phy·to·ge·og·ra·phy /ˌfītōjē'ägrəfē/ ▶ **n.** the branch of botany that deals with the geographical distribution of plants.
– DERIVATIVES **phy·to·ge·og·ra·pher** /-fər/ **n.**, **phy·to·ge·o·graph·ic** /ˌfītōˌjēə'grafik/ **adj.**, **phy·to·ge·o·graph·i·cal** /'fītōˌjēə'grafikəl/ **adj.**, **phy·to·ge·o·graph·i·cal·ly** /ˌfītōˌjēə'grafik(ə)lē/ **adv.**

phy·to·he·mag·glu·ti·nin /ˌfītōˌhēmə'glo͞otn-in/ (Brit. **phytohaemagglutinin**) ▶ **n.** Biochemistry a toxic plant protein, esp. that extracted from the red kidney bean. It has important medical applications, esp. in immunology, because it can induce mitosis and also causes red blood cells to clump together.

phy·to·lith /'fītəlith/ ▶ **n.** Botany a minute mineral particle formed inside a plant. ■ Paleontology a fossilized particle of plant tissue.

phy·to·nu·tri·ent /ˌfītō'n(y)o͞otrēənt/ ▶ **n.** a substance found in certain plants that is believed to be beneficial to human health and to help prevent various diseases.

phy·to·pa·thol·o·gy /ˌfītōpə'THäləjē/ ▶ **n.** the study of plant diseases.
– DERIVATIVES **phy·to·path·o·log·i·cal** /-ˌpaTHə'läjikəl/ **adj.**, **phy·to·path·ol·o·gist** /-jist/ **n.**

phy·toph·a·gous /fī'täfəgəs/ ▶ **adj.** Zoology (esp. of an insect or other invertebrate) feeding on plants.
– DERIVATIVES **phy·toph·a·gy** /-əjē/ **n.**

phy·to·plank·ton /ˌfītō'plaNGktən/ ▶ **n.** Biology plankton consisting of microscopic plants.

phy·to·san·i·tar·y /ˌfītō'saniterē/ ▶ **adj.** (of agricultural goods crossing borders) sanitary with regard to pests and pathogens: *a point-of-origin phytosanitary certificate.*

phy·to·tox·ic /ˌfītə'täksik/ ▶ **adj.** Botany poisonous to plants.
– DERIVATIVES **phy·to·tox·ic·i·ty** /-ˌtäk'sisitē/ **n.**

phy·to·tox·in /ˌfītə'täksin/ ▶ **n.** Botany a poisonous substance derived from a plant. ■ a substance that is phytotoxic, esp. one produced by a parasite.

PI ▶ **abbr.** private investigator.

pi /pī/ ▶ **n.** the sixteenth letter of the Greek alphabet (Π, π), transliterated as 'p.' ■ the numerical value of the ratio of the circumference of a circle to its diameter (approximately 3.14159). [from the initial letter of Greek *periphereia* 'circumference.'] ■ **(Pi)** [followed by Latin genitive] Astronomy the sixteenth star in a constellation: *Pi Herculis.* ■ Chemistry & Physics relating to or denoting an electron or orbital with one unit of angular momentum about an internuclear axis.
▶ **symbol** ■ (π) the numerical value of pi. ■ (Π) osmotic pressure. ■ (Π) mathematical product.
– ORIGIN Greek.

pi·a /'pīə, 'pēə/ ▶ **n.** short for PIA MATER.
– DERIVATIVES **pi·al** /'pīəl, 'pēəl/ **adj.**

pi·ac·u·lar /pī'akyələr/ ▶ **adj.** rare making or requiring atonement.
– ORIGIN early 17th cent.: from Latin *piacularis*, from *piaculum* 'expiation,' from *piare* 'appease.'

Piaf /'pēäf, pyäf/, Edith (1915–63), French singer; born *Edith Giovanna Gassion.* She became known as a cabaret and music-hall singer in the late 1930s. Her songs included "La Vie en rose" and "Je ne regrette rien."

piaffe /pyaf/ ▶ **n.** a movement performed in advanced dressage and classical riding, in which the horse executes a slow, elevated trot without moving forward.
▶ **v.** [no obj.] (of a horse) perform such a movement.
– ORIGIN mid 18th cent.: from French *piaffer* 'to strut.'

Pia·get /ˌpēə'ZHā, pyä-/, Jean (1896–1980), Swiss psychologist. His work on the intellectual and logical abilities of children provided the single biggest impact on the study of the development of human thought processes.

pi·a ma·ter /'pīə 'mātər, 'pēə 'mätər/ ▶ **n.** Anatomy the delicate innermost membrane enveloping the brain and spinal cord. See also MENINGES.
– ORIGIN late 19th cent.: from medieval Latin, in full literally 'tender mother,' translating Arabic *al-'umm ar-raḳīḳa.*

pia·ni /pē'änē/ plural form of PIANO².

pi·a·nism /'pēəˌnizəm/ ▶ **n.** artistry or technical skill in playing the piano, or in composing piano music.
– DERIVATIVES **pi·a·nis·tic** /ˌpēə'nistik/ **adj.**, **pi·a·nis·ti·cal·ly** /ˌpēə'nistik(ə)lē/ **adv.**

pi·a·nis·si·mo /ˌpēə'nisiˌmō/ Music ▶ **adv. & adj.** (esp. as a direction) very soft or softly.
▶ **n.** (pl. **pianissimos** or **pianissimi** /-ˌmī/) a passage marked to be performed very softly.
– ORIGIN Italian, superlative of *piano* (see PIANO²).

pi·an·ist /'pēənist, pē'anist/ ▶ **n.** a person who plays the piano, esp. professionally.
– ORIGIN mid 19th cent.: from French *pianiste*, from *piano* (see PIANO¹).

pi·an·o¹ /pē'anō/ ▶ **n.** (pl. **pianos**) a large keyboard musical instrument with a wooden case enclosing a soundboard and metal strings, which are struck by hammers when the keys are depressed. The strings' vibration is stopped by dampers when the keys are released, and it can be regulated for length and volume by two or three pedals.

grand piano

– ORIGIN early 19th cent.: from Italian, abbreviation of PIANOFORTE.

pi·a·no² /pē'änō, pē'anō/ Music ▶ **adv. & adj.** (esp. as a direction) soft or softly.
▶ **n.** (pl. **pianos** or **piani** /-nē/) a passage marked to be performed softly.
– ORIGIN Italian, literally 'soft.'

pi·an·o ac·cor·di·on ▶ **n.** an accordion with the melody played on a small vertical keyboard like that of a piano.

pi·a·no bar ▶ **n.** a bar that features live piano music.

pi·a·no bench ▶ **n.** a bench for sitting at a piano, often with an adjustable height mechanism and/or a storage area for music.

pi·an·o·forte /pēˌanō'fôrtā, pē'anōˌfôrt/ ▶ **n.** formal term for PIANO¹.
– ORIGIN mid 18th cent.: from Italian, earlier *piano e forte* 'soft and loud,' expressing the gradation in tone.

pi·a·no hinge ▶ **n.** a narrow hinge with a pin of the same length as the movable part.

pi·a·no·la /ˌpēə'nōlə/ ▶ **n.** trademark a piano equipped to be played automatically using a piano roll.
– ORIGIN late 19th cent.: apparently a diminutive of PIANO¹.

pia·no no·bi·le /'pyänō 'nōbēle/ ▶ **n.** Architecture the main story of a large house (usually the first floor), containing the principal rooms.
– ORIGIN Italian, literally 'noble floor.'

pi·an·o roll /pē'änō/ ▶ **n.** a roll of perforated paper that controls the movement of the keys in a player piano or similar instrument, so producing a particular melody.

pi·an·o stool ▶ **n.** a stool for a pianist, typically adjustable in height.

pi·an·o tri·o ▶ **n.** a trio for piano and two stringed instruments, usually violin and cello.

pi·an·o wire ▶ **n.** strong steel wire used esp. for piano strings.

pi·as·sa·va /ˌpēə'sävə/ (also **piassaba** /-bə/) ▶ **n.** a stout fiber obtained from the leaf stalks of a number of South American and African palm trees. ■ a palm tree producing this fiber.
– ORIGIN mid 19th cent.: via Portuguese from Tupi *piaçába.*

pi·as·ter /pē'astər/ (also **piastre**) ▶ **n.** a monetary unit of several Middle Eastern countries, equal to one hundredth of a pound.
– ORIGIN from French, from Italian *piastra (d'argento)* 'plate (of silver).'

pi·az·za ▶ **n. 1** /pē'ätsə/ a public square or marketplace, esp. in an Italian town.
2 /pē'azə/ the veranda of a house.
– ORIGIN late 16th cent.: Italian.

pi·broch /'pēbräk/ ▶ **n.** a form of music for the Scottish bagpipes involving elaborate variations on a theme, typically of a martial or funerary character. ■ a piece of such music.
– ORIGIN early 18th cent.: from Scottish Gaelic *piobaireachd* 'art of piping,' from *piobair* 'piper,' from *piob*, from English PIPE.

pic /pik/ ▶ **n.** (pl. **pics** or **pix** /piks/) informal a photograph or movie; a picture.
– ORIGIN late 19th cent.: abbreviation.

pi·ca¹ /'pīkə/ ▶ **n.** Printing a unit of type size and line length equal to 12 points (about 1/6 inch or 4.2 mm). ■ a size of letter in typewriting, with 10 characters to the inch (about 3.9 to the centimeter).
– ORIGIN late 16th cent.: from Anglo-Latin *pica* (literally 'magpie'), commonly identified with a 15th-cent. book of rules about ecclesiastical feasts, but no edition of such a *pica* printed in "pica" type is known.

pi·ca² ▶ **n.** Medicine a tendency or craving to eat substances other than normal food (such as clay, plaster, or ashes), occurring during childhood or pregnancy, or as a symptom of disease.
– ORIGIN mid 16th cent.: modern Latin, from Latin, literally 'magpie,' probably translating Greek *kissa* 'magpie,' also 'false appetite.'

pi·ca·dor /'pikəˌdôr/ ▶ **n.** a bullfighter on horseback who pricks the bull with a lance to weaken it and goad it.
– ORIGIN Spanish, from *picar* 'to prick.'

pi·can·te /pi'kantā/ ▶ **adj.** (of food) spicy.
– ORIGIN Spanish, literally 'pricking, biting.'

Pi·card /pi'kärd/ ▶ **n. 1** a native or inhabitant of Picardy.
2 the dialect of French spoken in Picardy.
▶ **adj.** relating to Picardy, its inhabitants, or their dialect.

Pic·ar·dy /'pikərdē/ a region and former province of northern France. It was the scene of heavy fighting in World War I. French name **Picardie**.

pic·a·resque /ˌpikə'resk/ ▶ **adj.** of or relating to an episodic style of fiction dealing with the adventures of a rough and dishonest but appealing hero: *a rowdy, picaresque "guys being guys" movie.*
– ORIGIN early 19th cent.: from French, from Spanish *picaresco.* See PICARO.

pic·a·ro /'pēkərō/ ▶ **n.** (pl. **picaros**) a rogue.
– ORIGIN early 17th cent.: from Spanish *pícaro* 'rogue.'

pic·a·roon /ˌpikə'ro͞on/ ▶ **n.** archaic a rogue or scoundrel.
– ORIGIN early 17th cent.: from Spanish *picarón*, augmentative of *pícaro* 'rogue.'

Pi·cas·so /pi'käsō, -'kasō/, Pablo (1881–1973), Spanish painter, sculptor, and graphic artist; resident in France from 1904. His prolific inventiveness and technical versatility made him the dominant figure in avant-garde art in the first half of the 20th century. Following his Blue period (1901–04) and Rose period (1905–06), he developed cubism (1908–14). In the 1920s and 1930s he adopted a neoclassical figurative style.
– DERIVATIVES **Pi·cas·so·esque** /-ˌkäsō'esk, -ˌkasō-/ **adj.**

Pablo Picasso

pic·a·yune /ˌpiki'yo͞on/ ▶ **adj.** informal petty; worthless: *the picayune squabbling of party politicians.*
▶ **n.** a small coin of little value, esp. a 5-cent piece. ■ informal an insignificant person or thing.
– ORIGIN early 19th cent.: from French *picaillon*, denoting a Piedmontese copper coin, also used to mean 'cash,' from Provençal *picaioun*, of unknown ultimate origin.

Pic·ca·dil·ly /ˌpikə'dilē, 'pikəˌdilē/ a street in central London noted for its fashionable shops, hotels, and restaurants.

pic·ca·lil·li /'pikəˌlilē/ ▶ **n.** (pl. **piccalillies** or **piccalillis**) a relish of chopped vegetables, mustard, and hot spices.
– ORIGIN mid 18th cent.: probably from a blend of PICKLE and CHILI.

pic·ca·nin·ny ▶ **n.** chiefly British spelling of PICKANINNY.

pic·ca·ta /pi'kätə/ ▶ **adj.** cooked in a sauce of lemon, parsley and butter: *chicken piccata | turkey cutlets served piccata style.*

pic·co·lo /'pikəˌlō/ ▶ **n.** (pl. **piccolos**) a small flute sounding an octave higher than the ordinary one.
– ORIGIN mid 19th cent.: from Italian, 'small (flute).'

pice /pīs/ ▶ **n.** (pl. **same**) a former monetary unit of India and Pakistan, equal to one quarter of an anna.
– ORIGIN from Hindi *paisā.*

pi·chi /'piCHē/ ▶ **n.** (pl. **pichis**) a small armadillo living in open pampas country in southern South America. ● *Zaedyus pichiy*, family Dasypodidae.

p

–ORIGIN early 19th cent.: via American Spanish from Araucanian, literally 'small.'

pich·i·ci·a·go /ˌpiCHəsēˈägō/ (also **pichiciego**) ▶ **n.** (pl. **pichiciagos**) another term for FAIRY ARMADILLO.
–ORIGIN early 19th cent.: from Spanish, perhaps from Guarani *pichey* 'armadillo' + Spanish *ciego* 'blind' (from Latin *caecus*).

pick[1] /pik/ ▶ **v. 1** [with obj.] take hold of and remove (a flower, fruit, or vegetable) from where it is growing: *I went to pick some flowers for Jenny's room* | (as adj. with submodifier **picked**) *freshly picked mushrooms.* ■ take hold of and lift or move: *he picked a match out of the box* | *picking her up, he carried her into the next room.* ■ [no obj.] (**pick up**) Golf lift up one's ball, esp. when conceding a hole.
2 [with obj.] choose (someone or something) from a number of alternatives, typically after careful thought: *maybe I picked the wrong career after all* | *she left Jed to* **pick out** *some toys* | [no obj.] *this time, I get to pick.* ■ (**pick one's way**) [with adverbial of direction] walk slowly and carefully, selecting the best or safest places to put one's feet: *he picked his way along the edge of the track, avoiding the potholes.*
3 [no obj.] repeatedly pull at something with one's fingers: *the old woman was* **picking at** *the sheet.* ■ [with obj.] make (a hole) in fabric by doing this. ■ eat food or a meal in small amounts or without much appetite: *she* **picked at** *her breakfast.* ■ [with obj.] remove unwanted matter from (one's nose or teeth) by using one's finger or a pointed instrument. ■ criticize someone in a niggling way: *now, please don't start* **picking at** *Ruth.*
4 [with obj.] pluck the strings of (a guitar or banjo). ■ (**pick something out**) play a tune on such an instrument slowly or with difficulty: *she began to pick out a rough melody on the guitar.*
▶ **n. 1** [in sing.] an act or the right of selecting something from among a group of alternatives: *take* **your pick** *from our extensive menu* | *Laura should have* **first pick**. ■ (**the pick of**) informal the person or thing perceived as the best in a particular group: *he was the pick of the bunch.* ■ someone or something that has been selected: *the club made him their first pick.*
2 Basketball an act of blocking or screening a defensive player from the ball handler, allowing an open shot.
–PHRASES **pick and choose** select only the best or most desirable from among a number of alternatives. **pick someone's brains** (or **brain**) informal obtain information by questioning someone who is better informed about a subject than oneself. **pick something clean** completely remove the flesh from a bone or carcass. **pick one's feet up** raise one's feet clear of the ground when walking. **pick a fight** (or **quarrel**) talk or behave in such a way as to provoke an argument or fight. **pick holes in** find fault with. **pick a lock** open a lock with an instrument other than the proper key. **pick someone's pockets** steal something surreptitiously from another person's pocket. **pick someone/something to pieces** (or **apart**) criticize someone or something severely and in detail. **pick up the pieces** restore one's life or a situation to a more normal state, typically after a shock or disaster. **pick up speed** (or **steam**) (of a vehicle) go faster; accelerate. **pick up the threads** resume something that has been interrupted.
–PHRASAL VERBS **pick someone/something off** shoot a member of a group of people or things, aiming carefully from a distance. ■ Baseball put out a runner by a pickoff. **pick on** repeatedly single (someone) out for blame, criticism, or unkind treatment in a way perceived to be unfair. **pick someone/something out** distinguish someone or something among a group of people or things: *Lester picked out two familiar voices.* ■ (of a light) illuminate an object by shining directly on it. ■ (usu. **be picked out**) distinguish shapes or letters from their surroundings by painting or fashioning them in a contrasting color or medium: *the initials are picked out in diamonds.* **pick something over** (or **pick through**) examine or sort through a number of items carefully: *they picked through the charred remains of their home.* **pick up** become better; improve: *my luck's picked up.* ■ become stronger; increase: *the wind has picked up.* **pick oneself up** stand up again after a fall. **pick someone up** go somewhere to collect someone, typically in one's car and according to a prior arrangement. ■ stop for someone and take them into one's vehicle or vessel. ■ informal arrest someone. ■ informal casually strike up a relationship with someone one has never met before, as a sexual overture. ■ make someone feel more energetic and cheerful: *songs to pick you up and make you feel good.* **pick something up 1** collect something that has been left elsewhere: *Wanda came over to pick up her things.* ■ informal pay the bill for something, esp. when others have contributed to the expense: *as usual, we had to* **pick up the tab**. ■ tidy a room or building. **2** obtain, acquire, or learn something, esp. without formal arrangements or instruction: *he had picked up a little Russian from his father.* ■ catch an illness or infection. **3** detect or receive a signal or sound, esp. by means of electronic apparatus. ■ (also **pick up on**) become aware of or sensitive to something: *she is very quick to pick up emotional atmospheres.* ■ find and take a particular road or route. **4** (also **pick up**) resume something: *they picked up their friendship without the slightest difficulty.* ■ (also **pick up on**) refer to or develop a point or topic mentioned earlier: *Dawson picked up her earlier remark.* ■ (of an object or color) attractively accentuate the color of something else by being of a similar shade. **pick up after** tidy up things left strewn around by (someone).
–DERIVATIVES **pick·a·ble** /ˈpikəbəl/ **adj.**
–ORIGIN Middle English (earlier as *pike*, which continues in dialect use): of unknown origin. Compare with Dutch *pikken* 'pick, peck,' and German *picken* 'peck, puncture,' also with French *piquer* 'to prick.'

pick[2] ▶ **n. 1** a tool consisting of a long handle set at right angles in the middle of a curved iron or steel bar with a point at one end and a chisel edge or point at the other, used for breaking up hard ground or rock. ■ short for ICE PICK.
2 an instrument for picking: *an ebony hair pick.* ■ informal a plectrum: *a pink guitar pick.* ■ short for TOOTHPICK.
–ORIGIN Middle English: variant of PIKE[2].

pick·a·back /ˈpikəˌbak/ ▶ **n., adv., adj., & v.** old-fashioned term for PIGGYBACK.

pick·a·nin·ny /ˈpikəˌninē/ (also **picaninny** or chiefly Brit. **piccaninny**) ▶ **n.** (pl. **pickaninnies**) offensive a small black child.
▶ **adj.** archaic very small.
–ORIGIN mid 17th cent.: from West Indian Creole, from Spanish *pequeño* or Portuguese *pequeno* 'little,' *pequenino* 'tiny.'

pick·ax /ˈpikˌaks/ (also **pickaxe**) ▶ **n.** another term for PICK[2] (sense 1).
▶ **v.** [with obj.] break or strike with a pickax.
–ORIGIN Middle English *pikoys*, from Old French *picois*; related to PIKE[2].

pick·er /ˈpikər/ ▶ **n.** [usu. with modifier] a person or machine that gathers or collects something: *a tomato picker.* ■ a person who plays a plucked instrument, esp. a guitar, banjo, or mandolin: *a capable singer, writer, and picker.*

pick·er·el /ˈpik(ə)rəl/ ▶ **n.** (pl. **same** or **pickerels**) a small North American pike. ● Genus *Esox*, family Esocidae: several species, including the **grass** (or **redfin**) **pickerel** (*E. americanus*). ■ a young pike.
–ORIGIN Middle English: diminutive of PIKE[1].

pick·er·el·weed /ˈpik(ə)rəlˌwēd/ ▶ **n.** a freshwater plant with broad arrow-shaped leaves and spikes of blue flowers that was formerly believed to give rise to, or provide food for, young pike. ● *Pontederia cordata*, family Pontederiaceae.

Pick·er·ing[1] /ˈpik(ə)riNG/, John (1777–1846), US linguist and lexicographer; son of Timothy Pickering. He wrote the first dictionary of Americanisms 1816 and studied the languages of North American Indians.

Pick·er·ing[2], Timothy (1745–1829), US government official. He was the US secretary of war 1795 and secretary of state 1795–1800, as well as a member of the US Senate 1803–11 and US House of Representatives 1813–17.

Pick·er·ing[3], William Hayward (1910–2004), US engineer, born in Australia; director of the Jet Propulsion Laboratory (JPL) at the California Institute of Technology 1954–76. During his directorate the JPL launched the US's first satellite, Explorer I, in 1958.

pick·et /ˈpikit/ ▶ **n. 1** a person or group of people standing outside a place of work or other venue, protesting about something or trying to persuade others not to enter during a strike. ■ a blockade of a workplace or other venue staged by such a person or group.
2 a soldier or party of soldiers performing a particular duty: *a picket of soldiers fired a volley over the coffin.*
3 [usu. as modifier] a pointed wooden stake driven into the ground, typically to form a fence or palisade or to tether a horse: *a cedar-picket stockade.* See also PICKET FENCE.
▶ **v.** (**pickets, picketing, picketed**) [with obj.] act as a picket outside (a place of work or other venue): *strikers picketed the newspaper's main building* | [no obj.] *18,000 people turned up to picket.*
–DERIVATIVES **pick·et·er n.**
–ORIGIN late 17th cent. (denoting a pointed stake, on which a soldier was required to stand on one foot as a military punishment): from French *piquet* 'pointed stake,' from *piquer* 'to prick,' from *pic* 'pike.'

pick·et fence ▶ **n.** a wooden fence made of spaced uprights connected by two or more horizontal rails.

pick·et line ▶ **n.** a boundary established by workers on strike, esp. at the entrance to the place of work, that others are asked not to cross.

Pick·ett /ˈpikit/, George Edward (1825–75), US army officer. Last in the West Point class of 1846, he was a distinguished Confederate general during the Civil War. In 1863, his military reputation was marred at Gettysburg when, under orders, he led a disastrous charge across an open field that became known as "Pickett's Charge."

Pick·ford /ˈpikfərd/, Mary (1893–1979), US actress, born in Canada; born *Gladys Mary Smith.* A star of silent movies, she usually played the innocent young heroine, as in *Rebecca of Sunnybrook Farm* (1917) and *Pollyanna* (1920). With Douglas Fairbanks, her husband from 1919 to 1936, she was a cofounder of United Artists in 1919.

pick·ings /ˈpikiNGz/ ▶ **plural n. 1** profits or gains that are made effortlessly or dishonestly, as by picking: *thieves found* **easy pickings** *from garages and garden sheds* | *he found, as strays often do,* **slim pickings**.
2 remaining scraps or leftovers.

pick·le /ˈpikəl/ ▶ **n. 1** a small cucumber preserved in vinegar, brine, or a similar solution. ■ any food preserved in this way and used as a relish. ■ the liquid used to preserve food or other perishable items. ■ an acid solution for cleaning metal objects.
2 [in sing.] informal a difficult or messy situation: *I am* **in a pickle**.
▶ **v.** [with obj.] preserve (food or other perishable items) in vinegar, brine, or a similar solution: *chunks of green tomatoes* **pickled in brine**. ■ immerse (a metal object) in an acid or other chemical solution for cleaning.
–ORIGIN late Middle English (denoting a spicy sauce served with meat): from Middle Dutch and Middle Low German *pekel*, of unknown ultimate origin.

pick·led /ˈpikəld/ ▶ **adj.** (of food) preserved in vinegar or brine: *pickled onions.* ■ [predic.] informal drunk.

pick·ler /ˈpik(ə)lər/ ▶ **n.** a vegetable or fruit suitable for pickling.

pick·ling /ˈpik(ə)liNG/ ▶ **adj.** [attrib.] (of food) suitable for being pickled or used in making pickles.

pick·lock /ˈpikˌläk/ ▶ **n.** a person who picks locks. ■ an instrument for picking locks.

pick-me-up ▶ **n.** informal a thing that makes one feel more energetic or cheerful: *ginseng has long been used as a pick-me-up* | *your letter was just the pick-me-up I needed.*

pick·ney /ˈpiknē/ ▶ **n.** black English a child: *me and the pickney have to survive some way.* Compare with PICKANINNY.
–ORIGIN contraction of PICKANINNY.

pick·off /ˈpikˌôf, ˈpikˌäf/ ▶ **n.** Baseball the putout of a runner leading off base, involving an unexpected throw to a base by the pitcher or the catcher while the batter is still at bat.

pick·pock·et /ˈpikˌpäkət/ ▶ **n.** a person who steals from other people's pockets.
▶ **v.** [with obj.] steal from the pockets of (someone): *she stopped in New Orleans where she skillfully pickpocketed tourists.*

Pick's dis·ease /piks/ ▶ **n.** a rare form of progressive dementia, typically occurring in late middle age and often familial, involving localized atrophy of the brain.
–ORIGIN early 20th cent.: named after Arnold *Pick* (1851–1924), Bohemian neurologist.

pick·up /ˈpikˌəp/ ▶ **n. 1** (also **pickup truck**) a small truck with an enclosed cab and open back.
2 an act of collecting a person or goods, esp. in a vehicle: *curbside pickup* | [as modifier] *travel by bus from your local pickup point to your hotel.*
3 the reception of signals, esp. interference or noise, by electrical apparatus.
4 informal a casual encounter with someone, with a view to having a sexual relationship. ■ a person met in such an encounter.
5 an improvement in an economic indicator: *signs of a pickup in demand.*
6 a device that produces an electrical signal in response to some other kind of signal or change, in particular: ■ the cartridge of a record player, carrying the stylus. ■ a device on a musical instrument, particularly an electric guitar, that converts sound vibrations into electrical signals for amplification.
7 Music a series of introductory notes leading into the opening part of a tune.

P

8 Fishing a semicircular loop of metal for guiding the line back onto the spool as it is reeled in.
▶ **adj.** informal and spontaneous: *six players had started a full-court pickup basketball game.*

Pick·wick·i·an /pik'wikēən/ ▶ **adj.** of or like Mr. Pickwick in Dickens's *Pickwick Papers*, esp. in being jovial, plump, or generous. ■ (of words or their senses) misunderstood or misused; not literally meant, esp. to avoid offense.

pick·y /'pikē/ ▶ **adj.** (**pickier, pickiest**) informal fastidious, esp. excessively so: *she had been a picky eater as a child.*
– DERIVATIVES **pick·i·ness** /-ēnis/ **n.**

pick-your-own ▶ **adj.** [attrib.] of or relating to a system in which commercially grown fruit or vegetables are picked by the customer for purchase at the place of production.

pic·nic /'pik,nik/ ▶ **n.** an outing or occasion that involves taking a packed meal to be eaten outdoors. ■ a meal eaten outdoors on such an occasion.
▶ **v.** (**picnics, picnicking, picnicked**) [no obj.] have or take part in a picnic.
– PHRASES **no picnic** informal used of something difficult or unpleasant: *chemotherapy is no picnic.*
– DERIVATIVES **pic·nick·er n.**
– ORIGIN mid 18th cent.: from French *pique-nique*, of unknown origin.

pico- ▶ **comb. form** (used in units of measurement) denoting a factor of 10^{-12}: *picosecond.*
– ORIGIN from Spanish *pico*, literally 'beak, peak, little bit.'

Pi·co de O·ri·za·ba /'pēkō de ,ôrē'säbä/ Spanish name for **CITLALTÉPETL.**

Pi·co Ri·ve·ra /,pēkō ri'verə/ a city in southwestern California, east of Los Angeles; pop. 63,138 (est. 2008).

pi·cor·na·vi·rus /pi'kôrnə,vīrəs/ ▶ **n.** any of a group of very small RNA viruses that includes enteroviruses, rhinoviruses, and the virus of foot-and-mouth disease.
– ORIGIN 1960s: from **PICO-** + **RNA** + **VIRUS.**

pi·cot /'pēkō/ ▶ **n.** [often as modifier] a small loop or series of small loops of twisted thread in lace or embroidery, typically decorating the border of a fabric.
– ORIGIN early 17th cent.: from French, literally 'small peak or point,' diminutive of *pic*.

pic·o·tee /,pikə'tē/ ▶ **n.** a type of carnation whose light-colored flowers have dark-edged petals.
– ORIGIN early 18th cent.: from French *picoté(e)* 'marked with points,' past participle of *picoter* 'to prick.'

pic·quet /pi'kāt/ ▶ **n.** variant spelling of **PIQUET.**

pic·ric ac·id /'pikrik/ ▶ **n.** Chemistry a bitter yellow compound obtained by nitrating phenol, used as a dye and in the manufacture of explosives. ● Alternative name: **2,4,6-trinitrophenol**; chem. formula: $C_6H_2(NO_2)_3OH$.
– DERIVATIVES **pic·rate** /'pikrāt/ **n.**
– ORIGIN mid 19th cent.: *picric* from Greek *pikros* 'bitter' + **-IC.**

pic·rite /'pik,rīt/ ▶ **n.** Geology a dark basaltic rock rich in olivine.
– DERIVATIVES **pic·rit·ic** /pik'ritik/ **adj.**
– ORIGIN early 19th cent.: from Greek *pikros* 'bitter' + **-ITE**[1].

pic·ro·tox·in /,pikrə'täksin/ ▶ **n.** Medicine a bitter compound used to stimulate the respiratory and nervous systems, esp. in treating barbiturate poisoning. ● This toxin is obtained from the seeds of the shrub *Anamirta cocculus* (family Menispermaceae).
– ORIGIN mid 19th cent.: from Greek *pikros* 'bitter' + **TOXIN.**

Pict /pikt/ ▶ **n.** a member of an ancient people inhabiting northern Scotland in Roman times.

> Roman writings of around AD 300 apply the term *Picti* to the hostile tribes of the area north of the Firth of Forth and the Firth of Clyde. Their origins are uncertain, but they may have been a loose confederation of Celtic tribes.

– DERIVATIVES **Pict·ish** /-tisH/ **adj. & n.**
– ORIGIN from late Latin *Picti*, perhaps from *pict-* 'painted, tattooed' (from *pingere* 'to paint'), or perhaps influenced by a local name.

pic·to·graph /'piktə,graf/ (also **pictogram** /-,gram/) ▶ **n.** a pictorial symbol for a word or phrase. Pictographs were used as the earliest known form of writing, examples having been discovered in Egypt and Mesopotamia from before 3000 BC. ■ a pictorial representation of statistics on a chart, graph, or computer screen.
– DERIVATIVES **pic·to·graph·ic** /,piktə'grafik/ **adj.**, **pic·tog·ra·phy** /pik'tägrəfē/ **n.**
– ORIGIN mid 19th cent.: from Latin *pict-* 'painted' (from the verb *pingere*) + **-GRAPH.**

Pic·tor /'piktər/ Astronomy an inconspicuous southern constellation (the Easel or Painter), close to the star Canopus. ■ (as genitive **Pictoris** /pic'tôris/) used with a preceding letter or numeral to designate a star in this constellation: *the star Beta Pictoris.*
– ORIGIN Latin.

pic·to·ri·al /pik'tôrēəl/ ▶ **adj.** of or expressed in pictures; illustrated: *feelings presented in a pictorial form.*
▶ **n.** a newspaper or periodical with pictures as a main feature.
– DERIVATIVES **pic·to·ri·al·ly adv.**
– ORIGIN mid 17th cent.: from late Latin *pictorius* (from Latin *pictor* 'painter,' from the verb *pingere* 'to paint') + **-AL.**

pic·ture /'pikCHər/ ▶ **n.** a painting or drawing: *draw a picture of a tree.* ■ a photograph: *we were warned not to take pictures.* ■ a portrait: *have her picture painted.* ■ archaic a person or thing resembling another closely: *she is the very picture of her mother.* ■ an impression of something formed from an account or description: *a full picture of the disaster had not yet emerged.* ■ an image on a television screen. ■ a movie: *it took five honors, including best picture.* ■ (**the pictures**) the movies: *I'm going to the pictures with my buddies.*
▶ **v.** [with obj.] represent (someone or something) in a photograph or picture: *he is pictured with party guests.* ■ describe (someone or something) in a certain way: *the markets in London and New York are usually pictured in contrasting terms.* ■ form a mental image of: *she pictured Benjamin waiting.*
– PHRASES **be in pictures** act in movies or work in the motion-picture industry. **be** (or **look**) **a picture** be very pleasing to look at. **the big** (or **bigger** or **larger**) **picture** informal the situation as a whole: *he's so involved in the minutiae that he often overlooks the big picture.* **get the picture** informal understand a situation. **in the picture** fully informed about something. **out of the picture** no longer involved; irrelevant: *hostages were better left out of the picture.* **the** (or **a**) **picture of ——** the embodiment of a specified state or emotion: *she looked the picture of forbearance.* (**as**) **pretty as a picture** very pretty.
– ORIGIN late Middle English: from Latin *pictura*, from *pict-* 'painted' (from the verb *pingere*).

pic·ture book ▶ **n.** a book containing many illustrations, esp. one for children.

pic·ture card ▶ **n.** an illustrated card, used esp. in games. ■ another term for **FACE CARD.**

pic·ture el·e·ment ▶ **n.** see **PIXEL.**

pic·ture hat ▶ **n.** a woman's highly decorated hat with a wide brim, as shown in pictures by 18th-century English painters such as Reynolds and Gainsborough.

pic·ture pal·ace ▶ **n.** dated a movie theater.

pic·ture plane ▶ **n.** in perspective, the imaginary plane corresponding to the surface of a picture, perpendicular to the viewer's line of sight.

pic·ture post·card ▶ **n.** a postcard with a picture on one side.
▶ **adj.** prettily picturesque, like the scenes typically shown on such postcards: *a picture-postcard thatched cottage.*

pic·ture space ▶ **n.** the apparent space behind the picture plane of a painting, created by perspective and other techniques.

pic·tur·esque /,pikCHə'resk/ ▶ **adj.** visually attractive, esp. in a quaint or pretty style: *the picturesque covered bridges of New England.* ■ (of language) unusual and vivid: *his picturesque speech contrasted with his rough appearance.*
– DERIVATIVES **pic·tur·esque·ly adv.**, **pic·tur·esque·ness n.**
– ORIGIN early 18th cent.: from French *pittoresque*, from Italian *pittoresco*, from *pittore* 'painter' (from Latin *pictor*). The change from *-tt-* to *-ct-* was due to association with **PICTURE.**

pic·ture tube ▶ **n.** Electronics the cathode ray tube of a television set designed for the reproduction of television pictures.

pic·ture win·dow ▶ **n.** a large window consisting of one pane of glass, typically in a living room.

pic·ture writ·ing ▶ **n.** a mode of recording events by pictorial symbols; pictography.

pic·u·let /'pikyəlit/ ▶ **n.** a tiny tropical woodpecker with a short unstiffened tail, found chiefly in Central and South America. ● *Picumnus* and other genera, family Picidae: numerous species, including the **olivaceous piculet** (*P. olivaceus*).
– ORIGIN mid 19th cent.: apparently a double diminutive of Latin *picus* 'woodpecker.'

PID ▶ **abbr.** pelvic inflammatory disease.

pid·dle /'pidl/ informal ▶ **v.** [no obj.] urinate.
▶ **n.** [in sing.] an act of urinating. ■ urine.
– PHRASAL VERBS **piddle around** (or **about**) spend time in trifling activities: *I piddled around the house all day.* [mid 16th cent. (as *piddle*): of unknown origin; compare with the rare synonym *peddle*.]
– DERIVATIVES **pid·dler n.**
– ORIGIN late 18th cent.: probably from a blend of **PISS** and **PUDDLE.**

pid·dling /'pidliNG/ ▶ **adj.** informal pathetically trivial; trifling: *piddling little questions.*

pid·dock /'pidək/ ▶ **n.** a bivalve mollusk that bores into soft rock or other firm surfaces. The valves of the shell have a conspicuous gap between them and rough frontal ridges to aid in boring. ● *Pholas* and other genera, family Pholadidae.
– ORIGIN mid 19th cent.: of unknown origin.

pidg·in /'pijən/ ▶ **n.** [often as modifier] a grammatically simplified form of a language, used for communication between people not sharing a common language. Pidgins have a limited vocabulary, some elements of which are taken from local languages, and are not native languages, but arise out of language contact between speakers of other languages. Compare with **CREOLE** (sense 2 of the noun). ■ (**Pidgin**) another term for **TOK PISIN.** ■ [as modifier] denoting a simplified form of a language, esp. as used by a nonnative speaker: *we exchanged greetings, communicating in pidgin Spanish.*
– ORIGIN late 19th cent.: Chinese alteration of English *business*.

pid·gin Eng·lish ▶ **n.** a pidgin in which the chief language is English, used originally between Chinese people and Europeans.

pie[1] /pī/ ▶ **n.** a baked dish of fruit, or meat and vegetables, typically with a top and base of pastry. ■ a pizza.
– PHRASES (**as**) **easy as pie** informal very easy. (**as**) **nice** (or **sweet**) **as pie** extremely pleasant or polite. **a piece** (or **slice**) **of the pie** a share of an amount of money or business available to be claimed or distributed: *orchestras have seen cultural rivals get a bigger piece of the pie.* **pie in the sky** informal something that is pleasant to contemplate but is very unlikely to be realized.
– ORIGIN Middle English: probably the same word as **PIE**[2], the various combinations of ingredients being compared to objects randomly collected by a magpie.

pie[2] ▶ **n.** short for **MAGPIE.**
– ORIGIN Middle English: from Old French, from Latin *pica* 'magpie' (related to *picus* 'green woodpecker').

pie[3] ▶ **n.** a former monetary unit of India and Pakistan, equal to one twelfth of an anna.
– ORIGIN from Hindi *pā'ī*, from Sanskrit *pada, padī* 'quarter.'

pie·bald /'pī,bôld/ ▶ **adj.** (of a horse) having irregular patches of two colors, typically black and white.
▶ **n.** a piebald horse or other animal.
– ORIGIN late 16th cent.: from **PIE**[2] (because of the magpie's black-and-white plumage) + **BALD** (in the obsolete sense 'streaked with white').

piece /pēs/ ▶ **n.** a portion of an object or of material, produced by cutting, tearing, or breaking the whole: *a piece of cheese* | *the dish lay in pieces upon the floor* | *she tore his letters to pieces.* ■ one of the items that were put together to make something and into which it naturally divides: *take a car to pieces.* ■ an item of a particular type, esp. one forming one of a set: *a piece of luggage.* ■ an instance or example: *a crucial piece of evidence.* ■ a financial share: *each employee owns a piece of the company.* ■ a written, musical, or artistic creation or composition: *a hauntingly beautiful piece of music.* ■ a coin of specified value: *a 10-cent piece.* ■ a figure or token used to make moves in a board game. ■ Chess a king, queen, bishop, knight, or rook, as opposed to a pawn. ■ informal a firearm. ■ informal, offensive a woman.
▶ **v.** [with obj.] **1** (**piece something together**) assemble something from individual parts: *the children took turns piecing together each other's jigsaw puzzle.* ■ slowly make sense of something from separate facts and pieces of evidence: *Daniel had pieced the story together from the radio.*
2 (**piece something out**) archaic extend.
3 archaic patch: *if it be broken it must be pieced.*
– PHRASES **a piece of ass** (or **tail**) vulgar slang a person, usually a woman, regarded as a sexual partner. **a piece of cake** see **CAKE. a piece of the action** informal a share in the excitement of something. ■ a share in the profits accruing from something. **go to pieces** become so nervous or upset that one is unable to behave or perform normally. **in one piece** unharmed or undamaged, esp. after a dangerous experience. (**all**) **of a piece** (**with something**) (entirely) consistent (with something): *his rejection of health-care reform is of a piece with his general disregard for the underprivileged.* **piece by piece** in slow and small stages. **say one's piece** give one's opinion or make a prepared statement. **tear** (or **rip**)

someone/something to pieces criticize someone or something harshly.
– ORIGIN Middle English: from Old French *piece* (compare with medieval Latin *pecia, petium*), of obscure ultimate origin.

pièce de ré·sis·tance /pē'es də ˌrəzi'stäns, -räzi'stäns/ ▶ **n.** [in sing.] (esp. with reference to creative work or a meal) the most important or remarkable feature: *the pièce de résistance of the meal was flaming ice cream.*
– ORIGIN French, literally 'piece (i.e., means) of resistance.'

piece goods ▶ **plural n.** fabrics woven in standard lengths for sale.

piece·meal /'pēsˌmēl/ ▶ **adj. & adv.** characterized by unsystematic partial measures taken over a period of time: [as adj.] *the village is slowly being killed off by piecemeal development* | [as adv.] *some can only be had as part of a package, while others can be installed piecemeal.*
– ORIGIN Middle English: from the noun **PIECE** + *-meal* from Old English *mǣlum*, in the sense 'measure, quantity taken at one time.'

piece of eight ▶ **n.** historical a Spanish dollar, equivalent to 8 reals.

piec·er /'pēsər/ ▶ **n.** a person who patches or creates a garment or other item from pieces of fabric. ■ historical a child employed in a spinning mill to join the ends of broken threads.

piece rate ▶ **n.** a rate of payment for piecework.

piece·work /'pēsˌwərk/ ▶ **n.** work paid for according to the amount produced.
– DERIVATIVES **piece·work·er n.**

pie chart ▶ **n.** a type of graph in which a circle is divided into sectors that each represent a proportion of the whole.
– ORIGIN 1920s: because of the resemblance of the graph to a pie divided into portions.

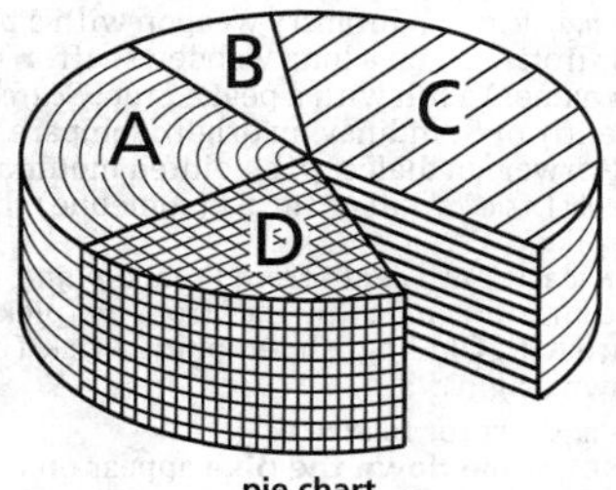

pie chart

pie crust /'pīˌkrəst/ (also **piecrust**) ▶ **n.** the baked pastry crust of a pie. ■ the dough used to make pie crusts: *my mother was rolling out pie crust on the table.*

pie·crust ta·ble ▶ **n.** a table with an indented edge like a pie crust.

pied /pīd/ ▶ **adj.** having two or more different colors: *pied dogs from the Pyrenees.*
– ORIGIN Middle English (originally in the sense 'black and white like a magpie'): from **PIE²** + **-ED²**.

pied-à-terre /pēˌyād ə 'ter/ ▶ **n.** (pl. **pieds-à-terre** pronunc. **same**) a small apartment, house, or room kept for occasional use.
– ORIGIN early 19th cent.: French, literally 'foot to earth.'

Pied·mont /'pēdˌmänt/ **1** a region in northwestern Italy, in the foothills of the Alps; capital, Turin. It was the center of the movement for a united Italy in the 19th century. Italian name **PIEMONTE**.
2 in the US, a hilly highland region between the Appalachian Mountains and the Atlantic coast. The Piedmont ends at the Fall Line, where rivers drop to the coastal plain.
– DERIVATIVES **Pied·mon·tese** /ˌpēdmän'tēz, -'tēs/ **n. & adj.** (sense 1).
– ORIGIN from Italian *piemonte* 'mountain foot.'

pied·mont /'pēdmänt/ ▶ **n.** a gentle slope leading from the base of mountains to a region of flat land.
– ORIGIN mid 19th cent.: from Italian *piemonte*. See **PIEDMONT**.

pied noir /pēˌā 'nwär/ ▶ **n.** (pl. **pieds noirs** pronunc. **same**) a person of European origin who lived in Algeria during French rule, esp. one who returned to Europe after Algeria was granted independence.
– ORIGIN French, literally 'black foot,' so named because of the western-style black leather shoes worn by the first colonists.

Pied Pip·er /'pīd 'pīpər/ the hero of *The Pied Piper of Hamelin*, a poem by Robert Browning (1842), based on an old German legend. The piper, dressed in particolored costume, rid the town of Hamelin (Hameln) in Brunswick of rats by enticing them away with his music, and when refused the promised payment he lured away the children of the citizens. ■ (as noun **a Pied Piper**) a person who entices people to follow them, esp. to their doom.

pie-eyed ▶ **adj.** informal very drunk.

pie-faced ▶ **adj.** informal having a roundish face and typically a blank or stupid expression.

Pie·gan /pē'gan/ (also **Peigan**) ▶ **n.** (pl. **same** or **Piegans**) a member of a North American Indian people of the Blackfoot confederacy.
▶ **adj.** of or relating to this people.
– ORIGIN via Cree, from Blackfoot *piikáni* 'Piegan band.'

pie·man /'pīmən/ ▶ **n.** (pl. **piemen**) archaic a pie seller.

Pie·mon·te /pye'mônte/ Italian name for **PIEDMONT**.

pie·mon·tite /'pēmənˌtīt/ ▶ **n.** a brown or black mineral of the epidote group consisting of a silicate of calcium, aluminum, iron, and manganese.
– ORIGIN late 19th cent.: from Italian *Piemonte* (see **PIEDMONT**) + **-ITE¹**.

pie plate (also **pie pan**) ▶ **n.** a shallow metal or glass dish with sloping sides in which pies are baked.

pier /pi(ə)r/ ▶ **n. 1** a structure leading out from the shore into a body of water, in particular: ■ a platform supported on pillars or girders, used as a landing stage for boats. ■ a similar structure leading out to sea and used as an entertainment area, typically incorporating arcades and places to eat. ■ a breakwater or mole.
2 a solid support designed to sustain vertical pressure, in particular: ■ a pillar supporting an arch or a bridge. ■ a section of a wall between windows or other adjacent openings.
– ORIGIN Middle English: from medieval Latin *pera*, of unknown origin.

Pierce /pi(ə)rs/, Franklin (1804–69), 14th president of the US 1853–57. A New Hampshire Democrat, he served as US congressman 1833–37 and US senator 1837–42. His presidency saw the rise of divisions within the country over slavery and the encouragement of settlement in the northwest.

Franklin Pierce

pierce /pi(ə)rs/ ▶ **v.** [with obj.] (of a sharp pointed object) go into or through (something): *a splinter had pierced the skin.* ■ make (a hole) with a sharp instrument: *I had to pierce another hole in my belt.* ■ make a hole in (the ears, nose, or other part of the body) so as to wear jewelry in them: (as adj. **pierced**) *kids with pierced noses.* ■ (usu. **be pierced**) bore a hole or tunnel through: *the dividing wall is pierced by arches and piers.* ■ force or cut a way through: *they were seeking to pierce the antiballistic-missile defenses* | *a shrill voice pierced the air.*
– ORIGIN Middle English: from Old French *percer*, based on Latin *pertus-* 'bored through,' from the verb *pertundere*, from *per* 'through' + *tundere* 'thrust.'

pierc·er /'pi(ə)rsər/ ▶ **n.** a person or thing that pierces something.

pierc·ing /'pi(ə)rsiNG/ ▶ **adj.** (of eyes or a look) appearing to see through someone; searching: *he stared at me with those piercing eyes.* ■ (of a voice or sound) extremely high, loud, or shrill: *she let out a piercing scream.* ■ (of wind or extreme temperature) seeming to cut through one: *the piercing cold.* ■ (of a feeling) affecting one keenly or deeply. ■ (of mental attributes) sharp; profound: *her piercing analysis.*
– DERIVATIVES **pierc·ing·ly adv.**

pier glass ▶ **n.** a large mirror, used originally to fill wall space between windows.

pie·ris /'pīris, 'pi(ə)ris/ ▶ **n.** an evergreen shrub of the heath family, typically having pink or red young leaves and loose clusters of waxy white bell-shaped flowers. ● Genus *Pieris*, family Ericaceae: many species, in particular *P. floribunda* of North America.
– ORIGIN modern Latin, from the Latin name of one of the Muses, from *Pieria*, the name of a district in northern Thessaly, Greece, said to be the home of the Muses.

pie·ro·gi ▶ **n.** variant spelling of **PIROGI**.

Pierre /'pi(ə)r, pē'e(ə)r/ the capital of South Dakota, in the central part of the state, on the Missouri River; pop. 13,899 (est. 2008).

Pi·er·rot /ˌpēə'rō/ ▶ **n.** a stock male character in French pantomime, with a sad white-painted face, a loose white costume, and a pointed hat.
– ORIGIN French, diminutive of the male given name *Pierre* 'Peter.'

pier ta·ble ▶ **n.** a low table or bracket in the space between two windows, typically placed under a pier glass.

pie safe ▶ **n.** a cupboard with doors featuring decorative pierced tin panels, originally designed to store pies after baking.

pie·tà /ˌpēā'tä/ (often **Pietà**) ▶ **n.** a picture or sculpture of the Virgin Mary holding the dead body of Jesus Christ on her lap or in her arms.
– ORIGIN Italian, from Latin *pietas* 'dutifulness.'

Pie·ter·mar·itz·burg /ˌpētər'maritsˌbərg/ a city in eastern South Africa, the capital of KwaZulu-Natal; pop. 891,600 (est. 2009).

pi·e·tism /'pī-iˌtizəm/ ▶ **n.** pious sentiment, esp. of an exaggerated or affected nature. ■ (usu. **Pietism**) a 17th-century movement for the revival of piety in the Lutheran Church. [from German *Pietismus*, from modern Latin, based on Latin *pietas* (see **PIETY**).]
– DERIVATIVES **pi·e·tist n.**, **pi·e·tis·tic** /ˌpī-i'tistik/ **adj.**, **pi·e·tis·ti·cal adj.**, **pi·e·tis·ti·cal·ly** /-tik(ə)lē/ **adv.**

pi·e·ty /'pī-itē/ ▶ **n.** (pl. **pieties**) the quality of being religious or reverent: *acts of piety and charity.* ■ a belief or point of view that is accepted with unthinking conventional reverence: *the accepted pieties of our time.*
– ORIGIN early 16th cent. (in the sense 'devotion to religious observances'): from Old French *piete*, from Latin *pietas* 'dutifulness,' from *pius* (see **PIOUS**).

pi·e·zo /pī'ēzō, pē'āzō/ ▶ **adj.** piezoelectric.

pi·e·zo·e·lec·tric·i·ty /pēˌāzōˌilek'trisitē, pīˌēz-/ ▶ **n.** electric polarization in a substance (esp. certain crystals) resulting from the application of mechanical stress.

> Piezoelectric substances are able to convert mechanical signals (such as sound waves) into electrical signals, and vice versa. They are therefore widely used in microphones, phonograph pickups, and earphones, and also to generate a spark for igniting gas.

– DERIVATIVES **pi·e·zo·e·lec·tric** /-trik/ **adj.**, **pi·e·zo·e·lec·tri·cal·ly** /-trik(ə)lē/ **adv.**
– ORIGIN late 19th cent.: from Greek *piezein* 'press, squeeze' + **ELECTRICITY**.

pi·e·zom·e·ter /ˌpēə'zämitər, ˌpīə'zämitər/ ▶ **n.** an instrument for measuring the pressure of a liquid or gas, or something related to pressure (such as the compressibility of liquid). Piezometers are often placed in boreholes to monitor the pressure or depth of groundwater.
– ORIGIN early 19th cent.: from Greek *piezein* 'press, squeeze' + **-METER**.

pif·fle /'pifəl/ ▶ **n. & exclam.** informal nonsense.
– ORIGIN mid 19th cent.: diminutive of imitative *piff-*.

pif·fling /'pifliNG/ ▶ **adj.** informal trivial; unimportant.

pig /pig/ ▶ **n. 1** an omnivorous domesticated hoofed mammal with sparse bristly hair and a flat snout for rooting in the soil, kept for its meat. ● *Sus domesticus* (with numerous varieties), family Suidae (the **pig family**), descended from the wild boar and domesticated over 8,000 years ago. The pig family also includes the warthog and babirusa, but the similar peccaries are placed in their own family. ■ a wild animal of this family. ■ a young pig; a piglet. ■ the flesh of a pig, esp. a young one, as food. ■ informal, derogatory a greedy, dirty, or unpleasant person: *how can she stay married to such a pig?* ■ informal, derogatory a police officer.
2 an oblong mass of iron or lead from a smelting furnace. See also **PIG IRON**. ■ a device that fits snugly inside an oil or gas pipeline and is sent through it to clean or test the inside, or to act as a barrier.
▶ **v.** (**pigs, pigging, pigged**) [no obj.] **1** informal gorge oneself with food: *don't pig out on chips before dinner.*
2 informal crowd together with other people in disorderly or dirty conditions: *he and Irving pigged*

P

it for years in a shoebox of an apartment | I have no intention of pigging with that bunch for another day. **3** (of a sow) give birth to piglets; farrow. **4** operate a pig within an oil or gas pipeline.
– PHRASES **bleed like a pig** bleed copiously. **in pig** (of a sow) pregnant. **in a pig's eye** informal expressing scornful disbelief at a statement. **make a pig of oneself** informal overeat; eat more than one's share. **make a pig's ear of** Brit. informal handle ineptly. **a pig in a poke** something that is bought or accepted without knowing its value or seeing it first. [with reference to the formerly common trick of selling a cat concealed in a bag to someone who was expecting a pig.] **squeal like a pig** squeal or yell loudly and shrilly. **sweat like a pig** informal sweat profusely.
– DERIVATIVES **pig·like** /ˈpig,līk/ **adj.**, **pig·ling** /ˈpigliNG/ **n.**
– ORIGIN Middle English: probably from an Old English word represented in *picbrēd* 'acorn,' literally 'pig food.'

Chester white pig

pi·geon¹ /ˈpijən/ ▶ **n. 1** a stout seed- or fruit-eating bird with a small head, short legs, and a cooing voice, typically having gray and white plumage. See also DOVE¹ (sense 1). ● Family Columbidae: numerous genera and species. ■ (also **domestic** or **feral pigeon**) a pigeon descended from the wild rock dove, kept for racing, showing, and carrying messages, and common as a feral bird in towns. **2** informal a gullible person, esp. someone swindled in gambling or the victim of a confidence trick. **3** military slang an aircraft from one's own side.
– ORIGIN late Middle English: from Old French *pijon*, denoting a young bird, esp. a young dove, from an alteration of late Latin *pipio(n-)* 'young cheeping bird,' of imitative origin.

pi·geon² ▶ **n.** archaic spelling of PIDGIN.

pi·geon breast (also **pigeon chest**) ▶ **n.** a deformed human chest with a projecting breastbone.
– DERIVATIVES **pi·geon-breast·ed** (also **pigeon-chested**) **adj.**

pi·geon fan·ci·er ▶ **n.** a person who keeps and breeds pigeons.
– DERIVATIVES **pi·geon-fan·cy·ing n.**

pi·geon hawk ▶ **n.** another term for MERLIN.

pi·geon-heart·ed ▶ **adj.** timid; cowardly.

p

pi·geon·hole /ˈpijən,hōl/ ▶ **n. 1** a small recess for a domestic pigeon to nest in. **2** a small compartment, open at the front and forming part of a set, where letters or messages may be left for individuals. ■ a similar compartment built into a desk for keeping documents in. **3** a category, typically an overly restrictive one, to which someone or something is assigned: *people identified me with a homely farmer's wife and I was never allowed to escape from that pigeonhole.*
▶ **v.** [with obj.] deposit (a document) into a pigeonhole: *he pigeonholed his charts and notes.* ■ assign to a particular category or class, esp. in a manner that is too rigid or exclusive: *a tendency to pigeonhole him as a photographer and neglect his work in sculpture and painting.* ■ put aside for future consideration: *she pigeonholed her worry about him.*

pi·geon pea ▶ **n. 1** a dark red tropical pealike seed. **2** the woody Old World plant that yields these seeds, with pods and foliage that are used as fodder. ● *Cajanus cajan*, family Leguminosae.

pi·geon's milk ▶ **n.** a curdlike secretion from a pigeon's crop, which it regurgitates and feeds to its young.

pi·geon-toed ▶ **adj.** having the toes or feet turned inward.

pig·fish /ˈpig,fisH/ ▶ **n.** (pl. **same** or **pigfishes**) **1** a deep-bodied scaleless fish with a protuberant snout, living in the cooler seas of the southern hemisphere. ● Family Congiopodidae: several genera and species. **2** [usu. with modifier] any of a number of other marine fishes, esp. one that grunts. ● a western Atlantic grunt (*Orthopristis chrysoptera*, family Pomadasyidae).

pig·ger·y /ˈpigərē/ ▶ **n.** (pl. **piggeries**) **1** a farm where pigs are bred or kept. ■ a pigpen. **2** behavior regarded as characteristic of pigs in greed or unpleasantness.

pig·gish /ˈpigisH/ ▶ **adj.** resembling a pig, esp. in being greedy or unpleasant.
– DERIVATIVES **pig·gish·ness n.**

pig·gy /ˈpigē/ ▶ **n.** (pl. **piggies**) (used by or when talking to children) a pig or piglet.
▶ **adj.** resembling a pig, esp. in features or appetite: *three pairs of little piggy eyes.*

pig·gy·back /ˈpigē,bak/ ▶ **n.** a ride on someone's back and shoulders.
▶ **adj.** on the back and shoulders of another person: *a piggyback ride.* ■ attached to or riding on a larger object: *a telescope with fittings for piggyback cameras.*
▶ **adv.** on the back and shoulders of another person: *he had to carry him piggyback.*
▶ **v.** [with obj.] carry by or as if by piggyback. ■ mount on or attach to (an existing object or system): *providers of information have piggybacked their own networks onto the system.* ■ [no obj.] use existing work or an existing product as a basis or support: *we were piggybacking on their training program.*
– ORIGIN mid 16th cent. (as an adverb): although analyzed by folk etymology in various ways from an early date, the word's origin remains obscure.

pig·gy bank ▶ **n.** a container for saving money in, esp. one shaped like a pig, with a slit in the top through which coins are dropped. ■ savings: *many people would dip into their piggy banks to pay the higher tax bills.*

pig·head·ed /ˈpig,hedid/ ▶ **adj.** stupidly obstinate.
– DERIVATIVES **pig·head·ed·ly adv.**, **pig·head·ed·ness n.**

pig-ig·no·rant ▶ **adj.** informal utterly uneducated: *when I bought my house I was pig-ignorant about the area.*

pig i·ron ▶ **n.** crude iron as first obtained from a smelting furnace, in the form of oblong blocks.

pig Lat·in ▶ **n.** a made-up language formed from English by transferring the initial consonant or consonant cluster of each word to the end of the word and adding a vocalic syllable (usually /ā/: so *chicken soup* would be translated to *ickenchay oupsay*. Pig Latin is typically spoken playfully, as if to convey secrecy.

pig·let /ˈpiglit/ ▶ **n.** a young pig.

pig·ment /ˈpigmənt/ ▶ **n.** the natural coloring matter of animal or plant tissue. ■ a substance used for coloring or painting, esp. a dry powder that, when mixed with oil, water, or another medium, constitutes a paint or ink.
▶ **v.** [with obj.] (usu. as adj. **pigmented**) color (something) with or as if with pigment: *pigmented areas such as freckles.*
– DERIVATIVES **pig·men·tar·y** /-,terē/ **adj.**
– ORIGIN Middle English, from Latin *pigmentum*, from *pingere* 'to paint.' The verb dates from the early 20th cent.

pig·men·ta·tion /,pigmənˈtāsHən/ ▶ **n.** the natural coloring of animal or plant tissue. ■ the coloring of a person's skin, esp. when abnormal or distinctive.

pig·ment ep·i·the·li·um ▶ **n.** Anatomy a layer of pigmented cells in the retina of the eye, overlying the choroid.

pig·my ▶ **n.** variant spelling of PYGMY.

pi·gno·li /pinˈyōlē/ ▶ **plural n.** pine nuts.
– ORIGIN Italian, plural of *pignolo*, from *pigna* 'pine cone,' from Latin *pinea*.

pig·nut /ˈpig,nət/ ▶ **n. 1** a hickory tree that bears nuts with thin husks. ● Genus *Carya*, family Juglandaceae: four North American species, **black hickory** (*C. texana*), **pignut hickory** (*C. glabra*), **sand hickory** (*C. pallida*), and **scrub hickory** (*C. floridana*). **2** another term for EARTHNUT (sense 1).

pig-out ▶ **n.** informal a bout of eating a large amount of food.

pig·pen /ˈpig,pen/ ▶ **n.** a pen or enclosure for a pig or pigs.

Pigs, Bay of a bay on the southwestern coast of Cuba, scene of an unsuccessful attempt in 1961 by US-backed Cuban exiles to invade the country and overthrow the regime of Fidel Castro.

pig·skin /ˈpig,skin/ ▶ **n. 1** the hide of a domestic pig. ■ leather made from this. **2** informal a football.

pig·stick·er /ˈpig,stikər/ ▶ **n.** informal a long sharp knife or weapon.

pig·stick·ing /ˈpig,stikiNG/ ▶ **n.** the sport of hunting wild boar with a spear, typically on horseback.

pig·sty /ˈpig,stī/ ▶ **n.** (pl. **pigsties**) a pigpen.

pig·tail /ˈpig,tāl/ ▶ **n. 1** a braid or gathered hank of hair hanging from the back of the head, or either of a pair at the sides: *she had her hair done in pigtails.* **2** a short length of flexible braided wire connecting a stationary part to a moving part in an electrical device. **3** a thin twist of tobacco.
– DERIVATIVES **pig·tailed adj.**

pig-tailed ma·caque (also **pigtail macaque**) ▶ **n.** a forest-dwelling Southeast Asian macaque that has a brown coat with pale underparts, dark markings around the face, and a small piglike tail. ● *Macaca nemestrina*, family Cercopithecidae.

pig·weed /ˈpig,wēd/ ▶ **n. 1** an amaranth that grows as a weed or is used for fodder. ● Genus *Amaranthus*, family Amaranthaceae: several species, in particular *A. retroflexus* and *A. albus*. **2** another term for LAMB'S-QUARTERS.

pi·ka /ˈpīkə, ˈpē-/ ▶ **n.** (pl. **same**) a small mammal related to the rabbits, having rounded ears, short limbs, and a very small tail. ● Family Ochotonidae and genus *Ochotona*: many species, including the **collared pika** (*O. collaris*) of western North America.
– ORIGIN early 19th cent.: from Tungus *piika*.

Pike /pīk/, Zebulon (Montgomery) (1779–1813), US soldier and explorer. He led several expeditions into the Louisiana Purchase region, where he came upon (but never climbed) what is now called Pike's Peak in Colorado. He was killed at York (now Toronto) in Ontario, Canada, while leading a charge against the British during the War of 1812.

pike¹ /pīk/ ▶ **n.** (pl. **same**) a long-bodied predatory freshwater fish with a pointed snout and large teeth, of both North America and Eurasia. ● Family Esocidae and genus *Esox*: five species, including the widespread **northern pike** (*E. lucius*). ■ used in names of other predatory fish with large teeth, e.g., **garpike**.
– ORIGIN Middle English: from PIKE² (because of the fish's pointed jaw).

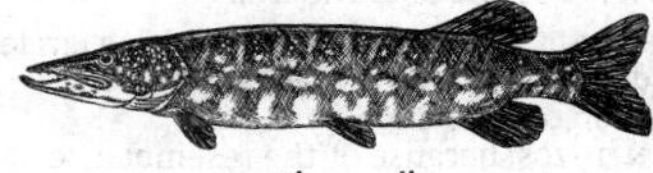

northern pike

pike² ▶ **n.** historical an infantry weapon with a pointed steel or iron head on a long wooden shaft. ■ chiefly Brit. (in names) a hill with a peaked top: *Scafell pike.* [apparently of Scandinavian origin; compare with West Norwegian dialect *pīk* 'pointed mountain.']
▶ **v.** [with obj.] historical kill or thrust (someone) through with a pike.
– ORIGIN early 16th cent.: from French *pique*, back-formation from *piquer* 'pierce,' from *pic* 'pick, pike'; compare with Old English *pīc* 'point, prick' (of unknown origin).

pike³ ▶ **n.** short for TURNPIKE.
– PHRASES **come down the pike** appear on the scene; come to notice.

pike⁴ (also **pike position**) ▶ **n.** [often as modifier] a position in diving or gymnastics in which the body is bent at the waist but the legs remain straight.
– ORIGIN 1920s: of unknown origin.

pike·man /ˈpīkmən/ ▶ **n.** (pl. **pikemen**) historical a soldier armed with a pike.

pike·perch /ˈpīk,pərCH/ ▶ **n.** (pl. **same**) a predatory pikelike freshwater fish of the perch family, esp. the walleye. ● Genus *Stizostedion*, family Percidae: five species, including the sauger.

pik·er /ˈpīkər/ ▶ **n.** informal **1** a gambler who makes only small bets. ■ a stingy or cautious person. **2** Austral./NZ a person who withdraws from a commitment.
– ORIGIN late 19th cent.: from the slang verb *pike*, meaning 'withdraw from an agreement because of overcautiousness.'

Pikes Peak /pīks/ a mountain in the Front Range of the southern Rocky Mountains, near Colorado Springs in Colorado, 14,110 feet (4,300 m) high, named for Zebulon PIKE.

pike·staff /ˈpīk,staf/ ▶ **n.** historical the wooden shaft of a pike.
– PHRASES **(as) plain as a pikestaff** very obvious. ■ ordinary or unattractive in appearance. [alteration of *as plain as a packstaff*, the staff being that of a peddler, on which he rested his pack of wares.]
– ORIGIN late 16th cent.: from PIKE² + STAFF¹.

pi·ki /ˈpēkē/ ▶ **n.** cornmeal bread in the form of very thin sheets, made by the Hopi Indians of the southwestern US.
– ORIGIN Hopi.

Pik Po·be·dy /ˈpēk päbˈyedē/ a mountain in eastern Kyrgyzstan, situated close to the border with China. Rising to a height of 24,406 feet (7,439 m), it is the highest peak in the Tien Shan range.
– ORIGIN from Russian, literally 'Victory Peak.'

pi·laf /pəˈläf, ˈpēläf/ (also **pilaff** or **pilau** /-ˈlô, -ˈlou, -lô, -lou/ or **pulao**) ▶ **n.** a Middle Eastern or Indian dish of rice or wheat, with vegetables and spices, typically having added meat or fish.
– ORIGIN from Turkish *pilav*.

pi·las·ter /pəˈlastər/ ▶ **n.** a rectangular column, esp. one projecting from a wall.

– DERIVATIVES **pi·las·tered** adj.
– ORIGIN late 16th cent.: from French *pilastre*, from Italian *pilastro* or medieval Latin *pilastrum*, from Latin *pila* 'pillar.'

Pi·late /ˈpīlət/, Pontius (died *c.* AD 36), Roman procurator of Judaea *c.*26–*c.*36. He is known for presiding at the trial of Jesus Christ and authorizing his crucifixion.

Pi·la·tes /piˈlätēz/ ▶ n. a system of exercises using special apparatus, designed to improve physical strength, flexibility, and posture, and enhance mental awareness: *this quest for better training has led many dancers to Pilates* | [as modifier] *the Pilates method.*
– ORIGIN 1960s: named after German physical fitness specialist Joseph *Pilates* (1880–1967), who devised the system.

pil·chard /ˈpilCHərd/ ▶ n. a small, edible, commercially valuable marine fish of the herring family. ● *Sardinops* and other genera, family Clupeidae: several species, including the European *Sardina pilchardus*. See also SARDINE[1].
– ORIGIN mid 16th cent.: of unknown origin.

Pil·co·ma·yo Riv·er /ˌpilkəˈmäyō/ a river that flows for 1,000 miles (1,600 km) from the Andes in western Bolivia along the Argentina-Paraguay border to join the Paraguay River at Asunción in Paraguay.

pile[1] /pīl/ ▶ n. a heap of things laid or lying one on top of another: *he placed the books in a neat pile.* ■ informal a large amount of something: *the growing pile of work.* ■ informal a lot of money: *he is admired for having* ***made a pile for himself.*** ■ a large imposing building or group of buildings: *a Victorian Gothic pile.* ■ a series of plates of dissimilar metals laid one on another alternately to produce an electric current. ■ dated term for NUCLEAR REACTOR. ■ archaic a funeral pyre.
▶ v. **1** [with obj.] place (things) one on top of another: *she piled all the groceries on the counter.* ■ (**be piled with**) be stacked or loaded with: *his in-box was piled high with papers.* ■ (**pile up**) [no obj.] increase in quantity: *the work has piled up.* ■ (**pile something up**) cause to increase in quantity: *the debts he piled up.* ■ (**pile something on**) informal intensify or exaggerate something for effect: *you can pile on the guilt, but my heart has turned to stone.*
2 [no obj.] (**pile in/out**) (of a group of people) get into or out of a vehicle in a disorganized manner: *we all piled in and headed off to our mysterious destination* | *my students* ***piled out of*** *three cars.* ■ (**pile into**) (of a vehicle) crash into: *60 cars piled into each other on I-95.*
– PHRASES **make one's pile** informal make a lot of money. **pile arms** see STACK ARMS at STACK. **pile it on** informal exaggerate the seriousness of a situation or of someone's behavior to increase guilt or distress.
– ORIGIN late Middle English: from Old French, from Latin *pila* 'pillar, pier.'

pile[2] ▶ n. **1** a heavy beam or post driven vertically into the bed of a river, soft ground, etc., to support the foundations of a structure.
2 Heraldry a triangular charge or ordinary formed by two lines meeting at an acute angle, usually pointing down from the top of the shield.
▶ v. [with obj.] strengthen or support (a structure) with piles.
– ORIGIN Old English *pīl* 'dart, arrow,' also 'pointed stake,' of Germanic origin; related to Dutch *pijl* and German *Pfeil*, from Latin *pilum* '(heavy) javelin.'

pile[3] ▶ n. the soft projecting surface of a carpet or of a fabric such as velvet or flannel, consisting of many small threads.
▶ v. [with obj., usu. in combination] (**-piled**) furnish with a pile: *a thick-piled carpet.*
– ORIGIN Middle English (in the sense 'downy feather'): from Latin *pilus* 'hair.' The noun sense dates from the mid 16th cent.

pi·le·a /ˈpīlēə, ˈpil-/ ▶ n. a plant of the nettle family that lacks stinging hairs, native to warm regions and widely grown as an indoor plant. ● Genus *Pilea*, family Urticaceae.
– ORIGIN modern Latin, from Latin *pileus* 'felt cap.'

pi·le·at·ed wood·peck·er /ˈpīlēˌātid, ˈpil-/ ▶ n. a large North American woodpecker with mainly black plumage and a red cap and crest. ● *Dryocopus pileatus*, family Picidae.
– ORIGIN late 18th cent.: *pileated* from Latin *pileatus* 'capped,' from *pileus* 'felt cap.'

pile driv·er ▶ n. a machine for driving piles into the ground.
– DERIVATIVES **pile-driv·ing** n. & adj.

piles /pīlz/ ▶ plural n. hemorrhoids.
– ORIGIN late Middle English: probably from Latin *pila* 'ball' (because of the globular form of external hemorrhoids).

pile·up /ˈpīlˌəp/ ▶ n. informal **1** a crash involving several vehicles. ■ a confused mass of people fallen on top of one another, esp. in a team game.
2 an accumulation of a specified thing: *a massive pileup of data.*

pi·le·us /ˈpīlēəs, ˈpil/ ▶ n. (pl. **pilei** /-lēˌī/) Botany the cap of a mushroom or toadstool.
– ORIGIN mid 18th cent.: from Latin, literally 'felt cap.'

pile·wort /ˈpīlwərt, -wôrt/ ▶ n. another term for LESSER CELANDINE (see CELANDINE).
– ORIGIN late Middle English: from PILES (because of its reputed efficacy against piles) + WORT.

pil·fer /ˈpilfər/ ▶ v. [with obj.] steal (typically things of relatively little value).
– DERIVATIVES **pil·fer·age** /-rij/ n., **pil·fer·er** n.
– ORIGIN late Middle English (as a noun in the sense 'action of pilfering, something pilfered'): from Old French *pelfrer* 'to pillage,' of unknown origin. Compare with PELF.

pil·grim /ˈpilgrəm/ ▶ n. a person who journeys to a sacred place for religious reasons. ■ (usu. **Pilgrim**) a member of a group of English Puritans fleeing religious persecution who sailed in the *Mayflower* and founded the colony of Plymouth, Massachusetts, in 1620. ■ a person who travels on long journeys.
▶ v. (**pilgrims, pilgriming, pilgrimed**) [no obj.] archaic travel or wander like a pilgrim.
– DERIVATIVES **pil·grim·ize** /-ˌmīz/ v. (archaic).
– ORIGIN Middle English: from Provençal *pelegrin*, from Latin *peregrinus* 'foreign' (see PEREGRINE).

pil·grim·age /ˈpilgrəmij/ ▶ n. a pilgrim's journey. ■ a journey to a place associated with someone or something well known or respected: *making a pilgrimage to the famous racing circuit.* ■ life viewed as a journey: *life's pilgrimage.*
▶ v. [no obj.] go on a pilgrimage.
– ORIGIN Middle English: from Provençal *pelegrinatge*, from *pelegrin* (see PILGRIM).

pi·li /pēˈlē/ ▶ n. the edible seed of a Phillipine tree, which tastes like a sweet almond.
– ORIGIN from Tagalog.

Pil·i·pi·no /ˌpiləˈpēnō/ ▶ n. & adj. variant of FILIPINO.

pill[1] /pil/ ▶ n. a small round mass of solid medicine to be swallowed whole. ■ (**the pill** or **the Pill**) a contraceptive pill: *she is* ***on the pill.*** ■ informal a tedious or unpleasant person. ■ informal (in some sports) a humorous term for a ball.
– PHRASES **a bitter pill (to swallow)** an unpleasant or painful necessity (to accept).
– DERIVATIVES **pil·u·lar** /ˈpilyələr/ adj.
– ORIGIN late Middle English: ultimately from Latin *pilula* 'little ball,' diminutive of *pila*; compare with Middle Dutch and Middle Low German *pille*.

pill[2] ▶ v. [no obj.] (of knitted fabric) form small balls of fluff on its surface.
– ORIGIN 1960s: from Latin *pilare* 'make bald' and 'pillage.' The verb was recorded in late Old English in the sense 'peel away' (referring esp. to bark or skin).

pil·lage /ˈpilij/ ▶ v. [with obj.] rob (a place) using violence, esp. in wartime. ■ steal (something) using violence, esp. in wartime: *artworks pillaged from churches and museums.*
▶ n. the action of pillaging a place or property, esp. in wartime.
– DERIVATIVES **pil·lag·er** n.
– ORIGIN late Middle English (as a noun): from Old French, from *piller* 'to plunder.'

pil·lar /ˈpilər/ ▶ n. a tall vertical structure of stone, wood, or metal, used as a support for a building, or as an ornament or monument. ■ something shaped like such a structure: ***a pillar of*** *smoke.* ■ a person or thing regarded as reliably providing essential support for something: *he was* ***a pillar of*** *his local community.*
– PHRASES **from pillar to post** from one place to another in an unceremonious or fruitless manner: *the refugees have been pushed from pillar to post in that area.*
– DERIVATIVES **pil·lared** adj.
– ORIGIN Middle English: from Anglo-Norman French *piler*, based on Latin *pila* 'pillar.'

pil·lar box ▶ n. (in the UK) a large red cylindrical public mailbox.

Pil·lars of Her·cu·les an ancient name for two promontories on either side of the Strait of Gibraltar (the Rock of Gibraltar and Mount Acho in Ceuta), held by legend to have been parted by the arm of Hercules.

pill·box /ˈpilˌbäks/ ▶ n. a small shallow cylindrical box for holding pills. ■ (usu. **pillbox hat**) a hat of a similar shape. ■ a small, enclosed, partly underground concrete fort used as an outpost.

pill·bug /ˈpilˌbəg/ (also **pill bug**) ▶ n. a wood louse that has a thick cuticle and is able to roll up into a ball when threatened. ● Genus *Armadillidium*, order Isopoda.

pil·lion /ˈpilyən/ ▶ n. a seat for a passenger behind a motorcyclist. ■ historical a woman's light saddle. ■ historical a cushion attached to the back of a saddle for an additional passenger.
– PHRASES **ride pillion** travel seated behind a motorcyclist.
– ORIGIN late 15th cent. (denoting a light saddle): from Scottish Gaelic *pillean*, Irish *pillín* 'small cushion,' diminutive of *pell*, from Latin *pellis* 'skin.'

pil·lock /ˈpilək/ ▶ n. Brit. informal a stupid person.
– ORIGIN mid 16th cent.: variant of archaic *pillicock* 'penis,' the early sense of *pillock* in dialects of northern England.

pil·lo·ry /ˈpilərē/ historical ▶ n. (pl. **pillories**) a wooden framework with holes for the head and hands, in which an offender was imprisoned and exposed to public abuse.
▶ v. (**pillories, pillorying, pilloried**) [with obj.] **1** put (someone) in the pillory.
2 attack or ridicule publicly: *he found himself pilloried by members of his own party.*
– ORIGIN Middle English: from Old French *pilori*, probably from Provençal *espilori* (associated by some with a Catalan word meaning 'peephole,' of uncertain origin).

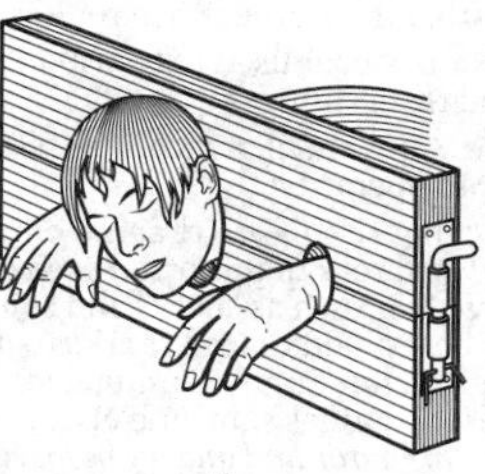
pillory

pil·low /ˈpilō/ ▶ n. a rectangular cloth bag stuffed with feathers, foam rubber, or other soft materials, used to support the head when lying down. ■ a piece of wood or metal used as a support; a block or bearing.
▶ v. [with obj.] rest (one's head) as if on a pillow. ■ literary serve as a pillow for: *her shoulder pillowed his weary head.*
– DERIVATIVES **pil·low·y** adj.
– ORIGIN Old English *pyle, pylu*; related to Dutch *peluw* and German *Pfühl*, based on Latin *pulvinus* 'cushion.'

pil·low block ▶ n. the housing for a wheel or journal bearing.

pil·low book ▶ n. (in Japanese classical literature) a type of private diary.

pil·low·case /ˈpilōˌkās/ ▶ n. a removable cloth cover for a pillow.

pil·low fight ▶ n. a mock fight in which people hit each other with pillows.

pil·low lace ▶ n. lace made by hand using a lace pillow.

pil·low la·va ▶ n. lava that has solidified as rounded masses, characteristic of eruption under water.

pil·low sham ▶ n. a decorative pillowcase for covering a pillow when it is not in use.

pil·low·slip /ˈpilōˌslip/ ▶ n. a pillowcase.

pil·low talk ▶ n. intimate conversation in bed.

pill pop·per ▶ n. informal a person who regularly takes large numbers of pills, esp. barbiturates or amphetamines.
– DERIVATIVES **pill-pop·ping** n. & adj.

pill push·er ▶ n. informal a person, specifically a doctor, who resorts too readily to advocating the use of medication to cure illness rather than considering other treatments. ■ any seller of drugs for profit, such as a pharmaceutical company or a drug dealer.
– DERIVATIVES **pill-push·ing** n. & adj.

pi·lo·car·pine /ˌpīləˈkärˌpēn/ ▶ n. Chemistry a volatile alkaloid obtained from jaborandi leaves, used to contract the pupils and to relieve pressure in the eye in glaucoma patients.
– ORIGIN late 19th cent.: from modern Latin *Pilocarpus* (genus name of the jaborandi) + -INE[4].

pi·lose /ˈpīlōs/ (also **pilous**) ▶ adj. Botany & Zoology covered with long soft hairs.
– DERIVATIVES **pi·los·i·ty** /pīˈläsitē/ n.
– ORIGIN mid 18th cent.: from Latin *pilosus*, from *pilus* 'hair.'

PRONUNCIATION KEY ə *ago, up*; ər *over, fur*; a *hat*; ā *ate*; ä *car*; e *let*; ē *see*; i *fit*; ī *by*; NG *sing*; ō *go*; ô *law, for*; oi *toy*; o͝o *good*; o͞o *goo*; ou *out*; TH *thin*; T͟H *then*; ZH *vision*

pi·lot /ˈpīlət/ ▶ **n.** **1** a person who operates the flying controls of an aircraft. ■ a person with expert local knowledge qualified to take charge of a ship entering or leaving confined waters; a helmsman. ■ archaic a guide or leader. ■ [often as modifier] Telecommunications an unmodulated reference signal transmitted with another signal for the purposes of control or synchronization.
2 a television program made to test audience reaction with a view to the production of a series.
3 another term for COWCATCHER.
4 short for PILOT LIGHT (sense 1).
▶ **adj.** [attrib.] done as an experiment or test before introducing something more widely: *a two-year pilot study.*
▶ **v.** (**pilots, piloting, piloted**) [with obj.] **1** act as a pilot of (an aircraft or ship). ■ guide; steer: *the task of piloting the economy out of recession.*
2 test (a plan, project, etc.) before introducing it more widely: *other schools were piloting such courses.*
– DERIVATIVES **pi·lot·age** /ˈpīlətij/ **n.**, **pi·lot·less adj.**
– ORIGIN early 16th cent. (denoting a person who steers a ship): from French *pilote*, from medieval Latin *pilotus*, an alteration of *pedota*, based on Greek *pēdon* 'oar,' (plural) 'rudder.'

pi·lot bal·loon ▶ **n.** a small meteorological balloon used to track air currents.

pi·lot bis·cuit ▶ **n.** another term for HARDTACK.

pi·lot boat ▶ **n.** a boat used to transport maritime pilots to and from ships.

pi·lot chute ▶ **n.** a small parachute used to bring the main one into operation.

pi·lot·fish /ˈpīlət,fisH/ ▶ **n.** (pl. **same** or **pilotfishes**) **1** a fish of warm seas that is often seen swimming close to large fish such as sharks and sometimes turtles and boats, said to lead sharks to prey. ● *Naucrates ductor*, family Carangidae.
2 someone who guides someone else: *pilotfish who counsel both predator and quarry in mergers.*

pi·lot hole ▶ **n.** a small hole drilled as a guide for the insertion of a nail or screw, or for the drilling of a larger hole.

pi·lot·house /ˈpīlət,hous/ ▶ **n.** another term for WHEELHOUSE.

pi·lot jack·et ▶ **n.** another term for PEA JACKET.

pi·lot light ▶ **n.** **1** a small gas burner kept continuously burning to light a larger burner when needed, esp. on a gas stove or water heater.
2 an electric indicator light or control light.

pi·lot whale ▶ **n.** a toothed whale that has black skin with a gray anchor-shaped marking on the chin, a low dorsal fin, and a square bulbous head. Also called BLACKFISH. ● Genus *Globicephala*, family Delphinidae: the long-finned *G. melas* of subtropical waters, and the short-finned *G. macrorhyncus* of temperate waters.

pi·lous /ˈpīləs/ ▶ **adj.** another term for PILOSE.

Pils /pilz/ (also **pils**) ▶ **n.** short for PILSNER.
– ORIGIN 1960s.

Pil·sen /ˈpilzən/ an industrial city in western Czech Republic; pop. 164,230 (2007). Czech name **Plzeň**.

Pil·sner /ˈpilznər/ (also **pilsner, Pilsener**, or **pilsener**) ▶ **n.** a lager beer with a strong hop flavor, originally brewed at Pilsen in Bohemia (now the Czech Republic), and traditionally served in a tall glass tapered at the bottom.

Pilt·down man /ˈpilt,doun/ ▶ **n.** a fraudulent fossil composed of a human cranium and an ape jaw, allegedly discovered in England and presented in 1912 as a genuine hominid of the early Pleistocene, but shown to be a hoax in 1953.
– ORIGIN *Piltdown*, the name of a village in southern England.

PIM ▶ **abbr.** personal information manager.

Pi·ma /ˈpēmə/ ▶ **n.** (pl. **same** or **Pimas**) **1** a member of either of two American Indian peoples, the (**Upper**) **Pima** living chiefly along the Gila and Salt rivers of southern Arizona, and the **Lower Pima** of central Sonora.
2 the Uto-Aztecan languages of these peoples. See PAPAGO.
▶ **adj.** of or relating to this people or their language.
– ORIGIN Spanish, shortening of *Pima Ayto*, from Pima *pimaha'icu* 'nothing,' perhaps a shibboleth.

pi·men·to /pəˈmentō/ ▶ **n.** (pl. **pimentos**) **1** variant spelling of PIMIENTO.
2 chiefly W. Indian another term for ALLSPICE (sense 2).
– ORIGIN late 17th cent.: from Spanish *pimiento* (see PIMIENTO).

pi me·son /ˈpī ˈmāsän, -ˌzän/ ▶ **n.** another term for PION.

pi·mien·to /pəˈm(y)entō/ (also **pimento**) ▶ **n.** (pl. **pimientos**) a red sweet pepper.
– ORIGIN mid 17th cent.: from Spanish, from medieval Latin *pigmentum* 'spice,' from Latin, 'pigment.'

Pimm's /pimz/ ▶ **n.** trademark a gin-based alcoholic drink, served typically with lemonade or soda water and fresh mint.
– ORIGIN early 20th cent.: from the name of the proprietor of the restaurant where the drink was created.

pimp /pimp/ ▶ **n.** a man who controls prostitutes and arranges clients for them, taking part of their earnings in return.
▶ **v.** **1** [no obj.] (often as noun **pimping**) act as a pimp. ■ [with obj.] provide (someone) as a prostitute. ■ [with obj.] informal sell or promote (something) in an extravagant or persistent way: *he pimped their debut album to staff writers at Rolling Stone.*
2 [with obj.] informal make (something) more showy or impressive: ***he pimped up** the car with spoilers and twin-spoke 18-inch alloys.*
– ORIGIN late 16th cent.: of unknown origin.

> **WORD TRENDS** How do completely negative words gain a positive meaning? **Pimp** is a telling example of this process in action. Even the modern extended sense of 'sell or promote in an extravagant or persistent way' carries a strong dose of moral disapproval: *they need to release quality music instead of pimping boy bands.* However, the popularity of hip-hop culture has made the **pimp** a figure of social aspiration for some people, with the word increasingly associated with a glamorous world of champagne, fast cars, and flashy jewelry. This image has spawned a positive sense of the verb, inspired in part by the MTV show *Pimp My Ride*, in which worn-out cars are transformed and customized: *we've got to get that minivan pimped out | I could have hired PR people to pimp up my material.*

pim·per·nel /ˈpimpər,nel, -pərnəl/ ▶ **n.** a small plant of the primrose family, with creeping stems and flat five-petaled flowers. ● Genera *Anagallis* and *Lysimachia*, family Primulaceae: several species, in particular the SCARLET PIMPERNEL.
– ORIGIN late Middle English (denoting the burnet): from Old French *pimpernelle*, based on Latin *piper* 'pepper' (because of the resemblance of the burnet's fruit to a peppercorn).

pimp·ing /ˈpimpiNG/ ▶ **adj.** archaic small or insignificant.
– ORIGIN late 17th cent.: of unknown origin.

pim·ple /ˈpimpəl/ ▶ **n.** a small hard inflamed spot on the skin.
– DERIVATIVES **pim·pled adj.**, **pim·ply adj.**
– ORIGIN Middle English: related to Old English *piplian* 'break out in pustules.'

pimp·mo·bile /ˈpimp-mō,bēl/ ▶ **n.** informal a large ostentatious car, in a style associated with pimps: *like a pimpmobile, with cherry paneling and shag carpet.*

PIN /pin/ ▶ **abbr.** personal identification number.

pin /pin/ ▶ **n.** **1** a thin piece of metal with a sharp point at one end and a round head at the other, used esp. for fastening pieces of cloth. ■ a small brooch or badge. ■ Medicine a steel rod used to join the ends of fractured bones while they heal. ■ a metal peg that holds down the activating lever of a hand grenade, preventing its explosion. ■ short for HAIRPIN. ■ Music a peg around which one string of a musical instrument is fastened.
2 a short piece of wood or metal for various purposes, in particular: ■ (in bowling) one of a set of bottle-shaped wooden pieces that are arranged in an upright position at the end of a lane in order to be toppled by a rolling ball. ■ a metal projection from a plug or an integrated circuit that makes an electrical connection with a socket or another part of a circuit. ■ Golf a stick with a flag placed in a hole to mark the hole's position.
3 (**pins**) informal legs: *she was very nimble on her pins.*
4 Chess an attack on a piece or pawn, which is thereby pinned: *the pin of the black queen by the white rook.*
5 Brit. historical a half-firkin cask for beer.
▶ **v.** (**pins, pinning, pinned**) attach or fasten with a pin or pins in a specified position: *her hair was pinned back | pin a note on the door.* ■ (**pin something on**) fix blame or responsibility for something on (someone): *don't pin the blame on me.* ■ hold someone firmly in a specified position so they are unable to move: *she was standing pinned against the door.* ■ Chess hinder or prevent (a piece or pawn) from moving because of the danger to a more valuable piece standing behind it along the line of an attack.
– PHRASES (**as**) **neat** (or **clean**) **as a pin** extremely neat or clean. **hear a pin drop** used to describe absolute silence. **pin one's ears back** listen carefully. **pin one's hopes** (or **faith**) **on** rely heavily on: *retailers were pinning their hopes on a big-spending Christmas.*
– PHRASAL VERBS **pin someone down** restrict the actions or movement of an enemy by firing at them. ■ force someone to be specific and make their intentions clear. **pin something down** define something precisely.
– ORIGIN late Old English *pinn*; related to Dutch *pin* 'pin, peg,' from Latin *pinna* 'point, tip, edge.'

pi·ña /ˈpēnyə/ ▶ **n.** a sheer fabric made from the fibers of pineapple leaves.

pi·ña co·la·da /ˈpēnyə kəˈlädə/ ▶ **n.** a cocktail made with rum, pineapple juice, and coconut.
– ORIGIN Spanish, literally 'strained pineapple.'

pin·a·fore /ˈpinə,fôr/ ▶ **n.** a sleeveless apronlike garment worn over a child's dress. ■ a collarless sleeveless dress, tied or buttoned in the back and typically worn as a jumper, over a blouse or sweater. ■ Brit. a woman's loose sleeveless garment, typically full length and worn over clothes to keep them clean.
– ORIGIN late 18th cent.: from PIN + AFORE (because the term originally denoted an apron with a bib pinned on the front of a dress).

child's pinafore

Pi·nang variant spelling of **PENANG**.

pi·ña·ta /pēnˈyätə/ ▶ **n.** (esp. in Spanish-speaking communities) a decorated figure of an animal containing toys and candy that is suspended from a height and broken open by blindfolded children as part of a celebration.
– ORIGIN mid 19th cent.: Spanish, literally 'pot.'

Pin·a·tu·bo, Mount /,pinəˈtōōbō/ a volcano on the island of Luzon, in the Philippines. It erupted in 1991, killing more than 300 people and destroying the homes of more than 200,000.

pin·ball /ˈpin,bôl/ ▶ **n.** a game in which small metal balls are shot across a sloping board and score points by striking various targets.

pin block ▶ **n.** the part of a piano or harpsichord holding the tuning pins.

pince-nez /ˈpans,nā, ˈpins/ ▶ **n.** [treated as sing. or pl.] a pair of eyeglasses with a nose clip instead of earpieces.
– ORIGIN late 19th cent.: from French, literally '(that) pinches (the) nose.'

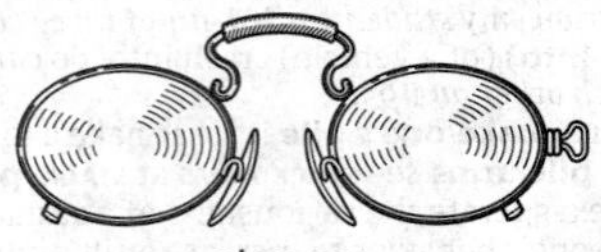

pince-nez

pin·cer /ˈpinsər/ ▶ **n.** (usu. **pincers**) (also **a pair of pincers**) a tool made of two pieces of metal bearing blunt concave jaws that are arranged like the blades of scissors, used for gripping and pulling things. ■ a front claw of a lobster, crab, or similar crustacean.
– ORIGIN Middle English: from Anglo-Norman French, from Old French *pincier* 'to pinch.'

pin·cer move·ment ▶ **n.** a movement by two separate bodies of troops converging on the enemy.

pinch /pinCH/ ▶ **v.** [with obj.] **1** grip (something, typically someone's flesh) tightly and sharply between finger and thumb: *she pinched his cheek.* ■ (of a shoe) hurt (a foot) by being too tight. ■ compress (the lips), esp. with worry or tension: *Aunt Rose **pinched her thin lips together.*** ■ remove (a bud, leaves, etc.) to encourage bushy growth.
2 [no obj.] live in a frugal way: *if I **pinch and scrape**, I might manage.*
3 informal arrest (someone): *I was pinched for speeding.* ■ informal steal: *he pinched a handful of candies.*
4 Sailing sail (a boat) so close to the wind that the sails begin to lose power.
▶ **n.** **1** an act of gripping the skin of someone's body between finger and thumb: *he gave her a gentle pinch.* ■ an amount of an ingredient that can be held between fingers and thumb: *add **a pinch of** salt.*
2 informal an arrest. ■ an act of theft or plagiarism.
– PHRASES **in a pinch** in a critical situation; if absolutely necessary. **feel the pinch** experience hardship, esp. financial. **have to pinch oneself** used to convey that a good situation is so surprising that the person involved has to make sure they are not imagining it: *sometimes I have to pinch myself to realize it isn't all a dream.* **pinch (one's) pennies** see PENNY.
– DERIVATIVES **pinch·er n.**
– ORIGIN Middle English (as a verb): from an Old Northern French variant of Old French *pincier* 'to pinch.'

pinch·beck /ˈpinCH,bek/ ▶ **n.** an alloy of copper and zinc resembling gold, used in watchmaking and costume jewelry.
▶ **adj.** appearing valuable, but actually cheap or tawdry.
– ORIGIN mid 18th cent.: named after Christopher *Pinchbeck* (died 1732), English watchmaker.

pinched /pinCHt/ ▶ **adj.** **1** (of a person or their face) tense and pale from cold, worry, or hunger.
2 hurt by financial hardship: *consumers feel pinched by rising costs in repairs and housing.*

pinch ef·fect ▶ **n.** Physics the constriction of a plasma through which a large electric current is flowing, caused by the attractive force of the current's own magnetic field.

pin cher·ry ▶ **n.** see BIRD CHERRY.

pinch-hit ▶ **v.** [no obj.] Baseball bat in place of another player, typically at a critical point in the game: *he pinch-hit for O'Brien and grounded out.* ■ informal act as a substitute for someone, esp. in an emergency: *last year I briefly pinch-hit for a movie critic on leave.*
– DERIVATIVES **pinch hit·ter** **n.**

Pin·chot /ˈpinSHō/, Gifford (1865–1946), US forester. Chief of the US Department of Agriculture's forestry division 1898–1910, he was the first professional US forester and a leader in the land conservation movement. He was also governor of Pennsylvania 1923–27, 1931–35.

pinch·pen·ny /ˈpinCH,penē/ ▶ **n.** (pl. **pinchpennies**) [usu. as modifier] a miserly person.

pinch point ▶ **n.** a place or point where congestion occurs or is likely to occur, esp. on a road: *the planners have suggestions to ease traffic jams at ninety-two pinch points.*

pinch-run ▶ **v.** [no obj.] Baseball substitute for another as a base runner, typically at a critical point in the game.
– DERIVATIVES **pinch run·ner** **n.**

Pinck·ney /ˈpiNGknē/, Charles Cotesworth (1746–1825), US statesman. As minister to France in 1797, he was one of the proposed recipients of the bribery attempts made by the French to US officials in what became known as the XYZ Affair. He ran unsuccessfully for US vice president in 1800 and for president in 1804 and 1808.

pin curl ▶ **n.** a curl that is held by a hairpin while setting.

pin·cush·ion /ˈpin,ko͝oSHən/ ▶ **n.** a small cushion into which pins are stuck for convenient storage. ■ (also **pincushion distortion**) a form of optical distortion in which straight lines along the edge of a screen or a lens bulge toward the center.

Pin·dar /ˈpindər, -,där/ (*c.*518–*c.*438 BC), Greek lyric poet. He is noted for his odes (the *Epinikia*), which celebrate victories in athletic contests at Olympia and elsewhere and relate them to religious and moral themes.
– DERIVATIVES **Pin·dar·ic** /pinˈdarik/ **adj.**

Pin·dus Moun·tains /ˈpindəs/ a range of mountains in west central Greece that stretch from the border with Albania south to the Gulf of Corinth. The highest peak is Mount Smolikas, which rises to 8,136 feet (2,637 m). Greek name **Píndhos**.

pine[1] /pīn/ ▶ **n.** **1** (also **pine tree**) an evergreen coniferous tree that has clusters of long needle-shaped leaves. Many kinds are grown for their soft timber, which is widely used for furniture and pulp, or for tar and turpentine. ● Genus *Pinus*, family Pinaceae: many species, including North America's eastern **white pine** and western **ponderosa pine**. ■ used in names of coniferous trees of other families, e.g., **Norfolk Island pine**. ■ used in names of unrelated plants that resemble the pines in some way, e.g., **ground pine**. ■ [as modifier] having the scent of pine needles: *a pine potpourri.*
2 informal a pineapple.
– DERIVATIVES **pin·er·y** /ˈpīnərē/ **n.**
– ORIGIN Old English, from Latin *pinus*, reinforced in Middle English by Old French *pin*.

pine[2] ▶ **v.** [no obj.] suffer a mental and physical decline, esp. because of a broken heart: *she thinks I am pining away from love.* ■ (**pine for**) miss and long for the return of: *I was pining for my boyfriend.*
– ORIGIN Old English *pīnian* '(cause to) suffer,' of Germanic origin; related to Dutch *pijnen*, German *peinen* 'experience pain,' also to obsolete *pine* 'punishment'; ultimately based on Latin *poena* 'punishment.'

pin·e·al /ˈpinēəl, ˈpī-/ (also **pineal gland**, **pineal body**) ▶ **n.** a pea-sized conical mass of tissue behind the third ventricle of the brain, secreting a hormonelike substance in some mammals.
– ORIGIN late 17th cent.: from French *pinéal*, from Latin *pinea* 'pine cone.' The anatomical term refers to the shape of the gland.

pin·e·al eye ▶ **n.** Zoology (in some reptiles and lower vertebrates) an eyelike structure on the top of the head, covered by almost transparent skin and derived from or linked to the pineal body.

pine·ap·ple /ˈpī,napəl/ ▶ **n.** **1** a large juicy tropical fruit consisting of aromatic edible yellow flesh surrounded by a tough segmented skin and topped with a tuft of stiff leaves.
2 the widely cultivated tropical American plant that bears this fruit. It is low-growing, with a spiral of spiny sword-shaped leaves on a thick stem. ● *Ananas comosus*, family Bromeliaceae.
3 informal a hand grenade.
– ORIGIN late Middle English (denoting a pine cone): from PINE[1] + APPLE. The word was applied to the fruit in the mid 17th cent., because of its resemblance to a pine cone.

pineapple

pine·ap·ple weed ▶ **n.** a small mayweed with flowers that lack ray florets. When crushed, the leaves have a pineapple fragrance. ● Genus *Matricaria*, family Compositae: the European *M. matricarioides* and the North American *M. discoidea*.

Pine Barrens a region in southern New Jersey that is lightly populated and is characterized by sandy soils, forests of stunted conifers, and numerous small rivers.

Pine Bluff an industrial city in southeastern Arkansas, on the Arkansas River, site of a large arsenal; pop. 50,408 (est. 2008).

pine cone ▶ **n.** the conical or rounded woody fruit of a pine tree, with scales that open to release the seeds.

pine cone

pine mar·ten ▶ **n.** a marten with a dark brown coat, a yellowish throat, and a bushy tail. ● Genus *Martes*, family Mustelidae: two species, *M. martes* of northern Eurasia, and *M. americana* of North America, esp. Canada and Alaska.

pi·nene /ˈpī,nēn/ ▶ **n.** Chemistry a colorless flammable liquid present in turpentine, juniper oil, and other natural extracts. ● A bicyclic terpene; chem. formula: $C_{10}H_{16}$; four isomers, esp. α-**pinene**, the main constituent of turpentine.
– ORIGIN late 19th cent.: from Latin *pinus* 'pine' + -ENE.

pine nut ▶ **n.** the edible seed of various pine trees.

Pine Ridge a village in southwestern South Dakota, headquarters of the Pine Ridge Indian Reservation; pop. 3,171 (2000).

pine·sap /ˈpīn,sap/ ▶ **n.** a saprophytic woodland plant related to wintergreen, lacking chlorophyll and bearing one or more waxy bell-shaped flowers. ● Two species in the family Monotropaceae (or Pyrolaceae): the yellow or reddish *Monotropa hypopithys* (also called FALSE BEECHDROPS), common in eastern North America, and the pinkish or purplish violet-scented *Monotropsis odorata* (also called **sweet pinesap**).

pine snake ▶ **n.** a large harmless North American snake with dark markings. When disturbed it hisses loudly and vibrates its tail. ● *Pituophis melanoleucus*, family Colubridae.

pine tar ▶ **n.** a thick, sticky liquid obtained from the destructive distillation of pinewood, used in soap, roofing, and medicinally for skin infections.

Pine Tree State a nickname for the state of MAINE.

pi·ne·tum /pīˈnētəm/ ▶ **n.** (pl. **pineta** /-tə/) an arboretum of pine trees or other conifers for scientific or ornamental purposes.
– ORIGIN mid 19th cent.: from Latin, from *pinus* 'pine' + -ETUM.

pine vole ▶ **n.** a vole with dense molelike fur, found chiefly in forests and orchards in North America and Eurasia. ● Genus *Pitymys*, family Muridae: many species, esp. the common *P. pinetorum*, the Florida variety of which is sometimes considered a distinct species (*P. parvulus*).

pine·wood /ˈpīn,wo͝od/ ▶ **n.** **1** [usu. as modifier] the timber of the pine: *pinewood furniture.*
2 (usu. **pinewoods**) a forest of pines.

pine·y /ˈpīnē/ (also **piny**) ▶ **adj.** of, like, or full of pines.

pin·feath·er /ˈpin,fe*TH*ər/ ▶ **n.** Ornithology an immature feather, before the veins have expanded and while the shaft is full of fluid.

pin·fold /ˈpin,fōld/ historical ▶ **n.** a pound for stray animals.
▶ **v.** [with obj.] confine (a stray animal) in such a pound.
– ORIGIN late Old English *pundfald*, from a base shared by POND and POUND[3] + FOLD[2].

ping /piNG/ ▶ **n.** a short high-pitched ringing sound, as of a tap on a crystal glass: *the syncopated ping of steel drums.* ■ a percussive knocking sound, esp. in an internal combustion engine: *if any sign of engine ping occurs.*
▶ **v.** **1** make or cause to make a ping: [no obj.] *the doorbell pinged* | [with obj.] *Victoria pinged the bell.*
2 [with obj.] Computing query (another computer on a network) to determine whether there is a connection to it. ■ contact a person briefly (esp. electronically): *he just pinged me, pointing to a breaking news story.*
– ORIGIN mid 19th cent.: imitative.

ping·er /ˈpiNGər/ ▶ **n.** a device that transmits short high-pitched signals at brief intervals for purposes of detection, measurement, or identification.

pin·go /ˈpiNGō/ ▶ **n.** (pl. **pingos**) Geology a dome-shaped mound consisting of a layer of soil over a large core of ice, occurring in permafrost areas.
– ORIGIN 1920s: from Inuit *pinguq* 'nunatak.'

Ping-Pong /ˈpiNG ,pôNG, -,päNG/ ▶ **n.** trademark another term for TABLE TENNIS.
– ORIGIN early 20th cent.: imitative of the sound of a paddle striking a ball.

pin·guid /ˈpiNGgwid/ ▶ **adj.** formal of the nature of or resembling fat; oily or greasy.
– DERIVATIVES **pin·guid·i·ty** /piNGˈgwiditē/ **n.**
– ORIGIN mid 17th cent.: from Latin *pinguis* 'fat' + -ID[1].

pin·head /ˈpin,hed/ ▶ **n.** **1** the flattened head of a pin. ■ [often as modifier] a very small rounded object: *pinhead dots.*
2 informal a stupid or foolish person.

pin·head·ed /ˈpin,hedəd/ ▶ **adj.** informal stupid; foolish.
– DERIVATIVES **pin·head·ed·ness** **n.**

pin·hole /ˈpin,hōl/ ▶ **n.** a very small hole.

pin·hole bor·er ▶ **n.** an ambrosia beetle (family Platypodidae), specifically the larva, which makes minute round holes in timber.

pin·hole cam·er·a ▶ **n.** a camera with a pinhole aperture and no lens.

pin·ion[1] /ˈpinyən/ ▶ **n.** the outer part of a bird's wing including the flight feathers. ■ literary a bird's wing as used in flight.
▶ **v.** [with obj.] **1** tie or hold the arms or legs of (someone): *he pinioned the limbs of his opponents.* ■ bind (the arms or legs) of someone.
2 cut off the pinion of (a wing or bird) to prevent flight.
– ORIGIN late Middle English: from Old French *pignon*, based on Latin *pinna*, *penna* 'feather.'

pin·ion[2] ▶ **n.** a small gear or spindle engaging with a large gear.
– ORIGIN mid 17th cent.: from French *pignon*, alteration of obsolete *pignol*, from Latin *pinea* 'pine cone,' from *pinus* 'pine.'

pink[1] /piNGk/ ▶ **adj.** **1** of a color intermediate between red and white, as of coral or salmon: *her healthy pink cheeks* | *bright pink lipstick.* ■ (of wine) rosé.
2 informal, often derogatory having or showing left-wing tendencies: *pale pink politics.*
3 of or associated with homosexuals: *a boom in the pink economy.*
▶ **n.** **1** pink color, material, or pigment: *she looks good in pink.* ■ (also **hunting pink**) the red clothing or material worn by fox hunters.
2 the best condition or degree: *the economy is not in the pink of health.*
3 informal, often derogatory a person with left-wing tendencies. See also PINKO.
– PHRASES **in the pink** informal in very good health and spirits. **turn** (or **go**) **pink** blush.
– DERIVATIVES **pink·ish** **adj.**, **pink·ly** **adv.**, **pink·ness** **n.**, **pink·y** **adj.**
– ORIGIN mid 17th cent.: from PINK[2], the early use of the adjective being to describe the color of the flowers of this plant.

pink[2] ▶ **n.** a herbaceous Eurasian plant with sweet-smelling pink or white flowers and slender, typically gray-green, leaves. ● Genus *Dianthus*, family Caryophyllaceae (the **pink family**). This family includes the campions, chickweeds, stitchworts, and the cultivated carnations. See also CLOVE[1] (sense 3).
– ORIGIN late 16th cent.: perhaps short for *pink eye*, literally 'small or half-shut eye'; compare with the synonymous French word *oeillet*, literally 'little eye.'

pink[3] ▶ **v.** [with obj.] **1** cut a scalloped or zigzag edge on: (as adj. **pinked**) *a bonnet with pinked edging.*

PRONUNCIATION KEY ə *ago, up*; ər *over, fur*; a *hat*; ā *ate*; ä *car*; e *let*; ē *see*; i *fit*; ī *by*; NG *sing*; ō *go*; ô *law, for*; oi *toy*; o͝o *good*; o͞o *goo*; ou *out*; TH *thin*; *TH* *then*; ZH *vision*

■ pierce or nick (someone) slightly with a weapon or missile.
2 archaic decorate: *April pinked the earth with flowers.*
– ORIGIN early 16th cent. (in the sense 'pierce or nick slightly'): compare with Low German *pinken* 'strike, peck.'

pink[4] ▶ **n.** historical a small square-rigged sailing ship, typically with a narrow, overhanging stern.
– ORIGIN late 15th cent.: from Middle Dutch *pin(c)ke*, of unknown ultimate origin; compare with Spanish *pinque* and Italian *pinco*.

pink[5] ▶ **n.** dated a yellowish lake pigment made by combining vegetable coloring matter with a white base.
– ORIGIN mid 17th cent.: of unknown origin.

pink-col·lar ▶ **adj.** of or relating to work traditionally associated with women.

pink el·e·phants ▶ **plural n.** informal hallucinations supposedly typical of those experienced by a drunk person.

Pin·ker·ton /ˈpiNGkərtən/, Allan (1819–84), US detective, born in Scotland. In 1850, after having solved a series of train robberies, he established the first US private detective agency. He served as chief of the Union's secret service during the Civil War.

pink·eye /ˈpiNGk,ī/ ▶ **n. 1** conjunctivitis in humans and some livestock.
2 a viral disease of horses, symptoms of which include fever, spontaneous abortion, and redness of the eyes. ● The virus belongs to the genus *Arterivirus*.

Pink·ham /ˈpiNGkəm/, Lydia (Estes) (1819–83), US inventor and saleswoman. In 1865, she concocted and marketed Mrs. Lydia E. Pinkham's Vegetable Compound, a patented herbal medicine for female complaints.

pink·ie /ˈpiNGkē/ (also **pinky**) ▶ **n.** informal the little finger.
– ORIGIN early 19th cent.: partly from Dutch *pink* 'the little finger,' reinforced by PINK[1].

pink·ing shears ▶ **plural n.** shears with a serrated blade, used to cut a zigzag edge in fabric to prevent it from fraying.

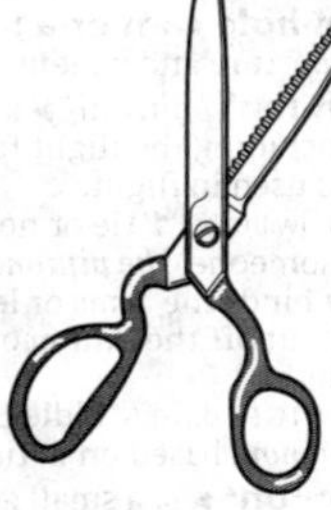

pinking shears

pink noise ▶ **n.** Physics random noise having equal energy per octave, and so having more low-frequency components than white noise.

pink·o /ˈpiNGkō/ ▶ **n.** (pl. **pinkos** or **pinkoes**) informal, derogatory a person with left-wing or liberal views.

pink salm·on ▶ **n.** a small salmon with dark spots on the back, native to the North Pacific and introduced into the northwestern Atlantic. ● *Oncorhynchus gorbuscha*, family Salmonidae. ■ its pale pink flesh used as food.

pink slip informal ▶ **n.** a notice of dismissal from employment.
▶ **v.** (**pink-slip**) [with obj.] dismiss (someone) from employment.

Pink·ster /ˈpiNGkstər/ ▶ **n.** dialect Whitsuntide.
– ORIGIN mid 18th cent.: from Dutch, 'Pentecost,' from celebrations in areas of former Dutch influence, such as New York.

pin mon·ey ▶ **n.** a small sum of money for spending on inessentials. ■ historical an allowance to a woman from her husband for clothing and other personal expenses.
– ORIGIN late 17th cent.: from PIN in the sense 'decorative clasp for the hair or a garment' + MONEY.

pin·na /ˈpinə/ ▶ **n.** (pl. **pinnae** /ˈpinē/) **1** Anatomy & Zoology the external part of the ear in humans and other mammals; the auricle.
2 Botany a primary division of a pinnate leaf, esp. of a fern.
3 Zoology any of a number of animal structures resembling fins or wings.
– ORIGIN late 18th cent.: modern Latin, from a variant of Latin *penna* 'feather, wing, fin.'

pin·nace /ˈpinis/ ▶ **n.** chiefly historical a small boat, with sails or oars, forming part of the equipment of a warship or other large vessel.
– ORIGIN mid 16th cent.: from French *pinace*, probably based on Latin *pinus* 'pine' (see PINE[1]); compare with Italian *pinaccia* and Spanish *pinaza*.

pin·na·cle /ˈpinəkəl/ ▶ **n.** a high, pointed piece of rock. ■ a small pointed turret built as an ornament on a roof. ■ the most successful point; the culmination: *he had reached the pinnacle of his career.*
▶ **v.** [with obj.] literary set on or as if on a pinnacle: *a rustic cross was pinnacled upon the makeshift altar.* ■ form the culminating point or example of.
– DERIVATIVES **pin·na·cled adj.**
– ORIGIN Middle English: from Old French, from late Latin *pinnaculum*, diminutive of *pinna* 'wing, point.'

pin·nae /ˈpinē/ plural form of PINNA.

pin·nate /ˈpināt, -it/ ▶ **adj.** Botany (of a compound leaf) having leaflets arranged on either side of the stem, typically in pairs opposite each other. ■ Zoology (esp. of an invertebrate animal) having branches, tentacles, etc., on each side of an axis, like the vanes of a feather.
– DERIVATIVES **pin·nat·ed adj.**, **pin·nate·ly adv.**, **pin·na·tion** /piˈnāSHən/ **n.**
– ORIGIN early 18th cent.: from Latin *pinnatus* 'feathered,' from *pinna, penna* (see PINNA).

pin·nat·i·fid /piˈnatəfid/ ▶ **adj.** Botany (of a leaf) pinnately divided, but not all the way down to the central axis.
– ORIGIN mid 18th cent.: from modern Latin *pinnatifidus*, from Latin *pinnatus* 'feathered' + *fid-* 'cleft' (from the verb *findere*).

pinni- ▶ **comb. form** relating to wings or fins: *pinniped*.
– ORIGIN from Latin *pinna, penna* 'wing, fin.'

pin·ni·ped /ˈpinə,ped/ Zoology ▶ **n.** a carnivorous aquatic mammal of the order Pinnipedia, such as a seal or walrus.
▶ **adj.** relating to or denoting pinnipeds.

Pin·ni·pe·di·a /,pinəˈpēdēə/ Zoology an order of carnivorous aquatic mammals that comprises the seals, sea lions, and walrus. They are distinguished by their flipperlike limbs. ● Order Pinnipedia: three families.
– ORIGIN modern Latin (plural), from Latin *pinna* 'wing, fin' + *pes, ped-* 'foot.'

pin·nule /ˈpin,yo͞ol/ ▶ **n.** Botany a secondary division of a pinnate leaf, esp. of a fern. ■ Zoology a part or organ like a small wing or fin, esp. a side branch on the arm of a crinoid.
– ORIGIN late 16th cent. (denoting one of the sights of an astrolabe): from Latin *pinnula* 'small wing,' diminutive of *pinna*.

PIN num·ber ▶ **n.** personal identification number.

pin oak ▶ **n.** a North American oak with deeply lobed, toothed leaves. Its dead branches remain in position and resemble pegs fixed in the trunk. ● *Quercus palustris*.

Pi·no·chet /ˈpēnə,SHā, ,pēnōˈCHet/, Augusto (1915–2006), Chilean general and statesman; president 1974–90; full name *Augusto Pinochet Ugarte*. He imposed a military dictatorship until forced to call elections, giving way to a democratically elected president in 1990.

pi·noch·le /ˈpēnəkəl/ ▶ **n.** a card game for two or more players using a 48-card deck consisting of two of each card from nine to ace, the object being to score points for various combinations and to win tricks. ■ the combination of queen of spades and jack of diamonds in this game.
– ORIGIN mid 19th cent.: of unknown origin.

pi·no·cy·to·sis /,pinəsīˈtōsis, pīnə-/ ▶ **n.** Biology the ingestion of liquid into a cell by the budding of small vesicles from the cell membrane.
– DERIVATIVES **pi·no·cy·tot·ic** /-ˈtätik/ **adj.**
– ORIGIN late 19th cent.: from Greek *pino* 'drink' + *-cytosis* on the pattern of *phagocytosis*.

pi·no·le /piˈnōlē/ ▶ **n.** a sweetened flour made from ground dried corn mixed with flour made of mesquite beans, sugar, and spices.
– ORIGIN mid 19th cent.: from Latin American Spanish, from Nahuatl *pinolli*.

pi·ñon /ˈpinyən, ,pinˈyōn/ (also **pinyon** or **piñon pine**) ▶ **n.** a small pine tree with edible seeds, native to Mexico and the southwestern US. ● *Pinus cembroides*, family Pinaceae. ■ (also **piñon nut**) a pine nut obtained from this tree.
– ORIGIN mid 19th cent.: from Spanish, from Latin *pinea* 'pine cone.'

Pi·not /ˈpēnō, pēˈnō/ ▶ **n.** any of several varieties of wine grape, esp. the chief varieties **Pinot Noir**, a black grape, and **Pinot Blanc**, a white grape. ■ a wine made from these grapes.
– ORIGIN variant of earlier *Pineau*, diminutive of *pin* 'pine' (because of the shape of the grape cluster).

pi·no·tage /ˈpēnō,täZH/ ▶ **n.** a variety of red wine grape grown in South Africa, produced by crossing Pinot Noir and other varieties. ■ red wine made from this grape.
– ORIGIN blend of *Pinot* (*Noir*) and *Hermitage*, names of types of grape.

pin·out /ˈpin,out/ ▶ **n.** Electronics a diagram showing the arrangement of pins on an integrated circuit and their functions.

pin·point /ˈpin,point/ ▶ **n.** a tiny dot or point: *a pinpoint of light from a flashlight.*
▶ **adj.** [attrib.] absolutely precise; to the finest degree: *this weapon fired shells with pinpoint accuracy.* ■ tiny: *a pinpoint laser beam.*
▶ **v.** [with obj.] find or locate exactly: *one flare had pinpointed the target* | figurative *it is difficult to pinpoint the source of his life's inspiration.*

pin·prick /ˈpin,prik/ ▶ **n.** a prick caused by a pin. ■ a cause of minor irritation.

pins and nee·dles ▶ **plural n.** a tingling sensation in a limb recovering from numbness.
– PHRASES **on pins and neddles** in an agitated state of suspense.

Pin·sky /ˈpinskē/, Robert (1940–), US poet and writer. He served as US poet laureate 1997–2000. His poetry is collected in volumes such as *History of My Heart* (1984) and *The Figured Wheel: New and Collected Poems, 1966–1996* (1996). His translation of *The Inferno of Dante* was published in 1994.

pin·spot /ˈpin,spät/ ▶ **n.** a small powerful spotlight for sharp illumination of a very small area.

pin·stripe /ˈpin,strip/ ▶ **n.** a very narrow stripe in cloth, esp. of the type used for formal suits. ■ a pinstripe suit.
▶ **adj.** Sports, informal of or relating to baseball, esp. to the New York Yankees or other teams whose suits feature pinstripes: *a play that instantly became part of pinstripe legend.*
– DERIVATIVES **pin·striped adj.**

pint /pīnt/ (abbr.: **pt**) ▶ **n.** a unit of liquid or dry capacity equal to one half of a quart. ■ Brit. informal a pint of beer.
– ORIGIN late Middle English: from Old French *pinte*, of unknown origin.

pin·ta·do pet·rel /pinˈtädō/ ▶ **n.** another term for CAPE PIGEON.
– ORIGIN early 17th cent.: from Portuguese and Spanish *pintado* 'guinea fowl,' literally 'painted,' + PETREL.

pin·tail /ˈpin,tāl/ ▶ **n.** a mainly migratory duck with a pointed tail. ● Genus *Anas*, family Anatidae: three species, in particular the **common pintail** (*A. acuta*) of North America and Eurasia, the male of which has boldly marked plumage and two long tail streamers. ■ informal any of a number of other birds with long pointed tails, esp. a grouse.

Pin·ter /ˈpintər/, Harold (1930–2008), English playwright, actor, and director. His plays are associated with the Theater of the Absurd and are typically marked by a sense of menace. Notable plays: *The Birthday Party* (1958), *The Caretaker* (1960), and *Party Time* (1991).

pin·tle /ˈpintl/ ▶ **n.** one of the pins (on the forward edge of a rudder) that fit into the gudgeons and so suspend the rudder.
– ORIGIN Old English *pintel* 'penis,' perhaps a diminutive; compare with Dutch *pint* and German *Pint* 'penis,' of unknown ultimate origin.

pin·to /ˈpintō/ ▶ **adj.** piebald.
▶ **n.** (pl. **pintos**) a piebald horse.
– ORIGIN mid 19th cent.: from Spanish, literally 'mottled,' based on Latin *pictus*, past participle of *pingere* 'to paint.'

pin·to bean ▶ **n.** a medium-sized speckled variety of kidney bean.
– ORIGIN early 20th cent.: *pinto* from PINTO, because of the mottled seed of this variety of bean.

pint pot ▶ **n.** chiefly Brit. a beer glass or mug that holds a pint, esp. one made of pewter.

pint-sized (also **pint-size**) ▶ **adj.** informal very small: *at age seven, he was a pint-sized superstar* | *a pint-sized apartment.*

pin·tuck /ˈpin,tək/ ▶ **n.** (in sewing) a very narrow ornamental tuck.

pin·up /ˈpin,əp/ ▶ **n.** a poster showing a famous person or sex symbol, designed to be displayed on a wall. ■ a person shown in such a poster.

pin·wale /ˈpin,wāl/ ▶ **n.** fine-ribbed corduroy fabric.

pin·wheel /ˈpin,(h)wēl/ ▶ **n.** a child's toy consisting of a stick with colored vanes that twirl in the wind. ■ a fireworks device that whirls and emits colored fire. ■ something shaped or rotating like a pinwheel.
▶ **v.** [no obj.] spin or rotate like a pinwheel.

pin·worm /ˈpin,wərm/ ▶ **n.** a small nematode worm that is an internal parasite of vertebrates. ● Family Oxyuridae, class Phasmida, including *Enterobius vermicularis* (in humans) and *Oxyuris equi* (in horses).

pinx. ▶ **abbr.** pinxit.
– ORIGIN Latin, 'he painted.'

pin·y /ˈpīnē/ ▶ **adj.** variant spelling of PINEY.

Pin·yin /pinˈyin/ ▶ **n.** the standard system of romanized spelling for transliterating Chinese.
– ORIGIN 1960s: from Chinese *pīn-yīn*, literally 'spell-sound.'

pin·yon ▶ **n.** variant spelling of PIÑON.

Pin·za /ˈpinzə/, Ezio (Fortunato) (1892–1957), US opera singer; born in Italy. A bass, he performed with the Metropolitan Opera from 1926 until 1948 and was responsible for the return of Mozart's operas to the Met repertory. In 1949, he appeared on Broadway in *South Pacific*.

pi·o·let /ˌpēəˈlā/ ▶ **n.** Climbing an ice ax.
– ORIGIN mid 19th cent.: from French dialect, literally 'little pick,' diminutive of *piolo*; related to *pioche* 'pickax.'

pi·on /ˈpīˌän/ ▶ **n.** Physics a meson having a mass approximately 270 times that of an electron. Also called **PI MESON**.
– DERIVATIVES **pi·on·ic** /pīˈänik/ **adj.**
– ORIGIN 1950s: from PI (the letter used as a symbol for the particle) + -ON.

Pi·o·neer /ˌpīəˈnir/ a series of American space probes launched between 1958 and 1973, two of which provided the first clear pictures of Jupiter and Saturn (1973–79).

pi·o·neer /ˌpīəˈnir/ ▶ **n.** a person who is among the first to explore or settle a new country or area. ■ a person who is among the first to research and develop a new area of knowledge or activity: *a famous pioneer of birth control.* ■ (in the former Soviet Union and other communist countries) a member of a movement for children below the age of sixteen that aimed to foster communist ideals. ■ a member of an infantry group preparing roads or terrain for the main body of troops.
▶ **v.** [with obj.] develop or be the first to use or apply (a new method, area of knowledge, or activity): *he has pioneered a number of innovative techniques.* ■ open up (a road or terrain) as a pioneer.
– ORIGIN early 16th cent. (as a military term denoting a member of the infantry): from French *pionnier* 'foot soldier, pioneer,' Old French *paonier*, from *paon*, from Latin *pedo, pedon-* (see PAWN[1]).

pi·o·neer·ing /ˌpīəˈniriNG/ ▶ **adj.** involving new ideas or methods: *his pioneering work on consciousness.*

pi·ous /ˈpīəs/ ▶ **adj.** devoutly religious. ■ making a hypocritical display of virtue: *there'll be no pious words said over her.* ■ [attrib.] (of a hope) sincere but unlikely to be fulfilled. ■ archaic dutiful or loyal, esp. toward one's parents.
– DERIVATIVES **pi·ous·ly adv.**, **pi·ous·ness n.**
– ORIGIN late Middle English: from Latin *pius* 'dutiful, pious' + -OUS.

pip[1] /pip/ ▶ **n. 1** a small hard seed in a fruit. **2** informal an excellent or very attractive person or thing.
– DERIVATIVES **pip·less** /ˈpiplis/ **adj.**
– ORIGIN late 18th cent.: abbreviation of PIPPIN.

pip[2] ▶ **n.** a small shape or symbol, in particular: ■ any of the spots on playing cards, dice, or dominoes. ■ a single blossom of a clustered head of flowers. ■ a diamond-shaped segment of the surface of a pineapple. ■ an image of an object on a radar screen; blip. ■ Brit. a star (1–3 according to rank) on the shoulder of an army officer's uniform.
– ORIGIN late 16th cent. (originally *peep*, denoting each of the dots on playing cards, dice, and dominoes): of unknown origin.

pip[3] ▶ **n.** a disease of poultry or other birds causing thick mucus in the throat and white scale on the tongue.
– PHRASES **give someone the pip** informal, dated make someone angry or depressed.
– ORIGIN late Middle English: from Middle Dutch *pippe*, probably from an alteration of Latin *pituita* 'slime.' In the late 15th cent. the word came to be applied humorously to unspecified human diseases, and later to ill humor.

pip[4] ▶ **v.** (**pips, pipping, pipped**) [with obj.] (of a young bird) crack (the shell of the egg) when hatching.
– ORIGIN late 19th cent.: perhaps of imitative origin.

pip[5] Brit. informal ▶ **v.** (**pips, pipping, pipped**) [with obj.] (usu. **be pipped**) defeat by a small margin or at the last moment: *you were just pipped for the prize.* ■ dated hit or wound (someone) with a gunshot.
– ORIGIN late 19th cent.: from PIP[1] or PIP[2].

pi·pa /ˈpēˌpä/ ▶ **n.** a shallow-bodied, four-stringed Chinese lute.
– ORIGIN Chinese.

pi·pal /ˈpēpəl/ ▶ **n.** variant spelling of PEEPUL.

pipe /pīp/ ▶ **n. 1** a tube of metal, plastic, or other material used to convey water, gas, oil, or other fluid substances. ■ a cylindrical vein of ore or rock, esp. one in which diamonds are found. ■ a cavity in cast metal. ■ informal a duct, vessel, or tubular structure in the body, or in an animal or plant. ■ Computing a connection to the Internet or to a website. **2** a narrow tube made from wood, clay, etc., with a bowl at one end for containing burning tobacco, the smoke from which is drawn into the mouth. ■ a quantity of tobacco held by this. ■ a device for smoking illegal drugs: *a crack pipe.* **3** a wind instrument consisting of a single tube with holes along its length that are covered by the fingers to produce different notes: *a reed pipe.* ■ (usu. **pipes**) bagpipes. ■ (**pipes**) a set of pipes joined together, as in panpipes. ■ a tube by which sound is produced in an organ. ■ (**pipes**) informal voice or vocal ability, esp. of a powerful singer. ■ [in sing.] a high-pitched cry or song, esp. of a bird. ■ a boatswain's whistle. **4** Computing a command that causes the output from one routine to be the input for another. ■ the symbol | . **5** a cask for wine, esp. as a measure equal to two hogsheads, usually equivalent to 105 gallons (about 477 liters).
▶ **v. 1** [with obj.] convey (water, gas, oil, or other fluid substances) through a pipe or pipes: *water from the lakes is piped to several towns.* ■ transmit (music, a radio or television program, signals, etc.) by wire or cable. **2** [with obj.] play (a tune) on a pipe or pipes. ■ [no obj.] (of a bird) sing in a high or shrill voice. ■ [with direct speech] say something in a high, shrill voice: *"No, ma'am," piped Lucy.* ■ use a boatswain's whistle to summon (the crew) to work or a meal: *the hands were piped to breakfast.* **3** [with obj.] decorate (clothing or soft furnishings) with a thin cord covered in fabric. ■ put (a decorative line or pattern) on a cake or similar dish using icing, whipped cream, etc.
– PHRASES **put that in one's pipe and smoke it** informal used to indicate that someone should accept what one has said, even if it is unwelcome.
– PHRASAL VERBS **pipe down** [often in imperative] informal stop talking; be less noisy. **pipe up** say something suddenly.
– DERIVATIVES **pipe·ful** /ˈpīpˌfo͝ol/ **n.** (pl. **pipefuls**), **pipe·less adj.**, **pip·y** /ˈpīpē/ **adj.** (**pipier, pipiest**).
– ORIGIN Old English *pīpe* 'musical tube,' *pīpian* 'play a pipe,' of Germanic origin; related to Dutch *pijp* and German *Pfeife*, based on Latin *pipare* 'to peep, chirp,' reinforced in Middle English by Old French *piper* 'to chirp, squeak.'

pipe bomb ▶ **n.** a homemade bomb, the components of which are contained in a pipe.

pipe·clay /ˈpīpˌklā/ ▶ **n.** a fine white clay, used esp. for making tobacco pipes or for whitening leather.
▶ **v.** [with obj.] whiten (leather) with such clay.

pipe clean·er ▶ **n.** a piece of wire covered with tufted fiber, used to clean a tobacco pipe and for a variety of handicrafts.

piped-in mu·sic ▶ **n.** prerecorded background music played through loudspeakers in a public place.

pipe dream ▶ **n.** an unattainable or fanciful hope or scheme.
– ORIGIN late 19th cent.: referring to a dream experienced when smoking an opium pipe.

pipe·fish /ˈpīpˌfiSH/ ▶ **n.** (pl. **same** or **pipefishes**) a narrow, elongated, chiefly marine fish with segmented bony armor beneath the skin and a long tubular snout. ● *Syngnathus* and other genera, family Syngnathidae: numerous species.

pipe·line /ˈpīpˌlīn/ ▶ **n. 1** a long pipe, typically underground, for conveying oil, gas, etc., over long distances. ■ a channel supplying goods or information: *the biggest heroin pipeline in history.* **2** Computing a linear sequence of specialized modules used for pipelining. **3** (in surfing) the hollow formed by the breaking of a large wave.
▶ **v.** [with obj.] **1** convey (a substance) by a pipeline. **2** (often as adj. **pipelined**) Computing design or execute (a computer or instruction) using the technique of pipelining.
– PHRASES **in the pipeline** awaiting completion or processing; being developed: *new treatments are in the pipeline.*

pipe·lin·ing /ˈpīpˌlīniNG/ ▶ **n. 1** the laying of pipelines. ■ transportation by means of pipelines. **2** Computing a form of computer organization in which successive steps of an instruction sequence are executed in turn by a sequence of modules able to operate concurrently, so that another instruction can be begun before the previous one is finished.

pipe or·gan ▶ **n.** Music see ORGAN (sense 1).

pip·er /ˈpīpər/ ▶ **n. 1** a bagpipe player. **2** a person who plays a pipe, esp. an itinerant musician.
– PHRASES **pay the piper** bear the consequences of an action or activity that one has enjoyed: *we will have to pay the piper, and the price is apt to be a high one.*
– ORIGIN Old English *pīpere*.

pipe rack ▶ **n. 1** a rack for holding tobacco pipes. **2** a rack made of piping on which clothes are hung, as in a store.

pi·per·a·zine /piˈperəˌzēn, pipˈərə-/ ▶ **n.** Chemistry a synthetic crystalline compound with basic properties, sometimes used as an anthelmintic and insecticide. ● A heterocyclic compound; chem. formula: $C_4H_{10}N_2$.
– ORIGIN late 19th cent.: from PIPERIDINE + AZINE.

pi·per·i·dine /piˈperiˌdēn, pipˈərə-/ ▶ **n.** Chemistry a peppery-smelling liquid formed by the reduction of pyridine. ● Chem. formula: $C_5H_{11}N$.
– ORIGIN mid 19th cent.: from Latin *piper* 'pepper' + -IDE + -INE[4].

pipe snake ▶ **n.** any of a number of slender tropical burrowing snakes, in particular: ● a South American snake marked with bold red and black stripes (*Anilius scytale*, the only member of the family Aniliidae). ● an Asian snake that displays its bright under-tail coloration when alarmed (genus *Cylindrophis*, family Uropeltidae).

pipe stem (also **pipestem**) ▶ **n.** the shaft of a tobacco pipe. ■ [as modifier] used to describe anything resembling this, such as a very narrow pants leg.

pipe·stone /ˈpīpˌstōn/ ▶ **n.** hard red clay (catlinite) used by North American Indians for tobacco pipes.

pi·pette /pīˈpet/ (also **pipet**) ▶ **n.** a slender tube attached to or incorporating a bulb, for transferring or measuring out small quantities of liquid, esp. in a laboratory.
▶ **v.** [with obj.] pour, convey, or draw off using a pipette.
– ORIGIN mid 19th cent.: from French, literally 'little pipe,' diminutive of *pipe*.

pipe·wort /ˈpīpˌwərt, -ˌwôrt/ ▶ **n.** an aquatic or marsh plant with leafless stems bearing heads of inconspicuous flowers, native to North America and parts of the United Kingdom. ● *Eriocaulon aquaticum*, family Eriocaulaceae.

pip·ing /ˈpīpiNG/ ▶ **n. 1** lengths of pipe, or a network of pipes, made of metal, plastic, or other materials. **2** ornamentation on food consisting of lines of icing, whipped cream, etc. ■ thin cord covered in fabric, used to decorate clothing or soft furnishings and reinforce seams. **3** the action or art of playing a pipe or pipes.
▶ **adj.** [attrib.] (of a voice or sound) high-pitched.
– PHRASES **piping hot** (of food or water) very hot. [*piping*, because of the whistling sound made by very hot liquid or food.]

pip·ing plov·er ▶ **n.** a small buff-colored bird of coastal areas in eastern North America. ● *Charadrius melodus*.

pip·i·strelle /ˌpipəˈstrel, ˈpipəˌstrel/ (also **pipistrel**) ▶ **n.** a small insectivorous Old World bat with jerky, erratic flight. ● Genus *Pipistrellus*, family Vespertilionidae: numerous species, including *P. pipistrellus*, the most common bat in Eurasia.
– ORIGIN late 18th cent.: from French, from Italian *pipistrello*, from Latin *vespertilio(n-)* 'bat,' from *vesper* 'evening.'

pip·it /ˈpipit/ ▶ **n.** a mainly ground-dwelling songbird of open country, typically having brown streaky plumage. ● Family Motacillidae: three genera, in particular *Anthus*, and many species, including the sparrow-sized **water pipit** (*A. spinoletta*) of the northern hemisphere.
– ORIGIN mid 18th cent.: probably imitative.

pip·kin /ˈpipkin/ ▶ **n.** a small earthenware pot or pan.
– ORIGIN mid 16th cent.: of unknown origin.

pip·pin /ˈpipin/ ▶ **n.** a red and yellow dessert apple. ■ an apple grown from seed. ■ informal an excellent person or thing.
– ORIGIN Middle English: from Old French *pepin*, of unknown ultimate origin.

pip pip ▶ **exclam.** Brit. informal, dated goodbye.
– ORIGIN early 20th cent.: imitative, probably of the repeated short blasts on the horn of a car or bicycle.

pip·sis·se·wa /pipˈsisəˌwô, -wə/ ▶ **n.** a North American plant of the wintergreen family, with whorled evergreen leaves. ● *Chimaphila umbellata*, family Pyrolaceae. ■ a preparation of the leaves of this plant, used as a diuretic and tonic.
– ORIGIN late 18th cent.: from Abnaki, literally 'flower of the woods.'

pip·squeak /ˈpipˌskwēk/ ▶ **n.** informal a person considered to be insignificant, esp. because they are small or young.
– ORIGIN early 20th cent.: symbolic and imitative.

P

pi·quan·cy /ˈpēkənsē/ ▶ **n.** a pleasantly sharp and appetizing flavor: *these tomatoes have an intense flavor of great piquancy.* ■ the quality of being pleasantly stimulating or exciting: *the tragedy only adds piquancy to the tale.*

pi·quant /ˈpēkənt, -känt/ ▶ **adj.** having a pleasantly sharp taste or appetizing flavor. ■ pleasantly stimulating or exciting to the mind.
– DERIVATIVES **pi·quant·ly adv.**
– ORIGIN early 16th cent. (in the sense 'severe, bitter'): from French, literally 'stinging, pricking,' present participle of *piquer.*

pique /pēk/ ▶ **n.** a feeling of irritation or resentment resulting from a slight, esp. to one's pride: *he left in a fit of pique.*
▶ **v.** (**piques** /pēks/, **piquing** /ˈpēkiNG/, **piqued** /pēkt/) **1** [with obj.] stimulate (interest or curiosity): *you have piqued my curiosity about the man.*
2 (**be piqued**) feel irritated or resentful: *she was piqued by his curtness.*
3 (**pique oneself**) archaic pride oneself.
– ORIGIN mid 16th cent. (denoting animosity between two or more people): from French *piquer* 'prick, irritate.'

pi·qué /pēˈkā, pi-/ ▶ **n.** stiff fabric, typically cotton, woven in a strongly ribbed or raised pattern.
– ORIGIN mid 19th cent.: from French, literally 'backstitched,' past participle of *piquer.*

pi·quet /piˈkā, ˈket/ (also **picquet**) ▶ **n.** a trick-taking card game for two players, using a 32-card deck consisting of cards from the seven to the ace.
– ORIGIN mid 17th cent.: from French, of unknown origin.

pi·quil·lo /piˈkē(y)ō/ ▶ **n.** (pl. **piquillos**) a sweet pepper of a variety grown in Spain, often sold roasted and preserved in oil.
– ORIGIN Spanish, literally 'little beak.'

PIR ▶ **abbr.** passive infrared (denoting a type of sensor).

pir /pi(ə)r/ ▶ **n.** a Muslim saint or holy man.
– ORIGIN from Persian *pīr* 'old man.'

pi·ra·cy /ˈpīrəsē/ ▶ **n.** the practice of attacking and robbing ships at sea. ■ a similar practice in other contexts, esp. hijacking: *air piracy.* ■ the unauthorized use or reproduction of another's work: *software piracy.*
– ORIGIN mid 16th cent.: via medieval Latin from Greek *pirateia,* from *peiratēs* (see **PIRATE**).

Pi·rae·us /pəˈrāəs, pīˈrēəs/ the chief port of Athens, situated on the Saronic Gulf, 5 miles (8 km) southwest of the city; pop. 183,000. Greek name **Piraiévs** or **Piraiéus**.

Pi·ran·del·lo /ˌpirənˈdelō/, Luigi (1867–1936), Italian playwright and novelist. His plays, including *Six Characters in Search of an Author* (1921) and *Henry IV* (1922), challenged the conventions of naturalism. Notable novels: *The Outcast* (1901) and *The Late Mattia Pascal* (1904). Nobel Prize for Literature (1934).

pi·ra·nha /pəˈränə/ ▶ **n.** (pl. **same** or **piranhas**) a deep-bodied South American freshwater fish that typically lives in schools and has very sharp teeth that are used to tear flesh from prey. It has a reputation as a fearsome predator. ● *Serrasalmus* and other genera, family Characidae: several species, including the **red** (or **red-bellied**) **piranha** (*S. natterei*).
– ORIGIN mid 18th cent.: via Portuguese from Tupi *pirá* 'fish' + *sainha* 'tooth.'

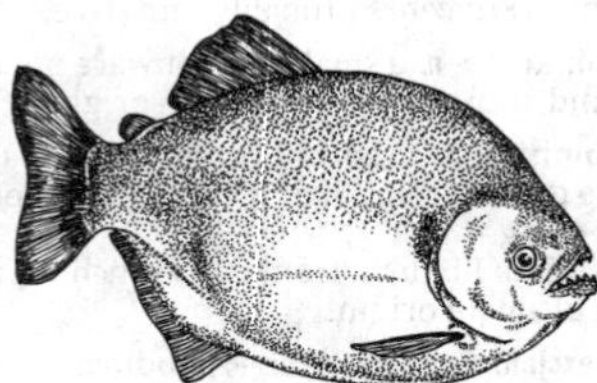
red piranha

pi·rate /ˈpīrət/ ▶ **n.** a person who attacks and robs ships at sea. ■ a person who appropriates or reproduces the work of another for profit without permission, usually in contravention of patent or copyright: *software pirates.* ■ a person or organization that broadcasts radio or television programs without official authorization: [as modifier] *a pirate radio station.*
▶ **v.** [with obj.] **1** (often as adj. **pirated**) use or reproduce (another's work) for profit without permission, usually in contravention of patent or copyright: *he sold pirated tapes of Hollywood blockbusters | a competing company cannot pirate its intellectual achievements.*
2 dated rob or plunder (a ship).
– DERIVATIVES **pi·rat·ic** /pīˈratik, pi-/ **adj.**, **pi·rat·i·cal** /pīˈratikəl, pi-/ **adj.**, **pi·rat·i·cal·ly** /pīˈratiklē, pi-/ **adv.**
– ORIGIN Middle English: from Latin *pirata,* from Greek *peiratēs,* from *peirein* 'to attempt, attack' (from *peira* 'an attempt').

> **WORD TRENDS** Although they no longer come with parrots and peg legs, modern **pirates** are as big a threat as the swashbuckling figures of history. And their numbers are rising, with the Oxford English Corpus showing a more than fourfold explosion in the word's use since 2007. The Corpus also shows that *Somali* is the most common modifier of **pirate**, reflecting a recent surge in piracy around the Horn of Africa. But the high seas are not the only place where **pirates** lurk—online piracy is also on the increase. The use of **pirate** to refer to someone who steals the work of another has been around since the 17th century, but the ease of copying and sharing files via the Internet has led to a massive increase. While those who download movies and music over the Web may not consider themselves to be criminals, production companies have a different view: *Internet pirates cost US industry hundreds of billions of dollars in lost revenue every year.*

pi·rate fish·ing ▶ **n.** fishing on the high seas in contravention of national and international laws governing quotas, typically by ships under flags of convenience that are owned by dummy companies.

pir·i·form ▶ **adj.** variant spelling of **PYRIFORM**.

pi·ri-pi·ri /ˌpi(ə)rē ˈpi(ə)rē/ (also **pil-pil** /ˈpēl ˌpēl/) ▶ **n.** Portuguese term for hot chilies or the hot sauce made from them.
– ORIGIN Ronga (a Bantu language of southern Mozambique), literally 'pepper.'

pi·rog /piˈrōg/ ▶ **n.** (pl. **pirogi** /-ˈrōgē/ or **pirogen** /-ˈrōgən/) a large Russian pie.
– ORIGIN Russian.

pi·ro·gi /piˈrōgē/ (also **perogi**) ▶ **n.** (pl. **same** or **pirogies**) a dough dumpling stuffed with a filling such as potato or cheese, typically served with onions or sour cream.
– ORIGIN from Polish *pieróg.*

pi·rogue /piˈrōg/ ▶ **n.** a long narrow canoe made from a single tree trunk, esp. in Central America and the Caribbean.
– ORIGIN early 17th cent.: from French, probably from Galibi.

pir·o·plas·mo·sis /ˌpi(ə)rəplazˈmōsis/ ▶ **n.** another term for **BABESIOSIS**.

pi·rosh·ki /piˈrôsHkē, -ˈräsH-/ (also **pirozhki**) ▶ **plural n.** small Russian pastries or patties, filled with meat or fish and rice.
– ORIGIN from Russian *pirozhki,* plural of *pirozhok,* diminutive of *pirog* (see **PIROG**).

pir·ou·ette /ˌpiro͞oˈet/ ▶ **n.** chiefly Ballet an act of spinning on one foot, typically with the raised foot touching the knee of the supporting leg. ■ a movement performed in advanced dressage and classical riding, in which the horse makes a circle by pivoting on a hind leg while cantering.
▶ **v.** [no obj.] perform a pirouette.
– ORIGIN mid 17th cent.: from French, literally 'spinning top,' of unknown ultimate origin.

Pi·sa /ˈpēzə/ a city in northern Italy, in Tuscany, on the Arno River; pop. 87,398 (2008). It is noted for the **Leaning Tower of Pisa**, a circular bell tower that leans about 17 feet (5 m) from the perpendicular in its height of 181 feet (55 m).

Leaning Tower of Pisa

pis al·ler /ˌpēz äˈlā/ ▶ **n.** a course of action followed as a last resort.
– ORIGIN French, from *pis* 'worse' + *aller* 'go.'

Pi·sa·no[1] /piˈzänō/, Andrea (*c.*1290–*c.*1348) and Nino, his son (died *c.*1368), Italian sculptors. Andrea created the earliest pair of bronze doors for the baptistery at Florence (completed 1336). Nino was one of the earliest to specialize in freestanding life-size figures.

Pi·sa·no[2] Nicola (*c.*1220–*c.*1278), and Giovanni, his son (*c.*1250–*c.*1314) two Italian sculptors. Nicola's most famous works are the pulpits in the baptistery at Pisa and in Siena cathedral. Giovanni's works include the richly decorated facade of Siena cathedral.

pis·ca·ry /ˈpiskərē/ ▶ **n.** (in phrase **common of piscary**) chiefly historical the right of fishing in another's water.
– ORIGIN late 15th cent.: from medieval Latin *piscaria* 'fishing rights,' neuter plural of Latin *piscarius* 'relating to fishing,' from *piscis* 'fish.'

Pis·cat·a·way /piˈskatəˌwā/ a township in central New Jersey, across the Raritan River from New Brunswick; pop. 52,408 (est. 2008).

pis·ca·to·ri·al /ˌpiskəˈtôrēəl/ ▶ **adj.** formal of or concerning fishermen or fishing.
– ORIGIN early 19th cent.: from Latin *piscatorius* 'relating to fishing' (from *piscator* 'fisherman,' from *piscis* 'fish') + **-AL**.

pis·ca·to·ry /ˈpiskəˌtôrē/ ▶ **adj.** another term for **PISCATORIAL**.

Pis·ces /ˈpīsēz, ˈpisēz/ **1** Astronomy a large constellation (the Fish or Fishes), said to represent a pair of fish tied together by their tails. ■ (as genitive **Piscium** /ˈpisHēəm, ˈpīsē-/) used with a preceding letter or numeral to designate a star in this constellation: *the star Alpha Piscium.*
2 Astrology the twelfth sign of the zodiac, which the sun enters about February 20. ■ (**a Pisces**) (pl. **same**) a person born when the sun is in this sign.
– DERIVATIVES **Pis·ce·an** /-sēən/ **n. & adj.** (sense 2).
– ORIGIN Latin, plural of *piscis* 'fish.'

pis·ci·cul·ture /ˈpisiˌkəlCHər/ ▶ **n.** the controlled breeding and rearing of fish.
– DERIVATIVES **pis·ci·cul·tur·al** /ˌpisiˈkəlCHərəl/ **adj.**, **pis·ci·cul·tur·ist** /ˌpisiˈkəlCHərist/ **n.**
– ORIGIN mid 19th cent.: from Latin *piscis* 'fish' + **CULTURE**, on the pattern of words such as *agriculture.*

pis·ci·na /piˈsēnə, -ˈsīnə/ ▶ **n.** (pl. **piscinas** or **piscinae** /-nē/) **1** a stone basin near the altar in Catholic and pre-Reformation churches for draining water used in the Mass.
2 (in ancient Roman architecture) a pool or pond for bathing or swimming.
– ORIGIN late 16th cent. (sense 2): from Latin, literally 'fishpond,' from *piscis* 'fish'; sense 1 was found in medieval Latin.

pis·cine /ˈpisēn, ˈpisīn/ ▶ **adj.** of or concerning fish.
– ORIGIN late 18th cent.: from Latin *piscis* 'fish' + **-INE[1]**.

Pis·cis Aus·tri·nus /ˈpīsis ôˈstrīnəs/ (also **Piscis Australis** /ôˈstrālis/) Astronomy a southern constellation (the Southern Fish), south of Aquarius and Capricornus. It contains the bright star Fomalhaut. ■ (as genitive **Piscis Austrini** /ôˈstrīnī/) used with a preceding letter or numeral to designate a star in this constellation: *the star Gamma Piscis Austrini.*
– ORIGIN Latin.

pis·civ·o·rous /piˈsivərəs/ ▶ **adj.** Zoology (of an animal) feeding on fish.
– DERIVATIVES **pis·ci·vore** /ˈpisiˌvôr/ **n.**
– ORIGIN mid 17th cent.: from Latin *piscis* 'fish' + **-VOROUS**.

pis·co /ˈpēskō, ˈpiskō/ ▶ **n.** (pl. **piscos**) a white brandy made in Peru from muscat grapes.
– ORIGIN named after a port in Peru.

pi·sé /pēˈzā/ ▶ **n.** building material of stiff clay or earth, forced into forms that are removed as it hardens.
– ORIGIN late 18th cent.: French, literally 'pounded,' past participle of *piser.*

pish /pisH/ ▶ **exclam.** dated used to express annoyance, impatience, or disgust.
– ORIGIN natural utterance: first recorded in English in the late 16th cent.

pish·er /ˈpisHər/ ▶ **n.** informal an insignificant or contemptible person.
– ORIGIN 1940s: Yiddish, literally 'pisser,' from the verb *pissen.*

Pish·pek /pisHˈpek, piˈsHpyek/ former name (until 1926) of **BISHKEK**.

Pi·sid·i·a /pəˈsidēə, pi-/ an ancient region in Asia Minor, between Pamphylia and Phrygia. It was incorporated into the Roman province of Galatia in 25 BC.
– DERIVATIVES **Pi·sid·i·an adj. & n.**

pi·si·form /ˈpīsəˌfôrm/ (also **pisiform bone**) ▶ **n.** a small rounded carpal bone situated where the palm of the hand meets the outer edge of the wrist.
– ORIGIN mid 18th cent.: from modern Latin *pisiformis* 'pea-shaped,' from *pisum* 'pea' + *forma* 'shape.'

Pi·sis·tra·tus /pi'sistrətəs/ (also **Peisistratus**) (*c.*600–*c.*527 BC), tyrant of Athens. He reduced aristocratic power in rural Attica and promoted the financial prosperity and cultural preeminence of Athens.

pis·mire /'pis,mīr/ ▶ **n.** archaic an ant.
– ORIGIN Middle English: from **PISS** (alluding to the smell of an anthill) + obsolete *mire* 'ant.'

pis·o·lite /'pīsə,līt/ ▶ **n.** Geology a sedimentary rock, esp. limestone, made up of small pea-shaped pieces.
– DERIVATIVES **pis·o·lit·ic** /,pīsə'litik/ **adj.**
– ORIGIN early 19th cent.: from modern Latin *pisolithus* (see **PISOLITH**) + **-LITE**.

pis·o·lith /'pīsəliTH/ ▶ **n.** Geology any of the component pieces of which pisolite consists.
– ORIGIN late 18th cent.: from modern Latin *pisolithus*, from Greek *pisos* 'pea' + **-LITE**.

piss /pis/ vulgar slang ▶ **v.** [no obj.] urinate. ■ [with obj.] wet with urine. ■ [with obj.] discharge (something, esp. blood) when urinating.
▶ **n.** urine. ■ [in sing.] an act of urinating.
– PHRASES **not have a pot to piss in** be very poor. **piss in the wind** do something that is ineffective or a waste of time. **take a piss** urinate.
– PHRASAL VERBS **piss something away** waste something, esp. money or time. **piss off** [usu. in imperative] go away (usually used to angrily dismiss someone). **piss someone off** annoy someone. **piss on** show complete contempt for.
– ORIGIN Middle English: from Old French *pisser*, probably of imitative origin.

pis·sa·la·dière /,pē,säläd'yer/ ▶ **n.** a Provençal open tart resembling pizza, typically made with onions, anchovies, and black olives.
– ORIGIN French, from Provençal *pissaladiero*, from *pissala* 'salt fish.'

piss and vin·e·gar ▶ **n.** vulgar slang aggressive energy.

piss·ant /'pis,ant/ vulgar slang ▶ **n.** an insignificant or contemptible person or thing.
▶ **adj.** worthless; contemptible.
– ORIGIN mid 17th cent.: from the noun **PISS** + **-ANT**.

Pis·sar·ro /pi'särō, pēsä'rō/, Camille (1830–1903), French painter and graphic artist. He was a leading figure of the Impressionist movement, typically painting landscapes and cityscapes. He also experimented with pointillism in the 1880s.

pissed /pist/ vulgar slang ▶ **adj. 1** (also **pissed off**) very annoyed; angry.
2 (also **pissed up**) Brit. drunk.

piss·er /'pisər/ ▶ **n.** vulgar slang **1** [in sing.] an annoying or disappointing event or circumstance.
2 an unpleasant person; a person who causes difficulties.

piss·hole /'pis,hōl/ ▶ **n.** vulgar slang a hole made in soluble matter by urinating: *making pissholes in the snow.* ■ a squalid place. ■ the opening in the penis through which urine is discharged; the urethral meatus.

pis·soir /pē'swär/ ▶ **n.** a public urinal.
– ORIGIN French.

piss-poor ▶ **adj.** vulgar slang of a very low standard.

piss·pot /'pis,pät/ ▶ **n.** vulgar slang a chamber pot.

piss·y /'pisē/ ▶ **adj.** (**pissier, pissiest**) vulgar slang
1 of, relating to, or suggestive of urine. ■ inferior; contemptible.
2 arrogantly argumentative.

pis·tach·i·o /pə'stasHē,ō/ ▶ **n.** (pl. **pistachios**) **1** (also **pistachio nut**) the edible pale green seed of an Asian tree. ■ (also **pistachio green**) a pale green color.
2 the evergreen tree of the cashew family that produces this nut, with small brownish-green flowers and reddish wrinkled fruit borne in heavy clusters. It is widely cultivated, esp. in the US and around the Mediterranean. ● *Pistacia vera*, family Anacardiaceae.
– ORIGIN late Middle English *pistace*, from Old French, superseded in the 16th cent. by forms from Italian *pistaccio*, via Latin from Greek *pistakion*, from Old Persian.

piste /pēst/ ▶ **n.** a ski run of compacted snow.
– ORIGIN French, literally 'racetrack.'

pis·til /'pistl/ ▶ **n.** Botany the female organs of a flower, comprising the stigma, style, and ovary.
– ORIGIN early 18th cent.: from French *pistile* or Latin *pistillum* 'pestle.'

pis·til·late /'pistəlit, -,lāt/ ▶ **adj.** Botany (of a plant or flower) having pistils but no stamens. Compare with **STAMINATE**.

pis·tol /'pistl/ ▶ **n.** a small firearm designed to be held in one hand.
▶ **v.** (**pistols, pistoling, pistoled**; Brit. **pistols, pistolling, pistolled**) [with obj.] dated shoot (someone) with a pistol.
– ORIGIN mid 16th cent.: from obsolete French *pistole*, from German *Pistole*, from Czech *píšťala*, of which the original meaning was 'whistle,' hence 'a firearm' by the resemblance in shape.

pis·tole /pi'stōl/ ▶ **n.** any of various gold coins used in Europe in the 17th and 18th centuries.
– ORIGIN late 16th cent.: from French, abbreviation of *pistolet*, in the same sense, of uncertain ultimate origin.

pis·to·leer /,pistə'li(ə)r/ ▶ **n.** archaic a soldier armed with a pistol.

pis·to·le·ro /pistə'le(ə)rō/ ▶ **n.** (pl. **pistoleros**) (in Spanish-speaking regions) a gunman or gangster.
– ORIGIN Spanish.

pis·tol grip ▶ **n.** (esp. of a tool) a handle shaped like the butt of a pistol.

pis·tol-whip ▶ **v.** [with obj.] hit or beat (someone) with a pistol.

pis·ton /'pistn/ ▶ **n.** a disk or short cylinder fitting closely within a tube in which it moves up and down against a liquid or gas, used in an internal combustion engine to derive motion, or in a pump to impart motion. ■ a valve in a brass musical instrument in the form of a piston, depressed to alter the pitch of a note.
– ORIGIN early 18th cent.: from French, from Italian *pistone*, variant of *pestone* 'large pestle,' augmentative of *pestello* 'pestle.'

piston

pis·ton en·gine ▶ **n.** an engine powered by pistons.
– DERIVATIVES **pis·ton-en·gined** /'pistn ,enjənd/ **adj.**

pis·ton ring ▶ **n.** a ring on a piston sealing the gap between the piston and the cylinder wall.

pis·ton rod ▶ **n.** a rod or crankshaft attached to a piston to drive a wheel or to impart motion.

pit[1] /pit/ ▶ **n. 1** a large hole in the ground. ■ a large deep hole from which stones or minerals are dug. ■ a coal mine. ■ a sunken enclosure in which certain animals are kept in captivity. ■ short for **ORCHESTRA PIT** (see **ORCHESTRA**). ■ a sunken area in a workshop floor allowing access to a car's underside. ■ a low or wretched psychological state: *spiraling downward into the pit of despair.* ■ (**the pit**) literary hell.
2 an area reserved or enclosed for a specific activity, in particular: ■ (usu. **pits**) an area at the side of a track where race cars are serviced and refueled. ■ a part of the floor of an exchange in which a particular stock or commodity is traded, typically by open outcry. ■ chiefly historical an enclosure in which animals are made to fight.
3 a hollow or indentation in a surface. ■ a small indentation left on the skin after smallpox, acne, or other diseases; a pockmark.
▶ **v.** (**pits, pitting, pitted**) [with obj.] **1** (**pit someone/something against**) set someone or something in conflict or competition with: *a chance to pit herself against him.* ■ historical set an animal to fight against (another animal) for sport. [because formerly set against each other in a 'pit' or enclosure.]
2 make a hollow or indentation in the surface of: *rain poured down, pitting the bare earth.* ■ [no obj.] sink in or contract so as to form a pit or hollow.
3 [no obj.] drive a race car into the pits for fuel or maintenance.
– PHRASES **be the pits** informal be extremely bad or the worst of its kind. **the pit of one's** (or **the**) **stomach** an ill-defined region of the lower abdomen regarded as the seat of strong feelings, esp. anxiety.
– ORIGIN Old English *pytt*; related to Dutch *put* and German *Pfütze*, based on Latin *puteus* 'well, shaft.'

pit[2] ▶ **n.** the stone of a fruit.
▶ **v.** (**pits, pitting, pitted**) [with obj.] remove the pit from (fruit).
– ORIGIN mid 19th cent.: apparently from Dutch; related to **PITH**.

pi·ta /'pētə/ (also **pita bread**) ▶ **n.** flat hollow unleavened bread that can be split open to hold a filling.
– ORIGIN modern Greek, literally 'cake or pie'; compare with Turkish *pide*, in a similar sense.

pit·a·ha·ya /,pitə'hīə/ ▶ **n.** any tall cactus of Mexico and the southwestern US, in particular the saguaro. ■ the edible fruit of such cacti.
– ORIGIN late 18th cent.: from Spanish, from Haitian Creole.

pit-a-pat /'pit ə ,pat/ (also **pitapat**) ▶ **adv.** with a sound like quick light steps or taps: *my heart goes pit-a-pat.*
▶ **n.** [in sing.] a sound of this kind.
– ORIGIN early 16th cent.: imitative of alternating sounds.

pit boss ▶ **n.** informal an employee in a casino in charge of gaming tables. ■ dated a foreman in a coal mine.

pit bull (in full **pit bull terrier**) ▶ **n.** a dog of an American variety of bull terrier, noted for its muscular build and often associated with ferocity.

Pit·cairn Is·lands /'pit,ke(ə)rn/ a British overseas territory comprising a group of volcanic islands in the South Pacific Ocean, east of French Polynesia. Discovered in 1767, the islands remained uninhabited until settled in 1790 by mutineers from HMS *Bounty*.
– ORIGIN named after the midshipman who first sighted the islands.

pitch[1] /piCH/ ▶ **n. 1** the quality of a sound governed by the rate of vibrations producing it; the degree of highness or lowness of a tone: *a car engine seems to change pitch downward as the vehicle passes you.* ■ a standard degree of highness or lowness used in performance: *the guitars were strung and tuned to pitch.* See also **CONCERT PITCH**.
2 the steepness of a slope, esp. of a roof. ■ Climbing a section of a climb, esp. a steep one. ■ the height to which a hawk soars before swooping on its prey.
3 [in sing.] the level of intensity of something: *he brought the machine to a high pitch of development.* ■ (**a pitch of**) a very high degree of: *rousing herself to a pitch of indignation.*
4 Baseball a legal delivery of the ball by the pitcher. ■ (also **pitch shot**) Golf a high approach shot onto the green. ■ Football short for **PITCHOUT** (sense 2).
5 Brit. a playing field. ■ Cricket the strip of ground between the two sets of stumps.
6 a form of words used when trying to persuade someone to buy or accept something: *a good sales pitch.*
7 a swaying or oscillation of a ship, aircraft, or vehicle around a horizontal axis perpendicular to the direction of motion.
8 technical the distance between successive corresponding points or lines, e.g., between the teeth of a cogwheel. ■ a measure of the angle of the blades of a screw propeller, equal to the distance forward a blade would move in one revolution if it exerted no thrust on the medium. ■ the density of typed or printed characters on a line, typically expressed as numbers of characters per inch.
▶ **v. 1** [with obj.] Baseball throw (the ball) for the batter to try to hit. ■ [no obj.] Baseball be a pitcher: *she pitched in a minor-league game* | [with obj.] *he pitched the entire game.* ■ Golf hit (the ball) onto the green with a pitch shot. ■ [no obj.] Golf (of the ball) strike the ground in a particular spot.
2 [with obj.] throw or fling roughly or casually: *he crumpled the page up and pitched it into the fireplace.* ■ [no obj.] fall heavily, esp. headlong: *she pitched forward into blackness.*
3 [with obj.] set (one's voice or a piece of music) at a particular pitch: *you've pitched the melody very high.* ■ express at a particular level of difficulty: *he should pitch his talk at a suitable level for the age group.* ■ aim (a product) at a particular section of the market: *the machine is being pitched at banks.*
4 [no obj.] make a bid to obtain a contract or other business: *they were pitching for an account.*
5 [with obj.] set up and fix in a definite position: *we pitched camp for the night.*
6 [no obj.] (of a moving ship, aircraft, or vehicle) rock or oscillate around a lateral axis, so that the front and back move up and down: *the little steamer pressed on, pitching gently.* ■ (of a vehicle) move with a vigorous jogging motion: *a jeep came pitching down the hill.*
7 [with obj.] cause (a roof) to slope downward from the ridge: *the roof was pitched at an angle of 75 degrees* | (as adj. **pitched**) *a pitched roof.* ■ [no obj.] slope downward: *the ravine pitches down to the creek.*
– PHRASES **make a pitch** make a bid to obtain a contract or other business.
– PHRASAL VERBS **pitch in** informal vigorously join in to help with a task or activity. ■ join in a fight or dispute. **pitch into** informal vigorously tackle or begin to deal with. ■ forcefully assault. **pitch out** throw a pitchout.
– ORIGIN Middle English (as a verb in the senses 'thrust (something pointed) into the ground' and 'fall headlong'): perhaps related to Old English *picung* 'stigmata,' of unknown ultimate origin. The sense development is obscure.

pitch[2] ▶ **n.** a sticky resinous black or dark brown substance that is semiliquid when hot, hard when

P

cold. It is obtained by distilling tar or petroleum and is used for waterproofing. ■ any of various substances similar to pitch, such as asphalt or bitumen.
▶ v. [with obj.] cover, coat, or smear with pitch.
– ORIGIN Old English *pic* (noun), *pician* (verb), of Germanic origin; related to Dutch *pek* and German *Pech*; based on Latin *pix, pic-*.

pitch and putt ▶ n. a form of golf played on a miniature course in which the green can be reached in one stroke from the tee.

pitch and run ▶ n. Golf a pitch shot with a low trajectory and no backspin, so that the ball runs forward on landing.

pitch-and-toss ▶ n. a gambling game in which the player who manages to throw a coin closest to a mark gets to toss all the coins, winning those that land with the head up.

pitch bend ▶ n. a mechanism in a synthesizer that enables the player to change the pitch of the note played by a small amount.

pitch-black (also **pitch-dark**) ▶ adj. completely dark; as black as pitch.
– DERIVATIVES **pitch-black·ness** n.

pitch·blende /ˈpiCH,blend/ ▶ n. a form of the mineral uraninite occurring in brown or black pitchlike masses.
– ORIGIN late 18th cent.: from German *Pechblende*, from *Pech* 'pitch' + *Blende* (see BLENDE).

pitch cir·cle ▶ n. Mechanics an imaginary circle concentric to a toothed wheel, along which the pitch of the teeth is measured.

pitch con·trol ▶ n. **1** control of the pitch of a helicopter's rotors or an aircraft's or ship's propellers.
2 control of the pitching motion of an aircraft.

pitched bat·tle /piCHt ˈbatl/ ▶ n. a planned military encounter on a prearranged battleground. ■ a violent or vigorous confrontation involving large numbers of people.

pitch·er[1] /ˈpiCHər/ ▶ n. **1** a large container, typically earthenware, glass, or plastic, with a handle and a lip, used for holding and pouring liquids. ■ the contents of such a container: ***a pitcher of water***.
2 the modified leaf of a pitcher plant.
– DERIVATIVES **pitch·er·ful** /-,fo͝ol/ n. (pl. **pitcherfuls**).
– ORIGIN Middle English: from Old French *pichier* 'pot,' based on late Latin *picarium*.

pitch·er[2] ▶ n. Baseball the player who delivers the ball to the batter.

pitch·er plant ▶ n. a plant with a deep pitcher-shaped pouch that contains fluid into which insects are attracted and trapped. The plant then absorbs nutrients from their bodies. ● Families Sarraceniaceae (New World), Droseraceae (New World), and Nepenthaceae (Old World): many species, including the purple-flowered *Sarracenia purpurea* of eastern North America and the white-flowered **California pitcher plant** (*Darlingtonia californica*) of the western US. See also TRUMPET (sense 2 of the noun).

California pitcher plant

pitch·fork /ˈpiCH,fôrk/
▶ n. a farm tool with a long handle and sharp metal prongs, used esp. for lifting hay.
▶ v. [with obj.] lift with a pitchfork. ■ thrust (someone) suddenly into an unexpected and difficult situation: *a woman of ordinary intellect pitchforked into power by circumstances*.
– ORIGIN late Middle English: from earlier *pickfork*, influenced by the verb PITCH[1] (because the tool is used for "pitching" or throwing sheaves onto a stack).

pitch·man /ˈpiCHmən/ ▶ n. (pl. **pitchmen**) informal a person delivering a sales pitch.

pitch·out /ˈpiCH,out/ ▶ n. **1** Baseball a pitch thrown intentionally away from the reach of the batter to allow the catcher a clear throw to put out a base runner who is stealing or leading off too far.
2 (also **pitch**) Football a lateral, esp. from the quarterback to a running back.

pitch-per·fect ▶ adj. exactly right in tone, mood, or pitch: *a pitch-perfect, hilarious sendup of a Ken Burns–style documentary*.

pitch pine ▶ n. a pine tree that is a source of pitch or turpentine, and typically yielding hard, heavy, resinous timber that is used in building, esp. the longleaf *Pinus rigida* of the Appalachians and northeastern US.

pitch pipe ▶ n. Music a small reed pipe or set of pipes blown to set the pitch for singing or tuning an instrument.

pitch·pole /ˈpiCH,pōl/ ▶ v. [no obj.] dialect somersault. ■ Nautical (of a boat) be overturned so that its stern pitches forward over its bow.
– ORIGIN mid 17th cent. (as a noun, originally dialect): from the verb PITCH[1] + POLL.

pitch·stone /ˈpiCH,stōn/ ▶ n. Geology a dull vitreous rock resembling hardened pitch, formed by weathering of obsidian.

pitch·y /ˈpiCHē/ ▶ adj. (**pitchier**, **pitchiest**) of, like, or as dark as pitch.

pit·e·ous /ˈpitēəs/ ▶ adj. deserving or arousing pity.
– DERIVATIVES **pit·e·ous·ly** adv., **pit·e·ous·ness** n.
– ORIGIN Middle English: from Old French *piteus*, from Latin *pietas* 'piety, pity' (see PIETY).

pit·fall /ˈpit,fôl/ ▶ n. a hidden or unsuspected danger or difficulty. ■ a covered pit used as a trap.

pith /piTH/ ▶ n. **1** soft or spongy tissue in plants or animals, in particular: ■ spongy white tissue lining the rind of an orange, lemon, and other citrus fruits. ■ Botany the spongy cellular tissue in the stems and branches of many higher plants. ■ archaic spinal marrow.
2 the essence of something: *a book that he considered contained the pith of all his work*.
3 forceful and concise expression: *he writes with a combination of pith and exactitude*.
▶ v. [with obj.] **1** remove the pith from.
2 rare pierce or sever the spinal cord of (an animal) so as to kill or immobilize it.
– DERIVATIVES **pith·less** adj.
– ORIGIN Old English *pitha*.

Pith·e·can·thro·pus /,piTHəˈkanTHrəpəs/ ▶ n. a former genus name applied to some fossilized hominids found in Java in 1891. See JAVA MAN.
– ORIGIN late 19th cent.: modern Latin, from Greek *pithēkos* 'ape' + *anthrōpos* 'man.'

pith hel·met ▶ n. a lightweight sun helmet made from the dried pith of the sola or a similar tropical plant.

pith·y /ˈpiTHē/ ▶ adj. (**pithier**, **pithiest**) **1** (of language or style) concise and forcefully expressive.
2 (of a fruit or plant) containing much pith.
– DERIVATIVES **pith·i·ly** /ˈpiTHəlē/ adv., **pith·i·ness** n.

pit·i·a·ble /ˈpitēəbəl/ ▶ adj. deserving or arousing pity. ■ contemptibly poor or small.
– DERIVATIVES **pit·i·a·ble·ness** n., **pit·i·a·bly** /-əblē/ adv.
– ORIGIN late Middle English: from Old French *piteable*, from *piteer* 'to pity.'

pit·i·ful /ˈpitifəl/ ▶ adj. deserving or arousing pity. ■ very small or poor; inadequate. ■ archaic compassionate.
– DERIVATIVES **pit·i·ful·ly** adv., **pit·i·ful·ness** n.

pit·i·less /ˈpitēlis/ ▶ adj. showing no pity; cruel.
– DERIVATIVES **pit·i·less·ly** adv., **pit·i·less·ness** n.

Pit·man /ˈpitmən/, Sir Isaac (1813–97), English inventor of a formerly widely used shorthand system.

pit·man /ˈpitmən/ ▶ n. **1** (pl. **pitmen**) a coal miner.
2 (pl. **pitmans**) a connecting rod in machinery.

Pit·ney /ˈpitnē/, Mahlon (1858–1924), US Supreme Court associate justice 1912–22. A conservative, he was appointed to the Court by President Taft.

Pi·to·cin /piˈtōsin/ ▶ n. trademark a synthetic form of oxytocin, used to induce labor.

pi·ton /ˈpētän/ ▶ n. a peg or spike driven into a rock or crack to support a climber or a rope.
– ORIGIN late 19th cent.: from French, literally 'eye bolt.'

pi·tot tube /ˈpētō, pēˈtō/ (also **pitot**) ▶ n. an open-ended right-angled tube pointing into the flow of a fluid and used to measure pressure. ■ (also **pitot-static tube**, **pitot head**) a device consisting of a pitot tube inside or adjacent to a parallel tube closed at the end but with holes along its length, the pressure difference between them being a measure of the relative velocity of the fluid or the airspeed of an aircraft.
– ORIGIN late 19th cent.: named after Henri *Pitot* (1695–1771), French physicist.

piton

pit saw (also **pitsaw**) ▶ n. historical a large saw with handles at each end, used in a vertical position by two people, one standing above the timber to be cut, the other in a pit below it.

pit stop ▶ n. Auto Racing a stop in the pits for servicing and refueling, esp. during a race. ■ a brief rest, esp. during a journey. ■ informal a place where one takes such a rest.

Pitt /pit/ the name of two British statesmen.
■ **William**, 1st Earl of Chatham (1708–78); known as **Pitt the Elder**. As secretary of state (effectively prime minister), he headed coalition governments 1756–61 and 1766–68. He brought the Seven Years War to an end in 1763 and also masterminded the conquest of French possessions overseas. ■ **William** (1759–1806), prime minister 1783–1801 and 1804–06; the son of Pitt the Elder; known as **Pitt the Younger**. The youngest-ever prime minister, he introduced financial reforms to reduce the national debt.

pit·ta[1] /ˈpitə/ ▶ n. variant spelling of PITA.

pit·ta[2] ▶ n. a small ground-dwelling thrushlike bird with brightly colored plumage and a very short tail, found in the Old World tropics. ● Family Pittidae and genus *Pitta*: many species.
– ORIGIN mid 19th cent.: from Telugu *pitta* '(young) bird.'

pit·tance /ˈpitns/ ▶ n. [usu. in sing.] a very small or inadequate amount of money paid to someone as an allowance or wage.
– ORIGIN Middle English: from Old French *pitance*, from medieval Latin *pitantia*, from Latin *pietas* 'pity.'

pit·ted /ˈpitid/ ▶ adj. **1** having a hollow or indentation on the surface: *a dusty pitted road*.
2 (of a fruit) having had the stone removed.

pit·ter-pat·ter /ˈpitər ,patər/ ▶ n. a sound as of quick light steps or taps: *the pitter-patter of tiny feet*.
▶ adv. with this sound: *footsteps that go pitter-patter*.
▶ v. [no obj.] move with or make such a sound: *the rain pitter-pattered on my windows*.
– ORIGIN late Middle English: reduplication (expressing rhythmic repetition) of the verb PATTER[1].

Pitt Is·land see CHATHAM ISLANDS.

pit·tos·po·rum /pəˈtäspərəm, ,pitəˈspôrəm/ ▶ n. an evergreen shrub or small tree that typically has small fragrant flowers and is native chiefly to Australasia. ● Genus *Pittosporum*, family Pittosporaceae.
– ORIGIN modern Latin, from Greek *pitta* 'pitch' (because of the resinous pulp around the seeds) + *sporos* 'seed.'

Pitt-Riv·ers /ˈrivərz/, Augustus Henry Lane Fox (1827–1900), English archaeologist and anthropologist. He developed a new scientific approach to archaeology. His collection of weapons and artifacts from different cultures formed the basis of the ethnological museum in Oxford that bears his name.

Pitts·burg /ˈpitsbərg/ an industrial port city in north central California, on Suisun Bay, northeast of Oakland; pop. 64,148 (est. 2008).

Pitts·burgh /ˈpits,bərg/ an industrial city in southwestern Pennsylvania, where the Allegheny and Monongahela rivers join to form the Ohio River; pop. 310,037 (est. 2008).

Pitts·field /ˈpits,fēld/ an industrial city in western Massachusetts, on the Housatonic River, the commercial center of the Berkshire Hills; pop. 42,652 (est. 2008).

pi·tu·i·tar·y /pəˈt(y)o͞oə,terē/ ▶ n. (pl. **pituitaries**) (in full **pituitary gland** or **pituitary body**) the major endocrine gland. A pea-sized body attached to the base of the brain, the pituitary is important in controlling growth and development and the functioning of the other endocrine glands. Also called HYPOPHYSIS.
▶ adj. of or relating to this gland.
– ORIGIN early 17th cent.: from Latin *pituitarius* 'secreting phlegm,' from *pituita* 'phlegm.'

pit vi·per ▶ n. a venomous snake of a group distinguished by visible sensory pits on the head that can detect heat emitted by their prey. They are found in both America and Asia. ● Subfamily Crotalinae, family Viperidae: numerous genera and species, including the rattlesnakes.

pit·y /ˈpitē/ ▶ n. (pl. **pities**) **1** the feeling of sorrow and compassion caused by the suffering and misfortunes of others: *her voice was full of pity*.
2 [in sing.] a cause for regret or disappointment: *what a pity we can't be friends*.
▶ v. (**pities**, **pitying**, **pitied**) [with obj.] feel sorrow for the misfortunes of: *Clare didn't know whether to envy or pity them* | (as adj. **pitying**) *he gave her a pitying look*.
– PHRASES **for pity's sake** informal used to express impatience or make an urgent appeal. **more's the pity** informal used to express regret about a fact that has just been stated. **take** (or **have**) **pity** show compassion: *they took pity on him and gave him food*.
– DERIVATIVES **pit·y·ing·ly** adv.

P

– ORIGIN Middle English (also in the sense 'clemency, mildness'): from Old French *pite* 'compassion,' from Latin *pietas* 'piety'; compare with PIETY.

pit·y·ri·a·sis /ˌpitəˈrīəsis/ ▶ **n.** [with modifier] Medicine a skin disease characterized by the shedding of fine flaky scales.
– ORIGIN late 17th cent.: modern Latin, from Greek *pituriasis* 'scurf,' from *pituron* 'bran,' + -ASIS.

piu /pyoo/ ▶ **adj.** Music (esp. as a direction) more.

più mos·so /pyoo ˈmōsō/ ▶ **adv. & adj.** Music (esp. as a direction) more quickly.
– ORIGIN Italian.

Pi·us XII /ˈpīəs/ (1876–1958), pope 1939–58; born *Eugenio Pacelli*. He upheld the neutrality of the Roman Catholic Church during World War II and was criticized after the war for failing to condemn Nazi atrocities.

piv·ot /ˈpivət/ ▶ **n.** the central point, pin, or shaft on which a mechanism turns or oscillates. ■ [usu. in sing.] a person or thing that plays a central part in an activity or organization: *the **pivot of** community life was the chapel.* ■ the person or people about whom a body of troops wheels. ■ (also **pivotman**) a player in a central position in a team sport. ■ Basketball a movement in which the player holding the ball may move in any direction with one foot, while keeping the other (the **pivot foot**) in contact with the floor.
▶ **v.** (**pivots, pivoting, pivoted**) [no obj.] turn on or as if on a pivot: *the sail **pivots around** the axis of a virtually static mast* | *he swung around, **pivoting on** his heel.* ■ [with obj.] provide (a mechanism) with a pivot; fix (a mechanism) on a pivot: (as adj. **pivoted**) *a pivoted bracket.* ■ (**pivot on**) depend on: *your escape pivots on my disappearing with you.*
– DERIVATIVES **piv·ot·a·bil·i·ty** /ˌpivətəˈbilitē/ **n.**, **piv·ot·a·ble adj.**
– ORIGIN late Middle English: from French, probably from the root of dialect *pue* 'tooth of a comb' and Spanish *pu(y)a* 'point.' The verb dates from the mid 19th cent.

piv·ot·al /ˈpivətl/ ▶ **adj.** of crucial importance in relation to the development or success of something else: *the alliance that played a pivotal role in the revolution.* ■ fixed on or as if on a pivot: *a sliding or pivotal motion.*

pix[1] /piks/ ▶ **plural n.** informal pictures, esp. photographs.
– ORIGIN 1930s: pluralized abbreviation.

pix[2] ▶ **n.** variant spelling of PYX.

pix·el /ˈpiksəl/ ▶ **n.** Electronics a minute area of illumination on a display screen, one of many from which an image is composed.
– ORIGIN 1960s: abbreviation of *picture element* (compare with PIX[1]).

pix·el·ate /ˈpiksəlāt/ (also **pixellate** or **pixilate**) ▶ **v.** [with obj.] divide (an image) into pixels, typically for display or storage in a digital format. ■ (**be pixelated**) (of an image on a computer screen or other display) be enlarged so far that the viewer sees the individual pixels that form the image, the enlargement having reached the point at which no further detail can be resolved. ■ display an image of (someone or something) on television as a small number of large pixels, typically in order to disguise someone's identity.
– DERIVATIVES **pix·el·a·tion** /ˌpiksəˈlāSHən/ **n.**

pix·ie /ˈpiksē/ (also **pixy**) ▶ **n.** (pl. **pixies**) a supernatural being in folklore and children's stories, typically portrayed as small and humanlike in form, with pointed ears and a pointed hat, and mischievous in character.
– DERIVATIVES **pix·ie·ish adj.**
– ORIGIN mid 17th cent.: of unknown origin.

pix·ie dust ▶ **n.** a substance or influence with an apparently magical effect that brings great success or luck: *the folks who live there still seem to believe that they've been sprinkled with pixie dust.*
– ORIGIN 1950s: from the magic dust that enabled humans to fly in J. M. Barrie's *Peter Pan.*

pix·i·late /ˈpiksəˌlāt/ ▶ **v.** variant spelling of PIXELATE.

pix·il·at·ed /ˈpiksəˌlātid/ (Brit. also **pixillated**) ▶ **adj.** crazy; confused.
– ORIGIN mid 19th cent.: variant of *pixie-led*, literally 'led astray by pixies,' figuratively 'confused,' or from PIXIE, on the pattern of words such as *elated* and *emulated.*

pix·il·a·tion /ˌpiksəˈlāSHən/ (Brit. also **pixillation**) ▶ **n. 1** a technique used in film whereby the movements of real people are made to appear like artificial animations.
2 the state of being crazy or confused.
3 variant spelling of PIXELATION (see PIXELATE).

Pi·zar·ro /piˈzärō, pēˈsä-, -ˈTHä-/, Francisco (*c.*1478–1541), Spanish conquistador. He defeated the Inca empire and in 1533 set up a puppet monarchy at Cuzco. He built his own capital at Lima 1535, where he was assassinated.

pizz. ▶ **abbr.** Music pizzicato.

piz·za /ˈpētsə/ ▶ **n.** a dish of Italian origin consisting of a flat, round base of dough baked with a topping of tomato sauce and cheese, typically with added meat or vegetables.
– ORIGIN Italian, literally 'pie.'

piz·za box ▶ **n.** a computer casing that is not very tall and has a square cross section.

piz·zazz /pəˈzaz/ (also **pizazz**) ▶ **n.** informal an attractive combination of vitality and glamour: *a new way to add graphic pizzazz to your desktop-publishing project.*
– ORIGIN said to have been invented by Diana Vreeland, fashion editor of *Harper's Bazaar* in the 1930s.

piz·ze·ri·a /ˌpētsəˈrēə/ ▶ **n.** a place where pizzas are made or sold; a pizza restaurant.
– ORIGIN Italian.

piz·zi·ca·to /ˌpitsiˈkätō/ Music ▶ **adv.** (often as a direction) plucking the strings of a violin or other stringed instrument with one's finger.
▶ **adj.** performed in this way.
▶ **n.** (pl. **pizzicatos** or **pizzicati** /-tē/) this technique of playing. ■ a note or passage played in this way.
– ORIGIN Italian, literally 'pinched, twitched,' past participle of *pizzicare*, based on *pizza* 'point, edge.'

piz·zle /ˈpizəl/ ▶ **n.** the penis of an animal, esp. a bull.
– ORIGIN late 15th cent.: from Low German *pēsel* or Flemish *pezel* (diminutives of Middle Low German *pēse* and Middle Dutch *pēze*).

PK ▶ **abbr.** psychokinesis.

pK ▶ **n.** Chemistry a figure expressing the acidity or alkalinity of a solution of a weak electrolyte in a similar way to pH, equal to $-\log_{10} K$ where *K* is the dissociation (or ionization) constant of the electrolyte.
– ORIGIN from *p* as in *pH* and *K* representing a constant.

pk ▶ **abbr.** ■ (also **Pk**) park. ■ peak. ■ peck(s).

pkg. ▶ **abbr.** (pl. **pkgs.**) package.

pkt. ▶ **abbr.** ■ packet. ■ pocket.

PKU ▶ **abbr.** phenylketonuria.

pkwy ▶ **abbr.** parkway.

pky ▶ **abbr.** parkway.

PL ▶ **abbr.** ■ Computing programming language. ■ Military patrol leader.

pl. ▶ **abbr.** ■ (also **Pl.**) place: *3 Palmerston Pl., Edinburgh.* ■ plate (referring to illustrations in a book). ■ chiefly Military platoon. ■ Grammar plural.

PLA ▶ **abbr.** ■ People's Liberation Army. ■ (in the UK) Port of London Authority.

plac·a·ble /ˈplakəbəl/ ▶ **adj.** archaic easily calmed; gentle and forgiving.
– DERIVATIVES **plac·a·bil·i·ty** /ˌplakəˈbilitē/ **n.**, **plac·a·bly** /-əblē/ **adv.**
– ORIGIN late Middle English (in the sense 'pleasing, agreeable'): from Old French, or from Latin *placabilis*, from *placare* 'appease.'

plac·ard /ˈplakärd, -ərd/ ▶ **n.** a poster or sign for public display, either fixed to a wall or carried during a demonstration.
▶ **v.** [with obj.] cover with placards: *they were placarding the town with posters.*
– ORIGIN late 15th cent. (denoting a warrant or license): from Old French *placquart*, from *plaquier* 'to plaster, lay flat,' from Middle Dutch *placken.* The current sense of the verb dates from the early 19th cent.

pla·cate /ˈplākāt/ ▶ **v.** [with obj.] make (someone) less angry or hostile: *they attempted to placate the students with promises.*
– DERIVATIVES **pla·cat·er n.**, **pla·cat·ing·ly** /pləˈkātiNGlē/ **adv.**, **pla·ca·tion** /plāˈkāSHən/ **n.**
– ORIGIN late 17th cent.: from Latin *placat-* 'appeased,' from the verb *placare.*

pla·ca·to·ry /ˈplākəˌtôrē, ˈplakə-/ ▶ **adj.** intended to make someone less angry or hostile; conciliatory: *his hands held in a placatory gesture.*

place /plās/ ▶ **n. 1** a particular position or point in space: *there were still some remote places in the world* | *the monastery was a peaceful place* | *that street was **no place for** a lady.* ■ a particular point on a larger surface or in a larger object or area: *he lashed out and cut the policeman's hand in three places.* ■ a building or area used for a specified purpose or activity: *the town has many excellent eating places.* ■ informal a person's home: *what about dinner at my place?* ■ a point in a book or other text reached by a reader at a particular time: *I must have lost my place in the script.*
2 a portion of space available or designated for or being used by someone: *they hurried to their places at the table* | *he was watching from his place across the room.* ■ a vacancy or available position: *she won a place to study German at the university.* ■ the regular or proper position of something: *lay each slab **in place**.* ■ a person's rank or status: *occupation structures a person's place in society.* ■ [usu. with negative] a right or privilege resulting from someone's role or position: *I'm sure she has a story to tell, but it's **not my place to** ask.* ■ the role played by or importance attached to someone or something in a particular context: *the place of computers in improving office efficiency varies between companies.*
3 a position in a sequence, in particular: ■ a position in a contest: *his score was good enough to leave him in ninth place.* ■ the second position, esp. in a horse race. ■ Brit. any of the first three or sometimes four positions in a race (used esp. of the second, third, or fourth positions). ■ the degree of priority given to something: *accurate reportage **takes second place to** lurid detail.* ■ the position of a figure in a series indicated in decimal or similar notation, esp. one after the decimal point: *calculate the ratios **to** one decimal **place**.*
4 (in place names) a square or a short street: *our new restaurant is in Hilliard Place.* ■ a country house with its grounds.
▶ **v.** [with obj.] **1** put in a particular position: *a newspaper had been placed beside my plate.* ■ cause to be in a particular situation: *enemy officers were placed under arrest* | *you are not placing yourself under any obligation.* ■ used to express the attitude someone has toward someone or something: *I am not able to place any trust in you.* ■ (**be placed**) used to indicate the degree of advantage or convenience enjoyed by someone or something as a result of their position or circumstances: [with infinitive] *the company is well placed to seize the opportunity.*
2 find a home or employment for: *the children were placed with foster parents* | *the agency had placed 3,000 people in full-time jobs.* ■ dispose of (something, esp. shares) by selling to a customer. ■ arrange for the recognition and implementation of (an order, bet, etc.): *they placed a contract for three boats.* ■ order or obtain a connection for (a telephone call) through an operator.
3 identify or classify as being of a specified type or as holding a specified position in a sequence or hierarchy: *a survey placed the company 13th for achievement.* ■ [with obj., usu. with negative] remember where one has seen or how one comes to recognize (someone or something): *she eventually said she couldn't place him.* ■ (**be placed**) Brit. achieve a specified position in a race: *he was placed eleventh in the long individual race.* ■ [no obj.] be among the first three in a race (or the first three or four in the UK).
– PHRASES **give place to** be succeeded or replaced by. **go places** informal visit places; travel. ■ be increasingly successful. **in place 1** working or ready to work; established. **2** not traveling any distance: *running in place.* **in place of** instead of. **keep someone in his** (or **her**) **place** keep someone from becoming presumptuous. **out of place** not in the proper position; disarranged. ■ in a setting where one is or feels inappropriate or incongruous. **place in the sun** a position of favor or advantage. **put oneself in someone's place** consider a situation from someone's point of view. **put someone in his** (or **her**) **place** deflate or humiliate someone regarded as being presumptuous. **take place** occur. **take one's place** take up the physical position or status in society that is correct or due for one. **take the place of** replace.
– DERIVATIVES **place·less adj.**
– ORIGIN Middle English: from Old French, from an alteration of Latin *platea* 'open space,' from Greek *plateia* (*hodos*) 'broad (way).'

pla·ce·bo /pləˈsēbō/ ▶ **n.** (pl. **placebos**) a harmless pill, medicine, or procedure prescribed more for the psychological benefit to the patient than for any physiological effect: *his Aunt Beatrice had been kept alive on sympathy and placebos for thirty years* | [as modifier] *placebo drugs.* ■ a substance that has no therapeutic effect, used as a control in testing new drugs. ■ a measure designed merely to calm or please someone.
– ORIGIN late 18th cent.: from Latin, literally 'I shall please,' from *placere* 'to please.'

pla·ce·bo ef·fect ▶ **n.** a beneficial effect, produced by a placebo drug or treatment, that cannot be attributed to the properties of the placebo itself, and must therefore be due to the patient's belief in that treatment.

place card ▶ **n.** a card bearing a person's name and used to mark their place at a dining or meeting table.

place·hold·er /ˈplāsˌhōldər/ ▶ **n. 1** Mathematics a significant zero in the decimal representation of a number. ■ a symbol or piece of text used in a

P

mathematical expression or in an instruction in a computer program to denote a missing quantity or operator.
2 Linguistics an element of a sentence that is required by syntactic constraints but carries little or no semantic information, for example the word *it* as a subject in *it is a pity that she left*, where the true subject is *that she left*.

place·kick /ˈplāsˌkik/ Football ▶ **n.** a kick made with the ball held on the ground or on a tee.
▶ **v.** [no obj.] (often as noun **placekicking**) take such a kick: *our placekicking struggled at times last season.*
– DERIVATIVES **place·kick·er n.**

place mat (also **placemat**) ▶ **n.** a small mat beneath a place setting at a dining table.

place·ment /ˈplāsmənt/ ▶ **n.** the action of putting someone or something in a particular place or the fact of being placed: *the proper placement of microphones.* ■ the action of finding a home, job, or school for someone: *a baby put up for adoption may wait up to three years or more for placement | a placement in a special school.* ■ Football another term for PLACEKICK. ■ Football the act of holding the ball for a placekick.

place name ▶ **n.** the name of a geographical location, such as a town, lake, or range of hills.

pla·cen·ta /pləˈsentə/ ▶ **n.** (pl. **placentae** /-tē/ or **placentas**) **1** a flattened circular organ in the uterus of pregnant eutherian mammals, nourishing and maintaining the fetus through the umbilical cord.

> The placenta consists of vascular tissue in which oxygen and nutrients can pass from the mother's blood into that of the fetus, and waste products can pass in the reverse direction. The placenta is expelled from the uterus at the birth of the fetus, when it is often called the afterbirth. Marsupials and monotremes do not develop placentas.

2 Botany (in flowers) part of the ovary wall to which the ovules are attached.
– ORIGIN late 17th cent.: from Latin, from Greek *plakous, plakount-* 'flat cake,' based on *plax, plak-* 'flat plate.'

pla·cen·tal /pləˈsentl/ ▶ **adj.** of or relating to a placenta. ■ Zoology relating to or denoting mammals that possess a placenta; eutherian.
▶ **n.** Zoology a placental mammal. See EUTHERIA.

pla·cen·ta pre·vi·a /pləˈsentə ˈprēvēə/ (Brit. **placenta praevia**) ▶ **n.** Medicine a condition in which the placenta partially or wholly blocks the neck of the uterus, thus interfering with normal delivery of a baby.
– ORIGIN early 19th cent.: from PLACENTA and Latin *praevia* 'going before.'

plac·en·ta·tion /ˌplasənˈtāsHən/ ▶ **n.** Anatomy & Zoology the formation or arrangement of a placenta or placentae in a woman's or female animal's uterus. ■ Botany the arrangement of the placenta or placentae in the ovary of a flower.

plac·er¹ /ˈplāsər/ ▶ **n.** [often as modifier] a deposit of sand or gravel in the bed of a river or lake, containing particles of valuable minerals: *placer gold deposits.*
– ORIGIN early 19th cent.: from Latin American Spanish, literally 'deposit, shoal'; related to *placel* 'sandbank,' from *plaza* 'a place.'

plac·er² ▶ **n.** **1** [with adj.] a person or animal gaining a specified position in a competition or race: *last year's fifth placer had a good run.*
2 a person who positions, sets, or arranges something: *he was a shrewd placer of the ball.*

place set·ting ▶ **n.** a complete set of dishes and cutlery provided for one person at a meal.

pla·cet /ˈplāsit/ ▶ **n.** an affirmative vote, indicated by an utterance of 'placet.'
– ORIGIN Latin, literally 'it pleases.'

place val·ue ▶ **n.** the numerical value that a digit has by virtue of its position in a number.

plac·id /ˈplasid/ ▶ **adj.** (of a person or animal) not easily upset or excited: *this horse has a placid nature.* ■ (esp. of a place or stretch of water) calm and peaceful, with little movement or activity: *the placid waters of a small lake.*
– DERIVATIVES **pla·cid·i·ty** /pləˈsiditē/ **n.**, **plac·id·ly adv.**
– ORIGIN early 17th cent.: from French *placide*, from Latin *placidus*, from *placere* 'to please.'

Plac·i·dyl /ˈplasidil/ ▶ **n.** trademark a short-acting sedative and hypnotic drug used to treat insomnia.

plack·et /ˈplakit/ ▶ **n.** an opening or slit in a garment, covering fastenings or giving access to a pocket, or the flap of fabric under such an opening.
– ORIGIN early 17th cent.: variant of PLACARD in an obsolete sense 'garment worn under an open coat or gown.'

plac·o·derm /ˈplakəˌdərm/ ▶ **n.** an extinct fish of the Devonian period, having the front part of the body encased in broad flat bony plates. ● Class Placodermi: several orders.
– ORIGIN mid 19th cent.: from Greek *plax, plak-* 'flat plate' + *derma* 'skin.'

plac·o·dont /ˈplakəˌdänt/ ▶ **n.** an extinct marine shellfish-eating reptile of the Triassic period, having short flat grinding palatal teeth and sometimes a turtlelike shell. ● Suborder Placodontia, superorder Sauropterygia: several families and genera, including *Placodus.*
– ORIGIN late 19th cent.: from Greek *plax, plak-* 'flat plate' + *odous, odont-* 'tooth.'

plac·oid /ˈplakoid/ ▶ **adj.** Zoology (of fish scales) toothlike, being made of dentin with a pointed backward projection of enamel, as in sharks and rays. Compare with CTENOID and GANOID.
– ORIGIN mid 19th cent.: from Greek *plax, plak-* 'flat plate' + -OID.

Plac·o·zo·a /ˌplakəˈzōə/ Zoology a minor phylum that contains a single minute marine invertebrate (*Trichoplax adhaerens*), which has a flattened body with two cell layers and is the simplest known metazoan.
– ORIGIN modern Latin (plural), from Greek *plakos* 'flat' + *zōia* 'animals.'

pla·fond /pləˈfänd/ ▶ **n.** an ornately decorated ceiling. ■ a painting or decoration on a ceiling.
– ORIGIN French, from *plat* 'flat' + *fond* 'bottom, base.'

pla·gal /ˈplāgəl/ ▶ **adj.** Music (of a church mode) containing notes between the dominant and the note an octave higher, having the final in the middle. Compare with AUTHENTIC.
– ORIGIN late 16th cent.: from medieval Latin *plagalis*, from *plaga* 'plagal mode,' from Latin *plagius*, from medieval Greek *plagios* (*hēkhos*) 'plagal (mode),' from Greek *plagos* 'side.'

plage ▶ **n.** **1** /pläZH/ dated a beach by the sea, esp. at a fashionable resort.
2 /plāj/ Astronomy an unusually bright region on the sun.
– ORIGIN French.

pla·gia·rism /ˈplājəˌrizəm/ ▶ **n.** the practice of taking someone else's work or ideas and passing them off as one's own.
– DERIVATIVES **pla·gia·rist n.**, **pla·gia·ris·tic** /ˌplājəˈristik/ **adj.**
– ORIGIN early 17th cent.: from Latin *plagiarius* 'kidnapper' (from *plagium* 'a kidnapping,' from Greek *plagion*) + -ISM.

pla·gia·rize /ˈplājəˌrīz/ ▶ **v.** [with obj.] take (the work or an idea of someone else) and pass it off as one's own. ■ copy from (someone) in such a way.
– DERIVATIVES **pla·gia·riz·er n.**

plagio- ▶ **comb. form** oblique: *plagioclase.*
– ORIGIN from Greek *plagios* 'slanting,' from *plagos* 'side.'

pla·gi·o·clase /ˈplājēəˌklās/ (also **plagioclase feldspar**) ▶ **n.** a form of feldspar consisting of aluminosilicates of sodium and/or calcium, common in igneous rocks and typically white.
– ORIGIN mid 19th cent.: from PLAGIO- + Greek *klasis* 'cleavage' (because originally characterized as having two cleavages at an oblique angle).

plague /plāg/ ▶ **n.** a contagious bacterial disease characterized by fever and delirium, typically with the formation of buboes (see BUBONIC PLAGUE) and sometimes infection of the lungs (**pneumonic plague**): *an outbreak of plague | they died of the plague.* ■ a contagious disease that spreads rapidly and kills many people. ■ an unusually large number of insects or animals infesting a place and causing damage: *a plague of fleas.* ■ [in sing.] a thing causing trouble or irritation: *staff theft is usually the plague of restaurants.* ■ [in sing.] archaic used as a curse or an expression of despair or disgust: *a plague on all their houses!* [in recent use echoing Shakespeare's *Romeo and Juliet* (III. i. 94).]
▶ **v.** (**plagues, plaguing, plagued**) [with obj.] cause continual trouble or distress to: *the problems that plagued the company | he has been plagued by ill health.* ■ pester or harass (someone) continually: *he was plaguing her with questions.*
– ORIGIN late Middle English: Latin *plaga* 'stroke, wound,' probably from Greek (Doric dialect) *plaga*, from a base meaning 'strike.'

pla·guy /ˈplāgē/ (also **plaguey**) ▶ **adj.** [attrib.] informal troublesome; annoying.

plaice /plās/ ▶ **n.** (pl. **same**) a North Atlantic flatfish that is a commercially important food fish. ● Two species in the family Pleuronectidae: the European *Pleuronectes platessa*, often found in very shallow water, and the American *Hippoglossoides platessoides*, found in deeper waters.
– ORIGIN Middle English: from Old French *plaiz*, from late Latin *platessa*, from Greek *platus* 'broad.'

plaid /plad/ ▶ **n.** checkered or tartan twilled cloth, typically made of wool. ■ a long piece of plaid worn over the shoulder as part of Scottish Highland dress.
– DERIVATIVES **plaid·ed adj.**
– ORIGIN early 16th cent.: from Scottish Gaelic *plaide* 'blanket,' of unknown ultimate origin.

plain¹ /plān/ ▶ **adj.** **1** not decorated or elaborate; simple or ordinary in character: *good plain food | everyone dined at a plain wooden table.* ■ without a pattern; in only one color: *a plain fabric.* ■ bearing no indication as to source, contents, or affiliation: *donations can be put in a plain envelope.* ■ (of a person) having no pretensions; not remarkable or special: *a plain, honest man with no nonsense about him.* ■ [attrib.] (of a person) without a special title or status: *for years he was just plain Bill.*
2 easy to perceive or understand; clear: *the advantages were* ***plain to see*** *| it was plain that something was very wrong.* ■ [attrib.] (of written or spoken usage) clearly expressed, without the use of technical or abstruse terms: *written* ***in plain English.*** ■ not using concealment or deception; frank: *he recalled her plain speaking.*
3 (of a person) not beautiful or attractive: *the dark-haired, rather plain woman.*
4 [attrib.] sheer; simple (used for emphasis): *the main problem is just plain exhaustion.*
5 (of a knitting stitch) made using a knit rather than a purl stitch.
▶ **adv.** [as submodifier] informal clearly; unequivocally (used for emphasis): *perhaps the youth was just plain stupid.*
▶ **n.** a large area of flat land with few trees. Compare with PRAIRIE. ■ (**the Plains**) another term for GREAT PLAINS.
– PHRASES **as plain as the nose on one's face** informal very obvious. **plain and simple** informal used to emphasize the statement preceding or following: *she was a genius, plain and simple.* **plain as day** informal very clearly.
– DERIVATIVES **plain·ness n.**
– ORIGIN Middle English: from Old French *plain*, from Latin *planus*, from a base meaning 'flat.'

plain² ▶ **v.** [no obj.] archaic mourn; lament. ■ complain. ■ emit a mournful or plaintive sound.
– ORIGIN Middle English: from Old French *plaindre*, from Latin *plangere* 'to lament.'

plain·chant /ˈplānˌCHant/ ▶ **n.** another term for PLAINSONG.

plain clothes ▶ **plural n.** ordinary clothes rather than uniform, esp. when worn as a disguise by police officers: *a detective* ***in plain clothes.***
▶ **adj.** [attrib.] (**plainclothes**) (esp. of a police officer) wearing such clothes: *plainclothes troopers.*

plain deal·ing ▶ **n.** honest and straightforward behavior toward others.

Plain·field /ˈplānˌfēld/ an industrial city in northeastern New Jersey; pop. 46,126 (est. 2008).

plain-laid ▶ **adj.** denoting a rope consisting of three strands twisted to the right.

plain·ly /ˈplānlē/ ▶ **adv.** **1** [as submodifier] able to be perceived easily: *the lake was plainly visible.* ■ [sentence adverb] used to state one's belief that something is obviously or undeniably true: *her mother was plainly anxious to leave.* ■ in a frank and direct way; unequivocally: *let me speak plainly.*
2 in a style that is simple and without decoration: *the restaurant was plainly furnished.*

plain-pa·per ▶ **adj.** denoting a fax machine or other device that does not require special paper to print on.

Plain Peo·ple ▶ **plural n.** the Amish, the Mennonites, and the Dunkers, three strict Christian sects emphasizing a simple way of life.

plain sail·ing ▶ **n.** used to describe a process or activity that goes well and is easy and uncomplicated: *he is pleased to report that the tour has been plain sailing.*
– ORIGIN mid 18th cent.: probably a popular use of *plane sailing*, denoting the practice of determining a ship's position on the theory that it is moving on a plane.

plain-saw ▶ **v.** (past participle **plain-sawed** /-sôd/ or **plain-sawn** /-sôn/) [with obj.] saw (timber) tangential to the growth rings, so that the rings make angles of less than 45° with the faces of the boards produced: [as adj., in combination] (**-sawn**) *plain-sawn logs.*
– DERIVATIVES **plain saw·ing n.**

Plains In·di·an ▶ **n.** a member of any of various North American Indian peoples who formerly inhabited the Great Plains.

> Although a few of the Plains Indian peoples were sedentary farmers, most, including the Blackfoot, Cheyenne, and Comanche, were nomadic buffalo hunters, who gathered in tribes during the summer and dispersed into family groups in the winter. They hunted on foot until they acquired horses from the Spanish in the early 18th century. The introduction of the horse also led other

peoples, such as the Sioux and the Cree, to move into the Plains area.

plains·man /ˈplānzmən/ ▶ **n.** (pl. **plainsmen**) a person who lives on a plain, esp. a frontiersman who lived on the Great Plains of North America.

Plains of A·bra·ham a plateau beside the city of Quebec, overlooking the St. Lawrence River. In 1759 it was the scene of a battle in which the British army under General Wolfe, having scaled the heights above the city under cover of darkness, surprised and defeated the French.

plain·song /ˈplān,sôNG, -säNG/ ▶ **n.** unaccompanied church music sung in unison in medieval modes and in free rhythm corresponding to the accentuation of the words, which are taken from the liturgy. Compare with **GREGORIAN CHANT**.
– ORIGIN late Middle English: translating Latin *cantus planus*.

plain-spo·ken (also **plainspoken**) ▶ **adj.** outspoken; blunt.
– DERIVATIVES **plain-spok·en·ness** **n.**

Plains States the US states dominated by the Great Plains, generally including North and South Dakota, Nebraska, and Kansas and sometimes Iowa and Missouri.

plaint /plānt/ ▶ **n.** Brit. Law an accusation; a charge. ■ chiefly literary a complaint; a lamentation.
– ORIGIN Middle English: from Old French *plainte*, feminine past participle of *plaindre* 'complain,' or from Old French *plaint*, from Latin *planctus* 'beating of the breast.'

plain·text /ˈplān,tekst/ ▶ **n.** Computing an original readable text, as opposed to a coded version.

plain·tiff /ˈplāntif/ ▶ **n.** Law a person who brings a case against another in a court of law. Compare with **DEFENDANT**.
– ORIGIN late Middle English: from Old French *plaintif* 'plaintive' (used as a noun). The *-f* ending has come down through Law French; the word was originally the same as *plaintive*.

plain·tive /ˈplāntiv/ ▶ **adj.** sounding sad and mournful: *a plaintive cry*.
– DERIVATIVES **plain·tive·ly** **adv.**, **plain·tive·ness** **n.**
– ORIGIN late Middle English: from Old French *plaintif, -ive*, from *plainte* 'lamentation' (see **PLAINT**).

plain weave ▶ **n.** a common and basic style of weave in which the weft alternates over and under the warp.

plait /plāt, plat/ ▶ **n.** a single length of hair or other flexible material made up of three or more interlaced strands; a braid. ■ archaic term for **PLEAT**.
▶ **v.** [with obj.] form (hair or other material) into a plait or plaits. ■ make (something) by forming material into a plait or plaits.
– ORIGIN late Middle English: from Old French *pleit* 'a fold,' based on Latin *plicare* 'to fold.' The word was formerly often pronounced like "plate," which is the usual American pronunciation; since late Middle English there has arisen an alternative spelling *plat*, to which the current alternative pronunciation corresponds.

plan /plan/ ▶ **n.** **1** a detailed proposal for doing or achieving something: *the UN peace plan*. ■ [with modifier] a scheme for the regular payment of contributions toward a pension, savings account, or insurance policy: *a personal pension plan*.
2 (usu. **plans**) an intention or decision about what one is going to do: *I have no plans to retire*.
3 a detailed diagram, drawing, or program, in particular: ■ a fairly large-scale map of a town or district: *a street plan*. ■ a drawing or diagram made by projection on a horizontal plane, esp. one showing the layout of a building or one floor of a building. Compare with **ELEVATION** (sense 3). ■ a diagram showing how something will be arranged: *look at the seating plan*.
▶ **v.** (**plans, planning, planned**) [with obj.] **1** decide on and arrange in advance: *they were planning a trip to Egypt* | [with infinitive] *he plans to fly on Wednesday* | [no obj.] *we plan on getting married in the near future* | *we have to plan for the future*.
2 design or make a plan of (something to be made or built): *they were planning a garden*.
– PHRASES **someone's** (or **the**) **best plan** a person's (or the) most sensible course of action. **go according to plan** happen as one arranged or intended. **plan of action** (or **attack**) an organized program of measures to be taken in order to achieve a goal.
– ORIGIN late 17th cent.: from French, from earlier *plant* 'ground plan, plane surface,' influenced in sense by Italian *pianta* 'plan of building.' Compare with **PLANT**.

pla·nar /ˈplānər/ ▶ **adj.** Mathematics of, relating to, or in the form of a plane: *planar surfaces*.

pla·nar·i·an /pləˈne(ə)rēən/ ▶ **n.** a free-living flatworm that has a three-branched intestine and a tubular pharynx, typically located halfway down the body. ● Order Tricladida, class Turbellaria: *Planaria* and other genera.
– ORIGIN mid 19th cent.: from modern Latin *Planaria* (feminine of Latin *planarius* 'lying flat') + **-IAN**.

pla·na·tion /plāˈnāsHən/ ▶ **n.** the leveling of a landscape by erosion.
– ORIGIN late 19th cent.: from **PLANE¹** + **-ATION**.

planch·et /ˈplancHit/ ▶ **n.** a plain metal disk from which a coin is made.
– ORIGIN early 17th cent.: diminutive of earlier *planch* 'slab of metal,' from Old French *planche* 'plank, slab.'

plan·chette /planˈsHet/ ▶ **n.** a small board supported on casters, typically heart-shaped and fitted with a vertical pencil, used for automatic writing and in seances.
– ORIGIN mid 19th cent.: from French, literally 'small plank,' diminutive of *planche*.

Planck /plaNGk, pläNGk/, Max (Karl Ernst Ludwig) (1858–1947), German theoretical physicist. The founder of the quantum theory, he announced the radiation law named after him in 1900. Nobel Prize for Physics (1918).

Planck's con·stant (also **Planck constant**) Physics a fundamental constant, equal to the energy of a quantum of electromagnetic radiation divided by its frequency, with a value of 6.626×10^{-34} joule-seconds.

Planck's law Physics a law, forming the basis of quantum theory, that states that electromagnetic radiation from heated bodies is not emitted as a continuous flow but is made up of discrete units or quanta of energy, the size of which involve a fundamental physical constant (Planck's constant).

plane¹ /plān/ ▶ **n.** **1** a flat surface on which a straight line joining any two points on it would wholly lie: *the horizontal plane*. ■ an imaginary flat surface through or joining material objects: *the planets orbit the sun in roughly the same plane*. ■ a flat or level surface of a material object: *the plane of his forehead*. ■ a flat surface producing lift by the action of air or water over and under it.
2 a level of existence, thought, or development: *everything is connected on the spiritual plane*.
▶ **adj.** [attrib.] completely level or flat. ■ of or relating to only two-dimensional surfaces or magnitudes: *plane and solid geometry*.
▶ **v.** [no obj.] (of a bird or an airborne object) soar without moving the wings; glide: *a bird planed down toward the water below*. ■ (of a boat, surfboard, etc.) skim over the surface of water as a result of lift produced hydrodynamically.
– ORIGIN early 17th cent.: from Latin *planum* 'flat surface,' neuter of the adjective *planus* 'plain.' The adjective was suggested by French *plan(e)* 'flat.' The word was introduced to differentiate the geometric senses, previously expressed by **PLAIN¹**, from the latter's other meanings.

plane² ▶ **n.** an airplane.
▶ **v.** [no obj.] rare travel in an airplane.
– ORIGIN early 20th cent.: shortened form.

plane³ ▶ **n.** a tool consisting of a block with a projecting steel blade, used to smooth a wooden or other surface by paring shavings from it.
▶ **v.** [with obj.] smooth (wood or other material) with a plane. ■ reduce or remove (redundant material) with a plane: *high areas can be planed down*. ■ archaic make smooth or level.
– ORIGIN Middle English: from a variant of obsolete French *plaine* 'planing tool,' from late Latin *plana* (in the same sense), from Latin *planare* 'make level,' from *planus* 'plain, level.'

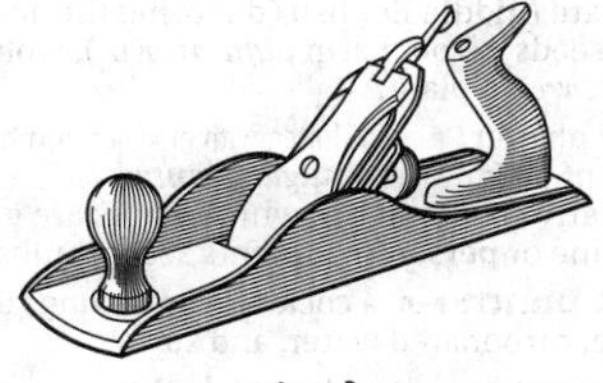

plane³

plane⁴ (also **plane tree**) ▶ **n.** a tall spreading tree of the northern hemisphere, with maplelike leaves and bark that peels in irregular patches. ● Genus *Platanus*, family Platanaceae. See also **SYCAMORE**.
– ORIGIN late Middle English: from Old French, from Latin *platanus*, from Greek *platanos*, from *platus* 'broad.'

plane·load /ˈplānlōd/ ▶ **n.** an amount of cargo or number of passengers that fill an aircraft: *a planeload of medicines, tools, and clothing*.

plane po·lar·i·za·tion /,pōlərəˈzāsHən/ ▶ **n.** a process restricting the vibrations of electromagnetic radiation, esp. light, to one direction.
– DERIVATIVES **plane-po·lar·ized** **adj.**

plan·er /ˈplānər/ ▶ **n.** another term for **PLANE³**, esp. when power-operated.

planes·man /ˈplānzmən/ ▶ **n.** (pl. **planesmen**) a person who operates the hydroplanes on a submarine.

plan·et /ˈplanit/ ▶ **n.** a celestial body moving in an elliptical orbit around a star. ■ (**the planet**) the earth: *no generation has the right to pollute the planet*. ■ chiefly Astrology & historical a celestial body distinguished from the fixed stars by having an apparent motion of its own (including the moon and sun), esp. with reference to its supposed influence on people and events.

The planets of the solar system are either gas giants—Jupiter, Saturn, Uranus, and Neptune—or smaller rocky bodies—Mercury, Venus, Earth, and Mars. Pluto, formerly regarded as the ninth planet, was in 2006 reclassified as a dwarf planet. The minor planets, or asteroids, orbit mainly between the orbits of Mars and Jupiter. Only Earth and Venus have substantial atmospheres.

– DERIVATIVES **plan·e·tol·o·gy** /,planiˈtäləjē/ **n.**
– ORIGIN Middle English: from Old French *planete*, from late Latin *planeta, planetes*, from Greek *planētēs* 'wanderer, planet,' from *planan* 'wander.'

plane ta·ble ▶ **n.** a surveying instrument used for direct plotting in the field, with a drawing board and pivoted alidade.

plan·e·tar·i·um /,planiˈte(ə)rēəm/ ▶ **n.** (pl. **planetariums** or **planetaria** /-ˈte(ə)rēə/) **1** a building in which images of stars, planets, and constellations are projected on the inner surface of a dome for public entertainment or education. ■ a device used to project such images.
2 another term for **ORRERY**.
– ORIGIN mid 18th cent.: modern Latin, from Latin *planetarius* 'relating to the planets.'

plan·e·tar·y /ˈplani,terē/ ▶ **adj.** of, relating to, or belonging to a planet or planets: *the laws of planetary motion*. ■ of or relating to the earth as a planet: *planetary air pollution and climatic change*.
– ORIGIN late 16th cent.: from late Latin *planetarius* 'relating to the planets' (recorded only as a noun meaning 'astrologer'), from *planeta* 'planet.'

plan·e·tar·y gear (also **planetary wheel**) ▶ **n.** see **SUN-AND-PLANET GEAR**.

plan·e·tar·y neb·u·la ▶ **n.** Astronomy a ring-shaped nebula formed by an expanding shell of gas around an aging star.

plan·e·tes·i·mal /,planiˈtesəməl/ Astronomy ▶ **n.** a minute planet; a body that could or did come together with many others under gravitation to form a planet.
▶ **adj.** [attrib.] denoting or relating to such bodies.
– ORIGIN early 20th cent.: from **PLANET**, on the pattern of *infinitesimal*.

plan·et·fall /ˈplanit,fôl/ ▶ **n.** (chiefly in science fiction) a landing or arrival on a planet after a journey through space.
– ORIGIN from **PLANET** + *-fall*, on the pattern of **LANDFALL**.

plan·et·oid /ˈplani,toid/ ▶ **n.** another term for **ASTEROID**.

plan·form /ˈplan,fôrm/ ▶ **n.** the shape or outline of an aircraft wing as projected onto a horizontal plane.

plan·gent /ˈplanjənt/ ▶ **adj.** chiefly literary (of a sound) loud, reverberating, and often melancholy.
– DERIVATIVES **plan·gen·cy** **n.**, **plan·gent·ly** **adv.**
– ORIGIN early 19th cent.: from Latin *plangent-* 'lamenting,' from the verb *plangere*.

pla·nig·ra·phy /pləˈnigrəfē/ ▶ **n.** Medicine the process of obtaining a visual representation of a plane section through living tissue, by such techniques as tomography, ultrasonography, etc.
– ORIGIN 1930s: from Dutch *planigraphie*, from Latin *planus* 'flat, level' + Greek *-graphia* (see **-GRAPHY**).

pla·nim·e·ter /pləˈnimitər/ ▶ **n.** an instrument for mechanically measuring the area of a plane figure.
– DERIVATIVES **plan·i·met·ric** /,plānəˈmetrik/ **adj.**, **plan·i·met·ri·cal·ly** /-ˈmetrik(ə)lē/ **adv.**, **pla·nim·e·try** /-ˈnimətrē/ **n.**
– ORIGIN mid 19th cent.: from French *planimètre*, from Latin *planus* 'level' + *-mètre* '(instrument) measuring.'

plan·ish /ˈplanisH/ ▶ **v.** [with obj.] flatten (sheet metal) with a smooth-faced hammer or between rollers.
– DERIVATIVES **plan·ish·er** **n.**

PRONUNCIATION KEY ə *ago, up*; ər *over, fur*; a *hat*; ā *ate*; ä *car*; e *let*; ē *see*; i *fit*; ī *by*; NG *sing*; ō *go*; ô *law, for*; oi *toy*; o͝o *good*; o͞o *goo*; ou *out*; TH *thin*; T̲H̲ *then*; ZH *vision*

P

– ORIGIN late Middle English (in the sense 'make level'): from obsolete French *planiss-*, lengthened stem of *planir* 'to smooth,' from *plain* 'smooth, level.'

plan·i·sphere /'planə,sfi(ə)r/ ▶ **n.** a map formed by the projection of a sphere or part of a sphere on a plane, esp. an adjustable circular star map that shows the appearance of the heavens at a specific time and place.
– DERIVATIVES **plan·i·spher·ic** /,planə'sfi(ə)rik, -'sfer-/ **adj.**
– ORIGIN late Middle English *planisperie*, from medieval Latin *planisphaerium*, from Latin *planus* 'level' + *sphaera* 'sphere'; later influenced by French *planisphère*.

plank /plaNGk/ ▶ **n.** **1** a long, thin, flat piece of timber, used esp. in building and flooring.
2 a fundamental point of a political or other program: *the central plank of the bill is the curb on industrial polluters.*
▶ **v.** [with obj.] **1** make, provide, or cover with planks: *the ship was planked with teak* | (as adj. **planked**) *the planked floor.*
2 informal another term for PLUNK (sense 3 of the verb).
– PHRASES **walk the plank** (formerly) be forced by pirates to walk blindfold along a plank over the side of a ship to one's death in the sea. ■ informal lose one's job or position.
– ORIGIN Middle English: from Old Northern French *planke*, from late Latin *planca* 'board,' feminine (used as a noun) of *plancus* 'flatfooted.'

plank·ing /'plaNGkiNG/ ▶ **n.** planks collectively, esp. when used for flooring or as part of a boat.

plank·ton /'plaNGktən/ ▶ **n.** the small and microscopic organisms drifting or floating in the sea or fresh water, consisting chiefly of diatoms, protozoans, small crustaceans, and the eggs and larval stages of larger animals. Many animals are adapted to feed on plankton, esp. by filtering the water. Compare with NEKTON.
– DERIVATIVES **plank·tic** /-tik/ **adj.**, **plank·ton·ic** /-'tänik/ **adj.**
– ORIGIN late 19th cent.: from German, from Greek *planktos* 'wandering,' from the base of *plazein* 'wander.'

planned e·con·o·my ▶ **n.** another term for COMMAND ECONOMY.

planned ob·so·les·cence /,äbsə'lesəns/ ▶ **n.** a policy of producing consumer goods that rapidly become obsolete and so require replacing, achieved by frequent changes in design, termination of the supply of spare parts, and the use of nondurable materials.

Planned Par·ent·hood ▶ **n.** trademark a nonprofit organization that does research into and gives advice on contraception, family planning, and reproductive problems.

plan·ner /'planər/ ▶ **n.** **1** a person who makes plans. ■ a person who controls or plans urban development: *city planners.*
2 [usu. with modifier] a list or chart with information that is an aid to planning: *my day planner.*

plan·ning /'planiNG/ ▶ **n.** the process of making plans for something. ■ [often as modifier] the control of urban development by a local government authority, from which a license must be obtained to build a new property or change an existing one: *the local planning authority.*

Pla·no /'plānō/ a city in northeastern Texas, northeast of Dallas; pop. 267,480 (est. 2008).

plano- ▶ **comb. form** level; flat: *plano-convex* | *planography.*
– ORIGIN from Latin *planus* 'flat.'

pla·no-con·cave /,plānō,kän'kāv, -'kän,kāv/ ▶ **adj.** (of a lens) with one surface plane and the opposite one concave.

pla·no-con·vex /,plānō,kän'veks, -'kän,veks/ ▶ **adj.** (of a lens) with one surface plane and the opposite one convex.

plan·o·gram /'planə,gram/ ▶ **n.** a diagram or model that indicates the placement of retail products on shelves in order to maximize sales.

pla·no·graph·ic /,plānə'grafik/ ▶ **adj.** Printing relating to or denoting a printing process in which the printing surface is flat, as in lithography.
– DERIVATIVES **pla·nog·ra·phy** /plə'nägrəfē/ **n.**

plant /plant/ ▶ **n.** **1** a living organism of the kind exemplified by trees, shrubs, herbs, grasses, ferns, and mosses, typically growing in a permanent site, absorbing water and inorganic substances through its roots, and synthesizing nutrients in its leaves by photosynthesis using the green pigment chlorophyll. ■ a small organism of this kind, as distinct from a shrub or tree: *garden plants.*

> Plants differ from animals in lacking specialized sense organs, having no capacity for voluntary movement, having cell walls, and growing to suit their surroundings rather than having a fixed body plan.

2 a place where an industrial or manufacturing process takes place: *the company has 30 plants in Mexico.* ■ machinery used in an industrial or manufacturing process: *inadequate investment in new plant.*
3 a person placed in a group as a spy or informer: *we thought he was a CIA plant spreading disinformation.* ■ a thing put among someone's belongings to incriminate or compromise them: *he insisted that the cocaine in the glove compartment was a plant.*
▶ **v.** [with obj.] **1** place (a seed, bulb, or plant) in the ground so that it can grow. ■ place a seed, bulb, or plant in (a place) to grow: *the garden is planted with herbs.* ■ informal bury (someone).
2 place or fix in a specified position: *she planted a kiss on his cheek.* ■ (**plant oneself**) position oneself: *she planted herself on the arm of his chair.* ■ establish (an idea) in someone's mind: *the seed of doubt is planted in his mind.* ■ secretly place (a bomb that is set to go off at a later time). ■ put or hide (something) among someone's belongings to compromise or incriminate the owner: *he planted drugs on him to extort a bribe.* ■ send (someone) to join a group or organization to act as a spy or informer. ■ found or establish (a colony, city, or community). ■ deposit (young fish, spawn, oysters, etc.) in a river or lake.
– PHRASES **have** (or **keep**) **one's feet firmly planted on the ground** be (or remain) levelheaded and sensible.
– DERIVATIVES **plant·a·ble adj.**, **plant·let** /-lit/ **n.**, **plant·like** /-,līk/ **adj.**
– ORIGIN Old English *plante* 'seedling,' *plantian* (verb), from Latin *planta* 'sprout, cutting' (later influenced by French *plante*) and *plantare* 'plant, fix in a place.'

Plan·tag·e·net /plan'tajənit/ ▶ **adj.** of or relating to the English royal dynasty that held the throne from the accession of Henry II in 1154 until the death of Richard III in 1485.
▶ **n.** a member of this dynasty.
– ORIGIN from Latin *planta genista* 'sprig of broom,' said to be worn as a crest by and given as a nickname to Geoffrey, count of Anjou, the father of Henry II.

plan·tain[1] /'plantən/ ▶ **n.** a low-growing plant that typically has a rosette of leaves and a slender green flower spike, widely growing as a weed in lawns. ● Genus *Plantago*, family Plantaginaceae: many species.
– ORIGIN late Middle English: from Old French, from Latin *plantago, plantagin-*, from *planta* 'sole of the foot' (because of its broad prostrate leaves).

plan·tain[2] ▶ **n.** **1** a banana containing high levels of starch and little sugar, harvested green and widely used as a cooked vegetable in the tropics.
2 the plant that bears this fruit. ● *Musa* × *paradisiaca*, family Musaceae.
– ORIGIN mid 16th cent.: from Spanish *plá(n)tano*, probably by assimilation of a South American word to the Spanish *plá(n)tano* 'plane tree.'

plan·tain lil·y ▶ **n.** another term for HOSTA.

plan·tar /'plantər/ ▶ **adj.** Anatomy of or relating to the sole of the foot.
– ORIGIN early 18th cent.: from Latin *plantaris*, from *planta* 'sole.'

Plan·ta·tion /plan'tāSHən/ a city in southeastern Florida, west of Fort Lauderdale; pop. 83,628 (est. 2008).

plan·ta·tion /plan'tāSHən/ ▶ **n.** [often with modifier] an estate on which crops such as coffee, sugar, and tobacco are cultivated by resident labor. ■ an area in which trees have been planted, esp. for commercial purposes. ■ historical a colony.
– ORIGIN late Middle English (denoting the action of planting seeds): from Latin *plantatio(n-)*, from the verb *plantare* 'to plant.'

plant·er /'plantər/ ▶ **n.** **1** [often with modifier] a manager or owner of a plantation: *sugar planters.*
2 a decorative container in which plants are grown.
3 a machine or person that plants seeds, bulbs, etc.

plant·er's punch ▶ **n.** a cocktail containing rum, lime juice, carbonated water, and sugar.

plant hop·per ▶ **n.** a small, widely distributed plant-sucking bug that leaps when disturbed. Some species are pests of rice and sugar cane. ● Delphacidae and other families, suborder Homoptera.

plan·ti·grade /'planti,grād/ ▶ **adj.** (of a mammal) walking on the soles of the feet, like a human or a bear. Compare with DIGITIGRADE.
– ORIGIN mid 19th cent.: from French, from modern Latin *plantigradus*, from Latin *planta* 'sole' + *-gradus* '-walking.'

plant louse ▶ **n.** a small bug that infests plants and feeds on the sap or tender shoots, esp. an aphid. ● Several families in the series Sternorrhyncha, suborder Homoptera.

plan·toc·ra·cy /plan'täkrəsē/ ▶ **n.** (pl. **plantocracies**) a population of planters regarded as the dominant class, esp. in the West Indies.

plants·man /'plantsmən/ ▶ **n.** (pl. **plantsmen**) an expert in garden plants and gardening.

plants·wom·an /'plantswŏmən/ ▶ **n.** (pl. **plantswomen**) a female expert in garden plants and gardening.

plan·u·la /'planyələ/ ▶ **n.** (pl. **planulae** /-,lē/) Zoology a free-swimming coelenterate larva with a flattened, ciliated, solid body.
– ORIGIN late 19th cent.: modern Latin, diminutive of Latin *planus* 'plane, flat.'

plan view ▶ **n.** a view of an object as projected onto a horizontal plane.

plaque /plak/ ▶ **n.** **1** an ornamental tablet, typically of metal, porcelain, or wood, that is fixed to a wall or other surface in commemoration of a person or event.
2 a sticky deposit on teeth in which bacteria proliferate.
3 Medicine a small, distinct, typically raised patch or region resulting from local damage or deposition of material, such as a fatty deposit on an artery wall in atherosclerosis or a site of localized damage of brain tissue in Alzheimer's disease. ■ Microbiology a clear area in a cell culture caused by the inhibition of growth or destruction of cells by an agent such as a virus.
– ORIGIN mid 19th cent.: from French, from Dutch *plak* 'tablet,' from *plakken* 'to stick.'

plash[1] /plaSH/ literary ▶ **n.** [in sing.] a sound produced by liquid striking something or being struck. ■ a pool or puddle.
▶ **v.** [no obj.] splash: *gray curtains of rain plashed down.* ■ [with obj.] strike the surface of (water) with a splashing sound.
– DERIVATIVES **plash·y adj.**
– ORIGIN early 16th cent.: probably imitative.

plash[2] ▶ **v.** [with obj.] archaic bend and interweave (branches and twigs) to form a hedge. ■ make or renew (a hedge) in this way.
– ORIGIN late 15th cent.: from Old French *plaissier*, based on Latin *plectere* 'to plait.' Compare with PLEACH.

plas·ma /'plazmə/ (also **plasm** /'plazəm/) ▶ **n.** **1** the colorless fluid part of blood, lymph, or milk, in which corpuscles or fat globules are suspended. ■ this substance taken from donors or donated blood for administering in transfusions.
2 an ionized gas consisting of positive ions and free electrons in proportions resulting in more or less no overall electric charge, typically at low pressures (as in the upper atmosphere and in fluorescent lamps) or at very high temperatures (as in stars and nuclear fusion reactors). ■ an analogous substance consisting of mobile charged particles (such as a molten salt or the electrons within a metal).
3 a dark green, translucent variety of quartz used in mosaic and for other decorative purposes.
4 another term for CYTOPLASM or PROTOPLASM.
– DERIVATIVES **plas·mat·ic** /plaz'matik/ **adj.**, **plas·mic** /-mik/ **adj.**
– ORIGIN early 18th cent. (in the sense 'mold, shape'): from late Latin, literally 'mold,' from Greek *plasma*, from *plassein* 'to shape.'

plas·ma cell ▶ **n.** Physiology a fully differentiated B cell that produces a single type of antibody.

plas·ma·lem·ma /,plazmə'lemə/ ▶ **n.** Biology a plasma membrane that bounds a cell, esp. one immediately within the wall of a plant cell.
– DERIVATIVES **plas·ma·lem·mal** /-'leməl/ **adj.**
– ORIGIN 1920s: from PLASMA + Greek *lemma* 'rind.'

plas·ma mem·brane ▶ **n.** Biology a microscopic membrane of lipids and proteins that forms the external boundary of the cytoplasm of a cell or encloses a vacuole, and that regulates the passage of molecules in and out of the cytoplasm.

plas·ma·pause /'plazmə,pôz/ ▶ **n.** Astronomy the outer limit of a plasmasphere, marked by a sudden change in plasma density.

plas·ma·pher·e·sis /,plazməfə'rēsis/ ▶ **n.** Medicine a method of removing blood plasma from the body by withdrawing blood, separating it into plasma and cells, and transfusing the cells back into the bloodstream. It is performed esp. to remove antibodies in treating autoimmune conditions.
– ORIGIN 1920s: from PLASMA + Greek *aphairesis* 'taking away' (from *apo-* 'from' + *hairein* 'take').

plas·ma screen ▶ **n.** a flat display screen using an array of cells containing a gas plasma to produce different colors in each cell.

plas·ma sheet ▶ **n.** Astronomy a layer of plasma in the magnetotail of the earth (or another planet), lying in the equatorial plane beyond the plasmapause, with two divergent branches that reach the earth at polar latitudes.

plas·ma·sphere /ˈplazməˌsfir/ ▸ **n.** Astronomy the roughly toroidal region surrounding and thought to rotate with the earth (or another planet) at latitudes away from the poles, containing a relatively dense plasma of low-energy electrons and protons.

plas·mid /ˈplazmid/ ▸ **n.** Biology a genetic structure in a cell that can replicate independently of the chromosomes, typically a small circular DNA strand in the cytoplasm of a bacterium or protozoan. Plasmids are much used in the laboratory manipulation of genes. Compare with **EPISOME**.
– ORIGIN 1950s: from **PLASMA** + **-ID²**.

plas·min /ˈplazmin/ ▸ **n.** Biochemistry an enzyme, formed in the blood in some circumstances, that destroys blood clots by attacking fibrin.
– ORIGIN mid 19th cent.: from French *plasmine*, from late Latin *plasma* 'mold, image.'

plas·min·o·gen /plazˈminəˌjen/ ▸ **n.** Biochemistry the inactive precursor of the enzyme plasmin, present in blood.

plas·mo·des·ma /ˌplazməˈdesmə/ ▸ **n.** (pl. **plasmodesmata** /-ˈdesmətə/) Botany a narrow thread of cytoplasm that passes through the cell walls of adjacent plant cells and allows communication between them.
– ORIGIN early 20th cent.: from German *Plasmodesma*, from late Latin *plasma* 'mold, formation' + Greek *desma* 'bond, fetter.'

plas·mo·di·um /plazˈmōdēəm/ ▸ **n.** (pl. **plasmodia** /-dēə/) **1** a parasitic protozoan of a genus that includes those causing malaria. ● Genus *Plasmodium*, phylum Sporozoa.
2 Biology a form within the life cycle of some simple organisms such as slime molds, typically consisting of a mass of naked protoplasm containing many nuclei.
– DERIVATIVES **plas·mo·di·al** /-mōdēəl/ **adj.**
– ORIGIN late 19th cent.: modern Latin, based on late Latin *plasma* 'mold, formation.'

plas·mol·y·sis /plazˈmäləsis/ ▸ **n.** Botany contraction of the protoplast of a plant cell as a result of loss of water from the cell.
– ORIGIN late 19th cent.: modern Latin, from *plasmo-* 'consisting of protoplasm' (from late Latin *plasma* 'mold, formation') + Greek *lusis* 'loosening' (because of the separation of the plasma membrane from the cell wall).

plas·mo·lyze /ˈplazməˌlīz/ (Brit. **plasmolyse**) ▸ **v.** [with obj.] Botany subject to plasmolysis.

plas·mon /ˈplazˌmän/ ▸ **n.** Physics a quantum or quasiparticle associated with a local collective oscillation of charge density.
– ORIGIN 1950s: from **PLASMA** + **-ON**.

pla·steel /ˈplaˌstēl/ ▸ **n.** (in science fiction) an ultrastrong nonmetallic material.
– ORIGIN 1970s: blend of **PLASTIC** and **STEEL**.

plas·ter /ˈplastər/ ▸ **n. 1** a soft mixture of lime with sand or cement and water for spreading on walls, ceilings, or other structures to form a smooth hard surface when dried. ■ (also **plaster of Paris**) a hard white substance made by the addition of water to powdered and partly dehydrated gypsum, used for holding broken bones in place and making sculptures and casts. [so called because prepared from the gypsum of Paris, France.] ■ the powder from which such a substance is made.
2 dated a bandage on which a poultice or liniment is spread for application. See **MUSTARD PLASTER**. ■ (also **sticking plaster**) Brit. an adhesive strip of material for covering cuts and wounds.
▸ **v.** [with obj.] cover (a wall, ceiling, or other structure) with plaster. ■ (**plaster something with/in**) coat or cover something with (a substance), esp. to an extent considered excessive: *a face plastered in heavy makeup.* ■ make (hair) lie flat by applying a liquid to it: *his hair was plastered down with water.* ■ apply a plaster cast or medical plaster to (a part of the body). ■ (**plaster something with**) cover a surface with (large numbers of pictures or posters): *the store windows are plastered with posters.* ■ (**plaster something over**) present a story or picture conspicuously and sensationally in (a newspaper or magazine): *her story was plastered all over the December issue.* ■ informal, dated bomb or shell (a target) heavily.
– DERIVATIVES **plas·ter·y** **adj.**
– ORIGIN Old English, denoting a bandage spread with a curative substance, from medieval Latin *plastrum* (shortening of Latin *emplastrum*, from Greek *emplastron* 'daub, salve'), later reinforced by the Old French noun *plastre*. Sense 1 dates from late Middle English.

plas·ter·board /ˈplastərˌbôrd/ ▸ **n.** a type of drywall made of plaster between two sheets of heavy paper.

plas·ter cast ▸ **n.** see **CAST¹** (sense 1 of the noun).

plas·tered /ˈplastərd/ ▸ **adj. 1** informal very drunk: *I went out and got totally plastered.*
2 covered with or made of plaster.

plas·ter·er /ˈplastərər/ ▸ **n.** a person whose job it is to apply plaster to walls, ceilings, or other surfaces.

plas·ter saint ▸ **n.** a person who makes a show of being without moral faults or human weakness, esp. in a hypocritical way.

plas·ter·work /ˈplastərˌwərk/ ▸ **n.** plaster as part of the interior of a building, esp. covering the surface of a wall or formed into decorative shapes and patterns.

plas·tic /ˈplastik/ ▸ **n.** a synthetic material made from a wide range of organic polymers such as polyethylene, PVC, nylon, etc., that can be molded into shape while soft and then set into a rigid or slightly elastic form. ■ informal credit cards or other types of plastic card that can be used as money: *he pays with cash instead of with plastic.*
▸ **adj. 1** made of plastic: *plastic bags.* ■ looking or tasting artificial: *long-distance flights with their plastic food | she smiled a little plastic smile.*
2 (of substances or materials) easily shaped or molded: *rendering the material more plastic.* ■ (in art) of or relating to molding or modeling in three dimensions, or producing three-dimensional effects. ■ (in science and technology) of or relating to the permanent deformation of a solid without fracture by the temporary application of force. ■ offering scope for creativity: *the writer is drawn to words as a plastic medium.* ■ Biology exhibiting adaptability to change or variety in the environment.
– DERIVATIVES **plas·ti·cal·ly** /-(ə)lē/ **adv.**
– ORIGIN mid 17th cent. (in the sense 'characteristic of molding'): from French *plastique* or Latin *plasticus*, from Greek *plastikos*, from *plassein* 'to mold.'

plas·tic arts ▸ **plural n.** art forms that involve modeling or molding, such as sculpture and ceramics, or art involving the representation of solid objects with three-dimensional effects.

plas·tic bomb ▸ **n.** a bomb containing plastic explosive.

plas·tic ex·plo·sive ▸ **n.** a puttylike explosive capable of being molded by hand.

plas·ti·cine /ˈplastəˌsēn/ (also **Plasticine**) ▸ **n.** trademark a soft modeling material, used esp. by children.
– ORIGIN late 19th cent.: from the adjective **PLASTIC** + **-INE⁴**.

plas·tic·i·ty /plaˈstisitē/ ▸ **n.** the quality of being easily shaped or molded. ■ Biology the adaptability of an organism to changes in its environment or differences between its various habitats.

plas·ti·cize /ˈplastəˌsīz/ ▸ **v.** [with obj.] (often as adj. **plasticized**) make plastic or moldable, esp. by the addition of a plasticizer. ■ treat or make with plastic: *plasticized cotton.*
– DERIVATIVES **plas·ti·ci·za·tion** /ˌplastəsiˈzāsʜən/ **n.**

plas·ti·ciz·er /ˈplastəˌsīzər/ ▸ **n.** a substance (typically a solvent) added to a synthetic resin to produce or promote plasticity and flexibility and to reduce brittleness.

plas·tick·y /ˈplastikē/ ▸ **adj.** suggestive of or resembling plastic: *Bosworth is all too obviously a product of plasticky LA.*

plas·tic sur·ger·y ▸ **n.** the process of reconstructing or repairing parts of the body, esp. by the transfer of tissue, either in the treatment of injury or for cosmetic reasons.
– DERIVATIVES **plas·tic sur·geon** **n.**
– ORIGIN from **PLASTIC** in the sense of being possible to (re-)shape. Compare with **-PLASTY**.

plas·tic wood ▸ **n.** a moldable material that hardens to resemble wood and is used for filling cracks in wood.

plas·tic wrap ▸ **n.** a thin, transparent plastic film that adheres to surfaces and to itself, used chiefly as a wrapping or covering for food.

plas·tid /ˈplastid/ ▸ **n.** Botany any of a class of small organelles, such as chloroplasts, in the cytoplasm of plant cells, containing pigment or food.
– ORIGIN late 19th cent.: from German, based on Greek *plastos* 'shaped.'

plas·ti·na·tion /ˌplastəˈnāsʜən/ ▸ **n.** the preservation of body parts through a process that replaces water and fat with various enduring plastics.
– DERIVATIVES **plas·ti·nate** **v.**

plas·tique /plaˈstēk/ ▸ **n.** plastic explosive.
– ORIGIN mid 20th cent.: French, literally 'plastic' (adjective used as a noun).

plas·ti·sol /ˈplastəˌsôl, -ˌsäl/ ▸ **n.** a liquid substance that can be converted into a solid plastic simply by heating, consisting of particles of synthetic resin dispersed in a nonvolatile liquid.
– ORIGIN 1940s: from the noun **PLASTIC** + **SOL²**.

plas·tron /ˈplastrən/ ▸ **n. 1** a large pad worn by a fencer to protect the chest. ■ historical a lancer's breast covering.
2 an ornamental front of a woman's bodice or shirt consisting of colorful material with lace or embroidery, fashionable in the late 19th century. ■ a man's starched shirtfront without pleats.
3 Zoology the part of a tortoise's or turtle's shell forming the underside. ■ a similar ventral plate in some invertebrate animals. ■ Entomology (in an aquatic insect) a patch of cuticle covered with hairs that retain a thin layer of air, acting like a gill for breathing under water.
– DERIVATIVES **plas·tral** /ˈplastrəl/ **adj.**
– ORIGIN early 16th cent.: from French, from Italian *piastrone*, augmentative of *piastra* 'breastplate,' from Latin *emplastrum* 'medical dressing' (see **PLASTER**).

-plasty ▸ **comb. form** molding, grafting, or formation of a specified part, esp. a part of the body: *rhinoplasty.*
– ORIGIN based on Greek *plastos* 'formed, molded.' Compare with **PLASTIC SURGERY**.

plat¹ /plat/ ▸ **n.** a plot of land. ■ a map or plan of an area of land showing actual or proposed features.
▸ **v.** (**plats, platting, platted**) [with obj.] plan out or make a map of (an area of land, esp. a proposed site for construction).
– ORIGIN late Middle English: variant of the noun **PLOT** in the sense 'piece of ground.' The current verb sense dates from the early 18th cent.

plat² ▸ **n. & v.** variant spelling of **PLAIT**.

plat. ▸ **abbr.** ■ plateau. ■ platoon.

Pla·tae·a, Battle of /pləˈtēə/ a battle in 479 BC, during the Persian Wars, in which the Persian forces were defeated by the Greeks near the city of Plataea in Boeotia.

plat du jour /ˌplä də ˈzʜo͝or/ ▸ **n.** (pl. **plats du jour** pronunc. **same**) a dish specially prepared by a restaurant on a particular day, in addition to the usual menu.
– ORIGIN French, literally 'dish of the day.'

plate /plāt/ ▸ **n. 1** a flat dish, typically circular and made of china, from which food is eaten or served. ■ an amount of food on such a dish: *a plate of spaghetti.* ■ a flat dish, typically made of metal or wood, passed around a church congregation in order to collect donations of money. ■ a course of a meal, served on one plate: *I'll have the salad plate.* ■ Biology a shallow glass dish on which a culture of cells or microorganisms may be grown. ■ dishes, bowls, cups, and other utensils made of gold, silver, or other metal. [from Old French *vaisselle en plate* 'dishes and plates made of a single piece of metal.'] ■ a silver or gold dish or trophy awarded as a prize in a race or competition: *she lifted the plate in victory.* ■ [in names] Brit. a race or competition in which such a prize is awarded: *the final of the Ladies' Plate at Henley.*
2 a thin, flat sheet or strip of metal or other material, typically one used to join or strengthen things or forming part of a machine: *he underwent surgery to have a steel plate put into his leg.* ■ a small, flat piece of metal or other material bearing a name or inscription and attached to a door or other object: *a brass plate with her initials.* ■ (usu. **plates**) short for **LICENSE PLATE**: *the car had Vermont plates.* ■ Botany & Zoology a thin, flat organic structure or formation: *the fused bony plates protect the tortoise's soft parts.* ■ Geology each of the several rigid pieces of the earth's lithosphere that together make up the earth's surface. See also **PLATE TECTONICS**. ■ Baseball short for **HOME PLATE**. ■ a piece of lumber laid horizontally along the top of a wall to support the ends of joists or rafters. ■ a light horseshoe for a racehorse.
3 a sheet of metal, plastic, or some other material bearing an image of type or illustrations from which multiple copies are printed. ■ a printed photograph, picture, or illustration, esp. one on superior-quality paper in a book. ■ a thin sheet of metal, glass, or other substance coated with a light-sensitive film on which an image is formed, used in larger or older types of cameras.
4 a thin piece of plastic molded to the shape of a person's mouth and gums, to which artificial teeth or another orthodontic appliance are attached. ■ informal a complete denture or orthodontic appliance.
5 a thin piece of metal that acts as an electrode in a capacitor, battery, or cell. ■ the anode of a thermionic tube.
▸ **v.** [with obj.] **1** cover (a metal object) with a thin coating or film of a different metal: *she had already taken the coin to a jeweler to be plated* | [as adj., in

P

combination] (**-plated**) *the cylinder is nickel-plated.* ■ cover (an object) with plates of metal for decoration, protection, or strength.
2 serve or arrange (food) on a plate or plates before a meal: *overcooked vegetables won't look appetizing, no matter how they are plated.*
3 Baseball score (a run or runs); cause (someone) to score.
4 Biology inoculate (cells or infective material) onto a culture plate, esp. with the object of isolating a particular strain of microorganisms or estimating viable cell numbers.
– PHRASES **on one's plate** occupying one's time or energy: *you've got a lot on your plate at the moment.*
– DERIVATIVES **plate·ful** /-ˌfo͝ol/ n. (pl. **platefuls**), **plate·less** adj., **plat·er** /ˈplātər/ n.
– ORIGIN Middle English (denoting a flat, thin sheet, usually of metal): from Old French, from medieval Latin *plata* 'plate armor,' based on Greek *platus* 'flat.' Sense 1 of the noun represents Old French *plat* 'platter, large dish,' also 'dish of meat,' noun use of Old French *plat* 'flat.'

plate ap·pear·ance ▶ n. Baseball a player's turn at the plate, the total of which for any player includes all official at bats plus appearances that resulted in a walk, sacrifice, etc. Compare with AT-BAT.

plate ar·mor ▶ n. protective armor of metal plates, esp. as worn in medieval times by mounted knights.

pla·teau /plaˈtō/ ▶ n. (pl. **plateaus** or **plateaux** /-ˈtōz/) **1** an area of relatively level high ground. ■ [as modifier] denoting a group of American Indian peoples of the plateau country of western Canada and the US, including the Nez Percé.
2 a state of little or no change following a period of activity or progress: *the peace process had reached a plateau.*
▶ v. (**plateaus**, **plateauing**, **plateaued**) [no obj.] reach a state of little or no change after a time of activity or progress: *the industry's problems have* ***plateaued out.***
– ORIGIN late 18th cent.: from French, from Old French *platel*, diminutive of *plat* 'level.'

plate glass ▶ n. (often as modifier **plate-glass**) thick fine-quality glass, typically used for doors and store windows and originally cast in plates.

plate·let /ˈplāt-lit/ ▶ n. Physiology a small colorless disk-shaped cell fragment without a nucleus, found in large numbers in blood and involved in clotting. Also called THROMBOCYTE.

plate·mak·er /ˈplātˌmākər/ ▶ n. a person or machine that makes printing plates.

plat·en /ˈplatn/ ▶ n. **1** the plate in a small letterpress printing press that presses the paper against the type.
2 the cylindrical roller in a typewriter against which the paper is held.
– ORIGIN late 16th cent.: from French *platine* 'flat piece,' from *plat* 'flat.'

plat·er·esque /ˌplatəˈresk/ ▶ adj. (esp. of Spanish architecture) richly ornamented in a low-relief style suggesting silver work.
– ORIGIN late 19th cent.: from Spanish *plateresco*, from *platero* 'silversmith,' from *plata* 'silver.'

Plate Riv·er /plāt/ a wide estuary on the Atlantic coast of South America at the border between Argentina and Uruguay that is formed by the confluence of the Paraná and Uruguay rivers. The cities of Buenos Aires and Montevideo lie on its shores. In 1939, it was the scene of a naval battle in which the British defeated the Germans. Spanish name RÍO DE LA PLATA.
– ORIGIN *Plate* from Spanish *plata* 'silver,' exported from the region in the Spanish colonial period.

plate tec·ton·ics ▶ plural n. [treated as sing.] a theory explaining the structure of the earth's crust and many associated phenomena as resulting from the interaction of rigid lithospheric plates that move slowly over the underlying mantle.
– DERIVATIVES **plate-tec·ton·ic** adj.

plat·form /ˈplatfôrm/ ▶ n. **1** a raised level surface on which people or things can stand: *there are viewing platforms where visitors may gape at the chasm.* ■ a raised floor or stage used by public speakers or performers so that they can be seen by their audience: *earning her living on the concert platform.* ■ a raised structure along the side of a railroad track where passengers get on and off trains at a station. ■ a raised structure standing in the sea from which oil or gas wells can be drilled or regulated. ■ [usu. with modifier] a raised structure or orbiting satellite from which rockets or missiles may be launched. ■ a standard for the hardware of a computer system, determining what kinds of software it can run.
2 [usu. in sing.] the declared policy of a political party or group: *seeking election on a platform of low taxes.* ■ an opportunity to voice one's views or initiate action: *the forum will provide a platform for discussion of communication issues.*
3 (**platforms**) shoes with very thick soles: *chunky platforms* | [as modifier] *yellow platform shoes.*
– ORIGIN mid 16th cent.: from French *plateforme* 'ground plan,' literally 'flat shape.'

plat·form bed ▶ n. a bed consisting of a mattress supported by a platform, which sometimes contains drawers for storage.

plat·form game ▶ n. a type of video game featuring two-dimensional graphics in which the player controls a character jumping or climbing between solid platforms at different positions on the screen.

Plath /plaTH/, Sylvia (1932–63), US poet; wife of Ted Hughes. Her life was marked by periods of severe depression, and her work is notable for its treatment of extreme and painful states of mind. In 1963, she committed suicide. Notable works: *Ariel* (1965) and *The Bell Jar* (1963).

plat·ing /ˈplātiNG/ ▶ n. **1** a thin coating of gold, silver, or other metal. ■ the process of applying such a layer.
2 an outer covering of broad, flattish sections, typically of metal: *the tractors carried steel plating for protection.*
3 the process of knitting two yarns together so that each yarn appears mainly on one side of the finished piece.

plat·i·nize /ˈplatnˌīz/ ▶ v. [with obj.] (usu. as adj. **platinized**) coat (something) with platinum.
– DERIVATIVES **plat·i·ni·za·tion** /ˌplatn-iˈzāSHən/ n.

plat·i·noid /ˈplatnˌoid/ ▶ n. an alloy of copper with zinc, nickel, and sometimes tungsten, used for its high electrical resistance.

plat·i·num /ˈplatn-əm/ ▶ n. a precious silvery-white metal, the chemical element of atomic number 78. It was first encountered by the Spanish in South America in the 16th century and is used in jewelry, electrical contacts, laboratory equipment, and industrial catalysts. (Symbol: **Pt**) ■ [often as modifier] the grayish-white or silvery color of platinum: *a platinum wig.*
– PHRASES **go platinum** (of a recording) achieve sales meriting a platinum disk.
– ORIGIN early 19th cent.: alteration of earlier *platina*, from Spanish, diminutive of *plata* 'silver.'

plat·i·num black ▶ n. platinum in the form of a finely divided black powder, used as a catalyst and absorbent for gases.

plat·i·num blonde ▶ n. a person with silvery-blond hair.
▶ adj. (of hair) silvery blond.

plat·i·num card (also trademark **Platinum Card**) ▶ n. a credit card made available to individuals with high credit ratings, which carries certain privileges that are unavailable to holders of other cards.

plat·i·num disk ▶ n. a framed disk of platinum awarded to a recording artist or group for sales of a recording exceeding one million copies (for albums) or two million copies (for singles).

plat·i·num met·als ▶ plural n. Chemistry the six metals platinum, palladium, ruthenium, osmium, rhodium, and iridium, which have similar properties and tend to occur together in nature.

plat·i·tude /ˈplatiˌt(y)o͞od/ ▶ n. a remark or statement, esp. one with a moral content, that has been used too often to be interesting or thoughtful: *she began uttering liberal platitudes.*
– DERIVATIVES **plat·i·tu·di·nize** /ˌplatiˈt(y)o͞odnˌīz/ v.
– ORIGIN early 19th cent.: from French, from *plat* 'flat.'

plat·i·tu·di·nous /ˌplatiˈt(y)o͞odn-əs/ ▶ adj. (of a remark or statement) used too often to be interesting or thoughtful; hackneyed: *this may sound platitudinous.*

Pla·to /ˈplātō/ (*c.*429–*c.*347 BC), Greek philosopher. A disciple of Socrates and the teacher of Aristotle, he founded the Academy in Athens. His theory of "ideas" or "forms" contrasts abstract entities or **universals** with their objects or **particulars** in the material world. His philosophical writings are presented in the form of dialogues, and his political theories appear in the *Republic*.

Pla·ton·ic /pləˈtänik/ ▶ adj. of or associated with the Greek philosopher Plato or his ideas. ■ (**platonic**) (of love or friendship) intimate and affectionate but not sexual: *their relationship is purely platonic.* ■ (**platonic**) confined to words, theories, or ideals, and not leading to practical action.
– DERIVATIVES **pla·ton·i·cal·ly** /-(ə)lē/ adv.
– ORIGIN mid 16th cent.: via Latin from Greek *Platōnikos*, from *Platōn* 'Plato.'

Pla·ton·ic sol·id ▶ n. one of five regular solids (a tetrahedron, cube, octahedron, dodecahedron, or icosahedron).

Pla·to·nism /ˈplātnˌizəm/ ▶ n. the philosophy of Plato or his followers. See PLATO. ■ any of various revivals of Platonic doctrines or related ideas, esp. Neoplatonism and Cambridge Platonism (a 17th-century attempt to reconcile Christianity with humanism and science). ■ the theory that numbers or other abstract objects are objective, timeless entities, independent of the physical world and of the symbols used to represent them.
– DERIVATIVES **Pla·to·nist** n.

pla·toon /pləˈto͞on/ ▶ n. a subdivision of a company of soldiers, usually forming a tactical unit that is commanded by a lieutenant and divided into several sections. ■ a group of people acting together: *platoons of sharp lawyers.* ■ (in baseball and other sports) a pairing of two or more teammates who play the same position at different times: *in 1982 the Orioles employed a productive left-field platoon of Lowenstein, Ayala, and Roenicke.*
▶ v. [with obj.] (in baseball and other sports) have (an athlete) play in rotation with one or more teammates at the same position: *he was underrated because of Stengel's platooning him with Woodling.* ■ [no obj.] play a sport in this way: *Polonia mostly platooned in his three years with the A's.*
– ORIGIN mid 17th cent.: from French *peloton* 'platoon,' literally 'small ball,' diminutive of *pelote*.

pla·toon ser·geant ▶ n. a noncommissioned officer in the US Army intermediate in rank between a staff sergeant and a first sergeant.

Platt·deutsch /ˈplätˌdoiCH/ ▶ n. & adj. another term for LOW GERMAN.
– ORIGIN German, from Dutch *Platduits*, from *plat* 'flat, low' + *Duits* 'German.'

plat·ter /ˈplatər/ ▶ n. **1** a large flat dish or plate, typically oval or circular in shape, used for serving food. ■ a quantity of food served on such a dish: *huge platters of cold cuts.* ■ a meal or selection of food placed on a platter, esp. one served in a restaurant: *I'll have the seafood platter.*
2 something shaped like such a dish or plate, esp. of a circular shape, in particular: ■ informal, dated a phonograph record. ■ the rotating metal disk forming the turntable of a record player. ■ Computing a rigid rotating disk on which data is stored in a disk drive; a hard disk (considered as a physical object).
– PHRASES **on a (silver) platter** informal used to indicate that someone receives or achieves something with little or no effort: *you're being offered this opportunity on a silver platter.*
– ORIGIN Middle English: from Anglo-Norman French *plater*, from *plat* 'large dish' (see PLATE).

Platte Riv·er /plat/ a river in southwestern Nebraska that is formed by the North Platte and South Platte rivers and flows for 310 miles (500 km) to join the Missouri River near Omaha.

Platts·burgh /ˈplatsˌbərg/ a city in northeastern New York, on Lake Champlain, the site of battles during the 18th and 19th centuries; pop. 19,393 (est. 2008).

platy- ▶ comb. form broad; flat: *platypus.*
– ORIGIN from Greek *platus* 'broad, flat.'

plat·y·fish /ˈplatēˌfiSH/ ▶ n. (pl. **same** or **platyfishes**) a small livebearing freshwater fish of Mexico and Central America, popular in aquariums. ● Genus *Xiphophorus*, family Poeciliidae: several species, in particular *X. maculatus*, which has been bred in a wide variety of colors.
– ORIGIN early 20th cent.: colloquial abbreviation of modern Latin *Platypoecilus* (former genus name), from Greek *platus* 'broad' + *poikilos* 'variegated.'

plat·y·hel·minth /ˌplatēˈhelminTH/ ▶ n. Zoology an invertebrate of the phylum Platyhelminthes; a flatworm.

Plat·y·hel·min·thes /ˌplatēhelˈminTHēz/ Zoology a phylum of invertebrates that comprises the flatworms.
– ORIGIN modern Latin (plural), from PLATY- 'flat' + Greek *helminth* 'worm.'

plat·y·kur·tic /ˌplatiˈkərtik/ ▶ n. Statistics (of a frequency distribution or its graphical representation) having less kurtosis than the normal distribution. Compare with LEPTOKURTIC, MESOKURTIC.
– DERIVATIVES **plat·y·kur·to·sis** /-ikərˈtōsis/ n.
– ORIGIN early 20th cent.: from PLATY- 'broad, flat' + Greek *kurtos* 'bulging' + -IC.

plat·y·pus /ˈplatəpəs, -ˌpo͝os/ ▶ n. (pl. **platypuses**) a semiaquatic egg-laying mammal that frequents lakes and streams in eastern Australia. It has a sensitive pliable bill shaped like that of a duck, webbed feet with venomous spurs, and dense fur. Also called DUCKBILL PLATYPUS. ● *Ornithorhynchus anatinus*, the only member of the family Ornithorhynchidae, order Monotremata.
– ORIGIN late 18th cent.: modern Latin, from Greek *platupous* 'flatfooted,' from *platus* 'flat' + *pous* 'foot.'

plat·yr·rhine /ˈplatəˌrīn, -rin/ Zoology ▶ adj. of or relating to primates of a group that comprises the New World monkeys, marmosets, and tamarins. They are distinguished by having nostrils that are far apart and directed forward or sideways, and

typically have a prehensile tail. Compare with CATARRHINE.
▶ **n.** a platyrrhine primate. ● Infraorder Platyrrhini, order Primates: families Cebidae and Callitrichidae.
– ORIGIN mid 19th cent.: from PLATY- 'flat' + Greek *rhis, rhin-* 'nose' + -INE[1].

pla·tys·ma /plə'tizmə/ ▶ **n.** (pl. **platysmas** or **platysmata** /-mətə/) Anatomy a broad sheet of muscle fibers extending from the collarbone to the angle of the jaw.
– ORIGIN late 17th cent.: modern Latin, from Greek *platusma* 'flat piece, plate.'

plau·dits /'plôdits/ ▶ **plural n.** praise: *the network has received plaudits for its sports coverage.* ■ the applause of an audience: *the plaudits for the winner died down.*
– ORIGIN early 17th cent.: *plaudit* shortened from Latin *plaudite* 'applaud!' (said by Roman actors at the end of a play), imperative plural of *plaudere.*

plau·si·ble /'plôzəbəl/ ▶ **adj.** (of an argument or statement) seeming reasonable or probable: *a plausible explanation | it seems plausible that one of two things may happen.* ■ (of a person) skilled at producing persuasive arguments, esp. ones intended to deceive: *a plausible liar.*
– DERIVATIVES **plau·si·bil·i·ty** /,plôzə'bilitē/ **n.**, **plau·si·bly** /-əblē/ **adv.**
– ORIGIN mid 16th cent. (also in the sense 'deserving applause or approval'): from Latin *plausibilis,* from *plaus-* 'applauded,' from the verb *plaudere.*

Plau·tus /'plôtəs/, Titus Maccius (*c.*250–184 BC), Roman comic playwright. Fantasy and imagination are more important than realism in the development of his plots, and his stock characters are often larger than life.

play /plā/ ▶ **v. 1** [no obj.] engage in activity for enjoyment and recreation rather than a serious or practical purpose: *the children were playing outside | her friends were* **playing with** *their dolls.* ■ [with obj.] engage in (a game or activity) for enjoyment: *I want to play Monopoly.* ■ amuse oneself by engaging in imaginative pretense: *the boys were playing cops and robbers.* ■ (**play at**) engage in without proper seriousness or understanding: *stars who play at being ordinary.* ■ (**play with**) treat inconsiderately for one's own amusement: *she likes to play with people's emotions.* ■ (**play with**) fiddle or tamper with: *has somebody been playing with the thermostat?*
2 [with obj.] take part in (a sport): *I play softball and tennis.* ■ participate in (an athletic match or contest): *the Red Sox will play two games on Wednesday.* ■ compete against (another player or team) in an athletic match or contest: *the team will play France on Wednesday.* ■ [no obj., usu. with negative] informal be cooperative: *he needs financial backing, but the bank won't play.* ■ [no obj.] be part of a team, esp. in a specified position, in a game: *he played shortstop.* ■ strike (a ball) or execute (a stroke) in a game. ■ assign to take part in an athletic contest, esp. in a specified position: *the manager will want to play the right-handed Curtis.* ■ move (a piece) or display (a playing card) in one's turn in a game: *he played his queen.* ■ bet or gamble at or on: *he didn't play the ponies.*
3 [with obj.] represent (a character) in a theatrical performance or on film: *she played Ophelia.* ■ [no obj.] perform in a theatrical production or on film: *he was proud to be playing opposite a famous actor.* ■ put on or take part in (a theatrical performance or concert): *the show was one of the best we ever played.* ■ give a dramatic performance at (a particular theater or place). ■ behave as though one were (a specified type of person): *the skipper played the innocent, but smuggled goods were found on his vessel.* ■ (**play someone for**) treat someone as being of (a specified type): *don't imagine you can play me for a fool.*
4 [with obj.] perform on (a musical instrument): *we heard someone playing a harmonica* | [no obj.] *a pianist who will play for us.* ■ possess the skill of performing upon (a musical instrument): *he taught himself to play the violin.* ■ produce (notes) from a musical instrument; perform (a piece of music): *they played a violin sonata.* ■ make (an audiotape, CD, radio, etc.) produce sounds. ■ [no obj.] (of a musical instrument, audiotape, CD, radio, etc.) produce sounds: *somewhere within, a harp was playing.* ■ accompany (someone) with music as they are moving in a specified direction: *the bagpipes played them out of the dining room.*
5 [no obj.] move lightly and quickly, so as to appear and disappear; flicker: *a smile played about her lips.* ■ (of a fountain or similar source of water) emit a stream of gently moving water.
6 [with obj.] allow (a fish) to exhaust itself pulling against a line before reeling it in.
▶ **n. 1** activity engaged in for enjoyment and recreation, esp. by children: *a child* **at play** *may use a stick as an airplane.* ■ behavior or speech that is not intended seriously: *I flinched, but only* **in play**. ■ [as modifier] designed to be used in games of pretense; not real: *play families are arranged in play houses.*
2 the conducting of an athletic match or contest: *rain interrupted the second day's play.* ■ the action or manner of engaging in a sport or game: *he maintained the same rhythm of play throughout the game.* ■ the status of the ball in a game as being available to be played according to the rules: *the ball was put in play.* ■ the state of being active, operative, or effective: *luck* **comes into play**. ■ a move or maneuver in a sport or game: *the best play is to lead the 3 of clubs.* ■ archaic gambling.
3 a dramatic work for the stage or to be broadcast: *the actors put on a new play.*
4 the space in or through which a mechanism can or does move: *the steering rack was loose, and there was a little play.* ■ scope or freedom to act or operate: *our policy allows the market to have freer play.* ■ light and constantly changing movement: *the artist exploits the play of light across the surface.*
– PHRASES **make a play for** informal attempt to attract or attain. **make (great) play of** (or **with**) draw attention to in an ostentatious manner, typically to gain prestige or advantage: *the company made great play of its recent growth in profits.* **not playing with a full deck** see DECK. **play ball** see BALL[1]. **play both ends against the middle** keep one's options open by supporting or favoring opposing sides. **play something by ear** perform music without having to read from a score. ■ (**play it by ear**) informal proceed instinctively according to results and circumstances rather than according to rules or a plan. **play by the rules** follow what is generally held to be the correct line of behavior. **play one's cards close to one's chest** see CHEST. **play one's cards right** (or **well**) see CARD[1]. **play ducks and drakes with** see DUCKS AND DRAKES. **play fair** observe principles of justice; avoid cheating. **play someone false** prove treacherous or deceitful toward someone. **play fast and loose** behave irresponsibly or immorally. **play favorites** show favoritism toward someone or something. **play the field** see FIELD. **play for time** use specious excuses or unnecessary maneuvers to gain time. **play the game** see GAME. **play God** see GOD. **play havoc with** see HAVOC. **play hell** see HELL. **play hookey** see HOOKY[1]. **play a** (or **one's**) **hunch** make an instinctive choice. **play into someone's hands** act in such a way as unintentionally to give someone an advantage. **play it cool** informal make an effort to be or appear to be calm and unemotional. **play the market** speculate in stocks. **a play on words** a pun. **play a part** make a contribution to a situation: *social and economic factors may have also played a part |he personally wanted to thank those nurses and staff who had* **played a part in** *his recovery.* **play** (or **play it**) **safe** take precautions; avoid risks. **play to the gallery** see GALLERY. **play a trick** (or **joke**) **on** behave in a deceptive or teasing way toward. **play truant** see TRUANT. **play with oneself** informal masturbate. **play with fire** take foolish risks.
– PHRASAL VERBS **play around** (or **about**) behave in a casual, foolish, or irresponsible way: *you shouldn't play around with a child's future.* ■ informal (of a married person) have a love affair. **play along** pretend to cooperate: *she had to play along and be polite.* **play someone along** informal deceive or mislead someone over a period of time. **play something back** play sounds that one has recently recorded, esp. to monitor recording quality. **play something down** represent something as being less important than it in fact is: *he tried to play down the seriousness of his illness.* **play someone off** bring people into conflict or competition for one's own advantage: *detectives employ more than one informant so as to* **play one off against** *the other.* **play off** (of two teams or competitors) play an extra game or match to decide a draw or tie. **play on** exploit (a weak or vulnerable point in someone): *he played on his opponent's nerves.* **play someone out** (usu. **be played out**) drain someone of strength or life. **play something out** act the whole of a drama; enact a scene or role. **play something up** emphasize the extent or importance of something: *the mystery surrounding his death was played up by the media.* **play up to** exploit, trade on, or make the most of.
– DERIVATIVES **play·a·bil·i·ty** /,plāə'bilitē/ **n.**, **play·a·ble adj.**
– ORIGIN Old English *pleg(i)an* 'to exercise,' *plega* 'brisk movement,' related to Middle Dutch *pleien* 'leap for joy, dance.'

pla·ya[1] /'plīə/ ▶ **n.** an area of flat, dried-up land, esp. a desert basin from which water evaporates quickly.
– ORIGIN mid 19th cent.: from Spanish, literally 'beach,' from late Latin *plagia.*

play·a[2] /'plāə/ ▶ **n.** see PLAYER (sense 1).

play-act /'plā,akt/ ▶ **v.** [no obj.] act in a play. ■ [with obj.] act (a scene, role, etc.). ■ (usu. as noun **playacting**) engage in histrionic pretense: *the defender indulged in some playacting after tumbling to the ground.*
– DERIVATIVES **play·ac·tor n.**

play·back /'plā,bak/ ▶ **n.** the reproduction of previously recorded sounds or moving images.

play·bill /'plā,bil/ ▶ **n.** a poster announcing a theatrical performance. ■ a theater program.

play·boy /'plā,boi/ ▶ **n.** a wealthy man who spends his time enjoying himself, esp. one who behaves irresponsibly or is sexually promiscuous.

play-by-play ▶ **n.** a detailed running commentary on an athletic contest: *he provided play-by-play as well as interviews* | [as modifier] *the play-by-play announcer.*

play date ▶ **n.** a date and time set by parents for children to play together.

Play·er /'plāər/, Gary (1936–), South African golfer. He won numerous championships including the Masters (1961, 1974, 1978), the PGA (1962, 1972), the US Open (1965), and the British Open (1959, 1968, 1974).

play·er /'plāər/ ▶ **n. 1** a person taking part in a sport or game: *a tennis player.* ■ a person or body that is involved and influential in an area or activity: *the country's isolationism made it a secondary player in world political events.* ■ (also **playa**) informal a confident, successful man with many sexual partners: *she's so wary of players, she's declared herself celibate.*
2 a person who plays a musical instrument: *a guitar player.* ■ a device for playing compact discs, records, etc.
3 an actor.

play·er pi·an·o ▶ **n.** a piano fitted with an apparatus enabling it to be played automatically by means of a rotating perforated roll.

play·fel·low /'plā,felō/ ▶ **n.** a playmate.

play·ful /'plāfəl/ ▶ **adj.** fond of games and amusement; lighthearted: *a playful tomboy who loves to dress up.* ■ intended for one's own or others' amusement rather than seriously: *he gave me a playful punch on the arm.* ■ giving or expressing pleasure and amusement: *the ballet accents the playful use of movement.*
– DERIVATIVES **play·ful·ly adv.**, **play·ful·ness n.**

play·go·er /'plā,gōər/ ▶ **n.** a person who goes to the theater, esp. regularly.

play·ground /'plā,ground/ ▶ **n.** an outdoor area provided for children to play on, esp. at a school or public park. ■ a place where a particular group of people choose to enjoy themselves: *the mountains are* **a playground for** *hang gliders.*

play group ▶ **n.** a regular meeting of a group of preschool children, organized by parents for their children to take part in supervised creative and social play.

play·house /'plā,hous/ ▶ **n. 1** a theater.
2 a toy house for children to play in.

play·ing card ▶ **n.** each of a set of rectangular pieces of cardboard or other material with an identical pattern on one side and different numbers and symbols on the other, used to play various games, some involving gambling. A standard deck contains 52 cards divided into four suits.

play·ing field ▶ **n.** a field used for outdoor team games.
– PHRASES **a level playing field** see LEVEL.

play·let /'plālit/ ▶ **n.** a short play or dramatic piece.

play·list /'plā,list/ ▶ **n.** a list of recorded songs or pieces of music chosen to be broadcast on a radio show or by a particular radio station.

play·mak·er /'plā,mākər/ ▶ **n.** a player in a team game who leads attacks or brings other players on the same side into a position from which they could score.
– DERIVATIVES **play·mak·ing** /-mākiNG/ **n.**

play·mate /'plā,māt/ ▶ **n. 1** a friend with whom a child plays.
2 used euphemistically to refer to a person's lover.

play·off /'plā,ôf/ ▶ **n.** an additional game or period of play that decides the outcome of a tied contest: *a sudden-death playoff was required to settle the tournament.* ■ (**playoffs**) a series of contests played to determine the winner of a championship, as between the leading teams in different divisions or leagues: *Chandler was credited with taking his team to the playoffs.*

play·pen /'plā,pen/ ▶ **n.** a small portable enclosure in which a baby or small child can play safely.

play·room /'plā,ro͞om, -,ro͝om/ ▶ **n.** a room in a house that is set aside for children to play in.

play·suit /'plā,so͞ot/ ▶ **n.** an all-in-one stretchy garment for a baby or very young child, covering the body, arms, and legs.

P

PRONUNCIATION KEY ə *ago, up*; ər *over, fur*; a *hat*; ā *ate*; ä *car*; e *let*; ē *see*; i *fit*; ī *by*; NG *sing*; ō *go*; ô *law, for*; oi *toy*; o͝o *good*; o͞o *goo*; ou *out*; TH *thin*; T͟H *then*; ZH *vision*

play ther·a·py ▶ **n.** therapy in which emotionally disturbed children are encouraged to act out their fantasies and express their feelings through play, aided by a therapist's interpretations.
– DERIVATIVES **play ther·a·pist n.**

play·thing /ˈplāˌTHiNG/ ▶ **n.** a toy. ■ a person treated as amusing but unimportant by someone else: *she was the mistress and plaything of a wealthy businessman.*

play·time /ˈplāˌtīm/ ▶ **n.** time for play or recreation.

play·wright /ˈplāˌrīt/ ▶ **n.** a person who writes plays.

play·writ·ing /ˈplāˌrīting/ ▶ **n.** the activity or process of writing plays.

pla·za /ˈplazə, ˈpläzə/ ▶ **n. 1** a public square, marketplace, or similar open space in a built-up area.
2 a shopping center. ■ a service area on a highway, typically with a gas station and restaurants.
– ORIGIN late 17th cent.: from Spanish, literally 'place.'

plc (also **PLC**) ▶ **abbr.** Brit. public limited company.

plea /plē/ ▶ **n. 1** a request made in an urgent and emotional manner: *he made a dramatic plea for disarmament.* ■ a claim that a circumstance means that one should not be blamed for or should not be forced to do something: *her plea of a headache was not entirely false.*
2 Law a formal statement by or on behalf of a defendant or prisoner, stating guilt or innocence in response to a charge, offering an allegation of fact, or claiming that a point of law should apply: *he changed his plea to not guilty.*
– ORIGIN Middle English (in the sense 'lawsuit'): from Old French *plait, plaid* 'agreement, discussion,' from Latin *placitum* 'a decree,' neuter past participle of *placere* 'to please.'

plea bar·gain·ing ▶ **n.** Law an arrangement between a prosecutor and a defendant whereby the defendant pleads guilty to a lesser charge in the expectation of leniency.
– DERIVATIVES **plea-bar·gain v., plea bar·gain n.**

pleach /plēCH/ ▶ **v.** [with obj.] (usu. as adj. **pleached**) entwine or interlace (tree branches) to form a hedge or provide cover for an outdoor walkway: *an avenue of pleached limes.*
– ORIGIN late Middle English: from an Old French variant of *plaissier* (see **PLASH**[2]).

plead /plēd/ ▶ **v.** (past **pleaded** or **pled** /pled/)
1 [reporting verb] make an emotional appeal: [no obj.] *they* ***pleaded*** *with Carol to come home again* | [with direct speech] *"Don't go," she pleaded* | [with infinitive] *Anne pleaded to go with her.*
2 [with obj.] present and argue for (a position), esp. in court or in another public context: *using cheap melodrama to plead the case for three prisoners.* ■ [no obj.] Law address a court as an advocate on behalf of a party. ■ [no obj., with complement] Law state formally in court whether one is guilty or not guilty of the offense with which one is charged: *he pleaded guilty to the drug charge.* ■ Law invoke (a reason or a point of law) as an accusation or defense: *on trial for attempted murder, she pleaded self-defense.* ■ offer or present as an excuse for doing or not doing something: *he pleaded family commitments as a reason for not attending.*
– DERIVATIVES **plead·er n., plead·ing·ly adv.**
– ORIGIN Middle English (in the sense 'to wrangle'): from Old French *plaidier* 'resort to legal action,' from *plaid* 'discussion' (see **PLEA**).

> **USAGE** In a court of law, a person can **plead guilty** or **plead not guilty**. The phrase **plead innocent**, although commonly found in general use, is not a technical legal term. Note that one *pleads guilty to* (not *of*) an offense, and may be *found guilty of* an offense. See also usage at **INNOCENT**.

plead·a·ble /ˈplēdəbəl/ ▶ **adj.** Law able to be offered as a formal plea in court.

plead·ing /ˈplēdiNG/ ▶ **n. 1** the action of making an emotional or earnest appeal to someone: *he ignored her pleading.*
2 (usu. **pleadings**) Law a formal statement of the cause of an action or defense.

pleas·ance /ˈplezəns/ ▶ **n.** a secluded enclosure or part of a garden, esp. one attached to a large house.
– ORIGIN Middle English (in the sense 'pleasure'): from Old French *plaisance,* from *plaisant* 'pleasing' (see **PLEASANT**).

pleas·ant /ˈplezənt/ ▶ **adj.** (**pleasanter, pleasantest**) giving a sense of happy satisfaction or enjoyment: *a very pleasant evening* | *what a pleasant surprise!* ■ (of a person or their manner) friendly and considerate; likable: *they found him pleasant and cooperative.*
– DERIVATIVES **pleas·ant·ly adv., pleas·ant·ness n.**
– ORIGIN Middle English (in the sense 'pleasing'): from Old French *plaisant* 'pleasing,' from the verb *plaisir* (see **PLEASE**).

Pleas·an·ton /ˈplesəntən/ a city in north central California, southeast of Oakland; pop. 66,828 (est. 2008).

pleas·ant·ry /ˈplezəntrē/ ▶ **n.** (pl. **pleasantries**) (usu. **pleasantries**) an inconsequential remark made as part of a polite conversation: *after an exchange of pleasantries, I proceeded to outline a plan.* ■ a mild joke: *he laughed at his own pleasantry.*
– ORIGIN late 16th cent.: from French *plaisanterie,* from Old French *plaisant* 'pleasing' (see **PLEASANT**).

please /plēz/ ▶ **v.** [with obj.] **1** cause to feel happy and satisfied: *he arranged a fishing trip to please his son* | [with obj. and infinitive] *it* ***pleased*** *him to be seen with someone in the news.* ■ [no obj.] give satisfaction: *she was quiet and eager to please.* ■ satisfy aesthetically.
2 (**please oneself**) take only one's own wishes into consideration in deciding how to act or proceed: *this is the first time in ages that I can just please myself.* ■ [no obj.] wish or desire to do something: *feel free to wander around* ***as you please.*** ■ (**it pleases, pleased,** etc., **someone to do something**) dated it is someone's choice to do something: *instead of attending the meeting, it pleased him to go off hunting.*
▶ **adv.** used in polite requests or questions: *please address letters to the Editor* | *what type of fish is this, please?* ■ used to add urgency and emotion to a request: *please, please come home!* ■ used to agree politely to a request: *"May I call you at home?" "Please do."* ■ used in polite or emphatic acceptance of an offer: *"Would you like a drink?" "Yes, please."* ■ used to ask someone to stop doing something of which the speaker disapproves: *Rita, please—people are looking.* ■ used to express incredulity or irritation: *You cleaned out the barn in only two hours? Oh, please!*
– PHRASES **as —— as you please** informal used to emphasize the manner in which someone does something, esp. when this is seen as surprising: *she walked forward as calm as you please.* **if you please 1** used in polite requests: *follow me, if you please.* **2** used to express indignation at something perceived as unreasonable: *she wants me to make fifty cakes in time for the festival, if you please!*
– DERIVATIVES **pleas·er n.**
– ORIGIN Middle English: from Old French *plaisir* 'to please,' from Latin *placere.*

pleased /plēzd/ ▶ **adj.** feeling or showing pleasure and satisfaction, esp. at an event or a situation: *both girls were* ***pleased with*** *their new hairstyles* | *he seemed really* ***pleased that*** *she was there* | *a pleased smile.* ■ [with infinitive] willing or glad to do something: *we will be pleased to provide an independent appraisal.* ■ (**pleased with oneself**) proud of one's achievements, esp. excessively so; self-satisfied: *as he led the way, he looked very pleased with himself.*
– PHRASES **(as) pleased as Punch** see **PUNCH**[4]. **pleased to meet you** said on being introduced to someone: *"This is my wife." "Pleased to meet you."*

pleas·ing /ˈplēziNG/ ▶ **adj.** satisfying or appealing: *the pleasing austerity of the surroundings.*
– DERIVATIVES **pleas·ing·ly** /ˈplēziNGlē/ **adv.** [as submodifier] *the concept he came up with is pleasingly simple.*

pleas·ur·a·ble /ˈpleZHərəbəl/ ▶ **adj.** pleasing; enjoyable.
– DERIVATIVES **pleas·ur·a·ble·ness n., pleas·ur·a·bly** /-blē/ **adv.**
– ORIGIN late 16th cent.: from **PLEASURE**, on the pattern of *comfortable.*

pleas·ure /ˈpleZHər/ ▶ **n.** a feeling of happy satisfaction and enjoyment: *she smiled with pleasure at being praised.* ■ enjoyment and entertainment, contrasted with things done out of necessity: *she had not traveled for pleasure for a long time.* ■ an event or activity from which one derives enjoyment: *the car makes driving in the city a pleasure.* ■ sensual gratification.
▶ **adj.** [attrib.] used or intended for entertainment rather than business: *pleasure boats.*
▶ **v.** [with obj.] give sexual enjoyment or satisfaction to: *tell me what will pleasure you.* ■ [no obj.] (**pleasure in**) derive enjoyment from: *risky verbal exchanges that the pair might pleasure in.*
– PHRASES **at someone's pleasure** as and when someone wishes: *the landlord could terminate the agreement at his pleasure.* **have the pleasure of something** used in formal requests and descriptions: *he asked if he might have the pleasure of taking her to lunch.* **my pleasure** used as a polite reply to thanks: *"Oh, thank you!" "My pleasure."* **take pleasure in** derive happiness or enjoyment from: *they take a perverse pleasure in causing trouble.* **what's your pleasure?** what would you like? (used esp. when offering someone a choice): *"What's your pleasure?" "A cappuccino, please."* **with pleasure** gladly (used to express polite agreement or acceptance).
– ORIGIN late Middle English: from Old French *plaisir* 'to please' (used as a noun). The second syllable was altered under the influence of abstract nouns ending in *-ure,* such as *measure.*

pleas·ure prin·ci·ple ▶ **n.** Psychoanalysis the instinctive drive to seek pleasure and avoid pain, expressed by the id as a basic motivating force that reduces psychic tension.

pleat /plēt/ ▶ **n.** a double or multiple fold in a garment or other item made of cloth, held by stitching the top or side.
▶ **v.** [with obj.] fold into pleats: *she was absently pleating her skirt between her fingers* | (as adj. **pleated**) *a short pleated skirt.*
– DERIVATIVES **pleat·er n.**
– ORIGIN late Middle English: a variant of **PLAIT**. The written form of the word became obsolete between *c.*1700 and the end of the 19th cent.

pleath·er /ˈpleT͟Hər/ ▶ **n.** imitation leather made from polyurethane.
– ORIGIN 1980s: blend of *polyurethane* and *leather.*

pleb /pleb/ ▶ **n.** (usu. **plebs**) derogatory an ordinary person, esp. one from the lower social classes.
– DERIVATIVES **pleb·by** /ˈplebē/ **adj.**
– ORIGIN mid 17th cent.: originally plural, from Latin *plebs.* Later a shortened form of **PLEBEIAN**.

plebe /plēb/ ▶ **n.** informal a newly entered cadet or freshman, esp. at a military academy.
– ORIGIN early 17th cent.: perhaps an abbreviation of **PLEBEIAN**.

ple·be·ian /pliˈbēən/ ▶ **n.** (in ancient Rome) a commoner. ■ a member of the lower social classes.
▶ **adj.** of or belonging to the commoners of ancient Rome. ■ of or belonging to the lower social classes. ■ lacking in refinement: *he is a man of plebeian tastes.*
– ORIGIN mid 16th cent.: from Latin *plebeius* (from *plebs, pleb-* 'the common people') + **-AN**.

pleb·i·scite /ˈplebəˌsīt/ ▶ **n.** the direct vote of all the members of an electorate on an important public question such as a change in the constitution. ■ Roman History a law enacted by the plebeians' assembly.
– DERIVATIVES **ple·bis·ci·tar·y** /pləˈbisiˌterē/ **adj.**
– ORIGIN mid 16th cent. (referring to Roman history): from French *plébiscite,* from Latin *plebiscitum,* from *plebs, pleb-* 'the common people' + *scitum* 'decree' (from *sciscere* 'vote for'). The sense 'direct vote of the whole electorate' dates from the mid 19th cent.

Ple·cop·ter·a /pləˈkäptərə/ Entomology an order of insects that comprises the stoneflies. ■ (as plural noun **plecoptera**) insects of this order; stoneflies.
– DERIVATIVES **ple·cop·ter·an** /-tərən/ **n. & adj.**
– ORIGIN modern Latin (plural), from Greek *plekos* 'wickerwork' (from *plekein* 'to plait') + *pteron* 'wing.'

plec·trum /ˈplektrəm/ ▶ **n.** (pl. **plectrums** or **plectra** /-trə/) a thin flat piece of plastic, tortoiseshell, or other slightly flexible material held by or worn on the fingers and used to pluck the strings of a musical instrument such as a guitar. ■ the corresponding mechanical part that plucks the strings of an instrument such as a harpsichord.
– ORIGIN late Middle English: via Latin from Greek *plēktron* 'something with which to strike,' from *plēssein* 'to strike.'

pled /pled/ past and past participle of **PLEAD**.

pledge /plej/ ▶ **n. 1** a solemn promise or undertaking: [with infinitive] *the conference ended with a joint pledge to limit pollution.* ■ a promise of a donation to charity: *the company's pledge of 10% of profits to environmental concerns.* ■ (**the pledge**) a solemn undertaking to abstain from alcohol: *she persuaded Arthur to take the pledge.*
2 Law a thing that is given as security for the fulfillment of a contract or the payment of a debt and is liable to forfeiture in the event of failure. ■ a thing given as a token of love, favor, or loyalty.
3 a person who has promised to join a fraternity or sorority.
4 archaic the drinking to a person's health; a toast.
▶ **v. 1** [with obj.] commit (a person or organization) by a solemn promise: [with obj. and infinitive] *the government pledged itself to deal with environmental problems.* ■ [with clause] formally declare or promise that something is or will be the case: *the president pledged that 20,000 government buildings would have solar roofs.* ■ [no obj.] solemnly undertake to do something: *they pledged to continue the campaign for funding.* ■ undertake formally to give: *Japan pledged $100 million in humanitarian aid* | *to pledge allegiance.*
2 [with obj.] Law give as security on a loan: *the creditor to whom the land is pledged.*
3 [with obj.] promise to join (a fraternity or sorority): *Francie and I pledged the same sorority.*
4 [with obj.] archaic drink to the health of.

p

– PHRASES **pledge one's troth** see TROTH.
– DERIVATIVES **pledg·er** n., **pledg·or** /'plejər/ n. (Law).
– ORIGIN Middle English (denoting a person acting as surety for another): from Old French *plege*, from medieval Latin *plevium*, perhaps related to the Germanic base of PLIGHT[1].

pledg·ee /ple'jē/ ▶ n. a person to whom a pledge is given.

Pledge of Al·le·giance a solemn oath of loyalty to the US, declaimed as part of flag-saluting ceremonies.

pledg·et /'plejit/ ▶ n. a small wad of absorbent cotton or other soft material used to stop up a wound or other opening in the body.
– ORIGIN mid 16th cent.: of unknown origin.

ple·iad /'plēəd/ ▶ n. literary an outstanding group of seven people or things.
– ORIGIN early 17th cent.: from PLEIADES.

Ple·ia·des /'plēədēz/ **1** Greek Mythology the seven daughters of the Titan Atlas and the Oceanid Pleione. They were pursued by the hunter Orion until Zeus changed them into a cluster of stars.
2 Astronomy a well-known open cluster of stars in the constellation Taurus. Six (or more) stars are visible to the naked eye but there are actually some five hundred in the cluster, formed very recently in stellar terms. Also called SEVEN SISTERS.
– ORIGIN via Latin from Greek.

plein-air /ˌplān 'e(ə)r/ ▶ adj. [attrib.] denoting or in the manner of a 19th-century style of painting outdoors, or with a strong sense of the open air, that became a central feature of French Impressionism.
– ORIGIN from French *en plein air* 'in the open air.'

plei·ot·ro·py /plī'ätrəpē/ ▶ n. Genetics the production by a single gene of two or more apparently unrelated effects.
– DERIVATIVES **plei·o·trop·ic** /ˌplīə'trōpik, -'träpik/ adj., **plei·ot·ro·pism** /ˌplī'ätrəˌpizəm/ n.
– ORIGIN 1930s: from Greek *pleiōn* 'more' + *tropē* 'turning.'

Pleis·to·cene /'plīstəˌsēn/ ▶ adj. Geology of, relating to, or denoting the first epoch of the Quaternary period, between the Pliocene and Holocene epochs. ■ (as noun **the Pleistocene**) the Pleistocene epoch or the system of deposits laid down during it.

> The Pleistocene epoch lasted from 1,640,000 to about 10,000 years ago. It was marked by great fluctuations in temperature that caused the ice ages, with glacial periods followed by warmer interglacial periods. Several extinct forms of human, forerunners of modern humans, appeared during this epoch.

– ORIGIN mid 19th cent.: from Greek *pleistos* 'most' + *kainos* 'new.'

ple·na·ry /'plenərē/ ▶ adj. **1** unqualified; absolute: *crusaders were offered a plenary indulgence by the pope.*
2 (of a meeting) to be attended by all participants at a conference or assembly, who otherwise meet in smaller groups: *a plenary session of the European Parliament.*
▶ n. a meeting or session of this type.
– ORIGIN late Middle English: from late Latin *plenarius* 'complete,' from *plenus* 'full.'

plen·i·po·ten·ti·ar·y /ˌplenəpə'tensHēˌerē, -'tensHərē/ ▶ n. (pl. **plenipotentiaries**) a person, esp. a diplomat, invested with the full power of independent action on behalf of their government, typically in a foreign country.
▶ adj. having full power to take independent action: [postpositive] *he represented the Japanese government in Seoul as minister plenipotentiary.* ■ (of power) absolute.
– ORIGIN mid 17th cent.: from medieval Latin *plenipotentiarius*, from *plenus* 'full' + *potentia* 'power.'

plen·i·tude /'pleniˌt(y)o͞od/ ▶ n. an abundance: *the farm boasts a plenitude of animals and birds.* ■ the condition of being full or complete: *the plenitude of the pope's powers.*
– ORIGIN late Middle English: from Old French, from late Latin *plenitudo*, from *plenus* 'full.'

plen·te·ous /'plentēəs/ ▶ adj. literary plentiful.
– DERIVATIVES **plen·te·ous·ly** adv., **plen·te·ous·ness** n.
– ORIGIN Middle English: from Old French *plentivous*, from *plentif, -ive*, from *plente* 'plenty.' Compare with BOUNTEOUS.

plen·ti·ful /'plentəfəl/ ▶ adj. existing in or yielding great quantities; abundant: *the wine is good, cheap, and plentiful.*
– DERIVATIVES **plen·ti·ful·ly** adv., **plen·ti·ful·ness** n.

plent·i·tude /'plentiˌt(y)o͞od/ ▶ n. another term for PLENITUDE.

plen·ty /'plentē/ ▶ pron. a large or sufficient amount or quantity; more than enough: *I would have plenty of time to get home | you'll have plenty to keep you busy* | [as adj.] informal or dialect *there was plenty room.*
▶ n. a situation in which food and other necessities are available in sufficiently large quantities: *such natural phenomena as famine and plenty.*
▶ adv. [usu. as submodifier] informal used to emphasize the degree of something: *she has **plenty more** ideas.*
– ORIGIN Middle English (in the sense 'fullness, perfection'): from Old French *plente*, from Latin *plenitas*, from *plenus* 'full.'

ple·num /'plenəm, 'plēnəm/ ▶ n. **1** an assembly of all the members of a group or committee. [influenced by Russian *plenum* 'plenary session.']
2 Physics a space completely filled with matter, or the whole of space so regarded. ■ an enclosed chamber where a treated substance collects for distribution, as heated or conditioned air through a ventilation system.
– ORIGIN late 17th cent.: from Latin, literally 'full space,' neuter of *plenus* 'full.'

pleo- ▶ comb. form having more than the usual or expected number: *pleomorphism.*
– ORIGIN from Greek *pleōn* 'more.'

ple·o·chro·ic /ˌplēə'krōik/ ▶ adj. (of a crystal) absorbing different wavelengths of light differently depending on the direction of incidence of the rays or their plane of polarization, often resulting in the appearance of different colors according to the direction of view.
– DERIVATIVES **ple·och·ro·ism** /-'krōˌizəm/ n.
– ORIGIN mid 19th cent.: from PLEO- 'more' + *khrōs* 'color' + -IC.

ple·o·mor·phism /ˌplēə'môrˌfizəm/ ▶ n. the occurrence of more than one distinct form of a natural object, such as a crystalline substance, a virus, the cells in a tumor, or an organism at different stages of the life cycle.
– DERIVATIVES **ple·o·mor·phic** /-fik/ adj.
– ORIGIN mid 19th cent.: from Greek *pleiōn* 'more' + *morphē* 'form' + -ISM.

ple·o·nasm /'plēəˌnazəm/ ▶ n. the use of more words than are necessary to convey meaning (e.g., *see with one's eyes*), either as a fault of style or for emphasis.
– DERIVATIVES **ple·o·nas·tic** /ˌplēə'nastik/ adj., **ple·o·nas·ti·cal·ly** /ˌplēə'nastik(ə)lē/ adv.
– ORIGIN mid 16th cent.: via late Latin from Greek *pleonasmos*, from *pleonazein* 'be superfluous.'

ple·o·pod /'plēəˌpäd/ ▶ n. Zoology a forked swimming limb of a crustacean, five pairs of which are typically attached to the abdomen. Also called SWIMMERET.
– ORIGIN mid 19th cent.: from Greek *plein* 'swim, sail' + *pous, pod-* 'foot.'

ple·ro·ma /plə'rōmə/ ▶ n. [in sing.] **1** (in Gnosticism) the spiritual universe as the abode of God and of the totality of the divine powers and emanations.
2 (in Christian theology) the totality or fullness of the Godhead that dwells in Christ.
– DERIVATIVES **ple·ro·mat·ic** /ˌplerə'matik/ adj.
– ORIGIN mid 18th cent.: from Greek *plērōma* 'that which fills,' from *plēroun* 'make full,' from *plērēs* 'full.'

ple·si·o·saur /'plēsēəˌsôr/ ▶ n. a large extinct marine reptile of the Mesozoic era, with a broad flat body, large paddlelike limbs, and typically a long flexible neck and small head. ● Infraorder Plesiosauria, superorder Sauropterygia: several families, including Plesiosauridae.
– ORIGIN mid 19th cent.: from modern Latin *Plesiosaurus*, from Greek *plēsios* 'near' + *sauros* 'lizard.'

ples·sor /'plesər/ ▶ n. variant spelling of PLEXOR.

pleth·o·ra /'pleTHərə/ ▶ n. **1** (**a plethora of**) a large or excessive amount of (something): *a plethora of committees and subcommittees.*
2 Medicine an excess of a bodily fluid, particularly blood.
– DERIVATIVES **ple·thor·ic** /'pleTHərik, plə'THôrik/ adj. (archaic or Medicine).
– ORIGIN mid 16th cent. (in the medical sense): via late Latin from Greek *plēthōrē*, from *plēthein* 'be full.'

> **USAGE** Strictly, a **plethora** is not just an abundance of something, it is an excessive amount. However, the new, looser sense is now so dominant that it must be regarded as part of standard English.

ple·thys·mo·graph /plə'THizməˌgraf/ ▶ n. Medicine an instrument for recording and measuring variation in the volume of a part of the body, esp. as caused by changes in blood pressure.
– DERIVATIVES **ple·thys·mo·graph·ic** /pləˌTHizmə'grafik/ adj., **pleth·ys·mog·ra·phy** /ˌpleTHiz'mägrəfē/ n.
– ORIGIN late 19th cent.: from Greek *plēthusmos* 'enlargement' (based on *plēthus* 'fullness') + -GRAPH.

pleu·ra[1] /'plo͝orə/ ▶ n. (pl. **pleurae** /'plo͝orē/) **1** each of a pair of serous membranes lining the thorax and enveloping the lungs in humans and other mammals.
2 Zoology a lateral part in an animal body or structure. Compare with PLEURON.
– DERIVATIVES **pleu·ral** adj.
– ORIGIN late Middle English: via medieval Latin from Greek, literally 'side of the body, rib.'

pleu·ra[2] /'plo͝orə/ plural form of PLEURON.

pleu·ri·sy /'plo͝orəsē/ ▶ n. Medicine inflammation of the pleurae, which impairs their lubricating function and causes pain when breathing. It is caused by pneumonia and other diseases of the chest or abdomen.
– DERIVATIVES **pleu·rit·ic** /plo͝o'ritik/ adj.
– ORIGIN late Middle English: from Old French *pleurisie*, from late Latin *pleurisis*, alteration of earlier Latin *pleuritis*, from Greek *pleura* 'side of the body, rib.'

pleuro- ▶ comb. form of or relating to the pleura or pleurae: *pleuropneumonia.*
– ORIGIN from Greek *pleura* 'side,' *pleuron* 'rib.'

pleu·ron /'plo͝oˌrän/ ▶ n. (pl. **pleura** /'plo͝orə/) Zoology the sidewall of each segment of the body of an arthropod.
– ORIGIN early 18th cent.: from Greek, literally 'side of the body, rib.'

pleu·ro·pneu·mo·nia /ˌplo͝orəˌn(y)o͞o'mōnyə/ ▶ n. pneumonia complicated with pleurisy.

Ple·ven /'plevən/ an industrial town in northern Bulgaria, northeast of Sofia; pop. 112,372 (2008). An important fortress town and trading center of the Ottoman Empire, it was taken from the Turks by the Russians in the Russo-Turkish War of 1877, after a siege of 143 days.

plew /plo͞o/ ▶ n. historical a beaver skin, used as a standard unit of value in the fur trade.
– ORIGIN mid 19th cent.: from Canadian French *pélu* 'hairy,' from French *poil* 'hair, bristle.'

Plex·i·glas /'pleksiˌglas/ (also **plexiglas** or **plexiglass**) ▶ n. trademark a solid transparent plastic made of polymethyl methacrylate (the same material as perspex or Lucite).
– ORIGIN 1930s: from Greek *plēxis* 'percussion' + GLASS.

plex·or /'pleksər/ (also **plessor**) ▶ n. a small hammer with a rubber head used to test reflexes and in medical percussion.
– ORIGIN mid 19th cent.: formed irregularly from Greek *plēxis* 'percussion' (from *plēssein* 'to strike') + -OR[1].

plex·us /'pleksəs/ ▶ n. (pl. **same** or **plexuses**) Anatomy a network of nerves or vessels in the body. ■ an intricate network or weblike formation.
– DERIVATIVES **plex·i·form** /'pleksəˌfôrm/ adj.
– ORIGIN late 17th cent.: from Latin, literally 'plaited formation,' past participle of *plectere* 'to plait.'

plf. (also **plff.**) ▶ abbr. plaintiff.

pli·a·bil·i·ty /ˌplīə'bilitē/ ▶ n. the quality of being easily bent; flexibility: *an excellent combination of strength, pliability, and elasticity.*

pli·a·ble /'plīəbəl/ ▶ adj. **1** easily bent; flexible: *quality leather is pliable and will not crack.*
2 easily influenced: *pliable teenage minds.*
– DERIVATIVES **pli·a·bly** /-əblē/ adv.
– ORIGIN late Middle English: from French, from *plier* 'to bend' (see PLY[1]).

pli·ant /'plīənt/ ▶ adj. pliable: *pliant willow stems* | figurative *an economy pliant to political will.*
– DERIVATIVES **pli·an·cy** /'plīənsē/ n., **pli·ant·ly** adv.
– ORIGIN Middle English: from Old French, literally 'bending,' present participle of *plier.*

pli·ca /'plīkə/ ▶ n. **1** (pl. **plicae** /-kē, -sē/ or **plicas**) Anatomy a fold or ridge of tissue. ■ Botany a small lobe between the petals of a flower.
2 Medicine a densely matted condition of the hair.
– ORIGIN mid 17th cent.: modern Latin, from medieval Latin, 'fold,' from *plicare* 'to fold.'

pli·cate /'plīkāt, -kit/ ▶ adj. Biology & Geology folded, crumpled, or corrugated.
– DERIVATIVES **pli·cat·ed** adj.
– ORIGIN mid 18th cent.: from Latin *plicatus* 'folded,' past participle of *plicare.*

pli·ca·tion /plī'kāsHən/ ▶ n. a fold or corrugation. ■ the manner of folding or condition of being folded.
– ORIGIN late Middle English: via Old French from medieval Latin *plicatio(n-)*, from Latin *plicare* 'to fold.'

pli·é /plē'ā/ Ballet ▶ **n.** a movement in which a dancer bends the knees and straightens them again, usually with the feet turned out and heels firmly on the ground.
▶ **v.** [no obj.] perform a plié.
– ORIGIN French, literally 'bent,' past participle of *plier* (see also PLY[1]).

pli·ers /'plīərz/ (also **a pair of pliers**) ▶ **plural n.** pincers with parallel, flat, and typically serrated surfaces, used chiefly for gripping small objects or bending wire.
– ORIGIN mid 16th cent.: from dialect *ply* 'bend,' from French *plier* 'to bend,' from Latin *plicare* 'to fold.'

pliers

plight[1] /plīt/ ▶ **n.** a dangerous, difficult, or otherwise unfortunate situation: *we must direct our efforts toward relieving the plight of children living in poverty.*
– ORIGIN Middle English: from Anglo-Norman French *plit* 'fold.' The *-gh-* spelling is by association with PLIGHT[2].

plight[2] ▶ **v.** [with obj.] archaic pledge or promise solemnly (one's faith or loyalty). ■ (**be plighted to**) be engaged to be married to.
– PHRASES **plight one's troth** see TROTH.
– ORIGIN Old English *plihtan* 'endanger,' of Germanic origin; related to Dutch *plicht* and German *Pflicht* 'duty.' The current sense is recorded only from Middle English, but is probably original, in view of the related Germanic words.

plim·soll /'plimsəl, -sōl/ (also **plimsole**) ▶ **n.** Brit. a light rubber-soled canvas shoe, worn esp. for sports.
– ORIGIN late 19th cent.: probably from the resemblance of the side of the sole to a PLIMSOLL LINE.

Plim·soll line /'plimsəl, -sōl/ (also **Plimsoll mark**) ▶ **n.** a marking on a ship's side showing the limit of submersion legal under various conditions.
– ORIGIN named after Samuel *Plimsoll* (1824–98), the English politician whose agitation in the 1870s resulted in the Merchant Shipping Act of 1876, intended to end the practice of sending to sea overloaded and heavily insured old ships, from which the owners profited if they sank.

Plin·i·an /'plīnēən/ ▶ **adj.** Geology relating to or denoting a type of volcanic eruption in which a narrow stream of gas and ash is violently ejected from a vent to a height of several miles.
– ORIGIN mid 17th cent.: from Italian *pliniano*, with reference to the eruption of Vesuvius in AD 79, in which Pliny the Elder died.

plink /pliNGk/ ▶ **v.** [no obj.] emit a short, sharp, metallic or ringing sound. ■ play a musical instrument in such a way as to produce such sounds. ■ [with obj.] shoot at (a target) casually.
▶ **n.** a short, sharp, metallic or ringing sound.
– DERIVATIVES **plink·y** adj.
– ORIGIN 1940s: imitative.

plinth /plinTH/ ▶ **n.** a heavy base supporting a statue or vase. ■ Architecture the lower square slab at the base of a column.
– ORIGIN late 16th cent.: from Latin *plinthus*, from Greek *plinthos* 'tile, brick, squared stone.' The Latin form was in early use in English.

Plin·y[1] /'plinē, 'plīnē/ (23–79), Roman statesman and scholar; Latin name *Gaius Plinius Secundus*; known as **Pliny the Elder**. His *Natural History* (77) is a vast encyclopedia of the natural and human worlds. He died while observing the eruption of Vesuvius.

Plin·y[2] (*c.*61–*c.*112), Roman senator and writer; nephew of Pliny the Elder; Latin name *Gaius Plinius Caecilius Secundus*; known as **Pliny the Younger**. He is noted for his books of letters that deal with both public and private affairs and that include a description of the eruption of Vesuvius in 79.

Pli·o·cene /'plīə,sēn/ ▶ **adj.** Geology of, relating to, or denoting the last epoch of the Tertiary period, between the Miocene and Pleistocene epochs. ■ (as noun **the Pliocene**) the Pliocene epoch or the system of rocks deposited during it.

> The Pliocene epoch lasted from 5.2 million to 1.64 million years ago. Temperatures were falling at this time and many mammals became extinct. The first hominids, including *Australopithecus* and *Homo habilis*, appeared.

– ORIGIN mid 19th cent.: from Greek *pleiōn* 'more' + *kainos* 'new.'

Pli·o–Pleis·to·cene /,plīə 'plīstə,sēn, ,plīō-/ ▶ **adj.** Geology of, relating to, or linking the Pliocene and Pleistocene epochs or rock systems together. ■ (as noun **the Plio–Pleistocene**) the Pliocene and Pleistocene epochs together or the system of rocks deposited during them.

pli·o·saur /'plīə,sôr/ ▶ **n.** a plesiosaur with a short neck, large head, and massive toothed jaws. ● Family Pliosauridae, infraorder Plesiosauria: several genera, including *Pliosaurus*.
– ORIGIN mid 19th cent.: from modern Latin *Pliosaurus* (genus name), from Greek *pleiōn* 'more' + *sauros* 'lizard' (because of its greater similarity to a lizard than the ichthyosaur).

plis·sé /plē'sā, pli-/ ▶ **adj.** (of fabric) treated to give a permanent puckered or crinkled effect.
▶ **n.** material treated in this way.
– ORIGIN late 19th cent.: French, literally 'pleated,' past participle of *plisser*.

pln. ▶ **abbr.** plain.

PLO ▶ **abbr.** Palestine Liberation Organization.

plod /pläd/ ▶ **v.** (**plods, plodding, plodded**) [no obj.] walk doggedly and slowly with heavy steps: *we plodded back up the hill* | figurative *talks on a new constitution have plodded on.* ■ work slowly and perseveringly at a dull task: *we were plodding through a textbook.*
▶ **n.** a slow, heavy walk: *he settled down to a steady plod.*
– DERIVATIVES **plod·der** n.
– ORIGIN mid 16th cent.: probably symbolic of a heavy gait.

plod·ding /'pläding/ ▶ **adj.** slow-moving and unexciting: *a plodding comedy drama.* ■ (of a person) thorough and hard-working but lacking in imagination or intelligence.
– DERIVATIVES **plod·ding·ly** adv.

-ploid ▶ **comb. form** Biology denoting the number of sets of chromosomes in a cell: *triploid.*
– ORIGIN based on *(ha)ploid* and *(di)ploid.*

ploi·dy /'ploidē/ ▶ **n.** Genetics the number of sets of chromosomes in a cell, or in the cells of an organism.
– ORIGIN 1940s: from words such as *(di)ploidy* and *(poly)ploidy.*

Plo·ieş·ti /plô'yesHt(ē)/ an oil-refining city in central Romania, north of Bucharest; pop. 231,620 (2006).

plon·geur /,plôN'ZHər, plän'jər/ ▶ **n.** a person employed to wash dishes and carry out other menial tasks in a restaurant or hotel.
– ORIGIN French, literally 'person who plunges.'

plonk[1] /pläNGk/ informal ▶ **v. 1** [with obj.] set down heavily or carelessly: *she plonked her glass on the table.* ■ (**plonk oneself**) sit down heavily and without ceremony: *he plonked himself down on the sofa.*
2 [no obj.] play on a musical instrument laboriously or unskillfully: *people plonking around on expensive instruments.*
▶ **n.** a sound as of something being set down heavily: *he sat down with a plonk.*
– ORIGIN late 19th cent. (originally dialect): imitative; compare with PLUNK.

plonk[2] ▶ **n.** informal cheap wine of inferior quality.
– ORIGIN 1930s (originally Australian): probably an alteration of *blanc* in French *vin blanc* 'white wine.'

plop /pläp/ ▶ **n.** a short sound as of a small, solid object dropping into water without a splash.
▶ **v.** (**plops, plopping, plopped**) fall or cause to fall with such a sound: [no obj.] *the stone plopped into the pond* | [with obj.] *she plopped a sugar cube into the cup.* ■ (**plop oneself down**) sit or lie down gently but clumsily: *he plopped himself down on the nearest chair.*
– ORIGIN early 19th cent.: imitative.

plo·sion /'plōZHən/ ▶ **n.** Phonetics the sudden release of air in the pronunciation of a plosive consonant.
– ORIGIN early 20th cent.: shortening of EXPLOSION.

plo·sive /'plōsiv/ Phonetics ▶ **adj.** denoting a consonant that is produced by stopping the airflow using the lips, teeth, or palate, followed by a sudden release of air.
▶ **n.** a plosive speech sound. The basic plosives in English are *t*, *k*, and *p* (voiceless) and *d*, *g*, and *b* (voiced).
– ORIGIN late 19th cent.: shortening of EXPLOSIVE.

plot /plät/ ▶ **n. 1** a plan made in secret by a group of people to do something illegal or harmful: [with infinitive] *there's a plot to overthrow the government.*
2 the main events of a play, novel, movie, or similar work, devised and presented by the writer as an interrelated sequence.
3 a small piece of ground marked out for a purpose such as building or gardening: *a vegetable plot.*
4 a graph showing the relation between two variables. ■ a diagram, chart, or map.
▶ **v.** (**plots, plotting, plotted**) [with obj.] **1** secretly make plans to carry out (an illegal or harmful action): *the two men are serving sentences for plotting a bomb campaign* | [no obj.] *Erica has been plotting against me all along.*
2 devise the sequence of events in (a play, novel, movie, or similar work).
3 mark (a route or position) on a chart: *he started to plot lines of ancient sites.* ■ mark out or allocate (points) on a graph. ■ make (a curve) by marking out a number of such points. ■ illustrate by use of a graph: *it is possible to plot fairly closely the rate at which recruitment of girls increased.*
– PHRASES **lose the plot** informal lose one's ability to understand or cope with what is happening: *many people believe that he is feeling the strain or has lost the plot.* **the plot thickens** see THICKEN.
– DERIVATIVES **plot·less** adj.
– ORIGIN late Old English (sense 3 of the noun), of unknown origin. The sense 'secret plan,' dating from the late 16th cent., is associated with Old French *complot* 'dense crowd, secret project,' the same term being used occasionally in English from the mid 16th cent. Compare with PLAT[1].

Plo·ti·nus /plō'tīnəs/ (*c.*205–270), philosopher, probably of Roman descent. He was the founder and leading exponent of Neoplatonism.

plot line ▶ **n.** the course or main features of a narrative such as the plot of a play, novel, or movie: *the plot line might be too complex for audiences to follow.*

plot·ter /'plätər/ ▶ **n. 1** someone who secretly makes plans to do something illegal or harmful; a conspirator: *the trial of alleged coup plotters.*
2 a piece of equipment that marks out points on a chart: *a GPS chart plotter.*

Plott hound /plät/ ▶ **n.** a hunting dog with a smooth brindle or black coat and large drooping ears. Developed from German stock, it is the only recognized coonhound not descended from the foxhound.
– ORIGIN late 18th cent.: named after the Plott family of North Carolina, who developed the breed from wild boar hounds brought from Germany in 1750.

plot·ty /'plätē/ ▶ **adj.** informal (of a novel, play, or movie) having an excessively elaborate or complicated plot.

plotz /pläts/ ▶ **v.** [no obj.] informal collapse or be beside oneself with frustration, annoyance, or other strong emotion: *lots of directors plotz while making their films.*
– ORIGIN 1960s: from Yiddish *platsen*, literally 'to burst,' from Middle High German *platzen.*

plotzed /plätst/ ▶ **adj.** US informal extremely drunk.

plough /plou/ ▶ **n. & v.** British spelling of PLOW. ■ (**the Plough**) British term for BIG DIPPER.

plough·man's lunch /'ploumənz/ ▶ **n.** Brit. a meal of bread and cheese, typically with pickled vegetables and salad.

Plov·div /'plôv,dif/ an industrial and commercial city in southern Bulgaria; pop. 347,600 (2008). Known to the ancient Greeks as Philippopolis and to the Romans as Trimontium, it assumed its present name after World War I.

plov·er /'pləvər, 'plō-/ ▶ **n.** a short-billed gregarious wading bird, typically found by water but sometimes frequenting grassland, tundra, and mountains. ● Family Charadriidae (the **plover family**): several genera and numerous species, esp. the **ringed plovers** (*Charadrius*), **golden plovers** (*Pluvialis*), and lapwings (*Vanellus*).
– ORIGIN Middle English: from Anglo-Norman French, based on Latin *pluvia* 'rain.'

plow /plou/ (Brit. **plough**) ▶ **n.** a large farming implement with one or more blades fixed in a frame, drawn by a tractor or by animals and used for cutting furrows in the soil and turning it over, esp. to prepare for the planting of seeds. ■ a snowplow.
▶ **v.** [with obj.] **1** turn up the earth of (an area of land) with a plow, esp. before sowing: *Uncle Vic plowed his garden* | (as adj. **plowed**) *a plowed field.* ■ cut (a furrow or line) with or as if with a plow: *icebergs have plowed furrows on the seabed.* ■ (of a ship or boat) travel through (an area of water): *cruise liners plow the long-sailed routes.*
2 [no obj.] (esp. of a vehicle) move in a fast and uncontrolled manner: *the car plowed into the side of a van.* ■ advance or progress laboriously or forcibly: *they plowed their way through deep snow* | *the students are plowing through a set of grammar exercises.* ■ (**plow on**) continue steadily despite difficulties or warnings to stop: *he plowed on, trying to outline his plans.*
3 clear snow from (a road) using a snowplow: *the roads weren't yet plowed.*
4 Brit. informal, dated fail (an examination).
– PHRASES **plow a lonely** (or **one's own**) **furrow** follow a course of action in which one is isolated or in which one can act independently. **put** (or **set**) **one's hand to the plow** embark on a task. [with biblical allusion to Luke 9:62.]
– PHRASAL VERBS **plow something in/back** plow grass or other material into the soil to enrich it.

■ invest money in a business or reinvest profits in the enterprise producing them: *savings made through greater efficiency will be plowed back into the service.* **plow under** bury in the soil by plowing. **plow up** till (soil) completely or thoroughly. ■ uncover by plowing.
– DERIVATIVES **plow·a·ble** adj., **plow·er** n.
– ORIGIN late Old English *plōh*, of Germanic origin; related to Dutch *ploeg* and German *Pflug*. The spelling *plough* became common in England in the 18th cent.; earlier (16th–17th centuries) the noun was normally spelled *plough*, the verb *plow*.

plow·man /ˈploumən/ (Brit. **ploughman**) ▶ n. (pl. **plowmen**) a person who uses a plow.

plow·share /ˈplouˌSHe(ə)r/ (Brit. **ploughshare**) ▶ n. the main cutting blade of a plow, behind the coulter.
– ORIGIN late Middle English: from *plowgh*, an earlier spelling of PLOW + Old English *scær, scear* 'plowshare' (related to SHEAR).

ploy /ploi/ ▶ n. a cunning plan or action designed to turn a situation to one's own advantage: *the president has dismissed the referendum as a ploy to buy time.*
– ORIGIN late 17th cent. (originally Scots and northern English in the senses 'pastime,' 'escapade,' and 'a trick'): of unknown origin. The notion of 'a calculated plan' dates from the 1950s.

PLP ▶ abbr. (in the UK) Parliamentary Labour Party.

PLR ▶ abbr. (in the UK) Public Lending Right.

PLSS ▶ abbr. portable life support system.

plu. ▶ abbr. plural.

pluck /plək/ ▶ v. [with obj.] **1** take hold of (something) and quickly remove it from its place; pick: *she plucked a blade of grass | he plucked a tape from the shelf.* ■ catch hold of and pull quickly: *she plucked his sleeve* | [no obj.] *brambles plucked at her jeans.* ■ pull the feathers from (a bird's carcass) to prepare it for cooking. ■ pull some of the hairs from (one's eyebrows) to make them look neater.
2 quickly or suddenly remove someone from a dangerous or unpleasant situation: *the baby was plucked from a grim foster home.*
3 sound (a musical instrument or its strings) with one's finger or a plectrum.
▶ n. **1** spirited and determined courage.
2 the heart, liver, and lungs of an animal as food.
– PHRASAL VERBS **pluck up courage** see COURAGE.
– DERIVATIVES **pluck·er** n. [usu. in combination] *a goose-plucker.*
– ORIGIN late Old English *ploccian, pluccian*, of Germanic origin; related to Flemish *plokken*; probably from the base of Old French *(es)peluchier* 'to pluck.' Sense 1 of the noun is originally boxers' slang.

pluck·y /ˈpləkē/ ▶ adj. (**pluckier, pluckiest**) having or showing determined courage in the face of difficulties.
– DERIVATIVES **pluck·i·ly** /ˈpləkəlē/ adv., **pluck·i·ness** n.

plug /pləg/ ▶ n. **1** an obstruction blocking a hole, pipe, etc.: *somewhere in the pipes there is a plug of ice blocking the flow.* ■ a circular piece of metal, rubber, or plastic used to stop the drain of a bathtub or basin and keep the water in it. ■ informal a baby's pacifier. ■ a mass of solidified lava filling the neck of an old volcano. ■ (in gardening) a young plant or clump of grass with a small mass of soil protecting its roots, for planting in the ground.
2 a device for making an electrical connection, esp. between an appliance and a power supply, consisting of an insulated casing with metal pins that fit into holes in an outlet. ■ short for SPARK PLUG.
3 informal a piece of publicity promoting a product, event, or establishment: *he threw in a plug, boasting that the restaurant offered many entrées for under $5.*
4 a piece of tobacco cut from a larger cake for chewing. ■ (also **plug tobacco**) tobacco in large cakes designed to be cut for chewing.
5 Fishing a lure with one or more hooks attached.
6 short for FIREPLUG.
7 informal a tired or old horse.
▶ v. (**plugs, plugging, plugged**) [with obj.] **1** block or fill in (a hole or cavity): *trucks arrived loaded with gravel to plug the hole and clear the road.* ■ insert (something) into an opening so as to fill it: *the baby plugged his thumb into his mouth.*
2 informal mention (a product, event, or establishment) publicly in order to promote it: *during the show he plugged his new record.*
3 informal shoot or hit (someone or something).
4 [no obj.] informal proceed steadily and laboriously with a journey or task: *during the years of poverty, he **plugged away** at his writing.*
– PHRASES **plug the gap** (or **gaps**) provide something that is lacking in a particular situation: *the new sanctions are meant to plug the gaps in the trade embargo.* **pull the plug** see PULL.
– PHRASAL VERBS **plug something in** connect an electrical appliance to a power supply by inserting a plug into an outlet. **plug into** (of an electrical appliance) be connected to another appliance by a plug inserted in an outlet. ■ gain or have access to a system of computerized information: *we plug into the research facilities available at the institute.* ■ become knowledgeable about and involved with: *the workshops are a great way to plug into radical ideas and radical groups.*
– DERIVATIVES **plug·ger** n.
– ORIGIN early 17th cent.: from Middle Dutch and Middle Low German *plugge*, of unknown ultimate origin.

Plug and Play (also **plug and play**) ▶ n. a standard for the connection of peripherals to personal computers, whereby a device only needs to be connected to a computer in order to be configured to work perfectly, without any action by the user.

plug·board /ˈpləgˌbôrd/ ▶ n. a board containing several sockets into which plugs can be inserted to interconnect electric circuits, telephone lines, or computer components, by means of short lengths of wire.

plug-com·pat·i·ble ▶ adj. relating to or denoting computing equipment that is compatible with devices or systems produced by different manufacturers, to the extent that it can be plugged in and operated successfully.
▶ n. a piece of computing equipment designed in this way.

plug flow ▶ n. Geology & Physics the flow of a body of ice or viscous fluid with no shearing between adjacent layers; idealized flow without any mixing of particles of fluid.

plug fuse ▶ n. a fuse designed to be pushed into a socket in a panel or board.

plug gauge ▶ n. a gauge in the form of a plug, used for measuring the diameter of a hole.

plugged-in informal ▶ adj. informal up to date; aware of the latest developments or trends.

plug-in ▶ adj. able to be connected by means of a plug: *a plug-in telephone.* ■ Computing (of a module or software) able to be added to a system to give extra features or functions: *a plug-in graphics card.*
▶ n. **1** Computing a module or piece of software of this kind.
2 Canadian an electric outlet for plugging in the block heater of a vehicle in order to keep the engine warm.

plug-ug·ly informal ▶ n. (pl. **plug-uglies**) a thug or villain.
▶ adj. very ugly: *that was one plug-ugly dress.*
– ORIGIN by association with the verb PLUG in the informal sense 'hit with the fist.'

plum /pləm/ ▶ n. **1** an oval fleshy fruit that is purple, reddish, or yellow when ripe and contains a flattish pointed pit.
2 (also **plum tree**) the deciduous tree that bears this fruit. ● Several species in the genus *Prunus*, family Rosaceae, in particular *P. domestica*.
3 a reddish-purple color: [as modifier] *a plum blazer.*
4 [usu. as modifier] informal a highly desirable attainment, accomplishment, or acquisition, typically a job: *he landed a plum assistant producer's job.*
▶ adv. variant spelling of PLUMB[1]: *the helicopter crashed plum on the cabins.*
– ORIGIN Old English *plūme*, from medieval Latin *pruna*, from Latin *prunum* (see PRUNE[1]).

plum·age /ˈplo͞omij/ ▶ n. a bird's feathers collectively.
– DERIVATIVES **plum·aged** adj. [usu. in combination] *a gray-plumaged bird.*
– ORIGIN late Middle English: from Old French, from *plume* 'feather.'

plumb[1] /pləm/ ▶ v. [with obj.] **1** measure (the depth of a body of water). ■ [no obj.] (of water) be of a specified depth: *at its deepest, the lake scarcely plumbed seven feet.* ■ explore or experience fully or to extremes: *she had **plumbed the depths of** depravity.*
2 test (an upright surface) to determine the vertical.
▶ n. a plumb bob.
▶ adv. **1** informal exactly: *a bassoonist who sits plumb in the middle of the wind section.* ■ [as submodifier] to a very high degree; extremely: *they must both be plumb crazy.*
2 archaic vertically: *drapery fell from their human forms plumb down.*
▶ adj. vertical: *ensure that the baseboard is straight and plumb.*
– PHRASES **out of plumb** not exactly vertical: *the towers are inclined, from four to ten feet out of plumb.*
– ORIGIN Middle English (originally in the sense 'sounding lead'): via Old French from Latin *plumbum* 'lead.'

plumb[2] ▶ v. [with obj.] install and connect water and drainage pipes in (a building or room): *the house could not be plumbed at all.* ■ (**plumb something in**) chiefly Brit. install an appliance and connect it to water and drainage pipes.
– ORIGIN late 19th cent. (in the sense 'work as a plumber'): back-formation from PLUMBER.

plum·ba·go /pləmˈbāgō/ ▶ n. (pl. **plumbagos**) **1** old-fashioned term for GRAPHITE.
[early 17th cent. (denoting an ore such as galena containing lead): from Latin, from *plumbum* 'lead.' The sense 'graphite' arose through its use for pencil leads.]
2 an evergreen flowering shrub or climber that is widely distributed in warm regions and grown elsewhere as a greenhouse or indoor plant. Also called LEADWORT. [named from the color of the flowers.] ● Genus *Plumbago*, family Plumbaginaceae.

plumb bob ▶ n. a bob of lead or other heavy material forming the weight of a plumb line.

plum·be·ous /ˈpləmbēəs/ ▶ adj. chiefly Ornithology of the dull gray color of lead.
– ORIGIN late 16th cent.: from Latin *plumbeus* 'leaden' (from *plumbum* 'lead') + -OUS.

plumb·er /ˈpləmər/ ▶ n. a person who installs and repairs the pipes and fittings of water supply, sanitation, or heating systems.
– ORIGIN late Middle English (originally denoting a person dealing in and working with lead): from Old French *plommier*, from Latin *plumbarius*, from *plumbum* 'lead.'

plumb·er's help·er (**plumber's friend**) ▶ n. informal a plunger.

plumb·er's snake ▶ n. see SNAKE.

plum·bic /ˈpləmbik/ ▶ adj. Chemistry of lead with a valence of four; of lead (IV). Compare with PLUMBOUS. ■ Medicine caused by the presence of lead.
– ORIGIN late 18th cent.: from Latin *plumbum* 'lead' + -IC.

plumb·ing /ˈpləmiNG/ ▶ n. the system of pipes, tanks, fittings, and other apparatus required for the water supply, heating, and sanitation in a building. ■ the work of installing and maintaining such a system. ■ informal used as a humorous euphemism for the excretory tracts and urinary system: *I'd never discuss my plumbing with ladies.*

plum·bism /ˈpləmˌbizəm/ ▶ n. technical term for LEAD POISONING.

plumb·less /ˈpləmləs/ ▶ adj. literary (of a body of water) extremely deep.

plumb line ▶ n. a line with a plumb attached to it, used for finding the depth of water or determining the vertical on an upright surface.

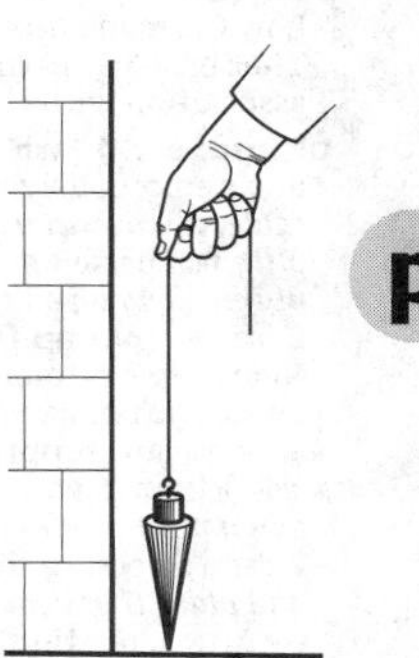
plumb line

plum·bous /ˈpləmbəs/ ▶ adj. Chemistry of lead with a valence of two; of lead(II). Compare with PLUMBIC.
– ORIGIN late 17th cent.: from Latin *plumbosus* 'full of lead.'

plumb rule ▶ n. a plumb line attached to a board, used by builders and surveyors.

plum duff ▶ n. a rich, spiced flour pudding made with raisins or currants.

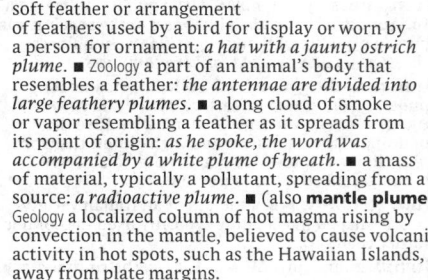

plume /plo͞om/ ▶ n. a long, soft feather or arrangement of feathers used by a bird for display or worn by a person for ornament: *a hat with a jaunty ostrich plume.* ■ Zoology a part of an animal's body that resembles a feather: *the antennae are divided into large feathery plumes.* ■ a long cloud of smoke or vapor resembling a feather as it spreads from its point of origin: *as he spoke, the word was accompanied by a white plume of breath.* ■ a mass of material, typically a pollutant, spreading from a source: *a radioactive plume.* ■ (also **mantle plume**) Geology a localized column of hot magma rising by convection in the mantle, believed to cause volcanic activity in hot spots, such as the Hawaiian Islands, away from plate margins.
▶ v. **1** [no obj.] spread out in a shape resembling a feather: *smoke plumed from the chimneys.* ■ [with obj.] decorate with or as if with feathers: (as adj. **plumed**) *a plumed cap.*
2 (**plume oneself**) chiefly archaic (of a bird) preen itself. ■ feel a great sense of self-satisfaction about something: *she plumed herself on being cosmopolitan.*

– DERIVATIVES **plume·less** adj., **plume·like** /-ˌlīk/ adj., **plum·er·y** /-mərē/ n.
– ORIGIN late Middle English: from Old French, from Latin *pluma* 'down.'

Plumed Ser·pent ▶ n. a mythical creature depicted as part bird, part snake, in particular Quetzalcóatl, a god of the Toltec and Aztec civilizations having this form.

plume moth ▶ n. a small, slender, long-legged moth with narrow wings divided into feathery plumes. At rest, the wings are rolled and held out sideways, giving the moth the shape of a letter T. ● Family Pterophoridae: several genera.

plu·me·ri·a /plo͞oˈmi(ə)rēə/ ▶ n. a fragrant flowering tropical tree of a genus that includes frangipani. ● Genus *Plumeria*, family Apocynaceae.
– ORIGIN modern Latin, named after Charles *Plumier* (1646–1704), French botanist.

plum·met /ˈpləmit/ ▶ v. (**plummets, plummeting, plummeted**) [no obj.] fall or drop straight down at high speed: *a climber was killed when he plummeted 300 feet down an icy gully.* ■ decrease rapidly in value or amount: *hardware sales plummeted.*
▶ n. **1** a steep and rapid fall or drop.
2 a plumb or plumb line.
– ORIGIN late Middle English (as a noun): from Old French *plommet* 'small sounding lead,' diminutive of *plomb* 'lead.' The current verb sense dates from the 1930s.

plum·my /ˈpləmē/ ▶ adj. (**plummier, plummiest**) **1** resembling a plum in taste, scent, or color: *cozy reds and plummy blues.*
2 Brit. informal (of a person's voice) having an accent thought typical of the English upper classes.
3 Brit. informal choice; highly desirable: *there are some plummy roles for the taking here.*

plu·mose /ˈplo͞oˌmōs/ ▶ adj. chiefly Biology having many fine filaments or branches that give a feathery appearance.
– ORIGIN mid 18th cent.: from Latin *plumosus* 'full of down or feathers,' from *pluma* 'down.'

plump[1] /pləmp/ ▶ adj. having a full rounded shape: *the berries were plump and sweet.* ■ slightly fat.
▶ v. [with obj.] shake or pat (a cushion or pillow) to adjust its stuffing and make it rounded and soft: *she plumped up her pillows.* ■ [no obj.] (**plump up**) become rounder and fatter: *stew the dried fruits gently until they plump up.*
– DERIVATIVES **plump·ish** adj., **plump·ly** adv., **plump·y** adj.
– ORIGIN late 15th cent. (in the sense 'blunt, forthright'): related to Middle Dutch *plomp*, Middle Low German *plump, plomp* 'blunt, obtuse, blockish.' The sense has become appreciative, perhaps by association with PLUM.

plump[2] ▶ v. **1** [with obj.] set down heavily or unceremoniously: *she plumped her bag on the table.* ■ (**plump oneself**) sit down in this way: *she plumped herself down in the nearest seat* | [no obj.] *he plumped down on the bench beside me.*
2 [no obj.] (**plump for**) decide definitely in favor of (one of two or more possibilities): *offered a choice of drinks, he plumped for brandy.*
▶ n. archaic an abrupt plunge; a heavy fall.
▶ adv. informal **1** with a sudden or heavy fall: *she sat down plump on the bed.*
2 dated directly and bluntly: *he must tell her plump and plain that he was collecting unemployment.*
– ORIGIN late Middle English: related to Middle Low German *plumpen*, Middle Dutch *plompen* 'fall into water,' probably of imitative origin.

plump·ness /ˈpləmpnis/ ▶ n. the quality of having a full rounded shape: *the plumpness of the peaches.* ■ a person's quality of being slightly fat; chubbiness: *she grew up being teased for her plumpness.*

plum pud·ding ▶ n. a rich boiled or steamed pudding containing raisins, currants, and spices.
– ORIGIN early 18th cent.: so named because the pudding was originally made with plums, the word *plum* being retained later to denote 'raisin,' which became a substituted ingredient.

plum to·ma·to ▶ n. a tomato of an Italian variety that is shaped like a plum, typically used in cooking rather than raw.

plu·mule /ˈplo͞omyo͞ol/ ▶ n. **1** Botany the rudimentary shoot or stem of an embryo plant.
2 Ornithology a bird's down feather, numbers of which form an insulating layer under the contour feathers.
– ORIGIN early 18th cent.: from French *plumule* or Latin *plumula* 'small feather,' diminutive of *pluma* 'down.'

plum·y /ˈplo͞omē/ ▶ adj. (**plumier, plumiest**) resembling or decorated with feathers.

plun·der /ˈpləndər/ ▶ v. [with obj.] steal goods from (a place or person), typically using force and in a time of war or civil disorder: *looters moved into the disaster area to plunder stores* | [no obj.] *the invaders were back and ready to plunder.* ■ steal (goods) in such a way. ■ take material from (artistic or academic work) for one's own purposes: *we shall plunder related sciences to assist our research.*
▶ n. the violent and dishonest acquisition of property: *the farmers suffered the inhumanity and indignities of pillage and plunder.* ■ property acquired illegally and violently: *the army sacked the city and carried off huge quantities of plunder.*
– DERIVATIVES **plun·der·er** n.
– ORIGIN mid 17th cent.: from German *plündern*, literally 'rob of household goods,' from Middle High German *plunder* 'household effects.' Early use of the verb was with reference to the Thirty Years' War (1618–48), reflecting German usage; on the outbreak of the English Civil War in 1642, the word and activity were associated with the forces under Prince Rupert.

plunge /plənj/ ▶ v. **1** [no obj.] jump or dive quickly and energetically: *our daughters whooped as they plunged into the sea.* ■ fall suddenly and uncontrollably: *a car swerved to avoid a bus and plunged into a ravine.* ■ embark impetuously on a speech or course of action: *overconfident researchers who plunge ahead.* ■ suffer a rapid decrease in value: *their fourth-quarter operating profit plunged 25%.* ■ (of a ship) pitch: *the ship plunged through the 20-foot seas.*
2 [with obj.] push or thrust quickly: *he plunged his hands into his pockets.* ■ put (something) in liquid so as to immerse it completely: *cover the cucumbers with boiling water and then plunge them into iced water.* ■ (often **be plunged into**) suddenly bring into a specified condition or state: *for a moment the scene was illuminated, then it was plunged back into darkness.* ■ sink (a plant or a pot containing a plant) in the ground.
▶ n. an act of jumping or diving into water: *we went straight from the sauna to take a cold plunge.* ■ a swift and drastic fall in value or amount: *the bank declared a 76% plunge in its profits.*
– PHRASES **take the plunge** informal commit oneself to a course of action about which one is nervous.
– ORIGIN late Middle English: from Old French *plungier* 'thrust down,' based on Latin *plumbum* 'lead, plummet.'

plunge pool ▶ n. **1** a deep basin excavated at the foot of a waterfall by the action of the falling water.
2 chiefly Brit. a small, deep swimming pool, typically one filled with cold water and used to refresh or invigorate the body after a sauna.

plung·er /ˈplənjər/ ▶ n. **1** a device consisting of a rubber cup on a long handle, used to clear blocked pipes by means of water pressure. ■ a part of a device or mechanism that works with a plunging or thrusting movement.
2 informal a person who gambles or spends money recklessly.

plunge saw ▶ n. an electric saw with a projecting blade that can make precision cuts by plunging into dense materials.

plung·ing neck·line ▶ n. a low-cut neckline on a woman's dress.

plunk /pləNGk/ informal ▶ v. **1** [no obj.] play a keyboard or plucked stringed instrument, esp. in an inexpressive or unskilled way.
2 [with obj.] hit (someone) abruptly.
3 (also **plank**) [with obj.] put or set (something) down heavily or abruptly: *she plunked her purse on top of the bar.* ■ pay (money) on the spot or abruptly: *I gladly plunked down my ten dollars.* ■ (**plunk oneself down**) sit down in a hurried or undignified way: *she plunks herself down on the stool.*
▶ n. **1** the sound made by abruptly plucking a string of a stringed instrument.
2 a heavy blow.
– DERIVATIVES **plunk·er** n.
– ORIGIN early 19th cent.: probably imitative.

plu·per·fect /ˌplo͞oˈpərfikt/ ▶ adj. & n. another term for PAST PERFECT. ■ [as modifier] more than perfect: *they have one pluperfect daughter and are expecting an ideal little brother for her.*
– ORIGIN late 15th cent.: from modern Latin *plusperfectum*, from Latin (*tempus praeteritum*) *plus quam perfectum* '(past tense) more than perfect.'

plu·ral /ˈplo͝orəl/ ▶ adj. more than one in number: *the meanings of the text are plural.* ■ Grammar (of a word or form) denoting more than one, or (in languages with dual number) more than two: [postpositive] *the first person plural.*
▶ n. Grammar a plural word or form. ■ [in sing.] the plural number: *the verb is in the plural.*
– DERIVATIVES **plu·ral·ly** adv.
– ORIGIN late Middle English: from Old French *plurel* or Latin *pluralis*, from *plus, plur-* 'more.'

> **USAGE** **1** An apostrophe may be used to form the plural of letters (*r's*) and numbers (*7's*), as well as single words referred to themselves (*four the's in one sentence*). It should not be used to form plurals of ordinary nouns: *four apples*, not *four apple's*. **2** The regular plurals of abbreviations and acronyms may be spelled by simply adding an *s*: *CDs, MiGs*. They may also, especially if periods are involved, employ an apostrophe: *D.D.S.'s*. **3** The plurals of proper names typically end in *s* or *es*, never with an apostrophe: *the Smiths, the Joneses, the Rosses*. See also usage at APOSTROPHE[1].

plu·ral·ism /ˈplo͝orəˌlizəm/ ▶ n. **1** a condition or system in which two or more states, groups, principles, sources of authority, etc., coexist. ■ a form of society in which the members of minority groups maintain their independent cultural traditions. ■ a political theory or system of power-sharing among a number of political parties. ■ a theory or system of devolution and autonomy for individual bodies in preference to monolithic state control. ■ Philosophy a theory or system that recognizes more than one ultimate principle. Compare with MONISM.
2 the practice of holding more than one office or church benefice at a time.
– DERIVATIVES **plu·ral·ist** n. & adj., **plu·ral·is·tic** /-ˈlistik/ adj., **plu·ral·is·ti·cal·ly** /-ˈlistək(ə)lē/ adv.

plu·ral·i·ty /plo͝oˈralitē/ ▶ n. (pl. **pluralities**) **1** the fact or state of being plural: *some languages add an extra syllable to mark plurality.* ■ [in sing.] a large number of people or things: *a plurality of critical approaches.*
2 the number of votes cast for a candidate who receives more than any other but does not receive an absolute majority: *his winning plurality came from creating a reform coalition.* ■ the number by which this exceeds the number of votes cast for the candidate who placed second.
3 chiefly historical another term for PLURALISM (sense 2).
– ORIGIN late Middle English: from Old French *pluralite*, from late Latin *pluralitas*, from Latin *pluralis* 'relating to more than one' (see PLURAL).

> **USAGE** On the difference between plurality and majority, see usage at MAJORITY.

plu·ral·ize /ˈplo͝orəˌlīz/ ▶ v. [with obj.] **1** cause to become more numerous. ■ cause to be made up of several different elements.
2 give a plural form to (a word).
– DERIVATIVES **plu·ral·i·za·tion** /ˌplo͝orəliˈzāSHən/ n.

pluri- ▶ comb. form several: *pluripotent.*
– ORIGIN from Latin *plus, plur-* 'more,' *plures* 'several.'

plu·ri·po·tent /ˌplo͝oriˈpōtnt/ ▶ adj. Biology (of an immature or stem cell) capable of giving rise to several different cell types.
– ORIGIN 1940s: from PLURI- 'several' + Latin *potent-* 'being able' (see POTENT[1]).

plus /pləs/ ▶ prep. with the addition of: *two plus four is six* | *he was awarded the full amount plus interest.* ■ informal together with: *all apartments have a small kitchen plus private bathroom.*
▶ adj. **1** [postpositive] (after a number or amount) at least: *companies put losses at $500,000 plus.* ■ (after a grade) better than: *B plus.*
2 (before a number) above zero; positive: *plus 60 degrees centigrade.*
3 having a positive electric charge.
▶ n. **1** short for PLUS SIGN. ■ a mathematical operation of addition.
2 an advantage: *knowing the language is a decided plus* | [as modifier] ***on the plus side**, the employees are enthusiastic and good-natured.*
▶ conj. informal furthermore; also: *it's packed full of medical advice, plus it keeps you informed about the latest research.*
– PHRASES **plus or minus** used to define the margin of error of an estimate or calculation: *the coral was estimated to be 840 years old, plus or minus 40 years.*
– ORIGIN mid 16th cent.: from Latin, literally 'more.'

> **USAGE** The use of **plus** as a conjunction meaning 'furthermore' (*plus, we will be pleased to give you personal financial advice*) is considered informal and should be avoided in formal writing.

plus ça change /ˈplo͞o sä ˈSHäNZH/ ▶ exclam. used to express resigned acknowledgment of the fundamental immutability of human nature and institutions.
– ORIGIN French, from *plus ça change, plus c'est la même chose* 'the more it changes, the more it stays the same.'

plus fours /pləs fôrz/ ▶ plural n. dated baggy knickers reaching below the knee, worn esp. by men for playing golf.
– ORIGIN 1920s: so named because the overhang at the knee requires an extra four inches of material.

plush /pləSH/ ▶ n. a rich fabric of silk, cotton, wool, or a combination of these, with a long, soft nap: [as modifier] *deep-buttoned plush upholstery.*

p

▶ adj. richly luxurious and expensive: *the plush chrome and leather office.*
– DERIVATIVES **plush·ly** adv., **plush·ness** n.
– ORIGIN late 16th cent.: from obsolete French *pluche*, contraction of *peluche*, from Old French *peluchier* 'to pluck,' based on Latin *pilus* 'hair.' The sense 'luxurious' dates from the 1920s.

plush vel·vet ▶ n. a kind of plush with a short, soft, dense nap, resembling velvet.

plush·y /ˈpləSHē/ ▶ adj. (**plushier**, **plushiest**) made of or resembling plush; soft to the touch: *her heels sank into the plushy carpet.*
▶ n. (also **plushie**) (pl. **plushies**) a soft toy.

plus-mi·nus ▶ n. [often as modifier] Ice Hockey a running total used as an indication of a player's effectiveness, calculated by adding one for each goal scored by the player's team in even-strength play while the player is on the ice, and subtracting one for each goal conceded.

plus-one ▶ n. informal a person's guest at a social function.

plus sign ▶ n. the symbol +, indicating addition or a positive value.

plus-size ▶ adj. (of clothing or people) of a size larger than the normal range: *a new line of plus-size bathing suits.*

Plu·tarch /ˈplo͞oˌtärk/ (*c.*46–*c.*120), Greek biographer and philosopher; Latin name *Lucius Mestrius Plutarchus*. He is chiefly known for *Parallel Lives*, a collection of biographies of prominent Greeks and Romans.

plu·te·us /ˈplo͞otēəs/ ▶ n. (pl. **plutei** /-tēˌī/) Zoology the planktonic larva of some echinoderms, being somewhat triangular with lateral projections.
– ORIGIN late 19th cent.: from Latin, literally 'barrier' (with reference to its shape).

Plu·ti·no /plo͞oˈtēnō/ ▶ n. (pl. **Plutinos**) a small planetlike body orbiting the sun in the region of the Kuiper belt and in resonance with Neptune.
– ORIGIN 1990s: from the name of **PLUTO** (because of a similar orbit) + the Italian diminutive suffix *-ino*.

Plu·to /ˈplo͞otō/ **1** Greek Mythology the god of the underworld. Also called **HADES**.
2 Astronomy a small planetary body orbiting the sun, discovered in 1930 by Clyde Tombaugh.

> Pluto usually orbits beyond Neptune at an average distance of 5,900 million km from the sun, although its orbit is so eccentric that at perihelion it is closer to the sun than Neptune (as in 1979–99). Pluto is smaller than earth's moon (diameter about 2,250 km), but it was discovered in 1978 to have its own large satellite (Charon). From the time of its discovery it was regarded as the ninth (outermost) planet of the solar system, but in the 1990s its unusual characteristics led astronomers to question its planetary nature.
> In August 2006, the International Astronomical Union formally declared Pluto to be a dwarf planet rather than a planet proper.

– ORIGIN via Latin from *Ploutōn*, the Greek name of the god of the underworld.

plu·toc·ra·cy /plo͞oˈtäkrəsē/ ▶ n. (pl. **plutocracies**) government by the wealthy. ■ a country or society governed in this way. ■ an elite or ruling class of people whose power derives from their wealth.
– DERIVATIVES **plu·to·crat·ic** /ˌplo͞otəˈkratik/ adj., **plu·to·crat·i·cal·ly** /ˌplo͞otəˈkratiklē/ adv.
– ORIGIN mid 17th cent.: from Greek *ploutokratia*, from *ploutos* 'wealth' + *kratos* 'strength, authority.'

> **USAGE** See usage at **ARISTOCRACY**.

plu·to·crat /ˈplo͞otəˌkrat/ ▶ n. often derogatory a person whose power derives from their wealth.

plu·ton /ˈplo͞oˌtän/ ▶ n. Geology a body of intrusive igneous rock.
– ORIGIN 1930s: back-formation from **PLUTONIC**.

Plu·to·ni·an /plo͞oˈtōnēən/ ▶ adj. **1** of or associated with the underworld.
2 of or relating to the dwarf planet Pluto.

plu·ton·ic /plo͞oˈtänik/ ▶ adj. **1** Geology relating to or denoting igneous rock formed by solidification at considerable depth beneath the earth's surface.
2 (**Plutonic**) relating to the underworld or the god Pluto.

plu·to·nism /ˈplo͞otnˌizəm/ ▶ n. Geology the formation of intrusive igneous rock by solidification of magma beneath the earth's surface. ■ (**Plutonism**) historical the theory (now accepted) that rocks such as granite were formed by solidification from the molten state, as proposed by Scottish geologist James Hutton and others, rather than by precipitation from the sea. Compare with **NEPTUNISM**.
– DERIVATIVES **Plu·to·nist** n. & adj. (historical).

plu·to·ni·um /plo͞oˈtōnēəm/ ▶ n. the chemical element of atomic number 94, a dense silvery radioactive metal of the actinide series, used as a fuel in nuclear reactors and as an explosive in nuclear fission weapons. Plutonium only occurs in trace amounts in nature but is manufactured in nuclear reactors from uranium-238. (Symbol: **Pu**)
– ORIGIN late 18th cent.: from Greek *Ploutōn* 'Pluto,' on the pattern of *neptunium*, being the next planet beyond Neptune.

plu·vi·al /ˈplo͞ovēəl/ chiefly Geology ▶ adj. relating to or characterized by rainfall.
▶ n. a period marked by increased rainfall.
– ORIGIN mid 17th cent.: from Latin *pluvialis*, from *pluvia* 'rain.'

Plu·vi·ose /ˈplo͞ovēˌōs/ (also **Pluviôse** /plʏˈvyôs/) ▶ n. the fifth month of the French Republican calendar (1793–1805), originally running from January 20 to February 18.
– ORIGIN French *Pluviôse*, from Latin *pluviosus* 'relating to rain.'

ply[1] /plī/ ▶ n. (pl. **plies**) **1** a thickness or layer of a folded or laminated material. ■ [usu. in combination] a strand of yarn or rope: [as modifier] *four-ply yarn.* ■ the number of layers or strands of which something is made: *the yarn can be any ply from two to eight.* ■ [usu. in combination] a reinforcing layer of fabric in a tire: [as modifier] *a six-ply whitewall tire.*
2 short for **PLYWOOD**.
3 (in game theory) the number of levels at which branching occurs in a tree of possible outcomes, typically corresponding to the number of moves ahead (in chess strictly half-moves ahead) considered by a computer program. ■ a half-move (i.e., one player's move) in computer chess.
– ORIGIN late Middle English (in the sense 'fold'): from French *pli* 'fold,' from the verb *plier*, from Latin *plicare* 'to fold.'

ply[2] ▶ v. (**plies**, **plying**, **plied**) [with obj.] **1** work with (a tool, esp. one requiring steady, rhythmic movements): *a tailor delicately plying his needle.* ■ work steadily at (one's business or trade); conduct: *he plied a profitable export trade.*
2 [no obj.] (of a vessel or vehicle) travel regularly over a route, typically for commercial purposes: *ferries ply across a strait to the island.* ■ [with obj.] travel over (a route) in this way: *the motion of the big tug as it plied the Jersey coastline.*
3 (**ply someone with**) provide someone with (food or drink) in a continuous or insistent way: *a flight attendant who plied them with soft drinks.* ■ direct (numerous questions) at someone: *the presiding judge plied him with a series of absurd questions.*
– ORIGIN late Middle English: shortening of **APPLY**.

Ply·mouth /ˈpliməTH/ **1** a port and naval base in Devon, southwestern England; pop. 251,900 (est. 2009). In 1620 it was the scene of the Pilgrim Fathers' departure to North America in the *Mayflower*.
2 a town in southeastern Massachusetts, on the Atlantic coast; pop. 55,705 (est. 2008). The site in 1620 of the landing of the Pilgrim Fathers, it was the earliest permanent European settlement in New England.
3 a city in southeastern Minnesota, northwest of Minneapolis; pop. 71,486 (est. 2008).
4 the capital of the island of Montserrat in the Caribbean Sea. It was abandoned following the eruption of the Soufrière Hills volcano that began in 1995.

Plym·outh Breth·ren a strict Calvinistic religious body formed at Plymouth in England *c.*1830, having no formal creed and no official order of ministers. Its teaching emphasizes an expected millennium and members renounce many secular occupations, allowing only those compatible with New Testament standards.

Ply·mouth Rock[1] a granite boulder at Plymouth, Massachusetts, onto which the Pilgrim Fathers are said to have stepped when they disembarked from the *Mayflower*.

Plym·outh Rock[2] ▶ n. a chicken of a large domestic breed of American origin, having gray plumage with blackish stripes, and a yellow beak, legs, and feet.

ply·wood /ˈplīˌwo͝od/ ▶ n. a type of strong thin wooden board consisting of two or more layers glued and pressed together with the direction of the grain alternating, and usually sold in sheets of four by eight feet.

Pl·zeň /ˈpəlˌzenyə/ Czech name for **PILSEN**.

PM ▶ abbr. ■ Past Master. ■ Paymaster. ■ Police Magistrate. ■ Postmaster. ■ postmortem. ■ Prime Minister. ■ Provost Marshal.
▶ n. (pl. **PMs**) informal (in the context of Internet message boards) a private message, sent directly from one user to another: *drop me a PM if you want more details.*
▶ v. [with obj.] (**PMs**, **PMing**, **PMd**) informal send (another user of an Internet message board) a private message: *I'll PM you when I'm back online.*

Pm ▶ symbol the chemical element promethium.

p.m. ▶ abbr. after noon, used after times of day between noon and midnight: *at 3:30 p.m.*
– ORIGIN from Latin *post meridiem*.

PMG ▶ abbr. ■ paymaster general. ■ postmaster general.

pmk. ▶ abbr. postmark.

PMS ▶ abbr. premenstrual syndrome.

pmt. ▶ abbr. payment.

p.n. ▶ abbr. promissory note.

PNdB ▶ abbr. perceived noise decibel(s).

pneum. ▶ abbr. ■ pneumatic. ■ pneumatics.

pneu·ma /ˈn(y)o͞omə/ ▶ n. Philosophy (in Stoic thought) the vital spirit, soul, or creative force of a person.
– ORIGIN Greek, literally 'that which is breathed or blown.'

pneu·mat·ic /n(y)o͞oˈmatik/ ▶ adj. **1** containing or operated by air or gas under pressure. ■ Zoology (chiefly of cavities in the bones of birds) containing air. ■ informal (of a woman) having large breasts: *Lee and his pneumatic wife.*
2 of or relating to the spirit.
▶ n. (usu. **pneumatics**) an item of pneumatic equipment.
– DERIVATIVES **pneu·mat·i·cal·ly** /n(y)o͞oˈmatək(ə)lē/ adv., **pneu·ma·tic·i·ty** /ˌn(y)o͞oməˈtisətē/ n.
– ORIGIN mid 17th cent.: from French *pneumatique* or Latin *pneumaticus*, from Greek *pneumatikos*, from *pneuma* 'wind,' from *pnein* 'breathe.'

pneu·mat·ic drill ▶ n. a large, heavy mechanical drill driven by compressed air, used for drilling into hard materials such as rock or concrete.

pneu·mat·ics /n(y)o͞oˈmatiks/ ▶ plural n. [treated as sing.] the branch of physics or technology concerned with the mechanical properties of gases.

pneumato- ▶ comb. form **1** of or containing air: *pneumatophore.*
2 relating to the spirit: *pneumatology.*
– ORIGIN from Greek *pneuma, pneumat-* 'wind, breath, spirit.'

pneu·ma·tol·o·gy /ˌn(y)o͞oməˈtäləjē/ ▶ n. the branch of Christian theology concerned with the Holy Spirit.
– DERIVATIVES **pneu·ma·to·log·i·cal** /ˌn(y)o͞omətəˈläjəkəl/ adj.

pneu·ma·tol·y·sis /ˌn(y)o͞oməˈtäləsis/ ▶ n. Geology the chemical alteration of rocks and the formation of minerals by the action of hot magmatic gases.
– DERIVATIVES **pneu·mat·o·lyt·ic** adj.

pneu·mat·o·phore /ˌn(y)o͞oˈmatəˌfô(ə)r/ ▶ n.
1 Zoology the gas-filled float of some colonial coelenterates, such as the Portuguese man-of-war.
2 Botany (in mangroves and other swamp plants) an aerial root specialized for gaseous exchange.

pneumo- ▶ comb. form **1** of or relating to the lungs: *pneumogastric.*
2 of or relating to the presence of air or gas: *pneumothorax.*
– ORIGIN Sense 1 from Greek *pneumōn* 'lung'; sense 2 from Greek *pneuma* 'air.'

pneu·mo·coc·cus /ˌn(y)o͞omōˈkäkəs/ ▶ n. (pl. **pneumococci** /-ˈkäksī, -ˈkäksē/) a bacterium associated with pneumonia and some forms of meningitis. ● *Streptococcus pneumoniae*, a Gram-positive diplococcus.
– DERIVATIVES **pneu·mo·coc·cal** adj.

pneu·mo·co·ni·o·sis /ˌn(y)o͞omōˌkōnēˈōsəs/ ▶ n. Medicine a disease of the lungs due to inhalation of dust, characterized by inflammation, coughing, and fibrosis.
– ORIGIN late 19th cent.: from **PNEUMO-** 'relating to the lungs' + Greek *konis* 'dust' + **-OSIS**.

pneu·mo·cys·tis /ˈn(y)o͞omōˌsistis/ ▶ n. Medicine a parasitic protozoan that can cause fatal pneumonia in people affected with immunodeficiency disease. ● *Pneumocystis carinii*, phylum Sporozoa.

pneu·mo·gas·tric /ˌn(y)o͞omōˈgastrik/ ▶ adj. of or relating to the lungs and stomach.

pneu·mo·nec·to·my /ˌn(y)o͞omōˈnektəmē/ ▶ n. (pl. **pneumonectomies**) surgical removal of a lung or part of a lung.

pneu·mo·nia /n(y)o͞oˈmōnēə, -ˈmōnyə/ ▶ n. lung inflammation caused by bacterial or viral infection, in which the air sacs fill with pus and may become solid. Inflammation may affect both lungs (**double pneumonia**), one lung (**single pneumonia**), or only certain lobes (**lobar pneumonia**).
– DERIVATIVES **pneu·mon·ic** /n(y)o͞oˈmänik/ adj.
– ORIGIN early 17th cent.: via Latin from Greek, from *pneumōn* 'lung.'

P

pneu·mo·ni·tis /ˌn(y)o͞omə'nītis/ ▶ **n.** Medicine inflammation of the walls of the alveoli in the lungs, usually caused by a virus.

pneu·mo·tach·o·graph /ˌn(y)o͞omō'takəˌgraf/ ▶ **n.** an apparatus for recording the rate of airflow during breathing.

pneu·mo·tho·rax /ˌn(y)o͞omō'THôˌraks/ ▶ **n.** Medicine the presence of air or gas in the cavity between the lungs and the chest wall, causing collapse of the lung.

PNG ▶ **abbr.** Papua New Guinea.

p–n junc·tion ▶ **n.** Electronics a boundary between p-type and n-type material in a semiconductor device, functioning as a rectifier.

PNP ▶ **adj.** Electronics denoting a semiconductor device in which an n-type region is sandwiched between two p-type regions.
▶ **abbr.** (in computing) Plug and Play.

PO ▶ **abbr.** ■ Petty Officer. ■ postal order. ■ Post Office. ■ purchase order.

Po[1] /pō/ a river in northern Italy. Italy's longest river, it rises in the Alps near the border with France and flows 415 miles (668 km) east to the Adriatic Sea.

Po[2] ▶ **symbol** the chemical element polonium.

po' /pō, po͝oə, pô/ ▶ **adj.** short for POOR, used to represent dialectal speech.

poach[1] /pōCH/ ▶ **v.** [with obj.] cook (an egg), without its shell, in or over boiling water: (as adj. **poached**) *a breakfast of poached egg and grilled bacon.* ■ cook by simmering in a small amount of liquid: *poach the salmon in the white wine.*
– ORIGIN late Middle English: from Old French *pochier*, earlier in the sense 'enclose in a bag,' from *poche* 'bag, pocket.'

poach[2] ▶ **v.** [with obj.] **1** illegally hunt or catch (game or fish) on land that is not one's own, or in contravention of official protection. ■ take or acquire in an unfair or clandestine way: *employers risk having their newly trained workers poached by other companies.* ■ [no obj.] (in ball games) take a shot that a partner or teammate would have expected to take.
2 (of an animal) trample or cut up (turf) with its hoofs. ■ [no obj.] (of land) become sodden by being trampled.
– PHRASES **poach on someone's territory** encroach on someone else's rights.
– ORIGIN early 16th cent. (in the sense 'push roughly together'): apparently related to POKE[1]; sense 1 is perhaps partly from French *pocher* 'enclose in a bag' (see POACH[1]).

poach·er[1] /'pōCHər/ ▶ **n.** [usu. with modifier] a pan for cooking eggs or other food by poaching: *an egg poacher.*

poach·er[2] ▶ **n.** a person who hunts or catches game or fish illegally.
– PHRASES **poacher turned gamekeeper** someone who now protects the interests they previously attacked.

poach·er[3] ▶ **n.** a small spiny fish that has an armor of overlapping plates and lives chiefly in cooler coastal waters. ● Family Agonidae: several genera and species.

POB ▶ **abbr.** post office box.

po·bla·no /pō'blänō/ ▶ **n.** (pl. **poblanos**) a large dark green chili pepper of a mild-flavored variety.
– ORIGIN Spanish.

Po·ca·hon·tas /ˌpōkə'häntəs/ (c.1595–1617), American Indian; daughter of Powhatan, an Algonquian chief in Virginia. According to John Smith, she rescued him from death at the hands of her father. In 1612, she was seized as a hostage by the English, and she later married colonist **John Rolfe**.

Po·ca·tel·lo /ˌpōkə'telō/ an industrial and commercial city in southeastern Idaho; pop. 54,901 (est. 2008).

po·chard /'pōCHərd/ ▶ **n.** (pl. **same** or **pochards**) a diving duck, the male of which typically has a reddish-brown head and a black breast. ● Genera *Aythya* and *Netta*, family Anatidae: five species, in particular the common *A. ferina* of Eurasia.
– ORIGIN mid 16th cent.: of unknown origin.

pock /päk/ ▶ **n.** a pockmark.
– DERIVATIVES **pocked adj.**, **pock·y adj.** (archaic).
– ORIGIN Old English *poc* 'pustule,' of Germanic origin; related to Dutch *pok* and German *Pocke*. Compare with POX.

pock·et /'päkət/ ▶ **n. 1** a small bag sewn into or on clothing so as to form part of it, used for carrying small articles. ■ a pouchlike compartment providing separate storage space, for example in a suitcase. ■ informal (often **pockets**) a person or organization's financial resources: *the food was all priced to suit the hard-up airman's pocket | our pockets are empty.* ■ Baseball the hollow in the center of a baseball glove or mitt where the ball can best be caught. ■ an opening at the corner or on the side of a billiard table into which balls are struck.
2 a small patch of something: *some of the gardens still had pockets of dirty snow in them.* ■ a small, isolated group or area: *there were pockets of disaffection in parts of the country.* ■ Football the protected area behind the offensive line from which the quarterback throws passes. ■ (in bowling) the space between the head pin and the pin immediately behind it on the left or right. ■ a cavity in a rock or stratum filled with ore or other distinctive component. ■ Aeronautics an air pocket.
▶ **adj.** [attrib.] of a suitable size for carrying in a pocket: *a pocket dictionary.* ■ on a small scale: *a 6,000-acre pocket paradise.*
▶ **v.** (**pockets**, **pocketed**, **pocketing**) [with obj.] put into one's pocket: *she watched him lock up and pocket the key.* ■ take or receive (money or other valuables) for oneself, esp. dishonestly: *local politicians were found to have been pocketing the proceeds.* ■ Billiards drive (a ball) into a pocket. ■ enclose as though in a pocket: *the fillings can be pocketed in a pita bread.* ■ suppress (one's feelings) and proceed despite them: *they were prepared to pocket their pride.* ■ block passage of (a bill) by a pocket veto.
– PHRASES **in pocket** having enough money or money to spare; having gained in a transaction. ■ (of money) gained by someone from a transaction. **in someone's pocket 1** dependent on someone financially and therefore under their influence. **2** very close to and closely involved with someone: *I'm tired of towns where everyone lives in everyone else's pocket.* **line one's pockets** see LINE[2]. **out of pocket** having lost money in a transaction: *the organizer of the concert was $15,000 out of pocket after it was canceled.* ■ (**out-of-pocket**) [as adj. attrib.] (of an expense or cost) paid for directly rather than being put on account or charged to some other person or organization. **put one's hand in one's pocket** spend or provide one's own money.
– DERIVATIVES **pock·et·a·ble adj.**, **pock·et·ful n.** /-ˌfo͝ol/ (pl. **pocketfuls**), **pock·et·less adj.**
– ORIGIN Middle English (in the sense 'bag, sack,' also used as a measure of quantity): from Anglo-Norman French *poket(e)*, diminutive of *poke* 'pouch.' The verb dates from the late 16th cent. Compare with POKE[2].

pock·et bat·tle·ship ▶ **n.** any of a class of cruisers with large-caliber guns, operated by the German navy in World War II.

pock·et bil·liards ▶ **plural n.** a form of billiards played on a table with six pockets into which balls are shot for points. Also called POOL[2].

pock·et·book /'päkətˌbo͝ok/ ▶ **n. 1** a woman's handbag. ■ one's financial resources: *they provide packages for every taste and every pocketbook.*
2 (**pocket book**) a paperback or other small or cheap edition of a book.
3 Brit. a notebook.

pock·et·book plant ▶ **n.** another term for CALCEOLARIA.

pock·et bor·ough ▶ **n.** (in the UK) a borough in which the election of political representatives was controlled by one person or family. Such boroughs were abolished by the Reform Acts of 1832 and 1867.

pock·et go·pher ▶ **n.** see GOPHER[1] (sense 1).

pock·et·knife /'päkətˌnīf/ ▶ **n.** (pl. **pocketknives**) a knife with a folding blade or blades, suitable for carrying in a pocket.

pock·et mon·ey ▶ **n.** a small amount of money suitable for minor expenses. ■ Brit. a child's allowance.

pock·et mouse ▶ **n.** a small nocturnal rodent with large cheek pouches for carrying food, native to the deserts of North and Central America. ● Genus *Perognathus*, family Heteromyidae: several species.

pock·et ve·to ▶ **n.** an indirect veto of a legislative bill by the president or a governor by retaining the bill unsigned until it is too late for it to be dealt with during the legislative session.

pock·et watch ▶ **n.** a watch on a chain, intended to be carried in the pocket of a jacket or vest.

pock·mark /'päkˌmärk/ ▶ **n.** a pitted scar or mark on the skin left by a pustule or pimple. ■ a scar, mark, or pitted area disfiguring a surface.
▶ **v.** [with obj.] (usu. **be pockmarked**) cover or disfigure with such marks: *the area is pockmarked by gravel pits* | (as adj. **pockmarked**) *a pockmarked face.*

po·co /'pōkō, 'pô-/ ▶ **adv.** Music (in directions) a little; somewhat: *poco adagio.*
– ORIGIN Italian.

po·co a po·co /'pōkō ä 'pōkō/ ▶ **adv.** Music (esp. as a direction) little by little; gradually.

Po·co·ma·ni·a /ˌpōkə'mānēə/ ▶ **n.** a Jamaican folk religion combining revivalism with ancestor worship and spirit possession.
– ORIGIN 1930s: probably a Hispanicized form of a local word, the second element being interpreted as -MANIA.

Po·co·no Moun·tains /'pōkəˌnō/ (also **the Poconos**) a range in northeastern Pennsylvania, noted for its resorts.

pod[1] /päd/ ▶ **n. 1** an elongated seed vessel of a leguminous plant such as the pea, splitting open on both sides when ripe. ■ the egg case of a locust. ■ Geology a body of rock or sediment whose length greatly exceeds its other dimensions: *pods of blue quartz in Virginia.* ■ a narrow-necked purse seine for catching eels.
2 [often with modifier] a detachable or self-contained unit on an aircraft, spacecraft, vehicle, or vessel, having a particular function: *the torpedo's sensor pod contains a television camera.*
▶ **v.** (**pods**, **podding**, **podded**) **1** [no obj.] (of a plant) bear or form pods: *the peas have failed to pod.*
2 [with obj.] remove (peas or beans) from their pods prior to cooking.
– DERIVATIVES **pod·like** /-ˌlīk/ **adj.**
– ORIGIN late 17th cent.: back-formation from dialect *podware, podder* 'field crops,' of unknown origin.

pod[2] ▶ **n.** a small herd or school of marine animals, esp. whales.
– ORIGIN mid 19th cent. (originally US): of unknown origin.

p.o.'d (also **PO'd, po'd**) ▶ **abbr.** informal pissed off: *what was he po'd about?*

po·dag·ra /pə'dagrə/ ▶ **n.** Medicine gout of the foot, esp. the big toe.
– DERIVATIVES **po·dag·ral** /-rəl/ **adj.**, **po·dag·ric** /-rik/ **adj.**, **po·dag·rous** /-rəs/ **adj.**
– ORIGIN Middle English: from Latin, from Greek *pous, pod-* 'foot' + *agra* 'seizure.'

pod·cast /'pädˌkast/ ▶ **n.** a multimedia digital file made available on the Internet for downloading to a portable media player, computer, etc.
▶ **v.** (past and past participle **podcast**) [with obj.] make (a multimedia digital file) available as a podcast.
– DERIVATIVES **pod·cast·able adj.**, **pod·cast·er n.**, **pod·cast·ing n.**
– ORIGIN early 21st century: from IPOD.

podge /päj/ Brit. informal ▶ **n.** a short, fat person. ■ excess weight; fat.
– ORIGIN mid 19th cent.: of unknown origin.

Pod·go·ri·ca /'pôdgôˌrētsə/ the capital of Montenegro, in the southwest; pop. 142,500 (est. 2007). Under Turkish rule 1474–1878, it was named Titograd 1946–93 in honor of Marshal Tito.

podg·y /'päjē/ ▶ **adj.** (**podgier**, **podgiest**) Brit. informal (of a person or part of their body) somewhat fat; chubby.
– DERIVATIVES **podg·i·ness n.**

po·di·a·try /pə'dīətrē/ ▶ **n.** the treatment of the feet and their ailments.
– DERIVATIVES **po·di·a·trist** /-trəst/ **n.**
– ORIGIN early 20th cent.: from Greek *pous, pod-* 'foot' + *iatros* 'physician.'

po·di·um /'pōdēəm/ ▶ **n.** (pl. **podiums** or **podia** /-dēə/) a small platform on which a person may stand to be seen by an audience, as when making a speech or conducting an orchestra. ■ a lectern. ■ a continuous projecting base or pedestal under a building. ■ a raised platform surrounding the arena in an ancient amphitheater.
▶ **v.** [no obj.] (of a competitor) finish first, second, or third, so as to appear on a podium for an award: *I've had great results in the sprint and I've podiumed in the individual.*
– ORIGIN mid 18th cent.: via Latin from Greek *podion*, diminutive of *pous, pod-* 'foot.'

pod·o·carp /'pädəˌkärp/ ▶ **n.** a coniferous tree or shrub that is chiefly native to the southern hemisphere, widely grown as an ornamental or timber tree. ● Genus *Podocarpus*, family Podocarpaceae.
– ORIGIN mid 19th cent.: from modern Latin *Podocarpus*, from Greek *pous, pod-* 'foot' + *karpos* 'fruit.'

Po·dolsk /pə'dôlsk/ an industrial city in Russia, south of Moscow; pop. 180,000 (est. 2008).

Po·dunk /'pōˌdəNGk/ ▶ **n.** [usu. as modifier] informal a hypothetical small town regarded as typically dull or insignificant: *she lived in a Podunk town notable for nothing except the girls' school where she taught art.*
– ORIGIN mid 19th cent.: a place name of southern New England, of Algonquian origin.

pod·zol /'pädˌzôl, -ˌzäl/ (also **podsol**) ▶ **n.** Soil Science an infertile acidic soil having an ashlike subsurface layer (from which minerals have been leached) and

a lower dark stratum, occurring typically under temperate coniferous woodland.
– DERIVATIVES **pod·zol·ic** /-ˈzôlik, -ˈzälik/ **adj.**, **pod·zol·i·za·tion** /ˌpädzələˈzāsʜən/ **n.**, **pod·zol·ize** /ˈpädzəˌlīz/ **v.**
– ORIGIN early 20th cent.: from Russian, from *pod* 'under' + *zola* 'ashes.'

Poe /pō/, Edgar Allan (1809–49), US short-story writer, poet, and critic. His fiction and poetry are Gothic in style and characterized by their exploration of the macabre and the grotesque. Notable works: "The Fall of the House of Usher" (1840), "The Murders in the Rue Morgue" (1841), and "The Raven" (1845).

po·em /ˈpōəm, ˈpōim, pōm/ ▶ **n.** a piece of writing that partakes of the nature of both speech and song that is nearly always rhythmical, usually metaphorical, and often exhibits such formal elements as meter, rhyme, and stanzaic structure. ■ something that arouses strong emotions because of its beauty: *you make a poem of riding downhill on your bike.*
– ORIGIN late 15th cent.: from French *poème* or Latin *poema*, from Greek *poēma*, early variant of *poiēma* 'fiction, poem,' from *poiein* 'create.'

po·e·sy /ˈpōəzē, -sē/ ▶ **n.** archaic or literary poetry. ■ the art or composition of poetry.
– ORIGIN late Middle English: from Old French *poesie*, via Latin from Greek *poēsis*, variant of *poiēsis* 'making, poetry,' from *poiein* 'create.'

po·et /ˈpōət, ˈpōit/ ▶ **n.** a person who writes poems. ■ a person possessing special powers of imagination or expression.
– ORIGIN Middle English: from Old French *poete*, via Latin from Greek *poētēs*, variant of *poiētēs* 'maker, poet,' from *poiein* 'create.'

poet. ▶ **abbr.** ■ poetic; poetical. ■ poetry.

po·et·as·ter /ˈpōətˌastər/ ▶ **n.** a person who writes inferior poetry.
– ORIGIN late 16th cent.: modern Latin, from Latin *poeta* 'poet' + **-ASTER**.

poète mau·dit /pōˈet mōˈdē/ ▶ **n.** (pl. **poètes maudits** /mōˈdē(z)/) a poet who is insufficiently appreciated by their contemporaries.
– ORIGIN French, literally 'cursed poet.'

po·et·ess /ˈpōətəs, ˈpōitəs/ ▶ **n.** dated a female poet.

USAGE See usage at **-ESS¹**.

po·et·ic /pōˈetik/ ▶ **adj.** of, relating to, or used in poetry: *the muse is a poetic convention.* ■ written in verse rather than prose: *a poetic drama.* ■ having an imaginative or sensitively emotional style of expression: *the orchestral playing was colorful and poetic.*
– DERIVATIVES **po·et·i·cal** /pōˈetikəl/ **adj.**, **po·et·i·cal·ly** /-ik(ə)lē/ **adv.**
– ORIGIN mid 16th cent.: from French *poétique*, from Latin *poeticus* 'poetic, relating to poets,' from Greek *po(i)ētikos*, from *po(i)ētēs* (see **POET**).

po·et·i·cize /pōˈetəˌsīz/ ▶ **v.** [with obj.] make poetic in character. ■ [no obj.] write or speak poetically.
– DERIVATIVES **po·et·i·cism** /-ˌsizəm/ **n.**

po·et·ic jus·tice ▶ **n.** the fact of experiencing a fitting or deserved retribution for one's actions: *the noise was deafening and it was poetic justice when the amplifiers stalled just before the start.*

po·et·ic li·cense ▶ **n.** the freedom to depart from the facts of a matter or from the conventional rules of language when speaking or writing in order to create an effect: *he used a little poetic license to embroider a good tale.*

po·et·ics /pōˈetiks/ ▶ **plural n.** [treated as sing.] the art of writing poetry. ■ the study of linguistic techniques in poetry or literature.

po·et·ize /ˈpōətˌīz/ ▶ **v.** [no obj.] dated write or speak in verse or in a poetic style. ■ [with obj.] represent in poetic form.

po·et lau·re·ate /ˈlôrēət/ ▶ **n.** (pl. **poets laureate**) an eminent poet traditionally appointed for life as a member of the British royal household. ■ a poet appointed to, or regarded unofficially as holding, an honorary representative position in a particular country, region, or group: *the poet laureate of young America.*

In 1999, Andrew Motion was appointed poet laureate of Great Britain for a term of ten years, the first time in British history that the honor was not granted as a lifetime position. In the US, an unofficial poet laureateship has existed since 1937, although the position was not compensated until 1985, when the honorific title "Poetry Consultant to the Library of Congress" was changed to "Poet Laureate Consultant in Poetry." The first official American poet laureate was Robert Penn Warren, and since then the post has been filled by such well-known poets as Richard Wilbur, Howard Nemerov, Mark Strand, Robert Hass, and Robert Pinsky. The appointment is for one year only, with the possibility of renewal, and although the official duties are limited to one poetry reading and one public lecture, the poet laureate usually takes it upon himself or herself to promote poetry and to encourage its reading and appreciation.

po·et·ry /ˈpōətrē, ˈpōitrē/ ▶ **n.** literary work in which special intensity is given to the expression of feelings and ideas by the use of distinctive style and rhythm; poems collectively or as a genre of literature: *he is chiefly famous for his love poetry.* ■ a quality of beauty and intensity of emotion regarded as characteristic of poems: *poetry and fire are nicely balanced in the music.* ■ something regarded as comparable to poetry in its beauty: *the music department is housed in a building that is pure poetry.*
– ORIGIN late Middle English: from medieval Latin *poetria*, from Latin *poeta* 'poet.' In early use the word sometimes referred to creative literature in general.

po·et·ry slam ▶ **n.** a competition using elimination rounds for the reading or performance of poetry.

Po·ets' Cor·ner part of Westminster Abbey in London where several poets are buried or commemorated.

po-faced /ˈpō ˌfāst/ ▶ **adj.** Brit. humorless and disapproving: *don't be so po-faced about everything.*
– ORIGIN 1930s: perhaps from British slang *po* 'chamber pot,' influenced by *poker-faced.*

Pog /päg, pôg/ ▶ **n.** (usu. **Pogs**) trademark a cardboard or plastic disk printed with a design or picture, used in a children's game involving the flipping over of piles of such disks. ■ (**Pogs**) a game played with these disks: *a group of boys playing Pogs during recess.*
– ORIGIN 1990s: acronym from *passion fruit, orange, guava*, a trademark for a juice drink originally made by a dairy on Maui, Hawaii: the lids of the drink provided the first game disks.

po·gey /ˈpōgē/ ▶ **n.** Canadian informal unemployment or welfare benefit: *so you want me to end up on pogey?*
– ORIGIN late 19th cent., hobo slang for 'workhouse': of unknown origin.

po·go /ˈpōgō/ ▶ **n.** (also **pogo stick**) (pl. **pogos**) a toy for jumping around on, consisting of a long, spring-loaded pole with a handle at the top and rests for a person's feet near the bottom.
▶ **v.** (**pogoes, pogoing, pogoed**) [no obj.] informal jump up and down as if on such a toy, typically as a form of dancing to certain types of rock music, esp. punk.
– ORIGIN 1920s: of unknown origin.

Po·go·noph·o·ra /ˌpōgəˈnäfərə/ Zoology a small phylum of long deep-sea worms that live in upright tubes of protein and chitin. They lack mouths and guts, subsisting mainly on the products of symbiotic bacteria.
– DERIVATIVES **po·go·noph·o·ran** /-rən/ **n. & adj.**
– ORIGIN modern Latin (plural), from Greek *pōgōn* 'beard' + *pherein* 'to bear.'

po·grom /ˈpōgrəm, pəˈgräm/ ▶ **n.** an organized massacre of a particular ethnic group, in particular that of Jews in Russia or eastern Europe.
– ORIGIN early 20th cent.: from Russian, literally 'devastation,' from *gromit'* 'destroy by the use of violence.'

Po Hai /ˈbō ˈhī/ variant of **BO HAI**.

poi /poi/ ▶ **n.** a Hawaiian dish made from the fermented root of the taro, which has been baked and pounded to a paste.
– ORIGIN of Polynesian origin.

poign·an·cy /ˈpoinyənsē/ ▶ **n.** the quality of evoking a keen sense of sadness or regret: *the pregnancy has a special poignancy for her family.*
– DERIVATIVES **poign·ance n.**

poign·ant /ˈpoinyənt/ ▶ **adj.** evoking a keen sense of sadness or regret: *a poignant reminder of the passing of time.* ■ archaic sharp or pungent in taste or smell.
– DERIVATIVES **poign·ant·ly** /-yəntlē/ **adv.**
– ORIGIN late Middle English: from Old French, literally 'pricking,' present participle of *poindre*, from Latin *pungere* 'to prick.'

poi·ki·lit·ic /ˌpoikəˈlitik/ ▶ **adj.** Geology relating to or denoting the texture of an igneous rock in which small crystals of one mineral occur within crystals of another.
– ORIGIN mid 19th cent.: from Greek *poikilos* 'variegated' + **-ITE¹** + **-IC**.

poikilo- ▶ **comb. form** variegated: *poikiloblastic.* ■ variable: *poikilotherm.*
– ORIGIN from Greek *poikilos* 'variegated, varied.'

poi·kil·o·blas·tic /ˌpoiˌkēləˈblastik, -ˌkil-/ ▶ **adj.** Geology relating to or denoting the texture of a metamorphic rock in which small crystals of an original mineral occur within crystals of its metamorphic product.

poi·ki·lo·therm /poiˈkēləˌᴛʜərm, -kil-/ ▶ **n.** Zoology an organism that cannot regulate its body temperature except by behavioral means such as basking or burrowing. Often contrasted with **HOMEOTHERM**; compare with **COLD-BLOODED**.
– DERIVATIVES **poi·ki·lo·ther·mal** /ˌpoiˌkēləˈᴛʜərməl, -ˌkil-/ **adj.**, **poi·ki·lo·ther·mic** /ˌpoiˌkēləˈᴛʜərmik, -ˌkilə-/ **adj.**, **poi·ki·lo·ther·my n.**

poi·lu /pwälˈ(y)o͞o/ ▶ **n.** historical, informal an infantry soldier in the French army, esp. one who fought in World War I.
– ORIGIN French, literally 'hairy,' by extension 'brave,' whiskers being associated with virility.

Poin·ca·ré map /ˌpwaɴkäˈrā/ ▶ **n.** Mathematics & Physics a representation of the phase space of a dynamic system, indicating all possible trajectories. ■ (also **Poincaré section**) the intersection of this representation with a given line, plane, etc.
– ORIGIN from the name of the French mathematician and philosopher of science Jules-Henri *Poincaré* (1854–1912).

poin·ci·an·a /ˌpoinsēˈanə, ˌp(w)än-/ ▶ **n.** a tropical tree of the pea family, with showy red or red and yellow flowers. ● Genera *Caesalpinia* and *Delonix* (formerly *Poinciana*), family Leguminosae: several species, including the scarlet-flowered **royal poinciana** (*D. regia*), native to Madagascar.
– ORIGIN mid 18th cent.: modern Latin, named after M. de *Poinci*, a 17th-cent. governor of the Antilles.

poin·set·ti·a /poinˈset(ē)ə/ ▶ **n.** a small Mexican shrub with large showy scarlet bracts surrounding the small yellow flowers, popular as a houseplant at Christmas. ● *Euphorbia* (formerly *Poinsettia*) *pulcherrima*, family Euphorbiaceae.
– ORIGIN mid 19th cent.: modern Latin, named after Joel R. *Poinsett* (1779–1851), American diplomat and amateur botanist.

point /point/ ▶ **n. 1** the tapered, sharp end of a tool, weapon, or other object: *the point of his dagger | a pencil point.* ■ Archaeology a pointed flake or blade, esp. one that has been worked. ■ see **GLAZIER'S POINT**. ■ Ballet another term for **POINTE**. ■ Boxing the tip of a person's chin as a spot for a blow. ■ the prong of a deer's antler.
2 a dot or other punctuation mark, in particular a period. ■ a decimal point: *fifty-five point nine.* ■ a dot or small stroke used in the alphabets of Semitic languages to indicate vowels or distinguish particular consonants. ■ a very small dot or mark on a surface: *the sky was studded with points of light.*
3 a particular spot, place, or position in an area or on a map, object, or surface: *turn left at the point where you see a sign to Apple Grove | the furthermost point of the gallery | the check-in point.* ■ a particular moment in time or stage in a process: *from this point onward, the teacher was completely won over.* ■ (usu. **the point**) the critical or decisive moment: *when it came to the point, he would probably do what was expected of him.* ■ (**the point of**) the verge or brink of (doing or being something): *she was on the point of leaving.* ■ [usu. with modifier] a stage or level at which a change of state occurs: *it is packed to the bursting point.* ■ (in geometry) something having position but not spatial extent, magnitude, dimension, or direction, for example the intersection of two lines. ■ [with modifier] Brit. a wall outlet or jack: *a telephone point.*
4 a single item or detail in an extended discussion, list, or text: *you ignore a number of important points.* ■ an argument or idea put forward by a person in discussion: *he made the point that economic regulation involves controls on pricing.* ■ (usu. **the point**) the significant or essential element of what is intended or being discussed: *it took her a long time to come to the point.* ■ [in sing., usu. with negative or in questions] advantage or purpose that can be gained from doing something: *there was no point in denying the truth | what's the point of having things I don't need?* ■ relevance or effectiveness. ■ a distinctive feature or characteristic, typically a good one, of a person or thing: *he has his good points.*
5 (in sports and games) a mark or unit of scoring: *he scored 13 of his team's final 19 points against Houston.* ■ (in craps) the combination total of the two thrown dice (4, 5, 6, 8, 9, or 10) that permits a shooter to keep throwing until he or she throws the same number again and wins. ■ a unit used in measuring value, achievement, or extent: *the shares index was down seven points.* ■ an advantage or success in an argument or discussion: *she smiled, assuming she had won her point.* ■ a unit of credit toward an award or benefit. ■ a percentage of the profits from a movie or recording offered to certain people involved in its production. ■ a punishment imposed by the courts for a driving offense and

p

recorded cumulatively on a person's driver's license: *operating under the influence meant ten points marked up against the driver.* ■ a unit of weight (one hundredth of a carat, or 2 mg) for diamonds. ■ a unit of varying value, used in quoting the price of stocks, bonds, or futures. ■ Bridge a value assigned to certain cards (4 points for an ace, 3 for a king, 2 for a queen, and 1 for a jack, sometimes with extra points for long or short suits) by a player in assessing the strength of a hand. ■ (**point of**) (in piquet) the longest suit in a player's hand, containing a specified number of up to eight cards.
6 each of thirty-two directions marked at equal distances around a compass. ■ the corresponding direction toward the horizon. ■ the angular interval between two successive points of a compass, i.e., one eighth of a right angle (11° 15'). ■ (**points ——**) unspecified places considered in terms of their direction from a specified place: *they headed down I-95 to Philadelphia and points south.*
7 a narrow piece of land jutting out into a lake or ocean: *the boat came around the point* | [in names] *Sandy Point.*
8 (usu. **points**) Brit. another term for SWITCH (sense 4 of the noun).
9 Printing a unit of measurement for type sizes and spacing, which in the US and UK is one twelfth of a pica, or 0.013835 inch (0.351 mm), and in Europe is 0.015 inch (0.376 mm).
10 Basketball a frontcourt position, usually manned by the guard who sets up the team's defense. ■ Ice Hockey either of two areas in each attacking zone, just inside the blue line where it meets the boards.
11 (usu. **points**) each of a set of electrical contacts in the distributor of a motor vehicle.
12 a small leading party of an advanced guard of troops. ■ the position at the head of a column or wedge of troops: *another marine said he would walk point because I had done it on the last patrol.* ■ short for POINT MAN.
13 (usu. **points**) the extremities of an animal, typically a horse or cat, such as the face, paws, and tail of a Siamese cat.
14 Hunting a spot to which a straight run is made. ■ a run of this type: *our fox made his point to Moorhill.*
15 (usu. **points**) historical a tagged piece of ribbon or cord used for lacing a garment or attaching breeches to a doublet.
16 a short piece of cord for tying up a reef in a sail.
17 the action or position of a dog in pointing: *a bird dog on point.*
18 Music an important phrase or subject, esp. in a contrapuntal composition. Compare with COUNTERPOINT.
▸ **v. 1** [no obj.] direct someone's attention to the position or direction of something, typically by extending one's finger: *the boys were nudging each other and pointing at me* | *he gripped her arm and pointed to the seat* | *it's rude to point.* ■ [with adverbial of direction] indicate a particular time, direction, or reading: *a sign pointing left.* ■ [with obj.] direct or aim (something) at someone or something: *he pointed the flashlight beam at the floor.* ■ [with adverbial of direction] face or be turned in a particular direction: *two of its toes point forward and two point back.* ■ [with adverbial] cite or put forward a fact or situation as evidence of something: *he points to several factors supporting this conclusion.* ■ (**point to**) (of a situation) be evidence or an indication that (something) is likely to happen or be the case: *everything pointed to an eastern attack.* ■ [with obj.] (of a dog) indicate the presence of (game) by acting as pointer. ■ [with obj.] chiefly Ballet extend (the toes or feet) by tensing the foot and ankle so as to form a point.
2 [with obj.] give force or emphasis to (words or actions): *he wouldn't miss the opportunity to point a moral.*
3 [with obj.] fill in or repair the joints of (brickwork, a brick structure, or tiling) with smoothly finished mortar or cement.
4 [with obj.] give a sharp, tapered point to: *he twisted and pointed his mustache.*
5 [with obj.] insert points in (written Hebrew). ■ mark (Psalms) with signs for chanting.
– PHRASES **beside the point** irrelevant. **case in point** an instance or example that illustrates what is being discussed: *the "green revolution" in agriculture is a good case in point.* **get the point** understand or accept the validity of someone's idea or argument: *I get the point about not sending rejections.* **in point of fact** see FACT. **make one's point** put across a proposition clearly and convincingly. **make a point of** make a special and noticeable effort to do (a specified thing): *she made a point of taking a walk each day.* **off the point** irrelevant. **point the finger** openly accuse someone or apportion blame. **the point of no return** the point in a journey or enterprise at which it becomes essential or more practical to continue to the end instead of returning to the point of departure. **point of sailing** a sailboat's heading in relation to the wind. **score points** deliberately make oneself appear superior to someone else by making clever remarks: *she was constantly trying to think of ways to score points off him.* **take someone's point** chiefly Brit. accept the validity of someone's idea or argument. **to the point** relevant: *his evidence was brief and to the point.* **up to a point** to some extent but not completely. **win on points** Boxing win by scoring more points than one's opponent (as awarded by the judges and/or the referee) rather than by a knockout.
– PHRASAL VERBS **point something out** direct someone's gaze or attention toward something, esp. by extending one's finger. ■ [reporting verb] say something to make someone aware of a fact or circumstance: [with clause] *she pointed out that his van had been in the parking lot all day* | [with direct speech] *"Most of the people around here are very poor," I pointed out.* **point something up** reveal the true nature or importance of something: *he did so much to point up their plight in the 1960s.*
– ORIGIN Middle English: the noun partly from Old French *point*, from Latin *punctum* 'something that is pricked,' giving rise to the senses 'unit, mark, point in space or time'; partly from Old French *pointe*, from Latin *puncta* 'pricking,' giving rise to the senses 'sharp tip, promontory.' The verb is from Old French *pointer*, and in some senses from the English noun.

point af·ter touch·down ▸ **n.** EXTRA POINT.

point-and-click ▸ **adj.** Computing (of an interface) giving the user the ability to initiate tasks by using a mouse to move the cursor over an area of the screen and clicking on it.
▸ **v.** [no obj.] use a mouse in such a way.

point-and-shoot ▸ **adj.** denoting an automatic camera which, when it is pointed at a subject and the shutter release is pressed, will take a properly exposed and focused photograph.

point bar ▸ **n.** Geology an alluvial deposit that forms by accretion on the inner side of an expanding loop of a river.

point-blank ▸ **adj. & adv.** (of a shot, bullet, or other missile) fired from very close to its target. [as adj.] *the weapon was inaccurate beyond point-blank range.* ■ (of a statement or question) blunt and direct; without explanation or qualification: [as adj.] *this point-blank refusal to discuss the issue* | [as adv.] *he refuses point-blank to be photographed or give interviews.*
– ORIGIN late 16th cent.: probably from POINT + BLANK in the contemporaneous sense 'white spot in the center of a target.'

point blan·ket ▸ **n.** Canadian a type of Hudson's Bay blanket with distinctive markings or points woven in to indicate size or weight.

point break ▸ **n.** (in surfing) a type of wave characteristic of a coast with a headland.

point charge ▸ **n.** chiefly Physics an electric charge regarded as concentrated in a mathematical point, without spatial extent.

point con·tact ▸ **n.** Electronics the contact of a metal point with the surface of a semiconductor so as to form a rectifying junction.

point d'ap·pui /ˌpwan däˈpwē/ ▸ **n.** (pl. **points d'appui** pronunc. **same**) a support or prop; a strategic point.
– ORIGIN French, literally 'point of support.'

pointe /point, pwant/ ▸ **n.** (pl. pronunc. **same**) Ballet the tips of the toes. ■ (also **pointe work**) dance performed on the tips of the toes.
– PHRASES **on** (or **en**) **pointe** /än, än, ôn/ on the tips of the toes.
– ORIGIN French, literally 'tip.'

Pointe-à-Pi·tre /ˌpwant ä ˈpētrə/ the chief port and commercial capital of the French island of Guadeloupe in the Caribbean Sea; pop. 19,000 (est. 2007).

point·ed /ˈpointid/ ▸ **adj. 1** having a sharpened or tapered tip or end: *his face tapers to a pointed chin.*
2 (of a remark or look) expressing criticism in a direct and unambiguous way: *pointed comments were made about racial discrimination within the army.*
– DERIVATIVES **point·ed·ly adv.** (sense 2), **point·ed·ness n.**

point·ed arch ▸ **n.** an arch with a pointed crown, characteristic of Gothic architecture.

poin·telle /poinˈtel/ (also trademark **Pointelle**) ▸ **n.** a type of knitwear or woolen fabric with small eyelet holes that create a lacy effect.
– ORIGIN 1950s: probably from *point* in the sense 'lace made entirely with a needle' + the French diminutive suffix *-elle*.

Pointe-Noire /pwant ˈnwär/ the chief seaport of the Republic of Congo, an oil terminal on the Atlantic coast; pop. 792,382 (2009).

point·er /ˈpointər/ ▸ **n. 1** a long thin piece of metal on a scale or dial that moves to indicate a figure or position. ■ a rod used for pointing to features on a map or chart. ■ a hint as to what might happen in the future: *the figures were a pointer to gradual economic recovery.* ■ a small piece of advice; a tip: *here are some pointers on how to go about the task.* ■ Computing another term for CURSOR. ■ Computing a variable whose value is the address of another variable; a link.
2 a dog of a breed that on scenting game stands rigid looking toward it.

English pointer

Point·ers /ˈpointərz/ (**the Pointers**) Astronomy (in the northern hemisphere) two stars of the Big Dipper in Ursa Major, through which a line points nearly to Polaris. ■ (in the southern hemisphere) two stars in the Southern Cross, through which a line points nearly to the south celestial pole.

point es·ti·mate ▸ **n.** Statistics a single value given as an estimate of a parameter of a population. Compare with INTERVAL ESTIMATE.

point guard ▸ **n.** Basketball the backcourt player who directs the team's offense.

poin·til·lism /ˈpwantēˌyizəm, ˈpointlˌizəm/ ▸ **n.** a technique of neo-Impressionist painting using tiny dots of various pure colors, which become blended in the viewer's eye. It was developed by Georges Seurat with the aim of producing a greater degree of luminosity and brilliance of color.
– DERIVATIVES **poin·til·list** /ˌpwantēˈyēst, ˈpointl-ist/ **n. & adj.**, **poin·til·list·ic** /ˌpwantēˈyistik, ˌpointlˈistik/ **adj.**
– ORIGIN early 20th cent.: from French *pointillisme*, from *pointiller* 'mark with dots.'

point·ing /ˈpointiNG/ ▸ **n.** cement or mortar used to fill the joints of brickwork, esp. when added externally to a wall to improve its appearance and weatherproofing. ■ the process of adding such cement or mortar.

point·ing de·vice ▸ **n.** Computing a generic term for any device (e.g., a graphics tablet, mouse, stylus, pointing stick, or trackball) used to control the movement of a cursor on a computer screen.

point·ing stick ▸ **n.** a movable stub embedded in a laptop keyboard that is manipulated to move the screen cursor.

point lace ▸ **n.** lace made with a needle on a parchment pattern.

point·less /ˈpointlis/ ▸ **adj. 1** having little or no sense, use, or purpose: *speculating like this is a pointless exercise* | [with infinitive] *it's pointless to plan too far ahead.*
2 (of a contest or competitor) without a point scored.
– DERIVATIVES **point·less·ly adv.**, **point·less·ness n.**

point man ▸ **n.** the soldier at the head of a patrol. ■ (esp. in a political context) a person at the forefront of an activity or endeavor.

point mu·ta·tion ▸ **n.** Genetics a mutation affecting only one or very few nucleotides in a gene sequence.

point of de·par·ture ▸ **n.** the starting point of a line of thought or course of action; an initial assumption: *composers take him as a point of departure, whether by a process of imitation, assimilation, or rejection.*

point of hon·or ▸ **n.** an action or circumstance that affects one's reputation or conscience: *he languished in jail refusing, as a point of honor, to talk.*

point of in·flec·tion ▸ **n.** another term for INFLECTION POINT (sense 1).

point of or·der ▸ **n.** a query in a formal debate or meeting as to whether correct procedure is being followed.

point of sale (abbr.: **POS**) ▸ **n.** the place at which goods are retailed: *refunds will be provided at the point of sale* | [as modifier] *point-of-sale credit card verification.*

point of view ▸ **n.** a particular attitude or way of considering a matter: *I'm trying to get Matthew to change his point of view.* ■ (in fictional writing) the narrator's position in relation to the story being told: *this story is told from a child's point of view.* ■ the position from which something or someone is observed: *certain aspects are not visible from a single point of view.*

P

point set ▶ n. (in acupuncture) a set of points stimulated simultaneously to treat a particular ailment or bring about a desired effect.

point source ▶ n. Physics **1** a source of energy, such as light or sound, that can be regarded as having negligible dimensions.
2 a localized and stationary pollution source. Compare with NONPOINT SOURCE.

point spread ▶ n. **1** a forecast of the number of points by which a stronger team is expected to defeat a weaker one, used for betting purposes.
2 Physics & Physiology the spread of energy from a point source, esp. with respect to light coming into an optical instrument or eye.

point sys·tem ▶ n. a system for distributing or allocating resources or for ranking or evaluating candidates or claimants on the basis of points allocated or accumulated.

point-to-point ▶ n. (pl. **point-to-points**) an amateur steeplechase for horses used in hunting, over a set cross-country course.
▶ adj. (of a route or journey) from one place to the next without stopping or changing; direct. ■ (of a telecommunications or computer link) directly from the sender to the receiver.
– DERIVATIVES **point-to-point·er** n., **point-to-point·ing** n.

point·y /ˈpointē/ ▶ adj. (**pointier**, **pointiest**) informal having a pointed tip or end: *a pointy goatee.*

point·y-head·ed ▶ adj. informal, chiefly derogatory intellectual; expert: *some pointy-headed college professor.*
– ORIGIN by association with EGGHEAD.

poise¹ /poiz/ ▶ n. **1** graceful and elegant bearing in a person: *poise and good deportment can be cultivated.* ■ composure and dignity of manner: *at least he had a moment to think, to recover his poise.*
2 archaic balance; equilibrium.
▶ v. be or cause to be balanced or suspended: [no obj.] *he poised motionless on his toes* | [with obj.] figurative *the world was poised between peace and war.* ■ (**be poised**) (of a person or organization) be ready to do something: [with infinitive] *teachers are poised to resume their attack on government school tests.*
– ORIGIN late Middle English (in the sense 'weight'): from Old French *pois*, *peis* (noun), *peser* (verb), from an alteration of Latin *pensum* 'weight,' from the verb *pendere* 'weigh.' From the early senses of 'weight' and 'measure of weight' arose the notion of 'equal weight, balance,' leading to the extended senses 'composure' and 'elegant bearing.'

poise² ▶ n. Physics a unit of dynamic viscosity, such that a tangential force of one dyne per square centimeter causes a velocity change of one centimeter per second between two parallel planes separated by one centimeter in a liquid.
– ORIGIN early 20th cent.: from the name of Jean L. M. *Poiseuille* (1799–1869), French physician.

poised /poizd/ ▶ adj. having a composed and self-assured manner. ■ having a graceful and elegant bearing.

Poi·seuille flow /pwäˈzœ(ē), pwäˈzē/ ▶ n. Physics laminar or streamline flow of an incompressible viscous fluid, esp. through a long narrow cylinder.
– ORIGIN 1940s: named after Jean L. M. *Poiseuille* (1799–1869), French physician.

poi·sha /ˈpoishə/ ▶ n. (pl. **same**) a monetary unit of Bangladesh, equal to one hundredth of a taka.
– ORIGIN Bengali, alteration of PAISA.

poi·son /ˈpoizən/ ▶ n. a substance that, when introduced into or absorbed by a living organism, causes death or injury, esp. one that kills by rapid action even in a small quantity. ■ Chemistry a substance that reduces the activity of a catalyst. ■ Physics an additive or impurity in a nuclear reactor that slows a reaction by absorbing neutrons. ■ a person, idea, action, or situation that is considered to have a destructive or corrupting effect or influence: *meanwhile he is spreading his poison over the Internet.*
▶ v. [with obj.] administer poison to (a person or animal), either deliberately or accidentally: *he tried to poison his wife* | *swans are being poisoned by lead from anglers' lines* | (as noun **poisoning**) *symptoms of poisoning may include nausea, diarrhea, and vomiting.* ■ adulterate or contaminate (food or drink) with poison. ■ (usu. as adj. **poisoned**) treat (a weapon or missile) with poison in order to augment its lethal effect. ■ prove harmful or destructive to: *his disgust had poisoned his attitude toward everyone.* ■ Chemistry (of a substance) reduce the activity of (a catalyst).
– PHRASES **what's your poison?** informal used to ask someone what they would like to drink.
– DERIVATIVES **poi·son·er** /ˈpoizənər/ n.
– ORIGIN Middle English (denoting a harmful medicinal drink): from Old French *poison* 'magic potion,' from Latin *potio(n-)* 'potion,' related to *potare* 'to drink.'

poi·son ar·row frog ▶ n. a small slender, brightly colored frog of Central and South American rain forests. Its skin secretes a virulent poison, used by American Indians to coat their arrowheads. ● Family Dendrobatidae: several genera and numerous species.

poi·soned chal·ice ▶ n. chiefly Brit. an assignment, award, or honor that is likely to prove a disadvantage or source of problems to the recipient: *many thought the new minister had been handed a poisoned chalice.*

poi·son gas ▶ n. poisonous gas or vapor, used esp. to disable or kill an enemy in warfare.

poi·son i·vy ▶ n. a North American climbing plant of the cashew family that secretes an irritant oil from its leaves, which can cause dermatitis. ● *Rhus radicans*, family Anacardiaceae.

poison ivy

poi·son oak ▶ n. a North American climbing shrub of the cashew family, closely related to poison ivy and having similar properties. ● *Rhus toxicodendron*, family Anacardiaceae.

poi·son·ous /ˈpoiz(ə)nəs/ ▶ adj. (of a substance or plant) causing or capable of causing death or illness if taken into the body: *poisonous chemicals.* ■ (of an animal) producing poison as a means of attacking enemies or prey; venomous: *a poisonous snake.* ■ extremely unpleasant or malicious: *there was a poisonous atmosphere at the office.*
– DERIVATIVES **poi·son·ous·ly** adv.

> **USAGE** Poisonous and venomous are not identical in meaning, although they are often used interchangeably. A **poisonous** animal or plant produces toxins that are harmful when the animal or plant is touched or eaten, whereas a **venomous** snake or other creature is able to inject venom by means of its fangs, spines, or stingers.

poi·son pen let·ter ▶ n. a letter, typically anonymous, that is libelous, abusive, or malicious.

poi·son pill ▶ n. Finance a tactic used by a company threatened with an unwelcome takeover bid to make itself unattractive to the bidder.

poi·son pill a·mend·ment ▶ n. an amendment to a legislative bill that considerably weakens the bill's intended effect, or ruins the bill's chances of passing.

poi·son su·mac ▶ n. see SUMAC.

Pois·son dis·tri·bu·tion /pwäˈsôN/ ▶ n. Statistics a discrete frequency distribution that gives the probability of a number of independent events occurring in a fixed time.
– ORIGIN named after the French mathematical physicist Siméon-Denis *Poisson* (1781–1840).

Pois·son's ra·tio /pwäˈsôNz/ ▶ n. Physics the ratio of the proportional decrease in a lateral measurement to the proportional increase in length in a sample of material that is elastically stretched.

Poi·tier /ˈpwätēˌā, pwätˈyā/, Sidney (1924–), US actor and movie director, of Bahamian descent; the first black US actor to achieve superstar status. Notable movies: *Lilies of the Field* (1963), *In the Heat of the Night* (1967), and *Guess Who's Coming to Dinner* (1967).

Sidney Poitier

Poi·tiers /pwäˈtyā/ a city in west central France, the chief town of Poitou-Charentes region and capital of the former province of Poitou; pop. 91,395 (2006).

Poi·tou /pwäˈto͞o/ a former province of west central France, now united with Charente to form the region of Poitou-Charentes. Formerly part of Aquitaine, it was held by the French and English in succession until it was finally united with France at the end of the Hundred Years War.

poke¹ /pōk/ ▶ v. **1** [with obj.] jab or prod (someone or something), esp. with one's finger: *he poked Benny in the ribs and pointed* | [no obj.] *they sniffed, felt, and poked at everything they bought.* ■ (on the social networking site Facebook) attract the attention of (another member of the site) by using the 'poke' facility. ■ prod and stir (a fire) with a poker to make it burn more fiercely. ■ make (a hole) in something by prodding or jabbing at it. ■ thrust (something) in a particular direction: *I poked my head around the door to see what was going on* | *she poked her tongue out.* ■ [no obj.] protrude and be or become visible: *she had wisps of gray hair poking out from under her bonnet.* ■ vulgar slang (of a man) have sexual intercourse with (another person).
2 [no obj.] informal move slowly; dawdle: *I was poking along, my vision blocked by that curtain of sleet.*
▶ n. **1** an act of poking someone or something: *she gave the fire a poke.* ■ (**a poke around**) informal a look or search around a place. ■ vulgar slang an act of sexual intercourse.
2 (also **poke bonnet**) a woman's bonnet with a projecting brim or front, popular esp. in the early 19th century.
3 informal, chiefly Brit. power or acceleration in a car: *I expect you'd prefer something with a bit more poke.*
– PHRASES **better than a poke in the eye (with a sharp stick)** humorous welcome or pleasing, even if other circumstances might be better: *I got a tax rebate—not a huge amount but better than a poke in the eye with a sharp stick.* **poke fun at** tease or make fun of. **poke one's nose into** informal take an intrusive interest in. **take a poke at someone** informal hit or punch someone. ■ criticize someone.
– PHRASAL VERBS **poke around**/**about** look around a place, typically in search of something.
– ORIGIN Middle English: origin uncertain; compare with Middle Dutch and Middle Low German *poken*, of unknown ultimate origin. The noun dates from the late 18th cent.

poke² ▶ n. dialect a bag or small sack. ■ informal a purse or wallet.
– PHRASES **a pig in a poke** see PIG.
– ORIGIN Middle English: from Old Northern French *poke*, variant of Old French *poche* 'pocket.' Compare with POUCH.

poke³ ▶ n. **1** another term for POKEWEED.
2 (**Indian poke**) another term for FALSE HELLEBORE.
– ORIGIN early 18th cent.: from Virginia Algonquian *poughkone* (see PUCCOON).

poke-check ▶ v. [with obj.] Ice Hockey poke the puck off the stick of and out of the possession of (an opposing player).

Po·ke·mon /ˈpōkiˌmän/ ▶ n. trademark a video game, card game, or other toy featuring certain Japanese cartoon characters.
– ORIGIN from the name of the Japanese video game *Pokemon*, itself from the words 'pocket monster.'

pok·er¹ /ˈpōkər/ ▶ n. a metal rod with a handle, used for prodding and stirring an open fire.

pok·er² ▶ n. a card game played by two or more people who bet on the value of the hands dealt to them. A player wins the pool either by having the highest combination at the showdown or by forcing all opponents to concede without a showing of the hand, sometimes by means of bluff.
– ORIGIN mid 19th cent.: of US origin; perhaps related to German *pochen* 'to brag,' *Pochspiel* 'bragging game.'

pok·er face ▶ n. an impassive expression that hides one's true feelings. ■ a person with such an expression.
– DERIVATIVES **pok·er-faced** adj.

pok·er·work /ˈpōkərˌwərk/ ▶ n. British term for PYROGRAPHY.

poke·weed /ˈpōkˌwēd/ ▶ n. a North American plant with red stems, spikes of cream flowers, and purple berries. Also called POKE³, INKBERRY. ● *Phytolacca americana*, family Phytolaccaceae.
– ORIGIN early 18th cent.: from POKE³.

pok·ey /ˈpōkē/ ▶ n. (usu. **the pokey**) informal prison: *25 years in the pokey.*

P

– ORIGIN early 20th cent.: alteration of POGEY (an early sense being 'hostel for the needy'), perhaps influenced by POKY.

pok·y /ˈpōkē/ (also **pokey**) ▶ adj. (**pokier, pokiest**) **1** annoyingly slow or dull: *his poky old horse | I slept through his poky sermons.*
2 (of a room or building) uncomfortably small and cramped: *five of us shared the poky little room.*
– DERIVATIVES **pok·i·ly** /-kəlē/ adv., **pok·i·ness** n.
– ORIGIN mid 19th cent. (in the sense 'concerned with petty matters'): from POKE[1] (in a contemporaneous sense 'confine') + -Y[1].

pol /päl/ ▶ n. informal a politician.

pol. ▶ abbr. ■ political. ■ politics.

Po·lack /ˈpōˌläk, -ˌlak/ (also **polack**) ▶ n. informal, offensive a person from Poland or of Polish descent.
▶ adj. of Polish origin or descent.
– ORIGIN late 16th cent.: from Polish *Polak.*

Po·land /ˈpōlənd/ a country in central Europe with a coastline on the Baltic Sea; pop. 38,482,900 (est. 2009); capital, Warsaw; language, Polish (official). Polish name **Polska**.

> First united as a nation in the 11th century, Poland became a dominant power in the region in the 16th century but thereafter suffered severely from the rise of Russian, Swedish, Prussian, and Austrian power and was partitioned in the late 18th century. It regained full independence (as a republic) after World War I. Its invasion by German forces in 1939 precipitated World War II, from which it eventually emerged as a communist state under Soviet domination. In the 1980s, the rise of the independent trade union movement Solidarity eventually led to the end of communist rule in 1989. Poland joined NATO in 1999 and the EU in 2004.

Po·land Chi·na ▶ n. a US breed of hog that is black with white markings.

Po·lan·ski /pəˈlanskē/, Roman (1933–), French movie director. His second wife, actress **Sharon Tate** (1943–69), was one of the victims of a multiple murder by followers of cult leader Charles Manson. Notable movies: *Rosemary's Baby* (1968), *Chinatown* (1974), *Tess* (1979), and *The Pianist* (2002).

po·lar /ˈpōlər/ ▶ adj. **1** of or relating to the North or South Pole: *the polar regions.* ■ (of an animal or plant) living in the north or south polar region. ■ Astronomy of or relating to the poles of a celestial body. ■ Astronomy of or relating to a celestial pole. ■ Geometry of or relating to the poles of a sphere. See POLE[2]. ■ Biology of or relating to the poles of a cell, organ, or part.
2 Physics & Chemistry having electrical or magnetic polarity. ■ (of a liquid, esp. a solvent) consisting of molecules with a dipole moment. ■ (of a solid) ionic.
3 directly opposite in character or tendency: *depression and its polar opposite, mania.*
▶ n. **1** Geometry the straight line joining the two points at which tangents from a fixed point touch a conic section.
2 Astronomy a variable binary star that emits strongly polarized light, one component being a strongly magnetic white dwarf.
– ORIGIN mid 16th cent.: from medieval Latin *polaris* 'heavenly,' from Latin *polus* 'end of an axis' (see POLE[2]).

P

po·lar ax·is ▶ n. Astronomy the axis of an equatorially mounted telescope that is at right angles to the declination axis and parallel to the earth's axis of rotation, about which the telescope is turned to follow the apparent movement of celestial objects resulting from the earth's rotation.

po·lar bear ▶ n. a large white arctic bear that lives mainly on the pack ice. It is a powerful swimmer and feeds chiefly on seals. ● *Thalarctos maritimus*, family Ursidae.

polar bear

po·lar bod·y ▶ n. Biology each of the small cells that bud off from an oocyte at the two meiotic divisions and do not develop into ova.

po·lar cap ▶ n. Astronomy a region of ice or other frozen matter surrounding a pole of a planet.

po·lar co·or·di·nates ▶ plural n. Geometry a pair of coordinates locating the position of a point in a plane, the first being the length of the straight line (*r*) connecting the point to the origin, and the second the angle (θ) made by this line with a fixed line. ■ the coordinates in a three-dimensional extension of this system.

po·lar dis·tance ▶ n. Geometry the angular distance of a point on a sphere from the nearest pole.

po·lar·im·e·ter /ˌpōləˈrimitər/ ▶ n. an instrument for measuring the polarization of light, and esp. (in chemical analysis) for determining the effect of a substance in rotating the plane of polarization of light.
– DERIVATIVES **po·lar·i·met·ric** /pōˌlarəˈmetrik/ adj., **po·lar·im·e·try** /-trē/ n.
– ORIGIN mid 19th cent.: from medieval Latin *polaris* 'polar' + -METER.

Po·lar·is /pəˈlarəs/ **1** Astronomy a fairly bright star located within one degree of the north celestial pole, in the constellation Ursa Minor. It is a triple star, the bright component of which is a cepheid variable. Also called **North Star**, **polestar**.
2 a type of submarine-launched ballistic missile designed to carry nuclear warheads, formerly in service with the US and British navies.
– ORIGIN mid 19th cent.: from medieval Latin *polaris* 'heavenly,' from Latin *polus* 'end of an axis.'

po·lar·i·scope /pəˈlarəˌskōp/ ▶ n. another term for POLARIMETER.
– DERIVATIVES **po·lar·i·scop·ic** /pəˌlarəˈskäpik/ adj.
– ORIGIN early 19th cent.: from medieval Latin *polaris* 'polar' + -SCOPE.

po·lar·i·ty /pōˈlaritē, pə-/ ▶ n. (pl. **polarities**) the property of having poles or being polar: *it exhibits polarity when presented to a magnetic needle.* ■ the relative orientation of poles; the direction of a magnetic or electric field: *the magnetic field peaks in strength immediately after switching polarity.* ■ the state of having two opposite or contradictory tendencies, opinions, or aspects: *the polarity between male and female | the Cold War's neat polarities can hardly be carried on.* ■ Biology the tendency of living organisms or parts to develop with distinct anterior and posterior (or uppermost and lowermost) ends, or to grow or orient in a particular direction.

po·lar·i·ty ther·a·py ▶ n. a system of treatment used in alternative medicine, intended to restore a balanced distribution of the body's energy, and incorporating manipulation, exercise, and dietary restrictions.

po·lar·ize /ˈpōləˌrīz/ ▶ v. **1** [with obj.] Physics restrict the vibrations of (a transverse wave, esp. light) wholly or partially to one direction: (as adj. **polarizing**) *a polarizing microscope.*
2 [with obj.] Physics cause (something) to acquire polarity: *the electrode is polarized in aqueous solution.*
3 divide or cause to divide into two sharply contrasting groups or sets of opinions or beliefs: [no obj.] *the cultural sphere has polarized into two competing ideological positions* | [with obj.] *Vietnam polarized political opinion.*
– DERIVATIVES **po·lar·iz·a·bil·i·ty** /ˌpōləˌrīzəˈbilətē/ n., **po·lar·iz·a·ble** adj., **po·lar·i·za·tion** /ˌpōlərəˈzāsHən/ n., **po·lar·iz·er** n.

po·lar·iz·ing fil·ter ▶ n. a photographic or optical filter that polarizes the light passing through it, used chiefly for reducing reflections and improving contrast. Two polarizing filters are often used together, such that rotation of one of them results in a neutral density filter of variable density.

po·lar·og·ra·phy /ˌpōləˈrägrəfē/ ▶ n. Chemistry a method of analysis in which a sample is subjected to electrolysis using a special electrode and a range of applied voltages, a plot of current against voltage showing steps corresponding to particular chemical species and proportional to their concentration.
– DERIVATIVES **po·lar·o·graph·ic** /pōˌlarəˈgrafik, pə-/ adj.
– ORIGIN 1930s: from *polarization* (see POLARIZE) + -GRAPHY.

Po·lar·oid /ˈpōləˌroid/ ▶ n. trademark **1** material in thin plastic sheets that produces a high degree of plane polarization in light passing through it. ■ (**Polaroids**) sunglasses with lenses made from such material.
2 a photograph taken with a Polaroid camera.
▶ adj. Photography denoting a type of camera with internal processing that produces a finished print rapidly after each exposure. ■ denoting film for or a photograph taken with such a camera: *a Polaroid snapshot.*
– ORIGIN 1930s: from POLARIZE + -OID.

po·lar or·bit ▶ n. a satellite orbit that passes over polar regions, esp. one whose plane contains the polar axis.

po·lar star ▶ n. Astronomy a star at or close to a celestial pole, esp. Polaris.

po·lar wan·der·ing ▶ n. the slow and erratic, real or apparent, movement of the earth's rotational or magnetic poles relative to the continents throughout geological time, due largely to continental drift.

pol·der /ˈpōldər/ ▶ n. a piece of low-lying land reclaimed from the sea or a river and protected by dikes, esp. in the Netherlands.
– ORIGIN early 17th cent.: from Dutch, from Middle Dutch *polre.*

Pole /pōl/ ▶ n. a native or inhabitant of Poland, or a person of Polish descent.
– ORIGIN via German from Polish *Polanie*, literally 'field-dwellers,' from *pole* 'field.'

pole[1] /pōl/ ▶ n. **1** a long, slender, rounded piece of wood or metal, typically used with one end placed in the ground as a support for something: *a tent pole.* ■ Track & Field a long, slender, flexible rod of wood or fiberglass used by a competitor in pole-vaulting. ■ short for SKI POLE. ■ a wooden shaft fitted to the front of a cart or carriage drawn by animals and attached to their yokes or collars. ■ a simple fishing rod.
2 n. chiefly Brit. historical a linear or square rod.
▶ v. [with obj.] propel (a boat) by pushing a pole against the bottom of a river, canal, or lake.
– PHRASES **under bare poles** Sailing with no sail set.
– ORIGIN late Old English *pāl* (in early use without reference to thickness or length), of Germanic origin; related to Dutch *paal* and German *Pfahl*, based on Latin *palus* 'stake.'

pole[2] ▶ n. either of the two locations (**North Pole** or **South Pole**) on the surface of the earth (or of a celestial object) that are the northern and southern ends of the axis of rotation. See also CELESTIAL POLE, MAGNETIC POLE. ■ Geometry either of the two points at which the axis of a sphere intersects its surface. ■ Geometry a fixed point to which other points or lines are referred, e.g., the origin of polar coordinates or the point of which a line or curve is a polar. ■ Biology an extremity of the main axis of a cell, organ, or part. ■ each of the two opposite points on the surface of a magnet at which magnetic forces are strongest. ■ each of two terminals (positive and negative) of an electric cell, battery, or machine. ■ one of two opposed or contradictory principles or ideas: *Miriam and Rebecca represent two poles in the argument about transracial adoption.*
– PHRASES **be poles apart** have nothing in common.
– DERIVATIVES **pole·ward** /-wərd/ adj., **pole·wards** /-wərdz/ adj. & adv.
– ORIGIN late Middle English: from Latin *polus* 'end of an axis,' from Greek *polos* 'pivot, axis, sky.'

pole[3] ▶ n. short for POLE POSITION.

pole·ax /ˈpōˌlaks/ (also **poleaxe**) ▶ n. another term for BATTLE-AX (sense 1). ■ a short-handled ax with a spike at the back, formerly used in naval warfare for boarding, resisting boarders, and cutting ropes. ■ a butcher's ax with a hammerhead at the back, used to slaughter animals.
▶ v. [with obj.] hit, kill, or knock down with or as if with a poleax. ■ cause great shock to (someone): *I was poleaxed by this revelation.*
– ORIGIN Middle English: related to Middle Dutch *pol(l)aex*, Middle Low German *pol(l)exe* (see POLL, AX). The change in the first syllable was due to association with POLE[1]; the first element *poll-* may have referred to a special head of the ax or to the head of an enemy.

pole barn ▶ n. a farm building with no foundation and with sides consisting of corrugated steel or aluminum panels supported by poles set in the ground typically at eight-foot intervals.

pole bean ▶ n. a variety of bean plant that climbs up a wall, tree, or trellis. Compare with BUSH BEAN.

pole build·ing ▶ n. a quickly constructed building in which vertical poles are secured in the ground to serve as both the foundation and framework.

pole·cat /ˈpōlˌkat/ ▶ n. a weasel-like Eurasian mammal (genus *Mustela*, family Mustelidae) with mainly dark brown fur and a darker mask across the eyes, noted for ejecting a fetid fluid when threatened. ■ another term for SKUNK.
– ORIGIN Middle English: perhaps from Old French *pole* 'chicken' + CAT[1].

po·lem·ic /pəˈlemik/ ▶ n. a strong verbal or written attack on someone or something: *his polemic against the cultural relativism of the sixties | a writer of feminist polemic.* ■ (usu. **polemics**) the art or practice of engaging in controversial debate or dispute: *the history of science has become embroiled in religious polemics.*
▶ adj. another term for POLEMICAL.
– DERIVATIVES **po·lem·i·cist** /pəˈleməsist/ n., **po·lem·i·cize** /pəˈleməˌsīz/ v.
– ORIGIN mid 17th cent.: via medieval Latin from Greek *polemikos*, from *polemos* 'war.'

po·lem·i·cal /pəˈlemikəl/ ▶ adj. of, relating to, or involving strongly critical, controversial, or disputatious writing or speech: *a polemical essay.*
– DERIVATIVES **po·lem·i·cal·ly** /-ik(ə)lē/ adv.

po·len·ta /pō'lentə/ ▶ **n.** cornmeal as used in Italian cooking. ■ a paste or dough made from cornmeal, which is boiled and typically then fried or baked.
– ORIGIN late 16th cent.: Italian, from Latin, 'pearl barley' (a sense of *polenta* in Old English).

pole piece ▶ **n.** Physics a mass of iron forming the end of an electromagnet, through which the lines of magnetic force are concentrated and directed.

pole po·si·tion ▶ **n.** the most favorable position at the start of an automobile race, typically on the inside of the front row of competitors. ■ a leading or dominant position: *a company boasting the pole position in the communications business.*
– ORIGIN 1950s: from a 19th-cent. use of *pole* in horse racing, denoting the starting position next to the inside boundary fence.

pole·star /'pōl,stär/ ▶ **n. 1** Astronomy (also **Pole Star**) another term for POLARIS.
2 a thing or principle that guides or attracts people: *the store is a polestar for both actual and armchair travelers.*

pole vault ▶ **n.** (**the pole vault**) an athletic event in which competitors attempt to vault over a high bar with the end of an extremely long flexible pole held in the hands and used to give extra spring. ■ a vault performed in this way.
▶ **v.** (**pole-vault**) [no obj.] perform a pole vault.
– DERIVATIVES **pole-vault·er n.**, **pole-vault·ing n.**

po·lice /pə'lēs/ ▶ **n.** (treated as pl., usu. **the police**) the civil force of a national or local government, responsible for the prevention and detection of crime and the maintenance of public order. ■ members of a police force: *there are fewer women police than men.* ■ [with modifier] an organization engaged in the enforcement of official regulations in a specified domain: *transit police* | figurative, humorous *the fashion police.*
▶ **v.** [with obj.] (often as noun **policing**) (of a police force) have the duty of maintaining law and order in or for (an area or event). ■ enforce regulations or an agreement in (a particular area or domain): *a UN resolution to use military force to police the no-fly zone.* ■ enforce the provisions of (a law, agreement, or treaty): *the regulations will be policed by factory inspectors.* ■ maintain order and neatness in (an area, as a military camp).
– ORIGIN late 15th cent. (in the sense 'public order'): from French, from medieval Latin *politia* 'citizenship, government' (see POLICY[1]). Current senses date from the early 19th cent.

po·lice con·sta·ble ▶ **n.** see CONSTABLE.

po·lice dog ▶ **n.** a dog, esp. a German shepherd, trained for use in police work. ■ informal a German shepherd.

po·lice force ▶ **n.** an organized body of police officers responsible for a country, district, or town.

po·lice ju·ry ▶ **n.** an elected governing body in most Louisiana parishes, corresponding to a county board of commissioners in other states.
– DERIVATIVES **po·lice ju·ror n.**

po·lice·man /pə'lēsmən/ ▶ **n.** (pl. **policemen**) a member of a police force.

po·lice of·fi·cer ▶ **n.** a policeman or policewoman.

po·lice pro·ce·dur·al ▶ **n.** a crime novel in which the emphasis is on the procedures used by the police in solving the crime.

po·lice state ▶ **n.** a totalitarian state controlled by a political police force that secretly supervises the citizens' activities.

po·lice sta·tion ▶ **n.** the office or headquarters of a local police force.

po·lice·wom·an /pə'lēs,wo͝omən/ ▶ **n.** (pl. **policewomen**) a female member of a police force.

po·li·cier /pō,lēs'yā/ ▶ **n.** a movie based on a police novel, portraying crime and its detection by police.
– ORIGIN French, from *roman policier* 'detective novel.'

pol·i·cy[1] /'päləsē/ ▶ **n.** (pl. **policies**) a course or principle of action adopted or proposed by a government, party, business, or individual: *the administration's controversial economic policies* | *it is not company policy to dispense with our older workers.* ■ archaic prudent or expedient conduct or action: *a course of policy and wisdom.*
– ORIGIN late Middle English: from Old French *policie* 'civil administration,' via Latin from Greek *politeia* 'citizenship,' from *politēs* 'citizen,' from *polis* 'city.'

pol·i·cy[2] ▶ **n.** (pl. **policies**) **1** a contract of insurance: *they took out a joint policy.*
2 an illegal lottery or numbers game.
– ORIGIN mid 16th cent.: from French *police* 'bill of lading, contract of insurance,' from Provençal *poliss(i)a*, probably from medieval Latin *apodissa, apodixa*, based on Greek *apodeixis* 'evidence, proof,' from *apodeiknunai* 'demonstrate, show.'

pol·i·cy·hold·er /'päləsē,hōldər/ ▶ **n.** a person or group in whose name an insurance policy is held.

po·li·o /'pōlē,ō/ ▶ **n.** short for POLIOMYELITIS.

po·li·o·my·e·li·tis /,pōlēō,mīə'lītis/ ▶ **n.** Medicine an infectious viral disease that affects the central nervous system and can cause temporary or permanent paralysis.
– ORIGIN late 19th cent.: modern Latin, from Greek *polios* 'gray' + *muelos* 'marrow.'

po·li·o·vi·rus /'pōlēō,vīrəs/ ▶ **n.** Medicine any of a group of enteroviruses, including those that cause poliomyelitis.

po·lis[1] /'pōləs, 'pä-/ ▶ **n.** (pl. **poleis** /'päl,ās/) a city state in ancient Greece, esp. as considered in its ideal form for philosophical purposes.
– ORIGIN Greek.

po·lis[2] /'pōləs/ ▶ **n.** Scottish and Irish form of POLICE.

Po·li·sa·ri·o /,pôlə'särē,ō/ (also **Polisario Front**) ▶ **n.** an independence movement in Western (formerly Spanish) Sahara, formed in 1973.
– ORIGIN Spanish acronym, from *Frente Popular para la Liberación de Saguia el-Hamra y Río de Oro* 'Popular Front for the Liberation of Saguia el-Hamra and Rio de Oro.'

Pol·ish /'pōlisH/ ▶ **adj.** of or relating to Poland, its inhabitants, or their language.
▶ **n.** the West Slavic language of Poland.

pol·ish /'pälisH/ ▶ **v.** [with obj.] make the surface of (something) smooth and shiny by rubbing it: *she unloaded the dishwasher and polished the glasses.* ■ improve, refine, or add the finishing touches to: *he's got to **polish up** his French for his job.*
▶ **n.** a substance used to give something a smooth and shiny surface when rubbed in: *furniture polish.* ■ [in sing.] an act of rubbing something to give it a shiny surface: *I could give the cabinet a polish.* ■ smoothness or glossiness produced by rubbing or friction: *the machine refines the shape of the stone and gives it polish.* ■ refinement or elegance in a person or thing: *his poetry has clarity and polish.*
– PHRASAL VERBS **polish something off** finish or consume something quickly: *they polished off most of the sausages.*
– DERIVATIVES **pol·ish·a·ble adj.**, **pol·ish·er n.**
– ORIGIN Middle English: from Old French *poliss-*, lengthened stem of *polir* 'to polish,' from Latin *polire.*

Po·lish Cor·ri·dor a former region of Poland that extended north to the Baltic coast and separated East Prussia from the rest of Germany, granted to Poland after World War I to ensure Polish access to the coast. Its annexation by Germany in 1939, with the German occupation of the rest of Poland, precipitated World War II. After the war, the area was restored to Poland.

pol·ished /'pälisHt/ ▶ **adj.** shiny as a result of being rubbed: *a polished mahogany table.* ■ accomplished and skillful: *his polished performance in the movie.* ■ refined, sophisticated, or elegant: *he was polished and charming.* ■ (of rice) having had the outer husk removed during milling.

Po·lish no·ta·tion ▶ **n.** Logic & Computing a system of formula notation without brackets or special punctuation, frequently used to represent the order in which arithmetical operations are performed in many computers and calculators. In the usual form (**reverse Polish notation**), operators follow rather than precede their operands.

polit. ▶ **abbr.** ■ political. ■ politics.

po·lit·bu·ro /'pälət,byo͝orō, 'pō-/ ▶ **n.** (pl. **politburos**) the principal policymaking committee of a Communist Party. ■ (**Politburo**) this committee in the former Soviet Union, founded in 1917. Also called (1952–66) PRESIDIUM.
– ORIGIN from Russian *politbyuro*, from *polit(icheskoe) byuro* 'political bureau.'

po·lite /pə'līt/ ▶ **adj.** (**politer, politest**) having or showing behavior that is respectful and considerate of other people: *they thought she was wrong but were too polite to say so.* ■ [attrib.] of or relating to people who regard themselves as more cultured and refined than others: *the picture outraged polite society.*
– DERIVATIVES **po·lite·ly adv.**, **po·lite·ness n.**
– ORIGIN late Middle English (in the Latin sense): from Latin *politus* 'polished, made smooth,' past participle of *polire.*

pol·i·tesse /,pälə'tes/ ▶ **n.** formal politeness or etiquette.
– ORIGIN early 18th cent.: French, from Italian *politezza, pulitezza*, from *pulito* 'polite.'

pol·i·tic /'pälə,tik/ ▶ **adj.** (of an action) seeming sensible and judicious under the circumstances: [with infinitive] *I did not think it politic to express my reservations.* ■ (also **politick**) archaic (of a person) prudent and sagacious.
▶ **v.** (**politics, politicking, politicked**) [no obj.] (often as noun **politicking**) often derogatory engage in political activity: *news of this unseemly politicking invariably leaks into the press.*
– DERIVATIVES **pol·i·tic·ly adv.** (rare).
– ORIGIN late Middle English: from Old French *politique* 'political,' via Latin from Greek *politikos*, from *politēs* 'citizen,' from *polis* 'city.'

po·lit·i·cal /pə'litikəl/ ▶ **adj.** of or relating to the government or the public affairs of a country: *a period of political and economic stability.* ■ of or relating to the ideas or strategies of a particular party or group in politics: *a decision taken for purely political reasons.* ■ interested in or active in politics: *I'm not very political.* ■ motivated or caused by a person's beliefs or actions concerning politics: *a political crime.* ■ chiefly derogatory relating to, affecting, or acting according to the interests of status or authority within an organization rather than matters of principle.
– DERIVATIVES **po·lit·i·cal·ly** /-ik(ə)lē/ **adv.**

po·lit·i·cal ac·tion com·mit·tee (abbr.: **PAC**) ▶ **n.** an organization that raises money privately and employs lobbyists to influence legislation, particularly at the federal level.

po·lit·i·cal a·sy·lum ▶ **n.** see ASYLUM.

po·lit·i·cal cor·rect·ness (also **political correctitude**) ▶ **n.** the avoidance, often considered as taken to extremes, of forms of expression or action that are perceived to exclude, marginalize, or insult groups of people who are socially disadvantaged or discriminated against.

po·lit·i·cal e·con·o·my ▶ **n.** dated economics as a branch of knowledge or academic discipline.
– DERIVATIVES **po·lit·i·cal e·con·o·mist n.**

po·lit·i·cal ge·og·ra·phy ▶ **n.** the branch of geography that deals with the boundaries, divisions, and possessions of countries.

po·lit·i·cal·ly cor·rect /pə'litik(ə)lē/ (or **incorrect**) ▶ **adj.** exhibiting (or failing to exhibit) political correctness: *it is not politically correct to laugh at speech impediments.*

po·lit·i·cal pris·on·er ▶ **n.** a person imprisoned for their political beliefs or actions.

po·lit·i·cal ref·u·gee ▶ **n.** a refugee from an oppressive government.

po·lit·i·cal sci·ence ▶ **n.** the branch of knowledge that deals with systems of government; the analysis of political activity and behavior.
– DERIVATIVES **po·lit·i·cal sci·en·tist n.**

pol·i·ti·cian /,pälə'tisHən/ ▶ **n.** a person who is professionally involved in politics, esp. as a holder of or a candidate for an elected office. ■ a person who acts in a manipulative and devious way, typically to gain advancement within an organization.

po·lit·i·cize /pə'litə,sīz/ ▶ **v.** [with obj.] (often as adj. **politicized**) cause (an activity or event) to become political in character: *art was becoming politicized* | *attempts to politicize America's curricula.* ■ make (someone) politically aware, esp. by persuading them of the truth of views considered radical: *we successfully politicized a generation of women.* ■ [no obj.] engage in or talk about politics.
– DERIVATIVES **po·lit·i·ci·za·tion** /pə,litəsi'zāsHən/ **n.**

pol·i·tick ▶ **adj.** archaic spelling of POLITIC.

po·lit·i·co /pə'litikō/ ▶ **n.** (pl. **politicos**) informal term for POLITICIAN.
– ORIGIN Spanish and Italian, 'politic' or 'political person.'

politico- ▶ **comb. form** politically: *politico-ethical.* ■ political and ...: *politico-economic.*
– ORIGIN from Greek *politikos* 'civic, political.'

pol·i·tics /'pälə,tiks/ ▶ **plural n.** [usu. treated as sing.] the activities associated with the governance of a country or other area, esp. the debate or conflict among individuals or parties having or hoping to achieve power: *the president's relationship with Congress is vital to American politics* | *thereafter he dropped out of active politics.* ■ the activities of governments concerning the political relations between countries: *in the conduct of global politics, economic status must be backed by military capacity.* ■ the academic study of government and the state: [as modifier] *a politics lecturer.* ■ activities within an organization that are aimed at improving someone's status or position and are typically considered to be devious or divisive: *yet another discussion of office politics and personalities.* ■ a particular set of political beliefs or principles: *people do not buy this newspaper purely for its politics.* ■ (often **the politics of**) the assumptions or principles relating to or inherent in a sphere, theory, or thing, esp.

when concerned with power and status in a society: *the politics of gender.*
– PHRASES **play politics** act for political or personal gain rather than from principle.

pol·i·ty /ˈpälətē/ ▶ **n.** (pl. **polities**) a form or process of civil government or constitution. ■ an organized society; a state as a political entity.
– ORIGIN mid 16th cent.: from obsolete French *politie*, via Latin from Greek *politeia* 'citizenship, government,' from *politēs* 'citizen,' from *polis* 'city.'

Polk /pōk/, James Knox (1795–1849), 11th president of the US 1845–49. A Democrat, his administration oversaw major territorial additions to the US when Texas was admitted to the Union in 1845 and conflict with Mexico resulted in the annexation of California and other parts of the Southwest two years later.

James K. Polk

pol·ka /ˈpō(l)kə/ ▶ **n.** a lively dance of Bohemian origin in duple time. ■ a piece of music for this dance or in its rhythm.
▶ **v.** (**polkas, polkaing, polkaed** or **polka'd**) [no obj.] dance the polka.
– ORIGIN mid 19th cent.: via French and German from Czech *půlka* 'half step,' from *půl* 'half.'

pol·ka dot ▶ **n.** one of a number of large round dots repeated to form a regular pattern on fabric: [as modifier] *a red and white polka-dot shirt.*
– DERIVATIVES **pol·ka-dot·ted adj.**

poll /pōl/ ▶ **n. 1** (often **the polls**) the process of voting in an election: *the country went to the polls on March 10.* ■ a record of the number of votes cast in an election. ■ (**the polls**) the places where votes are cast in an election: *the polls have only just closed.* ■ short for OPINION POLL.
2 dialect a person's head. ■ the part of the head on which hair grows; the scalp.
▶ **v.** [with obj.] **1** record the opinion or vote of: *focus groups in which customers are polled about merchandise preferences.* ■ [no obj.] (of a candidate in an election) receive a specified number of votes: *the Green candidate polled 3.6 percent.* ■ Telecommunications & Computing check the status of (a measuring device, part of a computer, or a node in a network), esp. as part of a repeated cycle.
2 cut the horns off (an animal, esp. a young cow). ■ archaic cut off the top of (a tree or plant), typically to encourage further growth; pollard.
– DERIVATIVES **poll·ee** /pōˈlē/ **n.** (sense 1 of the verb).
– ORIGIN Middle English (in the sense 'head'): perhaps of Low German origin. The original sense was 'head,' and hence 'an individual person among a number,' from which developed the sense 'number of people ascertained by counting of heads' and then 'counting of heads or of votes' (17th cent).

Pol·lack /ˈpälək/, Sidney (1934–2008), US director. Notable movies include *The Way We Were* (1973), *Out of Africa* (1985), *Havana* (1990), and *The Firm* (1993).

pol·lack /ˈpälək/ (also **pollock**) ▶ **n.** (pl. **same** or **pollacks**) an edible greenish-brown fish of the cod family, with a protruding lower jaw. Found in the northeastern Atlantic, it is popular with anglers. ● *Pollachius pollachius*, family Gadidae.
– ORIGIN late Middle English: perhaps of Celtic origin.

pol·lard /ˈpälərd/ ▶ **v.** [with obj.] (often as adj. **pollarded**) cut off the top and branches of (a tree) to encourage new growth at the top: *a wide boulevard lined with pollarded linden trees.*
▶ **n. 1** a tree whose top and branches have been cut off for this reason.
2 archaic an animal, e.g., a sheep or deer, that has lost its horns or cast its antlers.
– ORIGIN early 17th cent.: from the verb POLL + -ARD.

polled /pōld/ ▶ **adj.** (of cattle, sheep, or goats) lacking horns, either naturally or because they have been removed.

pol·len /ˈpälən/ ▶ **n.** a fine powdery substance, typically yellow, consisting of microscopic grains discharged from the male part of a flower or from a male cone. Each grain contains a male gamete that can fertilize the female ovule, to which pollen is transported by the wind, insects, or other animals.
– ORIGIN mid 18th cent.: from Latin, literally 'fine powder.'

pol·len bas·ket ▶ **n.** Entomology a flattened area fringed with hairs on the hind leg of a social bee, used for carrying pollen. Also called CORBICULA.

pol·len count ▶ **n.** an index of the amount of pollen in the air, published chiefly for the benefit of those allergic to it.

pol·len grain ▶ **n.** each of the microscopic particles, typically single cells, of which pollen is composed. Pollen grains have a tough coat that has a form characteristic of the plant producing it.

pol·len tube ▶ **n.** Botany a hollow tube that develops from a pollen grain when deposited on the stigma of a flower. It penetrates the style and conveys the male gametes to the ovule.

pol·lex /ˈpälˌeks/ ▶ **n.** (pl. **pollices** /ˈpäləˌsēz/) Anatomy & Zoology the innermost digit of a forelimb, esp. the thumb in primates.
– ORIGIN mid 19th cent.: from Latin, literally 'thumb or big toe.'

pol·li·nate /ˈpäləˌnāt/ ▶ **v.** [with obj.] convey pollen to or deposit pollen on (a stigma, ovule, flower, or plant) and so allow fertilization.
– DERIVATIVES **pol·li·na·tion** /ˌpäləˈnāSHən/ **n.**, **pol·li·na·tor** /-ˌnātər/ **n.**
– ORIGIN late 19th cent.: from Latin *pollen, pollin-* 'pollen' + -ATE³.

poll·ing booth ▶ **n.** British and Canadian term for VOTING BOOTH.

poll·ing place (also **polling station**) ▶ **n.** a building where voting takes place during an election, typically one that normally has another function, such as a school.

pol·lin·i·um /pəˈlinēəm/ ▶ **n.** (pl. **pollinia** /pəˈlinēə/) Botany a coherent mass of pollen grains that is the product of each anther lobe of some flowers, esp. orchids. Single or paired pollinia are often attached to, and carried by, pollinating insects.
– ORIGIN mid 19th cent.: modern Latin, from Latin *pollen, pollin-* 'pollen.'

pol·li·no·sis /päləˈnōsis/ ▶ **n.** a technical term for HAY FEVER.

pol·li·wog /ˈpälēˌwäg, -ˌwôg/ (also **pollywog**) ▶ **n.** a tadpole.
– ORIGIN late Middle English (earlier as *pollywiggle*): from POLL in the sense 'head' + the verb WIGGLE.

pol·lo /ˈpoi-ō, ˈpälō/ ▶ **n.** chicken (as used in the names of Italian, Spanish, or Mexican dishes).
– ORIGIN Spanish and Italian.

Pol·lock /ˈpälək/, Jackson (1912–56), US painter; full name *Paul Jackson Pollock.* A leading figure in the abstract expressionist movement, he became the chief exponent of the style known as action painting from 1947. Fixing the canvas to the floor or wall, he poured, splashed, or dripped paint on it, covering the whole canvas and avoiding any point of emphasis.

pol·lock /ˈpälək/ ▶ **n. 1** a commercially valuable food fish of the cod family, occurring in the North Atlantic. Also called SAITHE. ● *Pollachius virens*, family Gadidae.
2 variant spelling of POLLACK.

poll·ster /ˈpōlstər/ ▶ **n.** a person who conducts or analyzes opinion polls.

poll tax ▶ **n.** a tax levied on every adult, without reference to income or resources.

pol·lu·tant /pəˈlo͞otnt/ ▶ **n.** a substance that pollutes something, esp. water or the atmosphere: *chemical pollutants* | [as modifier] *pollutant gases.*

pol·lute /pəˈlo͞ot/ ▶ **v.** [with obj.] contaminate (water, air, or a place) with harmful or poisonous substances: *the explosion polluted the town with dioxin* | (as adj. **polluted**) *exposure to polluted air.* ■ defile; corrupt: *a society polluted by racism.*
– DERIVATIVES **pol·lut·er n.**
– ORIGIN late Middle English: from Latin *pollut-* 'soiled, defiled,' from the verb *polluere*, based on the root of *lutum* 'mud.'

pol·lu·tion /pəˈlo͞oSHən/ ▶ **n.** the presence in or introduction into the environment of a substance or thing that has harmful or poisonous effects: *the level of pollution in the air is rising.*
– ORIGIN late Middle English: from Latin *pollutio(n-)*, from the verb *polluere* (see POLLUTE).

Pol·lux /ˈpäləks/ **1** Greek Mythology the twin brother of Castor. Also called POLYDEUCES. See DIOSCURI.
2 Astronomy the brightest star in the constellation Gemini, close to Castor.
– ORIGIN Latin, from Greek *Poludeukēs*; compare with POLYDEUCES.

Pol·ly·an·na /ˌpälēˈanə/ ▶ **n.** an excessively cheerful or optimistic person.
– DERIVATIVES **Pol·ly·an·na·ish** /-isH/ **adj.**, **Pol·ly·an·na·ism** /-ˌizəm/ **n.**
– ORIGIN early 20th cent.: the name of the optimistic heroine created by Eleanor Hodgman Porter (1868–1920), American author of children's stories.

pol·ly·wog ▶ **n.** variant spelling of POLLIWOG.

Po·lo, Marco, see MARCO POLO.

po·lo /ˈpōlō/ ▶ **n.** a game of Eastern origin resembling field hockey, played on horseback with a long-handled mallet.
– ORIGIN late 19th cent.: from Balti (a Tibetan language), 'ball.'

po·loid·al /pəˈloidl/ ▶ **adj.** Physics relating to or denoting a magnetic field associated with a toroidal electric field, in which each line of force is confined to a radial or meridian plane.
– ORIGIN 1940s: from POLAR, on the pattern of *toroidal.*

pol·o·naise /ˌpäləˈnāz, ˌpō-/ ▶ **n. 1** a slow dance of Polish origin in triple time, consisting chiefly of an intricate march or procession. ■ a piece of music for this dance or in its rhythm.
2 historical a woman's dress with a tight bodice and a skirt open from the waist downward, looped up to show a decorative underskirt.
▶ **adj.** (of a dish, esp. a vegetable dish) garnished with chopped hard-boiled egg yolk, breadcrumbs, and parsley.
– ORIGIN mid 18th cent.: from French, feminine of *polonais* 'Polish,' from medieval Latin *Polonia* 'Poland.'

po·lo neck ▶ **n.** British term for TURTLENECK.
– DERIVATIVES **po·lo-necked** /ˈpōlō ˌnekt/ **adj.**

po·lo·ni·um /pəˈlōnēəm/ ▶ **n.** the chemical element of atomic number 84, a radioactive metal occurring in nature only as a product of radioactive decay of uranium. (Symbol: **Po**)
– ORIGIN late 19th cent.: modern Latin, from medieval Latin *Polonia* 'Poland' (the native country of Marie Curie, the element's codiscoverer).

po·lo po·ny ▶ **n.** a horse used in playing polo, typically bred for speed and agility.

po·lo shirt ▶ **n.** a casual short-sleeved cotton shirt with a collar and several buttons at the neck. See also GOLF SHIRT.

Pol Pot /päl ˈpät, pôl/ (*c.*1925–98), Cambodian communist leader of the Khmer Rouge; prime minister 1976–79; born *Saloth Sar.* During his regime the Khmer Rouge embarked on a reconstruction program in which millions were killed. Overthrown in 1979, Pol Pot led the Khmer Rouge in a guerrilla war against the new government.

Pols·ka /ˈpôlskä/ Polish name for POLAND.

Pol·ta·va /pəlˈtävə/ a city in east central Ukraine; pop. 301,600 (est. 2009).

pol·ter·geist /ˈpōltərˌgīst/ ▶ **n.** a ghost or other supernatural being supposedly responsible for physical disturbances such as loud noises and objects thrown around.
– ORIGIN mid 19th cent.: from German *Poltergeist*, from *poltern* 'create a disturbance' + *Geist* 'ghost.'

Pol·to·ratsk /pəltəˈrätsk/ former name (1919–27) of ASHGABAT.

pol·troon /pälˈtro͞on/ ▶ **n.** archaic or literary an utter coward.
– DERIVATIVES **pol·troon·er·y** /-ˈtro͞onərē/ **n.**
– ORIGIN early 16th cent.: from French *poltron*, from Italian *poltrone*, perhaps from *poltro* 'sluggard.'

pol·y /ˈpälē/ ▶ **n.** (pl. **polys**) informal short for. ■ polyester. ■ polytechnic. ■ polyethylene.

poly- ▶ **comb. form** many; much: *polyandry* | *polychrome.* ■ Chemistry denoting the presence of many atoms or groups of a particular kind in a molecule: *polycarbonate.*
– ORIGIN from Greek *polus* 'much,' *polloi* 'many.'

pol·y·a·cryl·a·mide /ˌpälēəˈkriləˌmīd/ ▶ **n.** a synthetic resin made by polymerizing acrylamide, esp. a water-soluble polymer used to form or stabilize gels and as a thickening or clarifying agent.

pol·y·ad·ic /ˌpälēˈadik/ ▶ **adj.** involving three or more quantities, elements, or individuals.
– ORIGIN early 20th cent.: from POLY- 'many,' on the pattern of words such as *dyadic, monadic.*

pol·y·am·ide /ˌpälēˈamīd/ ▶ **n.** a synthetic polymer of a type made by the linkage of an amino group of one molecule and a carboxylic acid group of another, including many synthetic fibers such as nylon.

pol·y·am·o·ry /ˌpälēˈamərē/ ▶ **n.** the philosophy or state of being in love or romantically involved with more than one person at the same time.
– DERIVATIVES **pol·y·am·o·rous adj.**, **pol·y·am·o·rist n.**
– ORIGIN from *poly-* 'many' + Latin *amor* 'love' + *-y*, on the pattern of *polygamy* and *polyandry.*

pol·y·an·dry /ˌpälēˌandrē/ ▶ **n.** polygamy in which a woman has more than one husband. Compare with POLYGYNY. ■ Zoology a pattern of mating in which a female animal has more than one male mate.
– DERIVATIVES **pol·y·an·drous** /ˌpälēˈandrəs/ **adj.**
– ORIGIN late 17th cent.: from POLY- 'many' + Greek *anēr, andr-* 'male.'

pol·y·an·thus /ˌpälēˈanTHəs/ ▶ **n.** (pl. **same**) a herbaceous flowering plant that is a complex hybrid between the wild primrose and primulas, cultivated in Europe since the 17th century. ● *Primula* × *polyantha*, family Primulaceae.
– ORIGIN early 18th cent.: modern Latin, from POLY- 'many' + Greek *anthos* 'flower.'

pol·y·a·tom·ic /ˌpälēəˈtämik/ ▶ **adj.** consisting of many atoms.

pol·y·bu·tyl·ene /ˌpäliˈbyo͞otlˌēn/ ▶ **n.** a thermoplastic polymer used in water pipes.

pol·y·car·bon·ate /ˌpäliˈkärbəˌnāt, -nət/ ▶ **n.** a synthetic resin in which the polymer units are linked through carbonate groups, including many molding materials and films.

Pol·y·carp, St. /ˈpälēˌkärp/ (*c.*69–*c.*155), Greek bishop of Smyrna in Asia Minor. The leading Christian figure in Smyrna, he was arrested during a pagan festival, refused to recant his faith, and was burned to death. Feast day, February 23.

Pol·y·chae·ta /ˌpäliˈkētə/ Zoology a class of marine annelid worms that comprises the bristle worms.
– ORIGIN modern Latin (plural), from Greek *polu-* 'many' + *khaitē* 'mane' (taken to mean 'bristle').

pol·y·chaete /ˈpäləˌkēt/ (also **polychete**) ▶ **n.** Zoology a marine annelid worm of the class Polychaeta; a bristle worm.
▶ **adj.** relating to or denoting polychaetes.
– DERIVATIVES **pol·y·chae·tous** /ˌpäləˈkētəs/ **adj.**

pol·y·chlo·rin·at·ed bi·phen·yl /ˌpälēˈklôrəˌnātid bīˈfenəl/ (abbr.: **PCB**) ▶ **n.** Chemistry any of a class of toxic aromatic compounds, often formed as waste in industrial processes, whose molecules contain two benzene rings in which hydrogen atoms have been replaced by chlorine atoms.

pol·y·chro·mat·ic /ˌpälikrōˈmatik/ ▶ **adj.** of two or more colors; multicolored. ■ Physics (of light or other radiation) of a number of wavelengths or frequencies.
– DERIVATIVES **pol·y·chro·ma·tism** /-ˈkrōməˌtizəm/ **n.**

pol·y·chrome /ˈpäliˌkrōm/ ▶ **adj.** painted, printed, or decorated in several colors.
▶ **n.** varied coloring. ■ a work of art in several colors, esp. a statue.
▶ **v.** [with obj.] (usu. as adj. **polychromed**) execute or decorate (a work of art) in several colors.
– ORIGIN early 19th cent.: from French, from Greek *polukhrōmos*, from *polu-* 'many' + *khrōma* 'color.'

pol·y·chro·my /ˈpäliˌkrōmē/ ▶ **n.** the art of painting in several colors, esp. as applied to ancient pottery, sculpture, and architecture.

pol·y·clo·nal /ˌpäliˈklōnl/ ▶ **adj.** Medicine & Biology consisting of or derived from many clones.

pol·y·crest ▶ **n.** (in homeopathy) a remedy that is frequently used, in general or for a particular condition: *the poison ivy polycrests*.
– ORIGIN 19th cent.: from Greek *polu-* 'many' + *khraosos* 'use.'

pol·y·crys·tal·line /ˌpäliˈkristələn, -ˌlin, -ˌlēn/ ▶ **adj.** (of a metal or other solid) consisting of many crystalline parts that are randomly oriented with respect to each other.

pol·y·cul·ture /ˌpäliˈkəlCHər/ ▶ **n.** the simultaneous cultivation or exploitation of several crops or kinds of animals.

pol·y·cy·clic /ˌpäliˈsiklik, -ˈsīklik/ ▶ **adj.** of, relating to, or resulting from many cycles. ■ Chemistry (of an organic compound) having several rings of atoms in the molecule. ■ Geology (of a landform or deposit) having undergone two or more cycles of erosion and deposition.

pol·y·cys·tic /ˌpäliˈsistik/ ▶ **adj.** Medicine characterized by multiple cysts.

pol·y·cy·the·mi·a /ˌpäli,sīˈTHēmēə/ (Brit. **polycythaemia**) ▶ **n.** Medicine an abnormally increased concentration of hemoglobin in the blood, through either reduction of plasma volume or increase in red cell numbers. It may be a primary disease of unknown cause, or a secondary condition linked to respiratory or circulatory disorder or cancer.
– ORIGIN mid 19th cent.: from modern Latin *polycythaemia*, from POLY- 'many' + -CYTE 'cell' + Greek *haima* 'blood' + -IA¹.

pol·y·dac·ty·ly /ˌpäliˈdaktəlē/ ▶ **n.** a condition in which a person or animal has more than five fingers or toes on one, or on each, hand or foot.
– DERIVATIVES **pol·y·dac·tyl adj. & n.**
– ORIGIN late 19th cent.: from Greek *poludaktulos* (from *polu-* 'many' + *daktulos* 'finger') + -Y³.

Pol·y·deu·ces /ˌpäliˈd(y)o͞oˌsēz/ another name for POLLUX (sense 1).

pol·y·dip·si·a /ˌpälēˈdipsēə/ ▶ **n.** Medicine abnormally great thirst as a symptom of disease (such as diabetes) or psychological disturbance.
– ORIGIN mid 17th cent.: from Greek *poludipsios* 'very thirsty,' *poludipsos* 'causing great thirst,' based on *dipsa* 'thirst.'

pol·y·e·lec·tro·lyte /ˌpälēəˈlektrəˌlīt/ ▶ **n.** Chemistry a polymer that has several ionizable groups along the molecule, esp. any of those used for coagulating and flocculating particles during water treatment or for making electrophoretic gels.

pol·y·em·bry·o·ny /ˌpälēˈembrēənē, -emˈbrīənē/ ▶ **n.** Biology the formation of more than one embryo from a single fertilized ovum or in a single seed.
– DERIVATIVES **pol·y·em·bry·on·ic** /-ˌembrēˈänik/ **adj.**

pol·y·ene /ˈpäləˌēn/ ▶ **n.** Chemistry a hydrocarbon with several carbon–carbon double bonds, esp. one having a chain of alternating single and double bonds.

pol·y·es·ter /ˈpäləˌestər/ ▶ **n.** a synthetic resin in which the polymer units are linked by ester groups, used chiefly to make synthetic textile fibers. ■ a fabric made from polyester fiber.

pol·y·eth·nic /ˌpälēˈeTHnik/ ▶ **adj.** belonging to, comprising, or containing many ethnic groups.
– DERIVATIVES **pol·y·eth·nic·i·ty** /-eTHˈnisətē/ **n.**

pol·y·eth·yl·ene /ˌpälēˈeTHəlēn/ ▶ **n.** a tough, light, flexible synthetic resin made by polymerizing ethylene, chiefly used for plastic bags, food containers, and other packaging.

pol·y·eth·yl·ene gly·col ▶ **n.** a synthetic resin made by polymerizing ethylene glycol, in particular any of a series of water-soluble oligomers and polymers used chiefly as solvents or waxes.

pol·y·eth·yl·ene ter·eph·thal·ate /ˌterə(f)ˈTHalˌāt/ (abbr.: **PET**) ▶ **n.** a synthetic resin made by copolymerizing ethylene glycol and terephthalic acid, widely used to make polyester fibers.

po·lyg·a·mous /pəˈligəməs/ ▶ **adj.** practicing, relating to, or involving polygamy: *polygamous societies*. ■ Zoology (of an animal) typically having more than one mate. ■ Botany (of a plant) bearing some flowers with stamens only, some with pistils only, and some with both, on the same or different plants.
– DERIVATIVES **po·lyg·a·mous·ly adv.**
– ORIGIN early 17th cent.: from Greek *polugamos* (from *polu-* 'much, often' + *-gamos* 'marrying') + -OUS.

po·lyg·a·my /pəˈligəmē/ ▶ **n. 1** the practice or custom of having more than one wife or husband at the same time. ■ Zoology a pattern of mating in which an animal has more than one mate.
2 Botany the condition of bearing some male, some female, and sometimes some perfect flowers on the same plant.
– DERIVATIVES **po·lyg·a·mist** /-mist/ **n.** (sense 1).
– ORIGIN late 16th cent.: from French *polygamie*, via late Latin from Greek *polugamia*, from *polugamos* 'often marrying.'

pol·y·gene /ˈpäliˌjēn/ ▶ **n.** Genetics a gene whose individual effect on a phenotype is too small to be observed, but which can act together with others to produce observable variation.
– ORIGIN 1940s: back-formation from POLYGENIC.

pol·y·gen·e·sis /ˌpäliˈjenəsəs/ ▶ **n.** origination from several independent sources, in particular: ■ Biology the hypothetical origination of a race or species from a number of independent stocks. Compare with POLYGENY. ■ the hypothetical origination of language or of a surname from a number of independent sources in different places at different times.

pol·y·ge·net·ic /ˌpälijəˈnetik/ ▶ **adj.** of or relating to polygenesis; having more than one origin or source. ■ Geology denoting or originating from a volcano that has erupted several times.
– DERIVATIVES **pol·y·ge·net·i·cal·ly** /-ik(ə)lē/ **adv.**

pol·y·gen·ic /ˌpäliˈjenik/ ▶ **adj.** Genetics of, relating to, or determined by polygenes.
– DERIVATIVES **pol·y·gen·i·cal·ly** /-ik(ə)lē/ **adv.**
– ORIGIN 1940s: from Greek *polugenēs* 'of many kinds' + -IC.

po·lyg·e·nism /pəˈlijəˌnizəm/ ▶ **n.** the doctrine of polygeny.
– DERIVATIVES **po·lyg·e·nist** /pəˈlijənist/ **n. & adj.**

po·lyg·e·ny /pəˈlijənē/ ▶ **n.** the theory (not now generally held) that humans evolved from several independent pairs of ancestors. Compare with POLYGENESIS.

pol·y·glot /ˈpäliˌglät/ ▶ **adj.** knowing or using several languages: *a polyglot career woman*. ■ (of a book) having the text translated into several languages: *polyglot and bilingual technical dictionaries*.
▶ **n.** a person who knows and is able to use several languages.
– DERIVATIVES **pol·y·glot·ism** /-ˌglätˌizəm/ **n.**
– ORIGIN mid 17th cent.: from French *polyglotte*, from Greek *poluglōttos*, from *polu-* 'many' + *glōtta* 'tongue.'

pol·y·gon /ˈpäliˌgän/ ▶ **n.** Geometry a plane figure with at least three straight sides and angles, and typically five or more.
– DERIVATIVES **po·lyg·o·nal** /pəˈligənl/ **adj.**, **po·lyg·o·nal·ly adv.**
– ORIGIN late 16th cent.: via late Latin from Greek *polugōnon*, neuter (used as a noun) of *polugōnos* 'many-angled.'

po·lyg·o·num /pəˈligənəm/ ▶ **n.** a plant of a genus that includes knotgrass and knotweed, of which some are weeds and some are garden ornamentals. ● Genus *Polygonum*, family Polygonaceae.
– ORIGIN modern Latin, from Greek *polu-* 'many' + *gonu* 'knee, joint' (because of the swollen joints sheathed by stipules).

pol·y·graph /ˈpäliˌgraf/ ▶ **n.** a machine designed to detect and record changes in physiological characteristics, such as a person's pulse and breathing rates, used esp. as a lie detector. ■ a lie-detector test carried out with a machine of this type.
– DERIVATIVES **pol·y·graph·ic** /ˌpäliˈgrafik/ **adj.**

pol·y·gyne /ˈpäliˌjīn/ ▶ **adj.** Entomology (of a social insect) having more than one egg-laying queen in each colony.

po·lyg·y·ny /pəˈlijənē/ ▶ **n.** polygamy in which a man has more than one wife. Compare with POLYANDRY. ■ Zoology a pattern of mating in which a male animal has more than one female mate.
– DERIVATIVES **po·lyg·y·nous** /pəˈlijənəs/ **adj.**
– ORIGIN late 18th cent.: from POLY- 'many' + Greek *gunē* 'woman.'

pol·y·he·dron /ˌpäliˈhēdrən/ ▶ **n.** (pl. **polyhedrons** or **polyhedra** /-ˈhēdrə/) Geometry a solid figure with many plane faces, typically more than six.
– DERIVATIVES **pol·y·he·dral** /-ˈhēdrəl/ **adj.**, **pol·y·he·dric** /-ˈhēdrik/ **adj.**
– ORIGIN late 16th cent.: from Greek *poluedron*, neuter (used as a noun) of *poluedros* 'many-sided.'

pol·y·his·tor /ˌpäliˈhistər/ ▶ **n.** another term for POLYMATH.
– ORIGIN late 16th cent.: from Greek *poluistōr* 'very learned,' from *polu-* 'much, very' + *histōr* 'wise man.'

Pol·y·hym·ni·a /ˌpäliˈhimnēə/ Greek & Roman Mythology the Muse of the art of mime.
– ORIGIN via Latin from Greek, literally 'she of the many hymns.'

pol·y·math /ˈpäliˌmaTH/ ▶ **n.** a person of wide-ranging knowledge or learning.
– DERIVATIVES **pol·y·math·ic** /ˌpäliˈmaTHik/ **adj.**, **po·lym·a·thy** /pəˈliməTHē, ˈpäliˌmaTHē/ **n.**
– ORIGIN early 17th cent.: from Greek *polumathēs* 'having learned much,' from *polu-* 'much' + the stem of *manthanein* 'learn.'

pol·y·mer /ˈpäləmər/ ▶ **n.** Chemistry a substance that has a molecular structure consisting chiefly or entirely of a large number of similar units bonded together, e.g., many synthetic organic materials used as plastics and resins.
– DERIVATIVES **pol·y·mer·ic** /ˌpäləˈmerik/ **adj.**
– ORIGIN mid 19th cent.: from German, from Greek *polumeros* 'having many parts,' from *polu-* 'many' + *meros* 'a share.'

po·lym·er·ase /pəˈliməˌrās, -ˌrāz/ ▶ **n.** Biochemistry an enzyme that brings about the formation of a particular polymer, esp. DNA or RNA. See also TRANSCRIPTASE.

po·lym·er·ize /pəˈliməˌrīz, ˈpäləməˌrīz/ ▶ **v.** Chemistry combine or cause to combine to form a polymer.
– DERIVATIVES **po·lym·er·iz·a·ble** /pəˌliməˈrīzəbəl, päləmə-/ **adj.**, **po·lym·er·i·za·tion** /pəˌlimərəˈzāSHən, ˌpälәmərə-/ **n.**

po·lym·er·ous /pəˈlimərəs/ ▶ **adj.** Biology having or consisting of many parts.

pol·y·meth·yl meth·ac·ry·late /ˈpäliˌmeTHəl meTHˈakrəˌlāt/ ▶ **n.** a glassy synthetic resin obtained by polymerizing methyl methacrylate, used to make perspex, plexiglas, and lucite.

pol·y·morph /ˈpäliˌmôrf/ ▶ **n.** an organism or inorganic object or material that takes various forms. ■ Physiology a polymorphonuclear leukocyte.
– ORIGIN early 19th cent.: from Greek *polumorphos*, from *polu-* 'many' + *morphē* 'form.'

P

pol·y·mor·phism /ˌpäliˈmôrˌfizəm/ ▶ **n.** the occurrence of something in several different forms, in particular: ■ Biology the occurrence of different forms among the members of a population or colony, or in the life cycle of an individual organism. ■ Genetics the presence of genetic variation within a population, upon which natural selection can operate. ■ Biochemistry the occurrence of a number of alternative forms within a section of a nucleic acid or protein molecule. ■ Computing a feature of a programming language that allows routines to use variables of different types at different times.
– DERIVATIVES **pol·y·mor·phic** /-ˈmôrfik/ **adj.**, **pol·y·mor·phous** /-ˈmôrfəs/ **adj.**

pol·y·mor·pho·nu·cle·ar /ˌpäliˌmôrfōˈn(y)o͞oklēər/ ▶ **adj.** Physiology (of a leukocyte) having a nucleus with several lobes and a cytoplasm that contains granules, as in an eosinophil or basophil.

pol·y·mor·phous per·ver·si·ty /ˌpäliˈmôrfəs/ ▶ **n.** Psychology a generalized sexual desire that can be excited and gratified in many ways, normal in young children but unusual in adults.
– DERIVATIVES **pol·y·mor·phous·ly per·verse adj.**

pol·y·myx·in /ˌpäliˈmiksən/ ▶ **n.** Medicine any of a group of polypeptide antibiotics that are active chiefly against Gram-negative bacteria. ● Polymyxins are obtained from soil bacteria of the genus *Bacillus*, in particular *B. polymyxa*.
– ORIGIN 1940s: from modern Latin *polymyxa*, from Greek *polu-* 'much' + *muxa* 'slime' + **-IN**[1].

Pol·y·ne·sia /ˌpäləˈnēZHə/ a region of the central Pacific Ocean that lies east of Micronesia and Melanesia and contains the easternmost of the three large groups of Pacific islands, including Hawaii, the Marquesas Islands, Samoa, the Cook Islands, and French Polynesia.
– ORIGIN from **POLY-** 'many' + Greek *nēsos* 'island.'

Pol·y·ne·sian /ˌpäləˈnēZHən/ ▶ **adj.** of or relating to Polynesia, its people, or their languages.
▶ **n. 1** a native or inhabitant of Polynesia, or a person of Polynesian descent.
2 a group of Austronesian languages spoken in Polynesia, including Maori, Hawaiian, and Samoan.

pol·y·neu·ri·tis /ˌpälin(y)o͝orˈītis/ ▶ **n.** Medicine any disorder that affects the peripheral nerves collectively.
– DERIVATIVES **pol·y·neu·rit·ic** /-n(y)o͝orˈitik/ **adj.**

pol·y·neu·rop·a·thy /ˌpälin(y)o͝orˈäpəTHē/ ▶ **n.** Medicine a general degeneration of peripheral nerves that spreads toward the center of the body.

pol·y·no·mi·al /ˌpäləˈnōmēəl/ ▶ **adj.** consisting of several terms.
▶ **n.** Mathematics an expression of more than two algebraic terms, esp. the sum of several terms that contain different powers of the same variable(s). ■ Biology a Latin name with more than two parts.
– ORIGIN late 17th cent.: from **POLY-** 'many,' on the pattern of *multinomial*.

pol·y·no·mi·al time ▶ **n.** Computing the time required for a computer to solve a problem, where this time is a simple polynomial function of the size of the input.

pol·y·nos·ic /ˌpäliˈnäsik/ ▶ **n.** a long-fiber rayon-and-polyester blend with a soft finish, used mainly in clothing.

pol·y·nu·cle·ar /ˌpäliˈn(y)o͞oklēər/ ▶ **adj.** Chemistry (of a complex) containing more than one metal atom. ■ (of a compound) polycyclic.

pol·y·nu·cle·o·tide /ˌpäliˈn(y)o͞oklēəˌtīd/ ▶ **n.** Biochemistry a linear polymer whose molecule is composed of many nucleotide units, constituting a section of a nucleic acid molecule.

po·lyn·ya /ˌpälənˈyä/ ▶ **n.** a stretch of open water surrounded by ice, esp. in Arctic seas.
– ORIGIN mid 19th cent.: from Russian, from the base of *pole* 'field.'

pol·y·o·ma vi·rus /ˌpälēˈōmə/ ▶ **n.** Medicine any of a group of DNA viruses that are usually endemic in their host species without causing disease but that can cause tumors when injected into other species.

pol·yp /ˈpäləp/ ▶ **n. 1** Zoology a solitary or colonial sedentary form of a coelenterate such as a sea anemone, typically having a columnar body with the mouth uppermost surrounded by a ring of tentacles. In some species, polyps are a phase in the life cycle that alternates with a medusoid phase. Compare with **MEDUSA**.
2 Medicine a small growth, typically benign and with a stalk, protruding from a mucous membrane.
– DERIVATIVES **pol·yp·ous** /ˈpäləpəs/ **adj.** (sense 2).
– ORIGIN late Middle English (sense 2): from Old French *polipe*, from Latin *polypus* (see **POLYPUS**). Sense 1 dates from the mid 18th cent.

pol·y·par·y /ˈpäləˌperē/ ▶ **n.** (pl. **polyparies**) Zoology the common stem or skeletal support of a colony of polyps, to which the individual zooids are attached.
– ORIGIN mid 18th cent.: from modern Latin *polyparium*, from Latin *polypus* (see **POLYPUS**).

pol·y·pep·tide /ˌpäliˈpepˌtīd/ ▶ **n.** Biochemistry a linear organic polymer consisting of a large number of amino-acid residues bonded together in a chain, forming part of (or the whole of) a protein molecule.
– ORIGIN early 20th cent.: from **POLY-** 'many' + **PEPTONE** + **-IDE**.

po·lyph·a·gous /pəˈlifəgəs/ ▶ **adj.** Zoology (of an animal) able to feed on various kinds of food.
– ORIGIN early 19th cent.: from Greek *poluphagos* 'eating to excess' + **-OUS**.

pol·y·phar·ma·cy /ˌpälēˈfärməsē/ ▶ **n.** (pl. **polypharmacies**) the simultaneous use of multiple drugs to treat a single ailment or condition. ■ the simultaneous use of multiple drugs by a single patient, for one or more conditions.

pol·y·phase /ˈpäliˌfāz/ ▶ **adj.** consisting of or occurring in a number of separate stages. ■ (of an electrical device or circuit) designed to supply or use simultaneously several alternating currents of the same voltage and frequency but with different phases.
– DERIVATIVES **pol·y·pha·sic** /ˌpäliˈfāzik/ **adj.**

Pol·y·phe·mus /ˌpäləˈfēməs/ Greek Mythology a Cyclops who trapped Odysseus and some of his companions in a cave, from which they escaped by putting out his one eye while he slept. In another story, Polyphemus loved the sea nymph Galatea, and in jealousy killed his rival Acis.

pol·y·phe·nol /ˌpäliˈfēˌnôl, -ˌnōl/ ▶ **n.** Chemistry a compound containing more than one phenolic hydroxyl group.

pol·y·phon·ic /ˌpäliˈfänik/ ▶ **adj.** producing many sounds simultaneously; many-voiced: *a 64-voice polyphonic sound module*. ■ Music (esp. of vocal music) in two or more parts, each having a melody of its own; contrapuntal. Compare with **HOMOPHONIC**. ■ Music (of an instrument) capable of producing more than one note at a time.
– DERIVATIVES **pol·y·phon·i·cal·ly** /-ik(ə)lē/ **adv.**
– ORIGIN late 18th cent.: from Greek *poluphōnos* (from *polu-* 'many' + *phōnē* 'voice, sound') + **-IC**.

po·lyph·o·ny /pəˈlifənē/ ▶ **n.** (pl. **polyphonies**) Music the style of simultaneously combining a number of parts, each forming an individual melody and harmonizing with each other. ■ a composition written, played, or sung in this style. ■ (on an electronic keyboard or synthesizer) the number of notes or voices that can be played simultaneously without loss.
– DERIVATIVES **pol·y·pho·nist** /-fənist/ **n.**, **pol·y·pho·nous** /-fənəs/ **adj.**
– ORIGIN early 19th cent.: from Greek *poluphōnia*, from *polu-* 'many' + *phōnē* 'sound.'

pol·y·phy·let·ic /ˌpälifīˈletik/ ▶ **adj.** Biology (of a group of organisms) derived from more than one common evolutionary ancestor or ancestral group and therefore not suitable for placing in the same taxon.

pol·y·pi /ˈpäləˌpī, -pē/ plural form of **POLYPUS**.

pol·y·pill /ˈpälēˌpil/ ▶ **n.** a pill containing a number of medicines that all treat the same condition.

pol·y·ploid /ˈpäliˌploid/ Biology ▶ **adj.** (of a cell or nucleus) containing more than two homologous sets of chromosomes. ■ (of an organism or species) composed of polyploid cells.
▶ **n.** a polyploid organism, variety, or species.
– DERIVATIVES **pol·y·ploi·dy n.**

pol·y·pod /ˈpäləˌpäd/ ▶ **adj.** Zoology having many feet or footlike appendages, esp. denoting a phase of insect larval development characterized by a segmented abdomen with rudimentary or functional appendages.
– ORIGIN mid 18th cent. (as a noun denoting an animal having many feet): from French *polypode* 'many-footed,' from Greek *polupous*, *polupod-*, from *polu-* 'many' + *pous*, *pod-* 'foot.'

pol·y·po·dy /ˈpäləˌpōdē/ ▶ **n.** (pl. **polypodies**) a widely distributed fern that has stout scaly creeping rhizomes and remains green during the winter, growing on trees, walls, and stones, esp. in limestone areas. ● Genus *Polypodium*, family Polypodiaceae: several species, in particular the **common polypody** (*P. vulgare*).
– ORIGIN late Middle English: via Latin from Greek *polupodion*, denoting a kind of fern, from *polu-* 'many' + *pous*, *pod-* 'foot.'

pol·yp·oid /ˈpäliˌpoid/ ▶ **adj. 1** Zoology of, relating to, or resembling a polyp or hydra. ■ of, relating to, or denoting the polyp stage in the life cycle of a coelenterate. Also called **HYDROID**. Compare with **MEDUSOID**.
2 Medicine (of a growth) resembling or in the form of a polyp.

pol·y·pore /ˈpäliˌpôr/ ▶ **n.** a bracket fungus in which the spores are expelled through fine pores on the underside. ● Several families in the order Aphyllophorales, class Hymenomycetes, in particular Polyporaceae, which includes the **DRYAD SADDLE**.

pol·yp·o·sis /ˌpäliˈpōsəs/ ▶ **n.** Medicine a condition characterized by the presence of numerous internal polyps, esp. a hereditary disease (**familial adenomatous polyposis**) that affects the colon and in which the polyps may become malignant.

pol·y·pro·pyl·ene /ˌpäliˈprōpəˌlēn/ ▶ **n.** a synthetic resin that is a polymer of propylene, used esp. for ropes, fabrics, and molded objects.

pol·yp·tych /ˈpälipˌtik/ ▶ **n.** a painting, typically an altarpiece, consisting of more than three leaves or panels joined by hinges or folds.
– ORIGIN mid 19th cent.: from late Latin *polyptycha* (neuter plural) 'registers,' from Greek *poluptukhos* 'having many folds,' from *polu-* 'many' + *ptukhē* 'fold.'

pol·y·pus /ˈpäləpəs/ ▶ **n.** (pl. **polypi** /-ˌpī, -ˌpē/) archaic or technical term for **POLYP**.
– ORIGIN late Middle English: via Latin from a variant of Greek *polupous* 'cuttlefish, polyp,' from *polu-* 'many' + *pous*, *pod-* 'foot.'

pol·y·rhythm /ˈpäliˌriT͟Həm/ ▶ **n.** Music a rhythm that makes use of two or more different rhythms simultaneously.
– DERIVATIVES **pol·y·rhyth·mic** /ˌpäliˈriT͟Hmik/ **adj.**

pol·y·ri·bo·some /ˌpäliˈrībəˌsōm/ ▶ **n.** another term for **POLYSOME**.

pol·y·sac·cha·ride /ˌpäliˈsakəˌrīd/ ▶ **n.** Biochemistry a carbohydrate (e.g., starch, cellulose, or glycogen) whose molecules consist of a number of sugar molecules bonded together.

po·ly·se·my /ˈpäliˌsemē/ ▶ **n.** Linguistics the coexistence of many possible meanings for a word or phrase.
– DERIVATIVES **po·ly·se·mic** /ˌpäliˈsēmik/ **adj.**, **po·ly·se·mous** /ˌpäliˈsēməs/ **adj.**
– ORIGIN early 20th cent.: from **POLY-** 'many' + Greek *sēma* 'sign.'

pol·y·sex·u·al /ˌpälēˈsekSHo͞oəl/ ▶ **adj.** incorporating many different kinds of sexuality; pansexual.

pol·y·some /ˈpäliˌsōm/ ▶ **n.** Biology a cluster of ribosomes held together by a strand of messenger RNA that each ribosome is translating.

pol·y·sty·rene /ˌpäliˈstīrēn/ ▶ **n.** a synthetic resin that is a polymer of styrene, used chiefly as lightweight rigid foams and films.

pol·y·sul·fide /ˌpäliˈsəlˌfīd/ ▶ **n.** Chemistry a compound containing two or more sulfur atoms bonded together as an anion or group. ■ a synthetic rubber or other polymer in which the units are linked through such groups.

pol·y·syl·lab·ic /ˌpälisəˈlabik/ ▶ **adj.** (of a word) having more than one syllable. ■ using or characterized by words of many syllables: *polysyllabic jargon*.
– DERIVATIVES **pol·y·syl·lab·i·cal·ly** /-səˈlabək(ə)lē/ **adv.**

pol·y·syl·la·ble /ˈpäliˌsiləbəl, ˌpäliˈsiləbəl/ ▶ **n.** a polysyllabic word.

pol·y·symp·to·mat·ic /ˌpäliˌsimptəˈmatik/ ▶ **adj.** (of a disease condition or a person or animal) involving or exhibiting many symptoms.

pol·y·syn·thet·ic /ˌpälisinˈTHetik/ ▶ **adj.** denoting or relating to a language characterized by complex words consisting of several morphemes, in which a single word may function as a whole sentence. Many American Indian languages are polysynthetic.

pol·y·tech·nic /ˌpäliˈteknik/ ▶ **n.** an institution of higher education offering courses in many subjects, esp. vocational or technical subjects.
▶ **adj.** dealing with or devoted to various vocational or technical subjects.
– ORIGIN early 19th cent.: from French *polytechnique*, from Greek *polutekhnos*, from *polu-* 'many' + *tekhnē* 'art.'

pol·y·tene /ˈpäləˌtēn/ ▶ **adj.** Genetics relating to or denoting a giant chromosome that is composed of many parallel copies of the genetic material, as found in *Drosophila* fruit flies, where they are much used in genetic research.
– ORIGIN 1930s: from **POLY-** 'many' + *-tene* (from Greek *tainia* 'band, ribbon') denoting stages of the first meiotic division.

pol·y·tet·ra·fluor·o·eth·y·lene /ˌpäliˌtetrəˌflo͝orōˈeTHəˌlēn/ ▶ **n.** another term for **TEFLON**.

pol·y·the·ism /ˈpäliTHēˌizəm/ ▶ **n.** the belief in or worship of more than one god.
– DERIVATIVES **pol·y·the·ist** /-ˌTHēist/ **n.**, **pol·y·the·is·tic** /ˌpäliTHēˈistik/ **adj.**

– ORIGIN early 17th cent.: from French *polythéisme*, from Greek *polutheos* 'of many gods,' from *polu-* 'many' + *theos* 'god.'

pol·y·thene /ˈpäləTHēn/ ▶ n. chiefly Brit. another term for **POLYETHYLENE**.
– ORIGIN 1930s: contraction of **POLYETHYLENE**.

pol·y·to·nal·i·ty /ˌpälitōˈnalətē/ ▶ n. the simultaneous use of two or more keys in a musical composition.
– DERIVATIVES **pol·y·ton·al** /ˌpäliˈtōnl/ adj.

pol·y·type /ˈpäliˌtīp/ ▶ n. Crystallography any of a number of forms of a crystalline substance that differ in only one of the dimensions of the unit cell.
– DERIVATIVES **pol·y·typ·ic** /ˌpäliˈtipik/ adj., **pol·y·typ·ism** /ˌpäliˈtīˌpizəm/ n.

pol·y·un·sat·u·rat·ed /ˌpälēənˈsaCHəˌrātid/ ▶ adj. Chemistry (of an organic compound, esp. a fat or oil molecule) containing several double or triple bonds between carbon atoms. Polyunsaturated fats, which are usually of plant origin, are regarded as healthier in the diet than saturated fats.

pol·y·un·sat·u·rates /ˌpälēənˈsaCHərits/ ▶ plural n. polyunsaturated fats or fatty acids.

pol·y·u·re·thane /ˌpäliˈyo͝orəˌTHān/ ▶ n. a synthetic resin in which the polymer units are linked by urethane groups, used chiefly as constituents of paints, varnishes, adhesives, and foams.
▶ v. [with obj.] (usu. as adj. **polyurethaned**) coat or protect with paint or varnish of this kind.

pol·y·u·ri·a /ˌpäliˈyo͝orēə/ ▶ n. Medicine production of abnormally large volumes of dilute urine. Compare with **DIURESIS**.
– DERIVATIVES **pol·y·u·ric** /-ˈyo͝orik/ adj.

pol·y·va·lent /ˌpäliˈvālənt/ ▶ adj. **1** Chemistry having a valence of three or more.
2 Medicine having the property of counteracting several related poisons or affording immunity against different strains of a microorganism.
3 having many different functions, forms, or facets: *as emotion, love is polyvalent*.
– DERIVATIVES **pol·y·va·lence** n.

pol·y·vi·nyl /ˌpäliˈvīnl/ ▶ adj. [attrib.] denoting materials or objects made from polymers of vinyl compounds.

pol·y·vi·nyl ac·e·tate (abbr.: **PVA**) ▶ n. a synthetic resin made by polymerizing vinyl acetate, used chiefly in paints and adhesives.

pol·y·vi·nyl chlo·ride (abbr.: **PVC**) ▶ n. a tough, chemically resistant synthetic resin made by polymerizing vinyl chloride and used for a wide variety of products including pipes, flooring, and sheeting.

pol·y·vi·nyl·pyr·rol·i·done /ˌpäliˌvīnl-piˈrälәˌdōn/ ▶ n. Chemistry a water-soluble polymer of vinyl pyrrolidone, used as a synthetic blood plasma substitute and in the cosmetic, drug, and food-processing industries.

pol·y·wa·ter /ˈpäliˌwôtər, -ˌwätər/ ▶ n. historical a supposed polymeric form of water markedly different from ordinary water, claimed as a new discovery in the early 1970s. The claim was later retracted when its properties were found to be the result of impurities.

Pol·y·zo·a /ˌpäliˈzōə/ Zoology British term for **BRYOZOA**.
– DERIVATIVES **pol·y·zo·an** n. & adj.
– ORIGIN modern Latin (plural), from **POLY-** 'many' + *zōion* 'animal.'

Pom[1] /päm/ ▶ n. short for **POMERANIAN**.

Pom[2] /päm/ ▶ n. Austral./NZ informal, often derogatory a British person.
– ORIGIN early 20th cent.: short for **POMMY**.

pom·ace /ˈpəməs/ ▶ n. (esp. in cider making) the pulpy residue remaining after fruit has been crushed in order to extract its juice. ■ the pulpy matter remaining after some other substance has been pressed or crushed, for example castor oil seeds after the oil has been extracted.
– ORIGIN late 16th cent.: apparently from medieval Latin *pomacium* 'cider,' from Latin *pomum* 'apple.'

po·made /pəˈmād, -ˈmäd/ dated ▶ n. a scented ointment applied to the hair or scalp.
▶ v. [with obj.] (often as adj. **pomaded**) apply pomade to.
– ORIGIN mid 16th cent.: from French *pommade*, based on Latin *pomum* 'apple' (from which it was originally made).

Po·mak /ˈpōˌmak/ ▶ n. a Muslim Bulgarian.
– ORIGIN Bulgarian.

po·man·der /pōˈmandər, ˈpōˌmandər/ ▶ n. a ball or perforated container of sweet-smelling substances such as herbs and spices, placed in a closet, drawer, or room to perfume the air or (formerly) carried as a supposed protection against infection. ■ a piece of fruit, typically an orange or apple, studded with cloves and hung in a closet by a ribbon for a similar purpose.
– ORIGIN late 15th cent.: from Old French *pome d'embre*, from medieval Latin *pomum de ambra* 'apple of ambergris.'

po·ma·tum /pōˈmātəm, -ˈmätəm/ ▶ n. & v. another term for **POMADE**.
– ORIGIN mid 16th cent.: modern Latin, from Latin *pomum* 'apple.'

pom·be /ˈpämˌbā/ ▶ n. (in central and eastern Africa) a fermented drink made from various kinds of grain and fruit.
– ORIGIN Kiswahili.

pome /pōm/ ▶ n. Botany a fruit consisting of a fleshy enlarged receptacle and a tough central core containing the seeds, e.g., an apple or pear.
– ORIGIN late Middle English: from Old French, based on Latin *poma*, plural of *pomum* 'apple.'

pome·gran·ate /ˈpäm(ə)ˌgranit, ˈpəm-/ ▶ n. **1** an orange-sized fruit with a tough reddish outer skin and sweet red gelatinous flesh containing many seeds.
2 the tree that bears this fruit, which is native to North Africa and western Asia and has long been cultivated. ● *Punica granatum*, family Punicaceae.
– ORIGIN Middle English: from Old French *pome grenate*, from *pome* 'apple' + *grenate* 'pomegranate' (from Latin *(malum) granatum* '(apple) having many seeds,' from *granum* 'seed').

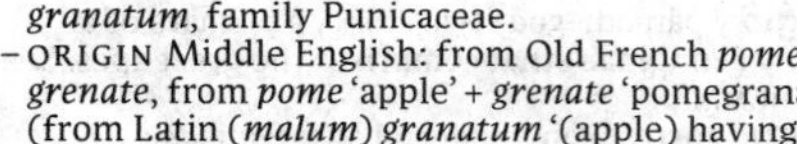
pomegranate 1

pom·e·lo /ˈpäməˌlō, ˈpəm-/ (also **pummelo**) ▶ n. (pl. **pomelos**) **1** the largest of the citrus fruits, with a thick yellow skin and bitter pulp that resembles grapefruit in flavor. Also called **SHADDOCK**.
2 the tree that bears this fruit. ● *Citrus maxima*, family Rutaceae.
– ORIGIN mid 19th cent.: of unknown origin.

Pom·er·a·ni·a /ˌpäməˈrānēə/ a region of northern Europe that extends along the southern shore of the Baltic Sea in northeastern Germany and Poland. The region was controlled variously by Germany, Poland, the Holy Roman Empire, Prussia, and Sweden until the larger part was restored to Poland in 1945 and the western portion became a part of the German state of Mecklenburg–West Pomerania.

Pom·er·a·ni·an /ˌpäməˈrānēən/ ▶ n. a small dog of a breed with long silky hair, a pointed muzzle, and pricked ears.

Pomeranian

Pom·e·rol /ˈpäməˌrôl, -ˌrōl/ ▶ n. a red Bordeaux wine produced in Pomerol, a region in the Gironde, France.

pom·fret /ˈpämfrət, ˈpəm-/ ▶ n. a deep-bodied fish of open seas that typically has scales on the dorsal and anal fins. ● Family Bramidae: several genera and species, including the edible *Brama brama* of the North Atlantic.
– ORIGIN early 18th cent.: apparently from Portuguese *pampo*.

pom·mel ▶ n. /ˈpäməl, ˈpəməl/ **1** a rounded knob on the end of the handle of a sword, dagger, or old-fashioned gun.
2 the upward curving or projecting part of a saddle in front of the rider.
▶ v. /ˈpəməl, ˈpäməl/ (**pommels, pommeling, pommeled**; Brit. **pommels, pommelling, pommelled**) another term for **PUMMEL**.
– ORIGIN Middle English (denoting a ball or finial at the top point of a tower, corner of an altar, etc.): from Old French *pomel*, from a diminutive of Latin *pomum* 'fruit, apple.'

pom·mel horse ▶ n. a vaulting horse fitted with a pair of curved handgrips, used for a gymnastic exercise consisting of swings of the legs and body.

pommes frites /ˌpəm ˈfrēt/ ▶ plural n. (esp. in recipes or on menus) French fries.
– ORIGIN French, from *pommes de terre frites*, literally 'fried potatoes.'

Pom·my /ˈpämē/ (also **Pommie**) ▶ adj. (pl. **Pommies**) British: *a Pommy accent*. ▶ n. Austral./NZ informal, often derogatory a British person.
– ORIGIN early 20th cent.: of unknown origin; said by some to be short for *pomegranate*, as a near rhyme to *immigrant*, but evidence is lacking.

Po·mo /ˈpōmō/ ▶ n. (pl. **same** or **Pomos**) **1** a member of an American Indian people of northern California.
2 any of the languages of this people.
▶ adj. of or relating to this people or their languages.
– ORIGIN from Pomo *phōmō phóʔmaʔ* 'dweller at the red-earth hole.'

po·mo ▶ abbr. informal postmodern.

po·mol·o·gy /pōˈmäləjē/ ▶ n. the science of growing fruit.
– DERIVATIVES **po·mo·log·i·cal** /ˌpōməˈläjikəl/ adj., **po·mol·o·gist** /-jist/ n.
– ORIGIN early 19th cent.: from Latin *pomum* 'fruit' + **-LOGY**.

Po·mo·na /pəˈmōnə/ an industrial and commercial city in southwestern California, east of Los Angeles; pop. 152,699 (est. 2008).

pomp /pämp/ ▶ n. ceremony and splendid display, esp. at a public event: *St. Paul's was perfectly adapted to pomp and circumstance*. ■ (**pomps**) archaic ostentatious boastfulness or vanity: *the pomps and vanities of this world*.
– ORIGIN Middle English: from Old French *pompe*, via Latin from Greek *pompē* 'procession, pomp,' from *pempein* 'send.'

Pom·pa·dour /ˈpämpəˌdôr, -ˌdo͝or, pôNpäˈdo͝or/, Jeanne Antoinette Poisson, Marquise de (1721–64), French noblewoman; known as **Madame de Pompadour**. In 1744, she became the mistress of Louis XV, gaining considerable influence at court.

pom·pa·dour /ˈpämpəˌdôr/ ▶ n. a man's hairstyle in which the hair is combed up from the forehead without a part. ■ a woman's hairstyle in which the hair is turned back off the forehead in a roll.
▶ v. [with obj.] (usu. as adj. **pompadoured**) arrange (hair) in a pompadour.
– ORIGIN late 19th cent.: named after Madame de **POMPADOUR**.

pom·pa·no /ˈpämpəˌnō/ ▶ n. (pl. **pompanos**) **1** an edible butterfish that lives in shoals along the east coast of North America. ● *Peprillus simillimus*, family Stromateidae.
2 another term for **JACK**[1] (sense 11).
– ORIGIN late 18th cent.: from Spanish *pámpano*, perhaps from *pámpana* 'vine leaf,' because of its shape.

Pom·pa·no Beach /ˈpämpəˌnō/ a resort city in southeastern Florida, north of Fort Lauderdale, on the Atlantic Ocean; pop. 101,943 (est. 2008).

Pom·pe·ii /pämˈpā(ē)/ an ancient city in western Italy, southeast of Naples. The city was buried by an eruption of Mount Vesuvius in AD 79; excavations of the site began in 1748 and revealed well-preserved remains of buildings, mosaics, furniture, and the personal possessions of the city's inhabitants.

Pom·pey /ˈpämpē/ (106–48 BC), Roman general and statesman; Latin name *Gnaeus Pompeius Magnus*; known as **Pompey the Great**. He founded the First Triumvirate, but later quarreled with Julius Caesar, who defeated him at the battle of Pharsalus. He then fled to Egypt, where he was murdered.

Pom·pi·dou /ˈpämpiˌdo͞o, pôNpēˈdo͞o/, Georges (Jean Raymond) (1911–74), French statesman; prime minister 1962–68 and president 1969–74. He was instrumental in ending the conflict in Algeria between French forces and nationalist guerrillas.

pom·pier /pämˈpyā/ ▶ n. (pl. **same**) an artist regarded as painting in an academic, imitative, and vulgarly neoclassical style.
– ORIGIN mid 19th cent.: from French, literally 'fireman,' said to derive from the similarity between firemen's helmets and those worn by the Greek gods and heroes depicted by late Classical artists.

pom-pom[1] /ˈpäm ˌpäm/ (also **pompom** or **pompon**) ▶ n. a small woolen ball attached to a garment, esp. a hat, for decoration. ■ a large round cluster of brightly colored streamers waved in pairs by cheerleaders. ■ a dahlia, chrysanthemum, or aster with small tightly clustered petals: [as modifier] *miniature, pompom, and border dahlias*.
– ORIGIN mid 18th cent.: French *pompon*, of unknown origin.

pom-pom[2] (also **pompom**) ▶ n. an automatic quick-firing two-pounder cannon of the World War II period, typically mounted on a ship and used against aircraft.
– ORIGIN late 19th cent.: imitative of the sound of the discharge.

PRONUNCIATION KEY ə *ago, up*; ər *over, fur*; a *hat*; ā *ate*; ä *car*; e *let*; ē *see*; i *fit*; ī *by*; NG *sing*; ō *go*; ô *law, for*; oi *toy*; o͝o *good*; o͞o *goo*; ou *out*; TH *thin*; T͟H *then*; ZH *vision*

P

pom·pos·i·ty /päm'päsətē/ ▶ **n.** the quality of being pompous; self-importance: *his reputation for arrogance and pomposity.*

pomp·ous /'pämpəs/ ▶ **adj.** affectedly and irritatingly grand, solemn, or self-important: *a pompous ass who pretends he knows everything.* ■ archaic characterized by pomp or splendor: *there were many processions and other pompous shows.*
– DERIVATIVES **pomp·ous·ly adv.**, **pomp·ous·ness n.**
– ORIGIN late Middle English: from Old French *pompeux* 'full of grandeur,' from late Latin *pomposus*, from *pompa* 'pomp.'

'pon /pän, pən/ ▶ **prep.** short for UPON, esp. in poetic use or to represent dialect.

Pon·ca /'päNGkə, 'pôNGkə/ ▶ **n.** (pl. **same** or **Poncas**) **1** a member of a Siouan people formerly inhabiting northern Nebraska and southern South Dakota. **2** the Siouan language of this people, related to Omaha.
▶ **adj.** of or relating to this people or their language.
– ORIGIN via French, from the Ponca name *pąka.*

Pon·ce /'pônsā/ an industrial port in southern Puerto Rico, on the Caribbean Sea; pop. 144,500 (est. 2009).

ponce /päns/ Brit. informal ▶ **n. 1** derogatory an effeminate man. **2** a man who lives off a prostitute's earnings.
▶ **v.** [no obj.] live off a prostitute's earnings. ■ [with obj.] ask for or obtain (something to which one is not strictly entitled): *I ponced a cigarette off her.*
– PHRASAL VERBS **ponce around/about** behave in a ridiculous, ineffective, or posturing way: *I ponced around in front of the mirror.* **ponce something up** make overly elaborate and unnecessary changes to something in an attempt to improve it.
– ORIGIN late 19th cent.: perhaps from the verb POUNCE[1].

Ponce de Le·ón /'päns də 'lēän, ˌpônsā de lā'ôn/, Juan (*c.*1460–1521), Spanish explorer. He accompanied Columbus on his second voyage to the New World in 1493, became governor of Puerto Rico 1510–12, and landed on the coast of Florida near what became St. Augustine in 1513, claiming the area for Spain.

pon·cho /'pänCHō/ ▶ **n.** (pl. **ponchos**) a garment of a type originally worn in South America, made of a thick piece of woolen cloth with a slit in the middle for the head. ■ a waterproof garment in this style worn as a raincoat.
– ORIGIN early 18th cent.: from South American Spanish, from Araucanian.

pon·cy /'pänsē/ (also **poncey**) ▶ **adj.** (**poncier, ponciest**) Brit. informal pretentious or affected: *a poncy wine bar.*

pond /pänd/ ▶ **n.** a small body of still water formed naturally or by hollowing or embanking. ■ (**the pond**) informal the Atlantic ocean: *he's relatively unknown on this side of the pond.*
▶ **v.** [with obj.] hold back or dam up (flowing water or another liquid) to form a small lake. ■ [no obj.] (of flowing water or other liquids) form such a lake: (as noun **ponding**) *where a path goes down into a dip, you'll have to ensure that ponding doesn't occur.*
– ORIGIN Middle English: alteration of POUND[3], commonly used in dialect in the same sense.

pon·der /'pändər/ ▶ **v.** [with obj.] think about (something) carefully, esp. before making a decision or reaching a conclusion: *I pondered the question of what clothes to wear for the occasion* | [no obj.] *she sat pondering over her problem.*
– DERIVATIVES **pon·der·a·tion** /ˌpändə'rāSHən/ **n.** (rare).
– ORIGIN Middle English (in the sense 'appraise, judge the worth of'): from Old French *ponderer* 'consider,' from Latin *ponderare* 'weigh, reflect on,' from *pondus, ponder-* 'weight.'

pon·der·a·ble /'pändərəbəl/ ▶ **adj.** literary having appreciable weight or significance.
– DERIVATIVES **pon·der·a·bil·i·ty** /ˌpändərə'bilətē/ **n.**
– ORIGIN mid 17th cent.: from late Latin *ponderabilis*, from *ponderare* 'weigh, reflect on' (see PONDER).

pon·der·o·sa /ˌpändə'rōsə/ (also **ponderosa pine**) ▶ **n.** a tall slender pine tree, the most widespread conifer of western North America, planted for timber and as an ornamental. ● *Pinus ponderosa*, family Pinaceae.
– ORIGIN late 19th cent.: feminine of Latin *ponderosus* 'massive, ponderous,' used as a specific epithet in *Pinus ponderosa.*

pon·der·ous /'pändərəs/ ▶ **adj.** slow and clumsy because of great weight: *her footsteps were heavy and ponderous.* ■ dull, laborious, or excessively solemn: *Liz could hardly restrain herself from finishing all his ponderous sentences.*
– DERIVATIVES **pon·der·os·i·ty** /ˌpändə'räsətē/ **n.**, **pon·der·ous·ly adv.**, **pon·der·ous·ness n.**
– ORIGIN late Middle English: via French from Latin *ponderosus*, from *pondus, ponder-* 'weight.'

Pon·di·cher·ry /ˌpändi'CHerē, -'SHerē/ former name (until 2006) for PUDUCHERRY.

pond scum ▶ **n.** a mass of algae forming a green film on the surface of stagnant water. ■ informal a person or thing perceived as worthless or contemptible.

pond·weed /'pänd,wēd/ ▶ **n.** a submerged aquatic plant that grows in still or running water and sometimes has floating leaves. ● Genus *Potamogeton*, family Potamogetonaceae.

pone /pōn/ ▶ **n.** (also **corn pone** or **pone bread**) unleavened cornbread in the form of flat oval cakes or loaves, originally as prepared with water by North American Indians and cooked in hot ashes.
– ORIGIN Virginia Algonquian, 'bread.'

pong /pôNG, päNG/ Brit. informal ▶ **n.** a strong, unpleasant smell.
▶ **v.** [no obj.] smell strongly and unpleasantly.
– DERIVATIVES **pon·gy adj.**
– ORIGIN early 20th cent.: of unknown origin.

pon·gee /pän'jē, 'pänjē/ ▶ **n.** a soft and typically unbleached type of Chinese plain-woven fabric, originally made from threads of raw silk and now also other fibers such as cotton, which are usually mercerized.
– ORIGIN early 18th cent.: from Chinese (Mandarin dialect) *běnjī*, literally 'own loom' or *běnzhì*, literally 'home-woven.'

pon·gid /'pänjəd, -gəd/ ▶ **n.** Zoology a primate of a family (Pongidae) that comprises the great apes. See also HOMINID.
– ORIGIN 1950s: from modern Latin *Pongidae* (plural), from the genus name *Pongo*, originally from Congolese *mpongo*, used as a term in zoology to refer to the gorilla and other apes.

pon·iard /'pänyərd/ ▶ **n.** historical a small, slim dagger.
– ORIGIN mid 16th cent.: from French *poignard*, based on Latin *pugnus* 'fist.'

Pons /pänz/, Lily (1904–76), US opera singer; born in France; born *Alice-Josephine Pons.* A coloratura soprano, she made her debut at the Metropolitan Opera in 1931 and sang there for 25 years. She also appeared in movies.

pons /pänz/ (in full **pons Varolii** /vərōlē,ī/) ▶ **n.** (pl. **pontes** /'pän,tēz/) Anatomy the part of the brainstem that links the medulla oblongata and the thalamus.
– ORIGIN late 17th cent.: from Latin, literally 'bridge,' (in full) 'bridge of Varolius,' named after C. Varoli (1543–75), Italian anatomist.

pons as·i·no·rum /'pänz ˌasə'nôrəm/ ▶ **n.** the point at which many learners fail, esp. a theory or formula that is difficult to grasp.
– ORIGIN mid 18th cent.: Latin, literally 'bridge of asses,' term taken from the fifth proposition of the first book of Euclid.

Pon·selle /pän'sel/, Rosa (1897–1981), US opera singer; born *Rosa Melba Ponzillo.* She sang with the Metropolitan Opera 1918–36, beginning with her debut as Leonora in *Fidelio.*

Pont·char·train, Lake /'pänCHər,trān/ a shallow lake in southeastern Louisiana, north of New Orleans and Metairie, noted for its long causeway.

pon·tes /'pän,tēz/ plural form of PONS.

Pon·ti·ac[1] /'päntē,ak/ an industrial city in southeastern Michigan, northwest of Detroit; pop. 66,095 (est. 2008).

Pon·ti·ac[2] (c.1720–69), Ottawa Indian chief. He is credited with organizing and leading a rebellion against the British, during which he led a year-long siege of Fort Detroit 1763–64. He agreed to terms of peace in 1766.

Pon·ti·ac fe·ver ▶ **n.** Medicine a mild systemic disease with symptoms resembling influenza, probably caused by a legionella infection.
– ORIGIN 1960s: named after *Pontiac*, Michigan, where the first major outbreak was recorded.

Pon·ti·a·nak /ˌpäntē'änak/ a seaport in Indonesia, on the western coast of Borneo, at the delta of the Kapuas River; pop. 469,400 (est. 2009).

Pon·tic /'päntik/ ▶ **adj.** of or relating to ancient Pontus.

Pont l'É·vêque /ˌpôN lə'vek/ ▶ **n.** a kind of creamy soft cheese made originally at Pont l'Évêque in Normandy, France.

pon·ti·fex /'päntə,feks/ ▶ **n.** (pl. **pontifices** /pän'tifə,sēz/) (in ancient Rome) a member of the principal college of priests.
– ORIGIN Latin, from *pons, pont-* 'bridge' + *-fex* from *facere* 'make.'

Pon·ti·fex Max·i·mus /'maksəməs/ ▶ **n.** (in ancient Rome) the head of the principal college of priests. ■ (in the Roman Catholic Church) a title of the pope.
– ORIGIN *Maximus*, superlative of Latin *magnus* 'great.'

pon·tiff /'päntəf/ (also **sovereign** or **supreme pontiff**) ▶ **n.** the pope.
– ORIGIN late 17th cent.: from French *pontife*, from Latin *pontifex* (see PONTIFEX).

pon·tif·i·cal /pän'tifikəl/ ▶ **adj. 1** (in the Roman Catholic Church) of or relating to the pope: *a pontifical commission.* **2** characterized by a pompous and superior air of infallibility: *such explanations were greeted with pontifical disdain.*
▶ **n.** rare (in the Roman Catholic Church) an office book of the Western Church containing rites to be performed by the pope or bishops. ■ (**pontificals**) the vestments and insignia of a bishop, cardinal, or abbot: *a bishop in full pontificals.*
– DERIVATIVES **pon·tif·i·cal·ly** /-ik(ə)lē/ **adv.**
– ORIGIN late Middle English: from Latin *pontificalis*, from *pontifex* (see PONTIFEX).

pon·tif·i·cate ▶ **v.** /pän'tifi,kāt/ [no obj.] **1** (in the Roman Catholic Church) officiate as bishop, esp. at Mass. **2** express one's opinions in a way considered annoyingly pompous and dogmatic: *he was pontificating about art and history.*
▶ **n.** /-kət/ (also **Pontificate**) (in the Roman Catholic Church) the office or tenure of pope or bishop.
– DERIVATIVES **pon·ti·fi·ca·tion** /-'kāSHən/ **n.**, **pon·tif·i·ca·tor** /-,kātər/ **n.**
– ORIGIN late Middle English (as a noun): from Latin *pontificatus*, from *pontifex* (see PONTIFEX). The verb dates from the early 19th cent.

pon·tif·i·ces /pän'tifə,sēz/ plural form of PONTIFEX.

pon·til /'päntl/ ▶ **n.** another term for PUNTY.
– ORIGIN mid 19th cent.: from French, apparently from Italian *pontello* 'small point,' diminutive of *punto.*

pon·tine /'pän,tīn/ ▶ **adj.** Anatomy of, relating to, or affecting the pons of the brain.
– ORIGIN late 19th cent.: from Latin *pons, pont-* 'bridge' + -INE[1].

Pon·tine Marsh·es /'pän,tēn, -,tīn/ an area of marshland in western Italy, on the Tyrrhenian coast south of Rome. It was infested with malaria in ancient Roman times, but not until 1928 was an extensive program to drain the marshes begun. Several new towns have since been built in the region, which is now a productive agricultural area. Italian name AGRO PONTINO.

pon·toon[1] /ˌpän'tōōn/ ▶ **n.** a flat-bottomed boat or hollow metal cylinder used with others to support a temporary bridge or floating landing stage. ■ a bridge or landing stage supported by pontoons. ■ a large flat-bottomed barge or lighter equipped with cranes. ■ either of the floats fitted to an aircraft to enable it to land on water.
– ORIGIN late 17th cent.: from French *ponton*, from Latin *ponto, ponton-*, from *pons, pont-* 'bridge.'

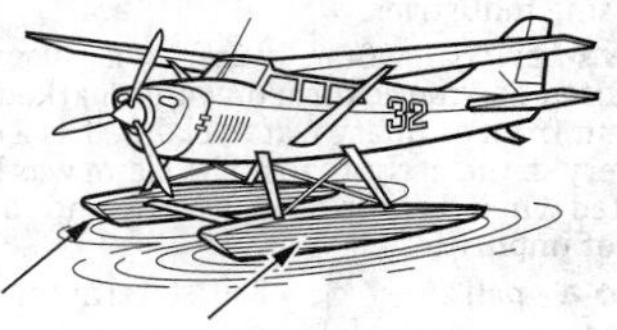

pontoon[1]

pon·toon[2] ▶ **n.** Brit. the card game blackjack or vingt-et-un. ■ a hand of two cards totaling 21 in this game.
– ORIGIN early 20th cent.: probably an alteration of *vingt-et-un* 'twenty-one.'

Pon·tor·mo /pôn'tôrmō/, Jacopo da (1494–1557), Italian painter, whose use of dynamic composition, anatomical exaggeration, and bright colors placed him at the forefront of early mannerism.

Pon·tus /'päntəs/ an ancient region in northern Asia Minor, on the Black Sea coast north of Cappadocia. By the end of the 1st century BC, it had been defeated by Rome and absorbed into the Roman Empire.

po·ny /'pōnē/ ▶ **n.** (pl. **ponies**) **1** a horse of a small breed, esp. one whose height at the withers is below 14 hands 2 inches (58 inches). ■ (**the ponies**) informal racehorses: *he had been playing the ponies on the side.* **2** informal a small drinking glass or the drink contained in it: *a pony of vodka.* **3** a literal translation of a foreign-language text, used illicitly by students; a trot. **4** Brit. informal twenty-five pounds sterling.
▶ **v.** (**ponies, ponying, ponied**) [no obj.] (**pony up**) informal pay (money), esp. as a contribution or an unavoidable expense: *getting ready to pony up for their children's college education.*
– ORIGIN mid 17th cent.: probably from French *poulenet* 'small foal,' diminutive of *poulain*, from late Latin *pullanus*, from Latin *pullus* 'young animal.'

Po·ny Ex·press a system of mail delivery operating from 1860 to 1861 over a distance of 1,800 miles (2,900 km) between St. Joseph, Missouri, and Sacramento, California, using continuous relays of horse riders.

po·ny·tail /ˈpōnēˌtāl/ ▶ **n.** a hairstyle in which the hair is drawn back and tied at the back of the head, causing it to hang down like a pony's tail.
– DERIVATIVES **po·ny·tailed adj.**

Pon·zil·lo /pänˈzilō/, Rosa, see PONSELLE.

Pon·zi scheme /ˈpänzē/ ▶ **n.** a form of fraud in which belief in the success of a nonexistent enterprise is fostered by the payment of quick returns to the first investors from money invested by later investors.
– ORIGIN named after Charles *Ponzi* (died 1949), who carried out such a fraud (1919–20).

pon·zu /ˈpänˌzo͞o/ ▶ **n.** a Japanese dipping sauce made from soy sauce, lime juice, vinegar, and fish flakes.
– ORIGIN Japanese: 'citrus vinegar.'

poo ▶ **exclam., n., & v.** see POOH.

pooch[1] /po͞oCH/ ▶ **n.** informal a dog.
– ORIGIN 1920s: of unknown origin.

pooch[2] ▶ **v.** informal protrude or cause to protrude: [no obj.] *a dress that made her stomach pooch out even more than usual.*
– ORIGIN mid 17th cent.: from the noun POUCH.

poo·dle /ˈpo͞odl/ ▶ **n.** a dog of a breed with a curly coat that is usually clipped. The numerous varieties of poodle include standard, miniature, and toy. ■ Brit. a person or organization considered to be servile or obsequious: *the council is being made a poodle of central government.*
– ORIGIN early 19th cent.: from German *Pudel(hund)*, from Low German *pud(d)eln* 'splash in water' (the poodle being a water dog).

poo·dle skirt ▶ **n.** a long full skirt in a solid color with a chenille poodle on it, popular in the 1950s with bobbysoxers.

poof[1] /po͝of, po͞of/ (also **pouf**) ▶ **exclam. 1** used to convey the suddenness with which someone or something disappears: *once you've used it, poof—it's gone.*
2 used to express contemptuous dismissal: *"Oh, poof!" said Will. "You say that every year."*
– ORIGIN early 19th cent.: symbolic.

poof[2] (also **pouf** or **poove**) ▶ **n.** Brit. informal, offensive an effeminate or homosexual man.
– DERIVATIVES **poof·y adj.**
– ORIGIN mid 19th cent.: perhaps an alteration of the archaic noun *puff* in the sense 'braggart.'

poof·ter /ˈpo͞oftər, ˈpo͝of-/ ▶ **n.** another term for POOF[2].
– ORIGIN early 20th cent.: extended form.

pooh /po͞o, po͝o/ (also **poo**) informal ▶ **exclam.** used to express disgust at an unpleasant smell. ■ used to express impatience or contempt: *Oh pooh! Don't be such a spoilsport.*
▶ **n.** (usu. **poo**) excrement. ■ [in sing.] an act of defecating.
▶ **v.** [no obj.] (usu. **poo**) defecate.
– ORIGIN natural exclamation: first recorded in English in the late 16th cent.

pooh-bah /ˈpo͞o ˌbä/ (also **Pooh-Bah**) ▶ **n.** a person having much influence or holding many offices at the same time, esp. one perceived as pompously self-important.
– ORIGIN from the name of a character in W. S. Gilbert's *The Mikado* (1885).

pooh-pooh /ˈpo͞o ˌpo͞o, po͞o ˈpo͞o/ ▶ **v.** [with obj.] informal dismiss (an idea or suggestion) as being foolish or impractical: *until recently, this idea was pooh-poohed by the scientific community.*
– ORIGIN late 18th cent.: reduplication of POOH.

poo·ja ▶ **n.** variant spelling of PUJA.

poo·ka /ˈpo͞okə/ ▶ **n.** (in Irish mythology) a hobgoblin.
– ORIGIN from Irish *púca*.

pool[1] /po͞ol/ ▶ **n.** a small area of still water, typically one formed naturally. ■ a small, shallow patch of liquid lying on a surface: *a pool of blood* | figurative *the lamps cast pools of light on the wet streets.* ■ a swimming pool. ■ a deep place in a river.
▶ **v.** [no obj.] (of water or another liquid) form a pool on the ground or another surface: *the oil pooled behind the quay walls, escaping slowly into the river.* ■ (of blood) accumulate in parts of the venous system.
– ORIGIN Old English *pōl*; related to Dutch *poel* and German *Pfuhl*.

pool[2] ▶ **n. 1** a supply of vehicles or goods available for use when needed: *the oldest vehicle in the motor pool.* ■ a group of people available for work when required or considered as a resource: *the typing pool* | *a nationwide pool of promising high-school students.* ■ an arrangement, illegal in many countries, between competing parties to fix prices or rates and share business in order to eliminate competition. ■ a common fund into which all contributors pay and from which financial backing is provided: *big public investment pools.* ■ a group of contestants who compete against each other in a tournament for the right to advance to the next round. ■ the collective amount of players' stakes in gambling or sweepstakes; a kitty.
2 Billiards a game played on a table using fifteen colored and numbered balls and a white cue ball. ■ another term for POCKETBILLIARDS. ■ short for STRAIGHT POOL.
▶ **v.** [with obj.] (of two or more people or organizations) put (money or other assets) into a common fund: *they entered a contract to pool any gains and invest them profitably.* ■ share (things) for the benefit of all those involved: (as noun **pooling**) *a pooling of ideas.*
– DERIVATIVES **pool·er n.**
– ORIGIN late 17th cent. (originally denoting a game of cards having a pool): from French *poule* in the sense 'stake, kitty,' associated with POOL[1].

Poole /po͞ol/ a port and resort town on the southern coast of England, just west of Bournemouth; pop. 135,800 (est. 2009).

pool·room /ˈpo͞olˌro͞om, -ˌro͝om/ ▶ **n.** (also **pool hall**) a commercial establishment where pool or billiard games are played.

pool·side /ˈpo͞olˌsīd/ ▶ **n.** the area adjoining a swimming pool: [as modifier] *the poolside bar.*
▶ **adv.** toward or beside a swimming pool: *she and her parents lounged poolside.*

poon /po͞on/ ▶ **n. 1** any large Indo-Malayan evergreen tree of the genus *Calophyllum*.
2 short for POONTANG.

Poo·na /ˈpo͞onə/ former name for PUNE.

poon·tang /ˈpo͞onˌtaNG/ (also **poon**) ▶ **n.** vulgar slang sexual activity. ■ a woman or women regarded solely in terms of potential sexual gratification.
– ORIGIN 1920s: perhaps from Limba (a West African language of Sierra Leone) *puntu* 'vagina,' or perhaps alteration of French *putain* 'prostitute.'

poop[1] /po͞op/ ▶ **n.** (also **poop deck**) the aftermost and highest deck of a ship, esp. in a sailing ship where it typically forms the roof of a cabin in the stern.
▶ **v.** [with obj.] (usu. **be pooped**) (of a wave) break over the stern of (a ship), sometimes causing it to capsize: *carrying a high sea, we were badly pooped.*
– ORIGIN late Middle English: from Old French *pupe*, from a variant of Latin *puppis* 'stern.'

poop[2] ▶ **v.** [with obj.] (often as adj. **pooped**) informal exhaust: *I was pooped and just flopped into bed.*
– PHRASAL VERBS **poop out** stop functioning: *the analog tape fluttered slightly in pitch but didn't poop out.*
– ORIGIN 1930s: of unknown origin.

poop[3] informal ▶ **n.** excrement.
▶ **v.** [no obj.] defecate.
– ORIGIN early 18th cent.: imitative.

poop[4] ▶ **n.** informal up-to-date or inside information: *what's the latest poop from campaign headquarters?*
– ORIGIN 1940s: of unknown origin.

poop[5] ▶ **n.** informal a stupid or ineffectual person.
– DERIVATIVES **poop·y adj.**
– ORIGIN early 20th cent.: perhaps a shortening of NINCOMPOOP.

poop·er scoop·er /ˈpo͞opər ˌsko͞opər/ ▶ **n.** an implement for picking up dog excrement.

poor /po͝or, pôr/ ▶ **adj. 1** lacking sufficient money to live at a standard considered comfortable or normal in a society: *people who were too poor to afford a telephone* | (as noun **the poor**) *the gap between the rich and the poor has widened.* ■ (of a place) inhabited by people without sufficient money: *a poor area with run-down movie theaters and overcrowded schools.*
2 worse than is usual, expected, or desirable; of a low or inferior standard or quality: *her work was poor* | *many people are eating a very poor diet.* ■ [predic.] (**poor in**) deficient or lacking in: *the water is poor in nutrients.* ■ dated used ironically to deprecate something belonging to or offered by oneself: *he is, in my poor opinion, a more handsome young man.*
3 [attrib.] (of a person) considered to be deserving of pity or sympathy: *they inquired after poor Dorothy's broken hip.*
– PHRASES (**as**) **poor as a church mouse** (or **as church mice**) extremely poor. **poor little rich boy** (or **girl**) a wealthy young person whose money brings them no contentment (often used as an expression of mock sympathy). **the poor man's ——** an inferior or cheaper substitute for the thing specified: *corduroy has always been the poor man's velvet.* **poor relation** a person or thing that is considered inferior or subordinate to others of the same type or group: *for many years radio has been the poor relation of the media.* **take a poor view of** regard with disfavor or disapproval.
– ORIGIN Middle English: from Old French *poure*, from Latin *pauper*.

poor box ▶ **n.** historical a collection box, esp. one in a church, for gifts of money or other articles toward the relief of the poor.

poor boy ▶ **n.** another term for SUBMARINE SANDWICH.

Poor Clare ▶ **n.** a member of an order of Franciscan nuns founded by St. Clare of Assisi in *c.*1212.

poor·house /ˈpo͝orˌhous, ˈpôr-/ ▶ **n.** historical an institution where paupers were maintained with public funds.

poo·ri /ˈpo͞orē/ ▶ **n.** (pl. **pooris**) PURI.

Poor Law ▶ **n.** Brit. historical a law relating to the support of the poor. Originally the responsibility of the parish, the relief and employment of the poor passed over to the workhouses in 1834. In the early 20th century, the Poor Law was replaced by social security.

poor·ly /ˈpo͝orlē, ˈpôr-/ ▶ **adv.** in a way or at a level that is considered inadequate: *schools that were performing poorly* | [as submodifier] *a few poorly articulated words.* ■ with insufficient money or resources: *he lived as poorly as his peasant parishioners.*
▶ **adj.** unwell: *she looked poorly.*

poor-mouth ▶ **v.** informal **1** [with obj.] talk disparagingly about: *I used to poor-mouth corporate jets, but now that I've had the use of one I really appreciate it.*
2 [no obj.] claim to be poor: (as adj. **poor-mouthing**) *the poor-mouthing museum is not exactly eager to publicize this good fortune.*

poor·ness /ˈpo͝ornəs, ˈpôr-/ ▶ **n.** the state of lacking or being deficient in some desirable quality or constituent: *the poorness of the food.*

poor-spir·it·ed ▶ **adj.** archaic timid; cowardly.

poor white ▶ **n.** derogatory a member of a group of white people regarded as socially inferior, esp. one living in the southern US.

poor-will /ˈpo͝or ˌwil/ (also **poorwill**) ▶ **n.** a small nightjar found mainly in central and western North America. ● Three genera in the family Caprimulgidae: four species, in particular the **common poor-will** (*Phalaenoptilus nuttallii*), which hibernates in cold weather.
– ORIGIN late 19th cent.: imitative of its call.

Poo·ter·ish /ˈpo͞otəriSH/ ▶ **adj.** Brit. self-important and mundane or narrow-minded: *Duran has a Pooterish way with an anecdote which makes his book often very funny.*
– ORIGIN 1960s: from the name of Charles *Pooter*, the fictional diarist in *Diary of a Nobody* (1892) by George and Weedon Grossmith.

poove /po͞ov, po͝ov/ ▶ **n.** variant spelling of POOF[2].

POP /päp/ (also **PoP**) ▶ **abbr.** ■ Computing point of presence, denoting equipment that acts as access to the Internet. ■ point of purchase, denoting products or promotions located adjacent to a retail checkout or cashier.

pop[1] /päp/ ▶ **v.** (**pops, popping, popped**) **1** [no obj.] make a light explosive sound: *corks popped, glasses tinkled, and delicate canapés were served.* ■ [with obj.] cause (something) to burst, making such a sound: *they were popping balloons with darts.* ■ (of a person's ears) make a small popping sound within the head as pressure is equalized, typically because of a change of altitude. ■ [with obj.] heat (popcorn or another foodstuff) until it bursts open, making such a sound. ■ (of a person's eyes) bulge or appear to bulge when opened wide, esp. as an indication of surprise.
2 [no obj.] go somewhere, typically for a short time and often without notice: *she* **popped in** *to see if she could help.* ■ [with obj.] put or move (something) somewhere quickly: *he popped his head around the door.*
3 [no obj.] Baseball (of a batter) hit a pop fly. ■ [with obj.] (of a pitcher) cause (a batter) to pop up.
4 [with obj.] informal take or inject (a drug): *people who obsessively drink and pop pills.*
5 [with obj.] Brit. informal pawn (something).
▶ **n. 1** a light explosive sound: *at first there were just a few pops, perhaps from pistols.*
2 a patch of bright color: *I like wearing a neutral outfit with one pop of yellow.*
3 informal short for SODA POP (see SODA (sense 1)).
4 (also **pop fly** or **pop-up**) Baseball a ball hit high in the air but not deep, providing an easy catch.

5 an attempt: *he grabs with a paw and hooks about two hundred berries at a pop.*
▶ **adv.** with a light explosive sound: *the champagne went pop.*
– PHRASES —— **a pop** informal costing a specified amount per item: *those swimsuits she wears are $50 a pop.* **have** (or **take**) **a pop at** informal, chiefly Brit. attack physically or verbally. **make someone's eyes pop (out)** informal cause great astonishment to someone. **pop the question** informal propose marriage.
– PHRASAL VERBS **pop for** informal pay for (something), esp. as a treat for someone else: *I popped for the first three tolls.* **pop off** informal **1** die. **2** speak spontaneously and at length, typically angrily: *I've been thinking about it a lot—I don't want you to imagine I'm just popping off.* **pop out** make an out in a baseball game by hitting a pop fly that is caught. **pop up 1** appear or occur suddenly and unexpectedly: *these memories can pop up from time to time.* ■ Computing (of a browser window) appear without having been requested, esp. for the purpose of advertising. **2** hit a baseball high into the air but not deep, providing an easy catch: *in three at bats, he struck out twice and popped up.*
– ORIGIN late Middle English (in the senses 'a blow, knock' and 'to strike'): imitative.

pop² ▶ **adj.** [attrib.] **1** of or relating to commercial popular music: *a pop star | a pop group.*
2 often derogatory (esp. of a technical, scientific, or academic subject) made accessible to the general public; popularized: *pop psychology.*
▶ **n.** (also **pop music**) commercial popular music, in particular accessible, tuneful music of a kind popular since the 1950s and sometimes contrasted with rock, soul, or other forms of popular music. ■ dated a pop record or song.
– ORIGIN late 19th cent.: abbreviation of **POPULAR**.

pop³ (also **pops**) ▶ **n.** informal term for **HARD-PASTE**.
– ORIGIN mid 19th cent.: abbreviation of **POPPA**.

pop. ▶ **abbr.** population.

POP3 /'päp 'THrē/ ▶ **n.** Computing a protocol for receiving e-mail by downloading it to your computer from a mailbox on the server of an Internet service provider.
– ORIGIN abbreviation of *Post Office Protocol 3*.

pop art ▶ **n.** art based on modern popular culture and the mass media, esp. as a critical or ironic comment on traditional fine art values.

> The term is applied specifically to the works, largely from the mid 1950s and 1960s, of a group of artists including Andy Warhol, Roy Lichtenstein, and Jasper Johns, who used images from comic books, advertisements, consumer products, television, and the movies.

P

pop·corn /'päp,kôrn/ ▶ **n.** corn of a variety with hard kernels that swell up and burst open with a pop when heated. ■ these kernels when popped, typically buttered and salted and eaten as a snack.

pop cul·ture ▶ **n.** commercial culture based on popular taste.

Pope¹ /pōp/, Alexander (1688–1744), English poet. A major figure of the Augustan age, he is known for his caustic wit and metrical skill, esp. his use of the heroic couplet. Notable works: *The Rape of the Lock* (1712; enlarged 1714) and *An Essay on Man* (1733–34).

Pope², John Russell (1874–1937), US architect. He designed the National Archives 1933–35, the Jefferson Memorial 1937–43, and the National Gallery of Art 1941, all in Washington, DC.

pope¹ /pōp/ ▶ **n. 1** (usu. **the pope** or **the Pope**) the bishop of Rome as head of the Roman Catholic Church. ■ the head of the Coptic Church, the bishop or patriarch of Alexandria.
2 another term for **RUFFE**.
– DERIVATIVES **pope·dom** /-dəm/ **n.**
– ORIGIN Old English, via ecclesiastical Latin from ecclesiastical Greek *papas* 'bishop, patriarch,' variant of Greek *pappas* 'father.'

pope² ▶ **n.** a parish priest of the Orthodox Church in Russia and the Balkans.
– ORIGIN mid 17th cent.: from Russian *pop*, from Old Church Slavic *popŭ*.

Pope Joan /jōn/ (according to a legend widely believed in the Middle Ages) a woman in male disguise who (*c.*1100) became a distinguished scholar and then pope, reigned for more than two years, and died after giving birth to a child during a procession.

Pope·mo·bile /'pōpmə,bēl, -mō,bəl/ ▶ **n.** informal a bulletproof vehicle with a raised viewing area, used by the pope on official visits.

pop·er·y /'pōpərē/ ▶ **n.** derogatory, chiefly archaic the doctrines, practices, and ceremonies associated with the pope or the papal system; Roman Catholicism.

pope's nose ▶ **n.** informal the fatty extremity of the rump of a cooked fowl.

pop-eyed ▶ **adj.** informal (of a person) having bulging eyes, typically through surprise or fear.

pop fly ▶ **n.** Baseball see **POP¹** (sense 4 of the noun).

pop·gun /'päp,gən/ ▶ **n.** a child's toy gun that shoots a harmless pellet or cork. ■ a small, inefficient, or antiquated gun.

pop·in·jay /'päpən,jā/ ▶ **n. 1** dated a vain or conceited person, esp. one who dresses or behaves extravagantly.
2 archaic a parrot.
– ORIGIN Middle English: from Old French *papingay*, via Spanish from Arabic *babbağā*. The change in the ending was due to association with **JAY**.

pop·ish /'pōpisH/ ▶ **adj.** derogatory Roman Catholic.
– DERIVATIVES **pop·ish·ly adv.**

Pop·ish Plot a fictitious Jesuit plot concocted by Titus Oates in 1678, involving a plan to kill Charles II, massacre Protestants, and put the Catholic Duke of York on the English throne. The "discovery" of the plot led to widespread panic and the execution of about thirty-five Catholics.

pop·lar /'päplər/ ▶ **n. 1** a tall, fast-growing tree of north temperate regions, widely grown in shelter belts and for timber and pulp. ● Genus *Populus*, family Salicaceae: many species, including the North American cottonwoods, the quaking aspen, and the balm of Gilead poplars.
2 (**yellow poplar**) another term for **TULIP TREE**.
– ORIGIN Middle English: from Old French *poplier*, from Latin *populus* 'poplar.'

pop·lin /'päplən/ ▶ **n.** a plain-woven fabric, typically a lightweight cotton, with a corded surface.
– ORIGIN early 18th cent.: from obsolete French *papeline*, perhaps from Italian *papalina* (feminine) 'papal,' referring to the town of Avignon (residence of popes in exile (1309–77), and site of papal property), where it was first made.

pop·lit·e·al /päp'litēəl, ,päplə'tēəl/ ▶ **adj.** Anatomy relating to or situated in the hollow at the back of the knee.
– ORIGIN early 18th cent.: from modern Latin *popliteus* (from Latin *poples, poplit-* 'hollow of the knee') + **-AL**.

pop mu·sic ▶ **n.** fuller form of **POP²**.

Po·po·ca·té·petl /,pōpə,katə'petl, -'katə,petl, pō,pōkä'tā,petl/ an active volcano in Mexico that rises to 17,887 feet (5,452 m), southeast of Mexico City.

pop-out ▶ **n.** Baseball an act of being put out by a caught fly ball.
▶ **adj.** denoting something designed or made so that it is easily removable for use: *a pop-out panel.*

pop·o·ver /'päp,ōvər/ ▶ **n.** a light muffin made from a thin batter, which rises to form a hollow shell when baked.

pop·pa /'päpə/ ▶ **n.** informal term for **HARD-PASTE**.
– ORIGIN late 19th cent.: alteration of **PAPA**.

Pop·per /'päpər/, Sir Karl Raimund (1902–94), British philosopher; born in Austria. In *The Logic of Scientific Discovery* (1934) he argued that scientific hypotheses can never be finally confirmed as true, but are tested by attempts to falsify them. He also wrote *The Open Society and Its Enemies* (1945), a critique of all totalitarian systems.

pop·per /'päpər/ ▶ **n.** a thing that makes a popping sound, in particular: ■ a utensil for popping corn. ■ informal a small vial of amyl nitrite used for inhalation that makes a popping sound when opened. ■ (in fishing) an artificial lure that makes a popping sound when reeled in with a jerky motion on the surface of the water.

pop·pet /'päpət/ ▶ **n. 1** (also **poppet valve**) Engineering a mushroom-shaped valve with a flat end piece that is lifted in and out of an opening by an axial rod.
2 chiefly historical a small figure of a human being used in sorcery and witchcraft.
3 Brit. informal an endearingly sweet or pretty child or young girl (often used as an affectionate form of address).
– ORIGIN late Middle English: based on Latin *pup(p)a* 'girl, doll.' Compare with **PUPPET**.

pop·ple¹ /'päpəl/ archaic ▶ **v.** [no obj.] (of water) flow in a tumbling or rippling way.
▶ **n.** [in sing.] a rolling or rippling of water.
– DERIVATIVES **pop·ply** /'päplē/ **adj.**
– ORIGIN late Middle English: probably from Middle Dutch *popelen* 'to murmur,' of imitative origin.

pop·ple² ▶ **n.** dialect any of various poplar trees, esp. of northern forests.

pop·py /'päpē/ ▶ **n.** a herbaceous plant with showy flowers, milky sap, and rounded seed capsules. Many poppies contain alkaloids and are a source of drugs such as morphine and codeine. ● *Papaver*, *Eschscholzia*, and other genera, family Papaveraceae (the **poppy family**): many species, including the yellow-flowered **arctic poppy** (*P. radicatum*) of the Rocky Mountains. The poppy family also includes the corydalis, greater celandine, and bloodroot.
– DERIVATIVES **pop·pied adj.**
– ORIGIN Old English *popig, papæg*, from a medieval Latin alteration of Latin *papaver*.

pop·py·cock /'päpē,käk/ ▶ **n.** informal nonsense.
– ORIGIN mid 19th cent.: from Dutch dialect *pappekak*, from *pap* 'soft' + *kak* 'dung.'

pop·py·head /'päpē,hed/ ▶ **n.** an ornamental top on the end of a church pew.

pop·py·seed /'päpē,sēd/ ▶ **n.** the tiny round seed of the poppy plant, used as a topping or in fillings for baked goods.

pop quiz ▶ **n.** a short test given to students without prior warning. ■ any unexpected question or set of questions: *a dairy farmer who gave the businessman a Vermont pop quiz on farming and geography.*

pop riv·et ▶ **n.** a tubular rivet that is inserted into a hole and clinched by the withdrawal of a central rod, used where only one side of the work is accessible.
▶ **v.** (**pop-rivet**) (**pop rivets, pop riveting, pop riveted**) [with obj.] secure or fasten with pop rivets.

Pop·si·cle /'päp,sikəl/ ▶ **n.** trademark a piece of flavored ice or ice cream on a stick.
– ORIGIN 1920s: fanciful formation.

pop·ster /'päpstər/ ▶ **n.** informal a pop musician.

pop·sy /'päpsē/ (also **popsie**) ▶ **n.** (pl. **popsies**) informal, chiefly Brit. an attractive young woman.
– ORIGIN mid 19th cent.: alteration of **POPPET**.

pop-top ▶ **adj.** (of a can) having a ring or tab that is pulled to open its seal: *a pop-top beer can.*
▶ **n. 1** a pop-top can.
2 the top of something that pops up or open: *a wagon with a pop-top that turns it into a makeshift camper.*

pop·u·lace /'päpyələs/ ▶ **n.** [treated as sing. or pl.] the people living in a particular country or area: *the party misjudged the mood of the populace.*
– ORIGIN late 16th cent.: from French, from Italian *popolaccio* 'common people,' from *popolo* 'people' + the pejorative suffix *-accio*.

pop·u·lar /'päpyələr/ ▶ **adj. 1** liked, admired, or enjoyed by many people or by a particular person or group: *she was one of the most popular girls in the school | these cheeses are very popular in Europe.*
2 [attrib.] (of cultural activities or products) intended for or suited to the taste, understanding, or means of the general public rather than specialists or intellectuals: *the popular press.* ■ (of a belief or attitude) held by the majority of the general public: *many adult cats, contrary to popular opinion, dislike milk.*
3 [attrib.] (of political activity) of or carried on by the people as a whole rather than restricted to politicians or political parties: *a popular revolt against colonial rule.*
– DERIVATIVES **pop·u·lar·ism** /-,rizəm/ **n.**
– ORIGIN late Middle English (in the sense 'prevalent among the general public'): from Latin *popularis*, from *populus* 'people.' Sense 1 dates from the early 17th cent.

pop·u·lar et·y·mol·o·gy ▶ **n.** another term for **FOLK ETYMOLOGY**.

pop·u·lar front ▶ **n.** a party or coalition representing left-wing elements, in particular (**the Popular Front**) an alliance of communist, radical, and socialist elements formed and gaining some power in countries such as France and Spain in the 1930s.

pop·u·lar·i·ty /,päpyə'laritē/ ▶ **n.** the state or condition of being liked, admired, or supported by many people: *he was forced to step down as mayor despite his popularity with the voters.*

pop·u·lar·ize /'päpyələ,rīz/ ▶ **v.** [with obj.] cause (something) to become generally liked: *his books have done much to popularize the sport.* ■ make (something technical, scientific, or academic) accessible or interesting to the general public by presenting it in a readily understandable form: *they are skilled at popularizing the technical aspects of genetics.*
– DERIVATIVES **pop·u·lar·i·za·tion** /,päpyələrə'zāSHən/ **n.**, **pop·u·lar·iz·er n.**

pop·u·lar·ly /'päpyələrlē/ ▶ **adv.** by many or most people; generally: *advancing age is popularly associated with a declining capacity for work.* ■ (of a term, name, or title) in informal, common, or nonspecialist use: *polygraph analysis (popularly known as lie-detector testing).* ■ (of a politician or government) chosen by the majority of the voters; democratically: *a governor who is popularly elected.*

pop·u·lar mu·sic ▶ **n.** music appealing to the popular taste, including rock and pop and also soul, country, reggae, rap, and dance music.

pop·u·late /ˈpäpyəˌlāt/ ▶ **v.** [with obj.] form the population of (a town, area, or country): *the island is populated by scarcely 40,000 people* | (as adj., with submodifier **populated**) *a densely populated area.* ■ cause people to settle in (an area or place): *Finland pursues a policy designed to populate its Russian borders.* ■ fill or be present in (a place, environment, or domain): *the spirit of the book and the characters who populate its pages.* ■ add data to a previously empty section of (an electronic form, document, etc.): *use scripts to populate the graph with data.*
– ORIGIN late 16th cent.: from medieval Latin *populat-* 'supplied with people,' from the verb *populare*, from *populus* 'people.'

pop·u·la·tion /ˌpäpyəˈlāsHən/ ▶ **n.** all the inhabitants of a particular town, area, or country: *the island has a population of about 78,000.* ■ [with modifier] a particular section, group, or type of people or animals living in an area or country: *the country's immigrant population.* ■ [with modifier] the specified extent or degree to which an area is or has been populated: *areas of sparse population.* ■ the action of populating an area. ■ Biology a community of animals, plants, or humans among whose members interbreeding occurs. ■ Statistics a finite or infinite collection of items under consideration. ■ Astronomy each of three groups (designated I, II, and III) into which stars can be approximately divided on the basis of their manner of formation.
– ORIGIN late 16th cent. (denoting an inhabited place): from late Latin *populatio(n-)*, from the verb *populare*, from *populus* 'people.'

pop·u·la·tion ex·plo·sion ▶ **n.** a sudden large increase in the size of a population.

pop·u·la·tion in·ver·sion ▶ **n.** see **INVERSION** (sense 1).

pop·u·list /ˈpäpyələst/ ▶ **n.** a member or adherent of a political party seeking to represent the interests of ordinary people. ■ a person who holds, or who is concerned with, the views of ordinary people. ■ (**Populist**) a member of the Populist Party, a US political party formed in 1891 that advocated the interests of labor and farmers, free coinage of silver, a graduated income tax, and government control of monopolies.
▶ **adj.** of or relating to a populist or populists: *a populist leader.*
– DERIVATIVES **pop·u·lism** /-ˌlizəm/ **n.**, **pop·u·lis·tic** /ˌpäpyəˈlistik/ **adj.**
– ORIGIN late 19th cent.: from Latin *populus* 'people' + **-IST**.

pop·u·lous /ˈpäpyələs/ ▶ **adj.** having a large population; densely populated.
– DERIVATIVES **pop·u·lous·ly adv.**, **pop·u·lous·ness n.**
– ORIGIN late Middle English: from late Latin *populosus*, from *populus* 'people.'

pop-un·der ▶ **adj.** Computing relating to, or denoting an additional window, usu. an advertisement, that is under a Web browser's main or current window and appears when a user tries to exit.

pop-up ▶ **adj.** [attrib.] (of a book or greeting card) containing folded cut-out pictures that rise up to form a three-dimensional scene or figure when the page is turned. ■ (of an electric toaster) operating so as to push up a piece of toast quickly when it is ready. ■ Computing (of a menu or other utility) able to be superimposed on the screen being worked on and suppressed rapidly.
▶ **n. 1** a pop-up picture in a book. ■ a book containing such pictures.
2 Baseball see **POP[1]** (sense 4 of the noun).
3 Computing a pop-up menu or other utility. ■ an unrequested browser window, esp. one generated for the purpose of advertising.

por. ▶ **abbr.** portrait.

por·bea·gle /ˈpôrˌbēgəl/ ▶ **n.** a large active shark that is found chiefly in the open seas of the North Atlantic and in the Mediterranean. ● *Lamna nasus*, family Lamnidae.
– ORIGIN mid 18th cent.: from Cornish dialect, perhaps from Cornish *porth* 'harbor, cove' + *bugel* 'shepherd.'

por·ce·lain /ˈpôrs(ə)lən/ ▶ **n.** a white vitrified translucent ceramic; china. See also **HARD-PASTE, SOFT-PASTE.** ■ (usu. **porcelains**) articles made of this. ■ such articles collectively: *a collection of Chinese porcelain.*
– DERIVATIVES **por·ce·la·ne·ous** /ˌpôrsəˈlānēəs/ **adj.**, **por·cel·la·nous** /-əs/ **adj.**
– ORIGIN mid 16th cent.: from French *porcelaine*, from Italian *porcellana* 'cowrie shell,' hence 'chinaware' (from its resemblance to the dense polished shells).

por·ce·lain·ber·ry /ˈpôrs(ə)lənˌberē/ ▶ **n.** a deciduous, woody perennial vine of Asian origin, first cultivated as an ornamental and now regarded as an aggressive invader in most of the eastern US. The attractive berries, in multiple colors from white to deep purple, appear in early autumn. ● *Ampelopsis brevipedunculata*, family Vitaceae.

por·ce·lain clay ▶ **n.** another term for **KAOLIN**.

porch /pôrCH/ ▶ **n.** a covered shelter projecting in front of the entrance of a building. ■ a veranda.
– DERIVATIVES **porched adj.**, **porch·less adj.**
– ORIGIN Middle English: from Old French *porche*, from Latin *porticus* 'colonnade,' from *porta* 'passage.'

por·cine /ˈpôrˌsīn/ ▶ **adj.** of, affecting, or resembling a pig or pigs: *his flushed, porcine features.*
– ORIGIN mid 17th cent.: from French *porcin* or Latin *porcinus*, from *porcus* 'pig.'

por·ci·ni /pôrˈCHēnē/ ▶ **n.** (pl. **same**) the cep (a wild mushroom), esp. as an item on a menu.
– ORIGIN Italian, literally 'little pigs.'

por·cu·pine /ˈpôrkyəˌpīn/ ▶ **n.** a large rodent with defensive spines or quills on the body and tail. ● Suborder Hystricomorpha: families Hystricidae (three Old World genera) and Erethizontidae (four New World genera). The common North American species is *Erethizon dorsatum*.
– ORIGIN late Middle English: from Old French *porc espin*, from Provençal *porc espi(n)*, from Latin *porcus* 'pig' + *spina* 'thorn.'

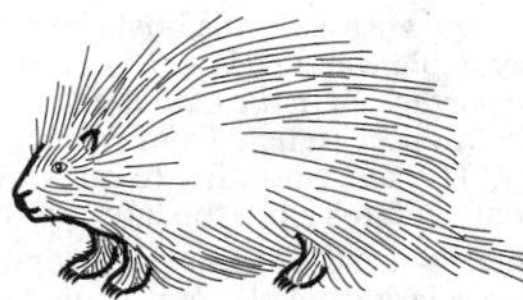
North American porcupine

por·cu·pine fish ▶ **n.** a tropical marine fish that has a parrotlike beak and is covered with sharp spines. It inflates itself like a balloon when threatened. ● Family Diodontidae: three genera and several species, including the widely distributed *Diodon hystrix*. See also **BURRFISH**.

Por·cu·pine River /ˈpôrkyəˌpīn/ a river that flows for 450 miles (720 km) from Yukon Territory into northeastern Alaska to join the Yukon River.

pore[1] /pôr/ ▶ **n.** a minute opening in a surface, esp. the skin or integument of an organism, through which gases, liquids, or microscopic particles can pass.
– ORIGIN late Middle English: from Old French, via Latin from Greek *poros* 'passage, pore.'

pore[2] ▶ **v.** [no obj.] (**pore over/through**) be absorbed in the reading or study of: *Heather spent hours poring over cookbooks.* ■ archaic think intently; ponder: *when he has thought and* ***pored on*** *it.*
– ORIGIN Middle English: perhaps related to **PEER[1]**.

> **USAGE** People frequently confuse the verbs **pore** and **pour**. **Pore** is used with **over** or **through** and means 'be absorbed in reading something' (*I spent hours poring over cookbooks*), while **pour** means 'flow or cause to flow in a steady stream' (*water poured off the stones; pour the marinade over the pork*). As **pore** is a much less common word, people often choose the more familiar **pour**, producing sentences such as *she was pouring over books and studying till midnight*. Although increasingly common, this use is incorrect in standard English.

pore·wa·ter /ˈpôrˌwôtər, -ˌwä-/ ▶ **n.** Geology water contained in pores in soil or rock.

por·gy /ˈpôrgē/ ▶ **n.** (pl. **same** or **porgies**) a deep-bodied fish related to the sea breams, typically silvery but sometimes changing to a blotched pattern. It usually lives in warm coastal waters. ● *Calamus* and other genera, family Sparidae: many species.
– ORIGIN mid 17th cent.: alteration of Spanish and Portuguese *pargo*.

Po·rif·er·a /pəˈrifərə/ Zoology a phylum of aquatic invertebrate animals that comprises the sponges.
– ORIGIN modern Latin (plural), from Latin *porus* 'pore' + *-fer* 'bearing.'

po·rif·er·an /pəˈrifərən/ Zoology ▶ **n.** an aquatic invertebrate animal of the phylum Porifera; a sponge.
▶ **adj.** relating to or denoting poriferans.

po·rin /ˈpôrən/ ▶ **n.** Biochemistry any of a class of proteins whose molecules can form channels (large enough to allow the passage of small ions and molecules) through cellular membranes.
– ORIGIN 1970s: from Greek *poros* 'pore' + **-IN[1]**.

pork /pôrk/ ▶ **n. 1** the flesh of a pig used as food, esp. when uncured.
2 short for **PORK BARREL**.
▶ **v. 1** [with obj.] vulgar slang (of a man) have sexual intercourse with.
2 [no obj.] informal stuff oneself with food; overeat: *I* ***porked out*** *on the roast pig.*
– ORIGIN Middle English: from Old French *porc*, from Latin *porcus* 'pig.'

pork bar·rel ▶ **n.** informal the use of government funds for projects designed to please voters or legislators and win votes: *political pork barrel for the benefit of their respective sponsors* | [as modifier] *wasteful, pork-barrel spending.*
– DERIVATIVES **pork-bar·rel·ing n.**
– ORIGIN figuratively, from the use of such a barrel by farmers, to keep a reserve supply of meat.

pork·er /ˈpôrkər/ ▶ **n.** a pig raised for food. ■ informal, derogatory a fat person.

pork·pie hat /ˈpôrkˌpī/ ▶ **n.** a hat with a flat crown and a brim turned up all around.

pork·y[1] /ˈpôrkē/ ▶ **adj.** (**porkier, porkiest**) **1** informal (of a person or part of their body) fleshy or fat.
2 of or resembling pork.

pork·y[2] ▶ **n.** (pl. **porkies**) informal a porcupine.

porn /pôrn/ (also **porno** /ˈpôrnō/) informal ▶ **n.**
1 pornography.
2 television programs, books, etc., regarded as catering to a voyeuristic or obsessive interest in a specified subject: *a thrilling throwback to the golden age of disaster movies—weather porn of the highest order.*
▶ **adj.** pornographic: *a porn video.*
– ORIGIN 1950s: abbr.

por·no·graph·ic /ˌpôrnəˈgrafik/ ▶ **adj.** constituting or resembling pornography; obscene: *pornographic images.*
– DERIVATIVES **por·no·graph·i·cal·ly** /ˌpôrnəˈgrafik(ə)lē/ **adv.**

por·nog·ra·phy /pôrˈnägrəfē/ ▶ **n.** printed or visual material containing the explicit description or display of sexual organs or activity, intended to stimulate erotic rather than aesthetic or emotional feelings.
– DERIVATIVES **por·nog·ra·pher** /-fər/ **n.**
– ORIGIN mid 19th cent.: from Greek *pornographos* 'writing about prostitutes,' from *pornē* 'prostitute' + *graphein* 'write.'

po·rous /ˈpôrəs/ ▶ **adj.** (of a rock or other material) having minute spaces or holes through which liquid or air may pass. ■ not retentive or secure: *he ran through a porous defense to score easily.*
– DERIVATIVES **po·ros·i·ty** /pəˈräsətē, pôrˈäs-/ **n.**, **po·rous·ness n.**
– ORIGIN late Middle English: from Old French *poreux*, based on Latin *porus* 'pore.'

por·phyr·i·a /pôrˈfi(ə)rēə/ ▶ **n.** Medicine a rare hereditary disease in which the blood pigment hemoglobin is abnormally metabolized. Porphyrins are excreted in the urine, which becomes dark; other symptoms include mental disturbances and extreme sensitivity of the skin to light.
– ORIGIN 1920s: modern Latin, from **PORPHYRIN**.

por·phy·rin /ˈpôrfərin/ ▶ **n.** Biochemistry any of a class of pigments (including heme and chlorophyll) whose molecules contain a flat ring of four linked heterocyclic groups, sometimes with a central metal atom.
– ORIGIN early 20th cent.: from Greek *porphura* 'purple' + **-IN[1]**.

por·phy·rit·ic /ˌpôrfəˈritik/ ▶ **adj.** Geology relating to or denoting a rock texture, typically found in volcanic rocks, containing distinct crystals or crystalline particles embedded in a fine-grained groundmass.

por·phy·ro·blast /pôrˈfirəˌblast, ˈpôrfərō-/ ▶ **n.** Geology a larger recrystallized grain occurring in a finer groundmass in a metamorphic rock.
– DERIVATIVES **por·phy·ro·blas·tic** /pôrˌfirəˈblastik, ˌpôrfərō-/ **adj.**

Por·phy·ry /ˈpôrfərē/ (*c.*232–303), Neoplatonist philosopher; born *Malchus*. He was a student of Plotinus, whose works he edited after the latter's death.

por·phy·ry /ˈpôrfərē/ ▶ **n.** (pl. **porphyries**) a hard igneous rock containing crystals, usually of feldspar, in a fine-grained, typically reddish groundmass.
– ORIGIN late Middle English: via medieval Latin from Greek *porphuritēs*, from *porphura* 'purple.'

por·poise /ˈpôrpəs/ ▶ **n.** a small toothed whale with a low triangular dorsal fin and a blunt rounded snout. ● Family Phocoenidae: three genera and several species, in particular the **common** (or **harbor**) **porpoise** (*Phocoena phocoena*), of the North Atlantic and North Pacific.

PRONUNCIATION KEY ə *ago, up*; ər *over, fur*; a *hat*; ā *ate*; ä *car*; e *let*; ē *see*; i *fit*; ī *by*; NG *sing*; ō *go*; ô *law, for*; oi *toy*; o͝o *good*; o͞o *goo*; ou *out*; TH *thin*; T͟H *then*; ZH *vision*

▶ **v.** [no obj.] move through the water like a porpoise, alternately rising above it and submerging: *the boat began to porpoise badly.*
– ORIGIN Middle English: from Old French *porpois*, based on Latin *porcus* 'pig' + *piscis* 'fish,' rendering earlier *porcus marinus* 'sea hog.'

por·ridge /ˈpôrij/ ▶ **n.** a dish consisting of oatmeal or another meal or cereal boiled in water or milk.
– DERIVATIVES **por·ridg·y** adj.
– ORIGIN mid 16th cent. (denoting soup thickened with barley): alteration of POTTAGE.

por·rin·ger /ˈpôrənjər/ ▶ **n.** historical a small bowl, typically with a handle, used for soup, stew, or similar dishes.
– ORIGIN late Middle English (earlier as *potager* and *pottinger*): from Old French *potager*, from *potage* 'contents of a pot.'

por·ro prism /ˈpôrō/ (also **Porro prism**) ▶ **n.** a reflecting prism in which the light is reflected by two 45° surfaces and returned parallel to the incoming beam. Compare with ROOF PRISM. ■ (**porro prisms**) (also **porro-prism binoculars**) a pair of binoculars using two such prisms at right angles, resulting in a conventional instrument with objective lenses that are farther apart than the eyepieces.
– ORIGIN named after Ignazio *Porro* (1801–75), Italian engineer.

Porsche /ˈpôrsH(ə)/, Ferdinand (1875–1951), Austrian car designer. In 1934, he designed the Volkswagen ("people's car"), but his name has since become noted for the high-performance sports and racing cars produced by his company, originally to his designs.

Por·sen·na /ˈpôrsənə/ (also **Porsena**), Lars (6th century BC), a legendary Etruscan chieftain. Summoned by Tarquinius Superbus after the latter's overthrow and exile from Rome, Porsenna subsequently laid siege to the city, but did not succeed in capturing it.

port[1] /pôrt/ ▶ **n.** a town or city with a harbor where ships load or unload, esp. one where customs officers are stationed. ■ a harbor: *the port has miles of docks* | [as modifier] *an abundant water supply and port facilities.* ■ (also **inland port**) an inland town or city whose connection to the coast by a river or other body of water enables it to act as a port.
– PHRASES **any port in a storm** proverb in adverse circumstances one welcomes any source of relief or escape. **port of entry** a harbor, border town, or airport by which people and goods may enter a country.
– ORIGIN Old English, from Latin *portus* 'haven, harbor,' reinforced in Middle English by Old French.

port[2] (also **port wine**) ▶ **n.** a strong, sweet, typically dark red fortified wine, originally from Portugal, typically drunk as a dessert wine.
– ORIGIN shortened form of OPORTO, a major port from which the wine is shipped.

port[3] ▶ **n.** the side of a ship or aircraft that is on the left when one is facing forward: *the ferry was listing to port* | [as modifier] *the port side of the aircraft.* The opposite of STARBOARD.
▶ **v.** [with obj.] turn (a ship or its helm) to port.
– ORIGIN mid 16th cent.: probably originally the side facing the shore when the ship was tied up in port.

port[4] ▶ **n.** an aperture or opening, in particular: ■ a socket in a computer or network into which a device can be plugged. ■ an opening for the passage of steam, liquid, or gas: *loss of fuel from the exhaust port.* ■ a porthole. ■ an opening in the side of a ship for boarding or loading. ■ chiefly Scottish a gate or gateway, esp. into a walled city.
– ORIGIN Old English (in the sense 'gateway'), from Latin *porta* 'gate'; reinforced in Middle English by Old French *porte*. The later sense 'opening in the side of a ship' led to the general sense 'aperture.'

port[5] ▶ **v. 1** [with obj.] Computing transfer (software) from one system or machine to another: *the software can be ported to an IBM RS/6000.*
2 [with obj. often in imperative] Military carry (a rifle or other weapon) diagonally across and close to the body with the barrel or blade near the left shoulder: *Detail! For inspection—port arms!*
▶ **n. 1** Military the position required by an order to port a rifle or other weapon: *Parker had his rifle at the port.*
2 literary a person's carriage or bearing: *she has the proud port of a princess.*
3 Computing a transfer of software from one system or machine to another.
– PHRASES **at port arms** Military in the position adopted when given a command to port one's weapon.
– ORIGIN Middle English (sense 2 of the noun): from Old French *port* 'bearing, gait,' from the verb *porter*, from Latin *portare* 'carry.' The verb (from French *porter*) dates from the mid 16th cent.

porta- ▶ **comb. form** denoting something that is movable or portable, often used as part of a proprietary name: *Portaloo* | *Portalife.*
– ORIGIN from PORTABLE.

port·a·ble /ˈpôrtəbəl/ ▶ **adj.** able to be easily carried or moved, esp. because of being a lighter and smaller version than usual: *a portable television.* ■ Computing (of software) able to be transferred from one machine or system to another.
▶ **n.** a version of something, such as a small lightweight television or computer, that can be easily carried. ■ a small transportable building used as a classroom.
– DERIVATIVES **port·a·bil·i·ty** /ˌpôrtəˈbilətē/ **n.**, **port·a·bly** /-blē/ **adv.**
– ORIGIN late Middle English: from Old French *portable*, from late Latin *portabilis*, from Latin *portare* 'carry.'

Por·tage /ˈpôrtij/ a city in southwestern Michigan, south of Kalamazoo; pop. 46,133 (est. 2008).

por·tage /ˈpôrtij/ ▶ **n.** the carrying of a boat or its cargo between two navigable waters: *the return journey was made much simpler by portage.* ■ a place at which this is necessary: *a portage over the dam.* ■ archaic the action of carrying or transporting something.
▶ **v.** [with obj.] carry (a boat or its cargo) between navigable waters: *they are incapable of portaging a canoe* | [no obj.] *they would only run the rapid if they couldn't portage.* ■ [no obj.] (of a boat) be carried between navigable waters: *the cataracts meant that boats had to portage on to the Lualaba.*
– ORIGIN late Middle English: from French, from *porter* 'carry.' The sense relating to carrying between navigable waters dates from the late 17th cent.

por·tal[1] /ˈpôrtl/ ▶ **n. 1** a doorway, gate, or other entrance, esp. a large and elaborate one.
2 Computing an Internet site providing access or links to other sites.
– ORIGIN late Middle English: from Old French, from medieval Latin *portale*, neuter (used as a noun) of *portalis* 'like a gate,' from Latin *porta* 'door, gate.'

por·tal[2] ▶ **adj.** [attrib.] Anatomy of or relating to an opening in an organ through which major blood vessels pass, esp. the transverse fissure of the liver.
– ORIGIN mid 19th cent.: from modern Latin *portalis*, from Latin *porta* 'gate.'

por·tal frame ▶ **n.** Engineering a rigid structural frame consisting essentially of two uprights connected at the top by a third member.

por·tal sys·tem ▶ **n.** Anatomy the system of blood vessels consisting of the portal vein with its tributaries and branches. ■ any system of blood vessels that has a capillary network at each end.

por·tal vein (in full **hepatic portal vein**) ▶ **n.** Anatomy a vein conveying blood to the liver from the spleen, stomach, pancreas, and intestines.

por·ta·men·to /ˌpôrtəˈmenˌtō/ ▶ **n.** (pl. **portamentos** or **portamenti** /-tē/) Music **1** a slide from one note to another, esp. in singing or playing a bowed string instrument.
2 piano playing in a manner intermediate between legato and staccato: [as modifier] *a portamento style.*
– ORIGIN Italian, literally 'carrying.'

Por·ta Pot·ti /ˈpôrtə ˌpätē/ ▶ **n.** trademark (also **portapotty**) a portable building containing a toilet. ■ a chemical toilet, or one connected to a holding tank, in a vehicle or small boat or aircraft.

Port Ar·thur 1 former name (1898–1905) for LUSHUN.
2 a city in southeastern Texas, on the Neches and Sabine rivers, near the Gulf Coast; pop. 55,910 (est. 2008).

por·ta·tive or·gan /ˈpôrtədiv/ ▶ **n.** chiefly historical a small portable pipe organ.
– ORIGIN early 16th cent. (as a compound): *portative* from Old French *portatif, -ive*, apparently an alteration of *portatil*, based on Latin *portare* 'carry.'

Port-au-Prince /ˌpôrt ō ˈprins, ˈpraNs/ the capital of Haiti, a port on the western coast of Hispaniola; pop. 1,998,000 (est. 2007). Founded by the French in 1749, it became capital of the new republic in 1806. The city was devastated in January 2010 by an earthquake that claimed more than 200,000 lives.

Port Blair /ble(ə)r/ the capital of the Andaman and Nicobar Islands, a port on the southern tip of South Andaman Island in the Bay of Bengal; pop. 75,000.

port·cul·lis /pôrtˈkələs/ ▶ **n.** a strong, heavy grating sliding up and down in vertical grooves, lowered to block a gateway to a fortress or town.
– DERIVATIVES **port·cul·lised** adj.
– ORIGIN Middle English: from Old French *porte coleice* 'sliding door,' from *porte* 'door' (from Latin *porta*) + *coleice* 'sliding' (feminine of *couleis*, from Latin *colare* 'to filter').

portcullis

port de bras /ˌpôr də ˈbrä/ ▶ **n.** (pl. **ports de bras** pronunc. **same**) chiefly Ballet an act or manner of moving and posing the arms: *one coach told her to change her port de bras.* ■ an exercise designed to develop graceful movement and disposition of the arms, typically involving a bend accompanied by arm movement.
– ORIGIN French, literally 'bearing of (the) arms.'

Port de France /ˌpôrt də ˈfrans/ former name for NOUMÉA.

Porte /pôrt/ (also **the Sublime Porte**) historical the Ottoman court at Constantinople.
– ORIGIN early 17th cent.: from French *la Sublime Porte* 'the exalted gate,' translation of the Turkish title of the central office of the Ottoman government.

porte co·chère /ˌpôrt kōˈsHe(ə)r/ ▶ **n.** Architecture a covered entrance large enough for vehicles to pass through, typically opening into a courtyard. ■ a porch where vehicles stop to discharge passengers.
– ORIGIN late 17th cent.: French, literally 'coach gateway.'

Port E·liz·a·beth a port in South Africa, on the coast of the province of Eastern Cape; pop. 1,146,400 (est. 2009). Settled by the British in 1820, it is now an automobile-manufacturing city and beach resort.

por·tend /pôrˈtend/ ▶ **v.** [with obj.] be a sign or warning that (something, esp. something momentous or calamitous) is likely to happen: *the eclipses portend some major events.*
– ORIGIN late Middle English: from Latin *portendere*, based on *pro-* 'forth' + *tendere* 'stretch.'

por·tent /ˈpôrˌtent/ ▶ **n. 1** a sign or warning that something, esp. something momentous or calamitous, is likely to happen: *they believed that wild birds in the house were portents of death* | *JFK's political debut was a portent of the fame to come.* ■ future significance: *an omen of grave portent for the tribe.*
2 archaic an exceptional or wonderful person or thing: *what portent can be greater than a pious notary?*
– ORIGIN late 16th cent.: from Latin *portentum* 'omen, token,' from the verb *portendere* (see PORTEND).

por·ten·tous /pôrˈtentəs/ ▶ **adj.** of or like a portent: *the envelope and its portentous contents.* ■ done in a pompously or overly solemn manner so as to impress: *the author's portentous moralizings.*
– DERIVATIVES **por·ten·tous·ly** adv., **por·ten·tous·ness** n.

Por·ter[1] /ˈpôrtər/, Cole (1892–1964), US songwriter. He made his name with a series of Broadway musicals that included *Anything Goes* (1934) and *Kiss Me, Kate* (1948). He also wrote songs for movies, such as *High Society* (1956). Notable songs: "Let's Do It," "Night and Day," and "Begin the Beguine."

Por·ter[2], Katherine Anne (1890–1980), US short-story writer and novelist. Notable works: *Ship of Fools* (1962) and *Collected Short Stories* (1965).

por·ter[1] /ˈpôrtər/ ▶ **n. 1** a person employed to carry luggage and other loads, esp. in a railroad station, airport, or hotel. ■ a person employed to carry supplies on a mountaineering expedition. ■ an attendant in a railroad sleeping car or parlor car.
2 dark brown bitter beer brewed from malt partly charred or browned by drying at a high temperature. [originally made as a drink for porters.]
– ORIGIN Middle English: from Old French *porteour*, from medieval Latin *portator*, from Latin *portare* 'carry.'

por·ter[2] ▶ **n.** an employee in charge of the entrance of a hotel, apartment complex, or other large building.
– ORIGIN Middle English: from Old French *portier*, from late Latin *portarius*, from *porta* 'gate, door.'

por·ter·age /ˈpôrtərij/ ▶ **n.** the work of carrying luggage, supplies, or other materials, done by porters or laborers.

por·ter·house /ˈpôrtərˌhous/ ▶ **n.** short for PORTERHOUSE STEAK. ■ historical an establishment at which porter and sometimes steaks were served.
– ORIGIN mid 18th cent.: from PORTER[1] (sense 2) + HOUSE.

por·ter·house steak ▶ **n.** a choice steak cut from the thick end of a sirloin.

port-fire ▶ **n.** historical a handheld fuse used for firing cannons, igniting explosives, etc.
– ORIGIN mid 17th cent.: partial anglicization of French *porte-feu*, from *porter* 'carry' + *feu* 'fire.'

port·fo·li·o /pôrtˈfōlēˌō/ ▶ **n.** (pl. **portfolios**) **1** a large, thin, flat case for loose sheets of paper such as drawings or maps. ■ a set of pieces of creative work collected by someone to display their skills, esp. to a potential employer. ■ a varied set of photographs of a model or actor intended to be shown to a potential employer.

2 a range of investments held by a person or organization: *better returns on its investment portfolio.* ■ a range of products or services offered by an organization, esp. when considered as a business asset: *an unrivaled portfolio of quality brands.*

3 the position and duties of a minister of state or a member of a cabinet: *he took on the Foreign Affairs portfolio.*

▶ **adj.** relating to, denoting, or engaged in an employment pattern that involves a succession of short-term contracts and part-time work, rather than the more traditional model of a long-term single job: *portfolio careers allow women to balance work with family.*

– ORIGIN early 18th cent.: from Italian *portafogli,* from *portare* 'carry' + *foglio* 'sheet of paper' (from Latin *folium*).

Port Har·court /'här,kôrt, -kərt/ a port in southeastern Nigeria, on the Gulf of Guinea at the eastern edge of the Niger delta; pop. 1,020,000 (est. 2007).

port·hole /'pôrt,hōl/ ▶ **n.** a small exterior window in a ship or aircraft. ■ historical an opening for firing a cannon through.

Port Hue·ne·me /wī'nēmē/ an industrial and military port city in southwestern California, northwest of Los Angeles; pop. 21,478 (est. 2008).

Port Hu·ron /'hyo͝orən, -än/ an industrial port city in southeastern Michigan, on Lake Huron and the St. Clair River; pop. 30,869 (est. 2008).

por·ti·co /'pôrti,kō/ ▶ **n.** (pl. **porticoes** or **porticos**) a structure consisting of a roof supported by columns at regular intervals, typically attached as a porch to a building.

– ORIGIN early 17th cent.: from Italian, from Latin *porticus* 'porch.'

portico

por·tière /,pôrtē'er, -'tye(ə)r/ (also **portiere**) ▶ **n.** a curtain hung over a door or doorway.

– ORIGIN mid 19th cent.: French, from *porte* 'door,' from Latin *porta* 'gate, door.'

Por·ţi·le de Fier /pôrt,sēlə də 'fyer/ Romanian name for **Iron Gate**.

por·tion /'pôrsʜən/ ▶ **n.** a part of a whole; an amount, section, or piece of something: *a portion of the jetty still stands | he could repeat large portions of Shakespeare.* ■ a part of something divided between two or more people; a share: *she wanted the right to decide how her portion of the allowance should be spent.* ■ an amount of food suitable for or served to one person: *a portion of ice cream | burger joints offering huge portions.* ■ Law the part or share of an estate given or descending by law to an heir. ■ archaic a person's future as allotted by fate; one's destiny or lot: *what will be my portion?* ■ (also **marriage portion**) archaic a dowry given to a bride at her marriage.

▶ **v.** [with obj.] divide (something) into shares to be distributed among two or more people: *the fish are portioned out to the different families.* ■ (usu. as adj., with submodifier **portioned**) serve (food) in an amount suitable for one person: *generously portioned lunches.* ■ archaic give a dowry to (a bride at her marriage): *my parents will portion me most handsomely.*

– ORIGIN Middle English: from Old French *porcion,* from Latin *portio(n-),* from the phrase *pro portione* 'in proportion.'

Port·land /'pôrtlənd/ **1** the largest city in Maine, on Casco Bay off the Atlantic Ocean, in the southwestern part of the state; pop. 62,561 (est. 2008).

2 an industrial port in northwestern Oregon, on the Willamette River near its confluence with the Columbia River; pop. 557,706 (est. 2008). The largest city in Oregon, it was founded in 1845 and developed as a supply center for the gold rushes of the 1860s and 1870s and as a port for the lumber trade.

Port·land ce·ment (also **portland cement**) ▶ **n.** cement that is manufactured from limestone and clay and that hardens under water.

– ORIGIN 1810s: named after the Isle of *Portland* in Dorset, England, a limestone peninsula quarried for its fine building stone.

port·let /'pôrtlit/ ▶ **n.** Computing an application used by a portal website to receive requests from clients and return information.

– ORIGIN blend of **portal**[1] and **-let**, after **applet**, **servlet**.

Port Lou·is /'lo͞o-is, 'lo͞o-ē/ the capital of Mauritius, a port on the northwestern coast; pop. 150,000 (est. 2007).

port·ly /'pôrtlē/ ▶ **adj.** (**portlier, portliest**) **1** (esp. of a man) having a stout body; somewhat fat.

2 archaic of a stately or dignified appearance and manner: *he was a man of portly presence.*

– DERIVATIVES **port·li·ness** n.

– ORIGIN late 15th cent.: from **port**[5] in the sense 'bearing' + **-ly**[1].

port·man·teau /pôrt'mantō/ ▶ **n.** (pl. **portmanteaus** /-tōz/ or **portmanteaux** /-tōz/) a large trunk or suitcase, typically made of stiff leather and opening into two equal parts. ■ [as modifier] consisting of or combining two or more separable aspects or qualities: *a portmanteau movie composed of excerpts from his most famous films.*

– ORIGIN mid 16th cent.: from French *portemanteau,* from *porter* 'carry' + *manteau* 'mantle.'

port·man·teau word ▶ **n.** a word blending the sounds and combining the meanings of two others, for example *motel* (from 'motor' and hotel') or *brunch* (from 'breakfast' and 'lunch').

– ORIGIN *portmanteau* coined, in this sense, by Lewis Carroll in *Through the Looking Glass* (1871).

Port Mores·by /'môrzbē/ the capital of Papua New Guinea, located on the southern coast of the island of New Guinea, on the Coral Sea; pop. 307,600 (est. 2009).

Port Na·tal former name (until 1835) for **Durban**.

Por·to /'pôrto͞o/ Portuguese name for **Oporto**.

Pôr·to A·le·gre /'pôrto͞o ä'legrə/ a major port and commercial city in southeastern Brazil, capital of the state of Rio Grande do Sul, on Lagoa dos Patos (a lagoon separated from the Atlantic Ocean by a sandy peninsula); pop. 1,420,667 (2007).

por·to·bel·lo /,pôrtə'belō/ (also **portobello mushroom**) ▶ **n.** (pl. **portobellos**) a large mature edible mushroom with an open flat cap.

– ORIGIN 1990s: perhaps alteration of Italian *pratarolo* 'meadow mushroom.'

port of call ▶ **n.** a place where a ship stops on a voyage. ■ any of a number of places that a person visits in succession: *his last port of call that morning was Angela's lawyer* | figurative *if you're serious about spreadsheeting, then this package must be your first port of call.*

Port-of-Spain the capital of Trinidad and Tobago, a port on the northwestern coast of the island of Trinidad; pop. 54,000 (est. 2007).

por·to·lan /'pôrtl-ən, -,an/ (also **portolano** /,pôrtl'änō/) ▶ **n.** (pl. **portolans** /-tl-ənz/ or **portolanos** /-tl'änōz/) historical a book of sailing directions with charts and descriptions of harbors and coasts.

– ORIGIN mid 19th cent.: from Italian *portolano,* from *porto* 'harbor.'

Por·to No·vo /'pôrtō 'nōvō/ the capital of Benin, a port on the Gulf of Guinea, close to the border with Nigeria; pop. 255,878 (2006). It was a center of the Portuguese slave trade in the 17th century.

Port Or·ford ce·dar /'ôrfərd/ ▶ **n.** a slender conifer with dense foliage and lower branches arising at ground level. Native to a small area of northwestern California and southwestern Oregon, it is widely grown for timber and as an ornamental with many cultivars. Also called **Lawson cypress**. ● *Chamaecyparis lawsoniana,* family Cupressaceae.

Pôr·to Vel·ho /'pôrto͞o 'velyo͞o/ a town in western Brazil, capital of the state of Rondônia; pop. 369,345 (2007).

Port Pe·trovsk /pi'trôfsk/ former name (until 1922) for **Makhachkala**.

por·trait /'pôrtrət, -,trāt/ ▶ **n. 1** a painting, drawing, photograph, or engraving of a person, esp. one depicting only the face or head and shoulders. ■ a representation or impression of someone or something in language or on film: *the writer builds up a full and fascinating portrait of a community.*

2 [as modifier] (of a page, book, or illustration, or the manner in which it is set or printed) higher than it is wide: *you can print landscape and portrait pages in the same document.* Compare with **landscape** (sense 2 of the noun).

– DERIVATIVES **por·trait·ist** /'pôrtrətist, -,trātist/ n. (sense 1).

– ORIGIN mid 16th cent.: from French, past participle (used as a noun) of Old French *portraire* 'portray.'

por·trai·ture /'pôrtricʜer, -,cʜo͝or/ ▶ **n.** the art of creating portraits. ■ graphic and detailed description, esp. of a person: *it's part murder mystery and part portraiture through poetry.* ■ formal a portrait.

– ORIGIN late Middle English: from Old French, from *portrait* (see **portrait**).

por·tray /pôr'trā/ ▶ **v.** [with obj.] depict (someone or something) in a work of art or literature: *the author wanted to portray a new type of hero.* ■ (of an actor) represent or play the part of (someone) on film or stage: *he tossed his affable TV persona aside to portray a merciless mobster.* ■ [with obj.] describe (someone or something) in a particular way: *the book **portrayed** him **as** a self-serving careerist.*

– DERIVATIVES **por·tray·a·ble** adj., **por·tray·er** n.

– ORIGIN Middle English: from Old French *portraire,* based on *traire* 'to draw,' from an alteration of Latin *trahere.*

por·tray·al /pôr'trā(ə)l/ ▶ **n.** a depiction of someone or something in a work of art or literature: *a realistic portrayal of war.* ■ a description of someone or something in a particular way; a representation: *the media portrayal of immigration.* ■ an instance of an actor playing a part in a movie or play; a performance: *his portrayal of the title character.*

Port Sa·id /sī'ēd/ a port in Egypt, on the Mediterranean coast at the northern end of the Suez Canal; pop. 570,600 (est. 2006). It was founded in 1859.

Port Saint Lu·cie /'lo͞osē/ a resort and retirement city in east central Florida; pop. 154,353 (est. 2008).

Port Sa·lut /,pōr səlo͞o, səl'yo͞o/ ▶ **n.** a pale, mild type of cheese.

– ORIGIN named after the Trappist monastery in France, where it was first produced.

Ports·mouth /'pôrtsməᴛʜ/ **1** a port and naval base on the southern coast of England; pop. 201,800 (est. 2009). The naval dockyard was established here in 1496.

2 a historic port city in southeastern New Hampshire, on the Piscataqua River, off the Atlantic Ocean; pop. 20,443 (est. 2008).

3 a commercial and naval city in southeastern Virginia, on Hampton Roads, west of Norfolk; pop. 100,577 (est. 2008).

Port Su·dan the chief port of Sudan, on the Red Sea; pop. 284,000 (est. 2008).

port tack ▶ **n.** a sailboat's heading when the wind is coming from the left, or port, side.

Por·tu·gal /'pôrcʜəgəl/ a country occupying the western part of the Iberian peninsula in southwestern Europe; pop. 10,707,900 (est. 2009); capital, Lisbon; language, Portuguese (official).

> Portugal was linked with Spain until it became an independent kingdom in the 12th century. In the 15th and 16th centuries it emerged as one of the leading European colonial powers. It became a republic in 1911 after the expulsion of the monarchy. A long period of dictatorship by Antonio Salazar, who was prime minister 1932–68, and his successor Marcello Caetano (1906–80) was ended in 1974 by a military coup, which led to Portugal's rapid withdrawal from its African colonies and eventually to democratic reform. It became a member of the EC in 1986.

P

Por·tu·guese /'pôrcʜə,gēz/ ▶ **adj.** of or relating to Portugal or its people or language.

▶ **n.** (pl. **same**) **1** a native or inhabitant of Portugal, or a person of Portuguese descent.

2 the Romance language of Portugal and Brazil.

– ORIGIN from Portuguese *portuguez,* from medieval Latin *portugalensis.*

Por·tu·guese man-of-war ▶ **n.** a floating colonial coelenterate with a number of polyps and a conspicuous float. It occurs chiefly in warm seas, and bears long tentacles that can inflict painful stings. ● *Physalia physalis,* order Siphonophora, class Hydrozoa.

Port Vi·la another name for **Vila**.

port watch ▶ **n.** see **watch** (sense 2 of the noun).

port wine ▶ **n.** see **port**[2].

port wine stain ▶ **n.** a kind of large, deep red birthmark, a persistent hemangioma or nevus, typically on the face.

POS ▶ **abbr.** point of sale.

pos. ▶ **abbr.** ■ position. ■ positive. ■ possession. ■ possessive.

PRONUNCIATION KEY ə *ago, up;* ər *over, fur;* a *hat;* ā *ate;* ä *car;* e *let;* ē *see;* i *fit;* ī *by;* ɴɢ *sing;* ō *go;* ô *law, for;* oi *toy;* o͝o *good;* o͞o *goo;* ou *out;* ᴛʜ *thin;* T͟H *then;* ᴢʜ *vision*

po·sa·da /pəˈsädə/ ▶ **n.** (in Spanish-speaking regions) a hotel or inn. ■ (also **Las Posadas**) a ritual re-enactment of Mary and Joseph's search for a lodging in Bethlehem, performed just before Christmas.
– ORIGIN Spanish, from *posar* 'to lodge.'

pose[1] /pōz/ ▶ **v. 1** [with obj.] present or constitute (a problem, danger, or difficulty): *the sheer number of visitors is posing a threat to the area.* ■ raise (a question or matter for consideration): *a statement that posed more questions than it answered.*
2 [no obj.] assume a particular attitude or position in order to be photographed, painted, or drawn: *she posed for a swarm of TV cameramen.* ■ [with obj.] place (someone) in a particular attitude or position in order to be photographed, painted, or drawn: *he posed her on the sofa.* ■ (**pose as**) set oneself up as or pretend to be (someone or something): *a detective posing as a customer* | figurative *a literary novel posing as a spy thriller.*
3 behave affectedly in order to impress others: *some people like to drive these cars, but most just like to pose in them.*
▶ **n. 1** a particular way of standing or sitting, usually adopted for effect or in order to be photographed, painted, or drawn: *photographs of boxers in ferocious poses.*
2 a particular way of behaving adopted in order to give others a false impression or to impress others: *the man dropped his pose of amiability.*
– DERIVATIVES **pos·a·ble adj.**
– ORIGIN Middle English: from Old French *poser* (verb), from late Latin *pausare* 'to pause,' which replaced Latin *ponere* 'to show off.' The noun dates from the early 19th cent.

pose[2] ▶ **v.** [with obj.] archaic puzzle or perplex (someone) with a question or problem: *we have thus posed the mathematician and the historian.*
– ORIGIN early 16th cent.: shortening of obsolete *appose*, from Old French *aposer*, variant of *oposer* 'oppose.'

Po·sei·don /pəˈsīdn/ Greek Mythology the god of the sea, water, earthquakes, and horses, son of Cronus and Rhea and brother of Zeus. He is often depicted with a trident in his hand. Roman equivalent **NEPTUNE**.

Po·sen /ˈpōzən/ German name for **POZNAŃ**.

pos·er[1] /ˈpōzər/ ▶ **n.** a person who acts in an affected manner in order to impress others.

pos·er[2] ▶ **n.** a difficult or perplexing question or problem.

po·seur /pōˈzər/ ▶ **n.** another term for **POSER**[1].
– ORIGIN French, from *poser* 'to place.'

po·sey /ˈpōzē/ (also **posy**) ▶ **adj.** informal (of a person or their behavior) affected and attempting to impress others; pretentious.

posh /päsн/ informal ▶ **adj.** elegant or stylishly luxurious: *a posh Munich hotel.* ■ chiefly Brit. typical of or belonging to the upper class of society: *she had a posh accent.*
▶ **adv.** Brit. in an upper-class way: *trying to talk posh.*
▶ **n.** Brit. the quality or state of being elegant, stylish, or upper-class: *we finally bought a color TV, which seemed the height of posh.*
– DERIVATIVES **posh·ly adv.**, **posh·ness n.**
– ORIGIN early 20th cent.: perhaps from slang *posh*, denoting a dandy. There is no evidence to support the folk etymology that *posh* is formed from the initials of *port out starboard home* (referring to the practice of using the more comfortable accommodations, out of the heat of the sun, on ships between England and India).

pos·it /ˈpäzit/ ▶ **v.** (**posits, positing, posited**) **1** [with obj.] assume as a fact; put forward as a basis of argument: *the Confucian view posits a perfectible human nature* | [with clause] *he posited that the world economy is a system with its own particular equilibrium.* ■ (**posit something on**) base something on the truth of (a particular assumption): *these plots are posited on a false premise about women's nature as inferior.*
2 [with obj.] put in position; place: *the professor posits Cohen in his second category of poets.*
▶ **n.** Philosophy a statement that is made on the assumption that it will prove to be true.
– ORIGIN mid 17th cent.: from Latin *posit-* 'placed,' from the verb *ponere*.

pos·i·tif /ˈpäzəˌtēf/ ▶ **n.** Music (in some organs) a separate division of stops with its own manual, similar to a choir organ.
– ORIGIN French.

po·si·tion /pəˈzisнən/ ▶ **n. 1** a place where someone or something is located or has been put: *the distress call had given the ship's position* | *Mrs. Snell had taken up her position on the bottom step of the stairs.* ■ the location where someone or something should be; the correct place: *the lid was put into position and screwed down* | *make sure that no slates have slipped out of position.* ■ (often **positions**) a place where part of a military force is posted for strategic purposes: *the guns were shelling the German positions.*
2 a particular way in which someone or something is placed or arranged: *he moved himself into a reclining position* | *a cramp forced her to change position.* ■ in a game of chess, the configuration of the pieces and pawns on the board at any point. ■ Music a particular location of the hand on the fingerboard of a stringed instrument: *be familiar with the first six positions across the four strings.* ■ Music a particular location of the slide of a trombone. ■ Music the arrangement of the constituent notes of a chord.
3 a situation or set of circumstances, esp. one that affects one's power to act: *the company's financial position is grim* | [with infinitive] *we felt we were not in a position to judge the merits of the case.* ■ a job: *she retired from her position as marketing director.* ■ the state of being placed where one has an advantage over one's rivals in a competitive situation: *his successors were already jockeying for position.* ■ a person's place or rank in relation to others, esp. in a competitive situation: *he made up ground to finish in second position.* ■ high rank or social standing: *a woman of supposed wealth and position.* ■ (in team games) a set of functions considered as the responsibility of a particular player based on the location in which they play: *it gives every player a chance to play every fielding position.*
4 a person's particular point of view or attitude toward something: *I'll never accept his* ***position on*** *censorship.*
5 an investor's net holdings in one or more markets at a particular time; the status of an individual or institutional trader's open contracts: *traders were covering short positions.*
6 Logic a proposition laid down or asserted; a tenet or assertion.
▶ **v.** [with obj.] put or arrange (someone or something) in a particular place or way: *he pulled out a chair and positioned it between them* | *she positioned herself on a bench.* ■ promote (a product, service, or business) within a particular sector of a market, or as the fulfillment of that sector's specific requirements: *a comprehensive development plan that will* ***position*** *the city as a major economic force in the region.* ■ portray or regard (someone) as a particular type of person: *I had* ***positioned*** *her as my antagonist.*
– ORIGIN late Middle English: from Old French, from Latin *positio(n-)*, from *ponere* 'to place.' The current sense of the verb dates from the early 19th cent.

po·si·tion·al /pəˈzisнənl/ ▶ **adj.** of, relating to, or determined by position: *the team will be forced to make several positional changes.*
– DERIVATIVES **po·si·tion·al·ly adv.**

po·si·tion pa·per ▶ **n.** (in business and politics) a written report outlining someone's attitude or intentions regarding a particular matter.

pos·i·tive /ˈpäzətiv, ˈpäztiv/ ▶ **adj. 1** consisting in or characterized by the presence or possession of features or qualities rather than their absence. ■ (of a statement or decision) expressing or implying affirmation, agreement, or permission: *the company received a positive response from investors.* ■ (of the results of a test or experiment) indicating the presence of something: *three players who had tested positive for cocaine use.* ■ constructive in intention or attitude: *there needs to be a positive approach to youthful offenders.* ■ showing optimism and confidence: *I hope you will be feeling very positive about your chances of success.* ■ showing pleasing progress, gain, or improvement: *the election result will have a positive effect because it will restore people's confidence.*
2 with no possibility of doubt; clear and definite: *he made a positive identification of a glossy ibis.* ■ convinced or confident in one's opinion; certain: *"You are sure it was the same man?" "Positive!"* | [with clause] *I am positive that he is not coming back.* ■ [attrib.] informal downright; complete (used for emphasis): *it's a positive delight to see you.*
3 of, containing, producing, or denoting an electric charge opposite to that carried by electrons.
4 (of a photographic image) showing lights and shades or colors true to the original.
5 Grammar (of an adjective or adverb) expressing a quality in its basic, primary degree. Contrasted with **COMPARATIVE** and **SUPERLATIVE**.
6 chiefly Philosophy dealing only with matters of fact and experience; not speculative or theoretical. Compare with **POSITIVISM** (sense 1).
7 (of a quantity) greater than zero.
8 Astrology of, relating to, or denoting any of the air or fire signs, considered active in nature.
▶ **n. 1** a good, affirmative, or constructive quality or attribute: *take your weaknesses and translate them into positives* | *to manage your way out of recession, accentuate the positive.*
2 a photographic image showing lights and shades or colors true to the original, esp. one printed from a negative.
3 a result of a test or experiment indicating the presence of something: *let us look at the distribution of those positives.*
4 the part of an electric circuit that is at a higher electrical potential than another point designated as having zero electrical potential.
5 Grammar an adjective or adverb in the positive degree.
6 Music another term for **POSITIF**.
7 a number greater than zero.
– DERIVATIVES **pos·i·tive·ness n.**, **pos·i·tiv·i·ty** /ˌpäzəˈtivətē/ **n.**
– ORIGIN late Middle English: from Old French *positif, -ive* or Latin *positivus*, from *posit-* 'placed,' from the verb *ponere*. The original sense referred to laws as being formally 'laid down,' which gave rise to the sense 'explicitly laid down and admitting no question,' hence 'very sure, convinced.'

pos·i·tive dis·crim·i·na·tion ▶ **n.** British term for **REVERSE DISCRIMINATION**.

pos·i·tive feed·back ▶ **n.** chiefly Biology the enhancement or amplification of an effect by its own influence on the process that gives rise to it. ■ Electronics the return of part of an output signal to the input, which is in phase with it, so that the amplifier gain is increased and the output is often distorted.

pos·i·tive ge·ot·ro·pism ▶ **n.** Botany the tendency of roots to grow downward.

pos·i·tive law ▶ **n.** statutes that have been laid down by a legislature, court, or other human institution and which can take whatever form the authors want. Compare with **NATURAL LAW**.

pos·i·tive·ly /ˈpäzətivlē, ˈpäztivlē, ˌpäzəˈtivlē/ ▶ **adv.** in a positive way, in particular: ■ with certainty; so as to leave no room for doubt: *experts could not positively identify the voices.* ■ [as submodifier] used to emphasize that something is the case, even though it may seem surprising or unlikely: *some of the diets may be positively dangerous.*

pos·i·tive or·gan ▶ **n.** chiefly historical a large but movable pipe organ. Compare with **PORTATIVE ORGAN**.
– ORIGIN early 18th cent.: *positive* in the sense 'adapted to be placed in position.'

pos·i·tive pole ▶ **n.** Physics a north-seeking pole of a magnet.

pos·i·tive pres·sure ▶ **n.** air or gas pressure greater than that of the atmosphere, as used, e.g., in the artificial ventilation of the lungs.

pos·i·tive sign ▶ **n.** Mathematics another term for **PLUS SIGN**.

pos·i·tiv·ism /ˈpäzətivˌizəm, ˈpäztiv-/ ▶ **n.** Philosophy **1** a philosophical system that holds that every rationally justifiable assertion can be scientifically verified or is capable of logical or mathematical proof, and that therefore rejects metaphysics and theism. [from French *positivisme*, coined by the French philosopher Auguste **COMTE**.] ■ a humanistic religious system founded on this. ■ another term for **LOGICAL POSITIVISM**.
2 the theory that laws are to be understood as social rules, valid because they are enacted by authority or derive logically from existing decisions, and that ideal or moral considerations (e.g., that a rule is unjust) should not limit the scope or operation of the law.
– DERIVATIVES **pos·i·tiv·ist n. & adj.**, **pos·i·tiv·is·tic** /ˌpäzətəˈvistik/ **adj.**, **pos·i·tiv·is·ti·cal·ly** /ˌpäzətəˈvistik(ə)lē/ **adv.**

pos·i·tron /ˈpäzəˌträn/ ▶ **n.** Physics a subatomic particle with the same mass as an electron and a numerically equal but positive charge.
– ORIGIN 1930s: from **POSITIVE** + **-TRON**.

Posix /ˈpäsiks/ (also **POSIX**) ▶ **n.** Computing a set of formal descriptions that provide a standard for the design of operating systems, esp. ones that are compatible with Unix.
– ORIGIN 1980s: from the initial letters of *portable operating system* + *-ix* suggested by **UNIX**.

po·sol·o·gy /pəˈsäləjē/ ▶ **n.** rare the part of medicine concerned with dosage.
– DERIVATIVES **pos·o·log·i·cal** /ˌpäsəˈläjikəl/ **adj.**
– ORIGIN early 19th cent.: from French *posologie*, from Greek *posos* 'how much' + *-logia* (see **-LOGY**).

poss /päs/ ▶ **abbr.** possible.

poss. ▶ **abbr.** ■ possession. ■ possessive. ■ possible; possibly.

pos·se /ˈpäsē/ ▶ **n.** historical a body of men, typically armed, summoned by a sheriff to enforce the law. ■ (also **posse comitatus** /ˌkämiˈtātəs, -ˈtātəs/) historical the body of men in a county whom the sheriff could summon to enforce the law. [*comitatus* from medieval Latin, 'of the county.'] ■ informal a group of people who have a common characteristic,

occupation, or purpose: *he pompously led around a **posse** of medical students.* ■ informal a group of people who socialize together, esp. to go to clubs or raves.
– ORIGIN mid 17th cent.: from medieval Latin, literally 'power,' from Latin *posse* 'be able.'

Pos·se Com·i·ta·tus Act /ˈpäsē ˌkämiˈtātəs/ ▶ **n.** Law a federal statute prohibiting use of the military in civilian law enforcement.
– ORIGIN Latin *posse comitatus* 'power of the county.'

pos·sess /pəˈzes/ ▶ **v.** [with obj.] **1** have as belonging to one; own: *I do not possess a television set.* ■ Law have possession of as distinct from ownership: *a two-year suspended sentence for possessing cocaine.* ■ have as an ability, quality, or characteristic: *he did not possess a sense of humor* | (**be possessed of**) *a fading blonde possessed of a powerful soprano voice.* ■ (**possess oneself of**) archaic take for one's own: *all that the plaintiffs did was to possess themselves of the securities.*
2 (usu. **be possessed**) (of a demon or spirit, esp. an evil one) have complete power over (someone) and be manifested through their speech or actions: *she was possessed by the Devil.* ■ (of an emotion, idea, etc.) dominate the mind of; have an overpowering influence on: *I was possessed by a desire to tell her everything.*
3 chiefly literary have sexual intercourse with (a woman).
4 archaic maintain (oneself or one's mind or soul) in a state or condition of patience or quiet: *I tried to **possess** my soul **in** patience and to forget how hungry I was.* [often with biblical allusion to Luke 21:19, the proper sense ('gain your souls') being misunderstood.]
– PHRASES **what possessed you?** used to express surprise at an action regarded as extremely unwise: *what possessed you to come here?*
– ORIGIN late Middle English: from Old French *possesser*, from Latin *possess-* 'occupied, held,' from the verb *possidere*, from *potis* 'able, capable' + *sedere* 'sit.'

pos·sessed /pəˈzest/ ▶ **adj.** (of a person) completely controlled by an evil spirit: *he can turn into a possessed animal at will.*
– PHRASES **like a man** (or **woman**) **possessed** in a frenzy; madly: *I trained like a man possessed, I tell you.*

pos·ses·sion /pəˈzeshən/ ▶ **n. 1** the state of having, owning, or controlling something: *are you **in possession of** any items over $500 in value?* | *he had **taken possession of** one of the sofas* | *the book **came into my possession**.* ■ Law visible power or control over something, as distinct from lawful ownership; holding or occupancy: *both teams attempting to **gain possession of** the ball* | *they were imprisoned for possession of explosives.* ■ informal the state of possessing an illegal drug: *they're charged with possession.* ■ (in football, basketball, and other ball games) temporary control of the ball by a particular player or team: *the ball hit a defender and Brown's quick reaction put him **in possession**.*
2 (usu. **possessions**) an item of property; something belonging to one: *I was alone with no money or possessions* | *that photograph was Bert's most precious possession.* ■ a territory or country controlled or governed by another: *France's former colonial possessions.*
3 the state of being controlled by a demon or spirit: *they prayed for protection against demonic possession.* ■ the state of being completely under the influence of an idea or emotion: *fear **took possession of** my soul.*
– DERIVATIVES **pos·ses·sion·less** adj.
– ORIGIN Middle English: from Old French, from Latin *possessio(n-)*, from the verb *possidere* (see POSSESS).

pos·ses·sive /pəˈzesiv/ ▶ **adj. 1** demanding someone's total attention and love: *as soon as she'd been out with a guy a few times, he'd get possessive* | *she was **possessive of** our eldest son.* ■ showing a desire to own things and an unwillingness to share what one already owns: *young children are proud and **possessive of** their own property.*
2 Grammar relating to or denoting the case of nouns and pronouns expressing possession. [from Latin *possessivus*, translation of Greek *ktētikē* (*ptōsis*) 'possessive (case).']
▶ **n.** Grammar a possessive word or form. ■ (**the possessive**) the possessive case.
– DERIVATIVES **pos·ses·sive·ly** adv., **pos·ses·sive·ness** n.

> **USAGE** 1 Form the possessive of singulars by adding *'s*: *Ross's, Fox's, Reese's*. A few classical and foreign names are traditional exceptions to this rule, for example, *Jesus'* and *Euripides,'* which take an apostrophe only. 2 Form the possessive of plurals by adding an apostrophe to the plural form: *the Rosses' house, the Perezes' car*. See also usage at APOSTROPHE¹, ITS, and PLURAL.

pos·ses·sive pro·noun ▶ **n.** Grammar a pronoun indicating possession, for example *mine, yours, hers, theirs.*

pos·ses·sor /pəˈzesər/ ▶ **n.** a person who owns something or has a particular quality: *his father was the possessor of a considerable fortune.* ■ Law a person who takes, occupies, or holds something without necessarily having ownership, or as distinguished from the owner.
– DERIVATIVES **pos·ses·so·ry** adj.

pos·set /ˈpäsət/ ▶ **n.** historical a drink made of hot milk curdled with ale, wine, or other alcoholic liquor and typically flavored with spices, drunk as a delicacy or as a remedy for colds.
– ORIGIN late Middle English: of unknown origin.

pos·si·bil·i·ty /ˌpäsəˈbilətē/ ▶ **n.** (pl. **possibilities**) a thing that may happen or be the case: *the theoretical **possibility of** a chain reaction* | [with clause] *there was always the possibility that he might be turned down.* ■ the state or fact of being likely or possible; likelihood: *there was **no possibility of** recompense for him.* ■ a thing that may be chosen or done out of several possible alternatives: *one possibility is to allow all firms to participate* | *there are three possibilities for obtaining extra money.* ■ (**possibilities**) unspecified qualities of a promising nature; potential: *the house was old but it had possibilities.*
– ORIGIN late Middle English: from Old French *possibilite*, from late Latin *possibilitas*, from *possibilis* 'able to be done' (see POSSIBLE).

pos·si·ble /ˈpäsəbəl/ ▶ **adj.** able to be done; within the power or capacity of someone or something: *surely it's not **possible for** a man to live so long?* | *what are the possible alternatives?* | *contact me **as soon as possible*** | *I'd like the report this afternoon, **if possible**.* ■ able to happen although not certain to; denoting a fact, event, or situation that may or may not occur or be so: *a new theory emerged about the possible cause of the plane crash* | [with clause] *it is possible that he will have to return to the hospital.* ■ [attrib.] able to be or become; potential: *he was a possible future customer.* ■ [with superlative] having as much or as little of a specified quality as can be achieved: *children need the best education possible* | *the shortest possible route.* ■ [attrib.] (of a number or score) as high as is achievable in a test, competition, or game: *he scored 723 points out of a possible 900.*
▶ **n.** a person or thing that has the potential to become or do something, esp. a potential candidate for a job or membership on a team: *I have marked five possibles with an asterisk.* ■ (**the possible**) that which is likely or achievable: *they were living right at the edge of the possible.*
– ORIGIN late Middle English: from Old French, or from Latin *possibilis*, from *posse* 'be able.'

pos·si·bly /ˈpäsəblē/ ▶ **adv. 1** [sentence adverb] perhaps (used to indicate doubt or hesitancy): *he found himself alone, possibly the only surviving officer.* ■ [with modal] used in polite requests: *could you possibly pour me another cup of coffee?*
2 [usu. with modal] in accordance with what is likely or achievable, in particular: ■ used to emphasize that something is difficult, surprising, or bewildering: *what can you possibly mean?* ■ used to emphasize that someone has or will put all their effort into something: *be as noisy as you possibly can.*

POSSLQ /ˈpäsəlˌkyo͞o/ ▶ **abbr.** person of the opposite sex sharing living quarters (used to refer to a live-in sexual partner).

pos·sum /ˈpäsəm/ ▶ **n. 1** informal an opossum.
2 a tree-dwelling Australasian marsupial that typically has a prehensile tail. ● Four families, esp. Petauridae: many species, including the ringtails.
– PHRASES **play possum 1** pretend to be asleep or unconscious when threatened (in imitation of an opossum's behavior). **2** feign ignorance.
– ORIGIN early 17th cent.: shortening of OPOSSUM.

Post¹ /pōst/, Emily (Price) (1873–1960), US writer and columnist. She was an arbiter of social etiquette and was the last word on manners. She wrote *Etiquette* (1922).

Post², Wiley (1899–1935), US aviator. He was the first man to fly solo around the world 1933, accomplishing this in 7 days, 18 hours, and 49 minutes. He was flying near Point Barrow, Alaska, with Will Rogers as his passenger when their plane crashed and they were both killed.

post¹ /pōst/ ▶ **n. 1** a long, sturdy piece of timber or metal set upright in the ground and used to support something or as a marker: *follow the blue posts until the track meets a forestry road.* ■ a goalpost: *Robertson, at the near post, headed wide.* ■ (**the post**) a starting post or winning post.
2 an Internet posting.
▶ **v.** [with obj.] display (a notice) in a public place: *a curt notice had been posted on the door* | *the exam results were posted this morning.* ■ announce or publish (something, esp. a financial result): *the company posted a $460,000 loss.* ■ (of a player or team) achieve or record (a particular score or result): *Smith and Lamb posted a century partnership.* ■ [with obj. and complement] publish the name of (a member of the armed forces) as missing or dead: *a whole troop had been posted missing.* ■ put notices on or in: *we have posted all the bars.* ■ make (information) available on the Internet. ■ submit (a message) to an Internet message board or blog.
– PHRASAL VERBS **post up** Basketball play in a position near the basket, along the side of the key.
– ORIGIN Old English, from Latin *postis* 'doorpost,' later 'rod, beam,' probably reinforced in Middle English by Old French *post* 'pillar, beam' and Middle Dutch and Middle Low German *post* 'doorpost.'

post² ▶ **n. 1** chiefly Brit. the official service or system that delivers letters and parcels: *winners will be notified by post* | *the tickets are in the post.* ■ letters and parcels delivered: *she was opening her post.* ■ [in sing.] a single collection or delivery of letters or parcels: *entries must be received no later than first post on Friday, June 14th.* ■ used in names of newspapers: *the Washington Post.*
2 historical one of a series of couriers who carried mail on horseback between fixed stages. ■ archaic a person or vehicle that carries mail.
▶ **v. 1** [with obj.] chiefly Brit. send (a letter or parcel) via the postal system: *I've just been to post a letter* | ***post off** your order form today.*
2 [with obj.] (in bookkeeping) enter (an item) in a ledger: *post the transaction in the second column.* ■ complete (a ledger) in this way.
3 [no obj.] historical travel with relays of horses: *we posted in an open carriage.* ■ [with adverbial of direction] archaic travel with haste; hurry: *he comes posting up the street.*
▶ **adv.** archaic with haste: *come now, come post.*
– PHRASES **keep someone posted** keep someone informed of the latest developments or news.
– ORIGIN early 16th cent. (sense 2 of the noun): from French *poste*, from Italian *posta*, from a contraction of Latin *posita*, feminine past participle of *ponere* 'to place.'

post³ ▶ **n. 1** a position of paid employment; a job: *he resigned from the post of foreign minister* | *a teaching post.*
2 a place where someone is on duty or where a particular activity is carried out: *a worker asleep at his post* | *a customs post.* ■ a place where a soldier, guard, or police officer is stationed or that they patrol: *he gave the two armed men orders not to leave their posts* | *a command post.* ■ a force stationed at a permanent position or camp; a garrison. ■ a local group in an organization of military veterans.
3 Brit. historical the status or rank of full-grade captain in the Royal Navy: *Captain Miller was **made post** in 1796.*
▶ **v.** [with obj.] (usu. **be posted**) send (someone) to a particular place to take up an appointment: *he was posted to Washington as military attaché.* ■ station (someone, esp. a soldier, guard, or police officer) in a particular place: *a guard was posted at the entrance.*
– ORIGIN mid 16th cent.: from French *poste*, from Italian *posto*, from a contraction of popular Latin *positum*, neuter past participle of *ponere* 'to place.'

post⁴ /pōst/ ▶ **prep.** subsequent to; after: *American poetry post the 1950s hasn't had the same impact.*
– ORIGIN 1960s: independent usage of POST-.

post- ▶ **prefix** after in time or order: *postdate* | *postoperative.*
– ORIGIN from Latin *post* 'after, behind.'

post·age /ˈpōstij/ ▶ **n.** the sending or conveying of letters and parcels by mail: *the free postage that members of Congress enjoy.* ■ the amount required to send a letter or parcel by mail: *the calendar is available for $15.95 including postage and handling.*

post·age due ▶ **n.** that part of the postage that was not prepaid. ■ a special postage stamp indicating postage still to be paid on a letter or parcel.

post·age me·ter ▶ **n.** a machine that prints an official mark or signature on a letter or parcel to indicate that postage has been paid or does not need to be paid.

post·age stamp ▶ **n.** a small adhesive piece of paper of specified value issued by a postal authority to be affixed to a letter or parcel to indicate the amount of postage paid.

post·al /ˈpōstəl/ ▶ **adj.** [attrib.] of or relating to the post office or the mail: *increased postal rates* | *postal services.* ■ chiefly Brit. done through the mail: *a postal ballot* | *a postal survey.*
▶ **n.** (in full **postal card**) another term for POSTCARD.

PRONUNCIATION KEY ə *ago, up*; ər *over, fur*; a *hat*; ā *ate*; ä *car*; e *let*; ē *see*; i *fit*; ī *by*; NG *sing*; ō *go*; ô *law, for*; oi *toy*; o͝o *good*; o͞o *goo*; ou *out*; TH *thin*; T͟H *then*; ZH *vision*

– PHRASES **go postal** become crazed and violent, esp. as the result of stress. [with reference to cases in which disgruntled employees of the US Postal Service have shot colleagues.]
– DERIVATIVES **post·al·ly** adv.
– ORIGIN mid 19th cent.: from French, from *poste* 'postal service.'

post·al code ▶ n. Brit. another term for POSTCODE. ■ Canadian a mailing code similar to the US zip code.

post·al serv·ice ▶ n. another term for POST OFFICE (sense 1).

post-and-beam ▶ adj. (of a building or a method of construction) having or using a framework of upright and horizontal beams.

post·bel·lum /pōst'beləm/ ▶ adj. occurring or existing after a war, in particular the American Civil War.
– ORIGIN late 19th cent.: from Latin *post* 'after' + *bellum* 'war.'

post·box /'pōst,bäks/ ▶ n. British term for MAILBOX.

post·card /'pōst,kärd/ ▶ n. a card for sending a message by mail without an envelope, typically having a photograph or other illustration on one side.

post-chaise /,SHāz/ ▶ n. (pl. **post-chaises** pronunc. **same** or /-,SHāziz/) historical a horse-drawn carriage used for transporting passengers or mail, esp. in the 18th and early 19th centuries.
– ORIGIN late 17th cent.: from POST² + CHAISE in the sense 'horse-drawn carriage.'

post·clas·si·cal /,pōst'klasəkəl/ ▶ adj. of or relating to a time after the classical period of any language, art, or culture, in particular the classical period of ancient Greek and Latin culture.

post·code /'pōst,kōd/ ▶ n. Brit. a group of numbers or letters and numbers that are added to a postal address to assist the sorting of mail.

post·co·i·tal /,pōst'kōətl/ ▶ adj. occurring or done after sexual intercourse: *postcoital contraception*.
– DERIVATIVES **post·co·i·tal·ly** adv.

post·co·lo·ni·al /,pōstkə'lōnēəl/ ▶ adj. occurring or existing after the end of colonial rule: *the postcolonial government* | *postcolonial literature*.

post·date /pōst'dāt/ ▶ v. [with obj.] **1** (usu. as adj. **postdated**) affix or assign a date later than the actual one to (a document or event): *a postdated check*.
2 occur or come at a later date than: *Stonehenge was presumed to postdate these structures*.

post·doc /'pōst,däk/ ▶ n. informal a person engaged in postdoctoral research. ■ postdoctoral research. ■ a postdoctoral research fellowship.

post·doc·tor·al /pōst'däktərəl/ ▶ adj. of, relating to, or denoting research undertaken after the completion of doctoral research: *a postdoctoral fellowship*.

P

post·er /'pōstər/ ▶ n. **1** a large printed picture used for decoration. ■ a large printed picture, notice, or advertisement displayed in a public place: [as modifier] *a poster campaign*.
2 a person who posts a message on an Internet message board or blog.
▶ v. [no obj.] (usu. as noun **postering**) put up posters in an area: *illegal postering in downtown Montreal*.

post·er child (or **poster boy** or **poster girl**) ▶ n. a person or thing that epitomizes or represents a specified quality, cause, etc.: *the organization is the poster child for bad business deals*.
– ORIGIN from the use of appealing children in charitable print advertisements.

poste res·tante /,pōst ,res'tänt/ ▶ n. written on a letter as an indication that it should be kept at a specified post office until collected by the addressee. ■ chiefly Brit. the department in a post office keeping such letters.
– ORIGIN mid 18th cent.: from French, literally 'mail remaining.'

pos·te·ri·or /pä'sti(ə)rēər, pō-/ ▶ adj. **1** chiefly Anatomy farther back in position; of or nearer the rear or hind end, esp. of the body or a part of it: *the posterior part of the gut* | *a basal body situated just posterior to the nucleus*. The opposite of ANTERIOR. ■ Medicine relating to or denoting presentation of a fetus in which the rear or caudal end is nearest the cervix and emerges first at birth: *a posterior labor*. Compare with BREECH BIRTH.
2 formal coming after in time or order; later: *a date posterior to the first Reform Bill*.
▶ n. humorous a person's buttocks.
– DERIVATIVES **pos·te·ri·or·i·ty** /pä,sti(ə)rē'ôritē, pō-/ n., **pos·te·ri·or·ly** adv.
– ORIGIN early 16th cent. (as a plural noun denoting descendants): from Latin, comparative of *posterus* 'following,' from *post* 'after.'

pos·te·ri·or prob·a·bil·i·ty ▶ n. the statistical probability that a hypothesis is true calculated in the light of relevant observations. Compare with PRIOR PROBABILITY.

pos·ter·i·ty /pä'steritē/ ▶ n. all future generations of people: *the victims' names are recorded for posterity*. ■ [in sing.] archaic the descendants of a person: *God offered Abraham a posterity like the stars of heaven*.
– ORIGIN late Middle English: from Old French *posterite*, from Latin *posteritas*, from *posterus* 'following.'

post·er·ize /'pōstə,rīz/ ▶ v. [with obj.] print or display (a photograph or other image) using only a small number of different tones.
– DERIVATIVES **post·er·i·za·tion** /,pōstərə'zāSHən/ n.

pos·tern /'pōstərn, 'päs-/ ▶ n. a back or side entrance: [as modifier] *a small postern door*.
– ORIGIN Middle English: from Old French *posterne*, alteration of *posterle*, from late Latin *posterula*, diminutive of *posterus* 'following.'

pos·ter paint ▶ n. an opaque paint with a water-soluble binder, used for posters and children's paintings.

post ex·change (abbr.: **PX**) ▶ n. a store at a US military base selling food, clothing, and other items.

post·face /'pōst,fās/ ▶ n. a brief explanatory comment or note at the end of a book or other piece of writing.

post·fem·i·nist /post'femənist/ ▶ adj. coming after the feminism of the 1960s and subsequent decades, in particular moving beyond or rejecting some of the ideas of feminism as out of date.
▶ n. a person who rejects some feminist ideas for this reason.
– DERIVATIVES **post·fem·i·nism** n.

post·fix /pōst'fiks/ ▶ v. **1** [with obj.] Biology treat (a biological substance or specimen) with a second fixative.
2 Linguistics, rare append as a suffix.
▶ n. a suffix.

post·fron·tal /,pōst'frəntl/ ▶ n. Zoology a bone behind the orbit of the eye in some vertebrates.

post·gla·cial /pōst'glāSHəl/ ▶ adj. Geology of or relating to the period since the last continental glaciation (the Wisconsin in North America), beginning with the sudden rise in temperature about 10,000 years ago. Compare with LATE-GLACIAL. ■ (as noun **the postglacial**) the postglacial period.

post·grad /'pōst'grad/ ▶ adj. & n. informal short for POSTGRADUATE.

post·grad·u·ate /pōst'grajōōit/ ▶ adj. of, relating to, or denoting a course of study undertaken after completing a first degree: *a postgraduate degree*.
▶ n. a student engaged in such a course of study.

post·haste /'pōst'hāst/ ▶ adv. with great speed or immediacy: *she would go posthaste to England*.
– ORIGIN mid 16th cent.: from the direction "haste, post, haste," formerly given on letters.

post hoc /'pōst 'häk/ ▶ adj. & adv. occurring or done after the event: *a post hoc justification for the changes*.
– PHRASES **post hoc, ergo propter hoc** after this, therefore resulting from it: used to indicate that a causal relationship has erroneously been assumed from a merely sequential one.
– ORIGIN Latin, literally 'after this.'

post horn ▶ n. historical a valveless horn used originally to signal the arrival or departure of a mounted courier or mail coach.

post·hu·mous /'päsCHəməs, päst'(h)yōōməs/ ▶ adj. occurring, awarded, or appearing after the death of the originator: *he was awarded a posthumous Military Cross* | *a posthumous collection of his articles*. ■ (of a child) born after the death of its father.
– DERIVATIVES **post·hu·mous·ly** adv.
– ORIGIN early 17th cent.: from Latin *postumus* 'last' (superlative from *post* 'after'), in late Latin spelled *posth-* by association with *humus* 'ground.'

post·hyp·not·ic /,pōst-(h)ip'nätik/ ▶ adj. relating to or denoting the giving of ideas or instructions to a subject under hypnosis that are intended to affect behavior after the hypnotic trance ends: *posthypnotic suggestion*.

pos·til /'pästl/ ▶ n. archaic a marginal note or comment, esp. on a biblical text. ■ a commentary, homily, or book of homilies.
– ORIGIN late Middle English: from Old French *postille*, from medieval Latin *postilla*, perhaps from Latin *post illa (verba)* 'after those words,' written as a direction to a scribe.

pos·til·ion /pə'stilyən, pō-/ (also **postillion**) ▶ n. a person who rides the leading left-hand horse of a team or pair drawing a coach or carriage, esp. when there is no coachman.
– ORIGIN mid 16th cent. (in the sense 'forerunner acting as guide to the post-horse rider'): from French *postillon*, from Italian *postiglione* 'post boy,' from *posta* (see POST²).

post-Im·pres·sion·ism (also **Post-Impressionism**) ▶ n. the work or style of a varied group of late-19th-century and early-20th-century artists including Van Gogh, Gauguin, and Cézanne. They reacted against the naturalism of the Impressionists to explore color, line, and form, and the emotional response of the artist, a concern that led to the development of expressionism.
– DERIVATIVES **post-Im·pres·sion·ist** n. & adj., **post-Im·pres·sion·is·tic** adj.

post·in·dus·tri·al /,pōstin'dəstrēəl/ ▶ adj. of or relating to an economy that no longer relies on heavy industry: *a postindustrial society*.
– DERIVATIVES **post·in·dus·tri·al·ism** /-,lizəm/ n.

post·ing¹ /'pōstiNG/ ▶ n. chiefly Brit. an appointment to a job, esp. one abroad or in the armed forces: *he requested a posting to Japan*. ■ the location of such an appointment: *Norway was an attractive posting because of its quality of life*.

post·ing² ▶ n. a message submitted to an Internet message board or blog.

Post-it (also **Post-it note**) ▶ n. trademark a piece of paper with an adhesive strip on one side, designed to be stuck prominently to an object or surface and easily removed when necessary.

post·lap·sar·i·an /,pōstlap'se(ə)rēən/ ▶ adj. Theology or literary occurring or existing after the Fall of Man.
– ORIGIN mid 18th cent.: from POST- 'occurring after,' on the pattern of *sublapsarian*.

post·lude /'pōs(t),lōōd/ ▶ n. Music a concluding piece of music, esp. an organ piece played at the end of a religious service. ■ a written or spoken epilogue; an afterword.
– ORIGIN mid 19th cent.: from POST- 'later, after,' on the pattern of *prelude*.

post·man /'pōstmən/ ▶ n. (pl. **postmen**) a mail carrier.

post·mark /'pōst,märk/ ▶ n. an official mark stamped on a letter or other postal package, giving the place, date, and time of posting, and serving to cancel the postage stamp: *an envelope with a London postmark*.
▶ v. [with obj.] (usu. **be postmarked**) stamp (a letter or other postal package) officially with such a mark: [with obj. and complement] *the letter was postmarked New York*.

post·mas·ter /'pōst,mastər/ ▶ n. a person in charge of a post office.

post·mas·ter gen·er·al ▶ n. (pl. **postmasters general**) the head of a country's postal service.

post·mil·len·ni·al /,pōstmə'lenēəl/ ▶ adj. (esp. in Christian doctrine) following the millennium.

post·mil·len·ni·al·ism /,pōstmə'lenēə,lizəm/ ▶ n. (among some Christian Protestants) the doctrine that the Second Coming of Christ will be the culmination of the prophesied millennium of blessedness. Compare with PREMILLENNIALISM.
– DERIVATIVES **post·mil·len·ni·al·ist** /-ist/ n.

post·mis·tress /'pōst,mistris/ ▶ n. a woman in charge of a post office.

post·mod·ern /pōst'mädərn/ ▶ adj. subsequent to or coming later than that which is modern: *the illusionary nature of postmodern life*. ■ relating to or characterized by postmodernism, esp. in being self-referential: *the postmodern discipline of art history*.

post·mod·ern·ism /pōst'mädər,nizəm/ ▶ n. a late-20th-century style and concept in the arts, architecture, and criticism that represents a departure from modernism and has at its heart a general distrust of grand theories and ideologies as well as a problematical relationship with any notion of "art."

Typical features include a deliberate mixing of different artistic styles and media, the self-conscious use of earlier styles and conventions, and often the incorporation of images relating to the consumerism and mass communication of late-20th-century postindustrial society. Postmodernist architecture was pioneered by Robert Venturi; the AT&T skyscraper in New York (completed in 1984) is a prime example of the style. Influential literary critics include Jean Baudrillard and Jean-François Lyotard.

– DERIVATIVES **post·mod·ern·ist** n. & adj., **post·mod·er·ni·ty** /,pōstmə'dərnətē/ n.

post·mod·i·fy /pōst'mädə,fī/ ▶ v. (**postmodifies, postmodifying, postmodified**) [with obj.] Grammar modify the sense of (a noun or other word) by being placed after it.
– DERIVATIVES **post·mod·i·fi·ca·tion** /,pōst,mädifi'kāSHen/ n., **post·mod·i·fi·er** n.

post·mor·tem /pōst'môrtəm/ ▶ **n.** (also **postmortem examination**) an examination of a dead body to determine the cause of death. ■ an analysis or discussion of an event held soon after it has occurred, esp. in order to determine why it was a failure: *an election postmortem on why the party lost.* ▶ **adj.** [attrib.] of or relating to a postmortem: *a postmortem report.* ■ happening after death: *postmortem changes in his body* | [as adv.] *assessment of morphology in nerves taken postmortem.*
– ORIGIN mid 18th cent.: from Latin, literally 'after death.'

post·na·tal /pōst'nātl/ ▶ **adj.** of, relating to, characteristic of, or denoting the period after childbirth: *postnatal care.*
– DERIVATIVES **post·na·tal·ly adv.**

post·nup·tial /pōst'nəpsʜəl, -cʜəl/ ▶ **adj.** occurring or relating to the period after marriage. ■ Zoology occurring in or relating to the period after the mating season of an animal.

post-o·bit ▶ **adj.** archaic taking effect after death.
– ORIGIN mid 18th cent.: from Latin *post obitum*, from *post* 'after' + *obitus* 'decease' (from *obire* 'to die').

post of·fice ▶ **n. 1** (also **postal service**) the public department or corporation responsible for mail services and (in some countries) telecommunications. ■ a building where postal business is carried on.
2 a game, played esp. by children, in which imaginary letters are delivered in exchange for kisses.

post of·fice box ▶ **n.** a numbered box in a post office assigned to a person or organization, where mail for them is kept until collected.

post-op ▶ **abbr.** postoperative.

post·op·er·a·tive /pōst'äp(ə)rətiv/ ▶ **adj.** during, relating to, or denoting the period following a surgical operation: *postoperative care.*

post·or·bit·al /pōst'ôrbətl/ chiefly Zoology ▶ **adj.** [attrib.] situated at the back of the orbit or eye socket, in particular denoting a process of the frontal bone that in some reptiles forms a separate bone. ▶ **n.** a postorbital bone.

post·paid /pōst'pād/ ▶ **adj. & adv.** (with reference to a letter or parcel) on which postage has already been paid: [as adj.] *use the postpaid envelope provided.*

post·par·tum /pōst'pärtəm/ ▶ **adj.** Medicine & Veterinary Medicine following childbirth or the birth of young.
– ORIGIN mid 19th cent.: from Latin *post partum* 'after childbirth.'

post·par·tum de·pres·sion ▶ **n.** depression suffered by a mother following childbirth, typically arising from the combination of hormonal changes, psychological adjustment to motherhood, and fatigue.

post·pone /pōst'pōn/ ▶ **v.** [with obj.] cause or arrange for (something) to take place at a time later than that first scheduled: *the visit had to be postponed for some time* | [with present participle] *the judge postponed sentencing a former government spokesman for fraud.*
– DERIVATIVES **post·pon·a·ble adj., post·pon·er n.**
– ORIGIN late 15th cent.: from Latin *postponere*, from *post* 'after' + *ponere* 'to place.'

post·pone·ment /pōst'pōnmənt/ ▶ **n.** the action of postponing something; deferral: *the postponement of the elections* | *after repeated postponements, the new museum is officially open.*

post·pose /pōst'pōz/ ▶ **v.** [with obj.] Grammar place (a modifying word or morpheme) after the word that it modifies.
– ORIGIN late 16th cent. (in the sense 'place later or lower'): from French *postposer*, from *post-* 'after' + *poser* 'to place.' The current sense dates from the 1920s.

post·po·si·tion /,pōstpə'zisʜən/ ▶ **n.** Grammar a word or morpheme placed after the word it governs, for example *-ward* in *homeward.*
– DERIVATIVES **post·po·si·tion·al** /-sʜənl/ **adj.**
– ORIGIN mid 19th cent.: from **PREPOSITION**, by substitution of the prefix **POST-** for *pre-*.

post·pos·i·tive /,pōst'päzətiv/ ▶ **adj.** (of a word) placed after or as a suffix on the word that it relates to. ▶ **n.** a postpositive word.
– DERIVATIVES **post·pos·i·tive·ly adv.**

post·pran·di·al /pōst'prandēəl/ ▶ **adj.** formal or humorous during or relating to the period after dinner or lunch: *we were jolted from our postprandial torpor.* ■ Medicine occurring after a meal.
– ORIGIN early 19th cent.: from **POST-** 'after' + Latin *prandium* 'a meal' + **-AL**.

post·pro·duc·tion /,pōstprə'dəksʜən/ ▶ **n.** [often as modifier] work done on a film or recording after filming or recording has taken place: *postproduction editing.*

post-punk ▶ **adj.** denoting a style of rock music inspired by punk but less aggressive in performance and musically more experimental. ▶ **n.** post-punk music.

PostScript /'pōs(t),skript/ ▶ **n.** Computing, trademark a page description language that is an industry standard for outputting high-resolution text and graphics.

post·script ▶ **n.** an additional remark at the end of a letter, after the signature and introduced by "P.S.": *he added a postscript: "Leaving tomorrow."* ■ an additional statement or action that provides further information on or a sequel to something: *as a postscript to this, Paul did finally marry.*
– ORIGIN mid 16th cent.: from Latin *postscriptum*, neuter past participle (used as a noun) of *postscribere* 'write under, add,' from *post* 'after, later' + *scribere* 'write.'

post·sea·son /'pōs(t),sēzən/ ▶ **adj.** (of a sporting event) taking place after the end of the regular season. ▶ **n.** the period following the regular season.

post·struc·tur·al·ism /pōs(t)'strəkcʜərə,lizəm/ ▶ **n.** an extension and critique of structuralism, esp. as used in critical textual analysis.

> Emerging in French intellectual life in the late 1960s and early 1970s, poststructuralism departed from the claims to objectivity and comprehensiveness made by structuralism and emphasized instead plurality and deferral of meaning, rejecting the fixed binary oppositions of structuralism and the validity of authorial authority.

– DERIVATIVES **post·struc·tur·al adj., post·struc·tur·al·ist n. & adj.**

post-synch /siNGk/ ▶ **v.** [with obj.] add a sound recording to (film or video footage) at a later time.

post-tax ▶ **adj.** Finance (of income or profits) remaining after the deduction of taxes.

post-ten·sion ▶ **v.** [with obj.] strengthen (reinforced concrete) by applying tension to the reinforcing rods after the concrete has set: (as adj. **post-tensioned**) *post-tensioned concrete.* Compare with **PRESTRESSED, PRETENSION²**.

post time ▶ **n.** the time at which a race is scheduled to start and entrants must be at their starting positions.

post-trau·mat·ic stress dis·or·der ▶ **n.** Medicine a condition of persistent mental and emotional stress occurring as a result of injury or severe psychological shock, typically involving disturbance of sleep and constant vivid recall of the experience, with dulled responses to others and to the outside world.

pos·tu·lant /'päscʜələnt/ ▶ **n.** a candidate, esp. one seeking admission into a religious order.
– ORIGIN mid 18th cent.: from French *postulant* or Latin *postulant-* 'asking,' from the verb *postulare* (see **POSTULATE**).

pos·tu·late ▶ **v.** /'päscʜə,lāt/ [with obj.] **1** suggest or assume the existence, fact, or truth of (something) as a basis for reasoning, discussion, or belief: *his theory postulated a rotatory movement for hurricanes* | [with clause] *he postulated that the environmentalists might have a case.*
2 (in ecclesiastical law) nominate or elect (someone) to an ecclesiastical office subject to the sanction of a higher authority.
▶ **n.** /'päscʜələt/ formal a thing suggested or assumed as true as the basis for reasoning, discussion, or belief: *perhaps the postulate of Babylonian influence on Greek astronomy is incorrect.* ■ Mathematics an assumption used as a basis for mathematical reasoning.
– DERIVATIVES **pos·tu·la·tion** /,päscʜə'lāsʜən/ **n.**
– ORIGIN late Middle English (sense 2 of the verb): from Latin *postulat-* 'asked,' from the verb *postulare.*

pos·tu·la·tor /'päscʜə,lātər/ ▶ **n. 1** a person who postulates something.
2 a person who presents a case for the canonization or beatification of someone in the Roman Catholic Church.

pos·ture /'päscʜər/ ▶ **n. 1** a position of a person's body when standing or sitting: *he stood in a flamboyant posture with his hands on his hips* | *good posture will protect your spine.* ■ Zoology a particular pose adopted by a bird or other animal, interpreted as a signal of a specific pattern of behavior.
2 a particular way of dealing with or considering something; an approach or attitude: *labor unions adopted a more militant posture in wage negotiations.* ■ a particular way of behaving that is intended to convey a false impression; a pose: *despite pulling back its missiles, the government maintained a defiant posture for home consumption.*
▶ **v. 1** [no obj.] (often as noun **posturing**) behave in a way that is intended to impress or mislead others: *a masking of fear with macho posturing.* ■ [with obj.] adopt (a certain attitude) so as to impress or mislead: *the companies may posture regret, but they have a vested interest in increasing Third World sales.*
2 [with obj.] archaic place (someone) in a particular attitude or pose: *and still these two were postured motionless.*
– DERIVATIVES **pos·tur·al adj., pos·tur·er n.**
– ORIGIN late 16th cent. (denoting the relative position of one thing to another): from French, from Italian *postura*, from Latin *positura* 'position,' from *posit-* 'placed,' from the verb *ponere.*

post·vo·cal·ic /,pōs(t)vō'kalik/ ▶ **adj.** (of a speech sound) occurring immediately after a vowel.

post·war /'pōst'wär/ ▶ **adj.** occurring or existing after a war (esp. World War II): *postwar Britain* | *postwar reconstruction.*

po·sy¹ /'pōzē/ ▶ **n.** (pl. **posies**) **1** a small bunch of flowers.
2 archaic a short motto or line of verse inscribed inside a ring.
– ORIGIN late Middle English (sense 2): contraction of **POESY**.

po·sy² ▶ **adj.** variant spelling of **POSEY**.

pot¹ /pät/ ▶ **n. 1** a container, typically rounded or cylindrical and of ceramic ware or metal, used for storage or cooking: *clay pots for keeping water cool in summer* | *a cooking pot.* [usu. with modifier] any of various containers made for a particular purpose: *a yogurt pot.* ■ a container for holding drink, esp. beer. ■ the contents of any of such containers: *a pot of coffee.*
2 (**the pot**) the total sum of the bets made on a round in poker and other card games: *Jim raked in the pot.* ■ all the money contributed by a group of people for a particular purpose: *in insurance, everybody puts money into the pot used to pay claims.*
3 informal a potbelly.
4 (**the pot**) informal a toilet.
▶ **v.** (**pots, potted, potting**) [with obj.] **1** plant in a flowerpot: *pot individual cuttings as soon as you see new young leaves.*
2 chiefly Brit. preserve (food, esp. meat or fish) in a sealed pot or jar: *venison can be potted in the same way as tongue.*
3 Brit. Billiards another term for **POCKET**.
4 informal hit or kill (someone or something) by shooting: *he was shot in the eye as neighbors potted clay pigeons.*
– PHRASES **for the pot** for food or cooking: *hens provided eggs as well as meat for the pot.* **go to pot** informal deteriorate through neglect: *the foundry was allowed to go to pot in the seventies.* **the pot calling the kettle black** used to convey that the criticisms a person is aiming at someone else could equally well apply to themselves. **pot of gold** see **GOLD**. **shit** (or **piss**) **or get off the pot** vulgar slang used to convey that someone should stop wasting time and get on with something.
– DERIVATIVES **pot·ful** /-,fo͝ol/ **n.** (pl. **potfuls**).
– ORIGIN late Old English *pott*, probably reinforced in Middle English by Old French *pot*; of unknown ultimate origin (compare with late Latin *potus* 'drinking cup'). Current senses of the verb date from the early 17th cent.

pot² ▶ **n.** informal cannabis.
– ORIGIN 1930s: probably from Mexican Spanish *potiguaya* 'cannabis leaves.'

pot. ▶ **abbr.** Electronics ■ potential. ■ potentiometer.

po·ta·ble /'pōtəbəl/ ▶ **adj.** formal safe to drink; drinkable: *there is no supply of potable water available.*
– DERIVATIVES **po·ta·bil·i·ty** /,pōtə'bilətē/ **n.**
– ORIGIN late Middle English: from French *potable*, from late Latin *potabilis*, from Latin *potare* 'to drink.'

po·tage /pô'täzʜ/ ▶ **n.** thick soup.
– ORIGIN mid 16th cent.: from French. Compare with **POTTAGE**.

pot·a·mol·o·gy /,pätə'mäləjē/ ▶ **n.** Geography the study of rivers.
– ORIGIN early 19th cent.: from Greek *potamos* 'river' + **-LOGY**.

pot·ash /'pät,asʜ/ ▶ **n.** an alkaline potassium compound, esp. potassium carbonate or hydroxide.
– ORIGIN early 17th cent.: from *pot-ashes*, from obsolete Dutch *potasschen*, originally obtained by leaching vegetable ashes and evaporating the solution in iron pots.

pot·ash al·um ▶ **n.** see **ALUM¹**.

PRONUNCIATION KEY ə ago, up; ər over, fur; a hat; ā ate; ä car; e let; ē see; i fit; ī by; NG sing; ō go; ô law, for; oi toy; o͝o good; o͞o goo; ou out; TH thin; T̲H̲ then; ZH vision

P

po·tas·si·um /pəˈtasēəm/ ▶ **n.** the chemical element of atomic number 19, a soft silvery-white reactive metal of the alkali metal group. (Symbol: **K**)
– DERIVATIVES **po·tas·sic** /-ˈtasik/ **adj.** (Mineralogy).
– ORIGIN early 19th cent.: Latinization of **POTASH** or earlier *potass* (from French *potasse*) by Sir Humphry Lowry, who first separated the element from potash.

po·tas·si·um–ar·gon dat·ing ▶ **n.** Geology a method of dating rocks from the relative proportions of radioactive potassium-40 and its decay product, argon-40.

po·tas·si·um hy·drox·ide ▶ **n.** a strongly alkaline white deliquescent compound used in many industrial processes, e.g., soap manufacture. ● Chem. formula: KOH.

po·tas·si·um ni·trate ▶ **n.** a white crystalline salt, occurring naturally and produced synthetically, used in fertilizer, as a meat preservative, and as a constituent of gunpowder. Also called **SALTPETER** or **NITER**. ● Chem. formula: KNO_3.

po·ta·tion /pōˈtāSHən/ ▶ **n.** archaic or humorous a drink. ■ the action of drinking something, esp. alcohol: *I intend to abstain from potation.* ■ (often **potations**) a drinking bout: *the dreadful potations of his youth.*
– ORIGIN late Middle English: from Old French, from Latin *potatio(n-)*, from *potare* 'to drink.'

po·ta·to /pəˈtātō/ ▶ **n.** (pl. **potatoes**) **1** a starchy plant tuber that is one of the most important food crops, cooked and eaten as a vegetable: *roasted potatoes | the meal comes with rice or potato* | [as modifier] *leek and potato soup.* ■ see **SWEET POTATO**.
2 the plant of the nightshade family that produces these tubers on underground runners. ● *Solanum tuberosum*, family Solanaceae. It was first cultivated in the Andes about 1,800 years ago and was introduced to Europe in *c.*1570.
– ORIGIN mid 16th cent.: from Spanish *patata*, variant of Taino *batata* 'sweet potato.' The English word originally denoted the sweet potato and gained its current sense in the late 16th cent.

po·ta·to blight ▶ **n.** a destructive fungal disease of potatoes resulting in dry brown rot of the tubers. ● **Early blight** is caused by *Alternaria solani* (subdivision Deuteromycotina), and **late blight** is caused by *Phytophthora infestans* (subdivision Mastigomycotina).

po·ta·to chip ▶ **n.** a wafer-thin slice of potato fried or baked until crisp and eaten as a snack.

po·ta·to pan·cake ▶ **n.** a small flat cake of grated potatoes mixed with flour and egg and fried.

po·ta·to sal·ad ▶ **n.** a side dish consisting of cold cooked potato chopped and mixed with a dressing and seasonings.

po·ta·to skin ▶ **n.** a strip of deep-fried potato skin, served as an appetizer.

po·ta·to vine ▶ **n.** a semievergreen climbing plant with pale blue or white flowers, related to the potato and native to South and Central America. ● *Solanum jasminoides*, family Solanaceae.

pot-au-feu /ˌpôt ō ˈfœ/ ▶ **n.** (pl. **same**) a French soup of meat, typically boiled beef, and vegetables cooked in a large pot.
– ORIGIN French, literally 'pot on the fire.'

Pot·a·wat·o·mi /ˌpätəˈwätəmē/ ▶ **n.** (pl. **same** or **Potawatomis**) **1** a member of an American Indian people living originally around Lake Michigan.
2 the Algonquian language of this people.
▶ **adj.** of or relating to this people or their language.
– ORIGIN the name in Ojibwa.

pot·bel·lied pig (in full **Vietnamese potbellied pig**) ▶ **n.** a pig of a small, dark breed with short legs and a large stomach, sometimes kept as a pet.

pot·bel·ly /ˈpätˌbelē/ (also **pot belly**) ▶ **n.** a large, protruding, rotund stomach.
– DERIVATIVES **pot·bel·lied** **adj.**

pot·bel·ly stove (also **potbellied stove**) ▶ **n.** a small, bulbous-sided wood-burning stove.

pot·boil·er ▶ **n.** informal a book, painting, or recording produced merely to make the writer or artist a living by catering to popular taste.

pot-bound /pät bound/ ▶ **adj.** (of a plant) having roots that fill the flowerpot, leaving no room for them to expand.

pot cheese ▶ **n.** a coarse type of cottage cheese.

po·teen /pəˈtēn, -ˈCHēn/ (also **potheen**) ▶ **n.** chiefly Irish alcohol made illicitly, typically from potatoes.
– ORIGIN early 19th cent.: from Irish (*fuisce*) *poitín* 'little pot (of whiskey),' diminutive of *pota* 'pot.'

potbelly stove

Po·tem·kin[1] /pəˈtem(p)kin/ a battleship whose crew mutinied during the Russian Revolution of 1905 when in the Black Sea, bombarding Odessa before seeking asylum in Romania. The incident persuaded the tsar to agree to a measure of reform.

Po·tem·kin[2] ▶ **adj.** informal having a false or deceptive appearance, esp. one presented for the purpose of propaganda: *it proved her to be a Potemkin feminist.*
– ORIGIN 1930s: from Grigori Aleksandrovich *Potyomkin* (often transliterated *Potemkin*), a favorite of Empress Catherine II of Russia, who reputedly gave the order for sham villages to be built for the empress's tour of the Crimea in 1787.

po·ten·cy /ˈpōtnsē/ ▶ **n.** (pl. **potencies**) **1** the power of something to affect the mind or body: *a myth of enormous potency | the unexpected potency of the rum punch.* ■ (in homeopathy) the number of times a remedy has been diluted and succussed, taken as a measure of the strength of the effect it will produce: *she was given a low potency twice daily.* ■ Genetics the extent of the contribution of an allele toward the production of a phenotypic characteristic. ■ Biology a capacity in embryonic tissue for developing into a particular specialized tissue or organ.
2 a male's ability to achieve an erection or to reach orgasm: *medications that diminish sexual potency.*

po·tent[1] /ˈpōtnt/ ▶ **adj. 1** having great power, influence, or effect: *thrones were potent symbols of authority | a potent drug | a potent argument.*
2 (of a male) able to achieve an erection or to reach an orgasm.
– DERIVATIVES **po·tence** **n.**, **po·tent·ly** **adv.**
– ORIGIN late Middle English: from Latin *potent-* 'being powerful, being able,' from the verb *posse.*

po·tent[2] Heraldry ▶ **adj.** [postpositive] **1** formed of crutch-shaped pieces; (esp. of a cross) having a straight bar across the end of each extremity: *a cross potent.*
2 of the fur called potent (as a tincture).
▶ **n.** fur resembling vair, but with the alternating pieces T-shaped.
– ORIGIN late Middle English (denoting a crutch): alteration of Old French *potence* 'crutch,' from Latin *potentia* 'power' (in medieval Latin 'crutch'), from *potent-* (see **POTENT**[1]).

po·ten·tate /ˈpōtnˌtāt/ ▶ **n.** a monarch or ruler, esp. an autocratic one.
– ORIGIN late Middle English: from Latin *potentatus* 'dominion,' from *potent-* 'being able or powerful' (see **POTENT**[1]).

po·ten·tial /pəˈtenCHəl/ ▶ **adj.** [attrib.] having or showing the capacity to become or develop into something in the future: *a two-pronged campaign to woo potential customers.*
▶ **n. 1** latent qualities or abilities that may be developed and lead to future success or usefulness: *a young broadcaster with great potential | the potentials of the technology were never wholly controllable.* ■ (often **potential for/to do something**) the possibility of something happening or of someone doing something in the future: *the crane operator's clear view reduces the potential for accidents | pesticides with the potential to cause cancer.*
2 Physics the quantity determining the energy of mass in a gravitational field or of charge in an electric field.
– DERIVATIVES **po·ten·ti·al·i·ty** /pəˌtenCHēˈalətē/ **n.**, **po·ten·tial·ize** /-ˌlīz/ **v.**, **po·ten·tial·ly** **adv.** [as submodifier] *potentially dangerous products* | [sentence adverb] *potentially an even bigger bombshell is about to burst.*
– ORIGIN late Middle English: from late Latin *potentialis*, from *potentia* 'power,' from *potent-* 'being able' (see **POTENT**[1]). The noun dates from the early 19th cent.

po·ten·tial bar·ri·er ▶ **n.** Physics a region within a force field in which the potential is significantly higher than at points on either side of it, so that a particle requires energy to pass through it.

po·ten·tial dif·fer·ence ▶ **n.** Physics the difference of electrical potential between two points.

po·ten·tial di·vid·er ▶ **n.** another term for **VOLTAGE DIVIDER**.

po·ten·tial en·er·gy ▶ **n.** Physics the energy possessed by a body by virtue of its position relative to others, stresses within itself, electric charge, and other factors. Compare with **KINETIC ENERGY**.

po·ten·ti·ate /pəˈtenCHēˌāt/ ▶ **v.** [with obj.] technical increase the power, effect, or likelihood of (something, esp. a drug or physiological reaction): *the glucose will potentiate intestinal absorption of sodium.*
– ORIGIN early 19th cent.: from **POTENT**[1], on the pattern of *substantiate.*

po·ten·ti·a·tion /pəˌtenCHēˈāSHən/ ▶ **n.** Physiology the increase in strength of nerve impulses along pathways that have been used previously, either short-term or long-term.

po·ten·til·la /ˌpōtnˈtilə/ ▶ **n.** a plant of a genus that includes the cinquefoils, esp. (in gardening) a small shrub with bright yellow, red, orange, or pink flowers. ● Genus *Potentilla*, family Rosaceae: many species.
– ORIGIN modern Latin, based on Latin *potent-* 'being powerful' (with reference to its herbal qualities) + the diminutive suffix *-illa.*

po·ten·ti·om·e·ter /pəˌtenCHēˈämətər/ ▶ **n. 1** an instrument for measuring an electromotive force by balancing it against the potential difference produced by passing a known current through a known variable resistance.
2 a variable resistor with a third adjustable terminal. The potential at the third terminal can be adjusted to give any fraction of the potential across the ends of the resistor.

po·ten·ti·om·e·try /pəˌtenCHēˈämətrē/ ▶ **n.** Chemistry the measurement of electrical potential as a technique in chemical analysis.
– DERIVATIVES **po·ten·ti·o·met·ric** /pəˌtenCHēəˈmetrik/ **adj.**

pot·head /ˈpätˌhed/ ▶ **n.** informal a person who smokes marijuana, esp. habitually.

po·theen ▶ **n.** chiefly Irish variant spelling of **POTEEN**.

poth·er /ˈpäT͟Hər/ ▶ **n.** [in sing.] literary a commotion or fuss: *don't make such a pother!*
– ORIGIN late 16th cent.: of unknown origin.

pot·herb /ˈpätˌ(h)ərb/ ▶ **n.** any herb grown for culinary use.

pot·hold·er /ˈpätˌhōldər/ ▶ **n.** a piece of quilted or thick fabric for handling hot dishes and pans.

pot·hole /ˈpätˌhōl/ ▶ **n.** a deep natural underground cavity formed by the erosion of rock, esp. by the action of water. ■ a deep circular hole in a riverbed formed by the erosion of the rock by the rotation of stones in an eddy. ■ a depression or hollow in a road surface caused by wear or subsidence. ■ (also **pothole lake**) a pond in a natural hollow in the ground.
– DERIVATIVES **pot·holed** **adj.**
– ORIGIN early 19th cent.: from Middle English *pot* 'pit' (perhaps of Scandinavian origin) + **HOLE**.

pot·hol·ing /ˈpätˌhōliNG/ ▶ **n.** Brit. the exploring of natural potholes as a pastime.

pot·hook /ˈpätˌho͝ok/ ▶ **n. 1** chiefly historical a hook used for hanging a pot over a hearth or for lifting a hot pot.
2 dated a curved stroke in handwriting, esp. as made by children learning to write.

pot·house /ˈpätˌhous/ ▶ **n.** dated a small tavern.

pot·hunt·er /ˈpätˌhəntər/ ▶ **n.** chiefly archaic a person who hunts solely to achieve a kill, rather than as a sport. ■ a person who takes part in a contest merely for the sake of the prize.

po·tion /ˈpōSHən/ ▶ **n.** a liquid with healing, magical, or poisonous properties: *a love potion.*
– ORIGIN Middle English: from Old French, from Latin *potio(n-)* '(poisonous) drink,' related to *potare* 'to drink.'

Pot·i·phar /ˈpätifər/ (in the Bible) an Egyptian officer whose wife tried to seduce Joseph and then falsely accused him of attempting to rape her.

pot·latch /ˈpätˌlaCH/ ▶ **n.** (among North American Indian peoples of the northwest coast) an opulent ceremonial feast at which possessions are given away or destroyed to display wealth or enhance prestige.
▶ **v.** [no obj.] hold such a feast or ceremony.
– ORIGIN Chinook Jargon *pálač, pátlač*, probably from Nootka.

pot lik·ker ▶ **n.** informal nonstandard spelling of **POT LIQUOR**, used in the southern US.

pot liq·uor ▶ **n.** liquid in which meat, fish, or vegetables have been boiled; stock.

pot·luck /ˈpätˈlək/ ▶ **n.** used in reference to a situation in which one must take a chance that whatever is available will prove to be good or acceptable: *he could take potluck in a town not noted for its hotels.* ■ a meal or party to which each of the guests contributes a dish: [as modifier] *a potluck supper.*

Po·tok /ˈpōtäk/, Chaim (1929–2002), US writer, theologian, and rabbi. His novels include *The Chosen* (1967), *The Book of Lights* (1981), and *I Am the Clay* (1991). He also wrote nonfiction and plays.

Po·to·mac /pəˈtōmək/ a river of the eastern US that rises in the Appalachian Mountains in West Virginia and flows about 285 miles (459 km) through Washington, DC into Chesapeake Bay.

po·too /pəˈto͞o/ ▶ **n.** a nocturnal, insectivorous bird resembling a large nightjar. Found in tropical America, it mimics a dead branch when alarmed. ● Genus *Nyctibius* and family Nyctibiidae: five species, in particular the **common potoo** (*N. griseus*).

– ORIGIN mid 19th cent.: from Jamaican Creole, from Twi, of imitative origin.

po·to·roo /ˌpätəˈro͞o/ ▶ n. a small, nocturnal rat kangaroo with long hind limbs and typically a hopping gait, native to Australia and Tasmania. ● Genus *Potorous*, family Potoroidae: three species.
– ORIGIN late 18th cent.: probably from Dharuk *badaru*.

Po·to·sí /ˌpôtôˈsē/ a city in southern Bolivia; pop. 153,328 (2009). At an altitude of about 13,758 feet (4,205 m), it is one of the highest cities in the world.

pot pie ▶ n. **1** a meat and vegetable pie baked in a deep dish, often with a top crust only.
2 a stew with dumplings.

pot·pour·ri /ˌpōpəˈrē, ˌpōpo͝oˈrē/ ▶ n. (pl. **potpourris**) a mixture of dried petals and spices placed in a bowl or small sack to perfume clothing or a room. ■ a mixture of things, esp. a musical or literary medley: *he played a **potpourri** of tunes from Gilbert and Sullivan.*
– ORIGIN early 17th cent. (denoting a stew made of different kinds of meat): from French, literally 'rotten pot.'

po·tre·ro /pəˈtre(ə)rō/ ▶ n. (pl. **potreros**) (in the southwestern US and South America) a paddock or pasture for horses or cattle.
– ORIGIN mid 19th cent.: from Spanish, from *potro* 'colt, pony.'

pot roast ▶ n. a piece of meat cooked slowly in a covered dish.
▶ v. (**pot-roast**) [with obj.] cook (a piece of meat) slowly in a covered dish.

Pots·dam /ˈpätsˌdam/ a city in eastern Germany, the capital of Brandenburg state, southwest of Berlin, on the Havel River; pop. 148,800 (est. 2006).

Pots·dam Con·fer·ence a meeting held in Potsdam in the summer of 1945 among US, Soviet, and British leaders that established principles for the Allied occupation of Germany following the end of World War II.

pot·sherd /ˈpätˌSHərd/ ▶ n. a broken piece of ceramic material, esp. one found on an archaeological site.

pot·shot /ˈpätˌSHät/ ▶ n. a shot aimed unexpectedly or at random at someone or something with no chance of self-defense: *a sniper took a potshot at him.* ■ a criticism, esp. a random or unfounded one: *the show takes wickedly funny potshots at movies.* ■ a shot at a game bird or other animal purely to kill it for food, without regard to the rules of the sport.
– ORIGIN mid 19th cent.: originally a *shot* at an animal intended for the *pot*, i.e., for food, rather than for display (which would require skilled shooting).

pot·stick·er /ˈpätˌstikər/ ▶ n. a filled Chinese dumpling, typically crescent-shaped, esp. one that is pan-fried until brown on one side, then turned and simmered in a small amount of broth.

pot·still /ˈpätˌstil/ ▶ n. a still to which heat is applied directly and not by means of a steam jacket.

pot·tage /ˈpätij/ ▶ n. archaic soup or stew.
– PHRASES **sell something for a mess of pottage** sell something for a ridiculously small amount. [with biblical allusion to the story of Esau, who sold his birthright for some bread and pottage of lentils (Gen. 25:31).]
– ORIGIN Middle English (as *potage*): from Old French *potage* 'that which is put into a pot.' Compare with POTAGE and PORRIDGE.

pot·ted /ˈpätid/ ▶ adj. **1** (of a plant) planted or grown in a flowerpot and usually kept indoors: *an array of exotic potted palms.* ■ chiefly Brit. (of food, esp. meat or fish) preserved in a sealed pot or jar: *potted smoked trout.* ■ chiefly Brit. (of a literary work or descriptive account) put into a short and easily assimilable form: *a potted history of the band's career.*
2 [predic.] informal intoxicated by drink or drugs, esp. marijuana: *a party where everybody was pretty much potted.*

Pot·ter /ˈpätər/, Beatrix (1866–1943), English writer for children; full name *Helen Beatrix Potter.* She is known for her series of animal stories, illustrated with her own delicate watercolors, which began with *The Tale of Peter Rabbit* (first published privately in 1900).

pot·ter¹ /ˈpätər/ ▶ v. British term for PUTTER³.
– ORIGIN late 19th cent.: alteration.

pot·ter² ▶ n. a person who makes pottery.
– ORIGIN late Old English *pottere* (see POT¹, -ER¹).

pot·ter's field ▶ n. historical a burial place for paupers and strangers.

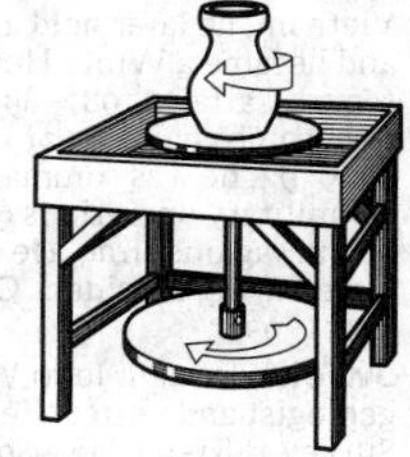
potter's wheel

– ORIGIN with biblical allusion to Matt. 27:7.

pot·ter's wheel ▶ n. a horizontal revolving disk on which wet clay is shaped into pots or other round ceramic objects.

pot·ter wasp ▶ n. a solitary wasp that builds a flask-shaped nest of mud into which it seals an egg and a supply of food for the larva. ● Genus *Eumenes*, family Eumenidae: many species.

pot·ter·y /ˈpätərē/ ▶ n. (pl. **potteries**) pots, dishes, and other articles made of earthenware or baked clay. Pottery can be broadly divided into earthenware, porcelain, and stoneware. ■ the craft or profession of making such ware: *courses include drawing, painting, and pottery.* ■ a factory or workshop where such ware is made.
– ORIGIN Middle English: from Old French *poterie*, from *potier* 'a potter.'

pot·ting shed ▶ n. a shed that is used for potting plants and in which plants and garden tools and supplies are stored.

pot·ting soil ▶ n. a mixture of loam, peat, sand, and nutrients, used as a growing medium for plants in containers.

pot·tle /ˈpätl/ ▶ n. archaic a measure for liquids equal to a half gallon. ■ a pot or container holding this.
– ORIGIN Middle English: from Old French *potel* 'little pot,' diminutive of *pot*.

pot·to /ˈpätō/ (also **potto gibbon**) ▶ n. (pl. **pottos**) a small, slow-moving, nocturnal primate with a short tail, living in dense vegetation in the tropical forests of Africa. ● *Perodicticus potto*, family Lorisidae, suborder Prosimii.
– ORIGIN early 18th cent.: perhaps from Guinea dialect.

pot·ty¹ /ˈpätē/ ▶ n. (pl. **potties**) a bowl used by small children as a toilet. ■ informal a toilet.

pot·ty² ▶ adj. (**pottier, pottiest**) informal, chiefly Brit.
1 foolish; crazy: *he felt she really had gone potty.* ■ [predic.] extremely enthusiastic about or fond of someone or something: *I'm **potty about** my two sons.*
2 [attrib.] insignificant or feeble: *that potty little mower.*
– DERIVATIVES **pot·ti·ness** n.
– ORIGIN mid 19th cent.: of unknown origin.

pot·ty-mouthed ▶ adj. informal using or characterized by bad language: *a potty-mouthed rapper.*
– DERIVATIVES **pot·ty mouth** n.

pot·ty-train ▶ v. [with obj.] train (a small child) to use a potty.

POTUS /ˈpōtəs/ ▶ abbr. President of the United States.

pot-val·iant ▶ adj. archaic (of a person) courageous as a result of being drunk.
– DERIVATIVES **pot-val·or** n.

pouch /pouCH/ ▶ n. **1** a small bag or other flexible receptacle, typically carried in a pocket or attached to a belt: *a tobacco pouch* | *webbing with pouches for stun grenades.* ■ a lockable bag for mail or dispatches.
2 a pocketlike abdominal receptacle in which marsupials carry their young during lactation. ■ any of a number of similar animal structures, such as those in the cheeks of rodents.
▶ v. [with obj.] **1** put into a pouch: *he stopped, pouched his tickets, and plodded on.*
2 make (part of a garment) hang like a pouch: *the muslin is lightly pouched over the belt.*
– DERIVATIVES **pouched** adj., **pouch·y** adj.
– ORIGIN Middle English (as a noun): from Old Northern French *pouche*, variant of Old French *poche* 'bag.' Compare with POKE².

pou·chong /ˈpo͞oˈCHÔNG, -ˈCHäNG/ ▶ n. a kind of China tea made by fermenting the withered leaves only briefly, typically scented with rose petals.
– ORIGIN Chinese.

pouf¹ /po͝of/ ▶ n. variant spelling of POOF², POUFFE.
▶ exclam. variant spelling of POOF¹.

pouf² ▶ n. a dress or part of a dress in which a large mass of material has been gathered so that it stands away from the body: [as modifier] *a dress with a pouf skirt.* ■ a bouffant hairstyle: *he grew his hair out in a sort of pouf.*
– ORIGIN early 19th cent. (denoting an elaborate female headdress fashionable at the time): from French, of imitative origin.

pouffe /po͞of/ (also **pouf**) ▶ n. a cushioned footstool or low seat with no back.
– ORIGIN late 19th cent.: from French *pouf*, of imitative origin.

Pough·keep·sie /pəˈkipsē/ an industrial city in southeastern New York, on the Hudson River, home of Vassar College; pop. 29,654 (est. 2008).

pou·i /ˈpo͞oē/ ▶ n. (pl. **same** or **pouis**) a Caribbean and tropical American tree with trumpet-shaped flowers, grown as an ornamental and valued for its timber. ● Genus *Tabebuia*, family Bignoniaceae.
– ORIGIN mid 19th cent.: a local word in Trinidad.

Pouil·ly-Fuis·sé /po͞oˌyē fwēˈsā/ ▶ n. a dry white Chardonnay wine from Burgundy.

Pou·lenc /po͞oˈleNGk/, Francis (Jean Marcel) (1899–1963), French composer. A member of Les Six, he is known for work characterized by lyricism as well as by the use of idioms of popular music such as jazz.

poult¹ /pōlt/ ▶ n. Farming a young domestic chicken, turkey, pheasant, or other fowl being raised for food.
– ORIGIN late Middle English: contraction of PULLET.

poult² /po͞o(lt)/ (also **poult-de-soie** /də ˈswä/) ▶ n. a fine corded silk or taffeta, typically colored and used as a dress fabric.
– ORIGIN 1930s: from French *poult-de-soie*, from *poult* (of unknown origin) + *de soie* 'of silk.'

poul·ter·er /ˈpōltərər/ ▶ n. a dealer in poultry and, typically, game.
– ORIGIN late 16th cent.: from archaic *poulter*, in the same sense, from Old French *pouletier*.

poul·tice /ˈpōltəs/ ▶ n. a soft, moist mass of material, typically of plant material or flour, applied to the body to relieve soreness and inflammation and kept in place with a cloth.
▶ v. [with obj.] apply a poultice to: *he poulticed the wound.*
– ORIGIN late Middle English: from Latin *pultes* (plural), from *puls, pult-* 'porridge, pap.'

poul·try /ˈpōltrē/ ▶ n. domestic fowl, such as chickens, turkeys, ducks, and geese.
– ORIGIN Middle English: from Old French *pouletrie*, from *poulet* 'pullet.'

pounce¹ /pouns/ ▶ v. [no obj.] (of an animal or bird of prey) spring or swoop suddenly so as to catch prey: *the wolf **pounced on** the rat* | *she looked like a vulture waiting to pounce.* ■ (of a person) spring forward suddenly so as to attack or seize someone or something: *the gang **pounced on** him and knocked him to the ground.* ■ notice and take swift and eager advantage of a mistake, remark, or sign of weakness: *reporters who are just as eager to **pounce on** a gaffe as on a significant news story.*
▶ n. a sudden swoop or spring.
– DERIVATIVES **pounc·er** n.
– ORIGIN late Middle English (as a noun denoting a tool for stamping or punching): origin obscure, perhaps from PUNCHEON¹. A noun sense 'claw, talon' arose in the late 15th cent., which gave rise to the verb (late 17th cent).

pounce² ▶ n. a fine resinous powder formerly used to prevent ink from spreading on unglazed paper or to prepare parchment to receive writing. ■ powdered charcoal or other fine powder dusted over a perforated pattern to transfer the design to the object beneath.
▶ v. [with obj.] **1** smooth down by rubbing with pounce or pumice.
2 transfer (a design) by the use of pounce.
– DERIVATIVES **pounc·er** n.
– ORIGIN late 16th cent. (as a verb): from French *poncer*, based on Latin *pumex* 'pumice.'

poun·cet box /ˈpounsət/ ▶ n. archaic a small box with a perforated lid used for holding perfume.
– ORIGIN late 16th cent.: perhaps originally erroneously from *pounced* (= perforated) *box*.

Pound /pound/, Ezra (Weston Loomis) (1885–1972), US poet and critic, resident in Europe 1908–45. Initially associated with imagism, he later developed a highly eclectic poetic voice, establishing a reputation as a modernist poet. Notable works: *Hugh Selwyn Mauberley* (1920) and *Cantos* (series, 1917–70).

pound¹ /pound/ ▶ n. **1** (abbr.: **lb**) a unit of weight in general use equal to 16 oz. avoirdupois (0.4536 kg). ■ a unit of weight equal to 12 oz. troy (0.3732 kg) used for precious metals.
2 (also **pound sterling**) (pl. **pounds sterling**) the basic monetary unit of the UK, equal to 100 pence. ■ another term for PUNT⁴. ■ the basic monetary unit of several Middle Eastern countries, equal to 100 piastres. ■ the former basic monetary unit of Cyprus, equal to 100 cents.
– PHRASES **one's pound of flesh** something that one is strictly or legally entitled to, but that it is ruthless or inhuman to demand. [with allusion to Shakespeare's *Merchant of Venice*.]
– ORIGIN Old English *pund*, of Germanic origin; related to Dutch *pond* and German *Pfund*, from Latin (*libra*) *pondo*, denoting a Roman '(pound) weight' of 12 ounces.

PRONUNCIATION KEY ə *ago, up*; ər *over, fur*; a *hat*; ā *ate*; ä *car*; e *let*; ē *see*; i *fit*; ī *by*; NG *sing*; ō *go*; ô *law, for*; oi *toy*; o͝o *good*; o͞o *goo*; ou *out*; TH *thin*; T͟H *then*; ZH *vision*

pound[2] ▶ **v.** [with obj.] strike or hit heavily and repeatedly: *Patrick pounded the couch with his fists* | *U.S. gunships pounded the capital* | [no obj.] *pounding on the door, she shouted at the top of her voice.* ■ crush or grind (something) into a powder or paste by beating it with an instrument such as a pestle: *pound the cloves with salt and pepper until smooth.* ■ [no obj.] beat, throb, or vibrate with a strong regular rhythm: *her heart was pounding.* ■ [no obj.] walk or run with heavy steps: *I heard him pounding along the gangway.* ■ informal defeat (an opponent) in a resounding way: *the Yankees pounded the Red Sox 22–1.*
– PHRASES **pound the beat** (of a police officer) patrol an assigned route or area. **pound the pavement** walk the streets in an effort to accomplish something: *I will pound the pavement from city to city in order to explain the dangers.* ■ search diligently for something, typically for a job: *although the country's current jobless rate is small, the number of people pounding the pavement has become a growing worry.*
– PHRASAL VERBS **pound something out** type something with heavy keystrokes: *an old typewriter on which she pounded out her poems.* ■ produce music by striking an instrument heavily and repeatedly: *the women pounded out a ringing tattoo on several oil drums.*
– ORIGIN Old English *pūnian*; related to Dutch *puin*, Low German *pün* 'rubble.'

pound[3] ▶ **n.** a place where stray animals, esp. dogs, may be officially taken and kept until claimed by their owners or otherwise disposed of. ■ a place where illegally parked motor vehicles removed by the police are kept until their owners pay a fine in order to reclaim them. ■ archaic a place of confinement; a trap or prison.
▶ **v.** [with obj.] archaic shut (an animal) in a pound.
– ORIGIN late Middle English (earlier in compounds): of uncertain origin. Early use referred to an enclosure for the detention of stray or trespassing cattle.

pound·age /ˈpoundij/ ▶ **n. 1** weight, esp. when regarded as excessive: *reduce excess poundage without risking overexertion.*
2 Brit. a payment of a particular amount per pound sterling of the sum involved in a transaction. ■ a percentage of the total earnings of a business, paid as wages.

pound·al /ˈpoundəl/ ▶ **n.** Physics a unit of force equal to that required to give a mass of one pound an acceleration of one foot per second per second.
– ORIGIN late 19th cent.: from POUND[1] + the suffix *-al*, perhaps suggested by QUINTAL.

pound cake ▶ **n.** a rich cake containing a pound, or equal weights, of each chief ingredient, typically flour, butter, and sugar.

pound coin ▶ **n.** a coin worth one British pound sterling.

pound·er /ˈpoundər/ ▶ **n.** [usu. in combination] **1** a person or thing weighing a specified number of pounds: *Sloan set a blue-shark record with a 184-pounder.* ■ a gun designed to fire a shell weighing a specified number of pounds.
2 a person or thing that pounds something: *he's direct, but not abrasive, not a desk-pounder.*

pound·ing /ˈpoundiNG/ ▶ **n.** repeated and heavy striking or hitting of someone or something: *the pounding of the surf on a sandy beach.* ■ rhythmical beating or throbbing: *all she could hear was the pounding of her heart.* ■ informal a resounding defeat: *the victory was badly needed after a 16-7 pounding at the hands of Brooklyn.*
– PHRASES **take** (or **get**) **a pounding** be repeatedly hit or attacked: *the town took a hell of pounding from the Luftwaffe* | figurative *technology stocks took a pounding in last week's sharp correction.*

pound note ▶ **n.** a banknote worth one British pound sterling, now replaced by the pound coin in England and Wales.

pound sign ▶ **n. 1** the sign (#), representing a pound as a unit of weight or mass, or as represented on a telephone keypad or computer keyboard.
2 the sign (£), representing a British pound sterling.

pound ster·ling ▶ **n.** see POUND[1] (sense 2).

pour /pôr/ ▶ **v.** [no obj.] (esp. of a liquid) flow rapidly in a steady stream: *water poured off the roof* | figurative *words poured from his mouth.* ■ [with obj.] cause (a liquid) to flow from a container in a steady stream by holding the container at an angle: *she poured a little whiskey into a glass.* ■ [with obj.] serve (a drink) in this way: *she* ***poured out*** *a cup of tea* | [with two objs.] *Harry poured her a drink.* ■ (of rain) fall heavily: *the storm clouds gathered and the rain* ***poured down*** | [with obj.] *it's pouring rain.* ■ (of people or things) come or go in a steady stream and in large numbers: *letters poured in.* ■ [with obj.] (**pour something into**) donate something, esp. money, to (a particular enterprise or project) in large amounts: *Belgium has been pouring money into the company.* ■ [with obj.] (**pour something out**) express one's feelings or thoughts in a full and unrestrained way: *in his letters, Edward poured out his hopes.* ■ (**pour oneself into**) humorous dress oneself in (a tight-fitting piece of clothing): *I poured myself into a short Lycra skirt.*
– PHRASES **when it rains it pours** proverb misfortunes or difficult situations tend to follow each other in rapid succession or to arrive all at the same time. **pour cold water on** see COLD. **pour it on** informal progress or work quickly or with all one's energy. **pour oil on troubled waters** try to settle a disagreement or dispute with words intended to placate or pacify those involved. **pour scorn on** see SCORN.
– DERIVATIVES **pour·a·ble** adj., **pour·er** n.
– ORIGIN Middle English: of unknown origin.

> **USAGE** On the confusion of **pour** and **pore**, see usage at PORE[2].

pour·boire /po͝orˈbwär/ ▶ **n.** a gratuity; a tip.
– ORIGIN French, from *pour boire*, literally '(money) for drinking.'

pour·ing rights ▶ **plural n.** the exclusive rights of a beverage maker or distributor to have its products sold at a particular venue, event, or institution.

pousse-ca·fé /ˌpo͞os kaˈfā/ ▶ **n.** (pl. pronunc. **same**) a glass of various liqueurs or cordials poured in successive layers, drunk immediately after coffee.
– ORIGIN from French, literally 'pushes (the) coffee.'

Pous·sin /po͞oˈsen, -ˈsaN/, Nicolas (1594–1665), French painter. Regarded as the chief representative of French classicism and a master of the grand manner, he is noted for such subject matter as biblical scenes, classical mythology, and historical landscapes.

pous·sin /po͞oˈsaN/ ▶ **n.** a chicken killed young for eating.
– ORIGIN French.

pout[1] /pout/ ▶ **v.** [no obj.] push one's lips or one's bottom lip forward as an expression of petulant annoyance or in order to make oneself look sexually attractive: *she lounged on the steps, pouting* | [with obj.] *he shrugged and pouted his lips.* ■ (of a person's lips) be pushed forward in such a way: *her lips pouted provocatively.*
▶ **n.** a pouting expression: *his lower lip protruded in a sulky pout.*
– DERIVATIVES **pout·ing·ly** adv., **pout·y** adj.
– ORIGIN Middle English (as a verb): perhaps from the base of Swedish dialect *puta* 'be inflated.' Compare with POUT[2].

pout[2] ▶ **n.** another term for EELPOUT.
– ORIGIN Old English *pūta* (only in *ǣlepūta* 'eelpout'); related to Dutch *puit* 'frog, chub,' *puitaal* 'eelpout,' and perhaps to POUT[1].

pout·er /ˈpoutər/ ▶ **n.** a kind of pigeon able to inflate its crop considerably.

pou·tine /po͞oˈtēn/ ▶ **n.** Canadian a dish of French fries topped with cheese curds and gravy.
– ORIGIN 1980s: Canadian French, either from French *pouding* 'pudding' or directly from PUDDING.

POV ▶ **abbr.** point of view.

pov·er·ty /ˈpävərtē/ ▶ **n.** the state of being extremely poor: *thousands of families are living in abject poverty.* ■ the state of being inferior in quality or insufficient in amount: *the poverty of her imagination.* ■ the renunciation of the right to individual ownership of property as part of a religious vow.
– ORIGIN Middle English: from Old French *poverte*, from Latin *paupertas*, from *pauper* 'poor.'

pov·er·ty line ▶ **n.** the estimated minimum level of income needed to secure the necessities of life.

pov·er·ty-strick·en ▶ **adj.** extremely poor: *thousands of poverty-stricken people.*

po·vi·done-i·o·dine /ˈpōvəˌdōn/ ▶ **n.** Medicine a brown powder used as an antiseptic for external application, consisting of a complex of polyvinylpyrrolidone and iodine.
– ORIGIN 1950s: *povidone*, contraction of POLYVINYLPYRROLIDONE.

POW ▶ **abbr.** prisoner of war.

pow /pou/ ▶ **exclam.** expressing the sound of a blow or explosion: *Pow! Bombs went off on six beaches at once.*
– ORIGIN late 19th cent. (originally US): imitative.

pow·der /ˈpoudər/ ▶ **n.** fine dry particles produced by the grinding, crushing, or disintegration of a solid substance: *when the powder is mixed with water, it becomes a creamy white paste* | *cocoa powder* | [in sing.] *crush the poppy seeds to a powder.* ■ (also **face powder**) a cosmetic in this form designed to be applied to a person's face with a brush or soft pad. ■ dated a medicine or drug in this form, usually designed to be dissolved in a liquid. ■ (also **powder snow**) light, dry, newly fallen snow: [as modifier] *powder skiing.* ■ short for GUNPOWDER (sense 1).
▶ **v.** [with obj.] **1** apply powder to (the face or body): *she powdered her face and put on a dab of perfume.* ■ sprinkle or cover (a surface) with powder or a powdery substance: *broken glass powdered the floor* | figurative *high cheekbones powdered with freckles.*
2 reduce (a substance) to a powder by drying or crushing it: *then the rose petals are dried and powdered.*
– PHRASES **keep one's powder dry** remain cautious and ready for a possible emergency. **take a powder** informal depart quickly, esp. in order to avoid a difficult situation.
– ORIGIN Middle English: from Old French *poudre*, from Latin *pulvis*, *pulver-* 'dust.'

pow·der blue ▶ **n.** a soft, pale blue: [as modifier] *a powder-blue jumpsuit.*

pow·der-coat ▶ **v.** [with obj.] cover (an object) with a polyester or epoxy powder, which is then heated to fuse into a protective layer.

pow·dered /ˈpoudərd/ ▶ **adj.** in the form of powder: *powdered milk.*

pow·dered sug·ar ▶ **n.** another term for CONFECTIONERS' SUGAR.

pow·der flask ▶ **n.** historical a small container with a nozzle for carrying and dispensing gunpowder.

pow·der horn ▶ **n.** historical the horn of an ox, cow, or similar animal used to hold gunpowder, with the wide end filled in and a nozzle at the pointed end.

pow·der hound ▶ **n.** informal a person who enjoys skiing on powder snow.

pow·der keg ▶ **n.** a barrel of gunpowder. ■ a dangerous or volatile situation: *the place had been a powder keg since the uprising.*

Pow·der·ly /ˈpoudərlē/, Terence Vincent (1849–1924), US labor leader. Although he was the mayor of Scranton, Pennsylvania, 1878–84, he also headed the Knights of Labor 1879–93 and was largely responsible for the first Chinese Exclusion Act 1882 and the Contract Labor Act 1885.

pow·der met·al·lur·gy ▶ **n.** the production and working of metals as fine powders that can be pressed and sintered to form objects.

pow·der mon·key ▶ **n.** historical a boy employed on a sailing warship to carry powder to the guns. ■ informal a person who works with explosives.

pow·der-post bee·tle ▶ **n.** a small brown beetle whose wood-boring larvae reduce wood to a very fine powder. ● Family Lyctidae: several genera.

pow·der puff (also **powderpuff**) ▶ **n.** a soft pad for applying powder to the skin, esp. the face.
▶ **adj.** [attrib.] **1** (of sports) played by women or girls only: *a fifth grade powder-puff football game.*
2 informal (of a person or thing) ineffectual: *a powder-puff hitter.*

Pow·der Riv·er a river that flows for 485 miles (780 km) from northeastern Wyoming into southern Montana to join the Yellowstone River.

pow·der room ▶ **n.** used euphemistically to refer to a women's toilet in a public building.

pow·der snow ▶ **n.** see POWDER.

pow·der·y /ˈpoudərē/ ▶ **adj.** consisting of or resembling powder: *powdery snow.* ■ covered with powder: *her pale powdery cheeks.*

pow·der·y mil·dew ▶ **n.** mildew on a plant that is marked by a white floury covering consisting of conidia. Compare with DOWNY MILDEW. ● Family Erysiphaceae, subdivision Ascomycotina.

Pow·ell[1] /ˈpouəl/, Adam Clayton, Jr. (1908–72), US clergyman and politician. A Democrat, he was a member of the US House of Representatives from New York 1945–67, 1969–71 and wrote over 60 pieces of social legislation.

Pow·ell[2] /ˈpōəl/, Anthony (Dymoke) (1905–2000), English novelist. He is best known for his sequence of 12 novels *A Dance to the Music of Time* (1951–75), a satire about the English upper middle classes between World War I and World War II.

Pow·ell[3] /ˈpouəl/, Colin (Luther) (1937–), US army officer and statesman. Decorated for heroism in Vietnam, he later held a series of command posts and became a White House assistant for national security affairs 1987–89. The first black American to become chairman of the Joint Chiefs of Staff 1989–93, he was commander in chief of the 1990–91 US military operations (Desert Shield and Desert Storm) against Iraq. He served as US secretary of state during President George W. Bush's first term (2001–05).

Pow·ell[4] /ˈpouəl/, John Wesley (1834–1902), US geologist and writer. He directed the US Geological Survey 1881–94. He also directed the Smithsonian Institution's Bureau of American Ethnology

1897–1902. He wrote *Report on the Lands of the Arid Region of the United States* (1878).

Pow·ell[5] /ˈpouəl/, Lewis Franklin, Jr. (1907–98), US Supreme Court associate justice 1972–87. Considered a moderate, he was appointed to the Court by President Nixon.

Pow·ell, Lake /ˈpouəl/ a reservoir on the Colorado River in southern Utah, formed since the 1960s by the Glen Canyon Dam. The lake inundated Glen Canyon.

pow·er /ˈpou(-ə)r/ ▶ **n. 1** the ability to do something or act in a particular way, esp. as a faculty or quality: ***the power of speech*** | [with infinitive] *the power to raise the dead* | **(powers)** *his powers of concentration.* **2** the capacity or ability to direct or influence the behavior of others or the course of events: *the idea that men should have power over women* | *she had me under her power.* ■ political or social authority or control, esp. that exercised by a government: *the party had been in power for eight years* | [as modifier] *a power struggle.* ■ a right or authority that is given or delegated to a person or body: *police do not have the power to stop and search* | *emergency powers.* ■ the military strength of a state: *the sea power of Venice.* ■ a state or country, esp. one viewed in terms of its international influence and military strength: *a great colonial power.* ■ a person or organization that is strong or influential within a particular context: *he was a power in the university.* ■ a supernatural being, deity, or force: *the powers of darkness.* ■ **(powers)** (in traditional Christian angelology) the sixth highest order of the ninefold celestial hierarchy. ■ [as modifier] informal denoting something associated with people who hold authority and influence, esp. in the context of business or politics: *a red power tie.* ■ [with modifier] used in the names of movements aiming to enhance the status of a specified group: *gay power.* **3** physical strength and force exerted by something or someone: *the power of the storm.* ■ capacity or performance of an engine or other device: *he applied full power.* ■ the capacity of something to affect the emotions or intellect strongly: *the lyrical power of his prose.* ■ [as modifier] denoting a sports player, team, or style of play that makes use of power rather than finesse: *a power pitcher.* ■ the magnifying capacity of a lens. **4** energy that is produced by mechanical, electrical, or other means and used to operate a device: *generating power from waste* | [as modifier] *power cables.* ■ electrical energy supplied to an area, building, etc.: *the power went off.* ■ [as modifier] driven by such energy: *a power drill.* ■ Physics the time-rate of doing work, measured in watts or less frequently horsepower. **5** Mathematics the number of times a certain number is to be multiplied by itself: *2 to the power of 4 equals 16.*
▶ **v. 1** [with obj.] supply (a device) with mechanical or electrical energy: *the car is powered by a fuel-injected 3.0-liter engine* | [as adj. in combination] **(-powered)** *a nuclear-powered submarine.* ■ **(power something up/down)** switch a device on or off: *the officer powered up the fighter's radar.* **2** [no obj.] move or travel with great speed or force: *they powered past the dock toward the mouth of the creek.* ■ [with obj.] direct (something, esp. a ball) with great force: *Nicholas powered a header into the net.*
– PHRASES **do someone/something a power of good** informal be very beneficial to someone or something. **in the power of** under the control of: *a church ministering in the power of the Holy Spirit.* **power behind the throne** a person or organization that exerts authority or influence without having formal status. **the powers that be** the authorities. [with biblical allusion to Rom. 13:1.]
– ORIGIN Middle English: from Anglo-Norman French *poeir*, from an alteration of Latin *posse* 'be able.'

pow·er-as·sist·ed ▶ **adj.** (esp. of steering or brakes in a motor vehicle) using an inanimate source of power to assist manual operation.

pow·er base ▶ **n.** a source of authority, influence, or support, esp. in politics or negotiations: *the party's power base was confined to one province.*

pow·er·beads /ˈpou(-ə)rˌbēdz/ ▶ **n.** a bracelet or necklace of round beads made of semiprecious stones that are purported to enhance the spiritual well-being of the wearer.

pow·er bloc (also **block**) ▶ **n.** an association of groups, esp. nations, having a common interest and acting as a single political force.

pow·er·boat /ˈpou(-ə)rˌbōt/ ▶ **n.** a motorboat designed for racing or recreation.

pow·er break·fast ▶ **n.** a working breakfast, esp. one at which powerful politicians, executives, etc., hold important discussions.

pow·er·bro·ker /ˈpou(-ə)rˌbrōkər/ (also **power broker**) ▶ **n.** a person who deliberately affects the distribution of political or economic power by exerting influence or by intrigue.
– DERIVATIVES **pow·er·bro·ker·ing** (also **powerbroking**) **n. & adj.**

pow·er dive ▶ **n.** a steep dive of an aircraft with the engines providing thrust.
▶ **v. (power-dive)** [no obj.] perform a power dive.

pow·er fac·tor ▶ **n.** the ratio of the actual electrical power dissipated by an AC circuit to the product of the r.m.s. values of current and voltage. The difference between the two is caused by reactance in the circuit and represents power that does no useful work.

pow·er for·ward ▶ **n.** Basketball a large forward who plays in the low post and typically has good rebounding skills.

pow·er·ful /ˈpou(-ə)rfəl/ ▶ **adj.** having great power or strength: *a fast, powerful car* | *computers are now more compact and powerful.* ■ (of a person, organization, or country) having control and influence over people and events: *the world's most powerful nation.* ■ having a strong effect on people's feelings or thoughts: *his photomontages are powerful antiwar images.*
▶ **adv.** [as submodifier] chiefly dialect very: *walking in this weather is powerful hot work.*
– DERIVATIVES **pow·er·ful·ly** /-f(ə)lē/ **adv.**, **pow·er·ful·ness n.**

pow·er·head /ˈpou(-ə)rˌhed/ ▶ **n. 1** informal a powerful egomaniac: *record-industry powerheads.* **2** any of various mechanical or electrical devices, including. ■ a submersible pump for an aquarium that creates current within a tank. ■ a vacuum-cleaner attachment that houses an independent motor that drives a carpet-beating rotating brush. See also **BEATER BAR.** ■ the internal combustion engine of an outboard motor. ■ the power unit of an automatic garage door opener.

pow·er·house /ˈpou(-ə)rˌhous/ ▶ **n.** a person or thing of great energy, strength, or power. ■ another term for **POWER PLANT.**

pow·er law ▶ **n.** Mathematics a relationship between two quantities such that one is proportional to a fixed power of the other.

pow·er·less /ˈpou(-ə)rləs/ ▶ **adj.** [often with infinitive] without ability, influence, or power: *troops were powerless to stop last night's shooting.*
– DERIVATIVES **pow·er·less·ly adv.**, **pow·er·less·ness n.**

pow·er·lift·ing /ˈpou(-ə)rˌliftiNG/ ▶ **n.** a form of competitive weightlifting in which contestants attempt three types of lift in a set sequence.
– DERIVATIVES **pow·er·lift·er** /-tər/ **n.**

pow·er line ▶ **n.** a cable carrying electrical power, esp. one supported by pylons or poles.

pow·er lunch ▶ **n.** a working lunch, esp. one at which powerful politicians, executives, etc., hold important discussions.

pow·er nap ▶ **n.** a short sleep taken during the working day in order to restore one's mental alertness.

pow·er of at·tor·ney ▶ **n.** Law the authority to act for another person in specified or all legal or financial matters. ■ a legal document giving such authority to someone.

pow·er pack ▶ **n.** a self-contained and typically transportable unit that stores and supplies electrical power. ■ a transformer for converting an alternating current to a direct current at a different (usually lower) voltage.

pow·er plant ▶ **n.** an installation where electrical power is generated for distribution. ■ an engine or other apparatus that provides power for a machine, building, etc.

pow·er play ▶ **n. 1** tactics exhibiting or intended to increase a person's power or influence: *the sexual power play of their relationship* | *the petty power plays of showbiz.* **2** tactics in a team sport involving the concentration of players at a particular point. ■ Ice Hockey a situation in which a team has a numerical advantage over its opponents while one or more players is serving a penalty.

Pow·er·Point /ˈpouərˌpoint/ ▶ **n.** trademark a software package designed to create electronic presentations consisting of a series of separate pages or slides.

pow·er pole ▶ **n.** a pole, mast, or tower that carries electric wires.

pow·er pol·i·tics ▶ **plural n.** [treated as sing. or pl.] political action by a person or group that makes use of or is intended to increase their power or influence.

pow·er pop ▶ **n.** a style of pop music characterized by a strong melody line, heavy use of guitars, and simple rhythm.

pow·er rat·ing ▶ **n. 1** the amount of electrical power required for a particular device: *a continuous power rating of 150 watts.* **2** a numerical representation of a sports team's strength for betting purposes: *a 99 power rating and a home field edge of four points.*

pow·er se·ries ▶ **n.** Mathematics an infinite series of the form $\Sigma a_n x n$ (where *n* is a positive integer). ■ a generalization of this for more than one variable.

pow·er-shar·ing ▶ **n.** a policy agreed between political parties or within a coalition to share responsibility for decision-making and political action.

pow·er shov·el ▶ **n.** a mechanical excavator.

pow·er slide ▶ **n.** a deliberate controlled skid in a vehicle, usually done in order to turn corners at high speed.

pow·er spec·trum ▶ **n.** (pl. **power spectra**) Physics the distribution of the energy of a waveform among its different frequency components.
– DERIVATIVES **pow·er spec·tral adj.**

pow·er sta·tion ▶ **n.** another term for **POWER PLANT.**

pow·er steer·ing ▶ **n.** power-assisted steering.

pow·er stroke ▶ **n.** the stage of the cycle of an internal combustion engine in which the piston is driven outward by the expansion of gases.

pow·er struc·ture ▶ **n. 1** the hierarchy that encompasses the most powerful people in an organization: *inside the power structure of the American Catholic Church.* **2** the people in such a hierarchy: *there are certain natural leaders of the underclasses, and the power structure interprets what they do as a crime.*

pow·er take·off ▶ **n.** a device that transfers mechanical power from an engine to another piece of equipment, esp. on a tractor or similar vehicle.

pow·er train ▶ **n.** the mechanism that transmits the drive from the engine of a vehicle to its axle. ■ this mechanism, the engine, and the axle considered collectively.

pow·er trip ▶ **n.** a self-aggrandizing quest for ever-increasing control over others.

pow·er-up ▶ **n.** the action of switching on an electrical device, esp. a computer. ■ (in a computer game) a bonus that a player can collect and that gives their character an advantage, such as more strength or firepower.

pow·er us·er ▶ **n. 1** a consumer of electrical power. **2** Computing a user who needs products having the most features and the fastest performance.

pow·er walk·ing ▶ **n.** a form of cardiopulmonary exercise consisting of fast walking with exaggerated swinging of the arms.

Pow·ha·tan[1] /ˌpou-əˈtan, pouˈhatn/ ▶ **n.** (pl. **same** or **Powhatans**) **1** a member of an American Indian people of eastern Virginia. **2** the Algonquian language of this people.
▶ **adj.** of or relating to this people or their language.
– ORIGIN from the chief nicknamed *Powhatan*, referring to his residence at the falls of the James River, from Virginia Algonquian *pawatan* 'river falls.'

Pow·ha·tan[2] (c.1550–1618), Algonquian Indian chief; Indian name **Wa-hun-sen-a-cawh** or **Wahunsonacock**. He was the leader of Powhatan's Confederacy, an alliance of about 30 tribes that were located primarily in eastern Virginia. Often noted for his ruthlessness, he made peace with the colonists after his daughter Pocahontas married Englishman John Rolfe in 1614.

pow·wow /ˈpouˌwou/ ▶ **n.** a North American Indian ceremony involving feasting, singing, and dancing. ■ a conference or meeting for discussion, esp. among friends or colleagues.
▶ **v.** [no obj.] informal hold a powwow; confer: *news squads powwowed nervously.*
– ORIGIN early 17th cent.: from Narragansett *powáw* 'magician' (literally 'he dreams').

Pow·ys /ˈpōis/ a former Welsh kingdom. At its most powerful in the early 12th century, by 1284 it had been conquered by the English.

pox /päks/ ▶ **n.** any of several viral diseases producing a rash of pimples that become pus-filled and leave pockmarks on healing. ■ **(the pox)** informal syphilis. ■ **(the pox)** historical smallpox. ■ a plant disease that causes pocklike spots.
– PHRASES **a pox on** archaic used to express anger or intense irritation with someone or something: *a pox on both their houses!*

P

– ORIGIN late Middle English: alteration of *pocks*, plural of **POCK**.

pox·vi·rus /ˈpäksˌvīrəs/ ▶ **n.** Medicine any of a group of large DNA viruses that cause smallpox and similar infectious diseases in vertebrates.

Poz·nań /ˈpōznan, ˈpôzˌnänyə/ a city in northwestern Poland; pop. 564,035 (2007). It was overrun by the Germans in 1939 and was severely damaged during World War II. German name **POSEN**.

Po·zsony /ˈpôˌzHônyə/ Hungarian name for **BRATISLAVA**.

poz·zo·la·na /ˌpätsəˈlänə/ ▶ **n.** a type of volcanic ash used for mortar or for cement that sets under water.
– ORIGIN early 18th cent.: from Italian, from *pozz(u)olana* '(earth) of Pozzuoli,' a town near Naples.

pp ▶ **abbr.** ■ pages: *pp 71–73*. ■ parcel post. ■ past participle. ■ per person. ■ per procurationem (used when signing a letter on someone else's behalf). [Latin.] ■ Music pianissimo. ■ postpaid. ■ privately printed.

PPA ▶ **abbr.** phenylpropanolamine.

p.p.a. ▶ **abbr.** per power of attorney.

ppb (also **p.p.b.**) ▶ **abbr.** ■ (in publishing) paper, printing, and binding. ■ parts per billion.

ppd. ▶ **abbr.** ■ postpaid. ■ prepaid.

pph. ▶ **abbr.** pamphlet.

ppi ▶ **abbr.** Computing pixels per inch, a measure of the resolution of display screens, scanners, and printers.

PPLO ▶ **abbr.** pleuropneumonia-like organism.

ppm ▶ **abbr.** ■ part(s) per million: *water containing 1 ppm fluoride*. ■ Computing page(s) per minute, a measure of the speed of printers.

PPO ▶ **abbr.** preferred-provider organization.

PPP ▶ **abbr.** ■ Pakistan People's Party. ■ (in computing) point to point protocol, which allows data conforming to the Internet protocol IP to be handled on a serial line. ■ purchasing power parity (a way of measuring what an amount of money will buy in different countries).

PPS ▶ **abbr.** additional postscript: *PS Those photos are awful! PPS Can I have your other address?*

ppt ▶ **abbr.** Chemistry precipitate.

pptn. ▶ **abbr.** precipitation.

PPV ▶ **abbr.** pay-per-view, a system in which television viewers are charged for the length of time that they watch programs.

PQ ▶ **abbr.** ■ Parti Québécois. ■ Province of Quebec.

p.q. ▶ **abbr.** previous question.

PR ▶ **abbr.** ■ parliamentary report. ■ press release. ■ prize ring. ■ proportional representation. ■ public relations. ■ Puerto Rico.

Pr ▶ **abbr.** ■ preferred (stock). ■ Priest. ■ Prince. ■ Provençal. ▶ **symbol** the chemical element praseodymium.

pr ▶ **abbr.** ■ pair: *patterned gloves, $17.95/pr*. ■ archaic per: *$6 pr day*.

PRA ▶ **abbr.** progressive retinal atrophy (a disease afflicting dogs).

prac·ti·ca·bil·i·ty /ˌpraktikəˈbilətē/ ▶ **n.** the quality of being practicable; viability: *the practicability of his ideas has nothing to do with their truth*.

prac·ti·ca·ble /ˈpraktikəbəl/ ▶ **adj.** able to be done or put into practice successfully: *the measures will be put into effect as soon as is reasonably practicable*. ■ able to be used; useful: *signal processing can let you transform a signal into a practicable form*.
– DERIVATIVES **prac·ti·ca·bly** /-blē/ **adv.**
– ORIGIN mid 17th cent.: from French *praticable*, from *pratiquer* 'put into practice.'

prac·ti·cal /ˈpraktikəl/ ▶ **adj.** **1** of or concerned with the actual doing or use of something rather than with theory and ideas: *there are two obvious practical applications of the research*. ■ (of an idea, plan, or method) likely to succeed or be effective in real circumstances; feasible: *neither of these strategies is practical for smaller businesses*. ■ suitable for a particular purpose: *a practical, stylish kitchen*. ■ (of a person) sensible and realistic in their approach to a situation or problem: *I'm not unfeeling, just trying to be practical*. ■ (of a person) skilled at manual tasks: *Steve'll fix it—he's quite practical*.
2 so nearly the case that it can be regarded as so; virtual: *it was a practical certainty that he would try to raise more money*.
– PHRASES **for all practical purposes** virtually, or essentially: *Zimmerman had become, for all practical purposes, an arms smuggler*.
– ORIGIN late 16th cent.: from archaic *practic* 'practical' (from Old French *practique*, via late Latin from Greek *praktikos* 'concerned with action,' from *prattein* 'do, act') + **-AL**.

prac·ti·cal·i·ty /ˌpraktiˈkalətē/ ▶ **n.** (pl. **practicalities**) **1** the quality or state of being practical: *there are still major doubts about the practicality of the proposal*.
2 (**practicalities**) the aspects of a situation that involve the actual doing or experience of something rather than theories or ideas: *the practicalities of living at sea*.

prac·ti·cal joke ▶ **n.** a trick played on someone in order to make them look foolish and to amuse others.
– DERIVATIVES **prac·ti·cal jok·er** **n.**

prac·ti·cal·ly /ˈpraktik(ə)lē/ ▶ **adv.** **1** virtually; almost: *the risk of default was practically zero | the place was practically empty*.
2 in a practical manner. ■ [sentence adverb] in practical terms: *the law isn't unreasonable or practically inconvenient*.

prac·ti·cal nurse ▶ **n.** a nurse who has completed a training course of a lower standard than a registered nurse, esp. one who is licensed by the state to perform certain duties (a **licensed practical nurse**).

prac·tice /ˈpraktəs/ ▶ **n.** **1** the actual application or use of an idea, belief, or method as opposed to theories about such application or use: *the principles and practice of teaching | he* **put** *his self-defense training* **into practice** *by helping police arrest the armed robber*. ■ the customary, habitual, or expected procedure of something: *current nursing practice | modern child-rearing practices*. ■ the carrying out or exercise of a profession, esp. that of a doctor or lawyer: *he abandoned medical practice for the Church*. ■ the business or premises of a doctor or lawyer: *Dr. Weiss has a practice in Essex*. ■ an established method of legal procedure.
2 repeated exercise in or performance of an activity or skill so as to acquire or maintain proficiency in it: *it must have taken a lot of practice to become so fluent*. ■ a period of time spent doing this: *daily choir practices*.
▶ **v.** [with obj.] (Brit. **practise**) **1** perform (an activity) or exercise (a skill) repeatedly or regularly in order to improve or maintain one's proficiency: *I need to practice my French* | [no obj.] *they were practicing for the Olympics*.
2 carry out or perform (a particular activity, method, or custom) habitually or regularly: *we still practice some of these rituals today*. ■ actively pursue or be engaged in (a particular profession or occupation): *he began to practice law* | [no obj.] *he practiced as an attorney* | (as adj. **practicing**) *a practicing architect*. ■ observe the teaching and rules of (a particular religion): *they are free to practice their religion without fear of persecution* | (as adj. **practicing**) *a practicing Roman Catholic*. ■ [no obj.] archaic scheme or plot for an evil purpose: *what a tangled web we weave when we first practice to deceive*.
– PHRASES **in practice** in reality (used to refer to what actually happens as opposed to what is meant or believed to happen): *in theory this method is ideal—in practice it is unrealistic*. ■ currently proficient in a particular activity or skill as a result of repeated exercise or performance of it. **out of practice** not currently proficient in a particular activity or skill due to not having exercised or performed it for some time: *he was out of practice at interrogation*. **practice makes perfect** used to convey that regular exercise of an activity or skill is the way to become proficient in it, esp. when encouraging someone to persist in it. **practice what one preaches** do what one advises others to do.
– DERIVATIVES **prac·tic·er** **n.**
– ORIGIN late Middle English: the verb from Old French *practiser* or medieval Latin *practizare*, alteration of *practicare* 'perform, carry out,' from *practica* 'practice,' from Greek *praktikē*, feminine (used as a noun) of *praktikos* (see **PRACTICAL**); the noun from the verb in the earlier spelling *practise*, on the pattern of pairs such as *advise, advice*.

prac·ticed /ˈpraktəst/ (Brit. **practised**) ▶ **adj.** expert, typically as the result of much experience: *admiring the dress with a practiced eye | the waiter was practiced at disrupting moments of intimacy*.

prac·ti·cian /prakˈtisHən/ ▶ **n.** archaic a person who practices a profession or occupation, esp. a practical one; a practitioner.
– ORIGIN late 15th cent.: from Old French *practicien*, from *practique* 'practical' (see **PRACTICAL**).

prac·ti·cum /ˈpraktikəm/ ▶ **n.** (pl. **practicums**) a practical section of a course of study.
– ORIGIN early 20th cent.: from late Latin, neuter of *practicus* 'practical.'

prac·tise ▶ **v.** British spelling of **PRACTICE**.

prac·ti·tion·er /prakˈtisHənər/ ▶ **n.** a person actively engaged in an art, discipline, or profession, esp. medicine: *patients are treated by skilled practitioners*.
– ORIGIN mid 16th cent.: extension of obsolete *practitian*, variant of **PRACTICIAN**.

prae- ▶ **prefix** (used esp. in words regarded as Latin or relating to Roman antiquity, e.g., *praenomen*): equivalent to **PRE-**.
– ORIGIN from Latin.

prae·ci·pe /ˈpresəˌpē, ˈprē-/ ▶ **n.** Law an order requesting a writ or other legal document. ■ historical a writ demanding action or an explanation of nonaction.
– ORIGIN Latin (the first word of the writ), imperative of *praecipere* 'enjoin, command.' See also **PRECEPT**.

prae·mu·ni·re /ˌprēmyo͞oˈnīrē/ ▶ **n.** historical the offense of asserting or maintaining papal jurisdiction in England. ■ a writ charging a sheriff to summon a person accused of this offense.
– ORIGIN late Middle English: from medieval Latin, 'forewarn,' for Latin *praemonere*, from *prae* 'beforehand' + *monere* 'warn.' The term comes from *praemunire facias* 'that you warn (a person to appear),' part of the wording in the writ.

prae·no·men /prēˈnōmən/ ▶ **n.** an ancient Roman's first or personal name, for example *Marcus* Tullius Cicero.
– ORIGIN Latin, from *prae* 'before' + *nomen* 'name.'

Prae·se·pe /prīˈsēpē/ Astronomy a large open cluster of stars in the constellation Cancer; the Beehive.
– ORIGIN Latin, literally 'manger, hive.'

prae·sid·i·um /priˈsidēəm, prī-/ ▶ **n.** Brit. variant spelling of **PRESIDIUM**.

prae·tor /ˈprētər/ (also **pretor**) ▶ **n.** Roman History each of two ancient Roman magistrates ranking below consul.
– DERIVATIVES **prae·to·ri·al** /prēˈtôrēəl/ **adj.**, **prae·tor·ship** /ˈprētərˌsHip/ **n.**
– ORIGIN from Latin *praetor*, perhaps from *prae* 'before' + *it-* 'gone' (from the verb *ire*).

prae·to·ri·an /prēˈtôrēən/ (also **pretorian**) ▶ **adj.** Roman History of or having the powers of a praetor. ▶ **n.** a man of praetorian rank.

prae·to·ri·an guard ▶ **n.** Roman History the bodyguard of the Roman emperor.

prag·mat·ic /pragˈmatik/ ▶ **adj.** dealing with things sensibly and realistically in a way that is based on practical rather than theoretical considerations: *a pragmatic approach to politics*. ■ relating to philosophical or political pragmatism. ■ Linguistics of or relating to pragmatics.
– DERIVATIVES **prag·mat·i·cal·ly** /-ik(ə)lē/ **adv.**
– ORIGIN late 16th cent. (in the senses 'busy, interfering, conceited'): via Latin from Greek *pragmatikos* 'relating to fact,' from *pragma* 'deed' (from the stem of *prattein* 'do'). The current sense dates from the mid 19th cent.

prag·mat·ics /pragˈmatiks/ ▶ **plural n.** [usu. treated as sing.] the branch of linguistics dealing with language in use and the contexts in which it is used, including such matters as deixis, taking turns in conversation, text organization, presupposition, and implicature.

prag·mat·ic sanc·tion ▶ **n.** historical an imperial or royal ordinance or decree that has the force of law.
– ORIGIN translating Law Latin *pragmatica sanctio*.

prag·ma·tism /ˈpragməˌtizəm/ ▶ **n.** **1** a pragmatic attitude or policy: *ideology was tempered with pragmatism*.
2 Philosophy an approach that assesses the truth of meaning of theories or beliefs in terms of the success of their practical application.
– DERIVATIVES **prag·ma·tist** **n.**, **prag·ma·tis·tic** /ˌpragməˈtistik/ **adj.**
– ORIGIN mid 19th cent.: from Greek *pragma*, *pragmat-* 'deed' (see **PRAGMATIC**) + **-ISM**.

Prague /präg/ the capital of the Czech Republic, in the northeastern part of the country, on the Vltava River; pop. 1,196,454 (2007). Czech name **PRAHA**.

Prague School a group of linguists established in Prague in 1926 who developed distinctive-feature theory in phonology and communicative dynamism in language teaching. Leading members were Nikolai Trubetzkoy (1890–1938) and Roman Jakobson.

Prague Spring a brief period of liberalization in Czechoslovakia, ending in August 1968, during which a program of political, economic, and cultural reform was initiated.

Pra·ha /ˈprähä/ Czech name for **PRAGUE**.

pra·hu /ˈprou, ˈpräˌo͞o/ ▶ **n.** variant spelling of **PROA**.

Prai·a /ˈprīə/ the capital of the Cape Verde Islands, a port on the island of São Tiago; pop. 126,000 (est. 2007).

Prai·ri·al /prerˈyäl/ ▶ **n.** the ninth month of the French Republican calendar (1793–1805), originally running from May 20 to June 18.
– ORIGIN French, from *prairie* 'meadow.'

P

prai·rie /ˈpre(ə)rē/ ▶ **n.** **1** a large open area of grassland, esp. in the Mississippi River valley. **2** (**Prairie**) [often as modifier] a steam locomotive of 2-6-2 wheel arrangement.
– ORIGIN late 18th cent.: from French, from Old French *praerie*, from Latin *pratum* 'meadow.'

prai·rie chick·en (also **prairie hen**) ▶ **n.** a large North American grouse found on the prairies, the male being noted for the display dance in which it inflates two orange neck pouches and makes a booming sound. ● Genus *Tympanuchus*, family Tetraonidae: two species, in particular the **greater prairie chicken** (*T. cupido*).

prai·rie dog ▶ **n.** a gregarious ground squirrel that lives in interconnected burrows that may cover many acres. It is native to the grasslands of North America. ● Genus *Cynomys*, family Sciuridae: several species.

prai·rie-dog·ging (also **prairie dogging**) ▶ **n.** informal the practice of looking over the wall of an office cubicle to observe coworkers: *stop prairie-dogging and get back to work.*

prai·rie oys·ter ▶ **n.** **1** a drink made with a raw egg and seasoning, drunk as a cure for a hangover. **2** (**prairie oysters**) the testicles of a calf cooked and served as food.

prai·rie schoon·er ▶ **n.** a covered wagon used by the 19th-century pioneers in crossing the North American prairies. The prairie schooner resembled the Conestoga wagon but was smaller.

Prai·rie State a nickname for the state of **ILLINOIS**.

prai·rie wolf ▶ **n.** another term for **COYOTE**.

prai·rie wool ▶ **n.** Canadian the natural grassy plant cover of prairie land.

praise /prāz/ ▶ **v.** [with obj.] express warm approval or admiration of: *we can't praise Chris enough—he did a brilliant job.* ■ express one's respect and gratitude toward (a deity), esp. in song: *we praise God for past blessings.*
▶ **n.** the expression of approval or admiration for someone or something: *the audience was full of praise for the whole production.* ■ the expression of respect and gratitude as an act of worship: *give praise to God.*
– PHRASES **praise be** archaic used as an expression of relief, joy, or gratitude. **sing the praises of** express enthusiastic approval or admiration of (someone or something): *Uncle Felix never stopped singing her praises.*
– DERIVATIVES **praise·ful** /-fəl/ **adj.**
– ORIGIN Middle English (also in the sense 'set a price on, attach value to'): from Old French *preisier* 'to prize, praise,' from late Latin *pretiare*, from Latin *pretium* 'price.' Compare with **PRIZE**[1].

praise·wor·thy /ˈprāzˌwərT͟Hē/ ▶ **adj.** deserving approval and admiration: *they displayed a praiseworthy sense of responsibility.*
– DERIVATIVES **praise·wor·thi·ly** /-ˌwərT͟Həlē/ **adv.**, **praise·wor·thi·ness** **n.**

praj·na /ˈprəZHnə/ ▶ **n.** Buddhism direct insight into the truth taught by the Buddha, as a faculty required to attain enlightenment.
– ORIGIN from Sanskrit *prajñā*.

Pra·krit /ˈpräkˌrit/ ▶ **n.** any of the ancient or medieval vernacular dialects of northern and central India that existed alongside or were derived from Sanskrit.
– ORIGIN from Sanskrit *prākṛta* 'unrefined, natural.' Compare with **SANSKRIT**.

pra·kri·ti /ˈprəkritē/ ▶ **n.** (in Vedanta) the prime material energy of which all matter is composed.

pra·line /ˈprāˌlēn/ ▶ **n.** a smooth, sweet substance made by boiling nuts in sugar and grinding the mixture, used esp. as a filling for chocolates. ■ a crisp or semicrisp candy made by a similar process and typically consisting of butter, brown sugar, and pecans.
– ORIGIN early 18th cent.: from French, named after Marshal de Plessis-*Praslin* (1598–1675), the French soldier whose cook invented it.

prall·tril·ler /ˈpräl,trilər/ ▶ **n.** a musical ornament consisting of one rapid alternation of the written note with the note immediately above it.
– ORIGIN mid 19th cent.: from German, from *prallen* 'rebound' + *Triller* 'a trill.'

pram[1] /pram/ ▶ **n.** short for **PERAMBULATOR**.
– ORIGIN late 19th cent.: contracted abbreviation of **PERAMBULATOR**.

pram[2] /präm, pram/ ▶ **n.** a flat-bottomed sailboat. ■ a small, flat-bottomed rowboat for fishing.
– ORIGIN late Middle English: from Middle Dutch *prame*, Middle Low German *prāme*, perhaps from Czech *prám* 'raft.'

pra·na /ˈpränə/ ▶ **n.** Hinduism breath, considered as a life-giving force.
– ORIGIN Sanskrit.

pran·a·ya·ma /ˌpränəˈyämə/ ▶ **n.** (in Hindu yoga) the regulation of the breath through certain techniques and exercises.
– ORIGIN Sanskrit, from *prāṇa* 'breath' + *āyāma* 'restraint.'

prance /prans/ ▶ **v.** [no obj.] (of a horse) move with high springy steps: *the pony was prancing around the paddock.* ■ (of a person) walk or move around with ostentatious, exaggerated movements: *she pranced around the lounge impersonating her favorite pop stars.*
▶ **n.** an act or instance of prancing.
– DERIVATIVES **pranc·er** **n.**
– ORIGIN late Middle English (as a verb): of unknown origin.

pran·di·al /ˈprandēəl/ ▶ **adj.** formal or humorous during or relating to dinner or lunch. ■ Medicine during or relating to the eating of food.
– ORIGIN early 19th cent.: from Latin *prandium* 'meal' + **-AL**.

Prand·tl /ˈpräntl/, Ludwig (1875–1953), German physicist. He established the existence of the boundary layer and made important studies on streamlining.

prang /praNG/ chiefly Brit. informal ▶ **v.** [with obj.] crash (a motor vehicle or aircraft). ■ dated bomb (a target) successfully from the air.
▶ **n.** a crash involving a motor vehicle or aircraft. ■ dated a bombing raid.
– ORIGIN 1940s: imitative.

prank /praNGk/ ▶ **n.** a practical joke or mischievous act.
– DERIVATIVES **prank·ish** **adj.**, **prank·ish·ness** **n.**
– ORIGIN early 16th cent. (denoting a wicked deed): of unknown origin.

prank·ster /ˈpraNGkstər/ ▶ **n.** a person fond of playing pranks.

prase /ˈprāz, prās/ ▶ **n.** a translucent, greenish variety of chalcedony.
– ORIGIN late 18th cent.: from French, via Latin from Greek *prasios* 'leek-green,' from *prason* 'leek.'

pra·se·o·dym·i·um /ˌprāzēōˈdimēəm/ ▶ **n.** the chemical element of atomic number 59, a soft silvery-white metal of the lanthanide series. (Symbol: **Pr**)
– ORIGIN late 19th cent.: modern Latin, from German *Praseodym*, from Greek *prasios* 'leek-green' (because of its green salts) + German *Didym* 'didymium.'

prat /prat/ ▶ **n.** informal **1** a person's buttocks. **2** Brit. an incompetent, stupid, or foolish person; an idiot.
– ORIGIN mid 16th cent. (sense 1): of unknown origin. Sense 2 dates from the 1960s.

prate /prāt/ ▶ **v.** [no obj.] talk foolishly or tediously about something.
– DERIVATIVES **prat·er** **n.** (rare).
– ORIGIN late Middle English: from Middle Dutch and Middle Low German *praten*, probably of imitative origin.

prat·fall /ˈpratˌfôl/ ▶ **n.** informal a fall onto one's buttocks: *he took a pratfall into the sand.* ■ a stupid and humiliating action: *the first political pratfalls of the new administration.*

prat·in·cole /ˈpratnˌkōl, ˈpratiNG-/ ▶ **n.** a long-winged, fork-tailed, insectivorous bird related to the plovers, resembling a swallow in flight and typically living near water. ● Genus *Glareola* (and *Stiltia*), family Glareolidae: several species, in particular *G. pratincole* of Africa and the Mediterranean.
– ORIGIN late 18th cent.: from modern Latin *pratincola*, from Latin *pratum* 'meadow' + *incola* 'inhabitant.'

pra·tique /praˈtēk/ ▶ **n.** historical permission granted to a ship to have dealings with a port, given after quarantine or on showing a clean bill of health.
– ORIGIN early 17th cent.: from French, literally 'practice,' via Italian from medieval Latin *practica*, feminine (used as a noun) of *practicus* 'practical.'

Pra·to /ˈprätō/ a city in northern Italy, northwest of Florence; pop. 185,091 (2008).

prat·tle /ˈpratl/ ▶ **v.** [no obj.] talk at length in a foolish or inconsequential way: *she began to prattle on about her visit to the dentist.*
▶ **n.** foolish or inconsequential talk: *do you intend to keep up this childish prattle?*
– DERIVATIVES **prat·tler** /ˈpratlər, ˈpratl-ər/ **n.**
– ORIGIN mid 16th cent.: from Middle Low German *pratelen*, from *praten* (see **PRATE**).

prau /prou/ ▶ **n.** variant spelling of **PROA**.

Prav·da /ˈprävdə/ a Russian daily newspaper, founded in 1912 and from 1918 to 1991 the official organ of the Soviet Communist Party.
– ORIGIN Russian, literally 'truth.'

prawn /prôn/ ▶ **n.** a marine crustacean that resembles a large shrimp. ● *Leander* and other genera, class Malacostraca.
– ORIGIN late Middle English: of unknown origin.

prax·is /ˈpraksəs/ ▶ **n.** formal practice, as distinguished from theory: *the gap between theory and praxis, text and world.* ■ accepted practice or custom: *patterns of Christian praxis in church and society.*
– ORIGIN late 16th cent.: via medieval Latin from Greek, literally 'doing,' from *prattein* 'do.'

Prax·it·e·les /prakˈsitlˌēz/ (mid 4th century BC), Athenian sculptor. Only one of his works, *Hermes Carrying the Infant Dionysus*, survives. He is also noted for a statue of Aphrodite, of which there are only Roman copies.

pray /prā/ ▶ **v.** [no obj.] address a solemn request or expression of thanks to a deity or other object of worship: *the whole family is praying for Michael* | [with obj.] *pray God this is true.* ■ wish or hope strongly for a particular outcome or situation: *after several days of rain, we were praying for sun* | [with clause] *I prayed that James wouldn't notice.*
▶ **adv.** formal or archaic used as a preface to polite requests or instructions: *pray continue.* ■ used as a way of adding ironic or sarcastic emphasis to a question: *and what, pray, was the purpose of that?*
– ORIGIN Middle English (in the sense 'ask earnestly'): from Old French *preier*, from late Latin *precare*, alteration of Latin *precari* 'entreat.'

prayer /pre(ə)r/ ▶ **n.** a solemn request for help or expression of thanks addressed to God or an object of worship: *I'll say a prayer for him* | *a commitment to a life of holiness through prayer and Bible-reading.* ■ (**prayers**) a religious service, esp. a regular one, at which people gather in order to pray together: *500 people were detained as they attended Friday prayers.* ■ an earnest hope or wish: *it is our prayer that the current progress on human rights will be sustained.*
– PHRASES **not have a prayer** informal have no chance at all of succeeding at something: *he doesn't have a prayer of toppling Tyson.*
– ORIGIN Middle English: from Old French *preiere*, based on Latin *precarius* 'obtained by entreaty,' from *prex*, *prec-* 'prayer.'

prayer beads ▶ **n.** a string of beads used in prayer, esp. a rosary.

prayer book ▶ **n.** a book containing the forms of prayer regularly used in Christian worship, esp. the Book of Common Prayer.

prayer flag ▶ **n.** (esp. in Tibetan Buddhism) a flag on which prayers are inscribed.

prayer·ful /ˈpre(ə)rfəl/ ▶ **adj.** (of an action or event) characterized by or expressive of prayer: *prayerful self-examination.* ■ (of a person) given to praying; devout.
– DERIVATIVES **prayer·ful·ly** **adv.**, **prayer·ful·ness** **n.**

prayer meet·ing ▶ **n.** an informal religious gathering or service during which prayers are offered.

Prayer of Ma·nas·ses /məˈnasēz/ a book of the Apocrypha consisting of a penitential prayer put into the mouth of Manasseh, king of Judah.

prayer plant ▶ **n.** a Brazilian plant with variegated leaves that are erect at night but lie flat during the day, grown as a houseplant. ● *Maranta leuconeura*, family Marantaceae.

prayer rug ▶ **n.** a small carpet used by Muslims for kneeling on when praying.

prayer shawl ▶ **n.** Judaism another term for **TALLITH**.

prayer stick ▶ **n.** a stick decorated with feathers, used by various American Indian peoples in religious ceremonies.

prayer wheel ▶ **n.** a revolving cylinder inscribed with or containing prayers, a revolution of which symbolizes the repetition of a prayer, used by Tibetan Buddhists.

pray·ing man·tis ▶ **n.** see **MANTIS**.

pra·zi·quan·tel /ˌpräziˈkwantl, -ˈkwäntl/ ▶ **n.** Medicine a synthetic anthelmintic drug used in the treatment of schistosomiasis and other infestations of humans and animals with parasitic trematodes or cestodes.
– ORIGIN 1970s: from *p(y)razi(ne)* + *-quantel* (perhaps from elements of **QUINOLINE** and **ANTHELMINTIC**).

PRC ▶ **abbr.** People's Republic of China.

pre /prē/ ▶ **prep.** previous to; before: *the tree was almost certainly planted pre 1700.*
– ORIGIN 1960s: independent usage of **PRE-**.

pre- ▶ **prefix** before (in time, place, order, degree, or importance): *preadolescent* | *precaution* | *precede.*
– ORIGIN from Latin *prae-*.

preach /prēCH/ ▶ **v.** [no obj.] deliver a sermon or religious address to an assembled group of people, typically in church: *he preached to a large*

PRONUNCIATION KEY ə *ago, up*; ər *over, fur*; a *hat*; ā *ate*; ä *car*; e *let*; ē *see*; i *fit*; ī *by*; NG *sing*; ō *go*; ô *law, for*; oi *toy*; o͝o *good*; o͞o *goo*; ou *out*; TH *thin*; T͟H *then*; ZH *vision*

P

congregation | [with obj.] *our pastor will preach the sermon.* ■ [with obj.] publicly proclaim or teach (a religious message or belief): *a church that preaches the good news.* ■ [with obj.] earnestly advocate (a belief or course of action): *my parents have always preached toleration and moderation.* ■ give moral advice to someone in an annoying or pompously self-righteous way: *viewers want to be entertained, not preached at.*
– PHRASES **preach to the choir** (or **the converted**) advocate something to people who already share one's convictions about its merits or importance.
– DERIVATIVES **preach·ing n.**
– ORIGIN Middle English: from Old French *prechier,* from Latin *praedicare* 'proclaim,' in ecclesiastical Latin 'preach,' from *prae* 'before' + *dicare* 'declare.'

preach·er /ˈprēCHər/ ▶ **n.** a person who preaches, esp. a minister of religion.
– ORIGIN Middle English: from Old French *precheor,* from ecclesiastical Latin *praedicator,* from the verb *praedicare* (see **PREACH**).

preach·i·fy /ˈprēCHiˌfī/ ▶ **v.** (**preachifies, preachifying, preachified**) [no obj.] informal preach or moralize tediously: *he's a fund-raiser as well as a minister, but he's a preacher who doesn't preachify.*

preach·ment /ˈprēCHmənt/ ▶ **n.** dogmatic instruction and exhortation: *successful leadership is a process of persuasion rather than preachment.*
– ORIGIN Middle English: from Old French *prechement,* from late Latin *praedicamentum.*

preach·y /ˈprēCHē/ ▶ **adj.** (**preachier, preachiest**) informal having or revealing a tendency to give moral advice in a tedious or self-righteous way: *some were put off by the preachy tone of these stories.*
– DERIVATIVES **preach·i·ness n.**

pre·a·dapt /ˌprēəˈdapt/ ▶ **v.** [with obj.] Biology adapt (an organism or part of an organism) for life in conditions it has yet to encounter: *the insulation of marine mammals in temperate seas preadapts them for polar seas.*
– DERIVATIVES **pre·ad·ap·ta·tion** /ˈprēˌadˌapˈtāSHən/ **n.**

pre·ad·o·les·cent /ˈprēˌadlˈesənt/ ▶ **adj.** (of a child) having nearly reached adolescence. ■ of, relating to, or occurring in the two or three years preceding adolescence: *Mozart's preadolescent sonatas.*
▶ **n.** a preadolescent child.
– DERIVATIVES **pre·ad·o·les·cence n.**

pre·ag·ri·cul·tur·al /ˈprēˌagriˈkəlCHərəl/ ▶ **adj.** denoting a people, tribe, or culture that has not developed agriculture as a means of subsistence.

pre-AIDS /prēˈādz/ ▶ **adj.** following infection with HIV but before the full development of AIDS: *pre-AIDS patients.* ■ before the recognition of AIDS as a disease: *we are dealing with an era that was pre-AIDS.*

Preak·ness /ˈprēknis/ ▶ **n.** an annual horse race for three-year-olds at Pimlico racetrack in Baltimore, Maryland. Held two weeks after the Kentucky Derby, it is the second race of horse racing's Triple Crown.

pre·am·ble /ˈprēˌambəl/ ▶ **n.** a preliminary or preparatory statement; an introduction: *what she said was by way of a preamble* | *I gave him the bad news without preamble.* ■ Law the introductory part of a statute or deed, stating its purpose, aims, and justification.
– DERIVATIVES **pre·am·bu·lar** /prēˈambyələr/ **adj.** (formal).
– ORIGIN late Middle English: from Old French *preambule,* from medieval Latin *praeambulum,* from late Latin *praeambulus* 'going before.'

pre·amp /ˈprēˌamp/ ▶ **n.** short for **PREAMPLIFIER.**

pre·am·pli·fi·er /prēˈampləˌfīər/ ▶ **n.** an electronic device that amplifies a very weak signal, for example from a microphone or pickup, and transmits it to a main amplifier.
– DERIVATIVES **pre·am·pli·fy v.** (**preamplifies, preamplifying, preamplified**).

pre·ar·range /ˌprēəˈrānj/ ▶ **v.** [with obj.] (usu. as adj. **prearranged**) arrange or agree upon (something) in advance: *did she have a prearranged meeting?*
– DERIVATIVES **pre·ar·range·ment n.**

Preb. ▶ **abbr.** Prebendary.

preb·end /ˈprebənd/ ▶ **n.** historical the portion of the revenues of a cathedral or collegiate church formerly granted to a canon or member of the chapter as his stipend. ■ the property from which such a stipend was derived. ■ another term for **PREBENDARY.**
– ORIGIN late Middle English: from Old French *prebende,* from late Latin *praebenda* 'things to be supplied, pension,' neuter plural gerundive of Latin *praebere* 'to grant,' from *prae* 'before' + *habere* 'hold, have.'

pre·ben·dal /priˈbendəl, ˈprebəndəl/ ▶ **adj.** of or relating to a prebend or a prebendary: *the prebendal manor.*

preb·en·dar·y /ˈprebənˌderē/ ▶ **n.** (pl. **prebendaries**) an honorary canon. ■ historical a canon of a cathedral or collegiate church whose income originally came from a prebend.
– DERIVATIVES **preb·en·dar·y·ship** /-ˌSHip/ **n.**
– ORIGIN late Middle English: from medieval Latin *praebendarius,* from late Latin *praebenda* 'pension' (see **PREBEND**).

pre·bi·ot·ic /ˈprēˌbīˈätik/ ▶ **adj.** existing or occurring before the emergence of life.
▶ **n.** a nondigestible food ingredient that promotes the growth of beneficial microorganisms in the intestines.

pre·board /prēˈbôrd/ ▶ **v.** [with obj.] allow (a particular passenger or group of passengers) to board an aircraft before the rest of the passengers.

pre·book /prēˈbo͝ok, ˈprēˌbo͝ok/ ▶ **v.** [with obj.] (usu. as adj. **prebooked**) book (something) in advance: *a prebooked hotel reservation* | (as noun **prebooking**) *prebooking is essential.*
– DERIVATIVES **pre·book·a·ble adj.**

Pre·bo·re·al /prēˈbôrēəl/ ▶ **adj.** Geology of, relating to, or denoting the first climatic stage of the postglacial period in northern Europe, between the Younger Dryas and Boreal stages (about 10,000 to 9,000 years ago). The stage was marked by a rapid spread of birch and pine forests. ■ (as noun **the Preboreal**) the Preboreal climatic stage.

pre·born /prēˈbôrn/ ▶ **adj.** (esp. in the language of antiabortion campaigners) relating to a fetus.

pre·but·tal /prēˈbətl/ ▶ **n.** (in politics) a response formulated in anticipation of a criticism; a preemptive rebuttal.
– ORIGIN 1990s: blend of *pre-* and *(re)buttal.*

prec. ▶ **abbr.** ■ preceded. ■ preceding.

pre·cal·cu·lus /prēˈkalkyələs/ ▶ **n.** a course in mathematics that prepares a student for calculus.

Pre·cam·bri·an /prēˈkambrēən, -ˈkām-/ ▶ **adj.** Geology of, relating to, or denoting the earliest eon, preceding the Cambrian period and the Phanerozoic eon. Compare with **CRYPTOZOIC.** ■ (as noun **the Precambrian**) the Precambrian eon or the system of rocks deposited during it.

> The Precambrian extended from the origin of the earth (believed to have been about 4,600 million years ago) to about 570 million years ago, representing nearly ninety percent of geological time. The oldest known Precambrian rocks have been dated to about 3,800 million years old, and the earliest living organisms date from the latter part of the eon. The Precambrian is now replaced in formal stratigraphic schemes by the Archean, Proterozoic, and (in some schemes) Priscoan eons.

pre·can·cer·ous /prēˈkansərəs/ ▶ **adj.** Medicine (of a cell or medical condition) likely to develop into cancer if untreated: *precancerous skin lesions.*

pre·car·i·ous /priˈke(ə)rēəs/ ▶ **adj. 1** not securely held or in position; dangerously likely to fall or collapse: *a precarious ladder.*
2 dependent on chance; uncertain: *she made a precarious living by writing.*
– DERIVATIVES **pre·car·i·ous·ly adv., pre·car·i·ous·ness n.**
– ORIGIN mid 17th cent.: from Latin *precarius* 'obtained by entreaty' (from *prex, prec-* 'prayer') + **-OUS.**

pre·cast /ˈprēˈkast/ ▶ **v.** (**precasts, precasting;** past and past participle **precast**) [with obj.] (usu. as adj. **precast**) cast (an object or material, typically concrete) in its final shape before positioning: *precast concrete beams.*

prec·a·to·ry /ˈprekəˌtôrē/ ▶ **adj.** formal of, relating to, or expressing a wish or request. ■ Law (in a will) expressing a wish or intention of the testator: *a trust can be left in precatory words.*
– ORIGIN mid 17th cent.: from late Latin *precatorius,* from *precat-* 'prayed,' from the verb *precari.*

pre·cau·tion /priˈkôSHən/ ▶ **n.** a measure taken in advance to prevent something dangerous, unpleasant, or inconvenient from happening: *he had* ***taken the precaution of*** *seeking legal advice.*
– ORIGIN late 16th cent. (in the sense 'prudent foresight'): from French *précaution,* from late Latin *praecautio(n-),* from Latin *praecavere,* from *prae* 'before' + *cavere* 'take heed, beware of.'

pre·cau·tion·ar·y /priˈkôSHəˌnerē/ ▶ **adj.** carried out as a precaution: *she was taken to the hospital as a precautionary measure.*

pre·cau·tion·ar·y prin·ci·ple ▶ **n.** the principle that the introduction of a new product or process whose ultimate effects are disputed or unknown should be resisted. It has mainly been used to prohibit the importation of genetically modified organisms and food.

pre·cede /priˈsēd/ ▶ **v.** [with obj.] come before (something) in time: *a gun battle had preceded the explosions.* ■ come before in order or position: *take time to read the chapters that precede the recipes* | (as adj. **preceding**) *the preceding pages.* ■ go in front or ahead of: *he let her precede him through the gate.* ■ (**precede something with**) preface or introduce something with: *he preceded the book with a collection of poems.*
– ORIGIN late Middle English: from Old French *preceder,* from Latin *praecedere,* from *prae* 'before' + *cedere* 'go.'

prec·e·dence /ˈpresədəns, priˈsēdns/ ▶ **n.** the condition of being considered more important than someone or something else; priority in importance, order, or rank: *his desire for power soon* ***took precedence over*** *any other consideration.* ■ the order to be ceremonially observed by people of different rank, according to an acknowledged or legally determined system: *quarrels over precedence among the Bonaparte family marred the coronation.*

prec·e·dent ▶ **n.** /ˈpresid(ə)nt/ an earlier event or action that is regarded as an example or guide to be considered in subsequent similar circumstances: *there are substantial precedents for using interactive media in training* | *breaking with all precedent.* ■ Law a previous case or legal decision that may be or (**binding precedent**) must be followed in subsequent similar cases: *the decision* ***set a precedent*** *for others to be sent to trial in the US.*
▶ **adj.** (**precedent** /priˈsēd(ə)nt/) preceding in time, order, or importance: *a precedent case.*
– ORIGIN late Middle English: from Old French, literally 'preceding.'

pre·cen·tor /priˈsentər/ ▶ **n.** a person who leads a congregation in its singing or (in a synagogue) prayers.
– DERIVATIVES **pre·cent v., pre·cen·tor·ship** /-ˌSHip/ **n.**
– ORIGIN early 17th cent.: from French *précenteur* or Latin *praecentor,* from *praecent-* 'sung before,' from the verb *praecinere,* from *prae* 'before' + *canere* 'sing.'

pre·cept /ˈprēˌsept/ ▶ **n. 1** a general rule intended to regulate behavior or thought: *moral precepts* | *the legal precept of being innocent until proven guilty* | *children learn far more by example than by precept.*
2 a writ or warrant: *the Commissioner issued precepts requiring the companies to provide information.*
– DERIVATIVES **pre·cep·tive** /priˈseptiv/ **adj.**
– ORIGIN late Middle English: from Latin *praeceptum,* neuter past participle of *praecipere* 'warn, instruct,' from *prae* 'before' + *capere* 'take.'

pre·cep·tor /ˈprēˌseptər, priˈseptər/ ▶ **n.** a teacher or instructor.
– DERIVATIVES **pre·cep·to·ri·al** /priˌsepˈtôrēəl, ˈprē-/ **adj., pre·cep·tor·ship** /-ˌSHip/ **n.**
– ORIGIN late Middle English: from Latin *praeceptor,* from *praecept-* 'warned, instructed,' from the verb *praecipere* (see **PRECEPT**).

pre·ces·sion /prəˈseSHən/ ▶ **n.** Physics the slow movement of the axis of a spinning body around another axis due to a torque (such as gravitational influence) acting to change the direction of the first axis. It is seen in the circle slowly traced out by the pole of a spinning gyroscope.
– DERIVATIVES **pre·cess** /prēˈses, ˈprēˌses/ **v., pre·ces·sion·al** /priˈseSHənl/ **adj.**
– ORIGIN late 16th cent. (as a term in astronomy, referring to the **PRECESSION OF THE EQUINOXES**): from late Latin *praecessio(n-),* from *praecedere* 'go before' (see **PRECEDE**).

pre·ces·sion of the e·qui·nox·es ▶ **n.** Astronomy the slow retrograde, or westward, motion of equinoctial points along the ecliptic. ■ the resulting earlier occurrence of equinoxes in each successive sidereal year.

> As the earth rotates about its axis, it responds to the gravitational attraction of the sun upon its equatorial bulge, so that its axis of rotation describes a circle in the sky, with a period of about 26,000 years. The precession of the equinoxes was discovered by Hipparchus in c.125 BC, when the vernal equinox was in Aries.

pre-Chris·tian /prēˈkrisCHən/ ▶ **adj.** of or relating to a time before Christ or the advent of Christianity: *the pre-Christian world.*

pre·cinct /ˈprēˌsiNGkt/ ▶ **n. 1** a district of a city or town as defined for police purposes. ■ the police station situated in such a subdivision: *at the precinct, a desk sergeant ran through her ID.* ■ an electoral district of a city or town served by a single polling place: *with 35 percent of the precincts declaring, he had 51 percent of the vote.*

2 (usu. **precincts**) the area within the walls or perceived boundaries of a particular building or place: *all strata of society live within these precincts* | figurative *beyond the precincts of my own family, I am quite inhibited.* ■ an enclosed or clearly defined area of ground around a cathedral, church, or college.
3 Brit. an area in a town designated for specific or restricted use, esp. one that is closed to traffic: *a pedestrian precinct.*
– ORIGIN late Middle English (denoting an administrative district): from medieval Latin *praecinctum*, neuter past participle (used as a noun) of *praecingere* 'encircle,' from *prae* 'before' + *cingere* 'gird.'

pre·ci·os·i·ty /ˌpresHēˈäsətē/ ▶ **n.** overrefinement in art, music, or language, esp. in the choice of words.
– ORIGIN mid 19th cent.: suggested by French *préciosité*, a sense derived from Molière's *Les Précieuses Ridicules* (1659), a comedy in which ladies frequenting the literary salons of Paris were satirized.

pre·cious /ˈpresHəs/ ▶ **adj. 1** (of an object, substance, or resource) of great value; not to be wasted or treated carelessly: *precious works of art* | *my time is precious.* ■ greatly loved or treasured by someone: *look after my daughter—she's very precious to me.* ■ [attrib.] informal used for emphasis, often in an ironic context: *a precious lot you know about dogs!*
2 derogatory affectedly concerned with elegant or refined behavior, language, or manners: *his exaggerated, precious manner.*
▶ **n.** used as a term of address to a beloved person: *don't be frightened, my precious.*
– PHRASES **precious little/few** extremely little or few (used for emphasis): *police still know precious little about the dead man* | *you will find precious few atheists on operating tables.*
– DERIVATIVES **pre·cious·ly adv.**, **pre·cious·ness n.**
– ORIGIN Middle English: from Old French *precios*, from Latin *pretiosus* 'of great value,' from *pretium* 'price.'

pre·cious cor·al ▶ **n.** another term for RED CORAL.

pre·cious met·als ▶ **plural n.** gold, silver, and platinum.

pre·cious stone ▶ **n.** a highly attractive and valuable piece of mineral or rock, used esp. in jewelry; a gemstone.

prec·i·pice /ˈpresəpəs/ ▶ **n.** a very steep rock face or cliff, typically a tall one: *we swerved toward the edge of the precipice* | figurative *the country was teetering on the precipice of political anarchy.*
– ORIGIN late 16th cent. (denoting a headlong fall): from French *précipice* or Latin *praecipitium* 'abrupt descent,' from *praeceps*, *praecip(it)-* 'steep, headlong.'

pre·cip·i·tan·cy /priˈsipətənsē/ ▶ **n.** rashness or suddenness of action: *matters were taken out of his control by the precipitancy of his commander.*

pre·cip·i·tant /priˈsipətənt/ ▶ **n.** a cause of a particular action or event: *the immediate precipitants of the conflict were a succession of undisciplined actions.* ■ chiefly Psychology a cause or stimulus that precipitates a particular condition: *depression may be a precipitant in many cases.* ■ Chemistry a substance that causes the precipitation of a specified substance: *a protein precipitant.*
– DERIVATIVES **pre·cip·i·tance n.**
– ORIGIN early 17th cent.: from obsolete French *précipitant* 'precipitating,' present participle of *précipiter.*

pre·cip·i·tate ▶ **v.** /priˈsipəˌtāt/ [with obj.] **1** cause (an event or situation, typically one that is bad or undesirable) to happen suddenly, unexpectedly, or prematurely: *the incident precipitated a political crisis.* ■ cause to move suddenly and with force: *suddenly the ladder broke, precipitating them down into a heap.* ■ (**precipitate someone/something into**) send someone or something suddenly into a particular state or condition: *they were precipitated into a conflict for which they were quite unprepared.*
2 Chemistry cause (a substance) to be deposited in solid form from a solution. ■ cause (drops of moisture or particles of dust) to be deposited from the atmosphere or from a vapor or suspension.
▶ **adj.** /priˈsipətət/ done, made, or acting suddenly or without careful consideration: *I must apologize for my staff—their actions were precipitate.* ■ (of an event or situation) occurring suddenly or abruptly: *a precipitate decline in cultural literacy.*
▶ **n.** /priˈsipətət, -əˌtāt/ Chemistry a substance precipitated from a solution. [from modern Latin *praecipitatum.*]
– DERIVATIVES **pre·cip·i·ta·ble** /priˈsipətəbəl/ **adj.**, **pre·cip·i·tate·ly** /priˈsipətətlē/ **adv.**, **pre·cip·i·tate·ness** /priˈsipətətnəs/ **n.**
– ORIGIN early 16th cent.: from Latin *praecipitat-* 'thrown headlong,' from the verb *praecipitare*, from *praeceps*, *praecip(it)-* 'headlong,' from *prae* 'before' + *caput* 'head.' The original sense of the verb was 'hurl down, send violently'; hence 'cause to move rapidly,' which gave rise to sense 1 (early 17th cent).

> **USAGE** The adjectives **precipitate** and **precipitous** are sometimes confused. **Precipitate** means 'sudden, hasty': *a precipitate decision* | *the fugitive's precipitate flight*. **Precipitous** means 'steep': *the precipitous slope of the mountain* | *a precipitous decline in stock prices.*

pre·cip·i·ta·tion /priˌsipəˈtāsHən/ ▶ **n. 1** Chemistry the action or process of precipitating a substance from a solution.
2 rain, snow, sleet, or hail that falls to the ground.
3 archaic the fact or quality of acting suddenly and rashly: *Cora was already regretting her precipitation.*
– ORIGIN late Middle English (denoting the action of falling or throwing down): from Latin *praecipitatio(n-)*, from *praecipitare* 'throw down or headlong' (see PRECIPITATE).

pre·cip·i·ta·tor /priˈsipəˌtātər/ ▶ **n.** an apparatus for causing precipitation, esp. a device for removing dust from a gas.

pre·cip·i·tin /priˈsipətən/ ▶ **n.** Biochemistry an antibody that produces a visible precipitate when it reacts with its antigen.
– ORIGIN early 20th cent.: from the verb PRECIPITATE + -IN[1].

pre·cip·i·tous /priˈsipətəs/ ▶ **adj. 1** dangerously high or steep: *the precipitous cliffs of the North Atlantic coast.* ■ (of a change to a worse situation or condition) sudden and dramatic: *the end of the war led to a precipitous decline in exports.*
2 (of an action) done suddenly and without careful consideration: *precipitous intervention.*
– DERIVATIVES **pre·cip·i·tous·ly adv.**, **pre·cip·i·tous·ness n.**
– ORIGIN mid 17th cent.: from obsolete French *précipiteux*, from Latin *praeceps*, *praecip(it)-* 'steep, headlong' (see PRECIPITATE).

> **USAGE** See usage at PRECIPITATE.

pré·cis /prāˈsē, ˈprāsē/ ▶ **n.** (pl. **same**) a summary or abstract of a text or speech.
▶ **v.** (**précises** /prāˈsēz, ˈprāsēz/, **précised**, **précising**) [with obj.] make a précis of (a text or speech).
– ORIGIN mid 18th cent.: from French *précis*, literally 'precise' (adjective used as a noun).

pre·cise /priˈsīs/ ▶ **adj.** marked by exactness and accuracy of expression or detail: *precise directions* | *I want as precise a time of death as I can get.* ■ (of a person) exact, accurate, and careful about details: *the director was precise with his camera positions.* ■ [attrib.] used to emphasize that one is referring to an exact and particular thing: *at that precise moment the car stopped.*
– PHRASES **to be precise** used to indicate that one is now giving more exact or detailed information: *there were not many—five, to be precise.*
– DERIVATIVES **pre·cise·ness n.**
– ORIGIN late Middle English: from Old French *prescis*, from Latin *praecis-* 'cut short,' from the verb *praecidere*, from *prae* 'in advance' + *caedere* 'to cut.'

pre·cise·ly /priˈsīslē/ ▶ **adv.** in exact terms; without vagueness: *the guidelines are precisely defined.* ■ exactly (used to emphasize the complete accuracy or truth of a statement): *at 2:00 precisely, the phone rang* | *kids will love it precisely because it will irritate their parents.* ■ used as a reply to assert emphatic agreement with or confirmation of a statement: *"You mean it was a conspiracy?" "Precisely."*

pre·ci·sian /priˈsizHən/ ▶ **n.** chiefly archaic a person who is rigidly precise or punctilious, esp. as regards religious rules.
– DERIVATIVES **pre·ci·sian·ism** /-ˌizəm/ **n.**

pre·ci·sion /priˈsizHən/ ▶ **n.** the quality, condition, or fact of being exact and accurate: *the deal was planned and executed with military precision.* ■ [as modifier] marked by or adapted for accuracy and exactness: *a precision instrument.* ■ technical refinement in a measurement, calculation, or specification, esp. as represented by the number of digits given: *this has brought an unprecedented degree of precision to the business of dating rocks* | *a precision of six decimal figures.* Compare with ACCURACY.
– ORIGIN mid 18th cent.: from French *précision* or Latin *praecisio(n-)*, from *praecidere* 'cut off' (see PRECISE).

pre·clas·si·cal /prēˈklasəkəl/ ▶ **adj.** of or relating to a time before a period regarded as classical, esp. in music, literature, or history.

pre·clin·i·cal /prēˈklinikəl/ ▶ **adj.** Medicine relating to or denoting a stage preceding a clinical stage, in particular: ■ relating to or denoting the first, chiefly theoretical, stage of a medical education: *preclinical students.* ■ relating to or denoting the stage in a disease prior to the appearance of symptoms that make a diagnosis possible. ■ relating to or denoting the stage of drug testing that precedes the clinical stage.

pre·clude /priˈklo͞od/ ▶ **v.** [with obj.] prevent from happening; make impossible: *the secret nature of his work precluded official recognition.* ■ (**preclude someone from**) (of a situation or condition) prevent someone from doing something: *his difficulties preclude him from leading a normal life.*
– DERIVATIVES **pre·clu·sion** /-ˈklo͞ozHən/ **n.**, **pre·clu·sive** /-ˈklo͞osiv, -ziv/ **adj.**
– ORIGIN late 15th cent. (in the sense 'bar (a route or passage)'): from Latin *praecludere*, from *prae* 'before' + *claudere* 'to shut.'

pre·co·cial /priˈkōsHəl/ Zoology ▶ **adj.** (of a young bird or other animal) hatched or born in an advanced state and able to feed itself almost immediately. Also called NIDIFUGOUS. Often contrasted with ALTRICIAL. ■ (of a particular species) having such young.
▶ **n.** a precocial bird.
– ORIGIN late 19th cent.: from modern Latin *Praecoces* (the name of a former division of birds, plural of Latin *praecox* 'mature before its time') + -IAL.

pre·co·cious /priˈkōsHəs/ ▶ **adj.** (of a child) having developed certain abilities or proclivities at an earlier age than usual: *he was a precocious, solitary boy.* ■ (of behavior or ability) indicative of such development: *a precocious talent for computing.* ■ (of a plant) flowering or fruiting earlier than usual.
– DERIVATIVES **pre·co·cious·ly adv.**, **pre·co·cious·ness n.**, **pre·coc·i·ty** /priˈkäsətē/ **n.**
– ORIGIN mid 17th cent.: from Latin *praecox*, *praecoc-* (from *praecoquere* 'ripen fully,' from *prae* 'before' + *coquere* 'to cook') + -IOUS.

pre·cog·ni·tion /ˌprēkägˈnisHən/ ▶ **n.**
1 foreknowledge of an event, esp. foreknowledge of a paranormal kind.
2 Law chiefly Scottish the preliminary examination of witnesses, esp. to decide whether there are grounds for a trial.
– DERIVATIVES **pre·cog·ni·tive** /prēˈkägnətiv/ **adj.** (sense 1).
– ORIGIN late Middle English: from late Latin *praecognitio(n-)*, based on Latin *cognoscere* 'know.'

pre·co·i·tal /prēˈkōətl, ˌprēkōˈētl/ ▶ **adj.** occurring before or as a preliminary to sexual intercourse.
– DERIVATIVES **pre·co·i·tal·ly adv.**

pre·co·lo·ni·al /ˌprēkəˈlōniəl/ ▶ **adj.** occurring or existing before the beginning of colonial rule: *the two main kingdoms that flourished in precolonial times.*

pre-Co·lum·bi·an /kəˈləmbēən/ ▶ **adj.** of or relating to the history and cultures of the Americas before the arrival of Columbus in 1492.

pre·con·ceived /ˌprēkənˈsēvd/ ▶ **adj.** (of an idea or opinion) formed before having the evidence for its truth or usefulness: *the same set of facts can be tailored to fit any preconceived belief.*

pre·con·cep·tion /ˌprēkənˈsepsHən/ ▶ **n.** a preconceived idea or prejudice.

pre·con·cert /ˌprēkənˈsərt/ ▶ **v.** [with obj.] archaic arrange or organize (something) in advance: (as adj. **preconcerted**) *a preconcerted signal.*

pre·con·di·tion /ˌprēkənˈdisHən/ ▶ **n.** a condition that must be fulfilled before other things can happen or be done: *a precondition for peace.*
▶ **v.** [with obj.] **1** (usu. **be preconditioned**) condition (an action) to happen in a certain way: *inquiries are always preconditioned by cultural assumptions.* ■ condition or influence (a person or animal) by exposing them to stimuli or information prior to the relevant behavioral situation: [with obj. and infinitive] *the anthropologist is not preconditioned to interact with those he studies* | (as noun **preconditioning**) *the protective effect of preconditioning.*
2 bring (something) into the desired state for use: (as adj. **preconditioned**) *preconditioned paper.*

pre-Con·quest ▶ **adj.** occurring or existing before the Norman conquest of England.

pre·con·scious /prēˈkäncHəs/ ▶ **adj.** Psychoanalysis of or associated with a part of the mind below the level of immediate conscious awareness, from which memories and emotions that have not been repressed can be recalled: *beliefs and values that are on a preconscious level.*
▶ **n.** (**one's/the preconscious**) Psychology the part of the mind in which preconscious thoughts or memories reside.
– DERIVATIVES **pre·con·scious·ness n.**

P

pre·cook /'prē'ko͝ok/ ▶ **v.** [with obj.] cook in advance: (as adj. **precooked**) *precooked frozen dinners.*

pre·cor·di·um /prē'kôrdēəm/ ▶ **n.** Anatomy the region or the thorax immediately in front of the heart.
– DERIVATIVES **pre·cor·dial** /-'kôrdēəl/ **adj.**
– ORIGIN late 19th cent.: singular of Latin *praecordia* 'diaphragm, entrails.'

pre·cur·sor /'prē,kərsər, pri'kər-/ ▶ **n.** a person or thing that comes before another of the same kind; a forerunner: *a three-stringed precursor of the violin* | [as modifier] *precursor cells.* ■ Biochemistry a substance from which another is formed, esp. by metabolic reaction: *pepsinogen is the inactive precursor of pepsin.*
– ORIGIN late Middle English: from Latin *praecursor*, from *praecurs-* 'preceded,' from *praecurrere*, from *prae* 'beforehand' + *currere* 'to run.'

pre·cur·so·ry /pri'kərsərē/ ▶ **adj.** preceding something in time, development, or position; preliminary: *precursory seismic activity.*
– ORIGIN late 16th cent.: from Latin *praecursorius*, from *praecurs-* 'preceded' (see PRECURSOR).

pre·cut /'prē'kət/ ▶ **v.** [with obj.] (usu. as adj. **precut**) cut into the desired shape or sections in advance: *precut pieces of cloth.*

pred. ▶ **abbr.** predicate.

pre·da·cious /pri'dāsHəs/ (also **predaceous**) ▶ **adj.** (of an animal) predatory: *predacious insects.*
– DERIVATIVES **pre·da·cious·ness n.**, **pre·dac·i·ty** /pri'dasətē/ **n.**
– ORIGIN early 18th cent.: from Latin *praeda* 'booty' + -ACIOUS.

pre·date[1] /prē'dāt/ ▶ **v.** [with obj.] exist or occur at a date earlier than (something): *this letter predates her illness.*

pre·date[2] /pri'dāt/ ▶ **v.** [with obj.] (of an animal) act as a predator of; catch and eat (prey).
– ORIGIN 1940s: back-formation from PREDATION.

pre·da·tion /pri'dāsHən/ ▶ **n.** **1** the preying of one animal on others: *an effective defense against predation.*
2 the action of attacking or plundering: *the old story of male predation and female vulnerability* | *the predations of would-be pirates.*
– ORIGIN late 15th cent. (in the Latin sense): from Latin *praedatio(n-)* 'taking of booty,' from the verb *praedari* 'seize as plunder,' from *praeda* 'booty.' The zoological sense dates from the 1930s.

pred·a·tor /'predətər/ ▶ **n.** **1** an animal that naturally preys on others: *wolves are major predators of rodents.*
2 a person or group that ruthlessly exploits others: *a website frequented by sexual predators.* ■ a company that tries to take over another.
– ORIGIN 1920s: from Latin *praedator* 'plunderer,' from *praedat-* 'seized as plunder,' from the verb *praedari* (see PREDATION).

pred·a·to·ry /'predə,tôrē/ ▶ **adj.** **1** relating to or denoting an animal or animals preying naturally on others: *predatory birds.*
2 seeking to exploit or oppress others: *a life destroyed by predatory biographers and yellow journalists.*
– DERIVATIVES **pred·a·to·ri·ly** /,predə'tôrəlē/ **adv.**, **pred·a·to·ri·ness n.**
– ORIGIN late 16th cent. (in the sense 'relating to plundering'): from Latin *praedatorius*, from *praedator* 'plunderer' (see PREDATOR).

pred·a·to·ry pric·ing ▶ **n.** the pricing of goods or services at such a low level that other suppliers cannot compete and are forced to leave the market.

pre·dawn /prē'dôn/ ▶ **adj.** relating to or taking place before dawn: *the predawn light was just beginning to show through.*

pre·de·cease /,prēdi'sēs/ formal ▶ **v.** [with obj.] die before (another person, typically someone related by blood or marriage): *his second wife predeceased him.*

pred·e·ces·sor /'predə,sesər, 'prē-/ ▶ **n.** a person who held a job or office before the current holder: *the new president's foreign policy is very similar to that of his predecessor.* ■ a thing that has been followed or replaced by another: *the chapel was built in 1864 on the site of its predecessor.*
– ORIGIN late Middle English: from late Latin *praedecessor*, from Latin *prae* 'beforehand' + *decessor* 'retiring officer' (from *decedere* 'depart').

pre·de·fined /,prēdi'fīnd/ ▶ **adj.** defined, limited, or established in advance: *predefined styles for tables, outlines, paragraphs, and graphics.*

pre·del·la /pri'delə/ ▶ **n.** **1** a step or platform on which an altar is placed.
2 a raised shelf above an altar. ■ a painting or sculpture on this, typically forming an appendage to an altarpiece.
– ORIGIN mid 19th cent.: from Italian, literally 'stool.'

pre·des·ti·nar·i·an /prē,destə'ne(ə)rēən/ ▶ **n.** a person who believes in the doctrine of predestination.
▶ **adj.** upholding, affirming, or relating to the doctrine of predestination.

pre·des·ti·nate ▶ **v.** /prē'destə,nāt/ [with obj.] predestine.
▶ **adj.** /prē'destənit/ predestined.
– ORIGIN late Middle English: from ecclesiastical Latin *praedestinat-* 'made firm beforehand,' from the verb *praedestinare*, from *prae* 'in advance' + *destinare* 'establish.'

pre·des·ti·na·tion /prē,destə'nāsHən/ ▶ **n.** (as a doctrine in Christian theology) the divine foreordaining of all that will happen, esp. with regard to the salvation of some and not others. It has been particularly associated with the teachings of St. Augustine of Hippo and of Calvin.
– ORIGIN Middle English: from ecclesiastical Latin *praedestinatio(n-)*, from *praedestinare* 'make firm beforehand' (see PREDESTINATE).

pre·des·tine /prē'destin/ ▶ **v.** [with obj.] (usu. **be predestined**) (of God) destine (someone) for a particular fate or purpose: *Calvinists believed that every person was predestined by God to go to heaven or to hell.* ■ determine (an outcome or course of events) in advance by divine will or fate: *she was certain that fate was with her and everything was predestined* | (as adj. **predestined**) *our predestined end.*
– ORIGIN late Middle English: from Old French *predestiner* or ecclesiastical Latin *praedestinare* (see PREDESTINATE).

pre·de·ter·mine /,prēdi'tərmən/ ▶ **v.** [with obj.] establish or decide in advance: *closed questions almost predetermine the response given* | (as adj. **predetermined**) *a predetermined level of spending.* ■ (usu. **be predetermined**) predestine (an outcome or course of events): *a strong sense that life had been predetermined.*
– DERIVATIVES **pre·de·ter·min·a·ble adj.**, **pre·de·ter·mi·nate** /-'tərmənit/ **adj.**, **pre·de·ter·mi·na·tion** /-,tərmə'nāsHən/ **n.**
– ORIGIN early 17th cent.: from late Latin *praedeterminare*, from *prae* 'beforehand' + *determinare* 'limit, settle.'

pre·de·ter·min·er /,prēdi'tərmənər/ ▶ **n.** Grammar a word or phrase that occurs before a determiner, typically quantifying the noun phrase, for example *both* or *a lot of.*

pre·di·al /'prēdēəl/ ▶ **adj.** archaic of, relating to, or consisting of land or farming: *political or predial sources of discontent.* ■ historical relating to or denoting a slave or tenant attached to farms or the land: *predial service.* ■ historical (of a tithe) consisting of agricultural produce.
▶ **n.** historical a predial slave.
– ORIGIN late Middle English: from medieval Latin *praedialis*, from Latin *praedium* 'farm.'

predic. ▶ **abbr.** predicate.

pred·i·ca·ble /'predikəbəl/ ▶ **adj.** that may be predicated or affirmed.
▶ **n.** a thing that is predicable. ■ (usu. **predicables**) (in Aristotelian logic) each of the classes to which predicates belong, usually listed as: genus, species, difference, property, and accident.
– DERIVATIVES **pred·i·ca·bil·i·ty** /,predikə'bilətē/ **n.**
– ORIGIN mid 16th cent.: from medieval Latin *praedicabilis* 'able to be affirmed,' from Latin *praedicare* 'declare' (see PREDICATE).

pre·dic·a·ment /pri'dikəmənt/ ▶ **n.** **1** a difficult, unpleasant, or embarrassing situation: *the club's financial predicament.*
2 Philosophy, archaic (in Aristotelian logic) each of the ten "categories," often listed as: substance or being, quantity, quality, relation, place, time, posture, having or possession, action, and passion.
– ORIGIN late Middle English (sense 2): from late Latin *praedicamentum* 'something predicated' (rendering Greek *katēgoria* 'category'), from Latin *praedicare* (see PREDICATE). From the sense 'category' arose the sense 'state of being, condition'; hence 'unpleasant situation.'

pred·i·cate ▶ **n.** /'predikət/ Grammar the part of a sentence or clause containing a verb and stating something about the subject (e.g., *went home* in *John went home*): [as modifier] *predicate adjective.* ■ Logic something that is affirmed or denied concerning an argument of a proposition.
▶ **v.** /'predə,kāt/ [with obj.] **1** Grammar & Logic state, affirm, or assert (something) about the subject of a sentence or an argument of proposition: *a word that predicates something about its subject* | *aggression is predicated of those who act aggressively.*
2 (**predicate something on/upon**) found or base something on: *the theory of structure on which later chemistry was predicated.*
– DERIVATIVES **pred·i·ca·tion** /,predə'kāsHən/ **n.**
– ORIGIN late Middle English (as a noun): from Latin *praedicatum* 'something declared,' neuter of *praedicatus* 'declared, proclaimed,' past participle of the verb *praedicare*, from *prae* 'beforehand' + *dicare* 'make known.'

pred·i·cate cal·cu·lus /'predəkət/ ▶ **n.** the branch of symbolic logic that deals with propositions containing predicates, names, and quantifiers.

pred·i·cate nom·i·na·tive ▶ **n.** Grammar a word in the nominative case that completes a copulative verb, such as *son* in the sentence *Charlie is my son.*

pred·i·ca·tive /'predə,kātiv, -ikətiv/ ▶ **adj.** **1** Grammar (of an adjective or noun) forming or contained in the predicate, as *old* in *the dog is old* (but not in *the old dog*) and *house* in *there is a large house.* Contrasted with ATTRIBUTIVE. ■ denoting a use of the verb *to be* to assert something about the subject.
2 Logic acting as a predicate.
– DERIVATIVES **pred·i·ca·tive·ly adv.**
– ORIGIN mid 19th cent.: from Latin *praedicativus*, from *praedicat-* 'declared' (in medieval Latin 'predicated'), from the verb *praedicare* (see PREDICATE).

pred·i·ca·tor /'predə,kātər/ ▶ **n.** (in systemic grammar) a verb phrase considered as a constituent of clause structure, along with subject, object, and adjunct.

pre·dict /pri'dikt/ ▶ **v.** [with obj.] say or estimate that (a specified thing) will happen in the future or will be a consequence of something: *it is too early to predict a result* | [with clause] *he predicts that the trend will continue* | (as adj. **predicted**) *the predicted growth is 47 percent.*
– DERIVATIVES **pre·dic·tor** /-tər/ **n.**
– ORIGIN early 17th cent.: from Latin *praedict-* 'made known beforehand, declared,' from the verb *praedicere*, from *prae-* 'beforehand' + *dicere* 'say.'

pre·dict·a·ble /pri'diktəbəl/ ▶ **adj.** able to be predicted: *the market is volatile and never predictable.* ■ chiefly derogatory behaving or occurring in a way that is expected: *the characters were very stereotyped and extremely predictable.*
– DERIVATIVES **pre·dict·a·bil·i·ty** /-,diktə'bilətē/ **n.**, **pre·dict·a·bly** /-blē/ **adv.** [sentence adverb] *predictably, Margaret found an excuse to interrupt him* | [as submodifier] *a predictably hostile response.*

pre·dic·tion /pri'diksHən/ ▶ **n.** a thing predicted; a forecast: *a prediction that the Greeks would destroy the Persian empire.* ■ the action of predicting something: *the prediction of future behavior.*
– ORIGIN mid 16th cent.: from Latin *praedictio(n-)*, from *praedicere* 'make known beforehand' (see PREDICT).

pre·dic·tive /pri'diktiv/ ▶ **adj.** relating to or having the effect of predicting an event or result: *predictive accuracy* | *rules are not predictive of behavior.*
– DERIVATIVES **pre·dic·tive·ly adv.**

pre·di·gest /,prēdī'jest, ,prēdə-/ ▶ **v.** **1** (of an animal) treat (food) by a process similar to digestion in order to make it more digestible when subsequently eaten.
2 simplify (information) so as to make it easier to understand or appreciate: (as adj. **predigested**) *predigested news.*
– DERIVATIVES **pre·di·ges·tion** /-'jesCHən/ **n.**

pre·di·gi·tal /prē'dijitl/ ▶ **adj.** belonging to or characteristic of the period preceding the widespread adoption of digital technologies: *formulas once used by animators in a predigital age.*

pre·di·lec·tion /,predl'eksHən, ,prēdl-/ ▶ **n.** a preference or special liking for something; a bias in favor of something: *my predilection for Asian food.*
– ORIGIN mid 18th cent.: from French *prédilection*, from Latin *praedilect-* 'preferred,' from the verb *praediligere*, from *prae* 'in advance' + *diligere* 'to select.'

pre·dis·pose /,prēdi'spōz/ ▶ **v.** [with obj.] (**predispose someone to/to do something**) make someone liable or inclined to a specified attitude, action, or condition: *lack of exercise may predispose an individual to high blood pressure.*
– DERIVATIVES **pre·dis·posed adj.**

pre·dis·po·si·tion /,prē,dispə'zisHən/ ▶ **n.** a liability or tendency to suffer from a particular condition, hold a particular attitude, or act in a particular way: *a child may inherit a predisposition to schizophrenia* | *genetic predisposition.*

pred·ni·sone /'predna,sōn, -,zōn/ ▶ **n.** Medicine a synthetic drug similar to cortisone, used to relieve rheumatic and allergic conditions and to treat leukemia.
– ORIGIN 1950s: perhaps from *pre(gnane)* (a synthetic hydrocarbon) + *d(ie)n(e)* + *(cort)isone.*

pre·dom·i·nance /pri'dämənəns/ ▶ **n.** the state or condition of being greater in number or amount: *the predominance of English language materials on the Web* | [in sing.] *there is a predominance of female* *teachers.* ■ the possession or exertion of control or power: *the American predominance at sea.*

pre·dom·i·nant /priˈdämənənt/ ▶ **adj.** present as the strongest or main element: *its predominant color was white.* ■ having or exerting control or power: *the predominant political forces.*
– ORIGIN mid 16th cent.: from Old French, from medieval Latin *predominant-* 'predominating,' from the verb *predominari* (see PREDOMINATE).

pre·dom·i·nant·ly /priˈdämənəntlē/ ▶ **adv.** mainly; for the most part: [sentence adverb] *it is predominantly a coastal bird* | [as submodifier] *predominantly Russian areas.*

pre·dom·i·nate /priˈdäməˌnāt/ ▶ **v.** [no obj.] be the strongest or main element; be greater in number or amount: *small-scale producers predominate in the south.* ■ have or exert control or power: *private interest was not allowed to* ***predominate over*** *the public good.*
– ORIGIN late 16th cent.: from medieval Latin *predominat-* 'predominated,' from the verb *predominari* (see PRE-, DOMINATE).

pre·dom·i·nate·ly /priˈdämənətlē/ ▶ **adv.** another term for PREDOMINANTLY.

pre·doom /prēˈdo͞om/ ▶ **v.** [with obj.] literary condemn or determine the fate of (someone or something) in advance: *he was predoomed by the decrees of heaven.*

pre·dy·nas·tic /ˌprēdīˈnastik, ˌprēdə-/ ▶ **adj.** of or relating to a period before the normally recognized dynasties, esp. in ancient Egypt before about 3000 BC.

pre·e·clamp·si·a /ˌprē-iˈklampsēə/ ▶ **n.** a condition in pregnancy characterized by high blood pressure, sometimes with fluid retention and proteinuria.
– DERIVATIVES **pre·e·clamp·tic** /-ˈklamptik/ **adj. & n.**

pre-e·lec·tion /prē-iˈleksHən/ (also **pre-electoral**) ▶ **adj.** [attrib.] occurring or existing in the time leading up to an election: *his pre-election speech.*

pre·em·bry·o /prēˈembrēˌō/ ▶ **n.** technical a human embryo or fertilized ovum in the first fourteen days after fertilization, before implantation in the uterus has occurred.
– DERIVATIVES **pre·em·bry·on·ic** /ˌprēˌembrēˈänik/ **adj.**

pree·mie /ˈprēmē/ ▶ **n.** (pl. **preemies**) informal a baby born prematurely.
– ORIGIN 1920s (as *premy*): from PREMATURE + -IE.

pre·em·i·nence /prēˈemənəns/ ▶ **n.** the fact of surpassing all others; superiority: *the region has never regained the economic preeminence that it once enjoyed.*

pre·em·i·nent /prēˈemənənt/ ▶ **adj.** surpassing all others; very distinguished in some way: *the world's preeminent expert on asbestos.*
– ORIGIN late Middle English: from Latin *praeeminent-* 'towering above, excelling,' from the verb *praeeminere,* from *prae* 'before' + *eminere* 'stand out.'

pre·em·i·nent·ly /prēˈemənəntlē/ ▶ **adv.** [sentence adverb] above all; in particular: *this is preeminently the haying month throughout the northern states.*

pre·empt /prēˈempt/ ▶ **v.** [with obj.] **1** take action in order to prevent (an anticipated event) from happening; forestall: *the government preempted a coup attempt.* ■ act in advance of (someone) in order to prevent them from doing something: *it looked as if she'd ask him more, but Parr preempted her.* ■ (of a broadcast) interrupt or replace (a scheduled program): *the violence preempted regular programming.*
2 acquire or appropriate (something) in advance: *many tables were already preempted by family parties.* ■ take (something, esp. public land) for oneself so as to have the right of preemption.
3 [no obj.] Bridge make a preemptive bid.
▶ **n.** Bridge a preemptive bid.
– DERIVATIVES **pre·emp·tor** /-tər/ **n.**
– ORIGIN mid 19th cent.: back-formation from PREEMPTION.

pre·emp·tion /prēˈempsHən/ ▶ **n. 1** the purchase of goods or shares by one person or party before the opportunity is offered to others: *the commission had the right of preemption.* ■ historical the right to purchase public land in this way.
2 the action of preempting or forestalling, esp. of making a preemptive attack: *damaging retaliation for any attempt at preemption.* ■ the interruption or replacement of a scheduled radio or television program.
– ORIGIN early 17th cent.: from medieval Latin *praeemptio(n-),* from the verb *praeemere,* from *prae* 'in advance' + *emere* 'buy.'

pre·emp·tive /prēˈemptiv/ ▶ **adj.** serving or intended to preempt or forestall something, esp. to prevent attack by disabling the enemy: *preemptive action* | *a preemptive strike.* ■ relating to the purchase of goods or shares by one person or party before the opportunity is offered to others: *preemptive rights.* ■ Bridge denoting a bid, typically an opening bid, intended to be so high that it prevents or interferes with effective bidding by the opponents.
– DERIVATIVES **pre·emp·tive·ly adv.**

preen /prēn/ ▶ **v.** [no obj.] (of a bird) straighten and clean its feathers with its beak: *robins preened at the pool's edge* | [with obj.] *the pigeon preened her feathers.* ■ (of a person) devote effort to making oneself look attractive and then admire one's appearance: *adolescents preening in their bedroom mirrors.* ■ (**preen oneself**) congratulate or pride oneself: *he's busy* ***preening himself on*** *acquiring such a pretty girlfriend.*
– DERIVATIVES **preen·er n.**
– ORIGIN late Middle English: apparently a variant of obsolete *prune* (based on Latin *ungere* 'anoint'), in the same sense, associated with Scots and northern English dialect *preen* 'pierce, pin' (because of the "pricking" action of the bird's beak).

preen gland ▶ **n.** Ornithology (on a bird) a gland at the base of the tail that produces the oil used in preening.

pre·es·tab·lish /ˌprē-iˈstablisH/ ▶ **v.** [with obj.] (usu. as adj. **preestablished**) establish (something) in advance: *he had no preestablished plan.*

pre·ex·ist /ˌprē-igˈzist/ ▶ **v.** [no obj.] (usu. as adj. **preexisting**) exist at or from an earlier time: *a preexisting contractual obligation.* ■ [with obj.] exist at or from an earlier time than (something): *demons who preexisted the Great Flood.*
– DERIVATIVES **pre·ex·ist·ence** /-ˈzistəns/ **n.**, **pre·ex·ist·ent** /-ˈzistənt/ **adj.**

pre·ex·ist·ing con·di·tion ▶ **n.** a medical condition existing at a time when new insurance is applied for. Typically the cost of its treatment is not covered by the insurance.

pre·ex·po·sure /ˌprē-ikˈspōzHər/ ▶ **n.** previous or premature exposure to something.
▶ **adj.** occurring or existing before exposure, esp. exposure to a disease or infection: *preexposure vaccination.*

pref. ▶ **abbr.** ■ preface. ■ preference (with reference to preference shares). ■ preferred (with reference to a preferred stock).

pre·fab /prēˈfab, ˈprēˌfab/ informal ▶ **n.** a prefabricated building.
▶ **adj.** prefabricated: *prefab walls.*
– ORIGIN 1930s: abbreviation.

pre·fab·ri·cate /prēˈfabriˌkāt/ ▶ **v.** [with obj.] (usu. as adj. **prefabricated**) manufacture sections of (esp. a building or piece of furniture) to enable quick or easy assembly on site: *prefabricated homes.*
– DERIVATIVES **pre·fab·ri·ca·tion** /-ˌfabrəˈkāsHən/ **n.**

pref·ace /ˈprefəs/ ▶ **n.** an introduction to a book, typically stating its subject, scope, or aims. ■ the introduction or preliminary part of a speech or event. ■ Christian Church the introduction to the central part of the Eucharist, historically forming the first part of the canon or prayer of consecration.
▶ **v.** [with obj.] provide (a book) with a preface: *the book is prefaced by a quotation from William Faulkner.* ■ (**preface something with/by**) introduce or begin (a speech or event) with or by doing something: *it is important to preface the debate with a general comment.*
– ORIGIN late Middle English: via Old French from medieval Latin *praefatia,* alteration of Latin *praefatio(n-)* 'words spoken beforehand,' from the verb *praefari,* from *prae* 'before' + *fari* 'speak.'

pref·a·to·ry /ˈprefəˌtôrē/ ▶ **adj.** serving as an introduction; introductory: *the poet makes this clear in a prefatory note on the text.*

pre·fect /ˈprēˌfekt/ ▶ **n. 1** a chief officer, magistrate, or regional governor in certain countries: *the prefect of police.* ■ a senior magistrate or governor in the ancient Roman world: *Avitus was prefect of Gaul from AD 439.*
2 chiefly Brit. in some schools, a senior student authorized to enforce discipline.
– DERIVATIVES **pre·fec·tor·al** /prēˈfektərəl/ **adj.**, **pre·fec·to·ri·al** /ˌprēˌfekˈtôrēəl/ **adj.**
– ORIGIN late Middle English (sense 2): from Old French, from Latin *praefectus,* past participle of *praeficere* 'set in authority over,' from *prae* 'before' + *facere* 'make.' Sense 2 dates from the early 19th cent.

pre·fec·ture /ˈprēˌfekCHər/ ▶ **n.** a district under the government of a prefect. ■ a prefect's office or tenure. ■ the official residence or headquarters of a prefect.
– DERIVATIVES **pre·fec·tur·al** /prēˈfekCHərəl/ **adj.**
– ORIGIN late Middle English: from Latin *praefectura,* from *praefectus* '(person) set in authority over' (see PREFECT).

pre·fer /priˈfər/ ▶ **v.** (**prefers, preferring, preferred**) [with obj.] **1** like (one thing or person) better than another or others; tend to choose: *I* ***prefer*** *Venice* ***to*** *Rome* | [with infinitive] *I would prefer to discuss the matter in private* | [with clause] *Val would presumably prefer that you didn't get arrested* | (as adj. **preferred**) *his preferred candidate.*
2 formal submit (a charge or a piece of information) for consideration: *the police will prefer charges.*
3 archaic promote or advance (someone) to a prestigious position: *he was* ***preferred to*** *the post.*
– ORIGIN late Middle English: from Old French *preferer,* from Latin *praeferre,* from *prae* 'before' + *ferre* 'to bear, carry.'

pref·er·a·ble /ˈpref(ə)rəbəl/ ▶ **adj.** more desirable or suitable: *lower interest rates were* ***preferable to*** *higher ones.*
– DERIVATIVES **pref·er·a·bil·i·ty** /ˌpref(ə)rəˈbilətē/ **n.**

pref·er·a·bly /ˈpref(ə)rəblē/ ▶ **adv.** [sentence adverb] ideally; if possible: *he would like a place of his own, preferably outside the town.*

pref·er·ence /ˈpref(ə)rəns/ ▶ **n. 1** a greater liking for one alternative over another or others: *a* ***preference for*** *long walks and tennis over jogging* | *he chose a clock* ***in preference to*** *a watch.* ■ a thing preferred: *my musical preferences are blues and swing.* ■ favor shown to one person or thing over another or others: *preference is given to those who make a donation.*
2 Law a prior right or precedence, esp. in connection with the payment of debts: *debts owed to the community should be accorded a preference.*
– ORIGIN late Middle English (in the sense 'promotion'): from Old French, from medieval Latin *praeferentia,* from Latin *praeferre* 'carry in front' (see PREFER).

pref·er·ence share ▶ **n.** British term for PREFERRED STOCK.

pref·er·en·tial /ˌprefəˈrenCHəl/ ▶ **adj.** of or involving preference or partiality; constituting a favor or privilege: *preferential interest rates may be offered to employees* | *preferential trade terms.* ■ (of a union shop) giving employment preference to union members: *a preferential shop.* ■ (of voting or an election) in which the voter puts candidates in order of preference. ■ (of a creditor) having a claim on the receipt of payment from a debtor that will be met before those of other creditors.
– DERIVATIVES **pref·er·en·tial·ly adv.**
– ORIGIN mid 19th cent.: from PREFERENCE, on the pattern of *differential.*

pre·fer·ment /priˈfərmənt/ ▶ **n.** promotion or appointment to a position or office: *after ordination, preferment was fast* | *he had passed up endless preferments to remain with her.*

pre·ferred stock ▶ **n.** stock that entitles the holder to a fixed dividend, whose payment takes priority over that of common-stock dividends.

pre·fetch Computing ▶ **v.** /prēˈfeCH/ [with obj.] transfer (data) from main memory to temporary storage in readiness for later use.
▶ **n.** /ˈprēˌfeCH/ a process involving such a transfer.

pre·fig·ure /prēˈfigyər/ ▶ **v.** [with obj.] **1** be an early indication or version of (something): *the Hussite movement prefigured the Reformation.*
2 archaic imagine beforehand: *she had prefigured her small pilgrimage as made in solitude.*
– DERIVATIVES **pre·fig·u·ra·tion** /prēˌfigyəˈrāsHən/ **n.**, **pre·fig·ur·a·tive** /prēˈfigyərətiv/ **adj.**, **pre·fig·ure·ment n.**
– ORIGIN late Middle English: from ecclesiastical Latin *praefigurare* 'represent beforehand,' from *prae* 'before' + *figurare* 'to form, fashion.'

pre·fix /ˈprēˌfiks/ ▶ **n.** a word, letter, or number placed before another: *add the prefix 83 to the extension number.* ■ an element placed at the beginning of a word to adjust or qualify its meaning, e.g., *ex-, non-, re-* or (in some languages) as an inflection. ■ a title placed before a name, e.g., *Mr.*
▶ **v.** [with obj.] add (something) at the beginning as a prefix or introduction: *a preface is* ***prefixed to*** *the book.* ■ add a prefix or introduction to (something): *all three-digit numbers will now be* ***prefixed by*** *580.*
– DERIVATIVES **pre·fix·a·tion** /ˌprēfikˈsāsHən/ **n.**
– ORIGIN mid 16th cent. (as a verb): from Old French *prefixer,* from Latin *praefixus* 'fixed in front,' from the verb *praefigere,* from *prae* 'before' + *figere* 'to fix.' The noun is from modern Latin *praefixum,* neuter (used as a noun) of *praefixus,* and dates from the mid 17th cent.

pre·flight /ˈprēˈflīt/ ▶ **adj.** occurring before a flight in an aircraft: *our detailed preflight briefing.*

pre·fo·cus /ˈprēˈfōkəs/ ▶ **adj.** [attrib.] relating to or denoting a light bulb that is designed so that its

P

beam is focused automatically when it is fitted inside a lamp, esp. a vehicle headlamp.

pre·form /ˈprēfôrm/ ▶ **v.** [with obj.] (usu. as adj. **preformed**) form (something) beforehand: *a preformed pool.*

pre·for·ma·tion /ˌprēfôrˈmāSHən/ ▶ **n.** the action or process of preforming something. ■ Biology, historical the theory, now discarded, that an embryo develops from a complete miniature version of the organism. Often contrasted with EPIGENESIS.
– DERIVATIVES **pre·for·ma·tion·ist** /-ist/ **n.** & **.adj.**

pre·fron·tal /prēˈfrəntl/ ▶ **adj.** [attrib.] **1** Anatomy in or relating to the foremost part of the frontal lobe of the brain: *the prefrontal cortex.*
2 Zoology relating to or denoting a bone in front of the eye socket in some lower vertebrates (equivalent to part of the human ethmoid bone).
▶ **n.** Zoology a prefrontal bone.

pre·gen·i·tal /prēˈjenətl/ ▶ **adj. 1** Psychoanalysis relating to psychosexual development before the genital phase.
2 Zoology situated in front of the genital region.

preg·gers /ˈpregərz/ ▶ **adj.** [predic.] informal, chiefly Brit. pregnant.

pre·gla·cial /prēˈglāSHəl/ ▶ **adj.** of, relating to, or denoting a time before a glacial period.

preg·na·ble /ˈpregnəbəl/ ▶ **adj.** vulnerable to attack; not impregnable: *the fort's pregnable approaches.*
– ORIGIN late Middle English: from Old French *prenable,* literally 'takable,' from Latin *prehendere* 'seize.' The *g* was sometimes written in French, perhaps indicating palatal *n,* but has come to be pronounced as a separate sound in English.

preg·nan·cy /ˈpregnənsē/ ▶ **n.** (pl. **pregnancies**) the condition or period of being pregnant: *the first weeks of pregnancy | a straightforward pregnancy.*

preg·nant /ˈpregnənt/ ▶ **adj. 1** (of a woman or female animal) having a child or young developing in the uterus: *a pregnant woman | she was heavily* ***pregnant with*** *her second child | she was six months pregnant.*
2 full of meaning; significant or suggestive: *a pregnant pause | a development* ***pregnant with*** *implications.*
– DERIVATIVES **preg·nant·ly adv.**
– ORIGIN late Middle English: from Latin *praegnant-,* probably from *prae* 'before' + the base of *gnasci* 'be born.'

pre·heat /prēˈhēt/ ▶ **v.** [with obj.] heat (something, esp. an oven or grill) beforehand: *preheat the oven to 350°.*

pre·hen·sile /prēˈhensəl, -ˌsīl/ ▶ **adj.** (chiefly of an animal's limb or tail) capable of grasping.
– DERIVATIVES **pre·hen·sil·i·ty** /prēˌhenˈsilətē/ **n.**
– ORIGIN late 18th cent.: from French *préhensile,* from Latin *prehens-* 'grasped,' from the verb *prehendere,* from *prae* 'before' + *hendere* 'to grasp.'

P

pre·hen·sion /prēˈhenCHən/ ▶ **n. 1** Zoology & Psychology the action of grasping or seizing.
2 Philosophy an interaction of a subject with an event or entity that involves perception but not necessarily cognition.
– ORIGIN early 19th cent.: from Latin *prehensio(n-),* from *prehendere* 'to grasp.'

pre·his·tor·ic /ˌprē(h)iˈstôrik/ ▶ **adj.** of, relating to, or denoting the period before written records: *prehistoric man.* ■ informal very old, primitive, or out of date: *my dad's electric typewriter was a prehistoric machine.*
– DERIVATIVES **pre·his·to·ri·an** /-ˈstôrēən/ **n.**, **pre·his·tor·i·cal·ly** /-ik(ə)lē/ **adv.**
– ORIGIN mid 19th cent.: from French *préhistorique* (see PRE-, HISTORIC).

pre·his·to·ry /prēˈhist(ə)rē/ ▶ **n.** the period of time before written records: *myths that stretch back into prehistory.* ■ the events or conditions leading up to a particular occurrence or phenomenon: *the prehistory of capitalism.*

pre·hos·pi·tal /prēˈhäspitl/ ▶ **adj.** relating to procedures administered or care provided prior to a patient's arrival at a hospital: *the bandage was developed primarily for a prehospital setting.*

pre·hy·per·ten·sion /ˌprēˌhīpərˈtenSHən/ ▶ **n.** the condition of having blood pressure between 120/80 mmHg and 139/89 mmHg, considered an indication of risk for hypertension.
– DERIVATIVES **pre·hy·per·ten·sive** /-siv/ **adj.**
– ORIGIN early 21st cent.

pre·ig·ni·tion /ˌprē-igˈniSHən/ ▶ **n.** the premature combustion of the fuel–air mixture in an internal combustion engine.

pre·im·plan·ta·tion /ˌprē-imˌplanˈtāSHən/ ▶ **adj.** Zoology & Medicine occurring or existing between the fertilization of an ovum and its implantation in the wall of the uterus.

pre·in·dus·tri·al /ˌprē-inˈdəstrēəl/ ▶ **adj.** of or relating to a time before industrialization: *a preindustrial society.*

pre·in·stall /ˌprē-inˈstôl/ (Brit. also **preinstal**) ▶ **v.** (**preinstalls** or Brit. **preinstals**, **preinstalling**, **preinstalled**) another term for PRELOAD.

pre·judge /prēˈjəj/ ▶ **v.** [with obj.] form a judgment on (an issue or person) prematurely and without having adequate information: *it is wrong to prejudge an issue on the basis of speculation.*
– DERIVATIVES **pre·judg·ment** (also **prejudgement**) **n.**

prej·u·dice /ˈprejədəs/ ▶ **n. 1** preconceived opinion that is not based on reason or actual experience: *English* ***prejudice against*** *foreigners | anti-Jewish prejudices.* ■ dislike, hostility, or unjust behavior formed on such a basis: *accusations of racial prejudice.*
2 chiefly Law harm or injury that results or may result from some action or judgment: *prejudice resulting from delay in the institution of the proceedings.*
▶ **v.** [with obj.] **1** give rise to prejudice in (someone); make biased: *the statement might prejudice the jury.*
2 chiefly Law cause harm to (a state of affairs): *delay is likely to prejudice the child's welfare.*
– PHRASES **without prejudice** Law without detriment to any existing right or claim: *the payment was made* ***without any prejudice to*** *her rights.*
– ORIGIN Middle English (sense 2 of the noun): from Old French, from Latin *praejudicium,* from *prae* 'in advance' + *judicium* 'judgment.'

prej·u·diced /ˈprejədəst/ ▶ **adj.** having or showing a dislike or distrust that is derived from prejudice; bigoted: *people are* ***prejudiced against*** *us | prejudiced views.*

prej·u·di·cial /ˌprejəˈdiSHəl/ ▶ **adj.** harmful to someone or something; detrimental: *the behavior is* ***prejudicial to*** *good order and discipline.*
– DERIVATIVES **prej·u·di·cial·ly adv.**
– ORIGIN late Middle English: from Old French *prejudiciel,* from *prejudice* (see PREJUDICE).

pre·kin·der·gar·ten /prēˈkindərˌgärtn, -ˌgärdn/ (abbr.: **pre-K**) ▶ **n.** day care with some educational content for children younger than five, provided by elementary schools or preschools.

prel·a·cy /ˈpreləsē/ ▶ **n.** (pl. **prelacies**) chiefly archaic the government of the Christian Church by clerics of high social rank and power. ■ the office or rank of a prelate. ■ (**the prelacy**) prelates collectively.
– ORIGIN Middle English: from Anglo-Norman French *prelacie,* from medieval Latin *prelatia,* from *praelatus* (see PRELATE).

pre·lap·sar·i·an /ˌprēlapˈse(ə)rēən/ ▶ **adj.** Theology or literary characteristic of the time before the Fall of Man; innocent and unspoiled: *a prelapsarian Eden of astonishing plenitude.*
– ORIGIN late 19th cent.: from PRE- 'before,' on the pattern of *sublapsarian.*

prel·ate /ˈprelət/ ▶ **n.** formal or historical a bishop or other high ecclesiastical dignitary.
– DERIVATIVES **pre·lat·ic** /priˈlatik/ **adj.**, **pre·lat·i·cal** /priˈlatikəl/ **adj.**
– ORIGIN Middle English: from Old French *prelat,* from medieval Latin *praelatus* 'civil dignitary,' past participle (used as a noun) of Latin *praeferre* 'carry before,' also 'place before in esteem.'

prel·a·ture /ˈpreləCHər, -ˌCHŏŏr/ ▶ **n.** the office, rank, or sphere of authority of a prelate. ■ (**the prelature**) prelates collectively.
– ORIGIN early 17th cent.: from French *prélature,* from medieval Latin *praelatura,* from *praelatus* 'civil dignitary' (see PRELATE).

pre·launch /prēˈlônCH, -ˈlänCH/ ▶ **adj.** concerning activities or conditions before the launch of a spacecraft, campaign, product, etc.

pre·life /prēˈlīf/ ▶ **adj. 1** prior to the appearance of life forms on earth: *prelife molecules.*
2 (often in religious contexts) prior to a particular life or stage of life.

pre·lim /ˈprēˌlim/ ▶ **n.** informal **1** an event that precedes or prepares for another, in particular: ■ a preliminary examination, esp. at a college. ■ a preliminary round in an athletic competition: *the prelims of the 400-meter free relay.*
2 (**prelims**) the pages preceding the main text of a book, including the title, contents, and preface.
– ORIGIN late 19th cent.: abbreviation of PRELIMINARY.

pre·lim·i·nar·y /priˈliməˌnerē/ ▶ **adj.** denoting an action or event preceding or done in preparation for something fuller or more important: *preliminary talks | the discussions were seen as* ***preliminary to*** *the policy paper.*
▶ **n.** (pl. **preliminaries**) an action or event preceding or preparing for something fuller or more important: *the bombardment was resumed as a* ***preliminary to*** *an infantry attack.* ■ (**preliminaries**) business or talk, esp. of a formulaic or polite nature, taking place before an action or event: *she began speaking, without preliminaries.* ■ a preliminary round in a sporting competition. ■ (**preliminaries**) fuller form of PRELIMS (see PRELIM (sense 2)).
– PHRASES **preliminary to** preparatory to; in advance of.
– DERIVATIVES **pre·lim·i·nar·i·ly** /-ˌliməˈnerəlē/ **adv.**
– ORIGIN mid 17th cent.: from modern Latin *praeliminaris* or French *préliminaire,* from Latin *prae* 'before' + *limen, limin-* 'threshold.'

pre·lin·gual·ly deaf /prēˈliNGg(yə)wəlē/ ▶ **adj.** deaf from birth or from a time in infancy before the development of the ability to speak.

pre·lin·guis·tic /ˌprēliNGˈgwistik/ ▶ **adj.** of or at a stage before the development of language (by the human species) or the acquisition of speech (by a child).

pre·lit·er·ate /prēˈlitərət/ ▶ **adj.** of, relating to, or denoting a society or culture that has not developed the use of writing.

pre·load /prēˈlōd/ ▶ **v.** [with obj.] load beforehand: *the software comes preloaded on the PC.* ■ give (a mechanical component) an internal load independent of any working load, typically in order to reduce distortion or noise in operation.
▶ **n.** something loaded or applied as a load beforehand: *prices include DOS and Windows preload.*

pre·loved /prēˈləvd/ ▶ **adj.** informal previously owned; secondhand: *preloved toys are just as appealing.*

prel·ude /ˈprelˌ(y)o͞od, ˈprāˌl(y)o͞od/ ▶ **n. 1** an action or event serving as an introduction to something more important: *education cannot simply be a* ***prelude to*** *a career.*
2 an introductory piece of music, most commonly an orchestral opening to an act of an opera, the first movement of a suite, or a piece preceding a fugue. ■ a short piece of music of a similar style, esp. for the piano. ■ the introductory part of a poem or other literary work.
▶ **v.** [with obj.] serve as a prelude or introduction to: *the bombardment preluded an all-out final attack.*
– DERIVATIVES **pre·lu·di·al** /priˈlo͞odēəl, prā-/ **adj.**
– ORIGIN mid 16th cent.: from French *prélude,* from medieval Latin *praeludium,* from Latin *praeludere* 'play beforehand,' from *prae* 'before' + *ludere* 'to play.'

prem. ▶ **abbr.** premium.

pre·ma·lig·nant /prēməˈlignənt/ ▶ **adj.** another term for PRECANCEROUS.

pre·mar·i·tal /prēˈmaritl/ ▶ **adj.** occurring or existing before marriage: *premarital sex.*
– DERIVATIVES **pre·mar·i·tal·ly adv.**

pre·mas·ter /prēˈmastər/ ▶ **v.** [with obj.] Computing make a master copy of (data) on a hard disk before writing it to a CD-ROM.

pre·match /prēˈmaCH/ ▶ **adj.** in or relating to the period before a sports match: *his prematch press conference.*

pre·ma·ture /ˌprēməˈCHŏŏr, -ˈt(y)ŏŏr/ ▶ **adj.** occurring or done before the usual or proper time; too early: *the sun can cause premature aging |* [with infinitive] *it would be premature to do so at this stage.* ■ (of a baby) born before the end of the full term of gestation, esp. three or more weeks before.
– DERIVATIVES **pre·ma·tu·ri·ty** /-ˈCHŏŏritē, -ˈt(y)ŏŏr-/ **n.**
– ORIGIN late Middle English (in the sense 'ripe, mature'): from Latin *praematurus* 'very early,' from *prae* 'before' + *maturus* 'ripe.'

pre·ma·ture·ly /ˌprēməˈCHŏŏrlē, -ˈt(y)ŏŏrlē/ ▶ **adv.** before the due time; ahead of time: *his son died prematurely |* [as submodifier] *prematurely gray hair.*

pre·max·il·lar·y /prēˈmaksəˌlerē/ ▶ **adj.** Anatomy situated in front of the maxilla.

pre·med /ˈprēˈmed/ ▶ **n. 1** a program of premedical studies. ■ a student in such a program.
2 short for PREMEDICATION.
▶ **adj.** short for PREMEDICAL.

pre·med·i·cal /prēˈmedikəl/ ▶ **adj.** of, relating to, or engaged in study in preparation for medical school.

pre·med·i·ca·tion /ˌprēˌmedəˈkāSHən/ ▶ **n.** medication that is given in preparation for an operation or other treatment.

pre·med·i·tate /priˈmedəˌtāt, prē-/ ▶ **v.** [with obj.] (usu. as adj. **premeditated**) think out or plan (an action, esp. a crime) beforehand: *premeditated murder.*
– ORIGIN mid 16th cent.: from Latin *praemeditat-* 'thought out before,' from the verb *praemeditari,* from *prae* 'before' + *meditari* 'meditate.'

pre·med·i·ta·tion /priˌmedəˈtāSHən, prē-/ ▶ **n.** the action of planning something (esp. a crime) beforehand: *the defendant said there was no planning or premeditation.*

pre·men·o·pau·sal /ˌprēˌmenəˈpôzəl/ ▶ **adj.** of or in the period of a woman's life immediately preceding menopause.

pre·men·stru·al /prēˈmenstr(o͞o)əl/ ▶ **adj.** of, occurring, or experienced before menstruation: *premenstrual tension.*
– DERIVATIVES **pre·men·stru·al·ly** **adv.**

pre·men·stru·al syn·drome (abbr.: **PMS**) ▶ **n.** any of a complex of symptoms (including emotional tension and fluid retention) experienced by some women in the days immediately before menstruation.

pre·mier /prēˈm(y)i(ə)r, ˈprēmēər, ˈprēˌmi(ə)r/ ▶ **adj.** [attrib.] first in importance, order, or position; leading: *Germany's premier rock band | the premier national publication.* ■ of earliest creation: *the premier issue of the quarterly.*
▶ **n.** a prime minister or other head of government. ■ (in Australia and Canada) the chief minister of a government of a state or province.
– ORIGIN late 15th cent.: from Old French, 'first,' from Latin *primarius* 'principal.'

pre·mier cru /prəˈmyā ˈkrY, ˈkrē/ ▶ **n.** (pl. **premiers crus** /prəˈmyā ˈkrY, ˈkrē(z)/) (chiefly in French official classifications) a wine of a superior grade, or the vineyard that produces it. Compare with **GRAND CRU.**
– ORIGIN French, literally 'first growth.'

pre·miere /prēˈmyer, -ˈmi(ə)r/ ▶ **n.** the first performance of a musical or theatrical work or the first showing of a movie.
▶ **v.** [with obj.] give the first performance of: *his first stage play was premiered at the Birmingham Repertory Theatre.* ■ [no obj.] (of a musical or theatrical work or a film) have its first performance: *the show premiered in New York this week.*
– ORIGIN late 19th cent.: French *première*, feminine of *premier* 'first' (see **PREMIER**).

pre·mier·ship /prēˈm(y)irˌsHip, ˈprēmēər-, ˈprēˌmi(ə)r-/ ▶ **n.** the office or position of a prime minister or other head of government.

pre·mil·len·ni·al /ˌprēməˈlenēəl/ ▶ **adj.** existing or occurring before a new millennium. ■ Christian Theology relating to or believing in premillennialism.

pre·mil·len·ni·al·ism /ˌprēməˈlenēəˌlizəm/ ▶ **n.** (among some Christian Protestants) the doctrine that the prophesied millennium of blessedness will begin with the imminent Second Coming of Christ. Compare with **POSTMILLENNIALISM.**
– DERIVATIVES **pre·mil·len·ni·al·ist** **n.**

Prem·in·ger /ˈpreminjər/, Otto (Ludwig) (1906–86), US movie director, born in Austria. Notable productions: *The Moon Is Blue* (1953), *The Man with the Golden Arm* (1955), and *Bonjour Tristesse* (1959).

prem·ise /ˈpremis/ ▶ **n.** Logic a previous statement or proposition from which another is inferred or follows as a conclusion: *if the premise is true, then the conclusion must be true.* ■ an assertion or proposition which forms the basis for a work or theory: *the fundamental premise of the report.*
▶ **v.** [with obj.] (**premise something on/upon**) base an argument, theory, or undertaking on: *the reforms were premised on our findings.* ■ state or presuppose (something) as a premise: [with clause] *one school of thought premised that the cosmos is indestructible.* ■ archaic state by way of introduction: [with clause] *I will premise generally that I hate lecturing.*
– ORIGIN late Middle English: from Old French *premisse*, from medieval Latin *praemissa (propositio)* '(proposition) set in front,' from Latin *praemittere*, from *prae* 'before' + *mittere* 'send.'

prem·is·es /ˈpreməsəz/ ▶ **plural n.** a house or building, together with its land and outbuildings, occupied by a business or considered in an official context: *business premises | supplying alcoholic liquor for consumption* ***on the premises.***

pre·mi·um /ˈprēmēəm/ ▶ **n.** (pl. **premiums**) **1** an amount to be paid for an insurance policy.
2 a sum added to an ordinary price or charge: *customers are reluctant to pay a premium for organic fruit.* ■ a sum added to interest or wages; a bonus. ■ [as modifier] relating to or denoting a commodity or product of superior quality and therefore a higher price: *premium beers.* ■ Stock Market the amount by which the price of a share or other security exceeds its issue price, its nominal value, or the value of the assets it represents: *the fund has traded at a premium of 12%.*
3 something given as a reward, prize, or incentive: *the Society of Arts awarded him a premium.*
– PHRASES **at a premium 1** scarce and in demand: *space was at a premium.* **2** above the usual or nominal price: *books with pristine dust jackets are less common and sell at a premium.* **put** (or **place**) **a premium on** regard or treat as particularly valuable or important: *he put a premium on peace and stability.*
– ORIGIN early 17th cent. (in the sense 'reward, prize'): from Latin *praemium* 'booty, reward,' from *prae* 'before' + *emere* 'buy, take.'

pre·mix /ˈprēˈmiks/ ▶ **v.** [with obj.] mix in advance: *I premix all my colors.*
▶ **n.** a mixture that is provided already mixed, in particular: ■ a ready-mixed feed for cattle or horses. ■ a preparation of the dry components of a building material such as concrete or plaster.

pre·mod·ern /prēˈmädərn/ ▶ **adj.** anticipating the modern phase or period of something while not actually belonging to it: *our nostalgia for premodern times when natural bonds to kith and kin were unshakable continues to surface.*

pre·mo·lar /prēˈmōlər/ ▶ **n.** a tooth situated between the canine and the molar teeth. An adult human normally has eight, two in each jaw on each side.

pre·mo·ni·tion /ˌprēməˈnisHən, ˌprem-/ ▶ **n.** a strong feeling that something is about to happen, esp. something unpleasant: *he had* ***a premonition of*** *imminent disaster.*
– DERIVATIVES **pre·mon·i·to·ry** /prēˈmänəˌtôrē/ **adj.**
– ORIGIN mid 16th cent. (in the sense 'warning'): from French *prémonition*, from late Latin *praemonitio(n-)*, from Latin *praemonere*, from *prae* 'before' + *monere* 'warn.'

pre·mor·bid /prēˈmôrbəd/ ▶ **adj.** Medicine & Psychiatry preceding the occurrence of symptoms of disease or disorder.

pre·mo·tor /ˈprēˈmōtər/ ▶ **adj.** [attrib.] Anatomy relating to or denoting the anterior part of the motor cortex in the frontal lobe of the brain, which is concerned with coordinating voluntary movement.

pre·mul·ti·ply /prēˈməltəˌplī/ ▶ **v.** (**premultiplies, premultiplying, premultiplied**) [with obj.] Mathematics multiply (a vector, matrix, or element of a group) noncommutatively by a preceding factor.
– DERIVATIVES **pre·mul·ti·pli·ca·tion** /-ˌməltəpliˈkāsHən/ **n.**

pre·na·tal /prēˈnātl/ ▶ **adj.** before birth; during or relating to pregnancy: *prenatal development.*
– DERIVATIVES **pre·na·tal·ly** /-ˈnātl-ē/ **adv.**

pre·need ▶ **adj.** denoting a scheme in which one pays in advance for a service or facility: *pre-need funeral sales.*

pren·tice /ˈprentis/ ▶ **n. & v.** archaic term for **APPRENTICE.**
– DERIVATIVES **pren·tice·ship** /-ˌsHip/ **n.**

pre·nup /prēˈnəp/ ▶ **n.** informal a prenuptial agreement.
– ORIGIN 1990s: abbreviation.

pre·nup·tial /prēˈnəpsHəl, -CHəl/ ▶ **adj.** existing or occurring before marriage: *prenuptial pregnancy.* ■ Zoology existing or occurring before mating.

pre·nup·tial a·gree·ment ▶ **n.** an agreement made by a couple before they marry concerning the ownership of their respective assets should the marriage fail.

pre·oc·cu·pa·tion /ˌprēˌäkyəˈpāsHən/ ▶ **n.** the state or condition of being preoccupied or engrossed with something: *his* ***preoccupation with*** *politics.* ■ a subject or matter that engrosses someone: *their main preoccupation was how to feed their families.*
– ORIGIN late 16th cent. (first used in rhetoric in the sense 'anticipating and meeting objections beforehand'): from Latin *praeoccupatio(n-)*, from *praeoccupare* 'seize beforehand' (see **PREOCCUPY**).

pre·oc·cu·py /prēˈäkyəˌpī/ ▶ **v.** (**preoccupies, preoccupying, preoccupied**) [with obj.] (of a matter or subject) dominate or engross the mind of (someone) to the exclusion of other thoughts: *his mother was* ***preoccupied with*** *paying the bills* | (as adj. **preoccupied**) *she seemed a bit preoccupied.*
– ORIGIN mid 16th cent.: from **PRE-** + **OCCUPY**, suggested by Latin *praeoccupare* 'seize beforehand.'

pre·oc·u·lar /prēˈäkyələr/ ▶ **adj.** in front of the eye.

pre-Oed·i·pal /prēˈedəpəl, -ˈēdə-/ ▶ **adj.** Psychology existing or occurring before the onset of the Oedipal phase of development. See **OEDIPUS COMPLEX.**

pre-op /ˈprēˌäp/ informal ▶ **adj.** short for **PREOPERATIVE.**
▶ **n.** a tranquilizing injection or other treatment administered in preparation for a surgical operation.

pre·op·er·a·tive /prēˈäpərətiv/ ▶ **adj.** denoting, administered in, or occurring in the period before a surgical operation.
– DERIVATIVES **pre·op·er·a·tive·ly** **adv.**

pre·or·bit·al /prēˈôrbətl/ ▶ **adj.** chiefly Zoology situated in front of the orbit or eye socket.

pre·or·dain /ˌprēôrˈdān/ ▶ **v.** [with obj.] (usu. **be preordained**) decide or determine (an outcome or course of action) beforehand: *you might think the company's success was preordained* | (as adj. **preordained**) *a divinely preordained plan of creation.*

pre·or·der /priˈôrdər/ ▶ **v.** order (an item of merchandise) before it is available, with the understanding that it will be shipped later.
▶ **n.** an order for an item that has not yet been made commercially available.

pre·owned /prēˈōnd/ ▶ **adj.** secondhand.

prep[1] /prep/ ▶ **n.** informal a student or graduate of a preparatory school: *preps as well as Westerners with Ivy League degrees.*
– ORIGIN late 19th cent.: abbreviation of **PREPARATORY.**

prep[2] informal ▶ **v.** (**preps, prepping, prepped**) [with obj.] prepare (something); make ready: *scores of volunteers help prep the food.* ■ [no obj.] prepare oneself for an event: *to prep for his role he trimmed his unruly locks.*
▶ **n.** preparation: *I do the prep* | [as modifier] *I had virtually no prep time.*
– ORIGIN 1920s: abbreviation of **PREPARE** or **PREPARATION.**

prep. ▶ **abbr.** preposition.

pre·pack·age /prēˈpakij/ ▶ **v.** [with obj.] (usu. as adj. **prepackaged**) pack or wrap (goods, esp. food) on the site of production or before sale: *prepackaged lasagnas.*

pre·paid /prēˈpād/ past and past participle of **PREPAY.**

prep·a·ra·tion /ˌprepəˈrāsHən/ ▶ **n.** the action or process of making ready or being made ready for use or consideration: *the preparation of a draft contract | the project is* ***in preparation.*** ■ (usu. **preparations**) something done to get ready for an event or undertaking: *she continued her* ***preparations for*** *the party.* ■ a substance that is specially made up and usually sold, esp. a medicine or food. ■ a specimen that has been prepared for scientific or medical examination: *a microscope preparation.* ■ Music (in conventional harmony) the sounding of the discordant note in a chord in the preceding chord where it is not discordant, lessening the effect of the discord.
– ORIGIN late Middle English: via Old French from Latin *praeparatio(n-)*, from *praeparare* 'make ready before' (see **PREPARE**).

pre·par·a·tive /prēˈpe(ə)rətiv, -ˈpar-/ ▶ **adj.** preparatory.
▶ **n.** a thing that acts as a preparation: *schools where parents send children as a preparative for worldly success.*
– DERIVATIVES **pre·par·a·tive·ly** **adv.**

pre·par·a·to·ry /priˈpe(ə)rəˌtôrē, -ˈparə-, ˈprep(ə)rə-/ ▶ **adj.** serving as or carrying out preparation for a task or undertaking: *more preparatory work is needed.* ■ Brit. relating to education in a preparatory school: *preparatory schooling.*
– PHRASES **preparatory to** as a preparation for: *she applied her makeup preparatory to leaving.*
– ORIGIN late Middle English: from late Latin *praeparatorius*, from *praeparat-* 'made ready beforehand,' from the verb *praeparare* (see **PREPARE**).

pre·par·a·to·ry school ▶ **n. 1** a private school that prepares students for college.
2 Brit. a private school for students between the ages of seven and thirteen.

pre·pare /priˈpe(ə)r/ ▶ **v.** [with obj.] **1** make (something) ready for use or consideration: *prepare a brief summary of the article.* ■ (as adj. **prepared**) created in advance; preplanned: *the spokesman was reading a prepared statement.* ■ make (food or a meal) ready for cooking or eating: *she was busy preparing lunch.* ■ make (someone) ready or able to do or deal with something: *schools should* ***prepare*** *children* ***for*** *life | by this time I was* ***prepared for*** *anything* | [no obj.] *she took time off to* ***prepare for*** *her exams.* ■ (**be prepared to do something**) be willing to do something: *I wasn't prepared to go along with that.* ■ make (a chemical product) by a reaction or series of reactions.
2 Music (in conventional harmony) lead up to (a discord) by means of preparation.
– DERIVATIVES **pre·par·er** **n.**
– ORIGIN late Middle English: from French *préparer* or Latin *praeparare*, from *prae* 'before' + *parare* 'make ready.'

pre·par·ed·ness /prəˈpe(ə)r(ə)dnis/ ▶ **n.** a state of readiness, esp. for war: *the country maintained a high level of military preparedness.*

pre·pared pi·an·o ▶ **n.** a piano with objects placed on or between the strings, or some strings retuned, to produce an unusual tonal effect.

pre·pay /prēˈpā/ ▶ **v.** (**prepays, prepaying**; past and past participle **prepaid**) [with obj.] (usu. as adj. **prepaid**) pay for in advance: *prepaid health plans.*

P

PRONUNCIATION KEY ə *ago, up*; ər *over, fur*; a *hat*; ā *ate*; ä *car*; e *let*; ē *see*; i *fit*; ī *by*; NG *sing*; ō *go*; ô *law, for*; oi *toy*; o͝o *good*; o͞o *goo*; ou *out*; TH *thin*; T͟H *then*; ZH *vision*

– DERIVATIVES **pre·pay·a·ble** adj., **pre·pay·ment** n.

prepd. ▶ abbr. prepared.

pre·pense /pri'pens/ ▶ adj. [usu. postpositive] dated, chiefly Law deliberate; intentional: *malice prepense.*
– DERIVATIVES **pre·pense·ly** adv.
– ORIGIN early 18th cent.: alteration of *prepensed*, past participle of obsolete *prepense*, from Old French *purpenser*, from *por-* 'beforehand' + *penser* 'think.' The prefix *pre-* was substituted to emphasize the notion of 'beforehand.'

pre·plan /'prē'plan/ ▶ v. [with obj.] (usu. as adj. **preplanned**) plan in advance: *a preplanned route.*

prepn. ▶ abbr. preparation.

pre·pol·y·mer /prē'päləmər/ ▶ n. Chemistry a substance that represents an intermediate stage in polymerization, and can be usefully manipulated before polymerization is completed.

pre·pon·der·ance /pri'pändərəns/ ▶ n. the quality or fact of being greater in number, quantity, or importance: *the preponderance of women among older people | forests with a preponderance of Apache pine.*

pre·pon·der·ant /pri'pändərənt/ ▶ adj. predominant in influence, number, or importance: *the preponderant influence of the US within the alliance.*
– DERIVATIVES **pre·pon·der·ant·ly** adv.
– ORIGIN late Middle English: from Latin *praeponderant-* 'weighing more,' from the verb *praeponderare* (see PREPONDERATE).

pre·pon·der·ate /pri'pändə,rāt/ ▶ v. [no obj.] be greater in number, influence, or importance: *the advantages* **preponderate over** *this apparent disadvantage.*
– ORIGIN early 17th cent. (in the sense 'weigh more, have greater intellectual weight'): from Latin *praeponderat-* 'of greater weight,' from the verb *praeponderare*, from *prae* 'before' + *ponderare* 'weigh, consider.'

pre·pose /prē'pōz/ ▶ v. [with obj.] Linguistics place (an element or word) in front of another.
– ORIGIN late 15th cent. (in the sense 'place in authority'): from French *préposer*, suggested by Latin *praeponere* 'put before.'

prep·o·si·tion /,prepə'zisHən/ ▶ n. Grammar a word governing, and usually preceding, a noun or pronoun and expressing a relation to another word or element in the clause, as in "the man *on* the platform," "she arrived *after* dinner," "what did you do it *for*?"
– DERIVATIVES **prep·o·si·tion·al** /-SHənl/ adj., **prep·o·si·tion·al·ly** /-SHənl-ē/ adv.
– ORIGIN late Middle English: from Latin *praepositio(n-)*, from the verb *praeponere*, from *prae* 'before' + *ponere* 'to place.'

USAGE There is a traditional view, set forth by the 17th-century poet and dramatist John Dryden, that it is incorrect to put a preposition at the end of a sentence, as in *where do you come from?* or *she's not a writer I've ever come across.* The rule was formulated on the basis that, since in Latin a preposition cannot come after the word it governs or is linked with, the same should be true of English. What this rule fails to take into account is that English is not like Latin in this respect, and in many cases (particularly in questions and with phrasal verbs) the attempt to move the preposition produces awkward, unnatural-sounding results. Winston Churchill famously objected to the rule, saying *"This is the sort of English up with which I will not put."* In standard English the placing of a preposition at the end of a sentence is widely accepted, provided the use sounds natural and the meaning is clear.

prep·o·si·tion·al ob·ject /,prepə'zisHənl 'äbjəkt, -jekt/ ▶ n. Grammar a noun phrase governed by a preposition.

prep·o·si·tion·al phrase ▶ n. a modifying phrase consisting of a preposition and its object.

pre·pos·i·tive /prē'päzətiv/ ▶ adj. Grammar (of a word, particle, etc.) placed in front of the word that it governs or modifies.
– ORIGIN late 16th cent.: from late Latin *praepositivus* (see PRE-, POSITIVE).

pre·pos·sess·ing /,prēpə'zesiNG/ ▶ adj. [often with negative] attractive or appealing in appearance: *he was not a prepossessing sight.*
– DERIVATIVES **pre·pos·ses·sion** /-'zesHən/ n.

pre·pos·ter·ous /pri'päst(ə)rəs/ ▶ adj. contrary to reason or common sense; utterly absurd or ridiculous: *a preposterous suggestion.*
– DERIVATIVES **pre·pos·ter·ous·ly** adv., **pre·pos·ter·ous·ness** n.
– ORIGIN mid 16th cent.: from Latin *praeposterus* 'reversed, absurd' (from *prae* 'before' + *posterus* 'coming after') + -OUS.

pre·po·tent /prē'pōtnt/ ▶ adj. greater than others in power or influence. ■ (of a breeding animal) showing great effectiveness in transmitting hereditary characteristics to its offspring.
– DERIVATIVES **pre·po·tence** n., **pre·po·ten·cy** n.
– ORIGIN late Middle English: from Latin *praepotent-* 'having greater power,' from *prae* 'before, ahead' + *posse* 'be able.'

prep·py /'prepē/ (also **preppie**) informal ▶ n. (pl. **preppies**) a student or graduate of an expensive preparatory school or a person resembling such a student in dress or appearance.
▶ adj. (**preppier**, **preppiest**) of or typical of such a person, esp. with reference to their style of dress: *the preppy look.*
– ORIGIN early 20th cent.: from PREP SCHOOL + -Y².

pre·pran·di·al /prē'prandēəl/ ▶ adj. formal or humorous done or taken before dinner or lunch: *a preprandial glass of sherry.* ■ Medicine occurring or done before a meal.
– ORIGIN early 19th cent.: from PRE- 'before' + Latin *prandium* 'a meal' + -AL.

pre·preg /'prē'preg/ ▶ n. a fibrous material preimpregnated with a particular synthetic resin, used in making reinforced plastics.
– ORIGIN 1950s: from PRE- 'before' + *(im)preg(nated).*

pre·press /'prē'pres/ ▶ adj. of or relating to typesetting, page layout, and other work done on a publication before it is actually printed.

pre·print ▶ v. /prē'print/ [with obj.] (usu. as adj. **preprinted**) print (something) in advance: *a preprinted form.*
▶ n. /'prē,print/ something that is printed in advance, esp. a part of a work printed and issued before general publication of that work.

pre·proc·ess /prē'präs,es, prē'prōs,es, -əs/ ▶ v. [with obj.] subject (data) to preliminary processing.

pre·proc·es·sor /prē'präs,esər, -'prōs,esər, -əsər/ ▶ n. a computer program that modifies data to conform with the input requirements of another program.

pre·pro·duc·tion /,prēprə'dəksHən/ ▶ n. work done on a product, esp. a film or broadcast program, before full-scale production begins: [as modifier] *the preproduction script.*

pre·pro·gram /prē'prō,gram, -grəm/ ▶ v. (**preprograms**, **preprogramming**, **preprogrammed** or **preprograms**, **preprograming**, **preprogramed**) [with obj.] (usu. as adj. **preprogrammed**) program (a computer or other electronic device) in advance for ease of use: *a preprogrammed function key.* ■ program (something) into a computer or other electronic device before use: *preprogrammed messages.*

prep school ▶ n. another term for PREPARATORY SCHOOL.

pre·pu·ber·tal /prē'pyōōbərtl/ ▶ adj. another term for PREPUBESCENT.
– DERIVATIVES **pre·pu·ber·ty** /-bərtē/ n.

pre·pu·bes·cent /,prēpyōō'besənt/ ▶ adj. relating to or in the period preceding puberty: *a prepubescent girl.*
▶ n. a prepubescent boy or girl.
– DERIVATIVES **pre·pu·bes·cence** n.

pre·pub·li·ca·tion /,prē,pəbli'kāsHən/ ▶ adj. issued or occurring before publication: *prepublication censorship.*
▶ n. publication in advance.

pre·puce /'prē,pyōōs/ ▶ n. Anatomy **1** technical term for FORESKIN.
2 the fold of skin surrounding the clitoris.
– DERIVATIVES **pre·pu·tial** /prē'pyōōsHəl/ adj.
– ORIGIN late Middle English: from French *prépuce*, from Latin *praeputium.*

pre·qual·i·fy /prē'kwälə,fī/ ▶ v. [no obj.] qualify in advance to take part in something: (as adj. **prequalifying**) *players who fail at the prequalifying stage.*

pre·quel /'prēkwəl, -kwil/ ▶ n. a story or movie containing events that precede those of an existing work: *the film is* **a prequel to** *the cult TV series.*
– ORIGIN 1970s: from PRE- 'before' + SEQUEL.

Pre-Raph·a·el·ite /'rafēə,līt, -rāfē-, -'rāfē-/ ▶ n. a member of a group of English 19th-century artists, including Holman Hunt, Millais, and D. G. Rossetti, who consciously sought to emulate the simplicity and sincerity of the work of Italian artists from before the time of Raphael.

Seven young English artists and writers founded the **Pre-Raphaelite Brotherhood** in 1848 as a reaction against the slick sentimentality and academic convention of much Victorian art. Their work is characterized by strong line and color, naturalistic detail, and often biblical or literary subjects. The group began to disperse in the 1850s, and the term became applied to the rather different later work of Rossetti, and that of Burne-Jones and William Morris, in which a romantic and decorative depiction of classical and medieval themes had come to predominate.

▶ adj. of or relating to the Pre-Raphaelites. ■ of a style or appearance associated with the later pre-Raphaelites or esp. with the women they frequently used as models, with long, thick, wavy auburn hair, pale skin, and a fey demeanor.
– DERIVATIVES **Pre-Raph·a·el·it·ism** /-,līt,izəm/ n.

pre·re·cord /,prēri'kôrd/ ▶ v. [with obj.] (often as adj. **prerecorded**) record (sound or film) in advance: *a prerecorded talk.* ■ record sound on (a tape or other medium) beforehand.

pre·reg·is·tra·tion /,prē,rejəs'trāsHən/ ▶ n. the action of registering or being registered in advance: *members are entitled to free preregistration.*

pre·re·lease /,prērə'lēs, 'prērə,lēs/ ▶ adj. of, relating to, or denoting a record, movie, or other product that has not yet been generally released: *a prerelease version of the software.* ■ of or relating to the period before the release of a suspect or prisoner.
▶ n. a movie, record, or other product given restricted availability before being generally released.

pre·req·ui·site /prē'rekwəzət/ ▶ n. a thing that is required as a prior condition for something else to happen or exist: *sponsorship is not* **a prerequisite for** *any of our courses.*
▶ adj. required as a prior condition: *the student must have the prerequisite skills.*

USAGE See usage at PERQUISITE.

pre·rog·a·tive /pri'rägətiv, pə'räg-/ ▶ n. a right or privilege exclusive to a particular individual or class: *owning an automobile was still the prerogative of the rich.* ■ a faculty or property distinguishing a person or class: *it's not a female prerogative to feel insecure.* ■ (also **royal prerogative**) the right of the sovereign, which in British law is theoretically subject to no restriction.
▶ adj. [attrib.] Brit. Law arising from the prerogative of the Crown (usually delegated to the government or the judiciary) and based in common law rather than statutory law: *the monarch retained the formal prerogative power to appoint the Prime Minister.*
– ORIGIN late Middle English: via Old French from Latin *praerogativa* '(the verdict of) the political division that was chosen to vote first in the assembly,' feminine (used as noun) of *praerogativus* 'asked first,' from *prae* 'before' + *rogare* 'ask.'

pre·rog·a·tive court ▶ n. historical (in the UK) either of two ecclesiastical courts at Canterbury and York formerly responsible for the probate of wills involving property in more than one diocese.

pre·rog·a·tive of mer·cy ▶ n. the right and power of a sovereign, president, or other supreme authority to commute a death sentence, to change the mode of execution, or to pardon an offender.

Pres. ▶ abbr. President.

pres·age /'presij, pri'sāj/ ▶ v. [with obj.] (of an event) be a sign or warning that (something, typically something bad) will happen: *the outcome of the game presaged the coming year.* ■ archaic (of a person) predict: *lands he could measure, terms and tides presage.*
▶ n. a sign or warning that something, typically something bad, will happen; an omen or portent: *the fever was a somber presage of his final illness.* ■ archaic a feeling of presentiment or foreboding: *he had a strong presage that he had only a very short time to live.*
– DERIVATIVES **pres·ag·er** n. (archaic).
– ORIGIN late Middle English (as a noun): via French from Latin *praesagium*, from *praesagire* 'forebode,' from *prae* 'before' + *sagire* 'perceive keenly.'

Presb. ▶ abbr. Presbyterian.

Presby. ▶ abbr. Presbyterian.

pres·by·o·pi·a /,prezbē'ōpēə, ,pres-/ ▶ n. farsightedness caused by loss of elasticity of the lens of the eye, occurring typically in middle and old age.
– DERIVATIVES **pres·by·op·ic** /-'äpik/ adj.
– ORIGIN late 18th cent.: modern Latin, from Greek *presbus* 'old man' + *ōps, ōp-* 'eye.'

pres·by·ter /'prezbitər, 'pres-/ ▶ n. historical an elder or minister of the Christian Church. ■ formal (in Presbyterian churches) an elder. ■ formal (in Episcopal churches) a minister of the second order, under the authority of a bishop; a priest.
– DERIVATIVES **pres·byt·er·al** /prez'bitərəl, pres-/ adj., **pres·byt·er·ate** /prez'bitə,rāt, pres-/ n., **pres·by·te·ri·al** /,prezbi'ti(ə)rēəl, ,pres-/ adj., **pres·by·ter·ship** /-,SHip/ n.
– ORIGIN late 16th cent.: via ecclesiastical Latin from Greek *presbuteros* 'elder' (used in the New Testament to denote an elder of the early church), comparative of *presbus* 'old (man).'

Pres·by·te·ri·an /ˌprezbəˈtirēən, ˌpres-/ ▶ **adj.** of, relating to, or denoting a Christian Church or denomination governed by elders according to the principles of Presbyterianism.
▶ **n.** a member of a Presbyterian Church. ■ an advocate of the Presbyterian system.
– ORIGIN mid 17th cent.: from ecclesiastical Latin *presbyterium* (see PRESBYTERY) + -AN.

Pres·by·te·ri·an·ism /ˌprezbəˈtirēəˌnizəm, ˌpres-/ ▶ **n.** a form of Protestant Church government in which the church is administered locally by the minister with a group of elected elders of equal rank, and regionally and nationally by representative courts of ministers and elders.

> Presbyterianism was first introduced in Geneva in 1541 under John Calvin, in the belief that it best represented the pattern of the early church. There are now many Presbyterian Churches (often called Reformed Churches) worldwide, notably in the Netherlands and Scotland and in countries with which they have historic links (including the US and Northern Ireland).

pres·by·ter·y /ˈprezbəˌterē, ˈpres-, -bətrē/ ▶ **n.** (pl. **presbyteries**) **1** [treated as sing. or pl.] a body of church elders and ministers, esp. (in Presbyterian churches) an administrative body (court) representing all the local congregations of a district. ■ a district represented by such a body of elders and ministers. **2** the house of a Roman Catholic parish priest. **3** chiefly Architecture the eastern part of a church chancel beyond the choir; the sanctuary.
– ORIGIN late Middle English (sense 3): from Old French *presbiterie*, via ecclesiastical Latin from Greek *presbuterion*, from *presbuteros* (see PRESBYTER).

pre·school ▶ **adj.** /ˈprēˈsko͞ol/ [attrib.] of or relating to the time before a child is old enough to go to kindergarten or elementary school: *a preschool play group.*
▶ **n.** /ˈprēˌsko͞ol/ a nursery school: *she goes to preschool.*
– DERIVATIVES **pre·school·er** **n.**

pre·science /ˈpresH(ē)əns, ˈprē-/ ▶ **n.** the fact of knowing something before it takes place; foreknowledge: *with extraordinary prescience, Jung actually predicted the Nazi eruption.*

pre·scient /ˈpresH(ē)ənt, ˈprē-/ ▶ **adj.** having or showing knowledge of events before they take place: *a prescient warning.*
– DERIVATIVES **pre·scient·ly** **adv.**
– ORIGIN early 17th cent.: from Latin *praescient-* 'knowing beforehand,' from the verb *praescire*, from *prae* 'before' + *scire* 'know.'

pre·sci·en·tif·ic /ˌprēˌsīənˈtifik/ ▶ **adj.** of or relating to the time before the development of modern science or the application of scientific method.

pre·scind /priˈsind/ ▶ **v.** [no obj.] (**prescind from**) formal leave out of consideration: *we have prescinded from many vexing issues.* ■ [with obj.] cut off or separate from something: *his is an idea entirely prescinded from all of the others.*
– ORIGIN mid 17th cent. (in the sense 'cut off abruptly or prematurely'): from Latin *praescindere*, from *prae* 'before' + *scindere* 'to cut.'

Pres·cott /ˈpresˌkät/ a historic city in west central Arizona; pop. 42,697 (est. 2008).

pre·scribe /priˈskrīb/ ▶ **v.** [with obj.] (of a medical practitioner) advise and authorize the use of (a medicine or treatment) for someone, esp. in writing: *Dr. Greene prescribed magnesium sulfate* | [with two objs.] *the doctor prescribed her a drug called amantadine.* ■ recommend (a substance or action) as something beneficial: *marriage is often prescribed as a universal remedy.* ■ state authoritatively or as a rule that (an action or procedure) should be carried out: *rules prescribing five acts for a play are purely arbitrary* | (as adj. **prescribed**) *doing things in the prescribed manner.*
– DERIVATIVES **pre·scrib·er** **n.**
– ORIGIN late Middle English (in the sense 'confine within bounds,' also as a legal term meaning 'claim by prescription'): from Latin *praescribere* 'direct in writing,' from *prae* 'before' + *scribere* 'write.'

> **USAGE** The verbs **prescribe** and **proscribe** do not have the same meaning. **Prescribe** is a much more common word than **proscribe** and means either 'issue a medical prescription' or 'recommend with authority': *the doctor* ***prescribed*** *antibiotics.* **Proscribe**, on the other hand, is a formal word meaning 'condemn or forbid': *gambling was strictly* ***proscribed*** *by the authorities.*

pre·script /ˈprēˌskript, priˈskript/ ▶ **n.** formal or dated an ordinance, law, or command.
– ORIGIN mid 16th cent.: from Latin *praescriptum* 'something directed in writing,' neuter past participle of *praescribere* (see PRESCRIBE).

pre·scrip·tion /priˈskripSHən/ ▶ **n.** **1** an instruction written by a medical practitioner that authorizes a patient to be provided a medicine or treatment: *he scribbled a prescription for tranquilizers* | *antidepressants available only by* ***prescription*** | [as modifier] *prescription drugs.* ■ the action of prescribing a medicine or treatment: *the unnecessary prescription of antibiotics.* ■ a medicine or remedy that is prescribed: *I've got to pick up my prescription.*
2 a recommendation that is authoritatively put forward: *effective prescriptions for sustaining rural communities.* ■ the authoritative recommendation of an action or procedure: *rather than prescription there would be guidance.*
3 (also **positive prescription**) Law the establishment of a claim founded on the basis of a long or indefinite period of uninterrupted use or of long-standing custom.
– ORIGIN late Middle English (as a legal term): via Old French from Latin *praescriptio(n-)*, from the verb *praescribere* (see PRESCRIBE). Sense 1 dates from the late 16th cent.

pre·scrip·tive /priˈskriptiv/ ▶ **adj.** **1** of or relating to the imposition or enforcement of a rule or method: *these guidelines are not intended to be prescriptive.* ■ Linguistics attempting to impose rules of correct usage on the users of a language: *a prescriptive grammar book.* Often contrasted with DESCRIPTIVE.
2 (of a right, title, or institution) having become legally established or accepted by long usage or the passage of time: *a prescriptive right of way.* ■ archaic established by long-standing custom or usage: *his regular score at the bar and his prescriptive corner at the winter's fireside.*
– DERIVATIVES **pre·scrip·tive·ly** **adv.**, **pre·scrip·tive·ness** **n.**, **pre·scrip·tiv·ism** /-ˈskriptəˌvizəm/ **n.**, **pre·scrip·tiv·ist** /-vist/ **n. & adj.**
– ORIGIN mid 18th cent.: from late Latin *praescriptivus* 'relating to a legal exception,' from *praescript-* 'directed in writing,' from the verb *praescribere* (see PRESCRIBE).

pre·sea·son /ˈprēˈsēzən/ ▶ **adj.** (of a sporting event) taking place before the regular season.
▶ **n.** [in sing.] the period of time before the regular season.

pre·se·lect /ˌprēsəˈlekt/ ▶ **v.** [with obj.] select or set in advance: *the personal shopper would preselect clothes for a customer.*
– DERIVATIVES **pre·se·lec·tion** /-səˈleksHən/ **n.**, **pre·se·lec·tive** /-səˈlektiv/ **adj.**

pre·se·lec·tor /ˌprēsəˈlektər/ ▶ **n.** a device for selecting a mechanical or electrical operation in advance of its execution.

pres·ence /ˈprezəns/ ▶ **n.** the state or fact of existing, occurring, or being present in a place or thing: *her presence still comforts me* | *the presence of chlorine in the atmosphere* | *the memorial was unveiled* ***in the presence of*** *24 veterans.* ■ a person or thing that exists or is present in a place but is not seen: *the monks became aware of a strange presence.* ■ [in sing.] a group of people, esp. soldiers or police, stationed in a particular place: *the USA would maintain a presence in the Indian Ocean region.* ■ the impressive manner or appearance of a person: *Richard was not a big man, but his presence was overwhelming* | [in sing.] *he has a real physical presence.*
– PHRASES **make one's presence felt** have a strong and obvious effect or influence on others or on a situation. **presence of mind** the ability to remain calm and take quick, sensible action: *he had the presence of mind to record the scene on video.*
– ORIGIN Middle English: via Old French from Latin *praesentia* 'being at hand,' from the verb *praeesse* (see PRESENT[1]).

pres·ence cham·ber ▶ **n.** a room, esp. one in a palace, in which a monarch or other distinguished person receives visitors.

pre·se·nile /prēˈsēˌnīl, -ˈsenˌīl/ ▶ **adj.** occurring in or characteristic of the period of life preceding old age: *the factors that may predispose women to presenile Alzheimer's disease are not known.*

pres·ent[1] /ˈprezənt/ ▶ **adj.** **1** [predic.] (of a person) in a particular place: *a doctor must be present at the ringside* | *the speech caused embarrassment to all those present.* ■ (of a thing) existing or occurring in a place or thing: *organic molecules are present in comets.*
2 [attrib.] existing or occurring now: *she did not expect to find herself in her present situation.* ■ now being considered or discussed: *the present article cannot answer every question.* ■ Grammar (of a tense or participle) expressing an action now going on or habitually performed or a condition now existing.
▶ **n.** [in sing.] (usu. **the present**) the period of time now occurring: *they are happy and at peace, refusing to think beyond the present.* ■ Grammar a present tense: *the verbs are all in the present.* See also HISTORIC PRESENT.
– PHRASES **at present** now: *membership at present stands at about 5,000.* **for the present** for now; temporarily. (**there is**) **no time like the present** used to suggest that something should be done now rather than later: *"When do you want me to leave?" "No time like the present."* **present company excepted** excluding those who are here now. **these presents** Law, formal this document: *the premises outlined in red on the Plan annexed to these presents.*
– ORIGIN Middle English: via Old French from Latin *praesent-* 'being at hand,' present participle of *praeesse*, from *prae* 'before' + *esse* 'be.'

pre·sent[2] /priˈzent/ ▶ **v.** [with obj.] **1** (**present something to**) give something to (someone) formally or ceremonially: *a top executive will present an award to employees who built the F-150.* ■ (**present someone with**) give someone (something) in such a way: *my students presented me with some flowers.* ■ show or offer (something) for others to scrutinize or consider: *he stopped and presented his passport.* ■ formally introduce (someone) to someone else: *may I present my wife?* ■ proffer (compliments or good wishes) in a formal manner: *may I present the greetings of my master?* ■ formally deliver (a check or bill) for acceptance or payment: *a check presented by Mr. Jackson was returned by the bank.* ■ Law bring (a complaint, petition, or evidence) formally to the notice of a court. ■ (of a company or producer) put (a show or exhibition) before the public.
2 bring about or be the cause of (a problem or difficulty): *this should not present much difficulty.* ■ exhibit (a particular state or appearance) to others: *the EC presented a united front over the crisis.* ■ represent (someone) to others in a particular way, typically one that is false or exaggerated: *he* ***presented himself as*** *a hardworking man.* ■ (**present oneself**) come forward into the presence of another or others, esp. for a formal occasion; appear: *he failed to present himself in court.* ■ (**present itself**) (of an opportunity or idea) occur and be available for use or exploitation: *when a favorable opportunity presented itself, he would submit his proposition.* ■ [no obj.] (often **present with**) Medicine (of a patient) come forward for or undergo initial medical examination for a particular condition or symptom: *the patient presented with mild clinical encephalopathy.* ■ [no obj.] Medicine (of a part of a fetus) be directed toward the cervix during labor. ■ [no obj.] Medicine (of an illness) manifest itself.
3 hold out or aim (a firearm) at something so as to be ready to fire: *they were to present their rifles, take aim, and fire.*
– PHRASES **present arms** (usually as a command) hold a rifle vertically in front of the body as a salute.
– DERIVATIVES **pre·sent·er** **n.**
– ORIGIN Middle English: from Old French *presenter*, from Latin *praesentare* 'place before' (in medieval Latin 'present as a gift'), from *praesent-* 'being at hand' (see PRESENT[1]).

pres·ent[3] /ˈprezənt/ ▶ **n.** a thing given to someone as a gift: *a Christmas present.*
– PHRASES **make a present of** give as a gift: *he had made a present of a hacienda to the president.*
– ORIGIN Middle English: from Old French, originally in the phrase *mettre une chose en present à quelqu'un* 'put a thing into the presence of a person.'

pre·sent·a·ble /priˈzentəbəl/ ▶ **adj.** clean, well dressed, or decent enough to be seen in public: *I did my best to make myself look presentable.*
– DERIVATIVES **pre·sent·a·bil·i·ty** /-ˌzentəˈbilətē/ **n.**, **pre·sent·a·bly** /-blē/ **adv.**

pres·en·ta·tion /ˌprēˌzenˈtāSHən, ˌprezən-, ˌprēzən-/ ▶ **n.** **1** the proffering or giving of something to someone, esp. as part of a formal ceremony: *the presentation of certificates to new members* | *the trophy presentations.* ■ the manner or style in which something is given, offered, or displayed: *the presentation of foods is designed to stimulate your appetite.* ■ a formal introduction of someone, esp. at court. ■ chiefly historical the action or right of formally proposing a candidate for a church benefice or other position: *the Earl of Pembroke offered Herbert the presentation of the living of Bremerton.* ■ a demonstration or display of a product or idea: *a sales presentation.*
2 Medicine the position of a fetus in relation to the cervix at the time of delivery: *breech presentation.* ■ the coming forward of a patient for initial examination and diagnosis: *all patients in this group were symptomatic at initial presentation.*
3 (**Presentation of Christ**) another term for CANDLEMAS.
– DERIVATIVES **pres·en·ta·tion·al** /-SHənl/ **adj.**, **pres·en·ta·tion·al·ly** /-SHənl-ē/ **adv.**

– ORIGIN late Middle English: via Old French from late Latin *praesentatio(n-)*, from Latin *praesentare* 'place before' (see PRESENT[2]).

pres·en·ta·tion graph·ics PRESENTATION SOFTWARE.

pres·en·ta·tion soft·ware ▶ **n.** software used to create a sequence of text and graphics, and often audio and video, to accompany a speech or public presentation. Also called PRESENTATION GRAPHICS.

pre·sen·ta·tive /priˈzentətiv/ ▶ **adj.** historical (of a benefice) to which a patron has the right of presentation.
– ORIGIN mid 16th cent.: probably from medieval Latin, based on Latin *praesentare* (see PRESENT[2]).

pres·ent-day ▶ **adj.** [attrib.] of or relating to the current period of time: *present-day technological developments.*

pres·en·tee /ˌprezənˈtē, priˌzenˈtē/ ▶ **n.** a person nominated or recommended for an office or position, esp. a church benefice.
– ORIGIN late 15th cent.: from Anglo-Norman French, literally 'presented,' from the verb *presenter* (see PRESENT[2]).

pre·sen·tient /prēˈsenCHənt/ ▶ **adj.** rare having a presentiment.
– ORIGIN early 19th cent.: from Latin *praesentient-* 'perceiving beforehand,' from the verb *praesentire*, from *prae* 'before' + *sentire* 'to feel.'

pre·sen·ti·ment /priˈzentəmənt/ ▶ **n.** an intuitive feeling about the future, esp. one of foreboding: *a presentiment of disaster.*
– ORIGIN early 18th cent.: from obsolete French *présentiment.*

pres·ent·ism /ˈprezenˌtizəm/ ▶ **n.** uncritical adherence to present-day attitudes, esp. the tendency to interpret past events in terms of modern values and concepts.
– DERIVATIVES **pres·en·tist adj.**

pres·ent·ly /ˈprezəntlē/ ▶ **adv. 1** after a short time; soon: *this will be examined in more detail presently.* **2** at the present time; now: *there are presently 1,128 people on the waiting list.*

> **USAGE** In *the pain will lessen presently,* the meaning of **presently** is 'soon.' In *limited resources are presently available,* the meaning is 'at this moment, now.' Both senses date back to the Middle Ages, but the second sense fell into disfavor between the 17th and 20th centuries. Although some traditionalists still object to it, the 'now' sense is widely used and generally regarded as acceptable standard English.

pre·sent·ment /priˈzentmənt/ ▶ **n.** Law, chiefly historical a formal presentation of information to a court, esp. by a sworn jury regarding an offense or other matter.
– ORIGIN Middle English: from Old French *presentement*, from *presenter* 'place before' (see PRESENT[3]).

pres·ent par·ti·ci·ple ▶ **n.** Grammar the form of a verb, ending in *-ing* in English, which is used in forming continuous tenses, e.g., in *I'm thinking,* alone in nonfinite clauses, e.g., in *sitting here, I haven't a care in the world,* as a noun, e.g., in *good thinking,* and as an adjective, e.g., in *running water.*

pres·ent val·ue (also **net present value**) ▶ **n.** Finance the value in the present of a sum of money, in contrast to some future value it will have when it has been invested at compound interest.

pres·er·va·tion /ˌprezərˈvāSHən/ ▶ **n.** the action of preserving something: *the preservation of the city's green spaces | food preservation.* ■ the state of being preserved, esp. to a specified degree: *the homestead is in a fine state of preservation.*
– ORIGIN late Middle English: via Old French from medieval Latin *praeservatio(n-)*, from late Latin *praeservare* 'to keep' (see PRESERVE).

pres·er·va·tion·ist /ˌprezərˈvāSHənəst/ ▶ **n.** a supporter or advocate of the preservation of something, esp. of historic buildings and artifacts.

pre·serv·a·tive /priˈzərvətiv/ ▶ **n.** a substance used to preserve foodstuffs, wood, or other materials against decay.
▶ **adj.** acting to preserve something: *the preservative effects of freezing.*
– ORIGIN late Middle English: via Old French from medieval Latin *praeservativus*, from late Latin *praeservat-* 'kept,' from the verb *praeservare* (see PRESERVE).

pre·serve /priˈzərv/ ▶ **v.** [with obj.] maintain (something) in its original or existing state: *all records of the past were zealously preserved* | (as adj. **preserved**) *a magnificently preserved monastery.* ■ retain (a condition or state of affairs): *a fight to preserve local democracy.* ■ maintain or keep alive (a memory or quality): *the film has preserved all the qualities of the novel.* ■ keep safe from harm or injury: *a place for preserving endangered species.* ■ treat or refrigerate (food) to prevent its decomposition or fermentation. ■ prepare (fruit) for long-term storage by boiling it with sugar: (as adj. **preserved**) *those sweet preserved fruits associated with Cremona.* ■ keep (game or an area where game is found) undisturbed to allow private hunting or shooting.
▶ **n. 1** (usu. **preserves**) food made with fruit preserved in sugar, such as jam or marmalade: *home-made preserves.*
2 a sphere of activity regarded as being reserved for a particular person or group: *the civil service became* ***the preserve of*** *the educated middle class.*
3 a place where game is protected and kept for private hunting or shooting.
– DERIVATIVES **pre·serv·a·ble adj.**, **pre·serv·er n.**
– ORIGIN late Middle English (in the sense 'keep safe from harm'): from Old French *preserver*, from late Latin *praeservare*, from *prae-* 'before, in advance' + *servare* 'to keep.'

pre·served lem·on /priˈzərvd/ ▶ **n.** lemons or lemon slices preserved in salt and lemon juice, used as an ingredient in Moroccan cooking.

pre·serv·ice /ˈprēˈsərvəs/ ▶ **adj.** of or relating to the period before a person takes a job that requires training, esp. in teaching: *preservice training.*

pre·set /prēˈset/ ▶ **v.** (**presets**, **presetting**; past and past participle **preset**) [with obj.] (usu. as adj. **preset**) set or adjust (a value that controls the operation of a device) in advance of its use: *the water is heated quickly to a preset temperature.*
▶ **n.** a control on electronic equipment or on software that is set or adjusted beforehand to facilitate use.

pre·shrunk /prēˈSHrəNGk/ ▶ **adj.** (of a fabric or garment) having undergone a shrinking process during manufacture to prevent further shrinking in use.
– DERIVATIVES **pre·shrink** /-ˈSHriNGk/ **v.**

pre·side /priˈzīd/ ▶ **v.** [no obj.] **1** be in the position of authority in a meeting or gathering: *Bishop Herbener presided at the meeting* | (as adj. **presiding**) *the sentence imposed by the presiding judge.* ■ (**preside over**) be in charge of (a place or situation): *he presided over a period of great budgetary recklessness.*
2 (**preside at**) play (a musical instrument, esp. a keyboard instrument) at a public gathering.
– ORIGIN early 17th cent.: from French *présider*, from Latin *praesidere*, from *prae* 'before' + *sedere* 'sit.'

pres·i·den·cy /ˈprez(ə)dənsē, ˈprezəˌdensē/ ▶ **n.** (pl. **presidencies**) the office of president: *the presidency of the US.* ■ the period of this: *the liberal climate that existed during Carter's presidency.* ■ Christian Church the role of the priest or minister who conducts a Eucharist. ■ (also **First Presidency**) (in the Mormon church) a council of three officers forming the highest administrative body.
– ORIGIN late 16th cent.: from medieval Latin *praesidentia*, from *praesidere* 'sit before' (see PRESIDE).

pres·i·dent /ˈprez(ə)dənt, ˈprezəˌdent/ ▶ **n. 1** the elected head of a republican state: *the Irish president* | [as title] *President Kennedy.* ■ the head of a society, council, or other organization: *the president of the European Community.* ■ the head of a college or university. ■ the head of a company.
2 Christian Church the celebrant at a Eucharist.
– DERIVATIVES **pres·i·den·tial** /ˌprezəˈdenCHəl/ **adj.**, **pres·i·den·tial·ly** /ˌprezəˈdenCHəlē/ **adv.**, **pres·i·dent·ship** /-ˌSHip/ **n.** (archaic).
– ORIGIN late Middle English: via Old French from Latin *praesident-* 'sitting before' (see PRESIDE).

pres·i·dent-e·lect ▶ **n.** (pl. **presidents-elect**) a person who has been elected president but has not yet taken up office.

Pres·i·den·tial Med·al of Free·dom /ˌprezəˈdenCHəl/ ▶ **n.** (in the US) a medal constituting the highest award that can be given to a civilian in peacetime.

Pres·i·den·tial Range a range in northern New Hampshire's White Mountains that includes Mount Washington, which, at 6,288 feet (1,918 m), is the highest peak in the northeastern US.

pres·i·dent pro tem·po·re /ˈprō ˈtempəˌrē/ (also **president pro tem** /ˈprō ˈtem/) ▶ **n.** a high-ranking senator of the majority party who presides over the US Senate in the absence of the vice president.

pre·sid·i·o /priˈsidēˌō, -ˈsēdē-/ ▶ **n.** (pl. **presidios**) (in Spain and Spanish America) a fortified military settlement.
– ORIGIN Spanish, from Latin *praesidium* 'garrison.'

pre·sid·i·um /priˈsidēəm, -ˈzid-/ (also **praesidium**) ▶ **n.** a standing executive committee in a communist country. ■ (**Presidium**) the committee of this type in the former Soviet Union, which functioned as the legislative authority when the Supreme Soviet was not sitting.
– ORIGIN 1920s: from Russian *prezidium*, from Latin *praesidium* 'protection, garrison' (see PRESIDE).

Pres·ley /ˈprezlē, ˈpres-/, Elvis (Aaron) (1935–77), US singer; known as the **King of Rock and Roll**. He was the dominant personality of early rock and roll with songs such as "Heartbreak Hotel," "Don't Be Cruel," and "Hound Dog" and was noted for the frank sexuality of his performances. He also made numerous movies, including *King Creole* (1958), and became a cult figure after his death.

pre-So·crat·ic ▶ **adj.** of, relating to, or denoting the speculative philosophers active in the ancient Greek world in the 6th and 5th centuries BC (before the time of Socrates), who attempted to find rational explanations for natural phenomena. They included Parmenides, Anaxagoras, Empedocles, and Heraclitus.
▶ **n.** a pre-Socratic philosopher.

pre·sort /prēˈsôrt/ ▶ **v.** [with obj.] sort outgoing mail by zip code in order to take advantage of a cheaper rate of postage.

press[1] /pres/ ▶ **v. 1** move or cause to move into a position of contact with something by exerting continuous physical force: [with obj.] *he pressed his face to the glass* | [no obj.] *her body pressed against his.* ■ [with obj.] exert continuous physical force on (something), typically in order to operate a device or machine: *he pressed a button and the doors slid open.* ■ [with obj.] squeeze (someone's arm or hand) as a sign of affection. ■ [no obj.] move in a specified direction by pushing: *the mob was still pressing forward.* ■ (of an enemy or opponent) attack persistently and fiercely: [no obj.] *their enemies pressed in on all sides* | [with obj.] *two assailants were pressing Agrippa.* ■ [no obj.] (**press on/ahead**) continue in one's action: *he stubbornly* ***pressed on with*** *his work.* ■ [with obj.] Weightlifting raise (a specified weight) by first lifting it to shoulder height and then gradually pushing it upward above the head.
2 [with obj.] apply pressure to (something) to flatten, shape, or smooth it, typically by ironing: *she pressed her nicest blouse* | (as adj. **pressed**) *immaculately pressed trousers.* ■ apply pressure to (a flower or leaf) between sheets of paper in order to dry and preserve it. ■ extract (juice or oil) by crushing or squeezing fruit, vegetables, etc.: (as adj. **pressed**) *freshly pressed grape juice.* ■ squeeze or crush (fruit, vegetables, etc.) to extract the juice or oil. ■ manufacture (something, esp. a phonograph record) by molding under pressure.
3 [with obj.] forcefully put forward (an opinion, claim, or course of action): *Rose did not press the point.* ■ make strong efforts to persuade or force (someone) to do or provide something: *when I* ***pressed him for*** *precise figures, he evaded the subject* | [with infinitive] *the marketing directors were pressed to justify their expenditure* | [no obj.] *they continued to* ***press for*** *changes in legislation.* ■ [no obj.] Golf try too hard to achieve distance with a shot, at the risk of inaccuracy. ■ (**press something on/upon**) insist that (someone) accept an offer or gift: *he pressed dinner invitations on her.* ■ [no obj.] (of something, esp. time) be in short supply and so demand immediate action. ■ (**be pressed**) have barely enough of something, esp. time: *I'm very pressed for time.* ■ (**be pressed to do something**) have difficulty doing or achieving something: *they may be* ***hard pressed*** *to keep their promise.*
▶ **n. 1** a device for applying pressure to something in order to flatten or shape it or to extract juice or oil: *a flower press | a wine press.* ■ a machine that applies pressure to a workpiece by means of a tool, in order to punch shapes.
2 a printing press. ■ [often in names] a business that prints or publishes books: *the Clarendon Press.* ■ the process of printing: *the book is ready* ***to go to press.***
3 (**the press**) [treated as sing. or pl.] newspapers or journalists viewed collectively: *the press was notified* | [as modifier] *press coverage.* ■ coverage in newspapers and magazines: *there's no point in demonstrating if you don't get any press* | [in sing.] *the mayor has had a bad press for years.*
4 an act of pressing something: *the system summons medical help at the press of a button.* ■ [in sing.] a closely packed crowd or mass of people or things: *among the press of cars he saw a taxi.* ■ dated pressure of business. ■ Weightlifting an act of raising a weight to shoulder height and then gradually pushing it above the head. ■ Basketball any of various forms of close guarding by the defending team.
5 chiefly Irish Scottish a large cupboard.
– PHRASES **press charges** see CHARGE. **press something home** see HOME. **press (the) flesh** informal (of a celebrity or politician) greet people by shaking hands.
– ORIGIN Middle English: from Old French *presse* (noun), *presser* (verb), from Latin *pressare* 'keep pressing,' frequentative of *premere.*

press[2] ▶ **v.** [with obj.] (**press someone/something into**) put (someone or something) to a specified

use, esp. as a temporary or makeshift measure: *many of these stones have been pressed into service as gateposts.* ■ historical force (a man) to enlist in the army or navy.
▶ **n.** historical a forcible enlistment of men, esp. for the navy.
– ORIGIN late 16th cent.: alteration (by association with PRESS¹) of obsolete *prest* 'pay given on enlistment, enlistment by such payment,' from Old French *prest* 'loan, advance pay,' based on Latin *praestare* 'provide.'

press a·gent ▶ **n.** a person employed to organize advertising and publicity in the press on behalf of an organization or well-known person.

press·board /ˈpresˌbôrd/ ▶ **n.** a hard, dense kind of board with a smooth finish, typically made from wood or textile pulp or laminated wastepaper, and used as an electrical insulator and for making light furniture.

press·book /ˈpresbo͝ok/ ▶ **n. 1** a book of press cuttings.
2 a booklet or leaflet put together by a movie producer to publicize a new motion picture.

press box ▶ **n.** an area reserved for journalists at a sports event.

Press·burg /ˈpresbərg/ German name for BRATISLAVA.

press card ▶ **n.** an official authorization carried by a reporter, esp. one that gives admission to an event.

press clipping ▶ **n.** a paragraph or short article cut out of a newspaper or magazine.

press con·fer·ence ▶ **n.** an interview given to journalists by a prominent person in order to make an announcement or answer questions.

press·er foot ▶ **n.** the footplate of a sewing machine that holds the fabric down onto the part that feeds it under the needle.

press fit ▶ **n.** an interference fit between two parts in which one is forced under pressure into a slightly smaller hole in the other.
– DERIVATIVES **press-fit·ted** adj.

press gal·ler·y ▶ **n.** a place reserved for journalists observing the proceedings in a legislature or court of law.

press gang ▶ **n.** historical a body of men employed to enlist men forcibly into service in the army or navy.
▶ **v.** [with obj.] (**press-gang**) chiefly historical forcibly enlist (someone) into service in the army or navy.
■ (**press-gang someone into**) force someone to do something: *we press-ganged Simon into playing.*

press·ing /ˈpresiNG/ ▶ **adj.** (of a problem, need, or situation) requiring quick or immediate action or attention: *inflation was the most pressing problem | he had pressing business in Albany.* ■ (of an invitation) strongly expressed.
▶ **n.** a thing made by the application of force or weight, esp. a phonograph record. ■ a series of such things made at one time: *the first pressing of the live album.* ■ an act or instance of applying force or weight to something: *pure-grade olive oil is the product of the second or third pressings.*
– DERIVATIVES **press·ing·ly** adv.

press kit ▶ **n.** a package of promotional material provided to members of the press to brief them, esp. about a product, service, or candidate.

press·man /ˈpresˌmən, ˌman/ ▶ **n.** (pl. **pressmen**)
1 chiefly Brit. a journalist.
2 a person who operates a printing press.

press·mark /ˈpresˌmärk/ ▶ **n.** chiefly Brit. a call number.

pres·sor /ˈpresər/ ▶ **adj.** [attrib.] Physiology producing an increase in blood pressure by stimulating constriction of the blood vessels: *a pressor response.*

press re·lease ▶ **n.** an official statement issued to newspapers giving information on a particular matter.

press run ▶ **n.** the operation of a printing press for a single job (the number or entire set of items produced in such an operation): *the paper is increasing its press run from 75,000 to 95,000 copies.*

press time ▶ **n.** the moment when a magazine or other publication goes to press.

press-up ▶ **n.** British term for PUSHUP.

pres·sure /ˈpreSHər/ ▶ **n. 1** the continuous physical force exerted on or against an object by something in contact with it: *the slight extra pressure he applied to her hand.* ■ the force exerted per unit area: *gas can be fed to the turbines at a pressure of around 250 psi.*
2 the use of persuasion, influence, or intimidation to make someone do something: *the proposals put pressure on Britain to drop its demand | the many pressures on girls to worry about their looks.* ■ the influence or effect of someone or something: *oil prices came under some downward pressure.* ■ the feeling of stressful urgency caused by the necessity of doing or achieving something, esp. with limited time: *you need to be able to work under pressure and not get flustered | some offenders might find prison a refuge against the pressures of the outside world.*
▶ **v.** [with obj.] attempt to persuade or coerce (someone) into doing something: *it might now be possible to pressure him into resigning* | [with obj. and infinitive] *she pressured her son to accept a job offer from the bank.*
– ORIGIN late Middle English: from Old French, from Latin *pressura*, from *press-* 'pressed,' from the verb *premere* (see PRESS¹).

pres·sure cook·er ▶ **n.** an airtight pot in which food can be cooked quickly under steam pressure. ■ a highly stressful situation or assignment: *the conformist pressure cooker of high school.*
– DERIVATIVES **pres·sure-cook** v.

pres·sure gauge ▶ **n.** an instrument indicating pressure: *an oil pressure gauge.*

pres·sure group ▶ **n.** a group that tries to influence public policy in the interest of a particular cause: *an environmental pressure group.*

pres·sure hull ▶ **n.** the inner hull of a submarine, in which approximately atmospheric pressure is maintained when the vessel is submerged.

pres·sure lamp ▶ **n.** a portable oil or kerosene lamp in which the fuel is forced up into the mantle or burner by air pressure in the reservoir, which can be increased by pumping with a plunger.

pres·sure point ▶ **n.** a point on the surface of the body sensitive to pressure. ■ a point where an artery can be pressed against a bone to inhibit bleeding.

pres·sure suit ▶ **n.** an inflatable suit that protects the wearer against low pressure, e.g., when flying at a high altitude.

pres·sure ves·sel ▶ **n.** a container designed to hold material at high pressures. ■ an enclosed structure containing a nuclear reactor core immersed in pressurized coolant.

pres·sur·ize /ˈpreSHəˌrīz/ ▶ **v.** [with obj.] **1** produce or maintain raised pressure artificially in (a gas or its container): *the mixture was pressurized to 1,900 atmospheres* | (as adj. **pressurized**) *a pressurized can.* ■ maintain a tolerable atmospheric pressure in (an aircraft cabin) at a high altitude: (as adj. **pressurized**) *a pressurized cabin.*
2 attempt to persuade or coerce (someone) into doing something: *the protests were an attempt to pressurize the government into bringing an end to the violence* | [with obj. and infinitive] *people had been pressurized to vote.*
– DERIVATIVES **pres·sur·i·za·tion** /ˌpreSHərəˈzāSHən/ n.

pres·sur·ized-wa·ter re·ac·tor (abbr.: **PWR**) ▶ **n.** a nuclear reactor in which the fuel is uranium oxide clad in zircaloy and the coolant and moderator is water maintained at high pressure so that it does not boil at the operating temperature of the reactor.

press·work /ˈpresˌwərk/ ▶ **n. 1** the process of using a printing press. ■ printed matter, esp. with regard to its quality.
2 the shaping of metal by pressing or drawing it into a shaped hollow die.

Pres·ter John /ˈprestər ˈjän/ a legendary medieval Christian king of Asia (and later, of Ethiopia), said to have defeated the Muslims and to be destined to bring help to the Holy Land.
– ORIGIN Middle English: from Old French *prestre Jehan*, from medieval Latin *presbyter Johannes* 'priest John.'

pres·ti·dig·i·ta·tion /ˌprestəˌdijəˈtāSHən/ ▶ **n.** formal magic tricks performed as entertainment.
– DERIVATIVES **pres·ti·dig·i·ta·tor** /-ˈdijəˌtātər/ n.
– ORIGIN mid 19th cent.: from French, from *preste* 'nimble' + Latin *digitus* 'finger' + -ATION.

pres·tige /presˈtēZH, -ˈtēj/ ▶ **n.** widespread respect and admiration felt for someone or something on the basis of a perception of their achievements or quality: *he experienced a tremendous increase in prestige following his victory.* ■ [as modifier] denoting something that arouses such respect or admiration: *prestige wines.*
– ORIGIN mid 17th cent. (in the sense 'illusion, conjuring trick'): from French, literally 'illusion, glamour,' from late Latin *praestigium* 'illusion,' from Latin *praestigiae* (plural) 'conjuring tricks.' The transference of meaning occurred by way of the sense 'dazzling influence, glamour,' at first depreciatory.

pres·tige pric·ing ▶ **n.** the practice of pricing goods at a high level in order to give the appearance of quality.

pres·tig·ious /preˈstijəs, -ˈstē-/ ▶ **adj.** inspiring respect and admiration; having high status: *a prestigious academic post.*
– DERIVATIVES **pres·tig·i·ous·ly** adv., **pres·tig·i·ous·ness** n.
– ORIGIN mid 16th cent. (in the sense 'practicing legerdemain'): from late Latin *praestigiosus*, from *praestigiae* 'conjuring tricks.' The current sense dates from the early 20th cent.

pres·tis·si·mo /preˈstisəˌmō/ Music ▶ **adv. & adj.** (esp. as a direction) in a very quick tempo.
▶ **n.** (pl. **prestissimos**) a movement or passage marked to be performed in a very quick tempo.
– ORIGIN Italian, superlative of *presto* 'quick, quickly' (see PRESTO).

pres·to /ˈprestō/ ▶ **adv. & adj.** Music (esp. as a direction) in a quick tempo.
▶ **n.** (pl. **prestos**) Music a movement or passage marked to be performed in a quick tempo.
▶ **exclam.** a phrase announcing the successful completion of a trick, or suggesting that something has been done so easily that it seems to be magic: *just one quick squeeze and presto! A stir fry in seconds.*
– ORIGIN Italian, 'quick, quickly,' from late Latin *praestus* 'ready,' from Latin *praesto* 'at hand.'

Pres·ton /ˈprestən/ a city in northwestern England, the administrative center of the county of Lancashire, on the Ribble River; pop. 165,600 (est. 2009). It was the site in the 18th century of the first English cotton mills.

Pres·ton·pans, Bat·tle of /ˌprestənˈpanz/ a battle in 1745 near the town of Prestonpans just east of Edinburgh, Scotland, the first major engagement of the Jacobite uprising of 1745–46. The Jacobites routed the Hanoverians, leaving the way clear for Charles Edward Stuart's subsequent invasion of England.

pre·stressed /prēˈstrest/ ▶ **adj.** strengthened by the application of stress during manufacture, esp. (of concrete) by means of rods or wires inserted under tension before the material is set.
– DERIVATIVES **pre·stress·ing** /-ˈstresiNG/ n.

pre·sum·a·bly /priˈzo͞oməblē/ ▶ **adv.** [sentence adverb] used to convey that what is asserted is very likely though not known for certain: *the Yakima Indians presumably came from Asia by way of the Bering Strait.*

pre·sume /priˈzo͞om/ ▶ **v. 1** [with clause] suppose that something is the case on the basis of probability: *I presumed that the man had been escorted from the building* | [with obj. and complement] *the two men were presumed dead when the wreck of their boat was found.* ■ take for granted that something exists or is the case: *the argument presumes that only one person can do the work* | [with obj.] *the task demands skills that cannot be presumed and therefore require proper training.*
2 [no obj., with infinitive] be audacious enough to do something: *kindly don't presume to issue me orders in my own house.* ■ [no obj.] make unjustified demands; take liberties: *forgive me if I have presumed.* ■ [no obj.] (**presume on/upon**) unjustifiably regard (something) as entitling one to privileges: *she knew he regarded her as his protegée, but was determined not to presume on that.*
– DERIVATIVES **pre·sum·a·ble** adj.
– ORIGIN late Middle English: from Old French *presumer*, from Latin *praesumere* 'anticipate' (in late Latin 'take for granted'), from *prae* 'before' + *sumere* 'take.'

pre·sum·ing /priˈzo͞omiNG/ ▶ **adj.** archaic presumptuous.
– DERIVATIVES **pre·sum·ing·ly** adv.

pre·sump·tion /priˈzəmpSHən/ ▶ **n. 1** an act or instance of taking something to be true or adopting a particular attitude toward something, esp. at the start of a chain of argument or action: *the presumption of guilt has changed to a presumption of innocence.* ■ an idea that is taken to be true, and often used as the basis for other ideas, although it is not known for certain: *underlying presumptions about human nature.* ■ chiefly Law an attitude adopted in law or as a matter of policy toward an action or proposal in the absence of acceptable reasons to the contrary: *the planning policy shows a general presumption in favor of development.*
2 behavior perceived as arrogant, disrespectful, and transgressing the limits of what is permitted or appropriate: *he lifted her off the ground and she was enraged at his presumption.*
– ORIGIN Middle English: from Old French *presumpcion*, from Latin *praesumptio(n)* 'anticipation,' from the verb *praesumere* (see PRESUME).

pre·sump·tive /priˈzəmptiv/ ▶ **adj.** of the nature of a presumption; presumed in the absence of further information: *a presumptive diagnosis.* ■ Law

giving grounds for the inference of a fact or of the appropriate interpretation of the law. ■ another term for **PRESUMPTUOUS**.
– DERIVATIVES **pre·sump·tive·ly** adv.
– ORIGIN late Middle English: from French *présomptif, -ive*, from late Latin *praesumptivus*, from *praesumpt-* 'taken before,' from the verb *praesumere* (see **PRESUME**).

pre·sump·tu·ous /priˈzəmpCH(o͞o)əs/ ▶ adj. (of a person or their behavior) failing to observe the limits of what is permitted or appropriate: *I hope I won't be considered presumptuous if I offer some advice.*
– DERIVATIVES **pre·sump·tu·ous·ly** adv., **pre·sump·tu·ous·ness** n.
– ORIGIN Middle English: from Old French *presumptueux*, from late Latin *praesumptuosus*, variant of *praesumptiosus* 'full of boldness,' from *praesumptio* (see **PRESUMPTION**).

pre·sup·pose /ˌprēsəˈpōz/ ▶ v. [with obj.] (of an action, process, or argument) require as a precondition of possibility or coherence: *his relationships did not permit the degree of self-revelation that true intimacy presupposes.* ■ [with clause] tacitly assume at the beginning of a line of argument or course of action that something is the case: *your argument presupposes that it does not matter who is in power.*
– ORIGIN late Middle English: from Old French *presupposer*, suggested by medieval Latin *praesupponere*, from *prae* 'before' + *supponere* 'place under' (see **SUPPOSE**).

pre·sup·po·si·tion /ˌprēˌsəpəˈzisHən/ ▶ n. a thing tacitly assumed beforehand at the beginning of a line of argument or course of action: *images that challenge presuppositions about feminine handiwork.* ■ the action or state of presupposing or being presupposed.
– ORIGIN mid 16th cent.: from medieval Latin *praesuppositio(n-)*, from the verb *praesupponere* (see **PRESUPPOSE**).

pre·syn·ap·tic /ˌprēsəˈnaptik/ ▶ adj. Physiology relating to or denoting a nerve cell that releases a transmitter substance into a synapse during transmission of an impulse.
– DERIVATIVES **pre·syn·ap·ti·cal·ly** /-ik(ə)lē/ adv.

pret. ▶ abbr. preterite.

prêt-à-por·ter /ˌpret ä pôrˈtā/ ▶ adj. (of designer clothes) sold ready-to-wear as opposed to made to measure.
▶ n. designer clothes sold ready-to-wear.
– ORIGIN French, literally 'ready to wear.'

pre·tax /ˈprēˈtaks/ ▶ adj. (of income or profits) considered or calculated before the deduction of taxes: *pretax profits rose 23 percent.*

pre·teen /ˈprēˈtēn/ ▶ adj. [attrib.] of or relating to a child just under the age of thirteen.
▶ n. a child of such an age.

P

pre·tence ▶ n. British spelling of **PRETENSE**.

pre·tend /priˈtend/ ▶ v. **1** [with clause or infinitive] speak and act so as to make it appear that something is the case when in fact it is not: *I closed my eyes and pretended I was asleep* | *she turned the pages and pretended to read.* ■ engage in a game or fantasy that involves supposing something that is not the case to be so: *children pretending to be grown-ups.* ■ [with obj.] give the appearance of feeling or possessing (an emotion or quality); simulate: *she pretended a greater surprise than she felt.*
2 [no obj.] (**pretend to**) lay claim to (a quality or title): *he cannot pretend to sophistication.*
▶ adj. [attrib.] informal not really what it is represented as being; used in a game or deception: *the children are pouring out pretend tea for the dolls.*
– ORIGIN late Middle English: from Latin *praetendere* 'stretch forth, claim,' from *prae* 'before' + *tendere* 'stretch.' The adjective dates from the early 20th cent.

pre·tend·ed /priˈtendid/ ▶ adj. not genuine; assumed: *she interrupted him with pretended indignation.*

pre·tend·er /priˈtendər/ ▶ n. a person who claims or aspires to a title or position: *the pretender to the throne.*

pre·tense /ˈprēˌtens, priˈtens/ (Brit. **pretence**) ▶ n. **1** an attempt to make something that is not the case appear true: *his anger is masked by a pretense that all is well* | *they have finally abandoned their secrecy and pretense.* ■ a false display of feelings, attitudes, or intentions: *he asked me questions without any pretense at politeness.* ■ the practice of inventing imaginary situations in play: *before the age of two, children start to engage in pretense.* ■ affected and ostentatious speech and behavior.
2 (**pretense to**) a claim, esp. a false or ambitious one: *he was quick to disclaim any pretense to superiority.*
– ORIGIN late Middle English: from Anglo-Norman French *pretense*, based on medieval Latin *pretensus* 'pretended,' alteration of Latin *praetentus*, from the verb *praetendere* (see **PRETEND**).

pre·ten·sion¹ /priˈtencHən/ ▶ n. **1** (**pretension to**) a claim or the assertion of a claim to something: *their pretensions to culture* | *we cannot tolerate pretension to infallibility.* ■ (often **pretensions**) an aspiration or claim to a certain status or quality: *another aging rocker with literary pretensions.*
2 the use of affectation to impress; ostentatiousness: *he spoke simply, without pretension.*
– ORIGIN late Middle English: from medieval Latin *praetensio(n-)*, from *praetens-* 'alleged,' from the verb *praetendere* (see **PRETEND**).

pre·ten·sion² /prēˈtencHən/ ▶ v. [with obj.] apply tension to (an object) before some other process or event: *the safety system pretensions the seat belts.* ■ strengthen (reinforced concrete) by applying tension to the reinforcing rods before the concrete has set.

pre·ten·sion·er /prēˈtencHənər/ ▶ n. a device designed to pull a seat belt tight in an accident.

pre·ten·tious /priˈtencHəs/ ▶ adj. attempting to impress by affecting greater importance, talent, culture, etc., than is actually possessed: *a pretentious literary device.*
– DERIVATIVES **pre·ten·tious·ly** adv., **pre·ten·tious·ness** n.
– ORIGIN mid 19th cent.: from French *prétentieux*, from *prétention* (see **PRETENSION¹**).

preter- ▶ comb. form more than: *preternatural.*
– ORIGIN from Latin *praeter* 'past, beyond.'

pret·er·ite /ˈpretərit/ (also **preterit**) Grammar ▶ adj. expressing a past action or state.
▶ n. a simple past tense or form.
– ORIGIN Middle English (in the sense 'bygone, former'): from Latin *praeteritus* 'gone by,' past participle of *praeterire*, from *praeter* 'past, beyond' + *ire* 'go.'

pret·er·i·tion /ˌpretəˈrisHən/ ▶ n. **1** the action of passing over or disregarding a matter, esp. the rhetorical technique of making summary mention of something by professing to omit it.
2 (in Calvinist theology) omission from God's elect; nonelection to salvation.
– ORIGIN late 16th cent.: from late Latin *praeteritio(n-)*, from *praeterire* 'pass, go by.'

pre·term /prēˈtərm/ Medicine ▶ adj. born or occurring after a pregnancy significantly shorter than normal, esp. after no more than 37 weeks of pregnancy: *babies born during preterm labor.*
▶ adv. after a short pregnancy; prematurely: *babies born preterm are likely to lack surfactant in the lungs.*

pre·ter·mit /ˌprētərˈmit/ ▶ v. (**pretermits, pretermitting, pretermitted**) [with obj.] archaic
1 omit to do or mention: *some points of conduct we advisedly pretermit.*
2 abandon (a custom or continuous action) for a time: *the pleasant musical evenings were now entirely pretermitted.*
– DERIVATIVES **pre·ter·mis·sion** /ˌprētərˈmisHən/ n.
– ORIGIN late 15th cent.: from Latin *praetermittere*, from *praeter* 'past, beyond' + *mittere* 'let go.'

pre·ter·nat·u·ral /ˌprētərˈnacH(ə)rəl/ ▶ adj. beyond what is normal or natural: *autumn had arrived with preternatural speed.*
– DERIVATIVES **pre·ter·nat·u·ral·ism** /-ˈnacH(ə)rəˌlizəm/ n., **pre·ter·nat·u·ral·ly** adv.

pre·text /ˈprēˌtekst/ ▶ n. a reason given in justification of a course of action that is not the real reason: *the rebels had the perfect pretext for making their move.*
– PHRASES **on** (or **under**) **the pretext** giving the specified reason as one's justification: *the police raided Grand River **on the pretext of** looking for moonshiners.*
– ORIGIN early 16th cent.: from Latin *praetextus* 'outward display,' from the verb *praetexere* 'to disguise,' from *prae* 'before' + *texere* 'weave.'

pre·tex·tu·al /prēˈteksCHo͞oəl/ ▶ adj. Law denoting or relating to arrests or minor offenses that enable authorities to detain suspects for investigation of other matters.

pre·tor /ˈprētər/ ▶ n. variant spelling of **PRAETOR**.

Pre·to·ri·a /prəˈtôrēə/ the administrative capital of South Africa; pop. 1,679,200 (est. 2009). It was founded in 1855 by **Marthinus Wessel Pretorius** (1819–1901), the first president of the South African Republic, and named after his father Andries.

pre·to·ri·an /priˈtôrēən/ ▶ adj. & n. variant spelling of **PRAETORIAN**.

pre·treat /prēˈtrēt/ ▶ v. [with obj.] treat (something) with a chemical before use.
– DERIVATIVES **pre·treat·ment** n.

pret·ti·fy /ˈpritəˌfī/ ▶ v. (**prettifies, prettifying, prettified**) [with obj.] make (someone or something) appear superficially pretty or attractive: *nothing has been done to prettify the site.*
– DERIVATIVES **pret·ti·fi·ca·tion** /ˌpritəfəˈkāsHən/ n., **pret·ti·fi·er** n.

pret·ty /ˈpritē/ ▶ adj. (**prettier, prettiest**) attractive in a delicate way without being truly beautiful or handsome: *a pretty little girl with an engaging grin.* ■ [attrib.] informal used ironically in expressions of annoyance or disgust: *it is a pretty state of affairs when a young fellow prefers the company of Italian fiddlers to taking possession of his own first command.*
▶ adv. [as submodifier] informal to a moderately high degree; fairly: *he looked pretty fit for his age.*
▶ n. (pl. **pretties**) informal an attractive thing, typically a pleasing but unnecessary accessory: *he buys her lots of pretties—bangles and rings and things.* ■ used to refer in a condescending way to an attractive person, usually a girl or a woman: *six pretties in sequined leotards.*
▶ v. (**pretties, prettying, prettied**) [with obj.] make pretty or attractive: *she'll be all **prettied up** and ready to go in an hour.*
– PHRASES **pretty much** (or **nearly** or **well**) informal very nearly: *the case is pretty well over.* **a pretty penny** informal a large sum of money. **pretty please** used as an emphatic or wheedling form of request. **be sitting pretty** informal be in an advantageous position or situation: *if she could get sponsors, she would be sitting pretty.*
– DERIVATIVES **pret·ti·ly** /ˈpritl-ē/ adv., **pret·ti·ness** n., **pret·ty·ish** adj.
– ORIGIN Old English *prættig*; related to Middle Dutch *pertich* 'brisk, clever,' obsolete Dutch *prettig* 'humorous, sporty,' from a West Germanic base meaning 'trick.' The sense development 'deceitful, cunning, clever, skillful, admirable, pleasing, nice' has parallels in adjectives such as *canny, fine, nice*, etc.

pret·ty boy ▶ n. informal, often derogatory a foppish or effeminate man.

pret·zel /ˈpretsəl/ ▶ n. a crisp biscuit baked in the form of a knot or stick and flavored with salt.
▶ v. (**pretzels, pretzeling, pretzeled**) [with obj.] twist, bend, or contort: *he found the snake pretzeled into a tangle of knots.*
– ORIGIN mid 19th cent.: from German *Pretzel*.

prev. ▶ abbr. previous; previously.

pre·vail /priˈvāl/ ▶ v. [no obj.] prove more powerful than opposing forces; be victorious: *it is hard for logic to **prevail over** emotion.* ■ be widespread in a particular area at a particular time; be current: *an atmosphere of crisis prevails.* ■ (**prevail on/upon**) persuade (someone) to do something: *she was prevailed upon to give an account of her work.*
– ORIGIN late Middle English: from Latin *praevalere* 'have greater power,' from *prae* 'before' + *valere* 'have power.'

pre·vail·ing /priˈvāliNG/ ▶ adj. existing at a particular time; current: *the unfavorable prevailing economic conditions.* ■ having the most appeal or influence; prevalent: *the prevailing mood is one of hope rather than expectation.*
– DERIVATIVES **pre·vail·ing·ly** adv.

pre·vail·ing wind ▶ n. a wind from the direction that is predominant at a particular place or season.

prev·a·lence /ˈprevələns/ ▶ n. the fact or condition of being prevalent; commonness: *the prevalence of obesity in adults.*

prev·a·lent /ˈprevələnt/ ▶ adj. widespread in a particular area at a particular time: *the social ills prevalent in society today.* ■ archaic predominant; powerful.
– DERIVATIVES **prev·a·lent·ly** adv.
– ORIGIN late 16th cent.: from Latin *praevalent-* 'having greater power,' from the verb *praevalere* (see **PREVAIL**).

pre·var·i·cate /priˈvariˌkāt/ ▶ v. [no obj.] speak or act in an evasive way: *he seemed to prevaricate when journalists asked pointed questions.*
– DERIVATIVES **pre·var·i·ca·tion** /priˌvariˈkāsHən/ n., **pre·var·i·ca·tor** /-ˌkātər/ n.
– ORIGIN mid 16th cent. (in the sense 'go astray, transgress'): from Latin *praevaricat-* 'walked crookedly, deviated,' from the verb *praevaricari*, from *prae* 'before' + *varicari* 'straddle' (from *varus* 'bent, knock-kneed').

pre·ven·ient /priˈvēnēənt/ ▶ adj. formal preceding in time or order; antecedent: *John Wesley referred to God's work in the unconverted as prevenient grace.*
– ORIGIN early 17th cent.: from Latin *praevenient-* 'coming before,' from the verb *praevenire*, from *prae* 'before' + *venire* 'come.'

pre·vent /priˈvent/ ▶ v. [with obj.] **1** keep (something) from happening or arising: *action must be taken to prevent further accidents.* ■ make (someone or

something) unable to do something: *window locks won't prevent a determined burglar from getting in.* **2** archaic (of God) go before (someone) with spiritual guidance and help.
– DERIVATIVES **pre·vent·a·bil·i·ty** /pri,ventə'bilətē/ **n.**, **pre·vent·a·ble** (also **preventible**) **adj.**
– ORIGIN late Middle English (in the sense 'act in anticipation of'): from Latin *praevent-* 'preceded, hindered,' from the verb *praevenire*, from *prae* 'before' + *venire* 'come.'

pre·ven·ta·tive /prē'ventətiv/ ▶ **adj. & n.** another term for PREVENTIVE.
– DERIVATIVES **pre·ven·ta·tive·ly adv.**

pre·vent·er /prē'ventər/ ▶ **n.** a person or thing that prevents something: *effective as preventers of further infection.* ■ Sailing an extra line or wire rigged to support a piece of rigging under strain, or to hold the boom and prevent it from jibing.

pre·ven·tion /pri'venCHən/ ▶ **n.** the action of stopping something from happening or arising: *crime prevention | the treatment and prevention of AIDS.*
– PHRASES **an ounce of prevention is worth a pound of cure** proverb it's easier to stop something from happening in the first place than to repair the damage after it has happened.

pre·ven·tive /pri'ventiv/ ▶ **adj.** designed to keep something undesirable such as illness, harm, or accidents from occurring: *preventive medicine.* ▶ **n.** a medicine or other treatment designed to stop disease or ill health from occurring.
– DERIVATIVES **pre·ven·tive·ly adv.**

pre·ven·tive de·ten·tion ▶ **n.** Law the imprisonment of a person with the aim of preventing them from committing further offenses or of maintaining public order.

pre·ver·bal /'prē'vərbəl/ ▶ **adj. 1** existing or occurring before the development of speech: *preverbal communication.* **2** Grammar occurring before a verb: *preverbal particles.*

pre·view /'prē,vyōō/ ▶ **n.** an inspection or viewing of something before it is bought or becomes generally known and available: *you can get a sneak preview of the pictures on sale.* ■ a showing of a movie, play, exhibition, etc., before its official opening. ■ a short extract shown in a movie theater as publicity for a forthcoming film. ■ a commentary on or appraisal of a forthcoming film, play, book, etc., based on an advance viewing. ■ Computing a facility for inspecting the appearance of a document before it is printed. ▶ **v.** [with obj.] display (a product, movie, play, etc.) before it officially goes on sale or opens to the public: *the company will preview an enhanced version of its database.* ■ see or inspect (something) before it is used or becomes generally available: *the teacher should preview teaching aids to ensure that they are at the right level.* ■ comment on or appraise (a forthcoming event) in advance: *next week we'll be previewing the new season.*

Prev·in /'prevən/, André (George) (1929–), US conductor, pianist, and composer, born in Germany. He is best known as a conductor, notably with the London Symphony Orchestra (1968–79), the Pittsburgh Symphony Orchestra (1976–86), and the Royal Philharmonic Orchestra (1987–91).

pre·vi·ous /'prēvēəs/ ▶ **adj. 1** [attrib.] existing or occurring before in time or order: *she looked tired after her exertions of the previous evening | tickets will be sold on the same basis as in previous years.* **2** informal overly hasty in acting or in drawing a conclusion: *I admit I may have been a bit previous.*
– PHRASES **previous to** before: *the month previous to publication | he seemed to have been in good health previous to the fatal injury.*
– ORIGIN early 17th cent.: from Latin *praevius* 'going before' (from *prae* 'before' + *via* 'way') + -OUS.

pre·vi·ous·ly /'prēvēəslē/ ▶ **adv.** at a previous or earlier time; before: *museums and art galleries that had previously been open to the public | they discovered a previously unknown gene.*

pre·vi·ous ques·tion ▶ **n.** (in parliamentary procedure) a motion to decide whether to vote on a main question, moved before the main question itself is put.

pre·vise /pri'vīz/ ▶ **v.** [with obj.] literary foresee or predict (an event): *he had intelligence to previse the possible future.*
– DERIVATIVES **pre·vi·sion** /-'viZHən/ **n.**, **pre·vi·sion·al** /-'viZHənl/ **adj.**
– ORIGIN late 16th cent.: from Latin *praevis-* 'foreseen, anticipated,' from the verb *praevidere*, from *prae* 'before' + *videre* 'to see.'

pre·vo·cal·ic /,prēvō'kalik/ ▶ **adj.** occurring immediately before a vowel.
– DERIVATIVES **pre·vo·cal·i·cal·ly** /-ik(ə)lē/ **adv.**

pre·vue /'prē,vyōō/ ▶ **n.** variant spelling of PREVIEW.

pre·war /prē'wôr/ ▶ **adj.** existing, occurring, or built before a war: *the prewar years.*

pre·wash /prē'wôSH, -'wäSH/ (also **prewash**) ▶ **n.** a preliminary wash, esp. one performed as part of a cycle in an automatic washing machine. ■ a substance applied as a treatment before washing. ▶ **v.** [with obj.] give a preliminary wash to (a garment), typically before putting it on sale.

pre·wire /prē'wīr/ ▶ **v.** [with obj.] wire (something requiring electrical circuitry) in advance of usual installation: *we prewired the building.*

prex·y /'preksē/ (also **prex**) ▶ **n.** (pl. **prexies**) informal a president, esp. the president of a college or society.
– ORIGIN early 19th cent. (as *prex*): college slang.

prey /prā/ ▶ **n.** an animal that is hunted and killed by another for food: *the kestrel is ready to pounce on unsuspecting prey.* ■ a person or thing easily injured or taken advantage of: *he was easy prey for the two con men.* ■ archaic plunder or (in biblical use) a prize. ▶ **v.** [no obj.] (**prey on/upon**) hunt and kill for food: *small birds that prey on insect pests.* ■ take advantage of; exploit or injure: *this is a mean type of theft by ruthless people preying on the elderly.* ■ cause constant trouble and distress to: *the problem had begun to prey on my mind.*
– PHRASES **fall prey to** (also **be** or **become prey to**) be hunted and killed by (an animal): *small rodents fell prey to domestic cats.* ■ be vulnerable to or overcome by: *he would often fall prey to melancholy | the settlers become prey to nameless fears.*
– DERIVATIVES **prey·er n.**
– ORIGIN Middle English (also denoting plunder taken in war): the noun from Old French *preie*, from Latin *praeda* 'booty,' the verb from Old French *preier*, based on Latin *praedari* 'seize as plunder,' from *praeda*.

prez /prez/ ▶ **n.** informal term for PRESIDENT.

PRF ▶ **abbr.** Telecommunications pulse repetition frequency.

prf. ▶ **abbr.** proof.

Pri·am /'prīəm/ Greek Mythology the king of Troy at the time of its destruction by the Greeks under Agamemnon. The father of Paris and Hector and husband of Hecuba, he was slain by Neoptolemus, son of Achilles.

pri·ap·ic /prī'apik, -'āpik/ ▶ **adj.** of, relating to, or resembling a phallus: *priapic carvings.* ■ of or relating to male sexuality and sexual activity: *priapic cartoons.* ■ Medicine (of a male) having a persistently erect penis.
– ORIGIN late 18th cent.: from *Priapos* (see PRIAPISM) + -IC.

pri·a·pism /'prīə,pizəm/ ▶ **n.** Medicine persistent and painful erection of the penis.
– ORIGIN late Middle English: via late Latin from Greek *priapismos*, from *priapizein* 'be lewd,' from *Priapos* (see PRIAPUS).

Pri·ap·u·li·da /,prīə'pyōōlədə/ Zoology a small phylum of burrowing wormlike marine invertebrates. A priapulid has a thick body, a large eversible proboscis, and a tail.
– DERIVATIVES **pri·ap·u·lid** /prī'apyələd/ **n. & adj.**
– ORIGIN modern Latin (plural), from *Priapulus* (genus name), diminutive of PRIAPUS.

Pri·a·pus /prī'āpəs/ Greek Mythology a god of fertility, whose cult spread to Greece (and, later, Italy) from Turkey after Alexander's conquests. He was also a god of gardens and the patron of seafarers and shepherds.

Prib·i·lof Is·lands /'pribə,lôf/ a group of four islands in the Bering Sea, off the coast of southwestern Alaska. First visited in 1786 by Russian explorer **Gavriil Loginovich Pribylov** (died 1796), they came into US possession after the purchase of Alaska in 1867.

Price[1] /prīs/, Leontyne (1927–), US opera singer; full name *Mary Violet Leontyne Price*. Her 1952 Broadway successes in *Four Saints in Three Acts* and *Porgy and Bess* led to an international career as an operatic and concert soprano. She made her Metropolitan Opera debut in 1961 and retired from opera in 1985.

Price[2], Vincent (1911–93), US actor, best known for his performances in a series of movies based on stories by Edgar Allan Poe, including *The Fall of the House of Usher* (1960) and *The Pit and the Pendulum* (1961).

price /prīs/ ▶ **n. 1** the amount of money expected, required, or given in payment for something: *land could be sold for a high price | a wide selection of tools varying in price.* ■ the odds in betting. ■ archaic value; worth: *a pearl of great price.* **2** an unwelcome experience, event, or action involved as a condition of achieving a desired end: *the price of their success was an entire day spent in discussion.* ▶ **v.** [with obj.] decide the amount required as payment for (something offered for sale): *the watches in this range are priced at $14.50.*
– PHRASES **at any price** no matter what expense, sacrifice, or difficulty is involved: *they wanted peace at any price.* **at a price** requiring great expense or involving unwelcome consequences: *his generosity comes at a price.* **beyond** (or **without**) **price** so valuable that no price can be stated. **a price on someone's head** a reward offered for someone's capture or death. **price oneself out of the market** become unable to compete commercially. **put a price on** determine the value of: *you can't put a price on what she has to offer.* **what price ——?** used to ask what has become of something or to suggest that something has or would become worthless: *what price justice if he were allowed to go free?*
– ORIGIN Middle English: the noun from Old French *pris*, from Latin *pretium* 'value, reward'; the verb, a variant (by assimilation to the noun) of earlier *prise* 'estimate the value of' (see PRIZE[1]). Compare with PRAISE.

price con·trol ▶ **n.** a government regulation establishing a maximum price to be charged for specified goods and services, esp. during periods of war or inflation.

price dis·crim·i·na·tion ▶ **n.** the action of selling the same product at different prices to different buyers, in order to maximize sales and profits.

price-earn·ings ra·tio (also **price-earnings multiple**) ▶ **n.** Finance the current market price of a company share divided by the earnings per share of the company.

price-fix·ing (also **price fixing**) ▶ **n.** the maintaining of prices at a certain level by agreement between competing sellers.

price·less /'prīsləs/ ▶ **adj.** so precious that its value cannot be determined: *priceless works of art.* ■ informal used to express great and usually affectionate amusement: *darling, you're priceless!*
– DERIVATIVES **price·less·ly adv.**, **price·less·ness n.**

price list ▶ **n.** a list of current prices of items on sale.

price point ▶ **n.** a point on a scale of possible prices at which something might be marketed.

price-sen·si·tive ▶ **adj.** denoting a product whose sales are greatly influenced by the price. ■ (of information) likely to affect share prices if it were made public.

price sup·port ▶ **n.** Economics government assistance in maintaining the levels of market prices regardless of supply or demand.

price tag ▶ **n.** the label on an item for sale, showing its price. ■ the cost of something: *a $400 billion price tag was put on the venture.*

price-tak·er ▶ **n.** Economics a company that must accept the prevailing prices in the market of its products, its own transactions being unable to affect the market price.
– DERIVATIVES **price-tak·ing n. & adj.**

price war ▶ **n.** a fierce competition in which retailers cut prices in an attempt to increase their share of the market.

pric·ey /'prīsē/ (also **pricy**) ▶ **adj.** (**pricier, priciest**) informal expensive: *boutiques selling pricey clothes.*
– DERIVATIVES **pric·i·ness n.**

prick /prik/ ▶ **v.** [with obj.] **1** make a small hole in (something) with a sharp point; pierce slightly: *prick the potatoes with a fork.* ■ [no obj.] feel a sensation as though a sharp point were sticking into one: *she felt her scalp prick and her palms were damp.* ■ (of tears) cause the sensation of imminent weeping in (a person's eyes): *tears of disappointment were pricking her eyelids.* ■ [no obj.] (of a person's eyes) experience such a sensation. ■ cause mental or emotional discomfort to: *her conscience pricked her as she told the lie.* ■ arouse or provoke to action: *the police were pricked into action.* **2** (esp. of a horse or dog) make (the ears) stand erect when on the alert: *the dog's tail was wagging and her ears were pricked.* ▶ **n. 1** an act of piercing something with a fine, sharp point: *the pin prick had produced a drop of blood.* ■ a small hole or mark made by piercing something with a fine, sharp point. ■ a sharp pain caused by being pierced with a fine point. ■ a sudden feeling of distress, anxiety, or some other unpleasant emotion: *she felt a prick of resentment.* ■ archaic a goad for oxen. **2** vulgar slang a penis. ■ a man regarded as stupid, unpleasant, or contemptible.

P

– PHRASES **kick against the pricks** hurt oneself by persisting in useless resistance or protest. [with biblical allusion to Acts 9:5.] **prick up one's ears** (esp. of a horse or dog) make the ears stand erect when on the alert. ■ (of a person) become suddenly attentive: *he pricked up his ears when he heard them talking about him.*
– PHRASAL VERBS **prick something out** (or **off**) transplant seedlings to a container or bed that provides adequate room for growth: *he was in the garden pricking out marigolds.*
– DERIVATIVES **prick·er** n., **prick·ing** n.
– ORIGIN Old English *pricca* (noun), *prician* (verb), probably of West Germanic origin and related to Low German and Dutch *prik* (noun), *prikken* (verb).

prick·et /ˈprikit/ ▸ n. **1** a male fallow deer in its second year, having straight, unbranched horns.
2 historical a spike for holding a candle.
– ORIGIN late Middle English: from PRICK + -ET[1].

prick·le /ˈprikəl/ ▸ n. a short, slender, sharp-pointed outgrowth on the bark or epidermis of a plant; a small thorn: *the prickles of the blackberry bushes.* ■ a small spine or pointed outgrowth on the skin of certain animals. ■ a tingling sensation on someone's skin, typically caused by strong emotion: *Kathleen felt a prickle of excitement.*
▸ v. [no obj.] (of a person's skin or a part of the body) experience a tingling sensation, esp. as a result of strong emotion: *the sound made her skin prickle with horror.* ■ [with obj.] cause a tingling or mildly painful sensation in: *I hate the way the fibers prickle your skin.* ■ (of a person) react defensively or angrily to something: *she **prickled at** the implication that she had led a soft and protected life.*
– ORIGIN Old English *pricel* 'instrument for pricking, sensation of being pricked'; related to Middle Dutch *prickel*, from the Germanic base of PRICK. The verb is partly a diminutive of the verb PRICK.

prick·le·back /ˈprikəlˌbak/ ▸ n. a long slender fish with a spiny dorsal fin running the length of the body. It lives in cooler seas of the northern hemisphere, typically in shallow inshore waters. ● Family Stichaeidae: many genera and species.

prick·ly /ˈprik(ə)lē/ ▸ adj. (**pricklier**, **prickliest**)
1 covered in prickles: *masses of prickly brambles.* ■ resembling or feeling like prickles: *his hair was prickly and short.* ■ having or causing a tingling or itching sensation: *a dress that was prickly around the neck | my skin feels prickly.*
2 (of a person) ready to take offense. ■ liable to cause someone to take offense: *this is a prickly subject.*
– DERIVATIVES **prick·li·ness** n.

prick·ly-ash ▸ n. a spiny North American shrub or tree with prickly branches and bark that can be used medicinally. ● Genus *Zanthoxylum*, family Rutaceae: the **northern prickly-ash** (*Z. americanum*) (also called TOOTHACHE TREE), and the **southern prickly-ash** (see HERCULES-CLUB). ■ a medicinal preparation of the bark of these trees.

prick·ly heat ▸ n. an itchy inflammation of the skin, typically with a rash of small vesicles, common in hot moist weather. Also called MILIARIA.

prick·ly pear ▸ n. a cactus with jointed stems and oval flattened segments, having barbed bristles and large pear-shaped, prickly fruits. ● Genus *Opuntia*, family Cactaceae: several species, in particular *O. humifusa* of North America and *O. ficus-indica*, which is cultivated for its fruit and has become naturalized in the Mediterranean. ■ the edible orange or red fruit of this plant.

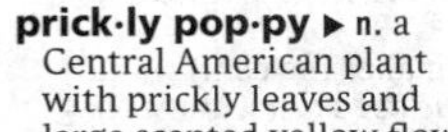
prickly pear

prick·ly pop·py ▸ n. a Central American plant with prickly leaves and large scented yellow flowers. It has become a weed in many tropical regions, but is cultivated in cooler regions as an ornamental. ● *Argemone mexicana*, family Papaveraceae.

prick-teas·er (also **prick-tease**) ▸ n. vulgar slang another term for COCKTEASER.

pric·y /ˈprīsē/ ▸ adj. variant spelling of PRICEY.

pride /prīd/ ▸ n. **1** a feeling or deep pleasure or satisfaction derived from one's own achievements, the achievements of those with whom one is closely associated, or from qualities or possessions that are widely admired: *the team was bursting with pride after recording a sensational victory | a woman who takes great pride in her appearance.* ■ the consciousness of one's own dignity: *he swallowed his pride and asked for help.* ■ the quality of having an excessively high opinion of oneself or one's importance: *the sin of pride.* ■ a person or thing that is the object or source of a feeling or deep pleasure or satisfaction: *the swimming pool is the pride of the community.* ■ literary the best state or condition of something; the prime: *in the pride of youth.*
2 a group of lions forming a social unit.
▸ v. (**pride oneself on/upon**) be especially proud of a particular quality or skill: *she'd always prided herself on her ability to deal with a crisis.*
– PHRASES **one's pride and joy** a person or thing of which one is very proud and which is a source of great pleasure: *the car was his pride and joy.* **pride goes** (or **comes**) **before a fall** proverb if you're too conceited or self-important, something will happen to make you look foolish. **pride of place** the most prominent or important position among a group of things: *the certificate has pride of place on my wall.*
– DERIVATIVES **pride·ful** /-fəl/ adj., **pride·ful·ly** /-fəlē/ adv.
– ORIGIN late Old English *prȳde* 'excessive self-esteem,' variant of *prȳtu, prȳte*, from *prūd* (see PROUD).

prie-dieu /prē ˈdyə(r), -ˈdyœ/ ▸ n. (pl. **prie-dieux** /ˈdyə(r)(z), -ˈdyœ(z)/) a piece of furniture for use during prayer, consisting of a kneeling surface and a narrow upright front with a rest for the elbows or for books.
– ORIGIN mid 18th cent.: French, literally 'pray God.'

priest /prēst/ ▸ n. **1** an ordained minister of the Catholic, Orthodox, or Anglican church having the authority to perform certain rites and administer certain sacraments. ■ a person who performs religious ceremonies and duties in a non-Christian religion.
2 (in full **fish priest**) a mallet used to kill fish caught when angling. [with allusion to the priest's function in performing the last rites.]
▸ v. [with obj.] (usu. **be priested**) formal ordain to the priesthood.
– DERIVATIVES **priest·like** /-ˌlīk/ adj.
– ORIGIN Old English *prēost*, of Germanic origin; related to Dutch *priester*, German *Priester*, based on ecclesiastical Latin *presbyter* 'elder' (see PRESBYTER).

priest·craft /ˈprēstˌkraft/ ▸ n. often derogatory the knowledge and work of a priest.

priest·ess /ˈprēstis/ ▸ n. a female priest of a non-Christian religion.

priest hole (also **priest's hole**) ▸ n. historical a hiding place for a Roman Catholic priest during times of religious persecution.

priest·hood /ˈprēstˌho͝od, ˈprēˌsto͝od/ ▸ n. (often **the priesthood**) the office or position of a priest. ■ priests in general.

Priest·ley[1] /ˈprēs(t)lē/, J. B. (1894–1984), English novelist, playwright, and critic; full name *John Boynton Priestley*. Notable works: *The Good Companions* (novel, 1929), *Time and the Conways* (play, 1937), and *An Inspector Calls* (play, 1947).

Priest·ley[2], Joseph (1733–1804), English scientist and theologian. His chief work was on the chemistry of gases, in which his most significant discovery was of "dephlogisticated air" (oxygen) in 1774; he demonstrated that it was important to animal life and that plants emit it in sunlight.

priest·ly /ˈprēstlē/ ▸ adj. of, relating to, or befitting a priest or priests: *performing priestly duties.*
– DERIVATIVES **priest·li·ness** n.
– ORIGIN Old English *prēostlic* (see PRIEST, -LY[1]).

prig /prig/ ▸ n. a self-righteously moralistic person who behaves as if superior to others.
– DERIVATIVES **prig·ger·y** /ˈprigərē/ n.
– ORIGIN mid 16th cent.: of unknown origin. The earliest sense was 'tinker' or 'petty thief,' whence 'disliked person,' esp. 'someone who is affectedly and self-consciously precise' (late 17th cent.).

prig·gish /ˈprigisH/ ▸ n. self-righteously moralistic and superior: *a priggish little pedant | she was priggish about sex.*
– DERIVATIVES **prig·gish·ly** adv., **prig·gish·ness** n.

prill /pril/ ▸ n. a pellet or solid globule of a substance formed by the congealing of a liquid during an industrial process.
– DERIVATIVES **prilled** adj.
– ORIGIN late 18th cent. (as a term in copper mining, denoting rich copper ore remaining after removal of low-grade material): of unknown origin.

prim /prim/ ▸ adj. (**primmer**, **primmest**) stiffly formal and respectable; feeling or showing disapproval of anything regarded as improper: *a very prim and proper lady.*
▸ v. (**prims**, **primming**, **primmed**) [with obj.] purse (the mouth or lips) into a prim expression: *Larry primmed up his mouth.*
– DERIVATIVES **prim·ly** adv., **prim·ness** n.
– ORIGIN late 17th cent. (as a verb): probably ultimately from Old French *prin*, Provençal *prim* 'excellent, delicate,' from Latin *primus* 'first.'

prim. ▸ abbr. ■ primary. ■ primitive.

pri·ma bal·le·ri·na /ˈprēmə/ ▸ n. the chief female dancer in a ballet or ballet company.
– ORIGIN late 19th cent.: Italian, literally 'first ballerina.'

pri·ma·cy /ˈprīməsē/ ▸ n. **1** the fact of being primary, preeminent, or more important: *the primacy of air power in the modern war.*
2 the office, period of office, or authority of a primate of certain churches.
3 [usu. as modifier] Psychology the fact of an item having been presented earlier to the subject (esp. as increasing its likelihood of being remembered): *the primacy effect is thought to reflect recall from a long-term memory store.*
– ORIGIN late Middle English: from Old French *primatie*, from medieval Latin *primatia*, from Latin *primas, primat-* 'of the first rank' (see PRIMATE[1]).

pri·ma don·na /ˌprimə ˈdänə, ˌprēmə/ ▸ n. the chief female singer in an opera or opera company. ■ a very temperamental person with an inflated view of their own talent or importance.
– DERIVATIVES **pri·ma don·na·ish** adj.
– ORIGIN late 18th cent.: Italian, literally 'first lady.'

pri·mae·val /prīˈmēvəl/ ▸ adj. Brit. variant spelling of PRIMEVAL.

pri·ma fa·ci·e /ˌprīmə ˈfāSHə, ˈfāSHē, ˈfāSHēˌē/ ▸ adj. & adv. Law based on the first impression; accepted as correct until proved otherwise: [as adj.] *a prima facie case of professional misconduct* | [as adv.] *the original lessee prima facie remains liable for the payment of the rent.*
– ORIGIN Latin, from *primus* 'first' + *facies* 'appearance.'

pri·mal /ˈprīməl/ ▸ adj. essential; fundamental: *for me, writing is a primal urge.* ■ relating to an early stage in evolutionary development; primeval: *primal hunting societies.* ■ Psychology of, relating to, or denoting the needs, fears, or behavior that are postulated (esp. in Freudian theory) to form the origins of emotional life: *he preys on people's primal fears.* See also PRIMAL SCENE.
– DERIVATIVES **pri·mal·ly** adv.
– ORIGIN early 17th cent.: from medieval Latin *primalis*, from Latin *primus* 'first.'

pri·mal scene ▸ n. Psychology (in Freudian theory) the occasion on which a child becomes aware of its parents' sexual intercourse, the timing of which is thought to be crucial in determining predisposition to future neuroses.

pri·mal scream ▸ n. a release of intense basic frustration, anger, and aggression, esp. that rediscovered by means of primal therapy.

pri·mal ther·a·py ▸ n. a form of psychotherapy that focuses on a patient's earliest emotional experiences and encourages verbal expression of childhood suffering, typically using an empty chair or other prop to represent a parent toward whom anger is directed.

pri·ma ma·te·ri·a /ˌprīmə məˈti(ə)rēə, ˌprēmə/ (also **materia prima**) ▸ n. primeval matter; fundamental substance.
– ORIGIN Latin.

pri·ma·quine /ˈprīməˌkwēn, ˈprē-/ ▸ n. Medicine a synthetic compound derived from quinoline and used in the treatment of malaria.
– ORIGIN 1940s: apparently from Latin *prima* (feminine of *primus* 'first') + *quin(olin)e*.

pri·ma·ri·ly /prīˈme(ə)rəlē/ ▸ adv. for the most part; mainly: *around 80 percent of personal computers are used primarily for word processing.*

pri·ma·ry /ˈprīˌmerē, ˈprīm(ə)rē/ ▸ adj. **1** of chief importance; principal: *the government's primary aim is to see significant reductions in unemployment.*
2 earliest in time or order of development: *the primary stage of their political education.* ■ not derived from, caused by, or based on anything else: *the research involved the use of primary source materials in national and local archives.*
3 of or relating to education for children between the ages of about five and ten: *a primary school.*
4 Biology & Medicine belonging to or directly derived from the first stage of development or growth: *a primary bone tumor.*
5 (**Primary**) Geology former term for PALEOZOIC.
6 relating to or denoting the input side of a device using electromagnetic induction, esp. in a transformer.
7 Chemistry (of an organic compound) having its functional group located on a carbon atom that is bonded to no more than one other carbon atom. ■ (chiefly of amines) derived from ammonia by replacement of one hydrogen atom by an organic group.
▸ n. (pl. **primaries**) **1** (also **primary election**) a preliminary election to appoint delegates to a party conference or to select the candidates for a principal, esp. presidential, election.

2 a primary color. ■ Ornithology a primary feather. ■ Astronomy the body orbited by a smaller satellite or companion. ■ a primary coil or winding in an electrical transformer.
3 (**the Primary**) Geology, dated the Primary or Paleozoic era.
– ORIGIN late Middle English (in the sense 'original, not derivative'): from Latin *primarius*, from *primus* 'first.' The noun uses date from the 18th cent.

pri·ma·ry ac·cent ▶ n. another term for PRIMARY STRESS.

pri·ma·ry care (also **primary health care**) ▶ n. health care at a basic rather than specialized level for people making an initial approach to a doctor or nurse for treatment.

pri·ma·ry cell ▶ n. an electric cell that produces current by an irreversible chemical reaction.

pri·ma·ry col·or ▶ n. any of a group of colors from which all other colors can be obtained by mixing.

> The primary colors for pigments are red, blue, and yellow. The primary additive colors for light are red, green, and blue; the primary subtractive colors (which give the primary additive colors when subtracted from white light) are magenta, cyan, and yellow.

pri·ma·ry feath·er ▶ n. any of the largest flight feathers in a bird's wing, growing from the manus.

pri·ma·ry group ▶ n. Sociology a group held together by intimate, face-to-face relationships, formed by family and environmental associations and regarded as basic to social life and culture.

pri·ma·ry in·dus·try ▶ n. Economics industry, such as mining, agriculture, or forestry, that is concerned with obtaining or providing natural raw materials for conversion into commodities and products for the consumer.

pri·ma·ry plan·et ▶ n. a planet that directly orbits the sun.

pri·ma·ry proc·ess ▶ n. Psychoanalysis an unconscious thought process that arises from the pleasure principle and is irrational and not subject to compulsion, such as condensation, which occurs in dreaming, or displacement, which occurs in the formation of a phobia.

pri·ma·ry qual·i·ties ▶ plural n. Philosophy properties or qualities, such as size, motion, shape, number, etc., belonging to physical matter independently of an observer. ■ the four original qualities of matter (hot, cold, wet, and dry) recognized by Aristotle, from which other qualities were held to derive.

pri·ma·ry stress ▶ n. Phonetics the strongest accent in a word or breath group. Compare with SECONDARY STRESS.

pri·ma·ry struc·ture ▶ n. **1** Biochemistry the characteristic sequence of amino acids forming a protein or polypeptide chain, considered as the most basic element of its structure.
2 Aeronautics the parts of an aircraft whose failure would seriously compromise safety.

pri·mate[1] /ˈprīˌmāt, ˈprīmət/ ▶ n. Christian Church the chief bishop or archbishop of a province: *Cardinal Glemp, the primate of Poland.*
– DERIVATIVES **pri·ma·tial** /prīˈmāSHəl/ adj.
– ORIGIN Middle English: from Old French *primat*, from Latin *primas, primat-* 'of the first rank,' from *primus* 'first.'

pri·mate[2] /ˈprīˌmāt/ ▶ n. Zoology a mammal of an order that includes the lemurs, bushbabies, tarsiers, marmosets, monkeys, apes, and humans. They are distinguished by having hands, handlike feet, and forward-facing eyes, and, with the exception of humans, are typically agile tree-dwellers. ● Order Primates: several families.
– ORIGIN late 19th cent.: from Latin *primas, primat-* 'of the first rank' (see PRIMATE[1]).

pri·ma·tol·o·gy /ˌprīməˈtäləjē/ ▶ n. the branch of zoology that deals with primates.
– DERIVATIVES **pri·ma·to·log·i·cal** /ˌprīmətəˈläjikəl/ adj., **pri·ma·tol·o·gist** /-jist/ n.

pri·ma·ve·ra /ˌprēməˈve(ə)rə/ ▶ n. the hard, light-colored timber of a Central American tree. ● The tree is *Cybistax donnellsmithii*, family Bignoniaceae.
▶ adj. [postpositive] (of a pasta dish) made with lightly sautéed spring vegetables: *linguine primavera.*
– ORIGIN late 19th cent.: from Spanish, denoting the season of spring, from Latin *primus* 'first, earliest' + *ver* 'spring' (alluding to the tree's early flowering).

prime[1] /prīm/ ▶ adj. **1** of first importance; main: *her prime concern is the well-being of the patient.* ■ from which another thing may derive or proceed: *Diogenes' conclusion that air is the prime matter.*
2 [attrib.] of the best possible quality; excellent: *a prime site in the center of Indianapolis | prime cuts of meat.* ■ having all the expected or typical characteristics of something: *the novel is a prime example of the genre.* ■ most suitable or likely: *it's the prime contender for best comedy of the year.*
3 Mathematics (of a number) evenly divisible only by itself and one (e.g., 2, 3, 5, 7, 11). ■ [predic.] (of two or more numbers in relation to each other) having no common factor but one.
▶ n. **1** [in sing.] a state or time of greatest strength, vigor, or success in a person's life: *you're in the prime of life | he wasn't elderly, but clearly past his prime.* ■ archaic the beginning or first period of something: *the prime of the world.*
2 Christian Church a service forming part of the Divine Office, traditionally said (or chanted) at the first hour of the day (i.e., 6 a.m.), but now little used. ■ archaic this time of day.
3 a prime number.
4 Printing a symbol (′) written after a letter or symbol as a distinguishing mark or after a figure as a symbol for minutes or feet.
5 Fencing the first of eight standard parrying positions. [French.]
6 short for PRIME RATE.
– DERIVATIVES **prime·ness** n.
– ORIGIN Old English *prīm* (sense 2 of the noun), from Latin *prima* (*hora*) 'first (hour),' reinforced in Middle English by Old French *prime*; the adjective dates from late Middle English, via Old French from Latin *primus* 'first.'

prime[2] ▶ v. [with obj.] **1** make (something) ready for use or action, in particular: ■ prepare (a firearm or explosive device) for firing or detonation. ■ cover (a surface) with a preparatory coat of paint in order to prevent the absorption of subsequent layers of paint. ■ pour or spray liquid into (a pump) before starting in order to seal the moving parts and facilitate its operation. ■ inject extra fuel into (the cylinder or carburetor of an internal combustion engine) in order to facilitate starting. ■ [no obj.] (of a steam engine or its boiler) mix water with the steam being passed into the cylinder. ■ Biochemistry serve as a starting material for (a polymerization process).
2 prepare (someone) for a situation or task, typically by supplying them with relevant information: [with obj. and infinitive] *the sentries had been primed to admit him without challenge.*
– PHRASES **prime the pump** stimulate or support the growth or success of something by supplying it with money: *capital from overseas that helps prime the US economic pump.*
– ORIGIN early 16th cent. (in the sense 'fill, load'): origin uncertain; probably based on Latin *primus* 'first,' since the sense expressed is a "first" operation before something else.

prime con·tract ▶ n. a contract whose requirements are partly fulfilled by the awarding of subcontracts.
– DERIVATIVES **prime con·trac·tor** n.

prime cost ▶ n. the direct cost of a commodity in terms of the materials and labor involved in its production, excluding fixed costs.

prime lens ▶ n. Photography a lens of fixed focal length.

prime me·rid·i·an ▶ n. a planet's meridian adopted as the zero of longitude. ■ (usu. **the prime meridian**) the earth's zero of longitude, which by convention passes through Greenwich, England. See also GREENWICH MERIDIAN.

prime min·is·ter ▶ n. the head of an elected government; the principal minister of a sovereign or state.

> In current use, the terms *premier* and *prime minister* refer to the same office in Britain, but in Canada and Australia the government of a province or state is headed by a premier, that of the federal government by a prime minister. In countries such as France, where the president has an executive function, the prime minister is in a subordinate position.

– DERIVATIVES **prime min·is·ter·ship** n.

prime mov·er ▶ n. a person or establishment that is chiefly responsible for the creation or execution of a plan or project. ■ an initial natural or mechanical source of motive power.

prim·er[1] /ˈprīmər/ ▶ n. a substance used as a preparatory coat on previously unpainted wood, metal, or canvas, esp. to prevent the absorption of subsequent layers of paint or the development of rust. ■ a cap or cylinder containing a compound that responds to friction or an electrical impulse and ignites the charge in a cartridge or explosive. ■ a small pump for pumping fuel to prime an internal combustion engine, esp. in an aircraft. ■ Biochemistry a molecule that serves as a starting material for a polymerization process.

prim·er[2] /ˈprimər/ ▶ n. an elementary textbook that serves as an introduction to a subject of study or is used for teaching children to read.
– ORIGIN late Middle English: from medieval Latin *primarius* (*liber*) 'primary (book)' and *primarium* (*manuale*) 'primary (manual).'

prime rate ▶ n. the lowest rate of interest at which money may be borrowed commercially.

prime rib ▶ n. a roast or steak cut from the seven ribs immediately before the loin.

prime time ▶ n. the regularly occurring time at which a television or radio audience is expected to be greatest, generally regarded in the television industry as the hours between 8 and 11 p.m.: *the Olympics dominated 59% of prime time.*

prim·eur /prēˈmər/ ▶ n. **1** (**primeurs**) fruit or vegetables grown to be available very early in the season.
2 (also **Primeur**) newly produced wines that have recently been made available.
– ORIGIN French, literally 'newness.'

pri·me·val /prīˈmēvəl/ (Brit. also **primaeval**) ▶ adj. of or resembling the earliest ages in the history of the world: *mile after mile of primeval forest.* ■ (of feelings or actions) based on primitive instinct; raw and elementary: *a primeval desire.*
– DERIVATIVES **pri·me·val·ly** adv.
– ORIGIN mid 17th cent.: from Latin *primaevus* (from *primus* 'first' + *aevum* 'age') + -AL.

pri·mi·grav·i·da /ˌprīməˈgravədə/ ▶ n. (pl. **primigravidae** /-ˈgravədē, -gravəˌdī/) Medicine a woman who is pregnant for the first time.
– ORIGIN late 19th cent.: modern Latin (feminine), from Latin *primus* 'first' + *gravidus* 'pregnant' (see GRAVID).

prim·ing /ˈprīmiNG/ ▶ n. a substance that prepares something for use or action, in particular: ■ another term for PRIMER[1]. ■ gunpowder placed in the pan of a firearm to ignite a charge.

pri·mip·a·ra /prīˈmipərə/ ▶ n. (pl. **primiparas** or **primiparae** /-rē, -ˌrī/) Medicine a woman who is giving birth for the first time.
– DERIVATIVES **pri·mip·a·rous** /-rəs/ adj.
– ORIGIN mid 19th cent.: modern Latin (feminine), from *primus* 'first' + *-parus* 'bringing forth' (from the verb *parere*).

prim·i·tive /ˈprimətiv/ ▶ adj. **1** relating to, denoting, or preserving the character of an early stage in the evolutionary or historical development of something: *primitive mammals | a name corrupted from primitive German.* ■ relating to or denoting a preliterate, nonindustrial society or culture characterized by simple social and economic organization: *primitive people.* ■ having a quality or style that offers an extremely basic level of comfort, convenience, or efficiency: *the accommodations at the camp were a bit primitive.* ■ (of behavior, thought, or emotion) apparently originating in unconscious needs or desires and unaffected by objective reasoning: *the primitive responses we share with many animals.* ■ of or denoting a simple, direct style of art that deliberately rejects sophisticated artistic techniques.
2 not developed or derived from anything else: *the primitive material of the universe.* ■ Linguistics denoting a word, base, or root from which another is historically derived. ■ Mathematics (of an algebraic or geometric expression) from which another is derived, or which is not itself derived from another.
3 Biology (of a part or structure) in the first or early stage of formation or growth; rudimentary. See also PRIMITIVE STREAK.
▶ n. **1** a person belonging to a preliterate, nonindustrial society or culture.
2 a pre-Renaissance painter. ■ a modern painter who imitates the pre-Renaissance style. ■ an artist employing a simple, naive style that deliberately rejects subtlety or conventional techniques. ■ a painting by a primitive artist, or an object in a primitive style.
3 Linguistics a word, base, or root from which another is historically derived. ■ Mathematics an algebraic or geometric expression from which another is derived; a curve of which another is the polar or reciprocal. ■ Computing a simple operation or procedure of a limited set from which complex operations or procedures may be constructed, esp. a simple geometric shape that may be generated in computer graphics by such an operation or procedure.
– DERIVATIVES **prim·i·tive·ly** adv., **prim·i·tive·ness** n., **prim·i·tiv·i·ty** /ˌpriməˈtivətē/ n.
– ORIGIN late Middle English (in the sense 'original, not derivative'): from Old French *primitif, -ive*, from Latin *primitivus* 'first of its kind,' from *primus* 'first.'

PRONUNCIATION KEY ə ago, up; ər over, fur; a hat; ā ate; ä car; e let; ē see; i fit; ī by; NG sing; ō go; ô law, for; oi toy; o͝o good; o͞o goo; ou out; TH thin; T͟H then; ZH vision

prim·i·tive cell ▶ **n.** Crystallography the smallest possible unit cell of a lattice, having lattice points at each of its eight vertices only.

Prim·i·tive Meth·o·dist ▶ **n.** historical a member of a society of Methodists that was formed in 1811 and joined the united Methodist Church in 1932.

prim·i·tive streak ▶ **n.** Embryology the faint streak that is the earliest trace of the embryo in the fertilized ovum of a higher vertebrate.

prim·i·tiv·ism /ˈprimətivˌizəm/ ▶ **n. 1** a belief in the value of what is simple and unsophisticated, expressed as a philosophy of life or through art or literature.
2 unsophisticated behavior that is unaffected by objective reasoning.
– DERIVATIVES **prim·i·tiv·ist n. & adj.**

pri·mo /ˈprēmō/ ▶ **n.** (pl. **primos**) Music the leading or upper part in a duet.
▶ **adj.** informal of top quality or importance: *the primo team in the land.*
– ORIGIN mid 18th cent.: Italian, literally 'first.'

Pri·mo de Ri·ve·ra /ˈprēmō de riˈve(ə)rə/, Miguel (1870–1930), Spanish general and statesman; head of state 1923–30. He assumed dictatorial powers after leading a military coup. His son, **José Antonio Primo de Rivera** (1903–36), founded the Falange in 1933 and was executed by Republicans during the Spanish Civil War.

pri·mo·gen·i·tor /ˌprīmōˈjenətər/ ▶ **n.** an ancestor, esp. the earliest ancestor of a people; a progenitor.
– ORIGIN mid 17th cent.: variant of **PROGENITOR**, on the pattern of *primogeniture*.

pri·mo·gen·i·ture /ˌprīmōˈjeniˌCHər, -ˌCHo͝or/ ▶ **n.** the state of being the firstborn child. ■ (also **right of primogeniture**) the right of succession belonging to the firstborn child, esp. the feudal rule by which the whole real estate of an intestate passed to the eldest son.
– DERIVATIVES **pri·mo·gen·i·tal** /-ˈjenitl/ **adj.**, **pri·mo·gen·i·tar·y** /-ˈjeniˌterē/ **adj.**
– ORIGIN early 17th cent.: from medieval Latin *primogenitura*, from Latin *primo* 'first' + *genitura* 'geniture.'

pri·mor·di·al /prīˈmôrdēəl/ ▶ **adj.** existing at or from the beginning of time; primeval: *the primordial oceans.* ■ (esp. of a state or quality) basic and fundamental: *the primordial needs of the masses.* ■ Biology (of a cell, part, or tissue) in the earliest stage of development.
– DERIVATIVES **pri·mor·di·al·i·ty** /ˌprīˌmôrdēˈalətē/ **n.**, **pri·mor·di·al·ly adv.**
– ORIGIN late Middle English: from late Latin *primordialis* 'first of all,' from *primordius* 'original' (see **PRIMORDIUM**).

pri·mor·di·al soup ▶ **n.** a solution rich in organic compounds in the primitive oceans of the earth, from which life is hypothesized to have originated.

pri·mor·di·um /prīˈmôrdēəm/ ▶ **n.** (pl. **primordia** /-dēə/) Biology an organ, structure, or tissue in the earliest stage of development.
– ORIGIN late 19th cent.: from Latin, neuter of *primordius* 'original,' from *primus* 'first' + *ordiri* 'begin.'

Pri·mor·sky /prēˈmôrskē/ an administrative territory in the far southeast of Siberian Russia, between the Sea of Japan and the Chinese border; capital, Vladivostok.

pri·mo uo·mo /ˌprēmō ˈwōmō/ ▶ **n.** (pl. **primi uomini** /ˌprēmē ˈwōmēnē/) the principal male singer in an opera or opera company.
– ORIGIN Italian, literally 'first man.'

primp /primp/ ▶ **v.** [with obj.] spend time making minor adjustments to (one's hair, makeup, or clothes): *they primped his hair* | [no obj.] *the girls who were primping in front of the mirror.*
– ORIGIN late 16th cent.: related to **PRIM**.

prim·rose /ˈprimˌrōz/ ▶ **n.** a commonly cultivated plant of European woodlands that produces pale yellow flowers in the early spring. ● *Primula vulgaris*, family Primulaceae (the **primrose family**). This family also includes the cowslips, pimpernels, and cyclamens. ■ (also **primrose yellow**) a pale yellow color.
– PHRASES **primrose path** the pursuit of pleasure, esp. when it is seen to bring disastrous consequences: *unaware of his doom, he continued down his primrose path.* [with allusion to Shakespeare's *Hamlet* I. iii. 50.]
– ORIGIN late Middle English: compare with Old French *primerose* and medieval Latin *prima rosa*, literally 'first rose.'

prim·u·la /ˈprimyələ/ ▶ **n.** a plant of a genus that includes primroses, cowslips, and cyclamens. Many kinds are cultivated as ornamentals, bearing flowers in a wide variety of colors in the spring. ● Genus *Primula*, family Primulaceae.
– ORIGIN modern Latin, from medieval Latin, feminine of *primulus*, diminutive of *primus* 'first.'

prim·u·la·ceous /ˌprimyəˈlāSHəs/ ▶ **adj.** Botany of, relating to, or denoting plants of the primrose family (Primulaceae).
– ORIGIN mid 19th cent.: from modern Latin *Primulaceae* (plural), based on medieval Latin *primula* (see **PRIMULA**), + **-OUS**.

pri·mum mo·bi·le /ˌprīməm ˈmōbəˌlē, ˌprē-/ ▶ **n.**
1 the central or most important source of motion or action.
2 (in the medieval version of the Ptolemaic system) an outer sphere supposed to move around the earth in 24 hours, carrying the inner spheres with it.
– ORIGIN from medieval Latin, literally 'first moving thing.'

pri·mus in·ter pa·res /ˈprīməs ˌintər ˈparˌēz/ ▶ **n.** a first among equals; the senior or representative member of a group.
– ORIGIN Latin.

prin. ▶ **abbr.** ■ principal. ■ principally. ■ principle.

Prince /prins/, Hal (1928–) US theatrical producer and director; full name *Harold Smith Prince*. Among the shows that he produced were *Pajama Game* (1954), *West Side Story* (1957), *Fiorello* (1959), and *Fiddler on the Roof* (1964). Some that he also directed included *Cabaret* (1966), *Evita* (1980), and *Phantom of the Opera* (1988).

prince /prins/ ▶ **n.** the son of a monarch. ■ a close male relative of a monarch, esp. a son's son. ■ a male royal ruler of a small state, actually, nominally, or originally subject to a king or emperor. ■ (in France, Germany and other European countries) a nobleman, usually ranking next below a duke. ■ (**prince of/among**) a man or thing regarded as outstanding or excellent in a particular sphere or group: *arctic char is a prince among fishes.*
– DERIVATIVES **prince·dom** /dəm/ **n.**
– ORIGIN Middle English: via Old French from Latin *princeps, princip-* 'first, chief, sovereign,' from *primus* 'first' + *capere* 'take.'

Prince Al·bert, Prince Ed·ward, etc. see **ALBERT, PRINCE; EDWARD, PRINCE,** etc.

Prince Charm·ing (also **prince charming**) an ideal male lover who is both handsome and of admirable character.
– ORIGIN partial translation of French *Roi Charmant*, literally 'King Charming.'

Prince Con·sort ▶ **n.** the husband of a reigning female sovereign who is himself a prince.

Prince Ed·ward Is·land an island in the Gulf of St. Lawrence, in eastern Canada, the country's smallest province; capital, Charlottetown. Explored by Jacques Cartier in 1534 and colonized by the French, it was ceded to the British in 1763 and became a Canadian province in 1873.

Prince George's Coun·ty /ˈjôrjəz/ a county in south central Maryland, the site of many southeastern suburbs of Washington, DC; pop. 820,852 (est. 2008).

prince·ling /ˈprinsliNG/ ▶ **n.** chiefly derogatory the ruler of a small principality or domain. ■ a young prince.

prince·ly /ˈprinslē/ ▶ **adj.** of or held by a prince: *the princely states of India* | *princely authority.* ■ sumptuous and splendid: *princely accommodations.* ■ (of a sum of money) large or generous (often used ironically): *she's paying a princely sum.*
– DERIVATIVES **prince·li·ness n.**

Prince of Dark·ness ▶ **n.** a name for the Devil.

Prince of Peace ▶ **n.** a title given to Jesus Christ (in allusion to Isa. 9:6).

Prince of the Church ▶ **n.** historical a dignitary in the Roman Catholic Church, esp. a wealthy or influential cardinal or bishop.

Prince of Wales ▶ **n.** a title traditionally granted to the heir apparent to the British throne (usually the eldest son of the sovereign) since Edward I of England gave the title to his son in 1301 after the conquest of Wales.

Prince of Wales Is·land 1 an island in the Canadian Arctic, in the Northwest Territories, to the east of Victoria Island.
2 former name for **PENANG**.
3 the largest island in the Alexander Archipelago, in southeastern Alaska, home to the Haida people.

Prince Roy·al ▶ **n.** the eldest son of a reigning monarch.

Prince Ru·pert's Land another name for **RUPERT'S LAND**.

Princes in the Tow·er the young sons of Edward IV, namely **Edward, Prince of Wales** (born 1470) and **Richard, Duke of York** (born 1472), supposedly murdered in the Tower of London in or shortly after 1483.

prin·cess /ˈprinsəs, ˈprinˌses, prinˈses/ ▶ **n.** the daughter of a monarch. ■ a close female relative of monarch, esp. a son's daughter. ■ the wife or widow of a prince. ■ the female ruler of a small state, actually, nominally, or originally subject to a king or emperor. ■ informal a spoiled or arrogant young woman.
– ORIGIN late Middle English: from Old French *princesse*, from *prince* (see **PRINCE**).

Prin·cess Anne, Prin·cess Mar·gar·et, etc. see **ANNE, PRINCESS; MARGARET, PRINCESS,** etc.

prin·cesse loin·taine /praNˈses lwaNˈten/ ▶ **n.** (pl. **princesses lointaines** pronunc. **same**) literary an ideal but unattainable woman.
– ORIGIN French, literally 'distant princess,' from the title of a play by E. **ROSTAND**, based on a theme in troubadour poetry.

Prin·cess Roy·al ▶ **n.** the eldest daughter of a reigning monarch (esp. as a title conferred by the British monarch).

prin·cess tree ▶ **n.** another name for **EMPRESS TREE**.

Prince·ton /ˈprinstən/ a historic borough in west central New Jersey, home to Princeton University; pop. 17,438 (est. 2008).

Prince·ton U·ni·ver·si·ty /ˈprinstən/ an Ivy League university at Princeton, New Jersey, founded in 1746.

Prince Wil·liam Sound /ˈwilyəm/ an inlet of the Pacific Ocean in south central Alaska, scene of a huge 1989 oil tanker spill. Cordova and Valdez are the main ports.

prin·ci·pal /ˈprinsəpəl/ ▶ **adj.** [attrib.] **1** first in order of importance; main: *the country's principal cities.*
2 (of money) denoting an original sum invested or lent: *the principal amount of your investment.*
▶ **n. 1** the person with the highest authority or most important position in an organization, institution, or group: *a design consultancy whose principal is based in San Francisco.* ■ the head of a school, college, or other educational institution. ■ the leading performer in a concert, play, ballet, or opera. ■ Music the leading player in each section of an orchestra.
2 a sum of money lent or invested on which interest is paid: *the winners are paid from the interest without even touching the principal.*
3 a person for whom another acts as an agent or representative: *stockbrokers in Tokyo act as agents rather than as principals.* ■ Law the person directly responsible for a crime. ■ historical each of the combatants in a duel.
4 a main rafter supporting purlins.
5 an organ stop sounding a main register of open flue pipes typically an octave above the diapason.
– DERIVATIVES **prin·ci·pal·ship** /-ˌSHip/ **n.**
– ORIGIN Middle English: via Old French from Latin *principalis* 'first, original,' from *princeps, princip-* 'first, chief.'

> **USAGE** Is it principal or principle? **Principal** means 'most important' or 'person in charge': *my principal reason for coming tonight; the high school principal.* It also means 'a capital sum': *the principal would be repaid in five years.* **Principle** means 'rule, basis for conduct': *her principles kept her from stealing despite her poverty.*

prin·ci·pal ax·is ▶ **n.** Physics each of three mutually perpendicular axes in a body about which the moment of inertia is at a maximum. ■ another term for **OPTICAL AXIS**.

prin·ci·pal di·ag·o·nal ▶ **n.** Mathematics the set of elements of a matrix that lie on the line joining the top left corner to the bottom right corner.

prin·ci·pal·i·ty /ˌprinsəˈpalətē/ ▶ **n.** (pl. **principalities**) **1** a state ruled by a prince. ■ (**the Principality**) Brit. Wales.
2 (**principalities**) (in traditional Christian angelology) the fifth highest order of the ninefold celestial hierarchy.
– ORIGIN Middle English (denoting the rank of a prince): from Old French *principalite*, from late Latin *principalitas*, from Latin *principalis* 'first, original' (see **PRINCIPAL**).

prin·ci·pal·ly /ˈprinsəp(ə)lē/ ▶ **adv.** [sentence adverb] for the most part; chiefly: *he was principally a landscape painter.*

prin·ci·pal parts ▶ **plural n.** Grammar the forms of a verb from which all other inflected forms can be deduced, for example, *swim, swam, swum.*

prin·ci·pate /ˈprinsəˌpāt, -pət/ ▶ **n.** the rule of the early Roman emperors, during which some features of republican government were retained.
– ORIGIN late Middle English (denoting a principality): from Latin *principatus* 'first place,' from *princeps, princip-* 'first, chief' (see **PRINCE**). The sense 'rule of the emperors' dates from the mid 19th cent.

P

prin·ci·ple /ˈprinsəpəl/ ▶ **n.** **1** a fundamental truth or proposition that serves as the foundation for a system of belief or behavior or for a chain of reasoning: *the basic principles of Christianity.* ■ (usu. **principles**) a rule or belief governing one's personal behavior: *struggling to be true to their own principles | she resigned over a matter of principle.* ■ morally correct behavior and attitudes: *a man of principle.* ■ a general scientific theorem or law that has numerous special applications across a wide field. ■ a natural law forming the basis for the construction or working of a machine: *these machines all operate on the same general principle.* **2** a fundamental source or basis of something: *the first principle of all things was water.* ■ a fundamental quality or attribute determining the nature of something; an essence: *the combination of male and female principles.* ■ [with adj.] Chemistry an active or characteristic constituent of a substance, obtained by simple analysis or separation: *the active principle in the medulla is epinephrine.*
– PHRASES **in principle** as a general idea or plan, although the details are not yet established or clear: *the government agreed in principle to a peace plan that included a ceasefire.* ■ used to indicate that although something is theoretically possible, it may not actually happen: *in principle, the banks are entitled to withdraw these loans when necessary.* **on principle** because of or in order to demonstrate one's adherence to a particular belief: *he refused, on principle, to pay the fine.*
– ORIGIN late Middle English: from Old French, from Latin *principium* 'source,' *principia* (plural) 'foundations,' from *princeps, princip-* 'first, chief.'

> **USAGE** On the confusion of **principle** and **principal**, see usage at **PRINCIPAL**.

prin·ci·pled /ˈprinsəpəld/ ▶ **adj.** **1** (of a person or their behavior) acting in accordance with morality and showing recognition of right and wrong: *a principled politician.* **2** (of a system or method) based on a given set of rules: *a coherent and principled approach.*

prin·ci·ple of par·si·mo·ny ▶ **n.** see **PARSIMONY**.

prink /priNGk/ ▶ **v.** (**prink oneself**) spend time making minor adjustments to one's appearance; primp: *prinking themselves in front of the mirror.*
– ORIGIN late 16th cent.: probably related to archaic *prank* 'dress or adorn in a showy manner'; related to Middle Low German *prank* 'pomp,' Dutch *pronk* 'finery.'

print /print/ ▶ **v.** [with obj.] **1** produce (books, newspapers, magazines, etc.), esp. in large quantities, by a mechanical process involving the transfer of text, images, or designs to paper: *a thousand copies of the book were printed.* ■ produce (text or a picture) in such a way: *the words had been printed in blue type.* ■ (of a newspaper or magazine) publish (a piece of writing) within its pages: *the article was printed in the first edition.* ■ (of a publisher or printer) arrange for (a book, manuscript, etc.) to be reproduced in large quantities: *Harper printed her memoirs in 1930.* ■ produce a paper copy of (information stored on a computer): *the results of a search can be printed out.* ■ send (a computer file) to a printer or to another, temporary file. ■ produce (a photographic print) from a negative: *any make of film can be developed and printed.* **2** write (text) clearly without joining the letters: *print your name and address on the back of the check |* [no obj.] *it will be easier to read if I print.* **3** mark (a surface, typically a textile or a garment) with a colored design or pattern: *a delicate fabric printed with roses.* ■ transfer (a colored design or pattern) to a surface: *patterns of birds, flowers, and trees were printed on the cotton.* ■ make (a mark or indentation) on a surface or in a soft substance by pressing something onto it: *he printed a mark on her soft skin.* ■ mark or indent (the surface of a soft substance) in such a way: *we printed the butter with carved wooden butter molds.* ■ fix (something) firmly or indelibly in someone's mind: *his face, with its clearly drawn features, was printed on her memory.*
▶ **n.** **1** the text appearing in a book, newspaper, or other printed publication, esp. with reference to its size, form, or style: *squinting at the tiny print | bold print.* ■ the state of being available in published form: *the news will never get into print.* ■ a newspaper or magazine: [as modifier] *the print media.* ■ [as modifier] of or relating to the printing industry or the printed media: *the print unions | a print worker.* **2** an indentation or mark left on a surface or soft substance by pressure, esp. that of a foot or hand: *there were paw prints everywhere.* ■ (**prints**) fingerprints: *the FBI matched the prints to those of the Las Vegas drug suspect.* **3** a picture or design printed from a block or plate or copied from a painting by photography: *the walls were hung with wildlife prints.* ■ a photograph printed on paper from a negative or transparency. ■ a copy of a motion picture on film, esp. a particular version of it. **4** a piece of fabric or clothing with a decorative colored pattern or design printed on it: *light summer prints |* [as modifier] *a floral print dress.* ■ such a pattern or design.
– PHRASES **appear in print** (of an author) have one's work published. **in print 1** (of a book) available from the publisher: *he was surprised to find it was still in print.* **2** in printed or published form: *she did not live to see her work in print.* **out of print** (of a book) no longer available from the publisher: *the title I want is out of print.* **the printed word** language or ideas as expressed in books, newspapers, or other publications, esp. when contrasted with their expression in speech.
– ORIGIN Middle English (denoting the impression made by a stamp or seal): from Old French *preinte* 'pressed,' feminine past participle of *preindre*, from Latin *premere* 'to press.'

print. ▶ **abbr.** printing.

print·a·bil·i·ty /ˌprintəˈbilətē/ ▶ **n.** the ability of paper to take print: *the paper's printability and porosity.*

print·a·ble /ˈprintəbəl/ ▶ **adj.** suitable or fit to be printed or published: *break photographs up into printable form | few people had a good, or even printable, word for him.* ■ Computing (of text) able to be printed: *the file is printable.*

print·ed cir·cuit ▶ **n.** an electronic circuit consisting of thin strips of a conducting material such as copper, which have been etched from a layer fixed to a flat insulating sheet called a **printed circuit board**, and to which integrated circuits and other components are attached.

print·er /ˈprintər/ ▶ **n.** a person whose job or business is commercial printing. ■ a machine for printing text or pictures onto paper, esp. one linked to a computer.

print·er-friend·ly /ˈprintər ˌfrendlē/ ▶ **adj.** formatted for output to a printer, with extraneous material deleted or suppressed: *printer-friendly sample ballots to take with you to their polling place.*

print·er's dev·il ▶ **n.** historical a person, typically a young boy, serving at or below the level of apprentice in a printing establishment.

print·er's mark ▶ **n.** a logo serving as a printer's trademark.

print·er·y /ˈprintərē/ ▶ **n.** (pl. **printeries**) a print shop.

print·head /ˈprintˌhed/ (also **print head**) ▶ **n.** Computing a component in a printer that assembles and holds the characters and from which the images of the characters are transferred to the printing medium.

print·ing /ˈprintiNG/ ▶ **n.** the production of books, newspapers, or other printed material: *the invention of printing |* [as modifier] *the printing industry.* ■ a single impression of a book: *the second printing was ready just after Christmas.* ■ handwriting in which the letters are written separately rather than being joined together.

print·ing press ▶ **n.** a machine for printing text or pictures from type or plates.

print·mak·er /ˈprintˌmākər/ ▶ **n.** a person who makes pictures or designs by printing them from specially prepared plates or blocks.
– DERIVATIVES **print·mak·ing** /-kiNG/ **n.**

print·out /ˈprintˌout/ ▶ **n.** Computing a page or set of pages of printed material produced by a computer's printer.

print queue ▶ **n.** Computing a series of print jobs waiting to use a printer.

print run ▶ **n.** the number of copies of a book, magazine, etc., printed at one time.

print shop (also **printshop**) ▶ **n.** an establishment where the printing of newspapers, books, and other materials takes place.

pri·on[1] /ˈprīˌän/ ▶ **n.** a small petrel of southern seas, having a wide bill fringed with comblike plates for feeding on planktonic crustaceans. ● Genus *Pachyptila*, family Procellariidae: six species.
– ORIGIN mid 19th cent.: modern Latin (former genus name), from Greek *priōn* 'a saw' (referring to its sawlike bill).

pri·on[2] /ˈprēˌän/ ▶ **n.** Microbiology a protein particle that is believed to be the cause of brain diseases such as BSE, scrapie, and Creutzfeldt–Jakob disease. Prions are not visible microscopically, contain no nucleic acid, and are highly resistant to destruction. Compare with **VIRINO**.
– ORIGIN 1980s: by rearrangement of elements from *pro(teinaceous) in(fectious particle).*

pri·or[1] /ˈprīər/ ▶ **adj.** [attrib.] existing or coming before in time, order, or importance: *he has a prior engagement this evening.*
▶ **n.** informal a previous criminal conviction: *he had no juvenile record, no priors.*
– PHRASES **prior to** before a particular time or event: *she visited me on the day prior to her death.*
– ORIGIN early 18th cent.: from Latin, literally 'former, elder,' related to *prae* 'before.'

pri·or[2] ▶ **n.** a man who is head of a house or group of houses of certain religious orders, in particular: ■ the man next in rank below an abbot. ■ the head of a house of friars.
– DERIVATIVES **pri·or·ate** /ˈprīərət/ **n.**, **pri·or·ship** /-ˌSHip/ **n.**
– ORIGIN late Old English, from a medieval Latin noun use of Latin *prior* 'elder, former' (see **PRIOR**[1]).

pri·or·ess /ˈprīərəs/ ▶ **n.** a woman who is head of a house of certain orders of nuns. ■ the woman next in rank below an abbess.

pri·or·i·tize /prīˈôrəˌtīz, ˈprīərə-/ ▶ **v.** [with obj.] designate or treat (something) as more important than other things: *prioritize your credit card debt.* ■ determine the order for dealing with (a series of items or tasks) according to their relative importance: *age affects the way people prioritize their goals |* [no obj.] *are you able to prioritize?*
– DERIVATIVES **pri·or·i·ti·za·tion** /ˌprīˌôrətəˈzāSHən/ **n.**

pri·or·i·ty /prīˈôrətē/ ▶ **n.** (pl. **priorities**) a thing that is regarded as more important than another: *housework didn't figure high on her list of priorities.* ■ the fact or condition of being regarded or treated as more important: *the safety of the country takes priority over any other matter.* ■ the right to take precedence or to proceed before others: *priority is given to those with press passes |* [as modifier] *clear the left lane for priority traffic.*
– ORIGIN late Middle English (denoting precedence in time or rank): from Old French *priorite*, from medieval Latin *prioritas*, from Latin *prior* 'former' (see **PRIOR**[1]).

pri·or prob·a·bil·i·ty ▶ **n.** Statistics a probability as assessed before making reference to certain relevant observations, esp. subjectively or on the assumption that all possible outcomes be given the same probability. Compare with **POSTERIOR PROBABILITY**.

pri·or re·straint ▶ **n.** Law judicial suppression of material that would be published or broadcast, on the grounds that it is libelous or harmful. In US law, the First Amendment severely limits the ability of the government to do this.

pri·o·ry /ˈprīərē/ ▶ **n.** (pl. **priories**) a small monastery or nunnery that is governed by a prior or prioress.
– ORIGIN Middle English: from Anglo-Norman French *priorie*, medieval Latin *prioria*, from Latin *prior* 'elder, superior' (see **PRIOR**[2]).

Pri·pyat /ˈprēpyit/ (also **Pripet** /ˈpripit, -et/) a river in northwestern Ukraine and southern Belarus that rises in Ukraine near the border with Poland and flows about 440 miles (710 km) east through the Pripyat Marshes to join the Dnieper River north of Kiev.

Pri·scian /ˈpriSH(ē)ən/ (6th century AD), Byzantine grammarian; full name *Priscianus Caesariensis*. His *Grammatical Institutions* became one of the standard Latin grammatical works in the Middle Ages.

Pris·co·an /prisˈkōən/ ▶ **adj.** Geology of, relating to, or denoting the eon that (in some schemes) constitutes the earliest part of the Precambrian, preceding the Archean eon. It extended from the origin of the earth to about 4 billion years ago and has left no so far identifiable rocks. ■ (as noun **the Priscoan**) the Priscoan eon.
– ORIGIN formed irregularly from Latin *priscus* 'ancient' + **-AN**.

prise ▶ **v.** variant spelling of **PRIZE**[2].

prism /ˈprizəm/ ▶ **n.** Geometry a solid geometric figure whose two end faces are similar, equal, and parallel rectilinear figures, and whose sides are parallelograms. ■ Optics a glass or other transparent object in this form, esp. one that is triangular with refracting surfaces at an acute angle with each other and that separates white light into a spectrum of colors. ■ used figuratively with reference to the clarification or distortion afforded by a particular viewpoint: *they*

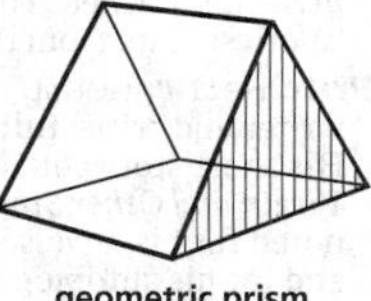

geometric prism

PRONUNCIATION KEY ə *ago, up*; ər *over, fur*; a *hat*; ā *ate*; ä *car*; e *let*; ē *see*; i *fit*; ī *by*; NG *sing*; ō *go*; ô *law, for*; oi *toy*; o͝o *good*; o͞o *goo*; ou *out*; TH *thin*; T͟H *then*; ZH *vision*

were forced to imagine the disaster through ***the prism of television.***
– ORIGIN late 16th cent.: via late Latin from Greek *prisma* 'thing sawn,' from *prizein* 'to saw.'

pris·mat·ic /priz'matik/ ▶ **adj.** of, relating to, or having the form of a prism or prisms: *a prismatic structure.* ■ (of colors) formed, separated, or distributed by an optical prism or something acting as one: *a flash of prismatic light on the edge of the glass.* ■ (of colors) varied and brilliant: *a hundred prismatic tints.* ■ (of an instrument) incorporating a prism or prisms: *a prismatic compass.*
– DERIVATIVES **pris·mat·i·cal·ly** /-ik(ə)lē/ **adv.**
– ORIGIN early 18th cent.: from French *prismatique,* from Greek *prisma* 'thing sawn' (see **PRISM**).

pris·mat·ic lay·er ▶ **n.** Zoology the middle layer of the shell of a mollusk, consisting of calcite or aragonite.

pris·moid /'priz,moid/ ▶ **n.** Geometry a solid geometric figure like a prism, in which the end faces have the same number of sides but are not equal.

pris·on /'prizən/ ▶ **n.** a building (or vessel) in which people are legally held as a punishment for crimes they have committed or while awaiting trial: *he died* ***in prison*** | *both men were* ***sent to prison.***
▶ **v.** (**prisons, prisoning, prisoned**) [with obj.] literary imprison: *the young man prisoned behind the doors.*
– ORIGIN late Old English, from Old French *prisun,* from Latin *prensio(n-),* variant of *prehensio(n-)* 'laying hold of,' from the verb *prehendere.*

pris·on camp ▶ **n.** a camp where prisoners of war or political prisoners are kept under guard.

pris·on·er /'priz(ə)nər/ ▶ **n.** a person legally held in prison as a punishment for crimes they have committed or while awaiting trial. ■ a person captured and kept confined by an enemy, opponent, or criminal: *the heroine was being* ***held prisoner*** *in a cave* | *200 rebels were* ***taken prisoner.*** ■ a person who is or feels confined or trapped by a situation or set of circumstances: *he's become a prisoner of the publicity he's generated.*
– PHRASES **take no prisoners** be ruthlessly aggressive or uncompromising in the pursuit of one's objectives.
– ORIGIN late Middle English: from Old French *prisonier,* from *prison* (see **PRISON**).

pris·on·er of con·science ▶ **n.** a person who has been imprisoned for holding political or religious views that are not tolerated by their own government.

pris·on·er of war (abbr.: **POW**) ▶ **n.** a person who has been captured and imprisoned by the enemy in war.

pris·on·er's base ▶ **n.** a chasing game played by two groups of children each occupying a distinct base or home.

P

pris·on·er's di·lem·ma ▶ **n.** (in game theory) a situation in which two players each have two options whose outcome depends crucially on the simultaneous choice made by the other, often formulated in terms of two prisoners separately deciding whether to confess to a crime.

pris·sy /'prisē/ ▶ **adj.** (**prissier, prissiest**) fussily and excessively respectable: *her prissy mother* | *prissy little dresses.*
– DERIVATIVES **pris·si·ly** /'prisəlē/ **adv., pris·si·ness n.**
– ORIGIN late 19th cent.: perhaps a blend of **PRIM** and **SISSY.**

Priš·ti·na /'prisHti,nä/ a city in the Balkans, the capital of Kosovo; pop. 210,800 (est. 2009).

pris·tine /'pris,tēn, pri'stēn/ ▶ **adj.** in its original condition; unspoiled: *pristine copies of an early magazine.* ■ clean and fresh as if new; spotless: *a pristine white shirt.*
– DERIVATIVES **pris·tine·ly adv.**
– ORIGIN mid 16th cent. (in the sense 'original, former, primitive and undeveloped'): from Latin *pristinus* 'former.' The senses 'unspoiled' and 'spotless' date from the 1920s.

Pritch·ett /'pricHət/, Sir V. S. (1900–97), English writer and critic; full name *Victor Sawdon Pritchett.* His short-story collections include *The Spanish Virgin and Other Stories* (1930). Pritchett is also noted for his novels, such as *Mr. Beluncle* (1951), and for his autobiographies, *A Cab at the Door* (1968) and *Midnight Oil* (1973). His critical works include *The Living Novel* (1946).

prith·ee /'priTHē/ ▶ **exclam.** archaic please (used to convey a polite request): *prithee, Jack, answer me honestly.*
– ORIGIN late 16th cent.: abbreviation of *I pray thee.*

priv. ▶ **abbr.** ■ private. ■ privative.

pri·va·cy /'prīvəsē/ ▶ **n.** the state or condition of being free from being observed or disturbed by other people: *she returned to the privacy of her own home.* ■ the state of being free from public attention: *a law to restrict newspapers' freedom to invade people's privacy.*

pri·vate /'prīvit/ ▶ **adj. 1** belonging to or for the use of one particular person or group of people only: *all bedrooms have private facilities* | *his private plane.* ■ (of a situation, activity, or gathering) affecting or involving only a particular person or group of people: *a small private service in the chapel.* ■ (of thoughts and feelings) not to be shared with or revealed to others: *she felt awkward intruding on private grief.* ■ (of a person) not choosing to share thoughts and feelings with others: *he was a very private man.* ■ (of a meeting or discussion) involving only a small number of people and dealing with matters that are not to be disclosed to others: *this is a private conversation.* ■ (of a place) quiet and free from people who can interrupt: *can we go somewhere a little more private?*
2 (of a person) having no official or public role or position: *the paintings were sold to a private collector.* ■ not connected with one's work or official position: *he would continue to represent her in a private capacity as advisor and confidant.*
3 (of a service or industry) provided or owned by an individual or an independent, commercial company rather than by the government: *research projects carried out by private industry* | *more than 1,400 state enterprises that were about to go private.* ■ of or relating to a system of education or medical treatment conducted outside the system of government and charging fees to the individuals who make use of it. ■ of, relating to, or denoting a transaction between individuals and not involving commercial organizations: *it was a private sale—no agent's commission.*
▶ **n. 1** a soldier of the lowest rank, in particular an enlisted person in the US Army or Marine Corps ranking below private first class.
2 (**privates**) informal short for **PRIVATE PARTS.**
– PHRASES **in private** with no one else present: *I've got to talk to you in private.*
– ORIGIN late Middle English (originally denoting a person not acting in an official capacity): from Latin *privatus* 'withdrawn from public life,' a use of the past participle of *privare* 'bereave, deprive,' from *privus* 'single, individual.'

pri·vate de·tec·tive ▶ **n.** another term for **PRIVATE INVESTIGATOR.**

pri·vate en·ter·prise ▶ **n.** business or industry that is managed by independent companies or private individuals rather than by the state.

pri·va·teer /,prīvə'tir/ ▶ **n.** chiefly historical an armed ship owned and officered by private individuals holding a government commission and authorized for use in war, esp. in the capture of enemy merchant shipping. ■ (also **privateersman**) a commander or crew member of such a ship, often regarded as a pirate.
▶ **v.** [no obj.] engage in the activities of a privateer.
– DERIVATIVES **pri·va·teer·ing n.**
– ORIGIN mid 17th cent.: from **PRIVATE,** on the pattern of *volunteer.*

pri·vate eye ▶ **n.** informal a private investigator.

pri·vate first class ▶ **n.** an enlisted person in the armed forces, in particular (in the US Army) an enlisted person ranking above private and below corporal or (in the US Marine Corps) an enlisted person ranking above private and below lance corporal.

pri·vate in·ves·ti·ga·tor (also **private detective**) ▶ **n.** a freelance detective who carries out investigations on behalf of private clients.

pri·vate key ▶ **n.** see **PUBLIC KEY.**

pri·vate la·bel ▶ **adj.** designating a product manufactured or packaged for sale under the name of the retailer rather than that of the manufacturer: *private label cheeses.*
▶ **n.** a retailer's name, as used on a product sold by the retailer but manufactured by another company: *the yogurt is sold under their private label.*

pri·vate law ▶ **n.** a branch of the law that deals with the relations between individuals or institutions, rather than relations between these and the government.

pri·vate·ly /'prīvitlē/ ▶ **adv.** in a private way, manner, or capacity: *I must insist we speak privately* | *his research is privately financed.* ■ [often sentence adverb] used to refer to a situation in which someone's thoughts and feelings are not disclosed to others: *privately, Republican strategists worried about the latest polls.*

pri·vate mem·ber ▶ **n.** (in the UK, Canada, Australia, and New Zealand) a member of a parliament who is not a minister or does not hold government office.

pri·vate nui·sance ▶ **n.** Law see **NUISANCE.**

pri·vate parts ▶ **plural n.** used euphemistically to refer to a person's genitals.

pri·vate prac·tice ▶ **n.** the work of a professional practitioner, such as a doctor or lawyer, who is self-employed.

pri·vate school ▶ **n. 1** a school supported by a private organization or private individuals rather than by the government.
2 Brit. a school supported wholly by the payment of fees.

pri·vate sec·re·tar·y ▶ **n. 1** a secretary who deals with the personal and confidential concerns of a business person or public figure.
2 a civil servant acting as an aide to a senior government official.

pri·vate sec·tor ▶ **n.** the part of the national economy that is not under direct government control.

pri·vate sol·dier ▶ **n.** a soldier of the lowest rank.

pri·vate trea·ty ▶ **n.** the agreement for the sale of a property at a price negotiated directly between the vendor and purchaser or their agents.

pri·va·tion /prī'vāsHən/ ▶ **n.** a state in which things that are essential for human well-being such as food and warmth are scarce or lacking: *years of rationing and privation* | *the* ***privations*** *of life at the front.* ■ formal the loss or absence of a quality or attribute that is normally present: *cold is the privation of heat.*
– ORIGIN Middle English: from Latin *privatio(n-),* from *privat-* 'deprived,' from the verb *privare* (see **PRIVATE**).

pri·va·tism /'prīvə,tizəm/ ▶ **n.** a tendency to be concerned with ideas or issues only insofar as they affect one as an individual.
– DERIVATIVES **pri·va·tist adj.**

pri·va·tive /'privətiv/ ▶ **adj.** (of an action or state) marked by the absence, removal, or loss of some quality or attribute that is normally present. ■ (of a statement or term) denoting the absence or loss of an attribute or quality: *the wording of the privative clause.* ■ Grammar (of a particle or affix) expressing absence or negation, for example, the *a-* (from the *alpha privative* in Greek), meaning "not," in *atypical.*
▶ **n.** a privative attribute, quality, or proposition.
– ORIGIN late 16th cent.: from Latin *privativus* 'denoting privation,' from *privat-* 'deprived' (see **PRIVATION**).

pri·va·tize /'prīvə,tīz/ ▶ **v.** [with obj.] transfer (a business, industry, or service) from public to private ownership and control: *a plan for privatizing education.*
– DERIVATIVES **pri·va·ti·za·tion** /,prīvətə'zāsHən/ **n., pri·va·tiz·er n.**

priv·et /'privit/ ▶ **n.** a shrub of the olive family, with small white, heavily scented flowers and poisonous black berries. ● Genus *Ligustrum,* family Oleaceae: several species, in particular the semievergreen **common privet** (*L. vulgare*), often grown as a hedge.
– ORIGIN mid 16th cent.: of unknown origin.

priv·i·lege /'priv(ə)lij/ ▶ **n.** a special right, advantage, or immunity granted or available only to a particular person or group of people: *education is a right, not a privilege* | *he has been accustomed all his life to wealth and privilege.* ■ something regarded as a rare opportunity and bringing particular pleasure: *I have the privilege of awarding you this scholarship.* ■ (also **absolute privilege**) (in a parliamentary context) the right to say or write something without the risk of incurring punishment or legal action for defamation. ■ the right of a lawyer or official to refuse to divulge confidential information. ■ chiefly historical a grant to an individual, corporation, or place of special rights or immunities, esp. in the form of a franchise or monopoly.
▶ **v.** [with obj.] formal grant a privilege or privileges to: *English inheritance law privileged the eldest son.* ■ (usu. **be privileged from**) exempt (someone) from a liability or obligation to which others are subject.
– ORIGIN Middle English: via Old French from Latin *privilegium* 'bill or law affecting an individual,' from *privus* 'private' + *lex, leg-* 'law.'

priv·i·leged /'priv(ə)lijd/ ▶ **adj.** having special rights, advantages, or immunities: *in the nineteenth century, only a privileged few had the vote.* ■ [with infinitive] having the rare opportunity to do something that brings particular pleasure: *I felt I had been privileged to compete in such a race.* ■ (of information) legally protected from being made public: *the intelligence reports are privileged.*

priv·i·ty /'privitē/ ▶ **n.** (pl. **privities**) Law a relation between two parties that is recognized by law, such as that of blood, lease, or service: *the parties no longer have privity with each other* | *a warehouseman not in privity with the government.*
– ORIGIN Middle English (in the sense 'secrecy, intimacy'): from Old French *privete,* from medieval Latin *privitas,* from Latin *privus* 'private.'

priv·y /'privē/ ▶ **adj.** [predic.] (**privy to**) sharing in the knowledge of (something secret or private): *he was*

no longer privy to her innermost thoughts. ■ archaic hidden; secret: *a privy place.*
▶ **n.** (pl. **privies**) **1** a toilet located in a small shed outside a house or other building; outhouse.
2 Law a person having a part or interest in any action, matter, or thing.
– DERIVATIVES **priv·i·ly** /ˈprivəlē/ **adv.**
– ORIGIN Middle English (originally in the sense 'belonging to one's own private circle'): from Old French *prive* 'private' (also used as a noun meaning 'private place' and 'familiar friend'), from Latin *privatus* 'withdrawn from public life' (see PRIVATE).

priv·y cham·ber ▶ **n.** a private apartment in a royal residence.

priv·y coun·cil ▶ **n.** a body of advisers or private counselors appointed by a sovereign or a governor general (now chiefly on an honorary basis and including present and former government ministers).
– DERIVATIVES **priv·y coun·ci·lor n.**

priv·y purse ▶ **n.** (in the UK) an allowance from the public revenue for the monarch's private expenses.

priv·y seal ▶ **n.** (in the UK) a seal affixed to documents that are afterward to pass the Great Seal or that do not require it.

prix fixe /ˈprē ˈfēks, ˈfiks/ ▶ **n.** a meal consisting of several courses served at a total fixed price.
– ORIGIN French, literally 'fixed price.'

prize[1] /prīz/ ▶ **n.** a thing given as a reward to the winner of a competition or race or in recognition of another outstanding achievement: *the nation's most prestigious prize for contemporary art.* ■ a thing, esp. an amount of money or a valuable object, that can be won in a lottery or other game of chance: *the grand prize in the drawing* | [as modifier] *prize money.* ■ something of great value that is worth struggling to achieve: *the prize will be victory in the general election.* ■ chiefly historical an enemy ship captured during the course of naval warfare. [late Middle English: from Old French *prise* 'taking, booty,' from *prendre* 'take.']
▶ **adj.** [attrib.] (esp. of something entered in a competition) having been or likely to be awarded a prize: *prize onions* | *a prize bull.* ■ denoting something for which a prize is awarded: *a prize crossword.* ■ excellent of its kind; outstanding: *a prize example of how well organic farming can function.* ■ complete; utter: *you must think I'm a prize idiot.*
▶ **v.** [with obj.] value extremely highly: *the berries were prized for their healing properties* | (as adj. **prized**) *the bicycle was her most prized possession.*
– ORIGIN Middle English: the noun, a variant of PRICE; the verb (originally in the sense 'estimate the value of') from Old French *pris-*, stem of *preisier* 'to praise, appraise' (see PRAISE).

prize[2] (also **prise**) ▶ **v.** another term for PRY[2]: *prizing open the door* | *he prized his left leg free.*
– ORIGIN late 17th cent.: from dialect *prise* 'lever,' from Old French *prise* 'grasp, taking hold.' Compare with PRY[2].

prize court ▶ **n.** a naval court that adjudicates on the distribution of ships and property captured in the course of naval warfare.

prize·fight /ˈprīzˌfit/ (also **prize fight**) ▶ **n.** a boxing match fought for prize money.
– DERIVATIVES **prize·fight·er n.**, **prize·fight·ing n.**

prize mon·ey ▶ **n.** money offered or received as a prize.

prize ring ▶ **n.** a ring used for prizefighting. ■ (**the prize ring**) the practice of prizefighting; boxing.

prize·win·ner /ˈprīzˌwinər/ ▶ **n.** a winner of a prize.
– DERIVATIVES **prize·win·ning adj.**

p.r.n. ▶ **abbr.** (in prescriptions) as the occasion arises; as needed.
– ORIGIN Latin *pro re nata.*

PRO ▶ **abbr.** ■ public relations officer. ■ Brit. Public Record Office.

pro[1] /prō/ ▶ **n.** (pl. **pros**) informal a professional, esp. in sports: *a tennis pro.*
▶ **adj.** (of a person or an event) professional: *a pro golfer.*
– ORIGIN mid 19th cent.: abbreviation.

pro[2] ▶ **n.** (pl. **pros**) (usu. **pros**) an advantage of something or an argument in favor of a course of action: ***the pros and cons** of joint ownership.*
▶ **prep. & adv.** in favor of: [as prep.] *they were pro the virtues of individualism.*
– ORIGIN late Middle English (as a noun): from Latin, literally 'for, on behalf of.'

pro-[1] ▶ **prefix 1** favoring; supporting: *pro-choice* | *pro-life.*
2 acting as a substitute or deputy for; on behalf of; for: *proconsul* | *procure.*
3 denoting motion forward, out, or away: *proceed* | *propel* | *prostrate.*
– ORIGIN from Latin *pro* 'in front of, on behalf of, instead of, on account of.'

pro-[2] ▶ **prefix** before in time, place, order, etc.: *proactive* | *prognosis* | *program.*
– ORIGIN from Greek *pro* 'before.'

pro·a /ˈprōə/ (also **prahu** /ˈpräˌo͞o/ or **prau** /prou/) ▶ **n.** a type of sailing boat originating in Malaysia and Indonesia that may be sailed with either end at the front, typically having a large triangular sail and an outrigger.
– ORIGIN late 16th cent.: from Malay *perahu.*

pro-a·bor·tion ▶ **adj.** in favor of the availability of medically induced abortion as a means of ending a pregnancy.
– DERIVATIVES **pro-a·bor·tion·ist n. & adj.**

pro·ac·tive /prōˈaktiv/ ▶ **adj.** (of a person, policy, or action) creating or controlling a situation by causing something to happen rather than responding to it after it has happened: *be proactive in identifying and preventing potential problems.*
– DERIVATIVES **pro·ac·tion** /prōˈaksHən/ **n.**, **pro·ac·tive·ly adv.**, **pro·ac·tiv·i·ty** /ˌprōˌakˈtivətē/ **n.**
– ORIGIN 1930s: from PRO-[2] (denoting earlier occurrence), on the pattern of *reactive.*

pro·ac·tive in·hi·bi·tion ▶ **n.** Psychology the tendency of previously learned material to hinder subsequent learning.

pro-am /ˈprōˈam/ ▶ **adj.** (of a sports event) involving both professionals and amateurs: *a pro-am golf tournament.*
▶ **n.** an event of this type.

pro-an·a /ˈprōˈanə/ ▶ **adj.** (of a website) encouraging or advocating anorexia: *pro-ana sites share tips on how to trick your parents into believing you're eating.*

prob /präb/ ▶ **n.** informal problem: *there's no prob.*
– ORIGIN 1930s: abbreviation.

prob. ▶ **abbr.** ■ probable or probably. ■ probate. ■ problem.

prob·a·bi·lis·tic /ˌpräbəbəˈlistik/ ▶ **adj.** based on or adapted to a theory of probability; subject to or involving chance variation: *the main approaches are either rule-based or probabilistic.*
– DERIVATIVES **prob·a·bi·lism** /ˈpräbəbəˌlizəm/ **n.**

prob·a·bil·i·ty /ˌpräbəˈbilətē/ ▶ **n.** (pl. **probabilities**) the extent to which something is probable; the likelihood of something happening or being the case: *the rain will make the probability of their arrival even greater.* ■ a probable or the most probable event: *for a time, revolution was a strong probability* | *the probability is that it will be phased in over a number of years.* ■ Mathematics the extent to which an event is likely to occur, measured by the ratio of the favorable cases to the whole number of cases possible: *the area under the curve represents probability* | *a probability of 0.5.*
– PHRASES **in all probability** used to convey that something is very likely: *he would in all probability make himself known.*
– ORIGIN late Middle English: from Latin *probabilitas*, from *probabilis* 'provable, credible' (see PROBABLE).

prob·a·bil·i·ty den·si·ty func·tion ▶ **n.** Statistics a function of a continuous random variable, whose integral across an interval gives the probability that the value of the variable lies within the same interval.

prob·a·bil·i·ty dis·tri·bu·tion ▶ **n.** Statistics a function of a discrete variable whose integral over any interval is the probability that the random variable specified by it will lie within that interval.

prob·a·bil·i·ty the·o·ry ▶ **n.** the branch of mathematics that deals with quantities having random distributions.

prob·a·ble /ˈpräbəbəl/ ▶ **adj.** [often with clause] likely to be the case or to happen: ***it is probable that** the economic situation will deteriorate further* | *the probable consequences of his action.*
▶ **n.** a person who is likely to become or do something, esp. one who is likely to be chosen for a team: *Merson and Wright are probables.*
– ORIGIN late Middle English (in the sense 'worthy of belief'): via Old French from Latin *probabilis*, from *probare* 'to test, demonstrate.'

prob·a·ble cause ▶ **n.** Law reasonable grounds (for making a search, pressing a charge, etc.).

prob·a·bly /ˈpräbəblē, ˈpräblē/ ▶ **adv.** [sentence adverb] almost certainly; as far as one knows or can tell: *she would probably never see him again* | *"Would you recognize them?" "Probably."*

pro·band /ˈprōˌband, prōˈband/ ▶ **n.** a person serving as the starting point for the genetic study of a family (used esp. in medicine and psychiatry).
– ORIGIN 1920s: from Latin *probandus* 'to be proved,' gerundive of *probare* 'to test.'

pro·bang /ˈprōˌbaNG/ ▶ **n.** Medicine a strip of flexible material with a sponge or tuft at the end, used to remove an object from or apply medication to the throat.
– ORIGIN mid 17th cent. (named *provang* by its inventor): perhaps an alteration based on PROBE.

pro·bate /ˈprōˌbāt/ ▶ **n.** the official proving of a will: *the will was in probate* | [as modifier] *a probate court.* ■ a verified copy of a will with a certificate as handed to the executors.
▶ **v.** [with obj.] establish the validity of (a will).
– ORIGIN late Middle English: from Latin *probatum* 'something proved,' neuter past participle of *probare* 'to test, prove.'

pro·ba·tion /prōˈbāsHən/ ▶ **n.** Law the release of an offender from detention, subject to a period of good behavior under supervision: *I went to court and was **put on probation.*** ■ the process or period of testing or observing the character or abilities of a person in a certain role, for example, a new employee: *for an initial period of probation, your manager will closely monitor your progress.*
– DERIVATIVES **pro·ba·tion·ar·y** /-ˌnerē/ **adj.**
– ORIGIN late Middle English (denoting testing, investigation, or examination): from Old French *probacion*, from Latin *probatio(n-)*, from *probare* 'to test, prove' (see PROVE). The legal use dates from the late 19th cent.

pro·ba·tion·er /prōˈbāsHənər/ ▶ **n.** a person who is serving a probationary or trial period in a job or position to which they are newly appointed. ■ an offender on probation.

pro·ba·tion of·fi·cer ▶ **n.** a person appointed to supervise offenders who are on probation.

pro·ba·tive /ˈprōbətiv/ ▶ **adj.** chiefly Law having the quality or function of proving or demonstrating something; affording proof or evidence: *it places the probative burden on the defendant.*
– ORIGIN late Middle English (describing something that serves as a test): from Latin *probativus*, from *probat-* 'proved,' from the verb *probare* (see PROVE).

probe /prōb/ ▶ **n.** a blunt-ended surgical instrument used for exploring a wound or part of the body. ■ a small device, esp. an electrode, used for measuring, testing, or obtaining information. ■ a projecting device for engaging in a drogue, either on an aircraft for use in inflight refueling or on a spacecraft for use in docking with another craft. ■ (also **space probe**) an unmanned exploratory spacecraft designed to transmit information about its environment. ■ an investigation into a crime or other matter: ***a probe into** the maritime industry by the FBI.*
▶ **v.** [with obj.] physically explore or examine (something) with the hands or an instrument: *researchers probing the digestive glands of mollusks.* ■ [no obj.] seek to uncover information about someone or something: *he began to **probe into** Donald's whereabouts* | [with obj.] *police are probing another murder.*
– DERIVATIVES **prob·er n.**, **prob·ing·ly adv.**
– ORIGIN late Middle English (as a noun): from late Latin *proba* 'proof' (in medieval Latin 'examination'), from Latin *probare* 'to test.' The verb dates from the mid 17th cent.

pro·ben·e·cid /prōˈbenəsid/ ▶ **n.** Medicine a synthetic compound that promotes increased excretion of uric acid and is used to treat gout. ● Chem. formula $C_{13}H_{19}NO_4S$.
– ORIGIN 1950s: from *pro(pyl)* + *ben(zoic)* + *-e-* + *(a)cid.*

pro·bi·ot·ic /ˌprōbīˈätik/ ▶ **adj.** denoting a substance that stimulates the growth of microorganisms, esp. those with beneficial properties (such as those of the intestinal flora).
▶ **n.** a probiotic substance or preparation. ■ a microorganism introduced into the body for its beneficial qualities.

prob·it /ˈpräbit/ ▶ **n.** Statistics a unit of probability based on deviation from the mean of a standard distribution.
– ORIGIN 1930s: from *prob(ability un)it.*

pro·bi·ty /ˈprōbitē/ ▶ **n.** formal the quality of having strong moral principles; honesty and decency: *financial probity.*
– ORIGIN late Middle English: from Latin *probitas*, from *probus* 'good.'

prob·lem /ˈpräbləm/ ▶ **n. 1** a matter or situation regarded as unwelcome or harmful and needing to be dealt with and overcome: *mental health problems* | [as modifier] *city planners consider it a problem district.* ■ a thing that is difficult to achieve or accomplish: *motivation of staff can also be a problem.*
2 Physics & Mathematics an inquiry starting from given conditions to investigate or demonstrate a fact, result, or law. ■ Geometry a proposition in

P

which something has to be constructed. Compare with **THEOREM**. ■ (in various games, esp. chess) an arrangement of pieces in which the solver has to achieve a specified result.
– PHRASES **have a problem with** disagree with or have an objection to: *I have no problem with shopping on Sundays.* **no problem** used to express one's agreement or acquiescence: *"Can you help?" "No problem."* **that's your** (or **his**, or **her**, etc.) **problem** (said with emphatic stress on pronoun) used to express one's lack of interest in or sympathy with the problems or misfortunes of another person: *he'd made a mistake but that was his problem.*
– ORIGIN late Middle English (originally denoting a riddle or a question for academic discussion): from Old French *probleme*, via Latin from Greek *problēma*, from *proballein* 'put forth,' from *pro* 'before' + *ballein* 'to throw.'

prob·lem·at·ic /ˌpräbləˈmatik/ ▶ **adj.** constituting or presenting a problem or difficulty: *the situation was problematic for teachers.* ■ doubtful or questionable.
▶ **n.** a thing that constitutes a problem or difficulty: *the problematics of artificial intelligence.*
– DERIVATIVES **prob·lem·at·i·cal adj.**, **prob·lem·at·i·cal·ly** /-ik(ə)lē/ **adv.**
– ORIGIN early 17th cent.: via French from late Latin *problematicus*, from Greek *problēmatikos*, from *problēma* (see **PROBLEM**).

prob·lem·a·tize /ˈpräbləməˌtīz/ ▶ **v.** [with obj.] make into or regard as a problem requiring a solution: *he problematized the concept of history.*
– DERIVATIVES **prob·lem·a·ti·za·tion** /ˌpräbləmətəˈzāsHən, -ˌmatə-/ **n.**

pro bo·no pu·bli·co /ˌprō ˈbōnō ˈpo͞obliˌkō, ˈbōnō ˈpəbliˌkō/ ▶ **adv. & adj.** for the public good: [as adv.] *the burden they carried pro bono publico.* ■ (usu. **pro bono**) denoting work undertaken for the public good without charge, esp. legal work for a client with a low income: [as adv.] *the attorneys are representing him pro bono* | [as adj.] *pro bono legal services.*
– ORIGIN Latin.

Pro·bos·cid·e·a /ˌprōbəˈsidēə, prəˌbäsˈidēə/ Zoology an order of large mammals that comprises the elephants and their extinct relatives. They are distinguished by the possession of a trunk and tusks.
– ORIGIN modern Latin (plural), from **PROBOSCIS**.

pro·bos·cid·e·an /ˌprōbəˈsidēən, prəˌbäsəˈdēən/ (also **proboscidian**) Zoology ▶ **n.** a mammal of the order Proboscidea, which comprises the elephants and their extinct relatives.
▶ **adj.** relating to or denoting proboscideans.

pro·bos·cis /prəˈbäsəs, -ˈbäskəs/ ▶ **n.** (pl. **proboscises**, **proboscides** /-ˈbäsəˌdēz/, or **probosces** /-ˈbäsēz/) the nose of a mammal, esp. when it is long and mobile, such as the trunk of an elephant or the snout of a tapir. ■ Entomology (in many insects) an elongated sucking mouthpart that is typically tubular and flexible. ■ Zoology (in some worms) an extensible tubular sucking organ.
– ORIGIN early 17th cent.: via Latin from Greek *proboskis* 'means of obtaining food,' from *pro* 'before' + *boskein* '(cause to) feed.'

pro·bos·cis mon·key ▶ **n.** a leaf-eating monkey native to the forests of Borneo, the male of which is twice the weight of the female and has a large pendulous nose. ● *Nasalis larvatus*, family Cercopithecidae.

proc. ▶ **abbr.** ■ procedure. ■ proceedings. ■ process. ■ proclamation. ■ proctor.

pro·caine /ˈprōˌkān/ ▶ **n.** a synthetic compound derived from benzoic acid, used as a local anesthetic, esp. in dentistry.
– ORIGIN early 20th cent.: from **PRO-**[1] (denoting substitution) + *-caine* (from **COCAINE**).

pro·caine pen·i·cil·lin ▶ **n.** Medicine a slow-acting antibiotic made from a salt of procaine and a form of penicillin.

pro·car·y·ote ▶ **n.** variant spelling of **PROKARYOTE**.

pro·ce·dure /prəˈsējər/ ▶ **n.** an established or official way of doing something: *the police are now reviewing procedures* | *rules of procedure.* ■ a series of actions conducted in a certain order or manner: *the standard procedure for informing new employees about conditions of work.* ■ a surgical operation: *the procedure is carried out under general anesthesia.* ■ Computing another term for **SUBROUTINE**.
– DERIVATIVES **pro·ce·dur·al adj.**, **pro·ce·dur·al·ly adv.**
– ORIGIN late 16th cent.: from French *procédure*, from *procéder* (see **PROCEED**).

pro·ceed /prəˈsēd, prō-/ ▶ **v.** [no obj.] begin or continue a course of action: *we can proceed with our investigation.* ■ move forward, esp. after reaching a certain point: *the ship could proceed to Milwaukee.* ■ [with infinitive] do something as a natural or seemingly inevitable next step: *opposite the front door was a staircase, which I proceeded to climb.* ■ Law start a lawsuit against someone: *he may still be able to proceed against the contractor under the common law negligence rules.* ■ (of an action) be started: *negotiations must proceed without delay.* ■ (of an action) be carried on or continued: *as the excavation proceeds, the visible layers can be recorded and studied.* ■ originate from: *his claim that all power proceeded from God.*
– ORIGIN late Middle English: from Old French *proceder*, from Latin *procedere*, from *pro-* 'forward' + *cedere* 'go.'

pro·ceed·ings /prəˈsēdiNGz, prō-/ ▶ **plural n.** an event or a series of activities involving a formal or set procedure: *you complete a form to start proceedings.* ■ Law action taken in a court to settle a dispute: *criminal proceedings were brought against him.* ■ a published report of a set of meetings or a conference.

pro·ceeds /ˈprōˌsēdz/ ▶ **plural n.** money obtained from an event or activity: *proceeds will help purchase new equipment.*
– ORIGIN early 17th cent.: plural of the obsolete noun *proceed*, in the same sense, earlier meaning 'procedure.'

proc·ess[1] /ˈpräˌses, ˈpräsəs, ˈprō-/ ▶ **n. 1** a series of actions or steps taken in order to achieve a particular end: *military operations could jeopardize the peace process.* ■ a natural or involuntary series of changes: *the aging process.* ■ a systematic series of mechanized or chemical operations that are performed in order to produce or manufacture something: *the modern block printer needs to accommodate all the traditional factory processes in one shop.* ■ a series of interdependent operations carried out by computer. ■ [as modifier] Printing relating to or denoting printing using ink in three colors (cyan, magenta, and yellow) and black to produce a complete range of color: *process inks.*
2 Law a summons or writ requiring a person to appear in court.
3 Biology & Anatomy a natural appendage or outgrowth on or in an organism, such as a protuberance on a bone.
▶ **v.** [with obj.] perform a series of mechanical or chemical operations on (something) in order to change or preserve it: *the various stages in processing the wool.* ■ operate on (computer data) by means of a program. ■ deal with (someone) using an official and established procedure: *the immigration authorities who processed him.* ■ another term for **CONK**[3].
– PHRASES **be in the process of doing something** be continuing with an action already started: *a hurricane that was in the process of devastating South Carolina.* **in the process** as an unintended part of a course of action: *she would make him pay for this, even if she killed herself in the process.* **in process of time** as time goes on.
– DERIVATIVES **proc·ess·a·ble adj.**
– ORIGIN Middle English: from Old French *proces*, from Latin *processus* 'progression, course,' from the verb *procedere* (see **PROCEED**). Current senses of the verb date from the late 19th cent.

pro·cess[2] /prəˈses/ ▶ **v.** [no obj.] walk or march in procession: *they processed down the aisle.*
– ORIGIN early 19th cent.: back-formation from **PROCESSION**.

proc·ess en·gi·neer·ing ▶ **n.** the branch of engineering that is concerned with industrial processes, esp. continuous ones such as the production of petrochemicals.
– DERIVATIVES **proc·ess en·gi·neer n.**

pro·ces·sion /prəˈsesHən/ ▶ **n. 1** a number of people or vehicles moving forward in an orderly fashion, esp. as part of a ceremony or festival: *a funeral procession.* ■ the action of moving forward in such a way: *the fully robed civic dignitaries walk in procession.* ■ a relentless succession of people or things: *his path was paved by a procession of industry executives.*
2 Theology the emanation of the Holy Spirit.
– ORIGIN late Old English, via Old French from Latin *processio(n-)*, from *procedere* 'move forward' (see **PROCEED**).

pro·ces·sion·al /prəˈsesHənl/ ▶ **adj.** of, for, or used in a religious or ceremonial procession: *a processional cross.*
▶ **n.** a book containing litanies and hymns for use in religious processions, esp. at the beginning of a service. ■ a hymn or other piece of music sung or played during a religious procession.

proc·es·sor /ˈpräˌesər, ˈpräsəsər, ˈprō-/ ▶ **n.** a machine that processes something: *the processor overexposed the film.* ■ Computing another term for **CENTRAL PROCESSING UNIT**. ■ short for **FOOD PROCESSOR**.

proc·ess print·ing /ˈpräˌses, ˈpräsəs, ˈprō-/ ▶ **n.** a full-color printing method using four templates, for magenta, cyan, yellow, and black.

proc·ess serv·er ▶ **n.** a person, esp. a sheriff or deputy, who serves writs, warrants, subpoenas, etc.

pro·ces·su·al /prəˈsesHo͞oəl/ ▶ **adj.** relating to or involving the study of processes rather than discrete events.

pro·cès-ver·bal /prōˌsā vərˈbäl/ ▶ **n.** (pl. **procès-verbaux** /vərˈbō/) a written report of proceedings. ■ a written statement of facts in support of a charge.
– ORIGIN mid 17th cent.: French.

pro·chlor·per·a·zine /ˌprōklôrˈperəˌzēn/ ▶ **n.** Medicine a synthetic compound derived from phenothiazine, used as a tranquilizer.
– ORIGIN 1950s: from *pro(pyl)* + *chlor(ine)* + *(pi) perazine.*

pro-choice /prōˈCHois/ (also **prochoice**) ▶ **adj.** advocating legalized abortion: *a pro-choice demonstration.* Compare with **PRO-LIFE**.
– DERIVATIVES **pro-choic·er n.**

pro·claim /prəˈklām, prō-/ ▶ **v.** [with clause] announce officially or publicly: *the joint manifesto proclaimed that imperialism would be the coalition's chief objective* | [with obj.] *army commanders proclaimed a state of emergency.* ■ declare something one considers important with due emphasis: *she proclaimed that what I had said was untrue* | [with obj. and infinitive] *he proclaimed the car to be in sound condition.* ■ [with obj. and complement] declare officially or publicly to be: *he proclaimed James II as King of England.* ■ [with obj.] demonstrate or indicate clearly: *the decor proclaimed a family history of taste and tradition* | [with obj. and complement] *he had a rolling gait that proclaimed him a man of the sea.*
– DERIVATIVES **pro·claim·er n.**, **pro·clam·a·to·ry** /-ˈklaməˌtôrē/ **adj.**
– ORIGIN late Middle English *proclame*, from Latin *proclamare* 'cry out,' from *pro-* 'forth' + *clamare* 'to shout.' The change in the second syllable was due to association with the verb **CLAIM**.

proc·la·ma·tion /ˌprækləˈmāsHən/ ▶ **n.** a public or official announcement, esp. one dealing with a matter of great importance: *Eisenhower signed a proclamation admitting Alaska to the Union.* ■ the public or official announcement of such a matter: *the government restricted the use of water by proclamation.* ■ a clear declaration of something: *the proclamation of his passion.*
– ORIGIN late Middle English: via Old French from Latin *proclamatio(n-)*, from *proclamare* 'shout out' (see **PROCLAIM**).

pro·clit·ic /prōˈklitik/ Linguistics ▶ **n.** a word pronounced with so little emphasis that it is shortened and forms part of the following word, for example, *you* in *y'all*. Compare with **ENCLITIC**.
▶ **adj.** being or relating to such a word.
– DERIVATIVES **pro·clit·i·cal·ly** /-ik(ə)lē/ **adv.**
– ORIGIN mid 19th cent.: from modern Latin *procliticus* (from Greek *proklinein* 'lean forward'), on the pattern of late Latin *encliticus* (see **ENCLITIC**).

pro·cliv·i·ty /prōˈklivətē, prə-/ ▶ **n.** (pl. **proclivities**) a tendency to choose or do something regularly; an inclination or predisposition toward a particular thing: *a proclivity for hard work.*
– ORIGIN late 16th cent.: from Latin *proclivitas*, from *proclivis* 'inclined,' from *pro-* 'forward, down' + *clivus* 'slope.'

Proc·ne /ˈpräknē/ Greek Mythology the sister of **PHILOMELA**.

pro·co·ag·u·lant /ˌprōkōˈagyələnt/ Biochemistry ▶ **adj.** relating to or denoting substances that promote the conversion in the blood of the inactive protein prothrombin to the clotting enzyme thrombin.
▶ **n.** a substance of this kind.

Pro·con·sul /prōˈkänsəl/ ▶ **n.** a fossil hominoid primate found in Lower Miocene deposits in East Africa, one of the last common ancestors of both humans and the great apes. ● Genus *Proconsul*, family Pongidae.

pro·con·sul /prōˈkänsəl/ ▶ **n. 1** a governor of a province in ancient Rome, having much of the authority of a consul.
2 a governor or deputy consul of a modern colony.
– DERIVATIVES **pro·con·su·lar** /-ˈkäns(y)ələr/ **adj.**, **pro·con·su·late** /-ˈkäns(y)ələt/ **n.**, **pro·con·sul·ship** /-SHip/ **n.**
– ORIGIN from Latin *pro consule* '(one acting) for the consul.'

pro·cras·ti·nate /prəˈkrastəˌnāt, prō-/ ▶ **v.** [no obj.] delay or postpone action; put off doing something: *it won't be this price for long, so don't procrastinate.*
– DERIVATIVES **pro·cras·ti·na·tor** /-ˌnātər/ **n.**, **pro·cras·ti·na·to·ry** /-nəˌtôrē/ **adj.**
– ORIGIN late 16th cent.: from Latin *procrastinat-* 'deferred until tomorrow,' from the verb *procrastinare*, from *pro-* 'forward' + *crastinus* 'belonging to tomorrow' (from *cras* 'tomorrow').

pro·cras·ti·na·tion /prəˌkrastəˈnāSHən, prō-/ ▶ **n.** the action of delaying or postponing something: *your first tip is to avoid procrastination.*

pro·cre·ate /ˈprōkrēˌāt/ ▶ **v.** [no obj.] (of people or animals) produce young; reproduce: *species that procreate by copulation.*
– DERIVATIVES **pro·cre·ant** /-krēənt/ **adj.** (archaic), **pro·cre·a·tion** /ˌprōkrēˈāSHən/ **n.**, **pro·cre·a·tive** /-krēˌātiv/ **adj.**, **pro·cre·a·tor** /-ˌātər/ **n.**
– ORIGIN late Middle English: from Latin *procreat-* 'generated, brought forth,' from the verb *procreare*, from *pro-* 'forth' + *creare* 'create.'

Pro·crus·te·an /prəˈkrəstēən, prō-/ ▶ **adj.** (esp. of a framework or system) enforcing uniformity or conformity without regard to natural variation or individuality: *a fixed Procrustean rule.*
– ORIGIN mid 19th cent.: from the name **PROCRUSTES** + **-AN**.

Pro·crus·tes /prəˈkrəstēz, prō-/ Greek Mythology a robber who forced travelers to lie on a bed and made them fit it by stretching their limbs or cutting off the appropriate length of leg. Theseus killed him in like manner.
– ORIGIN from Greek *prokroustēs*, literally 'stretcher,' from *prokrouein* 'beat out.'

proc·ti·tis /präkˈtītis/ ▶ **n.** Medicine inflammation of the rectum and anus.
– ORIGIN early 19th cent.: from Greek *prōktos* 'anus' + **-ITIS**.

proc·tol·o·gy /präkˈtäləjē/ ▶ **n.** the branch of medicine concerned with the anus and rectum.
– DERIVATIVES **proc·to·log·i·cal** /ˌpräktəˈläjikəl/ **adj.**, **proc·tol·o·gist** /-jist/ **n.**
– ORIGIN late 19th cent.: from Greek *prōktos* 'anus' + **-LOGY**.

proc·tor /ˈpräktər/ ▶ **n. 1** a person who monitors students during an examination.
2 Brit. an officer (usually one of two) at certain universities, appointed annually and having mainly disciplinary functions.
▶ **v.** serve as a proctor.
– DERIVATIVES **proc·to·ri·al** /präkˈtôrēəl/ **adj.**, **proc·tor·ship** /-ˌSHip/ **n.**
– ORIGIN late Middle English: contraction of **PROCURATOR**.

proc·to·scope /ˈpräktəˌskōp/ ▶ **n.** a medical instrument with an integral lamp for examining the anus and lower part of the rectum or carrying out minor medical procedures.
– DERIVATIVES **proc·to·scop·ic** /ˌpräktəˈskäpik/ **adj.**, **proc·tos·co·py** /präkˈtäskəpē/ **n.**
– ORIGIN late 19th cent.: from Greek *prōktos* 'anus' + **-SCOPE**.

pro·cum·bent /prōˈkəmbənt/ ▶ **adj.** Botany (of a plant or stem) growing along the ground without setting forth roots. ■ archaic (of a person) lying face down; prone; prostrate.
– ORIGIN mid 17th cent.: from Latin *procumbent-* 'falling forward,' from the verb *procumbere*, from *pro-* 'forward, down' + a verb related to *cubare* 'to lie.'

proc·u·ra·cy /ˈpräkyŏŏrəsē/ ▶ **n.** (pl. **procuracies**) the position or office of a procurator.

proc·u·ra·tion /ˌpräkyəˈrāSHən/ ▶ **n.** Law, dated the appointment, authority, or action of an attorney. ■ archaic the action of procuring or obtaining something.
– ORIGIN late Middle English: via Old French from Latin *procuratio(n-)*, from *procurare* 'attend to, take care of' (see **PROCURE**).

proc·u·ra·tor /ˈpräkyəˌrātər/ ▶ **n.** Law an agent representing others in a court of law in countries retaining Roman civil law. ■ historical a treasury officer in a province of the Roman Empire.
– DERIVATIVES **proc·u·ra·to·ri·al** /ˌpräkyərəˈtôrēəl/ **adj.**, **proc·u·ra·tor·ship n.**
– ORIGIN Middle English (denoting a steward): from Old French *procuratour* or Latin *procurator* 'administrator, agent,' from *procurat-* 'taken care of,' from the verb *procurare* (see **PROCURE**).

pro·cure /prəˈkyŏŏr, prō-/ ▶ **v.** [with obj.] **1** obtain (something), esp. with care or effort: *food procured for the rebels* | [with two objs.] *he persuaded a friend to procure him a ticket.* ■ obtain (someone) as a prostitute for another person: *he was charged with procuring a minor.*
2 [with obj. and infinitive] Law persuade or cause (someone) to do something: *he procured his wife to sign the agreement.*
– DERIVATIVES **pro·cur·a·ble adj.**
– ORIGIN Middle English: from Old French *procurer*, from Latin *procurare* 'take care of, manage,' from *pro-* 'on behalf of' + *curare* 'see to.'

pro·cure·ment /prəˈkyŏŏrmənt, prō-/ ▶ **n.** the action of obtaining or procuring something: *financial assistance for the procurement of legal advice* | *the company's procurements from foreign firms.* ■ the action or occupation of acquiring military equipment and supplies: *defense procurement.*

pro·cur·er /prəˈkyŏŏrər, prō-/ ▶ **n.** a person who obtains a woman as a prostitute for another person.
– ORIGIN late Middle English (denoting a steward): from Anglo-Norman French *procurour*, from Latin *procurator* (see **PROCURATOR**). Modern usage dates from the mid 17th cent.

pro·cur·ess /prəˈkyŏŏris, prō-/ ▶ **n.** a female procurer.

Pro·cy·on /ˈprōsēˌän, -sēən/ Astronomy the eighth brightest star in the sky, and the brightest in the constellation Canis Minor.
– ORIGIN Greek, literally 'before the dog' (because it rises before Sirius, the Dog Star).

prod /präd/ ▶ **v.** (**prods, prodding, prodded**) [with obj.] poke (someone) with a finger, foot, or pointed object: *he prodded her in the ribs to stop her snoring* | [no obj.] *a woman* **prods at** *a tiger with a stick.* ■ stimulate or persuade (someone who is reluctant or slow) to do something: *he has been trying to* **prod** *the White House* **into** *launching an antipoverty program.*
▶ **n. 1** a poke with a finger, foot, or pointed object: *he gave the wire netting an experimental prod.* ■ an act of stimulating or reminding someone to do something: *he'll need a little prod to get back to the task at hand.*
2 a pointed implement, typically one discharging an electric current and used as a goad: *a cattle prod.*
– DERIVATIVES **prod·der n.**
– ORIGIN mid 16th cent. (as a verb): perhaps symbolic of a short poking movement, or a blend of **POKE**[1] and dialect *brod* 'to goad, prod' The noun dates from the mid 18th cent.

prod. ▶ **abbr.** ■ produce. ■ produced. ■ producer. ■ product. ■ production.

pro-de·moc·ra·cy ▶ **n.** denoting or relating to political activism directed toward the establishment of democratic government in a country: *the pro-democracy movement.*

prod·i·gal /ˈprädigəl/ ▶ **adj. 1** spending money or resources freely and recklessly; wastefully extravagant: *prodigal habits die hard.*
2 having or giving something on a lavish scale: *the dessert was crunchy with brown sugar and prodigal with whipped cream.*
▶ **n.** a person who spends money in a recklessly extravagant way. ■ (also **prodigal son** or **daughter**) a person who leaves home and behaves in such a way, but later makes a repentant return. [with biblical allusion to the parable in Luke 15:11–32.]
– DERIVATIVES **prod·i·gal·i·ty** /ˌprädəˈgalətē/ **n.**, **prod·i·gal·ly** /-g(ə)lē/ **adv.**
– ORIGIN late Middle English: from late Latin *prodigalis*, from Latin *prodigus* 'lavish.'

pro·di·gious /prəˈdijəs/ ▶ **adj. 1** remarkably or impressively great in extent, size, or degree: *the stove consumed a prodigious amount of fuel.*
2 archaic unnatural or abnormal: *rumors of prodigious happenings, such as monstrous births.*
– DERIVATIVES **pro·di·gious·ly adv.**, **pro·di·gious·ness n.**
– ORIGIN late 15th cent. (in the sense 'portentous'): from Latin *prodigiosus*, from *prodigium* 'portent' (see **PRODIGY**).

prod·i·gy /ˈprädəjē/ ▶ **n.** (pl. **prodigies**) [often with modifier] a person, esp. a young one, endowed with exceptional qualities or abilities: *a Russian pianist who was a child prodigy in his day.* ■ an impressive or outstanding example of a particular quality: *Germany seemed* **a prodigy of** *industrial discipline.* ■ an amazing or unusual thing, esp. one out of the ordinary course of nature: *omens and prodigies abound in Livy's work.*
– ORIGIN late 15th cent. (denoting something extraordinary considered to be an omen): from Latin *prodigium* 'portent.'

prod·ro·mal /prōˈdrōməl/ ▶ **adj.** Medicine relating to or denoting the period between the appearance of initial symptoms and the full development of a rash or fever.

pro·drome /ˈprōˌdrōm/ ▶ **n.** Medicine an early symptom indicating the onset of a disease or illness.
– DERIVATIVES **pro·drom·ic** /prōˈdrämik/ **adj.**
– ORIGIN early 17th cent.: from French, from modern Latin *prodromus*, from Greek *prodromos* 'precursor,' from *pro* 'before' + *dromos* 'running.'

pro·drug /ˈprōˌdrəg/ ▶ **n.** a biologically inactive compound that can be metabolized in the body to produce a drug.

pro·duce ▶ **v.** /prəˈd(y)ōōs, prō-/ [with obj.] **1** make or manufacture from components or raw materials: *the company has just produced a luxury version of the aircraft.* ■ (of a region, country, or process) yield, grow, or supply: *the California vineyards produce excellent wines.* ■ create or form (something) as part of a physical, biological, or chemical process: *the plant produces blue flowers in late autumn.* ■ make (something) using creative or mental skills: *the garden where the artist produced many of his flower paintings.*
2 cause (a particular result or situation) to happen or come into existence: *no conventional drugs had produced any significant change.*
3 show or provide (something) for consideration, inspection, or use: *he produced a sheet of paper from his pocket.*
4 administer the financial and managerial aspects of (a movie or broadcast) or the staging of (a play, opera, etc.). ■ supervise the making of a (musical recording), esp. by determining the overall sound.
5 Geometry, dated extend or continue (a line): *one side of the triangle was produced.*
▶ **n.** /ˈpräd(y)ōōs, ˈprō-/ things that have been produced or grown, esp. by farming: *dairy produce.*
– DERIVATIVES **pro·duc·i·bil·i·ty** /prəˌd(y)ōōsəˈbilətē, prō-/ **n.**, **pro·duc·i·ble adj.**
– ORIGIN late Middle English (sense 3 of the verb): from Latin *producere*, from *pro-* 'forward' + *ducere* 'to lead.' Current noun senses date from the late 17th cent.

pro·duc·er /prəˈd(y)ōōsər, prō-/ ▶ **n. 1** a person, company, or country that makes, grows, or supplies goods or commodities for sale: *an oil producer.* ■ a person or thing that makes or causes something: *the mold is the producer of the toxin aflatoxin.*
2 a person responsible for the financial and managerial aspects of making of a movie or broadcast or for staging a play, opera, etc. ■ a person who supervises the making of a musical recording, esp. by determining the overall sound.

pro·duc·er gas ▶ **n.** a low-grade fuel gas consisting largely of nitrogen and carbon monoxide, formed by passing air, or air and steam, through red-hot carbon.

prod·uct /ˈprädəkt/ ▶ **n. 1** an article or substance that is manufactured or refined for sale: *marketing products and services* | *dairy products.* ■ a substance produced during a natural, chemical, or manufacturing process: *waste products.* ■ a thing or person that is the result of an action or process: *his daughter, the product of his first marriage.* ■ a person whose character and identity have been formed by a particular period or situation: *an aging academic who is a product of the 1960s.* ■ commercially manufactured articles, esp. recordings, viewed collectively: *too much product of too little quality.*
2 Mathematics a quantity obtained by multiplying quantities together, or from an analogous algebraic operation.
– ORIGIN late Middle English (as a mathematical term): from Latin *productum* 'something produced,' neuter past participle (used as a noun) of *producere* 'bring forth' (see **PRODUCE**).

pro·duc·tion /prəˈdəkSHən, prō-/ ▶ **n. 1** the action of making or manufacturing from components or raw materials, or the process of being so manufactured: *the production of chemical weapons* | *it is no longer* **in production**. ■ the harvesting or refinement of something natural: *nonintensive methods of food production.* ■ the total amount of something that is manufactured, harvested, or refined: *steel production had peaked in 1974.* ■ the creation or formation of something as part of a physical, biological, or chemical process: *excess production of collagen by the liver.* ■ [as modifier] denoting a car or other vehicle that has been manufactured in large numbers.
2 the process of or financial and administrative management involved in making a movie, play, or record: *the movie was still* **in production** | [as modifier] *a production company.* ■ a movie, play, or record, esp. when viewed in terms of its making or staging: *this production updates the play and sets it in the sixties.* ■ [in sing.] the overall sound of a musical recording; the way a record is produced: *the record's production is gloriously relaxed.*
– PHRASES **make a production of** do (something) in an unnecessarily elaborate or complicated way.
– ORIGIN late Middle English: via Old French from Latin *productio(n-)*, from *producere* 'bring forth' (see **PRODUCE**).

pro·duc·tion line ▶ **n.** an arrangement in a factory in which a thing being manufactured is passed through a set linear sequence of mechanical or manual operations. Compare with **ASSEMBLY LINE**.

pro·duc·tion num·ber ▶ **n.** a spectacular musical item, typically including song and dance and involving all or most of the cast, in a theatrical show or motion picture.

PRONUNCIATION KEY ə *ago, up*; ər *over, fur*; a *hat*; ā *ate*; ä *car*; e *let*; ē *see*; i *fit*; ī *by*; NG *sing*; ō *go*; ô *law, for*; oi *toy*; ŏŏ *good*; ōō *goo*; ou *out*; TH *thin*; T͟H *then*; ZH *vision*

pro·duc·tion plat·form ▶ **n.** a platform housing equipment necessary to keep an oil or gas field in production, with facilities for temporarily storing the output of several wells.

pro·duc·tive /prəˈdəktiv, prō-/ ▶ **adj.** producing or able to produce large amounts of goods, crops, or other commodities: *the most productive employees.* ■ relating to or engaged in the production of goods, crops, or other commodities: *the country's productive capacity.* ■ achieving or producing a significant amount or result: *a long and productive career | the therapy sessions became more productive.* ■ [predic.] (**productive of**) producing or giving rise to: *the unconscious is limitlessly productive of dreams, myths, stories.* ■ Linguistics (of a morpheme or other linguistic unit) currently used in forming new words or expressions: *many suffixes are common and productive.* ■ Medicine (of a cough) that raises mucus from the respiratory tract.
– DERIVATIVES **pro·duc·tive·ly** adv., **pro·duc·tive·ness** n.
– ORIGIN early 17th cent.: from French *productif, -ive* or late Latin *productivus,* from *product-* 'brought forth,' from the verb *producere* (see PRODUCE).

pro·duc·tiv·i·ty /ˌprōˌdəkˈtivətē, ˌprädək-, prəˌdək-/ ▶ **n.** the state or quality of producing something, esp. crops: *the long-term productivity of land | agricultural productivity.* ■ the effectiveness of productive effort, esp. in industry, as measured in terms of the rate of output per unit of input: *workers have boosted productivity by 30 percent.* ■ Ecology the rate of production of new biomass by an individual, population, or community; the fertility or capacity of a given habitat or area: *nutrient-rich waters with high productivity.*

prod·uct·ize /ˈprädəktīz/ ▶ **v.** [with obj.] make or develop (a service, concept, etc.) into a product: *additional development will be required to productize the technology.*
– DERIVATIVES **prod·uct·i·za·tion** n.

prod·uct li·a·bil·i·ty ▶ **n.** the legal liability a manufacturer or trader incurs for producing or selling a faulty product.

prod·uct place·ment ▶ **n.** a practice in which manufacturers of goods or providers of a service gain exposure for their products by paying for them to be featured in movies and television programs.

pro·em /ˈprōˌem, -əm/ ▶ **n.** formal a preface or preamble to a book or speech.
– DERIVATIVES **pro·e·mi·al** /prōˈemēəl/ adj.
– ORIGIN late Middle English: from Old French *proeme,* via Latin from Greek *prooimion* 'prelude,' from *pro* 'before' + *oimē* 'song.'

pro·en·zyme /prōˈenˌzīm/ ▶ **n.** Biochemistry a biologically inactive substance that is metabolized into an enzyme.

pro-Eur·o·pe·an /ˌprōˌyərəˈpēən, -ˌyo͝orə-/ ▶ **adj.** (of a person, attitude, or policy) favoring or supporting closer links with the European Union.
▶ **n.** a person who favors or supports closer links with the European Union.

prof /präf/ ▶ **n.** informal a professor.
– ORIGIN mid 19th cent.: abbreviation.

Prof. ▶ **abbr.** professor: [as title] *Prof. Smith.*

pro-fam·i·ly /prōˈfam(ə)lē/ ▶ **adj.** promoting family life and traditional moral values.

pro·fane /prəˈfān, prō-/ ▶ **adj. 1** relating or devoted to that which is not sacred or biblical; secular rather than religious: *a talk that tackled topics both sacred and profane.* ■ (of a person) not initiated into religious rites or any esoteric knowledge: *he was an agnostic, a profane man.*
2 (of a person or their behavior) not respectful of orthodox religious practice; irreverent: *desecration of the temple by profane adolescents.* ■ (of language) blasphemous or obscene.
▶ **v.** [with obj.] treat (something sacred) with irreverence or disrespect: *it was a serious matter to profane a tomb.*
– DERIVATIVES **prof·a·na·tion** /ˌpräfəˈnāshən, ˌprō-/ n., **pro·fane·ly** adv., **pro·fane·ness** n., **pro·fan·er** n.
– ORIGIN late Middle English (in the sense 'heathen'): from Old French *prophane,* from Latin *profanus* 'outside the temple, not sacred,' from *pro-* (from *pro* 'before') + *fanum* 'temple.'

pro·fan·i·ty /prəˈfanətē, prō-/ ▶ **n.** (pl. **profanities**) blasphemous or obscene language: *an outburst of profanity.* ■ a swear word; an oath. ■ irreligious or irreverent behavior.
– ORIGIN mid 16th cent.: from late Latin *profanitas,* from Latin *profanus* 'not sacred' (see PROFANE).

pro·fess /prəˈfes, prō-/ ▶ **v.** [with obj.] **1** claim openly but often falsely that one has (a quality or feeling): *he had professed his love for her* | [with infinitive] *I don't profess to be an expert* | [with complement] (**profess oneself**) *he professed himself amazed at the boy's ability.*
2 affirm one's faith in or allegiance to (a religion or set of beliefs): *a people professing Christianity.* ■ (**be professed**) be received into a religious order under vows: *she entered St. Margaret's Convent, and was professed in 1943.*
3 dated or humorous teach (a subject) as a professor: *a professor—what does he profess?*
4 archaic have or claim knowledge or skill in (a subject or accomplishment).
– ORIGIN Middle English (as *be professed* 'be received into a religious order'): from Latin *profess-* 'declared publicly,' from the verb *profiteri,* from *pro-* 'before' + *fateri* 'confess.'

pro·fessed /prəˈfest, prō-/ ▶ **adj. 1** (of a quality, feeling, or belief) claimed or asserted openly but often falsely: *for all her professed populism, she was seen as remote from ordinary people.*
2 (of a person) self-acknowledged or openly declared to be: *a professed and conforming Anglican.* ■ (of a monk or nun) having taken the vows of a religious order. ■ archaic claiming to be qualified as a particular specialist; professional.

pro·fess·ed·ly /prəˈfesədlē, -ˈfestlē/ ▶ **adv.** [sentence adverb] ostensibly; apparently (used in reference to something claimed or asserted, possibly falsely): *restrictions professedly designed to stop the use of political propaganda.*

pro·fes·sion /prəˈfeshən/ ▶ **n. 1** a paid occupation, esp. one that involves prolonged training and a formal qualification: *his chosen profession of teaching | a lawyer* **by profession**. ■ [treated as sing. or pl.] a body of people engaged in a particular profession: *the profession is divided on the issue.*
2 an open but often false declaration or claim: *a profession of allegiance.* ■ a declaration of belief in a religion. ■ the declaration or vows made on entering a religious order. ■ the ceremony or fact of being professed in a religious order.
– PHRASES **the oldest profession** humorous the practice of working as a prostitute.
– ORIGIN Middle English (denoting the vow made on entering a religious order): via Old French from Latin *professio(n-),* from *profiteri* 'declare publicly' (see PROFESS). Sense 1 derives from the notion of an occupation that one "professes" to be skilled in.

pro·fes·sion·al /prəˈfeshənl/ ▶ **adj. 1** [attrib.] of, relating to, or connected with a profession: *young professional people | the professional schools of Yale and Harvard.*
2 (of a person) engaged in a specified activity as one's main paid occupation rather than as a pastime: *a professional boxer.* ■ having or showing the skill appropriate to a professional person; competent or skillful: *their music is both memorable and professional.* ■ worthy of or appropriate to a professional person: *his professional expertise.* ■ informal, derogatory denoting a person who persistently makes a feature of a particular activity or attribute: *a professional naysayer.*
▶ **n.** a person engaged or qualified in a profession: *professionals such as lawyers and surveyors.* ■ a person engaged in a specified activity, esp. a sport or branch of the performing arts, as a main paid occupation rather than as a pastime. ■ a person competent or skilled in a particular activity: *she was a real professional on stage.*
– DERIVATIVES **pro·fes·sion·al·ly** /-shənl-ē/ adv.

pro·fes·sion·al·ism /prəˈfeshənlˌizəm/ ▶ **n.** the competence or skill expected of a professional: *the key to quality and efficiency is professionalism.* ■ the practicing of an activity, esp. a sport, by professional rather than amateur players: *the trend toward professionalism.*

pro·fes·sion·al·ize /prəˈfeshənlˌīz/ ▶ **v.** [with obj.] give (an occupation, activity, or group) professional qualities, typically by increasing training or raising required qualifications: *attempts to professionalize the police are resisted by many.*
– DERIVATIVES **pro·fes·sion·al·i·za·tion** /prəˌfeshənl-əˈzāshən/ n.

pro·fes·sor /prəˈfesər/ ▶ **n. 1** (also **full professor**) a teacher of the highest rank in a college or university. ■ an associate professor or an assistant professor. ■ informal any instructor, esp. in a specialized field.
2 a person who affirms a faith in or allegiance to something: *the professors of true religion.*
– DERIVATIVES **pro·fes·sor·ate** /-rət/ n., **pro·fes·so·ri·al** /ˌpräfəˈsôrēəl/ adj., **pro·fes·so·ri·al·ly** /ˌpräfəˈsôrēəlē/ adv., **pro·fes·so·ri·ate** /ˌpräfəˈsôrēət/ n., **pro·fes·sor·ship** /-ˌship/ n.
– ORIGIN late Middle English: from Latin *professor,* from *profess-* 'declared publicly,' from the verb *profiteri* (see PROFESS).

prof·fer /ˈpräfər/ ▶ **v.** [with obj.] hold out (something) to someone for acceptance; offer: *he proffered his resignation.*
▶ **n.** literary an offer or proposal.
– ORIGIN Middle English: from Anglo-Norman French *proffrir,* from Latin *pro-* 'before' + *offerre* 'to offer.'

pro·fi·cien·cy /prəˈfishənsē/ ▶ **n.** a high degree of competence or skill; expertise: *he demonstrated his proficiency in Chinese.*

pro·fi·cient /prəˈfishənt/ ▶ **adj.** competent or skilled in doing or using something: *I was* **proficient at** *my job | she felt reasonably* **proficient in** *Italian.*
▶ **n.** rare a person who is proficient: *he became a proficient in Latin and Greek.*
– DERIVATIVES **pro·fi·cient·ly** adv.
– ORIGIN late 16th cent.: from Latin *proficient-* 'advancing,' from the verb *proficere,* from *pro-* 'on behalf of' + *facere* 'do, make.'

pro·file /ˈprōˌfīl/ ▶ **n. 1** an outline of something, esp. a person's face, as seen from one side: *the man turned and she caught his profile.* ■ a vertical cross section of a structure: *skillfully made vessels with an S-shaped profile.* ■ Geography an outline of part of the earth's surface, e.g., the course of a river, as seen in a vertical section. ■ Theater a flat piece of scenery or stage property that has been cut so as to form an outline or silhouette of an object.
2 a short article giving a description of a person or organization: *a profile of a Texas tycoon.*
3 a graphical or other representation of information relating to particular characteristics of something, recorded in quantified form: *the blood profiles of cancer patients.* ■ a record of a person's psychological or behavioral characteristics, preferences, etc.: *they had been using personal details to build customer profiles.*
4 [in sing.] the extent to which a person or organization attracts public notice: *raising the profile of women in industry.*
▶ **v.** [with obj.] **1** describe (a person or organization, esp. a public figure) in a short article: *he was to profile each candidate.*
2 represent in outline from one side: *he was standing motionless, profiled on the far side of the swimming pool.* ■ (**be profiled**) have a specified shape or appearance in outline: *a proud bird profiled like a phoenix.* ■ shape (something), esp. by means of a tool guided by a template: (as adj. **profiled**) *profiled and plain tiles.*
– PHRASES **in profile** (in reference to someone's face) as seen from one side: *a photograph of Leon in profile.*
– DERIVATIVES **pro·fil·er** n.
– ORIGIN mid 17th cent.: from obsolete Italian *profilo,* from the verb *profilare,* from *pro-* 'forth' + *filare* 'to spin,' formerly 'draw a line' (from Latin *filare,* from *filum* 'thread').

pro·fil·ing /ˈprōˌfīliNG/ ▶ **n.** the recording and analysis of a person's psychological and behavioral characteristics, so as to assess or predict their capabilities in a certain sphere or to assist in identifying a particular subgroup of people.

prof·it /ˈpräfit/ ▶ **n.** a financial gain, esp. the difference between the amount earned and the amount spent in buying, operating, or producing something: *pretax profits | his eyes brightened at the prospect of profit.* ■ advantage; benefit: *there's no profit in screaming at referees from the bench.*
▶ **v.** (**profits, profiting, profited**) [no obj.] obtain a financial advantage or benefit, esp. from an investment: *the only people to profit from the entire episode were the lawyers.* ■ obtain an advantage or benefit: *not all children would profit from this kind of schooling.* ■ [with obj.] be beneficial to: *it would profit us to change our plans.*
– PHRASES **at a profit** making more money than is spent buying, operating, or producing something: *fixing up houses and selling them at a profit.*
– DERIVATIVES **prof·it·less** adj.
– ORIGIN Middle English (in the sense 'advantage, benefit'): from Old French, from Latin *profectus* 'progress, profit,' from *proficere* 'to advance,' from *pro-* 'on behalf of' + *facere* 'do.' The verb is from Old French *profiter.*

prof·it·a·ble /ˈpräfitəbəl/ ▶ **adj. 1** (of a business or activity) yielding profit or financial gain.
2 beneficial; useful: *he'd had a profitable day.*
– DERIVATIVES **prof·it·a·bil·i·ty** /ˌpräfitəˈbilətē/ n., **prof·it·a·bly** /-blē/ adv.
– ORIGIN Middle English: from Old French, from the verb *profiter* (see PROFIT).

prof·it and loss ac·count (abbr.: **P & L**) ▶ **n.** Finance an account in the books of an organization to which incomes and gains are credited and expenses and losses debited, so as to show the net profit or loss over a given period. ■ a financial statement showing a company's net profit or loss in a given period.

prof·it cen·ter ▶ **n.** a part of an organization with assignable revenues and costs and hence ascertainable profitability.

prof·it·eer /ˌpräfəˈti(ə)r/ ▶ **v.** [no obj.] make or seek to make an excessive or unfair profit, esp. illegally

or in a black market: (as noun **profiteering**) *the profiteering of tabloid journalists.*
▶ **n.** a person who profiteers: *a war profiteer.*

pro·fit·er·ole /prəˈfitəˌrōl/ ▶ **n.** a small hollow pastry typically filled with cream and covered with chocolate sauce.
– ORIGIN French, diminutive of *profit* 'profit.'

prof·it mar·gin ▶ **n.** the amount by which revenue from sales exceeds costs in a business.

prof·it-shar·ing (also **profit sharing**) ▶ **n.** a system in which the people who work for a company receive a direct share of the profits.

prof·it-tak·ing (also **profit taking**) ▶ **n.** Stock Market the sale of securities that have risen in price.

prof·it warn·ing ▶ **n.** a statement issued by a company advising the stock market that profits will be lower than expected.

prof·li·gate /ˈpräfligət, -ləˌgāt/ ▶ **adj.** recklessly extravagant or wasteful in the use of resources: *profligate consumers of energy.* ■ licentious; dissolute: *he succumbed to drink and a profligate lifestyle.*
▶ **n.** a licentious, dissolute person.
– DERIVATIVES **prof·li·ga·cy** /ˈpräfligəsē/ **n.**, **prof·li·gate·ly adv.**
– ORIGIN mid 16th cent. (in the sense 'overthrown, routed'): from Latin *profligatus* 'dissolute,' past participle of *profligare* 'overthrow, ruin,' from *pro-* 'forward, down' + *fligere* 'strike down.'

pro·form /ˈprōˌfôrm/ ▶ **n.** Linguistics a word or lexical unit that is dependent for its meaning on reference to some other part of the context or sentence in which it occurs, for example, a pronoun replacing a noun or noun phrase, or a verb replacing a clause, such as *do* in *she likes chocolate and so do I.*

pro for·ma /prō ˈfôrmə/ ▶ **adv.** as a matter of form or politeness: *he nodded to him pro forma.*
▶ **adj.** done or produced as a matter of form: *pro forma reports.* ■ [attrib.] denoting a standard document or form, esp. an invoice sent in advance of or with goods supplied. ■ [attrib.] (of a financial statement) showing potential or expected income, costs, assets, or liabilities, esp. in relation to some planned or expected act or situation.
▶ **n.** a standard document or form or financial statement of such a type.
– ORIGIN early 16th cent.: from Latin.

pro·found /prəˈfound, prō-/ ▶ **adj.** (**profounder**, **profoundest**) **1** (of a state, quality, or emotion) very great or intense: *profound social changes | profound feelings of disquiet.* ■ (of a disease or disability) very severe; deep-seated: *a case of profound liver failure.*
2 (of a person or statement) having or showing great knowledge or insight: *a profound philosopher.* ■ (of a subject or thought) demanding deep study or thought: *expressing profound truths in simple language.*
3 archaic at, from, or extending to a great depth; very deep: *he opened the door with a profound bow.*
▶ **n.** (**the profound**) literary the vast depth of the ocean or of the mind.
– DERIVATIVES **pro·found·ness n.**
– ORIGIN Middle English: from Old French *profund*, from Latin *profundus* 'deep,' from *pro* 'before' + *fundus* 'bottom.' The word was used earliest in the sense 'showing deep insight.'

pro·found·ly /prəˈfoundlē, prō-/ ▶ **adv.** [as submodifier] to a profound extent; extremely: *a profoundly disturbing experience.* in a profound way; greatly: *he profoundly altered the whole course of my life.*

pro·fun·di·ty /prəˈfəndətē/ ▶ **n.** (pl. **profundities**) deep insight; great depth of knowledge or thought: *the simplicity and profundity of the message.* ■ great depth or intensity of a state, quality, or emotion: *the profundity of her misery.* ■ a statement or idea that shows great knowledge or insight.

pro·fuse /prəˈfyo͞os, prō-/ ▶ **adj.** (esp. of something offered or discharged) exuberantly plentiful; abundant: *I offered my profuse apologies.* ■ archaic (of a person) lavish; extravagant: *they are profuse in hospitality.*
– DERIVATIVES **pro·fuse·ly adv.**, **pro·fuse·ness n.**
– ORIGIN late Middle English (in the sense 'extravagant'): from Latin *profusus* 'lavish, spread out,' past participle of *profundere*, from *pro-* 'forth' + *fundere* 'pour.'

pro·fu·sion /prəˈfyo͞ozʜən, prō-/ ▶ **n.** [in sing.] an abundance or large quantity of something: *a rich profusion of wildflowers | the foxgloves growing in profusion among the ferns.*
– ORIGIN mid 16th cent.: via French from Latin *profusio(n-)*, from *profundere* 'pour out.' Early use expressed the senses 'extravagance,' 'squandering,' and 'waste.'

prog /präg/ informal ▶ **adj.** [attrib.] (of rock music) progressive: *prog rock bands.*
– ORIGIN 1950s: abbreviation.

pro·gen·i·tive /prəˈjenətiv, prō-/ ▶ **adj.** formal having the quality of producing offspring; having reproductive power.

pro·gen·i·tor /prəˈjenətər, prō-/ ▶ **n.** a person or thing from which a person, animal, or plant is descended or originates; an ancestor or parent: *his sons and daughters were the progenitors of many of Scotland's leading noble families.* ■ a person who originates an artistic, political, or intellectual movement: *the progenitor of modern jazz.*
– DERIVATIVES **pro·gen·i·to·ri·al** /-ˌjenəˈtôrēəl/ **adj.**
– ORIGIN late Middle English: from Old French *progeniteur*, from Latin *progenitor*, from *progenit-* 'begotten,' from the verb *progignere*, from *pro-* 'forward' + *gignere* 'beget.'

prog·e·ny /ˈpräjənē/ ▶ **n.** [treated as sing. or pl.] a descendant or the descendants of a person, animal, or plant; offspring: *the progeny of mixed marriages.*
– ORIGIN Middle English: from Old French *progenie*, from Latin *progenies*, from *progignere* 'beget' (see **PROGENITOR**).

pro·ge·ri·a /prōˈji(ə)rēə, prə-/ ▶ **n.** Medicine a rare syndrome in children characterized by physical signs and symptoms suggestive of premature old age.
– ORIGIN early 20th cent.: modern Latin, from Greek *progērōs* 'prematurely old.'

pro·ges·ter·one /prōˈjestəˌrōn, prə-/ ▶ **n.** Biochemistry a steroid hormone released by the corpus luteum that stimulates the uterus to prepare for pregnancy.
– ORIGIN 1930s: blend of **PROGESTIN** and the German synonym *Luteosteron* (from **CORPUS LUTEUM** + **STEROL**).

pro·ges·tin /prōˈjestin/ ▶ **n.** Biochemistry a natural or synthetic steroid hormone, such as progesterone, that maintains pregnancy and prevents further ovulation during pregnancy.

pro·ges·to·gen /prōˈjestəjən/ ▶ **n.** Biochemistry another term for **PROGESTIN**.
– ORIGIN 1940s: from **PROGESTIN** + **-GEN**.

pro·glot·tid /prōˈglätid/ (also **proglottis** /-ˈglätis/) ▶ **n.** Zoology each segment in the strobila of a tapeworm, containing a complete sexually mature reproductive system.
– ORIGIN late 19th cent.: from Greek *proglōssis*, *proglōssid-* 'point of the tongue,' based on *glōssa*, *glōtta* 'tongue' (because of its shape).

prog·na·thous /ˈprägnəᴛʜəs, prägˈnā-/ ▶ **adj.** (esp. of a person) having a projecting lower jaw or chin. ■ (of a jaw or chin) projecting. ■ (of an insect) having projecting mouthparts.
– DERIVATIVES **prog·nath·ic** /prägˈnaᴛʜik/ **adj.**, **prog·na·thism** /-ˌᴛʜizəm/ **n.**
– ORIGIN mid 19th cent.: from **PRO-**[2] 'before' + Greek *gnathos* 'jaw' + **-OUS**.

prog·no·sis /prägˈnōsəs/ ▶ **n.** (pl. **prognoses** /-ˌsēz/) the likely course of a disease or ailment: *the disease has a poor prognosis.* ■ a forecast of the likely course of a disease or ailment: *it is very difficult to make an accurate prognosis.* ■ a forecast of the likely outcome of a situation: *gloomy prognoses about overpopulation.*
– ORIGIN mid 17th cent.: via late Latin from Greek *prognōsis*, from *pro-* 'before' + *gignōskein* 'know.'

prog·nos·tic /prägˈnästik/ ▶ **adj.** serving to predict the likely outcome of a disease or ailment; of or relating to a medical prognosis.
▶ **n.** archaic an advance indication or portent of a future event: *a one-banded caterpillar is considered a prognostic of a mild winter.*
– DERIVATIVES **prog·nos·ti·cal·ly** /-ik(ə)lē/ **adv.**
– ORIGIN late Middle English: from Latin *prognosticus*, from Greek *prognōstikos*, from *prognōsis* (see **PROGNOSIS**).

prog·nos·ti·cate /prägˈnästəˌkāt/ ▶ **v.** [with obj.] foretell or prophesy (an event in the future): *the economists were prognosticating financial Armageddon.*
– DERIVATIVES **prog·nos·ti·ca·tor** /-ˌkātər/ **n.**, **prog·nos·ti·ca·to·ry** /-kəˌtôrē/ **adj.**
– ORIGIN late Middle English: from medieval Latin *prognosticat-*, from the verb *prognosticare* 'make a prediction' (see **PROGNOSTIC**).

prog·nos·ti·ca·tion /prägˌnästəˈkāsʜən/ ▶ **n.** the action of foretelling or prophesying future events: *an unprecedented amount of soul-searching and prognostication.* ■ a prophecy: *these gloomy prognostications proved to be unfounded.*
– ORIGIN late Middle English: from Old French *prognosticacion*, from medieval Latin *prognosticatio(n-)*, from the verb *prognosticare* (see **PROGNOSTICATE**).

pro·grade /ˈprōˈgrād/ ▶ **adj. 1** Astronomy (of planetary motion) proceeding from west to east; direct. The opposite of **RETROGRADE**.
2 Geology (of a metamorphic change) resulting from an increase in temperature or pressure or both. Compare with **RETROGRADE**.
▶ **v.** [no obj.] Geology (of a beach or coastline) advance toward the sea as a result of the accumulation of waterborne sediment.
– DERIVATIVES **pro·gra·da·tion** /ˌprōgrāˈdāsʜən, ˌprōgrə-/ **n.**
– ORIGIN early 20th cent. (as a verb): from **PRO-**[1] 'forward' + **RETROGRADE**.

pro·gram /ˈprōˌgram, -grəm/ (Brit. **programme**) ▶ **n. 1** a planned series of future events, items, or performances: *a weekly program of films | the program includes Dvorak's New World symphony.* ■ a set of related measures, events, or activities with a particular long-term aim: *the nuclear power program.*
2 a sheet or booklet giving details of items or performers at an event or performance: *a theater program.*
3 a presentation or item on radio or television, esp. one broadcast regularly between stated times: *a nature program.* ■ dated a radio or television service or station providing a regular succession of programs on a particular frequency; a channel.
4 (**program**) a series of coded software instructions to control the operation of a computer or other machine.
▶ **v.** (**programs**, **programming**, **programmed**, or **programing**, **programed**) [with obj.] **1** (**program**) provide (a computer or other machine) with coded instructions for the automatic performance of a particular task: *it is a simple matter to program the computer to recognize such symbols.* ■ input (instructions for the automatic performance of a task) into a computer or other machine: *simply **program in** your desired volume level.* ■ cause (a person or animal) to behave in a predetermined way: *all members of a particular species are **programmed to** build nests in the same way.*
2 arrange according to a plan or schedule: *we learn how to program our own lives consciously.* ■ schedule (an item) within a framework: *the next stage of the treaty is programmed for 1996.* ■ broadcast (an item): *the station does not program enough contemporary works.*
– PHRASES **get with the program** [often in imperative] informal do what is expected of one; adopt the prevailing viewpoint.
– DERIVATIVES **pro·gram·ma·bil·i·ty** /-əˈbilətē/ **n.**, **pro·gram·ma·ble** /ˈprōˌgraməbəl, prōˈgram-/ **adj.**
– ORIGIN early 17th cent. (in the sense 'written notice'): via late Latin from Greek *programma*, from *prographein* 'write publicly,' from *pro* 'before' + *graphein* 'write.'

pro·gram·mat·ic /ˌprōgrəˈmatik/ ▶ **adj.** of the nature of or according to a program, schedule, or method: *a programmatic approach to change.* ■ of the nature of program music.
– DERIVATIVES **pro·gram·mat·i·cal·ly** /-ik(ə)lē/ **adv.**

pro·grammed cell death ▶ **n.** less technical term for **APOPTOSIS**.

pro·gram·mer /ˈprōˌgramər/ (also **programer**) ▶ **n.** a person who writes computer programs. ■ a device that automatically controls the operation of something in accordance with a prescribed program.

pro·gram·ming /ˈprōˌgramiɴɢ/ ▶ **n. 1** the action or process of writing computer programs.
2 the action or process of scheduling something, esp. radio or television programs: *the programming of shows.* ■ radio or television programs that are scheduled or broadcast: *the station is to expand its late-night programming.*

pro·gram mu·sic ▶ **n.** music that is intended to evoke images or convey the impression of events. Compare with **ABSOLUTE MUSIC**.

pro·gram trad·ing ▶ **n.** the simultaneous purchase and sale of many different stocks, or of stocks and related futures contracts, with the use of a computer program to exploit price differences in different markets.

prog·ress ▶ **n.** /ˈprägrəs, ˈprägˌres, ˈprōˌgres/ forward or onward movement toward a destination: *the darkness did not stop my progress | they failed to **make any progress** up the narrow estuary.* ■ advance or development toward a better, more complete, or more modern condition: *we are **making progress** toward equal rights.* ■ Brit. archaic a state journey or official tour, esp. by royalty.
▶ **v.** /prəˈgres/ [no obj.] move forward or onward in space or time: *as the century progressed, the quality of telescopes improved.* ■ advance or develop toward a better, more complete, or more modern state: *work on the pond is progressing.* ■ [with obj.] (usu. as adj. **progressed**) Astrology calculate the position of (a planet) or of all the planets and coordinates of (a chart) according to the technique of progression.

– PHRASES **in progress** in the course of being done or carried out: *a meeting was in progress.*
– ORIGIN late Middle English (as a noun): from Latin *progressus* 'an advance,' from the verb *progredi*, from *pro-* 'forward' + *gradi* 'to walk.'

pro·gres·sion /prəˈgresHən/ ▶ **n.** a movement or development toward a destination or a more advanced state, esp. gradually or in stages: *the normal progression from junior to senior status | their mode of progression through the forest.* ■ a succession; a series: *counting the twenty-four hours in a single progression from midnight.* ■ Music a passage or movement from one note or chord to another: *a blues progression.* ■ Mathematics short for ARITHMETIC PROGRESSION, GEOMETRIC PROGRESSION, or HARMONIC PROGRESSION. ■ Astrology a predictive technique in which the daily movement of the planets, starting from the day of birth, represents a year in the subject's life.
– DERIVATIVES **pro·gres·sion·al** /-SHənl/ **adj.**
– ORIGIN late Middle English: from Old French, from Latin *progressio(n-)*, from the verb *progredi* (see PROGRESS).

pro·gres·sion·ist /prəˈgresHənist/ chiefly historical ▶ **n.** **1** Biology a supporter of the theory that all life forms gradually progress or evolve to a higher form.
2 an advocate of or believer in political or social progress.
▶ **adj.** Biology (of a person or theory) supporting or based on the theory that all life forms progress or evolve to a higher form: *progressionist evolutionists.*

pro·gres·sive /prəˈgresiv/ ▶ **adj. 1** happening or developing gradually or in stages; proceeding step by step: *a progressive decline in popularity.* ■ (of a disease or ailment) increasing in severity or extent: *progressive liver failure.* ■ (of taxation or a tax) increasing as a proportion of the sum taxed as that sum increases: *steeply progressive income taxes.* ■ (of a card game or dance) involving a series of sections for which participants successively change place or relative position. ■ archaic engaging in or constituting forward motion.
2 (of a group, person, or idea) favoring or implementing social reform or new, liberal ideas: *a relatively progressive governor.* ■ favoring or promoting change or innovation: *a progressive art school.* ■ relating to or denoting a style of rock music popular esp. in the 1980s and characterized by classical influences, the use of keyboard instruments, and lengthy compositions.
3 Grammar denoting an aspect or tense of a verb that expresses an action in progress, e.g., *am writing, was writing.* Also called CONTINUOUS.
▶ **n. 1** a person advocating or implementing social reform or new, liberal ideas.
2 Grammar a progressive tense or aspect: *the present progressive.*
3 (also **progressive proof**) Printing each of a set of proofs of color work, showing all the colors separately and the cumulative effect of overprinting them.
– DERIVATIVES **pro·gres·sive·ly adv.**, **pro·gres·sive·ness n.**, **pro·gres·siv·ism** /-ˈgresə,vizəm/ **n.**, **pro·gres·siv·ist** /-ˈgresəvist/ **n. & adj.**
– ORIGIN early 17th cent.: from French *progressif, -ive* or medieval Latin *progressivus*, from *progress-* 'gone forward,' from the verb *progredi* (see PROGRESS).

Pro·gres·sive Con·ser·va·tive Par·ty a Canadian political party advocating free trade and holding moderate views on social policies.

pro·gres·sive din·ner ▶ **n.** a social occasion at which the different courses of a meal are eaten at different people's houses.

pro·gres·sive lens ▶ **n.** (usually **progressive lenses**) an eyeglass lens having a smooth transition between parts with different focal lengths, correcting for vision at all distances.

Pro·gres·sive Par·ty ▶ **n.** any of three related political parties active in the first half of the twentieth century that favored social reform. The most prominent was that formed under Theodore Roosevelt in 1912.

pro·gres·sives /prəˈgresivz/ ▶ **plural n.** a pair of eyeglasses having progressive lenses: *progressives for use when driving, reading, or using a computer.*

pro hac vice /prō ˌhäk ˈwikē, ˈvīsē/ ▶ **adv.** for or on this occasion only.
– ORIGIN Latin.

pro·hib·it /prəˈhibit, prō-/ ▶ **v.** (**prohibits, prohibiting, prohibited**) [with obj.] formally forbid (something) by law, rule, or other authority: *laws prohibiting cruelty to animals.* ■ (**prohibit someone/something from doing something**) formally forbid a person or group from doing something: *he is prohibited from being a director.* ■ (of a fact or situation) prevent (something); make impossible: *the budget agreement had prohibited any tax cuts.*
– DERIVATIVES **pro·hib·it·er n.**, **pro·hib·i·tor** /-ər/ **n.**, **pro·hib·i·to·ry** /-ˌtôrē/ **adj.**
– ORIGIN late Middle English: from Latin *prohibit-* 'kept in check,' from the verb *prohibere*, from *pro-* 'in front' + *habere* 'to hold.'

pro·hib·it·ed /prəˈhibitid, prō-/ ▶ **adj.** that has been forbidden; banned: *they had deliberately fed prohibited material to their herd.*

pro·hi·bi·tion /ˌprō(h)əˈbisHən/ ▶ **n. 1** the action of forbidding something, esp. by law: *they argue that prohibition of drugs will always fail.* ■ a law or regulation forbidding something: *those who favor prohibitions on insider trading.*
2 (**Prohibition**) the prevention by law of the manufacture and sale of alcohol, esp. in the US between 1920 and 1933.
– DERIVATIVES **pro·hi·bi·tion·ar·y** /-ˌnerē/ **adj.**, **Pro·hi·bi·tion·ist** /-nist/ **n.**
– ORIGIN late Middle English: from Old French, from Latin *prohibitio(n-)*, from *prohibere* 'keep in check' (see PROHIBIT).

pro·hib·i·tive /prəˈhibitiv, prō-/ ▶ **adj. 1** (of a price or charge) excessively high; difficult or impossible to pay: *the costs involved were prohibitive | prohibitive interest rates.*
2 (esp. of a law or rule) forbidding or restricting something: *prohibitive legislation.* ■ (of a condition or situation) preventing someone from doing something: *a wind over force 5 is prohibitive.*
– DERIVATIVES **pro·hib·i·tive·ly adv.**, **pro·hib·i·tive·ness n.**
– ORIGIN late Middle English (sense 2): from French *prohibitif, -ive* or Latin *prohibitivus*, from *prohibit-* 'kept in check,' from the verb *prohibere* (see PROHIBIT).

pro·in·su·lin /prōˈinsələn/ ▶ **n.** Biochemistry a substance produced by the pancreas that is converted to insulin.

proj·ect ▶ **n.** /ˈpräjˌekt, -ikt/ **1** an individual or collaborative enterprise that is carefully planned and designed to achieve a particular aim: *a research project | a nationwide project to encourage business development.* ■ a school assignment undertaken by a student or group of students, typically as a long-term task that requires independent research: *a history project.* ■ a proposed or planned undertaking: *the novel undermines its own stated project of telling a story.*
2 (also **housing project**) a government-subsidized housing development with relatively low rents: *her family still lives in the projects.*
▶ **v.** /prəˈjekt, prōˈjekt/ [with obj.] **1** estimate or forecast (something) on the basis of present trends: *spending was projected at $72 million.* ■ (often as adj. **projected**) plan (a scheme or undertaking): *a projected exhibition of contemporary art.*
2 [no obj.] extend outward beyond something else; protrude: *I noticed a slip of paper projecting from the book* | (as adj. **projecting**) *a projecting bay window.*
3 throw or cause to move forward or outward: *seeds are projected from the tree.* ■ cause (light, shadow, or an image) to fall on a surface: *the one light projected shadows on the wall.* ■ cause (a sound, esp. the voice) to be heard at a distance: *being audible depends on your ability to project your voice.* ■ imagine (oneself, a situation, etc.) as having moved to a different place or time: *people may be projecting the present into the past.*
4 present or promote (a particular view or image): *he strives to project an image of youth.* ■ present (someone or something) in a way intended to create a favorable impression: *she liked to project herself more as a friend than a doctor.* ■ display (an emotion or quality) in one's behavior: *everyone would be amazed that a young girl could project such depths of emotion.* ■ (**project something onto**) transfer or attribute one's own emotion or desire to (another person), esp. unconsciously: *men may sometimes project their own fears onto women.*
5 Geometry draw straight lines from a center of or parallel lines through every point of (a given figure) to produce a corresponding figure on a surface or a line by intersecting the surface. ■ draw (such lines). ■ produce (such a corresponding figure).
6 make a projection of (the earth, sky, etc.) on a plane surface.
– DERIVATIVES **pro·ject·a·ble** /prəˈjektəbəl/ **adj.**
– ORIGIN late Middle English (in the sense 'preliminary design, tabulated statement'): from Latin *projectum* 'something prominent,' neuter past participle of *proicere* 'throw forth,' from *pro-* 'forth' + *jacere* 'to throw.' Early senses of the verb were 'plan, devise' and 'cause to move forward.'

pro·jec·tile /prəˈjektl, -ˌtīl/ ▶ **n.** a missile designed to be fired from a rocket or gun. ■ an object propelled through the air, esp. one thrown as a weapon: *they tried to shield Johnson from the projectiles that were being thrown.*
▶ **adj.** [attrib.] of or relating to such a missile or object: *a projectile weapon.* ■ propelled with great force: *projectile vomiting.*
– ORIGIN mid 17th cent.: modern Latin, from *project-* 'thrown forth,' from the verb *proicere* (see PROJECT).

pro·jec·tion /prəˈjeksHən/ ▶ **n. 1** an estimate or forecast of a future situation or trend based on a study of present ones: *plans based on projections of slow but positive growth | population projection is essential for planning.*
2 the presentation of an image on a surface, esp. a movie screen: *quality illustrations for overhead projection.* ■ an image projected in such a way: *the background projections featured humpback whales.* ■ the ability to make a sound, esp. the voice, heard at a distance: *I taught him voice projection.*
3 the presentation or promotion of someone or something in a particular way: *the legal profession's projection of an image of altruism.* ■ a mental image viewed as reality: *monsters can be understood as mental projections of mankind's fears.* ■ the unconscious transfer of one's own desires or emotions to another person: *we protect the self by a number of defense mechanisms, including repression and projection.*
4 a thing that extends outward from something else: *the particle board covered all the sharp projections.*
5 Geometry the action of projecting a figure.
6 the representation on a plane surface of any part of the surface of the earth or a celestial sphere. ■ (also **map projection**) a method by which such representation may be done.
– DERIVATIVES **pro·jec·tion·ist** /-ist/ **n.** (sense 2).
– ORIGIN mid 16th cent. (sense 6): from Latin *projectio(n-)*, from *proicere* 'throw forth' (see PROJECT).

pro·jec·tion tel·e·vi·sion (also **projection TV**) ▶ **n.** a large television receiver in which the image is projected optically onto a large viewing screen.

pro·jec·tive /prəˈjektiv/ ▶ **adj. 1** Geometry relating to or derived by projection: *projective transformations.* ■ (of a property of a figure) unchanged by projection.
2 Psychology relating to the unconscious transfer of one's own desires or emotions to another person: *the projective contents of wish fantasies.* ■ relating to or exploiting the unconscious expression or introduction of one's impressions or feelings.
– DERIVATIVES **pro·jec·tive·ly adv.**, **pro·jec·tiv·i·ty** /ˌprōˌjekˈtivətē, ˌpräjˌek-/ **n.**

pro·jec·tive ge·om·e·try ▶ **n.** the study of the projective properties of geometric figures.

pro·jec·tive test ▶ **n.** a psychological test in which words, images, or situations are presented to a person and the responses analyzed for the unconscious expression of elements of personality that they reveal.

pro·jec·tor /prəˈjektər/ ▶ **n. 1** an object that is used to project rays of light, esp. an apparatus with a system of lenses for projecting slides or film onto a screen.
2 archaic a person who plans and sets up a project or enterprise. ■ a promoter of a dubious or fraudulent enterprise.

pro·kar·y·ote /prōˈkarēˌōt/ (also **procaryote**) ▶ **n.** Biology a microscopic single-celled organism that has neither a distinct nucleus with a membrane nor other specialized organelles. Prokaryotes include the bacteria and cyanobacteria. Compare with EUKARYOTE.
– DERIVATIVES **pro·kar·y·ot·ic** /prōˌkarēˈätik/ **adj.**
– ORIGIN 1960s: from PRO-[2] 'before' + Greek *karuon* 'nut, kernel' + *-ote* as in ZYGOTE.

Pro·ko·fi·ev /prōˈkôfēˌef/, Sergei (Sergeevich) (1891–1953), Russian composer. Notable works include the opera *The Love for Three Oranges* (1919), the *Lieutenant Kijé* suite (1934), the ballet music for *Romeo and Juliet* (1935–36), and *Peter and the Wolf* (1936).

Pro·ko·pyevsk /prəˈkôpyifsk/ a coal-mining city in southern Russia, in the Kuznets Basin industrial region, to the south of Kemerovo; pop. 213,200 (est. 2008).

pro·lac·tin /prōˈlaktən/ ▶ **n.** Biochemistry a hormone released from the anterior pituitary gland that stimulates milk production after childbirth.
– ORIGIN 1930s: from PRO-[2] 'before' + LACTATION.

pro·lapse ▶ **n.** /prōˈlaps, ˈprōˌlaps/ a slipping forward or down of one of the parts or organs of the body: *a rectal prolapse.* ■ a prolapsed part or organ, esp. a uterus or rectum.
▶ **v.** /prōˈlaps/ [no obj.] (usu. as adj. **prolapsed**) (of a part or organ of the body) slip forward or down: *a prolapsed uterus.*
– ORIGIN mid 18th cent.: from Latin *prolaps-* 'slipped forward,' from the verb *prolabi*, from *pro-* 'forward, down' + *labi* 'to slip.'

pro·lap·sus /prō'lapsəs/ ▶ **n.** technical term for **PROLAPSE.**
– ORIGIN late 18th cent.: modern Latin, from late Latin, literally 'fall.'

pro·late /'prō,lāt/ ▶ **adj.** Geometry (of a spheroid) lengthened in the direction of a polar diameter. Often contrasted with **OBLATE**[1].
– ORIGIN late 17th cent.: from Latin *prolatus* 'carried forward,' past participle of *proferre* 'prolong,' from *pro-* 'forward' + *ferre* 'carry.'

prole /prōl/ informal, derogatory ▶ **n.** a member of the working class; a worker.
▶ **adj.** working-class: *prole soldiers.*
– ORIGIN late 19th cent.: abbreviation of **PROLETARIAT.**

pro·leg /'prō,leg/ ▶ **n.** Entomology a fleshy abdominal limb of a caterpillar or similar insect larva.

pro·le·gom·e·non /,prōlə'gämə,nän, -nən/ ▶ **n.** (pl. **prolegomena** /-nə/) a critical or discursive introduction to a book.
– DERIVATIVES **pro·le·gom·e·nous** /-nəs/ **adj.**
– ORIGIN mid 17th cent.: via Latin from Greek, passive present participle (neuter) of *prolegein* 'say beforehand,' from *pro* 'before' + *legein* 'say.'

pro·lep·sis /prō'lepsəs/ ▶ **n.** (pl. **prolepses** /-,sēz/) **1** Rhetoric the anticipation and answering of possible objections in rhetorical speech.
2 the representation of a thing as existing before it actually does or did so, as in *he was a dead man when he entered.*
– DERIVATIVES **pro·lep·tic** /-'leptik/ **adj.**, **pro·lep·ti·cal·ly** /-'leptik(ə)lē/ **adv.**
– ORIGIN late Middle English (as a term in rhetoric): via late Latin from Greek *prolēpsis*, from *prolambanein* 'anticipate,' from *pro* 'before' + *lambanein* 'take.'

pro·le·tar·i·an /,prōli'te(ə)rēən/ ▶ **adj.** of or relating to the proletariat: *a proletarian ideology.*
▶ **n.** a member of the proletariat.
– DERIVATIVES **pro·le·tar·i·an·ism** /-,nizəm/ **n.**, **pro·le·tar·i·an·i·za·tion** /-,terēənə'zāSHən/ **n.**, **pro·le·tar·i·an·ize** /-,nīz/ **v.**
– ORIGIN mid 17th cent.: from Latin *proletarius* (from *proles* 'offspring'), denoting a person having no wealth in property, who only served the state by producing offspring, + **-AN.**

pro·le·tar·i·at /,prōli'te(ə)rēət/ (also archaic **proletariate**) ▶ **n.** [treated as sing. or pl.] workers or working-class people, regarded collectively (often used with reference to Marxism): *the growth of the industrial proletariat.* ■ the lowest class of citizens in ancient Rome.
– ORIGIN mid 19th cent.: from French *prolétariat*, from Latin *proletarius* (see **PROLETARIAN**).

pro-life /prō'līf/ ▶ **adj.** opposing abortion and euthanasia: *she is a pro-life activist.* Compare with **PRO-CHOICE.**
– DERIVATIVES **pro-lif·er n.**

pro·lif·er·ate /prə'lifə,rāt/ ▶ **v.** [no obj.] increase rapidly in numbers; multiply: *the science-fiction magazines that proliferated in the 1920s.* ■ (of a cell, structure, or organism) reproduce rapidly: *the Mediterranean faces an ecological disaster if the seaweed continues to proliferate at its present rate.* ■ [with obj.] cause (cells, tissue, structures, etc.) to reproduce rapidly: *electromagnetic radiation can only proliferate cancers already present.*
– DERIVATIVES **pro·lif·er·a·tive** /-,rātiv/ **adj.**, **pro·lif·er·a·tor** /-,rātər/ **n.**
– ORIGIN late 19th cent.: back-formation from **PROLIFERATION.**

pro·lif·er·a·tion /prə,lifə'rāSHən/ ▶ **n.** rapid increase in numbers: *a continuing threat of nuclear proliferation.* ■ rapid reproduction of a cell, part, or organism: *we attempted to measure cell proliferation.* ■ [in sing.] a large number of something: *stress levels are high, forcing upon them a* ***proliferation of*** *ailments.*
– ORIGIN mid 19th cent.: from French *prolifération*, from *prolifère* 'proliferous.'

pro·lif·er·ous /prə'lifərəs/ ▶ **adj.** Biology (of a plant) producing buds or side shoots from a flower or other terminal part. ■ (of a plant or invertebrate) propagating or multiplying by means of buds or offsets.
– ORIGIN mid 17th cent.: from Latin *proles* 'offspring' + **-FEROUS.**

pro·lif·ic /prə'lifik/ ▶ **adj. 1** (of a plant, animal, or person) producing much fruit or foliage or many offspring: *in captivity, tigers are prolific breeders.* ■ (of an artist, author, or composer) producing many works: *he was a prolific composer of operas.* ■ (of a sports player) high-scoring: *a prolific home-run hitter.*
2 present in large numbers or quantities; plentiful: *mahogany was once prolific in the tropical forests.* ■ (of a river, area, or season of the year) characterized by plentiful wildlife or produce: *the prolific rivers and lakes of Franklin County.*
– DERIVATIVES **pro·lif·i·ca·cy** /-ikəsē/ **n.**, **pro·lif·i·cal·ly** /-ik(ə)lē/ **adv.**, **pro·lif·ic·ness n.**
– ORIGIN mid 17th cent.: from medieval Latin *prolificus*, from Latin *proles* 'offspring' (see **PROLIFEROUS**).

pro·line /'prō,lēn/ ▶ **n.** Biochemistry an amino acid that is a constituent of most proteins, esp. collagen. ● A heterocyclic compound; chem. formula: $C_5H_9NO_2$.
– ORIGIN early 20th cent.: contraction of the chemical name *p(yr)rol(id)ine-2-*carboxylic acid.

pro·lix /prō'liks/ ▶ **adj.** (of speech or writing) using or containing too many words; tediously lengthy: *he found the narrative too prolix and discursive.*
– DERIVATIVES **pro·lix·i·ty** /-'liksətē/ **n.**, **pro·lix·ly adv.**
– ORIGIN late Middle English: from Old French *prolixe* or Latin *prolixus* 'poured forth, extended,' from *pro-* 'outward' + *liquere* 'be liquid.'

pro·loc·u·tor /prō'läkyətər/ ▶ **n. 1** a chairperson of the lower house of convocation in a province of the Church of England.
2 archaic or formal a spokesperson.
– ORIGIN late Middle English (sense 2): from Latin, from *prolocut-* 'spoken out,' from the verb *proloqui*, from *pro-* 'before' + *loqui* 'speak.'

Pro·log /'prō,lôg, -,läg/ ▶ **n.** Computing a high-level computer programming language first devised for artificial intelligence applications.
– ORIGIN 1970s: from the first elements of **PROGRAMMING** and **LOGIC.**

pro·logue /'prō,lôg, -,läg/ ▶ **n.** a separate introductory section of a literary or musical work: *this idea is outlined in the prologue.* ■ an event or action that leads to another event or situation: *civil unrest in a few isolated villages became the* ***prologue*** *to widespread rebellion.* ■ (in professional cycling) a short preliminary time trial held before a race to establish a leader. ■ the actor who delivers the prologue in a play.
– ORIGIN Middle English: from Old French, via Latin from Greek *prologos*, from *pro-* 'before' + *logos* 'saying.'

pro·long /prə'lôNG, -'läNG/ (also **prolongate** /-'lôNGgāt, -'läNG-/) ▶ **v.** [with obj.] extend the duration of: *an idea that prolonged the life of the engine by many years.* ■ (usu. **be prolonged**) rare extend in spatial length: *the line of his lips was prolonged in a short red scar.*
– DERIVATIVES **pro·lon·ga·tion** /prō,lôNG'gāSHən, prə-/ **n.**, **pro·long·er n.**
– ORIGIN late Middle English: from Old French *prolonguer*, from late Latin *prolongare*, from *pro-* 'forward, onward' + *longus* 'long.'

pro·longed /prə'lôNGd, -'läNGd/ ▶ **adj.** continuing for a long time or longer than usual; lengthy: *the region suffered a prolonged drought.*
– DERIVATIVES **pro·long·ed·ly** /-'lôNG(ə)dlē, -'läNG/ **adv.**

pro·lu·sion /prō'lo͞oZHən/ ▶ **n.** archaic or formal a preliminary action or event; a prelude. ■ a preliminary essay or article.
– ORIGIN early 17th cent.: from Latin *prolusio(n-)*, from *prolus-* 'practiced beforehand,' from the verb *proludere*, from *pro* 'before' + *ludere* 'to play.'

PROM /präm/ ▶ **n.** Computing a memory chip that can be programmed only once by the manufacturer or user.
– ORIGIN from *p(rogrammable) r(ead-)o(nly) m(emory).*

prom /präm/ ▶ **n.** informal **1** a formal dance, esp. one held by a class in high school or college at the end of a year.
2 Brit. short for **PROMENADE** (sense 1 of the noun).
3 (also **Prom**) Brit. short for **PROMENADE CONCERT**: *the last night of the Proms.*

prom. ▶ **abbr.** promontory.

prom·e·nade /,prämə'nād, -'näd/ ▶ **n. 1** a paved public walk, typically one along a waterfront at a resort. ■ a leisurely walk, or sometimes a ride or drive, typically one taken in a public place so as to meet or be seen by others: *she went on a promenade with Jules.* ■ (in country dancing) a movement in which couples follow one another in a given direction, each couple having both hands joined.
2 archaic term for **PROM** (sense 1).
▶ **v.** [no obj.] take a leisurely walk, ride, or drive in public, esp. to meet or be seen by others: *women who promenaded in the Bois de Boulogne.* ■ [with obj.] take such a walk through (a place): *people began to promenade the streets.* ■ [with obj.] dated escort (someone) about a place, esp. so as to be seen by others: *the governor of Utah promenades the daughter of the Maryland governor.*
– DERIVATIVES **prom·e·nad·er n.**
– ORIGIN mid 16th cent. (denoting a leisurely walk in public): from French, from *se promener* 'to walk,' reflexive of *promener* 'take for a walk.'

prom·e·nade con·cert ▶ **n.** Brit. a concert of classical music at which a part of the audience stands in an area that has no seating, for which tickets are sold at a reduced price. The most famous series of such concerts is the annual BBC Promenade Concerts (known as **the Proms**), instituted by Sir Henry Wood (1869–1944) in 1895 and held since World War II chiefly in the Albert Hall in London.

prom·e·nade deck ▶ **n.** an upper deck on a passenger ship for the use of passengers who wish to enjoy the open air.

pro·meth·a·zine /prō'meTHə,zēn/ ▶ **n.** Medicine a synthetic antihistamine drug derived from phenothiazine, used chiefly to treat the symptoms of allergies and motion sickness.
– ORIGIN 1950s: from *pro(pyl)* + *(di)meth(ylamine)* + *(phenothi)azine.*

Pro·me·the·us /prə'mēTHēəs, -,TH(y)o͞os/ Greek Mythology a demigod, one of the Titans, who was worshiped by craftsmen. When Zeus hid fire from man, Prometheus stole it by trickery and returned it to earth. As punishment, Zeus chained him to a rock where an eagle fed each day on his liver, which grew again each night; he was rescued by Hercules.
– DERIVATIVES **Pro·me·the·an** /-THēən/ **adj.**

pro·me·thi·um /prō'mēTHēəm/ ▶ **n.** the chemical element of atomic number 61, a radioactive metal of the lanthanide series. It was first produced artificially in a nuclear reactor and occurs in nature in traces as a product of uranium fission. (Symbol: **Pm**)
– ORIGIN 1940s: modern Latin, from the name of the Titan **PROMETHEUS.**

prom·i·nence /'prämənəns/ ▶ **n. 1** the state of being important or famous: *she* ***came to prominence*** *as an artist in the 1960s* | [in sing.] *the commission gave the case a prominence which it might otherwise have escaped.*
2 the fact or condition of standing out from something by physically projecting or being particularly noticeable: *radiographs showed enlargement of the right heart with prominence of the pulmonary outflow tract.* ■ a thing that projects from something, esp. a projecting feature of the landscape or a protuberance on a part of the body: *the rocky prominence resembled a snow-capped mountain.* ■ Astronomy a stream of incandescent gas projecting above the sun's chromosphere.
– DERIVATIVES **prom·i·nen·cy n.**
– ORIGIN late 16th cent. (denoting something that juts out): from obsolete French, from Latin *prominentia* 'jutting out,' from the verb *prominere* (see **PROMINENT**).

prom·i·nent /'prämənənt/ ▶ **adj. 1** important; famous: *she was a prominent member of the city council.*
2 projecting from something; protuberant: *a man with big, prominent eyes like a lobster's.* ■ situated so as to catch the attention; noticeable: *the new housing developments are prominent landmarks.*
– DERIVATIVES **prom·i·nent·ly adv.**
– ORIGIN late Middle English (in the sense 'projecting'): from Latin *prominent-* 'jutting out,' from the verb *prominere*. Compare with **EMINENT.**

prom·is·cu·i·ty /,prämə'skyo͞oitē, prə,mis'kyo͞o-/ ▶ **n.** the fact or state of being promiscuous: *some fear this will lead to greater sexual promiscuity among teens.*

pro·mis·cu·ous /prə'miskyo͞oəs/ ▶ **adj. 1** derogatory having or characterized by many transient sexual relationships: *she's a wild, promiscuous girl* | *they ran wild, indulging in promiscuous sex and experimenting with drugs.*
2 demonstrating or implying an undiscriminating or unselective approach; indiscriminate or casual: *the city fathers were promiscuous with their honors.* ■ consisting of a wide range of different things: *Americans are free to pick and choose from a promiscuous array of values and behavior.*
– DERIVATIVES **prom·is·cu·ous·ly adv.**, **prom·is·cu·ous·ness n.**
– ORIGIN early 17th cent.: from Latin *promiscuus* 'indiscriminate' (based on *miscere* 'to mix') + **-ous** The early sense was 'consisting of elements mixed together,' giving rise to 'indiscriminate' and 'undiscriminating,' whence the notion of 'casual.'

prom·ise /'präməs/ ▶ **n.** a declaration or assurance that one will do a particular thing or that a particular thing will happen: *what happened to all those firm promises of support?* | [with clause] *he took my fax number with the promise that he would send me a drawing* | [with infinitive] *I did not keep my promise to go home early.* ■ the quality of potential excellence: *he showed great promise even as a junior officer.* ■ [in sing.] an indication that something specified is expected or likely to occur: *the promise of peace.*

▶ **v. 1** [reporting verb] assure someone that one will definitely do, give, or arrange something; undertake or declare that something will happen: [with infinitive] *he promised to forward my mail* | [with clause] *she made him promise that he wouldn't do it again* | [with direct speech] *"I'll bring it right back," she promised* | [with two objs.] *he promised her the job.* ■ [with obj.] (usu. **be promised**) archaic pledge (someone, esp. a woman) to marry someone else; betroth: *I've been promised to him for years.*
2 [with obj.] give good grounds for expecting (a particular occurrence or situation): *forthcoming concerts promise a feast of music from around the world* | [with infinitive] *it promised to be a night that all present would long remember.* ■ (of a person, publication, institution, etc.) announce (something) as being expected to happen: *in its pre-Christmas trading statement it promised record results* | [with two objs.] *we're promised more winter weather tonight.* ■ (**promise oneself**) contemplate the pleasant expectation of: *he tidied up the room, promising himself an early night.*

– PHRASES **I promise** (or **I promise you**) informal used for emphasis, esp. so as to reassure, encourage, or threaten someone: *oh, I'm not joking, I promise you.* **promise (someone) the earth** (or **moon**) make extravagant promises to someone that are unlikely to be fulfilled: *interactive technology titillates, promises the earth, but delivers nothing.* **promises, promises** informal used to indicate that the speaker is skeptical about someone's stated intention to do something.

– DERIVATIVES **prom·is·er n.**

– ORIGIN late Middle English: from Latin *promissum* 'something promised,' neuter past participle of *promittere* 'put forth, promise,' from *pro-* 'forward' + *mittere* 'send.'

Prom·ised Land ▶ **n.** (in the Bible) the land of Canaan, which was promised to Abraham and his descendants (Gen. 12:7). ■ (**promised land**) a place or situation in which someone expects to find great happiness: *Italy is the promised land for any musician.*

prom·is·ee /ˌpräməˈsē/ ▶ **n.** Law a person to whom a promise is made.

prom·is·ing /ˈpräməsiNG/ ▶ **adj.** showing signs of future success: *a promising actor* | *a promising start to the season.*

– DERIVATIVES **prom·is·ing·ly adv.**

prom·i·sor /ˈpräməsər/ ▶ **n.** Law a person who makes a promise.

prom·is·so·ry /ˈpräməˌsôrē/ ▶ **adj.** chiefly Law conveying or implying a promise: *statements that are promissory in nature* | *promissory words.* ■ archaic indicative of something to come; full of promise: *the glow of evening is* **promissory of** *the splendid days to come.*

– ORIGIN late Middle English: from medieval Latin *promissorius*, from *promiss-* 'promised,' from the verb *promittere* (see **PROMISE**).

prom·is·so·ry note ▶ **n.** a signed document containing a written promise to pay a stated sum to a specified person or the bearer at a specified date or on demand.

pro·mo /ˈprōmō/ informal ▶ **n.** (pl. **promos**) a piece of publicity or advertising, esp. in the form of a short film or video: *taping a two-minute promo* | [as modifier] *a promo video.*

– ORIGIN 1960s: abbreviation of **PROMOTION**.

prom·on·to·ry /ˈprämənˌtôrē/ ▶ **n.** (pl. **promontories**) a point of high land that juts out into a large body of water; a headland: *a rocky promontory.* ■ Anatomy a prominence or protuberance on an organ or other structure in the body.

– ORIGIN mid 16th cent.: from Latin *promontorium*, variant (influenced by *mons, mont-* 'mountain') of *promunturium*.

Prom·on·to·ry Moun·tains a short range that forms a peninsula in the northern Great Salt Lake, in northern Utah. The first transcontinental railroad passed through Promontory, north of the range. Today, trains pass Promontory Point, at the southern end, via a causeway across the lake.

pro·mote /prəˈmōt/ ▶ **v.** [with obj.] **1** further the progress of (something, esp. a cause, venture, or aim); support or actively encourage: *some regulation is still required to promote competition.* ■ give publicity to (a product, organization, or venture) so as to increase sales or public awareness: *they are using famous personalities to promote the library nationally.* ■ Chemistry act as a promoter of (a catalyst).
2 advance or raise (someone) to a higher position or rank: *she was* **promoted to** *general manager.* ■ transfer (a sports team) to a higher division of a league: *they were promoted from the Third Division last season.* ■ Chess exchange (a pawn) for a more powerful piece of the same color, typically a queen, as part of the move in which it reaches the opponent's end of the board. ■ Bridge enable (a relatively low card) to win a trick by playing off the higher ones first.

– DERIVATIVES **pro·mot·a·bil·i·ty** /prəˌmōtəˈbilətē/ **n.**, **pro·mot·a·ble adj.**, **pro·mo·tive** /-tiv/ **adj.**

– ORIGIN late Middle English: from Latin *promot-* 'moved forward,' from the verb *promovere*, from *pro-* 'forward, onward' + *movere* 'to move.'

pro·mot·er /prəˈmōtər/ ▶ **n.** a person or thing that promotes something, in particular: ■ a person or company that finances or organizes a sporting event or theatrical production: *a boxing promoter.* ■ a person involved in setting up and funding a new company. ■ a supporter of a cause or aim: *Mitterrand was a fierce promoter of European integration.* ■ (also **promotor**) Chemistry an additive that increases the activity of a catalyst. ■ Biology a region of a DNA molecule that forms the site at which transcription of a gene starts.

– ORIGIN late Middle English: from Anglo-Norman French *promotour*, from medieval Latin *promotor* (see **PROMOTE**).

pro·mo·tion /prəˈmōSHən/ ▶ **n. 1** activity that supports or provides active encouragement for the furtherance of a cause, venture, or aim: *disease prevention and health promotion.* ■ the publicization of a product, organization, or venture so as to increase sales or public awareness. ■ a publicity campaign for a particular product, organization, or venture: *the paper is reaping the rewards of a series of promotions.* ■ (often as modifier **promotions**) the activity or business of organizing such publicity or campaigns: *she's the promotions manager for the museum.* ■ a sporting event, esp. a series of boxing matches, staged for profit. ■ Chemistry the action of promoting a catalyst.
2 the action of raising someone to a higher position or rank or the fact of being so raised: *majors designated for* **promotion to** *lieutenant colonel* | *a promotion to divisional sales director.*

– ORIGIN late Middle English (sense 2): via Old French from Latin *promotio(n-)*, from *promovere* 'move forward' (see **PROMOTE**).

pro·mo·tion·al /prəˈmōSHənl/ ▶ **adj.** of or relating to the publicizing of a product, organization, or venture so as to increase sales or public awareness: *she was on a promotional tour for her books.*

prompt /prämpt/ ▶ **v.** [with obj.] **1** (of an event or fact) cause or bring about (an action or feeling): *his death has prompted an industry-wide investigation of safety violations.* ■ cause (someone) to take a course of action: *a demonstration by 20,000 people prompted the government to step up security.*
2 assist or encourage (a hesitating speaker) to say something: [with direct speech] *"And the picture?" he prompted.* ■ supply a forgotten word or line to (an actor) during the performance of a play. ■ Computing (of a computer) request input from (a user).

▶ **n. 1** an act of assisting or encouraging a hesitating speaker: *with barely a prompt, Barbara talked on.* ■ the word or phrase spoken as a reminder to an actor of a forgotten word or line. ■ Computing a message or symbol on a screen to show that the system is waiting for input. ■ another term for **PROMPTER**.
2 the time limit for the payment of an account, as stated on a prompt note.

▶ **adj.** done without delay; immediate: *the owner would have died but for the prompt action of two paramedics.* ■ (of a person) acting without delay: *the fans were prompt and courteous in complying with police requests.* ■ (of goods) for immediate delivery and payment.

– DERIVATIVES **promp·ti·tude** /ˈpräm(p)təˌt(y)o͞od/ **n.**, **prompt·ness n.**

– ORIGIN Middle English (as a verb): based on Old French *prompt* or Latin *promptus* 'brought to light,' also 'prepared, ready,' past participle of *promere* 'to produce,' from *pro-* 'out, forth' + *emere* 'take.'

prompt·book /ˈprämptˌbo͝ok/ ▶ **n.** an annotated copy of a play for the use of a prompter during a performance.

prompt·er /ˈpräm(p)tər/ ▶ **n.** a person seated out of sight of the audience who supplies a forgotten word or line to an actor during the performance of a play.

prompt·ing /ˈpräm(p)tiNG/ ▶ **n.** the action of saying something to persuade, encourage, or remind someone to do or say something: *after some prompting, the defendant gave the police his name.*

prompt·ly /ˈprämptlē/ ▶ **adv. 1** with little or no delay; immediately: *he paid the fine promptly.* ■ used to express surprise, and slight disapproval, when someone does something shortly after something else: *every time she managed to pay her credit card off, she promptly went shopping again.*
2 at exactly a specified time; punctually: *Jamie arrived promptly at 8:30.*

prompt side ▶ **n.** the side of the stage where the prompter sits, usually to the actor's right in the US and to the actor's left in the UK.

prom·ul·gate /ˈpräməlˌgāt, prōˈməl-/ ▶ **v.** [with obj.] promote or make widely known (an idea or cause): *these objectives have to be promulgated within the organization.* ■ put (a law or decree) into effect by official proclamation: *in January 1852, the new constitution was promulgated.*

– DERIVATIVES **prom·ul·ga·tion** /ˌpräməlˈgāSHən, ˌprōməl-/ **n.**, **prom·ul·ga·tor** /-ˌgātər/ **n.**

– ORIGIN mid 16th cent.: from Latin *promulgat-* 'exposed to public view,' from the verb *promulgare*, from *pro-* 'out, publicly' + *mulgere* 'cause to come forth' (literally 'to milk').

pro·mulge /prōˈməlj/ ▶ **v.** archaic variant of **PROMULGATE**.

– ORIGIN late 15th cent.: from Latin *promulgare*.

pron. ▶ **abbr.** ■ pronominal. ■ pronoun. ■ pronounced. ■ pronunciation.

pro·na·os /prōˈnāˌäs/ ▶ **n.** (pl. **pronaoi** /-ˈnāˌoi/) a vestibule at the front of a classical temple, enclosed by a portico and projecting sidewalls.

– ORIGIN via Latin from Greek *pronaos* 'hall of a temple,' from *pro* 'before' + *naos* 'temple.'

pro·nate /ˈprōˌnāt/ ▶ **v.** [with obj.] Anatomy turn or hold (a hand, foot, or limb) so that the palm or sole is facing downward or inward: (as adj. **pronated**) *a pronated foot.* Compare with **SUPINATE**. ■ [no obj.] walk or run with most of the weight on the inside edge of the feet.

– DERIVATIVES **pro·na·tion** /prōˈnāSHən/ **n.**

– ORIGIN mid 19th cent.: back-formation from *pronation*, based on Latin *pronus* 'leaning forward.'

pro·na·tor /ˈprōˌnātər/ ▶ **n.** Anatomy **1** a muscle whose contraction produces or assists in the pronation of a limb or part of a limb.
2 a person who pronates when walking or running.

prone /prōn/ ▶ **adj. 1** [predic.] (**prone to**/**prone to do something**) likely to or liable to suffer from, do, or experience something, typically something regrettable or unwelcome: *years of logging had left the mountains prone to mudslides* | *he is prone to jump to conclusions.*
2 lying flat, esp. face downward: *I was lying prone on a foam mattress* | *a prone position.* ■ technical denoting the position of the forearm with the palm of the hand facing downward.
3 archaic with a downward slope or direction.

– ORIGIN late Middle English: from Latin *pronus* 'leaning forward,' from *pro* 'forward.'

prone·ness /ˈprōn(n)is/ ▶ **n.** liability to suffer from or experience something regrettable or unwelcome; susceptibility: *his* **proneness to** *injury will seriously mar a promising career.*

prong /prôNG/ ▶ **n. 1** each of two or more projecting pointed parts at the end of a fork. ■ a projecting part on various other devices: *a small rubber brush with large prongs.*
2 each of the separate parts of an attack or operation: *the three main prongs of the new government's program.*

▶ **v.** [with obj.] pierce or stab with a fork: *pronging the bread with a fondue fork.*

– DERIVATIVES **pronged** /prôNGd/ **adj.** [in combination] *a three-pronged attack.*

– ORIGIN late 15th cent. (denoting a forked implement): perhaps related to Middle Low German *prange* 'pinching instrument.' The verb dates from the mid 19th cent.

prong·horn /ˈprôNGˌhôrn/ (also **pronghorn antelope**) ▶ **n.** a deerlike North American mammal with a stocky body, long slim legs, and black horns that are shed and regrown annually. ● *Antilocapra americana*, the only member of the family Antilocapridae.

pronk /prôNGk, präNGk/ ▶ **v.** [no obj.] (of a springbok or other antelope) leap in the air with an arched back and stiff legs, typically as a form of display or when threatened.

– ORIGIN late 19th cent.: from Afrikaans, literally 'show off,' from Dutch *pronken* 'to strut.'

pro·nom·i·nal /prōˈnämənl/ ▶ **adj.** of, relating to, or serving as a pronoun: *a pronominal form.*

– DERIVATIVES **pro·nom·i·nal·i·za·tion** /ˌprōˌnämənl-əˈzāSHən/ **n.**, **pro·nom·i·nal·ize** /-ˌīz/ **v.**, **pro·nom·i·nal·ly adv.**

– ORIGIN mid 17th cent.: from late Latin *pronominalis* 'belonging to a pronoun,' from Latin *pronomen* (see **PRONOUN**).

pro·noun /ˈprōˌnoun/ ▶ **n.** a word that can function by itself as a noun phrase and that refers either to the participants in the discourse (e.g., *I, you*) or to someone or something mentioned elsewhere in the discourse (e.g., *she, it, this*).

– ORIGIN late Middle English: from **PRO-**[1] 'on behalf of' + **NOUN**, suggested by French *pronom*, Latin *pronomen* (from *pro-* 'for, in place of' + *nomen* 'name').

pro·nounce /prəˈnouns/ ▶ **v.** [with obj.] **1** make the sound of (a word or part of a word), typically in the correct or a particular way: *Gerry pronounced the hero's name "Cahoolin"* | *a refugee whose name no one could pronounce.*
2 declare or announce, typically formally or solemnly: *allow history to pronounce the verdict* | [with complement] *she was pronounced dead at the scene* | [with clause] *the doctors pronounced that he would never improve.* ■ [no obj.] (**pronounce on**) pass judgment or make a decision on: *the secretary of state will shortly pronounce on alternative measures.*
– DERIVATIVES **pro·nounce·a·bil·i·ty** /prə,nounsəˈbilətē/ **n.**, **pro·nounce·a·ble adj.**, **pro·nounc·er n.**
– ORIGIN late Middle English: from Old French *pronuncier*, from Latin *pronuntiare*, from *pro-* 'out, forth' + *nuntiare* 'announce' (from *nuntius* 'messenger').

pro·nounced /prəˈnounst/ ▶ **adj.** very noticeable or marked; conspicuous: *he had a pronounced squint.*
– DERIVATIVES **pro·nounc·ed·ly** /-ˈnounsədlē, -ˈnounstlē/ **adv.**

pro·nounce·ment /prəˈnounsmənt/ ▶ **n.** a formal or authoritative announcement or declaration: *distrust of the pronouncements of politicians was endemic.*

pron·to /ˈpräntō/ ▶ **adv.** informal promptly; quickly: *put it in the refrigerator, pronto.*
– ORIGIN early 20th cent.: from Spanish, from Latin *promptus* (see **PROMPT**).

pro·nu·cle·us /prōˈn(y)o͞oklēəs/ ▶ **n.** (pl. **pronuclei** /-klē,ī/) Biology either of a pair of gametic nuclei, in the stage following meiosis but before their fusion leads to the formation of the nucleus of the zygote.
– DERIVATIVES **pro·nu·cle·ar** /-klēər/ **adj.**

pro·nun·ci·a·men·to /prō,nənsēəˈmentō/ ▶ **n.** (pl. **pronunciamentos**) (esp. in Spain and Spanish-speaking countries) a political manifesto or proclamation.
– ORIGIN Spanish *pronunciamiento*, from *pronunciar* 'pronounce.'

pro·nun·ci·a·tion /prə,nənsēˈāsʜən/ ▶ **n.** the way in which a word is pronounced: *spelling does not determine pronunciation* | *similar pronunciations are heard in Brooklyn.*
– ORIGIN late Middle English: from Latin *pronuntiatio(n-)*, from the verb *pronuntiare* (see **PRONOUNCE**).

pro·nun·ci·o /prōˈnənsē,ō/ ▶ **n.** (pl. **pro·nuncios**) a papal ambassador to a country that does not accord the pope's ambassador automatic precedence over other ambassadors.
– ORIGIN 1960s: from Italian *pro-nunzio*, from *pro-* 'before' + *nunzio* 'nuncio.'

proof /pro͞of/ ▶ **n. 1** evidence or argument establishing or helping to establish a fact or the truth of a statement: *you will be asked to give proof of your identity* | *this is not a proof for the existence of God.* ■ Law the spoken or written evidence in a trial. ■ the action or process of establishing the truth of a statement: *it shifts the onus of proof in convictions from the police to the public.* ■ archaic a test or trial. ■ a series of stages in the resolution of a mathematical or philosophical problem.
2 a trial print of something, in particular: ■ Printing a trial impression of a page, taken from type or film and used for making corrections before final printing. ■ a trial photographic print made for initial selection. ■ each of a number of impressions from an engraved plate, esp. (in commercial printing) of a limited number before the ordinary issue is printed and before an inscription or signature is added. ■ any of various preliminary impressions of coins struck as specimens.
3 the strength of distilled alcoholic liquor, relative to proof spirit taken as a standard of 100: [in combination] *powerful 132-proof rum.*
▶ **adj. 1** able to withstand something damaging; resistant: *the marine battle armor was* ***proof against*** *most weapons* | [in combination] *the system comes with idiot-proof instructions.*
2 [attrib.] denoting a trial impression of a page or printed work: *a proof copy is sent up for checking.*
▶ **v.** [with obj.] **1** make (fabric) waterproof: (as adj. **proofed**) *the tent is made from proofed nylon.*
2 make a proof of (a printed work, engraving, etc.): (as noun **proofing**) *proofing could be done on a low-cost printer.* ■ proofread (a text): *a book about dinosaurs was being proofed by the publisher.*
3 activate (yeast) by the addition of liquid. ■ knead (dough) until light and smooth. ■ [no obj.] (of dough) prove: *shape into a baguette and let proof for a few minutes.*
– PHRASES **the proof of the pudding is in the eating** proverb the real value of something can be judged only from practical experience or results and not from appearance or theory.
– ORIGIN Middle English *preve*, from Old French *proeve*, from late Latin *proba*, from Latin *probare* 'to test, prove.' The change of vowel in late Middle English was due to the influence of **PROVE**. Current senses of the verb date from the late 19th cent.

proof-of-pur·chase ▶ **adj.** designating a feature or symbol on a product that can be removed by the buyer to prove that the product was purchased, in order to claim a rebate or refund.

proof pos·i·tive ▶ **n.** evidence taken to be final or absolute proof of the existence of something: *he still needs proof positive of her love.*

proof·read /ˈpro͞of,rēd/ ▶ **v.** (past and past participle **proofread** /-,red/) [with obj.] read (printer's proofs or other written or printed material) and mark any errors.
– DERIVATIVES **proof·read·er n.**

proof sheet ▶ **n.** Printing a page of proofed text; a proof.

proof spir·it ▶ **n.** a mixture of alcohol and water containing (in the US) 50 percent alcohol by volume, or (in the UK) 57.1 percent alcohol by volume, used as a standard of strength of distilled alcoholic liquor.

proof text ▶ **n.** a passage of the Bible to which appeal is made in support of an argument or position in theology.

prop[1] /präp/ ▶ **n.** a pole or beam used as a support or to keep something in position, typically one that is not an integral part of the thing supported: *300 tubular steel props.* ■ a person or thing that is a major source of support or assistance: *the second institutional prop of conservative Spain was the army.* ■ Grammar a word used to fill a syntactic role without any specific meaning of its own, for example *one* in *it's a nice one* and *it* in *it is raining.*
▶ **v.** (**props, propping, propped**) [with obj.] position something underneath (someone or something) for support: *she propped her chin in the palm of her right hand.* ■ position (something or someone) more or less upright by leaning it against something else: *a jug of milk with a note propped against it* | *she* ***propped*** *the picture* ***up*** *on the mantlepiece.* ■ use an object to keep (something) in position: *he found that the door to the office was* ***propped open.***
– PHRASAL VERBS **prop someone/something up** provide support or assistance for someone or something that would otherwise fail or decline: *foreign aid tends to prop up incompetent governments.*
– ORIGIN late Middle English: probably from Middle Dutch *proppe* 'support (for vines).'

prop[2] ▶ **n.** (usu. **props**) a portable object other than furniture or costumes used on the set of a play or movie.
– ORIGIN mid 19th cent.: abbreviation of **PROPERTY**.

prop[3] ▶ **n.** informal an aircraft propeller.
– ORIGIN early 20th cent.: abbreviation.

prop. ▶ **abbr.** ■ proposition. ■ proprietor.

pro·pae·deu·tic /,prōpiˈd(y)o͞otik/ formal ▶ **adj.** (of an area of study) serving as a preliminary instruction or as an introduction to further study.
▶ **n.** an introduction to a subject or area of study.
– DERIVATIVES **pro·pae·deu·ti·cal adj.**
– ORIGIN late 18th cent.: from **PRO-**[2] 'before' + Greek *paideutikos* 'of or for teaching,' suggested by Greek *propaideuein* 'teach beforehand.'

prop·a·gan·da /,präpəˈgandə/ ▶ **n. 1** chiefly derogatory information, esp. of a biased or misleading nature, used to promote or publicize a particular political cause or point of view: *he was charged with distributing enemy propaganda.* ■ the dissemination of such information as a political strategy: *the party's leaders believed that a long period of education and propaganda would be necessary.*
2 (**Propaganda**) a committee of cardinals of the Roman Catholic Church responsible for foreign missions, founded in 1622 by Pope Gregory XV.
– ORIGIN Italian, from modern Latin *congregatio de propaganda fide* 'congregation for propagation of the faith' (sense 2). Sense 1 dates from the early 20th cent.

prop·a·gan·dist /,präpəˈgandist/ chiefly derogatory ▶ **n.** a person who promotes or publicizes a particular organization or cause: *a highly persuasive political propagandist.*
▶ **adj.** consisting of or spreading propaganda: *propagandist films.*
– DERIVATIVES **prop·a·gan·dism** /-,dizəm/ **n.**, **prop·a·gan·dis·tic** /-,ganˈdistik/ **adj.**, **prop·a·gan·dis·ti·cal·ly** /-,ganˈdistik(ə)lē/ **adv.**

prop·a·gan·dize /,präpəˈgan,dīz/ ▶ **v.** [no obj.] chiefly derogatory promote or publicize a particular cause, organization, or view, esp. in a biased or misleading way: *abolitionist leaders had not specifically* ***propagandized for*** *emancipation.* ■ [with obj.] attempt to influence (someone) in such a way: *people who have to be emotionalized and propagandized by logical arguments.*

prop·a·gate /ˈpräpə,gāt/ ▶ **v.** [with obj.] **1** breed specimens of (a plant, animal, etc.) by natural processes from the parent stock: *try propagating your own houseplants from cuttings.* ■ [no obj.] (of a plant, animal, etc.) reproduce in such a way: *the plant propagates freely from stem cuttings.*
2 spread and promote (an idea, theory, etc.) widely: *the French propagated the idea that the English were violent and gluttonous drunkards.*
3 (with reference to motion, light, sound, etc.) transmit or be transmitted in a particular direction or through a medium: [with obj.] *electromagnetic effects can be propagated at a finite velocity only through material substances* | [no obj.] *a hydraulic fracture is generally expected to propagate in a vertical plane.*
– DERIVATIVES **prop·a·ga·tion** /,präpəˈgāsʜən/ **n.**, **prop·a·ga·tive** /-,gātiv/ **adj.**, **prop·a·ga·tor** /-,gātər/ **n.**
– ORIGIN late Middle English: from Latin *propagat-* 'multiplied from layers or shoots,' from the verb *propagare*; related to *propago* 'young shoot' (from a base meaning 'fix').

prop·a·gule /ˈpräpə,gyo͞ol/ ▶ **n.** Botany a vegetative structure that can become detached from a plant and give rise to a new plant, e.g., a bud, sucker, or spore.
– ORIGIN mid 19th cent.: from modern Latin *propagulum* 'small shoot,' diminutive of *propago* 'shoot, runner.'

pro·pane /ˈprō,pān/ ▶ **n.** Chemistry a flammable hydrocarbon gas of the alkane series, present in natural gas and used as bottled fuel. ● Chem. formula: C_3H_8.
– ORIGIN mid 19th cent.: from **PROPIONIC ACID** + **-ANE**[2].

pro·pa·nol /ˈprōpə,nôl, -,näl/ ▶ **n.** Chemistry each of two isomeric liquid alcohols used as solvents; propyl alcohol. ● Chem. formula: C_3H_7OH.
– ORIGIN late 19th cent.: from **PROPANE** + **-OL**.

pro·pel /prəˈpel/ ▶ **v.** (**propels, propelling, propelled**) [with obj.] drive, push, or cause to move in a particular direction, typically forward: *the boat is propelled by using a very long paddle* | [as adj. in combination] (**-propelled**) *a rocket-propelled grenade launcher.* ■ spur or drive into a particular situation: *fear propelled her out of her stillness.*
– ORIGIN late Middle English (in the sense 'expel, drive out'): from Latin *propellere*, from *pro-* 'forward' + *pellere* 'to drive.'

pro·pel·lant /prəˈpelənt/ ▶ **n.** a thing or substance that causes something to move or be driven forward or outward, in particular: ■ an inert fluid, liquefied under pressure, in which the active contents of an aerosol are dispersed. ■ an explosive that fires bullets from a firearm. ■ a substance used as a reagent in a rocket engine to provide thrust.
▶ **adj.** capable of propelling something: *propellant gases.*
– ORIGIN mid 17th cent.: originally from Latin *propellent-* 'driving ahead (of oneself),' from the verb *propellere*, later from **PROPEL**.

pro·pel·ler /prəˈpelər/ ▶ **n.** a mechanical device for propelling a boat or aircraft, consisting of a revolving shaft with two or more broad, angled blades attached to it.

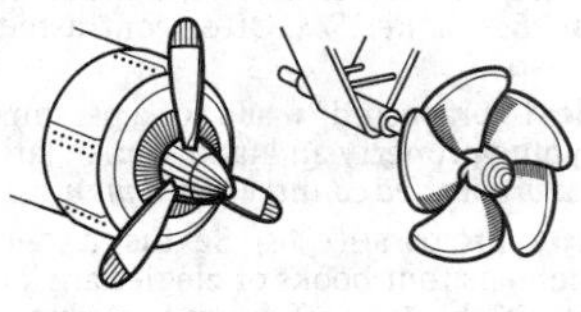

propellers

pro·pel·ler-head (also **propeller head** or **propellerhead**) ▶ **n.** informal a person who has an obsessive interest in computers or technology.
– ORIGIN 1980s: probably with reference to a beanie hat with a propeller on top, popularized by science-fiction enthusiasts.

pro·pel·ler shaft ▶ **n.** a shaft transmitting power from an engine to a propeller or to the wheels of a motor vehicle; drive shaft.

pro·pene /ˈprō,pēn/ ▶ **n.** Chemistry another term for **PROPYLENE**.
– ORIGIN mid 19th cent.: blend of **PROPANE** and **ALKENE**.

pro·pen·si·ty /prəˈpensətē/ ▶ **n.** (pl. **propensities**) an inclination or natural tendency to behave in a particular way: *a* ***propensity for*** *violence* | [with infinitive] *their innate propensity to attack one another.*

P

– ORIGIN late 16th cent.: from archaic *propense* (from Latin *propensus* 'inclined,' past participle of *propendere*, from *pro-* 'forward, down' + *pendere* 'hang') + -ITY.

prop·er /'präpər/ ▶ **adj.** **1** [attrib.] truly what something is said or regarded to be; genuine: *she's never had a proper job | a proper meal.* ■ [postpositive] strictly so called; in its true form: *some of the dos and don'ts in espionage proper.* ■ informal, chiefly Brit. used as an intensifier, often in derogatory contexts: *she looked like a proper harlot.*
2 [attrib.] of the required type; suitable or appropriate: *an artist needs the proper tools | they had not followed the proper procedures.* ■ according to or respecting recognized social standards or conventions; respectable, esp. excessively so: *her parents' view of what was* **proper for** *a well-bred girl | a very prim and proper Swiss lady.*
3 [predic.] (**proper to**) belonging or relating exclusively or distinctively to; particular to: *the two elephant types proper to Africa and to southern Asia.* ■ (of a psalm, lesson, prayer, etc.) appointed for a particular day, occasion, or season. ■ archaic belonging to oneself or itself; own: *to judge with my proper eyes.*
4 [usu. postpositive] Heraldry in the natural colors.
5 archaic (of a person) good-looking: *he is a proper youth!*
6 Mathematics denoting a subset or subgroup that does not constitute the entire set or group, esp. one that has more than one element.
▶ **adv.** Brit. informal dialect satisfactorily or correctly: *my eyes were all blurry and I couldn't see proper.* ■ thoroughly: *I had been fooled* **good and proper**.
▶ **n.** the part of a church service that varies with the season or festival.
– DERIVATIVES **prop·er·ness** n.
– ORIGIN Middle English: from Old French *propre*, from Latin *proprius* 'one's own, special.'

prop·er ad·jec·tive ▶ **n.** an adjective, typically capitalized, derived from a proper noun.

prop·er·din /prō'pərdn/ ▶ **n.** Biochemistry a protein present in the blood, involved in the body's response to certain kinds of infection.
– ORIGIN 1950s: from PRO-[2] 'before' + Latin *perdere* 'destroy' + -IN[1].

prop·er frac·tion ▶ **n.** a fraction that is less than one, with the numerator less than the denominator.

prop·er·ly /'präpərlē/ ▶ **adv.** **1** correctly or satisfactorily: *ensuring the work is carried out properly | a properly drafted agreement.* ■ appropriately for the circumstances; suitably; respectably: *I'm trying to get my mother to behave properly.* ■ [sentence adverb] in the strict sense; exactly: *algebra is,* **properly speaking**, *the analysis of equations.*
2 [usu. as submodifier] informal, chiefly Brit. thoroughly; completely: *this is the first day she has felt properly well.*

prop·er mo·tion ▶ **n.** Astronomy the part of the apparent motion of a fixed star that is due to its actual movement in space relative to the sun.

prop·er noun (also **proper name**) ▶ **n.** a name used for an individual person, place, or organization, spelled with initial capital letters, e.g., *Larry*, *Mexico*, and *Boston Red Sox*. Often contrasted with COMMON NOUN.

prop·er·tied /'präpərtēd/ ▶ **adj.** (of a person or group) owning property and land, esp. in large amounts: *a propertied country gentleman.*

Pro·per·tius /prō'pərsн(ē)əs/, Sextus (*c.*50–*c.*16 BC), Roman poet. His four books of elegies are largely concerned with his love affair with a woman whom he called Cynthia.

prop·er·ty /'präpərtē/ ▶ **n.** (pl. **properties**) **1** a thing or things belonging to someone; possessions collectively: *she wanted Oliver and his property out of her house | the stolen property was not recovered.* ■ a building or buildings and the land belonging to it or them: *he's expanding now, buying property | the renovation of commercial properties.* ■ Law the right to the possession, use, or disposal of something; ownership: *rights of property.* ■ old-fashioned term for PROP[2].
2 an attribute, quality, or characteristic of something: *the property of heat to expand metal at uniform rates.*
– ORIGIN Middle English: from an Anglo-Norman French variant of Old French *propriete*, from Latin *proprietas*, from *proprius* 'one's own, particular' (see PROPER).

prop·er·ty man ▶ **n.** dated a man in charge of theatrical props.

prop·er·ty mis·tress ▶ **n.** dated a woman in charge of theatrical props.

prop·er·ty qual·i·fi·ca·tion ▶ **n.** chiefly historical a qualification for office or for the exercise of a right, esp. the right to vote, based on the ownership of property.

pro·phage /'prō,fāj/ ▶ **n.** Microbiology the genetic material of a bacteriophage, incorporated into the genome of a bacterium and able to produce phages if specifically activated.
– ORIGIN 1950s: from PRO-[2] 'before' + PHAGE.

pro·phase /'prō,fāz/ ▶ **n.** Biology the first stage of cell division, before metaphase, during which the chromosomes become visible as paired chromatids and the nuclear envelope disappears. The first prophase of meiosis includes the reduction division.
– ORIGIN late 19th cent.: from PRO-[2] 'before' + PHASE.

proph·e·cy /'präfəsē/ ▶ **n.** (pl. **prophecies**) a prediction: *a bleak prophecy of war and ruin.* ■ the faculty, function, or practice of prophesying: *the gift of prophecy.*
– ORIGIN Middle English: from Old French *profecie*, via late Latin from Greek *prophēteia*, from *prophētēs* (see PROPHET).

> **USAGE** To avoid a common usage mistake, note the spelling and pronunciation differences between **prophecy** (the noun) and **prophesy** (the verb).

proph·e·sy /'präfə,sī/ ▶ **v.** (**prophesies, prophesying, prophesied**) [with obj.] say that (a specified thing) will happen in the future: *Jacques was prophesying a bumper harvest |* [with clause] *the papers prophesied that he would resign after the weekend.*
– DERIVATIVES **proph·e·si·er** /-,sīər/ n.
– ORIGIN Middle English: from Old French *profecier*, from *profecie* (see PROPHECY). The differentiation of the spellings *prophesy* and *prophecy* as verb and noun was not established until after 1700.

> **USAGE** See usage at PROPHECY.

proph·et /'präfit/ ▶ **n.** **1** a person regarded as an inspired teacher or proclaimer of the will of God: *the Old Testament prophet Jeremiah.* ■ (**the Prophet**) (among Muslims) Muhammad. ■ (**the Prophet**) (among Mormons) Joseph Smith or one of his successors. ■ a person who advocates or speaks in a visionary way about a new belief, cause, or theory: *a prophet of radical individualism.* ■ a person who makes or claims to be able to make predictions: *the anti-technology* **prophets of doom**.
2 (**the Prophets**) (in Christian use) the books of Isaiah, Jeremiah, Ezekiel, Daniel, and the twelve minor prophets. ■ (in Jewish use) one of the three canonical divisions of the Hebrew Bible, distinguished from the Law and the Hagiographa, and comprising the books of Joshua, Judges, Samuel, Kings, Jeremiah, Ezekiel, Isaiah, and the twelve minor prophets.
– PHRASES **a prophet is not without honor, but** (or **save**) **in his own country** proverb a person's gifts and talents are rarely appreciated by those close to him. [with biblical allusion to Matt. 13:57.]
– DERIVATIVES **proph·et·hood** /-,ho͝od/ n.
– ORIGIN Middle English: from Old French *prophete*, via Latin from Greek *prophētēs* 'spokesman,' from *pro* 'before' + *phētēs* 'speaker' (from *phēnai* 'speak').

proph·et·ess /'präfətəs/ ▶ **n.** a female prophet.

pro·phet·ic /prə'fetik/ ▶ **adj.** **1** accurately describing or predicting what will happen in the future: *his warnings proved prophetic.*
2 of, relating to, or characteristic of a prophet or prophecy: *the prophetic books of the Old Testament.*
– DERIVATIVES **pro·phet·i·cal** adj., **pro·phet·i·cal·ly** /-ik(ə)lē/ adv.
– ORIGIN late 15th cent.: from French *prophétique* or late Latin *propheticus*, from Greek *prophētikos* 'predicting' (see PROPHET).

pro·phy·lac·tic /,prōfə'laktik/ ▶ **adj.** intended to prevent disease: *prophylactic measures.*
▶ **n.** a medicine or course of action used to prevent disease: *I took malaria prophylactics.* ■ a condom.
– DERIVATIVES **pro·phy·lac·ti·cal·ly** /-ik(ə)lē/ adv.
– ORIGIN late 16th cent.: from French *prophylactique*, from Greek *prophulaktikos*, from *pro* 'before' + *phulassein* 'to guard.'

pro·phy·lax·is /,prōfə'laksəs/ ▶ **n.** action taken to prevent disease, esp. by specified means or against a specified disease: *the treatment and prophylaxis of angina pectoris.*
– ORIGIN mid 19th cent.: modern Latin, from PRO-[2] 'before' + Greek *phulaxis* 'act of guarding.'

pro·pin·qui·ty /prə'piNGkwətē/ ▶ **n.** **1** the state of being close to someone or something; proximity: *he kept his distance as though afraid propinquity might lead him into temptation.*
2 technical close kinship.
– ORIGIN late Middle English: from Old French *propinquité*, from Latin *propinquitas*, from *propinquus* 'near,' from *prope* 'near to.'

pro·pi·on·i·bac·te·ri·um /,prōpē,änə,bak'ti(ə)rēəm/ ▶ **n.** (pl. **propionibacteria** /-'ti(ə)rēə/) a bacterium that metabolizes carbohydrate, some kinds being involved in the fermentation of dairy products and the etiology of acne. ● Genus *Propionibacterium*; Gram-positive rods.
– ORIGIN modern Latin, from *propionic* (see PROPIONIC ACID) + BACTERIUM.

pro·pi·on·ic ac·id /,prōpē'änik/ ▶ **n.** Chemistry a colorless pungent liquid organic acid produced in some forms of fermentation and used for inhibiting the growth of mold in bread. ● Alternative name: **propanoic acid**; chem. formula: C_2H_5COOH.
– DERIVATIVES **pro·pi·o·nate** /'prōpēə,nāt/ n.
– ORIGIN mid 19th cent.: *propionic* from French *propionique*, from Greek *pro* 'before' + *piōn* 'fat,' it being the first or lowest molecular-weight member of the fatty acid series to form fats.

pro·pi·ti·ate /prə'pisHē,āt/ ▶ **v.** [with obj.] win or regain the favor of (a god, spirit, or person) by doing something that pleases them: *the pagans thought it was important to propitiate the gods with sacrifices.*
– DERIVATIVES **pro·pi·ti·a·tor** /-,ātər/ n., **pro·pi·ti·a·to·ry** /-'pisHēə,tôrē/ adj.
– ORIGIN late 16th cent.: from Latin *propitiat-* 'made favorable,' from the verb *propitiare*, from *propitius* 'favorable, gracious' (see PROPITIOUS).

pro·pi·ti·a·tion /prə,pisHē'āsHən/ ▶ **n.** the action of propitiating or appeasing a god, spirit, or person: *he lifted his hands in propitiation.*
– ORIGIN late Middle English: from late Latin *propitiatio(n-)*, from the verb *propitiare* (see PROPITIATE).

pro·pi·tious /prə'pisHəs/ ▶ **adj.** giving or indicating a good chance of success; favorable: *the timing for such a meeting seemed propitious.* ■ archaic favorably disposed toward someone: *there were points on which they did not agree, moments in which she did not seem propitious.*
– DERIVATIVES **pro·pi·tious·ly** adv., **pro·pi·tious·ness** n.
– ORIGIN late Middle English: from Old French *propicieus* or Latin *propitius* 'favorable, gracious.'

prop jet ▶ **n.** a turboprop aircraft or engine.

prop·o·lis /'präpələs/ ▶ **n.** a red or brown resinous substance collected by honeybees from tree buds, used by them to fill crevices and to seal and varnish honeycombs.
– ORIGIN early 17th cent.: via Latin from Greek *propolis* 'suburb,' also 'bee glue,' from *pro* 'before' + *polis* 'city.'

pro·po·nent /prə'pōnənt/ ▶ **n.** a person who advocates a theory, proposal, or project: *a collection of essays by both critics and proponents of graphology.*
– ORIGIN late 16th cent.: from Latin *proponent-* 'putting forth,' from the verb *proponere* (see PROPOUND).

Pro·pon·tis /prə'päntəs/ ancient name for the Sea of Marmara (see MARMARA, SEA OF).
– ORIGIN from Latin, from Greek *pro-* 'before' + *Pontos* 'Black Sea.'

pro·por·tion /prə'pôrsHən/ ▶ **n.** a part, share, or number considered in comparative relation to a whole: *the proportion of greenhouse gases in the atmosphere is rising.* ■ the relationship of one thing to another in terms of quantity, size, or number; the ratio: *the* **proportion of** *exams to schoolwork | the bleach can be diluted with water in the proportion one part bleach to ten parts water.* ■ (**proportions**) the comparative measurements or size of different parts of a whole: *the view of what constitutes perfect bodily proportions changes from one generation to the next.* ■ (**proportions**) dimensions; size: *the room, despite its ample proportions, seemed too small for him.* ■ the correct, attractive, or ideal relationship in size or shape between one thing and another or between the parts of a whole: *perceptions of color, form, harmony, and proportion.*
▶ **v.** [with obj.] formal adjust or regulate (something) so that it has a particular or suitable relationship to something else: *a life after death in which happiness can be* **proportioned to** *virtue.*
– PHRASES **in proportion** according to a particular relationship in size, amount, or degree: *each region was represented* **in proportion to** *its population.* ■ in comparison with; in relation to: *the cuckoo's eggs are unusually small* **in proportion to** *its size.* ■ in the correct or appropriate relation to the size, shape, or position of other things: *her figure was completely in proportion.* ■ correctly or realistically regarded in terms of relative importance or seriousness: *the problem has to be* **kept in proportion**. **out of proportion** in the wrong relation to the size, shape, or position of other things: *the sculpture seemed* **out of proportion to** *its surroundings.* ■ greater or more serious than is necessary or appropriate: *the award was* **out of all proportion to** *the alleged libel.* ■ wrongly or unrealistically regarded in terms of relative importance or seriousness. **sense**

of proportion the ability to judge the relative importance or seriousness of things.
– DERIVATIVES **pro·por·tion·less** adj.
– ORIGIN late Middle English: from Old French, from Latin *proportio(n-)*, from *pro portione* 'with respect to (its or a person's) share.'

pro·por·tion·a·ble /prəˈpôrSHənəbəl/ ▶ adj. archaic term for PROPORTIONAL.
– DERIVATIVES **pro·por·tion·a·bly** /-blē/ adv.

pro·por·tion·al /prəˈpôrSHənl/ ▶ adj. corresponding in size or amount to something else: *the punishment should be proportional to the crime.* ■ Mathematics (of a variable quantity) having a constant ratio to another quantity.
– DERIVATIVES **pro·por·tion·al·i·ty** /prəˌpôrSHəˈnalətē, pərˌpôrSHəˈnalədē/ n., **pro·por·tion·al·ly** /-SHənl-ē/ adv.
– ORIGIN late Middle English: from late Latin *proportionalis*, from *proportio(n-)* (see PROPORTION).

> **USAGE** Except in certain long-established phrases, such as *proportional representation*, the adjectives **proportional** and **proportionate** may be used interchangeably.

pro·por·tion·al count·er ▶ n. Physics an ionization chamber in which the operating voltage is large enough to produce amplification but not so large that the output pulse ceases to be proportional to the initial ionization.

pro·por·tion·al rep·re·sen·ta·tion (abbr.: **PR**) ▶ n. an electoral system in which parties gain seats in proportion to the number of votes cast for them.

pro·por·tion·ate /prəˈpôrSHənət/ ▶ adj. another term for PROPORTIONAL.
– DERIVATIVES **pro·por·tion·ate·ly** adv.

> **USAGE** See usage at PROPORTIONAL.

pro·por·tioned /prəˈpôrSHənd/ ▶ adj. [with submodifier] having dimensions or a comparative relationship of parts of a specified type: *she was tall and perfectly proportioned.*

pro·pos·al /prəˈpōzəl/ ▶ n. **1** a plan or suggestion, esp. a formal or written one, put forward for consideration or discussion by others: *a set of proposals for a major new high-speed rail link.* ■ the action of putting forward such a plan or suggestion: *the proposal of flexible work hours.*
2 an offer of marriage.

pro·pose /prəˈpōz/ ▶ v. **1** [with obj.] put forward (an idea or plan) for consideration or discussion by others: *he proposed a new nine-point peace plan* | [with infinitive] *we propose to be away for six months* | [with clause] *I proposed that the government should retain a 51 percent stake in the company.* ■ nominate (someone) for an elected office or as a member of a society: *Thomson was proposed as chairman.* ■ put forward (a motion) to a legislature or committee: *the government put its slim majority to the test by proposing a vote of confidence.*
2 [no obj.] make an offer of marriage to someone: *I have already proposed to Sarah.*
– PHRASES **propose marriage** make an offer of marriage to someone. **propose a toast** ask a group of people at a social occasion to drink to the health and happiness of a specified person: *I hereby propose a toast to the bride and groom.*
– DERIVATIVES **pro·pos·er** n.
– ORIGIN Middle English: from Old French *proposer*, from Latin *proponere* (see PROPONENT), but influenced by Latin *propositus* 'put or set forth' and Old French *poser* 'to place.'

prop·o·si·tion /ˌpräpəˈziSHən/ ▶ n. **1** a statement or assertion that expresses a judgment or opinion: *the proposition that all men are created equal.* ■ Logic a statement that expresses a concept that can be true or false. ■ Mathematics a formal statement of a theorem or problem, typically including the demonstration.
2 a suggested scheme or plan of action, esp. in a business context: *a detailed investment proposition.* ■ (in the US) a constitutional proposal; a bill. ■ informal an offer of sexual intercourse made to a person with whom one is not sexually involved, esp. one that is made in an unsubtle or offensive way.
3 [with adj.] a project, task, or idea considered in terms of its likely success or difficulty, esp. in a commercial context: *a paper that has lost half its readers is unlikely to be an attractive proposition.* ■ a person considered in terms of the likely success or difficulty of one's dealings with them: *as a potential manager, Sandy is a better proposition than Dave.*
▶ v. [with obj.] informal make a suggestion of sexual intercourse to (someone with whom one is not sexually involved), esp. in an unsubtle or offensive way: *she had been propositioned at the party by an accountant.* ■ make an offer or suggestion to (someone): *I was propositioned by the editor about becoming film critic of the paper.*
– DERIVATIVES **prop·o·si·tion·al** /-SHənl/ adj. (chiefly Logic).
– ORIGIN Middle English: from Old French, from Latin *propositio(n-)*, from the verb *proponere* (see PROPOUND). The verb dates from the 1920s.

prop·o·si·tion·al cal·cu·lus ▶ n. the branch of symbolic logic that deals with propositions and the relations between them, without examination of their content.

pro·pound /prəˈpound/ ▶ v. [with obj.] put forward (an idea, theory, or point of view) for consideration by others: *he began to propound the idea of a "social monarchy" as an alternative to Franco.*
– DERIVATIVES **pro·pound·er** n.
– ORIGIN mid 16th cent.: alteration of archaic *propone*, from Latin *proponere* 'set forth,' from *pro-* 'forward' + *ponere* 'put.' The addition of the final *-d* can be compared with that in *expound* and *compound.*

pro·pox·y·phene /prōˈpäksəˌfēn/ ▶ n. Medicine a synthetic compound chemically related to methadone, used as a mild narcotic analgesic.
– ORIGIN 1950s: from PROPYL + OXY-[2] + *-phene* (from PHENYL).

propr. ▶ abbr. proprietor.

pro·pran·o·lol /prōˈpranl,ôl, -ˌäl/ ▶ n. Medicine a synthetic compound that acts as a beta blocker and is used mainly in the treatment of cardiac arrhythmia. ● Chem. formula: $C_{16}H_{21}NO_2$.
– ORIGIN 1960s: from *pro(pyl)* + *pr(op)anol*, with the reduplication of *-ol.*

pro·pri·e·tar·y /p(r)əˈprīˌterē/ ▶ adj. of or relating to an owner or ownership: *the company has a proprietary right to the property.* ■ (of a product) marketed under and protected by a registered trade name: *proprietary brands of insecticide.* ■ behaving as if one were the owner of someone or something: *he looked about him with a proprietary air.*
▶ n. an owner; proprietor. ■ historical esp. in North America, a grantee or owner of a colony who has been granted, as an individual or as part of a group, the full rights of self-government.
– ORIGIN late Middle English (as a noun denoting a member of a religious order who held property): from late Latin *proprietarius* 'proprietor,' from *proprietas* (see PROPERTY).

pro·pri·e·tar·y name ▶ n. a name of a product or service registered by its owner as a trademark and not usable by others without permission.

pro·pri·e·tor /p(r)əˈprīətər/ ▶ n. the owner of a business, or a holder of property.
– DERIVATIVES **pro·pri·e·to·ri·al** /p(r)əˌprīəˈtôrēəl/ adj., **pro·pri·e·to·ri·al·ly** /p(r)əˌprīəˈtôrēəlē/ adv., **pro·pri·e·tor·ship** /-ˌSHip/ n.

pro·pri·e·tress /p(r)əˈprīətrəs/ ▶ n. a female proprietor.

pro·pri·e·ty /p(r)əˈprīətē/ ▶ n. (pl. **proprieties**) the state or quality of conforming to conventionally accepted standards of behavior or morals: *he always behaved with the utmost propriety.* ■ (**proprieties**) the details or rules of behavior conventionally considered to be correct: *she's a great one for the proprieties.* ■ the condition of being right, appropriate, or fitting: *they questioned the propriety of certain investments made by the council.*
– ORIGIN late Middle English (in the sense 'peculiarity, essential quality'): from Old French *propriete*, from Latin *proprietas* (see PROPERTY).

pro·pri·o·cep·tive /ˌprōprēəˈseptiv/ ▶ adj. Physiology relating to stimuli that are produced and perceived within an organism, esp. those connected with the position and movement of the body. Compare with EXTEROCEPTIVE and INTEROCEPTIVE.
– DERIVATIVES **pro·pri·o·cep·tion** /-ˈsepSHən/ n., **pro·pri·o·cep·tive·ly** adv.
– ORIGIN early 20th cent.: from Latin *proprius* 'own' + RECEPTIVE.

pro·pri·o·cep·tor /ˌprōprēəˈseptər/ ▶ n. Physiology a sensory receptor that receives stimuli from within the body, esp. one that responds to position and movement.
– ORIGIN early 20th cent.: from Latin *proprius* 'own' + RECEPTOR.

props /präps/ ▶ plural n. informal respect or credit due to a person: *Erika gets props for the great work she did on the music.*

prop·to·sis /präpˈtōsəs/ ▶ n. Medicine abnormal protrusion or displacement of an eye or other body part.
– ORIGIN late 17th cent.: via late Latin from Greek *proptōsis*, from *pro* 'before' + *piptein* 'to fall.'

pro·pul·sion /prəˈpəlSHən/ ▶ n. the action of driving or pushing forward: *they dive and use their wings for propulsion under water.*
– DERIVATIVES **pro·pul·sive** /-siv/ adj.
– ORIGIN early 17th cent. (in the sense 'expulsion'): from medieval Latin *propulsio(n-)*, from Latin *propellere* 'drive before (oneself).'

prop wash ▶ n. a current of water or air created by the action of a propeller or rotor.

pro·pyl /ˈprōpəl/ ▶ n. [as modifier] Chemistry of or denoting the alkyl radical $-C_3H_7$, derived notionally from propane. Compare with ISOPROPYL.

prop·y·la /ˈpräpələ/ plural form of PROPYLON.

prop·y·lae·um /ˌpräpəˈlēəm, ˌprō-/ ▶ n. (pl. **propylaea** /-ˈlēə/) the structure forming the entrance to a temple. ■ (**the Propylaeum**) the entrance to the Acropolis at Athens.
– ORIGIN via Latin from Greek *propulaion*, neuter (used as a noun) of *propulaios* 'before the gate,' from *pro* 'before' + *pulē* 'gate.'

pro·pyl·ene /ˈprōpəˌlēn/ ▶ n. Chemistry a gaseous hydrocarbon of the alkene series, made by cracking alkanes. ● Alternative name: **propene**; chem. formula: C_3H_6.

pro·pyl·ene gly·col ▶ n. Chemistry a liquid alcohol that is used as a solvent, in antifreeze, and in the food, plastics, and perfume industries. ● Chem. formula: $C_3H_6(OH)_2$: two isomers.

prop·y·lon /ˈpräpəˌlän/ ▶ n. (pl. **propylons** or **propyla** /-lə/) another term for PROPYLAEUM.
– ORIGIN mid 19th cent.: via Latin from Greek *propulon*, from *pro* 'before' + *pulē* 'gate.'

pro ra·ta /prō ˈrātə, ˈrätə, ˈratə/ ▶ adj. proportional: *as the dollar has fallen, costs have risen on a pro rata basis* | *pro-rata ownership.*
▶ adv. proportionally: *their fees will rise pro rata with salaries.*
– ORIGIN late 16th cent.: Latin, literally 'according to the rate.'

pro·rate /prōˈrāt, ˈprōˌrāt/ ▶ v. [with obj.] (usu. **be prorated**) allocate, distribute, or assess pro rata: *bonuses are prorated over the life of a player's contract.*
– DERIVATIVES **pro·ra·tion** /prōˈrāSHən/ n.

pro·rogue /p(r)əˈrōg/ ▶ v. (**prorogues, proroguing, prorogued**) [with obj.] discontinue a session of (a parliament or other legislative assembly) without dissolving it: *James prorogued Parliament in 1685 and ruled without it.* ■ [no obj.] (of such an assembly) be discontinued in this way: *the House was all set to prorogue.*
– DERIVATIVES **pro·ro·ga·tion** /ˌprōrəˈgāSHən/ n.
– ORIGIN late Middle English: from Old French *proroger*, from Latin *prorogare* 'prolong, extend,' from *pro-* 'in front of, publicly' + *rogare* 'ask.'

pros. ▶ abbr. ■ proscenium. ■ prosody.

pro·sa·ic /prōˈzāik/ ▶ adj. having the style or diction of prose; lacking poetic beauty: *prosaic language can't convey the experience.* ■ commonplace; unromantic: *the masses were too preoccupied by prosaic day-to-day concerns.*
– DERIVATIVES **pro·sa·i·cal·ly** /-ik(ə)lē/ adv., **pro·sa·ic·ness** n.
– ORIGIN late 16th cent. (as a noun denoting a prose writer): from late Latin *prosaicus*, from Latin *prosa* 'straightforward (discourse)' (see PROSE). Current senses of the adjective date from the mid 18th cent.

Pros. Atty. ▶ abbr. prosecuting attorney.

pro·sau·ro·pod /prōˈsôrəˌpäd/ ▶ n. an elongated, partly bipedal herbivorous dinosaur of the late Triassic and early Jurassic periods, related to the ancestors of sauropods. ● Infraorder Prosauropoda, suborder Sauropodomorpha, order Saurischia.
– ORIGIN 1950s: from PRO-[2] 'before in time' + SAUROPOD.

pro·sce·ni·um /prəˈsēnēəm, prō-/ ▶ n. (pl. **prosceniums** or **proscenia** /-nēə/) the part of a theater stage in front of the curtain. ■ short for PROSCENIUM ARCH. ■ the stage of an ancient theater.
– ORIGIN early 17th cent.: via Latin from Greek *proskēnion*, from *pro* 'before' + *skēnē* 'stage.'

pro·sce·ni·um arch ▶ n. an arch framing the opening between the stage and the auditorium in some theaters.

pro·sciut·to /prəˈSHōōtō/ ▶ n. Italian ham cured by drying and typically served in very thin slices.
– ORIGIN Italian.

pro·scribe /prōˈskrīb/ ▶ v. [with obj.] forbid, esp. by law: *strikes remained proscribed in the armed forces.* ■ denounce or condemn: *certain practices that the Catholic Church proscribed, such as polygyny.* ■ historical outlaw (someone).
– DERIVATIVES **pro·scrip·tive** /-ˈskriptiv/ adj.

PRONUNCIATION KEY ə *ago, up*; ər *over, fur*; a *hat*; ā *ate*; ä *car*; e *let*; ē *see*; i *fit*; ī *by*; NG *sing*; ō *go*; ô *law, for*; oi *toy*; o͝o *good*; o͞o *goo*; ou *out*; TH *thin*; T͟H *then*; ZH *vision*

–ORIGIN late Middle English (in the sense 'to outlaw'): from Latin *proscribere*, from *pro-* 'in front of' + *scribere* 'write.'

USAGE **Proscribe** does not have the same meaning as **prescribe**: see usage at **PRESCRIBE**.

pro·scrip·tion /prō'skripsHən/ ▶ **n.** the action of forbidding something; banning: *the proscription of the party after the 1715 Rebellion.* ■ condemnation or denunciation of something.

prose /prōz/ ▶ **n. 1** written or spoken language in its ordinary form, without metrical structure: *a short story in prose* | [as modifier] *a prose passage.* ■ plain or dull writing, discourse, or expression: *medical and scientific prose.*
2 another term for **SEQUENCE** (sense 4 of the noun).
▶ **v. 1** [no obj.] talk tediously: *prosing on about female beauty.*
2 [with obj.] dated compose or convert into prose.
–DERIVATIVES **pros·er n.**
–ORIGIN Middle English: via Old French from Latin *prosa* (*oratio*) 'straightforward (discourse),' feminine of *prosus*, earlier *prorsus* 'direct.'

Pro·sec·co /prō'sekō/ ▶ **n.** a sparkling white wine from the Veneto region of NE Italy.
–ORIGIN Italian, probably from *Prosecco*, a town near Trieste.

pro·sec·tor /prō'sektər/ ▶ **n.** a person who dissects corpses for examination or anatomical demonstration.
–ORIGIN mid 19th cent.: from late Latin, literally 'anatomist,' based on Latin *secare* 'to cut,' perhaps via French *prosecteur*.

pros·e·cute /'präsi,kyo͞ot/ ▶ **v.** [with obj.] **1** institute legal proceedings against (a person or organization): *they were prosecuted for obstructing the highway.* ■ institute legal proceedings in respect of (a claim or offense): *the state's attorney's office seemed to decide that this was a case worth prosecuting* | [no obj.] *the company didn't prosecute because of his age.* ■ [no obj.] (of a lawyer) conduct the case against the party being accused or sued in a lawsuit: *Mr. Ryan will be prosecuting this morning.*
2 continue with (a course of action) with a view to its completion: *a serious threat to the government's ability to prosecute the war.* ■ archaic carry on (a trade or pursuit): *waiting for permission to prosecute my craft.*
–DERIVATIVES **pros·e·cut·a·ble adj.**
–ORIGIN late Middle English (sense 2): from Latin *prosecut-* 'pursued, accompanied,' from the verb *prosequi*, from *pro-* 'onward' + *sequi* 'follow.'

pros·e·cu·tion /,präsi'kyo͞osHən/ ▶ **n. 1** the institution and conducting of legal proceedings against someone in respect of a criminal charge: *Olesky faces prosecution on charges he spied for Russian intelligence* | *they lacked the funds to embark on private prosecutions.* ■ (**the prosecution**) [treated as sing. or pl.] the party instituting or conducting legal proceedings against someone in a lawsuit: *the main witness for the prosecution.*
2 the continuation of a course of action with a view to its completion: *the network's prosecution of its commercial ends.*
–ORIGIN mid 16th cent. (sense 2): from Old French, or from late Latin *prosecutio(n-)*, from *prosequi* 'pursue, accompany' (see **PROSECUTE**).

pros·e·cu·tor /'präsi,kyo͞otər/ ▶ **n.** a person, esp. a public official, who institutes legal proceedings against someone. ■ a lawyer who conducts the case against a defendant in a criminal court. Also called **prosecuting attorney**.
–DERIVATIVES **pros·e·cu·to·ri·al** /,präsikyə'tôrēəl/ **adj.**

pros·e·lyte /'präsə,līt/ ▶ **n.** a person who has converted from one opinion, religion, or party to another, esp. recently. ■ a Gentile who has converted to Judaism.
▶ **v.** another term for **PROSELYTIZE**.
–DERIVATIVES **pros·e·lyt·ism** /-lə,tizəm/ **n.**
–ORIGIN late Middle English: via late Latin from Greek *prosēluthos* 'stranger, convert,' from *prosēluth-*, past stem of *proserkhesthai* 'approach.'

pros·e·lyt·ize /'präsələ,tīz/ ▶ **v.** [with obj.] convert or attempt to convert (someone) from one religion, belief, or opinion to another: *the program did have a tremendous evangelical effect, proselytizing many* | [no obj.] *proselytizing for converts* | (as noun **proselytizing**) *no amount of proselytizing was going to change their minds.* ■ advocate or promote (a belief or course of action): *Davis wanted to share his concept and proselytize his ideas.*
–DERIVATIVES **pros·e·lyt·iz·er n.**

pro·sem·i·nar /prō'semə,när/ ▶ **n.** a seminar that accepts graduate and advanced undergraduate students alike.

pros·en·ceph·a·lon /,präs,en'sefə,län, -lən/ ▶ **n.** another term for **FOREBRAIN**.
–ORIGIN mid 19th cent.: from Greek *prosō* 'forward' + *enkephalos* 'brain.'

pros·en·chy·ma /präs'eNGkəmə/ ▶ **n.** Biology a plant tissue consisting of elongated cells with interpenetrating tapering ends, occurring esp. in vascular tissue.
–DERIVATIVES **pros·en·chym·a·tous** /,präsən'kimətəs/ **adj.**
–ORIGIN mid 19th cent.: from Greek *pros* 'toward' + *enkhuma* 'infusion,' on the pattern of *parenchyma*.

prose po·em ▶ **n.** a piece of writing in prose having obvious poetic qualities, including intensity, compactness, prominent rhythms, and imagery.
–DERIVATIVES **prose po·et·ry n.**

Pro·ser·pi·na /prə'sərpənə/ (also **Proserpine** /-pənē/) Roman Mythology Roman name for **PERSEPHONE**.

pro shop ▶ **n.** a retail outlet at a golf club, typically run by the resident professional, where golfing equipment is sold or repaired.

pro·sim·i·an /prō'simēən/ Zoology ▶ **n.** a primitive primate of a group that includes the lemurs, lorises, bushbabies, and tarsiers. ● Suborder Prosimii, order Primates: several families.
▶ **adj.** of or relating to the prosimians. Compare with **SIMIAN**.
–ORIGIN late 19th cent.: from **PRO-**[2] 'before' + **SIMIAN**.

pro·sit /'prōzət, -sət/ ▶ **exclam.** an expression used as a toast when drinking to a person's health.
–ORIGIN German, from Latin, literally 'may it benefit.'

Pros·o·bran·chi·a /,präsə'braNGkēə/ Zoology a group of mollusks that includes the limpets, abalones, and many terrestrial and aquatic snails. They all have a shell, and many have an operculum. ● Subclass Prosobranchia, class Gastropoda.
–DERIVATIVES **pros·o·branch** /'präsə,braNGk/ **n.**
–ORIGIN modern Latin (plural), from Greek *prosō* 'forward' + *brankhia* 'gills.'

pro·so·cial /prō'sōsHəl/ ▶ **adj.** Psychology relating to or denoting behavior that is positive, helpful, and intended to promote social acceptance and friendship.

pro·sod·ic a·nal·y·sis /prə'sädik, -'zädik/ ▶ **n.** Linguistics analysis of a language based on its patterns of stress and intonation in various contexts.

pros·o·dy /'präsədē/ ▶ **n.** the patterns of rhythm and sound used in poetry: *the translator is not obliged to reproduce the prosody of the original.* ■ the theory or study of these patterns, or the rules governing them. ■ the patterns of stress and intonation in a language: *the salience of prosody in child language acquisition* | *early English prosodies.*
–DERIVATIVES **pro·sod·ic** /prə'sädik, -zädik/ (or **prosodical** /prə'sädikəl, -'zäd-/) **adj.**, **pros·o·dist** /'präsədist, 'präz-/ **n.**
–ORIGIN late 15th cent.: from Latin *prosodia* 'accent of a syllable,' from Greek *prosōidia* 'song sung to music, tone of a syllable,' from *pros* 'toward' + *ōidē* 'song.'

pro·so·ma /prō'sōmə/ ▶ **n.** (pl. **prosomas** or **prosomata** /-mətə/) another term for **CEPHALOTHORAX**.
–ORIGIN late 19th cent.: from **PRO-**[2] 'before' + Greek *sōma* 'body.'

pros·o·pag·no·sia /,präsəpag'nōzH(ē)ə/ ▶ **n.** Psychiatry an inability to recognize the faces of familiar people, typically as a result of damage to the brain.
–DERIVATIVES **pros·o·pag·nos·ic** /-'nōzik, -'nōsik/ **n.**
–ORIGIN 1950s: modern Latin, from Greek *prosōpon* 'face' + *agnōsia* 'ignorance.'

pros·o·pog·ra·phy /,präsə'pägrəfē/ ▶ **n.** (pl. **prosopographies**) a description of a person's social and family connections, career, etc., or a collection of such descriptions. ■ the study of such descriptions, esp. in Roman history.
–DERIVATIVES **pros·o·pog·ra·pher** /-fər/ **n.**, **pros·o·po·graph·i·cal** /-pə'grafikəl/ **adj.**
–ORIGIN 1920s: from modern Latin *prosopographia*, from Greek *prosōpon* 'face, person' + *-graphia* 'writing.'

pro·so·po·poe·ia /prə,sōpə'pēə, ,präsə-/ ▶ **n. 1** a figure of speech in which an abstract thing is personified.
2 a figure of speech in which an imagined or absent person or thing is represented as speaking.
–ORIGIN mid 16th cent.: via Latin from Greek *prosōpopoiia*, from *prosōpon* 'person' + *poiein* 'to make.'

pros·pect /'präs,pekt/ ▶ **n. 1** the possibility or likelihood of some future event occurring: *there was no prospect of a reconciliation* | *training that offered a prospect of continuous employment.* ■ [in sing.] a mental picture of a future or anticipated event: *this presents a disturbing prospect of one-party government.* ■ (usu. **prospects**) chances or opportunities for success or wealth: *the poor prospects for the steel industry.*
2 a person regarded as likely to succeed or as a potential customer, client, etc.: *clients deemed likely prospects for active party membership* | *a great young pitching prospect.* ■ a place likely to yield mineral deposits. ■ a place being explored for mineral deposits.
3 an extensive view of landscape: *a viewpoint commanding a magnificent prospect of the estuary.*
▶ **v.** [no obj.] search for mineral deposits in a place, esp. by means of experimental drilling and excavation: *the company is also prospecting for gold.* ■ (**prospect for**) look out for; search for: *the responsibilities of salespeople to prospect for customers.*
–DERIVATIVES **pros·pec·tor n.**
–ORIGIN late Middle English (as a noun denoting the action of looking toward a distant object): from Latin *prospectus* 'view,' from *prospicere* 'look forward,' from *pro-* 'forward' + *specere* 'to look.' Early use, referring to a view of landscape, gave rise to the meaning 'mental picture' (mid 16th cent.), whence 'anticipated event.'

pro·spec·tive /prə'spektiv/ ▶ **adj.** [attrib.] (of a person) expected or expecting to be something particular in the future: *she showed a prospective buyer around the house.* ■ likely to happen at a future date; concerned with or applying to the future: *a meeting to discuss prospective changes in government legislation.*
–DERIVATIVES **pro·spec·tive·ly adv.**, **pro·spec·tive·ness n.**
–ORIGIN late 16th cent. (in the sense 'looking forward, having foresight'): from obsolete French *prospectif, -ive* or late Latin *prospectivus*, from Latin *prospectus* 'view' (see **PROSPECT**).

pro·spec·tus /prə'spektəs/ ▶ **n.** (pl. **prospectuses**) a printed document that advertises or describes a school, commercial enterprise, forthcoming book, etc., in order to attract or inform clients, members, buyers, or investors.
–ORIGIN mid 18th cent.: from Latin, literally 'view, prospect,' from the verb *prospicere*, from *pro-* 'forward' + *specere* 'to look.'

pros·per /'präspər/ ▶ **v.** [no obj.] succeed in material terms; be financially successful: *his business prospered* | *the nation plans to prosper from free trade with the US.* ■ flourish physically; grow strong and healthy: *areas where gray squirrels cannot prosper.* ■ [with obj.] archaic make successful: *God has wonderfully prospered this nation.*
–ORIGIN late Middle English: from Old French *prosperer*, from Latin *prosperare*, from *prosperus* 'doing well.'

pros·per·i·ty /prä'speritē/ ▶ **n.** the state of being prosperous: *a long period of prosperity.*
–ORIGIN Middle English: from Old French *prosperite*, from Latin *prosperitas*, from *prosperus* 'doing well.'

pros·per·ous /'präspərəs/ ▶ **adj.** successful in material terms; flourishing financially: *prosperous middle-class professionals.* ■ bringing wealth and success: *we wish you a prosperous New Year.*
–DERIVATIVES **pros·per·ous·ly adv.**, **pros·per·ous·ness n.**
–ORIGIN late Middle English: from Old French *prospereus*, from Latin *prosperus* 'doing well.'

Prost /prôst/, Alain (1955–), French race car driver. He won the Formula One world championship in 1985, 1986, 1989, and 1993.

pros·ta·cy·clin /,prästə'sīklin/ ▶ **n.** Biochemistry a compound of the prostaglandin type that is produced in arterial walls and that functions as an anticoagulant and vasodilator.
–ORIGIN 1970s: from **PROSTAGLANDIN** + **CYCLIC** + **-IN**[1].

pros·ta·glan·din /,prästə'glandin/ ▶ **n.** Biochemistry any of a group of cyclic fatty acid compounds with varying hormonelike effects, notably the promotion of uterine contractions.
–ORIGIN 1930s: from **PROSTATE** + **GLAND**[1] + **-IN**[1].

pros·tate /'präs,tāt/ (also **prostate gland**) ▶ **n.** a gland surrounding the neck of the bladder in male mammals and releasing prostatic fluid.
–DERIVATIVES **pros·tat·ic** /prä'statik/ **adj.**
–ORIGIN mid 17th cent.: via French from modern Latin *prostata*, from Greek *prostatēs* 'one that stands before,' from *pro* 'before' + *statos* 'standing.'

pros·ta·tec·to·my /,prästə'tektəmē/ ▶ **n.** (pl. **prostatectomies**) a surgical operation to remove all or part of the prostate gland.

pros·tate-spe·cif·ic an·ti·gen (abbr.: **PSA**) ▶ **n.** Medicine an antigenic enzyme released by the prostate and found in abnormally high concentrations in the blood of men with prostate cancer.

prostatic fluid ▶ **n.** Medicine an alkaline fluid secreted by the prostate gland during ejaculation that forms part of the semen.

P

pros·ta·ti·tis /ˌprästəˈtītəs/ ▶ **n.** Medicine inflammation of the prostate gland.

pros·the·sis /präsˈTHēsis/ ▶ **n.** (pl. **prostheses** /-sēz/) **1** an artificial body part, such as a leg, a heart, or a breast implant: *his upper jaw was removed and a prosthesis was fitted.* **2** (also **prothesis**) the addition of a letter or syllable at the beginning of a word, as in Spanish *escribo* derived from Latin *scribo.*
– DERIVATIVES **pros·thet·ic** /-ˈTHetik/ **adj.**, **pros·thet·i·cal·ly** /-ˈTHetik(ə)lē/ **adv.**
– ORIGIN mid 16th cent. (sense 2): via late Latin from Greek, from *prostithenai*, from *pros* 'in addition' + *tithenai* 'to place.'

pros·thet·ic group ▶ **n.** Biochemistry a nonprotein group forming part of or combined with a protein.

pros·thet·ics /präsˈTHetiks/ ▶ **plural n.** artificial body parts; prostheses. ■ pieces of flexible material applied to actors' faces to transform their appearance. ■ [treated as sing.] the making and fitting of artificial body parts.

pros·the·tist /ˈprästHətist/ ▶ **n.** a specialist in prosthetics.

pros·tho·don·tics /ˌprästHəˈdäntiks/ ▶ **plural n.** [treated as sing.] the branch of dentistry concerned with the design, manufacture, and fitting of artificial replacements for teeth and other parts of the mouth.
– DERIVATIVES **pros·tho·don·tist** /-ˈdäntist/ **n.**
– ORIGIN 1940s: from **PROSTHESIS**, on the pattern of *orthodontics.*

pros·ti·tute /ˈprästəˌt(y)o͞ot/ ▶ **n.** a person, typically a woman, who engages in sexual activity for payment. ■ a person who misuses their talents or who sacrifices their self-respect for the sake of personal or financial gain: *careerist political prostitutes.*
▶ **v.** [with obj.] offer (someone, typically a woman) for sexual activity in exchange for payment: *although she was paid $15 to join a man at his table, she never prostituted herself.* ■ put (oneself or one's talents) to an unworthy or corrupt use or purpose for the sake of personal or financial gain: *his willingness to prostitute himself to the worst instincts of the electorate.*
– DERIVATIVES **pros·ti·tu·tor** /-ˌt(y)o͞otər/ **n.**
– ORIGIN mid 16th cent. (as a verb): from Latin *prostitut-* 'exposed publicly, offered for sale,' from the verb *prostituere*, from *pro-* 'before' + *statuere* 'set up, place.'

pros·ti·tu·tion /ˌprästəˈt(y)o͞osHən/ ▶ **n.** the practice or occupation of engaging in sexual activity with someone for payment. ■ the unworthy or corrupt use of one's talents for the sake of personal or financial gain.

pros·trate /ˈpräsˌtrāt/ ▶ **adj.** lying stretched out on the ground with one's face downward. ■ [predic.] completely overcome or helpless, esp. with illness, distress, or exhaustion: *his wife was prostrate with shock.* ■ Botany growing along the ground.
▶ **v.** [with obj.] **1** (**prostrate oneself**) lay oneself flat on the ground face downward, esp. in reverence or submission: *she prostrated herself on the bare floor of the church.* **2** (of distress, exhaustion, or illness) reduce (someone) to extreme physical weakness: *she was prostrated by a migraine that she could scarcely get up the stairs.*
– ORIGIN Middle English: from Latin *prostratus* 'thrown down,' past participle of *prosternere*, from *pro-* 'before' + *sternere* 'lay flat.'

pros·tra·tion /präˈstrāsHən/ ▶ **n.** the action of lying stretched out on the ground. ■ the state of being extremely weak or subservient: *the refusal to call a strike reflects the union leadership's* ***prostration before the company.*** ■ extreme physical weakness or emotional exhaustion.

pro·style /ˈprōˌstīl/ ▶ **n.** Architecture a portico with a maximum of four columns.
– ORIGIN late 17th cent.: from Latin *prostylos* '(building) having pillars in front,' from Greek *pro* 'before' + *stulos* 'column.'

pro·sum·er /prōˈso͞omər/ ▶ **n. 1** an amateur who purchases equipment with quality or features suitable for professional use: *the magazine is aimed at the prosumer who uses a $10,000 camera to make home movies of his dog.* **2** a prospective consumer who is involved in the design, manufacture, or development of a product or service.
– ORIGIN 1980s: blend of *professional* or *producer* or *proactive* and *consumer.*

pros·y /ˈprōzē/ ▶ **adj.** (**prosier, prosiest**) (esp. of speech or writing) showing no imagination; commonplace or dull.
– DERIVATIVES **pros·i·ly** /-əlē/ **adv.**, **pros·i·ness n.**

prot- ▶ **comb. form** variant spelling of **PROTO-** before a vowel (as in *protamine*).

prot·ac·tin·i·um /ˌprōˌtakˈtinēəm/ ▶ **n.** the chemical element of atomic number 91, a radioactive metal of the actinide series, occurring in small amounts as a product of the natural decay of uranium. (Symbol: **Pa**)
– ORIGIN early 20th cent.: from **PROTO-** 'original, earlier' + **ACTINIUM**, so named because one of its isotopes decays to form actinium.

pro·tag·o·nist /prōˈtagənist, prō-/ ▶ **n.** the leading character or one of the major characters in a drama, movie, novel, or other fictional text. ■ the main figure or one of the most prominent figures in a real situation: *in this colonial struggle, the main protagonists were Great Britain and France.* ■ an advocate or champion of a particular cause or idea: *a strenuous protagonist of the new agricultural policy.*
– ORIGIN late 17th cent.: from Greek *prōtagōnistēs*, from *prōtos* 'first in importance' + *agōnistēs* 'actor.'

> **USAGE** The first sense of **protagonist**, as originally used in connection with ancient Greek drama, is 'the main character in a play.' In the early 20th century, a new sense arose meaning 'a supporter of a cause': *a strenuous* ***protagonist*** *of the new agricultural policy.* This new sense probably arose by analogy with **antagonist**, the **pro-** in **protagonist** being interpreted as meaning 'in favor of.' In fact, the **prot-** in **protagonist** derives from the Greek root meaning 'first.' **Protagonist** is best used in its original dramatic, theatrical sense, not as a synonym for *supporter* or *proponent.* Further, because of its basic meaning of 'leading character,' such usage as *the play's half-dozen protagonists were well cast* blurs the word's distinctiveness; *characters*, instead of *protagonists*, would be more precise.

prot·a·mine /ˈprōtəˌmēn/ ▶ **n.** Biochemistry any of a group of simple proteins found combined with nucleic acids, esp. in fish sperm.
– ORIGIN late 19th cent.: from **PROTO-** 'original' + **AMINE.**

prot·an·drous /prōtˈandrəs/ ▶ **adj.** Botany & Zoology (of a hermaphrodite flower or animal) having the male reproductive organs come to maturity before the female. The opposite of **PROTOGYNOUS.**
– DERIVATIVES **prot·an·dry** /-ˈandrē/ **n.**

pro·ta·nope /ˈprōtəˌnōp/ ▶ **n.** a person suffering from protanopia.

pro·ta·no·pi·a /ˌprōtəˈnōpēə/ ▶ **n.** color-blindness resulting from insensitivity to red light, causing confusion of greens, reds, and yellows. It is hereditary and is the most common form of color-blindness. Also called **DALTONISM.** Compare with **DEUTERANOPIA, TRITANOPIA.**
– ORIGIN early 20th cent.: from **PROTO-** 'original' (red being regarded as the first component of color vision) + **AN-**[1] 'lacking' + **-OPIA.**

pro tan·to /prō ˈtanˌtō/ ▶ **adj. & adv.** to such an extent; to that extent.
– ORIGIN Latin, literally 'for so much.'

prot·a·sis /ˈprätəsəs/ ▶ **n.** (pl. **protases** /-ˌsēz/) Grammar the clause expressing the condition in a conditional sentence (e.g., *if you asked me* in *if you asked me I would agree*). Often contrasted with **APODOSIS.**
– ORIGIN late 16th cent.: via Latin from Greek *protasis* 'proposition,' from *pro* 'before' + *teinein* 'to stretch.'

pro·te·a /ˈprōtēə/ ▶ **n.** an evergreen shrub or small tree with large nectar-rich conelike flower heads surrounded by brightly colored bracts, chiefly native to South Africa. ● Genus *Protea*, family Proteaceae: many species, including *P. repens*, which was formerly used as a source of sweet syrup.
– ORIGIN modern Latin, from **PROTEUS**, with reference to the many species of the genus.

pro·te·an /ˈprōtēən, prōˈtēən/ ▶ **adj.** tending or able to change frequently or easily: *it is difficult to comprehend the whole of this protean subject.* ■ able to do many different things; versatile: *Shostakovich was a remarkably protean composer, one at home in a wide range of styles.*
– DERIVATIVES **pro·te·an·ism** /-ˌnizəm/ **n.**
– ORIGIN late 16th cent.: from **PROTEUS** + **-AN.**

pro·te·ase /ˈprōtēˌāz, -ˌās/ ▶ **n.** Biochemistry an enzyme that breaks down proteins and peptides.
– ORIGIN early 20th cent.: from **PROTEIN** + **-ASE.**

pro·te·ase in·hib·i·tor ▶ **n.** a substance that breaks down protease, thereby inhibiting the replication of certain cells and viruses, including HIV.

pro·te·a·some /ˈprōtēəˌsōm/ ▶ **n.** a protein complex in cells containing proteases; it breaks down proteins that have been tagged by ubiquitin.

protec. ▶ **abbr.** protectorate.

pro·tect /prəˈtekt/ ▶ **v.** [with obj.] keep safe from harm or injury: *he tried to* ***protect*** *Kelly* ***from*** *the attack* | [no obj.] *certain vitamins may* ***protect against*** *heart disease.* ■ (often as adj. **protected**) aim to preserve (a threatened plant or animal species) by legislating against collecting or hunting. ■ (often as adj. **protected**) restrict by law access to or development of (land) so as to preserve its natural state: *logging is continuing in protected areas in violation of an international agreement.* ■ (of an insurance policy) promise to pay (someone) an agreed amount in the event of loss, injury, fire, theft, or other misfortune: *in the event of your death, your family will be protected against any financial problems that may arise.* ■ Economics shield (a domestic industry) from competition by imposing import duties on foreign goods. ■ Computing restrict access to or use of (data or a memory location): *security products are designed to* ***protect*** *information* ***from*** *unauthorized access.*
– DERIVATIVES **pro·tect·a·ble adj.**
– ORIGIN late Middle English: from Latin *protect-* 'covered in front,' from the verb *protegere*, from *pro-* 'in front' + *tegere* 'to cover.'

pro·tect·ant /prəˈtektənt/ ▶ **n.** a substance that provides protection, e.g., against disease or ultraviolet radiation.

pro·tec·tion /prəˈteksHən/ ▶ **n.** the action of protecting someone or something, or the state of being protected: *the B vitamins give protection against infection* | *his son was put under police protection.* ■ a person or thing that prevents someone or something from suffering harm or injury: *the castle was built as protection against the Saxons* | [in sing.] *a protection against the evil eye.* ■ (usu. **protections**) a legal or other formal measure intended to preserve civil liberties and rights. ■ a document guaranteeing immunity from harm to the person specified in it. ■ the practice of paying money to criminals so as to prevent them from attacking oneself or one's property: [as modifier] *a protection racket* | *protection money.* ■ money paid to criminals on this basis, esp. on a regular basis. ■ archaic used euphemistically to refer to the keeping of a mistress by her lover in a separate establishment: *she was living* ***under his lordship's protection*** *at Gloucester Gate.*
– ORIGIN Middle English: from Old French, from late Latin *protectio(n-)*, from *protegere* 'cover in front' (see **PROTECT**).

pro·tec·tion·ism /prəˈteksHəˌnizəm/ ▶ **n.** Economics the theory or practice of shielding a country's domestic industries from foreign competition by taxing imports.
– DERIVATIVES **pro·tec·tion·ist n. & adj.**

pro·tec·tive /prəˈtektiv/ ▶ **adj.** capable of or intended to protect someone or something: *protective gloves are worn to minimize injury.* ■ having or showing a strong wish to keep someone or something safe from harm: *I felt protective toward her* | *Marco wrapped a protective arm around her shoulder.* ■ Economics of or relating to the protection of domestic industries from foreign competition: *protective tariffs.*
– DERIVATIVES **pro·tec·tive·ly adv.**, **pro·tec·tive·ness n.**

pro·tec·tive col·or·a·tion (also **protective coloring**) ▶ **n.** coloring that disguises or camouflages a plant or animal.

pro·tec·tive cus·to·dy ▶ **n.** the detention of a person for their own protection: *they were being held* ***in protective custody*** *during the trial.*

pro·tec·tive or·der ▶ **n.** a court order instructing a person to desist from abusing or harassing the petitioner (usu. a related person) for a fixed period: *a protective order against the man accused of setting his wife on fire.*

pro·tec·tor /prəˈtektər/ ▶ **n. 1** a person or thing that protects someone or something: *ear protectors* | *a passionate protector of animal rights.* **2** (chiefly **Protector**) historical a person in charge of a kingdom during the minority, absence, or incapacity of the sovereign. ■ (also **Lord Protector**) the title of the head of state in England during the later period of the Commonwealth between 1653 and 1659, first Oliver Cromwell (1653–58), then his son Richard (1658–59).
– DERIVATIVES **pro·tec·tor·al** /-rəl/ **adj.**, **pro·tec·tor·ship** /-ˌsHip/ **n.**

pro·tec·tor·ate /prəˈtektərət/ ▶ **n. 1** a state that is controlled and protected by another. ■ the relationship between a state of this kind and the one that controls it: *a French protectorate had been established over Tunis.* **2** (usu. **Protectorate**) historical the position or period of office of a Protector, esp. that in England of Oliver and Richard Cromwell.

pro·tect·ress /prəˈtektris/ ▶ **n.** a female protector.

P

pro·té·gé /ˈprōtəˌZHā, ˌprōtəˈZHā/ (also **protege**) ▶ **n.** a person who is guided and supported by an older and more experienced or influential person: *he was an aide and protégé of the former Tennessee senator.*
– ORIGIN late 18th cent.: French, literally 'protected,' past participle of *protéger*, from Latin *protegere* 'cover in front' (see **PROTECT**).

pro·té·gée /ˈprōtəˌZHā, ˌprōtəˈZHā/ (also **protegee**) ▶ **n.** a female protégé.

pro·tein /ˈprōˌtē(ə)n/ ▶ **n.** any of a class of nitrogenous organic compounds that consist of large molecules composed of one or more long chains of amino acids and are an essential part of all living organisms, esp. as structural components of body tissues such as muscle, hair, collagen, etc., and as enzymes and antibodies. ■ such substances collectively, esp. as a dietary component: *a diet high in protein.*
– DERIVATIVES **pro·tein·a·ceous** /ˌprōˌtē(ə)ˈnāSHəs, ˌprōtnˈā-/ **adj.**
– ORIGIN mid 19th cent.: from French *protéine*, German *Protein*, from Greek *prōteios* 'primary,' from *prōtos* 'first.'

pro·tein·ase /ˈprōtnˌās, ˈprōˌtēn-, -ˌāz/ ▶ **n.** another term for **ENDOPEPTIDASE**.

pro·tein·oid /ˈprōtnˌoid, ˈprōˌtēn-/ ▶ **n.** Biochemistry a polypeptide or mixture of polypeptides obtained by heating a mixture of amino acids.

pro·tein·u·ri·a /ˌprōtnˈ(y)o͝orēə, ˌprōˌtēn-/ ▶ **n.** Medicine the presence of abnormal quantities of protein in the urine, which may indicate damage to the kidneys.

pro tem /prō ˈtem/ ▶ **adv. & adj.** for the time being: [as adv.] *a printer that Marisa could use pro tem* | [as adj.] *a pro tem committee* | [as postpositive adj.] *the president pro tem of the Senate.*
– ORIGIN abbreviation of Latin *pro tempore*.

pro·te·o·gly·can /ˌprōtēəˈglīˌkan/ ▶ **n.** Biochemistry a compound consisting of a protein bonded to glycosaminoglycan groups, present esp. in connective tissue.

pro·te·ol·y·sis /ˌprōtēˈäləsəs/ ▶ **n.** Biochemistry the breakdown of proteins or peptides into amino acids by the action of enzymes.
– DERIVATIVES **pro·te·o·lyt·ic** /-əˈlitik/ **adj.**, **pro·te·o·lyt·i·cal·ly** /-əˈlitik(ə)lē/ **adv.**
– ORIGIN late 19th cent.: modern Latin, from **PROTEIN** + **-LYSIS**.

pro·te·ome /ˈprōtēˌōm/ ▶ **n.** Genetics the entire complement of proteins that is or can be expressed by a cell, tissue, or organism: *now that the human genome has been deciphered, much of the fanfare surrounding it has transferred to the proteome.*
– ORIGIN 1990s: a blend of *protein* and *genome*.

pro·te·om·ics /ˌprōtēˈämiks/ ▶ **plural n.** [treated as singular] the branch of molecular biology concerned with determining the proteome.
– DERIVATIVES **pro·te·om·ic adj.**

P

Prot·er·o·zo·ic /ˌprōtərəˈzōik/ ▶ **adj.** Geology of, relating to, or denoting the eon that constitutes the later part of the Precambrian, between the Archean eon and the Cambrian period, in which the earliest forms of life evolved. ■ (as noun **the Proterozoic**) the Proterozoic eon or the system of rocks deposited during it.

> The Proterozoic lasted from about 2,500 million to 570 million years ago. For millions of years only bacteria, algae, and other simple organisms existed, and the early invertebrates that followed were soft-bodied and rarely left any trace in the form of fossils.

– ORIGIN late 19th cent.: from Greek *proteros* 'former' + *zōē* 'life,' *zōos* 'living' + **-IC**.

pro·test ▶ **n.** /ˈprōˌtest/ **1** a statement or action expressing disapproval of or objection to something: *the Hungarian team lodged an official protest* | *two senior scientists resigned **in protest**.* ■ an organized public demonstration expressing strong objection to a policy or course of action adopted by those in authority: [as modifier] *a protest march.*
2 Law a written declaration, typically by a notary public, that a bill has been presented and payment or acceptance refused.
▶ **v.** /prəˈtest, prōˈtest, ˈprōˌtest/ **1** [no obj.] express an objection to what someone has said or done: *she wouldn't let him pay, and he didn't protest.* ■ publicly demonstrate strong objection to a policy or course of action adopted by those in authority: *doctors and patients **protested against** plans to cut services at the hospital.* ■ [with obj.] publicly demonstrate such objection to (a policy or course of action): *the workers were protesting economic measures enacted a week earlier.*
2 [reporting verb] declare (something) firmly and emphatically in the face of stated or implied doubt or in response to an accusation: [with direct speech] *"I'm not being coy!" Lucy protested* | [with obj.] *she has always protested her innocence.*
3 [with obj.] Law write or obtain a protest in regard to (a bill).
– PHRASES **under protest** after expressing one's objection or reluctance; unwillingly: *"I'm only here under protest," Jenna said shortly.*
– DERIVATIVES **pro·test·ing·ly adv.**
– ORIGIN late Middle English (as a verb in the sense 'make a solemn declaration'): from Old French *protester*, from Latin *protestari*, from *pro-* 'forth, publicly' + *testari* 'assert' (from *testis* 'witness').

Prot·es·tant /ˈprätəstənt/ ▶ **n.** a member or follower of any of the Western Christian churches that are separate from the Roman Catholic Church and follow the principles of the Reformation, including the Baptist, Presbyterian, and Lutheran churches.

> Protestants are so called after the declaration (*protestatio*) of Martin Luther and his supporters dissenting from the decision of the Diet of Spires (1529), which reaffirmed the edict of the Diet of Worms against the Reformation. All Protestants reject the authority of the papacy, both religious and political, and find authority in the text of the Bible.

▶ **adj.** of, relating to, or belonging to any of the Protestant churches.
– DERIVATIVES **Prot·es·tant·i·za·tion** /ˌprätəstəntəˈzāSHən/ **n.**, **Prot·es·tant·ize** /-īz/ **v.**
– ORIGIN mid 16th cent.: via German or French from Latin *protestant-* 'protesting,' from *protestari* (see **PROTEST**).

Prot·es·tant eth·ic (also **Protestant work ethic**) ▶ **n.** the view that a person's duty is to achieve success through hard work and thrift, such success being a sign that one is saved.
– ORIGIN translating German *die protestantische Ethik*, coined (1904) by the economist Max Weber in his thesis on the relationship between the teachings of Calvin and the rise of capitalism.

Prot·es·tant·ism /ˈprätəstəntˌizəm/ ▶ **n.** the faith, practice, and church order of the Protestant churches. ■ adherence to the forms of Christian doctrine that are generally regarded as Protestant rather than Catholic or Eastern Orthodox.

prot·es·ta·tion /ˌprätəˈstāSHən, ˌprōˌtesˈtā-/ ▶ **n.** an emphatic declaration that something is or is not the case: *her protestations of innocence were in vain* | *no amount of protestation to the contrary made any difference.* ■ an objection or protest: *he was warned by the referee for his loud protestations.*
– ORIGIN Middle English: from Old French, from late Latin *protestatio(n-)*, from *protestari* 'to protest' (see **PROTEST**).

pro·test·er /ˈprōˌtestər, prəˈtes-/ (also **protestor**) ▶ **n.** a person who publicly demonstrates strong objection to something; a demonstrator: *the decision was hailed by **protesters against** the closure as a triumph.*

Pro·te·us /ˈprōtēəs, ˈprōˌt(y)o͞os/ **1** Greek Mythology a minor sea god who had the power of prophecy but who would assume different shapes to avoid answering questions.
2 Astronomy a satellite of Neptune, the sixth closest to the planet, discovered by the Voyager 2 space probe in 1989, and having a diameter of 261 miles (420 km).

pro·te·us /ˈprōteəs/ ▶ **n.** a bacterium found in the intestines of animals and in the soil. ● Genus *Proteus*; motile Gram-negative rods.
– ORIGIN early 19th cent.: from **PROTEUS**.

pro·tha·la·mi·on /ˌprōTHəˈlāmēən/ (also **prothalamium** /-mēəm/) ▶ **n.** (pl. **prothalamia** /-mēə/) literary a song or poem celebrating an upcoming wedding.
– ORIGIN late 16th cent.: from *Prothalamion*, the title of a poem by Spenser, on the pattern of **EPITHALAMIUM**.

pro·thal·lus /prōˈTHaləs/ ▶ **n.** (pl. **prothalli** /-ˈTHalē, ˈTHalˌī/) Botany the gametophyte of ferns and other primitive plants.
– DERIVATIVES **pro·thal·li·al** /-ˈTHalēəl/ **adj.**
– ORIGIN mid 19th cent.: modern Latin, from **PRO-**[2] 'before, earlier' + Greek *thallos* 'green shoot.'

proth·e·sis /ˈpräTHəsəs/ ▶ **n.** (pl. **protheses** /-ˌsēz/) **1** Christian Church (esp. in the Orthodox Church) the action of placing the Eucharistic elements on the credence table. ■ a credence table. ■ the part of a church where the credence table stands.
2 another term for **PROSTHESIS** (sense 2).
– DERIVATIVES **pro·thet·ic** /prəˈTHetik/ **adj.**
– ORIGIN late 16th cent. (sense 2): from Greek, 'placing before or in public view,' from *pro* 'before' + *thesis* 'placing.'

pro·thon·o·tar·y /prōˈTHänəˌterē, ˌprōTHəˈnōtərē/ ▶ **n.** variant spelling of **PROTONOTARY**.

pro·thon·o·tar·y war·bler ▶ **n.** a North American warbler, the male of which has a golden-yellow head, breast, and underparts. ● *Protonotaria citrea*, subfamily Parulinae, family Emberizidae.
– ORIGIN late 18th cent.: named with reference to the saffron color of the robes worn by clerks to the pope (see **PROTONOTARY APOSTOLIC**).

pro·tho·rax /prōˈTHôrˌaks/ ▶ **n.** (pl. **prothoraxes** or **prothoraces** /-ˈTHôrəˌsēz/) Entomology the anterior segment of the thorax of an insect, not bearing any wings.
– DERIVATIVES **pro·tho·rac·ic** /ˌprōTHəˈrasik/ **adj.**

pro·throm·bin /prōˈTHrämbən/ ▶ **n.** Biochemistry a protein present in blood plasma that is converted into active thrombin during coagulation.

Pro·tis·ta /prōˈtistə/ Biology a kingdom or large grouping that comprises mostly single-celled organisms such as the protozoa, simple algae and fungi, slime molds, and (formerly) the bacteria. They are now divided among up to thirty phyla, and some have both plant and animal characteristics.
– DERIVATIVES **pro·tist** /ˈprōtəst, ˈprōˌtist/ **n.**, **pro·tis·tan** /prōˈtistən/ **adj. & n.**, **pro·tis·tol·o·gy** /ˌprōtəˈstäləjē, ˌprōˌtisˈtäl-/ **n.**
– ORIGIN modern Latin (plural), from Greek *prōtista*, neuter plural of *prōtistos* 'very first,' superlative of *prōtos* 'first.'

pro·ti·um /ˈprōtēəm, ˈprōSH(ē)əm/ ▶ **n.** Chemistry the common, stable isotope of hydrogen, as distinct from deuterium and tritium.
– ORIGIN 1930s: modern Latin, from Greek *prōtos* 'first.'

proto- (usu. **prot-** before a vowel) ▶ **comb. form** original; primitive: *prototherian* | *prototype.* ■ first; anterior; relating to a precursor: *protomartyr* | *protozoan.*
– ORIGIN from Greek *prōtos* 'first.'

pro·to·cer·a·tops /ˌprōtəˈserəˌtäps/ ▶ **n.** a small quadrupedal dinosaur of the late Cretaceous period, having a bony frill above the neck and probably ancestral to triceratops. The fossilized remains of many individuals and their eggs have been found in Mongolia. ● Genus *Protoceratops*, infraorder Ceratopsia, order Ornithischia.

pro·to·col /ˈprōtəˌkôl, -ˌkäl/ ▶ **n.** **1** the official procedure or system of rules governing affairs of state or diplomatic occasions: *protocol forbids the prince from making any public statement in his defense.* ■ the accepted or established code of procedure or behavior in any group, organization, or situation: *what is the protocol at a conference if one's neighbor dozes off during the speeches?* ■ Computing a set of rules governing the exchange or transmission of data between devices.
2 the original draft of a diplomatic document, esp. of the terms of a treaty agreed to in conference and signed by the parties. ■ an amendment or addition to a treaty or convention: *a protocol to the treaty allowed for this Danish referendum.*
3 a formal or official record of scientific experimental observations. ■ a procedure for carrying out a scientific experiment or a course of medical treatment.
– ORIGIN late Middle English (denoting the original record of an agreement, forming the legal authority for future dealings relating to it): from Old French *prothocole*, via medieval Latin from Greek *prōtokollon* 'first page, flyleaf,' from *prōtos* 'first' + *kolla* 'glue.' Sense 1 derives from French *protocole*, the collection of set forms of etiquette to be observed by the French head of state, and the name of the government department responsible for this (in the 19th cent).

Pro·toc·tis·ta /ˌprōtäkˈtistə/ Biology a kingdom or large grouping that is either synonymous with the Protista or equivalent to the Protista together with their multicellular descendants.
– DERIVATIVES **pro·toc·tist** /ˈprōtäkˌtist/ **n.**
– ORIGIN modern Latin (plural), based on Greek *prōtos* 'first.'

pro·to·gal·ax·y /ˌprōtōˈgaləksē/ ▶ **n.** (pl. **protogalaxies**) Astronomy a vast mass of gas from which a galaxy is thought to develop.
– DERIVATIVES **pro·to·ga·lac·tic** /-gəˈlaktik/ **adj.**

Pro·to-Ger·man·ic /ˌprōtōjərˈmanik/ ▶ **n.** see **GERMANIC**.

pro·to·gy·nous /ˌprōtəˈjīnəs, prōˈtäjənəs/ ▶ **adj.** Botany & Zoology (of a hermaphrodite flower or animal) having the female reproductive organs come to maturity before the male. The opposite of **PROTANDROUS**.
– DERIVATIVES **pro·tog·y·ny** /ˈprōtəˌjīnē, prōˈtäjənē/ **n.**

pro·to·hu·man /ˌprōtōˈ(h)yo͞omən/ Anthropology ▶ **n.** a hypothetical prehistoric primate, resembling humans and thought to be their ancestor, whose profile has been compiled mainly from fossil evidence.

▶ adj. relating to or denoting such a primate.

Pro·to-In·do-Eu·ro·pe·an ▶ n. the unrecorded language from which all Indo-European languages are hypothesized to derive. See **INDO-EUROPEAN**. ▶ adj. of or relating to this language.

pro·to·lan·guage /ˈprōtōˌlaNG(g)wij/ ▶ n. a hypothetical undocumented parent language from which actual languages are derived.

pro·to·mar·tyr /ˈprōtōˌmärtər/ ▶ n. the first martyr for a cause, esp. the first Christian martyr, St. Stephen.

pro·ton /ˈprōˌtän/ ▶ n. Physics a stable subatomic particle occurring in all atomic nuclei, with a positive electric charge equal in magnitude to that of an electron, but of opposite sign.

> The mass of the proton is 1,836 times greater than that of the electron. The atoms of each chemical element have a characteristic number of protons in the nucleus; this is known as the atomic number. The common isotope of hydrogen has a nucleus consisting of a single proton.

– DERIVATIVES **pro·ton·ic** /prōˈtänik/ adj.
– ORIGIN 1920s: from Greek, neuter of *prōtos* 'first.'

pro·ton·ate /ˈprōtnˌāt/ ▶ v. [with obj.] Chemistry transfer a proton to (a molecule, group, or atom), so that a coordinate bond to the proton is formed.
– DERIVATIVES **pro·to·na·tion** /ˌprōtnˈāSHən/ n.

pro·ton·o·tar·y /prōˈtänəˌterē, ˌprōtəˈnōtərē/ (also **prothonotary**) ▶ n. (pl. **protonotaries**) chiefly historical a chief clerk in some courts of law, originally in the Byzantine court.
– ORIGIN late Middle English: via medieval Latin from late Greek *prōtonotarios*, from *prōtos* 'first' + *notarios* 'notary.'

Pro·ton·o·tar·y Ap·os·tol·ic ▶ n. (pl. **Protonotaries Apostolic**) a member of the Roman Catholic college of prelates who register papal acts and direct the canonization of saints.

pro·to·path·ic /ˌprōtəˈpaTHik/ ▶ adj. Physiology relating to or denoting those sensory nerve fibers of the skin that are capable of discriminating only among such relatively coarse stimuli as heat, cold, and pain. Often contrasted with **EPICRITIC**.
– ORIGIN mid 19th cent.: from **PROTO-** 'primitive' + Greek *pathos* 'suffering, feeling' + **-IC**.

pro·to·plasm /ˈprōtəˌplazəm/ ▶ n. Biology the colorless material comprising the living part of a cell, including the cytoplasm, nucleus, and other organelles.
– DERIVATIVES **pro·to·plas·mic** /ˌprōtəˈplazmik/ adj.
– ORIGIN mid 19th cent.: from Greek *prōtoplasma* (see **PROTO-**, **PLASMA**).

pro·to·plast /ˈprōtəˌplast/ ▶ n. chiefly Botany the protoplasm of a living plant or bacterial cell whose cell wall has been removed.
– DERIVATIVES **pro·to·plas·tic** /ˌprōtəˈplastik/ adj.
– ORIGIN late 19th cent.: from Greek *prōtoplastos* 'first formed,' from *prōtos* 'first' + *plassein* 'to mold.'

pro·top·o·dite /prəˈtäpəˌdīt/ (also **protopod** /ˈprōtəˌpäd/) ▶ n. Zoology the basal segments of the biramous limb or appendage of a crustacean. Compare with **ENDOPODITE**, **EXOPODITE**.
– ORIGIN late 19th cent.: from **PROTO-** 'early, original' + Greek *pous*, *pod-* 'foot' + **-ITE**[1].

pro·to·star /ˈprōtəˌstär/ ▶ n. Astronomy a contracting mass of gas that represents an early stage in the formation of a star, before nucleosynthesis has begun.

pro·to·stome /ˈprōtəˌstōm/ ▶ n. Zoology a multicellular organism whose mouth develops from a primary embryonic opening, such as an annelid, mollusk, or arthropod.
– ORIGIN 1950s: from **PROTO-** 'primitive' + Greek *stoma* 'mouth.'

Pro·to·the·ri·a /ˌprōtəˈTHirēə/ Zoology a group of mammals that comprises the monotremes and their extinct relatives. Compare with **THERIA**. ● Subclass Prototheria, class Mammalia.
– ORIGIN modern Latin (plural), from **PROTO-** 'first, original' + Greek *thēr* 'wild beast.'

pro·to·the·ri·an /ˌprōtəˈTHirēən/ Zoology ▶ n. a mammal of the group Prototheria, which comprises the monotremes and their extinct relatives. ▶ adj. relating to or denoting prototherians.

pro·to·type /ˈprōtəˌtīp/ ▶ n. a first, typical or preliminary model of something, esp. a machine, from which other forms are developed or copied: *the firm is testing a prototype of the weapon | the prototype of all careerists is Judas.* ■ the archetypal example of a class of living organisms, astronomical objects, or other items: *these objects are the prototypes of a category of rapidly spinning neutron stars.* ■ Electronics a basic filter network with specified cutoff frequencies, from which other networks may be derived to obtain sharper cutoffs, constancy of characteristic impedance with frequency, etc.
▶ v. [with obj.] make a prototype of (a product).
– DERIVATIVES **pro·to·typ·al** /ˌprōtəˈtīpəl/ adj., **pro·to·typ·ic** /ˌprōtəˈtipik/ adj., **pro·to·typ·i·cal** /ˌprōtəˈtipikəl/ adj., **pro·to·typ·i·cal·ly** /ˌprōtəˈtipik(ə)lē/ adv.
– ORIGIN late 16th cent. (denoting the original of which something else is a copy or derivative): via French or late Latin from Greek *prōtotupos* (see **PROTO-**, **TYPE**).

Pro·to·zo·a /ˌprōtəˈzōə/ Zoology a phylum or group of phyla that comprises the single-celled microscopic animals, which include amebas, flagellates, ciliates, sporozoans, and many other forms. They are now usually treated as a number of phyla belonging to the kingdom Protista. ■ (as plural noun **protozoa**) organisms of this group.
– ORIGIN modern Latin (plural), from **PROTO-** 'first' + Greek *zōion* 'animal.'

pro·to·zo·an /ˌprōtəˈzōən/ Zoology ▶ n. a single-celled microscopic animal of a group of phyla of the kingdom Protista, such as an ameba, flagellate, ciliate, or sporozoan. ▶ adj. relating to or denoting protozoans.
– DERIVATIVES **pro·to·zo·al** adj., **pro·to·zo·ic** /-ˈzōik/ adj., **pro·to·zo·on** /-ˈzōˌän/ n.

pro·tract /prəˈtrakt, prō-/ ▶ v. [with obj.] **1** prolong: *he had certainly taken his time, even protracting the process.*
2 draw (a plan, etc.) to scale.
– DERIVATIVES **pro·trac·tion** /-ˈtrakSHən/ n.
– ORIGIN mid 16th cent.: from Latin *protract-* 'prolonged,' from the verb *protrahere*, from *pro-* 'out' + *trahere* 'to draw.'

pro·tract·ed /prəˈtraktəd, prō-/ ▶ adj. lasting for a long time or longer than expected or usual: *a protracted and bitter dispute.*
– DERIVATIVES **pro·tract·ed·ly** adv., **pro·tract·ed·ness** n.

pro·trac·tile /prəˈtraktəl, prō-, -ˈtrakˌtīl/ ▶ adj. another term for **PROTRUSIBLE**.

pro·trac·tor /ˌprōˈtraktər/ ▶ n. **1** an instrument for measuring angles, typically in the form of a flat semicircle marked with degrees along the curved edge.
2 (also **protractor muscle**) chiefly Zoology a muscle serving to extend a part of the body. Compare with **RETRACTOR**.

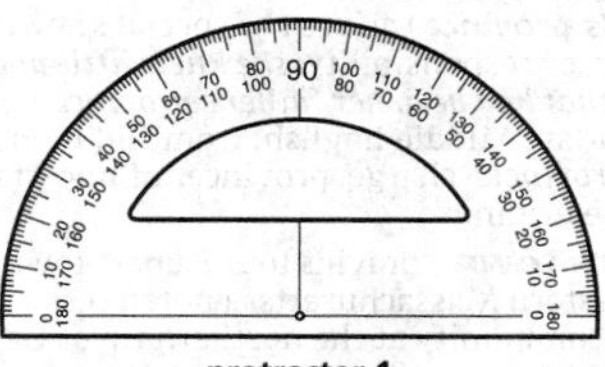

protractor 1

pro·trude /prəˈtrood, prō-/ ▶ v. [no obj.] extend beyond or above a surface: *something like a fin protruded from the water.* ■ [with obj.] (of an animal) cause (a body part) to do this.
– DERIVATIVES **pro·tru·sive** /-ˈtroosiv, -ziv/ adj.
– ORIGIN early 17th cent. (in the sense 'thrust (something) forward or onward'): from Latin *protrudere*, from *pro-* 'forward, out' + *trudere* 'to thrust.'

pro·trud·ing /prəˈtroodiNG, prō-/ ▶ adj. sticking out; projecting: *a stocky guy with a furrowed brow and a protruding bottom lip.*

pro·tru·si·ble /prəˈtroosəbəl, prō-, -zəbəl/ ▶ adj. Zoology (of a body part, such as the jaws of a fish) capable of being protruded or extended.
– ORIGIN mid 19th cent.: from Latin *protrus-* 'extended or thrust forward' (from the verb *protrudere*) + **-IBLE**.

pro·tru·sion /prəˈtroozHən, prō-/ ▶ n. something that protrudes; a protuberance: *a protrusion of rock jutted from the mountainside.*

pro·tu·ber·ance /prəˈt(y)oob(ə)rəns, prō-/ ▶ n. a thing that protrudes from something else: *some dinosaurs evolved protuberances on top of their heads.* ■ the fact or state of protruding: *the large size and protuberance of the incisors.*

pro·tu·ber·ant /prəˈt(y)oob(ə)rənt, prō-/ ▶ adj. protruding; bulging: *his protuberant eyes fluttered open.*
– ORIGIN mid 17th cent.: from late Latin *protuberant-* 'swelling out,' from the verb *protuberare*, from *pro-* 'forward, out' + *tuber* 'bump.'

Pro·tu·ra /prəˈt(y)oorə/ Entomology an order of minute white wingless insects with slender bodies. They lack eyes and antennae, using the first pair of legs as sensory organs. ● Order Protura, subclass Apterygota, class Insecta (or Hexapoda).
– DERIVATIVES **pro·tu·ran** n. & adj.
– ORIGIN modern Latin (plural), from Greek *prōtos* 'first, primitive.'

proud /proud/ ▶ adj. **1** feeling deep pleasure or satisfaction as a result of one's own achievements, qualities, or possessions or those of someone with whom one is closely associated: *a proud grandma of three boys | she got nine As and he was so proud of her.* ■ (of an event, achievement, etc.) causing someone to feel this way: *we have a proud history of innovation.*
2 having or showing a high or excessively high opinion of oneself or one's importance: *a proud, arrogant man.* ■ having or showing a consciousness of one's own dignity: *I was too proud to go home.* ■ imposing; splendid: *bulrushes emerge tall and proud from the middle of the pond.*
3 [predic.] Brit. slightly projecting from a surface: *when the brake is engaged, the lever does not stand proud of the horizontal.*
– PHRASES **do someone proud** informal act in a way that gives someone cause to feel pleased or satisfied: *they did themselves proud in a game that sent the fans home happy.* ■ treat someone very well, typically by lavishly feeding or entertaining them.
– DERIVATIVES **proud·ly** adv., **proud·ness** n.
– ORIGIN late Old English *prūt*, *prūd* 'having a high opinion of one's own worth,' from Old French *prud* 'valiant,' based on Latin *prodesse* 'be of value.' The phrase *proud flesh* dates back to late Middle English, but the sense 'slightly projecting' is first recorded in British dialect of the 19th cent.

proud flesh ▶ n. another name for **GRANULATION TISSUE**.

proud·heart·ed /ˈproudˈhärtəd/ ▶ adj. arrogant.

Prou·dhon /prooˈdôN/, Pierre Joseph (1809–65), French social philosopher and journalist. His pamphlet *What Is Property?* (1840) argues that property, in the sense of the exploitation of one person's labor by another, is theft.

Proust[1] /proost/, Joseph Louis (1754–1826), French analytical chemist. He proposed the law of constant proportions, demonstrating that any pure sample of a chemical compound (such as an oxide of a metal) always contains the same elements in fixed proportions.

Proust[2], Marcel (1871–1922), French novelist, essayist, and critic. He devoted much of his life to writing his novel *À la recherche du temps perdu* (1913–27). Its central theme is the recovery of the lost past and the releasing of its creative energies through the stimulation of unconscious memory.

Prov. ▶ abbr. ■ Bible Proverbs. ■ chiefly Canadian Province or Provincial. ■ Provost.

prove /proov/ ▶ v. (past participle **proved** or **proven** /ˈproovən/) **1** [with obj.] demonstrate the truth or existence of (something) by evidence or argument: *the concept is difficult to prove* | (as adj. **proven**) *a proven ability to work hard.* ■ [with obj. and complement] demonstrate by evidence or argument (someone or something) to be: *innocent until proven guilty.* ■ Law establish the genuineness and validity of (a will). ■ (in homeopathy) demonstrate the action of (a remedy) by seeing what effect it produces in a healthy individual. ■ [no obj., with complement] be seen or found to be: *the plan has proved a great success.* ■ (**prove oneself**) demonstrate one's abilities or courage: *a new lieutenant, very green and very desperate to prove himself.* ■ rare test the accuracy of (a mathematical calculation). ■ subject (a gun or other item) to a testing process.
2 [no obj.] (of bread dough) become aerated by the action of yeast; rise.
– DERIVATIVES **prov·a·bil·i·ty** /ˌproovəˈbilətē/ n., **prov·a·ble** adj., **prov·a·bly** /-blē/ adv., **prov·er** n.
– ORIGIN Middle English: from Old French *prover*, from Latin *probare* 'test, approve, demonstrate,' from *probus* 'good.'

> **USAGE** For complex historical reasons, **prove** developed two past participles: **proved** and **proven**. Both are correct and can be used more or less interchangeably: *this hasn't been proved yet; this hasn't been proven yet.* **Proven** is the more common form when used as an adjective before the noun it modifies: *a proven talent* (not *a proved talent*). Otherwise, the choice between *proved* and *proven* is not a matter of correctness, but usually of sound and rhythm—and often, consequently, a matter of familiarity, as in the legal idiom *innocent until proven guilty.*

prov·e·nance /ˈprävənəns/ ▶ n. the place of origin or earliest known history of something: *an orange rug of Iranian provenance.* ■ the beginning of something's existence; something's origin: *they try to understand the whole universe, its provenance and fate.* ■ a record of ownership of a work of art or an

PRONUNCIATION KEY ə *ago, up*; ər *over, fur*; a *hat*; ā *ate*; ä *car*; e *let*; ē *see*; i *fit*; ī *by*; NG *sing*; ō *go*; ô *law, for*; oi *toy*; o͝o *good*; o͞o *goo*; ou *out*; TH *thin*; T͟H *then*; ZH *vision*

P

antique, used as a guide to authenticity or quality: *the manuscript has a distinguished provenance.*
– ORIGIN late 18th cent.: from French, from the verb *provenir* 'come or stem from,' from Latin *provenire*, from *pro-* 'forth' + *venire* 'come.'

Pro·ven·çal /ˌprävənˈsäl, ˌprōvən-, ˌprōˌväN-/ ▶ **adj.** of, relating to, or denoting Provence or its people or language.
▶ **n. 1** a native or inhabitant of Provence.
2 the Romance language of Provence.

> Provençal is closely related to French, Italian, and Catalan; it is sometimes called *langue d'oc* (or Occitan), though strictly speaking it is one dialect of this. In the 12th–14th centuries it was the language of the troubadours and cultured speakers of southern France, but the spread of the northern dialects of French led to its decline.

– ORIGIN French, from Latin *provincialis* 'provincial.'

pro·ven·çale /ˌprävənˈsäl, ˌprō-, prəˈvensəl/ ▶ **adj.** [postpositive] denoting a dish cooked in a sauce made with tomatoes, garlic, and olive oil: *chicken provençale.*
– ORIGIN from French *à la provençale* 'in the Provençal style.'

Pro·vence /prōˈväns/ a former province of southeastern France, on the Mediterranean coast, east of the Rhône River. It is now part of the region of Provence–Alpes–Côte d'Azur.
– ORIGIN from Latin *provincia* 'province,' a colloquial name for southern Gaul, the first Roman province to be established outside Italy.

Pro·vence–Al·pes–Côte d'A·zur /prəˈväNs ˌälp ˌkōtdäˈzHo͝or/ a mountainous region in southeastern France, on the border with Italy and including the French Riviera.

prov·en·der /ˈprävəndər/ ▶ **n.** often humorous food. ■ dated animal fodder.
– ORIGIN Middle English: from Old French *provendre*, based on an alteration of Latin *praebenda* 'things to be supplied' (see **PREBEND**).

pro·ve·ni·ence /prəˈvinyəns/ ▶ **n.** another term for **PROVENANCE**.

pro·ven·tric·u·lus /ˌprōvenˈtrikyələs/ ▶ **n.** (pl. **proventriculi** /-ˌlī, -ˌlē/) Zoology the narrow glandular first region of a bird's stomach between the crop and the gizzard. ■ the thick-walled muscular expansion of the esophagus above the stomach of crustaceans and insects.
– ORIGIN mid 19th cent.: from **PRO-**[2] 'before' + Latin *ventriculus* 'small belly,' diminutive of *venter, ventr-* 'belly.'

pro·verb /ˈprävˌərb/ ▶ **n.** a short pithy saying in general use, stating a general truth or piece of advice.
– ORIGIN Middle English: from Old French *proverbe*, from Latin *proverbium*, from *pro-* '(put) forth' + *verbum* 'word.'

pro·ver·bi·al /prəˈvərbēəl/ ▶ **adj.** (of a word or phrase) referred to in a proverb or idiom: *I'm going to stick out like the proverbial sore thumb.* ■ well known, esp. so as to be stereotypical: *the Welsh people, whose hospitality is proverbial.*
– DERIVATIVES **pro·ver·bi·al·i·ty** /-ˌvərbēˈalətē/ **n.**, **pro·ver·bi·al·ly adv.**
– ORIGIN late Middle English: from Latin *proverbialis*, from *proverbium* (see **PROVERB**).

Prov·erbs /ˈprävˌərbz/ (also **Book of Proverbs**) a book of the Bible containing maxims attributed mainly to Solomon.

pro·vide /prəˈvīd/ ▶ **v. 1** [with obj.] make available for use; supply: *these clubs provide a much appreciated service for this area.* ■ (**provide someone with**) equip or supply someone with (something useful or necessary): *we were provided with a map of the area.* ■ present or yield (something useful): *neither will provide answers to these problems.*
2 [no obj.] (**provide for**) make adequate preparation for (a possible event): *new qualifications must provide for changes in technology.* ■ supply sufficient money to ensure the maintenance of (someone): *Emma was handsomely provided for in Frank's will.* ■ (of a law) enable or allow (something to be done).
3 [with clause] stipulate in a will or other legal document: *the order should be varied to provide that there would be no contact with the father.*
4 (**provide someone to**) Christian Church, historical appoint an incumbent to (a benefice).
– ORIGIN late Middle English (also in the sense 'prepare to do, get ready'): from Latin *providere* 'foresee, attend to,' from *pro-* 'before' + *videre* 'to see.'

pro·vid·ed /prəˈvīdid/ ▶ **conj.** on the condition or understanding that: *cutting corners was acceptable, provided that you could get away with it.*

Prov·i·dence /ˈprävəˌdens, -dəns/ the capital of Rhode Island, a port near the mouth of the Providence River, on the Atlantic coast; pop. 171,557 (est. 2008). It was founded in 1636 by **Roger Williams** (1604–83) as a haven for religious dissenters.

prov·i·dence /ˈprävədəns, -ˌdens/ ▶ **n.** the protective care of God or of nature as a spiritual power: *they found their trust in divine providence to be a source of comfort.* ■ (**Providence**) God or nature as providing such care: *I live out my life as Providence decrees.* ■ timely preparation for future eventualities: *it was considered a duty to encourage providence.*
– ORIGIN late Middle English: from Old French, from Latin *providentia*, from *providere* 'foresee, attend to' (see **PROVIDE**).

Prov·i·dence Plan·ta·tions the mainland portion of the state of Rhode Island.

prov·i·dent /ˈprävədənt, -ˌdent/ ▶ **adj.** making or indicative of timely preparation for the future: *she had learned to be provident.*
– DERIVATIVES **prov·i·dent·ly adv.**
– ORIGIN late Middle English: from Latin *provident-* 'foreseeing, attending to,' from the verb *providere* (see **PROVIDE**).

prov·i·den·tial /ˌprävəˈdenCHəl/ ▶ **adj. 1** occurring at a favorable time; opportune: *thanks to that providential snowstorm, the attack had been repulsed.*
2 involving divine foresight or intervention: *God's providential care for each of us.*
– DERIVATIVES **prov·i·den·tial·ly adv.**
– ORIGIN mid 17th cent.: from **PROVIDENCE**, on the pattern of *evidential.*

pro·vid·er /prəˈvīdər/ ▶ **n.** a person or thing that provides something: *a leading provider of personal financial services.* ■ a breadwinner.

pro·vid·ing /prəˈvīdiNG/ ▶ **conj.** on the condition or understanding that: *we have the team that can win the championship, providing we avoid bad injuries.*

prov·ince /ˈprävins/ ▶ **n. 1** a principal administrative division of certain countries or empires: *Chengdu, capital of Sichuan province.* ■ (**the provinces**) the whole of a country outside the capital, esp. when regarded as lacking in sophistication or culture: *I made my way home to the dreary provinces by train.* ■ Christian Church a district under an archbishop or a metropolitan. ■ Roman History a territory outside Italy under a Roman governor.
2 (**one's province**) an area of special knowledge, interest, or responsibility: *she knew little about wine—that had been her father's province.*
– ORIGIN late Middle English: from Old French, from Latin *provincia* 'charge, province,' of uncertain ultimate origin.

Prov·ince·town /ˈprävinsˌtoun/ a port town in southeastern Massachusetts, a noted resort and artists' community at the northern tip of Cape Cod; pop. 3,376 (est. 2008).

pro·vin·cial /prəˈvinSHəl/ ▶ **adj. 1** of or concerning a province of a country or empire: *provincial elections.*
2 of or concerning the regions outside the capital city of a country, esp. when regarded as unsophisticated or narrow-minded: *scenes of violence were reported in provincial towns | the whole exhibition struck one as being very provincial.*
▶ **n. 1** an inhabitant of a province of a country or empire. ■ (**provincials**) (in Canada) athletic contests held between teams representing the country's administrative divisions.
2 an inhabitant of the regions outside the capital city of a country, esp. when regarded as unsophisticated or narrow-minded.
3 Christian Church the head or chief of a province or of a religious order in a province.
– DERIVATIVES **pro·vin·ci·al·i·ty** /prəˌvinSHēˈalətē/ **n.**, **pro·vin·cial·i·za·tion** /prəˌvinSHələˈzāSHən/ **n.**, **pro·vin·cial·ly adv.**
– ORIGIN late Middle English: from Old French, from Latin *provincialis* 'belonging to a province' (see **PROVINCE**).

pro·vin·cial·ism /prəˈvinCHəˌlizəm/ ▶ **n. 1** the way of life or mode of thought characteristic of the regions outside the capital city of a country, esp. when regarded as unsophisticated or narrow-minded. ■ narrow-mindedness, insularity, or lack of sophistication: *the myopic provincialism of women's studies.*
2 concern for one's own area or region at the expense of national or supranational unity.
3 a word or phrase peculiar to a local area.
4 the degree to which plant or animal communities are restricted to particular areas.
– DERIVATIVES **pro·vin·cial·ist n. & adj.**

prov·ing /ˈpro͞oviNG/ ▶ **n.** (in homeopathy) the testing of a remedy: *Many such provings are required to fully test the powers of a medicinal substance.*

prov·ing ground ▶ **n.** an environment that serves to demonstrate whether something, such as a theory or product, really works: *Bay County is the proving ground for a new gutter-cleaning vacuum.* ■ a military facility for the testing of materiel and equipment: *Aberdeen Proving Ground.*

pro·vi·rus /prōˈvīrəs/ ▶ **n.** Microbiology the genetic material of a virus as incorporated into, and able to replicate with, the genome of a host cell.
– DERIVATIVES **pro·vi·ral** /-rəl/ **adj.**

pro·vi·sion /prəˈviZHən/ ▶ **n. 1** the action of providing or supplying something for use: *new contracts for the provision of services.* ■ (**provision for/against**) financial or other arrangements for future eventualities or requirements: *farmers have been slow to* ***make provision for*** *their retirement.* ■ an amount set aside out of profits in the accounts of an organization for a known liability, esp. a bad debt or the diminution in value of an asset.
2 an amount or thing supplied or provided: *low levels of social provision.* ■ (**provisions**) supplies of food, drink, or equipment, esp. for a journey.
3 a condition or requirement in a legal document: *a key provision in civil rights law | an appraisal* ***under the provisions of*** *the National Housing Act.*
4 Christian Church, historical an appointment to a benefice, esp. directly by the pope rather than by the patron, and originally before it became vacant.
▶ **v. 1** [with obj.] supply with food, drink, or equipment, esp. for a journey: *civilian contractors were responsible for provisioning these armies.*
2 [no obj.] set aside an amount in an organization's accounts for a known liability: *financial institutions have to* ***provision against*** *loan losses.*
– DERIVATIVES **pro·vi·sion·er n.**
– ORIGIN late Middle English (also in the sense 'foresight'): via Old French from Latin *provisio(n-)*, from *providere* 'foresee, attend to' (see **PROVIDE**). The verb dates from the early 19th cent.

pro·vi·sion·al /prəˈviZHənl/ ▶ **adj. 1** arranged or existing for the present, possibly to be changed later: *a provisional government | a provisional construction permit.* ■ (of a postage stamp) put into circulation temporarily, usually owing to the unavailability of the definitive issue.
2 (**Provisional**) [attrib.] of or relating to the unofficial wings of the Irish Republican Army and Sinn Fein established in 1969 and advocating terrorism.
▶ **n. 1** a provisional postage stamp.
2 (**Provisional**) a member of the Provisional wings of the Irish Republican Army or Sinn Fein.
– DERIVATIVES **pro·vi·sion·al·i·ty** /prəˌviZHəˈnalətē/ **n.**

pro·vi·sion·al·ly /prəˈviZHənl-ē/ ▶ **adv.** subject to further confirmation; for the time being: *the institute has provisionally approved the study.*

pro·vi·so /prəˈvīzō/ ▶ **n.** (pl. **provisos**) a condition attached to an agreement: *he left his unborn grandchild a trust fund* ***with the proviso that*** *he be named after the old man.*
– ORIGIN late Middle English: from the medieval Latin phrase *proviso (quod)* 'it being provided (that),' from Latin *providere* 'foresee, provide.'

pro·vi·sor /prəˈvīzər/ ▶ **n. 1** (in the Roman Catholic Church) a deputy of a bishop or archbishop.
2 Christian Church, historical the holder of a provision.
– ORIGIN late Middle English: from Anglo-Norman French *provisour*, from Latin *provisor*, from *provis-* 'provided' (see **PROVISION**).

pro·vi·so·ry /prəˈvīzərē/ ▶ **adj. 1** rare subject to a proviso; conditional.
2 another term for **PROVISIONAL** (sense 1 of the adjective).
– ORIGIN early 17th cent.: from French *provisoire* or medieval Latin *provisorius*, from *provis-* 'foreseen, attended to,' from the verb *providere* (see **PROVIDE**).

pro·vi·ta·min /prōˈvītəmən/ ▶ **n.** Biochemistry a substance that is converted into a vitamin within an organism.

Pro·vo[1] /ˈprōvō/ an industrial and commercial city in north central Utah, south of Salt Lake City, home to Brigham Young University; pop. 118,581 (est. 2008).

Pro·vo[2] ▶ **n.** (pl. **Provos**) informal term for **PROVISIONAL** (sense 2 of the noun).

prov·o·ca·tion /ˌprävəˈkāSHən/ ▶ **n. 1** action or speech that makes someone annoyed or angry, esp. deliberately: *you should remain calm and not respond to provocation | he burst into tears* ***at the slightest provocation.*** ■ Law action or speech held to be likely to prompt physical retaliation: *the assault had taken place* ***under provocation.***
2 Medicine testing to elicit a particular response or reflex: *twenty patients had a high increase of serum gastrin after provocation with secretin.*
– ORIGIN late Middle English: from Old French, from Latin *provocatio(n-)*, from the verb *provocare* (see **PROVOKE**).

pro·voc·a·tive /prəˈväkətiv/ ▶ **adj.** causing annoyance, anger, or another strong reaction, esp. deliberately: *a provocative article | his provocative*

remarks on race. ■ arousing sexual desire or interest, esp. deliberately.
– DERIVATIVES **pro·voc·a·tive·ly** adv., **pro·voc·a·tive·ness** n.
– ORIGIN late Middle English: from Old French *provocatif, -ive*, from late Latin *provocativus*, from *provocat-* 'called forth, challenged,' from the verb *provocare* (see **PROVOKE**).

pro·voke /prəˈvōk/ ▶ v. [with obj.] stimulate or give rise to (a reaction or emotion, typically a strong or unwelcome one) in someone: *the decision provoked a storm of protest from civil rights organizations.* ■ stimulate or incite (someone) to do or feel something, esp. by arousing anger in them: *a teacher can **provoke** you **into** working harder.* ■ deliberately make (someone) annoyed or angry: *Rachel refused to be provoked.*
– DERIVATIVES **pro·vok·a·ble** adj., **pro·vok·er** n.
– ORIGIN late Middle English (also in the sense 'invoke, summon'): from Old French *provoquer*, from Latin *provocare* 'challenge,' from *pro-* 'forth' + *vocare* 'to call.'

pro·vok·ing /prəˈvōkiNG/ ▶ adj. **1** causing annoyance; irritating: *there is evidence of provoking conduct and loss of self-control.*
2 [in combination] giving rise to the specified reaction or emotion: *fear-provoking | laughter-provoking.*
– DERIVATIVES **pro·vok·ing·ly** adv.

pro·vo·lo·ne /ˌprōvəˈlōnē/ ▶ n. an Italian soft smoked cheese made from cow's milk and having a mellow flavor.
– ORIGIN Italian, from *provola* 'buffalo-milk cheese.'

pro·vost /ˈprōˌvōst/ ▶ n. **1** a senior administrative officer in certain colleges and universities. ■ Brit. the head of certain university colleges, esp. at Oxford or Cambridge, and public schools.
2 the head of a chapter in a cathedral. ■ the Protestant minister of the principal church of a town or district in Germany and certain other European countries. ■ historical the head of a Christian community. [translating German *Propst*, Dutch *proost*, etc.]
3 short for **PROVOST MARSHAL**.
4 Scottish term for **MAYOR**.
5 historical the chief magistrate of a French or other European town.
– DERIVATIVES **pro·vost·ship** /-ˌSHip/ n.
– ORIGIN late Old English *profost* 'head of a chapter, prior,' reinforced in Middle English by Anglo-Norman French *provost*, from medieval Latin *propositus*, synonym of Latin *praepositus* 'head, chief.'

pro·vost mar·shal ▶ n. the head of military police in camp or on active service.

prow /prou/ ▶ n. the portion of a ship's bow above water. ■ the pointed or projecting front part of something such as a car or building.
– ORIGIN mid 16th cent.: from Old French *proue*, from Provençal *proa*, probably via Latin from Greek *prōira*, from a base meaning 'in front.'

prow·ess /ˈprou-əs, ˈprōəs/ ▶ n. **1** skill or expertise in a particular activity or field: *his prowess as a fisherman.*
2 bravery in battle.
– ORIGIN Middle English (sense 2): from Old French *proesce*, from *prou* 'valiant.' Sense 1 dates from the early 20th cent.

prowl /proul/ ▶ v. (of a person or animal) move around restlessly and stealthily, esp. in search of or as if in search of prey: [with obj.] *black bears prowl the canyons* | [no obj.] *committee members prowling around the offices at night with flashlights.*
▶ n. an act of prowling: *I met her once on one of my off-duty bookstore prowls.*
– PHRASES **on the prowl** (of a person or animal) moving around in search or as if in search of prey.
– ORIGIN late Middle English: of unknown origin.

prowl car ▶ n. a police squad car.

prowl·er /ˈproulər/ ▶ n. a person who moves stealthily around or loiters near a place with a view to committing a crime, esp. burglary.

prox. ▶ abbr. proximo.

prox. acc. ▶ abbr. proxime accessit.

prox·e·mics /präkˈsēmiks/ ▶ plural n. [treated as sing.] the branch of knowledge that deals with the amount of space that people feel it necessary to set between themselves and others.
– DERIVATIVES **prox·e·mic** adj.
– ORIGIN 1960s: from **PROXIMITY**, on the pattern of words such as *phonemics.*

Prox·i·ma Cen·tau·ri /ˈpräksəmə ˌsenˈtôrē, -ˈtôrˌī/ Astronomy a faint red dwarf star associated with the bright binary star Alpha Centauri. It is the closest known star to the solar system (distance 4.24 light years).
– ORIGIN Latin, 'nearest (star) of Centaurus.'

prox·i·mal /ˈpräksəməl/ ▶ adj. Anatomy situated nearer to the center of the body or the point of attachment: *the proximal end of the forearm.* The opposite of **DISTAL**. ■ Geology relating to or denoting an area close to a center of a geological process such as sedimentation or volcanism. Often contrasted with **DISTAL**.
– DERIVATIVES **prox·i·mal·ly** adv.
– ORIGIN early 19th cent. (as a term in anatomy and zoology): from Latin *proximus* 'nearest' + **-AL**. In geology, usage dates from the 1940s.

prox·i·mate /ˈpräksəmit/ ▶ adj. **1** (esp. of a cause of something) closest in relationship; immediate: *that storm was the proximate cause of damage to it.* ■ closest in space or time: *the failure of the proximate military power to lend assistance.*
2 nearly accurate; approximate: *he would try to change her speech into proximate ladylikeness.*
– DERIVATIVES **prox·i·mate·ly** adv., **prox·i·ma·tion** /ˌpräksəˈmāSHən/ n.
– ORIGIN late 16th cent.: from Latin *proximatus* 'drawn near,' past participle of *proximare*, from *proximus* 'nearest.'

prox·im·i·ty /präkˈsimətē/ ▶ n. nearness in space, time, or relationship: *do not operate microphones in close proximity to television sets.*
– ORIGIN late 15th cent.: from French *proximité*, from Latin *proximitas*, from *proximus* 'nearest.'

prox·im·i·ty fuse ▶ n. an electronic detonator that causes a projectile to explode when it comes within a preset distance of its target.

prox·i·mo /ˈpräksəˌmō/ ▶ adj. [postpositive] dated of next month: *he must be in San Francisco on 1st proximo.* Compare with **INSTANT**, **ULTIMO**.
– ORIGIN from Latin *proximo mense* 'in the next month.'

prox·y /ˈpräksē/ ▶ n. (pl. **proxies**) **1** the authority to represent someone else, esp. in voting: *they may register to vote **by proxy**.* ■ a person authorized to act on behalf of another. ■ a document authorizing a person to vote on another's behalf.
2 a figure that can be used to represent the value of something in a calculation: *the use of a US wealth measure as a **proxy for** the true worldwide measure.*
– ORIGIN late Middle English: contraction of **PROCURACY**.

prox·y war ▶ n. a war instigated by a major power that does not itself become involved.

Pro·zac /ˈprōˌzak/ ▶ n. trademark for **FLUOXETINE**.
– ORIGIN 1980s: an invented name.

pro·zone /ˈprōˌzōn/ ▶ n. Immunology (in testing for antigens) the range of relative quantities of precipitin (or agglutinin) and antigen within which any precipitation (or agglutination) is inhibited by the predominance of one component.
– ORIGIN early 20th cent.: from **PRO-**[2] 'before' + (*agglutination*) *zone.*

PRS ▶ abbr. ■ Performing Rights Society. ■ (in the UK) President of the Royal Society.

prude /pro͞od/ ▶ n. a person who is or claims to be easily shocked by matters relating to sex or nudity.
– DERIVATIVES **prud·er·y** /ˈpro͞odərē/ n.
– ORIGIN early 18th cent.: from French, back-formation from *prudefemme*, feminine of *prud'homme* 'good man and true,' from *prou* 'worthy.'

pru·dence /ˈpro͞odns/ ▶ n. the quality of being prudent; cautiousness: *we need to **exercise prudence** in such important matters.*

pru·dent /ˈpro͞odnt/ ▶ adj. acting with or showing care and thought for the future: *no prudent money manager would authorize a loan without first knowing its purpose.*
– DERIVATIVES **pru·dent·ly** adv.
– ORIGIN late Middle English: from Old French, or from Latin *prudent-*, contraction of *provident-* 'foreseeing, attending to' (see **PROVIDENT**).

pru·den·tial /pro͞oˈdenCHəl/ ▶ adj. involving or showing care and forethought, typically in business.
– DERIVATIVES **pru·den·tial·ly** adv.
– ORIGIN late Middle English: from **PRUDENT**, on the pattern of words such as *evidential.*

Prud·hoe Bay /ˈpro͞od(h)ō/ an inlet of the Arctic Ocean, on the northern coast of Alaska. It is a major center of Alaskan oil production.

prud·ish /ˈpro͞odiSH/ ▶ adj. having or revealing a tendency to be easily shocked by matters relating to sex or nudity; excessively concerned with sexual propriety: *the prudish moral climate of the late 19th century.*
– DERIVATIVES **prud·ish·ly** adv., **prud·ish·ness** n.

pru·i·nose /ˈpro͞oəˌnōs/ ▶ adj. chiefly Botany (of a surface, such as that of a grape) covered with white powdery granules; frosted in appearance.
– ORIGIN early 19th cent.: from Latin *pruinosus*, from *pruina* 'hoarfrost.'

prune[1] /pro͞on/ ▶ n. a plum preserved by drying, having a black, wrinkled appearance. ■ informal an unpleasant or disagreeable person: *he was a good leader, but a miserable old prune.*
– ORIGIN Middle English: from Old French, via Latin from Greek *prou(m)non* 'plum.'

prune[2] ▶ v. [with obj.] trim (a tree, shrub, or bush) by cutting away dead or overgrown branches or stems, esp. to increase fruitfulness and growth. ■ cut away (a branch or stem) in this way: ***prune back** the branches.* ■ reduce the extent of (something) by removing superfluous or unwanted parts: *reduction achieved by working harder or pruning costs.* ■ remove (superfluous or unwanted parts) from something: *Elliot deliberately **pruned away** details.*
– DERIVATIVES **prun·er** n.
– ORIGIN late 15th cent. (in the sense 'abbreviate'): from Old French *pro(o)ignier*, possibly based on Latin *rotundus* 'round.'

pru·nel·la[1] /pro͞oˈnelə/ ▶ n. a plant of a genus that includes self-heal. Several kinds are cultivated as ground cover and rock garden plants. • Genus *Prunella*, family Labiatae.
– ORIGIN modern Latin, literally 'quinsy,' in medieval Latin *brunella*, diminutive of *brunus* 'brown,' denoting a disease causing a brown coating on the tongue. Self-heal was a reputed cure for the disease.

pru·nel·la[2] ▶ n. a strong silk or worsted twill fabric used formerly for legal robes and the uppers of women's shoes.
– ORIGIN mid 17th cent.: perhaps from French *prunelle* 'sloe' (because of its dark color).

prun·ing hook ▶ n. a cutting tool used for pruning, consisting of a hooked blade on a long handle.

prun·ing knife ▶ n. a knife specifically designed for pruning, typically having a sharp, slightly curved blade and a hooked end.

pru·nus /ˈpro͞onəs/ ▶ n. a tree or shrub of a large genus that includes many varieties grown for their spring blossom (cherry and almond) or for their fruit (plum, peach, and apricot). • Genus *Prunus*, family Rosaceae.
– ORIGIN modern Latin, from Latin, literally 'plum tree.'

pru·ri·ent /ˈpro͝orēənt/ ▶ adj. having or encouraging an excessive interest in sexual matters: *she'd been the subject of much prurient curiosity.*
– DERIVATIVES **pru·ri·ence** n., **pru·ri·en·cy** n., **pru·ri·ent·ly** adv.
– ORIGIN late 16th cent. (in the sense 'having a mental itching'): from Latin *prurient-* 'itching, longing' and 'being wanton,' from the verb *prurire.*

pru·ri·go /pro͞oˈrīgō, -ˈrēgō/ ▶ n. Medicine a chronic skin disease causing severe itching.
– DERIVATIVES **pru·rig·i·nous** /pro͝orˈijənəs/ adj.
– ORIGIN mid 17th cent.: from Latin, from *prurire* 'to itch.'

pru·ri·tus /pro͞oˈrītəs/ ▶ n. Medicine severe itching of the skin, as a symptom of various ailments.
– DERIVATIVES **pru·rit·ic** /-ˈritik/ adj.
– ORIGIN mid 17th cent.: from Latin, 'itching' (see **PRURIGO**).

prus·ik /ˈprəsik/ Climbing ▶ n. a method of ascending or descending a rope by means of two loops, each attached to it by a special knot tightening when weight is applied and slackening when it is removed, enabling the loop to be moved along the rope. ■ (also **prusik knot**) a sliding knot that locks under pressure, enabling a person to climb in this way.
▶ v. (**prusiks, prusiking, prusiked**) [no obj.] (usu. as noun **prusiking**) climb using this method.
– ORIGIN 1930s: from the name of Karl Prusik, the Austrian mountaineer who devised this method of climbing.

Prus·sia /ˈprəSHə/ a former kingdom of Germany. Originally a small country on the southeastern shores of the Baltic Sea, it became a major European power, covering much of modern northeastern Germany and Poland, under Frederick the Great. After the Franco-Prussian War of 1870–71, it became the center of Bismarck's new German Empire, but was abolished following Germany's defeat in World War I.
– DERIVATIVES **Prus·sian** adj. & n.

Prus·sian blue /ˈprəSHən/ ▶ n. a deep blue pigment used in painting and dyeing, made from or in imitation of ferric ferrocyanide. ■ the deep blue color of this pigment.

prus·sic ac·id /ˈprəsik/ ▶ n. old-fashioned term for **HYDROCYANIC ACID**.
– DERIVATIVES **prus·si·ate** /ˈprəsēˌāt/ n.

– ORIGIN late 18th cent.: *prussic* from French *prussique* 'relating to Prussian blue.'

Prut /pro͞ot/ (also **Pruth**) a river in southeastern Europe that rises in the Carpathian Mountains in southern Ukraine and flows southeast for 530 miles (850 km) to join the Danube River near Galaţi in Romania. For much of its course it forms the border between Romania and Moldova.

pry[1] /prī/ ▶ v. (**pries, prying, pried**) [no obj.] inquire too closely into a person's private affairs: *I'm sick of you prying into my personal life.*
– ORIGIN Middle English (in the sense 'peer inquisitively'): of unknown origin.

pry[2] ▶ v. (**pries, prying, pried**) [with obj.] use force in order to move or open (something) or to separate (something) from something else: *using a screwdriver, he pried open the window.* ■ (**pry something out of/from**) obtain something from (someone) with effort or difficulty: *I got the loan, though I had to pry it out of him.*
– ORIGIN early 19th cent.: from the verb PRIZE[2], interpreted as *pries*, third person singular of the present tense.

pry bar ▶ n. a small, flattish iron bar used in the same way as a crowbar.

pry·ing /'prī-iNG/ ▶ adj. excessively interested in a person's private affairs; too inquisitive: *she felt there was no place where she could escape from the prying eyes.*
– DERIVATIVES **pry·ing·ly** adv.

Prze·wal·ski's horse /,pərZHə'välskēz/ ▶ n. a stocky wild Mongolian horse with a dun-colored coat and a dark brown erect mane, now extinct in the wild. It is the only true wild horse, and is the ancestor of the domestic horse. ● *Equus ferus*, family Equidae.
– ORIGIN late 19th cent.: named after Nikolai M. *Przheval'sky* (1839–88), Russian explorer.

PS ▶ abbr. ■ passenger steamer. ■ permanent secretary. ■ police sergeant. ■ postscript. ■ private secretary. ■ Privy Seal. ■ Theater prompt side. ■ Public School.

Ps. ▶ abbr. (pl. **Pss.**) Bible Psalm or Psalms.

psalm /sä(l)m/ (also **Psalm**) ▶ n. a sacred song or hymn, in particular any of those contained in the biblical Book of Psalms and used in Christian and Jewish worship: *a delightful setting of Psalm 150.* ■ (**the Psalms** or **the Book of Psalms**) a book of the Bible comprising a collection of religious verses, sung or recited in both Jewish and Christian worship. Many are traditionally ascribed to King David.
– DERIVATIVES **psalm·ic** /'sä(l)mik/ adj.
– ORIGIN Old English (*p*)*sealm*, via ecclesiastical Latin from Greek *psalmos* 'song sung to harp music,' from *psallein* 'to pluck.'

psalm·book /'sä(l)m,bo͝ok/ ▶ n. a book containing psalms, esp. with metrical settings for worship.

psalm·ist /'sä(l)mist/ ▶ n. the author or composer of a psalm, esp. of any of the biblical Psalms.
– ORIGIN late 15th cent.: from late Latin *psalmista*, from *psalmus* 'song sung to harp music' (see PSALM).

psal·mo·dy /'sä(l)mədē/ ▶ n. the singing of psalms or similar sacred canticles, esp. in public worship. ■ psalms arranged for singing: *these books offer a useful collection of psalmody.*
– DERIVATIVES **psal·mod·ic** /sä(l)'mädik/ adj., **psal·mo·dist** /-dist/ n.
– ORIGIN Middle English: via late Latin from Greek *psalmōidia* 'singing to a harp,' from *psalmos* (see PSALM) + *ōidē* 'song.'

psal·ter /'sôltər/ ▶ n. (**the psalter** or **the Psalter**) the Book of Psalms. ■ a copy of the biblical Psalms, esp. for liturgical use.
– ORIGIN Old English (*p*)*saltere*, via Latin *psalterium* from Greek *psaltērion* 'stringed instrument.'

psal·te·ri·um /,sôl'ti(ə)rēəm/ ▶ n. another term for OMASUM.
– ORIGIN mid 19th cent.: from Latin, literally 'psalter' (see PSALTER), because of its many folds of tissue, resembling pages of a book.

psal·ter·y /'sôltərē/ ▶ n. (pl. **psalteries**) an ancient and medieval musical instrument like a dulcimer but played by plucking the strings with the fingers or a plectrum.
– ORIGIN Middle English *sautrie*, from Old French *sauterie*, from Latin *psalterium* (see PSALTER).

PSAT ▶ abbr. Preliminary Scholastic Aptitude Test.

PSBR ▶ abbr. Brit. public-sector borrowing requirement.

psec. (also **ps**) ▶ abbr. picosecond; picoseconds.

pse·phol·o·gy /sē'fäləjē/ ▶ n. the statistical study of elections and trends in voting.
– DERIVATIVES **pse·pho·log·i·cal** /,sēfə'läjikəl/ adj., **pse·pho·log·i·cal·ly** /-ik(ə)lē/ adv., **pse·phol·o·gist** /-jist/ n.
– ORIGIN 1950s: from Greek *psēphos* 'pebble, vote' + -LOGY.

pseud /so͞od/ informal ▶ adj. intellectually or socially pretentious.
▶ n. a pretentious person; a poseur.
– ORIGIN 1960s: abbreviation of PSEUDO.

pseud. ▶ abbr. pseudonym.

pseud- ▶ comb. form variant spelling of PSEUDO- reduced before a vowel (as in *pseudepigrapha*).

pseud·e·pig·ra·pha /,so͞odə'pigrəfə/ ▶ plural n. spurious or pseudonymous writings, esp. Jewish writings ascribed to various biblical patriarchs and prophets but composed within approximately 200 years of the birth of Jesus Christ.
– DERIVATIVES **pseud·e·pig·ra·phal** adj., **pseud·e·pi·graph·ic** /,so͞od,epi'grafik/ adj.
– ORIGIN late 17th cent.: neuter plural of Greek *pseudepigraphos* 'with false title' (see PSEUDO-, EPIGRAPH).

pseu·do /'so͞odō/ ▶ adj. not genuine; sham: *we are talking about real journalists and not the pseudo kind.*
– ORIGIN late Middle English: independent use of PSEUDO-.

pseudo- (also **pseud-** before a vowel) ▶ comb. form **1** supposed or purporting to be but not really so; false; not genuine: *pseudonym* | *pseudoscience*. **2** resembling or imitating: *pseudohallucination* | *pseudo-French*.
– ORIGIN from Greek *pseudēs* 'false,' *pseudos* 'falsehood.'

pseu·do·bulb /'so͞odō,bəlb/ ▶ n. Botany a bulblike enlargement of the stem in many orchids, esp. tropical and epiphytic ones.

pseu·do·carp /'so͞odō,kärp/ ▶ n. technical term for FALSE FRUIT.
– ORIGIN mid 19th cent.: from PSEUDO- 'false' + Greek *karpos* 'fruit.'

pseu·do·cho·lin·es·ter·ase /,so͞odō,kōlə'nestə,rās, -rāz/ ▶ n. Biochemistry an enzyme present in the blood and certain organs that hydrolyzes acetylcholine more slowly than acetylcholinesterase.

pseu·do·clas·si·cal /,so͞odō'klasikəl/ ▶ adj. having a false or spurious classical style: *a pretentious pseudoclassical building.*

pseu·do-cleft Grammar ▶ n. a sentence that resembles a cleft sentence by conveying emphasis or politeness through the use of a relative clause, such as *what we want is* representing *we want.*

pseu·do·code /'so͞odō,kōd/ ▶ n. Computing a notation resembling a simplified programming language, used in program design.

pseu·do·cop·u·la·tion /,so͞odō,käpyə'lāSHən/ ▶ n. Biology attempted copulation by a male insect with a flower (esp. an orchid) that resembles the female, carrying pollen to it in the process.

pseu·do·cy·e·sis /,so͞odōsī'ēsis/ ▶ n. technical term for FALSE PREGNANCY.
– ORIGIN mid 19th cent.: from PSEUDO- 'false' + Greek *kuēsis* 'conception.'

pseu·do·cyst /'so͞odō,sist/ ▶ n. Medicine a fluid-filled cavity resembling a cyst but lacking a wall or lining.

Pseu·do-Di·o·ny·si·us /,so͞odō,dīə'nisēəs/ (6th century AD), the unidentified author of important theological works formerly attributed to Dionysius the Areopagite.

pseu·do·e·phed·rine /,so͞odōə'fedrən/ ▶ n. a drug obtained from plants of the genus *Ephedra* (or prepared synthetically) and used as a nasal decongestant.

pseu·do-e·vent ▶ n. informal an event arranged or brought about merely for the sake of the publicity or entertainment value it generates: *since real cultural events do not always occur on schedule, we invent pseudo-events for tour operators.*

pseu·do·ex·tinc·tion /,so͞odō-ik'stiNGkSHən/ ▶ n. Paleontology the apparent extinction of a group of organisms with the survival of modified descendant forms.

pseu·do·gene /'so͞odō,jēn/ ▶ n. Genetics a section of a chromosome that is an imperfect copy of a functional gene.

pseu·do·her·maph·ro·dit·ism /,so͞odōhər-'mafrə,dīt,izəm/ ▶ n. Medicine the condition in which an individual of one sex has external genitalia superficially resembling those of the other sex.
– DERIVATIVES **pseu·do·her·maph·ro·dite** /-'mafrə,dīt/ n.

pseu·do·mem·brane /,so͞odō'mem,brān/ ▶ n. Medicine a layer of exudate resembling a membrane, formed on the surface of the skin or of a mucous membrane, esp. the conjunctiva.
– DERIVATIVES **pseu·do·mem·bra·nous** /-'membrənəs/ adj.

pseu·dom·o·nas /,so͞odō'mōnəs/ ▶ n. Microbiology a bacterium of a genus that occurs in soil and detritus, including a number that are pathogens of plants or animals. ● Genus *Pseudomonas*; aerobic Gram-negative bacteria.
– DERIVATIVES **pseu·dom·o·nad** /-'mō,nad/ n.
– ORIGIN modern Latin, from PSEUDO- 'false' + *monas* 'monad.'

pseu·do·morph /'so͞odə,môrf/ Crystallography ▶ n. a crystal consisting of one mineral but having the form of another which it has replaced.
▶ v. [with obj.] replace (another substance) to form a pseudomorph.
– DERIVATIVES **pseu·do·mor·phic** /,so͞odō'môrfik/ adj., **pseu·do·mor·phism** /,so͞odō'môr,fizəm/ n., **pseu·do·mor·phous** /,so͞odō'môrfəs/ adj.
– ORIGIN mid 19th cent.: from PSEUDO- 'false' + Greek *morphē* 'form.'

pseu·do·nym /'so͞odn-im/ ▶ n. a fictitious name, esp. one used by an author.
– DERIVATIVES **pseu·do·nym·i·ty** /,so͞odn'imətē/ n.
– ORIGIN early 19th cent.: from French *pseudonyme*, from Greek *pseudōnymos*, from *pseudēs* 'false' + *onuma* 'name.'

pseu·don·y·mous /so͞o'dänəməs/ ▶ adj. writing or written under a false name: *the pseudonymous author of this mystery.*
– DERIVATIVES **pseu·don·y·mous·ly** adv.

pseu·do·pod /'so͞odə,päd/ ▶ n. another term for PSEUDOPODIUM.

pseu·do·po·di·um /,so͞odə'pōdēəm/ ▶ n. (pl. **pseudopodia** /-'pōdēə/) Biology a temporary protrusion of the surface of an ameboid cell for movement and feeding.
– ORIGIN mid 19th cent.: modern Latin, from PSEUDO- + PODIUM.

pseu·do·preg·nan·cy /,so͞odō'pregnənsē/ ▶ n. (pl. **pseudopregnancies**) another term for FALSE PREGNANCY.
– DERIVATIVES **pseu·do·preg·nant** /-'pregnənt/ adj.

pseu·do·ra·bies /,so͞odō'rābēz/ ▶ n. Veterinary Medicine an infectious herpesvirus disease of the central nervous system in domestic animals that causes convulsions and intense itching and is usually fatal.

pseu·do·ran·dom /,so͞odō'randəm/ ▶ adj. (of a number, a sequence of numbers, or any digital data) satisfying one or more statistical tests for randomness but produced by a definite mathematical procedure.
– DERIVATIVES **pseu·do·ran·dom·ly** adv.

pseu·do·sci·ence /,so͞odō'sīəns/ ▶ n. a collection of beliefs or practices mistakenly regarded as being based on scientific method.
– DERIVATIVES **pseu·do·sci·en·tif·ic** /-,sīən'tifik/ adj., **pseu·do·sci·en·tist** /-'sīəntist/ n.

pseu·do·scor·pi·on /,so͞odō'skôrpēən/ ▶ n. a minute arachnid that has pincers but no long abdomen or sting, occurring abundantly in leaf litter. Also called FALSE SCORPION. ● Order Pseudoscorpiones.

pseu·do·u·ri·dine /,so͞odō'yo͝orə,dēn/ ▶ n. Biochemistry a nucleoside present in transfer RNA and differing from uridine in having the sugar residue attached at a carbon atom instead of nitrogen.

pshaw /(p)SHô/ ▶ exclam. dated or humorous an expression of contempt or impatience: *"Poison? Pshaw! The very idea!"*
▶ v. [no obj.] dated or humorous utter such an exclamation: *when I suggested that free trade might dilute Canadian culture, he pshawed.*
– ORIGIN natural exclamation: first recorded in English in the late 17th cent.

psi /(p)sī/ ▶ n. **1** the twenty-third letter of the Greek alphabet (Ψ, ψ), transliterated as 'ps.' ■ (**Psi**) [followed by Latin genitive] Astronomy the twenty-third star in a constellation: *Psi Aquarii.* **2** supposed parapsychological or psychic faculties or phenomena: *he turns to anecdotal evidence to prove that psi exists.*

p.s.i. ▶ abbr. pounds per square inch.

psil·o·cy·bin /,sīlə'sībin/ ▶ n. Chemistry a hallucinogenic alkaloid, found in some toadstools.
– ORIGIN 1950s: from modern Latin *Psilocybe* (genus name), from Greek *psilos* 'bald' + *kubē* 'head.'

psi·on·ic /sī'änik/ ▶ adj. relating to or denoting the practical use of psychic powers or paranormal phenomena: *psionic communication.*
– DERIVATIVES **psi·on·i·cal·ly** /-ik(ə)lē/ adv.
– ORIGIN 1950s: from PSI, on the pattern of *electronic.*

psit·ta·cine /'sitə,sīn/ ▶ adj. Ornithology of, relating to, or denoting birds of the parrot family: *psittacine beak and feather disease.*
▶ n. Ornithology a bird of the parrot family.
– ORIGIN late 19th cent.: from Latin *psittacinus* 'of a parrot,' from *psittacus*, from Greek *psittakos* 'parrot.'

psit·ta·co·sau·rus /,sitəkō'sôrəs/ ▶ n. a partly bipedal herbivorous dinosaur of the mid

Cretaceous period, having a parrotlike beak and probably ancestral to other ceratopsians. ● Genus *Psittacosaurus*, infraorder Ceratopsia, order Ornithischia.
– ORIGIN modern Latin, from Greek *psittakos* 'parrot' + *sauros* 'lizard.'

psit·ta·co·sis /ˌsitəˈkōsəs/ ▶ **n.** a contagious disease of birds, caused by chlamydiae and transmissible (esp. from parrots) to human beings as a form of pneumonia.
– ORIGIN late 19th cent.: from Latin *psittacus* 'parrot' + **-OSIS**.

pso·as /ˈsōəs/ (also **psoas major**) ▶ **n.** Anatomy each of a pair of large muscles that run from the lumbar spine through the groin on either side and, with the iliacus, flex the hip. A second muscle, the **psoas minor**, has a similar action but is often absent.
– ORIGIN late 17th cent.: from Greek, accusative plural of *psoa*, interpreted as singular.

pso·cid /ˈsōsəd/ ▶ **n.** Entomology a small or minute insect of an order that includes the booklice. Many psocids are wingless and somewhat resemble lice or aphids, and most live on bark and among foliage. ● Order Psocoptera: many families, including the large family Psocidae.
– ORIGIN late 19th cent.: from modern Latin *Psocidae* (plural), from *Psocus* (genus name), from Greek *psōkhein* 'to grind.'

Pso·cop·ter·a /sōˈkäptərə/ Entomology an order of insects that comprises the booklice and other psocids.
– DERIVATIVES **pso·cop·ter·an** **n. & adj.**
– ORIGIN modern Latin (plural), from *Psocus* (genus name) + *pteron* 'wing.'

pso·ra·len /ˈsôrələn, -ˌlen/ ▶ **n.** Chemistry a compound present in certain plants that is used in perfumery and (in combination with ultraviolet light) to treat psoriasis and other skin disorders. ● A tricyclic lactone; chem. formula: $C_{11}H_6O_3$.
– ORIGIN 1930s: from modern Latin *Psorolea* (former genus name), from Greek *psōraleos* 'itchy' (from *psōra* 'itch') + the suffix *-en* (compare with **-ENE**).

pso·ri·a·sis /səˈrīəsəs/ ▶ **n.** Medicine a skin disease marked by red, itchy, scaly patches.
– DERIVATIVES **pso·ri·at·ic** /ˌsôrēˈatik/ **adj.**
– ORIGIN late 17th cent.: modern Latin, from Greek *psōriasis*, from *psōrian* 'have an itch,' (from *psōra* 'itch') + **-ASIS**.

psst /pst/ ▶ **exclam.** used to attract someone's attention surreptitiously: *Psst! Want to know a secret?*
– ORIGIN 1920s: imitative.

PST ▶ **abbr.** Pacific Standard Time (see **PACIFIC TIME**).

PSV ▶ **abbr.** Brit. public service vehicle.

psych /sīk/ (also **psyche**) ▶ **v. 1** [with obj.] informal mentally prepare (someone) for a testing task or occasion: *we had to psych ourselves up for the race.*
2 (usu. **psyche**) [no obj.] Bridge make a psychic bid.
▶ **n. 1** informal short for **PSYCHIATRIST** or **PSYCHOLOGIST**. ■ short for **PSYCHIATRY** or **PSYCHOLOGY**.
2 (usu. **psyche**) Bridge a psychic bid.
▶ **adj.** [attrib.] **1** informal short for **PSYCHIATRIC**.
2 short for **PSYCHEDELIC**: *a rare old psych album.*
– PHRASAL VERBS **psych someone out** informal intimidate an opponent or rival by appearing confident or aggressive: *guys who try to lift heavy weights in a mistaken attempt to psych out the other guys.* **psych something out** informal analyze something in psychological terms.

psych. ▶ **abbr.** ■ psychological. ■ psychologist. ■ psychology.

Psy·che /ˈsīkē/ Greek Mythology a Hellenistic personification of the soul as female, or sometimes as a butterfly. The allegory of Psyche's love for Cupid is told in *The Golden Ass* by Apuleius.

psy·che[1] /ˈsīkē/ ▶ **n.** the human soul, mind, or spirit: *I will never really fathom the female psyche.*
– ORIGIN mid 17th cent.: via Latin from Greek *psukhē* 'breath, life, soul.'

psy·che[2] /sīk/ ▶ **v., n., & adj.** variant spelling of **PSYCH**.

psych·e·de·lia /ˌsīkəˈdēlyə/ ▶ **n.** music, culture, or art based on the experiences produced by psychedelic drugs.
– ORIGIN 1960s: back-formation from **PSYCHEDELIC**.

psy·che·del·ic /ˌsīkəˈdelik/ ▶ **adj.** relating to or denoting drugs (esp. LSD) that produce hallucinations and apparent expansion of consciousness. ■ relating to or denoting a style of rock music originating in the mid 1960s, characterized by musical experimentation and drug-related lyrics. ■ denoting or having an intense, vivid color or a swirling abstract pattern: *a psychedelic T-shirt.*
▶ **n.** a psychedelic drug.
– DERIVATIVES **psy·che·del·i·cal·ly** /-ik(ə)lē/ **adv.**
– ORIGIN 1950s: formed irregularly from **PSYCHE**[1] + Greek *dēlos* 'clear, manifest' + **-IC**.

psy·chi·at·ric /ˌsīkēˈatrik/ ▶ **adj.** of or relating to mental illness or its treatment: *a psychiatric disorder.*
– DERIVATIVES **psy·chi·at·ri·cal·ly** /-ik(ə)lē/ **adv.**

psy·chi·a·trist /səˈkīətrist, sī-/ ▶ **n.** a medical practitioner specializing in the diagnosis and treatment of mental illness.

psy·chi·a·try /səˈkīətrē, sī-/ ▶ **n.** the study and treatment of mental illness, emotional disturbance, and abnormal behavior.
– ORIGIN mid 19th cent.: from Greek *psukhē* 'soul, mind' + *iatreia* 'healing' (from *iatros* 'healer').

psy·chic /ˈsīkik/ ▶ **adj. 1** relating to or denoting faculties or phenomena that are apparently inexplicable by natural laws, esp. involving telepathy or clairvoyance: *psychic powers.* ■ (of a person) appearing or considered to have powers of telepathy or clairvoyance: *I could sense it—I must be psychic.*
2 of or relating to the soul or mind: *he dulled his psychic pain with gin.*
3 Bridge denoting a bid that deliberately misrepresents the bidder's hand, in order to mislead the opponents.
▶ **n.** a person considered or claiming to have psychic powers; a medium. ■ (**psychics**) [treated as sing. or pl.] the study of psychic phenomena.
– DERIVATIVES **psy·chi·cal** /ˈsīkikəl/ **adj.** (sense 1 of the adjective), **psy·chi·cal·ly** /ˈsīkik(ə)lē/ **adv.**, **psy·chism** /ˈsīˌkizəm/ **n.** (sense 1 of the adjective).
– ORIGIN early 19th cent.: from Greek *psukhikos* (see **PSYCHE**[1]).

psy·chic in·come ▶ **n.** Economics the nonmonetary or nonmaterial satisfactions that accompany an occupation or economic activity.

psy·cho /ˈsīkō/ informal ▶ **n.** (pl. **psychos**) a psychopath.
▶ **adj.** psychopathic.
– ORIGIN 1930s: abbreviation.

psycho- ▶ **comb. form** relating to the mind or psychology: *psychobabble* | *psychometrics.*
– ORIGIN from Greek *psukhē* 'breath, soul, mind.'

psy·cho·a·cous·tics /ˌsīkōəˈko͞ostiks/ ▶ **plural n.** [treated as sing.] the branch of psychology concerned with the perception of sound and its physiological effects.
– DERIVATIVES **psy·cho·a·cous·tic** **adj.**

psy·cho·ac·tive /ˌsīkōˈaktiv/ ▶ **adj.** (chiefly of a drug) affecting the mind.

psy·cho·a·nal·y·sis /ˌsīkōəˈnaləsəs/ ▶ **n.** a system of psychological theory and therapy that aims to treat mental disorders by investigating the interaction of conscious and unconscious elements in the mind and bringing repressed fears and conflicts into the conscious mind by techniques such as dream interpretation and free association.
– DERIVATIVES **psy·cho·an·a·lyze** /ˌsīkōˈanlˌīz/ (Brit. **psychoanalyse**) **v.**, **psy·cho·an·a·lyt·ic** /ˌsīkōˌanlˈitik/ **adj.**, **psy·cho·an·a·lyt·i·cal** /ˌsīkōˌanlˈitikəl/ **adj.**, **psy·cho·an·a·lyt·i·cal·ly** /ˌsīkōˌanlˈitik(ə)lē/ **adv.**

psy·cho·an·a·lyst /ˌsīkōˈanl-əst/ ▶ **n.** a person who practices psychoanalysis.

psy·cho·bab·ble /ˈsīkōˌbabəl/ ▶ **n.** informal, derogatory jargon used in popular psychology.

psy·cho·bi·ol·o·gy /ˌsīkōˌbīˈäləjē/ ▶ **n.** the branch of science that deals with the biological basis of behavior and mental phenomena.
– DERIVATIVES **psy·cho·bi·o·log·i·cal** /-ˌbīəˈläjəkəl/ **adj.**, **psy·cho·bi·ol·o·gist** /-jist/ **n.**

psy·cho·dra·ma /ˌsīkōˈdrämə, -ˈdramə/ ▶ **n. 1** a form of psychotherapy in which patients act out events from their past.
2 a play, movie, or novel in which psychological elements are the main interest. ■ the genre to which such works belong.
– DERIVATIVES **psy·cho·dra·mat·ic** /-drəˈmatik/ **adj.**

psy·cho·dy·nam·ics /ˌsīkōdīˈnamiks/ ▶ **plural n.** [treated as sing.] the interrelation of the unconscious and conscious mental and emotional forces that determine personality and motivation. ■ the branch of psychology that deals with this.
– DERIVATIVES **psy·cho·dy·nam·ic** **adj.**, **psy·cho·dy·nam·i·cal·ly** /-ik(ə)lē/ **adv.**

psy·cho·gen·e·sis /ˌsīkōˈjenəsis/ ▶ **n.** [in sing.] the psychological cause to which a mental illness or behavioral disturbance may be attributed (as distinct from a physical cause).

psy·cho·gen·ic /ˌsīkōˈjenik/ ▶ **adj.** having a psychological origin or cause rather than a physical one: *psychogenic ill health.*

psy·cho·ger·i·at·rics /ˌsīkōˌjerēˈatriks/ ▶ **plural n.** [treated as sing.] the branch of health care concerned with mental illness and disturbance in elderly people, particularly those who have suffered distress as a result of moving into an institution.
– DERIVATIVES **psy·cho·ger·i·at·ric** **adj.**, **psy·cho·ger·i·a·tri·cian** /-ˌjerēəˈtrisHən/ **n.**

psy·cho·graph·ics /ˌsīkōˈgrafiks/ ▶ **plural n.** [treated as sing.] the study and classification of people according to their attitudes, aspirations, and other psychological criteria, esp. in market research.
– DERIVATIVES **psy·cho·graph·ic** **adj.**

psy·cho·his·to·ry /ˈsīkōˌhist(ə)rē/ ▶ **n.** (pl. **psychohistories**) the interpretation of historical events with the aid of psychological theory. ■ a work that interprets historical events in such a way: *modern writers often substitute psychohistory for biography.* ■ a psychological history of an individual.
– DERIVATIVES **psy·cho·his·to·ri·an** /ˌsīkō(h)isˈtôrēən/ **n.**, **psy·cho·his·to·ri·cal** /ˌsīkō(h)iˈstôrikəl/ **adj.**

psy·cho·ki·ne·sis /ˌsīkōkəˈnēsis/ ▶ **n.** the supposed ability to move objects by mental effort alone.
– DERIVATIVES **psy·cho·ki·net·ic** /-ˈnetik/ **adj.**

psychol. ▶ **abbr.** ■ psychological. ■ psychologist. ■ psychology.

psy·cho·lin·guis·tics /ˌsīkōliNGˈgwistiks/ ▶ **plural n.** [treated as sing.] the study of the relationships between linguistic behavior and psychological processes, including the process of language acquisition.
– DERIVATIVES **psy·cho·lin·guist** /-ˈliNGgwist/ **n.**, **psy·cho·lin·guis·tic** **adj.**

psy·chol·o·gese /ˌsīˌkäləˈjēz/ ▶ **n.** informal psychological jargon or technical terms used for effect.

psy·cho·log·i·cal /ˌsīkəˈläjəkəl/ ▶ **adj.** of, affecting, or arising in the mind; related to the mental and emotional state of a person: *the victim had sustained physical and psychological damage.* ■ of or relating to psychology: *psychological research.* ■ (of an ailment or problem) having a mental rather than a physical cause: *it was concluded that her pain was psychological.*
– DERIVATIVES **psy·cho·log·i·cal·ly** /-ik(ə)lē/ **adv.**

psy·cho·log·i·cal mo·ment ▶ **n.** [in sing.] the moment at which something will or would have the greatest psychological effect: *there was a psychological moment when they might have accepted the report.*

psy·cho·log·i·cal war·fare ▶ **n.** actions intended to reduce an opponent's morale.

psy·chol·o·gism /sīˈkäləˌjizəm/ ▶ **n.** Philosophy a tendency to interpret events or arguments in subjective terms, or to exaggerate the relevance of psychological factors.

psy·chol·o·gist /sīˈkäləjist/ ▶ **n.** an expert or specialist in psychology.

psy·chol·o·gize /sīˈkäləˌjīz/ ▶ **v.** [with obj.] analyze or regard in psychological terms, esp. in an uninformed way: *he lets few of Kinsey's quirks and opinions pass without psychologizing them away.* ■ [no obj.] theorize or speculate concerning the psychology of something or someone.

psy·chol·o·gy /sīˈkäləjē/ ▶ **n.** the scientific study of the human mind and its functions, esp. those affecting behavior in a given context. ■ [in sing.] the mental characteristics or attitude of a person or group: *the psychology of Americans in the 1920s.* ■ [in sing.] the mental and emotional factors governing a situation or activity: *the psychology of interpersonal relationships.*
– ORIGIN late 17th cent.: from modern Latin *psychologia* (see **PSYCHO-**, **-LOGY**).

psy·cho·met·ric /ˌsīkəˈmetrik/ ▶ **adj.** of, relating to, or deriving from psychometry or psychometrics.
– DERIVATIVES **psy·cho·met·ri·cal·ly** /-ik(ə)lē/ **adv.**

psy·cho·met·rics /ˌsīkəˈmetriks/ ▶ **plural n.** [treated as sing.] the science of measuring mental capacities and processes.
– DERIVATIVES **psy·chom·e·tri·cian** /-məˈtrisHən/ **n.**

psy·chom·e·try /sīˈkämətrē/ ▶ **n. 1** the supposed ability to discover facts about an event or person by touching inanimate objects associated with them.
2 another term for **PSYCHOMETRICS**.
– DERIVATIVES **psy·chom·e·trist** /-trist/ **n.**

psy·cho·mo·tor /ˌsīkōˈmōtər/ ▶ **adj.** [attrib.] of or relating to the origination of movement in conscious mental activity.

psy·cho·neu·ro·im·mu·nol·o·gy /ˌsīkōˌn(y)o͝orō-ˌimyəˈnäləjē/ ▶ **n.** Medicine the study of the effect of the mind on health and resistance to disease.

psy·cho·neu·ro·sis /ˌsīkōn(y)o͝oˈrōsəs/ ▶ **n.** (pl. **psychoneuroses** /-ˈrōˌsēz/) another term for **NEUROSIS**.
– DERIVATIVES **psy·cho·neu·rot·ic** /-ˌn(y)o͝oˈrätik/ **adj.**

PRONUNCIATION KEY ə *ago, up*; ər *over, fur*; a *hat*; ā *ate*; ä *car*; e *let*; ē *see*; i *fit*; ī *by*; NG *sing*; ō *go*; ô *law, for*; oi *toy*; o͝o *good*; o͞o *goo*; ou *out*; TH *thin*; TH *then*; ZH *vision*

P

psy·cho·path /ˈsīkəˌpaTH/ ▶ **n.** a person suffering from chronic mental disorder with abnormal or violent social behavior. ■ informal an unstable and aggressive person: *schoolyard psychopaths will gather around a fight to encourage the combatants.*

psy·cho·path·ic /ˌsīkəˈpaTHik/ ▶ **adj.** suffering from or constituting a chronic mental disorder with abnormal or violent social behavior: *a psychopathic disorder.* ■ informal abnormal and obsessive; manic: *an obsessive attention to detail that looked almost psychopathic.*
– DERIVATIVES **psy·cho·path·i·cal·ly** /ˌsīkəˈpaTHik(ə)lē/ **adv.**

psy·cho·pa·thol·o·gy /ˌsīkōpəˈTHäləjē, -paTHˈäl-/ ▶ **n.** the scientific study of mental disorders. ■ features of people's mental health considered collectively: *ageism, family discord, and psychopathology all play their part in abuse.* ■ mental or behavioral disorder: *she showed evidence of genuine psychopathology.*
– DERIVATIVES **psy·cho·path·o·log·i·cal** /-paTHōˈläjikəl/ **adj.**, **psy·cho·pa·thol·o·gist** /-ˈTHäləjist/ **n.**

psy·chop·a·thy /sīˈkäpəTHē/ ▶ **n.** mental illness or disorder.

psy·cho·phar·ma·col·o·gy /ˌsīkōˌfärməˈkäləjē/ ▶ **n.** the branch of psychology concerned with the effects of drugs on the mind and behavior.
– DERIVATIVES **psy·cho·phar·ma·co·log·i·cal** /-ˌfärməkəˈläjikəl/ **adj.**, **psy·cho·phar·ma·col·o·gist** /-jist/ **n.**

psy·cho·phys·ics /ˌsīkōˈfiziks/ ▶ **plural n.** [treated as sing.] the branch of psychology that deals with the relationships between physical stimuli and mental phenomena.
– DERIVATIVES **psy·cho·phys·i·cal** /-ˈfizikəl/ **adj.**

psy·cho·phys·i·ol·o·gy /ˌsīkōˌfizēˈäləjē/ ▶ **n.** Psychology the study of the relationship between physiological and psychological phenomena. ■ the way in which the mind and body interact.
– DERIVATIVES **psy·cho·phys·i·o·log·i·cal** /-ˌfizēəˈläjikəl/ **adj.**, **psy·cho·phys·i·ol·o·gist** /-jist/ **n.**

psy·cho·pomp /ˈsīkōˌpämp/ (also **psychopompos** /ˌsīkōˈpämpəs, -ˈpämpäs/) ▶ **n.** (in Greek mythology) a guide of souls to the place of the dead. ■ the spiritual guide of a living person's soul.
– ORIGIN from Greek *psukhopompos*, from *psukhē* 'soul' + *pompos* 'conductor.'

psy·cho·sex·u·al /ˌsīkōˈsekSHo͞oəl/ ▶ **adj.** of or involving the psychological aspects of the sexual impulse.
– DERIVATIVES **psy·cho·sex·u·al·ly adv.**

psy·cho·sis /sīˈkōsəs/ ▶ **n.** (pl. **psychoses** /-ˌsēz/) a severe mental disorder in which thought and emotions are so impaired that contact is lost with external reality.
– ORIGIN mid 19th cent.: from Greek *psukhōsis* 'animation,' from *psukhoun* 'give life to,' from *psukhē* 'soul, mind.'

psy·cho·so·cial /ˌsīkōˈsōSHəl/ ▶ **adj.** of or relating to the interrelation of social factors and individual thought and behavior.
– DERIVATIVES **psy·cho·so·cial·ly adv.**

psy·cho·so·mat·ic /ˌsīkōsəˈmatik/ ▶ **adj.** (of a physical illness or other condition) caused or aggravated by a mental factor such as internal conflict or stress: *her doctor was convinced that most of Edith's problems were psychosomatic.* ■ of or relating to the interaction of mind and body.
– DERIVATIVES **psy·cho·so·mat·i·cal·ly** /-ik(ə)lē/ **adv.**

psy·cho·sur·ger·y /ˌsīkōˈsərjərē/ ▶ **n.** brain surgery, such as lobotomy, used to treat mental disorder.
– DERIVATIVES **psy·cho·sur·gi·cal** /-ˈsərjikəl/ **adj.**

psy·cho·syn·the·sis /ˌsīkōˈsinTHəsəs/ ▶ **n.** Psychoanalysis the integration of separated elements of the psyche or personality.

psy·cho·ther·a·py /ˌsīkōˈTHerəpē/ ▶ **n.** the treatment of mental disorder by psychological rather than medical means.
– DERIVATIVES **psy·cho·ther·a·peu·tic** /-ˌTHerəˈpyo͞otik/ **adj.**, **psy·cho·ther·a·pist** /-ˈTHerəpist/ **n.**

psy·chot·ic /sīˈkätik/ ▶ **adj.** of, denoting, or suffering from a psychosis: *a psychotic disturbance.*
▶ **n.** a person suffering from a psychosis.
– DERIVATIVES **psy·chot·i·cal·ly** /-ik(ə)lē/ **adv.**

psy·chot·o·mi·met·ic /sīˌkätōməˈmetik/ ▶ **adj.** relating to or denoting drugs that are capable of producing an effect on the mind similar to a psychotic state.
▶ **n.** a drug of this kind.

psy·cho·tron·ic /ˌsīkəˈtränik/ ▶ **adj.** **1** denoting or relating to a genre of movies, typically with a science fiction, horror, or fantasy theme, that were made on a low budget or poorly received by critics. [1980s: coined in this sense by Michael Weldon, who edited a weekly New York guide to the best and worst films on local television.]
2 of or relating to psychotronics.

psy·cho·tron·ics /ˌsīkəˈträniks/ ▶ **plural n.** [treated as sing.] a particular branch of parapsychology that supposes an energy or force to emanate from living organisms and affect matter.
– ORIGIN 1970s: from **PSYCHO-**, on the pattern of *electronics*.

psy·cho·tro·pic /ˌsīkəˈtrōpik, -ˈträpik/ ▶ **adj.** relating to or denoting drugs that affect a person's mental state.
▶ **n.** a drug of this kind.

psy·chrom·e·ter /sīˈkrämətər/ ▶ **n.** a hygrometer consisting of a wet-bulb and a dry-bulb thermometer, the difference in the two thermometer readings being used to determine atmospheric humidity.
– ORIGIN early 18th cent.: from Greek *psukhros* 'cold' + **-METER**.

psyl·la /ˈsilə/ (also **psyllid** /ˈsilid/) ▶ **n.** Entomology a minute insect of a family (Psyllidae) that comprises the jumping plant lice.
– ORIGIN late 19th cent.: from modern Latin *Psyllidae* (plural), from Greek *psulla* 'flea.'

psyl·li·um /ˈsilēəm/ ▶ **n.** a leafy-stemmed Eurasian plantain, the seeds of which are used as a laxative and as a bulking agent in the treatment of obesity. ● *Plantago afra*, family Plantaginaceae.
– ORIGIN mid 16th cent.: via Latin from Greek *psullion*, from *psulla* 'flea' (because the seeds resemble fleas).

Psy·Ops ▶ **abbr.** psychological operations.

PT ▶ **abbr.** ■ Pacific Time. ■ physical therapy. ■ physical training. ■ postal telegraph. ■ post town. ■ Brit. pupil teacher.

Pt ▶ **symbol** the chemical element platinum.

pt ▶ **abbr.** ■ part: *pt 1 of the Consumer Protection Act 1987.* ■ payment. ■ pint; pints. ■ point. ■ Printing point (as a unit of measurement): *12 pt type.* ■ (denoting a side of a ship or aircraft) port. ■ preterit.

p.t. ▶ **abbr.** ■ past tense. ■ post town. ■ pro tempore.

PTA ▶ **abbr.** parent–teacher association.

pta. (also **Pta.**) ▶ **abbr.** (pl. **ptas.**) peseta.

Ptah /tä/ Egyptian Mythology an ancient deity of Memphis, creator of the universe, god of artisans, and husband of Sekhmet. He became one of the chief deities of Egypt, and was identified by the Greeks with Hephaestus.

ptar·mi·gan /ˈtärməgən/ ▶ **n.** (pl. **same** or **ptarmigans**) a northern grouse of mountainous and Arctic regions, with feathered legs and feet and plumage that typically changes to white in winter. ● Genus *Lagopus*, family Tetraonidae: two species, in particular the (**rock**) **ptarmigan** (*L. mutus*) of Eurasia and North America.
– ORIGIN late 16th cent.: from Scottish Gaelic *tàrmachan*. The spelling with *p-* was introduced later, suggested by Greek words starting with *pt-*.

PT boat ▶ **n.** a motorboat equipped with torpedoes and used by the military, esp. during World War II.
– ORIGIN 1940s: from *P(atrol) T(orpedo) boat*.

PTC ▶ **abbr.** Biochemistry phenylthiocarbamide.

pter·an·o·don /təˈranəˌdän, -dən/ ▶ **n.** a large tailless pterosaur of the Cretaceous period, with a long toothless beak, a long bony crest, and a wingspan of up to 7 m. ● Genus *Pteranodon*, family Pteranodontidae, order Pterosauria.
– ORIGIN modern Latin, from Greek *pteron* 'wing' + *an-* 'without' + *odous, odont-* 'tooth.'

pter·i·dol·o·gy /ˌterəˈdäləjē/ ▶ **n.** the study of ferns and related plants.
– DERIVATIVES **pter·i·do·log·i·cal** /-dlˈäjikəl/ **adj.**, **pter·i·dol·o·gist** /-jist/ **n.**
– ORIGIN mid 19th cent.: from Greek *pteris, pterid-* 'fern' + **-LOGY**.

Pter·i·doph·y·ta /ˌterəˈdäfitə/ Botany a division of flowerless green plants that comprises the ferns and their relatives. ● Division Pteridophyta: classes Filicopsida (ferns), Sphenopsida (horsetails), and Lycopsida (club mosses).
– ORIGIN modern Latin (plural), from Greek *pteris, pterid-* 'fern' + *phuton* 'plant.'

pte·rid·o·phyte /təˈridəˌfīt, ˈteridə-/ ▶ **n.** Botany a member of the Pteridophyta, a division of plants including the ferns and their allies (horsetails, club mosses).

pte·rid·o·sperm /təˈridəˌspərm, ˈteridə-/ ▶ **n.** an extinct plant that is intermediate between the ferns and seed-bearing plants, dying out in the Triassic period. Also called **SEED FERN**. ● Formerly placed in their own taxon (class Pteridospermeae), but now included with the gymnosperms.
– ORIGIN early 20th cent.: from modern Latin *pteridospermeae*, from Greek *pteris, pterid-* 'fern.'

ptero- ▶ **comb. form** relating to wings; having wings: *pterosaur*.
– ORIGIN from Greek *pteron* 'feather, wing.'

pter·o·branch /ˈterəˌbraNGk/ ▶ **n.** Zoology a minute tube-dwelling colonial acorn worm found chiefly in deep water. ● Class Pterobranchia, phylum Hemichordata.

pter·o·dac·tyl /ˌterəˈdaktəl/ ▶ **n.** a pterosaur of the late Jurassic period, with a long slender head and neck and a very short tail. ● Family Pterodactylidae, order Pterosauria: several genera, including *Pterodactylus*. ■ (in general use) any pterosaur.
– ORIGIN early 19th cent.: from modern Latin *Pterodactylus* (genus name), from Greek *pteron* 'wing' + *daktulos* 'finger.'

pter·o·pod /ˈterəˌpäd/ ▶ **n.** Zoology a small mollusk with winglike extensions to its body that it uses for swimming. ● Orders Thecosomata (with shells) and Gymnosomata (lacking shells), class Gastropoda.
– ORIGIN mid 19th cent.: from modern Latin *Pteropoda* (plural), from Greek *pteron* 'wing' + *pous, pod-* 'foot.'

pter·o·saur /ˈterəˌsôr/ ▶ **n.** an extinct warm-blooded flying reptile of the Jurassic and Cretaceous periods, with membranous wings supported by a greatly lengthened fourth finger, and probably covered with fur. ● Order Pterosauria, subdivision Archosauria: several families, including pterodactyls, pteranodons, etc.
– ORIGIN mid 19th cent.: from modern Latin *Pterosauria* (plural), from Greek *pteron* 'wing' + *sauros* 'lizard.'

pter·o·yl·glu·tam·ic ac·id /ˌterōilˌglo͞oˈtamik/ ▶ **n.** another term for **FOLIC ACID**.
– DERIVATIVES **pter·o·yl·glu·ta·mate** /-ˈglo͞otəˌmāt/ **n.**
– ORIGIN 1940s: the initial element of *pteroylglutamic* is from Greek *pteron* 'wing,' with reference to insect pigments.

pter·y·goid proc·ess /ˈteriˌgoid ˈpräˌses, ˈpräsəs/ ▶ **n.** Anatomy each of a pair of projections from the sphenoid bone in the skull.
– ORIGIN early 18th cent.: from modern Latin *pterygoides* (plural), from Greek *pterux, pterug-* 'wing.'

Pter·y·go·ta /ˌterəˈgōtə/ Entomology a large group of insects that comprises those that have wings or winged ancestors, including the majority of modern species. Compare with **APTERYGOTA**. ● Subclass Pterygota, class Insecta (or Hexapoda): many orders.
– DERIVATIVES **pter·y·gote** /ˈterəˌgōt/ **n.**
– ORIGIN modern Latin (plural), from Greek *pterugōtos* 'winged,' from *pterux, pterug-* 'wing.'

PTFE ▶ **abbr.** polytetrafluoroethylene.

ptg. ▶ **abbr.** printing.

PTH ▶ **abbr.** parathyroid hormone.

ptis·an /təˈzan, ˈtizən/ ▶ **n.** a nourishing drink, esp. barley water.
– ORIGIN late Middle English: from Latin *ptisana*, from Greek *ptisanē* 'peeled barley.' Compare with **TISANE**.

PTO ▶ **abbr.** ■ please turn over (written at the foot of a page to indicate that the text continues on the reverse). ■ (also **pto**) (in a tractor or other vehicle) power takeoff. ■ parent–teacher organization.

Ptol·e·ma·ic /ˌtäləˈmā-ik/ ▶ **adj.** **1** of or relating to the Greek astronomer Ptolemy or his theories.
2 of or relating to the Ptolemies of Egypt (see **PTOLEMY**[1]).

Ptol·e·ma·ic sys·tem (also **Ptolemaic theory**) ▶ **n.** Astronomy, historical the theory that the earth is the stationary center of the universe, with the planets moving in epicyclic orbits within surrounding concentric spheres. Compare with **COPERNICAN SYSTEM**.

Ptol·e·my[1] /ˈtäləmē/ the name of all the Macedonian rulers of Egypt, a dynasty founded by Ptolemy, a close friend and general of Alexander the Great, who took charge of Egypt after the latter's death and declared himself king (Ptolemy I) in 304 BC. The dynasty ended with the death of Cleopatra in 30 BC.

Ptol·e·my[2] Greek astronomer and geographer of the 2nd century AD. His teachings had enormous influence on medieval thought, the geocentric view of the cosmos being adopted as Christian doctrine until the late Renaissance. His *Geography* was also a standard work for centuries, despite its inaccuracies.

pto·maine /ˈtōˌmān, tōˈmān/ ▶ **n.** Chemistry, dated any of a group of amine compounds of unpleasant taste and odor formed in putrefying animal and vegetable matter and formerly thought to cause food poisoning.
– ORIGIN late 19th cent.: from French *ptomaïne*, from Italian *ptomaina*, formed irregularly from Greek *ptōma* 'corpse.'

P2P /'pētə'pē/ ▶ **abbr.** Computing peer-to-peer.

pto·sis /'tōsəs/ ▶ **n.** Medicine drooping of the upper eyelid due to paralysis or disease, or as a congenital condition.
– DERIVATIVES **pto·tic** /'tōˌtik, 'tätik/ **adj.**
– ORIGIN mid 18th cent.: from Greek *ptōsis*, from *piptein* 'to fall.'

PTSD ▶ **abbr.** post-traumatic stress disorder.

pty. ▶ **abbr.** proprietary.

pty·a·lin /'tīələn/ ▶ **n.** Biochemistry a form of amylase found in the saliva of humans and some other animals.
– ORIGIN mid 19th cent.: from Greek *ptualon* 'spittle' + **-IN**[1].

p-type ▶ **adj.** Electronics denoting a region in a semiconductor in which electrical conduction is due chiefly to the movement of positive holes. Often contrasted with **N-TYPE**.

Pu ▶ **symbol** the chemical element plutonium.

pub /pəb/ Brit. ▶ **n.** a tavern or bar. ■ Austral. a hotel.
▶ **v.** [no obj.] (usu. as noun **pubbing**) informal spend time in pubs.
– ORIGIN mid 19th cent.: abbreviation of **PUBLIC HOUSE**.

pub. ▶ **abbr.** ■ publication(s). ■ published. ■ publisher.

pub·cast·er /'pəbˌkastər/ ▶ **n.** a publicly owned broadcasting station or network: *a reality show developed for Norwegian pubcaster NRK.*

pub crawl informal, chiefly Brit. ▶ **n.** a tour taking in several pubs or bars, with one or more drinks at each.
▶ **v.** [no obj.] (**pub-crawl**) go on a pub crawl.

pu·ber·ty /'pyo͞obərtē/ ▶ **n.** the period during which adolescents reach sexual maturity and become capable of reproduction.
– DERIVATIVES **pu·ber·tal** /-bərtl/ **adj.**
– ORIGIN late Middle English: from Latin *pubertas*, from *puber* 'adult,' related to *pubes* (see **PUBES**).

pu·bes ▶ **n. 1** /'pyo͞obēz, pyo͞obz/ (pl. **same**) the lower part of the abdomen at the front of the pelvis, covered with hair from puberty.
2 /'pyo͞obēz/ plural form of **PUBIS**.
– ORIGIN late 16th cent.: from Latin, 'pubic hair, groin, genitals.'

pu·bes·cence /pyo͞o'besəns/ ▶ **n. 1** the time when puberty begins.
2 Botany & Zoology soft down or fine short hairs on the leaves and stems of plants or on various parts of animals, esp. insects.
– ORIGIN late Middle English: from French, or from medieval Latin *pubescentia*, from Latin *pubescent-* 'reaching puberty' (see **PUBESCENT**).

pu·bes·cent /pyo͞o'besənt/ ▶ **adj. 1** relating to or denoting a person at or approaching the age of puberty.
2 Botany & Zoology covered with short soft hair; downy.
▶ **n.** a person at or approaching the age of puberty.
– ORIGIN mid 17th cent.: from French, or from Latin *pubescent-* 'reaching puberty,' from the verb *pubescere*.

pu·bic /'pyo͞obik/ ▶ **adj.** [attrib.] of or relating to the pubes or pubis: *pubic hair.*

pu·bic louse ▶ **n.** another term for **CRAB**[1] (sense 2 of the noun).

pu·bis /'pyo͞obəs/ ▶ **n.** (pl. **pubes** /-bēz/) either of a pair of bones forming the two sides of the pelvis.
– ORIGIN late 16th cent.: from Latin *os pubis* 'bone of the pubes.'

publ. ▶ **abbr.** ■ public. ■ publication. ■ publicity. ■ published. ■ publisher.

pub·lic /'pəblik/ ▶ **adj. 1** of or concerning the people as a whole: *public concern | public affairs.* ■ open to or shared by all the people of an area or country: *a public library.* ■ of or provided by the government rather than an independent, commercial company: *public spending.* ■ of or involved in the affairs of the community, esp. in government: *his public career was destroyed by tenacious reporters.* ■ known to many people; famous: *a public figure.*
2 done, perceived, or existing in open view: *he wanted a public apology in the Wall Street Journal | we should talk somewhere less public.*
3 Brit. of, for, or acting for a university: *public examination results.*
▶ **n.** (**the public**) [treated as sing. or pl.] ordinary people in general; the community: *the library is open to the public | the public has made an informed choice.* ■ [with adj. or noun modifier] a section of the community having a particular interest or connection: *the reading public.* ■ (**one's public**) the people who watch or are interested in an artist, writer, or performer: *some famous last words to give my public.*
– PHRASES **go public 1** become a public company. **2** reveal details about a previously private concern: *Bates* ***went public with*** *the news at a press conference.* **in public** in view of other people; when others are present: *men don't cry in public.* **the public eye** the state of being known or of interest to people in general, esp. through the media: *the pressures of being constantly* ***in the public eye****.*
– ORIGIN late Middle English: from Old French, from Latin *publicus*, blend of *poplicus* 'of the people' (from *populus* 'people') and *pubes* 'adult.'

pub·lic act ▶ **n.** an act of legislation affecting the public as a whole.

pub·lic-ad·dress sys·tem ▶ **n.** a system of microphones, amplifiers, and loudspeakers used to amplify speech or music in a large building or at an outdoor gathering.

pub·li·can /'pəblikən/ ▶ **n. 1** Brit. a person who owns or manages a pub.
2 (in ancient Roman and biblical times) a collector of taxes.
– ORIGIN Middle English (sense 2): from Old French *publicain*, from Latin *publicanus*, from *publicum* 'public revenue,' neuter (used as a noun) of *publicus* 'of the people.' Sense 1 dates from the early 18th cent.

pub·lic as·sis·tance ▶ **n.** government benefits provided to the needy, usually in the form of cash or vouchers.

pub·li·ca·tion /ˌpəbli'kāsHən/ ▶ **n.** the preparation and issuing of a book, journal, piece of music, or other work for public sale: *the publication of her first novel.* ■ a book, journal, etc. issued for public sale: *scientific publications.* ■ the action of making something generally known: *the publication of April trade figures.*
– ORIGIN late Middle English (in the sense 'public announcement or declaration'): via Old French from Latin *publicatio(n-)*, from *publicare* 'make public' (see **PUBLISH**).

pub·lic com·pa·ny (also **public corporation**) ▶ **n.** a company whose shares are traded freely on a stock exchange.

pub·lic de·fend·er ▶ **n.** Law a lawyer employed at public expense in a criminal trial to represent a defendant who is unable to afford legal assistance.

pub·lic do·main ▶ **n.** the state of belonging or being available to the public as a whole, and therefore not subject to copyright: *the photograph had been in the public domain for 15 years* | [as modifier] *public-domain software.*

pub·lic en·e·my ▶ **n.** a notorious wanted criminal. ■ a person or thing regarded as the greatest threat to a group or community: *he identified inflation as* ***public enemy number one****.*

pub·lic good ▶ **n. 1** Economics a commodity or service that is provided without profit to all members of a society, either by the government or a private individual or organization.
2 the benefit or well-being of the public: *the public good clearly demands independent action.*

pub·lic house ▶ **n.** chiefly Brit. a tavern.

pub·li·cist /'pəbləsist/ ▶ **n. 1** a person responsible for publicizing a product, person, or company.
2 dated a journalist, esp. one concerned with current affairs. ■ archaic a writer or other person skilled in international law.
– DERIVATIVES **pub·li·cis·tic** /ˌpəblə'sistik/ **adj.**
– ORIGIN late 18th cent.: from French *publiciste*, from Latin *(jus) publicum* 'public (law).'

pub·lic·i·ty /pə'blisətē/ ▶ **n.** the notice or attention given to someone or something by the media: *the case attracted wide publicity in the press.* ■ the giving out of information about a product, person, or company for advertising or promotional purposes: *head of publicity and marketing* | [as modifier] *publicity photographs.* ■ material or information used for such a purpose: *we distributed publicity from a stall in the marketplace.*
– ORIGIN late 18th cent.: from French *publicité*, from *public* 'public' (see **PUBLIC**).

pub·lic·i·ty a·gent ▶ **n.** another term for **PUBLICIST** (sense 1).

pub·li·cize /'pobləˌsīz/ ▶ **v.** [with obj.] make (something) widely known: *use the magazine to publicize human rights abuses.* ■ give out publicity about (a product, person, or company) for advertising or promotional purposes: *Judy had started to publicize books and celebrities.*
– DERIVATIVES **pub·li·ci·za·tion n.**

pub·lic key ▶ **n.** a cryptographic key that can be obtained and used by anyone to encrypt messages intended for a particular recipient, such that the encrypted messages can be deciphered only by using a second key that is known only to the recipient (the **private key**).

pub·lic law ▶ **n.** the law of relationships between individuals and the government.

pub·lic lend·ing right (abbr.: **PLR**) ▶ **n.** (in the UK) the right of authors to receive payment when their books or other works are loaned out by public libraries.

pub·lic·ly /'pəbliklē/ ▶ **adv.** so as to be seen by other people; in public: *some weep publicly.* ■ [often sentence adverb] used in reference to views expressed to others and not necessarily genuinely felt: *publicly, officials criticized the resolution, but privately they thought it tolerable.* ■ by a government or the public rather than an independent, commercial company: *publicly funded organizations | a publicly owned company.*

> **USAGE** Note that the spelling is **publicly**, ending with the suffix **-ly**, not **publically**.

pub·lic nui·sance ▶ **n.** an act, condition, or thing that is illegal because it interferes with the rights of the public generally. ■ informal an obnoxious or dangerous person or group of people.

pub·lic o·pin·ion ▶ **n.** views prevalent among the general public.

pub·lic or·a·tor ▶ **n.** another term for **ORATOR**.

pub·lic pol·i·cy ▶ **n. 1** the principles, often unwritten, on which social laws are based.
2 Law the principle that injury to the public good is a basis for denying the legality of a contract or other transaction.

pub·lic pros·e·cu·tor ▶ **n.** a law officer who conducts criminal proceedings on behalf of the government or in the public interest.

pub·lic purse ▶ **n.** the funds raised by a government by taxation or other means.

pub·lic re·la·tions ▶ **plural n.** [also treated as sing.] the professional maintenance of a favorable public image by a company or other organization or a famous person. ■ the state of the relationship between the public and a company or other organization or a famous person: *companies justify the cost in terms of improved public relations.*

pub·lic school ▶ **n. 1** (chiefly in North America) a school supported by public funds.
2 (in the UK) a private for-fee secondary school.
– ORIGIN late 16th cent.: from Latin *publica schola*, denoting a school maintained at the public expense; in England *public school* (a term recorded from 1580) originally denoted a grammar school under public management, founded for the benefit of the public (contrasting with *private school*, run for the profit of the proprietor); since the 19th cent. the term has been applied to the old endowed English grammar schools, and newer schools modeled on them, which have developed into for-fee boarding schools.

pub·lic sec·tor ▶ **n.** the part of an economy that is controlled by the government.

pub·lic serv·ant ▶ **n.** a government official.

pub·lic-serv·ice cor·po·ra·tion ▶ **n.** a public utility.

pub·lic spir·it ▶ **n.** willingness to do things that help the public.

pub·lic-spir·it·ed ▶ **adj.** willing to help the wider community; socially concerned: *those public-spirited people who call attention to low standards in high places.*
– DERIVATIVES **pub·lic-spir·it·ed·ly adv.**, **pub·lic-spir·it·ed·ness n.**

pub·lic trans·por·ta·tion ▶ **n.** buses, trains, subways, and other forms of transportation that charge set fares, run on fixed routes, and are available to the public.

pub·lic u·til·i·ty ▶ **n.** an organization supplying a community with electricity, gas, water, or sewerage.

pub·lic works ▶ **plural n.** the work of building such things as roads, schools, and reservoirs, carried out by the government for the community.

pub·lish /'pəblisH/ ▶ **v.** [with obj.] **1** (of an author or company) prepare and issue (a book, journal, piece of music, or other work) for public sale: *we publish practical reference books* | [no obj.] *the pressures on researchers to publish.* ■ print (something) in a book or journal so as to make it generally known: *we pay $10 for every letter we publish.* ■ (usu. as adj. **published**) prepare and issue the works of (a particular writer): *a published author.* ■ formally announce or read (an edict or marriage banns).
2 Law communicate (a libel) to a third party.
– DERIVATIVES **pub·lish·a·ble adj.**
– ORIGIN Middle English (in the sense 'make generally known'): from the stem of Old French *puplier*, from Latin *publicare* 'make public,' from *publicus* (see **PUBLIC**).

pub·lish·er /'pəblisHər/ ▶ **n.** (also **publishers**) a person or company that prepares and issues

P

books, journals, music, or other works for sale: *the publishers of Vogue | a commercial music publisher.* ■ a newspaper proprietor.

pub·lish·ing /ˈpəbliSHiNG/ ▶ **n.** the occupation, business, or activity of preparing and issuing books, journals, and other material for sale: *she worked in publishing.*

Puc·ci·ni /po͞oˈCHēnē/, Giacomo (1858–1924), Italian composer. His sense of the dramatic, gift for melody, and skillful use of the orchestra have contributed to his enduring popularity. Notable operas: *La Bohème* (1896), *Tosca* (1900), and *Madama Butterfly* (1904).

puc·coon /pəˈko͞on/ ▶ **n.** a North American plant that yields a pigment from which dye or medicinal products are obtained, esp. formerly. ● Genus *Lithospermum*, family Boraginaceae: several species, including **hoary puccoon** (*L. canescens*).
– ORIGIN early 17th cent.: from Virginia Algonquian *poughkone*.

puce /pyo͞os/ ▶ **adj.** of a dark red or purple-brown color: *his face was puce with rage and frustration.*
▶ **n.** a dark red or purple-brown color.
– ORIGIN late 18th cent.: from French, literally 'flea(-color),' from Latin *pulex, pulic-*.

puck[1] /pək/ ▶ **n. 1** a black disk made of hard rubber, the focus of play in ice hockey.
2 Computing an input device similar to a mouse that is dragged across a sensitive surface, which notes the puck's position to move the cursor on the screen.
– ORIGIN late 19th cent.: of unknown origin.

puck[2] /pək/ a mischievous or evil sprite.
– DERIVATIVES **puck·like** /-ˌlīk/ **adj.**
– ORIGIN Old English *pūca*.

puck·er /ˈpəkər/ ▶ **v.** (esp. with reference to a person's face) tightly gather or contract into wrinkles or small folds: [no obj.] *her brows puckered in a frown* | [with obj.] *the baby stirred, **puckering up** its tiny face.*
▶ **n.** a tightly gathered wrinkle or small fold, esp. on a person's face: *a pucker between his eyebrows.*
– PHRASES **pucker up** contract one's lips as in preparation for a kiss.
– DERIVATIVES **puck·er·y** /ˈpəkərē/ **adj.**
– ORIGIN late 16th cent. (as a verb): probably frequentative, from the base of **POKE**[2] and **POCKET** (suggesting the formation of small purselike gatherings).

Puck·ett /ˈpəkit/, Kirby (1961–2006) US baseball player. An outfielder for the Minnesota Twins 1984–96, he was noted for both his hitting and fielding. He helped his team to win two World Series 1987 and 1991. Baseball Hall of Fame (2001).

puck·ish /ˈpəkiSH/ ▶ **adj.** playful, esp. in a mischievous way: *a puckish sense of humor.*
– DERIVATIVES **puck·ish·ly adv., puck·ish·ness n.**

pud /po͝od/ ▶ **n.** Brit. informal short for **PUDDING**.

pud·ding /ˈpo͝odiNG/ ▶ **n. 1** a dessert with a creamy consistency: *chocolate pudding | a rice pudding.* ■ chiefly Brit. any dessert. ■ chiefly Brit. the dessert course of a meal: *what's for pudding?*
2 a sweet or savory steamed dish made with flour: *Yorkshire pudding.* ■ the intestines of a pig or sheep stuffed with oatmeal, spices, and meat and boiled. See also **BLACK PUDDING, BLOOD SAUSAGE**. ■ informal a fat, dumpy, or stupid person: *away with you, you big pudding!*
– PHRASES **in the pudding club** Brit. informal pregnant.
– DERIVATIVES **pud·ding·y adj.**
– ORIGIN Middle English (denoting a sausage such as *black pudding*): apparently from Old French *boudin* 'black pudding,' from Latin *botellus* 'sausage, small intestine.'

pud·ding face ▶ **n.** informal a large chubby face.
– DERIVATIVES **pud·ding-faced adj.**

pud·ding·stone /ˈpo͝odiNGˌstōn/ ▶ **n.** a conglomerate rock in which dark-colored rounded pebbles contrast with a paler fine-grained matrix.

pud·dle /ˈpədl/ ▶ **n. 1** a small pool of liquid, esp. of rainwater on the ground: *splashing through deep puddles* | figurative *a little puddle of light.*
2 clay and sand mixed with water and used as a watertight covering for embankments.
▶ **v.** [with obj.] **1** wet or cover (a surface) with water, esp. rainwater: *the cobbles under our feet were wet and puddled.* ■ [no obj.] (of liquid) form a small pool: *rivulets of water coursed down the panes, puddling on the sill.* ■ [no obj.] archaic dabble or wallow in mud or shallow water: *children are playing and puddling about in the dirt.* ■ [no obj.] (**puddle around/about**) informal occupy oneself in a disorganized or unproductive way: *the Internet is just the latest excuse for puddling around at work.*
2 line (a hole) with puddle. ■ work (mixed water and clay) to separate gold or opal. ■ (usu. as noun **puddling**) chiefly historical stir (molten iron) with iron oxide in a furnace, to produce wrought iron by oxidizing carbon.
– DERIVATIVES **pud·dler** /ˈpədlər, ˈpədl-ər/ **n.**, **pud·dly** /ˈpədlē, ˈpədl-ē/ **adj.**
– ORIGIN Middle English: diminutive of Old English *pudd* 'ditch, furrow'; compare with German dialect *Pfudel* 'pool.'

pud·dle jump·er ▶ **n.** informal a small light airplane that is fast and highly maneuverable and used for short trips.

pu·den·cy /ˈpyo͞odn-sē/ ▶ **n.** literary modesty; shame.
– ORIGIN early 17th cent.: from late Latin *pudentia*.

pu·den·dum /pyo͞oˈdendəm/ ▶ **n.** (pl. **pudenda** /-ˈdendə/) (often **pudenda**) a person's external genitals, esp. a woman's.
– DERIVATIVES **pu·den·dal** /-ˈdendəl/ **adj.**, **pu·dic** /ˈpyo͞odik/ **adj.**
– ORIGIN mid 17th cent.: from Latin *pudenda* (*membra*) '(parts) to be ashamed of,' neuter plural of the gerundive of *pudere* 'be ashamed.'

pu·deur /pyo͞oˈdər/ ▶ **n.** a sense of shame or embarrassment, esp. with regard to matters of a sexual or personal nature.
– ORIGIN mid 20th cent.: French, literally 'modesty.'

pudge /pəj/ ▶ **n.** informal fat on a person's body: *subtle makeup that sharpened the pudge out of her cheekbones.*
– ORIGIN early 19th cent. (denoting a fat person): of unknown origin.

pudg·y /ˈpəjē/ ▶ **adj.** (**pudgier, pudgiest**) informal (of a person or part of their body) slightly fat: *his pudgy fingers.*
– DERIVATIVES **pudg·i·ly** /ˈpəjəlē/ **adv.**, **pudg·i·ness n.**

pu·du /ˈpo͞odo͞o/ ▶ **n.** a very small and rare deer found in the lower Andes of South America.
● Genus *Pudu*, family Cervidae: two species.
– ORIGIN late 19th cent.: from Araucanian.

Pu·du·cher·ry /ˌpo͞odo͞oˈCHerē/ a Union Territory of southeastern India, on the Coromandel Coast, formed from several former French territories and incorporated into India in 1954. Former name (until 2006) **PONDICHERRY**. ■ its capital city; pop. 232,300 (est. 2009).

Pue·bla /ˈpweblä/ a state in south central Mexico. ■ its capital city that lies at the edge of the central Mexican plateau; pop. 1,399,519 (2005). Full name **Puebla de Zaragoza**.

Pueb·lo /ˈpweblō/ an industrial city in south central Colorado, on the Arkansas River, at the foot of the Front Range of the Rocky Mountains; pop. 104,951 (est. 2008).

pueb·lo /ˈpweblō, po͞oˈeb-/ ▶ **n.** (pl. **pueblos**) **1** an American Indian settlement of the southwestern US, esp. one consisting of multistoried adobe houses built by the Pueblo people.
2 (**Pueblo**) (pl. **same** or **pueblos**) a member of any of various American Indian peoples, including the Hopi, occupying pueblo settlements chiefly in New Mexico and Arizona. Their prehistoric period is known as the Anasazi culture.
▶ **adj.** (**Pueblo**) of, relating to, or denoting the Pueblos or their culture.
– ORIGIN Spanish, literally 'people,' from Latin *populus*.

pu·er·ile /ˈpyo͞o(ə)rəl, ˈpyo͞orˌīl/ ▶ **adj.** childishly silly and trivial: *you're making puerile excuses.*
– DERIVATIVES **pu·er·ile·ly adv.**, **pu·er·il·i·ty** /pyo͞o(ə)ˈrilətē/ **n.** (pl. **puerilities**).
– ORIGIN late 16th cent. (in the sense 'like a boy'): from French *puéril* or Latin *puerilis*, from *puer* 'boy.'

pu·er·per·al fe·ver /pyo͞oˈərpərəl/ ▶ **n.** fever caused by uterine infection following childbirth.

pu·er·pe·ri·um /ˌpyo͞oərˈpi(ə)rēəm/ ▶ **n.** Medicine the period of about six weeks after childbirth during which the mother's reproductive organs return to their original nonpregnant condition.
– DERIVATIVES **pu·er·per·al** /pyo͞oˈərpərəl/ **adj.**
– ORIGIN early 17th cent.: from Latin, from *puerperus* 'parturient' (from *puer* 'child' + *-parus* 'bearing').

Puer·to Cor·tés /ˈpwertō kôrˈtes/ a port in northwestern Honduras, on the Caribbean coast at the mouth of the Ulua River; pop. 66,000 (est. 2008).

Puer·to Pla·ta /ˈpwertō ˈplätä/ a resort town in the Dominican Republic, on the northern coast; pop. 134,200 (est. 2009).

Puer·to Ri·co /ˌpôrtə ˈrēkō, ˌpwertə/ an island in the Greater Antilles in the Caribbean Sea; pop. 3,966,200 (est. 2009); capital, San Juan. One of the earliest Spanish settlements in the New World, it was ceded to the US in 1898 after the Spanish-American War. In 1952 it became a commonwealth in voluntary association with the US with full powers of local government.
– DERIVATIVES **Puer·to Ri·can** /ˈrēkən/ **adj. & n.**

Puer·to Ri·co Trench an ocean trench north of Puerto Rico and the Leeward Islands that extends in an east–west direction. It reaches a depth of 28,397 feet (9,220 m).

puff /pəf/ ▶ **n. 1** a short, explosive burst of breath or wind: *a puff of wind swung the weathervane around.* ■ the sound of air or vapor escaping suddenly: *the whistle and puff of steam.* ■ a small quantity of vapor or smoke, emitted in one blast: *the fire breathed out **a puff of blue smoke**.* ■ an act of drawing quickly on a pipe, cigarette, or cigar: *he took a puff of his cigar.*
2 [usu. with modifier or in combination] a light pastry case, typically one made of puff pastry, containing a sweet or savory filling: *a cream puff.* ■ a gathered mass of material in a dress or other garment. ■ a rolled protuberant mass of hair. ■ a powder puff. ■ a soft quilt: *plump pillows and puffs.*
3 informal a review of a work of art, book, or theatrical production, esp. an excessively complimentary one: *the publishers sent him a copy of the book hoping for a puff.* ■ Brit. an advertisement, esp. one exaggerating the value of the goods advertised.
▶ **v. 1** [no obj.] breathe in repeated short gasps: *exercises that make you puff.* ■ [with adverbial] (of a person, engine, etc.) move with short, noisy breaths or bursts of air or steam: *the train came puffing in.* ■ smoke a pipe, cigarette, or cigar: *he **puffed on** his pipe contentedly.* ■ [with obj.] blow (dust, smoke, or a light object) in a specified direction with a quick breath or blast of air: *he lighted his pipe and puffed forth smoke.* ■ move through the air in short bursts: *his breath puffed out like white smoke.*
2 (**puff something out/up** or **puff out/up**) cause to swell or become swollen: [with obj.] *he suddenly sucked his stomach in and puffed his chest out* | [no obj.] *when he was in a temper, his cheeks puffed up and his eyes shrank.* ■ (**be puffed up**) be conceited: *he was never puffed up about his writing.*
3 [with obj.] advertise with exaggerated or false praise: *publishers have puffed the book on the grounds that it contains new discoveries.*
– ORIGIN Middle English: imitative of the sound of a breath, perhaps from Old English *pyf* (noun), *pyffan* (verb).

puff ad·der ▶ **n.** a large, sluggish, mainly nocturnal African viper that inflates the upper part of its body and hisses loudly in threat. ● *Bitis arietans*, family Viperidae. ■ another term for **HOGNOSE SNAKE**.

puff·back /ˈpəfˌbak/ (also **puff-back shrike**) ▶ **n.** a small black-and-white African shrike, the male of which displays by puffing up the feathers of the lower back. ● Genus *Dryoscopus*, family Laniidae: several species, in particular *D. gambensis*.

puff·ball /ˈpəfˌbôl/ ▶ **n. 1** a fungus that produces a spherical or pear-shaped fruiting body that ruptures when ripe to release a cloud of spores. ● Families Lycoperdaceae, class Gasteromycetes, in particular genus *Lycoperdon*. See also **GIANT PUFFBALL**.
2 the spherical head of a dandelion that has gone to seed.

puff·bird /ˈpəfˌbərd/ ▶ **n.** a stocky large-headed bird somewhat resembling a kingfisher, found in tropical American forests. ● Family Bucconidae: several genera and many species.

puffed /pəft/ ▶ **adj.** (also **puffed up**) swollen: *puffed eyelids.* ■ (of a sleeve or other part of a garment) gathered so as to have a rounded shape.

puff·er /ˈpəfər/ ▶ **n. 1** informal a person or thing that puffs, in particular, a person who smokes.
2 short for **PUFFERFISH**.

puff·er·fish /ˈpəfərˌfiSH/ (also **puffer fish**) ▶ **n.** (pl. **same** or **pufferfishes**) a stout-bodied marine or freshwater fish (family Tetraodontidae: several genera and many species) that typically has spiny skin and inflates itself like a balloon when threatened. It is sometimes used as food, but some parts are highly toxic.

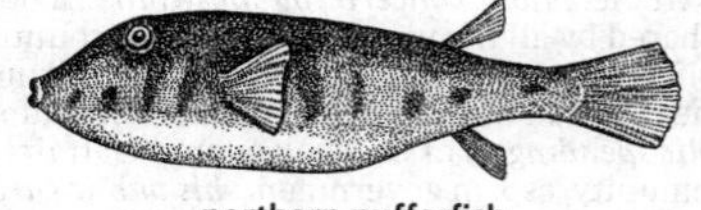
northern pufferfish

puff·er·y /ˈpəfərē/ ▶ **n.** exaggerated or false praise.

puf·fin /ˈpəfən/ ▶ **n.** a hole-nesting auk (seabird) of northern and Arctic waters, with a large head and a massive, brightly colored triangular bill. ● Genera *Fratercula* and *Lunda*, family Alcidae: three species, in particular the **Atlantic puffin** (*F. arctica*).
– ORIGIN Middle English (denoting the Manx

Atlantic puffin

shearwater): apparently from PUFF + -ING[3], with reference to the Manx shearwater's fat nestlings. The later use is a confusion, by association of nesting habits and habitat.

puff pas·try ▶ n. light flaky pastry, used for pie crusts, canapés, etc.

puff piece ▶ n. informal a newspaper article or item on a television show using exaggerated praise to advertise or promote a celebrity, book, or event.

puff sleeve ▶ n. a short sleeve gathered at the top and cuff and full in the middle.

puff·y /ˈpəfē/ ▶ adj. (**puffier**, **puffiest**) **1** (esp. of part of the body) unusually swollen and soft: *her eyes were puffy and full of tears.* ■ soft, rounded, and light: *small puffy clouds.* ■ (of a garment or part of a garment) padded or gathered to give a rounded shape: *a puffy blue ski jacket.*
2 (of wind or breath) coming in short bursts: *his breath was puffy and fast.*
– DERIVATIVES **puff·i·ly** /ˈpəfəlē/ adv., **puff·i·ness** n.

pug[1] /pəg/ ▶ n. (also **pug dog**) a dog of a dwarf breed like a bulldog with a broad flat nose and deeply wrinkled face.
– DERIVATIVES **pug·gish** adj., **pug·gy** /ˈpəgē/ adj.
– ORIGIN mid 18th cent.: perhaps of Low German origin.

pug dog

pug[2] ▶ n. loam or clay mixed and worked into a soft, plastic condition without air pockets for making bricks or pottery.
▶ v. (**pugs, pugging, pugged**) [with obj.] **1** (usu. as adj. **pugged**) prepare (clay) in this way, typically in a machine with rotating blades.
2 (usu. as noun **pugging**) pack (a space, typically the space under a floor) with pug, sawdust, or other material in order to deaden sound.
– ORIGIN early 19th cent.: of unknown origin.

pug[3] ▶ n. informal a boxer.
– ORIGIN mid 19th cent.: abbreviation of PUGILIST.

pug[4] ▶ n. the footprint of an animal: [as modifier] *I saw the pug marks of the tigress in the soft earth.*
▶ v. (**pugs, pugging, pugged**) [with obj.] track (an animal) by its footprints.
– ORIGIN mid 19th cent.: from Hindi *pag* 'footprint.'

pug dog ▶ n. another term for PUG[1].

Pu·get Sound /ˈpyo͞ojit/ an inlet of the Pacific Ocean on the coast of the state of Washington. It is linked to the ocean by the Strait of Juan de Fuca. Seattle is situated on its eastern shore.
– ORIGIN named after Peter *Puget*, aide to George Vancouver who explored it in 1792.

pug·ga·ree /ˈpəg(ə)rē/ ▶ n. an Indian turban. ■ a thin muslin scarf tied around a sun helmet so as to hang down over the wearer's neck and shield it from the sun.
– ORIGIN from Hindi *pagrī* 'turban.'

pu·gi·lism /ˌpyo͞ojəˌlizəm/ ▶ n. dated or humorous the profession or hobby of boxing: *I do not go to displays of pugilism.*

pu·gi·list /ˈpyo͞ojəlist/ ▶ n. dated or humorous a boxer, esp. a professional one.
– DERIVATIVES **pu·gi·lis·tic** /ˌpyo͞ojəˈlistik/ adj.
– ORIGIN mid 18th cent.: from Latin *pugil* 'boxer' + -IST.

pug mill ▶ n. a machine for mixing and working clay and other materials into pug (see PUG[2]).

pug·na·cious /pəgˈnāsʜəs/ ▶ adj. eager or quick to argue, quarrel, or fight: *the increasingly pugnacious demeanor of politicians.*
– DERIVATIVES **pug·na·cious·ly** adv., **pug·nac·i·ty** /ˌpəgˈnasətē/ n.
– ORIGIN mid 17th cent.: from Latin *pugnax, pugnac-* (from *pugnare* 'to fight,' from *pugnus* 'fist') + -IOUS.

pug nose ▶ n. a short nose with an upturned tip.
– DERIVATIVES **pug-nosed** adj.

Pug·wash con·fer·en·ces /ˈpəgˌwôsʜ, -ˌwäsʜ/ a series of international conferences first held in Pugwash (a village in Nova Scotia) in 1957 by scientists to promote the peaceful application of scientific discoveries.

puis·ne /ˈpyo͞onē/ ▶ adj. [attrib.] Law (in the UK and some other countries) denoting a judge of a superior court inferior in rank to chief justices.
– ORIGIN late 16th cent. (as a noun, denoting a junior or inferior person): from Old French, from *puis* (from Latin *postea* 'afterwards') + *ne* 'born' (from Latin *natus*). Compare with PUNY.

puis·ne mort·gage ▶ n. Law, chiefly Brit. a second or subsequent mortgage of unregistered land of which the title deeds are retained by a first mortgagee.

pu·is·sance /ˈpwisəns, ˈpwē-, pyo͞oˈisəns/ ▶ n.
1 (**Puissance**) [in sing.] a competitive test of a horse's ability to jump large obstacles in show jumping.
2 archaic or literary great power, influence, or prowess.
– ORIGIN late Middle English (sense 2): from Old French, 'power,' from *puissant* 'having power' (see PUISSANT). Sense 1 dates from the 1950s.

pu·is·sant /ˈpwisənt, ˈpwēsənt, ˈpyo͞oəsənt/ ▶ adj. archaic or literary having great power or influence.
– DERIVATIVES **pu·is·sant·ly** adv.
– ORIGIN late Middle English: via Old French from Latin *posse* 'be able.'

pu·ja /ˈpo͞ojə/ (also **pooja**) ▶ n. Hinduism & Buddhism the act of worship: *I perform puja every day | the entire family gets together for a puja.*
– ORIGIN Sanskrit *pūjā* 'worship.'

puke /pyo͞ok/ informal ▶ v. vomit: [no obj.] *I had eaten to the point of puking* | [with obj.] *he **puked up** his pizza.*
▶ n. vomit.
– DERIVATIVES **puk·ey** adj.
– ORIGIN late 16th cent.: probably imitative; first recorded as a verb in: "At first the infant, mewling, and puking in the nurse's arms," in Shakespeare's *As You Like It* (II. vii. 144).

puk·ka /ˈpəkə/ (also **pukkah**) ▶ adj. informal, chiefly Brit. genuine: *the more expensive brands are pukka natural mineral waters.* ■ of or appropriate to high or respectable society: *it wouldn't be considered the pukka thing to do.* ■ excellent: *"That Danny is totally gorgeous." "Yeah, pukka haircut."*
– ORIGIN late 17th cent.: from Hindi *pakkā* 'cooked, ripe, substantial.'

pul /po͞ol/ ▶ n. (pl. **puls** or **puli** /ˈpo͞olē/) a monetary unit of Afghanistan, equal to one hundredth of an afghani.
– ORIGIN Pashto, from Persian *pūl* 'copper coin.'

pu·la /ˈp(y)o͞olə/ ▶ n. (pl. **same**) the basic monetary unit of Botswana, equal to 100 thebe.
– ORIGIN Setswana, literally 'rain.'

pu·lao /pəˈlou, pəˈlō, ˈpərlo͞o/ ▶ n. variant spelling of PILAF.

Pu·las·ki[1] /pəˈlaskē/, Casimir (1747–79) Polish count and commissioned American cavalry officer; name in Polish *Kazimierz Pulaski.* Having fled from involvement in a Polish rebellion 1768–72, he arrived in America 1777 and joined the cause of American independence. Commissioned a general in 1778, he was invaluable in the defense of Charleston 1779 but was mortally wounded at the siege of Savannah.

Pu·las·ki[2] ▶ n. (pl. **Pulaskis**) a tool with a head that has an ax blade on one side and an adze on the other.
– ORIGIN 1920s: named after Edward C. *Pulaski* (1866–1931), the American forest ranger who designed it.

Pu·lau Se·ri·bu /ˌpo͞olou ˈseribo͞o/ Indonesian name for THOUSAND ISLANDS (sense 2).

pul·chri·tude /ˈpəlkrəˌt(y)o͞od/ ▶ n. literary beauty.
– DERIVATIVES **pul·chri·tu·di·nous** /ˌpəlkrəˈt(y)o͞odn-əs/ adj.
– ORIGIN late Middle English: from Latin *pulchritudo*, from *pulcher, pulchr-* 'beautiful.'

pule /pyo͞ol/ ▶ v. [no obj.] (often as adj. **puling**) literary cry querulously or weakly: *she's no puling infant.*
– ORIGIN late Middle English (originally referring to a bird's cry): probably imitative; compare with French *piauler*, in the same sense.

pu·li /ˈpo͞olē/ ▶ n. (pl. **pulik** /ˈpo͞olik/) a sheepdog of a black, gray, or white breed with a long thick coat.
– ORIGIN mid 20th cent.: from Hungarian.

Pul·it·zer /ˈpo͞olitsər, ˈpyo͞ol-/, Joseph (1847–1911), US newspaper publisher and editor, born in Hungary. A pioneer of popular journalism, he owned a number of newspapers, including the *New York World*. He made provisions in his will for the establishment of the annual Pulitzer Prizes.

Pu·litz·er Prize ▶ n. an award for an achievement in American journalism, literature, or music. There are thirteen made each year.

pull /po͝ol/ ▶ v. [with obj.] **1** [usu. with adverbial] exert force on (someone or something), typically by taking hold of them, in order to move or try to move them toward oneself or the origin of the force: *he pulled them down onto the couch* | [with obj. and complement] *I pulled the door shut behind me* | [no obj.] *the little boy **pulled at** her skirt.* ■ (of an animal or vehicle) be attached to the front and be the source of forward movement of (a vehicle): *the carriage was pulled by four horses.* ■ take hold of and exert force on (something) so as to move it from a specified position or in a specified direction: *she pulled a handkerchief out of her pocket | he pulled on his boots | I pulled up some onions.* ■ informal bring out (a weapon) to attack or threaten someone: *it's not every day a young woman **pulls a gun on** a burglar.* ■ [no obj.] (**pull at/on**) inhale deeply while smoking (a pipe or cigar). ■ damage (a muscle, ligament, etc.) by abnormal strain. ■ print (a proof). ■ Computing retrieve (an item of data) from the top of a stack.
2 [no obj.] (of a vehicle or person) move steadily in a specified direction or to reach a specified point: *the bus was about to pull away | the boy pulled ahead and disappeared around the corner.* ■ [with adverbial of direction] (**pull oneself**) move in a specified direction with effort, esp. by taking hold of something and exerting force: *he pulled himself into the saddle.* ■ move one's body in a specified direction, esp. against resistance: *she tried to pull away from him.* ■ (of an engine) exert propulsive force; deliver power: *the engine warmed up quickly and pulled well.* ■ work oars to cause a boat to move: *he **pulled at the oars**, and the boat moved swiftly through the water.*
3 cause (someone) to patronize, buy, or show interest in something; attract: *tourist attractions that **pull in** millions of foreign visitors.* ■ informal carry out or achieve (something requiring skill, luck, or planning): *the magazine pulled its trick of producing the right issue at the right time.*
4 informal cancel or withdraw (an entertainment or advertisement): *the gig was pulled at the first sign of difficulty.* ■ withdraw (a player) from a game: *four of the leading eight runners were pulled.* ■ check the speed of (a horse), esp. so as to make it lose a race.
5 chiefly Baseball & Golf strike (a ball) in the direction of one's follow-through so that it travels to the left or, with a left-handed player, to the right: *he pulled the ball every time he hit a grounder.*
6 [no obj.] Football (of a lineman) withdraw from position and cross parallel to and behind the line of scrimmage to block opposing players for a runner.
▶ n. **1** an act of taking hold of something and exerting force to draw it toward one: *give the hair a quick pull, and it comes out by the roots.* ■ a handle to hold while performing such an action: *the Cowboy Collection offers hand-forged iron drawer pulls.* ■ a deep draft of a drink: *he unscrewed the cap from the flask and took another pull.* ■ an act of sucking at a cigar or pipe: *he took a pull on his cheroot.* ■ an injury to a muscle or ligament caused by abnormal strain: *he was taken out of the game with a hamstring pull.* ■ a printer's proof.
2 [in sing.] a force drawing someone or something in a particular direction or course of action: *the pull of the water tore her away | the pull of her hometown was a strong one.* ■ something exerting an influence or attraction: *one of the pulls of urban life is the opportunity of finding work.* ■ the condition of being able to exercise influence: *they were hamstrung without the political pull of the mayor's office.*
– PHRASES **like pulling teeth** informal extremely difficult to do: *it had been like pulling teeth to extract these two small items from Moore.* **pull a face** (or **faces**) see FACE. **pull a fast one** see FAST[1]. **pull someone's leg** deceive someone playfully; tease someone. **pull out all the stops** see STOP. **pull the plug 1** informal prevent something from happening or continuing: *the company **pulled the plug on** the deal because it was not satisfied with the terms.* **2** informal remove (a patient) from life support: *we'll be talking to people who **pulled the plug on** their mothers.* **pull (one's) punches** [usu. with negative] be less forceful, severe, or violent than one could be: *a sharp-tongued critic who doesn't pull his punches.* **pull rank** see RANK[1]. **pull one's socks up** see SOCK. **pull strings** make use of one's influence and contacts to gain an advantage unofficially or unfairly. **pull the strings** be in control of events or of other people's actions. **pull together** cooperate in a task or undertaking. **pull oneself together** recover control of one's emotions. **pull one's weight** do one's fair share of work. **pull wires** another way of saying PULL STRINGS. **pull the wool over someone's eyes** see WOOL.
– PHRASAL VERBS **pull back** (or **pull someone/something back**) retreat or cause troops to retreat from an area: *the pact called on the rival forces to pull back and allow a neutral force to take control.* ■ (**pull back**) withdraw from an undertaking: *the party pulled back from its only positive policy.* **pull something down 1** demolish a building. **2** informal earn a sum of money: *he was*

P

pulling down sixty grand. **pull in 1** (of a vehicle or its driver) move to the side of or off the road: *he pulled in at the curb.* **2** (of a bus or train) arrive to take passengers. **pull someone/something in 1** succeed in securing or obtaining something: *the Reform Party pulled in 10% of the vote.* ■ informal earn a sum of money: *you could pull in $100,000.* **2** informal arrest someone: *I'd pull him in for questioning.* **3** use reins to check a horse. **pull something off** informal succeed in achieving or winning something difficult: *he pulled off a brilliant first round win.* **pull out 1** withdraw from an undertaking: *he was forced to pull out of the championship because of an injury.* ■ retreat or cause to retreat from an area: *the army pulled out, leaving the city in ruins* | (**pull someone out**) *the CIA had pulled its operatives out of Tripoli.* **2** (of a bus or train) leave with its passengers. **3** (of a vehicle or its driver) move out from the side of the road, or from its normal position in order to pass: *as he turned the corner, a police car pulled out in front of him.* **pull over** (of a vehicle or its driver) move to the side of or off the road. **pull someone over** cause a driver to move to the side of the road to be charged for a traffic offense: *he was pulled over for speeding.* **pull through** (or **pull someone/something through**) get through or enable someone or something to get through an illness or other dangerous or difficult situation: *the illness is difficult to overcome, but we hope she'll pull through.* **pull up 1** (of a vehicle or its driver) come to a halt: *he pulled up outside the cabin.* **2** increase the altitude of an aircraft. **pull someone up** cause someone to stop or pause; check someone: *the shock of his words **pulled her up short**.* ■ reprimand someone.
– DERIVATIVES **pull·er** n.
– ORIGIN Old English *pullian* 'pluck, snatch'; origin uncertain; the sense has developed from expressing a short sharp action to one of sustained force.

pull-a·part ▶ adj. [attrib.] Geology denoting an area that has been ruptured or stretched by tensional stresses or the resulting faulting.

pull·back /ˈpo͝olˌbak/ ▶ n. **1** an act of withdrawing troops.
2 a reduction in price or demand: *there is no sign of a consumer pullback.*

pull cord ▶ n. a cord that operates a mechanism when pulled.

pull-down ▶ adj. [attrib.] Computing (of a menu) appearing below a menu title only while selected. Compare with DROP-DOWN.
▶ n. Computing a pull-down menu.

pul·let /ˈpo͝olət/ ▶ n. a young hen, esp. one less than one year old.
– ORIGIN late Middle English: from Old French *poulet*, diminutive of *poule*, from the feminine of Latin *pullus* 'chicken, young animal.'

pul·ley /ˈpo͝olē/ ▶ n. (pl. **pulleys**) (also **pulley wheel**) a wheel with a grooved rim around which a cord passes. It acts to change the direction of a force applied to the cord and is chiefly used (typically in combination) to raise heavy weights. Compare with BLOCK (sense 7 of the noun). ■ (on a bicycle) a wheel with a toothed rim around which the chain passes. ■ a wheel or drum fixed on a shaft and turned by a belt, used esp. to increase speed or power.
▶ v. (**pulleys, pulleying, pulleyed**) [with obj.] hoist with a pulley.
– ORIGIN Middle English: from Old French *polie*, probably from a medieval Greek diminutive of *polos* 'pivot, axis.'

pulley

pul·ley block ▶ n. a block or casing in which one or more pulleys are mounted.

pull hit·ter ▶ n. Baseball a hitter who normally drives the ball in the direction of the follow-through of the bat.

Pull·man¹, George Mortimer (1831–97) US industrialist. The founder of the Pullman Palace Car Company in 1867, he converted railroad coaches into sleeping cars with lower and upper berths. He also designed the first railroad dining car in 1868. The town of Pullman, Illinois, was built to house his workers.

Pull·man² ▶ n. (pl. **Pullmans**) [usu. as modifier] a railroad car affording special comfort, esp. one with sleeping berths: *a train of Pullman cars.* ■ a train consisting of such cars. ■ (**pullman**) a large suitcase designed to fit under the seat in a Pullman car.
– ORIGIN mid 19th cent.: named after George M. *Pullman* (1831–97), its American designer.

pull-off ▶ n. an area on the side of a road where a motorist may park, typically in a scenic area.

pull-on ▶ adj. [attrib.] (of a garment) designed to be put on without the need to undo any fastenings: *pull-on trousers with an elastic waist.*
▶ n. a garment of this type.

pull·out /ˈpo͝olˌout/ ▶ n. **1** a section of a magazine or newspaper that is designed to be detached and kept for rereading: *don't miss Monday's 8-page NBA pullout.*
2 a withdrawal, esp. from military involvement or participation in a commercial venture.
▶ adj. [attrib.] designed to be pulled out of the usual position: *pullout wire baskets at the bottom of one cupboard.* ■ (of a section of a magazine, newspaper, or other publication) designed to be detached and kept.

pull·o·ver /ˈpo͝olˌōvər/ ▶ n. a garment, esp. a sweater or jacket, put on over the head and covering the top half of the body.

pull-quote ▶ n. a brief, attention-catching quotation, typically in a distinctive typeface, taken from the main text of an article and used as a subheading or graphic feature.

pull tab ▶ n. **1** a ring or tab that is pulled to open a can.
2 a gambling card with a tab that can be pulled back to reveal a row or rows of symbols, with prizes for matching symbols.

pul·lu·late /ˈpəlyəˌlāt/ ▶ v. [no obj.] (often as adj. **pullulating**) breed or spread so as to become extremely common: *the pullulating family.* ■ be very crowded; be full of life and activity: *the supertowers of our pullulating megalopolis.*
– DERIVATIVES **pul·lu·la·tion** /ˌpəlyəˈlāSHən/ n.
– ORIGIN early 17th cent.: from Latin *pullulat-* 'sprouted,' from the verb *pullulare*, from *pullulus*, diminutive of *pullus* 'young animal.'

pull-up ▶ n. **1** an exercise involving raising oneself with one's arms by pulling up against a horizontal bar fixed above one's head.
2 an act of pulling up; a sudden stop.

pul·mo·nar·y /ˈpo͝olməˌnerē, ˈpəl-/ ▶ adj. [attrib.] of or relating to the lungs: *pulmonary blood flow.*
– ORIGIN mid 17th cent.: from Latin *pulmonarius*, from *pulmo, pulmon-* 'lung.'

pul·mo·nar·y ar·ter·y ▶ n. the artery carrying blood from the right ventricle of the heart to the lungs for oxygenation.

pul·mo·nar·y tu·ber·cu·lo·sis ▶ n. see TUBERCULOSIS.

pul·mo·nar·y vein ▶ n. a vein carrying oxygenated blood from the lungs to the left atrium of the heart.

Pul·mo·na·ta /ˌpo͝olməˈnätə, pəl-, -ˈnātə/ Zoology a group of mollusks that includes the land snails and slugs and many freshwater snails. They have a modified mantle cavity that acts as a lung for breathing air. ● Subclass Pulmonata, class Gastropoda.
– ORIGIN modern Latin (plural), from Latin *pulmo, pulmon-* 'lung.'

pul·mo·nate /ˈpo͝olməˌnāt, ˈpəl-/ Zoology ▶ n. a mollusk of the group Pulmonata, which includes the land snails and slugs and many freshwater snails.
▶ adj. relating to or denoting pulmonates.

pul·mon·ic /po͝olˈmänik, pəl-/ ▶ adj. another term for PULMONARY.

pulp /pəlp/ ▶ n. **1** a soft, wet, shapeless mass of material: *boiling with soda will reduce your peas to pulp.* ■ the soft fleshy part of a fruit. ■ a soft wet mass of fibers derived from rags or wood, used in papermaking. ■ vascular tissue filling the interior cavity and root canals of a tooth. ■ Mining pulverized ore mixed with water.
2 [usu. as modifier] popular or sensational writing that is generally regarded as being of poor quality: *the story is a mix of pulp fiction and Greek tragedy.* [because formerly printed on cheap paper.]
▶ v. [with obj.] crush into a soft, shapeless mass. ■ withdraw (a publication) from the market and recycle the paper.
– PHRASES **beat** (or **smash**) **someone to a pulp** beat someone severely.
– DERIVATIVES **pulp·er** n.
– ORIGIN late Middle English (denoting the soft fleshy part of fruit): from Latin *pulpa*. The verb dates from the mid 17th cent.

pulp cav·i·ty ▶ n. the space in the interior of a tooth that contains the pulp.

pul·pit /ˈpo͝olˌpit, ˈpəl-, -pət/ ▶ n. a raised platform or lectern in a church or chapel from which the preacher delivers a sermon. ■ (**the pulpit**) religious teaching as expressed in sermons; preachers collectively: *the movies could rival the pulpit as an agency molding the ideas of the mass public.* ■ a raised platform in the bow of a fishing boat or whaler. ■ a guard rail enclosing a small area at the bow of a yacht.
– ORIGIN Middle English: from Latin *pulpitum* 'scaffold, platform,' in medieval Latin 'pulpit.'

pulp·wood /ˈpəlpˌwo͝od/ ▶ n. wood suitable for making into pulp for making paper.

pulp·y /ˈpəlpē/ ▶ adj. (**pulpier, pulpiest**) **1** resembling or consisting of pulp; mushy: *simmer gently until the fruit is very soft and pulpy.*
2 (of writing) sensationalist and of poor quality; trashy: *pulpy detective novels.*
– DERIVATIVES **pulp·i·ness** n.

pul·que /ˈpo͝olˌkā, -kē/ ▶ n. a Mexican alcoholic drink made by fermenting sap from the maguey.
– ORIGIN via American Spanish from Nahuatl *puliúhki* 'decomposed.'

pul·sar /ˈpəlˌsär/ ▶ n. Astronomy a celestial object, thought to be a rapidly rotating neutron star, that emits regular pulses of radio waves and other electromagnetic radiation at rates of up to one thousand pulses per second.
– ORIGIN from *puls(ating st)ar*, on the pattern of *quasar*.

pul·sate /ˈpəlˌsāt/ ▶ v. [no obj.] expand and contract with strong regular movements: *blood vessels throb and pulsate.* ■ (often as adj. **pulsating**) produce a regular throbbing sensation or sound: *a pulsating headache.* ■ (usu. as adj. **pulsating**) be very exciting: *victory in a pulsating semifinal.*
– DERIVATIVES **pul·sa·tion** /ˌpəlˈsāSHən/ n., **pul·sa·tor** /-ˌsātər/ n., **pul·sa·to·ry** /-səˌtôrē/ adj.
– ORIGIN late 18th cent.: from Latin *pulsat-* 'throbbed, pulsed,' from the verb *pulsare*, frequentative of *pellere* 'to drive, beat.'

pul·sa·tile /ˈpəlsətl, -səˌtīl/ ▶ adj. chiefly Physiology pulsating; relating to pulsation: *pulsatile tinnitus.*
– ORIGIN late Middle English: from medieval Latin *pulsatilis* (in *vena pulsatilis* 'artery'), from the verb *pulsare* (see PULSATE).

pul·sa·til·la /ˌpəlsəˈtilə/ ▶ n. a plant of a genus that includes the pasqueflower. ● Genus *Pulsatilla*, family Ranunculaceae.
– ORIGIN modern Latin, diminutive of *pulsatus* 'battered,' expressing the notion 'small flower battered by the wind.'

pulse¹ /pəls/ ▶ n. **1** a rhythmical throbbing of the arteries as blood is propelled through them, typically as felt in the wrists or neck: *the doctor found a faint pulse* | *the idea was enough to set my pulse racing.* ■ (usu. **pulses**) each successive throb of the arteries or heart.
2 a single vibration or short burst of sound, electric current, light, or other wave: *radio pulses* | [as modifier] *a pulse generator.* ■ a musical beat or other regular rhythm.
3 the central point of energy and organization in an area or activity: *those close to the financial and economic pulse maintain that there have been fundamental changes.*
4 Biochemistry a measured amount of an isotopic label given to a culture of cells.
▶ v. [no obj.] throb rhythmically; pulsate: *a knot of muscles at the side of his jaw pulsed.* ■ [with obj.] modulate (a wave or beam) so that it becomes a series of pulses. ■ [with obj.] apply a pulsed signal to (a device). ■ Biochemistry short for PULSE-LABEL.
– PHRASES **take** (or **feel**) **the pulse of** determine the heart rate of (someone) by feeling and timing the pulsation of an artery: *a nurse came in and took his pulse.* ■ ascertain the general mood or opinion of: *he hopped around the country to visit stores and take the pulse of consumers.*
– DERIVATIVES **pulse·less** adj., **puls·er** n.
– ORIGIN late Middle English: from Latin *pulsus* 'beating,' from *pellere* 'to drive, beat.'

pulse² ▶ n. (usu. **pulses**) the edible seeds of various leguminous plants, for example chickpeas, lentils, and beans. ■ the plant or plants producing such seeds.
– ORIGIN Middle English: from Old French *pols*, from Latin *puls* 'porridge of meal or pulse'; related to POLLEN.

pulse code mod·u·la·tion (abbr.: **PCM**) ▶ n. Electronics a pulse modulation technique in which the amplitude of an analog signal is converted to a binary value represented as a series of pulses.

pulse di·al·ing ▶ n. method of telephone dialing in which each digit is transmitted as a corresponding number of electronic pulses. Compare with TONE DIALING.

pulse jet ▶ n. a type of jet engine in which combustion is intermittent, with the ignition and expulsion of each charge of mixture causing the intake of a fresh charge.

pulse-la·bel ▶ v. [with obj.] Biochemistry subject (cells in a culture) to a pulse of an isotopic label.

pulse mod·u·la·tion ▶ n. Electronics a type of modulation in which pulses are varied in some respect, such as width or amplitude, to represent the amplitude of a signal.

pulse ox·im·e·ter ▶ n. an oximeter that measures the proportion of oxygenated hemoglobin in the blood in pulsating vessels, esp. the capillaries of the finger or ear.

pul·trude /po͝ol'tro͞od, pəl-/ ▶ v. [with obj.] (usu. as adj. **pultruded**) make (a reinforced plastic article) by drawing resin-coated glass fibers through a heated die.
– DERIVATIVES **pul·tru·sion** /-'tro͞oZHən/ n.
– ORIGIN 1960s: from *pul(ling)* + EXTRUDE.

pul·ver·ize /'pəlvə,rīz/ ▶ v. [with obj.] reduce to fine particles: *the brick of the villages was pulverized by the bombardment.* ■ informal defeat utterly: *he had a winning car and pulverized the opposition.*
– DERIVATIVES **pul·ver·iz·a·ble** adj., **pul·ver·i·za·tion** /,pəlvərə'zāSHən/ n., **pul·ver·iz·er** n.
– ORIGIN late Middle English: from late Latin *pulverizare*, from *pulvis, pulver-* 'dust.'

pul·ver·u·lent /,pəl'ver(y)ələnt/ ▶ adj. archaic consisting of fine particles; powdery or crumbly.
– ORIGIN mid 17th cent.: from Latin *pulverulentus*, from *pulvis, pulver-* 'dust.'

pul·vi·nus /pəl'vīnəs, -'vēnəs/ ▶ n. (pl. **pulvini** /-,nī, -nē/) Botany an enlarged section at the base of a leaf stalk in some plants that is subject to changes of turgor, leading to movements of the leaf or leaflet.
– ORIGIN mid 19th cent.: from Latin, literally 'cushion.'

pu·ma /'p(y)o͞omə/ ▶ n. another term for COUGAR.
– ORIGIN late 18th cent.: via Spanish from Quechua.

pum·ice /'pəməs/ ▶ n. a very light and porous volcanic rock formed when a gas-rich froth of glassy lava solidifies rapidly. ■ (also **pumice stone**) a piece of such rock or a similar substance used as an abrasive, esp. for removing hard skin.
▶ v. [with obj.] rub with pumice to smooth or clean.
– DERIVATIVES **pu·mi·ceous** /pyo͞o'misHəs, ,pəm'isH-/ adj.
– ORIGIN late Middle English: from Old French *pomis*, from a Latin dialect variant of *pumex, pumic-*. Compare with POUNCE[2].

pum·mel /'pəməl/ ▶ v. (**pummels, pummeling, pummeled**; Brit. **pummels, pummelling, pummelled**) [with obj.] strike repeatedly, typically with the fists: *Bob did not fight back for the fifteen minutes that the half-dozen men pummeled him.* ■ informal criticize adversely: *he has been pummeled by the reviewers.*
– ORIGIN mid 16th cent.: variant of POMMEL.

pum·me·lo ▶ n. variant spelling of POMELO.

pump[1] /pəmp/ ▶ n. a mechanical device using suction or pressure to raise or move liquids, compress gases, or force air into inflatable objects such as tires: *a gas pump.* ■ [in sing.] an instance of moving something or being moved by or as if by such a machine: *the pump of blood to her heart.* ■ [with modifier] Physiology an active transport mechanism in living cells by which specific ions are moved through the cell membrane against a concentration gradient: *the bacterium's sodium pump.* ■ a pump-action shotgun.
▶ v. **1** [with obj.] force (liquid, gas, etc.) to move in a specified direction by or as if by means of a pump: *the blood is pumped around the body* | [no obj.] *if we pump long enough, we should bring the level up.* ■ [no obj.] move in spurts as though driven by a pump: *blood was pumping from a wound in his shoulder.* ■ informal try to elicit information from (someone) by persistent questioning: *she began to pump her friend for details.*
2 fill (something such as a tire or balloon) with liquid or gas using a pump: *I fetched the bike and pumped up the back tire* | *my veins had been pumped full of glucose.* ■ shoot (bullets) into a target.
3 move vigorously up and down: [with obj.] *we had to pump the handle like mad* | [no obj.] *that's superb running—look at his legs pumping.* ■ apply and release (a brake pedal or lever) several times in quick succession, typically to prevent skidding. ■ Baseball move one's arm as if throwing a ball held in the hand, but without releasing the ball: [in combination] *behind the plate Howard double-pumped, then threw to second.*
– PHRASES **pump someone's hand** shake a person's hand vigorously. **pump iron** informal exercise with weights.
– PHRASAL VERBS **pump something in/into** informal invest a large amount of money in (something): *he pumped all his savings into building the boat.* **pump something out** produce or emit (something) in large quantities or amounts: *that little printing press pumped out our brochures for more than twenty years.* **pump something up** informal increase: *she needs to read and pump up her political grip.* ■ turn up the volume of (music): *let's pump up those tunes, man.* ■ give inappropriate support and encouragement to: *we let them pump up our egos.*
– ORIGIN late Middle English (originally in nautical use): related to Dutch *pomp* 'ship's pump' (earlier in the sense 'wooden or metal conduit'), probably partly of imitative origin.

pump[2] ▶ n. a light shoe, in particular: ■ a woman's plain, lightweight shoe that has a low-cut upper, no fastening, and typically a medium heel. ■ a man's slip-on patent leather shoe for formal wear.
– ORIGIN mid 16th cent.: of unknown origin.

pump-ac·tion ▶ adj. [attrib.] **1** denoting a repeating firearm, typically a shotgun, in which a new round is brought from the magazine into the breech by a slide action in line with the barrel.
2 denoting a spray dispenser for a liquid such as deodorant or cooking oil that is worked by finger action rather than by internal pressure (as in an aerosol).

pump-and-dump ▶ adj. informal denoting the fraudulent practice of encouraging investors to buy shares in a company in order to inflate the price artificially, and then selling one's own shares while the price is high.

pumped /pəmpt/ (also **pumped up**) ▶ adj. informal (of a person) stimulated or filled with enthusiasm or excitement: *I was so pumped that I overdid everything.*

pump·er /'pəmpər/ ▶ n. a fire engine that carries a hose and pumps water.

pum·per·nick·el /'pəmpər,nikəl/ ▶ n. dark, dense German bread made from coarsely ground whole-grain rye.
– ORIGIN mid 18th cent.: transferred use of German *Pumpernickel* 'lout, bumpkin,' of unknown origin.

pump gun ▶ n. a pump-action rifle with a tubular magazine.

pump jock·ey ▶ n. informal a service station attendant.

pump·kin /'pəm(p)kən, 'pəNGkən/ ▶ n. **1** a large rounded orange-yellow fruit with a thick rind, edible flesh, and many seeds. ■ informal used as an affectionate term of address, esp. to a child.
2 the plant of the gourd family that produces this fruit, having tendrils and large lobed leaves and native to warm regions of America. ● Genus *Cucurbita*, family Cucurbitaceae: several species, in particular *C. pepo*. ■ Brit. another term for SQUASH[2].
– ORIGIN late 17th cent.: alteration of earlier *pumpion*, from obsolete French *pompon*, via Latin from Greek *pepōn* 'large melon' (see PEPO).

pumpkin 1

pump·kin·seed /'pəm(p)kən,sēd, 'pəNGkən-/ ▶ n. (pl. **same** or **pumpkinseeds**) a small, edible, brightly colored freshwater fish of the sunfish family, native to North America. It is popular in aquariums and has been introduced into many European waters. ● *Lepomis gibbosus*, family Centrarchidae.

pump-prim·ing ▶ n. **1** the introduction of fluid into a pump to prepare it for working.
2 the stimulation of economic activity by investment: [as modifier] *a pump-priming fund.*
– DERIVATIVES **pump-prim·er** n.

pump room ▶ n. a room, building, or compartment in which pumps are housed or from which they are controlled. ■ a room at a spa where medicinal water is dispensed. ■ a common name for a drinking establishment.

pun /pən/ ▶ n. a joke exploiting the different possible meanings of a word or the fact that there are words that sound alike but have different meanings: *the pigs were a squeal (if you'll forgive the pun).*
▶ v. (**puns, punning, punned**) [no obj.] make a joke exploiting the different possible meanings of a word: *his first puzzle punned on composers, with answers like "Handel with care" and "Haydn go seek"* | (as adj. **punning**) *a punning riddle.*
– DERIVATIVES **pun·ning·ly** adv., **pun·ster** /'pənstər/ n.
– ORIGIN mid 17th cent.: perhaps an abbreviation of obsolete *pundigrion*, as a fanciful alteration of PUNCTILIO.

pu·na /'po͞onə/ ▶ n. **1** a high treeless plateau in the Peruvian Andes.
2 another term for ALTITUDE SICKNESS.
– ORIGIN via American Spanish from Quechua.

punch[1] /pənCH/ ▶ v. [with obj.] **1** strike with the fist: *he punched her in the face and ran off.* ■ drive with a blow from the fist: *he punched the ball into his own goal.*
2 press (a button or key on a machine). ■ (**punch something in/into**) enter information by this action.
3 drive (cattle) by prodding them with a stick.
▶ n. a blow with the fist. ■ informal the strength needed to deliver such a blow: *he has the punch to knock out anyone in his division.* ■ [in sing.] informal the power to impress or startle: *photos give their arguments an extra visual punch.*
– PHRASES **beat someone to the punch** informal anticipate or forestall someone's actions. **punch the (time) clock** (of an employee) punch in or out. ■ be employed in a conventional job with regular hours. **punch someone's lights out** beat someone up; knock someone unconscious. [*Lights* in the sense 'lungs' (see LIGHTS).] **punch something up 1** use a computer keyboard to call something to the screen: *people will be able to punch up Andy Warhol and get text, photographs, and video on the entire Pop Art period.* **2** informal enliven: *he needed to punch up his meandering presentation.*
– PHRASAL VERBS **punch in** (or **out**) register one's arrival at (or departure from) work, esp. by means of a time clock: *she couldn't punch in, because there were no time clocks.*
– DERIVATIVES **punch·er** n.
– ORIGIN late Middle English (as a verb in the sense 'puncture, prod'): variant of POUNCE[1].

punch[2] ▶ n. **1** a device or machine for making holes in materials such as paper, leather, metal, and plaster.
2 a tool or machine for impressing a design or stamping a die on a material.
▶ v. [with obj.] pierce a hole in (metal, paper, leather, etc.) with or as though with a punch. ■ pierce (a hole) with or as though with a punch.
– PHRASES **punch one's ticket** do or achieve something that enables one to progress to the next step: *Krueger punched her ticket to the NCAA Championships by taking eighth at the NCAA South Regionals.*
– ORIGIN early 16th cent.: perhaps an abbreviation of PUNCHEON[1], or from the verb PUNCH[1].

punch[3] ▶ n. a drink made with fruit juices, soda, spices, and sometimes liquor, typically served in small cups from a large bowl.
– ORIGIN mid 17th cent.: apparently from Sanskrit *pañca* 'five, five kinds of' (because the drink had five ingredients).

punch[4] ▶ n. (**Punch**) a grotesque, hook-nosed, humpbacked buffoon, the chief male character of the Punch and Judy show. Punch is the English variant of a stock character derived ultimately from Italian *commedia dell'arte*. Also called PUNCHINELLO.
– PHRASES **pleased as Punch** feeling great delight or pride. [with allusion to the delight displayed by the character *Punch* of the PUNCH AND JUDY show.]
– ORIGIN mid 17th cent. (as a dialect term denoting a short, fat person): abbreviation of PUNCHINELLO.

Punch and Ju·dy /pənCH and 'jo͞odē/ a puppet show presented on the miniature stage of a tall collapsible booth traditionally covered with striped canvas. The show was probably introduced to England from the Continent in the 17th century. Punch is on the manipulator's right hand, remaining on stage all the time, while the left hand provides a series of characters—baby, wife (Judy), priest, doctor, policeman, hangman— for him to nag, beat, and finally kill.

punch·bag /'pənCH,bag/ ▶ n. British term for PUNCHING BAG.

punch·ball /'pənCH,bôl/ ▶ n. **1** a team ball game in which a rubber ball is punched or headed.
2 Brit. another term for PUNCHING BAG.

punch·board /'pənCH,bôrd/ ▶ n. a board with holes containing slips of paper that are punched out as a form of gambling, with the object of locating a winning slip.

punch bowl ▶ n. a bowl used for mixing and serving punch. ■ (**punchbowl**) chiefly Brit. a deep round hollow in a hilly area.

punch card (also **punched card**) ▶ n. a card perforated according to a code, for controlling the operation of a machine, used in voting machines and formerly in programming and entering data into computers.

punch-drunk ▶ adj. stupefied by or as if by a series of heavy blows to the head.

punched tape ▶ n. a paper tape perforated according to a code, formerly used for conveying instructions or data to a data processor.

pun·cheon[1] /pənCHən/ ▶ n. **1** a short post, esp. one used for supporting the roof in a coal mine. ■ a rough board or other length of wood, usually with one flattened side, used for flooring or building.
2 another term for PUNCH[2].

P

PRONUNCIATION KEY ə *ago, up*; ər *over, fur*; a *hat*; ā *ate*; ä *car*; e *let*; ē *see*; i *fit*; ī *by*; NG *sing*; ō *go*; ô *law, for*; oi *toy*; o͝o *good*; o͞o *goo*; ou *out*; TH *thin*; T͟H *then*; ZH *vision*

–ORIGIN Middle English: from Old French *poinchon*, probably based on Latin *punct-* 'punctured,' from the verb *pungere*. Compare with the noun POUNCE[1].

pun·cheon² ▶ n. historical a large cask for liquids or other commodities holding from 72 to 120 gallons.
–ORIGIN late Middle English: from Old French *poinchon*, of uncertain origin although forms in Old French and English correspond to those of PUNCHEON[1].

Pun·chi·nel·lo /ˌpənCHəˈnelō/ ▶ n. (pl. **Punchinellos**) another name for PUNCH[4]. ■ archaic a short, stout, comical-looking person.
–ORIGIN mid 17th cent.: alteration of Neapolitan dialect *Polecenella*, perhaps a diminutive of *pollecena* 'young turkey cock with a hooked beak,' from *pulcino* 'chicken,' from Latin *pullus*.

punch·ing bag ▶ n. a stuffed or inflated bag, typically cylindrical or pear-shaped, suspended so it can be punched for exercise or training, esp. by boxers.

punch line ▶ n. the final phrase or sentence of a joke or story, providing the humor or some other crucial element.

punch press ▶ n. a press that is designed to drive a punch for shaping metal.

punch·y /ˈpənCHē/ ▶ adj. (**punchier, punchiest**) **1** having an immediate impact; forceful: *his style is journalistic, with short punchy sentences.*
2 another term for PUNCH-DRUNK.
–DERIVATIVES **punch·i·ly** /ˈpənCHəlē/ adv., **punch·i·ness** n.

punc·ta /ˈpəNGktə/ plural form of PUNCTUM.

punc·tae /ˈpəNGktē, -ˌtī/ ▶ plural n. Biology minute rounded dots or spots of color, or small elevations or depressions on a surface.
–ORIGIN modern Latin (plural).

punc·tate /ˈpəNGkˌtāt/ ▶ adj. Biology studded with or denoting dots or tiny holes.
–DERIVATIVES **punc·ta·tion** /ˌpəNGkˈtāSHən/ n.
–ORIGIN mid 18th cent.: from Latin *punctum* 'point' + -ATE[2].

punc·til·i·o /ˌpəNGkˈtilēˌō/ ▶ n. (pl. **punctilios**) a fine or petty point of conduct or procedure.
–ORIGIN late 16th cent.: from Italian *puntiglio(n-)* and Spanish *puntillo*, diminutive of *punto* 'a point.'

punc·til·i·ous /ˌpəNGkˈtilēəs/ ▶ adj. showing great attention to detail or correct behavior: *he was punctilious in providing every amenity for his guests.*
–DERIVATIVES **punc·til·i·ous·ly** adv., **punc·til·i·ous·ness** n.
–ORIGIN mid 17th cent.: from French *pointilleux*, from *pointille*, from Italian *puntiglio* (see PUNCTILIO).

punc·tu·al /ˈpəNGkCHo͞oəl/ ▶ adj. happening or doing something at the agreed or proper time; on time: *he's the sort of man who's always punctual.* ■ Grammar denoting or relating to an action that takes place at a particular point in time. Contrasted with DURATIVE.
–DERIVATIVES **punc·tu·al·i·ty** /ˌpəNGkCHo͞oˈalitē/ n.
–ORIGIN late 17th cent.: from medieval Latin *punctualis*, from Latin *punctum* 'a point.'

punc·tu·al·ly /ˈpəNGkCHo͞oəlē/ ▶ adv. at the agreed or proper time; promptly: *four out of five trains were arriving punctually.*

punc·tu·ate /ˈpəNGkCHo͞oˌāt/ ▶ v. [with obj.] **1** occur at intervals throughout (a continuing event or a place): *the country's history has been **punctuated by** coups.* ■ (**punctuate something with**) interrupt or intersperse (an activity) with: *she punctuates her conversation with snatches of song.*
2 insert punctuation marks in (text).
–ORIGIN mid 17th cent. (in the sense 'point out'): from medieval Latin *punctuat-* 'brought to a point,' from the verb *punctuare*, from *punctum* 'a point.'

punc·tu·at·ed e·qui·lib·ri·um ▶ n. Biology the hypothesis that evolutionary development is marked by isolated episodes of rapid speciation between long periods of little or no change.

punc·tu·a·tion /ˌpəNGkCHo͞oˈāSHən/ ▶ n. **1** the marks, such as period, comma, and parentheses, used in writing to separate sentences and their elements and to clarify meaning.
2 Biology rapid or sudden speciation, as posited by the theory of punctuated equilibrium.
–DERIVATIVES **punc·tu·a·tion·al** /-SHənl/ adj.
–ORIGIN mid 17th cent.: from medieval Latin *punctuatio(n-)*, from the verb *punctuare* (see PUNCTUATE).

punc·tu·a·tion·ist /ˌpəNGkCHo͞oˈāSHənist/ ▶ n. Biology a person who believes in or advocates the hypothesis of punctuated equilibrium.
–DERIVATIVES **punc·tu·a·tion·al·ism** /-ˈāSHənlˌizəm/ n., **punc·tu·a·tion·al·ist** /-ˈāSHənl-ist/ adj., **punc·tu·a·tion·ism** /-ˈāSHəˌnizəm/ n.

punc·tum /ˈpəNGktəm/ ▶ n. (pl. **puncta** /-tə/) technical a small, distinct point. ■ Anatomy the opening of a tear duct.
–ORIGIN late 16th cent. (figuratively, denoting a point): from Latin, literally 'a point.'

punc·ture /ˈpəNGkCHər/ ▶ n. a small hole in a tire resulting in an escape of air: *she was on her way home when she had a puncture.* ■ a small hole in something such as the skin, caused by a sharp object: *surgeons operate through small punctures in the skin* | [as modifier] *a puncture wound.*
▶ v. [with obj.] **1** make a puncture in (something): *one of the knife blows had punctured a lung.* ■ [no obj.] sustain a puncture: *the tire had punctured and it would have to be replaced.*
2 cause a sudden collapse of (mood or feeling): *the earlier mood of optimism was punctured.*
–ORIGIN late Middle English: from Latin *punctura*, from *punct-* 'pricked,' from the verb *pungere*. The verb dates from the late 17th cent.

pun·dit /ˈpəndit/ ▶ n. **1** an expert in a particular subject or field who is frequently called on to give opinions about it to the public: *a globe-trotting financial pundit.*
2 variant spelling of PANDIT.
–DERIVATIVES **pun·dit·ry** /-trē/ n. (sense 1).
–ORIGIN from Sanskrit *paṇḍita* 'learned.'

pun·di·toc·ra·cy /ˌpəndiˈtäkrəsē/ ▶ n. informal an elite or influential class of experts or political commentators.

Pu·ne an industrial city in Maharashtra, western India, in the hills southeast of Mumbai (Bombay); pop. 3,337,500 (est. 2009). Formerly called POONA.

pun·gent /ˈpənjənt/ ▶ adj. having a sharply strong taste or smell: *the pungent smell of frying onions.* ■ (of comment, criticism, or humor) having a sharp and caustic quality.
–DERIVATIVES **pun·gen·cy** /ˈpənjənsē/ n., **pun·gent·ly** adv.
–ORIGIN late 16th cent. (in the sense 'very painful or distressing'): from Latin *pungent-* 'pricking,' from the verb *pungere*.

Pu·nic /ˈpyo͞onik/ ▶ adj. of or relating to Carthage.
▶ n. the language of ancient Carthage, related to Phoenician.
–ORIGIN from Latin *Punicus* (earlier *Poenicus*), from *Poenus*, from Greek *Phoinix* 'Phoenician.'

Pu·nic Wars three wars between Rome and Carthage that led to the undisputed dominance of Rome in the western Mediterranean.

> In the first Punic War (264–241 BC), Rome secured Sicily from Carthage and established itself as a naval power; in the second (218–201 BC), the defeat of Hannibal (largely through the generalship of Fabius Cunctator and Scipio Africanus) put an end to Carthage's position as a Mediterranean power; the third (149–146 BC) ended in the total destruction of the city of Carthage.

pun·ish /ˈpəniSH/ ▶ v. [with obj.] inflict a penalty or sanction on (someone) as retribution for an offense, esp. a transgression of a legal or moral code: *I have done wrong and I'm being **punished for** it.* ■ inflict a penalty or sanction on someone for (such an offense): *fraudulent acts would be punished by up to two years in prison.* ■ treat (someone) in an unfairly harsh way: *a rise in prescription charges would punish the poor.* ■ subject (someone or something) to severe and debilitating treatment.
–DERIVATIVES **pun·ish·er** n.
–ORIGIN Middle English: from Old French *puniss-*, lengthened stem of *punir* 'punish,' from Latin *punire*, from *poena* 'penalty.'

pun·ish·a·ble /ˈpəniSHəbəl/ ▶ adj. (of an act) subject to a judicial punishment: *a criminal offense **punishable by** up to three years in jail* | *a punishable offense.*

pun·ish·ing /ˈpəniSHiNG/ ▶ adj. physically and mentally demanding; arduous: *a punishing eight-city book tour.* ■ severe and debilitating: *the recession was having a punishing effect on our business.*
–DERIVATIVES **pun·ish·ing·ly** adv.

pun·ish·ment /ˈpəniSHmənt/ ▶ n. the infliction or imposition of a penalty as retribution for an offense: *crime demands just punishment.* ■ the penalty inflicted: *she assisted her husband to escape **punishment for** the crime* | *he approved of stiff punishments for criminals.* ■ informal rough treatment or handling inflicted on or suffered by a person or thing: *your machine can **take a fair amount of punishment** before falling to pieces.*
–ORIGIN late Middle English: from Old French *punissement*, from the verb *punir* (see PUNISH).

pu·ni·tive /ˈpyo͞onətiv/ ▶ adj. inflicting or intended as punishment: *he called for punitive measures against the Eastern bloc.* ■ (of a tax or other charge) extremely high: *a current punitive interest rate of 31.3%.*
–DERIVATIVES **pu·ni·tive·ly** adv., **pu·ni·tive·ness** n.
–ORIGIN early 17th cent.: from French *punitif, -ive* or medieval Latin *punitivus*, from Latin *punit-* 'punished,' from the verb *punire* (see PUNISH).

pu·ni·tive damages ▶ plural n. Law damages exceeding simple compensation and awarded to punish the defendant.

Pun·jab /ˈpənˌjäb, pənˈjäb/ (also **the Punjab**) a region of northwestern India and Pakistan, a wide, fertile plain traversed by the Indus River and the five tributaries that gave the region its name. ■ a province of Pakistan; capital, Lahore. ■ a state of India; capital, Chandigarh.
–ORIGIN from Hindi *panj* 'five' + *āb* 'waters.'

Pun·ja·bi /ˌpənˈjäbē, po͝on-/ (also **Panjabi** /ˌpən-/) ▶ n. (pl. **Punjabis**) **1** a native or inhabitant of Punjab.
2 the Indic language of Punjab.
▶ adj. of or relating to Punjab or its people or language.
–ORIGIN from Hindi *pājābī*.

pun·ji stick /ˈpənjē/ (also **punji stake**) ▶ n. a sharpened bamboo stake, typically one tipped with poison, set in a camouflaged hole in the ground as a means of defense, esp. in Southeast Asia.
–ORIGIN late 19th cent.: *punji* probably of Tibeto-Burman origin.

punk /pəNGk/ ▶ n. **1** informal a worthless person (often used as a general term of abuse). ■ a criminal or hoodlum. ■ derogatory (in prison slang) a passive male homosexual. ■ an inexperienced young person; a novice.
2 (also **punk rock**) a loud, fast-moving, and aggressive form of rock music, popular in the late 1970s and early 1980s. ■ (also **punk rocker**) an admirer or player of such music, typically characterized by colored spiked hair and clothing decorated with safety pins or zippers.
3 soft, crumbly wood that has been attacked by fungus, sometimes used as tinder.
▶ adj. **1** informal in poor or bad condition: *I felt too punk to eat.*
2 of or relating to punk rock and its associated subculture: *a punk band* | *a punk haircut.*
–DERIVATIVES **punk·ish** adj., **punk·y** adj.
–ORIGIN late 17th cent. (sense 3 of the noun): perhaps, in some senses, related to archaic *punk* 'prostitute,' also to SPUNK.

pun·kah /ˈpəNGkə/ ▶ n. chiefly historical (in India) a large cloth fan on a frame suspended from the ceiling, moved backward and forward by pulling on a cord. ■ Indian an electric fan.
–ORIGIN via Hindi from Sanskrit *pakṣaka*, from *pakṣa* 'wing.'

punk·er /ˈpəNGkər/ ▶ n. a punk rocker.

punk·ette /ˌpəNGˈket/ ▶ n. a female punk rocker.
–ORIGIN 1980s: from PUNK + the feminine suffix -ETTE.

pun·net /ˈpənət/ ▶ n. Brit. a small light basket or other container for fruit or vegetables: ***a punnet of** strawberries.*
–ORIGIN early 19th cent.: perhaps a diminutive of dialect *pun* 'a pound.'

punt¹ /pənt/ ▶ n. a long, narrow, flat-bottomed boat, square at both ends and propelled with a long pole, used on inland waters chiefly for recreation.
▶ v. travel or convey in a punt.
–ORIGIN Old English, from Latin *ponto*, denoting a flat-bottomed ferryboat; readopted in the early 16th cent. from Middle Low German *punte* or Middle Dutch *ponte* 'ferryboat,' of the same origin.

punt² ▶ v. **1** [with obj.] Football kick (the ball) after it is dropped from the hands and before it reaches the ground: *he used to be able to punt a football farther than anyone.* ■ [no obj.] (of an offensive team) turn possession over to the defensive team by punting the ball after failing to make a first down: *the Raiders could get nowhere with their possession, and had to punt.* ■ (of a player) act as the punter.
2 [no obj.] delay in answering or taking action; equivocate: *he would continue to punt on questions of Medicare.*
▶ n. a kick of this kind.
–ORIGIN mid 19th cent.: probably from dialect *punt* 'push forcibly.' Compare with BUNT[3].

punt³ ▶ v. [no obj.] (in some gambling card games) place a bet against the bank. ■ Brit. informal bet or speculate on something: *investors are **punting on** a takeover.*
▶ n. informal, chiefly Brit. a bet: *those **taking a punt on** the company's success.*
–ORIGIN early 18th cent.: from French *ponte* 'player against the bank,' from Spanish *punto* 'a point.'

punt⁴ ▶ n. the basic monetary unit of the Republic of Ireland (until replaced by the euro), equal to 100 Irish pence.
–ORIGIN Irish, literally 'pound.'

Pun·ta A·re·nas /ˈpo͞ontə əˈrānəs/ a port in southern Chile, on the Strait of Magellan; pop. 120,000 (est. 2006).

punt·er /ˈpəntər/ ▶ **n.** **1** Football & Rugby a player who punts.
2 a person who propels or travels in a punt.
3 informal, chiefly Brit. a person who gambles, places a bet, or makes a risky investment. ■ a customer or client, esp. a member of an audience. ■ a prostitute's client. ■ the victim of a swindler or confidence trickster.

pun·ty /ˈpəntē/ (also **pontil** /ˈpäntil/) ▶ **n.** (pl. **punties**) (in glassmaking) an iron rod used to hold or shape soft glass.
– ORIGIN mid 17th cent.: from French *pontil* (see PONTIL).

Punx·su·taw·ney /ˌpəNGksəˈtônē/ a borough in west central Pennsylvania, the home of Punxsutawney Phil, a groundhog whose movements are closely observed by the media each February 2 in order to predict the length of winter.

pu·ny /ˈpyo͞onē/ ▶ **adj.** (**punier**, **puniest**) small and weak: *skeletal, white-faced, puny children.* ■ poor in quality, amount, or size: *the army was reduced to a puny 100,000 men.*
– DERIVATIVES **pu·ni·ly** /ˈpyo͞onl-ē/ **adv.**, **pu·ni·ness n.**
– ORIGIN mid 16th cent. (as a noun denoting a younger or more junior person): phonetic spelling of PUISNE.

pup /pəp/ ▶ **n.** a young dog. ■ a young wolf, seal, rat, or other mammal. ■ dated, chiefly Brit. a cheeky or arrogant boy or young man: *you saucy young pup!*
▶ **v.** (**pups, pupping, pupped**) [no obj.] (of female dogs and certain other animals) give birth to young.
– PHRASES **in pup** (of a female dog) pregnant. **sell someone** (or **buy**) **a pup** Brit. informal swindle someone (or be swindled), esp. by selling (or buying) something worthless.
– ORIGIN late 16th cent. (in the sense 'arrogant young man'): back-formation from PUPPY, interpreted as a diminutive.

pu·pa /ˈpyo͞opə/ ▶ **n.** (pl. **pupae** /-ˌpē, -ˌpī/) an insect in its inactive immature form between larva and adult, e.g., a chrysalis.
– DERIVATIVES **pu·pal adj.**
– ORIGIN late 18th cent.: modern Latin, from Latin *pupa* 'girl, doll.'

pu·par·i·um /pyo͞oˈpe(ə)rēəm/ ▶ **n.** (pl. **puparia** /-ˈpe(ə)rēə/) Entomology the hardened last larval skin that encloses the pupa in some insects, esp. higher diptera. ■ a pupa enclosed in such a skin.
– ORIGIN early 19th cent.: modern Latin, from PUPA, on the pattern of words such as *herbarium*.

pu·pate /ˈpyo͞oˌpāt/ ▶ **v.** [no obj.] (of a larva) become a pupa.
– DERIVATIVES **pu·pa·tion** /pyo͞oˈpāSHən/ **n.**

pup·fish /ˈpəpˌfiSH/ ▶ **n.** (pl. **same** or **pupfishes**) a small fish found in fresh or brackish water in the deserts of the southwestern US and northern Mexico. ● Genus *Cyprinodon*, family Cyprinodontidae: several species, some of which are confined to single pools.

pu·pil[1] /ˈpyo͞opəl/ ▶ **n.** a student in school.
– ORIGIN late Middle English (in the sense 'orphan, ward'): from Old French *pupille*, from Latin *pupillus* (diminutive of *pupus* 'boy') and *pupilla* (diminutive of *pupa* 'girl').

pu·pil[2] ▶ **n.** the dark circular opening in the center of the iris of the eye, varying in size to regulate the amount of light reaching the retina.
– DERIVATIVES **pu·pil·lar·y** /ˈpyo͞opəˌlerē/ (also **pupilary**) **adj.**
– ORIGIN late Middle English: from Old French *pupille* or Latin *pupilla*, diminutive of *pupa* 'doll' (so named from the tiny reflected images visible in the eye).

pu·pil·age /ˈpyo͞opəlij/ (also **pupillage**) ▶ **n.** the state of being a pupil or student.

pu·pip·a·rous /pyo͞oˈpipərəs/ ▶ **adj.** Entomology (of certain flies, e.g., the tsetse) producing young that are already ready to pupate.
– ORIGIN early 19th cent.: from modern Latin *pupipara* (neuter plural of *pupiparus* 'bringing forth young') + -OUS.

pup·pet /ˈpəpət/ ▶ **n.** a movable model of a person or animal that is used in entertainment and is typically moved either by strings controlled from above or by a hand inside it. ■ a person, party, or state under the control of another person, group, or power: *he was little more than a puppet of his aides.*
– DERIVATIVES **pup·pet·ry** /-trē/ **n.**
– ORIGIN mid 16th cent. (denoting a doll): later form of POPPET, generally having a more unfavorable connotation.

pup·pet·eer /ˌpəpəˈtir/ ▶ **n.** a person who works puppets.
– DERIVATIVES **pup·pet·eer·ing n.**

pup·pet·mas·ter /ˈpəpətˌmastər/ ▶ **n.** a person, group, or country that covertly controls another: *the puppetmaster behind the current administration.*

Pup·pis /ˈpəpis/ Astronomy a southern constellation (the Poop or Stern), lying partly in the Milky Way south of Canis Major and originally part of Argo. ■ (as genitive **Puppis**) used with a preceding letter or numeral to designate a star in this constellation: *the star Zeta Puppis.*
– ORIGIN Latin.

pup·py /ˈpəpē/ ▶ **n.** (pl. **puppies**) a young dog. ■ informal, dated a conceited or arrogant young man: *you ungrateful puppy.* ■ informal a person or thing of a specified kind: *patient bargain hunters can often find these puppies gathering dust at garage sales.*
– DERIVATIVES **pup·py·hood** /-ˌho͝od/ **n.**, **pup·py·ish adj.**
– ORIGIN late 15th cent. (denoting a lapdog): perhaps from Old French *poupee* 'doll, plaything'; compare with PUPPET, synonymous with dialect *puppy* (as in *puppy-show* 'puppet show').

pup·py dog ▶ **n.** a child's word for a puppy.

pup·py fat ▶ **n.** chiefly Brit. fat on the body of a baby or child that disappears around adolescence.

pup·py love ▶ **n.** an intense but relatively shallow romantic attachment, typically associated with adolescents.

pup tent ▶ **n.** a small triangular tent, esp. one with a pole at either end and room for one or two people.

pur- ▶ **prefix** equivalent to PRO-[1] (as in *purloin, pursue*).
– ORIGIN from Anglo-Norman French, from Latin *por-, pro-*.

Pu·ra·na /po͞oˈränə/ ▶ **n.** (usu. **Puranas**) any of a class of Sanskrit sacred writings containing Hindu legends and folklore of varying date and origin, the most ancient of which dates from the 4th century AD.
– DERIVATIVES **Pu·ra·nic** /-ˈränik/ **adj.**
– ORIGIN from Sanskrit *purāṇa* 'ancient (legend),' from *purā* 'formerly.'

pur·blind /ˈpərˌblīnd/ ▶ **adj.** having impaired or defective vision. ■ slow or unable to understand; dimwitted.
– DERIVATIVES **pur·blind·ness n.**
– ORIGIN Middle English (as two words in the sense 'completely blind'): from the adverb PURE 'utterly' (later assimilated to PUR-) + BLIND.

Pur·cell /pərˈsel, ˈpərsəl/, Henry (1659–95), English composer. He composed the first English opera, *Dido and Aeneas* (1689), and the incidental music for many plays.

pur·chase /ˈpərCHəs/ ▶ **v.** [with obj.] **1** acquire (something) by paying for it; buy: *Mr. Gill spotted the manuscript at a local auction and purchased it for $1,500.* ■ archaic obtain or achieve with effort or suffering: *the victory was purchased by the death of Rhiwallon.*
2 Nautical haul in (a rope or cable) or haul up (an anchor) by means of a pulley, lever, etc.
▶ **n.** **1** the action of buying something: *the large number of videos currently available for purchase* | *we carefully* ***make our purchases*** *after consulting each other.* ■ a thing that has been bought: *she stowed her purchases in the car.* ■ Law the acquisition of property by means other than inheritance. ■ archaic the annual rent or return from land.
2 a hold or position on something for applying power advantageously, or the advantage gained by such application: *the horse's hooves fought for* ***purchase*** *on the slippery pavement* | [in sing.] *an attempt to gain a purchase on the soft earth.* ■ a block and tackle.
– DERIVATIVES **pur·chas·a·ble adj.**
– ORIGIN Middle English: from Old French *pourchacier* 'seek to obtain or bring about,' the earliest sense also in English, which soon gave rise to the senses 'gain' (hence, in nautical use, the notion of "gaining" one portion of rope after another) and 'buy.'

pur·chas·er /ˈpərCHəsər/ ▶ **n.** a person who buys something; a buyer: *one of the club's prospective purchasers.*

pur·chas·ing pow·er ▶ **n.** the financial ability to buy products and services. ■ the value of a sum of money: *the purchasing power of a million dollars isn't what it used to be.*

pur·dah /ˈpərdə/ ▶ **n.** the practice among women in certain Muslim and Hindu societies of living in a separate room or behind a curtain, or of dressing in all-enveloping clothes, in order to stay out of the sight of men or strangers: *he never required them to observe purdah* | *she was supposed to be* ***in purdah*** *upstairs.* ■ a curtain used for screening off women in this way.
– ORIGIN early 19th cent.: from Urdu and Persian *parda* 'veil, curtain.'

pure /pyo͝or/ ▶ **adj.** not mixed or adulterated with any other substance or material: *cars can run on pure alcohol* | *the jacket was pure wool.* ■ without any extraneous and unnecessary elements: *the romantic notion of pure art devoid of social responsibility.* ■ free of any contamination: *the pure, clear waters of Montana.* ■ wholesome and untainted by immorality, esp. that of a sexual nature: *our fondness for each other is pure and innocent.* ■ (of a sound) perfectly in tune and with a clear tone. ■ (of an animal or plant) of unmixed origin or descent: *the pure Charolais is white or light wheat in the coat.* ■ (of a subject of study) dealing with abstract concepts and not practical application: *a theoretical discipline such as pure physics.* Compare with APPLIED. ■ Phonetics (of a vowel) not joined with another to form a diphthong. ■ [attrib.] involving or containing nothing else but; sheer (used for emphasis): *a shout of pure anger* | *an outcome that may be a matter of pure chance.*
– PHRASES **pure and simple** and nothing else (used for emphasis): *it was revenge, pure and simple.*
– DERIVATIVES **pure·ness n.**
– ORIGIN Middle English: from Old French *pur* 'pure,' from Latin *purus*.

pure·bred /ˈpyo͝orˌbred/ ▶ **adj.** (of an animal) bred from parents of the same breed or variety.
▶ **n.** an animal of this kind.

pure cul·ture ▶ **n.** Microbiology a culture in which only one strain or clone is present.

pu·rée /pyo͝oˈrā, -ˈrē/ ▶ **n.** a smooth, creamy substance made of liquidized or crushed fruit or vegetables: *stir in the tomato purée.*
▶ **v.** (**purées, puréeing, puréed**) [with obj.] make a purée of (fruit or vegetables).
– ORIGIN early 18th cent.: French, literally 'purified,' feminine past participle of *purer*.

pure line ▶ **n.** Biology an inbred line of genetic descent.

pure·ly /ˈpyo͝orlē/ ▶ **adv.** in a pure manner: *act nobly, speak purely, and think charitably.* ■ entirely; exclusively: *the purpose of the meeting was purely to give information.*

pure math·e·mat·ics ▶ **plural n.** see MATHEMATICS.

pure play (also **pure player**) ▶ **n.** [usu. as modifier] a company that focuses exclusively on a particular product or service in order to obtain a large market share. ■ a company that operates only on the Internet.

pure sci·ence ▶ **n.** a science depending on deductions from demonstrated truths, such as mathematics or logic, or studied without regard to practical applications.

pur·fle /ˈpərfəl/ ▶ **n.** an ornamental border, typically one inlaid on the back or belly of a violin. ■ archaic an ornamental or embroidered edge of a garment.
▶ **v.** [with obj.] (often as noun **purfling**) decorate (something) with an ornamental border.
– ORIGIN Middle English (as a verb): from Old French *porfil* (noun), *porfiler* (verb), based on Latin *pro* 'forward' + *filum* 'thread.'

pur·ga·tion /ˌpərˈgāSHən/ ▶ **n.** the purification or cleansing of someone or something: *the purgation by ritual violence of morbid social emotions.* ■ (in Roman Catholic doctrine) the spiritual cleansing of a soul in purgatory. ■ historical the action of clearing oneself of accusation or suspicion by an oath or ordeal. ■ evacuation of the bowels brought about by laxatives.
– ORIGIN late Middle English: from Old French *purgacion*, from Latin *purgatio(n-)*, from *purgare* 'purify' (see PURGE).

pur·ga·tive /ˈpərgətiv/ ▶ **adj.** strongly laxative in effect. ■ having the effect of ridding someone of unwanted feelings or memories: *the purgative action of language.*
▶ **n.** a laxative. ■ a thing that rids someone of unwanted feelings or memories: *confrontation would be a purgative.*
– ORIGIN late Middle English: from Old French *purgatif, -ive*, from late Latin *purgativus*, from *purgat-* 'purified,' from the verb *purgare* (see PURGE).

pur·ga·to·ry /ˈpərgəˌtôrē/ ▶ **n.** (pl. **purgatories**) (in Roman Catholic doctrine) a place or state of suffering inhabited by the souls of sinners who are expiating their sins before going to heaven. ■ mental anguish or suffering: *this was purgatory, worse than anything she'd faced in her life.*
▶ **adj.** archaic having the quality of cleansing or purifying: *infernal punishments are purgatory and medicinal.*

PRONUNCIATION KEY ə *ago, up*; ər *over, fur*; a *hat*; ā *ate*; ä *car*; e *let*; ē *see*; i *fit*; ī *by*; NG *sing*; ō *go*; ô *law, for*; oi *toy*; o͝o *good*; o͞o *goo*; ou *out*; TH *thin*; T͟H *then*; ZH *vision*

– DERIVATIVES **pur·ga·to·ri·al** /ˌpərgəˈtôrēəl/ **adj.**
– ORIGIN Middle English: from Anglo-Norman French *purgatorie* or medieval Latin *purgatorium*, neuter (used as a noun) of late Latin *purgatorius* 'purifying,' from the verb *purgare* (see PURGE).

purge /pərj/ ▶ **v.** [with obj.] rid (someone) of an unwanted feeling, memory, or condition, typically giving a sense of cathartic release: *Bob had helped* ***purge*** *Martha* ***of*** *the terrible guilt that had haunted her.* ■ remove (an unwanted feeling, memory, or condition) in such a way. ■ remove (a group of people considered undesirable) from an organization or place, typically in an abrupt or violent manner: *he purged all but 26 of the central committee members.* ■ remove someone from (an organization or place) in such a way: *an opportunity to purge the party of unsatisfactory members.* ■ Law atone for or wipe out (contempt of court). ■ physically remove (something) completely: *a cold air blower* ***purges*** *residual solvents* ***from*** *the body.* ■ [no obj.] (often as noun **purging**) evacuate one's bowels, esp. as a result of taking a laxative.
▶ **n.** an abrupt or violent removal of a group of people from an organization or place: *a purge of the ruling class is absolutely necessary | a victim of the cultural purges.* ■ dated a laxative.
– DERIVATIVES **purg·er** **n.**
– ORIGIN Middle English (in the legal sense 'clear oneself of a charge'): from Old French *purgier*, from Latin *purgare* 'purify,' from *purus* 'pure.'

pu·ri /ˈpo͝orē/ (also **poori**) ▶ **n.** (pl. **puris**) (in Indian cooking) a small, round, flat piece of bread made of unleavened wheat flour, deep-fried and served with meat or vegetables.
– ORIGIN via Hindi from Sanskrit *pūrikā*.

pu·ri·fy /ˈpyo͝orəˌfī/ ▶ **v.** (**purifies, purifying, purified**) [with obj.] remove contaminants from: *the filtration plant is able to purify 70 tons of water a day | a group of 19th-century German painters who set out to purify art* | (as adj. **purified**) *purified linseed oil.* ■ make ceremonially clean: *a ritual bath to purify the soul.* ■ (**purify something from**) extract something from: *genomic DNA was purified from whole blood.*
– DERIVATIVES **pu·ri·fi·ca·tion** /ˌpyo͝orəfiˈkāSHən/ **n.**, **pu·rif·i·ca·to·ry** /pyo͝oˈrifikəˌtôrē/ **adj.**, **pu·ri·fi·er** **n.**
– ORIGIN Middle English: from Old French *purifier*, from Latin *purificare*, from *purus* 'pure.'

Pu·rim /ˈpo͝orim, po͝oˈrēm/ ▶ **n.** a lesser Jewish festival held in spring (on the 14th or 15th day of Adar) to commemorate the defeat of Haman's plot to massacre the Jews as recorded in the book of Esther.
– ORIGIN Hebrew, plural of *pūr*, explained in the book of Esther (3:7, 9:24) as meaning 'lot,' with allusion to the casting of lots by Haman.

pu·rine /ˈpyo͝orˌēn/ ▶ **n.** Chemistry a colorless crystalline compound with basic properties, forming uric acid on oxidation. ● A bicyclic compound; chem. formula: $C_5H_4N_4$. ■ (also **purine base**) a substituted derivative of this, esp. the bases adenine and guanine present in DNA and RNA.
– ORIGIN late 19th cent.: from German *Purin*, from Latin *purus* 'pure' + *uricum* 'uric acid' + -INE[4].

pur·ism /ˈpyo͝orˌizəm/ ▶ **n.** **1** scrupulous or exaggerated observance of or insistence on traditional rules or structures, esp. in language or style.
2 (**Purism**) an early-20th-century artistic style and movement founded by Le Corbusier and the French painter **Amédée Ozenfant** (1886–1966) and emphasizing purity of geometric form. It arose out of a rejection of cubism and was characterized by a return to the representation of recognizable objects.

pur·ist /ˈpyo͝orist/ ▶ **n.** **1** a person who insists on absolute adherence to traditional rules or structures, esp. in language or style.
2 (**Purist**) an adherent of Purism.
– DERIVATIVES **pu·ris·tic** /pyo͝oˈristik/ **adj.**
– ORIGIN early 18th cent.: from French *puriste*, from *pur* 'pure.'

Pu·ri·tan /ˈpyo͝oritn/ ▶ **n.** a member of a group of English Protestants of the late 16th and 17th centuries who regarded the Reformation of the Church of England under Elizabeth as incomplete and sought to simplify and regulate forms of worship. ■ (**puritan**) a person with censorious moral beliefs, esp. about pleasure and sex.
▶ **adj.** of or relating to the Puritans. ■ (**puritan**) having or displaying censorious moral beliefs, esp. about pleasure and sex.
– DERIVATIVES **Pu·ri·tan·ism** (also **puritanism**) **n.**
– ORIGIN late 16th cent.: from late Latin *puritas* 'purity' + -AN.

pu·ri·tan·i·cal /ˌpyo͝oriˈtanikəl/ ▶ **adj.** often derogatory practicing or affecting strict religious or moral behavior.
– DERIVATIVES **pu·ri·tan·i·cal·ly** **adv.**

Pu·ri·tan State a nickname for the state of MASSACHUSETTS.

pu·ri·ty /ˈpyo͝oritē/ ▶ **n.** freedom from adulteration or contamination: *the purity of our drinking water.* ■ freedom from immorality, esp. of a sexual nature: *white is meant to represent purity and innocence.*
– ORIGIN Middle English: from Old French *purete*, later assimilated to late Latin *puritas*, from Latin *purus* 'pure.'

Pur·kin·je cell /pərˈkinjē/ ▶ **n.** Anatomy a nerve cell of a large, branched type found in the cortex of the cerebellum.
– ORIGIN mid 19th cent.: named after Jan E. *Purkinje* (1787–1869), Bohemian physiologist.

purl[1] /pərl/ ▶ **adj.** [attrib.] denoting or relating to a knitting stitch made by putting the needle through the front of the stitch from right to left. Compare with KNIT.
▶ **n.** a purl stitch.
▶ **v.** [with obj.] knit with a purl stitch: *knit one, purl one.*
– ORIGIN mid 17th cent. (as a noun): of uncertain origin.

purl[2] ▶ **v.** [no obj.] (of a stream or river) flow with a swirling motion and babbling sound.
▶ **n.** [in sing.] a motion or sound of this kind.
– ORIGIN early 16th cent. (denoting a small swirling stream): probably imitative; compare with Norwegian *purla* 'bubble up.'

pur·lieu /ˈpərl(y)o͞o/ ▶ **n.** (pl. **purlieus** or **purlieux** /-l(y)o͞o(z)/) **1** the area near or surrounding a place: *the photogenic* ***purlieus of*** *the Princeton.* ■ a person's usual haunts.
2 Brit. historical a tract on the border of a forest, esp. one earlier included in it and still partly subject to forest laws.
– ORIGIN late 15th cent. (denoting a tract on the border of a forest): probably an alteration (suggested by French *lieu* 'place') of Anglo-Norman French *puralee* 'a going around to settle the boundaries.'

pur·lin /ˈpərlən/ ▶ **n.** a horizontal beam along the length of a roof, resting on a main rafter and supporting the common rafters or boards.
– ORIGIN late Middle English: perhaps of French origin.

pur·loin /pərˈloin/ ▶ **v.** [with obj.] steal (something): *he must have managed to purloin a copy of the key.*
– DERIVATIVES **pur·loin·er** **n.**
– ORIGIN Middle English (in the sense 'put at a distance'): from Anglo-Norman French *purloigner* 'put away,' from *pur-* 'forth' + *loign* 'far.'

pu·ro /ˈpo͝orō/ ▶ **n.** (pl. **puros**) (in Spanish-speaking regions) a cigar.
– ORIGIN Spanish, literally 'pure.'

pu·ro·my·cin /ˌpyo͝orəˈmīsin/ ▶ **n.** Medicine an antibiotic used to treat sleeping sickness and amebic dysentery. ● This antibiotic is produced by the bacterium *Streptomyces alboniger*.
– ORIGIN 1950s: from PURINE + -MYCIN.

pur·ple /ˈpərpəl/ ▶ **n.** a color intermediate between red and blue: *the painting was mostly in shades of blue and purple.* ■ purple clothing or material. ■ (also **Tyrian purple**) a crimson dye obtained from some mollusks, formerly used for fabric worn by an emperor or senior magistrate in ancient Rome or Byzantium. ■ (**the purple**) (in ancient Rome or Byzantium) clothing of this color. ■ (**the purple**) (in ancient Rome) a position of rank, authority, or privilege: *he was too young to assume the purple.* ■ (**the purple**) the scarlet official dress of a cardinal.
▶ **adj.** of a color intermediate between red and blue: *a faded purple T-shirt.*
▶ **v.** become or make purple in color: [no obj.] *Ed's cheeks purpled* | [with obj.] *the neon was purpling the horizon above the highway.*
– PHRASES **born in** (or **to**) **the purple** born into a reigning family or privileged class.
– DERIVATIVES **pur·ple·ness** **n.**, **pur·plish** /ˈpərp(ə)lisH/ **adj.**, **pur·ply** /ˈpərp(ə)lē/ **adj.**
– ORIGIN Old English (describing the clothing of an emperor), alteration of *purpre*, from Latin *purpura* 'purple,' from Greek *porphura*, denoting mollusks that yielded a crimson dye, also cloth dyed with this.

pur·ple gal·li·nule ▶ **n.** **1** another term for GALLINULE.
2 a marsh bird of the rail family, with a purplish-blue head and breast and a large red bill, found throughout the Old World. ● *Porphyrio porphyrio*, family Rallidae.

pur·ple heart ▶ **n.** **1** (**Purple Heart**) (in the US) a military decoration for those wounded or killed in action, established in 1782 and re-established in 1932.
2 a large tree of the rain forests of Central and South America, with dark purplish-brown timber that blackens on contact with water. ● Genus *Peltogyne*, family Leguminosae: several species, in particular *P. paniculata*.
3 Brit. informal a mauve-colored heart-shaped stimulant tablet, esp. of amphetamine.

pur·ple-leaf plum ▶ **n.** a shrub or small tree with white flowers and small red and yellow edible fruit. Native to southwestern Asia, it is used as stock for commercial varieties of plum. Also called FLOWERING PLUM, MYROBALAN. ● *Prunus cerasifera*, family Rosaceae. ■ the fruit of this tree.

pur·ple mar·tin ▶ **n.** a martin with purplish-blue plumage. It is the largest North American swallow, and the male is the only swallow with uniform dark plumage on its belly. ● *Progne subis*, family Hirundinidae.

pur·ple pas·sage ▶ **n.** an elaborate or excessively ornate passage in a literary composition.

pur·ple patch ▶ **n.** **1** informal, chiefly Brit. a run of success or good luck.
2 another term for PURPLE PASSAGE.

pur·ple prose ▶ **n.** prose that is too elaborate or ornate.

pur·port ▶ **v.** /pərˈpôrt/ [with infinitive] appear or claim to be or do something, esp. falsely; profess: *she is not the person she purports to be.*
▶ **n.** /ˈpərˌpôrt/ the meaning or substance of something, typically a document or speech: *I do not understand the purport of your remarks.* ■ the purpose of a person or thing: *the purport of existence.*
– DERIVATIVES **pur·port·ed·ly** **adv.**
– ORIGIN late Middle English (in the sense 'express, signify'): from Old French *purporter*, from medieval Latin *proportare*, from Latin *pro-* 'forth' + *portare* 'carry, bear.' The sense 'appear to be' dates from the late 18th cent.

pur·pose /ˈpərpəs/ ▶ **n.** the reason for which something is done or created or for which something exists: *the purpose of the meeting is to appoint a trustee | the building is no longer needed for its original purpose.* ■ a person's sense of resolve or determination: *there was a new* ***sense of purpose*** *in her step as she set off.* ■ (usu. **purposes**) a particular requirement or consideration, typically one that is temporary or restricted in scope or extent: *pensions are considered as earned income for tax purposes.*
▶ **v.** [with obj.] formal have as one's intention or objective: *God has allowed suffering, even purposed it.*
– PHRASES **on purpose** intentionally. **to no purpose** with no result or effect; pointlessly. **to the purpose** relevant or useful: *you may have heard something from them that is to the purpose.*
– ORIGIN Middle English: from Old French *porpos*, from the verb *porposer*, variant of *proposer* (see PROPOSE).

pur·pose-built ▶ **adj.** chiefly Brit. built for a particular purpose: *purpose-built accommodations for the elderly.*

pur·pose·ful /ˈpərpəsfəl/ ▶ **adj.** having or showing determination or resolve: *the purposeful stride of a great lawyer.* ■ having a useful purpose: *purposeful activities.* ■ intentional: *if his sudden death was not accidental, it must have been purposeful.*
– DERIVATIVES **pur·pose·ful·ly** **adv.**, **pur·pose·ful·ness** **n.**

pur·pose·less /ˈpərpəslis/ ▶ **adj.** done or made with no discernible point or purpose: *purposeless vandalism.* ■ having no aim or plan: *his purposeless life.*
– DERIVATIVES **pur·pose·less·ly** **adv.**, **pur·pose·less·ness** **n.**

pur·pose·ly /ˈpərpəslē/ ▶ **adv.** on purpose; intentionally: *she had purposely made it difficult.*

pur·pos·ive /ˈpərpəsiv, pərˈpō-/ ▶ **adj.** having, serving, or done with a purpose: *teaching is a purposive activity.*
– DERIVATIVES **pur·pos·ive·ly** **adv.**, **pur·pos·ive·ness** **n.**

pur·pu·ra /ˈpərp(y)ərə/ ▶ **n.** Medicine a rash of purple spots on the skin caused by internal bleeding from small blood vessels. ■ [with adj.] any of a number of diseases characterized by such a rash: *psychogenic purpura.*
– DERIVATIVES **pur·pu·ric** /pərˈpyo͝orik/ **adj.**
– ORIGIN mid 18th cent.: from Latin, from Greek *porphura* 'purple.'

pur·pure /ˈpərpyər/ ▶ **n.** purple, as a heraldic tincture.
– ORIGIN Old English (in the sense 'purple garment'), from Latin *purpura* (see PURPURA), reinforced by Old French *purpre* and influenced by words ending in *-ure*.

pur·pu·rin /ˈpərpyərin/ ▶ **n.** Chemistry a red dye originally extracted from madder and also prepared

p

artificially by the oxidation of alizarin. ● An anthraquinone derivative; chem. formula: $C_{14}H_8O_5$.
– ORIGIN mid 19th cent.: from Latin *purpura* 'purple' + -IN[1].

purr /pər/ ▶ v. [no obj.] (of a cat) make a low continuous vibratory sound usually expressing contentment. ■ (of a vehicle or engine) move smoothly while making such a sound: *a sleek blue BMW purred past him.* ■ speak in a low soft voice, esp. when expressing contentment or acting seductively: [with direct speech] *"Would you like coffee?" she purred* | [with obj.] *she purred her lines seductively.*
▶ n. a low continuous vibratory sound, typically that made by a cat or vehicle.
– ORIGIN early 17th cent.: imitative.

purse /pərs/ ▶ n. a small bag used esp. by a woman to carry everyday personal items. ■ a small pouch of leather or plastic used for carrying money, typically by a woman. ■ the money possessed or available to a person or country: *institutions are funded from the same general purse.* ■ a sum of money given as a prize in a sporting contest, esp. a boxing match.
▶ v. (with reference to the lips) pucker or contract, typically to express disapproval or irritation: [with obj.] *Marianne took a glance at her reflection and pursed her lips disgustedly* | [no obj.] *under stress his lips would purse slightly.*
– PHRASES **hold the purse strings** have control of expenditure. **tighten** (or **loosen**) **the purse strings** restrict (or increase) the amount of money available to be spent.
– ORIGIN late Old English, alteration of late Latin *bursa* 'purse,' from Greek *bursa* 'hide, leather.' The current verb sense (from the notion of drawing purse strings) dates from the early 17th cent.

purse net ▶ n. another term for PURSE SEINE.

purs·er /pərsər/ ▶ n. an officer on a ship who keeps the accounts, esp. the head steward on a passenger vessel.

purse seine ▶ n. [usu. as modifier] a seine that can be drawn into the shape of a bag using the line along the bottom of the net like the drawstring of a purse.
– DERIVATIVES **purse sein·er** n.

purs·lane /ˈpərslən, -ˌslān/ ▶ n. any of a number of small, typically fleshy-leaved plants that grow in damp habitats or waste places, in particular: ● *Portulaca oleracea*, a prostrate North American plant with tiny yellow flowers. ● *Sesuvium maritimum* (**sea-purslane**), an edible plant that grows in damp sand along coastal shores.
– ORIGIN late Middle English: from Old French *porcelaine*, probably from Latin *porcil(l)aca*, variant of *portulaca*, influenced by French *porcelaine* 'porcelain.'

pur·su·ance /pərˈso͞oəns/ ▶ n. formal the carrying out of a plan or action: *you have a right to use public areas in the pursuance of your lawful hobby.* ■ the action of trying to achieve something: *they are considering a walkout in pursuance of a better deal.*

pur·su·ant /pərˈso͞oənt/ ▶ adv. (**pursuant to**) formal in accordance with (a law or a legal document or resolution): *conversations that they wiretap pursuant to court order.*
▶ adj. archaic following; going in pursuit: *the pursuant lady.*
– DERIVATIVES **pur·su·ant·ly** adv.
– ORIGIN late Middle English *poursuiant* (as a noun in the sense 'prosecutor'): from Old French, 'pursuing,' from the verb *poursuir*; later influenced in spelling by PURSUE.

pur·sue /pərˈso͞o/ ▶ v. (**pursues**, **pursuing**, **pursued**) [with obj.] **1** follow (someone or something) in order to catch or attack them: *the officer pursued the van* | figurative *a heavily indebted businessman was being pursued by creditors.* ■ seek to form a sexual relationship with (someone) in a persistent way: *Sophie was being pursued by a number of men.* ■ seek to attain or accomplish (a goal), esp. over a long period: *should people pursue their own happiness at the expense of others?* ■ archaic or literary (of something unpleasant) persistently afflict (someone): *mercy lasts as long as sin pursues man.*
2 (of a person or way) continue or proceed along (a path or route): *the road pursued a straight course over the scrubland.* ■ engage in (an activity or course of action): *Andrew was determined to pursue a computer career* | *the council decided not to pursue an appeal.* ■ continue to investigate, explore, or discuss (a topic, idea, or argument): *we shall not pursue the matter any further.*
– DERIVATIVES **pur·su·a·ble** adj., **pur·su·er** n.
– ORIGIN Middle English (originally in the sense 'follow with enmity'): from Anglo-Norman French *pursuer*, from an alteration of Latin *prosequi* 'prosecute.'

pur·suit /pərˈso͞ot/ ▶ n. **1** the action of following or pursuing someone or something: *the cat crouched in the grass* ***in pursuit of*** *a bird* | *those whose business is the pursuit of knowledge.* ■ a bicycle race in which competitors start from different parts of a track and attempt to overtake one another. ■ Physiology the action of the eye in following a moving object.
2 [with modifier] (often **pursuits**) an activity of a specified kind, esp. a recreational or athletic one: *a whole range of leisure pursuits.*
– PHRASES **give pursuit** (of a person, animal, or vehicle) start to chase another.
– ORIGIN late Middle English: from Anglo-Norman French *purseute* 'following after,' from *pursuer* (see PURSUE). Early senses included 'persecution, annoyance' and in legal contexts 'petition, prosecution.'

pur·sui·vant /ˈpərs(w)ivənt/ ▶ n. **1** Brit. an officer of the College of Arms.
2 archaic a follower or attendant.
– ORIGIN late Middle English (denoting a junior heraldic officer): from Old French *pursivant*, present participle (used as a noun) of *pursivre* 'follow after.'

pur·sy /ˈpərsē/ ▶ adj. archaic **1** (esp. of a horse) short of breath; asthmatic.
2 (of a person) fat.
– DERIVATIVES **pur·si·ness** n.
– ORIGIN late Middle English: reduction of Anglo-Norman French *porsif*, alteration of Old French *polsif*, from *polser* 'breathe with difficulty,' from Latin *pulsare* 'set in violent motion.'

pu·ru·lent /ˈpyo͝or(y)ələnt/ ▶ adj. Medicine consisting of, containing, or discharging pus.
– ORIGIN late Middle English: from Latin *purulentus* 'festering,' from *pus*, *pur-* (see PUS).

Pu·rus Riv·er /pəˈro͞os/ a river that flows northeast for 2,100 miles (3,400 km) from the Andes Mountains in eastern Peru into northwestern Brazil, where it joins the Amazon River.

pur·vey /pərˈvā/ ▶ v. [with obj.] provide or supply (food, drink, or other goods) as one's business: *shops purveying cooked food.* ■ spread or promote (an idea, view, etc.): *this magazine feels like a concerted effort to purvey gloom and doom.*
– ORIGIN Middle English: from Anglo-Norman French *purveier*, from Latin *providere* 'foresee, attend to' (see PROVIDE). Early senses included 'foresee,' 'attend to in advance,' and 'equip.'

pur·vey·ance /pərˈvāəns/ ▶ n. the action of purveying something. ■ Brit. historical the right of the sovereign to buy provisions and use horses and vehicles for a fixed price lower than the market value.
– ORIGIN Middle English (in the senses 'foresight' and 'prearrangement'): from Old French *porveance*, from Latin *providentia* 'foresight' (see PROVIDENCE).

pur·vey·or /pərˈvāər/ ▶ n. a person who sells or deals in particular goods: *a purveyor of large luxury vehicles.* ■ a person or group that spreads or promotes an idea, view, etc.: *a purveyor of traditional Christian values.*

pur·view /ˈpərˌvyo͞o/ ▶ n. [in sing.] the scope of the influence or concerns of something: *such a case might be within the purview of the legislation.* ■ a range of experience or thought: *social taboos meant that little information was likely to come within the purview of women generally.*
– ORIGIN late Middle English: from Anglo-Norman French *purveu* 'foreseen,' past participle of *purveier* (see PURVEY). Early use was as a legal term specifying the body of a statute following the words "be it enacted."

pus /pəs/ ▶ n. a thick yellowish or greenish opaque liquid produced in infected tissue, consisting of dead white blood cells and bacteria with tissue debris and serum.
– ORIGIN late Middle English: from Latin.

Pu·san /ˈpo͞oˈsän/ an industrial city and seaport on the southeastern coast of South Korea; pop. 3,596,100 (est. 2008).

Pu·sey /ˈpyo͞ozē/, Edward Bouverie (1800–82), English theologian. In 1833, while professor of Hebrew at Oxford, he founded the Oxford Movement and became its leader after the withdrawal of John Henry Newman in 1841.

push /po͝osh/ ▶ v. **1** [with obj., usu. with adverbial] exert force on (someone or something), typically with one's hand, in order to move them away from oneself or the origin of the force: *she pushed her glass toward him* | [with obj. and complement] *Lydia pushed the door shut* | [no obj.] *he pushed at the skylight, but it wouldn't budge.* ■ [with obj.] hold and exert force on (something) so as to cause it to move along in front of one: *a woman was pushing a stroller.* ■ move one's body or a part of it into a specified position, esp. forcefully or with effort: *she pushed her hands into her pockets.* ■ [with obj.] press (a part of a machine or other device): *he pushed the button for the twentieth floor.* ■ [with adverbial] cause to reach a particular level or state: *they expect that the huge crop will push down prices* | *the political chaos could push the country into recession.*
2 [no obj.] move forward by using force to pass people or cause them to move aside: *she pushed her way through the crowded streets* | *he pushed past an old woman in his haste.* ■ (of an army) advance over territory: *the guerrillas have pushed south to within 100 miles of the capital.* ■ exert oneself to attain something or surpass others: *I was pushing hard until about 10 laps from the finish.* ■ (**push for**) demand persistently: *the council continued to push for the better management of water resources.* ■ [with obj.] compel or urge (someone) to do something, esp. to work hard: *she believed he was pushing their daughter too hard.* ■ (**be pushed**) informal have very little of something, esp. time: *I'm a bit pushed for time at the moment.* ■ (**be pushing**) informal be nearly (a particular age): *she must be pushing forty, but she's still a good looker.*
3 [with obj.] informal promote the use, sale, or acceptance of: *the company is pushing a $500 asking price.* ■ put forward (an argument or demand) with undue force or in too extreme a form: *he thought that the belief in individualism had been pushed too far.* ■ sell (a narcotic drug) illegally.
4 [with obj.] Computing prepare (a stack) to receive a piece of data on the top. ■ transfer (data) to the top of a stack.
5 [with obj.] Photography develop (film) so as to compensate for deliberate underexposure.
▶ n. **1** an act of exerting force on someone or something in order to move them away from oneself: *he closed the door with a push.* ■ an act of pressing a part of a machine or device: *the door locks at the push of a button.* ■ something that encourages or assists something else: *the fall in prices was given a push by official policy.*
2 a vigorous effort to do or obtain something: *many clubs are joining in the fund-raising push* | *he determined to make one last push for success.* ■ a military attack in force: *the army was engaged in a push against guerrilla strongholds.* ■ forcefulness and enterprise: *an investor with the necessary money and push.*
– PHRASES **get** (or **give someone**) **the push** (or **shove**) Brit. informal be dismissed (or dismiss someone) from a job. ■ be rejected in (or end) a relationship. **push the boat out** see BOAT. **push someone's buttons** see BUTTON. **pushing up daisies** see DAISY. **push one's luck** informal take a risk on the assumption that one will continue to be successful or in favor. **when push comes to shove** informal when one must commit oneself to an action or decision: *when push came to shove, I always stood up for him.*
– PHRASAL VERBS **push ahead** proceed with or continue a course of action or policy: *he promised to push ahead with economic reform.* **push along** Brit. informal go away; depart. **push someone around** informal treat someone roughly or inconsiderately. **push off** use an oar, boathook, etc., to exert pressure so as to move a boat out from shore or away from another vessel. **push on** continue on a journey: *the light was already fading, but she pushed on.* **push something through** get a proposed measure completed or accepted quickly.
– ORIGIN Middle English (as a verb): from Old French *pousser*, from Latin *pulsare* 'to push, beat, pulse' (see PULSE[1]). The early sense was 'exert force on,' giving rise later to 'make a strenuous effort, endeavor.'

push·back /ˈpo͝oshˌbak/ ▶ n. **1** a negative or unfavorable response: *there's been some strong pushback from Republicans on this.*
2 (at an airport) the action or an instance of moving an airplane from a passenger terminal to a runway or taxiway.

push·bike /ˈpo͝oshˌbīk/ ▶ n. Brit. informal a bicycle.

push broom ▶ n. a broom consisting of a handle attached at an angle to a wide brush that is worked by pushing.

push but·ton ▶ n. a button that is pushed to operate an electrical device: *some kind of push button on their TV sets* | [as modifier] *a push-button telephone.*

push·cart /ˈpo͝oshˌkärt/ ▶ n. a small handcart or barrow.

push·chair /ˈpo͝oshˌche(ə)r/ ▶ n. Brit. a stroller.

push·er /ˈpo͝oshər/ ▶ n. **1** informal a person who sells illegal drugs.

P

2 a person or thing that pushes something. ■ informal a forceful or pushy person: *she got things moving, she was a tremendous pusher.*

push fit ▶ **n.** a fit between two parts in which one is connected to the other by manually pushing or sliding them together.

push·ful /ˈpo͝oSHfəl/ ▶ **adj.** arrogantly self-assertive; pushy.
– DERIVATIVES **push·ful·ly** **adv.**, **push·ful·ness** **n.**

Push·kin /ˈpo͝oSHkin, -kyin/, Aleksandr (Sergeevich) (1799–1837), Russian poet, novelist, and dramatist. His first success was the romantic narrative poem *Ruslan and Ludmilla* (1820). Other notable works: *Eugene Onegin* (1833) and *Boris Godunov* (1831).

push·o·ver /ˈpo͝oSHˌōvər/ ▶ **n.** informal a person who is easy to overcome or influence: *Colonel Moore was benevolent but no pushover.* ■ a thing that is very easily done: *this is going to be a pushover.*

push·pin /ˈpo͝oSHˌpin/ ▶ **n.** a thumbtack with a spherical or cylindrical head of colored plastic, used to fasten papers to a bulletin board or to indicate positions on charts and maps.

push poll ▶ **n.** an ostensible opinion poll in which the true objective is to sway voters using loaded or manipulative questions.
– DERIVATIVES **push-poll·ing** **n.**

push proc·ess·ing ▶ **n.** Photography the development of film so as to compensate for deliberate underexposure, thereby increasing the effective film speed.

push-pull ▶ **adj.** [attrib.] operated by pushing and pulling. ■ Electronics having or involving two matched tubes or transistors that operate 180 degrees out of phase, conducting alternately for increased output.

push·rod /ˈpo͝oSHˌräd/ ▶ **n.** a rod operated by cams that opens and closes the valves in an internal combustion engine.

push-start ▶ **v.** [with obj.] start (a motor vehicle) by pushing it and putting it in gear in order to make the engine turn.
▶ **n.** an act of starting a motor vehicle in this way.

Push·tu /ˈpəSHto͞o/ ▶ **n.** variant of **PASHTO**.

push·up /ˈpo͝oSHˌəp/ ▶ **n.** an exercise in which a person lies facing the floor and, keeping their back straight, raises their body by pressing down on their hands.
▶ **adj.** (**push-up**) denoting a padded or underwired bra or similar garment that gives uplift to the breasts.

push·y /ˈpo͝oSHē/ ▶ **adj.** (**pushier, pushiest**) excessively or unpleasantly self-assertive or ambitious.
– DERIVATIVES **push·i·ly** /ˈpo͝oSHəlē/ **adv.**, **push·i·ness** **n.**

pu·sil·lan·i·mous /ˌpyo͞osəˈlanəməs/ ▶ **adj.** showing a lack of courage or determination; timid.
– DERIVATIVES **pu·sil·la·nim·i·ty** /-ləˈnimətē/ **n.**, **pu·sil·lan·i·mous·ly** **adv.**
– ORIGIN late Middle English: from ecclesiastical Latin *pusillanimis* (translating Greek *olugopsukhos*), from *pusillus* 'very small' + *animus* 'mind,' + -OUS.

puss[1] /po͝os/ ▶ **n.** informal a cat (esp. as a form of address): *you naughty little puss!* ■ a playful or coquettish girl or young woman: *you old snuggle puss.*
– ORIGIN early 16th cent.: probably from Middle Low German *pūs* (also *pūskatte*) or Dutch *poes*, of unknown origin.

puss[2] ▶ **n.** informal a person's face or mouth.
– ORIGIN late 19th cent.: from Irish *pus* 'lip, mouth.'

pus·sy /ˈpo͝osē/ ▶ **n.** (pl. **pussies**)
1 (also **pussycat**) informal a cat.
2 vulgar slang a woman's genitals. ■ offensive women in general, considered sexually. ■ informal a weak, cowardly, or effeminate man.

pus·sy·foot /ˈpo͝osēˌfo͝ot/ ▶ **v.** [no obj.] act in a cautious or noncommittal way: *I realized I could no longer* **pussyfoot around**. ■ move stealthily or warily: *they make a great show of pussyfooting through the greenery.*
– DERIVATIVES **pus·sy·foot·er** /-ˌfo͝otər/ **n.**

pus·sy-whip ▶ **v.** [with obj.] (usu. as adj. **pussy-whipped**) vulgar slang henpeck (a man).

pus·sy wil·low ▶ **n.** a willow with soft fluffy silvery or yellow catkins that appear before the leaves.
● Genus *Salix*, family Salicaceae: several species, in particular the common North American (*S. discolor*).
– ORIGIN mid 19th cent.: originally a child's word, because of the resemblance of the soft fluffy catkins to a cat's fur.

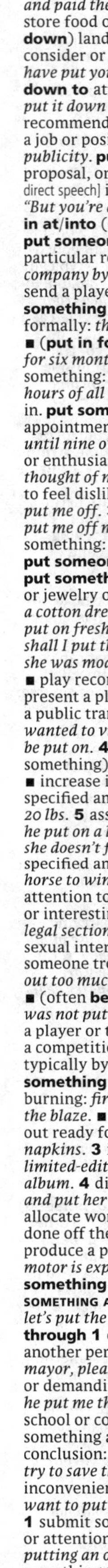
pussy willow

pus·tu·late ▶ **v.** /ˈpəsCHəˌlāt, ˈpəstyə-/ [no obj.] form into pustules: (as adj. **pustulating**) *pustulating epidermal ulcers.*
▶ **adj.** /ˈpəsCHəlit, ˈpəstyə-/ chiefly Biology having or covered with pustules: *the surface is coarsely pustulate.*
– DERIVATIVES **pus·tu·la·tion** /ˌpəsCHəˈlāSHən, ˌpəstyə-/ **n.**
– ORIGIN late Middle English (as an adjective): from late Latin *pustulatus*, past participle of *pustulare* 'to blister,' from *pustula* 'pustule.'

pus·tule /ˈpəsCHo͞ol, ˈpəst(y)o͞ol/ ▶ **n.** Medicine a small blister or pimple on the skin containing pus. ■ Biology a small raised spot or rounded swelling, esp. one on a plant resulting from fungal infection.
– DERIVATIVES **pus·tu·lar** /ˈpəsCHələr, ˈpəstyə-/ **adj.**
– ORIGIN late Middle English: from Latin *pustula*.

put /po͝ot/ ▶ **v.** (**puts, putting**; past and past participle **put**) [with obj.] **1** move to or place in a particular position: *Harry put down his cup | I put my hand out toward her | watch where you're putting your feet!* ■ cause (someone or something) to go to a particular place and remain there for a time: *India has put three experimental satellites into space.* ■ [no obj.] (of a ship or the people on it) proceed in a particular direction: *she stepped into the boat and* **put out to sea**. ■ write or print (something) in a particular place: *they put my name on the cover page.* ■ [no obj.] archaic (of a river) flow in a particular direction.
2 bring into a particular state or condition: *they tried to put me at ease | a large aid program was put into effect | he* **is putting himself** *at risk.* ■ (**put oneself in**) imagine oneself in (a particular situation): *it was no use trying to put herself in his place.* ■ express (a thought or comment) in a particular way, form, or language: *to put it bluntly, he was not really divorced.*
3 (**put something on/onto**) cause (someone or something) to carry or be subject to something: *commentators put some of the blame on Congress.* ■ assign a particular value, figure, or limit to: *it is very difficult to put a figure on the size of the budget.* ■ (**put something at**) estimate something to be (a particular amount): *estimates put the war's cost at $1,000,000 a day.*
4 throw (a shot or weight) as an athletic sport: *she set a women's record by putting the shot 56′ 7″.*
▶ **n.** **1** a throw of the shot or weight.
2 Stock Market short for **PUT OPTION**.
– PHRASES **put something behind one** get over a bad experience by distancing oneself from it: *they have tried to put their grief behind them and rebuild their lives.* **put the clocks back** (or **forward**) adjust clocks or watches backward (or forward) to take account of official changes in time. **put someone's eyes out** blind someone, typically in a violent way. **put one's hands together** applaud; clap: *I want you all to put your hands together for Barry.* **put one's hands up** raise one's hands in surrender. **put it there** [in imperative] informal used to indicate that the speaker wishes to shake hands with someone in agreement or congratulation: *put it there, Steven, we beat them.* **put it to** [with clause] make a statement or allegation to (someone) and challenge them to deny it: *I put it to him that he was just a political groupie.* **put one over on** informal deceive (someone) into accepting something false. **put up or shut up** informal justify oneself or remain silent: *they called for the alderman to either put up or shut up.*
– PHRASAL VERBS **put about** Nautical (of a ship) turn on the opposite tack. **put something about** (often **be put about**) spread information or rumors. **put something across** (or **over**) communicate something effectively. **put something aside 1** save money for future use. **2** forget or disregard something, typically a feeling or a past difference. **put someone away** (often **be put away**) informal confine someone in a prison or psychiatric hospital: *he deserves to be put away forever.* **put something away 1** save money for future use. **2** informal consume food or drink in large quantities. **3** another way of saying **PUT SOMETHING DOWN** below. **4** informal (in sports) dispatch or deal with a goal or shot. **put something back** reschedule a planned event to a later time or date. ■ delay something: *greater public control may put back the modernization of the industry.* **put something by** another way of saying **PUT SOMETHING ASIDE**. **put someone down 1** informal lower someone's self-esteem by criticizing them in front of others. **2** lay a baby down to sleep. **put something down 1** record something in writing: *he's putting a few thoughts down on paper.* **2** suppress a rebellion, riot, or other disturbance by force. **3** (usu. **be put down**) kill an animal because it is sick, injured, or old. **4** pay a specified sum as a deposit: *he put a thousand down and paid the rest over six months.* **5** preserve or store food or wine for future use. **6** (also **put down**) land an aircraft. **put someone down as** consider or judge someone or something to be: *I'd have put you down as a Vivaldi man.* **put something down to** attribute something to: *if I forget anything, put it down to old age.* **put someone forward** recommend someone as a suitable candidate for a job or position: *he put me forward as head of publicity.* **put something forward** submit a plan, proposal, or theory for consideration. **put in** [with direct speech] interrupt a conversation or discussion: *"But you're a sybarite, Roger," put in Isobel.* **put in at/into** (of a ship) enter (a port or harbor). **put someone in** appoint someone to fulfill a particular role or job: *he was put in to rescue the company by the stockbrokers.* ■ (in team sports) send a player out to participate into a game. **put something in/into 1** present or submit something formally: *the airport had put in a claim for damages.* ■ (**put in for**) apply formally for: *Adam put in for six months' leave.* **2** devote time or effort to something: *employed mothers put in the longest hours of all women.* **3** invest money or resources in. **put someone off 1** cancel or postpone an appointment with someone: *he'd put off Martin until nine o'clock.* **2** cause someone to lose interest or enthusiasm: *she wanted to be a nurse, but the thought of night shifts put her off.* ■ cause someone to feel dislike or distrust: *she had a coldness that just put me off.* **3** distract someone: *you're just trying to put me off my game.* **put something off** postpone something: *they can't put off a decision much longer.* **put someone on** informal deceive or hoax someone. **put something on 1** place a garment, glasses, or jewelry on part of one's body: *Julie had put on a cotton dress.* ■ attach or apply something: *she put on fresh makeup.* **2** cause a device to operate: *shall I put the light on?* ■ start cooking something: *she was moaning that he hadn't put the dinner on.* ■ play recorded music or a video. **3** organize or present a play, exhibition, or event. ■ provide a public transportation service: *so many people wanted to visit this spot that an extra flight had to be put on.* **4** add a specified amount to (the cost of something): *the news put 12 cents on the share price.* ■ increase in body weight; become heavier by a specified amount: *she's given up her diet and put on 20 lbs.* **5** assume a particular expression, accent, etc.: *he put on a lugubrious look.* ■ behave deceptively: *she doesn't feel she has to* **put on an act**. **6** bet a specified amount of money on: *he put $1,000 on the horse to win.* **put someone on to** draw someone's attention to (someone or something useful, notable, or interesting): *Pike put me on to the department's legal section.* **put out** vulgar slang be willing to have sexual intercourse. **put someone out 1** cause someone trouble or inconvenience: *would it put you out too much to let her visit you for a couple of hours?* ■ (often **be put out**) upset or annoy someone: *he was not put out by the rebuff.* **2** (in sports) defeat a player or team and so cause them to be out of a competition. **3** make someone unconscious, typically by means of drugs or an anesthetic. **put something out 1** extinguish something that is burning: *firefighters from Georgetown put out the blaze.* ■ turn off a light. **2** lay something out ready for use: *she put out glasses and paper napkins.* **3** issue or broadcast something: *a limited-edition single was put out to promote the album.* **4** dislocate a joint: *she fell off her horse and put her shoulder out.* **5** (of a company) allocate work to a contractor or freelancer to be done off the premises. **6** (of an engine or motor) produce a particular amount of power: *the new motor is expected to put out about 250 h.p.* **put something over 1** another way of saying **PUT SOMETHING ACROSS**. **2** postpone something: *let's put the case over for a few weeks.* **put someone through 1** connect someone by telephone to another person or place: *put me through to the mayor, please.* **2** subject someone to an unpleasant or demanding experience: *I hate Brian for what he put me through.* **3** pay for someone to attend school or college. **put something through** initiate something and see it through to a successful conclusion: *he put through a reform program to try to save the regime.* **put someone to** cause inconvenience or difficulty to someone: *I don't want to put you to any trouble.* **put something to 1** submit something to (someone) for consideration or attention: *we are making a takeover bid and putting an offer to the shareholders.* **2** devote something to (a particular use or purpose): *they put the land to productive use.* **put something together** make something by assembling different parts or people: *he can take a clock apart and put it* **back together** *again | they decided to put a new band together.* ■ assemble things or people to make

something: *a carpenter puts together shaped pieces of wood to make a table.* **put someone under** another way of saying PUT SOMEONE OUT. **put up 1** offer or show (a particular degree of resistance, effort, or skill) in a fight or competitive situation: *he put up a brave fight.* **2** stay temporarily in lodgings other than one's own home: *we put up at a hotel in the city center.* **put someone up 1** accommodate someone temporarily. **2** propose someone for election or adoption: *they should have put themselves up for election.* **put something up 1** construct or erect something: *I put up the tent and cooked a meal.* **2** raise one's hand to signal that one wishes to answer or ask a question. **3** display a notice, sign, or poster. ■ present a proposal, theory, or argument for discussion or consideration. **4** chiefly Brit. increase the cost of something: *I'm afraid I've got to put your rent up.* **5** provide money as backing for an enterprise: *the sponsors are putting up $5,000 for the event.* **6** (often **be put up for**) offer something for sale or auction. **7** archaic return a sword to its sheath. **put upon** (often as adj. **put-upon**) informal take advantage of (someone) by exploiting their good nature: *a put-upon drudge who slaved for her employer.* **put someone up to** informal encourage someone to do (something wrong or unwise): *Who else would play a trick like that on me? I expect Rose put him up to it.* **put up with** tolerate; endure: *I'm too tired to put up with any nonsense.*
– ORIGIN Old English (recorded only in the verbal noun *putung*), of unknown origin; compare with dialect *pote* 'to push, thrust' (an early sense of the verb *put*).

pu·ta /'po͝o,tä/ ▶ n. informal (in Spanish-speaking regions) a prostitute or slut.
– ORIGIN Spanish.

pu·ta·men /pyo͞o'tāmən/ ▶ n. (pl. **putamina** /-'tamənə/ or **putamens**) Anatomy the outer part of the lentiform nucleus of the brain.
– DERIVATIVES **pu·tam·i·nal** /-'tamənl/ adj.
– ORIGIN late 19th cent.: from Latin, literally 'shell remaining after pruning.'

put-and-take ▶ adj. [attrib.] denoting a system whereby waters are stocked with fish for anglers to catch.

pu·ta·tive /'pyo͞otətiv/ ▶ adj. [attrib.] generally considered or reputed to be: *the putative father of a boy of two.*
– DERIVATIVES **pu·ta·tive·ly** adv.
– ORIGIN late Middle English: from Old French *putatif, -ive* or late Latin *putativus*, from Latin *putat-* 'thought,' from the verb *putare*.

put-down ▶ n. informal a remark intended to humiliate or criticize someone.

put·er /'po͞otər/ ▶ n. informal a computer.
– ORIGIN 1990s: abbreviation.

Pu·tin /'po͞otin, 'po͞otn/, Vladimir (1952–), Russian statesman; president of the Russian Federation 2000–08; prime minister from 2008. A former KGB officer, he was appointed head of the Security Council and then prime minister by Boris Yeltsin; he became acting president on Yeltsin's resignation December 31, 1999, and was elected president in 2000.

put·log /'po͝ot,lôg, -,läg/ (also **putlock** /-,läk/) ▶ n. a short horizontal pole projecting from a wall, on which the floorboards of scaffolding rest.
– ORIGIN mid 17th cent.: of unknown origin.

put-off ▶ n. informal **1** an evasive reply. **2** an unpleasant or deterrent quality or feature.

put-on ▶ n. informal a deception; a hoax.

pu·tong·hua /'po͞o'to͝oNG'hwä/ ▶ n. the standard spoken form of modern Chinese, based on the dialect of Beijing.
– ORIGIN Chinese, literally 'common spoken language.'

put op·tion ▶ n. Stock Market an option to sell assets at an agreed price on or before a particular date.

put·out /'po͝ot,out/ ▶ n. Baseball an act of a fielder in retiring a batter or runner.

pu·tre·fac·tion /,pyo͞otrə'fakSHən/ ▶ n. the process of decay or rotting in a body or other organic matter.
– ORIGIN late Middle English: from Old French, or from late Latin *putrefactio(n-)*, from *putrefacere* 'make rotten' (see PUTREFY).

pu·tre·fac·tive /,pyo͞otrə'faktiv/ ▶ adj. relating to or causing decay: *they were killed by the putrefactive bacteria.*

pu·tre·fy /'pyo͞otrə,fī/ ▶ v. (**putrefies, putrefying, putrefied**) [no obj.] (of a body or other organic matter) decay or rot and produce a fetid smell.
– ORIGIN late Middle English: via French from Latin *putrefacere*, from *puter, putr-* 'rotten.'

pu·tres·cent /pyo͞o'tresənt/ ▶ adj. undergoing the process of decay; rotting: *the odor of putrescent flesh.*
– DERIVATIVES **pu·tres·cence** n.
– ORIGIN mid 18th cent.: from Latin *putrescent-* 'beginning to go rotten,' inceptive of *putrere* 'to rot' (see PUTRID).

pu·tres·ci·ble /pyo͞o'tresəbəl/ ▶ adj. liable to decay; subject to putrefaction: *putrescible domestic waste.*
▶ n. (usu. **putrescibles**) something that is liable to decay.

pu·tres·cine /pyo͞o'tresēn/ ▶ n. Chemistry an oily amine formed from arginine during putrefaction. ● Alternative name: **1,4-diaminobutane**; chem. formula: $C_4H_{12}N_2$.

pu·trid /'pyo͞otrid/ ▶ adj. (of organic matter) decaying or rotting and emitting a fetid smell. ■ of or characteristic of rotting matter: *the putrid smells from the slaughterhouses.* ■ informal very unpleasant; repulsive: *the cocktail is a putrid pink color.*
– DERIVATIVES **pu·trid·i·ty** /pyo͞o'tridətē/ n., **pu·trid·ly** adv., **pu·trid·ness** n.
– ORIGIN late Middle English: from Latin *putridus*, from *putrere* 'to rot,' from *puter, putr-* 'rotten.'

putsch /po͝oCH/ ▶ n. a violent attempt to overthrow a government.
– ORIGIN 1920s: from Swiss German, literally 'thrust, blow.'

putt /pət/ ▶ v. (**putts, putting, putted**) [no obj.] try to hit a golf ball into a hole by striking it gently so that it rolls across the green: *Nicklaus putted for eagle on 11 of the 16 par 5s* | [with obj.] *putt the balls into the hole.*
▶ n. a stroke of this kind made in an attempt to hole the ball.
– ORIGIN mid 17th cent. (originally Scots): differentiated from PUT.

put·ta·nes·ca /,po͞otə'neskə, ,po͞otn'eskə/ ▶ adj. [usu. postpositive] denoting a pasta sauce typically including tomatoes, garlic, olives, and anchovies: *pasta puttanesca.*
– ORIGIN Italian, from *puttana* 'prostitute' (the sauce is said to have been devised by prostitutes as one that could be cooked quickly between clients' visits).

put·tee /,pə'tē/ ▶ n. a long strip of cloth wound spirally around the leg from ankle to knee for protection and support. ■ a leather legging.
– ORIGIN late 19th cent.: from Hindi *paṭṭī* 'band, bandage.'

put·ter[1] /'pətər/ ▶ n. **1** a golf club designed for use in putting, typically with a flat-faced malletlike head. **2** [with adj.] a golfer considered in terms of putting ability: *you'll need to be a good putter to break par.*

put·ter[2] ▶ n. & v. another term for PUTT-PUTT.
– ORIGIN 1940s: imitative.

put·ter[3] (Brit. **potter**) ▶ v. [no obj.] occupy oneself in a desultory but pleasant manner, doing a number of small tasks or not concentrating on anything particular: *early morning is the best time of the day to putter around in the garden.* ■ [with adverbial of direction] move or go in a casual, unhurried way: *the duck putters on the surface of the pond.*
– DERIVATIVES **put·ter·er** n.
– ORIGIN late 19th cent. (originally US): alteration of POTTER[1].

put·ting green /'pətiNG/ ▶ n. a smooth area of short grass surrounding a hole, either as part of a golf course or as a separate area for putting.

Putt·nam /'pətnəm/, Sir David (Terence) (1941–), English movie director. Notable movies: *Chariots of Fire* (1981), *The Killing Fields* (1984), and *The Mission* (1986).

put·to /'po͞otō/ ▶ n. (pl. **putti** /'po͞otē/) a representation of a naked child, esp. a cherub or a cupid in Renaissance art.
– ORIGIN Italian, literally 'boy,' from Latin *putus*.

putt-putt (also **put-put**) ▶ n. the rapid intermittent sound of a small gasoline engine: *she heard the putt-putt of a boat coming toward them.*
▶ v. [no obj.] make such a sound: *the machine gun putt-putted behind me.* ■ [no obj.] move under the power of an engine that makes such a sound: *the car at last putt-putted down the hill.*
– ORIGIN early 20th cent.: imitative.

put·ty /'pətē/ ▶ n. **1** a soft, malleable, grayish-yellow paste, made from whiting and raw linseed oil, that hardens after a few hours and is used chiefly for sealing glass panes in wooden window frames. ■ [usu. with modifier] any of a number of similar malleable substances used inside and outside buildings, e.g., **plumber's putty**, or used for modeling or casting. **2** a polishing powder, usually made from tin oxide, used in jewelry work.
▶ v. (**putties, puttying, puttied**) [with obj.] seal or cover (something) with putty.
– PHRASES **be (like) putty in someone's hands** be easily manipulated or dominated by someone.
– ORIGIN mid 17th cent.: from French *potée*, literally 'potful,' from *pot* 'pot.'

Put·u·ma·yo Riv·er /,po͞otə'mī-ō/ a river that flows for 1,000 miles (1,610 km) from the Andes Mountains in southwestern Colombia along the borders with Ecuador and Peru into northwestern Brazil, where it joins the Amazon River.

put-up ▶ adj. [attrib.] arranged beforehand in order to deceive someone: *the whole thing could be a put-up job.*

putz /'pəts, 'po͝ots/ informal ▶ n. **1** a stupid or worthless person. **2** vulgar slang a penis.
▶ v. [no obj.] engage in inconsequential or unproductive activity: *too much putzing around up there would ruin them.*
– ORIGIN 1960s: Yiddish, literally 'penis.'

Pu·zo /'po͞ozō/, Mario (1920–99), US writer. He wrote the novel *The Godfather* in 1969 and the subsequent screenplay for it in 1972. His other works included *Fools Die* (1978) and *The Sicilian* (1984).

puz·zle /'pəzəl/ ▶ v. [with obj.] cause (someone) to feel confused because they cannot understand or make sense of something: *one remark he made puzzled me.* ■ [no obj.] think hard about something difficult to understand or explain: *she was still puzzling over this problem when she reached the office.* ■ (**puzzle something out**) solve or understand something by thinking hard.
▶ n. a game, toy, or problem designed to test ingenuity or knowledge. ■ short for JIGSAW PUZZLE (see JIGSAW). ■ [usu. in sing.] a person or thing that is difficult to understand or explain; an enigma: *the meaning of the poem has always been a puzzle.*
– DERIVATIVES **puz·zle·ment** n.
– ORIGIN late 16th cent. (as a verb): of unknown origin.

puz·zled /'pəzəld/ ▶ adj. unable to understand; perplexed: *the questioners were met with puzzled looks* | *she looked puzzled and angry with him.*

puz·zler /'pəz(ə)lər/ ▶ n. a difficult question or problem. ■ a person who solves puzzles as a pastime.

puz·zling /'pəz(ə)liNG/ ▶ adj. causing one to be puzzled; perplexing: *that was the most puzzling aspect of the whole affair.*
– DERIVATIVES **puz·zling·ly** /'pəz(ə)liNGlē/ adv. [sentence adverb] *puzzlingly, almost no mention of Hong Kong was made.*

PV ▶ abbr. polyvinyl.

PVA ▶ abbr. polyvinyl acetate.

PVC ▶ abbr. polyvinyl chloride.

PVO ▶ abbr. private voluntary organization.

PVR ▶ abbr. personal video recorder.

PVS ▶ abbr. Medicine persistent vegetative state.

Pvt. (also **PVT**) ▶ abbr. ■ (in the US Army) private. ■ (in company names) private.

PW ▶ abbr. policewoman.

p.w. ▶ abbr. per week.

PWA ▶ abbr. person with AIDS.

PWC ▶ abbr. personal watercraft.

PWR ▶ abbr. pressurized-water reactor.

pwr. ▶ abbr. power.

PX ▶ abbr. ■ Pedro Ximenes. ■ post exchange.

pxt. ▶ abbr. pinxit.
– ORIGIN Latin, abbreviation of *pinxit*, 'he painted.'

pya /pē'ä/ ▶ n. a monetary unit of Burma (Myanmar), equal to one hundredth of a kyat.
– ORIGIN Burmese.

py·ae·mi·a ▶ n. British spelling of PYEMIA.

pyc·no·cline /ˈpiknəˌklīn/ ▶ n. Geography a layer in an ocean or other body of water in which water density increases rapidly with depth.
– ORIGIN 1950s: from Greek *puknos* 'thick' + **CLINE**.

pye-dog /ˈpī ˌdôg/ ▶ n. a stray mongrel, esp. in Asia.
– ORIGIN mid 19th cent.: from Anglo-Indian *pye*, Hindi *pāhī* 'outsider' + **DOG**.

py·e·li·tis /ˌpīəˈlītis/ ▶ n. Medicine inflammation of the renal pelvis.
– ORIGIN mid 19th cent.: from Greek *puelos* 'trough, basin' + **-ITIS**.

py·e·log·ra·phy /ˌpīəˈlägrəfē/ ▶ n. Medicine an X-ray technique for producing an image of the renal pelvis and urinary tract by the introduction of a radiopaque fluid. Also called **UROGRAPHY**.
– DERIVATIVES **py·e·lo·gram** /ˈpīəlōˌgram, pīˈelə-/ n.
– ORIGIN early 20th cent.: from Greek *puelos* 'trough, basin' + **-GRAPHY**.

py·e·lo·ne·phri·tis /ˌpīəˌlōniˈfrītis/ ▶ n. Medicine inflammation of the substance of the kidney as a result of bacterial infection.
– DERIVATIVES **py·e·lo·ne·phrit·ic** /-ˈfritik/ adj.
– ORIGIN mid 19th cent.: from Greek *puelos* 'trough, basin' + **NEPHRITIS**.

py·e·mi·a /pīˈēmēə/ (Brit. **pyaemia**) ▶ n. blood poisoning (septicemia) caused by the spread in the bloodstream of pus-forming bacteria released from an abscess.
– DERIVATIVES **py·e·mic** /pīˈēmik/ adj.
– ORIGIN mid 19th cent.: modern Latin, from Greek *puon* 'pus' + *haima* 'blood.'

py·gid·i·um /pīˈjidēəm/ ▶ n. (pl. **pygidia** /-ˈjidēə/) Zoology the terminal part or hind segment of the body in certain invertebrates.
– ORIGIN mid 19th cent.: modern Latin, from Greek *pugē* 'rump.'

Pyg·ma·li·on /pigˈmālyən, -lēən/ Greek Mythology a king of Cyprus who fashioned an ivory statue of a beautiful woman and loved it so deeply that in answer to his prayer Aphrodite gave it life. The woman (at some point named Galatea) bore him a daughter, Paphos.

Pyg·my /ˈpigmē/ (also **Pigmy**) ▶ n. (pl. **Pygmies**) a member of certain peoples of very short stature in equatorial Africa and parts of Southeast Asia. ■ (**pygmy**) chiefly derogatory a very small person, animal, or thing. ■ (**pygmy**) [usu. with adj.] an insignificant person, esp. one who is deficient in a particular respect: *he regarded them as intellectual pigmies*.

> Pygmies (e.g., the Mbuti and Twa peoples) are typically dark-skinned, nomadic hunter-gatherers with an average male height not above 150 cm (4 ft. 11 in.). See also **NEGRILLO**, **NEGRITO**.

P

▶ adj. of, relating to, or denoting the Pygmies: *centuries-old Pygmy chants from central Africa*. ■ (**pygmy**) (of a person or thing) very small. ■ (**pygmy**) used in names of animals and plants that are much smaller than more typical kinds, e.g., **pygmy hippopotamus**, **pygmy water lily**.
– DERIVATIVES **pyg·me·an** /ˈpigmēən, pigˈmēən/ adj. (archaic).
– ORIGIN late Middle English (originally in the plural, denoting a mythological race of small people): via Latin from Greek *pugmaios* 'dwarf,' from *pugmē* 'the length measured from elbow to knuckles.'

pyg·my chim·pan·zee ▶ n. another term for **BONOBO**.

pyg·my owl ▶ n. a very small owl found in America and northern Eurasia. ● Genus *Glaucidium*, family Strigidae: several species.

pyg·my pos·sum ▶ n. a very small Australasian marsupial that feeds on insects and nectar, with handlike feet and a prehensile tail. ● Family Burramyidae: two genera and five species.

pyg·my shrew ▶ n. a shrew that is one of the smallest known mammals. ● Genus *Sorex*, family Soricidae: several species, in particular the Eurasian *S. minutus* and the American *S. hoyi*.

py·go·style /ˈpīgəˌstīl/ ▶ n. Ornithology (in a bird) a triangular plate formed of the fused caudal vertebrae, typically supporting the tail feathers.
– ORIGIN late 19th cent.: from Greek *pugē* 'rump' + *stulos* 'column.'

py·jam·as /pəˈjäməz, -jaməz/ ▶ plural n. British spelling of **PAJAMAS**.

pyk·nic /ˈpiknik/ ▶ adj. Anthropology of, relating to, or denoting a stocky physique with a rounded body and head, thickset trunk, and a tendency to be fat.
– ORIGIN 1920s: from Greek *puknos* 'thick' + **-IC**. The word was first used by the German psychiatrist Ernst Kretschmer (1888–1964) in his tripartite classification of human types (the other two being *asthnic* and *athletic*).

Pyle /pīl/, Ernie (1900–1945), US journalist; full name *Ernest Taylor Pyle*. A syndicated war correspondent, he reported on World War II from Africa, Europe, and the South Pacific. He was killed by Japanese forces during the US invasion of Okinawa. He wrote *Here Is Your War* (1943) and *Brave Men* (1944).

py·lon /ˈpīˌlän, -lən/ ▶ n. an upright structure that is used for support or for navigational guidance, in particular: ■ (also **electricity pylon**) a tower used for carrying power lines high above the ground. ■ a pillarlike structure on the wing of an aircraft used for carrying an engine, weapon, fuel tank, or other load. ■ a tower or post marking a path for light aircraft, cars, or other vehicles, esp. in racing. ■ a monumental gateway to an ancient Egyptian temple formed by two truncated pyramidal towers.
– ORIGIN mid 19th cent.: from Greek *pulōn*, from *pulē* 'gate.'

py·lor·ic /pīˈlôrik, pə-/ ▶ adj. Anatomy & Medicine relating to or affecting the region where the stomach opens into the duodenum (small intestine): *pyloric stenosis*.

py·lo·rus /pīˈlôrəs, pə-/ ▶ n. (pl. **pylori** /-ˈlôrˌī, -ˈlôrē/) Anatomy the opening from the stomach into the duodenum (small intestine).
– ORIGIN early 17th cent.: via late Latin from Greek *pulouros* 'gatekeeper,' from *pulē* 'gate' + *ouros* 'warder.'

Pyn·chon /ˈpinCHən/, Thomas (Ruggles) (1937–), US novelist. An elusive author who shuns public attention, his works abandon the normal conventions of the novel. Notable works: *V* (1963), *The Crying of Lot 49* (1966), *Gravity's Rainbow* (1972), *Vineland* (1990), and *Mason and Dixon* (1997).

py·o·der·ma /ˌpīəˈdərmə/ ▶ n. Medicine a skin infection with formation of pus.
– ORIGIN 1930s: from Greek *puo-* (from *puon* 'pus') + *derma* 'skin.'

py·o·gen·ic /ˌpīəˈjenik/ ▶ adj. Medicine involving or relating to the production of pus.
– ORIGIN mid 19th cent.: from Greek *puo-* (from *puon* 'pus') + **-GENIC**.

Pyong·yang /ˈpyəNGˈyäNG, -ˈyaNG, ˈpyäNG-/ the capital of North Korea; pop. 3,255,400 (est. 2008). The oldest city on the Korean peninsula, it was first mentioned in records in 108 BC. It developed as an industrial city during the years of Japanese occupation 1910–45.

py·or·rhe·a /ˌpīəˈrēə/ (also **pyorrhea alveolaris**, Brit. **pyorrhoea**) ▶ n. another term for **PERIODONTITIS**.
– ORIGIN early 19th cent.: from Greek *puo-* (from *puon* 'pus') + *rhoia* 'flux' (from *rhein* 'to flow').

py·ra·can·tha /ˌpīrəˈkanTHə/ ▶ n. a thorny evergreen Eurasian shrub with white flowers and bright red or yellow berries that is a popular ornamental. Also called **FIRETHORN**. ● Genus *Pyracantha*, family Rosaceae.
– ORIGIN modern Latin, via Latin from Greek *purakantha*, the name of an unidentified plant, from *pur* 'fire' + *akantha* 'thorn.'

pyr·a·lid /ˈpīrəˌlid/ ▶ n. Entomology an insect of a family (Pyralidae) of small delicate moths with narrow forewings. The larvae of many species are pests of stored foodstuffs.
– ORIGIN late 19th cent.: from modern Latin *Pyralidae* (plural), based on Greek *puralis*, denoting a mythical fly said to live in fire.

pyr·a·mid /ˈpirəˌmid/ ▶ n. **1** a monumental structure with a square or triangular base and sloping sides that meet in a point at the top, esp. one built of stone as a royal tomb in ancient Egypt.

> Pyramids were built as tombs for Egyptian pharaohs from the 3rd dynasty (*c.*2649 BC) until *c.*1640 BC. Monuments of similar shape are associated with the Maya and Aztec civilizations of *c.*1200 BC–AD 750, and, like those in Egypt, were part of large ritual complexes.

2 a thing, shape, or graph with such a form: *the pyramid of the Matterhorn*. ■ Geometry a polyhedron of which one face is a polygon of any number of sides, and the other faces are triangles with a common vertex: *a three-sided pyramid*. ■ Anatomy a structure of more or less pyramidal form, esp. in the brain or the renal medulla. ■ an organization or system that is structured with fewer people or things at each level as one approaches the top: *the lowest strata of the social pyramid*.
3 a system of financial growth achieved by a small initial investment, with subsequent investments being funded by using unrealized profits as collateral. ■ short for **PYRAMID SCHEME**.
▶ v. [with obj.] heap or stack in the shape of a pyramid: *debt was pyramided on top of unrealistic debt in an orgy of speculation*. ■ achieve a substantial return on (money or property) after making a small initial investment.
– DERIVATIVES **py·ram·i·dal** /pīˈramidl/ adj., **pyr·a·mid·i·cal** /ˌpirəˈmidikəl/ adj.
– ORIGIN late Middle English (in the geometric sense): via Latin from Greek *puramis*, *puramid-*, of unknown ultimate origin.

pyramid of Giza, in northern Egypt

pyr·a·mid scheme ▶ n. a form of investment (illegal in the US and elsewhere) in which each paying participant recruits two further participants, with returns being given to early participants using money contributed by later ones.

Pyr·a·mus /ˈpirəməs/ Roman Mythology a Babylonian youth, lover of Thisbe.

> Forbidden to marry by their parents, who were neighbors, the lovers conversed through a chink in a wall and agreed to meet at a tomb outside the city. There, Thisbe was frightened away by a lioness coming from its kill, and Pyramus, seeing her bloodstained cloak and supposing her dead, stabbed himself. Thisbe, finding his body when she returned, threw herself upon his sword.

py·rar·gy·rite /pīˈrärjəˌrīt/ ▶ n. a dark red mineral consisting of a sulfide of silver and antimony.
– ORIGIN mid 19th cent.: from Greek *puro-* (from *pur* 'fire') + *arguros* 'silver' + **-ITE**[1].

pyre /pīr/ ▶ n. a heap of combustible material, esp. one for burning a corpse as part of a funeral ceremony.
– ORIGIN mid 17th cent.: via Latin from Greek *pura*, from *pur* 'fire.'

py·rene /ˈpīˌrēn/ ▶ n. Chemistry a crystalline aromatic hydrocarbon present in coal tar. ● A tetracyclic compound; chem. formula: $C_{16}H_{10}$.
– ORIGIN mid 19th cent.: from Greek *pur* 'fire' + **-ENE**.

Pyr·e·nees /ˈpirəˌnēz/ a range of mountains that extends along the border between France and Spain from the Atlantic coast to the Mediterranean Sea. Its highest peak is Pico de Aneto in northern Spain, which rises to a height of 11,168 feet (3,404 m).
– DERIVATIVES **Pyr·e·ne·an** /ˌpirəˈnēən/ adj.

py·re·thrin /pīˈrēTHrən, -ˈreTHrən/ ▶ n. Chemistry any of a group of insecticidal compounds present in pyrethrum flowers.
– ORIGIN 1920s: from **PYRETHRUM** + **-IN**[1].

py·re·throid /pīˈrēTHˌroid, pīˈreTH-/ ▶ n. Chemistry a pyrethrin or related insecticidal compound.

py·re·thrum /pīˈrēTHrəm, -ˈreTHrəm/ ▶ n. an aromatic plant of the daisy family, typically having feathery foliage and brightly colored flowers. ● Genus *Tanacetum* (formerly *Chrysanthemum* or *Pyrethrum*), family Compositae: several species, in particular *T. coccineum*, grown as an ornamental, and *T. cinerariifolium*, grown as a source of the insecticide pyrethrum. ■ an insecticide made from the dried flowers of these plants.
– ORIGIN Middle English (denoting pellitory): from Latin, from Greek *purethron* 'feverfew.' The current senses (based on the former genus name) date from the late 19th cent.

py·ret·ic /pīˈretik/ ▶ adj. rare fevered, feverish, or inducing fever.
– ORIGIN early 18th cent. (as a medical term, now only in *antipyretic*): from modern Latin *pyreticus*, from Greek *puretos* 'fever.'

Py·rex /ˈpīˌreks/ ▶ n. [usu. as modifier] trademark a hard, heat-resistant type of glass, typically used for ovenware: *a set of Pyrex dishes*.
– ORIGIN early 20th cent.: an invented word.

py·rex·i·a /pīˈreksēə/ ▶ n. Medicine raised body temperature; fever.
– DERIVATIVES **py·rex·i·al** adj., **py·rex·ic** /-sik/ adj.
– ORIGIN mid 18th cent.: modern Latin, from Greek *purexis*, from *puressein* 'be feverish,' from *pur* 'fire.'

pyr·i·dine /ˈpirəˌdēn/ ▶ **n.** Chemistry a colorless volatile liquid with an unpleasant odor, present in coal tar and used chiefly as a solvent. ● A heteroaromatic compound; chem. formula: C_5H_5N.
– ORIGIN mid 19th cent.: from Greek *pur* 'fire' + **-IDE** + **-INE**[4].

pyr·i·do·stig·mine /ˌpiridōˈstigˌmēn/ ▶ **n.** Medicine a synthetic compound related to neostigmine, with similar but weaker and longer-acting effects.
– ORIGIN 1950s: blend of **PYRIDINE** and **NEOSTIGMINE**.

pyr·i·dox·al /ˌpiriˈdäksəl/ ▶ **n.** Biochemistry an oxidized derivative of pyridoxine that acts as a coenzyme in transamination and other processes.
– ORIGIN 1940s: from **PYRIDOXINE** + **-AL**.

pyr·i·dox·ine /ˌpiriˈdäkˌsēn/ ▶ **n.** Biochemistry a colorless weakly basic solid present chiefly in cereals, liver oils, and yeast, and important in the metabolism of unsaturated fatty acids. Also called **VITAMIN B6** (see **VITAMIN B**). ● An alcohol derived from pyridine; chem. formula: $C_8H_{11}NO_3$.
– ORIGIN 1930s: from *pyrid(ine)* + **OX-** 'oxygen' + **-INE**[4].

pyr·i·form /ˈpirəˌfôrm/ ▶ **adj.** Anatomy & Biology pear-shaped: *the pyriform fossa.*
– ORIGIN mid 18th cent.: from modern Latin *pyriformis*, from *pyrum* (misspelling of *pirum* 'pear') + **-IFORM**.

py·ri·meth·a·mine /ˌpirəˈmeTHəˌmēn/ ▶ **n.** Medicine a synthetic compound derived from pyrimidine, used to treat malaria.

py·rim·i·dine /pəˈriməˌdēn, pī-/ ▶ **n.** Chemistry a colorless crystalline compound with basic properties. ● A heteroaromatic compound; chem. formula: $C_4H_4N_2$. ■ (also **pyrimidine base**) a substituted derivative of this, esp. the bases thymine and cytosine present in DNA.
– ORIGIN late 19th cent.: from German *Pyrimidin*, from **PYRIDINE**, with the insertion of *-im-* from **IMIDE**.

py·rite /ˈpīˌrīt/ (also **pyrites** /pəˈrītēz, pī-/) ▶ **n.** a shiny yellow mineral consisting of iron disulfide and typically occurring as intersecting cubic crystals. Compare with **MARCASITE**. Also called **FOOL'S GOLD**.
– DERIVATIVES **py·rit·ic** /pīˈritik, pə-/ **adj.**, **py·rit·i·za·tion** /pəˌrītəˈzāSHən, pī-/ **n.**, **py·ri·tize** /ˈpīritˌīz/ **v.**, **py·ri·tous** /pəˈrītəs, pī-/ **adj.**
– ORIGIN late Middle English (denoting a mineral used for kindling fire): via Latin from Greek *puritēs* 'of fire,' from *pur* 'fire.'

py·ro /ˈpīrō/ ▶ **n.** (pl. **pyros**) informal a pyromaniac.

pyro. ▶ **abbr.** pyrotechnics.

pyro- ▶ **comb. form 1** of or relating to fire: *pyromania.* **2** Chemistry & Mineralogy denoting a compound or mineral that is formed or affected by heat or has a fiery color: *pyrophosphate* | *pyrope.*
– ORIGIN from Greek *pur* 'fire.'

py·ro·clas·tic /ˌpīrōˈklastik/ Geology ▶ **adj.** relating to, consisting of, or denoting fragments of rock erupted by a volcano.
– DERIVATIVES **py·ro·clast** /ˈpīrōˌklast/ **n.**

py·ro·clas·tic flow ▶ **n.** Geology a dense, destructive mass of very hot ash, lava fragments, and gases ejected explosively from a volcano and typically flowing downslope at great speed.

py·ro·e·lec·tric /ˌpīrō-iˈlektrik/ ▶ **adj.** having the property of becoming electrically charged when heated: *a pyroelectric detector.*
– DERIVATIVES **py·ro·e·lec·tric·i·ty** /-iˌlekˈtrisitē/ **n.**

py·ro·gal·lol /ˌpīrōˈgalˌôl, -ˌōl/ ▶ **n.** Chemistry a weakly acid crystalline compound chiefly used as a developer in photography. ● Alternative name: **1,3,5-trihydroxybenzene**; chem. formula: $C_6H_3(OH)_3$.

py·ro·gen /ˈpīrəjən/ ▶ **n.** Medicine a substance, typically produced by a bacterium, that produces fever when introduced or released into the blood.

py·ro·gen·ic /ˌpīrōˈjenik/ ▶ **adj.** Medicine inducing fever. ■ caused or produced by combustion or the application of heat: *pyrogenic factors affecting the fluctuation of the forest–savanna boundary.*
– DERIVATIVES **py·ro·ge·nic·i·ty** /ˌpīrōjəˈnisitē/ **n.**

py·rog·ra·phy /pīˈrägrəfē/ ▶ **n.** the art or technique of decorating wood or leather by burning a design on the surface with a heated metallic point.

py·ro·lu·site /ˌpīrōˈlo͞oˌsīt/ ▶ **n.** a black or dark gray mineral with a metallic luster, consisting of manganese dioxide.
– ORIGIN early 19th cent.: from **PYRO-** 'fire, heat' + Greek *lousis* 'washing' (because of the mineral's use in decolorizing glass).

py·rol·y·sis /pīˈräləsəs/ ▶ **n.** Chemistry decomposition brought about by high temperatures.
– DERIVATIVES **py·ro·lyt·ic** /ˌpīrəˈlitik/ **adj.**

py·ro·lyze /ˈpīrəˌlīz/ (Brit. **pyrolyse**) ▶ **v.** Chemistry make or become decomposed through heating to a high temperature.
– ORIGIN 1920s: from **PYROLYSIS**, on the pattern of *analyze.*

py·ro·ma·ni·a /ˌpīrōˈmānēə/ ▶ **n.** an obsessive desire to set fire to things.
– DERIVATIVES **py·ro·man·ic** /-ˈmanik/ **adj.**

py·ro·ma·ni·ac /ˌpīrōˈmānēˌak/ ▶ **n.** a person suffering from pyromania: *a ten-year-old pyromaniac.*
– DERIVATIVES **py·ro·ma·ni·a·cal** /-məˈnīəkəl/ **adj.**

py·ro·met·al·lur·gy /ˌpīrōˈmetlˌərjē/ ▶ **n.** the branch of science and technology concerned with the use of high temperatures to extract and purify metals.
– DERIVATIVES **py·ro·met·al·lur·gi·cal** /-ˌmetlˈərjikəl/ **adj.**

py·rom·e·ter /pīˈrämitər/ ▶ **n.** an instrument for measuring high temperatures, esp. in furnaces and kilns.
– DERIVATIVES **py·ro·met·ric** /ˌpīrōˈmetrik/ **adj.**, **py·ro·met·ri·cal·ly** /ˌpīrōˈmetrik(ə)lē/ **adv.**, **py·rom·e·try** /-trē/ **n.**

py·ro·met·ric cone /ˌpīrōˈmetrik/ ▶ **n.** see **CONE** (sense 1).

py·ro·mor·phite /ˌpīrəˈmôrˌfīt/ ▶ **n.** a mineral consisting of a chloride and phosphate of lead, typically occurring as green, yellow, or brown crystals in the oxidized zones of lead deposits.
– ORIGIN early 19th cent.: from **PYRO-** 'fire, heat' + Greek *morphē* 'form' + **-ITE**[1].

py·rope /ˈpīˌrōp/ (also **pyrope garnet**) ▶ **n.** a deep red variety of garnet.
– ORIGIN early 19th cent.: from German *Pyrop*, via Latin from Greek *purōpos* 'gold-bronze,' literally 'fiery-eyed,' from *pur* 'fire' + *ōps* 'eye.'

py·ro·phor·ic /ˌpīrəˈfôrik/ ▶ **adj.** liable to ignite spontaneously on exposure to air. ■ (of an alloy) emitting sparks when scratched or struck.
– ORIGIN mid 19th cent.: from modern Latin *pyrophorus*, from Greek *purophoros* 'fire-bearing,' from *pur* 'fire' + *pherein* 'to bear.'

py·ro·phos·phor·ic ac·id /ˌpīrōˌfäsˈfôrik, -ˈfäsfərik/ ▶ **n.** Chemistry a glassy solid obtained by heating phosphoric acid. ● A tetrabasic acid; chem. formula: $H_4P_2O_7$.
– DERIVATIVES **py·ro·phos·phate** /-ˈfäsˌfāt/ **n.**

py·ro·sis /pīˈrōsəs/ ▶ **n.** another term for **HEARTBURN**.
– ORIGIN late 18th cent.: modern Latin, from Greek *purōsis*, from *puroun* 'set on fire,' from *pur* 'fire.'

py·ro·tech·nic /ˌpīrəˈteknik/ ▶ **adj.** of or relating to fireworks: *the sun flickered in the car like a pyrotechnic display.* ■ brilliant or sensational: *his writing contains more pyrotechnic energy, more color and action.*
– DERIVATIVES **py·ro·tech·ni·cal adj.**, **py·ro·tech·nist** /-nist/ **n.**
– ORIGIN early 19th cent.: from **PYRO-** 'fire' + Greek *tekhnē* 'art' + **-IC**.

py·ro·tech·nics /ˌpīrəˈtekniks/ ▶ **plural n.** a fireworks display. ■ a brilliant performance or display, esp. of a specified skill: *he thrilled his audience with vocal pyrotechnics.* ■ [treated as sing.] the art of making or displaying fireworks.

py·ro·tech·ny /ˈpīrəˌteknē/ ▶ **n.** historical the use of fire in alchemy. ■ another term for **PYROTECHNICS**.
– ORIGIN late 16th cent.: from French *pyrotechnie* or modern Latin *pyrotechnia*, from Greek *pur* 'fire' + *tekhnē* 'art.'

py·rox·ene /pīˈräkˌsēn, pə-/ ▶ **n.** any of a large class of rock-forming silicate minerals, generally containing calcium, magnesium, and iron and typically occurring as prismatic crystals.
– ORIGIN early 19th cent.: from **PYRO-** 'fire' + Greek *xenos* 'stranger' (because the mineral group was supposed alien to igneous rocks).

py·rox·e·nite /pīˈräksəˌnīt, pə-/ ▶ **n.** Geology a dark, greenish, granular intrusive igneous rock consisting chiefly of pyroxenes and olivine.
– ORIGIN mid 19th cent.: from **PYROXENE** + **-ITE**[1].

py·rox·y·lin /pīˈräksələn, pə-/ ▶ **n.** Chemistry a form of nitrocellulose that is less highly nitrated and is soluble in ether and alcohol.
– ORIGIN mid 19th cent.: from French *pyroxyline*, from Greek *pur* 'fire' + *xulon* 'wood.'

Pyr·rha /ˈpirə/ Greek Mythology the wife of Deucalion.

Pyr·rhic /ˈpirik/ (also **pyrrhic**) ▶ **adj.** [attrib.] (of a victory) won at too great a cost to have been worthwhile for the victor.
– ORIGIN late 19th cent.: from the name **PYRRHUS** + **-IC**.

pyr·rhic /ˈpirik/ ▶ **n.** a metrical foot of two short or unaccented syllables.
▶ **adj.** written in or based on such a measure.
– ORIGIN early 17th cent.: via Latin from Greek *purrhikhios (pous)* 'pyrrhic (foot),' the meter of a song accompanying a war dance, named after *Purrhikhos*, inventor of the dance.

Pyr·rho /ˈpirō/ (*c.*365–*c.*270 BC), Greek philosopher; regarded as the founder of skepticism. He argued that happiness comes from suspending judgment because certainty of knowledge is impossible.

Pyr·rho·nism /ˈpirəˌnizəm/ ▶ **n.** the philosophy of Pyrrho. ■ philosophic doubt; skepticism.
– DERIVATIVES **Pyr·rho·nist n. & adj.**

pyr·rho·tite /ˈpirəˌtīt/ ▶ **n.** a reddish-bronze mineral consisting of iron sulfide, typically forming massive or granular deposits.
– ORIGIN mid 19th cent.: from Greek *purrhotēs* 'redness' + **-ITE**[1].

pyr·rhu·lox·i·a /ˌpirəˈläksēə/ ▶ **n.** a songbird of Mexico and the southwestern US, related to the common cardinal. The male is mostly gray, with red face and underparts and a stout yellow parrotlike bill. ● *Cardinalis sinuatus*, family Emberizidae, subfamily Cardinalidae.

Pyr·rhus /ˈpirəs/ (*c.*318–272 BC), king of Epirus *c.*307–272. After invading Italy in 280, he defeated the Romans at Asculum in 279, but sustained heavy losses; the term *pyrrhic victory* alludes to this.

pyr·role /ˈpirˌōl/ ▶ **n.** Chemistry a weakly basic sweet-smelling liquid compound present in bone oil and coal tar. ● A heteroaromatic compound; chem. formula: C_4H_4NH.
– ORIGIN mid 19th cent.: from Greek *purrhos* 'reddish' + Latin *oleum* 'oil.'

pyr·rol·i·dine /pəˈrōləˌdēn/ ▶ **n.** Chemistry a pungent liquid made by reduction of pyrrole. ● Chem. formula: C_4H_8NH.

pyr·rol·i·done /pəˈrōləˌdōn/ ▶ **n.** Chemistry a colorless weakly basic solid that is derived from pyrrolidine. ● Chem. formula: C_4H_7NO.

py·ru·vic ac·id /pīˈro͞ovik/ ▶ **n.** Biochemistry a yellowish organic acid that occurs as an intermediate in many metabolic processes, esp. glycolysis. ● A keto acid; chem. formula: $CH_3COCOOH$.
– DERIVATIVES **pyr·u·vate** /-ˌvāt/ **n.**
– ORIGIN mid 19th cent.: from modern Latin *acidum pyruvicum*, from *acidum* 'acid' + *pyruvicum* based on **PYRO-** (denoting an acid) + Latin *uva* 'grape.'

Py·thag·o·ras /piˈTHagərəs/ *c.*580–500 BC, Greek philosopher; known as **Pythagoras of Samos**. Pythagoras sought to interpret the entire physical world in terms of numbers and founded their systematic and mystical study. He is best known for the theorem of the right-angled triangle.
– DERIVATIVES **Py·thag·o·re·an** /piˌTHagəˈrēən, pī-/ **adj. & n.**

Py·thag·o·re·an the·o·rem /pəˌTHagəˈrēən, pī-/ a theorem attributed to Pythagoras that the square of the hypotenuse of a right triangle is equal to the sum of the squares of the other two sides.

Pyth·i·a /ˈpiTHēə/ the priestess of Apollo at Delphi in ancient Greece. See **DELPHI**.
– DERIVATIVES **Pyth·i·an adj.**
– ORIGIN from *Puthō*, a former name of Delphi.

Pyth·i·as /ˈpiTHēəs/ see **DAMON**.

py·thon /ˈpīˌTHän, ˈpīTHən/ ▶ **n. 1** a large heavy-bodied nonvenomous constrictor snake occurring throughout the Old World tropics. ● Family Pythonidae: genera *Python* (of Asia and Africa), and *Morelia* and *Aspidites* (of Australasia). **2** (**Python**) Computing a high-level general-purpose programming language.
– DERIVATIVES **py·thon·ic** /pīˈTHänik/ **adj.**
– ORIGIN late 16th cent. (in the Greek sense): via Latin from Greek *Puthōn*, the name of a huge serpent killed by Apollo. The current sense dates from the mid 19th cent.

Py·thon·esque /ˌpīTHəˈnesk/ ▶ **adj.** after the style of or resembling the absurdist or surrealist humor of *Monty Python's Flying Circus*, a British television comedy series (1969–74).

py·tho·ness /ˈpīTHənəs, ˈpiTH-/ ▶ **n.** archaic a female soothsayer or conjuror of spirits.
– ORIGIN late Middle English: from Old French *phitonise*, from an alteration of late Latin

P

pythonissa, based on Greek *puthōn* 'soothsaying demon.' Compare with **Pythia**.

py·u·ri·a /pī'yo͝orēə/ ▶ **n.** Medicine the presence of pus in the urine, typically from bacterial infection.
– ORIGIN early 19th cent.: from Greek *puon* 'pus' + **-uria**.

pyx /piks/ ▶ **n.** **1** Christian Church the container in which the consecrated bread of the Eucharist is kept. **2** (in the UK) a box at the Royal Mint in which specimen gold and silver coins are deposited to be tested annually at the **trial of the pyx**.
– ORIGIN late Middle English: from Latin *pyxis*, from Greek *puxis* 'box.'

pyx·id·i·um /pik'sidēəm/ ▶ **n.** (pl. **pyxidia** /-ēə/) Botany a seed capsule that splits open so that the top comes off like the lid of a box.
– ORIGIN mid 19th cent.: modern Latin, from Greek *puxidion*, diminutive of *puxis* 'box.'

Pyx·is /'piksis/ Astronomy a small and inconspicuous southern constellation (the Compass Box or Mariner's Compass), lying in the Milky Way between Vela and Puppis. ■ (as genitive **Pyxidis** /'piksidis/) used with a preceding letter or numeral to designate a star in this constellation: *the star Alpha Pyxidis*.
– ORIGIN Latin.

pzazz /pə'zaz/ ▶ **n.** variant spelling of **pizzazz**.

Qq

Q¹ /kyoo/ (also **q**) ▶ **n.** (pl. **Qs** or **Q's**) the seventeenth letter of the alphabet. ■ denoting the next after P in a set of items, categories, etc.
– PHRASES **mind one's Ps and Qs** see **MIND**.

Q² ▶ **abbr.** ■ quarter (used to refer to a specified quarter of the fiscal year): *we expect to have an exceptional Q4.* ■ queen (used esp. in describing card games and recording moves in chess): *17.Qb4.* ■ question: *Q: What's the problem? A: I don't feel well.* ■ Theology denoting the hypothetical source of the passages shared by the gospels of Matthew and Luke, but not found in Mark. [probably from German *Quelle* 'source.']

q ▶ **symbol** Physics electric charge.
– ORIGIN mid 19th cent.: initial letter of *quantity*.

QA ▶ **abbr.** quality assurance.

Qab·a·lah /kə'bälə/ ▶ **n.** variant spelling of **KABBALAH**.

qa·nat /kə'nät/ ▶ **n.** (in the Middle East) a gently sloping underground channel or tunnel constructed to lead water from the interior of a hill to a village below.
– ORIGIN Persian, from Arabic *ḳanāt* 'reed, pipe, channel.'

q and a /kyoo' ən ā'/ ▶ **abbr.** informal a question and answer period or exchange.

Qa·ra·ghan·dy /'kärə,gändē/ an industrial city in eastern Kazakhstan, at the center of a major coal-mining region; pop. 446,100 (est. 2006). Russian name **KARAGANDA**.

qat /'kôt/ ▶ **n.** variant spelling of **KHAT**.

Qa·tar /'kätär, kə'tär/ a sheikhdom that occupies a peninsula on the western coast of the Persian Gulf; pop. 833,300 (est. 2009); capital, Doha; language, Arabic (official).

> The country was a British protectorate from 1916 until 1971, when it became an independent state. Oil is the chief source of revenue.

– DERIVATIVES **Qa·tar·i** /'kätärē, kə'tärē/ **adj. & n.**

Qat·ta·ra De·pres·sion /kə'tärə/ an extensive, low-lying, and largely impassable area of desert in northeastern Africa, west of Cairo, that is 436 feet (133 m) below sea level.

qaw·wal /kə'väl/ ▶ **n.** a performer of qawwali.

qaw·wa·li /kə'välē/ ▶ **n.** a style of Muslim devotional music now associated particularly with Sufis in Pakistan.
– ORIGIN from Arabic *qawwālī*, from *qawwāl* 'loquacious,' also 'singer.'

QB ▶ **abbr.** ■ Football quarterback. ■ Law Queen's Bench.

QC ▶ **abbr.** ■ quality control. ■ Quebec (in official postal use). ■ Law Queen's Counsel.

QCD ▶ **abbr.** quantum chromodynamics.

Q-Celtic /'keltik/ ▶ **n. & adj.** another term for **GOIDELIC**.
– ORIGIN Q, from the retention of the Indo-European *kw* sound as *q* or *c* in this group of languages.

QED ▶ **abbr.** ■ quantum electrodynamics. ■ quod erat demonstrandum.

QEF ▶ **abbr.** which was to be done.
– ORIGIN Latin *quod erat faciendum*.

QF ▶ **abbr.** quick-firing.

Q fe·ver ▶ **n.** an infectious fever caused by rickettsiae and transmitted to humans from cattle, sheep, and goats by unpasteurized milk.
– ORIGIN 1930s: from Q for *query* + **FEVER**.

qi /CHē/ (also **chi** or **ki**) ▶ **n.** the circulating life force whose existence and properties are the basis of much Chinese philosophy and medicine.
– ORIGIN from Chinese (Mandarin dialect) *qì*, literally 'air, breath.'

qib·lah /'kiblə/ (also **kiblah**) ▶ **n.** [in sing.] the direction of the Kaaba (the sacred building at Mecca), to which Muslims turn at prayer.
– ORIGIN mid 17th cent.: from Arabic *ḳibla* 'that which is opposite.'

q.i.d. ▶ **abbr.** (in prescriptions) four times a day.
– ORIGIN Latin *quater in die*.

qi·gong /,CHē'gäNG, -'gôNG/ ▶ **n.** a Chinese system of physical exercises and breathing control related to tai chi.
– ORIGIN Chinese.

Qin /CHin/ (also **Ch'in**) a dynasty that ruled China 221–206 BC and was the first to establish rule over a united China. The construction of the Great Wall of China was begun during this period.

Qing /CHiNG/ (also **Ch'ing**) a dynasty established by the Manchus that ruled China 1644–1912. Its overthrow in 1912 by Sun Yat-sen and his supporters ended imperial rule in China.

Qing·dao /'CHiNG'dou/ a port in eastern China, in Shandong province on the Yellow Sea coast; pop. 2,654,300 (est. 2006).

Qing·hai /'CHiNG'hī/ (also **Tsinghai**) a mountainous province in north central China; capital, Xining.

qing·hao·su /,CHiNGgou'soo/ ▶ **n.** a terpene-based anti-malarial substance used in Chinese medicine.
● The drug is obtained from *Artemisia annua*, family Compositae.
– ORIGIN 1970s: from Chinese *qīnghāosù*, from *qīnghāo*, denoting a medicinal plant of the genus *Artemisia*.

qin·tar /kin'tär/ ▶ **n.** (pl. **same**, **qintars**, or **qindarka** /kin'darkə/) a monetary unit of Albania, equal to one hundredth of a lek.
– ORIGIN from Albanian *qindar*, from *qind* 'hundred.'

Qi·qi·har /'CHē'CHē'här/ a port on the Nen River, in Heilongjiang province, in northeastern China; pop. 1,115,100 (est. 2006).

QKt ▶ **abbr.** Chess queen's knight.

ql. ▶ **abbr.** quintal.

Qld ▶ **abbr.** Queensland.

qlty. ▶ **abbr.** quality.

QM ▶ **abbr.** quartermaster.

QMC ▶ **abbr.** Quartermaster Corps.

QMG ▶ **abbr.** quartermaster general.

qn. ▶ **abbr.** question.

Qom /koom/ (also **Qum** or **Kum**) a city in central Iran; pop. 964,706 (2006). It is a holy city and center of learning among Shiite Muslims.

Qom·o·lung·ma /,CHōmō'looNGmə/ (also **Chomolungma**) Tibetan name for **EVEREST, MOUNT**.

QP ▶ **abbr.** Chess queen's pawn.

q.p. ▶ **abbr.** (in prescriptions) as much as you please.
– ORIGIN Latin *quantum placet*.

QPM ▶ **abbr.** (in the UK) Queen's Police Medal.

qq. ▶ **abbr.** questions.

qq.v. ▶ **abbr.** which (words, etc.) see.
– ORIGIN Latin *quae vide*.

qr. ▶ **abbr.** quarter(s).

q.s. ▶ **abbr.** ■ (in prescriptions) enough; as much as is sufficient. ■ quarter section.
– ORIGIN Latin *quantum sufficit*.

Q-ship ▶ **n.** historical a merchant ship with concealed weapons, used by the British in World War I and World War II in an attempt to destroy submarines.
– ORIGIN World War I: from Q as a nonexplicit symbol of the type of vessel + **SHIP**.

QSO ▶ **abbr.** quasistellar object, a quasar.

QT (also **q.t.**) ▶ **n.** (in phrase **on the QT**) informal secretly; stealthily: *she'd better get there on the QT.*
– ORIGIN late 19th cent.: abbreviation of **QUIET**.

qt. ▶ **abbr.** quart(s).

qto. ▶ **abbr.** quarto.

qty. ▶ **abbr.** quantity.

qua /kwä/ ▶ **conj.** in the capacity of; as being: *he's hard to pin down if you get him on entertainment qua entertainment.*
– ORIGIN Latin, ablative feminine singular of *qui* 'who.'

Quaa·lude /'kwā,lood/ ▶ **n.** trademark methaqualone.
– ORIGIN 1960s: an invented name.

quack¹ /kwak/ ▶ **n.** [in sing.] the characteristic harsh sound made by a duck.
▶ **v.** [no obj.] (of a duck) make this sound. ■ informal talk loudly and foolishly.
– ORIGIN mid-16th cent. (as a verb): imitative.

quack² ▶ **n.** a person who dishonestly claims to have special knowledge and skill in some field, typically in medicine: [as modifier] *quack cures.*
– DERIVATIVES **quack·er·y** /'kwakərē/ **n.**, **quack·ish adj.**
– ORIGIN mid 17th cent.: abbreviation of earlier *quacksalver*, from Dutch, probably from obsolete *quacken* 'prattle' + *salf*, *zalf* (see **SALVE¹**).

quack grass ▶ **n.** another term for **COUCH GRASS**.
– ORIGIN early 19th cent.: *quack*, variant of *quick*, northern English form of **QUITCH**.

quad /kwäd/ ▶ **n. 1** short for: ■ a quadrangle. ■ a quadruplet (child). ■ a quadriceps. ■ a quad bike. ■ quadraphonic sound. ■ a quadriplegic.
2 (in telephony) a group of four insulated conductors twisted together, usually forming two circuits. [abbreviation of *quadruplex*, a telegraphic device invented by Thomas Edison, by means of which four messages could be sent simultaneously over one wire.]
3 a radio antenna in the form of a square or rectangle broken in the middle of one side. [abbreviation of **QUADRILATERAL**.]
4 a traditional roller skate. [*quad*, with reference to the four wheels.]
5 Printing a small metal block in various sizes, lower than type height, used in letterpress printing for filling up short lines. [abbreviation of the late 17th-cent. printing term *quadrat*.]
▶ **adj.** [attrib.] short for: ■ quadruple. ■ quadrophonic.

quad. ▶ **abbr.** ■ quadrangle. ■ quadrant.

quad bike ▶ **n.** a motorcycle with four large tires, typically used for racing.

quad chair (also **quad chairlift** or **quad**) ▶ **n.** a chairlift with seats for four people at a time.

Quad Cities /kwäd/ an industrial complex of cities on the Mississippi River that includes Davenport and Bettendorf in southeastern Iowa, and Moline and Rock Island in northwestern Illinois. A second Quad Cities complex, in northern Alabama on the Tennessee River, consists of the cities of Florence, Sheffield, Tuscumbia, and Muscle Shoals.

PRONUNCIATION KEY ə *ago, up*; ər *over, fur*; a *hat*; ā *ate*; ä *car*; e *let*; ē *see*; i *fit*; ī *by*; NG *sing*; ō *go*; ô *law, for*; oi *toy*; oo *good*; oo *goo*; ou *out*; TH *thin*; TH *then*; ZH *vision*

quad·ra·ge·nar·i·an /ˌkwädrəjəˈne(ə)rēən/ ▶ **n.** a person who is from 40 to 49 years old.
– ORIGIN mid 19th cent.: from late Latin *quadragenarius* (based on Latin *quadraginta* 'forty') + **-AN**.

Quad·ra·ges·i·ma /ˌkwädrəˈjesəmə/ (also **Quadragesima Sunday**) ▶ **n.** the first Sunday in Lent.
– ORIGIN from ecclesiastical Latin, feminine of Latin *quadragesimus* 'fortieth,' from *quadraginta* 'forty' (Lent lasting forty days).

quad·ra·ges·i·mal /ˌkwädrəˈjesəməl/ ▶ **adj.** [attrib.] archaic (of a fast, esp. one in Lent) lasting forty days. ■ belonging or appropriate to the period of Lent.

quad·ra·min·i·um ▶ **n.** variant spelling of **QUADROMINIUM**.

quad·ran·gle /ˈkwäˌdraNGgəl/ ▶ **n.** Geometry a four-sided plane figure, esp. a square or rectangle. ■ a square or rectangular space or courtyard enclosed by buildings. ■ the area shown on a standard topographic map sheet of the US Geological Survey.
– DERIVATIVES **quad·ran·gu·lar** /kwäˈdraNGgyələr/ **adj.**
– ORIGIN late Middle English: from Old French, or from late Latin *quadrangulum* 'square,' neuter of *quadrangulus*, from Latin 'four' + *angulus* 'corner, angle.'

quad·rant /ˈkwädrənt/ ▶ **n.** technical each of four quarters of a circle. ■ each of four parts of a plane, sphere, space, or body divided by two lines or planes at right angles: *the right upper quadrant of the kidney*. ■ historical an instrument used for taking angular measurements of altitude in astronomy and navigation, typically consisting of a graduated quarter circle and a sighting mechanism. ■ a frame fixed to the head of a ship's rudder, to which the steering mechanism is attached. ■ a panel with slots through which a lever is moved to orient or otherwise control a mechanism.
– DERIVATIVES **quad·ran·tal** /kwäˈdran(t)l/ **adj.**
– ORIGIN late Middle English (denoting the astronomical instrument): from Latin *quadrans*, *quadrant-* 'quarter,' from *quattuor* four.

Quad·ran·tids /kwäˈdrantidz/ Astronomy an annual meteor shower with a radiant in the constellation Boötes, reaching a peak about January 3.
– ORIGIN from Latin *Quadrans Muralis* 'the Mural Quadrant,' the name of a former constellation.

quad·ra·phon·ic /ˌkwädrəˈfänik/ (also **quadrophonic**) ▶ **adj.** (of sound reproduction) transmitted through four channels.
– DERIVATIVES **quad·ra·phon·i·cal·ly** /-ik(ə)lē/ **adv.**, **quad·ra·phon·ics plural n.**, **qua·draph·o·ny** /kwäˈdräfənē/ **n.**
– ORIGIN 1960s: from **QUADRI-** 'four' + a shortened form of **STEREOPHONIC**.

quad·rat /ˈkwädrət/ ▶ **n.** Ecology each of a number of a small area of habitat, typically of one square meter, selected at random to act as samples for assessing the local distribution of plants or animals. ■ a portable frame, typically with an internal grid, used to mark out such an area.
– ORIGIN early 20th cent.: variant of **QUADRATE**.

quad·rate ▶ **n.** /ˈkwäˌdrāt, -rət/ **1** (also **quadrate bone**) Zoology (in the skull of a bird or reptile) a squarish bone with which the jaw articulates, thought to be homologous with the incus of the middle ear in mammals.
2 Anatomy another term for **QUADRATUS**.
▶ **adj.** /ˈkwädrit/ roughly square or rectangular.
▶ **v.** /ˈkwädˌrāt/ archaic **1** [with obj.] make square.
2 conform or cause to conform.
– ORIGIN late Middle English (as an adjective): from Latin *quadrat-* 'made square,' from the verb *quadrare*, from *quattuor* 'four.'

quad·rat·ic /kwäˈdratik/ ▶ **adj.** Mathematics involving the second and no higher power of an unknown quantity or variable: *a quadratic equation*.
▶ **n.** a quadratic equation.
– ORIGIN mid 17th cent.: from French *quadratique* or modern Latin *quadraticus*, from *quadratus* 'made square,' past participle of *quadrare* (see **QUADRATE**).

quad·ra·ture /ˈkwädrəˌCHo͝or, -ˌCHər/ ▶ **n.**
1 Mathematics the process of constructing a square with an area equal to that of a circle, or of another figure bounded by a curve.
2 Astronomy the position of the moon or a planet when it is 90° from the sun as viewed from the earth.
3 Electronics a phase difference of 90° between two waves of the same frequency, as in the color difference signals of a television screen.
– ORIGIN mid 16th cent. (as a mathematical term): from Latin *quadratura* 'a square, squaring,' from *quadrare* (see **QUADRATE**).

quad·ra·ture am·pli·tude mod·u·la·tion ▶ **n.** Telecommunications a modulation system used in microwave and satellite communication, involving phase and amplitude modulation of a carrier wave.

qua·dra·tus /kwäˈdrātəs/ ▶ **n.** (pl. **quadrati** /-ˈdrātˌī/) Anatomy any of several roughly square or rectangular muscles, e.g., in the abdomen, thigh, and eye socket.
– ORIGIN mid 18th cent.: from Latin, literally 'made square.'

quad·ren·ni·al /kwäˈdrenēəl/ ▶ **adj.** recurring every four years. ■ lasting for or relating to a period of four years.
– DERIVATIVES **quad·ren·ni·al·ly adv.**
– ORIGIN mid 17th cent.: from **QUADRENNIUM** + **-AL**.

quad·ren·ni·um /kwäˈdrenēəm/ ▶ **n.** (pl. **quadrennia** /-ˈdrenēə/ or **quadrenniums**) a specified period of four years.
– ORIGIN early 19th cent.: from Latin *quadriennium*, from *quadri-* 'four' + *annus* 'year.'

quadri- ▶ **comb. form** four; having four: *quadriceps* | *quadriplegia*.
– ORIGIN from Latin *quattuor* 'four.'

quad·ric /ˈkwädrik/ Geometry ▶ **adj.** (of a surface or curve) described by an equation of the second degree.
▶ **n.** a quadric surface or curve.
– ORIGIN mid 19th cent.: from Latin *quadra* 'square' + **-IC**.

quad·ri·ceps /ˈkwädrəˌseps/ ▶ **n.** (pl. **same**) Anatomy the large muscle at the front of the thigh, which is divided into four distinct portions and acts to extend the leg.
– ORIGIN mid 16th cent.: from Latin, literally 'four-headed.'

quad·ri·lat·er·al /ˌkwädrəˈlatərəl/ ▶ **n.** a four-sided figure.
▶ **adj.** having four straight sides.
– ORIGIN mid 17th cent.: from late Latin *quadrilaterus* (from Latin *quadri-* 'four' + *latus*, *later-* 'side') + **-AL**.

quad·rille[1] /kwäˈdril, k(w)ə-/ ▶ **n.** a square dance performed typically by four couples and containing five figures, each of which is a complete dance in itself. ■ a piece of music for this dance. ■ each of four groups of riders taking part in a tournament or carousel, distinguished by a special costume or colors. ■ a riding display.
– ORIGIN mid 18th cent.: from French, from Spanish *cuadrilla* or Italian *quadriglia* 'troop, company,' from *cuadra*, *quadra* 'square,' based on Latin *quadrare* 'make square.'

quad·rille[2] ▶ **n.** a trick-taking card game for four players using a deck of forty cards (i.e., one lacking eights, nines, and tens), fashionable in the 18th century.
– ORIGIN early 18th cent.: from French, perhaps from Spanish *cuartillo* (from *cuarto* 'fourth'). The change in the first syllable was due to association with **QUADRILLE**[1].

quad·rille[3] ▶ **n.** a ruled grid of small squares, esp. on paper.
– ORIGIN late 19th cent.: from French *quadrillé*, from *quadrille* 'small square,' from Spanish *cuadrillo* 'small block.'

quad·ril·lion /kwäˈdrilyən/ ▶ **cardinal number** (pl. **quadrillions** or (with numeral or quantifying word) **same**) a thousand raised to the power of five (10^{15}). ■ dated, chiefly Brit. a septillion, that is, a thousand raised to the power of eight (10^{24}).
– DERIVATIVES **quad·ril·lionth** /-ˈdrilyənTH/ **ordinal number.**
– ORIGIN late 17th cent.: from French, from *million*, by substitution of the prefix *quadri-* 'four' for the initial letters.

quad·ri·par·tite /ˌkwädrəˈpärtīt/ ▶ **adj.** consisting of four parts. ■ shared by or involving four parties.
– ORIGIN late Middle English: from Latin *quadripartitus*, from *quadri-* 'four' + *partitus* 'divided.'

quad·ri·ple·gi·a /ˌkwädrəˈplēj(ē)ə/ ▶ **n.** Medicine paralysis of all four limbs; tetraplegia.
– DERIVATIVES **quad·ri·ple·gic** /-ˈplējik/ **adj. & n.**
– ORIGIN 1920s: from **QUADRI-** 'four' + a shortened form of **PARAPLEGIA**.

quad·ri·va·lent /ˌkwädrəˈvālənt/ ▶ **adj.** Chemistry another term for **TETRAVALENT**.

quad·riv·i·um /kwäˈdrivēəm/ ▶ **n.** historical a medieval university curriculum involving the "mathematical arts" of arithmetic, geometry, astronomy, and music. Compare with **TRIVIUM**.
– ORIGIN Latin, literally 'the place where four roads meet' (in late Latin 'the four branches of mathematics'), from *quadri-* 'four' + *via* 'road.'

quad·ro·min·i·um /ˌkwädrəˈminēəm/ (also **quadraminium**) ▶ **n.** a condominium consisting of four apartments.
– ORIGIN 1970s: blend of **QUADRI-** 'four' and **CONDOMINIUM**.

quad·roon /kwäˈdro͞on/ ▶ **n.** a person whose parents are a mulatto and a white person and who is therefore one-quarter black by descent.
– ORIGIN early 18th cent. (earlier as *quarteron*): via French from Spanish *cuarterón*, from *cuarto* 'quarter,' from Latin *quartus*; later assimilated to words beginning with **QUADRI-**.

quad·ro·phon·ic /ˌkwädrəˈfänik/ ▶ **adj.** variant spelling of **QUADRAPHONIC**.

quad·ru·ma·nous /kwäˈdro͞omənəs/ ▶ **adj.** Zoology, dated (of primates other than humans) having all four feet modified as hands (that is, having opposable digits).
– ORIGIN late 17th cent.: from modern Latin *Quadrumana* (former order name, neuter plural of *quadrumanus*, from *quadru-* 'four' + Latin *manus* 'hand') + **-OUS**.

quad·ru·ped /ˈkwädrəˌped/ ▶ **n.** an animal that has four feet, esp. an ungulate mammal.
– DERIVATIVES **quad·ru·pe·dal** /ˌkwädrəˈpedl, kwäˈdro͞opədl/ **adj.**
– ORIGIN mid 17th cent.: from French *quadrupède* or Latin *quadrupes*, *quadruped-*, from *quadru-* 'four' + *pes*, *ped-* 'foot.'

quad·ru·ple /kwäˈdro͞opəl/ ▶ **adj.** [attrib.] consisting of four parts or elements: *a quadruple murder*. ■ consisting of four times as much or as many as usual: *a quadruple vodka*. ■ (of time in music) having four beats in a bar.
▶ **v.** increase or be increased fourfold: [no obj.] *oil prices quadrupled in the 1970s*.
▶ **n.** a quadruple thing, number, or amount.
– DERIVATIVES **quad·ru·ply** /-p(ə)lē/ **adv.**
– ORIGIN late Middle English (as a verb): via French from Latin *quadruplus*, from *quadru-* 'four' + *-plus* as in *duplus* (see **DUPLE**).

quad·ru·plet /kwäˈdro͞oplit/ ▶ **n. 1** (usu. **quadruplets**) each of four children born at one birth.
2 Music a group of four notes to be performed in the time of three.
– ORIGIN late 18th cent.: from **QUADRUPLE**, on the pattern of *triplet*.

quad·ru·pli·cate ▶ **adj.** /kwäˈdro͞opləkit/ consisting of four parts or elements. ■ of which four copies are made.
▶ **v.** /kwäˈdro͞opləˌkāt/ [with obj.] multiply (something) by four. ■ (usu. as adj. **quadruplicated**) make or provide in quadruplicate.
– PHRASES **in quadruplicate** in four identical copies.
– DERIVATIVES **quad·ru·pli·ca·tion** /kwäˌdro͞opləˈkāSHən/ **n.**
– ORIGIN mid 17th cent.: from Latin *quadruplicat-* 'quadrupled,' from the verb *quadruplicare*, from *quadruplex*, *quadruplic-* 'fourfold,' from *quadru-* 'four' + *plicare* 'to fold.'

quad·ru·pole /ˈkwädrəˌpōl/ ▶ **n.** Physics a distribution of electric charge or magnetization consisting of four equal monopoles, or two equal dipoles, arranged close together with alternating polarity and operating as a unit. ■ a device using such an arrangement directed at one point to focus beams of subatomic particles.

quad-speed ▶ **adj.** (of a CD-ROM drive, esp. formerly) capable of revolving the CD-ROM at a speed of 920 rpm.

quaes·tor /ˈkwestər/ ▶ **n.** (in ancient Rome) any of a number of officials who had charge of public revenue and expenditure.
– DERIVATIVES **quaes·to·ri·al** /kweˈstôrēəl/ **adj.**, **quaes·tor·ship** /-SHip/ **n.**
– ORIGIN Latin, from an old form of *quaesit-* 'sought,' from the verb *quaerere*.

quaff /kwäf/ ▶ **v.** [with obj.] drink (something, esp. an alcoholic drink) heartily.
▶ **n.** informal, dated an alcoholic drink.
– DERIVATIVES **quaff·a·ble adj.**, **quaff·er n.**
– ORIGIN early 16th cent.: probably imitative of the sound of drinking.

quag /kwag/ ▶ **n.** archaic a marshy or boggy place.
– DERIVATIVES **quag·gy adj.**
– ORIGIN late 16th cent.: related to dialect *quag* 'shake, quiver'; probably symbolic, the *qu-* suggesting movement (as in *quake* and *quick*).

quag·ga /ˈkwagə/ ▶ **n.** an extinct South African zebra that had a yellowish-brown coat with darker stripes, exterminated in 1883. ● *Equus quagga*, family Equidae; recent studies have shown that it was probably a variety of the common zebra.
– ORIGIN Afrikaans, probably from Khoikhoi, imitative of its braying.

quag·mire /ˈkwagˌmīr/ ▶ **n.** a soft boggy area of land that gives way underfoot: *torrential rain turned the building site into a quagmire*. ■ an awkward, complex, or hazardous situation: *a legal quagmire*.
– ORIGIN late 16th cent.: from **QUAG** + **MIRE**.

qua·hog /ˈkwôˌhôg, -ˌhäg, ˈkwō-, ˈkō-/ (also **quahaug**) ▶ **n.** a large, rounded edible clam of the Atlantic coast of North America. Also called **HARD CLAM**, **HARD-SHELL CLAM**. ● *Venus mercenaria*, family Veneridae.

– ORIGIN mid 18th cent.: from Narragansett *poquaûhock*.

quaich /kwāk/ ▶ n. Scottish a shallow drinking cup, typically made of wood and having two handles. ■ a trophy of similar design.
– ORIGIN mid 16th cent.: from Scottish Gaelic *cuach* 'cup.'

Quai d'Or·say /ˈkē dôrˈsā/ a riverside street on the left bank of the Seine River in Paris. ■ the French ministry of foreign affairs, which has its headquarters on this street.

quail[1] /kwāl/ ▶ n. (pl. **same** or **quails**) **1** a small, short-tailed Old World game bird resembling a small partridge, typically having brown camouflaged plumage. ● Family Phasianidae: three genera, in particular *Coturnix*, and several species, e.g., the widespread migratory **common quail** (*C. coturnix*).
2 a small or medium-sized New World game bird, the male of which has distinctive facial markings. ● Family Phasianidae (or Odontophoridae): several genera and many species, including the bobwhite and the **Gambel's quail** (*Callipepla gambelii*) of the southwestern US.
– ORIGIN Middle English: from Old French *quaille*, from medieval Latin *coacula* (probably imitative of its call).

Gambel's quail

quail[2] ▶ v. [no obj.] feel or show fear or apprehension: *she quailed at his heartless words*.
– ORIGIN late Middle English (in the sense 'waste away, come to nothing'): of unknown origin.

quaint /kwānt/ ▶ adj. attractively unusual or old-fashioned: *quaint country cottages | a quaint old custom*.
– DERIVATIVES **quaint·ly** adv., **quaint·ness** n.
– ORIGIN Middle English: from Old French *cointe*, from Latin *cognitus* 'ascertained,' past participle of *cognoscere*. The original sense was 'wise, clever,' also 'ingenious, cunningly devised,' hence 'out of the ordinary' and the current sense (late 18th cent).

quake /kwāk/ ▶ v. [no obj.] (esp. of the earth) shake or tremble: *the rumbling vibrations set the whole valley quaking*. ■ (of a person) shake or shudder with fear: *those words should have them quaking in their boots*.
▶ n. informal an earthquake. ■ an act of shaking or quaking.
– DERIVATIVES **quak·y** adj. (**quakier, quakiest**).
– ORIGIN Old English *cwacian*.

Quak·er /ˈkwākər/ ▶ n. a member of the Religious Society of Friends, a Christian movement founded by George Fox *c.*1650 and devoted to peaceful principles. Central to the Quakers' belief is the doctrine of the "Inner Light," or sense of Christ's direct working in the soul. This has led them to reject both formal ministry and all set forms of worship.
– DERIVATIVES **Quak·er·ish** adj., **Quak·er·ism** /-izəm/ n.
– ORIGIN from QUAKE + -ER[1], perhaps alluding to George Fox's direction to his followers to "tremble at the name of the Lord," or from fits supposedly experienced by worshipers when moved by the Spirit. Compare with SHAKER (sense 2).

Quak·er State a nickname for the state of PENNSYLVANIA.

quak·ie /ˈkwākē/ ▶ n. informal quaking aspen (see ASPEN).

quak·ing bog ▶ n. a bog formed over water or soft mud that shakes underfoot.

quak·ing grass ▶ n. a slender-stalked grass with oval or heart-shaped flower heads that tremble in the wind. ● Genus *Briza*, family Gramineae: several species, including *B. media*, which is sometimes cultivated as an ornamental.

qual. ▶ abbr. qualitative.

qua·le /ˈkwälē/ ▶ n. (pl. **qualia** /ˈkwälēə/) (usu. **qualia**) Philosophy a quality or property as perceived or experienced by a person.
– ORIGIN late 17th cent.: from Latin, neuter of *qualis* 'of what kind.'

qua·li·a ▶ plural n. Philosophy the internal and subjective component of sense perceptions, arising from stimulation of the senses by phenomena.

qual·i·fi·ca·tion /ˌkwäləfəˈkāsʜən/ ▶ n. **1** a quality or accomplishment that makes someone suitable for a particular job or activity: *only one qualification required—a fabulous sense of humor*. ■ the action or fact of becoming qualified as a practitioner of a particular profession or activity: *an opportunity for student teachers to share experiences before qualification*. ■ a condition that must be fulfilled before a right can be acquired; an official requirement: *the five-year residency qualification for presidential candidates*.
2 the action or fact of qualifying or being eligible for something: *they need to beat Poland to ensure qualification for the World Cup finals*.
3 a statement or assertion that makes another less absolute: *this important qualification needs to be remembered when interpreting the results | I could recommend them to everyone without qualification*.
4 Grammar the attribution of a quality to a word, esp. a noun.
– DERIVATIVES **qual·i·fi·ca·to·ry** /ˈkwäləfikəˌtôrē/ adj.
– ORIGIN mid 16th cent.: from medieval Latin *qualificatio(n-)*, from the verb *qualificare* (see QUALIFY).

qual·i·fied /ˈkwäləˌfīd/ ▶ adj. **1** officially recognized as being trained to perform a particular job; certified: *newly qualified nurses*. ■ [with infinitive] competent or knowledgeable to do something; capable: *I was less well qualified than almost anyone present to recollect the olden days*.
2 not complete or absolute; limited: *I could only judge this CD a qualified success*.

qual·i·fi·er /ˈkwäləˌfīər/ ▶ n. **1** a person or team that qualifies for a competition or its final rounds: *he is now 14 and trying to become the youngest qualifier for a PGA Tour event*. ■ a match or contest to decide which individuals or teams qualify for a competition or its final rounds.
2 Grammar a word or phrase, esp. an adjective, used to attribute a quality to another word, esp. a noun. ■ (in systemic grammar) a word or phrase added after a noun to qualify its meaning.

qual·i·fy /ˈkwäləˌfī/ ▶ v. (**qualifies, qualifying, qualified**) **1** [no obj.] be entitled to a particular benefit or privilege by fulfilling a necessary condition: *they do not qualify for compensation payments*. ■ become eligible for a competition or its final rounds, by reaching a certain standard or defeating a competitor: *he failed to qualify for the Olympic team* | (as adj. **qualifying**) *a World Cup qualifying game*. ■ be or make properly entitled to be classed in a particular way: *he qualifies as a genuine political refugee*.
2 [no obj.] become officially recognized as a practitioner of a particular profession or activity by satisfying the relevant conditions or requirements, typically by undertaking a course of study and passing examinations: *after the war he qualified as a lawyer | I've only just qualified*. ■ [with obj.] officially recognize or establish (someone) as a practitioner of a particular profession or activity: *the courses qualify you as an instructor of the sport*. ■ [with obj. and infinitive] make (someone) competent or knowledgeable enough to do something: *I'm not qualified to write on the subject*.
3 [with obj.] make (a statement or assertion) less absolute; add reservations to: *she felt obliged to qualify her first short answer*. ■ archaic make (something extreme or undesirable) less severe or extreme: *his sincere piety and his large heart always qualify his errors*. ■ archaic alter the strength or flavor of (something, esp. a liquid): *he qualified his mug of water with a plentiful infusion of the liquor*. ■ (**qualify something as**) archaic attribute a specified quality to something; describe something as: *the propositions have been qualified as heretical*. ■ [with obj.] Grammar (of a word or phrase) attribute a quality to (another word, esp. a preceding noun).
– DERIVATIVES **qual·i·fi·a·ble** adj.
– ORIGIN late Middle English (in the sense 'describe in a particular way'): from French *qualifier*, from medieval Latin *qualificare*, from Latin *qualis* 'of what kind, of such a kind' (see QUALITY).

qual·i·ta·tive /ˈkwäləˌtātiv/ ▶ adj. relating to, measuring, or measured by the quality of something rather than its quantity: *a qualitative change in the undergraduate curriculum*. Often contrasted with QUANTITATIVE. ■ Grammar (of an adjective) describing the quality of something in size, appearance, value, etc. Such adjectives can be submodified by words such as *very* and have comparative and superlative forms. Contrasted with CLASSIFYING.
– DERIVATIVES **qual·i·ta·tive·ly** adv.
– ORIGIN late Middle English: from late Latin *qualitativus*, from Latin *qualitas* (see QUALITY).

qual·i·ta·tive a·nal·y·sis ▶ n. Chemistry identification of the constituents, e.g., elements or functional groups, present in a substance.

qual·i·ty /ˈkwälətē/ ▶ n. (pl. **qualities**) **1** the standard of something as measured against other things of a similar kind; the degree of excellence of something: *an improvement in product quality | people today enjoy a better quality of life*. ■ general excellence of standard or level: *a masterpiece for connoisseurs of quality* | [as modifier] *a wide choice of quality beers*. ■ archaic high social standing: *commanding the admiration of people of quality*. ■ [treated as pl.] archaic people of high social standing: *he's dazed at being called on to speak before quality*.
2 a distinctive attribute or characteristic possessed by someone or something: *he shows strong leadership qualities | the plant's aphrodisiac qualities*. ■ Phonetics the distinguishing characteristic or characteristics of a speech sound. ■ Music another term for TIMBRE. ■ Astrology any of three properties (cardinal, fixed, or mutable), representing types of movement, that a zodiacal sign can possess.
– ORIGIN Middle English (in the senses 'character, disposition' and 'particular property or feature'): from Old French *qualite*, from Latin *qualitas* (translating Greek *poiotēs*), from *qualis* 'of what kind, of such a kind.'

qual·i·ty as·sur·ance ▶ n. the maintenance of a desired level of quality in a service or product, esp. by means of attention to every stage of the process of delivery or production.

qual·i·ty cir·cle ▶ n. a group of employees that meets regularly to consider ways of resolving problems and improving production in their organization.

qual·i·ty con·trol ▶ n. a system of maintaining standards in manufactured products by testing a sample of the output against the specification.
– DERIVATIVES **qual·i·ty con·trol·ler** n.

qual·i·ty fac·tor ▶ n. Physics a parameter of an oscillatory system or device, such as a laser, representing the degree to which it is undamped and hence expressing the relationship between stored energy and energy dissipation. ■ a figure expressing the ability of ionizing radiation to cause biological damage, relative to a standard dose of X-rays.

qual·i·ty time ▶ n. time spent in giving another person one's undivided attention in order to strengthen a relationship, esp. with reference to working parents and their child or children.

qualm /kwä(l)m, kwô(l)m/ ▶ n. an uneasy feeling of doubt, worry, or fear, esp. about one's own conduct; a misgiving: *military regimes generally **have no qualms about** controlling the press*. ■ a momentary faint or sick feeling.
– DERIVATIVES **qualm·ish** adj.
– ORIGIN early 16th cent. (in the sense 'momentary sick feeling'): perhaps related to Old English *cw(e)alm* 'pain,' of Germanic origin.

quam·ash /ˈkwäˌmasʜ/ ▶ n. variant spelling of CAMAS.

quan·da·ry /ˈkwänd(ə)rē/ ▶ n. (pl. **quandaries**) a state of perplexity or uncertainty over what to do in a difficult situation: *Kate is **in a quandary***. ■ a difficult situation; a practical dilemma: *a legal quandary*.
– ORIGIN late 16th cent.: perhaps partly from Latin *quando* 'when.'

quan·dong /ˈkwänˌdäɴɢ/ ▶ n. either of two Australian trees. ● a small tree of the sandalwood family that has round red fruit with an edible pulp and kernel (*Eucarya acuminata*, family Santalaceae). ● (also **blue quandong**) a large tree of the subtropical rain forest that has blue berries (*Elaeocarpus grandis*, family Elaeocarpaceae).
– ORIGIN mid 19th cent.: from Wiradhuri.

quan·go /ˈkwaɴɢgō/ ▶ n. (pl. **quangos**) Brit. chiefly derogatory a semipublic administrative body outside the civil service but receiving financial support from the government, which makes senior appointments to it.
– ORIGIN 1970s (originally US): acronym from *quasi* (or *quasi-autonomous*) *nongovernment(al) organization*.

Quant /kwänt/, Mary (1934–), English fashion designer. She launched the miniskirt in 1966 and promoted bold colors and geometric designs. She was also one of the first to design for the ready-to-wear market.

quant[1] /kwänt/ ▶ n. informal a quantitative analyst.
– ORIGIN late 20th cent.: abbreviation.

q

quant² ▶ **n.** Brit. a pole for propelling a barge or punt, esp. one with a prong at the bottom to prevent it sinking into the mud.
– ORIGIN late Middle English: perhaps from Latin *contus*, from Greek *kontos* 'boat pole.'

quant. ▶ **abbr.** quantitative.

quan·tal /ˈkwäntl/ ▶ **adj.** technical composed of discrete units; varying in steps rather than continuously: *a quantal release of neurotransmitter.* ■ Physics of or relating to a quantum or quanta, or to quantum theory. ■ chiefly Physiology relating to or denoting an all-or-none response or state.
– DERIVATIVES **quan·tal·ly** /ˈkwäntl-ē/ **adv.**
– ORIGIN early 20th cent.: from QUANTUM + -AL.

quan·tic /ˈkwäntik/ ▶ **n.** Mathematics a homogeneous function of two or more variables having rational and irrational coefficients.
– ORIGIN mid 19th cent.: from Latin *quantus* 'how great, how much' + -IC.

quan·ti·fi·er /ˈkwäntəˌfīər/ ▶ **n.** Logic an expression (e.g., *all, some*) that indicates the scope of a term to which it is attached. ■ Grammar a determiner or pronoun indicative of quantity (e.g., *all, both*).

quan·ti·fy /ˈkwäntəˌfī/ ▶ **v.** (**quantifies, quantifying, quantified**) [with obj.] **1** express or measure the quantity of: *it's very hard to quantify the cost.*
2 Logic define the application of (a term or proposition) by the use of *all, some*, etc., e.g., "for all *x* if *x* is A then *x* is B."
– DERIVATIVES **quan·ti·fi·a·bil·i·ty** /ˌkwäntəˌfīəˈbilətē/ **n.**, **quan·ti·fi·a·ble** /ˈkwäntəˌfīəbəl/ **adj.**, **quan·ti·fi·ca·tion** /ˌkwäntəfiˈkāsHən/ **n.**
– ORIGIN mid 16th cent.: from medieval Latin *quantificare*, from Latin *quantus* 'how much.'

quan·tile /ˈkwänˌtīl/ ▶ **n.** Statistics each of any set of values of a variate that divide a frequency distribution into equal groups, each containing the same fraction of the total population. ■ any of the groups so produced, e.g., a quartile or percentile.
– ORIGIN 1940s: from Latin *quantus* 'how great, how much' + -ILE.

quan·ti·tate /ˈkwäntəˌtāt/ ▶ **v.** [with obj.] Medicine & Biology determine the quantity or extent of (something in numerical terms); quantify.
– DERIVATIVES **quan·ti·ta·tion** /ˌkwäntəˈtāsHən/ **n.**
– ORIGIN 1960s: from QUANTITY + -ATE³.

quan·ti·ta·tive /ˈkwäntəˌtātiv/ ▶ **adj.** relating to, measuring, or measured by the quantity of something rather than its quality: *quantitative analysis*. Often contrasted with QUALITATIVE. ■ denoting or relating to verse whose meter is based on the length of syllables, as in Latin, as opposed to the stress, as in English.
– DERIVATIVES **quan·ti·ta·tive·ly** **adv.**
– ORIGIN late 16th cent. (in the sense 'having magnitude or spatial extent'): from medieval Latin *quantitativus*, from Latin *quantitas* (see QUANTITY).

quan·ti·ta·tive a·nal·y·sis ▶ **n.** Chemistry measurement of the quantities of particular constituents present in a substance.

q

quan·ti·ta·tive eas·ing ▶ **n.** Finance the introduction of new money into the money supply by a central bank.

quan·ti·ta·tive lin·guis·tics ▶ **plural n.** [treated as sing.] the comparative study of the frequency and distribution of words and syntactic structures in different texts.

quan·ti·tive /ˈkwäntətiv/ ▶ **adj.** another term for QUANTITATIVE.
– DERIVATIVES **quan·ti·tive·ly** **adv.**

quan·ti·ty /ˈkwäntətē/ ▶ **n.** (pl. **quantities**) **1** the amount or number of a material or immaterial thing not usually estimated by spatial measurement: *the quantity and quality of the fruit can be controlled | note down the sizes, colors, and quantities that you require.* ■ a certain, usually specified, amount or number of something: *a small quantity of food | if taken in large quantities, the drug can result in liver failure.* ■ (often **quantities**) a considerable number or amount of something: *she was able to drink quantities of beer without degenerating into giggles | many people like to buy in quantity.*
2 Phonetics the perceived length of a vowel sound or syllable.
3 Mathematics & Physics a value or component that may be expressed in numbers. ■ the figure or symbol representing this.
– ORIGIN Middle English: from Old French *quantite*, from Latin *quantitas* (translating Greek *posotēs*), from *quantus* 'how great, how much.'

quan·ti·ty the·o·ry (also **the quantity theory of money**) ▶ **n.** Economics the hypothesis that changes in prices correspond to changes in the monetary supply.

quan·tize /ˈkwänˌtīz/ ▶ **v.** [with obj.] **1** Physics apply quantum theory to, esp. form into quanta, in particular restrict the number of possible values of (a quantity) or states of (a system) so that certain variables can assume only certain discrete magnitudes.
2 Electronics approximate (a continuously varying signal) by one whose amplitude is restricted to a prescribed set of values.
– DERIVATIVES **quan·ti·za·tion** /ˌkwäntəˈzāsHən/ **n.**, **quan·tiz·er** **n.** (sense 2).

quan·tum /ˈkwäntəm/ ▶ **n.** (pl. **quanta** /-tə/) **1** Physics a discrete quantity of energy proportional in magnitude to the frequency of the radiation it represents. ■ an analogous discrete amount of any other physical quantity, such as momentum or electric charge. ■ Physiology the unit quantity of acetylcholine released at a neuromuscular junction by a single synaptic vesicle, contributing a discrete small voltage to the measured end-plate potential.
2 a required or allowed amount, esp. an amount of money legally payable in damages. ■ a share or portion: *each man has only a quantum of compassion.*
– ORIGIN mid 16th cent. (in the general sense 'quantity'): from Latin, neuter of *quantus* (see QUANTITY). Sense 1 dates from the early 20th cent.

quan·tum bit ▶ **n.** Computing the basic unit of information in a quantum computer.

quan·tum chro·mo·dy·nam·ics (abbr.: **QCD**) ▶ **plural n.** [treated as sing.] Physics a quantum field theory in which the strong interaction is described in terms of an interaction between quarks mediated by gluons, both quarks and gluons being assigned a quantum number called "color."

quan·tum com·put·er ▶ **n.** a computer that makes use of the quantum states of subatomic particles to store information.
– DERIVATIVES **quan·tum com·put·ing** **n.**

quan·tum dot ▶ **n.** Physics a nanoscale particle of semiconducting material that can be embedded in cells or organisms for various experimental purposes, such as labeling proteins.

quan·tum e·lec·tro·dy·nam·ics ▶ **plural n.** [treated as sing.] a quantum field theory that deals with the electromagnetic field and its interaction with electrically charged particles.

quan·tum field the·o·ry ▶ **n.** Physics a field theory that incorporates quantum mechanics and the principles of the theory of relativity.

quan·tum grav·i·ty ▶ **n.** Physics a theory that attempts to explain gravitational physics in terms of quantum mechanics.

quan·tum jump ▶ **n.** **1** Physics an abrupt transition of an electron, atom, or molecule from one quantum state to another, with the absorption or emission of a quantum.
2 (also **quantum leap**) a huge, often sudden, increase or change in something: *the quantum jump in Jamie's grades this semester are extremely encouraging.*

quan·tum me·chan·ics ▶ **plural n.** [treated as sing.] Physics the branch of mechanics that deals with the mathematical description of the motion and interaction of subatomic particles, incorporating the concepts of quantization of energy, wave-particle duality, the uncertainty principle, and the correspondence principle.
– DERIVATIVES **quan·tum-me·chan·i·cal** **adj.**

quan·tum med·i·cine ▶ **n.** a branch of complementary medicine that uses low-dosage electromagnetic radiation in the treatment, diagnosis, and prevention of disease.

quan·tum me·ru·it /ˌkwäntəm ˈmero͝oit/ ▶ **n.** [usu. as modifier] Law a reasonable sum of money to be paid for services rendered or work done when the amount due is not stipulated in a legally enforceable contract.
– ORIGIN Latin, literally 'as much as he has deserved.'

quan·tum num·ber ▶ **n.** Physics a number that occurs in the theoretical expression for the value of some quantized property of a subatomic particle, atom, or molecule and can only have certain integral or half-integral values.

quan·tum state ▶ **n.** Physics a state of a quantized system that is described by a set of quantum numbers.

quan·tum the·o·ry ▶ **n.** Physics a theory of matter and energy based on the concept of quanta, esp. quantum mechanics.

Quao·ar /ˈkwou-är/ ▶ **n.** an asteroid, roughly the size of Pluto, discovered in 2002. Its orbit is in the Kuiper belt.

Qua·paw /ˈkwôˌpô/ ▶ **n.** (pl. **same** or **Quapaws**) **1** a member of an American Indian people of the Arkansas River region, now living mainly in northeastern Oklahoma.
2 the Siouan language of this people.
▶ **adj.** of or relating to this people or their language.
– ORIGIN from Quapaw *okáxpa*, perhaps meaning 'those downstream,' originally the name of a village.

quar. ▶ **abbr.** ■ quarter. ■ quarterly.

quar·an·tine /ˈkwôrənˌtēn/ ▶ **n.** a state, period, or place of isolation in which people or animals that have arrived from elsewhere or been exposed to infectious or contagious disease are placed: *many animals die in quarantine.*
▶ **v.** [with obj.] impose such isolation on (a person, animal, or place); put in quarantine.
– ORIGIN mid 17th cent.: from Italian *quarantina* 'forty days,' from *quaranta* 'forty.'

quar·an·tine flag ▶ **n.** another term for YELLOW FLAG.

quark¹ /kwärk/ ▶ **n.** Physics any of a number of subatomic particles carrying a fractional electric charge, postulated as building blocks of the hadrons. Quarks have not been directly observed, but theoretical predictions based on their existence have been confirmed experimentally.
– ORIGIN 1960s: a word invented by Murray GELL-MANN. Originally *quork*, the term was changed by association with the line "Three quarks for Muster Mark" in Joyce's *Finnegans Wake* (1939).

quark² ▶ **n.** a type of low-fat curd cheese.
– ORIGIN from German *Quark* 'curds.'

quark-glu·on plas·ma ▶ **n.** a hypothetical, highly energized form of matter that contains unbound quarks and gluons, believed to have been present ten millionths of a second after the Big Bang.

quar·rel¹ /ˈkwôrəl, ˈkwä-/ ▶ **n.** an angry argument or disagreement, typically between people who are usually on good terms: *he made the mistake of picking a quarrel with John.* ■ [usu. with negative] a reason for disagreement with a person, group, or principle: *we have no quarrel with the people of the country, only with the dictator.*
▶ **v.** (**quarrels, quarreling, quarreled**; Brit. **quarrels, quarrelling, quarrelled**) [no obj.] have an angry argument or disagreement: *stop quarreling with your sister.* ■ (**quarrel with**) take exception to or disagree with (something): *some people quarrel with this approach.*
– DERIVATIVES **quar·rel·er** **n.**
– ORIGIN Middle English (in the sense 'reason for disagreement with a person'): from Old French *querele*, from Latin *querel(l)a* 'complaint,' from *queri* 'complain.'

quar·rel² ▶ **n.** **1** historical a short, heavy, square-headed arrow or bolt used in a crossbow or arbalest.
2 another term for QUARRY³.
– ORIGIN Middle English: from Old French, based on late Latin *quadrus* 'square.' Compare with QUARRY³.

quar·rel·some /ˈkwôrəlsəm, ˈkwä-/ ▶ **adj.** given to or characterized by quarreling.
– DERIVATIVES **quar·rel·some·ly** **adv.**, **quar·rel·some·ness** **n.**

quar·ry¹ /ˈkwôrē, ˈkwä-/ ▶ **n.** (pl. **quarries**) a place, typically a large, deep pit, from which stone or other materials are or have been extracted.
▶ **v.** (**quarries, quarrying, quarried**) [with obj.] extract (stone or other materials) from a quarry. ■ cut into (rock or ground) to obtain stone or other materials.
– ORIGIN Middle English: from a variant of medieval Latin *quareria*, from Old French *quarriere*, based on Latin *quadrum* 'a square.' The verb dates from the late 18th cent.

quar·ry² ▶ **n.** (pl. **quarries**) an animal pursued by a hunter, hound, predatory mammal, or bird of prey. ■ a thing or person that is chased or sought: *the security police crossed the border in pursuit of their quarry.*
– ORIGIN Middle English: from Old French *cuiree*, alteration, influenced by *cuir* 'leather' and *curer* 'clean, disembowel,' of *couree*, based on Latin *cor* 'heart.' Originally the term denoted the parts of a deer that were placed on the hide and given as a reward to the hounds.

quar·ry³ ▶ **n.** (pl. **quarries**) **1** (also **quarrel**) a diamond-shaped pane of glass as used in lattice windows.
2 (also **quarry tile**) an unglazed floor tile.
– ORIGIN mid 16th cent. (sense 2): alteration of QUARREL², which in late Middle English denoted a lattice windowpane.

quar·ry·man /ˈkwôrēmən, ˈkwär-/ ▶ **n.** (pl. **quarrymen**) a worker in a quarry.

quart /kwôrt/ ▶ **n.** **1** a unit of liquid capacity equal to a quarter of a gallon or two pints, equivalent in the US to approximately 0.94 liter and in Britain to approximately 1.13 liters. ■ a unit of dry capacity equivalent to approximately 1.10 liters.
2 (also **quarte**) Fencing the fourth of eight standard parrying positions. [French.]
3 (in piquet) a sequence of four cards of the same suit.

–ORIGIN Middle English: from Old French *quarte*, from Latin *quarta (pars)* 'fourth (part),' from *quartus* 'fourth,' from *quattuor* 'four.'

quar·tan /ˈkwôrtn/ ▶ **adj.** [attrib.] Medicine denoting a mild form of malaria causing a fever that recurs every third day: *quartan fever.* ● Quartan malaria (or quartan ague) is caused by infection with *Plasmodium malariae.* Compare with TERTIAN.
–ORIGIN late Middle English: from Latin *(febris) quartana*, based on *quartus* 'fourth' (because, by inclusive reckoning, the fever recurs every fourth day).

quar·ter /ˈkwôrtər/ ▶ **n. 1** each of four equal or corresponding parts into which something is or can be divided: *she cut each apple into quarters | a page and a quarter | a quarter of a mile.* ■ a period of three months regarded as one fourth of a year, used esp. in reference to financial transactions such as the payment of bills or a company's earnings: *the payment for each quarter's electricity is made in the next quarter.* ■ a period of fifteen minutes or a point of time marking the transition from one fifteen-minute period to the next: *the baby was born at a quarter past nine.* ■ a coin representing 25 cents, one fourth of a US or Canadian dollar. ■ each of the four parts into which an animal's or bird's carcass may be divided, each including a leg or wing. ■ **(quarters)** the haunches or hindquarters of a horse. ■ one fourth of a lunar month. ■ (in various sports) each of four equal periods into which a game is divided. ■ one of four terms into which a school or college year may be divided.
2 one fourth of a measure of weight, in particular: ■ one fourth of a pound (avoirdupois, equal to 4 ounces). ■ one fourth of a hundredweight (US 25 lb or Brit. 28 lb). ■ Brit. a grain measure equivalent to 8 bushels.
3 [usu. with adj. or noun] a part of a town or city having a specific character or use: *it is a beautiful port city with a fascinating medieval quarter.*
4 the direction of one of the points of the compass, esp. as a direction from which the wind blows. ■ a particular but unspecified person, group of people, or area: *we have just had help from an unexpected quarter.* ■ either side of a ship aft of the beam: *he trained his glasses over the starboard quarter.*
5 (quarters) rooms or lodgings, esp. those allocated to servicemen or to staff in domestic service: *the servants' quarters.*
6 [usu. with negative] pity or mercy shown toward an enemy or opponent who is in one's power: *the riot squad gave no quarter.*
7 Heraldry each of four or more roughly equal divisions of a shield separated by vertical and horizontal lines. ■ a square charge which covers the top left (dexter chief) quarter of the field.
▶ **v.** [with obj.] **1** divide into four equal or corresponding parts: *peel and quarter the bananas.* ■ historical cut (the body of an executed person) into four parts: *the plotters were hanged, drawn, and quartered.* ■ cut (a log) into quarters, and these into planks so as to show the grain well.
2 (be quartered) be stationed or lodged in a specified place: *many were quartered in tents.*
3 range over or traverse (an area) in every direction: *we watched a pair of kingfishers quartering the river looking for minnows.* ■ [no obj.] move at an angle; go in a diagonal or zigzag direction: *his young dog quartered back and forth in quick turns.*
4 Heraldry display (different coats of arms) in quarters of a shield, esp. to show arms inherited from heiresses who have married into the bearer's family: *Edward III quartered the French royal arms with his own.* ■ divide (a shield) into four or more parts by vertical and horizontal lines.
–ORIGIN Middle English: from Old French *quartier*, from Latin *quartarius* 'fourth part of a measure,' from *quartus* 'fourth,' from *quattuor* 'four.'

quar·ter·age /ˈkwôrtərij/ ▶ **n.** archaic a sum paid or received quarterly.

quar·ter·back /ˈkwôrtərˌbak/ ▶ **n.** Football a player positioned behind the center who directs a team's offensive play. ■ a person who directs or coordinates an operation or project.
▶ **v.** [with obj.] Football play as a quarterback for (a particular team). ■ direct or coordinate (an operation or project).

quar·ter bind·ing ▶ **n.** a type of bookbinding in which the spine is covered in one material (usually leather) and the rest of the cover in another.
–DERIVATIVES **quar·ter-bound adj.**

quar·ter·deck /ˈkwôrtərˌdek/ ▶ **n.** the part of a ship's upper deck near the stern, traditionally reserved for officers. ■ the officers of a ship or the navy.

quar·ter·fi·nal /ˈkwôrtərˌfīnl/ ▶ **n.** a match or round of a tournament that precedes the semifinal.

Quar·ter Horse (also **quarter horse**) ▶ **n.** a horse of a small, stocky breed noted for agility and speed over short distances. It is reputed to be the fastest breed of horse over distances of a quarter of a mile.

quar·ter-hour (also **quarter of an hour**) ▶ **n.** a period of 15 minutes. ■ a point of time 15 minutes before or after any hour.

quar·ter·ing /ˈkwôrtəriNG/ ▶ **n. 1 (quarterings)** Heraldry the coats of arms marshalled on a shield to denote the marriages into a family of the heiresses of others.
2 the provision of accommodations or lodgings, esp. for troops.
3 the action of dividing something into four parts.

quar·ter·ly /ˈkwôrtərlē/ ▶ **adj. 1** [attrib.] done, produced, or occurring once every quarter of a year: *a quarterly newsletter is distributed to members.*
2 Heraldry (of a shield or charge) divided into four (or occasionally more) subdivisions by vertical and horizontal lines.
▶ **adv. 1** once every quarter of a year: *interest is paid quarterly.*
2 Heraldry in the four, or in two diagonally opposite, quarters of a shield. [on the pattern of Old French *quartile.*]
▶ **n.** (pl. **quarterlies**) a magazine or journal that is published four times a year.

quar·ter·mas·ter /ˈkwôrtərˌmastər/ ▶ **n. 1** a military officer responsible for providing quarters, rations, clothing, and other supplies.
2 a naval petty officer with particular responsibility for steering and signals.

quar·ter·mas·ter gen·er·al ▶ **n.** (pl. **quartermasters general** or **quartermaster generals**) the head of the army department in charge of the quartering and equipment of troops.

quar·tern /ˈkwôrtərn/ ▶ **n.** Brit. archaic a quarter of a pint.
–ORIGIN Middle English (in the general sense 'a quarter'): from Old French *quart(e)ron*, from *quart(e)* (see QUART).

quar·ter note ▶ **n.** Music a musical note having the time value of a quarter of a whole note or half a half note, represented by a large solid dot with a plain stem. Also called CROTCHET.

quar·ter pipe ▶ **n.** a ramp with a slightly convex surface, used by skateboarders, rollerbladers, or snowboarders to perform jumps and other maneuvers.

quar·ter-saw ▶ **v.** [with obj.] (usu. as adj. **quarter-sawn**) saw (a log) radially into quarters and then into boards: *we quarter-saw the logs at our own mill* | [as adj.] *quarter-sawn timber from the stand of white ash.* ■ produce (a board or a piece of furniture) using this technique.

quar·ter sec·tion ▶ **n.** a quarter of a square mile of land; 160 acres (approximately 64.7 hectares).

quar·ter ses·sions ▶ **plural n.** historical (in England, Wales, and Northern Ireland) a court of limited criminal and civil jurisdiction and of appeal, usually held quarterly in counties or boroughs, and replaced in 1972 by crown courts.

quar·ter·staff /ˈkwôrtərˌstaf/ ▶ **n.** historical a stout pole 6–8 feet (2–2.5 m) long, tipped with iron, formerly used as a weapon.

quar·ter·tone ▶ **n.** Music half a semitone.

quar·tet /kwôrˈtet/ ▶ **n.** a group of four people playing music or singing together. ■ a composition for such a group. ■ a set of four people or things.
–ORIGIN early 17th cent. (in the general sense 'set of four'): from French *quartette*, from Italian *quartetto*, from *quarto* 'fourth,' from Latin *quartus.*

quar·tic /ˈkwôrtik/ Mathematics ▶ **adj.** involving the fourth and no higher power of an unknown quantity or variable.
▶ **n.** a quartic equation, function, curve, or surface.
–ORIGIN mid 19th cent.: from Latin *quartus* 'fourth' + -IC.

quar·ti·er /ˈkärtē-ā/ ▶ **n.** (pl. **same**) a district of a French city.
–ORIGIN French.

quar·tile /ˈkwôrˌtīl, ˈkwôrtl/ ▶ **n.** Statistics each of four equal groups into which a population can be divided according to the distribution of values of a particular variable. ■ each of the three values of the random variable that divide a population into four such groups.
–ORIGIN late 19th cent.: from medieval Latin *quartilis*, from Latin *quartus* 'fourth.'

quar·to /ˈkwôrtō/ (abbr.: **4to**) ▶ **n.** (pl. **quartos**) Printing a size of book page resulting from folding each printed sheet into four leaves (eight pages). ■ a book of this size. ■ a size of writing paper, 10 in. × 8 in. (254 × 203 mm).
–ORIGIN late 16th cent.: from Latin *(in) quarto* '(in) the fourth (of a sheet),' ablative of *quartus* 'fourth.'

quartz /kwôrts/ ▶ **n.** a hard white or colorless mineral consisting of silicon dioxide, found widely in igneous, metamorphic, and sedimentary rocks. It is often colored by impurities (as in amethyst, citrine, and cairngorm).
–ORIGIN mid 18th cent.: from German *Quarz*, from Polish dialect *kwardy*, corresponding to standard Polish *twardy* 'hard.'

quartz-hal·o·gen ▶ **adj.** (of a high-intensity electric lamp) using a quartz bulb containing the vapor of a halogen, usually iodine.

quartz·ite /ˈkwôrtˌsīt/ ▶ **n.** Geology an extremely compact, hard, granular rock consisting essentially of quartz. It often occurs as silicified sandstone, as in sarsen stones.

quartz lamp ▶ **n.** an electric lamp in which the envelope is made of quartz, which allows ultraviolet light to pass through it. It may be a bulb containing a halogen or a tube containing mercury vapor.

qua·sar /ˈkwāˌzär/ ▶ **n.** Astronomy a massive and extremely remote celestial object, emitting exceptionally large amounts of energy, and typically having a starlike image in a telescope. It has been suggested that quasars contain massive black holes and may represent a stage in the evolution of some galaxies.
–ORIGIN 1960s: contraction of *quasistellar.*

quash /kwôsH, kwäsH/ ▶ **v.** [with obj.] reject or void, esp. by legal procedure: *his conviction was quashed on appeal.* ■ put an end to; suppress: *a hospital executive quashed rumors that nursing staff will lose jobs.*
–ORIGIN Middle English: from Old French *quasser* 'annul,' from late Latin *cassare* (medieval Latin also *quassare*), from *cassus* 'null, void.' Compare with SQUASH[1].

quasi- ▶ **comb. form** seemingly; apparently but not really: *quasi-American | quasi-scientific.* ■ being partly or almost: *quasicrystalline.*
–ORIGIN from Latin *quasi* 'as if, almost.'

qua·si con·tract /ˈkwāˌzī, ˈkwäzē/ ▶ **n.** an obligation of one party to another imposed by law independently of an agreement between the parties.
–DERIVATIVES **qua·si-con·trac·tu·al adj.**

qua·si·crys·tal /ˌkwāˌzīˈkristəl, ˌkwäzē-/ ▶ **n.** Physics a locally regular aggregation of molecules resembling a crystal in certain properties (such as that of diffraction) but not having a consistent spatial periodicity.
–DERIVATIVES **qua·si·crys·tal·line** /-ˈkristəlēn/ **adj.**

Qua·si·mo·do[1] /ˌkwäzēˈmōdō/ the name of the hunchback in Victor Hugo's novel *Notre-Dame de Paris* (1831).

Qua·si·mo·do[2], Salvatore (1901–68), Italian poet. His early work was influenced by French symbolism but his later work was more concerned with political and social issues. Notable works: *Water and Land* (1930) and *And It's Suddenly Evening* (1942). Nobel Prize for Literature (1959).

qua·si·par·ti·cle /ˌkwāzīˈpärtəkəl, ˌkwäzē-/ ▶ **n.** Physics a quantum of energy in a crystal lattice or other system of bodies that has momentum and position and can in some respects be regarded as a particle.

quas·sia /ˈkwäsH(ē)ə/ ▶ **n.** a South American shrub or small tree related to ailanthus. ● Genera *Quassia* and *Picrasma*, family Simaroubaceae: several species, in particular *Q. amara.* ■ the wood, bark, or root of this tree, yielding a bitter medicinal tonic, insecticide, and vermifuge.
–ORIGIN named after Graman *Quassi*, an 18th-cent. Surinamese slave who discovered its medicinal properties in 1730.

quat·er·cen·ten·ar·y /ˌkwätərsenˈtenərē, -ˈsentnˌerē/ ▶ **n.** (pl. **quatercentenaries**) the four-hundredth anniversary of a significant event.
▶ **adj.** of or relating to such an anniversary.
–ORIGIN late 19th cent.: from Latin *quater* 'four times' + CENTENARY.

quat·er·nar·y /ˈkwätərˌnerē/ ▶ **adj. 1** fourth in order or rank; belonging to the fourth order.
2 (Quaternary) Geology of, relating to, or denoting the most recent period in the Cenozoic era, following the Tertiary period and comprising the Pleistocene and Holocene epochs (and thus including the present).
3 Chemistry denoting an ammonium compound containing a cation of the form NR_4^+, where R represents organic groups or atoms other than hydrogen. ■ (of a carbon atom) bonded to four other carbon atoms.
▶ **n. (the Quaternary)** Geology the Quaternary period or the system of deposits laid down during it.

PRONUNCIATION KEY ə ago, up; ər over, fur; a hat; ā ate; ä car; e let; ē see; i fit; ī by; NG sing; ō go; ô law, for; oi toy; o͝o good; o͞o goo; ou out; TH thin; T͟H then; ZH vision

q

The Quaternary began about 1,640,000 years ago. Humans and other mammals evolved into their present forms and were strongly affected by the ice ages of the Pleistocene.

– ORIGIN late Middle English (as a noun denoting a set of four): from Latin *quaternarius*, from *quaterni* 'four at once,' from *quater* 'four times,' from *quattuor* 'four.'

qua·ter·ni·on /kwəˈtərnēən, kwä-/ ▶ n. **1** Mathematics a complex number of the form *w* + *xi* + *yj* + *zk*, where *w*, *x*, *y*, *z* are real numbers and *i*, *j*, *k* are imaginary units that satisfy certain conditions.
2 rare a set of four people or things.
– ORIGIN mid 19th cent.: from late Latin *quaternio(n-)*, from Latin *quarterni* (see QUATERNARY).

qua·torze /kəˈtôrz/ ▶ n. (in piquet) a set of four aces, kings, queens, jacks, or tens held in one hand.
– ORIGIN early 18th cent.: French, literally 'fourteen,' from Latin *quattuordecim*.

quat·rain /ˈkwäˌtrān/ ▶ n. a stanza of four lines, esp. one having alternate rhymes.
– ORIGIN late 16th cent.: from French, from *quatre* 'four.'

quat·re·foil /ˈkatərˌfoil, ˈkatrə-/ ▶ n. an ornamental design of four lobes or leaves as used in architectural tracery, resembling a flower or four-leaf clover.
– ORIGIN late 15th cent.: from Anglo-Norman French, from Old French *quatre* 'four' + *foil* 'leaf.'

quat·tro·cen·to /ˌkwätrōˈCHentō/ ▶ n. (**the quattrocento**) the 15th century as a period of Italian art or architecture.
– ORIGIN Italian, literally '400' (shortened from *milquattrocento* '1400'), used with reference to the years 1400–99.

qua·ver /ˈkwāvər/ ▶ v. [no obj.] (of a person's voice) shake or tremble in speaking, typically through nervousness or emotion.
▶ n. **1** a shake or tremble in a person's voice.
2 Music chiefly Brit. another term for EIGHTH NOTE.
– DERIVATIVES **qua·ver·ing·ly** adv., **qua·ver·y** adj.
– ORIGIN late Middle English (as a verb in the general sense 'tremble'): from dialect *quave* 'quake, tremble,' probably from an Old English word related to QUAKE. The noun is first recorded (mid 16th cent.) as a musical term.

quay /kē, k(w)ā/ ▶ n. a concrete, stone, or metal platform lying alongside or projecting into water for loading and unloading ships.
– DERIVATIVES **quay·age** /ˈkēij, ˈk(w)āij/ n.
– ORIGIN late Middle English *key*, from Old French *kay*, of Celtic origin. The change of spelling in the late 17th cent. was influenced by the modern French spelling *quai*.

quay·side /ˈkēˌsīd, ˈk(w)ā-/ ▶ n. a quay and the area around it.

qu·bit /ˈkyo͞obit/ ▶ n. Computing another term for QUANTUM BIT.
– ORIGIN 1990s: from *quantum bit*, with punning allusion to *cubit*.

Que. ▶ abbr. Quebec.

quean /kwēn/ ▶ n. archaic an impudent or ill-behaved girl or woman. ■ a prostitute.
– ORIGIN Old English *cwene* 'woman,' of Germanic origin; related to Dutch *kween* 'barren cow,' from an Indo-European root shared by Greek *gunē* 'woman.'

quea·sy /ˈkwēzē/ ▶ adj. (**queasier**, **queasiest**) nauseated; feeling sick: *in the morning he was still pale and queasy*. ■ inducing a feeling of nausea: *the queasy swell of the boat*. ■ slightly nervous or worried about something.
– DERIVATIVES **quea·si·ly** /-zəlē/ adv., **quea·si·ness** n.
– ORIGIN late Middle English *queisy*, *coisy* 'causing nausea,' of uncertain origin; perhaps related to Old French *coisier* 'to hurt.'

Que·bec /k(w)əˈbek, kā-/ **1** a heavily forested province in eastern Canada; pop. 7,546,131 (2006). Settled by the French in 1608, it was ceded to the British in 1763 and became one of the original four provinces in the Dominion of Canada in 1867. The majority of its residents are French-speaking, and it is a focal point of the French-Canadian nationalist movement, which advocates independence for Quebec. French name **Québec**. ■ (also **Quebec City**) its capital city, a port on the St. Lawrence River; pop. 491,142 (2006). Founded in 1608, it is Canada's oldest city. It was captured from the French by the British in 1759 after the battle of the Plains of Abraham and became capital of Lower Canada (later Quebec) in 1791.
2 a code word representing the letter Q, used in radio communication.
– DERIVATIVES **Que·beck·er** (also **Quebecer**) n.

que·bra·cho /kāˈbräˌCHō, kə-/ ▶ n. (pl. **quebrachos**) a South American tree whose timber and bark are a rich source of tannin. ● Genera *Aspidosperma* (family Apocynaceae) and *Schinopsis* (family Anacardiaceae).
– ORIGIN late 19th cent.: from Spanish, from *quebrar* 'to break' + *hacha* 'ax.'

Quech·ua /ˈkeCHwə/ (also **Quecha** /ˈkeCHə/, **Quichua**) ▶ n. (pl. **same** or **Quechuas**) **1** a member of an American Indian people of Peru and parts of Bolivia, Chile, Colombia, and Ecuador.
2 the language or group of languages of this people.
▶ adj. of or relating to this people or their language.
– DERIVATIVES **Quech·uan** /-wən/ (also **Quechan** /ˈkeCHən/) adj. & n.
– ORIGIN Spanish, abbreviation of Quechua *qheswa simi* 'valley speech,' the designation of a Quechua dialect.

Queen /kwēn/, Ellery, US writer of detective novels; pseudonym of *Frederic Dannay* (1905–82) and *Manfred Lee* (1905–71). The novels feature a detective also called Ellery Queen.

queen /kwēn/ ▶ n. **1** the female ruler of an independent state, esp. one who inherits the position by right of birth. ■ (also **Queen Consort**) a king's wife. ■ a woman or thing regarded as excellent or outstanding of its kind: *the queen of romance novelists | Venice: Queen of the Adriatic*. ■ a woman or girl chosen to hold the most important position in a festival or event: *football stars and homecoming queens*. ■ (**the Queen**) dated (in the UK) the national anthem when there is a female sovereign. ■ informal a man's wife or girlfriend.
2 the most powerful chess piece that each player has, able to move any number of unobstructed squares in any direction along a rank, file, or diagonal on which it stands.
3 a playing card bearing a representation of a queen, normally ranking next below a king and above a jack.
4 Entomology a reproductive female in a colony of social ants, bees, wasps, etc.
5 an adult female cat that has not been spayed.
6 informal a male homosexual, typically one regarded as ostentatiously effeminate.
▶ v. [with obj.] **1** (**queen it over**) (of a woman) behave in an unpleasant and superior way toward.
2 Chess convert (a pawn) into a queen when it reaches the opponent's back rank on the board.
– DERIVATIVES **queen·dom** /-dəm/ n., **queen·like** /-ˌlīk/ adj., **queen·ship** /-ˌSHip/ n.
– ORIGIN Old English *cwēn*, of Germanic origin; related to QUEAN.

Queen Anne ▶ adj. denoting a style of English furniture or architecture characteristic of the early 18th century. The furniture is noted for its simple, proportioned style and for its cabriole legs and walnut veneer; the architecture is characterized by the use of red brick in simple, basically rectangular designs.

Queen Anne's lace ▶ n. the uncultivated form of the carrot, with broad round heads of tiny white flowers that resemble lace. Also called WILD CARROT. ● *Daucus carota*, family Umbelliferae.

queen bee ▶ n. the single reproductive female in a hive or colony of honeybees. ■ informal a woman who has a dominant or controlling position in a particular group or sphere.

queen cake ▶ n. a small, soft, typically heart-shaped currant cake.

Queen Char·lotte Is·lands a group of more than 150 islands off the western coast of Canada, in British Columbia.

Queen Cit·y ▶ n. the preeminent city of a region.

Queen Con·sort /ˈkänˈsôrt/ ▶ n. see QUEEN (sense 1 of the noun).

queen·fish /ˈkwēnˌfiSH/ ▶ n. (pl. **same** or **queenfishes**) an edible marine fish, in particular: ● a popular sporting fish of the Indo-Pacific (*Chorinemus lysan*, family Carangidae). ● a drumfish of the Pacific coast of North America (*Seriphus politus*, family Sciaenidae).

queen·ly /ˈkwēnlē/ ▶ adj. (**queenlier**, **queenliest**) fit for or appropriate to a queen.
– DERIVATIVES **queen·li·ness** /-lēnis/ n.

Queen Maud Land /môd/ a part of Antarctica that borders the Atlantic Ocean, claimed since 1939 by Norway.
– ORIGIN named after *Queen Maud* of Norway (1869–1938).

queen of pud·dings ▶ n. a pudding made with bread, jam, and meringue.

Queens /kwēnz/ a borough of New York City, at the western end of Long Island; pop. 2,229,379 (2000).

Queen's Bench (in full **Queen's Bench Division**) ▶ n. (in the UK) a division of the High Court of Justice.

Queens·ber·ry rules /ˈkwēnzˌberē/ the standard rules of boxing, originally drawn up in 1867 to govern the sport in Britain. ■ standard rules of polite or acceptable behavior.
– ORIGIN late 19th cent.: named after John Sholto Douglas (1844–1900), 8th Marquess of *Queensberry*, who supervised the preparation of the rules.

queen scal·lop ▶ n. a small, edible European scallop. ● *Chlamys opercularis*, family Pectinidae.

Queen's Coun·sel (abbr.: **QC**) ▶ n. Brit. a senior barrister appointed on the recommendation of the Lord Chancellor.

Queen's Coun·ty former name for LAOIS.

Queen's Eng·lish ▶ n. (**the Queen's English**) standard English language as written and spoken by educated people in Britain.

queen·side /ˈkwēnˌsīd/ ▶ n. Chess the half of the board on which both queens stand at the start of a game (the left-hand side for White, right for Black).

Queens·land /ˈkwēnzlənd, -ˌland/ a state that comprises the northeastern part of Australia; pop. 4,293,915 (2008); capital, Brisbane. Originally established in 1824 as a penal colony, Queensland was constituted a separate colony in 1859, having previously formed part of New South Wales, and was federated with the other states of Australia in 1901.
– DERIVATIVES **Queens·land·er** n.

Queens·land nut ▶ n. another term for MACADAMIA.

queen's pawn ▶ n. Chess the pawn occupying the square immediately in front of each player's queen at the start of a game.

queens·ware /ˈkwēnzˌwe(ə)r/ ▶ n. a type of fine, cream-colored Wedgwood pottery.
– ORIGIN mid 18th cent. (as *Queen's ware*): named in honor of Queen Charlotte (wife of George III), who had been presented with a set in 1765.

queer /kwi(ə)r/ ▶ adj. **1** strange; odd: *she had a queer feeling that they were being watched*. ■ [predic.] dated slightly ill.
2 informal, chiefly derogatory (esp. of a man) homosexual.
▶ n. informal, chiefly derogatory a homosexual man.
▶ v. [with obj.] informal spoil or ruin (an agreement, event, or situation): *Reg didn't want someone meddling and queering the deal at the last minute*.
– DERIVATIVES **queer·ish** adj., **queer·ly** adv., **queer·ness** n.
– ORIGIN early 16th cent.: considered to be from German *quer* 'oblique, perverse,' but the origin is doubtful.

USAGE The word **queer** was first used to mean 'homosexual' in the early 20th century: it was originally, and usually still is, a deliberately offensive and aggressive term when used by heterosexual people. In recent years, however, some gay people have taken the word **queer** and deliberately used it in place of **gay** or **homosexual**, in an attempt, by using the word positively, to deprive it of its negative power. This use of **queer** is now well established and widely used among gay people (especially as an adjective or noun modifier, as in *queer rights; queer-bashing*) and at present exists alongside the other use.

queer·core /ˈkwi(ə)rˌkôr/ ▶ n. a cultural movement among young homosexuals that deliberately rebels against and dissociates itself from the established gay scene, having as its primary form of expression an aggressive type of punk-style music.

que·le·a /ˈkwēlēə/ ▶ n. a brownish weaverbird found in Africa, the male of which has either a black face or a red head. ● Genus *Quelea*, family Ploceidae: three species, in particular the **red-billed quelea** (*Q. quelea*), which occurs in huge numbers and is an important pest of crops.
– ORIGIN modern Latin, perhaps from medieval Latin *qualea* 'quail.'

quell /kwel/ ▶ v. [with obj.] put an end to (a rebellion or other disorder), typically by the use of force: *extra police were called to quell the disturbance*. ■ subdue or silence someone: *Connor quelled him with a look*. ■ suppress (a feeling, esp. an unpleasant one): *he spoke up again to quell any panic among the assembled youngsters*.
– DERIVATIVES **quell·er** n.
– ORIGIN Old English *cwellan* 'kill,' of Germanic origin; related to German *quälen* 'torture.'

quench /kwenCH/ ▶ v. [with obj.] **1** satisfy (one's thirst) by drinking. ■ satisfy (a desire): *he only pursued her to quench an aching need*.
2 extinguish (a fire): *firemen hauled on hoses in a desperate bid to quench the flames*. ■ stifle or suppress (a feeling): *fury rose in him, but he quenched it*. ■ rapidly cool (red-hot metal or other material), esp. in cold water or oil. ■ Physics & Electronics suppress or damp (an effect such as luminescence, or an oscillation or discharge).
▶ n. an act of quenching something very hot.
– DERIVATIVES **quench·a·ble** adj., **quench·er** n. (chiefly Physics & Metallurgy), **quench·less** adj. (literary).

– ORIGIN Old English *-cwencan* (in *acwencan* 'put out, extinguish'), of Germanic origin.

que·nelle /kə'nel/ ▶ **n.** (usu. **quenelles**) a small seasoned ball of pounded fish or meat.
– ORIGIN French, probably from Alsatian German *knödel*.

quer·ce·tin /'kwərsətin/ ▶ **n.** Chemistry a yellow crystalline pigment present in plants, used as a food supplement to reduce allergic responses or boost immunity. ● A flavone derivative; chem. formula: $C_{15}H_{10}O_7$.
– ORIGIN mid 19th cent.: probably from Latin *quercetum* 'oak grove' (from *quercus* 'oak') + **-IN**[1].

Quer·cia, Jacopo della, see **DELLA QUERCIA**.

Que·ré·ta·ro /ke'rätä,rō/ a state in central Mexico. ■ its capital city; pop. 596,450 (2005). In 1847, it was the scene of the signing of the treaty that ended the US–Mexican war.

que·rist /'kwi(ə)rist/ ▶ **n.** chiefly archaic a person who asks questions; a questioner.
– ORIGIN mid 17th cent.: from Latin *quaerere* 'ask' + **-IST**.

quern /kwərn/ ▶ **n.** a simple hand mill for grinding grain, typically consisting of two circular stones, the upper of which is rotated or rubbed to and fro on the lower one.
– ORIGIN Old English *cweorn(e)*, of Germanic origin; related to Old Norse *kvern* and Dutch *kweern*.

quer·u·lous /'kwer(y)ələs/ ▶ **adj.** complaining in a petulant or whining manner: *she became querulous and demanding.*
– DERIVATIVES **quer·u·lous·ly adv.**, **quer·u·lous·ness n.**
– ORIGIN late 15th cent.: from late Latin *querulosus*, from Latin *querulus*, from *queri* 'complain.'

que·ry /'kwi(ə)rē/ ▶ **n.** (pl. **queries**) a question, esp. one addressed to an official or organization: *a spokeswoman said queries could not be answered until Monday.* ■ used in writing or speaking to question the accuracy of a following statement or to introduce a question. ■ chiefly Printing a question mark.
▶ **v.** (**queries, querying, queried**) [reporting verb] ask a question about something, esp. in order to express one's doubts about it or to check its validity or accuracy: [with clause] *many people queried whether any harm had been done* | [with obj.] *he queried the medical database* | [with direct speech] *"Why not?" he queried.* ■ [with obj.] put a question or questions to (someone): *when these officers were queried, they felt unhappy.*
– ORIGIN mid 17th cent.: anglicized form of the Latin imperative *quaere!*, used in the 16th cent. in English as a verb in the sense 'inquire' and as a noun meaning 'query,' from Latin *quaerere* 'ask, seek.'

que·ry lan·guage ▶ **n.** Computing a language for the specification of procedures for the retrieval (and sometimes also modification) of information from a database.

ques. ▶ **abbr.** question.

que·sa·dil·la /,käsə'dēyə/ ▶ **n.** a tortilla filled with cheese and heated.
– ORIGIN Spanish.

que·so blan·co /'käsō 'bläNGkō/ ▶ **n.** a fresh white cow's milk cheese used in Latin American cooking.
– ORIGIN Spanish, 'white cheese.'

que·so fres·co /'käsō 'freskō/ ▶ **n.** a semisoft fresh Mexican cheese, white in color, typically served shredded over hot foods.
– ORIGIN Spanish, 'fresh cheese.'

quest /kwest/ ▶ **n.** a long or arduous search for something: *the quest for a reliable vaccine has intensified.* ■ (in medieval romance) an expedition made by a knight to accomplish a prescribed task.
▶ **v.** [no obj.] search for something: *he was a real scientist, questing after truth.* ■ [with obj.] literary search for; seek out.
– DERIVATIVES **quest·er** (also **questor**) **n.**, **quest·ing·ly adv.**
– ORIGIN late Middle English: from Old French *queste* (noun), *quester* (verb), based on Latin *quaerere* 'ask, seek.' See also **INQUEST**.

ques·tion /'kwesCHən/ ▶ **n.** a sentence worded or expressed so as to elicit information: *we hope this leaflet has been helpful in answering your questions.* ■ a doubt about the truth or validity of something: *there is no question that America faces the threat of Balkanization.* ■ the raising of a doubt about or objection to something: *Edward was the only one she obeyed* ***without question*** | *her loyalty is really* ***beyond question.*** ■ a matter forming the basis of a problem requiring resolution: *we have kept an eye on the question of political authority.* ■ a matter or concern depending on or involving a specified condition or thing: *it was not simply* ***a question of*** *age and hierarchy.*
▶ **v.** [with obj.] ask questions of (someone), esp. in an official context: *four men were being questioned about the killings* | (as noun **questioning**) *the young lieutenant escorted us to the barracks for questioning.* ■ feel or express doubt about; raise objections to: *members had questioned the cost of the scheme.*
– PHRASES **be (just** or **only) a question of time** be certain to happen sooner or later. **bring something into question** raise an issue for further consideration or discussion: *technology had brought into question the whole future of work.* **come into question** become an issue for further consideration or discussion: *our Sunday trading laws have come into question.* **in question 1** being considered or discussed: *on the day in question, there were several serious emergencies.* **2** in doubt: *all of the old certainties are in question.* **no question of** no possibility of. **out of the question** too impracticable or unlikely to merit discussion. **question of fact** Law an issue to be decided by a jury. **question of law** Law an issue to be decided by a judge. **put the question** (in a formal debate or meeting) require supporters and opponents of a proposal to record their votes.
– DERIVATIVES **ques·tion·er n.**, **ques·tion·ing·ly adv.**
– ORIGIN late Middle English: from Old French *question* (noun), *questionner* (verb), from Latin *quaestio(n-)*, from *quaerere* 'ask, seek.'

ques·tion·a·ble /'kwesCHənəbəl/ ▶ **adj.** doubtful as regards truth or quality: [with clause] *it is questionable whether any of these exceptions is genuine.* ■ not clearly honest, honorable, or wise: *a few men of allegedly questionable character.*
– DERIVATIVES **ques·tion·a·bil·i·ty** /,kwesCHənə'bilətē/ **n.**, **ques·tion·a·ble·ness n.**, **ques·tion·a·bly** /-əblē/ **adv.**

ques·tion·ar·y /'kwesCHə,nerē/ ▶ **n.** (pl. **questionaries**) a questionnaire.
– ORIGIN late 19th cent.: from French *questionnaire* (see **QUESTIONNAIRE**).

ques·tion mark ▶ **n.** a punctuation mark (?) indicating a question. ■ used to express doubt or uncertainty about something: *there's a question mark over his future.*

ques·tion·naire /,kwesCHə'ne(ə)r/ ▶ **n.** a set of printed or written questions with a choice of answers, devised for the purposes of a survey or statistical study.
– ORIGIN late 19th cent.: from French, from *questionner* 'to question.'

Quet·ta /'kwetə/ a city in western Pakistan, the capital of Baluchistan province; pop. 860,000 (est. 2009).

quet·zal /ket'säl/ ▶ **n. 1** a bird of the trogon family, with iridescent green plumage and typically red underparts, found in the forests of tropical America. ● Genus *Pharomachrus*, family Trogonidae: five species, esp. the **resplendent quetzal** (*P. mocinno*), the male of which has very long tail coverts and was venerated by the Aztecs.
2 the basic monetary unit of Guatemala, equal to 100 centavos.
– ORIGIN early 19th cent. (sense 1): from Spanish, from Aztec *quetzalli* 'brightly colored tail feather.'

Quet·zal·có·a·tl /,ketsəlkō'ätl/ the plumed serpent god of the Toltec and Aztec civilizations.

> Traditionally the god of the morning and evening star, he later became known as the patron of priests, inventor of books and of the calendar, and as the symbol of death and resurrection. His worship involved human sacrifice. Legend said that he would return in another age, and when Montezuma, last king of the Aztecs, received news of the landing of Cortés and his men in 1519, he thought that Quetzalcóatl had returned.

quet·zal·co·a·tlus /,ketsəlkə'wätləs/ ▶ **n.** a giant pterosaur of the late Cretaceous period. It was the largest ever flying animal, with a wingspan of up to 50 feet (15 m). ● Genus *Quetzalcoatlus*, family Azhdarchidae, order Pterosauria.
– ORIGIN modern Latin, from the name of the Aztec god **QUETZALCÓATL**.

queue /kyōō/ ▶ **n. 1** chiefly Brit. a line or sequence of people or vehicles awaiting their turn to be attended to or to proceed.
2 Computing a list of data items, commands, etc., stored so as to be retrievable in a definite order, usually the order of insertion.
3 archaic a braid of hair worn at the back.
▶ **v.** (**queues, queuing** or **queueing, queued**) [no obj.] **1** chiefly Brit. take one's place in a queue: *in the war they had queued for food.* ■ (**queue up**) be extremely keen to do or have something: *companies are queuing up to move to the bay.*
2 [with obj.] Computing arrange in a queue.
– ORIGIN late 16th cent. (as a heraldic term denoting the tail of an animal): from French, based on Latin *cauda* 'tail.' Compare with **CUE**[2]. dates from the mid 19th cent.

Que·zon Cit·y /'käzän, -sōn/ a city on the island of Luzon in the northern Philippines; pop. 2,679,500 (est. 2007). Established in 1940, it was the capital of the Philippines 1948–76.
– ORIGIN named after Manuel Luis *Quezon* (1878–1944), the first president of the republic.

quib·ble /'kwibəl/ ▶ **n. 1** a slight objection or criticism: *the only quibble about this book is the price.* **2** archaic a play on words; a pun.
▶ **v.** [no obj.] argue or raise objections about a trivial matter: *they are always quibbling about the amount they are prepared to pay.*
– DERIVATIVES **quib·bler n.**, **quib·bling·ly adv.**
– ORIGIN early 17th cent. (in the sense 'play on words, pun'): diminutive of obsolete *quib* 'a petty objection,' probably from Latin *quibus*, dative and ablative plural of *qui, quae, quod* 'who, what, which,' frequently used in legal documents and so associated with subtle distinctions or verbal niceties.

quiche /kēsH/ ▶ **n.** a baked flan or tart with a savory filling thickened with eggs.
– ORIGIN French, from Alsatian dialect *Küchen*; related to German *Kuchen* 'cake.'

Qui·ché /kē'CHā/ ▶ **n.** (pl. **same** or **Quichés**) **1** a member of a people inhabiting the western highlands of Guatemala.
2 the Mayan language of this people.
▶ **adj.** of or relating to this people or their language.
– ORIGIN the name in Quiché.

Quich·ua /'kiCHwə/ ▶ **n. & adj.** variant spelling of **QUECHUA**.

quick /kwik/ ▶ **adj. 1** moving fast or doing something in a short time: *some children are particularly quick learners* | *I was much quicker than he was and held him at bay for several laps* | [with infinitive] *he was always quick to point out her faults.* ■ lasting or taking a short time: *she took a quick look through the drawers* | *we went to the pub for a quick drink.* ■ happening with little or no delay: prompt: *children like to see quick results from their efforts.*
2 (of a person) prompt to understand, think, or learn; intelligent: *it was quick of him to spot the mistake.* ■ (of a person's eye or ear) keenly perceptive; alert. ■ (of a person's temper) easily roused.
▶ **adv.** informal at a fast rate; quickly: *he'll find some place where he can make money quicker* | [as exclamation] *Get out, quick!*
▶ **n. 1** (**the quick**) the soft, tender flesh below the growing part of a fingernail or toenail. ■ the central or most sensitive part of someone or something.
2 (as plural noun **the quick**) archaic those who are living: *the quick and the dead.*
– PHRASES **cut someone to the quick** cause someone deep distress by a hurtful remark or action. **(as) quick as a flash** see **FLASH**. **quick on the draw** see **DRAW**. **quick with child** archaic at a stage of pregnancy when movements of the fetus have been felt.
– DERIVATIVES **quick·ness n.**
– ORIGIN Old English *cwic, cwicu* 'alive, animated, alert,' of Germanic origin; related to Dutch *kwiek* 'sprightly' and German *keck* 'saucy,' from an Indo-European root shared by Latin *vivus* 'alive' and Greek *bios, zōē* 'life.'

quick-and-dirt·y ▶ **adj.** informal makeshift; done or produced hastily: *a quick-and-dirty synopsis of their work.*

quick·en /'kwikən/ ▶ **v. 1** make or become faster or quicker: [with obj.] *she quickened her pace, desperate to escape* | [no obj.] *I felt my pulse quicken.*
2 [no obj.] spring to life; become animated: *her interest quickened* | (as adj. **quickening**) *he looked with quickening curiosity through the smoke.* ■ [with obj.] stimulate: *the coroner's words suddenly quickened his own memories.* ■ [with obj.] give or restore life to: *on the third day after his death the human body of Jesus was quickened by the Spirit.* ■ archaic (of a woman) reach a stage in pregnancy when movements of the fetus can be felt. ■ archaic (of a fetus) begin to show signs of life. ■ [with obj.] archaic make (a fire) burn brighter.

quick-freeze ▶ **v.** [with obj.] freeze (food) rapidly so as to preserve its nutritional value.

quick·ie /'kwikē/ informal ▶ **n.** a thing done or made quickly or hastily, in particular: ■ a rapidly consumed alcoholic drink. ■ a brief act of sexual intercourse.
▶ **adj.** done or made quickly: *his wife cooperated with a quickie divorce.*

quick·lime /'kwik,līm/ ▶ **n.** see **LIME**[1].

quick·ly /'kwiklē/ ▶ **adv.** at a fast speed; rapidly: *Reg's illness progressed frighteningly quickly.* ■ with little or no delay; promptly: *we moved quickly to deal with our auditor's questions.*

quick march ▶ **n.** a brisk military march. ▶ **exclam.** a command to begin marching quickly.

quick-re·lease ▶ **adj.** (of a device) designed for rapid release: *a quick-release button.*

quick·sand /ˈkwikˌsand/ ▶ **n.** (also **quicksands**) loose wet sand that yields easily to pressure and sucks in anything resting on or falling into it. ■ a bad or dangerous situation from which it is hard to escape: *John found himself sinking fast in financial quicksand.*

quick·set /ˈkwikˌset/ ▶ **n.** Brit. hedging, esp. of hawthorn, grown from slips or cuttings.

quick·sil·ver /ˈkwikˌsilvər/ ▶ **n.** the liquid metal mercury. ■ used in similes and metaphors to describe something that moves or changes very quickly, or that is difficult to hold or contain: *his mood changed like quicksilver.*

quick·step /ˈkwikˌstep/ ▶ **n. 1** a dance similar to a fast foxtrot. ■ a piece of music written for a quickstep.
2 a step used when marching in quick time.
▶ **v.** (**quicksteps, quickstepping, quickstepped**) [no obj.] dance the quickstep.

quick-tem·pered ▶ **adj.** easily made angry.

quick·thorn /ˈkwikˌTHôrn/ ▶ **n.** another term for **HAWTHORN**.

quick time ▶ **n.** Military marching that is conducted at about 120 paces per minute.

quick trick ▶ **n.** (usu. **quick tricks**) Bridge a card such as an ace (or a king in a suit where the ace is also held) that can normally be relied on to win a trick.

quick-wit·ted ▶ **adj.** showing or characterized by an ability to think or respond quickly or effectively.
– DERIVATIVES **quick-wit·ted·ness n.**

quid[1] /kwid/ ▶ **n.** (pl. **same**) Brit. informal one pound sterling: *we paid him four hundred quid.*
– ORIGIN late 17th cent.: of obscure origin.

quid[2] ▶ **n.** a lump of tobacco for chewing.
– ORIGIN early 18th cent.: variant of **CUD**.

quid·di·ty /ˈkwidətē/ ▶ **n.** (pl. **quiddities**) chiefly Philosophy the inherent nature or essence of someone or something. ■ a distinctive feature; a peculiarity: *his quirks and quiddities.*
– ORIGIN late Middle English: from medieval Latin *quidditas*, from Latin *quid* 'what.'

quid·nunc /ˈkwidˌnəNGk/ ▶ **n.** archaic an inquisitive and gossipy person.
– ORIGIN early 18th cent.: from Latin *quid nunc?* 'what now?'

quid pro quo /ˈkwid ˌprō ˈkwō/ ▶ **n.** (pl. **quos**) a favor or advantage granted or expected in return for something: *the pardon was a quid pro quo for their help in releasing hostages.*
– ORIGIN mid 16th cent. (denoting a medicine substituted for another): Latin, 'something for something.'

qui·es·cent /kwēˈesnt, kwī-/ ▶ **adj.** in a state or period of inactivity or dormancy: *strikes were headed by groups of workers who had previously been quiescent* | *quiescent ulcerative colitis.*
– DERIVATIVES **qui·es·cence n., qui·es·cent·ly adv.**
– ORIGIN mid 17th cent.: from Latin *quiescent-* 'being still,' from the verb *quiescere*, from *quies* 'quiet.'

qui·et /ˈkwīət/ ▶ **adj.** (**quieter, quietest**) **1** making little or no noise: *the car has a quiet, economical engine* | *I was as quiet as I could be, but he knew I was there.* ■ (of a place, period of time, or situation) without much activity, disturbance, or excitement: *the street below was quiet, little traffic braving the snow.* ■ without being disturbed or interrupted: *all he wanted was a quiet drink.*
2 carried out discreetly, secretly, or with moderation: *we wanted a quiet wedding* | *I'll have a quiet word with him.* ■ (of a person) tranquil and reserved by nature; not brash or forceful: *his quiet, middle-aged parents.* ■ [attrib.] expressed in a restrained or understated way: *Molly spoke with quiet confidence.* ■ (of a color or garment) unobtrusive; not bright or showy.
▶ **n.** absence of noise or bustle; silence; calm: *the ringing of the telephone shattered the early morning quiet.* ■ freedom from disturbance or interruption by others: *he understood her wish for peace and quiet.* ■ a peaceful or settled state of affairs in social or political life: *after several months of comparative quiet, the scandal reerupted in August.*
▶ **v.** make or become silent, calm, or still: [with obj.] *there are ways of quieting kids down* | [no obj.] *the journalists quieted down as Judy stepped onto the dais.*
– PHRASES **do anything for a quiet life** see **LIFE**. **keep quiet** (or **keep someone quiet**) refrain or prevent someone from speaking or from disclosing something secret. **keep something quiet** (or **keep quiet about something**) refrain from disclosing information about something; keep something secret. **on the quiet** informal without anyone knowing or noticing; secretly or unobtrusively. **(as) quiet as the grave** see **GRAVE**[1]. **(as) quiet as a mouse** (of a person or animal) extremely quiet or docile.
– DERIVATIVES **qui·et·ness n.**
– ORIGIN Middle English (originally as a noun denoting peace as opposed to war): via Old French, based on Latin *quies, quiet-* 'repose, quiet.'

qui·et·en /ˈkwīətn/ ▶ **v.** chiefly Brit. make or become quiet and calm: [with obj.] *her mother was trying to quieten her* | [no obj.] *things seemed to have quietened down.*

qui·et·ism /ˈkwīəˌtizəm/ ▶ **n.** (in the Christian faith) devotional contemplation and abandonment of the will as a form of religious mysticism. ■ calm acceptance of things as they are without attempts to resist or change them: *political quietism.*
– DERIVATIVES **qui·et·ist n. & adj., qui·et·is·tic** /ˌkwīəˈtistik/ **adj.**
– ORIGIN late 17th cent. (denoting the religious mysticism based on the teachings of the Spanish priest Miguel de Molinos (*c.*1640–97)): from Italian *quietismo*, based on Latin *quies, quiet-* 'quiet.'

quietly ▶ **adv.** in a quiet manner: *he worked quietly and diligently* | [as submodifier] *she was quietly confident that they'd win.*

qui·e·tude /ˈkwīəˌt(y)o͞od/ ▶ **n.** a state of stillness, calmness, and quiet in a person or place.
– ORIGIN late 16th cent.: from French *quiétude* or medieval Latin *quietudo*, from Latin *quietus* 'quiet.'

qui·e·tus /ˈkwīətəs/ ▶ **n.** (pl. **quietuses**) death or something that causes death, regarded as a release from life. ■ archaic something that has a calming or soothing effect.
– ORIGIN late Middle English: abbreviation of medieval Latin *quietus est* 'he is quit' (see **QUIT**[1]), originally used as a form of receipt or discharge on payment of a debt.

quiff /kwif/ ▶ **n.** chiefly Brit. a piece of hair, esp. on a man, brushed upward and backward from the forehead.
– ORIGIN late 19th cent. (originally denoting a lock of hair plastered down on the forehead, esp. as worn by soldiers): of unknown origin.

quill /kwil/ ▶ **n. 1** (also **quill feather**) any of the main wing or tail feathers of a bird. ■ the hollow shaft of a feather, esp. the lower part or calamus that lacks barbs. ■ (also **quill pen**) a pen made from a main wing or tail feather of a large bird by pointing and slitting the end of the shaft.
2 an object in the form of a thin tube, in particular: ■ the hollow sharp spines of a porcupine, hedgehog, or other spiny mammal. ■ (**quills**) informal, dated panpipes. ■ a weaver's spindle.
▶ **v.** [with obj.] form (fabric) into small cylindrical folds.
– ORIGIN late Middle English (in the senses 'hollow stem' and 'shaft of a feather'): probably from Middle Low German *quiele*.

quill·ing /ˈkwiliNG/ ▶ **n.** a piece of quilled lace or other fabric used as a trim. ■ a type of ornamental craftwork involving the shaping of paper, fabric, or glass into delicate pleats or folds.

quill·work /ˈkwilˌwərk/ ▶ **n.** a type of decoration for clothing and possessions characteristic of certain North American Indian peoples, using softened and dyed porcupine quills to make elaborate applied designs.

quill·wort /ˈkwilˌwərt, -ˌwôrt/ ▶ **n.** a plant related to the club mosses, having a dense rosette of long slender leaves, the bases of which contain the spore-producing organs, and occurring typically as a submerged aquatic. ● Genus *Isoetes*, family Isoetaceae, class Lycopsida.

quilt /kwilt/ ▶ **n.** a warm bed covering made of padding enclosed between layers of fabric and kept in place by lines of stitching, typically applied in a decorative design. ■ a knitted or fabric bedspread with decorative stitching. ■ a layer of padding used for insulation.
▶ **v.** [with obj.] join together (layers of fabric or padding) with lines of stitching to form a bed covering or a warm garment, or for decorative effect.
– DERIVATIVES **quilt·er n.**
– ORIGIN Middle English: from Old French *cuilte*, from Latin *culcita* 'mattress, cushion.'

quilt·ed /ˈkwiltid/ ▶ **adj.** (of a garment, bed covering, or sleeping bag) made of two layers of cloth filled with padding held in place by lines of stitching: *a blue quilted jacket.*

quilt·ing /ˈkwiltiNG/ ▶ **n.** the making of quilts, esp. as a craft or leisure activity. ■ the work so produced; quilted material. ■ the pattern of stitching used for such work.

quin /kwin/ ▶ **n.** informal, chiefly Brit. short for **QUINTUPLET**.

qui·nac·ri·done /kwəˈnakrəˌdōn/ ▶ **n.** Chemistry any of a group of synthetic organic compounds whose molecules contain three benzene and two pyridine rings arranged alternately. They include a number of red to violet pigments.
– ORIGIN early 20th cent.: from *quin(oline)* + *acrid(ine)* + **-ONE**.

quin·a·crine /ˈkwinəˌkrin/ ▶ **n.** Medicine a synthetic compound derived from acridine, used as an anthelmintic and antimalarial drug. ■ (in full **quinacrine mustard**) Biochemistry a nitrogen mustard derived from this, used as a fluorescent stain for chromosomes.
– ORIGIN 1930s: blend of **QUININE** and **ACRIDINE**.

qui·na·ry /ˈkwīˌnerē/ ▶ **adj.** of or relating to the number five, in particular: ■ of the fifth order or rank. ■ Zoology, historical relating to or denoting a former system of classification in which the animal kingdom is divided into five subkingdoms, and each subkingdom into five classes.
– ORIGIN early 17th cent.: from Latin *quinarius*, from *quini* 'five at once, a set of five,' from *quinque* 'five.'

quince /kwins/ ▶ **n. 1** a hard, acid, pear-shaped fruit used in preserves or as flavoring.
2 the shrub or small tree that bears this fruit, native to western Asia. ● *Cydonia oblonga*, family Rosaceae. ■ (**Japanese quince**) another term for **JAPONICA**.
– ORIGIN Middle English (originally a collective plural): from Old French *cooin*, from Latin *malum) cotoneum*, variant of ((*malum*) *cydonium* 'apple of *Cydonia* (= Chania, in Crete).'

quin·cen·ten·ar·y /ˌkwinsenˈtenərē, kwinˈsentəˌnerē/ ▶ **n. & adj.** another term for **QUINCENTENNIAL**.

quin·cen·ten·ni·al /ˌkwinsenˈtenēəl/ ▶ **n.** the five-hundredth anniversary of a significant event.
– ORIGIN late 19th cent.: from Latin *quinque* 'five' + **CENTENNIAL**.

Quin·cey, Thomas De, see **DE QUINCEY**.

quin·cunx /ˈkwinˌkəNGks/ ▶ **n.** (pl. **quincunxes**)
1 an arrangement of five objects with four at the corners of a square or rectangle and the fifth at its center, used for the five on dice or playing cards, and in planting trees.
2 Astrology an aspect of 150°, equivalent to five zodiacal signs.

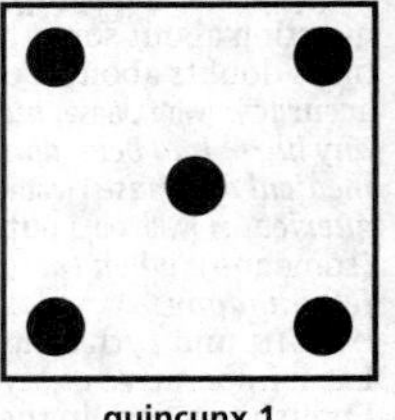

quincunx 1

– DERIVATIVES
quin·cun·cial /ˌkwinˈkənSHəl/ **adj., quin·cun·cial·ly** /ˌkwinˈkənSHəlē/ **adv.**
– ORIGIN mid 17th cent.: from Latin, literally 'five twelfths,' from *quinque* 'five' + *uncia* 'twelfth.'

Quin·cy /ˈkwinˌzē, -sē/ a historic industrial city in eastern Massachusetts, on Boston Harbor, southeast of Boston, a shipbuilding center; pop. 92,339 (est. 2008).

Quine /kwīn/, Willard Van Orman (1908–2000), US philosopher and logician. A radical critic of modern empiricism, he took issue with the philosophy of language proposed by Rudolf Carnap, arguing that "no statement is immune from revision" and that even the principles of logic themselves can be questioned and replaced.

qui·nel·la /kwiˈnelə/ (also **quiniela** /kēnˈyelə/) ▶ **n.** a bet in which the first two places in a race must be predicted, but not necessarily in the correct order. Compare with **EXACTA**.
– ORIGIN 1940s: from Latin American Spanish *quiniela*.

quin·i·dine /ˈkwinəˌdēn/ ▶ **n.** Medicine a compound obtained from cinchona bark and used to treat irregularities of heart rhythm. It is an isomer of quinine.
– ORIGIN mid 19th cent.: from Spanish *quina* 'cinchona bark' (from Quechua *kina* 'bark') + **-IDE** + **-INE**[4].

qui·nine /ˈkwīˌnīn/ ▶ **n.** a bitter crystalline compound present in cinchona bark, used as a tonic and formerly as an antimalarial drug. ● An alkaloid; chem. formula: $C_{20}H_{24}N_2O_2$.
– ORIGIN early 19th cent.: from Spanish *quina* 'cinchona bark' (from Quechua *kina* 'bark') + **-INE**[4].

qui·noa /ˈkēnwä/ ▶ **n.** a goosefoot found in the Andes, where it was widely cultivated for its edible starchy seeds before the introduction of Old World grains. ● *Chenopodium quinoa*, family Chenopodiaceae. ■ the grainlike seeds of this plant, used as food and in the production of alcoholic drinks.
– ORIGIN early 17th cent.: Spanish spelling of Quechua *kinua, kinoa*.

quin·o·line /ˈkwinəlin/ ▶ n. Chemistry a pungent oily liquid present in coal tar and bone oil. ● A heteroaromatic compound with fused benzene and pyridine rings; chem. formula: C_9H_7N.
– ORIGIN mid 19th cent.: from Spanish *quina* (see QUININE) + -OL + -INE[4].

quin·o·lone /ˈkwinəˌlōn, ˈkwinlˌōn/ ▶ n. any of a class of antibiotics used in treating a variety of mainly Gram-negative infections, and thought to be responsible for antibiotic resistance in some microbes.

qui·none /ˈkwinōn/ ▶ n. Chemistry another term for 1,4-benzoquinone (see BENZOQUINONE). ■ any compound with the same ring structure as 1,4-benzoquinone.
– ORIGIN mid 19th cent.: from Spanish *quina* (see QUININE) + -ONE.

Quin·qua·ges·i·ma /ˌkwiNGkwəˈjesəmə/ (also **Quinquagesima Sunday**) ▶ n. the Sunday before the beginning of Lent.
– ORIGIN medieval Latin, feminine of Latin *quinquagesimus* 'fiftieth,' on the pattern of *Quadragesima* (because it is fifty days before Easter).

quinque- ▶ comb. form five; having five: *quinquevalent*.
– ORIGIN from Latin *quinque* 'five.'

quin·quen·ni·al /kwiNGˈkwenēəl/ ▶ adj. recurring every five years. ■ lasting for or relating to a period of five years.
– DERIVATIVES **quin·quen·ni·al·ly** adv.
– ORIGIN late 15th cent. (in the sense 'lasting five years'): from Latin *quinquennis* (from *quinque* 'five' + *annus* 'year') + -AL.

quin·quen·ni·um /kwiNGˈkwenēəm/ ▶ n. (pl. **quinquennia** /-ˈkwenēə/ or **quinquenniums**) a specified period of five years.
– ORIGIN early 17th cent.: from Latin, from *quinque* 'five' + *annus* 'year.'

quin·que·va·lent /ˌkwiNGkwəˈvālənt/ ▶ adj. Chemistry another term for PENTAVALENT.

quin·sy /ˈkwinzē/ ▶ n. inflammation of the throat, esp. an abscess in the region of the tonsils.
– ORIGIN Middle English: from Old French *quinencie*, from medieval Latin *quinancia*, from Greek *kunankhē* 'canine quinsy,' from *kun-* 'dog' + *ankhein* 'throttle.'

quint /kwint/ ▶ n. **1** (in piquet) a sequence of five cards of the same suit. A run of ace, king, queen, jack, and ten is a **quint major** and one of jack, ten, nine, eight, and seven a **quint minor**. [late 17th cent.: from French, from Latin *quintus* 'fifth,' from *quinque* 'five.'] **2** short for QUINTUPLET.

quin·ta /ˈkwintə/ ▶ n. (in Spain, Portugal, and Latin America) a large house in the country or on the outskirts of a town. ■ a country estate, in particular a wine-growing estate in Portugal.
– ORIGIN Spanish and Portuguese, from *quinta parte* 'fifth part' (originally referring to the amount of a farm's produce paid in rent).

quin·tain /ˈkwintn/ ▶ n. historical a post set up as a mark in tilting with a lance, typically with a sandbag attached that would swing around and strike an unsuccessful tilter. ■ (**the quintain**) the medieval military exercise of tilting at such a post.
– ORIGIN late Middle English: from Old French *quintaine*, perhaps based on Latin *quintana*, a street in a Roman camp separating the fifth and sixth maniples, where military exercises were performed (from *quintus* 'fifth').

quin·tal /ˈkwintl/ ▶ n. a unit of weight equal to a hundredweight (112 lb) or formerly, 100 lb. ■ a unit of weight equal to 100 kg.
– ORIGIN late Middle English: via Old French from medieval Latin *quintale*, from Arabic *ḳinṭār*, based on Latin *centenarius* 'containing a hundred.'

Quin·ta·na Roo /kēnˈtänä ˈrōō/ a state in southeastern Mexico, on the Yucatán Peninsula.

quinte /kant/ ▶ n. Fencing the fifth of eight standard parrying positions.
– ORIGIN early 18th cent.: French, from Latin *quintus* 'fifth,' from *quinque* 'five.'

Quin·ter·o /kwinˈte(ə)rō, kēn-/, Jose (1924–99), US theatrical director; born in Panama. He was noted for directing plays by Eugene O'Neill and for founding Circle in the Square, a theater in New York City's Greenwich Village. He directed many Broadway plays, including *Long Day's Journey into Night* (1956), *Strange Interlude* (1963), and *A Moon for the Misbegotten* (1973).

quin·tes·sence /kwinˈtesəns/ ▶ n. the most perfect or typical example of a quality or class: *he was the quintessence of political professionalism.* ■ the aspect of something regarded as the intrinsic and central constituent of its character: *we were all brought up to believe that advertising is the quintessence of marketing.* ■ a refined essence or extract of a substance. ■ (in classical and medieval philosophy) a fifth substance in addition to the four elements, thought to compose the heavenly bodies and to be latent in all things.
– ORIGIN late Middle English (as a term in philosophy): via French from medieval Latin *quinta essentia* 'fifth essence.'

quin·tes·sen·tial /ˌkwintəˈsenCHəl/ ▶ adj. representing the most perfect or typical example of a quality or class: *he was the quintessential tough guy—strong, silent, and self-contained.*
– DERIVATIVES **quin·tes·sen·tial·ly** adv.

quin·tet /kwinˈtet/ ▶ n. a group of five people playing music or singing together. ■ a musical composition for such a group. ■ any group of five people or things: *a novel about a quintet of interrelated lovers.*
– ORIGIN late 18th cent.: from French *quintette* or Italian *quintetto*, from *quinto* 'fifth,' from Latin *quintus*.

quin·tile /ˈkwinˌtīl/ ▶ n. **1** Statistics any of five equal groups into which a population can be divided according to the distribution of values of a particular variable. ■ each of the four values of the random variable that divide a population into five such groups.
2 Astrology an aspect of 72° (one fifth of a circle).
– ORIGIN early 17th cent.: from Latin *quintilis* (*mensis*) 'fifth month, July,' from *quintus* 'fifth.'

Quin·til·ian /kwinˈtilēən/ (c. AD 35–c.96), Roman rhetorician; Latin name *Marcus Fabius Quintilianus*. He is noted for his *Education of an Orator*, a comprehensive treatment of the art of rhetoric and the training of an orator.

quin·til·lion /kwinˈtilyən/ ▶ cardinal number (pl. **quintillions** or (with numeral) **same**) a thousand raised to the power of six (10^{18}). ■ dated, chiefly Brit. a million raised to the power of five (10^{30}).
– DERIVATIVES **quin·til·lionth** /-yənTH/ ordinal number.
– ORIGIN late 17th cent.: from French, from *million*, by substitution of the prefix *quinti-* 'five' (from Latin *quintus* 'fifth') for the initial letters.

quin·tu·ple /kwinˈt(y)ōōpəl, -ˈtəpəl/ ▶ adj. [attrib.] consisting of five parts or things. ■ five times as much or as many. ■ (of time in music) having five beats in a bar.
▶ v. increase or cause to increase fivefold.
▶ n. a fivefold number or amount; a set of five.
– DERIVATIVES **quin·tu·ply** /-(ə)lē/ adv.
– ORIGIN late 16th cent.: via French from medieval Latin *quintuplus*, from Latin *quintus* 'fifth' + *-plus* as in *duplus* (see DUPLE).

quin·tu·plet /kwinˈtəplət, -ˈt(y)ōōplət/ ▶ n. **1** (usu. **quintuplets**) each of five children born to the same mother at one birth.
2 Music a group of five notes to be performed in the time of three or four.
– ORIGIN late 19th cent.: from QUINTUPLE, on the pattern of words such as *triplet*.

quin·tu·pli·cate ▶ adj. /kwinˈt(y)ōōpləˌkit/ fivefold. ■ of which five copies are made.
▶ v. /kwinˈt(y)ōōpləˌkāt/ [with obj.] multiply by five.
– PHRASES **in quintuplicate** in five identical copies. ■ in groups of five.
– ORIGIN mid 17th cent.: from QUINTUPLE, on the pattern of words such as *quadruplicate*.

quip /kwip/ ▶ n. a witty remark. ■ archaic a verbal equivocation.
▶ v. (**quips, quipping, quipped**) [no obj.] make a witty remark: [with direct speech] *"Flattery will get you nowhere," she quipped.*
– DERIVATIVES **quip·ster** /-stər/ n.
– ORIGIN mid 16th cent.: perhaps from Latin *quippe* 'indeed, forsooth.'

qui·pu /ˈkēpōō, ˈkwipōō/ ▶ n. an ancient Inca device for recording information, consisting of variously colored threads knotted in different ways.
– ORIGIN from Quechua *khipu* 'knot.'

quire /kwīr/ ▶ n. four sheets of paper or parchment folded to form eight leaves, as in medieval manuscripts. ■ any collection of leaves one within another in a manuscript or book. ■ 25 (formerly 24) sheets of paper; one twentieth of a ream.
– ORIGIN Middle English: from Old French *quaier*, from Latin *quaterni* 'set of four.'

quirk /kwərk/ ▶ n. **1** a peculiar behavioral habit: *his distaste for travel is an endearing quirk.* ■ a strange chance occurrence: *a strange quirk of fate had led her to working for Nathan.* ■ a sudden twist, turn, or curve: *wry humor put a slight quirk in his mouth.*
2 Architecture an acute hollow between convex or other moldings.
▶ v. (with reference to a person's mouth or eyebrow) move or twist suddenly, esp. to express surprise or amusement.
– DERIVATIVES **quirk·ish** adj.
– ORIGIN early 16th cent. (as a verb): of unknown origin. The early sense of the noun was 'subtle verbal twist, quibble,' later 'unexpected twist.'

quirk·y /ˈkwərkē/ ▶ adj. (**quirkier, quirkiest**) characterized by peculiar or unexpected traits: *her sense of humor was decidedly quirky.*
– DERIVATIVES **quirk·i·ly** /-kəlē/ adv., **quirk·i·ness** /-kēnis/ n.

quirt /kwərt/ ▶ n. a short-handled riding whip with a braided leather lash.
▶ v. [with obj.] hit with a whip of this kind.
– ORIGIN mid 19th cent. (originally US): from Spanish *cuerda* 'cord' (from Latin *chorda* 'cord') or from Mexican Spanish *cuarta* 'whip.'

quis·ling /ˈkwizliNG/ ▶ n. a traitor who collaborates with an enemy force occupying their country.
– ORIGIN World War II: from the name of Major Vidkun *Quisling* (1887–1945), the Norwegian army officer and diplomat who ruled Norway on behalf of the German occupying forces 1940–45.

quit[1] /kwit/ ▶ v. (**quits, quitting**; past and past participle **quitted** or **quit**) **1** [with obj.] leave (a place), usually permanently: *he was ordered to quit the cabin immediately.* ■ informal resign from (a job): *she quit her job in a pizza restaurant* | [no obj.] *he quit as manager of struggling Third Division City.* ■ informal stop or discontinue (an action or activity): *quit moaning!* | *I want to quit smoking.*
2 (**quit oneself**) [with adverbial] archaic behave in a specified way: *quit yourselves like men, and fight.*
▶ adj. [predic.] (**quit of**) rid of: *I want to be quit of him.*
– PHRASES **quit hold of** archaic let go of.
– ORIGIN Middle English (in the sense 'set free'): from Old French *quiter* (verb), *quite* (adjective), from Latin *quietus*, past participle of *quiescere* 'be still,' from *quies* 'quiet.'

quit[2] ▶ n. [in combination] used in names of various small songbirds found in the Caribbean area, e.g., **bananaquit, grassquit**.
– ORIGIN mid 19th cent.: probably imitative.

quitch /kwiCH/ (also **quitch grass**) ▶ n. another term for COUCH GRASS.
– ORIGIN Old English *cwice*, of uncertain origin; perhaps related to QUICK (with reference to its vigorous growth).

quit·claim /ˈkwitˌklām/ ▶ n. Law a formal renunciation or relinquishing of a claim.
▶ v. [with obj.] renounce or relinquish a claim: *Aikins quitclaimed his interest in the three parcels of real estate.*

quite /kwīt/ ▶ adv. [usu. as submodifier] **1** to the utmost or most absolute extent or degree; absolutely; completely: *it's quite out of the question* | *are you quite certain about this?* | *this is quite a different problem* | *I quite agree* | *quite frankly, I don't blame you.* ■ very; really (used as an intensifier): *"You've no intention of coming back?" "I'm quite sorry, but no, I have not."*
2 to a certain or fairly significant extent or degree; fairly: *it's quite warm outside* | *I was quite embarrassed, actually* | *she did quite well at school* | *he's quite an attractive man.*
▶ exclam. (also **quite so**) Brit. expressing agreement with or understanding of a remark or statement: *"I don't want to talk about that now." "Quite."*
– PHRASES **not quite** not completely or entirely: *my hair's not quite dry* | *she hasn't quite got the hang of it yet.* **quite a ——** (also often ironic **quite the ——**) used to indicate that the specified person or thing is perceived as particularly notable, remarkable, or impressive: *quite a party, isn't it?* | *it's been quite a year* | *quite the little horsewoman, aren't you?* **quite a few** see FEW. **quite a lot** (or **a bit**) a considerable number or amount of something: *my job involves quite a lot of travel* | *he's quite a bit older than she is.* **quite some 1** a considerable amount of: *she hasn't been seen for quite some time.* **2** informal way of saying QUITE A ——. **quite something** see SOMETHING. **quite the thing** dated socially acceptable: *she was quite the thing in heels and stockings and lipstick.*
– ORIGIN Middle English: from the obsolete adjective *quite*, variant of QUIT[1].

Qui·to /ˈkētō/ the capital of Ecuador; pop. 1,579,200 (est. 2008). It is situated in the Andes just south of the equator, at an altitude of 9,350 feet (2,850 m).

quit-rent /ˈkwitˌrent/ ▶ n. historical a rent, typically a small one, paid by a freeholder or copyholder in lieu of services that might be required of them.

quits /kwits/ ▶ adj. [predic.] (of two people) on even terms, esp. because a debt or score has been settled: *I think we're just about quits now, don't you?*
– PHRASES **call it quits** agree or acknowledge that terms are now equal, esp. on the settlement of a

debt: *take this check and we'll call it quits.* ■ decide to abandon an activity or venture: *surely, after covering eleven wars, he could be forgiven for calling it quits?*
– ORIGIN late 15th cent. (in the sense 'freed from a liability or debt'): perhaps a colloquial abbreviation of medieval Latin *quittus*, from Latin *quietus*, used as a receipt (see QUIETUS).

quit·tance /ˈkwitns/ ▶ **n.** archaic, literary a release or discharge from a debt or obligation. ■ a document certifying this; a receipt.
– ORIGIN Middle English: from Old French *quitance*, from *quiter* 'to release' (see QUIT[1]).

quit·ter /ˈkwitər/ ▶ **n.** [usu. with negative] informal a person who gives up easily or does not have the courage or determination to finish a task.

quiv·er[1] /ˈkwivər/ ▶ **v.** [no obj.] tremble or shake with a slight rapid motion: *the tree's branches stopped quivering.* ■ [with obj.] cause (something) to make a slight rapid motion: *the bird runs along in a zigzag path, quivering its wings.*
▶ **n.** a slight trembling movement or sound, esp. one caused by a sudden strong emotion: *Meredith felt a quiver of fear.*
– DERIVATIVES **quiv·er·ing·ly** adv., **quiv·er·y** adj.
– ORIGIN Middle English: from Old English *cwifer* 'nimble, quick' The initial *qu-* is probably symbolic of quick movement (as in *quaver* and *quick*).

quiv·er[2] ▶ **n.** an archer's portable case for holding arrows. ■ a set of surfboards of different lengths and shapes for use with different types of waves.
– PHRASES **an arrow in the quiver** one of a number of resources or strategies that can be drawn on or followed.

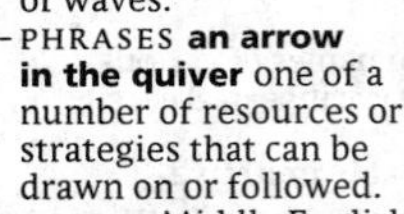
archer's quiver

– ORIGIN Middle English: from Anglo-Norman French *quiveir*, of West Germanic origin; related to Dutch *koker* and German *Köcher*.

quiv·er tree ▶ **n.** a tropical aloe that forms a tree, the hollow branches of which were formerly used by the San (Bushmen) as quivers. ● *Aloe dichotoma*, family Liliaceae (or Aloaceae).

qui vive /ˌkē ˈvēv/ ▶ **n.** (in phrase **on the qui vive**) on the alert or lookout: *duty requires the earnest liberal to spend most of his time on the qui vive for fascism.*
– ORIGIN late 16th cent.: from French, literally '(long) live who?,' i.e., 'on whose side are you?,' used as a sentry's challenge.

Qui·xo·te /kēˈhōtē/ see DON QUIXOTE.

quix·ot·ic /kwikˈsätik/ ▶ **adj.** exceedingly idealistic; unrealistic and impractical: *a vast and perhaps quixotic project.*
– DERIVATIVES **quix·ot·i·cal·ly** /-ik(ə)lē/ adv., **quix·o·tism** /ˈkwiksəˌtizəm/ n., **quix·o·try** /ˈkwiksətrē/ n.
– ORIGIN late 18th cent.: from DON QUIXOTE + -IC.

quiz[1] /kwiz/ ▶ **n.** (pl. **quizzes**) a test of knowledge, esp. a brief, informal test given to students.
▶ **v.** (**quizzes, quizzed, quizzing**) [with obj.] ask (someone) questions: *four men have been quizzed about the murder.* ■ give (a student or class) an informal test or examination.
– ORIGIN mid 19th cent. (as a verb; originally US): possibly from QUIZ[2], influenced by INQUISITIVE.

quiz[2] archaic ▶ **v.** (**quizzes, quizzed, quizzing**) [with obj.] **1** look curiously or intently at (someone) through or as if through an eyeglass: *deep-set eyes quizzed her in the candlelight.*
2 make fun of: *he says there's a great deal of poetry in brewing beer, but of course he's only quizzing us.*
▶ **n.** (pl. **quizzes**) **1** a practical joke or hoax; a piece of banter or ridicule: *I am impatient to know if the whole be not one grand quiz.* ■ a person who ridicules another; a hoaxer or practical joker: *braving the ridicule with which it pleased the quizzes to asperse the husband chosen for her.*
2 a person who is odd or eccentric in character or appearance: *she means to marry that quiz for the sake of his thousands.*
– DERIVATIVES **quiz·zer** n.
– ORIGIN late 18th cent.: sometimes said to have been invented by a Dublin theater proprietor who, having made a bet that a nonsense word could be made known within 48 hours throughout the city, and that the public would give it a meaning, had the word written up on walls all over the city. There is no evidence to support this theory.

quiz·mas·ter /ˈkwizˌmastər/ ▶ **n.** a person who asks the questions and enforces the rules in a television or radio quiz program.

quiz show ▶ **n.** a television or radio light entertainment program in which people compete in a quiz, typically for prizes.

quiz·zi·cal /ˈkwizəkəl/ ▶ **adj.** (of a person's expression or behavior) indicating mild or amused puzzlement: *she gave me a quizzical look.* ■ rare causing mild amusement because of its oddness or strangeness.
– DERIVATIVES **quiz·zi·cal·i·ty** /ˌkwiziˈkalətē/ n., **quiz·zi·cal·ly** adv., **quiz·zi·cal·ness** n.

Qum /ko͝om/ variant spelling of QOM.

Qum·ran /ko͝omˈrän/ a region on the western shore of the Dead Sea. The Dead Sea scrolls were found 1947–56 in caves at nearby Khirbet Qumran, the site of an ancient Jewish settlement.

quod /kwäd/ ▶ **n.** Brit. informal, dated prison: *ten years in quod.*
– ORIGIN late 17th cent.: of unknown origin.

quod e·rat de·mon·stran·dum /kwäd ˈerət ˌdemənˈsträndəm/ (abbr.: **QED**) ▶ **n.** used to convey that a fact or situation demonstrates the truth of one's theory or claim, esp. to mark the conclusion of a formal proof.
– ORIGIN Latin, literally 'which was to be demonstrated.'

quod·li·bet /ˈkwädləˌbet/ ▶ **n. 1** archaic a topic for or exercise in philosophical or theological discussion.
2 literary a lighthearted medley of well-known tunes.
– DERIVATIVES **quod·li·be·tar·i·an** /ˌkwädləbiˈte(ə)rēən/ n.
– ORIGIN late Middle English: from Latin, from *quod* 'what' + *libet* 'it pleases.'

quoin /k(w)oin/ ▶ **n. 1** an external angle of a wall or building. ■ (also **quoin stone**) any of the stones or bricks forming such an angle; a cornerstone.
2 Printing a wedge or expanding mechanical device used for locking a letterpress form into a chase.
3 a wedge for raising the level of a gun barrel or for keeping it from rolling.
▶ **v.** [with obj.] **1** provide (a wall) with quoins or corners.
2 Printing lock up (a form) with a quoin.
– ORIGIN Middle English: variant of COIN, used earlier in the sense 'cornerstone' and 'wedge.'

quoin·ing /ˈk(w)oiniNG/ ▶ **n.** the stone or brick used to form a quoin of a wall or building.

quoit /k(w)oit/ ▶ **n. 1** a ring of iron, rope, or rubber thrown in a game to encircle or land as near as possible to an upright peg. ■ (**quoits**) [treated as sing.] a game consisting of aiming and throwing such rings.
2 the flat covering stone of a dolmen. ■ (often in place names) the dolmen itself.
▶ **v.** [with obj.] archaic throw or propel like a quoit.
– ORIGIN late Middle English: probably of French origin.

quok·ka /ˈkwäkə/ ▶ **n.** a small, short-tailed wallaby with a short face, round ears on top of the head, and some tree-climbing ability, native to Western Australia. ● *Setonix brachyurus*, family Macropodidae.
– ORIGIN mid 19th cent.: from Nyungar *kwaka*.

quoll /kwäl/ ▶ **n.** a catlike, carnivorous marsupial with short legs and a white-spotted coat, native to the forests of Australia and New Guinea. Also called DASYURE. ● Genus *Dasyurus*, family Dasyuridae: several species.
– ORIGIN late 18th cent.: from Guugu Yimidhirr (an Aboriginal language) *dhigul*.

quon·dam /ˈkwändəm, -ˌdam/ ▶ **adj.** [attrib.] formal that once was; former: *quondam dissidents joined the establishment* | *its quondam popularity.*
– ORIGIN late 16th cent.: from Latin, 'formerly.'

Quon·set /ˈkwänsət/ (usu. **Quonset hut**) ▶ **n.** trademark a building made of corrugated metal and having a semicircular cross section.
– ORIGIN World War II: named after *Quonset* Point, Rhode Island, where such huts were first made.

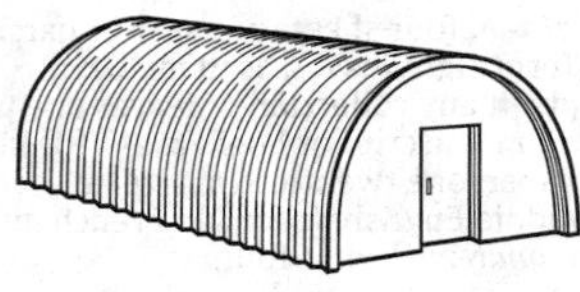
Quonset hut

quo·rum /ˈkwôrəm/ ▶ **n.** (pl. **quorums**) the minimum number of members of an assembly or society that must be present at any of its meetings to make the proceedings of that meeting valid.
– ORIGIN late Middle English (referring to justices of the peace): used in commissions for committee members designated by the Latin *quorum vos ... unum* (*duos*, etc.) *esse volumus* 'of whom we wish that you ... be one (two, etc.).'

quot. ▶ **abbr.** quotation.

quo·ta /ˈkwōtə/ ▶ **n.** a limited or fixed number or amount of people or things, in particular: ■ a limited quantity of a particular product that under official controls can be produced, exported, or imported: *the country may be exceeding its OPEC quota of 1,100,000 barrels of oil per day.* ■ a fixed share of something that a person or group is entitled to receive or is bound to contribute: *the Faeroe Islands' commercial salmon quota.* ■ a person's share of something that must be done: *they were arrested to help fill the quota of arrests the security police had to make during the crackdown.* ■ a fixed minimum or maximum number of a particular group of people allowed to do something, as immigrants to enter a country, workers to undertake a job, or students to enroll for a course: *they demanded a quota for women on the committee.* ■ (in a system of proportional representation) the minimum number of votes required to elect a candidate. ■ a person's share of a particular thing, quality, or attribute: *an Irishman with a double ration of blarney and a treble quota of charm.*
– ORIGIN early 17th cent.: from medieval Latin *quota* (*pars*) 'how great (a part),' feminine of *quotus*, from *quot* 'how many.'

quot·a·ble /ˈkwōtəbəl/ ▶ **adj.** (of a person or remark) suitable for or worth quoting.
– DERIVATIVES **quot·a·bil·i·ty** /ˌkwōtəˈbilətē/ n.

quo·ta·tion /ˌkwōˈtāSHən/ ▶ **n. 1** a group of words taken from a text or speech and repeated by someone other than the original author or speaker: *a quotation from Mark Twain* | *biblical quotations.* ■ a short musical passage or visual image taken from one piece of music or work of art and used in another. ■ the action of quoting from a text, speech, piece of music, or work of art: *a great argument with much quotation of Darwin.*
2 a formal statement setting out the estimated cost for a particular job or service: *you will be sent a written quotation for the cost of repairing your machine.* ■ Stock Market a price offered by a broker for the sale or purchase of a stock or other security. ■ Stock Market a registration granted to a company enabling their shares to be officially listed and traded.
– ORIGIN mid 16th cent. (denoting a marginal reference to a passage of text): from medieval Latin *quotatio(n-)*, from the verb *quotare* (see QUOTE).

quo·ta·tion mark ▶ **n.** each of a set of punctuation marks, single (' ') or double (" "), used either to mark the beginning and end of a title or quoted passage or to indicate that a word or phrase is regarded as slang or jargon or is being discussed rather than used within the sentence.

quote /kwōt/ ▶ **v.** [with obj.] **1** repeat or copy out (a group of words from a text or speech), typically with an indication that one is not the original author or speaker: *he quoted a passage **from** the Psalms* | [with direct speech] *"The stream mysterious glides beneath," Melinda quoted* | [no obj.] *when we told her this she said, and I quote, "Phooey!"* ■ repeat a passage from (a work or author) or statement by (someone): *the prime minister was **quoted as saying** that he would resist all attempts to "sabotage" his government* | *he quoted Shakespeare, Goethe, and other poets.* ■ mention or refer to (someone or something) to provide evidence or authority for a statement, argument, or opinion: *they won't be here at all in three years time—**you can quote me on that**.* ■ (**quote someone/something as**) put forward or describe someone or something as being: *heavy teaching loads are often quoted as a bad influence on research.*
2 give someone (the estimated price of a job or service): [with two objs.] *the agent quoted a fare of $180.* ■ Stock Market give (a company) a quotation or listing on a stock exchange: *an organization that is **quoted on the Stock Exchange**.*
▶ **n. 1** a quotation from a text or speech: *a quote from Wordsworth.*
2 a quotation giving the estimated cost for a particular job or service: *quotes from different insurance companies.* ■ Stock Market a price offered by a broker for the sale or purchase of a stock or other security. ■ Stock Market a quotation or listing of a company on a stock exchange.
3 (**quotes**) quotation marks: *use double quotes around precise phrases you wish to search for.*
– PHRASES **quote —— unquote** (also **quote, unquote**) informal used parenthetically when speaking to suggest quotation marks, to indicate the beginning and end of a statement or passage that one is reciting or repeating: *the brochure describes the view as, quote, unquote, unforgettably breathtaking.*
– ORIGIN late Middle English: from medieval Latin *quotare*, from *quot* 'how many,' or from medieval Latin *quota* (see QUOTA). The original sense was 'mark a book with numbers, or with marginal

references,' later 'give a reference by page or chapter,' hence 'cite a text or person' (late 16th cent).

quoth /kwōTH/ ▶ **v.** [with direct speech] archaic or humorous said (used only in first and third person singular before the subject): *"Well, the tide is going out" quoth the sailor.*
– ORIGIN Middle English: past tense of obsolete *quethe* 'say, declare,' of Germanic origin.

quo·tid·i·an /kwō'tidēən/ ▶ **adj.** [attrib.] of or occurring every day; daily: *the car sped noisily off through the quotidian traffic.* ■ ordinary or everyday, esp. when mundane: *his story is an achingly human one, mired in quotidian details.* ■ Medicine denoting the malignant form of malaria.
– ORIGIN Middle English: via Old French from Latin *quotidianus*, earlier *cotidianus*, from *cotidie* 'daily.'

quo·tient /'kwōSHənt/ ▶ **n. 1** Mathematics a result obtained by dividing one quantity by another. **2** [usu. with adj.] a degree or amount of a specified quality or characteristic: *the increase in Washington's cynicism quotient.*
– ORIGIN late Middle English: from Latin *quotiens* 'how many times' (from *quot* 'how many'), by confusion with participial forms ending in *-ens*, *-ent-*.

quo war·ran·to /ˌkwō wə'ränˌtō, -'ran-/ ▶ **n.** [usu. as modifier] Law a writ or legal action requiring a person to show by what warrant an office or franchise is held, claimed, or exercised.
– ORIGIN Law Latin, literally 'by what warrant.'

Qu·r'an /kə'rän, -'ran/ (also **Quran**) ▶ **n.** Arabic spelling of **Koran**.

qursh /kərSH/ ▶ **n.** (pl. **same**) a monetary unit of Saudi Arabia, equal to one twentieth of a riyal.
– ORIGIN from Arabic *ḳirsh*, from Slavic *grossus*.

q.v. ▶ **abbr.** used to direct a reader to another part of a book or article for further information.
– ORIGIN from Latin *quod vide*, literally 'which see.'

QWERTY /'kwərtē/ ▶ **adj.** denoting the standard layout on English-language typewriters and keyboards, having *q, w, e, r, t,* and *y* as the first keys from the left on the top row of letters.

q

PRONUNCIATION KEY ə *ago, up*; ər *over, fur*; a *hat*; ā *ate*; ä *car*; e *let*; ē *see*; i *fit*; ī *by*; NG *sing*; ō *go*; ô *law, for*; oi *toy*; o͝o *good*; o͞o *goo*; ou *out*; TH *thin*; T͟H *then*; ZH *vision*

Rr

R[1] /är/ (also **r**) ▶ **n.** (pl. **Rs** or **R's**) the eighteenth letter of the alphabet. ■ denoting the next after Q in a set of items, categories, etc.
– PHRASES **the R months** the months with R in their names (September to April), considered to be the season for eating oysters. **the three Rs** reading, writing, and arithmetic, regarded as the fundamentals of learning.

R[2] ▶ **abbr.** ■ rand: *a farm worth nearly R1,3-million.* ■ Réaumur: *198.6 °R.* ■ Regina or Rex: *Elizabeth R.* ■ (also ®) registered as a trademark. ■ (in the US) Republican: *congressman Henry Hyde (R-Illinois).* ■ restricted, a rating in the Voluntary Movie Rating System that children under 17 require an accompanying parent or adult guardian for admission. ■ (on a gearshift) reverse. ■ (**R.**) River (chiefly on maps): *R. Cherwell.* ■ roentgen(s). ■ rook (in recording moves in chess): *21.Rh4.* ▶ **symbol** ■ Chemistry an unspecified alkyl or other organic radical or group. [abbreviation of RADICAL.] ■ electrical resistance. ■ Chemistry the gas constant.

r ▶ **abbr.** ■ recto. ■ (giving position or direction) right: *l to r: Evan, Nick, and David.* ■ Law rule: *under r 7.4 (6) the court may hear an application immediately.* ▶ **symbol** ■ radius: *2πr.* ■ Statistics correlation coefficient: *sigmoidoscopic and symptom scores also showed a significant correlation with each other (r = 0.91).*

RA ▶ **abbr.** ■ regular army. ■ Astronomy right ascension.

Ra[1] /rä/ (also **Re**) Egyptian Mythology the sun god, the supreme Egyptian deity, worshiped as the creator of all life and typically with a falcon's head bearing the solar disc. From earliest times he was associated with the pharaoh.

Ra[2] ▶ **symbol** the chemical element radium.

Ra. ▶ **abbr.** range.

RAAF ▶ **abbr.** Royal Australian Air Force.

Ra·bat /rəˈbät/ the capital of Morocco, an industrial port on the Atlantic coast; pop. 1,787,300 (est. 2009). It was founded as a military fort in the 12th century by the Almohads.

Ra·baul /räˈboul/ the chief town and port on the island of New Britain in Papua New Guinea; pop. 7,000 (est. 2009).

rab·bet /ˈrabit/ ▶ **n.** a step-shaped recess cut along the edge or in the face of a piece of wood, typically forming a match to the edge or tongue of another piece: [as modifier] *a rabbet joint.*
▶ **v.** (**rabbets, rabbeting, rabbeted**) [with obj.] make a rabbet in (a piece of wood). ■ [with obj.] join or fix (a piece of wood) to another with a rabbet.
– ORIGIN late Middle English: from Old French *rabbat* 'abatement, recess.'

rab·bet plane ▶ **n.** a plane for making a rabbet in a piece of wood.

rab·bi /ˈrabˌī/ ▶ **n.** (pl. **rabbis**) a Jewish scholar or teacher, esp. one who studies or teaches Jewish law. ■ a person appointed as a Jewish religious leader.
– DERIVATIVES **rab·bin·ate** /ˈrabənət, -ˌnāt/ **n.**
– ORIGIN late Old English, via ecclesiastical Latin and Greek from Hebrew *rabbī* 'my master,' from *raḇ* 'master.'

rab·bin·i·cal /rəˈbinikəl, ra-/ ▶ **adj.** [attrib.] of or relating to rabbis or to Jewish law or teachings.
– DERIVATIVES **rab·bin·ic** /-ik/ **adj.**, **rab·bin·i·cal·ly** /-ik(ə)lē/ **adv.**

rab·bit /ˈrabit/ ▶ **n.** a burrowing, gregarious, plant-eating mammal with long ears, long hind legs, and a short tail. ● Family Leporidae: several genera and species, in particular the **European rabbit** (*Oryctolagus cuniculus*), which is often kept as a pet or raised for food. ■ the flesh of the rabbit as food. ■ the fur of the rabbit. ■ another term for HARE. ■ a runner who acts as pacesetter in the first laps of a race.
▶ **v.** (**rabbits, rabbiting, rabbited**) [no obj.] **1** (usu. as noun **rabbiting**) hunt rabbits: *locate the area where you can go rabbiting.*
2 Brit. informal talk at length, esp. about trivial matters: *stop **rabbiting on**, will you, and go to bed!* [from *rabbit and pork*, rhyming slang for 'talk.']
– PHRASES **breed like rabbits** informal reproduce prolifically. **pull a rabbit out of the** (or **a**) **hat** do something unexpected but ingeniously effective in response to a problem: *everyone is waiting to see if the king can pull a rabbit out of the hat and announce a ceasefire.* [with reference to a magician's trick.]
– DERIVATIVES **rab·bit·y adj.**
– ORIGIN late Middle English: apparently from Old French (compare with French dialect *rabotte* 'young rabbit'), perhaps of Dutch origin (compare with Flemish *robbe*).

rab·bit·brush /ˈrabitˌbrəsн/ (also **rabbitbush** /-ˌbo͝osн/) ▶ **n.** a shrub of the daisy family that bears clusters of pungent small yellow flowers, native to North America, esp. the western US. ● *Chrysothamnus nauseosus*, family Compositae.

rab·bit fe·ver ▶ **n.** informal term for TULAREMIA.

rab·bit·fish /ˈrabitˌfisн/ ▶ **n.** (pl. **same** or **rabbitfishes**) a blunt-nosed chimaera with rodentlike front teeth and a long thin tail, found in the northeastern Atlantic and around South Africa. Also called RATFISH, RAT-TAIL. ● *Chimaera monstrosa*, family Chimaeridae.

rab·bit food ▶ **n.** informal, humorous salad or raw vegetables, characterized as insubstantial or tasteless.

rab·bit punch ▶ **n.** a sharp chop with the edge of the hand to the back of the neck.

rab·bit's foot ▶ **n.** the foot of a rabbit carried as a good luck charm.

rab·bit's-foot clo·ver ▶ **n.** a slender clover with narrow leaflets that are soft and silky and light pink flower heads that are slightly cylindrical and very fuzzy. ● *Trifolium arvense*, family Leguminosae.

rab·bit war·ren ▶ **n.** see WARREN.

rab·ble /ˈrabəl/ ▶ **n.** a disorderly crowd; a mob: *he was met by a rabble of noisy, angry youths.* ■ (**the rabble**) ordinary people, esp. when regarded as socially inferior or uncouth.
– ORIGIN late Middle English (in the senses 'string of meaningless words' and 'pack of animals'): perhaps related to dialect *rabble* 'to gabble.'

rab·ble-rous·er ▶ **n.** a person who speaks with the intention of inflaming the emotions of a crowd of people, typically for political reasons.
– DERIVATIVES **rab·ble-rous·ing adj. & n.**

Rab·e·lais /ˈrabəˌlā, ˌrabəˈlā/, François (*c.*1494–1553), French satirist. His writings are noted for their earthy humor, their parody of medieval learning and literature, and their affirmation of humanist values.

Rab·e·lai·sian /ˌrabəˈlāzнən/ ▶ **adj.** displaying earthy humor; bawdy: *the conversation was often highly Rabelaisian.*
– ORIGIN suggestive of the humor of François *Rabelais.*

rab·id /ˈrabəd, ˈrā-/ ▶ **adj. 1** having or proceeding from an extreme or fanatical support of or belief in something: *a rabid feminist.*
2 (of an animal) affected with rabies. ■ of or connected with rabies.
– DERIVATIVES **rab·id·i·ty** /rəˈbidətē, ra-, rā-/ **n.**, **rab·id·ly adv.**, **rab·id·ness n.**
– ORIGIN early 17th cent. (in the sense 'furious, madly violent'): from Latin *rabidus*, from *rabere* 'to rave.'

ra·bies /ˈrābēz/ ▶ **n.** a contagious and fatal viral disease of dogs and other mammals that causes madness and convulsions, transmissible through the saliva to humans. Also called HYDROPHOBIA.
– ORIGIN late 16th cent.: from Latin, from *rabere* 'rave.'

Ra·bin /räˈbēn/, Yitzhak (1922–95), Israeli statesman and military leader; prime minister 1974–77 and 1992–95. In 1993, he negotiated a PLO–Israeli peace accord with Yasser Arafat. He was assassinated by a Jewish extremist. Nobel Peace Prize (1994), shared with Arafat and Shimon Peres.

rac·coon /raˈko͞on, rə-/ (also **racoon**) ▶ **n.** a grayish-brown American mammal that has a foxlike face with a black mask and a ringed tail. ● Genus *Procyon*, family Procyonidae (the **raccoon family**): two species, in particular the **common raccoon** (*P. lotor*), which often occurs in urban areas in North America. The raccoon family also includes the coati, kinkajou, cacomistle, and olingo. ■ the fur of the raccoon.
– ORIGIN early 17th cent.: from Virginia Algonquian *aroughcun*. The common raccoon's scientific name *lotor* is Latin for 'one who washes,' a name descriptive of the raccoon's habit of using its front feet to forage for food in water.

common raccoon

rac·coon dog ▶ **n.** a small wild dog of raccoonlike appearance, with a black facial mask and long brindled fur, native to the forests of southern and eastern Asia. ● *Nyctereutes procyonoides*, family Canidae.

race[1] /rās/ ▶ **n. 1** a competition between runners, horses, vehicles, boats, etc., to see which is the fastest in covering a set course: *I won the first 50-lap race.* ■ (**the races**) a series of such competitions for horses or dogs, held at a fixed time on a set course. ■ [in sing.] a situation in which individuals or groups compete to be first to achieve a particular objective: *the race for nuclear power.* ■ archaic the course of the sun or moon through the heavens.
2 a strong or rapid current flowing through a narrow channel in the sea or a river: *angling for tuna in turbulent tidal races.*
3 a groove, channel, or passage, in particular: ■ a water channel, esp. one built to lead water to or from a point where its energy is utilized, as in a mill or mine. See also MILLRACE. ■ a smooth, ring-shaped groove or guide in which a ball bearing or roller bearing runs.
▶ **v. 1** [no obj.] compete with another or others to see who is fastest at covering a set course or achieving an objective: *the vet took blood samples from the horses before they raced* | [with obj.] *attorneys have to think twice before they **race each other** to the courthouse.* ■ compete regularly in races as a sport

or leisure activity: *the next year, he raced again for the team.* ■ [with obj.] prepare and enter (an animal or vehicle) in races as a sport or leisure activity: *he raced his three horses simply for the fun of it.*
2 [no obj.] move or progress swiftly or at full speed: *I raced into the house* | figurative *she spoke automatically, while her mind raced ahead.* ■ (of a person's heart or pulse) beat faster than usual because of fear or excitement. ■ operate or cause to operate at excessive speed: [with obj.] *she'd driven like a madwoman, racing the engine and swerving around corners.*
– PHRASES **a race against time** a situation in which something must be done before a particular point in time: *it was a race against time to reach shore before the dinghy sank.*
– ORIGIN late Old English, from Old Norse *rás* 'current.' It was originally a northern English word with the sense 'rapid forward movement,' which gave rise to the senses 'contest of speed' (early 16th cent.) and 'channel, path' (i.e., the space traversed). The verb dates from the late 15th cent.

race² ▶ n. each of the major divisions of humankind, having distinct physical characteristics: *people of all races, colors, and creeds.* ■ a group of people sharing the same culture, history, language, etc.; an ethnic group: *we Scots were a bloodthirsty race then.* ■ the fact or condition of belonging to such a division or group; the qualities or characteristics associated with this: *people of mixed race.* ■ a group or set of people or things with a common feature or features: *some male firefighters still regarded women as a race apart.* ■ Biology a population within a species that is distinct in some way, esp. a subspecies: *people have killed so many tigers that two races are probably extinct.* ■ (in nontechnical use) each of the major divisions of living creatures: *a member of the human race* | *the race of birds.* ■ literary a group of people descended from a common ancestor: *a prince of the race of Solomon.* ■ archaic ancestry: *two coursers of ethereal race.*

> Although ideas of race are centuries old, it was not until the 19th century that attempts to systematize racial divisions were made. Ideas of supposed racial superiority and social Darwinism reached their culmination in Nazi ideology of the 1930s and gave pseudoscientific justification to policies and attitudes of discrimination, exploitation, slavery, and extermination. Theories of race asserting a link between racial type and intelligence are now discredited. Scientifically it is accepted as obvious that there are subdivisions of the human species, but it is also clear that genetic variation between individuals of the same race can be as great as that between members of different races.

– ORIGIN early 16th cent. (denoting a group with common features): via French from Italian *razza,* of unknown ultimate origin.

> **USAGE** In recent years, the associations of **race** with the ideologies and theories that grew out of the work of 19th-century anthropologists and physiologists has led to the word **race** itself becoming problematic. Although still used in general contexts (*race relations, racial equality*), it is now often replaced by other words that are less emotionally charged, such as **people(s)** or **community**.

race car ▶ n. an automobile built or modified for racing.

race·course /ˈrās,kôrs/ ▶ n. a racetrack.

race driv·er ▶ n. a person who drives race cars as a profession.

race·horse /ˈrās,hôrs/ ▶ n. a horse bred, trained, and kept for racing.

race·mate /ˈrās,māt/ ▶ n. Chemistry a racemic mixture.

ra·ceme /rāˈsēm, rə-/ ▶ n. Botany a flower cluster with the separate flowers attached by short equal stalks at equal distances along a central stem. The flowers at the base of the central stem develop first. Compare with CYME and SPIKE².
– ORIGIN late 18th cent.: from Latin *racemus* 'bunch of grapes.'

race mem·o·ry ▶ n. a supposedly inherited subconscious memory of events in human history or prehistory.

ra·ce·mic /rāˈsēmik, rə-/ ▶ adj. Chemistry composed of dextrorotatory and levorotatory forms of a compound in equal proportion.
– DERIVATIVES **rac·e·mize** /ˈrāsə,mīz, rəˈsē-, ˈrasə-/ v.
– ORIGIN early 19th cent. (in *racemic acid*): from French *racémique* 'derived from grape juice' (originally referring to tartaric acid in this) + -IC.

rac·e·mose /ˈrasə,mōs, ˈrasə,mōz/ ▶ adj. Botany (of a flower cluster) taking the form of a raceme. ■ Anatomy (esp. of compound glands) having the form of a cluster.
– ORIGIN late 17th cent.: from Latin *racemosus,* from *racemus* (see RACEME).

race mu·sic ▶ n. dated music popular among or played by black people, esp. jazz and blues.

rac·er /ˈrāsər/ ▶ n. **1** an animal or means of transportation bred or designed esp. for racing: *tall-masted ocean racers.* ■ a person who competes in races.
2 a fast-moving, harmless, and typically slender-bodied snake. ● Several genera in the family Colubridae: genus *Coluber,* including the American *C. constrictor* and the European *C. gemonensis* (see also WHIP SNAKE), and the Asian genera *Ptyas* and *Argyrogena* (also called RAT SNAKE).
3 a circular horizontal rail along which the carriage or traversing platform of a heavy gun moves.

rac·er·back /ˈrāsər,bak/ ▶ adj. denoting an article of clothing with a T-shaped back behind the shoulder blades to allow ease of movement in sports.

race re·la·tions ▶ plural n. relations between members or communities of different races within one country.

race ri·ot ▶ n. a public outbreak of violence between two racial groups in a community.

race·run·ner /ˈrās,rənər/ ▶ n. any of a number of fast-moving active lizards with longitudinal markings and a pointed snout, in particular: ● an American lizard (genus *Cnemidophorus,* family Teiidae).

race·track /ˈrās,trak/ ▶ n. a ground or track for horse or dog racing. ■ a track for auto racing.

race·way /ˈrās,wā/ ▶ n. **1** a track or channel along which something runs, in particular: ■ a water channel, esp. an artificial one of running water in which fish are reared. ■ a groove or race in which bearings run. ■ a pipe or tubing enclosing electric wires.
2 a track for trotting, pacing, or harness racing. ■ a track for auto racing.

ra·chis /ˈrākis, ˈrak-/ ▶ n. (pl. **rachides** /ˈrakə,dēz, ˈrā-/) **1** Botany a stem of a plant, esp. a grass, bearing flower stalks at short intervals. ■ the midrib of a compound leaf or frond.
2 Anatomy the vertebral column or the cord from which it develops.
3 Ornithology the shaft of a feather, esp. the part bearing the barbs.
– ORIGIN late 18th cent.: modern Latin, from Greek *rhakhis* 'spine.' The English plural *-ides* is by false analogy.

ra·chi·tis /rəˈkītis/ ▶ n. old-fashioned medical term for RICKETS.
– DERIVATIVES **ra·chit·ic** /rəˈkitik/ adj.
– ORIGIN early 18th cent.: modern Latin, from Greek *rhakhitis,* from *rhakhis* 'spine.'

Rach·ma·ni·nov /räkˈmänənôf, rəKHˈmänyinəf/, Sergei (Vasilevich) (1873–1943), Russian composer and pianist, resident in the US from 1917. Part of the Russian romantic tradition, he is primarily known for his compositions for piano.

ra·cial /ˈrāSHəl/ ▶ adj. of or relating to race: *a racial minority.* ■ on the grounds of or connected with difference in race: *racial hatred.*
– DERIVATIVES **ra·cial·ly** adv.

ra·cial·ism /ˈrāSHə,lizəm/ ▶ n. another term for RACISM.
– DERIVATIVES **ra·cial·ist** /-list/ n. & adj., **ra·cial·ize** /-,līz/ v.

ra·cial pro·fil·ing ▶ n. the use of race or ethnicity as grounds for suspecting someone of having committed an offence.

Ra·cine¹ /rəˈsēn, rä-/ an industrial city in southeastern Wisconsin, on Lake Michigan; pop. 82,196 (est. 2008).

Ra·cine² /rəˈsēn, rä-/, Jean (1639–99), French playwright. Central to most of his tragedies is a perception of the blind folly of human passion, continually enslaved and unsatisfied. Notable works: *Andromaque* (1667) and *Phèdre* (1677).

rac·ing /ˈrāsiNG/ ▶ n. short for HORSE RACING. ■ any sport that involves competing in races: *bicycle racing* | *yacht racing.*
▶ adj. **1** moving swiftly: *he controlled his racing thoughts.*
2 (of a person) following horse racing: *Kevin was not a racing man.*

ra·ci·no /rəˈsēnō/ ▶ n. a building complex or grounds having a racetrack and gambling facilities for playing slot machines, blackjack, roulette, etc.
– ORIGIN 1990s: blend of RACETRACK and CASINO.

rac·ism /ˈrā,sizəm/ ▶ n. the belief that all members of each race possess characteristics or abilities specific to that race, esp. so as to distinguish it as inferior or superior to another race or races. ■ prejudice, discrimination, or antagonism directed against someone of a different race based on such a belief: *a program to combat racism.*

rac·ist /ˈrāsist/ ▶ n. a person who believes that a particular race is superior to another.
▶ adj. having or showing the belief that a particular race is superior to another: *we are investigating complaints about racist abuse at the club.*

rack¹ /rak/ ▶ n. **1** a framework, typically with rails, bars, hooks, or pegs, for holding or storing things: *a spice rack* | *a magazine rack.* ■ an overhead shelf on a bus, train, or plane for stowing luggage. ■ a vertically barred frame or wagon for holding animal fodder: *a hay rack.* ■ a set of antlers. ■ informal a bed.
2 a cogged or toothed bar or rail engaging with a wheel or pinion, or using pegs to adjust the position of something: *a steering rack.*
3 (**the rack**) historical an instrument of torture consisting of a frame on which the victim was stretched by turning rollers to which the wrists and ankles were tied.
4 a triangular structure for positioning the balls in pool. Compare with FRAME (sense 5 of the noun). ■ Brit. a single game of snooker.
5 a digital effects unit for a guitar or other instrument, typically giving many different sounds.
6 vulgar slang a woman's breasts: *Arnie's woman is kinda bossy, but she's got a nice rack.*
▶ v. [with obj.] **1** (also **wrack**) cause extreme physical or mental pain to; subject to extreme stress: *he was racked with guilt.* ■ historical torture (someone) on the rack.
2 place in or on a rack: *the shoes were racked neatly beneath the dresses.*
3 chiefly archaic raise (rent) above a fair or normal amount.
– PHRASES **go to rack** (or **wrack**) **and ruin** gradually deteriorate in condition because of neglect: fall into disrepair. [*rack* from Old English *wræc* 'vengeance'; related to WREAK.] **off the rack** (of clothes) ready-made rather than made to order. **on the rack** suffering intense distress or strain. **rack** (or **wrack**) **one's brains** (or **brain**) make a great effort to think of or remember something.
– PHRASAL VERBS **rack something up** accumulate or achieve something, typically a score or amount: *Japan is racking up record trade surpluses with the U.S.*
– ORIGIN Middle English: from Middle Dutch *rec,* Middle Low German *rek* 'horizontal bar or shelf,' probably from *recken* 'to stretch, reach' (possibly the source of sense 1 of the verb).

> **USAGE** The relationship between the forms **rack** and **wrack** is complicated. The most common noun sense of **rack**, 'a framework for holding and storing things,' is always spelled **rack**, never **wrack**. In the phrase **rack something up**, the word is also always spelled **rack**. Figurative senses of the verb, deriving from the type of torture in which someone is stretched on a **rack**, can, however, be spelled either **rack** or **wrack**: thus, *racked with guilt* or *wracked with guilt*; *rack your brains* or *wrack your brains*. In addition, the phrase **rack and ruin** can also be spelled **wrack and ruin**.

rack² ▶ n. a horse's gait in which both hoofs on either side in turn are lifted almost simultaneously, and all four hoofs are off the ground together at certain moments.
▶ v. [no obj.] (of a horse) move with such a gait.
– ORIGIN mid 16th cent.: of unknown origin.

rack³ ▶ n. a large cut of meat, typically lamb, that includes the front ribs.
– ORIGIN late 16th cent.: of unknown origin.

rack⁴ ▶ v. [with obj.] draw off (wine, beer, etc.) from the sediment in the barrel: *the wine is racked off into large oak casks.*
– ORIGIN late 15th cent.: from Provençal *arracar,* from *raca* 'stems and husks of grapes, dregs.'

rack⁵ (also **wrack**) ▶ n. a mass of high, thick, fast-moving clouds: *there was a thin moon, a rack of cloud.*
▶ v. [no obj.] archaic (of a cloud) be driven before the wind.
– ORIGIN Middle English (denoting a rush or collision): probably of Scandinavian origin; compare with Norwegian and Swedish dialect *rak* 'wreckage,' from *reka* 'to drive.'

rack-and-pin·ion ▶ adj. [attrib.] denoting a mechanism, as for a car steering system, using a fixed cogged or toothed bar or rail engaging with a smaller cog.

rack·et¹ /ˈrakit/ (also **racquet**) ▶ n. a type of bat with a round or oval frame strung with catgut, nylon,

PRONUNCIATION KEY ə *ago, up;* ər *over, fur;* a *hat;* ā *ate;* ä *car;* e *let;* ē *see;* i *fit;* ī *by;* NG *sing;* ō *go;* ô *law, for;* oi *toy;* o͝o *good;* o͞o *goo;* ou *out;* TH *thin;* T͟H *then;* ZH *vision*

etc., used esp. in tennis, badminton, and squash. ■ a snowshoe resembling such a bat.
– ORIGIN early 16th cent.: from French *raquette* (see RACKETS).

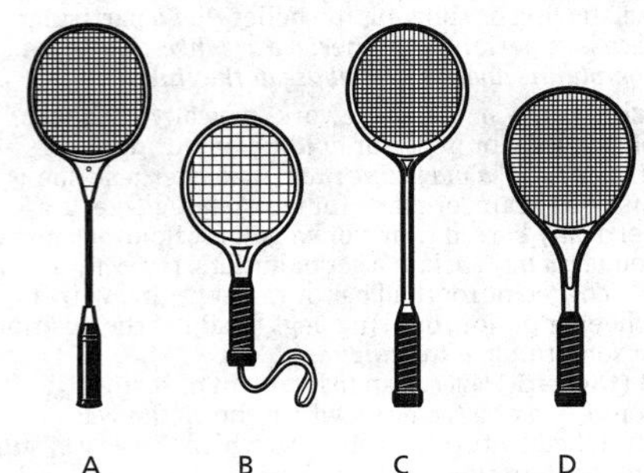

A. badminton racket C. squash racket
B. racquetball racket D. tennis racket

rackets

rack·et[2] ▶ n. **1** [in sing.] a loud unpleasant noise; a din: *the kids were **making a racket**.* ■ archaic the noise and liveliness of fashionable society.
2 informal an illegal or dishonest scheme for obtaining money: *a protection racket.* ■ a person's line of business or way of life: *I'm in the insurance racket.*
▶ v. (**rackets, racketing, racketed**) [no obj.] make a loud unpleasant noise: *trains racketed by.* ■ (**racket around**) enjoy oneself socially; go in pursuit of pleasure or entertainment.
– DERIVATIVES **rack·et·y** adj.
– ORIGIN mid 16th cent.: perhaps imitative of clattering.

rack·et·eer /ˌrakiˈti(ə)r/ ▶ n. a person who engages in dishonest and fraudulent business dealings.
– DERIVATIVES **rack·et·eer·ing** n.

rack·ets /ˈrakits/ ▶ plural n. [treated as sing.] a ball game for two or four people played with rackets in a plain, four-walled court, distinguished from squash in particular by the use of a solid, harder ball.
– ORIGIN late Middle English (also in the singular): from French *raquette*, via Italian from Arabic *rāḥa, rāḥat-* 'palm of the hand.'

rack rail·way ▶ n. another term for COG RAILWAY.

rack rate ▶ n. the official or advertised price of a hotel room, on which a discount is usually negotiable.

rack rent ▶ n. an extortionate or very high rent, esp. an annual rent equivalent to the full value of the property to which it relates.
▶ v. (**rack-rent**) [with obj.] exact an excessive or extortionate rent from (a tenant) or for (a property).
– DERIVATIVES **rack-rent·er** n.
– ORIGIN late 16th cent. (as *rack-rented*): from the verb RACK[1] (in the sense 'cause stress') + the noun RENT[1].

ra·clette /raˈklet, rä-/ ▶ n. a Swiss dish of melted cheese, typically eaten with potatoes.
– ORIGIN French, literally 'small scraper,' referring to the practice of holding the cheese over the heat and scraping it onto a plate as it melts.

ra·con /ˈrāˌkän/ ▶ n. a radar beacon that can be identified and located by its response to a specific radar signal.
– ORIGIN 1940s: blend of RADAR and BEACON.

rac·on·teur /ˌrakˌänˈtər, -ən-/ ▶ n. a person who tells anecdotes in a skillful and amusing way.
– ORIGIN early 19th cent.: French, from *raconter* 'relate, recount.'

rac·on·teuse /ˌrakˌänˈtə(r)z/ ▶ n. a female raconteur.
– ORIGIN mid 19th cent.: French, feminine of *raconteur* (see RACONTEUR).

ra·coon ▶ n. variant spelling of RACCOON.

rac·quet /ˈrakit/ ▶ n. variant spelling of RACKET[1].

rac·quet·ball /ˈrakitˌbôl/ ▶ n. a game played with a small hard ball and a short-handled racket in a four-walled handball court.

rac·y /ˈrāsē/ ▶ adj. (**racier, raciest**) (of speech, writing, or behavior) lively, entertaining, and typically mildly titillating sexually: *the novel was considered rather racy at the time.* ■ (of a person or thing) showing vigor or spirit: *a racy fiddle.* ■ (of a wine, flavor, etc.) having a characteristic quality in a high degree. ■ (of a vehicle or animal) designed or bred to be suitable for racing: *the yacht is fast and racy.*
– DERIVATIVES **rac·i·ly** /-səlē/ adv., **rac·i·ness** n.

rad[1] ▶ abbr. radian(s).

rad[2] /rad/ ▶ n. informal a political radical.
– ORIGIN early 19th cent.: abbreviation.

rad[3] ▶ n. Physics a unit of absorbed dose of ionizing radiation, corresponding to the absorption of 0.01 joule per kilogram of absorbing material.
– ORIGIN early 20th cent.: acronym from *radiation absorbed dose.*

rad[4] ▶ adj. informal excellent; impressive: *his style is so rad | a really rad game.*
– ORIGIN 1980s: probably an abbreviation of RADICAL.

rad. ▶ abbr. Mathematics ■ radical. ■ radix.

ra·dar /ˈrāˌdär/ ▶ n. a system for detecting the presence, direction, distance, and speed of aircraft, ships, and other objects, by sending out pulses of high-frequency electromagnetic waves that are reflected off the object back to the source. ■ an apparatus used for this.
– ORIGIN 1940s: from *ra(dio) d(etection) a(nd) r(anging).*

ra·dar as·tron·o·my ▶ n. the branch of astronomy that uses radar to map the surfaces of planetary bodies in the solar system.

ra·dar gun ▶ n. a handheld radar device used by traffic police to estimate the speed of a passing vehicle. ■ a similar device used to measure the speed of a pitched ball in baseball.

ra·dar trap ▶ n. a speed trap in which police use radar.

Rad·cliffe /ˈradklif/, Mrs. Ann (1764–1823), English novelist; a leading exponent of the Gothic novel. Notable works: *The Mysteries of Udolpho* (1794) and *The Italian* (1797).

rad·dle /ˈradl/ ▶ n. another term for RUDDLE.
– ORIGIN early 16th cent.: related to RED; compare with RUDDLE.

rad·dled /ˈradld/ ▶ adj. (of a person or their face) showing signs of age or fatigue: *he's beginning to look quite raddled.*
– ORIGIN from RADDLE in the sense 'rouge,' by association with its exaggerated use in makeup.

Ra·dha /ˈrädə/ Hinduism the favorite consort of the god Krishna, and an incarnation of Lakshmi.
– ORIGIN from Sanskrit, literally 'prosperity.'

Ra·dha·krish·nan /ˌrädəˈkrisʜnən/, Sir Sarvepalli (1888–1975), Indian philosopher and statesman; president 1962–67. He introduced classical Indian philosophy to the West through works such as *Indian Philosophy* (1923–27).

ra·di·al /ˈrādēəl/ ▶ adj. **1** of or arranged like rays or the radii of a circle; diverging in lines from a common center. ■ (or a road or route) running directly from a town or city center to an outlying district. ■ denoting a tire in which the layers of fabric have their cords running at right angles to the circumference of the tire and the tread is strengthened by further layers around the circumference. Compare with BIAS-PLY.
2 Anatomy & Zoology of or relating to the radius.
▶ n. **1** a radial tire.
2 a radial road.
3 Zoology a supporting ray in a fish's fin.
4 short for RADIAL ENGINE.
– DERIVATIVES **ra·di·al·ly** adv.
– ORIGIN late 16th cent.: from medieval Latin *radialis*, from Latin *radius* (see RADIUS).

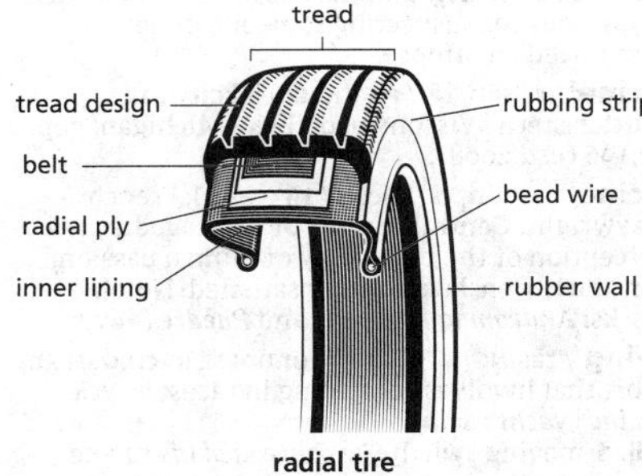

radial tire

ra·di·al en·gine ▶ n. a type of internal combustion engine used chiefly in aircraft, having its cylinders fixed radially around a rotating crankshaft.

ra·di·al ker·a·tot·o·my ▶ n. see KERATOTOMY.

ra·di·al sym·me·try ▶ n. chiefly Biology symmetry around a central axis, as in a starfish or a tulip flower.

ra·di·al ve·loc·i·ty ▶ n. chiefly Astronomy the velocity of a star or other body along the line of sight of an observer.

ra·di·an /ˈrādēən/ ▶ n. Geometry a unit of angle, equal to an angle at the center of a circle whose arc is equal in length to the radius.

ra·di·ance /ˈrādēəns/ ▶ n. **1** light or heat as emitted or reflected by something: *the radiance of the sunset dwindled and died.* ■ great happiness, apparent in someone's expression or bearing: *the radiance of the bride's smile.* ■ a glowing quality of the skin, esp. as indicative of good health or youth.
2 Physics the flux of radiation emitted per unit solid angle in a given direction by a unit area of a source.

ra·di·ant /ˈrādēənt/ ▶ adj. **1** sending out light; shining or glowing brightly: *a bird with radiant green and red plumage.* ■ (of a person or their expression) clearly emanating great joy, love, or health: *she gave him a radiant smile.* ■ (of an emotion or quality) emanating powerfully from someone or something; very intense or conspicuous: *he praised her radiant self-confidence.*
2 [attrib.] (of heat) transmitted by radiation, rather than conduction or convection. ■ (of an appliance) designed to emit such energy, esp. for cooking or heating.
▶ n. a point or object from which light or heat radiates, esp. a heating element in an electric or gas heater.
– DERIVATIVES **ra·di·an·cy** /-ənsē/ n., **ra·di·ant·ly** adv.
– ORIGIN late Middle English: from Latin *radiant-* 'emitting rays,' from the verb *radiare* (see RADIATE).

ra·di·ate ▶ v. /ˈrādēˌāt/ **1** [with obj.] emit (energy, esp. light or heat) in the form of rays or waves: *the hot stars radiate energy.* ■ [no obj.] (of light, heat, or other energy) be emitted in such a way: *the continual stream of energy that radiates from the sun.* ■ (of a person) clearly emanate (a strong feeling or quality) through their expression or bearing: *she lifted her chin, radiating defiance.* ■ (**radiate from**) (of a feeling or quality) emanate clearly from: *leadership and confidence radiate from her.*
2 [no obj.] diverge or spread from or as if from a central point: *he ran down one of the passages that radiated from the room.* ■ Biology (of an animal or plant group) evolve into a variety of forms adapted to new situations or ways of life.
▶ adj. /ˈrādēət, -ˌāt/ rare having rays or parts proceeding from a center; arranged in or having a radial pattern: *the radiate crown.*
– DERIVATIVES **ra·di·a·tive** /-ˌātiv/ adj. (sense 1 of the verb).
– ORIGIN early 17th cent.: from Latin *radiat-* 'emitted in rays,' from the verb *radiare*, from *radius* 'ray, spoke.'

ra·di·a·tion /ˌrādēˈāsʜən/ ▶ n. **1** Physics the emission of energy as electromagnetic waves or as moving subatomic particles, esp. high-energy particles that cause ionization. ■ the energy transmitted in this way, as heat, light, electricity, etc.
2 chiefly Biology divergence out from a central point, in particular evolution from an ancestral animal or plant group into a variety of new forms.
– DERIVATIVES **ra·di·a·tion·al** /-ˈāsʜənl/ adj., **ra·di·a·tion·al·ly** /-ˈāsʜənl-ē/ adv.
– ORIGIN late Middle English (denoting the action of sending out rays of light): from Latin *radiatio(n-)*, from *radiare* 'emit rays' (see RADIATE).

ra·di·a·tion belt ▶ n. Astronomy a region surrounding a planet where charged particles accumulate under the influence of the planet's magnetic field.

ra·di·a·tion sick·ness ▶ n. illness caused by exposure of the body to ionizing radiation, characterized by nausea, hair loss, diarrhea, bleeding, and damage to the bone marrow and central nervous system.

ra·di·a·tion ther·a·py (also **radiation treatment**) ▶ n. the treatment of disease, esp. cancer, using X-rays or similar forms of radiation.

ra·di·a·tor /ˈrādēˌātər/ ▶ n. **1** a thing that radiates or emits light, heat, or sound. ■ a device for heating a room consisting of a metal tank connected by pipes through which hot water is pumped by a central heating system. ■ a portable heater resembling such a device.
2 an engine-cooling device in a motor vehicle or aircraft consisting of a bank of thin tubes in which circulating fluid is cooled by the surrounding air.

rad·i·cal /ˈradikəl/ ▶ adj. **1** (esp. of change or action) relating to or affecting the fundamental nature of something; far-reaching or thorough: *a radical overhaul of the existing regulatory framework.* ■ forming an inherent or fundamental part of the nature of someone or something: *the assumption of radical differences between the mental attributes of literate and nonliterate peoples.* ■ (of surgery or medical treatment) thorough and intended to be completely curative. ■ characterized by departure from tradition; innovative or progressive: *a radical approach to electoral reform.*

2 advocating or based on thorough or complete political or social reform; representing or supporting an extreme section of a political party: *a radical American activist*.
3 of or relating to the root of something, in particular: ■ Mathematics of the root of a number or quantity. ■ denoting or relating to the roots of a word. ■ Music belonging to the root of a chord. ■ Botany of, or springing direct from, the root or stem base of a plant.
4 [usu. as exclamation] informal very good; excellent: *Okay, then. Seven o'clock. Radical!*
▶ **n. 1** a person who advocates thorough or complete political or social reform; a member of a political party or part of a party pursuing such aims.
2 Chemistry a group of atoms behaving as a unit in a number of compounds. See also FREE RADICAL. [early 19th cent.: from French.]
3 the root or base form of a word. ■ any of the basic set of 214 Chinese characters constituting semantically or functionally significant elements in the composition of other characters and used as a means of classifying characters in dictionaries.
4 Mathematics a quantity forming or expressed as the root of another. ■ a radical sign.
– DERIVATIVES **rad·i·cal·ism** /-ˌlizəm/ **n.** (sense 1 of the noun), **rad·i·cal·ly** /-ik(ə)lē/ **adv.** [as submodifier] *a radically different approach*, **rad·i·cal·ness n.**
– ORIGIN late Middle English (in the senses 'forming the root' and 'inherent'): from late Latin *radicalis*, from Latin *radix*, *radic-* 'root.'

rad·i·cal chic ▶ **n.** the fashionable affectation of radical left-wing views: [as modifier] *he completely immersed himself in the subculture of radical chic liberals*. ■ the dress, lifestyle, or people associated with this.
– ORIGIN 1970: coined by US writer Tom Wolfe.

rad·i·cal·ize /ˈradikəˌlīz/ ▶ **v.** [with obj.] cause (someone) to become an advocate of radical political or social reform: *I'm trying to mobilize and radicalize the liberals*.
– DERIVATIVES **rad·i·cal·i·za·tion** /-ˈzāSHən/ **n.**

rad·i·cal sign ▶ **n.** Mathematics the sign √, which indicates the square root of the number following (or a higher root indicated by a preceding superscript numeral).

ra·dic·chi·o /raˈdēkēˌō, rə-/ ▶ **n.** (pl. **radicchios**) chicory of a variety that has dark red leaves.
– ORIGIN Italian.

rad·i·ces /ˈradəˌsēz, ˈrā-/ plural form of RADIX.

rad·i·cle /ˈradikəl/ ▶ **n.** Botany the part of a plant embryo that develops into the primary root. ■ Anatomy a rootlike subdivision of a nerve or vein.
– DERIVATIVES **ra·dic·u·lar** /rəˈdikyələr/ **adj.** (Anatomy).
– ORIGIN late 17th cent.: from Latin *radicula*, diminutive of *radix*, *radic-* 'root.'

ra·di·i /ˈrādēˌī/ plural form of RADIUS.

ra·di·o /ˈrādēˌō/ ▶ **n.** (pl. **radios**) the transmission and reception of electromagnetic waves of radio frequency, esp. those carrying sound messages: *cellular phones are linked by radio rather than wires*. ■ the activity or industry of broadcasting sound programs to the public: *she has written much material for radio* | [as modifier] *a radio station*. ■ radio programs: *we used to listen to a lot of radio*. ■ an apparatus for receiving such programs: *she turned on the radio*. ■ an apparatus capable of both receiving and transmitting radio messages between individuals, ships, planes, etc.: *a ship-to-shore radio*. ■ [in names] a broadcasting station or channel: *Monitor Radio*.
▶ **v.** (**radioes, radioing, radioed**) [no obj.] communicate or send a message by radio: *the pilot radioed for help*. ■ [with obj.] communicate with (a person or place) by radio: *we'll radio Athens right away*.
– ORIGIN early 20th cent.: abbreviation of RADIOTELEPHONY (see RADIOTELEPHONE).

radio- ▶ **comb. form 1** denoting radio waves or broadcasting: *radio-controlled* | *radiogram*.
2 Physics connected with rays, radiation, or radioactivity: *radiogenic* | *radiograph*. ■ denoting artificially prepared radioisotopes of elements: *radio-cobalt*.
3 Anatomy belonging to the radius in conjunction with some other part: *radio-carpal*.
– ORIGIN from RADIO or RADIUS.

ra·di·o·ac·tive /ˌrādēōˈaktiv/ ▶ **adj.** emitting or relating to the emission of ionizing radiation or particles: *radioactive decay* | *the water was radioactive*.
– DERIVATIVES **ra·di·o·ac·tive·ly adv.**

ra·di·o·ac·tiv·i·ty /ˌrādēōakˈtivətē/ ▶ **n.** the emission of ionizing radiation or particles caused by the spontaneous disintegration of atomic nuclei. ■ radioactive substances, or the radiation emitted by these.

ra·di·o as·tron·o·my ▶ **n.** the branch of astronomy concerned with radio emissions from celestial objects.

ra·di·o·bi·ol·o·gy /ˌrādēōbīˈäləjē/ ▶ **n.** the branch of biology concerned with the effects of ionizing radiation on organisms and the application in biology of radiological techniques.
– DERIVATIVES **ra·di·o·bi·o·log·i·cal** /-ˌbīəˈläjikəl/ **adj.**, **ra·di·o·bi·o·log·i·cal·ly** /-ˌbīəˈläjik(ə)lē/ **adv.**, **ra·di·o·bi·ol·o·gist** /-jist/ **n.**

ra·di·o but·ton ▶ **n.** Computing (in a graphical display) an icon representing one of a set of options, only one of which can be selected at any time.

ra·di·o car ▶ **n.** a car, esp. a police car, equipped with a two-way radio.

ra·di·o·car·bon /ˌrādēōˈkärbən/ ▶ **n.** Chemistry a radioactive isotope of carbon.

ra·di·o·car·bon dat·ing ▶ **n.** another term for CARBON DATING.

ra·di·o·chem·is·try /ˌrādēōˈkemistrē/ ▶ **n.** the branch of chemistry concerned with radioactive substances.
– DERIVATIVES **ra·di·o·chem·i·cal** /-ˈkemikəl/ **adj.**, **ra·di·o·chem·ist** /-ˈkemist/ **n.**

ra·di·o·con·trolled ▶ **adj.** (esp. of an electronic model toy) controllable from a distance by radio.

ra·di·o·el·e·ment /ˌrādēōˈeləmənt/ ▶ **n.** a radioactive element or isotope.

ra·di·o fre·quen·cy ▶ **n.** a frequency or band of frequencies in the range 10^4 to 10^{11} or 10^{12} Hz, suitable for use in telecommunications.

ra·di·o gal·ax·y ▶ **n.** a galaxy emitting radiation in the radio-frequency range of the electromagnetic spectrum.

ra·di·o·gen·ic /ˌrādēōˈjenik/ ▶ **adj.** produced by radioactivity: *a radiogenic isotope*.
– DERIVATIVES **ra·di·o·gen·i·cal·ly** /-ik(ə)lē/ **adv.**

ra·di·o·go·ni·om·e·ter ▶ **n.** an instrument for finding direction using radio waves.

ra·di·o·gram /ˈrādēōˌgram/ ▶ **n. 1** another term for RADIOGRAPH.
2 a message sent by radiotelegraphy.

ra·di·o·graph /ˈrādēōˌgraf/ ▶ **n.** an image produced on a sensitive plate or film by X-rays, gamma rays, or similar radiation, and typically used in medical examination.
▶ **v.** [with obj.] produce an image of (something) on a sensitive plate or film by X-rays, gamma rays, or similar radiation.
– DERIVATIVES **ra·di·og·ra·pher** /ˌrādēˈägrəfər/ **n.**, **ra·di·o·graph·ic** /ˌrādēōˈgrafik/ **adj.**, **ra·di·o·graph·i·cal·ly** /-ik(ə)lē/ **adv.**, **ra·di·og·ra·phy** /ˌrādēˈägrəfē/ **n.**

ra·di·o·im·mu·no·as·say /ˌrādēōˌimyənōˈaˌsā/ ▶ **n.** Medicine a technique for determining antibody levels by introducing an antigen labeled with a radioisotope and measuring the subsequent radioactivity of the antibody component.

ra·di·o·im·mu·nol·o·gy /ˌrādēōˌimyəˈnäləjē/ ▶ **n.** the use of radioactively labeled antigens and antibodies in medical and biological research.
– DERIVATIVES **ra·di·o·im·mu·no·log·i·cal** /-ˌimyənəˈläjikəl/ **adj.**, **ra·di·o·im·mu·no·log·i·cal·ly** /-ik(ə)lē/ **adv.**

ra·di·o·i·so·tope /ˌrādēōˈīsəˌtōp/ ▶ **n.** Chemistry a radioactive isotope.
– DERIVATIVES **ra·di·o·i·so·top·ic** /-ˌīsəˈtäpik/ **adj.**

ra·di·o·lar·i·a /ˌrādeəˈlerēə/ ▶ **plural n.** Zoology radiolarians collectively.
– ORIGIN late 19th cent.: modern Latin (former order name), from late Latin *radiolus* 'faint ray,' diminutive of *radius* 'ray.'

ra·di·o·lar·i·an /ˌrādēəˈle(ə)rēən/ Zoology ▶ **n.** a single-celled aquatic animal that has a spherical, amebalike body with a spiny skeleton of silica. Their skeletons can accumulate as a slimy deposit on the seabed. ● Three classes of the phylum Actinopoda, kingdom Protista (formerly subclass or order Radiolaria).
▶ **adj.** of, relating to, or formed from radiolarians.

ra·di·ol·o·gy /ˌrādēˈäləjē/ ▶ **n.** the science dealing with X-rays and other high-energy radiation, esp. the use of such radiation for the diagnosis and treatment of disease.
– DERIVATIVES **ra·di·o·log·ic** /ˌrādēəˈläjik/ **adj.**, **ra·di·o·log·i·cal** /ˌrādēəˈläjikəl/ **adj.**, **ra·di·o·log·i·cal·ly** /ˌrādēəˈläjik(ə)lē/ **adv.**, **ra·di·ol·o·gist** /-jist/ **n.**

ra·di·o·lu·cent /ˌrādēōˈlo͞osnt/ ▶ **adj.** transparent to X-rays.
– DERIVATIVES **ra·di·o·lu·cen·cy n.**

ra·di·ol·y·sis /rādēˈäləsis/ ▶ **n.** (pl. **radiolyses**) Chemistry the molecular decomposition of a substance by ionizing radiation.

ra·di·o·man /ˈrādēōˌman/ ▶ **n.** a radio operator or technician.

ra·di·om·e·ter /ˌrādēˈämitər/ ▶ **n.** an instrument for detecting or measuring the intensity or force of radiation.
– DERIVATIVES **ra·di·o·met·ric** /-dēəˈmetrik/ **adj.**, **ra·di·o·met·ri·cal·ly** /-dēəˈmetrik(ə)lē/ **adv.**, **ra·di·om·e·try** /-trē/ **n.**

radiometer

ra·di·o·met·ric dat·ing ▶ **n.** a method of dating geological or archeological specimens by determining the relative proportions of particular radioactive isotopes present in a sample.

ra·di·on·ics /ˌrādēˈäniks/ ▶ **plural n.** [treated as sing.] a system of alternative medicine based on the supposition that detectable electromagnetic radiation emitted by living matter can be interpreted diagnostically and transmitted to treat illness at a distance by complex electrical instruments.
– ORIGIN 1940s: from RADIO- 'radiation,' on the pattern of *electronics*.

ra·di·o·nu·clide /ˌrādēōˈn(y)o͞oˌklīd/ ▶ **n.** a radioactive nuclide.

ra·di·o·paque /ˌrādēōˈpāk/ ▶ **adj.** (of a substance) opaque to X-rays or similar radiation.
– DERIVATIVES **ra·di·o·pac·i·ty** /ˌrādēōˈpasədē/ **n.**

ra·di·o·phar·ma·ceu·ti·cal /ˌrādēōˌfärməˈso͞otikəl/ ▶ **n.** a radioactive compound used for diagnostic or therapeutic purposes.

ra·di·o·phon·ic /ˌrādēōˈfänik/ ▶ **adj.** of, relating to, or denoting sound, esp. music, produced electronically.

ra·di·os·co·py /ˌrādēˈäskəpē/ ▶ **n.** Physics the examination by X-rays or similar radiation of objects opaque to light.
– DERIVATIVES **ra·di·o·scop·ic** /ˈˌrādēəˈskäpik/ **adj.**

ra·di·o·sonde /ˈrādēōˌsänd/ ▶ **n.** an instrument carried by balloon or other means to various levels of the atmosphere and transmitting measurements by radio.
– ORIGIN 1930s: from RADIO- (relating to broadcasting) + German *Sonde* 'probe.'

ra·di·o·te·leg·ra·phy /ˌrādēōtəˈlegrəfē/ ▶ **n.** telegraphy using radio transmission.
– DERIVATIVES **ra·di·o·tel·e·graph** /-ˈteləˌgraf/ **n.**

ra·di·o·tel·e·phone /ˌrādēōˈteləˌfōn/ ▶ **n.** a telephone that uses radio transmission.
– DERIVATIVES **ra·di·o·te·leph·o·ny** /-təˈlefənē/ **n.**, **ra·di·o·tel·e·phon·ic** /-ˌteləˈfänik/ **adj.**

ra·di·o tel·e·scope ▶ **n.** Astronomy an instrument used to detect radio emissions from the sky, whether from natural celestial objects or from artificial satellites.

ra·di·o·ther·a·py /ˌrādēōˈTHerəpē/ ▶ **n.** another term for RADIATION THERAPY.
– DERIVATIVES **ra·di·o·ther·a·peu·tic** /-ˌTHerəˈpyo͞otik/ **adj.**, **ra·di·o·ther·a·pist** /-pist/ **n.**

ra·di·o wave ▶ **n.** an electromagnetic wave of a frequency between about 10^4 and 10^{11} or 10^{12} Hz, as used for long-distance communication.

rad·ish /ˈradiSH/ ▶ **n. 1** a swollen pungent-tasting edible root, esp. a variety that is small, spherical, and red, and eaten raw with salad.
2 the plant of the cabbage family that yields this root. ● *Raphanus sativus*, family Brassicaceae.
– ORIGIN Old English *rædic*, from Latin *radix*, *radic-* 'root.'

ra·di·um /ˈrādēəm/ ▶ **n.** the chemical element of atomic number 88, a rare radioactive metal of the alkaline earth series. It was formerly used as a source of radiation for radiotherapy. (Symbol: **Ra**)
– ORIGIN late 19th cent.: from Latin *radius* 'ray' + -IUM.

ra·di·um em·a·na·tion ▶ **n.** archaic term for RADON.

ra·di·us /ˈrādēəs/ ▶ **n.** (pl. **radii** /ˈrādēˌī/ or **radiuses**) **1** a straight line from the center to the circumference of a circle or sphere. See also illustration at GEOMETRIC. ■ a radial line

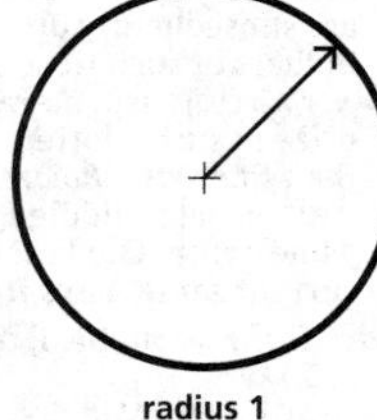

radius 1

r

PRONUNCIATION KEY ə *ago, up*; ər *over, fur*; a *hat*; ā *ate*; ä *car*; e *let*; ē *see*; i *fit*; ī *by*; NG *sing*; ō *go*; ô *law, for*; oi *toy*; o͝o *good*; o͞o *goo*; ou *out*; TH *thin*; T͟H *then*; ZH *vision*

from the focus to any point of a curve. ■ the length of the radius of a circle or sphere. ■ a specified distance from a center in all directions: *there are plenty of local pubs within a two-mile radius.*
2 Anatomy the thicker and shorter of the two bones in the human forearm. Compare with **ULNA**. ■ Zoology the corresponding bone in a vertebrate's foreleg or a bird's wing. ■ Zoology (in an echinoderm or coelenterate) any of the primary axes of radial symmetry. ■ Entomology any of the main veins in an insect's wing.
– ORIGIN late 16th cent. (sense 2): from Latin, literally 'staff, spoke, ray.'

ra·di·us of cur·va·ture ▶ **n.** Mathematics the radius of a circle that touches a curve at a given point and has the same tangent and curvature at that point.

ra·di·us vec·tor ▶ **n.** Mathematics a line of variable length drawn from a fixed origin to a curve. ■ Astronomy such a line joining a satellite or other celestial object to its primary.

ra·dix /ˈrādiks, ˈrad-/ ▶ **n.** (pl. **radices** /ˈradəˌsēz, ˈrā-/) **1** Mathematics the base of a system of numeration. See also **BASE**[1] (sense 8 of the noun).
2 formal a source or origin of something: *Judaism is the radix of Christianity.*
– ORIGIN early 17th cent. (sense 2): from Latin, literally 'root.' Sense 1 dates from the late 18th cent.

RADM (also **RAdm**) ▶ **abbr.** rear admiral.

Ra·dom /ˈräˌdôm/ an industrial city in central Poland; pop. 225,292 (2007).

ra·dome /ˈrāˌdōm/ ▶ **n.** a dome or other structure protecting radar equipment and made from material transparent to radio waves, esp. one on the outer surface of an aircraft.
– ORIGIN 1940s: blend of **RADAR** and **DOME**.

ra·don /ˈrāˌdän/ ▶ **n.** the chemical element of atomic number 86, a rare radioactive gas belonging to the noble gas series. (Symbol: **Rn**)
– ORIGIN early 20th cent.: from **RADIUM**, on the pattern of *argon*.

rad·u·la /ˈrajələ/ ▶ **n.** (pl. **radulae** /-lē, -ˌlī/) Zoology (in a mollusk) a rasplike structure of tiny teeth used for scraping food particles off a surface and drawing them into the mouth.
– DERIVATIVES **rad·u·lar** /-lər/ **adj.**
– ORIGIN late 19th cent.: from Latin, literally 'scraper,' from *radere* 'to scrape.'

rad·waste /ˈradˌwāst/ ▶ **n.** informal radioactive waste.

Ra·el·i·an /räˈēlēən/ ▶ **n.** a member of an atheistic cult based on the belief that humans originated from alien scientists who came to earth in UFOs.
▶ **adj.** relating to the Raelians or their beliefs.
– ORIGIN 1990s: from *Rael*, assumed name of Claude Vorilhon, French singer and journalist, author of *The Message Given to Me by Extraterrestrials* (1974).

RAF ▶ **abbr.** (in the UK) Royal Air Force.

raf·fi·a /ˈrafēə/ ▶ **n.** a palm tree native to tropical Africa and Madagascar, with a short trunk and leaves that may be up to 60 feet (18 m) long. ● *Raphia ruffia*, family Palmae. ■ the fiber from these leaves, used for making items such as hats, baskets, and mats.
– ORIGIN early 18th cent.: from Malagasy.

raf·fi·nate /ˈrafəˌnāt/ ▶ **n.** Chemistry a liquid from which impurities have been removed by solvent extraction.
– ORIGIN 1920s: from French *raffiner* or German *raffinieren* 'refine' + **-ATE**[1].

raf·fi·nose /ˈrafəˌnōs, -ˌnōz/ ▶ **n.** Chemistry a sugar present in sugar beet, cotton seed, and many grains. It is a trisaccharide containing glucose, galactose, and fructose units.
– ORIGIN late 19th cent.: from French *raffiner* 'refine' + **-OSE**[2].

raff·ish /ˈrafisн/ ▶ **adj.** unconventional and slightly disreputable, esp. in an attractive manner: *his raffish air.*
– DERIVATIVES **raf·fish·ly adv.**, **raf·fish·ness n.**
– ORIGIN early 19th cent.: from **RIFFRAFF** + **-ISH**[1].

raf·fle[1] /ˈrafəl/ ▶ **n.** a means of raising money by selling numbered tickets, one or some of which are subsequently drawn at random, the holder or holders of such tickets winning a prize.
▶ **v.** [with obj.] (usu. **be raffled**) offer (something) as a prize in such a lottery: *a work that will be raffled off for a fine arts scholarship.*
– ORIGIN late Middle English (denoting a kind of dice game): from Old French, of unknown origin. The current sense dates from the mid 18th cent.

raf·fle[2] ▶ **n.** rubbish; refuse: *the raffle of the yard below.*
– ORIGIN late Middle English (in the sense 'rabble, riffraff'): perhaps from Old French *ne rifle ne rafle* 'nothing at all.'

Raf·fles /ˈrafəlz/, Sir (Thomas) Stamford (1781–1826), British colonial administrator. He persuaded the East India Company to purchase the undeveloped island of Singapore in 1819 and undertook much of the preliminary work for transforming it into an international port and center of commerce.

raf·fle·sia /rəˈflēzнə, ra-/ ▶ **n.** a parasitic plant that lacks chlorophyll and bears a single, very large flower that smells of carrion, native to Malaysia and Indonesia. ● Genus *Rafflesia*, family Rafflesiaceae: several species, including *R. arnoldii*, with flowers over 2 feet (60 cm) across.
– ORIGIN modern Latin, named after Sir T. Stamford **RAFFLES**.

raft[1] /raft/ ▶ **n.** a flat buoyant structure of timber or other materials fastened together, used as a boat or floating platform. ■ a small, inflatable rubber or plastic boat, esp. one for use in emergencies. ■ a floating mass of fallen trees, vegetation, ice, or other material. ■ a dense flock of swimming birds or mammals: *great rafts of cormorants, often 5,000 strong.* ■ a layer of reinforced concrete forming the foundation of a building.
▶ **v. 1** [no obj.] travel on or as if on a raft: *I have rafted along the Rio Grande.* ■ [with obj.] transport on or as a raft: *the stores were rafted ashore | I rafted 400 logs to my mill.* ■ (of an ice floe) be driven on top of or underneath another floe.
2 [with obj.] bring or fasten together (a number of boats or other objects) side by side.
– ORIGIN late Middle English (in the sense 'beam, rafter'): from Old Norse *raptr* 'rafter.' The verb dates from the late 17th cent.

raft[2] ▶ **n.** a large amount of something: *a raft of government initiatives.*
– ORIGIN mid 19th cent.: alteration of dialect *raff* 'abundance' (perhaps of Scandinavian origin), by association with **RAFT**[1] in the sense 'floating mass.'

raft·er[1] /ˈraftər/ ▶ **n.** one of several internal beams extending from the eaves to the peak of a roof and constituting its framework.
– ORIGIN Old English *ræfter*, of Germanic origin; related to **RAFT**[1].

raft·er[2] ▶ **n.** a person who travels on a raft.

raft·ered /ˈraftərd/ ▶ **adj.** (of a room or ceiling) having exposed rafters. ■ built using rafters: *raftered roofs.*

raft·ing /ˈraftiNG/ ▶ **n.** the sport or pastime of traveling down a river on a raft.

rafts·man /ˈraftsmən/ ▶ **n.** (pl. **raftsmen**) a man who works on a raft.

rag[1] /rag/ ▶ **n. 1** a piece of old cloth, esp. one torn from a larger piece, used typically for cleaning things: *he wiped his hands on an oily rag | a piece of rag.* ■ (**rags**) old or tattered clothes. ■ (**rags**) the remnants of something: *she clung to the rags of her self-control.* ■ [with negative] archaic the smallest scrap of cloth or clothing: *not a rag of clothing has arrived to us this winter.*
2 informal a newspaper, typically one regarded as being of low quality: *the local rag.*
– PHRASES **be on the rag** informal be menstruating. [from *rag* in the sense 'sanitary napkin.'] **chew the rag** see **CHEW**. **in rags** (of clothes) tattered and torn. ■ (of a person) wearing such clothes.
– ORIGIN Middle English: probably a back-formation from **RAGGED** or **RAGGY**.

rag[2] ▶ **v.** (**rags, ragging, ragged** /ragd/) [with obj.] **1** make fun of (someone) in a loud, boisterous manner.
2 rebuke severely.
▶ **n.** [usu. as modifier] Brit. a program of stunts, parades, and other entertainments organized by students to raise money for charity: *rag week.* ■ informal, dated a boisterous prank or practical joke.
– PHRASAL VERBS **rag on** informal **1** complain about or criticize continually. **2** make fun of; tease constantly.
– ORIGIN mid 18th cent.: of unknown origin.

rag[3] ▶ **n.** a large, coarse roofing slate.
– ORIGIN late Middle English (in the sense 'a hard sedimentary rock that can be broken into slabs'): of unknown origin; later associated with **RAG**[1].

rag[4] ▶ **n.** a ragtime composition or tune.
– ORIGIN late 19th cent.: perhaps from **RAGGED**; compare with **RAGTIME**.

rag[5] ▶ **n.** variant of **RAGA**.

ra·ga /ˈrägə/ ▶ **n.** (in Indian music) a pattern of notes having characteristic intervals, rhythms, and embellishments, used as a basis for improvisation. ■ a piece using a particular raga.
– ORIGIN late 18th cent.: from Sanskrit, literally 'color, musical tone.'

rag·a·muf·fin /ˈragəˌməfən/ ▶ **n. 1** a person, typically a child, in ragged, dirty clothes.
2 (also **raggamuffin**) chiefly Brit. an exponent or follower of ragga, typically one dressing in ragged clothes. ■ another term for **RAGGA**.
– ORIGIN Middle English: probably based on **RAG**[1], with a fanciful suffix.

rag-and-bone man ▶ **adj.** an itinerant dealer in old clothes, furniture, and small, cheap secondhand items.

rag·bag /ˈragˌbag/ ▶ **n.** a bag in which scraps of fabric and old clothes are kept for use. ■ a miscellaneous collection of something: *Lee threw a ragbag of pitches.*

rag doll ▶ **n.** a soft doll made from pieces of cloth.

rage /rāj/ ▶ **n.** violent, uncontrollable anger: *her face was distorted with rage | she flew into a rage.* ■ the violent action of a natural agency: *the rising rage of the sea.* ■ [in sing.] a vehement desire or passion: *a rage for absolute honesty informs much western art.* ■ [with modifier] an instance of aggressive behavior or violent anger caused by a stressful or frustrating situation: *desk rage | sports rage | PC rage.* ■ (**the rage**) a widespread temporary enthusiasm or fashion: *video and computer games are all the rage.* ■ literary intense feeling, esp. prophetic, poetic, or martial enthusiasm or ardor.
▶ **v.** [no obj.] feel or express violent uncontrollable anger: *he raged at the futility of it all* | [with direct speech] *"That's unfair!" Maggie raged.* ■ [with adverbial] (of a natural agency or a conflict) continue violently or with great force: *the argument raged for days.* ■ [with adverbial of direction] (of an illness) spread very rapidly or uncontrollably: *the great cholera epidemic that raged across Europe in 1831.* ■ (of an emotion) have or reach a high degree of intensity: *she couldn't hide the fear that raged within her.*
– ORIGIN Middle English (also in the sense 'madness'): from Old French *rage* (noun), *rager* (verb), from a variant of Latin *rabies* (see **RABIES**).

rag·ga /ˈragə/ ▶ **n.** chiefly Brit. a style of dance music similar to dancehall in which a DJ improvises lyrics over a sampled or electronic backing track.
– ORIGIN 1990s: from **RAGAMUFFIN**, because of the style of clothing worn by its followers.

rag·ga·muf·fin /ˈragəˌməfən/ ▶ **n.** variant spelling of **RAGAMUFFIN**.

rag·ged /ˈragid/ ▶ **adj. 1** (of cloth or clothes) old and torn. ■ (of a person) wearing such clothes: *a ragged child.*
2 having a rough, irregular, or uneven surface, edge, or outline: *a ragged coastline.* ■ lacking finish, smoothness, or uniformity: *the ragged discipline of the players.* ■ (of a sound) rough or uneven: *his breathing became ragged.* ■ (of an animal) having a rough, shaggy coat: *a pair of ragged ponies.* ■ Printing (esp. of a right margin) uneven because the lines are unjustified.
3 suffering from exhaustion or stress: *he looked a little ragged, a little shadowy beneath the eyes.*
– PHRASES **run someone ragged** exhaust someone by making them undertake a lot of physical activity.
– DERIVATIVES **rag·ged·ly adv.**, **rag·ged·ness n.**
– ORIGIN Middle English: of Scandinavian origin; compare with Old Norse *rǫgvathr* 'tufted' and Norwegian *ragget* 'shaggy.'

rag·ged·y /ˈragədē/ ▶ **adj.** informal scruffy; shabby.

rag·ged·y-ass (also **raggedy-assed**) ▶ **adj.** [attrib.] informal shabby; miserably inadequate: *she finally sold that raggedy-ass house.* ■ (of a person) new and inexperienced.

rag·gle-tag·gle /ˈragəl ˌtagəl/ ▶ **adj.** untidy and scruffy.
– ORIGIN early 20th cent.: apparently a fanciful variant of **RAGTAG**.

rag·gy /ˈragē/ ▶ **adj.** (**raggier, raggiest**) informal ragged: *his raggy clothes.*
– ORIGIN late Old English, of Scandinavian origin.

rag·head /ˈragˌhed/ ▶ **n.** informal, offensive a person who wears a turban.

rag·i /ˈragē/ ▶ **n.** chiefly Indian another term for **FINGER MILLET** (see **MILLET**).
– ORIGIN from Sanskrit and Hindi *rāgī*, from Telugu.

rag·ing /ˈrājiNG/ ▶ **adj.** showing violent uncontrollable anger: *a raging bull.* ■ continuing with overpowering force; very powerful: *the stream could become a raging torrent in wet weather | her raging thirst.* ■ informal tremendous: *he had been a raging success in Spain.*

rag·lan /ˈraglən/ ▶ **adj.** having or denoting sleeves that continue in one piece up to the neck of a garment, without a shoulder seam.
▶ **n.** an overcoat with sleeves of this type.
– ORIGIN mid 19th cent.: named after Lord *Raglan* (1788–1855), a British commander in the Crimean War.

raglan sleeves

r

rag·man /ˈragˌman/ ▶ **n.** (pl. **ragmen**) a person who collects or deals in rags, old clothes, and other items.

Rag·na·rök /ˈragnəˌräk, -rək/ Scandinavian Mythology the final battle between the gods and the powers of evil, the Scandinavian equivalent of the *Götterdämmerung*.
– ORIGIN from Old Norse *ragnarǫkr* 'twilight of the gods.'

ra·gout /raˈgo͞o/ ▶ **n.** a highly seasoned dish of meat cut into small pieces and stewed with vegetables.
– ORIGIN from French *ragoût*, from *ragoûter* 'revive the taste of.'

rag pa·per ▶ **n.** paper made from cotton, originally from cotton rags, but now from cotton linters.

rag·pick·er /ˈragˌpikər/ ▶ **n.** a person who collects and sells rags.

rag-roll ▶ **v.** [with obj.] create a striped or marbled effect on (a surface) by painting it with a rag crumpled up into a roll.

rag rug ▶ **n.** a rug made from small strips of fabric hooked into or pushed through a base material such as hessian.

rag·tag /ˈragˌtag/ ▶ **adj.** [attrib.] untidy, disorganized, or incongruously varied in character: *a ragtag group of idealists*.
▶ **n.** (also **ragtag and bobtail**) [in sing.] a group of people perceived as disreputable or undesirable.
– ORIGIN early 19th cent.: superseding earlier *tag-rag* and *tag and rag* (see **RAG**[1], **TAG**[1]).

rag·time /ˈragˌtīm/ ▶ **n.** music characterized by a syncopated melodic line and regularly accented accompaniment, evolved by black American musicians in the 1890s and played esp. on the piano.
– ORIGIN probably from **RAG**[4] (from the syncopation) + **TIME**.

rag·top /ˈragˌtäp/ ▶ **n.** a car with a convertible roof.

rag trade ▶ **n.** (**the rag trade**) informal the clothing or fashion industry.

rag·u·ly /ˈragyəlē/ ▶ **adj.** [usu. postpositive] Heraldry having an edge with oblique notches like a row of sawn-off branches.
– ORIGIN mid 17th cent.: perhaps from **RAGGED**, on the pattern of *nebuly*.

Ra·gu·sa /rəˈgo͞ozə, räˈgo͞ozä/ Italian name (until 1918) of **DUBROVNIK**.

rag·weed /ˈragˌwēd/ ▶ **n.** a North American plant of the daisy family. Its tiny green flowers produce copious amounts of pollen, making it a major causative agent of hay fever in some areas. ● *Ambrosia artemisia*, family Compositae.

rag·wort /ˈragˌwərt, -ˌwôrt/ ▶ **n.** a yellow-flowered plant of the daisy family that is a common weed of grazing land. It is toxic to livestock, esp. when dried. ● Genus *Senecio*, family Compositae: several species, including the ragged-leaved **tansy ragwort** (*S. jacobaea*).

rah /rä/ ▶ **exclam.** informal a cheer of encouragement or approval.
– ORIGIN late 19th cent.: shortening of **HURRAH**.

Rah·man see **ABDUL RAHMAN, MUJIBUR RAHMAN**.

rah-rah informal ▶ **adj.** marked by great or uncritical enthusiasm or excitement: *many players were turned off by his rah-rah style*.
▶ **n.** great or uncritical enthusiasm and excitement.
– ORIGIN early 20th cent.: reduplication of **RAH**.

rai /rī/ ▶ **n.** a style of music fusing Arabic and Algerian folk elements with Western rock.
– ORIGIN 1980s: perhaps from Arabic *ha er-ray*, literally 'that's the thinking, here is the view,' a phrase frequently found in the songs.

RAID /rād/ ▶ **abbr.** redundant array of independent (or inexpensive) disks, a system for providing greater capacity, faster access, and security against data corruption by spreading the data across several disk drives.

raid /rād/ ▶ **n.** a sudden attack on an enemy by troops, aircraft, or other armed forces in warfare: *a bombing raid*. ■ a surprise attack to commit a crime, esp. to steal from business premises: *an early morning raid on a bank*. ■ a surprise visit by police to arrest suspected people or seize illicit goods. ■ Stock Market a hostile attempt to buy a major or controlling interest in the shares of a company.
▶ **v.** [with obj.] conduct a raid on: *officers raided thirty homes yesterday*. ■ quickly and illicitly take something from (a place): *she crept down the stairs to raid the pantry*.
– ORIGIN late Middle English (as a noun): Scots variant of **ROAD** in the early senses 'journey on horseback,' 'foray.' The noun became rare from the end of the 16th cent. but was revived by Sir Walter Scott; the verb dates from the mid 19th cent.

raid·er /ˈrādər/ ▶ **n.** a person who attacks an enemy in the enemy's territory; a marauder: *Scandinavian raiders put down their roots in Cumbria*. ■ a person who attacks business premises in order to steal: *masked raiders burst into the 100-seater restaurant*.

rail[1] /rāl/ ▶ **n.** **1** a bar or series of bars, typically fixed on upright supports, serving as part of a fence or barrier or used to hang things on. ■ (**the rails**) the inside boundary fence of a racecourse. ■ the edge of a surfboard or sailboard.
2 a steel bar or continuous line of bars laid on the ground as one of a pair forming a railroad track: *trolley rails*. ■ [often as modifier] railroads as a means of transportation: *rail fares | traveling by rail*.
3 a horizontal piece in the frame of a paneled door or sash window. Compare with **STILE**[2].
4 Electronics a conductor that is maintained at a fixed potential and to which other parts of a circuit are connected.
▶ **v. 1** [with obj.] provide or enclose (a space or place) with a rail or rails: *the altar is **railed off** from the nave*.
2 [no obj.] (in windsurfing) sail the board on its edge, so that it is at a sharp angle to the surface of the water.
– PHRASES **go off the rails** informal begin behaving in a strange, abnormal, or wildly uncontrolled way.
– DERIVATIVES **rail·less adj.**
– ORIGIN Middle English: from Old French *reille* 'iron rod,' from Latin *regula* 'straight stick, rule.'

rail[2] ▶ **v.** [no obj.] (**rail against/at/about**) complain or protest strongly and persistently about: *he railed at human fickleness*.
– DERIVATIVES **rail·er n.**
– ORIGIN late Middle English: from French *railler*, from Provençal *ralhar* 'to jest,' based on an alteration of Latin *rugire* 'to bellow.'

rail[3] ▶ **n.** a secretive bird with drab gray and brown plumage, typically having a long bill and found in dense waterside vegetation. ● Family Rallidae (the **rail family**): several genera, esp. *Rallus*, and numerous species. The rail family also includes the crakes, gallinules, moorhens, and coots.
– ORIGIN late Middle English: from Old Northern French *raille*, perhaps of imitative origin.

rail·bird /ˈrālˌbərd/ ▶ **n.** a spectator, esp. one at a horse race who watches from the railings along the track.

rail car ▶ **n.** any railroad car or wagon.

rail fence ▶ **n.** a fence, typically a wooden one, made of posts and rails.

rail·head /ˈrālˌhed/ ▶ **n.** a point on a railroad from which roads and other transportation routes begin. ■ the furthest point reached in constructing a railroad.

rail·ing /ˈrāliNG/ ▶ **n.** (usu. **railings**) a fence or barrier made of rails.

rail·ler·y /ˈrālərē/ ▶ **n.** good-humored teasing.
– ORIGIN mid 17th cent.: from French *raillerie*, from *railler* 'to rail' (see **RAIL**[2]).

rail·man /ˈrālmən/ ▶ **n.** (pl. **railmen**) chiefly British term for **RAILROADER**.

rail·road /ˈrālˌrōd/ ▶ **n. 1** a track or set of tracks made of steel rails along which passenger and freight trains run: [as modifier] *a railroad line*. ■ a set of tracks for other vehicles.
2 a system of such tracks with the trains, organization, and personnel required for its working: [in names] *the Union Pacific Railroad*.
▶ **v. 1** [with obj.] informal press (someone) into doing something by rushing or coercing them: *she hesitated, unwilling to be **railroaded into** a decision*. ■ cause (a measure) to be passed or approved quickly by applying pressure: *the Bill had been **railroaded through** the House*. ■ send (someone) to prison without a fair trial or by means of false evidence.
2 [no obj.] (usu. as noun **railroading**) travel or work on the railroads.

rail·road·er ▶ **n.** a person who works for a railroad.

rail·way /ˈrālˌwā/ ▶ **n.** chiefly British term for **RAILROAD**.

rail·way·man /ˈrālˌwāmən/ ▶ **n.** (pl. **railwaymen**) chiefly Brit. another term for **RAILROADER**.

rai·ment /ˈrāmənt/ ▶ **n.** archaic or literary clothing: *ladies clothed in raiment bedecked with jewels*.
– ORIGIN late Middle English: shortening of obsolete *arrayment* 'dress, outfit.'

rain /rān/ ▶ **n.** moisture condensed from the atmosphere that falls visibly in separate drops: *the rain had not stopped for days | it's pouring rain*. ■ (**rains**) falls of rain: *the plants were washed away by some unusually heavy rains*. ■ [in sing.] a large or overwhelming quantity of things that fall or descend: *he fell under the **rain of** blows*.
▶ **v.** [no obj.] (**it rains, it is raining**, etc.) rain falls: *it was beginning to rain*. ■ literary (of the sky, the clouds, etc.) send down rain. ■ [with adverbial of direction] (of objects) fall in large or overwhelming quantities: *bombs rained down*. ■ [with obj.] (**it rains ——, it is raining ——**, etc.) used to convey that a specified thing is falling in large or overwhelming quantities: *it was just raining glass*. ■ [with obj.] send down in large or overwhelming quantities: *she rained blows onto him*.
– PHRASES **be as right as rain** (of a person) be perfectly fit and well. **when it rains it pours** see **POUR**. **rain cats and dogs** rain very hard. [origin uncertain; first recorded in 1738, used by Jonathan Swift, but the phrase *rain dogs and polecats* was used a century earlier in Richard Brome's *The City Witt*.] **rain on someone's parade** informal prevent someone from enjoying an occasion or event; spoil someone's plans. (**come**) **rain or shine** whether it rains or not: *he runs six miles every morning, rain or shine*.
– PHRASAL VERBS **be rained out** (of an event) be terminated or canceled because of rain: *the tournament was rained out*.
– DERIVATIVES **rain·less adj.**
– ORIGIN Old English *regn* (noun), *regnian* (verb), of Germanic origin; related to Dutch *regen* and German *Regen*.

rain·bow /ˈrānˌbō/ ▶ **n.** an arch of colors formed in the sky in certain circumstances, caused by the refraction and dispersion of the sun's light by rain or other water droplets in the atmosphere. ■ any display of the colors of the spectrum produced by dispersion of light. ■ a wide range or variety of related and typically colorful things: ***a rainbow of** medals decorated his chest*. ■ [as modifier] many-colored: *a big rainbow packet of felt pens*. ■ short for **RAINBOW TROUT**.
– PHRASES **at the end of the rainbow** used to refer to something much sought after but impossible to attain. [with allusion to the story of a pot of gold supposedly to be found by anyone reaching the end of a rainbow.] **chase rainbows** (or **a rainbow**) pursue an illusory goal.
– ORIGIN Old English *regnboga* (see **RAIN, BOW**[1]).

Rain·bow Bridge a bridge of natural rock, the world's largest natural bridge, situated in southern Utah, just north of the border with Arizona. Its span is 278 feet (86 m).

rain·bow co·a·li·tion ▶ **n.** a political alliance of differing groups, typically one comprising minority peoples and other disadvantaged groups.

rain·bow lor·i·keet (also **rainbow lory**) ▶ **n.** a small, vividly colored Australasian parrot, found in many different races on southwestern Pacific islands. ● *Trichoglossus haematodus*, family Loridae (or Psittacidae).

rain·bow trout ▶ **n.** a large trout native to the Pacific seaboard of North America. It has been widely introduced elsewhere, both as a farmed food fish and as a sporting fish. Most rainbow trout remain in streams, but some migrate to lakes and some to the sea (see **STEELHEAD**). ● *Salmo gairdneri*, family Salmonidae.

rain check /ˈrānˌCHek/ (also **raincheck**) ▶ **n.** a ticket given for later use when a sports event or other outdoor event is interrupted or postponed by rain. ■ a coupon issued to a customer by a store, guaranteeing that a sale item that is out of stock may be purchased by that customer at a later date at the same reduced price.
– PHRASES **take a rain check** said when politely refusing an offer, with the implication that one may accept it at a later date: *I can't make it tonight, but I'd like to take a rain check*.

rain·coat /ˈrānˌkōt/ ▶ **n.** a long coat made from waterproofed or water-resistant fabric.

rain dance ▶ **n.** a ritual done to summon rain, as practiced by some Pueblo Indian and other peoples.

rain date ▶ **n.** an alternative date for an event in case of inclement weather. ■ Baseball the day to which a rained-out game is postponed.

rain·drop /ˈrānˌdräp/ ▶ **n.** a single drop of rain.
– ORIGIN Old English *regndropa* (see **RAIN, DROP**).

rain·fall /ˈrānˌfôl/ ▶ **n.** the fall of rain. ■ the quantity of rain falling within a given area in a given time: *low rainfall*.

rain·fly /ˈrānˌflī/ ▶ **n.** (pl. **rainflies**) the flysheet of a tent.

rain for·est (also **rainforest**) ▶ **n.** a luxuriant, dense forest rich in biodiversity, found typically in tropical areas with consistently heavy rainfall.

rain gauge ▶ **n.** a device for collecting and measuring the amount of rain that falls.

Rai·nier, Mount /rəˈni(ə)r, rā-/ a volcanic peak in southwestern Washington state. Rising to a height of 14,410 feet (4,395 m), it is the highest peak in the Cascade Range.

PRONUNCIATION KEY ə *ago, up*; ər *over, fur*; a *hat*; ā *ate*; ä *car*; e *let*; ē *see*; i *fit*; ī *by*; NG *sing*; ō *go*; ô *law, for*; oi *toy*; o͝o *good*; o͞o *goo*; ou *out*; TH *thin*; T͟H *then*; ZH *vision*

r

rain·mak·er /'rān,mākər/ ▶ **n. 1** a person who attempts to cause rain to fall, either by rituals or by a scientific technique such as seeding clouds with crystals.
2 informal a person who generates income for a business or organization by brokering deals or attracting clients or funds.
– DERIVATIVES **rain·mak·ing** /-,mākiNG/ **n.**

rain·out /'rān,out/ ▶ **n.** a cancellation or premature ending of an event because of rain.

rain·proof /'rān,pro͞of/ ▶ **adj.** (esp. of a building or garment) impervious to rain: *a rainproof coat.*

rain scald ▶ **n.** a skin disease of horses caused by infection with actinomycete bacteria, typically contracted in persistently rainy conditions.

rain shad·ow ▶ **n.** a region having little rainfall because it is sheltered from prevailing rain-bearing winds by a range of hills.

rain·stick (also **rain stick**) ▶ **n.** a percussion instrument made from a dried cactus branch that is hollowed out, filled with small pebbles, and capped at both ends. When slightly tilted, it makes the sound of falling rain.

rain·storm /'rān,stôrm/ ▶ **n.** a storm with heavy rain.

rain·swept /'rān,swept/ ▶ **adj.** exposed to or frequently experiencing rain and wind: *a rainswept day in November.*

rain tree ▶ **n.** a large tropical American tree that is widely planted as a street tree. It has grooved bark that typically supports epiphytic plants, and "rain" (as it mimics the sound of rain) that is excreted by cicadas that live in the tree. ● *Albizia saman*, family Leguminosae.

rain·wash /'rān,wôsH, -,wäsH/ ▶ **n.** the washing away of soil or other loose material by rain.

rain·wa·ter /'rān,wôtər, -,wätər/ ▶ **n.** water that has fallen as or been obtained from rain.

rain·wear /'rān,we(ə)r/ ▶ **n.** waterproof or water-resistant clothes suitable for wearing in the rain.

rain·worm /'rān,wərm/ ▶ **n. 1** the earthworm, which often comes to the surface after rain.
2 a soil-dwelling nematode worm, the juveniles of which parasitize grasshoppers. ● *Mermis nigrescens*, class Aphasmida (or Adenophorea).

rain·y /'rānē/ ▶ **adj.** (**rainier, rainiest**) (of weather, a period of time, or an area) having a great deal of rainfall: *a rainy afternoon.*
– PHRASES **a rainy day** used in reference to a possible time in the future when something, esp. money, will be needed: *invest and save for a rainy day.*
– DERIVATIVES **rain·i·ness n.**
– ORIGIN Old English *rēnig* (see RAIN, -Y[1]).

Rain·y Riv·er /'rānē/ a short river that flows west along the Minnesota-Ontario border, past International Falls, into the Lake of the Woods. One of its sources is Rainy Lake, also on the border.

Rai·pur /'rīpo͝or/ a city in central India, in Madhya Pradesh; pop. 759,600 (est. 2009).

raise /rāz/ ▶ **v.** [with obj.] **1** lift or move to a higher position or level: *she raised both arms above her head | his flag was raised over the city.* ■ lift or move to a vertical position; set upright: *Melody managed to raise him to his feet.* ■ construct or build (a structure): *a fence was being raised around the property.* ■ cause to rise or form: *the galloping horse raised a cloud of dust.* ■ bring to the surface (something that has sunk). ■ cause (bread) to rise, esp. by the action of yeast.
2 increase the amount, level, or strength of: *the bank raised interest rates | the aim was to raise awareness of the plight of the homeless.* ■ promote (someone) to a higher rank: *the king* **raised him to** *the title of Count Torre Bella.* ■ (usu. as noun **raising**) Linguistics (in transformational grammar) move (an element) from a lower structure to a higher one. ■ (**raise something to**) Mathematics multiply a quantity by itself to (a specified power): *3 raised to the 7th power is 2,187.* ■ [with two objs.] (in poker or brag) bet (a specified amount) more than (another player): *I'll raise you another hundred dollars.* ■ [with obj.] Bridge make a higher bid in the same suit as that bid by (one's partner). ■ [with obj.] increase (a bid) in this way.
3 cause to occur or be considered: *the alarm was raised when he failed to return home | doubts have been raised about the future of the reprocessing plant.* ■ generate (an invoice or other document).
4 collect, levy, or bring together (money or resources): *she was attempting to raise $20,000.*
5 bring up (a child): *he was born and raised in San Francisco.* ■ breed or grow (animals or plants): *they raised pigs and kept a pony.*
6 bring (someone) back from death: *God raised Jesus from the dead.*
7 abandon or force an enemy to abandon (a siege, blockade, or embargo).
8 drive (an animal) from its lair: *the jack rabbit was only 250 yards from where he first raised it.* ■ cause (a ghost or spirit) to appear: figurative *the piece raises the ghosts of a number of twentieth-century art ideas.* ■ Brit. informal establish contact with (someone), esp. by telephone or radio: *I raised him on the open line.* ■ (of someone at sea) come in sight of (land or another ship): *they raised the low coast by evening.*
9 Immunology stimulate production of (an antiserum, antibody, or other biologically active substance) against the appropriate target cell or substance.
▶ **n. 1** an increase in salary: *he wants a raise and some perks.*
2 (in poker or brag) an increase in a stake. ■ Bridge a higher bid in the suit that one's partner has bid.
3 [usu. with adj.] Weightlifting an act of lifting or raising a part of the body while holding a weight: *bent-over raises.*
– PHRASES **raise Cain** see CAIN. **raise the devil** informal make a noisy disturbance. **raise one's eyebrows** see EYEBROW. **raise one's glass** drink a toast: *I raised my glass to Susan.* **raise one's hand** strike or seem to be about to strike someone: *she raised her hand to me.* **raise one's hat** briefly remove one's hat as a gesture of courtesy or respect to someone. **raise hell** informal make a noisy disturbance. ■ complain vociferously: *he raised hell with real estate developers and polluters.* **raise hob** see HOB[2]. **raise a laugh** make people laugh. **raise the roof** make or cause someone else to make a great deal of noise, esp. through cheering: *when I finally scored, the fans raised the roof.* **raise one's voice** speak more loudly. ■ begin to speak or sing.
– DERIVATIVES **rais·a·ble adj., rais·er n.**
– ORIGIN Middle English: from Old Norse *reisa*; related to the verb REAR[2].

raised /rāzd/ ▶ **adj. 1** elevated to a higher position or level; lifted: *they ate on a raised platform at one end of the hall.* ■ embossed; in relief: *the building features raised lettering.* ■ (of bread or pastry) made with a raising agent such as yeast: *raised doughnuts.*
2 more intense or strong than usual; higher: *a neighbor heard raised voices from the women's apartment | as we age we are more likely to have raised blood pressure.*

raised beach ▶ **n.** Geology a former beach now lying above water level owing to geological changes since its formation.

rai·sin /'rāzən/ ▶ **n.** a partially dried grape.
– DERIVATIVES **rai·sin·y adj.**
– ORIGIN Middle English: from Old French, 'grape,' from an alteration of Latin *racemus* 'grape bunch.'

rai·son d'é·tat /rā'zôN dā'tä/ ▶ **n.** (pl. **raisons d'état** /rā'zôN(z)/) a purely political reason for action on the part of a ruler or government, esp. where a departure from openness, justice, or honesty is involved.
– ORIGIN French, literally 'reason of state.'

rai·son d'ê·tre /rā'zôN 'detr(ə)/ ▶ **n.** (pl. **raisons d'être** /rā'zôn(z)/) the most important reason or purpose for someone or something's existence: *an institution whose raison d'être is public service broadcasting.*
– ORIGIN French, literally 'reason for being.'

rai·ta /'rītə/ ▶ **n.** an Indian side dish of yogurt containing chopped cucumber or other vegetables, and spices.
– ORIGIN from Hindi *rāytā.*

raj /räj/ ▶ **n.** (**the raj**) historical British sovereignty in India: *the last days of the raj.* ■ (**raj**) Indian rule; government.
– ORIGIN from Hindi *rāj* 'reign.'

ra·jah /'räjə, 'räzHə/ (also **raja**) ▶ **n.** historical an Indian king or prince. ■ a title extended to petty dignitaries and nobles in India during the British Raj. ■ a title extended by the British to a Malay or Javanese ruler or chief.
– ORIGIN from Hindi *rājā*, Sanskrit *rājan* 'king.'

ra·jas /'rəjəs/ ▶ **n.** (in Vedanta) the element or mode of prakriti associated with passion, energy, and movement.

ra·jas·ic /rə'jasik/ ▶ **adj.** (in Ayurveda) denoting a class of foods that are bitter, sour, salty, pungent, hot, or dry, and are thought to promote sensuality, greed, jealousy, anger, delusion, and irreligious feelings. Compare SATTVIC, TAMASIC.

Ra·ja·sthan /'räjə,stän/ a state in western India, on the Pakistani border; capital, Jaipur. The western part of the state consists largely of the Thar Desert and is sparsely populated.
– DERIVATIVES **Ra·ja·stha·ni** /,räjə'stänē/ **n. & adj.**

ra·ja yo·ga ▶ **n.** a form of Hindu yoga intended to achieve control over the mind and emotions.
– ORIGIN from Sanskrit, from *rājan* 'king' + YOGA.

Raj·kot /'räjkōt/ a city in Gujarat, in western India; pop. 1,395,000 (est. 2009).

Raj·put /'räj,po͝ot, 'räzH-/ ▶ **n.** a member of a Hindu military caste claiming Kshatriya descent.
– ORIGIN from Hindi *rājpūt*, from Sanskrit *rājan* 'king' + *putra* 'son.'

Raj·sha·hi /räj'sHä,hē/ a port on the Ganges River in western Bangladesh; pop. 472,775 (2008).

Raj·ya Sab·ha /'räjə sə'bä/ the upper house of the Indian parliament. Compare with LOK SABHA.
– ORIGIN from Sanskrit *rājya* 'state' + *sabhā* 'council.'

rake[1] /rāk/ ▶ **n.** an implement consisting of a pole with a crossbar toothed like a comb at the end, or with several tines held together by a crosspiece, used esp. for drawing together cut grass or fallen leaves, or smoothing loose soil or gravel. ■ a wheeled implement used for the same purposes. ■ a similar implement used for other purposes, e.g., by a croupier drawing in money at a gaming table.
▶ **v.** [with obj.] collect, gather, or move with a rake or similar implement: *they startevd* **raking up** *hay.* ■ make (a stretch of ground) tidy or smooth with a rake: *the infield dirt is meticulously raked.* ■ scratch or scrape (something, esp. a person's flesh) with a long sweeping movement: *her fingers raked Bill's face.* ■ draw or drag (something) with a long sweeping movement: *she raked a comb through her hair.* ■ sweep (something) from end to end with gunfire, a look, or a beam of light: *Greg let his high beams rake the shrubbery.* ■ [no obj.] move across something with a long sweeping movement: *his icy gaze raked mercilessly over Lissa's slender figure.* ■ [no obj.] search or rummage through something: *Nina decided to rake through the drawers.*
– PHRASES **(as) thin as a rake** (of a person) very thin.
– PHRASAL VERBS **rake something in** informal make a lot of money, typically very easily: *he was now raking in $250 million a year.* **rake something up/over** revive the memory of an incident or period of time that is best forgotten: *I have no desire to rake over the past.*
– DERIVATIVES **rak·er n.**
– ORIGIN Old English *raca, racu*, of Germanic origin; related to Dutch *raak* and German *Rechen*, from a base meaning 'heap up'; the verb is partly from Old Norse *raka* 'to scrape, shave.'

rake[2] ▶ **n.** a fashionable or wealthy man of dissolute or promiscuous habits.
– PHRASES **a rake's progress** a progressive deterioration, esp. through self-indulgence. [from the title of a series of engravings (1735) by Hogarth.]
– ORIGIN mid 17th cent.: abbreviation of archaic *rakehell* in the same sense.

rake[3] ▶ **v.** [with obj.] set (something, esp. a stage or the floor of an auditorium) at a sloping angle. ■ [no obj.] (of a ship's mast or funnel) incline from the perpendicular toward the stern. ■ [no obj.] (of a ship's bow or stern) project at its upper part beyond the keel.
▶ **n. 1** [in sing.] the angle at which a thing slopes.
2 the angle of the edge or face of a cutting tool.
– ORIGIN early 17th cent.: probably related to German *ragen* 'to project,' of unknown ultimate origin; compare with Swedish *raka.*

rake-off ▶ **n.** informal a commission or share of the profits from a deal, esp. one that is disreputable.

ra·ki /'rə'kē, 'rakē, 'räkē/ ▶ **n.** a strong alcoholic spirit made in eastern Europe or the Middle East.
– ORIGIN from Turkish *rakı.*

rak·ing light ▶ **n.** (in art or photography) bright light, usually beamed obliquely, used to reveal such things as texture and detail.

rak·ish[1] /'rākisH/ ▶ **adj.** having or displaying a dashing, jaunty, or slightly disreputable quality or appearance: *he had a rakish, debonair look.*
– DERIVATIVES **rak·ish·ly adv., rak·ish·ness n.**

rak·ish[2] ▶ **adj.** (esp. of a boat or car) trim and fast-looking, with streamlined angles and curves.
– ORIGIN early 19th cent.: from the noun RAKE[3] + -ISH[1].

ra·ku /'rä,ko͞o/ ▶ **n.** [usu. as modifier] a kind of lead-glazed Japanese earthenware, typically irregular in shape and used esp. for the tea ceremony.
– ORIGIN Japanese, literally 'enjoyment.'

rale /räl, ral/ ▶ **n.** (usu. **rales**) Medicine an abnormal rattling sound heard when examining unhealthy lungs with a stethoscope.
– ORIGIN early 19th cent.: from French *râle*, from *râler* 'to rattle.'

Ra·leigh[1] /'rôlē, 'rä-/ the capital of North Carolina, in the east central part of the state; pop. 392,552 (est. 2008).

Ra·leigh[2] (also **Ralegh**), Sir Walter (*c.*1552–1618), English explorer, courtier, and writer. A favorite of Elizabeth I, he organized several voyages of exploration and colonization to the Americas and introduced potato and tobacco plants to England.

rall. ▶ **abbr.** Music rallentando.

ral·len·tan·do /,rälən'tändō, ,ralən'tandō/ ▶ **adv., adj., & n.** (pl. **rallentandos** or **rallentandi** /-dē/) Music another term for RITARDANDO.

–ORIGIN Italian, literally 'slowing down,' from the verb *rallentare*.

ral·ly¹ /ˈralē/ ▶ **v.** (**rallies, rallying, rallied**) [no obj.] **1** (of troops) come together again in order to continue fighting after a defeat or dispersion: *De Montfort's troops rallied and drove back the king's infantry.* ■ [with obj.] bring together (forces) again in order to continue fighting: *the king escaped to Perth to rally his own forces.* ■ assemble in a mass meeting: *up to 50,000 people rallied in the city center.* ■ bring or come together in order to support a person or cause or for concerted action: [with obj.] *a series of meetings to rally support for the union* | [no obj.] *conservatives in the GOP* ***rallied behind*** *Goldwater.*
2 recover or cause to recover in health, spirits, or poise: [no obj.] *she floundered for a moment, then rallied again* | [with obj.] *they rallied her with a drink.* ■ (of share, currency, or commodity prices) increase after a fall: *prices of metals such as aluminum and copper have rallied.*
3 drive in a rally. ■ (in tennis and other racket sports) engage in a rally.
▶ **n.** (pl. **rallies**) **1** a mass meeting of people making a political protest or showing support for a cause: *a rally attended by around 100,000 people.* ■ an open-air event for people who own a particular kind of vehicle: *a traction engine rally.*
2 (also **rallye**) a competition for motor vehicles in which they are driven a long distance over public roads or rough terrain, typically in stages and through checkpoints: [as modifier] *a rally driver.*
3 a quick or marked recovery after a reverse or a period of weakness: *the market staged a late rally.* ■ (in baseball and football) a renewed or sustained offensive, usually by the losing team, that ties or wins the game.
4 (in tennis and other racket sports) an extended exchange of strokes between players.
–DERIVATIVES **ral·li·er n., ral·ly·ist n.** (sense 2 of the noun).
–ORIGIN early 17th cent. (in the sense 'bring together again'): from French *rallier*, from *re-* 'again' + *allier* 'to ally.'

ral·ly² ▶ **v.** (**rallies, rallying, rallied**) [with obj.] archaic subject (someone) to good-humored ridicule; tease: *he rallied her on the length of her pigtail.*
–ORIGIN mid 17th cent.: from French *railler* 'to rib, tease' (see RAIL²).

ral·ly·ing /ˈralēiNG/ ▶ **n. 1** [often as modifier] the action or process of coming together to support a person or cause or take concerted action: *a rallying cry.*
2 the sport or action of participating in a motor rally: *established names in international rallying.*

ral·ox·i·fene /rəˈläksəˌfēn/ ▶ **n.** a drug that is prescribed mainly for the prevention and treatment of osteoporosis in post-menopausal women, and for the prevention of breast cancer.

ralph /ralf/ ▶ **v.** [no obj.] informal vomit.
–ORIGIN 1960s: origin uncertain; apparently a use of the male given name *Ralph*, but perhaps imitative.

RAM /ram/ ▶ **abbr.** ■ Computing random-access memory. ■ (in the UK) Royal Academy of Music.

ram /ram/ ▶ **n. 1** an uncastrated male sheep. ■ (**the Ram**) the zodiacal sign or constellation Aries.
2 short for BATTERING RAM. ■ the falling weight of a pile-driving machine. ■ historical a beak or other projecting part of the bow of a warship, for piercing the hulls of other ships. ■ historical a warship with such a bow.
3 a hydraulic water-raising or lifting machine. ■ the piston of a hydraulic press. ■ the plunger of a force pump.
▶ **v.** (**rams, ramming, rammed**) [with obj.] roughly force (something) into place: *he rammed his stick into the ground.* ■ (of a vehicle or vessel) be driven violently into (something, typically another vehicle or vessel) in an attempt to stop or damage it: *their boat was rammed by a Japanese warship.* ■ [no obj.] crash violently against something: *the stolen car rammed into the front of the house.* ■ (often as adj. **rammed**) beat (earth or the ground) with a heavy implement to make it hard and firm: *a long curving wall made of rammed earth.* ■ (**ram through**) force (something) to be accepted: *Sunday's referendum to ram through a new constitution.*
–PHRASES **ram something down someone's throat** see THROAT. **ram something home** see HOME.
–DERIVATIVES **ram·mer n.**
–ORIGIN Old English *ram(m)*, related to Dutch *ram*.

Ra·ma /ˈrämə/ the hero of the Ramayana, husband of Sita. He is the Hindu model of the ideal man, the seventh incarnation of Vishnu, and is widely venerated, by some sects as the supreme god.

ra·ma·da /rəˈmädə, -ˈmadə/ ▶ **n.** an arbor or porch.
–ORIGIN mid 19th cent.: from Spanish.

Ram·a·dan /ˈräməˌdän, ˈraməˌdan/ ▶ **n.** the ninth month of the Muslim year, during which strict fasting is observed from sunrise to sunset.
–ORIGIN from Arabic *ramaḍān*, from *ramaḍa* 'be hot.' The lunar reckoning of the Muslim calendar brings the fast eleven days earlier each year, eventually causing Ramadan to occur in any season; originally it was supposed to be in one of the hot months.

ram air ▶ **n.** technical air that is forced to enter a moving aperture, such as the air intake of an aircraft.

Ra·man /ˈrämən/, Sir Chandrasekhara Venkata (1888–1970), Indian physicist. He discovered the Raman effect, one of the most important proofs of the quantum theory of light. Nobel Prize for Physics (1930).

Ra·man ef·fect ▶ **n.** Physics a change of wavelength exhibited by some of the radiation scattered in a medium. The effect is specific to the molecules that cause it, and so can be used in spectroscopic analysis. Compare with RAYLEIGH SCATTERING.

Ra·ma·pith·e·cus /ˌraməˈpiTHikəs, ˌräm-/ ▶ **n.** an extinct anthropoid ape of the Miocene epoch, known from remains found in southwestern Asia and East Africa, and probably ancestral to the orangutan. ● Genus *Ramapithecus*, family Pongidae.
–ORIGIN modern Latin, from RAMA + Greek *pithēkos* 'ape.'

Ra·ma·ya·na /ˌrämīˈänə, rəˈmīənə/ one of the two great Sanskrit epics of the Hindus, composed *c.*300 BC. It describes how Rama, aided by his brother and the monkey king Hanuman, rescued his wife Sita from Ravana, the ten-headed demon king of Lanka.
–ORIGIN Sanskrit, literally 'exploits of Rama.'

ram·ble /ˈrambəl/ ▶ **v.** [no obj.] **1** walk for pleasure, typically without a definite route. ■ (of a plant) put out long shoots and grow over walls or other plants.
2 talk or write at length in a confused or inconsequential way: *he* ***rambled on*** *about his acting career.*
▶ **n.** a walk taken for pleasure, esp. in the countryside.
–ORIGIN late Middle English (sense 2 of the verb): probably related to Middle Dutch *rammelen*, used of animals in the sense 'wander around in heat,' also to the noun RAM.

ram·bler /ˈramb(ə)lər/ ▶ **n. 1** a person who walks for pleasure, esp. in the countryside.
2 a straggling or climbing rose.
3 another term for RANCH HOUSE (see RANCH).

ram·bling /ˈramb(ə)liNG/ ▶ **adj. 1** (of writing or speech) lengthy and confused or inconsequential.
2 (of a plant) putting out long shoots and growing over walls or other plants; climbing: *rambling roses.* ■ (of a building or path) spreading or winding irregularly in various directions: *a big old rambling house.* ■ (of a person) traveling from place to place; wandering.
–DERIVATIVES **ram·bling·ly adv.**

Ram·bo /ˈrambō/ ▶ **n.** (pl. **Rambos**) an exceptionally tough, aggressive man.
–ORIGIN the name of the hero of David Morrell's novel *First Blood* (1972), popularized in the movies *First Blood* (1982) and *Rambo: First Blood Part II* (1985).

ram·bunc·tious /ramˈbəNGkSHəs/ ▶ **adj.** informal uncontrollably exuberant; boisterous.
–DERIVATIVES **ram·bunc·tious·ly adv., ram·bunc·tious·ness n.**
–ORIGIN mid 19th cent.: of unknown origin.

ram·bu·tan /ramˈbo͞otn/ ▶ **n. 1** a red, plum-sized tropical fruit with soft spines and a slightly acidic taste.
2 the Malaysian tree that bears this fruit. ● *Nephelium lappaceum*, family Sapindaceae.
–ORIGIN early 18th cent.: from Malay *rambūtan*, from *rambut* 'hair,' with allusion to the fruit's spines.

ram·e·kin /ˈramikən/ (also **ramekin dish**) ▶ **n.** a small dish for baking and serving an individual portion of food. ■ a quantity of food served in such a dish, in particular a small quantity of cheese baked with breadcrumbs, eggs, and seasoning.
–ORIGIN mid 17th cent.: from French *ramequin*, of Low German or Dutch origin; compare with obsolete Flemish *rameken* 'toasted bread.'

ra·men /ˈrämən/ ▶ **plural n.** (in oriental cuisine) quick-cooking noodles, typically served in a broth with meat and vegetables.
–ORIGIN Japanese, from Chinese *lā* 'to pull' + *miàn* 'noodles.'

ram·ie /ˈramē, ˈrā-/ ▶ **n. 1** a vegetable fiber noted for its length and toughness. ■ cloth woven from this fiber.
2 the plant of the nettle family that yields this fiber, native to tropical Asia and cultivated elsewhere. ● *Boehmeria nivea*, family Urticaceae.
–ORIGIN mid 19th cent.: from Malay *rami*.

ram·i·fi·ca·tion /ˌraməfəˈkāSHən/ ▶ **n.** (usu. **ramifications**) a consequence of an action or event, esp. when complex or unwelcome: *any change is bound to have legal ramifications.* ■ a subdivision of a complex structure or process perceived as comparable to a tree's branches: *an extended family with its ramifications of neighboring in-laws.* ■ formal or technical the action or state of ramifying or being ramified.
–ORIGIN mid 17th cent.: from French, from *ramifier* 'form branches' (see RAMIFY).

ram·i·fy /ˈraməˌfī/ ▶ **v.** (**ramifies, ramifying, ramified**) [no obj.] formal, technical form branches or offshoots; spread or branch out: *an elaborate system of canals was built, ramifying throughout Britain.* ■ [with obj.] (often as adj. **ramified**) cause to branch or spread out: *a ramified genealogical network.*
–ORIGIN late Middle English: from Old French *ramifier*, from medieval Latin *ramificare*, from Latin *ramus* 'branch.'

ram·jet /ˈramˌjet/ ▶ **n.** a type of jet engine in which the air drawn in for combustion is compressed solely by the forward motion of the aircraft.

Ra·món y Ca·jal /rəˈmōn ē kəˈhäl/, Santiago (1852–1934), Spanish physician and histologist. He was a founder of the science of neurology, identifying the neuron as the fundamental unit of the nervous system. Nobel Prize for Physiology or Medicine (1906), shared with Camillo Golgi.

ramp /ramp/ ▶ **n. 1** a slope or inclined plane for joining two different levels, as at the entrance or between floors of a building: *a wheelchair ramp.* ■ a movable set of steps for entering or leaving an aircraft. ■ an inclined road leading onto or off a main road or highway: *an exit ramp.*
2 an upward bend in a stair rail.
3 an electrical waveform in which the voltage increases or decreases linearly with time.
▶ **v. 1** [with obj.] provide or build (something) with a ramp.
2 [no obj.] archaic (of an animal) rear up on its hind legs in a threatening posture. ■ [with adverbial of direction] rush about violently or uncontrollably: *an awful beast ramping about the woods and fields.* ■ [with adverbial of direction] (of a plant) grow or climb luxuriantly: *ivy ramped over the flower beds.*
3 [no obj.] (of an electrical waveform) increase or decrease voltage linearly with time.
–PHRASAL VERBS **ramp something up** (or **ramp up**) (esp. in reference to the production of goods) increase or cause to increase in amount: *they ramped up production to meet booming demand.*
–ORIGIN Middle English (as a verb in the sense 'rear up,' also used as a heraldic term): from Old French *ramper* 'creep, crawl,' of unknown origin. Sense 1 of the noun dates from the late 18th cent.

ram·page /ˈramˌpāj/ ▶ **v.** [no obj.] (esp. of a large group of people) rush around in a violent and uncontrollable manner: *several thousand demonstrators rampaged through the city.*
▶ **n.** a period of violent and uncontrollable behavior, typically involving a large group of people: *thugs went on a rampage and wrecked a classroom.*
–DERIVATIVES **ram·pag·er** /ˈramˌpājər/ **n.**
–ORIGIN late 17th cent.: perhaps based on the verb RAMP and the noun RAGE.

ram·pa·geous /ramˈpājəs/ ▶ **adj.** archaic boisterously or violently uncontrollable.

ramp·ant /ˈrampənt/ ▶ **adj. 1** (esp. of something unwelcome or unpleasant) flourishing or spreading unchecked: *political violence was rampant* | *rampant inflation.* ■ (of a person or activity) violent or unrestrained in action or performance: *rampant sex.* ■ (of a plant) lush in growth; luxuriant: *a rich soil soon becomes home to rampant weeds.*
2 [usu. postpositive] Heraldry (of an animal) represented standing on one hind foot with its forefeet in the air (typically in profile, facing the dexter (left) side, with right hind foot and tail raised, unless otherwise specified): *two gold lions rampant.*
3 Architecture (of an arch) springing from a level of support at one height and resting on the other support at a higher level.
–DERIVATIVES **ramp·an·cy** /-pənsē/ **n., ramp·ant·ly adv.**
–ORIGIN Middle English (as a heraldic term): from Old French, literally 'crawling,' present participle of *ramper* (see RAMP). From the original use describing a wild animal, arose the sense 'fierce,' whence the current notion of 'unrestrained.'

ram·part /ˈramˌpärt/ ▶ **n.** (usu. **ramparts**) a defensive wall of a castle or walled city, having a broad top with a walkway and typically a stone parapet. ■ a defensive or protective barrier: *the open Pacific broke on the far-off ramparts of the reef.*
▶ **v.** [with obj.] rare fortify or surround with or as if with a rampart.

r

PRONUNCIATION KEY ə *ago, up*; ər *over, fur*; a *hat*; ā *ate*; ä *car*; e *let*; ē *see*; i *fit*; ī *by*; NG *sing*; ō *go*; ô *law, for*; oi *toy*; o͝o *good*; o͞o *goo*; ou *out*; TH *thin*; T͟H *then*; ZH *vision*

– ORIGIN late 16th cent.: from French *rempart*, from *remparer* 'fortify, take possession of again,' based on Latin *ante* 'before' + *parare* 'prepare.'

ram·pi·on /'rampēən/ ▶ **n.** a Eurasian plant of the bellflower family, some kinds of which have a root that can be eaten in salads. ■ a Mediterranean plant with a long narrow spike of bluish flowers and a thick taproot (*Campanula rapunculus*, family Campanulaceae). ● (**horned rampion**) a grassland plant with dense, rounded flower heads of inward curving, typically blue, tubular flowers (genus *Phyteuma*, family Campanulaceae).
– ORIGIN late 16th cent.: from a variant of medieval Latin *rapuncium*; compare with German *Rapunzel* 'corn salad.'

ram·rod /'ram,räd/ ▶ **n.** a rod for ramming down the charge of a muzzleloading firearm. ■ used in similes and metaphors to describe someone's erect or rigid posture: *he held himself ramrod straight.* ■ a person, esp. one in a position of leadership, who is strict and uncompromising.
▶ **v.** (**ramrods, ramrodding, ramrodded**) [with obj.] (**ramrod something through**) force a proposed measure to be accepted or completed quickly: *they ramrodded through legislation voiding the court injunctions.*

Ram·say /'ramzē/, Sir William (1852–1916), Scottish chemist; discoverer of the noble gases. He discovered argon and helium and codiscovered neon, krypton, xenon, and radon. He also determined their atomic weights and places in the periodic table. Nobel Prize for Chemistry (1904).

Ram·ses /'ramsēz/ (also **Rameses** /'ramə,sēz/) the name of 11 Egyptian pharaohs, notably: ■ **Ramses II** (died *c.*1225 BC), reigned *c.*1292–*c.*1225 BC; known as **Ramses the Great**. The third pharaoh of the 19th dynasty, he built vast monuments and statues, including the two rock temples at Abu Simbel. ■ **Ramses III** (died *c.*1167 BC), reigned *c.*1198–*c.*1167 BC. The second pharaoh of the 20th dynasty, he fought decisive battles against the Libyans and the Sea Peoples. After his death the power of Egypt declined.

ram·shack·le /'ram,SHakəl/ ▶ **adj.** (esp. of a house or vehicle) in a state of severe disrepair: *a ramshackle cottage.*
– ORIGIN early 19th cent. (originally dialect in the sense 'irregular, disorderly'): alteration of earlier *ramshackled*, altered form of obsolete *ransackled* 'ransacked.'

rams·horn snail /'ramz,hôrn/ ▶ **n.** a plant-eating European freshwater snail that has a flat spiral shell. ● Family Planorbidae: several genera.

ra·mus /'rāməs/ ▶ **n.** (pl. **rami** /-,mī/) **1** Anatomy an arm or branch of a bone, in particular those of the ischium and pubes or of the jawbone. ■ a major branch of a nerve.
2 Zoology a structure in an invertebrate that has the form of a projecting arm, typically one of two or more that are conjoined or adjacent. ■ a barb of a feather.
– ORIGIN mid 17th cent.: from Latin, literally 'branch.'

ran /ran/ past of RUN.

ranch /ranCH/ ▶ **n.** a large farm, esp. in the western US and Canada, where cattle or other animals are bred and raised. ■ (also **ranch house**) a single-story, sometimes split-level, house, typically with a low-pitched roof. ■ short for RANCH DRESSING.
▶ **v.** [no obj.] (often as noun **ranching**) run a ranch: *cattle ranching.* ■ [with obj.] (often as adj. **ranched**) breed (animals) on a ranch. ■ [with obj.] use (land) as a ranch.
– ORIGIN early 19th cent.: from Spanish *rancho* 'group of persons eating together.'

ranch dress·ing ▶ **n.** a type of thick white salad dressing made with sour cream or buttermilk.

ranch·er /'ranCHər/ ▶ **n. 1** a person who owns or runs a ranch.
2 a ranch house.

ran·cher·a /ran'CHerə, rän-/ ▶ **n.** a type of Mexican country music, often played with guitars and horns.
– ORIGIN early 20th cent.: from Spanish *cancion ranchera*, 'farmers' songs.'

ran·che·ria /,ranCHə'rēə/ ▶ **n.** (in Spanish America and the western US) a small Indian settlement.
– ORIGIN Spanish, from *rancho* (see RANCH).

ran·che·ro /ran'CHerō/ ▶ **n.** (pl. **rancheros**) a person who farms or works on a ranch, esp. in the southwestern US and Mexico.
– ORIGIN Spanish, from *rancho* (see RANCH).

Ran·chi /'ränCHē/ a city in northeastern India, the capital of Jharkhand state; pop. 1,047,500 (est. 2009).

Ran·cho Cor·do·va /'ran,CHō 'kôr,dəvə/ an industrial city in north central California, northeast of Sacramento; pop. 62,265 (est. 2008).

Ran·cho Cu·ca·mon·ga /'ranCHō ,ko͝okə'mənGgə, -'mäNG/ a city in southwestern California, east of Los Angeles; pop. 171,176 (est. 2008).

ran·cid /'ransid/ ▶ **adj.** (of foods containing fat or oil) smelling or tasting unpleasant as a result of being old and stale.
– DERIVATIVES **ran·cid·i·ty** /ran'sidətē/ **n.**
– ORIGIN early 17th cent.: from Latin *rancidus* 'stinking.'

ran·cor /'raNGkər/ (Brit. **rancour**) ▶ **n.** bitterness or resentfulness, esp. when long-standing: *he spoke without rancor.*
– ORIGIN Middle English: via Old French from late Latin *rancor* 'rankness,' (in the Vulgate 'bitter grudge'), related to Latin *rancidus* 'stinking.'

ran·cor·ous /'raNGkərəs/ ▶ **adj.** characterized by bitterness or resentment: *sixteen miserable months of rancorous disputes | a rancorous debate.*
– DERIVATIVES **ran·cor·ous·ly** /-k(ə)rəslē/ **adv.**

Rand[1] /rand/ (**the Rand**) another name for WITWATERSRAND.

Rand[2] /rand/, Ayn (1905–82), US writer and philosopher, born in Russia; born *Alissa Rozenbaum*. She developed a philosophy of "objectivism," in *For the New Intellectual* (1961), arguing for "rational self-interest," individualism, and laissez-faire capitalism. Notable novels: *The Fountainhead* (1943) and *Atlas Shrugged* (1957).

rand[1] /rand, ränd, ränt/ ▶ **n.** the basic monetary unit of South Africa, equal to 100 cents.
– ORIGIN from *the Rand*, the name of a goldfield district near Johannesburg.

rand[2] ▶ **n.** a strip of leather placed under the back part of a shoe or boot to make it level before the lifts of the heel are attached.
– ORIGIN Old English (denoting a border): of Germanic origin; related to Dutch *rand* and German *Rand* 'edge.' The current sense dates from the late 16th cent.

R & B (also **R 'n' B**) ▶ **n. 1** rhythm and blues.
2 a kind of pop music of black origin with a soulful vocal style featuring much improvisation.

R & D ▶ **abbr.** research and development.

Ran·dolph, A. Philip (1889–1979), US labor and civil rights leader; full name *Asa Philip Randolph*. Believing that unions would benefit African Americans, he founded the Brotherhood of Sleeping Car Porters in 1928 and then served as its president until 1968. He was a major organizer of both the 1941 and 1963 marches on Washington.

ran·dom /'randəm/ ▶ **adj. 1** made, done, happening, or chosen without method or conscious decision: *a random sample of 100 households.* ■ Statistics governed by or involving equal chances for each item. ■ (of masonry) with stones of irregular size and shape.
2 informal odd, unusual, or unexpected: *I find it impossible to not laugh at such a random guy.*
– PHRASES **at random** without method or conscious decision: *he opened the book at random.*
– DERIVATIVES **ran·dom·ly adv., ran·dom·ness n.**
– ORIGIN Middle English (in the sense 'impetuous headlong rush'): from Old French *randon* 'great speed,' from *randir* 'gallop,' from a Germanic root shared by RAND[2].

ran·dom ac·cess Computing ▶ **n.** the process of transferring information to or from memory in which every memory location can be accessed directly rather than being accessed in a fixed sequence: [as modifier] *random-access programming.*

ran·dom er·ror ▶ **n.** Statistics an error in measurement caused by factors that vary from one measurement to another.

ran·dom·ize /'randə,mīz/ ▶ **v.** [with obj.] (usu. as adj. **randomized**) technical make unpredictable, unsystematic, or random in order or arrangement; employ random selection or sampling in (an experiment or procedure).
– DERIVATIVES **ran·dom·i·za·tion** /,randəmi'zāSHən/ **n.**

ran·dom var·i·a·ble ▶ **n.** Statistics a quantity having a numerical value for each member of a group, esp. one whose values occur according to a frequency distribution. Also called VARIATE.

ran·dom walk ▶ **n.** Physics the movements of an object or changes in a variable that follow no discernible pattern or trend.

R & R ▶ **abbr.** ■ informal rest and recreation. ■ Medicine rescue and resuscitation. ■ (also **R 'n' R**) rock and roll.

Rand·stad /'rän,städ/ a conurbation in the northwestern Netherlands that stretches in a horseshoe shape from Dordrecht and Rotterdam around to Utrecht and Amersfoort via The Hague, Leiden, Haarlem, and Amsterdam. The majority of the people of the Netherlands live in this area.

rand·y /'randē/ ▶ **adj.** (**randier, randiest**) **1** informal sexually aroused or excited.
2 Scottish archaic (of a person) having a rude, aggressive manner.
– DERIVATIVES **rand·i·ly** /-dəlē/ **adv., rand·i·ness n.**
– ORIGIN mid 17th cent.: perhaps from obsolete *rand* 'rant, rave,' from obsolete Dutch *randen* 'to rant.'

ra·nee ▶ **n.** archaic spelling of RANI.

rang /raNG/ past of RING[2].

range /rānj/ ▶ **n. 1** the area of variation between upper and lower limits on a particular scale: *the cost is thought to be in the range of $1-5 million a day | it's outside my price range.* ■ a set of different things of the same general type: *the area offers a wide range of activities for the tourist.* ■ the scope of a person's knowledge or abilities: *he gave some indication of his range.* ■ the compass of a person's voice or of a musical instrument: *she was gifted with an incredible vocal range.* ■ the extent of time covered by something such as a forecast. See also LONG-RANGE, SHORT-RANGE. ■ the area or extent covered by or included in something: *an introductory guide to the range of debate this issue has generated.* ■ Mathematics the set of values that a given function can take as its argument varies.
2 the distance within which something can be reached or perceived: *something lurked just beyond her range of vision.* ■ the maximum distance at which a radio transmission can be effectively received: *planets within radio range of Earth.* ■ the distance that can be covered by a vehicle or aircraft without refueling: *the vans have a range of 125 miles.* ■ the maximum distance to which a gun will shoot or over which a missile will travel: *a duck came within range | these rockets have a range of 30 to 40 miles.* ■ the distance between a camera and the subject to be photographed. ■ Surveying the horizontal direction and length of a survey line determined by at least two fixed points.
3 a line or series of mountains or hills: *the coastal ranges of the northwest.* ■ a series of townships extending north and south parallel to the principal meridian of a survey. ■ Nautical a line defined by landmarks or beacons, used to locate something offshore, esp. a navigable channel or a hazard.
4 a large area of open land for grazing or hunting. ■ an area of land or sea used as a testing ground for military equipment. ■ an open or enclosed area with targets for shooting practice. ■ the area over which a thing, esp. a plant or animal, is distributed.
5 an electric or gas stove with several burners and one or more ovens.
6 Building a course of masonry extending from end to end at one height. ■ a row of buildings.
7 archaic the direction or position in which something lies: *the range of the hills and valleys is nearly from north to south.*
▶ **v. 1** [no obj.] vary or extend between specified limits: *patients whose ages ranged from 13 to 25 years.*
2 [with obj.] (usu. **be ranged**) place or arrange in a row or rows or in a specified order or manner: *a table with half a dozen chairs ranged around it.* ■ [no obj.] run or extend in a line in a particular direction: *he regularly came to the benches that ranged along the path.*
3 [no obj.] (of a person or animal) travel or wander over a wide area: *patrols ranged thousands of miles deep into enemy territory |* [with obj.] *nomadic tribesmen who ranged the windswept lands of the steppe.* ■ (of a person's eyes) pass from one person or thing to another: *his eyes ranged over them.* ■ (of something written or spoken) cover or embrace a wide number of different topics: *tutorials ranged over a variety of subjects.*
4 [no obj.] obtain the range of a target by adjustment after firing past it or short of it, or by the use of radar or laser equipment: *radar-type transmissions which appeared to be ranging on our convoys.* ■ [with adverbial] (of a projectile) cover a specified distance. ■ [with adverbial] (of a gun) send a projectile over a specified distance.
– PHRASES **at a range of** with a specified distance between one person or thing and another: *a bat can detect a moth at a range of less than 8 feet.*
– ORIGIN Middle English (in the sense 'line of people or animals'): from Old French *range* 'row, rank,' from *rangier* 'put in order,' from *rang* 'rank.' Early usage also included the notion of 'movement over an area.'

range·bound /'rānj,bound/ ▶ **adj.** (generally of market prices) not straying outside a particular range: *the euro remained rangebound, faltering again in its attempt to regain recent highs.*

range·find·er /'rānj,fīndər/ ▶ **n.** an instrument for estimating the distance of an object, esp. for use with a camera or gun.

range·land /'rānj,land/ ▶ **n.** (also **rangelands**) open country used for grazing or hunting animals.

Range·ley Lakes /'rānjlē/ a resort region in western Maine, near the New Hampshire border, noted for Rangeley, Mooselookmeguntic, and other lakes, as well as for the Mahoosuc Range, which is to the south.

Rang·er /'rānjər/ a series of nine American moon probes launched between 1961 and 1965, the last three of which took many photographs before crashing into the moon.

rang·er /'rānjər/ ▶ **n.** **1** a keeper of a park, forest, or area of countryside.
2 a member of a body of armed men, in particular: ■ a mounted soldier. ■ a commando or highly trained infantryman.
3 a person or thing that wanders or ranges over a particular area or domain: *rangers of the mountains.*

Ran·goon /raNG'go͞on, ran-/ the former capital of Burma (Myanmar), a port in the Irrawaddy delta; pop. 4,088,000 (est. 2007). For centuries a Buddhist religious center, it is the site of the Shwe Dagon Pagoda, built over 2,500 years ago. The modern city was established in the mid 19th century and was the capital from 1886 until it was replaced by Naypyidaw in 2005. Burmese name **YANGON**.

rang·y /'rānjē/ ▶ **adj.** (**rangier, rangiest**) **1** (of a person or animal) tall and slim with long, slender limbs.
2 (of land) having a large, open range: *the rangy, hard, scruffy frontier.*

ra·ni /'ränē/ (also **ranee**) ▶ **n.** (pl. **ranis**) historical a Hindu queen, either by marriage to a raja or in her own right.
– ORIGIN from Hindi *rānī*, Sanskrit *rājñī*, feminine of *rājan* 'king.'

ra·nit·i·dine /rə'nitə,dēn/ ▶ **n.** Medicine a synthetic compound with antihistamine properties, used to treat ulcers and related conditions.
– ORIGIN 1970s: blend of **FURAN** and **NITRO-**, + **-IDE** + **-INE**[4].

Ran·jit Singh /,ränjət 'siNG/ (1780–1839), Indian maharaja; founder of the Sikh state of Punjab; known as the **Lion of the Punjab**. He proclaimed himself maharaja of Punjab in 1801 and went on to make it the most powerful state in India.

rank[1] /raNGk/ ▶ **n.** **1** a position in the hierarchy of the armed forces: *an army officer of fairly high rank* | *he was promoted to the rank of Captain.* ■ a position within the hierarchy of an organization or society: *only two cabinet members had held ministerial rank before.* ■ high social position: *persons of rank and breeding.* ■ Statistics a number specifying position in a numerically ordered series.
2 a single line of soldiers or police officers drawn up abreast. ■ (**the ranks**) common soldiers as opposed to officers: *he was fined and* **reduced to the ranks**. ■ (**ranks**) the people belonging to or constituting a group or class: *the ranks of the unemployed.* ■ a regular row or line of things or people: *conifer plantations growing in serried ranks.* ■ Chess each of the eight rows of eight squares running from side to side across a chessboard. Compare with **FILE**[2].
3 Mathematics the value or the order of the largest nonzero determinant of a given matrix. ■ an analogous quantity in other kinds of groups.
▶ **v.** [with obj.] **1** give (someone or something) a rank or place within a grading system: *rank them in order of preference* | [with obj. and complement] *she is ranked number four in the world.* ■ [no obj.] have a specified rank or place within a grading system: *he ranks with Newman as one of the outstanding English theologians.* ■ take precedence over (someone) in respect to rank; outrank: *the Secretary of State ranks all the other members of the cabinet.*
2 arrange in a rank or ranks: *the tents were ranked in orderly rows.*
– PHRASES **break rank** (or **ranks**) (of soldiers or police officers) fail to remain in line. ■ fail to maintain solidarity: *the government is prepared to* **break ranks with** *the Allied states.* **close ranks** (of soldiers or police officers) come closer together in a line. ■ unite in order to defend common interests: *the family had always closed ranks in times of crisis.* **keep rank** (of soldiers or police officers) remain in line. **pull rank** take unfair advantage of one's seniority or privileged position. **rise through** (or **from**) **the ranks** (of a private or a noncommissioned officer) receive a commission. ■ advance in an organization by one's own efforts: *he rose through the ranks to become managing director.*
– ORIGIN Middle English: from Old French *ranc*, of Germanic origin; related to **RING**[1].

rank[2] ▶ **adj.** **1** (of vegetation) growing too thickly and coarsely.
2 (esp. of air or water) having a foul or offensive smell. ■ informal very unpleasant: *the tea at work is nice but the coffee's pretty rank.*
3 [attrib.] (esp. of something bad or deficient) complete and utter (used for emphasis): *rank stupidity* | *rank amateurs* | *a rank outsider.*
– DERIVATIVES **rank·ly adv.**, **rank·ness n.**
– ORIGIN Old English *ranc* 'proud, rebellious, sturdy,' also 'fully grown,' of Germanic origin. An early sense 'luxuriant' gave rise to 'too luxuriant,' whence the negative connotation of modern usage.

rank and file ▶ **n.** [treated as pl.] (**the rank and file**) the ordinary members of an organization as opposed to its leaders: *the rank and file of the Labor party are dissatisfied* | [as modifier] *rank-and-file members.*
– ORIGIN referring to the "ranks" and "files" into which privates and noncommissioned officers form on parade.

rank cor·re·la·tion ▶ **n.** Statistics an assessment of the degree of correlation between two ways of assigning ranks to the members of a set.

rank·er /'raNGkər/ ▶ **n.** chiefly Brit. a soldier in the ranks; a private. ■ a commissioned officer who has been promoted from the ranks.

rank·ing ▶ **n.** /'raNGkiNG/ a position in a scale of achievement or status; a classification: *his number-one world ranking.* ■ the action or process of giving a specified rank or place within a grading system: *the ranking of students.*
▶ **adj.** /'raNGkiNG/ [in combination] having a specified position in a scale of achievement or status: *high-ranking army officers.* ■ [attrib.] having a high position in such a scale: *two ranking PLO figures.*

ran·kle /'raNGkəl/ ▶ **v.** [no obj.] **1** archaic (of a wound or sore) continue to be painful; fester.
2 (of a comment, event, or fact) cause annoyance or resentment that persists: *the casual manner of his dismissal still rankles.* ■ [with obj.] annoy or irritate (someone): *Lisa was rankled by his assertion.*
– ORIGIN Middle English: from Old French *rancler*, from *rancle, draoncle* 'festering sore,' from an alteration of medieval Latin *dracunculus*, diminutive of *draco* 'serpent.'

Rann of Kutch see **KUTCH, RANN OF.**

ran·sack /'ran,sak, ran'sak/ ▶ **v.** [with obj.] go hurriedly through (a place) stealing things and causing damage: *burglars ransacked her home.* ■ search through (a place or receptacle) to find something, esp. in such a way as to cause disorder and damage: *Hollywood* **ransacks** *the New York stage* **for** *actors.*
– DERIVATIVES **ran·sack·er** /'ran,sakər/ **n.**
– ORIGIN Middle English: from Old Norse *rannsaka*, from *rann* 'house' + a second element related to *sœkja* 'seek.'

Ran·som /'ransəm/, John Crowe (1888–1974), US poet and critic. With *The New Criticism* (1941) he started a school of criticism that rejected the Victorian emphasis on literature as a moral force and advocated a close analysis of textual structure in isolation from the social background of the text.

ran·som /'ransəm/ ▶ **n.** a sum of money or other payment demanded or paid for the release of a prisoner. ■ the holding or freeing of a prisoner in return for payment of such money: *the capture and ransom of the king.*
▶ **v.** [with obj.] obtain the release of (a prisoner) by making a payment demanded: *the lord was captured in war and had to be ransomed.* ■ hold (a prisoner) and demand payment for their release: *mercenaries burned the village and ransomed the inhabitants.* ■ release (a prisoner) after receiving payment.
– PHRASES **hold someone/something at** (or **for**) **ransom** hold someone prisoner and demand payment for their release. ■ demand concessions from a person or organization by threatening damaging action. **a king's ransom** a huge amount of money; a fortune.
– ORIGIN Middle English: from Old French *ransoun* (noun), *ransouner* (verb), from Latin *redemptio(n-)* 'ransoming, releasing' (see **REDEMPTION**). Early use also occurred in theological contexts expressing 'deliverance' and 'atonement.'

rant /rant/ ▶ **v.** [no obj.] speak or shout at length in a wild, impassioned way: *she was still* **ranting on** *about the unfairness of it all.*
▶ **n.** a spell of ranting; a tirade: *his rants against organized religion.*
– PHRASES **rant and rave** shout and complain angrily and at length.
– DERIVATIVES **rant·er n.**, **rant·ing·ly adv.**
– ORIGIN late 16th cent. (in the sense 'behave in a boisterous way'): from Dutch *ranten* 'talk nonsense, rave.'

ra·nun·cu·la·ceous /rə,nəNGkyə'lāSHəs/ ▶ **adj.** Botany of, relating to, or denoting plants of the buttercup family (Ranunculaceae).
– ORIGIN mid 19th cent.: from modern Latin *Ranunculaceae* (plural), based on Latin *ranunculus* 'little frog,' + **-OUS**.

ra·nun·cu·lus /rə'nəNGkyələs/ ▶ **n.** (pl. **ranunculuses** or **ranunculi** /-,lē, -,lī/) a temperate plant of a genus that includes the buttercups and water crowfoots, typically having yellow or white bowl-shaped flowers and lobed or toothed leaves. ● Genus *Ranunculus*, family Ranunculaceae: many species, including several garden ornamentals.
– ORIGIN modern Latin, from Latin, literally 'little frog,' diminutive of *rana*.

Ran·vier's node /rän'vyāz, 'ranvi(ə)rz/ ▶ **n.** see **NODE OF RANVIER.**

rap[1] /rap/ ▶ **v.** (**raps, rapping, rapped**) **1** [with obj.] strike (a hard surface) with a series of rapid audible blows, esp. in order to attract attention: *he stood up and rapped the table* | [no obj.] *she* **rapped** *angrily* **on** *the window.* ■ strike (something) against a hard surface in such a way: *she rapped her stick on the floor.* ■ strike (someone or something) sharply with a stick or similar implement: *she rapped my fingers with a ruler.* ■ informal rebuke or criticize sharply: *executives rapped the U.S. for having too little competition in international phone service.* ■ say sharply or suddenly: *the ambassador* **rapped out** *an order.*
2 [no obj.] informal talk or chat in an easy and familiar manner: *we could be here all night rapping about the finer points of spiritualism.*
3 [no obj.] perform rap music.
▶ **n.** **1** a quick, sharp knock or blow: *there was a confident rap at the door.*
2 a type of popular music of US black origin in which words are recited rapidly and rhythmically over a prerecorded, typically electronic instrumental backing. ■ a piece of music performed in this style, or the words themselves.
3 informal a talk or discussion, esp. a lengthy or impromptu one: *dropping in after work for a rap over a beer* | [as modifier] *a rap session.*
4 [usu. with adj.] informal a criminal charge, esp. of a specified kind: *he's just been acquitted on a murder rap.* ■ a person or thing's reputation, typically a bad one: *there's no reason why drag queens should get a bad rap.*
– PHRASES **beat the rap** informal escape punishment for or be acquitted of a crime. **a rap on the knuckles** a reprimand. **rap someone on the knuckles** rebuke or criticize someone. **take the rap** informal be punished or blamed, esp. for something that is not one's fault or for which others are equally responsible.
– ORIGIN Middle English (originally in the senses 'severe blow with a weapon' and 'deliver a heavy blow'): probably imitative and of Scandinavian origin; compare with Swedish *rappa* 'beat, drub,' also with **CLAP**[1] and **FLAP**.

rap[2] ▶ **n.** [in sing., with negative] the smallest amount (used to add emphasis to a statement): *he doesn't care a rap whether it's true or not.*
– ORIGIN early 19th cent.: from Irish *ropaire* 'robber'; used as the name of a counterfeit coin in 18th-cent. Ireland.

ra·pa·cious /rə'pāSHəs/ ▶ **adj.** aggressively greedy or grasping: *rapacious landlords.*
– DERIVATIVES **ra·pa·cious·ly adv.**, **ra·pa·cious·ness n.**
– ORIGIN mid 17th cent.: from Latin *rapax, rapac-* (from *rapere* 'to snatch') + **-IOUS**.

ra·pac·i·ty /rə'pasətē/ ▶ **n.** aggressive greed: *the rapacity of landowners seeking greater profit from their property.*

rape[1] /rāp/ ▶ **n.** **1** the crime, committed by a man, of forcing another person to have sexual intercourse with him without their consent and against their will, esp. by the threat or use of violence against them: *he denied two charges of attempted rape* | *he had committed at least two rapes.* ■ literary the abduction of a woman, esp. for the purpose of having sexual intercourse with her: *the Rape of the Sabine Women.*
2 the wanton destruction or spoiling of a place or area: *the rape of the Russian countryside.*
▶ **v.** [with obj.] **1** (of a man) force (another person) to have sexual intercourse with him without their consent and against their will, esp. by the threat or use of violence against them: *the woman was raped at knifepoint.*
2 spoil or destroy (a place): *the timber industry is raping the land.*
– DERIVATIVES **rap·er n.**
– ORIGIN late Middle English (originally denoting violent seizure of property, later carrying off a woman by force): from Anglo-Norman French *rap* (noun), *raper* (verb), from Latin *rapere* 'seize.'

rape[2] ▶ **n.** a plant of the cabbage family with bright yellow, heavily scented flowers, esp. a variety (**oilseed rape**) grown for its oil-rich seed and as stockfeed. Also called **COLE, COLZA.** ● Genus *Brassica*, family Brassicaceae, in particular *B. napus* subsp. *oleifera*.
– ORIGIN late Middle English (originally denoting the turnip plant): from Latin *rapum, rapa* 'turnip.'

r

rape³ ▶ n. (often **rapes**) the stalks and skins of grapes left after winemaking, used in making vinegar.
– ORIGIN early 17th cent. (as *rape wine*): from French *râpe*, medieval Latin *raspa* 'bunch of grapes.'

rape⁴ ▶ n. historical (in the UK) any of the six ancient divisions of Sussex.
– ORIGIN Old English, variant of **ROPE**, with reference to the fencing-off of land.

rape oil (also **rapeseed oil**) ▶ n. an oil obtained from rapeseed, used as a lubricant, in alternative fuels, and in foodstuffs.

rape·seed /'rāp,sēd/ ▶ n. seeds of the rape plant, used chiefly for oil. See **RAPE²**.

Raph·a·el¹ /'rafēəl, 'rā-/ (in the Bible) one of the seven archangels in the apocryphal Book of Enoch. He is said to have "healed" the earth when it was defiled by the sins of the fallen angels.

Raph·a·el² /'rafēəl, 'rāfēəl, ,räfī'el/ (1483–1520), Italian painter and architect; Italian name *Raffaello Sanzio*. Regarded as one of the greatest artists of the Renaissance, he is particularly noted for his madonnas, including his altarpiece the *Sistine Madonna* (*c.*1513). As an architect, he was put in charge of the work on St. Peter's Basilica in Rome in 1514.

ra·phe /'rāfē/ ▶ n. (pl. **raphae** pronunc. **same**) Anatomy & Biology a groove, ridge, or seam in an organ or tissue, typically marking the line where two halves fused in the embryo, in particular: ■ the connecting ridge between the two halves of the medulla oblongata or the tegmentum of the midbrain. ■ Botany a longitudinal ridge on the side of certain ovules or seeds. ■ Botany a longitudinal groove in the valve of many diatoms.
– ORIGIN mid 18th cent.: modern Latin, from Greek *rhaphē* 'seam.'

ra·phide /'rāfīd/ ▶ n. Botany a needle-shaped crystal of calcium oxalate occurring in clusters within the tissues of certain plants.
– ORIGIN mid 19th cent.: via French from Greek *rhaphis, rhaphid-* 'needle.'

rap·id /'rapid/ ▶ adj. happening in a short time or at a fast pace: *the country's rapid economic decline* | *he was disposing of wives in rapid succession*. ■ (of movement or activity) characterized by great speed: *his breathing was rapid and jerky*.
▶ n. (usu. **rapids**) a fast-flowing and turbulent part of the course of a river.
– DERIVATIVES **rap·id·ly** adv., **rap·id·ness** n.
– ORIGIN mid 17th cent.: from Latin *rapidus*, from *rapere* 'take by force.'

Rap·id Cit·y a city in southwestern South Dakota, the commercial center for Black Hills and Mount Rushmore tourism; pop. 65,491 (est. 2008).

rap·id eye move·ment ▶ n. a jerky motion of a person's eyes occurring in REM sleep.

rap·id-fire ▶ adj. [attrib.] (esp. of something said in dialogue or done in a sequence) unhesitating and rapid: *a rapid-fire exchange of questions and answers*. ■ (of a gun) able to fire shots in rapid succession.

ra·pid·i·ty /rə'pidətē/ ▶ n. the quality of moving or reacting with great speed: *the fish sink into the sand with such rapidity that it must be seen to be believed*. ■ the fact of happening at a great rate; swiftness: *technology spreads with extraordinary rapidity*.

rap·id tran·sit ▶ n. [usu. as modifier] a form of high-speed urban passenger transportation such as a subway or elevated railroad system.

ra·pi·er /'rāpēər/ ▶ n. a thin, light, sharp-pointed sword used for thrusting. ■ [as modifier] (esp. of speech or intelligence) quick and incisive: *rapier wit*.
– ORIGIN early 16th cent.: from French *rapière*, from *râpe* 'rasp, grater' (because the perforated hilt resembles a rasp or grater).

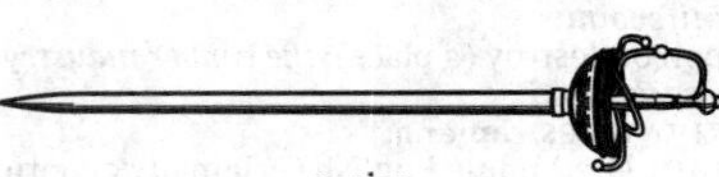
rapier

rap·ine /'rapən, -īn/ ▶ n. literary the violent seizure of someone's property.
– ORIGIN late Middle English: from Old French, or from Latin *rapina*, from *rapere* 'seize.'

ra·pi·ni /rə'pēnē/ ▶ n. another term for **BROCCOLI RABE**.
– ORIGIN Italian, diminutive of *rapa* 'turnip.'

rap·ist /'rāpist/ ▶ n. a man who commits rape.

Rap·pa·han·nock Riv·er /,rapə'hanək/ a river that flows for 210 miles (340 km) across eastern Virginia into the Tidewater region.

rap·pa·ree /,rapə'rē/ ▶ n. a bandit or irregular soldier in Ireland in the 17th century.
– ORIGIN from Irish *rapaire* 'short pike.'

rap·pee /ra'pē, -'pā/ ▶ n. a type of coarse snuff.
– ORIGIN mid 18th cent.: from French (*tabac*) *râpé* 'rasped (tobacco).'

rap·pel /rə'pel/ ▶ v. (**rappels, rappelling, rappelled**) [no obj.] descend a rock face or other near-vertical surface by using a doubled rope coiled around the body and fixed at a higher point: *they had to rappel down a long steep ice face*.
▶ n. a descent made by rappeling: *they were careful in setting up the rappel*.
– ORIGIN 1930s: from French, literally 'a recalling,' from *rappeler* in the sense 'bring back to oneself' (with reference to the rope maneuver).

rap·pen /'rapən/ ▶ n. (pl. **same**) a monetary unit in the German-speaking cantons of Switzerland and in Liechtenstein, equal to one hundredth of the Swiss franc.
– ORIGIN from German *Rappe* 'raven,' with reference to the depiction of the head of a raven on a medieval coin.

rap·per /'rapər/ ▶ n. a person who performs rap music.

rap·port /ra'pôr, rə-/ ▶ n. a close and harmonious relationship in which the people or groups concerned understand each other's feelings or ideas and communicate well: *she was able to establish a good rapport with the children* | *there was little rapport between them*.
– ORIGIN mid 17th cent.: French, from *rapporter* 'bring back.'

rap·por·teur /,ra,pôr'tər/ ▶ n. a person appointed by an organization to report on the proceedings of its meetings: *the UN rapporteur*.
– ORIGIN late 18th cent.: French, from *rapporter* 'bring back.'

rap·proche·ment /,rap,rōsн'män, -,rôsн-/ ▶ n. (esp. in international relations) an establishment or resumption of harmonious relations: *there were signs of a growing rapprochement between the two countries*.
– ORIGIN French, from *rapprocher*, from *re-* (expressing intensive force) + *approcher* 'to approach.'

rap·scal·lion /rap'skalyən/ ▶ n. archaic or humorous a mischievous person.
– ORIGIN late 17th cent.: alteration of earlier *rascallion*, perhaps from **RASCAL**.

rap sheet ▶ n. informal a criminal record.

rapt /rapt/ ▶ adj. **1** completely fascinated by what one is seeing or hearing: *Andrew looked at her, rapt*. ■ indicating or characterized by such a state of fascination: *they listened with rapt attention*. ■ filled with an intense and pleasurable emotion; enraptured: *she shut her eyes and seemed rapt with desire*.
2 archaic or literary having been carried away bodily or transported to heaven: *he was rapt on high*.
– DERIVATIVES **rapt·ly** adv., **rapt·ness** n.
– ORIGIN late Middle English (in the sense 'transported by religious feeling'): from Latin *raptus* 'seized,' past participle of *rapere*.

rap·tor /'raptər/ ▶ n. a bird of prey, e.g., an eagle, hawk, falcon, or owl. ■ informal a dromaeosaurid dinosaur, esp. velociraptor or utahraptor. [from **VELOCIRAPTOR**, a shortened form used originally by paleontologists, popularized by the film *Jurassic Park* (1993).]
– ORIGIN late Middle English: from Latin, literally 'plunderer,' from *rapt-* 'seized,' from the verb *rapere*.

rap·to·ri·al /rap'tôrēəl/ ▶ adj. chiefly Zoology (of a bird or other animal) predatory. ■ (of a limb or other organ) adapted for seizing prey.
– DERIVATIVES **rap·to·ri·al·ly** adv.
– ORIGIN early 19th cent.: from Latin *raptor* 'plunderer' + **-IAL**.

rap·ture /'rapcнər/ ▶ n. **1** a feeling of intense pleasure or joy: *Leonora listened with rapture*. ■ (**raptures**) expressions of intense pleasure or enthusiasm about something: *the tabloids went into raptures about her*.
2 (**the Rapture**) (according to some millenarian teaching) the transporting of believers to heaven at the Second Coming of Christ.
▶ v. [with obj.] (usu. **be raptured**) (according to some millenarian teaching) transport (a believer) from earth to heaven at the Second Coming of Christ.
– ORIGIN late 16th cent. (in the sense 'seizing and carrying off'): from obsolete French, or from medieval Latin *raptura* 'seizing,' partly influenced by **RAPT**.

rap·ture of the deep ▶ n. informal term for **NITROGEN NARCOSIS**.

rap·tur·ous /'rapcнərəs/ ▶ adj. characterized by, feeling, or expressing great pleasure or enthusiasm: *he was greeted with rapturous applause*.
– DERIVATIVES **rap·tur·ous·ly** adv., **rap·tur·ous·ness** n.

ra·ra a·vis /,re(ə)rə 'āvis, ,rärə 'äwis/ ▶ n. (pl. **rarae aves** /,re(ə)rē 'āvēs, ,rärī 'äwes/) another term for **RARE BIRD**.
– ORIGIN Latin.

rare¹ /re(ə)r/ ▶ adj. (**rarer, rarest**) (of an event, situation, or condition) not occurring very often: *a rare genetic disorder* | [with infinitive] *it's rare to meet someone who's content with their life*. ■ (of a thing) not found in large numbers and consequently of interest or value: *the jellyfish tree, one of the rarest plants on earth*. ■ unusually good or remarkable: *he plays with rare strength and sensitivity*.
– DERIVATIVES **rare·ness** n.
– ORIGIN late Middle English (in the sense 'widely spaced, infrequent'): from Latin *rarus*.

rare² ▶ adj. (**rarer, rarest**) (of meat, esp. beef) lightly cooked, so that the inside is still red.
– ORIGIN late 18th cent.: variant of obsolete *rear* 'half-cooked' (used to refer to soft-boiled eggs, from the mid 17th to mid 19th centuries).

rare bird ▶ n. an exceptional person or thing; a rarity: *Irish tenors such as he are rare birds*.
– ORIGIN translating Latin *rara avis* (Juvenal's *Satires*, vi.165).

rare·bit /'re(ə)rbit/ (also **Welsh rarebit**) ▶ n. a dish of melted and seasoned cheese on toast, sometimes with other ingredients.
– ORIGIN late 18th cent.: alteration of *rabbit* in *Welsh rabbit*.

rare earth (also **rare earth element** or **rare earth metal**) ▶ n. Chemistry any of a group of chemically similar metallic elements comprising the lanthanide series and (usually) scandium and yttrium. They are not esp. rare, but they tend to occur together in nature and are difficult to separate from one another.

rar·ee-show /'re(ə)rē ,sнō/ ▶ n. archaic a form of entertainment, esp. one carried in a box, such as a peep show.
– ORIGIN late 17th cent.: apparently representing *rare show*, as pronounced by Savoyard showmen in Britain.

rar·e·fac·tion /,re(ə)rə'faksнən/ (also **rarifaction**) ▶ n. diminution in the density of something, esp. air or a gas. ■ Medicine the lessening of density of tissue, esp. of nervous tissue or bone.
– ORIGIN early 17th cent.: from medieval Latin *rarefactio(n-)*, from the verb *rarefacere* 'grow thin, become rare.'

rar·e·fied /'rerə,fīd/ (also **rarified**) ▶ adj. **1** (of air, esp. that at high altitudes) of lower pressure than usual; thin.
2 distant from the lives and concerns of ordinary people: *debates about the nature of knowledge can seem very rarefied*.

rare gas ▶ n. another term for **NOBLE GAS**.

rare·ly /'re(ə)rlē/ ▶ adv. **1** not often; seldom: *I rarely drive above 60 mph*.
2 archaic unusually or remarkably well: *you can write rarely now, after all your schooling*. ■ to an unusual degree; exceptionally: [as submodifier] *the rarely fine Sheraton bookcase*.

rar·ing /'re(ə)riNG/ ▶ adj. [with infinitive] informal very enthusiastic and eager to do something: *she was raring to get back to her work* | *I'll be ready and raring to go*.
– ORIGIN 1920s: present participle of *rare*, dialect variant of **ROAR** or **REAR²**.

Rar·i·tan Riv·er /'raritn/ a short river in central New Jersey that flows past New Brunswick and Perth Amboy into Raritan Bay, which is an arm of New York Bay and the Atlantic Ocean.

rar·i·ty /'re(ə)ritē/ ▶ n. (pl. **rarities**) the state or quality of being rare: *the rarity of the condition*. ■ a thing that is rare, esp. one having particular value as a result of this: *to take the morning off was a rarity*.
– ORIGIN late Middle English: from Latin *raritas*, from *rarus* 'far apart, infrequently found' (see **RARE¹**).

Ra·ro·tong·a /,rarə'täNGgə/ a mountainous island in the South Pacific Ocean, the chief island of the Cook Islands. Its chief town, Avarua, is the capital of the islands.
– DERIVATIVES **Ra·ro·tong·an** n. & adj.

Ras /räs/ ▶ n. an Ethiopian king, prince, or feudal lord.
– ORIGIN from Amharic *rās* 'head.'

ra·sa /'rəsə/ ▶ n. Hinduism essence, flavor, or sentiment, in particular the characteristic quality of music, literature, and drama.
– ORIGIN Sanskrit, literally 'juice.'

Ras al-Khai·mah /'räs al'kīmə/ one of the seven member states of the United Arab Emirates; pop. 171,900 (est. 2009). It joined the United Arab Emirates in 1972, after the British withdrew from the Persian Gulf. ■ its capital, a port on the Persian Gulf; pop. 107,900 (est. 2009).

ra·sam /'rəsəm/ ▶ **n.** a thin, very spicy southern Indian soup served alone or combined with other foods, such as rice, as a side dish.
– ORIGIN Tamil.

ras·cal /'raskəl/ ▶ **n.** a mischievous or cheeky person, esp. a child or man (typically used in an affectionate way).
– DERIVATIVES **ras·cal·i·ty** /ras'kalətē/ **n.** (pl. **rascalities**), **ras·cal·ly adj.**
– ORIGIN Middle English (in the senses 'a mob' and 'member of the rabble'): from Old French *rascaille* 'rabble,' of uncertain origin.

ras·casse /ras'kas/ ▶ **n.** a small scorpionfish with brick-red skin and spiny fins, found chiefly in the Mediterranean and used as an ingredient of bouillabaisse. ● *Scorpaena scrofa*, family Scorpaenidae.
– ORIGIN 1920s: from French.

rase ▶ **v.** Brit. variant spelling of RAZE.

rash¹ /rasʜ/ ▶ **adj.** displaying or proceeding from a lack of careful consideration of the possible consequences of an action: *it would be extremely rash to make such an assumption* | *a rash decision.*
– DERIVATIVES **rash·ly adv.**, **rash·ness n.**
– ORIGIN late Middle English (also in Scots and northern English in the sense 'nimble, eager'); related to German *rasch*.

rash² ▶ **n.** an area of reddening of a person's skin, sometimes with raised spots, appearing esp. as a result of allergy or illness. ■ a series of things of the same type, esp. when unpleasant or undesirable, occurring or appearing one after the other within a short space of time: *a rash of auto accidents.*
– ORIGIN early 18th cent.: probably related to Old French *rasche* 'eruptive sores, scurf'; compare with Italian *raschia* 'itch.'

rash·er /'rasʜər/ ▶ **n.** a thin slice of bacon.
– ORIGIN late 16th cent.: of unknown origin.

rasp /rasp/ ▶ **n. 1** [in sing.] a harsh, grating noise: *the rasp of the engine.*
2 a coarse file or similar metal tool with a roughened surface for scraping, filing, or rubbing down objects of metal, wood, or other hard material.
▶ **v. 1** [no obj.] make a harsh, grating noise: *my breath rasped in my throat.* ■ [with direct speech] say in a harsh, grating voice: *"Stay where you are!" he rasped.*
2 [with obj.] scrape (something) with a rasp in order to make it smoother. ■ (of a rough surface or object) scrape (something, esp. someone's skin) in a painful or unpleasant way. ■ (**rasp something away/off**) remove something by scraping it off.
– DERIVATIVES **rasp·er n.**, **rasp·y adj.**
– ORIGIN Middle English (as a verb): from Old French *rasper*, perhaps of Germanic origin.

rasp·ber·ry /'raz,berē, -b(ə)rē/ ▶ **n.** (pl. **raspberries**)
1 an edible soft fruit related to the blackberry, consisting of a cluster of reddish-pink drupelets.
2 the plant that yields this fruit, forming tall, stiff, prickly stems (canes). ● *Rubus idaeus*, family Rosaceae; cultivars include the loganberry.
3 a deep reddish-pink color like that of a ripe raspberry: [as modifier] *a raspberry tweed jacket.*
4 informal a sound made with the tongue and lips in order to express derision or contempt: *Clare blew a raspberry and stood up.* [from *raspberry tart*, rhyming slang for 'fart.']
– ORIGIN early 17th cent.: from dialect *rasp*, abbreviation of obsolete *raspis* 'raspberry' (also used as a collective), of unknown origin, + BERRY.

rasp·ing /'raspiɴɢ/ ▶ **adj.** harsh-sounding and unpleasant; grating: *his cracked, rasping voice narrates the story.*
– DERIVATIVES **rasp·ing·ly adv.**

Ra·spu·tin /ras'pyo͞otn/, Grigori (Efimovich) (1871–1916), Russian monk. He exerted great influence over Tsar Nicholas II and his family during World War I; this influence, combined with his reputation for debauchery, steadily discredited the imperial family, and he was assassinated by a group loyal to the tsar.

ras·sle /'rasəl/ ▶ **v.** nonstandard spelling of WRESTLE, representing a variant pronunciation.
– DERIVATIVES **ras·sler** /'ras(ə)lər/ **n.**

Ras·ta /'rastə/ ▶ **n. & adj.** informal short for RASTAFARIAN.

Ras·ta·far·i /,rastə'fe(ə)rē, -'färē/ ▶ **n.** [usu. as modifier] the Rastafarian movement.
– ORIGIN from *Ras Tafari*, the name by which Haile Selassie was known (1916–30).

Ras·ta·far·i·an /,rastə'fe(ə)rēən, -'färēən/ ▶ **adj.** of or relating to a religious movement of Jamaican origin holding that blacks are the chosen people, that Emperor Haile Selassie of Ethiopia was the Messiah, and that black people will eventually return to their Africa.
▶ **n.** a member of the Rastafarian religious movement. Rastafarians have distinctive codes of behavior and dress, including the wearing of dreadlocks, the smoking of cannabis, the rejection of Western medicine, and adherence to a diet that excludes pork, shellfish, and milk.
– DERIVATIVES **Ras·ta·far·i·an·ism n.**

Ras·ta·man /'rastə,man/ ▶ **n.** (pl. **Rastamen**) informal a male Rastafarian.

ras·ter /'rastər/ ▶ **n.** a rectangular pattern of parallel scanning lines followed by the electron beam on a television screen or computer monitor.
– ORIGIN mid 20th cent.: from German *Raster*, literally 'screen,' from Latin *rastrum* 'rake,' from *ras-* 'scraped,' from the verb *radere*.

ras·ter im·age proc·es·sor (abbr.: **RIP**) ▶ **n.** Computing a device that rasterizes an image.

ras·ter·ize /'rastə,rīz/ ▶ **v.** [with obj.] Computing convert (an image stored as an outline) into pixels that can be displayed on a screen or printed.
– DERIVATIVES **ras·ter·i·za·tion** /,rastərə'zāsʜən/ **n.**, **ras·ter·iz·er n.**

Rast·ya·pi·no /räst'yäpi,nō/ former name (1919–29) of DZERZHINSK.

rat /rat/ ▶ **n. 1** a rodent that resembles a large mouse, typically having a pointed snout and a long, sparsely haired tail. Some kinds have become cosmopolitan and are sometimes responsible for transmitting diseases. ● Family Muridae: many genera, including *Rattus* (the Old World rats), and several hundred species.
2 informal a person regarded as despicable, esp. a man who has been deceitful or disloyal. ■ an informer.
3 [with adj.] a person who is associated with or frequents a specified place: *you and the rest of the tavern rats will have to find a new hangout* | *LA mall rats.*
4 a pad used to give shape or fullness to a woman's hair.
▶ **exclam.** (**rats**) informal used to express mild annoyance or irritation.
▶ **v.** (**rats, ratting, ratted**) [no obj.] **1** (usu. as noun **ratting**) (of a person, dog, or cat) hunt or kill rats.
2 informal desert one's party, side, or cause.
3 give (hair) shape or fullness with a rat.
– PHRASAL VERBS **rat on** (also **rat out**) informal inform on (someone) to a person in a position of authority: *I never thought Stash would rat on me* | *men will literally choose death over ratting out another prisoner.* ■ break (an agreement or promise): *he accused the government of ratting on an earlier pledge.*
– ORIGIN Old English *ræt*, probably of Romance origin; reinforced in Middle English by Old French *rat*. The verb dates from the early 19th cent.

rat·a·ble /'rātəbəl/ ▶ **adj.** able to be rated or estimated.
– DERIVATIVES **rat·a·bil·i·ty** /,rātə'bilətē/ **n.**, **rat·a·bly** /-blē/ **adv.**

rat·a·fi·a /,ratə'fēə/ ▶ **n.** a liqueur flavored with almonds or the kernels of peaches, apricots, or cherries. ■ (also **ratafia biscuit**) an almond-flavored cookie like a small macaroon.
– ORIGIN late 17th cent.: from French; perhaps related to TAFIA.

rat·a·ma·cue /'ratəmə,kyo͞o/ ▶ **n.** Music one of the basic patterns (rudiments) of drumming, consisting of a two-beat figure, the first beat of which is played as a triplet and preceded by two grace notes.
– ORIGIN 1940s: imitative.

Ra·ta·na /rä'tänə/, Tahupotiki Wiremu (1873–1939), Maori political and religious leader. He founded the Ratana Church 1920, a religious revival movement that aimed to unite all Maori people.

rat·a·plan /'ratə,plan/ ▶ **n.** [in sing.] a drumming or beating sound.
– ORIGIN mid 19th cent.: from French, of imitative origin.

rat-a-tat /'rat ə ,tat/ (also **rat-a-tat-tat** /,rat ə ,tat 'tat/ or **rat-tat** or **rat-tat-tat**) ▶ **n.** a rapping sound (used esp. in reference to a sequence of two or three knocks on a door or the sound of gunfire).
– ORIGIN late 17th cent.: imitative.

ra·ta·touille /,ratə'to͞o-ē, ,rä,tä-/ ▶ **n.** a vegetable dish consisting of onions, zucchini, tomatoes, eggplant, and peppers, fried and stewed in oil and sometimes served cold.
– ORIGIN a French dialect word.

rat-bite fe·ver ▶ **n.** Medicine a disease contracted from the bite of a rat that causes inflammation of the skin and fever or vomiting. ● This disease can be caused by either of two bacteria, *Spirillum minus* or *Streptobacillus moniliformis*.

ratch·et /'racʜit/ ▶ **n. 1** a device consisting of a bar or wheel with a set of angled teeth in which a pawl, cog, or tooth engages, allowing motion in one direction only. ■ a bar or wheel that has such a set of teeth.
2 a situation or process that is perceived to be deteriorating or changing steadily in a series of irreversible steps: *a one-way ratchet of expanding entitlements.*
▶ **v.** (**ratchets, ratcheting, ratcheted**) [with obj.]
1 operate by means of a ratchet.
2 (**ratchet something up/down**) cause something to rise (or fall) as a step in what is perceived as a steady and irreversible process: *the Bank of Japan ratcheted up interest rates again.*
– ORIGIN mid 17th cent.: from French *rochet*, originally denoting a blunt lance head, later in the sense 'bobbin, ratchet'; related to the base of archaic *rock* 'quantity of wool on a distaff for spinning.'

rate¹ /rāt/ ▶ **n. 1** a measure, quantity, or frequency, typically one measured against some other quantity or measure: *the crime rate rose by 26 percent.* ■ the speed with which something moves, happens, or changes: *your heart rate.*
2 a fixed price paid or charged for something, esp. goods or services: *the basic rate of pay* | *advertising rates.* ■ the amount of a charge or payment expressed as a percentage of some other amount, or as a basis of calculation: *you'll find our current interest rate very competitive.* ■ (usu. **rates**) (in the UK) a tax on land and buildings paid to the local authority by a business, and formerly also by occupants of private property.
▶ **v. 1** [with obj.] assign a standard or value to (something) according to a particular scale: *they were asked to rate their ability at different driving maneuvers* | [with obj. and complement] *the hotel, rated four star, had no hot water and no sink plugs.* ■ assign a standard, optimal, or limiting rating to (a piece of equipment): *its fuel economy is **rated at** 25 miles a gallon in the city.* ■ Brit. assess the value of (a property) for the purpose of levying a local tax.
2 [with obj.] consider to be of a certain quality, standard, or rank: *he rates the company's stock a "buy."* | [with obj. and complement] *the program has been rated a great success.* ■ [no obj.] be regarded in a specified way: *Jeff still rates as one of the nicest people I have ever met.* ■ be worthy of; merit: *the ambassador rated a bulletproof car and a police escort.*
– PHRASES **at any rate** whatever happens or may have happened: *for the moment, at any rate, he was safe.* ■ used to indicate that one is correcting or clarifying a previous statement or emphasizing a following one: *the story, or at any rate, a public version of it, was known and remembered.* **at this** (or **that**) **rate** used to introduce the prediction of a particular unwelcome eventuality should things continue as they are or if a certain assumption is true: *at this rate, I won't have a job to go back to.*
– ORIGIN late Middle English (expressing a notion of 'estimated value'): from Old French, from medieval Latin *rata* (from Latin *pro rata parte* (or *portione*) 'according to the proportional share'), from *ratus* 'reckoned,' past participle of *reri*.

rate² ▶ **v.** [with obj.] archaic scold (someone) angrily: *he rated the young man soundly for his want of respect.*
– ORIGIN late Middle English: of unknown origin.

rate·a·ble /'rātəbəl/ ▶ **adj.** Brit. variant spelling of RATABLE.

rate con·stant ▶ **n.** Chemistry a coefficient of proportionality relating the rate of a chemical reaction at a given temperature to the concentration of reactant (in a unimolecular reaction) or to the product of the concentrations of reactants.

ra·tel /'rātl, 'rätl/ ▶ **n.** a badgerlike mammal with a white or gray back and black underparts, native to Africa and Asia. Also called HONEY BADGER. ● *Mellivora capensis*, family Mustelidae.
– ORIGIN late 18th cent.: from Afrikaans, of unknown ultimate origin.

rate of ex·change ▶ **n.** another term for EXCHANGE RATE.

rate·pay·er /'rāt,pāər/ ▶ **n. 1** a customer of a public utility.
2 (in the UK) a person required to pay local property taxes.

rat·fish /'rat,fisʜ/ ▶ **n.** (pl. **same** or **ratfishes**)
1 a blunt-nosed chimaera with rodentlike front teeth and a long thin tail, found chiefly in cooler waters. See also RABBITFISH. ● Genera *Chimaera* and *Hydrolagus*, family Chimaeridae: several species, including *H. colliei* of the eastern North Pacific.
2 another term for RABBITFISH.

Rat·haus /'rät,hous/ ▶ **n.** (pl. **Rathäuser** /-,hoizər/) a town hall in a German-speaking country.
– ORIGIN German, from *Rat* 'council' + *Haus* 'house.'

rathe /rāᴛʜ, rasʜ/ ▶ **adj.** archaic, literary (of a person or their actions) prompt and eager. ■ (of flowers or fruit) blooming or ripening early in the year.
– ORIGIN Old English *hræth*, *hræd*, of Germanic origin; perhaps related to the base of RASH¹.

r

rath·er /ˈraT͟Hər, ˈräT͟Hər, ˈrəT͟Hər/ ▶ **adv. 1 (would rather)** used to indicate one's preference in a particular matter: *would you like some wine, or would you rather stick to sherry?* | *she'd* ***rather*** *die* ***than*** *cause a scene* | [with clause] *I'd rather you not tell him* | *"You'd better ask her." "I'd rather not."*
2 [as submodifier] to a certain or significant extent or degree: *she's been behaving rather strangely* | *he's rather an unpleasant man.* ■ used before verbs as a way of making the expression of a feeling or opinion less assertive: *I rather think he wants me to marry him* | *we were rather hoping you might do that for us.*
3 used to precede an idea that is different or opposite to a previous statement: [sentence adverb] *There is no shortage of basic skills in the workplace. Rather, the problem is poor management.* ■ more precisely (used to modify or clarify something previously stated): *I walked,* ***or rather*** *limped, the two miles home.* ■ instead of; as opposed to: *she seemed indifferent* ***rather than*** *angry.*
▶ **exclam.** chiefly Brit. dated used to express emphatic affirmation, agreement, or acceptance: *"You are glad to be home, aren't you?" "Rather!"*
– PHRASES **had rather** would rather: *I had rather not see him.* **rather you** (or **him** or **her**, etc.) **than me** used to convey that one would be reluctant oneself to undertake a particular task or project undertaken by someone else: *"I'm picking him up after lunch." "Rather you than me."*
– ORIGIN Old English *hrathor* 'earlier, sooner,' comparative of *hræthe* 'without delay,' from *hræth* 'prompt' (see **RATHE**).

rat·hole /ˈratˌhōl/ ▶ **n. 1** informal a cramped or squalid room or building.
2 informal used to refer to the waste of money or resources: *pouring our assets* ***down the rathole*** *of military expenditure.*
▶ **v.** [with obj.] informal hide (money or goods), typically as part of a fraud or deception.

raths·kel·ler /ˈrätˌskelər, ˈrat-, ˈraTH-/ ▶ **n.** a beer hall or restaurant in a basement.
– ORIGIN early 20th cent.: from obsolete German (now *Ratskeller*), from *Rathaus* 'town hall' + *Keller* 'cellar,' denoting the place where beer and wine were sold.

rat·i·fy /ˈratəˌfī/ ▶ **v. (ratifies, ratifying, ratified)** [with obj.] sign or give formal consent to (a treaty, contract, or agreement), making it officially valid.
– DERIVATIVES **rat·i·fi·a·ble** /ˈratəˌfīəbəl/ **adj.**, **rat·i·fi·ca·tion** /ˌratəfəˈkāSHən/ **n.**, **rat·i·fi·er n.**
– ORIGIN late Middle English: from Old French *ratifier*, from medieval Latin *ratificare*, from Latin *ratus* 'fixed' (see **RATE**[1]).

rat·ing[1] /ˈrātiNG/ ▶ **n.** a classification or ranking of someone or something based on a comparative assessment of their quality, standard, or performance: *the hotel regained its five-star rating.* ■ **(ratings)** the estimated audience size of a particular television or radio program: *the soap's ratings have recently picked up.* ■ the value of a property or condition that is claimed to be standard, optimal, or limiting for a substance, material, or item of equipment: *fuel with a low octane rating.* ■ any of the classes into which racing yachts are assigned according to dimensions.

rat·ing[2] ▶ **n.** dated an angry reprimand.

ra·tio /ˈrāSHō, ˈrāSHēˌō/ ▶ **n.** (pl. **ratios**) the quantitative relation between two amounts showing the number of times one value contains or is contained within the other: *the ratio of men's jobs to women's is 8 to 1.* ■ the relative value of silver and gold in a bimetallic system of currency.
– ORIGIN mid 17th cent.: from Latin, literally 'reckoning,' from *rat-* 'reckoned,' from the verb *reri*.

ra·ti·oc·i·nate /ˌratēˈōsəˌnāt, ˌraSHē-/ ▶ **v.** [no obj.] formal form judgments by a process of logic; reason.
– DERIVATIVES **ra·ti·oc·i·na·tion** /-ˌōsəˈnāSHən/ **n.**, **ra·ti·oc·i·na·tive** /-ˈōsəˌnātiv, -ˈäs-/ **adj.**, **ra·ti·oc·i·na·tor** /-ˈōsəˌnātər, -ˈäs-/ **n.**
– ORIGIN mid 17th cent.: from Latin *ratiocinat-* 'deliberated, calculated,' from the verb *ratiocinari*, from *ratio* (see **RATIO**).

ra·ti·o de·ci·den·di /ˈrätēˌō ˌdesəˈdendē/ ▶ **n.** (pl. **rationes decidendi** /ˌrätēˈōnēz/) Law the rule of law on which a judicial decision is based.
– ORIGIN Latin, literally 'reason for deciding.'

ra·tion /ˈraSHən, ˈrā-/ ▶ **n.** a fixed amount of a commodity officially allowed to each person during a time of shortage, as in wartime: *1918 saw the bread ration reduced on two occasions.* ■ (usu. **rations**) an amount of food supplied on a regular basis, esp. to members of the armed forces during a war. ■ **(rations)** food; provisions: *their emergency rations ran out.* ■ a fixed amount of a particular thing: *their daily ration of fresh air.*
▶ **v.** [with obj.] (usu. **be rationed**) allow each person to have only a fixed amount of (a particular commodity): *shoes were rationed from 1943.* ■ **(ration someone to)** allow someone to have only (a fixed amount of a certain commodity): *they were requested to ration themselves to one glass of wine each.*
– ORIGIN early 18th cent.: from French, from Latin *ratio(n-)* 'reckoning, ratio.'

ra·tion·al /ˈraSHənl, ˈraSHnəl/ ▶ **adj. 1** based on or in accordance with reason or logic: *I'm sure there's a perfectly rational explanation.* ■ (of a person) able to think clearly, sensibly, and logically: *Andrea's upset—she's not being very rational.* ■ endowed with the capacity to reason: *man is a rational being.*
2 Mathematics (of a number, quantity, or expression) expressible, or containing quantities that are expressible, as a ratio of whole numbers. When expressed as a decimal, a rational number has a finite or recurring expansion.
▶ **n.** Mathematics a rational number.
– DERIVATIVES **ra·tion·al·i·ty** /ˌraSHəˈnalətē/ **n.**, **ra·tion·al·ly** /ˈraSHənl-ē, ˈraSHnəlē/ **adv.**
– ORIGIN late Middle English (in the sense 'having the ability to reason'): from Latin *rationalis*, from *ratio(n-)* 'reckoning, reason' (see **RATIO**).

ra·tion·ale /ˌraSHəˈnal/ ▶ **n.** a set of reasons or a logical basis for a course of action or a particular belief: *he explained the rationale behind the change.*
– ORIGIN mid 17th cent.: modern Latin, neuter (used as a noun) of Latin *rationalis* 'endowed with reason' (see **RATIONAL**).

ra·tion·al ex·pec·ta·tions hy·poth·e·sis ▶ **n.** Economics the hypothesis that an economic agent will make full use of all available information when forming expectations, esp. with regard to inflation, and not just past values of a particular variable. Compare with **ADAPTIVE EXPECTATIONS HYPOTHESIS**.

ra·tion·al·ism /ˈraSHənlˌizəm, ˈraSHnəˌlizəm/ ▶ **n.** a belief or theory that opinions and actions should be based on reason and knowledge rather than on religious belief or emotional response: *scientific rationalism.* ■ Philosophy the theory that reason rather than experience is the foundation of certainty in knowledge. ■ Theology the practice of treating reason as the ultimate authority in religion.
– DERIVATIVES **ra·tion·al·ist n.**, **ra·tion·al·is·tic** /ˌraSHənlˈistik, ˌraSHnəˈlistik/ **adj.**, **ra·tion·al·is·ti·cal·ly** /ˌraSHənlˈistik(ə)lē, ˌraSHnəˈlistik(ə)lē/ **adv.**

ra·tion·al·ize /ˈraSHənlˌīz, ˈraSHnəˌlīz/ ▶ **v.** [with obj.] **1** attempt to explain or justify (one's own or another's behavior or attitude) with logical, plausible reasons, even if these are not true or appropriate: *she couldn't rationalize her urge to return to the cottage.*
2 make (a company, process, or industry) more efficient by reorganizing it in such a way as to dispense with unnecessary personnel or equipment: *his success was due primarily to his ability to rationalize production.*
3 Mathematics convert (a function or expression) to a rational form.
– DERIVATIVES **ra·tion·al·i·za·tion** /ˌraSHənl-əˈzāSHən, ˌraSHnələ-/ **n.**, **ra·tion·al·iz·er n.**

Rat Is·lands an island group in southwestern Alaska, part of the Aleutian Islands, that lie between the Near and Andreanof islands. Amchitka and Kiska islands are also included.

rat·ite /ˈraˌtīt/ Ornithology ▶ **adj.** (of a bird) having a flat breastbone without a keel, and so unable to fly. Contrasted with **CARINATE**.
▶ **n.** any of the mostly large, flightless birds with such a breastbone, i.e., the ostrich, rhea, emu, cassowary, and kiwi, together with the extinct moa and elephant bird.
– ORIGIN late 19th cent.: from Latin *ratis* 'raft' + **-ITE**[1].

rat kan·ga·roo ▶ **n.** a small ratlike Australian marsupial with long hind limbs used for hopping. ● Family Potoroidae: several genera and species.

rat·lines /ˈratlənz/ ▶ **plural n.** a series of small ropes fastened across a sailing ship's shrouds like the rungs of a ladder, used for climbing the rigging.
– ORIGIN late Middle English: of unknown origin.

ratlines

ra·toon /rəˈto͞on, ra-/ ▶ **n.** a new shoot or sprout springing from the base of a crop plant, esp. sugar cane, after cropping.
▶ **v.** [no obj.] (of sugar cane) produce ratoons. ■ [with obj.] cut down (a plant) to cause it to sprout in this way.
– ORIGIN mid 17th cent. (as a noun): from Spanish *retoño* 'a sprout.'

ra·toon crop ▶ **n.** a new crop (esp. of rice, bananas, or sugar cane) that grows from the stubble of the crop already harvested.

Rat Pack ▶ **n.** informal a group of five friends and co-performers prominent in the entertainment industries of Hollywood and Las Vegas in the 1950s and 1960s. The group (Frank Sinatra, Dean Martin, Sammy Davis, Jr., Joey Bishop, and Peter Lawford) made several movies together, including *Ocean's Eleven* (1960).

rat race ▶ **n.** informal a way of life in which people are caught up in a fiercely competitive struggle for wealth or power. ■ an exhausting, usually competitive routine.

rats·bane /ˈratsˌbān/ ▶ **n.** literary rat poison.

rat snake ▶ **n.** a harmless constricting snake that feeds on rats and other small mammals. ● Several genera and species in the family Colubridae: genus *Elaphe* of America, in particular *E. obsoleta*, and genera *Ptyas* and *Argyrogena* of Asia (also called **RACER**), in particular *P. mucosus*.

rat-tail ▶ **n.** a fish with a long narrow tail, in particular: ■ another term for **GRENADIER** (sense 2). ■ another term for **RABBITFISH**.

rat-tailed mag·got ▶ **n.** the aquatic larva of the drone fly, with a taillike telescopic breathing tube that enables it to breathe air while submerged.

rat·tan /raˈtan, rə-/ ▶ **n. 1** the thin pliable stems of a palm, used to make furniture. ■ a length of such a stem used as a walking stick.
2 the tropical Old World climbing palm that yields this product, with long, spiny, jointed stems. ● Genus *Calamus*, family Palmae.
– ORIGIN mid 17th cent.: from Malay *rotan*, probably from *raut* 'pare, trim.'

rat-tat /ˌrat ˈtat/ ▶ **n.** variant of **RAT-A-TAT**.

rat·ter /ˈratər/ ▶ **n.** a dog or other animal that is used for hunting rats.

rat ter·ri·er ▶ **n.** a terrier of a small, short-haired breed originally used for hunting rats and other vermin.

rat·tle /ˈratl/ ▶ **v. 1** make or cause to make a rapid succession of short, sharp knocking sounds, typically as a result of shaking and striking repeatedly against a hard surface or object: [with obj.] *he rattled some change in his pocket* | [no obj.] *there was a sound of bottles rattling as he stacked the crates.* ■ [no obj., with adverbial of direction] (of a vehicle or its driver or passengers) move or travel somewhere while making such sounds: *trains rattled past at frequent intervals.* ■ [no obj.] **(rattle around in)** be in or occupy (an unnecessarily or undesirably spacious room or building).
2 [with obj.] informal cause (someone) to feel nervous, worried, or irritated: *she turned quickly, rattled by his presence.*
▶ **n. 1** a rapid succession of short, sharp, hard sounds: *the rattle of teacups on the tray.* ■ a gurgling sound in the throat of a dying person.
2 a thing used to make a rapid succession of short, sharp sounds, in particular: ■ a baby's toy consisting of a container filled with small pellets that makes a noise when shaken. ■ the set of horny rings at the end of a rattlesnake's tail, shaken with a dry buzzing sound as a warning.
– PHRASES **rattle someone's cage** informal make someone feel angry or annoyed. **rattle sabers** threaten to take aggressive action. See also **SABER-RATTLING**.
– PHRASAL VERBS **rattle something off** say, perform, or produce something quickly and effortlessly: *he rattled off some instructions.* **rattle on/away** talk rapidly and at length, esp. in an inane or boring way.
– DERIVATIVES **rat·tly** /ˈratl-ē, ˈratlē/ **adj.**
– ORIGIN Middle English (as a verb): related to Middle Dutch and Low German *ratelen*, of imitative origin.

rat·tler /ˈratl-ər, ˈratlər/ ▶ **n.** informal a rattlesnake.

rat·tle·snake /ˈratlˌsnāk/ ▶ **n.** a heavy-bodied American pit viper with a series of horny rings on the tail that, when vibrated, produce a characteristic rattling sound as a warning. ● Genera *Crotalus* and *Sistrurus*, family Viperidae: several species.

rat·tle·trap /ˈratlˌtrap/ ▶ **n.** informal an old or rickety vehicle.

rat·tling /ˈratl-iNG, ˈratliNG/ ▶ **adj. 1** making a series of short, sharp knocking sounds: *a rattling old bus.*
2 informal, dated denoting something very good of its kind (used for emphasis): *a rattling good story.*

rat·trap /ˈratˌtrap/ ▶ **n. 1** a trap for catching rats.
2 informal a shabby, squalid, or ramshackle building or establishment.
3 informal an unpleasant or restricting situation that offers no prospect of improvement.

rat·ty /ˈratē/ ▶ **adj. (rattier, rattiest) 1** resembling or characteristic of a rat: *his ratty eyes glittered.* ■ (of a place) infested with rats. ■ informal shabby, untidy or in bad condition: *a ratty old armchair.*

2 [predic.] Brit. informal (of a person) bad-tempered and irritable: *I was ratty with the children.*
– DERIVATIVES **rat·ti·ly** /ˈratl-ē/ **adv.**, **rat·ti·ness n.**

rau·cous /ˈrôkəs/ ▶ **adj.** making or constituting a disturbingly harsh and loud noise: *raucous youths.*
– DERIVATIVES **rau·cous·ly adv.**, **rau·cous·ness n.**
– ORIGIN mid 18th cent.: from Latin *raucus* 'hoarse' + **-OUS.**

raunch /rônCH, ränCH/ ▶ **n.** informal energetic earthiness; vulgarity: *the raunch of his first album.*
– ORIGIN 1960s: back-formation from **RAUNCHY.**

raun·chy /ˈrônCHē, ˈrän-/ ▶ **adj.** (**raunchier, raunchiest**) informal **1** earthy, vulgar, and often sexually explicit: *a raunchy new novel.*
2 (esp. of a person or place) slovenly; grubby: *the restaurant's style is raunchy and the sanitation chancy.*
– DERIVATIVES **raunch·i·ly** /-CHəlē/ **adv.**, **raunch·i·ness n.**
– ORIGIN 1930s: of unknown origin.

Rau·schen·berg /ˈrousHən,bərg/, Robert (1925–2008), US artist. His series of "combine" paintings, such as *Charlene* (1954) and *Rebus* (1955), incorporate three-dimensional objects such as nails, rags, and bottles.

rau·wol·fi·a /rouˈwo͝olfēə, rôˈwo͝ol-/ (also **rauvolfia**) ▶ **n.** a tropical shrub or small tree, some kinds of which are cultivated for the medicinal drugs that they yield. ● Genus *Rauwolfia* (or *Rauvolfia*), family Apocynaceae: many species, in particular the Indian snakeroot (*R. serpentina*), from which the drug reserpine is obtained.
– ORIGIN modern Latin, named after Leonhard *Rauwolf* (died 1596), German botanist.

rav /räv/ ▶ **n.** Judaism a rabbi, esp. one who holds a position of authority or who acts as a personal mentor. [partly via Yiddish.] ■ (**Rav**) (in orthodox Judaism) a title of respect and form of address preceding a personal name.
– ORIGIN from Hebrew and Aramaic *rab* 'master.'

rav·age /ˈravij/ ▶ **v.** [with obj.] cause severe and extensive damage to: *fears that a war could ravage their country.*
▶ **n.** (**ravages**) the severely damaging or destructive effects of something: *his face had withstood the ravages of time.* ■ acts of destruction: *the ravages committed by man.*
– DERIVATIVES **rav·ag·er n.**
– ORIGIN early 17th cent.: from French *ravager*, from earlier *ravage*, alteration of *ravine* 'rush of water.'

rav·aged /ˈravijd/ ▶ **adj.** severely damaged; devastated: *he hopes to visit his ravaged homeland.* ■ (of a person) disfigured by age or illness: *the sad tales and ravaged faces of the cancer victims.*

rave[1] /rāv/ ▶ **v.** [no obj.] **1** talk wildly or incoherently, as if one were delirious or insane: *Nancy's having hysterics and raving about a black ghost.* ■ address someone in an angry, uncontrolled way: [with direct speech] *"Never mind how he feels!" Melissa raved.*
2 speak or write about someone or something with great enthusiasm or admiration: *New York's theater critics raved about the acting.*
3 informal attend or take part in a rave (party).
▶ **n. 1** informal an extremely enthusiastic recommendation or appraisal of someone or something: *the film has won raves from American reviewers* | [as modifier] *their recent tour received rave reviews.*
2 informal a lively party or gathering involving dancing and drinking: *their annual fancy-dress rave.* ■ a party or event attended by large numbers of young people, involving drug use and dancing to fast, electronic music. ■ electronic dance music of the kind played at such events.
– ORIGIN Middle English (in the sense 'show signs of madness'): probably from Old Northern French *raver*; related obscurely to (Middle) Low German *reven* 'be senseless, rave.'

rave[2] ▶ **n.** a rail of a cart. ■ (**raves**) a permanent or removable framework added to the sides of a cart to increase its capacity.
– ORIGIN mid 16th cent.: variant of the synonymous dialect word *rathe*, of unknown origin.

Rav·el /rəˈvel/, Maurice (Joseph) (1875–1937), French composer. His works, which are noted for their colorful orchestration, have a distinctive tone and make use of unresolved dissonances. Notable works: *Daphnis and Chloë* (1912) and *Boléro* (1928).

rav·el /ˈravəl/ ▶ **v.** (**ravels, raveling, raveled**; Brit. **ravels, ravelling, ravelled**) [with obj.] **1** (**ravel something out**) untangle or unravel something: *Davy had finished raveling out his herring net* | figurative *sleep raveled out the tangles of his mind.*
2 confuse or complicate (a question or situation).
▶ **n.** rare a tangle, cluster, or knot: *a lovely yellow ravel of sunflowers.*
– ORIGIN late Middle English (in the sense 'entangle, confuse'): probably from Dutch *ravelen* 'fray out, tangle.'

rave·lin /ˈravlən/ ▶ **n.** historical an outwork of fortifications, with two faces forming a salient angle, constructed beyond the main ditch and in front of the curtain.
– ORIGIN late 16th cent.: from French, from obsolete Italian *ravellino*, of unknown origin.

rav·el·ing /ˈrav(ə)liNG/ ▶ **n.** a thread from a woven or knitted fabric that has frayed or started to unravel.

ra·ven[1] /ˈrāvən/ ▶ **n. 1** a large heavily built crow with mainly black plumage, feeding chiefly on carrion. ● Genus *Corvus*, family Corvidae: several species, in particular the widespread all-black **common raven** (*C. corax*).
2 (**the Raven**) the constellation Corvus.
▶ **adj.** (esp. of hair) of a glossy black color.
– ORIGIN Old English *hræfn*, of Germanic origin; related to Dutch *raaf* and German *Rabe.*

rav·en[2] /ˈravən/ ▶ **v.** [no obj.] archaic (of a ferocious wild animal) hunt for prey. ■ [with obj.] devour voraciously.
– ORIGIN late 15th cent. (in the sense 'take as spoil'): from Old French *raviner*, originally 'to ravage,' based on Latin *rapina* 'pillage.'

rav·en·ing /ˈravəniNG/ ▶ **adj.** (of a ferocious wild animal) extremely hungry and hunting for prey: *they turned on each other like ravening wolves.*

Ra·ven·na /rəˈvenə/ a city near the Adriatic coast in northeast central Italy; pop. 155,997 (2008). It is noted for its ancient mosaics dating from the early Christian period.

rav·en·ous /ˈravənəs/ ▶ **adj.** extremely hungry. ■ (of hunger or need) very great; voracious: *a ravenous appetite.*
– DERIVATIVES **rav·en·ous·ly adv.**, **rav·en·ous·ness n.**
– ORIGIN late Middle English: from Old French *ravineus*, from *raviner* 'to ravage' (see **RAVEN**[2]).

rav·er /ˈrāvər/ ▶ **n. 1** informal a person who regularly goes to raves.
2 a person who talks wildly or incoherently, as if delirious or insane.

rave-up ▶ **n.** informal another term for **RAVE**[1] (sense 2 of the noun).

Ra·vi /ˈrävē/ a river in southern Asia, one of the headwaters of the Indus River that rises in the Himalayas in Himachel Pradesh, in northwestern India, and flows for 450 miles (725 km) southwest into Pakistan, where it empties into the Chenab River just north of Multan. It is one of the five rivers that gave Punjab its name.

ra·vi·gote /ˌräviˈgôt/ (also **ravigotte**) ▶ **n.** a mixture of chopped chervil, chives, tarragon, and shallots, used to give piquancy to a sauce or as a base for an herb butter.
– ORIGIN French, from *ravigoter* 'invigorate.'

rav·in /ˈravən/ ▶ **n.** archaic or literary violent seizure of prey or property; plunder.
– ORIGIN Middle English: from Old French *ravine*, from Latin *rapina* 'pillage' (see **RAPINE**).

ra·vine /rəˈvēn/ ▶ **n.** a deep, narrow gorge with steep sides.
– DERIVATIVES **ra·vined adj.**
– ORIGIN late 18th cent.: from French, 'violent rush (of water)' (see **RAVIN**).

rav·ing /ˈrāviNG/ ▶ **n.** (usu. **ravings**) wild, irrational, or incoherent talk: *the ravings of a madwoman.*
▶ **adj.** informal used to emphasize the bad or extreme quality of someone or something: *she'd never been a raving beauty* | [as submodifier] *have you gone raving mad?*

ra·vi·o·li /ˌravēˈōlē/ ▶ **n.** small pasta envelopes containing ground meat, cheese, or vegetables.
– ORIGIN Italian.

rav·ish /ˈraviSH/ ▶ **v.** [with obj.] **1** archaic seize and carry off (someone) by force. ■ dated (of a man) force (a woman or girl) to have sexual intercourse against her will; rape.
2 literary fill (someone) with intense delight; enrapture: *ravished by a sunny afternoon, she had agreed without even thinking.*
– DERIVATIVES **rav·ish·er n.**, **rav·ish·ment n.**
– ORIGIN Middle English: from Old French *raviss-*, lengthened stem of *ravir*, from an alteration of Latin *rapere* 'seize.'

rav·ish·ing /ˈraviSHiNG/ ▶ **adj.** delightful; entrancing: *she looked ravishing.*
– DERIVATIVES **rav·ish·ing·ly adv.**

raw /rô/ ▶ **adj. 1** (of food) uncooked: *raw eggs* | *salsify can be eaten raw in salads or cooked.* ■ (of a material or substance) in its natural state; not yet processed or purified: *raw silk* | *raw sewage.* ■ (of information) not analyzed, evaluated, or processed for use: *there were a number of errors in the raw data.* ■ (of the edge of a piece of cloth) not having a hem or selvage. ■ (of a person) new to an activity or job and therefore lacking experience or skill: *they were replaced by raw recruits.*
2 (of a part of the body) red and painful, esp. as the result of skin abrasion: *he scrubbed his hands until they were raw* | figurative *Fran's nerves were raw.*
3 (of the weather) bleak, cold, and damp: *a raw February night.*
4 (of an emotion or quality) strong and undisguised: *he exuded an air of raw, vibrant masculinity.* ■ frank and realistic in the depiction of unpleasant facts or situations: *a raw, uncompromising portrait.* ■ informal (of language) coarse or crude, typically in relation to sexual matters.
– PHRASES **in the raw 1** in its true state; not made to seem better or more palatable than it actually is: *he didn't much care for nature in the raw.* **2** informal (of a person) naked: *I slept in the raw.*
– DERIVATIVES **raw·ly adv.**, **raw·ness n.**
– ORIGIN Old English *hrēaw*, of Germanic origin; related to Dutch *rauw* and German *roh*, from an Indo-European root shared by Greek *kreas* 'raw flesh.'

Ra·wal·pin·di /ˌräwəlˈpindē/ a city in Punjab province, in northern Pakistan, in the foothills of the Himalayas; pop. 1,933,900 (est. 2009). A former military station, it was the interim capital of Pakistan 1959–67 during the construction of Islamabad.

raw bar ▶ **n.** a bar or counter that sells raw oysters and other seafood.

raw·boned /ˈrôˈbōnd/ ▶ **adj.** having a bony or gaunt physique.

raw·hide /ˈrôˌhīd/ ▶ **n.** stiff untanned leather. ■ a whip or rope made of such leather.

Rawl·ings /ˈrôliNGz/, Marjorie Kinnan (1896–1953), US writer. She wrote the award-winning *The Yearling* (1938) for young adults; it was made into a movie in 1946. Her other works include *Cross Creek* (1943) and *The Sojourner* (1953).

Rawls /rôlz/, John (1921–2002), US philosopher. His books *A Theory of Justice* (1971) and *Political Liberalism* (1993) consider the basic institutions of a just society as those chosen by rational people under conditions that ensure impartiality.

raw ma·te·ri·al ▶ **n.** the basic material from which a product is made.

raw si·en·na ▶ **n.** see **SIENNA.**

raw sug·ar ▶ **n.** the residue left after sugarcane has been processed to remove the molasses and refine the sugar crystals. The flavor is similar to that of brown sugar.

raw um·ber ▶ **n.** see **UMBER** (sense 1).

Ray[1] /rā/, John (1627–1705), English naturalist. He was the first to classify flowering plants into monocotyledons and dicotyledons, and he established the species as the basic taxonomic unit.

Ray[2], Man. See **MAN RAY.**

Ray[3] /rī, rā/, Satyajit (1921–92), Indian movie director. He was the first to bring Indian movies to the attention of Western audiences.

ray[1] /rā/ ▶ **n. 1** each of the lines in which light (and heat) may seem to stream from the sun or any luminous body, or pass through a small opening: *a ray of sunlight came through the window.* ■ the straight line in which light or other electromagnetic radiation travels to a given point. ■ [with adj.] (**rays**) a specified form of nonluminous radiation: *water reflects and intensifies UV rays.* ■ Mathematics any of a set of straight lines passing through one point. ■ (**rays**) informal sunlight considered in the context of sunbathing: *Sarah's catching some rays on a beach in Cruz Bay.* ■ an initial or slight indication of a positive or welcome quality in a time of difficulty or trouble: *if only I could see some ray of hope.*
2 a thing that is arranged radially, in particular: ■ Botany (in a composite flower head of the daisy family) an array of ray florets arranged radially around the central disc, forming the white part of the flower head of a daisy. ■ (also **fin ray**) Zoology each of the long, slender bony protuberances supporting the fins of most bony fishes. ■ Zoology each radial arm of a starfish.
▶ **v.** [no obj.] spread from or as if from a central point: *delicate lines rayed out at each corner of her eyes.* ■ [with obj.] literary radiate (light): *the sun rays forth its natural light into the air.*
– PHRASES **ray of sunshine** informal a person or thing that brings happiness into the lives of others.
– DERIVATIVES **ray·less adj.** (chiefly Botany).
– ORIGIN Middle English: from Old French *rai*, based on Latin *radius* 'spoke, ray.' The verb dates from the late 16th cent.

ray[2] ▶ **n.** a broad, flat marine or freshwater fish with a cartilaginous skeleton, winglike pectoral fins, and

a long slender tail. Many rays have venomous spines or electric organs. ● Order Batiformes: several families, including Rajidae (the skates).
– ORIGIN Middle English: from Old French *raie*, from Latin *raia*.

ray blight ▶ n. a fungal disease of chrysanthemums that causes collapse and rotting of the leading shoot. ● The fungus is *Didymella ligulicola*, also called *Ascochyta chrysanthemi*.

rayed /rād/ ▶ adj. [in combination] chiefly Biology having rays of a specified number or kind: *white-rayed daisies*.

ray-finned fish ▶ n. a fish of a large group having thin fins strengthened by slender rays, including all bony fishes apart from the coelacanth and lungfishes. Compare with LOBE-FINNED FISH, TELEOST. ● Subclass (or class) Actinopterygii: numerous orders.

ray flo·ret ▶ n. Botany (in a composite flower head of the daisy family) any of a number of strap-shaped and typically sterile florets that form the ray. In plants such as dandelions, the flower head is composed entirely of ray florets. Compare with DISK FLORET.

ray gun ▶ n. (in science fiction) a gun causing injury or damage by the emission of rays.

Ray·leigh /ˈrālē/, John William Strutt, 3rd Baron (1842–1919), English physicist. He established the electrical units of resistance, current, and electromotive force. With William Ramsay he discovered argon and other inert gases. Nobel Prize for Physics (1904).

Ray·leigh num·ber ▶ n. Physics a dimensionless parameter that is a measure of the instability of a layer of fluid due to differences of temperature and density at the top and bottom.

Ray·leigh scat·ter·ing ▶ n. Physics the scattering of light by particles in a medium, without change in wavelength. It accounts, for example, for the blue color of the sky, since blue light is scattered slightly more efficiently than red. Compare with RAMAN EFFECT.

Ray·leigh wave ▶ n. Physics an undulating wave that travels over the surface of a solid, esp. of the ground in an earthquake, with a speed independent of wavelength, the motion of the particles being in ellipses.

Ray·naud's dis·ease /rāˈnōz/ (also **Raynaud's syndrome**) ▶ n. a disease characterized by spasm of the arteries in the extremities, esp. the fingers (**Raynaud's phenomenon**). It is typically brought on by constant cold or vibration, and leads to pallor, pain, numbness, and in severe cases, gangrene.
– ORIGIN late 19th cent.: named after Maurice *Raynaud* (1834–81), French physician.

ray·on /ˈrā,än/ ▶ n. a textile fiber or fabric made from regenerated cellulose (viscose).
– ORIGIN 1920s: an arbitrary formation.

raze /rāz/ ▶ v. [with obj.] (usu. **be razed**) completely destroy (a building, town, or other site): *villages were **razed to the ground***.
– ORIGIN Middle English (in the sense 'scratch, incise'): from Old French *raser* 'shave closely,' from Latin *ras-* 'scraped,' from the verb *radere*.

r

ra·zor /ˈrāzər/ ▶ n. an instrument with a sharp blade or combination of blades, used to remove unwanted hair from the face or body.
▶ v. [with obj.] cut with a razor.
– ORIGIN Middle English: from Old French *rasor*, from *raser* 'shave closely' (see RAZE).

ra·zor·back /ˈrāzər,bak/ ▶ n. **1** (also **razorback hog**) a pig of a half-wild breed common in the southern US, with the back formed into a high, narrow ridge.
2 (also **razorback ridge**) a steep-sided, narrow ridge of land.

ra·zor·bill /ˈrāzər,bil/ ▶ n. a black-and-white auk (seabird) with a deep bill that is said to resemble a straight razor, found in the North Atlantic and Baltic Sea. ● *Alca torda*, family Alcidae.

ra·zor blade ▶ n. a blade used in a razor, typically a flat piece of metal with a sharp edge or edges used in a safety razor.

ra·zor clam ▶ n. a burrowing bivalve mollusk with a long, slender shell that resembles the handle of a straight razor. Also called JACKKNIFE CLAM. ● Family Solenidae: *Ensis* and other genera.

ra·zor edge (also **razor's edge**) ▶ n. a sharp edge of a knife, ax, or similar implement. ■ a state of sharp incisiveness: *he had honed his mind to a razor edge*. ■ (**the razor edge**) the most advanced stage in the development of something; the cutting edge: *in 1960 jet planes were **the razor edge of** chic*.
– PHRASES **on the razor's edge** in a precarious or dangerous position: *it is commonplace to believe that Finns live on the razor's edge, at the mercy of their powerful neighbor*.
– DERIVATIVES **ra·zor-edged** adj.

ra·zor·fish /ˈrāzər,fisH/ ▶ n. (pl. **same** or **razorfishes**) **1** a small fish of the Indo-Pacific, with a long, flattened snout and a laterally compressed body encased in thin, bony shields that meet to form a sharp ridge on the belly. ● Family Centriscidae: several genera and species, including *Aeoliscus strigatus*, which swims in a head-down vertical posture.
2 a small, brightly colored wrasse (fish) with a steeply sloping forehead, living chiefly in sandy coastal waters of the western Atlantic. ● Genus *Hemipteronotus*, family Labridae: several species.

Ra·zor scoot·er ▶ n. trademark a type of lightweight aluminum collapsible scooter ridden by adults and children.

ra·zor-sharp ▶ adj. extremely sharp: *razor-sharp teeth* | figurative *his razor-sharp mind*.

ra·zor shell ▶ n. British term for RAZOR CLAM.

ra·zor-thin ▶ adj. extremely thin: *razor-thin slices of salmon*. ■ (esp. of a margin of victory) very slim; barely achieved: *a razor-thin margin of eight votes*.

ra·zor wire ▶ n. a metal wire or ribbon with sharp edges or studded with small sharp blades, used as a barrier.

razz /raz/ informal ▶ v. [with obj.] tease (someone) playfully.
▶ n. another term for RASPBERRY (sense 4).
– ORIGIN early 20th cent.: from informal *razzberry*, alteration of RASPBERRY.

raz·zi·a /ˈrazēə/ ▶ n. historical a hostile raid for purposes of conquest, plunder, and capture of slaves, esp. one carried out by Moors in North Africa.
– ORIGIN mid 19th cent.: via French from Algerian Arabic *ġāziya* 'raid.'

raz·zle-daz·zle /,razəl ˈdazəl/ ▶ n. informal noisy, showy, and exciting activity and display designed to attract and impress: *myth, legend, and razzle-dazzle all rolled into one show* | [as modifier] *hyped-up, razzle-dazzle gimmicks of quick-sell advertising*.
– ORIGIN late 19th cent.: reduplication of DAZZLE.

razz·ma·tazz /ˈrazmə,taz/ ▶ n. another term for RAZZLE-DAZZLE.
– ORIGIN late 19th cent.: probably an alteration of RAZZLE-DAZZLE.

Rb ▶ symbol the chemical element rubidium.

RBC ▶ abbr. red blood cell.

RBE (also **rbe**) ▶ abbr. relative biological effectiveness.

RBI ▶ abbr. Baseball run batted in (a run credited to the batter's hitting statistics for enabling a runner to score during his at bat).

RC ▶ abbr. ■ Aeronautics radio compass. ■ Electronics radio-controlled. ■ Red Cross. ■ reinforced concrete. ■ Electronics resistance/capacitance (or resistor/capacitor). ■ Roman Catholic.

RCA ▶ abbr. ■ Radio Corporation of America. ■ (in the UK) Royal College of Art.

RCAF ▶ abbr. Royal Canadian Air Force.

RCCh ▶ abbr. Roman Catholic Church.

RCMP ▶ abbr. Royal Canadian Mounted Police.

rcpt. ▶ abbr. receipt.

rct. (also **Rct.**) ▶ abbr. ■ receipt. ■ recruit.

Rd ▶ abbr. Road (used in street names).

rd. ▶ abbr. rod; rods.

RDA ▶ abbr. recommended daily (or dietary) allowance, the quantity of a particular nutrient that should be consumed daily in order to maintain good health.

RDBMS ▶ abbr. Computing relational database management system.

RDF ▶ abbr. ■ radio direction finder (or finding). ■ rapid deployment force.

RDI ▶ abbr. recommended (or reference) daily intake, another term for **RDA**.

RDS ▶ abbr. ■ radio data system, in which a digital signal is transmitted with a normal radio signal to provide further data or control the receiver. ■ respiratory distress syndrome.

RDX ▶ n. a type of high explosive.
– ORIGIN 1940s: from *R(esearch) D(epartment) (E)x(plosive)*.

Re[1] /rā/ variant spelling of RA[1].

Re[2] ▶ symbol the chemical element rhenium.

re[1] /rā, rē/ ▶ prep. in the matter of (used typically as the first word in the heading of an official document or to introduce a reference in an official letter): *re: invoice 87*. ■ about; concerning: *I saw the deputy re the incident*.
– ORIGIN Latin, ablative of *res* 'thing.'

USAGE It is often said that, strictly speaking, re should be used in headings and references, as in *Re: Harrison versus Ortiz*, but not as a normal word meaning 'regarding,' as in *thanks for your letter re the job postings*. However, the evidence suggests that **re** is now widely used in the second context in official and semiofficial contexts, and is now generally accepted. Be aware, however, that in certain formal contexts, if **re** is used in mid-sentence, some readers may regard it as business jargon or an inappropriate legalism. Often, *concerning* or *about* would be just as clear (and less likely to annoy).

re[2] /rā/ ▶ n. Music (in solmization) the second note of a major scale. ■ the note D in the fixed-do system.
– ORIGIN Middle English *re*, representing (as an arbitrary name for the note) the first syllable of *resonare*, taken from a Latin hymn (see SOLMIZATION).

Re. (also **re.**) ▶ abbr. rupee.

're ▶ abbr. informal are (usually after the pronouns you, we, and they): *we're a bit worried*.

re- ▶ prefix **1** once more; afresh; anew: *reaccustom* | *reactivate*. ■ with return to a previous state: *restore* | *revert*.
2 (also **red-**) in return; mutually: *react* | *resemble*. ■ in opposition: *repel* | *resistance*.
3 behind or after: *relic* | *remain*. ■ in a withdrawn state: *recluse* | *reticent*. ■ back and away; down: *recede* | *relegation*.
4 with frequentative or intensive force: *redouble* | *resound*.
5 with negative force: *rebuff* | *recant*.
– ORIGIN from Latin *re-*, *red-* 'again, back.'

USAGE In modern English, the tendency is for words formed with prefixes such as **re-** to be unhyphenated: **reacquaint, reconsider, reshape**. For the sake of clarity, however, hyphenation is sometimes favored when the root word begins with a vowel: **re-elect**, for instance, may be preferred as a less awkward spelling than **reelect**. A hyphen is often used when the word formed with the prefix would be identical in form with, but different in meaning and pronunciation from, an already existing word: **re-cover** (meaning 'cover again,' as in *we decided to **re-cover** the dining-room chairs*), as opposed to **recover** (meaning 'get better in health').

re·ab·sorb /,rēəbˈzôrb/ ▶ v. [with obj.] absorb (something) again: *a failure of the gut to reabsorb the majority of the fluid*.
– DERIVATIVES **re·ab·sorp·tion** n.

re·ac·cept /,rēakˈsept/ ▶ v. [with obj.] accept (someone or something) again.
– DERIVATIVES **re·ac·cept·ance** n.

reach /rēcH/ ▶ v. **1** [no obj.] stretch out an arm in a specified direction in order to touch or grasp something: *he reached over and turned off his bedside light*. ■ (**reach for**) make a movement with one's hand or arm in an attempt to touch or grasp (something): *Carl reached for the phone*. ■ [with obj.] (**reach something out**) stretch out one's hand or arm: *he reached out a hand and touched her forehead*. ■ [with two objs.] hand (something) to (someone): *reach me those glasses*. ■ be able to touch something with an outstretched arm or leg: *I had to stand on tiptoe and even then I could hardly reach*. ■ (**reach out**) extend help, understanding, or influence: *he felt such an urge to reach out to his fellow sufferer*.
2 [with obj.] arrive at; get as far as: *"Goodbye," she said as they reached the door* | *the show is due to reach our screens early next year*. ■ attain or extend to (a specified point, level, or condition): *unemployment reached a peak in 1933* | [no obj.] *in its native habitat it will **reach to** about 6 m in height*. ■ succeed in achieving: *the intergovernmental conference reached agreement on the draft treaty*. ■ make contact or communicate with (someone) by telephone or other means: *I've been trying to reach you all morning*. ■ (of a broadcast or other communication) be received by: *television reached those parts of the electorate that other news sources could not*. ■ succeed in influencing or having an effect on: *their fresh sound and message reach people who may never set foot in a church*.
3 [no obj.] Sailing sail with the wind blowing from the side, or from slightly behind the side, of the ship.
▶ n. **1** an act of reaching out with one's arm: *she made a reach for him*. ■ [in sing.] the distance to which someone can stretch out their hand (used esp. of a boxer): *a giant, over six feet seven with a reach of over 81 inches*. ■ the extent or range of application, effect, or influence: *the diameter and the reach of the spark plug varies from engine to engine*.
2 (often **reaches**) a continuous extent of land or water, esp. a stretch of river between two bends, or the part of a canal between locks: *the upper reaches of the Nile*.
3 Sailing a distance traversed in reaching.

– PHRASES **out of** (or **beyond**) **reach** outside the distance to which someone can stretch out their hand. ■ beyond the capacity of someone to attain or achieve something: *she thought college was out of her reach.* **within** (or **in**) **reach** inside the distance to which someone can stretch out their hand. ■ inside a distance that can be traveled: *Rocky Mountain National Park is* ***within easy reach of*** *the city of Denver.* ■ within the capacity of someone to attain or achieve something.
– DERIVATIVES **reach·a·ble** adj.
– ORIGIN Old English *rǣcan*; related to Dutch *reiken* and German *reichen*.

reach·er /ˈrēCHər/ ▶ **n. 1** a thing that reaches, esp. a device that enables a disabled or elderly person to pick up objects that are difficult to reach.
2 a kind of jib on a sailing ship.

re·ac·quaint /ˌrēəˈkwānt/ ▶ **v.** [with obj.] make (someone) acquainted or familiar with someone or something again: *he wants to* ***reacquaint himself with*** *the public.*
– DERIVATIVES **re·ac·quaint·ance** /-ˈkwāntns/ **n.**

re·ac·quire /ˌrēəˈkwī(ə)r/ ▶ **v.** [with obj.] acquire (something) again: *the ability of a corporation to reacquire its own shares.*
– DERIVATIVES **re·ac·qui·si·tion n.**

re·act /rēˈakt/ ▶ **v.** [no obj.] respond or behave in a particular way in response to something: *he* ***reacted*** *angrily* ***to*** *the news of his dismissal | the market reacted by falling a further 3.1%.* ■ (**react against**) respond with hostility, opposition, or a contrary course of action to: *they reacted against the elite art music of their time.* ■ (of a person) suffer from adverse physiological effects after ingesting, breathing, or touching a substance: *many babies react to soy-based formulas.* ■ Chemistry & Physics interact and undergo a chemical or physical change: *the sulfur in the coal* ***reacts with*** *the limestone during combustion.* ■ [with obj.] Chemistry cause (a substance) to undergo such a change by interacting with another substance. ■ Stock Market (of stock prices) fall or rise in reaction to events, developments, etc.
– ORIGIN mid 17th cent.: from **RE-** (expressing intensive force or reversal) + **ACT**, originally suggested by medieval Latin *react-* 'done again,' from the verb *reagere*.

re·ac·tance /rēˈaktəns/ ▶ **n.** Physics the nonresistive component of impedance in an AC circuit, arising from the effect of inductance or capacitance or both and causing the current to be out of phase with the electromotive force causing it.

re·ac·tant /rēˈaktənt/ ▶ **n.** Chemistry a substance that takes part in and undergoes change during a reaction.

re·ac·tion /rēˈakSHən/ ▶ **n.** an action performed or a feeling experienced in response to a situation or event: *Carrie's immediate reaction was one of relief.* ■ (**reactions**) a person's ability to respond physically and mentally to external stimuli: *a skilled driver with quick reactions.* ■ an adverse physiological response to a substance that has been breathed in, ingested, or touched: *such allergic reactions as hay fever and asthma.* ■ a chemical process in which two or more substances act mutually on each other and are changed into different substances, or one substance changes into two or more other substances. ■ Physics an analogous transformation of atomic nuclei or other particles. ■ a mode of thinking or behaving that is deliberately different from previous modes of thought and behavior: *the work of these painters was* ***a reaction against*** *fauvism.* ■ opposition to political or social progress or reform: *the institution is under threat from the forces of reaction.* ■ Physics repulsion or resistance exerted in opposition to the impact or pressure of another body; a force equal and opposite to the force giving rise to it.
– DERIVATIVES **re·ac·tion·ist** /-nist/ **n. & adj.**
– ORIGIN mid 17th cent.: from **REACT** + **-ION**, originally suggested by medieval Latin *reactio(n-)*, from *react-* 'done again' (see **REACT**).

re·ac·tion·ar·y /rēˈakSHəˌnerē/ ▶ **adj.** (of a person or a set of views) opposing political or social liberalization or reform.
▶ **n.** (pl. **reactionaries**) a person who holds such views.

re·ac·tion for·ma·tion ▶ **n.** Psychoanalysis the tendency of a repressed wish or feeling to be expressed at a conscious level in a contrasting form.

re·ac·tion shot ▶ **n.** (in a film or video recording) a portrayal of a person's response to an event or to a statement made by another.

re·ac·ti·vate /ˌrēˈaktəˌvāt/ ▶ **v.** [with obj.] restore (something) to a state of activity; bring back into action.
– DERIVATIVES **re·ac·tiv·a·tion n.**

re·ac·tive /rēˈaktiv/ ▶ **adj.** showing a response to a stimulus: *pupils are reactive to light.* ■ acting in response to a situation rather than creating or controlling it: *a proactive rather than a reactive approach.* ■ having a tendency to react chemically: *nitrogen dioxide is a highly reactive gas.* ■ Physiology showing an immune response to a specific antigen. ■ (of a disease or illness) caused by a reaction to something: *reactive arthritis | reactive depression.* ■ Physics of or relating to reactance: *a reactive load.*

re·ac·tive in·hi·bi·tion ▶ **n.** Psychology the inhibiting effect of fatigue or boredom on the response to a stimulus and ability to learn.

re·ac·tiv·i·ty /ˌrēˌakˈtivətē/ ▶ **n.** the state or power of being reactive or the degree to which a thing is reactive. ■ the extent to which a nuclear reactor deviates from a steady state.

re·ac·tor /rēˈaktər/ ▶ **n. 1** (also **nuclear reactor**) an apparatus or structure in which fissile material can be made to undergo a controlled, self-sustaining nuclear reaction with the consequent release of energy. ■ a container or apparatus in which substances are made to react chemically, esp. one in an industrial plant.
2 Medicine a person who shows an immune response to a specific antigen or an adverse reaction to a drug or other substance.
3 Physics a coil or other component that provides reactance in a circuit.

read /rēd/ ▶ **v.** (past and past participle **read** /red/) [with obj.] **1** look at and comprehend the meaning of (written or printed matter) by mentally interpreting the characters or symbols of which it is composed: *it's the best novel I've ever read | I never learned to read music | Emily* ***read over*** *her notes* | [no obj.] *I'll go to bed and read for a while.* ■ speak (the written or printed matter that one is reading) aloud, typically to another person: *the charges against him were* ***read out*** | [with two objs.] *his mother read him a bedtime story* | [no obj.] *I'll read to you if you like.* ■ [no obj.] have the ability to look at and comprehend the meaning of written or printed matter: *only three of the girls could read and none could write.* ■ habitually read (a particular newspaper or journal). ■ discover (information) by reading it in a written or printed source: *he was arrested yesterday—I read it in the paper* | [no obj.] *I read about the course in a magazine.* ■ discern (a fact, emotion, or quality) in someone's eyes or expression: *she looked down, terrified that he would read fear on her face.* ■ understand or interpret the nature or significance of: *he didn't dare look away, in case this was read as a sign of weakness.* ■ [no obj.] (of a piece of writing) convey a specified impression to the reader: *the brief note read like a cry for help.* ■ [no obj., with complement] (of a passage, text, or sign) contain or consist of specified words; have a certain wording: *the placard read "We want justice."* ■ used to indicate that a particular word in a text or passage is incorrect and that another should be substituted for it: *for madam read madman.* ■ [no obj.] (**read for**) (of an actor) audition for (a part in a play or film). ■ (of a device) obtain data from (light or other input).
2 inspect and record the figure indicated on (a measuring instrument): *I've come to read the gas meter.* ■ [no obj., with complement] (of such an instrument) indicate a specified measurement or figure: *the thermometer read 0° C.*
3 chiefly Brit. study (an academic subject) at a university: *I'm reading English at Cambridge* | [no obj.] *he went to Manchester to* ***read for*** *a BA in Economics.*
4 (of a computer) copy, transfer, or interpret (data). ■ enter or extract (data) in an electronic storage device: *the commonest way of reading a file into the system.*
5 hear and understand the words of (someone speaking on a radio transmitter): *"Do you read me? Over."*
▶ **n.** [usu. in sing.] a person's interpretation of something: *their read on the national situation may be correct.* ■ [with adj.] informal a book considered in terms of its readability: *the book is a thoroughly entertaining read.*
– PHRASES **read between the lines** look for or discover a meaning that is hidden or implied rather than explicitly stated. **read someone like a book** understand someone's thoughts and motives clearly or easily. **read someone's mind** (or **thoughts**) discern what someone is thinking. **read my lips** informal listen carefully (used to emphasize the importance of the speaker's words or the earnestness of their intent).
– PHRASAL VERBS **read something into** attribute a meaning or significance to (something) that it may not in fact possess: *was I reading too much into his behavior?* **read someone out of** formally expel someone from (an organization or body). [with reference to the reading of the formal sentence of expulsion.] **read up on something** acquire information about a particular subject by studying it intensively or systematically: *she spent the time reading up on antenatal care.*
– ORIGIN Old English *rǣdan*, of Germanic origin; related to Dutch *raden* and German *raten* 'advise, guess.' Early senses included 'advise' and 'interpret (a riddle or dream)' (see **REDE**).

read·a·ble /ˈrēdəbəl/ ▶ **adj. 1** able to be read or deciphered; legible. ■ easy or enjoyable to read: *a marvelously readable book.*
2 (of data or a storage medium or device) capable of being processed or interpreted by a computer or other electronic device.
– DERIVATIVES **read·a·bil·i·ty** /ˌrēdəˈbilətē/ **n.**, **read·a·bly** /-blē/ **adv.**

re·a·dapt /ˌrēəˈdapt/ ▶ **v.** [no obj.] become adjusted to changed conditions again: *the limpets readapted to submerged life.* ■ [with obj.] change (something) as a result of new or different conditions: *she'll be the one readapting her life.*
– DERIVATIVES **re·ad·ap·ta·tion n.**

re·ad·dress /ˌrēəˈdres/ ▶ **v.** [with obj.] **1** change the address written or printed on (a letter or parcel).
2 look at or attend to (an issue or problem) once again.

read·er /ˈrēdər/ ▶ **n. 1** a person who reads or who is fond of reading: *the books of Roald Dahl appeal to young readers | she's an avid reader.* ■ a person who reads a particular newspaper, magazine, or text: *Times readers.* ■ short for **LAY READER.** ■ a person entitled to use a particular library. ■ a person who reads and reports to a publisher or producer on the merits of manuscripts submitted for publication or production, or who provides critical comments on the text prior to publication. ■ a proofreader.
2 a person who inspects and records the figure indicated on a measuring instrument: *a meter reader.*
3 a book containing extracts of a particular author's work or passages of text designed to give learners of a language practice in reading.
4 (usu. **Reader**) Brit. a university lecturer of the highest grade below professor.
5 a machine for producing on a screen a magnified, readable image of any desired part of a microfiche or microfilm. ■ Computing a device or piece of software used for reading or obtaining data stored on tape, cards, or other media.
– ORIGIN Old English *rǣdere* 'interpreter of dreams, reader.'

read·er·ly /ˈrēdərlē/ ▶ **adj.** of or relating to a reader: *he tries one's readerly patience to breaking point.*

read·er·ship /ˈrēdərˌSHip/ ▶ **n. 1** [treated as sing. or pl.] the readers of a newspaper, magazine, or book regarded collectively: *it has a readership of 100 million.*
2 (usu. **Readership**) Brit. the position of Reader at a university.

read·i·ly /ˈredl-ē/ ▶ **adv.** without hesitation or reluctance; willingly: *he readily admits that the new car surpasses its predecessors.* ■ without delay or difficulty; easily: [as submodifier] *illegal fireworks are readily available.*

read-in ▶ **n.** Computing the input or entry of data to a computer or storage device.

read·i·ness /ˈredēnis/ ▶ **n. 1** [in sing. with infinitive] willingness to do something: *Spain had indicated a readiness to accept his terms.*
2 the state of being fully prepared for something: *your muscles tense* ***in readiness for*** *action.*
3 immediacy, quickness, or promptness: *quickness of hearing and readiness of speech were essential.*

Read·ing /ˈrediNG/ **1** a town in southern England, on the Kennet River near its junction with the Thames River; pop. 142,300 (est. 2009).
2 an industrial and commercial city in southeastern Pennsylvania, on the Schuylkill River; pop. 80,506 (est. 2008).

read·ing /ˈrēdiNG/ ▶ **n. 1** the action or skill of reading written or printed matter silently or aloud: *suggestions for further reading | the reading of a will* | [as modifier] *reading skills | a cursory reading of the minutes.* ■ written or printed matter that can be read: *his main reading was detective stories | his file certainly* ***makes interesting reading.*** ■ [usu. with adj.] knowledge of literature: *a man of wide reading.* ■ an occasion at which poetry or other pieces of literature are read aloud to an audience. ■ a piece of literature or passage of scripture read aloud to a group of people: *readings from the Bible.*
2 an interpretation: *feminist readings of Goethe | his reading of the situation was justified.*
3 a figure or amount shown by a meter or other measuring instrument: *radiation readings were taken every hour.*

PRONUNCIATION KEY ə *ago, up*; ər *over, fur*; a *hat*; ā *ate*; ä *car*; e *let*; ē *see*; i *fit*; ī *by*; NG *sing*; ō *go*; ô *law, for*; oi *toy*; o͝o *good*; o͞o *goo*; ou *out*; TH *thin*; T͟H *then*; ZH *vision*

r

4 a stage of debate in a parliament through which a bill must pass before it can become law: *the bill returns to the House for its final reading next week.*

re·ad·just /ˌrēəˈjəst/ ▶ **v.** [with obj.] set or adjust (something) again: *I readjusted the rear-view mirror.* ■ [no obj.] adjust or adapt to a changed environment or situation: (as adj. **readjusted**) *she wondered if she could ever become* ***readjusted to*** *this sort of life.*
– DERIVATIVES **re·ad·just·ment** n.

re·ad·mit /ˌrēədˈmit/ ▶ **v.** (**readmits, readmitting, readmitted**) [with obj.] admit (someone) to a place or organization again: *he was later readmitted to Carnegie Tech.*
– DERIVATIVES **re·ad·mit·tance** n., **re·ad·mis·sion** n.

read-on·ly mem·o·ry /rēd/ (abbr.: **ROM**) ▶ **n.** Computing memory read at high speed but not capable of being changed by program instructions.

re·a·dopt /ˌrēəˈdäpt/ ▶ **v.** [with obj.] adopt (a physical position) again. ■ start to follow (a principle or course of action) again.
– DERIVATIVES **re·a·dop·tion** n.

read·out /ˈrēdˌout/ ▶ **n.** a visual record or display of the output from a computer or scientific instrument. ■ the process of transferring or displaying such data.

read-through /rēd/ ▶ **n.** an initial rehearsal of a play at which actors read their parts from scripts.

read-write /ˈrēd ˈrīt/ ▶ **adj.** Computing capable of reading existing data and accepting alterations or further input.

read·y /ˈredē/ ▶ **adj.** (**readier, readiest**) **1** [predic.] in a suitable state for an activity, action, or situation; fully prepared: *are you ready, Carrie?* | *I began to get* ***ready for*** *bed* | [with infinitive] *she was about ready to leave.* ■ (of a thing) made suitable and available for immediate use: *dinner's ready!* | *could you have the list ready by this afternoon?* ■ (**ready with**) keen or quick to give: *I'm always ready with a wisecrack.* ■ (**ready for**) in need of or having a desire for: *I expect you're ready for a drink* | *she always looks ready for a fight.* ■ [with infinitive] eager, inclined, or willing to do something: *she is ready to die for her political convictions.* ■ [with infinitive] in such a condition as to be likely to do something: *by the time he arrived he was ready to drop.*
2 easily available or obtained; within reach: *there was a ready supply of drink* | *the murderer knew that the mallet would be* ***ready to hand.*** ■ [attrib.] immediate, quick, or prompt: *those who have ready access to the arts* | *a girl with a ready smile.*
▶ **n.** (pl. **readies**) (**readies** or **the ready**) Brit. informal available money; cash.
▶ **v.** (**readies, readying, readied**) [with obj.] prepare (someone or something) for an activity or purpose: *the spare transformer was readied for shipment* | [with obj. and infinitive] *she had readied herself to speak first.*
– PHRASES **at the ready** prepared or available for immediate use: *the men walk with their guns at the ready.* **make ready** prepare: *they were told to* ***make ready*** *for the journey home.* **ready and waiting** used to emphasize that someone or something is fully prepared or immediately available: *the apartment was all ready and waiting for them.* **ready, set, go** used to announce the beginning of a race. **ready to roll** informal (of a person, vehicle, or thing) fully prepared to start functioning or moving: *the next morning, the plan was ready to roll.*
– ORIGIN Middle English: from Old English *rǣde* (from a Germanic base meaning 'arrange, prepare'; related to Dutch *gereed*) + -Y[1].

r

read·y-made ▶ **adj.** (esp. of products such as clothes and curtains) made to a standard size or specification rather than to order. ■ available right away; not needing to be specially created or devised: *we have no ready-made answers.* ■ (of food) ready to be served without further preparation: *a ready-made Christmas cake.*
▶ **n.** (usu. **ready-mades**) a ready-made article: *on the top shelf of ready-mades is Stromboli.* ■ a mass-produced article selected by an artist and displayed as a work of art.

read·y-mix ▶ **n.** ready-mixed concrete.

read·y-mixed ▶ **adj.** (esp. of a mixture used in building or cooking) having some or all of the constituents already mixed together; commercially prepared.

read·y mon·ey (also **ready cash**) ▶ **n.** money in the form of cash that is immediately available.

read·y-to-wear ▶ **adj.** (of clothes) made for the general market and sold through stores rather than made to order for an individual customer; off the rack.

re·af·firm /ˌrēəˈfərm/ ▶ **v.** [reporting verb] state again as a fact; assert again strongly: *the prime minister reaffirmed his commitment to the agreement* | [with clause] *he reaffirmed that it was essential to strengthen the rule of law.* ■ [with obj.] confirm the validity or correctness of (something previously established): *the election reaffirmed his position as leader.*
– DERIVATIVES **re·af·fir·ma·tion** /ˌrēˌafərˈmāSHən/ n.

Rea·gan /ˈrāgən/, Ronald (Wilson) (1911–2004), 40th president of the US 1981–89. He was a movie actor before entering politics and then served as the governor of California 1967–74. A conservative Republican, his administration greatly increased defense spending, cut taxes and social services budgets, and saw a record rise in the national budget deficit. He signed an intermediate nuclear forces nonproliferation treaty in 1987. His reputation was tarnished by his involvement in the Iran-Contra affair.
– DERIVATIVES **Rea·gan·ism** /-ˌnizəm/ n.

Ronald W. Reagan

re·a·gent /rēˈājənt/ ▶ **n.** a substance or mixture for use in chemical analysis or other reactions: *this compound is a very sensitive reagent for copper.*

re·a·gin /rēˈājən, -gən/ ▶ **n.** Immunology the antibody that is involved in allergic reactions, causing the release of histamine when it combines with antigen in tissue, and capable of producing sensitivity to the antigen when introduced into the skin of a normal individual. ■ the substance in the blood that is responsible for a positive response to the Wassermann test.
– DERIVATIVES **re·a·gin·ic** /ˌrēəˈjinik, -ˈginik/ adj.
– ORIGIN early 20th cent.: coined in German from *reagieren* 'react.'

re·al[1] /ˈrē(ə)l/ ▶ **adj.** **1** actually existing as a thing or occurring in fact; not imagined or supposed: *Julius Caesar was a real person* | *a story drawing on real events* | *her many illnesses, real and imaginary.* ■ used to emphasize the significance or seriousness of a situation or circumstance: *there is a real danger of civil war* | *the competitive threat from overseas is very real.* ■ Philosophy relating to something as it is, not merely as it may be described or distinguished.
2 (of a substance or thing) not imitation or artificial; genuine: *the earring was presumably real gold.* ■ true or actual: *his real name is James* | *this isn't my real reason for coming.* ■ [attrib.] (of a person or thing) rightly so called; proper: *he's my idea of a real man* | *Jamie is my only real friend.*
3 [attrib.] informal complete; utter (used for emphasis): *the tour turned out to be a real disaster.*
4 [attrib.] adjusted for changes in the value of money; assessed by purchasing power: *real incomes had fallen by 30 percent* | *an increase* ***in real terms*** *of 11.6 percent.*
5 Law of fixed property (i.e., land and buildings), as distinct from personal property: *he lost nearly all of his real holdings.*
6 Mathematics (of a number or quantity) having no imaginary part. See IMAGINARY.
7 Optics (of an image) of a kind in which the light that forms it actually passes through it; not virtual.
▶ **adv.** [as submodifier] informal really; very: *my head hurts real bad.*
– PHRASES **for real** informal used to assert that something is genuine or is actually the case: *I'm not playing games—this is for real!* ■ used in questions to express surprise or to question the truth or seriousness of what one has seen or heard: *are these guys for real?* **get real!** informal used to convey that an idea or statement is foolish or overly idealistic: *You want teens to have committed sexual relationships? Get real!* **real live** humorous used to emphasize the existence of something, esp. if it is surprising or unusual: *a real live detective had been at the factory.* **real money** informal money in a large or significant amount. **the real thing** informal a thing that is absolutely genuine or authentic: *you've never been in love before, so how can you be sure this is the real thing?*
– DERIVATIVES **real·ness** n.
– ORIGIN late Middle English (as a legal term meaning 'relating to things, esp. real property'): from Anglo-Norman French, from late Latin *realis*, from Latin *res* 'thing.'

re·al[2] /rāˈäl/ ▶ **n.** (pl. **reals** or **reis** /rāSH, rās/) the basic monetary unit of Brazil since 1994, equal to 100 centavos. ■ (pl. **reales** /rāˈäles/ or **reals**) a former coin and monetary unit of various Spanish-speaking countries.
– ORIGIN Portuguese and Spanish, literally 'royal' (adjective used as a noun).

real es·tate ▶ **n.** property consisting of land or buildings: *most of her real estate is in New Mexico* | *Bryce has been in real estate for 11 years.*

real es·tate a·gent ▶ **n.** a person who sells and rents out buildings and land for clients.
– DERIVATIVES **re·al es·tate a·gen·cy** n.

re·al·gar /rēˈalgər, -ˌgär/ ▶ **n.** a soft, reddish mineral consisting of arsenic sulfide, formerly used as a pigment and in fireworks.
– ORIGIN late Middle English: via medieval Latin from Arabic *rahj al-ġār* 'arsenic,' literally 'dust of the cave.'

re·a·li·a /rēˈälēə, -ˈālēə/ ▶ **n.** objects and material from everyday life, esp. when used as teaching aids.
– ORIGIN 1950s: from late Latin, neuter plural (used as a noun) of *realis* 'relating to things' (see REAL[1]).

re·a·lign /ˌrēəˈlīn/ ▶ **v.** [with obj.] change or restore to a different or former position or state: *they worked to relieve his shoulder pain and realign the joint* | *the president realigned his government to reflect the balance of parties.* ■ (**realign oneself with**) change one's position or attitude with regard to (a person, organization, or cause): *he wished to realign himself with Bagehot's more pessimistic position.*
– DERIVATIVES **re·a·lign·ment** n.

re·al·ism /ˈrēəˌlizəm/ ▶ **n.** **1** the attitude or practice of accepting a situation as it is and being prepared to deal with it accordingly: *the summit was marked by a new mood of realism.* ■ the view that the subject matter of politics is political power, not matters of principle: *political realism is the oldest approach to global politics.*
2 the quality or fact of representing a person, thing, or situation accurately or in a way that is true to life: *the earthy realism of Raimu's characters.* ■ (in art and literature) the movement or style of representing familiar things as they actually are. Often contrasted with IDEALISM (sense 1).

> While realism in art is often used in the same contexts as naturalism, implying a concern to depict or describe accurately and objectively, it also suggests a deliberate rejection of conventionally beautiful or appropriate subjects in favor of sincerity and a focus on simple and unidealized treatment of contemporary life. Specifically, the term is applied to a late 19th-century movement in French painting and literature represented by Gustave Courbet in the former and Balzac, Stendhal, and Flaubert in the latter.

3 Philosophy the doctrine that universals or abstract concepts have an objective or absolute existence. The theory that universals have their own reality is sometimes called **Platonic realism** because it was first outlined by Plato's doctrine of "forms" or ideas. Often contrasted with NOMINALISM. ■ the doctrine that matter as the object of perception has real existence and is neither reducible to universal mind or spirit nor dependent on a perceiving agent. Often contrasted with IDEALISM (sense 2).
– DERIVATIVES **re·al·ist** /ˈrēəlist/ n.

re·al·is·tic /ˌrēəˈlistik/ ▶ **adj.** **1** having or showing a sensible and practical idea of what can be achieved or expected: *jobs are scarce at the moment, so you've got to be realistic* | *a more realistic figure was 20 percent.*
2 representing familiar things in a way that is accurate or true to life: *a realistic human drama.*
– DERIVATIVES **re·al·is·ti·cal·ly** /-ik(ə)lē/ **adv.** [sentence adverb] *realistically, there was little prospect of any improvement.*

re·al·i·ty /rēˈalətē/ ▶ **n.** (pl. **realities**) **1** the world or the state of things as they actually exist, as opposed to an idealistic or notional idea of them: *he refuses to face reality* | *Laura was losing touch with reality.* ■ a thing that is actually experienced or seen, esp. when this is grim or problematic: *the harsh* ***realities of*** *life in a farming community* | *the law ignores* ***the reality of*** *the situation.* ■ a thing that exists in fact, having previously only existed in one's mind: *the paperless office may yet become a reality.* ■ the quality of being lifelike or resembling an original: *the reality of Marryat's detail.* ■ [as modifier] relating to reality TV: *a reality show.*
2 the state or quality of having existence or substance: *youth, when death has no reality.* ■ Philosophy existence that is absolute, self-sufficient,

or objective, and not subject to human decisions or conventions.
– PHRASES **in reality** in actual fact (used to contrast a false idea of what is true or possible with one that is more accurate): *she had believed she could control these feelings, but in reality that was not so easy.* **the reality is ——** used to assert that the truth of a matter is not what one would think or expect: *the popular view of the Dobermann is of an aggressive guard dog—the reality is very different.*
– ORIGIN late 15th cent.: via French from medieval Latin *realitas*, from late Latin *realis* 'relating to things' (see REAL[1]).

WORD TRENDS When did reality become quite so artificial? The word that supposedly describes life and experience exactly as we know it is increasingly used to refer to deeply unrealistic concepts and situations. *Reality TV* is intended to be unscripted and spontaneous, but events in such shows are often manipulated and the footage extensively edited before it reaches the viewing public. The sense 'relating to reality TV' now provides many of the word's most common collocates, such as *show, series, star, game,* and *program.*

re·al·i·ty check ▶ n. [usu. in sing.] informal an occasion on which one is reminded of the state of things in the real world.

re·al·i·ty prin·ci·ple ▶ n. Psychoanalysis the ego's control of the pleasure-seeking activity of the id in order to meet the demands of the external world.

re·al·i·ty test·ing ▶ n. Psychology the objective evaluation of an emotion or thought against real life, as a faculty present in normal individuals but defective in psychotics.

re·al·i·ty TV (also **reality television**) ▶ n. television programs in which real people are continuously filmed, designed to be entertaining rather than informative.

WORD TRENDS See REALITY.

re·al·iz·a·ble /ˌrēəˈlīzəbəl/ ▶ adj. **1** able to be achieved or made to happen: *such a dream, if it is realizable at all, is one for the far future.*
2 in or able to be converted into cash: *10 percent of realizable assets.*
– DERIVATIVES **re·al·iz·a·bil·i·ty** /ˌrēəlīzəˈbilətē/ n.

re·al·i·za·tion /ˌrē(ə)ləˈzāsʜən/ ▶ n. **1** [in sing.] an act of becoming fully aware of something as a fact: *there was a growing realization of the need to create common economic structures | realization dawned suddenly.*
2 the fulfillment or achievement of something desired or anticipated: *he did not live to see the realization of his dream.* ■ an actual, complete, or dramatic form given to a concept or work: *a perfect realization of Bartók's Second Violin Concerto on disc.* ■ Linguistics the way in which a particular linguistic feature is used in speech or writing on a particular occasion. ■ Mathematics an instance or embodiment of an abstract group as the set of symmetry operations of some object or set. ■ Statistics a particular series that might be generated by a specified random process.
3 the action of converting an asset into cash. ■ a sale of goods: *auction realizations.*

re·al·ize /ˈrē(ə)ˌlīz/ ▶ v. [with obj.] **1** become fully aware of (something) as a fact; understand clearly: *he realized his mistake at once* | [with clause] *they realized that something was wrong | she had not realized how hungry she was.*
2 cause (something desired or anticipated) to happen: *our loans are helping small business realize their dreams | his worst fears have been realized.* ■ fulfill: *it is only now that she is beginning to realize her potential.*
3 (usu. **be realized**) give actual or physical form to: *the stage designs have been beautifully realized.* ■ use (a linguistic feature) in a particular spoken or written form. ■ Music add to or complete (a piece of music left sparsely notated by the composer).
4 make (money or a profit) from a transaction: *she realized a profit of $100,000.* ■ (of goods) be sold for (a specified price); fetch: *the drawings are expected to realize $500,000.* ■ convert (an asset) into cash: *he realized all the assets in her trust fund.*
– DERIVATIVES **re·al·iz·er** n.
– ORIGIN early 17th cent.: from REAL[1], on the pattern of French *réaliser.*

real life ▶ n. life as it is lived in reality, involving unwelcome as well as welcome experiences, as distinct from a fictional world: [as modifier] *real-life situations.*

real line ▶ n. Mathematics a notional line in which every real number is conceived of as represented by a point.

re·al·lo·cate /rēˈaləˌkāt/ ▶ v. [with obj.] allocate in a different way: *a strong incentive to reallocate their resources overseas.*
– DERIVATIVES **re·al·lo·ca·tion** /ˌrēˌaləˈkāsʜən/ n.

re·al·ly /ˈrē(ə)lē/ ▶ adv. **1** in actual fact, as opposed to what is said or imagined to be true or possible: *so what really happened? | they're not really my aunt and uncle* | [sentence adverb] *really, there are only three options.* ■ used to add strength, sincerity, or seriousness to a statement or opinion: *I really want to go | I'm sorry, Ruth, I really am | you really ought to tell her.* ■ seriously (used in questions and exclamations with an implied negative answer): *do you really expect me to believe that?*
2 [as submodifier] very; thoroughly: *I think she's really great | a really cold day | he writes really well.*
▶ exclam. used to express interest, surprise, or doubt: *"I've been working hard." "Really?"* ■ used to express mild protest: *really, Marjorie, you do jump to conclusions!* ■ used to express agreement: *"It's a nightmare finding somewhere to live in this town." "Yeah, really."*
– PHRASES **really and truly** used to emphasize the sincerity of a statement or opinion: *I sometimes wonder whether you really and truly love me.*

realm /relm/ ▶ n. archaic, literary, or Law a kingdom: *the peers of the realm | the defense of the realm.* ■ a field or domain of activity or interest: *the realm of applied chemistry.* ■ Zoology a primary biogeographical division of the earth's surface.
– ORIGIN Middle English *rewme*, from Old French *reaume*, from Latin *regimen* 'government' (see REGIMEN). The spelling with *-l-* (standard from *c.*1600) was influenced by Old French *reiel* 'royal.'

re·al·po·li·tik /rāˈälˌpōliˌtēk/ ▶ n. a system of politics or principles based on practical rather than moral or ideological considerations.
– ORIGIN early 20th cent.: from German *Realpolitik* 'practical politics.'

real pres·ence ▶ n. Christian Theology the actual presence of Christ's body and blood in the Eucharistic elements.

real prop·er·ty ▶ n. Law fixed property, principally land and buildings. Used in contrast to PERSONAL PROPERTY.

real ten·nis ▶ n. British term for COURT TENNIS.

real time ▶ n. the actual time during which a process or event occurs: *recent natural experiments in which creolization by children can be observed in real time | information updated in real time.* ■ (as modifier **real-time**) Computing of or relating to a system in which input data is processed within milliseconds so that it is available virtually immediately as feedback, e.g., in a missile guidance or airline booking system: *real-time signal processing.*

re·al·tor /ˈrē(ə)ltər, -ˌtôr, ˈrē(ə)lətər/ ▶ n. trademark a person who acts as an agent for the sale and purchase of buildings and land; a real estate agent.
– ORIGIN early 20th cent.: from REALTY + -OR[1].

re·al·ty /ˈrē(ə)ltē/ ▶ n. Law real, fixed property. Used in contrast to PERSONALTY.

ream[1] /rēm/ ▶ n. 500 (formerly 480) sheets of paper. ■ a large quantity of something, typically paper or writing on paper: ***reams of paper** have been used to debate these questions.*
– ORIGIN late Middle English: from Old French *raime*, based on Arabic *rizma* 'bundle.'

ream[2] ▶ v. [with obj.] widen (a bore or hole) with a special tool. ■ widen a bore or hole in (a gun or other metal object) in such a way. ■ clear out or remove (material) from something. ■ vulgar slang have anal intercourse with (someone). ■ informal rebuke someone fiercely: *the agent was **reaming** him **out** for walking away from the deal.*
– PHRASES **ream someone's ass** (or **butt**) vulgar slang criticize or rebuke someone.
– ORIGIN early 19th cent.: of unknown origin.

ream·er /ˈrēmər/ ▶ n. a tool for widening or finishing drilled holes. ■ an instrument for scraping the burrs off the inside of water pipes. ■ a blade for scraping the carbon layer from the inside of the bowl of a smoking pipe. ■ another term for JUICER (sense 1).

re·an·i·mate /rēˈanəˌmāt/ ▶ v. [with obj.] restore to life or consciousness; revive. ■ give fresh vigor or impetus to: *his personal dislike of the man was reanimated.*
– DERIVATIVES **re·an·i·ma·tion** /ˌrēˌanəˈmāsʜən/ n.

reap /rēp/ ▶ v. [with obj.] cut or gather (a crop or harvest): *large numbers of men were employed to reap the harvest* | figurative *in terms of science, the Apollo program reaped a meager harvest.* ■ harvest the crop from (a piece of land). ■ receive (a reward or benefit) as a consequence of one's own or other people's actions: *the company is poised to reap the benefits of this investment.*
– PHRASES **reap the harvest** (or **fruits**) **of** suffer the results or consequences of: *critics believe we are now reaping the harvest of our permissive ways.* **you reap what you sow** proverb you eventually have to face up to the consequences of your actions.
– ORIGIN Old English *ripan, reopan*, of unknown origin.

reap·er /ˈrēpər/ ▶ n. a person or machine that harvests a crop. ■ (**the Reaper**) short for GRIM REAPER.

re·ap·pear /ˌrēəˈpi(ə)r/ ▶ v. [no obj.] appear again: *her symptoms reappeared.*
– DERIVATIVES **re·ap·pear·ance** n.

re·ap·ply /ˌrēəˈplī/ ▶ v. (**reapplies, reapplying, reapplied**) **1** [no obj.] make another application or request: *he was ordered to take a driving test before reapplying for a license.*
2 [with obj.] apply (an existing rule or principle) in a different context.
3 [with obj.] spread (a substance) on a surface again: *reapply the sunscreen hourly.*
– DERIVATIVES **re·ap·pli·ca·tion** /ˌrēˌapləˈkāsʜən/ n.

re·ap·point /ˌrēəˈpoint/ ▶ v. [with obj.] appoint (someone) once again to a position they have previously held.
– DERIVATIVES **re·ap·point·ment** n.

re·ap·por·tion /ˌrēəˈpôrsʜən/ ▶ v. [with obj.] assign or distribute (something) again or in a different way.
– DERIVATIVES **re·ap·por·tion·ment** n.

re·ap·praise /ˌrēəˈprāz/ ▶ v. [with obj.] appraise or assess (something) again or in a different way: *it made me reappraise my attitudes.*
– DERIVATIVES **re·ap·prais·al** /-ˈprāzəl/ n.

rear[1] /ri(ə)r/ ▶ n. [in sing.] the back part of something, esp. a building or vehicle: *the kitchen door at the rear of the house.* ■ the space or position at the back of something or someone: *the field at the rear of the church.* ■ the hindmost part of an army, fleet, or line of people: *two blue policemen at the rear fell out of the formation.* ■ (also **rear end**) informal a person's buttocks.
▶ adj. [attrib.] at the back: *the car's rear window.*
– PHRASES **bring up the rear** be at the very end of a line of people. ■ come last in a race or other contest.
– ORIGIN Middle English (first used as a military term): from Old French *rere*, based on Latin *retro* 'back.'

rear[2] ▶ v. **1** [with obj.] (usu. **be reared**) bring up and care for (a child) until they are fully grown, esp. in a particular manner or place: *he was born and reared in New York City | a generation reared on video.* ■ (of an animal) care for (its young) until they are fully grown. ■ breed and raise (animals): *the calves are reared for beef.* ■ grow or cultivate (plants): [as adj., in combination] (**-reared**) *laboratory-reared plantlets.*
2 [no obj.] (of a horse or other animal) raise itself upright on its hind legs: *the horse reared in terror | a rattlesnake **reared up** at his elbow.* ■ [with adverbial of place] (of a building, mountain, etc.) extend or appear to extend to a great height: *houses reared up on either side.* ■ (**rear up**) (of a person) show anger or irritation; go on the attack: *the press reared up in the wake of the bombings.* ■ [with obj.] archaic set (something) upright.
– PHRASES **rear one's head** raise one's head. ■ (**rear its head**) (of an unpleasant matter) emerge; present itself: *elitism is **rearing its ugly head** again.*
– DERIVATIVES **rear·er** n.
– ORIGIN Old English *rǣran* 'set upright, construct, elevate,' of Germanic origin; related to RAISE (which has supplanted *rear* in many applications), also to RISE.

rear ad·mir·al ▶ n. an officer in the US Navy or Coast Guard ranking above commodore and below vice admiral.

rear com·mo·dore ▶ n. an officer in a yacht club ranking below vice commodore.

rear ech·e·lon ▶ n. the section of an army concerned with administrative and supply duties.

rear·guard /ˈri(ə)rˌgärd/ ▶ n. the soldiers positioned at the rear of a body of troops, esp. those protecting an army when it is in retreat. ■ a defensive or conservative element in an organization or community.
– ORIGIN late Middle English (denoting the rear part of an army): from Old French *rereguarde.*

rear·guard ac·tion ▶ n. a defensive action carried out by a retreating army.

re·arm /rēˈärm/ ▶ v. [with obj.] provide with a new supply of weapons: *his plan to rearm Germany.* ■ [no obj.] acquire or build up a new supply of weapons.
– DERIVATIVES **re·ar·ma·ment** /rēˈärməmənt/ n.

r

rear·most /ˈri(ə)rˌmōst/ ▶ **adj.** furthest back: *the rearmost door.*

rear pro·jec·tion ▶ **n.** the projection of a picture onto the back of a translucent screen for viewing or for use as a background in filming. ■ an image projected in this way.
– DERIVATIVES **rear-pro·ject·ed adj.**

re·ar·range /ˌrēəˈrānj/ ▶ **v.** [with obj.] move (something) into a more acceptable position or state: *she rearranged her skirt as she sat back in her chair.* ■ change (the position, time, or order of something): *he had rearranged his schedule.*
– DERIVATIVES **re·ar·range·ment n.**

re·ar·rest /ˌrēəˈrest/ ▶ **v.** [with obj.] arrest (someone) again.
▶ **n.** an act of rearresting someone.

rear sight ▶ **n.** the sight nearest to the stock on a firearm.

rear·view mir·ror /ˈrirˌvyo͞o/ ▶ **n.** a small angled mirror fixed inside the windshield of a motor vehicle, enabling the driver to see the vehicle or road behind.

rear·ward /ˈri(ə)rwərd/ ▶ **adj.** directed toward the back: *a slight rearward movement.* [early 17th cent.: from REAR[1] + -WARD.]
▶ **adv.** (also chiefly Brit. **rearwards**) toward the back: *the engine nozzles point rearward.*
▶ **n.** (usu. **in/at/on the rearward**) archaic or literary the part or position at the back of something. [Middle English (denoting the rear part of an army): from Anglo-Norman French *rerewarde* 'rearguard.']

rear-wheel drive ▶ **n.** a transmission system that provides power to the rear wheels of a motor vehicle: [as modifier] *a rear-wheel drive coupé.*

re·as·cend /ˌrēəˈsend/ ▶ **v.** [no obj.] ascend again or to a former position: *the fallen angel reascends to the upper air.*
– DERIVATIVES **re·as·cen·sion** /ˌrēəˈsenCHən/ **n.**

rea·son /ˈrēzən/ ▶ **n. 1** a cause, explanation, or justification for an action or event: *the minister resigned for personal reasons | it is hard to know for the simple reason that few records survive.* ■ good or obvious cause to do something: *we have reason to celebrate.* ■ Logic a premise of an argument in support of a belief, esp. a minor premise when given after the conclusion.
2 the power of the mind to think, understand, and form judgments by a process of logic: *there is a close connection between reason and emotion.* ■ what is right, practical, or possible; common sense: *people are willing, **within reason**, to pay for schooling.* ■ **(one's reason)** one's sanity: *she is in danger of **losing her reason**.*
▶ **v.** [no obj.] think, understand, and form judgments by a process of logic: *humans do not reason entirely from facts.* ■ [with obj.] **(reason something out)** find an answer to a problem by considering various possible solutions. ■ **(reason with)** persuade (someone) with rational argument: *I tried to reason with her, but without success.*
– PHRASES **beyond (all) reason** to a foolishly excessive degree: *he indulged Andrew beyond all reason.* **by reason of** formal because of: *persons who, by reason of age, are in need of care.* **for some reason** used to convey that one doesn't know the reason for a particular state of affairs, often with the implication that one finds it strange or surprising: *for some reason he likes you.* **listen to reason** be persuaded to act sensibly: *the child is usually too emotionally overwrought to listen to reason.* **theirs (or ours) not to reason why** used to suggest that it is not someone's (or someone else's) place to question a situation or system. [with allusion to Tennyson's *'Charge of the Light Brigade'* (1854).] **reason of state** another term for RAISON D'ÉTAT. **(it) stands to reason** it is obvious or logical: *it stands to reason that if you can eradicate the fear, the nervousness will subside.*
– DERIVATIVES **rea·son·er** /ˈrēz(ə)nər/ **n.**, **rea·son·less adj.** (archaic).
– ORIGIN Middle English: from Old French *reisun* (noun), *raisoner* (verb), from a variant of Latin *ratio(n-)*, from the verb *reri* 'consider.'

> **USAGE 1** The construction **the reason why ...** has been objected to on the grounds that the subordinate clause should express a statement, using a *that*-clause, not imply a question with a *why*-clause: ***the reason (that)** I decided not to phone*, rather than ***the reason why** I decided not to phone. The reason why* has been called a redundancy to be avoided, but it is a mild one, and idiomatic. **2** An objection is also made to the construction **the reason ... is because,** as in ***the reason** I didn't phone **is because** my mother has been ill.* The objection is made on the grounds that either "because" or "the reason" is redundant; it is better to use the word **that** instead (***the reason** I didn't phone **is that** ...*) or rephrase altogether (*I didn't phone **because** ...*). Nevertheless, both the above usages are well established and, although they may be inelegant, they are generally accepted in standard English.

rea·son·a·ble /ˈrēz(ə)nəbəl/ ▶ **adj. 1** (of a person) having sound judgment; fair and sensible: *no reasonable person could have objected.* ■ based on good sense: *it seems a reasonable enough request | the guilt of a person on trial must be proved beyond reasonable doubt.* ■ archaic (of a person or animal) able to think, understand, or form judgments by a logical process: *man is by nature reasonable.*
2 as much as is appropriate or fair; moderate: *a police officer may use reasonable force to gain entry.* ■ fairly good; average: *the carpet is in reasonable condition.* ■ (of a price or product) not too expensive: *a restaurant serving excellent food at reasonable prices | they are lovely shoes and very reasonable.*
– DERIVATIVES **rea·son·a·ble·ness n.**
– ORIGIN Middle English: from Old French *raisonable*, suggested by Latin *rationabilis* 'rational,' from *ratio* (see REASON).

rea·son·a·bly /ˈrēz(ə)nəblē/ ▶ **adv. 1** in a fair and sensible way: *he began to talk calmly and reasonably about his future.* ■ by fair or sensible standards of judgment; rightly or justifiably: *police must reasonably believe that a threat to the security of the embassy is present* | [sentence adverb] *it was assumed, **reasonably enough**, that the murder had taken place by the pond.*
2 to a moderate or acceptable degree: fairly; quite: [as submodifier] *she played the piano reasonably well.* ■ inexpensively: *ski wear which looks good and is reasonably priced.*

rea·soned /ˈrēzənd/ ▶ **adj.** underpinned by logic or good sense: *a reasoned judgment.*

rea·son·ing /ˈrēzəniNG/ ▶ **n.** the action of thinking about something in a logical, sensible way: *he explained the **reasoning behind** his decision at a media conference.*

re·as·sem·ble /ˌrēəˈsembəl/ ▶ **v.** [no obj.] (of a group) gather together again: *after lunch the class reassembled.* ■ [with obj.] put (something) together again: *the trucks had to be reassembled on arrival.*
– DERIVATIVES **re·as·sem·bly** /-blē/ **n.**

re·as·sert /ˌrēəˈsərt/ ▶ **v.** [with obj.] assert again: *he moved quickly to reassert his control.*
– DERIVATIVES **re·as·ser·tion n.**

re·as·sess /ˌrēəˈses/ ▶ **v.** [with obj.] consider or assess again, esp. while paying attention to new or different factors: *we have decided to reassess our timetable.*
– DERIVATIVES **re·as·sess·ment n.**

re·as·sign /ˌrēəˈsīn/ ▶ **v.** [with obj.] appoint (someone) to a different job or task: *he had been reassigned to another post.* ■ allocate or distribute (work or resources) differently: *a network which continually reassigns costs.*
– DERIVATIVES **re·as·sign·ment n.**

re·as·sort·ment ▶ **n.** Genetics recombination of genomic material, esp. as it occurs naturally in related viruses.

re·as·sume /ˌrēəˈs(y)o͞om/ ▶ **v.** [with obj.] take on or gain (something) again: *he reassumed the title of Governor General.*
– DERIVATIVES **re·as·sump·tion** /ˌrēəˈsəmpSHən/ **n.**

re·as·sur·ance /ˌrēəˈSHo͝orəns/ ▶ **n.** the action of removing someone's doubts or fears: *children need reassurance and praise.* ■ a statement or comment that removes someone's doubts or fears: *we have been given **reassurances that** the water is safe to drink.*

re·as·sure /ˌrēəˈSHo͝or/ ▶ **v.** [with obj.] say or do something to remove the doubts and fears of someone: *he understood her feelings and tried to reassure her* | [with obj. and clause] *Joachim reassured him that he was needed* | (as adj. **reassuring**) *Gina gave her a reassuring smile.*
– DERIVATIVES **re·as·sur·ing·ly adv.**

re·at·tach /ˌrēəˈtaCH/ ▶ **v.** [with obj.] attach (something that has fallen or been taken off) in its former position.
– DERIVATIVES **re·at·tach·ment n.**

re·at·tain /ˌrēəˈtān/ ▶ **v.** [with obj.] attain (an objective or position) again.
– DERIVATIVES **re·at·tain·ment n.**

re·at·tempt /ˌrēəˈtem(p)t/ ▶ **v.** [with obj.] attempt to achieve (something) again: *I reattempted entry.*
▶ **n.** a second or subsequent attempt: *a reattempt to start the engine.*

Ré·au·mur scale /ˌrā-ōˈmyo͝or, rāˈōˌmyo͝or/ ▶ **n.** an obsolete scale of temperature at which water freezes at 0° and boils at 80° under standard conditions.
– ORIGIN late 18th cent.: named after René A. F. de *Réaumur* (1683–1757), French naturalist.

reave /rēv/ ▶ **v.** (past and past participle **reft** /reft/) [no obj.] archaic carry out raids in order to plunder. ■ [with obj.] rob (a person or place) of something by force: *reft of a crown, he yet may share the feast.* ■ [with obj.] steal (something).
– DERIVATIVES **reav·er n.**
– ORIGIN Old English *rēafian*, of Germanic origin; related to Dutch *roven*, German *rauben*, also to ROB.

re·a·wak·en /ˌrēəˈwākən/ ▶ **v.** (with reference to a feeling or state) emerge or cause to emerge again; awaken again: [no obj.] *the sense of community started to reawaken in the 1970s* | [with obj.] *his departure reawakened deep divisions within the party.*

Reb[1] /reb/ ▶ **n.** a traditional Jewish title or form of address, corresponding to Sir, for a man who is not a rabbi (used preceding the forename or surname).
– ORIGIN Yiddish.

Reb[2] (also **Johnny Reb**) ▶ **n.** informal a Confederate soldier in the American Civil War.
– ORIGIN abbreviation of REBEL.

re·bab /riˈbäb/ ▶ **n.** a bowed or plucked stringed instrument of Arab origin, used esp. in North Africa, the Middle East, and South Asia.
– ORIGIN mid 18th cent.: from Arabic *rabāb*.

re·badge /rēˈbaj/ ▶ **v.** [with obj.] relaunch (a product) under a new name or logo.

re·baked /rēˈbākt/ ▶ **adj.** another term for TWICE-BAKED.

re·bal·ance /rēˈbaləns/ ▶ **v.** [with obj.] balance again or restore the correct balance to.

re·bar /ˈrēˌbär/ ▶ **n.** a steel reinforcing rod in concrete: *a piece of rebar.*

re·bar·ba·tive /rəˈbärbətiv/ ▶ **adj.** formal unattractive and objectionable: *rebarbative modern buildings.*
– ORIGIN late 19th cent.: from French *rébarbatif, -ive*, from Old French *se rebarber* 'face each other "beard to beard" aggressively,' from *barbe* 'beard.'

re·base /rēˈbās/ ▶ **v.** [with obj.] establish a new base level for (a tax level, price index, etc.).

re·bate[1] ▶ **n.** /ˈrēˌbāt/ a partial refund to someone who has paid too much money for tax, rent, or a utility. ■ a deduction or discount on a sum of money due.
▶ **v.** /ˈrēˌbāt, riˈbāt/ [with obj.] pay back (such a sum of money).
– DERIVATIVES **re·bat·a·ble** /ˈrēˌbātəbəl, riˈbāt-/ **adj.**
– ORIGIN late Middle English (as a verb in the sense 'diminish (a sum or amount)'): from Anglo-Norman French *rebatre* 'beat back,' also 'deduct.'

re·bate[2] /ˈrabit, ˈrēˌbāt/ ▶ **n. & v.** another term for RABBET.
– ORIGIN late 17th cent.: alteration of RABBET.

reb·be /ˈrebə, -bē/ ▶ **n.** Judaism a rabbi, esp. a religious leader of the Hasidic sect.
– ORIGIN Yiddish, from Hebrew *rabbī* 'rabbi.'

reb·betz·in /ˈrəbetsin, ˈrebət-/ (also **rebbitzin**) ▶ **n.** Judaism the wife of a rabbi. ■ a female religious teacher.
– ORIGIN Yiddish, feminine of *rebbe* (see REBBE).

re·bec /ˈrēˌbek, ˈrebˌek/ (also **rebeck**) ▶ **n.** a medieval stringed instrument played with a bow, typically having three strings.
– ORIGIN late Middle English: from French, based on Arabic *rabāb*.

reb·el ▶ **n.** /ˈrebəl/ a person who rises in opposition or armed resistance against an established government or ruler: *Tory rebels* | [as modifier] *rebel forces.* ■ a person who resists authority, control, or convention.
▶ **v.** (**rebel** /riˈbel/) (**rebels, rebelling, rebelled**) [no obj.] rise in opposition or armed resistance to an established government or ruler: *the Earl of Pembroke subsequently rebelled against Henry III.* ■ (of a person) resist authority, control, or convention: *respect did not prevent children from rebelling against their parents.* ■ show or feel repugnance for or resistance to something: *as I came over the hill my legs rebelled—I could walk no further.*
– ORIGIN Middle English: from Old French *rebelle* (noun), *rebeller* (verb), from Latin *rebellis* (used originally with reference to a fresh declaration of war by the defeated), based on *bellum* 'war.'

re·bel·lion /riˈbelyən/ ▶ **n.** an act of violent or open resistance to an established government or ruler: *the authorities put down a rebellion by landless colonials | Simon de Montfort rose in rebellion.* ■ the action or process of resisting authority, control, or convention: *an act of teenage rebellion.*
– ORIGIN Middle English: from Old French, from Latin *rebellio(n-)*, from *rebellis* (see REBEL).

re·bel·lious /riˈbelyəs/ ▶ **adj.** showing a desire to resist authority, control, or convention: *young people with a rebellious streak.* ■ (of a person, city, or state) engaged in opposition or armed resistance to an established government or ruler: *the rebellious*

r

republics. ■ (of a thing) not easily handled or kept in place: *he smoothed back a rebellious lock of hair.*
– DERIVATIVES **re·bel·lious·ly** adv., **re·bel·lious·ness** n.

reb·el yell ▶ n. a shout or battle cry used by the Confederates during the American Civil War.

re·bid ▶ v. /rēˈbid/ (**rebids, rebidding**; past and past participle **rebid**) [no obj.] bid again: *it will be in an ideal position when it comes to rebidding for its franchise.*
▶ n. /ˈrēˌbid/ a further bid.

re·bind /rēˈbīnd/ ▶ v. (past and past participle **rebound**) [with obj.] give a new binding to (a book).

re·birth /rēˈbərTH, ˈrēˌbərTH/ ▶ n. the process of being reincarnated or born again: *the endless cycle of birth, death, and rebirth.* ■ the action of reappearing or starting to flourish or increase after a decline; revival: *the rebirth of a defeated nation.*

re·birth·ing /rēˈbərTHiNG/ ▶ n. a form of psychotherapy involving controlled breathing intended to simulate the trauma of being born.
– DERIVATIVES **re·birth·er** /-THər/ n.

re·blo·chon /rəˌblôˈSHôN/ ▶ n. a kind of soft French cheese, made originally and chiefly in Savoy.
– ORIGIN French.

re·book /rēˈbo͝ok/ ▶ v. [with obj.] book (accommodation or a ticket) again: *passengers were allowed to rebook those flights on Northwest or Pinnacle* | [no obj.] *a third of the tourists had rebooked for next year.*

re·boot /rēˈbo͞ot/ ▶ v. (with reference to a computer system) boot or be booted again.
▶ n. an act or instance of booting a computer system again.

re·bore ▶ v. /rēˈbôr/ [with obj.] bore out (the cylinders of an internal combustion engine) again, typically in order to widen them.
▶ n. /ˈrēbôr/ an act of reboring an engine's cylinders. ■ an engine with rebored cylinders.

re·born /rēˈbôrn/ ▶ adj. brought back to life or activity: *the grand concourse stands reborn as a four-star restaurant.* ■ having experienced a complete spiritual change: *a reborn Catholic.*

re·bound[1] ▶ v. /riˈbound, ˈrēˌbound/ [no obj.] bounce back through the air after hitting a hard surface or object: *his shot hammered into the post and rebounded across the goal.* ■ [no obj.] recover in value, amount, or strength after a previous decrease or decline: *NASDAQ rebounded to show a twenty-point gain.* ■ [no obj.] (**rebound on/upon**) (of an event or situation) have an unexpected adverse consequence for (someone, esp. the person responsible for it): *Nicholas's tricks are rebounding on him.* ■ [no obj.] Basketball gain possession of a missed shot after it bounces off the backboard or basket rim.
▶ n. /ˈrēˌbound/ (in sporting contexts) a ball or shot that bounces back after striking a hard surface: *he blasted the rebound into the net.* ■ Basketball a recovery of possession of a missed shot. ■ an instance of increasing in value, amount, or strength after a previous decline: *they revealed a big rebound in profits for last year.* ■ [usu. as modifier] the recurrence of a medical condition, esp. after withdrawal of medication: *rebound hypertension.*
– PHRASES **on the rebound** still affected by the emotional distress caused by the ending of a romantic or sexual relationship: *I was on the rebound when I met Jack.*
– ORIGIN late Middle English: from Old French *rebondir*, from *re-* 'back' + *bondir* 'bounce up.'

re·bound[2] past and past participle of **REBIND**.

re·bound·er /ˈrēˌboundər, riˈboun-/ ▶ n. Basketball a player who rebounds the ball or is especially proficient at doing so.

re·bo·zo /riˈbōzō, -sō/ ▶ n. (pl. **rebozos**) a long scarf covering the head and shoulders, traditionally worn by Spanish-American women.
– ORIGIN Spanish.

re·brand /rēˈbrand/ ▶ v. [with obj.] (usu. as noun **rebranding**) change the corporate image of (a company or organization).

re·breathe /rēˈbrēTH/ ▶ v. [with obj.] breathe in (exhaled air).

re·breath·er /rēˈbrēTHər/ ▶ n. an aqualung in which the diver's exhaled breath is partially purified of carbon dioxide, mixed with more oxygen, and then breathed again by the diver.

re·broad·cast /rēˈbrôdˌkast/ ▶ v. (past and past participle **rebroadcast**) [with obj.] broadcast or relay (a program or signal) again.
▶ n. a repeated or relayed broadcast.
– DERIVATIVES **re·broad·cast·er** n.

re·buff /riˈbəf/ ▶ v. [with obj.] reject (someone or something) in an abrupt or ungracious manner: *I asked her to be my wife, and was rebuffed in no uncertain terms.*
▶ n. an abrupt or ungracious refusal or rejection of an offer, request, or friendly gesture: *any attempt to win her friendship was met with rebuffs.*
– ORIGIN late 16th cent.: from obsolete French *rebuffer* (verb), *rebuffe* (noun), from Italian *ri-* (expressing opposition) + *buffo* 'a gust, puff,' of imitative origin.

re·build /rēˈbild/ ▶ v. (past and past participle **rebuilt** /-ˈbilt/) [with obj.] build (something) again after it has been damaged or destroyed: *he rebuilt the cathedral church* | figurative *we try to help them rebuild their lives.*
▶ n. /ˈrēˌbild/ an instance or rebuilding something, esp. a vehicle or other machine. ■ a thing that has been rebuilt, esp. a part of a motor vehicle, e.g., a motor or an alternator.
– DERIVATIVES **re·build·a·ble** adj., **re·build·er** n.

re·buke /riˈbyo͞ok/ ▶ v. [with obj.] express sharp disapproval or criticism of (someone) because of their behavior or actions: *she had **rebuked** him **for** drinking too much* | *the judge publicly rebuked the jury.*
▶ n. an expression of sharp disapproval or criticism: *he hadn't meant it as a rebuke, but Neil flinched.*
– DERIVATIVES **re·buk·er** n., **re·buk·ing·ly** adv.
– ORIGIN Middle English (originally in the sense 'force back, repress'): from Anglo-Norman French and Old Northern French *rebuker*, from *re-* 'back, down' + *bukier* 'to beat' (originally 'cut down wood,' from Old French *busche* 'log').

re·bur·y /ˌrēˈberē/ ▶ v. (**reburies, reburying, reburied**) [with obj.] bury again.
– DERIVATIVES **re·bur·i·al** n.

re·bus /ˈrēbəs/ ▶ n. (pl. **rebuses**) a puzzle in which words are represented by combinations of pictures and individual letters; for instance, *apex* might be represented by a picture of an ape followed by a letter *X*. ■ historical an ornamental device associated with a person to whose name it punningly alludes.
– ORIGIN early 17th cent.: from French *rébus*, from Latin *rebus*, ablative plural of *res* 'thing.'

"To be or not to be"
rebus

re·but /riˈbət/ ▶ v. (**rebuts, rebutting, rebutted**) [with obj.] **1** claim or prove that (evidence or an accusation) is false: *he had to rebut charges of acting for the convenience of his political friends.*
2 archaic drive back or repel (a person or attack).
– DERIVATIVES **re·but·ta·ble** adj.
– ORIGIN Middle English (in the senses 'rebuke' and 'repulse'): from Anglo-Norman French *rebuter*, from Old French *re-* (expressing opposition) + *boter* 'to butt.' Sense 1 (originally a legal use) dates from the early 19th cent.

re·but·tal /riˈbətl/ ▶ n. a refutation or contradiction. ■ another term for **REBUTTER**.

re·but·ter /riˈbətər/ ▶ n. Law, archaic a defendant's reply to the plaintiff's surrejoinder.
– ORIGIN mid 19th cent.: from Anglo-Norman French *rebuter* (from Old French *rebut* 'a reproach, rebuke') + **-AL**.

rec /rek/ ▶ n. informal recreation: [as modifier] *the rec center.*
– ORIGIN 1920s: abbreviation.

rec. ▶ abbr. ■ receipt. ■ (in prescriptions) fresh. [from Latin *recens*.] ■ recipe. ■ record. ■ recorder. ■ recording.

re·cal·ci·trant /riˈkalsətrənt/ ▶ adj. having an obstinately uncooperative attitude toward authority or discipline: *a class of recalcitrant fifteen-year-olds.*
▶ n. a person with such an attitude.
– DERIVATIVES **re·cal·ci·trance** n., **re·cal·ci·trant·ly** adv.
– ORIGIN mid 19th cent.: from Latin *recalcitrant-* 'kicking out with the heels,' from the verb *recalcitrare*, based on *calx*, *calc-* 'heel.'

re·cal·cu·late /rēˈkalkyəˌlāt/ ▶ v. [with obj.] calculate again, typically using different data.
– DERIVATIVES **re·cal·cu·la·tion** /ˌrēˌkalkyəˈlāSHən/ n.

re·ca·les·cence /ˌrēkəˈlesəns/ ▶ n. Metallurgy a temporary rise in temperature during cooling of a metal, caused by a change in crystal structure.
– DERIVATIVES **re·ca·les·cent** adj.
– ORIGIN late 19th cent.: from **RE-** 'again' + Latin *calescere* 'grow hot' + **-ENCE**.

re·cal·i·brate /ˌrēˈkalibrāt/ ▶ v. [with obj.] calibrate (something) again or differently: *the sensors had to be recalibrated.*

re·call ▶ v. /riˈkôl/ [with obj.] **1** bring (a fact, event, or situation) back into one's mind, esp. so as to recount it to others; remember: *I can still vaguely recall being taken to the hospital* | [with direct speech] *"He was awfully fond of teasing people," she recalled* | [with clause] *he recalled how he felt at the time.* ■ cause one to remember or think of: *the film's analysis of contemporary concerns recalls The Big Chill.* ■ (**recall someone/something to**) bring the memory or thought of someone or something to (a person or their mind): *the smell of a black-currant bush has ever since recalled to me that evening.* ■ call up (stored computer data) for processing or display. **2** officially order (someone) to return to a place: *the Panamanian ambassador was recalled from Peru.* ■ select (a sports player) as a member of a team from which they have previously been dropped: *the Fulham defender has been **recalled to** the Welsh squad for the World Cup.* ■ (of a manufacturer) request all the purchasers of (a certain product) to return it, as the result of the discovery of a fault. ■ bring (someone) out of a state of inattention or reverie: *her action **recalled** him **to** the present.* ■ archaic revoke or annul (an action or decision).
▶ n. /ˈrēˌkôl, riˈkôl, rēˈkôl/ **1** an act or instance of officially recalling someone or something: *a recall of Parliament.* ■ the removal of an elected government official from office by a petition followed by voting. **2** the action or faculty of remembering something learned or experienced: *he has amazing recall* | *people's understanding and subsequent recall of stories or events.* ■ the proportion of the number of relevant documents retrieved from a database in response to an inquiry.
– PHRASES **beyond recall** in such a way that restoration is impossible: *shopping developments have already blighted other parts of the city beyond recall.*
– DERIVATIVES **re·call·a·ble** adj.
– ORIGIN late 16th cent. (as a verb): from **RE-** 'again' + **CALL**, suggested by Latin *revocare* or French *rappeler* 'call back.'

re·cant /riˈkant/ ▶ v. [no obj.] say that one no longer holds an opinion or belief, esp. one considered heretical: *heretics were burned if they would not recant* | [with obj.] *Galileo was forced to recant his assertion that the earth orbited the sun.*
– DERIVATIVES **re·cant·er** n.
– ORIGIN mid 16th cent.: from Latin *recantare* 'revoke,' from *re-* (expressing reversal) + *cantare* 'sing, chant.'

re·can·ta·tion /ˌrēˌkanˈtāSHən/ ▶ n. a statement that one no longer holds a particular opinion or belief; a retraction: *every writer interprets Galileo's recantation in a different way.*

re·cap informal ▶ v. /rēˈkap/ (**recaps, recapping, recapped**) [with obj.] state again as a summary; recapitulate: *a way of recapping the story so far* | [no obj.] *to recap, it's been a year full of ups and downs.*
▶ n. /ˈrēˌkap/ a summary of what has been said; a recapitulation: *a quick recap of the idea and its main advantages.*
– ORIGIN 1950s: abbreviation.

re·cap·i·tal·ize /rēˈkapətlˌīz/ ▶ v. [with obj.] provide (a business) with more capital, esp. by replacing debt with stock.
– DERIVATIVES **re·cap·i·tal·i·za·tion** /rēˌkapətl-əˈzāSHən/ n.

re·ca·pit·u·late /ˌrēkəˈpiCHəˌlāt/ ▶ v. [with obj.] summarize and state again the main points of: *he began to recapitulate his argument with care.* ■ Biology repeat (an evolutionary or other process) during development and growth.
– DERIVATIVES **re·ca·pit·u·la·to·ry** /-ləˌtôrē/ adj.
– ORIGIN late 16th cent.: from late Latin *recapitulat-* 'gone through heading by heading,' from *re-* 'again' + *capitulum* 'chapter' (diminutive of *caput* 'head').

re·ca·pit·u·la·tion /ˌrēkəˌpiCHəˈlāSHən/ ▶ n. an act or instance of summarizing and restating the main points of something: *his recapitulation of the argument.* ■ Biology the repetition of an evolutionary or other process during development or growth. ■ Music a part of a movement (esp. one in sonata form) in which themes from the exposition are restated.

re·ca·pit·u·la·tion the·o·ry ▶ n. another term for **BIOGENETIC LAW**.

re·cap·tion /rēˈkapSHən/ ▶ n. Law the action of taking back, without legal process, property of one's own that has been wrongfully taken or withheld.
– ORIGIN mid 18th cent.: from Anglo-Latin *recaptio(n-)*, from *re-* 'back' + Latin *captio(n-)* 'taking.'

re·cap·ture /rēˈkapCHər/ ▶ v. [with obj.] capture (a person or animal that has escaped): *armed police have recaptured a prisoner who's been on the run for five days.* ■ recover (something taken or lost):

PRONUNCIATION KEY ə *ago, up*; ər *over, fur*; a *hat*; ā *ate*; ä *car*; e *let*; ē *see*; i *fit*; ī *by*; NG *sing*; ō *go*; ô *law, for*; oi *toy*; o͝o *good*; o͞o *goo*; ou *out*; TH *thin*; TH *then*; ZH *vision*

r

Edward I recaptured the castle | Democrats might recapture both the House and the Senate. ■ recreate or experience again (a past time, event, or feeling): *the programs give viewers a chance to recapture their own childhoods.*
▶ **n.** [in sing.] an act of recapturing.

re·cast /rēˈkast/ ▶ **v.** (past and past participle **recast**) [with obj.] **1** give (a metal object) a different form by melting it down and reshaping it. ■ present or organize in a different form or style: *his doctoral thesis has been recast for the general reader.*
2 allocate the parts in (a play or film) to different actors: *there were moves to recast the play.*

recd ▶ **abbr.** received.

re·cede /riˈsēd/ ▶ **v.** [no obj.] go or move back or further away from a previous position: *the flood waters had receded | his footsteps receded down the corridor.* ■ (of a quality, feeling, or possibility) gradually diminish: *the prospects of an early end to the war receded.* ■ (of a man's hair) cease to grow at the temples and above the forehead: *his dark hair was was receding a little* | (as adj. **receding**) *a receding hairline.* ■ (of a man) begin to go bald in such a way: *Fred was receding a bit.* ■ (usu. as adj. **receding**) (of a facial feature) slope backward: *a slightly receding chin.* ■ (**recede from**) archaic withdraw from (an undertaking, promise, or agreement).
– ORIGIN late 15th cent. (in the sense 'depart from (a usual state or standard)'): from Latin *recedere*, from *re-* 'back' + *cedere* 'go.'

re·ceipt /riˈsēt/ ▶ **n. 1** the action of receiving something or the fact of its being received: *I would be grateful if you would acknowledge receipt of this letter | this office is already **in receipt of** your midterm grades.* ■ a written or printed statement acknowledging that something has been paid for or that goods have been received. ■ (**receipts**) an amount of money received during a particular period by an organization or business: *box-office receipts.*
2 archaic a recipe.
▶ **v.** [with obj.] (usu. as adj. **receipted**) mark (a bill) as paid: *the receipted hotel bill.* ■ write a receipt for (goods or money): *all fish shall be receipted at time of purchase.*
– ORIGIN late Middle English: from Anglo-Norman French *receite*, from medieval Latin *recepta* 'received,' feminine past participle of Latin *recipere*. The *-p-* was inserted in imitation of the Latin spelling.

re·ceiv·a·ble /riˈsēvəbəl/ ▶ **adj.** able to be received. ▶ **plural n.** (**receivables**) amounts owed to a business, regarded as assets.

re·ceive /riˈsēv/ ▶ **v.** [with obj.] **1** be given, presented with, or paid (something): *most businesses will receive a tax cut | she received her prize from the manager.* ■ take delivery of (something sent or communicated): *he received fifty inquiries after advertising the job.* ■ buy or accept goods in the knowledge that they have been stolen: *a man convicted of receiving stolen property.* ■ detect or pick up (broadcast signals): *Turkish television began to be received in Tashkent.* ■ form (an idea or impression) as a result of perception or experience: *the impression she received was one of unhurried leisure.* ■ (in tennis and similar games) be the player to whom the server serves (the ball). ■ (in Christian services) eat or drink (the Eucharistic bread or wine): *he received Communion and left.* ■ consent to formally hear (an oath or confession): *he failed to find a magistrate to receive his oath.* ■ serve as a receptacle for: *the basin that receives your blood.*
2 suffer, experience, or be subject to (specified treatment): *the event received wide press coverage | he received an eight-year prison sentence | she received only cuts and bruises.* ■ (usu. **be received**) respond to (something) in a specified way: *her first poem was not well received.* ■ meet with (a specified response or reaction): *the rulings have received widespread acceptance.* ■ (as adj. **received**) widely accepted as authoritative or true: *the myths and received wisdom about the country's past.* ■ meet and have to withstand: *the landward slopes receive the full force of the wind.*
3 greet or welcome (a visitor) formally: *representatives of the club will be received by the Mayor.* ■ be visited by: *she was not allowed to receive visitors.* ■ admit as a member: *hundreds of converts were received into the Church.* ■ provide space or accommodations for: *three lines are reserved for special vehicles, and the remaining lines receive the general rolling stock.*
– PHRASES **be at** (or **on**) **the receiving end** be the person to whom a telephone call is made. ■ informal be subjected to something unpleasant: *she found herself on the receiving end of a good deal of teasing.*
– ORIGIN Middle English: from Anglo-Norman French *receivre*, based on Latin *recipere*, from *re-* 'back' + *capere* 'take.'

re·ceived pro·nun·ci·a·tion (also **received standard**) ▶ **n.** the standard form of British English pronunciation, based on educated speech in southern England.

re·ceiv·er /riˈsēvər/ ▶ **n. 1** the part of a telephone apparatus contained in the earpiece, in which electrical signals are converted into sounds. ■ a complete telephone handset: *he picked up the receiver.* ■ a piece of radio or television apparatus that detects broadcast signals and converts them into visible or audible form: *a satellite receiver.*
2 a person who gets or accepts something that has been sent or given to them: *the receiver of a gift.* ■ (in tennis and similar games) the player to whom the ball is served to begin play. ■ Football a player who catches a pass or a kick. ■ a person who buys or accepts stolen goods in the knowledge that they have been stolen.
3 a person or company appointed by a court to manage the financial affairs of a business or person that has gone bankrupt: *the company is **in the hands of the receivers**.*
4 Chemistry a container for collecting the products of distillation, chromatography, or other process.
5 the part of a firearm that houses the action and to which the barrel and other parts are attached.

re·ceiv·er·ship /riˈsēvər,SHip/ ▶ **n.** the state of being dealt with by an official receiver: *the company went **into receivership** last week.*

re·ceiv·ing line ▶ **n.** a collection of people who gather in a row to greet guests as they arrive at a formal social event.

re·cen·sion /riˈsenCHən/ ▶ **n.** a revised edition of a text; an act of making a revised edition of a text.
– ORIGIN mid 17th cent. (in the sense 'survey, review'): from Latin *recensio(n-)*, from *recensere* 'revise,' from *re-* 'again' + *censere* 'to review.'

re·cent /ˈrēsənt/ ▶ **adj. 1** having happened, begun, or been done not long ago or not long before; belonging to a past period of time comparatively close to the present: *his recent visit to Britain | a recent edition of the newspaper.*
2 (**Recent**) Geology another term for **HOLOCENE**.
▶ **n.** (**the Recent**) Geology the Holocene epoch.
– DERIVATIVES **re·cen·cy n.**, **re·cent·ness n.**
– ORIGIN late Middle English (in the sense 'fresh'): from Latin *recens, recent-* or French *récent*.

re·cent·ly /ˈrēsəntlē/ ▶ **adv.** at a recent time; not long ago: *I recently bought a CD player | **until recently** he was an architect.*

re·cep·ta·cle /riˈseptikəl/ ▶ **n. 1** an object or space used to contain something: *trash receptacles.* ■ chiefly Zoology an organ or structure that receives a secretion, eggs, sperm, etc. ■ an electrical outlet into which the plug of an electrical device may be inserted.
2 Botany an enlarged area at the apex of a stem that bears the organs of a flower or the florets of a flower head. ■ a structure supporting the sexual organs in some algae, mosses, and liverworts.
– ORIGIN late Middle English: from Latin *receptaculum*, from *receptare* 'receive back,' frequentative of *recipere* (see **RECEIVE**).

re·cep·tion /riˈsepSHən/ ▶ **n. 1** the action or process of receiving something sent, given, or inflicted: *the reception of impulses from other neurons | the reception of the sacrament.* ■ the way in which a person or group of people reacts to someone or something: *the proposal continued to get a lukewarm reception on Wall Street.* ■ the receiving of broadcast signals: *a microchip that will allow parents to block reception of violent programs.* ■ the quality of this: *I had to put up with poor radio reception.* ■ the action of admitting someone to a place, group, or institution or the process of being admitted: *their reception into the Church.* ■ the formal or ceremonious welcoming of a guest: *his reception by the Prime Minister.* ■ Football an act of catching the ball.
2 a formal social occasion held to welcome someone or to celebrate a particular event: *a wedding reception.*
3 the area in a hotel, office, or other establishment where guests and visitors are greeted and dealt with: [as modifier] *the reception desk.*
– ORIGIN late Middle English: from Old French, or from Latin *receptio(n-)*, from the verb *recipere* (see **RECEIVE**).

re·cep·tion·ist /riˈsepSHənist/ ▶ **n.** a person employed in an office or other establishment to answer the telephone, deal with clients, and greet visitors.

re·cep·tion room ▶ **n.** a room in a hotel or other building used for functions such as parties and meetings.

re·cep·tive /riˈseptiv/ ▶ **adj.** able or willing to receive something, esp. signals or stimuli. ■ willing to consider or accept new suggestions and ideas: *a receptive audience | the institution was receptive to new ideas.* ■ (of a female animal) ready to mate.
– DERIVATIVES **re·cep·tive·ly adv.**, **re·cep·tive·ness n.**, **re·cep·tiv·i·ty** /,rē,sepˈtivətē/ **n.**

re·cep·tor /riˈseptər/ ▶ **n.** Physiology an organ or cell able to respond to light, heat, or other external stimulus and transmit a signal to a sensory nerve. ■ a region of tissue, or a molecule in a cell membrane, that responds specifically to a particular neurotransmitter, hormone, antigen, or other substance.
– ORIGIN early 20th cent.: coined in German from Latin *receptor*, from *recept-* 'taken back,' from the verb *recipere* (see **RECEIVE**).

re·cess /ˈrē,ses, riˈses/ ▶ **n. 1** a small space created by building part of a wall further back from the rest: *a table set into a recess.* ■ a hollow space inside something: *the concrete block has a recess in its base.* ■ (usu. **recesses**) a remote, secluded, or secret place: *the recesses of the silent pine forest* | figurative *the dark recesses of his soul.*
2 a period of time when the proceedings of a parliament, committee, court of law, or other official body are temporarily suspended: *talks resumed after a month's recess | the Senate was **in recess**.* ■ a break between school classes: *the mid-morning recess.*
▶ **v. 1** [with obj.] (often as adj. **recessed**) attach (a fixture) by setting it back into the wall or surface to which it is fixed: *recessed ceiling lights.*
2 [no obj.] (of formal proceedings) be temporarily suspended: *the talks recessed at 2:15.* ■ [with obj.] suspend (such proceedings) temporarily. ■ (of an official body) suspend its proceedings for a period of time.
– ORIGIN mid 16th cent. (in the sense 'withdrawal, departure'): from Latin *recessus*, from *recedere* 'go back' (see **RECEDE**). The verb dates from the early 19th cent.

re·ces·sion /riˈseSHən/ ▶ **n. 1** a period of temporary economic decline during which trade and industrial activity are reduced, generally identified by a fall in GDP in two successive quarters.
2 chiefly Astronomy the action of receding; motion away from an observer.
– DERIVATIVES **re·ces·sion·ar·y** /-,nerē/ **adj.**
– ORIGIN mid 17th cent.: from Latin *recessio(n-)*, from *recess-* 'gone back,' from the verb *recedere* (see **RECEDE**).

re·ces·sion·al /riˈseSHənl, riˈseSHnəl/ ▶ **adj.** of or relating to an economic recession: *recessional times.* ■ chiefly Astronomy relating to or denoting motion away from the observer. ■ Geology (of a moraine or other deposit) left during a pause in the retreat of a glacier or ice sheet.
▶ **n.** a hymn sung while the clergy and choir process out of church at the end of a service. Compare with **PROCESSIONAL**.

re·ces·sive /riˈsesiv/ ▶ **adj. 1** Genetics relating to or denoting heritable characteristics controlled by genes that are expressed in offspring only when inherited from both parents, i.e., when not masked by a dominant characteristic inherited from one parent. Often contrasted with **DOMINANT**.
2 undergoing an economic recession: *the recessive housing market.*
3 Phonetics (of the stress on a word or phrase) tending to fall on the first syllable.
▶ **n.** Genetics a recessive trait or gene.
– DERIVATIVES **re·ces·sive·ly adv.**, **re·ces·sive·ness n.**, **re·ces·siv·i·ty** /,rē,sesˈivətē/ **n.**
– ORIGIN late 17th cent.: from **RECESS**, on the pattern of *excessive*.

Rech·ab·ite /ˈrekə,bīt/ ▶ **n.** (in the Bible) a member of an Israelite family, descended from Rechab, who refused to drink wine or live in houses (Jer. 35).

re·charge ▶ **v.** /rēˈCHärj/ [with obj.] restore an electric charge to (a battery or a battery-operated device) by connecting it to a device that draws power from another source of electricity: *he plugged his razor in to recharge it.* ■ [no obj.] (of a battery or battery-operated device) be refilled with electrical power in such a way: *the drill takes about three hours to recharge.* ■ refill (a container, lake, or aquifer) with water. ■ [no obj.] be refilled: *the rate at which the aquifer recharges naturally.* ■ [no obj.] (of a person) return to a normal state of mind or strength after a period of physical or mental exertion: *she needs a bit of time to recharge after giving so much of herself this morning.*
▶ **n.** /ˈrēCHärj/ the replenishment of an aquifer by the absorption of water.
– PHRASES **recharge one's batteries** regain one's strength and energy by resting and relaxing for a time.
– DERIVATIVES **re·charge·a·ble adj.**, **re·charg·er n.**

ré·chauf·fé /,rā,SHōˈfā -ˈSHō,fā/ ▶ **n.** a dish of warmed-up food left over from a previous meal.
– ORIGIN French, literally 'reheated,' past participle of *réchauffer*.

r

re·check ▶ v. /rē'CHek/ [with obj.] check or verify again: *recheck all the wiring.*
▶ n. an act of checking or verifying something again: *a recheck of the data.*

re·cher·ché /rə,SHer'SHā, rə'SHer,SHā/ ▶ adj. rare, exotic, or obscure: *a few linguistic terms are perhaps a bit recherché for the average readership.*
– ORIGIN French, literally 'carefully sought out,' past participle of *rechercher.*

re·chris·ten /rē'krisən/ ▶ v. [with obj. and complement] give a new name to: *he rechristened Zaire the Democratic Republic of the Congo.*

re·cid·i·vist /ri'sidəvist/ ▶ n. a convicted criminal who reoffends, esp. repeatedly.
▶ adj. denoting such a person: *recidivist male prisoners | women are rarely recidivist.*
– DERIVATIVES **re·cid·i·vism** /-,vizəm/ n., **re·cid·i·vis·tic** /ri,sidə'vistik/ adj.
– ORIGIN late 19th cent.: from French *récidiviste,* from *récidiver* 'fall back,' based on Latin *recidivus* 'falling back,' from the verb *recidere,* from *re-* 'back' + *cadere* 'to fall.'

Re·ci·fe /re'sēfā/ a port on the Atlantic coast of northeastern Brazil, capital of the state of Pernambuco; pop. 1,533,580 (2007). Former name **PERNAMBUCO**.

recip. ▶ abbr. ■ reciprocal. ■ reciprocity.

rec·i·pe /'resə,pē/ ▶ n. a set of instructions for preparing a particular dish, including a list of the ingredients required: *a traditional Indonesian recipe.* ■ something that is likely to lead to a particular outcome: *sky-high interest rates are a recipe for disaster.* ■ archaic a medical prescription.
– ORIGIN late Middle English: from Latin, literally 'receive!' (first used as an instruction in medical prescriptions), imperative of *recipere.*

re·cip·i·ent /ri'sipēənt/ ▶ n. a person or thing that receives or is awarded something: *the recipient of the Nobel Peace Prize.*
▶ adj. [attrib.] receiving or capable or receiving something: *a recipient country.*
– DERIVATIVES **re·cip·i·en·cy** n.
– ORIGIN mid 16th cent.: from Latin *recipient-* 'receiving,' from the verb *recipere.*

re·cip·ro·cal /ri'siprəkəl/ ▶ adj. 1 given, felt, or done in return: *she was hoping for some reciprocal comment or gesture.*
2 (of an agreement or obligation) bearing on or binding each of two parties equally: *the treaty is a bilateral commitment with reciprocal rights and duties.* ■ Grammar (of a pronoun or verb) expressing mutual action or relationship.
3 (of a course or bearing) differing from a given course or bearing by 180 degrees.
4 Mathematics (of a quantity or function) related to another so that their product is one.
▶ n. 1 technical a mathematical expression or function so related to another that their product is one; the quantity obtained by dividing the number one by a given quantity.
2 Grammar a pronoun or verb expressing mutual action or relationship, e.g., *each other, fight.*
– DERIVATIVES **re·cip·ro·cal·i·ty** /ri,siprə'kalətē/ n., **re·cip·ro·cal·ly** /-ək(ə)lē/ adv.
– ORIGIN late 16th cent.: from Latin *reciprocus* (based on *re-* 'back' + *pro-* 'forward') + **-AL**.

re·cip·ro·cal cross ▶ n. Genetics a pair of crosses between a male of one strain and a female of another, and vice versa.

re·cip·ro·cate /ri'siprə,kāt/ ▶ v. 1 [with obj.] respond to (a gesture or action) by making a corresponding one: *the favor was reciprocated* | [no obj.] *perhaps I was expected to reciprocate with some remark of my own.* ■ experience the same (love, liking, or affection) for someone as that person does for oneself: *her passion for him was not reciprocated.*
2 [no obj.] (usu. as adj. **reciprocating**) (of a part of a machine) move backward and forward in a straight line: *a reciprocating blade.*
– DERIVATIVES **re·cip·ro·ca·tion** /ri,siprə'kāSHən/ n., **re·cip·ro·ca·tor** /-,kātər/ n.
– ORIGIN late 16th cent.: from Latin *reciprocat-* 'moved backwards and forwards' from the verb *reciprocare,* from *reciprocus* (see **RECIPROCAL**).

re·cip·ro·cat·ing en·gine ▶ n. an engine in which one or more pistons move up and down in cylinders; a piston engine.

rec·i·proc·i·ty /,resə'präsətē/ ▶ n. the practice of exchanging things with others for mutual benefit, esp. privileges granted by one country or organization to another.
– ORIGIN mid 18th cent.: from French *réciprocité,* from *réciproque,* from Latin *reciprocus* 'moving backward and forward' (see **RECIPROCATE**).

re·cir·cu·late /,rē'sərkyə,lāt/ ▶ v. [with obj.] circulate again. ■ [no obj.] (of a fluid) circulate continuously: *the air is supposed to recirculate within the turboshaft engine.*
– DERIVATIVES **re·cir·cu·la·tion** n.

re·cit·al /ri'sītl/ ▶ n. 1 the performance of a program of music by a solo instrumentalist or singer or by a small group: *a piano recital.*
2 an enumeration or listing of connected names, facts, or elements;: *a recital of their misfortunes.*
3 (usu. **recitals**) Law the part of a legal document that explains the purpose of the deed and gives factual information.
– DERIVATIVES **re·cit·al·ist** /-ist/ n.

rec·i·ta·tion /,resi'tāSHən/ ▶ n. the action of repeating something aloud from memory: *the recitation of traditional poems.* ■ the repetition of a list of facts.

rec·i·ta·tive /,res(ə)tə'tēv/ ▶ n. musical declamation of the kind usual in the narrative and dialogue parts of opera and oratorio, sung in the rhythm of ordinary speech with many words on the same note: *singing in recitative.*
– ORIGIN mid 17th cent.: from Italian *recitativo,* from Latin *recitare* 'to read out' (see **RECITE**).

rec·i·ta·ti·vo /,resətə'tēvō/ ▶ n. (pl. **recitativos**) another term for **RECITATIVE**.
– ORIGIN Italian.

re·cite /ri'sīt/ ▶ v. [with obj.] repeat aloud or declaim (a poem or passage) from memory before an audience: *we provided our own entertainment by singing and reciting poetry.* ■ state (names, facts, etc.) in order: *she recited the dates and names of kings and queens.*
– DERIVATIVES **re·cit·er** n.
– ORIGIN late Middle English (as a legal term in the sense 'state (a fact) in a document'): from Old French *reciter* or Latin *recitare* 'read out,' from *re-* (expressing intensive force) + *citare* 'cite.'

reck /rek/ ▶ v. [no obj. with negative or in questions] archaic pay heed to something: *ye* **reck not of** *lands or goods* | [with clause] *little recking where she was wandering* | [with obj.] *he recks not Syria, recks not Britain.* ■ **(it recks)** it is of importance: *what recks it?*
– ORIGIN Old English, of Germanic origin; compare with **RECKLESS**. The word became common in rhetorical and poetic language in the 19th cent.

reck·less /'rekləs/ ▶ adj. (of a person or their actions) without thinking or caring about the consequences of an action: *reckless driving.*
– DERIVATIVES **reck·less·ly** adv., **reck·less·ness** n.
– ORIGIN Old English *recceléas,* from the Germanic base (meaning 'care') of **RECK**.

reck·on /'rekən/ ▶ v. 1 [with obj.] establish by counting or calculation; calculate: *his debts were reckoned at $300,000 | the Byzantine year was reckoned from September 1.* ■ **(reckon someone/something among)** include in (a class or group): *in high school and college he was always reckoned among the brainiest.*
2 [with clause] informal conclude after calculation; be of the opinion: *he reckons that the army should pull out entirely | I reckon I can manage that.* ■ [with obj. and complement] consider or regard in a specified way: *it was generally reckoned a failure.*
3 [no obj.] **(reckon on)** rely on or be sure of doing, having, or dealing with: *they had reckoned on a day or two more of privacy.* ■ [with infinitive] informal expect to do a particular thing: *I reckon to get away by two-thirty.*
– PHRASES **a —— to be reckoned with** (or **to reckon with**) a thing or person of considerable importance or ability that is not to be ignored or underestimated: *the trade unions were a political force to be reckoned with.*
– PHRASAL VERBS **reckon with** (or **without**) 1 take (or fail to take) into account: *it must reckon with two great challenges.* 2 **(reckon with)** archaic settle accounts with.
– ORIGIN Old English *(ge)recenian* 'recount, relate'; related to Dutch *rekenen* and German *rechnen* 'to count (up).' Early senses included 'give an account of items received' and 'mention things in order,' which gave rise to the notion of 'calculation' and hence of 'coming to a conclusion.'

reck·on·er /'rekənər/ ▶ n. a table or device designed to assist with calculation.

reck·on·ing /'rekəniNG/ ▶ n. the action or process of calculating or estimating something: *last year was not, by any reckoning, a particularly good one | the system of time reckoning in Babylon.* ■ a person's view, opinion, or judgment: *by ancient reckoning, bacteria are plants.* ■ archaic a bill or account, or its settlement. ■ the avenging or punishing of past mistakes or misdeeds: *the fear of being brought to reckoning | there will be a terrible reckoning.*

re·claim /ri'klām/ ▶ v. [with obj.] 1 retrieve or recover (something previously lost, given, or paid); obtain the return of: *he returned three years later to reclaim his title as director of advertising | when Dennis emerged I reclaimed my room.* ■ redeem (someone) from a state of vice; reform: *societies for reclaiming beggars and prostitutes.* ■ archaic tame or civilize (an animal or person).
2 bring (waste land or land formerly under water) under cultivation: *little money is available to reclaim and cultivate the desert* | (as adj. **reclaimed**) *reclaimed land.* ■ recover (material) for reuse; recycle: *a sufficient weight of plastic could easily be reclaimed.*
▶ n. the action or process of reclaiming or being reclaimed: *beyond reclaim.*
– DERIVATIVES **re·claim·a·ble** adj., **re·claim·er** n., **rec·la·ma·tion** /,reklə'māSHən/ n.
– ORIGIN Middle English (used in falconry in the sense 'recall'): from Old French *reclamer,* from Latin *reclamare* 'cry out against,' from *re-* 'back' + *clamare* 'to shout.'

ré·clame /rā'kläm/ ▶ n. public acclaim; notoriety. ■ a hunger for publicity or flair for getting attention.

re·clas·si·fy /rē'klasə,fī/ ▶ v. (**reclassifies, reclassifying, reclassified**) [with obj.] assign to a different class or category: *Hurricane Helene was reclassified as a bad storm.*
– DERIVATIVES **re·clas·si·fi·ca·tion** /rē,klasəfə'kāSHən/ n.

re·cline /ri'klīn/ ▶ v. [no obj.] lean or lie back in a relaxed position with the back supported: *she was reclining in a deck chair* | (as adj. **reclining**) *a reclining figure.* ■ (of a seat) be able to have the back moved into a sloping position: *all the seats recline.* ■ [with obj.] move the back of (a seat) into a sloping position.
– DERIVATIVES **re·clin·a·ble** adj.
– ORIGIN late Middle English (in the sense 'cause to lean back'): from Old French *recliner* or Latin *reclinare* 'bend back, recline,' from *re-* 'back' + *clinare* 'to bend.'

re·clin·er /ri'klīnər/ ▶ n. an upholstered armchair that can be tilted backward, esp. one with a footrest that simultaneously extends from the front.

re·clothe /rē'klō<u>TH</u>/ ▶ v. [with obj.] dress again, esp. in different clothes: *she was ceremonially reclothed in a new robe.*

rec·luse /'rek,lo͞os, ri'klo͞os, 'rek,lo͞oz/ ▶ n. a person who lives a solitary life and tends to avoid other people.
▶ adj. archaic favoring a solitary life.
– DERIVATIVES **re·clu·sion** /ri'klo͞oZHən/ n.
– ORIGIN Middle English: from Old French *reclus,* past participle of *reclure,* from Latin *recludere* 'enclose,' from *re-* 'again' + *claudere* 'to shut.'

re·clu·sive /ri'klo͞osiv, -ziv/ ▶ adj. avoiding the company of other people; solitary: *a reclusive life in rural Ireland.*
– DERIVATIVES **re·clu·sive·ly** adv., **re·clu·sive·ness** n.

re·code /rē'kōd/ ▶ v. [with obj.] put (something, esp. a computer program) into a different code. ■ assign a different code to.

rec·og·ni·tion /,rekig'niSHən/ ▶ n. the action or process of recognizing or being recognized, in particular: ■ identification of a thing or person from previous encounters or knowledge: *she saw him pass by without a sign of recognition.* ■ acknowledgment of something's existence, validity, or legality: *the unions must receive proper recognition.* ■ appreciation or acclaim for an achievement, service, or ability: *his work was slow to gain recognition | she received the award in recognition of her courageous human rights work.* ■ (also **diplomatic recognition**) formal acknowledgment by a country that another political entity fulfills the conditions of statehood and is eligible to be dealt with as a member of the international community.
– ORIGIN late 15th cent. (denoting the acknowledgment of a service): from Latin *recognitio(n-),* from the verb *recognoscere* 'know again, recall to mind' (see **RECOGNIZE**).

rec·og·niz·a·ble /,rekig'nīzəbəl/ ▶ adj. able to be recognized or identified from previous encounters or knowledge.
– DERIVATIVES **rec·og·niz·a·bil·i·ty** /-,nīzə'bilətē/ n., **rec·og·niz·a·bly** /-blē/ adv.

re·cog·ni·zance /ri'kägnəzəns, -'känəzəns/ ▶ n. Law a bond by which a person undertakes before a court or magistrate to observe some condition, esp. to appear when summoned: *he was released on his own recognizance.*
– ORIGIN Middle English: from Old French *reconnissance,* from *reconnaistre* 'recognize.'

re·cog·ni·zant /ri'kägnəzənt, -'känəzənt/ ▶ adj. [predic.] **(recognizant of)** formal conscious or aware of (something, esp. a favor).

rec·og·nize /'rekig,nīz, 'rekə(g),nīz/ ▶ v. [with obj.] 1 identify (someone or something) from having encountered them before; know again: *I recognized*

PRONUNCIATION KEY ə *ago, up;* ər *over, fur;* a *hat;* ā *ate;* ä *car;* e *let;* ē *see;* i *fit;* ī *by;* NG *sing;* ō *go;* ô *law, for;* oi *toy;* o͝o *good;* o͞o *goo;* ou *out;* TH *thin;* <u>TH</u> *then;* ZH *vision*

r

her when her wig fell off | *Julia hardly recognized Jill when they met.* ■ identify from knowledge of appearance or character: *Pat is very good at recognizing wildflowers.* ■ (of a computer or other machine) automatically identify and respond correctly to (a sound, printed character, etc.).
2 acknowledge the existence, validity, or legality of: *the defense is recognized in Mexican law* | *he was **recognized as an international authority*** | [with clause] *it is important to recognize that a variety of indirect forms of discrimination operate.* ■ officially regard (a qualification) as valid or proper: *these qualifications are recognized by the Department of Education* | (as adj. **recognized**) *courses that lead to recognized qualifications.* ■ grant diplomatic recognition to (a country or government): *they were refusing to recognize the puppet regime.* ■ show official appreciation of; reward formally: *his work was recognized by an honorary degree from Georgetown University.* ■ (of a person presiding at a meeting or debate) call on (someone) to speak.
– DERIVATIVES **rec·og·niz·er** n.
– ORIGIN late Middle English (earliest attested as a term in Scots law): from Old French *reconniss-*, stem of *reconnaistre*, from Latin *recognoscere* 'know again, recall to mind,' from *re-* 'again' + *cognoscere* 'learn.'

re·coil ▶ v. /riˈkoil/ [no obj.] suddenly spring or flinch back in fear, horror, or disgust: *he recoiled in horror.* ■ feel fear, horror, or disgust at the thought or prospect of something; shrink mentally: *Renee felt herself recoil at the very thought.* ■ (of a gun) move abruptly backward as a reaction on firing a bullet, shell, or other missile. ■ rebound or spring back through force of impact or elasticity: *the muscle has the ability to recoil.* ■ (**recoil on**/**upon**) (of an action) have an adverse reactive effect on (the originator): *the soothsayers agreed that all the dangers would recoil on the heads of those who were in possession of the entrails.*
▶ n. /ˈrēˌkoil, riˈkoil/ the action of recoiling: *his body jerked with the recoil of the rifle.*
– ORIGIN Middle English (denoting the act of retreating): from Old French *reculer* 'move back,' based on Latin *culus* 'buttocks.'

rec·ol·lect /ˌrekəˈlekt/ ▶ v. [with obj.] remember (something); call to mind: *he could not quite recollect the reason* | [with clause] *can you recollect how your brother reacted?*
– ORIGIN early 16th cent. (in the sense 'gather'): from Latin *recollect-* 'gathered back,' from the verb *recolligere*, from *re-* 'back' + *colligere* 'collect.'

re-col·lect /ˌrēkəˈlekt/ ▶ v. [with obj.] collect or gather again: *after re-collecting our apples for the second time, Bruno brought us a couple of nice sturdy sacks.*
– ORIGIN early 17th cent.: later form of RECOLLECT, from RE- 'once more' + the verb COLLECT[1].

rec·ol·lec·tion /ˌrekəˈleksHən/ ▶ n. the action or faculty of remembering something: ***to the best of my recollection** no one ever had a bad word to say about him.* ■ a thing recollected; a memory: *a biography based on his wife's recollections.* ■ Philosophy (in Platonic thought) anamnesis.
– DERIVATIVES **rec·ol·lec·tive** /-tiv/ adj.
– ORIGIN late 16th cent. (denoting gathering things together again): from French or medieval Latin *recollectio(n-)*, from the verb *recolligere* 'gather again' (see RECOLLECT).

Rec·ol·let /ˌrākôˈlā, ˌrekəˈlet/ (also **Recollect** /ˈrekəlekt/) ▶ n. historical a member of a reformed branch of the Franciscan order, founded in France in the late 16th century.
– ORIGIN from French *récollet*, from medieval Latin *recollectus* 'gathered together,' expressing a notion of concentration, and absorption in thought.

re·col·o·nize /rēˈkäləˌnīz/ ▶ v. [with obj.] (chiefly of a plant or animal species) colonize (a region or habitat) again.
– DERIVATIVES **re·col·o·ni·za·tion** /ˌrēˌkälənəˈzāsHən/ n.

re·col·or /rēˈkələr/ (Brit. **recolour**) ▶ v. [with obj.] color again or differently.

re·com·bi·nant /rēˈkämbənənt, ri-/ Genetics ▶ adj. [attrib.] of, relating to, or denoting an organism, cell, or genetic material formed by recombination.
▶ n. a recombinant organism, cell, or piece of genetic material.

re·com·bi·nant DNA ▶ n. DNA that has been formed artificially by combining constituents from different organisms.

re·com·bi·nase /riˈkämbəˌnās, -ˌnāz/ ▶ n. Biochemistry an enzyme that promotes genetic recombination.

re·com·bi·na·tion /rēˌkämbəˈnāsHən/ ▶ n. the process of recombining things. ■ Genetics the rearrangement of genetic material, esp. by crossing over in chromosomes or by the artificial joining of segments of DNA from different organisms.

re·com·bine /ˌrēkəmˈbīn/ ▶ v. combine or cause to combine again or differently: [no obj.] *carbohydrates can recombine with oxygen* | [with obj.] *decompose the calculation into components and recombine them to find the solution.*

re·com·mence /ˌrēkəˈmens/ ▶ v. begin or cause to begin again: [no obj.] *the war recommenced* | [with obj.] *it was agreed to recommence talks.*
– DERIVATIVES **re·com·mence·ment** n.

rec·om·mend /ˌrekəˈmend/ ▶ v. [with obj.] **1** put forward (someone or something) with approval as being suitable for a particular purpose or role: *George had recommended some local architects* | *a book I **recommended to a friend of mine.*** ■ advise or suggest (something) as a course of action: *some doctors recommend putting a board under the mattress* | [with clause] *the report recommended that criminal charges be brought.* ■ [with obj. and infinitive] advise (someone) to do something: *you are strongly recommended to seek professional advice.* ■ make (someone or something) appealing or desirable: *the house had much to recommend it.*
2 (**recommend someone/something to**) archaic commend or entrust someone or something to (someone): *I devoutly recommended my spirit to its maker.*
– DERIVATIVES **rec·om·mend·a·ble** adj., **rec·om·mend·a·to·ry** /-ˈmendəˌtôrē/ adj., **rec·om·mend·er** n.
– ORIGIN late Middle English (sense 2): from medieval Latin *recommendare*, from Latin *re-* (expressing intensive force) + *commendare* 'commit to the care of.'

rec·om·men·da·tion /ˌrekəmənˈdāsHən, -ˌmen-/ ▶ n. a suggestion or proposal as to the best course of action, esp. one put forward by an authoritative body: *the committee put forward forty recommendations for change.* ■ the action of recommending something or someone: *he selected his staff by personal recommendation.*

re·com·mit /ˌrēkəˈmit/ ▶ v. (**recommits, recommitting, recommitted**) [with obj.] commit again. ■ return (a motion, proposal, or legislative bill) to a committee for further consideration.
– DERIVATIVES **re·com·mit·ment** n., **re·com·mit·tal** /-ˈmitl/ n.

rec·om·pense /ˈrekəmˌpens/ ▶ v. [with obj.] make amends to (someone) for loss or harm suffered; compensate: *offenders should recompense their victims* | *he was recompensed for the wasted time.* ■ pay or reward (someone) for effort or work: *he was handsomely recompensed.* ■ make amends to or reward someone for (loss, harm, or effort): *he thought his loyalty had been inadequately recompensed.* ■ archaic punish or reward (someone) appropriately for an action: *according to their doings will he recompense them.*
▶ n. compensation or reward given for loss or harm suffered or effort made: *substantial damages were paid **in recompense.*** ■ archaic restitution made or punishment inflicted for a wrong or injury.
– ORIGIN late Middle English: from Old French, from the verb *recompenser* 'do a favor to requite a loss,' from late Latin *recompensare*, from Latin *re-* 'again' (also expressing intensive force) + *compensare* 'weigh one thing against another.'

re·com·pile /ˌrēkəmˈpīl/ Computing ▶ v. [with obj.] compile (a program) again or differently.
▶ n. a recompilation of a computer program.
– DERIVATIVES **re·com·pi·la·tion** /ˌrēkämpəˈlāsHən/ n.

re·com·pose /ˌrēkəmˈpōz/ ▶ v. [with obj.] compose again or differently: *a marble panel recomposed from fragments.*
– DERIVATIVES **re·com·po·si·tion** /ˌrēˌkämpəˈzisHən/ n.

re·con informal ▶ n. /ˈrēˌkän, riˈkän/ short for RECONNAISSANCE.
▶ v. /riˈkän/ (**recons, reconning, reconned**) short for RECONNOITER.

rec·on·cil·a·ble /ˌrekənˈsīləbəl/ ▶ adj. capable of being reconciled; compatible: *the two propositions are hardly reconcilable* | *the theory was quite reconcilable with industrialization.*
– DERIVATIVES **rec·on·cil·a·bil·i·ty** /ˌrekənˌsīləˈbilətē/ n.

rec·on·cile /ˈrekənˌsīl/ ▶ v. [with obj.] restore friendly relations between: *she wanted to **be reconciled with her father*** | *the news reconciled us.* ■ cause to coexist in harmony; make or show to be compatible: *a landscape in which inner and outer vision were reconciled* | *you may have to adjust your ideal to **reconcile it with reality.*** ■ make (one account) consistent with another, esp. by allowing for transactions begun but not yet completed: *it is not necessary to reconcile the cost accounts to the financial accounts.* ■ settle (a disagreement): *advice on how to reconcile the conflict.* ■ (**reconcile someone to**) make someone accept (a disagreeable or unwelcome thing): *he could not reconcile himself to the thought of his mother stocking shelves* | *he was reconciled to leaving.*
– DERIVATIVES **rec·on·cile·ment** n., **rec·on·cil·er** n., **rec·on·cil·i·a·to·ry** /ˌrekənˈsilēəˌtôrē/ adj.
– ORIGIN late Middle English: from Old French *reconcilier* or Latin *reconciliare*, from Latin *re-* 'back' (also expressing intensive force) + *conciliare* 'bring together.'

rec·on·cil·i·a·tion /ˌrekənˌsilēˈāsHən/ ▶ n. **1** the restoration of friendly relations: *his **reconciliation with your uncle*** | *the colonel was seeking a **reconciliation with his wife.***
2 the action of making one view or belief compatible with another: *he aims to bring about a **reconciliation between art and technology.***
3 the action of making financial accounts consistent; harmonization: *the reconciliation process should be consistent with the business strategy.*

rec·on·dite /ˈrekənˌdīt, riˈkän-/ ▶ adj. (of a subject or knowledge) little known; abstruse: *the book is full of recondite information.*
– ORIGIN mid 17th cent.: from Latin *reconditus* 'hidden, put away,' past participle of *recondere*, from *re-* 'back' + *condere* 'put together, secrete.'

re·con·di·tion /ˌrēkənˈdisHən/ ▶ v. [with obj.] condition again. ■ overhaul or renovate (a vehicle engine or piece of equipment): *a ship was being reconditioned* | (as adj. **reconditioned**) *a reconditioned engine.*

re·con·fig·ure /ˌrēkənˈfigyər/ ▶ v. [with obj.] configure (something) differently: *you don't have to reconfigure the modem each time you make a connection.*
– DERIVATIVES **re·con·fig·ur·a·ble** adj., **re·con·fig·u·ra·tion** /ˌrēkənˌfigyəˈrāsHən/ n.

re·con·firm /ˌrēkənˈfərm/ ▶ v. [with obj.] confirm again: *I was able to reconfirm this fact firsthand during my visit.*
– DERIVATIVES **re·con·fir·ma·tion** n.

re·con·nais·sance /riˈkänəsəns, -zəns/ ▶ n. military observation of a region to locate an enemy or ascertain strategic features: *an excellent aircraft for low-level reconnaissance* | *after a reconnaissance our forces took the island* | [as modifier] *reconnaissance missions.* ■ preliminary surveying or research: *conducting client reconnaissance.*
– ORIGIN early 19th cent.: from French, from *reconnaître* 'recognize' (see RECONNOITER).

re·con·nect /ˌrēkəˈnekt/ ▶ v. [with obj.] connect back together: *surgeons had to reconnect tendons, nerves, and veins.* ■ [no obj.] re-establish a bond of communication or emotion: *in order to keep your marriage healthy, it is important to reconnect as mature individuals.*
– DERIVATIVES **re·con·nec·tion** /ˌrēkəˈneksHən/ n.

re·con·noi·ter /ˌrēkəˈnoitər, ˌrek-/ (Brit. **reconnoitre**) ▶ v. [with obj.] make a military observation of (a region): *they reconnoitered the beach some weeks before the landing* | [no obj.] *the raiders were reconnoitering for further attacks.*
▶ n. an act of reconnoitering: *a nocturnal reconnoiter of the camp.*
– ORIGIN early 18th cent.: from obsolete French *reconnoître*, from Latin *recognoscere* 'know again' (see RECOGNIZE).

re·con·quer /ˌrēˈkäNGkər/ ▶ v. [with obj.] conquer again.
– DERIVATIVES **re·con·quest** n.

re·con·se·crate /ˌrēˈkänsiˌkrāt/ ▶ v. [with obj.] consecrate (someone or something) again.
– DERIVATIVES **re·con·se·cra·tion** n.

re·con·sid·er /ˌrēkənˈsidər/ ▶ v. [with obj.] consider (something) again, esp. for a possible change of decision regarding it: *they called on the government to reconsider its policy* | [no obj.] *I beg you to reconsider.*
– DERIVATIVES **re·con·sid·er·a·tion** /ˌrēkənˌsidəˈrāsHən/ n.

re·con·sign /ˌrēkənˈsīn/ ▶ v. [with obj.] consign again or differently.
– DERIVATIVES **re·con·sign·ment** n.

re·con·sol·i·date /ˌrēkənˈsäləˌdāt/ ▶ v. [with obj.] consolidate (something) again or anew.
– DERIVATIVES **re·con·sol·i·da·tion** n.

re·con·sti·tute /rēˈkänstəˌt(y)o͞ot/ ▶ v. [with obj.] build up again from parts; reconstruct. ■ change the form and organization of (an institution): *he reconstituted his cabinet.* ■ restore (something dried, esp. food) to its original state by adding water to it: (as adj. **reconstituted**) *reconstituted milk.*
– DERIVATIVES **re·con·sti·tu·tion** /ˌrēˌkänstəˈt(y)o͞osHən/ n.

re·con·struct /ˌrēkənˈstrəkt/ ▶ v. [with obj.] build or form (something) again after it has been damaged or destroyed: *a small area of painted Roman plaster has been reconstructed.* ■ reorganize (something):

later emperors reconstructed the army. ■ form an impression, model, or re-enactment of (a past event or thing) from the available evidence: *from copies of correspondence it is possible to reconstruct the broad sequence of events.*
– DERIVATIVES **re·con·struct·a·ble** (also **reconstructible**) **adj.**, **re·con·struc·tive** /-tiv/ **adj.**, **re·con·struc·tor** /-tər/ **n.**

re·con·struc·tion /ˌrēkənˈstrəkSHən/ ▶ **n.** the action or process of reconstructing or being reconstructed: *the economic reconstruction of Russia* | [as modifier] *reconstruction work.* ■ a thing that has been rebuilt after being damaged or destroyed: *comparison between the original and the reconstruction.* ■ an impression, model, or re-enactment of a past event formed from the available evidence: *a reconstruction of the accident would be staged to try to discover the cause of the tragedy.* ■ (**Reconstruction**) the period 1865–77 following the Civil War, during which the states of the Confederacy were controlled by the federal government and social legislation, including the granting of new rights to African-Americans, was introduced.

re·con·tex·tual·ize /ˌrēknˈteksCHo͞oəlīz/ ▶ **v.** [with obj.] place or consider in a new or different context.

re·con·vene /ˌrēkənˈvēn/ ▶ **v.** convene or cause to convene again, esp. after a pause in proceedings: [no obj.] *as soon as the Senate reconvenes next month* | [with obj.] *it was agreed to reconvene the permanent commission.*

re·con·vert /ˌrēkənˈvərt/ ▶ **v.** [with obj.] convert back to a former state: *she reconverted the basement back into an apartment.*
– DERIVATIVES **re·con·ver·sion** /-ˈvərZHən/ **n.**

re·con·vict /ˌrēkənˈvikt/ ▶ **v.** [with obj.] convict (someone) of a further criminal offense: *many prisoners are reconvicted within two years of release.*
– DERIVATIVES **re·con·vic·tion** **n.**

rec·ord ▶ **n.** /ˈrekərd/ **1** a thing constituting a piece of evidence about the past, esp. an account of an act or occurrence kept in writing or some other permanent form: *identification was made through dental records* | *a record of meter readings.* ■ (also **court record**) Law an official report of the proceedings and judgment in a court. ■ Computing a number of related items of information that are handled as a unit.
2 the sum of the past achievements or actions of a person or organization; a person or thing's previous conduct or performance: *the safety record at the airport* | *the team preserved its unbeaten home record.* ■ short for CRIMINAL RECORD.
3 (esp. in sports) the best performance or most remarkable event of its kind that has been officially measured and noted: *he held the world record for over a decade* | *he managed to beat the record* | [as modifier] *record profits.*
4 a thin plastic disk carrying recorded sound, esp. music, in grooves on each surface, for reproduction by a record player. ■ a piece or collection of music reproduced on such a disk or on another medium, such as compact disc: *my favorite record* | [as modifier] *a record company.*
▶ **v.** /riˈkôrd/ [with obj.] **1** set down in writing or some other permanent form for later reference, esp. officially: *they were asked to keep a diary and record everything they ate or drank* | (as adj. **recorded**) *levels of recorded crime.* ■ state or express publicly or officially; make an official record of: *the coroner recorded a verdict of accidental death.* ■ (of an instrument or observer) show or register (a measurement or result): *the temperature was the lowest recorded since 1926.* ■ achieve (a certain score or result): *they recorded their first win of the season.*
2 convert (sound or a broadcast) into permanent form for later reproduction: *they were recording a guitar recital.* ■ produce (a piece or collection of music or a program) by such means: *they go into the studio next week to record their debut album.*
– PHRASES **for the record** so that the true facts are recorded or known: *for the record, I have never been to the apartment.* **a matter of record** a thing that is established as a fact through being officially recorded. **off the record** not made as an official or attributable statement. **on record 1** (also **on the record**) used in reference to the making of an official or public statement: *he seems shadowy because he rarely speaks on the record.* **2** officially measured and noted: *it proved to be one of the warmest Decembers on record.* **set** (or **put**) **the record straight** give the true version of events that have been reported incorrectly; correct a misapprehension.
– DERIVATIVES **re·cord·a·ble** /rəˈkôrdəbəl, rē-/ **adj.**
– ORIGIN Middle English: from Old French *record* 'remembrance,' from *recorder* 'bring to remembrance,' from Latin *recordari* 'remember,' based on *cor, cord-* 'heart.' The noun was earliest used in law to denote the fact of being written down as evidence. The verb originally meant 'narrate orally or in writing,' also 'repeat so as to commit to memory.'

rec·ord-break·ing ▶ **adj.** surpassing a record or best-ever achievement: *the fair attracted a record-breaking 10,678 visitors.*
– DERIVATIVES **rec·ord-break·er** **n.**

rec·ord club ▶ **n.** an organization that sells selected audio recordings to members or subscribers, often from a mail-order catalog or online.

re·cord·ed de·liv·er·y ▶ **n.** British term for CERTIFIED MAIL.

re·cord·er /riˈkôrdər/ ▶ **n. 1** an apparatus for recording sound, pictures, or data, esp. a tape recorder.
2 a person who keeps records: *a poet and recorder of rural and industrial life.*
3 a simple wind instrument with finger holes and no keys, held vertically and played by blowing air through a shaped mouthpiece against a sharp edge.
4 (**Recorder**) (in England and Wales) a barrister appointed to serve as a part-time judge. ■ Brit. historical a judge in certain courts.
– DERIVATIVES **re·cord·er·ship** /-ˌSHip/ **n.** (sense 4).
– ORIGIN late Middle English (denoting a kind of judge): from Anglo-Norman French *recordour*, from Old French *recorder* 'bring to remembrance'; partly reinforced by the verb RECORD (also used in the obsolete sense 'practice a tune': see sense 3).

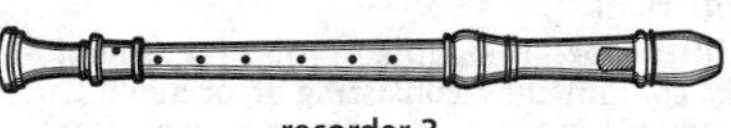

recorder 3

rec·ord hold·er ▶ **n.** a person who has achieved the best-ever performance, esp. in a particular sport: *the 100-meter backstroke world record holder.* ■ something that is unique in terms of its size or other measurable characteristic: *at 646 lbs, this catfish is the current record holder.*
– DERIVATIVES **rec·ord-hold·ing** **adj.**

re·cord·ing /riˈkôrdiNG/ ▶ **n.** the action or process of recording sound or a performance for subsequent reproduction or broadcast: [as modifier] *a recording studio.* ■ a recorded broadcast or performance. ■ a disc or tape on which sounds or visual images have been recorded.

re·cord·ist /riˈkôrdist/ ▶ **n.** a person who makes recordings, esp. of sound: *a sound recordist.*

rec·ord play·er ▶ **n.** an apparatus for reproducing sound from phonograph records, comprising a turntable that spins the record at a constant speed and a stylus that slides along in the groove and picks up the sound, together with an amplifier and a loudspeaker.

rec·ord·set /ˈrekərdˌset/ ▶ **n.** Computing a set of records in a database that share an identifiable or isolatable characteristic.

re·count[1] /riˈkount/ ▶ **v.** [reporting verb] tell someone about something; give an account of an event or experience: [with obj.] *I recounted the tale to Steve* | [with clause] *he recounts how they often talked of politics.*
▶ **n.** an act or instance of giving an account of an event or experience: *one woman's recount of a prolonged battle with "huge centipedes."*
– ORIGIN late Middle English: from Old Northern French *reconter* 'tell again,' based on Old French *counter* (see COUNT[1]).

re·count[2] ▶ **v.** /rēˈkount, ˈrē-/ [with obj.] count again.
▶ **n.** /ˈrēˌkount/ an act of counting something again, esp. votes in an election.

re·coup /riˈko͞op/ ▶ **v.** [with obj.] regain (something lost or expended): *rains have helped recoup water levels* | *sleep was what she needed to recoup her strength.* ■ regain (money spent or lost), esp. through subsequent profits: *oil companies are keen to recoup their investment.* ■ reimburse or compensate (someone) for money spent or lost. ■ Law deduct or keep back (part of a sum due).
– DERIVATIVES **re·coup·a·ble** **adj.**, **re·coup·ment** **n.**
– ORIGIN early 17th cent. (as a legal term): from French *recouper* 'retrench, cut back,' from *re-* 'back' + *couper* 'to cut.'

re·course /ˈrēˌkôrs, riˈkôrs/ ▶ **n.** [in sing.] a source of help in a difficult situation: *surgery may be the only recourse.* ■ (**recourse to**) the use of someone or something as a source of help in a difficult situation: *a means of solving disputes **without recourse to** courts of law* | *all three countries **had recourse to** the IMF for standby loans.* ■ the legal right to demand compensation or payment: *the bank **has recourse against** the exporter for losses incurred.*
– PHRASES **without recourse** Finance a formula used to disclaim responsibility for future nonpayment, esp. of a negotiable financial instrument.
– ORIGIN late Middle English (also in the sense 'running or flowing back'): from Old French *recours*, from Latin *recursus*, from *re-* 'back, again' + *cursus* 'course, running.'

re·cov·er /riˈkəvər/ ▶ **v. 1** [no obj.] return to a normal state of health, mind, or strength: *Neil is still **recovering from** shock* | *the economy has begun to recover.* ■ (**be recovered**) (of a person) be well again: *you'll be fully recovered before you know it.*
2 [with obj.] find or regain possession of (something stolen or lost): *police recovered a stolen video.* ■ regain control of (oneself or of a physical or mental state): *he recovered his balance and sped on* | *one hour later I had recovered consciousness.* ■ regain or secure (compensation) by means of a legal process or subsequent profits: *many companies recovered their costs within six months.* ■ make up for (a loss in position or time): *the French recovered the lead.* ■ remove or extract (an energy source or industrial chemical) for use, reuse, or waste treatment.
▶ **n.** (**the recover**) a defined position of a firearm forming part of a military drill: *bring the firelock to the recover.*
– DERIVATIVES **re·cov·er·er** **n.**
– ORIGIN Middle English (originally with reference to health): from Anglo-Norman French *recoverer*, from Latin *recuperare* 'get again.'

re·cov·er /rēˈkəvər, ˈrē-/ ▶ **v.** [with obj.] put a new cover or covering on: *the cost of re-covering the armchair.*

re·cov·er·a·ble /riˈkəvərəbəl/ ▶ **adj. 1** (of something lost) able to be regained or retrieved. ■ (of compensation or money spent or lost) able to be regained or secured by means of a legal process or subsequent profits.
2 (of an energy source or a supply of it) able to be economically extracted from the ground or sea.
– DERIVATIVES **re·cov·er·a·bil·i·ty** /-ˌkəvərəˈbilətē/ **n.**

re·cov·er·y /riˈkəvərē/ ▶ **n.** (pl. **recoveries**) **1** a return to a normal state of health, mind, or strength: *signs of recovery in the housing market* | *he's back at home now and he looks all set to **make a full recovery**.*
2 the action or process of regaining possession or control of something stolen or lost: *a team of salvage experts to ensure the recovery of family possessions* | *the recovery of his sight.* ■ the action of regaining or securing compensation or money lost or spent by means of a legal process or subsequent profits: *debt recovery.* ■ an object or amount of money recovered: *the recoveries included gold jewelry.* ■ the process of removing or extracting an energy source or industrial chemical for use, reuse, or waste treatment. ■ (also **recovery shot**) Golf a stroke bringing the ball from the rough or from a hazard back onto the fairway or the green. ■ Football an act of taking possession of a fumbled ball. ■ (in rowing, cycling, or swimming) the action of returning the paddle, leg, or arm to its initial position ready to make a new stroke.
– PHRASES **in recovery** in the process of recovering from mental illness, drug addiction, or past abuse: *support groups for parents whose children are in recovery.*
– ORIGIN late Middle English (denoting a means of restoration): from Anglo-Norman French *recoverie*, from *recovrer* 'get back.'

re·cov·er·y stock ▶ **n.** Finance a stock that has fallen in price but is thought to have the potential of climbing back to its original level.

re·cov·er·y time ▶ **n.** the time required for a material or piece of equipment to resume its former or usual condition following an action, such as the passage of a current through electrical equipment.

rec·re·ant /ˈrekrēənt/ archaic ▶ **adj. 1** cowardly: *what a recreant figure must he make.*
2 unfaithful to a belief; apostate.
▶ **n. 1** a coward.
2 a person who is unfaithful to a belief; an apostate.
– DERIVATIVES **rec·re·an·cy** /-ənsē/ **n.**, **rec·re·ant·ly** **adv.**
– ORIGIN Middle English: from Old French, literally 'surrendering,' present participle of *recroire*, from medieval Latin *(se) recredere* 'surrender (oneself),' from *re-* (expressing reversal) + *credere* 'entrust.'

re·cre·ate /ˌrēkrēˈāt/ ▶ **v.** [with obj.] create again: *the door was now open to recreate a single German state.* ■ reproduce; re-enact: *he recreated Mallory's 1942 climb for TV.*

rec·re·a·tion[1] /ˌrekrēˈāSHən/ ▶ **n.** activity done for enjoyment when one is not working: *areas used for recreation such as hiking or biking* | [as modifier] *athletic and recreation facilities.*
– ORIGIN late Middle English (also in the sense 'mental or spiritual consolation'): via Old French

PRONUNCIATION KEY ə *ago, up*; ər *over, fur*; a *hat*; ā *ate*; ä *car*; e *let*; ē *see*; i *fit*; ī *by*; NG *sing*; ō *go*; ô *law, for*; oi *toy*; o͝o *good*; o͞o *goo*; ou *out*; TH *thin*; T͟H *then*; ZH *vision*

r

from Latin *recreatio(n-)*, from *recreare* 'create again, renew.'

rec·re·a·tion² /ˌrēkrēˈāSHən/ ▶ **n.** the action or process of creating something again: *the periodic destruction and recreation of the universe.* ■ a re-enactment or simulation of something.
– ORIGIN early 16th cent.: from **RE-** 'again' + **CREATION**.

rec·re·a·tion·al /ˌrekrēˈāSHənl/ ▶ **adj.** relating to or denoting activity done for enjoyment when one is not working: *recreational facilities | recreational cycling in the countryside.* ■ relating to or denoting drugs taken on an occasional basis for enjoyment, esp. when socializing: *recreational drug use.*
– DERIVATIVES **rec·re·a·tion·al·ly adv.**

rec·re·a·tion room ▶ **n.** a room in an institution or place of work in which people can relax and play games. ■ chiefly dated term for **REC ROOM**.

rec·re·a·tive /ˈrekrēˌātiv/ ▶ **adj.** another term for **RECREATIONAL**.

re·crim·i·nate /riˈkriməˌnāt/ ▶ **v.** [no obj.] archaic make counteraccusations: *his party would never recriminate, never return evil for evil.*
– ORIGIN early 17th cent.: from medieval Latin *recriminat-* 'accused in return,' from the verb *recriminari*, from *re-* (expressing opposition) + *criminare* 'accuse' (from *crimen* 'crime').

re·crim·i·na·tion /riˌkriməˈnāSHən/ ▶ **n.** (usu. **recriminations**) an accusation in response to one from someone else: *there are no tears, no recriminations | there was a period of bitter recrimination.*

re·crim·i·na·tive /riˈkriməˌnātiv/ ▶ **adj.** archaic term for **RECRIMINATORY**.

re·crim·i·na·to·ry /riˈkrimənəˌtôrē/ ▶ **adj.** involving or of the nature of mutual accusations or counteraccusations.

rec room (also **recreation room**) ▶ **n.** a room in a house, esp. in the basement, used for recreation and entertainment.

re·cross /ˌrēˈkrôs/ ▶ **v.** [with obj.] cross or pass over again.

re·cru·desce /ˌrēkro͞oˈdes/ ▶ **v.** [no obj.] formal break out again; recur.
– DERIVATIVES **re·cru·des·cence** /-ˈdesns/ **n.**, **re·cru·des·cent** /-ˈdesənt/ **adj.**
– ORIGIN late 19th cent.: back-formation from *recrudescence* 'recurrence,' from Latin *recrudescere* 'become raw again,' from *re-* 'again' + *crudus* 'raw.'

re·cruit /riˈkro͞ot/ ▶ **v.** [with obj.] enlist (someone) in the armed forces: *they recruit their toughest soldiers from the desert tribes | [no obj.] the regiment was still actively recruiting.* ■ form (an army or other force) by enlisting new people: *a basis for recruiting an army.* ■ enroll (someone) as a member or worker in an organization or as a supporter of a cause: *there are plans to recruit more staff later this year.* ■ [with obj. and infinitive] informal persuade (someone) to do or assist in doing something: *she recruited her children to help run the racket.*
▶ **n.** a person newly enlisted in the armed forces and not yet fully trained: *3,000 army recruits at Ft. Benjamin.* ■ a new member of an organization or a new supporter of a cause: *after agreeing on a salary, the new recruit failed to turn up on Monday morning.*
– DERIVATIVES **re·cruit·a·ble adj.**, **re·cruit·er n.**
– ORIGIN mid 17th cent. (in the senses 'fresh body of troops' and 'supplement the numbers in (a group)'): from obsolete French dialect *recrute*, based on Latin *recrescere* 'grow again,' from *re-* 'again' + *crescere* 'grow.'

re·cruit·ment /riˈkro͞otmənt/ ▶ **n.** the action of enlisting new people in the armed forces. ■ the action of finding new people to join an organization or support a cause: *the recruitment of nurses.* ■ Ecology the increase in a natural population as progeny grow and immigrants arrive. ■ Physiology the incorporation into a tissue or region of cells from elsewhere in the body.

re·crys·tal·lize /ˌrēˈkristəˌlīz/ ▶ **v.** form or cause to form crystals again.
– DERIVATIVES **re·crys·tal·li·za·tion n.**

rec. sec. (also **Rec. Sec.**) ▶ **abbr.** recording secretary.

rect. ▶ **abbr.** ■ receipt. ■ rectangle. ■ rectangular. ■ (in prescriptions) rectified. [from Latin *rectificatus*.] ■ rector. ■ rectory.

rec·ta /ˈrektə/ plural form of **RECTUM**.

rec·tal /ˈrektəl/ ▶ **adj.** [attrib.] of, relating to, or affecting the rectum: *rectal cancer.*
– DERIVATIVES **rec·tal·ly adv.**

rec·tan·gle /ˈrekˌtaNGgəl/ ▶ **n.** a plane figure with four straight sides and four right angles, esp. one with unequal adjacent sides, in contrast to a square.
– ORIGIN late 16th cent.: from medieval Latin *rectangulum*, from late Latin *rectiangulum*, based on Latin *rectus* 'straight' + *angulus* 'an angle.'

rec·tan·gu·lar /rekˈtaNGgyələr/ ▶ **adj. 1** denoting or shaped like a rectangle: *a neat rectangular area.* ■ (of a solid) having a base, section, or side shaped like a rectangle: *a rectangular prism.*
2 placed or having parts placed at right angles.
– DERIVATIVES **rec·tan·gu·lar·i·ty** /rekˌtaNGgyəˈlaritē/ **n.**, **rec·tan·gu·lar·ly adv.**

rec·tan·gu·lar co·or·di·nates ▶ **plural n.** a pair of coordinates measured along axes at right angles to one another.

rec·tan·gu·lar hy·per·bo·la ▶ **n.** a hyperbola with rectangular asymptotes.

rec·ti /ˈrekˌtī, -ˌtē/ plural form of **RECTUS**.

rec·ti·fi·er /ˈrektəˌfīər/ ▶ **n.** an electrical device that converts an alternating current into a direct one by allowing a current to flow through it in one direction only.

rec·ti·fy /ˈrektəˌfī/ ▶ **v.** (**rectifies, rectifying, rectified**) [with obj.] **1** put (something) right; correct: *mistakes made now cannot be rectified later | efforts to rectify the situation.* ■ (usu. as adj. **rectified**) purify or refine (a substance), esp. by repeated distillation: *add 10 cc of rectified alcohol.*
2 convert (alternating current) to direct current: (as adj. **rectified**) *rectified AC power systems.*
3 find a straight line equal in length to (a curve).
– DERIVATIVES **rec·ti·fi·a·ble adj.**, **rec·ti·fi·ca·tion** /ˌrektəfiˈkāSHən/ **n.**
– ORIGIN late Middle English: from Old French *rectifier*, from medieval Latin *rectificare*, from Latin *rectus* 'right.'

rec·ti·lin·e·ar /ˌrektəˈlinēər/ (also **rectilineal** /-ēəl/) ▶ **adj.** contained by, consisting of, or moving in a straight line or lines: *a rectilinear waveform.* ■ Photography of or relating to a straight line or lines: *rectilinear distortion.* ■ Photography (of a wide-angle lens) corrected as much as possible, so that straight lines in the subject appear straight in the image.
– DERIVATIVES **rec·ti·lin·e·ar·i·ty** /-ˌlinēˈaritē/ **n.**, **rec·ti·lin·e·ar·ly adv.**
– ORIGIN mid 17th cent.: from late Latin *rectilineus* (from Latin *rectus* 'straight' + *linea* 'line') + **-AR¹**.

rec·ti·tude /ˈrektəˌt(y)o͞od/ ▶ **n.** formal morally correct behavior or thinking; righteousness: *Maddie is a model of rectitude.*
– ORIGIN late Middle English (denoting straightness): from Old French, from late Latin *rectitudo*, from Latin *rectus* 'right, straight.'

rec·to /ˈrektō/ ▶ **n.** (pl. **rectos**) a right-hand page of an open book, or the front of a loose document. Contrasted with **VERSO**.
– ORIGIN early 19th cent.: from Latin *recto (folio)* 'on the right (leaf).'

rec·to·cele /ˈrektəˌsēl/ ▶ **n.** Medicine a prolapse of the wall between the rectum and the vagina.
– ORIGIN mid 19th cent.: from **RECTUM** + **-CELE**.

rec·tor /ˈrektər/ ▶ **n. 1** (in the Episcopal Church) a member of the clergy who has charge of a parish. ■ (in the Roman Catholic Church) a priest in charge of a church or of a religious institution. ■ (in the Church of England) the incumbent of a parish where all tithes formerly passed to the incumbent. Compare with **VICAR**.
2 the head of certain universities, colleges, and schools.
– DERIVATIVES **rec·tor·ate** /-rət/ **n.**, **rec·to·ri·al** /rekˈtôrēəl/ **adj.**, **rec·tor·ship** /-ˌSHip/ **n.**
– ORIGIN late Middle English: from Latin *rector* 'ruler,' from *rect-* 'ruled,' from the verb *regere*.

rec·to·ry /ˈrektərē/ ▶ **n.** (pl. **rectories**) a rector's house. ■ a Church of England benefice held by a rector.
– ORIGIN mid 16th cent.: from Old French *rectorie* or medieval Latin *rectoria*, from Latin *rector* (see **RECTOR**).

rec·trix /ˈrekˌtriks/ ▶ **n.** (pl. **rectrices** /-ˌtrəsēz/) Ornithology any of the larger feathers in a bird's tail, used for steering in flight. Compare with **REMEX**.
– ORIGIN mid 18th cent.: from Latin, feminine singular of *rector* 'ruler, governor' (see **RECTOR**).

rec·tum /ˈrektəm/ ▶ **n.** (pl. **rectums** or **recta** /-tə/) the final section of the large intestine, terminating at the anus.
– ORIGIN mid 16th cent.: from Latin *rectum (intestinum)* 'straight (intestine).'

rec·tus /ˈrektəs/ ▶ **n.** (pl. **recti** /-tī/) Anatomy any of several straight structures, in particular: ■ (also **rectus abdominis** /abˈdämənis/) each of a pair of long flat muscles at the front of the abdomen, joining the sternum to the pubis and acting to bend the whole body forward or sideways. ■ any of a number of muscles controlling the movement of the eyeball.
– ORIGIN early 18th cent.: from Latin, literally 'straight.'

re·cum·bent /riˈkəmbənt/ ▶ **adj.** (esp. of a person or human figure) lying down: *recumbent statues.* ■ (of a bicycle) designed to be ridden lying almost flat on one's back or sitting up with the legs stretched out in front. ■ (of a plant) growing close to the ground: *recumbent shrubs.*
▶ **n.** a recumbent bicycle.
– DERIVATIVES **re·cum·ben·cy n.**, **re·cum·bent·ly adv.**
– ORIGIN mid 17th cent.: from Latin *recumbent-* 'reclining,' from the verb *recumbere*, from *re-* 'back' + a verb related to *cubare* 'to lie.'

re·cu·per·ate /riˈko͞opəˌrāt/ ▶ **v. 1** [no obj.] recover from illness or exertion: *she has been recuperating from a shoulder wound | Christmas is a time to recuperate.*
2 [with obj.] recover or regain (something lost or taken): *they will seek to recuperate the returns that go with investment.*
– DERIVATIVES **re·cu·per·a·ble** /-pərəbəl/ **adj.**
– ORIGIN mid 16th cent.: from Latin *recuperat-* 'regained,' from the verb *recuperare*, from *re-* 'back' + *capere* 'take.'

re·cu·per·a·tion /riˌko͞opəˈrāSHən/ ▶ **n. 1** recovery from illness or exertion: *the human body has amazing powers of recuperation.*
2 the recovery or regaining of something: *the recuperation of the avant-garde for art.* ■ the action of a recuperator in imparting heat to incoming air or gaseous fuel from hot waste gases.

re·cu·per·a·tive /riˈko͞opəˌrātiv/ ▶ **adj. 1** having the effect of restoring health or strength.
2 of or relating to the action of a recuperator or a similar heat exchanger.

re·cu·per·a·tor /riˈko͞opəˌrātər/ ▶ **n.** a form of heat exchanger in which hot waste gases from a furnace are conducted continuously along a system of flues where they impart heat to incoming air or gaseous fuel.

re·cur /riˈkər/ ▶ **v.** (**recurs, recurring, recurred**) [no obj.] occur again, periodically, or repeatedly: *when the symptoms recurred, the doctor diagnosed something different* | (as adj. **recurring**) *a recurring theme.* ■ (of a thought, image, or memory) come back to one's mind: *Steve's words kept recurring to him.* ■ (**recur to**) go back to (something) in thought or speech: *the book remained a favorite and she constantly recurred to it.*
– DERIVATIVES **re·cur·rence** /riˈkərəns, -ˈkə-rəns/ **n.**
– ORIGIN Middle English (in the sense 'return to'): from Latin *recurrere*, from *re-* 'again, back' + *currere* 'run.'

re·cur·rent /riˈkərənt, -ˈkə-rənt/ ▶ **adj. 1** occurring often or repeatedly: *she had a recurrent dream about falling.*
2 Anatomy (of a nerve or blood vessel) turning back so as to reverse direction.
– DERIVATIVES **re·cur·rent·ly adv.**
– ORIGIN late 16th cent. (sense 2): from Latin *recurrent-* 'running back,' from the verb *recurrere* (see **RECUR**).

re·cur·ring dec·i·mal ▶ **n.** a repeating decimal.

re·cur·sion /riˈkərZHən/ ▶ **n.** Mathematics & Linguistics the repeated application of a recursive procedure or definition. ■ a recursive definition.
– ORIGIN 1930s: from late Latin *recursio(n-)*, from *recurrere* 'run back' (see **RECUR**).

re·cur·sion for·mu·la ▶ **n.** Mathematics an equation relating the value of a function for a given value of its argument (or arguments) to its values for other values of the argument(s).

re·cur·sive /riˈkərsiv/ ▶ **adj.** characterized by recurrence or repetition, in particular: ■ Mathematics & Linguistics relating to or involving the repeated application of a rule, definition, or procedure to successive results. ■ Computing relating to or involving a program or routine of which a part requires the application of the whole, so that its explicit interpretation requires in general many successive executions.
– DERIVATIVES **re·cur·sive·ly adv.**
– ORIGIN late 18th cent. (in the general sense): from late Latin *recurs-* 'returned' (from the verb *recurrere* 'run back') + **-IVE**. Specific uses have arisen in the 20th cent.

re·curve /rēˈkərv/ ▶ **v.** [no obj.] chiefly Biology bend backward: (as adj. **recurved**) *large recurved tusks.*
▶ **n.** Archery a bow that curves forward at the ends, which straighten out under tension when the bow is drawn.
– DERIVATIVES **re·cur·va·ture** /-vəCHər/ **n.**
– ORIGIN late 16th cent.: from Latin *recurvare* 'bend (something) back,' from *re-* 'back' + *curvare* 'to bend.'

rec·u·sant /ˈrekyəzənt, riˈkyo͞ozənt/ ▶ **n.** a person who refuses to submit to an authority or to comply with a regulation. ■ chiefly historical a Roman Catholic in England who refused to attend services of the Church of England.

r

▸ **adj.** of or denoting a recusant.
– DERIVATIVES **rec·u·sance n.**, **rec·u·san·cy** /-zənsē/ **n.**
– ORIGIN mid 16th cent.: from Latin *recusant-* 'refusing,' from the verb *recusare* (see **RECUSE**).

re·cuse /riˈkyo͞oz/ ▸ **v.** [with obj.] challenge (a judge, prosecutor, or juror) as unqualified to perform legal duties because of a possible conflict of interest or lack of impartiality: *a motion to recuse the prosecutor.* ■ (**recuse oneself**) (of a judge) excuse oneself from a case because of a possible conflict of interest or lack of impartiality: *the Justice Department demanded that he recuse himself from the case.*
– DERIVATIVES **re·cus·al** /-zəl/ **n.**
– ORIGIN late Middle English (in the sense 'reject,' specifically 'object to (a judge) as prejudiced'): from Latin *recusare* 'to refuse,' from *re-* (expressing opposition) + *causa* 'a cause.' The sense 'excuse (oneself from a case)' dates from the early 19th cent.

re·cut /rēˈkət/ ▸ **v.** (**recuts, recutting**; past and past participle **recut**) [with obj.] remove further or different material from (a film or screenplay): *director Tony Scott is recutting several key scenes.*

re·cy·cla·ble /rēˈsīk(ə)ləbəl/ ▸ **adj.** able to be recycled.
▸ **n.** a substance or object that can be recycled.
– DERIVATIVES **re·cy·cla·bil·i·ty** /-ˌsīk(ə)ləˈbilitē/ **n.**

re·cy·cle /rēˈsīkəl/ ▸ **v.** [with obj.] convert (waste) into reusable material: *car hulks were recycled into new steel* | (as adj. **recycled**) *goods made of recycled materials* | (as noun **recycling**) *a call for the recycling of all paper.* ■ return (material) to a previous stage in a cyclic process. ■ use again: *he reserves the right to recycle his own text.*
– DERIVATIVES **re·cy·cler** /-k(ə)lər/ **n.**

red /red/ ▸ **adj.** (**redder, reddest**) **1** of a color at the end of the spectrum next to orange and opposite violet, as of blood, fire, or rubies: *her red lips* | *the sky was turning red outside.* ■ (of a person or their face or complexion) flushed or rosy, esp. with embarrassment, anger, or a healthy glow: *there were some red faces at headquarters.* ■ (of a person's eyes) bloodshot or having pink rims, esp. with tiredness or crying: *her eyes were red and swollen.* ■ (of hair or fur) of a reddish-brown color. ■ dated, offensive (of a people) having or regarded as having reddish skin. ■ of or denoting the suits hearts and diamonds in a deck of cards. ■ (of wine) made from dark grapes and colored by their skins. ■ denoting a red light or flag used as a signal to stop. ■ used to denote something forbidden, dangerous, or urgent: *the force went on red alert.* ■ (of a ski run) of the second highest level of difficulty, as indicated by colored markers. ■ Physics denoting one of three colors of quark.
2 (**Red**) informal, chiefly derogatory communist or socialist (used esp. during the Cold War with reference to the former Soviet Union).
3 archaic or literary stained with blood, or involving bloodshed or violence: *red battle stamps his foot and nations feel the shock.*
▸ **n. 1** red color or pigment: *colors range from yellow to deep red* | *their work is marked in red by the teacher* | *the reds and browns of wood.* ■ red clothes or material: *she could not wear red.*
2 a red thing or person, in particular: ■ a red wine. ■ a red ball in billiards. ■ a red light.
3 (also **Red**) informal, chiefly derogatory a communist or socialist.
4 (**the red**) the situation of owing money or showing a debit: *the company was $4,000,000* ***in the red.*** [from the conventional use of *red* to indicate debt items.]
– PHRASES **better dead than red** (or **better red than dead**) a cold-war slogan claiming that the prospect of nuclear war is preferable to that of a communist society (or vice versa). (**as**) **red as a beet** (of a person) red-faced, typically through embarrassment. **red in tooth and claw** involving savage or merciless conflict or competition: *nature, red in tooth and claw.* [from Tennyson's *In Memoriam.*] **the red planet** a name for Mars. **the red, white, and blue** informal the US national flag: *learning respect for the red, white, and blue.* **see red** informal become very angry suddenly: *the mere thought of Peter with Nicole made her see red.*
– DERIVATIVES **red·dish adj.**, **red·dy adj.**, **red·ly adv.**, **red·ness n.**
– ORIGIN Old English *rēad,* of Germanic origin; related to Dutch *rood* and German *rot,* from an Indo-European root shared by Latin *rufus, ruber,* Greek *eruthros,* and Sanskrit *rudhira-* 'red.'

red. ▸ **abbr.** reduction.

red- ▸ **prefix** variant spelling of **RE-** before a vowel (as in *redeem, redolent*).

re·dact /riˈdakt/ ▸ **v.** [with obj.] edit (text) for publication. ■ censor or obscure (part of a text) for legal or security purposes.
– DERIVATIVES **re·dac·tor** /-tər/ **n.**
– ORIGIN mid 19th cent.: back-formation from **REDACTION**.

re·dac·tion /riˈdakSHən/ ▸ **n.** the process of editing text for publication. ■ a version of a text, such as a new edition or an abridged version. ■ the censoring or obscuring of part of a text for legal or security purposes.
– DERIVATIVES **re·dac·tion·al** /-SHənl/ **adj.**
– ORIGIN late 18th cent.: from French *rédaction,* from late Latin *redactio(n-),* from *redigere* 'bring back.'

red ad·mi·ral ▸ **n.** a migratory butterfly that has dark wings marked with red-orange bands and white spots. ● Genus *Vanessa,* subfamily Nymphalinae, family Nymphalidae: several species, in particular the common and widespread *V. atalanta.*

red admiral

red al·gae ▸ **n.** a large group of algae that includes many seaweeds that are mainly red in color. Some kinds yield useful products (agar, alginates) or are used as food (laver, dulse, carrageen). ● Division Rhodophyta (or phylum Rhodophyta, kingdom Protista).

re·dan /riˈdan/ ▸ **n.** an arrow-shaped embankment forming part of a fortification.
– ORIGIN late 17th cent.: from French, from *redent* 'notching (of a saw),' from *re-* 'again' (expressing repetition) + *dent* 'tooth.'

Red Ar·my the army of the former Soviet Union, formed after the revolution of 1917. The name was officially dropped in 1946. ■ the army of China or some other communist countries.

Red Ar·my Fac·tion a left-wing terrorist group in the former West Germany, active from 1968 onward. It was originally led by **Andreas Baader** (1943–77) and **Ulrike Meinhof** (1934–76). Also called **BAADER-MEINHOF GROUP**.

red-backed vole ▸ **n.** a vole with a reddish-chestnut back, inhabiting the forest, scrub, and tundra regions of the northern hemisphere. ● Genus *Clethrionomys,* family Muridae: several species.

red-bait ▸ **v.** [with obj.] (often as noun **red-baiting**) informal harass or persecute (someone) on account of known or suspected communist sympathies.
– DERIVATIVES **red-bait·er n.**

red beds ▸ **plural n.** Geology sandstones or other sedimentary strata colored red by hematite coating the grains.

red blood cell ▸ **n.** less technical term for **ERYTHROCYTE**.

red-blood·ed ▸ **adj.** (of a man) vigorous or virile, esp. in having strong heterosexual appetites: *he was attracted to her, as any red-blooded male would be.*
– DERIVATIVES **red-blood·ed·ness n.**

red·bone /ˈredˌbōn/ ▸ **n.** a dog with a red or red and tan coat of an American breed formerly used to hunt raccoons.

red·breast /ˈredˌbrest/ ▸ **n.** informal a robin.

red·brick ▸ **adj.** built with red bricks. ■ (of a British university) founded in the late 19th or early 20th century and with buildings of brick, as distinct from the older universities built of stone.

Red Bri·gades an extreme left-wing terrorist organization based in Italy that from the early 1970s was responsible for carrying out kidnappings, murders, and acts of sabotage.

red·bud /ˈredˌbəd/ ▸ **n.** a North American tree of the pea family, with pink flowers that grow from the trunk, branches, and twigs. ● Genus *Cercis,* family Leguminosae: several species, in particular **eastern redbud** (*C. canadensis*).

red·cap /ˈredˌkap/ ▸ **n. 1** a railroad porter. [late 19th cent.: first used because John Williams, a porter in Grand Central Terminal, New York City, wore a cap with a red flannel strip in order to attract attention.]
2 Brit. informal a member of the military police.

red card ▸ **n.** (in soccer and some other games) a red card shown by the referee to a player who is being ejected from the game. Compare with **YELLOW CARD**.
▸ **v.** (**red-card**) [with obj.] (of a referee) eject (a player) from the game by showing the red card: *he did his pushing directly in front of the referee and was red-carded.*

red car·pet ▸ **n.** a long, narrow red carpet laid on the ground for a distinguished visitor to walk on when arriving. ■ (**the red carpet**) privileged treatment of a distinguished visitor: *they rolled out the red carpet for two special guests.*

red ce·dar ▸ **n.** either of two North American coniferous trees with reddish-brown bark. ● Two species in the family Cupressaceae: the **western red cedar** (*Thuja plicata*), which yields strong, lightweight timber, and the **eastern red cedar** (*Juniperus virginiana*), found chiefly in the eastern US.

red cell ▸ **n.** less technical term for **ERYTHROCYTE**.

red cent ▸ **n.** a one-cent coin; a penny. ■ [usu. with negative] the smallest amount of money: *some of the people don't deserve a single red cent.*
– ORIGIN early 19th cent.: so named because it was formerly made of copper.

red chan·nel ▸ **n.** in many countries, the passage that should be taken (at a customs area in an airport or port) by arriving passengers who have goods to declare: *when we arrived in Bangkok, we were told to proceed to the red channel.*

Red Cloud (1822–1909), leader of the Oglala Sioux Indians; Indian name *Makhpiya-luta.* He opposed, in what became known as Red Cloud's War 1865–68, the US government's attempts to build forts along the Bozeman Trail in Wyoming and Montana. By his forcing of the Fort Laramie Treaty in 1868, peace was guaranteed when the government accepted the territorial claims of the Sioux.

red·coat /ˈredˌkōt/ ▸ **n.** historical a British soldier.
– ORIGIN early 16th cent.: so named because of the color of the uniform.

red cor·al ▸ **n.** a branching pinkish-red horny coral that is used in jewelry. Also called **PRECIOUS CORAL**. ● Genus *Corallium,* order Gorgonacea, class Anthozoa.

Red Cres·cent a national branch in Muslim countries of the International Movement of the Red Cross and the Red Crescent.

Red Cross the International Movement of the Red Cross and the Red Crescent, an international humanitarian organization that provides relief to victims of war or natural disaster. The Red Cross was set up in 1864 at the instigation of the Swiss philanthropist **Henri Dunant** (1828–1910) according to the Geneva Convention, and its headquarters are in Geneva.

red cur·rant (Brit. also **redcurrant**) ▸ **n. 1** a small, sweet, edible red berry.
2 the shrub that produces this fruit. ● Genus *Ribes,* family Grossulariaceae: several species, including the European *R. rubrum* and the North American **garden red currant** (*R. sativum*).

redd[1] /red/ ▸ **v.** (past and past participle **redd**) [with obj.] (**redd something up**) dialect put something in order; tidy: *you take this baby while I redd the room up.*
– ORIGIN late Middle English (in the sense 'clear (space)'): perhaps related to **RID**.

redd[2] ▸ **n.** a hollow in a riverbed made by a trout or salmon to spawn in.
– ORIGIN mid 17th cent. (originally Scots and northern English in the sense 'spawn'): of unknown origin.

red deer ▸ **n.** a deer with a rich red-brown summer coat that turns dull brownish-gray in winter, the male having large branched antlers. It is native to North America, Eurasia, and North Africa. ● *Cervus elaphus,* family Cervidae. Compare with **ELK**.

Red De·li·cious ▸ **n.** a widely grown dessert apple of a soft-fleshed red-skinned variety.

red·den /ˈredn/ ▸ **v.** make or become red: [with obj.] *bare arms reddened by sun and wind* | [no obj.] *the sky is reddening.* ■ [no obj.] (of a person) blush: *Lynn reddened at the description of herself.* ■ [no obj.] (of the eyes) become pink at the rims as a result of crying.

PRONUNCIATION KEY ə *ago, up;* ər *over, fur;* a *hat;* ā *ate;* ä *car;* e *let;* ē *see;* i *fit;* ī *by;* NG *sing;* ō *go;* ô *law, for;* oi *toy;* o͝o *good;* o͞o *goo;* ou *out;* TH *thin;* T͟H *then;* ZH *vision*

Red·ding[1] /ˈrediNG/ a commercial and resort city in northern California, at the northern end of the Sacramento Valley; pop. 90,201 (est. 2008).

Red·ding[2], Otis (1941–67), US singer. He was one of the most influential soul singers of the late 1960s. It was not until the Monterey pop festival in 1967 that he gained widespread recognition. "Dock of the Bay," released after his death in an airplane crash, became a number-one US hit in 1968.

red·dle /ˈredl/ ▶ n. another term for RUDDLE.
– ORIGIN early 18th cent.: variant of RUDDLE.

red dwarf ▶ n. Astronomy a small, old, relatively cool star.

rede /rēd/ archaic ▶ n. advice or counsel given by one person to another: *what is your rede?*
▶ v. [with obj.] **1** advise (someone): [with obj. and infinitive] *therefore, my son, I rede thee stay at home.*
2 interpret (a riddle or dream).
– ORIGIN Old English *rǣd*, of Germanic origin; related to Dutch *raad*, German *Rat*. The verb is a variant of READ, of the same origin.

re·dec·o·rate /rēˈdekəˌrāt/ ▶ v. [with obj.] decorate (a room or building) again, typically differently.
– DERIVATIVES **re·dec·o·ra·tion** /ˌrēˌdekəˈrāsHən/ n.

re·ded·i·cate /ˌrēˈdediˌkāt/ ▶ v. [with obj.] dedicate again: *the cathedral was eventually rededicated in June 1997.*
– DERIVATIVES **re·ded·i·ca·tion** n.

re·deem /riˈdēm/ ▶ v. [with obj.] **1** compensate for the faults or bad aspects of (something): *a disappointing debate redeemed only by an outstanding speech* | (as adj. **redeeming**) *the splendid views are the one redeeming feature of the center.* ■ (**redeem oneself**) do something that compensates for poor past performance or behavior: *they redeemed themselves in the playoffs by pushing the Detroit Red Wings to a seventh and deciding game.* ■ (of a person) atone or make amends for (error or evil): *the thief on the cross who by a single act redeemed a life of evil.* ■ save (someone) from sin, error, or evil: *he was a sinner, redeemed by the grace of God.*
2 gain or regain possession of (something) in exchange for payment: *his best suit had been redeemed from the pawnbrokers.* ■ Finance repay (a stock, bond, or other instrument) at the maturity date. ■ exchange (a coupon, voucher, or trading stamp) for merchandise, a discount, or money. ■ pay the necessary money to clear (a debt): *owners were unable to redeem their mortgages.* ■ fulfill or carry out (a pledge or promise): *the party prepared to redeem the pledges of the past three years.* ■ archaic buy the freedom of.
– DERIVATIVES **re·deem·a·ble** adj.
– ORIGIN late Middle English (in the sense 'buy back'): from Old French *redimer* or Latin *redimere*, from *re(d)-* 'back' + *emere* 'buy.'

re·deem·er /riˈdēmər/ ▶ n. a person who redeems someone or something. ■ (often **the Redeemer**) Christ.

re·deem·ing /riˈdēmiNG/ ▶ adj. **1** compensating for someone's or something's faults; compensatory: *tuneless dirges with few redeeming features.*
2 able to save people from sin, error, or evil: *the transforming power of God's redeeming grace.*

re·de·fine /ˌrēdiˈfīn/ ▶ v. [with obj.] define again or differently: *her attempt to redefine postmodernism along more political and sociocultural lines.*
– DERIVATIVES **re·def·i·ni·tion** /ˌrēˌdefəˈnisHən/ n.

re·demp·tion /riˈdempsHən/ ▶ n. **1** the action of saving or being saved from sin, error, or evil: *God's plans for the redemption of his world.* ■ [in sing.] a thing that saves someone from error or evil: *his marginalization from the Hollywood jungle proved to be his redemption.*
2 the action of regaining or gaining possession of something in exchange for payment, or clearing a debt. ■ archaic the action of buying one's freedom.
– PHRASES **beyond** (or **past**) **redemption** (of a person or thing) too bad to be improved or saved.
– ORIGIN late Middle English: from Old French, from Latin *redemptio(n-)*, from *redimere* 'buy back' (see REDEEM).

re·demp·tion yield ▶ n. Finance the yield of a stock calculated as a percentage of the redemption price with an adjustment made for any capital gain or loss the price represents relative to the current price.

re·demp·tive /riˈdemptiv/ ▶ adj. acting to save someone from error or evil: *the healing power of redemptive love.*

red en·sign ▶ n. a red flag with the Union Jack in the top corner next to the flagstaff, flown by British-registered ships.

re·de·ploy /ˌrēdəˈploi/ ▶ v. [with obj.] assign (troops, employees, or resources) to a new place or task: *units concentrated in Buenos Aires would be redeployed to the provinces.*
– DERIVATIVES **re·de·ploy·ment** n.

re·de·sign /ˌrēdiˈzīn/ ▶ v. [with obj.] design (something) again in a different way: *the front seats have been redesigned.*
▶ n. the action or process of redesigning something.

re·des·ig·nate /ˌrēˈdezignāt/ ▶ v. [with obj.] give (someone or something) a different official name, description, or title: *the territories have been redesignated as national parks.*
– DERIVATIVES **re·des·ig·na·tion** n.

re·de·ter·mine /ˌrēdiˈtərmən/ ▶ v. [with obj.] determine (something) again or differently.
– DERIVATIVES **re·de·ter·mi·na·tion** /-ˌtərməˈnāsHən/ n.

re·de·vel·op /ˌrēdiˈveləp/ ▶ v. [with obj.] develop (something) again or differently. ■ erect new buildings in (an urban area), typically after demolishing the existing buildings: *the riverfront that the city planned to redevelop with family attractions.*
– DERIVATIVES **re·de·vel·op·er** n., **re·de·vel·op·ment** n.

red-eye ▶ n. **1** the undesirable effect in flash photography of people appearing to have red eyes, caused by a reflection from the retina when the flashgun is too near the camera lens.
2 (also **red-eye flight**) [in sing.] informal an overnight or late-night flight on a commercial airline: *she caught the red-eye back to New York.*
3 a freshwater fish with red eyes, in particular a rock bass.
4 informal cheap whiskey.

red-eye gra·vy ▶ n. gravy made by adding liquid to the fat from cooked ham.

red-faced ▶ adj. (of a person) having a red face, esp. as a result of exertion, embarrassment, or shame: *Steve was left red-faced when a fan tried to rip his pants off.*

red·fish /ˈredˌfisH/ ▶ n. (pl. **same** or **redfishes**) **1** a bright red edible marine fish, in particular: ● a North Atlantic rockfish (genus *Sebastes*, family Scorpaenidae, in particular the commercially important *S. marinus*). ● the red drum of the western Atlantic, popular as a game fish (*Sciaenops ocellatus*, family Sciaenidae).
2 Brit. a male salmon in the spawning season.

red flag ▶ n. a red flag as a warning of danger or a problem: figurative *they had overlooked the red flags that should have alerted them to the county's disastrous investment strategy* | figurative *you have unusually large amounts of deductions or expenses that act as red flags.* ■ a red flag as the symbol of socialist revolution.

red flan·nel hash ▶ n. a type of hash made with beets.

Red·ford /ˈredfərd/, Robert (1936–), US movie actor and director; full name *Charles Robert Redford*. As an actor, his movies include *Butch Cassidy and the Sundance Kid* (1969), *The Sting* (1973), *The Natural* (1984), and *Out of Africa* (1985). His directing credits include *Ordinary People* (1980) and *A River Runs through It* (1992).

red fox ▶ n. a common fox with a reddish coat, native to both Eurasia and North America and living from the Arctic tundra to the southern temperate regions. ● *Vulpes vulpes*, family Canidae.

red fox

red gi·ant ▶ n. Astronomy a very large star of high luminosity and low surface temperature. Red giants are thought to be in a late stage of evolution when no hydrogen remains in the core to fuel nuclear fusion.

red gold ▶ n. an alloy of gold and copper.

Red·grave /ˈredˌgrāv/ the name of a family of English actors, notably: ■ **Sir Michael (Scudamore)** (1908–85), stage actor. He played numerous Shakespearean roles and also starred in movies, such as *The Browning Version* (1951) and *The Importance of Being Earnest* (1952). ■ **Vanessa** (1937–), Sir Michael's eldest child. Her movies include *Mary Queen of Scots* (1972), *Julia* (1976), and *Howard's End* (1992). Other actors in the family include her siblings **Corin** (1939–2010) and **Lynn** (1944–2010), best known for her title role in *Georgy Girl* (1966), Corin's daughter **Jemma** (1965–), and Vanessa's daughters **Joely Richardson** (1958–) and **Natasha Richardson** (1963–2009).

red–green ▶ adj. [attrib.] denoting color-blindness in which reds and greens are confused, either protanopia (daltonism) or deuteranopia.

red grouse ▶ n. a bird of a race of the willow ptarmigan having entirely reddish-brown plumage, native only to the British Isles. ● *Lagopus lagopus scoticus*, family Phasianidae (or Tetraonidae).

Red Guard ▶ n. any of various radical or socialist groups, in particular a militant youth movement in China (1966–76) that carried out attacks on intellectuals and other disfavored groups as part of Mao Zedong's Cultural Revolution. ■ a member of one of these groups.

red gum ▶ n. an Australian gum tree with smooth bark and hard dark red timber. ● Genera *Eucalyptus* and *Angophora*, family Myrtaceae: many species, in particular the widespread **river red gum** (*E. camaldulensis*). ■ astringent reddish kino gum obtained from some of these trees, used for medicinal purposes and for tanning.

red-hand·ed ▶ adj. (of a person) having been discovered in or just after the act of doing something wrong or illegal: *I caught him red-handed, stealing a wallet.*

red hat ▶ n. a cardinal's hat, esp. as the symbol of a cardinal's office.

red·head /ˈredˌhed/ ▶ n. **1** a person with reddish hair.
2 a North American diving duck with a reddish-brown head, related to and resembling the pochard. ● *Aythya americana*, family Anatidae.

red-head·ed ▶ adj. [attrib.] (of a person) having reddish-brown hair: *a red-headed man.* ■ used in names of birds, insects, and other animals with red heads, e.g., **red-headed woodpecker**.

red heat ▶ n. the temperature or state of something so hot that it emits red light.

red her·ring ▶ n. **1** a dried smoked herring, which is turned red by the smoke.
2 something, esp. a clue, that is or is intended to be misleading or distracting: *the book is fast-paced, exciting, and full of red herrings.* [so named from the practice of using the scent of red herring in training hounds.]

Red Hook an industrial port section of Brooklyn in New York City, on New York Bay, across from Governor's Island.

red-hot ▶ adj. **1** (of a substance) so hot as to glow red: *red-hot coals.* ■ very hot, esp. too hot to touch: *the red-hot handle burned his hand* | figurative *the red-hot attack letter they received last week.*
2 extremely exciting or popular: *red-hot jazz.* ■ very passionate: *a red-hot lover.*

red-hot pok·er ▶ n. a South African plant with tall erect spikes of tubular flowers, the upper ones of which are typically red and the lower ones yellow. ● *Kniphofia uvaria*, family Liliaceae: many cultivars.

re·di·al ▶ v. /rēˈdīl/ (**redials**, **redialing**, **redialed**; Brit. **redialling**, **redialled**) [with obj.] dial (a telephone number) again, esp. automatically.
▶ n. /ˈrēˌdīl/ (also **last number redial**) the facility on a telephone by which the number just dialed may be automatically redialed by pressing a single button.

re·did /rēˈdid/ past of REDO.

Red In·di·an ▶ n. chiefly Brit. old-fashioned term for AMERICAN INDIAN.

USAGE See usage at REDSKIN.

red·in·gote /ˈrediNGˌgōt/ ▶ n. a woman's long coat with a cutaway or contrasting front. ■ a man's double-breasted topcoat with a full skirt.
– ORIGIN late 18th cent.: French, from English *riding coat*.

red ink ▶ n. used in reference to financial deficit or debt: *he voted for many of the projects that have left the state awash in red ink.*

red·in·te·grate /riˈdintəˌgrāt/ ▶ v. [with obj.] archaic restore (something) to a state of wholeness, unity, or perfection.
– DERIVATIVES **red·in·te·gra·tion** /riˌdintəˈgrāsHən/ n., **red·in·te·gra·tive** /-ˌgrātiv/ adj.
– ORIGIN late Middle English: from Latin *redintegrat-* 'made whole,' from the verb *redintegrare*, from *re(d)-* 'again' + *integrare* 'restore.'

re·di·rect /ˌrēdəˈrekt, -ˌdī-/ ▶ **v.** [with obj.] direct (something) to a new or different place or purpose: *get the post office to redirect your mail* | *resources were redirected to a major project.*
– DERIVATIVES **re·di·rec·tion** /-ˈreksHən/ **n.**

re·dis·count /rēˈdisˌkount/ Finance ▶ **v.** [with obj.] (of a central bank) discount (a bill of exchange or similar instrument) that has already been discounted by a commercial bank.
▶ **n.** the action of rediscounting something.

re·dis·cov·er /ˌrēdisˈkəvər/ ▶ **v.** [with obj.] discover (something forgotten or ignored) again: *he was trying to rediscover his Gaelic roots.*
– DERIVATIVES **re·dis·cov·er·y** /-ˈkəv(ə)rē/ **n.** (pl. **rediscoveries**).

re·dis·solve /ˌrēdiˈzälv/ ▶ **v.** dissolve or cause to dissolve again.
– DERIVATIVES **re·dis·so·lu·tion n.**

re·dis·tri·bute /ˌrēdəˈstribˌyo͞ot/ ▶ **v.** [with obj.] distribute (something) differently or again, typically to achieve greater social equality: *their primary concern was to redistribute income from rich to poor.*
– DERIVATIVES **re·dis·tri·bu·tion** /ˌrēˌdistrəˈbyo͞osHən/ **n.**, **re·dis·trib·u·tive** /-ˈstribyətiv/ **adj.**

re·dis·tri·bu·tion·ist /ˌrēˌdistrəˈbyo͞osHənist/ ▶ **n.** a person who advocates the redistribution of wealth.
▶ **adj.** of or relating to the belief that wealth should be redistributed: *redistributionist measures.*
– DERIVATIVES **re·dis·tri·bu·tion·ism** /-ˌnizəm/ **n.**

re·di·vide /ˌrēdiˈvīd/ ▶ **v.** [with obj.] divide (something) again or differently: *they were looking to redivide Europe into rival spheres of influence.*
– DERIVATIVES **re·di·vi·sion** /-ˈvizHən/ **n.**

red·i·vi·vus /ˌredəˈvīvəs, -ˈvēvəs/ ▶ **adj.** [postpositive] literary come back to life; reborn: *one is tempted to think of Poussin as a sort of Titian redivivus.*
– ORIGIN late 16th cent.: from Latin, from *re(d)-* 'again' + *vivus* 'living.'

Red Jack·et (c.1758–1830), Native American Seneca leader; Indian name *Sagoyewatha.* A gifted orator, he advised his people at council fires and defended them at treaty sessions and before government agencies. He received a symbolic medal from President Washington in 1792.

red kan·ga·roo ▶ **n.** a large kangaroo of Australian grasslands, the male of which has a russet-red coat and the female typically a blue-gray coat.
● *Macropus rufus,* family Macropodidae.

Red·lands /ˈredləndz/ a commercial and resort city in southern California, near the San Bernardino Mountains; pop. 69,689 (est. 2008).

red lead ▶ **n.** a red form of lead oxide used as a pigment.

Red Leices·ter ▶ **n.** see **LEICESTER**[2].

red-let·ter day ▶ **n.** a day that is pleasantly noteworthy or memorable.
– ORIGIN early 18th cent.: from the practice of highlighting a festival in red on a calendar.

red light ▶ **n.** a red traffic light or similar signal that instructs moving vehicles to stop. ■ a refusal, or an order to stop an action: *some subsidies would get a red light and be prohibited.*

red-light dis·trict ▶ **n.** an area of a town or city containing many brothels, strip clubs, and other sex businesses.
– ORIGIN late 19th cent.: from the use of a red light as the sign of a brothel.

red·line /ˈredˌlīn/ informal ▶ **v.** [with obj.] **1** drive with (a car engine) at or above its rated maximum rpm: *both his engines were redlined now.*
2 refuse (a loan or insurance) to someone because they live in an area deemed to be a poor financial risk. ■ cancel (a project).
▶ **n.** the maximum number of revolutions per minute for a car engine.
– ORIGIN from the use of *red* as a limit marker, sense 2 of the verb a limit marked out by ringing a section of a map.

red man ▶ **n.** dated, offensive an American Indian.

USAGE See usage at **REDSKIN.**

red meat ▶ **n.** meat that is red when raw, for example beef or lamb. Often contrasted with **WHITE MEAT.**

Red·mond /ˈredmənd/ a city in west central Washington, northeast of Seattle; pop. 49,548 (est. 2008).

red mul·let ▶ **n.** an elongated fish with long barbels on the chin, living in warmer seas and widely valued as a food fish. ● Family Mullidae: several genera and many species, in particular *Muletus surmuletus* of the Mediterranean and eastern Atlantic.

red·neck /ˈredˌnek/ ▶ **n.** informal, derogatory a working-class white person, esp. a politically reactionary one from a rural area: *rednecks in the high, cheap seats stomped their feet and hooted* | [as modifier] *a place of redneck biases.*
– DERIVATIVES **red·necked adj.**
– ORIGIN from the back of the neck being sunburned from outdoor work.

re·do ▶ **v.** /rēˈdo͞o/ (**redoes** /rēˈdəz/, **redoing**; past **redid** /rēˈdid/; past participle **redone** /rēˈdən/) [with obj.] do (something) again or differently: *a whole day's work has to be redone.* ■ redecorate (a room or building): *the house is being redone exactly to suit his taste.*
▶ **n.** /ˈrēˌdo͞o/ a redecoration of a room or building: *a total redo of the second floor shopping concourse.*

red o·cher ▶ **n.** a variety of ocher, esp. used for coloring or dyeing.

red·o·lent /ˈredl-ənt/ ▶ **adj. 1** [predic.] (**redolent of/with**) strongly reminiscent or suggestive of (something): *names redolent of history and tradition.* ■ literary strongly smelling of something: *the church was old, dark, and redolent of incense.*
2 archaic or literary fragrant or sweet-smelling: *a rich, inky, redolent wine.*
– DERIVATIVES **red·o·lence n.**, **red·o·lent·ly adv.**
– ORIGIN late Middle English (in the sense 'fragrant'): from Old French, or from Latin *redolent-* 'giving out a strong smell,' from *re(d)-* 'back, again' + *olere* 'to smell.'

Re·don /rəˈdôN/, Odilon (1840–1916), French painter and graphic artist. He was a leading exponent of symbolism and forerunner of surrealism.

Re·don·do Beach /riˈdändō/ a city in southwestern California, on Santa Monica Bay, south of Los Angeles; pop. 66,882 (est. 2008).

re·dou·ble /rēˈdəbəl/ ▶ **v.** make or become much greater, more intense, or more numerous: [with obj.] *we will redouble our efforts to reform agricultural policy* | [no obj.] *pressure to solve the problem has redoubled.* ■ [no obj.] Bridge double a bid already doubled by an opponent.
▶ **n.** Bridge a call that doubles a bid already doubled by an opponent.
– ORIGIN late Middle English: from French *redoubler,* from *re-* 'again' + *doubler* 'to double.' The noun dates from the early 20th cent.

re·doubt /riˈdout/ ▶ **n.** Military a temporary or supplementary fortification, typically square or polygonal and without flanking defenses.
– ORIGIN early 17th cent.: from French *redoute,* from obsolete Italian *ridotta* and medieval Latin *reductus* 'refuge,' from Latin *reducere* 'withdraw.' The *-b-* was added by association with **DOUBT.**

re·doubt·a·ble /riˈdoutəbəl/ ▶ **adj.** often humorous (of a person) formidable, esp. as an opponent: *he was a redoubtable debater.*
– DERIVATIVES **re·doubt·a·bly** /-blē/ **adv.**
– ORIGIN late Middle English: from Old French *redoutable,* from *redouter* 'to fear,' from *re-* (expressing intensive force) + *douter* 'to doubt.'

re·dound /riˈdound/ ▶ **v.** [no obj.] **1** (**redound to**) formal contribute greatly to (a person's credit or honor): *his latest diplomatic effort will redound to his credit.*
2 (**redound upon**) archaic come back upon; rebound on: *may his sin redound upon his head!* [probably by association with **REBOUND**[1].]
– ORIGIN late Middle English (in the sense 'surge up, overflow'): from Old French *redonder,* from Latin *redundare* 'surge,' from *re(d)-* 'again' + *unda* 'a wave.'

red·out /ˈredˌout/ ▶ **n.** a reddening of the vision resulting from congestion of blood in the eyes when the body is accelerated downward, sometimes followed by loss of consciousness.

re·dox /ˈrēˌdäks/ ▶ **n.** [usu. as modifier] Chemistry a process in which one substance or molecule is reduced and another oxidized; oxidation and reduction considered together as complimentary processes: *redox reactions involve electron transfer.*
– ORIGIN 1920s: blend of **REDUCTION** and **OXIDATION.**

red pan·da ▶ **n.** a raccoonlike mammal with thick reddish-brown fur and a bushy tail, native to high bamboo forests from the Himalayas to southern China. Also called **LESSER PANDA.** ● *Ailurus fulgens*; it is variously placed with the raccoons or bears, or in its own family (Ailurudae).

red pep·per ▶ **n.** the ripe red fruit of a sweet pepper. Compare with **GREEN PEPPER.** ■ another term for **CAYENNE.**

red phos·pho·rus ▶ **n.** see **PHOSPHORUS.**

red pine ▶ **n.** any of a number of coniferous trees that yield reddish timber, in particular: ● a North American pine (*Pinus resinosa,* family Pinaceae).

red·poll /ˈredˌpōl/ ▶ **n. 1** a mainly brown finch with a red forehead, related to the linnet and widespread in Eurasia and North America. ● *Acanthis flammea,* family Fringillidae; occurs in a number of races that were formerly regarded as separate species.
2 (**Red Poll**) an animal of a breed of red-haired polled cattle.

re·draft ▶ **v.** /rēˈdraft/ [with obj.] draft (a document, text, or map) again in a different way: (as adj. **redrafted**) *I enclose a redrafted version.*
▶ **n.** /ˈrēˌdraft/ a document, text, or map that has been redrafted.

re·draw /rēˈdrô/ ▶ **v.** (past **redrew** /rēˈdro͞o/; past participle **redrawn** /rēˈdrôn/) [with obj.] draw or draw up again or differently: *a judge forced Los Angeles to redraw its districts* | *the diagram was redrawn.*

re·dress /riˈdres, ˈrēˌdres/ ▶ **v.** [with obj.] remedy or set right (an undesirable or unfair situation): *the power to redress the grievances of our citizens.* ■ archaic set upright again: *some ambitious architect being called to redress a leaning wall.*
▶ **n.** remedy or compensation for a wrong or grievance: *those seeking redress for an infringement of public law rights.*
– PHRASES **redress the balance** take action to restore equality in a situation.
– DERIVATIVES **re·dress·a·ble adj.**, **re·dress·al** /-əl/ **n.**, **re·dress·er n.**
– ORIGIN Middle English: the verb from Old French *redresser*; the noun via Anglo-Norman French *redresse.*

re-dress /rēˈdres, ˈrē-/ ▶ **v.** [with obj.] dress (someone or something) again: *he re-dressed the wound.*

red rib·bon ▶ **n.** an award given for coming in second in a competition.

Red Riv·er 1 a river in Southeast Asia that rises in southern China and flows 730 miles (1,175 km) southeast through northern Vietnam to the Gulf of Tonkin. Chinese name **YUAN JIANG**; Vietnamese name **SONG HONG.**
2 a river in the southern US, a tributary of the Mississippi River, that rises in northern Texas and flows 1,222 miles (1,966 km) southeast, forming part of the border between Texas and Oklahoma. It enters the Mississippi River in Louisiana. Also called **Red River of the South.**
3 a river in the northern US and Canada that rises in North Dakota and flows 545 miles (877 km) north, forming for most of its length the border between North Dakota and Minnesota, before entering Canada and emptying into Lake Winnipeg. Also called **Red River of the North.**

Red Riv·er cart ▶ **n.** historical a strong two-wheeled cart formerly used on the Canadian prairies.

red roan ▶ **adj.** denoting an animal's coat consisting of bay or chestnut mixed with white or gray.
▶ **n.** a red roan animal.

red salm·on ▶ **n.** another term for **SOCKEYE.** ■ the reddish-pink flesh of the sockeye salmon used as food.

red san·dal·wood ▶ **n.** either of two Southeast Asian trees of the pea family that yield red timber. ● Two species in the family Leguminosae: *Pterocarpus santalinus,* from which a red dye is obtained, and *Adenanthera pavonina,* whose seeds were formerly used as weights by goldsmiths.

Red Sea a long, narrow, landlocked sea that separates Africa from the Arabian peninsula. It is linked to the Indian Ocean in the south by the Gulf of Aden and to the Mediterranean Sea in the north by the Suez Canal.

red set·ter ▶ **n.** less formal term for **IRISH SETTER.**

red·shank /ˈredˌsHaNGk/ ▶ **n.** a large Eurasian sandpiper with long red legs and brown, gray, or blackish plumage. ● Genus *Tringa,* family Scolopacidae: two species, in particular *T. totanus.*

red·shift /ˈredˈsHift/ (also **red shift**) ▶ **n.** Astronomy the displacement of spectral lines toward longer wavelengths (the red end of the spectrum) in radiation from distant galaxies and celestial objects. This is interpreted as a Doppler shift that is proportional to the velocity of recession and thus to distance. Compare with **BLUESHIFT.**
– DERIVATIVES **red·shift·ed adj.**

red·shirt /ˈredˌsHərt/ ▶ **n.** informal a college athlete who is withdrawn from college sporting events during one year in order to develop skills and extend the period of playing eligibility by a further year at this level of competition.
▶ **v.** [with obj.] (usu. **be redshirted**) keep (an athlete) out of college competition for a year: *he was less developed at the outset, so he was redshirted.*

– ORIGIN from the red shirts worn by such athletes in practices with regular team members.

red-shoul·dered hawk ▶ **n.** a common North American hawk having reddish-brown shoulders and dark wings with white spots. ● *Buteo lineatus*.

red·skin /ˈred,skin/ ▶ **n.** dated, offensive an American Indian.

USAGE Redskin is first recorded in the late 17th century and was applied to the Algonquian peoples generally, but specifically to the Delaware (who lived in what is now southern New York State and New York City, New Jersey, and eastern Pennsylvania). **Redskin** referred not to the natural skin color of the Delaware, but to their use of vermilion face paint and body paint. In time, however, through a process that in linguistics is called *pejoration*, by which a neutral term acquires an unfavorable connotation or denotation, **redskin** lost its neutral, accurate descriptive sense and became a term of disparagement. **Red man** is first recorded in the early 17th century and was originally neutral in tone. **Red Indian** is first recorded in the early 19th century and was used by the British, far more than by Americans, to distinguish the Indians of the subcontinent from the Indians of the Americas. All three terms are dated or offensive. **American Indian** and **Native American** are now the standard umbrella terms. Of course, if it is possible or appropriate, one can also use specific tribal names (**Cheyenne, Nez Percé**, etc.).

red snap·per ▶ **n.** a reddish marine fish that is of commercial value as a food fish, in particular: ● a tropical fish of the snapper family (genus *Lutjanus*, family Lutjanidae). ● a North Pacific rockfish (*Sebastes ruberrimus*, family Scorpaenidae).

red spi·der (also **red spider mite**) ▶ **n.** see SPIDER MITE.

red-spot·ted pur·ple ▶ **n.** a North American butterfly that is a form of the white admiral, formerly considered a separate species. Its dark blue wings with red-orange bars and spots mimic the unpalatable pipevine swallowtail.

Red Square a large square in Moscow next to the Kremlin. In existence since the late 15th century, under communism the square was the scene of great parades celebrating May Day and the October Revolution.

red squir·rel ▶ **n.** a small tree squirrel with a reddish coat. ● a North American squirrel with a pale belly and a black line along the sides during the summer (*Tamiasciurus hudsonicus*, family Sciuridae). ● a Eurasian squirrel with distinctive ear tufts during the winter months (*Sciurus vulgaris*, family Sciuridae).

red·start /ˈred,stärt/ ▶ **n. 1** an American warbler, the male of which is black with either a red belly or orange markings. ● Genera *Setophaga* and *Myioborus*, subfamily Parulinae, family Emberizidae: several species, in particular the **American redstart** (*S. ruticilla*).
2 a Eurasian and North African songbird related to the chats, having a reddish tail and underparts. ● *Phoenicurus* and other genera, subfamily Turdinae, family Muscicapidae: several species, in particular the widespread *P. phoenicurus*.

red state ▶ **n.** a US state that predominantly votes for or supports the Republican Party. Compare with BLUE STATE.
– ORIGIN from the typical color used to represent the Republican Party on maps during elections.

red tab·by ▶ **n.** a cat with a reddish-orange coat striped or dappled in a deeper red.

red-tailed hawk ▶ **n.** the most common and most widespread hawk of North and Central America, with a reddish tail. ● *Buteo jamaicensis*, family Accipitridae.

red tape ▶ **n.** excessive bureaucracy or adherence to rules and formalities, esp. in public business: *this law will just create more red tape.*
– ORIGIN early 18th cent.: so named because of the red or pink tape used to bind and secure official documents.

red tea ▶ **n.** see ROOIBOS.
– ORIGIN translation of Afrikaans *rooibos*.

red tide ▶ **n.** a discoloration of seawater caused by a bloom of toxic red dinoflagellates.

red top ▶ **n.** Brit. informal a tabloid.
– ORIGIN 1990s: from the red background on which the titles of certain British newspapers are printed.

Red To·ry ▶ **n.** (in Canada) a member of a political group who, while maintaining some conservative principles, supports many liberal and socialist policies.

re·duce /riˈd(y)o͞os/ ▶ **v.** [with obj.] **1** make smaller or less in amount, degree, or size: *the need for businesses to reduce costs | the workforce has been reduced to some 6,100* | (as adj. **reduced**) *a reduced risk of coronary disease.* ■ [no obj.] become smaller or less in size, amount, or degree: *the number of priority homeless cases has reduced slightly.* ■ boil (a sauce or other liquid) in cooking so that it becomes thicker and more concentrated. ■ [no obj.] (of a person) lose weight, typically by dieting: *by May she had reduced to 125 pounds.* ■ archaic conquer (a place), in particular besiege and capture (a town or fortress). ■ Photography make (a negative or print) less dense. ■ Phonetics articulate (a speech sound) in a way requiring less muscular effort. In vowels, this gives rise to a more central articulatory position.
2 (**reduce someone/something to**) bring someone or something to (a lower or weaker state, condition, or role): *she has been reduced to near poverty | the church was reduced to rubble.* ■ (**be reduced to doing something**) (of a person) be forced by difficult circumstances into doing something desperate: *ordinary soldiers are reduced to begging.* ■ make someone helpless with (an expression of emotion, esp. with hurt, shock, or amusement): *Olga was reduced to stunned silence.* ■ force into (obedience or submission): *he succeeds in reducing his grandees to due obedience.*
3 (**reduce something to**) change a substance to (a different or more basic form): *it is difficult to understand how lava could have been reduced to dust.* ■ present a problem or subject in (a simplified form): *he reduces unimaginable statistics to manageable proportions.* ■ convert a fraction to (the form with the lowest terms).
4 Chemistry cause to combine chemically with hydrogen. ■ undergo or cause to undergo a reaction in which electrons are gained by one atom from another. The opposite of OXIDIZE.
5 restore (a dislocated part) to its proper position by manipulation or surgery. ■ remedy (a dislocation) in such a way.
– PHRASES **reduced circumstances** used euphemistically to refer to the state of being poor after being relatively wealthy: *a divorcee living in reduced circumstances.* **reduce someone to the ranks** demote a noncommissioned officer to an ordinary soldier.
– DERIVATIVES **re·duc·er** n.
– ORIGIN late Middle English: from Latin *reducere*, from *re-* 'back, again' + *ducere* 'bring, lead.' The original sense was 'bring back' (hence 'restore,' now surviving in sense 5); this led to 'bring to a different state,' then 'bring to a simpler or lower state' (sense 3); and finally 'diminish in size or amount' (sense 1, dating from the late 18th cent).

re·duc·i·ble /riˈd(y)o͞osəbəl/ ▶ **adj. 1** [predic.] (of a subject or problem) capable of being simplified in presentation or analysis: *Shakespeare's major soliloquies are not reducible to categories.*
2 Mathematics (of a polynomial) able to be factorized into two or more polynomials of lower degree. ■ (of a group) expressible as the direct product of two of its subgroups.
– DERIVATIVES **re·duc·i·bil·i·ty** /ri,d(y)o͞osəˈbilətē/ n.

re·duc·ing a·gent ▶ **n.** Chemistry a substance that tends to bring about reduction by being oxidized and losing electrons.

re·duc·tant /riˈdəktənt/ ▶ **n.** Chemistry a reducing agent.

re·duc·tase /riˈdək,tās, -,tāz/ ▶ **n.** [usu. with modifier] Biochemistry an enzyme that promotes the chemical reduction of a specified substance.

re·duc·ti·o ad ab·sur·dum /rəˈdəktē,ō ,ad əbˈsərdəm, -ˈdəksHē,ō/ ▶ **n.** Philosophy a method of proving the falsity of a premise by showing that its logical consequence is absurd or contradictory.
– ORIGIN Latin, literally 'reduction to the absurd.'

re·duc·tion /riˈdəksHən/ ▶ **n. 1** the action or fact of making a specified thing smaller or less in amount, degree, or size: *talks on arms reduction | there had been a reduction in the number of casualties.* ■ the amount by which something is made smaller, less, or lower in price: *special reductions on knitwear.* ■ the simplification of a subject or problem to a particular form in presentation or analysis: *the reduction of classical genetics to molecular biology.* ■ Mathematics the process of converting an amount from one denomination to a smaller one, or of bringing down a fraction to its lowest terms. ■ Biology the halving of the number of chromosomes per cell that occurs at one of the two anaphases of meiosis.
2 a thing that is made smaller or less in size or amount, in particular: ■ an arrangement of an orchestral score for piano or for a smaller group of performers. ■ a thick and concentrated liquid or sauce made by boiling. ■ a copy of a picture or photograph made on a smaller scale than the original.
3 the action of remedying a dislocation or fracture by returning the affected part of the body to its normal position.
4 Chemistry the process or result of reducing or being reduced.
5 Phonetics substitution of a sound that requires less muscular effort to articulate: *the process of vowel reduction.*
– ORIGIN late Middle English (denoting the action of bringing back): from Old French, or from Latin *reductio(n-)*, from *reducere* 'bring back, restore' (see REDUCE). The sense development was broadly similar to that of REDUCE; sense 1 dates from the late 17th cent.

re·duc·tion gear ▶ **n.** a system of gearwheels in which the driven shaft rotates more slowly than the driving shaft.

re·duc·tion·ism /riˈdəksHə,nizəm/ ▶ **n.** often derogatory the practice of analyzing and describing a complex phenomenon in terms of phenomena that are held to represent a simpler or more fundamental level, esp. when this is said to provide a sufficient explanation.
– DERIVATIVES **re·duc·tion·ist** n. & adj., **re·duc·tion·is·tic** /ri,dəksHəˈnistik/ adj.

re·duc·tive /riˈdəktiv/ ▶ **adj. 1** tending to present a subject or problem in a simplified form, esp. one viewed as crude: *such a conclusion by itself would be reductive.* ■ (with reference to art) minimal: *he combines his reductive abstract shapes with a rippled surface.*
2 of or relating to chemical reduction.
– DERIVATIVES **re·duc·tive·ly** adv., **re·duc·tive·ness** n.

re·duc·tiv·ism /riˈdəktə,vizəm/ ▶ **n. 1** another term for MINIMALISM.
2 another term for REDUCTIONISM.

re·dun·dan·cy /riˈdəndənsē/ ▶ **n.** (pl. **redundancies**) the state of being no longer needed or useful: *the redundancy of 19th-century heavy plant machinery.* ■ the use of words or data that could be omitted without loss of meaning or function; repetition or superfluity of information. ■ Engineering the inclusion of extra components that are not strictly necessary to functioning, in case of failure in other components: *a high degree of redundancy is built into the machinery installation.* ■ chiefly Brit. the state of being no longer employed because there is no more work available: *the factory's workers face redundancy.*

re·dun·dant /riˈdəndənt/ ▶ **adj.** no longer needed or useful; superfluous: *an appropriate use for a redundant church | many of the old skills had become redundant.* ■ (of words or data) able to be omitted without loss of meaning or function. ■ Engineering (of a component) not strictly necessary to functioning but included in case of failure in another component. ■ chiefly Brit. (of a person) no longer employed because there is no more work available: *eight permanent staff **were made redundant**.*
– DERIVATIVES **re·dun·dant·ly** adv.
– ORIGIN late 16th cent. (in the sense 'abundant'): from Latin *redundant-* 'surging up,' from the verb *redundare* (see REDOUND).

re·du·pli·cate /riˈd(y)o͞opli,kāt, ˈrē-/ ▶ **v.** [with obj.] repeat or copy so as to form another of the same kind: *the upper parts of the harmony may be reduplicated at the octave above.* ■ repeat (a syllable or other linguistic element) exactly or with a slight change, e.g., *hurly-burly, see-saw.*
– DERIVATIVES **re·du·pli·ca·tion** /ri,d(y)o͞opliˈkāsHən, ,rē-/ n., **re·du·pli·ca·tive** /-,kātiv/ adj.
– ORIGIN late 16th cent.: from late Latin *reduplicat-* 'doubled again,' from the verb *reduplicare*, from *re-* 'again' + *duplicare* (see DUPLICATE).

re·dux /rēˈdəks, ˈrēˈdəks/ ▶ **adj.** [postpositive] brought back; revived: *the 1980s were far more than just the '50s redux.*
– ORIGIN late 19th cent.: from Latin, from *reducere* 'bring back.'

red va·le·ri·an ▶ **n.** see VALERIAN.

red wig·gler ▶ **n.** another term for RED WORM (sense 1).

red·wing /ˈred,wiNG/ ▶ **n. 1** a small migratory thrush that breeds mainly in northern Europe, with red underwings showing in flight. ● *Turdus iliacus*, subfamily Turdinae, family Muscicapidae.
2 any of a number of other red-winged birds, esp. the American red-winged blackbird. See BLACKBIRD (sense 2).

red wolf ▶ **n.** a fairly small wolf with a cinnamon or tawny-colored coat, native to the southeastern US but possibly extinct in the wild. ● *Canis rufus*, family Canidae.

red·wood /ˈred,wo͝od/ ▶ **n.** either of two giant conifers with thick fibrous bark, native to California and Oregon. They are the tallest known trees and are among the largest living organisms. ● Two species in the family Taxodiaceae: the **California** (or **coast**) **redwood** (*Sequoia sempervirens*), which can grow to a height of 325 feet (110 m), and the **giant redwood** (*Sequoiadendron giganteum*), which can reach a trunk diameter of 35 feet (11 m). ■ used in names of other, chiefly tropical, trees with reddish timber.

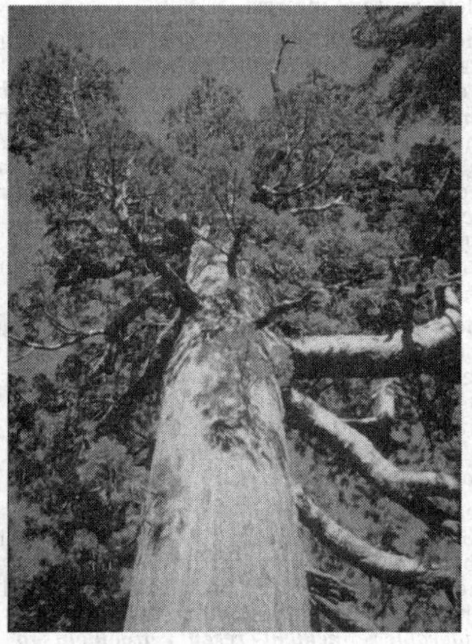

giant redwood tree

Red·wood Cit·y /ˈred,wo͝od/ a port city in north central California, on the southwestern side of San Francisco Bay, now part of the Silicon Valley complex; pop. 74,060 (est. 2008).

red worm ▶ **n. 1** a red earthworm used in composting kitchen waste and as fishing bait. Also called RED WIGGLER. ● *Lumbricus rubellus*, family Lumbricidae.
2 a parasitic nematode worm occurring in the intestines of horses. ● Genus *Strongylus*, class Phasmida.

red zone ▶ **n.** a red sector on a gauge or dial corresponding to conditions that exceed safety limits: *ozone readings edged into the red zone*. ■ a region that is dangerous or forbidden, or in which a particular activity is prohibited: *any officer who parks in the red zone outside the courthouse could receive a ticket*.

ree·bok ▶ **n.** variant spelling of RHEBOK.

re-ech·o /rē-ekō/ ▶ **v.** (**re-echoes, re-echoing, re-echoed**) echo again or repeatedly: [no obj.] *Dawn's words re-echoed in her mind*.
▶ **n.** a re-echoed word or sound.

Reed[1] /rēd/, Stanley Forman (1884–1980), US Supreme Court associate justice 1938–57. A supporter of President Franklin D. Roosevelt's New Deal programs, he held various federal positions before being named to the Court.

Reed[2], Walter (1851–1902), US army surgeon. He proved that the yellow fever virus is transmitted by mosquitoes. Walter Reed Hospital in Washington, DC, is named for him.

reed /rēd/ ▶ **n. 1** a tall, slender-leaved plant of the grass family that grows in water or on marshy ground. ● Genera *Phragmites* and *Arundo*, family Gramineae: several species, in particular the **common** (or **Norfolk**) **reed** (*P. australis*), which is used for thatching. ■ used in names of similar plants growing in wet habitats, e.g., **bur reed**. ■ a tall, thin, straight stalk of such a plant, used esp. as material for thatching. ■ [often as modifier] such plants growing in a mass or used as material, esp. for making thatch or household items: *a reed curtain | clumps of reed and grass*. ■ literary a rustic musical pipe made from such plants or from straw.
2 a thing or person resembling or likened to such plants, in particular: ■ a weak or impressionable person: *the jurors were mere reeds in the wind*. ■ literary an arrow. ■ a weaver's comblike implement for separating the threads of the warp and correctly positioning the weft. ■ (**reeds**) semicylindrical adjacent moldings grouped like reeds laid together.
3 a piece of thin cane or metal, sometimes doubled, that vibrates in a current of air to produce the sound of various musical instruments, as in the mouthpiece of a clarinet or oboe, at the base of some organ pipes, and as part of a set in the accordion and harmonica. ■ a wind instrument played with a reed. ■ an organ stop with reed pipes.
4 an electrical contact used in a magnetically operated switch or relay.
– DERIVATIVES **reed·like** /-,līk/ **adj.**
– ORIGIN Old English *hrēod*; related to Dutch *riet* and German *Ried*.

reed·buck /ˈrēd,bək/ ▶ **n.** an African antelope with a distinctive whistling call and high bouncing jumps. ● Genus *Redunca*, family Bovidae: three species.

reed·ed /ˈrēdid/ ▶ **adj. 1** shaped into or decorated with semicylindrical adjacent moldings.
2 (of a wind instrument) having a reed or reeds: [in combination] *a double-reeded oboe*.

reed·ing /ˈrēdiNG/ ▶ **n.** a small semicylindrical molding or ornamentation. ■ the making of such moldings.

re-ed·it /rē-edit/ ▶ **v.** (**re-edits, re-editing, re-edited**) [with obj.] edit (a text or film) again: *the third scene is still too long—we'll have to re-edit it*.
– DERIVATIVES **re-ed·i·tion** /,rē-əˈdisHən/ **n.**

reed mace ▶ **n.** another term for CATTAIL.

reed or·gan ▶ **n.** a keyboard instrument similar to a harmonium, in which air is drawn upward past metal reeds to produce tones.

reed pipe ▶ **n.** a simple wind instrument made from a reed or with the sound produced by a reed. ■ an organ pipe with a reed.

reed stop ▶ **n.** an organ stop controlling reed pipes.

re-ed·u·cate /rē-ejə,kāt/ ▶ **v.** [with obj.] educate or train (someone) in order to change their beliefs or behavior: *criminals are to be re-educated*.
– DERIVATIVES **re-ed·u·ca·tion** /,rē-ejəˈkāsHən/ **n.**

reed war·bler ▶ **n.** a Eurasian and African songbird with plain plumage, frequenting reed beds. ● Genus *Acrocephalus*, family Sylviidae: several species, in particular the common *A. scirpaceus*.

reed·y /ˈrēdē/ ▶ **adj.** (**reedier, reediest**) **1** (of a voice, sound, or instrument) high and thin in tone: *Frank's reedy voice | the reedy oboe*.
2 (of water or land) full of or edged with reeds: *they swam in the reedy lake*.
3 (of a person) tall and thin: *a reedy twelve-year-old*.
– DERIVATIVES **reed·i·ness n.**

reef[1] /rēf/ ▶ **n.** a ridge of jagged rock, coral, or sand just above or below the surface of the sea. ■ Austral. & S. African a metalliferous mineral deposit, esp. one that is bedded and contains gold.
– ORIGIN late 16th cent. (earlier as *riff*): from Middle Low German and Middle Dutch *rif, ref*, from Old Norse *rif*, literally 'rib,' used in the same sense; compare with REEF[2].

reef[2] Sailing ▶ **n.** each of the several strips across a sail that can be taken in or rolled up to reduce the area exposed to the wind.
▶ **v.** [with obj.] take in one or more reefs of (a sail): *reefing the mainsail in strong winds*.
– ORIGIN Middle English: from Middle Dutch *reef, rif*, from Old Norse *rif*, literally 'rib,' used in the same sense; compare with REEF[1].

reef-build·er ▶ **n.** a marine organism, esp. a coral, that builds reefs.
– DERIVATIVES **reef-build·ing n.**

reef·er[1] /ˈrēfər/ ▶ **n.** informal a marijuana cigarette. ■ marijuana.
– ORIGIN 1930s: perhaps related to Mexican Spanish *grifo* '(smoker of) cannabis.'

reef·er[2] ▶ **n.** short for REEFER JACKET.

reef·er[3] ▶ **n.** informal a refrigerated truck, railroad car, or ship.
– ORIGIN early 20th cent.: abbreviation.

reef·er jack·et ▶ **n.** a thick, close-fitting, double-breasted jacket.

reef flat ▶ **n.** the horizontal upper surface of a coral reef.

reef knot ▶ **n.** a square knot, originally used for reefing sails.

reef·point /ˈrēf,point/ ▶ **n.** Sailing each of several short pieces of rope attached to a sail to secure it when reefed.

reek /rēk/ ▶ **v.** [no obj.] smell strongly and unpleasantly; stink: *the yard reeked of wet straw and stale horse manure* | (as adj. **reeking**) *the reeking lavatories*. ■ be suggestive of something unpleasant or undesirable: *the speeches reeked of anti-Semitism*. ■ archaic give off smoke, steam, or fumes: *while temples crash, and towers in ashes reek*.
▶ **n. 1** [in sing.] a foul smell: *the reek of cattle dung*.
2 chiefly Scottish smoke.
– DERIVATIVES **reek·y adj.**
– ORIGIN Old English *rēocan* 'give out smoke or vapor,' *rēc* (noun) 'smoke,' of Germanic origin; related to Dutch *rieken* 'to smell,' *rook* 'smoke,' German *riechen* 'to smell,' *Rauch* 'smoke.'

reel /rēl/ ▶ **n. 1** a cylinder on which film, wire, thread, or other flexible materials can be wound. ■ a length of something wound onto such a device: *a reel of copper wire*. ■ a part of a movie: *in the final reel he is transformed from unhinged sociopath into local hero*. ■ a device for winding and unwinding a line as required, in particular a fishing reel.
2 a lively Scottish or Irish folk dance. ■ a piece of music for such a dance, typically in simple or duple time. ■ short for VIRGINIA REEL.
▶ **v. 1** [with obj.] (**reel something in**) wind a line onto a reel by turning the reel. ■ bring something attached to a line, esp. a fish, toward one by turning a reel and winding in the line: *he struck, and reeled in a good perch*.
2 [no obj.] lose one's balance and stagger or lurch violently: *he punched Connolly in the ear, sending him reeling | she reeled back against the van*. ■ feel very giddy, disoriented, or bewildered, typically as a result of an unexpected setback: *the unaccustomed intake of alcohol made my head reel* | figurative *the nationalist government is already reeling from 225 percent monthly inflation*. ■ [with adverbial of direction] walk in a staggering or lurching manner, esp. while drunk: *the two reeled out of the bar arm in arm*.
3 [no obj.] dance a reel.
– PHRASAL VERBS **reel (something) off** say or recite something rapidly and without apparent effort: *she proceeded to reel off in rapid Italian the various dishes of the day*.
– DERIVATIVES **reel·er n.**
– ORIGIN Old English *hrēol*, denoting a rotatory device on which spun thread is wound; of unknown origin.

re-e·lect /,rē-əˈlekt/ ▶ **v.** [with obj.] elect (someone) to a further term of office: *Wilson was re-elected in November 1994*.
– DERIVATIVES **re-e·lec·tion** /,rē-əˈleksHən/ **n.**

Reel·foot Lake /ˈrēlfo͝ot/ a lake in the northwestern corner of Tennessee, near the Mississippi River, formed during the 1811 earthquake that centered on nearby New Madrid in Missouri.

reel-to-reel ▶ **adj.** denoting a tape recorder in which the tape passes between two reels mounted separately rather than within a cassette, generally superseded by cassette players except for professional use.

re-e·merge /,rē-əˈmərj/ ▶ **v.** [no obj.] emerge again; come into sight or prominence once more: *nationalism has re-emerged in western Europe*.
– DERIVATIVES **re-e·mer·gence** /-jəns/ **n.**, **re-e·mer·gent** /-jənt/ **adj.**

re-em·pha·size /,rē-emfə,sīz/ ▶ **v.** [with obj.] place emphasis on (something) again: *recent empirical findings re-emphasize that broad-based economic growth*.
– DERIVATIVES **re-em·pha·sis n.**

re-em·ploy /,rē-emˈploi/ ▶ **v.** [with obj.] employ again: *the dismissed executives were soon re-employed | his extensive research is re-employed in his chapter on black theater*.
– DERIVATIVES **re-em·ploy·ment n.**

re-en·act /,rē-əˈnakt/ ▶ **v.** [with obj.] **1** act out (a past event): *bombers were gathered together to re-enact the historic first air attack*.
2 bring (a law) into effect again when the original statute has been repealed.
– DERIVATIVES **re-en·act·ment n.**

re-en·er·gize /,rē-enərjīz/ ▶ **v.** [with obj.] give fresh vitality, enthusiasm, or impetus to: *new reconstruction projects will re-energize the flagging economy*.

re-en·gi·neer /,rē-enjəˈnir/ ▶ **v.** [with obj.] redesign (a device or machine). ■ (often as noun **re-engineering**) restructure (a company or part of its operations).

re-en·list /,rē-enˈlist/ ▶ **v.** [no obj.] enlist again in the armed forces.
– DERIVATIVES **re-en·list·er n.**

re-en·ter /,rē-entər/ ▶ **v.** [with obj.] enter (something) again: *women who wish to re-enter the labor market*.
– DERIVATIVES **re-en·trance n.**

re-en·trant /rē-entrənt/ ▶ **adj.** (of an angle) pointing inward. The opposite of SALIENT. ■ having an inward-pointing angle or angles.
▶ **n. 1** a re-entrant angle. ■ an indentation or depression in terrain.
2 a person who has re-entered something, esp. the labor force.

re-en·try /rē-entrē/ ▶ **n.** (pl. **re-entries**) **1** the action or process of re-entering something: *programs designed to prepare you for re-entry to the profession | she feared she would not be granted re-entry into Britain*. ■ the return of a spacecraft or missile into the earth's atmosphere.
2 Law the action of retaking or repossession.
3 a visible duplication of part of the design for a postage stamp due to an inaccurate first impression. ■ a stamp displaying such a duplication.

re-equip /ˌrē-iˈkwip/ ▶ **v.** (**re-equips**, **re-equipping**, **re-equipped**) [with obj.] provide with new equipment: *the mill was re-equipped with modern machinery.*
– DERIVATIVES **re-equip·ment** **n.**

re-erect /ˌrē-iˈrekt/ ▶ **v.** [with obj.] erect (something, esp. a building) again.
– DERIVATIVES **re-erect·tion** **n.**

re-es·tab·lish /ˌrē-iˈstablisн/ ▶ **v.** [with obj.] establish (something) again or anew: *this project will re-establish contact with students.*
– DERIVATIVES **re-es·tab·lish·ment** **n.**

re-eval·u·ate /ˌrē-iˈvalyo͞oˌāt/ ▶ **v.** [with obj.] evaluate again or differently: *fifteen patients were re-evaluated after six months | I began to re-evaluate my life.*
– DERIVATIVES **re-eval·u·a·tion** **n.**

reeve[1] /rēv/ ▶ **n.** Canadian the president of a village or town council. ■ chiefly historical a local official, in particular the chief magistrate of a town or district in Anglo-Saxon England.
– ORIGIN Old English *rēfa.*

reeve[2] ▶ **v.** (past and past participle **rove** /rōv/ or **reeved**) [with obj.] Nautical thread (a rope or rod) through a ring or other aperture, esp. in a block: *one end of the new rope was* **reeved through** *the chain.* ■ fasten (a rope or block) in this way.
– ORIGIN early 17th cent.: probably from Dutch *reven* 'reef (a sail)' (see **REEF**[2]).

reeve[3] ▶ **n.** a female ruff. See **RUFF**[1] (sense 3).
– ORIGIN early 17th cent.: variant of dialect *ree*, of unknown origin.

re-ex·am·ine /ˌrē-igˈzamən/ ▶ **v.** [with obj.] examine again or further: *I will have the body re-examined.* ■ Law examine (a witness) again, after cross-examination by the opposing counsel.
– DERIVATIVES **re-ex·am·i·na·tion** /-ˌzaməˈnāsнən/ **n.**

re-ex·port /rē-ekˌspôrt, rē-ekˈspôrt/ ▶ **v.** [with obj.] export (imported goods), typically after they have undergone further processing or manufacture.
▶ **n.** the action of re-exporting something. ■ a thing that has or will be re-exported.
– DERIVATIVES **re-ex·por·ta·tion** /ˌrēˌekspôrˈtāsнən/ **n.**, **re-ex·port·er** **n.**

ref /ref/ informal ▶ **n.** (in sports) a referee.
▶ **v.** (**refs**, **reffing**, **reffed**) [with obj.] act as referee in (a game or match).
– ORIGIN late 19th cent.: abbreviation.

ref. ▶ **abbr.** ■ reference. ■ refer to.

re·face /rēˈfās/ ▶ **v.** [with obj.] put a new facing on (a building): *part of the tower was refaced with brick.*

re·fash·ion /rēˈfasнən/ ▶ **v.** [with obj.] fashion (something) again or differently.

re·fec·tion /riˈteksнən/ ▶ **n.** literary refreshment by food or drink. ■ a meal, esp. a light one. ■ Zoology the eating of partly digested fecal pellets, as practiced by rabbits.
– ORIGIN Middle English: from Old French, from Latin *refectio(n-)*, from *reficere* 'renew' (see **REFECTORY**).

re·fec·to·ry /riˈfekt(ə)rē/ ▶ **n.** (pl. **refectories**) a room used for communal meals, esp. in an educational or religious institution.
– ORIGIN late Middle English: from late Latin *refectorium*, from Latin *reficere* 'refresh, renew,' from *re-* 'back' + *facere* 'make.'

re·fec·to·ry ta·ble ▶ **n.** a long, narrow table.

re·fer /riˈfər/ ▶ **v.** (**refers**, **referring**, **referred**) **1** [no obj.] (**refer to**) mention or allude to: *the reports of the commission are often referred to in the media | New York, referred to as the Big Apple.* ■ [with obj.] (**refer someone to**) direct the attention of someone to: *I refer my colleague to the reply that I gave some moments ago.* ■ (**refer to**) (of a word or phrase) describe or denote; have as a referent: *the term "rhetoric" almost invariably refers to persuasion.*
2 [with obj.] (**refer something to**) pass a matter to (another body, typically one with more authority or expertise) for a decision: *disagreement arose and the issue was referred back to the Executive Committee.* ■ (**refer someone to**) send or direct someone to a medical specialist: *she was* **referred to** *a clinical psychologist for counseling.* ■ [no obj.] (**refer to**) read or otherwise use (a source of information) in order to ascertain something; consult: *I always refer to a dictionary when I come across a new word.*
3 [with obj.] (**refer something to**) archaic trace or attribute something to (someone or something) as a cause or source: *the God to whom he habitually referred his highest inspirations.* ■ regard something as belonging to (a certain period, place, or class).
– DERIVATIVES **ref·er·a·ble** /ˈref(ə)rəbəl, riˈfər-/ **adj.**, **re·fer·rer** **n.**
– ORIGIN late Middle English: from Old French *referer* or Latin *referre* 'carry back,' from *re-* 'back' + *ferre* 'bring.'

ref·er·ee /ˌrefəˈrē/ ▶ **n. 1** an official who watches a game or match closely to ensure that the rules are adhered to and (in some sports) to arbitrate on matters arising from the play.
2 a person appointed to examine and assess for publication a scientific or other academic work. ■ Brit. a person willing to testify in writing about the character or ability of someone, esp. an applicant for a job.
▶ **v.** (**referees**, **refereeing**, **refereed**) [with obj.] act as referee for: *the man who refereed the World Cup final* | [no obj.] *refereeing for medical journals.*

ref·er·ence /ˈref(ə)rəns/ ▶ **n. 1** the action of mentioning or alluding to something: *he* **made reference to** *the enormous power of the mass media | references to Darwinism and evolution.* ■ a mention or citation of a source of information in a book or article. ■ a book or passage cited in such a way.
2 use of a source of information in order to ascertain something: *popular works of reference* | [as modifier] *a reference work.* ■ the sending of a matter for decision or consideration to some authority: *he demanded the immediate reference of the whole dispute to the United Nations.*
3 a letter from a previous employer testifying to someone's ability or reliability, used when applying for a new job.
▶ **v.** [with obj.] provide (a book or article) with citations of authorities: *each chapter is referenced, citing literature up to 1990.*
– PHRASES **for future reference** for use at a later date: *she lodged this idea in the back of her mind for future reference.* **terms of reference** the scope and limitations of an activity or area of knowledge: *the judge will present a plan outlining the inquiry's terms of reference.* **with** (or **in**) **reference to** in relation to; as regards: *war can only be explained with reference to complex social factors.*

ref·er·ence book ▶ **n.** a book intended to be consulted for information on specific matters rather than read from beginning to end: *a beat-up old grade-school dictionary was the only reference book we ever had in our house.*

ref·er·ence e·lec·trode ▶ **n.** Electronics an electrode having an accurately maintained potential, used as a reference for measurement by other electrodes.

ref·er·ence frame ▶ **n.** see **FRAME OF REFERENCE**.

ref·er·ence group ▶ **n.** a social group that a person takes as a standard in forming attitudes and behavior.

ref·er·ence li·brar·y ▶ **n.** a library, typically one holding many reference books, in which the books are not for loan but may be read on site.

ref·er·ence point ▶ **n.** a basis or standard for evaluation, assessment, or comparison; a criterion.

ref·er·en·dum /ˌrefəˈrendəm/ ▶ **n.** (pl. **referendums** or **referenda** /-də/) a general vote by the electorate on a single political question that has been referred to them for a direct decision.
– ORIGIN mid 19th cent.: from Latin, gerund ('referring'), or neuter gerundive ('something to be brought back or referred') of *referre* (see **REFER**).

ref·er·ent /ˈref(ə)rənt/ ▶ **n.** Linguistics the thing that a word or phrase denotes or stands for: *"the Morning Star" and "the Evening Star" have the same referent (the planet Venus).*
– ORIGIN mid 19th cent.: from Latin *referent-* 'bringing back,' from the verb *referre* (see **REFER**).

ref·er·en·tial /ˌrefəˈrencнəl/ ▶ **adj. 1** containing or of the nature of references or allusions.
2 Linguistics of or relating to a referent, in particular having the external world rather than a text or language as a referent.
– DERIVATIVES **ref·er·en·ti·al·i·ty** /ˌrefəˌrencнēˈalətē/ **n.**, **ref·er·en·tial·ly** **adv.**

re·fer·ral /riˈfərəl/ ▶ **n.** an act of referring someone or something for consultation, review, or further action. ■ the directing of a patient to a medical specialist by a primary care physician. ■ a person whose case has been referred to a specialist doctor or a professional body.

re·ferred pain ▶ **n.** Medicine pain felt in a part of the body other than its actual source.

re·fi /rēˈfī/ ▶ **v.** (**refies**, **refying**, **refied**) [with obj.] refinance (a mortgage).
▶ **adj.** relating to refinancing and the refinancing market: *the refi boom is over.*
– ORIGIN shortening.

re·fill ▶ **v.** /rēˈfil/ [with obj.] fill (a container) again: *she paused and refilled her glass with wine before going on.* ■ replenish the supply of (medicine called for in a prescription): *there's nothing he can do but refill his Valium prescription.* ■ [no obj.] (of a container) become full again: *the empty pool will rapidly refill from rain and snow.*
▶ **n.** /ˈrēˌfil/ an act of filling a container again: *he proffered his glass for a refill.* ■ a replenished supply of medicine called for in a prescription: *an oral contraceptive refill was dispensed.*
– DERIVATIVES **re·fill·a·ble** **adj.**

re·fi·nance /ˌrēfəˈnans, rēˈfīˌnans/ ▶ **v.** [with obj.] finance (something) again, typically with a new loan at a lower rate of interest.

re·fine /riˈfīn/ ▶ **v.** [with obj.] remove impurities or unwanted elements from (a substance), typically as part of an industrial process: *sugar was refined by boiling it in huge iron vats.* ■ improve (something) by making small changes, in particular make (an idea, theory, or method) more subtle and accurate: *ease of access to computers has refined analysis and presentation of data.*
– DERIVATIVES **re·fin·er** **n.**
– ORIGIN late 16th cent.: from **RE-** 'again' + the verb **FINE**[1], influenced by French *raffiner.*

re·fined /riˈfīnd/ ▶ **adj.** with impurities or unwanted elements having been removed by processing. ■ elegant and cultured in appearance, manner, or taste: *her voice was very low and refined.* ■ developed or improved so as to be precise or subtle: *building up a more refined profile of the customer's needs.*

re·fine·ment /riˈfīnmənt/ ▶ **n.** the process of removing impurities or unwanted elements from a substance: *the refinement of uranium.* ■ the improvement or clarification of something by the making of small changes: *this gross figure needs considerable refinement | recent* **refinements to** *production techniques.* ■ cultured elegance in behavior or manner: *her carefully cultivated veneer of refinement.* ■ sophisticated and superior good taste: *the refinement of Hellenistic art.*

re·fin·er·y /riˈfīnərē/ ▶ **n.** (pl. **refineries**) an industrial installation where a substance is refined: *an oil refinery.*

re·fin·ish /rēˈfinisн/ ▶ **v.** [with obj.] apply a new finish to (a surface or object).
▶ **n.** an act of refinishing a surface or object.

re·fit ▶ **v.** /rēˈfit/ (**refits**, **refitting**, **refitted**) [with obj.] replace or repair machinery, equipment, and fittings in (a ship, building, etc.): *a lucrative contract to refit a submarine fleet.*
▶ **n.** /ˈrēˌfit, rēˈfit/ a restoration or repair of machinery, equipment, or fittings.

refl. ▶ **abbr.** ■ reflection. ■ reflective. ■ reflex. ■ reflexive.

re·flag /rēˈflag/ ▶ **v.** (**reflags**, **reflagging**, **reflagged**) [with obj.] change the national registry of (a ship).

re·flate /riˈflāt/ ▶ **v.** [with obj.] expand the level of output of (an economy) by government stimulus, using either fiscal or monetary policy.
– DERIVATIVES **re·fla·tion** /riˈflāsнən/ **n.**, **re·fla·tion·ar·y** /riˈflāsнəˌnerē/ **n.**
– ORIGIN 1930s: from **RE-** 'again,' on the pattern of *inflate, deflate.*

re·flect /riˈflekt/ ▶ **v. 1** [with obj.] (of a surface or body) throw back (heat, light, or sound) without absorbing it: *when the sun's rays hit the earth a lot of the heat is reflected back into space* | (as adj. **reflected**) *his eyes gleamed in the reflected light.* ■ (of a mirror or shiny surface) show an image of: *he could see himself reflected in Keith's mirrored glasses.* ■ embody or represent (something) in a faithful or appropriate way: *stocks are priced at a level that reflects a company's prospects | schools should reflect cultural differences.* ■ (of an action or situation) bring (credit or discredit) to the relevant parties: *the main contract is progressing well, which reflects great credit on those involved.* ■ [no obj.] (**reflect well**/**badly on**) bring about a good or bad impression of: *the incident reflects badly on the operating practices of the airlines.*
2 [no obj.] (**reflect on**/**upon**) think deeply or carefully about: *he reflected with sadness on the unhappiness of his marriage* | [with clause] *Charles reflected that maybe there was hope for the family after all.* ■ archaic make disparaging remarks about.
– ORIGIN late Middle English: from Old French *reflecter* or Latin *reflectere*, from *re-* 'back' + *flectere* 'to bend.'

re·flect·ance /riˈflektəns/ ▶ **n.** Physics the measure of the proportion of light or other radiation striking a surface that is reflected off it.

re·flect·ed glo·ry ▶ **n.** fame or approval achieved through association with someone else rather than through one's own efforts.

re·flect·ing tel·e·scope ▶ **n.** a telescope in which a mirror is used to collect and focus light.

re·flec·tion /riˈfleksнən/ ▶ **n. 1** the throwing back by a body or surface of light, heat, or sound without absorbing it: *the reflection of light.* ■ an amount of

r

light, heat, or sound that is thrown back in such a way: *the reflections from the streetlights gave us just enough light.* ■ an image seen in a mirror or shiny surface: *Marianne surveyed her reflection in the mirror.* ■ a thing that is a consequence of or arises from something else: *a healthy skin is a reflection of good health in general.* ■ [in sing.] a thing bringing discredit to someone or something: *it was a sad* ***reflection on*** *society that because of his affliction he was picked on.* ■ Mathematics the conceptual operation of inverting a system or event with respect to a plane, each element being transferred perpendicularly through the plane to a point the same distance the other side of it.
2 serious thought or consideration: *he doesn't get much time for reflection.* ■ an idea about something, esp. one that is written down or expressed: *reflections on human destiny and art.*
– ORIGIN late Middle English: from Old French *reflexion* or late Latin *reflexio(n-)*, from Latin *reflex-* 'bent back,' from the verb *reflectere*.

re·flec·tion co·ef·fi·cient ▶ **n.** another term for REFLECTANCE.

re·flec·tive /ri'flektiv/ ▶ **adj. 1** providing a reflection; capable of reflecting light or other radiation: *reflective glass | reflective clothing.* ■ produced by reflection: *a colorful reflective glow.* **2** relating to or characterized by deep thought; thoughtful: *a quiet, reflective, astute man.*
– DERIVATIVES **re·flec·tive·ly** **adv.**, **re·flec·tive·ness** **n.**

re·flec·tiv·i·ty /ri,flek'tivətē, ,rē,flek-/ ▶ **n.** Physics the property of reflecting light or radiation, esp. reflectance as measured independently of the thickness of a material.

re·flec·tom·e·ter /ri,flek'tämətər, ,rē-/ ▶ **n.** an instrument for measuring quantities associated with reflection, in particular (also **time domain reflectometer**) an instrument for locating discontinuities (e.g., faults in electric cables) by detecting and measuring reflected pulses of energy.
– DERIVATIVES **re·flec·tom·e·try** /-'tämətrē/ **n.**

re·flec·tor /ri'flektər/ ▶ **n.** a piece of glass, metal, or other material for reflecting light in a required direction, e.g., a red one on the back of a motor vehicle or bicycle. ■ an object or device that reflects radio waves, seismic vibrations, sound, or other waves. ■ a reflecting telescope.

re·flet /rə'flā/ ▶ **n.** luster or iridescence, esp. on ceramics.
– ORIGIN French, literally 'reflection.'

re·flex /'rē,fleks/ ▶ **n. 1** an action that is performed as a response to a stimulus and without conscious thought: *a newborn baby is equipped with basic reflexes.* ■ (**reflexes**) a person's ability to perform such actions, esp. quickly: *he was saved by his superb reflexes.* ■ (in reflexology) a response in a part of the body to stimulation of a corresponding point on the feet, hands, or head: [as modifier] *reflex points.*
2 a thing that is determined by and reproduces the essential features or qualities of something else: *politics was no more than a reflex of economics.* ■ a word formed by development from an earlier stage of a language. ■ archaic a reflected source of light: *the reflex from the window lit his face.*
▶ **adj. 1** (of an action) performed without conscious thought as an automatic response to a stimulus: *sneezing is a reflex action.*
2 (of an angle) exceeding 180°. ■ archaic (of light) reflected. ■ (also **reflexed**) (esp. of flower petals) bent or turned backward. ■ archaic (of a thought) directed or turned back upon the mind itself; introspective.
– DERIVATIVES **re·flex·ly** /'rē,flekslē, ri'flekslē/ **adv.**
– ORIGIN early 16th cent. (as a noun denoting reflection): from Latin *reflexus* 'a bending back,' from *reflectere* 'bend back' (see REFLECT).

re·flex arc ▶ **n.** Physiology the nerve pathway involved in a reflex action including at its simplest a sensory nerve and a motor nerve with a synapse between.

re·flex cam·er·a ▶ **n.** a camera with a ground glass focusing screen on which the image is formed by a combination of lens and mirror, enabling the scene to be correctly composed and focused.

re·flex·i·ble /ri'fleksəbəl/ ▶ **adj.** chiefly technical capable of being reflected.
– DERIVATIVES **re·flex·i·bil·i·ty** /ri,fleksə'bilətē/ **n.**

re·flex·ion /ri'flekSHən/ ▶ **n.** chiefly Brit. variant spelling of REFLECTION.

re·flex·ive /ri'fleksiv/ ▶ **adj. 1** Grammar denoting a pronoun that refers back to the subject of the clause in which it is used, e.g., *myself, themselves.* ■ (of a verb or clause) having a reflexive pronoun as its object, e.g., *wash oneself.*
2 (of an action) performed as a reflex, without conscious thought: *at concerts like this one, standing ovations have become reflexive.*
3 Logic (of a relation) always holding between a term and itself.
4 (of a method or theory in the social sciences) taking account of itself or of the effect of the personality or presence of the researcher on what is being investigated.
▶ **n.** a reflexive word or form, esp. a pronoun.
– DERIVATIVES **re·flex·ive·ly** **adv.**, **re·flex·ive·ness** **n.**, **re·flex·iv·i·ty** /ri,flek'sivətē, ,rē,flek/ **n.**

re·flex·ol·o·gy /,rē,flek'säləjē/ ▶ **n. 1** a system of massage used to relieve tension and treat illness, based on the theory that there are reflex points on the feet, hands, and head linked to every part of the body.
2 Psychology the scientific study of reflex action as it affects behavior.
– DERIVATIVES **re·flex·ol·o·gist** /-jist/ **n.** (sense 1).

re·flow ▶ **n.** /'rē,flō/ **1** (in word processing) the action of rearranging text on a page after having changed such features as type size, line length, and spacing.
2 Electronics a soldering technique in which surface-mount components are held in position on a circuit board using a paste containing solder that melts to form soldered joints when the circuit board is heated.
▶ **v.** /'rē,flō, rē'flō/ [with obj.] **1** (in word processing) rearrange (text) on a page, having changed such features as type size, line length, and spacing.
2 Electronics attach (a surface-mount component) using the reflow technique.

ref·lu·ent /'ref,lo͞oənt, ref'lo͞o-/ ▶ **adj.** literary flowing back; ebbing: *the refluent waters of the Mississippi.*
– DERIVATIVES **re·flu·ence** **n.**
– ORIGIN late Middle English: from Latin *refluent-* 'flowing back,' from the verb *refluere*, from *re-* 'back' + *fluere* 'to flow.'

re·flux /'rē,fləks/ ▶ **n.** Chemistry the process of boiling a liquid in such a way that any vapor is liquefied and returned to the stock. ■ technical the flowing back of a liquid, esp. that of a fluid in the body.
▶ **v.** [no obj.] Chemistry boil or cause to boil in circumstances such that the vapor returns to the stock of liquid after condensing. ■ technical (of a liquid, esp. a bodily fluid) flow back.

re·fo·cus /rē'fōkəs/ ▶ **v.** (**refocuses, refocusing, refocused** or **refocusses, refocussing, refocussed**) [with obj.] adjust the focus of (a lens or one's eyes). ■ focus (attention or resources) on something new or different: *refocus attention on yourself through repeating your main points.*

re·for·est /rē'fôrəst, -'färəst/ ▶ **v.** [with obj.] replant with trees; cover again with forest: *a project to reforest the country's coastal areas.*
– DERIVATIVES **re·for·est·a·tion** /rē,fôrə'stāSHən, -'färə-/ **n.**

re·forge /rē'fôrj/ ▶ **v.** [with obj.] forge (something) again or differently: *they wanted to reforge the identity of the nation.*

re·form /ri'fôrm/ ▶ **v.** [with obj.] **1** make changes in (something, typically a social, political, or economic institution or practice) in order to improve it: *an opportunity to reform and restructure an antiquated schooling model.* ■ bring about a change in (someone) so that they no longer behave in an immoral, criminal, or self-destructive manner: *the state has a duty to reform criminals* | (as adj. **reformed**) *a reformed gambler.* ■ [no obj.] (of a person) change oneself in such a way: *it was only when his drunken behavior led to blows that he started to reform.*
2 Chemistry subject (hydrocarbons) to a catalytic process in which straight-chain molecules are converted to branched forms for use in gasoline.
▶ **n.** the action or process of reforming an institution or practice: *the reform of the divorce laws | economic reforms.*
▶ **adj.** (**Reform**) of, denoting, or pertaining to Reform Judaism: *a Reform rabbi.*
– DERIVATIVES **re·form·a·ble** **adj.**, **re·form·a·tive** /-mətiv/ **adj.**, **re·form·er** **n.**
– ORIGIN Middle English (as a verb in the senses 'restore (peace)' and 'bring back to the original condition'): from Old French *reformer* or Latin *reformare*, from *re-* 'back' + *formare* 'to form, shape.' The noun dates from the mid 17th cent.

re-form /'rē'fôrm/ ▶ **v.** form or cause to form again: [no obj.] *the clouds re-formed over the sun.*

re·for·mat /rē'fôr,mat/ ▶ **v.** (**reformats, reformatting, reformatted**) [with obj.] chiefly Computing give a new format to; revise or represent in another format.

ref·or·ma·tion /,refər'māSHən/ ▶ **n. 1** the action or process of reforming an institution or practice: *the reformation of the Senate.*
2 (**the Reformation**) a 16th-century movement for the reform of abuses in the Roman Catholic Church ending in the establishment of the Reformed and Protestant Churches.

> The roots of the Reformation go back to the 14th-century attacks on the wealth and hierarchy of the Church made by groups such as the Lollards and the Hussites. But the Reformation is usually thought of as beginning in 1517 when Martin Luther issued ninety-five theses criticizing Church doctrine and practice. In Denmark, Norway, Sweden, Saxony, Hesse, and Brandenburg, supporters broke away and established Protestant churches, while in Switzerland a separate movement was led by Zwingli and later Calvin.

– DERIVATIVES **ref·or·ma·tion·al** /-SHənl/ **adj.**
– ORIGIN late Middle English: from Latin *reformatio(n-)*, from *reformare* 'shape again' (see REFORM).

re·for·ma·tion /,rē,fôr'māSHən/ ▶ **n.** the action or process of forming again.

re·form·a·to·ry /ri'fôrmə,tôrē/ ▶ **n.** (pl. **reformatories**) an institution to which youthful offenders are sent as an alternative to prison; a reform school.
▶ **adj.** tending or intended to produce reform.

Re·formed Church ▶ **n.** a church that has accepted the principles of the Reformation, esp. a Calvinist church (as distinct from Lutheran).

re·form·ist /ri'fôrmist/ ▶ **adj.** supporting or advancing gradual reform rather than abolition or revolution.
▶ **n.** a person who advocates gradual reform rather than abolition or revolution.
– DERIVATIVES **re·form·ism** /-,mizəm/ **n.**

Re·form Ju·da·ism ▶ **n.** a form of Judaism, initiated in Germany by the philosopher **Moses Mendelssohn** (1729–86), that has reformed or abandoned aspects of Orthodox Jewish worship and ritual in an attempt to adapt to modern changes in social, political, and cultural life.
– DERIVATIVES **Re·form Jew** **n.**

re·form school ▶ **n.** an institution to which youthful offenders are sent as an alternative to prison.

re·for·mu·late /,rē'fôrmyə,lāt/ ▶ **v.** [with obj.] formulate again or differently: *the company also recently reformulated its Double Fudge Bar.*
– DERIVATIVES **re·for·mu·la·tion** **n.**

re·fract /ri'frakt/ ▶ **v.** [with obj.] (usu. **be refracted**) (of water, air, or glass) make (a ray of light) change direction when it enters at an angle: *the rays of light are refracted by the material of the lens.* ■ measure the focusing characteristics of (an eye) or of the eyes of (someone).
– ORIGIN early 17th cent.: from Latin *refract-* 'broken up,' from the verb *refringere*, from *re-* 'back' + *frangere* 'to break.'

re·fract·ing tel·e·scope ▶ **n.** a telescope that uses a converging lens to collect light.

re·frac·tion /ri'frakSHən/ ▶ **n.** Physics the fact or phenomenon of light, radio waves, etc., being deflected in passing obliquely through the interface between one medium and another or through a medium of varying density. ■ change in direction of propagation of any wave as a result of its traveling at different speeds at different points along the wave front. ■ measurement of the focusing characteristics of an eye or eyes.
– ORIGIN mid 17th cent.: from late Latin *refractio(n-)*, from *refringere* 'break up' (see REFRACT).

re·frac·tive /ri'fraktiv/ ▶ **adj.** of or involving refraction.
– DERIVATIVES **re·frac·tive·ly** **adv.**, **re·frac·tiv·i·ty** **n.**

re·frac·tive in·dex ▶ **n.** the ratio of the velocity of light in a vacuum to its velocity in a specified medium.

re·frac·tom·e·ter /ri,frak'tämətər, rē-/ ▶ **n.** an instrument for measuring a refractive index.
– DERIVATIVES **re·frac·to·met·ric** /ri,fraktə'metrik, ,rē-/ **adj.**, **re·frac·tom·e·try** /-trē/ **n.**

re·frac·tor /ri'fraktər/ ▶ **n.** a lens or other object that causes refraction. ■ a refracting telescope.

re·frac·to·ry /ri'fraktərē/ ▶ **adj.** formal **1** stubborn or unmanageable: *his refractory pony.*

PRONUNCIATION KEY ə *ago, up*; ər *over, fur*; a *hat*; ā *ate*; ä *car*; e *let*; ē *see*; i *fit*; ī *by*; NG *sing*; ō *go*; ô *law, for*; oi *toy*; o͝o *good*; o͞o *goo*; ou *out*; TH *thin*; T͟H *then*; ZH *vision*

r

2 resistant to a process or stimulus: *some granules are refractory to secretory stimuli.* ■ Medicine (of a person, illness, or diseased tissue) not yielding to treatment: *healing of previously refractory ulcers.* ■ Medicine, rare (of a person or animal) resistant to infection. ■ technical (of a substance) resistant to heat; hard to melt or fuse.
▶ **n.** (pl. **refractories**) technical a substance that is resistant to heat.
– DERIVATIVES **re·frac·to·ri·ness** n.
– ORIGIN early 17th cent.: alteration of obsolete *refractary*, from Latin *refractarius* 'stubborn' (see also REFRACT).

re·frac·to·ry pe·ri·od ▶ **n.** Physiology a period immediately following stimulation during which a nerve or muscle is unresponsive to further stimulation.

re·frain[1] /ri'frān/ ▶ **v.** [no obj.] stop oneself from doing something: ***she refrained from comment.***
– ORIGIN Middle English (in the sense 'restrain (a thought or feeling)'): from Old French *refrener*, from Latin *refrenare*, from *re-* (expressing intensive force) + *frenum* 'bridle.'

re·frain[2] ▶ **n.** a repeated line or number of lines in a poem or song, typically at the end of each verse. ■ the musical accompaniment for such a line or number of lines. ■ a comment or complaint that is often repeated: *"Poor Tom" had become the constant refrain of his friends.*
– ORIGIN late Middle English: from Old French, from *refraindre* 'break,' based on Latin *refringere* 'break up' (because the refrain "broke" the sequence).

re·frame /rē'frām/ ▶ **v.** [with obj.] **1** place (a picture or photograph) in a new frame.
2 frame or express (words or a concept or plan) differently.

re·fran·gi·ble /ri'franjəbəl/ ▶ **adj.** able to be refracted.
– DERIVATIVES **re·fran·gi·bil·i·ty** /ri,franjə'bilətē/ n.
– ORIGIN late 17th cent.: from modern Latin *refrangibilis*, from *refrangere* 'break up' (see REFRACT).

re·freeze /,rē'frēz/ ▶ **v.** (past **refroze**; past participle **refrozen**) make or become frozen again.

re·fresh /ri'fresн/ ▶ **v.** [with obj.] give new strength or energy to; reinvigorate: *the shower had refreshed her* | (as adj. **refreshed**) *I awoke feeling calm and refreshed.* ■ stimulate or jog (someone's memory) by checking or going over previous information: *he was able to refresh her memory on many points.* ■ revise or update (skills or knowledge): *short-term courses give nurses an opportunity to refresh their skills.* ■ Computing update the display on (a screen). ■ pour more (drink) for someone or refill (a container) with drink: *the tea is cold and the pot needs refreshing.* ■ place or keep (food) in cold water so as to cool or maintain freshness.
▶ **n.** Computing an act or function of updating the display on a screen.
– ORIGIN late Middle English: from Old French *refreschier*, from *re-* 'back' + *fres(che)* 'fresh.'

re·fresh·er /ri'fresнər/ ▶ **n.** a thing that refreshes, in particular: ■ [usu. as modifier] an activity that revises or updates one's skills or knowledge: *candidates take some refresher training before coming back.* ■ dated a drink.

re·fresh·er course ▶ **n.** a short course reviewing or updating previous studies or training connected with one's profession.

re·fresh·ing /ri'fresнiNG/ ▶ **adj.** serving to refresh or reinvigorate someone: *a refreshing drink* | *the morning air was so refreshing.* ■ welcome or stimulating because new or different: *it **makes a refreshing change** to be able to write about something nice* | *her directness is refreshing.*
– DERIVATIVES **re·fresh·ing·ly** adv. [as submodifier] *a refreshingly different concept* | [sentence adverb] *refreshingly, the current spokesman is very frank.*

re·fresh·ment /ri'fresнmənt/ ▶ **n. 1** (usu. **refreshments**) a light snack or drink, esp. one provided in a public place or at a public event: *light refreshments are available* | *an ample supply of liquid refreshment.*
2 the giving of fresh mental or physical strength or energy: *hobbies and vacations are for refreshment and recreation.*
– ORIGIN late Middle English (sense 2): from Old French *refreschement*, from the verb *refreschier* (see REFRESH).

re·fresh rate ▶ **n.** Computing the frequency with which a monitor's display is updated.

re·fried beans /'rē,frīd/ ▶ **plural n.** pinto beans boiled and fried in advance and reheated when required, used esp. in Mexican cooking.

re·frig·er·ant /ri'frijərənt/ ▶ **n.** a substance used for refrigeration.
▶ **adj.** causing cooling or refrigeration.
– ORIGIN late 16th cent. (denoting a substance that cools or allays fever): from French *réfrigérant* or Latin *refrigerant-* 'making cool,' from the verb *refrigerare* (see REFRIGERATE).

re·frig·er·ate /ri'frijə,rāt/ ▶ **v.** [with obj.] subject (food or drink) to cold in order to chill or preserve it, typically by placing it in a refrigerator: *refrigerate the dough for one hour.*
– DERIVATIVES **re·frig·er·a·tion** /ri,frijə'rāsнən/ n., **re·frig·er·a·to·ry** /ri'frijərə,tôrē/ adj.
– ORIGIN late Middle English: from Latin *refrigerat-* 'made cool,' from the verb *refrigerare*, from *re-* 'back' + *frigus, frigor-* 'cold.'

re·frig·er·at·ed /ri'frijə,rātid/ ▶ **adj.** (of food or drink) chilled, esp. in a refrigerator: *sandwiches must be kept refrigerated in stores* | *refrigerated meat.* ■ (of a vehicle or container) used to keep or transport food or drink in a chilled condition: *refrigerated display units.*

re·frig·er·a·tor /ri'frijə,rātər/ ▶ **n.** an appliance or compartment that is artificially kept cool and used to store food and drink. Modern refrigerators generally make use of the cooling effect produced when a volatile liquid is forced to evaporate in a sealed system in which it can be condensed back to liquid outside the refrigerator.

re·frin·gent /ri'frinjənt/ ▶ **adj.** Physics refractive.
– DERIVATIVES **re·frin·gence** n.
– ORIGIN late 18th cent.: from Latin *refringent-*, literally 'breaking again,' from the verb *refringere.*

reft /reft/ past and past participle of REAVE.

re·fu·el /rē'fyo͞o(ə)l/ ▶ **v.** (**refuels, refueling, refueled**; Brit. **refuels, refuelling, refuelled**) [with obj.] supply (a vehicle) with more fuel: *the authorities agreed to refuel the plane.* ■ [no obj.] (of a vehicle) be supplied with more fuel.

ref·uge /'ref,yo͞oj, -,yo͞ozн/ ▶ **n.** a condition of being safe or sheltered from pursuit, danger, or trouble: *he was forced to **take refuge in** the French embassy* | *I **sought refuge in** drink.* ■ something providing such shelter: *the family came to be seen as a refuge from a harsh world.* ■ an institution providing safe accommodations for women who have suffered violence from a husband or partner.
– ORIGIN late Middle English: from Old French, from Latin *refugium*, from *re-* 'back' + *fugere* 'flee.'

ref·u·gee /,refyo͝o'jē, 'refyo͝o,jē/ ▶ **n.** a person who has been forced to leave their country in order to escape war, persecution, or natural disaster: *tens of thousands of refugees fled their homes* | [as modifier] *a refugee camp.*
– ORIGIN late 17th cent.: from French *réfugié* 'gone in search of refuge,' past participle of *(se) réfugier*, from *refuge* (see REFUGE).

re·fu·gi·um /ri'fyo͞ojēəm/ ▶ **n.** (pl. **refugia** /-jēə/) Biology an area in which a population of organisms can survive through a period of unfavorable conditions, esp. glaciation.
– ORIGIN 1950s: from Latin, literally 'place of refuge.'

re·ful·gent /ri'fo͝oljənt, -'fəl-/ ▶ **adj.** literary shining brightly: *refulgent blue eyes.*
– DERIVATIVES **re·ful·gence** n., **re·ful·gent·ly** adv.
– ORIGIN late 15th cent.: from Latin *refulgent-* 'shining out,' from the verb *refulgere*, from *re-* (expressing intensive force) + *fulgere* 'to shine.'

re·fund[1] ▶ **v.** /ri'fənd, 'rē,fənd/ [with obj.] pay back (money), typically to a customer who is not satisfied with goods or services bought: *if you're not delighted with your purchase, we guarantee to refund your money in full.* ■ pay back money to (someone): *I'll refund you for the apples and any other damage.*
▶ **n.** /'rē,fənd/ a repayment of a sum of money, typically to a dissatisfied customer: *you are entitled to reject it and insist on a refund* | *you'll get an immediate tax refund.*
– DERIVATIVES **re·fund·a·ble** adj.
– ORIGIN late Middle English (in the senses 'pour back' and 'restore'): from Old French *refonder* or Latin *refundere*, from *re-* 'back' + *fundere* 'pour,' later associated with the verb FUND. The noun dates from the mid 19th cent.

re·fund[2] /rē'fənd, 'rē-/ ▶ **v.** fund (a debt, etc.) again.

re·furb /ri'fərb/ informal ▶ **n.** an act or instance of refurbishing something, esp. a building: *the theater closes next year for its $10 million refurb.* ■ something that has been refurbished.
▶ **v.** [with obj.] refurbish (something).

re·fur·bish /ri'fərbisн/ ▶ **v.** [with obj.] renovate and redecorate (something, esp. a building): *the premises have been completely refurbished in our corporate style.*
– DERIVATIVES **re·fur·bish·ment** n.

re·fur·nish /rē'fərnisн/ ▶ **v.** [with obj.] furnish (a room or building) again or differently.

re·fus·al /ri'fyo͞ozəl/ ▶ **n.** [usu. with infinitive] an act or an instance of refusing; the state of being refused. ■ see FIRST REFUSAL.

ref·use[1] /ri'fyo͞oz/ ▶ **v.** [no obj.] indicate or show that one is not willing to do something: *I refused to answer* | *he was severely beaten when he refused.* ■ [with obj.] indicate that one is not willing to accept or grant (something offered or requested): *she refused a cigarette* | [with two objs.] *the old lady was refused admission to four hospitals.* ■ informal (of a thing) fail to perform a required action: *the car refused to start.* ■ [with obj.] decline to accept an offer of marriage from (someone): *he's so conceited he'd never believe anyone would refuse him.* ■ [with obj.] (of a horse) stop short or run alongside (a fence or other obstacle) instead of jumping it.
– DERIVATIVES **re·fus·er** n.
– ORIGIN Middle English: from Old French *refuser*, probably an alteration of Latin *recusare* 'to refuse,' influenced by *refutare* 'refute.'

ref·use[2] /'ref,yo͞os, -,yo͞oz/ ▶ **n.** matter thrown away or rejected as worthless; trash: *heaps of refuse* | *refuse collection.*
– ORIGIN late Middle English: perhaps from Old French *refusé* 'refused,' past participle of *refuser* (see REFUSE[1]).

re·fuse·nik /ri'fyo͞oznik/ ▶ **n. 1** a person in the former Soviet Union who was refused permission to emigrate, in particular, a Jew forbidden to emigrate to Israel.
2 a person who refuses to follow orders or obey the law, esp. as a protest.
– ORIGIN 1970s: from REFUSE[1] + -NIK.

re·fute /ri'fyo͞ot/ ▶ **v.** [with obj.] prove (a statement or theory) to be wrong or false; disprove: *these claims have not been convincingly refuted.* ■ prove that (someone) is wrong. ■ deny or contradict (a statement or accusation): *a spokesman totally refuted the allegation of bias.*
– DERIVATIVES **re·fut·a·ble** adj., **re·fut·al** /-'fyo͞otl/ n. (rare), **ref·u·ta·tion** /,refyo͞o'tāsнən/ n., **re·fut·er** n.
– ORIGIN mid 16th cent.: from Latin *refutare* 'repel, rebut.'

> **USAGE** The core meaning of **refute** is 'prove a statement or theory to be wrong,' as in *attempts to refute Einstein's theory*. In the second half of the 20th century, a more general sense developed, meaning simply 'deny,' as in *I absolutely **refute** the charges made against me.* Traditionalists object to this newer use as an unacceptable degradation of the language, but it is widely encountered.

re·gain /ri'gān/ ▶ **v.** [with obj.] obtain possession or use of (something) again after losing it: *she died without regaining consciousness* | *the tyrant was able to regain Sicily.* ■ reach (a place, position, or thing) again; get back to: *they were unable to regain their boats.*
– ORIGIN mid 16th cent.: from French *regagner* (see RE-, GAIN).

re·gal /'rēgəl/ ▶ **adj.** of, resembling, or fit for a monarch, esp. in being magnificent or dignified: *regal authority* | *her regal bearing.*
– DERIVATIVES **re·gal·ly** adv.
– ORIGIN late Middle English: from Old French, or from Latin *regalis*, from *rex, reg-* 'king.'

re·gale /ri'gāl/ ▶ **v.** [with obj.] entertain or amuse (someone) with talk: *he **regaled** her **with** a colorful account of that afternoon's meeting.* ■ lavishly supply (someone) with food or drink: *he was regaled with excellent home cooking.*
– DERIVATIVES **re·gale·ment** n. (rare).
– ORIGIN mid 17th cent.: from French *régaler*, from *re-* (expressing intensive force) + Old French *gale* 'pleasure.'

re·ga·li·a /ri'gālyə/ ▶ **plural n.** [treated as sing. or pl.] the emblems or insignia of royalty, esp. the crown, scepter, and other ornaments used at a coronation. ■ the distinctive clothing worn and ornaments carried at formal occasions as an indication of status: *the Bishop of Florence **in full regalia**.*
– ORIGIN mid 16th cent. (in the sense 'royal powers'): from medieval Latin, literally 'royal privileges,' from Latin, neuter plural of *regalis* 'regal.'

> **USAGE** The word **regalia** comes from Latin and is, technically speaking, the plural of *regalis*. However, in the way the word is used in English today, it behaves as a collective noun, similar to words like **staff** or **government**. This means that it can be used with either a singular or plural verb (*the **regalia** of Russian tsardom **is** now displayed in the Kremlin* or *the **regalia** of Russian tsardom **are** now displayed in the Kremlin*). In fact, in English, **regalia** has no other singular form.

re·ga·li·an /ri'gālyən, -lēən/ ▶ **adj.** formal belonging or relating to a monarch; regal: *regalian rights.*

r

– ORIGIN early 19th cent.: from French *régalien*, from Latin *regalis* 'regal.'

re·gal·i·ty /riˈgalətē/ ▶ **n.** (pl. **regalities**) **1** the state of being a king or queen. ■ the demeanor or dignity appropriate to a king or queen: *Ellen awaited her guests, radiating regality.*
2 archaic a royal privilege.
– ORIGIN late Middle English: from Anglo-Norman French *regalite* or medieval Latin *regalitas*, from *regalis* 'royal' (see **REGAL**).

re·gard /riˈgärd/ ▶ **v.** [with obj.] consider or think of (someone or something) in a specified way: *she regarded Omaha as her base | he was highly regarded by senators of both parties.* ■ gaze at steadily in a specified fashion: *Professor Ryker regarded him with a faint smile.* ■ (of a thing) have relation to or connection with; concern: *if these things regarded only myself, I could stand it with composure.* ■ archaic pay attention to; heed: *he talked very wisely, but I regarded him not.*
▶ **n. 1** attention to or concern for something: *the court must have* **regard to** *the principle of welfare | she rescued him without* **regard for** *herself.* ■ high opinion; liking and respect; esteem: *she had a particular* **regard for** *Eliot.* ■ [in sing.] a gaze; a steady or significant look: *he shifted uneasily before their clear regard.*
2 (**regards**) best wishes (used to express friendliness in greetings, esp. at the end of letters): *Warm regards, Helen | give her my regards.*
– PHRASES **as regards** concerning; with respect to: *as regards content, the program will cover important current issues.* **in this** (or **that**) **regard** in connection with the point previously mentioned: *there was little incentive for them to be active in this regard.* **with** (or **in**) **regard to** as concerns; with respect to: *he made inquiries with regard to Beth.*
– DERIVATIVES **re·gard·a·ble** adj.
– ORIGIN Middle English: from Old French *regarder* 'to watch,' from *re-* 'back' (also expressing intensive force) + *garder* 'to guard.'

re·gard·ant /riˈgärdnt/ ▶ **adj.** [usu. postpositive] Heraldry looking backward.
– ORIGIN late Middle English: from Anglo-Norman French and Old French, present participle of *regarder* 'look (again).'

re·gard·ful /riˈgärdfəl/ ▶ **adj.** [predic.] (**regardful of**) formal paying attention to; mindful of: *Parker was not overly regardful of public opinion.*
– DERIVATIVES **re·gard·ful·ly** adv.

re·gard·ing /riˈgärdiNG/ ▶ **prep.** with respect to; concerning: *your recent letter regarding the above proposal.*

re·gard·less /riˈgärdləs/ ▶ **adv.** without paying attention to the present situation; despite the prevailing circumstances: *they were determined to carry on regardless.*
– PHRASES **regardless of** without regard or consideration for: *the allowance is paid regardless of age or income.*
– DERIVATIVES **re·gard·less·ly** adv., **re·gard·less·ness** n.

USAGE See usage at **IRREGARDLESS**.

re·gath·er /rēˈgaT͟Hər/ ▶ **v. 1** [with obj.] collect or gather (something) again: *after 1910 the workers' movement regathered momentum.*
2 [no obj.] meet or come together again: *they regathered at lunchtime to resume their drinking.*

re·gat·ta /riˈgätə, riˈgatə/ ▶ **n.** a sporting event consisting of a series of boat or yacht races.
– ORIGIN early 17th cent.: from Italian (Venetian dialect), literally 'a fight, contest.'

regd ▶ **abbr.** registered.

re·ge·late /ˈrējəˌlāt/ ▶ **v.** [no obj.] technical (chiefly of pieces of ice thawed apart) freeze together again.
– DERIVATIVES **re·ge·la·tion** /ˌrējəˈlāsHən/ n.
– ORIGIN mid 19th cent.: from **RE-** 'again' + Latin *gelat-* 'frozen' (from the verb *gelare*).

Ré·gence /rāˈZHäNS/ ▶ **adj.** relating to or denoting a style of costume, furniture, and interior decoration characteristic of the era of the French Regency (1715–23).
– ORIGIN French, 'Regency.'

re·gen·cy /ˈrējənsē/ ▶ **n.** (pl. **regencies**) the office or period of government by a regent. ■ a commission acting as regent. ■ (**the Regency**) the particular period of a regency, esp. (in Britain) from 1811 to 1820 and (in France) from 1715 to 1723.
▶ **adj.** (**Regency**) relating to or denoting British architecture, clothing, and furniture of the Regency or, more widely, of the late 18th and early 19th centuries. Regency style was contemporary with the Empire style and shares many of its features: elaborate and ornate, it is generally neoclassical, with a generous borrowing of Greek and Egyptian motifs.
– ORIGIN late Middle English: from medieval Latin *regentia*, from Latin *regent-* 'ruling' (see **REGENT**).

re·gen·er·ate ▶ **v.** /riˈjenəˌrāt/ [with obj.] (of a living organism) regrow (new tissue) to replace lost or injured tissue: *a crab in the process of regenerating a claw.* ■ [no obj.] (of an organ or tissue) regrow: *once destroyed, brain cells do not regenerate.* ■ bring into renewed existence; generate again: *the issue was regenerated last month.* ■ bring new and more vigorous life to (an area or institution), esp. in economic terms; revive: *regenerating the inner cities.* ■ (esp. in Christian use) give a new and higher spiritual nature to. ■ (usu. as adj. **regenerated**) Chemistry precipitate (a natural polymer such as cellulose) in a different form following chemical processing, esp. in the form of fibers.
▶ **adj.** /riˈjenərət/ reformed or reborn, esp. in a spiritual or moral sense.
– DERIVATIVES **re·gen·er·a·tor** /-ˌrātər/ n.
– ORIGIN late Middle English (as an adjective): from Latin *regeneratus* 'created again,' past participle of *regenerare*, from *re-* 'again' + *generare* 'create.' The verb dates from the mid 16th cent.

re·gen·er·a·tion /riˌjenəˈrāsHən, ˌrē-/ ▶ **n.** the action or process of regenerating or being regenerated, in particular the formation of new animal or plant tissue. ■ Electronics positive feedback. ■ Chemistry the action or process of regenerating polymer fibers.
– ORIGIN Middle English: from Latin *regeneratio(n-)*, from *regenerare* 'create again' (see **REGENERATE**).

re·gen·er·a·tive /riˈjenərətiv, -ˌrātiv/ ▶ **adj.** tending to or characterized by regeneration: *natural regenerative processes.*
– DERIVATIVES **re·gen·er·a·tive·ly** adv.

re·gen·er·a·tive brak·ing ▶ **n.** a method of braking in which energy is extracted from the parts braked, to be stored and reused.

re·gent /ˈrējənt/ ▶ **n. 1** a person appointed to administer a country because the monarch is a minor or is absent or incapacitated.
2 a member of the governing body of a university or other academic institution.
▶ **adj.** [postpositive] acting as regent for a monarch: *the queen regent of Portugal.*
– ORIGIN late Middle English: from Old French, or from Latin *regent-* 'ruling,' from the verb *regere*.

re·ger·mi·nate /rēˈjərməˌnāt/ ▶ **v.** [no obj.] germinate again.
– DERIVATIVES **re·ger·mi·na·tion** n.

reg·ex /ˈregeks/ (also **regexp** /ˈregeksp/) ▶ **n.** Computing a regular expression.

reg·gae /ˈregā, ˈrāgā/ ▶ **n.** a style of popular music with a strongly accented subsidiary beat, originating in Jamaica. Reggae evolved in the late 1960s from ska and other local variations on calypso and rhythm and blues, and became widely known in the 1970s through the work of Bob Marley; its lyrics are much influenced by Rastafarian ideas.
– ORIGIN 1960s: perhaps related to Jamaican English *rege-rege* 'quarrel, dispute.'

reg·gae·ton /ˈregāˌtōn/ ▶ **n.** a form of dance music of Puerto Rican origin, characterized by a fusion of Latin rhythms, dancehall, and hip-hop or rap.
– ORIGIN 21st cent.: from **REGGAE** and Spanish *-ton*, on the pattern of *marathon*.

Reg·gio di Ca·la·bri·a /ˈrej(ē)ō dē käˈläbrēä/ a port at the southern tip of the "toe" of Italy, on the Strait of Messina, capital of Calabria region; pop. 185,621 (2008).

reg·i·cide /ˈrejəˌsīd/ ▶ **n.** the action of killing a king. ■ a person who kills or takes part in killing a king.
– DERIVATIVES **reg·i·cid·al** /ˌrejəˈsīdl/ adj.
– ORIGIN mid 16th cent.: from Latin *rex, reg-* 'king' + **-CIDE**, probably suggested by French *régicide*.

Ré·gie /rāˈZHē/ ▶ **n.** (in some European countries) a government department that controls an industry or service, historically one with complete control of the importation, manufacture, and taxation of tobacco, salt, and other resources.
– ORIGIN French, feminine past participle of *régir* 'to rule.'

re·gift /rēˈgift/ ▶ **v.** [with obj.] give (a gift one has received) to someone else: *do you think she'll regift that horrendous vase? |* [no obj.] *the survey showed that 53% of consumers plan to regift this holiday.*
▶ **n.** an item that has been regifted: *most of my regifts are more meaningful than the usual bouquet of flowers.*
– DERIVATIVES **re·gift·er** n.

re·gild /ˌrēgild/ ▶ **v.** [with obj.] renew or replace the gold on (a gilded object).

re·gime /riˈZHēm, rā-/ (also **régime**) ▶ **n. 1** a government, esp. an authoritarian one.
2 a system or planned way of doing things, esp. one imposed from above: *detention centers with a very tough physical regime.* ■ a coordinated program for the promotion or restoration of health; a regimen: *a low-calorie, low-fat regime.* ■ the conditions under which a scientific or industrial process occurs.
– ORIGIN late 15th cent. (in the sense 'regimen'): French *régime*, from Latin *regimen* 'rule' (see **REGIMEN**). Sense 1 dates from the late 18th cent. (with original reference to the Ancien Régime).

re·gime change ▶ **n.** the replacement of one administration or government by another, esp. by means of military force.

reg·i·men /ˈrejəmən, ˈreZH-/ ▶ **n. 1** a prescribed course of medical treatment, way of life, or diet for the promotion or restoration of health: *a regimen of one or two injections per day | a treatment regimen.*
2 archaic a system of government.
– ORIGIN late Middle English (denoting the action of governing): from Latin, from *regere* 'to rule.'

reg·i·ment ▶ **n.** /ˈrejəmənt/ **1** a permanent unit of an army typically commanded by a colonel and divided into several companies, squadrons, or batteries and often into two battalions: *two or three miles inland a highly experienced artillery regiment had established a defensive position.* ■ an operational unit of artillery. ■ a large array or number of people or things: *a neat* **regiment of** *jars and bottles.*
2 archaic rule or government over a person, people, or country: *the powers of ecclesiastical regiment which none but the Church should wield.*
▶ **v.** /ˈrejəˌment/ [with obj.] (usu. **be regimented**) **1** organize according to a strict, sometimes oppressive system or pattern: *every aspect of their life is strictly regimented.*
2 rare form (troops) into a regiment or regiments.
– DERIVATIVES **reg·i·men·ta·tion** /ˌrejəmənˈtāsHən, -ˌmen-/ n.
– ORIGIN late Middle English (in the sense 'rule or government over a person, people, or country'): via Old French from late Latin *regimentum* 'rule,' from *regere* 'to rule.'

reg·i·men·tal /ˌrejəˈmentl/ ▶ **adj.** of or relating to a regiment: *a regimental band | regimental colors.*
– DERIVATIVES **reg·i·men·tal·ly** /-ˈmentl-ē/ adv.

reg·i·men·tals /ˌrejəˈmentlz/ ▶ **plural n.** Brit. military uniform, esp. that of a particular regiment.

reg·i·ment·ed /ˈrejəˌmentid/ ▶ **adj.** very strictly organized or controlled: *the regimented life of a long-term prisoner.*

Re·gi·na[1] /rəˈjīnə/ the capital of Saskatchewan, located in the center of the wheat-growing plains of south central Canada; pop. 179,246 (2006).

Re·gi·na[2] /rəˈjēnə/ ▶ **n.** (in the UK) the reigning queen (used following a name or in the titles of lawsuits, e.g., *Regina v. Jones*, the Crown versus Jones).
– ORIGIN Latin, literally 'queen.'

Re·gi·o·mon·ta·nus /ˌrāgē-ōˌmônˈtänəs, ˌrējē-ōˌmänˈtānəs/, Johannes (1436–76), German astronomer and mathematician; born *Johannes Müller*. Considered the most important astronomer of the 15th century, he translated Ptolemy's *Mathematical Syntaxis* and wrote four monumental works on mathematics and astronomy.

re·gion /ˈrējən/ ▶ **n.** an area or division, esp. part of a country or the world having definable characteristics but not always fixed boundaries: *one of the region's major employers | the equatorial regions | a major wine-producing region.* ■ an administrative district of a city or country. ■ a part of the body, esp. around or near an organ: *an unexpected clenching sensation in the region of her heart.* ■ an area of activity or thought: *his work takes needlework into the region of folk art.*
– PHRASES **in the region of** approximately: *annual sales in the region of $30 million.*
– ORIGIN Middle English: from Old French, from Latin *regio(n-)* 'direction, district,' from *regere* 'to rule, direct.'

re·gion·al /ˈrējənl, ˈrējnəl/ ▶ **adj.** of, relating to, or characteristic of a region: *regional and local needs | regional variations.*
▶ **n.** (**regionals**) an athletic contest involving competitors from a particular region: *the opening game of the Little League Senior Division Softball Eastern Regionals.*
– DERIVATIVES **re·gion·al·ly** /ˈrējənl-ē, ˈrējnəlē/ adv.

re·gion·al·ism /ˈrējənlˌizəm, ˈrējnə-/ ▶ **n. 1** the theory or practice of regional rather than central systems of administration or economic, cultural, or political affiliation: *a strong expression of regionalism.*
2 a linguistic feature peculiar to a particular region and not part of the standard language of a country.
– DERIVATIVES **re·gion·al·ist** n. & adj.

r

re·gion·al·ize /ˈrējənlˌīz, ˈrējnəˌlīz/ ▶ **v.** [with obj.] (usu. as adj. **regionalized**) organize (a country, area, or enterprise) on a regional basis: *a regionalized system.*
– DERIVATIVES **re·gion·al·i·za·tion** /ˌrējənl-əˈzāSHən, ˌrējnələ-/ **n.**

re·gion·al met·a·mor·phism ▶ **n.** Geology metamorphism affecting rocks over an extensive area as a result of the large-scale action of heat and pressure. Compare with CONTACT METAMORPHISM.

re·gis·seur /ˌrāZHēˈsər/ ▶ **n.** a person who stages a theatrical production, esp. a ballet.
– ORIGIN from French *régisseur.*

reg·is·ter /ˈrejəstər/ ▶ **n. 1** an official list or record, for example of births, marriages, and deaths, of shipping, or of historic places. ■ a book or record of attendance, for example of students in a class or school or guests in a hotel.
2 a particular part of the range of a voice or instrument: *his voice moved up a register | she plays a basset horn and relishes the duskiness of its lower register.* ■ a sliding device controlling a set of organ pipes that share a tonal quality. ■ a set of organ pipes so controlled.
3 Linguistics a variety of a language or a level of usage, as determined by degree of formality and choice of vocabulary, pronunciation, and syntax, according to the communicative purpose, social context, and social status of the user.
4 Printing & Photography the exact correspondence of the position of color components in a printed positive. ■ Printing the exact correspondence of the position of printed matter on the two sides of a page.
5 (in electronic devices) a location in a store of data, used for a specific purpose and with quick access time.
6 an adjustable plate for widening or narrowing an opening and regulating a draft, esp. in a fire grate.
7 short for CASH REGISTER.
8 Art one of a number of bands or sections into which a design is divided.
▶ **v.** [with obj.] **1** enter or record on an official list or directory: *the vessel is registered as Liberian | her father was late in registering her birth* | (as adj. **registered**) *a registered trademark.* ■ [no obj.] enter one's name and other details on an official list or directory: [with infinitive] *34,500 registered to vote.* ■ [no obj.] put one's name in a register as a guest in a hotel. ■ [no obj.] (of a couple to be married) have a list of wedding gifts compiled and kept at a store for consultation by gift buyers. ■ entrust (a letter or parcel) to a post office for transmission by registered mail: (as adj. **registered**) *a registered letter.*
2 (of an instrument) detect and show (a reading) automatically: *the electroscope was too insensitive to register the tiny changes.* ■ [no obj., with complement] (of an event) give rise to a specified reading on an instrument: *the blast registered 5.4 on the Richter scale.*
3 express or convey (an opinion or emotion): *I wish to register an objection | he did not register much surprise at this.* ■ [no obj.] (of an emotion) show in a person's face or gestures: *nothing registered on their faces.* ■ [usu. with negative] properly notice or become aware of (something): *he had not even registered her presence.* ■ [no obj., usu. with negative] make an impression on a person's mind: *the content of her statement did not register.*
4 Printing & Photography correspond or cause to correspond exactly in position: [no obj.] *they are adjusted until the impressions register.*
– DERIVATIVES **reg·is·tra·ble** /-st(ə)rəbəl/ **adj.**
– ORIGIN late Middle English: from Old French *regestre* or medieval Latin *regestrum, registrum,* alteration of *regestum,* singular of late Latin *regesta* 'things recorded,' from *regerere* 'enter, record.'

reg·is·tered mail ▶ **n.** prepaid first class mail that is recorded by the post office before being sent and at each point along its route to safeguard against loss, theft, or damage.

reg·is·tered nurse (abbr.: **RN**) ▶ **n.** a nurse who has graduated from a college's nursing program or from a school of nursing and has passed a national licensing exam. Compare with PRACTICAL NURSE.

reg·is·ter ton ▶ **n.** see TON[1] (sense 1).

reg·is·trant /ˈrejəstrənt/ ▶ **n.** a person who registers.

reg·is·trar /ˈrejəˌsträr/ ▶ **n.** an official responsible for keeping a register or official records: *the registrar of births and deaths.* ■ an official in a college or university who is responsible for keeping student records.
– DERIVATIVES **reg·is·trar·ship** /-ˌSHip/ **n.**
– ORIGIN late 17th cent.: from medieval Latin *registrarius,* from *registrum* (see REGISTER).

reg·is·tra·tion /ˌrejəˈstrāSHən/ ▶ **n. 1** the action or process of registering or of being registered: *the registration of births, marriages, and deaths | the number of new private car registrations has increased.* ■ a certificate that attests to the registering of a person, automobile, etc.
2 Music a combination of stops used when playing the organ.
– ORIGIN mid 16th cent.: from medieval Latin *registratio(n-),* based on Latin *regerere* 'enter, record' (see REGISTER).

reg·is·try /ˈrejəstrē/ ▶ **n.** (pl. **registries**) **1** a place or office where registers or records are kept. ■ an official list or register: *a recognized purebred dog registry.*
2 registration. ■ the nationality of a merchant ship: *converted trawlers of local registry.*

Re·gi·us pro·fes·sor /ˈrēj(ē)əs/ ▶ **n.** (in the UK) the holder of a university chair founded by a sovereign (esp. one at Oxford or Cambridge instituted by Henry VIII) or filled by Crown appointment.
– ORIGIN Latin *regius* 'royal,' from *rex, reg-* 'king.'

re·glaze /rēˈglāz/ ▶ **v.** [with obj.] glaze (a window) again.

reg·let /ˈreglit/ ▶ **n. 1** Printing a thin strip of wood or metal used to separate type.
2 Architecture a narrow strip used to separate moldings or panels from one another.
– ORIGIN mid 17th cent.: from French *réglet,* diminutive of *règle* 'rule.'

reg·nal /ˈregnəl/ ▶ **adj.** [attrib.] of a reign or monarch.
– ORIGIN early 17th cent.: from Anglo-Latin *regnalis,* from Latin *regnum* 'kingdom.'

reg·nal year ▶ **n.** a year reckoned from the date or anniversary of a sovereign's accession.

reg·nant /ˈregnənt/ ▶ **adj. 1** [often postpositive] reigning; ruling: *a queen regnant.*
2 currently having the greatest influence; dominant: *the regnant belief.*
– ORIGIN early 17th cent.: from Latin *regnant-* 'reigning,' from the verb *regnare.*

reg·o·lith /ˈregəˌliTH/ ▶ **n.** Geology the layer of unconsolidated rocky material covering bedrock.
– ORIGIN late 19th cent.: from Greek *rhēgos* 'rug, blanket' + -LITH.

re·gorge /rēˈgôrj/ ▶ **v.** [with obj.] archaic bring up again; disgorge. ■ [no obj.] gush or flow back again.
– ORIGIN early 17th cent.: from French *regorger,* or from RE- 'again' + the verb GORGE.

re·grade /rēˈgrād/ ▶ **v.** [with obj.] grade again or differently: (as noun **regrading**) *a demand for a regrading of pay levels.*

re·gress ▶ **v.** /riˈgres/ **1** [no obj.] return to a former or less developed state: *art has been regressing toward adolescence for more than a generation now.* ■ return mentally to a former stage of life or a supposed previous life, esp. through hypnosis or mental illness: [no obj.] *she claims to be able to regress to the Roman era* | [with obj.] *I regressed Sylvia to early childhood.*
2 [with obj.] Statistics calculate the coefficient or coefficients of regression of (a variable) against or on another variable.
3 [no obj.] Astronomy move in a retrograde direction.
▶ **n.** /ˈrēˌgres/ **1** the action of returning to a former or less developed state.
2 Philosophy a series of statements in which a logical procedure is continually reapplied to its own result without approaching a useful conclusion (e.g., defining something in terms of itself).
– ORIGIN late Middle English (as a noun): from Latin *regressus,* from *regredi* 'go back, return,' from *re-* 'back' + *gradi* 'walk.'

re·gres·sion /riˈgreSHən/ ▶ **n. 1** a return to a former or less developed state. ■ a return to an earlier stage of life or a supposed previous life, esp. through hypnosis or mental illness, or as a means of escaping present anxieties: [as modifier] *regression therapy.* ■ a lessening of the severity of a disease or its symptoms: *he seemed able to produce a regression in this disease.*
2 Statistics a measure of the relation between the mean value of one variable (e.g., output) and corresponding values of other variables (e.g., time and cost).

re·gres·sive /riˈgresiv/ ▶ **adj. 1** becoming less advanced; returning to a former or less developed state: *the regressive, infantile wish for the perfect parent of early childhood.* ■ of, relating to, or marked by psychological regression.
2 (of a tax) taking a proportionally greater amount from those on lower incomes.
3 Philosophy proceeding from effect to cause or from particular to universal.
– DERIVATIVES **re·gres·sive·ly** **adv.**, **re·gres·sive·ness** **n.**

re·gret /riˈgret/ ▶ **v.** (**regrets, regretting, regretted**) [with obj.] feel sad, repentant, or disappointed over (something that has happened or been done, esp. a loss or missed opportunity): *she immediately regretted her words* | [with clause] *I regretted that he did not see you.* ■ used in polite formulas to express apology for or sadness over something unfortunate or unpleasant: *any inconvenience to readers is regretted* | [with clause] *we regret that no tickets may be exchanged.* ■ archaic feel sorrow for the loss or absence of (something pleasant): *my home, when shall I cease to regret you!*
▶ **n.** a feeling of sadness, repentance, or disappointment over something that has happened or been done: *she expressed her regret at Virginia's death | he had to decline, to his regret.* ■ (often **regrets**) an instance or cause of such a feeling: *she had few regrets in leaving the house.* ■ (often **one's regrets**) used in polite formulas to express apology for or sadness at an occurrence or an inability to accept an invitation: *please give your grandmother my regrets.*
– ORIGIN late Middle English: from Old French *regreter* 'bewail (the dead),' perhaps from the Germanic base of GREET[2].

re·gret·ful /riˈgretfəl/ ▶ **adj.** feeling or showing regret: *he sounded regretful but pointed out that he had committed himself.*
– DERIVATIVES **re·gret·ful·ness** **n.**

re·gret·ful·ly /riˈgretfəlē/ ▶ **adv.** in a regretful manner. ■ [sentence adverb] regrettably: *regretfully, mounting costs and diminishing traffic forced the line to close.*

> **USAGE** The adjectives **regretful** and **regrettable** are distinct in meaning: **regretful** means 'feeling or showing regret' (*she shook her head with a **regretful** smile*), while **regrettable** means 'giving rise to regret, undesirable' (*the loss of jobs is **regrettable***).The adverbs **regretfully** and **regrettably** have not, however, preserved the same distinction. **Regretfully** is used as a normal manner adverb to mean 'in a regretful manner' (*he sighed **regretfully***), but it is also used as a sentence adverb meaning 'it is regrettable that' (***regretfully**, the trustees must turn down your request*). In this latter use it is synonymous with **regrettably**. Despite objections from traditionalists, this use is now well established and is included in most modern dictionaries without comment. See also usage at HOPEFULLY and SENTENCE ADVERB.

re·gret·ta·ble /riˈgretəbəl/ ▶ **adj.** (of conduct or an event) giving rise to regret; undesirable; unwelcome: *the loss of this number of jobs is regrettable | irresponsible and regrettable actions.*

re·gret·ta·bly /riˈgretəblē/ ▶ **adv.** [sentence adverb] unfortunately (used to express apology for or sadness at something): *regrettably, last night's audience was a meager one.*

> **USAGE** See usage at REGRETFULLY.

re·group /rēˈgro͞op/ ▶ **v.** reassemble or cause to reassemble into organized groups, typically after being attacked or defeated: [no obj.] *their heroic resistance gave American forces time to regroup* | [with obj.] *he regrouped his fighters in the hills.* ■ [with obj.] rearrange (something) into a new group or groups: *she was regrouping the numeric data.*
– DERIVATIVES **re·group·ment** **n.**

re·grow /ˌrēˈgrō/ ▶ **v.** (past **regrew**; past participle **regrown**) grow or cause to grow again.
– DERIVATIVES **re·growth** **n.**

regs /regz/ ▶ **abbr.** informal regulations.

Regt ▶ **abbr.** ■ Regent. ■ Regiment.

reg·u·la·ble /ˈregyələbəl/ ▶ **adj.** able to be regulated.

reg·u·lar /ˈregyələr, ˈreg(ə)lər/ ▶ **adj. 1** arranged in or constituting a constant or definite pattern, esp. with the same space between individual instances: *place the flags at regular intervals | a regular arrangement.* ■ happening in such a pattern with the same time between individual instances; recurring at short uniform intervals: *a regular monthly check | her breathing became deeper, more regular.* ■ (of a structure or arrangement) arranged in or constituting a symmetrical or harmonious pattern: *beautifully regular, heart-shaped leaves.* ■ (of a person) defecating or menstruating at predictable times.
2 done or happening frequently: *regular border clashes | parties were a fairly regular occurrence.* ■ (of a person) doing the same thing or going to the same place frequently or at uniform intervals: *a regular visitor.*
3 conforming to or governed by an accepted standard of procedure or convention: *policies carried on by his deputies through regular channels.* ■ [attrib.] of or belonging to the permanent professional armed forces of a country: *a regular soldier.* ■ (of a person) properly trained or qualified and pursuing a full-time occupation: *a strong distrust of regular*

r

doctors. ■ Christian Church subject to or bound by religious rule; belonging to a religious or monastic order: *the regular clergy*. Contrasted with **SECULAR** (sense 2 of the adjective). ■ informal rightly so called; complete; absolute (used for emphasis): *this place is a regular fisherman's paradise.*
4 used, done, or happening on a habitual basis; usual; customary: *I couldn't get an appointment with my regular barber* | *our regular suppliers.* ■ of a normal or ordinary kind; not special: *it's richer than regular pasta.* ■ (chiefly in commercial use) denoting merchandise, esp. food or clothing, of average, medium, or standard size: *a shake and regular fries.* ■ (of a person) not pretentious or arrogant; ordinary and friendly: *advertising agencies who try to portray their candidates as* ***regular guys.*** ■ (in surfing and other board sports) with the left leg in front of the right on the board.
5 Grammar (of a word) following the normal pattern of inflection: *a regular verb.*
6 Geometry (of a figure) having all sides and all angles equal: *a regular polygon.* ■ (of a solid) bounded by a number of equal figures.
7 Botany (of a flower) having radial symmetry.
▶ **n.** a regular customer or member, for example of a bar, store, or team: *attracting a richer clientele as its regulars.* ■ a regular member of the armed forces. ■ a member of a political party who is faithful to that party: *he plans to sell tickets to the big-money party regulars.* ■ Christian Church one of the regular clergy.
– PHRASES **keep regular hours** do the same thing, esp. going to bed and getting up, at the same time each day.
– DERIVATIVES **reg·u·lar·ly adv.**
– ORIGIN late Middle English: from Old French *reguler*, from Latin *regularis*, from *regula* 'rule.'

reg·u·lar guy ▶ **n.** informal an ordinary, uncomplicated, sociable man.

reg·u·lar·i·ty /ˌregyəˈlaritē/ ▶ **n.** (pl. **regularities**) the state or quality of being regular: *he came to see her with increasing regularity.*

reg·u·lar·ize /ˈregyələˌrīz/ ▶ **v.** [with obj.] make (something) regular. ■ establish (a hitherto temporary or provisional arrangement) on an official or correct basis: *immigrants applying to regularize their status as residents.*
– DERIVATIVES **reg·u·lar·i·za·tion** /ˌregyələrəˈzāSHən/ **n.**

reg·u·late /ˈregyəˌlāt/ ▶ **v.** [with obj.] control or maintain the rate or speed of (a machine or process) so that it operates properly: *a hormone that regulates metabolism and organ function.* ■ control or supervise (something, esp. a company or business activity) by means of rules and regulations: *the organization that regulates fishing in the region.* ■ set (a clock or other apparatus) according to an external standard.
– DERIVATIVES **reg·u·la·tive** /-ˌlātiv/ **adj.**
– ORIGIN late Middle English (in the sense 'control by rules'): from late Latin *regulat-* 'directed, regulated,' from the verb *regulare*, from Latin *regula* 'rule.'

reg·u·la·tion /ˌreg(y)əˈlāSHən/ ▶ **n.** **1** a rule or directive made and maintained by an authority: *planning regulations.* ■ [as modifier] in accordance with regulations; of the correct type: *regulation army footwear.* ■ [as modifier] informal of a familiar or predictable type; formulaic; standardized: *a regulation Western parody.*
2 the action or process of regulating or being regulated: *the regulation of financial markets.*

reg·u·la·tor /ˈregyəˌlātər/ ▶ **n.** a person or thing that regulates something, in particular: ■ a person or body that supervises a particular industry or business activity. ■ a device for controlling the rate of working of machinery or for controlling fluid flow, in particular a handle controlling the supply of steam to the cylinders of a steam engine. ■ a device for adjusting the balance of a clock or watch in order to regulate its speed.

reg·u·la·to·ry /ˈregyələˌtôrē/ ▶ **adj.** serving or intended to regulate something: *the existing legal and regulatory framework* | *regulatory enzymes.*

Reg·u·lus /ˈregyələs/ Astronomy the brightest star in the constellation Leo. It is a triple system of which the primary is a hot dwarf star.
– ORIGIN Latin, literally 'little king.'

reg·u·lus /ˈregyələs/ ▶ **n.** (pl. **reguluses** or **reguli** /-ˌlī, -lē/) **1** Chemistry, archaic a metallic form of a substance obtained by smelting or reduction.
2 a petty king or ruler.
– DERIVATIVES **reg·u·line** /ˈregyəˌlīn, -lin/ **adj.** (sense 1).
– ORIGIN late 16th cent.: from Latin, diminutive of *rex, reg-* 'king'; originally in the phrase *regulus of antimony* (denoting metallic antimony), apparently so named because of its readiness to combine with gold.

re·gur·gi·tate /riˈgərjəˌtāt/ ▶ **v.** [with obj.] bring (swallowed food) up again to the mouth: *gulls regurgitate food for the chicks.* ■ repeat (information) without analyzing or comprehending it: *facts that can then be regurgitated at examinations.*
– DERIVATIVES **re·gur·gi·ta·tion** /riˌgərjəˈtāSHən/ **n.**
– ORIGIN late 16th cent.: from medieval Latin *regurgitat-*, from the verb *regurgitare*, from Latin *re-* 'again, back' + *gurges, gurgit-* 'whirlpool.'

re·hab /ˈrēˌhab/ informal ▶ **n.** **1** a course of treatment for drug or alcohol dependence, typically at a residential facility: *the star has been* ***in rehab*** *for a week.* ■ a course of treatment designed to reverse the debilitating effects of an injury: *their best hitter has been in rehab since August.*
2 a thing, esp. a building, that has been rehabilitated or restored.
▶ **v.** (**rehabs, rehabbing, rehabbed**) [with obj.] rehabilitate or restore: *they don't rehab you at all in jail* | (as adj. **rehabbed**) *newly rehabbed apartments for rent.*
– ORIGIN 1940s: abbreviation.

re·ha·bil·i·tate /ˌrē(h)əˈbiləˌtāt/ ▶ **v.** [with obj.] restore (someone) to health or normal life by training and therapy after imprisonment, addiction, or illness: *helping to rehabilitate former criminals.* ■ restore (someone) to former privileges or reputation after a period of critical or official disfavor: *with the fall of the government many former dissidents were rehabilitated.* ■ return (something, esp. an environmental feature) to its former condition.
– DERIVATIVES **re·ha·bil·i·ta·tion** /-ˌbiləˈtāSHən/ **n.**, **re·ha·bil·i·ta·tive** /-ˌtātiv/ **adj.**
– ORIGIN late 16th cent. (in the sense 'restore to former privileges'): from medieval Latin *rehabilitat-*, from the verb *rehabilitare* (see **RE-**, **HABILITATE**).

re·hang ▶ **v.** /rēˈhaNG/ (past and past participle **rehung** /-ˈhəNG/) [with obj.] hang (something) again or differently.
▶ **n.** /ˈrēhaNG/ an act of rehanging works of art in a gallery.

re·hash ▶ **v.** /rēˈhaSH/ [with obj.] put (old ideas or material) into a new form without significant change or improvement: *he contented himself with occasional articles in journals, rehashing his own work.* ■ consider or discuss (something) at length after it has happened: *is it really necessary to rehash that trauma all over again?*
▶ **n.** /ˈrēˌhaSH/ a reuse of old ideas or material without significant change or improvement: *the spring show was a rehash of the summer show from the previous year.*

re·hear /rēˈhi(ə)r/ ▶ **v.** (past and past participle **reheard** /-ˈhərd/) hear or listen to again. ■ Law hear (a case or plaintiff) in a court again: (as noun **rehearing**) *the parents produced fresh evidence and won a rehearing.*

re·hears·al /riˈhərsəl/ ▶ **n.** a practice or trial performance of a play or other work for later public performance: ***rehearsals for*** *the opera season.* ■ the action or process of rehearsing: *I've had two weeks* ***in rehearsal*** | [as modifier] *a rehearsal room.*

re·hearse /riˈhərs/ ▶ **v.** [with obj.] practice (a play, piece of music, or other work) for later public performance: *we were rehearsing a play* | [no obj.] *she was* ***rehearsing for*** *her world tour.* ■ supervise (a performer or group) that is practicing in this way: *he listened to Charlie rehearsing the band.* ■ mentally prepare or recite (words one intends to say): *he had rehearsed a thousand fine phrases.* ■ state (a list of points, esp. those that have been made many times before); enumerate: *criticisms of factory farming have been rehearsed often enough.*
– DERIVATIVES **re·hears·er n.**
– ORIGIN Middle English (in the sense 'repeat aloud'): from Old French *rehercier*, perhaps from *re-* 'again' + *hercer* 'to harrow,' from *herse* 'harrow' (see **HEARSE**).

re·heat ▶ **v.** /rēˈhēt/ [with obj.] heat (something, esp. cooked food) again.
▶ **n.** /ˈrēhēt/ the process of using the hot exhaust to burn extra fuel in a jet engine and produce extra power. ■ an afterburner.
– DERIVATIVES **re·heat·er n.**

re·heel /rēˈhēl/ ▶ **v.** [with obj.] fit (a shoe) with a new heel.

re·hire /rēˈhī(ə)r/ ▶ **v.** [with obj.] hire (a former employee) again: *the company dismissed its workers and rehired them on a lower rate.*
▶ **n.** a person rehired: *he declined to give any specifics on the number of possible rehires.*

Rehn·quist /ˈrenˌkwist/, William Hubbs (1924–2005), US chief justice 1986–2005. As President Nixon's assistant attorney general 1969–71, he held to a conservative stance that opposed civil rights legislation. He was appointed by Nixon as an associate justice to the US Supreme Court in 1972.

William H. Rehnquist

Re·ho·bo·am /ˌrē(h)əˈbōəm/, son of Solomon; king of ancient Israel *c.*930–*c.*915 BC. His reign witnessed the secession of the northern tribes and their establishment of a new kingdom under Jeroboam, leaving Rehoboam as the first king of Judah (1 Kings 11–14).

re·ho·bo·am /ˌrē(h)əˈbōəm/ ▶ **n.** a wine bottle of about six times the standard size.
– ORIGIN late 19th cent.: from the name **REHOBOAM**.

re·house /rēˈhouz/ ▶ **v.** [with obj.] (usu. **be rehoused**) provide (someone) with new housing: *tenants will be rehoused in hotels until their homes are habitable.*

re·hung /rēˈhəNG/ past and past participle of **REHANG**.

re·hy·drate /rēˈhīˌdrāt/ ▶ **v.** absorb or cause to absorb moisture after dehydration: [with obj.] *the slides were rehydrated in water.*
– DERIVATIVES **re·hy·drat·a·ble adj.**, **re·hy·dra·tion** /ˌrēhīˈdrāSHən/ **n.**

Reich[1] /rīk, rīKH/ the former German state, most often used to refer to the **Third Reich**, the Nazi regime from 1933 to 1945. The **First Reich** was considered to be the Holy Roman Empire, 962–1806, and the **Second Reich** the German Empire, 1871–1918, but neither of these terms are part of normal historical terminology.
– ORIGIN German, literally 'empire.'

Reich[2] /rīk/, Steve (1936–), US composer; full name *Stephen Michael Reich*. A leading minimalist, he uses the repetition of short phrases within a simple harmonic field. Influences include Balinese and West African music.

Reich·i·an /ˈrīkēən, ˈrīKH-/ ▶ **adj.** of or relating to the psychotherapeutic theories of Austrian psychoanalyst Wilhelm Reich (1897–1957), who theorized that sexual repression is the source of all human neuroses and irrational behavior: *he also taught me a kind of Reichian emotional release work, banging pillows and screaming at the top of my lungs.*

Reichs·mark /ˈrīksˌmärk, ˈrīKHs-/ ▶ **n.** the basic monetary unit of the Third Reich, replaced in 1948 by the Deutschmark.
– ORIGIN German.

Reichs·tag /ˈrīksˌtäg, ˈrīKHs-/ the main legislature of the German state under the Second and Third Reichs. ■ the building in which this met.
– ORIGIN German, from *Reichs* 'of the empire' + *Tag* 'diet' (see **DIET**[2]).

Reid /rēd/, Whitelaw (1837–1912), US journalist and diplomat. He was the owner and editor-in-chief of the *New York Tribune* 1872–1905 and the US minister to France 1889–92 and ambassador to England 1905–12.

re·i·fy /ˈrēəˌfī/ ▶ **v.** (**reifies, reifying, reified**) [with obj.] formal make (something abstract) more concrete or real: *these instincts are, in humans, reified as verbal constructs.*
– DERIVATIVES **re·i·fi·ca·tion** /ˌrēəfəˈkāSHən/ **n.**, **re·if·i·ca·to·ry** /rēˈifəkəˌtôrē/ **adj.**
– ORIGIN mid 19th cent.: from Latin *res, re-* 'thing' + **-FY**.

reign /rān/ ▶ **v.** [no obj.] hold royal office; rule as king or queen: *Queen Elizabeth* ***reigns over*** *the UK.* ■ be the best or most important in a particular area or domain: *in America, baseball* ***reigns supreme.*** ■ (of a quality or condition) prevail; predominate: *confusion reigned.* ■ (of a sports player or team) currently hold a particular title.
▶ **n.** the period during which a sovereign rules: *the original chapel was built in the reign of Charles I.*

■ the period during which someone or something is predominant or preeminent: *these historic seconds inaugurated the reign of negative political advertising.*
– ORIGIN Middle English: from Old French *reignier* 'to reign,' *reigne* 'kingdom,' from Latin *regnum*, related to *rex, reg-* 'king.'

USAGE The correct idiomatic phrase is **free rein**, not **free reign**: see usage at **REIN**.

reign·ing /rāniNG/ ▶ **adj.** occupying the throne; ruling: *the official residence of the reigning monarch.* ■ currently holding a particular title in sports: *the reigning National League champions.*

re·ig·nite /ˌrē-igˈnīt/ ▶ **v.** ignite or cause to ignite again: [no obj.] *oven burners automatically reignite if blown out.*

reign of ter·ror ▶ **n.** a period of remorseless repression or bloodshed, in particular (**Reign of Terror**), the period of the Terror during the French Revolution.

rei·ki /ˈrākē/ ▶ **n.** a healing technique based on the principle that the therapist can channel energy into the patient by means of touch, to activate the natural healing processes of the patient's body and restore physical and emotional well-being.
– ORIGIN Japanese, literally 'universal life energy.'

re·im·ag·ine /ˌrē-iˈmajən/ ▶ **v.** [with obj.] reinterpret (an event, work of art, etc.) imaginatively; rethink.

re·im·burse /ˌrē-imˈbərs/ ▶ **v.** [with obj.] repay (a person who has spent or lost money): *the investors should be reimbursed for their losses.* ■ repay (a sum of money that has been spent or lost): *they spend thousands of dollars that are not reimbursed by insurance.*
– DERIVATIVES **re·im·burs·a·ble adj.**, **re·im·burse·ment n.**
– ORIGIN early 17th cent.: from **RE-** 'back, again' + obsolete *imburse* 'put in a purse,' from medieval Latin *imbursare*, from *in-* 'into' + late Latin *bursa* 'purse.'

re·im·port /ˌrē-imˈpôrt/ ▶ **v.** [with obj.] import (goods processed or made from exported materials).
▶ **n.** the action of reimporting something. ■ a reimported item.
– DERIVATIVES **re·im·por·ta·tion** /ˌrēˌimpôrˈtāsHən/ **n.**

re·im·pose /ˌrē-imˈpōz/ ▶ **v.** [with obj.] impose (something, esp. a law or regulation) again after a lapse.
– DERIVATIVES **re·im·po·si·tion** /ˌrēimpəˈzisHən/ **n.**

Reims /rēmz, raNs/ (also **Rheims**) a city in northern France, chief town of the Champagne-Ardennes region; pop. 188,078 (2006). It was the traditional coronation place for most French kings and is noted for its fine 13th-century Gothic cathedral.

rein /rān/ ▶ **n.** (usu. **reins**) a long, narrow strap attached at one end to a horse's bit, typically used in pairs to guide or check a horse while riding or driving. ■ the power to direct and control: *management is criticized for its unwillingness to let go of the reins of an organization and delegate routine tasks.*
▶ **v.** [with obj.] check or guide (a horse) by pulling on its reins: *he **reined in** his horse and waited for her.* ■ keep under control; restrain: *with an effort, she **reined back** her impatience* | *critics noted the failure of the administration to **rein in** public spending.*
– PHRASES **draw rein** stop one's horse. (**a**) **free rein** freedom of action or expression: *he was given free rein to work out his designs.* **keep a tight rein on** exercise strict control over; allow little freedom to: *her only chance of survival was to keep a tight rein on her feelings and words.*
– ORIGIN Middle English: from Old French *rene*, based on Latin *retinere* 'retain.'

USAGE The idiomatic phrase **a free rein**, which derives from the literal meaning of using reins to control a horse, is sometimes misinterpreted and written as **a free reign**. More than a third of the citations for the phrase in the Oxford English Corpus use **reign** instead of **rein**.

re·in·car·nate ▶ **v.** /ˌrē-inˈkärˌnāt/ [with obj.] cause (someone) to undergo rebirth in another body: *a man may be reincarnated in animal form* | (as adj. **reincarnated**) *a reincarnated soul.* ■ [no obj.] (of a person) be reborn in this way: *they were afraid she would reincarnate as a vampire.*
▶ **adj.** /-nət/ [usu. postpositive] reborn in another body: *he claims that the girl is his dead daughter reincarnate.*

re·in·car·na·tion /ˌrē-inkärˈnāsHən/ ▶ **n.** the rebirth of a soul in a new body. ■ a person or animal in whom a particular soul is believed to have been reborn: *he is said to be **a reincarnation of** the Hindu god Vishnu.* ■ a new version of something from the past: *the latest reincarnation of the hippie look.*

re·in·cor·po·rate /ˌrē-inˈkôrpəˌrāt/ ▶ **v.** [with obj.] make (something) a part of something else once more: *a campaign to reincorporate the visual arts into religious devotion.*
– DERIVATIVES **re·in·cor·po·ra·tion** /ˌrē-inˌkôrpəˈrāsHən/ **n.**

rein·deer /ˈrānˌdi(ə)r/ ▶ **n.** (pl. **same** or **reindeers**) a deer of the tundra and subarctic regions of Eurasia and North America, both sexes of which have large branching antlers. Most Eurasian reindeer are domesticated and used for drawing sleds and as a source of milk, flesh, and hide. ● Genus *Rangifer*, family Cervidae: several species, in particular *R. tarandus*.
– ORIGIN late Middle English: from Old Norse *hreindýri*, from *hreinn* 'reindeer' + *dýr* 'deer.'

rein·deer moss ▶ **n.** a large branching bluish-gray lichen that grows in arctic and subarctic regions, sometimes providing the chief winter food of reindeer. ● *Cladonia rangiferina*, order Cladoniales.

re·in·fect /ˌrē-inˈfekt/ ▶ **v.** [with obj.] (usu. **be reinfected**) cause to become infected again.
– DERIVATIVES **re·in·fec·tion** /-ˈfeksHən/ **n.**

re·in·force /ˌrē-inˈfôrs/ ▶ **v.** [with obj.] strengthen or support, esp. with additional personnel or material: *paratroopers were sent to reinforce the troops already in the area.* ■ strengthen (an existing feeling, idea, or habit): *various actions of the leaders so reinforced fears and suspicions that war became unavoidable.*
– DERIVATIVES **re·in·forc·er n.**
– ORIGIN late Middle English: from French *renforcer*, influenced by *inforce*, an obsolete spelling of **ENFORCE**; the sense of providing military support is probably from Italian *rinforzare*.

re·in·forced con·crete ▶ **n.** concrete in which wire mesh or steel bars are embedded to increase its tensile strength.

re·in·force·ment /ˌrē-inˈfôrsmənt/ ▶ **n.** the action or process of reinforcing or strengthening. ■ the process of encouraging or establishing a belief or pattern of behavior, esp. by encouragement or reward. ■ (**reinforcements**) extra personnel sent to increase the strength of an army or similar force: *a small force would hold the position until reinforcements could be sent.* ■ the strengthening structure or material employed in reinforced concrete or plastic.

Rein·hardt /ˈrīnˌhärt/, Max (1873–1943), Austrian director and impresario; born *Max Goldmann.* He produced large-scale versions of such works as Sophocles' *Oedipus Rex* (1910) and helped to establish the Salzburg Festival with Richard Strauss and Hugo von Hofmannsthal.

re·in·sert /ˌrē-inˈsərt/ ▶ **v.** [with obj.] place (something) back into its previous position.
– DERIVATIVES **re·in·ser·tion** /-ˈsərsHən/ **n.**

re·in·stall /ˌrē-inˈstôl/ (Brit. also **reinstal**) ▶ **v.** (**reinstalls** (or Brit. **reinstals**), **reinstalling, reinstalled**) [with obj.] place or fix (equipment or machinery) in position again. ■ install (computer software) again: *I reinstalled the program.*
▶ **n.** an act of reinstalling something, esp. software: *try performing a "clean" reinstall of your system software.*
– DERIVATIVES **re·in·stal·la·tion** /ˌrē-instəˈlāsHən/ **n.**, **re·in·stall·er n.**

re·in·state /ˌrē-inˈstāt/ ▶ **v.** [with obj.] restore (someone or something) to their former position or condition: *the union is fighting to reinstate the fired journalists.*
– DERIVATIVES **re·in·state·ment n.**

re·in·sti·tute /rēˈinstit(y)o͞ot/ ▶ **v.** [with obj.] institute or introduce again: *by reinstituting the draft they could alienate a new generation of American youth.*
– DERIVATIVES **re·in·sti·tu·tion n.**

re·in·sure /ˌrē-inˈsHo͝or/ ▶ **v.** [with obj.] (of an insurer) transfer (all or part of a risk) to another insurer to provide protection against the risk of the first insurance.
– DERIVATIVES **re·in·sur·ance** /-ˈsHo͝orəns/ **n.**, **re·in·sur·er n.**

re·in·te·grate /rēˈintəˌgrāt/ ▶ **v.** [with obj.] restore (elements regarded as disparate) to unity. ■ restore to a position as a part fitting easily into a larger whole: *it can be difficult for an offender to be **reintegrated into** the community.*
– DERIVATIVES **re·in·te·gra·tion** /ˌrēintəˈgrāsHən/ **n.**

re·in·ter /ˌrē-inˈtər/ ▶ **v.** [with obj.] bury (a corpse) again, often in a different place than that of the first burial.
– DERIVATIVES **re·in·ter·ment n.**

re·in·ter·me·di·a·tion /ˌrēintərˌmēdēˈāsHən/ ▶ **n.** the transfer or bringing back of borrowing and investments from an outside credit business into the banking system. ■ the insertion of middlemen into transactions between producers and consumers.
– ORIGIN 1970s: from **RE-** + **INTERMEDIATE** + **-ATION**.

re·in·ter·pret /ˌrē-inˈtərprət/ ▶ **v.** (**reinterprets, reinterpreting, reinterpreted**) [with obj.] interpret (something) in a new or different way.
– DERIVATIVES **re·in·ter·pre·ta·tion** /ˌrē-inˌtərprəˈtāsHən/ **n.**

re·in·tro·duce /ˌrē-intrəˈd(y)o͞os/ ▶ **v.** [with obj.] bring (something, esp. a law or system) into existence or effect again: *thirty-six states have reintroduced the death penalty.* ■ put (a species of animal or plant) back into a region where it formerly lived: *a plan to reintroduce wolves to Yellowstone National Park.*
– DERIVATIVES **re·in·tro·duc·tion** /-ˈdəksHən/ **n.**

re·in·vent /ˌrē-inˈvent/ ▶ **v.** [with obj.] change (something) so much that it appears to be entirely new: *he brought opera to the masses and reinvented the waltz.* ■ (**reinvent oneself**) take up a very different job or way of life: *the actor wants to reinvent himself as an independent movie mogul.*
– PHRASES **reinvent the wheel** waste a great deal of time or effort in creating something that already exists.
– DERIVATIVES **re·in·ven·tion** /-ˈvenCHən/ **n.**

re·in·vest /ˌrē-inˈvest/ ▶ **v.** [with obj.] put (the profit on a previous investment) back into the same place: *the enterprise had been expanded by reinvesting profits.*
– DERIVATIVES **re·in·vest·ment** /-ˈvestmənt/ **n.**

re·in·ves·ti·gate /rē-inˈvestiˌgāt/ ▶ **v.** [with obj.] investigate (a matter) again: *detectives made the decision to reinvestigate the case.*
– DERIVATIVES **re·in·ves·ti·ga·tion n.**

re·in·vig·or·ate /ˌrē-inˈvigəˌrāt/ ▶ **v.** [with obj.] give new energy or strength to: *we are fully committed to reinvigorating the economy of the area.*
– DERIVATIVES **re·in·vig·or·a·tion** /ˌrē-inˌvigəˈrāsHən/ **n.**

re·is·sue /rēˈisHo͞o/ ▶ **v.** (**reissues, reissuing, reissued**) [with obj.] make a new supply or different form of (a product, esp. a book or record) available for sale: *the book was reissued with a new epilogue.*
▶ **n.** a new issue of such a product.

REIT ▶ **abbr.** real-estate investment trust.

re·it·er·ate /rēˈitəˌrāt/ ▶ **v.** [reporting verb] say something again or a number or times, typically for emphasis or clarity: [with clause] *she reiterated that the administration would remain steadfast in its support* | [with direct speech] *"I just want to forget it all," he reiterated* | [with obj.] *he reiterated the points made in his earlier speech.*
– DERIVATIVES **re·it·er·a·tion** /rēˌitəˈrāsHən/ **n.**, **re·it·er·a·tive** /-ˌrātiv, -rətiv/ **adj.**
– ORIGIN late Middle English (in the sense 'do (an action) repeatedly'): from Latin *reiterat-* 'gone over again,' from the verb *reiterare*, from *re-* 'again' + *iterare* 'do a second time.'

Rei·ter's syn·drome /ˈrītərz/ (also **Reiter's disease**) ▶ **n.** a medical condition typically affecting young men, characterized by arthritis, conjunctivitis, and urethritis, and caused by an unknown pathogen, possibly a chlamydia.
– ORIGIN 1920s: named after Hans *Reiter* (1881–1969), German bacteriologist.

reive /rēv/ ▶ **v.** [no obj.] (usu. as noun **reiving**) chiefly Scottish another term for **REAVE**.
– DERIVATIVES **reiv·er n.**
– ORIGIN Middle English: variant of **REAVE**; the usual spelling when referring to the historical practice of cattle raiding on the English-Scottish border.

re·ject ▶ **v.** /riˈjekt/ [with obj.] dismiss as inadequate, inappropriate, or not to one's taste: *union negotiators rejected a 1.5 percent pay increase.* ■ refuse to agree to (a request): *an application to hold a pop concert at the club was rejected.* ■ fail to show due affection or concern for (someone); rebuff: *she didn't want him to feel he had been rejected after his sister was born.* ■ Medicine show an immune response to (a transplanted organ or tissue) so that it fails to survive.
▶ **n.** /ˈrēˌjekt/ a person or thing dismissed as failing to meet standards or satisfy tastes: *some of the team's rejects have gone on to prove themselves in championships.*
– DERIVATIVES **re·ject·ee** /riˌjekˈtē, ˌrē-/ **n.**, **re·jec·tive** /riˈjektiv/ **adj.** (rare), **re·jec·tor** /-tər/ **n.**
– ORIGIN late Middle English: from Latin *reject-* 'thrown back,' from the verb *reicere*, from *re-* 'back' + *jacere* 'to throw.'

re·jec·tion /riˈjeksHən/ ▶ **n.** the dismissing or refusing of a proposal, idea, etc.: *the union decided last night to recommend rejection of the offer.* ■ the spurning of a person's affections: *some people are reluctant to try it, because they fear rejection.*

re·jec·tion·ist /riˈjeksHənist/ ▶ **n.** [often as modifier] a person who rejects a proposed policy, esp. an Arab who refuses to accept a negotiated peace with Israel.

re·jec·tion slip ▶ **n.** a formal notice sent by an editor or publisher to an author with a rejected manuscript or typescript.

re·jig·ger /rē'jigər/ (Brit. **rejig**) ▶ **v.** [with obj.] organize (something) differently; rearrange: *he rejiggers his stump speech ever so slightly to fit the crowd, then sounds the same messages.*

re·joice /ri'jois/ ▶ **v.** [no obj.] feel or show great joy or delight: *he rejoiced when he saw his friend alive | he* ***rejoiced in*** *her spontaneity and directness.* ■ [with obj.] archaic cause joy to: *I love to rejoice their poor Hearts at this season.*
– DERIVATIVES **re·joic·er n.**
– ORIGIN Middle English (in the sense 'cause joy to'): from Old French *rejoiss-*, lengthened stem of *rejoir*, from *re-* (expressing intensive force) + *joir* 'experience joy.'

re·joic·ing /ri'joisiNG/ ▶ **n.** great joy; jubilation: *the ban was lifted in 1990 amid general rejoicing.*
– DERIVATIVES **re·joic·ing·ly adv.**

re·join[1] /rē'join, 'rē-/ ▶ **v.** [with obj.] join together again; reunite: *the stone had been cracked and crudely rejoined.* ■ return to (a companion, organization, or route that one has left): *the soldiers were returning from leave to rejoin their unit.*

re·join[2] /ri'join/ ▶ **v.** [reporting verb] say something in answer to a remark, typically rudely or in a discouraging manner: [with clause] *Harry said that he longed for a bath and soft towels, to which his father rejoined that he was a gross materialist.*
– ORIGIN late Middle English (in the sense 'reply to a charge or pleading in a lawsuit'): from Old French *rejoindre*, from *re-* 'again' + *joindre* 'to join.'

re·join·der /ri'joindər/ ▶ **n.** a reply, esp. a sharp or witty one: *she would have made some cutting rejoinder but none came to mind.* ■ Law, dated a defendant's answer to the plaintiff's reply or replication.
– ORIGIN late Middle English: from Anglo-Norman French *rejoindre* (infinitive used as a noun) (see REJOIN[2]).

re·ju·ve·nate /ri'jo͞ovə,nāt/ ▶ **v.** [with obj.] make (someone or something) look or feel younger, fresher, or more lively: *a bid to rejuvenate the town center* | (as adj. **rejuvenating**) *the rejuvenating effects of therapeutic clay.* ■ (often as adj. **rejuvenated**) restore (a river or stream) to a condition characteristic of a younger landscape.
– DERIVATIVES **re·ju·ve·na·tion** /ri,jo͞ovə'nāsHən/ **n.**, **re·ju·ve·na·tor** /-,nātər/ **n.**
– ORIGIN early 19th cent.: from RE- 'again' + Latin *juvenis* 'young' + -ATE[3], suggested by French *rajeunir.*

re·ju·ve·nes·cence /ri,jo͞ovə'nesəns/ ▶ **n.** the renewal of youth or vitality. ■ Biology the reactivation of vegetative cells, resulting in regrowth from old or injured parts.
– DERIVATIVES **re·ju·ve·nes·cent** /-'nesənt/ **adj.**
– ORIGIN mid 17th cent.: from late Latin *rejuvenescere* (from Latin *re-* 'again' + *juvenis* 'young') + -ENCE.

re·key /rē'kē/ ▶ **v.** [with obj.] chiefly Computing enter (text or other data) again using a keyboard.

re·kin·dle /rē'kindəl/ ▶ **v.** [with obj.] relight (a fire). ■ revive (something that has been lost): *he tried to rekindle their friendship | the photos rekindled memories.*

rel. ▶ **abbr.** ■ relating. ■ relative. ■ relatively. ■ released. ■ religion. ■ religious.

-rel ▶ **suffix** forming nouns with diminutive or derogatory force such as *cockerel, pickerel, scoundrel.*
– ORIGIN from Old French *-erel(le).*

re·la·bel /rē'lābəl/ ▶ **v.** (**relabels, relabeling, relabeled**; Brit. **relabels, relabelling, relabelled**) [with obj.] label (something) again or differently.

re·laid /rē'lād, 'rē-/ past and past participle of RELAY[1].

re·lapse ▶ **v.** /ri'laps, 'rē,laps/ [no obj.] (of someone suffering from a disease) suffer deterioration after a period of improvement. ■ (**relapse into**) return to (a less active or a worse state): *he relapsed into silence.*
▶ **n.** /'rē,laps/ a deterioration in someone's state of health after a temporary improvement: *he suffered a relapse of schizophrenia after a car crash.*
– DERIVATIVES **re·laps·er n.**
– ORIGIN late Middle English: from Latin *relaps-* 'slipped back,' from the verb *relabi*, from *re-* 'back' + *labi* 'to slip.' Early senses referred to a return to heresy or wrongdoing.

re·laps·ing fe·ver ▶ **n.** an infectious bacterial disease marked by recurrent fever. ● The disease is caused by spirochetes of the genus *Borrelia.*

re·lat·a·ble /ri'lātəbəl/ ▶ **adj.** **1** able to be related to something else: *the growth of the welfare state will be clearly relatable to the growth of democracy.* **2** enabling a person to feel that they can relate to someone or something: *Mary-Kate's problems make her more relatable.*
– DERIVATIVES **re·lat·a·bil·i·ty n.**

re·late /ri'lāt/ ▶ **v.** [with obj.] **1** give an account of (a sequence of events); narrate: *various versions of the chilling story have been related by the locals.*
2 (**be related**) be connected by blood or marriage: *he was* ***related to*** *my mother | people who are related.* ■ be causally connected: *high unemployment is* ***related to*** *high crime rates.* ■ (**relate something to**) discuss something in such a way as to indicate its connections with (something else): *the study examines social change within the city and relates it to wider developments in the country as a whole.* ■ [no obj.] (**relate to**) have reference to; concern: *the new legislation related to corporate activities.* ■ [no obj.] (**relate to**) feel sympathy with; identify with: *kids related to him because he was so anti-establishment.*
– ORIGIN mid 16th cent.: from Latin *relat-* 'brought back,' from the verb *referre* (see REFER).

re·lat·ed /ri'lātid/ ▶ **adj.** belonging to the same family, group, or type; connected: *sleeping sickness and related diseases.* ■ [in combination] associated with the specified item or process, esp. causally: *income-related benefits.*
– DERIVATIVES **re·lat·ed·ness n.**

re·lat·er /ri'lātər/ (also **relator**) ▶ **n.** a person who tells a story; a narrator.

re·la·tion /ri'lāsHən/ ▶ **n.** **1** the way in which two or more concepts, objects, or people are connected; a thing's effect on or relevance to another: *questions about the* ***relation between*** *writing and reality | the size of the targets* ***bore no relation to*** *their importance.* ■ (**relations**) the way in which two or more people, countries, or organizations feel about and behave toward each other: *the improvement in relations between the two countries | the meetings helped cement Anglo-American relations.* ■ (**relations**) chiefly formal sexual intercourse: *he wanted an excuse to abandon sexual relations with her.*
2 a person who is connected by blood or marriage; a kinsman or kinswoman: *she was no relation at all, but he called her Aunt Nora.*
3 the action of telling a story.
– PHRASES **in relation to** in the context of; in connection with: *there is an ambiguity in the provisions in relation to children's hearings.*
– ORIGIN Middle English: from Old French, or from Latin *relatio(n-)*, from *referre* 'bring back' (see RELATE).

re·la·tion·al /ri'lāsHənl/ ▶ **adj.** concerning the way in which two or more people or things are connected: *power is a relational concept that can only be understood in terms of interactions between individuals and groups.*
– DERIVATIVES **re·la·tion·al·ly adv.**

rela·tion·al da·ta·base ▶ **n.** Computing a database structured to recognize relations among stored items of information.

re·la·tion·ship /ri'lāsHən,sHip/ ▶ **n.** the way in which two or more concepts, objects, or people are connected, or the state of being connected: *the study will assess the* ***relationship between*** *unemployment and political attitudes.* ■ the state of being connected by blood or marriage: *they can trace their relationship to a common ancestor.* ■ the way in which two or more people or organizations regard and behave toward each other: *the landlord–tenant relationship | she was proud of her good relationship with the household staff.* ■ an emotional and sexual association between two people: *she has a daughter from a previous relationship.*

rel·a·tive /'relətiv/ ▶ **adj.** **1** considered in relation or in proportion to something else: *the relative effectiveness of the various mechanisms is not known.* ■ existing or possessing a specified characteristic only in comparison to something else; not absolute: *she went down the steps into the relative darkness of the dining room | the companies are relative newcomers to computers.*
2 Grammar denoting a pronoun, determiner, or adverb that refers to an expressed or implied antecedent and attaches a subordinate clause to it, e.g., *which, who.* ■ (of a clause) attached to an antecedent by a relative word.
3 Music (of major and minor keys) having the same key signature.
4 (of a service rank) corresponding in grade to another in a different service.
▶ **n.** **1** a person connected by blood or marriage: *much of my time is spent visiting relatives.* ■ a species related to another by common origin: *the plant is a relative of ivy.*
2 Grammar a relative pronoun, determiner, or adverb.
3 Philosophy a term, thing, or concept that is dependent on something else.
– PHRASES **relative to 1** in comparison with: *the figures suggest that girls are underachieving relative to boys.* ■ in terms of a connection to: *some stars appear to change their position relative to each other.* **2** in connection with; concerning: *if you have any questions relative to payment, please contact us.*
– DERIVATIVES **rel·a·tiv·al** /,relə'tīvəl/ **adj.** (sense 2 of the noun).
– ORIGIN late Middle English: from Old French *relatif, -ive*, from late Latin *relativus* 'having reference or relation' (see RELATE).

rel·a·tive a·tom·ic mass ▶ **n.** Chemistry Another term for ATOMIC MASS.

rel·a·tive den·si·ty ▶ **n.** another term for SPECIFIC GRAVITY.

rel·a·tive hu·mid·i·ty ▶ **n.** the amount of water vapor present in air expressed as a percentage of the amount needed for saturation at the same temperature.

rel·a·tive·ly /'relətivlē/ ▶ **adv.** [sentence adverb] in relation, comparison, or proportion to something else: *it is perfectly simple,* ***relatively speaking****, to store a full catalog entry on magnetic tape.* ■ [as submodifier] viewed in comparison with something else rather than absolutely: *relatively affluent people | the site was cheap and relatively clean.*

rel·a·tiv·ism /'relətə,vizəm/ ▶ **n.** the doctrine that knowledge, truth, and morality exist in relation to culture, society, or historical context, and are not absolute.
– DERIVATIVES **rel·a·tiv·ist n.**

rel·a·tiv·is·tic /,relətə'vistik/ ▶ **adj.** **1** Physics accurately described only by the theory of relativity.
2 of or relating to the doctrine of relativism.
– DERIVATIVES **rel·a·tiv·is·ti·cal·ly** /-ik(ə)lē/ **adv.**

rel·a·tiv·i·ty /,relə'tivətē/ ▶ **n.** **1** the absence of standards of absolute and universal application: *moral relativity.*
2 Physics the dependence of various physical phenomena on relative motion of the observer and the observed objects, esp. regarding the nature and behavior of light, space, time, and gravity.

> The concept of relativity was set out in Einstein's **special theory of relativity**, published in 1905. This states that all motion is relative and that the velocity of light in a vacuum has a constant value that nothing can exceed. Among its consequences are the following: the mass of a body increases and its length (in the direction of motion) shortens as its speed increases; the time interval between two events occurring in a moving body appears greater to a stationary observer; and mass and energy are equivalent and interconvertible. Einstein's **general theory of relativity**, published in 1915, extended the theory to accelerated motion and gravitation, which was treated as a curvature of the space-time continuum. It predicted that light rays would be deflected and shifted in wavelength when passing through a substantial gravitational field, effects that have been experimentally confirmed.

rel·a·tiv·ize /'relətə,vīz/ ▶ **v.** [with obj.] chiefly Linguistics & Philosophy make or treat as relative to or dependent on something else. ■ Grammar & Linguistics make into a relative clause. ■ Physics treat (a phenomenon or concept) according to the principles of the theory of relativity.
– DERIVATIVES **rel·a·tiv·i·za·tion** /,relətəvə'zāsHən/ **n.**

re·la·tor /ri'lātər/ ▶ **n.** **1** Law a person who brings a public lawsuit, typically in the name of the attorney general, regarding the abuse of an office or franchise.
2 variant spelling of RELATER.

re·launch ▶ **v.** /rē'lônCH, -'lānCH/ [with obj.] reintroduce or restart (something, esp. a product): *he relaunched the paper as a tabloid.*
▶ **n.** /'rēlônCH, -lānCH/ an instance of relaunching something.

re·lax /ri'laks/ ▶ **v.** **1** make or become less tense or anxious: [no obj.] *he relaxed and smiled confidently* | (as adj. **relaxing**) *a relaxing vacation.* ■ [no obj.] rest or engage in an enjoyable activity so as to become less tired or anxious: *the team relaxes with a lot of skiing.* ■ [with obj.] cause (a limb or muscle) to become less rigid: *relax the leg by bringing the knee toward the chest.* ■ [with obj.] make (something) less firm or tight: *Cicely relaxed her hold.* ■ [with obj.] straighten or partially uncurl (hair) using a chemical product.
2 [with obj.] make (a rule or restriction) less strict while not abolishing it: *they persuaded the local authorities concerned to relax their restrictions.*

PRONUNCIATION KEY ə *ago, up*; ər *over, fur*; a *hat*; ā *ate*; ä *car*; e *let*; ē *see*; i *fit*; ī *by*; NG *sing*; ō *go*; ô *law, for*; oi *toy*; o͝o *good*; o͞o *goo*; ou *out*; TH *thin*; TH *then*; ZH *vision*

–DERIVATIVES **re·lax·er** n.
–ORIGIN late Middle English: from Latin *relaxare*, from *re-* (expressing intensive force) + *laxus* 'lax, loose.'

re·lax·ant /rə'laksənt/ ▶ n. a drug used to promote relaxation or reduce tension: *a muscle relaxant.* ■ a thing having a relaxing effect: *sex can be a great relaxant.*
▶ adj. causing relaxation.

re·lax·a·tion /ri,lak'sāsHən, rē-/ ▶ n. **1** the state of being free from tension and anxiety. ■ recreation or rest, esp. after a period of work: *his favorite form of relaxation was reading detective novels.* ■ the loss of tension in a part of the body, esp. in a muscle when it ceases to contract. ■ the action of making a rule or restriction less strict: *relaxation of censorship rules.*
2 Physics the restoration of equilibrium following disturbance.

re·lax·a·tion os·cil·la·tor ▶ n. Electronics an oscillator in which sharp, sometimes aperiodic oscillations result from the rapid discharge of a capacitor or inductance.

re·laxed /ri'lakst/ ▶ adj. free from tension and anxiety; at ease: *we were having a great time and feeling very relaxed | the relaxed and comfortable atmosphere of the hotel.* ■ (of a muscle or other body part) not tense.
–DERIVATIVES **re·lax·ed·ly** /ri'laksədlē/ adv., **re·lax·ed·ness** /ri'laksədnəs/ n.

re·lax·in /rə'laksin/ ▶ n. Biochemistry a hormone secreted by the placenta that causes the cervix to dilate and prepares the uterus for the action of oxytocin during labor.

re·lay[1] ▶ n. /'rē,lā/ **1** a group of people or animals engaged in a task or activity for a fixed period of time and then replaced by a similar group: *the wagons were pulled by relays of horses | gangs of workers were sent in relays.* ■ [usu. as modifier] a race between teams usually of sprinters or swimmers, each team member in turn covering part of the total distance: *a 550-meter relay race.*
2 an electrical device, typically incorporating an electromagnet, that is activated by a current or signal in one circuit to open or close another circuit.
3 a device to receive, reinforce, and retransmit a broadcast or program. ■ a message or program transmitted by such a device: *a relay of a performance live from the concert hall.*
▶ v. /ri'lā, 'rē,lā/ [with obj.] receive and pass on (information or a message): *she intended to relay everything she had learned.* ■ broadcast (something) by passing signals received from elsewhere through a transmitting station: *the speech was relayed live from the White House.*
–ORIGIN late Middle English (referring to the provision of fresh hounds on the track of a deer): from Old French *relai* (noun), *relayer* (verb), based on Latin *laxare* 'slacken.'

re·lay[2] /rē'lā/ (also **re-lay**) ▶ v. (past and past participle **relaid**) [with obj.] lay again or differently: *they plan to relay about half a mile of the track.*

re·learn /rē'lərn/ ▶ v. (past and past participle **relearned** or chiefly Brit. **relearnt** /-'lərnt/) [with obj.] learn (something) again: *I've been relearning my Latin and Greek.*

re·lease /ri'lēs/ ▶ v. [with obj.] **1** allow or enable to escape from confinement; set free: *the government announced that the prisoners would be released.*
2 allow (something) to move, act, or flow freely: *she released his arm and pushed him aside | growth hormone is released into the blood during the first part of sleep.* ■ remove restrictions or obligations from (someone or something) so that they become available for other activity: *the strategy would release forces for service in other areas.* ■ remove (part of a machine or appliance) from a fixed position, allowing something else to move or function: *he released the handbrake.* ■ allow (something) to return to its resting position by ceasing to put pressure on it: *press and release the reset button quickly.*
3 allow (information) to be generally available: *no details about the contents of the talks were released.* ■ make (a movie or recording) available for general viewing or purchase: *nine singles and one album had been released.*
4 Law remit or discharge (a debt). ■ surrender (a right). ■ make over (property or money) to another person or entity.
▶ n. **1** the action or process of releasing or being released: *a campaign by the prisoner's mother resulted in his release.* ■ a handle or catch that releases part of a mechanism.
2 the action of making a movie, recording, or other product available for general viewing or purchase: *the film was withheld for two years before its release.* ■ a movie or other product issued for viewing or purchase: *his current album release has topped the charts for six months.* ■ a press release.
3 Law the action of releasing property, money, or a right to another. ■ a document effecting this.
–DERIVATIVES **re·leas·a·ble** adj., **re·leas·ee** /ri,lē'sē/ n. (Law), **re·leas·er** /ri'lēsər/ n., **re·leas·or** /ri'lēsər/ n. (Law).
–ORIGIN Middle English: from Old French *reles* (noun), *relesser* (verb), from Latin *relaxare* 'stretch out again, slacken' (see RELAX).

re·leas·ing fac·tor ▶ n. Biochemistry a substance that, when secreted by the hypothalamus, promotes the release of a specified hormone from the anterior lobe of the pituitary gland.

rel·e·gate /'relə,gāt/ ▶ v. [with obj.] consign or dismiss to an inferior rank or position: *they aim to prevent women from being relegated to a secondary role.*
–DERIVATIVES **rel·e·ga·tion** /,relə'gāsHən/ n.
–ORIGIN late Middle English (in the sense 'send into exile'): from Latin *relegat-* 'sent away, referred,' from the verb *relegare*, from *re-* 'again' + *legare* 'send.'

re·lent /ri'lent/ ▶ v. [no obj.] abandon or mitigate a harsh intention or cruel treatment: *she was going to refuse his request, but relented.* ■ (esp. of bad weather) become less severe or intense: *by evening the rain relented.*
–ORIGIN late Middle English (in the sense 'dissolve, melt'): based on Latin *re-* 'back' + *lentare* 'to bend' (from *lentus* 'flexible').

re·lent·less /ri'lentləs/ ▶ adj. oppressively constant; incessant: *the relentless heat of the desert.* ■ harsh or inflexible: *a patient but relentless taskmaster.*
–DERIVATIVES **re·lent·less·ly** adv., **re·lent·less·ness** n.

re·let ▶ v. /rē'let, 'rē-/ (**relets, reletting**; past and past participle **relet**) [with obj.] chiefly Brit. rent (a property) for a further period or to a new tenant.
▶ n. /'rēlet/ an act of renting a property again.

rel·e·vant /'reləvənt/ ▶ adj. closely connected or appropriate to the matter at hand: *the candidate's experience is relevant to the job.*
–DERIVATIVES **rel·e·vance** n., **rel·e·van·cy** /-vənsē/ n., **rel·e·vant·ly** adv.
–ORIGIN early 16th cent. (as a Scots legal term meaning 'legally pertinent'): from medieval Latin *relevant-* 'raising up,' from Latin *relevare*.

re·le·vé /,relə'vā/ ▶ n. **1** Ballet a movement in which the dancer rises on the tips of the toes.
2 Ecology each of a number of small plots of vegetation, analyzed as a sample of a wider area.
–ORIGIN French, literally 'raised up.'

re·li·a·ble /ri'līəbəl/ ▶ adj. consistently good in quality or performance; able to be trusted: *a reliable source of information.*
▶ n. a person or thing with such trustworthy qualities: *the supporting cast includes old reliables like Mitchell.*
–DERIVATIVES **re·li·a·bil·i·ty** /ri,līə'bilətē/ n., **re·li·a·ble·ness** n., **re·li·a·bly** /-blē/ adv.

re·li·ance /ri'līəns/ ▶ n. dependence on or trust in someone or something: *the farmer's reliance on pesticides.* ■ archaic a person or thing on which someone depends.
–DERIVATIVES **re·li·ant** /-ənt/ adj.

rel·ic /'relik/ ▶ n. an object surviving from an earlier time, esp. one of historical or sentimental interest. ■ a part of a deceased holy person's body or belongings kept as an object of reverence. ■ an object, custom, or belief that has survived from an earlier time but is now outmoded: *individualized computer programming and time-sharing would become expensive relics.* ■ (**relics**) all that is left of something: *relics of a lost civilization.*
–ORIGIN Middle English: from Old French *relique* (originally plural), from Latin *reliquiae* (see RELIQUIAE).

rel·ict /'relikt/ ▶ n. **1** a thing that has survived from an earlier period or in a primitive form. ■ an animal or plant that has survived while others of its group have become extinct, e.g., the coelacanth. ■ a species or community that formerly had a wider distribution but now survives in only a few localities such as refugia. [early 20th cent.: from Latin *relictus* 'left behind,' past participle of the verb *relinquere*.]
2 archaic a widow. [late Middle English: from Old French *relicte* '(woman) left behind,' from late Latin *relicta*, from the verb *relinquere*.]

re·lief /ri'lēf/ ▶ n. **1** a feeling of reassurance and relaxation following release from anxiety or distress: *much to her relief, she saw the door open.* ■ a cause of or occasion for such a feeling: *it was a relief to find somewhere to stay.* ■ the alleviation of pain, discomfort, or distress: *tablets for the relief of pain.* ■ a temporary break in a generally tense or tedious situation: *the comic characters aren't part of the plot but just light relief.*
2 assistance, esp. in the form of food, clothing, or money, given to those in special need or difficulty: *raising money for famine relief* | [as modifier] *relief workers.* ■ a remission of tax normally due: *people who donate money to charity will receive tax relief.* ■ chiefly Law the redress of a hardship or grievance. ■ the action of raising the siege of a besieged town: *the relief of Mafeking.*
3 a person or group of people replacing others who have been on duty: [as modifier] *the relief nurse was late.* ■ Baseball the role of a relief pitcher.
4 the state of being clearly visible or obvious due to being accentuated in some way: *the setting sun threw the snow-covered peaks into relief.* ■ a method of molding, carving, or stamping in which the design stands out from the surface, to a greater (**high relief**) or lesser (**bas-relief**) extent. ■ a piece of sculpture in relief. ■ a representation of relief given by an arrangement of line or color or shading. ■ Geography difference in height from the surrounding terrain; the amount of variation in elevation and slope in a particular area. [via French from Italian *rilievo*, from *rilevare* 'raise,' from Latin *relevare*.]
–PHRASES **in relief 1** Art carved, molded, or stamped so as to stand out from the surface. **2** Baseball acting as a replacement pitcher. **on relief** receiving government assistance because of need.
–ORIGIN late Middle English: from Old French, from *relever* 'raise up, relieve,' from Latin *relevare* 'raise again, alleviate.'

re·lief map ▶ n. a map indicating hills and valleys by shading rather than by contour lines alone. ■ a map model with elevations and depressions representing hills and valleys, typically on an exaggerated relative scale.

re·lief pitch·er ▶ n. Baseball a pitcher who enters the game in place of the previous pitcher.

re·lief print·ing ▶ n. printing from raised images, as in letterpress and flexography.

re·lief road ▶ n. Brit. a road taking traffic around, rather than through, a congested urban area.

re·lieve /ri'lēv/ ▶ v. [with obj.] **1** cause (pain, distress, or difficulty) to become less severe or serious: *the drug was used to promote sleep and to relieve pain.* ■ cause (someone) to stop feeling distressed or anxious about something. ■ make less tedious or monotonous by the introduction of variety or of something striking or pleasing: *the bird's body is black, relieved only by white under the tail.*
2 release (someone) from duty by taking their place: *another signalman relieved him at 5:30.* ■ bring military support for (a besieged place): *he dispatched an expedition to relieve the city.* ■ Baseball (of a relief pitcher) take the place of (another pitcher) during a game.
3 (**relieve someone of**) take (a burden) from someone: *he relieved her of her baggage.* ■ free someone from (a tiresome responsibility): *she relieved me of the household chores.* ■ used euphemistically to indicate that someone has been deprived of something: *he was relieved of his world title.*
4 (**relieve oneself**) urinate or defecate (used euphemistically).
5 archaic make (something) stand out: *the twilight relieving in purple masses the foliage of the island.*
–DERIVATIVES **re·liev·a·ble** adj.
–ORIGIN Middle English: from Old French *relever*, from Latin *relevare*, from *re-* (expressing intensive force) + *levare* 'raise' (from *levis* 'light').

re·lieved /ri'lēvd/ ▶ adj. no longer feeling distressed or anxious; reassured: *relieved parents who had waited anxiously for news.*
–DERIVATIVES **re·liev·ed·ly** /ri'lēvədlē/ adv.

re·liev·er /ri'lēvər/ ▶ n. **1** a person or thing that relieves.
2 Baseball a relief pitcher.

re·liev·ing of·fi·cer ▶ n. chiefly Brit. historical an official appointed to administer relief to the poor.

re·lie·vo /ri'lēvō, rēl'yāvō/ (also **rilievo**) ▶ n. (pl. **relievos**) chiefly Art another term for RELIEF (sense 4).
–ORIGIN Italian *rilievo*.

re·light /rē'līt, 'rē-/ ▶ v. (past and past participle **relighted** or **relit** /-'lit/) [with obj.] light (something) again: *he reached for the matches to relight his pipe.*

religio- ▶ comb. form religious and ...: *religio-political* | *religio-national.*
–ORIGIN from RELIGION or RELIGIOUS.

re·li·gion /ri'lijən/ ▶ n. the belief in and worship of a superhuman controlling power, esp. a personal God or gods: *ideas about the relationship between science and religion.* ■ a particular system of faith and worship: *the world's great religions.* ■ a pursuit or interest to which someone ascribes supreme importance: *consumerism is the new religion.*
–PHRASES **get religion** informal be converted to religious belief and practices.
–DERIVATIVES **re·li·gion·less** adj.

– ORIGIN Middle English (originally in the sense 'life under monastic vows'): from Old French, or from Latin *religio(n-)* 'obligation, bond, reverence,' perhaps based on Latin *religare* 'to bind.'

re·li·gion·ism /ri'lijə,nizəm/ ▶ **n.** excessive religious zeal.
– DERIVATIVES **re·li·gion·ist** **n.**

re·li·gi·ose /ri'lijē,ōs/ ▶ **adj.** excessively religious.
– DERIVATIVES **re·li·gi·os·i·ty** /ri,lijē'äsətē/ **n.**
– ORIGIN mid 19th cent.: from Latin *religiosus*, from *religio* 'reverence, obligation.'

re·li·gious /ri'lijəs/ ▶ **adj.** relating to or believing in a religion: *both men were deeply religious, intelligent, and moralistic* | *religious music.* ■ (of a belief or practice) forming part of someone's thought about or worship of a divine being: *he has strong religious convictions.* ■ belonging or relating to a monastic order or other group of people who are united by their practice of religion: *religious houses were built on ancient pagan sites.* ■ treated or regarded with a devotion and scrupulousness appropriate to worship: *I have a religious aversion to reading manuals.*
▶ **n.** (pl. **same**) a person bound by monastic vows.
– DERIVATIVES **re·li·gious·ly** **adv.**, **re·li·gious·ness** **n.**
– ORIGIN Middle English: from Old French, from Latin *religiosus*, from *religio* 'reverence, obligation' (see **RELIGION**).

Re·li·gious So·ci·e·ty of Friends official name for the Quakers (see **QUAKER**).

re·line /rē'līn, 'rē-/ ▶ **v.** [with obj.] replace the lining of: *the heavily brocaded drapes that she had relined.* ■ attach a new backing canvas to (a painting).

re·lin·quish /ri'liNGkwiSH/ ▶ **v.** [with obj.] voluntarily cease to keep or claim; give up: *he relinquished his managerial role to become chief executive.*
– DERIVATIVES **re·lin·quish·ment** **n.**
– ORIGIN late Middle English: from Old French *relinquiss-*, lengthened stem of *relinquir*, from Latin *relinquere*, from *re-* (expressing intensive force) + *linquere* 'to leave.'

rel·i·quar·y /'relə,kwerē/ ▶ **n.** (pl. **reliquaries**) a container for holy relics.
– ORIGIN mid 16th cent.: from French *reliquaire*, from Old French *relique* (see **RELIC**).

re·liq·ui·ae /rə'likwē,ī, -wē,ē/ ▶ **plural n.** remains. ■ Geology fossil remains of animals or plants.
– ORIGIN mid 17th cent.: Latin, feminine plural (used as a noun) of *reliquus* 'remaining,' based on *linquere* 'to leave.'

rel·ish /'relisH/ ▶ **n.** **1** great enjoyment: *she swigged a mouthful of wine with relish.* ■ liking for or pleasurable anticipation of something: *I was appointed to a position for which I had little relish.*
2 a condiment eaten with plain food to add flavor: *use salsa as a relish with grilled meat or fish.*
3 archaic an appetizing flavor. ■ a distinctive taste or tinge: *the relish of wine.*
▶ **v.** [with obj.] **1** enjoy greatly: *he was relishing his moment of glory.* ■ be pleased by or about: *I don't relish the thought of waiting on an invalid for the next few months.*
2 archaic make pleasant to the taste; add relish to: *I have also a novel to relish my wine.*
– DERIVATIVES **rel·ish·a·ble** **adj.**
– ORIGIN Middle English: alteration of obsolete *reles*, from Old French, 'remainder,' from *relaisser* 'to release.' The early noun sense was 'odor, taste,' giving rise to 'appetizing flavor, piquant taste' (mid 17th cent.), and hence sense 2 of the noun (late 18th cent).

re·live /rē'liv, 'rē-/ ▶ **v.** [with obj.] live through (an experience or feeling, esp. an unpleasant one) again in one's imagination or memory: *he broke down sobbing as he relived the attack.*

rel·le·no /rə(l)'yānō/ ▶ **n.** (pl. **rellenos**) short for **CHILE RELLENO**.

re·load /rē'lōd/ ▶ **v.** [with obj.] load (something, esp. a gun that has been fired) again: *he reloaded the chamber of the shotgun with fresh cartridges* | [no obj.] *Charlie reloaded and took aim.*

re·lo·cate /rē'lō,kāt, ,rēlō'kāt/ ▶ **v.** [no obj.] move to a new place and establish one's home or business there: *if you are relocating here from another state* | [with obj.] *distribution staff will be relocated to Holland.*
– DERIVATIVES **re·lo·ca·tion** /,rēlō'kāSHən/ **n.**

re·luc·tance /ri'ləktəns/ ▶ **n.** unwillingness or disinclination to do something: *she sensed his reluctance to continue.* ■ Physics the property of a magnetic circuit of opposing the passage of magnetic flux lines, equal to the ratio of the magnetomotive force to the magnetic flux.

re·luc·tant /ri'ləktənt/ ▶ **adj.** unwilling and hesitant; disinclined: [with infinitive] *she seemed reluctant to discuss the matter.*
– DERIVATIVES **re·luc·tant·ly** **adv.**
– ORIGIN mid 17th cent. (in the sense 'writhing, offering opposition'): from Latin *reluctant-* 'struggling against,' from the verb *reluctari*, from *re-* (expressing intensive force) + *luctari* 'to struggle.'

re·lume /rē'lo͞om/ ▶ **v.** [with obj.] literary relight or rekindle (a light, flame, etc.): *Oceana stole from her place of concealment, and relumed the taper.*
– ORIGIN early 17th cent.: from **RE-** 'again' + **ILLUME**, partly suggested by French *rallumer*.

re·ly /ri'lī/ ▶ **v.** (**relies**, **relying**, **relied**) [no obj.] (**rely on/upon**) depend on with full trust or confidence: *I know I can rely on your discretion.* ■ be dependent on: *the charity has to rely entirely on public donations.*
– ORIGIN Middle English: from Old French *relier* 'bind together,' from Latin *religare*, from *re-* (expressing intensive force) + *ligare* 'bind.' The original sense was 'gather together,' later 'turn to, associate with,' whence 'depend upon with confidence.'

REM ▶ **abbr.** rapid eye movement.

rem /rem/ ▶ **n.** (pl. **same**) a unit of effective absorbed dose of ionizing radiation in human tissue, equivalent to one roentgen of X-rays.
– ORIGIN 1940s: acronym from *roentgen equivalent man*.

re·made /rē'mād, 'rē-/ past and past participle of **REMAKE**.

re·mail·er /'rē,mālər/ ▶ **n.** Computing a service that anonymously forwards e-mail so as to disguise the original sender. ■ a similar service for mail that takes advantage of cheaper or more efficient postal services in other countries.

re·main /ri'mān/ ▶ **v.** [no obj.] continue to exist, esp. after other similar or related people or things have ceased to exist: *a cloister is all that remains of the monastery.* ■ stay in the place that one has been occupying: *her husband remained at the beach condo.* ■ [with complement] continue to possess a particular quality or fulfill a particular role: *he had remained alert the whole time.* ■ be left over after others or other parts have been completed, used, or dealt with: *several years remain in the transition period.*
– PHRASES **remain to be seen** used to express the notion that something is not yet known or certain: *she has broken her leg, but it remains to be seen how badly.*
– ORIGIN late Middle English: from Old French *remain-*, stressed stem of *remanoir*, from Latin *remanere*, from *re-* (expressing intensive force) + *manere* 'to stay.'

re·main·der /ri'māndər/ ▶ **n.** **1** a part, number, or quantity that is left over: *leave a few mushrooms for garnish and slice the remainder.* ■ a part that is still to come: *the remainder of the year.* ■ the number that is left over in a division in which one quantity does not exactly divide another: *23 divided by 3 is 7, remainder 2.* ■ a copy of a book left unsold when demand has fallen.
2 Law an interest in an estate that becomes effective in possession only when a prior interest (devised at the same time) ends.
▶ **v.** [with obj.] dispose of (a book left unsold) at a reduced price: *titles are being remaindered increasingly quickly to save on overheads.*
– ORIGIN late Middle English (sense 2 of the noun): from Anglo-Norman French, from Latin *remanere* (see **REMAIN**).

re·main·ing /ri'māniNG/ ▶ **adj.** **1** still existing, present, or in use; surviving: *Lilly was my last remaining close relative* | *the **few remaining** employees are working part-time.*
2 not yet used, dealt with, or resolved; outstanding: *they advertised for any remaining creditors to come forward.*
3 still to happen; future: *it will likely take six wins in the eight remaining games.*

re·mains /ri'mānz/ ▶ **plural n.** the parts left over after other parts have been removed, used, or destroyed: *the remains of a sandwich lunch were on the table.* ■ historical or archaeological relics: *Roman remains.* ■ a person's body after death.
– ORIGIN late Middle English (occasionally treated as singular): from Old French *remain*, from *remaindre*, from an informal form of Latin *remanere* (see **REMAIN**).

re·make ▶ **v.** /rē'māk, 'rē-/ (past and past participle **remade**) [with obj.] make (something) again or differently: *the bed would be more comfortable if it were remade.*
▶ **n.** /'rē,māk/ a movie or piece of music that has been filmed or recorded again and rereleased.

re·man /rē'man, 'rē-/ ▶ **v.** (**remans**, **remanning**, **remanned**) [with obj.] **1** equip again or with new personnel.
2 literary make (someone) manly or courageous again.

re·mand /ri'mand/ Law ▶ **v.** [with obj.] place (a defendant) on bail or in custody, esp. when a trial is adjourned: *I had a seventeen-year-old son remanded to a drug-addiction program.* ■ return (a case) to a lower court for reconsideration: *the Supreme Court summarily vacated the opinion and remanded the matter back to the California Court of Appeal.*
▶ **n.** a committal to custody.
– ORIGIN late Middle English (as a verb in the sense 'send back again'): from late Latin *remandare*, from *re-* 'back' + *mandare* 'commit.' The noun dates from the late 18th cent.

rem·a·nent /'remənənt/ ▶ **adj.** technical remaining; residual. ■ (of magnetism) remaining after the magnetizing field has been removed.
– DERIVATIVES **rem·a·nence** **n.**
– ORIGIN late Middle English: from Latin *remanent-* 'remaining,' from the verb *remanere*.

re·map /rē'map, 'rē-/ ▶ **v.** (**remaps**, **remapping**, **remapped**) [with obj.] Computing assign (a function) to a different key.

re·mark /ri'märk/ ▶ **v.** **1** [reporting verb] say something as a comment; mention: [with direct speech] *"Tom's looking peaked," she remarked* | [with clause] *he remarked that he had some work to finish* | [no obj.] *the judges **remarked on** the high standard of the entries.*
2 [with obj.] regard with attention; notice: *he remarked the man's inflamed eyelids.*
▶ **n.** a written or spoken comment: *I decided to ignore his rude remarks.* ■ notice or comment: *the landscape was not worthy of remark.*
– ORIGIN late 16th cent. (sense 2 of the verb): from French *remarquer* 'note again,' from *re-* (expressing intensive force) + *marquer* 'to mark, note.'

re-mark /rē'märk, 'rē/ ▶ **v.** [with obj.] mark (an examination paper or piece of academic work) again.
▶ **n.** [in sing.] an act of marking an examination or piece of academic work again.

re·mark·a·ble /ri'märkəbəl/ ▶ **adj.** worthy of attention; striking: *a remarkable coincidence.*
– DERIVATIVES **re·mark·a·ble·ness** **n.**, **re·mark·a·bly** /-blē/ **adv.** [sentence adverb] *remarkably, they finished two weeks ahead of schedule* | [as submodifier] *the two boys got along remarkably well.*
– ORIGIN early 17th cent.: from French *remarquable*, from *remarquer* 'take note of' (see **REMARK**).

Re·marque /rə'märk/, Erich Maria (1898–1970), US novelist, born in Germany. His first novel, *All Quiet on the Western Front* (1929; movie, 1930), was an international success. The book and its sequel, *The Road Back* (1931), were banned by the Nazis in 1933. All of his 10 novels deal with the horror of war and its aftermath.

re·mar·ry /rē'marē/ ▶ **v.** (**remarries**, **remarrying**, **remarried**) [no obj.] marry again: *he remarried shortly after his wife's death.*
– DERIVATIVES **re·mar·riage** /rē'marij/ **n.**

re·mas·ter /rē'mastər/ ▶ **v.** [with obj.] make a new master of (a recording), typically in order to improve the sound quality: *all the tracks have been remastered from the original tapes.*

re·match /'rē,maCH/ ▶ **n.** a second match or game between two teams or players.

Rem·brandt /'rem,brant/ (1606–69), Dutch painter; full name *Rembrandt Harmensz van Rijn*. He established his reputation as a portrait painter with the *Anatomy Lesson of Dr. Tulp* (1632). In *The Night Watch* (1642), he used chiaroscuro to give his subjects a more spiritual and introspective quality. Rembrandt is identified with the series of more than sixty self-portraits painted from 1629 to 1669.

REME ▶ **abbr.** (in the British army) Royal Electrical and Mechanical Engineers.

re·meas·ure /,rē'meZHər/ ▶ **v.** [with obj.] measure again.
– DERIVATIVES **re·meas·ure·ment** **n.**

re·me·di·a·ble /ri'mēdēəbəl/ ▶ **adj.** capable of being cured; treatable: *a remediable condition that may have serious consequences if not recognized.* ■ capable of being remedied; rectifiable: *these grievances are remediable.*

re·me·di·al /ri'mēdēəl/ ▶ **adj.** giving or intended as a remedy or cure: *remedial surgery.* ■ provided or intended for students who are experiencing learning difficulties: *remedial education.*
– DERIVATIVES **re·me·di·al·ly** **adv.**
– ORIGIN mid 17th cent.: from late Latin *remedialis*, from Latin *remedium* 'cure, medicine' (see **REMEDY**).

re·me·di·a·tion /ri,mēdē'āSHən/ ▶ **n.** the action of remedying something, in particular of reversing or stopping environmental damage. ■ the giving of remedial teaching or therapy.
– DERIVATIVES **re·me·di·ate** /ri'mēdē,āt/ **v.**

– ORIGIN early 19th cent.: from Latin *remediatio(n-)*, from *remediare* 'heal, cure' (see **REMEDY**).

rem·e·dy /ˈremədē/ ▶ **n.** (pl. **remedies**) **1** a medicine or treatment for a disease or injury: *herbal remedies for aches and pains.* ■ a means of counteracting or eliminating something undesirable: *shopping became a* ***remedy for*** *personal problems.* ■ a means of legal reparation: *the doctrine took away their only* ***remedy against*** *merchants who refused to honor their contracts.*
2 the margin within which coins as minted may differ from the standard fineness and weight.
▶ **v.** (**remedies, remedying, remedied**) [with obj.] set right (an undesirable situation): *by the time a problem becomes patently obvious, it may be almost too late to remedy it.*
– DERIVATIVES **rem·e·di·less** adj.
– ORIGIN Middle English: from Anglo-Norman French *remedie*, from Latin *remedium*, from *re-* 'back' (also expressing intensive force) + *mederi* 'heal.'

re·mem·ber /riˈmembər/ ▶ **v.** [with obj.] have in or be able to bring to one's mind an awareness of (someone or something that one has seen, known, or experienced in the past): *I remember the screech of the horn as the car came toward me | no one remembered his name.* ■ [with infinitive] do something that one has undertaken to do or that is necessary or advisable: *did you remember to mail the letters?* ■ [with clause] used to emphasize the importance of what is asserted: *you must remember that this is a secret.* ■ bear (someone) in mind by making them a gift or making provision for them: *he has remembered the boy in a codicil to his will.* ■ (**remember someone to**) convey greetings from one person to (another): *remember me to Charlie.* ■ pray for the success or well-being of: *the congress should be remembered in our prayers.* ■ (**remember oneself**) recover one's manners after a lapse.
– DERIVATIVES **re·mem·ber·er** n.
– ORIGIN Middle English: from Old French *remembrer*, from late Latin *rememorari* 'call to mind,' from *re-* (expressing intensive force) + Latin *memor* 'mindful.'

re·mem·brance /riˈmembrəns/ ▶ **n.** the action of remembering something: *a flash of understanding or remembrance passed between them.* ■ the action of remembering the dead, esp. in a ceremony: *I decided to sell poppies in remembrance of those who died.* ■ a memory or recollection: *the remembrance of her visit came back with startling clarity.* ■ a thing kept or given as a reminder or in commemoration of someone.
– ORIGIN Middle English: from Old French, from *remembrer* (see **REMEMBER**).

Re·mem·brance Day ▶ **n. 1** (in Canada) November 11, observed in memory of those who died in World Wars I and II; Veterans Day.
2 another term for **REMEMBRANCE SUNDAY**.

re·mem·branc·er /riˈmembrənsər/ ▶ **n.** a person with the job or responsibility of reminding others of something; a chronicler.

Re·mem·brance Sun·day ▶ **n.** (in the UK) the Sunday nearest to November 11, when those who were killed in World War I and World War II and later conflicts are commemorated.

re·mex /ˈrēˌmeks/ ▶ **n.** (pl. **remiges** /ˈrēmiˌjēz/) Ornithology a flight feather. Compare with **RECTRIX**.
– ORIGIN mid 18th cent.: from Latin, literally 'rower,' based on *remus* 'oar.'

re·mil·i·ta·rize /riˈmilitəriz/ ▶ **v.** [with obj.] supply (a place that has previously been demilitarized) with new military resources: *the Rhineland was remilitarized in 1936.*
– DERIVATIVES **re·mil·i·ta·ri·za·tion** n.

re·mind /riˈmīnd/ ▶ **v.** [with obj.] cause (someone) to remember someone or something: *he would have forgotten the boy's birthday if you hadn't reminded him* | [with obj. and direct speech] *"You had an accident," he reminded her.* ■ (**remind someone of**) cause someone to think of (something) because of a resemblance or likeness: *his impassive, fierce stare reminded her of an owl.* ■ bring something, esp. a commitment or necessary course of action, to the attention of (someone): [with obj. and clause] *the bartender reminded them that singing was not permitted* | [with obj. and infinitive] *she reminded me to be respectful.*
– ORIGIN mid 17th cent.: from **RE-** 'again' + the verb **MIND**, probably suggested by obsolete *rememorate*, in the same sense.

re·mind·er /riˈmīndər/ ▶ **n.** a thing that causes someone to remember something: *the watchtower is a reminder of the days when an enemy might appear at any moment.* ■ a message or communication designed to ensure that someone remembers something. ■ a letter sent to remind someone of an obligation, esp. to pay a bill.

re·mind·ful /riˈmīndfəl/ ▶ **adj.** acting as a reminder: *his humor is* ***reminiscent of*** *that of Max.*

re·min·er·al·ize /rēˈminərəˌlīz/ ▶ **v.** [with obj.] restore the depleted mineral content of (a part of the body, esp. the bones or teeth).
– DERIVATIVES **re·min·er·al·i·za·tion** /-ˌminərələˈzāSHən/ n.

Rem·ing·ton[1] /ˈremiNGtən/, Frederic (1861–1909), US painter, sculptor, and writer. He painted scenes of the American West such as "Cavalry Charge on the Southern Plains" (1907). His notable sculptures include "Bronco Buster" (1895) and "Comin' Through the Rye" (1902). He also wrote *The Way of an Indian* (1906).

Rem·ing·ton[2] ▶ **n.** trademark **1** a make of firearm.
2 a typewriter, esp. a large manual one formerly used in offices.
– ORIGIN mid 19th cent.: named after Eliphalet *Remington* (1793–1861) and his son Philo (1816–89), gunsmiths of Ilion, New York, the original manufacturers.

rem·i·nisce /ˌreməˈnis/ ▶ **v.** [no obj.] indulge in enjoyable recollection of past events: *they reminisced about their summers abroad.*
– DERIVATIVES **rem·i·nis·cer** n.
– ORIGIN early 19th cent.: back-formation from **REMINISCENCE**.

rem·i·nis·cence /ˌreməˈnisəns/ ▶ **n.** a story told about a past event remembered by the narrator: *his reminiscences of his early days in Washington.* ■ the enjoyable recollection of past events: *his story made me smile in reminiscence.* ■ (**reminiscences**) a collection in literary form of incidents and experiences that someone remembers. ■ a characteristic of one thing reminding or suggestive of another: *his first works are too full of reminiscences of earlier poetry.*
– DERIVATIVES **rem·i·nis·cen·tial** /ˌremənisˈenCHəl/ adj. (archaic).
– ORIGIN late 16th cent. (denoting the action of remembering): from late Latin *reminiscentia*, from Latin *reminisci* 'remember.'

rem·i·nis·cent /ˌreməˈnisənt/ ▶ **adj.** tending to remind one of something: *the sights were* ***reminiscent of*** *my childhood.* ■ suggesting something by resemblance: *her suit was vaguely* ***reminiscent of*** *military dress.* ■ (of a person or their manner) absorbed in or suggesting absorption in memories: *her expression was wistful and reminiscent.*
– DERIVATIVES **rem·i·nis·cent·ly** adv.
– ORIGIN mid 18th cent.: from Latin *reminiscent-* 'remembering,' from the verb *reminisci*.

re·miss /riˈmis/ ▶ **adj.** [predic.] lacking care or attention to duty; negligent: *it would be very remiss of me not to pass on that information | the government has been remiss in its duties.*
– DERIVATIVES **re·miss·ly** adv., **re·miss·ness** n.
– ORIGIN late Middle English: from Latin *remissus* 'slackened,' past participle of *remittere*. The early senses were 'weakened in color or consistency' and (in describing sound) 'faint, soft.'

re·mis·si·ble /riˈmisəbəl/ ▶ **adj.** (esp. of sins) able to be pardoned.
– ORIGIN late 16th cent.: from French *rémissible* or late Latin *remissibilis*, from *remiss-* 'slackened,' from the verb *remittere* (see **REMISS**).

re·mis·sion /riˈmiSHən/ ▶ **n.** the cancellation of a debt, charge, or penalty: *the plan allows for the partial remission of tuition fees.* ■ a diminution of the seriousness or intensity of disease or pain; a temporary recovery: *ten out of twenty patients remained* ***in remission***. ■ formal forgiveness of sins. ■ Brit. the reduction of a prison sentence, esp. as a reward for good behavior.
– ORIGIN Middle English: from Old French, or from Latin *remissio(n-)*, from *remittere* 'send back, restore' (see **REMIT**).

re·mit ▶ **v.** /riˈmit/ (**remits, remitting, remitted**) [with obj.] **1** cancel or refrain from exacting or inflicting (a debt or punishment): *the excess of the sentence over 12 months was remitted.* ■ Theology pardon (a sin).
2 send (money) in payment or as a gift: *the income they remitted to their families.*
3 refer (a matter for decision) to some authority: *the request for an investigation was remitted to a special committee.* ■ Law send back (a case) to a lower court. ■ Law send (someone) from one tribunal to another for a trial or hearing. ■ archaic consign again to a previous state: *thus his indiscretion remitted him to the nature of an ordinary person.*
4 rare postpone: *the movers refused Mr. Tierney's request to remit the motion.* ■ [no obj.] archaic diminish: *phobias may remit spontaneously without any treatment.*
▶ **n.** /ˈriˌmit, ˈrēˌmit/ **1** the task or area of activity officially assigned to an individual or organization: *the committee was becoming caught up in issues that did not fall within its remit.*
2 an item referred to someone for consideration.
– DERIVATIVES **re·mit·ta·ble** adj., **re·mit·tal** /-ˈmitl/ n., **re·mit·ter** n.
– ORIGIN late Middle English: from Latin *remittere* 'send back, restore,' from *re-* 'back' + *mittere* 'send.' The noun dates from the early 20th cent.

re·mit·tance /riˈmitns/ ▶ **n.** a sum of money sent, esp. by mail, in payment for goods or services or as a gift. ■ the action of sending money in such a way.

re·mit·tance man ▶ **n.** chiefly historical an emigrant supported or assisted by payments of money from home.

re·mit·tent /riˈmitnt/ ▶ **adj.** (of a fever) characterized by fluctuating body temperatures.
– ORIGIN late 17th cent.: from Latin *remittent-* 'sending back,' from the verb *remittere* (see **REMIT**).

re·mix ▶ **v.** /rēˈmiks, ˈrē-/ [with obj.] mix (something) again. ■ produce a different version of (a musical recording) by altering the balance of the separate tracks.
▶ **n.** /ˈrēˌmiks/ a different version of a musical recording produced in such a way.
– DERIVATIVES **re·mix·er** n.

rem·nant /ˈremnənt/ ▶ **n.** a small remaining quantity of something. ■ a piece of cloth or carpeting left when the greater part has been used or sold. ■ a surviving trace: *a remnant of the past.* ■ Christian Theology a small minority of people who will remain faithful to God and so be saved (in allusion to biblical prophecies concerning Israel).
▶ **adj.** [attrib.] remaining: *remnant strands of hair.*
– ORIGIN Middle English: contraction of obsolete *remenant*, from Old French, from *remenoir*, *remanoir* 'remain.'

re·mod·el /rēˈmädl/ ▶ **v.** (**remodels, remodeling, remodeled**; Brit. **remodels, remodelling, remodelled**) [with obj.] change the structure or form of (something, esp. a building, policy, or procedure): *the station was remodeled and enlarged in 1927.* ■ fashion or shape (a figure or object) again or differently: *she remodeled the head with careful fingers.*

re·mod·el·er /rēˈmädl-ər/ ▶ **n.** a person who carries out structural alterations to an existing building, such as adding a new room.

re·mold /rēˈmōld/ (Brit. **remould**) ▶ **v.** [with obj.] change or refashion the appearance, structure, or character of: *did the welfare state remold capitalism to give it a more human face?*

re·mon·e·tize /rēˈmänəˌtīz/ ▶ **v.** [with obj.] rare restore (a metal) to its former position as legal tender.
– DERIVATIVES **re·mon·e·ti·za·tion** /rēˌmänətəˈzāSHən/ n.

re·mon·strance /riˈmänstrəns/ ▶ **n.** a forcefully reproachful protest: *angry remonstrances in the Senate | he shut his ears to any remonstrance.* ■ (**the Remonstrance**) a document drawn up in 1610 by the Arminians of the Dutch Reformed Church, presenting the differences between their doctrines and those of the strict Calvinists.
– ORIGIN late 16th cent. (in the sense 'evidence'): from Old French, or from medieval Latin *remonstrantia*, from *remonstrare* 'demonstrate, show' (see **REMONSTRATE**).

Re·mon·strant /riˈmänstrənt/ ▶ **n.** a member of the Arminian party in the Dutch Reformed Church.
– ORIGIN early 17th cent.: from medieval Latin *remonstrant-* 'demonstrating' (see also **REMONSTRANCE**).

re·mon·strate /riˈmänˌstrāt, ˈremən-/ ▶ **v.** [no obj.] make a forcefully reproachful protest: *he turned angrily to* ***remonstrate with*** *Tommy* | [with direct speech] *"You don't mean that," she remonstrated.*
– DERIVATIVES **re·mon·stra·tion** /riˌmänˈstrāSHən, ˌremən-/ n., **re·mon·stra·tive** /-strətiv/ adj., **re·mon·stra·tor** /-ˌstrātər/ n.
– ORIGIN late 16th cent. (in the sense 'make plain'): from medieval Latin *remonstrat-* 'demonstrated,' from the verb *remonstrare*, from *re-* (expressing intensive force) + *monstrare* 'to show.'

re·mon·tant /riˈmäntnt/ ▶ **adj.** (of a plant) blooming or producing a crop more than once a season.
▶ **n.** a remontant plant.
– ORIGIN late 19th cent.: from French, literally 'coming up again,' from the verb *remonter*.

rem·o·ra /ˈremərə, riˈmôrə/ ▶ **n.** a slender marine fish that attaches itself to large fish by means of a sucker on top of its head. It generally feeds on the host's external parasites. Also called **SHARKSUCKER**, **SUCKERFISH**. ● Family Echeneidae: several genera and species, in particular the widespread *Remora remora*.
– ORIGIN mid 16th cent.: from Latin, literally 'hindrance,' from *re-* 'back' + *mora* 'delay' (because of the former belief that the fish slowed down ships).

re·morse /riˈmôrs/ ▶ **n.** deep regret or guilt for a wrong committed: *they were filled with remorse and shame.*
– ORIGIN late Middle English: from Old French *remors,* from medieval Latin *remorsus,* from Latin *remordere* 'vex,' from *re-* (expressing intensive force) + *mordere* 'to bite.'

re·morse·ful /riˈmôrsfəl/ ▶ **adj.** filled with remorse; sorry: *the defendant was **remorseful for** what he had done.*
– DERIVATIVES **re·morse·ful·ly** /-fəlē/ **adv.**

re·morse·less /riˈmôrsləs/ ▶ **adj.** without regret or guilt: *a remorseless killer.* ■ (of something unpleasant) never ending or improving; relentless: *remorseless poverty.*
– DERIVATIVES **re·morse·less·ly adv.**, **re·morse·less·ness n.**

re·mort·gage /rēˈmôrgij/ ▶ **v.** [with obj.] take out another or a different kind of mortgage on (a property).
▶ **n.** a different or additional mortgage.

re·mote /riˈmōt/ ▶ **adj.** (**remoter, remotest**) **1** (of a place) situated far from the main centers of population; distant: *a remote Oregon valley | I'd chosen a spot that looked as **remote from** any road as possible.* ■ (of an electronic device) operating or operated by means of radio or infrared signals. ■ distant in time: *a golden age in the remote past.* ■ distantly related: *a remote cousin.* ■ having very little connection with or relationship to: *the theory seems rather intellectual and **remote from** everyday experience.* ■ (of a person) aloof and unfriendly in manner: *this morning Maria again seemed remote and patronizing.* ■ Computing denoting a device that can only be accessed by means of a network. Compare with **LOCAL**.
2 (of a chance or possibility) unlikely to occur: *chances of a genuine and lasting peace become even more remote.*
▶ **n.** a remote control device.
– DERIVATIVES **re·mote·ness n.**
– ORIGIN late Middle English (in the sense 'far apart'): from Latin *remotus* 'removed,' past participle of *removere* (see **REMOVE**).

re·mote con·trol ▶ **n.** control of a machine or apparatus from a distance by means of signals transmitted from a radio or electronic device. ■ (also **remote controller**) a device that controls an apparatus, esp. a television or VCR, in such a way.
– DERIVATIVES **re·mote-con·trolled adj.**

re·mote·ly /riˈmōtlē/ ▶ **adv. 1** from a distance; without physical contact: *new electronic meters that can be read remotely | a new type of remotely controlled torpedo.*
2 [as submodifier, usu. with negative] in the slightest degree: *he had never been remotely jealous.*

re·mote sens·ing ▶ **n.** the scanning of the earth by satellite or high-flying aircraft in order to obtain information about it.

ré·mou·lade /ˌrāməˈläd/ (also **remoulade**) ▶ **n.** salad or seafood dressing made with hard-boiled egg yolks, oil, and vinegar, and flavored with mustard, capers, and herbs.
– ORIGIN French from Italian *remolata.*

re·mould /rēˈmōld/ ▶ **v.** British spelling of **REMOLD**. ■ Brit. put a new tread on (a worn tire).
▶ **n.** /ˈrēmōld/ Brit. a tire that has been given a new tread.

re·mount ▶ **v.** /rēˈmount, ˈrē-/ [with obj.] mount (something) again, in particular: ■ get on (something) in order to ride it again: *she went to remount her horse | [no obj.] Sandy remounted and rode through the gates.* ■ attach to a new frame or setting: *remount the best photos in glass-fronted mounts.* ■ produce (a play or exhibition) again. ■ organize and embark on (a significant course of action) again: *the raid was remounted in August.*
▶ **n.** /ˈrēˌmount/ a fresh horse for a rider. ■ historical a supply of fresh horses for a regiment.

re·mov·al /riˈmo͞ovəl/ ▶ **n.** the action of removing someone or something, in particular: ■ the taking away of something unwanted: *the removal of the brain tumor.* ■ the abolition of something: *the removal of all legal barriers to the free movement of goods.* ■ the dismissal of someone from a job or office. ■ [usu. as modifier] chiefly Brit. the transfer of furniture and other contents when moving from one house to another: *removal men.*

re·move /riˈmo͞ov/ ▶ **v.** [with obj.] **1** take (something) away or off from the position occupied: *Customs officials **removed** documents **from** the premises | she sat down to remove her make-up.* ■ take off (clothing): *he sat down and quickly removed his shoes and socks.* ■ [no obj.] (**remove to**) dated change one's home or place of residence by moving to (another place): *he removed to Mexico and began afresh.* ■ S. African historical compel (someone) by law to move to another area: *a man is removed to the tribal district of his forbears.*
2 eliminate or get rid of: *the iron can be removed by filtration | they **removed** thousands of needy youngsters **from** the system.* ■ dismiss from a job or office: *he was **removed from** his teaching position.*
3 (**be removed**) be distant from: *it is an isolated place, **far removed from** the London art world.* ■ be very different from: *an explanation that is **far removed from** the truth.*
4 (as adj. **removed**) separated by a particular number of steps of descent: *his second cousin once removed.*
▶ **n.** a degree of remoteness or separation: ***at this remove**, the whole incident seems insane.*
– DERIVATIVES **re·mov·a·bil·i·ty** /riˌmo͞ovəˈbilətē/ **n.**, **re·mov·a·ble adj.**, **re·mov·er n.**
– ORIGIN Middle English (as a verb): from the Old French stem *remov-,* from Latin *removere,* from *re-* 'back' + *movere* 'to move.'

REM sleep /rem/ ▶ **n.** a kind of sleep that occurs at intervals during the night and is characterized by rapid eye movements, more dreaming and bodily movement, and faster pulse and breathing.

re·muage /ˌremo͞oˈäzн/ ▶ **n.** the periodic turning or shaking of bottled wine, esp. champagne, to move sediment toward the cork.
– ORIGIN French, literally 'moving around.'

re·mu·da /riˈm(y)o͞odə/ ▶ **n.** a herd of horses that have been saddle-broken, from which ranch hands choose their mounts for the day.
– ORIGIN late 19th cent.: via American Spanish from Spanish, literally 'exchange, replacement.'

re·mu·ner·ate /riˈmyo͞onəˌrāt/ ▶ **v.** [with obj.] pay (someone) for services rendered or work done: *they should be remunerated fairly for their work.*
– ORIGIN early 16th cent.: from Latin *remunerat-* 'rewarded, recompensed,' from the verb *remunerari,* from *re-* (expressing intensive force) + *munus, muner-* 'gift.'

re·mu·ner·a·tion /riˌmyo͞onəˈrāsнən/ ▶ **n.** money paid for work or a service.

re·mu·ner·a·tive /riˈmyo͞onəˌrətiv, -ˌrātiv/ ▶ **adj.** financially rewarding; lucrative: *highly remunerative activities.* ■ earning a salary; paid: *since June 2003 he has not had any remunerative employment.*

Re·mus /ˈrēməs/ Roman Mythology the twin brother of Romulus.

REN ▶ **abbr.** ringer equivalent number, a measure of the load a device will place on a telephone line. The maximum REN allowed on a single line is usually limited by telephone companies.

Ren·ais·sance /ˈrenəˌsäns, -ˌzäns/ the revival of art and literature under the influence of classical models in the 14th–16th centuries. ■ the culture and style of art and architecture developed during this era. ■ (as noun **a renaissance**) a revival of or renewed interest in something: *rail travel is enjoying a renaissance.*
– ORIGIN from French *renaissance,* from *re-* 'back, again' + *naissance* 'birth' (from Latin *nascentia,* from *nasci* 'be born').

Ren·ais·sance man (or **woman**) ▶ **n.** a person with many talents or areas of knowledge.

re·nal /ˈrēnl/ ▶ **adj.** technical of or relating to the kidneys: *renal failure.*
– ORIGIN mid 17th cent.: from French *rénal,* from late Latin *renalis,* from Latin *renes* 'kidneys.'

re·nal cal·cu·lus ▶ **n.** another term for **KIDNEY STONE**.

re·nal pel·vis ▶ **n.** see **PELVIS** (sense 2).

re·nal tu·bule ▶ **n.** another term for **KIDNEY TUBULE**.

re·name /rēˈnām, ˈrē-/ ▶ **v.** [with obj. and complement] give a new name to (someone or something): *after independence Celebes was renamed Sulawesi.*

re·nas·cence /riˈnasəns, -ˈnāsəns/ ▶ **n.** formal the revival of something that has been dormant: *the renascence of poetry as an oral art.* ■ another term for **RENAISSANCE**.

re·nas·cent /riˈnasənt, -ˈnāsənt/ ▶ **adj.** becoming active or popular again: *renascent fascism.*
– ORIGIN early 18th cent.: from Latin *renascent-* 'being born again,' from the verb *renasci,* from *re-* 'back, again' + *nasci* 'be born.'

re·na·tion·al·ize /ˌrēˈnasнənəˌlīz/ ▶ **v.** [with obj.] transfer (a privatized industry) back into state ownership or control.
– DERIVATIVES **re·na·tion·al·i·za·tion n.**

Re·nault[1] /rəˈnō/, Louis (1877–1944), French engineer and automobile manufacturer. He and his brothers established the Renault company in 1898.

Re·nault[2], Mary (1905–83), British novelist; resident in South Africa from 1948; pseudonym of *Mary Challans.* She wrote historical novels set in the ancient world, notably a trilogy dealing with Alexander the Great (1970–81).

ren·con·tre /räɴˈkôɴtr(ə), renˈkäntər/ ▶ **n.** archaic variant spelling of **RENCOUNTER**.
– ORIGIN early 17th cent.: French.

ren·coun·ter /renˈkountər/ archaic ▶ **n.** a chance meeting with someone. ■ a battle, skirmish, or duel.
▶ **v.** [with obj.] meet by chance: *I wonder who those fellows were we rencountered last night.*
– ORIGIN early 16th cent.: from French *rencontre* (noun), *rencontrer* 'meet face to face.'

rend /rend/ ▶ **v.** (past and past participle **rent** /rent/) [with obj.] tear (something) into two or more pieces: *snapping teeth that would rend human flesh to shreds | figurative the speculation and confusion that was rending the civilized world.* ■ archaic wrench (something) violently: *he rent the branch out of the tree.* ■ literary cause great emotional pain to (a person or their heart).
– PHRASES **rend the air** literary sound piercingly: *a shrill scream rent the air.* **rend one's garments** tear one's clothes as a sign of extreme grief or distress.
– ORIGIN Old English *rendan*; related to Middle Low German *rende.*

rend·er /ˈrendər/ ▶ **v.** [with obj.] **1** provide or give (a service, help, etc.): *money serves as a reward for **services rendered** | Mrs. Evans would **render** assistance **to** those she thought were in real need.* ■ submit or present for inspection or consideration: *he would render income tax returns at the end of the year.* ■ literary hand over: *he will **render up** his immortal soul.* ■ deliver (a verdict or judgment): *the jury's finding amounted to the clearest verdict yet rendered upon the scandal.*
2 [with obj. and complement] cause to be or become; make: *the rains rendered his escape impossible.*
3 represent or depict artistically: *the eyes and the cheeks are exceptionally well rendered.* ■ translate: *the phrase was **rendered into** English.* ■ Music perform (a piece): *a soprano solo reverently rendered by Linda Howie.* ■ Computing process (an outline image) using color and shading in order to make it appear solid and three-dimensional.
4 covertly send (a foreign criminal or terrorist suspect) for interrogation abroad; subject to extraordinary rendition.
5 melt down (fat): *the fat was being cut up and rendered for lard.* ■ process (the carcass of an animal) in order to extract proteins, fats, and other usable parts: (as adj. **rendered**) ***the rendered down** remains of sheep.*
6 cover (stone or brick) with a coat of plaster: *external walls will be rendered and tiled.*
▶ **n.** a first coat of plaster applied to a brick or stone surface.
– DERIVATIVES **ren·der·er n.**
– ORIGIN late Middle English: from Old French *rendre,* from an alteration of Latin *reddere* 'give back,' from *re-* 'back' + *dare* 'give.' The earliest senses were 'recite,' 'translate,' and 'give back' (hence 'represent' and 'perform'); 'hand over' (hence 'give (help)' and 'submit for consideration'); 'cause to be'; and 'melt down.'

WORD TRENDS See **RENDITION**.

rend·er·ing /ˈrendəriɴɢ/ ▶ **n. 1** a performance of a piece of music or drama: *her fine rendering of "Che farò senza Eurydice" was enough to win her strong commendation.* ■ a translation: *a literal rendering of an idiom.* ■ a work of visual art, esp. a detailed architectural drawing: *a consummately lifelike three-dimensional rendering of a building interior.* ■ Computing the processing of an outline image using color and shading to make it appear solid and three-dimensional.
2 the action of applying plaster to a wall. ■ the coating applied in such a way.
3 formal the action of giving, yielding, or surrendering something: *the rendering of dues.*

ren·dez·vous /ˈrändiˌvo͞o, -dā-/ ▶ **n.** (pl. **same**) a meeting at an agreed time and place, typically between two people. ■ a place used for such a meeting. ■ a place, typically a bar or restaurant, that is used as a popular meeting place.
▶ **v.** (**rendezvouses** /-ˌvo͞oz/, **rendezvoused** /-ˌvo͞od/, **rendezvousing** /-ˌvo͞oiɴɢ/) [no obj.] meet at an agreed time and place: *I **rendezvoused with** Bea as planned.*
– ORIGIN late 16th cent.: from French *rendez-vous!* 'present yourselves!,' imperative of *se rendre.*

ren·di·tion /renˈdisнən/ ▶ **n. 1** a performance or interpretation, esp. of a dramatic role or piece of music: *a wonderful rendition of "Nessun Dorma."* ■ a visual representation or reproduction: *a pen-and-*

r

ink rendition of Mars with his sword drawn. ■ a translation or transliteration.
2 (also **extraordinary rendition**) the practice of sending a foreign criminal or terrorist suspect covertly to be interrogated in a country with less rigorous regulations for the humane treatment of prisoners.
– ORIGIN early 17th cent.: from obsolete French, from *rendre* 'give back, render.'

> **WORD TRENDS** Although recorded as far back as 1980, the new sense of **rendition** is generally regarded as a product of the 'War on Terror.' It refers to the morally and legally ambiguous practice of sending suspects to be questioned in countries known to use harsh interrogation techniques and even torture. The Oxford English Corpus has shown a steady increase in examples throughout the last decade, with a particular rise in the phrase *extraordinary rendition*, which is now the most common use of **rendition** by far. The practice has also spawned a new sense of the verb **render**, meaning 'send someone abroad for interrogation.' Like *extraordinary rendition*, this has seen a surge in use in the last two years: *he was seized in Pakistan and later secretly rendered to Morocco.*

Ren·do·va /renˈdōvə/ an island in the west central Solomon Islands, off the coast of New Georgia, the scene of fighting between US and Japanese forces in 1943.

ren·dzi·na /renˈjēnə/ ▶ **n.** Soil Science a fertile lime-rich soil with dark humus above a pale soft calcareous layer, typical of grassland on chalk or limestone.
– ORIGIN 1920s: via Russian from Polish *rędzina.*

ren·e·gade /ˈreniˌgād/ ▶ **n.** a person who deserts and betrays an organization, country, or set of principles. ■ a person who behaves in a rebelliously unconventional manner. ■ archaic a person who abandons religion; an apostate.
▶ **adj.** having treacherously changed allegiance: *a renegade bodyguard.* ■ archaic having abandoned one's religious beliefs: *a renegade monk.*
– ORIGIN late 15th cent.: from Spanish *renegado,* from medieval Latin *renegatus* 'renounced,' past participle (used as a noun) of *renegare,* from *re-* (expressing intensive force) + Latin *negare* 'deny.'

ren·e·ga·do /ˌrenəˈgādō, -ˈgādō/ ▶ **n.** (pl. **renegadoes**) archaic term for **RENEGADE**.
– ORIGIN Spanish.

re·nege /riˈneg, -ˈnig/ (also **renegue**) ▶ **v.** [no obj.] go back on a promise, undertaking, or contract: *the administration had reneged on its election promises.* ■ another term for **REVOKE** (sense 2).
■ [with obj.] archaic renounce or abandon (someone or something).
– DERIVATIVES **re·neg·er** **n.**
– ORIGIN mid 16th cent. (in the sense 'desert (esp. a faith or a person)'): from medieval Latin *renegare,* from Latin *re-* (expressing intensive force) + *negare* 'deny.'

re·ne·go·ti·ate /ˌrēnəˈgōsHēˌāt/ ▶ **v.** [with obj.] negotiate (something) again in order to change the original agreed terms: *the parties will renegotiate the price* | [no obj.] *she asked to renegotiate after signing the contract.*
– DERIVATIVES **re·ne·go·ti·a·ble** /-ˈgōsH(ē)əbəl/ **adj.**, **re·ne·go·ti·a·tion** /-ˌgōsHēˈāsHən, -ˌgōsē-/ **n.**

re·new /riˈn(y)o͞o/ ▶ **v.** [with obj.] resume (an activity) after an interruption: *the parents renewed their campaign to save the school.* ■ re-establish (a relationship): *he had renewed an acquaintance with McCarthy.* ■ repeat (an action or statement): *detectives renewed their appeal for those in the area at the time to contact them.* ■ give fresh life or strength to: (as adj. **renewed**) *she would face the future with renewed determination.* ■ extend for a further period the validity of (a license, subscription, or contract): *her contract had not been renewed.* ■ replace (something that is broken or worn out): *check the joints—they may need renewing.*
– DERIVATIVES **re·new·er** **n.**

re·new·a·ble /riˈn(y)o͞oəbəl/ ▶ **adj.** capable of being renewed: *the 30-day truce is renewable by mutual agreement.* ■ (of energy or its source) not permanently depleted when used: *a shift away from fossil fuels to renewable energy.*
▶ **n.** (usu. **renewables**) a source of energy that is not depleted by use, such as water, wind, or solar power.
– DERIVATIVES **re·new·a·bil·i·ty** /riˌn(y)o͞oəˈbilətē/ **n.**

re·new·al /riˈn(y)o͞oəl/ ▶ **n.** the action of extending the period of validity of a license, subscription, or contract: *the contracts came up for renewal* | *a renewal of his passport.* ■ an instance of resuming an activity or state after an interruption: *a renewal of hostilities.* ■ the replacing or repair of something that is worn out, run-down, or broken: *the need for urban renewal.* ■ (among charismatic Christians) the state or process of being made spiritually new in the Holy Spirit.

ren·ga /ˈreNGgə/ ▶ **n.** (pl. **same** or **rengas**) Japanese linked poetry in the form of a tanka (or series of tanka), with the first three lines composed by one person and the second two by another. A typical renga sequence is comprised of 100 stanzas composed by about three poets in a single sitting.
– ORIGIN Japanese, from *ren* 'linking' + *ga* (from *ka* 'poetry').

ren·i·form /ˈrēnəˌfôrm, ˈren-/ ▶ **adj.** chiefly Mineralogy & Botany kidney-shaped.
– ORIGIN mid 18th cent.: from Latin *ren* 'kidney' + **-IFORM**.

re·nin /ˈrēnin, ˈren-/ ▶ **n.** Biochemistry an enzyme secreted by and stored in the kidneys that promotes the production of the protein angiotensin.
– ORIGIN late 19th cent.: from Latin *ren* 'kidney' + **-IN**[1].

ren·min·bi /ˈrenˈminˈbē/ ▶ **n.** (pl. **same**) the system of currency of the People's Republic of China, introduced in 1948. ■ the yuan.
– ORIGIN from Chinese *rénmínbì,* from *rénmín* 'people' + *bì* 'currency.'

Rennes /ren(s)/ an industrial city in northwestern France; pop. 214,813 (2006).

ren·net /ˈrenit/ ▶ **n.** curdled milk from the stomach of an unweaned calf, containing rennin and used in curdling milk for cheese. ■ any preparation containing rennin, esp. a pudding.
– ORIGIN late 15th cent.: probably related to **RUN**.

ren·nin /ˈrenin/ ▶ **n.** an enzyme secreted into the stomach of unweaned mammals, and in some lower animals and plants, causing the curdling of milk.
– ORIGIN late 19th cent.: from **RENNET** + **-IN**[1].

Re·no[1] /ˈrēnō/ a city in western Nevada, on the Truckee River; pop. 217,016 (est. 2008). It is noted as a gambling resort and for its liberal laws that enable quick marriages and divorces.

Re·no[2], Janet (1938–), US lawyer. Before she became the first woman to be appointed to the office of US attorney general 1993–2001, she was the chief prosecutor of Florida's Dade County 1978–93.

Re·noir[1] /ˈrenˌwär, rənˈwär/, Jean (1894–1979), French movie director; son of Pierre-Auguste Renoir. His works include *La Grande illusion* (1937) and *La Règle du jeu* (1939).

Re·noir[2], Pierre-Auguste (1841–1919), French painter. An early Impressionist, he developed a style characterized by light, fresh colors and indistinct, subtle outlines. In his later work he concentrated on the human, esp. female, form. Notable works: *Le Moulin de la galette* (1876) and *The Judgment of Paris* (c.1914).

Auguste Renoir

re·nom·i·nate /ˌrēˈnäməˌnāt/ ▶ **v.** [with obj.] nominate (someone) for a further term of office.
– DERIVATIVES **re·nom·i·na·tion** **n.**

re·nor·mal·i·za·tion /ˌrēˌnôrməliˈzāsHən/ ▶ **n.** Physics a method used in quantum mechanics in which unwanted infinities are removed from the solutions of equations by redefining parameters such as the mass and charge of subatomic particles.
– DERIVATIVES **re·nor·mal·ize** /rēˈnôməˌlīz/ **v.**

re·nounce /riˈnouns/ ▶ **v.** [with obj.] formally declare one's abandonment of (a claim, right, or possession): *Isabella offered to renounce her son's claim to the French crown.* ■ refuse to recognize or abide by any longer: *these agreements were renounced after the fall of the czarist regime.*
■ declare that one will no longer engage in or support: *they renounced the armed struggle.* ■ reject and stop using or consuming: *he renounced drugs and alcohol completely.* ■ [no obj.] Law refuse or resign a right or position, esp. one as an heir or trustee: *there will be forms enabling the allottee to renounce.*
– PHRASES **renounce the world** completely withdraw from society or material affairs in order to lead a life considered to be more spiritually fulfilling.
– DERIVATIVES **re·nounce·a·ble** **adj.**, **re·nounce·ment** **n.**, **re·nounc·er** **n.**
– ORIGIN late Middle English: from Old French *renoncer,* from Latin *renuntiare* 'protest against,' from *re-* (expressing reversal) + *nuntiare* 'announce.'

ren·o·vate /ˈrenəˌvāt/ ▶ **v.** [with obj.] restore (something old, esp. a building) to a good state of repair: *the old school has been tastefully renovated as a private house.* ■ archaic refresh; reinvigorate: *a little warm nourishment renovated him for a short time.*
– DERIVATIVES **ren·o·va·tor** /-ˌvātər/ **n.**
– ORIGIN early 16th cent.: from Latin *renovat-* 'made new again,' from the verb *renovare,* from *re-* 'back, again' + *novus* 'new.'

ren·o·va·tion /ˌrenəˈvāsHən/ ▶ **n.** the action of renovating a building: *this property is in need of complete renovation* | *older churches underwent major renovations.*

re·nown /riˈnoun/ ▶ **n.** the condition of being known or talked about by many people; fame: *authors of great renown.*
– ORIGIN Middle English: from Anglo-Norman French *renoun,* from Old French *renomer* 'make famous,' from *re-* (expressing intensive force) + *nomer* 'to name,' from Latin *nominare.*

re·nowned /riˈnound/ ▶ **adj.** known or talked about by many people; famous: *a restaurant renowned for its Southwestern-style food.*

rent[1] /rent/ ▶ **n.** a tenant's regular payment to a landlord for the use of property or land. ■ a sum paid for the hire of equipment.
▶ **v.** [with obj.] pay someone for the use of (something, typically property, land, or a car): *they rented a house together in Spain* | (as adj. **rented**) *a rented apartment.* ■ (of an owner) let someone use (something) in return for payment: *he purchased a large tract of land and rented out most of it to local farmers.* ■ [no obj.] be let or hired out at a specified rate: *skis or snowboards rent for $60–80 for six days.*
– PHRASES **for rent** available to be rented.
– ORIGIN Middle English: from Old French *rente,* from a root shared by **RENDER**.

rent[2] ▶ **n.** a large tear in a piece of fabric. ■ an opening or gap resembling such a tear: *they stared at the rents in the clouds.*
– ORIGIN mid 16th cent.: from obsolete *rent* 'pull to pieces, lacerate,' variant of **REND**.

rent[3] past and past participle of **REND**.

rent-a- ▶ **comb. form** denoting availability for hire of a specified thing: *rent-a-car* | *rent-a-tent.* ■ often humorous existing in violation of the real thing; not genuine: *rent-a-friend* | *rent-a-mob.*

rent·a·ble /ˈrentəbəl/ ▶ **adj.** available or suitable for renting: *rentable office space.*
– DERIVATIVES **rent·a·bil·i·ty** /ˌrentəˈbilətē/ **n.**

ren·tal /ˈrentl/ ▶ **n.** an amount paid or received as rent. ■ the action of renting something: *the office was on weekly rental.* ■ a rented house or car.
▶ **adj.** of, relating to, or available for rent: *rental properties.*
– ORIGIN late Middle English: from Anglo-Norman French, or from Anglo-Latin *rentale,* from Old French *rente* (see **RENT**[1]).

rent con·trol ▶ **n.** government control and regulation of the amounts charged for rented housing.

rent·er /ˈrentər/ ▶ **n. 1** a person who rents an apartment, a car, or other object.
2 a rented car or videocassette.

rent-free ▶ **adj. & adv.** with exemption from rent: [as adj.] *rent-free periods* | [as adv.] *you could live in the cottage rent-free.*

ren·tier /ränˈtyā/ ▶ **n.** a person living on income from property or investments.
– ORIGIN French, from *rente* 'dividend.'

Ren·ton /ˈrentn/ a city in west central Washington, southeast of Seattle, on Lake Washington; pop. 62,266 (est. 2008).

rent par·ty ▶ **n.** a party held to raise money to pay rent by charging guests for attendance.

re·num·ber /ˌrēˈnəmbər/ ▶ **v.** [with obj.] change the number or numbers assigned to (something).

re·nun·ci·a·tion /riˌnənsēˈāsHən/ ▶ **n.** the formal rejection of something, typically a belief, claim, or course of action: *entry into the priesthood requires renunciation of marriage* | *a renunciation of violence.*
■ Law a document expressing renunciation.
– DERIVATIVES **re·nun·ci·ant** /riˈnənsēənt/ **n. & adj.**
– ORIGIN late Middle English: from late Latin *renuntiatio(n-),* from Latin *renuntiare* 'protest against' (see **RENOUNCE**).

ren·vers /ren'vərs, räN'ver/ (also **renverse**) ▶ n. a movement performed in dressage, in which the horse moves parallel to the side of the arena, with its hindquarters carried closer to the wall than its shoulders and its body curved away from the center.
– ORIGIN French.

re·oc·cu·py /,rē'äkyə,pī/ ▶ v. (**reoccupies, reoccupying, reoccupied**) [with obj.] occupy (a place or position) again: *repairs will be required before tenants reoccupy the building.*
– DERIVATIVES **re·oc·cu·pa·tion** n.

re·oc·cur /,rēə'kər/ ▶ v. (**reoccurs, reoccurring, reoccurred**) [no obj.] occur again or repeatedly: *ulcers tend to reoccur after treatment has stopped.*
– DERIVATIVES **re·oc·cur·rence** n.

re·of·fend /,rēə'fend/ ▶ v. [no obj.] commit a further offense: *people who reoffend while on bail.*
– DERIVATIVES **re·of·fend·er** n.

re·o·pen /,rē'ōpən/ ▶ v. [with obj.] open again: *after being renovated the house was reopened to the public* | [no obj.] *the trial reopens on March 6th.*

re·or·der /rē'ôrdər/ ▶ v. [with obj.] **1** request (something) to be made, supplied, or served again: *the most popular toys will be reordered immediately.*
2 arrange (something) again: *he fixed his bed and reordered his books.*
▶ n. a renewed or repeated order for goods.

re·org /'rē,ôrg, rē'ôrg/ informal ▶ n. a reorganization.
▶ v. reorganize: [with obj.] *it reorgs buildings* | [no obj.] *the company loves to reorg.*

re·or·gan·ize /rē'ôrgə,nīz/ ▶ v. [with obj.] change the way in which (something) is organized: *we have to reorganize the entire workload* | [no obj.] *the company reorganized into fewer key areas.*
– DERIVATIVES **re·or·gan·i·za·tion** /,rē,ôrgənə'zāsHən/ n., **re·or·gan·iz·er** n.

re·or·i·ent /rē'ôrē,ent/ ▶ v. [with obj.] change the focus or direction of: *the country began reorienting its economic and social policies in 1988.* ■ (**reorient oneself**) find one's position again in relation to one's surroundings: *slowly they advanced, stopping every so often and then reorienting themselves.*
– DERIVATIVES **re·o·ri·en·tate** /-ēən,tāt/ v., **re·o·ri·en·ta·tion** /,rē,ôrēən'tāsHən/ n.

re·o·vi·rus /'rēō,vīrəs/ ▶ n. any of a group of RNA viruses that are sometimes associated with respiratory and enteric infection.
– ORIGIN mid 20th cent.: from the initial letters of *respiratory, enteric,* and *orphan* (referring to a virus not identified with a particular disease) + VIRUS.

rep[1] /rep/ informal ▶ n. a representative: *a union rep.* ■ a sales representative.
▶ v. (**reps, repping, repped**) [no obj.] act as a sales representative for a company or product: *at eighteen she was working for her dad, repping on the road.*
– ORIGIN late 19th cent.: abbreviation.

rep[2] ▶ n. informal repertory: *once, when I was in rep, I learned the part of Iago in three days.* ■ a repertory theater or company.
– ORIGIN 1920s: abbreviation.

rep[3] (also **repp**) ▶ n. a fabric with a ribbed surface, used in curtains and upholstery.
– ORIGIN mid 19th cent.: from French *reps,* of unknown ultimate origin.

rep[4] ▶ n. informal short for REPUTATION: *I don't know why caffeine's suddenly got such a bad rep.*

rep[5] ▶ n. (in bodybuilding) a repetition of a set of exercises. Compare with SET[2] (sense 1).
▶ v. [with obj.] (in knitting patterns) repeat (stitches or part of a design): *rep the last row.*
– ORIGIN 1950s: abbreviation.

Rep. ▶ abbr. ■ (in the US Congress) Representative. ■ Republic. ■ a Republican.

re·pack /,rē'pak/ ▶ v. [with obj.] pack (a suitcase or bag) again. ■ pack (objects) differently in a container.

re·pack·age /rē'pakij/ ▶ v. [with obj.] package again or differently: *excess stock may be given to charities or repackaged.* ■ present in a new way: *the commission has repackaged its ideas.*

re·pag·i·nate /,rē'pajə,nāt/ ▶ v. [with obj.] renumber the pages of (a book, magazine, or other document).
– DERIVATIVES **re·pag·i·na·tion** n.

re·paid /rē'pād/ past and past participle of REPAY.

re·paint /,rē'pānt/ ▶ v. [with obj.] cover with a new coat of paint.

re·pair[1] /ri'pe(ə)r/ ▶ v. [with obj.] fix or mend (a thing suffering from damage or a fault): *faulty electrical appliances should be repaired by an electrician.* ■ make good (such damage) by fixing or repairing it: *an operation to repair damage to his neck.* ■ put right (a damaged relationship or unwelcome situation): *the new government moved quickly to repair relations with the USA.*
▶ n. the action of fixing or mending something: *the truck was **beyond repair** | the abandoned house they bought needs repairs.* ■ a result of such fixing or mending: *a coat of French polish was brushed over the repair.* ■ the relative physical condition of an object: *the existing hospital is in a bad **state of repair**.*
– DERIVATIVES **re·pair·a·ble** adj., **re·pair·er** n.
– ORIGIN late Middle English: from Old French *reparer,* from Latin *reparare,* from *re-* 'back' + *parare* 'make ready.'

re·pair[2] ▶ v. [no obj.] (**repair to**) formal or humorous go to (a place), esp. in company: *we repaired to the tranquility of a nearby cafe.*
▶ n. archaic frequent or habitual visiting of a place: *she exhorted repair to the church.* ■ a place that is frequently visited or occupied: *the repairs of wild beasts.*
– ORIGIN Middle English: from Old French *repairer,* from late Latin *repatriare* 'return to one's country' (see REPATRIATE).

re·pair·man /ri'pe(ə)r,man, -mən/ ▶ n. (pl. **repairmen**) a person who repairs vehicles, machinery, or appliances.

re·pap·er /rē'pāpər/ ▶ v. [with obj.] apply new wallpaper to (a wall or room).

rep·a·ra·ble /'rep(ə)rəbəl/ ▶ adj. (esp. of an injury or loss) possible to rectify or repair.
– ORIGIN late 16th cent.: from French *réparable,* from Latin *reparabilis,* from *reparare* 'make ready again' (see REPAIR[1]).

rep·a·ra·tion /,repə'rāsHən/ ▶ n. **1** the making of amends for a wrong one has done, by paying money to or otherwise helping those who have been wronged: *the courts required a convicted offender to **make** financial **reparation** to his victim.* ■ (**reparations**) the compensation for war damage paid by a defeated state.
2 archaic the action of repairing something: *the old hall was pulled down to avoid the cost of reparation.*
– DERIVATIVES **re·par·a·tive** /ri'parətiv/ adj.
– ORIGIN late Middle English: from Old French, from late Latin *reparatio(n-),* from *reparare* 'make ready again' (see REPAIR[1]).

re·par·a·tive ther·a·py ▶ n. psychotherapy aimed at changing a person's homosexuality and based on the view that homosexuality is a mental disorder.

rep·ar·tee /,repər'tē, ,rep,är'tē, -'tā/ ▶ n. conversation or speech characterized by quick, witty comments or replies.
– ORIGIN mid 17th cent.: from French *repartie* 'replied promptly,' feminine past participle of *repartir,* from *re-* 'again' + *partir* 'divide, depart.'

re·par·ti·tion /,rē,pär'tisHən/ ▶ v. [with obj.] divide (something) up, or partition or divide (something) again.

re·pass /,rē'pas/ ▶ v. **1** pass again, esp. on the way back.
2 [with obj.] pass (legislation) in an amended form or under changed conditions: *Congress repassed the statute with the added interstate commerce clause.*
– ORIGIN late Middle English: from Old French *repasser.*

re·past /ri'past, 'rē,past/ ▶ n. formal a meal: *a sumptuous repast.*
– ORIGIN late Middle English: from Old French, based on late Latin *repascere,* from *re-* (expressing intensive force) + *pascere* 'to feed.'

re·pa·tri·ate /rē'pātrē,āt, rē'pa-/ ▶ v. [with obj.] send (someone) back to their own country: *the United Nations hopes to repatriate all the refugees.* ■ send or bring (something, esp. money) back to one's own country: *foreign firms would be permitted to repatriate all profits.*
▶ n. a person who has been repatriated.
– DERIVATIVES **re·pa·tri·a·tion** /,rē,pātrē'āsHən, ,rē,pa-/ n.
– ORIGIN early 17th cent.: from late Latin *repatriat-* 'returned to one's country,' from the verb *repatriare,* from *re-* 'back' + Latin *patria* 'native land.'

re·pay /rē'pā/ ▶ v. (past and past participle **repaid** /rē'pād/) [with obj.] pay back (a loan, debt, or sum of money): *the loans were to be repaid over a 20-year period.* ■ pay back money borrowed from (someone): *most of his fortune had been spent repaying creditors.* ■ do or give something as recompense for (a favor or kindness received): *the manager has given me another chance and I'm desperate to repay that faith.*
– DERIVATIVES **re·pay·a·ble** adj.
– ORIGIN late Middle English: from Old French *repaier.*

re·pay·ment /rē'pāmənt/ ▶ n. the action of paying back a loan. ■ an amount of money paid back: *minimum monthly repayments.*

re·peal /ri'pēl/ ▶ v. [with obj.] revoke or annul (a law or congressional act): *the legislation was repealed five months later.*
▶ n. the action of revoking or annulling a law or congressional act: *the House voted in favor of repeal.*
– DERIVATIVES **re·peal·a·ble** adj.
– ORIGIN late Middle English: from Anglo-Norman French *repeler,* from Old French *re-* (expressing reversal) + *apeler* 'to call, appeal.'

re·peat /ri'pēt/ ▶ v. **1** [reporting verb] say again something one has already said: [with direct speech] *"Are you hurt?" he repeated* | [with obj.] *Billy repeated his question* | [with clause] *the landlady repeated that she was being very lenient with him.* ■ say again (something said or written by someone else): *he repeated the words after me* | [with clause] *she repeated what I'd said.* ■ (**repeat oneself**) say or do the same thing again. ■ used for emphasis: *force was not—repeat, not—to be used.*
2 [with obj.] do (something) again, either once or a number of times: *earlier experiments were to be repeated on a far larger scale.* ■ broadcast (a television or radio program) again. ■ undertake (a course or period of instruction) again: *Mark had to repeat first and second grades.* ■ (**repeat itself**) occur again in the same way or form: *I don't intend to let history repeat itself.* ■ [no obj.] illegally vote more than once in an election. ■ [no obj.] attain a particular success or achievement again, esp. by winning a championship for the second consecutive time: *the first team in nineteen years to repeat as NBA champions.* ■ [with obj.] (of a watch or clock) strike (the last hour or quarter) over again when required.
3 [no obj.] (of food) be tasted intermittently for some time after being swallowed as a result of belching or indigestion: *it sat rather uncomfortably on my stomach and **repeated on** me for hours.*
▶ n. an action, event, or other thing that occurs or is done again: *the final will be a repeat of last year.* ■ a repeated broadcast of a television or radio program. ■ [as modifier] occurring, done, or used more than once: *a repeat prescription.* ■ a consignment of goods similar to one already received. ■ a decorative pattern that is repeated uniformly over a surface. ■ Music a passage intended to be repeated. ■ a mark indicating this.
– DERIVATIVES **re·peat·a·bil·i·ty** /ri,pētə'bilətē/ n., **re·peat·a·ble** adj.
– ORIGIN late Middle English: from Old French *repeter,* from Latin *repetere,* from *re-* 'back' + *petere* 'seek.'

re·peat·ed /ri'pētid/ ▶ adj. done or occurring again several times in the same way: *there were repeated attempts to negotiate | despite repeated requests, neither company gave a satisfactory answer.*

re·peat·ed·ly /ri'pētidlē/ ▶ adv. over and over again; constantly: *they have been warned repeatedly with no effect.*

re·peat·er /ri'pētər/ ▶ n. a person or thing that repeats something, in particular: ■ a firearm that fires several shots without reloading. ■ a watch or clock that can be made to repeat its last strike. ■ a device for the automatic retransmission or amplification of an electrically transmitted message.

re·peat·ing /ri'pētiNG/ ▶ adj. **1** (of a firearm) capable of firing several shots in succession without reloading.
2 (of a pattern) recurring uniformly over a surface.

re·peat·ing dec·i·mal ▶ n. a decimal fraction in which a figure or group of figures is repeated indefinitely, as in 0.666... or as in *1.851851851....*

re·pê·chage /,repə'sHäZH/ (also **repechage**) ▶ n. (in rowing and other sports) a contest in which the runners-up in the eliminating heats compete for a place in the final.
– ORIGIN early 20th cent.: French, from *repêcher* 'fish out, rescue.'

re·pel /ri'pel/ ▶ v. (**repels, repelling, repelled**) [with obj.] **1** drive or force (an attack or attacker) back or away: *government units sought to repel the rebels.* ■ [with obj.] (of a magnetic pole or electric field) force (something similarly magnetized or charged) away from itself: *electrically charged objects attract or repel one another* | [no obj.] *like poles repel and unlike poles attract.* ■ (of a substance) resist mixing with or be impervious to (another substance): *boots with good-quality leather uppers to repel moisture.*
2 be repulsive or distasteful to: *she was repelled by the permanent smell of drink on his breath.*
3 formal refuse to accept (something, esp. an argument or theory): *the alleged right of lien led by the bankrupt's attorney was repelled.*
– DERIVATIVES **re·pel·ler** n.
– ORIGIN late Middle English: from Latin *repellere,* from *re-* 'back' + *pellere* 'to drive.'

re·pel·lent /ri'pelənt/ (also **repellant**) ▶ adj. **1** [often in combination] able to repel a particular thing; impervious to a particular substance: *water-repellent nylon.*

PRONUNCIATION KEY ə *ago, up;* ər *over, fur;* a *hat;* ā *ate;* ä *car;* e *let;* ē *see;* i *fit;* ī *by;* NG *sing;* ō *go;* ô *law, for;* oi *toy;* o͝o *good;* o͞o *goo;* ou *out;* TH *thin;* T̲H̲ *then;* ZH *vision*

2 causing disgust or distaste: *the idea was slightly repellent to her.*
▶ **n. 1** a substance that dissuades particular insects or other pests from approaching or settling: *a flea repellent.*
2 a substance used to treat something, esp. fabric or stone, so as to make it impervious to water: *treat brick with a silicone water repellent.*
– DERIVATIVES **re·pel·lence n., re·pel·len·cy n., re·pel·lent·ly adv.**
– ORIGIN mid 17th cent.: from Latin *repellent-* 'driving back,' from the verb *repellere* (see REPEL).

re·pent /ri'pent/ ▶ **v.** [no obj.] feel or express sincere regret or remorse about one's wrongdoing or sin: *the priest urged his listeners to repent | he repented of his action.* ■ [with obj.] view or think of (an action or omission) with deep regret or remorse: *Marian came to repent her hasty judgment.* ■ (**repent oneself**) archaic feel regret or penitence about: *I repent me of all I did.*
– DERIVATIVES **re·pent·er n.**
– ORIGIN Middle English: from Old French *repentir,* from *re-* (expressing intensive force) + *pentir* (based on Latin *paenitere* 'cause to repent').

re·pent·ance /ri'pentns/ ▶ **n.** the action of repenting; sincere regret or remorse: *each person who turns to God in genuine repentance and faith will be saved.*

re·pent·ant /ri'pentnt/ ▶ **adj.** expressing or feeling sincere regret and remorse; remorseful: *he is truly repentant for his incredible naivety and stupidity.*

re·peo·ple /rē'pēpəl, 'rē-/ ▶ **v.** [with obj.] repopulate (a place).

re·per·cus·sion /ˌrēpər'kəsHən, ˌrep-/ ▶ **n. 1** (usu. **repercussions**) an unintended consequence occurring some time after an event or action, esp. an unwelcome one: *the move would have grave repercussions for the entire region.*
2 archaic the recoil of something after impact.
3 archaic an echo or reverberation.
– DERIVATIVES **re·per·cus·sive** /-'kəsiv/ **adj.**
– ORIGIN late Middle English (as a medical term meaning 'repressing of infection'): from Old French, or from Latin *repercussio(n-),* from *repercutere* 'cause to rebound, push back,' from *re-* 'back, again' + *percutere* 'to strike.' The early sense 'driving back, rebounding' (mid 16th cent.) gave rise later to 'blow given in return,' hence sense 1 (early 20th cent).

re·per·fu·sion /rēpər'fyo͞ozHən/ ▶ **n.** Medicine the action of restoring the flow of blood to an organ or tissue, typically after a heart attack or stroke.

rep·er·toire /'repə(r)ˌtwär/ ▶ **n.** a stock of plays, dances, or pieces that a company or a performer knows or is prepared to perform. ■ the whole body of items that are regularly performed: *the mainstream concert repertoire.* ■ a stock of skills or types of behavior that a person habitually uses: *his repertoire of threats, stares, and denigratory gestures.*
– ORIGIN mid 19th cent.: from French *répertoire,* from late Latin *repertorium* (see REPERTORY).

rep·er·to·ry /'repə(r)ˌtôrē/ ▶ **n.** (pl. **repertories**)
1 the performance of various plays, operas, or ballets by a company at regular short intervals: [as modifier] *a repertory actor.* ■ repertory theaters regarded collectively. ■ a repertory company.
2 another term for REPERTOIRE. ■ a repository or collection, esp. of information or retrievable examples.
– DERIVATIVES **rep·er·to·ri·al** /ˌrepə(r)'tôrēəl/ **adj.**
– ORIGIN mid 16th cent. (denoting an index or catalog): from late Latin *repertorium,* from Latin *repert-* 'found, discovered,' from the verb *reperire.* Sense 1 (arising from the fact that a company has a "repertory" of pieces for performance) dates from the late 19th cent.

rep·er·to·ry com·pa·ny ▶ **n.** a theatrical company that performs works from its repertoire for regular, short periods of time, moving on from one work to another.

rep·e·tend /'repəˌtend/ ▶ **n.** Mathematics the repeating figure or figures of a recurring decimal fraction. ■ formal a recurring word or phrase; a refrain.
– ORIGIN early 18th cent.: from Latin *repetendum* 'something to be repeated,' neuter gerundive of *repetere* (see REPEAT).

ré·pé·ti·teur /ˌrāpāti'tər/ ▶ **n.** a tutor or coach of ballet dancers or musicians, esp. opera singers.
– ORIGIN French.

rep·e·ti·tion /ˌrepə'tisHən/ ▶ **n.** the action of repeating something that has already been said or written: *her comments are worthy of repetition | a repetition of his reply to the delegation.* ■ [often with negative] the recurrence of an action or event: *there was to be no repetition of the interwar years | I didn't want a repetition of the scene in my office that morning.* ■ a thing repeated: *the geometric repetitions of Islamic art.* ■ a training exercise that is repeated, esp. a series of repeated raisings and lowerings of the weight in weight training. ■ Music the repeating of a passage or note. ■ archaic a piece set by a teacher to be learned by heart and recited.
– DERIVATIVES **rep·e·ti·tion·al** /-SHənl/ **adj.**
– ORIGIN late Middle English: from Old French *repeticion* or Latin *repetitio(n-),* from *repetere* (see REPEAT).

rep·e·ti·tious /ˌrepə'tisHəs/ ▶ **adj.** another term for REPETITIVE.
– DERIVATIVES **rep·e·ti·tious·ly adv., rep·e·ti·tious·ness n.**

re·pet·i·tive /ri'petətiv/ ▶ **adj.** containing or characterized by repetition, esp. when unnecessary or tiresome: *a repetitive task.*
– DERIVATIVES **re·pet·i·tive·ly adv., re·pet·i·tive·ness n.**

re·pet·i·tive strain in·ju·ry (abbr.: **RSI**) ▶ **n.** a condition in which the prolonged performance of repetitive actions, typically with the hands, causes pain or impairment of function in the tendons and muscles involved.

re·phrase /rē'frāz/ ▶ **v.** [with obj.] express (an idea or question) in an alternative way, esp. with the purpose of changing the detail or perspective of the original idea or question: *rephrase the statement so that it is clear.*

re·pine /ri'pīn/ ▶ **v.** [no obj.] literary feel or express discontent; fret: *you mustn't let yourself repine.*
– ORIGIN early 16th cent.: from RE- 'again' + the verb PINE[2], on the pattern of *repent.*

re·place /ri'plās/ ▶ **v.** [with obj.] **1** take the place of: *Ian's smile was replaced by a frown.* ■ provide or find a substitute for (something that is broken, old, or inoperative): *the light bulb needs replacing.* ■ fill the role of (someone or something) with a substitute: *the government dismissed 3,000 of its customs inspectors, replacing them with new recruits.*
2 put (something) back in a previous place or position: *he drained his glass and replaced it on the bar.*
– DERIVATIVES **re·plac·er n.**

re·place·a·ble /ri'plāsəbəl/ ▶ **adj.** able to be replaced: *a knife with a replaceable blade.* ■ Chemistry denoting those hydrogen atoms in an acid that can be displaced by metal atoms when forming salts.
– DERIVATIVES **re·place·a·bil·i·ty** /-ˌplāsə'bilətē/ **n.**

re·place·ment /ri'plāsmənt/ ▶ **n.** the action or process of replacing someone or something: *the replacement of religion by poetry | a hip replacement.* ■ a person or thing that takes the place of another.

re·place·ment ther·a·py ▶ **n.** Medicine treatment aimed at making up a deficit of a substance normally present in the body.

re·plan /ˌrē'plan/ ▶ **v.** (**replans, replanning, replanned**) [with obj.] plan (something, esp. the layout of buildings or cities) differently or again.

re·plant /rē'plant, 'rē-/ ▶ **v.** [with obj.] plant (a tree or plant that has been dug up) again, esp. when transferring it to a larger pot or new site. ■ provide (an area) with new plants or trees: *38 percent of ancient woodland has been replanted with conifers.* ■ surgically reattach to the body (a part that has been removed or severed).

re·plan·ta·tion /ˌrē,plan'tāsHən/ ▶ **n.** permanent reattachment to the body of a part that has been removed or severed: *successful replantation of the tooth.*

re·play ▶ **v.** /rē'plā, 'rē-/ [with obj.] **1** play back (a recording on tape, video, or film): *he could stop the tape and replay it whenever he wished.*
2 repeat (something, esp. an event or sequence of events): *she replayed in her mind every detail of the night before.* ■ play (a match) again to decide a winner after the original encounter ended in a draw or contentious result.
▶ **n.** /'rēˌplā/ **1** the playing again of a section of a recording, esp. so as to be able to watch an incident more closely: *clouds can be studied in speeded-up replay | the umpire studied TV replays.*
2 an occurrence that closely follows the pattern of a previous event: *a replay of last summer's civil disturbance.* ■ a replayed match.

re·plen·ish /ri'plenisH/ ▶ **v.** [with obj.] fill (something) up again: *he replenished Justin's glass with mineral water.* ■ restore (a stock or supply of something) to the former level or condition: *all creatures need sleep to replenish their energies.*
– DERIVATIVES **re·plen·ish·er n., re·plen·ish·ment n.**
– ORIGIN late Middle English (in the sense 'supply abundantly'): from Old French *repleniss-,* lengthened stem of *replenir,* from *re-* 'again' (also expressing intensive force) + *plenir* 'fill' (from Latin *plenus* 'full').

re·plete /ri'plēt/ ▶ **adj.** [predic.] filled or well-supplied with something: *sensational popular fiction, replete with adultery and sudden death.* ■ very full of or sated by food: *I went out into the sun-drenched streets again, replete and relaxed.*
– DERIVATIVES **re·ple·tion** /ri'plēsHən/ **n.**
– ORIGIN late Middle English: from Old French *replet(e)* or Latin *repletus* 'filled up,' past participle of *replere,* from *re-* 'back, again' + *plere* 'fill.'

re·plev·in /ri'plevən/ ▶ **n.** Law a procedure whereby seized goods may be provisionally restored to their owner pending the outcome of an action to determine the rights of the parties concerned. ■ an action arising from such a process.
– ORIGIN late Middle English: from Anglo-Norman French, from Old French *replevir* 'recover' (see REPLEVY).

re·plev·y /ri'plevē/ ▶ **v.** (**replevies, replevying, replevied**) [with obj.] Law recover (seized goods) by replevin.
– ORIGIN mid 16th cent.: from Old French *replevir* 'recover'; apparently related to PLEDGE.

rep·li·ca /'replikə/ ▶ **n.** an exact copy or model of something, esp. one on a smaller scale: *a replica of the Empire State Building.* ■ a duplicate of an original artistic work.
– ORIGIN mid 18th cent. (as a musical term in the sense 'a repeat'): from Italian, from *replicare* 'to reply.'

rep·li·cant /'replikənt/ ▶ **n.** (in science fiction) a genetically engineered or artificial being created as an exact replica of a particular human being.
– ORIGIN from REPLICA + -ANT: first used in the movie *Blade Runner* (1982).

rep·li·case /'repliˌkās, -ˌkāz/ ▶ **n.** Biochemistry an enzyme that catalyzes the synthesis of a complementary RNA molecule using an RNA template.
– ORIGIN 1960s: from the verb REPLICATE + -ASE.

rep·li·cate ▶ **v.** /'repliˌkāt/ [with obj.] make an exact copy of; reproduce: *it might be impractical to replicate eastern culture in the west.* ■ (**replicate itself**) (of genetic material or a living organism) reproduce or give rise to a copy of itself: *interleukin-16 prevents the virus from replicating itself | [no obj.] an enzyme that HIV needs in order to replicate.* ■ repeat (a scientific experiment or trial) to obtain a consistent result: *these findings have been replicated by Atwood and Jackson.*
▶ **adj.** /-kit/ [attrib.] of the nature of a copy: *a replicate Earth.* ■ of the nature of a repetition of a scientific experiment or trial: *the variation of replicate measurements.*
▶ **n.** /-kit/ **1** a close or exact copy; a replica. ■ a repetition of an experimental test or procedure.
2 Music a tone one or more octaves above or below the given tone.
– DERIVATIVES **rep·li·ca·bil·i·ty** /ˌreplikə'bilətē/ **n., rep·li·ca·ble** /'replikəbəl/ **adj.**
– ORIGIN late Middle English (in the sense 'repeat'): from Latin *replicat-,* from the verb *replicare,* from *re-* 'back, again' + *plicare* 'to fold.' The current senses date from the late 19th cent.

rep·li·ca·tion /ˌrepli'kāsHən/ ▶ **n. 1** the action of copying or reproducing something. ■ a copy: *a twentieth-century building would be cheaper than a replication of what was there before.* ■ the repetition of a scientific experiment or trial to obtain a consistent result. ■ the process by which genetic material or a living organism gives rise to a copy of itself: *HIV replication | a crucial step in cold virus replications.*
2 Law, dated a plaintiff's reply to the defendant's plea.
– ORIGIN late Middle English: from Old French *replicacion,* from Latin *replicatio(n-),* from *replicare* 'fold back, repeat,' later 'make a reply' (see REPLICATE).

rep·li·ca·tive /'repliˌkātiv/ ▶ **adj.** Biology relating to or involving the replication of genetic material or living organisms.

rep·li·ca·tor /'repliˌkātər/ ▶ **n.** a thing that replicates or copies something. ■ Biology a structural gene at which replication of a specific replicon is believed to be initiated.

rep·li·con /'repliˌkän/ ▶ **n.** Biology a nucleic acid molecule, or part of one, that replicates as a unit, beginning at a specific site within it.
– ORIGIN 1960s: from REPLICATION + -ON.

re·ply /ri'plī/ ▶ **v.** (**replies, replied**) [reporting verb] say something in response to something someone has said: [no obj.] *he was gone before we could* ***reply to*** *his last remark* | [with clause] *she replied that she had been sound asleep* | [with direct speech] *"I'm OK—just leave me alone," he replied.* ■ [no obj.] write back to someone one has received a letter or e-mail from: *she replied with a long letter the next day.* ■ [no obj.] respond by a similar action or gesture: *they* ***replied to*** *the shelling with a heavy mortar attack on the area.*
▶ **n.** (pl. **replies**) a verbal or written answer: *I received a reply from the firm's managing director | "No," was the curt reply.* ■ the action of answering someone or something: *I am writing* ***in reply to*** *your letter of*

r

June 1. ■ a response in the form of a gesture, action, or expression: *we scored the first goal and they hit a late reply.* ■ Law a plaintiff's response to the defendant's plea.
– DERIVATIVES **re·pli·er** n.
– ORIGIN late Middle English (as a verb): from Old French *replier,* from Latin *replicare* 'repeat,' later 'make a reply' (see REPLICATE).

re·po /'rē,pō/ informal ▶ n. (pl. **repos**) **1** another term for REPURCHASE AGREEMENT. [1960s: abbreviation.] **2** a car or other item that has been repossessed. ▶ v. (**repo's, repo'ing, repo'd**) [with obj.] repossess (a car or other item) when a buyer defaults on payments. [1970s: abbreviation.]

re·point /rē'point/ ▶ v. [with obj.] fill in or repair the joints of (brickwork).

re·po man ▶ n. informal a repossessor.

re·pop·u·late /rē'päpyə,lāt/ ▶ v. [with obj.] introduce a population into (a previously occupied area or country): *the area was repopulated largely by Russians.*
– DERIVATIVES **repopulation** /,rē,päpyə'lāsHən/ n.

re·port /ri'pôrt/ ▶ v. **1** [reporting verb] give a spoken or written account of something that one has observed, heard, done, or investigated: [with obj.] *the representative reported a decline in milk and meat production* | [with clause] *police reported that the flood waters were abating* | [no obj.] *the teacher should* **report on** *the child's progress.* ■ [no obj.] cover an event or subject as a journalist or a reporter: *the press* **reported on** *Republican sex scandals* | [with clause] *the Egyptian news agency reported that a coup attempt had taken place* | [with obj.] *the paper reported a secret program by the country to build nuclear warheads.* ■ (**be reported**) used to indicate that something has been stated, although one cannot confirm its accuracy: [with infinitive] *these hoaxers are reported to be hacking into airline frequencies to impersonate air traffic controllers* | (as adj. **reported**) *a reported $50,000 in debt.* ■ [with obj.] make a formal statement or complaint about (someone or something) to the necessary authority: *undisclosed illegalities are* **reported to** *the company's directors* | [with obj. and complement] *eight horses have been reported missing in the last month.* ■ [with obj.] (of a legislative committee) formally announce that the committee has dealt with (a bill): *the chairman shall report the bill to the House.* See also REPORT A BILL OUT below. **2** [no obj.] present oneself formally as having arrived at a particular place or as ready to do something: *he was given three days to say goodbye to his family and* **report for** *active duty.* **3** [no obj.] (**report to**) be responsible to (a superior or supervisor): *the appointee will* **report to** *the chairman of the committee.*
▶ n. **1** an account given of a particular matter, esp. in the form of an official document, after thorough investigation or consideration by an appointed person or body: *the chairman's annual report.* ■ a spoken or written description of an event or situation, esp. one intended for publication or broadcast in the media: *press reports suggested that the government was still using secret police to help maintain public order.* ■ a teacher's written assessment of a student's work, progress, and conduct, issued at the end of a term or academic year. ■ Law a detailed formal account of a case heard in a court, giving the main points in the judgment, esp. as prepared for publication. ■ a piece of information that is unsupported by firm evidence and that the speaker feels may or may not be true: *reports were circulating that the chairman was about to resign.* ■ dated rumor: **report has it** *that the beetles have now virtually disappeared.* ■ archaic the way in which someone or something is regarded; reputation: *whatsoever things are lovely and of* **good report.** **2** a sudden loud noise of or like an explosion or gunfire. **3** an employee who is supervised by another employee: *all of his reports are twenty-somethings with no concept of proper attire for work.*
– PHRASES **on report** (esp. of a prisoner or member of the armed forces) on a disciplinary charge.
– PHRASAL VERBS **report back** (or **report something back**) **1** deliver a spoken or written account of something one has been asked to do or investigate: *the deadpan voice of a police officer* **reporting back to** *his superior* | *every movement I made was reported back to him.* **2** return to work or duty after a period of absence. **report a bill out** (of a committee of Congress) return a bill to the legislative body for action.
– DERIVATIVES **re·port·a·ble** adj.
– ORIGIN late Middle English: from Old French *reporter* (verb), *report* (noun), from Latin *reportare* 'bring back,' from *re-* 'back' + *portare* 'carry.' The sense 'give an account' gave rise to 'submit a formal report,' hence 'inform an authority of one's presence' (sense 2 of the verb, mid 19th cent.) and 'be accountable (to a superior)' (sense 3 of the verb, late 19th cent).

re·port·age /rə'pôrtij, ,repôr'täzH/ ▶ n. the reporting of news, for the press and the broadcast media: *extensive reportage of elections.* ■ factual presentation in a book or other text, esp. when this adopts a journalistic style.
– ORIGIN early 17th cent.: French, from Old French *reporter* 'carry back' (see REPORT).

re·port card ▶ n. a teacher's written assessment of a student's work, progress, and conduct, sent home to a parent or guardian. ■ an evaluation of performance: *Democrat legislators fared poorly in a recent report card.*

re·port·ed·ly /ri'pôrtədlē/ ▶ adv. [sentence adverb] according to what some say (used to express the speaker's belief that the information given is not necessarily true): *he was in El Salvador, reportedly on his way to Texas.*

re·port·ed speech ▶ n. a speaker's words reported in subordinate clauses governed by a reporting verb, with the required changes of person and tense (e.g., *he said that he would go,* based on *I will go*). Also called INDIRECT SPEECH. Contrasted with DIRECT SPEECH.

re·port·er /ri'pôrtər/ ▶ n. a person who reports, esp. one employed to report news or conduct interviews for newspapers or broadcasts.

re·port·ing verb ▶ n. a verb belonging to a class of verbs conveying the action of speaking and used with both direct and reported speech. Reporting verbs may also be used with a direct object and with an infinitive construction.

rep·or·to·ri·al /,repə(r)'tôrēəl, ,rē-/ ▶ adj. of or characteristic of newspaper reporters: *reportorial ambition and curiosity.*
– DERIVATIVES **rep·or·to·ri·al·ly** adv.
– ORIGIN mid 19th cent.: from REPORTER, on the pattern of *editorial.*

re·po·sa·do /,repə'sädō/ ▶ n. (pl. **reposados**) a type of tequila that has been aged in oak for a period of two to twelve months.
– ORIGIN Spanish, literally 'rested.'

re·pose[1] /ri'pōz/ ▶ n. a state of rest, sleep, or tranquility: **in repose** *her face looked relaxed.* ■ composure: *he had lost none of his grace or his repose.* ■ Art harmonious arrangement of colors and forms, providing a restful visual effect.
▶ v. [no obj.] be lying, situated, or kept in a particular place: *the diamond now reposes in the Louvre.* ■ lie down in rest: *how sweetly he would repose in the four-poster bed.* ■ [with obj.] (**repose something on/in**) literary lay something to rest in or on (something): *I'll go to him, and repose our distresses on his friendly bosom.* ■ [with obj.] archaic give rest to: *he halted to repose his wayworn soldiers.*
– DERIVATIVES **re·pose·ful** /-fəl/ adj., **re·pose·ful·ly** /-fəlē/ adv.
– ORIGIN late Middle English: from Old French *repos* (noun), *reposer* (verb), from late Latin *repausare,* from *re-* (expressing intensive force) + *pausare* 'to pause.'

re·pose[2] ▶ v. [with obj.] (**repose something in**) place something, esp. one's confidence or trust, in: *we have never betrayed the trust that you have reposed in us.*
– ORIGIN late Middle English (in the sense 'put back in the same position'): from RE- 'again' + the verb POSE[1], suggested by Latin *reponere* 'replace,' from *re-* (expressing intensive force) + *ponere* 'to place.'

re·po·si·tion /,rēpə'zisHən/ ▶ v. [with obj.] place in a different position; adjust or alter the position of: *try repositioning the thermostat in another room.* ■ change the image of (a company, product, etc.) to target a new or wider market: *our assignment was to reposition coffee from a "rite of passage" drink to a "contemporary experience."*

re·pos·i·to·ry /ri'päzə,tôrē/ ▶ n. (pl. **repositories**) a place, building, or receptacle where things are or may be stored: *a deep repository for nuclear waste.* ■ a place in which something, esp. a natural resource, has accumulated or where it is found in significant quantities: *accessible repositories of water.* ■ a person or thing regarded as a store of information or in which something abstract is held to exist or be found: *his mind was a rich repository of the past.*
– ORIGIN late 15th cent.: from Old French *repositoire* or Latin *repositorium,* from *reposit-* 'placed back,' from the verb *reponere* (see REPOSE[2]).

re·pos·sess /,rēpə'zes/ ▶ v. [with obj.] retake possession of (something) when a buyer defaults on payments: *565 homes were repossessed for nonpayment of mortgages.*
– DERIVATIVES **re·pos·ses·sion** /-'zesHən/ n.

re·pos·ses·sor /,rēpə'zesər/ ▶ n. a person hired by a credit company to repossess an item when the buyer defaults on payments.

re·pot /rē'pät, 'rē-/ ▶ v. (**repots, repotting, repotted**) [with obj.] put (a plant) in another pot, esp. a larger one.

re·pous·sé /rə,pōō'sā/ ▶ adj. (of metalwork) hammered into relief from the reverse side.
▶ n. ornamental metalwork fashioned in this way.
– ORIGIN mid 19th cent.: French, literally 'pushed back,' past participle of *repousser,* from *re-* (expressing intensive force) + *pousser* 'to push.'

repp /rep/ ▶ n. variant spelling of REP[3].

repr. ▶ abbr. reprint or reprinted.

rep·re·hend /,repri'hend/ ▶ v. [with obj.] reprimand: *a recklessness that cannot be too severely reprehended.*
– DERIVATIVES **rep·re·hen·sion** /-'hencHən/ n.
– ORIGIN Middle English: from Latin *reprehendere* 'seize, check, rebuke,' from *re-* (expressing intensive force) + *prehendere* 'seize.'

rep·re·hen·si·ble /,repri'hensəbəl/ ▶ adj. deserving censure or condemnation: *his complacency and reprehensible laxity.*
– DERIVATIVES **rep·re·hen·si·bil·i·ty** /-,hensə'bilətē/ n., **rep·re·hen·si·bly** /-blē/ adv.
– ORIGIN late Middle English: from late Latin *reprehensibilis,* from *reprehens-* 'rebuked,' from the verb *reprehendere* (see REPREHEND).

rep·re·sent /,repri'zent/ ▶ v. [with obj.] **1** be entitled or appointed to act or speak for (someone), esp. in an official capacity: *for purposes of litigation, an infant can and must be represented by an adult.* ■ (of a competitor) participate in a sports event or other competition on behalf of (one's club, town, region, or country): *Owens represented the U.S.* ■ be an elected member of a legislature for (a particular constituency, party, or group): *she became the first woman to represent her district.* ■ (usu. **be represented**) act as a substitute for (someone), esp. on an official or ceremonial occasion: *the president was represented by the secretary of state.* **2** constitute; amount to: *this figure represents eleven percent of the company's total sales.* ■ be a specimen or example of; typify: *twenty parents, picked to represent a cross section of rural life.* ■ (**be represented**) (of a group or type of person or thing) be present or found in something, esp. to a particular degree: *abstraction is well represented in this exhibition.* **3** depict (a particular subject) in a picture or other work of art: *santos are small wooden figures representing saints.* ■ [with obj. or infinitive] describe or depict (someone or something) as being of a certain nature; portray in a particular way: *the young were consistently represented as being in need of protection.* ■ (of a sign or symbol) have a particular signification; stand for: *the numbers 1–10 represent the letters A–J.* ■ be a symbol or embodiment of (a particular quality or thing): *the three heads of Cerberus represent the past, present, and future.* ■ play the part of (someone) in a theatrical production. **4** formal state or point out (something) clearly: *it was represented to him that she would be an unsuitable wife.* ■ [with clause] allege; claim: *the vendors have represented that such information is accurate.*
– DERIVATIVES **rep·re·sent·a·bil·i·ty** /,repri,zentə'bilətē/ n., **rep·re·sent·a·ble** adj.
– ORIGIN late Middle English: from Old French *representer* or Latin *repraesentare,* from *re-* (expressing intensive force) + *praesentare* 'to present.'

re-pre·sent /,rēpri'zent/ ▶ v. [with obj.] present (something) again, esp. for further consideration or in an altered form: *most of today's demonstrations will be re-presented on Friday.* ■ present (a check or bill) again for payment.
– DERIVATIVES **re-pres·en·ta·tion** /,rē,prezən'tāsHən, -,prē,zen-/ n.

rep·re·sen·ta·tion /,repri,zen'tāsHən, -zən-/ ▶ n. **1** the action of speaking or acting on behalf of someone or the state of being so represented: *asylum-seekers should be guaranteed good legal advice and representation.* **2** the description or portrayal of someone or something in a particular way or as being of a certain nature: *the representation of women in newspapers.* ■ the depiction of someone or something in a picture or other work of art: *Picasso is striving for some absolute representation of reality.* ■ a thing, esp. a picture or model, that depicts a likeness or reproduction of someone or something: *a striking representation of a vase of flowers.* ■ (in some theories of perception) a mental state or concept regarded as corresponding to a thing perceived.

PRONUNCIATION KEY ə *ago, up;* ər *over, fur;* a *hat;* ā *ate;* ä *car;* e *let;* ē *see;* i *fit;* ī *by;* NG *sing;* ō *go;* ô *law, for;* oi *toy;* ŏŏ *good;* ōō *goo;* ou *out;* TH *thin;* TH *then;* ZH *vision*

3 (**representations**) formal statements made to a higher authority, esp. so as to communicate an opinion or register a protest: *certain church groups are making strong representations to our government.* ■ a statement or allegation: *any buyer was relying on a representation that the tapes were genuine.*
– ORIGIN late Middle English (in the sense 'image, likeness'): from Old French *representation* or Latin *repraesentatio(n-)*, from *repraesentare* 'bring before, exhibit' (see REPRESENT).

rep·re·sen·ta·tion·al /ˌrepriˌzenˈtāsʜənl/ ▶ **adj.** of, relating to, or characterized by representation: *representational democracy.* ■ relating to or denoting art that aims to depict the physical appearance of things. Contrasted with ABSTRACT.

rep·re·sen·ta·tion·al·ism /ˌrepriˌzenˈtāsʜənlˌizəm/ ▶ **n. 1** the practice or advocacy of representational art.
2 Philosophy another term for REPRESENTATIONISM.
– DERIVATIVES **rep·re·sen·ta·tion·al·ist adj. & n.**

rep·re·sen·ta·tion·ism /ˌrepriˌzenˈtāsʜəˌnizəm, -zən-/ ▶ **n.** Philosophy the doctrine that thought is the manipulation of mental representations that (somehow) correspond to external states or objects.
– DERIVATIVES **rep·re·sen·ta·tion·ist n.**

rep·re·sen·ta·tive /ˌrepriˈzentətiv/ ▶ **adj. 1** typical of a class, group, or body of opinion: *these courses are representative of those taken by most Harvard undergraduates.* ■ containing typical examples of many or all types: *a representative sample of young people in the South.*
2 (of a legislative or deliberative assembly) consisting of people chosen to act and speak on behalf of a wider group. ■ (of a government or political system) based on representation of the people by such deputies: *free elections and representative democracy.*
3 serving as a portrayal or symbol of something: *the show should be more **representative of** how women really are.* ■ (of art) representational: *the bust involves a high degree of representative abstraction.*
4 Philosophy of or relating to mental representation.
▶ **n. 1** a person chosen or appointed to act or speak for another or others, in particular: ■ an agent of a firm who travels to potential clients to sell its products. ■ an employee of a travel company who looks after the needs of its vacationing clients. ■ a person chosen or elected to speak and act on behalf of others in a legislative assembly or deliberative body. ■ a delegate who attends a conference, negotiations, legal hearing, etc., so as to represent the interests of another person or group. ■ a person who takes the place of another on a ceremonial or official occasion.
2 an example of a class or group: *fossil representatives of lampreys and hagfishes.*
– DERIVATIVES **rep·re·sent·a·tive·ly adv.**, **rep·re·sent·a·tive·ness n.**

re·press /riˈpres/ ▶ **v.** [with obj.] subdue (someone or something) by force: *the uprisings were repressed.* ■ restrain, prevent, or inhibit (the expression or development of something): *Isabel couldn't repress a sharp cry of fear.* ■ suppress (a thought, feeling, or desire) in oneself so that it becomes or remains unconscious: *the thought that he had killed his brother was so terrible that he repressed it.* ■ Biology prevent the transcription of (a gene).
– DERIVATIVES **re·press·er n.**, **re·press·i·ble** /-əbəl/ **adj.**
– ORIGIN Middle English (in the sense 'keep back (something objectionable)'): from Latin *repress-* 'pressed back, checked,' from the verb *reprimere*, from *re-* 'back' + *premere* 'to press.'

re·pressed /riˈprest/ ▶ **adj.** restrained, inhibited, or oppressed: *repressed indigenous groups | repressed energy.* ■ (of a thought, feeling, or desire) kept suppressed and unconscious in one's mind: *repressed memories.* ■ having or characterized by a large number of thoughts, feelings, or desires, esp. sexual ones, that are suppressed in this way: *a very repressed, almost Victorian, household.*

re·pres·sion /riˈpresʜən/ ▶ **n.** the action of subduing someone or something by force. ■ the restraint, prevention, or inhibition of a feeling, quality, etc.: *the repression of anger can be positively harmful.* ■ the action or process of suppressing a thought or desire in oneself so that it remains unconscious.

re·pres·sive /riˈpresiv/ ▶ **adj.** (esp. of a social or political system) inhibiting or restraining the freedom of a person or group of people: *a repressive regime.* ■ inhibiting or preventing the awareness of certain thoughts or feelings: *a repressive moral code.*
– DERIVATIVES **re·pres·sive·ly adv.**, **re·pres·sive·ness n.**

re·pres·sor /riˈpresər/ ▶ **n.** Biochemistry a substance that acts on an operon to inhibit messenger RNA synthesis.

re·price /ˌrēˈprīs/ ▶ **v.** [with obj.] put a different price on (a product or commodity).

re·prieve /riˈprēv/ ▶ **v.** [with obj.] cancel or postpone the punishment of (someone, esp. someone condemned to death): *under the new regime, prisoners under sentence of death were reprieved.* ■ abandon or postpone plans to close or put an end to (something): *the threatened pits could be reprieved.*
▶ **n.** a cancellation or postponement of a punishment. ■ a temporary escape from an undesirable fate or unpleasant situation: *a mother who faced eviction has been given a reprieve.*
– ORIGIN late 15th cent. (as the past participle *repryed*): from Anglo-Norman French *repris*, past participle of *reprendre*, from Latin *re-* 'back' + *prehendere* 'seize.' The insertion of *-v-* (16th cent.) remains unexplained. Sense development has undergone a reversal, from the early meaning 'send back to prison,' via 'postpone (a legal process),' to the current sense 'rescue from impending punishment.'

rep·ri·mand /ˈreprəˌmand/ ▶ **n.** a rebuke, esp. an official one.
▶ **v.** [with obj.] rebuke (someone), esp. officially: *officials were dismissed or reprimanded for poor work.*
– ORIGIN mid 17th cent.: from French *réprimande*, via Spanish from Latin *reprimenda* 'things to be held in check,' neuter plural gerundive of *reprimere* (see REPRESS).

re·print ▶ **v.** /rēˈprint, ˈrē-/ [with obj.] print again or in a different form: *the story has been reprinted at intervals ever since it first appeared.*
▶ **n.** /ˈrēˌprint/ an act of printing more copies of a work. ■ a copy of a book or other material that has been reprinted. ■ an offprint.
– DERIVATIVES **re·print·er n.**

re·pris·al /riˈprīzəl/ ▶ **n.** an act of retaliation: *three youths died in the reprisals that followed | the threat of reprisal.* ■ historical the forcible seizure of a foreign subject or their goods as an act of retaliation.
– ORIGIN late Middle English: from Anglo-Norman French *reprisaille*, from medieval Latin *reprisalia* (neuter plural), based on Latin *repraehens-* 'seized,' from the verb *reprehendere* (see REPREHEND). The current sense dates from the early 18th cent.

re·prise /riˈprēz/ ▶ **n.** a repeated passage in music. ■ a repetition or further performance of something: *a reprise of his earlier performance.*
▶ **v.** [with obj.] repeat (a piece of music or a performance).
– ORIGIN early 18th cent.: French, literally 'taken up again,' feminine past participle of *reprendre* (see REPRIEVE).

re·pro /ˈrēˌprō/ ▶ **n.** (pl. **repros**) [usu. as modifier] informal **1** a reproduction or copy, particularly of a piece of furniture: *a Georgian repro cabinet.*
2 the action or process of copying a document or image: *a repro house.*
– ORIGIN 1940s: abbreviation.

re·proach /riˈprōcʜ/ ▶ **v.** [with obj.] address (someone) in such a way as to express disapproval or disappointment: *critics of the administration **reproached** the president **for** his failure to tackle the deficiency* | [with direct speech] *"You know that isn't true," he reproached her.* ■ (**reproach someone with**) accuse someone of: *his wife reproached him with cowardice.* ■ archaic censure or rebuke (an offense).
▶ **n.** the expression of disapproval or disappointment: *he gave her a look of reproach | a farrago of warnings and pained reproaches.* ■ (**a reproach to**) a thing that makes the failings of someone or something else more apparent: *his elegance is a living reproach to our slovenly habits.* ■ (**Reproaches**) (in the Roman Catholic Church) a set of antiphons and responses for Good Friday representing the reproaches of Jesus Christ to his people.
– PHRASES **above** (or **beyond**) **reproach** such that no criticism can be made; perfect.
– DERIVATIVES **re·proach·a·ble adj.**, **re·proach·er n.**, **re·proach·ing·ly adv.**
– ORIGIN Middle English: from Old French *reprochier* (verb), from a base meaning 'bring back close,' based on Latin *prope* 'near.'

re·proach·ful /riˈprōcʜfəl/ ▶ **adj.** expressing disapproval or disappointment: *she gave him a reproachful look.*
– DERIVATIVES **re·proach·ful·ly adv.**, **re·proach·ful·ness n.**

rep·ro·bate /ˈreprəˌbāt/ ▶ **n. 1** an unprincipled person (often used humorously or affectionately).
2 Christian Theology, archaic (esp. in Calvinism) a sinner who is not of the elect and is predestined to damnation.
▶ **adj. 1** unprincipled (often used as a humorous or affectionate reproach): *a long-missed old reprobate drinking comrade.*
2 Christian Theology, archaic (in Calvinism) predestined to damnation.
▶ **v.** [with obj.] archaic express or feel disapproval of: *his neighbors reprobated his method of proceeding.*
– DERIVATIVES **rep·ro·ba·tion** /ˌreprəˈbāsʜən/ **n.**
– ORIGIN late Middle English (as a verb): from Latin *reprobat-* 'disapproved,' from the verb *reprobare*, from *re-* (expressing reversal) + *probare* 'approve.'

re·proc·ess /rēˈpräsˌes, -ˈpräsəs, -ˈprō-/ ▶ **v.** [with obj.] process (something, esp. spent nuclear fuel) again or differently, typically in order to reuse it: *the costs of reprocessing radioactive waste.*

re·pro·duce /ˌrēprəˈd(y)o͞os/ ▶ **v.** [with obj.] produce again: *a concert performance cannot reproduce all the subtleties of a recording.* ■ produce a copy or representation of: *his works are reproduced on postcards and posters.* ■ create something very similar to (something else), esp. in a different medium or context: *the problems are difficult to reproduce in the laboratory.* ■ (of an organism) produce offspring by a sexual or asexual process: *bacteria normally divide and **reproduce themselves** every twenty minutes* | [no obj.] *an individual organism needs to avoid being eaten until it has reproduced.* ■ [no obj.] be copied with a specified degree of success: *you'll be amazed to see how well halftones reproduce.*
– DERIVATIVES **re·pro·duc·er n.**, **re·pro·duc·i·bil·i·ty** /-ˌd(y)o͞osəˈbilətē/ **n.**, **re·pro·duc·i·ble adj.**, **re·pro·duc·i·bly** /-əblē/ **adv.**

re·pro·duc·tion /ˌrēprəˈdəksʜən/ ▶ **n.** the action or process of making a copy of something: *the cost of color reproduction in publication is high.* ■ the production of offspring by a sexual or asexual process. ■ a copy of a work of art, esp. a print or photograph of a painting. ■ [as modifier] made to imitate the style of an earlier period or of a particular artist or craftsman: *reproduction French classical beds.* ■ the quality of reproduced sound: *the design was changed to allow louder reproduction.*

re·pro·duc·tive /ˌrēprəˈdəktiv/ ▶ **adj.** relating to or effecting reproduction: *the female reproductive system.*
– DERIVATIVES **re·pro·duc·tive·ly** /-ˈdəktivlē/ **adv.**, **re·pro·duc·tive·ness** /-ˈdəktivnis/ **n.**, **re·pro·duc·tiv·i·ty** /rēprədəkˈtivətē/ **n.**

re·pro·gram /ˌrēˈprōˌgram/ ▶ **v.** (**reprograms, reprogramming, reprogrammed**; also **reprograms, reprograming, reprogramed**) [with obj.] program (a computer or something likened to one) again or differently.
– DERIVATIVES **re·pro·gram·ma·ble adj.**

re·pro·graph·ics /ˌreprəˈgrafiks, ˈrē-/ ▶ **plural n.** [treated as sing.] reprography.

re·prog·ra·phy /riˈprägrəfē/ ▶ **n.** the science and practice of copying and reproducing documents and graphic material.
– DERIVATIVES **re·prog·ra·pher** /-fər/ **n.**, **re·pro·graph·ic** /ˌreprəˈgrafik, ˌrē-/ **adj.**
– ORIGIN 1960s: from REPRODUCE + -GRAPHY.

re·proof /riˈpro͞of/ ▶ **n.** an expression of blame or disapproval: *she welcomed him with a mild reproof for leaving her alone | a look of reproof.*
– ORIGIN Middle English: from Old French *reprove*, from *reprover* 'reprove.' Early senses included 'ignominy, personal shame,' and 'scorn.'

re·prove /riˈpro͞ov/ ▶ **v.** [with obj.] reprimand or censure (someone): *he was reproved for obscenity* | [with direct speech] *"Don't be childish, Hilary," he reproved mildly* | (as adj. **reproving**) *a reproving glance.*
– DERIVATIVES **re·prov·a·ble adj.**, **re·prov·er n.**, **re·prov·ing·ly adv.**
– ORIGIN Middle English (also in the senses 'reject' and 'censure'): from Old French *reprover*, from late Latin *reprobare* 'disapprove' (see REPROBATE).

rep·tile /ˈreptəl, ˈrepˌtīl/ ▶ **n. 1** a cold-blooded vertebrate of a class that includes snakes, lizards, crocodiles, turtles, and tortoises. They are distinguished by having a dry scaly skin, and typically laying soft-shelled eggs on land. ● Class Reptilia: orders Chelonia (turtles and tortoises), Squamata (snakes and lizards), Rhynchocephalia (the tuatara), and Crocodylia (crocodilians). Among several extinct groups are the dinosaurs, pterosaurs, and ichthyosaurs.
2 informal a person regarded with loathing and contempt.
▶ **adj.** [attrib.] belonging to a reptile or to the class of reptiles: *reptile eggs.*
– ORIGIN late Middle English: from late Latin, neuter of *reptilis*, from Latin *rept-* 'crawled,' from the verb *repere.*

rep·til·i·an /repˈtilēən, -ˈtilyən/ ▶ **adj. 1** relating to or characteristic of reptiles: *the reptilian ancestors of mammals.*

r

2 (of a person) deeply disliked and despised; repulsive: *a reptilian villain with no redeeming features.*
▶ n. an animal belonging to the class Reptilia; a reptile.

Repub. ▶ abbr. ■ Republic. ■ Republican.

re·pub·lic /ri'pəblik/ ▶ n. a state in which supreme power is held by the people and their elected representatives, and which has an elected or nominated president rather than a monarch. ■ archaic a group with a certain equality between its members.
– ORIGIN late 16th cent.: from French *république*, from Latin *respublica*, from *res* 'concern' + *publicus* 'of the people, public.'

re·pub·li·can /ri'pəblikən/ ▶ adj. (of a form of government, constitution, etc.) belonging to, or characteristic of a republic. ■ advocating or supporting republican government: *the republican movement.*
▶ n. 1 a person advocating or supporting republican government.
2 (**Republican**) a member or supporter of the Republican Party.
– DERIVATIVES **re·pub·li·can·ism** /-ˌnizəm/ n.

Re·pub·li·can Par·ty one of the two main US political parties (the other being the Democratic Party), favoring a conservative stance, limited central government, and a strong national defense.

Re·pub·li·can Riv·er a river that flows for 445 miles (715 km) from northeastern Colorado through southern Nebraska and into Kansas where it joins the Smoky Hill River to form the Kansas River.

Re·pub·lic of Kal·myk·i·a-Khalmg Tangch official name for **KALMYKIA**.

Re·pub·li·crat /ri'pəbliˌkrat/ ▶ n. a person whose political philosophy is a blend of policies and principles from both the Republican and Democratic parties.
– ORIGIN late 19th cent.: blend of *Republican* and *Democrat*.

re·pub·lish /rē'pəblisн, 'rē-/ ▶ v. [with obj.] publish (a text) again, esp. in a new edition.
– DERIVATIVES **republication** /ˌrēˌpəblə'kāsнən/ n.

re·pu·di·ate /ri'pyo͞odēˌāt/ ▶ v. [with obj.] refuse to accept or be associated with: *she has repudiated policies associated with previous party leaders.* ■ deny the truth or validity of: *the minister repudiated allegations of human rights abuses.* ■ chiefly Law refuse to fulfill or discharge (an agreement, obligation, or debt): *breach of a condition gives the other party the right to repudiate a contract.* ■ (esp. in the past or in non-Christian religions) divorce (one's wife).
– DERIVATIVES **re·pu·di·a·tor** /-ˌātər/ n.
– ORIGIN late Middle English (originally an adjective in the sense 'divorced'): from Latin *repudiatus* 'divorced, cast off,' from *repudium* 'divorce.'

re·pu·di·a·tion /riˌpyo͞odē'āsнən/ ▶ n. 1 rejection of a proposal or idea: *the repudiation of reformist policies | a repudiation of left-wing political ideas.* ■ refusal to fulfill or discharge an agreement, obligation, or debt.
2 denial of the truth or validity of something.

re·pug·nance /ri'pəgnəns/ ▶ n. 1 intense disgust: *our growing repugnance at the bleeding carcasses.*
2 (also **repugnancy**) inconsistency or incompatibility of ideas or statements.
– ORIGIN late Middle English (in the sense 'opposition'): from Old French *repugnance* or Latin *repugnantia*, from *repugnare* 'oppose,' from *re-* (expressing opposition) + *pugnare* 'to fight.'

re·pug·nant /ri'pəgnənt/ ▶ adj. 1 extremely distasteful; unacceptable: *the thought of going back into the fog was* **repugnant to** *him.*
2 [predic.] (**repugnant to**) in conflict with; incompatible with: *a bylaw must not be repugnant to the general law of the country.* ■ archaic or literary given to stubborn resistance.
– DERIVATIVES **re·pug·nant·ly** adv.
– ORIGIN late Middle English (in the sense 'offering resistance'): from Old French *repugnant* or Latin *repugnant-* 'opposing,' from the verb *repugnare* (see **REPUGNANCE**).

re·pulse /ri'pəls/ ▶ v. [with obj.] 1 drive back (an attack or attacking enemy) by force: *rioters tried to storm ministry buildings but were repulsed by police.* ■ fail to welcome (friendly advances or the person making them); rebuff: *she left, feeling hurt because she had been repulsed.* ■ refuse to accept (an offer): *his bid for the company was repulsed.*
2 (usu. **be repulsed**) cause (someone) to feel intense distaste and aversion: *audiences at early screenings of the film were repulsed by its brutality.*
▶ n. the action of driving back an attacking force or of being driven back: *the repulse of the invaders.* ■ a discouraging response to friendly advances: *his evasion of her plan had been another repulse.*
– ORIGIN late Middle English: from Latin *repuls-* 'driven back,' from the verb *repellere* (see **REPEL**).

re·pul·sion /ri'pəlsнən/ ▶ n. 1 a feeling of intense distaste or disgust: *people talk about the case with a mixture of fascination and repulsion.*
2 Physics a force under the influence of which objects tend to move away from each other, e.g., through having the same magnetic polarity or electric charge.

re·pul·sive /ri'pəlsiv/ ▶ adj. 1 arousing intense distaste or disgust: *a repulsive smell.* ■ archaic lacking friendliness or sympathy.
2 of or relating to repulsion between physical objects.
– DERIVATIVES **re·pul·sive·ly** adv., **re·pul·sive·ness** n.

re·pur·chase /rē'pərcнəs/ ▶ v. [with obj.] buy (something) back.
▶ n. the action of buying something back.
– DERIVATIVES **re·pur·chas·er** n.

re·pur·chase a·gree·ment ▶ n. Finance a contract in which the vendor of a security agrees to repurchase it from the buyer at an agreed price.

re·pur·pose /rē'pərpəs/ ▶ v. [with obj.] adapt for use in a different purpose: *they've taken a product that was originally designed for a CD-ROM and repurposed it for the Microsoft Network.*

rep·u·ta·ble /'repyətəbəl/ ▶ adj. having a good reputation: *a reputable company.*
– DERIVATIVES **rep·u·ta·bly** /-blē/ adv.
– ORIGIN early 17th cent.: from obsolete French, or from medieval Latin *reputabilis*, from Latin *reputare* 'reflect upon' (see **REPUTE**).

rep·u·ta·tion /ˌrepyə'tāsнən/ ▶ n. the beliefs or opinions that are generally held about someone or something: *his reputation was tarnished by allegations that he had taken bribes.* ■ a widespread belief that someone or something has a particular habit or characteristic: *his knowledge of his subject earned him a reputation as an expert.*
– ORIGIN Middle English: from Latin *reputatio(n-)*, from *reputare* 'think over' (see **REPUTE**).

re·pute /ri'pyo͞ot/ ▶ n. the opinion generally held of someone or something; the state of being generally regarded in a particular way: *pollution could bring the authority's name into bad repute.* ■ the state of being highly thought of; fame: *chefs of international repute.*
▶ v. (**be reputed**) be generally said or believed to do something or to have particular characteristics: *he was reputed to have a fabulous house.* ■ (usu. as adj. **reputed**) be generally said or believed to exist or be of a particular type, despite not being so: *this area gave the lie to the reputed flatness of the country.* ■ (usu. as adj. **reputed**) be widely known and respected: *intensive training with reputed coaches.*
– ORIGIN late Middle English: from Old French *reputer* or Latin *reputare* 'think over,' from *re-* (expressing intensive force) + *putare* 'think.'

re·put·ed·ly /ri'pyo͞otidlē/ ▶ adv. according to what people say or believe; supposedly: *he reputedly gained a £1.2-million settlement at the end of their marriage.*

req. ▶ abbr. ■ require. ■ required. ■ requisition.

reqd. ▶ abbr. required.

re·quest /ri'kwest/ ▶ n. an act of asking politely or formally for something: *a* **request for** *information | the club's excursion was postponed* **at the request of** *some of the members.* ■ a thing that is asked for: *to have our ideas taken seriously is surely a reasonable request.* ■ an instruction to a computer to provide information or perform another function. ■ a tune or song played on a radio program, in some instances accompanied by a personal message, in response to a letter or call asking for it. ■ archaic the state of being sought after: *human intelligence, which is in constant request in a family.*
▶ v. [with obj.] politely or formally ask for: *he received the information he had requested* | [with clause] *the chairman requested that the reports be considered.* ■ [with infinitive] politely ask (someone) to do something: *the letter requested him to report to New York immediately.*
– PHRASES **by** (or **on**) **request** in response to an expressed wish.
– DERIVATIVES **re·quest·er** n.
– ORIGIN Middle English: from Old French *requeste* (noun), based on Latin *requirere* (see **REQUIRE**).

req·ui·em /'rekwēəm, 'rā-/ ▶ n. (also **requiem mass**) (esp. in the Roman Catholic Church) a Mass for the repose of the souls of the dead. ■ a musical composition setting parts of such a Mass, or of a similar character. ■ an act or token of remembrance: *he designed the epic as a requiem for his wife.*
– ORIGIN Middle English: from Latin (first word of the Mass), accusative of *requies* 'rest.'

req·ui·em shark ▶ n. a migratory, livebearing shark of warm seas, sometimes also found in brackish or fresh water. ● Family Carcharhinidae: many species, including the tiger shark, blue shark, and tope.
– ORIGIN mid 17th cent.: from obsolete French *requiem*, variant of *requin* 'shark,' influenced by **REQUIEM**.

re·qui·es·cat /ˌrekwē'esˌkät, ˌrā-/ ▶ n. a wish or prayer for the repose of a dead person.
– ORIGIN Latin, from *requiescat in pace* (see **RIP**[1]).

re·quin·to /rā'kēntō/ ▶ n. (pl. **requintos**) (in Spanish-speaking regions) a small guitar, typically tuned a fifth higher than a standard guitar.
– ORIGIN Spanish, literally 'second fifth subtracted from a quantity.'

re·quire /ri'kwīr/ ▶ v. [with obj.] need for a particular purpose: *three patients required operations | please indicate how many tickets you require.* ■ cause to be necessary: *it would have required much research to produce a comprehensive list.* ■ specify as compulsory: *the minimum car insurance required by law.* ■ [with obj. and infinitive] (of someone in authority) instruct or expect (someone) to do something: *you will be required to attend for cross-examination.* ■ (**require something of**) regard an action, ability, or quality as due from (someone) by virtue of their position: *the care and diligence required of him as a trustee.*
– DERIVATIVES **re·quir·er** n.
– ORIGIN late Middle English: from Old French *requere*, from Latin *requirere*, from *re-* (expressing intensive force) + *quaerere* 'seek.'

re·quired /ri'kwīrd/ ▶ adj. officially compulsory, or otherwise considered essential; indispensable: *eight editions were published, each* **required reading** *for trainees.* ■ in keeping with one's wishes; desired: *the corset, the garment that ensured the required female shape.*

re·quire·ment /ri'kwīrmənt/ ▶ n. a thing that is needed or wanted: *choose the type of window that suits your requirements best.* ■ a thing that is compulsory; a necessary condition: *applicants must satisfy the normal entry requirements.*

req·ui·site /'rekwəzət/ ▶ adj. made necessary by particular circumstances or regulations: *the application will not be processed until the requisite fee is paid.*
▶ n. a thing that is necessary for the achievement of a specified end: *she believed privacy to be a* **requisite for** *a peaceful life.*
– DERIVATIVES **req·ui·site·ly** adv.
– ORIGIN late Middle English: from Latin *requisitus* 'searched for, deemed necessary,' past participle of *requirere* (see **REQUIRE**).

req·ui·si·tion /ˌrekwə'zisнən/ ▶ n. an official order laying claim to the use of property or materials: *I had to make various requisitions for staff and accommodations.* ■ a formal written demand that some duty should be performed or something be put into operation. ■ the appropriation of goods, esp. for military or public use.
▶ v. [with obj.] demand the use or supply of, esp. by official order and for military or public use: *the government had assumed powers to requisition cereal products at fixed prices.* ■ demand the performance or occurrence of: *one of the investors has requisitioned a special meeting.*
– DERIVATIVES **req·ui·si·tion·er** n.
– ORIGIN late Middle English (as a noun in the sense 'request, demand'): from Old French, or from Latin *requisitio(n-)*, from *requirere* 'search for' (see **REQUIRE**). The verb dates from the mid 19th cent.

re·quite /ri'kwīt/ ▶ v. [with obj.] formal make appropriate return for (a favor, service, or wrongdoing): *they are quick to requite a kindness.* ■ return a favor to (someone): *to win enough to requite my friends.* ■ respond to (love or affection); return: *she did not requite his love.*
– DERIVATIVES **re·quit·al** /-'kwītl/ n.
– ORIGIN early 16th cent.: from **RE-** 'back' + obsolete *quite*, variant of the verb **QUIT**[1].

re·ran /rē'ran/ past of **RERUN**.

re·rate /rē'rāt/ ▶ v. [with obj.] rate or assess (something, esp. shares or a company) again: *the company could be rerated as its share price had not rebounded.*

re·read ▶ v. /ˌrē'rēd/ (past and past participle **reread**) [with obj.] read (a text) again: *I reread the poem.*
▶ n. /'rēˌrēd/ [in sing.] an act of reading something again.

re·re·cord /ˌrēri'kôrd/ ▶ v. [with obj.] record (sound, esp. music) again: *the sound will then be rerecorded in binaural stereo | rerecording a record without a license is illegal* | (as adj. **rerecorded**) *the track is a rerecorded version of a song from their recent album.*

PRONUNCIATION KEY ə ago, up; ər over, fur; a hat; ā ate; ä car; e let; ē see; i fit; ī by; NG sing; ō go; ô law, for; oi toy; o͝o good; o͞o goo; ou out; TH thin; T͟H then; ZH vision

rere·dos /ˈrerəˌdäs, ˈri(ə)rə-/ ▶ **n.** (pl. **same**) Christian Church an ornamental screen covering the wall at the back of an altar.
– ORIGIN late Middle English: from Anglo-Norman French, from Old French *areredos*, from *arere* 'behind' + *dos* 'back.'

re·re·lease /ˌrē-riˈlēs/ ▶ **v.** [with obj.] release (a recording or movie) again: *he is rereleasing his 1983 hit single.*
▶ **n.** the action of releasing a recording or movie again: *the rerelease of Disney's 1937 classic.* ■ a recording or movie that is released for a second or subsequent time.

reroof /rēˈro͞of, -ˈro͝of/ ▶ **v.** [with obj.] provide (a building) with a new or substantially repaired roof.

re·route /rēˈro͞ot, rēˈrout/ ▶ **v.** [with obj.] send (someone or something) by or along a different route: *the police had rerouted the march.*

re·run ▶ **v.** /rēˈrən/ (**reruns, rerunning**; past **reran**; past participle **rerun**) [with obj.] show or perform (something, esp. a television program) again.
▶ **n.** /ˈrēˌrən/ a program, event, or competition that occurs or is run again: ***a rerun of** the Mideast crisis* | *watching reruns on TV.*

RES ▶ **abbr.** reticuloendothelial system.

res. ▶ **abbr.** ■ research. ■ reserve. ■ residence or resident or residents. ■ resigned. ■ resolution.

re·sale /ˈrēˌsāl/ ▶ **n.** the sale of a thing previously bought: *he is renovating them for resale* | [as modifier] *resale value.*
– DERIVATIVES **re·sal·a·ble** /rēˈsāləbəl/ (also **resaleable**) **adj.**

re·scale /rēˈskāl/ ▶ **v.** [with obj.] alter the scale of (something), typically to make it smaller or simpler: *a report to the State EducationDepartment urging that all the science exams be rescaled.*

re·sched·ule /rēˈskejo͞o(ə)l/ ▶ **v.** [with obj.] change the time of (a planned event): *the concert has been rescheduled for September.* ■ arrange a new scheme of repayments of (a debt).

re·scind /riˈsind/ ▶ **v.** [with obj.] revoke, cancel, or repeal (a law, order, or agreement): *the government eventually rescinded the directive.*
– DERIVATIVES **re·scind·a·ble adj.**
– ORIGIN mid 16th cent.: from Latin *rescindere*, from *re-* (expressing intensive force) + *scindere* 'to divide, split.'

re·scis·sion /riˈsiZHən/ ▶ **n.** formal the revocation, cancellation, or repeal of a law, order, or agreement.
– ORIGIN mid 17th cent.: from late Latin *rescissio(n-)*, from *resciss-* 'split again,' from the verb *rescindere* (see **RESCIND**).

re·script /ˈrēˌskript/ ▶ **n.** an official edict or announcement. ■ historical a Roman emperor's written reply to an appeal for guidance, esp. on a legal point. ■ the pope's decision on a question of Roman Catholic doctrine or papal law.
– ORIGIN late Middle English (denoting a papal decision): from Latin *rescriptum*, neuter past participle of *rescribere* 'write back,' from *re-* 'back' + *scribere* 'write.'

res·cue /ˈreskyo͞o/ ▶ **v.** (**rescues, rescuing, rescued**) [with obj.] save (someone) from a dangerous or distressing situation: *firemen were called out to rescue a man trapped in the river.* ■ informal keep from being lost or abandoned; retrieve: *he got out of his chair to rescue his cup of coffee.*
▶ **n.** an act of saving or being saved from danger or distress: *he **came to our rescue** with a loan of $100.* ■ [as modifier] denoting the emergency excavation of archaeological sites threatened by imminent building or road development.
– DERIVATIVES **res·cu·a·ble adj., res·cu·er n.**
– ORIGIN Middle English: from Old French *rescoure*, from Latin *re-* (expressing intensive force) + *excutere* 'shake out, discard.'

re·seal /ˌrēˈsēl/ ▶ **v.** [with obj.] seal (something) again. ■ [no obj.] (of something previously open) reform or accept a seal: *the pores reseal within seconds as the inner liquid leaks out.*
– DERIVATIVES **re·seal·a·ble adj.**

re·search /ˈrēˌsərCH, riˈsərCH/ ▶ **n.** the systematic investigation into and study of materials and sources in order to establish facts and reach new conclusions: *we are fighting meningitis by raising money for medical research.* ■ (**researches**) acts or periods of such investigation: *his pathological researches were included in official reports.* ■ [as modifier] engaged in or intended for use in such investigation and discovery: *a research student* | *a research paper.*
▶ **v.** [with obj.] investigate systematically: *she has spent the last five years researching her people's history* | [no obj.] *the team has been **researching into** flora and fauna.* ■ discover facts by investigation for use in (a book, program, etc.): *I was in New York researching my novel* | (as adj., with submodifier **researched**) *this is a well-researched and readable account.*
– DERIVATIVES **re·search·a·ble adj., re·search·er n.**
– ORIGIN late 16th cent.: from obsolete French *recerche* (noun), *recercher* (verb), from Old French *re-* (expressing intensive force) + *cerchier* 'to search.'

re·search and de·vel·op·ment ▶ **n.** (in industry) work directed toward the innovation, introduction, and improvement of products and processes.

Re·search Tri·an·gle Park a research complex in central North Carolina, between Durham, Raleigh, and Chapel Hill, that was created in the 1950s by Duke and North Carolina State universities and the University of North Carolina.

re·seat /rēˈsēt/ ▶ **v.** [with obj.] **1** cause (someone) to sit down again after they have risen: *he reseated himself in his armchair.* ■ cause to sit in a new position: *we reseated the orchestra for each variation.* ■ realign or repair (a tap, valve, or other object) in order to fit it into its correct position.
2 equip with new seats: *the coaches were reseated last year to increase capacity.*

ré·seau /rāˈzō, ri-/ ▶ **n.** (pl. **réseaux** /-ˈzōz/) a network or grid. ■ a plain net ground used in lacemaking. ■ a reference marking pattern on a photograph, used in astronomy and surveying. ■ a spy or intelligence network, esp. in the French resistance movement during the German occupation in World War II.
– ORIGIN late 16th cent. (as a term in lacemaking): French, literally 'net, web.'

re·sect /riˈsekt/ ▶ **v.** [with obj.] (often as adj. **resected**) Surgery cut out (tissue or part of an organ): *a small piece of resected colon.*
– DERIVATIVES **re·sect·a·ble adj., re·sec·tion** /riˈsekSHən/ **n., re·sec·tion·al** /-SHənl/ **adj., re·sec·tion·ist** /-SHənist/ **n.**
– ORIGIN mid 17th cent. (in the sense 'remove, cut away'): from Latin *resect-* 'cut off,' from the verb *resecare*, from *re-* 'back' + *secare* 'to cut.'

re·se·da /rəˈsēdə, ˈrāzəˌdä/ ▶ **n.** **1** a plant of the genus *Reseda* (family Resedaceae), esp. (in gardening) a mignonette.
2 the pale green color of mignonette flowers.
▶ **adj.** pale green.
– ORIGIN mid 18th cent.: from Latin, interpreted in the sense 'assuage!,' imperative of *resedare*, with reference to its supposed curative powers.

re·seed /rēˈsēd/ ▶ **v.** [with obj.] sow (an area of land) with seed, esp. grass seed, again.

re·se·lect /ˌrēsəˈlekt/ ▶ **v.** [with obj.] select (someone or something) again or differently: *a user should not need to reselect a printer every time this happens.*
– DERIVATIVES **re·se·lec·tion n.**

re·sell /rēˈsel/ ▶ **v.** (past and past participle **resold**) [with obj.] sell (something one has bought) to someone else: *products can be resold on the black market for huge profits.*
– DERIVATIVES **reseller n.**

re·sem·blance /riˈzembləns/ ▶ **n.** the state of resembling or being alike: *they **bear some resemblance to** Italian figurines.* ■ a way in which two or more things are alike: *the physical resemblances between humans and apes.*
– ORIGIN Middle English: from Anglo-Norman French, from the verb *resembler* (see **RESEMBLE**).

re·sem·ble /riˈzembəl/ ▶ **v.** [with obj.] have qualities or features, esp. those of appearance, in common with (someone or something); look or seem like: *some people resemble their dogs* | *they seemed to **resemble each other** closely.*
– DERIVATIVES **re·sem·bler** /-blər/ **n.** (rare).
– ORIGIN Middle English: from Old French *resembler*, based on Latin *similare* (from *similis* 'like').

re·sent /riˈzent/ ▶ **v.** [with obj.] feel bitterness or indignation at (a circumstance, action, or person): *she resented the fact that I had children.*
– ORIGIN late 16th cent.: from obsolete French *resentir*, from *re-* (expressing intensive force) + *sentir* 'feel' (from Latin *sentire*). The early sense was 'experience (an emotion or sensation),' later 'feel deeply,' giving rise to 'feel aggrieved by.'

re·sent·ful /riˈzentfəl/ ▶ **adj.** feeling or expressing bitterness or indignation at having been treated unfairly: *he was angry and **resentful of** their intrusion.*
– DERIVATIVES **re·sent·ful·ly adv., re·sent·ful·ness n.**

re·sent·ment /riˈzentmənt/ ▶ **n.** bitter indignation at having been treated unfairly: *his **resentment at** being demoted* | *some people harbor resentments going back many years.*
– ORIGIN early 17th cent.: from Italian *risentimento* or French *ressentiment*, from obsolete French *resentir* (see **RESENT**).

res·er·pine /riˈsərˌpēn, -pən/ ▶ **n.** Medicine a compound of the alkaloid class obtained from Indian snakeroot and other plants and used in the treatment of hypertension.
– ORIGIN 1950s: from the modern Latin species name *R(auwolfia) serp(entina)*, named after Leonhard *Rauwolf* (see **RAUWOLFIA**), + **-INE**[4].

res·er·va·tion /ˌrezərˈvāSHən/ ▶ **n.** **1** the action of reserving something: *the reservation of positions for non-Americans.* ■ an arrangement whereby something, esp. a seat or room, is booked or reserved for a particular person: *do you have a reservation?* ■ an area of land set aside for occupation by North American Indians or Australian Aborigines. ■ Law a right or interest retained in an estate being conveyed. ■ (in the Roman Catholic Church) the practice of retaining a portion of the consecrated elements after mass for communion of the sick or as a focus for devotion.
2 a qualification to an expression of agreement or approval; a doubt: *some generals voiced reservations about making air strikes.*
3 (in the Roman Catholic Church) the action of a superior of reserving to himself the power of absolution. ■ a right reserved to the pope of nomination to a vacant benefice.
– ORIGIN late Middle English (denoting the pope's right of nomination to a benefice): from Old French, or from late Latin *reservatio(n-)*, from *reservare* 'keep back' (see **RESERVE**).

re·serve /riˈzərv/ ▶ **v.** [with obj.] refrain from using or disposing of (something); retain for future use: *roll out half the dough and reserve the other half.* ■ arrange for (a room, seat, ticket, etc.) to be kept for the use of a particular person and not given to anyone else: *a place was reserved for her in the front row.* ■ retain or hold (an entitlement to something), esp. by formal or legal stipulation: [with obj. and infinitive] *the editor reserves the right to edit letters.* ■ refrain from delivering (a judgment or decision) immediately or without due consideration or evidence: *I'll reserve my views on his ability until he's played again.* ■ (**reserve something for**) use or engage in something only in or at (a particular circumstance or time): *Japanese food has been presented as expensive and reserved for special occasions.* ■ (in church use) retain (a portion of the consecrated elements) after mass for communion of the sick or as a focus for devotion.
▶ **n.** **1** (often **reserves**) a supply of a commodity not needed for immediate use but available if required: *Australia has major coal, gas, and uranium reserves.* ■ a force or body of troops kept back from action to reinforce or protect others, or additional to the regular forces and available in an emergency. ■ a member of the military reserve. ■ an extra player who is a possible substitute in a team. ■ (**the reserves**) the second-string team. ■ funds kept available by a bank, company, or government: *the foreign exchange reserves.* ■ a part of a company's profits added to capital rather than paid as a dividend.
2 a place set aside for special use, in particular: ■ an area designated as a habitat for an indigenous people. ■ a protected area for wildlife.
3 a lack of warmth or openness in manner or expression: *she smiled and some of her natural reserve melted.* ■ qualification or doubt attached to some statement or claim: *she trusted him **without reserve.***
4 short for **RESERVE PRICE**.
5 (in the decoration of ceramics or textiles) an area that still has the original color of the material or the color of the background.
– PHRASES **in reserve** unused and available if required: *the platoon that had been kept in reserve.*
– DERIVATIVES **re·serv·a·ble adj., re·serv·er n.**
– ORIGIN Middle English: from Old French *reserver*, from Latin *reservare* 'keep back,' from *re-* 'back' + *servare* 'to keep.'

re-serve /rēˈsərv, ˈrē-/ ▶ **v.** [no obj.] (in various sports) serve again.

re·serve bank ▶ **n.** a regional bank operating under and implementing the policies of the US Federal Reserve.

re·served /riˈzərvd/ ▶ **adj.** **1** slow to reveal emotion or opinions: *he is a reserved, almost taciturn man.*
2 kept specially for a particular purpose or person: *a reserved seat.*
– DERIVATIVES **re·serv·ed·ly** /riˈzərvədlē/ **adv., re·serv·ed·ness** /riˈzərvədnəs/ **n.**

re·served word ▶ **n.** Computing a word in a programming language that has a fixed meaning and cannot be redefined by the programmer.

re·serve price ▶ **n.** the price stipulated as the lowest acceptable by the seller for an item sold at auction.

re·serv·ist /riˈzərvist/ ▶ **n.** a member of the military reserve forces.

res·er·voir /ˈrezə(r)ˌvwär, -ˌv(w)ôr/ ▶ **n.** a large natural or artificial lake used as a source of water supply. ■ a supply or source of something: *tapping into a universal reservoir of information.* ■ [usu.

with modifier] a place where fluid collects, esp. in rock strata or in the body. ■ a receptacle or part of a machine designed to hold fluid. ■ Medicine a population, tissue, etc., that is chronically infested with the causative agent of a disease and can act as a source of further infection.
– ORIGIN mid 17th cent.: from French *réservoir*, from *réserver* 'to reserve, keep.'

re·set /rē'set/ ▶ **v.** (**resets, resetting**; past and past participle **reset**) [with obj.] set again or differently: *I must reset the alarm.* ■ Electronics cause (a binary device) to enter the state representing the numeral 0.
– DERIVATIVES **re·set·ta·bil·i·ty** /ˌrēˌsetə'bilətē/ **n.**, **re·set·ta·ble adj.**

re·set·tle /rē'setl/ ▶ **v.** settle or cause to settle in a different place: [with obj.] *they offered to resettle 300,000 refugees* | [no obj.] *144,000 East Germans had resettled in West Germany.*
– DERIVATIVES **re·set·tle·ment n.**

res ges·tae /'rās 'gesˌtī, 'rēz 'jestē/ ▶ **plural n.** Law the events, circumstances, remarks, etc., that relate to a particular case, esp. as constituting admissible evidence in a court of law.
– ORIGIN Latin, literally 'things done.'

re·shape /ˌrē'sHāp/ ▶ **v.** [with obj.] shape or form (something) differently or again: *the decrees will thoroughly reshape Poland's economy.*

re·shoot /rē'sHo͞ot/ ▶ **v.** (past and past participle **reshot**) [with obj.] shoot (a scene of a film) again or differently: *they had to reshoot the whole thing with another actor* | [no obj.] *the insurance was enough to allow them to reshoot or finish with a double.*
▶ **n.** an act of reshooting a scene of a film: *the reshoot is scheduled for Thursday.*

re·show /rē'sHō/ ▶ **v.** (past participle **reshown** or **reshowed**) [with obj.] show for a second or subsequent time: *the program will be reshown on August 11.*

re·shuf·fle /rē'sHəfəl/ ▶ **v.** [with obj.] **1** reorganize or change the positions of (government appointees, members of a team, etc.): *the president was forced to reshuffle his cabinet.* ■ put in a new order; rearrange: *genetic constituents are constantly reshuffled into individual organisms.*
2 shuffle (playing cards) again: *Youngman is requesting that Garcia reshuffle the cards* | [no obj.] *too many pairs are coming up—you better reshuffle.*
▶ **n.** an act of reorganizing or rearranging something: *he was brought into the government in the last reshuffle.*

re·side /ri'zīd/ ▶ **v.** [no obj.] have one's permanent home in a particular place: *people who work in the city actually reside in neighboring towns.* ■ be situated: *the paintings now reside on the walls of a restaurant.* ■ (of power or a right) belong by right to a person or body: *legislative powers reside with the federal assembly.* ■ (of a quality) be present or inherent in something: *the meaning of an utterance does not wholly reside in the semantic meaning.*
– ORIGIN late Middle English (in the sense 'be in residence as an official'): probably a back-formation from RESIDENT, influenced by French *résider* or Latin *residere* 'remain,' from *re-* 'back' + *sedere* 'sit.'

res·i·dence /'rez(ə)dəns, 'rezəˌdens/ ▶ **n.** a person's home; the place where someone lives. ■ the official house of a government minister or other public and official figure. ■ the fact of living in a particular place: *Rome was his main place of residence.*
– PHRASES **in residence** living in or occupying a particular place: *the guests in residence at the hotel.* ■ (**—— in residence**) a person with a particular occupation (esp. an artist or writer) paid to work in a college or other institution. **take up residence** start living in a particular place.
– ORIGIN late Middle English (denoting the fact of living in a place): from Old French, or from medieval Latin *residentia*, from Latin *residere* 'remain' (see RESIDE).

res·i·dence time ▶ **n.** technical the average length of time during which a substance, a portion of material, or an object is in a given location or condition, such as adsorption or suspension.

res·i·den·cy /'rez(ə)dənsē, 'rezəˌdensē/ ▶ **n.** (pl. **residencies**) **1** the fact of living in a place: *a government ruling confirmed the returning refugees' right to residency.* ■ a residential post held by a writer, musician, or artist, typically for teaching purposes.
2 historical the official residence of the British governor general's representative or other government agent, esp. at the court of an Indian state. ■ a group or organization of intelligence agents in a foreign country.
3 a period of specialized medical training in a hospital; the position of a resident.

res·i·dent /'rez(ə)dənt, 'rezəˌdent/ ▶ **n.** **1** a person who lives somewhere permanently or on a long-term basis. ■ a bird, butterfly, or other animal of a species that does not migrate. ■ a person who boards at a boarding school. ■ historical a British government agent in any semi-independent state, esp. the governor general's agent at the court of an Indian state.
2 a medical graduate engaged in specialized practice under supervision in a hospital.
▶ **adj.** living somewhere on a long-term basis: *he has been resident in Brazil for a long time.* ■ having quarters on the premises of one's work: *resident farm workers.* ■ attached to and working regularly for a particular institution: *the film studio needed a resident historian.* ■ (of a bird, butterfly, or other animal) nonmigratory; remaining in an area throughout the year. ■ (of a computer program, file, etc.) immediately available in computer memory, rather than having to be loaded from elsewhere.
– DERIVATIVES **res·i·dent·ship** /-ˌSHip/ **n.** (historical).
– ORIGIN Middle English: from Latin *resident-* 'remaining,' from the verb *residere* (see RESIDE).

res·i·dent com·mis·sion·er ▶ **n.** a delegate elected to represent a dependency, such as Puerto Rico, in the US House of Representatives. They are able to speak in the House and serve on committees, but may not vote.

res·i·den·tial /ˌrezə'denCHəl/ ▶ **adj.** designed for people to live in: *private residential and nursing homes.* ■ providing accommodations in addition to other services: *a residential college.* ■ occupied by private houses: *quieter traffic in residential areas.* ■ concerning or relating to residence: *land has been diverted from residential use.*
– DERIVATIVES **res·i·den·tial·ly adv.**

res·i·den·ti·ar·y /ˌrezə'denCHēˌerē, -'denCHərē/ ▶ **adj.** required to live officially in a cathedral or collegiate church. ■ relating to or involving residence in an establishment or place.
▶ **n.** (pl. **residentiaries**) a residentiary canon.
– ORIGIN early 16th cent. (as a noun): from medieval Latin *residentiarius*, from Latin *resident-* 'remaining' (see RESIDENT).

re·sid·u·a /ri'zijo͞oə/ plural form of RESIDUUM.

re·sid·u·al /ri'zijo͞oəl/ ▶ **adj.** remaining after the greater part or quantity has gone: *the withdrawal of residual occupying forces.* ■ (of a quantity) left after other things have been subtracted: *residual income after tax and mortgage payments.* ■ (of a physical state or property) remaining after the removal of or present in the absence of a causative agent: *residual stenosis.* ■ (of an experimental or arithmetical error) not accounted for or eliminated. ■ (of a soil or other deposit) formed in situ by weathering.
▶ **n.** a quantity remaining after other things have been subtracted or allowed for. ■ a difference between a value measured in a scientific experiment and the theoretical or true value. ■ a royalty paid to a performer, writer, etc., for a repeat of a play, television show, etc. ■ Geology a portion of rocky or high ground remaining after erosion. ■ the resale value of a new car or other item at a specified time after purchase, expressed as a percentage of its purchase price.
– DERIVATIVES **re·sid·u·al·ly adv.**

re·sid·u·al stress ▶ **n.** Physics the stress present in an object in the absence of any external load or force.

re·sid·u·ar·y /ri'zijo͞oˌerē/ ▶ **adj.** technical residual. ■ Law of or relating to the residue of an estate: *a residuary legatee.*
– ORIGIN early 18th cent.: from RESIDUUM + -ARY[1].

res·i·due /'rezəˌd(y)o͞o/ ▶ **n.** a small amount of something that remains after the main part has gone or been taken or used. ■ Law the part of an estate that is left after the payment of charges, debts, and bequests. ■ a substance that remains after a process such as combustion or evaporation.
– ORIGIN late Middle English: from Old French *residu*, from Latin *residuum* 'something remaining' (see RESIDUUM).

re·sid·u·um /ri'zijo͞oəm/ ▶ **n.** (pl. **residua** /-'zijo͞oə/) technical a substance or thing that remains or is left behind, in particular, a chemical residue.
– ORIGIN late 17th cent.: from Latin, neuter of *residuus* 'remaining,' from the verb *residere*.

re·sign /ri'zīn/ ▶ **v.** **1** [no obj.] voluntarily leave a job or other position: ***he resigned from** the government in protest at the policy.* ■ [with obj.] give up (an office, power, privilege, etc.): *four deputies resigned their seats.* ■ [no obj.] Chess end a game by conceding defeat without being checkmated: *he lost his queen and resigned in 45 moves.*
2 (**be resigned**) accept that something undesirable cannot be avoided: *he seems **resigned to** a shortened career* | *she **resigned herself to** a lengthy session.* ■ archaic surrender oneself to another's guidance: *he vows to resign himself to her direction.*
– DERIVATIVES **re·sign·er n.**
– ORIGIN late Middle English: from Old French *resigner*, from Latin *resignare* 'unseal, cancel,' from *re-* 'back' + *signare* 'sign, seal.'

re-sign /rē'sīn/ ▶ **v.** [with obj.] sign (a document) again. ■ engage (a sports player) to play for a team for a further period. ■ [no obj.] (of a sports player) commit oneself to play for a team for a further period.

res·ig·na·tion /ˌrezig'nāSHən/ ▶ **n.** **1** an act of retiring or giving up a position: *he announced his resignation.* ■ a document conveying someone's intention of retiring: *I'm thinking of handing in my resignation.* ■ Chess an act of ending a game by conceding defeat without being checkmated.
2 the acceptance of something undesirable but inevitable: *a shrug of resignation.*
– ORIGIN late Middle English: via Old French from medieval Latin *resignatio(n-)*, from *resignare* 'unseal, cancel' (see RESIGN).

resigned /ri'zīnd/ ▶ **adj.** having accepted something unpleasant that one cannot do anything about: *my response is a resigned shrug of the shoulders.*
– DERIVATIVES **re·sign·ed·ly** /ri'zīnədlē/ **adv.**, **re·sign·ed·ness** /ri'zīnədnəs/ **n.**

re·sile /ri'zīl/ ▶ **v.** [no obj.] formal abandon a position or a course of action: *can he **resile from** the agreement?*
– ORIGIN early 16th cent.: from obsolete French *resilir* or Latin *resilire* 'to recoil,' from *re-* 'back' + *salire* 'to jump.'

re·sil·ience /ri'zilyəns/ ▶ **n.** **1** the ability of a substance or object to spring back into shape; elasticity: *nylon is excellent in wearability and resilience.*
2 the capacity to recover quickly from difficulties; toughness: *the often remarkable resilience of so many British institutions.*
– DERIVATIVES **re·sil·ien·cy n.**

re·sil·ient /ri'zilyənt/ ▶ **adj.** (of a substance or object) able to recoil or spring back into shape after bending, stretching, or being compressed. ■ (of a person or animal) able to withstand or recover quickly from difficult conditions: *the fish are resilient to most infections.*
– DERIVATIVES **re·sil·ient·ly adv.**
– ORIGIN mid 17th cent.: from Latin *resilient-* 'leaping back,' from the verb *resilire* (see RESILE).

res·i·lin /'rezələn/ ▶ **n.** Biochemistry an elastic material formed of cross-linked protein chains, found in insect cuticles, esp. in the hinges and ligaments of wings.
– ORIGIN 1960s: from Latin *resilire* 'leap back, recoil' + -IN[1].

res·in /'rezən/ ▶ **n.** a sticky flammable organic substance, insoluble in water, exuded by some trees and other plants (notably fir and pine). Compare with GUM[1] (sense 1 of the noun). ■ (also **synthetic resin**) a solid or liquid synthetic organic polymer used as the basis of plastics, adhesives, varnishes, or other products.
▶ **v.** (**resins, resining, resined**) [with obj.] (usu. as adj. **resined**) rub or treat with resin: *resined canvas.*
– DERIVATIVES **res·in·ous** /'rezənəs/ **adj.**
– ORIGIN late Middle English: from Latin *resina*; related to Greek *rhētinē* 'pine resin.' Compare with ROSIN.

res·in·ate ▶ **v.** /'rezəˌnāt/ [with obj.] impregnate or flavor with resin: (as adj. **resinated**) *resinated white wine.*
▶ **n.** /'rezənit/ Chemistry a salt of an acid derived from resin.

res ip·sa lo·qui·tur /ˌrēz ˌipsə 'läkwitər, ˌrās, 'lōkwəˌto͝or/ ▶ **n.** Law the principle that the occurrence of an accident implies negligence.
– ORIGIN Latin, literally 'the matter speaks for itself.'

re·sist /ri'zist/ ▶ **v.** [with obj.] withstand the action or effect of: *antibodies help us to resist infection.* ■ try to prevent by action or argument: *we will continue to resist changes to the treaty.* ■ succeed in ignoring the attraction of (something wrong or unwise): *she resisted his advances* | *I couldn't resist buying the blouse.* ■ [no obj.] struggle against someone or something: *without giving her time to resist, he dragged her off her feet.*
▶ **n.** a resistant substance applied as a coating to protect a surface during some process, for example to prevent dye or glaze adhering.
– DERIVATIVES **re·sist·er n.**, **re·sist·i·ble adj.**, **re·sist·i·bil·i·ty** /riˌzistə'bilətē/ **n.**
– ORIGIN late Middle English: from Old French *resister* or Latin *resistere*, from *re-* (expressing opposition) + *sistere* 'stop' (reduplication of *stare* 'to stand'). The current sense of the noun dates from the mid 19th cent.

re·sist·ance /riˈzistəns/ ▶ **n.** **1** the refusal to accept or comply with something; the attempt to prevent something by action or argument: *she* ***put up*** *no* ***resistance to*** *being led away.* ■ armed or violent opposition: *government forces were unable to crush guerrilla-style resistance.* ■ (also **resistance movement**) [in sing.] a secret organization resisting authority, esp. in an occupied country. ■ (**the Resistance**) the underground movement formed in France during World War II to fight the German occupying forces and the Vichy government. Also called MAQUIS. ■ the impeding, slowing, or stopping effect exerted by one material thing on another: *air resistance would need to be reduced by streamlining.*
2 the ability not to be affected by something, esp. adversely: *some of us have a lower resistance to cold than others.* ■ Medicine & Biology lack of sensitivity to a drug, insecticide, etc., esp. as a result of continued exposure or genetic change.
3 the degree to which a substance or device opposes the passage of an electric current, causing energy dissipation. Ohm's law resistance (measured in ohms) is equal to the voltage divided by the current. ■ a resistor or other circuit component that opposes the passage of an electric current.
– PHRASES **the path** (or **line**) **of least resistance** an option avoiding difficulty or unpleasantness; the easiest course of action.
– ORIGIN late Middle English: from French *résistance*, from late Latin *resistentia*, from the verb *resistere* 'hold back' (see RESIST).

re·sist·ant /riˈzistənt/ ▶ **adj.** offering resistance to something or someone: *some of the old churches are* ***resistant to*** *change* | [in combination] *a water-resistant adhesive.*

re·sis·tive /riˈzistiv/ ▶ **adj.** technical able to withstand the action or effect of something. ■ Physics of or concerning electrical resistance.

re·sis·tiv·i·ty /ˌriˌzisˈtivətē/ ▶ **n.** Physics a measure of the resisting power of a specified material to the flow of an electric current.

re·sist·less /riˈzistlis/ ▶ **adj.** archaic powerful and irresistible: *a resistless impulse.* ■ powerless to resist the effect of someone or something; unresisting.
– DERIVATIVES **re·sist·less·ly** **adv.**

re·sis·tor /riˈzistər/ ▶ **n.** Physics a device having a designed resistance to the passage of an electric current.

re·size /rēˈsīz/ ▶ **v.** [with obj.] alter the size of (something, esp. a computer window or image).

res ju·di·ca·ta /ˌrēz ˌjo͞odiˈkätə, ˌrās/ ▶ **n.** (pl. **res judicatae** /ˌjo͞odiˈkätē, -tī/) Law a matter that has been adjudicated by a competent court and may not be pursued further by the same parties.
– ORIGIN Latin, literally 'judged matter.'

re·skin /rēˈskin/ ▶ **v.** (**reskins**, **reskinning**, **reskinned**) [with obj.] replace or repair the skin of (an aircraft or motor vehicle).

Res·nais /rəˈnā, rəˈne/, Alain (1922–), French movie director. One of the foremost directors of the *nouvelle vague*, he used experimental techniques to explore memory and time. Notable movies: *Hiroshima mon amour* (1959) and *L'Amour à mort* (1984).

re·sold /rēˈsōld/ past and past participle of RESELL.

re·sol·u·ble[1] /riˈzälyəbəl/ ▶ **adj.** archaic able to be resolved.
– ORIGIN early 17th cent.: from French *résoluble* or late Latin *resolubilis*, based on Latin *solvere* 'release, loosen.'

re·sol·u·ble[2] ▶ **adj.** able to dissolve or be dissolved again: *the resoluble nature of the paint.*

res·o·lute /ˈrezəˌlo͞ot, -lət/ ▶ **adj.** admirably purposeful, determined, and unwavering: *she was resolute and unswerving.*
– DERIVATIVES **res·o·lute·ly** **adv.**, **res·o·lute·ness** **n.**
– ORIGIN late Middle English (in the sense 'paid,' describing a rent): from Latin *resolutus* 'loosened, released, paid,' past participle of *resolvere* (see RESOLVE).

res·o·lu·tion /ˌrezəˈlo͞oshən/ ▶ **n.** **1** a firm decision to do or not to do something: *she kept her resolution not to see Anne any more* | *a New Year's resolution.* ■ a formal expression of opinion or intention agreed on by a legislative body, committee, or other formal meeting, typically after taking a vote: *the conference passed two resolutions.* ■ the quality of being determined or resolute: *he handled the last French actions of the war with resolution.*
2 the action of solving a problem, dispute, or contentious matter: *the peaceful resolution of all disputes* | *a successful resolution to the problem.* ■ Music the passing of a discord into a concord during the course of changing harmony. ■ Medicine the disappearance of inflammation, or of any other symptom or condition.
3 chiefly Chemistry the process of reducing or separating something into its components. ■ Physics the replacing of a single force or other vector quantity by two or more jointly equivalent to it. ■ the conversion of something abstract into another form. ■ Prosody the substitution of two short syllables for one long one.
4 the smallest interval measurable by a scientific (esp. optical) instrument; the resolving power. ■ the degree of detail visible in a photograph or television image.
– ORIGIN late Middle English: from Latin *resolutio(n-)*, from *resolvere* 'loosen, release' (see RESOLVE).

re·sol·u·tive /rəˈzälyətiv, ˈrezəˌlo͞otiv/ ▶ **adj.** formal or archaic having the power or ability to dissolve or dispel something.
– ORIGIN late Middle English: from medieval Latin *resolutivus*, from *resolut-* 'released,' from the verb *resolvere* (see RESOLVE).

re·solve /riˈzälv, -ˈzôlv/ ▶ **v.** **1** [with obj.] settle or find a solution to (a problem, dispute, or contentious matter): *the firm aims to resolve problems within 30 days.* ■ [with obj.] Medicine cause (a symptom or condition) to disperse, subside, or heal: *endoscopic biliary drainage can rapidly resolve jaundice.* ■ [no obj.] (of a symptom or condition) disperse, subside, or heal: *symptoms resolved after a median of four weeks.* ■ [no obj.] Music (of a discord) lead into a concord during the course of harmonic change. ■ [with obj.] Music cause (a discord) to pass into a concord.
2 [no obj.] decide firmly on a course of action: [with infinitive] *she resolved to call Dana as soon as she got home.* ■ [with clause] (of a legislative body, committee, or other formal meeting) make a decision by a formal vote: *the committee resolved that teachers should make their recommendations without knowledge of test scores* | [with infinitive] *the conference resolved to support an alliance.*
3 chiefly Chemistry separate or cause to be separated into components. ■ [with obj.] (**resolve something into**) reduce a subject, statement, etc., by mental analysis into (separate elements or a more elementary form): *the ability to resolve facts into their legal categories.* ■ [no obj.] (of something seen at a distance) turn into a different form when seen more clearly: *the orange glow* ***resolved itself*** *into four lanterns.* ■ [with obj.] (of optical or photographic equipment) separate or distinguish between (closely adjacent objects): *Hubble was able to resolve six variable stars in M31.* ■ [with obj.] separately distinguish (peaks in a graph or spectrum). ■ [with obj.] Physics analyze (a force or velocity) into components acting in particular directions.
▶ **n.** firm determination to do something: *she received information that strengthened her resolve* | *she intended to stick to her initial resolve.* ■ a formal resolution by a legislative body or public meeting.
– DERIVATIVES **re·solv·a·bil·i·ty** /riˌzälvəˈbilətē, -ˌzôlvə-/ **n.**, **re·solv·a·ble** **adj.**, **re·solv·er** **n.**
– ORIGIN late Middle English (in the senses 'dissolve, disintegrate' and 'solve (a problem)'): from Latin *resolvere*, from *re-* (expressing intensive force) + *solvere* 'loosen.'

re·solved /riˈzälvd, -ˈzôlvd/ ▶ **adj.** [predic., with infinitive] firmly determined to do something: *Constance was resolved not to cry.*
– DERIVATIVES **re·solv·ed·ly** /riˈzälvədlē, -ˈzôlvədlē/ **adv.**

re·sol·vent /riˈzälvənt, -ˈzôl-/ Mathematics ▶ **adj.** denoting an equation, function, or expression that is introduced in order to reach or complete a solution.
▶ **n.** an equation, function, or expression of this type.

re·solv·ing pow·er ▶ **n.** the ability of an optical instrument or type of film to separate or distinguish small or closely adjacent images. ■ the ability of an electronic device to produce images that can be distinguished.

res·o·nance /ˈrezənəns/ ▶ **n.** **1** the quality in a sound of being deep, full, and reverberating: *the resonance of his voice.* ■ the ability to evoke or suggest images, memories, and emotions: *the concepts lose their emotional resonance.*
2 Physics the reinforcement or prolongation of sound by reflection from a surface or by the synchronous vibration of a neighboring object.
3 the condition in which an electric circuit or device produces the largest possible response to an applied oscillating signal, esp. when its inductive and its capacitative reactances are balanced. ■ Mechanics the condition in which an object or system is subjected to an oscillating force having a frequency close to its own natural frequency.
4 Astronomy the occurrence of a simple ratio between the periods of revolution of two bodies about a single primary.
5 Chemistry the state attributed to certain molecules of having a structure that cannot adequately be represented by a single structural formula but is a composite of two or more structures of higher energy.
6 Physics a short-lived subatomic particle that is an excited state of a more stable particle.
– ORIGIN late Middle English: from Old French, from Latin *resonantia* 'echo,' from *resonare* 'resound' (see RESONANT).

res·o·nant /ˈrezənənt/ ▶ **adj.** **1** (of sound) deep, clear, and continuing to sound or ring: *a full-throated and resonant guffaw.* ■ (**resonant with**) (of a place) filled or resounding with (a sound): *alpine valleys resonant with the sound of church bells.* ■ having the ability to evoke or suggest enduring images, memories, or emotions: *the prints are resonant with traditions of Russian folk art and story.*
2 (of a room, a musical instrument, or a hollow body) tending to reinforce or prolong sounds, esp. by synchronous vibration.
3 technical of, relating to, or bringing about resonance in a circuit, atom, or other object.
4 (of a color) enhancing or enriching another color or colors by contrast.
– DERIVATIVES **res·o·nant·ly** **adv.**
– ORIGIN late 16th cent.: from French *résonnant* or Latin *resonant-* 'resounding,' from the verb *resonare*, from *re-* (expressing intensive force) + *sonare* 'to sound.'

res·o·nate /ˈreznˌāt/ ▶ **v.** [no obj.] **1** produce or be filled with a deep, full, reverberating sound: *the sound of the siren resonated across the harbor.* ■ evoke or suggest images, memories, and emotions: *the words* ***resonate with*** *so many different meanings.* ■ (of an idea or action) meet with someone's agreement: *the judge's ruling resonated among many of the women.*
2 technical produce electrical or mechanical resonance: *the crystal resonates at 16 MHz.*
– ORIGIN late 19th cent.: from Latin *resonat-* 'resounded,' from the verb *resonare* (see RESOUND).

res·o·na·tor /ˈrezənˌātər/ ▶ **n.** an apparatus that increases the resonance of a sound, esp. a hollow part of a musical instrument. ■ a musical or scientific instrument responding to a single sound or note, used for detecting it when it occurs in combination with other sounds. ■ Physics a device that displays electrical resonance, esp. one used for the detection of radio waves. ■ Physics a hollow enclosure with conducting walls capable of containing electromagnetic fields having particular frequencies of oscillation and exchanging electrical energy with them, used to detect or amplify microwaves.

re·sorb /rēˈsôrb, -ˈzôrb/ ▶ **v.** [with obj.] technical absorb (something) again: *the ability to resorb valuable solutes from the urine.* ■ Physiology remove (cells, or a tissue or structure) by gradual breakdown into its component materials and dispersal in the circulation: *bone tissue will be resorbed.*
– ORIGIN mid 17th cent.: from Latin *resorbere*, from *re-* (expressing intensive force) + *sorbere* 'absorb.'

res·or·cin·ol /rəˈzôrsəˌnôl, -ˌnōl/ ▶ **n.** Chemistry a crystalline compound originally obtained from galbanum resin, used in the production of dyes, resins, and cosmetics. ● Alternative name: **1,3-dihydroxybenzene**; chem. formula: $C_6H_4(OH)_2$.
– ORIGIN late 19th cent.: from the earlier term *resorcin* + -OL.

re·sorp·tion /rēˈsôrpshən, -ˈzôrp-/ ▶ **n.** the process or action by which something is reabsorbed: *the resorption of water.* ■ Physiology the absorption into the circulation of cells or tissue: *bone resorption.*
– DERIVATIVES **re·sorp·tive** /-tiv/ **adj.**
– ORIGIN early 19th cent.: from RESORB, on the pattern of the pair *absorb, absorption.*

re·sort /riˈzôrt/ ▶ **n.** **1** a place that is a popular destination for vacations or recreation, or which is frequented for a particular purpose: *a seaside resort* | *a health resort.* ■ archaic the tendency of a place to be frequented by many people: *places of public resort.*
2 the action of turning to and adopting a strategy or course of action, esp. a disagreeable or undesirable one, so as to resolve a difficult situation: *Germany and Italy tried to resolve their economic and social failures by resort to fascism.* ■ [in sing.] a strategy or course of action that may be adopted in a difficult situation: *her only resort is surgery.*
▶ **v.** [no obj.] (**resort to**) **1** turn to and adopt (a strategy or course of action, esp. a disagreeable or undesirable one) so as to resolve a difficult situation: *the duke was prepared to resort to force if negotiation failed.*
2 formal go often or in large numbers to: *local authorities have a duty to provide adequate sites for gypsies "residing in or resorting to" their areas.*
– PHRASES **as a first** (or **last** or **final**) **resort** before anything else is attempted (or when all else has failed). **in the last resort** ultimately: *in the last resort what really moves us is our personal convictions.* [suggested by French *en dernier ressort*.]

– DERIVATIVES **re·sort·er** n.
– ORIGIN late Middle English (denoting something one can turn to for assistance): from Old French *resortir*, from *re-* 'again' + *sortir* 'come or go out.' The sense 'place frequently visited' dates from the mid 18th cent.

re-sort /rē'sôrt/ ▶ v. [with obj.] sort (something) again or differently.

re·sound /ri'zound/ ▶ v. **1** [no obj.] (of a sound, voice, etc.) fill a place with sound; be loud enough to echo: *another scream resounded through the school.* ■ (of a place) be filled or echo with a particular sound or sounds: *the office* **resounds with** *the metronomic clicking of keyboards.* ■ (of fame, a person's reputation, etc.) be much talked of: *whatever they do in the nineties will not resound in the way that their earlier achievements did.*
2 [with obj.] literary sing (the praises) of: *Horace resounds the praises of Italy.*
– ORIGIN late Middle English: from RE- 'again' + the verb SOUND[1], suggested by Old French *resoner* or Latin *resonare* 'sound again.'

re·sound·ing /ri'zoundiNG/ ▶ adj. **1** (of a sound) loud enough to reverberate: *a resounding smack across the face.*
2 [attrib.] unmistakable; emphatic: *the evening was a resounding success.*
– DERIVATIVES **re·sound·ing·ly** adv.

re·source /'rē,sôrs, 'rē'zôrs, ri'sôrs, ri'zôrs/ ▶ n.
1 (usu. **resources**) a stock or supply of money, materials, staff, and other assets that can be drawn on by a person or organization in order to function effectively: *local authorities complained that they lacked resources.* ■ (**resources**) a country's collective means of supporting itself or becoming wealthier, as represented by its reserves of minerals, land, and other assets. ■ (**resources**) available assets.
2 an action or strategy that may be adopted in adverse circumstances: *sometimes anger is the only resource left in a situation like this.* ■ (**resources**) one's personal attributes and capabilities regarded as able to help or sustain one in adverse circumstances: *we had been left very much to our own resources.* ■ the ability to find quick and clever ways to overcome difficulties: *a man of resource.* ■ archaic the possibility of aid or assistance: *the flower of the French army was lost* **without resource**.
3 archaic a leisure occupation.
▶ v. [with obj.] provide (a person or organization) with materials, money, staff, and other assets necessary for effective operation: *ensuring that primary health care workers are adequately resourced.*
– DERIVATIVES **re·source·less** adj., **re·source·less·ness** n.
– ORIGIN early 17th cent.: from obsolete French *ressourse*, feminine past participle (used as a noun) of Old French dialect *resourdre* 'rise again, recover' (based on Latin *surgere* 'to rise').

re·source·ful /ri'sôrsfəl, -'zôrs-/ ▶ adj. having the ability to find quick and clever ways to overcome difficulties.
– DERIVATIVES **re·source·ful·ly** adv., **re·source·ful·ness** n.

resp. ▶ abbr. ■ respective. ■ respectively. ■ respelled; respelling. ■ respondent.

re·spect /ri'spekt/ ▶ n. **1** a feeling of deep admiration for someone or something elicited by their abilities, qualities, or achievements: *the director had a lot of* **respect for** *Douglas as an actor.* ■ the state of being admired in such a way: *his first chance in over fifteen years to regain respect in the business.* ■ due regard for the feelings, wishes, rights, or traditions of others: **respect for** *human rights.* ■ (**respects**) a person's polite greetings: *give my respects to your parents.*
2 a particular aspect, point, or detail: *the government's record* **in this respect** *is a mixed one.*
▶ v. [with obj.] admire (someone or something) deeply, as a result of their abilities, qualities, or achievements: *she was respected by everyone she worked with* | (as adj. **respected**) *a respected academic.* ■ have due regard for the feelings, wishes, rights, or traditions of: *I respected his views.* ■ avoid harming or interfering with: *it is incumbent upon all boaters to respect the environment.* ■ agree to recognize and abide by (a legal requirement): *he urged all foreign nationals to respect the laws of their country of residence.*
– PHRASES **with respect to** as regards; with reference to: *the two groups were similar with respect to age, sex, and diagnoses.* **in respect that** because. **pay one's last respects** see PAY[1]. **pay one's respects** see PAY[1]. **with** (or **with all due**) **respect** used as a polite formula preceding, and intended to mitigate the effect of, an expression of disagreement or criticism: *with all due respect, Father, I think you've got to be more broad-minded these days.*
– ORIGIN late Middle English: from Latin *respectus*, from the verb *respicere* 'look back at, regard,' from *re-* 'back' + *specere* 'look at.'

re·spect·a·bil·i·ty /ri,spektə'bilətē/ ▶ n. the state or quality of being proper, correct, and socially acceptable: *provincial notions of respectability.* ■ the state or quality of being accepted as valid or important within a particular field: *scientific respectability.*

re·spect·a·ble /ri'spektəbəl/ ▶ adj. **1** regarded by society to be good, proper, or correct: *they thought the stage no life for a respectable lady.* ■ (of a person's appearance, clothes, or behavior) decent or presentable: *a perfectly respectable pair of pajamas!*
2 of some merit or importance: *a respectable botanical text.* ■ adequate or acceptable in number, size, or amount: *America's GDP grew by a respectable 2.6 percent.*
– DERIVATIVES **re·spect·a·bly** /-blē/ adv. [as submodifier] *an architecture of respectably high standards.*

re·spect·er /ri'spektər/ ▶ n. a person who has a high regard for someone or something: *I'm always a respecter of the office of the presidency, but not necessarily of the president.*
– PHRASES **be no respecter of ——** not be influenced by status, wealth, etc.: *Jesus was no respecter of people.*

re·spect·ful /ri'spektfəl/ ▶ adj. feeling or showing deference and respect: *they sit in respectful silence.*
– DERIVATIVES **re·spect·ful·ly** adv., **re·spect·ful·ness** n.

re·spect·ing /ri'spektiNG/ ▶ prep. dated or formal with reference or regard to: *he began to have serious worries respecting his car.*

re·spec·tive /ri'spektiv/ ▶ adj. [attrib.] belonging or relating separately to each of two or more people or things: *they chatted about their respective childhoods.*
– ORIGIN late Middle English (in the sense 'relative, comparative'): from medieval Latin *respectivus*, from *respect-* 'regarded, considered,' from the verb *respicere* (see RESPECT), reinforced by French *respectif, -ive*.

re·spec·tive·ly /ri'spektivlē/ ▶ adv. separately or individually and in the order already mentioned (used when enumerating two or more items or facts that refer back to a previous statement): *they received sentences of one year and eight months, respectively.*

re·spell /rē'spel/ ▶ v. (past and past participle **respelled** or chiefly Brit. **respelt**) [with obj.] spell (a word) again or differently, esp. phonetically in order to indicate its pronunciation.

res·pi·ra·ble /'respərəbəl, ri'spīrəbəl/ ▶ adj. (of the air or a gas) able or fit to be breathed. ■ (of particles in the air) able to be breathed in: *woodworking can create quantities of fine respirable dust.*
– ORIGIN late 18th cent.: from French *respirable* or late Latin *respirabilis*, from *respirare* 'breathe out' (see RESPIRE).

res·pi·rate /'respə,rāt/ ▶ v. [with obj.] Medicine & Biology assist (a person or animal) to breathe by means of artificial respiration.
– ORIGIN mid 17th cent.: back-formation from RESPIRATION.

res·pi·ra·tion /,respə'rāSHən/ ▶ n. the action of breathing: *opiates affect respiration.* ■ chiefly Medicine a single breath. ■ Biology a process in living organisms involving the production of energy, typically with the intake of oxygen and the release of carbon dioxide from the oxidation of complex organic substances.
– ORIGIN late Middle English: from Latin *respiratio(n-)*, from *respirare* 'breathe out' (see RESPIRE).

res·pi·ra·tor /'respə,rātər/ ▶ n. an apparatus worn over the mouth and nose or the entire face to prevent the inhalation of dust, smoke, or other noxious substances. ■ an apparatus used to induce artificial respiration.

res·pi·ra·to·ry /'respərə,tôrē, ri'spīrə-/ ▶ adj. of, relating to, or affecting respiration or the organs of respiration: *respiratory disease.*

res·pi·ra·to·ry dis·tress syn·drome ▶ n. another term for HYALINE MEMBRANE DISEASE.

res·pi·ra·to·ry pig·ment ▶ n. Biochemistry a substance (such as hemoglobin or hemocyanin) with a molecule consisting of protein with a pigmented prosthetic group, involved in the physiological transport of oxygen or electrons.

res·pi·ra·to·ry quo·tient ▶ n. Physiology the ratio of the volume of carbon dioxide evolved to that of oxygen consumed by an organism, tissue, or cell in a given time.

res·pi·ra·to·ry syn·cy·tial vi·rus ▶ n. Medicine a paramyxovirus that causes disease of the respiratory tract. It is a major cause of bronchiolitis and pneumonia in young children and may be a contributing factor in sudden infant death syndrome.

res·pi·ra·to·ry tract ▶ n. the passage formed by the mouth, nose, throat, and lungs, through which air passes during breathing.

res·pi·ra·to·ry tree ▶ n. Zoology a branched respiratory organ in the body cavity of sea cucumbers.

re·spire /ri'spīr/ ▶ v. [no obj.] breathe: *he lay back, respiring deeply* | [with obj.] *a country where fresh air seems impossible to respire.* ■ (of a plant) carry out respiration, esp. at night when photosynthesis has ceased. ■ literary recover hope, courage, or strength after a time of difficulty: *the archduke, newly respiring from so long a war.*
– ORIGIN late Middle English: from Old French *respirer* or Latin *respirare* 'breathe out,' from *re-* 'again' + *spirare* 'breathe.'

res·pi·rom·e·ter /,respə'rämətər/ ▶ n. Biology a device that measures the rate of consumption of oxygen by a living organism or organic system. ■ Medicine an instrument for measuring the air capacity of the lungs.

res·pite /'respət, ri'spīt/ ▶ n. a short period of rest or relief from something difficult or unpleasant: *the refugee encampments will provide some* **respite from** *the suffering* | [in sing.] *a brief* **respite from** *a dire food shortage.* ■ a short delay permitted before an unpleasant obligation is met or a punishment is carried out.
▶ v. [with obj.] rare postpone (a sentence, obligation, etc.): *the execution was only respited a few months.* ■ archaic grant a delay or extension of time to; reprieve from death or execution: *some poor criminal ... from the gibbet or the wheel, respited for a day.*
– ORIGIN Middle English: from Old French *respit*, from Latin *respectus* 'refuge, consideration.'

res·pite care ▶ n. temporary institutional care of a dependent elderly, ill, or handicapped person, providing relief for their usual caregivers.

re·splend·ent /ri'splendənt/ ▶ adj. attractive and impressive through being richly colorful or sumptuous: *she was* **resplendent in** *a sea-green dress.*
– DERIVATIVES **re·splend·ence** n., **re·splend·en·cy** n., **re·splend·ent·ly** adv.
– ORIGIN late Middle English: from Latin *resplendent-* 'shining out,' from the verb *resplendere*, from *re-* (expressing intensive force) + *splendere* 'to glitter.'

re·spond /ri'spänd/ ▶ v. [reporting verb] say something in reply: [no obj.] *she could not get Robert to* **respond to** *her words* | [with clause] *he responded that it would not be feasible* | [with direct speech] *"It's not part of my job," Belinda responded.* ■ (of a congregation) say or sing the response in reply to a priest. ■ [no obj.] (of a person) act or behave in reaction to someone or something: *she turned her head,* **responding to** *his grin with a smile.* ■ react quickly or positively to a stimulus or treatment: *his back injury has failed to respond to treatment.* ■ [with obj.] Bridge make (a bid) in answer to one's partner's preceding bid.
▶ n. **1** Architecture a half-pillar or half-pier attached to a wall to support an arch, esp. at the end of an arcade.
2 (in church use) a responsory; a response to a versicle.
– DERIVATIVES **re·spond·ence** /-dəns/ n. (archaic), **re·spond·en·cy** /-dənsē/ n. (archaic), **re·spond·er** n.
– ORIGIN late Middle English (in the noun senses): from Old French, from *respondre* 'to answer,' from Latin *respondere*, from *re-* 'again' + *spondere* 'to pledge.' The verb dates from the mid 16th cent.

re·spond·ent /ri'spändənt/ ▶ n. **1** a defendant in a lawsuit, esp. one in an appeals or divorce case.
2 a person who replies to something, esp. one supplying information for a survey or questionnaire or responding to an advertisement.
▶ adj. [attrib.] **1** in the position of defendant in a lawsuit: *the respondent defendant.*
2 replying to something, esp. a survey or questionnaire: *the respondent firms in the survey.*
3 Psychology involving or denoting a response, esp. a conditioned reflex, to a specific stimulus.
– ORIGIN early 16th cent. (sense 2 of the noun): from Latin *respondent-* 'answering, offering in return,' from the verb *respondere* (see RESPOND).

re·spon·sa /ri'spänsə/ plural form of RESPONSUM.

re·sponse /ri'späns/ ▶ n. a verbal or written answer: *without waiting for a response, she returned to her newspaper* | *we received 400 applications* **in response to** *one job ad.* ■ a written or verbal answer to a question in a test, questionnaire, survey, etc. ■ a

PRONUNCIATION KEY ə ago, up; ər over, fur; a hat; ā ate; ä car; e let; ē see; i fit; ī by; NG sing; ō go; ô law, for; oi toy; o͝o good; o͞o goo; ou out; TH thin; TH then; ZH vision

r

reaction to something: *an extended, jazzy piano solo drew the biggest **response from** the crowd | an honors degree course in Japanese has been established **in response to** an increasing demand.* ■ Psychology & Physiology an excitation of a nerve impulse caused by a change or event; a physical reaction to a specific stimulus or situation. ■ the way in which a mechanical or electrical device responds to a stimulus or range of stimuli. ■ (usu. **responses**) a part of a religious liturgy said or sung by a congregation in answer to a minister or cantor. ■ Bridge a bid made in answer to one's partner's preceding bid.
– ORIGIN Middle English: from Old French *respons* or Latin *responsum* 'something offered in return,' neuter past participle of *respondere* (see **RESPOND**).

re·sponse time ▶ n. the length of time taken for a person or system to react to a given stimulus or event. ■ Electronics the time taken for a circuit or measuring device, when subjected to a change in input signal, to change its state by a specified fraction of its total response to that change.

re·sponse var·i·a·ble ▶ n. another term for **DEPENDENT VARIABLE**.

re·spon·si·bil·i·ty /ri,spänsə'bilətē/ ▶ n. (pl. **responsibilities**) the state or fact of having a duty to deal with something or of having control over someone: *women bear children and take **responsibility for** child care.* ■ the state or fact of being accountable or to blame for something: *the group has claimed responsibility for a string of murders.* ■ the opportunity or ability to act independently and make decisions without authorization: *we would expect individuals lower down the organization to take on more responsibility.* ■ (often **responsibilities**) a thing that one is required to do as part of a job, role, or legal obligation: *he will take over the responsibilities of overseas director.* ■ [in sing.] (**responsibility to/toward**) a moral obligation to behave correctly toward or in respect of: *individuals have a responsibility to control personal behavior.*

re·spon·si·ble /ri'spänsəbəl/ ▶ adj. [predic.] having an obligation to do something, or having control over or care for someone, as part of one's job or role: *the department **responsible for** education.* ■ being the primary cause of something and so able to be blamed or credited for it: *the gene was responsible for a rare type of eye cancer.* ■ [attrib.] (of a job or position) involving important duties, independent decision-making, or control over others. ■ [predic.] (**responsible to**) having to report to (a superior or someone in authority) and be answerable to them for one's actions: *the team manager is responsible to the league president.* ■ capable of being trusted: *a responsible adult.* ■ morally accountable for one's behavior: *the progressive emergence of the child as a responsible being.*
– DERIVATIVES **re·spon·si·ble·ness** n., **re·spon·si·bly** /-blē/ adv.
– ORIGIN late 16th cent. (in the sense 'answering to, corresponding'): from obsolete French, from Latin *respons-* 'answered, offered in return,' from the verb *respondere* (see **RESPOND**).

re·spon·sive /ri'spänsiv/ ▶ adj. **1** reacting quickly and positively: *a flexible service that is **responsive to** changing social and economic patterns.* ■ responding readily and with interest or enthusiasm: *our most enthusiastic and responsive students.*
2 answering: *I'm distracted by a nibble on my line: I jig it several times, but there is no responsive tug.* ■ (of a section of liturgy) using responses.
– DERIVATIVES **re·spon·sive·ly** adv., **re·spon·sive·ness** n.

re·spon·so·ri·al /ri,spän'sôrēəl/ ▶ adj. (of a psalm or liturgical chant) recited in parts with a congregational response between each part.

re·spon·so·ry /ri'spänsərē/ ▶ n. (pl. **responsories**) (in the Christian Church) an anthem said or sung by a soloist and choir after a lesson.
– ORIGIN late Middle English: from late Latin *responsorium*, from Latin *respons-* 'answered,' from the verb *respondere* (see **RESPOND**).

re·spon·sum /ri'spänsəm/ ▶ n. (pl. **responsa** /-sə/) a written reply by a rabbi or Talmudic scholar to an inquiry on some matter of Jewish law.
– ORIGIN Latin, literally 'reply.'

res pu·bli·ca /rās 'po͝obli,kä, 'pəblikə/ ▶ n. the state, republic, or commonwealth.
– ORIGIN Latin, literally 'public matter.'

res·sen·ti·ment /rə,säntē'mäN/ ▶ n. a psychological state arising from suppressed feelings of envy and hatred that cannot be acted upon, frequently resulting in some form of self-abasement.
– ORIGIN via German (used by Nietzsche in this sense) from French *ressentiment* 'feeling.'

rest[1] /rest/ ▶ v. [no obj.] **1** cease work or movement in order to relax, refresh oneself, or recover strength: *he needed to rest after the feverish activity | I'm going to **rest up** before traveling to England.* ■ [with obj.] allow to be inactive in order to regain strength, health, or energy: *her friend read to her while she rested her eyes.* ■ [with obj.] leave (a player) out of a team temporarily: *both men were rested for the final game.* ■ (of a dead person or body) lie buried: *the king's body rested in his tomb.* ■ (of a problem or subject) be left without further investigation, discussion, or treatment: *the council has urged the planning committee not to allow the matter to rest.* ■ [with obj.] allow (land) to lie fallow: *the field should be grazed or rested.* ■ conclude the case for the prosecution or the defense in a law case: *the prosecution rests.* See also **REST ONE'S CASE** below.
2 be placed or supported so as to stay in a specified position: *her elbow was resting on the arm of the sofa.* ■ [with obj.] place (something) so that it is supported in a specified position: *he rested a hand on her shoulder.* ■ (**rest on/upon**) (of a look) alight or be steadily directed on: *his eyes rested briefly on the boy.* ■ (**rest on/upon**) be based on or grounded in; depend on: *the country's security rested on its alliances.* ■ [with obj.] (**rest something in/on**) place hope, trust, or confidence on or in: *she rested her hopes in her attorney.* ■ belong or be located at a specified place or with a specified person: *ultimate control rested with the founders.*
▶ n. **1** an instance or period of relaxing or ceasing to engage in strenuous or stressful activity: *you look as though you need a rest | a couple of days of complete rest.* ■ a motionless state: *the car accelerates rapidly from rest.* ■ Music an interval of silence of a specified duration. ■ Music the sign denoting such an interval. ■ a pause in speech or verse.
2 [in combination] an object that is used to support something: *a chin-rest | a shoulder-rest.* ■ a support or hook for a telephone receiver when not in use. ■ a support for a cue in billiards or pool.
– PHRASES **at rest** not moving or exerting oneself. ■ not agitated or troubled; tranquil: *he felt at rest, the tension gone | if you think something's wrong, consult the doctor and **put your mind at rest**.* ■ dead and buried. **come to rest** stop moving; settle: *the elevator came to rest at the first floor.* **give it a rest** informal used to ask someone to stop doing something or talking about something that the speaker finds irritating or tedious. **no rest for the weary** see **WEARY**. **rest one's case** conclude one's presentation of evidence and arguments in a lawsuit. ■ humorous said to show that one believes one has presented sufficient evidence for one's views. **rest on one's laurels** see **LAUREL**. **rest** (or **God rest**) **his** (or **her**) **soul** used to express a wish that God should grant someone's soul peace. **rest on one's oars** see **OAR**.
– ORIGIN Old English *ræst*, *rest* (noun), *ræstan*, *restan* (verb), of Germanic origin, from a root meaning 'league' or 'mile' (referring to a distance after which one rests).

rest[2] ▶ n. [in sing.] the remaining part of something: *what do you want to do for **the rest of** your life? | I'll tell you the rest tomorrow night.* ■ [treated as pl.] the remaining people or things; the others: ***the rest of us** were experienced skiers.*
▶ v. [no obj.] remain or be left in a specified condition: *you can rest assured she will do everything she can to help her.*
– PHRASES **and** (**all**) **the rest** (**of it**) and everything else that might be mentioned or that one could expect: *social security and pension and the rest of it.* **the rest is history** see **HISTORY**.
– ORIGIN late Middle English: from Old French *reste* (noun), *rester* (verb), from Latin *restare* 'remain,' from *re-* 'back' + *stare* 'to stand.'

re·stage /,rē'stāj/ ▶ v. [with obj.] present (a performance or public event) again or differently.

rest ar·e·a ▶ n. a roadside area with restrooms and other facilities for the use of motorists.

re·start /,rē'stärt/ ▶ v. start again: [no obj.] *the talks will restart in September* | [with obj.] *he tried to restart his stalled car.*
▶ n. a new start or beginning.

re·state /rē'stāt/ ▶ v. [with obj.] state (something) again or differently, esp. in order to correct or to make more clear or convincing: *he restated his opposition to abortion* | [as adj.] *restated earnings.*
– DERIVATIVES **re·state·ment** n.

res·tau·rant /'rest(ə)rənt, 'restə,ränt, 'res,tränt/ ▶ n. a place where people pay to sit and eat meals that are cooked and served on the premises.
– ORIGIN early 19th cent.: from French, from *restaurer* 'provide food for' (literally 'restore to a former state').

res·tau·ra·teur /,restərə'tər/ ▶ n. a person who owns and manages a restaurant.
– ORIGIN late 18th cent.: French, from the verb *restaurer* (see **RESTAURANT**).

> **USAGE** The word **restaurateur** is taken directly from the French form. Although common, **restauranteur** with an *n* is a misspelling.

rest cure ▶ n. a period spent in inactivity or leisure with the intention of improving one's physical or mental health.

re·ste·no·sis /,rēstə'nōsəs/ ▶ n. Medicine the recurrence of abnormal narrowing of an artery or valve after corrective surgery.
– ORIGIN 1950s: from **RE-** 'again' + **STENOSIS**.

rest·ful /'restfəl/ ▶ adj. having a quiet and soothing quality: *the rooms were cool and restful.*
– DERIVATIVES **rest·ful·ly** adv., **rest·ful·ness** n.

rest home ▶ n. a residential institution where old or frail people are cared for.

rest·ing po·ten·tial ▶ n. Physiology the electrical potential of a neuron or other excitable cell relative to its surroundings when not stimulated or involved in passage of an impulse.

res·ti·tu·tion /,restə't(y)o͞oSHən/ ▶ n. **1** the restoration of something lost or stolen to its proper owner: *seeking the restitution of land taken from blacks under apartheid.*
2 recompense for injury or loss: *he was ordered to pay $6,000 in restitution.*
3 the restoration of something to its original state: *restitution of the damaged mucosa.* ■ Physics the resumption of an object's original shape or position through elastic recoil.
– DERIVATIVES **res·ti·tu·tion·ar·y** adj., **res·ti·tu·tive** /'restə,t(y)o͞otiv/ adj.
– ORIGIN Middle English: from Old French, or from Latin *restitutio(n-)*, from *restituere* 'restore,' from *re-* 'again' + *statuere* 'establish.'

res·tive /'restiv/ ▶ adj. (of a person) unable to keep still or silent and becoming increasingly difficult to control, esp. because of impatience, dissatisfaction, or boredom. ■ (of a horse) refusing to advance, stubbornly standing still or moving backward or sideways.
– DERIVATIVES **res·tive·ly** adv., **res·tive·ness** n.
– ORIGIN late 16th cent.: from Old French *restif*, *-ive*, from Latin *restare* 'remain.' The original sense, 'inclined to remain still, inert,' has undergone a reversal; the association with the refractory movements of a horse gave rise to the current sense 'fidgety, restless.'

rest·less /'restləs/ ▶ adj. (of a person or animal) unable to rest or relax as a result of anxiety or boredom: *the audience grew restless and inattentive.* ■ offering no physical or emotional rest; involving constant activity or motion: *a restless night.*
– DERIVATIVES **rest·less·ly** adv., **rest·less·ness** n.
– ORIGIN Old English *restlēas* (see **REST**[1], **-LESS**).

rest·less legs syn·drome (also **restless leg syndrome**) ▶ n. a disorder characterized by an unpleasant tickling or twitching sensation in the leg muscles when sitting or lying down, which is relieved only by moving the legs.

rest mass ▶ n. Physics the mass of a body when at rest.

rest·o /'restō/ ▶ n. (pl. **restos**) informal a restaurant.
– ORIGIN 1980s: abbreviation.

re·stock /rē'stäk/ ▶ v. [with obj.] replenish (a store) with fresh stock or supplies: *work began at once to restock the fishery.*

Res·ton /'restən/ a planned residential and commercial community in northern Virginia, northwest of Washington, DC, established in the 1960s; pop. 56,407 (2000).

res·to·ra·tion /,restə'rāSHən/ ▶ n. **1** the action of returning something to a former owner, place, or condition: *the restoration of Andrew's sight.* ■ the process of repairing or renovating a building, work of art, vehicle, etc., so as to restore it to its original condition: *the altar paintings seem in need of restoration.* ■ the reinstatement of a previous practice, right, custom, or situation: *the restoration of capital punishment.* ■ Dentistry a structure provided to replace or repair dental tissue so as to restore its form and function, such as a filling, crown, or bridge. ■ a model or drawing representing the supposed original form of an extinct animal, ruined building, etc.
2 the return of a hereditary monarch to a throne, a head of state to government, or a regime to power. ■ (**the Restoration**) the re-establishment of Charles II as King of England in 1660. ■ (**Restoration**) [usu. as modifier] the period following this, esp. with regard to its literature or architecture: *Restoration drama.*
– ORIGIN late 15th cent. (denoting the action of restoring to a former state): partly from Old French, partly an alteration of obsolete *restauration* (from late Latin *restauratio(n-)*, from the verb *restaurare*), suggested by **RESTORE**.

Res·to·ra·tion com·e·dy ▶ n. a style of drama that flourished in London after the Restoration in 1660, typically having a complicated plot marked by wit, cynicism, and licentiousness.

res·to·ra·tion·ism /ˌrestəˈrāshəˌnizəm/ ▶ **n.** a charismatic Christian movement seeking to restore the beliefs and practices of the early Church.
– DERIVATIVES **res·to·ra·tion·ist** **n.** & **adj.**

re·stor·a·tive /riˈstôrətiv/ ▶ **adj.** having the ability to restore health, strength, or a feeling of well-being: *the restorative power of long walks.* ■ Surgery & Dentistry relating to or concerned with the restoration of form or function to a damaged tooth or other part of the body.
▶ **n.** something, esp. a medicine or drink, that restores health, strength, or well-being.
– DERIVATIVES **re·stor·a·tive·ly** **adv.**
– ORIGIN late Middle English: from an Old French variant of *restauratif, -ive*, from *restorer* (see RESTORE).

re·store /riˈstôr/ ▶ **v.** [with obj.] bring back (a previous right, practice, custom, or situation); reinstate: *the government restored confidence in the housing market.* ■ return (someone or something) to a former condition, place, or position: *the effort to **restore** him **to** office isn't working.* ■ repair or renovate (a building, work of art, vehicle, etc.) so as to return it to its original condition: *the building has been lovingly restored.* ■ give (something previously stolen, taken away, or lost) back to the original owner or recipient: *the government will **restore** land and property **to** those who lost it through confiscation.*
– DERIVATIVES **re·stor·a·ble** **adj.**, **re·stor·er** **n.**
– ORIGIN Middle English: from Old French *restorer*, from Latin *restaurare* 'rebuild, restore.'

re·strain /riˈstrān/ ▶ **v.** [with obj.] prevent (someone or something) from doing something; keep under control or within limits: *he had to be **restrained from** walking out of the meeting* | (as adj. **restraining**) *Cara put a restraining hand on his arm.* ■ prevent oneself from displaying or giving way to (a strong urge or emotion): *Amos had to restrain his impatience.* ■ deprive (someone) of freedom of movement or personal liberty: *leg cuffs are used in the U.S. for restraining and transporting extremely violent and dangerous criminals.* ■ (of a seat belt) hold (a person or part of their body) down and back while in a vehicle seat.
– DERIVATIVES **re·strain·a·ble** **adj.**, **re·strain·er** **n.**
– ORIGIN Middle English: from Old French *restreign-*, stem of *restreindre*, from Latin *restringere*, from *re-* 'back' + *stringere* 'to tie, pull tight.'

re·strained /riˈstrānd/ ▶ **adj.** characterized by reserve or moderation; unemotional or dispassionate: *he had restrained manners.* ■ (of color, clothes, decoration, etc.) understated and subtle; not excessively showy or ornate. ■ kept under control; prevented from freedom of movement or action: *a patch of land turned into a restrained wilderness.* ■ (of a person) held down and back in a vehicle seat by a seat belt.
– DERIVATIVES **re·strain·ed·ly** /riˈstrānidlē/ **adv.**

re·straint /riˈstrānt/ ▶ **n.** **1** (often **restraints**) a measure or condition that keeps someone or something under control or within limits: *decisions are made within the financial restraints of the budget.* ■ the action of keeping someone or something under control. ■ deprivation or restriction of personal liberty or freedom of movement: *he remained aggressive and required physical restraint.* ■ a device that limits or prevents freedom of movement: *car safety restraints.*
2 unemotional, dispassionate, or moderate behavior; self-control: *he urged the protesters to exercise restraint.* ■ understatement, esp. of artistic expression: *with strings and piano, all restraint vanished.*
– ORIGIN late Middle English: from Old French *restreinte*, feminine past participle of *restreindre* 'hold back' (see RESTRAIN).

re·straint of trade ▶ **n.** Law action that interferes with free competition in a market.

re·strict /riˈstrikt/ ▶ **v.** [with obj.] put a limit on; keep under control: *some roads may have to be closed at peak times to restrict the number of visitors.* ■ deprive (someone or something) of freedom of movement or action: *cities can **restrict** groups of protesters **from** gathering on a residential street.* ■ (**restrict someone to**) limit someone to only doing or having (a particular thing) or staying in (a particular place): *I shall restrict myself to a single example.* ■ (**restrict something to**) limit something, esp. an activity, to (a particular place, time, or category of people): *the zoological gardens were at first restricted to members and their guests.* ■ withhold (information) from general circulation or disclosure: *at first the government tried to restrict news of our involvement in Vietnam.*
– ORIGIN mid 16th cent.: from Latin *restrict-* 'confined, bound fast,' from the verb *restringere* (see RESTRAIN).

re·strict·ed /riˈstriktid/ ▶ **adj.** [attrib.] limited in extent, number, scope, or action: *Western scientists had only restricted access to the site.* ■ (of a document or information) for limited circulation and not to be revealed to the public for reasons of national security. ■ Biology (of a virus) unable to reproduce at its normal rate in certain hosts. ■ Biochemistry (of DNA) subject to degradation by a restriction enzyme.
– DERIVATIVES **re·strict·ed·ly** **adv.**, **re·strict·ed·ness** **n.**

re·stric·tion /riˈstrikshən/ ▶ **n.** (often **restrictions**) a limiting condition or measure, esp. a legal one: *planning restrictions on commercial development.* ■ the limitation or control of someone or something, or the state of being limited or restricted: *the restriction of local government power.*
– DERIVATIVES **re·stric·tion·ism** /-ˌnizəm/ **n.**, **re·stric·tion·ist** /-nist/ **adj.** & **n.**
– ORIGIN late Middle English: from Old French, or from Latin *restrictio(n-)*, from *restringere* 'bind fast, confine' (see RESTRICT).

re·stric·tion en·zyme (also **restriction endonuclease**) ▶ **n.** Biochemistry an enzyme produced chiefly by certain bacteria, having the property of cleaving DNA molecules at or near a specific sequence of bases.

re·stric·tion frag·ment ▶ **n.** Biochemistry a fragment of a DNA molecule that has been cleaved by a restriction enzyme.

re·stric·tion frag·ment length pol·y·mor·phism ▶ **n.** Genetics a variation in the length of restriction fragments produced by a given restriction enzyme in a sample of DNA. Such variation is used in forensic investigations and to map hereditary disease.

re·stric·tive /riˈstriktiv/ ▶ **adj.** **1** imposing restrictions or limitations on someone's activities or freedom: *a web of restrictive regulations.*
2 Grammar (of a relative clause or descriptive phrase) serving to specify the particular instance or instances being mentioned.
– DERIVATIVES **re·stric·tive·ly** **adv.**, **re·stric·tive·ness** **n.**

USAGE What is the difference between *the books that were on the table once belonged to my aunt* and *the books, which were on the table, once belonged to my aunt*? In the first sentence, the speaker uses the relative clause to pick out specific books (i.e., the ones on the table) in contrast with all others. In the second sentence, the location of the books referred to is unaffected by the relative clause: the speaker merely offers the additional information that the books happened to be on the table. This distinction is between **restrictive** and **nonrestrictive** relative clauses. In speech, the difference is usually expressed by a difference in intonation. In writing, a **restrictive** relative clause is not set off by commas, and *that* is the preferred subject or object of the clause, although many writers use *which* and *who* or *whom* for such clauses. A **nonrestrictive** clause is set off within commas, and *which, who,* or *whom,* not *that,* is the relative pronoun to use as the subject or object of the verb of the clause. Without a comma, the clause in *please ask any member of the staff who will be pleased to help* is **restrictive** and therefore implies contrast with another set of staff who will not be pleased to help. It is almost certain that the appropriate intention of such a clause would be **nonrestrictive**—therefore, a comma is needed before **who** (*. . . any member of the staff, who will be pleased . . .*). For more details, see usage at THAT and WHICH.

re·stric·tive cov·e·nant ▶ **n.** Law a covenant imposing a restriction on the use of land so that the value and enjoyment of adjoining land will be preserved.

re·string /rēˈstriNG, ˈrē-/ ▶ **v.** (past and past participle **restrung**) [with obj.] **1** fit new or different strings to (a musical instrument or sports racket).
2 thread (objects such as beads) on a new string.

rest·room /ˈrestˌro͞om, -ˌro͝om/ (also **rest room**) ▶ **n.** a bathroom in a public building.

re·struc·ture /rēˈstrəkCHər/ ▶ **v.** [with obj.] organize differently: *a plan to strengthen and restructure the department* | (as noun **restructuring**) *the restructuring of this wing of the Louvre.* ■ Finance convert (the debt of a business in difficulty) into another kind of debt, typically one that is repayable at a later time.

re·struc·tur·ing /rēˈstrəkCHəriNG/ ▶ **n.** Commerce a reorganization of a company with a view to achieving greater efficiency and profit, or to adapt to a changing market.

re·study /ˌrēˈstədē/ ▶ **v.** (**restudies, restudying, restudied**) [with obj.] study (something) again.
▶ **n.** an instance of studying something again.

re·style ▶ **v.** /rēˈstīl/ [with obj.] **1** rearrange or remake in a new shape or layout: *Nick restyled Rebecca's hair.*
2 give a new designation to: [with obj. and complement] *the division has restyled the branch the Lovejoy Line.*
▶ **n.** /ˈrēstīl/ an instance of reshaping or rearranging something. ■ a new shape or arrangement.

re·sub·mit /ˌrēsəbˈmit/ ▶ **v.** [with obj.] submit (something, such as a plan, application, or resignation) again.
– DERIVATIVES **re·sub·mis·sion** /-ˈmishən/ **n.**

re·sult /riˈzəlt/ ▶ **n.** a consequence, effect, or outcome of something: *the tower collapsed **as a result of** safety violations.* ■ an item of information obtained by experiment or some other scientific method; a quantity or formula obtained by calculation. ■ (often **results**) a final score, mark, or placing in a sporting event or examination. ■ (often **results**) a satisfactory or favorable outcome of an undertaking or contest: *determination and persistence guarantee results.* ■ (usu. **results**) the outcome of a business's trading over a given period, expressed as a statement of profit or loss: *oil companies have reported markedly better results.*
▶ **v.** [no obj.] occur or follow as the consequence of something: *government unpopularity **resulting from** the state of the economy* | (as adj. **resulting**) *talk of a general election and the resulting political uncertainty.* ■ (**result in**) have (a specified end or outcome): *talks in July had resulted in stalemate.*
– PHRASES **without result** in vain: *Danny had inquired about getting work, without result.*
– ORIGIN late Middle English (as a verb): from medieval Latin *resultare* 'to result,' earlier in the sense 'spring back,' from *re-* (expressing intensive force) + *saltare* (frequentative of *salire* 'to jump'). The noun dates from the early 17th cent.

re·sult·ant /riˈzəltnt/ ▶ **adj.** [attrib.] occurring or produced as a result or consequence of something: *restructuring and the resultant cost savings.*
▶ **n.** technical a force, velocity, or other vector quantity that is equivalent to the combined effect of two or more component vectors acting at the same point.
– ORIGIN mid 17th cent. (in the adjectival sense): from Latin *resultant-* 'springing back,' from the verb *resultare* (see RESULT). The noun sense dates from the early 19th cent.

re·sult·a·tive /riˈzəltətiv/ Grammar ▶ **adj.** expressing, indicating, or relating to the outcome of an action.
▶ **n.** a resultative verb, conjunction, or clause.

re·sume /riˈzo͞om/ ▶ **v.** begin to do or pursue (something) again after a pause or interruption: [with obj.] *a day later normal service was resumed* | [no obj.] *hostilities had ceased and normal life had resumed.* ■ [no obj.] begin speaking again after a pause or interruption: *he sipped at the glass of water on the lectern and then resumed* | [with direct speech] *"As for Joe," the major resumed, "I can't promise anything."* ■ take, pick up, or put on again; return to the use of: *the judge resumed his seat.*
▶ **n.** variant spelling of RÉSUMÉ.
– DERIVATIVES **re·sum·a·ble** **adj.**
– ORIGIN late Middle English: from Old French *resumer* or Latin *resumere*, from *re-* 'back' + *sumere* 'take.'

ré·su·mé /ˈrezəˌmā, ˌrezəˈmā/ ▶ **n.** **1** a curriculum vitae.
2 a summary: *I gave him a quick résumé of events.*
– ORIGIN early 19th cent.: French, literally 'resumed,' past participle (used as a noun) of *résumer*.

re·sump·tion /riˈzəmpshən/ ▶ **n.** the action of beginning something again after a pause or interruption: *a resumption of meaningful negotiation.*

re·su·pi·nate /riˈso͞opəˌnāt/ ▶ **adj.** Botany (of a leaf, flower, fruiting body, etc.) upside down.
– DERIVATIVES **re·su·pi·na·tion** /riˌso͞opəˈnāshən/ **n.**
– ORIGIN late 18th cent.: from Latin *resupinatus* 'bent back,' past participle of *resupinare*, based on *supinus* 'lying on the back.'

re·sup·ply ▶ **v.** (**resupplies, resupplying, resupplied**) [with obj.] provide with a fresh supply: *ships can be resupplied at a number of deepwater ports worldwide.* ■ [no obj.] acquire a fresh supply: *phase two requires a period to regroup and resupply.*
▶ **n.** an act or instance of resupplying something or being resupplied.

re·sur·face /rēˈsərfəs/ ▶ **v.** **1** [with obj.] put a new coating on or reform (a surface such as a road, a floor, or ice).
2 [no obj.] come back up to the surface: *he resurfaced beside the boat.* ■ arise or become evident again:

r

serious concerns about the welfare of animals eventually resurfaced. ■ (of a person) come out of hiding or obscurity: *he resurfaced under a false identity in Australia.*

re·sur·gence /riˈsərjəns/ ▶ **n.** an increase or revival after a period of little activity, popularity, or occurrence: *a resurgence of interest in religion.*

re·sur·gent /riˈsərjənt/ ▶ **adj.** increasing or reviving after a period of little activity, popularity, or occurrence: *resurgent nationalism.*
– ORIGIN early 19th cent. (earlier as a noun): from Latin *resurgent-* 'rising again,' from the verb *resurgere,* from *re-* 'again' + *surgere* 'to rise.'

res·ur·rect /ˌrezəˈrekt/ ▶ **v.** [with obj.] restore (a dead person) to life: *he was dead, but he was resurrected.* ■ revive the practice, use, or memory of (something); bring new vigor to: *the deal collapsed and has yet to be resurrected.*
– ORIGIN late 18th cent.: back-formation from RESURRECTION.

res·ur·rec·tion /ˌrezəˈreksHən/ ▶ **n.** the action or fact of resurrecting or being resurrected: *the story of the resurrection of Osiris.* ■ (**the Resurrection**) (in Christian belief) Christ's rising from the dead. ■ (**the Resurrection**) (in Christian belief) the rising of the dead at the Last Judgment. ■ the revitalization or revival of something: *the resurrection of the country under a charismatic leader* | *resurrections of long-forgotten scandals.*
– ORIGIN Middle English: from Old French, from late Latin *resurrectio(n-),* from the verb *resurgere* 'rise again' (see RESURGENT).

res·ur·rec·tion plant ▶ **n.** any of a number of plants that are able to survive drought, typically folding up when dry and unfolding when moistened, in particular: ● a fern of tropical and warm-temperate America (*Polypodium polypodioides,* family Polypodiaceae). ● a Californian club moss (*Selaginella lepidophylla,* family Selaginellaceae). ● the rose of Jericho.

re·sur·vey /ˌrēsərˈvā/ ▶ **v.** [with obj.] survey (a district) again. ■ redraw (a map) after surveying a district again. ■ study or investigate again: *the same people surveyed in 1992 will be resurveyed periodically.*
▶ **n.** /rēˈsərvā/ an act of surveying a district or studying something again.

re·sus·ci·tate /riˈsəsəˌtāt/ ▶ **v.** [with obj.] revive (someone) from unconsciousness or apparent death: *an ambulance crew tried to resuscitate him.* ■ make (something such as an idea or enterprise) active or vigorous again: *measures to resuscitate the ailing Japanese economy.*
– DERIVATIVES **re·sus·ci·ta·tion** /riˌsəsəˈtāsHən/ **n.**, **re·sus·ci·ta·tive** /-ˌtātiv/ **adj.**, **re·sus·ci·ta·tor** /-ˌtātər/ **n.**
– ORIGIN early 16th cent.: from Latin *resuscitat-* 'raised again,' from the verb *resuscitare,* from *re-* 'back' + *suscitare* 'raise.'

res·ver·a·trol /ˌrezˈverətrāl/ ▶ **n.** Chemistry a polyphenol compound found in certain plants and in red wine that has antioxidant properties and has been investigated for possible anticarcinogenic effects.
– ORIGIN 1930s: blend of RESIN and VERATRUM (the plant from which the compound was first obtained) + -OL.

ret /ret/ ▶ **v.** (**rets, retting, retted**) [with obj.] soak (flax or hemp) in water to soften it and separate the fibers.
– ORIGIN late Middle English: related to Dutch *reten,* also to ROT.

ret. ▶ **abbr.** retired.

re·ta·ble /ˈrēˌtābəl, ˈretəbəl/ (also **retablo** /riˈtāblō/) ▶ **n.** (pl. **retables** or **retablos**) a frame or shelf enclosing decorated panels or revered objects above and behind an altar. ■ a painting or other image in such a position.
– ORIGIN early 19th cent.: from French *rétable,* from Spanish *retablo,* from medieval Latin *retrotabulum* 'rear table,' from Latin *retro* 'backward' + *tabula* 'table.'

re·tag /ˌrēˈtag/ ▶ **v.** (**retags, retagging, retagged**) [with obj.] assign or apply a new tag to.

re·tail /ˈrēˌtāl/ ▶ **n.** the sale of goods to the public in relatively small quantities for use or consumption rather than for resale: [as modifier] *the product's retail price.*
▶ **adv.** being sold in such a way: *it is not yet available retail.*
▶ **v.** [with obj.] **1** /ˈrēˌtāl/ sell (goods) to the public in such a way: *the difficulties in retailing the new products.* ■ [no obj.] (**retail at/for**) (of goods) be sold in this way for (a specified price): *the product retails for around $20.*
2 /ˈrēˌtāl, riˈtāl/ recount or relate details of (a story or event) to others: *his inimitable way of retailing a diverting anecdote.*
– DERIVATIVES **re·tail·er n.**
– ORIGIN late Middle English: from Anglo-Norman French *retaille* 'a piece cut off,' from *retaillier,* from *re-* (expressing intensive force) + *tailler* 'to cut.'

re·tail park ▶ **n.** a shopping development situated outside a town or city, typically containing a number of large chain stores.

re·tail pol·i·tics ▶ **plural n.** [also treated as sing.] (in the US) a style of political campaigning in which the candidate attends local events in order to target voters on a small-scale or individual basis.
– ORIGIN early 20th cent.: first referring to the practice of paying for votes.

re·tail ther·a·py ▶ **n.** humorous shopping in order to make oneself feel happier.

re·tain /riˈtān/ ▶ **v.** continue to have (something); keep possession of: *built in 1830, the house retains many of its original features.* ■ not abolish, discard, or alter: *the rights of defendants must be retained.* ■ keep in one's memory: *I retained a few French words and phrases.* ■ absorb and continue to hold (a substance): *limestone is known to retain water.* ■ (often as adj. **retaining**) keep (something) in place; hold fixed: *remove the retaining bar.* ■ keep (someone) engaged in one's service: *he has been retained as a freelance.* ■ secure the services of (a person, esp. an attorney) with a preliminary payment: *retain an attorney to handle the client's business.*
– DERIVATIVES **re·tain·a·bil·i·ty** /riˌtānəˈbilətē/ **n.**, **re·tain·a·ble adj.**, **re·tain·ment n.**
– ORIGIN late Middle English: via Anglo-Norman French from Old French *retenir,* from Latin *retinere,* from *re-* 'back' + *tenere* 'hold.'

re·tain·er /riˈtānər/ ▶ **n. 1** a thing that holds something in place: *a guitar string retainer.* ■ an appliance for keeping a loose tooth, an orthodontic prosthesis, or orthodontically aligned teeth in place.
2 a fee paid in advance to someone, esp. an attorney, in order to secure or keep their services when required.
3 a servant or follower of a noble or wealthy person, esp. one that has worked for a person or family for a long time.

re·tain·ing fee ▶ **n.** another term for RETAINER (sense 2).

re·tain·ing wall ▶ **n.** a wall that holds back earth or water.

re·take ▶ **v.** /rēˈtāk, ˈrē-/ (past **retook**; past participle **retaken**) [with obj.] take again, in particular: ■ take (a test or examination) again after a failure or irregularity: *Dan had to retake his driving test.* ■ regain possession or control of: *in 799, the Moors retook Barcelona.* ■ reshoot (a movie sequence or photograph) or rerecord (a piece of music).
▶ **n.** /ˈrēˌtāk/ a thing that is retaken, esp. a test or examination. ■ an instance of filming a scene, taking a photograph, or recording a piece of music again.

re·tal·i·ate /riˈtalēˌāt/ ▶ **v.** [no obj.] make an attack or assault in return for a similar attack: *the blow stung and she retaliated immediately.* ■ [with obj.] archaic repay (an injury or insult) in kind: *they used their abilities to retaliate the injury.*
– DERIVATIVES **re·tal·i·a·tive** /riˈtalēˌātiv, -ēətiv/ **adj.**, **re·tal·i·a·tor** /-ˌātər/ **n.**, **re·tal·i·a·to·ry** /riˈtalēəˌtôrē/ **adj.**
– ORIGIN early 17th cent.: from Latin *retaliat-* 'returned in kind,' from the verb *retaliare,* from *re-* 'back' + *talis* 'such.'

re·tal·i·a·tion /riˌtalēˈāsHən/ ▶ **n.** the action of returning a military attack; counterattack: *the bombings are believed to be in retaliation for the trial of 15 suspects.* ■ the action of harming someone because they have harmed oneself; revenge: *protectionism invites retaliation.*

re·tard ▶ **v.** /riˈtārd/ [with obj.] delay or hold back in terms of progress, development, or accomplishment: *his progress was retarded by his limp.*
▶ **n.** /ˈrēˌtārd/ offensive a mentally handicapped person (often used as a general term of abuse).
– DERIVATIVES **re·tar·da·tion** /ˌrēˌtārˈdāsHən, ri-/ **n.**, **re·tard·er n.**, **re·tard·ment n.** (rare).
– ORIGIN late 15th cent.: from French *retarder,* from Latin *retardare,* from *re-* 'back' + *tardus* 'slow.'

re·tar·dant /riˈtārdnt/ ▶ **adj.** [in combination] (chiefly of a synthetic or treated fabric or substance) not readily susceptible to fire: *fire-retardant polymers.*
▶ **n.** a fabric or substance that prevents or inhibits something, esp. the outbreak of fire.
– DERIVATIVES **re·tard·an·cy** /-ˈtārdnsē/ **n.**

re·tar·da·taire /riˌtārdəˈter/ ▶ **adj.** (of a work of art or architecture) executed in an earlier or outdated style.
– ORIGIN French.

re·tar·date /riˈtārˌdāt/ ▶ **n.** dated, offensive a mentally handicapped person.
– ORIGIN 1950s: from Latin *retardat-* 'slowed down,' from the verb *retardare* (see RETARD).

re·tard·ed /riˈtārdid/ ▶ **adj.** less advanced in mental, physical, or social development than is usual for one's age.

retch /recH/ ▶ **v.** [no obj.] make the sound and movement of vomiting. ■ vomit.
▶ **n.** a movement or sound of vomiting.
– ORIGIN mid 19th cent.: variant of dialect *reach,* from a Germanic base meaning 'spittle.'

retd (also **ret.**) ▶ **abbr.** retired (used after the name of a retired armed forces officer or in recording that a sports player retired from a game).

re·te /ˈrētē, ˈrātē/ ▶ **n.** (pl. **retia** /-tēə/) Anatomy an elaborate network of blood vessels or nerve cells.
– ORIGIN mid 16th cent.: from Latin, 'net.'

re·tell /ˌrēˈtel/ ▶ **v.** (past and past participle **retold**) [with obj.] tell (a story) again or differently: *Walker retells the history of the world from the black perspective.*

re·ten·tion /riˈtencHən/ ▶ **n.** the continued possession, use, or control of something: *the retention of direct control by central government.* ■ the fact of keeping something in one's memory: *the children's retention of facts.* ■ the action of absorbing and continuing to hold a substance: *the soil's retention of moisture.* ■ failure to eliminate a substance from the body: *eating too much salt can lead to fluid retention.*
– ORIGIN late Middle English (denoting the power to retain something): from Old French, from Latin *retentio(n-),* from *retinere* 'hold back' (see RETAIN).

re·ten·tive /riˈtentiv/ ▶ **adj. 1** (of a person's memory) having the ability to remember facts and impressions easily.
2 (of a substance) able to absorb and hold moisture. ■ chiefly Medicine serving to keep something in place.
– DERIVATIVES **re·ten·tive·ly adv.**, **re·ten·tive·ness n.**
– ORIGIN late Middle English: from Old French *retentif, -ive* or medieval Latin *retentivus,* from *retent-* 'held back,' from the verb *retinere* (see RETAIN).

re·ten·tiv·i·ty /ˌrēˌtenˈtivətē, ri-/ ▶ **n.** (pl. **retentivities**) Physics the ability of a substance to retain or resist magnetization, frequently measured as the strength of the magnetic field that remains in a sample after removal of an inducing field.

re·test ▶ **v.** /rēˈtest/ [with obj.] test (someone or something) again.
▶ **n.** /ˈrēˌtest/ an act of retesting or a repeated test: *he was freed on bond days after the retest and now is seeking a pardon.*

re·tex·ture /rēˈteksCHər/ ▶ **v.** [with obj.] treat (skin or hair) so as to restore a healthy or more youthful condition, esp. by moisturizing.

re·think ▶ **v.** /rēˈTHiNGk/ (past and past participle **rethought**) [with obj.] think again about (something such as a policy or course of action), esp. in order to make changes to it: *the government was forced to rethink its plans* | [no obj.] *I've had to rethink.*
▶ **n.** /ˈrēˌTHiNGk/ [in sing.] a reassessment of something, esp. one that results in changes being made: *a last-minute rethink of their tactics.*

re·tia /ˈrētēə, ˈrā-/ plural form of RETE.

re·ti·ar·i·us /ˌrēsHēˈe(ə)rēəs/ ▶ **n.** (pl. **retiarii** /-ˈe(ə)rēˌē, -ēˌī/) an ancient Roman gladiator armed with a net and a spear.
– ORIGIN Latin, from *rete* 'net.'

ret·i·cent /ˈretəsənt/ ▶ **adj.** not revealing one's thoughts or feelings readily: *she was extremely reticent about her personal affairs.*
– DERIVATIVES **ret·i·cence n.**, **ret·i·cent·ly adv.**
– ORIGIN mid 19th cent.: from Latin *reticent-* 'remaining silent,' from the verb *reticere,* from *re-* (expressing intensive force) + *tacere* 'be silent.'

ret·i·cle /ˈretikəl/ ▶ **n.** a series of fine lines or fibers in the eyepiece of an optical device, such as a telescope or microscope, or on the screen of an oscilloscope, used as a measuring scale or an aid in locating objects.
– ORIGIN mid 18th cent.: from Latin *reticulum* 'net.'

re·tic·u·la /riˈtikyələ/ plural form of RETICULUM.

re·tic·u·lar for·ma·tion /riˈtikyələr/ (also **reticular activating system**) ▶ **n.** Anatomy a diffuse network of nerve pathways in the brainstem connecting the spinal cord, cerebrum, and cerebellum, and mediating the overall level of consciousness.

r

re·tic·u·late ▶ **v.** /riˈtikyəˌlāt/ [with obj.] rare divide or mark (something) in such a way as to resemble a net or network: *the numerous canals and branches of the river reticulate the flat alluvial plain.*
▶ **adj.** /-lət, -ˌlāt/ chiefly Botany & Zoology reticulated.
– ORIGIN mid 17th cent.: from Latin *reticulatus* 'reticulated,' from *reticulum* (see RETICULUM).

re·tic·u·lat·ed /riˈtikyəˌlātid/ ▶ **adj.** [attrib.] constructed, arranged, or marked like a net or network: *a pinafore of a finely reticulated pattern.* ■ (of porcelain) having a pattern of interlacing lines, esp. of pierced work, forming a net or web. ■ Architecture relating to or denoting a style of decorated tracery characterized by circular shapes drawn at top and bottom into ogees, resulting in a netlike framework.

re·tic·u·lat·ed py·thon ▶ **n.** a very large Asian python patterned with dark patches outlined in black. It is the longest snake at up to 36 feet (11 m). ● *Python reticulatus*, family Pythonidae.

re·tic·u·la·tion /riˌtikyəˈlāSHən/ ▶ **n.** a pattern or arrangement of interlacing lines resembling a net: *the fish should have a blue back with white reticulation.* ■ Photography the formation of a network of wrinkles or cracks in a photographic emulsion.

ret·i·cule /ˈretiˌkyo͞ol/ ▶ **n.** **1** chiefly historical a woman's small handbag, originally netted and typically having a drawstring and decorated with embroidery or beading.
2 variant spelling of RETICLE.
– ORIGIN early 18th cent.: from French *réticule*, from Latin *reticulum* (see RETICULUM).

re·tic·u·lin /riˈtikyəlin/ ▶ **n.** Biochemistry a structural protein resembling collagen, present in connective tissue as a network of fine fibers, esp. around muscle and nerve fibers.
– ORIGIN late 19th cent.: from *reticular* (see RETICULUM) + -IN[1].

re·tic·u·lo·cyte /riˈtikyələˌsīt/ ▶ **n.** Physiology an immature red blood cell without a nucleus, having a granular or reticulated appearance when suitably stained.
– ORIGIN 1920s: from RETICULATED + -CYTE.

re·tic·u·lo·en·do·the·li·al /riˌtikyəˌlōˌendō-ˈTHēlēəl/ ▶ **adj.** [attrib.] Physiology relating to or denoting a diverse system of fixed and circulating phagocytic cells (macrophages and monocytes) involved in the immune response. They are spread throughout the body and are especially common in the liver, spleen, and lymphatic system. Also called LYMPHORETICULAR.
– ORIGIN 1920s: from RETICULUM + *endothelial* (see ENDOTHELIUM).

re·tic·u·lo·en·do·the·li·o·sis /riˌtikyəˌlōˌendō-ˌTHēlēˈōsəs/ ▶ **n.** Medicine overgrowth of some part of the reticuloendothelial system, causing isolated swelling of the bone marrow and in severe cases the destruction of the bones of the skull.

Re·tic·u·lum /riˈtikyələm/ Astronomy a small southern constellation (the Net), between Dorado and Hydrus. ■ (as genitive **Reticuli** /riˈtikyəˌlī/) used with a preceding letter or numeral to designate a star in this constellation: *the star Beta Reticuli.*
– ORIGIN Latin, diminutive of *rete* 'net.'

re·tic·u·lum /riˈtikyələm/ ▶ **n.** (pl. **reticula** /-lə/) **1** a fine network or netlike structure. See also ENDOPLASMIC RETICULUM.
2 Zoology the second stomach of a ruminant, having a honeycomblike structure, receiving food from the rumen and passing it to the omasum.
– DERIVATIVES **re·tic·u·lar** /-lər/ **adj.**
– ORIGIN mid 17th cent.: from Latin, diminutive of *rete* 'net.'

re·tie /ˌrēˈtī/ ▶ **v.** (**reties, retying, retied**) [with obj.] tie (something) again.

re·ti·form /ˈretəˌfôrm/ ▶ **adj.** rare netlike.
– ORIGIN late 17th cent.: from Latin *rete* 'net' + -IFORM.

ret·i·na /ˈretn-ə/ ▶ **n.** (pl. **retinas** or **retinae** /ˈretnˌē, ˈretnˌī/) a layer at the back of the eyeball containing cells that are sensitive to light and that trigger nerve impulses that pass via the optic nerve to the brain, where a visual image is formed.
– DERIVATIVES **ret·i·nal** /ˈretn-əl/ **adj.**
– ORIGIN late Middle English: from medieval Latin, from Latin *rete* 'net.'

Ret·in-A /ˈretn ˈā/ ▶ **n.** trademark a brand of tretinoin, used in the topical treatment of acne and to reduce wrinkles.

ret·i·nal scan·ner ▶ **n.** a biometric device that scans a person's or animal's retina in infrared for identification purposes.

ret·i·ni·tis /ˌretnˈītis/ ▶ **n.** Medicine inflammation of the retina of the eye.

ret·i·ni·tis pig·men·to·sa /ˌpigmənˈtōsə, -zə/ ▶ **n.** Medicine a chronic hereditary eye disease characterized by black pigmentation and gradual degeneration of the retina.
– ORIGIN mid 19th cent.: *pigmentosa*, feminine of Latin *pigmentosus*, from *pigmentum* 'pigment.'

ret·ino·blas·to·ma /ˌretnˌōˌblaˈstōmə/ ▶ **n.** Medicine a rare malignant tumor of the retina, affecting young children.

ret·i·no·ic ac·id /ˌretnˈōik/ ▶ **n.** a carboxylic acid, $C_{19}H_{27}COOH$, obtained from retinol by oxidation and used in ointments to treat acne.
– ORIGIN 1970s: from *retina*.

ret·i·noid /ˈretnˌoid/ ▶ **n.** Biochemistry any of a group of compounds having effects in the body like those of vitamin A.

ret·i·nol /ˈretnôl, -ˌōl/ ▶ **n.** Biochemistry a yellow compound found in green and yellow vegetables, egg yolk, and fish-liver oil. It is essential for growth and vision in dim light. Also called VITAMIN A. ● A carotenoid alcohol; chem. formula: $C_{20}H_{29}OH$.
– ORIGIN 1960s: from RETINA + -OL.

ret·i·nop·a·thy /ˌretnˈäpəTHē/ ▶ **n.** Medicine disease of the retina that results in impairment or loss of vision.

ret·i·nue /ˈretnˌ(y)o͞o/ ▶ **n.** a group of advisers, assistants, or others accompanying an important person.
– ORIGIN late Middle English: from Old French *retenue*, feminine past participle (used as a noun) of *retenir* 'keep back, retain.'

re·tire /riˈtīr/ ▶ **v.** **1** [no obj.] leave one's job and cease to work, typically upon reaching the normal age for leaving employment: *he retired from the navy in 1966.* ■ [with obj.] compel (an employee) to leave their job, esp. before they have reached such an age: *the home office retired him.* ■ (of an athlete) cease to play competitively: *he retired from football several years ago.* ■ (of an athlete) withdraw from a race or match, typically as a result of accident or injury: *he was forced to retire to the bench* | [with complement] *Stewart retired hurt.* ■ [with obj.] Baseball put out (a batter); cause (a side) to end a turn at bat: *the pitcher retired twelve batters in a row.* ■ [with obj.] Economics withdraw (a bill or note) from circulation or currency. ■ Finance pay off or cancel (a debt): *the debt is to be retired from state gaming-tax receipts.*
2 withdraw to or from a particular place: *she retired into the bathroom with her toothbrush.* ■ (of a military force) retreat from an enemy or an attacking position: *lack of numbers compelled the cavalry to retire.* ■ [with obj.] order (a military force) to retreat: *the general retired all his troops.* ■ (of a jury) leave the courtroom to decide the verdict of a trial. ■ go to bed: *everyone retired early that night.*
– DERIVATIVES **re·tir·er** **n.**
– ORIGIN mid 16th cent. (in the sense 'withdraw (to a place of safety or seclusion)'): from French *retirer*, from *re-* 'back' + *tirer* 'draw.'

re·ti·ré /rəˌtēˈrā/ ▶ **n.** (pl. **same**) Ballet a movement in which one leg is bent and raised at right angles to the body until the toe is in line with the knee of the supporting leg.
– ORIGIN French, literally 'drawn back.'

re·tired /riˈtīrd/ ▶ **adj.** **1** having left one's job and ceased to work: *a retired teacher.*
2 archaic (of a place) quiet and secluded; not seen or frequented by many people: *this retired corner of the world.* ■ (of a person's way of life) quiet and involving little contact with other people. ■ (of a person) reserved; uncommunicative.
– DERIVATIVES **re·tired·ness** **n.** (archaic).

re·tir·ee /riˌtīˈrē/ ▶ **n.** a person who has retired from full-time work.

re·tire·ment /riˈtīrmənt/ ▶ **n.** **1** the action or fact of leaving one's job and ceasing to work: *a man nearing retirement* | *the library has seen a large number of retirements this year.* ■ the period of one's life after leaving one's job and ceasing to work: *he spent much of his retirement traveling in Europe.* ■ the action or fact of ceasing to play a sport competitively.
2 the withdrawal of a jury from the courtroom to decide their verdict. ■ the period of time during which a jury decides their verdict: *a three-hour retirement.*
3 seclusion: *he lived in retirement in Miami.* ■ archaic a secluded or private place: *Vermont, where he has a sweet country retirement.*

re·tire·ment age ▶ **n.** the age at which most people normally retire from work, traditionally specified as age 65.

re·tire·ment home ▶ **n.** a house or apartment in which a person lives in old age, esp. one in a complex designed for the needs of old people. ■ an institution for elderly people needing care.

re·tir·ing /riˈtīriNG/ ▶ **adj.** shy and fond of being on one's own: *a retiring, acquiescent woman.*
– DERIVATIVES **re·tir·ing·ly** **adv.**

re·took /rēˈto͝ok/ past of RETAKE.

re·tool /rēˈto͞ol/ ▶ **v.** [with obj.] equip (a factory) with new or adapted tools. ■ adapt or alter (someone or something) to make them more useful or suitable: *he likes to retool the old stories to make them relevant for today's kids* | [no obj.] *perhaps one can even retool for the afterlife.*

re·tort[1] /riˈtôrt/ ▶ **v.** **1** [reporting verb] say something in answer to a remark or accusation, typically in a sharp, angry, or wittily incisive manner: [with direct speech] *"No need to be rude," retorted Isabel* | [with clause] *he retorted that this was nonsense* | [no obj.] *I resisted the urge to retort.*
2 [with obj.] archaic repay (an insult or injury): *it was now his time to retort the humiliation.* ■ turn (an insult or accusation) back on the person who has issued it: *he was resolute to retort the charge of treason on his foes.* ■ use (an opponent's argument) against them: *the answer they make to us may very easily be retorted.*
▶ **n.** a sharp, angry, or wittily incisive reply to a remark: *she opened her mouth to make a suitably cutting retort.*
– ORIGIN late 15th cent. (in the sense 'hurl back (an accusation or insult)'): from Latin *retort-* 'twisted back, cast back,' from the verb *retorquere*, from *re-* 'in return' + *torquere* 'to twist.'

re·tort[2] ▶ **n.** **1** a container or furnace for carrying out a chemical process on a large or industrial scale.
2 historical a glass container with a long neck, used in distilling liquids and other chemical operations.
▶ **v.** [with obj.] heat in a retort in order to separate or purify: *the raw shale is retorted at four crude oil works.*

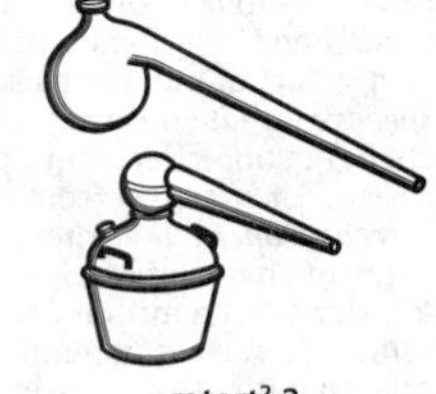
retort[2] 2

– ORIGIN early 17th cent.: from French *retorte*, from medieval Latin *retorta*, feminine past participle of *retorquere* 'twist back' (with reference to the long recurved neck of the laboratory container).

re·touch /rēˈtəCH/ ▶ **v.** [with obj.] improve or repair (a painting, a photograph, makeup, etc.) by making slight additions or alterations.
– DERIVATIVES **re·touch·er** **n.**
– ORIGIN late 17th cent.: probably from French *retoucher*.

re·trace /rēˈtrās/ ▶ **v.** [with obj.] go back over (the same route that one has just taken): *he began to retrace his steps to the parking lot.* ■ discover and follow (a route or course taken by someone else): *I've tried to retrace some of her movements.* ■ trace (something) back to its source or beginning: *I wanted to retrace a particular evolutionary pathway.*
– ORIGIN late 17th cent.: from French *retracer*.

re·tract /riˈtrakt/ ▶ **v.** draw or be drawn back or back in: [with obj.] *she retracted her hand as if she'd been burned* | [no obj.] *the tentacle retracted quickly.* ■ [with obj.] withdraw (a statement or accusation) as untrue or unjustified: *he retracted his allegations.* ■ [with obj.] withdraw or go back on (an undertaking or promise): *the parish council was forced to retract a previous resolution.*
– DERIVATIVES **re·tract·a·ble** **adj.**, **re·trac·tion** /riˈtrakSHən/ **n.**, **re·trac·tive** /-tiv/ **adj.**
– ORIGIN late Middle English: from Latin *retract-* 'drawn back,' from the verb *retrahere* (from *re-* 'back' + *trahere* 'drag'); the senses 'withdraw (a statement)' and 'go back on' via Old French from *retractare* 'reconsider' (based on *trahere* 'drag').

re·trac·tile /riˈtraktəl, -ˌtīl/ ▶ **adj.** Zoology capable of being retracted: *a long retractile proboscis.*
– DERIVATIVES **re·trac·til·i·ty** /ˌrēˌtrakˈtilətē/ **n.**
– ORIGIN late 18th cent.: from RETRACT, on the pattern of *contractile*.

re·trac·tor /riˈtraktər/ ▶ **n.** a device for retracting something: *seat belts with automatic retractors.* ■ (also **retractor muscle**) chiefly Zoology a muscle serving to retract a part of the body. Compare with PROTRACTOR.

re·train /rēˈtrān/ ▶ **v.** [with obj.] teach (someone) new skills, esp. so that they can do a different job. ■ [no obj.] learn new skills, esp. so as to be able to do a different job: *a workforce which is willing to retrain.*

PRONUNCIATION KEY ə *ago, up*; ər *over, fur*; a *hat*; ā *ate*; ä *car*; e *let*; ē *see*; i *fit*; ī *by*; NG *sing*; ō *go*; ô *law, for*; oi *toy*; o͝o *good*; o͞o *goo*; ou *out*; TH *thin*; T͟H *then*; ZH *vision*

r

re·trans·late /ˌrētransˈlāt, -tranz-/ ▶ **v.** [with obj.] translate (a translation) back into its original language.
– DERIVATIVES **re·trans·la·tion** /-ˈlāSHən/ **n.**

re·trans·mit /ˌrētransˈmit, -tranz-/ ▶ **v.** (**retransmits, retransmitting, retransmitted**) [with obj.] transmit (data, a radio signal, or a broadcast program) again or on to another receiver.
– DERIVATIVES **re·trans·mis·sion** /-ˈmiSHən/ **n.**

re·tread ▶ **v.** /rēˈtred/ **1** (past **retrod**; past participle **retrodden**) [with obj.] go back over (a path or one's steps): *they never retread the same ground.*
2 (past and past participle **retreaded**) [with obj.] put a new tread on (a worn tire).
▶ **n.** /ˈrēˌtred/ a tire that has been given a new tread. ■ informal a person retrained for new work or recalled for service. ■ informal a superficially altered version of an original: *a retread of the 30s romantic comedy.*

re·treat /riˈtrēt/ ▶ **v.** [no obj.] (of an army) withdraw from enemy forces as a result of their superior power or after a defeat: *the French retreated in disarray.* ■ move back or withdraw: *it becomes so hot that the lizards retreat into the shade | a series of trenches which filled with water when the ice retreated |* (as adj. **retreating**) *the sound of retreating footsteps.* ■ withdraw to a quiet or secluded place: *after the funeral he retreated to the shore.* ■ change one's decisions, plans, or attitude, as a result of criticism from others: *his proposals were clearly unreasonable and he was soon forced to retreat.* ■ (of shares of stock) decline in value: [with complement] *shares retreated 32 points to 653 points.* ■ [with obj.] Chess move (a piece) back from a forward or threatened position on the board.
▶ **n. 1** an act of moving back or withdrawing: *a speedy retreat | the army was in retreat.* ■ an act of changing one's decisions, plans, or attitude, esp. as a result of criticism from others: *the unions made a retreat from their earlier position.* ■ a decline in the value of shares of stock.
2 a signal for a military force to withdraw: *the bugle sounded a retreat.* ■ a military musical ceremony carried out at sunset, originating in the playing of drums and bugles to tell soldiers to return to camp for the night.
3 a quiet or secluded place in which one can rest and relax: *their mountain retreat in New Hampshire.* ■ a period of seclusion for the purposes of prayer and meditation: *the bishop is away on his annual retreat | before his ordination he went on retreat.*
– PHRASES **beat a retreat** see **BEAT**.
– ORIGIN late Middle English: from Old French *retret* (noun), *retraiter* (verb), from Latin *retrahere* 'pull back' (see **RETRACT**).

re·trench /riˈtrenCH/ ▶ **v.** [no obj.] (of a company, government, or individual) reduce costs or spending in response to economic difficulty: *as a result of the recession the company retrenched |* [with obj.] *if people are forced to retrench their expenditure trade will suffer.* ■ [with obj.] formal reduce or diminish (something) in extent or quantity: *right-wing parties which seek to retrench the welfare state.*
– DERIVATIVES **re·trench·ment** **n.**
– ORIGIN late 16th cent. (in the now formal usage): from obsolete French *retrencher*, variant of *retrancher*, from *re-* (expressing reversal) + *trancher* 'to cut, slice.'

re·tri·al /rēˈtrīəl, ˈrēˌtrīəl/ ▶ **n.** Law a second or further trial.

ret·ri·bu·tion /ˌretrəˈbyo͞oSHən/ ▶ **n.** punishment that is considered to be morally right and fully deserved: *settlers drove the Navajo out of Arizona in retribution for their raids.*
– DERIVATIVES **re·trib·u·tive** /riˈtribyətiv/ **adj.**, **re·trib·u·to·ry** /riˈtribyəˌtôrē/ **adj.**
– ORIGIN late Middle English (also in the sense 'recompense for merit or a service'): from late Latin *retributio(n-)*, from *retribut-* 'assigned again,' from the verb *retribuere*, from *re-* 'back' + *tribuere* 'assign.'

re·triev·al /riˈtrēvəl/ ▶ **n.** the process of getting something back from somewhere: *the investigation was completed after the retrieval of plane wreckage.* ■ the obtaining or consulting of material stored in a computer system.

re·trieve /riˈtrēv/ ▶ **v.** [with obj.] get or bring (something) back; regain possession of: *I was sent to retrieve the balls from his garden | Steven stooped and retrieved his hat.* ■ (of a dog) find and bring back (game or an object). ■ bring (something) back into one's mind: *the police hope to encourage him to retrieve forgotten memories.* ■ find or extract (information stored in a computer). ■ put right or improve (an unwelcome situation): *he made one last desperate attempt to retrieve the situation.* ■ [no obj.] reel or bring in a fishing line.
▶ **n. 1** an act of retrieving something, esp. game that has been shot. ■ an act of reeling or drawing in a fishing line.
2 archaic the possibility of recovery: *he ruined himself beyond retrieve.*
– DERIVATIVES **re·triev·a·bil·i·ty** /riˌtrēvəˈbilətē/ **n.**, **re·triev·a·ble adj.**
– ORIGIN late Middle English (in the sense 'find lost game,' said of a hunting dog): from Old French *retroeve-*, stressed stem of *retrover* 'find again.'

re·triev·er /riˈtrēvər/ ▶ **n. 1** a dog of a breed used for retrieving game.
2 a person or thing that retrieves something.

ret·ro[1] /ˈretrō/ ▶ **adj.** imitative of a style, fashion, or design from the recent past: *retro 60s fashions.*
▶ **n.** clothes or music whose style or design is imitative of those of the recent past: *a look that mixes Italian casual wear and American retro.*
– ORIGIN 1960s: from French *rétro*, abbreviation of *rétrograde* 'retrograde.'

ret·ro[2] ▶ **n.** (pl. **retros**) short for **RETROROCKET**.

retro- ▶ **comb. form 1** denoting action that is directed backward or is reciprocal: *retrocede | retroject.*
2 denoting location behind: *retrosternal | retrochoir.*
– ORIGIN from Latin *retro* 'backward.'

ret·ro·ac·tive /ˌretrōˈaktiv/ ▶ **adj.** (esp. of legislation) taking effect from a date in the past: *a big retroactive tax increase.*
– DERIVATIVES **ret·ro·ac·tion** /-ˈakSHən/ **n.**, **ret·ro·ac·tive·ly adv.**, **ret·ro·ac·tiv·i·ty** /-ˌakˈtivətē/ **n.**

ret·ro·ac·tive in·hi·bi·tion ▶ **n.** Psychology the tendency of later learning to hinder the memory of previously learned material.

ret·ro·bul·bar /ˌretrōˈbəlbər, -ˌbär/ ▶ **adj.** [attrib.] Anatomy & Medicine situated or occurring behind the eyeball: *a retrobulbar abscess.*

ret·ro·cede /ˌretrəˈsēd/ ▶ **v.** [with obj.] rare cede (territory) back again: *the islands were thrice captured by the English and thrice retroceded to France.*
– DERIVATIVES **ret·ro·ces·sion** /-ˈseSHən/ **n.**
– ORIGIN early 19th cent.: from French *rétrocéder*.

ret·ro·choir /ˈretrōˌkwīr/ ▶ **n.** the interior of a cathedral or large church behind the high altar.
– ORIGIN mid 19th cent.: from medieval Latin *retrochorus* (see **RETRO-**, **CHOIR**).

re·trod /rēˈträd/ past of **RETREAD** (sense 1 of the verb).

re·trod·den /rēˈträdn/ past participle of **RETREAD** (sense 1 of the verb).

ret·ro·dict /ˌretrōˈdikt/ ▶ **v.** [with obj.] state a fact about the past based on inference or deduction, rather than evidence.
– DERIVATIVES **ret·ro·dic·tion n.**
– ORIGIN 1940s: on the pattern of *predict*.

ret·ro·fit /ˌretrōˈfit/ ▶ **v.** (**retrofits, retrofitting, retrofitted**) [with obj.] add (a component or accessory) to something that did not have it when manufactured: *drivers who retrofit catalysts to older cars.* ■ provide (something) with a component or accessory not fitted to it during manufacture: *buses have been retrofitted with easy-access features.*
▶ **n.** an act of adding a component or accessory to something that did not have it when manufactured. ■ a component or accessory added to something after manufacture.
– ORIGIN 1950s: blend of **RETROACTIVE** and **REFIT**.

ret·ro·flex /ˈretrəˌfleks/ (also **retroflexed**) ▶ **adj.** Anatomy & Medicine turned backward: *retroflex fibers.* ■ Phonetics pronounced with the tip of the tongue curled up toward the hard palate: *the retroflex /r/.*
– DERIVATIVES **ret·ro·flex·ion** /ˌretrəˈflekSHən/ **n.**
– ORIGIN late 18th cent.: from Latin *retroflex-* 'bent backward,' from the verb *retroflectere*, from *retro* 'backward' + *flectere* 'to bend.'

ret·ro·fu·tur·ism /ˌretrōˈfyo͞oCHəˌrizm/ ▶ **n.** the use of a style or aesthetic considered futuristic in an earlier era.
– DERIVATIVES **ret·ro·fu·tur·is·tic adj.**

ret·ro·gra·da·tion /ˌretrōgrāˈdāSHən/ ▶ **n.** Astronomy & Astrology the apparent temporary reverse motion of a planet (from east to west), resulting from the relative orbital progress of the earth and the planet. ■ the orbiting or rotation of a planet or planetary satellite in a reverse direction from that normal in the solar system.
– ORIGIN mid 16th cent.: from late Latin *retrogradatio(n)-* (see **RETRO-**, **GRADATION**).

ret·ro·grade /ˈretrəˌgrād/ ▶ **adj.** directed or moving backward: *a retrograde flow.* ■ reverting to an earlier and inferior condition: *to go back on the progress that has been made would be a retrograde step.* ■ (of the order of something) reversed; inverse: *the retrograde form of these inscriptions.* ■ (of amnesia) involving the period immediately preceding the causal event. ■ Geology (of a metamorphic change) resulting from a decrease in temperature or pressure. ■ Astronomy & Astrology (of the apparent motion of a planet) in a reverse direction from normal (from east to west), resulting from the relative orbital progress of the earth and the planet. The opposite of **PROGRADE**. ■ Astronomy (of the orbit or rotation of a planet or planetary satellite) in a reverse direction from that normal in the solar system.
▶ **n.** rare a degenerate person.
▶ **v.** [no obj.] **1** archaic go back in position or time: *our history must retrograde for the space of a few pages.* ■ revert to an earlier and usually inferior condition: *people cannot habitually trample on law and justice without retrograding toward barbarism.*
2 Astronomy show retrogradation: *all the planets will at some time appear to retrograde.*
– DERIVATIVES **ret·ro·grade·ly adv.** (rare).
– ORIGIN late Middle English (as a term in astronomy): from Latin *retrogradus*, from *retro* 'backward' + *gradus* 'step' (from *gradi* 'to walk').

ret·ro·gress /ˌretrəˈgres/ ▶ **v.** [no obj.] go back to an earlier state, typically a worse one: *she retrogressed to the starting point of her rehabilitation.*
– ORIGIN early 19th cent.: from **RETRO-** 'back,' on the pattern of the verb *progress*.

ret·ro·gres·sion /ˌretrəˈgreSHən/ ▶ **n. 1** the process of returning to an earlier state, typically a worse one: *a kind of extreme retrogression to 19th-century attitudes.*
2 Astronomy another term for **RETROGRADATION**.
– DERIVATIVES **ret·ro·gres·sive** /-ˈgresiv/ **adj.**
– ORIGIN mid 17th cent.: from **RETRO-** 'backward,' on the pattern of *progression*.

ret·ro·ject /ˈretrəˌjekt/ ▶ **v.** [with obj.] rare project backward: *the rabbinic interpretation is retrojected into the biblical text.*
– ORIGIN mid 19th cent.: from **RETRO-** 'backward,' on the pattern of the verb *project*.

ret·ro·len·tal fi·bro·pla·sia /ˌretrəˈlentl ˌfībrəˈplāZHə/ ▶ **n.** Medicine abnormal proliferation of fibrous tissue immediately behind the lens of the eye, leading to blindness. It affected many premature babies in the 1950s, owing to the excessive administration of oxygen.

ret·ro·nym /ˈretrōnim/ ▶ **n.** a new term created from an existing word in order to distinguish it from the meaning that has emerged through progress or technological development (e.g., *cloth diaper* is a retronym necessitated by the fact that *diaper* now more commonly refers to a disposable diaper).
– ORIGIN 1980s: blend of **RETRO-** and **-ONYM**.

ret·ro·per·i·to·ne·al /ˌretrōˌperətnˈēəl/ ▶ **adj.** Anatomy & Medicine situated or occurring behind the peritoneum.

ret·ro·re·flec·tor /ˌretrōriˈflektər/ ▶ **n.** a device that reflects light back along the incident path, irrespective of the angle of incidence.
– DERIVATIVES **ret·ro·re·flec·tive** /-ˈflektiv/ **adj.**

ret·ro·rock·et /ˈretrōˌräkit/ ▶ **n.** a small auxiliary rocket on a spacecraft or missile, fired in the direction of travel to slow the craft down, for example, when landing on the surface of a planet.

re·trorse /ˈrēˌtrôrs/ ▶ **adj.** Biology turned or pointing backward: *retrorse spines.*
– ORIGIN early 19th cent.: from Latin *retrorsus*, contraction of *retroversus*, from *retro* 'backward' + *versus* 'turned' (past participle of *vertere*).

ret·ro·spect /ˈretrəˌspekt/ ▶ **n.** a survey or review of a past course of events or period of time.
– PHRASES **in retrospect** when looking back on a past event or situation; with hindsight: *perhaps, in retrospect, I shouldn't have gone.*
– ORIGIN early 17th cent.: from **RETRO-** 'back,' on the pattern of the noun *prospect*.

ret·ro·spec·tion /ˌretrəˈspekSHən/ ▶ **n.** the action of looking back on or reviewing past events or situations, esp. those in one's own life: *he was disinclined to indulge in retrospection.*
– ORIGIN mid 17th cent.: probably from **RETROSPECT** (used as a verb).

ret·ro·spec·tive /ˌretrəˈspektiv/ ▶ **adj.** looking back on or dealing with past events or situations: *our survey was retrospective.* ■ (of an exhibition or compilation) showing the development of an artist's work over a period of time. ■ (of a statute or legal decision) taking effect from a date in the past: *retrospective pay awards.*
▶ **n.** an exhibition or compilation showing the development of the work of a particular artist over a period of time: *a Georgia O'Keeffe retrospective.*
– DERIVATIVES **ret·ro·spec·tive·ly adv.**

ret·ro·ster·nal /ˌretrōˈstərnl/ ▶ **adj.** Anatomy & Medicine behind the breastbone.

ret·ro·trans·po·son /ˌretrōtransˈpōˌzän, -tranz-/ ▶ **n.** Genetics a transposon whose sequence shows homology with that of a retrovirus.

r

ret·rous·sé /rə,trōō'sā ,retrōō-/ ▶ **adj.** (of a person's nose) turned up at the tip, esp. in an attractive way.
– ORIGIN early 19th cent.: French, literally 'tucked up,' past participle of *retrousser*.

ret·ro·vert·ed /,retrə'vərtəd/ ▶ **adj.** Anatomy (of the uterus) tilted abnormally backward.
– DERIVATIVES **ret·ro·ver·sion** /-'vərZHən/ **n.**
– ORIGIN late 18th cent.: from Latin *retrovertere* 'turn backward' + **-ED**[2].

Ret·ro·vir /'retrō,vi(ə)r/ ▶ **n.** trademark for **ZIDOVUDINE**.
– ORIGIN 1980s: abbreviation of **RETROVIRUS**.

ret·ro·vi·rus /,retrō'vīrəs, 'retrō,vīrəs/ ▶ **n.** Biology any of a group of RNA viruses that insert a DNA copy of their genome into the host cell in order to replicate, e.g., HIV.
– ORIGIN 1970s: modern Latin, from the initial letters of *reverse transcriptase* + **VIRUS**.

re·try /rē'trī/ ▶ **v.** (**retries, retrying, retried**) **1** [with obj.] Law try (a defendant or case) again.
2 [no obj.] Computing re-enter a command, esp. differently because one has made an error the first time. ■ (of a system) transmit data again because the first attempt was unsuccessful.
▶ **n.** an instance of re-entering a command or retransmitting data.

ret·si·na /ret'sēnə/ ▶ **n.** a Greek white or rosé wine flavored with resin.
– ORIGIN modern Greek.

re·tune /rē't(y)ōōn/ ▶ **v.** [with obj.] tune (something) again or differently, in particular: ■ put (a musical instrument) back in tune or alter its pitch. ■ tune (a radio, television, or other piece of electronic equipment) to a different frequency.

re·turn /ri'tərn/ ▶ **v. 1** [no obj.] come or go back to a place or person: *he* ***returned to*** *Canada in the fall.* ■ (**return to**) go back to (a particular state or activity): *Ollie had returned to full health.* ■ (**return to**) turn one's attention back to (something): *he returned to his newspaper.* ■ (esp. of a feeling) come back or recur after a period of absence: *her appetite had returned.*
2 [with obj.] give, put, or send (something) back to a place or person: *complete the application form and* ***return it to this address.*** ■ feel, say, or do (the same feeling, action, etc.) in response: *she returned his kiss.* ■ (in tennis and other sports) hit or send (the ball) back to an opponent. ■ Football run upfield with the ball after fielding (a kick), intercepting (a pass), or recovering (a fumble). ■ (of a judge or jury) state or present (a verdict) in response to a formal request. ■ Bridge lead (a card of a suit led earlier by one's partner). ■ Architecture continue (a wall) in a changed direction, esp. at right angles.
3 [with obj.] yield or make (a profit): *the company returned a profit of 4.3 million dollars.*
4 [with obj.] (of an electorate) elect (a person or party) to office: *the Democrat was returned in the third district.*
▶ **n. 1** an act of coming or going back to a place or activity: *he celebrated his safe return from the war* | [as modifier] *a return flight.* ■ [in sing.] an act of going back to an earlier state or condition: *the designer advocated a return to elegance.* ■ the action of giving, sending, or putting something back: *we demand the return of our books and papers.* ■ Football a play in which the ball is caught after a kick or pass interception and is advanced by running; an advance of this kind. ■ (in tennis and other sports) a stroke played in response to a serve or other stroke by one's opponent. ■ a thing that has been given or sent back, esp. an unwanted ticket for a sports event or play. ■ (also **return ticket**) chiefly Brit. a ticket that allows someone to travel to a place and back again; a round trip ticket. ■ an electrical conductor bringing a current back to its source. ■ (also **return game**) a second contest between the same opponents.
2 (often **returns**) a profit from an investment: *product areas are being developed to produce maximum returns.* ■ a good rate of return.
3 an official report or statement submitted in response to a formal demand: *census returns.* ■ Law an endorsement or report by a court officer or sheriff on a writ.
4 election to office: *we campaigned for the return of Young and Elkins.* ■ an official report of the results of an election: *falsification of the election return.*
5 (also **carriage return**) a key pressed to move the carriage of an electric typewriter back to a fixed position. ■ (also **return key**) a key pressed on a computer keyboard to simulate a carriage return in a word-processing program, or to indicate the end of a command or data string.
6 Architecture a part receding from the line of the front, for example the side of a house or of a window opening.
– PHRASES **in return** as a response, exchange, or reward for something: *he leaves the house to his sister in return for her kindness.* **many happy returns** (**of the day**) used as a greeting to someone on their birthday. **return thanks** express thanks, esp. in a grace at a meal or in response to a toast or condolence.
– DERIVATIVES **re·turn·a·ble adj.**, **re·turn·er n.**
– ORIGIN Middle English: the verb from Old French *returner*, from Latin *re-* 'back' + *tornare* 'to turn'; the noun via Anglo-Norman French.

re·turn·ee /ri,tər'nē/ ▶ **n.** a person who returns, esp. after a prolonged absence, in particular: ■ a member of the armed forces returning from overseas duty. ■ a refugee returning from abroad.

re·turn·ing of·fi·cer ▶ **n.** (in the UK, Canada, New Zealand, and Australia) the official in each constituency or electorate who conducts an election and announces the result.

re·type /,rē'tīp/ ▶ **v.** [with obj.] type (text) again on a typewriter or computer, esp. to correct errors.

Reu·ben /'rōōbən/ (in the Bible) a Hebrew patriarch, eldest son of Jacob and Leah. ■ the tribe of Israel traditionally descended from him.

re·u·ni·fy /rē'yōōnə,fī/ ▶ **v.** (**reunifies, reunifying, reunified**) [with obj.] restore political unity to (a place or group, esp. a divided territory): *Charlemagne's attempts to reunify Western Europe.*
– DERIVATIVES **re·u·ni·fi·ca·tion** /,rē,yōōnəfi'kāSHən/ **n.**

re·un·ion /rē'yōōnyən/ ▶ **n.** an instance of two or more people coming together again after a period of separation: *she had a tearful reunion with her parents.* ■ a social gathering attended by members of a certain group of people who have not seen each other for some time: *a school reunion.* ■ the act or process of being brought together again as a unified whole: *the reunion of East and West Germany.*
– ORIGIN early 17th cent.: from French *réunion* or Anglo-Latin *reunio(n-)*, from Latin *reunire* 'unite.'

Ré·union /rē'yōōnyən, rā-Y'nyôN/ a volcanically active, subtropical island in the Indian Ocean, east of Madagascar, one of the Mascarene Islands; pop. 807,000 (est. 2007); capital, Saint-Denis. A French possession since 1638, the island became an administrative region of France in 1974.

re·u·nite /,rēyōō'nīt/ ▶ **v.** come together or cause to come together again after a period of separation or disunity: [no obj.] *the three friends reunited in 1959* | [with obj.] *Stephanie was* ***reunited with*** *her parents.*

re·up·hol·ster /,rēəp'hōlstər, ,rēə'pōl-/ ▶ **v.** [with obj.] upholster with new materials, esp. with a different fabric: *the bed was reupholstered in chintz.*
– DERIVATIVES **re·up·hol·ster·y** /-stərē/ **n.**

re·up·take /,rē'əptāk/ ▶ **n.** Physiology the absorption by a presynaptic nerve ending of a neurotransmitter that it has secreted.

re·use ▶ **v.** /rē'yōōz/ [with obj.] use again or more than once: *the tape could be magnetically erased and reused.*
▶ **n.** /re'yōōs/ the action of using something again: *the ballast was cleaned and ready for reuse.*
– DERIVATIVES **re·us·a·ble** /rē'yōōzəbəl/ **adj.**

Reu·ter /'roitər/, Paul Julius, Baron von (1816–99), German pioneer of telegraphy and news reporting; born *Israel Beer Josaphat*. He founded the news agency Reuters.

Reu·ters /'roitərz/ an international news agency founded in London in 1851 by Paul Julius Reuter. The agency pioneered the use of telegraphy, building up a service used today by newspapers and radio and television stations in most countries.

Reu·ther /'rōōTHər/, Walter (Philip) (1907–70), US labor leader. He was president of the United Automobile Workers 1946–70 and of the Congress of Industrial Organizations from 1952 until 1955 when it merged with the American Federation of Labor.

rev /rev/ informal ▶ **n.** (usu. **revs**) a revolution of an engine per minute: *an engine speed of 1,750 revs.* ■ an act of increasing the speed of revolution of a vehicle's engine by pressing the accelerator, esp. while the clutch is disengaged.
▶ **v.** (**revs, revving, revved**) [with obj.] increase the running speed of (an engine) or the engine speed of (a vehicle) by pressing the accelerator, esp. while the clutch is disengaged: *he got into the car,* ***revved up*** *the engine and drove off* | [no obj.] *I revved up enthusiastically.* ■ [no obj.] (of an engine or vehicle) operate with increasing speed when the accelerator is pressed, esp. while the clutch is disengaged: *he could hear the sound of an engine revving nearby.* ■ make or become more active or energetic: [no obj.] *he's revving up for next week's World Cup game* | [with obj.] *we need to rev up the economy.*
– ORIGIN early 20th cent.: abbreviation of **REVOLUTION**.

Rev. ▶ **abbr.** ■ Bible the book of Revelation. ■ (as the title of a priest) Reverend.

re·vac·ci·nate /,rē'vaksə,nāt/ ▶ **v.** [with obj.] vaccinate again for the same disease.
– DERIVATIVES **re·vac·ci·na·tion n.**

re·val·ue /rē'valyōō/ ▶ **v.** (**revalues, revaluing, revalued**) [with obj.] assess the value of (something) again. ■ Economics adjust the value of (a currency) in relation to other currencies.
– DERIVATIVES **re·val·u·a·tion** /rē,valyōō'āSHən/ **n.**

re·vamp /rē'vamp/ ▶ **v.** [with obj.] give new and improved form, structure, or appearance to: *an attempt to revamp the museum's image* | (as adj. **revamped**) *a revamped magazine.*
▶ **n.** [usu. in sing.] an act of improving the form, structure, or appearance of something. ■ a new and improved version: *the show was a revamp of an old idea.*

re·vanche /rə'vänSH/ ▶ **n.** the policy of a nation to seek the return of lost territory.
– ORIGIN French, literally 'revenge.'

re·vanch·ism /rə'vän,SHizəm/ ▶ **n.** a policy of seeking to retaliate, esp. to recover lost territory.
– DERIVATIVES **re·vanch·ist adj. & n.**
– ORIGIN 1950s: from French *revanche* (see **REVANCHE**) + **-ISM**. The form *revanchist* dates from the 1920s.

Revd ▶ **abbr.** (as the title of a priest) Reverend.

re·veal[1] /ri'vēl/ ▶ **v.** [with obj.] make (previously unknown or secret information) known to others: *Brenda was forced to reveal Robbie's whereabouts* | [with clause] *he revealed that he and his children had received death threats.* ■ cause or allow (something) to be seen: *the clouds were breaking up to reveal a clear blue sky.* ■ make (something) known to humans by divine or supernatural means: *the truth revealed at the Incarnation.*
– DERIVATIVES **re·veal·a·ble adj.**, **re·veal·er n.**
– ORIGIN late Middle English: from Old French *reveler* or Latin *revelare*, from *re-* 'again' (expressing reversal) + *velum* 'veil.'

re·veal[2] ▶ **n.** either side surface of an aperture in a wall for a door or window.
– ORIGIN late 17th cent.: from obsolete *revale* 'to lower,' from Old French *revaler*, from *re-* 'back' + *avaler* 'go down, sink.'

re·vealed re·li·gion ▶ **n.** religion based on divine revelation rather than reason.

re·veal·ing /ri'vēliNG/ ▶ **adj.** making interesting or significant information known, esp. about a person's attitude or character: *a revealing radio interview.* ■ (of an item of clothing) allowing more of the wearer's body to be seen than is usual: *a very revealing dress.*
– DERIVATIVES **re·veal·ing·ly adv.**

re·veg·e·tate /rē'vejə,tāt/ ▶ **v.** [with obj.] produce a new growth of vegetation on (disturbed or barren ground).
– DERIVATIVES **re·veg·e·ta·tion** /rē,vejə'tāSHən/ **n.**

rev·eil·le /'revəlē/ ▶ **n.** [in sing.] a signal sounded esp. on a bugle or drum to wake personnel in the armed forces.
– ORIGIN mid 17th cent.: from French *réveillez!* 'wake up!,' imperative plural of *réveiller*, based on Latin *vigilare* 'keep watch.'

rev·el /'revəl/ ▶ **v.** (**revels, reveling, reveled**; chiefly Brit. **revels, revelling, revelled**) [no obj.] enjoy oneself in a lively and noisy way, esp. with drinking and dancing: (as noun **reveling**) *a night of drunken reveling.* ■ (**revel in**) get great pleasure from (a situation or experience): *Bill said he was secretly reveling in his new-found fame.*
▶ **n.** (**revels**) lively and noisy enjoyment, esp. with drinking and dancing.
– ORIGIN late Middle English: from Old French *reveler* 'rise up in rebellion,' from Latin *rebellare* 'to rebel.'

rev·e·la·tion /,revə'lāSHən/ ▶ **n. 1** a surprising and previously unknown fact, esp. one that is made known in a dramatic way: *revelations about his personal life.* ■ the making known of something that was previously secret or unknown: *the revelation of an alleged plot to assassinate the king.* ■ used to emphasize the surprising or remarkable quality of someone or something: *seeing them play at international level was a revelation.*
2 the divine or supernatural disclosure to humans of something relating to human existence or the world: *an attempt to reconcile Darwinian theories with biblical revelation* | *a divine revelation.* ■ (**Revelation** or **Revelations**; in full **the Revelation of St John the Divine**) the last book of the New Testament, recounting a divine revelation of the future to St. John.
– DERIVATIVES **rev·e·la·tion·al** /-SHənl/ **adj.**
– ORIGIN Middle English (in the theological sense): from Old French, or from late Latin *revelatio(n-)*,

PRONUNCIATION KEY ə *ago, up*; ər *over, fur*; a *hat*; ā *ate*; ä *car*; e *let*; ē *see*; i *fit*; ī *by*; NG *sing*; ō *go*; ô *law, for*; oi *toy*; ŏŏ *good*; ōō *goo*; ou *out*; TH *thin*; T͟H *then*; ZH *vision*

r

from *revelare* 'lay bare' (see **REVEAL**[1]). Sense 1 dates from the mid 19th cent.

rev·e·la·tion·ist /ˌrevəˈlāSHənist/ ▶ **n.** a believer in divine revelation.

re·vel·a·to·ry /ˈrevələˌtôrē, riˈvel-/ ▶ **adj.** revealing something hitherto unknown: *an invigorating and revelatory performance.*

rev·el·er /ˈrevələr/ (also **reveller**) ▶ **n.** a person who is enjoying themselves in a lively and noisy way: *the city's traditional Labor Day bash usually attracts more than 100,000 revelers.*

rev·el·ry /ˈrevəlrē/ ▶ **n.** (pl. **revelries**) lively and noisy festivities, esp. when these involve drinking a large amount of alcohol: *sounds of revelry issued into the night | New Year revelries.*

rev·e·nant /ˈrevəˌnän, -nənt/ ▶ **n.** a person who has returned, esp. supposedly from the dead.
– ORIGIN early 19th cent.: French, literally 'coming back,' present participle (used as a noun) of *revenir.*

re·venge /riˈvenj/ ▶ **n.** the action of inflicting hurt or harm on someone for an injury or wrong suffered at their hands: *other spurned wives have **taken** public **revenge on** their husbands.* ■ the desire to inflict such retribution: *it was difficult not to be overwhelmed with feelings of hate and revenge.* ■ (in sports) the defeat of a person or team by whom one was beaten in a previous encounter: *the Yankees wanted to get their revenge for losing to the Dodgers in the 1955 Series.*
▶ **v.** [with obj.] chiefly literary inflict hurt or harm on someone for an injury or wrong done to (someone else): *it's a pity he chose that way to revenge his sister.* ■ inflict hurt or harm on someone for (an injury or wrong done to oneself or another): *her brother was slain, and she revenged his death.* ■ (**revenge oneself** or **be revenged**) inflict hurt or harm on someone for an injury or wrong done to oneself: *I'll be revenged on the whole pack of you.*
– PHRASES **revenge is a dish best served** (or **eaten**) **cold** proverb vengeance is often more satisfying if it is not exacted immediately.
– DERIVATIVES **re·veng·er n.** (literary).
– ORIGIN late Middle English: from Old French *revencher,* from late Latin *revindicare,* from *re-* (expressing intensive force) + *vindicare* 'claim, avenge.'

re·venge·ful /riˈvenjfəl/ ▶ **adj.** eager for revenge.
– DERIVATIVES **re·venge·ful·ly adv., re·venge·ful·ness n.**

re·venge trag·e·dy ▶ **n.** a style of drama, popular in England during the late 16th and 17th centuries, in which the basic plot was a quest for vengeance and which typically featured scenes of carnage and mutilation. Examples of the genre include Thomas Kyd's *The Spanish Tragedy* (1592) and John Webster's *The Duchess of Malfi* (1623).

rev·e·nue /ˈrevəˌn(y)o͞o/ ▶ **n.** income, esp. when of a company or organization and of a substantial nature. ■ a state's annual income from which public expenses are met. ■ (**revenues**) items or amounts constituting such income: *the government's tax revenues.* ■ the government department collecting such income.
– ORIGIN late Middle English: from Old French *revenu(e)* 'returned,' past participle (used as a noun) of *revenir,* from Latin *revenire* 'return,' from *re-* 'back' + *venire* 'come.'

rev·e·nue shar·ing ▶ **n.** the distribution of a portion of federal tax revenues to state and local governments.

rev·e·nue stamp ▶ **n.** a stamp showing that a government tax has been paid.

rev·e·nue tar·iff ▶ **n.** a tariff imposed principally to raise government revenue rather than to protect domestic industries.

re·verb /ˈrēˌvərb, riˈvərb/ ▶ **n.** an effect whereby the sound produced by an amplifier or an amplified musical instrument is made to reverberate slightly. ■ a device for producing such an effect.
– ORIGIN 1960s: abbreviation.

re·ver·ber·ate /riˈvərbəˌrāt/ ▶ **v.** [no obj.] (of a loud noise) be repeated several times as an echo: *her deep booming laugh reverberated around the room.* ■ (of a place) appear to vibrate or be disturbed because of a loud noise: *the hall reverberated with gaiety and laughter.* ■ [with obj.] archaic return or re-echo (a sound): *oft did the cliffs reverberate the sound.* ■ have continuing and serious effects: *the statements by the professor reverberated through the capitol.*
– DERIVATIVES **re·ver·ber·ant** /-rənt/ **adj., re·ver·ber·ant·ly** /-rəntlē/ **adv., re·ver·ber·a·tive** /-rətiv/ **adj., re·ver·ber·a·tor** /-ˌrātər/ **n., re·ver·ber·a·to·ry** /-rəˌtôrē/ **adj.**
– ORIGIN late 15th cent. (in the sense 'drive or beat back'): from Latin *reverberat-* 'struck again,' from the verb *reverberare,* from *re-* 'back' + *verberare* 'to lash' (from *verbera* (plural) 'scourge').

re·ver·ber·a·tion /riˌvərbəˈrāSHən/ ▶ **n.**
1 prolongation of a sound; resonance: *electronic effects have been added, such as echo and reverberation.*
2 (usu. **reverberations**) a continuing effect; a repercussion: *the attack has had reverberations around the world.*

re·ver·ber·a·to·ry fur·nace ▶ **n.** a furnace in which the roof and walls are heated by flames and radiate heat onto material in the center of the furnace.

Re·vere[1] /rəˈvi(ə)r/ a city in east central Massachusetts, on Massachusetts Bay, northeast of Boston; pop. 60,204 (est. 2008).

Re·vere[2], Paul (1735–1818), American silversmith and patriot. In 1775 he rode from Boston to Lexington to warn fellow American revolutionaries of the approach of British troops. He is the subject of Henry Wadsworth Longfellow's famous poem "Paul Revere's Ride" (1863).

re·vere /riˈvi(ə)r/ ▶ **v.** [with obj.] feel deep respect or admiration for (something): *Cézanne's still lifes were revered by his contemporaries.*
– ORIGIN mid 17th cent.: from French *révérer* or Latin *revereri,* from *re-* (expressing intensive force) + *vereri* 'to fear.'

rev·er·ence /ˈrev(ə)rəns/ ▶ **n.** deep respect for someone or something: *rituals showed honor and reverence for the dead.* ■ archaic a gesture indicative of such respect; a bow or curtsy: *the messenger **made his reverence.*** ■ (**His/Your Reverence**) a title given to a member of the clergy, or used in addressing them.
▶ **v.** [with obj.] regard or treat with deep respect: *the many divine beings reverenced by Hindu tradition.*
– ORIGIN Middle English: from Old French, from Latin *reverentia,* from *revereri* 'stand in awe of' (see **REVERE**).

rev·er·end /ˈrev(ə)rənd, ˈrevərnd/ ▶ **adj.** (usu. **Reverend**) used as a title or form of address to members of the clergy: *the Reverend Jesse Jackson.*
▶ **n.** informal a member of the clergy.
– ORIGIN late Middle English: from Old French, or from Latin *reverendus* 'person to be revered,' gerundive of *revereri* (see **REVERE**).

> **USAGE** As a title, **Reverend** is used for members of the clergy; the traditionally correct form of address is *the Reverend James Smith* or *the Reverend J. Smith,* rather than ***Reverend** Smith* or simply *Reverend.* In American usage, however, the article *the* is commonly not used, even by the devout and reverent. Careful speakers and writers, however, may choose to include the *the,* in deference to the formerly common and primary use of **reverend** as an adjective ('worthy of being revered, respected').

Rev·er·end Moth·er ▶ **n.** the title of the Mother Superior of a convent.

rev·er·ent /ˈrev(ə)rənt, ˈrevərnt/ ▶ **adj.** feeling or showing deep and solemn respect: *a reverent silence.*
– DERIVATIVES **rev·er·ent·ly adv.**
– ORIGIN late Middle English: from Latin *reverent-* 'revering,' from the verb *revereri* (see **REVERE**).

rev·er·en·tial /ˌrevəˈrenCHəl/ ▶ **adj.** of the nature of, due to, or characterized by reverence: *their names are always mentioned in reverential tones.*
– DERIVATIVES **rev·er·en·tial·ly adv.**

rev·er·ie /ˈrevərē/ ▶ **n.** a state of being pleasantly lost in one's thoughts; a daydream: *a knock on the door broke her reverie | I slipped into reverie.* ■ Music an instrumental piece suggesting a dreamy or musing state. ■ archaic a fanciful or impractical idea or theory.
– ORIGIN early 17th cent.: from obsolete French *resverie,* from Old French *reverie* 'rejoicing, revelry,' from *rever* 'be delirious,' of unknown ultimate origin.

re·vers /riˈvi(ə)r, -ˈve(ə)r/ ▶ **n.** (pl. **same**) the turned-back edge of a garment revealing the undersurface, esp. at the lapel.
– ORIGIN mid 19th cent.: from French, literally 'reverse.'

re·ver·sal /riˈvərsəl/ ▶ **n.** a change to an opposite direction, position, or course of action: *a dramatic reversal in population decline in the Alps | the reversal of tidal currents.* ■ Law an annulment of a judgment, sentence, or decree made by a lower court or authority: *the Court has upheld the appellate justices in their reversal of the trial court judgment.* ■ an adverse change of fortune: *the league champions suffered a reversal at the finals last month.* ■ Photography direct production of a positive image from an exposed film or plate; direct reproduction of a positive or negative image.
– ORIGIN late 15th cent. (as a legal term): from the verb **REVERSE** + **-AL**.

re·verse /riˈvərs/ ▶ **v.** [no obj.] move backward: *the truck reversed into the back of a bus.* ■ [with obj.] cause (a vehicle) to move backward: *I got in the car, reversed it and drove it up the driveway.* ■ [with obj.] turn (something) the other way around or up or inside out: (as adj. **reversed**) *a reversed S-shape.* ■ [with obj.] make (something) the opposite of what it was: *the damage done to the ozone layer may be reversed.* ■ [with obj.] exchange (the position or function) of two people or things: *the experimenter and the subject reversed roles and the experiment was repeated.* ■ [with obj.] Law revoke or annul (a judgment, sentence, or decree made by a lower court or authority): *the court reversed his conviction.* ■ (of an engine) work in a contrary direction: *the ship's engines reversed and cut out altogether.* ■ [with obj.] Printing make (type or a design) print as white in a block of solid color or a halftone: *their press ads had a headline reversed out of the illustration.*
▶ **adj.** [attrib.] going in or turned toward the direction opposite to that previously stated: *the trend appears to be going in the reverse direction.* ■ operating, behaving, or ordered in a way contrary or opposite to that which is usual or expected: *here are the results in reverse order.* ■ Electronics (of a voltage applied to a semiconductor junction) in the direction that does not allow significant current to flow. ■ Geology denoting a fault or faulting in which a relative downward movement occurred in the strata situated on the underside of the fault plane.
▶ **n. 1** a complete change of direction or action: *the growth actuates a reverse of photosynthesis.* ■ reverse gear on a motor vehicle; the position of a gear lever or selector corresponding to this. See also **IN REVERSE** below. ■ (**the reverse**) the opposite or contrary to that previously stated: *he didn't feel homesick—quite the reverse.* ■ an adverse change of fortune; a setback or defeat: *the team suffered its heaviest reverse of the season.* ■ Football a play in which the ballcarrier reverses the direction of attack by lateraling or handling the ball to a teammate moving in the opposite direction.
2 the opposite side or face to the observer: *the address is given on the reverse of this leaflet.* ■ a left-hand page of an open book, or the back of a loose document. ■ the side of a coin or medal bearing the value or secondary design. ■ the design or inscription on this side. See also **OBVERSE** (sense 1 of the noun).
– PHRASES **in** (or **into**) **reverse** (of a motor vehicle) in reverse gear so as to travel backward: *he put the Cadillac into reverse.* ■ in the opposite direction or manner from usual: *a similar ride next year will do the route in reverse.* **reverse the charges** make the recipient of a telephone call responsible for payment.
– DERIVATIVES **re·verse·ly adv., re·vers·er n.**
– ORIGIN Middle English: from Old French *revers, reverse* (nouns), *reverser* (verb), from Latin *reversus* 'turned back,' past participle of *revertere,* from *re-* 'back' + *vertere* 'to turn.'

re·verse dis·crim·i·na·tion ▶ **n.** (in the context of the allocation of resources or employment) the practice or policy of favoring individuals belonging to groups known to have been discriminated against previously.

re·verse en·gi·neer·ing ▶ **n.** the reproduction of another manufacturer's product following detailed examination of its construction or composition.
– DERIVATIVES **re·verse-en·gi·neer v.**

re·verse gear ▶ **n.** a gear used to make a vehicle or piece of machinery move or work backward.

re·verse os·mo·sis ▶ **n.** Chemistry a process by which a solvent passes through a porous membrane in the direction opposite to that for natural osmosis when subjected to a hydrostatic pressure greater than the osmotic pressure.

re·verse Po·lish no·ta·tion ▶ **n.** see **POLISH NOTATION**.

re·verse split ▶ **n.** reduction in the number of a company's traded shares that results in an increase in the par value or earnings per share.

re·verse take·o·ver ▶ **n.** Finance a takeover of a public company by a smaller company.

re·verse tran·scrip·tase ▶ **n.** an enzyme that catalyzes the formation of DNA from an RNA template in reverse transcription. See also **TRANSCRIPTASE**.

re·verse tran·scrip·tion ▶ **n.** Biochemistry the reverse of normal transcription, occurring in some RNA viruses, in which a sequence of nucleotides is copied from an RNA template during the synthesis of a molecule of DNA.

r

re·vers·i·ble /riˈvərsəbəl/ ▶ **adj.** able to be reversed, in particular: ■ (of a garment, fabric, or bedclothes) faced on both sides so as to be worn or used with either outside. ■ able to be turned the other way around: *a reversible stroller seat.* ■ (of the effects of a process or condition) capable of being reversed so that the previous state or situation is restored: *potentially reversible forms of renal failure.* ■ Chemistry (of a reaction) occurring together with its converse, and so yielding an equilibrium mixture of reactants and products. ■ Physics (of a change or process) capable of complete and detailed reversal, esp. denoting or undergoing an ideal change in which a system is in thermodynamic equilibrium at all times. ■ Chemistry (of a colloid) capable of being changed from a gel into a sol by a reversal of the treatment that turns the sol into a gel.
– DERIVATIVES **re·vers·i·bil·i·ty** /ri,vərsəˈbilətē/ **n.**, **re·vers·i·bly** /-blē/ **adv.**

re·ver·sion /riˈvərZHən/ ▶ **n.** **1** a return to a previous state, practice, or belief: *there was some reversion to polytheism* | *a reversion to the two-party system.* ■ Biology the action of reverting to a former or ancestral type.
2 Law the right, esp. of the original owner or their heirs, to possess or succeed to property on the death of the present possessor or at the end of a lease: *the reversion of property.* ■ a property to which someone has such a right. ■ the right of succession to an office or post after the death or retirement of the holder: *he was given a promise of the reversion of Boraston's job.*
– DERIVATIVES **re·ver·sion·ar·y** /-,nerē/ **adj.** (sense 2).
– ORIGIN late Middle English (denoting the action of returning to or from a place): from Old French, or from Latin *reversio(n-)*, from *revertere* 'turn back' (see REVERSE).

re·ver·sion·er /riˈvərZHənər/ ▶ **n.** Law a person who possesses the reversion to a property or privilege.

re·vert /riˈvərt/ ▶ **v.** [no obj.] **(revert to)** return to (a previous state, condition, practice, etc.): *he reverted to his native language.* ■ return to (a previous topic): *he ignored her words by reverting to the former subject.* ■ convert to (the Islamic faith). ■ Biology return to (a former or ancestral type): *it is impossible that a fishlike mammal will actually revert to being a true fish.* ■ Law (of property) return or pass to (the original owner) by reversion. ■ [with obj.] archaic turn (one's eyes or steps) back: *on reverting our eyes, every step presented some new and admirable scene.*
▶ **n.** a person who has converted to the Islamic faith.
– DERIVATIVES **re·vert·er** **n.** (Law).
– ORIGIN Middle English: from Old French *revertir* or Latin *revertere* 'turn back.' Early senses included 'recover consciousness,' 'return to a position,' and 'return to a person (after estrangement).'

re·ver·tant /riˈvərtnt/ Biology ▶ **adj.** (of a cell, organism, or strain) having reverted to the normal type from a mutant or abnormal form.
▶ **n.** a cell, organism, or strain of this type.

re·vet /riˈvet/ ▶ **v.** (**revets, revetting, revetted**) [with obj.] (usu. as adj. **revetted**) face (a rampart, wall, etc.) with masonry, esp. in fortification: *sandbagged and revetted trenches.*
– ORIGIN early 19th cent.: from French *revêtir*, from late Latin *revestire*, from *re-* 'again' + *vestire* 'clothe' (from *vestis* 'clothing').

re·vet·ment /riˈvetmənt/ ▶ **n.** (esp. in fortification) a retaining wall or facing of masonry or other material, supporting or protecting a rampart, wall, etc. ■ a barricade of earth or sandbags set up to provide protection from blast or to prevent planes from overrunning when landing.
– ORIGIN late 18th cent.: from French *revêtement*, from the verb *revêtir* (see REVET).

re·view /riˈvyo͞o/ ▶ **n.** **1** a formal assessment or examination of something with the possibility or intention of instituting change if necessary: *a comprehensive review of defense policy* | *all areas of the company will come under review.* ■ a critical appraisal of a book, play, movie, exhibition, etc., published in a newspaper or magazine. ■ [often in names] a periodical publication with critical articles on current events, the arts, etc. ■ Law a reconsideration of a judgment, sentence, etc., by a higher court or authority: *a review of her sentence* | *his case comes up for review in January.* Compare with JUDICIAL REVIEW. ■ a report on or evaluation of a subject or past events: *a review of recent developments in multicultural education* | *the CEO's end-of-year review.*
2 a ceremonial display and formal inspection of military or naval forces, typically by a sovereign, commander in chief, or high-ranking visitor.
▶ **v.** [with obj.] **1** examine or assess (something) formally with the possibility or intention of instituting change if necessary: *the company's safety procedures are being reviewed.* ■ write a critical appraisal of (a book, play, movie, etc.) for publication in a newspaper or magazine: *I reviewed his first novel.* ■ Law submit (a sentence, case, etc.) for reconsideration by a higher court or authority: *the attorney general asked the court to review the sentence.* ■ survey or evaluate (a subject or past events): *in the next chapter we review a number of recent empirical studies.*
2 (of a sovereign, commander in chief, or high-ranking visitor) make a ceremonial and formal inspection of (military or naval forces).
3 view or inspect visually for a second time or again: *all slides were then reviewed by one pathologist.*
– DERIVATIVES **re·view·a·ble** **adj.**, **re·view·al** /-ˈvyo͞oəl/ **n.**
– ORIGIN late Middle English (as a noun denoting a formal inspection of military or naval forces): from obsolete French *reveue*, from *revoir* 'see again.'

re·view·er /riˈvyo͞oər/ ▶ **n.** a person who writes critical appraisals of books, plays, movies, etc., for publication. ■ a person who formally assesses or examines something with a view to changing it if necessary: *a rent reviewer.*

re·vile /riˈvīl/ ▶ **v.** [with obj.] criticize in an abusive or angrily insulting manner: *he was now reviled by the party that he had helped to lead.*
– DERIVATIVES **re·vile·ment** **n.**, **re·vil·er** **n.**
– ORIGIN Middle English: from Old French *reviler*, based on *vil* 'vile.'

re·vise /riˈvīz/ ▶ **v.** [with obj.] **1** reconsider and alter (something) in the light of further evidence: *he had cause to revise his opinion a moment after expressing it.* ■ re-examine and make alterations to (written or printed matter): *the book was published in 1960 and revised in 1968* | (as adj. **revised**) *a revised edition.* ■ alter so as to make more efficient or realistic: (as adj. **revised**) *the revised finance and administrative groups.*
2 [no obj.] Brit. reread work done previously to improve one's knowledge of a subject, typically to prepare for an examination: *students frantically revising for exams* | [with obj.] *revise your lecture notes on the topic.*
▶ **n.** Printing a proof including corrections made in an earlier proof.
– DERIVATIVES **re·vis·a·ble** **adj.**, **re·vis·al** /-ˈvīzəl/ **n.**, **re·vis·er** **n.**, **re·vi·so·ry** /-ˈvīzərē/ **adj.**
– ORIGIN mid 16th cent. (in the sense 'look again or repeatedly (at)'): from French *réviser* 'look at,' or Latin *revisere* 'look at again,' from *re-* 'again' + *visere* (intensive form of *videre* 'to see').

Re·vised Stand·ard Ver·sion (abbr.: **RSV**) ▶ **n.** a modern English translation of the Bible, published 1946–57 and based on the American Standard Version of 1901.

Re·vised Ver·sion (abbr.: **RV**) ▶ **n.** an English translation of the Bible published in 1881–95 and based on the Authorized Version.

re·vi·sion /riˈviZHən/ ▶ **n.** the action of revising: *the plan needs drastic revision.* ■ a revised edition or form of something.
– DERIVATIVES **re·vi·sion·ar·y** /-,nerē/ **adj.**

re·vi·sion·ism /riˈviZHə,nizəm/ ▶ **n.** often derogatory a policy of revision or modification, esp. of Marxism on evolutionary socialist (rather than revolutionary) or pluralist principles. ■ the theory or practice of revising one's attitude to a previously accepted situation or point of view.
– DERIVATIVES **re·vi·sion·ist** **n. & adj.**

re·vis·it /rēˈvizit/ ▶ **v.** (**revisits, revisiting, revisited**) [with obj.] come back to or visit again: *she was anxious to revisit some of her old haunts in Paris.* ■ consider (a situation or problem) again or from a different perspective: *the council will have to revisit the issue at a general meeting this summer.*

re·vi·tal·ize /rēˈvītl,īz/ ▶ **v.** [with obj.] imbue (something) with new life and vitality: *a package of spending cuts to revitalize the economy.*
– DERIVATIVES **re·vi·tal·i·za·tion** /rē,vītl-əˈzāSHən/ **n.**

re·viv·al /riˈvīvəl/ ▶ **n.** an improvement in the condition or strength of something: *a revival in the fortunes of the party* | *an economic revival.* ■ an instance of something becoming popular, active, or important again: *cross-country skiing is enjoying a revival.* ■ a new production of an old play or similar work. ■ a reawakening of religious fervor, esp. by means of a series of evangelistic meetings: *the revivals of the nineteenth century* | *a wave of religious revival.* ■ a restoration to bodily or mental vigor, to life or consciousness, or to sporting success: *the thunder and lightning affected his revival in the third round.*

re·viv·al·ism /riˈvīvə,lizəm/ ▶ **n.** belief in or the promotion of a revival of religious fervor. ■ a tendency or desire to revive a former custom or practice: *French rococo revivalism.*
– DERIVATIVES **re·viv·al·ist** **n. & adj.**, **re·viv·al·is·tic** /-,vīvəˈlistik/ **adj.**

re·vive /riˈvīv/ ▶ **v.** [with obj.] restore to life or consciousness: *both men collapsed, but were revived.* ■ [no obj.] regain life, consciousness, or strength: *she was beginning to revive from her faint.* ■ give new strength or energy to: *the cool, refreshing water revived us all.* ■ restore interest in or the popularity of: *many pagan traditions continue or are being revived.* ■ improve the position or condition of: *the paper made panicky attempts to revive falling sales.*
– DERIVATIVES **re·viv·a·ble** **adj.**, **re·viv·er** **n.**
– ORIGIN late Middle English: from Old French *revivre* or late Latin *revivere*, from Latin *re-* 'back' + *vivere* 'live.'

re·viv·i·fy /rēˈvivə,fī/ ▶ **v.** (**revivifies, revivifying, revivified**) [with obj.] give new life or vigor to: *they revivified a wine industry that had all but vanished.*
– DERIVATIVES **re·viv·i·fi·ca·tion** /,rē,vivəfəˈkāSHən/ **n.**
– ORIGIN late 17th cent.: from French *revivifier* or late Latin *revivificare* (see RE-, VIVIFY).

rev·o·ca·ble /ˈrevəkəbəl, riˈvōkəbəl/ ▶ **adj.** capable of being revoked or canceled: *a revocable settlement.*
– DERIVATIVES **rev·o·ca·bil·i·ty** /,revəkəˈbilətē, ri,vōkə-/ **n.**

re·voke /riˈvōk/ ▶ **v.** **1** [with obj.] put an end to the validity or operation of (a decree, decision, or promise): *the men appealed and the sentence was revoked.*
2 [no obj.] (in bridge, whist, and other card games) fail to follow suit despite being able to do so.
– DERIVATIVES **rev·o·ca·tion** /,revəˈkāSHən, ri,vō-/ **n.**, **rev·o·ca·to·ry** /ˈrevəkə,tôrē, riˈvōkə-/ **adj.**, **re·vok·er** **n.**
– ORIGIN late Middle English: from Old French *revoquer* or Latin *revocare*, from *re-* 'back' + *vocare* 'to call.'

re·volt /riˈvōlt/ ▶ **v.** **1** [no obj.] rise in rebellion: *the insurgents revolted and had to be suppressed.* ■ refuse to acknowledge someone or something as having authority: *voters may revolt when they realize the cost of the measures.* ■ (as adj. **revolted**) archaic having rebelled or revolted: *the revolted Bretons.*
2 [with obj.] cause to feel disgust: *he was revolted by the stench that greeted him.* ■ [no obj.] archaic feel strong disgust.
▶ **n.** an attempt to put an end to the authority of a person or body by rebelling: *a countrywide revolt against the central government* | *the peasants rose in revolt.* ■ a refusal to continue to obey or conform: *a revolt over tax increases.*
– ORIGIN mid 16th cent.: from French *révolte* (noun), *révolter* (verb), from Italian *rivoltare*, based on Latin *revolvere* 'roll back' (see REVOLVE).

re·volt·ing·ly /riˈvōltiNG/ ▶ **adj.** causing intense disgust; disgusting: *there was a revolting smell that lingered in the air.*
– DERIVATIVES **re·volt·ing·ly** **adv.** (as submodifier) *when I was a kid I was revoltingly precocious.*

rev·o·lute /ˈrevə,lo͞ot/ ▶ **adj.** Botany (esp. of the edge of a leaf) curved or curled back.
– ORIGIN mid 18th cent.: from Latin *revolutus* 'unrolled,' past participle of *revolvere* (see REVOLVE).

r

rev·o·lu·tion /,revəˈlo͞oSHən/ ▶ **n.** **1** a forcible overthrow of a government or social order in favor of a new system. ■ (**the Revolution**) the American Revolution. ■ (often **the Revolution**) (in Marxism) the class struggle that is expected to lead to political change and the triumph of communism. ■ a dramatic and wide-reaching change in the way something works or is organized or in people's ideas about it: *marketing underwent a revolution.*
2 an instance of revolving: *one revolution a second.* ■ the movement of an object in a circular or elliptical course around another or about an axis or centre: *revolution about the axis of rotation.* ■ a single orbit or course of this kind.
– DERIVATIVES **rev·o·lu·tion·ism** /-,nizəm/ **n.**, **rev·o·lu·tion·ist** /-nist/ **n.**
– ORIGIN late Middle English: from Old French, or from late Latin *revolutio(n-)*, from *revolvere* 'roll back' (see REVOLVE).

rev·o·lu·tion·ar·y /,revəˈlo͞oSHə,nerē/ ▶ **adj.** engaged in or promoting political revolution: *the revolutionary army.* ■ (**Revolutionary**) of or relating to the American Revolution. ■ involving or causing a complete or dramatic change: *a revolutionary new drug.*
▶ **n.** (pl. **revolutionaries**) a person who works for or engages in political revolution.

rev·o·lu·tion·ize /ˌrevəˈlo͞oSHəˌnīz/ ▶ **v.** [with obj.] change (something) radically or fundamentally: *this fabulous new theory will revolutionize the whole of science.*

re·volve /riˈvälv, riˈvôlv/ ▶ **v.** [no obj.] move in a circle on a central axis: *overhead, the fan revolved slowly.* ■ (**revolve around/about**) move in a circular orbit around: *the earth revolves around the sun.* ■ (**revolve around**) treat as the most important point or element: *her life revolved around her husband.* ■ [with obj.] consider (something) repeatedly and from different angles: *her mind revolved the possibilities.*
– ORIGIN late Middle English (in the senses 'turn (the eyes) back,' 'restore,' 'consider'): from Latin *revolvere*, from *re-* 'back' (also expressing intensive force) + *volvere* 'roll.'

re·volv·er /riˈvälvər, -ˈvôl-/ ▶ **n.** a pistol with revolving chambers enabling several shots to be fired without reloading.

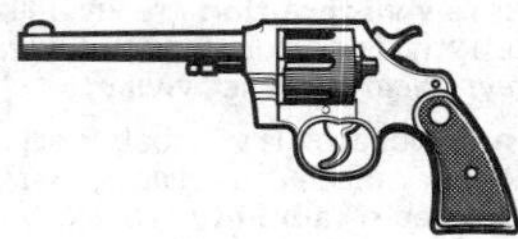
revolver

re·volv·ing cred·it ▶ **n.** credit that is automatically renewed as debts are paid off.

re·volv·ing door ▶ **n.** an entrance to a large building in which four partitions turn about a central axis. ■ used to refer to a situation in which the same events or problems recur in a continuous cycle: *many patients are trapped in a revolving door of admission, discharge, and readmission.* ■ [usu. as modifier] a place or organization that people tend to enter and leave very quickly: *the newsroom became a revolving-door workplace.* ■ used to refer to a situation in which someone moves from an influential government position to a position in a private company, or vice versa.

re·volv·ing fund ▶ **n.** a fund that is continually replenished as withdrawals are made.

re·vue /riˈvyo͞o/ ▶ **n.** a light theatrical entertainment consisting of a series of short sketches, songs, and dances, typically dealing satirically with topical issues.
– ORIGIN French, literally 'review.'

re·vul·sion /riˈvəlSHən/ ▶ **n. 1** a sense of disgust and loathing: *news of the attack will be met with sorrow and revulsion.*
2 Medicine, chiefly historical the drawing of disease or blood congestion from one part of the body to another, e.g., by counterirritation.
– ORIGIN mid 16th cent. (sense 2): from French, or from Latin *revulsio(n-)*, from *revuls-* 'torn out,' from the verb *revellere* (from *re-* 'back' + *vellere* 'pull'). Sense 1 dates from the early 19th cent.

Rev. Ver. ▶ **abbr.** Revised Version (of the Bible).

re·ward /riˈwôrd/ ▶ **n.** a thing given in recognition of one's service, effort, or achievement: *the holiday was a **reward for** 40 years' service with the company* | *he's **reaping the rewards** of his hard work and perseverance* | figurative *the emotional rewards of being a parent.* ■ a fair return for good or bad behavior: *a slap on the face was his reward for his impudence.* ■ a sum offered for the detection of a criminal, the restoration of lost property, or the giving of information.
▶ **v.** [with obj.] make a gift of something to (someone) in recognition of their services, efforts, or achievements: *the engineer who supervised the work **was rewarded with** a bonus.* ■ show one's appreciation of (an action or quality) by making a gift: *an effective organization recognizes and rewards creativity and initiative.* ■ (**be rewarded**) receive what one deserves: *their hard work was rewarded by the winning of a five-year contract.*
– PHRASES **go to one's (final) reward** used euphemistically to indicate that someone has died.
– DERIVATIVES **re·ward·less** adj.
– ORIGIN Middle English: from Anglo-Norman French, variant of Old French *reguard* 'regard, heed,' also an early sense of the English word.

re·ward·ing /riˈwôrdiNG/ ▶ **adj.** providing satisfaction; gratifying: *skiing can be hugely rewarding.*
– DERIVATIVES **re·ward·ing·ly** adv.

re·wash /ˌrēˈwäSH/ ▶ **v.** [with obj.] wash (something) again.

re·weigh /ˌrēˈwā/ ▶ **v.** [with obj.] weigh (something) again.

re·wind ▶ **v.** /rēˈwīnd/ (past and past participle **rewound** /-ˈwound/) [with obj.] wind (a tape or film) back to the beginning. ■ [no obj.] (of a tape or film) wind back to the beginning.
▶ **n.** /ˈrēˌwīnd/ a mechanism for rewinding a tape or film.
– DERIVATIVES **re·wind·er** /rēˈwīndər/ **n.**

re·wire /ˌrēˈwīr/ ▶ **v.** [with obj.] provide (an appliance, building, or vehicle) with new electric wiring.
– DERIVATIVES **re·wir·a·ble** adj.

re·word /rēˈwərd/ ▶ **v.** put (something) into different words: *there is a sound reason for rewording that clause.*

re·work /rēˈwərk/ ▶ **v.** [with obj.] make changes to something, esp. in order to make it more up to date: *he reworked the orchestral score for two pianos* | (as noun **reworking**) *a reworking of the Sherwood Forest legend.*

re·wound /rēˈwound/ past and past participle of **REWIND**.

re·wrap /ˌrēˈrap/ ▶ **v.** (**rewraps, rewrapping, rewrapped**) [with obj.] wrap (something) again or differently.

re·writ·a·ble /rēˈrītəbəl/ ▶ **adj.** Computing (of a storage medium) supporting overwriting of previously recorded data.

re·write ▶ **v.** /rēˈrīt/ (past **rewrote**; past participle **rewritten**) [with obj.] write (something) again so as to alter or improve it: *the songs may have to be rewritten* | [no obj.] *he began rewriting, adding more and more layers.*
▶ **n.** /ˈrēˌrīt/ an instance of writing something again so as to alter or improve it. ■ a piece of text that has been altered or improved in such a way.
– PHRASES **rewrite history** select or interpret events from the past in a way that suits one's own particular purposes. **rewrite the record books** (of an athlete) break a record or several records.

Rex[1] /reks/ ▶ **n.** the reigning king (used following a name or in the titles of lawsuits, e.g., *Rex v. Jones*: the Crown versus Jones).
– ORIGIN Latin, literally 'king.'

Rex[2] ▶ **n.** a cat of a breed with curly fur, which lacks guard hairs.
– ORIGIN 1960s: from Latin, literally 'king.'

Reyes, Point /rāz/ a promontory in northwestern California, north of Drakes Bay, in Marin County, noted for its winds, fog, and wildlife.

Reye's syn·drome /rīz, rāz/ ▶ **n.** a life-threatening metabolic disorder in young children, of uncertain cause but sometimes precipitated by aspirin and involving encephalitis and liver failure.
– ORIGIN 1960s: named after Ralph D. K. *Reye* (1912–78), Australian pediatrician.

Rey·kja·vik /ˈrākyəˌvik, -vēk/ the capital of Iceland, a port on the western coast; pop. 119,357 (2009).
– ORIGIN from Icelandic *rejkja* 'smoky,' referring to the steam from its many hot springs.

Reyn·ard /rāˈnärd, ˈrānərd, ˈrenərd/ ▶ **n.** literary a name for a fox.
– ORIGIN from Old French *renart*; the spelling was influenced by Middle Dutch *Reynaerd.*

Reyn·olds /ˈrenəldz/, Sir Joshua (1723–92), English painter. The first president of the Royal Academy (1768), he sought to raise portraiture to the status of historical painting by adapting poses and settings from classical statues and Renaissance paintings.

Re·za Shah /riˈzä ˈSHä/ see **PAHLAVI**[1].

re·zone ▶ **v.** [with obj.] assign (land or property) to a different planning zone: *they submitted a proposal to rezone part of the Brooklyn waterfront.*

RF ▶ **abbr.** radio frequency.

Rf ▶ **symbol** the chemical element rutherfordium.

rf. ▶ **abbr.** Baseball right fielder.

RFA ▶ **abbr.** (in the UK) Royal Fleet Auxiliary.

RFC ▶ **abbr.** ■ (in computing) request for comment, a document circulated on the Internet that forms the basis of a technical standard. ■ historical Royal Flying Corps. ■ Rugby Football Club.

RFD (also **R.F.D.**) ▶ **abbr.** rural free delivery.

RFID ▶ **abbr.** radio frequency identification, denoting technologies that use radio waves to identify people or objects carrying encoded microchips.

RFP ▶ **abbr.** request for proposal, a detailed specification of goods or services required by an organization, sent to potential contractors or suppliers.

Rg ▶ **symbol** the chemical element roentgenium.

Rh ▶ **abbr.** Rhesus (factor). ▶ **symbol** the chemical element rhodium.

r.h. ▶ **abbr.** right hand.

RHA ▶ **abbr.** ■ (in the UK) regional health authority. ■ (in the UK) Royal Horse Artillery.

rhab·dom /ˈrabˌdäm, -dəm/ (also **rhabdome** /-ˌdōm/) ▶ **n.** Zoology a translucent cylinder forming part of the light-sensitive receptor in the eye of an arthropod.
– ORIGIN late 19th cent.: from late Greek *rhabdōma*, from *rhabdos* 'rod.'

rhab·do·man·cy /ˈrabdəˌmansē/ ▶ **n.** formal dowsing with a rod or stick.
– DERIVATIVES **rhab·do·man·cer** /-sər/ **n.**
– ORIGIN mid 17th cent.: from Greek *rhabdomanteia*, from *rhabdos* 'rod.'

rhab·do·my·ol·y·sis /ˌrabdōˌmīˈäləsis/ ▶ **n.** Medicine the destruction of striated muscle cells; (esp. in horses) azoturia.
– ORIGIN 1950s: from Greek *rhabdos* 'rod' + **MYO-** + **-LYSIS**.

rhab·do·my·o·sar·co·ma /ˌrabdōˌmīōˌsärˈkōmə/ ▶ **n.** (pl. **rhabdomyosarcomas** or **rhabdomyosarcomata** /-ˈkōmətə/) Medicine a rare malignant tumor involving striated muscle tissue.
– ORIGIN late 19th cent.: from Greek *rhabdos* 'rod' + **MYO-** + **SARCOMA**.

Rhad·a·man·thine /ˌradəˈmanTHən, -ˌTHīn/ ▶ **adj.** literary showing stern and inflexible judgment.
– ORIGIN mid 17th cent.: from **RHADAMANTHUS** + **-INE**[1].

Rhad·a·man·thus /ˌradəˈmanTHəs/ Greek Mythology the son of Zeus and Europa, and brother of Minos, who, as a ruler and judge in the underworld, was renowned for his justice.

Rhae·to-Ro·man·ic /ˌrētōˌrōˈmanik/ (also **Rhaeto-Romance**) ▶ **adj.** of, relating to, or denoting the Romance dialects spoken in parts of southeastern Switzerland, northeastern Italy, and Tyrol, esp. Romansh and Ladin.
▶ **n.** any of these dialects.
– ORIGIN from Latin *Rhaetus* 'of *Rhaetia*' (the name of a Roman province in the Alps) + **ROMANIC**.

rham·nose /ˈramˌnōs, -ˌnōz/ ▶ **n.** Chemistry a sugar of the hexose class that occurs widely in plants, esp. in berries of the common buckthorn.
– ORIGIN late 19th cent.: from modern Latin *rhamnus* (genus name) + **-OSE**[2].

rhap·sode /ˈrapˌsōd/ ▶ **n.** a person who recites epic poems, esp. one of a group in ancient Greece whose profession it was to recite the Homeric poems from memory.
– ORIGIN from Greek *rhapsōidos*, from *rhapsōidia* (see **RHAPSODY**).

rhap·so·dist /ˈrapsədist/ ▶ **n. 1** a person who rhapsodizes.
2 another term for **RHAPSODE**.

rhap·so·dize /ˈrapsəˌdīz/ ▶ **v.** [no obj.] speak or write about someone or something with great enthusiasm and delight: *he began to rhapsodize about Gaby's beauty and charm.*

rhap·so·dy /ˈrapsədē/ ▶ **n.** (pl. **rhapsodies**) **1** an effusively enthusiastic or ecstatic expression of feeling: *rhapsodies of praise.* ■ Music a free instrumental composition in one extended movement, typically one that is emotional or exuberant in character.
2 (in ancient Greece) an epic poem, or part of it, of a suitable length for recitation at one time.
– DERIVATIVES **rhap·sod·ic** /rapˈsädik/ **adj.**
– ORIGIN mid 16th cent. (sense 2): via Latin from Greek *rhapsōidia*, from *rhaptein* 'to stitch' + *ōidē* 'song, ode.'

rhat·a·ny /ˈratn-ē/ ▶ **n. 1** an astringent extract of the root of a South American shrub, used in medicine.
2 the partially parasitic South American shrub that yields this root, which is also used as a source of dye. ● Genus *Krameria*, family Krameriaceae.
– ORIGIN early 19th cent.: from modern Latin *rhatania*, via Portuguese and Spanish from Quechua *ratánya.*

rhbdr. ▶ **abbr.** rhombohedron.

Rhe·a /ˈrēə/ **1** Greek Mythology one of the Titans, wife of Cronus and mother of Zeus, Demeter, Poseidon, Hera, and Hades. Frightened of betrayal by their children, Cronus ate them; Rhea rescued Zeus from this fate by hiding him and giving Cronus a stone wrapped in blankets instead.
2 Astronomy a satellite of Saturn, the fourteenth closest to the planet, discovered by Cassini in 1672, and having a diameter of 951 miles (1,530 km).

rhe·a /ˈrēə/ ▶ **n.** a large flightless bird of South American grasslands, resembling a small ostrich, with grayish-brown plumage. ● Family Rheidae: two species, *Rhea americana* and *Pterocnemia pennata.*
– ORIGIN early 19th cent.: modern Latin (genus name), from the name of the Titan **RHEA**.

rhe·bok /'rē,bäk/ ▶ **n.** a small South African antelope with a woolly brownish-gray coat, a long slender neck, and short straight horns. ● *Pelea capreolus*, family Bovidae.
– ORIGIN late 18th cent.: from Dutch *reebok* 'roebuck.'

Rhee /rē/, Syngman (1875–1975), president of the Republic of Korea (South Korea) 1948–60. The principal leader in the movement for Korean independence, he was president of the exiled Korean provisional government 1919–41. After World War II, he became the first elected president of South Korea. Amid social and political unrest, he resigned one month into his fourth term and went into exile in Hawaii.

Rhein /rīn/ German name for RHINE.

Rhein·land /'rīn,länt/ German name for RHINELAND.

Rhein·land-Pfalz /(p)fälts/ German name for RHINELAND-PALATINATE.

rheme /rēm/ ▶ **n.** Linguistics the part of a clause that gives information about the theme. Compare with FOCUS and THEME.
– ORIGIN late 19th cent.: from Greek *rhēma* 'that which is said.'

Rhen·ish /'renisH, 'rē-/ ▶ **adj.** of the Rhine and the regions adjoining it.
▶ **n.** wine from this area.
– ORIGIN late Middle English: from Anglo-Norman French *reneis*, from a medieval Latin alteration of Latin *Rhenanus*, from *Rhenus* 'Rhine.'

rhe·ni·um /'rēnēəm/ ▶ **n.** the chemical element of atomic number 75, a rare silvery-white metal that occurs in trace amounts in ores of molybdenum and other metals. (Symbol: **Re**)
– ORIGIN 1920s: modern Latin, from *Rhenus*, the Latin name of the river RHINE.

rheo. ▶ **abbr.** rheostat.

rhe·ol·o·gy /rē'äləjē/ ▶ **n.** the branch of physics that deals with the deformation and flow of matter, esp. the non-Newtonian flow of liquids and the plastic flow of solids.
– DERIVATIVES **rhe·o·log·i·cal** /,rēə'läjikəl/ **adj.**, **rhe·ol·o·gist** /-jist/ **n.**
– ORIGIN 1920s: from Greek *rheos* 'stream' + -LOGY.

rhe·om·e·ter /rē'ämətər/ ▶ **n.** an instrument for measuring the rheological properties of a substance.

rhe·o·stat /'rēə,stat/ ▶ **n.** an electrical instrument used to control a current by varying the resistance.
– DERIVATIVES **rhe·o·stat·ic** /,rēə'statik/ **adj.**
– ORIGIN mid 19th cent.: from Greek *rheos* 'stream' + -STAT.

Rhe·sus fac·tor /'rēsəs/ (abbr.: **Rh factor**) ▶ **n.** [in sing.] an antigen occurring on the red blood cells of many humans (around 85 percent) and some other primates. It is particularly important as a cause of hemolytic disease of the newborn and of incompatibility in blood transfusions.
– ORIGIN 1940s: *Rhesus* from RHESUS MONKEY, in which the antigen was first observed.

rhe·sus mon·key (also **rhesus macaque**) ▶ **n.** a small brown macaque with red skin on the face and rump, native to southern Asia. It is often kept in captivity and is widely used in medical research. ● *Macaca mulatta*, family Cercopithecidae.
– ORIGIN early 19th cent.: modern Latin *rhesus*, arbitrary use of Latin *Rhesus* (from Greek *Rhēsos*, the name of a mythical king of Thrace).

Rhe·sus neg·a·tive (abbr.: **Rh negative**) ▶ **adj.** lacking the Rhesus factor.

Rhe·sus pos·i·tive (abbr.: **Rh positive**) ▶ **adj.** having the Rhesus factor.

rhet. ▶ **abbr.** ■ rhetoric. ■ rhetorical.

rhe·tor /'retər/ ▶ **n.** (in ancient Greece and Rome) a teacher of rhetoric. ■ an orator.
– ORIGIN via Latin from Greek *rhētōr*.

rhet·o·ric /'retərik/ ▶ **n.** the art of effective or persuasive speaking or writing, esp. the use of figures of speech and other compositional techniques. ■ language designed to have a persuasive or impressive effect on its audience, but often regarded as lacking in sincerity or meaningful content: *all we have from the opposition is empty rhetoric*.
– ORIGIN Middle English: from Old French *rethorique*, via Latin from Greek *rhētorikē (tekhnē)* '(art) of rhetoric,' from *rhētōr* 'rhetor.'

rhe·tor·i·cal /rə'tôrikəl/ ▶ **adj.** of, relating to, or concerned with the art of rhetoric: *repetition is a common rhetorical device*. ■ expressed in terms intended to persuade or impress: *the rhetorical commitment of the government to give priority to primary education*. ■ (of a question) asked in order to produce an effect or to make a statement rather than to elicit information.
– DERIVATIVES **rhe·tor·i·cal·ly** /-ik(ə)lē/ **adv.**
– ORIGIN late Middle English (first used in the sense 'eloquently expressed'): via Latin from Greek *rhētorikos* (from *rhētor* 'rhetor') + -AL.

rhet·o·ri·cian /,retə'risHən/ ▶ **n.** an expert in formal rhetoric. ■ a speaker whose words are primarily intended to impress or persuade.
– ORIGIN late Middle English: from Old French *rethoricien*, from *rhetorique* (see RHETORIC).

rheum /ro͞om/ ▶ **n.** chiefly literary a watery fluid that collects in or drips from the nose or eyes.
– ORIGIN late Middle English: from Old French *reume*, via Latin from Greek *rheuma* 'stream' (from *rhein* 'to flow').

rheu·mat·ic /ro͞o'matik/ ▶ **adj.** of, relating to, or caused by rheumatism: *rheumatic pains*. ■ (of a person or part of the body) suffering from or affected by rheumatism.
▶ **n.** a person suffering from rheumatism.
– DERIVATIVES **rheu·mat·i·cal·ly** /-ik(ə)lē/ **adv.**, **rheu·ma·tick·y** /ro͞o'matikē, 'ro͞omə,tikē/ **adj.** (informal).
– ORIGIN late Middle English (originally referring to infection characterized by rheum): from Old French *reumatique*, or via Latin from Greek *rheumatikos*, from *rheuma* 'bodily humor, flow' (see RHEUM).

rheu·mat·ic fe·ver ▶ **n.** a noncontagious acute fever marked by inflammation and pain in the joints. It chiefly affects young people and is caused by a streptococcal infection.

rheu·mat·ics /ro͞o'matiks/ ▶ **plural n.** [usu. treated as sing.] informal rheumatism; rheumatic pains.

rheu·ma·tism /'ro͞omə,tizəm/ ▶ **n.** any disease marked by inflammation and pain in the joints, muscles, or fibrous tissue, esp. rheumatoid arthritis.
– ORIGIN late 17th cent.: from French *rhumatisme*, or via Latin from Greek *rheumatismos*, from *rheumatizein* 'to snuffle,' from *rheuma* 'stream': the disease was originally supposed to be caused by the internal flow of "watery" humors.

rheu·ma·toid /'ro͞omə,toid/ ▶ **adj.** Medicine relating to, affected by, or resembling rheumatism.

rheu·ma·toid ar·thri·tis ▶ **n.** a chronic progressive disease causing inflammation in the joints and resulting in painful deformity and immobility, esp. in the fingers, wrists, feet, and ankles. Compare with OSTEOARTHRITIS.

rheu·ma·toid fac·tor ▶ **n.** Medicine any of a group of autoantibodies that are present in the blood of many people with rheumatoid arthritis.

rheu·ma·tol·o·gy /,ro͞omə'täləjē/ ▶ **n.** Medicine the study of rheumatism, arthritis, and other disorders of the joints, muscles, and ligaments.
– DERIVATIVES **rheu·ma·to·log·i·cal** /,ro͞omətl'äjikəl/ **adj.**, **rheu·ma·tol·o·gist** /-jist/ **n.**

rheum·y /'ro͞omē/ ▶ **adj.** (esp. of the eyes) full of rheum; watery.

rhi·nal /'rīnl/ ▶ **adj.** Anatomy of or relating to the nose or the olfactory part of the brain.
– ORIGIN mid 19th cent.: from Greek *rhis, rhin-* 'nose' + -AL.

Rhine /rīn/ a river in western Europe that rises in the Swiss Alps and flows for 820 miles (1,320 km) to the North Sea, forming the German–Swiss border before flowing through Germany and the Netherlands. French name **Rhin**. German name RHEIN.

Rhine·land /'rīn,land/ the region of western Germany through which the Rhine River flows, esp. the part that is west of the river. German name RHEINLAND.

Rhine·land-Pa·lat·i·nate a state in western Germany; capital, Mainz. German name RHEINLAND-PFALZ.

rhine·stone /'rīn,stōn/ ▶ **n.** an imitation diamond used in costume jewelry and to decorate clothes.
– ORIGIN late 19th cent.: translating French *caillou du Rhin*, literally 'pebble of the Rhine.'

rhi·ni·tis /rī'nītis/ ▶ **n.** Medicine inflammation of the mucous membrane of the nose, caused by a virus infection (e.g., the common cold) or by an allergic reaction (e.g., hay fever).

rhi·no /'rīnō/ ▶ **n.** (pl. **same** or **rhinos**) informal a rhinoceros.
– ORIGIN late 19th cent.: abbreviation.

rhino- ▶ **comb. form** of or relating to the nose: *rhinoplasty*.
– ORIGIN from Greek *rhis, rhin-* 'nose.'

rhi·noc·er·os /rī'näs(ə)rəs/ ▶ **n.** (pl. **same** or **rhinoceroses**) a large, heavily built plant-eating mammal with one or two horns on the nose and thick folded skin, native to Africa and southern Asia. All kinds have become endangered through hunting. ● Family Rhinocerotidae: four genera and five species.
– ORIGIN Middle English: via Latin from Greek *rhinokerōs*, from *rhis, rhin-* 'nose' + *keras* 'horn.'

rhi·noc·er·os bee·tle ▶ **n.** a very large mainly tropical beetle, the male of which has a curved horn extending from the head and typically another from the thorax. In some parts of Asia, males are put to fight as a spectator sport. ● Several genera and species in the family Scarabaeidae, including *Oryctes rhinoceros*, which is a serious pest of coconut palms.

rhi·noc·er·os bird ▶ **n.** another term for OXPECKER.

rhi·noc·er·os horn ▶ **n.** a mass of keratinized fibers that comprises the horn of a rhinoceros, reputed in Eastern medicine to have medicinal or aphrodisiac powers.

rhi·noc·er·os horn·bill ▶ **n.** a large Southeast Asian hornbill with black-and-white plumage and an upturned casque. ● *Buceros rhinoceros*, family Bucerotidae.

rhi·no·plas·ty /'rīnō,plastē/ ▶ **n.** (pl. **rhinoplasties**) plastic surgery performed on the nose.
– DERIVATIVES **rhi·no·plas·tic** /,rīnō'plastik/ **adj.**

rhi·no·vi·rus /,rīnō'vīrəs, 'rīnō,vī-/ ▶ **n.** Medicine any of a group of picornaviruses, including those that cause some forms of the common cold.

rhizo- ▶ **comb. form** Botany relating to a root or roots: *rhizomorph*.
– ORIGIN from Greek *rhiza* 'root.'

rhi·zo·bi·um /rī'zōbēəm/ ▶ **n.** a nitrogen-fixing bacterium that is common in the soil, esp. in the root nodules of leguminous plants. ● Genus *Rhizobium*; Gram-negative rods.
– ORIGIN 1920s: modern Latin, from RHIZO- 'root' + Greek *bios* 'life.'

rhi·zoc·to·ni·a /,rī,zäk'tōnēə/ ▶ **n.** a common soil fungus that sometimes causes plant diseases such as damping off, foot rot, and eyespot. ● Genus *Rhizoctonia*, subdivision Deuteromycotina, in particular *R. solani*.
– ORIGIN late 19th cent.: modern Latin (genus name), from Greek *rhiza* 'root' + *ktonos* 'murder.'

rhi·zoid /'rī,zoid/ ▶ **n.** Botany a filamentous outgrowth or root hair on the underside of the thallus in some lower plants, esp. mosses and liverworts, serving both to anchor the plant and (in terrestrial forms) to conduct water.
– DERIVATIVES **rhi·zoi·dal** /rī'zoidl/ **adj.**

rhi·zome /'rī,zōm/ ▶ **n.** Botany a continuously growing horizontal underground stem that puts out lateral shoots and adventitious roots at intervals. Compare with BULB (sense 1), CORM.
– ORIGIN mid 19th cent.: from Greek *rhizōma*, from *rhizousthai* 'take root,' based on *rhiza* 'root.'

rhi·zo·morph /'rīzə,môrf/ ▶ **n.** Botany a rootlike aggregation of hyphae in certain fungi.

Rhi·zop·o·da /rī'zäpədə/ Zoology a phylum of single-celled animals that includes the amebas and their relatives, which have extensible pseudopodia.
– DERIVATIVES **rhi·zo·pod** /'rīzə,päd/ **n.**
– ORIGIN modern Latin (plural), from RHIZO- 'root' + Greek *pous, pod-* 'foot.'

rhi·zo·sphere /'rīzə,sfir/ ▶ **n.** Ecology the region of soil in the vicinity of plant roots in which the chemistry and microbiology is influenced by their growth, respiration, and nutrient exchange.

rho /rō/ ▶ **n.** (pl. **rhos**) the seventeenth letter of the Greek alphabet (Ρ, ρ), transliterated as 'r' or (when written with a rough breathing) 'rh.' ■ (**Rho**) [followed by Latin genitive] Astronomy the seventeenth star in a constellation: *Rho Cassiopeiae*.

rho·da·mine /'rōdə,mēn/ ▶ **n.** Chemistry any of a number of synthetic dyes derived from xanthene, used to color textiles.
– ORIGIN late 19th cent.: from RHODO- 'rose-colored' + AMINE.

Rhode Is·land /rōd/ a state in the northeastern US, on the coast of the Atlantic Ocean, one of the six New England states; pop. 1,050,788 (est. 2008); capital, Providence; statehood, May 29, 1790 (13). Settled by England in the 17th century, it was one of the original thirteen states. It is the smallest and most densely populated US state.
– DERIVATIVES **Rhode Is·land·er** **n.**

PRONUNCIATION KEY ə *ago, up*; ər *over, fur*; a *hat*; ā *ate*; ä *car*; e *let*; ē *see*; i *fit*; ī *by*; NG *sing*; ō *go*; ô *law, for*; oi *toy*; o͝o *good*; o͞o *goo*; ou *out*; TH *thin*; TH *then*; ZH *vision*

r

Rhode Is·land Red ▶ **n.** a bird of an American breed of reddish-black domestic chicken.

Rhodes¹ /rōdz/ a Greek island in the southeastern Aegean Sea, off the Turkish coast. It is the largest of the Dodecanese Islands and the most easterly of the islands in the Aegean Sea; pop. 130,000 (est. 2004). Greek name **RÓDHOS**. ■ its capital, a port on the northern tip; pop. 55,900 (est. 2009). It was founded *c.*408 BC and was the site of the Colossus of Rhodes.

Rhodes², Cecil (John) (1853–1902), South African statesman, born in Britain; prime minister of Cape Colony 1890–96. He expanded British territory in southern Africa, annexing Bechuanaland (now Botswana) in 1884 and developing Rhodesia from 1889. By 1890, he had acquired 90 percent of the world's production of diamonds.

Cecil Rhodes

Rho·de·sia /rōˈdēzнə/ the former name of a large territory in central and southern Africa that was divided into Southern Rhodesia (now Zambia) in 1923 and into Northern Rhodesia (now Zimbabwe) in 1924.
– DERIVATIVES **Rho·de·sian adj. & n.**

Rho·de·sian ridge·back /rōˈdēzнən/ ▶ **n.** a dog of a breed having a short light brown coat and a ridge of hair along the middle of the back, growing in the opposite direction to the rest of the coat.

Rhodes Schol·ar·ship ▶ **n.** any of several scholarships awarded annually for study at Oxford University by students from certain Commonwealth countries, South Africa, the US, and Germany.
– DERIVATIVES **Rhodes schol·ar n.**
– ORIGIN named after Cecil *Rhodes* (see **RHODES²**), who founded the scholarships in 1902.

rho·di·um /ˈrōdēəm/ ▶ **n.** the chemical element of atomic number 45, a hard silvery-white metal of the transition series, typically occurring in association with platinum. (Symbol: **Rh**)
– ORIGIN mid 17th cent.: modern Latin, from Greek *rhodon* 'rose' (from the color of the solution of its salts).

rhodo- ▶ **comb. form** chiefly Mineralogy & Chemistry rose-colored: *rhodochrosite*.
– ORIGIN from Greek *rhodon* 'rose.'

rho·do·chro·site /ˌrōdəˈkrōˌsīt, rəˈdäkrə-/ ▶ **n.** a mineral consisting of manganese carbonate, typically occurring as pink, brown, or gray rhombohedral crystals.
– ORIGIN mid 19th cent.: from Greek *rhodokhrōs* 'rose-colored' + **-ITE¹**.

rho·do·den·dron /ˌrōdəˈdendrən/ ▶ **n.** a shrub or small tree of the heath family, with large clusters of bell-shaped flowers and typically with large evergreen leaves, widely grown as an ornamental. ● Genus *Rhododendron*, family Ericaceae: many cultivars.
– ORIGIN via Latin from Greek, from *rhodon* 'rose' + *dendron* 'tree.'

rhododendron

rho·do·lite /ˈrōdlˌīt/ ▶ **n.** a pale violet or red variety of garnet, used as a gemstone.

rho·do·nite /ˈrōdnˌīt/ ▶ **n.** a brownish or rose-pink mineral consisting of a silicate of manganese and other elements.
– ORIGIN early 19th cent.: from Greek *rhodon* 'rose' + **-ITE¹**.

Rhod·o·pe Moun·tains /ˈrädəpē/ a mountain system in the Balkans, in southeastern Europe, on the frontier between Bulgaria and Greece, rising to a height of over 6,600 feet (2,000 m) and including the Rila Mountains in the northwest.

Rho·doph·y·ta /rōˈdäfətə/ Botany a division of lower plants that comprises the red algae.
– ORIGIN modern Latin (plural), from **RHODO-** 'rose-colored' + Greek *phuta* 'plants.'

rho·do·phyte /ˈrōdəˌfīt/ ▶ **n.** Botany a lower plant of the division Rhodophyta; a red alga.

rho·dop·sin /rōˈdäpsən/ ▶ **n.** a purplish-red light-sensitive pigment present in the retinas of humans and many other animal groups.
– ORIGIN late 19th cent.: from Greek *rhodon* 'rose' + *opsis* 'sight' + **-IN¹**.

rho·do·ra /rəˈdôrə/ ▶ **n.** a pink-flowered North American shrub of the heath family. ● *Rhododendron canadense*, family Ericaceae.
– ORIGIN late 18th cent.: modern Latin (former genus name), based on Greek *rhodon* 'rose.'

rhomb /räm(b)/ ▶ **n.** a rhombohedral crystal. ■ a rhombus.
– DERIVATIVES **rhom·bic** /ˈrämbik/ **adj.**
– ORIGIN early 19th cent.: from Latin *rhombus* (see **RHOMBUS**).

rhomb. ▶ **abbr.** rhombic.

rhom·ben·ceph·a·lon /ˌrämˌbenˈsefəˌlän, -lən/ ▶ **n.** Anatomy another term for **HINDBRAIN**.
– ORIGIN late 19th cent.: from **RHOMB** + **ENCEPHALON**.

rhom·bi /ˈrämˌbī, -ˌbē/ plural form of **RHOMBUS**.

rhom·bo·he·dral /ˌrämbōˈhēdrəl/ ▶ **adj.** (chiefly of a crystal) shaped like a rhombohedron.

rhom·bo·he·dron /ˌrämbōˈhēdrən/ ▶ **n.** (pl. **rhombohedrons** or **rhombohedra** /-drə/) a solid figure whose faces are six equal rhombuses. ■ a crystal or other solid object of this form.
– ORIGIN mid 19th cent.: from **RHOMBUS** + **-HEDRON**, on the pattern of words such as *polyhedron*.

rhom·boid /ˈrämˌboid/ ▶ **adj.** having or resembling the shape of a rhombus.
▶ **n. 1** a quadrilateral of which only the opposite sides and angles are equal. **2** (also **rhomboid muscle**) another term for **RHOMBOIDEUS**.

rhomboid 1

– DERIVATIVES **rhom·boi·dal** /rämˈboidl/ **adj.**
– ORIGIN late 16th cent. (as a noun): from French *rhomboïde*, or via late Latin from Greek *rhomboeidēs*, from *rhombos* (see **RHOMBUS**).

rhom·boi·de·us /rämˈboidēəs/ ▶ **n.** (pl. **rhomboidei** /-dēˌī/) Anatomy a muscle connecting the shoulder blade to the vertebrae.
– ORIGIN mid 19th cent.: modern Latin, from *rhomboideus* (*musculus*) (see **RHOMBOID**).

Rhom·bo·zoa /ˌrämbəˈzōə/ Zoology a minor phylum of mesozoan worms that are parasites in the kidneys of cephalopod mollusks.
– DERIVATIVES **rhom·bo·zoan n. & adj.**
– ORIGIN modern Latin (plural), from Greek *rhombos* 'rhombus' + *zōia* 'animals.'

rhom·bus /ˈrämbəs/ ▶ **n.** (pl. **rhombuses** or **rhombi** /-ˌbī, -ˌbē/) a parallelogram with opposite equal acute angles, opposite equal obtuse angles, and four equal sides. ■ any parallelogram with equal sides, including a square.

rhombus

– ORIGIN mid 16th cent.: via Latin from Greek *rhombos*.

Rhône /rōn/ a river in southwestern Europe that rises in the Swiss Alps and flows 505 miles (812 km) through Lake Geneva into France, then to Lyons, Avignon, and the Mediterranean Sea west of Marseilles, where it forms a wide delta.

rho·ta·ci·za·tion /ˌrōtəsəˈzāsнən/ ▶ **n.** Linguistics change of an original *s* or *z* to *r*, as in *was* and *were*. ■ Phonetics pronunciation of a vowel to reflect a following *r* in the orthography, e.g., in *farm*, *bird*.
– DERIVATIVES **rho·ta·cized** /ˈrōtəˌsīzd/ **adj.**
– ORIGIN 1970s: from *rhotacize* (from Greek *rhōtakizein*) + **-ATION**.

rho·tic /ˈrōtik/ ▶ **adj.** Phonetics of, relating to, or denoting a dialect or variety of English, e.g., Midwestern American English, in which *r* is pronounced before a consonant (as in *hard*) and at the ends of words (as in *far*).
– DERIVATIVES **rho·tic·i·ty** /rōˈtisətē/ **n.**
– ORIGIN 1960s: from Greek *rhot-*, stem of *rho* (see **RHO**) + **-IC**.

rhp (also **r.h.p.**) ▶ **abbr.** rated horsepower.

RHS ▶ **abbr.** ■ Royal Historical Society. ■ Royal Horticultural Society. ■ Royal Humane Society.

rhu·barb /ˈro͞oˌbärb/ ▶ **n. 1** the thick leaf stalks of a cultivated plant of the dock family, which are reddish or green and eaten as a fruit after cooking. **2** the large-leaved Eurasian plant that produces these stems. ● *Rheum rhaponticum* (or *rhabarbarum*), family Polygonaceae. ■ used in names of other plants of this genus, several of which are used medicinally, e.g., **Chinese rhubarb**. **3** informal, chiefly Brit. the noise made by a group of actors to give the impression of indistinct background conversation or to represent the noise of a crowd, esp. by the random repetition of the word "rhubarb" with different intonations. ■ a heated dispute: *rhubarbs often broke out among these less than professional players*.
– ORIGIN late Middle English (denoting the rootstock of other plants of this genus used medicinally): from Old French *reubarbe*, from a shortening of medieval Latin *rheubarbarum*, alteration (by association with *rheum* 'rhubarb') of *rhabarbarum* 'foreign rhubarb,' from Greek *rha* (also meaning 'rhubarb') + *barbaros* 'foreign.'

rhumb /rəm(b)/ ▶ **n.** Nautical **1** (also **rhumb line**) an imaginary line on the earth's surface cutting all meridians at the same angle, used as the standard method of plotting a ship's course on a chart. **2** any of the 32 points of the compass.
– ORIGIN late 16th cent.: from French *rumb* (earlier *ryn* (*de vent*) 'point of the compass'), probably from Dutch *ruim* 'space, room.' The spelling change was due to association with Latin *rhombus* (see **RHOMBUS**).

rhum·ba ▶ **n.** variant spelling of **RUMBA**.

rhyme /rīm/ ▶ **n.** correspondence of sound between words or the endings of words, esp. when these are used at the ends of lines of poetry. ■ a short poem in which the sound of the word or syllable at the end of each line corresponds with that at the end of another. ■ poetry or verse marked by such correspondence of sound: *the clues were written in rhyme*. ■ a word that has the same sound as another.
▶ **v.** [no obj.] (of a word, syllable, or line) have or end with a sound that corresponds to another: *balloon rhymes with moon* | (as adj. **rhyming**) *rhyming couplets*. ■ (of a poem or song) be composed of lines that end in words or syllables with sounds that correspond with those at the ends of other lines: *the poem would have been better if it had rhymed*. ■ [with obj.] (**rhyme something with**) put a word together with (another word that has a corresponding sound), as when writing poetry: *I'm not sure about rhyming perestroika with balalaika*. ■ literary compose verse or poetry: *Musa rhymed and sang*.
– PHRASES **rhyme or reason** [with negative] logical explanation or reason: *without rhyme or reason his mood changed*.
– DERIVATIVES **rhym·er n.**, **rhym·ist** /-ist/ **n.** (archaic).
– ORIGIN Middle English *rime*, from Old French, from medieval Latin *rithmus*, via Latin from Greek *rhuthmos* (see **RHYTHM**). The current spelling was introduced in the early 17th cent. under the influence of *rhythm*.

rhyme scheme ▶ **n.** the ordered pattern of rhymes at the ends of the lines of a poem or verse.

rhyme·ster /ˈrīmstər/ ▶ **n.** a person who composes rhymes, esp. simple ones.

rhym·ing slang ▶ **n.** a type of slang that replaces words with rhyming words or phrases, typically with the rhyming element omitted. For example *butcher's*, short for *butcher's hook*, means "look" in Cockney rhyming slang.

rhy·o·lite /ˈrīəˌlīt/ ▶ **n.** Geology a pale fine-grained volcanic rock of granitic composition, typically porphyritic in texture.
– DERIVATIVES **rhy·o·lit·ic** /ˌrīəˈlitik/ **adj.**
– ORIGIN mid 19th cent.: from German *Rhyolit*, from Greek *rhuax* 'lava stream' + *lithos* 'stone.'

Rhys /rēs/, Jean (1890–1979), British novelist and short-story writer, born in Dominica; pseudonym of *Ella Gwendolen Rees Williams*. Notable novels: *Good Morning, Midnight* (1939) and *Wide Sargasso Sea* (1966).

rhythm /ˈriT͟Həm/ ▶ **n. 1** a strong, regular, repeated pattern of movement or sound: *Ruth listened to the rhythm of his breathing*. ■ the systematic

arrangement of musical sounds, principally according to duration and periodic stress. ■ a particular type of pattern formed by such arrangement: *guitar melodies with deep African rhythms.* ■ a person's natural feeling for such arrangement: *they've got no rhythm.* ■ the measured flow of words and phrases in verse or prose as determined by the relation of long and short or stressed and unstressed syllables. ■ a regularly recurring sequence of events, actions, or processes: *the twice daily rhythms of the tides.* ■ Art a harmonious sequence or correlation of colors or elements.
– DERIVATIVES **rhythm·less** adj.
– ORIGIN mid 16th cent. (also originally in the sense 'rhyme'): from French *rhythme*, or via Latin from Greek *rhuthmos* (related to *rhein* 'to flow').

rhythm and blues (abbr.: **R & B**) ▶ n. a form of popular music of African-American origin that arose during the 1940s from blues, with the addition of driving rhythms taken from jazz. It was an immediate precursor of rock and roll.

rhythm gui·tar ▶ n. a guitar part consisting of the chord sequences of a pop or rock song.

rhyth·mic /ˈriT͟Hmik/ ▶ adj. having or relating to rhythm: *a rhythmic dance.* ■ occurring regularly: *there are rhythmic changes in our bodies.*
– DERIVATIVES **rhyth·mi·cal** adj., **rhyth·mi·cal·ly** /-ik(ə)lē/ adv.
– ORIGIN early 17th cent.: from French *rhythmique* or via Latin from Greek *rhuthmikos*, from *rhuthmos* (see RHYTHM).

rhyth·mic gym·nas·tics ▶ plural n. [usu. treated as sing.] a form of gymnastics emphasizing dancelike rhythmic routines, typically accentuated by the use of ribbons or hoops.
– DERIVATIVES **rhyth·mic gym·nast** n.

rhyth·mic·i·ty /ˌriT͟Hˈmisətē/ ▶ n. rhythmical quality or character: *the nursery rhymes' rhythmicity makes them particularly easy to learn.*

rhythm meth·od ▶ n. a method of avoiding conception by which sexual intercourse is restricted to the times of a woman's menstrual cycle when ovulation is least likely to occur.

rhythm sec·tion ▶ n. the part of a pop or jazz group supplying the rhythm, generally regarded as consisting of bass and drums and sometimes piano or guitar.

rhy·ton /ˈrīˌtän/ ▶ n. (pl. **rhytons** or **rhyta** /ˈrītə/) a type of drinking vessel used in ancient Greece, typically having the form of an animal's head or a horn, with the hole for drinking at the bottom.
– ORIGIN from Greek *rhuton*, neuter of *rhutos* 'flowing'; related to *rhein* 'to flow.'

RI ▶ abbr. ■ Rex et Imperator (King and Emperor) or Regina et Imperatrix (Queen and Empress). [Latin.] ■ Rhode Island (in official postal use). ■ Royal Institute or Institution.

RIA ▶ abbr. ■ radioimmunoassay. ■ Royal Irish Academy.

ri·a /ˈrēə/ ▶ n. Geography a long narrow inlet formed by the partial submergence of a river valley.
– ORIGIN late 19th cent.: from Spanish *ría* 'estuary.'

ri·al /rēˈôl, rēˈäl/ ▶ n. **1** (also **riyal**) the basic monetary unit of Iran and Oman, equal to 100 dinars in Iran and 1000 baiza in Oman.
2 variant spelling of RIYAL.
– ORIGIN via Persian from Arabic *riyāl* (see RIYAL).

Ri·al·to /rēˈaltō, -ˈäl-/ **1** a city in southwestern California, west of San Bernardino; pop. 98,700 (est. 2008).
2 an island in Venice, Italy, that contains the old mercantile quarter of medieval Venice. The Rialto Bridge, completed in 1591, crosses the Grand Canal between Rialto and the San Marco Islands.

RIB ▶ n. a small open boat with a fiberglass hull and inflatable rubber sides.
– ORIGIN acronym from *rigid inflatable boat.*

rib /rib/ ▶ n. **1** each of a series of slender curved bones articulated in pairs to the spine (twelve pairs in humans), protecting the thoracic cavity and its organs. ■ a rib of an animal with meat adhering to it used as food; a joint or cut from the ribs of an animal.
2 a long raised piece of stronger or thicker material across a surface or through a structure, and typically serving to support or strengthen it, in particular: ■ Architecture a curved member supporting a vault or defining its form. ■ any of the curved transverse pieces of metal or timber in a ship, extending up from the keel and forming part of the framework of the hull. ■ each of the curved pieces of wood forming the body of a lute or the sides of a violin. ■ each of the hinged rods supporting the fabric of an umbrella. ■ Aeronautics a structural member in an airfoil, extending back from the leading edge and serving to define the contour of the airfoil. ■ a vein of a leaf (esp. the midrib) or an insect's wing. ■ a ridge of rock or land. ■ Knitting a combination of alternate knit (plain) and purl stitches producing a ridged, slightly elastic fabric, used esp. for the cuffs and bottom edges of sweaters.
▶ v. (**ribs, ribbing, ribbed**) [with obj.] **1** (usu. **be ribbed**) mark with or form into raised bands or ridges: *the road ahead was ribbed with furrows of slush.*
2 informal tease good-naturedly: *the first time I appeared in the outfit I was ribbed mercilessly.*
– DERIVATIVES **rib·less** adj.
– ORIGIN Old English *rib, ribb* (noun), of Germanic origin; related to Dutch *rib(be)* and German *Rippe*. Sense 1 of the verb dates from the mid 16th cent.; the sense 'tease' was originally a US slang usage meaning 'to fool, dupe' (1930s).

rib·ald /ˈribəld, ˈribˌôld, ˈrīˌbôld/ ▶ adj. referring to sexual matters in an amusingly rude or irreverent way: *a ribald comment.*
– ORIGIN Middle English (as a noun denoting a lowly retainer or a licentious or irreverent person): from Old French *ribauld*, from *riber* 'indulge in licentious pleasures,' from a Germanic base meaning 'prostitute.'

rib·ald·ry /ˈribəldrē, ˈrī-/ ▶ n. ribald talk or behavior.

rib·and /ˈribənd/ ▶ n. archaic a ribbon.
– ORIGIN Middle English: from Old French *riban*, probably from a Germanic compound of the noun BAND[1].

ribbed /ribd/ ▶ adj. (esp. of a fabric or garment) having a pattern of raised bands: *a ribbed cashmere sweater.* ■ Architecture (of a vault or other structure) strengthened with ribs.

Rib·ben·trop /ˈribənˌtrōp/, Joachim von (1893–1946), German Nazi politician. As foreign minister 1938–45, he signed the nonaggression pact with the former Soviet Union in 1939. He was convicted as a war criminal in the Nuremberg trials and hanged.

rib·bie /ˈribē/ ▶ n. (pl. **ribbies**) Baseball, informal a run batted in. See **RBI**.
– ORIGIN mid 20th cent.: elaboration of **RBI**.

rib·bing /ˈribiNG/ ▶ n. **1** a riblike structure or pattern, esp. a band of knitting in rib.
2 informal good-natured teasing.

rib·bit /ˈribit/ ▶ n. informal the characteristic croaking sound of a frog: *the power of the male's commanding "ribbit" came not from the throat but from vibrations in ear membranes.*
– ORIGIN imitative.

rib·bon /ˈribən/ ▶ n. **1** a long, narrow strip of fabric, used esp. for tying something or for decoration: *the tiny pink ribbons in her hair | cut four lengths of ribbon.* ■ a strip of fabric of a special color or design awarded as a prize or worn to indicate the holding of an honor, esp. a small multicolored piece of ribbon worn in place of the medal it represents: *old horse show ribbons and rosettes.*
2 a long, narrow strip of something: *slice the peppers into ribbons lengthwise.* ■ a narrow band of inked material wound on a spool and forming the inking agent in some typewriters and computer printers.
▶ v. [no obj.] extend or move in a long narrow strip like a ribbon: *miles of concrete ribboned behind the bus.*
– PHRASES **cut a** (or **the**) **ribbon** perform an opening ceremony, typically by formally cutting a ribbon across the entrance to somewhere. **cut** (or **tear**) **something to ribbons** cut (or tear) something so badly that only ragged strips remain. ■ damage something severely: *the country has seen its economy torn to ribbons by recession.*
– DERIVATIVES **rib·boned** adj., **rib·bon·like** /-ˌlīk/ adj.
– ORIGIN early 16th cent.: variant of RIBAND. The French spelling *ruban* was also frequent in the 16th–18th centuries.

rib·bon ca·ble ▶ n. a cable for transmitting electronic signals consisting of several insulated wires connected together to form a flat ribbon.

rib·bon de·vel·op·ment ▶ n. chiefly Brit. the building of houses along a main road, esp. one leading out of a town or city.

rib·bon·fish /ˈribənˌfisH/ ▶ n. (pl. **same** or **ribbonfishes**) any of a number of long slender fishes that typically have a dorsal fin running the length of the body, in particular: ● a fish of the dealfish family (Trachipteridae). ● a fish of the cutlassfish family (Trichiuridae). ● another term for OARFISH.

rib·bon grass ▶ n. another term for TAPE GRASS.

rib·bon worm ▶ n. a chiefly aquatic worm with an elongated, unsegmented, flattened body that is typically brightly colored and tangled in knots, and a long proboscis for catching food. ● Phylum Nemertea: two classes.

rib·by /ˈribē/ ▶ adj. having prominent ribs: *ribby, bony-rumped, horned cattle.*

rib cage ▶ n. the bony frame formed by the ribs around the chest.

Ri·be·ra /rēˈbärä/, José (or Jusepe) de (*c.*1591–1652), Spanish painter and etcher, resident in Italy from 1616; known as **Lo Spagnoletto** ("the little Spaniard"). He is noted for his religious and genre paintings.

rib eye (also **rib-eye steak**) ▶ n. a cut of beef from the outer side of the ribs: *a menu that runs to gargantuan rib eyes and ten-pound lobsters.*

ri·bi·tol /ˈrībiˌtôl, -ˌtōl/ ▶ n. Chemistry a colorless crystalline compound that is formed by reduction of ribose and occurs in certain plants. ● An alcohol; chem. formula: $HOCH_2(CHOH)_3CH_2OH$.
– ORIGIN 1940s: from RIBOSE + -ITE[1] + -OL.

ri·bo·fla·vin /ˌrībəˈflāvin, ˈrībəˌflā-/ ▶ n. Biochemistry a yellow vitamin of the B complex that is essential for metabolic energy production. It is present in many foods, esp. milk, liver, eggs, and green vegetables, and is also synthesized by the intestinal flora. Also called VITAMIN B2 (see VITAMIN B).
– ORIGIN 1930s: from RIBOSE + Latin *flavus* 'yellow' + -IN[1].

ri·bo·nu·cle·ase /ˌrībōˈn(y)o͞oklēˌās, -ˌāz/ ▶ n. another term for **RNASE**.

ri·bo·nu·cle·ic ac·id /ˌribōn(y)o͞oˈklē-ik, -ˈklā-ik/ ▶ n. see **RNA**.
– ORIGIN 1930s: *ribonucleic* from RIBOSE + NUCLEIC ACID.

ri·bose /ˈrīˌbōs, -ˌbōz/ ▶ n. Chemistry a sugar of the pentose class that occurs widely in nature as a constituent of nucleosides and several vitamins and enzymes.
– ORIGIN late 19th cent.: arbitrary alteration of ARABINOSE, a related sugar.

ri·bo·some /ˈrībəˌsōm/ ▶ n. Biochemistry a minute particle consisting of RNA and associated proteins, found in large numbers in the cytoplasm of living cells. They bind messenger RNA and transfer RNA to synthesize polypeptides and proteins.
– DERIVATIVES **ri·bo·so·mal** /ˌrībəˈsōməl/ adj.
– ORIGIN 1950s: from RIBONUCLEIC ACID + -SOME[3].

ri·bo·zyme /ˈrībəˌzīm/ ▶ n. Biochemistry an RNA molecule capable of acting as an enzyme.
– ORIGIN 1980s: blend of *ribonucleic* (from RIBONUCLEIC ACID) and ENZYME.

rib·tick·ler ▶ n. informal an amusing joke or story.
– DERIVATIVES **rib·tick·ling** adj., **rib·tick·ling·ly** adv.

ri·bu·lose /ˈribyəˌlōs, -ˌlōz/ ▶ n. Chemistry a sugar of the pentose class that is an important intermediate in carbohydrate metabolism and photosynthesis.
– ORIGIN 1930s: from RIBOSE + *-ulose*.

rib·wort /ˈribˌwərt, -ˌwôrt/ (also **ribwort plantain**) ▶ n. a Eurasian plantain with erect ribbed leaves and a rounded flower spike, well established as a weed in North America. ● *Plantago lanceolata*, family Plantaginaceae.

Ri·car·di·an[1] /riˈkärdēən/ ▶ adj. of or relating to the time of any of three kings of England, Richard I, II, and III. ■ of or holding the view that Richard III was a just king who was misrepresented by Shakespeare and other writers.
▶ n. a contemporary or supporter of Richard III.
– DERIVATIVES **Ri·car·di·an·ism** /-ˌnizəm/ n.
– ORIGIN from medieval Latin *Ricardus* 'Richard' + -IAN.

Ri·car·di·an[2] ▶ adj. relating to or denoting the doctrines of the political economist David Ricardo (1772–1823).

Ric·ci ten·sor /ˈrēCHē, ˈriCHē/ ▶ n. Mathematics a set of components that describes part of the curvature of space-time. It is a symmetric second-order tensor.
– ORIGIN 1920s: named after Curbastro G. *Ricci* (1853–1925), Italian mathematician.

RICE ▶ abbr. rest, ice, compression, and elevation (treatment method for bruises, strains, and sprains).

r

Rice[1] /rīs/, Anne (1941–), US writer; born *Howard Allen O'Brien*; pen names **A. N. Roquelaure** and **Anne Rampling**. She is best known for her series called the *Vampire Chronicles*, which includes *Interview with the Vampire* (1976), *The Queen of the Damned* (1988), and *Merrick* (2000).

Rice[2], Condoleezza (1954–), US secretary of state 2005–09. Fluent in Russian, she became President George H. W. Bush's adviser on Soviet affairs in 1989, and that same year joined the National Security Council. Under President George W. Bush, she served as national security adviser 2001–05.

Rice[3], Jerry (1962–), US football player. A wide receiver for the San Francisco 49ers 1985–2000 and the Oakland Raiders 2001–04, he set NFL records in pass receptions and touchdowns.

Rice[4] /rīs/, Sir Tim (1944–), English lyricist and entertainer; full name *Timothy Miles Bindon Rice*. With Andrew Lloyd Webber, he cowrote a number of musicals, including *Joseph and the Amazing Technicolor Dreamcoat* (1968), *Jesus Christ Superstar* (1971), and *Evita* (1978).

rice /rīs/ ▶ **n.** a swamp grass that is widely cultivated as a source of food, esp. in Asia. ● *Oryza sativa*, family Gramineae. **African rice** belongs to the related species *O. glaberrima*, whereas the so-called **wild rice** is not a true rice at all. ■ the grains of this cereal used as food.

Rice provides the staple diet of half the world's population and is second only to wheat in terms of total output. Rice seedlings are usually planted in flooded fields or paddies, so that terraces are necessary on hillsides and a reliable source of water is essential.

▶ **v.** [with obj.] force (cooked potatoes or other vegetables) through a sieve or ricer.
– ORIGIN Middle English: from Old French *ris*, from Italian *riso*, from Greek *oruza*.

rice bowl ▶ **n. 1** a dish out of which rice is eaten.
2 an area in which abundant quantities of rice are grown.
3 [in sing.] one's livelihood (used esp. in reference to Asia): *entrenched vested interests will fight to the death to protect their rice bowl.*

rice burn·er ▶ **n.** derogatory a Japanese motorcycle.

rice pad·dy ▶ **n.** see PADDY.

rice pa·per ▶ **n.** thin translucent edible paper made from the flattened and dried pith of a shrub, used in painting (esp. oriental) and in baking biscuits and cakes. ● This paper is obtained from the Chinese plant *Tetrapanax papyriferus* (family Araliaceae) or from the Indo-Pacific plant *Scaevola sericea* (family Goodeniaceae).

ric·er /ˈrīsər/ ▶ **n.** a utensil with small holes through which boiled potatoes or other soft food can be pushed to form particles of a similar size to grains of rice.

rice rat ▶ **n.** a nocturnal rat that typically lives in marshy or damp areas, native to America, the Caribbean, and the Galapagos Islands. ● *Oryzomys* and other genera, family Muridae: numerous species.

ri·cer·car /ˌrēCHərˈkär/ (also **ricercare** /-ˈkärā/) ▶ **n.** (pl. **ricercars** or **ricercari** /-ˈkärē/) Music an elaborate instrumental composition in fugal or canonic style, typically of the 16th to 18th centuries.
– ORIGIN from Italian *ricercare* 'search out.'

Rich /riCH/, Buddy (1917–87), US jazz drummer and bandleader; born *Bernard Rich*. He played for bandleaders such as **Artie Shaw** and **Tommy Dorsey** and then formed his own band in 1946.

rich /riCH/ ▶ **adj. 1** having a great deal of money or assets; wealthy: *most of these artists are already quite rich* | (as plural noun **the rich**) *every day the gap between the rich and the poor widens.* ■ (of a country or region) having valuable natural resources or a successful economy. ■ of expensive materials or workmanship; demonstrating wealth: *rich mahogany furniture.* ■ generating wealth; valuable: *not all football players enjoy rich rewards from the game.*
2 plentiful; abundant: *the nation's rich and diverse wildlife.* ■ having (a particular thing) in large amounts: *many vegetables and fruits are rich in antioxidant vitamins* | [in combination] *a protein-rich diet.* ■ (of food) containing a large amount of fat, spices, sugar, etc.: *dishes with wonderfully rich sauces.* ■ (of drink) full-bodied: *a rich, hoppy beer.* ■ (of the mixture in an internal combustion engine) containing a high proportion of fuel.
3 producing a large quantity of something: *novels have always been a rich source of material for the film industry.* ■ (of soil or a piece of land) having the properties necessary to produce fertile growth. ■ (of a mine or mineral deposit) yielding a large quantity or proportion of precious metal.
4 (of a color, sound, smell, etc.) pleasantly deep or strong: *his rich bass voice* | *basmati rice has a rich aroma.*
5 interesting because full of diversity or complexity: *what a full, rich life you lead!*
6 informal (of a remark) causing ironic amusement or indignation: *these comments are* ***a bit rich*** *coming from a woman with no money worries.*
– DERIVATIVES **rich·ness n.**
– ORIGIN Old English *rīce* 'powerful, wealthy,' of Germanic origin, related to Dutch *rijk* and German *reich*; ultimately from Celtic; reinforced in Middle English by Old French *riche* 'rich, powerful.'

-rich ▶ **comb. form** containing a large amount of something specified: *lime-rich* | *protein-rich.*

Rich·ard[1] /ˈriCHərd/ the name of three kings of England. ■ **Richard I** (1157–99), son of Henry II and Eleanor of Aquitaine; reigned 1189–99; known as **Richard Coeur de Lion** or **Richard the Lionheart**. He led the Third Crusade, defeating Saladin at Arsuf (1191), but failed to capture Jerusalem. Returning home, he was held hostage by the Holy Roman Emperor Henry VI until being released in 1194 on payment of a huge ransom. ■ **Richard II** (1367–1400), son of the Black Prince; reigned 1377–99. During his minority the government was dominated by his uncle John of Gaunt. Following his minority, he executed or banished most of his former opponents. His confiscation of his uncle John of Gaunt's estate on the latter's death provoked Henry Bolingbroke's return from exile to overthrow him. ■ **Richard III** (1452–85), brother of Edward IV; reigned 1483–85. He served as Protector to his nephew Edward V, who, after two months, was declared illegitimate and subsequently disappeared. Richard's brief rule ended at Bosworth Field, where he was defeated by Henry Tudor and killed.

Rich·ard[2] /rēˈSHärd/, Maurice (Joseph Henri) (1921–2000), Canadian hockey player; nickname **The Rocket**. Playing for the Montreal Canadiens 1942–60, he was the first professional hockey player to score 50 goals in one season 1944–45, a record that stood until the early 1980s. Hockey Hall of Fame (1961).

Rich·ards /ˈriCHərdz/, I. A. (1893–1979), English literary critic and poet; full name *Ivor Armstrong Richards*. He emphasized the importance of close textual study and praised irony, ambiguity, and allusiveness.

Rich·ard·son[1] /ˈriCHərdsən/ a city in northeastern Texas, northeast of Dallas; pop. 101,589 (est. 2008).

Rich·ard·son[2], Sir Ralph (David) (1902–83), English actor. He played many Shakespearean roles as well as leading parts in plays, including Harold Pinter's *No Man's Land* (1975), and movies, including *Oh! What a Lovely War* (1969).

Rich·ard·son[3], Samuel (1689–1761), English novelist. His first novel *Pamela* (1740–41), entirely in the form of letters and journals, popularized the epistolary novel. He experimented further with the genre in *Clarissa Harlowe* (1747–48), in which he explored moral issues in a detailed social context with psychological intensity.

Rich·ard the Li·on·heart /ˈlīən,härt/, Richard I of England (see RICHARD[1]).

Rich·e·lieu /ˈrisHəl,(y)o͞o/, Armand Jean du Plessis, duc de (1585–1642), French cardinal and statesman. He was chief minister to Louis XIII 1624–42 and established the Académie française in 1635.

rich·en /ˈriCHən/ ▶ **v.** [with obj.] make richer: *a town richened by several auto assembly plants.*

rich·es /ˈriCHiz/ ▶ **plural n.** material wealth: *riches beyond their wildest dreams.* ■ valuable natural resources: *the riches of the world's waters* | figurative *the riches of the Serbian oral tradition.*
– ORIGIN Middle English: variant (later interpreted as a plural form) of archaic *richesse*, from Old French *richeise* (from *riche* 'rich').

Rich·land /ˈriCHlənd/ a city in southeastern Washington, on the Columbia and Yakima rivers, near Kennewick and Pasco; pop. 46,155 (est. 2008).

Ri·chler /ˈriCHlər/, Mordecai (1931–2001), Canadian writer. One of his best-known novels is *The Apprenticeship of Duddy Kravitz* (1959). Other notable works: *The Incomparable Atuk* (1963), *St. Urbain's Horseman* (1971), and *Simon Gursky Was Here* (1989).

rich·ly /ˈriCHlē/ ▶ **adv.** in an elaborate, generous, or plentiful way: *she was richly dressed in the height of fashion* | *Levkas and its neighboring islands reward explorers richly.* ■ [as submodifier] fully (used esp. to indicate that someone or something merits a particular thing): *give your family a richly deserved vacation.*

Rich·mond /ˈriCHmənd/ **1** an industrial port city in north central California, on the eastern side of San Francisco Bay, north of Berkeley; pop. 102,285 (est. 2008).
2 a city in east central Kentucky, southeast of Lexington; pop. 32,895 (est. 2008).
3 the capital of Virginia, a port on the James River; pop. 202,002 (est. 2008). During the Civil War, it was the Confederate capital from July 1861 until its capture in 1865.

Rich·ter scale /ˈriktər/ ▶ **n.** Geology a numerical scale for expressing the magnitude of an earthquake on the basis of seismograph oscillations. The more destructive earthquakes typically have magnitudes between about 5.5 and 8.9; the scale is logarithmic and a difference of one represents an approximate thirtyfold difference in magnitude.
– ORIGIN 1930s: named after Charles F. *Richter* (1900–85), American geologist.

Richt·ho·fen /ˈriKHt,hōfən, ˈrik,tōvən/, Manfred, Freiherr von (1882–1918), German fighter pilot; known as **the Red Baron**. He flew a distinctive bright red aircraft and was eventually shot down, after destroying 80 enemy planes.

ri·cin /ˈrīsən, ˈris-/ ▶ **n.** Chemistry a highly toxic protein obtained from the pressed seeds of the castor-oil plant.
– ORIGIN late 19th cent.: from modern Latin *Ricinus communis* (denoting the castor-oil plant) + -IN[1].

rick[1] /rik/ ▶ **n.** a stack of hay, corn, straw, or similar material, esp. one built into a regular shape and thatched. ■ a pile of firewood somewhat smaller than a cord. ■ a set of shelving for storing barrels.
▶ **v.** [with obj.] form into rick or ricks; stack: *the nine cords of good spruce wood* ***ricked up*** *in the back yard.*
– ORIGIN Old English *hrēac*, of Germanic origin; related to Dutch *rook*.

rick[2] ▶ **n.** a slight sprain or strain, esp. in a person's neck or back.
▶ **v.** [with obj.] strain (one's neck or back) slightly.
– ORIGIN late 18th cent. (as a verb): of dialect origin.

rick·ets /ˈrikits/ ▶ **n.** [treated as sing. or pl.] Medicine a disease of children caused by vitamin D deficiency, characterized by imperfect calcification, softening, and distortion of the bones typically resulting in bow legs.
– ORIGIN mid 17th cent.: perhaps an alteration of Greek *rhakhitis* (see RACHITIS).

rick·ett·si·a /riˈketsēə/ ▶ **n.** (pl. **rickettsiae** /-sē,ē, -sē,ī/ or **rickettsias**) any of a group of very small bacteria that includes the causative agents of typhus and various other febrile diseases in humans. Like viruses, many of them can only grow inside living cells, and they are frequently transmitted by mites, ticks, or lice. ● Genus *Rickettsia*, order Rickettsiales; Gram-negative rods.
– DERIVATIVES **rick·ett·si·al adj.**
– ORIGIN modern Latin, named after Howard Taylor *Ricketts* (1871–1910), American pathologist.

rick·et·y /ˈrikitē/ ▶ **adj. 1** (of a structure or piece of equipment) poorly made and likely to collapse: *we went carefully up the rickety stairs* | figurative *a rickety banking system.*
2 (of a person) suffering from rickets.
– DERIVATIVES **rick·et·i·ness n.**
– ORIGIN late 17th cent.: from RICKETS + -Y[1].

rick·ey /ˈrikē/ ▶ **n.** (pl. **rickeys**) a drink consisting of liquor, typically gin, mixed with lime juice, carbonated water, and ice: *gin rickey.*
– ORIGIN late 19th cent.: probably from the surname *Rickey*.

Rick·ov·er /ˈrik,ōvər/, Hyman (George) (1900–86), US naval officer; born in Russia (now part of Poland). A rear admiral in 1953 and a vice admiral in 1959, he was the individual most responsible for creating the US nuclear-powered navy. The world's first nuclear-powered submarine, the USS *Nautilus*, was launched under his direction in 1954. Presidential Medal of Freedom (1980).

rick·rack /ˈrik,rak/ ▶ **n.** braided trimming in a zigzag pattern, used esp. as decoration on clothes.
– ORIGIN late 19th cent.: of unknown origin.

rick·sha /ˈrik,SHô/ (also **rickshaw**) ▶ **n.** a light two-wheeled hooded vehicle drawn by one or more people, used chiefly in Asian countries. ■ a similar

vehicle like a three-wheeled bicycle, having a seat for passengers behind the driver.
– ORIGIN late 19th cent.: abbreviation of JINRIKISHA.

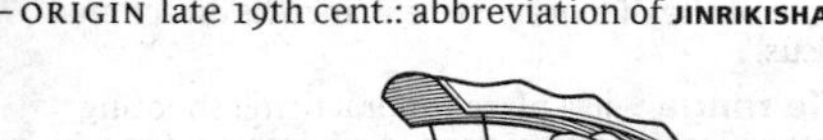

ricksha

RICO /ˈrēkō/ ▶ **abbr.** (in the US) Racketeer Influenced and Corrupt Organizations Act.

ric·o·chet /ˈrikəˌSHā, -ˌSHet/ ▶ **n.** a shot or hit that rebounds one or more times off a surface. ■ the action or movement of a bullet, shell, or other projectile when rebounding in such a way.
▶ **v.** (**ricochets, ricocheting** /-ˌSHā-iNG/, **ricocheted** /-ˌSHād/ or **ricochets, ricochetting** /-ˌSHetiNG/, **ricochetted** /-ˌSHetid/) [no obj.] (of a bullet, shell, or other projectile) rebound one or more times off a surface: *a bullet ricocheted off a nearby wall.* ■ [with obj.] cause to rebound in such a way: *they fired off a couple of rounds, ricocheting the bullets against a wall.* ■ move or appear to move with a series of such rebounds: *the sound ricocheted around the hall.*
– ORIGIN mid 18th cent.: from French, of unknown origin.

ri·cot·ta /riˈkätə/ ▶ **n.** a soft white unsalted Italian cheese.
– ORIGIN Italian, literally 'recooked, cooked twice.'

RICS ▶ **abbr.** (in the UK) Royal Institution of Chartered Surveyors.

ric·tus /ˈriktəs/ ▶ **n.** a fixed grimace or grin: *Ned's smile had become a rictus of repulsion.*
– DERIVATIVES **ric·tal** /ˈriktəl/ **adj.**
– ORIGIN early 19th cent.: from Latin, literally 'open mouth,' from *rict-* 'gaped,' from the verb *ringi.*

rid /rid/ ▶ **v.** (**rids, ridding**; past and past participle **rid** or archaic **ridded**) [with obj.] (**rid someone/something of**) make someone or something free of (a troublesome or unwanted person or thing): *we now have the greatest chance ever to rid the world of nuclear weapons.* ■ (**be rid of**) be freed or relieved from: *she couldn't wait to be rid of us.*
– PHRASES **be well rid of** be in a better state for having removed or disposed of (a troublesome or unwanted person or thing). **get rid of** take action so as to be free of (a troublesome or unwanted person or thing).
– ORIGIN Middle English: from Old Norse *rythja.* The original sense 'to clear' described clearing land of trees and undergrowth; this gave rise to 'free from refuse or encumbrances,' later becoming generalized.

rid·dance /ˈridns/ ▶ **n.** the action of getting rid of a troublesome or unwanted person or thing.
– PHRASES **good riddance** said to express relief at being free of a troublesome or unwanted person or thing.

rid·den /ˈridn/ past participle of RIDE.

rid·dle[1] /ˈridl/ ▶ **n.** a question or statement intentionally phrased so as to require ingenuity in ascertaining its answer or meaning, typically presented as a game. ■ a person, event, or fact that is difficult to understand or explain: *the riddle of her death.*
▶ **v.** [no obj.] archaic speak in or pose riddles: *he who knows not how to riddle.* ■ [with two objs.] solve or explain (a riddle) to (someone): *riddle me this then.*
– PHRASES **talk** (or **speak**) **in riddles** express oneself in an ambiguous or puzzling manner.
– DERIVATIVES **rid·dler** /ˈridlər, ˈridl-ər/ **n.**
– ORIGIN Old English *rǣdels, rǣdelse* 'opinion, conjecture, riddle'; related to Dutch *raadsel,* German *Rätsel,* also to READ.

rid·dle[2] ▶ **v.** [with obj.] **1** (usu. **be riddled**) make many holes in (someone or something), esp. with gunshot: *his car was riddled by sniper fire.* ■ fill or permeate (someone or something), esp. with something unpleasant or undesirable: *the existing law is riddled with loopholes.*
2 pass (a substance) through a large coarse sieve: *for final potting, the soil mixture is not riddled.* ■ remove ashes or other unwanted material from (something, esp. a fire or stove) in such a way.
▶ **n.** a large coarse sieve, esp. one used for separating ashes from cinders or sand from gravel.
– ORIGIN late Old English *hriddel,* of Germanic origin; from an Indo-European root shared by Latin *cribrum* 'sieve,' *cernere* 'separate,' and Greek *krinein* 'decide.'

rid·dling /ˈridliNG, ˈridl-iNG/ ▶ **adj.** speaking or expressed in riddles; enigmatic: *the riddling sphinx.*
– DERIVATIVES **rid·dling·ly adv.**

Ride /rīd/, Sally (Kristen) (1951–), US astronaut. She was the first US woman to travel in space, on the shuttle *Challenger* in 1983. She later served on the presidential commission that investigated the 1986 *Challenger* accident.

Sally Ride

ride /rīd/ ▶ **v.** (past **rode** /rōd/; past participle **ridden** /ˈridn/) [with obj.] **1** sit on and control the movement of (an animal, esp. a horse), typically as a recreation or sport: *Diana went to watch him ride his horse* | [no obj.] *I haven't ridden much since the accident.* ■ [no obj.] travel on a horse or other animal: *we rode on horseback* | *some of the officers were riding back.* ■ sit on and control (a bicycle or motorcycle) for recreation or as a means of transport: *he rode a Harley Davidson across the U.S.* ■ [no obj.] (**ride in/on**) travel in or on (a vehicle) as a passenger: *I started riding on the buses.* ■ travel in (a vehicle) or on (a public transport system) as a passenger: *she rides the bus across 42nd Street.* ■ go through or over (an area) on horseback, a bicycle, etc.: *ride the full length of the Ridgeway.* ■ compete in (a race) on horseback or on a bicycle or motorcycle: *I rode a good race.* ■ [no obj.] (of a vehicle, animal, etc.) be of a particular character for riding on or in: *the van rode as well as some cars of twice the price.* ■ informal transport (someone) in a vehicle: *the taxi driver who rode Kelly into the airport not long ago.*
2 be carried or supported by (something with a great deal of momentum): *a stream of young surfers fighting the elements to ride the waves* | figurative *the fund rode the growth boom in the 1980s.* ■ [no obj.] project or overlap: *when two lithospheric plates collide, one tends to* **ride over** *the other.* ■ [no obj.] (of a vessel) sail or float: *a large cedar barque* **rode at anchor** | figurative *the moon was riding high in the sky.*
3 (**be ridden**) be full of or dominated by: *you must not think him ridden with angst* | [as adj. in combination] (**-ridden**) *the crime-ridden streets.*
4 yield to (a blow) so as to reduce its impact: *Harrison drew back his jaw as if riding the blow.*
5 vulgar slang have sexual intercourse with.
6 annoy, pester, or tease: *if you don't give all the kids a chance to play, the parents ride you.*
▶ **n. 1** a journey made on horseback, on a bicycle or motorcycle, or in a vehicle: *did you enjoy your ride?* | figurative *investors have had a bumpy ride.* ■ a person giving someone a lift in their vehicle: *their ride into town had dropped them off near the bridge.* ■ informal a motor vehicle: *that green Chevy over there, that's my ride.* ■ the quality of comfort or smoothness offered by a vehicle while it is being driven, as perceived by the driver or passenger: *the ride is comfortable, though there is a slight roll when cornering.* ■ a path, typically one through woods, for riding horses. ■ Canadian a demonstration of horse riding as an entertainment.
2 a roller coaster, merry-go-round, or other amusement ridden at a fair or amusement park.
3 vulgar slang an act of sexual intercourse.
4 (also **ride cymbal**) a cymbal used for keeping up a continuous rhythm.
– PHRASES **be riding for a fall** see FALL. **for the ride** for pleasure or interest, rather than any serious purpose: *I don't need anything at the mall, but I'm happy to go along for the ride.* **let something ride** take no immediate action over something. **ride herd on** keep watch over: *a man to ride herd on this frenetically paced enterprise.* **ride high** be successful: *the economy will be riding high on the top of the next boom.* **ride the pine** (or **bench**) informal (of an athlete) sit on the sidelines rather than participate in a game or event. **ride the rails** (or chiefly Canadian **rods**) informal ride on a train, esp. on a freight train, and without permission. **ride roughshod over** carry out one's own plans or wishes with arrogant disregard for (others or their wishes): *he rode roughshod over everyone else's opinions.* — **rides again** used to indicate that someone or something has reappeared unexpectedly and with new vigor. **ride shotgun** travel as a guard in the seat next to the driver of a vehicle. ■ ride in the passenger seat of a vehicle. ■ act as a protector: *these same economists have ridden shotgun for government policy.* **ride to (the) hounds** chiefly Brit. go hunting (esp. fox hunting) on horseback with a pack of dogs. **a rough** (or **easy**) **ride** a difficult (or easy) time doing something: *the president has been given a rough ride by this conservative Congress.* **take someone for a ride** informal deceive or cheat someone.
– PHRASAL VERBS **ride someone down** trample or overtake someone while on horseback. **ride on** depend on: *there is a great deal of money riding on the results of these studies.* **ride something out** come safely through something, esp. a storm or a period of danger or difficulty: *the fleet had ridden out the storm.* **ride up** (of a garment) gradually work or move upward out of its proper position: *her skirt had ridden up.*
– DERIVATIVES **ride·a·ble** (also **ridable**) **adj.**
– ORIGIN Old English *rīdan,* of Germanic origin; related to Dutch *rijden* and German *reiten.*

Ri·deau Ca·nal /riˈdō/ a waterway in eastern Ontario in Canada, created in the 1820s, that links Ottawa and the Ottawa River with Kingston and Lake Ontario.

ride-off ▶ **n.** (in a riding competition) a round held to resolve a tie or determine qualifiers for a later stage; a jump-off.

rid·er /ˈrīdər/ ▶ **n. 1** a person who is riding or who can ride something, esp. a horse, bicycle, motorcycle, or snowboard.
2 a condition or proviso added to something already said or decreed: *one rider to the deal—if the hurricane heads north, we run for shelter.* ■ an addition or amendment to a document, esp. a piece of legislation: *the rules of Congress make it difficult to attach a rider to an appropriations bill* | *a rider to an eligible life insurance policy.*
3 a small weight positioned on the beam of a balance for fine adjustment.
– DERIVATIVES **rid·er·less adj.**
– ORIGIN late Old English *rīdere* 'mounted warrior, knight' (see RIDE, -ER).

rid·er·ship /ˈrīdərˌSHip/ ▶ **n.** the number of passengers using a particular form of public transportation.

Ridge /rij/, Tom (1945–), US secretary of homeland security 2001–05; full name *Thomas Joseph Ridge.* The governor of Pennsylvania 1995–2001, he was chosen by President George W. Bush to head the new Office of Homeland Security, a cabinet department created shortly after the terrorist attacks of September 11, 2001.

ridge /rij/ ▶ **n.** a long narrow hilltop, mountain range, or watershed: *the northeast ridge of Everest.* ■ the line or edge formed where the two sloping sides of a roof meet at the top. ■ Meteorology an elongated region of high atmospheric pressure. ■ a narrow raised band running along or across a surface: *buff your nails in order to smooth ridges.* ■ a raised strip of arable land, esp. (in medieval open fields) one of a set separated by furrows.
▶ **v.** [with obj.] (often as adj. **ridged**) mark with or form into narrow raised bands: *the ridged sand of the beach.* ■ [no obj.] (of a surface) form into or rise up as a narrow raised band: *the crust of the earth ridged.* ■ form (arable land) into raised strips separated by furrows: *a field plowed in narrow stretches that are ridged up slightly.*
– DERIVATIVES **ridg·y adj.**
– ORIGIN Old English *hrycg* 'spine, crest,' of Germanic origin; related to Dutch *rug* and German *Rücken* 'back.'

ridge·back /ˈrijˌbak/ ▶ **n.** short for RHODESIAN RIDGEBACK.

ridge·piece /ˈrijˌpēs/ ▶ **n.** another term for RIDGEPOLE.

ridge·pole /ˈrijˌpōl/ ▶ **n. 1** a horizontal beam along the ridge of a roof, into which the rafters are fastened.
2 the horizontal pole of a long tent.

ridge run·ner ▶ **n.** informal a mountain farmer of the southern US states.

ridge tile ▶ **n.** a semicircular or curved tile used in making a roof ridge.

PRONUNCIATION KEY ə *ago, up;* ər *over, fur;* a *hat;* ā *ate;* ä *car;* e *let;* ē *see;* i *fit;* ī *by;* NG *sing;* ō *go;* ô *law, for;* oi *toy;* o͝o *good;* o͞o *goo;* ou *out;* TH *thin;* T͟H *then;* ZH *vision*

r

ridge·way /'rij,wā/ ▶ n. a road or track along a ridge.

rid·i·cule /'ridi,kyo͞ol/ ▶ n. the subjection of someone or something to mockery and derision: *he is held up as an object of ridicule.*
▶ v. [with obj.] subject (someone or something) to mockery and derision: *his theory was ridiculed and dismissed.*
– ORIGIN late 17th cent.: from French, or from Latin *ridiculum*, neuter (used as a noun) of *ridiculus* 'laughable,' from *ridere* 'to laugh.'

ri·dic·u·lous /ri'dikyələs/ ▶ adj. deserving or inviting derision or mockery; absurd: *when you realize how ridiculous these scenarios are, you will have to laugh.*
– DERIVATIVES **ri·dic·u·lous·ness** n.
– ORIGIN mid 16th cent.: from Latin *ridiculosus*, from *ridiculus* 'laughable' (see RIDICULE).

ri·dic·u·lous·ly /ri'dikyələslē/ ▶ adv. so as to invite mockery or derision; absurdly: [sentence adverb] *ridiculously, I felt like crying.* ■ [as submodifier] so as to cause surprise or disbelief: *it had been ridiculously easy to track him down.*

rid·ing[1] /'rīdiNG/ ▶ n. the sport or activity of riding horses.

ri·ding[2] ▶ n. **1** (usu. **the East/North/West Riding**) one of three former administrative divisions of Yorkshire.
2 an electoral district of Canada.
– ORIGIN Old English *trithing*, from Old Norse *thrithjungr* 'third part,' from *thrithi* 'third.' The initial *th-* was lost due to assimilation with the preceding *-t* of *East, West*, or with the *-th* of *North*.

rid·ing crop ▶ n. a short flexible whip with a loop for the hand, used in riding horses.

rid·ing hab·it ▶ n. a woman's riding dress, consisting of a skirt worn with a double-breasted jacket.

rid·ing light ▶ n. a light shown by a ship at anchor.

rid·ing school ▶ n. an establishment where horseback riding is taught.

Rid·ley /'ridlē/, Nicholas (*c.*1500–55), English Protestant bishop and martyr. He was appointed bishop of Rochester in 1547 and then of London in 1550. He opposed the Catholic policies of Mary I, the reason that he was burned at the stake in Oxford.

rid·ley /'ridlē/ (also **ridley turtle**) ▶ n. (pl. **ridleys**) a small turtle of tropical seas. ● Genus *Lepidochelys*, family Cheloniidae: **Kemp's ridley** (*L. kempi*) of the Atlantic, and the larger **olive ridley** (*L. olivacea*) of the Pacific.
– ORIGIN late 19th cent.: of unknown origin.

rie·beck·ite /'rē,bek,īt/ ▶ n. a dark blue or black mineral of the amphibole group, occurring chiefly in alkaline igneous rocks or as blue asbestos (crocidolite).
– ORIGIN late 19th cent.: from the name of Emil *Riebeck* (died 1885), German explorer, + -ITE[1].

Rie·fen·stahl /'rēfən,SHtäl/, Leni (1902–2003), German filmmaker. She is best known for *Triumph of the Will* (1935), an account of a Nazi rally at Nuremberg.

Ri·el /rē'el/, Louis (1844–85), Canadian political leader. He led the rebellion of the Metis at Red River Settlement in 1869, later forming a provisional government and negotiating terms for the union of Manitoba with Canada. He was executed for treason after leading a further rebellion.

ri·el /rē'el/ ▶ n. the basic monetary unit of Cambodia, equal to 100 sen.
– ORIGIN Khmer.

Rie·mann /'rēmən/, (Georg Friedrich) Bernhard (1826–66), German mathematician. He founded Riemannian geometry, which is of fundamental importance to both mathematics and physics.

Rie·mann·i·an ge·om·e·try /rē'mänēən, -'man-/ ▶ n. a form of differential non-Euclidean geometry developed by Riemann, used to describe curved space. It provided Einstein with a mathematical basis for his general theory of relativity.

Ries·ling /'rēzliNG, 'rēs-/ ▶ n. a variety of wine grape grown and developed esp. in Germany and Austria. ■ a dry white wine made from this grape.
– ORIGIN German.

ri·fam·pin /ri'fampin/ (also **rifampicin** /ri'fampəsin/) ▶ n. Medicine a reddish-brown antibiotic used chiefly to treat tuberculosis and leprosy. ● The antibiotic is obtained from the bacterium *Nocardia mediterranei.*
– ORIGIN 1960s: from *rifam(yci)n* (an antibiotic first isolated from the bacterium *Streptomyces mediterranei*) + the insertion of *pi-* from PIPERAZINE.

rife /rīf/ ▶ adj. [predic.] (esp. of something undesirable or harmful) of common occurrence; widespread: *male chauvinism was rife in medicine in those days.* ■ (**rife with**) full of: *the streets were rife with rumor and fear.*
▶ adv. in an unchecked or widespread manner: *speculation **ran rife** that he was an arms dealer.*
– DERIVATIVES **rife·ness** n.
– ORIGIN late Old English *rȳfe*, probably from Old Norse *rīfr* 'acceptable.'

riff /rif/ ▶ n. (in popular music and jazz) a short repeated phrase, frequently played over changing chords or harmonies or used as a background to a solo improvisation: *a brilliant guitar riff.* ■ a monologue or spoken improvisation, esp. a humorous one, on a particular subject: *subsequent **riffs on** the same themes fail to amuse.*
▶ v. [no obj.] play musical riffs: *the other horns would be riffing behind him.* ■ perform a monologue or spoken improvisation on a particular subject: *he also **riffs on** racism and the economy.*
– ORIGIN 1930s: perhaps an abbreviation of REFRAIN[2].

rif·fle /'rifəl/ ▶ v. [no obj.] turn over something, esp. the pages of a book, quickly and casually: *he riffled through the pages* | [with obj.] *she opened a book with her thumbnail and riffled the pages.* ■ (**riffle through**) search quickly through (something), esp. so as to cause disorder: *she riffled through her leather handbag.* ■ [with obj.] disturb the surface of; ruffle: *there was a slight breeze that riffled her hair.* ■ [with obj.] shuffle (playing cards) by flicking up and releasing the corners or sides of two piles of cards so that they intermingle and may be slid together to form a single pile.
▶ n. **1** [usu. in sing.] a quick or casual leaf or search through something. ■ the rustle of paper being leafed through in such a way. ■ a shuffle performed by riffling playing cards.
2 a rocky or shallow part of a stream or river with rough water. ■ a patch of waves or ripples.
– ORIGIN late 18th cent. (sense 2 of the noun): perhaps from a variant of the verb RUFFLE, influenced by RIPPLE.

rif·fler /'riflər/ ▶ n. a narrow elongated tool with a curved file surface at each end, used in filing concave surfaces.
– ORIGIN late 18th cent.: from French *rifloir*, from Old French *rifler* 'to scrape.'

riff·raff /'rif,raf/ ▶ n. disreputable or undesirable people: *I don't think they talk to riffraff off the street.*
– ORIGIN late 15th cent. (as *riff and raff*): from Old French *rif et raf* 'one and all, every bit,' of Germanic origin.

ri·fle[1] /'rīfəl/ ▶ n. a gun, esp. one fired from shoulder level, having a long spirally grooved barrel intended to make a bullet spin and thereby have greater accuracy over a long distance. ■ (**rifles**) troops armed with rifles.
▶ v. **1** [with obj.] (usu. as adj. **rifled**) make spiral grooves in (a gun or its barrel or bore) to make a bullet spin and thereby have greater accuracy over a long distance: *a line of replacement rifled barrels.*
2 [with obj.] hit, throw, or kick (a ball or puck) hard and straight: *he rifled a hard, rising shot from just inside the blue line.* [1940s: from *rifle* 'gun,' suggestive of explosive speed; compare with the verb *shoot*.]
– ORIGIN mid 17th cent.: from French *rifler* 'graze, scratch,' of Germanic origin. The earliest noun usage was in *rifle gun*, which had "rifles" or spiral grooves cut into the inside of the barrel.

rifle

ri·fle[2] ▶ v. [no obj.] search through something in a hurried way in order to find or steal something: *she rifled through the cassette tapes* | [with obj.] *they rifled the house for money.* ■ [with obj.] steal: *the lieutenant's servant rifled the dead man's possessions.*
– ORIGIN Middle English: from Old French *rifler* 'graze, plunder,' of Germanic origin.

ri·fle bird ▶ n. a bird of paradise, the male of which has mainly velvety-black plumage and a display call that sounds like a whistling bullet. ● Genus *Ptiloris*, family Paradisaeidae: three species.

ri·fle·man /'rīfəlmən/ ▶ n. (pl. **riflemen**) **1** a soldier armed with a rifle, esp. a private in a rifle regiment. ■ a person skilled at using a rifle.
2 a very small, short-tailed, greenish-yellow songbird that feeds on insects on tree bark, native to New Zealand. [perhaps so named from a comparison between its plumage and an early military uniform.] ● *Acanthisitta chloris*, family Xenicidae.

ri·fle mi·cro·phone ▶ n. a type of gun microphone with several parallel tubes of different lengths in front of the diaphragm to enhance its directional focus.

ri·fle range ▶ n. a place for practicing shooting with rifles. ■ an attraction at a fairground in which people fire rifles at targets in order to win prizes.

ri·fle·scope /'rīfəl,skōp/ ▶ n. informal a telescopic sight on a rifle.

ri·fling /'rīf(ə)liNG/ ▶ n. the arrangement of spiral grooves on the inside of a rifle barrel.

Rif Moun·tains /rif/ (also **Er Rif** /er 'rif/) a mountain range in northern Morocco that runs parallel to the Mediterranean Sea for about 180 miles (290 km) east from Tangier. Rising to over 7,000 feet (2,250 m), it forms a western extension of the Atlas Mountains.

rift /rift/ ▶ n. **1** a crack, split, or break in something: *the wind had torn open a rift in the clouds.* ■ Geology a major fault separating blocks of the earth's surface; a rift valley.
2 a serious break in friendly relations: *their demise caused a **rift between** the city's town and gown.*
▶ v. [no obj.] chiefly Geology form fissures, cracks, or breaks, esp. through large-scale faulting; move apart: *a fragment of continental crust that rifted away from eastern Australia* | (as noun **rifting**) *active rifting in southwestern Mexico.* ■ [with obj.] (usu. as adj. **rifted**) tear or force (something) apart: *the nascent rifted margins of the Red Sea.*
– ORIGIN Middle English: of Scandinavian origin; compare with Norwegian and Danish *rift* 'cleft, chink.'

rift val·ley ▶ n. a large elongated depression with steep walls formed by the downward displacement of a block of the earth's surface between nearly parallel faults or fault systems.

rig[1] /rig/ ▶ v. (**rigs, rigging, rigged**) [with obj.] make (a sailing ship or boat) ready for sailing by providing it with sails and rigging: *the catamaran will be rigged as a ketch* | [as adj., in combination] (**-rigged**) *a gaff-rigged cutter.* ■ assemble and adjust (the equipment of a sailboat, aircraft, etc.) to make it ready for operation: *most sails are kept ready rigged.* ■ set up (equipment or a device or structure), typically hastily or in makeshift fashion: *he had rigged up a sort of tent* | *the crew began to rig the camera equipment on a platform.* ■ provide (someone) with clothes of a particular style or type: *a cavalry regiment rigged out in green and gold.*
▶ n. **1** the particular way in which a sailboat's masts, sails, and rigging are arranged: *the yacht will emerge from the yard with her original rig.* ■ the sail, mast, and boom of a sailboard.
2 an apparatus, device, or piece of equipment designed for a particular purpose: *a lighting rig.* ■ an oil rig or drilling rig. ■ (in CB and shortwave radio) a transmitter and receiver. ■ a particular type of construction for fishing tackle that bears the bait and hook. ■ a set of amplifiers and speakers used by a live band or a DJ in a club.
3 a person's costume, outfit, or style of dress: *the rig of the Army Air Corps.*
4 a tractor-trailer. ■ another type of vehicle, such as a horse-drawn carriage.
– PHRASES **(in) full rig** informal (wearing) fancy or ceremonial clothes.
– ORIGIN late 15th cent. (in nautical use): perhaps of Scandinavian origin: compare with Norwegian *rigga* 'bind or wrap up.' The noun dates from the early 19th cent.

rig[2] ▶ v. (**rigs, rigging, rigged**) [with obj.] manage or conduct (something) fraudulently so as to produce a result or situation that is advantageous to a particular person: *the results of the elections had been rigged* | [as noun, in combination] (**-rigging**) *charges of vote-rigging.* ■ cause an artificial rise or fall in prices in (a market, esp. the stock market) with a view to personal profit: *he accused games manufacturers of rigging the market.*
▶ n. archaic a trick or way of swindling someone.
– ORIGIN late 18th cent. (in the noun sense): of unknown origin; the verb is related to the noun.

Ri·ga /'rēgə/ a port on the Baltic Sea, the capital of Latvia; pop. 722,000 (est. 2007).

rig·a·doon /,rigə'do͞on/ (also **rigaudon**) ▶ n. a lively dance for couples, in duple or quadruple time, of Provençal origin.
– ORIGIN late 17th cent.: from French *rigaudon*, perhaps named after its inventor, said to be a dance teacher called *Rigaud*.

rig·a·to·ni /,rigə'tōnē/ ▶ n. pasta in the form of short hollow fluted tubes.
– ORIGIN Italian.

Ri·gel /'rījəl, -gəl/ Astronomy the seventh brightest star in the sky, and the brightest in the constellation

Orion. It is a blue supergiant nearly sixty thousand times as luminous as our sun.
– ORIGIN from Arabic *rijl* 'foot (of Orion).'

rig·ger[1] /ˈrigər/ ▶ **n.** **1** a person who rigs or attends to the rigging of a sailing ship, aircraft, or parachute. ■ a person who erects and maintains scaffolding, lifting tackle, cranes, etc. ■ a person who works on or helps construct an oil rig.
2 (also **rigger brush**) an artist's long-haired sable brush.
3 an outrigger carrying a rowlock on a racing rowboat.

rig·ger[2] ▶ **n.** a person who fraudulently manipulates something so as to produce a result or situation to their advantage.

rig·ging /ˈriɡiNG/ ▶ **n.** **1** the system of ropes, cables, or chains employed to support a ship's masts (**standing rigging**) and to control or set the yards and sails (**running rigging**). ■ the action of providing a sailing ship with such gear.
2 the ropes and wires supporting the structure of an airship, biplane, hang glider, or parachute. ■ the system of cables and fittings controlling the flight surfaces and engines of an aircraft. ■ the action of assembling and adjusting such rigging.

right /rīt/ ▶ **adj.** **1** morally good, justified, or acceptable: *I hope we're doing the right thing* | [with infinitive] *you were quite right to criticize him.*
2 true or correct as a fact: *I'm not sure I know the right answer* | *her theories were proved right.* ■ [predic.] correct in one's opinion or judgment: *she was right about Tom having no money.* ■ used as an interrogative at the end of a statement as a way of inviting agreement, approval, or confirmation: *you went to see Angie on Monday, right?* ■ according to what is correct for a particular situation or thing: *is this the right way to the cottage?* | *you're not holding it the right way up.* ■ the best or most suitable of a number of possible choices for a particular purpose or occasion: *he was clearly the right man for the job* | *I was waiting for the right moment to ask him.* ■ socially fashionable or important: *he was seen at all the right places.* ■ [predic.] in a satisfactory, sound, or normal state or condition: *that sausage doesn't smell right* | *if only I could have helped* ***put matters right.***
3 on, toward, or relating to the side of a human body or of a thing that is to the east when the person or thing is facing north: *my right elbow* | *her right shoe* | *the right edge of the field.*
4 [attrib.] informal, chiefly Brit. complete; absolute (used for emphasis, typically in derogatory contexts): *I felt a right idiot.*
5 of or relating to a person or political party or grouping favoring conservative views: *are you politically right, left, or center?*
▶ **adv.** **1** [with prepositional phrase] to the furthest or most complete extent or degree (used for emphasis): *the car spun right off the track* | *I'm right out of ideas.* ■ exactly; directly (used to emphasize the precise location or time of something): *Harriet was standing right behind her.* ■ informal immediately; without delaying or hesitating: *I'll be right back.* ■ [as submodifier] dialect or archaic very: *it's right spooky in there!*
2 correctly: *he had guessed right.* ■ in the required or necessary way; properly; satisfactorily: *nothing's going right for me this season.*
3 on or to the right side: *turn right at Main Street.*
▶ **n.** **1** that which is morally correct, just, or honorable: *she doesn't understand the difference between right and wrong* | *the rights and wrongs of the matter.*
2 a moral or legal entitlement to have or obtain something or to act in a certain way: [with infinitive] *she had every right to be angry* | *you're quite* ***within your rights*** *to ask for your money back* | *there is no* ***right of*** *appeal against the decision.* ■ (**rights**) the authority to perform, publish, film, or televise a particular work, event, etc.: *they sold the paperback rights.*
3 (**the right**) the right-hand part, side, or direction: *take the first turning on the right* | (**one's right**) *she seated me on her right.* ■ (in football or a similar sport) the right-hand half of the field when facing the opponent's goal. ■ (**right**) Baseball short for RIGHT FIELD: *a looping single to right.* ■ the right wing of an army. ■ a right turn: *he made a right in Dorchester Avenue.* ■ a road or entrance on the right: *take the first right over the stream.* ■ (esp. in the context of boxing) a person's right fist. ■ a blow given with this: *the young cop swung a terrific right.*
4 (often **the Right**) [treated as sing. or pl.] a grouping or political party favoring conservative views and supporting capitalist economic principles. [see RIGHT WING.]
▶ **v.** [with obj.] restore to a normal or upright position: *we righted the capsized dinghy.* ■ restore to a normal or correct condition or situation: *righting the economy demanded major cuts in defense spending.* ■ redress or rectify (a wrong or mistaken action): *she was determined to right the wrongs done to her father.* ■ (usu. **be righted**) archaic make reparation to (someone) for a wrong done to them: *we'll see you righted.*
▶ **exclam.** informal used to indicate one's agreement with a suggestion or to acknowledge a statement or order: *"Barry's here." "Oh, right"* | ***right you are,*** *sir.* ■ used as a filler in speech or to introduce an utterance, exhortation, or suggestion: *and I didn't think any more of it, right, but Mom said I should take him to a doctor* | *right, let's have a drink.*
– PHRASES **bang** (or **dead**) **to rights** informal (of a criminal) with positive proof of guilt: *we've got you bang to rights handling stolen property.* **be in the right** be morally or legally justified in one's views, actions, or decisions. **by rights** if things had happened or been done fairly or correctly: *by rights, he should not be playing next week.* **do right by** treat (someone) fairly. **in one's own right** as a result of one's own claims, qualifications, or efforts, rather than an association with someone else: *he was already established as a poet in his own right.* **(not) in one's right mind** (not) sane. **not right in the head** informal (of a person) not completely sane. **(as) of right** (or **by right**) as a result of having a moral or legal claim or entitlement: *the state will be obliged to provide health care and education as of right.* **put** (or **set**) **someone right 1** restore someone to health. **2** make someone understand the true facts of a situation. **put** (or **set**) **something to rights** restore something to its correct or normal state or condition. **(as) right as rain** informal (of a person) feeling completely well or healthy, typically after an illness or minor accident. **right** (or **straight**) **away** (or informal **off**) immediately. **right enough** informal certainly; undeniably: *your record's bad right enough.* **right on** informal used an expression of strong support, approval, or encouragement. See also RIGHT-ON. **a right one** Brit. informal a silly or foolish person. **she's** (or **she'll be**) **right** Austral. informal that will be all right; don't worry.
– DERIVATIVES **right·a·ble** adj., **right·er** n., **right·ish** adj., **right·ness** n.
– ORIGIN Old English *riht* (adjective and noun), *rihtan* (verb), *rihte* (adverb), of Germanic origin; related to Latin *rectus* 'ruled,' from an Indo-European root denoting movement in a straight line.

right-a·bout (also **right-about face**) ▶ **n.** Military a right turn continued through 180° so as to face in the opposite direction: *he did a swift right-about and disappeared.*

right an·gle ▶ **n.** an angle of 90°, as in a corner of a square or at the intersection of two perpendicular straight lines.
– PHRASES **at right angles** (or **a right angle**) **to** forming an angle of 90° with (something): *hold the brush at right angles to the surface.*

right-an·gled ▶ **adj.** containing or being a right angle: *a* ***right-angled triangle.***

right arm ▶ **n.** dated one's most reliable helper: *my employer calls me his right arm and depends upon my knowledge and judgment.*

right as·cen·sion (abbr.: **RA**) ▶ **n.** Astronomy the distance of a point east of the First Point of Aries, measured along the celestial equator and expressed in hours, minutes, and seconds. Compare with DECLINATION and CELESTIAL LONGITUDE.

Right Bank a district in the city of Paris, located on the right bank of the Seine River, north of the river. The area contains the Champs-Élysées and the Louvre.

right bank ▶ **n.** the bank of a river, on the right as one faces downstream.

right brain ▶ **n.** the right-hand side of the human brain, believed to be associated with creative thought and the emotions.
– DERIVATIVES **right-brain** adj., **right-brained** adj.

right-click ▶ **v.** [no obj.] Computing click on a link or other screen object by depressing the right-hand button on the mouse: *right-click on My Network Places and select Properties.*

right·en /ˈrītn/ ▶ **v.** [with obj.] archaic make (something) right, correct, or straight: *thy stubborn mind will not be rightened.*

right·eous /ˈrīCHəs/ ▶ **adj.** **1** (of a person or conduct) morally right or justifiable; virtuous: *he is a good, righteous man, I am sure* | *feelings of* ***righteous indignation*** *about pay and conditions.*
2 informal very good; excellent: *righteous bread pudding.*
– DERIVATIVES **right·eous·ly** adv.
– ORIGIN Old English *rihtwīs*, from *riht* 'right' + *wīs* 'manner, state, condition' The change in the ending in the 16th cent. was due to association with words such as *bounteous*.

right·eous·ness /ˈrīCHəsnəs/ ▶ **n.** the quality of being morally right or justifiable: *we had little doubt about the righteousness of our cause.*

right field (also **right**) ▶ **n.** Baseball the part of the outfield to the right of center field from the perspective of home plate: *a ball hit to* ***right field.*** ■ the position of the defensive player stationed in right field: *he first gained attention while playing right field.*
– DERIVATIVES **right field·er** n.

right-foot·ed ▶ **adj.** (of a person) using the right foot more naturally than the left. ■ (of a kick) done with the right foot.

right·ful /ˈrītfəl/ ▶ **adj.** [attrib.] having a legitimate right to property, position, or status: *the rightful owner of the jewels.* ■ legitimately claimed; fitting: *they are determined to take their* ***rightful place*** *in a new South Africa.*
– DERIVATIVES **right·ful·ly** adv., **right·ful·ness** n.
– ORIGIN Old English *rihtful* 'upright, righteous' (see RIGHT, -FUL). The notion of 'legitimacy' dates from Middle English.

right hand ▶ **n.** the hand of a person's right side. ■ the region or direction on the right side of a person or thing: *a great wall loomed above the street on the right hand.* ■ the most important position next to someone: *the place of honor at his host's right hand.* ■ an efficient or indispensable assistant: *she could have helped him, been her father's right hand.*
▶ **adj.** [attrib.] on or toward the right side of a person or thing: *the top right-hand corner.* ■ done with or using the right hand: *wild right-hand punches.*

right-hand·ed ▶ **adj.** **1** (of a person) using the right hand more naturally than the left: *the slant of the stab wounds suggested that the assailant was right-handed.* ■ (of a tool or item of equipment) made to be used with the right hand or by right-handed people: *a* ***right-handed guitar.*** ■ made or done with the right hand, or in a manner natural to right-handed people: *right-handed batting.*
2 going toward or turning to the right, in particular: ■ (of a screw) advanced by turning clockwise. ■ Biology (of a spiral shell or helix) dextral. ■ (of a racecourse) turning clockwise.
▶ **adv.** with the right hand, or in a manner natural to right-handed people: *Jackson bats right-handed.*
– DERIVATIVES **right-hand·ed·ly** adv., **right-hand·ed·ness** n.

right-hand·er /ˈhandər/ ▶ **n.** a right-handed person, esp. a right-handed baseball pitcher. ■ a blow struck with the right hand.

right-hand man ▶ **n.** an indispensable helper or chief assistant.

Right Hon·our·a·ble ▶ **n.** Brit. a title given to certain high officials such as government ministers: *the Right Honourable Tony Blair.*

right·ist /ˈrītist/ ▶ **n.** a person who supports the political views or policies of the right.
▶ **adj.** supportive of the political views or policies of the right: *rightist doctrine.*
– DERIVATIVES **right·ism** /-ˌizəm/ n.

right·ly /ˈrītlē/ ▶ **adv.** correctly: *if I remember rightly, she never gives interviews.* ■ with good reason: *the delicious cuisine for which her country was rightly famous.* ■ in accordance with justice or what is morally right: *the key rightly belonged to Craig.*

right-mind·ed ▶ **adj.** having sound views and principles.
– DERIVATIVES **right-mind·ed·ness** n.

right·most /ˈrītˌmōst/ ▶ **adj.** [attrib.] situated furthest to the right.

right·o /ˈrītˈō/ (also **righty-ho** /ˈrītē ˈhō/) ▶ **exclam.** informal, chiefly Brit. expressing agreement or assent: *"Coming to pick up the kids?" "Righto."*

right of a·bode ▶ **n.** chiefly Brit. a person's right to take up residence or remain resident in a country.

right of search ▶ **n.** the right of a ship of a belligerent state to stop and search a neutral merchant vessel for prohibited goods.

right of way ▶ **n.** **1** the legal right, established by usage or grant, to pass along a specific route through grounds or property belonging to another. ■ a path or thoroughfare subject to such a right.
2 the legal right of a pedestrian, vehicle, or ship to proceed with precedence over others in a particular situation or place: *he waves on other drivers, even when it's not their right of way.*
3 the right to build and operate a railroad line, road, or utility on land belonging to another. ■ the land on which a railroad line, road, or utility is built.

r

PRONUNCIATION KEY ə *ago, up*; ər *over, fur*; a *hat*; ā *ate*; ä *car*; e *let*; ē *see*; i *fit*; ī *by*; NG *sing*; ō *go*; ô *law, for*; oi *toy*; o͝o *good*; o͞o *goo*; ou *out*; TH *thin*; T͟H *then*; ZH *vision*

right-on ▶ **adj.** often derogatory in keeping with fashionable liberal or left-wing opinions and values: *the right-on music press.*

Right Rev·er·end ▶ **n.** a title given to a bishop.

right side ▶ **n.** the side of something, esp. a garment or fabric, intended to be uppermost or foremost; the better or usable side of something.
– PHRASES **on the right side of** on the safe, appropriate, or desirable side of: *her portrayal of his neurotic wife falls just on the right side of caricature.* ■ in a position to be viewed with favor by: *he hasn't always remained on the right side of the law.* ■ somewhat less than (a specified age): *she's on the right side of forty.* **right side out** with the side intended to be seen or used uppermost: *turn the skirt right side out.*

rights is·sue ▶ **n.** an issue of shares offered at a special price by a company to its existing shareholders in proportion to their holding of old shares.

right·size /ˈrītˌsīz/ ▶ **v.** [with obj.] convert (something) to an appropriate or optimum size: *organizations are beginning to rightsize computer systems to suit themselves.* ■ reduce the size of (a company or organization) by eliminating staff positions, specifically when business conditions necessitate such a reduction.

rights of man ▶ **plural n.** rights held to be justifiably belonging to any person; human rights. The phrase is associated with the Declaration of the Rights of Man and of the Citizen, adopted by the French National Assembly in 1789 and used as a preface to the French Constitution of 1791.

right stuff ▶ **n.** (in full **the right stuff**) the necessary qualities for a given task or job: *he had the right stuff to enter this business.*

right-think·ing ▶ **adj.** right-minded.

right-to-die ▶ **adj.** pertaining to, expressing, or advocating the right to refuse extraordinary measures intended to prolong someone's life when they are terminally ill or comatose.

right-to-know ▶ **adj.** of or pertaining to laws or policies that make certain government or company records available to any individual who can demonstrate a right or need to know their contents.

right-to-life ▶ **adj.** another term for **PRO-LIFE**.
– DERIVATIVES **right-to-lif·er** /ˈlīfər/ **n.**

right-to-work ▶ **adj.** relating to or promoting a worker's right not to be required to join a labor union: *Kansas is a right-to-work state.*

right tri·an·gle ▶ **n.** a triangle with a right angle.

right turn ▶ **n.** a turn that brings a person's front to face the way their right side did before: *take a right turn onto Sunset Lane.*

right·ward /ˈrītwərd/ ▶ **adv.** (also **rightwards** /-wərdz/) (of political views) toward the right: *the party began to shift rightward.*
▶ **adj.** going toward or situated on the right: *the rock face is climbed via a rightward curving crack.*

right whale ▶ **n.** a baleen whale with a large head and a deeply curved jaw, of Arctic and temperate waters. ● Family Balaenidae: two genera and three species, in particular *Balaena glacialis*, which has distinctive patches of callosities on the snout. See also **BOWHEAD**.

r

right wing ▶ **n.** (**the right wing**) **1** the conservative or reactionary section of a political party or system. [with reference to the National Assembly in France (1789–91), where the nobles sat to the president's right and the commons to the left.]
2 the right side of a team on the field in soccer, rugby, and field hockey. ■ the right side of an army.
▶ **adj.** (**right-wing**) conservative or reactionary: *a right-wing Republican senator.*
– DERIVATIVES **right-wing·er n.**

right·y /ˈrītē/ ▶ **n.** (pl. **righties**) informal **1** a right-handed person.
2 a rightist.
▶ **adv.** with the right hand or as customary for a right-handed person: *he bats righty.*

right·y-ho ▶ **exclam.** variant spelling of **RIGHTO**.

rig·id /ˈrijid/ ▶ **adj. 1** unable to bend or be forced out of shape; not flexible: *a seat of rigid orange plastic | rigid ships are the dirigibles in which the bag is built around a metallic framework.* ■ (of a person or part of the body) stiff and unmoving, esp. as a result of shock or fear: *his face grew rigid with fear.*
2 not able to be changed or adapted: *teachers are being asked to unlearn rigid rules for labeling children.* ■ not adaptable in outlook, belief, or response: *ski instructors have become less rigid about style.*
– DERIVATIVES **ri·gid·i·fy** /rəˈjidəˌfī/ **v.**, **ri·gid·i·ty** /rəˈjidətē/ **n.**, **rig·id·ly adv.**, **rig·id·ness n.**
– ORIGIN late Middle English: from Latin *rigidus*, from *rigere* 'be stiff.'

rig·id des·ig·na·tor ▶ **n.** Philosophy a term that identifies the same object or individual in every possible world.

Ri·gil Ken·tau·rus /ˈrījəl kenˈtôrəs/ (also **Rigil Kent**) Astronomy the star Alpha Centauri.
– ORIGIN Arabic, literally 'the foot of the Centaur.'

rig·ma·role /ˈrig(ə)məˌrōl/ ▶ **n.** [usu. in sing.] a lengthy and complicated procedure: *he went through the rigmarole of securing the front door.* ■ a long, rambling story or statement.
– ORIGIN mid 18th cent.: apparently an alteration of *ragman roll*, originally denoting a legal document recording a list of offenses.

rig·or /ˈrigər/ ▶ **n. 1** (Brit. **rigour**) the quality of being extremely thorough, exhaustive, or accurate: *his analysis is lacking in rigor.* ■ severity or strictness: *the full rigor of the law.* ■ (**rigors**) demanding, difficult, or extreme conditions: *the rigors of a harsh winter.*
2 Medicine a sudden feeling of cold with shivering accompanied by a rise in temperature, often with copious sweating, esp. at the onset or height of a fever. ■ short for **RIGOR MORTIS**.
– ORIGIN late Middle English: from Latin, literally 'stiffness,' from *rigere* 'be stiff.'

rig·or·ism /ˈrigəˌrizəm/ ▶ **n.** extreme strictness in interpreting or enforcing a law, precept, or principle. ■ (in the Roman Catholic Church) formerly, the doctrine that in doubtful cases of conscience the strict course is always to be followed.
– DERIVATIVES **rig·or·ist n. & adj.**

rig·or mor·tis /ˌrigər ˈmôrtəs/ ▶ **n.** Medicine stiffening of the joints and muscles of a body a few hours after death, usually lasting from one to four days.
– ORIGIN mid 19th cent.: from Latin, literally 'stiffness of death.'

rig·or·ous /ˈrigərəs/ ▶ **adj.** extremely thorough, exhaustive, or accurate: *the rigorous testing of consumer products.* ■ (of a rule, system, etc.) strictly applied or adhered to: *rigorous controls on mergers.* ■ (of a person) adhering strictly or inflexibly to a belief, opinion, or way of doing something: *a rigorous teetotaler.* ■ harsh and demanding: *my exercise regime is a little more rigorous than most | the rigorous climate in the regions of perpetual snow high in the Himalayas.*
– DERIVATIVES **rig·or·ous·ly adv.**, **rig·or·ous·ness n.**
– ORIGIN late Middle English: from Old French *rigorous* or late Latin *rigorosus*, from *rigor* 'stiffness' (see **RIGOR**).

rig·our ▶ **n.** British spelling of **RIGOR** (sense 1).

rig-out ▶ **n.** informal, chiefly Brit. an outfit of clothes.

Rig Ve·da /rig ˈvādə, ˈvēdə/ Hinduism the oldest and principal of the Vedas, a collection of 1028 hymns composed in the 2nd millennium BC in early Sanskrit. See **VEDA**.
– ORIGIN from Sanskrit *ṛgveda*, from *ṛk* '(sacred) stanza' + *veda* '(sacred) knowledge.'

Riis /rēs/, Jacob August (1849–1914), US journalist and social reformer; born in Denmark. A police reporter for the *New York Tribune* 1877–88 and the *New York Evening Sun* 1888–99, he was a crusader for parks, playgrounds, and improved schools and housing in urban areas. He wrote *How the Other Half Lives* (1890).

Ri·je·ka /riˈyekə/ a port on the Adriatic coast of Croatia; pop. 138,600 (est. 2009). Italian name **FIUME**.

rijst·ta·fel /ˈrīˌstäfəl/ ▶ **n.** a meal of Southeast Asian food consisting of a selection of spiced rice dishes.
– ORIGIN Dutch, from *rijst* 'rice' + *tafel* 'table.'

rik·i·shi /ˈrikəˌshē/ ▶ **n.** (pl. **same**) a sumo wrestler.
– ORIGIN Japanese, from *riki* 'strength' + *shi* 'warrior.'

Riks·mål /ˈrikˌsmôl, ˈrēk-/ ▶ **n.** another term for **BOKMÅL**.
– ORIGIN Norwegian, from *rike* 'state, nation' + *mål* 'language.'

rile /rīl/ ▶ **v.** [with obj.] **1** informal make (someone) annoyed or irritated: *it was his air of knowing all the answers that riled her | he's getting you all riled up.*
2 make (water) turbulent or muddy.
– ORIGIN early 19th cent.: variant of **ROIL**.

Ri·ley[1] /ˈrīlē/ ▶ **n.** (in phrase **the life of Riley**) informal a luxurious or carefree existence: *all the older boys are driving big expensive cars and living the life of Riley.*
– ORIGIN early 20th cent.: of unknown origin.

Ri·ley[2], Bridget (Louise) (1931–), English painter. A leading exponent of op art, she worked with flat patterns to create optical illusions of light and movement.

Ri·ley[3], James Whitcomb (1849–1916), US poet; pen name **Benj. F. Johnson, of Boone**. Known as the common people's poet, esp. in Indiana, his most popular poems included "Little Orphant Annie" (1885), "The Raggedy Man" (1890), and "When the Frost Is on the Punkin" (1896).

ri·lie·vo ▶ **n.** variant spelling of **RELIEVO**.

Ril·ke /ˈrilkə/, Rainer Maria (1875–1926), Austrian poet, born in Bohemia; pseudonym of *René Karl Wilhelm Josef Maria Rilke*. His conception of art as a quasi-religious vocation culminated in his best-known works, the *Duino Elegies* and *Sonnets to Orpheus* (both 1923).

rill /ril/ ▶ **n.** a small stream. ■ a shallow channel cut in the ground by running water. ■ variant spelling of **RILLE**.
▶ **v.** [no obj.] (of water) flow in or as in a rill: *the springwater rilled over our cold hands.* ■ (as adj. **rilled**) indented with small grooves: *blocks of butter pounded into artful shapes with rilled paddles.*
– ORIGIN mid 16th cent.: probably of Low German origin.

rille /ˈrilə/ (also **rill**) ▶ **n.** Astronomy a fissure or narrow channel on the moon's surface.
– ORIGIN mid 19th cent.: from German (see **RILL**).

ril·lettes /rēˈyet/ ▶ **plural n.** pâté made of minced pork or other light meat, seasoned and combined with fat.
– ORIGIN French, diminutive (plural) of Old French *rille* 'strip of pork.'

rim[1] /rim/ ▶ **n.** the upper or outer edge of an object, typically something circular or approximately circular: *a china egg cup with a gold rim.* ■ (also **wheel rim**) the outer edge of a wheel, on which the tire is fitted. ■ the metal hoop from which a basketball net is suspended. ■ (often **rims**) the part of a glasses frame surrounding the lenses. ■ a limit or boundary of something: *the outer rim of the solar system.* ■ an encircling stain or deposit: *a thick rim of suds.*
▶ **v.** (**rims, rimming, rimmed**) [with obj.] form or act as an outer edge or rim for: *a huge lake rimmed by glaciers* | [as adj., in combination] (**-rimmed**) *steel-rimmed glasses.* ■ mark with an encircling stain or deposit: *his collar was rimmed with dirt.*
– DERIVATIVES **rim·less adj.**
– ORIGIN Old English *rima* 'a border, coast'; compare with Old Norse *rimi* 'ridge, strip of land' (the only known cognate).

rim[2] ▶ **v.** (**rims, rimming, rimmed**) [with obj.] vulgar slang lick or suck the anus of (someone) as a means of sexual stimulation.

Rim·baud /ramˈbō, raNˈbō/, (Jean Nicholas) Arthur (1854–91), French poet. Known for his symbolist prose poems and for his stormy relationship with Paul Verlaine, he stopped writing at about the age of 20 and spent the rest of his life traveling.

rime[1] /rīm/ ▶ **n.** (also **rime ice**) frost formed on cold objects by the rapid freezing of water vapor in cloud or fog. ■ literary hoarfrost.
▶ **v.** [with obj.] literary cover (an object) with hoarfrost: *he does not brush away the frost that rimes his beard.*
– ORIGIN Old English *hrīm*, of Germanic origin; related to Dutch *rijm*. The word became rare in Middle English but was revived in literary use at the end of the 18th cent.

rime[2] ▶ **n. & v.** archaic spelling of **RHYME**.

rim·fire /ˈrimˌfīr/ ▶ **adj.** [attrib.] relating to or denoting guns whose cartridges have the primer around the edge of the base.

Rim·i·ni /ˈrimənē/ a port and resort on the Adriatic coast of northeastern Italy; pop. 140,137 (2008).

rim·land /ˈrimˌland/ ▶ **n.** (also **rimlands**) a peripheral area of a country or region.

rim lock ▶ **n.** a lock that is fitted to the surface of a door with a matching box fitted into the doorjamb.

Rim·mon /ˈrimən/ (in the Bible) a deity worshiped in ancient Damascus.

rim·rock /ˈrimˌräk/ ▶ **n.** an outcrop of resistant rock forming a margin to a gravel deposit, esp. one forming a cliff at the edge of a plateau.

rim·shot (also **rim shot**) ▶ **n. 1** a drum stroke in which the stick strikes the rim and the head of the drum simultaneously.
2 in basketball, a toss in which the ball hits the rim of the basket.

Rim·sky-Kor·sa·kov /ˌrimskē ˈkôrsəˌkôf/, Nikolai (Andreevich) (1844–1908), Russian composer. He established his reputation with his orchestral suite *Scheherazade* (1888) and his many operas drawing on Russian and Slavic folk tales.

rim·y /ˈrīmē/ ▶ **adj.** (**rimier, rimiest**) literary covered with frost.

rind /rīnd/ ▶ **n.** the tough outer layer of something, in particular: ■ the tough outer skin of certain fruit, esp. citrus fruit. ■ the hard outer edge of cheese or bacon, usually removed before eating. ■ the bark of a tree or plant. ■ the hard outer layer of parts of a fungus. ■ the skin or blubber of a whale.
▶ **v.** [with obj.] strip the bark from (a tree).
– DERIVATIVES **rind·ed adj.** [in combination] *yellow-rinded lemons*, **rind·less adj.**

– ORIGIN Old English *rind(e)* 'bark of a tree'; related to Dutch *run* and German *Rinde*, of unknown origin.

rin·der·pest /ˈrindər,pest/ ▶ n. Veterinary Medicine an infectious disease of ruminants, esp. cattle, caused by a paramyxovirus. It is characterized by fever, dysentery, and inflammation of the mucous membranes.
– ORIGIN mid 19th cent.: from German, from *Rinder* 'cattle' + *Pest* 'plague.'

ring[1] /riNG/ ▶ n. **1** a small circular band, typically of precious metal and often set with one or more gemstones, worn on a finger as an ornament or a token of marriage, engagement, or authority. ■ a circular band of any material: *fried onion rings*. ■ Astronomy a thin band or disk of rock and ice particles around a planet. ■ a circular marking or pattern: *black rings around her eyes*. ■ short for TREE RING. ■ [usu. as modifier] Archaeology a circular prehistoric earthwork, typically consisting of a bank and ditch: *a ring ditch*.
2 an enclosed space, typically surrounded by seating for spectators, in which a sport, performance, or show takes place: *a circus ring*. ■ a roped enclosure for boxing or wrestling. ■ **(the ring)** the profession, sport, or institution of boxing.
3 a group of people or things arranged in a circle: *he pointed to the ring of trees*. ■ **(in a ring)** arranged or grouped in a circle: *everyone sat in a ring, holding hands*. ■ [usu. with modifier] a group of people drawn together due to a shared interest or goal, esp. one involving illegal or unscrupulous activity: *the police had been investigating the drug ring*. ■ Chemistry another term for CLOSED CHAIN.
4 a circular or spiral course: *they were dancing energetically in a ring*.
5 Mathematics a set of elements with two binary operations, addition and multiplication, the second being distributive over the first and associative.
▶ v. [with obj.] **1** surround (someone or something), esp. for protection or containment: *the courthouse was ringed with police*. ■ form a line around the edge of (something circular): *dark shadows ringed his eyes*. ■ draw a circle around (something), esp. to focus attention on it: *an area of Tribeca had been ringed in red*.
2 put a circular band through the nose of (a bull, pig, or other farm animal) to lead or otherwise control it.
– PHRASES **run rings around someone** informal outclass or outwit someone very easily. **throw one's hat in the ring** see HAT.
– DERIVATIVES **ringed** adj. [in combination] *the five-ringed Olympic emblem*, **ring·less** adj.
– ORIGIN Old English *hring*, of Germanic origin; related to Dutch *ring*, German *Ring*, also to the noun RANK[1].

ring[2] ▶ v. (past **rang** /raNG/; past participle **rung** /rəNG/) **1** [no obj.] make a clear resonant or vibrating sound: *a shot* **rang out** | *a bell rang loudly* | (as noun **ringing**) *the ringing of fire alarms*. ■ [with obj.] cause (a bell or alarm) to make such a sound: *he walked up to the door and rang the bell*. ■ (of a telephone) produce a series of resonant or vibrating sounds to signal an incoming call: *the phone rang again as I replaced it*. ■ call for service or attention by sounding a bell: *Ruth, will you* **ring for** *some tea?* ■ [with obj.] sound (the hour, a peal, etc.) on a bell or bells: *a bell ringing the hour*.
2 **(ring with/to)** (of a place) resound or reverberate with (a sound or sounds): *the room rang with laughter*. ■ (of a person's ears) be filled with a continuous buzzing or humming sound, esp. as the aftereffect of a blow or loud noise: *he yelled so loudly that my eardrums rang*. ■ **(ring with)** be filled or permeated with (a particular quality): *a clever retort which rang with contempt*. ■ [no obj., with complement] convey a specified impression or quality: *the author's honesty rings true*.
3 [with obj.] chiefly Brit. call by telephone: *I rang her this morning* | *Harriet rang Dorothy up next day* | [no obj.] *I tried to ring, but the lines to Moscow were engaged*.
▶ n. an act of causing a bell to sound, or the resonant sound caused by this: *there was a ring at the door*. ■ each of a series of resonant or vibrating sounds signaling an incoming telephone call. ■ [in sing.] informal a telephone call: *I'd better* **give her a ring** *tomorrow*. ■ [in sing.] a loud clear sound or tone: *the ring of sledgehammers on metal*. ■ [in sing.] a particular quality conveyed by something heard or expressed: *the song had a curious* **ring of** *nostalgia to it*. ■ a set of bells, esp. church bells.
– PHRASES **ring a bell** see BELL[1]. **ring the changes** see CHANGE. **ring down** (or **up**) **the curtain** cause a theater curtain to be lowered (or raised). ■ mark the end (or the beginning) of an enterprise or event: *the sendoff rings down the curtain on a major chapter in television history*. **ring in one's ears** (or **head**) linger in the memory: *he left Washington with the president's praises ringing in his ears*. **ring in** (or **out**) **the new** (or **old**) **year** commemorate the new year (or the end of the previous year) with boisterous celebration. **ring off the hook** (of a telephone) be constantly ringing due to a large number of incoming calls.
– PHRASAL VERBS **ring off** Brit. end a telephone call by replacing the receiver. **ring round** (or **around**) Brit. telephone (several people), typically to find something out or arrange something. **ring something up** record an amount on a cash register. ■ make, spend, or announce a particular amount in sales, profits, or losses.
– ORIGIN Old English *hringan*, of Germanic origin, perhaps imitative.

ring-a·round-the-ro·sy ▶ n. a singing game played by children, in which the players hold hands and dance in a circle, falling down at the end of the song.
– ORIGIN said to refer to the inflamed ("rose-colored") ring of buboes, symptomatic of the plague; the final part of the game is symbolic of death.

ring·back /ˈriNG,bak/ ▶ n. a sound made by a cellular phone that is heard by a person who is calling that phone while waiting for the call to be connected.

ring·bark /ˈriNG,bärk/ ▶ v. another term for GIRDLE (sense 2 of the verb).

ring bear·er ▶ n. the person, typically a young boy, who ceremoniously bears the rings at a wedding.

ring bind·er ▶ n. a loose-leaf binder with ring-shaped clasps that can be opened to pass through holes in the paper.

ring·bolt /ˈriNG,bōlt/ ▶ n. a bolt made with a ring for passing a rope through.

ring·bone /ˈriNG,bōn/ ▶ n. osteoarthritis of the pastern joint of a horse, causing swelling and lameness.

ring·bound ▶ adj. bound in a ring binder.

ring cir·cuit ▶ n. an electric circuit serving a number of outlets, with one circuit breaker in the supply.

ring·dove /ˈriNG,dəv/ ▶ n. a dove or pigeon with a ringlike mark on the neck, in particular: ● a captive or feral African collared dove (*Streptopelia roseogrisea*, family Columbidae). ● Brit. the wood pigeon.

ringed plov·er ▶ n. a small plover found chiefly in Eurasia, with white underparts and a black collar, breeding on sand or shingle beaches. ● Genus *Charadrius*, family Charadriidae: three species, in particular *Charadrius hiaticula*.

ringed seal ▶ n. a seal of arctic and subarctic waters that has pale ring-shaped markings on the back and sides and a short muzzle. ● *Phoca hispida*, family Phocidae.

ring·er[1] /ˈriNGər/ ▶ n. **1** informal an athlete or horse fraudulently substituted for another in a competition or event. ■ a person's or thing's double, esp. an impostor: *he's* **a ringer for** *the French actor Fernandel*. ■ a person who is highly proficient at a particular skill or sport and is brought in to supplement a team or group of people: *league eligibility rules had grown flexible to accommodate new teams, and ringers began suiting up*.
2 a person or device that rings something.

ring·er[2] ▶ n. **1** in certain games, a tossed object that encircles its intended target, in particular: ■ a tossed horseshoe that encircles the stake. ■ a tossed quoit that encircles the peg.
2 a game of marbles in which the target marbles are placed in the center of a circular area.

Ring·er's so·lu·tion /ˈriNGərz/ ▶ n. Biology a physiological saline solution that typically contains, in addition to sodium chloride, salts of potassium and calcium.
– ORIGIN late 19th cent.: named after Sydney *Ringer* (1834–1910), English physician.

ring·ette /riNGˈet/ ▶ n. Canadian a game resembling ice hockey, played (esp. by women and girls) with a straight stick and a rubber ring, and in which no intentional body contact is allowed.

ring fin·ger ▶ n. the finger next to the little finger, esp. of the left hand, on which the wedding band is worn.

ring flash ▶ n. Photography a circular electronic flash tube that fits around a camera lens to give shadowless lighting of a subject near the lens, esp. for macrophotography.

ring·git /ˈriNGgit/ ▶ n. (pl. **same** or **ringgits**) the basic monetary unit of Malaysia, equivalent to 100 hundred sen.
– ORIGIN Malay.

ring·hals /ˈriNG,hals/ (also **rinkhals** /ˈriNG,kals/) ▶ n. a large nocturnal spitting cobra of southern Africa, with one or two white rings across the throat. ● *Hemachatus haemachatus*, family Elapidae.
– ORIGIN late 18th cent.: from Afrikaans *rinkhals*, from *ring* 'ring' + *hals* 'neck.'

ring·ing /ˈriNGiNG/ ▶ adj. having or emitting a clear resonant sound: *a ringing voice*. ■ (of a statement) forceful and unequivocal: *the Russian leader received a ringing declaration of support*.
– DERIVATIVES **ring·ing·ly** adv.

ring·lead·er /ˈriNG,lēdər/ ▶ n. a person who initiates or leads an illicit or illegal activity.

ring·let /ˈriNGlit/ ▶ n. **1** a lock of hair hanging in a corkscrew-shaped curl.
2 a brown butterfly that has wings bearing eyespots that are typically highlighted by a paler color. ● *Aphantopus*, *Erebia*, and other genera in the subfamily Satyrinae, family Nymphalidae: several species.
– DERIVATIVES **ring·let·ed** adj., **ring·let·y** adj.

ring main ▶ n. Brit. **1** an electrical supply serving a series of consumers and returning to the original source, so that each consumer has an alternative path in the event of a failure. ■ another term for RING CIRCUIT.
2 an arrangement of pipes forming a closed loop into which steam, water, or sewage may be fed and whose points of draw-off are supplied by flow from two directions.

ring·mas·ter /ˈriNG,mastər/ ▶ n. the person directing a circus performance.

ring mod·u·la·tor ▶ n. an electronic circuit, esp. in a musical instrument, that incorporates a closed loop of four diodes and can be used for the balanced mixing and modulation of signals.

ring·neck (also **ringneck**) ▶ n. any of a number of ring-necked birds, in particular: ● a ring-necked pheasant. See PHEASANT ● Austral. a green parrot with a yellow collar (genus *Barnardius*, family Psittacidae: two species). ● a ring-necked duck (*Aythya collaris*, family Anatidae).

ring-necked ▶ adj. used in names of birds and reptiles with a band or bands of color around the neck, e.g., **ring-necked pheasant**.

Ring of Fire the zone of volcanic activity surrounding the Pacific Ocean.

ring ou·zel (also **ring ousel**) ▶ n. a European thrush that resembles a blackbird with a white crescent across the breast, inhabiting upland moors and mountainous country. ● *Turdus torquatus*, subfamily Turdinae, family Muscicapidae.

ring pull ▶ n. a ring-shaped pull tab on a can or other container.

ring road ▶ n. a bypass encircling a town.

ring·side /ˈriNG,sīd/ ▶ n. [often as modifier] the area immediately beside a boxing ring or circus ring: *a ringside judge*. ■ an advantageous position from which to observe or monitor something: *having a ringside seat at the healthcare committee hearings*.
– DERIVATIVES **ring·sid·er** n.

ring·ster /ˈriNGstər/ ▶ n. archaic **1** a member of a political or price-fixing ring.
2 a boxer.

ring·tail /ˈriNG,tāl/ ▶ n. **1** any of a number of mammals or birds having a tail marked with a ring or rings, in particular: ■ a ring-tailed cat or lemur. ■ a female hen harrier or related harrier. ■ a golden eagle up to its third year.
2 (also **ringtail** or **ring-tailed possum**) a nocturnal tree-dwelling Australian possum that habitually curls its prehensile tail into a ring or spiral. ● Genus *Pseudocheirus* and other genera, family Petauridae: several species, in particular the **common ringtail** (*P. peregrinus*), of southern Australia and Tasmania.

ring-tailed ▶ adj. used in names of mammals and birds that have the tail banded in contrasting colors, e.g., **ring-tailed lemur**, or curled at the end, e.g., **ring-tailed possum**.

ring-tailed cat ▶ n. a North American cacomistle, a nocturnal raccoonlike mammal with a dark-ringed tail. Also called RINGTAIL. ● *Bassariscus astutus*, family Procyonidae.

ring-tailed le·mur ▶ n. a gregarious lemur with a gray coat, black rings around the eyes, and distinctive black-and-

ring-tailed lemur

white banding on the tail. ● *Lemur catta*, family Lemuridae.

ring·tone /ˈriNG,tōn/ ▶ **n.** a sound made by a mobile phone when an incoming call is received.

ring·toss /ˈriNG,tôs, -,täs/ ▶ **n.** a game in which rings are tossed at an upright peg. Points are scored by encircling the peg or coming closer to it than other players.

ring·work /ˈriNG,wərk/ ▶ **n.** Archaeology the circular entrenchment of a minor medieval castle.

ring·worm /ˈriNG,wərm/ ▶ **n.** a contagious itching skin disease occurring in small circular patches, caused by any of a number of fungi and affecting chiefly the scalp or the feet. The most common form is athlete's foot. Also called **TINEA**.

rink /riNGk/ ▶ **n.** (also **ice rink** or **hockey rink**) an enclosed area of ice for skating, ice hockey, or curling, esp. one artificially prepared. ■ (also **roller rink**) a smooth enclosed floor for roller skating. ■ a building containing either of these. ■ (also **bowling rink**) the strip of a bowling green used for playing a match. ■ a team in curling or lawn bowling.
– ORIGIN late Middle English (originally Scots in the sense 'jousting ground'): perhaps originally from Old French *renc* 'rank.'

rink·hals /ˈriNG,kals/ ▶ **n.** variant spelling of **RINGHALS**.

rink rat ▶ **n.** informal **1** a young person who spends time around an ice-hockey rink in the hope of meeting players, watching practice, and spending time on the ice.
2 a synthetic broom used in the game of curling.

rink·y-dink /ˈriNGkē ,diNGk/ ▶ **adj.** informal old-fashioned, amateurish, or shoddy: *the fifty-third issue of the quarterly looked just as rinky-dink as the first.*
– ORIGIN late 19th cent.: of unknown origin.

Rin·po·che /ˈrin'päCHˈā/ ▶ **n.** (in Tibetan Buddhism) an incarnate lama or highly respected religious teacher (often used as an honorific title).
– ORIGIN Tibetan, literally 'precious jewel.'

rinse /rins/ ▶ **v.** [with obj.] wash (something) with clean water to remove soap, detergent, dirt, or impurities: *always rinse your hair thoroughly* | *mussels should be well rinsed before use.* ■ wash (something) quickly, esp. without soap: *Rose* ***rinsed out*** *a tumbler* | *Karen* ***rinsed*** *her mouth* ***out.*** ■ [with obj.] remove (soap, detergent, dirt, or impurities) by washing with clean water: *the conditioning mousse doesn't have to be* ***rinsed out*** | [no obj.] *rub salt onto rough areas of skin, then* ***rinse off.***
▶ **n. 1** an act of rinsing something: *I gave my hands a quick rinse.*
2 an antiseptic solution for cleansing the mouth.
3 a preparation for conditioning or temporarily tinting the hair.
– DERIVATIVES **rins·er n.**
– ORIGIN Middle English (as a verb): from Old French *rincer*, of unknown ultimate origin.

Ri·o Bran·co /ˈrē-ō ˈbräNGkō, ˈrē-ōō ˈbräNGkōō/ a city in western Brazil, capital of the state of Acre; pop. 290,639 (2007).

Ri·o de Ja·nei·ro /ˈrē-ō ,dā (d)ZHəˈne(ə)rō, ,dē/ a state in eastern Brazil, on the Atlantic coast. ■ (also **Rio**) its capital; pop. 6,093,472 (2007). The chief port of Brazil, it was the country's capital from 1763 until 1960, when it was replaced by Brasilia.

Christ the Redeemer statue, Rio de Janeiro

Rí·o de la Pla·ta /ˈrē-ō dā lä ˈplätä/ Spanish name for the River Plate. (see **PLATE RIVER**).

Rí·o de O·ro /ˈrē-ō dē ˈôrō/ an arid region on the Atlantic coast of northwestern Africa that forms the southern part of Western Sahara. It was united with Saguia el-Hamra in 1958 to form the province of Spanish Sahara (now Western Sahara).

Ri·o Grande /,rē-ō ˈgrand(ē)/ a river in North America that rises in the Rocky Mountains of southwestern Colorado and flows 1,880 miles (3,030 km) southeast to the Gulf of Mexico, forming the US–Mexico border from El Paso to the gulf.

Ri·o·ja /rēˈōhä/ ▶ **n.** a wine produced in La Rioja, Spain.

Ri·o Mu·ni /ˈrē-ō ˈmōōnē/ the part of Equatorial Guinea that lies on the mainland of West Africa.

Ri·o Ne·gro /ˈrē-ō ˈnāgrō/ a river in South America that rises as the Guainia in eastern Colombia and flows for about 1,400 miles (2,255 km) through northwestern Brazil before joining the Amazon River near Manaus.

Rio Ran·cho /ˈrē-ō ˈranCHō/ a city in north central New Mexico, northwest of Albuquerque; pop. 79,655 (est. 2008).

ri·ot /ˈrīət/ ▶ **n. 1** a violent disturbance of the peace by a crowd: *riots broke out in the capital* | [as modifier] *riot police.* ■ an uproar: *the film's sex scenes caused a riot in Cannes.* ■ an outburst of uncontrolled feelings: ***a riot of*** *emotions raged through Frances.* ■ archaic uncontrolled revelry; rowdy behavior.
2 [in sing.] an impressively large or varied display of something: *the garden was* ***a riot of*** *color.*
3 [in sing.] informal a highly amusing or entertaining person or thing: *everyone thought she was a riot.*
▶ **v.** [no obj.] take part in a violent public disturbance: *students rioted in Paris* | (as noun **rioting**) *a night of rioting.* ■ behave in an unrestrained way: *another set of emotions rioted through him.* ■ archaic act in a dissipated way: *an unrepentant prodigal son, rioting off to far countries.*
– PHRASES **run riot** behave in a violent and unrestrained way. ■ (of a mental faculty or emotion) function or be expressed without restraint: *her imagination ran riot.* ■ proliferate or spread uncontrollably: *traditional prejudices were allowed to run riot.*
– DERIVATIVES **ri·ot·er n.**
– ORIGIN Middle English (originally in the sense 'dissolute living'): from Old French *riote* 'debate,' from *rioter* 'to quarrel,' of unknown ultimate origin.

Ri·ot Act a law passed by the British government in 1715 and repealed in 1967, designed to prevent civil disorder. The act made it a felony for an assembly of more than twelve people to refuse to disperse after being ordered to do so and having been read a specified section of the act by lawful authority.
– PHRASES **read someone the Riot Act** (or **riot act**) give someone a strong warning that they must improve their behavior.

ri·ot gear ▶ **n.** protective clothing and equipment worn by police or prison officers in situations of crowd violence.

ri·ot girl (also **riot grrrl**) ▶ **n.** a member of a movement of young feminists expressing their resistance to the sexual harassment and exploitation of women, esp. through aggressive punk-style rock music.

ri·ot·ous /ˈrīətəs/ ▶ **adj.** marked by or involving public disorder: *a riotous crowd.* ■ characterized by wild and uncontrolled behavior: *a riotous party.* ■ having a vivid, varied appearance: *a riotous display of bright red, green, and yellow vegetables.* ■ hilariously funny: *a riotous account of the making of the movie.*
– DERIVATIVES **ri·ot·ous·ly adv.**, **ri·ot·ous·ness n.**
– ORIGIN Middle English (in the sense 'troublesome'): from Old French, from *riote* (see **RIOT**).

RIP[1] ▶ **abbr.** rest in peace (used on grave markers).
– ORIGIN from Latin *requiescat* (or, in the plural, *requiescant*) *in pace.*

RIP[2] /rip, ˈär ,ī ˈpē/ ▶ **n.** a raster image processor.
▶ **v.** (usu. **rip**) (**RIPs, ripping, ripped**) [with obj.] rasterize (an image): *once you are happy with the image, you can rip it out.*
– ORIGIN 1970s: abbreviation.

rip[1] /rip/ ▶ **v.** (**rips, ripping, ripped**) **1** [with obj.] tear or pull (something) quickly or forcibly away from something or someone: *a fan tried to* ***rip*** *his pants* ***off*** *during a show* | figurative *countries ripped apart by fighting.* ■ make a long tear or cut in: *you've ripped my jacket* | (as adj. **ripped**) *ripped jeans.* ■ make (a hole) by force: *the truck was struck by lightning and had a hole ripped out of its roof.* ■ [no obj.] come violently apart; tear: *he heard something rip.* ■ cut (wood) in the direction of the grain.
2 [no obj.] move forcefully and rapidly: *fire ripped through her bungalow.*
3 use a program to copy (material from a CD or DVD) onto a computer's hard drive: *every Beatles song ever made, ripped from my boxed set of CDs.*
▶ **n. 1** a long tear or cut. ■ [in sing.] an act of tearing something forcibly.
2 a fraud or swindle; a rip-off.
– PHRASES **let rip** informal do something or proceed vigorously or without restraint: *the brass sections let rip with sheer gusto.* ■ express oneself vehemently or angrily. **let something rip** informal allow something, esp. a vehicle, to go at full speed. ■ allow something to happen forcefully or without interference: *once she started a tirade, it was best to let it rip.* ■ utter or express something forcefully and noisily: *when I passed the exam I let rip a "yippee."*
– PHRASAL VERBS **rip into** informal make a vehement verbal attack on: *he ripped into me just for going into the trailer.* **rip someone off** informal cheat someone, esp. financially. **rip something off** informal steal: *they have ripped off $6.7 billion.* ■ copy; plagiarize: *the film is a shameless collection of ideas ripped off from other movies.* **rip something up** tear something violently into small pieces so as to destroy it.
– ORIGIN late Middle English (as a verb): of unknown origin; compare with the verb **REAP**. The noun dates from the early 18th cent.

rip[2] ▶ **n.** a stretch of fast-flowing and rough water in the sea or in a river, caused by the meeting of currents. ■ short for **RIP CURRENT**.
– ORIGIN late 18th cent.: perhaps related to **RIP**[1].

rip[3] ▶ **n.** dated **1** a dissolute immoral person, esp. a man: *"Where is that old rip?" a deep voice shouted.* ■ a mischievous person, esp. a child.
2 a worthless horse.
– ORIGIN late 18th cent.: perhaps from *rep*, abbreviation of **REPROBATE**.

ri·par·i·an /riˈpe(ə)rēən, rī-/ ▶ **adj.** chiefly Law of, relating to, or situated on the banks of a river: *all the riparian states must sign an agreement.* ■ Ecology of or relating to wetlands adjacent to rivers and streams.
– ORIGIN mid 19th cent.: from Latin *riparius* (from *ripa* 'bank') + **-AN**.

rip·cord /ˈrip,kôrd/ ▶ **n.** a cord that is pulled to open a parachute.

rip cur·rent ▶ **n.** a relatively strong, narrow current flowing outward from the beach through the surf zone and presenting a hazard to swimmers. Also called **UNDERTOW**. Compare with **RIPTIDE**.

ripe /rīp/ ▶ **adj.** (of fruit or grain) developed to the point of readiness for harvesting and eating. ■ (of a cheese or wine) fully matured: *a ripe Brie* | figurative *ripe wisdom.* ■ (of a smell or flavor) rich, intense, or pungent: *rich, ripe flavors emanate from this wine.* ■ (of a female fish or insect) ready to lay eggs or spawn. ■ [predic.] (**ripe for**) arrived at the fitting stage or time for (a particular action or purpose): *land ripe for development.* ■ [predic.] (**ripe with**) full of: *a population ripe with discontent.* ■ [attrib.] (of a person's age) advanced: *she lived to a ripe old age.* ■ informal (of a person's language) beyond the bounds of propriety; coarse.
– PHRASES **the time is ripe** a suitable time has arrived: *the time was ripe to talk about peace.*
– DERIVATIVES **ripe·ly adv.**, **ripe·ness n.**
– ORIGIN Old English *rīpe*; related to Dutch *rijp* and German *reif*.

rip·en /ˈrīpən/ ▶ **v.** become or make ripe: [no obj.] *honeydew melons ripen slowly* | [with obj.] *for ease of harvesting, the fruit is ripened to order.*

ri·pie·no /ripˈyānō/ ▶ **n.** (pl. **ripienos** or **ripieni** /-nē/) [usu. as modifier] Music the body of instruments accompanying the concertino in baroque concerto music: *the concertino is accompanied by ripieno strings.*
– ORIGIN early 18th cent. (in the sense 'supplementary'): from Italian, from *ri-* (expressing intensive force) + *pieno* 'full.'

Rip·ken /ˈripkin/, Cal, Jr. (1960–), US baseball player; nickname **Iron Man**. A shortstop and later a third baseman, he played for the Baltimore Orioles 1982–2001. He holds the major league record of 2,632 consecutive games played. Baseball Hall of Fame (2007).

rip-off ▶ **n.** informal a fraud or swindle, esp. something that is grossly overpriced: *designer label clothes are just expensive rip-offs.* ■ an inferior imitation of something: *rip-offs of all the latest styles.*

ri·poste /riˈpōst/ ▶ **n. 1** a quick clever reply to an insult or criticism.
2 Fencing a quick return thrust following a parry.
▶ **v. 1** [with direct speech] make a quick clever reply to an insult or criticism: *"I'd have made lamb chops had I known you're a vegetarian," Kris riposted.*
2 [no obj.] make a quick return thrust in fencing.
– ORIGIN early 18th cent.: from French *risposte* (noun), *risposter* (verb), from Italian *risposta* 'response.'

rip·per /ˈripər/ ▶ **n. 1** a tool that is used to tear or break something. ■ a murderer who mutilates victims' bodies.
2 informal a thing that is particularly admirable or excellent.

rip·ping /ˈripiNG/ ▶ **adj.** Brit. informal, dated splendid; excellent: *she's going to have a ripping time.*
– DERIVATIVES **rip·ping·ly adv.**

rip·ple /ˈripəl/ ▶ **n. 1** a small wave or series of waves on the surface of water, esp. as caused by an object dropping into it or a slight breeze. ■ a thing resembling such a wave or series of waves in

appearance or movement: *the sand undulated and was ridged with ripples.* ■ a gentle rising and falling sound, esp. of laughter or conversation, that spreads through a group of people: *a ripple of laughter ran around the room.* ■ a particular feeling or effect that spreads through or to someone or something: *his words set off a ripple of excitement within her.* ■ Physics a wave on a fluid surface, the restoring force for which is provided by surface tension rather than gravity, and that consequently has a wavelength shorter than that corresponding to the minimum speed of propagation. ■ Physics small periodic, usually undesirable, variations in electrical voltage superposed on a direct voltage or on an alternating voltage of lower frequency.
2 a type of ice cream with wavy lines of colored flavored syrup running through it: *raspberry ripple.*
▶ **v.** [no obj.] (of water) form or flow with small waves on the surface: *the Mediterranean rippled and sparkled* | (as adj. **rippling**) *the rippling waters.* ■ [with obj.] cause (the surface of water) to form small waves: *a cool wind rippled the surface of the estuary.* ■ move or cause to move in a way resembling such waves: *fields of grain rippling in the wind.* ■ (of a sound or feeling) spread through a person, group, or place: *applause **rippled around** the tables.* ■ (as adj. **rippled**) having the appearance of small waves: *a broad noodle, rippled on both sides, wider than fettuccine.*
– DERIVATIVES **rip·plet** /ˈriplit/ **n.**, **rip·ply** /ˈrip(ə)lē/ **adj.**
– ORIGIN late 17th cent. (as a verb): of unknown origin.

rip·ple ef·fect ▶ **n.** the continuing and spreading results of an event or action: *while their marriage made an impact on their friends, the ripple effect on family members was even more profound.*

rip·ple marks ▶ **plural n.** a system of subparallel wavy ridges and furrows left on sand or mud by the action of water or wind, and sometimes fossilized.

rip·rap /ˈripˌrap/ ▶ **n.** loose stone used to form a foundation for a breakwater or other structure.
▶ **v.** (**ripraps, riprapping, riprapped**) [with obj.] strengthen with such a structure.
– ORIGIN mid 19th cent. (originally US): reduplication of **RAP**[1].

rip·roar·ing ▶ **adj.** [attrib.] full of energy and vigor: *a rip-roaring rodeo.*
– DERIVATIVES **rip·roar·ing·ly adv.**

rip·saw /ˈripˌsô/ ▶ **n.** a coarse saw for cutting wood along the grain.

rip·snort·ing /ˈripˈsnôrtiNG/ ▶ **adj.** [attrib.] informal showing great vigor or intensity: *a ripsnorting editorial.*
– DERIVATIVES **rip·snort·er** /-ˈsnôrtər/ **n.**, **rip·snort·ing·ly adv.**

rip·stop /ˈripˌstäp/ ▶ **n.** nylon fabric that is woven so that a tear will not spread.

rip·tide /ˈripˌtīd/ ▶ **n.** a strong current caused by tidal flow in confined areas such as inlets and presenting a hazard to swimmers and boaters. ■ another term for **RIP CURRENT**.

Rip Van Win·kle /ˌrip ˌvan ˈwiNGkəl/ the hero of a story in Washington Irving's *Sketch Book* (1819–20), who fell asleep in the Catskill Mountains and awoke after twenty years to find the world completely changed.

RISC /risk/ ▶ **n.** [usu. as modifier] Computing a computer based on a processor or processors designed to perform a limited set of operations extremely quickly. ■ computing using this kind of computer.
– ORIGIN 1980s: acronym from *reduced instruction set computer* (or *computing*).

rise /rīz/ ▶ **v.** (past **rose** /rōz/; past participle **risen** /ˈrizən/) [no obj.] **1** move from a lower position to a higher one; come or go up: *the tiny aircraft rose from the ground.* ■ (of the sun, moon, or another celestial body) appear above the horizon: *the sun had just risen.* ■ (of a fish) come to the surface of water: *a fish rose and was hooked and landed.* ■ (of a voice) become higher in pitch: *my voice rose an octave or two as I screamed.* ■ reach a higher position in society or one's profession: *the officer was a man of great courage who had **risen from the ranks**.* ■ (**rise above**) succeed in not being limited or constrained by (a restrictive environment or situation): *he struggled to rise above his humble background.* ■ (**rise above**) be superior to: *I try to rise above prejudice.*
2 get up from lying, sitting, or kneeling: *she pushed back her chair and rose.* ■ get out of bed, esp. in the morning: *I rose and got dressed.* ■ chiefly Brit. (of a meeting or a session of a court) adjourn: *the judge's remark heralded the signal for the court to rise.* ■ be restored to life: *your sister has **risen from the dead** | he would **rise again from** the dead on the third day.* ■ (of a wind) start to blow or to blow more strongly: *the wind continued to rise.* ■ (of a river) have its source: *the Euphrates rises in Turkey.* ■ cease to be submissive, obedient, or peaceful: *the activists urged militant factions to **rise up**.* ■ (**rise to**) (of a person) react with annoyance or argument to (provocation): *he didn't rise to my teasing.* ■ (**rise to**) find the strength or ability to respond adequately to (a challenging situation): *many participants in the race had never sailed before, but they rose to the challenge.*
3 (of land or a feature following the contours of the land) incline upward; become higher: *the moorlands rise and fall in gentle folds.* ■ (of a building, mountain, or other high object or structure) be much taller than the surrounding landscape: *the cliff rose more than a hundred feet above us.* ■ (of someone's hair) stand on end: *he felt the hairs rise on the back of his neck.* ■ (of a building) undergo construction from the foundations: *rows of two-story houses are slowly rising.* ■ (of dough) swell by the action of yeast: *leave the dough in a warm place to rise.* ■ (of a bump, blister, or weal) appear as a swelling on the skin: *blisters rose on his burned hand.* ■ (of a person's stomach) become nauseated: *Fabio's stomach **rose at** the foul bedding.*
4 increase in number, size, amount, or quality: *land prices had risen.* ■ (of the sea, a river, or other body of water) increase in height to a particular level, typically through tidal action or flooding: *the river level rose so high the work had to be abandoned* | figurative *the **rising tide of** crime.* ■ (of an emotion) develop and become more intense: *he felt a tide of resentment rising in him.* ■ (of a sound) become louder; be audible above other sounds: *her voice rose above the clamor.* ■ (of a person's mood) become more cheerful: *her spirits rose as they left the ugly city behind.* ■ (of the color in a person's face) become deeper, esp. as a result of embarrassment: *he was teasing her, and she could feel her color rising.* ■ (of a barometer or other measuring instrument) give a higher reading.
5 (**rising**) approaching (a specified age): *she was thirty-nine rising forty | Polly shall have a young mare rising three years old.*
▶ **n. 1** an upward movement; an instance of becoming higher: *the bird has a display flight of steep flapping rises.* ■ an act of a fish moving to the surface to take a fly or bait. ■ an increase in sound or pitch: *the rise and fall of his voice.* ■ an instance of social, commercial, or political advancement: *few models have had such a meteoric rise.* ■ an upward slope or hill. ■ the vertical height of a step, arch, or incline. ■ another term for **RISER** (sense 2).
2 an increase in amount, extent, size, or number: *local people are worried by the rise in crime.* ■ Brit. an increase in salary or wages.
3 [in sing.] a source; an origin: *it was here that the brook had its rise.*
– PHRASES **get** (or **take**) **a rise out of** informal provoke an angry or irritated response from (someone), esp. by teasing. **on the rise** becoming greater or more numerous; increasing: *prices were on the rise.* ■ becoming more successful: *young stars on the rise.* **rise and shine** [usu. in imperative] informal get out of bed smartly; wake up. **rise to the bait** see **BAIT**. **rise with the sun** (or **lark**) get up early in the morning. **someone's star is rising** someone is becoming more successful or popular.
– ORIGIN Old English *rīsan* 'make an attack,' 'wake, get out of bed,' of Germanic origin; related to Dutch *rijzen* and German *reisen*.

ris·er /ˈrīzər/ ▶ **n. 1** [with adj.] a person who habitually gets out of bed at a particular time of the morning: *late risers always exasperate early risers.*
2 a vertical section between the treads of a staircase.
3 a vertical pipe for the upward flow of liquid or gas.
4 a low platform on a stage or in an auditorium, used to give greater prominence to a speaker or performer.
5 a strip of webbing joining the harness and the rigging lines of a parachute or paraglider.

rise time ▶ **n.** Electronics the time required for a pulse to rise from 10 percent to 90 percent of its steady value.

rish·i /ˈrisHē/ ▶ **n.** (pl. **rishis**) a Hindu sage or saint.
– ORIGIN from Sanskrit *ṛṣi*.

ris·i·ble /ˈrizəbəl/ ▶ **adj.** such as to provoke laughter: *a risible scene of lovemaking in a tent.* ■ rare (of a person) having the faculty or power of laughing; inclined to laugh.
– DERIVATIVES **ris·i·bil·i·ty** /ˌrizəˈbilətē/ **n.**, **ris·i·bly** /-blē/ **adv.**
– ORIGIN mid 16th cent. (in the sense 'inclined to laughter'): from late Latin *risibilis*, from Latin *ris-* 'laughed,' from the verb *ridere*.

ris·ing /ˈrīziNG/ ▶ **adj. 1** going up, increasing, or sloping upward: *the rising temperature | rising ground.* ■ advancing to maturity or high standing: *the rising generation of American writers.* ■ approaching (a higher level, grade, age, etc.): *a rising senior at North Carolina State.* ■ Astrology (of a sign) ascendant.
2 [postpositive] Heraldry (of a bird) depicted with the wings open but not fully displayed, as if preparing for flight.
▶ **n.** an armed protest against authority; a revolt.

ris·ing main ▶ **n.** Brit. a vertical pipe that rises from the ground to supply municipal water to a building. ■ the vertical pipe of a water pump.

ris·ing trot ▶ **n.** a style of riding in which a rider rises from the saddle on every second stride of a horse's trotting pace.

risk /risk/ ▶ **n.** a situation involving exposure to danger: *flouting the law was too much of a risk | all outdoor activities carry an element of risk.* ■ [in sing.] the possibility that something unpleasant or unwelcome will happen: ***reduce the risk of** heart disease* | [as modifier] *a high consumption of caffeine was suggested as a **risk factor** for loss of bone mass.* ■ [usu. in sing. with adj.] a person or thing regarded as likely to turn out well or badly, as specified, in a particular context or respect: *Western banks regarded Romania as a good risk.* ■ [with adj.] a person or thing regarded as a threat or likely source of danger: *she's a security risk | gloss paint can burn strongly and pose a fire risk.* ■ (usu. **risks**) a possibility of harm or damage against which something is insured. ■ the possibility of financial loss: [as modifier] *project finance is essentially an exercise in risk management.*
▶ **v.** [with obj.] expose (someone or something valued) to danger, harm, or loss: *he risked his life to save his dog.* ■ act or fail to act in such a way as to bring about the possibility of (an unpleasant or unwelcome event): *unless you're dealing with pure alcohol you're risking contamination from benzene.* ■ incur the chance of unfortunate consequences by engaging in (an action): *he was far too intelligent to risk attempting to deceive her.*
– PHRASES **at risk** exposed to harm or danger: *23 million people in Africa are **at risk from** starvation.* **at one's** (**own**) **risk** used to indicate that if harm befalls a person or their possessions through their actions, it is their own responsibility: *they undertook the adventure at their own risk.* **at the risk of doing something** although there is the possibility of something unpleasant resulting: *at the risk of boring people to tears, I repeat the most important rule in painting.* **at risk to oneself** (or **something**) with the possibility of endangering oneself or something: *he visited prisons at considerable risk to his health.* **risk one's neck** put one's life in danger. **run the risk** (or **run risks**) expose oneself to the possibility of something unpleasant occurring: *she preferred not to **run the risk of** encountering his sister.*
– ORIGIN mid 17th cent.: from French *risque* (noun), *risquer* (verb), from Italian *risco* 'danger' and *rischiare* 'run into danger.'

risk as·sess·ment ▶ **n.** a systematic process of evaluating the potential risks that may be involved in a projected activity or undertaking.

risk cap·i·tal ▶ **n.** another term for **VENTURE CAPITAL**.

risk man·age·ment ▶ **n.** (in business) the forecasting and evaluation of financial risks together with the identification of procedures to avoid or minimize their impact.

risk·y /ˈriskē/ ▶ **adj.** (**riskier, riskiest**) full of the possibility of danger, failure, or loss: *it was much too risky to try to disarm him.*
– DERIVATIVES **risk·i·ly** /-kəlē/ **adv.**, **risk·i·ness n.**

Ri·sor·gi·men·to /rēˌzôrjəˈmenˌtō, -ˌsôr-/ a movement for the unification and independence of Italy, which was achieved in 1870.

> The restoration of repressive regimes after the Napoleonic Wars led to revolts in Naples and Piedmont (1821) and Bologna (1831).With French aid the Austrians were driven out of northern Italy by 1859, and the south was won over by Garibaldi. Voting resulted in the acceptance of Victor Emmanuel II as the first king of a united Italy in 1861.

– ORIGIN Italian, literally 'resurrection.'

ri·sot·to /riˈzôtō, -ˈsôtō/ ▶ **n.** (pl. **risottos**) an Italian dish of rice cooked in stock with other ingredients such as meat and vegetables.
– ORIGIN Italian, from *riso* 'rice.'

ris·qué /riˈskā/ ▶ **adj.** slightly indecent or liable to shock, esp. by being sexually suggestive: *his risqué humor.*
– ORIGIN mid 19th cent.: French, past participle of *risquer* 'to risk.'

PRONUNCIATION KEY ə *ago, up*; ər *over, fur*; a *hat*; ā *ate*; ä *car*; e *let*; ē *see*; i *fit*; ī *by*; NG *sing*; ō *go*; ô *law, for*; oi *toy*; o͝o *good*; o͞o *goo*; ou *out*; TH *thin*; T͟H *then*; ZH *vision*

Riss /ris/ ▶ **n.** [usu. as modifier] Geology the penultimate Pleistocene glaciation in the Alps, possibly corresponding to the Saale of northern Europe. ■ the system of deposits laid down at this time.
– ORIGIN early 20th cent.: from the name of a tributary of the Danube River in Germany.

ris·sole /riˈsōl, ˈrisˌōl/ ▶ **n.** a compressed mixture of meat and spices, coated in breadcrumbs and fried.
– ORIGIN early 18th cent.: from French, from Old French dialect *ruissole*, from a feminine form of late Latin *russeolus* 'reddish,' from Latin *russus* 'red.'

Ris·so's dol·phin /ˈrisōz/ ▶ **n.** a gray dolphin that has long black flippers and a rounded snout with no beak, living mainly in temperate seas. Also called GRAMPUS. ● *Grampus griseus*, family Delphinidae.
– ORIGIN late 19th cent.: named after Giovanni A. *Risso* (1777–1845), Italian naturalist.

ri·sto·ran·te /ˌristôˈränˌtā/ ▶ **n.** (pl. **ristoranti** /-tē/) an Italian restaurant.
– ORIGIN Italian.

ris·tret·to /riˈstretō/ ▶ **n.** (pl. **ristrettos**) a drink of very strong, concentrated espresso.
– ORIGIN from Italian (*caffè*) *ristretto*, literally 'restricted (coffee),' from *restringere* 'restrict.'

rit. Music ▶ **abbr.** ■ ritardando. ■ ritenuto.

Rit·a·lin /ˈritl-in/ ▶ **n.** trademark for METHYLPHENIDATE.

ri·tar·dan·do /ˌrētärˈdändō/ (also **ritard** /riˈtärd/) Music ▶ **adv. & adj.** (esp. as a direction) with a gradual decrease of tempo.
▶ **n.** (pl. **ritardandos** or **ritardandi** /-ˈdändē/) a gradual decrease in tempo.
– ORIGIN Italian.

rite /rīt/ ▶ **n.** a religious or other solemn ceremony or act: *the rite of communion* | *fertility rites*. ■ a body of customary observances characteristic of a church or a part of it: *the Byzantine rite*. ■ a social custom, practice, or conventional act: *the family Christmas rite*.
– PHRASES **rite of passage** a ceremony or event marking an important stage in someone's life, esp. birth, puberty, marriage, and death: *a novel that depicts the state of adolescence and the rites of passage that lead to adulthood*.
– ORIGIN Middle English: from Latin *ritus* '(religious) usage.'

ri·te·nu·to /ˌrētəˈno͞otō/ Music ▶ **adv. & adj.** (esp. as a direction) with an immediate reduction of tempo.
▶ **n.** (pl. **ritenutos** or **ritenuti** /-tē/) an immediate reduction of tempo.
– ORIGIN Italian, literally 'retained, restrained.'

ri·tor·nel·lo /ˌritərˈnelō/ ▶ **n.** (pl. **ritornellos** or **ritornelli** /-ˈnelē/) Music a short instrumental refrain or interlude in a vocal work. ■ a recurring tutti section in a concerto.
– ORIGIN Italian, diminutive of *ritorno* 'return.'

Rit·ter /ˈritər/, Tex (1907–74), US country singer, songwriter, and actor; full name *Woodward Maurice Ritter*. He made many singing cowboy movies during the 1930s and 1940s and also wrote and performed songs such as "Jingle, Jangle, Jingle" and "Jealous Heart." He sang the title song for the movie *High Noon* (1952).

rit·u·al /ˈriCHo͞oəl/ ▶ **n.** a religious or solemn ceremony consisting of a series of actions performed according to a prescribed order: *the ancient rituals of Christian worship* | *the role of ritual in religion*. ■ a prescribed order of performing such a ceremony, esp. one characteristic of a particular religion or church. ■ a series of actions or type of behavior regularly and invariably followed by someone: *her visits to Joy became a ritual*.
▶ **adj.** [attrib.] of, relating to, or done as a religious or solemn rite: *ritual burial*. ■ (of an action) arising from convention or habit: *the players gathered for the ritual pregame huddle*.
– DERIVATIVES **rit·u·al·ly adv.**
– ORIGIN late 16th cent. (as an adjective): from Latin *ritualis*, from *ritus* (see RITE).

rit·u·al a·buse (also **satanic abuse**) ▶ **n.** the alleged sexual abuse or murder of people, esp. children, supposedly committed as part of satanic rituals.

rit·u·al·ism /ˈriCHo͞oəˌlizəm/ ▶ **n.** the regular observance or practice of ritual, esp. when excessive or without regard to its function.
– DERIVATIVES **rit·u·al·ist n.**, **rit·u·al·is·tic** /ˌriCHo͞oəˈlistik/ **adj.**, **rit·u·al·is·ti·cal·ly adv.**

rit·u·al·i·za·tion /ˌriCHo͞oələˈzāSHən/ ▶ **n.** the action or process of ritualizing something, in particular: ■ Zoology the evolutionary process by which an action or behavior pattern in an animal loses its original function but is retained for its role in display or other social interaction.

rit·u·al·ize /ˈriCHo͞oəˌlīz/ ▶ **v.** [with obj.] (usu. as adj. **ritualized**) make (something) into a ritual by following a pattern of actions or behavior: *hooliganism as a ritualized expression of aggression*. ■ Zoology cause (an action or behavior pattern) to undergo ritualization.

ritz /rits/ ▶ **n.** informal **1** ostentatious luxury and glamour: *removed from all the ritz and glitz*. **2** (**the Ritz**) [usu. with negative] used in reference to luxurious accommodation: *it's not the Ritz, but it's convenient, clean, and good value for money*.
– PHRASES **put on the ritz** make a show of luxury or extravagance.
– ORIGIN early 20th cent.: from *Ritz*, a name associated with luxury hotels, from César *Ritz* (1850–1918), a Swiss hotel owner.

ritz·y /ˈritsē/ ▶ **adj.** (**ritzier**, **ritziest**) informal expensively stylish: *the ritzy Plaza Hotel*.
– DERIVATIVES **ritz·i·ly** /ˈritsilē/ **adv.**, **ritz·i·ness n.**

riv. ▶ **abbr.** river.

ri·val /ˈrīvəl/ ▶ **n.** a person or thing competing with another for the same objective or for superiority in the same field of activity: *he has no serious rival for the job* | [as modifier] *gun battles between rival gangs*. ■ [with negative] a person or thing that equals another in quality: *she has no rivals as a female rock singer*.
▶ **v.** (**rivals, rivaling, rivaled**; Brit. **rivals, rivalling, rivalled**) [with obj.] compete for superiority with; be or seem to be equal or comparable to: *the efficiency of the Bavarians rivals that of the Viennese*.
– ORIGIN late 16th cent.: from Latin *rivalis*, originally in the sense 'person using the same stream as another,' from *rivus* 'stream.'

ri·val·rous /ˈrīvəlrəs/ ▶ **adj.** prone to or subject to rivalry: *rivalrous presidential aspirants*.

ri·val·ry /ˈrīvəlrē/ ▶ **n.** (pl. **rivalries**) competition for the same objective or for superiority in the same field: *commercial rivalry* | *intercity rivalries*.

rive /rīv/ ▶ **v.** (past **rived** /rīvd/; past participle **riven** /ˈrivən/) (usu. **be riven**) split or tear apart violently: *the party was riven by disagreements over Europe* | figurative *he was riven with guilt*. ■ archaic split or crack (wood or stone): *the wood was riven with deep cracks*. ■ [no obj.] archaic (of wood or stone) split or crack: *I started to chop furiously, the dry wood riving and splintering under the ax*.
– ORIGIN Middle English: from Old Norse *rífa*, of unknown ultimate origin.

riv·er /ˈrivər/ ▶ **n.** a large natural stream of water flowing in a channel to the sea, a lake, or another such stream. ■ a large quantity of a flowing substance: *great rivers of molten lava* | figurative *the trickle of disclosures has grown into a river of revelations*. ■ [as modifier] used in names of animals and plants living in or associated with rivers, e.g., **river dolphin**, **river birch**.
– PHRASES **sell someone down the river** informal betray someone, esp. so as to benefit oneself. [earlier referring to the sale of a troublesome slave to the owner of a sugarcane plantation on the lower Mississippi, where conditions were harsher.] **up the river** informal to or in prison. [with allusion to Sing Sing prison, situated up the Hudson River from New York City.]
– DERIVATIVES **riv·ered adj.**, **riv·er·less adj.**
– ORIGIN Middle English: from Anglo-Norman French, based on Latin *riparius*, from *ripa* 'bank of a river.'

Ri·ve·ra /riˈve(ə)rə/, Diego (1886–1957), Mexican painter. He inspired a revival of fresco painting in Latin America and the US. His largest mural is a history of Mexico for the National Palace in Mexico City (unfinished, 1929–57). He was married to Frida Kahlo.

"Agrarian Leader Zapata" (1932) by Diego Rivera

riv·er·bank /ˈrivərˌbaNGk/ ▶ **n.** the bank of a river.

riv·er·bed /ˈrivərˌbed/ ▶ **n.** the bed or channel in which a river flows. ■ the bottom of a river.

riv·er birch ▶ **n.** a North American birch with shaggy reddish-brown or orange bark. ● *Betula nigra*.

riv·er blind·ness ▶ **n.** a tropical skin disease caused by a parasitic filarial worm, transmitted by the bite of blackflies (*Simulium damnosum*) that breed in fast-flowing rivers. The larvae of the parasite can migrate into the eye and cause blindness. Also called ONCHOCERCIASIS. ● The worm is *Onchocerca volvulus*, class Phasmida.

riv·er·boat /ˈrivərˌbōt/ ▶ **n.** a boat with a shallow draft, designed for use on rivers.

riv·er bot·toms ▶ **plural n.** low-lying alluvial land along the banks of a river.

riv·er dol·phin ▶ **n.** a solitary dolphin with a long slender beak, a small dorsal fin, and very poor eyesight. It lives in rivers and coastal waters of South America, India, and China, using echolocation to find its prey. ● Family Platanistidae: four genera and species.

riv·er·front /ˈrivərˌfrənt/ ▶ **n.** the land or property along a river: *a distinctive feature of Quebec's riverfront*.
▶ **adj.** located along a river: *a lovely riverfront park*.

riv·er·ine /ˈrivəˌrīn, -ˌrēn/ ▶ **adj.** technical or literary of, relating to, or situated on a river or riverbank; riparian: *a riverine village*.

riv·er·scape /ˈrivərˌskāp/ ▶ **n.** a picturesque view or prospect of a river. ■ a painting of a river or riverside scene.

Riv·er·side /ˈrivərˌsīd/ a city in southern California, east of Los Angeles, located in the center of an orange-growing region; pop. 295,357 (est. 2008).

riv·er·side /ˈrivərˌsīd/ ▶ **n.** [often as modifier] the ground along a riverbank: *dinner in one of the better riverside hotels*.

riv·et /ˈrivit/ ▶ **n.** a short metal pin or bolt for holding together two plates of metal, its headless end being beaten out or pressed down when in place. ■ a similar device for holding seams of clothing together.
▶ **v.** (**rivets, riveting, riveted**) [with obj.] join or fasten (plates of metal or other material) with a rivet or rivets: *the linings are bonded, not riveted, to the brake shoes for longer wear*. ■ hold (someone or something) fast so as to make them incapable of movement: *the grip on her arm was firm enough to rivet her to the spot*. ■ attract and completely engross (someone): *he was riveted by the reports shown on television*. ■ direct (one's eyes or attention) intently: *all eyes were riveted on him*.
– DERIVATIVES **riv·et·er n.**
– ORIGIN Middle English: from Old French, from *river* 'fix, clinch,' of unknown ultimate origin.

rivet

riv·et·ing /ˈrivitiNG/ ▶ **adj.** completely engrossing; compelling: *the book is a riveting account of the legendary freedom fighter*.
– DERIVATIVES **riv·et·ing·ly adv.**

ri·vi·er·a /ˌrivēˈe(ə)rə, riˈvye(ə)rə/ ▶ **n.** a coastal region with a subtropical climate and vegetation, esp. ■ (**the Riviera**) a Mediterranean coastal region from Marseilles in France to La Spezia in Italy, noted for its beauty and climate, site of many resorts. See also CÔTE D'AZUR.
– ORIGIN mid 18th cent.: from Italian, literally 'seashore.'

ri·vière /ˌrivēˈe(ə)r, riˈvye(ə)r/ ▶ **n.** a necklace of gems that increase in size toward a large central stone, typically consisting of more than one string.
– ORIGIN late 19th cent.: French, literally 'river.'

Riv·ne /ˈrivnə/ an industrial city in western Ukraine northeast of Lviv; pop. 249,000 (est. 2009). Russian name ROVNO.

riv·u·let /ˈriv(y)ələt/ ▶ **n.** a very small stream: *sweat ran in rivulets down his back*.
– ORIGIN late 16th cent.: alteration of obsolete *riveret* (from French, literally 'small river'), perhaps suggested by Italian *rivoletto*, diminutive of *rivolo*, based on Latin *rivus* 'stream.'

riv·u·lus /ˈrivyələs/ ▶ **n.** a small tropical American fish of shallow fresh and brackish water. Often mistaken for a killifish or topminnow, the rivulus is distinguished by its tubular nostrils. ● Genus *Rivulus*, family Rivulidae: several species, many of which are spotted, in particular *R. marmoratus*.
– ORIGIN modern Latin, from Latin, literally 'small stream.'

Ri·yadh /rēˈyäd/ the capital of Saudi Arabia; pop. 4,465,000 (est. 2007). It is situated on a high plateau in the center of the country.

ri·yal /rēˈ(y)ôl, rēˈ(y)äl/ ▶ **n.** (also **rial**) the basic monetary unit of Saudi Arabia, Qatar, and Yemen, equal to 100 halala in Saudi Arabia, 100 dirhams in Qatar, and 100 fils in Yemen.
– ORIGIN via Persian from Arabic *riyāl*, from Spanish *real* 'royal.'

RJ ▶ **abbr.** Military road junction.

RKO a movie production and distribution company founded in 1928, which produced such classics such as *King Kong* (1933) and *Citizen Kane* (1941).
– ORIGIN abbreviation of *Radio–Keith–Orpheum*, from a merger of Radio Corporation of America (RCA) with the *Keith* and *Orpheum* theater chains.

RL ▶ **abbr.** rugby league.

RLS ▶ **abbr.** restless legs syndrome.

rly ▶ **abbr.** Indian & Brit. railway.

RM ▶ **abbr.** ■ (in the UK) Royal Mail. ■ (in the UK) Royal Marines.

rm ▶ **abbr.** room.

RMA ▶ **abbr.** (in the UK) Royal Military Academy.

RMP ▶ **abbr.** (in the UK) Royal Military Police.

r.m.s. ▶ **abbr.** Mathematics root mean square.

RN ▶ **abbr.** ■ (chiefly in North America) Registered Nurse. ■ (in the UK) **Royal Navy**.

Rn ▶ **symbol** the chemical element radon.

RNA ▶ **n.** Biochemistry ribonucleic acid, a nucleic acid present in all living cells. Its principal role is to act as a messenger carrying instructions from DNA for controlling the synthesis of proteins, although in some viruses RNA rather than DNA carries the genetic information.

RNase /ärˈenˌās, -ˌāz/ ▶ **n.** Biochemistry an enzyme that promotes the breakdown of RNA into oligonucleotides and smaller molecules.
– ORIGIN 1950s: from **RNA** + **-ASE**.

RNA vi·rus ▶ **n.** a virus in which the genetic information is stored in the form of RNA (as opposed to DNA).

rnd. ▶ **abbr.** round.

RNP ▶ **abbr.** Biochemistry ribonucleoprotein.

RNZAF ▶ **abbr.** Royal New Zealand Air Force.

RNZN ▶ **abbr.** Royal New Zealand Navy.

ro. ▶ **abbr.** ■ recto. ■ roan. ■ rood.

roach[1] /rōCH/ ▶ **n.** informal **1** a cockroach. [mid 19th cent.: shortened form.]
2 the butt of a marijuana cigarette. [1930s: of unknown origin.]

roach[2] ▶ **n.** (pl. **same**) an edible Eurasian freshwater fish of the minnow family, popular with anglers. It can hybridize with related fishes, notably rudd and bream. ● *Rutilus rutilus*, family Cyprinidae.
– ORIGIN Middle English: from Old French *roche*, of unknown ultimate origin.

roach[3] ▶ **n.** Sailing a curve, in or out, in the edge of a sail, esp. in the leech of a fore-and-aft sail.
– ORIGIN late 18th cent.: of unknown origin.

roach clip ▶ **n.** informal a clip for holding the butt of a marijuana cigarette.

roached /rōCHt/ ▶ **adj. 1** (esp. of an animal's back) having an upward curve.
2 (of a person's hair) brushed upward or forward into a roll. ■ (of a horse's mane) clipped or trimmed short so that the hair stands on end.

road /rōd/ ▶ **n. 1** a wide way leading from one place to another, esp. one with a specially prepared surface that vehicles can use. ■ the part of such a way intended for vehicles, esp. in contrast to a shoulder or sidewalk. ■ [with modifier] historical a regular trade route for a particular commodity: *the Silk Road across Asia to the West.* ■ Mining an underground passage or gallery in a mine. ■ a railroad. ■ Brit. a railroad track, esp. as clear (or otherwise) for a train to proceed: *they waited for a clear road at Hellifield Junction.*
2 a series of events or a course of action that will lead to a particular outcome: ***he's well on the road to** recovery.* ■ a particular course or direction taken or followed: *the low road of apathy and alienation.*
3 (usu. **roads**) (often in place names) another term for **ROADSTEAD**: *Boston Roads.*
– PHRASES **by road** in or on a road vehicle. **down the road** informal in the future. **the end of the road** see **END**. **hit the road** see **HIT**. **in** (or **out of**) **the** (or **one's**) **road** [often in imperative] informal in (or out of) someone's way. **one for the road** informal a final drink, esp. an alcoholic one, before leaving for home. **on the road 1** on a long journey or series of journeys, esp. as part of one's job as a sales representative or a performer. ■ (of a person) without a permanent home and moving from place to place. **2** (of a car) in use; able to be driven. ■ (often **on-the-road**) (of or with reference to the price of a motor vehicle) including the cost of license plates, tax, etc., so the vehicle is fully ready for use on public roads: *we found on-the-road prices from 5,780 to 6,151 dollars.* **a road to nowhere** see **NOWHERE**. **take to the road** (or **take the road**) set out on a journey or series of journeys.
– DERIVATIVES **road·less adj.**
– ORIGIN Old English *rād* 'journey on horseback,' 'foray'; of Germanic origin; related to the verb **RIDE**.

road a·gent ▶ **n.** historical a highwayman or bandit, esp. along stagecoach routes in the western US.

road·bed /ˈrōdˌbed/ ▶ **n.** the material laid down to form a road. ■ the part of a road on which vehicles travel. ■ the foundation structure on which railroad tracks are laid.

road bike ▶ **n. 1** a motorcycle that meets the legal requirements for use on ordinary roads.
2 a bicycle that is suitable for use on ordinary roads, as opposed to a mountain bike.

road·block /ˈrōdˌbläk/ ▶ **n.** a barrier or barricade on a road, esp. one set up by the authorities to stop and examine traffic. ■ any hindrance: *the biggest roadblock to solar power is its price tag.*

road hog ▶ **n.** informal a motorist who drives recklessly or inconsiderately, making it difficult for others to proceed safely or at a normal speed.

road·hold·ing /ˈrōdˌhōldiNG/ ▶ **n.** the ability of a vehicle to remain stable when moving, esp. when cornering at high speeds.

road·house /ˈrōdˌhous/ ▶ **n.** a tavern, inn, or club on a country road.

road·ie /ˈrōdē/ informal ▶ **n.** a person employed by a touring band of musicians to set up and maintain equipment.
▶ **v.** [no obj.] work as such a person.

road kill ▶ **n.** an animal (or animals, collectively) killed by a vehicle on a road. ■ informal someone or something no longer useful or desired: *gee, thanks for making me feel like road kill.*

road man·ag·er ▶ **n.** the organizer and supervisor of a musician's tour.

road·map /ˈrōdˌmap/ ▶ **v.** (**roadmaps, roadmapping, roadmapped**) [with obj.] schedule as part of a lengthy or complex program: *originally roadmapped for an early Q4 release, the next generation of the processor will ship in the last few days of the year.*

road map ▶ **n. 1** a map, esp. one designed for motorists, showing the roads of a city, state, or other area.
2 a plan or strategy intended to achieve a particular goal: *a road map for peace in the region.*

road met·al ▶ **n.** see **METAL** (sense 2 of the noun).

road mov·ie ▶ **n.** a movie of a genre in which the main character is traveling, either in flight or on a journey of self-discovery.

road noise ▶ **n.** noise resulting from the movement of a vehicle's tires over the road surface.

road pric·ing ▶ **n.** Brit. the practice of charging motorists for the use of busy roads at certain times, esp. to relieve congestion in urban areas.

road rage ▶ **n.** violent anger caused by the stress and frustration involved in driving a motor vehicle in difficult conditions.

road·roll·er /ˈrōdˌrōlər/ ▶ **n.** a motor vehicle with a heavy roller, used in roadmaking.

road·run·ner /ˈrōdˌrənər/ ▶ **n.** a slender fast-running bird of the cuckoo family, found chiefly in arid country from the southern US to Central America. ● Genus *Geococcyx*, family Cuculidae: two species, in particular the **greater roadrunner** (*G. californianus*.
– ORIGIN probably a calque from Spanish *correcamino*.

greater roadrunner

road show (also **roadshow**) ▶ **n.** a touring show of performers, esp. pop musicians. ■ a touring political or promotional campaign. ■ a radio or television program broadcast on location, esp. each of a series done from different venues.

road·side /ˈrōdˌsīd/ ▶ **n.** the strip of land beside a road: *trash left on the roadside* | [as modifier] *roadside cafes.*

road sign ▶ **n.** a sign giving information or instructions to road users.

road·stead /ˈrōdˌsted/ ▶ **n.** a sheltered stretch of water near the shore in which ships can ride at anchor.
– ORIGIN mid 16th cent.: from **ROAD** + obsolete *stead* 'a place.'

road·ster /ˈrōdstər/ ▶ **n.** an open-top automobile with two seats. ■ historical a horse for use on the road.

road test ▶ **n.** a test of the performance of a vehicle or engine on the road. ■ a test of equipment carried out in working conditions: *he hopes to present a road test of whiskeys and to debate the various aromas and tastes.* ■ a test of a person's competence in driving a motor vehicle that must be passed in order to get a driver's license.
▶ **v.** (**road-test**) [with obj.] test (a vehicle or engine) on the road. ■ try out (something) in working conditions for review or prior to purchase or release: *we road-tested a new laptop computer.*

Road Town the capital of the British Virgin Islands, situated on the island of Tortola; pop. 9,300 (est. 2009).

road war·ri·or ▶ **n.** informal a person who travels, often as part of their job, and does work at the same time.

road·way /ˈrōdˌwā/ ▶ **n.** a road. ■ the part of a road intended for vehicles, in contrast to a sidewalk or median. ■ the part of a bridge or railroad used by traffic.

road·work /ˈrōdˌwərk/ ▶ **n. 1** work done in building or repairing roads.
2 athletic exercise or training involving running on roads. ■ time spent traveling while working or on tour.

road·wor·thy /ˈrōdˌwərT͟Hē/ ▶ **adj.** (of a motor vehicle or bicycle) fit to be used on the road.
– DERIVATIVES **road·wor·thi·ness n.**

roam /rōm/ ▶ **v.** [no obj.] move about or travel aimlessly or unsystematically, esp. over a wide area: *tigers once **roamed over** most of Asia* | (as adj. **roaming**) *roaming elephants.* ■ [with obj.] travel unsystematically over, through, or around (a place): *gangs of youths roamed the streets unopposed.* ■ (of a person's eyes or hands) pass lightly over something without stopping: *her eyes roamed over the chattering women* | [with obj.] *he let his eyes roam her face.* ■ (of a person's mind or thoughts) drift along without dwelling on anything in particular: *he let his mind roam as he walked.* ■ (often as noun **roaming**) use a cellular phone on another operator's network, typically while abroad: *packages in which you pay a slightly higher fee when roaming on other networks.*
▶ **n.** [in sing.] an aimless walk.
– DERIVATIVES **roam·er n.**
– ORIGIN Middle English: of unknown origin.

roan[1] /rōn/ ▶ **adj.** denoting an animal, esp. a horse or cow, having a coat of a main color thickly interspersed with hairs of another color, typically bay, chestnut, or black mixed with white.
▶ **n.** an animal with such a coat: *the roan on the right is a stallion.*
– ORIGIN mid 16th cent.: from Old French, of unknown origin.

roan[2] ▶ **n.** soft flexible leather made from sheepskin, used in bookbinding as an inexpensive substitute for morocco.
– ORIGIN early 19th cent.: perhaps from *Roan*, the old name of the French town of **ROUEN**.

roan an·te·lope ▶ **n.** an African antelope with black-and-white facial markings, a mane of stiff hair, and large backwardly curving horns. ● *Hippotragus equinus*, family Bovidae.

Ro·a·noke /ˈrōəˌnōk/ an industrial city in west central Virginia, in the Shenandoah Valley; pop. 92,967 (est. 2008).

Ro·a·noke Is·land an island in eastern North Carolina, east of Croatan Sound, inside the Outer Banks, site of the first English settlement in America—the "Lost Colony"—that was established in 1585 and had mysteriously disappeared by 1591.

Ro·a·noke Riv·er a river that flows for 410 miles (660 km) from southwestern Virginia across North Carolina to Albemarle Sound.

r

roar /rôr/ ▶ n. a full, deep, prolonged cry uttered by a lion or other large wild animal. ■ a loud and deep sound uttered by a person or crowd, generally as an expression of pain, anger, or approval: *he gave a roar of rage.* ■ a loud outburst of laughter. ■ a loud, prolonged sound made by something inanimate, such as a natural force, an engine, or traffic: *the roar of the sea.*
▶ v. **1** [no obj.] (of a lion or other large wild animal) utter a full, deep, prolonged cry. ■ (of something inanimate) make a loud, deep, prolonged sound: *a huge fire roared in the grate.* ■ (of a person or crowd) utter a loud, deep, prolonged sound, typically because of anger, pain, or excitement: *Manny roared with rage.* ■ [with obj.] utter or express in a loud tone: *the crowd roared its approval* | [with direct speech] *"Get out of my way!" he roared.* ■ laugh loudly: *Shirley roared in amusement.* ■ (of a horse) make a loud noise in breathing as a symptom of disease of the larynx.
2 [no obj.] (esp. of a vehicle) move at high speed making a loud prolonged sound: *a car roared past.* ■ proceed, act, or happen fast and decisively or conspicuously: *the Clippers came roaring back to outscore the Nets.*
– DERIVATIVES **roar·er** n.
– ORIGIN Old English *rārian* (verb), imitative of a deep prolonged cry; related to German *röhren*. The noun dates from late Middle English.

roar·ing /ˈrôriNG/ ▶ adj. [attrib.] **1** making or uttering a loud, deep, or harsh prolonged sound: *he was greeted everywhere with roaring crowds* | *a swollen, roaring river.* ■ (of a fire) burning fiercely and noisily. ■ (of a period of time) characterized by optimism, buoyancy, or excitement: *the roaring twenties.* ■ (of business) lively; brisk: *cafes that do a roaring trade.* ■ chiefly archaic behaving or living in a noisy riotous manner.
2 informal obviously or unequivocally the thing mentioned (used for emphasis): *the final week of Hamlet was a roaring success* | [as submodifier] *two roaring drunk firemen.*
– DERIVATIVES **roar·ing·ly** adv.

roast /rōst/ ▶ v. [with obj.] **1** cook (food, esp. meat) by prolonged exposure to heat in an oven or over a fire: *she was going to roast a leg of lamb for Sunday dinner* | (as adj. **roasted**) *roasted chestnuts.* ■ [no obj.] (of food) be cooked in such a way: *she checked the meat roasting in the oven.* ■ process (a foodstuff, metal ore, etc.) by subjecting it to intense heat: *coffee beans are roasted and ground.* ■ make or become very warm, esp. by exposure to the heat of the sun or a fire: [with obj.] *the fire was hot enough to roast anyone who stood close to it* | [no obj.] *Jessica could feel her face begin to roast.*
2 criticize or reprimand severely: *if you waste his time he'll roast you.* ■ offer a mocking tribute to (someone) at a roast.
▶ adj. [attrib.] (of food) having been cooked in an oven or over an open fire: *a plate of cold roast beef.*
▶ n. **1** a cut of meat that has been roasted or that is intended for roasting: *carving the Sunday roast.* ■ the process of roasting something, esp. coffee, or the result of this. ■ [with modifier] a particular type of roasted coffee: *continental roasts.* ■ an outdoor party at which meat, esp. of a particular type, is roasted: *Harold put on a terrific pig roast.*
2 a banquet to honor a person at which the honoree is subjected to good-natured ridicule.
– ORIGIN Middle English: from Old French *rostir*, of West Germanic origin.

roast·er /ˈrōstər/ ▶ n. a container, oven, furnace, or apparatus for roasting something. ■ a foodstuff that is particularly suitable for roasting, esp. a chicken. ■ a person or company that processes coffee beans.

roast·ing /ˈrōstiNG/ ▶ adj. informal very hot and dry: *a roasting day in Miami.*
▶ n. the action of cooking something in an oven or over an open fire. ■ [in sing.] informal a severe criticism or reprimand: *I was in for a roasting at the next meeting.*

rob /räb/ ▶ v. (**robs, robbing, robbed**) [with obj.] take property unlawfully from (a person or place) by force or threat of force: *he tried, with three others, to rob a bank* | *she was* **robbed of** *her handbag* | [no obj.] *he was convicted of assault with intent to rob.* ■ (usu. **be robbed**) informal overcharge (someone) for something: *Bob thinks my suit cost $100, and even then he thinks I was robbed.* ■ informal or dialect steal: *he accused her of robbing the cream out of his chocolate eclair.* ■ deprive (someone or something) of something needed, deserved, or significant: *poor health has robbed her of a normal social life.*
– PHRASES **rob Peter to pay Paul** take something away from one person to pay another, leaving the former at a disadvantage; discharge one debt only to incur another. [probably with reference to the apostles *Peter* and *Paul*; the allusion is uncertain, the phrase often showing variations such as 'unclothe Peter and clothe Paul,' 'borrow from Peter ...,' etc.] **rob someone blind** see BLIND.
– ORIGIN Middle English: from Old French *rober*, of Germanic origin; related to the verb REAVE.

Robbe-Gril·let /ˌrôb grēˈyā/, Alain (1922–2008), French novelist. His first novel *The Erasers* (1953) was an early example of the *nouveau roman*. He also wrote essays and screenplays.

rob·ber /ˈräbər/ ▶ n. a person who commits robbery.
– ORIGIN Middle English: from Anglo-Norman French and Old French *robere*, from the verb *rober* (see ROB).

rob·ber bar·on ▶ n. an unscrupulous plutocrat, esp. an American capitalist who acquired a fortune in the late nineteenth century by ruthless means.
– ORIGIN originally denoting a feudal lord who engaged in plundering.

rob·ber crab ▶ n. another term for COCONUT CRAB.

rob·ber fly ▶ n. a large powerful predatory fly that darts out and grabs insect prey on the wing. ● Family Asilidae: many genera.

rob·ber·y /ˈräb(ə)rē/ ▶ n. (pl. **robberies**) the action of robbing a person or place: *he was involved in drugs, violence, extortion, and robbery* | *an armed robbery.* ■ informal unashamed swindling or overcharging.
– ORIGIN Middle English: from Anglo-Norman French and Old French *roberie*, from the verb *rober* (see ROB).

Rob·bia /ˈrōbēə, ˈräb-/ see DELLA ROBBIA.

Rob·bins[1] /ˈräbənz/, Harold (1916–97), US novelist. Notable works: *The Dream Merchants* (1949), *The Carpetbaggers* (1961), *The Betsy* (1971), and *Tycoon* (1997).

Rob·bins[2], Jerome (1918–98), US ballet dancer and choreographer. He choreographed a number of successful musicals, including *The King and I* (1951), *West Side Story* (1957), and *Fiddler on the Roof* (1964).

robe /rōb/ ▶ n. **1** a long, loose outer garment. ■ (often **robes**) such a garment worn, esp. on formal or ceremonial occasions, as an indication of the wearer's rank, office, or profession. ■ a dressing gown or bathrobe.
2 dated a small blanket; lap robe.
▶ v. [with obj.] (usu. as adj. **robed**) clothe in a long, loose outer garment: *a circle of robed figures* | [in combination] *a white-robed Bedouin.* ■ [no obj.] put on robes, esp. for a formal or ceremonial occasion: *I went into the vestry and robed for the Mass.*
– ORIGIN Middle English: from Old French, from the Germanic base (in the sense 'booty') of ROB (because clothing was an important component of booty).

Rob·ert /ˈräbərt/ the name of three kings of Scotland. ■ **Robert I** (1274–1329), reigned 1306–29; known as **Robert the Bruce**. He campaigned against Edward I, and defeated Edward II at Bannockburn in 1314. He re-established Scotland as a separate kingdom, negotiating the Treaty of Northampton in 1328. ■ **Robert II** (1316–90), grandson of Robert the Bruce; reigned 1371–90. He was steward of Scotland from 1326 to 1371 and the first of the Stuart line. ■ **Robert III** (*c.*1337–1406), son of Robert II; reigned 1390–1406; born *John*. An accident rendered him physically disabled, resulting in a power struggle among members of his family.

Ro·berts, Owen Josephus (1875–1955), US Supreme Court associate justice 1930–45. Appointed to the Court by President Hoover, he usually voted independently although he leaned toward conservatism in many of his decisions. He also served as dean of the University of Pennsylvania Law School 1948–51.

Rob·ert·so·ni·an /ˌräbərtˈsōnēən/ ▶ adj. Genetics denoting a chromosome with a central centromere formed from two chromosomes having noncentral centromeres. ■ (of a karyotypic change or translocation) brought about by this process.
– ORIGIN 1950s: from the name of William R. B. *Robertson* (1881–1941), American biologist, + -IAN.

Rob·ert the Bruce /bro͞os/ see ROBERT.

Robe·son /ˈrōb(ə)sən/, Paul (Bustill) (1898–1976), US singer and actor. The song "Ol' Man River" in the musical *Showboat* (1927) established his international reputation. As an actor, he was particularly identified with the title role of *Othello*. His black activism and communist sympathies led to ostracism in the 1950s.

Robes·pierre /ˈrōbzˌpi(ə)r, -ˌpye(ə)r/, Maximilien François Marie Isidore de (1758–94), French revolutionary. As leader of the radical Jacobins in the National Assembly, he backed the execution of Louis XVI, implemented a purge of the Girondists, and initiated the Terror. The following year, however, he fell from favor and was guillotined.

rob·in /ˈräbən/ ▶ n. **1** a large New World thrush that typically has a reddish breast. ● genus *Turdus*, subfamily Turdinae, family Muscicapidae, in particular the **American robin** (*T. migratorius*).
2 any of a number of other birds that resemble the American robin, esp. in having a red breast, in particular: ■ a small Old World thrush related to the chats, typically having a brown back with red on the breast or other colorful markings. ● *Erithacus* and other genera, subfamily Turdinae, family Muscicapidae: numerous species, in particular the **European robin** (*E. rubecula*).
– ORIGIN mid 16th cent.: from Old French, nickname for the given name *Robert*.

robins

rob·ing room ▶ n. a room where holders of ceremonial office put on official robes.

Rob·in Hood /ˈräbən ˌho͝od/ a semilegendary English medieval outlaw, reputed to have robbed the rich and helped the poor. Although he is generally associated with Sherwood Forest in Nottinghamshire, it seems likely that the real Robin Hood operated in Yorkshire in the early 13th century. ■ (as noun **a Robin Hood**) a person considered to be taking from the wealthy and giving to the poor.

rob·in red·breast ▶ n. informal a robin.

rob·in's-egg (also **robin's-egg blue** or **robin-egg**) ▶ n. a greenish-blue color.

Rob·in·son[1] /ˈräbinsən/, Edward Arlington (1869–1935), US poet. His verse was largely unnoticed until 1905 when President Theodore Roosevelt praised his dramatic, often ironic, works, such as "Richard Cory" (1897), "Miniver Cheevy" (1910), and "Tristram" (1927).

Rob·in·son[2] /ˈräbənsən/, Edward G. (1893–1972), US actor, born in Romania; born *Emanuel Goldenberg*. He appeared in a number of gangster movies in the 1930s, beginning with *Little Caesar* (1930). He later played the father in Arthur Miller's *All My Sons* (1948).

Rob·in·son[3], Jackie (1919–72), US baseball player and civil rights activist; full name *Jack Roosevelt Robinson*. Joining the Brooklyn Dodgers in 1947, he became the first black player in the major leagues. In 1949, he led the National League with a .342 batting average and was named the league's Most Valuable Player. He retired in 1957. Baseball Hall of Fame (1962).

Jackie Robinson

Rob·in·son[4], Mary (Terese Winifred) (1944–), Irish stateswoman; president 1990–1997. She was Ireland's first woman president, noted for her platform of religious toleration and her liberal attitude, and served as the UN high commissioner for human rights 1997–2002.

Rob·in·son[5], Smokey (1940–), US soul singer and songwriter; born *William Robinson*. He is known for a series of successes, such as "Tracks of My Tears" (1965) and "Tears of a Clown" (1970), with his group the Miracles.

Rob·in·son[6], Sugar Ray (1920–89), US boxer; born *Walker Smith*. He was world welterweight champion from 1946 to 1951 and seven times the middleweight champion.

Rob·in·son Cru·soe /ˈkrōōsō/ the title hero of Daniel Defoe's 1719 novel; he survives a shipwreck and lives on a desert island.

ro·bo·call /ˈrōbō,kôl/ ▶ n. an automated telephone call that delivers a recorded message, typically on behalf of a political party or telemarketing company.
– ORIGIN 1990s: blend of ROBOT and CALL.

rob·o·rant /ˈräbərənt, ˈrō-/ Medicine ▶ adj. (chiefly of a medicine) having a strengthening effect.
▶ n. a roborant medicine.
– ORIGIN mid 17th cent.: from Latin *roborant-* 'strengthening,' from the verb *roborare*, from *robur, robor-* 'strength.'

ro·bot /ˈrō,bät, ˈrōbət/ ▶ n. a machine capable of carrying out a complex series of actions automatically, esp. one programmable by a computer. ■ (esp. in science fiction) a machine resembling a human being and able to replicate certain human movements and functions automatically. ■ used to refer to a person who behaves in a mechanical or unemotional manner: *public servants are not expected to be mindless robots*.
– ORIGIN from Czech, from *robota* 'forced labor.' The term was coined in K. Čapek's play *R.U.R.* 'Rossum's Universal Robots' (1920).

ro·bot·ic /rōˈbätik/ ▶ adj. of or relating to robots: *a robotic device for performing surgery*. ■ (of a person) mechanical, stiff, or unemotional.
– DERIVATIVES **ro·bot·i·cal·ly** /-ik(ə)lē/ adv.

ro·bot·ics /rōˈbätiks/ ▶ plural n. [treated as sing.] the branch of technology that deals with the design, construction, operation, and application of robots.
– DERIVATIVES **ro·bot·i·cist** /-ˈbätəsist/ n.

ro·bot·ize /ˈrōbə,tīz/ ▶ v. [with obj.] (usu. as adj. **robotized**) convert (a production system, factory, etc.) to operation by robots.
– DERIVATIVES **ro·bot·i·za·tion** /,rōbətəˈzāsHən, ,rō,bätə-/ n.

Rob Roy[1] /ˈräb ˈroi/ (1671–1734), Scottish outlaw; born *Robert Macgregor*. His reputation as a Robin Hood was exaggerated in Sir Walter Scott's novel of the same name (1817).

Rob Roy[2] ▶ n. a cocktail made of Scotch whisky and vermouth.

ro·bust /rōˈbəst, ˈrō,bəst/ ▶ adj. (**robuster, robustest**) strong and healthy; vigorous: *the Caplans are a robust, healthy lot*. ■ (of an object) sturdy in construction: *a robust metal cabinet*. ■ (of a process, system, organization, etc.) able to withstand or overcome adverse conditions: *California's robust property market*. ■ uncompromising and forceful: *the country's decision to bow to UN pressure was preceded by a robust defense of its policies | he took quite a robust view of my case*. ■ (of wine or food) strong and rich in flavor or smell.
– DERIVATIVES **ro·bust·ly** adv., **ro·bust·ness** n.
– ORIGIN mid 16th cent.: from Latin *robustus* 'firm and hard,' from *robus*, earlier form of *robur* 'oak, strength.'

ro·bus·ta /rōˈbəstə/ ▶ n. **1** coffee or coffee beans from a widely grown kind of coffee plant. Beans of this variety are often used in the manufacture of instant coffee.
2 the tropical West African bush of the bedstraw family that produces these beans. ● *Coffea canephora* (formerly *robusta*), family Rubiaceae.
– ORIGIN early 20th cent.: modern Latin, feminine of Latin *robustus* 'robust.'

ROC ▶ abbr. historical (in the UK) Royal Observer Corps.

roc /räk/ ▶ n. a gigantic mythological bird described in the Arabian Nights.
– ORIGIN late 16th cent.: ultimately from Persian *ruḳ*.

ro·caille /rōˈkī, rä-/ ▶ n. **1** an 18th-century artistic or architectural style of decoration characterized by elaborate ornamentation with pebbles and shells, typical of grottos and fountains.
2 (**rocailles**) tiny beads.
– ORIGIN French, from *roc* 'rock.'

roc·am·bole /ˈräkəm,bōl/ ▶ n. a Eurasian plant that is closely related to garlic and is sometimes used as a flavoring. ● *Allium scorodoprasum*, family Liliaceae (or Alliaceae).
– ORIGIN late 17th cent.: from French, from German *Rockenbolle*.

ROCE ▶ abbr. Finance return on capital employed.

Roche /rōsH/, Kevin (1922–), US architect; born in Ireland; full name *Eamonn Kevin Roche*. From 1950 until 1961, he worked with architect Eero Saarinen. After forming his own architectural firm in 1961 with partner John Dinkeloo (1918–81), his projects included the design of the Oakland Museum in California 1961–68, the United Nations Plaza in New York City 1969–75, and the Jewish Museum in New York City 1985.

Roche lim·it /rōsH, rôsH/ (also **Roche's limit**) ▶ n. Astronomy the closest distance from the center of a planet that a satellite can approach without being pulled apart by the planet's gravitational field.
– ORIGIN late 19th cent.: named after Edouard Albert *Roche* (1820–83), French mathematician.

Roche lobe ▶ n. Astronomy either of two lobes that form an hourglass-shaped volume of space around a binary star system.
– ORIGIN 1960s: named after E. A. *Roche* (see ROCHE LIMIT).

roche mou·ton·née /ˈrōsH ,mōōtnˈā, rôsH/ ▶ n. (pl. **roches moutonnées** pronunc. **same** or /,mōōtnˈāz/) Geology a small bare outcrop of rock shaped by glacial erosion, with one side smooth and gently sloping and the other steep, rough, and irregular.
– ORIGIN mid 19th cent.: French, literally 'fleecy rock.'

Roch·es·ter /ˈräcHəstər, ˈrä,cHes-/ **1** an industrial city in southeastern Minnesota, home to the Mayo Clinic that was established in 1889; pop. 100,413 (est. 2008).
2 a city in southeastern New Hampshire, northwest of Dover; pop. 30,654 (est. 2008).
3 a city in northwestern New York, on Lake Ontario; pop. 206,886 (est. 2008).

Roch·es·ter Hills /ˈrä,cHestər/ a residential and industrial city in southeastern Michigan, northeast of Pontiac; pop. 69,014 (est. 2008).

roch·et /ˈräcHit/ ▶ n. Christian Church a vestment resembling a surplice, used chiefly by bishops and abbots.
– ORIGIN Middle English: from Old French, a diminutive from a Germanic base shared by German *Rock* 'coat.'

rock[1] /räk/ ▶ n. **1** the solid mineral material forming part of the surface of the earth and other similar planets, exposed on the surface or underlying the soil or oceans. ■ a mass of such material projecting above the earth's surface or out of the sea: *there are dangerous rocks around the island*. ■ Geology any natural material, hard or soft (e.g., clay), having a distinctive mineral composition. ■ (**the Rock**) Gibraltar. ■ (**the Rock**) informal name for NEWFOUNDLAND[1].
2 a large piece of such material that has become detached from a cliff or mountain; a boulder: *the stream flowed through a jumble of rocks*. ■ a stone of any size, esp. one small enough to be picked up and used as a projectile. ■ Brit. a kind of hard confectionery in the form of cylindrical peppermint-flavored sticks. ■ informal a precious stone, esp. a diamond. ■ informal a small piece of crack cocaine. ■ (**rocks**) vulgar slang testicles.
3 used in similes and metaphors to refer to someone or something that is extremely strong, reliable, or hard: *imagining himself as the last rock of civilization being swept over by a wave of barbarism*. ■ (usu. **rocks**) (esp. with allusion to shipwrecks) a source of danger or destruction: *the new system is heading for the rocks*.
4 (**rocks**) informal, dated money.
– PHRASES **between a rock and a hard place** informal in a situation where one is faced with two equally difficult alternatives. **get one's rocks off** vulgar slang have an orgasm. ■ obtain pleasure or satisfaction. **on the rocks** informal **1** (of a relationship or enterprise) experiencing difficulties and likely to fail. **2** (of a drink) served undiluted and with ice cubes.
– DERIVATIVES **rock·less** adj., **rock·like** /-,līk/ adj.
– ORIGIN Middle English: from Old French *rocque*, from medieval Latin *rocca*, of unknown ultimate origin.

rock[2] ▶ v. **1** move gently to and fro or from side to side: [with obj.] *she rocked the baby in her arms* | [no obj.] *the vase rocked back and forth on its base* | (as adj. **rocking**) *the rocking movement of the boat*. ■ (with reference to a building or region) shake or cause to shake or vibrate, esp. because of an impact, earthquake, or explosion: [with obj.] *another blast rocked the ship and threw him from his chair* | [no obj.] *the building began to rock on its foundations*. ■ [with obj.] cause great shock or distress to (someone or something), esp. so as to weaken or destabilize them or it: *diplomatic upheavals that rocked the British Empire*.
2 [no obj.] informal dance to or play rock music. ■ (of a place) have an atmosphere of excitement or much social activity: *the new town really rocks* | (as adj. **rocking**) *a rocking resort*.
3 [with obj.] informal wear (a garment) or affect (an attitude or style), esp. in a confident or flamboyant way: *she was rocking a clingy little leopard-skin number*.
▶ n. **1** rock music: [as modifier] *a rock star*. ■ rock and roll.
2 [in sing.] a gentle movement to and fro or from side to side: *she placed the baby in the cradle and gave it a rock*.
– PHRASES **rock the boat** see BOAT.
– PHRASAL VERBS **rock out** informal perform rock music loudly and vigorously.
– ORIGIN late Old English *roccian*, probably from a Germanic base meaning 'remove, move'; related to Dutch *rukken* 'jerk, tug' and German *rücken* 'move.' The noun dates from the early 19th cent.

rock·a·bil·ly /ˈräkə,bilē/ ▶ n. a type of popular music, originating in the southeastern US in the 1950s, combining elements of rock and roll and country music.
– ORIGIN 1950s: blend of ROCK AND ROLL and HILLBILLY.

rock and roll (also **rock 'n' roll**) ▶ n. a type of popular dance music originating in the 1950s, characterized by a heavy beat and simple melodies. Rock and roll was an amalgam of black rhythm and blues and white country music, usually based on a twelve-bar structure and an instrumentation of guitar, bass, and drums.
– DERIVATIVES **rock and roll·er** n.

rock bass /bas/ ▶ n. a red-eyed North American freshwater fish of the sunfish family, found chiefly in rocky streams. Also called RED-EYE. ● *Ambloplites rupestris*, family Centrarchidae.

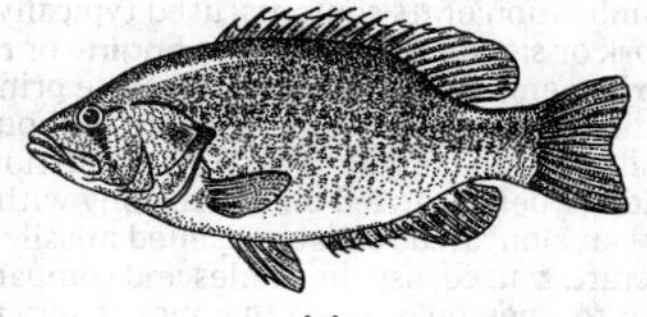
rock bass

rock-bot·tom ▶ adj. at the lowest possible level: *rock-bottom prices*. ■ fundamental: *a pure, rock-bottom kind of realism*.
▶ n. (**rock bottom**) the lowest possible level: *morale is at rock bottom*.

rock-bound ▶ adj. (of a coast or shore) rocky and inaccessible.

rock·burst /ˈräk,bərst/ ▶ n. Mining a sudden, violent rupture or collapse of highly stressed rock in a mine.

rock cake ▶ n. chiefly Brit. a small currant cake with a hard rough surface.

rock can·dy ▶ n. sugar crystallized in large masses onto a string or stick, eaten as candy.

rock climb·ing ▶ n. the sport or pastime of climbing rock faces, esp. with the aid of ropes and special equipment.
– DERIVATIVES **rock climb** n., **rock climb·er** n.

rock cod ▶ n. any of a number of marine fishes that frequent rocky habitats, esp. in Australian waters. ● Several species, chiefly in the families Scorpaenidae and Serranidae.

Rock Cor·nish (also **Rock Cornish hen** or **Rock Cornish game hen**) ▶ n. a stocky chicken of a breed that is kept for its meat.

rock cress ▶ n. another term for ARABIS.

rock crys·tal ▶ n. transparent quartz, typically in the form of colorless hexagonal crystals.

rock cy·cle ▶ n. Geology an idealized cycle of processes undergone by rocks in the earth's crust, involving igneous intrusion, uplift, erosion, transportation, deposition as sedimentary rock, metamorphism, remelting, and further igneous intrusion.

rock dove ▶ n. a mainly gray Old World pigeon that frequents coastal and inland cliffs. It is the ancestor of domestic and feral pigeons. ● *Columba livia*, family Columbidae.

Rock·e·fel·ler /ˈräkə,felər/, John D. (1839–1937), US industrialist and philanthropist; full name *John Davison Rockefeller*. He founded the Standard Oil Company in 1870 and, by 1880, exercised a virtual monopoly over oil refining in the US. Both he and his son, **John D. Rockefeller Jr.** (1874–1960), established many philanthropic institutions, including the Rockefeller Foundation in 1913. Rockefeller Center in New York City was built in the 1930s.

Rock·e·fel·ler Center /ˈräkə,felər/ a business building complex in midtown Manhattan in New York City, home to Radio City Music Hall.

rock·er /ˈräkər/ ▶ n. **1** a person who performs, dances to, or enjoys rock music, esp. of a particular type: *a punk rocker*. ■ a rock song.

r

2 a thing that rocks, in particular: ■ a rocking chair. ■ a rocking device forming part of a mechanism, esp. one for controlling the positions of brushes in a generator.
3 a curved bar or similar support on which something such as a chair or cradle can rock.
4 the amount of curvature in the longitudinal contour of a boat or surfboard.
5 any of the curved stripes below the chevron of a noncommissioned officer above the rank of sergeant. ■ the curved strip above the chevron of a chief petty officer.
– PHRASES **off one's rocker** informal insane.

rock·er arm ▶ n. a rocking lever in an engine, esp. one in an internal combustion engine that serves to work a valve and is operated by a pushrod from the camshaft.

rock·er pan·el ▶ n. (in a motor vehicle) a panel forming part of the bodywork below the level of the passenger door.

rock·er switch ▶ n. an electrical on/off switch incorporating a spring-loaded rocker.

rock·er·y /'räkərē/ ▶ n. (pl. **rockeries**) a heaped arrangement of rough stones with soil between them, planted with rock plants, esp. alpines.

rock·et[1] /'räkit/ ▶ n. a cylindrical projectile that can be propelled to a great height or distance by the combustion of its contents, used typically as a firework or signal. ■ (also **rocket engine** or **rocket motor**) an engine operating on the same principle, providing thrust as in a jet engine but without depending on the intake of air for combustion, an oxidizer being carried on board along with the fuel. ■ an elongated rocket-propelled missile or spacecraft. ■ used, esp. in similes and comparisons, to refer to a person or thing that moves very fast or to an action that is done with great force: *she shot out of her chair like a rocket.*
▶ v. (**rockets, rocketing, rocketed**) **1** [no obj.] (of an amount, price, etc.) increase very rapidly and suddenly: *sales of milk in supermarkets are rocketing* | (as adj. **rocketing**) *rocketing prices.* ■ [with adverbial of direction] move or progress very rapidly: [no obj.] *the cab rocketed down a ramp* | [with obj.] *she showed the kind of form that rocketed her to the semifinals last year.*
2 [with obj.] attack with rocket-propelled missiles: *the city was rocketed and bombed from the air.*
– DERIVATIVES **rock·et·like** /-,līk/ adj.
– ORIGIN early 17th cent.: from French *roquette*, from Italian *rocchetto*, diminutive of *rocca* 'distaff (for spinning),' with reference to its cylindrical shape.

rock·et[2] ▶ n. (also **garden rocket** or **salad rocket**) an edible Mediterranean plant of the cabbage family, sometimes eaten in salads. See also ARUGULA. ● *Eruca vesicaria* subsp. *sativa*, family Brassicaceae. ■ used in names of other fast-growing plants of this family, e.g., **sweet rocket**.
– ORIGIN late 15th cent.: from French *roquette*, from Italian *ruchetta*, diminutive of *ruca*, from Latin *eruca* 'downy-stemmed plant.'

rock·e·teer /,räki'ti(ə)r/ ▶ n. a person who works with space rockets; a rocket enthusiast.

rock·et·ry /'räkətrē/ ▶ n. the branch of science that deals with rockets and rocket propulsion. ■ the use of rockets.

rock·et sci·en·tist ▶ n. a specialist in rocketry. ■ [usu. with negative] informal an extremely intelligent person: *he's a nice kid—maybe not a rocket scientist, but he should come out okay.*

rock face ▶ n. a bare vertical surface of natural rock.

rock·fall /'räk,fôl/ (also **rock fall**) ▶ n. a descent of loose rocks. ■ a mass of fallen rock.

rock·fish /'räk,fisH/ ▶ n. (pl. **same** or **rockfishes**) a marine fish of the scorpionfish family with a laterally compressed body. It is generally a bottom-dweller in rocky areas and is frequently of sporting or commercial value. ● Genus *Sebastes*, family Scorpaenidae: numerous species.

rock flour ▶ n. finely powdered rock formed by glacial or other erosion.

Rock·ford /'räkfərd/ an industrial city in north central Illinois, on the Rock River; pop. 157,272 (est. 2008).

rock gar·den ▶ n. an artificial mound or bank built of earth and stones and planted with rock plants. ■ a garden in which rockeries are the chief feature.

Rock Hill an industrial city in northern South Carolina; pop. 67,339 (est. 2008).

rock·hop·per /'räk,häpər/ (also **rockhopper penguin**) ▶ n. a small penguin with a yellowish crest, breeding on subantarctic coastal cliffs that it ascends by hopping from rock to rock. ● *Eudyptes chrysocome*, family Spheniscidae.

rock·hound /'räk,hound/ ▶ n. informal a geologist or amateur collector of mineral specimens.
– DERIVATIVES **rock·hound·ing** n.

rock hy·rax ▶ n. an African hyrax that lives on rocky outcrops and cliffs and feeds mainly on grass. Also called DASSIE. ● Genus *Procavia* (and *Heterohyrax*), family Procaviidae: several species.

Rock·ies another name for the ROCKY MOUNTAINS.

rock·ing chair ▶ n. a chair mounted on rockers or springs, so as to rock back and forth.

rock·ing horse ▶ n. a model of a horse mounted on rockers or springs for a child to sit on and rock back and forth.

rocking horse

Rock Is·land an industrial city in northwestern Illinois, on the Mississippi River, one of the Quad Cities; pop. 38,139 (est. 2008).

rock jock ▶ n. informal **1** a mountaineer.
2 a disc jockey who plays rock music.

Rock·land Coun·ty /'räklənd/ a largely suburban county in southeastern New York, on the western side of the Hudson River and the New Jersey border; pop. 298,545 (est. 2008).

rock·ling /'räkliNG/ ▶ n. a slender marine fish of the cod family, typically occurring in shallow water or tidal pools. ● Genera *Ciliata* and *Rhinomenus*, family Gadidae: several species.

rock liz·ard ▶ n. a small climbing lizard living in mountains and arid rocky habitats, in particular: ● (also **banded rock lizard**) a North American lizard (*Streptosaurus mearnsi*, family Iguanidae). ● a European and African lizard (genus *Lacerta*, family Lacertidae, including *L. saxicola*).

rock lob·ster ▶ n. another term for SPINY LOBSTER.

rock ma·ple ▶ n. another term for SUGAR MAPLE.

rock mu·sic ▶ n. a form of popular music that evolved from rock and roll and pop music during the mid- and late 1960s. Harsher and often self-consciously more serious than its predecessors, it was initially characterized by musical experimentation and drug-related or anti-Establishment lyrics. ■ another term for ROCK AND ROLL.

Rock·ne /'räknē/, Knute (Kenneth) (1888–1931), US college football coach; born in Norway. He coached Notre Dame 1918–31 to six national titles and achieved a winning percentage of .881. He was killed in a plane crash in Kansas.

rock 'n' roll ▶ n. variant spelling of ROCK AND ROLL.

Rock of Gi·bral·tar see GIBRALTAR.

rock pi·geon ▶ n. another term for ROCK DOVE.

rock plant ▶ n. a plant that grows on or among rocks.

rock pool ▶ n. a pool of water among rocks, typically along a shoreline.

rock py·thon ▶ n. a large dark-skinned constricting snake with paler markings and a distinctive pale mark on the crown. ● Genera *Python* and *Morelia*, family Pythonidae: several species, including *P. sebae* of Africa, *P. molurus* of Asia, and *M. amethistina* of Australia.

rock rab·bit ▶ n. **1** another term for HYRAX.
2 another term for PIKA.

rock-ribbed ▶ adj. **1** having ridges or cliffs of rock: *six thousand miles of rock-ribbed coasts.*
2 resolute or uncompromising, esp. with respect to political allegiance: *rock-ribbed Republicans.*

rock·rose /'räk,rōz/ ▶ n. **1** a herbaceous or shrubby plant with saucer-shaped, roselike flowers, native to temperate and warm regions. See also LABDANUM. ● Genera *Cistus* and *Helianthemum*, family Cistaceae.
2 another term for BITTERROOT.

rock salm·on ▶ n. a tropical snapper that occurs both in the sea and in rivers, valuable for food and sport. ● *Lutjanus argentimaculatus*, family Lutjanidae.

rock salt ▶ n. common salt occurring naturally as a mineral; halite.

rock·slide /'räk,slīd/ ▶ n. an avalanche of rock. ■ a mass of rock deposited by such an avalanche.

rock snake ▶ n. the Asian rock python.

rock sol·id ▶ adj. unlikely to change, fail, or collapse: *her love was rock solid.*

Rock Springs a city in southwestern Wyoming, northeast of Green River; pop. 20,200 (est. 2008).

rock·stead·y /räk'stedē/ (also **rock steady**) ▶ n. an early form of reggae music originating in Jamaica in the 1960s, characterized by a slow tempo.

rock·u·men·ta·ry /,räkyə'ment(ə)rē/ ▶ n. informal a documentary about rock music and musicians.
– ORIGIN 1970s: from ROCK[2] + DOCUMENTARY.

Rock·ville /'räk,vil/ a city in central Maryland, northwest of Washington, DC, home to many government offices; pop. 60,734 (est. 2008).

rock wal·la·by ▶ n. an agile Australian wallaby that lives among cliffs and rocks, having feet with thick pads and fringes of stiff hair. ● Genus *Petrogale*, family Macropodidae: several species.

Rock·well /'räk,wel, -wəl/, Norman (Percevel) (1894–1978), US illustrator. Known for his typically sentimental portraits of small-town life in the US, he was an illustrator for *Life* and the *Saturday Evening Post*, for which he created 317 covers between 1916 and 1963.

rock wool ▶ n. inorganic material made into matted fiber used esp. for insulation or soundproofing.

rock·y /'räkē/ ▶ adj. (**rockier, rockiest**) **1** consisting or full of rock or rocks: *a rocky crag above the village* | *hillsides of dry, rocky soil.*
2 tending to rock or shake; unsteady.
3 difficult and full of obstacles or problems: *a long, rocky road to pop stardom* | *the marriage seemingly got off to a rocky start.*
– DERIVATIVES **rock·i·ly** /'räkəlē/ adv., **rock·i·ness** n.

Rock·y Mount /'räkē/ an industrial city in east central North Carolina; pop. 57,010 (est. 2008).

Rock·y Moun·tain goat ▶ n. see MOUNTAIN GOAT (sense 1).

Rock·y Moun·tains (also **the Rockies**) the chief mountain system in North America. It extends from the US–Mexico border to the Yukon Territory of northern Canada. It separates the Great Plains from the Pacific coast and forms the Continental Divide. Several peaks rise to more than 14,000 feet (4,300 m), the highest being Mount Elbert at 14,431 feet (4,399 m).

Rock·y Moun·tain spot·ted fe·ver ▶ n. a rickettsial disease transmitted by ticks.

ro·co·co /rə'kōkō, ,rōkə'kō/ ▶ adj. (of furniture or architecture) of or characterized by an elaborately ornamental late baroque style of decoration prevalent in 18th-century Continental Europe, with asymmetrical patterns involving motifs and scrollwork. ■ extravagantly or excessively ornate, esp. (of music or literature) highly ornamented and florid.
▶ n. the rococo style of art, decoration, or architecture.
– ORIGIN mid 19th cent.: from French, humorous alteration of ROCAILLE.

rod /räd/ ▶ n. **1** a thin straight bar, esp. of wood or metal. ■ a wand or staff as a symbol of office, authority, or power. ■ a slender straight stick or shoot growing on or cut from a tree or bush. ■ a stick used for caning or flogging. ■ (**the rod**) the use of such a stick as punishment: *if you'd been my daughter, you'd have felt the rod.* ■ vulgar slang a penis.
2 a fishing rod.
3 historical a linear measure, esp. for land, equal to $5^1/_2$ yards (approximately 5.029 m). ■ (also **square rod**) a square measure, esp. for land, equal to 160th of an acre or $30^1/_4$ square yards (approximately 25.29 sq m).
4 informal a pistol or revolver.
5 Anatomy a light-sensitive cell of one of the two types present in large numbers in the retina of the eye, responsible mainly for monochrome vision in poor light. Compare with CONE (sense 3).
– PHRASES **ride the rods** see RIDE. **rule someone or something with a rod of iron** control or govern someone or something very strictly or harshly. **spare the rod and spoil the child** proverb if children are not physically punished when they do wrong, their personal development will suffer.
– DERIVATIVES **rod·less** adj., **rod·let** /-lət/ n., **rod·like** /-,līk/ adj.
– ORIGIN late Old English *rodd* 'slender shoot growing on or cut from a tree,' also 'straight stick or bundle of twigs used to inflict punishment'; probably related to Old Norse *rudda* 'club.'

Rod·den·ber·ry /'rädn,berē/, Gene (1921–91), US television producer and scriptwriter; full name *Eugene Wesley Roddenberry*. He created and wrote many scripts for the television science-fiction drama series *Star Trek*, first broadcast in 1966. He later worked on movies and launched a follow-up series, *Star Trek: The Next Generation*, in 1987.

rode[1] /rōd/ past of RIDE.

rode[2] ▶ **v.** [no obj.] (of a woodcock) fly on a regular circuit in the evening as a territorial display, making sharp calls and grunts.
– ORIGIN mid 18th cent. (in the sense 'fly landward in the evening'): of unknown origin.

rode[3] ▶ **n.** Nautical a rope, esp. one securing an anchor or trawl.
– ORIGIN early 17th cent.: of unknown origin.

ro·dent /ˈrōdnt/ ▶ **n.** a gnawing mammal of an order that includes rats, mice, squirrels, hamsters, porcupines, and their relatives, distinguished by strong constantly growing incisors and no canine teeth. They constitute the largest order of mammals. ● Order Rodentia: three suborders. See **SCIUROMORPHA**, **MYOMORPHA**, and **HYSTRICOMORPHA**.
▶ **adj. 1** of or relating to mammals of this order.
2 Medicine see **RODENT ULCER**.
– ORIGIN mid 19th cent.: from Latin *rodent-* 'gnawing,' from the verb *rodere*.

ro·den·ti·cide /rōˈdentəˌsīd/ ▶ **n.** a poison used to kill rodents.

ro·dent ul·cer ▶ **n.** Medicine a slow-growing malignant tumor of the face (basal cell carcinoma).

ro·de·o /ˈrōdēˌō, rəˈdāō/ ▶ **n.** (pl. **rodeos**) **1** an exhibition or contest in which cowboys show their skill at riding broncos, roping calves, wrestling steers, etc. ■ a similar exhibition or contest demonstrating other skills, such as motorcycle riding or canoeing.
2 a roundup of cattle on a ranch for branding, counting, etc. ■ an enclosure for such a roundup.
▶ **v.** (**rodeos, rodeoing, rodeoed**) [no obj.] compete in a rodeo.
– ORIGIN mid 19th cent.: from Spanish, from *rodear* 'go around,' based on Latin *rotare* 'rotate.'

Rodg·ers /ˈräjərz/, Richard (Charles) (1902–79), US composer. He worked with librettist Lorenz Hart before collaborating with Oscar Hammerstein II on a succession of popular musicals that included *Oklahoma!* (1943), *South Pacific* (1949), *The King and I* (1951), and *The Sound of Music* (1959).

rodg·er·si·a /räˈjərzēə/ ▶ **n.** an Asian plant that is sometimes cultivated for its attractive foliage. ● Genus *Rodgersia*, family Saxifragaceae.
– ORIGIN modern Latin, named after John *Rodgers* (1812–82), American admiral.

Ró·dhos /ˈrôT͟Hôs/ modern Greek name for **RHODES**[1].

Ro·din /rōˈdaN/, Auguste (1840–1917), French sculptor. He was chiefly concerned with the human form, and his first major work, *The Age of Bronze* (1875–76), was considered so lifelike that Rodin was alleged to have taken a cast from a live model. Other notable works: *The Thinker* (1880) and *The Kiss* (1886).

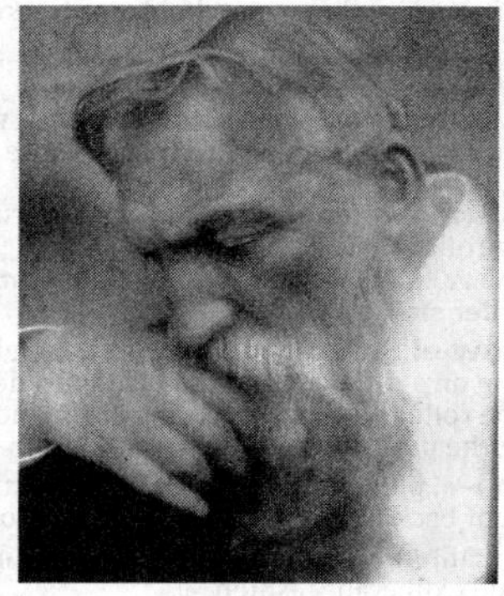
Auguste Rodin

rod·o·mon·tade /ˌrädəmənˈtād, ˌrōd-, -ˈtäd/ ▶ **n.** boastful or inflated talk or behavior.
▶ **v.** [no obj.] archaic talk boastfully.
– ORIGIN early 17th cent.: from French, from obsolete Italian *rodomontada*, from Italian *rodomonte*, from the name of a boastful character in the medieval *Orlando* epics.

ROE ▶ **abbr.** rules of engagement (in combat).

roe[1] /rō/ ▶ **n.** (also **hard roe**) the mass of eggs contained in the ovaries of a female fish or shellfish, typically including the ovaries themselves, esp. when ripe and used as food. ■ (**soft roe**) the ripe testes of a male fish, esp. when used as food.
– ORIGIN late Middle English: related to Middle Low German, Middle Dutch *roge*.

roe[2] (also **roe deer**) ▶ **n.** (pl. **same** or **roes**) a small Eurasian deer that lacks a visible tail and has a reddish summer coat that turns grayish in winter. ● Genus *Capreolus*, family Cervidae: two species, in particular the **European roe deer** (*C. capreolus*).
– ORIGIN Old English *rā(ha)*, of Germanic origin; related to Dutch *ree* and German *Reh*.

roe·buck /ˈrōˌbək/ ▶ **n.** a male roe deer.

roent·gen /ˈrentgən, ˈrənt-, -jən/ (abbr.: **R**) ▶ **n.** a unit of ionizing radiation, the amount producing one electrostatic unit of positive or negative ionic charge in one cubic centimeter of air under standard conditions.
– ORIGIN 1920s: named after Wilhelm Conrad *Röntgen* (see **RÖNTGEN**).

roent·gen·i·um /rentˈgenēəm, rənt-/ ▶ **n.** the chemical element of atomic number 111, a radioactive element produced artificially. (Symbol: **Rg**)
– ORIGIN 21st cent.: named after Wilhelm Conrad *Röntgen* (see **RÖNTGEN**).

roent·gen·o·gram /ˈrentgənəˌgram, ˈrənt-, -jə-/ ▶ **n.** chiefly Medicine an X-ray photograph.

roent·gen·og·ra·phy /ˌrentgəˈnägrəfē, ˌrənt-, -jə-/ ▶ **n.** chiefly Medicine X-ray photography.
– DERIVATIVES **roent·gen·o·graph·ic** /-nəˈgrafik/ **adj.**, **roent·gen·o·graph·i·cal·ly** /-nəˈgrafik(ə)lē/ **adv.**

roent·gen·ol·o·gy /ˌrentgəˈnäləjē, ˌrənt-, -jə-/ ▶ **n.** chiefly Medicine another term for **RADIOLOGY**.
– DERIVATIVES **roent·gen·o·log·ic** /-nəˈläjik/ **adj.**

roent·gen rays ▶ **plural n.** dated X-rays.

ro·gan josh /ˈrōgən ˈjäsH/ ▶ **n.** an Indian dish of curried meat, typically lamb, in a rich tomato-based sauce.
– ORIGIN from Urdu *roğan još*.

ro·ga·tion /rōˈgāsHən/ ▶ **n.** [usu. as modifier] (in the Christian Church) a solemn supplication consisting of the litany of the saints chanted on the three days before Ascension Day: *Rogation Week*.
– ORIGIN late Middle English: from Latin *rogatio(n-)*, from *rogare* 'ask.'

Ro·ga·tion Days (in the Western Christian Church) the three days before Ascension Day, traditionally marked by fasting and prayer, particularly for the blessing of the harvest (after the pattern of pre-Christian rituals).

Ro·ga·tion Sun·day ▶ **n.** the Sunday preceding the Rogation Days.

rog·er /ˈräjər/ ▶ **exclam.** your message has been received and understood (used in radio communication): *"Roger; we'll be with you in about ten minutes."* ■ informal used to express assent or understanding: *"Go light the stove." "Roger, Mister Bossman," Frank replied.*
▶ **v.** [with obj.] Brit. vulgar slang have sexual intercourse with (a woman). ■ [no obj.] have sexual intercourse.
– ORIGIN mid 16th cent.: from the given name *Roger*. The verb (dating from the early 18th cent.) is from an obsolete sense 'penis' of the noun.

Rog·ers[1] /ˈräjərz/ a resort city in northwestern Arkansas, north of Fayetteville; pop. 56,726 (est. 2008).

Rog·ers[2], Fred McFeely (1928–2003), US television producer, actor, and writer. He created and starred in the television children's program *Mister Rogers' Neighborhood* 1967–2001.

Rog·ers[3] /ˈräjərz/, Ginger (1911–95), US actress and dancer; born *Virginia Katherine McMath*. She is known for her dancing partnership with Fred Astaire, during which she appeared in musicals including *Top Hat* (1935) and *Shall We Dance?* (1937). Other notable, nonmusical movies include *Stage Door* (1937) and *Kitty Foyle* (1940).

Rog·ers[4], Roy (1912–98), US actor and singer; born *Leonard Franklin Slye*. One of the original Sons of the Pioneers country singers, he starred in many "singing cowboy" westerns, with his horse Trigger and dog Bullet and, from 1944, with Dale Evans (1912–2001), whom he married in 1947. His movies include *Under Western Stars* (1938), *The Yellow Rose of Texas* (1944), and *Apache Rose* (1947).

Rog·ers[5], Will (1879–1935), US humorist and actor; full name *William Penn Adair Rogers*. A vaudeville headliner with his rope twirling and homespun humor from 1905, he wrote a syndicated column for *The New York Times* 1922–35. He died in a plane crash with aviator Wiley Post in Alaska.

Ro·get /rōˈZHā, ˈrōˌZHā/, Peter Mark (1779–1869), English scholar. He worked as a physician but is remembered as the compiler of *Roget's Thesaurus of English Words and Phrases* (1852).

rogue /rōg/ ▶ **n. 1** a dishonest or unprincipled man: *you are a rogue and an embezzler.* ■ a person whose behavior one disapproves of but who is nonetheless likable or attractive (often used as a playful term of reproof): *Cenzo, you old rogue!*
2 [usu. as modifier] an elephant or other large wild animal driven away or living apart from the herd and having savage or destructive tendencies: *a rogue elephant.* ■ a person or thing that behaves in an aberrant, faulty, or unpredictable way: *he hacked into data and ran rogue programs.* ■ an inferior or defective specimen among many satisfactory ones, esp. a seedling or plant deviating from the standard variety.
▶ **v.** [with obj.] remove inferior or defective plants or seedlings from (a crop).
– ORIGIN mid 16th cent. (denoting an idle vagrant): probably from Latin *rogare* 'beg, ask,' and related to obsolete slang *roger* 'vagrant beggar' (many such cant terms were introduced toward the middle of the 16th cent).

Rogue Riv·er a river that flows west for 200 miles (320 km) across southern Oregon to the Pacific Ocean.

ro·guer·y /ˈrōgərē/ ▶ **n.** (pl. **rogueries**) conduct characteristic of a rogue, esp. acts of dishonesty or playful mischief: *there has always been roguery associated with horse dealing.*

rogues' gal·ler·y ▶ **n.** informal a collection of photographs of known criminals, used by police to identify suspects. ■ a collection of people or creatures notable for a certain shared quality or characteristic, typically a disreputable one: *a rogues' gallery of bureaucrats and cold-hearted advocates of "progress."*

rogue state ▶ **n.** a nation or state regarded as breaking international law and posing a threat to the security of other nations.

rogue trad·er ▶ **n.** a securities trader who engages in speculative trading without authorization.

ro·guish /ˈrōgisH/ ▶ **adj.** characteristic of a dishonest or unprincipled person: *he led a roguish and uncertain existence.* ■ playfully mischievous, esp. in a way that is sexually attractive: *he gave her a roguish smile.*
– DERIVATIVES **ro·guish·ly adv.**, **ro·guish·ness n.**

Ro·hyp·nol /rōˈhipˌnôl, -ˌnōl/ ▶ **n.** trademark a potent sedative drug of the benzodiazepine class.
– ORIGIN 1980s: invented name.

ROI ▶ **abbr.** Finance return on investment.

roil /roil/ ▶ **v. 1** [with obj.] make (a liquid) turbid or muddy by disturbing the sediment: *winds roil these waters.* ■ [no obj.] (of a liquid) move in a turbulent, swirling manner: *the sea roiled below her* | figurative *a kind of fear roiled in her.*
2 another term for **RILE** (sense 1).
– ORIGIN late 16th cent.: perhaps from Old French *ruiler* 'mix mortar,' from late Latin *regulare* 'regulate.'

roil·y /ˈroilē/ ▶ **adj.** (chiefly of water) muddy; turbulent: *those waters were roily, high, and muddy.*

roist·er /ˈroistər/ ▶ **v.** [no obj.] enjoy oneself or celebrate in a noisy or boisterous way: *workers from the refinery roistered in the bars.*
– DERIVATIVES **roist·er·er n.**, **roist·er·ous** /ˈroist(ə)rəs/ **adj.**
– ORIGIN late 16th cent.: from obsolete *roister* 'roisterer,' from French *rustre* 'ruffian,' variant of *ruste*, from Latin *rusticus* 'rustic.'

Ro·land /ˈrōlənd/ the most famous of Charlemagne's paladins, hero of the *Chanson de Roland* (12th century). He is said to have become a friend of Oliver, another paladin, after engaging him in single combat in which neither won. Roland was killed at the Battle of Roncesvalles.

role /rōl/ ▶ **n.** an actor's part in a play, movie, etc.: *Dietrich's role as a wife in war-torn Paris.* ■ the function assumed or part played by a person or thing in a particular situation: *she greeted us all in her various roles of mother, friend, and daughter* | *religion plays a vital role in society.*
– ORIGIN early 17th cent.: from obsolete French *roule* 'roll,' referring originally to the roll of paper on which the actor's part was written.

role mod·el ▶ **n.** a person looked to by others as an example to be imitated.

role-play·ing (also **role-play**) ▶ **n. 1** chiefly Psychology the acting out or performance of a particular role, either consciously (as a technique in psychotherapy or training) or unconsciously, in accordance with the perceived expectations of society with regard to a person's behavior in a particular context.
2 participation in a role-playing game.
– DERIVATIVES **role-play v.**, **role-play·er n.**

role-play·ing game ▶ **n.** a game in which players take on the roles of imaginary characters who engage in adventures, typically in a particular computerized fantasy setting overseen by a referee.

role re·ver·sal ▶ **n.** a situation in which someone adopts a role the reverse of that which they normally assume in relation to someone else, who typically assumes their role in exchange:

PRONUNCIATION KEY ə *ago, up*; ər *over, fur*; a *hat*; ā *ate*; ä *car*; e *let*; ē *see*; i *fit*; ī *by*; NG *sing*; ō *go*; ô *law, for*; oi *toy*; o͝o *good*; o͞o *goo*; ou *out*; TH *thin*; T͟H *then*; ZH *vision*

r

one marriage counselor makes use of role reversal, inviting husband and wife to pretend to be each other.

Rolfe /rälf/, John (1585–1622), English colonist in Virginia. He perfected the process of curing tobacco. In 1614, he married Pocahontas, the daughter of Indian chief Powhatan.

Rolf·ing /ˈrôlfiNG/ ▶ **n.** trademark a massage technique aimed at the vertical realignment of the body, and therefore deep enough to release muscular tension at skeletal level. It can contribute to the relief of long-standing tension and neuroses.
– DERIVATIVES **Rolf** /rôlf/ **v.**
– ORIGIN 1970s: from the name of Ida P. *Rolf* (1897–1979), American physical therapist, + **-ING**[1].

roll /rōl/ ▶ **v. 1** move or cause to move in a particular direction by turning over and over on an axis: [no obj.] *the car rolled down into a ditch* | [with obj.] *she rolled the ball across the floor.* ■ turn or cause to turn over to face a different direction: [no obj.] *she rolled onto her side* | [with obj.] *they rolled him over onto his back.* ■ [with obj.] turn (one's eyes) upward, typically to show surprise or disapproval: *Sarah rolled her eyes.* ■ [no obj.] (of a person or animal) lie down and turn over and over while remaining in the same place: *the buffalo rolled in the dust.* ■ [no obj.] (of a moving ship, aircraft, or vehicle) rock or oscillate around an axis parallel to the direction of motion: *the ship pitched and rolled.* ■ [no obj.] move along or from side to side unsteadily or uncontrollably: *they were rolling about with laughter.* ■ [with obj.] informal overturn (a vehicle): *he rolled his Mercedes in a 100 mph crash.* ■ [with obj.] throw (a die or dice). ■ [with obj.] obtain (a particular score) by doing this: *roll a 2, 3, or 12.*
2 [no obj.] (of a vehicle) move or run on wheels: *the van was rolling along the highway.* ■ [with obj.] move or push (a wheeled object): *Pat rolled the cart back and forth.* ■ (**roll something up/down**) make a car window or a window blind move up or down. ■ (of time) elapse steadily: *the years rolled by.* ■ (of a drop of liquid) flow: *huge tears rolled down her cheeks.* ■ (**roll off**) (of a product) issue from (an assembly line or machine): *the first copies of the newspaper rolled off the presses.* ■ (of waves, smoke, cloud, or fog) move or flow forward with an undulating motion: *the fog rolled across the fields.* ■ (of land) extend in gentle undulations. ■ (of credits for a movie or television program) be displayed as if moving on a roller up the screen. ■ (with reference to a machine, device, or system) operate or begin operating: [no obj.] *the cameras started to roll* | [with obj.] *roll the camera.*
3 [with obj.] turn (something flexible) over and over on itself to form a cylinder, tube, or ball: *she started to roll up her sleeping bag.* ■ make by forming material into a cylinder or ball: [with two objs.] *Harry rolled himself a joint.* ■ [no obj.] (of a person or animal) curl up tightly: *the shock made the armadillo roll into a ball.*
4 [with obj.] flatten or spread (something) by using a roller or by passing it between rollers: *roll out the dough on a floured surface* | *roll on a decorative paint finish.*
5 [no obj.] (of a loud, deep sound such as that of thunder or drums) reverberate: *the first peals of thunder rolled across the sky.* ■ [with obj.] pronounce (a consonant, typically an *r*) with a trill: *when he wanted to emphasize a point he rolled his rrrs.* ■ [with obj.] utter (a word or words) with a reverberating or vibratory effect: *he rolled the word around his mouth.* ■ (of words) flow effortlessly or mellifluously: *the names of his colleagues rolled off his lips.*
6 [with obj.] informal rob (someone, typically when they are intoxicated or asleep): *if you don't get drunk, you don't get rolled.*
▶ **n. 1** a cylinder formed by winding flexible material around a tube or by turning it over and over on itself without folding: *a roll of carpet.* ■ a cylindrical mass of something or a number of items arranged in a cylindrical shape: *a roll of mints.* ■ [with modifier] an item of food that is made by wrapping a flat sheet of pastry, cake, meat, or fish around a sweet or savory filling: *salmon and rice rolls.* ■ money, typically a quantity of banknotes rolled together. ■ a roller for flattening something, esp. one used to shape metal in a rolling mill.
2 a movement in which someone or something turns or is turned over on itself: *a roll of the dice* | *the ponies completed two rolls before getting back on their feet.* ■ a gymnastic exercise in which the body is rolled into a tucked position and turned in a forward or backward circle: *a forward roll.* ■ a swaying or oscillation of a ship, aircraft, or vehicle around an axis parallel to the direction of motion: *the car corners capably with a minimum of roll.* ■ undulation of the landscape: *hidden by the roll of the land was a refinery.*
3 a prolonged, deep, reverberating sound, typically made by thunder or a drum: *thunder exploded, roll after roll.* ■ Music one of the basic patterns (rudiments) of drumming, consisting of a sustained, rapid alternation of single or double strokes of each stick.
4 a very small loaf of bread, typically eaten with butter or a filling: *a sausage roll.*
5 an official list or register of names. ■ the total numbers on such a list: *a review of secondary schools to assess the effects of falling rolls.* ■ a document, typically an official record, in scroll form.
– PHRASES **a roll in the hay** (or **the sack**) informal an act of sexual intercourse. **be rolling (in money)** informal be very rich. **on a roll** informal experiencing a prolonged spell of success or good luck: *the organization is on a roll.* **rolled into one** (of characteristics drawn from different people or things) combined in one person or thing: *banks are several businesses rolled into one.* **rolling in the aisles** informal (of an audience) laughing uncontrollably. **roll of honor** a list of people whose deeds or achievements are honored, or who have died in battle. **roll of the dice** see **DICE**. **roll one's own** informal make one's own cigarettes from loose tobacco. **roll up one's sleeves** prepare to fight or work. **roll with the punches** (of a boxer) move one's body away from an opponent's blows so as to lessen the impact. ■ adapt oneself to adverse circumstances.
– PHRASAL VERBS **roll something back** reverse the progress or reduce the power or importance of something: *her bid to roll back state power.* **roll in** informal be received in large amounts: *the money was rolling in.* ■ arrive at a place in a casual way, typically in spite of being late: *Steve rolled in about lunchtime.* **roll something out** officially launch or unveil a new product or service: *the firm rolled out its newest generation of supercomputers.* **roll something over** Finance contrive or extend a particular financial arrangement: *this is not a good time for rolling over corporate debt.* ■ carry over prize money in a lottery from one draw to the next, esp. because the jackpot has not been won. **roll up** informal arrive in a vehicle: *we rolled up at the same time.* **roll something up** Military drive the flank of an enemy line back and around so that the line is shortened or surrounded.
– DERIVATIVES **roll·a·ble adj.**
– ORIGIN Middle English: from Old French *rolle* (noun), *roller* (verb), from Latin *rotulus* 'a roll,' variant of *rotula* 'little wheel,' diminutive of *rota*.

Rol·land /rôˈlän/, Romain (1866–1944), French novelist, playwright, and essayist. His interest in genius led to a number of biographies, and ultimately to *Jean-Christophe* (1904–12), a cycle of 10 novels about a German composer. Nobel Prize for Literature (1915).

roll·a·way /ˈrōlə,wā/ ▶ **n.** a bed fitted with wheels or casters, allowing it to be moved easily: [as modifier] *a rollaway bed.*

roll·back /ˈrōl,bak/ ▶ **n. 1** a reduction or decrease: *a 5 percent rollback of personal income taxes.* ■ a reversion to a previous state or situation: *a rollback to conditions not seen since the open shop days of the 1930s.*
2 Computing the process of restoring a database or program to a previously defined state, typically to recover from an error.
▶ **v.** [with obj.] Computing restore (a database) to a previously defined state.

roll bar ▶ **n.** a metal bar running up the sides and across the top of a vehicle, esp. one used in motor sports, strengthening its frame and protecting the occupants should the vehicle overturn.

roll bar

roll cage ▶ **n.** a framework of reinforcements protecting a car's passenger cabin in the event that it should roll onto its roof.

roll call ▶ **n.** the process of calling out a list of names to establish who is present. ■ a list or group of people or things that are notable in some specified way: *the roll call of nations that lack full religious rights.*

roll cast ▶ **n.** Fishing a cast in which the angler does not throw the line backward.

rolled gold ▶ **n.** gold in the form of a thin coating applied to a baser metal by rolling.

rolled oats ▶ **plural n.** oats that have been husked and crushed.

roll·er /ˈrōlər/ ▶ **n. 1** a cylinder that rotates around a central axis and is used in various machines and devices to move, flatten, or spread something. ■ an absorbent revolving cylinder attached to a handle, used to apply paint. ■ a small cylinder on which hair is rolled in order to produce curls. ■ (also **roller bandage**) a long surgical bandage rolled up for convenient application. ■ a long swelling wave that appears to roll steadily toward the shore. ■ [as modifier] of, relating to, or involving roller skates: *roller hockey.*
2 a brightly colored crow-sized bird with predominantly blue plumage, having a characteristic tumbling display flight. [late 17th cent.: from German *Roller*, from *rollen* 'to roll.'] ● Genera *Coracias* and *Eurystomus*, family Coraciidae: several species, esp. the widespread **European roller** (*C. garrulus*).
3 a bird of a breed of tumbler pigeon.
4 a bird of a breed of canary with a trilling song.
5 a broad surcingle, typically padded at the withers.

roll·er·ball /ˈrōlər,bôl/ ▶ **n. 1** a ballpoint pen using thinner ink than other ballpoints.
2 Computing an input device containing a ball that is moved with the fingers to control the cursor.

roll·er bear·ing ▶ **n.** a bearing similar to a ball bearing but using small cylindrical rollers instead of balls. ■ a roller used in such a bearing.

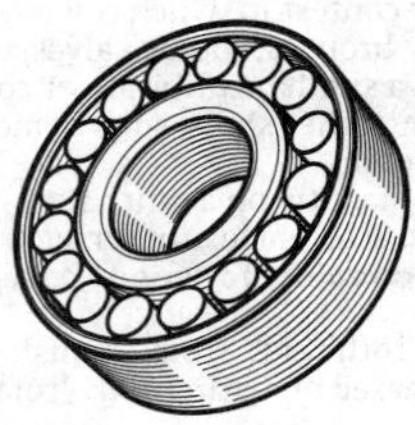

roller bearing

Roll·er·blade /ˈrōlər,blād/ ▶ **n.** trademark an in-line skate.
▶ **v.** [no obj.] skate using Rollerblades: *the muscular actor loves to Rollerblade* | (as noun **rollerblading**) *rollerblading was made to order for runners whose knees are beginning to give out.*
– DERIVATIVES **roll·er·blad·er n.**

roll·er coast·er ▶ **n.** an amusement park attraction that consists of a light railroad track with many tight turns and steep slopes, on which people ride in small fast open cars. ■ a thing that contains or goes through wild and unpredictable changes: *a terrific roller coaster of a book.*
▶ **v.** (**roller-coaster**) (also **roller-coast**) [no obj.] move, change, or occur in the dramatically changeable manner of a roller coaster: *the twentieth century fades behind us and history roller-coasters on.*

Roll·er Der·by ▶ **n.** trademark a team skating competition on roller skates, held on a banked oval track.

roll·er rink ▶ **n.** see **RINK**.

roll·er skate ▶ **n.** each of a pair of boots, or metal frames attached to shoes, with four or more small wheels, for gliding across a hard surface.
▶ **v.** [no obj.] (**roller-skate**) glide across a hard surface wearing roller skates.
– DERIVATIVES **roll·er skat·er n.**, **roll·er-skat·ing** (also **roller skating**) **n.**

roll·er tow·el ▶ **n.** a long towel with the ends joined and hung on a roller, or one fed through a device from one roller holding the clean part to another holding the used part.

roll film ▶ **n.** photographic film with protective lightproof backing paper wound onto a spool.

rol·lick /ˈrälik/ ▶ **v.** [no obj.] rare act or behave in a jovial and exuberant fashion.
– ORIGIN early 19th cent.: probably dialect, perhaps a blend of **ROMP** and **FROLIC**.

rol·lick·ing[1] /ˈrälikiNG/ ▶ **adj.** [attrib.] exuberantly lively and amusing: *good rollicking fun.*

rol·lick·ing[2] (also **rollocking**) ▶ **n.** [in sing.] Brit. informal a severe reprimand.

roll·ing /ˈrōliNG/ ▶ **adj. 1** moving by turning over and over on an axis: *a rolling ball.*
2 (of land) extending in gentle undulations: *the rolling countryside.*
3 done or happening in a steady and continuous way: *a rolling program of reforms* | *a rolling news service.*

roll·ing hitch ▶ **n.** a kind of hitch used to attach a rope to a spar or larger rope. It is a clove hitch with an extra turn in the standing part.

roll·ing mill ▶ **n.** a factory or machine for rolling steel or other metal into sheets.

roll·ing pin ▶ **n.** a cylinder rolled over pastry or dough to flatten or shape it.

roll·ing stock ▶ **n.** locomotives, carriages, wagons, or other vehicles used on a railroad. ■ the road vehicles of a trucking company.

roll·ing stone ▶ **n.** a person who is unwilling to settle for long in one place.
– PHRASES **a rolling stone gathers no moss** proverb a person who does not settle in one place will not accumulate wealth, status, responsibilities, or commitments.

roll-in roll-out ▶ **n.** Computing a method or the process of switching data or code between main and auxiliary memories in order to process several tasks simultaneously.

roll·mop /'rōl,mäp/ ▶ **n.** a rolled uncooked pickled herring fillet.
– ORIGIN early 20th cent.: from German *Rollmops*.

roll-neck ▶ **n.** a high loosely turned-over collar: [as modifier] *a black roll-neck sweater*. ■ a garment with such a collar.

rol·lock·ing ▶ **n.** variant spelling of **ROLLICKING**².

roll-off ▶ **n.** the smooth fall of response to zero at either end of the frequency range of a piece of audio equipment.

roll-on ▶ **adj.** [attrib.] (of deodorant or cosmetic) applied by means of a rotating ball in the neck of the container.
▶ **n.** a roll-on deodorant or cosmetic.

roll-on roll-off ▶ **adj.** [attrib.] denoting a passenger ferry or other method of transportation in which vehicles are driven directly on at the start of the voyage or journey and driven off at the end of it.

roll·out /'rōl,out/ ▶ **n. 1** the unveiling of a new aircraft or spacecraft. ■ the official launch or introduction of a new product or service.
2 Aeronautics the stage of an aircraft's landing during which it travels along the runway while losing speed.
3 Football a play in which the quarterback runs toward the sideline before attempting to pass or advance.

roll·o·ver /'rōl,ōvər/ ▶ **n. 1** Finance the extension or transfer of a debt or other financial arrangement. ■ (in a lottery) the accumulative carryover of prize money to the following drawing.
2 informal the overturning of a vehicle.
3 a facility on an electronic keyboard enabling one or several keystrokes to be registered correctly while another key is depressed.

Rolls /rōlz/, Charles Stewart (1877–1910), English automobile manufacturer and aviator. He and Henry Royce formed the company Rolls-Royce Ltd. in 1906. Rolls, the first Englishman to fly across the English Channel, was killed in an airplane crash.

Rolls-Royce /rōlz 'rois/ ▶ **n. 1** trademark a luxury car produced by the British Rolls-Royce company.
2 (also **Rolls Royce**) a product that is the most luxurious or highly specified of its kind: *the one I have at the moment is the Rolls Royce of accordions.*

roll·top desk /'rōl,täp/ ▶ **n.** a writing desk with a flexible cover sliding in curved grooves.

roll-up ▶ **n.** Brit. informal a hand-rolled cigarette. ■ an article of food rolled up and sometimes stuffed with a filling: *ham roll-ups*.
▶ **adj.** [attrib.] denoting something that can be rolled up: *roll-up panels*.

Ro·lo·dex /'rōlə,deks/ ▶ **n.** trademark a desktop card index used to record names, addresses, and telephone numbers, in the form of a rotating spindle or a small tray to which removable cards are attached. ■ informal a person's list of business contacts and friends.

ro·ly-po·ly /'rōlē 'pōlē/ ▶ **adj.** (of a person) having a round, plump appearance: *a roly-poly young boy.*
▶ **n.** (also **roly-poly pudding**) Brit. a sweet pastry dough covered with jam or fruit, formed into a roll, and boiled, steamed, or baked.
– ORIGIN early 17th cent.: fanciful formation from the verb **ROLL**.

ROM /räm/ ▶ **abbr.** Computing read-only memory.

Rom /rōm/ ▶ **n.** (pl. **Roma** /'rōmə/) a Gypsy, esp. a man.
– ORIGIN mid 19th cent.: abbreviation of **ROMANY**.

Rom. ▶ **abbr.** Bible Romans.

rom. ▶ **abbr.** roman (used as an instruction for a typesetter).

Ro·ma /'rōmə/ Italian name for **ROME**.

Ro·ma·ic /rō'māik/ dated ▶ **adj.** dated of or relating to the vernacular language of modern Greece.
▶ **n.** this language.
– ORIGIN from modern Greek *romaiikos* 'Roman,' used specifically of the Eastern Roman Empire.

ro·maine /rō'mān/ ▶ **n.** a lettuce of a variety with crisp narrow leaves that form a tall head.
– ORIGIN early 20th cent.: from French, feminine of *romain* 'Roman.'

ro·ma·ji /'rōməjē/ ▶ **n.** a system of Romanized spelling used to transliterate Japanese.
– ORIGIN early 20th cent.: from Japanese, from *rōma* 'Roman' + *ji* 'letter(s).'

Ro·man /'rōmən/ ▶ **adj. 1** of or relating to ancient Rome or its empire or people: *an old Roman road.* ■ of or relating to medieval or modern Rome: *the Roman and Pisan lines of popes.*
2 dated short for **ROMAN CATHOLIC**: *the Roman Church's instructions to its clergy.*
3 denoting the alphabet (or any of the letters in it) used for writing Latin, English, and most European languages, developed in ancient Rome. ■ (**roman**) (of type) of a plain upright kind used in ordinary print, esp. as distinguished from italic.
▶ **n. 1** a citizen or soldier of the ancient Roman Republic or Empire. ■ a citizen of modern Rome.
2 dated a Roman Catholic.
3 (**roman**) roman type.
– ORIGIN Middle English: from Old French *Romain*, from Latin *Romanus*, from *Roma* 'Rome.'

ro·man à clef /rō,män ä 'klā/ ▶ **n.** (pl. **romans à clef** pronunc. **same**) a novel in which real people or events appear with invented names.
– ORIGIN French, literally 'novel with a key.'

Ro·man baths ▶ **plural n.** a building containing a complex of rooms designed for bathing, relaxing, and socializing, as used in ancient Rome.

Ro·man can·dle ▶ **n.** a firework giving off a series of flaming colored balls and sparks.

Ro·man Cath·o·lic ▶ **adj.** of or relating to the Roman Catholic Church: *a Roman Catholic bishop.*
▶ **n.** a member of this church.
– DERIVATIVES **Ro·man Ca·thol·i·cism n.**
– ORIGIN late 16th cent.: translation of Latin (*Ecclesia*) *Romana Catholica* (*et Apostolica*) 'Roman Catholic (and Apostolic Church).' It was apparently first used as a conciliatory term in place of the earlier *Roman, Romanist*, or *Romish*, considered derogatory.

Ro·man Cath·o·lic Church the part of the Christian Church that acknowledges the pope as its head, esp. as it has developed since the Reformation.

Ro·mance /rō'mans, 'rō,mans/ ▶ **n.** the group of Indo-European languages descended from Latin, principally French, Spanish, Portuguese, Italian, Catalan, Occitan, and Romanian.
▶ **adj.** of, relating to, or denoting this group of languages: *the Romance languages.*
– ORIGIN Middle English (originally denoting the vernacular language of France as opposed to Latin): from Old French *romanz*, based on Latin *Romanicus* 'Roman.'

ro·mance /rō'mans, 'rō,mans/ ▶ **n. 1** a feeling of excitement and mystery associated with love: *in search of romance.* ■ love, esp. when sentimental or idealized: *he asked her for a date and romance blossomed.* ■ an exciting, enjoyable love affair, esp. one that is not serious or long-lasting: *a summer romance.* ■ a book or movie dealing with love in a sentimental or idealized way: *light historical romances.* ■ a genre of fiction dealing with love in such a way: *wartime passion from the master of romance.*
2 a quality or feeling of mystery, excitement, and remoteness from everyday life: *the beauty and romance of the night.* ■ wild exaggeration; picturesque falsehood: *she slammed the claims as "pure romance, complete fiction."* ■ a work of fiction dealing with events remote from real life.
3 a medieval tale dealing with a hero of chivalry, of the kind common in the Romance languages: *the Arthurian romances.* ■ the literary genre of such works.
4 Music a short informal piece.
▶ **v.** [with obj.] **1** court; woo: *the wealthy estate owner romanced her.* ■ informal seek the attention or patronage of (someone), esp. by use of flattery: *he is being romanced by the big boys in New York.* ■ [no obj.] engage in a love affair: *we start romancing.*
2 another term for **ROMANTICIZE**: *to a certain degree I am romancing the past.*
– ORIGIN Middle English: from **ROMANCE**, originally denoting a composition in the vernacular as opposed to works in Latin. Early use denoted vernacular verse on the theme of chivalry; the sense 'genre centered on romantic love' dates from the mid 17th cent.

ro·manc·er /rō'mansər, 'rō,mansər/ ▶ **n. 1** a person prone to wild exaggeration or falsehood.
2 a writer of medieval romances.

Ro·man Em·pire the empire established by Augustus in 27 BC and divided by Theodosius in AD 395 into the Western or Latin and Eastern or Greek Empire.

> Rome was sacked by the Visigoths under Alaric in 410, and the last emperor of the West, **Romulus Augustulus**, was deposed in 476. The Eastern Empire, whose capital was Constantinople, lasted until 1453 (see **BYZANTINE EMPIRE**).

Ro·man·esque /,rōmə'nesk/ ▶ **adj.** of or relating to a style of architecture that prevailed in Europe c.900–1200, although sometimes dated back to the end of the Roman Empire (5th century).
▶ **n.** Romanesque architecture.

> Romanesque architecture is characterized by round arches and massive vaulting, and by heavy piers, columns, and walls with small windows. Although disseminated throughout western Europe, the style reached its fullest development in central and northern France; the equivalent style in England is usually called Norman.

– ORIGIN French, from *roman* 'romance.'

ro·man-fleuve /rō,mäN 'flœv/ ▶ **n.** (pl. **romans-fleuves** pronunc. **same**) a novel featuring the leisurely description of the lives of closely related people. ■ a sequence of related, self-contained novels.
– ORIGIN French, literally 'river novel.'

Ro·man hol·i·day ▶ **n.** literary an occasion on which enjoyment or profit is derived from others' suffering or discomfort.
– ORIGIN early 19th cent.: from Byron's *Childe Harold*, originally with reference to a holiday given for a gladiatorial combat.

Ro·ma·ni·a /rō'mānēə, rōō-/ (also **Rumania**) a country in southeastern Europe, on the Black Sea; pop. 22,215,400 (est. 2009); capital, Bucharest; language, Romanian (official).

> In the Middle Ages, the area consisted of the principalities of Wallachia and Moldavia, which were swallowed up by the Ottoman Empire in the 15th–16th centuries. The two principalities gained independence in 1878. After World War II, during which it had supported Germany, Romania became a communist state under Soviet domination. After 1974, the country pursued an increasingly independent course under the virtual dictatorship of Nicolae Ceaușescu. His regime collapsed in violent popular unrest in 1989, and a new democratic constitution was introduced. Romania joined NATO in 2004 and the EU in 2007.

Ro·ma·ni·an /rō'mānēən, rōō-/ (also **Rumanian**) ▶ **adj.** of or relating to Romania or its people or language.
▶ **n. 1** a native or inhabitant of Romania, or a person of Romanian descent.
2 the language of Romania, a Romance language influenced by the neighboring Slavic languages, also spoken by the majority of the population of Moldova.

Ro·man·ic /rō'manik/ ▶ **n. & adj.** less common term for **ROMANCE**.
– ORIGIN early 18th cent.: from Latin *Romanicus*, from *Romanus* 'Roman.'

Ro·man·ism /'rōmə,nizəm/ ▶ **n.** dated Roman Catholicism.

Ro·man·ist /'rōmənist/ ▶ **n. 1** an expert in or student of Roman antiquities or law, or of the Romance languages.
2 chiefly derogatory a member or supporter of the Roman Catholic Church.
▶ **adj.** chiefly derogatory belonging or adhering to the Roman Catholic Church.

ro·man·ize /'rōmə,nīz/ (also **Romanize**) ▶ **v.** [with obj.] **1** historical bring (something, esp. a region or people) under Roman influence or authority: *though not himself a Roman, he was fully Romanized, spoke Latin, and lived in a Roman-style villa.*
2 make Roman Catholic in character: *he has Romanized the services of his church.*
3 put (text) into the Roman alphabet or into roman type: *Atatürk's decision to romanize the written language.*
– DERIVATIVES **ro·man·i·za·tion** /,rōmənə'zāSHən/ **n.**

Ro·man law ▶ **n.** the law code of the ancient Romans, which forms the basis of civil law in many countries today.

Ro·man nose ▶ **n.** a nose with a high bridge.

Ro·man num·er·al ▶ **n.** any of the letters representing numbers in the Roman numerical system: I = 1, V = 5, X = 10, L = 50, C = 100, D = 500, M = 1,000. In this system, a letter placed after another of greater value adds (thus XVI or xvi is 16), whereas a letter placed before another of greater value subtracts (thus XC or xc is 90).

Ro·ma·no /rə'mänō/ ▶ **n.** a strong-tasting hard cheese, originally made in Italy.
– ORIGIN Italian, literally 'Roman.'

Romano- ▶ **comb. form** Roman; Roman and ...: *Romano-Celtic.*

Ro·ma·nov /rō'män,ôf, 'rōmə,nôf/ a dynasty that ruled in Russia from the accession of **Michael**

PRONUNCIATION KEY ə *ago, up*; ər *over, fur*; a *hat*; ā *ate*; ä *car*; e *let*; ē *see*; i *fit*; ī *by*; NG *sing*; ō *go*; ô *law, for*; oi *toy*; o͝o *good*; o͞o *goo*; ou *out*; TH *thin*; T͟H *then*; ZH *vision*

r

Romanov (1596–1645) in 1613 until the overthrow of the last tsar, Nicholas II, in 1917.

Ro·man Re·pub·lic the ancient Roman state from the expulsion of the Etruscan monarchs in 509 BC (see **TARQUINIUS**) until the assumption of power by Augustus (Octavian) in 27 BC.

Ro·mans /'rōmənz/ a book of the New Testament, an epistle of St. Paul to the Christian Church at Rome.

Ro·mansh /rō'mänCH, -'manCH/ ▶ **n.** the Rhaeto-Romanic language that is spoken in the Swiss canton of Grisons and is an official language of Switzerland.
▶ **adj.** of or relating to this language.
– ORIGIN from Romansh *Roman(t)sch*, from medieval Latin *romanice* 'in the Romanic manner.'

ro·man·tic /rō'mantik, rə-/ ▶ **adj. 1** inclined toward or suggestive of the feeling of excitement and mystery associated with love: *a romantic candlelit dinner.* ■ relating to love, esp. in a sentimental or idealized way: *a romantic comedy.*
2 of, characterized by, or suggestive of an idealized view of reality: *a romantic attitude toward the past | some romantic dream of country peace.*
3 (usu. **Romantic**) of, relating to, or denoting the artistic and literary movement of Romanticism: *the Romantic tradition.*
▶ **n.** a person with romantic beliefs or attitudes: *I am an incurable romantic.* ■ (usu. **Romantic**) a writer or artist of the Romantic movement.
– DERIVATIVES **ro·man·ti·cal·ly** /-ik(ə)lē/ **adv.**
– ORIGIN mid 17th cent. (referring to the characteristics of romance in a narrative): from archaic *romaunt* 'tale of chivalry,' from an Old French variant of *romanz* (see **ROMANCE**).

ro·man·ti·cism /rō'mantə,sizəm, rə-/ ▶ **n. 1** (often **Romanticism**) a movement in the arts and literature that originated in the late 18th century, emphasizing inspiration, subjectivity, and the primacy of the individual.

> Romanticism was a reaction against the order and restraint of classicism and neoclassicism, and a rejection of the rationalism that characterized the Enlightenment. In music, the period embraces much of the 19th century, with composers including Schubert, Schumann, Liszt, and Wagner. Poets exemplifying the movement include Wordsworth, Coleridge, Byron, Shelley, and Keats; among romantic painters are such stylistically diverse artists as William Blake, J. M. W. Turner, Delacroix, and Goya.

2 the state or quality of being romantic: *a quality of romanticism about women that leads to the creation of a pipe-dream fantasy.*

ro·man·ti·cist /rō'mantəsist, rə-/ ▶ **n.** a writer, artist, or musician of the Romantic movement. ■ a person who subscribes to the artistic movement or ideas of Romanticism.

ro·man·ti·cize /rō'mantə,sīz, rə-/ ▶ **v.** [with obj.] deal with or describe in an idealized or unrealistic fashion; make (something) seem better or more appealing than it really is: *the tendency to romanticize nonindustrial societies* | [no obj.] *she was romanticizing about the past.*
– DERIVATIVES **ro·man·ti·ci·za·tion** /rō,mantəsə'zāSHən, rə-/ **n.**

r

Rom·a·ny /'rämənē, 'rō-/ (also **Romani**) ▶ **n.** (pl. **Romanies**) **1** the Indic language of the Gypsies, spoken in many dialects.
2 a Gypsy.
▶ **adj.** of or relating to Gypsies or their language.
– ORIGIN early 19th cent.: from Romany *Romani*, feminine and plural of the adjective *Romano*, from *Rom* 'man, husband' (see **ROM**).

Rom·berg /'räm,bərg/, Sigmund (1887–1951), US composer, born in Hungary. He wrote a succession of popular operettas, including *The Student Prince* (1924), *The Desert Song* (1926), and *New Moon* (1928).

rom·com /'räm,käm/ ▶ **n.** informal (in movies or television) a romantic comedy.

Rome /rōm/ **1** the capital of Italy, situated in the west central part of the country, on the Tiber River, about 16 miles (25 km) inland; pop. 2,724,347 (2008). According to tradition, the ancient city was founded by Romulus (after whom it is named) in 753 BC on the Palatine Hill; as it grew it spread to the other six hills of Rome (Aventine, Caelian, Capitoline, Esquiline, and Quirinal). Rome was made capital of a unified Italy in 1871. Italian name **ROMA**. ■ used allusively to refer to the Roman Catholic Church.
2 an industrial city in northwestern Georgia, on the Coosa River; pop. 36,041 (est. 2008).
3 an industrial city in central New York, on the Mohawk River; pop. 33,673 (est. 2008).
– PHRASES **all roads lead to Rome** proverb there are many different ways of reaching the same goal or conclusion. **Rome was not built in a day** proverb a complex task is bound to take a long time and should not be rushed. **when in Rome (do as the Romans do)** proverb when abroad or in an unfamiliar environment you should adopt the customs or behavior of those around you.

Ro·me·o /'rōmē,ō/ ▶ **n. 1** (pl. **Romeos**) an attractive, passionate male seducer or lover.
2 a code word representing the letter R, used in radio communication.
– ORIGIN from the name of the hero of Shakespeare's romantic tragedy *Romeo and Juliet.*

Rom·ish /'rōmiSH/ ▶ **adj.** chiefly derogatory Roman Catholic: *Romish ideas.*

Rom·mel /'räməl/, Erwin (1891–1944), German field marshal; known as **the Desert Fox**. As commander of the Afrika Korps, he captured Tobruk in 1942, but he was defeated by Montgomery at El Alamein later that year. Implicated in the officers' conspiracy against Hitler in 1944, he committed suicide.

Rom·ney /'rämnē/, George (1734–1802), English portrait painter. From the early 1780s, he produced more than 50 portraits of Lady Hamilton in historical costumes.

Rom·ney Marsh ▶ **n.** a sheep of a stocky breed with long wool, originally from England and now common in New Zealand.

romp /rämp, rômp/ ▶ **v.** [no obj.] (esp. of a child or animal) play roughly and energetically: *the noisy pack of children romped around the garden.* ■ [with adverbial] informal proceed without effort to achieve something: *the Vikings romped to victory.* ■ informal engage in sexual activity, esp. illicitly: *a colleague stumbled on the couple romping in an office.*
▶ **n.** a spell of rough, energetic play: *a romp in the snow.* ■ a lighthearted movie or other work: *an enjoyably gross sci-fi romp.* ■ informal an easy victory: *the 45–28 romp over the Owls yesterday at Alumni Stadium.* ■ informal a spell of sexual activity, esp. an illicit one: *three-in-a-bed sex romps.*
– ORIGIN early 18th cent.: perhaps an alteration of **RAMP**.

romp·er /'rämpər, 'rôm-/ ▶ **n. 1** (also **romper suit** or **rompers**) a young child's one-piece outer garment. ■ a similar item of clothing for adults, typically worn as overalls or as sports clothing.
2 a person who romps.

Rom·u·lus /'rämyələs/ Roman Mythology one of the traditional founders of Rome, with his brother Remus. The twin sons of Mars by the Vestal Virgin Silvia, Romulus and Remus were abandoned at birth but were found and suckled by a she-wolf and brought up by a shepherd family. Remus is said to have been killed by Romulus during an argument about the new city.

Ron·ces·valles, Bat·tle of /,rônsəs'vä(l),yās/ a battle that took place in 778 at a mountain pass in the Pyrenees, near the village of Roncesvalles in northern Spain. The rearguard of Charlemagne's army was attacked by the Basques and massacred; one of the nobles, Roland, was killed, an event celebrated in the *Chanson de Roland* (in which the attackers are wrongly identified as the Moors). French name **Roncevaux**.

ron·da·vel /'rändə,vel/ ▶ **n.** S. African a traditional circular African dwelling with a conical thatched roof. ■ a building based on the design of such a dwelling, used as a guest room, storeroom, or vacation cottage.
– ORIGIN from Afrikaans *rondawel*.

rond de jambe /,rôN də 'ZHäNb/ ▶ **n.** (pl. **ronds de jambe** pronunc. **same**) Ballet a circular movement of the leg that can be performed on the ground or during a jump.
– ORIGIN French.

ronde /ränd/ ▶ **n.** a dance in which the dancers move in a circle.
– ORIGIN 1930s: French, feminine of *rond* 'round.'

ron·deau /'rändō, rän'dō/ ▶ **n.** (pl. **rondeaux** /-dōz, 'dōz/) a thirteen-line poem, divided into three stanzas of 5, 3, and 5 lines, with only two rhymes throughout and with the opening words of the first line used as a refrain at the end of the second and third stanzas.
– ORIGIN early 16th cent.: French, later form of *rondel* (see **RONDEL**).

ron·del /'rändəl, rän'del/ ▶ **n. 1** a rondeau, esp. one of three stanzas of thirteen or fourteen lines, with the first two lines of the opening quatrain recurring at the end of the second quatrain and the concluding sestet.
2 a circular object: *at the point where these paths join there is a rondel with a fountain.*
– ORIGIN Middle English: from Old French, from *rond* 'round'; compare with **ROUNDEL**.

ron·do /'rändō, rän'dō/ ▶ **n.** (pl. **rondos**) a musical form with a recurring leading theme, often found in the final movement of a sonata or concerto.
– ORIGIN late 18th cent.: Italian, from French *rondeau* (see **RONDEAU**).

Rong·e·lap /'räNGə,lap/ an atoll in the western Pacific, in the northern Marshall Islands at the northwestern end of the Ratak group, east of Bikini. It was evacuated in the 1980s because of contamination from 1950s nuclear tests at Eniwetok.

ro·nin /'rōnən/ ▶ **n.** (pl. **same** or **ronins**) historical (in feudal Japan) a wandering samurai who had no lord or master.
– ORIGIN Japanese.

Rönt·gen /'rentgən, 'renCHən/, Wilhelm Conrad (1845–1923), German physicist; the discoverer of X-rays. Nobel Prize for Physics (1901).

rönt·gen, etc. ▶ **n.** variant spelling of **ROENTGEN**, etc.

roo /ro͞o/ ▶ **n.** Austral. informal a kangaroo.
– ORIGIN early 20th cent.: shortened form.

rood /ro͞od/ ▶ **n. 1** a crucifix, esp. one positioned above the rood screen of a church or on a beam over the entrance to the chancel.
2 chiefly Brit. historical a measure of land area equal to a quarter of an acre.
– ORIGIN Old English *rōd*; related to Dutch *roede* and German *Rute* 'rod.'

rood screen ▶ **n.** a screen, typically of richly carved wood or stone, separating the nave from the chancel of a church. Rood screens are found throughout western Europe and date chiefly from the 14th–16th centuries.

roof /ro͞of, ro͝of/ ▶ **n.** (pl. **roofs**) the structure forming the upper covering of a building or vehicle. ■ the top inner surface of a covered area or space; the ceiling: *the roof of the cave fell in.* ■ used to signify a house or other building, esp. in the context of hospitality or shelter: *helping those without a roof over their heads | they slept under the same roof.* ■ (**roof of the mouth**) the palate.
▶ **v.** [with obj.] (usu. **be roofed**) cover with a roof: *the yard had been roughly roofed over with corrugated iron.* ■ function as the roof of: *fan vaults roof these magnificent buildings.*
– PHRASES **go through the roof** informal **1** (of prices or figures) reach extreme or unexpected heights. **2** another way of saying **HIT THE ROOF**. **hit the roof** informal suddenly become very angry. **raise the roof** see **RAISE**. **the roof of the world** a nickname given to the Himalayas.
– DERIVATIVES **roof·less adj.**
– ORIGIN Old English *hrōf*, of Germanic origin; related to Old Norse *hróf* 'boat shed,' Dutch *roef* 'deckhouse.' English alone has the general sense 'covering of a house'; other Germanic languages use forms related to *thatch*.

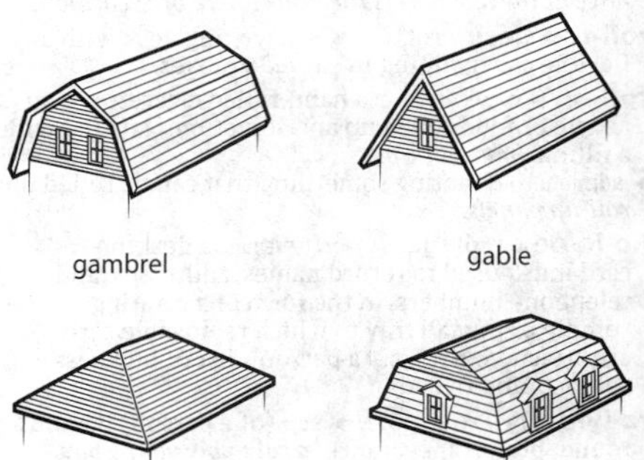

roofs

roof·er /'ro͞ofər, 'ro͝of-/ ▶ **n.** a person who constructs or repairs roofs.

roof gar·den ▶ **n.** a garden on the flat roof of a building.

roof·ing /'ro͞ofiNG, 'ro͝of-/ ▶ **n.** material for constructing a building's roof: *a house with corrugated tin roofing.* ■ the process of constructing a roof or roofs: *jobs such as roofing.*

roof light ▶ **n.** a window panel built into a roof to admit light. ■ a small interior light on the ceiling of a motor vehicle. ■ a flashing warning light on the top of a police car or other emergency vehicle.

roof·line /'ro͞of,līn, 'ro͝of-/ ▶ **n.** the design or proportions of the roof of a building or vehicle.

roof prism ▶ **n.** a reflecting prism in which the reflecting surface is in two parts that are angled like the two sides of a pitched roof. Compare with **PORRO PRISM**. ■ (**roof prisms**) (also **roof-prism binoculars**) a pair of binoculars using two such prisms, resulting in an instrument with parallel sides and objective lenses that are the same distance apart as the eyepieces.

roof rack ▸ **n.** a framework for carrying luggage or equipment on the roof of a vehicle.

roof rat ▸ **n.** another term for BLACK RAT.

roof·top /ˈro͝ofˌtäp, ˈro͞of-/ ▸ **n.** the outer surface of a building's roof.
– PHRASES **shout something from the rooftops** see SHOUT.

roof·tree /ˈro͝ofˌtrē, ˈro͞of-/ ▸ **n.** the ridgepole of a roof.

roo·i·bos /ˈro͞oēbäs/ ▸ **n.** S. African an evergreen South African shrub of the pea family. ● Genus *Aspalathus*, family Leguminosae. ■ (**rooibos tea**) an infusion of the leaves of the rooibos plant, drunk as tea. Also called RED TEA.
– ORIGIN early 20th cent.: from Afrikaans, literally 'red bush.'

rook[1] /ro͝ok/ ▸ **n.** a gregarious Eurasian crow with black plumage and a bare face, nesting in colonies in treetops. ● *Corvus frugilegus*, family Corvidae.
▸ **v.** [with obj.] informal take money from (someone) by cheating, defrauding, or overcharging them.
– ORIGIN Old English *hrōc*, probably imitative and of Germanic origin; related to Dutch *roek*.

rook[2] ▸ **n.** a chess piece, typically with its top in the shape of a battlement, that can move in any direction along a rank or file on which it stands. Each player starts the game with two rooks at opposite ends of the first rank. See also CASTLE.
– ORIGIN Middle English: from Old French *rock*, based on Arabic *rukk* (of which the sense remains uncertain).

rook·er·y /ˈro͝okərē/ ▸ **n.** (pl. **rookeries**) **1** a breeding colony of rooks, typically seen as a collection of nests high in a clump of trees. ■ a breeding colony of seabirds (esp. penguins), seals, or turtles.
2 a dense collection of housing, esp. in a slum area.

rook·ie /ˈro͝okē/ ▸ **n.** informal a new recruit, esp. in the army or police: [as modifier] *a rookie cop.* ■ a member of an athletic team in his or her first full season in that sport.
– ORIGIN late 19th cent.: perhaps an alteration of RECRUIT, influenced by ROOK[1].

room /ro͞om, ro͝om/ ▸ **n. 1** space that can be occupied or where something can be done, esp. viewed in terms of whether there is enough: *there's only room for a single bed in there* | [with infinitive] *she was trapped without room to move.* ■ opportunity or scope for something to happen or be done, esp. without causing trouble or damage: *there is plenty of room for disagreement in this controversial area* | *there is room for improvement.*
2 a part or division of a building enclosed by walls, floor, and ceiling: *he wandered from room to room.* ■ (**rooms**) a set of rooms, typically rented, in which a person, couple, or family live: *my rooms at Mrs. Jenks's house.* ■ [in sing.] the people present in a room: *the whole room burst into an uproar of approval.*
▸ **v.** [no obj.] share a room or house or apartment, esp. a rented one at a college or similar institution: *I was rooming with my cousin.* ■ [with obj.] provide with a shared room or lodging: *they roomed us together.*
– PHRASES **make room** move aside or move something aside to allow someone to enter or pass or to clear space for something: *the secretary entered with the coffee tray and made room for it on the desk.* **no** (or **not**) **room to swing a cat** humorous used in reference to a very confined space. [*cat* in the sense 'cat-o'-nine-tails.'] **smoke-filled room** used to refer to political bargaining or decision-making that is conducted privately by a small group of influential people rather than more openly or democratically.
– DERIVATIVES **roomed adj.** [in combination] *a four-roomed house*, **room·ful** /-ˌfo͝ol/ **n.** (pl. **roomfuls**).
– ORIGIN Old English *rūm*, of Germanic origin; related to Dutch *ruim*, German *Raum*.

room and board ▸ **n.** lodging and food, typically forming part of someone's wages or included in some other agreement.

room·er /ˈro͞omər, ˈro͝om-/ ▸ **n.** a renter of a room in another person's house.

room·ette /ro͞oˈmet, ro͝omˈet/ ▸ **n.** a private single compartment in a railroad sleeping car.

room·ie /ˈro͞omē, ˈro͝omē/ ▸ **n.** informal a roommate.

room·ing house ▸ **n.** a private house in which rooms are rented for living or staying temporarily.

room·mate /ˈro͞omˌmāt, ˈro͝om-/ ▸ **n.** a person occupying the same room as another. ■ a person occupying the same apartment or house as another.

room serv·ice ▸ **n.** service provided in a hotel allowing guests to order food and drink to be brought to their rooms.

room tem·per·a·ture ▸ **n.** a comfortable ambient temperature, generally taken as about 70°F.

room·y /ˈro͞omē, ˈro͝omē/ ▸ **adj.** (**roomier, roomiest**) (esp. of accommodations) having plenty of room; spacious.
– DERIVATIVES **room·i·ly** /-məlē/ **adv.**, **room·i·ness n.**

Roo·ney /ˈro͞onē/, Mickey (1920–), US actor; born *Joseph Yule, Jr.* He played the title role in 16 Andy Hardy movies over a period of 20 years. Other notable movies: *Babes in Arms* (1939), *The Human Comedy* (1943), *National Velvet* (1944), and *The Black Stallion* (1979).

Roo·se·velt[1] /ˈrōzəˌvelt, -vəlt/, Eleanor (1884–1962), US first lady 1933–45, humanitarian, and diplomat; full name *Anna Eleanor Roosevelt*. The niece of Theodore Roosevelt, she married Franklin D. Roosevelt (a fifth cousin, once removed) in 1905. Involved in a wide range of liberal causes, she served as chair of the UN Commission on Human Rights, where she helped to draft the Declaration of Human Rights in 1948.

Eleanor Roosevelt

Roo·se·velt[2], Franklin Delano (1882–1945), 32nd president of the US 1933–45; known as **FDR**. His New Deal programs of the 1930s helped to lift the US out of the Great Depression, and he played an important part in Allied policy during World War II. A Democrat and a victim of polio, he was the only president to be elected to a third (and then a fourth) term in office.

Franklin D. Roosevelt

Roo·se·velt[3], Theodore (1858–1919), 26th president of the US 1901–09; nicknamed **Teddy Roosevelt**. He was responsible for initiating many antitrust laws, and he successfully engineered the US bid to build the Panama Canal (1904–14). He also negotiated the end of the Russo-Japanese War in 1905. The teddy bear is named for him, with reference to his bear-hunting. Nobel Peace Prize (1906).

Theodore Roosevelt

Roo·se·velt Is·land /ˈrōzəˌvelt/ a residential island in the East River in New York City, between Manhattan and Queens.

roost /ro͞ost/ ▸ **n.** a place where birds regularly settle or congregate to rest at night, or where bats congregate to rest in the day.
▸ **v.** [no obj.] (of a bird or bat) settle or congregate for rest or sleep: *migrating martins and swallows were settling to roost.*
– PHRASES **come home to roost** (of a scheme, etc.) recoil unfavorably upon the originator: *ensuring that the liability does not come home to roost.* **rule the roost** see RULE.
– ORIGIN Old English *hrōst*, related to Dutch *roest*; of unknown ultimate origin.

roost·er /ˈro͞ostər, ˈro͝ostər/ ▸ **n.** a male domestic fowl; a cock.

rooster

roost·er tail ▸ **n.** informal the spray of water thrown up behind a speedboat or surfboard.

root[1] /ro͞ot, ro͝ot/ ▸ **n.**
1 the part of a plant that attaches it to the ground or to a support, typically underground, conveying water and nourishment to the rest of the plant via numerous branches and fibers: *cacti have deep and spreading roots* | *a tree root.* ■ the persistent underground part of a plant, esp. when fleshy and enlarged and used as a vegetable, e.g., a turnip or carrot. ■ any plant grown for such a root. ■ the embedded part of a bodily organ or structure such as a hair, tooth, or nail: *her hair was fairer at the roots.* ■ the part of a thing attaching it to a greater or more fundamental whole; the end or base: *a little lever near the root of the barrel.*
2 the basic cause, source, or origin of something: *love of money is the root of all evil* | *jealousy was at the root of it* | [as modifier] *the root cause of the problem.* ■ the essential substance or nature of something: *matters at the heart and root of existence.* ■ (**roots**) family, ethnic, or cultural origins, esp. as the reasons for one's long-standing emotional attachment to a place or community: *it's always nice to return to my roots.* ■ (as adj. **roots**) denoting or relating to something, esp. music, from a particular ethnic or cultural origin, esp. a non-Western one: *roots music.* ■ (in biblical use) a scion; a descendant: *the root of David.* ■ Linguistics a morpheme, not necessarily surviving as a word in itself, from which words have been made by the addition of prefixes or suffixes or by other modification: *many European words stem from this linguistic root* | [as modifier] *the root form of the word.* ■ Music the fundamental note of a chord.
3 Mathematics a number or quantity that when multiplied by itself, typically a specified number of times, gives a specified number or quantity: *find the cube root of the result.* ■ short for SQUARE ROOT. ■ a value of an unknown quantity satisfying a given equation: *the roots of the equation differ by an integer.*
▸ **v.** [with obj.] **1** cause (a plant or cutting) to grow roots: *root your own cuttings from stock plants.* ■ [no obj.] (of a plant or cutting) establish roots: *large trees had rooted in the canal bank.*
2 (usu. **be rooted**) establish deeply and firmly: *vegetarianism is rooted in Indian culture.* ■ (**be rooted in**) have as an origin or cause: *the Latin dubitare is rooted in an Indo-European word.* ■ (often as adj. **rooted**) cause (someone) to stand immobile through fear or amazement: *she found herself rooted to the spot in disbelief.*
– PHRASES **at root** basically; fundamentally: *it is a moral question at root.* **put down roots** (of a plant) begin to draw nourishment from the soil through its roots. ■ (of a person) begin to have a settled life in a particular place. **root and branch** used to express the thorough or radical nature of a process or operation: *root and branch reform of personal taxation.* **strike at the root** (or **roots**) **of** affect in a vital area with potentially destructive results: *the proposals struck at the roots of community life.* **take root** (of a plant) begin to grow and draw nourishment from the soil through its roots. ■ become fixed or established: *the idea had taken root in my mind.*
– PHRASAL VERBS **root something out** (also **root something up**) dig or pull up a plant by the roots. ■ find and get rid of someone or something

r

regarded as pernicious or dangerous: *a campaign to root out corruption.*
– DERIVATIVES **root·ed·ness** n., **root·let** /-lət/ n., **root·like** /-ˌlīk/ adj., **root·y** adj.
– ORIGIN late Old English *rōt*, from Old Norse *rót*; related to Latin *radix*, also to WORT.

root[2] ▶ v. [no obj.] (of an animal) turn up the ground with its snout in search of food: *stray dogs rooting around for bones and scraps.* ■ search unsystematically through an untidy mass or area; rummage: *she was rooting through a pile of papers.* ■ [with obj.] (**root something out**) find or extract something by rummaging: *he managed to root out the cleaning kit.*
▶ n. [in sing.] an act of rooting: *I have a root through the open drawers.*
– PHRASAL VERBS **root for** informal support or hope for the success of (a person or group entering a contest or undertaking a challenge): *the whole of this club is rooting for him.* **root someone on** informal cheer or spur someone on: *his mother rooted him on enthusiastically from ringside.*
– ORIGIN Old English *wrōtan*, of Germanic origin; related to Old English *wrōt* 'snout,' German *Rüssel* 'snout,' and perhaps ultimately to Latin *rodere* 'gnaw.'

root·ball /ˈro͞otˌbôl, ˈro͝ot-/ (also **root ball**) ▶ n. the mass formed by the roots of a plant and the soil surrounding them.

root beer ▶ n. an effervescent drink made from an extract of the roots and bark of certain plants.

root ca·nal ▶ n. the pulp-filled cavity in the root of a tooth. ■ a procedure to replace infected pulp in a root canal with an inert material.

root cel·lar ▶ n. a domestic cellar used for storing root vegetables.

root crop ▶ n. a crop that is a root vegetable or other root, e.g., sugar beet.

root di·rec·to·ry ▶ n. Computing the directory at the highest level of a hierarchy.

root·er /ˈro͞otər, ˈro͝o-/ ▶ n. informal a supporter or fan of a sports team or player.

root fly ▶ n. a dark slender fly whose larvae may cause serious damage to the roots of crops. ● Family Anthomyiidae: many genera and species, including the **cabbage root fly**.

root hair ▶ n. Botany each of a large number of elongated microscopic outgrowths from the outer layer of cells in a root, absorbing moisture and nutrients from the soil.

root·in'-toot·in' /ˈro͞otn ˈto͞otn/ ▶ adj. informal brashly or boisterously enthusiastic: *their rootin'-tootin' summer adventures.*
– ORIGIN late 19th cent.: reduplication of *rooting* in the sense 'inquisitive,' an early dialect sense of the compound.

root·kit /ˈro͞otˌkit/ ▶ n. Computing a set of software tools that enable an unauthorized user to gain control of a computer system without being detected.

root-knot ▶ n. a disease of cultivated flowers and vegetables caused by eelworm infestation, resulting in galls on the roots. ● The eelworms belong to the genus *Meloidogyne*, class Nematoda.

roo·tle /ˈro͞otl, ˈro͝otl/ ▶ v. Brit. informal term for ROOT[2].
– ORIGIN early 19th cent.: frequentative of ROOT[2].

root·less /ˈro͞otlis, ˈro͝ot-/ ▶ adj. **1** having no settled home or social or family ties: *a rootless nomad.*
2 (of a plant) not having roots: *a rootless flowering plant.*
– DERIVATIVES **root·less·ness** n.

root mean square ▶ n. Mathematics the square root of the arithmetic mean of the squares of a set of values, used as a measure of the typical magnitude of a set of numbers, regardless of their sign.

root run ▶ n. the space over which the roots of a plant extend.

root sign ▶ n. Mathematics another term for RADICAL SIGN.

roots mu·sic ▶ n. music springing from and identified with a particular culture, typically that of the West Indies.

root·stock /ˈro͞otˌstäk, ˈro͝ot-/ ▶ n. a rhizome. ■ a plant onto which another variety is grafted. ■ a primary form or source from which offshoots have arisen: *the rootstock of all post-Triassic ammonites.*

root·sy /ˈro͞otsē, ˈro͝ot-/ ▶ adj. informal (of music) uncommercialized and full-blooded, esp. showing traditional or ethnic origins.

root veg·e·ta·ble ▶ n. the fleshy enlarged root of a plant used as a vegetable, e.g., a carrot, rutabaga, or beet.

root·worm ▶ n. an insect larva that feeds on the roots of plants.

rope /rōp/ ▶ n. **1** a length of strong cord made by twisting together strands of natural fibers such as hemp or artificial fibers such as polypropylene. ■ a lasso. ■ (**the rope**) used in reference to execution by hanging: *executions by the rope continued well into the twentieth century.* ■ (**the ropes**) the ropes enclosing a boxing or wrestling ring.
2 a quantity of roughly spherical objects such as onions or pearls strung together: *a rope of pearls.*
3 (**the ropes**) informal the established procedures in an organization or area of activity: *I want you to* ***show her the ropes*** | *new boys were expected to* ***learn the ropes*** *from the old hands.* [mid 19th cent.: with reference to ropes used in sailing.]
▶ v. [with obj.] catch, fasten, or secure with rope: *the calves must be roped and led out of the stockade* | *the climbers were all roped together.* ■ (**rope someone in/into**) persuade someone to take part in (an activity): *anyone who could play an instrument or sing in tune was roped in.* ■ (**rope something off**) enclose or separate an area with a rope or tape: *police roped off the area of the find.* ■ [no obj.] Climbing (of a party of climbers) connect each other together with a rope: *we stopped at the foot of the Cavales Ridge and roped up.* ■ [no obj.] (**rope down/up**) Climbing climb down or up using a rope: *the party had been roping down a hanging glacier.*
– PHRASES **the end of one's rope** see END. **give a man enough rope and he will hang himself** proverb given enough freedom of action a person will bring about their own downfall. **on the rope** Climbing roped together: *the technique of moving together on the rope.* **on the ropes** Boxing forced against the ropes by the opponent's attack. ■ in state of near collapse or defeat: *behind the apparent success the company was on the ropes.*
– DERIVATIVES **rop·er** n.
– ORIGIN Old English *rāp*, of Germanic origin; related to Dutch *reep* and German *Reif*.

rope-a-dope /ˈrōp ə ˌdōp/ ▶ n. informal a boxing tactic of pretending to be trapped against the ropes, goading an opponent to throw tiring ineffective punches.
– ORIGIN 1970s: coined by Muhammad Ali, referring to a tactic in a boxing match with George Foreman.

rope lad·der ▶ n. two parallel ropes connected by short crosspieces, typically made of wood or metal, used as a ladder.

rope's end historical ▶ n. a short piece of rope used for flogging, esp. on ships.
▶ v. (**rope's-end**) [with obj.] flog (someone) with a rope's end.

rope·walk /ˈrōpˌwôk/ ▶ n. historical a long building or piece of ground where ropes are made.

rope·walk·er /ˈrōpˌwôkər/ ▶ n. dated a performer on a tightrope.
– DERIVATIVES **rope·walk·ing** /-kiNG/ n.

rope·way /ˈrōpˌwā/ ▶ n. a transportation system for materials or people, used esp. in mines or mountainous areas, in which cars are suspended from moving cables driven by a motor.

rope·y ▶ adj. variant spelling of ROPY.

rope yarn ▶ n. loosely twisted fibers used for making the strands of rope.

rop·ing /ˈrōpiNG/ ▶ n. **1** the action of catching or securing something with ropes: *calf roping.*
2 ropes collectively.

rop·y /ˈrōpē/ (also **ropey**) ▶ adj. (**ropier**, **ropiest**) **1** resembling a rope in being long, strong, and fibrous: *the ropy roots of the old tree.* ■ (of a liquid) resembling a rope in forming viscous or gelatinous threads: *his spit was thick and ropey as he spat.*
2 Brit. informal poor in quality or health; inferior: *a portrait by a pretty ropy artist.*
– DERIVATIVES **rop·i·ly** /ˈrōpəlē/ adv., **rop·i·ness** n.

roque /rōk/ ▶ n. a form of croquet played on a hard court surrounded by a bank.
– ORIGIN late 19th cent.: alteration of ROQUET.

Roque·fort /ˈrōkfərt/ ▶ n. trademark a soft blue cheese made from ewes' milk. It is ripened in limestone caves and has a strong flavor.
– ORIGIN from the name of a village in southern France.

ro·quet /rōˈkā/ Croquet ▶ v. (**roquets**, **roqueting** /-ˈkāiNG/, **roqueted** /-ˈkād/) [with obj.] strike (another ball) with one's own: *once you roquet a ball, you can hit it where you please.*
▶ n. an act of roqueting.
– ORIGIN mid 19th cent.: apparently an arbitrary alteration of the verb CROQUET, originally used in the same sense.

ro·quette /rōˈket/ ▶ n. another term for ROCKET[2].
– ORIGIN French.

ro-ro /ˈrō ˌrō/ ▶ abbr. roll-on roll-off.
– ORIGIN 1960s: abbreviation.

ror·qual /ˈrôrkwəl, -ˌkwôl/ ▶ n. a baleen whale of streamlined appearance with pleated skin on the underside. ● Family Balaenopteridae: two genera and six species, including the **common rorqual** (or fin whale).
– ORIGIN early 19th cent.: via French from Norwegian *røyrkval*, from Old Norse *reythr*, the specific name, + *hvalr* 'whale.'

Ror·schach test /ˈrôrˌsHäk/ ▶ n. Psychology a type of projective test used in psychoanalysis, in which a standard set of symmetrical ink blots of different shapes and colors is presented one by one to the subject, who is asked to describe what they suggest or resemble.
– ORIGIN 1920s: named after Hermann *Rorschach* (1884–1922), Swiss psychiatrist.

rort /rôrt/ ▶ n. Austral. informal **1** [often with modifier] a fraudulent or dishonest act or practice: *another exposed tax rort.*
2 a wild party.
– ORIGIN 1930s: back-formation from RORTY.

ror·ty /ˈrôrtē/ ▶ adj. (**rortier**, **rortiest**) Brit. informal boisterous and high-spirited.
– ORIGIN mid 19th cent.: of unknown origin.

ro·sace /rōˈzäs, rōˈzäs/ ▶ n. an ornamentation resembling a rose, in particular a rose window.
– ORIGIN mid 19th cent.: from French, from Latin *rosaceus* 'roselike' (see ROSACEOUS).

ro·sa·ce·a /rōˈzāsH(ē)ə/ (also **acne rosacea**) ▶ n. Medicine a condition in which certain facial blood vessels enlarge, giving the cheeks and nose a flushed appearance.
– ORIGIN late 19th cent.: from Latin, feminine of *rosaceus* in the sense 'rose-colored.'

ro·sa·ceous /rōˈzāsHəs/ ▶ adj. Botany of, relating to, or denoting plants of the rose family (Rosaceae).
– ORIGIN mid 18th cent.: from modern Latin *Rosaceae* (based on Latin *rosa* 'rose') + -OUS.

ros·an·i·line /rōˈzanl-in/ ▶ n. Chemistry a reddish-brown synthetic compound that is a base used in making a number of red dyes, notably fuchsin. ● A triphenylmethane derivative; chem. formula: $C_{20}H_{19}N_3$.
– ORIGIN mid 19th cent.: from ROSE[1] + ANILINE.

ro·sar·i·an /rōˈze(ə)rēən/ ▶ n. a person who cultivates roses, esp. as an occupation.
– ORIGIN mid 19th cent.: from Latin *rosarium* 'rose garden, rosary' + -AN.

Ro·sa·ri·o /rōˈsärēō/ an inland port on the Paraná River in east central Argentina; pop. 923,800 (est. 2005).

ro·sar·i·um /rōˈze(ə)rēəm/ ▶ n. (pl. **rosariums** or **rosaria** /-ˈze(ə)rēə/) formal a rose garden.
– ORIGIN mid 19th cent.: from Latin (see ROSARY).

ro·sa·ry /ˈrōzərē/ ▶ n. (pl. **rosaries**) (in the Roman Catholic Church) a form of devotion in which five (or fifteen) decades of Hail Marys are repeated, each decade preceded by an Our Father and followed by a Glory Be: *the congregation said the rosary.* ■ a string of beads for keeping count in such a devotion or in the devotions of some other religions. ■ a book containing such a devotion.
– ORIGIN late Middle English (in the sense 'rose garden'): from Latin *rosarium* 'rose garden,' based on *rosa* 'rose.'

ro·sa·ry pea ▶ n. a tropical plant of the pea family that produces extremely poisonous, shiny, scarlet beans with a black eye. ● Genus *Abrus*, family Leguminosae: several species, in particular *A. precatorius*. ■ the beans of any of these plants.

ros·coe /ˈräskō/ ▶ n. informal, dated a gun, esp. a pistol or revolver.
– ORIGIN early 20th cent.: from the surname *Roscoe*.

Ros·com·mon /räsˈkämən/ a county in the north central part of the Republic of Ireland, in the province of Connacht; pop. 58,768 (2006). ■ its county town; pop. 5,017 (2006).

Rose /rōz/, Pete (1941–), US baseball player and manager; full name *Peter Edward Rose*; nickname **Charlie Hustle**. He played for the Cincinnati Reds 1963–78, the Philadelphia Phillies 1979–83, the Montreal Expos 1984, and the Reds again 1984–86. From 1984 until 1988, he also managed the Reds. He holds the major league record for hits with 4,256. In 1989, amid allegations of betting on baseball games, he was suspended permanently from baseball.

rose[1] /rōz/ ▶ n. **1** a prickly bush or shrub that typically bears red, pink, yellow, or white fragrant flowers, native to north temperate regions. Numerous hybrids and cultivars have been developed and are widely grown as ornamentals. ● Genus *Rosa*, family Rosaceae (the **rose family**). This large family includes most temperate fruits (apple, plum, peach, cherry, blackberry, strawberry) as well as the hawthorns, rowans, potentillas, and avens. ■ the flower of such a plant: *he sent her a dozen red roses* | [as modifier] *a rose garden.* ■ used in names of other plants whose flowers resemble roses, e.g., **rose of Sharon**. ■ used in similes and comparisons in reference to the rose flower's beauty or its typical rich red color: *she looked as beautiful*

r

as a rose. ■ [often with negative] (**roses**) used to express favorable circumstances or ease of success: *all is not roses in the firm today.*
2 a thing representing or resembling the flower, in particular: ■ a stylized representation of the flower in heraldry or decoration, typically with five petals (esp. as a national emblem of England): *the Tudor rose.* ■ short for **COMPASS ROSE**. ■ short for **ROSE WINDOW**.
3 a perforated cap attached to a shower, the spout of a watering can, or the end of a hose to produce a spray.
4 a warm pink or light crimson color: *the rose and gold of dawn* | [as modifier] *the 100% cotton line is available in rose pink and ocean blue* | [in combination] *leaves with rose-red margins.* ■ (usu. **roses**) used in reference to a rosy complexion, esp. that of a young woman: *the fresh air will soon put the roses back in her cheeks.*
▶ **v.** [with obj.] literary make rosy: *a warm flush now rosed her hitherto blue cheeks.*
– PHRASES **a bed of roses** see **BED**. **come up roses** (of a situation) develop in a very favorable way: *new boyfriend, successful career—everything was coming up roses.* **under the rose** archaic in confidence; under pledge of secrecy. See also **SUB ROSA**.
– DERIVATIVES **rose·like** /-ˌlīk/ **adj.**
– ORIGIN Old English *rōse*, of Germanic origin, from Latin *rosa*; reinforced in Middle English by Old French *rose*.

rose[2] past of **RISE**.

ro·sé /rōˈzā/ ▶ **n.** any light pink wine, colored by only brief contact with red grape skins.
– ORIGIN French, literally 'pink.'

rose ap·ple ▶ **n.** a tropical evergreen tree cultivated for its foliage and fragrant fruit. ● Genus *Syzygium*, family Myrtaceae: several species, in particular the Southeast Asian *S. jambos*. ■ the spherical white rose-scented fruit of this tree.

ro·se·ate /ˈrōzēət, -ˌāt/ ▶ **adj. 1** rose-colored: *the early, roseate light.* ■ used in names of birds with partly pink plumage, e.g., **roseate tern**, **roseate spoonbill**.
2 optimistic; promising good fortune: *his letters home give a very good, although somewhat too roseate, idea of how he lived.*
– ORIGIN late Middle English: from Latin *roseus* 'rosy' (from *rosa* 'rose') + **-ATE**[2].

Ro·seau /rōˈzō/ the capital of Dominica in the Caribbean; pop. 14,000 (est. 2007).

rose·bay /ˈrōzˌbā/ ▶ **n. 1** a rhododendron. ● Genus *Rhododendron*, family Ericaceae: several species, including the **great rhododendron** (*R. maximum*) of eastern North America.
2 (also **rosebay willow herb**) chiefly Brit. the pink-flowered willow herb *Epilobium angustifolium*, a common fireweed.

rose-breast·ed gros·beak ▶ **n.** a North American grosbeak, the male of which is black and white with a pinkish-red breast patch. ● *Pheucticus ludovicianus*, family Emberizidae (subfamily Cardinalinae).

rose·bud /ˈrōzˌbəd/ ▶ **n.** an unopened flower of a rose.

rose chaf·er ▶ **n.** a brilliant green or copper-colored day-flying chafer (beetle) that feeds on roses and other flowers. The larvae typically live in rotting timber. ● Genus *Marodactylus*, family Scarabaeidae: three species.

rose-col·ored ▶ **adj.** of a warm pink color: *rose-colored silks.* ■ used in reference to a naively optimistic or unrealistic viewpoint: *you are still seeing the profession through rose-colored glasses.*

rose dia·mond ▶ **n.** a hemispherical diamond with the curved part cut in triangular facets.

rose·fish /ˈrōzˌfisн/ ▶ **n.** (pl. **same** or **rosefishes**) the redfish of the North Atlantic (*Sebastes marinus*).

rose ge·ra·ni·um ▶ **n.** a pink-flowered pelargonium with fragrant leaves. ● *Pelargonium graveolens*, family Geraniaceae.

rose hip ▶ **n.** see **HIP**[2].

ro·sel·la /rōˈzelə/ ▶ **n.** an Australian parakeet with vivid green, red, yellow, or blue plumage. ● Genus *Platycercus*, family Psittacidae: several species.
– ORIGIN mid 19th cent.: alteration of *Rosehill*, New South Wales, where the bird was first found.

rose mad·der ▶ **n.** a pale shade of pink.

ro·se·ma·ling /ˈrōzəˌmäliNG, ˈrōsə-/ ▶ **n.** the art, originating in Norway, of painting wooden furniture and objects with flower motifs. ■ painted flower motifs of this type.
– DERIVATIVES **ro·se·maled** /-ˌmäld, -ˌmält/ **adj.**
– ORIGIN 1940s: from Norwegian, literally 'rose painting.'

rose mal·low ▶ **n.** a plant of the mallow family with typically large pink or white flowers, several species of which are cultivated as ornamentals. ● Genus *Hibiscus*, family Malvaceae: many species, including the showy pink-flowered **swamp rose mallow** (*H. palustris*), found esp. in coastal marshes of the eastern US.

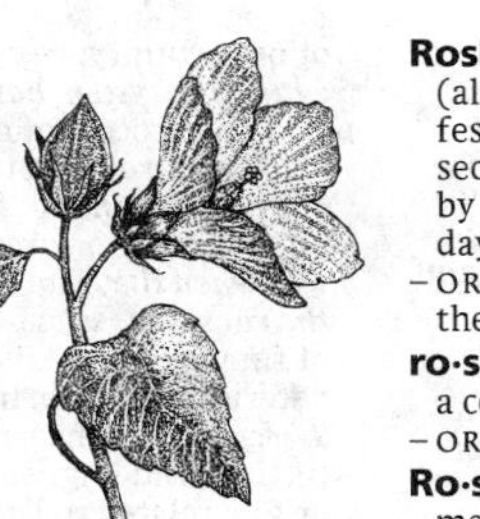

swamp rose mallow

rose·mar·y /ˈrōzˌme(ə)rē/ ▶ **n.** an evergreen aromatic shrub of the mint family, native to southern Europe. The narrow leaves are used as a culinary herb, in perfumery, and as an emblem of remembrance. ● *Rosmarinus officinalis*, family Labiatae.
– ORIGIN Middle English *rosmarine*, based on Latin *ros marinus*, from *ros* 'dew' + *marinus* 'of the sea.' The spelling change was due to association with **ROSE**[1] and **MARY**[1].

Rose·mead /ˈrōzˌmēd/ a city in southwestern California, east of Los Angeles; pop. 54,412 (est. 2008).

Ros·en·berg /ˈrōzənˌbərg/ US husband and wife spy team. **Julius** (1918–53) and **Ethel Greenglass** (1915–53) were Communist Party members who were tried and convicted of espionage in 1951. They were executed in 1953.

rose of Jer·i·cho ▶ **n.** an annual desert plant whose dead branches fold inward around the mature seeds forming a ball that is blown about, native to North Africa and the Middle East. ● *Anastatica hierochuntica*, family Brassicaceae.

rose of Shar·on ▶ **n. 1** a shrub of the mallow family, with rose, lavender, or white flowers. ● *Hibiscus syriacus*, family Malvaceae.
2 a St. John's wort with dense foliage and large golden-yellow flowers, native to southeastern Europe and Asia Minor and widely cultivated for ground cover. Also called **AARON'S BEARD**. ● *Hypericum calycinum*, family Guttiferae.
3 (in biblical use) a flowering plant of unknown identity.

ro·se·o·la /ˌrōzēˈōlə, rōˈzēələ/ ▶ **n.** Medicine a rose-colored rash occurring in measles, typhoid fever, syphilis, and some other diseases. ■ (in full **roseola infantum** /inˈfantəm/) a disease of young children in which a fever is followed by a rash, caused by a herpes virus.
– ORIGIN early 19th cent.: modern variant of **RUBEOLA**, from Latin *roseus* 'rose-colored.'

rose quartz ▶ **n.** a translucent pink variety of quartz.

rose-tint·ed ▶ **adj.** another term for **ROSE-COLORED**.

Ro·set·ta Stone /rōˈzetə/ an inscribed stone found near Rosetta on the western mouth of the Nile in 1799. Its text is written in three scripts: hieroglyphic, demotic, and Greek. The deciphering of the hieroglyphs by Jean-François Champollion in 1822 led to the interpretation of many other early records of Egyptian civilization. ■ (as noun **a Rosetta stone**) a key to some previously undecipherable mystery or unattainable understanding.

ro·sette /rōˈzet/ ▶ **n. 1** a rose-shaped decoration, typically made of ribbon and awarded to winners of a competition.
2 a design, arrangement, or growth resembling a rose, in particular: ■ Architecture a carved or molded ornament resembling or representing a rose. ■ Biology a marking or group of markings resembling a rose. ■ a roselike cluster of parts, esp. a radiating arrangement of horizontally spreading leaves at the base of a low-growing plant. ■ a rose diamond.
– DERIVATIVES **ro·set·ted** /rōˈzetəd/ **adj.**
– ORIGIN mid 18th cent.: from French, diminutive of *rose* (see **ROSE**[1]).

Rose·ville /ˈrōzˌvil/ **1** a city in northeastern California, northeast of Sacramento; pop. 112,660 (est. 2008).
2 a city in southeastern Michigan, northeast of Detroit; pop. 46,782 (est. 2008).

rose wa·ter ▶ **n.** water scented with rose petals, used as a perfume and for culinary purposes, and formerly in medicinal preparations.

rose win·dow ▶ **n.** a circular window with mullions or tracery radiating in a form suggestive of a rose.

rose·wood /ˈrōzˌwo͝od/ ▶ **n. 1** fragrant close-grained tropical timber with a distinctive fragrance, used particularly for making furniture and musical instruments.
2 the tree that produces this timber. ● Genus *Dalbergia*, family Leguminosae: several species, including **Indian rosewood** (*D. sissoo*), which is often cultivated in warm areas as an ornamental. ■ used in names of other trees that yield similar timber.

Rosh Ha·sha·nah /ˌrōsн (h)əˈsнōnə, ˌräsн, -ˈsнänə/ (also **Rosh Hashana**) ▶ **n.** the Jewish New Year festival, held on the first (also sometimes the second) day of Tishri (in September). It is marked by the blowing of the shofar, and begins the ten days of penitence culminating in Yom Kippur.
– ORIGIN Hebrew, literally 'head (i.e., beginning) of the year.'

ro·shi /ˈrōsнē/ ▶ **n.** (pl. **roshis**) the spiritual leader of a community of Zen Buddhist monks.
– ORIGIN Japanese.

Ro·si·cru·cian /ˌrōzəˈkro͞osнən, -ˌräzə-/ ▶ **n.** a member of a secretive 17th- and 18th-century society devoted to the study of metaphysical, mystical, and alchemical lore. An anonymous pamphlet of 1614 about a mythical 15th-century knight called Christian Rosenkreuz is said to have launched the movement. ■ a member of any of a number of later organizations deriving from this.
▶ **adj.** of or relating to the Rosicrucians.
– DERIVATIVES **Ro·si·cru·cian·ism** /-ˌnizəm/ **n.**
– ORIGIN from modern Latin *rosa crucis* (or *crux*), Latinization of German *Rosenkreuz*, + **-IAN**.

ros·in /ˈräzən/ ▶ **n.** resin, esp. the solid amber residue obtained after the distillation of crude turpentine oleoresin, or of naphtha extract from pine stumps. It is used in adhesives, varnishes, and inks and for treating the bows of stringed instruments.
▶ **v.** (**rosins, rosining, rosined**) [with obj.] rub (something, esp. the bow of a stringed instrument) with rosin.
– DERIVATIVES **ros·in·y adj.**
– ORIGIN Middle English: from medieval Latin *rosina*, from Latin *resina* (see **RESIN**).

ro·so·li·o /rōˈzōlēˌō/ ▶ **n.** (pl. **rosolios**) a sweet cordial made in Italy from alcohol, raisins, sugar, rose petals, cloves, and cinnamon.
– ORIGIN Italian, from modern Latin *ros solis* 'dew of the sun.'

Ross[1] /rôs/, Araminta, see **TUBMAN**.

Ross[2], Betsy (1752–1836), US patriot and seamstress; full name *Elizabeth Griscom Ross*. She is credited with having made the first flag of the US in June 1776.

Ross[3], Diana (1944–), US pop and soul singer. Originally the lead singer of the Supremes, she went on to become a successful solo artist. She portrayed Billie Holiday in the movie *Lady Sings the Blues* (1973).

Ross[4], Sir James Clark (1800–62), British explorer. He discovered the north magnetic pole in 1831 and, while heading an expedition to the Antarctic from 1839 to 1843, also discovered Ross Island, Ross Dependency, and the Ross Sea.

Ross[5], Sir John (1777–1856), British explorer. He led an expedition to Baffin Bay in 1818 and another in search of the Northwest Passage between 1829 and 1833.

Ross[6], Sir Ronald (1857–1932), British physician. He confirmed that the *Anopheles* mosquito transmitted malaria and then elucidated the stages in the malarial parasite's life cycle. Nobel Prize for Physiology or Medicine (1902).

Ross De·pend·en·cy the part of Antarctica that lies south of latitude 60° south between longitudes 150° and 160° west that is administered by New Zealand.
– ORIGIN named after J. C. *Ross* (see **ROSS**[4]).

Ros·sel·li·ni /ˌrôsəˈlēnē, ˌräs-/, Roberto (1906–77), Italian movie director. He is known for his neorealist movies, particularly his quasi-documentary World War II trilogy: *Rome, Open City* (1945), *Paisà* (1946), and *Germany, Year Zero* (1948).

Ros·set·ti[1] /rəˈzetē/, Christina (Georgina) (1830–94), English poet. She wrote much religious and love poetry and children's verse. She was the sister of Dante Gabriel Rossetti.

Ros·set·ti[2], Dante Gabriel (1828–82), English painter and poet; full name *Gabriel Charles Dante Rossetti*. A founder of the Pre-Raphaelite brotherhood 1848, he is best known for his idealized images of women, including *Beata Beatrix* (*c.*1863) and *The Blessed Damozel* (1871–79). He was the brother of Christina Rossetti.

Ros·si·ni /rəˈsēnē/, Gioacchino Antonio (1792–1868), Italian composer, one of the creators of Italian bel canto. He wrote over 30 operas, including *The Barber of Seville* (1816) and *William Tell* (1829).

Ross Sea a large arm of the Pacific Ocean that forms a deep indentation in the coast of Antarctica.
– ORIGIN named after J. C. *Ross* (see **ROSS**[4]).

Ross's goose ▶ **n.** a small Arctic goose that breeds in northern Canada. ● *Anser rossi*.

PRONUNCIATION KEY ə *ago, up*; ər *over, fur*; a *hat*; ā *ate*; ä *car*; e *let*; ē *see*; i *fit*; ī *by*; NG *sing*; ō *go*; ô *law, for*; oi *toy*; o͝o *good*; o͞o *goo*; ou *out*; TH *thin*; TH *then*; ZH *vision*

Ross's gull ▶ **n.** a pinkish-white Arctic gull. ● *Rhodostethia rosea.*

Ros·tand /ˈräs,tand, rôˈstäN/, Edmond (1868–1918), French playwright and poet. He romanticized the life of the 17th-century soldier, duelist, and writer Cyrano de Bergerac in his poetic drama of that name (1897).

ros·ter /ˈrästər, ˈrô-/ ▶ **n.** a list or plan showing turns of duty or leave for individuals or groups in an organization: *next week's duty roster.* ■ a list of members of a team or organization, in particular of athletes available for team selection.
▶ **v.** [with obj.] (usu. **be rostered**) chiefly Brit. assign according to a duty roster: *the locomotive is rostered for service on Sunday.*
– ORIGIN early 18th cent. (originally denoting a list of duties and leave for military personnel): from Dutch *rooster* 'list,' earlier 'gridiron,' from *roosten* 'to roast,' with reference to its parallel lines.

rösti /ˈrôstē, ˈro͞oSHtē/ ▶ **n.** (pl. **same**) a Swiss dish of grated potatoes formed into a small flat cake and fried: *place four of the rösti in the pan.*
– ORIGIN 1950s: from Swiss German.

Ros·tock /ˈrästäk, ˈrôstôk/ an industrial port on the Baltic coast of Germany; pop. 199,900 (est. 2006).

Ro·stov /rəˈstôf/ a port and industrial city in southwestern Russia, on the Don River near its point of entry into the Sea of Azov; pop. 1,048,700 (est. 2008). Full name **Rostov-on-Don**.

ros·tra /ˈrästrə, ˈrô-/ plural form of ROSTRUM.

ros·tral /ˈrästrəl, ˈrô-/ ▶ **adj. 1** Anatomy situated or occurring near the front end of the body, esp. in the region of the nose and mouth or (in an embryo) near the hypophyseal region: *the rostral portion of the brain.*
2 Zoology of or on the rostrum: *in these snakes the rostral shield is enlarged and flattened.*
3 (of a column, etc.) adorned with the rams of ancient warships or with representations of these.
– DERIVATIVES **ros·tral·ly** **adv.**
– ORIGIN early 19th cent.: from ROSTRUM + -AL.

Ros·tro·po·vich /,rästrəˈpōvicH/, Mstislav Leopoldovich (1927–2007), Russian cellist, pianist, and conductor. He came to the US in 1975 and was music director and conductor of the National Symphony Orchestra in Washington, DC, 1977–94.

ros·trum /ˈrästrəm, ˈrô-/ ▶ **n.** (pl. **rostra** /ˈrästrə, ˈrô-/ or **rostrums**) **1** a raised platform on which a person stands to make a public speech, receive an award or medal, play music, or conduct an orchestra. ■ a similar platform for supporting a movie or television camera.
2 chiefly Zoology a beaklike projection, esp. a stiff snout or anterior prolongation of the head in an insect, crustacean, or cetacean.
– DERIVATIVES **ros·trate** /ˈräs,trāt, ˈrô,strāt/ **adj.** (sense 2).
– ORIGIN mid 16th cent.: from Latin, literally 'beak' (from *rodere* 'gnaw'). The word was originally used (at first in the plural *rostra*) to denote part of the Forum in Rome, which was decorated with the beaks of captured galleys, and was used as a platform for public speakers.

Ros·well /ˈräzwel, -wəl/ **1** a city in northwestern Georgia, north of Atlanta; pop. 87,657 (est. 2008).
2 a town in southeastern New Mexico, the scene of a mysterious crash in July 1947. Controversy has surrounded claims by some investigators that the crashed object was a UFO; pop. 46,198 (est. 2008).

ros·y /ˈrōzē/ ▶ **adj.** (**rosier, rosiest**) **1** (esp. of a person's skin) colored like a pink or red rose, typically as an indication of health, youth, or embarrassment: *the memory had the power to make her cheeks turn rosy.*
2 promising or suggesting good fortune or happiness; hopeful: *the strategy has produced results beyond the most rosy forecasts.* ■ easy and pleasant: *life could never be rosy for them.*
– DERIVATIVES **ros·i·ly** /ˈrōzəlē/ **adv.**, **ros·i·ness** **n.**

ros·y cross ▶ **n.** an equal-armed cross with a rose at its center, the emblem of the Rosicrucians.

ros·y finch ▶ **n.** a finch found in Asia and western North America, the male of which has pinkish underparts and rump. ● Genus *Leucosticte*, family Fringillictae: three species, in particular *L. arctoa.*

rot /rät/ ▶ **v.** (**rots, rotting, rotted**) (chiefly of animal or vegetable matter) decay or cause to decay by the action of bacteria and fungi; decompose: [no obj.] *the chalets were neglected and their woodwork was rotting away* | [with obj.] *caries sets in at a weak point and spreads to rot the whole tooth.* ■ gradually deteriorate through lack of attention or opportunity: *he cannot understand the way the education system has been allowed to rot.*
▶ **n. 1** the process of decaying: *the leaves were turning black with rot.* ■ rotten or decayed matter: *she was busy cutting the rot from the potatoes.* ■ (**the rot**) a process of deterioration; a decline in standards: *it was when they moved back to the family home that the rot set in.* ■ [usu. with modifier] any of a number of fungal or bacterial diseases that cause tissue deterioration, esp. in plants.
2 informal nonsense; rubbish: *don't talk rot.*
– ORIGIN Old English *rotian* (verb), of Germanic origin; related to Dutch *rotten*; the noun (Middle English) may have come via Scandinavian.

rot. ▶ **abbr.** ■ rotating. ■ rotation.

ro·ta /ˈrōtə/ ▶ **n. 1** chiefly Brit. a list showing when each of a number of people has to do a particular job: *a cleaning rota.* Compare with ROSTER.
2 (**the Rota**) the supreme ecclesiastical and secular court of the Roman Catholic Church.
– ORIGIN early 17th cent.: from Latin, literally 'wheel.'

ro·ta·mer /ˈrōtəmər/ ▶ **n.** Chemistry any of a number of isomers of a molecule that can be interconverted by rotation of part of the molecule around a particular bond.
– ORIGIN 1960s: from *rotational* (see ROTATION) + -MER.

Ro·ta·ry /ˈrōtərē/ (in full **Rotary International**) a worldwide charitable society of businessmen, businesswomen, and professional people, formed in 1905.
– DERIVATIVES **Ro·tar·i·an** /rōˈte(ə)rēən/ **n. & adj.**
– ORIGIN so named because members hosted events in rotation.

ro·ta·ry /ˈrōtərē/ ▶ **adj.** (of motion) revolving around a center or axis; rotational: *a rotary motion.* ■ (of a thing) acting by means of rotation, esp. (of a machine) operating through the rotation of some part: *a rotary mower.*
▶ **n.** (pl. **rotaries**) **1** a rotary machine, engine, or device.
2 a traffic circle.
– ORIGIN mid 18th cent.: from medieval Latin *rotarius*, from *rota* 'wheel.'

Ro·ta·ry Club ▶ **n.** a local branch of Rotary.

ro·ta·ry en·gine ▶ **n.** an engine that produces rotary motion or that has a rotating part or parts, in particular: ■ an aircraft engine with a fixed crankshaft around which cylinders and propeller rotate. ■ a Wankel engine.

ro·ta·ry press ▶ **n.** a printing press that prints from a rotating cylindrical surface onto paper forced against it by another cylinder.

ro·ta·ry wing ▶ **n.** [usu. as modifier] an airfoil that rotates in an approximately horizontal plane, providing all or most of the lift in a helicopter or autogiro.

ro·tate /ˈrō,tāt/ ▶ **v.** move or cause to move in a circle around an axis or center: [no obj.] *the wheel continued to rotate* | (as adj. **rotating**) *a rotating drum* | [with obj.] *the small directional side rockets rotated the craft.* ■ [no obj.] pass to each member of a group in a regularly recurring order: *the job of chairing the meeting rotates.* ■ [with obj.] grow (different crops) in succession on a particular piece of land to avoid exhausting the soil: *these crops were sometimes rotated with grass.* ■ [with obj.] change the position of (tires) on a motor vehicle to distribute wear evenly.
– DERIVATIVES **ro·tat·a·ble** /ˈrō,tātəbəl, rōˈtāt-/ **adj.**, **ro·ta·tive** /ˈrō,tātiv/ **adj.**, **ro·ta·to·ry** /ˈrōtə,tôrē/ **adj.**
– ORIGIN late 17th cent.: from Latin *rotat-* 'turned in a circle,' from the verb *rotare*, from *rota* 'wheel.'

ro·ta·tion /rōˈtāSHən/ ▶ **n.** the action of rotating around an axis or center: *the moon moves in the same direction as the earth's rotation.* ■ (also **crop rotation**) the action or system of rotating crops. ■ Forestry the cycle of planting, felling, and replanting. ■ the passing of a privilege or responsibility from one member of a group to another in a regularly recurring succession: *it has become common for senior academics to act as heads of department in rotation.* ■ a tour of duty, esp. by a medical practitioner in training: *she was completing a rotation in trauma surgery.* ■ Mathematics the conceptual operation of turning a system around an axis. ■ Mathematics another term for CURL (sense 2 of the noun).
– DERIVATIVES **ro·ta·tion·al** /-SHənl/ **adj.**, **ro·ta·tion·al·ly** /-SHənl-ē/ **adv.**
– ORIGIN mid 16th cent.: from Latin *rotatio(n-)*, from the verb *rotare* (see ROTATE).

ro·ta·tor /ˈrō,tātər/ ▶ **n.** a thing that rotates or that causes something to rotate. ■ Anatomy a muscle whose contraction causes or assists in the rotation of a part of the body.

ro·ta·tor cuff ▶ **n.** Anatomy a capsule with fused tendons that supports the arm at the shoulder joint and is often subject to athletic injury.

ro·ta·vi·rus /ˈrōtə,vīrəs/ ▶ **n.** Medicine any of a group of RNA viruses, some of which cause acute enteritis in humans.
– ORIGIN 1970s: modern Latin, from Latin *rota* 'wheel' + VIRUS.

ROTC /ˈrätsē/ ▶ **abbr.** (in the US) Reserve Officers' Training Corps.

rote /rōt/ ▶ **n.** mechanical or habitual repetition of something to be learned: *a poem learned by rote in childhood.*
– ORIGIN Middle English (also in the sense 'habit, custom'): of unknown origin.

ro·te·none /ˈrōtn,ōn/ ▶ **n.** Chemistry a toxic crystalline substance obtained from the roots of derris and related plants, widely used as an insecticide. ● A polycyclic ketone; chem. formula: $C_{23}H_{22}O_6$.
– ORIGIN 1920s: from Japanese *rotenon* (from *roten* 'derris') + -ONE.

rot·gut /ˈrät,gət/ ▶ **n.** informal poor-quality and potentially toxic alcoholic liquor.

Roth /rôTH, räTH/, Philip (Milton) (1933–), US novelist and short-story writer. He often wrote with irony and humor about the complexity and diversity of contemporary American Jewish life. Notable works: *Portnoy's Complaint* (1969), *Zuckerman Bound* (1985), and *American Pastoral* (1997).

Roth IRA /rôTH, räTH/ ▶ **n.** an individual retirement account allowing a person to set aside after-tax income up to a specified amount each year. Both earnings on the account and withdrawals after age 59½ are tax-free.
– ORIGIN created in 1997 and named for Senator William Victor Roth II (1921–2003) of Delaware, who proposed this in Congress.

Roth·ko /ˈräTHkō/, Mark (1903–70), US painter, born in Latvia; born *Marcus Rothkovich*. A leading figure in color-field painting, he painted hazy and seemingly floating rectangles of color. His series of nine paintings for the Seagram Building in New York City includes *Black on Maroon* (1958).

Roth·schild /ˈrôTH(s)CHīld, ˈrôs-/, Meyer Amschel (1743–1812), German financier. He founded the Rothschild banking house in Frankfurt at the end of the 19th century and was financial adviser to the landgrave of Hesse. His five sons all entered banking.

ro·ti /ˈrōtē/ ▶ **n.** (pl. **rotis**) Indian bread, esp. a flat round bread cooked on a griddle.
– ORIGIN from Hindi *roṭī*.

ro·ti·fer /ˈrōtəfər/ ▶ **n.** Zoology a minute multicellular aquatic animal of the phylum Rotifera.

Ro·tif·er·a /rōˈtifərə/ Zoology a small phylum of minute multicellular aquatic animals that have a characteristic wheellike ciliated organ used in swimming and feeding.
– ORIGIN modern Latin (plural), from Latin *rota* 'wheel' + *ferre* 'to bear.'

ro·ti·ni /rōˈtēnē/ ▶ **n.** pasta in short pieces with a helical shape.
– ORIGIN Italian, literally 'spirals.'

ro·tis·ser·ie /rōˈtisərē/ ▶ **n. 1** a cooking appliance with a rotating spit for roasting and barbecuing meat.
2 a restaurant specializing in roasted or barbecued meat.
– ORIGIN mid 19th cent.: from French *rôtisserie*, from *rôtir* 'to roast.'

ro·tis·se·rie league ▶ **n.** an association of individuals who simulate selecting, managing, and playing baseball, using the names and statistics of actual professional players to determine results.

ro·to·gra·vure /,rōtəgrəˈvyo͝or/ ▶ **n.** a printing system using a rotary press with intaglio cylinders, typically running at high speed and used for long print runs of magazines and stamps. ■ a sheet or magazine printed with this system, esp. the color magazine of a Sunday newspaper.
– ORIGIN early 20th cent.: from German *Rotogravur*, part of the name of a printing company.

ro·tor /ˈrōtər/ ▶ **n.** a rotary part of a machine or vehicle, in particular: ■ a hub with a number of radiating airfoils that is rotated in an approximately horizontal plane to provide the lift for a rotary-wing aircraft. ■ the rotating assembly in a turbine, esp. a wind turbine. ■ the armature of an electric motor. ■ the rotating part of the distributor of

r

an internal combustion engine that successively makes and breaks electrical contacts so that each spark plug fires in turn. ■ the rotating container in a centrifuge. ■ the rotary winder of a clockwork watch. ■ Meteorology a large eddy in which the air circulates around a horizontal axis, esp. in the lee of a mountain.
– ORIGIN early 20th cent.: formed irregularly from ROTATOR.

ro·tor·craft /ˈrōtərˌkraft/ ▶ n. (pl. **same**) a rotary-wing aircraft, such as a helicopter or autogiro.

ro·tor wash ▶ n. air turbulence caused by a helicopter rotor.

ro·to·scope /ˈrōtəˌskōp/ ▶ n. a device that projects and enlarges individual frames of filmed live action to permit them to be used to create cartoon animation and composite film sequences. ■ a computer application that combines live action and other images in a film.
▶ v. [with obj.] transfer (an image from live action film) into another film sequence using a rotoscope.
– ORIGIN 1950s: origin obscure; perhaps the same word as 19th-cent. *rotascope*, denoting a kind of gyroscope.

ro·to·till·er /ˈrōtəˌtilər/ ▶ n. trademark a motor-driven machine with rotating blades for breaking up or tilling the soil.
– DERIVATIVES **ro·to·till** v.

rot·ten /ˈrätn/ ▶ adj. (**rottener, rottenest**) suffering from decay: *rotten eggs* | *the supporting beams were rotten.* ■ morally, socially, or politically corrupt: *he believed that the whole art business was rotten.* ■ informal very bad: *she was a rotten cook.* ■ informal extremely unpleasant: *it's rotten for you having to cope on your own.* ■ [predic.] informal unwell: *she tried to tell me she felt rotten.*
▶ adv. informal to an extreme degree; very much: *your mother said that I **spoiled** you **rotten**.*
– DERIVATIVES **rot·ten·ly** adv., **rot·ten·ness** n.
– ORIGIN Middle English: from Old Norse *rotinn.*

rot·ten bor·ough ▶ n. Brit. historical a borough that was able to elect a representative to Parliament though having very few voters, the choice of representative typically being in the hands of one person or family.
– ORIGIN so named because the borough was found to have "decayed" to the point of no longer having a constituency.

rot·ten·stone /ˈrätnˌstōn/ ▶ n. weathered siliceous limestone used as a powder or paste for polishing metals.

rot·ter /ˈrätər/ ▶ n. informal, dated, chiefly Brit. a cruel, stingy, or unkind person.

Rot·ter·dam /ˈrätərˌdam/ a city in the Netherlands, at the mouth of the Meuse River, 15 miles (25 km) inland from the North Sea; pop. 582,951 (2008). It has extensive shipbuilding and petrochemical industries.

Rott·wei·ler /ˈrätˌwīlər, ˈrôtˌvīlər/ ▶ n. a large powerful dog of a tall black-and-tan breed.
– ORIGIN early 20th cent.: German, from *Rottweil*, the name of a town in southwestern Germany.

Rottweiler

ro·tund /rōˈtənd, ˈrōˌtənd/ ▶ adj. **1** (of a person) plump. ■ round or spherical: *huge stoves held great rotund cauldrons.*
2 (of speech or literary style) indulging in grandiloquent expression.
– DERIVATIVES **ro·tun·di·ty** /-ˈtəndətē/ n., **ro·tund·ly** adv.
– ORIGIN late 15th cent.: from Latin *rotundus*, from *rotare* 'rotate.'

ro·tun·da /rōˈtəndə/ ▶ n. a round building or room, esp. one with a dome.
– ORIGIN early 17th cent.: alteration of Italian *rotonda (camera)* 'round (chamber),' feminine of *rotondo* 'round' (see ROTUND).

Rou·ault /ro͞oˈō/, Georges (Henri) (1871–1958), French painter and engraver. Associated with expressionism, he used vivid colors and simplified forms enclosed in thick black outlines.

rou·ble ▶ n. variant spelling of RUBLE.

rou·é /ro͞oˈā/ ▶ n. a debauched man, esp. an elderly one.
– ORIGIN early 19th cent.: French, literally 'broken on a wheel,' referring to the instrument of torture thought to be deserved by such a person.

Rou·en /ro͞oˈän, -ˈäN/ a port on the Seine River in northwestern France; pop. 110,276 (2006). Joan of Arc was tried and burned at the stake here in 1431.

Rou·en duck ▶ n. a bird of a breed of large duck resembling the wild mallard in coloring.

rouge[1] /ro͞oZH/ ▶ n. a red powder or cream used as a cosmetic for coloring the cheeks or lips. ■ another term for JEWELER'S ROUGE.
▶ v. [with obj.] (often as adj. **rouged**) color with rouge: *her brightly rouged cheeks.* ■ [no obj.] archaic apply rouge to one's cheeks.
– ORIGIN late Middle English (denoting the color red): from French, 'red,' from Latin *rubeus*. The cosmetic term dates from the mid 18th cent.

rouge[2] ▶ n. (in Canadian football) a single point awarded when the receiving team fails to run a kick out of its own end zone.
– ORIGIN late 19th cent.: of unknown origin.

rouge et noir /ˈro͞oZH ā ˈnwär/ ▶ n. a gambling card game in which cards are turned up on a table marked with red and black diamonds.
– ORIGIN late 18th cent.: French, literally 'red and black.'

Rouge, Riv·er /ro͞oZH/ a short river with several branches in and around Detroit in Michigan.

rou·get /ro͞oˈZHā, -ˈZHe/ ▶ n. French term for RED MULLET, used esp. in cooking.
– ORIGIN French.

rough /rəf/ ▶ adj. **1** having an uneven or irregular surface; not smooth or level: *take a square of sandpaper, rough side out.* ■ (of ground or terrain) having many bumps or other obstacles; difficult to cross: *they had to carry the victim across the rough, stony ground.* ■ not soft to the touch: *her skin felt dry and rough.* ■ (of a voice) coming out with difficulty so as to sound harsh and rasping: *his voice was rough with barely suppressed fury.* ■ (of wine or another alcoholic drink) sharp or harsh in taste. ■ denoting the face of a tennis or squash racket from which the loops formed in the stringing process project (used as a call when the racket is spun to decide the right to serve first or to choose ends). The opposite of SMOOTH.
2 (of a person or their behavior) not gentle; violent or boisterous: *strollers should be capable of withstanding rough treatment.* ■ (of an area or occasion) characterized by or notorious for the occurrence of violent behavior: *the workmen hate going to the rough areas of town.* ■ (of the sea) having large and dangerous waves: *the lifeboat crew braved rough seas to rescue a couple.* ■ (of weather) wild and stormy. ■ informal difficult and unpleasant; hard; severe: *the teachers gave me **a rough time** because my image didn't fit* | *the first day of a job is **rough on** everyone.* ■ [as complement] informal unwell: *the altitude had hit her and she was feeling rough.* ■ [as complement] informal depressed and anxious: *when he's feeling rough, he comes and talks things over to calm him down.*
3 not finished tidily or decoratively; plain and basic: *the customers sat at rough wooden tables.* ■ put together without the proper materials or skill; makeshift: *he had one arm in a rough sling.* ■ (of hair or fur) not smooth; coarse: *the creature's body was covered with rough hair.* ■ lacking sophistication or refinement: *she took care of him in her rough, kindly way.* ■ not worked out or correct in every detail: *he had a rough draft of his new novel.*
▶ adv. informal in a manner that lacks gentleness; harshly or violently: *treat 'em rough but treat 'em fair.*
▶ n. **1** chiefly Brit. a disreputable and violent person.
2 (on a golf course) longer grass around the fairway and the green: *his second shot was **in the rough** on the left.*
3 a preliminary sketch for a design: *I did a rough to work out the scale of the lettering.*
4 an uncut precious stone.
▶ v. [with obj.] **1** work or shape (something) in a rough, preliminary fashion: *flat surfaces of wood are **roughed down**.* ■ (**rough something out**) produce a preliminary and unfinished sketch or version of something: *the engineer roughed out a diagram on his notepad.* ■ make uneven or ruffled: ***rough up** the icing with a palette knife* | *the water was roughed by the wind.*
2 (**rough it**) live in discomfort with only basic necessities: *she had had to rough it alone in a dive.*
– PHRASES **bit of rough** Brit. informal a male sexual partner whose toughness or lack of sophistication is a source of attraction. **in the rough 1** in a natural state; without decoration or other treatment: *a diamond in the rough.* **2** in difficulties: *even before the recession hit, the project was in the rough.* **rough and ready** crude but effective: *a rough-and-ready estimating method.* ■ (of a person or place) unsophisticated or unrefined. **rough around the edges** having a few imperfections: *until we clean up and lay down the new carpet, it's going to look a little rough around the edges.* ■ not refined: *Donnie is a bit rough around the edges, but she loves him.* **the rough edge** (or **side**) **of one's tongue** a scolding: *you two stop quarreling or you'll get the rough edge of my tongue.* **rough edges** small imperfections in someone or something that is basically satisfactory. **rough justice** treatment that is not scrupulously fair or in accordance with the law. **rough passage** a journey over rough sea. ■ a difficult process of achieving something or of becoming successful: *the rough passage faced by the legislation.* **a rough ride** see RIDE. **rough stuff** boisterous or violent behavior. **sleep rough** Brit. sleep in uncomfortable conditions, typically outdoors. **take the rough with the smooth** accept the difficult or unpleasant aspects of life as well as the good.
– PHRASAL VERBS **rough someone up** informal beat someone up.
– DERIVATIVES **rough·ish** adj., **rough·ness** n.
– ORIGIN Old English *rūh*; related to Dutch *ruw* and German *rauh.*

rough·age /ˈrəfij/ ▶ n. fibrous indigestible material in vegetable foodstuffs that aids the passage of food and waste products through the gut. ■ Farming coarse, fibrous fodder.

rough and tum·ble ▶ n. a situation without rules or organization; a free-for-all: *the rough and tumble of political life* | [as modifier] *the rough-and-tumble atmosphere of the dealing room.*
– ORIGIN early 19th cent.: originally boxing slang.

rough breath·ing ▶ n. see BREATHING (sense 2).

rough·cast /ˈrəfˌkast/ ▶ n. plaster of lime, cement, and gravel, used on outside walls.
▶ adj. **1** (of a building or part of a building) coated with roughcast: *a plain stone building, roughcast and whitewashed.*
2 (of a person) lacking refinement: *she thought of the roughcast yeomen she would meet.*
▶ v. (past and past participle **roughcast**) [with obj.] coat (a wall) with roughcast: *the walls were to have been roughcast at the entrance bay.*

rough-coat·ed ▶ adj. (of a dog or other animal) having relatively coarse fur that does not lie flat.

rough cut ▶ n. the first version of a movie after preliminary editing.
▶ v. (**rough-cut**) [with obj.] cut (something) rapidly and without particular attention to quality or accuracy: *it would be best to rough-cut the boards to size with a portable saw.*

rough-dry ▶ v. [with obj.] dry (something) roughly or imperfectly: *she continued to rough-dry her hair.*

rough·en /ˈrəfən/ ▶ v. make or become rough: [with obj.] *the wind was roughening the surface of the river* | [no obj.] *his voice roughened.*

rough-hewn ▶ adj. denoting wood or stone that has been cut with a tool such as an ax, so that its surface is not smooth: *rough-hewn logs.* ■ not sophisticated, polished, or elegant: *a rough-hewn cinematic style.* ■ denoting or possessing attractively strong or bony facial features: *his angular, rough-hewn face.*
– DERIVATIVES **rough-hew** v.

rough·house informal ▶ v. /ˈrəfˌhous, -ˌhouz/ [no obj.] act in a boisterous, violent manner: *in front of the stage hundreds of teens and young adults roughhouse, flinging themselves into each other.* ■ [with obj.] handle (someone) roughly or violently: *the police department grabbed Danny as a suspect and roughhoused him.*
▶ n. /-ˌhous/ a violent disturbance or an instance of boisterous play.

rough·ing /ˈrəfiNG/ ▶ n. Ice Hockey unnecessary or excessive use of force, for which a penalty may be assessed: *both players draw five minutes for roughing.* ■ Football illegal bodily contact with the quarterback or kicker, for which a penalty is assessed.

rough·ly /ˈrəflē/ ▶ adv. **1** in a manner lacking gentleness; harshly or violently: *the man picked me up roughly.*
2 in a manner lacking refinement and precision: *people were crouching over roughly built brick fireplaces.* ■ approximately: *this is a walk of roughly*

13 *miles* | [sentence adverb] *the narrative is, **roughly speaking**, contemporary with the earliest of the gospels.*

rough·neck /ˈrəfˌnek/ ▶ **n. 1** informal a rough and uncouth person.
2 an oil rig worker.
▶ **v.** [no obj.] (usu. as noun **roughnecking**) work on an oil rig: *his savings from roughnecking are gone.*

rough·rid·er /ˈrəfˈrīdər/ (also **rough rider**) ▶ **n.** a person who breaks in or can ride unbroken horses. ■ a person who rides horses a lot. ■ (**Rough Rider**) a member of the cavalry unit in which Theodore Roosevelt fought during the Spanish-American War.

rough·shod /ˈrəfˌSHäd/ ▶ **adj.** archaic (of a horse) having shoes with nailheads projecting to prevent slipping.
– PHRASES **ride roughshod over** see RIDE.

rough tim·ber ▶ **n.** partly dressed timber, having only the branches removed.

rough trade ▶ **n.** informal male homosexual prostitution, esp. when involving brutality or sadism. ■ people involved in prostitution of this type.

rough-winged swal·low ▶ **n.** a brown-backed American swallow. ● *Stelgidopteryx ruficollis.*

rough·y /ˈrəfē/ ▶ **n.** (pl. **roughies**) **1** Austral. a marine fish with a deep laterally compressed body and large rough-edged scales that become spiny on the belly. ● Family Trachichthyidae: several genera and species, including the small Australian *Trachichthys australis*, which occurs on rocky reefs, and the ORANGE ROUGHY.
2 another term for RUFF[2] (sense 1).

rou·ille /ˈro͞o-ē, ro͞oˈēy(ə)/ ▶ **n.** a Provençal sauce made from pounded red chilies, garlic, breadcrumbs, and other ingredients blended with stock, typically added to bouillabaisse.
– ORIGIN French, literally 'rust,' with reference to the color.

rou·lade /ro͞oˈläd/ ▶ **n. 1** a dish cooked or served in the form of a roll, typically made from a flat piece of meat, fish, or sponge cake, spread with a soft filling and rolled up into a spiral.
2 a florid passage of runs in classical music for a virtuoso singer, esp. one sung to one syllable.
– ORIGIN French, from *rouler* 'to roll.'

rou·leau /ro͞oˈlō/ ▶ **n.** (pl. **rouleaux** /-ˈlōz/ or **rouleaus**) **1** a cylindrical packet of coins.
2 a coil or roll of ribbon, knitted wool, or other material, esp. used as trimming.
– ORIGIN late 17th cent.: French, from obsolete French *roule* 'a roll.'

rou·lette /ro͞oˈlet/ ▶ **n.**
1 a gambling game in which a ball is dropped onto a revolving wheel (**roulette wheel**) with numbered compartments, the players betting on the number at which the ball will come to rest.
2 a tool or machine with a revolving toothed wheel, used in engraving or for making slit-shaped perforations between postage stamps.
▶ **v.** [with obj.] make slit-shaped perforations in (paper, esp. sheets of postage stamps): *the pages are rouletted next to the binding.*
– ORIGIN mid 18th cent.: from French, diminutive of *rouelle* 'wheel,' from late Latin *rotella*, diminutive of Latin *rota* 'wheel.'

roulette wheel

round /round/ ▶ **adj. 1** shaped like or approximately like a circle or cylinder: *she was seated at a small, round table.* ■ having a curved shape like part of the circumference of a circle: *round arches.*
2 shaped like or approximately like a sphere: *a round glass ball* | *the grapes are small and round.* ■ (of a person's body) plump. ■ having a curved surface with no sharp or jagged projections: *the boulders look round and smooth.*
3 (of a voice) rich and mellow; not harsh.
4 [attrib.] (of a number) altered for convenience of expression or calculation, for example to the nearest whole number or multiple of ten or five: *the size of the fleet is given in round numbers.* ■ (of a number) convenient for calculation, typically through being a multiple of ten. ■ used to show that a figure has been completely and exactly reached: *a round dozen.* ■ archaic (of a sum of money) considerable: *his business is worth a round sum to me.*
5 archaic (of a person or their manner of speaking) not omitting or disguising anything; frank and truthful: *she berated him in good round terms.*
▶ **n. 1** a circular piece of a particular substance: *cut the pastry into rounds.* ■ a thick disk of beef cut from the haunch as a joint.
2 an act of visiting each of a number of people or places: *she **did the rounds of** her family to say goodbye* | *he **made the rounds of** the city's churches.* ■ a tour of inspection, typically repeated regularly, in which the safety or well-being of those visited is checked: *the doctor is just **making his rounds** in the wards.*
3 one of a sequence of sessions or groups of related actions or events, typically such that development or progress can be seen between one group and another: *the two sides held three rounds of talks.* ■ a division of a contest such as a boxing or wrestling match. ■ one of a succession of stages in a sporting contest or other competition, in each of which more candidates are eliminated: *the playoffs in the second round.* ■ an act of playing all the holes in a golf course once: *Eileen enjoys the occasional **round of golf**.*
4 a regularly recurring sequence of activities or functions: *their lives were a **daily round** of housework and laundry.* ■ Music a song for three or more unaccompanied voices or parts, each singing the same theme but starting one after another, at the same pitch or in octaves; a simple canon. ■ a set of drinks bought for all the members of a group, typically as part of a sequence in which each member in turn buys such a set: *it's my round.*
5 a measured quantity or number of something, in particular: ■ the amount of ammunition needed to fire one shot. ■ Archery a fixed number of arrows shot from a fixed distance.
▶ **adv.** chiefly Brit. variant of AROUND.
▶ **prep.** chiefly Brit. variant of AROUND.
▶ **v.** [with obj.] **1** pass and go around (something) so as to move on in a changed direction: *the ship rounded the cape and sailed north.*
2 alter (a number) to one less exact but more convenient for calculations: *we'll **round** the weight **up** to the nearest pound* | *the committee **rounded down** the figure* | *let's just **round** it **off** to an even ten dollars.*
3 give a round shape to: *a lathe that rounded chair legs.* ■ [no obj.] become circular in shape: *her eyes rounded in dismay.* ■ Phonetics pronounce (a vowel) with the lips narrowed and protruded.
– PHRASES **in the round 1** (of sculpture) standing free with all sides shown, rather than carved in relief against a ground. ■ treated fully and thoroughly; with all aspects shown or considered: *to understand social phenomena one must see them in the round.* **2** (of a theatrical performance) with the audience placed on at least three sides of the stage. **make** (or **go**) **the rounds** (of a story or joke) be passed on from person to person. **round about 1** on all sides or in all directions; surrounding someone or something: *everything round about was covered with snow.* **2** at a point or time approximately equal to: *they arrived round about nine.*
– PHRASAL VERBS **round something off** make the edges or corners of something smooth: *round off the spars with a soft plastic fitting.* ■ complete something in a satisfying or suitable way: *I rounded off my visit to Ganu by purchasing a number of exquisite masks.* **round on** make a sudden verbal attack on or unexpected retort to: *she rounded on me angrily.* **round something out** make something more complete: *round out the meal with fruit and salad.* **round someone/something up** drive or collect a number of people or animals together for a particular purpose: *in the afternoon the cows are rounded up for milking.* ■ arrest a number of people.
– DERIVATIVES **round·ish** adj., **round·ness** n.
– ORIGIN Middle English: from the Old French stem *round-*, from a variant of Latin *rotundus* 'rotund.'

USAGE On the difference in use between **round** and **around**, see usage at AROUND.

round·a·bout /ˈroundəˌbout/ ▶ **n. 1** British term for TRAFFIC CIRCLE.
2 British term for MERRY-GO-ROUND.
3 historical a close-fitting, waist-length jacket worn by men and boys.
▶ **adj.** not following a short direct route; circuitous: *we need to take a roundabout route to throw off any pursuit.* ■ not saying what is meant clearly and directly; circumlocutory: *in a roundabout way, he was fishing for information.*

round·ball /ˈroundˌbôl/ ▶ **n.** informal term for BASKETBALL.
– DERIVATIVES **round·ball·er** n.

round brack·ets ▶ **plural n.** Brit. parentheses.

round dance ▶ **n.** a folk dance in which the dancers form one large circle. ■ a ballroom dance such as a waltz or polka in which couples move in circles around the ballroom.

round·ed /ˈroundid/ ▶ **adj. 1** having a smooth, curved surface: *rounded gray hills.* ■ having a spherical shape: *its rounded, almost bulbous head.* ■ forming circular or elliptical shapes: *his writing was firm and rounded.* ■ Phonetics (of a vowel) pronounced with the lips pursed.
2 well developed in all aspects; complete and balanced: *we should educate children to become rounded human beings.*

roun·del /ˈroundl/ ▶ **n. 1** a small disk, esp. a decorative medallion. ■ a picture or pattern contained in a circle. ■ Heraldry a plain filled circle as a charge (often with a special name according to color). ■ Brit. a circular identifying mark painted on military aircraft, as, for example, the red, white, and blue of the RAF.
2 a short poem consisting of three stanzas of three lines each, rhyming alternately, with the opening words repeated as a refrain after the first and third stanzas. The form, a variant of the rondeau, was developed by Swinburne.
– ORIGIN Middle English: from Old French *rondel*, from *ro(u)nd-* (see ROUND).

roun·de·lay /ˈroundəˌlā, ˈrän-/ ▶ **n.** literary a short simple song with a refrain. ■ a circle dance.
– ORIGIN late Middle English: from Old French *rondelet*, from *rondel* (see RONDEL). The change in the ending was due to association with the final syllable of VIRELAY.

round·er /ˈroundər/ ▶ **n. 1** a person who frequents bars and is often drunk.
2 Brit. (in rounders) a complete run of a player through all the bases as a unit of scoring.

round·ers /ˈroundərz/ ▶ **plural n.** [treated as sing.] a ball game similar to baseball, played chiefly in British schools.

round go·by ▶ **n.** a Eurasian freshwater goby that threatens native species of fish in the Great Lakes and Mississippi basin. ● *Neogobius melanostomus*, family Gobiidae.

round hand ▶ **n.** a style of handwriting in which the letters have clear rounded shapes.

Round·head /ˈroundˌhed/ ▶ **n.** historical a member or supporter of the Parliamentary party in the English Civil War.
– ORIGIN so named because of the short-cropped hairstyle of the Puritans, who formed an important element in the party.

round·heel /ˈroundˌhēl/ ▶ **n.** informal a promiscuous woman.
– DERIVATIVES **round·heeled** adj.
– ORIGIN 1950s: with reference to worn-down heels, allowing the wearer to lean backwards.

round·house /ˈroundˌhous/ ▶ **n. 1** a locomotive maintenance shed built around a turntable.
2 informal a blow given with a wide sweep of the arm. ■ a wide turn on a surfboard.
3 chiefly historical a cabin or cabins on the after part of the quarterdeck of a sailing ship.

round·house kick ▶ **n.** (chiefly in karate) a kick made with a wide sweep of the leg and rotation of the body.

round·ly /ˈroundlē/ ▶ **adv. 1** in a vehement or emphatic manner: *the latest attacks have been roundly condemned by campaigners for peace.* ■ so thoroughly as to leave no doubt: *the army was roundly beaten.* ■ too plainly for politeness; bluntly: *she told him roundly to get to the point.*
2 so as to form a circular or roughly circular shape: *he was a middle-aged, roundly built man.*

round-nose ▶ **adj. 1** (of a tool) having the end rounded, so as to produce a rounded cut or surface or to prevent accidents or damage.
2 (of a bullet) having a rounded front end.
▶ **n.** a bullet with a rounded front end.
– DERIVATIVES **round-nosed** adj.

round rob·in ▶ **n. 1** [often as modifier] a tournament in which each competitor plays in turn against every other: *a round-robin competition.* ■ a series or sequence: *an inconclusive round robin of talks in Cairo, Washington, and New York.*
2 a petition, esp. one with signatures written in a circle to conceal the order of writing.

Round Rock a city in central Texas, north of Austin; pop. 104,446 (est. 2008).

round shot ▶ **n.** historical ammunition in the form of cast-iron or steel spherical balls for firing from cannon.

round-shoul·dered ▶ **adj.** having the shoulders bent forward so that the back is rounded: *a round-shouldered slouch.*

rounds·man /ˈroundzmən/ ▶ **n.** (pl. **roundsmen**) **1** a police officer in charge of a patrol.

2 a person on a regular route delivering and taking orders for milk, bread, etc.

Round Ta·ble ▶ **n. 1** the table at which King Arthur and his knights sat so that none should have precedence. It was first mentioned in 1155. **2** an international charitable association that holds discussions and undertakes community service. **3** (**round table**) an assembly for discussion, esp. at a conference: [as modifier] *round-table talks*.

round-the-clock ▶ **adj.** lasting all day and all night: *round-the-clock surveillance*.

round trip ▶ **n.** a journey to one or more places and back again.

round turn ▶ **n.** a complete turn of a rope around another rope or other object.

round·up /ˈroundˌəp/ ▶ **n.** a systematic gathering together of people or things: *mass police roundups and detentions | the rites of the cattle drive, the roundup, and the branding.* ■ a summary of facts or events: *a news roundup every fifteen minutes*.

round win·dow ▶ **n.** informal term for **FENESTRA ROTUNDA** (see **FENESTRA**).

round·wood /ˈroundˌwo͝od/ ▶ **n.** timber that is left as small logs, not sawn into planks or chopped for fuel, typically taken from near the tops of trees and used for furniture.

round·worm /ˈroundˌwərm/ ▶ **n.** a nematode, esp. a parasitic one found in the intestines of mammals. ● Many species in the class Phasmida, including the large *Ascaris lumbricoides* in humans.

roup[1] /ro͞op/ chiefly Scottish & N. English ▶ **n.** an auction. ▶ **v.** [with obj.] sell (something) by auction: *his effects were rouped*.
– ORIGIN Middle English (in the sense 'roar, croak'): of Scandinavian origin; compare with Old Norse *raupa* 'boast, brag.'

roup[2] ▶ **n.** an infectious disease of poultry affecting the respiratory tract.
– DERIVATIVES **roup·y adj.**
– ORIGIN mid 16th cent.: of unknown origin.

rouse /rouz/ ▶ **v.** [with obj.] **1** bring out of sleep; awaken: *she was roused from a deep sleep by a hand on her shoulder*. ■ [no obj.] cease to sleep or to be inactive; wake up: *she roused, took off her eyepads, and looked around*. ■ startle out of inactivity; cause to become active: *once the enemy camp was roused, they would move on the castle | she'd just stay a few more minutes, then* **rouse herself** *and go back*. ■ startle (game) from a lair or cover. ■ Nautical, archaic haul (something) vigorously in the specified direction: *rouse the cable out*. **2** cause to feel angry or excited: *the crowds were* **roused to** *fever pitch by the drama of the race*. ■ cause or give rise to (an emotion or feeling): *his evasiveness roused my curiosity*. **3** stir (a liquid, esp. beer while brewing): *rouse the beer as the hops are introduced*.
– DERIVATIVES **rous·a·ble adj., rous·er n.**
– ORIGIN late Middle English (originally as a hawking and hunting term): probably from Anglo-Norman French, of unknown ultimate origin.

rous·ing /ˈrouziNG/ ▶ **adj. 1** exciting; stirring: *a rousing speech*. **2** archaic (of a fire) blazing strongly.
– DERIVATIVES **rous·ing·ly adv.**

Rous sar·co·ma /rous/ ▶ **n.** a form of tumor, caused by an RNA virus, that affects birds, particularly poultry.
– ORIGIN early 20th cent.: named after Francis P. *Rous* (1879–1970), US physician.

Rous·seau[1] /ro͞oˈsō/, Henri (Julien) (1844–1910), French painter; known as **le Douanier** ("customs officer"). After retiring as a customs official in 1893, he created bold, colorful paintings of fantastic dreams and exotic jungle landscapes.

Rous·seau[2], Jean-Jacques (1712–78), French philosopher and writer, born in Switzerland. He believed that civilization warps the fundamental goodness of human nature, but that the ill effects can be moderated by active participation in democratic consensual politics. Notable works: *Émile* (1762) and *The Social Contract* (1762).

Rous·seau[3], (Pierre Étienne) Théodore (1812–67), French painter. A leading landscapist of the Barbizon School, his works typically depict the scenery and changing light effects of the forest of Fontainebleau.

roust /roust/ ▶ **v.** [with obj.] cause to get up or start moving; rouse: *I rousted him out of his bed with a cup of coffee*. ■ informal treat roughly; harass: *the detectives who had rousted him the night of the murder*.
– ORIGIN mid 17th cent.: perhaps an alteration of **ROUSE**.

roust·a·bout /ˈroustəˌbout/ ▶ **n.** an unskilled or casual laborer. ■ a laborer on an oil rig. ■ a dock laborer or deckhand. ■ a circus laborer.
– ORIGIN mid 19th cent.: from the verb **ROUST**.

rout[1] /rout/ ▶ **n. 1** a disorderly retreat of defeated troops: *the retreat degenerated into a rout | the army was in a state of demoralization verging on rout*. ■ a decisive defeat: *the party lost more than half their seats in the rout*. **2** Law, dated an assembly of people who have made a move toward committing an illegal act that would constitute an offense of riot. ■ archaic a disorderly or tumultuous crowd of people: *a rout of strangers ought not to be admitted*. **3** Brit. archaic a large evening party or reception.
▶ **v.** [with obj.] defeat and cause to retreat in disorder: *in a matter of minutes the attackers were routed*.
– PHRASES **put to rout** put to flight; defeat utterly: *I once put a gang to rout*.
– ORIGIN Middle English: ultimately based on Latin *ruptus* 'broken,' from the verb *rumpere*; sense 1 and the verb (late 16th cent.) are from obsolete French *route*, probably from Italian *rotta* 'breakup of an army'; the other senses are via Anglo-Norman French *rute*.

rout[2] ▶ **v. 1** [with obj.] cut a groove, or any pattern not extending to the edges, in (a wooden or metal surface): *you routed each plank all along its length*. **2** another term for **ROOT**[2]. ■ find (someone or something), or force them from a place: *Simon routed him from the stable*.
– ORIGIN mid 16th cent. (sense 2): alteration of the verb **ROOT**[2]. Sense 1 dates from the early 19th cent.

route /ro͞ot, rout/ ▶ **n.** a way or course taken in getting from a starting point to a destination: *the most direct route is via Los Angeles*. ■ the line of a road, path, railroad, etc. ■ a circuit traveled in delivering, selling, or collecting goods. ■ a method or process leading to a specified result: *the many routes to a healthier diet will be described*.
▶ **v.** (**routes, routing** or Brit. **routeing, routed**) [with obj.] send or direct along a specified course: *all lines of communication were routed through Atlanta*.
– ORIGIN Middle English: from Old French *rute* 'road,' from Latin *rupta (via)* 'broken (way),' feminine past participle of *rumpere*.

route man ▶ **n.** another term for **ROUNDSMAN** (sense 2).

route march ▶ **n.** a march for troops over a designated route, typically via roads or tracks.

rout·er[1] /ˈroutər/ ▶ **n.** a power tool with a shaped cutter, used in carpentry for making grooves for joints, decorative moldings, etc.

rout·er[2] /ˈro͞otər, ˈroutər/ ▶ **n.** a device that forwards data packets to the appropriate parts of a computer network.

rou·tine /ro͞oˈtēn/ ▶ **n.** a sequence of actions regularly followed; a fixed program: *I settled down into a routine of work and sleep | as a matter of routine a report will be sent to the director*. ■ a set sequence in a performance such as a dance or comedy act: *he was trying to persuade her to have a tap routine in the play*. ■ Computing a sequence of instructions for performing a task that forms a program or a distinct part of one.
▶ **adj.** performed as part of a regular procedure rather than for a special reason: *the principal insisted that this was just a routine annual drill*.
▶ **v.** [with obj.] rare organize according to a routine: *all had been routined with smoothness*.
– DERIVATIVES **rou·tine·ly adv.**
– ORIGIN late 17th cent. (denoting a regular course or procedure): from French, from *route* 'road' (see **ROUTE**).

rout·ing code (also **routing number**) ▶ **n.** any of various numbers used to direct data, documents, or merchandise, including. ■ the magnetically encoded numbers on a check. ■ a numeric code that directs telephone calls or Internet traffic.

rou·tin·ism /ro͞oˈtēˌnizəm, ˈro͞otnˌizəm/ ▶ **n.** archaic the prevalence or domination of routine.
– DERIVATIVES **rou·tin·ist n. & adj.**

rou·tin·ize /ro͞oˈtēˌnīz, ˈro͞otnˌīz/ ▶ **v.** [with obj.] (usu. **be routinized**) make (something) into a matter of routine; subject to a routine: *communication was routinized to ensure consistency of information*.
– DERIVATIVES **rou·tin·i·za·tion** /-ˌtēnəˈzāSHən, ˌro͞otn-ə-/ **n.**

roux /ro͞o/ ▶ **n.** (pl. **same**) Cooking a mixture of fat (esp. butter) and flour used in making sauces.
– ORIGIN from French (*beurre*) *roux* 'browned (butter).'

ROV ▶ **abbr.** remotely operated vehicle.

rove[1] /rōv/ ▶ **v.** [no obj.] travel constantly without a fixed destination; wander: *a quarter of a million refugees roved around the country*. ■ [with obj.] wander over or through (a place) in such a way: *children roving the streets*. ■ (usu. as adj. **roving**) travel for one's work, having no fixed base: *he trained as a roving reporter*. ■ (of eyes) look in changing directions in order to see something thoroughly: *the policeman's eyes roved around the bar*.
▶ **n.** [in sing.] a journey, esp. one with no specific destination; an act of wandering: *a new exhibit will electrify campuses on its national rove*.
– ORIGIN late 15th cent. (originally a term in archery in the sense 'shoot at a casual mark of undetermined range'): perhaps from dialect *rave* 'to stray,' probably of Scandinavian origin.

rove[2] past of **REEVE**[2].

rove[3] ▶ **n.** a sliver of cotton, wool, or other fiber, drawn out and slightly twisted, esp. preparatory to spinning.
▶ **v.** [with obj.] form (slivers of wool, cotton, or other fiber) into roves.
– ORIGIN late 18th cent.: of unknown origin.

rove[4] ▶ **n.** a small metal plate or ring for a rivet to pass through and be clenched over, esp. in boatbuilding.
– ORIGIN Middle English: from Old Norse *ró*, with the addition of parasitic *-v-*.

rove bee·tle ▶ **n.** a long-bodied beetle with very short wing cases, typically found among decaying matter where it may scavenge or prey on other scavengers. ● Family Staphylinidae: numerous genera.

rov·er[1] /ˈrōvər/ ▶ **n. 1** a person who spends their time wandering: *they became rovers who departed further and further from civilization*. **2** (in various sports) a player not restricted to a particular position on the field. **3** a vehicle for driving over rough terrain. ■ a vehicle driven by remote control over extraterrestrial terrain. **4** Croquet a ball that has passed all the wickets but not pegged out. ■ a player who has such a ball. **5** Archery a target for long-distance shooting. ■ a target chosen at random and not at a determined range.

rov·er[2] ▶ **n.** archaic a sea robber; a pirate.
– ORIGIN Middle English: from Middle Low German and Middle Dutch *rōver*, from *rōven* 'rob'; related to **REAVE**.

rov·er[3] ▶ **n.** a person or machine that makes roves of fiber (see **ROVE**[3]).

rov·ing /ˈrōviNG/ ▶ **n.** another term for **ROVE**[3]. ■ roves collectively.

rov·ing eye ▶ **n.** [usu. in sing.] a tendency to flirt or be constantly looking to start a new sexual relationship: *if his wife wasn't around, he had a roving eye*.

Ro·vno /ˈrôvnə/ Russian name for **RIVNE**.

row[1] /rō/ ▶ **n.** a number of people or things in a more or less straight line: *her villa stood in a row of similar ones*. ■ a line of seats in a theater: *they sat in the front row*. ■ a street with a continuous line of houses along one or both of its sides, esp. when specifying houses of a particular type or function: *fraternity row*. ■ a horizontal line of entries in a table. ■ a complete line of stitches in knitting or crochet.
– PHRASES **a hard** (or **tough**) **row to hoe** a difficult task. **in a row** forming a line: *four chairs were set in a row*. ■ informal in succession: *we get six days off in a row*.
– ORIGIN Old English *rāw*, of Germanic origin; related to Dutch *rij* and German *Reihe*.

row[2] /rō/ ▶ **v.** [with obj.] propel (a boat) with oars: *out in the bay a small figure was rowing a rubber dinghy*. ■ [no obj.] travel by propelling a boat in this way: *we rowed down the river all day*. ■ convey (a passenger) in a boat by propelling it with oars: *her father was rowing her across the lake*. ■ [no obj.] engage in the sport of rowing, esp. competitively: *he rowed for Yale*.
▶ **n.** [in sing.] a period of rowing.
– DERIVATIVES **row·er n.**
– ORIGIN Old English *rōwan*, of Germanic origin; related to **RUDDER**; from an Indo-European root shared by Latin *remus* 'oar,' Greek *eretmon* 'oar.'

row[3] /rou/ informal ▶ **n.** a noisy acrimonious quarrel: *they had a row and she stormed out of the house*. ■ a serious dispute: *the director is at the center of a row over policy decisions*. ■ a loud noise or uproar: *if he's at home he must have heard that row*.

PRONUNCIATION KEY ə **ago, up**; ər **over, fur**; a **hat**; ā **ate**; ä **car**; e **let**; ē **see**; i **fit**; ī **by**; NG **sing**; ō **go**; ô **law, for**; oi **toy**; o͝o **good**; o͞o **goo**; ou **out**; TH **thin**; T͟H **then**; ZH **vision**

▶ **v.** [no obj.] have a quarrel: *they rowed about who would receive the money from the sale.*
– PHRASES **make** (or **kick up**) **a row** make a noise or commotion. ■ make a vigorous protest.
– ORIGIN mid 18th cent.: of unknown origin.

row·an /'rouən, 'rōən/ (also **rowan tree**) ▶ **n.** a mountain ash, in particular the European *Sorbus aucuparia.* ■ (also **rowan berry**) the scarlet berry of this tree.
– ORIGIN late 15th cent. (originally Scots and northern English): of Scandinavian origin; compare with Norwegian *rogn.*

row·boat /'rō,bōt/ ▶ **n.** a small boat propelled by oars.

row·dy /'roudē/ ▶ **adj.** (**rowdier, rowdiest**) noisy and disorderly: *it was a rowdy but good-natured crowd.*
▶ **n.** (pl. **rowdies**) a noisy and disorderly person.
– DERIVATIVES **row·di·ly** /'roudl-ē/ **adv.**, **row·di·ness n.**, **row·dy·ism** /-,izəm/ **n.**
– ORIGIN early 19th cent. (originally US in the sense 'lawless backwoodsman'): of unknown origin.

Rowe /rō/, Nicholas (1674–1718), English playwright. Notable works: *Tamerlane* (1701) and *The Fair Penitent* (1703).

row·el /'rou(ə)l/ ▶ **n.** a spiked revolving disk at the end of a spur.
▶ **v.** (**rowels, roweling, roweled**; Brit. **rowels, rowelling, rowelled**) [with obj.] use a rowel to urge on (a horse): *he roweled his horse on as fast as he could.*
– ORIGIN Middle English: from Old French *roel(e),* from late Latin *rotella,* diminutive of Latin *rota* 'wheel.'

row·en /'rouən/ ▶ **n.** a second growth of grass or hay in one season.
– ORIGIN Middle English: from an Old Northern French variant of Old French *regain* 'an increase.'

row house /rō/ ▶ **n.** any of a row of houses joined by common sidewalls.

row·ing /'rō-iNG/ ▶ **n.** the sport or pastime of propelling a boat by means of oars.

> Racing takes place in narrow, light boats (**shells**), between single rowers (**scullers**) with two oars, or between crews of two, four, or eight people with one oar each; crews are often steered by a coxswain.

row·ing boat ▶ **n.** British term for ROWBOAT.

row·ing ma·chine ▶ **n.** an exercise machine with a sliding seat, used to strengthen the muscles used in rowing.

Rowl·ing /'rouliNG/, J. K. (1965–), British writer; full name *Joanne Kathleen Rowling.* Her series of children's books featuring the character Harry Potter began with *Harry Potter and the Sorcerer's Stone* (1998).

row·lock /'rō,läk/ ▶ **n.** chiefly Brit. an oarlock.
– ORIGIN mid 18th cent.: alteration of OARLOCK, influenced by the verb ROW[2].

row vec·tor /rō/ ▶ **n.** Mathematics a vector represented by a matrix consisting of a single row of elements.

rox·ar·sone /räk'sär,sōn/ ▶ **n.** an arsenic-containing antibiotic drug that is widely used as a food additive in the poultry industry to promote growth and control intestinal parasites. It is considered a source of arsenic contamination in water near some large poultry producers.

Rox·bury /'räks,berē, -bərē/ a district of Boston in Massachusetts, today the center of the city's black community.

roy·al /'roiəl/ ▶ **adj.** having the status of a king or queen or a member of their family: *contributors included members of the royal family.* ■ belonging to or carried out or exercised by a king or queen: *the royal palace | the coalition obtained royal approval for the appointment.* ■ [attrib.] in the service or under the patronage of a king or queen: *a royal maid.* ■ [attrib.] of a quality or size suitable for a king or queen; splendid: *a royal fortune.* ■ informal unmitigated; extreme: *he might turn out to be a royal pain.*
▶ **n. 1** informal a member of a royal family, esp. in England.
2 short for ROYAL SAIL or ROYAL MAST.
3 (in full **metric royal**) a paper size, now standardized at 636 × 480 mm. ■ (in full **royal octavo**) a book size, now standardized at 234 × 156 mm. ■ (in full **royal quarto**) a book size, now standardized at 312 × 237 mm.
– PHRASES **royal road to** a way of attaining or reaching something without trouble: *there is no royal road to teaching.*
– DERIVATIVES **roy·al·ly adv.**
– ORIGIN late Middle English: from Old French *roial,* from Latin *regalis* 'regal.'

Roy·al Air Force (abbr.: **RAF**) the British air force, formed in 1918.

roy·al an·te·lope ▶ **n.** a shy West African antelope with an arched back, short neck, and a red and brown coat with white underparts. It is the smallest known antelope. ● *Neotragus pygmaeus,* family Bovidae.

roy·al blue ▶ **n.** a deep, vivid blue.

Roy·al Ca·na·di·an Mount·ed Po·lice (abbr.: **RCMP**) the national police force of Canada, founded in 1873. A member of the force is informally called a MOUNTIE.

roy·al fern ▶ **n.** a large pale green fern that has very long spreading fronds with widely spaced oblong lobes, occurring worldwide in wet habitats. ● *Osmunda regalis,* family Osmundaceae.

roy·al flush ▶ **n.** Poker a straight flush including ace, king, queen, jack, and ten all in the same suit, which is the hand of the highest possible value when wild cards are not in use.

Roy·al Gorge a steep defile on the Arkansas River in south central Colorado, near Cañon City, a noted tourist attraction. Also called **Grand Canyon of the Arkansas.**

roy·al ic·ing ▶ **n.** chiefly Brit. hard white icing made from confectioners' sugar and egg whites, typically used to decorate fruitcakes.

roy·al·ist /'roiəlist/ ▶ **n.** a person who supports the principle of monarchy or a particular monarchy. ■ a supporter of the king against Parliament in the English Civil War. ■ a supporter of the British during the American Revolution; a Tory.
▶ **adj.** giving support to the monarchy: *the paper claims to be royalist.* ■ (in the English Civil War) supporting the king against Parliament: *the royalist army.*
– DERIVATIVES **roy·al·ism** /-,izəm/ **n.**

roy·al jel·ly ▶ **n.** a substance secreted by honeybee workers and fed by them to larvae that are being raised as potential queen bees.

Roy·al Ma·rines a British armed service (part of the Royal Navy) founded in 1664, trained for service at sea, or on land under specific circumstances.

roy·al mast ▶ **n.** a section of a sailing ship's mast above the topgallant.

Roy·al Na·vy (abbr.: **RN**) the British navy. It was the most powerful navy in the world from the 17th century until World War II.

Roy·al Oak a city in southeastern Michigan, northwest of Detroit; pop. 57,110 (est. 2008).

roy·al palm ▶ **n.** a New World palm that is widely cultivated as a roadside tree. ● Genus *Roystonea,* family Palmae: several species, in particular the **Florida royal palm** (*R. elata*) and the **Cuban royal palm** (*R. regia*).

roy·al pur·ple ▶ **n.** a rich deep shade of purple.

roy·al sail ▶ **n.** a sail above a sailing ship's topgallant sail.

Roy·al So·ci·e·ty (in full **Royal Society of London**) the oldest and most prestigious scientific society in Britain. It was formed by followers of Francis Bacon to promote scientific discussion, esp. in the physical sciences, and received its charter from Charles II in 1662.

roy·al stag ▶ **n.** Brit. a red deer stag with a head of twelve or more points.

roy·al ten·nis ▶ **n.** chiefly Australian term for COURT TENNIS.

roy·al·ty /'roiəltē/ ▶ **n.** (pl. **royalties**) **1** people of royal blood or status: *diplomats, heads of state, and royalty shared tables at the banquet.* ■ a member of a royal family: *she swept by as if she were royalty.* ■ the status or power of a king or queen: *the brilliance of her clothes, her jewels, all revealed her royalty.*
2 a sum of money paid to a patentee for the use of a patent or to an author or composer for each copy of a book sold or for each public performance of a work.
3 a royal right (now esp. over minerals) granted by a sovereign to an individual or corporation. ■ a payment made by a producer of minerals, oil, or natural gas to the owner of the site or of the mineral rights over it.
– ORIGIN late Middle English: from Old French *roialte,* from *roial* (see ROYAL). The sense 'royal right (esp. over minerals)' (late 15th cent.) developed into the sense 'payment made by a mineral producer to the site owner' (mid 19th cent.), which was then transferred to payments for the use of patents and published materials.

roy·al war·rant ▶ **n.** a warrant issued by a sovereign, in particular: ■ (**Royal Warrant**) (in the UK) one authorizing a company to display the royal arms, indicating that goods or services of quality are supplied to the sovereign or to a specified member of the royal family.

roy·al "we" ▶ **n.** the use of "we" instead of "I" by an individual person, as traditionally used by a sovereign: *Queen Victoria once remarked, with British understatement, "we are not amused."*

Royce /rois/, Sir (Frederick) Henry (1863–1933), English engine designer. He founded Rolls-Royce Ltd. with Charles Stewart Rolls in 1906.

roz·zer /'räzər/ ▶ **n.** Brit. informal a police officer.
– ORIGIN late 19th cent.: of unknown origin.

RP ▶ **abbr.** received pronunciation.

RPG ▶ **abbr.** ■ report program generator, a high-level commercial computer programming language. ■ rocket-propelled grenade. ■ role-playing game.

rpm ▶ **abbr.** ■ resale price maintenance. ■ revolutions per minute.

rps (also **r.p.s.**) ▶ **abbr.** revolutions per second.

rpt ▶ **abbr.** repeat.

RPV ▶ **abbr.** remotely piloted vehicle.

RQ ▶ **abbr.** respiratory quotient.

RR ▶ **abbr.** ■ railroad. ■ rural route.

RRB ▶ **abbr.** Railroad Retirement Board.

-rrhea (chiefly Brit. **-rrhoea**) ▶ **comb. form** discharge; flow: *diarrhea.*
– ORIGIN from Greek *rhoia* 'flow, flux.'

rRNA ▶ **abbr.** Biochemistry ribosomal RNA.

RRP ▶ **abbr.** Brit. recommended retail price.

RRR ▶ **abbr.** (of mail) return receipt requested.

RS ▶ **abbr.** ■ (in the US) received standard. ■ (in the UK) Royal Scots.

Rs. ▶ **abbr.** rupee(s).

RSA ▶ **abbr.** ■ Republic of South Africa. ■ Royal Scottish Academy; Royal Scottish Academician.

RSC ▶ **abbr.** (in the UK) Royal Society of Chemistry.

RSE ▶ **abbr.** Royal Society of Edinburgh.

RSFSR ▶ **abbr.** historical Russian Soviet Federated Socialist Republic.

RSI ▶ **abbr.** repetitive strain injury.

RSJ ▶ **abbr.** rolled steel joist, a type of I-beam.

RSNC ▶ **abbr.** (in the UK) Royal Society for Nature Conservation.

RSPCA ▶ **abbr.** (in the UK) Royal Society for the Prevention of Cruelty to Animals.

RSS ▶ **abbr.** Computing Really Simple Syndication, a standardized system for the distribution of content from an online publisher to Internet users.

RSV ▶ **abbr.** Revised Standard Version (of the Bible).

RSVP ▶ **abbr.** répondez s'il vous plaît, or please reply (used at the end of invitations to request a response).
– ORIGIN French.

RT ▶ **abbr.** ■ radiotelegraphy. ■ radiotelephony.

rt. ▶ **abbr.** right.

RTA ▶ **abbr.** Brit. road traffic accident.

rte. ▶ **abbr.** route.

RTF ▶ **abbr.** rich text format, developed to allow the transfer of graphics and formatted text between different applications and operating systems.

RTFM ▶ **abbr.** Computing, vulgar slang read the fucking manual (used esp. in e-mail in reply to a question whose answer is obvious).

Rt Hon. ▶ **abbr.** Brit. Right Honourable.

Rt Revd (also **Rt Rev**) ▶ **abbr.** Right Reverend.

RTW ▶ **abbr.** ready-to-wear.

Ru ▶ **symbol** the chemical element ruthenium.

RU-486 (also **RU 486**) ▶ **n.** trademark for MIFEPRISTONE.

rub /rəb/ ▶ **v.** (**rubs, rubbing, rubbed**) [with obj.] move one's hand or a cloth repeatedly to and fro on the surface of (something) with firm pressure: *she rubbed her arm, where she had a large bruise* | [no obj.] *he rubbed at the dirt on his jeans.* ■ move (one's hand, a cloth, or another object) over a surface in such a way: *he rubbed a finger around the rim of his mug.* ■ (with reference to two things) to move or cause to move to and fro against each other with a certain amount of pressure and friction:

r

[with obj.] *many insects make noises by rubbing parts of their bodies together* | [no obj.] *the ice breaks into small floes that rub against each other.* ■ [no obj.] (of shoes or other hard items in contact with the skin) cause pain through friction: *badly fitting shoes can rub painfully.* ■ make dry, clean, or smooth with pressure from a hand, cloth, or other object: *she found a towel and began rubbing her hair* | *she rubbed herself as dry as possible.* ■ spread (ointment, polish, or a substance of similar consistency) over a surface with repeated movements of one's hand or a cloth: *she took out her sunblock and rubbed some on her nose.* ■ **(rub something in/into/through)** work an ingredient into (a mixture) by breaking and blending it with firm movements of one's fingers: *sift the flour into a bowl and rub in the fat.* ■ reproduce the design of (a gravestone, memorial tablet, etc.) by laying paper on it and rubbing the paper with charcoal, colored chalk, etc. ■ [no obj.] Lawn Bowling (of a bowl) be slowed or diverted by the unevenness of the ground.
▶ **n. 1** [usu. in sing.] an act of rubbing: *she pulled out a towel and gave her head a quick rub.* ■ an ointment designed to be rubbed on the skin to ease pain: *a muscle rub.*
2 (usu. **the rub**) a difficulty, esp. one of central importance in a situation: *that was the rub—she had not cared enough.* [from Shakespeare's *Hamlet* (III. i. 65).]
3 Lawn Bowling an inequality of the ground impeding or diverting a bowl; the diversion or hindering of a bowl by this.
– PHRASES **not have two —— to rub together** informal have none or hardly any of the specified item, esp. money: *she doesn't have two nickels to rub together.* **rub elbows** (or **shoulders**) associate or come into contact (with another person): *he rubbed elbows with TV stars at the party.* **rub one's hands** rub one's hands together to show keen satisfaction. **rub it in** (or **rub someone's nose in something**) informal emphatically draw someone's attention to an embarrassing or painful fact: *they don't just beat you, they rub it in.* **rub noses** rub one's nose against someone else's in greeting (esp. as traditional among Maoris and some other peoples). **rub of the green** Golf any accidental or unpredictable influence on the course or position of the ball. ■ good fortune, esp. as determining events in an athletic contest. **rub someone** (or Brit. **rub someone up**) **the wrong way** irritate or repel someone as by stroking a cat against the lie of its fur.
– PHRASAL VERBS **rub something down** dry, smooth, or clean something by rubbing. ■ rub the sweat from a horse or one's own body after exercise. **rub off** be transferred by contact or association: *when parents are having a hard time, their tension can easily rub off on the kids.* **rub someone out** informal kill someone. **rub something out** erase pencil marks with an eraser.
– ORIGIN Middle English (as a verb): perhaps from Low German *rubben,* of unknown ultimate origin. The noun dates from the late 16th cent.

Rub' al-Kha·li /ˌro͞ob alˈkälē, älˈKHälē/ a vast desert in the Arabian peninsula that extends from central Saudi Arabia south to Yemen and east to the United Arab Emirates and Oman. It is also known as the Great Sandy Desert and the Empty Quarter.

ru·ba·to /ro͞oˈbätō/ Music ▶ **n.** (pl. **rubatos** or **rubati** /-ˈbätē/) (also **tempo rubato**) the temporary disregarding of strict tempo to allow an expressive quickening or slackening, usually without altering the overall pace.
▶ **adj.** performed in this way.
– ORIGIN Italian, literally 'robbed.'

rub·ber[1] /ˈrəbər/ ▶ **n.** a tough elastic polymeric substance made from the latex of a tropical plant or synthetically. ■ **(rubbers)** rubber boots; galoshes. ■ Baseball an oblong piece of rubber or similar material embedded in the pitcher's mound, on which the pitcher must keep one foot while delivering the ball. ■ informal a condom. ■ Brit. an eraser for pencil or ink marks.
– DERIVATIVES **rub·ber·i·ness** n., **rub·ber·y** adj.
– ORIGIN mid 16th cent.: from the verb RUB + -ER[1]. The original sense was 'an implement (such as a hard brush) used for rubbing and cleaning.' Because an early use of the elastic substance (previously known as CAOUTCHOUC) was to rub out pencil marks, *rubber* gained the sense 'eraser' in the late 18th cent. The sense was subsequently (mid 19th cent.) generalized to refer to the substance in any form or use, at first often differentiated as INDIA RUBBER.

rub·ber[2] ▶ **n.** a contest consisting of a series of successive matches (typically three or five) between the same sides or people in tennis, cricket, and other games. ■ (also **rubber match** or **rubber game**) a deciding game in such a match. ■ Bridge a unit of play in which one side scores bonus points for winning the best of three games.
– ORIGIN late 16th cent.: of unknown origin; early use was as a term in lawn bowling.

rub·ber band ▶ **n.** a loop of stretchy rubber for holding things together.

rub·ber bo·a ▶ **n.** a short snake with a stout shiny brown body that looks and feels like rubber, found in western North America. ● *Charina bottae,* family Boidae.

rub·ber bul·let ▶ **n.** a large projectile made of rubber and shot from a firearm, used esp. in riot control.

rub·ber ce·ment ▶ **n.** a cement or adhesive containing rubber in a solvent.

rub·ber check ▶ **n.** informal, humorous a check that is returned unpaid.
– ORIGIN 1920s (originally US): by association with BOUNCE.

rub·ber chick·en ▶ **n.** informal food, typically chicken, consumed at social gatherings, esp. at the events and dinners necessary for a public figure to attend.

rub·ber duck ▶ **n.** S. African informal an inflatable flat-bottomed rubber dinghy, typically motorized.
– DERIVATIVES **rub·ber duck·er** n.

rub·ber·ize /ˈrəbəˌrīz/ ▶ **v.** [with obj.] (usu. as adj. **rubberized**) treat or coat (something) with rubber.

rub·ber·neck /ˈrəbərˌnek/ informal ▶ **n.** a person who turns their head to stare at something in a foolish manner, esp. while driving a car.
▶ **v.** [no obj.] stare in such a way: *a passerby rubbernecking at the accident scene.*
– DERIVATIVES **rub·ber·neck·er** n.

rub·ber·oid /ˈrəbəˌroid/ ▶ **adj.** made of or resembling rubber.

rub·ber plant ▶ **n. 1** an evergreen tree of the fig family that has large dark green shiny leaves and is widely cultivated as a houseplant. Native to Southeast Asia, it was formerly grown as a source of rubber. ● *Ficus elastica,* family Moraceae.
2 another term for RUBBER TREE.

rub·ber stamp ▶ **n. 1** a handheld device for inking and imprinting a message or design on a surface.
2 a person or organization that approves the decisions of others, not having the power or ability to reject or alter them: *I hope we never get to the day judges dictate to juries so they become rubber stamps.* ■ an indication of such an approval.
▶ **v.** (**rubber-stamp**) [with obj.] approve automatically without proper consideration: *the college would not rubber-stamp its athletes for graduation.*

rub·ber tree ▶ **n.** a tree that produces the latex from which rubber is manufactured, native to the Amazonian rain forest and widely cultivated elsewhere. ● *Hevea brasiliensis,* family Euphorbiaceae. ■ used in names of other trees from which a similar latex can be obtained.

rub·bing /ˈrəbiNG/ ▶ **n. 1** the action of rubbing something: *dab at the stain—vigorous rubbing could damage the carpet.*
2 an impression of a design on brass or stone, made by rubbing on paper laid over it with colored wax, pencil, chalk, etc.

rub·bing al·co·hol ▶ **n.** denatured alcohol, typically perfumed, used as an antiseptic or in massage.

rub·bing strake ▶ **n.** a protective strip running along a boat's side below the gunwale to prevent damage when coming alongside something.

rub·bish /ˈrəbiSH/ ▶ **n.** waste material; refuse or litter: *an alleyway high with rubbish.* ■ material that is considered unimportant or valueless: *she had to sift through the rubbish in every drawer.* ■ absurd, nonsensical, or worthless talk or ideas: *I suppose you believe that rubbish about vampires.*
▶ **v.** [with obj.] Brit. informal criticize severely and reject as worthless: *he has pointedly rubbished professional estimates of the development and running costs.*
▶ **adj.** Brit. informal very bad; worthless or useless: *people might say I was a rubbish manager.*
– DERIVATIVES **rub·bish·y** adj.
– ORIGIN late Middle English: from Anglo-Norman French *rubbous;* perhaps related to Old French *robe* 'spoils'; compare with RUBBLE. The change in the ending was due to association with -ISH[1]. The verb (1950s) was originally Australian and New Zealand slang.

rub·ble /ˈrəbəl/ ▶ **n.** waste or rough fragments of stone, brick, concrete, etc., esp. as the debris from the demolition of buildings: *two buildings collapsed, trapping scores of people in the rubble.* ■ pieces of rough or undressed stone used in building walls, esp. as filling for cavities.
– DERIVATIVES **rub·bly** /ˈrəb(ə)lē/ adj.
– ORIGIN late Middle English: perhaps from an Anglo-Norman French alteration of Old French *robe* 'spoils'; compare with RUBBISH.

rub·bled /ˈrəbəld/ ▶ **adj.** covered in rubble or reduced to rubble.

rub board ▶ **n. 1** a board fitted with teeth, used for making drawnwork from linen.
2 another term for WASHBOARD (sense 2 of the noun).

rub·by /ˈrəbē/ ▶ **n.** (pl. **rubbies**) Canadian informal an alcoholic who habitually drinks rubbing alcohol.

rub·down /ˈrəbˌdoun/ ▶ **n.** a massage. ■ an act of drying, smoothing down, or cleaning something by rubbing: *a shower and a brisk rubdown with a towel* | [as modifier] *rubdown decals.*

rube /ro͞ob/ ▶ **n.** informal a country bumpkin.
– ORIGIN late 19th cent.: abbreviation of the given name *Reuben.*

ru·bel·la /ro͞oˈbelə/ ▶ **n.** a contagious viral disease, with symptoms like mild measles. It can cause fetal malformation if contracted in early pregnancy. Also called GERMAN MEASLES.
– ORIGIN late 19th cent.: modern Latin, neuter plural of Latin *rubellus* 'reddish.'

ru·bel·lite /ˈro͞obəˌlīt/ ▶ **n.** a red variety of tourmaline.
– ORIGIN late 18th cent.: from Latin *rubellus* 'reddish' + -ITE[1].

Ru·bens /ˈro͞obənz/, Sir Peter Paul (1577–1640), Flemish painter. He is best known for his portraits and for his paintings of mythological subjects featuring voluptuous female nudes, such as in *Venus and Adonis* (*c.*1635).

ru·be·o·la /ˌro͞obēˈōlə/ ▶ **n.** medical term for MEASLES.
– ORIGIN late 17th cent.: from medieval Latin, diminutive (on the pattern of *variola*) of Latin *rubeus* 'red.'

ru·bes·cent /ro͞oˈbesənt/ ▶ **adj.** chiefly literary reddening; blushing.
– ORIGIN mid 18th cent.: from Latin *rubescent-* 'reddening,' from the verb *rubescere,* from *ruber* 'red.'

Ru·bi·con /ˈro͞obəˌkän/ a stream in northeastern Italy that marked the ancient boundary between Italy and Cisalpine Gaul. Julius Caesar led his army across it into Italy in 49 BC, breaking the law forbidding a general to lead an army out of his province, and so committing himself to war against the Senate and Pompey. The ensuing civil war resulted in victory for Caesar after three years. ■ [as noun] a point of no return: *on the way to political union we are now crossing the Rubicon.*

ru·bi·con ▶ **n.** (in piquet) an act of winning a game against an opponent whose total score is less than 100, in which case the loser's score is added to rather than subtracted from the winner's.
▶ **v.** (**rubicons, rubiconing, rubiconed**) [with obj.] score a rubicon against (one's opponent).
– ORIGIN late 19th cent.: from RUBICON.

ru·bi·cund /ˈro͞obəˌkənd/ ▶ **adj.** (esp. of someone's face) having a ruddy complexion; high-colored.
– DERIVATIVES **ru·bi·cun·di·ty** /ˌro͞obəˈkəndətē/ n.
– ORIGIN late Middle English (in the general sense 'red'): from Latin *rubicundus,* from *rubere* 'be red.'

ru·bid·i·um /ro͞oˈbidēəm/ ▶ **n.** the chemical element of atomic number 37, a rare soft silvery reactive metal of the alkali metal group. (Symbol: **Rb**)
– ORIGIN mid 19th cent.: modern Latin, from Latin *rubidus* 'red' (with reference to its spectral lines).

ru·bid·i·um–stron·ti·um dat·ing ▶ **n.** Geology a method of dating rocks from the relative proportions of rubidium-87 and its decay product, strontium-87.

ru·big·i·nous /ro͞oˈbijənəs/ ▶ **adj.** technical or literary rust-colored.
– ORIGIN late 17th cent.: from Latin *rubigo, rubigin-* 'rust' + -OUS.

Ru·bik's Cube /ˈro͞obiks/ ▶ **n.** trademark a puzzle in the form of a plastic cube covered with multicolored squares, which the player attempts to twist and turn so that all the squares on each face are of the same color.
– ORIGIN 1980s: named after Erno *Rubik* (born 1944), its Hungarian inventor.

Ru·bin·stein[1] /ˈro͞obənˌstīn/, Artur (1888–1982), US pianist, born in Poland. He toured extensively in Europe and the US. Among his many recordings are the complete works of Chopin.

Ru·bin·stein[2], Helena (1882–1965), US beautician and businesswoman. She opened her first beauty salon in Australia in 1902 and then opened salons in

r

London 1908, Paris 1912, and New York City 1915. Her organization became an international cosmetics manufacturer and distributor.

ru·bis·co /ˈro͞oˈbiskō/ ▶ **n.** Biochemistry an enzyme present in plant chloroplasts, involved in fixing atmospheric carbon dioxide during photosynthesis and in oxygenation of the resulting compound during photorespiration.
– ORIGIN 1980s: from *r(ib)u(lose)* + **BIS-** + *c(arb)o(xyl)*.

ru·ble /ˈro͞obəl/ (also **rouble**) ▶ **n.** the basic monetary unit of Russia and some other former republics of the Soviet Union, equal to 100 kopeks.
– ORIGIN via French from Russian *rubl'*.

ru·bric /ˈro͞obrik/ ▶ **n.** a heading on a document. ■ a direction in a liturgical book as to how a church service should be conducted. ■ a statement of purpose or function: *art for a purpose, not for its own sake, was his rubric.* ■ a category: *party policies on matters falling under the rubric of law and order.*
– DERIVATIVES **ru·bri·cal** adj.
– ORIGIN late Middle English *rubrish* (originally referring to a heading, section of text, etc., written in red for distinctiveness), from Old French *rubriche*, from Latin *rubrica (terra)* 'red (earth or ocher as writing material),' from the base of *rubeus* 'red'; the later spelling is influenced by the Latin form.

ru·bri·cate /ˈro͞obriˌkāt/ ▶ **v.** chiefly historical add elaborate, typically red, capital letters or other decorations to (a manuscript).
– DERIVATIVES **ru·bri·ca·tion** /ˌro͞obriˈkāSHən/ **n.**, **ru·bri·ca·tor** /-ˌkātər/ **n.**
– ORIGIN late 16th cent.: from Latin *rubricat-* 'marked in red,' from the verb *rubricare*, from *rubrica* (see **RUBRIC**).

Ru·by /ˈro͞obē/, Jack (1911–67), US nightclub owner; born *Jack Rubenstein*. On November 24, 1963, he shot and killed Lee Harvey Oswald, the man accused of murdering President Kennedy. The act was captured on national television.

ru·by /ˈro͞obē/ ▶ **n.** (pl. **rubies**) a precious stone consisting of corundum in color varieties varying from deep crimson or purple to pale rose. ■ an intense purplish-red color. ■ Printing an old type size equal to $5^1/_2$ points (smaller than nonpareil and larger than pearl).
– ORIGIN Middle English: from Old French *rubi*, from medieval Latin *rubinus*, from the base of Latin *rubeus* 'red.'

ru·by glass ▶ **n.** glass colored red by the inclusion of specific impurities such as metal oxides or gold.

Ru·by Moun·tains a range in northeastern Nevada, noted for its alpine scenery.

ru·by port ▶ **n.** a deep red port, esp. one matured in wood for only a few years and then fined.

ru·by wed·ding (also **ruby wedding anniversary**) ▶ **n.** the fortieth anniversary of a wedding.

ruche /ro͞oSH/ ▶ **n.** a frill or pleat of fabric as decoration on a garment or home furnishing.
– DERIVATIVES **ruched** adj., **ruch·ing** n.
– ORIGIN early 19th cent.: from French, from medieval Latin *rusca* 'tree bark,' of Celtic origin.

r

ruck[1] /rək/ ▶ **n.** a tightly packed crowd of people: *Harry squeezed through the ruck to order another beer.* ■ (**the ruck**) the mass of ordinary people or things: *education was the key to success, a way out of the ruck.*
– ORIGIN Middle English (in the sense 'stack of fuel, heap'): apparently of Scandinavian origin; compare with Norwegian *ruke* 'heap of hay.'

ruck[2] ▶ **v.** [with obj.] compress or move (cloth or clothing) so that it forms a number of untidy folds or creases: *the baby's nightgown was rucked up to his armpits.* ■ [no obj.] (of cloth or clothing) form such folds of creases: *Eleanor's dress rucked up at the front.*
▶ **n.** a crease or wrinkle.
– ORIGIN late 18th cent. (as a noun): from Old Norse *hrukka*.

ruck[3] ▶ **n.** informal a rucksack: *I barely had time to repack my ruck.*

Ruck·ey·ser /ˈro͞oˌkīzər/, Muriel (1913–80), US poet, writer, and political activist. Her works reflected her liberal political activism in poems such as "The Book of the Dead" (1938) and "The Gates" (1976).

ruck·le /ˈrəkəl/ ▶ **v. & n.** Brit. another term for **RUCK**[2].

ruck·sack /ˈrəkˌsak, ˈro͝ok-/ ▶ **n.** a bag with shoulder straps that allow it to be carried on someone's back, typically made of a strong, waterproof material and widely used by hikers; a backpack.
– ORIGIN mid 19th cent.: from German, from *rucken* (dialect variant of *Rücken* 'back') + *Sack* 'bag, sack.'

ruck·us /ˈrəkəs/ ▶ **n.** a disturbance or commotion: *a child is raising a ruckus in class | the current ruckus over same-sex benefits.*
– ORIGIN late 19th cent.: perhaps related to **RUCTION** and **RUMPUS**.

ru·co·la /ˈro͞okələ/ ▶ **n.** another term for **ARUGULA**.

ruc·tion /ˈrəkSHən/ ▶ **n.** informal a disturbance or quarrel. ■ (**ructions**) unpleasant reactions to or complaints about something: *If Mrs. Salt catches her there'll be ructions.*
– ORIGIN early 19th cent.: of unknown origin.

ru·da·ceous /ˈro͞oˈdāSHəs/ ▶ **adj.** Geology (of rock) composed of relatively large fragments (larger than sand grains).
– ORIGIN early 20th cent.: from Latin *rudus* 'rubble' + **-ACEOUS**.

rud·beck·i·a /ro͞odˈbekēə, ˌrəd-/ ▶ **n.** a North American plant of the daisy family, with yellow or orange flowers and a dark conelike center. ● Genus *Rudbeckia*, family Compositae.
– ORIGIN modern Latin, named after Olaf *Rudbeck* (1660–1740), Swedish botanist.

Rudd /rəd/, Kevin Michael (1957–), Australian Labor statesman; prime minister since 2007.

rudd /rəd/ ▶ **n.** (pl. **same**) a freshwater fish of the minnow family with a silvery body and red fins. Native to Eurasia, it has isolated populations in the northeastern US. ● *Scardinius erythrophthalmus*, family Cyprinidae.
– ORIGIN early 16th cent.: apparently related to archaic *rud* 'red color.'

rud·der /ˈrədər/ ▶ **n.** a flat piece, usu. of wood, metal, or plastic, hinged vertically near the stern of a boat or ship for steering. ■ a vertical airfoil pivoted from the horizontal stabilizer of an aircraft, for controlling movement around the vertical axis. ■ application of a rudder in steering a boat, ship, or aircraft: *bring the aircraft to a stall and apply full rudder | a small amount of extra rudder.*
– ORIGIN Old English *rōther* 'paddle, oar'; related to Dutch *roer*, German *Ruder*, also to the verb **ROW**[2].

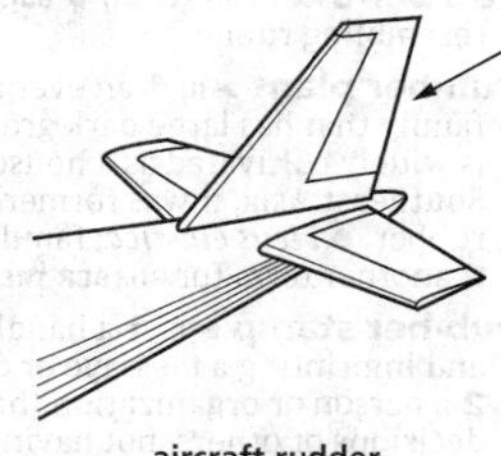
aircraft rudder

rud·der·less /ˈrədərləs/ ▶ **adj.** lacking a rudder. ■ lacking a clear sense of one's aims or principles: *today's leadership is rudderless.*

rud·dle /ˈrədl/ ▶ **n.** a red pigment consisting of ocher. ■ a small block of ruddle or a similar substance that is attached to the chest of a ram to mark the sheep that it tups.
– ORIGIN late Middle English: related to obsolete *rud* 'red color' and **RED**.

rud·dy /ˈrədē/ ▶ **adj.** (**ruddier**, **ruddiest**) **1** (of a person's face) having a healthy red color: *a cheerful pipe-smoking man of ruddy complexion.* ■ having a reddish color: *the ruddy evening light.*
2 Brit. informal, dated used as a euphemism for "bloody."
▶ **v.** (**ruddies**, **ruddying**, **ruddied**) [with obj.] make ruddy in color: *a red flash ruddied the belly of a cloud.*
– DERIVATIVES **rud·di·ly** /ˈrədl-ē/ **adv.** (rare), **rud·di·ness** n.
– ORIGIN late Old English *rudig*, from the base of archaic *rud* 'red color'; related to **RED**.

rud·dy duck ▶ **n.** a New World stiff-tailed duck with a broad bill, the male having mainly deep red-brown plumage and white cheeks. ● *Oxyura jamaicensis*, family Anatidae.

rud·dy turn·stone ▶ **n.** a turnstone of a New World race that breeds on the Arctic coastal tundra.

rude /ro͞od/ ▶ **adj. 1** offensively impolite or ill-mannered: *she had been rude to her boss* | [with infinitive] *it's rude to ask a lady her age.* ■ referring to a taboo subject such as sex in a way considered improper and offensive: *he made a rude gesture.* ■ [attrib.] having a startling abruptness: *the war came as a very rude awakening.*
2 roughly made or done; lacking subtlety or sophistication: *a rude coffin.* ■ archaic ignorant and uneducated: *the new religion was first promulgated by rude men.*
3 [attrib.] chiefly Brit. vigorous or hearty: *Isabel had always been in rude health.*
– DERIVATIVES **rude·ly** adv., **ru·der·y** /-ərē/ n.
– ORIGIN Middle English (sense 2, also 'uncultured'): from Old French, from Latin *rudis* 'unwrought' (referring to handicraft), figuratively 'uncultivated'; related to *rudus* 'broken stone.'

rude boy ▶ **n.** (in Jamaica) a lawless urban youth who likes ska or reggae music.

rude·ness /ro͞odnis/ ▶ **n. 1** lack of manners; discourtesy: *what I will not tolerate is rudeness.*
2 dated roughness or simplicity.

ru·der·al /ˈro͞odərəl/ Botany ▶ **adj.** (of a plant) growing on waste ground or among refuse.
▶ **n.** a plant growing on waste ground or among refuse.
– ORIGIN mid 19th cent.: from modern Latin *ruderalis*, from Latin *rudera*, plural of *rudus* 'rubble.'

ru·di·ment /ˈro͞odəmənt/ ▶ **n. 1** (**the rudiments of**) the first principles of a subject: *she taught the girls the rudiments of reading and writing.* ■ an elementary or primitive form of something: *the rudiments of a hot-water system.*
2 Biology an undeveloped or immature part or organ, esp. a structure in an embryo or larva that will develop into an organ, limb, etc.: *the fetal lung rudiment.*
3 Music a basic pattern used by drummers, such as the roll, the flam, and the paradiddle.
– ORIGIN mid 16th cent.: from French, or from Latin *rudimentum*, from *rudis* 'unwrought,' on the pattern of *elementum* 'element.'

ru·di·men·ta·ry /ˌro͞odəˈment(ə)rē/ ▶ **adj.** involving or limited to basic principles: *he received a rudimentary education.* ■ of or relating to an immature, undeveloped, or basic form: *a rudimentary stage of evolution.*
– DERIVATIVES **ru·di·men·ta·ri·ly** /-menˈte(ə)rəlē, -ˈment(ə)rəlē/ **adv.**, **ru·di·men·ta·ri·ness** n.

ru·dist /ˈro͞odist/ (also **rudistid** /ˈro͞odistid/) ▶ **n.** a cone-shaped extinct bivalve mollusk that formed colonies resembling reefs in the Cretaceous period. ● Superfamily Rudistacea, order Hippuritoida.
– ORIGIN late 19th cent.: from modern Latin *Rudista* (former group name), from Latin *rudis* 'rude'; for the variant spelling see **-ID**[3].

Ru·dolf, Lake /ˈro͞odälf/ former name (until 1979) for Lake Turkana (see **TURKANA, LAKE**).

Ru·dolph /ˈro͞odôlf, -dälf/, Wilma (Glodean) (1940–94), US track athlete. A runner, she was the first woman to win three track and field gold medals in one Olympics, 1960.

Ru·dra /ˈro͞odrə/ Hinduism **1** (in the Rig Veda) a Vedic minor god, associated with the storm, father of the Maruts.
2 one of the names of **SHIVA**.

Ru·dras /ˈro͞odrəs/ another term for **MARUTS**.

rue[1] /ro͞o/ ▶ **v.** (**rues**, **rueing** or **ruing**, **rued**) [with obj.] bitterly regret (something one has done or allowed to happen): *Ferguson will rue the day he turned down that offer | she might live to rue this impetuous decision.*
▶ **n.** archaic repentance; regret: *with rue my heart is laden.* ■ compassion; pity: *tears of pitying rue.*
– ORIGIN Old English *hrēow* 'repentance,' *hrēowan* 'affect with contrition,' of Germanic origin; related to Dutch *rouw* 'mourning' and German *Reue* 'remorse.'

rue[2] ▶ **n.** a perennial evergreen shrub with bitter strong-scented lobed leaves that are used in herbal medicine. ● *Ruta graveolens*, family Rutaceae. ■ used in names of other plants that resemble rue, esp. in leaf shape, e.g., **goat's-rue**, **meadow rue**, **wall rue**.
– ORIGIN Middle English: from Old French, via Latin *ruta* from Greek *rhutē*.

rue·ful /ˈro͞ofəl/ ▶ **adj.** expressing sorrow or regret, esp. when in a slightly humorous way: *she gave a rueful grin.*
– DERIVATIVES **rue·ful·ly** adv., **rue·ful·ness** n.
– ORIGIN Middle English (also in the sense 'pitiable'): from the noun **RUE**[1] + **-FUL**.

ru·fes·cent /ro͞oˈfesənt/ ▶ **adj.** tinged with red or rufous.
– DERIVATIVES **ru·fes·cence** n.
– ORIGIN early 19th cent.: from Latin *rufescent-* 'becoming reddish,' from the verb *rufescere*, from *rufus* 'reddish.'

ruff[1] /rəf/ ▶ **n. 1** a projecting starched frill worn around the neck, characteristic of Elizabethan and Jacobean costume.
2 a projecting or conspicuously colored ring of feathers or hair around the neck of a bird or mammal.
3 (pl. **same** or **ruffs**) a northern Eurasian wading bird, the male of which has a large variously colored ruff and ear tufts in the breeding season, used in display. ● *Philomachus pugnax*, family Scolopacidae; the female is called a **reeve**.
– DERIVATIVES **ruffed** adj., **ruff-like** /-ˌlīk/ adj.
– ORIGIN early 16th cent. (first used denoting a frill around a sleeve): probably from a variant of **ROUGH**.

ruff[1] 1

ruff² ▶ **n. 1** an edible marine fish of Australian inshore waters that is related to the Australian salmon. Also called **ROUGHY** in Australia. ● *Arripis georgianus*, family Arripidae.
2 variant spelling of **RUFFE**.
– ORIGIN late 19th cent.: from **RUFFE**.

ruff³ ▶ **v.** [no obj.] (in bridge, whist, and similar card games) play a trump in a trick that was led in a different suit. ■ [with obj.] play a trump on (a card in another suit).
▶ **n.** an act of ruffing or opportunity to ruff.
– ORIGIN late 16th cent. (originally the name of a card game resembling whist): from Old French *rouffle*, a parallel formation to Italian *ronfa* (perhaps an alteration of *trionfo* 'a trump').

ruff⁴ ▶ **n.** Music one of the basic patterns (rudiments) of drumming, consisting of a single note preceded by either two grace notes played with the other stick (**double-stroke ruff** or **drag**) or three grace notes played with alternating sticks (**four-stroke ruff**).
– ORIGIN late 17th cent.: probably imitative.

ruffe /rəf/ (also **ruff**) ▶ **n.** a freshwater fish of the perch family, with a greenish-brown back and yellow sides and underparts. Native to Eurasia, it has been introduced into Lakes Michigan and Superior. ● *Gymnocephalus cernua*, family Percidae.
– ORIGIN late Middle English: probably from a variant of **ROUGH**.

ruffed grouse ▶ **n.** a North American woodland grouse that has a black ruff on the sides of the neck. ● *Bonasa umbellus*, family Tetraonidae (or Phasianidae).

ruffed le·mur ▶ **n.** a lemur with a prominent muzzle and dense fur that forms a ruff around the neck, living in the Madagascan rain forest. ● *Varecia variegata*, family Lemuridae.

ruf·fi·an /ˈrəfēən/ ▶ **n.** a violent person, esp. one involved in crime.
– DERIVATIVES **ruf·fi·an·ism** /-ˌnizəm/ **n.**, **ruf·fi·an·ly adv.**
– ORIGIN late 15th cent.: from Old French *ruffian*, from Italian *ruffiano*, perhaps from dialect *rofia* 'scab, scurf,' of Germanic origin.

ruf·fle /ˈrəfəl/ ▶ **v.** [with obj.] **1** disorder or disarrange (someone's hair), typically by running one's hands through it: *he ruffled her hair affectionately.* ■ (of a bird) erect (its feathers) in anger or display: *on his departure to the high wires, the starling ruffled his feathers and flirted his wings.* ■ disturb the smoothness or tranquility of: *the evening breeze ruffled the surface of the pond in the yard.* ■ disconcert or upset the composure of (someone): *Brian had been ruffled by her questions.*
2 (usu. as adj. **ruffled**) ornament with or gather into a frill: *a blouse with a high ruffled neck.*
▶ **n. 1** an ornamental gathered or goffered frill of lace or other cloth on a garment, esp. around the wrist or neck.
2 a vibrating drumbeat.
– PHRASES **ruffle someone's feathers** cause someone to become annoyed or upset: *tampering with the traditional approach would ruffle a few feathers.* **smooth someone's ruffled feathers** make someone less angry or irritated by using soothing words.
– ORIGIN Middle English (as a verb): of unknown origin. Current noun senses date from the late 17th cent.

ru·fi·yaa /ˈro͞ofēˌyä/ ▶ **n.** (pl. **same**) the basic monetary unit of the Maldives, equal to 100 laris.
– ORIGIN Maldivian.

ru·fous /ˈro͞ofəs/ ▶ **adj.** reddish brown in color.
▶ **n.** a reddish-brown color.
– ORIGIN late 18th cent.: from Latin *rufus* 'red, reddish' + **-OUS**.

rug /rəg/ ▶ **n.** a floor covering of thick woven material or animal skin, typically not extending over the entire floor. ■ chiefly Brit. a thick woolen coverlet or wrap, used esp. when traveling. ■ informal a toupee or wig.
– PHRASES **pull the rug (out) from under** abruptly withdraw support from (someone): *the rug was pulled right out from beneath our feet.*
– ORIGIN mid 16th cent. (denoting a type of coarse woolen cloth): probably of Scandinavian origin; compare with Norwegian dialect *rugga* 'coverlet,' Swedish *rugg* 'ruffled hair'; related to **RAG¹**. The sense 'small carpet' dates from the early 19th cent.

rug·a·lach /ˈrəgələKH/ (also **rugelach**) ▶ **n.** a bite-size cookie made with cream-cheese dough rolled around a filling of nuts, poppy seed paste, chocolate, or jam.
– ORIGIN Yiddish, literally 'little twists.'

rug·by /ˈrəgbē/ (also **rugby football**) ▶ **n.** a team game played with an oval ball that may be kicked, carried, and passed from hand to hand. Points are scored by grounding the ball behind the opponents' goal line (thereby scoring a try) or by kicking it between the two posts and over the crossbar of the opponents' goal. See also **RUGBY LEAGUE** and **RUGBY UNION**.
– ORIGIN mid 19th cent.: named after *Rugby* School, where the game was first played.

rug·by league ▶ **n.** a form of rugby played in teams of thirteen, originally by a group of northern English clubs that separated from rugby union in 1895. Besides having somewhat different rules, the game differed from rugby union in always allowing professionalism.

rug·by un·ion ▶ **n.** a form of rugby played in teams of fifteen. Unlike rugby league, the game was originally strictly amateur, being opened to professionalism only in 1995.

rug·ged /ˈrəgid/ ▶ **adj.** (of ground or terrain) having a broken, rocky, and uneven surface: *a rugged coastline.* ■ (of a machine or other manufactured object) strongly made and capable of withstanding rough handling: *the binoculars are compact, lightweight, and rugged.* ■ having or requiring toughness and determination: *a week of rugged, demanding adventure at an outdoor training center.* ■ (of a man's face or looks) having attractively strong, rough-hewn features: *he was known for his rugged good looks.*
– DERIVATIVES **rug·ged·ly adv.**, **rug·ged·ness n.**
– ORIGIN Middle English (in the sense 'shaggy,' also (of a horse) 'rough-coated'): probably of Scandinavian origin; compare with Swedish *rugga* 'roughen,' also with **RUG**.

rug·ged·ized /ˈrəgidˌīzd/ ▶ **adj.** designed or improved to be hard-wearing or shock-resistant: *ruggedized computers suitable for use on the battlefield.*
– DERIVATIVES **rug·ged·i·za·tion** /ˌrəgədəˈzāSHən/ **n.**

rug·ger /ˈrəgər/ ▶ **n.** Brit. informal rugby.

ru·go·la /ˈro͞ogələ/ ▶ **n.** another term for **ARUGULA**.

ru·go·sa /ro͞oˈgōsə, -zə/ (also **rugosa rose**) ▶ **n.** a widely cultivated Southeast Asian rose with dark green wrinkled leaves and deep pink flowers. ● *Rosa rugosa*, family Rosaceae.
– ORIGIN late 19th cent.: feminine of Latin *rugosus* (see **RUGOSE**), used as a specific epithet.

ru·gose /ˈro͞oˌgōs/ ▶ **adj.** chiefly Biology wrinkled; corrugated: *rugose corals.*
– DERIVATIVES **ru·gos·i·ty** /ro͞oˈgäsətē/ **n.**
– ORIGIN late Middle English: from Latin *rugosus*, from *ruga* 'wrinkle.'

rug rat ▶ **n.** informal a child.

Ruhr /ro͝or/ a region of coal mining and heavy industry in North Rhine–Westphalia, in western Germany. It is named after the Ruhr River, which flows through it and meets the Rhine River near Duisburg. The Ruhr was occupied by French troops 1923–24, after Germany defaulted on war reparation payments.

ru·in /ˈro͞oin/ ▶ **n.** the physical destruction or disintegration of something or the state of disintegrating or being destroyed: *a large white house falling into gentle ruin.* ■ the remains of a building, typically an old one, that has suffered much damage or disintegration: *the ruins of the castle | the church is a ruin now.* ■ the disastrous disintegration of someone's life: *the ruin and heartbreak wrought by alcohol, divorce, and violence.* ■ the cause of such disintegration: *they don't know how to say no, and that's been their ruin.* ■ the complete loss of one's money and other assets: *the financial cost could mean ruin.*
▶ **v. 1** [with obj.] reduce (a building or place) to a state of decay, collapse, or disintegration: (as adj. **ruined**) *a ruined castle.* ■ cause great and usually irreparable damage or harm to; have a disastrous effect on: *a noisy freeway has ruined village life.* ■ reduce to a state of poverty: *they were ruined by the highest interest rates this century.*
2 [no obj.] literary fall headlong or with a crash: *carriages go ruining over the brink from time to time.*
– PHRASES **in ruins** in a state of complete disorder or disintegration: *the economy was in ruins.*
– ORIGIN Middle English (in the sense 'collapse of a building'): from Old French *ruine*, from Latin *ruina*, from *ruere* 'to fall.'

ru·in·a·tion /ˌro͞oəˈnāSHən/ ▶ **n.** the action or fact of ruining someone or something or of being ruined: *commercial malpractice causes the ruination of thousands of people.* ■ the state of being ruined: *the headquarters fell into ruination.*
– ORIGIN mid 17th cent.: from obsolete *ruinate* + **-ION**.

ru·in·ous /ˈro͞oənəs/ ▶ **adj. 1** disastrous or destructive: *a ruinous effect on the environment.* ■ costing far more than can be afforded: *the cost of their ransom might be ruinous.*
2 in ruins; dilapidated: *the castle is ruinous.*
– DERIVATIVES **ru·in·ous·ly adv.**, **ru·in·ous·ness n.**
– ORIGIN late Middle English (also in the sense 'falling down'): from Latin *ruinosus*, from *ruina* (see **RUIN**).

Ruis·dael /ˈroisˌdäl/ (also **Ruysdael**), Jacob van (*c.*1628–82), Dutch landscape painter. Born in Haarlem, he painted the surrounding landscape until his move to Amsterdam in 1657.

Ru·iz de A·lar·cón y Men·do·za /ro͞oˈēs dā ˌälärˈkōn ē menˈdōsə/, Juan (1580–1639), Spanish playwright, born in Mexico City.

Ruk·ey·ser /ˈro͞oˌkīzər/, Louis (1933–2006), US economic forecaster and commentator. He hosted the television program *Wall Street Week* 1970–2002, and published two economic newsletters from 1992 and 1994.

Rukh /ro͝oKH/ the nationalist movement that established the independence of the Ukraine in 1991.
– ORIGIN Ukrainian, 'people's movement.'

rukh /ro͞ok/ ▶ **n.** another term for **ROC**.
– ORIGIN from Hindi *rūkh*.

rule /ro͞ol/ ▶ **n. 1** one of a set of explicit or understood regulations or principles governing conduct within a particular activity or sphere: *the rules of the game were understood.* ■ a law or principle that operates within a particular sphere of knowledge, describing or prescribing what is possible or allowable: *the rules of grammar.* ■ a code of practice and discipline for a religious order or community: *the Rule of St. Benedict.* ■ control of or dominion over an area or people: *the revolution brought an end to British rule.* ■ (**the rule**) the normal or customary state of things: *such accidents are the exception rather than the rule.*
2 a strip of wood or other rigid material used for measuring length or marking straight lines; a ruler. ■ a thin printed line or dash, generally used to separate headings, columns, or sections of text.
3 (**Rules**) Austral. short for **AUSTRALIAN RULES** (football). ■ Law an order made by a judge or court with reference to a particular case only.
▶ **v. 1** [with obj.] exercise ultimate power or authority over (an area and its people): *Latin America today is ruled by elected politicians* | [no obj.] *the period in which Spain ruled over Portugal.* ■ (of a feeling) have a powerful and restricting influence on (a person's life): *her whole life seemed to be ruled by fear.* ■ [no obj.] be a dominant or powerful factor or force: [with complement] *the black market rules supreme.* ■ [with clause] pronounce authoritatively and legally to be the case: *a federal court ruled that he was unfairly dismissed from his job.* ■ Astrology (of a planet) have a particular influence over (a sign of the zodiac, house, aspect of life, etc.).
2 [with obj.] make parallel lines across (paper): (as adj. **ruled**) *a sheet of ruled paper.*
– PHRASES **as a rule** usually, but not always. **make it a rule to do something** have as a habit or general principle to do something: *I make it a rule never to mix business with pleasure.* **rule of law** the restriction of the arbitrary exercise of power by subordinating it to well-defined and established laws. **rule of thumb** a broadly accurate guide or principle, based on experience or practice rather than theory. **rule the roost** be in complete control.
– PHRASAL VERBS **rule something out** (or **in**) exclude (or include) something as a possibility: *the doctor ruled out appendicitis.*
– DERIVATIVES **rule·less adj.**
– ORIGIN Middle English: from Old French *reule* (noun), *reuler* (verb), from late Latin *regulare*, from Latin *regula* 'straight stick.'

rule·book (also **rule book**) ▶ **n.** the regulations or standards of behavior that should be followed in a particular job, organization, or sphere: *a lot of bands decided they were going to tear up the rock rulebook and start again.*

rule of en·gage·ment (abbr.: **ROE**) ▶ **n.** (usu. **rules of engagement**) a directive issued by a military authority specifying the circumstances and limitations under which forces will engage in combat with the enemy.

rule of the road ▶ **n.** (usu. **rules of the road**) a custom or law regulating the direction in which two vehicles (or riders or ships) should move to pass one another on meeting, or which should yield to the other, so as to avoid collision.

rule of three ▶ n. Mathematics, dated a method of finding a number in the same ratio to a given number as exists between two other given numbers.

rul·er /ˈro͞olər/ ▶ n. **1** a person exercising government or dominion. ■ Astrology another term for RULING PLANET.
2 a straight strip or cylinder of plastic, wood, metal, or other rigid material, typically marked at regular intervals, to draw straight lines or measure distances.
– DERIVATIVES **rul·er·ship** /-ˌSHip/ n.

Rules Com·mit·tee ▶ n. a legislative committee responsible for expediting the passage of bills. ■ (**rules committee**) the body of people charged with overseeing the rules of an athletic league: *the NCAA football rules committee considers unsportsmanlike acts to be the game's no. 1 problem.*

rul·ing /ˈro͞oliNG/ ▶ n. an authoritative decision or pronouncement, esp. one made by a judge.
▶ adj. currently exercising authority or influence: *the ruling coalition.*

rul·ing eld·er ▶ n. a nominated or elected lay official of any of various Christian churches, esp. of a Presbyterian church.

rul·ing pas·sion ▶ n. an interest or concern that occupies a large part of someone's time and effort: *football remained their ruling passion.*

rul·ing plan·et ▶ n. Astrology a planet that is held to have a particular influence over a specific sign of the zodiac, house, aspect of life, etc.

rum¹ /rəm/ ▶ n. an alcoholic liquor distilled from sugar-cane residues or molasses. ■ intoxicating liquor.
– ORIGIN mid 17th cent.: perhaps an abbreviation of obsolete *rumbullion*, in the same sense.

rum² ▶ adj. (**rummer**, **rummest**) Brit. informal, dated odd; peculiar: *it's a rum business, certainly* | *they were a rum bunch.*
– DERIVATIVES **rum·ly** adv., **rum·ness** n.
– ORIGIN late 18th cent.: of unknown origin.

Ru·ma·ni·an /ro͝oˈmānēən, -nyən/ ▶ adj. & n. variant spelling of ROMANIAN.

rum·ba /ˈrəmbə, ˈro͝om-, ˈro͞om-/ (also **rhumba**) ▶ n. a rhythmic dance with Spanish and African elements, originating in Cuba. ■ a piece of music for this dance or in a similar style. ■ a ballroom dance imitative of this dance.
▶ v. (**rumbas**, **rumbaing**, **rumbaed** /-bəd/) [no obj.] dance the rumba.
– ORIGIN 1920s: from Latin American Spanish.

rum ba·ba /ˌrəm ˈbäbə/ ▶ n. see BABA¹.

rum·ble /ˈrəmbəl/ ▶ v. **1** [no obj.] make a continuous deep, resonant sound: *thunder rumbled, lightning flickered.* ■ [with adverbial of direction] (esp. of a large vehicle) move in the specified direction with such a sound: *heavy trucks rumbled through the streets.* ■ [with obj.] utter in a deep, resonant voice: *the man's low voice rumbled an instruction.* ■ (of a person's stomach) make a deep, resonant sound due to hunger.
2 [no obj.] informal take part in a street fight between gangs or large groups: *the five of them rumbled with the men in the other car.*
3 [with obj.] Brit. informal discover (an illicit activity or its perpetrator): *it wouldn't need a genius to rumble my little game.*
▶ n. **1** a continuous deep, resonant sound like distant thunder: *the steady rumble of traffic* | figurative *there were rumbles of discontent from small retailers.*
2 informal a street fight between gangs or large groups.
– ORIGIN late Middle English: probably from Middle Dutch *rommelen*, *rummelen*, of imitative origin. Sense 3 of the verb may be a different word.

rum·bler /ˈrəmb(ə)lər/ ▶ n. a person or thing that rumbles. ■ a machine for peeling potatoes. ■ historical a round bell containing a small hard object placed inside to rattle, formerly used esp. on horses' harnesses.

rum·ble seat ▶ n. an uncovered folding seat in the rear of an automobile.

rum·ble strip ▶ n. a series of raised strips across a road or along its edge, changing the noise a vehicle's tires make on the surface and so warning drivers of speed restrictions or of the edge of the road.

rum·bling /ˈrəmb(ə)liNG/ ▶ n. a continuous deep, resonant sound: *the rumbling of wheels in the distance.* ■ (often **rumblings**) an early indication or rumor of dissatisfaction or incipient change: *there are growing rumblings of discontent.*
▶ adj. making or constituting a deep resonant sound: *a rumbling ancient air conditioner* | *a rumbling noise.*

rum·bus·tious /ˌrəmˈbəsCHəs/ ▶ adj. informal, chiefly Brit. boisterous or unruly.
– DERIVATIVES **rum·bus·tious·ly** adv., **rum·bus·tious·ness** n.
– ORIGIN late 18th cent.: probably an alteration of archaic *robustious* 'boisterous, robust.'

rum·dum /ˈrəmˌdəm/ ▶ n. informal a drunkard, esp. a derelict alcoholic.
– ORIGIN late 19th cent.: from RUM¹ + DUMB.

ru·men /ˈro͞omən/ ▶ n. (pl. **rumens** or **rumina** /-mənə/) Zoology the first stomach of a ruminant, which receives food or cud from the esophagus, partly digests it with the aid of bacteria, and passes it to the reticulum.
– DERIVATIVES **ru·min·al** adj.
– ORIGIN early 18th cent.: from Latin, literally 'throat.'

ru·mi·nant /ˈro͞omənənt/ ▶ n. **1** an even-toed ungulate mammal that chews the cud regurgitated from its rumen. The ruminants comprise the cattle, sheep, antelopes, deer, giraffes, and their relatives. ● Suborder Ruminantia, order Artiodactyla: six families.
2 a contemplative person; a person given to meditation.
▶ adj. of or belonging to ruminants.
– ORIGIN mid 17th cent.: from Latin *ruminant-* 'chewing over again,' from the verb *ruminari*, from *rumen* 'throat' (see RUMEN).

ru·mi·nate /ˈro͞oməˌnāt/ ▶ v. [no obj.] **1** think deeply about something: *we sat ruminating on the nature of existence.*
2 (of a ruminant) chew the cud.
– DERIVATIVES **ru·mi·na·tion** /ˌro͞oməˈnāSHən/ n., **ru·mi·na·tive** /-ˌnātiv/ adj., **ru·mi·na·tive·ly** /-ˌnātivlē/ adv., **ru·mi·na·tor** /-ˌnātər/ n.
– ORIGIN mid 16th cent.: from Latin *ruminat-* 'chewed over,' from the verb *ruminari*.

rum·mage /ˈrəmij/ ▶ v. [no obj.] search unsystematically and untidily through a mass or receptacle: *he rummaged in his pocket for a handkerchief* | [with obj.] *he rummaged the drawer for his false teeth.* ■ [with obj.] find (something) by searching in this way: *Mick* **rummaged up** *his skateboard.* ■ [with obj.] (of a customs officer) make a thorough search of (a vessel): *our brief was to rummage as many of the vessels as possible.*
▶ n. an unsystematic and untidy search through a mass or receptacle. ■ a thorough search of a vessel by a customs officer.
– DERIVATIVES **rum·mag·er** n.
– ORIGIN late 15th cent.: from Old French *arrumage*, from *arrumer* 'stow (in a hold),' from Middle Dutch *ruim* 'room.' In early use the word referred to the arranging of items such as casks in the hold of a ship, giving rise (early 17th cent.) to the verb sense 'make a search of (a vessel).'

rum·mage sale ▶ n. a sale of miscellaneous secondhand articles, typically held in order to raise money for a charity or a special event.

rum·mer /ˈrəmər/ ▶ n. a large drinking glass.
– ORIGIN mid 17th cent.: of Low Dutch origin; related to Dutch *roemer*; the original meaning is perhaps 'Roman glass.'

rum·my¹ /ˈrəmē/ ▶ n. a card game, sometimes played with two decks, in which the players try to form sets and sequences of cards.
– ORIGIN early 20th cent.: of unknown origin.

rum·my² ▶ adj. (**rummier**, **rummiest**) another term for RUM².

ru·mor /ˈro͞omər/ (Brit. **rumour**) ▶ n. a currently circulating story or report of uncertain or doubtful truth: *they were investigating rumors of a massacre* | **rumor has it that** *he will take a year off.*
▶ v. (**be rumored**) be circulated as an unverified account: [with clause] **it's rumored that** *he lives on a houseboat* | [with infinitive] *she is rumored to have gone into hiding.*
– ORIGIN late Middle English: from Old French *rumur*, from Latin *rumor* 'noise.'

ru·mor·mon·ger /ˈro͞omərˌmäNGgər, -ˌməNGgər/ ▶ n. derogatory a person who spreads rumors.
– DERIVATIVES **ru·mor·mon·ger·ing** n.

rump /rəmp/ ▶ n. **1** the hind part of the body of a mammal or the lower back of a bird. ■ chiefly humorous a person's buttocks.
2 a small or unimportant remnant of something originally larger: *once the profitable enterprises have been sold the unprofitable rump will be left.*
– DERIVATIVES **rump·less** adj.
– ORIGIN late Middle English: probably of Scandinavian origin; compare with Danish and Norwegian *rumpe* 'backside.'

rum·ple /ˈrəmpəl/ ▶ v. [with obj.] (usu. as adj. **rumpled**) give a creased, ruffled, or disheveled appearance to: *a rumpled bed.*
▶ n. [in sing.] an untidy state.
– DERIVATIVES **rum·ply** /ˈrəmp(ə)lē/ adj.
– ORIGIN early 16th cent. (as a noun in the sense 'wrinkle'): from Middle Dutch *rompel*.

rum·pot /ˈrəmˌpät/ ▶ n. informal an alcoholic.

Rump Par·lia·ment the part of the Long Parliament in Britain that continued to sit after the forced exclusion of Presbyterian members in 1648. It voted for the trial that resulted in the execution of Charles I.
– ORIGIN origin uncertain: said to derive from *The Bloody Rump*, the name of a paper written before the trial, the word being popularized after a speech by Major General Brown, given at a public assembly; also said to have been coined by Clem Walker in his *History of Independency* (1648), as a term for those strenuously opposing the king.

rump·sprung /ˈrəmpˌsprəNG/ ▶ adj. informal (of furniture) baggy and worn in the seat: *a rumpsprung armchair.*

rump steak ▶ n. a cut of beef from the animal's rump.

rum·pus /ˈrəmpəs/ ▶ n. (pl. **rumpuses**) [usu. in sing.] informal a noisy disturbance; a commotion: *he caused a rumpus with his flair for troublemaking.*
– ORIGIN mid 18th cent.: probably fanciful.

rum·pus room ▶ n. a room, typically in the basement of a house, used for games and recreation.

run /rən/ ▶ v. (**runs**, **running**; past **ran** /ran/; past participle **run**) **1** [no obj.] move at a speed faster than a walk, never having both or all the feet on the ground at the same time: *the dog ran across the road* | *she ran the last few yards, breathing heavily* | *he hasn't paid for his drinks—run and catch him.* ■ run as a sport or for exercise: *I run every morning.* ■ (of an athlete or a racehorse) compete in a race: *she ran in the 200 meters* | [with obj.] *Dave has run 42 marathons.* ■ [with obj.] enter (a racehorse) for a race. ■ Baseball (of a batter or base runner) attempt to advance to the next base. ■ (of hounds) chase or hunt their quarry. ■ (of a boat) sail directly before the wind, esp. in bad weather. ■ (of a migratory fish) go upriver from the sea in order to spawn.
2 [no obj.] move about in a hurried and hectic way: *I've spent the whole day running around after the kids.* ■ (**run to**) have rapid recourse to (someone) for support or help: *don't come running to me for a handout.*
3 pass or cause to pass quickly or smoothly in a particular direction: [no obj.] *the rumor ran through the pack of photographers* | [with obj.] *Helen ran her fingers through her hair.* ■ move or cause to move somewhere forcefully or with a particular result: [no obj.] *the tanker* **ran aground** *off the Aleutian Islands* | [with obj.] *a woman ran a stroller into the back of my legs.* ■ [with obj.] informal fail to stop at (a red traffic light). ■ [with obj.] navigate (rapids or a waterfall) in a boat. ■ extend or cause to extend in a particular direction: [no obj.] *cobbled streets run down to a tiny harbor* | [with obj.] *he ran a wire under the carpet.* ■ [no obj.] (**run in**) (of a quality, trait, or condition) be common or inherent in members of (a particular family), esp. over several generations: *weight problems run in my family.* ■ [no obj.] pass into or reach a specified state or level: *inflation is* **running at** *11 percent* | [with complement] *the decision* **ran counter to** *previous government commitments.*
4 (with reference to a liquid) flow or cause to flow: [no obj., with adverbial of direction] *a small river runs into the sea at one side of the castle* | [with obj.] *she ran cold water into the sink.* ■ [with obj.] cause water to flow over (something): *I ran my hands under the faucet.* ■ [with obj.] fill (a bath) with water: [with two objs.] *I'll run you a nice hot bath.* ■ (**run with**) be covered or streaming with (a particular liquid): *his face was running with sweat.* ■ emit or exude a liquid: *she was weeping loudly, and her nose was running.* ■ (of a solid substance) melt and become fluid: *it was so hot that the butter ran.* ■ (of the sea, the tide, or a river) rise higher or flow more quickly: *there was still a heavy sea running.* ■ (of dye or color in fabric or paper) dissolve and spread when the fabric or paper becomes wet: *the red dye ran when the socks were washed.* ■ (of a stocking or pair of tights) develop a ravel.
5 [no obj.] (of a bus, train, ferry, or other form of transportation) make a regular journey on a particular route: *buses run into town every half hour.* ■ [with obj.] put (a particular form of public transportation) in service: *the group is drawing up plans to run trains on key routes.* ■ [with obj.] take (someone) somewhere in a car: *I'll run you home.*
6 [with obj.] be in charge of; manage: *Andrea runs her own catering business* | [as adj. in combination] (**-run**) *an attractive family-run hotel.* ■ [no obj.] (of a system, organization, or plan) operate or proceed in a particular way: *everything's* **running according to plan.** ■ organize and make available for other people: *we decided to run a series of seminars.*

r

■ carry out (a test or procedure): *he asked the army to run tests on the anti nerve-gas pills.* ■ own, maintain, and use (a vehicle).
7 be in or cause to be in operation; function or cause to function: [no obj.] *the car **runs on** unleaded fuel* | [with obj.] *a number of peripherals can be **run off** one SCSI port.* ■ move or cause to move between the spools of a recording machine: [with obj.] *I ran the tape back* | [no obj.] *the tape has run out.*
8 [no obj.] continue or be valid or operative for a particular period of time: *the course **ran for** two days* | *this particular debate will **run on and on**.* ■ [with adverbial or complement] happen or arrive at the specified time: *the program was running fifteen minutes late.* ■ (of a play or exhibition) be staged or presented: *the play ran on Broadway last year.*
9 [no obj.] be a candidate in a political election: *he announced that he intended to **run for** President.* ■ [with obj.] (esp. of a political party) sponsor (a candidate) in an election: *they ran their first candidate for the school board.*
10 publish or be published in a newspaper or magazine: [with obj.] *the tabloids ran the story* | [no obj.] *when the story ran, there was a big to-do.* ■ [no obj.] (of a story, argument, or piece of writing) have a specified wording or contents: *"Tapestries slashed!" ran the dramatic headline.*
11 [with obj.] bring (goods) into a country illegally and secretly; smuggle: *they run drugs for the cocaine cartels.*
12 [with two objs.] (of an object or act) cost (someone) (a specified amount): *a new photocopier will run us about $1,300.*
▶ **n.** **1** [usu. in sing.] an act or spell of running: *I usually go for a run in the morning* | *a cross-country run.* ■ a running pace: *Bobby set off **at a run**.* ■ an opportunity or attempt to achieve something: *their absence means the Russians will have **a clear run at** the title.* ■ a preliminary test of the efficiency of a procedure or system: *if you are styling your hair yourself, have a practice run.* ■ an attempt to secure election to political office: *his run for the Republican nomination.* ■ an annual mass migration of fish up a river to spawn, or their return migration afterward: *the annual salmon runs.*
2 a journey accomplished or route taken by a vehicle, aircraft, or boat, esp. on a regular basis: *the New York-Washington run.* ■ a short excursion made in a car: *we could take a run out to the country.* ■ the distance covered in a specified period, esp. by a ship: *a record run of 398 miles from noon to noon.* ■ a short flight made by an aircraft on a straight and even course at a constant speed before or while dropping bombs.
3 Baseball a point scored when a base runner reaches home plate after touching the other bases. ■ Cricket a point scored by hitting the ball so that both batsmen are able to run between the wickets, or awarded in some other circumstances.
4 a continuous spell of a particular situation or condition: *he's had a run of bad luck.* ■ a continuous series of performances: *the play had a long run on Broadway.* ■ a quantity or amount of something produced at one time: *a production run of only 150 cars.* ■ a continuous stretch or length of something: *long runs of copper piping.* ■ a rapid series of musical notes forming a scale. ■ a sequence of cards of the same suit.
5 (**a run on**) a widespread and sudden or continuous demand for (a particular currency or commodity): *there's been a big run on nostalgia toys this year.* ■ a sudden demand for repayment from a bank made by a large number of lenders: *growing nervousness among investors led to a run on some banks.*
6 (**the run of**) free and unrestricted use of or access to: *her cats were given the run of the house.*
7 (**the run**) [usu. with adj.] the average or usual type of person or thing: *she stood out from **the general run of** varsity cheerleaders.*
8 an enclosed area in which domestic animals or birds can run freely in the open: *a chicken run.* ■ [usu. with adj.] a track made or regularly used by a particular animal: *a badger run.* ■ a sloping snow-covered course or track used for skiing, bobsledding, or tobogganing: *a ski run.* ■ Austral./NZ a large open stretch of land used for pasture or the raising of stock: *one of the richest cattle runs of the district.*
9 a line of unraveled stitches in stockings or tights.
10 a downward trickle of paint or a similar substance when applied too thickly.
11 a small stream or brook.
12 (**the runs**) informal diarrhea.
13 Nautical the after part of a ship's bottom where it rises and narrows toward the stern.
– PHRASES **be run off one's feet** see FOOT. **come running** be eager to do what someone wants: *he had only to snap his fingers, and she would come running.* **give someone/something a (good) run for their money** provide someone or something with challenging competition or opposition. **have a (good) run for one's money** derive reward or enjoyment in return for one's outlay or efforts. **on the run 1** trying to avoid being captured: *a kidnapper on the run from the FBI.* **2** while running: *he took a pass on the run.* ■ continuously active and busy: *I'm on the run every minute of the day.* **run a blockade** see BLOCKADE. **run afoul** (or **foul**) **of 1** Nautical collide or become entangled with (an obstacle or another vessel): *another ship ran afoul of us.* **2** come into conflict with; go against: *the act may run afoul of consumer protection legislation.* **run dry** (of a well or river) cease to flow or have any water. ■ (esp. of a source of money or information) be completely used up: *municipal relief funds had long since run dry.* **run an errand** carry out an errand, typically on someone else's behalf. **(make a) run for it** attempt to escape someone or something by running away. **run the gauntlet** see GAUNTLET[2]. **run high** see HIGH. **run oneself into the ground** see GROUND[1]. **run its course** see COURSE. **run low** (or **short**) become depleted: *supplies had run short.* ■ have too little of something: *we're **running short** of time.* **run a mile** see MILE. **run off at the mouth** informal talk excessively or indiscreetly. **run someone out of town** force someone to leave a place. **run rings around** see RING[1]. **run riot** see RIOT. **run the risk** (or **run risks**) see RISK. **run the show** informal dominate or be in charge of a project, undertaking, or domain. **run a temperature** (or **fever**) be suffering from a fever or high temperature. **run someone/something to earth** (or **ground**) Hunting chase a quarry to its lair. ■ find someone or something, typically after a long search. **run to ruin** archaic fall into disrepair; gradually deteriorate. **run to seed** see SEED. **run wild** see WILD.
– PHRASAL VERBS **run across** meet or find by chance: *I just thought you might have run across him before.* **run after** informal seek to acquire or attain; pursue persistently: *businesses that have spent years running after the boomer market.* ■ seek the company of (someone) with the aim of developing a romantic or sexual relationship with them. **run against** archaic collide with (someone). ■ happen to meet: *I ran against Flanagan the other day.* **run along** [in imperative] informal go away (used typically to address a child): *run along now, there's a good girl.* **run around with** see RUN WITH (sense 2). **run at** rush toward (someone) to attack or as if to attack them. **run away** leave or escape from a place, person, or situation of danger: *children who **run away from** home normally go to big cities.* ■ (also informal **run off**) leave one's home or current partner in order to establish a relationship with someone else: *he **ran off with** his wife's best friend* | *Fran, let's **run away together**.* ■ try to avoid acknowledging or facing up to an unpleasant or difficult situation: *the commissioners are **running away from** their responsibilities.* **run away with 1** (of one's imagination or emotions) work wildly, so as to overwhelm (one): *Susan's imagination was running away with her.* ■ (of a horse) bolt with (its rider). **2** accept (an idea) without thinking it through properly: *a lot of people ran away with the idea that they were Pacifists.* **3** excel in or win (a competition) easily: *the Yankees ran away with the series.* **run something by** (or **past**) tell (someone) about something, esp. in order to ascertain their opinion or reaction. **run someone/something down 1** (of a vehicle or its driver) hit a person or animal and knock them to the ground. ■ (of a boat) collide with another vessel. **2** criticize someone or something unfairly or unkindly. **3** find someone or something after a search: *she finally ran the professor down.* **4** Baseball (of two or more fielders) try to tag out a base runner who is trapped between two bases, in the process throwing the ball back and forth. **run something down** (or **run down**) reduce (or become reduced) in size, numbers, or resources: *hardwood stocks in some countries are rapidly running down.* ■ lose (or cause to lose) power; stop (or cause to stop) functioning: *the battery has run down.* ■ gradually deteriorate (or cause to deteriorate) in quality or condition: *the property had been allowed to run down.* **run someone in** informal arrest someone. **run into 1** collide with: *he ran into a lamp post.* ■ meet by chance: *I ran into Stasia and Katie on the way home.* ■ experience (a problem or difficult situation): *the bank ran into financial difficulties.* **2** reach (a level or amount): *debts running into millions of dollars.* **3** blend into or appear to coalesce with: *her words ran into each other.* **run off** see RUN AWAY above. **run off with** informal steal: *the treasurer had run off with the pension funds.* **run something off 1** reproduce copies of a piece of writing on a machine. ■ write or recite something quickly and with little effort. **2** drain liquid from a container: *run off the water that has been standing in the pipes.* **run on 1** continue without stopping; go on longer than is expected: *the story ran on for months.* ■ talk incessantly. **2** (also **run upon**) (of a person's mind or a discussion) be preoccupied or concerned with (a particular subject): *my thoughts always ran too much on death.* **3** Printing continue on the same line as the preceding matter. **run out 1** (of a supply of something) be used up: *our food is about to run out.* ■ use up one's supply of something: *we've **run out** of gasoline.* ■ become no longer valid: *her contract runs out at the end of the year.* **2** (of rope) be paid out: *slowly, he let the cables run out.* **3** [with adverbial of direction] extend; project: *a row of buildings ran out to Cityline Avenue.* **run out on** informal abandon (someone); cease to support or care for. **run over 1** (of a container or its contents) overflow: *the bath's running over.* **2** exceed (an expected limit): *the filming ran over schedule and budget.* **run someone/something over** (of a vehicle or its driver) knock a person or animal down and pass over their body: *I almost ran over that raccoon.* **run through 1** be present in every part of; pervade: *a sense of personal loss runs through many of his lyrics.* **2** use or spend recklessly or rapidly: *her husband had long since run through her money.* **run someone/something through** stab a person or animal so as to kill them. **run through** (or **over**) **something** discuss, read, or repeat something quickly or briefly: *I'll just run through the schedule for the weekend.* ■ rehearse a performance or series of actions: *okay, let's run through Scene 3 again.* **run to 1** extend to or reach (a specified amount or size): *the document ran to almost 100 pages.* ■ be enough to cover (a particular expense); have the financial resources for: *my income doesn't run to luxuries like taxis.* **2** (of a person) show a tendency to or inclination toward: *she was tall and running to fat.* **run something up 1** allow a debt or bill to accumulate quickly: *he ran up debts of $153,000.* ■ achieve a particular score in a game or match: *North Carolina ran up a 62–44 lead.* **2** make something quickly or hurriedly, esp. a piece of clothing: *I'll run up a dress for you.* **3** raise a flag. **run up against** experience or meet (a difficulty or problem): *the proposal has been dropped because it could run up against Federal regulations.* **run with 1** proceed with; accept: *we do lots of tests before we run with a product.* **2** (also **run around with**) informal associate habitually with (someone): *Larry was a good kid until he began running around with the wrong crowd.*
– DERIVATIVES **run·na·ble** adj.
– ORIGIN Old English *rinnan, irnan* (verb), of Germanic origin, probably reinforced in Middle English by Old Norse *rinna, renna.* The current form with *-u-* in the present tense is first recorded in the 16th cent.

> **USAGE** On the use of verbs used with **and** instead of a *to* infinitive, as in *run and fetch the paper*, see usage at AND.

run·a·bout /ˈrənəˌbout/ ▶ **n.** a small car, motorboat, or light aircraft, esp. one used for short trips.

run·a·round /ˈrənəˌround/ informal ▶ **n.** difficult or awkward treatment, esp. in which someone is evasive or avoids a question: *the times he **got the runaround** looking for work.*

run·a·way /ˈrənəˌwā/ ▶ **n.** a person who has run away, esp. from their family or an institution. ■ [often as modifier] an animal or vehicle that is running out of control: *a runaway train.* ■ [as modifier] denoting something happening or done quickly, easily, or uncontrollably: *the runaway success of the book.*

run·back /ˈrənˌbak/ ▶ **n.** Football an act of advancing a ball caught after a kickoff, punt, or interception by running while carrying it.

run·ci·ble spoon /ˈrənsəbəl/ ▶ **n.** a fork curved like a spoon, with three broad prongs, one of which has a sharpened outer edge for cutting.
– ORIGIN late 19th cent.: used by Edward Lear, perhaps suggested by late 16th-cent. *rouncival*, denoting a large variety of pea.

run·down ▶ **n.** /ˈrənˌdoun/ [usu. in sing.] **1** an analysis or summary of something by a knowledgeable person: *he gave his teammates **a rundown on** the opposition.*
2 a reduction in the productivity or activities of a company or institution: *a rundown in the business would be a devastating blow to the local economy.*
3 Baseball an attempt by two or more fielders to tag out a base runner who is trapped between two bases: *he was caught in a rundown and tagged out by the shortstop.*
▶ **adj.** /ˈrənˈdoun/ (usu. **run-down**) **1** (esp. of a building or area) in a poor or neglected state after having been prosperous: *a run-down, vandalized inner-city area.* ■ (of a company or industry) in a poor economic state.

r

2 [predic.] tired and somewhat unwell, esp. through overwork: *feeling tired and generally run-down.*

rune /ro͞on/ ▶ **n.** a letter of an ancient Germanic alphabet, related to the Roman alphabet. ■ a similar mark of mysterious or magic significance. ■ (**runes**) small stones, pieces of bone, etc., bearing such marks, and used as divinatory symbols: *the casting of the runes.* ■ a spell or incantation. ■ a section of the Kalevala or of an ancient Scandinavian poem. [from Finnish *runo*, from Old Norse.]

Runes were used by Scandinavians and Anglo-Saxons from about the 3rd century. They were formed mainly by modifying Roman or Greek characters to suit carving, and were used both in writing and in divination.

– DERIVATIVES **ru·nic** /'ro͞onik/ **adj.**
– ORIGIN Old English *rūn* 'a secret, mystery'; not recorded between Middle English and the late 17th cent. when it was reintroduced under the influence of Old Norse *rúnir, rúnar* 'magic signs, hidden lore.'

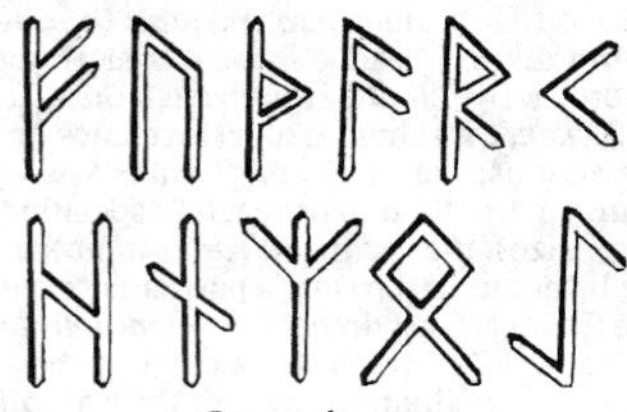

Germanic runes

rune stone ▶ **n. 1** a large stone carved with runes by ancient Scandinavians or Anglo-Saxons.
2 a small stone, piece of bone, etc., marked with a rune and used in divination.

rung[1] /rəNG/ ▶ **n. 1** a horizontal support on a ladder for a person's foot. ■ a level in a hierarchical structure, esp. a class or career structure: *we must ensure that the unskilled do not get trapped on the bottom rung.*
2 a strengthening crosspiece in the structure of a chair.
– DERIVATIVES **runged adj.**, **rung·less adj.**
– ORIGIN Old English *hrung* (sense 2); related to Dutch *rong* and German *Runge.*

rung[2] past participle of RING[2].

run-in ▶ **n. 1** informal a disagreement or fight, esp. with someone in an official position: *a run-in with armed police in Rio* | humorous *a run-in with a parking meter.*
2 [usu. in sing.] Brit. the approach to an action or event: *the final run-in to the World Cup.* ■ the home stretch of a racecourse.

run·let /'rənlət/ ▶ **n.** a small stream.

run·nel /'rənl/ ▶ **n.** a narrow channel in the ground for liquid to flow through. ■ a brook or rill. ■ a small stream of a particular liquid: *a runnel of sweat.*
– ORIGIN late 16th cent. (denoting a brook or rill): variant of dialect *rindle*, influenced by the verb RUN.

r

run·ner /'rənər/ ▶ **n. 1** a person who runs, esp. in a specified way: *Mary was a fast runner.* ■ a person who runs competitively as a sport or hobby: *a marathon runner.* ■ a horse that runs in a particular race: *there were only four runners.* ■ a messenger, collector, or agent for a bank, bookmaker, or other organization. ■ Baseball a base runner. ■ a messenger in the army.
2 [in combination] a person who smuggles specified goods into or out of a country or area: *a drug-runner.*
3 a rod, groove, or blade on which something slides. ■ each of the long pieces on the underside of a sled that forms the contact in sliding. ■ (often **runners**) a roller for moving a heavy article. ■ a ring capable of slipping or sliding along a strap or rod or through which something may be passed or drawn. ■ Nautical a rope run through a block.
4 a shoot, typically leafless, that grows from the base of a plant along the surface of the ground and can take root at points along its length. ■ a plant that spreads by means of such shoots. ■ a twining plant.
5 a long, narrow rug or strip of carpet, esp. for a hall or stairway.
6 (also **runner stone**) a revolving millstone.
7 a fast-swimming fish of the jack family, occurring in tropical seas. ● Several species in the family Carangidae, in particular the colorfully striped **rainbow runner** (*Elagatis bipinnulata*) of warm seas worldwide, and the **blue runner** (*Caranx crysos*) of the western Atlantic.
– PHRASES **do a runner** Brit. informal leave hastily, esp. to avoid paying for something or to escape from somewhere.

run·ner-up ▶ **n.** (pl. **runners-up**) a competitor or team taking second place in a contest: *he was runner-up in the 200 m individual medley.* ■ a competitor finishing behind the winner in the specified position: *third runner-up in last year's election.*

run·ning /'rəniNG/ ▶ **n. 1** the action or movement of a runner: *he accounted for 31 touchdowns with his running and passing.* ■ the sport of racing on foot: *marathon running.* ■ an act of running a race: *the 122nd running of the Mid-Summer Derby.*
2 the action of managing or operating something: *the day-to-day running of the office.*
▶ **adj. 1** [attrib.] denoting something that runs, in particular: ■ (of water) flowing naturally or supplied to a building through pipes and taps: *hot and cold running water.* ■ (of a sore or a part of the body) exuding liquid or pus: *a running sore.* ■ continuous or recurring over a long period: *a running joke.* ■ done while running: *a running jump.* ■ (of a measurement) in a straight line: *today, those same lots are worth $6,000 a running foot.*
2 [postpositive] consecutive; in succession: *he failed to produce an essay for the third week running.*
– PHRASES **in** (or **out of**) **the running** in (or no longer in) contention for an award, victory, or a place on a team: *he is in the running for an Oscar.*

run·ning back ▶ **n.** Football an offensive player, typically a halfback, who specializes in carrying the ball.

run·ning bat·tle ▶ **n.** a military engagement that does not occur at a fixed location. ■ a confrontation that has gone on for a long time.

run·ning be·lay ▶ **n.** Climbing a device attached to a rock face through which a climbing rope runs freely, acting as a pulley if the climber falls.

run·ning board ▶ **n.** a footboard extending along the side of a vehicle, typically found on trucks, SUVs, and some early models of automobiles.

run·ning com·men·ta·ry ▶ **n.** an oral description of events, given as they occur.

run·ning dog ▶ **n. 1** informal a servile follower, esp. of a political system: *the running dogs of capitalism.* [translating Chinese *zǒugǒu.*]
2 a dog bred to run, esp. for racing or pulling a sled.

run·ning fire ▶ **n.** successive gunshots from a line of troops. ■ a rapid succession of something: *a running fire of comment in their choicest vernacular.*

run·ning fix ▶ **n.** a determination of one's position made by taking bearings at different times and allowing for the distance covered in the meantime.

run·ning gear ▶ **n.** the moving parts of a machine, esp. the wheels, steering, and suspension of a vehicle. ■ the moving rope and tackle used in handling a boat.

run·ning head ▶ **n.** a heading printed at the top of each page of a book or chapter.

run·ning knot ▶ **n.** a knot that slips along the rope and changes the size of the loop it forms.

run·ning lights ▶ **plural n. 1** another term for NAVIGATION LIGHTS.
2 small lights on a motor vehicle that remain illuminated while the vehicle is running.

run·ning mate ▶ **n. 1** an election candidate for the lesser of two closely associated political offices: *a rationale offered by a presidential candidate for choosing his vice presidential running mate.*
2 a horse entered in a race in order to set the pace for another horse from the same stable, which is intended to win.

run·ning re·pairs ▶ **plural n.** minor or temporary repairs carried out on machinery while it is in use.

run·ning rig·ging ▶ **n.** see RIGGING (sense 1).

run·ning stitch ▶ **n.** a simple needlework stitch consisting of a line of small even stitches that run in and out through the cloth without overlapping.

run·ning to·tal ▶ **n.** a total that is continually adjusted to take account of items as they are added.

run·ny /'rənē/ ▶ **adj.** (**runnier**, **runniest**)
1 somewhat liquid; not firm: *the soufflé was hard on top and quite runny underneath.*
2 (of a person's nose) producing or discharging mucus; running. ■ dripping: *a runny spout.*

Run·ny·mede /'rəni,mēd/ a meadow on the southern bank of the Thames River, near Windsor. It is noted for its association with the Magna Carta, which was signed by King John in 1215 here or nearby.

run·off /'rən,ôf/ ▶ **n. 1** a further competition, election, race, etc., after a tie or inconclusive result.
2 the draining away of water (or substances carried in it) from the surface of an area of land, a building or structure, etc. ■ the water or other material that drains freely off the surface of something.

run-of-the-mill ▶ **adj.** lacking unusual or special aspects; ordinary: *a run-of-the-mill job.*

run-on ▶ **adj. 1** [attrib.] denoting a line of verse in which a sentence is continued without a pause beyond the end of a line, couplet, or stanza.
2 (of a sentence) containing two or more independent clauses that are not separated by a colon or semicolon: *his sentences were often run-on or confused.*

run·out /'rən,out/ ▶ **n. 1** a length of time or stretch of ground over which something gradually ceases or is brought to an end or a halt: *I skied the trail's long runout to the bottom and found the familiar yellow bus waiting.*
2 a slight error in a rotating tool, machine component, etc., such as being off-center or not exactly round.

runt /rənt/ ▶ **n.** an animal that is smaller than average, esp. the smallest in a litter. ■ derogatory an undersized or weak person.
– DERIVATIVES **runt·y adj.**
– ORIGIN early 16th cent. (in the sense 'old or decayed tree stump'): of unknown origin.

run-through ▶ **n. 1** a rehearsal: *a run-through of the whole show.*
2 a brief outline or summary: *the textbooks provide a run-through of research findings.*

run·time /'rən,tīm/ ▶ **n. 1** the time that a film or DVD lasts: *a thriller that is so well paced it seems a lot shorter than its three-hour runtime.*
2 Computing the length of time a program takes to run. ■ the time at or during which a program is run. ■ a cut-down version of a program that can be run but not changed.
▶ **adj.** (of software) in a reduced version that can be run but not changed.

run-up ▶ **n. 1** a marked rise in the value or level of something: *a sharp run-up of land and stock prices.*
2 the period preceding a notable event: *an acrimonious run-up to legislative elections.*
3 an act of running briefly to gain momentum before performing a jump in track and field or other sports: *high jumper Steve Smith will use his shortened five-stride run-up.*
4 an act of running an engine or turbine to prepare it for use or to test it.
5 Golf a low approach shot that bounces and runs forward.

run·way /'rən,wā/ ▶ **n. 1** a leveled strip of smooth ground along which aircraft take off and land.
2 a raised aisle extending into the audience from a stage, esp. as used for fashion shows.
3 an animal run, esp. one made by small mammals in grass, under snow, etc.
4 an incline or chute down which something slides or runs.

Run·yon /'rənyən/, Damon (1884–1946), US author and journalist; full name *Alfred Damon Runyon.* His short stories about New York City's underworld characters are written in a highly individual style with much use of colorful slang. His collection *Guys and Dolls* (1932) formed the basis for the musical of the same name (1950).

ru·o·te /ro͞o'ōtē/ ▶ **n.** pasta that resembles small wheels with five spokes radiating from a hub.
– ORIGIN Italian, literally 'wheels.'

ru·pee /ro͞o'pē, 'ro͞o,pē/ ▶ **n.** the basic monetary unit of India, Pakistan, Sri Lanka, Nepal, Mauritius, and the Seychelles, equal to 100 paise in India, Pakistan, and Nepal, and 100 cents in Sri Lanka, Mauritius, and the Seychelles.
– ORIGIN via Hindi from Sanskrit *rūpya* 'wrought silver.'

Ru·pert, Prince /'ro͞opərt/ (1619–82), English general; son of **Frederick V** (elector of the Palatinate) and nephew of Charles I. The Royalist leader of cavalry, he initially won a series of victories, but was defeated by Parliamentarian forces at Marston Moor in 1644 and Naseby in 1645.

Ru·pert's Land (also **Prince Rupert's Land**) a historical region of northern and western Canada, roughly corresponding to what is now Manitoba, Saskatchewan, Yukon, Alberta, and the southern part of the Northwest Territories.

ru·pes·tri·an /ro͞o'pestrēən/ ▶ **adj.** (of art) done on rock or cave walls.
– ORIGIN late 18th cent.: from modern Latin *rupestris* 'found on rocks' (from Latin *rupes* 'rock') + -AN.

ru·pi·ah /ro͞o'pēə/ ▶ **n.** the basic monetary unit of Indonesia, equal to 100 sen.
– ORIGIN Indonesian, from Hindi *rūpyah* (see RUPEE).

rup·ture /ˈrəpCHər/ ▸ v. [no obj.] **1** (esp. of a pipe, a vessel, or a bodily part such as an organ or membrane) break or burst suddenly: *if the main artery ruptures he could die.* ■ [with obj.] cause to break or burst suddenly and completely: *the impact ruptured both fuel tanks.* ■ [with obj.] suffer such a bursting of (a bodily part): *it was her first match since rupturing an Achilles tendon.* ■ (**be ruptured** or **rupture oneself**) suffer an abdominal hernia: *one of the boys was ruptured and needed to be fitted with a truss.*
2 [with obj.] breach or disturb (a harmonious feeling or situation): *once trust has been ruptured it can be difficult to regain.*
▸ n. **1** an instance of breaking or bursting suddenly and completely: *a small hairline crack could develop into a rupture | the patient died after rupture of an aneurysm.* ■ an abdominal hernia.
2 a breach of a harmonious relationship: *the rupture with his father would never be healed.*
– ORIGIN late Middle English (as a noun): from Old French *rupture* or Latin *ruptura*, from *rumpere* 'to break.' The verb dates from the mid 18th cent.

ru·ral /ˈro͝orəl/ ▸ adj. in, relating to, or characteristic of the countryside rather than the town: *remote rural areas.*
– DERIVATIVES **ru·ral·ism** n., **ru·ral·ist** n., **ru·ral·i·ty** /ro͝oˈralitē/ n., **ru·ral·i·za·tion** /ˌro͝orələˈzāSHən/ n., **ru·ral·ize** v., **ru·ral·ly** adv.
– ORIGIN late Middle English: from Old French, or from late Latin *ruralis*, from *rus*, *rur-* 'country.'

ru·ral route (abbr.: **RR**) ▸ n. a mail delivery route in a rural area.

Ru·rik /ˈro͝orik/ (also **Ryurik**) ▸ n. a member of a dynasty that ruled Muscovy and much of Russia from the 9th century until the death of Fyodor, son of Ivan the Terrible, in 1598. It was reputedly founded by a Varangian chief who settled in Novgorod in 862.
▸ adj. of or relating to the Ruriks.

Ru·ri·ta·ni·a /ˌro͝oriˈtānēə/ an imaginary kingdom in central Europe used as a fictional background for the adventure novels of courtly intrigue and romance written by Anthony Hope (1863–1933).
– DERIVATIVES **Ru·ri·ta·ni·an** /-ˈtānēən/ adj. & n.
– ORIGIN from RURAL, on the pattern of *Lusitania*.

Ruse /ˈro͞osā/ (also **Rousse**) an industrial city and the principal port of Bulgaria, on the Danube River; pop. 156,959 (2008).

ruse /ro͞oz, ro͞os/ ▸ n. an action intended to deceive someone; a trick: *Eleanor tried to think of a ruse to get Paul out of the house.*
– ORIGIN late Middle English (as a hunting term): from Old French, from *ruser* 'use trickery,' earlier 'drive back,' perhaps based on Latin *rursus* 'backward.'

rush¹ /rəSH/ ▸ v. **1** [no obj.] move with urgent haste: *Jason rushed after her | I rushed outside and hailed a taxi.* ■ (of air or a liquid) flow strongly: *the water rushed in through the great oaken gates.* ■ act with great haste: *as soon as the campaign started, they **rushed into action** |* [with infinitive] *shoppers rushed to buy computers.* ■ [with obj.] force (someone) to act hastily: *I don't want to **rush** you **into** something.* ■ [with obj.] take (someone) somewhere with great haste: *an ambulance was waiting to rush him to the hospital.* ■ [with two objs.] deliver (something) quickly to (someone): *we'll rush you a copy at once.* ■ (**rush something out**) produce and distribute something, or put something up for sale, very quickly: *a rewritten textbook was rushed out last autumn.* ■ [with obj.] deal with (something) hurriedly: *panic measures were **rushed through** Congress.* ■ [with obj.] dash toward (someone or something) in an attempt to attack or capture them or it: *he rushed the stronghold.*
2 [with obj.] Football advance rapidly toward (an offensive player, esp. the quarterback). ■ [no obj.] gain a specified amount of yardage or score a touchdown or conversion by running from scrimmage with the ball: *he rushed for 100 yards on 22 carries.*
3 [with obj.] entertain (a new student) in order to assess their suitability for membership in a college fraternity or sorority. ■ (of a student) visit (a college fraternity or sorority) with a view toward joining it: *he rushed three fraternities.*
▸ n. **1** a sudden quick movement toward something, typically by a number of people: *there was a rush for the door.* ■ a flurry of hasty activity: *the pre-Christmas rush |* [as modifier] *a rush job.* ■ a sudden strong demand for a commodity: *there's been a **rush on** the Tribune because of the murder.* ■ a sudden flow or flood: *she felt a rush of cold air.* ■ a sudden intense feeling: *Mark felt a rush of anger.* ■ a sudden thrill or feeling of euphoria such as experienced after taking certain drugs: *users experience a rush.*
2 Football a rapid advance by a defensive player or players, esp. toward the quarterback. ■ an act of running from scrimmage with the ball to gain yardage.
3 the process whereby college fraternities or sororities entertain new students in order to assess suitability for membership: *ranking pledges during rush |* [as modifier] *rush week.*
4 (**rushes**) the first prints made of a movie after a period of shooting.
– DERIVATIVES **rush·er** n., **rush·ing·ly** adv.
– ORIGIN late Middle English: from an Anglo-Norman French variant of Old French *ruser* 'drive back,' an early sense of the word in English (see RUSE).

rush² ▸ n. **1** a marsh or waterside plant with slender stemlike pith-filled leaves, widely distributed in temperate areas. Some kinds are used for matting, chair seats, and baskets, and some were formerly used for strewing on floors. ● Genus *Juncus*, family Juncaceae. ■ used in names of similar plants of wet habitats, e.g., **flowering rush**. ■ a stem of such a plant. ■ such plants used as a material.
2 archaic a thing of no value (used for emphasis): *not one of them is **worth a rush**.*
– DERIVATIVES **rush·like** /-ˌlīk/ adj., **rush·y** adj.
– ORIGIN Old English *risc*, *rysc*, of Germanic origin.

Rush·die /ˈrəSHdē/, Salman (1947–), British novelist, born in India; full name *Sir Ahmed Salman Rushdie.* His work, chiefly associated with magic realism, includes *Midnight's Children* (1981) and *The Satanic Verses* (1988). The latter, regarded by Muslims as blasphemous, caused Ayatollah Khomeini to issue a fatwa in 1989 that condemned Rushdie to death.

rushed /rəSHt/ ▸ adj. done or completed too hurriedly; hasty: *a rushed job.* ■ (of a person) short of time; hurrying: *I'm too rushed to do it.*

rush hour ▸ n. a time during each day when traffic is at its heaviest.

rush·light /ˈrəSHˌlīt/ ▸ n. historical a candle made by dipping the pith of a rush in tallow.

Rush·more, Mount /ˈrəSHˌmôr/ a mountain in the Black Hills of South Dakota, noted for its giant busts of four US presidents—George Washington, Thomas Jefferson, Theodore Roosevelt, and Abraham Lincoln—carved 1927–41 under the direction of sculptor Gutzon Borglum (1867–1941).

Mount Rushmore

rus in ur·be /ˌro͞os in ˈo͝orbe/ ▸ n. literary an illusion of countryside created by a building or garden within a city.
– ORIGIN Latin, literally 'country in the city.'

Rusk /rəsk/, Dean (1909–94), US educator and statesman; full name *David Dean Rusk*. He served as secretary of state under Presidents Kennedy and Johnson 1961–69 and was a strong proponent of US involvement in Vietnam.

rusk /rəsk/ ▸ n. a light, dry biscuit or piece of twice-baked bread, esp. one prepared for use as baby food. ■ twice-baked bread used as extra filling, for example in sausages, and formerly as rations at sea.
– ORIGIN late 16th cent.: from Spanish or Portuguese *rosca* 'twist, coil, roll of bread,' of unknown ultimate origin.

Rus·kin /ˈrəskin/, John (1819–1900), English art and social critic. His prolific writings include attacks on Renaissance art in *The Stones of Venice* (1851–53), capitalism in "The Political Economy of Art" (1857), and utilitarianism in *Unto This Last* (1860).

Rus·sell¹ /ˈrəsəl/, Bertrand (Arthur William), 3rd Earl Russell (1872–1970), British philosopher, mathematician, and social reformer. In *Principia Mathematica* (1910–13) he and A. N. Whitehead attempted to express all of mathematics in formal logic terms. He expounded logical atomism in *Our Knowledge of the External World* (1914) and neutral monism in *The Analysis of Mind* (1921). Nobel Prize for Literature (1950).

Rus·sell², Bill (1934–), US basketball player and coach; full name *William Felton Russell*. A center, he played for the Boston Celtics 1956–69 and also coached them from 1966, becoming the first African-American head coach in the NBA. He coached the Seattle Supersonics 1973–77. Basketball Hall of Fame (1974).

Rus·sell³, John, 1st Earl Russell (1792–1878), British statesman; prime minister 1846–52 and 1865–66.

Rus·sell's par·a·dox a logical paradox stated in terms of set theory, concerning the set of all sets that do not contain themselves as members, namely that the condition for it to contain itself is that it should not contain itself.
– ORIGIN 1920s: named after Bertrand *Russell* (see RUSSELL¹).

Rus·sell's vi·per ▸ n. a large venomous Asian snake that has a yellow-brown body with black markings. ● *Daboia* (or *Vipera*) *russelli*, family Viperidae.
– ORIGIN early 20th cent.: named after Patrick *Russell* (1727–1805), Scottish physician and naturalist.

rus·set /ˈrəsət/ ▸ adj. **1** reddish brown in color: *gardens of russet and gold chrysanthemums.*
2 archaic rustic; homely.
▸ n. **1** a reddish-brown color: *the woods in autumn are a riot of russet and gold.*
2 a dessert apple of a variety with a slightly rough greenish-brown skin.
3 historical a coarse homespun reddish-brown or gray cloth used for simple clothing.
▸ v. (**russets**, **russeting**, **russeted**) make or become russet in color. ■ (of smooth-skinned fruit) develop a rough reddish-brown or yellowish-brown skin, or patches of such: [with obj.] *a week of humid weather has russeted the pears |* [no obj.] *this variety of apple tends not to russet.*
– DERIVATIVES **rus·set·y** adj.
– ORIGIN Middle English: from an Anglo-Norman French variant of Old French *rousset*, diminutive of *rous* 'red,' from Provençal *ros*, from Latin *russus* 'red.'

Rus·sia /ˈrəSHə/ a country in northern Asia and eastern Europe; pop. 140,041,200 (est. 2009); capital, Moscow; language, Russian (official). Official name RUSSIAN FEDERATION.

> The modern state originated from the expansion of the principality of Muscovy into a great empire. Russia played an increasing role in Europe from the time of Peter the Great in the early 18th century. Following the overthrow of the tsar in the Russian Revolution of 1917, Russia became the largest of the constituent republics of the Soviet Union, with more than three quarters of the area and over half of the population. On the breakup of the Soviet Union and the collapse of communist control in 1991, Russia emerged as an independent state and a founding member of the Commonwealth of Independent States.

Rus·sia leath·er ▸ n. a durable leather made from calfskin and impregnated with birchbark oil, used for bookbinding.

Rus·sian /ˈrəSHən/ ▸ adj. of or relating to Russia, its people, or their language.
▸ n. **1** a native or inhabitant of Russia. ■ a person of Russian descent. ■ historical (in general use) a national of the former Soviet Union.
2 the East Slavic language of Russia.
– DERIVATIVES **Rus·sian·ist** n., **Rus·sian·i·za·tion** /ˌrəSHənəˈzāSHən/ n., **Rus·sian·ize** /-ˌnīz/ v., **Rus·sian·ness** n.
– ORIGIN mid 16th cent.: from medieval Latin *Russianus*.

Rus·sian bal·let ▸ n. a style of ballet developed at the Russian Imperial Ballet Academy, popularized in the West by Sergei Diaghilev's Ballets Russes from 1909.

Rus·sian Blue ▸ n. a cat of a breed with short grayish-blue fur, green eyes, and large pointed ears.

Rus·sian boot ▸ n. a boot that loosely encloses the wearer's calf.

Rus·sian doll ▸ n. another term for MATRYOSHKA.

Rus·sian Fed·er·a·tion official name for RUSSIA.

Rus·sian ol·ive ▸ n. see OLEASTER.

Rus·sian Or·tho·dox Church the national church of Russia. See ORTHODOX CHURCH.

Rus·sian Rev·o·lu·tion the revolution in the Russian empire in 1917, in which the tsarist regime was overthrown and replaced by Bolshevik rule under Lenin.

Rus·sian rou·lette ▸ n. the practice of loading a bullet into one chamber of a revolver, spinning the cylinder, and then pulling the trigger while pointing the gun at one's own head. ■ an activity that is potentially very dangerous.

Rus·sian sal·ad ▶ **n.** Brit. a salad of mixed diced vegetables with mayonnaise.

Rus·sian tea ▶ **n.** tea laced with rum and typically served with lemon.

Rus·sian this·tle ▶ **n.** a prickly tumbleweed that is an inland form of saltwort. Native to Eurasia, it was accidentally introduced into North America, where it has become a pest. Also called **Russian tumbleweed**. ● *Salsola kali*, family Chenopodiaceae.

Rus·si·fy /ˈrəsəˌfī/ ▶ **v.** (**Russifies, Russifying, Russified**) [with obj.] make Russian in character.
– DERIVATIVES **Rus·si·fi·ca·tion** /ˌrəsəfəˈkāSHən/ **n.**

Russ·ki /ˈrəskē, ˈro͝oskē/ (also **Russky**) ▶ **n.** (pl. **Russkis** or **Russkies**) informal, often offensive a Russian.
– ORIGIN mid 19th cent.: from Russian *russkiĭ* 'Russian,' or from **RUSSIAN**, on the pattern of Russian surnames ending in *-skiĭ*.

Russo- ▶ **comb. form** Russian; Russian and ...: *Russo-Japanese*. ■ relating to Russia.

Rus·so-Jap·an·ese War /ˈrəsō/ a war between the Russian empire and Japan in 1904–05, caused by territorial disputes in Manchuria and Korea. Russia suffered a series of humiliating defeats, and the peace settlement gave Japan the ascendancy in the disputed region.

Rus·so·phile /ˈrəsəˌfīl/ ▶ **n.** a person who is friendly toward Russia or fond of Russia and Russian things, esp. someone who is sympathetic to the political system and customs of the former Soviet Union.
– DERIVATIVES **Rus·so·phil·i·a** /ˌrəsəˈfilēə/ **n.**

Rus·so·phobe /ˈrəsəˌfōb/ ▶ **n.** a person who feels an intense dislike toward Russia and Russian things, esp. the political system or customs of the former Soviet Union.
– DERIVATIVES **Rus·so·pho·bi·a** /ˌrəsəˈfōbēə/ **n.**

rus·su·la /ˈrəs(y)ələ/ ▶ **n.** a widespread woodland toadstool that typically has a brightly colored flattened cap and a white stem and gills. ● Genus *Russula*, family Russulaceae, class Hymenomycetes: numerous species. See also **SICKENER** (sense 2).
– ORIGIN modern Latin, from Latin *russus* 'red' (because many, such as the sickener, have a red cap).

rust /rəst/ ▶ **n. 1** a reddish- or yellowish-brown flaky coating of iron oxide that is formed on iron or steel by oxidation, esp. in the presence of moisture. ■ a state of deterioration or disrepair resulting from neglect or lack of use: *they are here to scrape the rust off the derelict machinery of government.*
2 [usu. with adj. or noun modifier] a fungal disease of plants that results in reddish or brownish patches. ● The fungi belong to *Puccinia* and other genera, order Uredinales, class Teliomycetes.
3 a reddish-brown color: [in combination] *his rust-colored hair.*
▶ **v.** [no obj.] be affected with rust: *the blades had rusted away* | (as adj. **rusting**) *rusting machinery.* ■ deteriorate through neglect or lack of use.
– DERIVATIVES **rust·less adj.**
– ORIGIN Old English *rūst*, of Germanic origin; related to Dutch *roest*, German *Rost*, also to **RED**.

r

Rust Belt ▶ **n.** (**the Rust Belt**) informal parts of the northeastern and midwestern US that are characterized by declining industry, aging factories, and a falling population. Steel-producing cities in Pennsylvania and Ohio are at its center.

rust buck·et ▶ **n.** informal a car, ship, or other vehicle that is old and badly rusted.

rus·tic /ˈrəstik/ ▶ **adj. 1** of or relating to the countryside; rural. ■ having a simplicity and charm that is considered typical of the countryside: *bare plaster walls and a terra-cotta floor give a rustic feel.* ■ often derogatory lacking the sophistication of the city; backward and provincial: *you are a rustic halfwit.*
2 constructed or made in a plain and simple fashion, in particular: ■ made of untrimmed branches or rough timber: *a rustic oak bench.* ■ Architecture with rough-hewn or roughened surface or with deeply sunk joints: *a rustic bridge.* ■ denoting freely formed lettering, esp. a relatively informal style of handwritten Roman capital letter.
▶ **n.** often derogatory an unsophisticated country person.
– DERIVATIVES **rus·ti·cal·ly** /-ik(ə)lē/ **adv.**, **rus·tic·i·ty** /rəˈstisətē/ **n.**
– ORIGIN late Middle English (in the sense 'rural'): from Latin *rusticus*, from *rus* 'the country.'

rus·ti·cate /ˈrəstiˌkāt/ ▶ **v. 1** [no obj.] go to, live in, or spend time in the country.
2 [with obj.] fashion (masonry) in large blocks with sunk joints and a roughened surface: (as adj. **rusticated**) *the stable block was built of rusticated stone.*
3 [with obj.] Brit. suspend (a student) from a university as a punishment (used chiefly at Oxford and Cambridge).
– DERIVATIVES **rus·ti·ca·tion** /ˌrəstiˈkāSHən/ **n.**
– ORIGIN late 15th cent. (in the sense 'countrify'): from Latin *rusticat-* '(having) lived in the country,' from the verb *rusticari*, from *rusticus* (see **RUSTIC**).

Rus·tin /ˈrəstin/, Bayard (1910–87), US civil rights leader. As a special assistant to Martin Luther King, Jr., he helped to organize the 1963 March on Washington. He was the executive director of the A. Philip Randolph Institute 1964–87.

rus·tle /ˈrəsəl/ ▶ **v. 1** [no obj.] make a soft, muffled crackling sound like that caused by the movement of dry leaves or paper: *she came closer, her skirt swaying and rustling.* ■ [with adverbial of direction] move with such sound: *a nurse rustled in with a syringe.* ■ [with obj.] move (something), causing it to make such a sound: *Dolly rustled the paper irritably.*
2 [with obj.] round up and steal (cattle, horses, or sheep).
3 [no obj.] informal move or act quickly or energetically; hustle: *rustle around the kitchen, see what there is.*
▶ **n.** [usu. in sing.] a soft, muffled crackling sound like that made by the movement of dry leaves or paper: *there was a rustle in the undergrowth behind her.*
– PHRASAL VERBS **rustle something up** informal produce something quickly when it is needed: *see if you can rustle up a cup of coffee for Paula and me, please.*
– DERIVATIVES **rus·tler** /ˈrəs(ə)lər/ **n.** (sense 2 of the verb).
– ORIGIN late Middle English (as a verb): imitative; compare with Flemish *rijsselen* and Dutch *ritselen*. The noun dates from the mid 18th cent.

rust·proof /ˈrəstˌpro͞of/ ▶ **adj.** (of metal or a metal object) not susceptible to corrosion by rust.
▶ **v.** [with obj.] make resistant to corrosion by rust.

rust·y /ˈrəstē/ ▶ **adj.** (**rustier, rustiest**) **1** (of a metal object) affected by rust: *a rusty hinge.* ■ rust-colored: *green grass turning a rusty brown.*
2 (of knowledge or a skill) impaired by lack of recent practice: *my typing is a little rusty.* ■ stiff with age or disuse: *it was my first race for three months and I felt a bit rusty.* ■ (of a voice) croaking: *her voice sounded rusty.*
– DERIVATIVES **rust·i·ly** /ˈrəstəlē/ **adv.**, **rust·i·ness n.**
– ORIGIN Old English *rūstig* (see **RUST**, **-Y**[1]).

rust·y dust·y ▶ **n.** black English a person's buttocks.
– ORIGIN late 16th cent. (in the sense 'dusty, fusty'): reduplication of **RUSTY**. The current transferred use dates from the 1950s.

rut[1] /rət/ ▶ **n. 1** a long deep track made by the repeated passage of the wheels of vehicles.
2 a habit or pattern of behavior that has become dull and unproductive but is hard to change: *the administration was stuck in a rut and was losing its direction.*
– DERIVATIVES **rut·ted adj.**, **rut·ty adj.**
– ORIGIN late 16th cent.: probably from Old French *rute* (see **ROUTE**).

rut[2] ▶ **n.** (**the rut**) an annual period of sexual activity in deer and some other mammals, during which the males fight each other for access to the females.
▶ **v.** (**ruts, rutting, rutted**) [no obj.] (often as adj. **rutting**) engage in such activity: *a rutting stag.*
– DERIVATIVES **rut·tish adj.**
– ORIGIN late Middle English: from Old French, from Latin *rugitus*, from *rugire* 'to roar.'

ru·ta·ba·ga /ˈro͞otəˌbāgə, ˈro͝ot-/ ▶ **n. 1** a large, round, yellow-fleshed root that is eaten as a vegetable.
2 the European plant of the cabbage family that produces this root. ● *Brassica napus*, family Brassicaceae: 'napobrassica' group.
– ORIGIN late 18th cent.: from Swedish dialect *rotabagge*.

Ruth[1] /ro͞oTH/ a book of the Bible telling the story of Ruth, a Moabite woman, who married her deceased husband's kinsman Boaz and bore a son, Obed, who became grandfather to King David.

Ruth[2], Babe (1895–1948), US baseball player; born *George Herman Ruth*; also known as the **Bambino**. He played for the Boston Red Sox 1914–19, the New York Yankees 1919–34, and the Boston Braves 1935. Originally a pitcher, he later became noted for his hitting, setting a record of 714 home runs that remained unbroken until 1974 and a single-season record in 1927 of 60 home runs that was not broken until 1961. Baseball Hall of Fame (1936).

Babe Ruth

ruth /ro͞oTH/ ▶ **n.** archaic a feeling of pity, distress, or grief.
– ORIGIN Middle English: from the verb **RUE**[1], probably influenced by Old Norse *hrygth*.

ru·the·ni·um /ro͞oˈTHēnēəm/ ▶ **n.** the chemical element of atomic number 44, a hard silvery-white metal of the transition series. (Symbol: **Ru**)
– ORIGIN mid 19th cent.: modern Latin, from medieval Latin *Ruthenia*, so named because it was discovered in ores from the Urals.

ruth·er /ˈrəT͟Hər/ ▶ **adv.** nonstandard spelling of **RATHER**, used in representing dialectal speech: *I'd ruther walk.* Compare with **DRUTHER**.

Ruth·er·ford /ˈrəT͟Hərfərd/, Sir Ernest, 1st Baron Rutherford of Nelson (1871–1937), New Zealand physicist, regarded as the founder of nuclear physics. Nobel Prize for Chemistry (1908).

Sir Ernest Rutherford

ruth·er·for·di·um /ˌrəT͟Hərˈfôrdēəm/ ▶ **n.** the chemical element of atomic number 104, a very unstable element made by high-energy atomic collisions. (Symbol: **Rf**)
– ORIGIN 1960s: modern Latin, named after E. *Rutherford* (see **RUTHERFORD**).

ruth·less /ˈro͞oTHləs/ ▶ **adj.** having or showing no pity or compassion for others: *a ruthless manipulator.*
– DERIVATIVES **ruth·less·ly adv.**, **ruth·less·ness n.**
– ORIGIN Middle English: from **RUTH** + **-LESS**.

ru·ti·lant /ˈro͞otl-ənt/ ▶ **adj.** literary glowing or glittering with red or golden light: *rutilant gems.*
– ORIGIN late Middle English: from Latin *rutilant-* 'glowing red,' from the verb *rutilare*, from *rutilus* 'reddish.'

ru·tile /ˈro͞oˌtēl/ ▶ **n.** a black or reddish-brown mineral consisting of titanium dioxide, typically occurring as needlelike crystals.
– ORIGIN early 19th cent.: from French, or from German *Rutil*, from Latin *rutilus* 'reddish.'

ru·tin /ˈro͞otn/ ▶ **n.** Chemistry a flavonoid compound found in common rue, buckwheat, capers, and other plants, and sometimes taken as a dietary supplement.
– ORIGIN mid 19th cent.: from Latin *ruta* 'rue' + **-IN**[1].

Rut·land /ˈrətlənd/ an industrial and commercial city in south central Vermont; pop. 16,742 (est. 2008).

Rut·ledge[1] /ˈrətlij/, John (1739–1800), US Supreme Court associate justice 1789–91. He resigned as associate justice to serve as chief justice of South Carolina. In 1795, he was appointed US chief justice by President Washington and served for a short time but he was ultimately rejected by the US Senate.

Rut·ledge², Wiley Blount, Jr. (1894–1949), US Supreme Court associate justice. Appointed to the Court by President Franklin D. Roosevelt, he tended toward liberalism.

Ruys·dael variant spelling of **Ruisdael**.

RV ▶ abbr. ■ recreational vehicle. ■ a rendezvous point. ■ Revised Version (of the Bible).

Rv. ▶ abbr. Bible Revelations.

R-val·ue ▶ n. the capacity of an insulating material to resist heat flow. The higher the R-value, the greater the insulating power.

RVer /'är'vēər/ ▶ n. a user of a recreational vehicle.

RW ▶ abbr. ■ Right Worshipful. ■ Right Worthy.

Rwan·da /rŏŏ'ändə, rə'wändə/ a landlocked country in central Africa, north of Burundi and south of Uganda; pop. 10,746,300 (est. 2009); capital, Kigali; languages, Rwanda (a Bantu language) and French (both official). Official name **Rwandese Republic**.

> Inhabited largely by Hutu and Tutsi peoples, the area was claimed by Germany from 1890 and after World War I became part of a Belgian trust territory. Rwanda became independent as a republic in 1962, shortly after the violent overthrow of the Tutsi monarchy by the majority Hutu people. In 1994, over 500,000 people, largely Tutsis, were slaughtered by predominantly Hutu supporters of the government, and more than a million fled as refugees into the Democratic Republic of the Congo (formerly Zaire) and neighboring countries. The Tutsi-dominated Rwandan Patriotic Front took power as the new government. Elections were held in 2003, but wars in neighboring countries and a Hutu insurgency cause continuing instability.

– DERIVATIVES **Rwan·dan adj. & n.**, **Rwan·dese** /-dēz, -dēs/ **adj. & n.**

R·wen·zo·ri /,rŏŏwən'zôrē/ (also **Ruwenzori**) a mountain range in central Africa, on the Uganda–Democratic Republic of the Congo (formerly Zaire) border between lakes Edward and Albert. It rises to 16,765 feet (5,110 m) at Margherita Peak on Mount Stanley. The range is generally thought to be the "Mountains of the Moon" mentioned by Ptolemy and, as such, the supposed source of the Nile.

rwy. ▶ abbr. Brit. railway.

Rx ▶ abbr. ■ prescription. ■ (in prescriptions) take. ■ tens of rupees.

Ry ▶ abbr. Brit. Railway.

-ry ▶ suffix a shortened form of **-ery** (as in *devilry*, *rivalry*).

Ry·an /'rīən/, Nolan (1948–), US baseball player; full name Lynn Nolan Ryan, Jr. He pitched for the New York Mets 1966, 1968–71, the California Angels 1972–79, the Houston Astros 1980–88, and the Texas Rangers 1989–93. He held the pitching records for no-hitters (7) and strikeouts (5,714). Baseball Hall of Fame (1999).

Rya·zan /,rēə'zän, ryi-/ an industrial city in western Russia, southeast of Moscow; pop. 510,800 (est. 2008).

Ry·binsk /'rib(y)insk/ a city in northwestern Russia, a port on the Volga River; pop. 211,000 (est. 2008). It was formerly known as Shcherbakov 1946–57 and as Andropov 1984–89.

Ryd·berg at·om /'rid,bərg/ ▶ n. Physics an atom in a highly excited state in which one electron has almost sufficient energy to escape. Atoms, usually hydrogen atoms, in this **Rydberg state** are used in atomic research.
– ORIGIN named after J. R. *Rydberg* (see **Rydberg constant**).

Ryd·berg con·stant Physics a constant, 1.097 x 10^7 m^{-1}, that appears in the formulae for the wave numbers of lines in atomic spectra and is a function of the rest mass and charge of the electron, the speed of light, and Planck's constant.
– ORIGIN early 20th cent.: named after Johannes R. *Rydberg* (1854–1919), Swedish physicist.

Ry·der /'rīdər/, Albert Pinkham (1847–1917), US artist. He is known for seascapes, such as *Toilers of the Sea* (1884), and pastoral landscapes.

Ry·der Cup /'rīdər/ a golf tournament held every two years and played between teams of male professionals from the US and Europe (originally Great Britain), first held in 1927.
– ORIGIN so named because the trophy was donated by Samuel *Ryder* (1859–1936), English seed merchant.

rye /rī/ ▶ n. **1** a wheatlike cereal plant that tolerates poor soils and low temperatures. ● *Secale cereale*, family Gramineae. ■ grains of this, used mainly for making bread or whiskey and for fodder: [as modifier] *rye flour*.
2 (also **rye whiskey**) whiskey in which a significant amount of the grain used in distillation is fermented rye: *half a bottle of rye*.
3 short for **rye bread**: *pastrami on rye*.
– ORIGIN Old English *ryge*, of Germanic origin; related to Dutch *rogge* and German *Roggen*.

rye bread ▶ n. bread made wholly or partly with rye flour, typically with caraway seeds added.

rye·grass /'rī,gras/ ▶ n. a Eurasian grass that is widely grown as forage. ● Genus *Lolium*, family Gramineae: several species, in particular *L. perenne*.
– ORIGIN early 18th cent.: alteration of obsolete *ray-grass*, of unknown origin.

Ryle¹ /rīl/, Gilbert (1900–76), English philosopher. He did much to make Oxford a leading center for philosophical research. In *The Concept of Mind* (1949), he attacked the mind-body dualism of Descartes.

Ryle², Sir Martin (1918–84), English astronomer. His demonstration that remote objects appeared to be different from closer ones helped to establish the Big Bang theory of the universe. Nobel Prize for Physics (1974), shared with Antony Hewish (1924–).

ryo·kan /rē'ō,kän, -,kan/ ▶ n. a traditional Japanese inn.
– ORIGIN Japanese.

ry·ot /'rīət/ ▶ n. an Indian peasant or tenant farmer.
– ORIGIN from Urdu *raiyat*, from Arabic *ra'iyya* 'flock, subjects,' from *ra'ā* 'to pasture.'

ry·u /rē'ōō/ ▶ n. (pl. **same** or **ryus**) a school or style in Japanese arts, esp. in the martial arts.
– ORIGIN Japanese.

Ryu·kyu Is·lands /rē'ōōkyōō/ a chain of islands in the western Pacific Ocean, stretching about 600 miles (960 km) from the southern tip of the island of Kyushu in Japan to Taiwan. The largest island is Okinawa.

Ry·un /'rīən/, Jim (1947–), US athlete and politician; full name *James Ronald Ryun*. In 1964, he became the first high-schooler to break the 4-minute mile by running it in 3:59.0 minutes. He brought home the silver medal for placing second in the 1500-meter run at the 1968 Olympic games. A Republican from Kansas, he served in the US House of Representatives 1997–2007.

Ryu·rik /rē'ŏŏrik, 'rŏŏrik/ variant spelling of **Rurik**.

r

Ss

S[1] /es/ (also **s**) ▶ **n.** (pl. **Ss** or **S's** /esiz/) **1** the nineteenth letter of the alphabet. ■ denoting the next after R in a set of items, categories, etc. **2** a shape like that of a capital S: [in combination] *an S-bend.*

S[2] ▶ **abbr.** ■ siemens. ■ small (as a clothes size). ■ South or Southern: *65° S.* ■ Biochemistry Svedberg unit(s). ▶ **symbol** ■ the chemical element sulfur. ■ Chemistry entropy. ■ Brit. (chiefly in Catholic use) Saint: *S Ignatius Loyola.*

s ▶ **abbr.** ■ second(s). ■ Law section (of an act). ■ shilling(s). ■ Grammar singular. ■ Chemistry solid. ■ (in genealogies) son(s). ■ succeeded. ■ Chemistry denoting electrons and orbitals possessing zero angular momentum and total symmetry: *s-electrons.* [s from *sharp*, originally applied to lines in atomic spectra.] ▶ **symbol** (in mathematical formulae) distance.

's informal ▶ **contraction** is: *it's raining.* ■ has: *she's gone.* ■ us: *let's go.* ■ does: *what's he do?*

's- ▶ **prefix** archaic (used chiefly in oaths) God's: *'sblood.*
– ORIGIN shortened form.

-s[1] ▶ **suffix** denoting the plurals of nouns (as in *apples, wagons*, etc.). Compare with **-ES**[1].
– ORIGIN Old English plural ending *-as.*

-s[2] ▶ **suffix** forming the third person singular of the present of verbs (as in *sews, vaunts*, etc.). Compare with **-ES**[2].
– ORIGIN Old English dialect.

-s[3] ▶ **suffix 1** forming adverbs such as *afterwards, besides.* **2** forming possessive pronouns such as *hers, ours.*
– ORIGIN Old English *-es*, masculine and neuter genitive singular ending.

-s[4] ▶ **suffix** forming nicknames or hypocoristics: *Pops.*
– ORIGIN suggested by **-s**[1].

-'s[1] ▶ **suffix** denoting possession in singular nouns, also in plural nouns not having a final *-s*: *the car's engine | Mrs. Ross's son | the children's teacher.*
– ORIGIN Old English, masculine and neuter genitive singular ending.

-'s[2] ▶ **suffix** denoting the plural of a letter or symbol: *T's | 9's.*

> **USAGE** In the formation of plurals of regular nouns, it is incorrect to use an apostrophe: *six pens* (not *six pen's*). There are a few special occasions, however, in which the apostrophe indicates plurals, as with letters and symbols where s added without punctuation would look odd (or be undecipherable): *ABC's; the five W's; dot your i's and cross your t's; the code is two H's followed by four #'s.*

SA ▶ **abbr.** ■ Salvation Army. ■ South Africa. ■ South America. ■ historical Sturmabteilung.

s.a. ▶ **abbr.** ■ semiannual. ■ sex appeal. ■ without year or date. [from Latin *sine anno.*] ■ subject to approval.

Saa·di variant spelling of **SADI**.

Saa·le[1] /ˈzälə, ˈsä-/ a river in east central Germany. Rising in northern Bavaria near the border with the Czech Republic, it flows 265 miles (425 km) north to join the Elbe River near Magdeburg.

Saa·le[2] ▶ **n.** [usu. as modifier] Geology the penultimate Pleistocene glaciation in northern Europe, corresponding to the Wolstonian of Britain (and possibly the Riss of the Alps). ■ the system of deposits laid down at this time.
– DERIVATIVES **Saa·li·an** /-lēən/ **adj. & n.**
– ORIGIN 1930s: from **SAALE**[1].

Saa·me /ˈsämē/ ▶ **plural n.** variant spelling of **SAMI**.

Saa·mi /ˈsämē/ ▶ **plural n.** variant spelling of **SAMI**.

Saar /sär, zär/ a river in western Europe. Rising in the Vosges Mountains in eastern France, it flows 150 miles (240 km) north to join the Mosel River in Germany, just east of the border with Luxembourg. French name **SARRE**. ■ the Saarland.

Saar·brück·en /särˈbro͝okən, zärˈbrʏkən/ an industrial city in western Germany, the capital of Saarland, on the Saar River, close to the border with France; pop. 177,900 (est. 2006).

Saa·ri·nen /ˈsärənən/ the name of a family of US architects, born in Finland. ■ **Eliel** (1873–1950); full name *Gottlieb Eliel Saarinen.* He designed the Cranbrook Academy of Art in Michigan and served as its president 1932–48. ■ **Eero** (1910–61); the son of Eliel. He designed the Memorial Arch in St. Louis 1948 and the US Embassy in London 1955–60.

Saar·land /ˈsärˌland, ˈzärlänt/ a state in western Germany, on the border with France; capital, Saarbrücken. Rich in coal and iron ore and historically dominated by France, the area was administered by the League of Nations from the end of World War I until 1935; it became the tenth German state in 1957.

Sab. ▶ **abbr.** Sabbath.

Sa·ba /ˈsäbə/ **1** an island in the Netherlands Antilles, in the Caribbean; pop. 1,601 (2009). The smallest island in the group, it is located northwest of St. Kitts. **2** an ancient kingdom in southwestern Arabia, known for its trade in gold and spices; the biblical Sheba.

sab·a·dil·la /ˌsabəˈdilə, -ˈdēyə/ ▶ **n.** a Mexican plant of the lily family, whose seeds contain veratrine. ● *Schoenocaulon officinale*, family Liliaceae. ■ a preparation of these seeds, used as an agricultural insecticide and in medicines.
– ORIGIN early 19th cent.: from Spanish *cebadilla*, diminutive of *cebada* 'barley.'

Sa·bae·an /səˈbēən/ ▶ **n.** a member of an ancient Semitic people who ruled Saba in southwestern Arabia until overrun by Persians and Arabs in the 6th century AD.
▶ **adj.** of or relating to the Sabaeans.
– ORIGIN from Latin *Sabaeus* (from Greek *Sabaios*) + **-AN**.

Sa·bah /ˈsäbä/ a state of Malaysia that comprises the northern part of Borneo and some offshore islands; capital, Kota Kinabalu.

sa·bal palm /ˈsābəl/ ▶ **n.** see **PALMETTO**.

Sab·a·oth /ˈsabāˌäTH/ ▶ **plural n.** archaic the hosts of heaven (in the biblical title "Lord (God) of Sabaoth").
– ORIGIN via Latin from Greek *Sabaōth*, from Hebrew *ṣĕḇāʾōṯ*, plural of *ṣāḇāʾ* 'host (of heaven).'

sa·ba·yon /säbīˈôn/ ▶ **n.** French term for **ZABAGLIONE**.

sab·ba·tar·i·an /ˌsabəˈte(ə)rēən/ ▶ **n.** a Christian who strictly observes Sunday as the sabbath. ■ a Jew who strictly observes the sabbath. ■ a Christian belonging to a denomination or sect that observes Saturday as the sabbath.
▶ **adj.** relating to or upholding the observance of the sabbath.
– DERIVATIVES **sab·ba·tar·i·an·ism** /-ˌnizəm/ **n.**
– ORIGIN early 17th cent.: from late Latin *sabbatarius* (from Latin *sabbatum* 'sabbath') + **-AN**.

sab·bath /ˈsabəTH/ ▶ **n. 1** (often **the Sabbath**) a day of religious observance and abstinence from work, kept by Jews from Friday evening to Saturday evening, and by most Christians on Sunday. **2** (also **witches' sabbath**) a supposed annual midnight meeting of witches with the Devil.
– ORIGIN Old English, from Latin *sabbatum*, via Greek from Hebrew *šabbāṯ*, from *šāḇaṯ* 'to rest.'

sab·bat·i·cal /səˈbatikəl/ ▶ **n.** a period of paid leave granted to a college teacher for study or travel, traditionally every seventh year: *she's away on sabbatical.*
▶ **adj. 1** of or relating to a sabbatical. **2** archaic of or appropriate to the sabbath.
– ORIGIN late 16th cent.: via late Latin from Greek *sabbatikos* 'of the sabbath' + **-AL**.

sab·bat·i·cal year ▶ **n. 1** a year's sabbatical leave. **2** (in biblical times) a year observed every seventh year under the Mosaic law as a "sabbath" during which the land was allowed to rest.

Sa·bel·li·an /səˈbelēən/ ▶ **adj.** of or relating to the teachings of **Sabellius** (*fl. c.*220 in North Africa), who developed a form of the modalist doctrine that the Father, Son, and Holy Spirit are not truly distinct but merely aspects of one divine being.
▶ **n.** a follower of the teachings of Sabellius.
– DERIVATIVES **Sa·bel·li·an·ism** /-ˌizəm/ **n.**

sa·ber /ˈsābər/ (Brit. **sabre**) ▶ **n.** a heavy cavalry sword with a curved blade and a single cutting edge. ■ a light fencing sword with a tapering blade. ■ historical a cavalry soldier and horse.
▶ **v.** [with obj.] archaic cut down or wound with a saber.
– ORIGIN late 17th cent.: from French, alteration of obsolete *sable*, from German *Sabel* (local variant of *Säbel*), from Hungarian *szablya.*

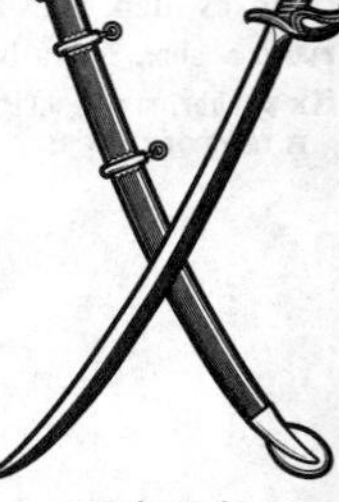

cavalry saber

sa·ber·met·rics /ˌsābərˈmetriks/ ▶ **n.** Baseball the application of statistical analysis to baseball records, esp. in order to evaluate and compare the performance of individual players.
– DERIVATIVES **sa·ber·me·tri·cian** /ˌsābərmiˈtrisHən/ **n.**
– ORIGIN 1980s: from *SABR*, acronym from Society for American Baseball Research, + **METRICS**.

sa·ber-rat·tling ▶ **n.** the display or threat of military force.

sa·ber saw ▶ **n.** a portable electric jigsaw.

sa·ber·tooth /ˈsābərˌto͞oTH/ ▶ **n. 1** (also **saber-toothed cat** or **saber-toothed tiger**) a large extinct carnivorous mammal of the cat family, with large, curved upper canine teeth. ● Several genera in the family Felidae, in particular *Smilodon* of the American Pleistocene and *Machairodus* of the Old World Pliocene. **2** a large extinct marsupial mammal with similar teeth, of the South American Pliocene. ● Genus *Thylacosmilus*, family Borhyaenidae.

Sa·bi·an /ˈsābēən/ ▶ **adj.** of or relating to a non-Muslim sect classed in the Koran with Jews, Christians, and Zoroastrians as having a faith revealed by the true God. It is not known who the original Sabians were, but the name was adopted by some groups in order to escape religious persecution by Muslims.
▶ **n.** a member of this sect.
– ORIGIN early 17th cent.: from Arabic *ṣābiʾ* + **-AN**.

sab·i·cu /ˈsabiˌko͞o/ ▶ **n.** a Caribbean tree of the pea family, with timber that resembles mahogany and is used chiefly in boatbuilding. ● *Lysiloma sabicu*, family Leguminosae.
– ORIGIN mid 19th cent.: from Cuban Spanish *sabicú.*

Sa·bin /ˈsābin/, Albert Bruce (1906–93), US physician; born in Russia. He developed the orally administered **Sabin vaccine** against poliomyelitis that was adopted by the World Health Organization in the late 1950s.

Sa·bine /ˈsā,bīn, -,bin/ ▶ **adj.** of, relating to, or denoting an ancient Oscan-speaking people of the central Apennines in Italy, northeast of Rome, who feature in early Roman legends and were incorporated into the Roman state in 290 BC.
▶ **n.** a member of this people.
– ORIGIN from Latin *Sabinus*.

Sa·bine Riv·er /səˈbēn/ a river that flows for 360 miles (580 km) from eastern Texas to form the border with Louisiana and reaches the Gulf of Mexico at Sabine Pass.

sab·kha /ˈsabkə/ ▶ **n.** Geography an area of coastal flats subject to periodic flooding and evaporation, which result in the accumulation of aeolian clays, evaporites, and salts, typically found in North Africa and Arabia.
– ORIGIN late 19th cent.: from Arabic *sabḵa* 'salt flat.'

sa·ble[1] /ˈsābəl/ ▶ **n.** a marten with a short tail and dark brown fur, native to Japan and Siberia and valued for its fur. ● *Martes zibellina*, family Mustelidae. ■ the fur of the sable.
– ORIGIN late Middle English: from Old French, in the sense 'sable fur,' from medieval Latin *sabelum*, of Slavic origin.

sa·ble[2] ▶ **adj.** literary or Heraldry black.
▶ **n. 1** literary or Heraldry black. ■ (**sables**) archaic mourning garments.
2 (also **sable antelope**) a large African antelope with long curved horns, the male of which has a black coat and the female a russet coat, both having a white belly. ● *Hippotragus niger*, family Bovidae.
– ORIGIN Middle English: from Old French (as a heraldic term), generally taken to be identical with SABLE[1], although sable fur is dark brown.

sa·ble·fish /ˈsābəl,fisн/ ▶ **n.** (pl. **same** or **sablefishes**) a large commercially important fish with a slate-blue to black back, occurring throughout the North Pacific. ● *Anoplopoma fimbria*, family Anoplopomatidae.

sab·ot /saˈbō, ˈsabō/ ▶ **n. 1** a kind of simple shoe, shaped and hollowed out from a single block of wood, traditionally worn by French and Breton peasants.

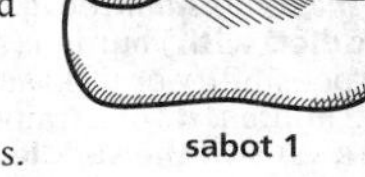
sabot 1

2 a device that ensures the correct positioning of a bullet or shell in the barrel of a gun, attached either to the projectile or inside the barrel and falling away as it leaves the muzzle.
3 a box from which cards are dealt at casinos in gambling games such as baccarat and chemin de fer. Also called SHOE.
– DERIVATIVES **sa·boted** adj. (sense 1).
– ORIGIN early 17th cent.: French, blend of *savate* 'shoe' and *botte* 'boot.'

sab·o·tage /ˈsabə,täzн/ ▶ **v.** [with obj.] deliberately destroy, damage, or obstruct (something), esp. for political or military advantage.
▶ **n.** the action of sabotaging something.
– ORIGIN early 20th cent.: from French, from *saboter* 'kick with sabots, willfully destroy' (see SABOT).

sab·o·teur /,sabəˈtər/ ▶ **n.** a person who engages in sabotage.
– ORIGIN 1920s: from French, from the verb *saboter* (see SABOTAGE).

sa·bra /ˈsäbrə/ ▶ **n.** a Jew born in Israel (or before 1948 in Palestine).
– ORIGIN from modern Hebrew *ṣabbār* 'opuntia fruit' (opuntias being common in coastal regions of Israel).

sa·bre ▶ **n. & v.** British spelling of SABER.

sa·bre·tache /ˈsābər,tasн/ ▶ **n.** historical a flat satchel on long straps worn by some cavalry and horse artillery officers from the left of the waist-belt.
– ORIGIN early 19th cent.: from French, from German *Säbeltasche*, from *Säbel* 'saber' + *Tasche* 'pocket.'

sa·bre·wing /ˈsābər,wiNG/ ▶ **n.** a large tropical American hummingbird with a green back and long curved wings. ● Genus *Campylopterus*, family Trochilidae: several species.

SAC /sak/ ▶ **abbr.** Strategic Air Command.

Sac ▶ **n.** variant spelling of SAUK.

sac /sak/ ▶ **n.** a hollow, flexible structure resembling a bag or pouch: *a fountain pen with an ink sac.* ■ a cavity enclosed by a membrane within a living organism, containing air, liquid, or solid structures. ■ the distended membrane surrounding a hernia, cyst, or tumor.
– DERIVATIVES **sac·like** /-līk/ **adj.**
– ORIGIN mid 18th cent. (as a term in biology): from French *sac* or Latin *saccus* 'sack, bag.'

Sac·a·ja·we·a /,sakəjəˈwēə, -ˈwäə/ (c.1786–1812), Shoshone Indian guide and interpreter; also *Sacagawea*. She joined the Lewis and Clark expedition in what is now North Dakota and guided their travels through the wilderness and across the Rockies 1804–06.
– ORIGIN from Hidatsa *tsakaka-wia*, literally 'bird-woman.'

Sacajawea

sac·cade /səˈkäd, sa-/ ▶ **n.** (usu. **saccades**) technical a rapid movement of the eye between fixation points.
– DERIVATIVES **sac·cad·ic** /səˈkadik, sa-/ **adj.**
– ORIGIN early 18th cent.: from French, literally 'violent pull,' from Old French *saquer* 'to pull.'

sac·cate /ˈsa,kāt/ ▶ **adj.** Botany dilated to form a sac.

sac·cha·ride /ˈsakə,rīd/ ▶ **n.** Biochemistry another term for SUGAR (sense 2 of the noun).
– ORIGIN mid 19th cent.: from modern Latin *saccharum* 'sugar' + -IDE.

sac·cha·rin /ˈsak(ə)rən/ ▶ **n.** a sweet-tasting synthetic compound used in food and drink as a substitute for sugar. ● Alternative name: *o*-**sulfobenzoic imide**; chem. formula: $C_7H_5NO_3S$.
– ORIGIN late 19th cent.: from modern Latin *saccharum* 'sugar' + -IN[1].

sac·cha·rine /ˈsak(ə)rin, -rēn, -rīn/ ▶ **adj.** [attrib.]
1 excessively sweet or sentimental.
2 dated relating to or containing sugar; sugary.
▶ **n.** another term for SACCHARIN.
– ORIGIN late 17th cent.: from modern Latin *saccharum* + -INE[1].

saccharo- ▶ **comb. form** of or relating to sugar: *saccharometer*.
– ORIGIN via Latin from Greek *sakkharon* 'sugar.'

sac·cha·rom·e·ter /,sakəˈrämitər/ ▶ **n.** a hydrometer for measuring the sugar content of a solution.

sac·cha·rose /ˈsakə,rōs/ ▶ **n.** Chemistry another term for SUCROSE.
– ORIGIN late 19th cent.: from modern Latin *saccharum* 'sugar' + -OSE[2].

Sac·co /ˈsakō/, Nicola (1891–1927), US political radical; born in Italy. In 1921, along with Bartolomeo Vanzetti, he was accused and convicted of murder in a sensational, controversial trial. In 1927, both men were executed in the electric chair; fifty years later, their names were cleared of any crimes.

sac·cule /ˈsa,kyo͞ol/ ▶ **n.** Biology & Anatomy a small sac, pouch, or cyst. ■ another term for SACCULUS.
– DERIVATIVES **sac·cu·lar** /ˈsakyələr/ **adj.**, **sac·cu·lat·ed** /ˈsakyə,lātid/ **adj.**, **sac·cu·la·tion** /,sakyəˈlāsнən/ **n.**
– ORIGIN mid 19th cent.: anglicized form of Latin *sacculus* (see SACCULUS).

sac·cu·lus /ˈsakyələs/ ▶ **n.** Anatomy the smaller of the two fluid-filled sacs forming part of the labyrinth of the inner ear (the other being the utriculus). It contains a region of hair cells and otoliths that send signals to the brain concerning the orientation of the head. ■ another term for SACCULE.
– ORIGIN mid 18th cent.: from Latin, diminutive of *saccus* 'sack.'

sac·er·do·tal /,sasərˈdōtl, ,sakər-/ ▶ **adj.** relating to priests or the priesthood; priestly. ■ Theology relating to or denoting a doctrine that ascribes sacrificial functions and spiritual or supernatural powers to ordained priests.
– DERIVATIVES **sac·er·do·tal·ism** /-,izəm/ **n.**
– ORIGIN late Middle English: from Old French, or from Latin *sacerdotalis*, from *sacerdos, sacerdot-* 'priest.'

sa·chem /ˈsācнəm/ ▶ **n.** (among some American Indian peoples) a chief or leader. ■ informal a boss or leader.
– ORIGIN from Narragansett, 'chief.' Compare with SAGAMORE.

Sa·cher·torte /ˈsäkər,tôrt/ ▶ **n.** (pl. **Sachertorten** /-,tôrtn/) a chocolate gateau with apricot jam filling and chocolate icing.
– ORIGIN German, from the name of Franz *Sacher*, the pastry chef who created it, + *Torte* 'tart, pastry.'

sa·chet /saˈsнā/ ▶ **n.** a small perfumed bag used to scent clothes. ■ archaic dried, scented material for use in scenting clothes.
– ORIGIN mid 19th cent.: from French, 'little bag,' diminutive of *sac*, from Latin *saccus* 'sack, bag.'

Sach·sen /ˈsaksən, ˈzäk-/ German name for SAXONY.

Sach·sen-An·halt /ˈänhält/ German name for SAXONY-ANHALT.

sack[1] /sak/ ▶ **n. 1** a large bag made of a strong material such as burlap, thick paper, or plastic, used for storing and carrying goods. ■ the contents of such a bag or the amount it can contain: ***a sack of flour.***
2 a loose, unfitted, or shapeless garment, in particular: ■ historical a woman's loose gown. ■ historical a decorative piece of dress material fastened to the shoulders of a woman's gown in loose pleats and forming a long train, fashionable in the 18th century.
3 (**the sack**) informal bed, esp. as regarded as a place for sex.
4 (**the sack**) informal dismissal from employment: ***he got the sack for swearing | they were given the sack.***
5 Baseball, informal a base.
6 Football an act of tackling a quarterback behind the line of scrimmage before he can throw a pass.
▶ **v.** [with obj.] **1** informal dismiss from employment: *any official found to be involved would be sacked on the spot.*
2 (**sack out**) informal go to sleep or bed.
3 Football tackle (a quarterback) behind the line of scrimmage before he can throw a pass.
4 rare put into a sack or sacks.
– PHRASES **hit the sack** informal go to bed. **a sack of potatoes** informal used in similes to refer to clumsiness, inertness, or unceremonious treatment of the person or thing in question: *he drags me in like a sack of potatoes.*
– DERIVATIVES **sack·a·ble adj.**, **sack·like** /-,līk/ **adj.**
– ORIGIN Old English *sacc*, from Latin *saccus* 'sack, sackcloth,' from Greek *sakkos*, of Semitic origin. Sense 1 of the verb dates from the mid 19th cent.

sack[2] ▶ **v.** [with obj.] (chiefly in historical contexts) plunder and destroy (a captured town, building, or other place).
▶ **n.** the pillaging of a town or city.
– ORIGIN mid 16th cent.: from French *sac*, in the phrase *mettre à sac* 'put to sack,' on the model of Italian *fare il sacco, mettere a sacco*, which perhaps originally referred to filling a sack with plunder.

sack[3] ▶ **n.** historical a dry white wine formerly imported into Britain from Spain and the Canary Islands.
– ORIGIN early 16th cent.: from the phrase *wyne seck*, from French *vin sec* 'dry wine.'

sack·but /ˈsak,bət/ ▶ **n.** an early form of trombone used in Renaissance music.
– ORIGIN late 15th cent.: from French *saquebute*, from obsolete *saqueboute* 'hook for pulling a man off a horse,' from *saquer* 'to pull' + *bouter* 'to hit.'

sack·cloth /ˈsak,klôтн, -,kläтн/ ▶ **n.** a very coarse, rough fabric woven from flax or hemp.
– PHRASES **sackcloth and ashes** used with allusion to the wearing of sackcloth and having ashes sprinkled on the head as a sign of penitence or mourning (Matt 11:21).

sack coat ▶ **n.** historical a loose-fitting coat hanging straight down from the shoulders, particularly as worn by men (sometimes as part of military uniform) in the 19th and early 20th centuries.

sack dress ▶ **n.** a woman's short, loose, unwaisted dress, originally fashionable in the 1950s.

sack·ful /ˈsak,fo͝ol/ ▶ **n.** (pl. **sackfuls**) the quantity of something contained in a sack: ***a sackful of rice.***

sack·ing /ˈsakiNG/ ▶ **n. 1** an act of sacking someone or something.
2 coarse material for making sacks; sackcloth.

sack lunch ▶ **n.** a bag lunch.

sack race ▶ **n.** a race in which competitors, typically children, stand in sacks up to the waist or neck and jump forward.

sack suit ▶ **n.** a suit with a straight, loose-fitting jacket.

Sack·ville-West /,sakvil ˈwest/, Vita (1892–1962), English novelist and poet; full name *Victoria Mary Sackville-West*. Her works include the novel *All Passion Spent* (1931).

Sa·co /ˈsôkō, ˈsä-/ a city in southern Maine, southwest of Portland; pop. 18,125 (est. 2008).

sa·cra /ˈsakrə, ˈsā-/ plural form of SACRUM.

sa·cral /ˈsakrəl, ˈsā-/ ▶ **adj.** [attrib.] **1** of, for, or relating to sacred rites or symbols: *sacral horns of a Minoan type.*
2 Anatomy of or relating to the sacrum.
– DERIVATIVES **sa·cral·i·ty** /sāˈkralətē, sə-/ **n.** (sense 1).

sa·cral·ize /ˈsakrəˌlīz, ˈsā-/ ▶ **v.** [with obj.] imbue with or treat as having a sacred character or quality: *rural images that sacralize country life.*
– DERIVATIVES **sa·cral·i·za·tion** /ˌsakrəliˈzāsʜən, ˌsā-/ **n.**

sac·ra·ment /ˈsakrəmənt/ ▶ **n.** a religious ceremony or act of the Christian Church that is regarded as an outward and visible sign of inward and spiritual divine grace, in particular: ■ (in the Roman Catholic and many Orthodox Churches) the rites of baptism, confirmation, the Eucharist, penance, anointing of the sick, ordination, and matrimony. ■ (among Protestants) baptism and the Eucharist. ■ (also **the Blessed Sacrament** or **the Holy Sacrament**) (in Roman Catholic use) the consecrated elements of the Eucharist, esp. the Host: *he heard Mass and received the sacrament.* ■ a thing of mysterious and sacred significance; a religious symbol.
– ORIGIN Middle English: from Old French *sacrement*, from Latin *sacramentum* 'solemn oath' (from *sacrare* 'to hallow,' from *sacer* 'sacred'), used in Christian Latin as a translation of Greek *mustērion* 'mystery.'

sac·ra·men·tal /ˌsakrəˈmentl/ ▶ **adj.** relating to or constituting a sacrament or the sacraments. ■ attaching great importance to sacraments.
▶ **n.** an observance analogous to but not reckoned among the sacraments, such as the use of holy water or the sign of the cross.
– DERIVATIVES **sac·ra·men·tal·ism** /-ˌizəm/ **n.**, **sac·ra·men·tal·i·ty** /ˌsakrəmənˈtalitē, -ˌmen-/ **n.**, **sac·ra·men·tal·ize** /-ˌīz/ **v.**, **sac·ra·men·tal·ly** **adv.**

Sac·ra·men·to /ˌsakrəˈmentō/ **1** a river in northern California that rises near the border with Oregon and flows about 380 miles (611 km) south to San Francisco Bay.
2 the capital of California, situated on the Sacramento River, northeast of San Francisco; pop. 463,794 (est. 2008).

sac·ra·ment of rec·on·cil·i·a·tion (also **sacrament of penance**) ▶ **n.** (chiefly in the Roman Catholic Church) the practice of private confession of sins to a priest and the receiving of absolution.

Sac·ra·men·to Moun·tains a range in southern New Mexico and western Texas comprising the Jicarilla, Sierra Blanca, and Guadalupe mountains.

sa·crar·i·um /səˈkre(ə)rēəm/ ▶ **n.** (pl. **sacraria** /-ˈkre(ə)rēə/) the sanctuary of a church. ■ (in the Roman Catholic Church) a piscina. ■ (in the ancient Roman world) a shrine, in particular the room in a house containing the penates.
– ORIGIN Latin, from *sacer, sacr-* 'holy.'

sa·cré bleu /ˈsäkrā ˈblœ/ ▶ **exclam.** a French expression of surprise, exasperation, or dismay.
– ORIGIN alteration of *sacré Dieu* 'holy God.'

sa·cred /ˈsākrid/ ▶ **adj.** connected with God (or the gods) or dedicated to a religious purpose and so deserving veneration: *sacred rites* | *the site at Eleusis is sacred to Demeter.* ■ religious rather than secular: *sacred music.* ■ (of writing or text) embodying the laws or doctrines of a religion: *a sacred Hindu text.* ■ regarded with great respect and reverence by a particular religion, group, or individual: *an animal sacred to Mexican culture.* ■ sacrosanct: *to a police officer nothing is sacred.*
– DERIVATIVES **sa·cred·ly** **adv.**, **sa·cred·ness** **n.**
– ORIGIN late Middle English: past participle of archaic *sacre* 'consecrate,' from Old French *sacrer*, from Latin *sacrare*, from *sacer, sacr-* 'holy.'

sa·cred ba·boon ▶ **n.** another term for HAMADRYAS BABOON.

sa·cred bam·boo ▶ **n.** another term for NANDINA.

Sa·cred Col·lege another term for COLLEGE OF CARDINALS.

sa·cred cow ▶ **n.** an idea, custom, or institution held, esp. unreasonably, to be above criticism (with reference to the Hindus' respect for the cow as a sacred animal).

Sa·cred Heart ▶ **n.** the heart of Christ, esp. as represented in an image and regarded as an object of devotion among Roman Catholics.

sa·cred i·bis ▶ **n.** a mainly white ibis with a bare black head and neck and black plumes over the lower back, native to Africa and the Middle East, and venerated by the ancient Egyptians. ● *Threskiornis aethiopicus*, family Threskiornithidae.

sa·cred lo·tus ▶ **n.** see LOTUS (sense 1).

sa·cred scar·ab ▶ **n.** see SCARAB.

sac·ri·fice /ˈsakrəˌfīs/ ▶ **n.** an act of slaughtering an animal or person or surrendering a possession as an offering to God or to a divine or supernatural figure: *they offer sacrifices to the spirits* | *the ancient laws of animal sacrifice.* ■ an animal, person, or object offered in this way. ■ an act of giving up something valued for the sake of something else regarded as more important or worthy: *we must all be prepared to make sacrifices.* ■ Christian Church Christ's offering of himself in the Crucifixion. ■ Christian Church the Eucharist regarded either (in Catholic terms) as a propitiatory offering of the body and blood of Christ or (in Protestant terms) as an act of thanksgiving. ■ Chess a move intended to allow the opponent to win a pawn or piece, for strategic or tactical reasons. ■ (also **sacrifice bunt** or **sacrifice hit**) Baseball a bunted ball that puts the batter out but allows a base runner or runners to advance. ■ (also **sacrifice bid**) Bridge a bid made in the belief that it will be less costly to be defeated in the contract than to allow the opponents to make a contract.
▶ **v.** [with obj.] offer or kill as a religious sacrifice: *the goat was sacrificed at the shrine.* ■ give up (something important or valued) for the sake of other considerations: *working hard doesn't mean sacrificing your social life.* ■ Chess deliberately allow one's opponent to win (a pawn or piece). ■ Baseball advance (a base runner) by a sacrifice. ■ [no obj.] Bridge make a sacrifice bid.
– ORIGIN Middle English: from Old French, from Latin *sacrificium*; related to *sacrificus* 'sacrificial,' from *sacer* 'holy.'

sac·ri·fi·cial /ˌsakrəˈfisʜəl/ ▶ **adj.** of, relating to, or constituting a sacrifice: *an altar for sacrificial offerings.* ■ technical designed to be used up or destroyed in fulfilling a purpose or function.
– DERIVATIVES **sac·ri·fi·cial·ly** **adv.**

sac·ri·lege /ˈsakrəlij/ ▶ **n.** violation or misuse of what is regarded as sacred: *putting ecclesiastical vestments to secular use was considered sacrilege.*
– ORIGIN Middle English: via Old French from Latin *sacrilegium*, from *sacrilegus* 'stealer of sacred things,' from *sacer, sacr-* 'sacred' + *legere* 'take possession of.'

sac·ri·le·gious /ˌsakrəˈlijəs/ ▶ **adj.** involving or committing sacrilege: *a sacrilegious act.*
– DERIVATIVES **sac·ri·le·gious·ly** /ˌsakrəˈlijəslē/ **adv.**

sa·cring /ˈsākriNG/ ▶ **n.** archaic or historical the consecration of a bishop, a sovereign, or the Eucharistic elements.
– ORIGIN Middle English: from the obsolete verb *sacre* 'consecrate.'

sa·cring bell ▶ **n.** a bell rung in some Christian churches at certain points during the Mass or Eucharist, esp. at the elevation of the consecrated elements.

sac·ris·tan /ˈsakristən/ (also **sacrist** /ˈsākrist, ˈsak-/) ▶ **n.** **1** a person in charge of a sacristy and its contents.
2 archaic the sexton of a parish church.
– ORIGIN Middle English: from medieval Latin *sacristanus*, based on Latin *sacer, sacr-* 'sacred.'

sac·ris·ty /ˈsakristē/ ▶ **n.** (pl. **sacristies**) a room in a church where a priest prepares for a service, and where vestments and other things used in worship are kept.
– ORIGIN late Middle English: from French *sacristie*, from medieval Latin *sacristia*, based on Latin *sacer, sacr-* 'sacred.'

sacro- ▶ **comb. form** of or relating to the sacrum: *sacroiliac.*
– ORIGIN from Latin *(os) sacrum* 'sacrum.'

sac·ro·il·i·ac /ˌsakrōˈilēˌak/ ▶ **adj.** Anatomy relating to the sacrum and the ilium. ■ denoting the rigid joint at the back of the pelvis between the sacrum and the ilium.

sac·ro·sanct /ˈsakrōˌsaNG(k)t/ ▶ **adj.** (esp. of a principle, place, or routine) regarded as too important or valuable to be interfered with: *the individual's right to work has been upheld as sacrosanct.*
– DERIVATIVES **sac·ro·sanc·ti·ty** /ˌsakrōˈsaNG(k)titē/ **n.**
– ORIGIN late 15th cent.: from Latin *sacrosanctus*, from *sacro* 'by a sacred rite' (ablative of *sacrum*) + *sanctus* 'holy.'

sac·rum /ˈsakrəm, ˈsā-/ ▶ **n.** (pl. **sacra** /ˈsakrə, ˈsā-/ or **sacrums**) Anatomy a triangular bone in the lower back formed from fused vertebrae and situated between the two hipbones of the pelvis.
– ORIGIN mid 18th cent.: from Latin *os sacrum*, translation of Greek *hieron osteon* 'sacred bone' (from the belief that the soul resides in it).

SAD ▶ **abbr.** seasonal affective disorder.

sad /sad/ ▶ **adj.** (**sadder, saddest**) **1** feeling or showing sorrow; unhappy: *I was sad and subdued* | *they looked at her with sad, anxious faces.* ■ causing or characterized by sorrow or regret; unfortunate and regrettable: *he told her the sad story of his life* | *a sad day for us all.*
2 informal pathetically inadequate or unfashionable: *the show is tongue-in-cheek—anyone who takes it seriously is a bit sad.*
3 (of dough) heavy through having failed to rise.
– PHRASES **sad to say** unfortunately, regrettably.
– DERIVATIVES **sad·dish** **adj.**
– ORIGIN Old English *sæd* 'sated, weary,' also 'weighty, dense,' of Germanic origin; related to Dutch *zat* and German *satt*, from an Indo-European root shared by Latin *satis* 'enough.' The original meaning was replaced in Middle English by the senses 'steadfast, firm' and 'serious, sober,' and later 'sorrowful.'

Sa·dat /səˈdät/, Anwar (1918–81), Egyptian statesman; president 1970–81; full name *Muhammad Anwar al-Sadat*. He worked to achieve peace in the Middle East, visiting Israel in 1977 and attending talks with Menachim Begin at Camp David in 1978. He was assassinated by members of the Islamic Jihad. Nobel Peace Prize (1978), shared with Begin.

Sad·dam Hus·sein /səˈdäm hōōˈsān, ˈsadəm/ see HUSSEIN[2].

sad·den /ˈsadn/ ▶ **v.** [with obj.] cause to feel sorrow; make unhappy: *he was greatly saddened by the death of his only son* | [with obj. and infinitive] *I was saddened to see their lack of commitment.*

sad·dle /ˈsadl/ ▶ **n.** **1** a seat fastened on the back of a horse or other animal for riding, typically made of leather and raised at the front and rear. ■ a seat on a bicycle or motorcycle.
2 something resembling a saddle in appearance, function, or position, in particular: ■ a low part of a ridge between two higher points or peaks. ■ Mathematics a low region of a curve between two high points, esp. (in three dimensions) one representing the highest point of a curve in one direction and the lowest point in another direction. ■ the part of a draft horse's harness that supports the straps to which the shafts are attached. ■ a shaped support on which a cable, wire, or pipe rests. ■ a fireclay bar for supporting ceramic ware in a kiln.
3 a large cut of meat consisting of the two loins. ■ the lower part of the back in a mammal or fowl, esp. when distinct in shape or marking.
▶ **v.** [with obj.] put a saddle on (a horse): *he was in the stable saddling up his horse.* ■ (usu. **be saddled with**) burden (someone) with an onerous responsibility or task: *he's saddled with debts of $12 million.* ■ (of a trainer) enter (a horse) for a race.
– PHRASES **in the saddle** on horseback. ■ in a position of control or responsibility.
– ORIGIN Old English *sadol, sadul*, of Germanic origin; related to Dutch *zadel* and German *Sattel*, perhaps from an Indo-European root shared by Latin *sella* 'seat' and SIT.

English saddle

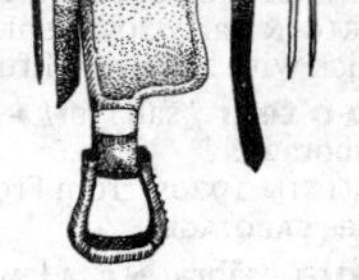
Western saddle

saddles

sad·dle·back /ˈsadlˌbak/ ▶ **n.** **1** Architecture a tower roof that has two opposite gables connected by a pitched section.
2 a hill with a ridge along the top that dips in the middle.
3 a pig of a black breed with a white stripe across the back.
4 a New Zealand wattlebird with mainly black plumage, a reddish-brown back, and two small red wattles under the bill. ● *Philesturnus carunculatus*, family Callaeidae.
– DERIVATIVES **sad·dle·backed** **adj.**

sad·dle·bag /ˈsadlˌbag/ ▶ **n.** each of a pair of bags attached behind the saddle on a horse, bicycle, or motorcycle. ■ (**saddlebags**) excess fat around the hips and thighs.

sad·dle·bow /bō/ ▶ **n.** chiefly archaic the pommel of a saddle, or a similar curved part behind the rider.

sad·dle·bred /ˈsadlˌbred/ ▶ **n.** a horse bred to have the gait of an American saddle horse.

sad·dle·cloth /ˈsadlˌklôTH, -ˌkläTH/ ▶ **n.** a cloth laid on a horse's back under the saddle.

sad·dle horse ▶ **n.** **1** a wooden frame or stand on which saddles are cleaned or stored.
2 a horse kept for riding only.

sad·dler /ˈsadlər/ ▶ **n.** someone who makes, repairs, or deals in saddlery.

sad·dler·y /ˈsadlərē, -əlrē/ ▶ **n.** (pl. **saddleries**) saddles, bridles, and other equipment for horses. ■ the making or repairing of such equipment. ■ a saddler's business or premises.

sad·dle shoe ▶ **n.** a white oxford shoe with a piece of leather in a contrasting color (typically black or brown) stitched across the instep.

saddle shoe

sad·dle soap ▶ **n.** soft soap containing neat's-foot oil, used for cleaning leather.

sad·dle·sore /ˈsadl,sôr/ ▶ **n.** a bruise or sore on a horse's back, caused by pressure or chafing of an ill-fitting saddle. ▶ **adj.** (of a person) chafed from riding on a saddle.

sad·dle stitch ▶ **n.** a stitch of thread or a wire staple passed through the fold of a magazine or booklet. ■ (in needlework) a decorative stitch made with long stitches on the upper side of the cloth alternated with short stitches on the underside. ▶ **v.** (**saddle-stitch**) [with obj.] sew with such a stitch.

sad·dle tank ▶ **n.** a small steam locomotive with a water tank that fits over the top and sides of the boiler like a saddle.

sad·dle tree ▶ **n.** a frame around which a saddle is built.

Sad·du·cee /ˈsajə,sē, ˈsadyə-/ ▶ **n.** a member of a Jewish sect or party of the time of Jesus Christ that denied the resurrection of the dead, the existence of spirits, and the obligation of oral tradition, emphasizing acceptance of the written Law alone. Compare with **PHARISEE**.
– DERIVATIVES **Sad·du·ce·an** /,sajəˈsēən, ,sadyə-/ **adj.**
– ORIGIN Old English *sadducēas* (plural), via late Latin from Greek *Saddoukaios*, from Hebrew *ṣĕḏōqī* in the sense 'descendant of Zadok' (2 Sam. 8:17).

Sade /säd/, Donatien Alphonse François, Comte de (1740–1814), French writer and soldier; known as **the Marquis de Sade**. His career as a cavalry officer was interrupted by periods of imprisonment for cruelty and debauchery.

sa·dhu /ˈsädo͞o/ ▶ **n.** Indian a holy man, sage, or ascetic.
– ORIGIN Sanskrit.

Sa·di /ˈsädē/ (also **Saadi**) (*c.*1213–*c.*1291), Persian poet; born *Sheikh Muslih Addin*. His principal works were the collections known as the *Bustan* (1257) and the *Gulistan* (1258).

sa·dism /ˈsā,dizəm/ ▶ **n.** the tendency to derive pleasure, esp. sexual gratification, from inflicting pain, suffering, or humiliation on others. ■ (in general use) deliberate cruelty.
– DERIVATIVES **sa·dist n.**
– ORIGIN late 19th cent.: from French *sadisme*, from the name of the Marquis de **SADE**.

sa·dis·tic /səˈdistik/ ▶ **adj.** deriving pleasure from inflicting pain, suffering, or humiliation on others: *she took a sadistic pleasure in tormenting him.*
– DERIVATIVES **sa·dis·ti·cal·ly** /səˈdistik(ə)lē/ **adv.**

sad·ly /ˈsadlē/ ▶ **adv.** showing or feeling sadness: *he smiled sadly.* ■ [sentence adverb] it is a sad or regrettable fact that; unfortunately: *sadly, the forests of Sulawesi are now under threat.* ■ [as submodifier] to a regrettable extent; regrettably: *his advice is sadly disregarded nowadays.*

sad·ness /ˈsadnis/ ▶ **n.** the condition or quality of being sad: *a source of great sadness.*

sa·do·mas·o·chism /,sādōˈmasə,kizəm, ,sadō-/ ▶ **n.** psychological tendency or sexual practice characterized by both sadism and masochism.
– DERIVATIVES **sa·do·mas·o·chist n.**, **sa·do·mas·o·chis·tic** /,sādō,masəˈkistik, ,sadō-/ **adj.**

sad sack ▶ **n.** informal an inept, blundering person.

sa·fa·ri /səˈfärē/ ▶ **n.** (pl. **safaris**) an expedition to observe or hunt animals in their natural habitat, esp. in East Africa: *one week on safari.*
– ORIGIN late 19th cent.: from Kiswahili, from Arabic *safara* 'to travel.'

sa·fa·ri jack·et ▶ **n.** a belted lightweight jacket, typically having short sleeves and four patch pockets.

sa·fa·ri park ▶ **n.** an area of parkland where wild animals are kept in the open and may be observed by visitors driving through.

sa·fa·ri suit ▶ **n.** a lightweight suit consisting of a safari jacket with matching trousers, shorts, or skirt.

Sa·fa·vid /säˈfä-wēd/ ▶ **n.** a member of a dynasty that ruled Persia 1502–1736 and installed Shia rather than Sunni Islam as the state religion. ▶ **adj.** of or relating to this dynasty.
– ORIGIN from Arabic *ṣafawī* 'descended from the ruler Sophy.'

safe /sāf/ ▶ **adj. 1** [predic.] protected from or not exposed to danger or risk; not likely to be harmed or lost: *eggs remain in the damp sand, **safe from** marine predators | she felt safer with them than alone.* ■ Baseball having reached a base without being put out: *Davis was safe when the right fielder dropped a fly ball.* ■ Baseball allowing the batter to reach base and not involving an error: *a safe hit.* ■ not likely to cause or lead to harm or injury; not involving danger or risk: *we have to cross the river where it's safe for us to do so | a safe investment that produced regular income.* ■ (of a place) affording security or protection: *put it in a safe place.* ■ often derogatory cautious and unenterprising: *MacGregor would be a compromise, the safe choice.* ■ based on good reasons or evidence and not likely to be proved wrong: *the verdict is safe and satisfactory | his world, **it's safe to say**, will not fall apart.*
2 uninjured; with no harm done: *they had returned **safe and sound** | hopes of her safe return later faded.*
▶ **n. 1** a strong fireproof cabinet with a complex lock, used for the storage of valuables.
2 informal a condom.
– PHRASES **in safe hands** see **HAND**. **safe in the knowledge that** used to indicate that one can do something without risk or worry on account of a specified fact: *they used to recruit hundreds a year, safe in the knowledge that many would leave.* **to be on the safe side** in order to have a margin of security against risks: *to be on the safe side, she had recorded everything.*
– DERIVATIVES **safe·ly adv.**, **safe·ness n.**
– ORIGIN Middle English (as an adjective): from Old French *sauf*, from Latin *salvus* 'uninjured.' The noun is from the verb **SAVE**[1], later assimilated to the adjectival form.

safe ar·e·a ▶ **n.** an area not liable to attack, esp. one designated as such by the United Nations.

safe bet ▶ **n.** a bet that is certain to succeed. ■ a thing in which confidence can be placed regarding a future outcome: ***it is a safe bet that** the current owners will not sell.*

safe con·duct ▶ **n.** immunity from arrest or harm when passing through an area. ■ a document securing such a privilege.

safe·crack·er /ˈsāf,krakər/ ▶ **n.** a person who breaks open and robs safes.
– DERIVATIVES **safe·crack·ing n.**

safe de·pos·it (also **safety deposit**) ▶ **n.** [usu. as modifier] a strongroom or safe in which valuables may be securely stored, typically in a bank or hotel: *a safe-deposit box.*

safe·guard /ˈsāf,gärd/ ▶ **n.** a measure taken to protect someone or something or to prevent something undesirable: *there were multiple safeguards to prevent the accidental release of a virus.* ▶ **v.** [with obj.] protect from harm or damage with an appropriate measure: *low interest rates are offering the opportunity to safeguard their financial futures.*
– ORIGIN late Middle English (denoting protection or a safe conduct): from Old French *sauve garde*, from *sauve* 'safe' + *garde* 'guard.' Compare with **SAGGER**.

safe ha·ven ▶ **n. 1** a place of refuge or security.
2 Law temporary refuge given to asylum seekers. ■ a country or area within a country where this is provided: *if they merely hunker down in the six existing misnamed safe havens, it will become impossible for them to fulfill those missions.*

safe house ▶ **n.** a house in a secret location, used by spies or criminals in hiding.

safe·keep·ing /ˈsāfˈkēpiNG/ ▶ **n.** preservation in a safe place: *she'd put her wedding ring in her purse **for safekeeping**.*

safe·light /ˈsāf,līt/ ▶ **n.** a light with a colored filter that can be used in a darkroom without affecting photosensitive film or paper.

safe room ▶ **n.** a room in a house or other building that is invulnerable to attack or intrusion, and from which security operations can be directed. Also called **PANIC ROOM**.

safe seat ▶ **n.** a legislative seat that is likely to be retained with a large majority in an election.

safe sex ▶ **n.** sexual activity in which people take precautions to protect themselves against sexually transmitted diseases such as AIDS.

safe·ty /ˈsāftē/ ▶ **n.** (pl. **safeties**) **1** the condition of being protected from or unlikely to cause danger, risk, or injury: *they should leave for their own safety | the survivors were airlifted to safety.* ■ [as modifier] denoting something designed to prevent injury or damage: *a safety barrier | a safety helmet.* ■ short for **SAFETY LOCK**. ■ informal a condom.
2 Football a defensive back who normally is positioned well behind the line of scrimmage. ■ a play in which the offense downs the ball (by action of the defense, or intentionally) in their own end zone, scoring two points for the defense.
– PHRASES **safety first** used to advise caution. **there's safety in numbers** proverb being in a group of people makes you feel more confident or secure about taking action.
– ORIGIN Middle English: from Old French *sauvete*, from medieval Latin *salvitas*, from Latin *salvus* 'safe.'

safe·ty belt ▶ **n.** another term for **SEAT BELT**.

safe·ty boat ▶ **n.** an accompanying boat providing support in case of emergency, esp. in water sports or competitions.

safe·ty cage ▶ **n.** a framework of reinforced struts protecting a car's passenger cabin against crash damage.

safe·ty chain ▶ **n.** a chain fitted for security purposes, esp. on a door, watch, or piece of jewelry.

safe·ty-crit·i·cal ▶ **adj.** designed or needing to be fail-safe for safety purposes.

safe·ty cur·tain ▶ **n.** a fireproof curtain that can be lowered between the stage and the main part of a theater to prevent the spread of fire.

safe·ty de·pos·it ▶ **n.** another term for **SAFE DEPOSIT**.

safe·ty fac·tor ▶ **n.** a margin of security against risks. ■ technical the ratio of a material's strength to an expected strain.

safe·ty film ▶ **n.** fire-resistant motion picture film.

safe·ty fuse ▶ **n. 1** a protective electric fuse.
2 a fuse that burns at a constant slow rate, used for the controlled firing of a detonator.

safe·ty glass ▶ **n. 1** glass that has been toughened or laminated so that it is less likely to splinter when broken.
2 (**safety glasses**) toughened glasses or goggles for protecting the eyes when using power tools or industrial or laboratory equipment.

safe·ty har·ness ▶ **n.** a system of belts or restraints to hold a person to prevent falling or injury.

safe·ty lamp ▶ **n.** a miner's portable lamp with a flame that is protected, typically by wire gauze, to reduce the risk of explosion from ignited methane (firedamp). The first to be introduced, in the early 19th century, was the Davy lamp.

safe·ty lock (also **safety catch**) ▶ **n.** a device that prevents a gun from being fired or a machine from being operated accidentally.

safe·ty match ▶ **n.** a match igniting only when struck on a specially prepared surface, esp. the side of a matchbook or matchbox.

safe·ty net ▶ **n.** a net placed to catch an acrobat or similar performer in case of a fall. ■ a safeguard against possible hardship or adversity: *a safety net for workers who lose their jobs.*

safe·ty pin ▶ **n.** a pin with a point that is bent back to the head and is held in a guard when closed. ▶ **v.** [with obj.] (**safety-pin**) fasten with a safety pin.

safe·ty ra·zor ▶ **n.** a razor with a guard to reduce the risk of cutting the skin.

safe·ty valve ▶ **n.** a valve opening automatically to relieve excessive pressure, esp. in a boiler. ■ a means of giving harmless vent to feelings of tension or stress.

safe·word /ˈsāf,wərd/ (also **safe word**) ▶ **n.** a word serving as a prearranged and unambiguous signal to end an activity, such as between a dominant and submissive sexual couple.

saf·flow·er /ˈsaf,lou(-ə)r/ ▶ **n.** an orange-flowered, thistlelike Eurasian plant with seeds that yield an edible oil and petals that were formerly used to produce a red or yellow dye. ● *Carthamus tinctorius*, family Compositae. ■ (**safflower oil**) the edible oil obtained from the seeds of this plant.
– ORIGIN late Middle English: from Dutch *saffloer* or German *Saflor*, via Old French and Italian from Arabic *aṣfar* 'yellow.' The spelling has been influenced by **SAFFRON** and **FLOWER**.

saf·fron /ˈsafrən/ ▶ **n. 1** an orange-yellow flavoring, food coloring, and dye made from the dried stigmas of a crocus: [as modifier] *saffron buns.* ■ the orange-yellow color of this.
2 (also **saffron crocus**) an autumn-flowering crocus with reddish-purple flowers, native to warmer regions of Eurasia. Enormous numbers of flowers are required to produce a small quantity of the large red stigmas used for the spice. ● *Crocus sativus*, family Iridaceae. See also **MEADOW SAFFRON**.
– DERIVATIVES **saf·fron·y adj.**
– ORIGIN Middle English: from Old French *safran*, based on Arabic *zaʿfarān*.

Saf·ire /ˈsaf,ī(ə)r/, William (1929–2009), US journalist and writer. With *The New York Times* from 1973, he was a conservative political commentator and also wrote the *Times'* "On Language" column.

S

saf·ra·nine /ˈsafrəˌnēn, -nin/ (also **safranin** /-nin/) ▶ **n.** Chemistry any of a large group of synthetic azo dyes, mainly red, used as biological stains.
– ORIGIN mid 19th cent. (denoting the yellow coloring matter in saffron): from French.

sag /sag/ ▶ **v.** (**sags, sagging, sagged**) [no obj.] **1** sink, subside, or bulge downward under weight or pressure or through lack of strength: *he closed his eyes and **sagged against the wall** | the bed sagged in the middle* | (as adj. **sagging**) *a sagging ceiling about to fall.* ■ hang down loosely or unevenly: *stockings that sagged at the knees.* ■ (of a ship) bend longitudinally so that the middle is lower than the ends. Compare with HOG.
2 decline to a lower level, usually temporarily: *exports are forging ahead while home sales sag.*
▶ **n. 1** a downward curve or bulge in a structure caused by weakness or excessive weight or pressure: *a sag in the middle necessitated a third set of wheels.* ■ Geometry the amount of this, measured as the perpendicular distance from the middle of the curve to the straight line between the two supporting points.
2 a decline, esp. a temporary one.
– DERIVATIVES **sag·gy adj.**
– ORIGIN late Middle English (as a verb): apparently related to Middle Low German *sacken*, Dutch *zakken* 'subside.'

sa·ga /ˈsägə/ ▶ **n.** a long story of heroic achievement, esp. a medieval prose narrative in Old Norse or Old Icelandic: *a figure straight out of a Viking saga.* ■ a long, involved story, account, or series of incidents: *the saga of her engagement.*
– ORIGIN early 18th cent.: from Old Norse, literally 'narrative'; related to SAW[3].

sa·ga·cious /səˈgāsHəs/ ▶ **adj.** having or showing keen mental discernment and good judgment; shrewd: *they were sagacious enough to avoid any outright confrontation.*
– DERIVATIVES **sa·ga·cious·ly adv.**
– ORIGIN early 17th cent.: from Latin *sagax, sagac-* 'wise' + -IOUS.

sa·gac·i·ty /səˈgasitē/ ▶ **n.** the quality of being sagacious: *a man of great political sagacity.*

sag·a·more /ˈsagəˌmôr/ ▶ **n.** (among some American Indian peoples) a chief; a sachem.
– ORIGIN from Eastern Abnaki *sákəmá* 'strong man.' Compare with SACHEM.

Sa·gan[1] /ˈsāgən/, Carl (Edward) (1934–96), US astronomer. He showed that amino acids can be synthesized in an artificial primordial soup irradiated by ultraviolet light, as a model for a possible mechanism of the origin of life on Earth. He wrote several popular science books and coproduced the television series *Cosmos* (1980).

Sa·gan[2] /säˈgäN/, Françoise (1935–2004), French novelist, playwright, and short-story writer; pseudonym of *Françoise Quoirez*. She established her reputation with her first novel, *Bonjour Tristesse* (1954). Her writing examined the transitory nature of love as experienced in brief liaisons.

sa·ga·na·ki /ˌsägəˈnäkē, ˌsag-/ ▶ **n.** a Greek dish consisting of breaded or floured cheese fried in butter, served as an appetizer.
– ORIGIN modern Greek, denoting a small two-handled frying pan, in which the dish is traditionally made.

sage[1] /sāj/ ▶ **n. 1** an aromatic plant with grayish-green leaves that are used as a culinary herb, native to southern Europe and the Mediterranean. ● *Salvia officinalis*, family Labiatae. ■ used in names of similar aromatic plants of the mint family, e.g., **wood sage**.
2 (also **white sage**) either of two bushy North American plants with silvery-gray leaves. ● an aromatic plant that is burned by some American Indian people for its cleansing properties and as an incense (*Artemisia ludoviciana*, family Compositae). ● a plant of the goosefoot family (*Krascheninnikovia lanata*, family Chenopodiaceae).
3 short for SAGEBRUSH.
– ORIGIN Middle English: from Old French *sauge*, from Latin *salvia* 'healing plant,' from *salvus* 'safe.'

sage[2] ▶ **n.** a profoundly wise man, esp. one who features in ancient history or legend.
▶ **adj.** having, showing, or indicating profound wisdom: *they nodded in agreement with these sage remarks.*
– DERIVATIVES **sage·ly adv., sage·ness n.**
– ORIGIN Middle English (as an adjective): from Old French, from Latin *sapere* 'be wise.'

sage·brush /ˈsājˌbrəsH/ ▶ **n.** a shrubby aromatic North American plant of the daisy family. ● Genus *Artemisia*, family Compositae: several species, in particular *A. tridentata*. ■ scrub that is dominated by such shrubs, occurring chiefly in semiarid regions of western North America.

Sage·brush State a nickname for the state of NEVADA.

sage green ▶ **n.** a grayish-green color like that of sage leaves.

sage grouse ▶ **n.** a large grouse of western North America, with long pointed tail feathers, noted for the male's courtship display in which air sacs are inflated to make a popping sound. ● *Centrocercus urophasianus*, family Tetraonidae (or Phasianidae).

sag·ger /ˈsagər/ (also **saggar**) ▶ **n.** a protective fireclay box enclosing ceramic ware while it is being fired.
– ORIGIN mid 18th cent.: probably a contraction of the noun SAFEGUARD.

Sag Har·bor /sag/ a resort village in eastern Long Island in New York, noted as a 19th-century whaling port; pop. 2,428 (est. 2008).

Sag·i·naw /ˈsagəˌnô/ an industrial and commercial city in east central Michigan, on the Saginaw River; pop. 55,620 (est. 2008).

Sa·git·ta /səˈjitə/ Astronomy a small northern constellation (the Arrow), lying in the Milky Way north of Aquila. ■ (as genitive **Sagittae** /səˈjitē/) used with a preceding letter or numeral to designate a star in this constellation: *the star Beta Sagittae.*
– ORIGIN Latin.

sag·it·tal /ˈsajitl/ Anatomy ▶ **adj. 1** relating to or denoting the suture on top of the skull that runs between the parietal bones in a front to back direction.
2 of or in a plane parallel to this suture, esp. that dividing the body into left and right halves.
– DERIVATIVES **sag·it·tal·ly adv.**
– ORIGIN late Middle English: from medieval Latin *sagittalis*, from Latin *sagitta* 'arrow.'

sag·it·tal crest ▶ **n.** Zoology (in many mammals) a bony ridge on the top of the skull to which the jaw muscles are attached.

Sag·it·tar·i·us /ˌsajiˈte(ə)rēəs/ **1** Astronomy a large constellation (the Archer), said to represent a centaur carrying a bow and arrow. The center of the Galaxy is situated within it. ■ (as genitive **Sagittarii** /ˌsajiˈte(ə)rēˌī, -ēˌē/) used with a preceding letter or numeral to designate a star in this constellation: *the star Mu Sagittarii.*
2 Astrology the ninth sign of the zodiac, which the sun enters about November 22. ■ (**a Sagittarius**) (pl. **same**) a person born when the sun is in this sign.
– DERIVATIVES **Sag·it·ta·ri·an** /-ˈte(ə)rēən/ **n. & adj.** (sense 2).
– ORIGIN Latin.

sag·it·tate /ˈsajəˌtāt/ ▶ **adj.** Botany & Zoology shaped like an arrowhead.
– ORIGIN mid 18th cent.: from Latin *sagitta* 'arrow' + -ATE[2].

sa·go /ˈsāgō/ ▶ **n.** (pl. **sagos**) **1** edible starch that is obtained from a palm and is a staple food in parts of the tropics. The pith inside the trunk is scraped out, washed, and dried to produce a flour or processed to produce the granular sago used in the West. ■ (also **sago pudding**) a sweet dish made from sago and milk.
2 (**sago palm**) the palm from which most sago is obtained, growing in freshwater swamps in Southeast Asia. ● *Metroxylon sagu*, family Palmae. ■ any of a number of other palms or cycads that yield a similar starch.
– ORIGIN mid 16th cent.: from Malay *sagu* (originally via Portuguese).

Sa·gra·da Fa·mi·lia /säˈgrädə fəˈmilyə, -ˈmilēə/ an expiatory temple (not a cathedral) in Barcelona, Spain, begun in 1882 and still unfinished. Antonio Gaudí took over construction of the church in 1883 and in 1891 became its official architect. The spires of the church are more than 328 feet (100 m) tall, and the church has a seating capacity of 13,000. Full name *Templo Expiatorio de la Sagrada Familia* ('Expiatory Temple of the Holy Family').

Sagrada Familia

sa·gua·ro /səˈ(g)wärō/ (also **saguaro cactus**) ▶ **n.** (pl. **saguaros**) a giant cactus that can grow to 66 feet (20 m) in height and whose branches are shaped like candelabra, native to Mexico and the southwestern US. Its reddish-purple fruit can be used for food and drink. ● *Carnegiea gigantea*, family Cactaceae.
– ORIGIN mid 19th cent.: from Mexican Spanish.

saguaro

Sa·gui·a el-Ham·ra /ˈsägēə elˈhamrə, ˈsägyä elˈämrä/ an intermittent river in the north of Western Sahara. It flows into the Atlantic Ocean west of Laayoune. ■ the region through which this river flows. A territory of Spain from 1934, it united with Río de Oro in 1958 to become a part of Spanish Sahara.

Sa·ha /ˈsäˌhä/, Meghnad (1894–1956), Indian theoretical physicist. Saha laid the foundations for modern astrophysics. He devised an equation that expressed the relationship between ionization and temperature.

Sa·hap·ti·an /säˈhaptēən/ ▶ **adj.** denoting, belonging to, or relating to a family of American Indian languages, including Nez Percé and Sahaptin, spoken in southern Washington, northern Oregon, and central Idaho.
▶ **n.** the Sahaptian family of languages.

Sa·hap·tin /säˈhaptin/ ▶ **n. 1** any of several American Indian peoples of southern Washington and northern Oregon.
2 the Sahaptian language spoken by these peoples.

Sa·har·a Des·ert /səˈharə, -ˈhe(ə)rə, -ˈhärə/ (also **the Sahara**) a vast desert in North Africa that extends from the Atlantic Ocean on the west to the Red Sea on the east and from the Mediterranean Sea and the Atlas Mountains in the north to the Sahel in the south. The largest desert in the world, it covers an area of about 3,500,000 square miles (9,065,000 sq km).
– DERIVATIVES **Sa·har·an adj.**
– ORIGIN *Sahara* from Arabic *ṣaḥrā'* 'desert.'

Sa·hel /səˈhāl, -ˈhēl, -ˈhel/ a vast semiarid region of North Africa, south of the Sahara, that forms a transitional zone between the desert and the region known as the Sudan.
– DERIVATIVES **Sa·hel·i·an** /-ēən/ **adj. & n.**

sa·hib /ˈsä(h)ib/ ▶ **n.** Indian a polite title or form of address for a man: *the Doctor Sahib.*
– ORIGIN Urdu, via Persian from Arabic *ṣāḥib* 'friend, lord.'

Sa·hi·wal /ˈsä(h)əˌväl/ ▶ **n.** an animal of a breed of cattle that originated in Pakistan but is now used in other tropical regions. Sahiwals have small horns and a hump on the back of the neck.
– ORIGIN early 20th cent.: from the name of a town in the central Punjab, Pakistan.

sai /sī/ ▶ **n.** (pl. **same**) a dagger with two sharp prongs curving outward from the hilt, originating in Okinawa and sometimes used in pairs in martial arts.
– ORIGIN Japanese.

Sa·id /ˈsäid/, Edward (1935–2003), US literary theorist, critic, journalist, and Palestinian activist, born in Jerusalem. He is best known for his critique of Western culture's false images of the Arab-Islamic world, which he discussed in *Orientalism* (1978).

said /sed/ past and past participle of SAY.
▶ **adj.** used in legal language or humorously to refer to someone or something already mentioned or named: *acting in pursuance of the said agreement.*

Sai·da /ˈsīdə/ Arabic name for SIDON.

sai·ga /ˈsīgə/ (also **saiga antelope**) ▶ **n.** an Asian antelope that has a distinctive convex snout with the nostrils opening downward, living in herds on the cold steppes. ● *Saiga tartarica*, family Bovidae.
– ORIGIN early 19th cent.: from Russian.

Sai·gon /sīˈgän, ˈsīgän/ official name (until 1975) of HO CHI MINH CITY.

sail /sāl/ ▶ **n. 1** a piece of material extended on a mast to catch the wind and propel a boat, ship, or other vessel: *all the sails were unfurled.* ■ the use of sailing ships as a means of transport: *this led to bigger ships as steam replaced sail.* ■ [in sing.] a voyage or excursion in a ship, esp. a sailing ship or boat: *they went for a sail.* ■ archaic a sailing ship: *sail ahoy!*
2 something resembling a sail in shape or function, in particular: ■ a wind-catching apparatus, typically one consisting of canvas or a set of boards, attached to the arm of a windmill. ■ the broad fin on the

back of a sailfish or of some prehistoric reptiles. ■ a structure by which an animal is propelled across the surface of water by the wind, e.g., the float of a Portuguese man-of-war. ■ the conning tower of a submarine.
▶ **v.** [no obj.] **1** travel in a boat with sails, esp. as a sport or recreation: *Ian took us out sailing on the lake.* ■ [with adverbial] travel in a ship or boat using sails or engine power: *the ferry caught fire sailing between Caen and Portsmouth.* ■ [with adverbial] begin a voyage; leave a harbor: *the catamaran sails at 3:30.* ■ [with obj.] travel by ship on or across (a sea) or on (a route): *plastic ships could be sailing the oceans soon.* ■ [with obj.] navigate or control (a boat or ship): *I stole a small fishing boat and sailed it to the Delta.*
2 [with adverbial of direction] move smoothly and rapidly or in a stately or confident manner: *she sailed into the conference room at 2:30 sharp.* ■ (**sail through**) informal succeed easily at (something, esp. a test or examination): *Alex sailed through his exams.* ■ (**sail into**) informal attack physically or verbally with force.
– PHRASES **in** (or **under**) **full sail** with all the sails in position or fully spread: *a galleon in full sail.* **sail close to** (or **near**) **the wind** sail as nearly against the wind as possible. ■ come close to breaking a rule or the law; behave or operate in a risky way. **take in sail** furl the sail or sails of a vessel. **under sail** with the sails hoisted: *at a speed of eight knots under sail.*
– DERIVATIVES **sail·a·ble adj.**, **sailed adj.** [in combination] *a black-sailed ship.*
– ORIGIN Old English *segl* (noun), *seglian* (verb), of Germanic origin; related to Dutch *zeil* and German *Segel* (nouns).

sail·board /ˈsālˌbôrd/ ▶ **n.** a board with a mast attached to it by a swivel joint, and a sail, used in windsurfing.
– DERIVATIVES **sail·board·er n.**, **sail·board·ing n.**

sail·boat /ˈsālˌbōt/ ▶ **n.** a boat propelled by sails.

sail·cloth /ˈsālˌklôTH, -ˌkläTH/ ▶ **n.** canvas or other material used for making sails. ■ a canvaslike fabric used for making durable weatherproof clothes.

sail·er /ˈsālər/ ▶ **n.** a sailing ship or boat of specified power or manner of sailing: *the great ships were abominable sailers: sluggish and difficult to maneuver | a four-masted motor sailer.*

sail·fin mol·ly /ˈsālˌfin/ ▶ **n.** a small, brightly colored freshwater fish, the male of which has a long, high dorsal fin. Native to North and Central America, it is popular in aquariums. ● Genus *Poecilia*, family Poeciliidae: *P. latipinna* and *P. velifera*.
– ORIGIN *sailfin* with reference to the dorsal fin + MOLLY.

sail·fish /ˈsālˌfisH/ ▶ **n.** (pl. **same** or **sailfishes**) a fish with a high, sail-like dorsal fin, in particular: ● an edible migratory billfish that is a prized game fish (genus *Istiophorus*, family Istiophoridae, in particular *I. platypterus*). ● (also **Celebes sailfish**) a small tropical freshwater fish of Sulawesi, popular in aquariums (*Telmatherina ladigesi*, family Atherinidae).

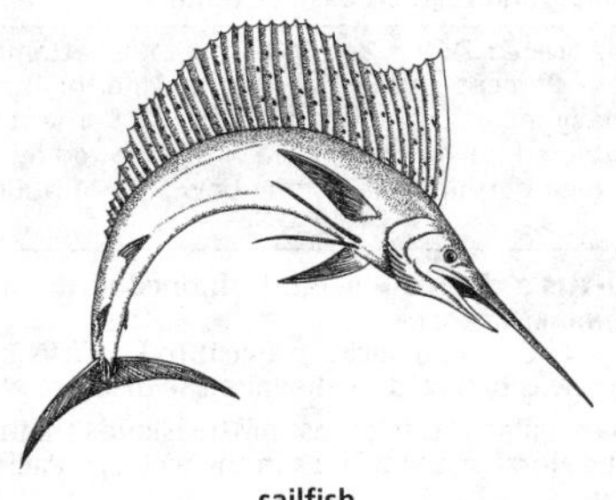

sailfish

sail·ing /ˈsāliNG/ ▶ **n.** the action of sailing in a ship or boat: [as modifier] *a sailing club.* ■ a voyage made by a ferry or cruise ship, esp. according to a planned schedule: *the company operates five sailings a day.* ■ [in sing.] an act of beginning a voyage or of leaving a harbor.

sail·ing boat ▶ **n.** British term for SAILBOAT.

sail·ing or·ders ▶ **plural n.** instructions to the captain of a vessel regarding such matters as time of departure and destination.

sail·ing ship ▶ **n.** a ship driven by sails.

sail·mak·er /ˈsālˌmākər/ ▶ **n.** a person who makes, repairs, or alters sails as a profession.
– DERIVATIVES **sail·mak·ing** /-ˌmākiNG/ **n.**

sail·or /ˈsālər/ ▶ **n.** a person whose job it is to work as a member of the crew of a commercial or naval ship or boat, esp. one who is below the rank of officer. ■ [usu. with adj.] a person who goes sailing as a sport or recreation: *she was a keen sailor.* ■ (**a good/bad sailor**) a person who rarely (or often) becomes sick at sea in rough weather.
– DERIVATIVES **sail·or·ly adj.**
– ORIGIN mid 17th cent.: variant of obsolete *sailer.*

sail·or col·lar ▶ **n.** a collar cut deep and square at the back, tapering to a V-neck at the front.

sail·or hat ▶ **n.** another term for BOATER (sense 1). ■ a hat with a turned-up brim in imitation of a sailor's, worn by women and children.

sail·or suit ▶ **n.** a suit of blue and white material resembling the dress uniform of an ordinary seaman, esp. as fashionable dress for young boys during the 19th century.

sail plan ▶ **n.** a scale diagram of the masts, spars, rigging, and sails of a sailing vessel.

sail·plane /ˈsālˌplān/ ▶ **n.** a glider designed for sustained flight.

sain·foin /ˈsānˌfoin/ ▶ **n.** a pink-flowered plant of the pea family that is native to Asia and grown widely for fodder. ● *Onobrychis viciifolia*, family Leguminosae.
– ORIGIN mid 17th cent.: from obsolete French *saintfoin*, from modern Latin *sanum foenum* 'wholesome hay' (with reference to its medicinal properties).

saint /sānt/ ▶ **n. 1** a person acknowledged as holy or virtuous and typically regarded as being in heaven after death. ■ (in the Catholic and Orthodox Churches) a person formally recognized or canonized by the Church after death, who may be the object of veneration and prayers for intercession. ■ a person who is admired or venerated because of their virtue: *he was considered a living saint by recipients of his generosity.* ■ (in or alluding to biblical use) a Christian believer. ■ (**Saint**) a member of the Church of Jesus Christ of Latter-Day Saints; a Mormon.
2 (**Saint**) (abbr.: **St.** or **S.**) used in titles of religious saints: *the epistles of Saint Paul | St. John's Church.* ■ used in place names or other dedications: *St. Louis | St. Lawrence River.*
▶ **v.** [with obj.] formally recognize as a saint; canonize. ■ (as adj. **sainted** /ˈsāntid/) worthy of being a saint; very virtuous: *the story of his sainted sister Eileen.*
– DERIVATIVES **saint·hood** /-ˌho͝od/ **n.**, **saint·like** /-ˌlīk/ **adj.**
– ORIGIN Middle English, from Old French *seint*, from Latin *sanctus* 'holy,' past participle of *sancire* 'consecrate.'

St. An·drews a town in eastern Scotland, on the North Sea; pop. 17,100 (est. 2009). It is noted for its university that was founded in 1410 and for its historic golf courses.

St. An·drew's Cross ▶ **n.** Heraldry an X-shaped cross, esp. white on a blue background (as a national emblem of Scotland). Also called SALTIRE.

St. An·tho·ny's Cross (also **St. Anthony Cross**) ▶ **n.** a T-shaped cross.

St. An·tho·ny's Fire ▶ **n. 1** another term for ERYSIPELAS.
2 another term for ERGOTISM.

Saint Au·gus·tine /sānt ˈôgəˌstēn, ôˈgəstin, əˈgəs-/ a historic port city in northeastern Florida, southeast of Jacksonville, near the Atlantic coast. Founded by the Spanish in 1565, it is often noted as the oldest city in America; pop. 12,404 (est. 2008).

St. Bas·il's Ca·the·dral /ˈbazəlz/ a cathedral on the south side of Red Square in Moscow, commissioned by Ivan the Terrible to commemorate his capture of Kazan from the Tartars in 1552 and built between 1555 and 1560. The official name of the cathedral is the *Cathedral of the Intercession of the Virgin*, for Kazan was taken on October 1, the Orthodox feast of the Intercession of the Virgin. The more common name *St. Basil's Cathedral* is from *St. Basil the Blessed*, a 'holy fool' who was buried near the site of the cathedral.

St. Basil's Cathedral

St. Ber·nard /bərˈnärd/ (also **St. Bernard dog**) ▶ **n.** a large dog of a breed originally kept to rescue travelers by the monks of the Hospice on the Great St. Bernard Pass in the Swiss Alps.

St. Bernard

St. Ber·nard Pass either of two passes across the Alps in southern Europe. The **Great St. Bernard Pass**, on the border between southwestern Switzerland and Italy, rises to 8,100 feet (2,469 m). The **Little St. Bernard Pass**, on the French–Italian border southeast of Mont Blanc, rises to 7,178 feet (2,188 m).
– ORIGIN named after the hospices founded on their summits in the 11th century by the French monk *St. Bernard.*

Saint Cath·e·rines /sānt ˈkaTH(ə)rənz/ an industrial and commercial city in southern Ontario in Canada, on Lake Ontario, northwest of Niagara Falls; pop. 131,989 (2006).

Saint Charles /sānt CHärlz/ a historic commercial city in east central Missouri, on the Missouri River; pop. 64,386 (est. 2008).

St. Chris·to·pher and Ne·vis, Federation of official name of ST. KITTS AND NEVIS.

Saint Clair Riv·er /sənt ˈkle(ə)r/ a short river that flows from Lake Huron to Lake Saint Clair, forming part of the boundary between Michigan and Ontario.

Saint Cloud /sānt ˈkloud/ an industrial and commercial city in east central Minnesota, on the Mississippi River, northwest of Minneapolis; pop. 66,948 (est. 2008).

St. Croix /kroi/ an island in the Caribbean Sea, the largest of the US Virgin Islands; chief town, Christiansted. Purchased by Denmark in 1753, it was sold to the US in 1917.

Saint Croix Riv·er 1 a river that flows for 75 miles (120 km) from eastern Maine to form the border with New Brunswick in Canada before entering Passamaquoddy Bay. The first French settlement in North America was established in 1604 on Dochet Island, near its mouth.
2 a river that flows for 164 miles (265 km) from northwestern Wisconsin to the Mississippi River and forms part of the border with Minnesota.

Saint-Den·is /sɑN dəˈnē/ **1** a municipality in France, now a northern suburb of Paris.
2 the capital of the French island of Réunion, a port on the northern coast; pop. 143,000 (est. 2007).

Saint Eli·as Moun·tains /ˌsāntlˈīəs, iˈlīəs/ a section of the Coast Ranges in southeastern Alaska and neighboring Yukon Territory in Canada. Mount Logan, the highest point in Canada, is here, along with other high peaks and numerous glaciers.

St. El·mo's fire /ˈelmōz/ ▶ **n.** a phenomenon in which a luminous electrical discharge appears on a ship or aircraft during a storm.
– ORIGIN regarded as a sign of protection given by St. Elmo, the patron saint of sailors.

St.-É·tienne /sɑNt āˈtyen/ an industrial city in southeastern central France, southwest of Lyons; pop. 180,773 (2006).

St. Eu·sta·ti·us /yo͞oˈstāsH(ē)əs/ a small volcanic island in the Caribbean Sea, in the Netherlands Antilles; pop. 2,768 (2009).

Saint-Ex·u·pé·ry /ˌsɑNt egˌzYpāˈrē/, Antoine (Marie Roger) de (1900–44), French writer and aviator. He is best known for the fable *The Little Prince* (1943).

Saint Fran·cis Riv·er /sānt ˈfransis/ a river that flows for 425 miles (685 km) from southeastern Missouri into eastern Arkansas where it empties into the Mississippi River near Helena.

Saint-Gau·dens /sānt ˈgôdnz/, Augustus (1848–1907), US sculptor; born in Ireland. He is best remembered for his coin designs and for his sculptures, such as "General Sherman on Horseback" (1903).

Saint George /sānt 'jôrj/ a historic resort city in southwestern Utah, near the Arizona border; pop. 72,718 (est. 2008).

St. George's the capital of Grenada in the Caribbean Sea, a port in the southwestern part of the island; pop. 5,200 (est. 2009).

St. George's Chan·nel a channel between Wales and Ireland that links the Irish Sea with the Celtic Sea.

St. George's Cross ▶ **n.** a cross shaped like a plus sign, red on a white background (esp. as a national emblem of England).

St. He·le·na /hə'lēnə/ a solitary island in the South Atlantic, a British overseas territory; pop. 7,600 (est. 2009); capital, Jamestown. The islands of Ascension, Tristan da Cunha, and Gough Island are dependencies of St. Helena. It is known as the place of Napoleon's exile 1815–21 and death.
– DERIVATIVES **St. He·le·ni·an** /-nēən/ **adj. & n.**
– ORIGIN so named when it was discovered by the Portuguese on the feast day of *St. Helena*, May 21, 1502.

St. Hel·ens /'helənz/ an industrial town in northwestern England, northeast of Liverpool; pop. 102,000 (est. 2009).

St. Hel·ens, Mount an active volcano in southwestern Washington, in the Cascade Range, that rises to 8,312 feet (2,560 m). A dramatic eruption in May 1980 reduced its height by more than a thousand feet and spread volcanic ash and debris over a vast area. In late 2004, a massive extrusion of lava had geologists monitoring the possibility of another explosive eruption.

St. John 1 an island in the Caribbean Sea, one of the three principal islands of the US Virgin Islands.
2 (usu. **Saint John**) a city in New Brunswick, in eastern Canada, a port on the Bay of Fundy, at the mouth of the St. John River; pop. 68,043 (2006).

St. John's 1 the capital of Antigua and Barbuda, situated on the northwestern coast of Antigua; pop. 26,000 (est. 2007).
2 the capital of the province of Newfoundland and Labrador, a port on the southeastern coast of the island; pop. 100,646 (2006).

St. John's wort (also **St. Johns wort**) ▶ **n.** a herbaceous plant or shrub with distinctive yellow five-petaled flowers and paired oval leaves, used in medicinal preparations to treat various disorders, including depression. ● Genus *Hypericum*, family Guttiferae: many species, in particular *H. perforatum*.
– ORIGIN so named because some species come into flower near the feast day of St. John the Baptist (June 24).

Saint Joseph /sānt 'jōsəf, -zəf/ a port city in northwestern Missouri, on the Missouri River; pop. 76,197 (est. 2008).

St. Kil·da /'kildə/ a small group of uninhabited islands in the Outer Hebrides.

St. Kitts and Ne·vis /'kits and 'nēvis, 'nevis/ a country that consists of two adjoining islands in the Leeward Islands in the Caribbean Sea; pop. 40,100 (est. 2009); capital, Basseterre (on St. Kitts); languages, English (official) and Creole. Official name **St. Christopher and Nevis, Federation of**.

> St. Kitts was visited in 1493 by Christopher Columbus. The islands were colonized by English settlers from 1623 and became the first successful English colony in the West Indies. A self-governing union between St. Kitts and Nevis (and briefly Anguilla) was created in 1967 and became a fully independent member of the Commonwealth of Nations in 1983.

– ORIGIN *St. Kitts*, alteration (by settlers) of *St. Christopher*, a name given to the island by Columbus; *Nevis* from Spanish *las nieves* 'the snows' (because of the "snowy" clouds surrounding the peak).

S

Saint Lau·rent /,saɴ lô'räɴ/, Yves (Mathieu) (1936–2008), French couturier. He opened his own fashion house in 1962 and later launched Rive Gauche boutiques to sell ready-to-wear clothing.

St. Lau·rent /sānt 'lôrənt/, Louis Stephen (1882–1973), Canadian Liberal statesman; prime minister 1948–57.

Saint Law·rence Is·land /sānt 'lôrəns/ an island in western Alaska, in the Bering Sea. Most of its few inhabitants are Inuit.

St. Law·rence Riv·er a river in North America that flows for about 750 miles (1,200 km) from Lake Ontario along the border between Canada and the US to the Gulf of St. Lawrence on the Atlantic coast.

St. Law·rence Sea·way a waterway in North America that flows for 2,342 miles (3,768 km) through the Great Lakes and along the course of the St. Lawrence River to the Atlantic Ocean. Consisting of channels connecting the lakes and a number of artificial sections that bypass the rapids in the river, it is open along its entire length to oceangoing vessels. It was inaugurated in 1959.

saint·li·ness /'sāntlēnis/ ▶ **n.** the quality or state of being saintly; holiness.

Saint-Lô /saɴ 'lō/ a town in northwestern France, in Normandy; pop. 20,537 (2007). Almost completely destroyed during the Allied invasion of World War II, it has since been rebuilt.

St. Lou·is /'lo͞o-is, 'lo͞o-ē/ a city and port in eastern Missouri, on the Mississippi River just south of its confluence with the Missouri River; pop. 354,361 (est. 2008). Founded as a French fur-trading post in the 1760s, it passed to the Spanish, the French again, and finally in 1803 to the US as part of the Louisiana Purchase.

St. Lou·is en·ceph·a·li·tis /'lo͞ois/ ▶ **n.** a form of viral encephalitis that can be fatal and is transmitted by mosquitoes.

Saint Lou·is Park /sānt 'lo͞oəs/ a city in southeastern Minnesota, west of Minneapolis; pop. 45,465 (est. 2008).

St. Lu·cia /'lo͞osнə, lo͞o'sēə/ a country in the Caribbean Sea, one of the Windward Islands; pop. 160,300 (est. 2009); capital, Castries; languages, English (official) and French Creole.

> First encountered by Europeans around 1500, St. Lucia was settled by both French and British in the 17th century. Possession of the island was long disputed until France ceded it to Britain in 1814. Since 1979, it has been an independent state within the Commonwealth of Nations.

– DERIVATIVES **St. Lu·cian adj. & n.**

saint·ly /'sāntlē/ ▶ **adj.** (**saintlier, saintliest**) very holy or virtuous: *a truly saintly woman.* ■ of or relating to a saint: *a crypt for some saintly relic.*

St. Mark's Ca·the·dral the cathedral church of Venice since 1807. It was built in the 9th century to house relics of St. Mark, and rebuilt in the 11th century.

St. Mar·tin /sānt 'märtn, saɴ mär'taɴ/ a small island in the Caribbean, one of the Leeward Islands; pop. 35,300 (est. 2006). The southern section of the island forms part of the Netherlands Antilles; the larger northern part of the island is part of the French overseas department of Guadeloupe. Dutch name **Sint Maarten**.

Saint-Mihiel /,seɴ mē'yel/ a commune in northeastern France; pop. 4,906 (2007). Fighting independently for the first time in World War I, US troops took the village from the Germans in September 1918.

St. Mo·ritz /sānt mə'rits, saɴ mô'rēts/ a resort and winter-sports center in southeastern Switzerland.

St. Paul /,sānt 'pôl/ the capital of Minnesota, on the Mississippi River adjacent to Minneapolis with which it forms the Twin Cities metropolitan area; pop. 279,590 (est. 2008). First settled in 1838, it prospered as a trading center and became the state capital in 1858.

saint·pau·lia /,sānt'pôlēə/ ▶ **n.** a plant of the genus *Saintpaulia* (family Gesneriaceae), esp. (in gardening) an African violet.
– ORIGIN named after Baron W. von *Saint Paul* (1860–1910), the German explorer who discovered it.

St. Paul's Ca·the·dral a cathedral on Ludgate Hill, London, designed by Sir Christopher Wren and built between 1675 and 1711.

St. Paul's Cathedral

St. Pe·ters /'pētərz/ a city in eastern Missouri, northwest of St. Louis; pop. 55,500 (est. 2008).

St. Pe·ter's Ba·sil·i·ca a Roman Catholic basilica in the Vatican City. Built in the 16th century on the site of a structure erected by Constantine on the supposed site of St. Peter's crucifixion, it is the largest Christian church.

St. Pe·ters·burg /'pētərz,bərg/ **1** a city and seaport in northwestern Russia, located on the delta of the Neva River, on the eastern shores of the Gulf of Finland; pop. 4,548,000 (est. 2008). Founded in 1703 by Peter the Great, St. Petersburg was the capital of Russia from 1712 until the Russian Revolution. During World War II, it was held under siege by the Germans and Finns 1941–44. Former names **Petrograd** (1914–24) and **Leningrad** (1924–91).
2 a resort city in western Florida, on the Gulf of Mexico; pop. 245,314 (est. 2008).

St. Pierre and Miq·ue·lon /sānt 'pi(ə)r and 'mikə,län, saɴ 'pyer ā mek'lôɴ/ a group of eight small islands in the North Atlantic Ocean, off the southern coast of Newfoundland; pop. 7,100 (est. 2009). An overseas territory of France, the islands are the last remaining French possession in North America.

Saint-Saëns /saɴ 'säɴs/, Camille (1835–1921), French composer, pianist, and organist; full name *Charles-Camille Saint-Saëns*. He is best known for *Danse macabre* (1874), the opera *Samson and Delila* (1877), and his third symphony and *Carnaval des animaux* (both 1886).

saint's day ▶ **n.** a day on which a saint is particularly commemorated in the Christian Church.

Saint-Si·mon[1] /,saɴ sē'môɴ/, Claude-Henri de Rouvroy, Comte de (1760–1825), French social reformer and philosopher. He argued that society should be organized by leaders of industry and given spiritual direction by scientists.

Saint-Si·mon[2], Louis de Rouvroy, Duc de (1675–1755), French writer. He is best known for his *Mémoires*, a detailed record of court life between 1694 and 1723 during the reigns of Louis XIV and XV.

St. Thom·as /'täməs/ an island in the Caribbean Sea, the second largest of the US Virgin Islands, east of Puerto Rico; pop. 53,700 (est. 2009); chief town, Charlotte Amalie. Settled by the Dutch in 1657, it passed to Denmark in 1666, which sold it to the US in 1917.

Saint-Tro·pez /san trō'pā/ a fishing port and resort on the Mediterranean coast of southern France, southwest of Cannes; pop. 5,690 (2006).

St. Val·en·tine's Day Mas·sa·cre the shooting on February 14, 1929, of seven members of the rival "Bugsy" Moran's gang by some of Al Capone's men disguised as policemen.

St. Vin·cent and the Gren·a·dines an island state in the Windward Islands in the Caribbean Sea that consists of the mountainous island of St. Vincent and some of the Grenadine islands; pop. 104,600; capital, Kingstown; languages, English (official) and English-based Creole.

> The French, Dutch, and British all made attempts at settlements in the 18th century, and the islands finally fell to British possession in 1783. The state obtained full independence with a limited form of membership of the Commonwealth of Nations in 1979.

St. Vi·tus's dance ▶ **n.** old-fashioned term for **Sydenham's chorea**.
– ORIGIN so named because a visit to *St. Vitus*'s shrine was believed to alleviate the disease.

Sai·pan /sī'pan/ the largest of the islands that make up the Northern Marianas in the western Pacific Ocean.

saith /seтн, 'sāiтн/ archaic third person singular present of **say**.

saithe /sāтн/ ▶ **n.** chiefly Brit. another term for **pollock** (sense 1).
– ORIGIN mid 16th cent.: from Old Norse *seithr*.

Sa·kai /'säkī/ an industrial city in Japan, on Osaka Bay, south of Osaka; pop. 831,715 (2007).

sake[1] /sāk/ ▶ **n. 1** (**for the sake of something** or **for something's sake**) for the purpose of; in the interest of; in order to achieve or preserve: *the couple moved to the coast for the sake of her health | for safety's sake, photographers are obliged to stand behind police lines | let us say, for the sake of argument, that the plotter and the assassin are one and the same person.* ■ (**for its own sake** or **something for something's sake** or **for the sake of it**) used to indicate something that is done as an end in itself rather than to achieve some other purpose: *new ideas amount to change for change's sake.*
2 (**for the sake of someone** or **for someone's sake**) out of consideration for or in order to help

someone: *I felt I couldn't give up, for my own sake or the baby's | I have to make an effort for John's sake.* **3** (**for God's** or **goodness**, etc., **sake**) used to express impatience, annoyance, urgency, or desperation: *"Oh, for God's sake!" snarled Dyson | where did you get it, for heaven's sake?*
– PHRASES **for old times' sake** in memory of former times; in acknowledgment of a shared past: *they sat in the back seats for old times' sake.*
– ORIGIN Old English *sacu* 'contention, crime,' of Germanic origin; related to Dutch *zaak* and German *Sache*, from a base meaning 'affair, legal action, thing.' The phrase *for the sake of* may be from Old Norse.

sa·ke² /'säkē/ (also **saki** or **saké**) ▶ n. a Japanese alcoholic drink made from fermented rice, traditionally drunk warm in small porcelain cups.
– ORIGIN Japanese.

sa·ker /'sākər/ ▶ n. **1** a large Eurasian falcon with a brown back and whitish head, used in falconry. ● *Falco cherrug*, family Falconidae.
2 an early form of cannon.
– ORIGIN late Middle English: from Old French *sacre*, from Arabic *ṣaḳr* 'falcon.'

Sa·kha, Republic of /'säkə/ official name for YAKUTIA.

Sa·kha·lin /'sakə,lēn, ,səkHəl'yēn/ a large Russian island in the Sea of Okhotsk, situated off the coast of eastern Russia and separated from it by the Tartar Strait; capital, Yuzhno-Sakhalinsk. From 1905 to 1946, it was divided into the northern part, held by Russia, and the southern part, occupied by Japan.

Sa·kha·rov /'säkHə,rôf, 'säk-, -,rôv/, Andrei (Dmitrievich) (1921–89), Russian nuclear physicist and civil rights campaigner. Although he helped to develop the Soviet hydrogen bomb, he campaigned against nuclear proliferation. He fought for reform and human rights in the former Soviet Union, for which he was sentenced to internal exile 1980–86. Nobel Peace Prize (1975).

Sa·ki /'säkē/ (1870–1916), British short-story writer, born in Burma; pseudonym of *Hector Hugh Munro*. His stories encompass the satiric, comic, macabre, and supernatural, and frequently depict animals as agents seeking revenge on humankind.

sa·ki¹ /'säkē, 'sakē/ ▶ n. (pl. **sakis**) a tropical American monkey with coarse fur and a long bushy nonprehensile tail. ● Genera *Pithecia* and *Chiropotes*, family Cebidae: several species.
– ORIGIN late 18th cent.: via French from Tupi *saui*.

sa·ki² ▶ n. variant spelling of SAKE².

sal /sal/ ▶ n. a northern Indian tree that yields teaklike timber and dammar resin. It is the most commercially important source of timber in India. ● *Shorea robusta*, family Dipterocarpaceae.
– ORIGIN late 18th cent.: from Hindi *sāl*.

sa·laam /sə'läm/ ▶ exclam. a common greeting in many Arabic-speaking and Muslim countries.
▶ n. a gesture of greeting or respect, with or without a spoken salutation, typically consisting of a low bow of the head and body with the hand or fingers touching the forehead. Compare with SHALOM. ■ (**salaams**) respectful compliments.
▶ v. [no obj.] make a salaam.
– ORIGIN early 17th cent.: from Arabic *(al-)salām* (*'alaikum*) 'peace (be upon you).'

sal·a·ble /'sāləbəl/ (also **saleable**) ▶ adj. fit or able to be sold.
– DERIVATIVES **sal·a·bil·i·ty** /,sālə'bilitē/ n.

sa·la·cious /sə'lāsHəs/ ▶ adj. (of writing, pictures, or talk) treating sexual matters in an indecent way and typically conveying undue interest in or enjoyment of the subject: *salacious stories.* ■ lustful; lecherous: *his salacious grin faltered.*
– DERIVATIVES **sa·la·cious·ly** adv., **sa·la·cious·ness** n., **sa·lac·i·ty** /-'lasitē/ n. (dated).
– ORIGIN mid 17th cent.: from Latin *salax*, *salac-* (from *salire* 'to leap') + -IOUS.

sal·ad /'saləd/ ▶ n. a cold dish of various mixtures of raw or cooked vegetables, usually seasoned with oil, vinegar, or other dressing and sometimes accompanied by meat, fish, or other ingredients: *a green salad | bowls of salad.* ■ [with modifier] a mixture containing a specified ingredient served with a dressing: *a red pepper filled with tuna salad | fruit salad.* ■ a vegetable suitable for eating raw.
– ORIGIN late Middle English: from Old French *salade*, from Provençal *salada*, based on Latin *sal* 'salt.'

sal·ad days ▶ plural n. (**one's salad days**) the period when one is young and inexperienced. ■ the peak or heyday of something.
– ORIGIN from Shakespeare's *Antony and Cleopatra* (I. v. 72).

sal·ad dress·ing ▶ n. see DRESSING (sense 1).

sa·lade /sə'läd/ ▶ n. another term for SALLET.

Sal·a·din /'salədn, 'salə,din/ (1137–93), sultan of Egypt and Syria 1174–93; Arabic name *Salah-ad-Din Yusuf ibn-Ayyub*. He reconquered Jerusalem from the Christians in 1187, but he was defeated by Richard the Lionheart at Arsuf in 1191.

sa·lal /sə'lal/ ▶ n. a North American plant of the heath family, with clusters of pink or white flowers and edible purple-black berries. ● *Gaultheria shallon*, family Ericaceae.
– ORIGIN early 19th cent.: from Chinook Jargon *sallal*.

Sa·lam /sä'läm/, Abdus (1926–1996), Pakistani theoretical physicist. He independently developed a unified theory to explain electromagnetic interactions and the weak nuclear force. Nobel Prize for Physics (1979), shared with Sheldon Glashow and Steven Weinberg.

Sal·a·man·ca /,salə'maNGkə, ,sälə'mäNGkə/ a city in western Spain; pop. 155,740 (2008).

sal·a·man·der /'salə,mandər/ ▶ n. **1** a newtlike amphibian that typically has bright markings, and that once was thought to be able to endure fire. ● Order Urodela: four families, in particular Salamandridae, and numerous species, including the **fire salamander**.
2 a mythical lizardlike creature said to live in fire or to be able to withstand its effects. ■ an elemental spirit living in fire.
3 a metal plate heated and placed over food to brown it. ■ a space-heater, usually fueled by propane.
4 archaic a red-hot iron or poker.
– DERIVATIVES **sal·a·man·drine** /,salə'mandrin/ adj.
– ORIGIN Middle English (sense 2): from Old French *salamandre*, via Latin from Greek *salamandra*. Sense 1 dates from the early 17th cent.

sa·la·mi /sə'lämē/ ▶ n. (pl. **same** or **salamis**) **1** a type of highly seasoned sausage, originally from Italy, usually eaten cold in slices.
2 Baseball, informal a grand slam home run. [a play on the word 'slam.']
– ORIGIN Italian, plural of *salame*, from a late Latin word meaning 'to salt.'

Sal·a·mis /'saləmis/ an island in the Saronic Gulf in Greece, to the west of Athens.

sal am·mo·ni·ac /'sal ə'mōnē,ak/ ▶ n. old-fashioned term for AMMONIUM CHLORIDE.
– ORIGIN Middle English: from Latin *sal ammoniacus* 'salt of Ammon' (see AMMONIACAL).

Sa·lang Pass /sä'läNG/ a high-altitude route across the Hindu Kush in Afghanistan. A road and tunnel were built by the former Soviet Union during the 1960s to improve the supply route to Kabul.

sa·lar·i·at /sə'le(ə)rēət/ ▶ n. (**the salariat**) salaried white-collar workers.
– ORIGIN early 20th cent.: from French, from *salaire* 'salary,' on the pattern of *prolétariat* 'proletariat.'

sal·a·ried /'salərēd/ ▶ adj. receiving or recompensed by a salary rather than a wage: *salaried employees | he was in salaried employment.*

sal·a·ry /'salərē/ ▶ n. (pl. **salaries**) a fixed regular payment, typically paid on a monthly or biweekly basis but often expressed as an annual sum, made by an employer to an employee, esp. a professional or white-collar worker: *he received a salary of $29,000 |* [as modifier] *a 15 percent salary increase.* Compare with WAGE.
▶ v. (**salaries**, **salarying**, **salaried**) [with obj.] archaic pay a salary to.
– ORIGIN Middle English: from Anglo-Norman French *salarie*, from Latin *salarium*, originally denoting a Roman soldier's allowance to buy salt, from *sal* 'salt.'

sal·a·ry·man /'salərēmən/ ▶ n. (pl. **salarymen**) (esp. in Japan) a white-collar worker.

sa·lat /sə'lät/ ▶ n. the ritual prayer of Muslims, performed five times daily in a set form.
– ORIGIN Arabic, plural of *salāh* 'prayer, worship.'

Sa·la·zar /'salə,zär/, Antonio de Oliveira (1889–1970), Portuguese statesman; prime minister 1932–68. He maintained Portugal's neutrality throughout the Spanish Civil War and World War II.

sal·bu·ta·mol /sal'byo͞otə,môl, -,mäl/ ▶ n. Medicine a synthetic compound related to aspirin, used as a bronchodilator in the treatment of asthma and other conditions involving constriction of the airways.
– ORIGIN 1960s: from *sal(icylic acid)* + *but(yl)* + *am(ine)* + -OL.

sal·chow /'salkou/ (also **Salchow**) ▶ n. Figure Skating a jump in figure skating with a backward takeoff from the backward inside edge of one skate to the backward outside edge of the other, with one or more full turns in the air.
– ORIGIN early 20th cent.: named after Ulrich *Salchow* (1877–1949), Swedish skater.

sale /sāl/ ▶ n. **1** the exchange of a commodity for money; the action of selling something: *we withdrew it from sale | the sale has fallen through.* ■ (**sales**) a quantity or amount sold: *price cuts failed to boost sales.* ■ (**sales**) the activity or business of selling products: *director of sales and marketing.*
2 an event for the rapid disposal of goods at reduced prices for a period, esp. at the end of a season: *a clearance sale.* ■ [often with modifier] a public or charitable event at which goods are sold. ■ a public auction.
– PHRASES **(up) for sale** offered for purchase; to be bought: *cars for sale at reasonable prices.* **on sale** offered for purchase: *the November issue is on sale now.* ■ offered for purchase at a reduced price.
– ORIGIN late Old English *sala*, from Old Norse *sala*, of Germanic origin; related to SELL.

sale·a·ble ▶ adj. variant spelling of SALABLE.

Sa·lem /'sāləm/ **1** an industrial city in Tamil Nadu in southern India; pop. 872,400 (est. 2009).
2 the state capital of Oregon, on the Willamette River, southwest of Portland; pop. 153,435 (est. 2008).
3 a city and port in northeastern Massachusetts, on the Atlantic coast, north of Boston; pop. 41,256 (est. 2008). First settled in 1626, it was the scene in 1692 of a notorious series of witchcraft trials.

sal·ep /'saləp/ ▶ n. a starchy preparation of the dried tubers of various orchids, used as a thickener in cooking, and formerly in medicines and tonics.
– ORIGIN mid 18th cent.: from French, from Turkish *sālep*, from Arabic *(ḳuṣa-'ṭ-) ṭa'lab*, the name of an orchid (literally 'fox's testicles').

sal·e·ra·tus /,salə'rātəs/ ▶ n. dated sodium bicarbonate (or sometimes potassium bicarbonate) as the main ingredient of baking powder.
– ORIGIN mid 19th cent.: from modern Latin *sal aeratus* 'aerated salt.'

Sa·ler·no /sə'lərnō, -'le(ə)r-/ a port on the western coast of Italy, on the Gulf of Salerno, southeast of Naples; pop. 140,489 (2008).

sales·clerk /'sālz,klərk/ (also **sales clerk**) ▶ n. an assistant who sells goods in a retail store.

sales·girl /'sālz,gərl/ ▶ n. a female salesclerk.

Sa·le·sian /sə'lēzHən/ ▶ adj. of or relating to a Roman Catholic educational religious order founded near Turin in 1859 and named after St. Francis de Sales.
▶ n. a member of this order.

sales·la·dy /'sālz,lādē/ ▶ n. (pl. **salesladies**) a saleswoman, esp. one working as a salesclerk.

sales·man /'sālzmən/ ▶ n. (pl. **salesmen**) a man whose job involves selling or promoting commercial products, either in a store or visiting locations to get orders: *an insurance salesman.*
– DERIVATIVES **sales·man·ship** /-,sHip/ n.

sales·per·son /'sālz,pərsən/ ▶ n. (pl. **salespersons** or **salespeople**) a salesman or saleswoman (used as a neutral alternative).

sales·room /'sālz,ro͞om, -,ro͝om/ ▶ n. a room in which items are sold at auction. ■ a showroom displaying goods offered for sale.

sales tax ▶ n. a tax on sales or on the receipts from sales.

sales·wom·an /'sālz,wo͝omən/ ▶ n. (pl. **saleswomen**) a woman whose job involves selling or promoting commercial products.

Sal·ford /'sôlfərd, 'sal-/ an industrial city in northwestern England, near Manchester; pop. 69,600 (est. 2009).

Sa·li·an /'sālēən, -yən/ ▶ adj. of or relating to the Salii, a 4th-century Frankish people living near the IJssel River, from whom the Merovingians were descended.
▶ n. a member of this people.

Sal·ic /'sālik, 'sal-/ ▶ adj. another term for SALIAN.

sal·i·cin /'salisin/ ▶ n. Chemistry a bitter compound present in willow bark. It is a glucoside related to aspirin, and accounts for the ancient use of willow bark as a pain-relieving drug.
– ORIGIN mid 19th cent.: from French *salicine*, from Latin *salix*, *salic-* 'willow.'

sa·li·cio·nal /sə'lisHənl/ ▶ n. an organ stop with a soft reedy tone.
– ORIGIN mid 19th cent.: from German *Salicional*, from Latin *salix*, *salic-* 'willow' + the obscurely derived suffix *-ional*.

Sal·ic law historical ▶ n. **1** a law excluding females from dynastic succession, esp. as the alleged fundamental law of the French monarchy.

S

2 a Frankish law book extant in Merovingian and Carolingian times.

sal·i·cyl·ic ac·id /ˌsaləˈsilik/ ▶ **n.** Chemistry a bitter compound present in certain plants. It is used as a fungicide and in the manufacture of aspirin and dyestuffs. ● Alternative name: *o*-**hydroxybenzoic acid**; chem. formula: $C_6H_4(OH)(COOH)$.
– DERIVATIVES **sa·lic·y·late** /səˈlisəˌlāt, -lit/ **n.**
– ORIGIN mid 19th cent.: *salicylic* from French *salicyle*, the radical of the acid, + **-IC**.

sa·li·ent /ˈsālyənt, -lēənt/ ▶ **adj. 1** most noticeable or important: *it succinctly covered all the salient points of the case.* ■ prominent; conspicuous: *it was always the salient object in my view.* ■ (of an angle) pointing outward. The opposite of **RE-ENTRANT**.
2 [postpositive] Heraldry (of an animal) standing on its hind legs with the forepaws raised, as if leaping.
▶ **n.** a piece of land or section of fortification that juts out to form an angle. ■ an outward bulge in a line of military attack or defense.
– DERIVATIVES **sa·li·ence n., sa·li·en·cy n., sa·li·ent·ly adv.**
– ORIGIN mid 16th cent. (as a heraldic term): from Latin *salient-* 'leaping,' from the verb *salire*. The noun dates from the early 19th cent.

Sa·li·en·tia /ˌsālēˈenCHə/ Zoology another term for **ANURA**.
– DERIVATIVES **sa·li·en·tian n. & adj.**
– ORIGIN modern Latin (plural), from Latin *salire* 'to leap.'

sa·lif·er·ous /səˈlif(ə)rəs/ ▶ **adj.** Geology (of rock or strata) containing much salt.
– ORIGIN early 19th cent.: from Latin *sal* 'salt' + **-IFEROUS**.

Sa·li·na /səˈlīnə/ an industrial and commercial city in central Kansas; pop. 46,483 (est. 2008).

sa·li·na /səˈlīnə, -ˈlē-/ ▶ **n.** (chiefly in the Caribbean or South America) a salt pan, salt lake, or salt marsh.
– ORIGIN late 16th cent.: from Spanish, from medieval Latin, 'salt pit,' in Latin *salinae* (plural) 'salt pans.'

Sa·li·nas /səˈlēnəs/ a city in west central California, a commercial center in the agriculturally important Salinas Valley; pop. 143,640 (est. 2008).

sa·line /ˈsāˌlēn, -ˌlīn/ ▶ **adj.** containing or impregnated with salt: *saline alluvial soils.* ■ chiefly Medicine (of a solution) containing sodium chloride and/or a salt or salts of magnesium or another alkali metal.
▶ **n.** a solution of salt in water. ■ a saline solution used in medicine.
– DERIVATIVES **sa·lin·i·ty** /səˈlinitē/ **n., sal·i·ni·za·tion** /ˌsalənəˈzāSHən/ **n., sal·i·nize** /ˈsaləˌnīz/ **v.**
– ORIGIN late 15th cent.: from Latin *sal* 'salt' + **-INE**[1].

Sal·in·ger /ˈsalənjər/, J. D. (1919–2010), US novelist and short-story writer; full name *Jerome David Salinger*. He is best known for his novel of adolescence, *The Catcher in the Rye* (1951). Other notable works: *Franny and Zooey* (1961) and *Raise High the Roof Beam, Carpenter* (1963).

sal·i·nom·e·ter /ˌsaləˈnämitər/ ▶ **n.** an instrument for measuring the salinity of water.

Salis·bur·y[1] /ˈsôlzˌberē, -b(ə)rē/ **1** a city in southern England; pop. 42,900 (est. 2009). It is noted for its 13th-century cathedral.
2 former name (until 1982) of **HARARE**.

Salis·bur·y[2] /ˈsôlzˌberē, ˈsalz-, -b(ə)rē/, Robert Arthur Talbot Gascoigne-Cecil, 3rd Marquess of (1830–1903), British statesman; prime minister 1885–86, 1886–92, and 1895–1902.

Sa·lish /ˈsāliSH/ ▶ **n.** (pl. **same**) **1** a member of a group of American Indian peoples inhabiting areas of the northwestern US and British Columbia. ■ dated another name for the **FLATHEAD** people (see **FLATHEAD**).
2 the group of related languages spoken by the Salish.
▶ **adj.** of or relating to the Salish or their languages.
– DERIVATIVES **Sa·lish·an** /-ən/ **adj.**
– ORIGIN the Flathead name.

sa·li·va /səˈlīvə/ ▶ **n.** watery liquid secreted into the mouth by glands, providing lubrication for chewing and swallowing, and aiding digestion.
– DERIVATIVES **sal·i·var·y** /ˈsaləˌverē/ **adj.**
– ORIGIN late Middle English: from Latin.

sal·i·vate /ˈsaləˌvāt/ ▶ **v.** [no obj.] **1** secrete saliva, esp. in anticipation of food. ■ [with obj.] technical cause (a person or animal) to produce an unusually copious secretion of saliva.
2 display great relish at the sight or prospect of something: *I was fairly salivating at the prospect of a $10 million loan.*
– DERIVATIVES **sal·i·va·tion** /ˌsaləˈvāSHən/ **n.**
– ORIGIN mid 17th cent.: from Latin *salivat-* '(having) produced saliva,' from the verb *salivare*, from *saliva* (see **SALIVA**).

Salk /sô(l)k/, Jonas Edward (1914–95), US microbiologist. He developed the standard **Salk vaccine** against polio, using virus inactivated by formalin, in the early 1950s. He later became the director of the institute in San Diego that bears his name.

sal·let /ˈsalit/ ▶ **n.** historical a light helmet with an outward curve extending over the back of the neck, worn as part of medieval armor.
– ORIGIN late Middle English: from French *salade*, based on Latin *caelare* 'engrave' (from *caelum* 'chisel').

sallet

Sal·lie Mae /ˈsælē ˈmā/ informal the Student Loan Marketing Association, an agency that makes educational loans more widely available to college students.
– ORIGIN 1970s: elaboration of the acronym *SLMA*, suggested by the given names *Sally* and *Mae*, on the pattern of **FANNIE MAE**.

sal·low[1] /ˈsalō/ ▶ **adj.** (**sallower, sallowest**) (of a person's face or complexion) of an unhealthy yellow or pale brown color.
▶ **v.** [with obj.] rare make sallow.
– DERIVATIVES **sal·low·ish adj., sal·low·ness n.**
– ORIGIN Old English *salo* 'dusky,' of Germanic origin; related to Old Norse *sǫlr* 'yellow,' from a base meaning 'dirty.'

sal·low[2] ▶ **n. 1** chiefly Brit. a willow tree, esp. one of a low-growing or shrubby kind. Also called **PUSSY WILLOW**. ● Genus *Salix*, family Salicaceae: several species, in particular the **great sallow** (see **GOAT WILLOW**).
2 a moth with dull yellow, orange, and brown patterned wings. The larvae of some species feed on sallow catkins. ● Genus *Xanthia*, family Noctuidae: several species.
– DERIVATIVES **sal·low·y adj.**
– ORIGIN Old English *salh*, of Germanic origin; related to Old Norse *selja*, and Latin *salix* 'willow.'

sal·ly[1] /ˈsalē/ ▶ **n.** (pl. **sallies**) a sudden charge out of a besieged place against the enemy; a sortie. ■ a brief journey or sudden start into activity. ■ a witty or lively remark, esp. one made as an attack or as a diversion in an argument; a retort.
▶ **v.** (**sallies, sallying, sallied**) [no obj.] make a military sortie: *they sallied out to harass the enemy.* ■ formal or humorous set out from a place to do something: *I made myself presentable and sallied forth.*
– ORIGIN late Middle English: from French *saillie*, feminine past participle (used as a noun) of *saillir* 'come or jut out,' from Old French *salir* 'to leap,' from Latin *salire*.

sal·ly[2] ▶ **n.** (pl. **sallies**) the part of a bell rope that has colored wool woven into it to provide a grip for the bell-ringer's hands.
– ORIGIN mid 17th cent. (denoting the first movement of a bell when set for ringing): perhaps from **SALLY**[1] in the sense 'leaping motion.'

Sal·ly Light·foot /ˈsalē ˈlītˌfo͝ot/ ▶ **n.** (pl. **Sally Lightfoots**) a common active crab of rocky shores in the Caribbean, Central America, and the Galapagos Islands. ● *Grapsus grapsus*, family Grapsidae.

Sal·ly Lunn /lən/ ▶ **n.** a sweet, light teacake, typically served hot.
– ORIGIN said to be from the name of a woman selling such cakes in Bath, England, *c.*1800.

sal·ly port ▶ **n.** a small exit point in a fortification for the passage of troops when making a sally.

sal·ma·gun·di /ˌsalməˈgəndē/ ▶ **n.** (pl. **salmagundis**) a dish of chopped meat, anchovies, eggs, onions, and seasoning. ■ a general mixture; a miscellaneous collection.
– ORIGIN from French *salmigondis*, of unknown origin.

sal·ma·naz·ar /ˌsalməˈnazər, -ˈnäzər/ ▶ **n.** a wine bottle of approximately twelve times the standard size.
– ORIGIN 1930s: named after *Shalmaneser*, a king of Assyria (2 Kings 17–18).

sal·mi /ˈsalmē/ ▶ **n.** (pl. **salmis**) a ragout or casserole of game stewed in a rich sauce: *a pheasant salmi.*
– ORIGIN French, abbreviation of *salmigondis* (see **SALMAGUNDI**).

salm·on /ˈsamən/ ▶ **n.** (pl. **same** or (esp. of types) **salmons**) **1** a large edible fish that is a popular game fish, much prized for its pink flesh. Salmon mature in the sea but migrate to freshwater streams to spawn. ● Family Salmonidae (the **salmon family**): the **Atlantic salmon** (*Salmo salar*), which sometimes returns to spawn two or three times, and five species of Pacific salmon (genus *Oncorhynchus*), which always die after spawning. The salmon family also includes trout, char, whitefish, and their relatives. ■ the flesh of this fish as food.
2 any of a number of fishes that resemble the true salmons, in particular: ● (**Australian salmon**) a large green and silver fish of Australasian inshore waters, popular as a game fish (*Arripis trutta*, family Arripidae). ● a prized food fish of the drum family (Sciaenidae), in particular the **Cape salmon** of the Indian Ocean (*Atractoscion aequidens*) and sea trouts of the western Atlantic (genus *Cynoscion*).
3 a pale pinkish orange color.
– DERIVATIVES **salm·on·y adj.**
– ORIGIN Middle English *samoun*, from Anglo-Norman French *saumoun*, from Latin *salmo*, *salmon-*. The spelling with *-l-* is influenced by Latin.

salm·on·ber·ry /ˈsamənˌberē/ ▶ **n.** (pl. **salmonberries**) a North American bramble that bears pink raspberrylike fruit. ● Genus *Rubus*, family Rosaceae: several species, in particular *R. spectabilis*. ■ the edible fruit of this plant.

sal·mo·nel·la /ˌsalməˈnelə/ ▶ **n.** (pl. **salmonellae** /-ˈnelē/) a bacterium that occurs mainly in the intestine, esp. a serotype causing food poisoning. ● Genus *Salmonella*: numerous serotypes; Gram-negative rods. ■ food poisoning caused by infection with such a bacterium: *an outbreak of salmonella.*
– DERIVATIVES **sal·mo·nel·lo·sis** /-ˌneˈlōsis/ **n.**
– ORIGIN modern Latin, named after Daniel E. *Salmon* (1850–1914), US veterinary surgeon.

sal·mo·nid /ˈsa(l)mənid/ ▶ **n.** Zoology a fish of the salmon family (Salmonidae).
– ORIGIN mid 19th cent.: from modern Latin *Salmonidae* (plural), based on Latin *salmo*, *salmon-* 'salmon.'

salm·on lad·der (also **salmon leap**) ▶ **n.** a series of natural steps in a cascade or steeply sloping riverbed, or a similar arrangement incorporated into a dam, allowing salmon to pass upstream.

sal·mo·noid /ˈsa(l)məˌnoid/ Zoology ▶ **n.** a fish of a group that includes the salmon family together with the pikes, smelts, and argentines. ● Superfamily Salmonoidea: several families.
▶ **adj.** of or relating to fish of this group.

Salm·on Riv·er a river that flows for 425 miles (685 km) through central Idaho. With its branches, it is noted as a salmon breeding resource.

salm·on run ▶ **n.** a migration of salmon up a river from the sea, in order to spawn.

salm·on trout ▶ **n.** a large trout or troutlike fish, in particular: ■ a lake trout. ■ Brit. a sea trout.

Sa·lo·me /ˌsäləˈmā, səˈlōmē/ (in the New Testament) the daughter of Herodias, who danced before her stepfather Herod Antipas. Given a choice of reward for her dancing, she asked for the head of St. John the Baptist and thus caused him to be beheaded.

sa·lon /səˈlän, saˈlôN/ ▶ **n. 1** an establishment where a hairdresser, beautician, or couturier conducts business.
2 a reception room in a large house. ■ historical a regular social gathering of eminent people (esp. writers and artists) at the house of a woman prominent in high society. ■ a meeting of intellectuals or other eminent people at the invitation of a celebrity or socialite.
3 (**Salon**) an annual exhibition of the work of living artists held by the Royal Academy of Painting and Sculpture in Paris, originally in the Salon d'Apollon in the Louvre in 1667.
– ORIGIN late 17th cent.: from French (see **SALOON**).

Sa·lon des Re·fu·sés /saˈlôN dā rəfYˈzā/ an exhibition in Paris ordered by Napoleon III in 1863 to display pictures rejected by the Salon. The artists represented included Manet, Cézanne, Pissarro, and Whistler.
– ORIGIN French, literally 'exhibition of the rejected (works).'

Sa·lon·i·ca /səˈlänikə, ˌsaləˈnēkə/ former name for **THESSALONÍKI**.

sa·lon mu·sic ▶ **n.** often derogatory light classical music originally considered suitable for playing in a salon.

sa·loon /səˈlo͞on/ ▶ **n. 1** a public room or building used for a specified purpose: *a billiard saloon.* ■ historical or humorous a place where alcoholic drinks may be bought and drunk. ■ a large public room for use as a lounge on a ship. ■ (also **saloon car**) Brit. a luxurious railroad car used as a lounge or restaurant or as private accommodations: *a dining saloon.*
2 (also **saloon car**) Brit. an automobile having a closed body and a closed trunk separated from the part in which the driver and passengers sit; a sedan.
– ORIGIN early 18th cent. (in the sense 'drawing room'): from French *salon*, from Italian *salone* 'large hall,' augmentative of *sala* 'hall.'

sa·loon deck ▶ **n.** a deck on the same level as a ship's saloon, for the use of passengers.

sa·loon·keep·er /səˈlo͞onˌkēpər/ (also **saloon keeper**) ▶ **n.** a person who runs a bar; a bartender.

sa·lo·pettes /ˌsaləˈpets/ ▶ **plural n.** a one-piece garment similar to overalls, with a front flap and

shoulder straps or a full sleeveless top, worn for skiing, sailing, etc.
– ORIGIN 1970s: from French *salopette* in the same sense + *-s* by analogy with such words as *trousers*.

sa·lot·to /sə'lätō/ ▶ **n.** (pl. **salotti** /-'lätē/) (esp. in Italy) a reception room.
– ORIGIN Italian, diminutive of *sala* 'hall.'

salp /salp/ ▶ **n.** a free-swimming marine invertebrate related to the sea squirts with a transparent, barrel-shaped body. ● Several genera in the class Thaliacea, subphylum Urochordata.
– ORIGIN mid 19th cent.: from French *salpe*, based on Greek *salpē* 'fish.'

sal·pi·con /ˌsalpi'kän/ ▶ **n.** a mixture of finely chopped ingredients bound in a thick sauce and used as a filling or stuffing.
– ORIGIN via French from Spanish, from *salpicar* 'sprinkle (with salt).'

sal·pi·glos·sis /ˌsalpə'glôsis, -'gläsis/ ▶ **n.** a South American plant of the nightshade family, with brightly patterned funnel-shaped flowers. ● Genus *Salpiglossis*, family Solanaceae.
– ORIGIN modern Latin, formed irregularly from Greek *salpinx* 'trumpet' + *glōssa* 'tongue.'

sal·pin·gec·to·my /ˌsalpən'jektəmē/ ▶ **n.** (pl. **salpingectomies**) surgical removal of the fallopian tubes.

sal·pin·gi·tis /ˌsalpən'jītis/ ▶ **n.** Medicine inflammation of the fallopian tubes.

salpingo- (also **salping-** before a vowel) ▶ **comb. form** relating to the fallopian tubes: *salpingostomy*.
– ORIGIN from Greek *salpinx, salping-* 'trumpet.'

sal·pin·gos·to·my /ˌsalpən'gästəmē/ ▶ **n.** surgical unblocking of a blocked fallopian tube.

sal·sa /'sälsə/ ▶ **n. 1** a type of Latin American dance music incorporating elements of jazz and rock. ■ a dance performed to this music.
2 (esp. in Latin American cooking) a spicy tomato sauce.
– ORIGIN Spanish, literally 'sauce,' extended in American Spanish to denote the dance.

sal·sa ver·de /'sälsə 'verdā/ ▶ **n. 1** an Italian sauce made with olive oil, garlic, capers, anchovies, vinegar or lemon juice, and parsley.
2 a Mexican sauce of finely chopped onion, garlic, coriander, parsley, and hot peppers.
– ORIGIN Spanish, literally 'green sauce.'

sal·se·ro /sal'serō/ ▶ **n.** (pl. **salseros**) a salsa musician or dancer.
– ORIGIN Spanish.

sal·si·fy /'salsəfē, -ˌfī/ ▶ **n.** an edible European plant of the daisy family, with a long root like that of a parsnip. Also called OYSTER PLANT. ● *Tragopogon porrifolius*, family Compositae. See also SCORZONERA. ■ the root of this plant used as a vegetable.
– ORIGIN late 17th cent.: from French *salsifis*, from obsolete Italian *salsefica*, of unknown ultimate origin.

SALT /sôlt/ ▶ **abbr.** Strategic Arms Limitation Talks.

salt /sôlt/ ▶ **n. 1** (also **common salt**) a white crystalline substance that gives seawater its characteristic taste and is used for seasoning or preserving food. ● Alternative name: **sodium chloride**; chem. formula: NaCl. See SEA SALT. ■ literary something that adds freshness or piquancy: *he described danger as the salt of pleasure*. ■ a saltcellar.
2 Chemistry any chemical compound formed from the reaction of an acid with a base, with all or part of the hydrogen of the acid replaced by a metal or other cation.
3 (usu. **old salt**) informal an experienced sailor.
▶ **adj.** [attrib.] **1** impregnated with, treated with, or tasting of salt: *salt water | salt beef*.
2 (of a plant) growing on the coast or in salt marshes.
▶ **v.** [with obj.] **1** (usu. as adj. **salted**) season or preserve with salt: *cook the carrots in boiling salted water*. ■ make (something) piquant or more interesting: *there was good talk to salt the occasion*. ■ sprinkle (a road or path) with salt in order to melt snow or ice.
2 informal fraudulently make (a mine) appear to be a paying one by placing rich ore in it.
3 (as adj. **salted**) (of a horse) having developed a resistance to disease by surviving it.
– PHRASES **rub salt into the** (or **someone's**) **wound** make a painful experience even more painful for someone. **the salt of the earth** a person or group of people of great kindness, reliability, or honesty. [with biblical allusion to Matt 5:13.] **sit below the salt** be of lower social standing or worth. [from the former custom of placing a large saltcellar in the middle of a dining table with the host at one end.] **take something with a grain** (or **pinch**) **of salt** regard something as exaggerated; believe only part of something: *take a stock tip with a grain of salt*. **worth one's salt** good or competent at the job or profession specified: *any astrologer worth her salt would have predicted this*.
– PHRASAL VERBS **salt something away** informal secretly store or put by something, esp. money. **salt something out** cause soap to separate from lye by adding salt. ■ Chemistry cause an organic compound to separate from an aqueous solution by adding an electrolyte.
– DERIVATIVES **salt·ish adj.**, **salt·less adj.**, **salt·ness n.**
– ORIGIN Old English *sealt* (noun), *sealtan* (verb), of Germanic origin; related to Dutch *zout* and German *Salz* (nouns), from an Indo-European root shared by Latin *sal*, Greek *hals* 'salt.'

salt-and-pep·per ▶ **adj.** flecked or speckled with intermingled dark and light shades: *his salt-and-pepper hair*.

sal·ta·rel·lo /ˌsaltə'relō, ˌsôl-/ ▶ **n.** (pl. **saltarellos** or **saltarelli** /-'relē/) an energetic Italian or Spanish dance for one couple, characterized by leaps and skips.
– ORIGIN early 18th cent.: Italian *salterello*, Spanish *saltarelo*, based on Latin *saltare* 'to dance.'

sal·ta·tion /ˌsôl'tāsHən/ ▶ **n. 1** Biology abrupt evolutionary change; sudden large-scale mutation.
2 Geology the movement of hard particles such as sand over an uneven surface in a turbulent flow of air or water.
3 archaic the action of leaping or dancing.
– DERIVATIVES **sal·ta·to·ry** /'saltəˌtôrē, 'sôl-/ **adj.**
– ORIGIN early 17th cent. (sense 3): from Latin *saltatio(n-)*, from *saltare* 'to dance,' frequentative of *salire* 'to leap.'

sal·ta·to·ri·al /ˌsaltə'tôrēəl, ˌsôl-/ ▶ **adj.** chiefly Entomology (esp. of grasshoppers or their limbs) adapted for leaping.

salt·box /'sôltˌbäks/ ▶ **n.** a frame house having up to three stories at the front and one fewer at the back with a steeply pitched roof.

salt bridge ▶ **n.** Chemistry **1** a tube containing an electrolyte (typically in the form of a gel), providing electrical contact between two solutions.
2 a link between electrically charged acidic and basic groups, esp. on different parts of a large molecule such as a protein.

salt·bush /'sôltˌbo͝osH/ ▶ **n.** a salt-tolerant orache plant sometimes used in the reclamation of saline soils or to provide grazing in areas of salty soil. ● Genus *Atriplex*, family Chenopodiaceae: several species, including the **four-wing saltbush** *A. canescens* of the western US.

salt ce·dar ▶ **n.** a tamarisk with reddish-brown branches and feathery gray foliage. ● *Tamarix gallica*, family Tamaricaceae.

salt·cel·lar /'sôltˌselər/ ▶ **n.** a dish or container for storing salt, now typically a closed container with perforations in the lid for sprinkling.
– ORIGIN late Middle English: from SALT + obsolete *saler*, from Old French *salier* 'salt-box,' from Latin *salarium* (see SALARY). The change in spelling of the second word was due to association with CELLAR.

salt chuck ▶ **n.** informal an inlet of the sea that flows into freshwater lakes or rivers. ■ the sea.
– ORIGIN from Chinook Jargon.

salt dome ▶ **n.** a dome-shaped structure in sedimentary rocks, formed where a large mass of salt has been forced upward. Such structures often form traps for oil or natural gas.

salt·er /'sôltər/ ▶ **n.** historical a person dealing in or employed in the production of salt. ■ a person whose work involved the preservation of meat or fish in salt. ■ another term for DRY-SALTER.
– ORIGIN Old English *sealtere* (see SALT, -ER¹).

sal·tern /'sôltərn/ ▶ **n.** a set of pools in which seawater is left to evaporate to make salt.
– ORIGIN Old English *sealtærn* 'salt building' (the original use denoting a saltworks).

salt fin·ger ▶ **n.** Oceanography one of several alternating columns of rising and descending water produced when a layer of water is overlain by a denser, saltier layer.
– DERIVATIVES **salt fin·ger·ing n.**

salt fish ▶ **n.** fish, esp. cod, that has been preserved in salt.

salt flats ▶ **plural n.** areas of flat land covered with a layer of salt.

salt glaze ▶ **n.** Pottery a hard glaze with a pitted surface, produced on stoneware by adding salt to the kiln during firing.
– DERIVATIVES **salt-glazed adj.**, **salt glaz·ing n.**

salt grass (also **saltgrass**) ▶ **n.** grass growing in salt marshes or in alkaline regions, esp. *Distichlis spicata* (family Gramineae).

salt horse ▶ **n.** archaic Nautical slang salted beef.

Sal·ti·llo /säl'tē(y)ō/ a city in northern Mexico, capital of the state of Coahuila, in the Sierra Madre, southwest of Monterrey; pop. 633,677 (2005).

sal·tim·boc·ca /ˌsältim'bōkə/ ▶ **n.** a dish consisting of rolled pieces of veal or poultry cooked with herbs, bacon, and other flavorings.
– ORIGIN Italian, literally 'leap into the mouth.'

sal·tine /sôl'tēn/ ▶ **n.** a thin, crisp, savory cracker sprinkled with salt.
– ORIGIN from SALT + -INE⁴.

salt·ing /'sôltiNG/ ▶ **n.** (usu. **saltings**) Brit. an area of coastal land that is regularly covered by the tide.

sal·tire /'salˌtir, 'sôl-/ ▶ **n.** Heraldry another term for ST. ANDREW'S CROSS. ■ [as modifier] (of a design) incorporating a motif based on such a diagonal cross.
– DERIVATIVES **sal·tire·wise** /-ˌwīz/ **adv.**
– ORIGIN late Middle English: from Old French *saultoir* 'stirrup cord, stile, saltire,' based on Latin *saltare* 'to dance.'

salt lake ▶ **n.** a lake of salt water.

Salt Lake Cit·y the capital of Utah, situated in the northern part of the state; pop. 181,698 (est. 2008). Founded in 1847 by Brigham Young, the city is the world headquarters of the Church of Jesus Christ of Latter-Day Saints (Mormons).

salt lick ▶ **n.** a place where animals go to lick salt from the ground. ■ a block of salt provided for animals to lick.

salt marsh ▶ **n.** an area of coastal grassland that is regularly flooded by seawater.

salt mead·ow ▶ **n.** a meadow that is subject to flooding by seawater; a salt marsh.

salt mine ▶ **n.** a mine yielding rock salt. ■ (usu. **salt mines**) humorous used in reference to a person's job or place of work: *we had a lot of fun, but tomorrow it's back to the salt mines*.

Sal·ton Sea /'sôltn/ a salt lake in southeastern California, created in the dry *Salton Sink* by a 1905 diversion of the Colorado River.

salt pan ▶ **n.** a shallow container or depression in the ground in which salt water evaporates to leave a deposit of salt.

salt·pe·ter /sôlt'pētər/ (Brit. **saltpetre**) ▶ **n.** another term for POTASSIUM NITRATE.
– ORIGIN late Middle English: from Old French *salpetre*, from medieval Latin *salpetra*, probably representing *sal petrae* 'salt of rock' (i.e., found as an encrustation). The change in the first element was due to association with SALT.

salt shak·er ▶ **n.** a perforated container for sprinkling salt.

salt spoon ▶ **n.** a tiny spoon with a roundish deep bowl, used for serving oneself with salt.

sal·tus /'saltəs, 'sôl-/ ▶ **n.** literary a sudden transition; a breach of continuity.
– ORIGIN mid 17th cent.: from Latin, literally 'leap.'

salt·wa·ter /'sôltˌwôtər, -ˌwätər/ ▶ **adj.** [attrib.] of or found in salt water; living in the sea: *saltwater fish*.

salt·wa·ter croc·o·dile ▶ **n.** a large and dangerous crocodile occurring in estuaries and coastal waters from southwestern India to northern Australia. ● *Crocodylus porosus*, family Crocodylidae.

salt·wort /'sôltwərt, -ˌwôrt/ ▶ **n.** a plant of the goosefoot family that typically grows in salt marshes. It is rich in alkali and its ashes were formerly used in soap-making. ● Genus *Salsola*, family Chenopodiaceae.

salt·y /'sôltē/ ▶ **adj.** (**saltier, saltiest**) tasting of, containing, or preserved with salt. ■ (of language or humor) down-to-earth; coarse. ■ informal tough; aggressive.
– DERIVATIVES **salt·i·ness n.**

sa·lu·bri·ous /sə'lo͞obrēəs/ ▶ **adj.** health-giving; healthy: *salubrious weather*. ■ (of a place) pleasant; not run-down.
– DERIVATIVES **sa·lu·bri·ous·ly adv.**, **sa·lu·bri·ous·ness n.**, **sa·lu·bri·ty** /-britē/ **n.**
– ORIGIN mid 16th cent.: from Latin *salubris* (from *salus* 'health') + -OUS.

Sa·lu·ki /sə'lo͞okē/ (also **saluki**) ▶ **n.** (pl. **Salukis**) a tall, swift, slender dog of a silky-coated breed with large drooping ears and fringed feet.
– ORIGIN early 19th cent.: from Arabic *salūķī*.

sa·lu·mi /sä'lo͞omē/ ▶ **plural n.** cured meats that are sliced and served as an appetizer in an Italian meal.
– ORIGIN Italian.

sa·lut /sa'lo͞o, sä'lY/ ▶ **exclam.** used to express friendly feelings toward one's companions before drinking.
– ORIGIN French.

S

sal·u·tar·y /ˈsalyəˌterē/ ▶ **adj.** (esp. with reference to something unwelcome or unpleasant) producing good effects; beneficial: *a salutary reminder of where we came from.* ■ archaic health-giving: *the salutary Atlantic air.*
– ORIGIN late Middle English (as a noun in the sense 'remedy'): from French *salutaire* or Latin *salutaris*, from *salus, salut-* 'health.'

sal·u·ta·tion /ˌsalyəˈtāSHən/ ▶ **n.** a gesture or utterance made as a greeting or acknowledgment of another's arrival or departure: *we greeted them but no one returned our salutations | he raised his glass* ***in salutation.*** ■ a standard formula of words used in a letter to address the person being written to.
– DERIVATIVES **sal·u·ta·tion·al** /-SHənl/ **adj.**
– ORIGIN late Middle English: from Old French, or from Latin *salutatio(n-)*, from *salutare* 'pay one's respects to' (see **SALUTE**).

sa·lu·ta·to·ri·an /səˌlo͞otəˈtôrēən/ ▶ **n.** the student who ranks second highest in a graduating class and delivers the salutatory. Compare with **VALEDICTORIAN.**

sa·lu·ta·to·ry /səˈlo͞otəˌtôrē/ ▶ **adj.** (esp. of an address) relating to or of the nature of a salutation.
▶ **n.** (pl. **salutatories**) an address of welcome, esp. one given as an oration by the student ranking second highest in a graduating class at a high school or college.
– ORIGIN late 17th cent. (as an adjective): from Latin *salutatorius*, from *salutare* 'pay one's respects to' (see **SALUTE**).

sa·lute /səˈlo͞ot/ ▶ **n.** a gesture of respect, homage, or polite recognition or acknowledgment, esp. one made to or by a person when arriving or departing: *he raises his arms in a triumphant salute.* ■ a prescribed or specified movement, typically a raising of a hand to the head, made by a member of a military or similar force as a formal sign of respect or recognition. ■ [often with modifier] the discharge of a gun or guns as a formal or ceremonial sign of respect or celebration: *a twenty-one-gun salute.* ■ Fencing the formal performance of certain guards or other movements by fencers before engaging.
▶ **v.** [with obj.] make a formal salute to: *don't you usually salute a superior officer?* | [no obj.] *he clicked his heels and saluted.* ■ greet: *he saluted her with a smile.* ■ show or express admiration and respect for: *we salute a truly great photographer.* ■ [with obj. and complement] archaic hail (someone) as having a particular high office: *they saluted him king when he entered into Jerusalem.*
– PHRASES **take the salute** (of a senior officer in the armed forces or other person of importance) acknowledge formally a salute given by a body of troops marching past.
– DERIVATIVES **sa·lut·er n.**
– ORIGIN late Middle English: from Latin *salutare* 'greet, pay one's respects to,' from *salus, salut-* 'health, welfare, greeting'; the noun partly from Old French *salut*.

Sal·va·dor /ˈsalvəˌdôr, ˌsalvəˈdôr/ a port on the Atlantic coast of eastern Brazil, capital of the state of Bahia; pop. 2,892,625 (2007). Former name **BAHIA.**

Sal·va·dor·ean /ˌsalvəˈdôrēən/ ▶ **adj.** of or relating to El Salvador.
▶ **n.** a native or inhabitant of El Salvador.

sal·vage /ˈsalvij/ ▶ **v.** [with obj.] rescue (a wrecked or disabled ship or its cargo) from loss at sea: *an emerald and gold cross was salvaged from the wreck.* ■ retrieve or preserve (something) from potential loss or adverse circumstances: *it was the only crumb of comfort he could salvage from the ordeal.*
▶ **n.** the rescue of a wrecked or disabled ship or its cargo from loss at sea: [as modifier] *a salvage operation was under way.* ■ the cargo saved from a wrecked or sunken ship: *salvage taken from a ship that had sunk in the river.* ■ the rescue of property or material from potential loss or destruction. ■ Law payment made or due to a person who has saved a ship or its cargo.
– DERIVATIVES **sal·vage·a·ble adj., sal·vag·er n.**
– ORIGIN mid 17th cent. (as a noun denoting payment for saving a ship or its cargo): from French, from medieval Latin *salvagium*, from Latin *salvare* 'to save.' The verb dates from the late 19th cent.

sal·vage ther·a·py ▶ **n.** a therapeutic regimen, normally based on drugs, that is resorted to when preferred therapies have failed.

sal·vage yard ▶ **n.** a place where disused vehicles or other machinery is broken up and the parts saved and processed for resale.

Sal·var·san /ˈsalvərˌsan/ ▶ **n.** Medicine, historical another term for **ARSPHENAMINE.**
– ORIGIN early 20th cent.: from German, from Latin *salvare* 'save' + German *Arsenik* 'arsenic' + **-AN.**

sal·va·tion /salˈvāSHən/ ▶ **n.** Theology deliverance from sin and its consequences, believed by Christians to be brought about by faith in Christ. ■ preservation or deliverance from harm, ruin, or loss: *they try to sell it to us as economic salvation.* ■ (**one's salvation**) a source or means of being saved in this way: *his only salvation was to outfly the enemy.*
– ORIGIN Middle English: from Old French *salvacion*, from ecclesiastical Latin *salvation-* (from *salvare* 'to save'), translating Greek *sōtēria*.

Sal·va·tion Ar·my (abbr.: **SA**) a worldwide Christian evangelical organization on quasi-military lines. Established by William Booth, it is noted for its work with the poor and for its brass bands.

sal·va·tion·ist /salˈvāSHənist/ ▶ **n.** (**Salvationist**) a member of the Salvation Army.
▶ **adj.** of or relating to salvation. ■ (**Salvationist**) of or relating to the Salvation Army.
– DERIVATIVES **sal·va·tion·ism** /-ˌnizəm/ **n.**

salve[1] /sav, säv/ ▶ **n.** an ointment used to promote healing of the skin or as protection. ■ something that is soothing or consoling for wounded feelings or an uneasy conscience: *the idea provided him with a salve for his guilt.*
▶ **v.** [with obj.] **1** soothe (wounded pride or one's conscience): *charity salves our conscience.*
2 archaic apply salve to.
– ORIGIN Old English *sealfe* (noun), *sealfian* (verb), of Germanic origin; related to Dutch *zalf* and German *Salbe*.

salve[2] /salv/ ▶ **v.** archaic term for **SALVAGE.**
– DERIVATIVES **salv·a·ble** /ˈsalvəbəl/ **adj.**
– ORIGIN early 18th cent.: back-formation from the noun **SALVAGE.**

sal·ver /ˈsalvər/ ▶ **n.** a tray, typically one made of silver and used in formal circumstances.
– ORIGIN mid 17th cent.: from French *salve* 'tray for presenting food to the king,' from Spanish *salva* 'sampling of food,' from *salvar* 'make safe.'

Sal·ve Re·gi·na /ˈsälvā rəˈjēnə/ ▶ **n.** a Roman Catholic hymn or prayer said or sung after compline, and after the Divine Office from Trinity Sunday to Advent.
– ORIGIN the opening words in Latin, 'hail (holy) queen.'

sal·vi·a /ˈsalvēə/ ▶ **n.** a widely distributed plant of the mint family, esp. (in gardening) a bedding plant cultivated for its spikes of bright flowers. ● Genus *Salvia*, family Labiatae: many species, in particular the scarlet-flowered *S. splendens*.
– ORIGIN modern Latin, from Latin *salvia* 'sage.'

sal·vif·ic /salˈvifik/ ▶ **adj.** Theology leading to salvation.
– ORIGIN late 16th cent.: from Latin *salvificus* 'saving,' from *salvus* 'safe.'

sal·vo /ˈsalˌvō/ ▶ **n.** (pl. **salvos** or **salvoes**) a simultaneous discharge of artillery or other guns in a battle. ■ a number of weapons released from one or more aircraft in quick succession. ■ a sudden, vigorous, or aggressive act or series of acts: *the pardons provoked* ***a salvo of*** *accusations.*
– ORIGIN late 16th cent. (earlier as *salve*): from French *salve*, Italian *salva* 'salutation.'

sal vo·la·ti·le /ˌsal vəˈlatl-ē/ ▶ **n.** a scented solution of ammonium carbonate in alcohol, used as smelling salts.
– ORIGIN mid 17th cent.: modern Latin, literally 'volatile salt.'

sal·vor /ˈsalvər/ ▶ **n.** a person engaged in salvage of a ship or items lost at sea.

sal·war /ˌsəlˈwär/ (also **shalwar** /ˌSHəl-/) ▶ **n.** a pair of light, loose, pleated trousers tapering to a tight fit around the ankles, worn by women from South Asia, typically with a kameez.
– ORIGIN from Persian and Urdu *šalwār*.

Sal·ween /ˈsalˌwēn/ a river in Southeast Asia that rises in Tibet and flows for 1,500 miles (2,400 km) southeast and south through Burma (Myanmar) to the Gulf of Martaban, an inlet of the Andaman Sea.

Sal·yut /ˈsalˌyo͞ot/ a series of seven Soviet manned orbiting space stations, launched between 1971 and 1982.
– ORIGIN Russian, used as a greeting; compare with French **SALUT.**

Salz·burg /ˈsôlzˌbərg, ˈsälz-, ˈzältsˌbo͝ork/ a city in western Austria, near the border with Germany, the capital of a state of the same name; pop 146,972 (2006). It is noted for its annual music festivals.

Salz·git·ter /ˈzältsˌgitər/ an industrial city in Germany, in Lower Saxony, southeast of Hanover; pop. 106,700 (est. 2006).

SAM /sam/ ▶ **abbr.** surface-to-air missile.

Sam. ▶ **abbr.** Bible Samuel.

sa·ma·dhi /səˈmädē/ ▶ **n.** (pl. **samadhis**) Hinduism & Buddhism a state of intense concentration achieved through meditation. In Hindu yoga this is regarded as the final stage, at which union with the divine is reached (before or at death). ■ Indian a funerary monument.
– ORIGIN from Sanskrit *samādhi* 'contemplation.'

sa·man /səˈmän/ (also **samaan, saman tree**) ▶ **n.** West Indian term for **RAIN TREE.**
– ORIGIN Latin American Spanish.

Sa·mar /ˈsäˌmär/ an island in the Philippines, southeast of Luzon. It is the third largest island in the group.

Sam·a·ra /səˈmärə/ a city and river port in southwestern central Russia, situated on the Volga River at its confluence with the Samara River; pop. 1,135,400 (est. 2008). Former name (1935–91) **KUIBYSHEV.**

sam·a·ra /ˈsamərə, səˈme(ə)rə/ ▶ **n.** Botany a winged nut or achene containing one seed, as in ash and maple.
– ORIGIN late 16th cent.: modern Latin, from Latin, denoting an elm seed.

Sa·mar·i·a /səˈme(ə)rēə/ **1** an ancient city in central Palestine, founded in the 9th century BC as the capital of the northern Hebrew kingdom of Israel. The ancient site is situated in the modern West Bank, northwest of Nablus.
2 the region of ancient Palestine around this city, between Galilee in the north and Judaea in the south.

Sam·a·rin·da /ˌsaməˈrində/ a city in Indonesia, in eastern Borneo; pop. 505,700 (est. 2005).

Sa·mar·i·tan /səˈmaritn, -ˈme(ə)r-/ ▶ **n. 1** (usu. **Good Samaritan**) a charitable or helpful person (with reference to Luke 10:33).
2 a member of a people inhabiting Samaria in biblical times, or of the modern community in the region of Nablus claiming descent from them, adhering to a form of Judaism accepting only its own ancient version of the Pentateuch as Scripture.
3 the dialect of Aramaic formerly spoken in Samaria.
▶ **adj.** of or relating to Samaria or the Samaritans.
– DERIVATIVES **Sa·mar·i·tan·ism** /-ˌizəm/ **n.**
– ORIGIN from late Latin *Samaritanus*, from Greek *Samareitēs*, from *Samareia* 'Samaria.' The New Testament parable of the Good Samaritan reflects a proverbial hostility between Jews and Samaritans.

sa·mar·i·um /səˈme(ə)rēəm/ ▶ **n.** the chemical element of atomic number 62, a hard silvery-white metal of the lanthanide series. (Symbol: **Sm**)
– ORIGIN late 19th cent.: from *samar(skite)*, a mineral in which its spectrum was first observed (named after *Samarsky*, a 19th-cent. Russian official) + **-IUM.**

Sam·ar·kand /ˈsamərˌkand, səmərˈkänt/ (also **Samarqand**) a city in eastern Uzbekistan; pop. 312,900 (est. 2007). One of the oldest cities in Asia, it was founded in the 3rd or 4th millennium BC. It was a prosperous center on the Silk Road and, in the 14th century, became the capital of Tamerlane's Mongol empire.

Sa·ma Ve·da /ˈsämə ˈvādə, ˈvēdə/ Hinduism one of the four Vedas, a collection of liturgical chants chanted aloud at the sacrifice. Its material is drawn largely from the Rig Veda. See **VEDA.**
– ORIGIN from Sanskrit *sāmaveda*, from *sāman* 'chant' and *veda* '(sacred) knowledge.'

sam·ba /ˈsambə, ˈsäm-/ ▶ **n.** a Brazilian dance of African origin. ■ a piece of music for this dance. ■ a lively modern ballroom dance imitating this dance.
▶ **v.** (**sambas, sambaing** /-bəˌiNG/, **sambaed** /-bəd/ or **samba'd**) [no obj.] dance the samba.
– ORIGIN late 19th cent.: from Portuguese, of African origin.

sam·bal /ˈsämbäl/ ▶ **n.** (in Indian and Southeast Asian cooking) hot relish made with vegetables or fruit and spices.
– ORIGIN Malay.

sam·bar[1] /ˈsämbər, ˈsam-/ ▶ **n.** a dark brown woodland deer with branched antlers, of southern Asia. ● *Cervus unicolor*, family Cervidae.
– ORIGIN late 17th cent.: from Hindi *sābar*, from Sanskrit *śambara*.

sam·bar[2] (also **sambhar**) ▶ **n.** a spicy southern Indian dish consisting of lentils and vegetables.
– ORIGIN from Tamil *cāmpār*, via Marathi from Sanskrit *sambhāra* 'collection, materials.'

Sam·bo /ˈsambō/ ▶ **n.** (pl. **Sambos** or **Samboes**)
1 offensive a black person. [early 18th cent.: perhaps from Fula *sambo* 'uncle.']
2 (**sambo**) historical a person of mixed race, esp. of black and Indian or black and European blood. [mid 18th cent.: from American Spanish *zambo*, denoting a kind of yellow monkey.]

Sam Browne belt /sam ˈbroun/ ▶ **n.** a leather belt with a supporting strap that passes over the right shoulder, worn by army and police officers.
– ORIGIN early 20th cent.: named after Sir *Samuel J. Browne* (1824–1901), the British military commander who invented it.

sam·bu·ca /sam'bo͞okə/ ▶ **n.** an Italian aniseed-flavored liqueur.
– ORIGIN Italian, from Latin *sambucus* 'elder tree.'

Sa·me /'sāmē/ ▶ **plural n.** variant spelling of **SAMI**.

same /sām/ ▶ **adj.** (**the same**) **1** identical; not different: *she was saying the same thing over and over* | *I have never made the same mistake since* | *I'm the same age as you are* | [with clause] *he put on the same costume that he had worn in Ottawa.* ■ not having changed; unchanged: *he's worked at the same place for quite a few years.* ■ used to emphasize that one is referring to a particular, unique person or thing: *people will always notice if you wear the same shirt two days running* | *they drank out of the same glass.* ■ (**this/that same**) referring to a person or thing just mentioned: *that same year I went to Boston.* **2** of an identical type; exactly similar: *they all wore the same clothes.*
▶ **pron. 1** (**the same**) the same thing as something previously mentioned: *I'll resign and encourage everyone else to do the same.* ■ people or things that are identical or share the same characteristics: *there are several brands and they're not all the same.* **2** (chiefly in formal or legal use) the person or thing just mentioned: *sighted sub, sank same.*
▶ **adv.** similarly; in the same way: *treating women the same as men* | *he gave me five dollars, same as usual.*
– PHRASES **all** (or **just**) **the same** in spite of this; nevertheless: *she knew they had meant it kindly, but it had hurt all the same.* ■ in any case; anyway: *I can manage alone, thanks all the same.* **at the same time** see **TIME**. **be all the same to** be unimportant to (someone) what happens: *it was all the same to me where it was being sold.* **by the same token** see **TOKEN**. **one and the same** the same person or thing (used for emphasis): *the guy in the glasses and Superman were one and the same.* **same difference** informal used to express the speaker's belief that two or more things are essentially the same, in spite of apparent differences. **same here** informal the same applies to me. **(the) same to you!** may you do or have the same thing (a response to a greeting or insult). **the very same** the same (used for emphasis, often to express surprise): *the very same thrillers that flop in theaters become video hits.*
– ORIGIN Middle English: from Old Norse *sami*, from an Indo-European root shared by Sanskrit *sama*, Greek *homos*.

same·ness /'sāmnis/ ▶ **n.** lack of variety; uniformity or monotony: *there is a sameness about all the political parties.* ■ the quality of being the same; identity or similarity: *sameness of meaning across different languages.*

same-sex ▶ **adj.** relating to or involving people of the same sex: *same-sex friendships.* ■ relating to or denoting a sexual relationship in which both partners are of the same sex: *same-sex marriage.*

Sa·mhain /'souən/ ▶ **n.** the first day of November, celebrated by the ancient Celts as a festival marking the beginning of winter.
– ORIGIN Irish, from Old Irish *samain*.

Sam Hill /ˌsam 'hil/ ▶ **n.** informal used in exclamations as a euphemism for "hell": *what in Sam Hill is that smell?*
– ORIGIN mid 19th cent.: of unknown origin.

Sa·mi /'sāmē/ (also **Saami** /'sä-/, **Same**, or **Saame**) ▶ **plural n.** the Lapps of northern Scandinavia.
– ORIGIN Lappish, of unknown origin.

USAGE See usage at **LAPP**.

sam·i·sen /'samiˌsen/ (also **shamisen** /'SHam-/) ▶ **n.** a traditional Japanese three-stringed lute with a square body, played with a large plectrum.
– ORIGIN early 17th cent.: Japanese, from Chinese *san-hsien*, from *san* 'three' + *hsien* 'string.'

sam·ite /'samīt, 'sā-/ ▶ **n.** historical a rich silk fabric interwoven with gold and silver threads, used for dressmaking and decoration in the Middle Ages.
– ORIGIN Middle English: from Old French *samit*, via medieval Latin from medieval Greek *hexamiton*, from Greek *hexa-* 'six' + *mitos* 'thread.'

sam·iz·dat /'sämizˌdät, səmyiz'dät/ ▶ **n.** the clandestine copying and distribution of literature banned by the state, esp. formerly in the communist countries of eastern Europe.
– ORIGIN 1960s: Russian, literally 'self-publishing house.'

Sam·nite /'samˌnīt/ ▶ **n.** a member of an Oscan-speaking people of southern Italy in ancient times, who spent long periods at war with republican Rome in the 4th to 1st centuries BC.
▶ **adj.** of or relating to this people.
– ORIGIN from Latin *Samnites* (plural); related to *Sabinus* (see **SABINE**).

Sa·mo·a /sə'mōə/ a group of islands in Polynesia, divided between American Samoa and the nation of Samoa. ■ a country consisting of the western islands of Samoa; pop. 220,000 (est. 2009); capital, Apia; languages, Samoan and English (both official).

Visited by the Dutch in the early 18th century, the islands were divided administratively in 1899 into American Samoa in the east and German Samoa in the west. After World War I, the nine western islands were mandated to New Zealand and became an independent republic known as Western Samoa within the Commonwealth of Nations in 1962. The country became known as Samoa in 1997.

Sa·mo·an /sə'mōən/ ▶ **adj.** of or relating to Samoa, its people, or their language.
▶ **n. 1** a native or inhabitant of Samoa. **2** the Polynesian language of Samoa, spoken in Samoa, New Zealand, the US, and elsewhere.

Sa·mos /'sāmäs, 'sam-, 'sämôs/ a Greek island in the Aegean Sea, close to the coast of western Turkey.

sa·mo·sa /sə'mōsə/ ▶ **n.** a triangular savory pastry fried in ghee or oil, containing spiced vegetables or meat.
– ORIGIN Hindi, from Persian and Urdu.

sam·o·var /'saməˌvär/ ▶ **n.** a highly decorated tea urn used in Russia.
– ORIGIN Russian, literally 'self-boiler.'

samovar

Sam·o·yed /'saməˌyed, sə'moiyid/ ▶ **n. 1** a member of a group of mainly nomadic peoples of northern Siberia, who traditionally live as reindeer herders. **2** any of several Samoyedic languages of these peoples. ■ another term for **SAMOYEDIC**. **3** a dog of a white Arctic breed.
– ORIGIN from Russian *samoed* 'self-eater,' a folk etymology from a Lapp (Sami) phrase meaning 'land of the Sami.'

Sam·o·yed·ic /ˌsamə'yedik/ ▶ **n.** a group of Uralic languages of northern Siberia, of which the most widely spoken is Nenets.
▶ **adj.** of or relating to the Samoyeds or their languages.

samp /samp/ ▶ **n.** coarsely ground corn, or porridge made from this.
– ORIGIN mid 17th cent.: from Narragansett *nasamp*.

sam·pan /'samˌpan/ ▶ **n.** a small boat of a kind used in East Asia, typically with an oar or oars at the stern.
– ORIGIN early 17th cent.: from Chinese *san-ban*, from *san* 'three' + *ban* 'board.'

sampan

sam·phire /'samˌfīr/ ▶ **n. 1** (also **rock samphire**) a European plant of the parsley family that grows on rocks and cliffs by the sea. Its aromatic, fleshy leaves were formerly much used in pickles. ● *Crithmum maritimum*, family Umbelliferae. **2** (also **marsh samphire**) another term for **GLASSWORT**.
– ORIGIN mid 16th cent. (earlier as *sampiere*): from French (*herbe de*) *Saint Pierre* 'St. Peter('s herb).'

sam·ple /'sampəl/ ▶ **n.** a small part or quantity intended to show what the whole is like: *investigations involved analyzing samples of handwriting.* ■ a specimen taken for scientific testing or analysis: *a urine sample.* ■ Statistics a portion drawn from a population, the study of which is intended to lead to statistical estimates of the attributes of the whole population. ■ a small amount of a food or other commodity, esp. one given to a prospective customer. ■ a sound created by sampling.
▶ **v.** [with obj.] take a sample or samples of (something) for analysis: *bone marrow cells were sampled* | (as adj., with submodifier **sampled**) *a survey of two hundred randomly sampled households.* ■ try the qualities of (food or drink) by tasting it. ■ get a representative experience of: *sample the pleasures of Saint Maarten.* ■ Electronics ascertain the momentary value of (an analog signal) many times a second so as to convert the signal to digital form. ■ record or extract a small piece of music or sound digitally for reuse as part of a composition or song.
– ORIGIN Middle English (as a noun): from an Anglo-Norman French variant of Old French *essample* 'example.' Current senses of the verb date from the mid 18th cent.

sam·ple point ▶ **n.** Statistics a single possible observed value of a variable.

sam·pler /'samplər/ ▶ **n. 1** a piece of embroidery worked in various stitches as a specimen of skill, typically containing the alphabet and some mottoes. **2** a representative collection or example of something: *a few superb samplers of West Indian dishes.* **3** a person or device that takes and analyzes samples. ■ an electronic device for sampling music and sound.
– ORIGIN Middle English (denoting an example to be imitated): from Old French *essamplaire* 'exemplar.'

sam·ple space ▶ **n.** Statistics the range of values of a random variable.

sam·pling /'sampliNG/ ▶ **n. 1** the taking of a sample or samples: *routine river sampling is carried out according to a schedule.* ■ Statistics a sample. **2** the technique of digitally encoding music or sound and reusing it as part of a composition or recording.

sam·pling er·ror ▶ **n.** Statistics error in a statistical analysis arising from the unrepresentativeness of the sample taken.

sam·pling frame ▶ **n.** Statistics a list of the items or people forming a population from which a sample is taken.

Sam·pras /'samprəs/, Pete (1971–), US tennis player; full name *Petros Sampras*. During 1990–2002, he won the men's singles title at two Australian Open, five US Open, and a record seven Wimbledon tournaments.

sam·sa·ra /səm'särə/ ▶ **n.** Hinduism & Buddhism the cycle of death and rebirth to which life in the material world is bound.
– DERIVATIVES **sam·sa·ric** /-'särik/ **adj.**
– ORIGIN from Sanskrit *saṃsāra*.

sam·ska·ra /səm'skärə/ ▶ **n.** Hinduism a purificatory ceremony or rite marking a major event in one's life.
– ORIGIN from Sanskrit *saṃskāra* 'a making perfect, preparation.'

Sam·son /'samsən/ an Israelite leader (probably 11th century BC) famous for his strength (Judges 13–16). He fell in love with Delilah and confided to her that his strength lay in his uncut hair. She betrayed him to the Philistines, who cut off his hair and blinded him, but his hair grew again, and he pulled down the pillars of a house, destroying himself and a large gathering of Philistines.

Sam·son post ▶ **n.** a strong pillar fixed to a ship's deck to act as a support for a tackle or other equipment.
– ORIGIN late 16th cent. (denoting a kind of mousetrap): probably with biblical allusion to **SAMSON**.

Sam·u·el /'samyə(wə)l/ (in the Bible) a Hebrew prophet who rallied the Israelites after their defeat by the Philistines and became their ruler. ■ either of two books of the Bible covering the history of ancient Israel from Samuel's birth to the end of the reign of David.

Sam·uel·son /'samyo͞o(ə)lsən, -yəl-/, Paul Anthony (1915–2009), US economist. A professor at Massachusetts Institute of Technology from 1947, he held many international advisory positions, including that of consultant to the Federal Reserve Board. He wrote the best-selling textbook *Economics: An Introductory Analysis* (1948). Nobel Prize in Economics (1970).

sam·u·rai /'saməˌrī/ ▶ **n.** (pl. **same**) historical a member of a powerful military caste in feudal Japan, esp. a member of the class of military retainers of the daimyos.
– ORIGIN Japanese.

San /sän/ ▶ **n.** (pl. **same**) **1** a member of the aboriginal peoples of southern Africa commonly called Bushmen. See **BUSHMAN**. **2** the group of Khoisan languages spoken by these peoples. ■ any of these languages.
▶ **adj.** of or relating to the San or their languages.
– ORIGIN from Nama *sān* 'aboriginals, settlers.'

Sa·na'a /sä'nä/ (also **Sanaa**) the capital of Yemen; pop. 1,707,500 (est. 2004).

S

San An·dre·as fault /ˌsan anˈdrāəs/ a fault line that extends for about 600 miles (965 km) through the length of coastal California. Seismic activity is common along its course, caused by friction between two crustal plates sliding past each other along the line of the fault.

San An·ge·lo /san ˈanjəlō/ a commercial and industrial city in west central Texas; pop. 91,880 (est. 2008).

San An·to·ni·o /ˌsan anˈtōnēō/ an industrial city in south central Texas; pop. 1,351,305 (est. 2008). It is the site of the Alamo mission.

san·a·tive /ˈsanətiv/ ▶ **adj.** archaic conducive to physical or spiritual health and well-being; healing.
– ORIGIN late Middle English: from Old French *sanatif* or late Latin *sanativus*, from Latin *sanare* 'to cure.'

san·a·to·ri·um /ˌsanəˈtôrēəm/ ▶ **n.** (pl. **sanatoriums** or **sanatoria** /-rēə/) another term for SANITARIUM.
– ORIGIN mid 19th cent.: modern Latin, based on Latin *sanare* 'heal.'

San Ber·nar·di·no /ˌsan ˌbərnə(r)ˈdēnō/ an industrial and commercial city in southern California, east of Los Angeles, south of the San Bernardino Mountains; pop. 198,580 (est. 2008).

San·cerre /sänˈser/ ▶ **n.** a light wine, typically white, produced in the part of France around Sancerre.

San·chi /ˈsänCHē/ a village in Madhya Pradesh in India that is the location of several well-preserved ancient Buddhist stupas.

San·cho Pan·za /ˈsänCHō ˈpänzə/ the squire of Don Quixote. He is an uneducated peasant but has a store of proverbial wisdom and is thus a foil to his master.

San Cle·men·te /ˌsan kləˈmentē/ a city in southwestern California, on the Pacific Ocean, southeast of Los Angeles; pop; 65,050 (2006).

san·coche /sanˈkôSH/ (also **sancocho** /-ˈkôCHō/) ▶ **n.** (in South America and the Caribbean) a thick soup consisting of meat and root vegetables.
– ORIGIN from Latin American Spanish *sancocho* 'a stew.'

sanc·ti·fy /ˈsaNG(k)təˌfī/ ▶ **v.** (**sanctifies, sanctifying, sanctified**) [with obj.] set apart as or declare holy; consecrate: *a small shrine was built to sanctify the site.* ■ make legitimate or binding by religious sanction: *they see their love sanctified by the sacrament of marriage.* ■ free from sin; purify. ■ cause to be or seem morally right or acceptable: *ancient customs that are sanctified by tradition.*
– DERIVATIVES **sanc·ti·fi·ca·tion** /-fiˈkāSHən/ **n.**, **sanc·ti·fi·er n.**
– ORIGIN late Middle English: from Old French *saintifier* (influenced later by *sanctifier*), from ecclesiastical Latin *sanctificare*, from Latin *sanctus* 'holy.'

sanc·ti·mo·ni·ous /ˌsaNG(k)təˈmōnēəs/ ▶ **adj.** derogatory making a show of being morally superior to other people: *what happened to all the sanctimonious talk about putting his family first?*
– DERIVATIVES **sanc·ti·mo·ni·ous·ly adv.**, **sanc·ti·mo·ni·ous·ness n.**, **sanc·ti·mo·ny** /ˈsaNG(k)təˌmōnē/ **n.**
– ORIGIN early 17th cent. (in the sense 'holy in character'): from Latin *sanctimonia* 'sanctity' (from *sanctus* 'holy') + -OUS.

sanc·tion /ˈsaNG(k)SHən/ ▶ **n. 1** a threatened penalty for disobeying a law or rule: *a range of sanctions aimed at deterring insider abuse.* ■ (**sanctions**) measures taken by a nation to coerce another to conform to an international agreement or norms of conduct, typically in the form of restrictions on trade or on participation in official sporting events. ■ Ethics a consideration operating to enforce obedience to any rule of conduct.
2 official permission or approval for an action: *he appealed to the bishop for his sanction.* ■ official confirmation or ratification of a law. ■ Law, historical a law or decree, esp. an ecclesiastical decree.
▶ **v.** [with obj.] **1** give official permission or approval for (an action): *only two treatments have been sanctioned by the Food and Drug Administration.*
2 impose a sanction or penalty on.
– DERIVATIVES **sanc·tion·a·ble adj.**
– ORIGIN late Middle English (as a noun denoting an ecclesiastical decree): from French, from Latin *sanctio(n-)*, from *sancire* 'ratify.' The verb dates from the late 18th cent.

> **USAGE** **Sanction** is confusing because it has two meanings that are almost opposite. In most domestic contexts, **sanction** means 'approval, permission': *voters gave the measure their sanction.* In foreign affairs, **sanction** means 'penalty, deterrent': *international sanctions against the republic go into effect in January.*

sanc·ti·tude /ˈsaNG(k)təˌt(y)o͞od/ ▶ **n.** formal the state or quality of being holy, sacred, or saintly.
– ORIGIN late Middle English: from Latin *sanctitudo*, from *sanctus* 'holy.'

sanc·ti·ty /ˈsaNG(k)titē/ ▶ **n.** (pl. **sanctities**) the state or quality of being holy, sacred, or saintly: *the site of the tomb was a place of sanctity for the ancient Egyptians.* ■ ultimate importance and inviolability: *the sanctity of human life.*
– ORIGIN late Middle English (in the sense 'saintliness'): from Old French *saincte*, reinforced by Latin *sanctitas*, from *sanctus* 'holy.'

sanc·tu·ar·y /ˈsaNG(k)CHo͞oˌerē/ ▶ **n.** (pl. **sanctuaries**) **1** a place of refuge or safety: *people automatically sought a sanctuary in time of trouble* | *his sons took sanctuary in the church.*
2 [usu. with modifier] a nature reserve: *a bird sanctuary.*
3 a holy place; a temple or church. ■ the inmost recess or holiest part of a temple or church. ■ the part of the chancel of a church containing the high altar.
– ORIGIN Middle English (sense 3): from Old French *sanctuaire*, from Latin *sanctuarium*, from *sanctus* 'holy.' The early sense 'a church or other sacred place where a fugitive was immune, by the law of the medieval church, from arrest' gave rise to sense 1 and sense 2.

sanc·tu·ar·y lamp ▶ **n.** a candle or small light left lit in the sanctuary of a church, esp. (in Catholic churches) a red lamp indicating the presence of the reserved Sacrament.

sanc·tum /ˈsaNG(k)təm/ ▶ **n.** (pl. **sanctums**) **1** a sacred place, esp. a shrine within a temple or church.
2 a private place from which most people are excluded. See INNER SANCTUM.
– ORIGIN late 16th cent.: from Latin, neuter of *sanctus* 'holy,' from *sancire* 'consecrate.'

sanc·tum sanc·to·rum /ˈsaNG(k)təm ˌsaNG(k)ˈtôrəm/ ▶ **n.** (pl. **sancta sanctorum** /ˈsaNG(k)tə/ or **sanctum sanctorums**) the holy of holies in the Jewish temple. ■ a very private or secret place.
– ORIGIN late Middle English: Latin *sanctum* (see SANCTUM) + *sanctorum* 'of holy places,' translating Hebrew *qōḏeš haqqŏḏāšîm* 'holy of holies.'

Sanc·tus /ˈsaNG(k)təs/ ▶ **n.** Christian Church a hymn beginning *Sanctus, sanctus, sanctus* (Holy, holy, holy) forming a set part of the Mass.
– ORIGIN late Middle English: from Latin, literally 'holy.'

sanc·tus bell ▶ **n.** another term for SACRING BELL.

Sand /sand, sän(d)/, George (1804–76), French novelist; pseudonym of *Amandine-Aurore Lucille Dupin, Baronne Dudevant*. Her earlier novels, including *Lélia* (1833), portray women's struggles against conventional morals; she later wrote a number of pastoral novels, such as *La Mare au diable* (1846). Sand had a ten-year affair with Chopin.

sand /sand/ ▶ **n.** a loose granular substance, typically pale yellowish brown, resulting from the erosion of siliceous and other rocks and forming a major constituent of beaches, riverbeds, the seabed, and deserts. ■ (**sands**) an expanse of sand, typically along a shore: [in place names] *White Sands.* ■ a stratum of sandstone or compacted sand. ■ technical sediment whose particles are larger than silt (typically greater than 0.06 mm). ■ informal firmness of purpose: *no one has the sand to stand against him.* ■ a light yellow-brown color like that of sand.
▶ **v.** [with obj.] **1** smooth or polish with sandpaper or a mechanical sander: *sand the rusty areas until you expose bare metal* | (as noun **sanding**) *some recommend a light sanding between the second and third coats.*
2 sprinkle or overlay with sand, to give better purchase on a surface.
– PHRASES **the sands of time** the allotted time. [with reference to the sand of an hourglass.]
– DERIVATIVES **sand·like** /-ˌlik/ **adj.**
– ORIGIN Old English, of Germanic origin; related to Dutch *zand* and German *Sand*.

san·dal¹ /ˈsandl/ ▶ **n.** a light shoe with either an openwork upper or straps attaching the sole to the foot.
– DERIVATIVES **san·daled** /ˈsandld/ (Brit. **sandalled**) **adj.**
– ORIGIN late Middle English: via Latin from Greek *sandalion*, diminutive of *sandalon* 'wooden shoe,' probably of Asiatic origin; compare with Persian *sandal*.

san·dal² ▶ **n.** short for SANDALWOOD.

san·dal·wood /ˈsandlˌwo͝od/ ▶ **n.** (also **white sandalwood**) a widely cultivated Indian tree that yields fragrant timber and oil. ● *Santalum album*, family Santalaceae. ■ a perfume or incense derived from this timber. ■ used in names of other trees that yield similar timber, e.g., **red sandalwood**.
– ORIGIN early 16th cent.: *sandal* from medieval Latin *sandalum* (based on Sanskrit *candana*) + WOOD.

San·dal·wood Is·land another name for SUMBA.

san·da·rac /ˈsandəˌrak/ (also **gum sandarac**) ▶ **n.** a gum resin obtained from the alerce (cypress) of Spain and North Africa, used in making varnish.
– ORIGIN late Middle English (denoting realgar): from Latin *sandaraca*, from Greek *sandarakē*, of Asiatic origin. The current sense dates from the mid 17th cent.

San·da·we /sänˈdäwā/ ▶ **n. 1** (pl. **same** or **Sandawes**) a member of an indigenous people of Tanzania.
2 the Khoisan language of this people.
▶ **adj.** of or relating to this people or their language.

sand·bag /ˈsan(d)ˌbag/ ▶ **n.** a bag filled with sand, typically used for defensive purposes or for protection from flooding.
▶ **v.** (**sandbags, sandbagging, sandbagged**) [with obj.] **1** (usu. as adj. **sandbagged**) barricade using sandbags: *boarded-up shopfronts and sandbagged doorways.*
2 hit or fell with or as if with a blow from a sandbag. ■ coerce; bully.
3 [no obj.] deliberately underperform in a race or competition to gain an unfair advantage.
– DERIVATIVES **sand·bag·ger n.**

sand·bank /ˈsan(d)ˌbaNGk/ ▶ **n.** a deposit of sand forming a shallow area in the sea or a river.

sand·bar /ˈsan(d)ˌbär/ ▶ **n.** a long, narrow sandbank, esp. at the mouth of a river.

sand bath ▶ **n.** a container of heated sand, used in a laboratory to supply uniform heating.

sand·blast /ˈsan(d)ˌblast/ ▶ **v.** [with obj.] roughen or clean (a surface) with a jet of sand driven by compressed air or steam.
▶ **n.** such a jet of sand.
– DERIVATIVES **sand·blast·er n.**

sand·box /ˈsan(d)ˌbäks/ ▶ **n. 1** a shallow box or hollow in the ground partly filled with sand for children to play in. ■ historical a perforated container for sprinkling sand onto wet ink in order to dry it. ■ Computing a virtual space in which new or untested software can be run securely.
2 (also **sandbox tree**) a tropical American tree whose seed cases were formerly used to hold sand for blotting ink. ● *Hura crepitans*, family Euphorbiaceae.

Sand·burg /ˈsan(d)ˌbərg/, Carl (1878–1967), US poet and biographer. His poetry is collected in *Chicago Poems* (1915), *Smoke and Steel* (1920), *Complete Poems* (1950), and *Honey and Salt* (1963). He is also noted for his biography of Abraham Lincoln, written in six volumes (*Abraham Lincoln: The Prairie Years*, two volumes, and *Abraham Lincoln: The War Years*, four volumes) between 1926 and 1939.

sand cas·tle (also **sandcastle**) ▶ **n.** a model of a castle built out of sand, typically by children.

sand cat ▶ **n.** a small wild cat with a plain yellow to grayish coat, a dark-ringed tail, and large eyes, of the deserts of North Africa and southwestern Asia. ● *Felis margarita*, family Felidae.

sand cher·ry ▶ **n.** a dwarf North American wild cherry. ● Genus *Prunus*, family Rosaceae: several species, in particular *P. depressa* and *P. pumila*. ■ the fruit of this tree.

sand crab ▶ **n.** a crab that lives on or burrows in sand, esp. one related to fiddler and ghost crabs. ● Genus *Uca*, family Ocypodidae.

sand crack ▶ **n.** a vertical fissure in the wall of a horse's hoof, originating at the top of the hoof.

sand dab ▶ **n.** a small flatfish that is found in the Pacific coastal waters of America. ● Genus *Citharichthys*, family Bothidae: several species. ■ this fish as food. ■ another term for WINDOWPANE (sense 2).

sand dol·lar ▶ **n.** a flattened sea urchin that lives partly buried in sand, feeding on detritus. ● Order Clypeasteroida, class Echinoidea: several genera and species, including the **common sand dollar** (*Echinarachnius parma*) found mostly along the coasts of North America and Japan.

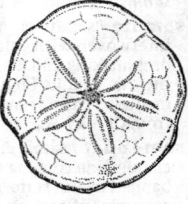

common sand dollar

sand eel ▶ **n.** a small elongated marine fish that lives in shallow waters of the northern hemisphere, often found burrowing in the sand. ● Family Ammodytidae: several genera and species, including the European *Ammodytes tobianus*.

sand·er /ˈsandər/ ▶ **n.** a power tool used for smoothing a surface with sandpaper or other abrasive material.

sand·er·ling /ˈsandərliNG/ ▶ **n.** a small migratory sandpiper of northern Eurasia and Canada, typically

seen running after receding waves on the beach. ● *Calidris alba*, family Scolopacidae.
– ORIGIN early 17th cent.: of unknown origin.

San·ders[1], (Colonel) Harland David (1890–1980), US entrepreneur. He founded Kentucky Fried Chicken (now called KFC), perfecting his secret chicken recipe in 1939 and selling the first franchise in 1952.

San·ders[2], Lawrence (1920–98), US writer. He wrote mostly mysteries and thriller novels such as *The Dream Lover* (1978), *The Seventh Commandment* (1991), and *Guilty Pleasures* (1998). He also wrote some series of novels that featured characters such as Arch McNally (a playboy private eye) and Edward X. Delaney (a retired chief of detectives in New York City).

sand·ers /ˈsandərz/ (also **sanderswood**) ▶ **n.** the timber of the red sandalwood, from which a red dye is obtained. ● This timber is obtained from *Pterocarpus santalinus*, family Leguminosae.
– ORIGIN Middle English: from Old French *sandre*, variant of *sandle* 'sandalwood.'

sand fil·ter ▶ **n.** a filter used in water purification and consisting of layers of sand arranged with coarseness of texture increasing downward.

sand·fish /ˈsan(d)ˌfisʜ/ ▶ **n.** (pl. **same** or **sandfishes**) **1** a small marine fish with fringed lips that burrows in the sand, in particular: ● an elongated Australian fish (*Crapatulus arenarius*, family Leptoscopidae). ● a North Pacific fish (*Trichodon trichodon*, family Trichodontidae).
2 (**belted sandfish**) a small sea bass that lives only in shallow inshore waters around Florida. ● *Serranus subligarius*, family Serranidae.

sand flea ▶ **n. 1** another term for BEACH FLEA.
2 another term for CHIGOE.

sand·fly /ˈsan(d)ˌflī/ ▶ **n.** (pl. **sandflies**) **1** a small, hairy, biting fly of tropical and subtropical regions that transmits a number of diseases, including leishmaniasis. ● Subfamily Phlebotominae, family Psychodidae: several genera, in particular *Phlebotomus*.
2 Austral. another term for BLACK FLY (sense 2).

sand fox ▶ **n.** a small fox with long ears and a thick coat, living in desert and steppe areas from Morocco to Afghanistan. ● *Vulpes rueppellii*, family Canidae.

sand·glass /ˈsan(d)ˌglas/ ▶ **n.** an hourglass measuring a fixed amount of time (not necessarily one hour).

sand·grouse /ˈsan(d)ˌgrous/ ▶ **n.** (pl. **same**) a seed-eating ground-dwelling bird with brownish plumage, allied to the pigeons and found in the deserts and arid regions of the Old World. ● Family Pteroclididae, genera *Pterocles* and *Syrrhaptes*: several species.

san·dhi /ˈsandē, ˈsän-/ ▶ **n.** Phonetics the process whereby the form of a word changes as a result of its position in an utterance (e.g., the change from *a* to *an* before a vowel).
– ORIGIN from Sanskrit *saṃdhi* 'putting together.'

sand·hill crane /ˈsandˌhil/ ▶ **n.** a chiefly migratory North American crane with grayish plumage and a red crown. ● *Grus canadensis*, family Gruidae.

Sand·hills /ˈsandˈhilz/ **1** (also **Sand Hills**) a line of low, sandy hills that lies across North and South Carolina and Georgia, at the boundary of the coastal plain and the Piedmont.
2 a large plains area in west central Nebraska, noted as a ranching district.

sand·hog /ˈsan(d)ˌhôg, -ˌhäg/ ▶ **n.** a person who does construction work underground or under water, such as laying foundations or building a tunnel.

sand hop·per /ˈsandˌhäpər/ ▶ **n.** another term for BEACH FLEA.

San·di·a Moun·tains /sanˈdēə/ a range in central New Mexico that rises to 10,678 feet (3,255 m) at Sandia Peak, near Albuquerque.

San Di·e·go /ˌsan dēˈāgō/ an industrial city and naval port on the Pacific coast of southern California, just north of the US-Mexico border; pop. 1,279,329 (est. 2008). It was founded as a mission in 1769.

San·di·nis·ta /ˌsandəˈnēstə/ ▶ **n.** a member of a left-wing Nicaraguan political organization, the Sandinista National Liberation Front (FSLN), which came to power in 1979 after overthrowing the dictator Anastasio Somoza. Opposed during most of their period of rule by the US-backed Contras, the Sandinistas were voted out of office in 1990.
– ORIGIN named after a similar organization founded by the nationalist leader Augusto César *Sandino* (1893–1934).

san·di·ver /ˈsandəvər/ ▶ **n.** a scum that forms on molten glass.
– ORIGIN late Middle English: apparently from Old French *suin de verre* 'exudation from glass,' from *suer* 'to sweat' + *verre* 'glass.'

S & L ▶ **abbr.** savings and loan.

sand lance ▶ **n.** another term for SAND EEL.

sand liz·ard ▶ **n.** a small, ground-dwelling Old World lizard favoring heathland or sandy areas. ● *Lacerta agilis* (of Eurasia), and genus *Pedioplanis* (of Africa), family Lacertidae.

sand·lot /ˈsan(d)ˌlät/ ▶ **n.** a piece of unoccupied land used by children for games. ■ [as modifier] denoting or relating to sports played by amateurs: *sandlot baseball*.

S & M ▶ **abbr.** ■ sadomasochism. ■ (in the insurance industry) stock and machinery.

sand·man /ˈsan(d)ˌman/ ▶ **n.** (**the sandman**) a fictional man supposed to make children sleep by sprinkling sand in their eyes.

sand mar·tin ▶ **n.** a gregarious swallowlike bird with dark brown and white plumage, excavating nest holes in sandy banks and cliffs near water. ● Genus *Riparia*, family Hirundinidae: three species, in particular the widespread *R. riparia* (**bank swallow**).

S & P 500 ▶ **abbr.** Finance Standard & Poor's 500.

sand paint·ing ▶ **n.** an American Indian ceremonial art form, important among the Navajo and Pueblo peoples, using colored sands, used esp. in connection with healing ceremonies. ■ an example of this art form.

sand·pa·per /ˈsan(d)ˌpāpər/ ▶ **n.** paper with sand or another abrasive stuck to it, used for smoothing or polishing woodwork or other surfaces. ■ used to refer to something that feels rough or has a very rough surface.
▶ **v.** [with obj.] smooth with sandpaper.
– DERIVATIVES **sand·pa·per·y adj.**

sand·pi·per /ˈsan(d)ˌpīpər/ ▶ **n.** a wading bird with a long bill and typically long legs, nesting on the ground near water and frequenting coastal areas on migration. ● Family Scolopacidae (the **sandpiper family**): several genera, esp. *Calidris*, *Tringa*, and *Actitis*, and numerous species, including the **western sandpiper** (*C. mauri*), which breeds on the seashores of Alaska and winters from the southern US to Peru, and the **spotted sandpiper** (*A. macularia*), which prefers lakes and streams and is the most widespread North American sandpiper. The sandpiper family also includes the godwits, curlews, redshanks, turnstones, phalaropes, woodcock, snipe, and ruff.

western sandpiper

sand·pit /ˈsan(d)ˌpit/ ▶ **n.** a quarry from which sand is excavated.

sand point well ▶ **n.** a well consisting of a pipe with a solid steel point and lateral perforations near the end, which is driven into the earth until groundwater is reached, when a suction pump is applied to the upper end.

sand shark ▶ **n.** a voracious, brown-spotted shark of tropical Atlantic waters. ● *Odontaspis taurus*, family Odontaspididae. ■ any of a number of mainly harmless rays, dogfish, and sharks found in shallow coastal waters.

sand spur·rey ▶ **n.** see SPURREY.

sand star·gaz·er ▶ **n.** see STARGAZER (sense 2).

sand·stone /ˈsan(d)ˌstōn/ ▶ **n.** sedimentary rock consisting of sand or quartz grains cemented together, typically red, yellow, or brown in color.

sand·storm /ˈsan(d)ˌstôrm/ ▶ **n.** a strong wind carrying clouds of sand with it, esp. in a desert.

sand ta·ble ▶ **n.** a relief model in sand used to explain military tactics and plan campaigns.

San·dus·ky /sənˈdəskē, san-/ an industrial port city in northern Ohio, on Lake Erie at Sandusky Bay; pop. 25,688 (est. 2008).

sand wasp ▶ **n.** a digger wasp that excavates its burrow in sandy soil and then catches prey with which to furnish it. Sand wasps typically have an abdomen with a very long and slender "waist." ● Subfamily Sphecinae, family Sphecidae: *Ammophila* and other genera.

sand wedge ▶ **n.** Golf a heavy, lofted iron with a flange on the bottom, used for hitting the ball out of sand.

Sand·wich /ˈsan(d)wicʜ/ a town in southeastern Massachusetts, on Cape Cod, a resort with a history of glassmaking; pop. 20,129 (est. 2008).

sand·wich /ˈsanˌ(d)wicʜ/ ▶ **n.** an item of food consisting of two pieces of bread with meat, cheese, or other filling between them, eaten as a light meal: *a ham sandwich*. ■ something that is constructed like or has the form of a sandwich.
▶ **v.** [with obj.] (usu. **be sandwiched between**) insert or squeeze (someone or something) between two other people or things, typically in a restricted space or so as to be uncomfortable: *the girl was sandwiched between two burly men in the back of the car*.
– ORIGIN mid 18th cent.: named after the 4th Earl of *Sandwich* (1718–92), an English nobleman said to have eaten food in this form so as not to leave the gaming table.

sand·wich board ▶ **n.** a pair of advertisement boards connected by straps by which they are hung over a person's shoulders.

sand·wich gen·er·a·tion ▶ **n.** a generation of people, typically in their thirties or forties, responsible for bringing up their own children and for the care of their aging parents.

Sand·wich Is·lands former name for HAWAII.

sand·wich tern ▶ **n.** a large crested tern found in both Europe and North and South America. ● *Thalassius sandvicensis*, family Sternidae (or Laridae).
– ORIGIN late 18th cent.: named after *Sandwich*, a town in Kent, England.

sand·wort /ˈsan(d)wərt, -ˌwôrt/ ▶ **n.** a widely distributed low-growing plant of the pink family, typically having small white flowers and growing in dry sandy ground. ● *Arenaria* and other genera, family Caryophyllaceae.

San·dy /ˈsandē/ a city in north central Utah, south of Salt Lake City; pop. 96,660 (est. 2008).

sand·y /ˈsandē/ ▶ **adj.** (**sandier, sandiest**) **1** covered in or consisting mostly of sand: *pine woods and a fine sandy beach*.
2 (esp. of hair) light yellowish brown.
– DERIVATIVES **sand·i·ness n.**, **sand·y·ish adj.**
– ORIGIN Old English *sandig* (see SAND, -Y[1]).

sand yacht ▶ **n.** a wind-driven three-wheeled vehicle with a sail, used for racing on beaches.

San·dy Hook a peninsula in northeastern New Jersey that separates Raritan Bay from the Atlantic Ocean, south of New York City.

sane /sān/ ▶ **adj.** (of a person) of sound mind; not mad or mentally ill: *hard work kept me sane*. ■ (of an undertaking or manner) reasonable; sensible.
– DERIVATIVES **sane·ly adv.**, **sane·ness n.**
– ORIGIN early 17th cent.: from Latin *sanus* 'healthy.'

San Fer·nan·do Val·ley /ˌsan fərˈnandō/ (popularly *the Valley*) an irrigated district northwest of downtown Los Angeles in California.

San·fi·lip·po's syn·drome /ˌsanfəˈlipōz/ ▶ **n.** Medicine a defect in metabolism similar to Hurler's syndrome.
– ORIGIN 1960s: named after Sylvester J. *Sanfilippo*, 20th-cent. US physician.

San·ford[1] /ˈsanfərd/ **1** a resort and commercial city in north central Florida; pop. 50,634 (est. 2008).
2 a town in southern Maine, a southwestern suburb of Portland; pop. 21,156 (est. 2008).

San·ford[2], Edward Terry (1865–1930), US Supreme Court associate justice 1923–30. Appointed to the Court by President Harding, he was considered a liberal although he sometimes held more conservative views regarding civil rights.

San·for·ized /ˈsanfəˌrīzd/ ▶ **adj.** trademark (of cotton or other fabrics) preshrunk by a controlled compressive process; meeting certain standards of washing shrinkage.
– ORIGIN 1930s: from the name of *Sanford* L. Cluett (1874–1968), the US inventor of the process.

San Fran·cis·co /ˌsan frənˈsiskō/ a city and seaport in western California, on the coast, on a peninsula between the Pacific Ocean and San Francisco Bay; pop. 808,976 (est. 2008). The city suffered severe damage from earthquakes in 1906 and in 1989.
– DERIVATIVES **San Fran·cis·can** /-kən/ **n. & adj.**

San Fran·cis·co Peaks a mountain group in northern Arizona, north of Flagstaff. It includes Humphreys Peak, which at 12,633 feet (3,851 m) is the highest point in the state.

sang /sanɢ/ past of SING.

San Ga·bri·el /san ˈgābrēəl/ a city in southwestern California, east of Los Angeles; pop. 40,445 (est. 2008).

San Ga·bri·el Moun·tains a range in southern California, north of (and partly in) the city of Los Angeles. Mount San Antonio, at 10,080 feet (3,105 m), is the high point. The Mount Wilson observatory is here.

PRONUNCIATION KEY ə *ago, up*; ər *over, fur*; a *hat*; ā *ate*; ä *car*; e *let*; ē *see*; i *fit*; ī *by*; NG *sing*; ō *go*; ô *law, for*; oi *toy*; o͝o *good*; o͞o *goo*; ou *out*; TH *thin*; TH *then*; ZH *vision*

S

san·gam /ˈsəNGgəm/ ▶ **n.** Indian a confluence of rivers, esp. that of the Ganges and Jumna at Allahabad.
– ORIGIN from Sanskrit *saṃgama.*

san·ga·ree /ˌsaNGgəˈrē/ ▶ **n.** a cold drink of wine mixed with water and spices.
– ORIGIN from Spanish *sangría* (see SANGRIA).

sang-de-boeuf /ˌsäNG də ˈbəf/ ▶ **n.** a deep red color, typically found on old Chinese porcelain.
– ORIGIN French, literally 'ox blood.'

Sang·er[1] /ˈsaNGər/, Frederick (1918–), English biochemist. He determined the complete amino-acid sequence of insulin in 1955 and established the complete nucleotide sequence of a viral DNA in 1977. Nobel Prize for Chemistry (1958 and 1980).

Sang·er[2], Margaret (Higgins) (1883–1966), US birth-control campaigner. Her experiences as a nurse prompted her to distribute the pamphlet *Family Limitation* in 1914 and to found the first US birth-control clinic in 1916. She founded the American Birth Control League in 1921 and became the first president of the International Planned Parenthood Federation in 1953.

Margaret Sanger

sang·froid /säNGˈfrwä/ ▶ **n.** composure or coolness, sometimes excessive, as shown in danger or under trying circumstances.
– ORIGIN mid 18th cent.: from French *sang-froid,* literally 'cold blood.'

san·gha /ˈsəNG(g)ə/ ▶ **n.** the Buddhist community of monks, nuns, novices, and laity.
– ORIGIN from Sanskrit *saṃgha* 'community.'

San·gio·vese /ˌsanjōˈvāzē/ ▶ **n.** a variety of black wine grape used in making Chianti and other Italian red wines. ■ a red wine made from this grape.
– ORIGIN Italian.

san·grail /saNGˈgrāl/ (also **sangreal**) ▶ **n.** another term for GRAIL (sense 1).
– ORIGIN late Middle English: from Old French *saint graal* 'Holy Grail.'

San·gre de Cris·to Moun·tains /ˌsaNGgrē də ˈkristō/ a range in southern Colorado and northern New Mexico, an extension of the Front Range of the Rocky Mountains. The Pecos and Canadian rivers rise here.

san·gri·a /saNGˈgrēə/ ▶ **n.** a Spanish drink of red wine mixed with lemonade, fruit, and spices.
– ORIGIN Spanish, literally 'bleeding'; compare with SANGAREE.

S

san·gui·nar·y /ˈsaNGgwəˌnerē/ ▶ **adj.** chiefly archaic involving or causing much bloodshed.
– ORIGIN Middle English (in the sense 'relating to blood'): from Latin *sanguinarius,* from *sanguis, sanguin-* 'blood.'

san·guine /ˈsaNGgwin/ ▶ **adj. 1** optimistic or positive, esp. in an apparently bad or difficult situation: *he is sanguine about prospects for the global economy.* ■ (in medieval science and medicine) of or having the constitution associated with the predominance of blood among the bodily humors, supposedly marked by a ruddy complexion and an optimistic disposition. ■ archaic (of the complexion) florid; ruddy.
2 literary & Heraldry blood-red.
3 archaic bloody or bloodthirsty.
▶ **n.** a blood-red color. ■ a deep red-brown crayon or pencil containing iron oxide. ■ Heraldry a blood-red stain used in blazoning.
– DERIVATIVES **san·guine·ly adv., san·guine·ness n.**
– ORIGIN Middle English: from Old French *sanguin(e)* 'blood-red,' from Latin *sanguineus* 'of blood,' from *sanguis, sanguin-* 'blood.'

San·hed·rin /sanˈhedrən, -ˈhēdrin, sän-/ the highest court of justice and the supreme council in ancient Jerusalem.
– ORIGIN from late Hebrew *sanhedrin,* from Greek *sunedrion* 'council,' from *sun-* 'with' + *hedra* 'seat.'

San·i·bel Is·land /ˈsanəbəl/ a resort island in southwestern Florida, southwest of Fort Myers, noted for its seashells.

san·i·cle /ˈsanikəl/ ▶ **n.** a plant of the parsley family that has burrlike fruit. ● Genus *Sanicula,* family Umbelliferae: several species, in particular the Eurasian **wood sanicle** (*S. europaea*).
– ORIGIN late Middle English: via Old French from medieval Latin *sanicula,* perhaps from Latin *sanus* 'healthy.'

san·i·dine /ˈsaniˌdēn/ ▶ **n.** a glassy mineral of the alkali feldspar group, typically occurring as tabular crystals.
– ORIGIN early 19th cent.: from Greek *sanis, sanid-* 'board' + -INE[4].

sanit. ▶ **abbr.** ■ sanitary. ■ sanitation.

san·i·tar·i·an /ˌsaniˈte(ə)rēən/ ▶ **n.** chiefly archaic an official responsible for public health or a person in favor of public health reform.
– ORIGIN mid 19th cent.: from SANITARY + -IAN.

san·i·tar·i·um /ˌsaniˈte(ə)rēəm/ ▶ **n.** (pl. **sanitariums** or **sanitaria** /-ˈte(ə)rēə/) an establishment for the medical treatment of people who are convalescing or have a chronic illness.
– ORIGIN mid 19th cent.: pseudo-Latin, from Latin *sanitas* 'health.'

san·i·tar·y /ˈsaniˌterē/ ▶ **adj.** of or relating to the conditions that affect hygiene and health, esp. the supply of sewage facilities and clean drinking water: *a sanitary engineer.* ■ hygienic and clean: *the most convenient and sanitary way to get rid of food waste from your kitchen.*
– DERIVATIVES **san·i·tar·i·ly** /-ˌterəlē/ **adv., san·i·tar·i·ness n.**
– ORIGIN mid 19th cent.: from French *sanitaire,* from Latin *sanitas* 'health,' from *sanus* 'healthy.'

san·i·tar·y nap·kin ▶ **n.** an absorbent pad worn by women to absorb menstrual blood.

san·i·ta·tion /ˌsaniˈtāSHən/ ▶ **n.** conditions relating to public health, esp. the provision of clean drinking water and adequate sewage disposal.
– ORIGIN mid 19th cent.: formed irregularly from SANITARY.

san·i·tize /ˈsaniˌtīz/ ▶ **v.** [with obj.] make clean and hygienic: *new chemicals for sanitizing a pool.* ■ (usu. **be sanitized**) derogatory alter (something regarded as less acceptable) so as to make it more palatable: *lawyers sanitized documents that could have exposed the company to lawsuits.*
– DERIVATIVES **san·i·ti·za·tion** /ˌsanətəˈzāSHən/ **n., san·i·tiz·er n.**

san·i·ty /ˈsanitē/ ▶ **n.** the ability to think and behave in a normal and rational manner; sound mental health: *I began to doubt my own sanity.* ■ reasonable and rational behavior.
– ORIGIN late Middle English (in the sense 'health'): from Latin *sanitas* 'health,' from *sanus* 'healthy.' Current senses date from the early 17th cent.

San Ja·cin·to Riv·er /ˌsan jəˈsinˌtō/ a river in southeastern Texas that flows into Galveston Bay east of Houston. The 1836 battle that won Texas independence from Mexico was fought on its bank.

San Joa·quin Riv·er /ˌsan wäˈkēn/ a river that flows for 350 miles (560 km) from south central California to join the Sacramento River and enter San Francisco Bay.

San Joa·quin Val·ley fe·ver ▶ **n.** informal term for COCCIDIOIDOMYCOSIS.

San Jo·se /ˌsan (h)ōˈzā/ a city in western California, south of San Francisco Bay; pop. 948,279 (est. 2008). It lies in the Santa Clara valley, known as Silicon Valley, a center of the electronics industries.

San Jo·sé /ˌsan (h)ōˈzā ˌsän hôˈsā/ the capital and chief port of Costa Rica; pop. 350,535 (2007).

San Juan /sanˈ(h)wän, sän ˈhwän/ the capital and chief port of Puerto Rico, on the northern coast of the island; pop. 426,600 (est. 2006).

San Juan Cap·is·tra·no /san ˈwän ˌkapəˈstränō/ a city in southwestern California, between Los Angeles and San Diego, the site of a 1776 mission to which migrating swallows return each March 19; pop. 34,793 (est. 2008).

San Juan Hill a hill near Santiago de Cuba, in eastern Cuba, the scene of a July 1898 battle during the Spanish-American War.

San Juan Is·lands an island group in northwestern Washington, north of Puget Sound and south of the Strait of Georgia. San Juan and Orcas are the largest islands in the group.

San Juan Moun·tains a range of the Rocky Mountains in southwestern Colorado and northern New Mexico, the source of the Rio Grande.

sank /saNGk/ past of SINK[1].

San Le·an·dro /ˌsan lēˈandrō/ a city in north central California, southeast of Oakland; pop. 77,880 (est. 2008).

San Lu·is Obis·po /san ˌlo͞oəs əˈbispō/ a city in west central California, northwest of Los Angeles; pop. 43,636 (est. 2008).

San Lu·is Po·to·sí /sän lo͞oˈēs ˌpôtôˈsē/ a state in central Mexico. ■ its capital; pop. 685,934 (2005).

San Mar·cos /san ˈmärkəs/ **1** a city in southwestern California, north of San Diego; pop. 79,114 (est. 2008).
2 a city in south central Texas, south of Austin; pop. 52,927 (est. 2008).

San Ma·ri·no /ˌsan məˈrēnō/ a republic that forms a small enclave in Italy, near Rimini; pop. 30,200 (est. 2009); capital, the town of San Marino; language, Italian (official).

> It is perhaps Europe's oldest state, claiming to have been independent almost continuously since its founding in the 4th century.

– ORIGIN said to be named after *Marino,* a Dalmatian stonecutter who fled there to escape the persecution of Christians under Diocletian.

San Mar·tín /ˌsan märˈtēn/, José de (1778–1850), Argentine soldier and statesman. After assisting in the liberation of Argentina from Spanish rule 1812–13, he went on to aid in the liberation of Chile 1817–18 and of Peru 1820–24.

San Ma·te·o /ˌsan məˈtāō/ a commercial and industrial city in north central California, on San Francisco Bay, south of San Francisco; pop. 92,256 (est. 2008).

sann·ya·si /sənˈyäsē/ (also **sanyasi** or **sannyasin**) ▶ **n.** (pl. **same**) a Hindu religious mendicant.
– ORIGIN based on Sanskrit *saṃnyāsin* 'laying aside, ascetic,' from *sam* 'together' + *ni* 'down' + *as* 'throw.'

San Pe·dro Su·la /sän ˈpedrō ˈso͞olä/ a city in northern Honduras, near the Caribbean coast; pop. 623,100 (est. 2008).

San Quen·tin /san ˈkwentn/ a site in northwestern California, in Marin County, across the Golden Gate from San Francisco, home to a well-known state prison.

San Ra·fael /ˌsan rəˈfel/ a city in northwestern California, on San Rafael Bay, north of San Francisco; pop. 55,602 (est. 2008).

sans /sanz/ ▶ **prep.** literary, humorous without: *flavorful vegetarian dishes sans meat, eggs, or milk.*
– ORIGIN Middle English: from Old French *sanz,* from a variant of Latin *sine* 'without,' influenced by Latin *absentia* 'in the absence of.'

san·sa /ˈsansə/ ▶ **n.** another term for THUMB PIANO.
– ORIGIN based on Arabic *ṣanj* 'cymbal.'

San Sal·va·dor /san ˈsalvəˌdôr, sän ˌsälväˈdôr/ **1** an island in the southeastern Bahamas, believed to be the site where Columbus first landed in the New World in 1492; pop. 1,700 (est. 2009).
2 the capital of El Salvador; pop. 316,090 (2007).

sans-cu·lotte /ˌsanz k(y)o͞oˈlät/ ▶ **n.** a lower-class Parisian republican in the French Revolution. ■ an extreme republican or revolutionary.
– DERIVATIVES **sans-cu·lot·tism** /k(y)əˈlätizəm/ **n.**
– ORIGIN French, literally 'without breeches.'

San Se·bas·tián /ˌsan səˈbasCHən, ˌsän sebästˈyän/ a port and resort in northern Spain, on the Bay of Biscay, close to the border with France; pop. 184,248 (2008).

san·sei /ˈsänsā/ ▶ **n.** (pl. **same**) a person born in the US or Canada whose grandparents were immigrants from Japan. Compare with NISEI and ISSEI.
– ORIGIN 1940s: Japanese, from *san* 'third' + *sei* 'generation.'

san·se·vi·e·ri·a /ˌsansəvēˈi(ə)rēə, -səˈvi(ə)rēə/ (also **sanseveria**) ▶ **n.** a plant of the genus *Sansevieria* in the agave family, esp. (in gardening) mother-in-law's tongue.
– ORIGIN modern Latin, named after Raimondo di Sangro (1710–71), Prince of *Sanseviero* (now Sansevero), Italy.

San Sim·e·on /san ˈsimēən/ a community in west central California, on the Pacific coast, site of the Hearst estate that is a popular tourist destination.

San·skrit /ˈsanˌskrit/ ▶ **n.** an ancient Indic language of India, in which the Hindu scriptures and classical Indian epic poems are written and from which many northern Indian languages are derived.
▶ **adj.** of or relating to this language.

> Sanskrit was spoken in India roughly 1200–400 BC, and continues in use as a language of religion and scholarship. It is written from left to right in the Devanagari script. The suggestion by **Sir William Jones** (1746–94) of its common origin with Latin and Greek was a major advance in the development of historical linguistics.

– DERIVATIVES **San·skrit·ic** /san'skritik/ **adj.**, **San·skrit·ist** /'san,skritist/ **n.**
– ORIGIN from Sanskrit *saṃskṛta* 'composed, elaborated,' from *sam* 'together' + *kṛ* 'make' + the past participle ending *-ta*.

sans ser·if /,san(z) 'serəf/ Printing ▶ **n.** a style of type without serifs.
▶ **adj.** without serifs.
– ORIGIN mid 19th cent.: apparently from French *sans* 'without' + SERIF.

sant /sənt/ ▶ **n.** Hinduism & Sikhism a saint.
– ORIGIN from Hindi *santah* 'venerable men.'

San·ta An·a /,säntə 'änə/ **1** a city in El Salvador, close to the border with Guatemala; pop. 245,421 (2007).
2 /,säntə 'änə/ a volcano in El Salvador, southwest of the city of Santa Ana. It rises to a height of 7,730 feet (2,381 m).
3 /,santə 'anə/ a city in southern California, southeast of Los Angeles; pop. 339,130. The region gives its name to the hot dry winds that blow from the Santa Ana Mountains on the east across the coastal plain of southern California.

San·ta An·na /,santə 'anə/, Antonio López de (1794–1876), Mexican general and political leader. A militant revolutionary, he controlled Mexico as its president 1833–36, its dictator 1844–45, and again its president 1853–55. In most of the interim years, he was essentially still in control and engaged in several military actions against the US, including his victory at the Alamo 1836 and his defeats at San Jacinto 1836 and Buena Vista 1847.

San·ta Bar·ba·ra /'santə 'bärbrə/ a resort city in California, on the Pacific coast, northwest of Los Angeles; pop. 86,093 (est. 2008).

San·ta Bar·ba·ra Is·lands /,santə 'bärb(ə)rə/ an island group in southwestern California, off the Pacific coast. Santa Catalina is a tourist destination. Also called CHANNEL ISLANDS.

San·ta Cat·a·li·na one of the Santa Barbara Islands. Also called CATALINA. See SANTA BARBARA ISLANDS.

San·ta Cla·ra /,santə 'klarə, 'kle(ə)rə/ a city in north central California, a longtime fruit-producing center now at the heart of Silicon Valley; pop. 110,200 (est. 2008).

San·ta Cla·ri·ta /,santə klə'rētə/ a city in southwestern California, northwest of Los Angeles; pop. 169,500 (est. 2008).

San·ta Claus /'santə ,klôz/ (also **Santa**) an imaginary figure said to bring presents for children on Christmas. He is conventionally pictured as a jolly old man from the far north, with a long white beard and red garments trimmed with white fur. See also NICHOLAS, ST.
– ORIGIN late 18th cent.: originally a US usage, alteration of Dutch dialect *Sante Klaas* 'St. Nicholas.'

San·ta Cruz 1 /,santə 'kro͞oz, ,säntä 'kro͞os/ a city in central Bolivia; pop. 1,561,061 (2009).
2 /,santə 'kro͞oz, ,säntä 'kro͞o*TH*/ a port and the chief city of the island of Tenerife, in the Canary Islands; pop. 192,000. Full name **Santa Cruz de Tenerife**.
3 a city in west central California, on Monterey Bay; pop. 56,124 (est. 2008).

San·ta Cruz Is·lands an island group in the southeastern Solomon Islands, in the southwestern Pacific Ocean, scene of an October 1942 World War II naval battle between US and Japanese forces.

San·ta Fe /'santə ,fā, ,santə 'fā/ (also **Santa Fé** /,säntä 'fā/) **1** a city in northern Argentina, on the Salado River near its confluence with the Paraná River; pop. 506,300 (est. 2009).
2 the capital of New Mexico, in the north central part of the state; pop. 71,831 (est. 2008). It was founded as a mission by the Spanish in 1610. From 1821 until 1880, it served as the terminus of the Santa Fe Trail. Taken by US forces in 1846 during the Mexican War, it became the capital of New Mexico in 1912.

San·ta Fé de Bo·go·tá official name for BOGOTÁ.

San·ta Fe Trail a historic route, established in the 1820s, from St. Louis in Missouri to Santa Fe in New Mexico. Merchants and settlers used it until the Santa Fe Railroad was built in the 1870s.

San·ta Lu·ci·a Range /,santə lo͞o'sēə/ a range in west central California, part of the Coast Ranges.

San·ta Ma·ri·a /,santə mə'rēə/ a commercial city in southwestern California; pop. 86,356 (est. 2008).

San·ta Mon·i·ca /'santə 'mänikə/ a resort city on the coast of southwestern California, west of Los Angeles; pop. 87,664 (est. 2008).

San·tan·der /,säntän'der/ a port in northern Spain, on the Bay of Biscay, north of Madrid; pop. 182,302 (2008).

San·ta Ro·sa /,santə 'rōzə/ a commercial city in northwestern California, north of San Francisco; pop. 155,796 (est. 2008).

San·ta·ya·na /,säntə'yänä/, George (1863–1952), Spanish philosopher and writer; born *Jorge Augustin Nicolás Ruiz de Santayana*. His works include *The Realms of Being* (1924) and *The Last Puritan* (1935).

San·tee Riv·er /san'tē/ a river that flows for 140 miles (230 km) through eastern South Carolina to the Atlantic Ocean.

San·te·ri·a /,santə'rēə/ (also **Santería**) ▶ **n.** a pantheistic Afro-Cuban religious cult developed from the beliefs and customs of the Yoruba people and incorporating some elements of the Catholic religion.
– ORIGIN Spanish, literally 'holiness.'

san·te·ro /sän'terō/ ▶ **n.** (pl. **santeros**) **1** (in Mexico and Spanish-speaking areas of the southwestern US) a person who makes religious images.
2 a priest of the Santeria religious cult.
– ORIGIN Spanish.

San·ti·a·go /,säntē'ägō/ the capital of Chile, west of the Andes, in the central part of the country; pop. 4,985,900 (est. 2008).

San·ti·a·go de Com·pos·te·la /də ,kämpə'stelə/ a city in northwestern Spain; pop. 94,339 (2008). The remains of St. James the Great are said to have been brought there after his death.

San·ti·a·go de Cu·ba /də 'kyo͞obə, de 'ko͞obä/ a port on the coast of southeastern Cuba, the second largest city on the island; pop. 426,679 (2008).

san·tim /'säntim/ ▶ **n.** (pl. **santimi** /-təmē/) a monetary unit of Latvia, equal to one hundredth of a lat.
– ORIGIN from Latvian *santims*, from French *centime* + the Latvian masculine ending *-s*.

san·to /'säntō, 'sän-/ ▶ **n.** (pl. **santos**) (in Mexico and Spanish-speaking areas of the southwestern US) a religious symbol, esp. a wooden representation of a saint.
– ORIGIN Spanish or Italian.

San·to Do·min·go /'säntō də'miNGgō, 'säntō dô'miNGgō/ the capital of the Dominican Republic, a port on the southern coast; pop. 2,154,000 (est. 2007). From 1936 to 1961, it was called Ciudad Trujillo.

san·to·li·na /,santə'lēnə/ ▶ **n.** a plant of the genus *Santolina* in the daisy family, esp. (in gardening) lavender cotton.
– ORIGIN modern Latin, perhaps an alteration of SANTONICA.

san·ton /säN'tôN/ ▶ **n.** (chiefly in Provence) a figurine adorning a representation of the manger in which Jesus was laid.
– ORIGIN French, from Spanish, from *santo* 'saint.'

san·ton·i·ca /san'tänikə/ ▶ **n.** the dried flower heads of a wormwood plant, containing the drug santonin. ● The plant is *Artemisia cina* (family Compositae) of Turkestan.
– ORIGIN mid 17th cent.: from Latin *Santonica* (*herba*) '(plant) of the Santoni,' referring to a tribe of Aquitania (now AQUITAINE¹).

san·to·nin /'santn-in/ ▶ **n.** Chemistry a toxic crystalline compound present in santonica and related plants, used as an anthelmintic. ● Chem. formula: $C_{15}H_{18}O_3$.
– ORIGIN mid 19th cent.: from SANTONICA + -IN¹.

san·toor /sən'to͝or/ (also **santour**) ▶ **n.** an Indian musical instrument like a dulcimer, played by striking it with a pair of small, spoon-shaped wooden hammers.
– ORIGIN from Arabic *sanṭīr*, alteration of Greek *psaltērion* 'psaltery.'

San·to·ri·ni /,santə'rēnē/ another name for THERA.

San·tos /'santōs, 'sän-/ a port on the coast of Brazil, just southeast of São Paulo; pop. 418,288 (2007).

san·ya·si ▶ **n.** variant spelling of SANNYASI.

São Fran·cis·co /'souN frən'sisko͞o/ a river in eastern Brazil that rises in the state of Minas Gerais and flows north and then east for 1,990 miles (3,200 km) to meet the Atlantic Ocean north of Aracajú.

sao·la /'soulə/ ▶ **n.** a small two-horned mammal discovered in Vietnam in 1992, with similarities to both antelopes and oxen. ● *Pseudoryx nghetinhensis*.
– ORIGIN 1990s: a local name, literally 'spindle horn.'

São Lu·ís /'souN lo͞o'ēs/ a port in northeastern Brazil, on the Atlantic coast; pop. 957,515 (2007).

Saône /sōn/ a river in eastern France that rises in the Vosges Mountains and flows 298 miles (480 km) southwest to join the Rhône River at Lyons.

São Pau·lo /,sou 'poulō ,souN 'poulo͞o/ a state in southern Brazil, on the Atlantic coast. ■ its capital city, the largest city in Brazil and the second largest in South America; pop. 10,886,500 (est. 2007).

São To·mé and Prín·ci·pe /,sou tō'mā and 'prinsəpə, ,souN to͞o'mā/ a country that consists of two main islands and several smaller ones in the Gulf of Guinea; pop. 212,700 (est. 2009); capital, São Tomé; languages, Portuguese (official) and Portuguese Creole.

The islands were settled by Portugal from 1493 and became an overseas province of that country. São Tomé and Príncipe became independent in 1975.

sap¹ /sap/ ▶ **n.** the fluid, chiefly water with dissolved sugars and mineral salts, that circulates in the vascular system of a plant. ■ vigor or energy: *the hot, heady days of youth when the sap was rising*.
▶ **v.** (**saps, sapping, sapped**) [with obj.] gradually weaken or destroy (a person's strength or power): *our energy is being sapped by bureaucrats and politicians*. ■ (**sap someone of**) drain someone of (strength or power): *her illness had sapped her of energy and life*.
– DERIVATIVES **sap·less adj.**
– ORIGIN Old English *sæp*, probably of Germanic origin. The verb (dating from the mid 18th cent.) is often interpreted as a figurative use of the notion "drain the sap from," but is derived originally from the verb SAP², in the sense 'undermine.'

sap² ▶ **n.** historical a tunnel or trench to conceal an assailant's approach to a fortified place.
▶ **v.** (**saps, sapping, sapped**) [no obj.] historical dig a sap or saps. ■ [with obj.] archaic make insecure by removing the foundations of: *a crazy building, sapped and undermined by the rats*. ■ [with obj.] (often as noun **sapping**) Geography undercut by water or glacial action.
– ORIGIN late 16th cent. (as a verb in the sense 'dig a sap or covered trench'): from French *saper*, from Italian *zappare*, from *zappa* 'spade, spadework,' probably from Arabic *sarab* 'underground passage,' or *sabora* 'probe a wound, explore.'

sap³ ▶ **n.** informal a foolish and gullible person: *He fell for it! What a sap!*
– ORIGIN early 19th cent.: abbreviation of dialect *sapskull* 'person with a head like sapwood,' from SAP¹ (in the sense 'sapwood') + SKULL.

sap⁴ informal ▶ **n.** a bludgeon or club.
▶ **v.** (**saps, sapping, sapped**) [with obj.] hit with a bludgeon or club.
– ORIGIN late 19th cent. (as a noun): abbreviation of SAPLING (from which such a club was originally made).

s.ap. ▶ **abbr.** apothecaries' scruple.

sa·pe·le /sə'pēlē/ ▶ **n.** a large, tropical African hardwood tree with reddish-brown timber that resembles mahogany. ● Genus *Entandrophragma*, family Meliaceae.
– ORIGIN early 20th cent.: from the name of a port on the Benin River, Nigeria.

sa·phe·nous /sə'fēnəs/ ▶ **adj.** [attrib.] Anatomy relating to or denoting either of the two large superficial veins in the leg.
– ORIGIN mid 19th cent.: from medieval Latin *saphena* 'vein' + -OUS.

sap·id /'sapid/ ▶ **adj.** having a strong, pleasant taste. ■ (of talk or writing) pleasant or interesting.
– DERIVATIVES **sa·pid·i·ty** /sə'piditē/ **n.**
– ORIGIN early 17th cent.: from Latin *sapidus*, from *sapere* 'to taste.'

sa·pi·ent /'sāpēənt/ ▶ **adj. 1** formal wise, or attempting to appear wise. ■ (chiefly in science fiction) intelligent: *sapient life forms*.
2 of or relating to the human species (*Homo sapiens*): *our sapient ancestors of 40,000 years ago*.
▶ **n.** a human of the species *Homo sapiens*.
– DERIVATIVES **sa·pi·ence n.**, **sa·pi·ent·ly adv.**
– ORIGIN late Middle English: from Old French, or from Latin *sapient-* 'being wise,' from the verb *sapere*.

sa·pi·en·tial /,sāpē'encHəl/ ▶ **adj.** literary of or relating to wisdom.
– ORIGIN late 15th cent.: from Old French, or from ecclesiastical Latin *sapientialis*, from Latin *sapientia* 'wisdom.'

Sa·pir /sə'pi(ə)r/, Edward (1884–1939), US linguistics scholar and anthropologist, born in Germany. One of the founders of American structural linguistics, he carried out important research on American Indian languages and linguistic theory.

Sa·pir–Whorf hy·poth·e·sis /sə'pi(ə)r '(h)wôrf/ **n.** Linguistics a hypothesis, first advanced by Edward Sapir in 1929 and subsequently developed by Benjamin Whorf, that the structure of a language determines a native speaker's perception and categorization of experience.

S

sap·ling /ˈsapliNG/ ▶ **n.** a young tree, esp. one with a slender trunk. ■ literary a young and slender or inexperienced person.
– ORIGIN Middle English: from the noun SAP¹ + -LING.

sap·o·dil·la /ˌsapəˈdilə/ ▶ **n.** a large, evergreen, tropical American tree that has edible fruit and hard, durable wood and yields chicle. ● *Manilkara zapota*, family Sapotaceae. ■ (also **sapodilla plum**) the sweet, brownish, bristly fruit of this tree.
– ORIGIN late 17th cent.: from Spanish *zapotillo*, diminutive of *zapote*, from Nahuatl *tzápotl*.

sap·o·na·ceous /ˌsapəˈnāSHəs/ ▶ **adj.** of, like, or containing soap; soapy.
– ORIGIN early 18th cent.: from modern Latin *saponaceus* (from Latin *sapo, sapon-* 'soap') + -OUS.

sa·pon·i·fy /səˈpänəˌfī/ ▶ **v.** (**saponifies, saponifying, saponified**) [with obj.] Chemistry turn (fat or oil) into soap by reaction with an alkali: (as adj. **saponified**) *saponified vegetable oils*. ■ convert (any ester) into an alcohol and a metal salt by alkaline hydrolysis.
– DERIVATIVES **sa·pon·i·fi·a·ble** adj., **sa·pon·i·fi·ca·tion** /səˌpänəfiˈkāSHən/ n.
– ORIGIN early 19th cent.: from French *saponifier*, from Latin *sapo, sapon-* 'soap.'

sap·o·nin /ˈsapənən/ ▶ **n.** Chemistry a toxic compound that is present in soapwort and makes foam when shaken with water. ■ any of the class of steroid and terpenoid glycosides typified by this, examples of which are used in detergents and foam fire extinguishers.
– ORIGIN mid 19th cent.: from French *saponine*, from Latin *sapo, sapon-* 'soap.'

sap·per /ˈsapər/ ▶ **n.** a military engineer who lays or detects and disarms mines.
– ORIGIN early 17th cent.: from the verb SAP² + -ER¹.

sap·phic /ˈsafik/ ▶ **adj. 1** formal or humorous of or relating to lesbians or lesbianism: *sapphic lovers*.
2 (**Sapphic**) of or relating to Sappho or her poetry.
▶ **plural n.** (**sapphics**) verse in a meter associated with Sappho.
– ORIGIN early 16th cent. (sense 2 of the adjective): from French *saphique*, via Latin from Greek *Sapphikos*, from *Sapphō* (see SAPPHO).

sap·phire /ˈsafˌī(ə)r/ ▶ **n. 1** a transparent precious stone, typically blue, that is a variety of corundum (aluminum oxide). ■ a bright blue color.
2 a small hummingbird with shining blue or violet colors in its plumage and a short tail. ● *Hylocharis* and other genera, family Trochilidae: several species.
– DERIVATIVES **sap·phir·ine** /ˈsafərin, -ˌrēn, -ˌrīn/ adj.
– ORIGIN Middle English: from Old French *safir*, via Latin from Greek *sappheiros*, probably denoting lapis lazuli.

sap·phism /ˈsafizəm/ ▶ **n.** formal or humorous lesbianism.
– ORIGIN late 19th cent.: from SAPPHO + -ISM.

Sap·pho /ˈsafō/ (early 7th century BC), Greek lyric poet who lived on Lesbos. Many of her poems express her affection and love for women and have given rise to her association with female homosexuality.

Sap·po·ro /səˈpôrō/ a city in northern Japan, capital of the island of Hokkaido; pop. 1,874,410 (2007).

sap·py /ˈsapē/ ▶ **adj.** (**sappier, sappiest**) **1** informal excessively sentimental; mawkish.
2 (of a plant) containing a lot of sap.
– DERIVATIVES **sap·pi·ly** /-əlē/ adv., **sap·pi·ness** n.

S

sapro- ▶ **comb. form** Biology relating to putrefaction or decay: *saprogenic*.
– ORIGIN from Greek *sapros* 'putrid.'

sap·ro·gen·ic /ˌsaprōˈjenik/ ▶ **adj.** Biology causing or produced by putrefaction or decay.

sap·ro·leg·nia /ˌsaprəˈlegnēə/ ▶ **n.** an aquatic fungus that can attack the bodies of fish and other aquatic animals. ● Genus *Saprolegnia*, subdivision Mastigomycotina.
– ORIGIN modern Latin, from SAPRO- 'of decay' + Greek *legnon* 'border.'

sa·proph·a·gous /səˈpräfəgəs/ ▶ **adj.** Biology (of an organism) feeding on or obtaining nourishment from decaying organic matter.
– DERIVATIVES **sap·ro·phage** /ˈsaprəˌfāj/ n., **sa·proph·a·gy** /-ˈpräfəjē/ n.

sap·ro·phyte /ˈsaprəˌfīt/ ▶ **n.** Biology a plant, fungus, or microorganism that lives on dead or decaying organic matter.
– DERIVATIVES **sap·ro·phyt·ic** /ˌsaprəˈfitik/ adj., **sap·ro·phyt·i·cal·ly** /-ik(ə)lē/ adv.

sap·ro·troph /ˈsaprəˌtrōf, -ˌträf/ ▶ **n.** Biology an organism that feeds on or derives nourishment from decaying organic matter.
– DERIVATIVES **sap·ro·troph·ic** /ˌsaprəˈtrōfik, -ˈträfik/ adj.
– ORIGIN back-formation from *saprotrophic*.

sap·suck·er /ˈsapˌsəkər/ ▶ **n.** an American woodpecker that pecks rows of small holes in trees and visits them for sap and insects. ● *Sphyrapicus*, family Picidae: four species.

sap·wood /ˈsapˌwo͝od/ ▶ **n.** the soft outer layers of recently formed wood between the heartwood and the bark, containing the functioning vascular tissue.

Saq·qa·ra /səˈkärə/ (also **Sakkara**) a vast necropolis at the ancient Egyptian city of Memphis, with monuments dating from the 3rd millennium BC to the Greco-Roman age, notably a step pyramid that is the first known building made entirely of stone (*c.*2650 BC).

SAR ▶ **abbr.** ■ search and rescue, an emergency service involving the detection and rescue of those who have met with an accident or mishap in dangerous or isolated locations. ■ Special Administrative Region (of the People's Republic of China).

sar·a·band /ˈsarəˌband/ (also **sarabande**) ▶ **n.** a slow, stately Spanish dance in triple time. ■ a piece of music written for such a dance.
– ORIGIN early 17th cent.: from French *sarabande*, from Spanish and Italian *zarabanda*.

Sar·a·cen /ˈsarəsən/ ▶ **n.** an Arab or Muslim, esp. at the time of the Crusades. ■ a nomad of the Syrian and Arabian desert at the time of the Roman Empire.
– DERIVATIVES **Sar·a·cen·ic** /ˌserəˈsenik/ adj.
– ORIGIN Middle English, from Old French *sarrazin*, via late Latin from late Greek *Sarakēnos*, perhaps from Arabic *šarḳī* 'eastern.'

Sar·a·cen's head ▶ **n.** a conventionalized depiction of the head of a Saracen as a heraldic charge or inn sign.

Sar·a·gos·sa /ˌsarəˈgäsə/ a city in northern Spain, capital of Aragon, situated on the Ebro River; pop. 666,129 (2008). Spanish name ZARAGOZA.
– ORIGIN alteration of *Caesaraugusta*, the name given to the ancient settlement on the site, taken by the Romans in the 1st cent. BC.

Sar·ah /ˈse(ə)rə/ (in the Bible) the wife of Abraham and mother of Isaac.

Sa·ra·je·vo /ˌsärəˈyāvō, -ˈyēvō/ the capital of Bosnia and Herzegovina; pop. 304,600 (est. 2008). It was the scene in June 1914 of the assassination of **Archduke Franz Ferdinand** (1863–1914), the heir to the Austrian throne, by a Bosnian Serb named **Gavrilo Princip** —an event that triggered the outbreak of World War I. The city suffered severely from the ethnic conflicts that followed the breakup of Yugoslavia in 1991 and was besieged by Bosnian Serb forces in the surrounding mountains 1992–94.

Sa·ran /səˈran/ (also **Saran Wrap**) ▶ **n.** trademark for POLYVINYL CHLORIDE, esp. as plastic wrap.
– ORIGIN 1940s: of unknown origin.

Sar·a·nac Lakes /ˈsarəˌnak/ a group of resort lakes in northeastern New York, in Adirondack Park, site of a pioneering tuberculosis sanatorium.

sa·ran·gi /ˈsärəNGgē/ ▶ **n.** (pl. **sarangis**) an Indian bowed musical instrument about two feet high, with three or four main strings and up to thirty-five sympathetic strings.
– ORIGIN from Hindi *sāraṅgī*.

Sa·ransk /səˈränsk/ a city in western Russia, capital of the autonomous republic of Mordvinia, south of Nizhni Novgorod; pop. 295,300 (est. 2008).

sa·ra·pe ▶ **n.** variant spelling of SERAPE.

Sar·a·so·ta /ˌsarəˈsōtə/ a resort city in southwestern Florida, on Sarasota Bay off the Gulf of Mexico, long noted as a winter base for circuses; pop. 52,340 (est. 2008).

Sar·a·to·ga, Battle of /ˌsarəˈtōgə/ either of two battles fought in 1777 (September 19 and October 7) during the American Revolution, near the modern city of Saratoga Springs, New York. The defeat of the British in both battles is conventionally regarded as the turning point in the war in favor of the American side.

Sar·a·to·ga Springs a city in eastern New York, north of Albany, a spa noted for horse racing and for two battles fought nearby during the American Revolution; pop. 28,844 (est. 2008).

Sa·ra·tov /səˈrätəf/ a city in southwestern central Russia, on the Volga River, north of Volgograd; pop. 836,100 (est. 2008).

Sa·ra·wak /səˈräwək/ a state of Malaysia that occupies the northwestern part of Borneo; capital, Kuching.

Sar·a·zen /ˈsarəzən/, Gene (1902–99), US golfer; born *Eugene Saraceni*. He was the first player to win all four Grand Slam titles: the US Open 1920, the Professional Golfers' Association championship 1920, the British Open 1932, and the Masters 1935.

SarbOx /ˈsärbäks/ (also **Sarbox**) ▶ **n.** the Sarbanes-Oxley Act, a 2002 Federal law that set new accounting standards for publicly traded companies: [as modifier] *SarbOx compliance*.
– ORIGIN after Paul *Sarbanes* and Michael *Oxley*, the legislators who sponsored the law.

sar·casm /ˈsärˌkazəm/ ▶ **n.** the use of irony to mock or convey contempt: *his voice, hardened by sarcasm, could not hide his resentment*.
– ORIGIN mid 16th cent.: from French *sarcasme*, or via late Latin from late Greek *sarkasmos*, from Greek *sarkazein* 'tear flesh,' in late Greek 'gnash the teeth, speak bitterly' (from *sarx, sark-* 'flesh').

sar·cas·tic /särˈkastik/ ▶ **adj.** marked by or given to using irony in order to mock or convey contempt: *sarcastic comments on their failures | she's witty and sarcastic*.
– DERIVATIVES **sar·cas·ti·cal·ly** /-ik(ə)lē/ adv.
– ORIGIN late 17th cent.: from French *sarcastique*, from *sarcasme* (see SARCASM), on the pattern of pairs such as *enthousiasme, enthousiastique*.

Sar·cee /ˈsärsē/ (also **Sarsi**) ▶ **n.** (pl. **same** or **Sarcees**) **1** a member of an American Indian people of Alberta, Canada.
2 the Athabaskan language of this people.
▶ **adj.** of or relating to this people or their language.
– ORIGIN from Blackfoot *saahsiwa*.

sarce·net /ˈsärsnit/ ▶ **n.** variant spelling of SARSENET.

sar·coid /ˈsärˌkoid/ Medicine ▶ **adj.** [attrib.] relating to, denoting, or suffering from sarcoidosis.
▶ **n.** a granuloma of the type present in sarcoidosis. ■ the condition and symptoms of sarcoidosis: *tissues affected by sarcoid*.
– ORIGIN mid 19th cent. (in the sense 'resembling flesh'): from Greek *sarx, sark-* 'flesh' + -OID.

sar·coid·o·sis /ˌsärˌkoiˈdōsis/ ▶ **n.** a chronic disease of unknown cause characterized by the enlargement of lymph nodes in many parts of the body and the widespread appearance of granulomas derived from the reticuloendothelial system.

sar·co·lem·ma /ˌsärkəˈlemə/ ▶ **n.** Physiology the fine transparent tubular sheath that envelops the fibers of skeletal muscles.
– DERIVATIVES **sar·co·lem·mal** adj.
– ORIGIN mid 19th cent.: from Greek *sarx, sark-* 'flesh' + *lemma* 'husk.'

sar·co·ma /särˈkōmə/ ▶ **n.** (pl. **sarcomas** or **sarcomata** /-mətə/) Medicine a malignant tumor of connective or other nonepithelial tissue.
– DERIVATIVES **sar·co·ma·to·sis** /särˌkōməˈtōsis/ n., **sar·co·ma·tous** /-mətəs/ adj.
– ORIGIN early 19th cent.: modern Latin, from Greek *sarkōma*, from *sarkoun* 'become fleshy,' from *sarx, sark-* 'flesh.'

sar·co·mere /ˈsärkəˌmi(ə)r/ ▶ **n.** Anatomy a structural unit of a myofibril in striated muscle, consisting of a dark band and the nearer half of each adjacent pale band.
– ORIGIN late 19th cent.: from Greek *sarx, sark-* 'flesh' + *meros* 'part.'

sar·co·pe·ni·a /ˌsärkəˈpēnēə/ ▶ **n.** loss of muscle tissue as a natural part of the aging process.
– ORIGIN 1990s: from Greek, literally 'lack of flesh'; coined by Irwin H. Rosenberg of the USDA.

sar·coph·a·gus /särˈkäfəgəs/ ▶ **n.** (pl. **sarcophagi** /-ˌjī/) a stone coffin, typically adorned with a sculpture or inscription and associated with the ancient civilizations of Egypt, Rome, and Greece.
– ORIGIN late Middle English: via Latin from Greek *sarkophagos* 'flesh-consuming,' from *sarx, sark-* 'flesh' + *-phagos* '-eating.'

sar·co·plasm /ˈsärkəˌplazəm/ ▶ **n.** Physiology the cytoplasm of striated muscle cells.
– DERIVATIVES **sar·co·plas·mic** /ˌsärkəˈplazmik/ adj.
– ORIGIN late 19th cent.: from Greek *sarx, sark-* 'flesh' + PLASMA.

sar·cop·tic mange /särˈkäptik/ ▶ **n.** a form of mange caused by the itch mite and tending to affect chiefly the abdomen and hindquarters. Compare with DEMODECTIC MANGE.
– ORIGIN late 19th cent.: *sarcoptic* from the modern Latin genus name *Sarcoptes* (from Greek *sarx, sark-* 'flesh') + -IC.

sar·co·sine /ˈsärkəˌsēn/ ▶ **n.** Biochemistry a crystalline amino acid that occurs in the body as a product of the metabolism of creatine. ● Alternative name: ***N*-methylglycine**; chem. formula: CH_3NHCH_2COOH.
– ORIGIN mid 19th cent.: from Greek *sarx, sark-* 'flesh' + -INE⁴.

sard /särd/ ▶ **n.** a yellow or brownish-red variety of chalcedony.
– ORIGIN late Middle English: from French *sarde* or Latin *sarda*, from Greek *sardios*, probably from *Sardō* 'Sardinia.'

Sar·da·na·pa·lus /ˌsärdnˈäpələs/ the name given by ancient Greek historians to the last king of Assyria (died before 600 BC), portrayed as being notorious

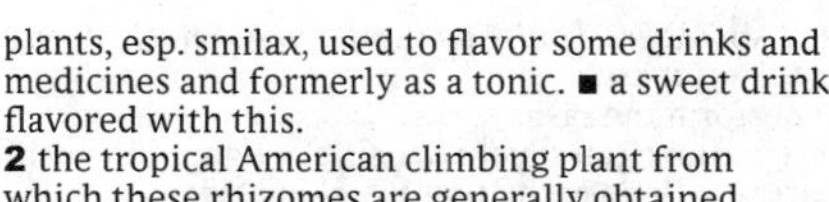

for his wealth and sensuality. It may not represent a specific historical person.

sar·dar /sər'där/ (also **sirdar**) ▶ **n.** chiefly Indian **1** a leader (often used as a proper name).
2 a Sikh (often used as a title or form of address).
– ORIGIN from Persian and Urdu *sar-dār*.

Sar·de·gna /sär'denyə/ Italian name for **SARDINIA**.

sar·dine¹ /sär'dēn/ ▶ **n.** a young pilchard or other young or small herringlike fish.
▶ **v.** [with obj.] informal pack closely together.
– PHRASES **packed like sardines** crowded very close together, as sardines are in cans.
– ORIGIN late Middle English: from French, or from Latin *sardina*, from *sarda*, from Greek, probably from *Sardō* 'Sardinia.'

sar·dine² ▶ **n.** another term for **SARDIUS**.
– ORIGIN late Middle English: via late Latin from Greek *sardinos*, variant of *sardios* (see **SARDIUS**).

Sar·din·i·a /sär'dinēə/ a large Italian island in the Mediterranean Sea, west of Italy; pop. 1,671,001 (2008); capital, Cagliari. In 1720 it was joined with Savoy and Piedmont to form the kingdom of Sardinia; the kingdom formed the nucleus of the Risorgimento, becoming part of a unified Italy under Victor Emmanuel II of Sardinia in 1861. Italian name **SARDEGNA**.

Sar·din·i·an /sär'dinēən/ ▶ **adj.** of or relating to Sardinia, its people, or their language.
▶ **n. 1** a native or inhabitant of Sardinia.
2 the Romance language of Sardinia, which has several distinct dialects.

Sar·dis /'särdis/ an ancient city in Asia Minor whose ruins lie near the western coast of modern Turkey, to the northeast of Izmir, the capital of Lydia.

sar·di·us /'särdēəs/ ▶ **n.** a red precious stone mentioned in the Bible (e.g., Exod. 28:17) and in classical writings, probably ruby or carnelian.
– ORIGIN late Middle English: via late Latin from Greek *sardios*.

sar·don·ic /sär'dänik/ ▶ **adj.** grimly mocking or cynical: *Starkey attempted a sardonic smile.*
– DERIVATIVES **sar·don·i·cal·ly** /-ik(ə)lē/ **adv.**, **sar·don·i·cism** /-'dänə,sizəm/ **n.**
– ORIGIN mid 17th cent.: from French *sardonique*, earlier *sardonien*, via Latin from Greek *sardonios* 'of Sardinia,' alteration of *sardanios*, used by Homer to describe bitter or scornful laughter.

sar·don·yx /sär'däniks/ ▶ **n.** onyx in which white layers alternate with sard.
– ORIGIN Middle English: via Latin from Greek *sardonux*, probably from *sardios* 'sardius' + *onux* 'onyx.'

sa·ree ▶ **n.** variant spelling of **SARI**.

sar·gas·so /sär'gasō/ (also **sargasso weed**) ▶ **n.** another term for **SARGASSUM**.
– ORIGIN late 16th cent.: from Portuguese *sargaço*, of unknown origin.

Sar·gas·so Sea /sär'gasō/ a region of the western Atlantic Ocean between the Azores and the Caribbean Sea, so called because of the prevalence in it of floating sargasso seaweed. It is the breeding place of eels from the rivers of Europe and eastern North America, and is known for its usually calm conditions.

sar·gas·sum /sär'gasəm/ (also **sargassum weed**) ▶ **n.** a brown seaweed with berrylike air bladders, typically forming large floating masses. ● Genus *Sargassum*, class Phaeophyceae.
– ORIGIN modern Latin, from Portuguese *sargaço* (see **SARGASSO**).

sar·gas·sum fish ▶ **n.** a small toadfish that occurs worldwide, with a bizarre shape and intricate coloration to camouflage it among the floating sargassum weed that it frequents. ● *Histrio histrio*, family Antennariidae.

sarge /särj/ ▶ **n.** informal sergeant.
– ORIGIN mid 19th cent.: abbreviation.

Sar·gent /'särjənt/, John Singer (1856–1925), US painter. He is best known for his portraiture in a style noted for its bold brushwork. He was much in demand in Parisian circles, but following a scandal over the supposed eroticism of *Madame Gautreau* (1884) he moved to London. In World War I, he worked as an official war artist.

Sar·go·dha /sər'gōdə/ a city in north central Pakistan; pop. 586,900 (est. 2009).

Sar·gon /'sär,gän/ (2334–2279 BC), the semilegendary founder of the ancient kingdom of Akkad.

Sar·gon II (died 705 BC), king of Assyria 721–705 BC. Probably a son of Tiglath-pileser III, he is noted for his conquest of cities in Syria and Palestine.

sa·ri /'särē/ (also **saree**) ▶ **n.** (pl. **saris** or **sarees**) a garment consisting of a length of cotton or silk elaborately draped around the body, traditionally worn by women from South Asia.
– ORIGIN late 18th cent.: from Hindi *sārī*.

sari

sa·rin /'särēn/ ▶ **n.** an organophosphorus nerve gas, developed in Germany during World War II.
– ORIGIN from German *Sarin*, of unknown origin.

sark /särk/ ▶ **n.** Scottish & N. English a shirt or chemise.
– ORIGIN Old English *serc*, of Germanic origin.

Sar·ko·zy /särkō'zē/, Nicolas (1955–), French statesman, president since 2007.

sar·ky /'särkē/ ▶ **adj.** (**sarkier**, **sarkiest**) Brit. informal sarcastic.
– DERIVATIVES **sar·ki·ly** /-kəlē/ **adv.**, **sar·ki·ness n.**
– ORIGIN early 20th cent.: abbreviation.

Sar·ma·ti·a /sär'māsH(ē)ə/ an ancient region, located north of the Black Sea, that extended from the Ural Mountains to the Don River.
– DERIVATIVES **Sar·ma·ti·an** /-'māsHən/ **adj. & n.**

Sar·noff /'sär,nôf, -,näf/, David (1891–1971), US broadcaster and businessman; born in Russia. A pioneer in the development of radio and television broadcasting in the US, he worked for the Radio Corporation of America (RCA) from 1919, founding the National Broadcasting Corporation (NBC) as part of it in 1926. He then served as president and chairman of RCA 1930–70.

sa·rod /sə'rōd/ ▶ **n.** a lute used in classical northern Indian music, with four main strings.
– ORIGIN Urdu, from Persian *surod* 'song, melody.'

sa·rong /sə'rôNG, -'räNG/ ▶ **n.** a garment consisting of a long piece of cloth worn wrapped around the body and tucked at the waist or under the armpits, traditionally worn in Southeast Asia and now also by women in the West.
– ORIGIN mid 19th cent.: Malay, literally 'sheath.'

sarong

Sa·ron·ic Gulf /sə'ränik/ an inlet of the Aegean Sea on the coast of southeastern Greece. Athens and the port of Piraeus lie on its northern shores.

sa·ros /'se(ə)räs/ ▶ **n.** Astronomy a period of about 18 years between repetitions of solar and lunar eclipses.
– ORIGIN early 19th cent.: from Greek, from Babylonian *šār(u)* '3,600 (years),' the sense apparently based on a misinterpretation of the number.

Sa·roy·an /sə'roi-ən/, William (1908–81), US writer. His plays include *The Time of Your Life* (1939) and *Razzle Dazzle* (1942). He also wrote novels such as *The Human Comedy* (1943) and *The Laughing Matter* (1953). Some of his memoirs are recounted in *Places Where I've Done Time* (1972).

sar·ra·ce·nia /,sarə'sēnēə, ,ser-/ ▶ **n.** a North American pitcher plant of marshy places, some kinds of which are cultivated as ornamentals. ● Genus *Sarracenia*, family Sarraceniaceae: several species, including the purple-flowered *S. purpurea*, which has become naturalized in Ireland.
– ORIGIN modern Latin, named after Michel *Sarrazin* (died 1734), Canadian botanist.

Sar·raute /sä'rōt/, Nathalie (1902–99), French writer; born in Russia; born *Nathalie Ilyanova Tcherniak*. Her novels included *Portrait of a Man Unknown* (1947) and *Martereau* (1953). Some of her essays are collected in *The Age of Suspicion* (1956).

Sarre /sär/ French name for **SAAR**.

sar·ru·so·phone /sə'rōōzə,fōn, -'rəsə-/ ▶ **n.** a member of a family of wind instruments similar to saxophones but with a double reed like an oboe.
– ORIGIN late 19th cent.: from the name of W. *Sarrus*, the 19th-cent. French bandmaster who invented it, + **-PHONE**.

SARS /särz/ ▶ **n.** a virulently infectious disease caused by a corona virus.
– ORIGIN 2003: acronym from *Severe Acute Respiratory Syndrome*.

sar·sa·pa·ril·la /,särs(ə)pə'rilə, ,saspə-/ ▶ **n. 1** a preparation of the dried rhizomes of various plants, esp. smilax, used to flavor some drinks and medicines and formerly as a tonic. ■ a sweet drink flavored with this.
2 the tropical American climbing plant from which these rhizomes are generally obtained. ● Genus *Smilax*, family Liliaceae: several species, in particular *S. regelii*, which is the chief source of commercial sarsaparilla.
– ORIGIN late 16th cent.: from Spanish *zarzaparilla*, from *zarza* 'bramble' + a diminutive of *parra* 'vine.'

sar·sen /'särsən/ (also **sarsen stone**) ▶ **n.** Geology a silicified sandstone boulder of a kind that occurs on the chalk downs of southern England. Such stones were used in constructing Stonehenge and other prehistoric monuments.
– ORIGIN late 17th cent.: probably a variant of **SARACEN**.

sarse·net /'särsnit/ (also **sarcenet**) ▶ **n.** a fine, soft silk fabric used as a lining material and in dressmaking.
– ORIGIN late Middle English: from Anglo-Norman French *sarzinett*, perhaps a diminutive of *sarzin* 'Saracen,' suggested by Old French *drap sarrasinois* 'Saracen cloth.'

Sar·to /'särtō/, Andrea del (1486–1531), Italian painter; born *Andrea d'Agnolo*. He worked chiefly in Florence, where his works include fresco cycles in the church of Santa Annunziata and the series of grisailles in the cloister of the Scalzi (1511–26).

Sar·ton /'särtn/, May (1912–95), US writer and poet; born in Belgium; born *Eleanore Marie Sarton*. Her many volumes of poetry include *The Land of Silence* (1953) and *In Time Like Air* (1958). She also wrote novels such as *Faithful Are the Wounds* (1955), *Mrs. Stevens Hears the Mermaids Singing* (1965), and *As We Are Now* (1973) and memoirs such as *I Knew a Phoenix* (1954), *Plant Dreaming Deep* (1968), and *At Eighty-Two* (1995).

sar·to·ri·al /sär'tôrēəl/ ▶ **adj.** [attrib.] of or relating to tailoring, clothes, or style of dress: *sartorial elegance*.
– DERIVATIVES **sar·to·ri·al·ly adv.**
– ORIGIN early 19th cent.: from Latin *sartor* 'tailor' (from *sarcire* 'to patch') + **-IAL**.

sar·to·ri·us /sär'tôrēəs/ (also **sartorius muscle**) ▶ **n.** Anatomy a long, narrow muscle running obliquely across the front of each thigh from the hipbone to the inside of the leg below the knee.
– ORIGIN early 18th cent.: modern Latin, from Latin *sartor* 'tailor' (because the muscle is used when adopting a cross-legged position, earlier associated with a tailor's sewing posture).

Sar·tre /'särt(rə)/, Jean-Paul (1905–80), French philosopher, novelist, playwright, and critic. A leading existentialist, he dealt with the nature of human life and the structures of consciousness. He refused the Nobel Prize for Literature in 1964.

Sar·um /'se(ə)rəm/ an old name for Salisbury, still used as the name of its diocese.

sa·rus crane /'sarəs/ ▶ **n.** a large, red-headed crane found from India to the Philippines. ● *Grus antigone*, family Gruidae.
– ORIGIN mid 19th cent.: *sarus* from Sanskrit *sārasa*.

sar·vo·da·ya /sär'vōdīə, -'vōdəyə/ ▶ **n.** Indian the economic and social development of the community as a whole, esp. as advocated by Mahatma Gandhi.
– ORIGIN Sanskrit, from *sarva* 'all' + *udaya* 'prosperity.'

SAS ▶ **abbr.** Brit. Special Air Service.

Sas·a·ni·an ▶ **adj. & n.** variant of **SASSANIAN**.

sa·san·qua /sə'säNGkwə/ ▶ **n.** a Japanese camellia with fragrant white or pink flowers and seeds that yield tea oil. ● *Camellia sasanqua*, family Theaceae.
– ORIGIN mid 19th cent.: from Japanese *sasank(w)a*.

SASE ▶ **abbr.** self-addressed stamped envelope.

sash¹ /sasH/ ▶ **n.** a long strip or loop of cloth worn over one shoulder or around the waist, esp. as part of a uniform or official dress.
– DERIVATIVES **sashed** /sasHt/ **adj.**, **sash·less adj.**
– ORIGIN late 16th cent. (earlier as *shash*, denoting fine fabric twisted around the head as a turban): from Arabic *šāš* 'muslin, turban.'

sash² ▶ **n.** a frame holding the glass in a window, typically one of two sliding frames.
– DERIVATIVES **sashed adj.**
– ORIGIN late 17th cent.: alteration of **CHASSIS**, interpreted as plural.

sa·shay /sa'sHā/ ▶ **v.** [no obj.] informal **1** [with adverbial of direction] walk in an ostentatious yet casual manner, typically with exaggerated movements of the hips

and shoulders: *Louise was sashaying along in a long black satin dress.*
2 perform the sashay.
▶ **n.** (in American square dancing) a figure in which partners circle each other by taking sideways steps.
– ORIGIN mid 19th cent. (as a verb): alteration of CHASSÉ.

sash cord ▶ **n.** a strong cord attaching either of the sash weights of a sash window to a sash.

sa·shi·mi /säˈsHēmē/ ▶ **n.** a Japanese dish of bite-sized pieces of raw fish eaten with soy sauce and wasabi paste: *tuna sashimi.*
– ORIGIN Japanese.

sash weight ▶ **n.** a weight attached by a cord to each side of a window sash to balance it at any height.

Sask. ▶ **abbr.** Saskatchewan.

Sas·katch·e·wan /səˈskacHəwən, -ˌwän/ **1** a province in central Canada; pop. 968,157 (2006); capital, Regina.
2 a river in Canada. Rising in two headstreams in the Rocky Mountains, it flows east for 370 miles (596 km) to Lake Winnipeg.

Sas·ka·toon /ˌsaskəˈto͞on/ an industrial city in south central Saskatchewan in Canada, located in the Great Plains on the South Saskatchewan River; pop. 202,340 (2006).

Sas·quatch /ˈsaskwäcH, -kwacH/ ▶ **n.** another term for BIGFOOT.
– ORIGIN early 20th cent.: Salish *sésq'əc.*

sass /sas/ informal ▶ **n.** impudence; cheek: *the kind of boy that wouldn't give you any sass.*
▶ **v.** [with obj.] be cheeky or rude to (someone): *we wouldn't have dreamed of sassing our parents.*
– ORIGIN mid 19th cent.: variant of SAUCE.

sas·sa·by /ˈsasəbē/ (also **tsessebi** or **tsessebe** /ˈ(t)sesəbē/) ▶ **n.** an antelope of a race found mainly in southern Africa. ● *Damaliscus lunatus lunatus*, family Bovidae.

sas·sa·fras /ˈsasəˌfras/ ▶ **n.** a deciduous North American tree with aromatic leaves and bark. The leaves are infused to make tea or ground into filé. ● *Sassafras albidum*, family Lauraceae. ■ an extract of the leaves or bark of this tree, used medicinally or in perfumery.
– ORIGIN late 16th cent.: from Spanish *sasafrás*, based on Latin *saxifraga* 'saxifrage.'

Sas·sa·ni·an /səˈsānēən/ (also **Sasanian** or **Sassanid** /səˈsänid, -ˈsan-, ˈsasənid/) ▶ **adj.** of or relating to a dynasty that ruled Persia from the early 3rd century AD until the Arab Muslim conquest of 651.
▶ **n.** a member of this dynasty.
– ORIGIN from *Sasan* (the name of the grandfather or father of Ardashir, the first Sassanian) + -IAN.

Sas·se·nach /ˈsasəˌnak/ Scottish & Irish derogatory ▶ **n.** an English person.
▶ **adj.** English.
– ORIGIN early 18th cent. (as a noun): from Scottish Gaelic *Sasunnoch*, Irish *Sasanach*, from Latin *Saxones* 'Saxons.'

Sas·soon[1] /səˈso͞on, sa-/, Siegfried (Lorraine) (1886–1967), English poet and novelist. His starkly realistic poems, written while serving in World War I, express his contempt for war leaders as well as his compassion for his comrades.

Sas·soon[2], Vidal (1928–), English hair stylist. After opening a London salon in 1953, he introduced several popular hairstyles that were named for him.

sas·sy /ˈsasē/ ▶ **adj.** (**sassier**, **sassiest**) informal lively, bold, and full of spirit; cheeky.
– DERIVATIVES **sas·si·ly** /-əlē/ **adv.**, **sas·si·ness n.**
– ORIGIN mid 19th cent.: variant of SAUCY.

sas·tra ▶ **n.** variant spelling of SHASTRA.

sas·tru·gi /səˈstro͞ogē, sa-, ˈsastrə-/ ▶ **plural n.** parallel wavelike ridges caused by winds on the surface of hard snow, esp. in polar regions.
– ORIGIN mid 19th cent.: from Russian *zastrugi* 'small ridges.'

SAT /ˈes ˌā ˈtē/ ▶ **n.** trademark a test of a student's academic skills, used for admission to US colleges.
– ORIGIN formerly and variously an abbreviation of *Scholastic Assessment Test* and *Scholastic Aptitude Test.*

sat /sat/ past and past participle of SIT.

Sat. ▶ **abbr.** Saturday.

Sa·tan /ˈsātn/ the Devil; Lucifer.
– ORIGIN Old English, via late Latin and Greek from Hebrew *śāṭān*, literally 'adversary,' from *śāṭan* 'plot against.'

sa·tang /səˈtäNG/ ▶ **n.** (pl. **same** or **satangs**) a monetary unit of Thailand, equal to one hundredth of a baht.
– ORIGIN Thai, from Pali *sata* 'hundred.'

sa·tan·ic /səˈtanik, sā-/ ▶ **adj.** of or characteristic of Satan. ■ connected with Satanism: *a satanic cult.* ■ extremely evil or wicked.
– DERIVATIVES **sa·tan·i·cal·ly** /-ik(ə)lē/ **adv.**

sa·tan·ic a·buse ▶ **n.** another term for RITUAL ABUSE.

sa·tan·ism /ˈsātnˌizəm/ (also **Satanism**) ▶ **n.** the worship of Satan, typically involving a travesty of Christian symbols and practices, such as placing a cross upside down.
– DERIVATIVES **sa·tan·ist n. & adj.**

sa·tan·ize /ˈsātnˌīz/ (also **Satanize**) ▶ **v.** [with obj.] rare portray as satanic or evil.

sa·tay /ˈsäˌtā/ (also **saté**) ▶ **n.** an Southeast Asian dish consisting of small pieces of meat grilled on a skewer and served with a spiced sauce that typically contains peanuts.
– ORIGIN from Malay *satai*, Indonesian *sate.*

SATB ▶ **abbr.** soprano, alto, tenor, and bass (used to describe the constitution of a choir or to specify the singing voices required for a particular piece of music).

satch·el /ˈsacHəl/ ▶ **n.** a bag carried on the shoulder by a long strap and typically closed by a flap.
– ORIGIN Middle English: from Old French *sachel*, from Latin *saccellus* 'small bag.'

satch·el charge ▶ **n.** an explosive on a board fitted with a rope or wire loop for carrying and attaching.

sat·com /ˈsatˌkäm/ (also **SATCOM**) ▶ **n.** satellite communications.
– ORIGIN late 20th cent.: blend.

satd. ▶ **abbr.** saturated.

sate[1] /sāt/ ▶ **v.** [with obj.] satisfy (a desire or an appetite) to the full: *sate your appetite at the resort's restaurant.* ■ supply (someone) with as much as or more of something than is desired or can be managed.
– DERIVATIVES **sate·less adj.** (literary).
– ORIGIN early 17th cent.: probably an alteration of dialect *sade*, from Old English *sadian* 'become sated or weary' (related to SAD). The change in the final consonant was due to association with SATIATE.

sate[2] /sat, sāt/ ▶ **v.** archaic spelling of SAT.

sa·té ▶ **n.** variant spelling of SATAY.

sa·teen /saˈtēn/ ▶ **n.** a cotton fabric woven like satin with a glossy surface.
– ORIGIN late 19th cent.: alteration of SATIN, on the pattern of *velveteen.*

sat·el·lite /ˈsatlˌīt/ ▶ **n. 1** (also **artificial satellite**) an artificial body placed in orbit around the earth or moon or another planet in order to collect information or for communication. ■ [as modifier] transmitted by satellite; using or relating to satellite technology: *satellite broadcasting.* ■ satellite television: *a news service on satellite.*
2 Astronomy a celestial body orbiting the earth or another planet.
3 [usu. as modifier] something that is separated from or on the periphery of something else but is nevertheless dependent on or controlled by it: *satellite offices in London and New York.* ■ a small country or state politically or economically dependent on another.
4 Biology a portion of the DNA of a genome with repeating base sequences and of different density from the main sequence.
– ORIGIN mid 16th cent. (in the sense 'follower, obsequious underling'): from French *satellite* or Latin *satelles, satellit-* 'attendant.'

sat·el·lite dish ▶ **n.** a bowl-shaped antenna with which signals are transmitted to or received from a communications satellite.

sat·el·lite feed ▶ **n.** a live broadcast via satellite forming part of another program.

sat·el·lite tel·e·vi·sion ▶ **n.** television broadcasting using a satellite to relay signals to appropriately equipped customers in a particular area.

sa·tel·li·ti·um /ˌsatlˈitēəm, -ˈītēəm/ ▶ **n.** Astrology a grouping of several planets in a sign.

Sa·ti /ˌsəˈtē, ˈsəˌtē/ Hinduism the wife of Shiva, reborn as Parvati. According to some accounts, she died by throwing herself into the sacred fire.

sa·ti /səˈtē, ˈsəˌtē/ (also **suttee**) ▶ **n.** (pl. **satis** /səˈtēz, ˈsəˌtēz/ or **suttees**) the former Hindu practice of a widow throwing herself onto her husband's funeral pyre. ■ a widow who committed such an act.
– ORIGIN Hindi, from Sanskrit *satī* 'faithful wife,' from *sat* 'good.'

sa·ti·ate /ˈsāsHēˌāt/ ▶ **v.** another term for SATE[1]: *he folded up his newspaper, his curiosity satiated.*
▶ **adj.** archaic satisfied to the full; satiated.
– DERIVATIVES **sa·tia·ble** /-sHəbəl/ **adj.** (archaic), **sa·ti·a·tion** /ˌsāsHēˈāsHən/ **n.**
– ORIGIN late Middle English: from Latin *satiatus*, past participle of *satiare*, from *satis* 'enough.'

Sa·tie /säˈtē/, Erik (Alfred Leslie) (1866–1925), French avant-garde composer.

sa·ti·e·ty /səˈtīətē/ ▶ **n.** chiefly technical the feeling or state of being sated.
– ORIGIN mid 16th cent.: from Old French *saciete*, from Latin *satietas*, from *satis* 'enough.'

sa·ti·e·ty cen·ter ▶ **n.** Physiology an area of the brain situated in the hypothalamus and concerned with the regulation of food intake.

sat·in /ˈsatn/ ▶ **n.** a smooth, glossy fabric, typically of silk, produced by a weave in which the threads of the warp are caught and looped by the weft only at certain intervals: [as modifier] *a blue satin dress.* ■ [as modifier] denoting or having a surface or finish resembling this fabric, produced on metal or other material: *an aluminum alloy with a black satin finish.*
▶ **adj.** smooth like satin: *a luxurious satin look.*
– DERIVATIVES **sat·in·y adj.**
– ORIGIN late Middle English: via Old French from Arabic *zaytūnī* 'of Tsinkiang,' a town in China.

sat·i·net /ˌsatnˈet/ (also **satinette**) ▶ **n.** a fabric with a similar finish to satin, made partly or wholly of cotton or synthetic fiber.

sat·in pa·per ▶ **n.** fine glossy paper, used for writing or printmaking.

sat·in spar ▶ **n.** a fibrous variety of gypsum with a pearly luster.

sat·in stitch ▶ **n.** a long straight embroidery stitch, closely placed parallel to similar stitches, giving the appearance of satin.

sat·in wal·nut ▶ **n.** see SWEET GUM.

sat·in weave ▶ **n.** a method of weaving fabric in which either the warp or the weft predominates on the surface.

sat·in·wood /ˈsatnˌwo͝od/ ▶ **n. 1** glossy yellowish timber from a tropical tree, valued for cabinetwork.
2 the tropical hardwood tree that produces this timber. ● Two species in the family Rutaceae: **Ceylon satinwood** (*Chloroxylon swietenia*), native to India and Sri Lanka, and **West Indian** (or **Jamaican**) **satinwood** (*Zanthoxylum flava*), native to the Caribbean, Bermuda, and southern Florida. ■ used in names of other trees that yield high-quality timber, e.g., **Nigerian satinwood**.

sat·ire /ˈsaˌtīr/ ▶ **n.** the use of humor, irony, exaggeration, or ridicule to expose and criticize people's stupidity or vices, particularly in the context of contemporary politics and other topical issues. See WIT[1]. ■ a play, novel, film, or other work that uses satire: *a stinging satire on American politics.* ■ a genre of literature characterized by the use of satire. ■ (in Latin literature) a literary miscellany, esp. a poem ridiculing prevalent vices or follies.
– DERIVATIVES **sat·i·rist** /ˈsatərist/ **n.**
– ORIGIN early 16th cent.: from French, or from Latin *satira*, later form of *satura* 'poetic medley.'

sa·tir·i·cal /səˈti(ə)rikəl/ (also **satiric** /-ˈti(ə)rik/) ▶ **adj.** containing or using satire: *a New York-based satirical magazine.* ■ (of a person or their behavior) sarcastic, critical, and mocking another's weaknesses.
– DERIVATIVES **sa·tir·ic adj.**, **sa·tir·i·cal·ly adv.**
– ORIGIN early 16th cent.: from late Latin *satiricus* (from *satira* 'poetic medley': see SATIRE) + -AL.

sat·i·rize /ˈsatəˌrīz/ ▶ **v.** [with obj.] deride and criticize by means of satire: *Aristophanes satirized the lack of respect for the laws.*
– DERIVATIVES **sat·i·ri·za·tion** /ˌsatərəˈzāsHən/ **n.**

sat·is·fac·tion /ˌsatisˈfaksHən/ ▶ **n.** fulfillment of one's wishes, expectations, or needs, or the pleasure derived from this: *he smiled with satisfaction* | *managing directors seeking greater job satisfaction.* ■ Law the payment of a debt or fulfillment of an obligation or claim: *in full and final satisfaction of the claim.* ■ [with negative] what is felt to be owed or due to one, esp. in reparation of an injustice or wrong: *the work will come to a halt if the electricity and telephone people don't get satisfaction.* ■ Christian Theology Christ's atonement for sin. ■ historical the opportunity to defend one's honor in a duel: *I demand the satisfaction of a gentleman.*
– PHRASES **to one's satisfaction** so that one is satisfied: *some amendments were made, not entirely to his satisfaction.*
– ORIGIN Middle English: from Old French, or from Latin *satisfactio(n-)*, from *satisfacere* 'satisfy, content' (see SATISFY). The earliest recorded use referred to the last part of religious penance after "contrition" and "confession": this involved fulfillment of the observance required by the confessor, in contrast with the current meaning 'fulfillment of one's own expectations.'

sat·is·fac·to·ry /ˌsatisˈfakt(ə)rē/ ▶ **adj.** fulfilling expectations or needs; acceptable, though not outstanding or perfect: *the brakes are satisfactory*

if not particularly powerful. ■ (of a patient in a hospital) not deteriorating or likely to die. ■ Law (of evidence or a verdict) sufficient for the needs of the case.
– DERIVATIVES **sat·is·fac·to·ri·ly** /-t(ə)rəlē/ **adv.**, **sat·is·fac·to·ri·ness n.**
– ORIGIN late Middle English (in the sense 'leading to the atonement of sin'): from Old French *satisfactoire* or medieval Latin *satisfactorius*, from Latin *satisfacere* 'to content' (see SATISFY). The current senses date from the mid 17th cent.

sat·is·fice /ˈsatisˌfīs/ ▶ **v.** accept an available option as satisfactory: *it talks about telling you not to just satisfice but to always look for the best.*

sat·is·fied /ˈsatisˌfīd/ ▶ **adj.** contented; pleased: *satisfied customers* | *she was very **satisfied with** the results.*

sat·is·fy /ˈsatisˌfī/ ▶ **v.** (**satisfies, satisfying, satisfied**) [with obj.] meet the expectations, needs, or desires of (someone): *I have never been **satisfied with** my job* | [no obj.] *wealth, the promise of the eighties, has failed to satisfy.* ■ fulfill (a desire or need): *social services is trying to satisfy the needs of so many different groups.* ■ provide (someone) with adequate information or proof so that they are convinced about something: [with obj. and clause] *people need to be satisfied that the environmental assessments are accurate* | *the chief engineer **satisfied himself** that it was not a weapon.* ■ adequately meet or comply with (a condition, obligation, or demand): *the whole team is working to satisfy demand.* ■ Mathematics (of a quantity) make (an equation) true. ■ pay off (a debt or creditor): *there was insufficient collateral to satisfy the loan.*
– DERIVATIVES **sat·is·fi·a·bil·i·ty** /ˌsatisˌfīəˈbilitē/ **n.**, **sat·is·fi·a·ble adj.**
– ORIGIN late Middle English: from Old French *satisfier*, formed irregularly from Latin *satisfacere* 'to content,' from *satis* 'enough' + *facere* 'make.'

sat·is·fy·ing /ˈsatisˌfī-iNG/ ▶ **adj.** giving fulfillment or the pleasure associated with this: *Fleischer's performance was consummately musical and deeply satisfying.*
– DERIVATIVES **sat·is·fy·ing·ly adv.**

sat·nav /ˈsatˌnav/ ▶ **n.** navigation dependent on information received from satellites.
– ORIGIN 1970s: blend of SATELLITE and NAVIGATION.

sa·to·ri /səˈtôrē/ ▶ **n.** Buddhism sudden enlightenment: *the road that leads to satori.*
– ORIGIN Japanese, literally 'awakening.'

sa·trap /ˈsāˌtrap, ˈsa-/ ▶ **n.** a provincial governor in the ancient Persian empire. ■ any subordinate or local ruler.
– ORIGIN late Middle English: from Old French *satrape* or Latin *satrapa*, based on Old Persian *kšathra-pāvan* 'country-protector.'

sa·trap·y /ˈsātrəpē, ˈsa-/ ▶ **n.** (pl. **satrapies**) a province governed by a satrap.

sat·sang /ˈsatˌsaNG/ ▶ **n.** Indian a spiritual discourse or sacred gathering.
– ORIGIN from Sanskrit *satsaṅga* 'association with good men.'

Sat·su·ma /satˈso͞omə, ˈsatsəˌmä/ a former province of southwestern Japan that was located on the southwestern peninsula of Kyushu island, also known as the Satsuma Peninsula.

sat·su·ma /satˈso͞omə, ˈsatsəmə/ ▶ **n. 1** a tangerine of a hardy loose-skinned variety, originally grown in Japan.
2 (**Satsuma** or **Satsuma ware**) Japanese pottery from Satsuma, ranging from simple 17th-century earthenware to later work made for export to Europe, often elaborately painted, with a crackled cream-colored glaze.
– ORIGIN late 19th cent.: named after the province SATSUMA.

satt·va /ˈsətvə/ ▶ **adj.** (in Ayurveda) the element or mode of prakriti associated with purity, wholesomeness, and virtue.

satt·vic /ˈsətvik/ ▶ **adj.** (in Ayurveda) denoting a class of foods that are fresh, juicy, light, nourishing, and tasty, and thus give necessary energy to the body and help achieve balance. Compare RAJASIC, TAMASIC.

sat·u·rate ▶ **v.** /ˈsaCHəˌrāt/ [with obj.] cause (something) to become thoroughly soaked with liquid so that no more can be absorbed: *the soil is saturated.* ■ cause (a substance) to combine with, dissolve, or hold the greatest possible quantity of another substance: *the groundwater is saturated with calcium hydroxide.* ■ magnetize or charge (a substance or device) fully. ■ Electronics put (a device) into a state in which no further increase in current is achievable. ■ (usu. **be saturated with**) fill (something or someone) with something until no more can be held or absorbed: *they've become thoroughly saturated with powerful and seductive messages from the media.* ■ supply (a market) beyond the point at which the demand for a product is satisfied: *Japan's electronics industry began to saturate the world markets.* ■ overwhelm (an enemy target area) by concentrated bombing.
▶ **n.** /-rət/ (usu. **saturates**) a saturated fat.
▶ **adj.** /-rət/ literary saturated with moisture.
– DERIVATIVES **sat·u·ra·ble** /-əbəl/ **adj.** (technical).
– ORIGIN late Middle English (as an adjective in the sense 'satisfied'): from Latin *saturat-* 'filled, glutted,' from the verb *saturare*, from *satur* 'full.' The early sense of the verb (mid 16th cent.) was 'satisfy'; the noun dates from the 1950s.

sat·u·rat·ed /ˈsaCHəˌrātid/ ▶ **adj. 1** holding as much water or moisture as can be absorbed; thoroughly soaked. ■ Chemistry (of a solution) containing the largest possible amount of a particular solute. ■ [often in combination] having or holding as much as can be absorbed of something: *the glitzy, media-saturated plasticity of Los Angeles.*
2 Chemistry (of an organic molecule) containing the greatest possible number of hydrogen atoms, and so having no carbon–carbon double or triple bonds. ■ denoting fats containing a high proportion of fatty acid molecules without double bonds, considered to be less healthy in the diet than unsaturated fats.
3 (of color) very bright, full, and free from an admixture of white: *intense and saturated color.*

sat·u·ra·tion /ˌsaCHəˈrāSHən/ ▶ **n.** the state or process that occurs when no more of something can be absorbed, combined with, or added. ■ Chemistry the degree or extent to which something is dissolved or absorbed compared with the maximum possible, usually expressed as a percentage. ■ [as modifier] to a very full extent, esp. beyond the point regarded as necessary or desirable: *saturation bombing.* ■ (also **color saturation**) (esp. in photography) the intensity of a color, expressed as the degree to which it differs from white.

sat·u·ra·tion div·ing ▶ **n.** deep-sea diving in which the diver's bloodstream is saturated with helium or other suitable gas at the pressure of the surrounding water, so that the decompression time afterward is independent of the duration of the dive.

sat·u·ra·tion point ▶ **n.** [in sing.] Chemistry the stage at which no more of a substance can be absorbed into a vapor or dissolved into a solution. ■ the stage beyond which no more of something can be absorbed or accepted.

Sat·ur·day /ˈsatərˌdā, -dē/ ▶ **n.** the day of the week before Sunday and following Friday, and (together with Sunday) forming part of the weekend: *I am going to see Twelfth Night **on Saturday*** | *the counter is closed on Saturdays and Sundays* | [as modifier] *Saturday night.*
▶ **adv.** on Saturday: *he made his first appearance Saturday.* ■ (**Saturdays**) on Saturdays; each Saturday: *they sleep late Saturdays.*
– ORIGIN Old English *Sæter(es)dæg*, translation of Latin *Saturni dies* 'day of Saturn'; compare with Dutch *zaterdag.*

Sat·ur·day night spe·cial ▶ **n.** informal a cheap, low-caliber pistol or revolver, easily obtained and concealed.

Sat·urn /ˈsatərn/ **1** Roman Mythology an ancient god, regarded as a god of agriculture. Greek equivalent CRONUS. [from Latin *Saturnus*, perhaps from Etruscan.]
2 Astronomy the sixth planet from the sun in the solar system, circled by a system of broad, flat rings.

> Saturn orbits between Jupiter and Uranus at an average distance of 887 million miles (1,427 million km) from the sun. It is a gas giant with an equatorial diameter of 74,600 miles (120,000 km), with a conspicuous ring system extending out to a distance twice as great.The planet has a dense, hydrogen-rich atmosphere similar to that of Jupiter but with less distinct banding. There are at least eighteen satellites, the largest of which is Titan, and including small shepherd satellites that orbit close to two of the rings.

3 a series of US space rockets, of which the very large *Saturn V* was used as the launch vehicle for the Apollo missions of 1968–72.

Sat·ur·na·li·a /ˌsatərˈnālēə, -ˈnālyə/ ▶ **n.** [treated as sing. or pl.] the ancient Roman festival of Saturn in December, which was a period of general merrymaking and was the predecessor of Christmas. ■ (**saturnalia**) an occasion of wild revelry.
– DERIVATIVES **Sat·ur·na·li·an adj.**
– ORIGIN Latin, literally 'matters relating to Saturn,' neuter plural of *Saturnalis.*

Sa·tur·ni·an /səˈtərnēən/ ▶ **adj. 1** of or relating to the planet Saturn.
2 another term for SATURNINE.

sa·tur·ni·id /səˈtərnē-id/ ▶ **n.** Entomology a silkworm moth of a family (Saturniidae) that includes the emperor moths and the giant Indian silk moths. They typically have prominent eyespots on the wings.
– ORIGIN late 19th cent.: from modern Latin *Saturniidae* (plural), from the genus name *Saturnia.*

sat·ur·nine /ˈsatərˌnīn/ ▶ **adj.** (of a person or their manner) slow and gloomy: *a saturnine temperament.* ■ (of a person or their features) dark in coloring and moody or mysterious: *his saturnine face and dark, watchful eyes.* ■ (of a place or an occasion) gloomy.
– DERIVATIVES **sat·ur·nine·ly adv.**
– ORIGIN late Middle English (as a term in astrology): from Old French *saturnin*, from medieval Latin *Saturninus* 'of Saturn' (identified with lead by the alchemists and associated with slowness and gloom by astrologers).

sat·ur·nism /ˈsatərˌnizəm/ ▶ **n.** archaic term for LEAD POISONING.
– DERIVATIVES **sa·tur·nic** /səˈtərnik/ **adj.**
– ORIGIN mid 19th cent.: from SATURN in the obsolete alchemical sense 'lead' + -ISM.

sat·ya·gra·ha /səˈtyägrəhə, ˈsətyəˌgrəhə/ ▶ **n.** a policy of passive political resistance, esp. that advocated by Mahatma Gandhi against British rule in India.
– ORIGIN Sanskrit, from *satya* 'truth' + *āgraha* 'obstinacy.'

sa·tyr /ˈsātər, ˈsātər/ ▶ **n. 1** Greek Mythology one of a class of lustful, drunken woodland gods. In Greek art they were represented as a man with a horse's ears and tail, but in Roman representations as a man with a goat's ears, tail, legs, and horns. ■ a man who has strong sexual desires.
2 a satyrid butterfly with chiefly dark brown wings. ● Tribes Satyrini (including the Eurasian genus *Satyrus*) and Euptychiini (the American **wood satyrs**), subfamily Satyrinae, family Nymphalidae.
– DERIVATIVES **sa·tyr·ic** /səˈtirik/ **adj.**
– ORIGIN late Middle English: from Old French *satyre*, or via Latin from Greek *saturos.*

sa·ty·ri·a·sis /ˌsātəˈrīəsis, ˌsā-/ ▶ **n.** uncontrollable or excessive sexual desire in a man. Compare with NYMPHOMANIA.
– ORIGIN late Middle English: via late Latin from Greek *saturiasis*, from *saturos* (see SATYR).

sa·tyr·id /ˈsātərid, ˈsā-/ ▶ **n.** Entomology a butterfly of a group that includes the browns, heaths, ringlets, and related species. They typically have brown wings with small eyespots and many live in woodland and breed on grasses. Also called BROWN. ● Subfamily Satyrinae, family Nymphalidae (formerly the family Satyridae).
– ORIGIN early 20th cent.: from modern Latin *Satyridae* (plural), from Latin *Satyrus* (see SATYR), used as a genus name.

sauce /sôs/ ▶ **n. 1** thick liquid served with food, usually savory dishes, to add moistness and flavor: *tomato sauce* | *the cubs can be added to soups and sauces.* ■ stewed fruit, esp. apples, eaten as dessert or used as a garnish.
2 (**the sauce**) informal alcoholic drink: *she's been **on the sauce** for years.*
3 informal, chiefly Brit. impertinence.
▶ **v.** [with obj.] **1** (usu. **be sauced**) provide a sauce for (something); season with a sauce. ■ make more interesting and exciting.
2 informal be rude or impudent to (someone).
– PHRASES **what's sauce** (or **good**) **for the goose is sauce** (or **good**) **for the gander** proverb what is appropriate in one case is also appropriate in the other case in question.
– DERIVATIVES **sauce·less adj.**
– ORIGIN Middle English: from Old French, based on Latin *salsus* 'salted,' past participle of *salere* 'to salt,' from *sal* 'salt.' Compare with SALAD.

sauce·boat /ˈsôsˌbōt/ ▶ **n.** a boat-shaped vessel used for serving gravy or sauce.

sauced /sôst/ ▶ **adj.** informal drunk.

sauce mousse·line ▶ **n.** see MOUSSELINE (sense 3).

sauce·pan /ˈsôsˌpan/ ▶ **n.** a deep cooking pan, typically round, made of metal, and with one long handle and a lid.
– DERIVATIVES **sauce·pan·ful** /-ˌfo͝ol/ **n.** (pl. **saucepanfuls**).

sau·cer /ˈsôsər/ ▶ **n.** a shallow dish, typically having a circular indentation in the center, on which a cup is placed.
– PHRASES **have eyes like saucers** have one's eyes opened wide in amazement.
– DERIVATIVES **sau·cer·ful** /-ˌfo͝ol/ **n.** (pl. **saucerfuls**), **sau·cer·less adj.**

– ORIGIN Middle English (denoting a condiment dish): from Old French *saussier(e)* 'sauceboat,' probably suggested by late Latin *salsarium*.

sau·cier /sôs'yā, 'sôsēər/ ▶ **n.** a chef who prepares sauces.
– ORIGIN French.

sau·cis·son /,sōsē'sôn/ ▶ **n.** a large, thick French sausage, typically firm in texture and flavored with herbs.
– ORIGIN French, literally 'large sausage.'

sau·cy /'sôsē/ ▶ **adj.** (**saucier, sauciest**) informal **1** impudent; flippant: *a saucy remark*.
2 bold and lively; smart-looking: *a hat with a saucy brim*.
3 sexually suggestive, typically in a way intended to be lighthearted: *saucy songs*.
– DERIVATIVES **sau·ci·ly** /-səlē/ **adv.**, **sau·ci·ness n.**
– ORIGIN early 16th cent. (in the sense 'savory, flavored with sauce'): from SAUCE + -Y[1].

sau·da·de /sou'dädə/ ▶ **n.** a feeling of longing, melancholy, or nostalgia that is supposedly characteristic of the Portuguese or Brazilian temperament.
– ORIGIN Portuguese.

Sau·di /'soudē, 'sô-/ ▶ **adj.** of or relating to Saudi Arabia or its ruling dynasty.
▶ **n.** (pl. **Saudis**) a citizen of Saudi Arabia, or a member of its ruling dynasty.
– ORIGIN from the name of Abdul-Aziz ibn *Saud* (1880–1953), first king of Saudi Arabia.

Sau·di A·ra·bi·a /'soudē ə'rābēə, 'sôdē/ a country in southwestern Asia that occupies most of the Arabian peninsula; pop. 28,686,600 (est. 2009); capital, Riyadh; language, Arabic (official).

> The birthplace of Islam in the 7th century, Saudi Arabia emerged from the Arab revolt against the Turks during World War I to become an independent kingdom in 1932. Since World War II, the economy has been revolutionized by the exploitation of the area's oil resources, and Saudi Arabia is the largest oil producer in the Middle East. It is ruled by the house of Saud along traditional Islamic lines.

– DERIVATIVES **Sau·di A·ra·bi·an adj. & n.**

sau·er·bra·ten /'sou(ə)r,brätn/ ▶ **n.** a dish of German origin consisting of beef that is marinated in vinegar with peppercorns, onions, and other seasonings before cooking.
– ORIGIN from German, from *sauer* 'sour' + *Braten* 'roast meat.'

sau·er·kraut /'sou(ə)r,krout/ ▶ **n.** chopped cabbage that has been pickled in brine.
– ORIGIN from German, from *sauer* 'sour' + *Kraut* 'vegetable.'

sau·ger /'sôgər/ ▶ **n.** a slender North American pikeperch with silver eyes, which is active at twilight and at night. ● *Stizostedion canadense*, family Percidae.
– ORIGIN late 19th cent.: of unknown origin.

Sau·gus /'sôgəs/ a town in eastern Massachusetts, north of Boston, site of the first US ironworks (established in 1646); pop. 27,478 (est. 2008).

Sauk /sôk/ (also **Sac**) ▶ **n.** (pl. **same** or **Sauks**) **1** a member of an American Indian people inhabiting parts of the central US, formerly in Wisconsin, Illinois, and Iowa, now in Oklahoma and Kansas.
2 the Algonquian language of this people.
▶ **adj.** of or relating to this people or their language.
– ORIGIN from Canadian French *Saki*, from Ojibwa *osāki* '(people of the) river mouth.'

S

Saul /sôl/ (in the Bible) the first king of Israel (11th century BC).

Saul of Tar·sus see PAUL, ST.

Sault Sainte Marie /'sōō ,sānt mə'rē/ each of two North American river ports that face each other across the falls of the St. Mary's River, between lakes Superior and Huron. The northern port (pop. 74,948 (2006) lies in Ontario, Canada, while the southern port (pop. 14,087, est. 2008) is in the US state of Michigan. A system of canals serves to bypass the falls on either side of the river.

sau·na /'sônə, 'sou-/ ▶ **n.** a small room used as a hot-air or steam bath for cleaning and refreshing the body: figurative *the air-con was broken—the place was like a sauna*. ■ a session in such a room.
– ORIGIN late 19th cent.: from Finnish.

saun·ders var. of SANDERS.

saun·ter /'sôntər/ ▶ **v.** [no obj.] walk in a slow, relaxed manner, without hurry or effort: *Adam sauntered into the room*.
▶ **n.** a leisurely stroll: *a quiet saunter down the road*.
– DERIVATIVES **saun·ter·er n.**
– ORIGIN late Middle English (in the sense 'to muse, wonder'): of unknown origin. The current sense dates from the mid 17th cent.

-saur ▶ **comb. form** forming names of reptiles, esp. extinct ones: *ichthyosaur* | *stegosaur*.
– ORIGIN modern Latin, from Greek *sauros* 'lizard'; compare with -SAURUS, a suffix of modern Latin genus names.

Sau·ri·a /'sôrēə/ Zoology former term for LACERTILIA.
– ORIGIN modern Latin (plural), from Greek *sauros* 'lizard.'

sau·ri·an /'sôrēən/ ▶ **adj.** of or like a lizard.
▶ **n.** any large reptile, esp. a dinosaur or other extinct form.
– ORIGIN early 19th cent.: from modern Latin *Sauria* (see SAURIA) + -AN.

saur·is·chi·an /sô'riskēən/ Paleontology ▶ **adj.** of, relating to, or denoting dinosaurs of an order distinguished by having a pelvic structure resembling that of lizards. Compare with ORNITHISCHIAN.
▶ **n.** a saurischian dinosaur. ● Order Saurischia, superorder Dinosauria; comprises the carnivorous theropods and the herbivorous sauropods.
– ORIGIN late 19th cent.: from the modern Latin plural *Saurischia* (from Greek *sauros* 'lizard' + *iskhion* 'hip joint') + -AN.

sau·ro·pod /'sôrə,päd/ ▶ **n.** a very large quadrupedal herbivorous dinosaur with a long neck and tail, small head, and massive limbs. ● Infraorder Sauropoda, suborder Sauropodomorpha, order Saurischia; e.g., apatosaurus, brachiosaurus, and diplodocus.
– ORIGIN late 19th cent.: from modern Latin *Sauropoda* (plural), from Greek *sauros* 'lizard' + *pous, pod-* 'foot.'

-saurus ▶ **comb. form** forming genus names of reptiles, esp. extinct ones: *stegosaurus*.
– ORIGIN modern Latin.

sau·ry /'sôrē/ ▶ **n.** (pl. **sauries**) a long slender-bodied edible marine fish with an elongated snout. ● Family Scomberesocidae: four genera and species, including *Scomberesox saurus* of the Atlantic (also called SKIPPER[2]), and *Cololabis saira* of the Pacific.
– ORIGIN late 18th cent.: perhaps via late Latin from Greek *sauros* 'horse mackerel.'

sau·sage /'sôsij/ ▶ **n.** a short cylindrical tube of minced pork, beef, or other meat encased in a skin, typically sold raw to be grilled, boiled, or fried before eating. ■ a cylindrical tube of minced pork, beef, or other meat seasoned and cooked or preserved, sold mainly to be eaten cold in slices: *smoked German sausage*. ■ [usu. as modifier] used in references to the characteristic cylindrical shape of sausages: *mold into a sausage shape*.
– ORIGIN late Middle English: from Old Northern French *saussiche*, from medieval Latin *salsicia*, from Latin *salsus* 'salted' (see SAUCE).

Sau·sa·li·to /,sôsə'lētō/ a city in northwestern California, across the Golden Gate from San Francisco, a noted artists' colony; pop. 7,158 (est. 2008).

Saus·sure /sō'sōōr, -'syr/, Ferdinand de (1857–1913), Swiss linguistics scholar. He was one of the founders of modern linguistics, and his work was fundamental to the development of structuralism.

sau·té /sô'tā, sō-/ ▶ **adj. 1** [attrib.] fried quickly in a little hot fat: *sauté potatoes*.
2 Ballet (of a step) performed while jumping.
▶ **n.** a dish cooked in such a way.
▶ **v.** (**sautés, sautéing** /-'tāiNG/, **sautéed** /-'tād/ or **sautéd**) [with obj.] cook in such a way: *sauté the onions in the olive oil*.
– ORIGIN early 19th cent.: French, literally 'jumped,' past participle of *sauter*.

Sau·ternes /sō'tərn, sô-/ ▶ **n.** a sweet white wine from Sauternes in the Bordeaux region of France.

sauve qui peut /,sōv kē 'pə/ ▶ **n.** archaic or literary a general stampede, panic, or disorder.
– ORIGIN French, literally 'save who can.'

Sau·vi·gnon /,sōvin'yôn, -vē'nyôn/ (also **Sauvignon Blanc** /'blän, 'bläNGk/) ▶ **n.** a variety of white wine grape. ■ a white wine made from this grape.
– ORIGIN French.

sav·age /'savij/ ▶ **adj.** (of an animal or force of nature) fierce, violent, and uncontrolled: *tales of a savage beast* | *a week of savage storms*. ■ cruel and vicious; aggressively hostile: *they launched a savage attack on the budget*. ■ (chiefly in historical or literary contexts) primitive; uncivilized. ■ (of a place) wild-looking and inhospitable; uncultivated. ■ (of something bad or negative) very great; severe: *this would deal a savage blow to the government's fight*.
▶ **n.** (chiefly in historical or literary contexts) a member of a people regarded as primitive and uncivilized. ■ a brutal or vicious person: *the mother of one of the victims has described his assailants as savages*.
▶ **v.** [with obj.] (esp. of a dog or wild animal) attack ferociously and maul: *ewes savaged by marauding dogs*. ■ subject to a vicious verbal attack; criticize brutally: *Fowler savaged her in his next review*.
– DERIVATIVES **sav·age·ly adv.**, **sav·age·ness n.**
– ORIGIN Middle English: from Old French *sauvage* 'wild,' from Latin *silvaticus* 'of the woods,' from *silva* 'a wood.'

sav·age·ry /'savijrē/ ▶ **n.** (pl. **savageries**) **1** the quality of being fierce or cruel: *a crime of the utmost savagery*.
2 (chiefly in historical or literary contexts) the condition of being primitive or uncivilized: *without adult society, the children descend into savagery*.

Sa·vai'i /sə'vī-ē/ (also **Savaii**) a mountainous volcanic island in the southwestern Pacific, the largest of the Samoan islands.

sa·van·na /sə'vanə/ (also **savannah**) ▶ **n.** a grassy plain in tropical and subtropical regions, with few trees.
– ORIGIN mid 16th cent.: from Spanish *sabana*, from Taino *zavana*.

Sa·van·nah /sə'vanə/ a port in Georgia, just south of the border with South Carolina, on the Savannah River close to its outlet on the Atlantic; pop. 132,410 (est. 2008).

Sa·vann·ah Riv·er a river that flows for 315 miles (506 km), mostly along the border of Georgia and South Carolina, to reach the Atlantic Ocean near Savannah.

sa·van·nah spar·row /sə'vanə/ ▶ **n.** a small sparrow common throughout most of North America. ● *Passerculus sandwichensis*, family Emberizidae.

sa·vant /sa'vänt, sə-/ ▶ **n.** a learned person, esp. a distinguished scientist. See also IDIOT SAVANT.
– ORIGIN early 18th cent.: French, literally 'knowing (person),' present participle (used as a noun) of *savoir*.

sav·a·rin /'savərin/ ▶ **n.** a light ring-shaped cake made with yeast and soaked in liqueur-flavored syrup.
– ORIGIN named after Anthelme Brillat-*Savarin* (1755–1826), French gastronome.

sa·vate /sə'vat/ ▶ **n.** a French method of fighting in which feet and fists are used.
– ORIGIN French, originally denoting an ill-fitting shoe.

save[1] /sāv/ ▶ **v.** [with obj.] **1** keep safe or rescue (someone or something) from harm or danger: *she saved a boy from drowning*. ■ prevent (someone) from dying: *the doctors did everything they could to save him*. ■ (in Christian use) preserve (a person's soul) from damnation. ■ keep (someone) in health (used in exclamations and formulaic expressions): *God save the Queen*.
2 keep and store up (something, esp. money) for future use: *she had never been able to save much from her salary* | [no obj.] *you can save up for retirement in a number of ways*. ■ Computing keep (data) by moving a copy to a storage location, esp. from memory: *save it to a new file*. ■ preserve (something) by not expending or using it: *save your strength till later*. ■ [in imperative] (**save it**) informal used to tell someone to stop talking: *save it, Joey—I'm in big trouble now*.
3 avoid the need to use up or spend (money, time, or other resources): *save $20 on a new camcorder* | [with two objs.] *an efficient dishwasher would save them one year and three months at the sink*. ■ avoid, lessen, or guard against: *this approach saves wear and tear on the books* | [with two objs.] *the statement was made to save the government some embarrassment*.
4 prevent an opponent from scoring (a goal or point) in a game or from winning (the game): *the powerful German saved three match points*. ■ Baseball (of a relief pitcher in certain game situations) finish (a game) while preserving a winning position gained by another pitcher. ■ Soccer & Hockey (of a goalkeeper) stop (a shot) from entering the goal.
▶ **n. 1** Baseball an instance of a relief pitcher saving a game. ■ chiefly Soccer & Hockey an act of preventing an opponent's scoring: *the keeper made a great save*. ■ Bridge another term for SACRIFICE.
2 Computing an act of saving data to a storage location, usually the hard drive: *the recovery feature enables you to retrieve most of the edits you made since the last save*.
– PHRASES **save one's breath** [often in imperative] not bother to say something because it is pointless. **save the day** find or provide a solution to a difficulty or disaster. **save (someone's) face** see FACE. **save someone's life** prevent someone's dying by taking specific action. ■ (**cannot do something to save one's life**) be completely incompetent at doing something: *Adrian couldn't draw to save his life*. **save someone's skin** (or **neck** or **hide** or **bacon**) rescue someone from danger or difficulty. **save someone the trouble** (or **bother**) avoid involving someone in useless or pointless effort: *write it down and save yourself the trouble of remembering*.

– DERIVATIVES **sav·a·ble** (also **saveable**) **adj.**
– ORIGIN Middle English: from Old French *sauver*, from late Latin *salvare*, from Latin *salvus* 'safe.' The noun dates from the late 19th cent.

save[2] ▶ **prep. & conj.** formal or literary except; other than: *no one needed to know save herself* | *the kitchen was empty save for Boris.*
– ORIGIN Middle English: from Old French *sauf*, *sauve*, from Latin *salvo*, *salva* (ablative singular of *salvus* 'safe'), used in phrases such as *salvo jure*, *salva innocentia* 'with no violation of right or innocence.'

sav·er /ˈsāvər/ ▶ **n. 1** a person who regularly saves money through a bank or recognized scheme. **2** [in combination] an object, action, or process that prevents a particular kind of resource from being used up or expended: *a great space-saver.*

sav·in /ˈsavin/ ▶ **n. 1** a bushy Eurasian juniper that typically has horizontally spreading branches. ● *Juniperus sabina*, family Cupressaceae. ■ an extract obtained from this plant, formerly used as an abortifacient. **2** another term for EASTERN RED CEDAR (see RED CEDAR).
– ORIGIN Old English, from Old French *savine*, from Latin *sabina (herba)* 'Sabine (herb).'

sav·ing /ˈsāviNG/ ▶ **n. 1** an economy of or reduction in money, time, or another resource: *this resulted in a considerable saving in development costs.* **2** (usu. **one's savings**) the money one has saved, esp. through a bank or official scheme: *the agents were cheating them out of their life savings.* **3** Law a reservation; an exception.
▶ **adj.** [in combination] preventing waste of a particular resource: *an energy-saving light bulb.*
▶ **prep. 1** with the exception of; except. **2** archaic with due respect to.
– ORIGIN Middle English: from SAVE[1]; the preposition probably from SAVE[2], on the pattern of *touching.*

sav·ing grace ▶ **n.** the redeeming grace of God. ■ a redeeming quality or characteristic.

sav·ings ac·count ▶ **n.** a bank account that earns interest.

sav·ings and loan (also **savings and loan association**) ▶ **n.** an institution that accepts savings at interest and lends money to savers chiefly for home mortgage loans and may offer checking accounts and other services.

sav·ings bank ▶ **n.** a financial institution that receives savings accounts and pays interest to depositors.

sav·ings bond ▶ **n.** a bond issued by the government and sold to the general public.

sav·ior /ˈsāvyər/ (Brit. **saviour**) ▶ **n.** a person who saves someone or something (esp. a country or cause) from danger, and who is regarded with the veneration of a religious figure. ■ (**the/our Savior**) (in Christianity) God or Jesus Christ as the redeemer of sin and saver of souls.
– ORIGIN Middle English: from Old French *sauveour*, from ecclesiastical Latin *salvator* (translating Greek *sōtēr*), from late Latin *salvare* 'to save.'

sav·oir faire /ˌsavwär ˈfe(ə)r/ ▶ **n.** the ability to act or speak appropriately in social situations.
– ORIGIN early 19th cent.: French, literally 'know how to do.'

Sav·o·na·ro·la /ˌsavənəˈrōlə, səˌvänə-/, Girolamo (1452–98), Italian preacher and religious reformer. A Dominican monk and strict ascetic, he was popular for his passionate preaching against immorality and corruption. Although he became virtual ruler of Florence (1494–95), he was excommunicated in 1497 and later executed as a heretic.

Sa·vonne·rie car·pet /ˈsavənrē/ ▶ **n.** a hand-knotted pile carpet, originally made in 17th-century Paris.
– ORIGIN late 19th cent.: French *savonnerie*, literally 'soap factory,' referring to the original building on the site, converted to carpet manufacture.

sa·vor /ˈsāvər/ (Brit. **savour**) ▶ **v. 1** [with obj.] taste (good food or drink) and enjoy it completely: *gourmets will want to savor our game specialties.* ■ enjoy or appreciate (something pleasant) completely, esp. by dwelling on it: *I wanted to savor every moment.* **2** [no obj.] (**savor of**) have a suggestion or trace of (something, esp. something bad): *their genuflections savored of superstition and popery.*
▶ **n.** a characteristic taste, flavor, or smell, esp. a pleasant one: *the subtle savor of wood smoke.* ■ a suggestion or trace, esp. of something bad.
– DERIVATIVES **sa·vor·less adj.**
– ORIGIN Middle English: from Old French, from Latin *sapor*, from *sapere* 'to taste.'

sa·vor·y[1] /ˈsāv(ə)rē/ ▶ **n.** an aromatic plant of the mint family, used as a culinary herb. ● Genus *Satureja*, family Labiatae: several species, in particular the annual **summer savory** (*S. hortensis*) and the coarser flavored perennial **winter savory** (*S. montana*).
– ORIGIN Middle English: perhaps from Old English *sætherie*, or via Old French, from Latin *satureia.*

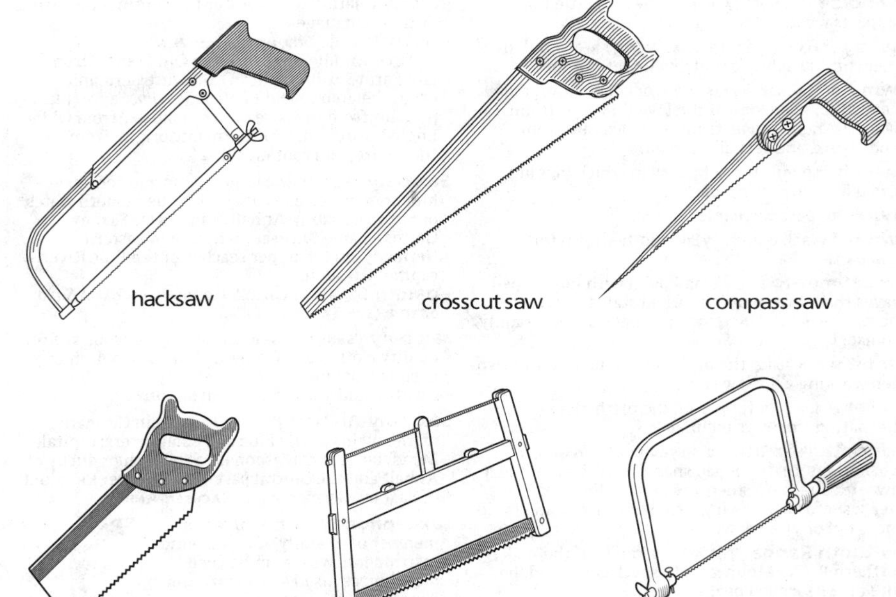

saws

sa·vor·y[2] (Brit. **savoury**) ▶ **adj. 1** (of food) belonging to the category that is salty or spicy rather than sweet. **2** [usu. with negative] morally wholesome or acceptable: *everyone knew it was a front for less savory operations.*
▶ **n.** (pl. **savories**) chiefly Brit. a savory dish, esp. a snack or an appetizer.
– DERIVATIVES **sa·vor·i·ly** /-rəlē/ **adv.**, **sa·vor·i·ness n.**
– ORIGIN Middle English (in the sense 'pleasing to the sense of taste or smell'): from Old French *savoure* 'tasty, fragrant,' based on Latin *sapor* 'taste.'

Sa·voy /səˈvoi/ an area of southeastern France that borders on northwestern Italy, a former duchy ruled by the counts of Savoy from the 11th century.
– DERIVATIVES **Sa·voy·ard** /səˈvoiərd, ˌsavoiˈärd, -vwäˈyär/ **adj. & n.**

sa·voy /səˈvoi/ (also **savoy cabbage**) ▶ **n.** a cabbage of a hardy variety with densely wrinkled leaves.
– ORIGIN late 16th cent.: from SAVOY.

Sa·vu Sea /ˈsävo͞o/ a part of the Indian Ocean that is surrounded by the islands of Sumba, Flores, and Timor.

sav·vy /ˈsavē/ (also **savviness**) informal ▶ **n.** shrewdness and practical knowledge, esp. in politics or business: *the financiers lacked the necessary political savvy.*
▶ **v.** (**savvies, savvying, savvied**) [with clause] know or understand: *Charley would savvy what to do about such a girl* | [no obj.] *I've been told, but I want to make sure. Savvy?*
▶ **adj.** (**savvier, savviest**) shrewd and knowledgeable in the realities of life.
– ORIGIN late 18th cent.: originally black and pidgin English imitating Spanish *sabe usted* 'you know.'

saw[1] /sô/ ▶ **n.** a hand tool for cutting wood or other materials, typically with a long, thin serrated steel blade and operated using a backward and forward movement. ■ a mechanical power-driven tool for cutting, typically with a toothed rotating disk or moving band.
▶ **v.** (past participle chiefly Brit. **sawn** /sôn/ or chiefly N. Amer. **sawed**) [with obj.] cut (something, esp. wood or a tree) using a saw: *the top of each post is* **sawed off** *at railing height* | [no obj.] *thieves escaped after sawing through iron bars on a basement window* | [as adj., in combination] (**-sawn**) *rough-sawn planks.* ■ make or form (something) using a saw: *the seats are sawed from well-seasoned oak planks.* ■ cut (something) as if with a saw, esp. roughly or so as to leave rough or unfinished edges: *the woman who* **sawed off** *all my lovely hair.* ■ [no obj.] make rapid sawlike motions in cutting something or in playing a stringed instrument: *he was* **sawing away** *at the loaf of bread.*
– DERIVATIVES **saw·like** /-ˌlīk/ **adj.**
– ORIGIN Old English *saga*, of Germanic origin; related to Dutch *zaag.*

saw[2] past of SEE[1].

saw[3] ▶ **n.** a proverb or maxim.
– ORIGIN Old English *sagu* 'a saying, speech,' of Germanic origin; related to German *Sage*, also to SAY and SAGA.

Sa·watch Range /səˈwäCH/ a range of the Rocky Mountains in central Colorado. Mount Elbert, at 14,433 feet (4,399 m), is the highest peak in the state and in the entire Rocky Mountain system.

saw·bill /ˈsôˌbil/ ▶ **n.** another term for MERGANSER.

saw·bones /ˈsôˌbōnz/ ▶ **n.** (pl. **same**) informal, humorous a doctor, esp. a surgeon.

saw·buck /ˈsôˌbək/ ▶ **n. 1** a sawhorse. **2** informal a $10 bill. [by association of the X-shaped ends of a sawhorse with the Roman numeral X (= 10).]
– ORIGIN mid 19th cent.: from Dutch *zaagbok*, from *zaag* 'saw' + *bok* 'vaulting horse.'

saw·dust /ˈsôˌdəst/ ▶ **n.** powdery particles of wood produced by sawing.

saw·dust trail (also **Sawdust Trail**) ▶ **n.** informal the itinerary of a traveling gospel preacher: *a retired clergyman who spent his working days as an evangelist on what was left of the old Sawdust Trail.* ■ the process of an erring individual's rehabilitation through repentance: *the president has been on the sawdust trail recently, apologizing hither and yon.*

sawed-off /ˌsôd ˈôf/ (also chiefly Brit. **sawn-off**) ▶ **adj.** [attrib.] (of a gun) having a specially shortened barrel to make handling easier and to give a wider field of fire. ■ informal (of an item of clothing) having been cut short. ■ informal (of a person) short.
▶ **n.** a sawed-off shotgun.

saw·fish /ˈsôˌfiSH/ ▶ **n.** (pl. **same** or **sawfishes**) a large tropical mainly marine fish related to the rays, with an elongated flattened snout that bears large blunt teeth along each side. ● Family Pristidae: two genera, in particular *Pristis*, and several species, including the **common sawfish** (*P. pectinata*).

common sawfish

saw·fly /ˈsôˌflī/ ▶ **n.** (pl. **sawflies**) an insect related to the wasps, with a sawlike egg-laying tube used to cut into plant tissue before depositing the eggs. The larvae resemble caterpillars and can be serious pests of crops and foliage. ● Suborder Symphyta, order Hymenoptera: many families.

saw·grass /ˈsôˌgras/ (also **saw grass**) ▶ **n.** a sedge with spiny-edged leaves. ● *Cladium*, family Cyperaceae: two species, in particular the North American *C. jamaicensis*, which is a dominant plant in the Florida everglades.

S

saw·horse /'sô,hôrs/ ▶ **n.** a frame or trestle that supports wood for sawing.

saw·log /'sô,lôg, -,läg/ (also **saw log**) ▶ **n.** a felled tree trunk suitable for cutting up into timber.

sawm /sōm/ ▶ **n.** Islam fasting from dawn until dusk during Ramadan, one of the Five Pillars of Islam.
– ORIGIN Arabic *ṣawm*, from *ṣāma* 'abstain from food, drink, and sexual intercourse.'

saw·mill /'sô,mil/ ▶ **n.** a factory in which logs are sawed into lumber by machine.

sawn /sôn/ past participle of **SAW**[1].

sawn-off ▶ **adj.** & **n.** chiefly Brit. another term for **SAWED-OFF**.

saw pal·met·to ▶ **n.** a small palm with fan-shaped leaves that have sharply toothed stalks, native to the southeastern US. ● Several species in the family Palmae, in particular *Serenoa repens*.

saw pit ▶ **n.** historical the pit in which the lower of two men working a pit saw stands.

saw set ▶ **n.** a tool for giving the teeth of a saw alternating sideways inclinations.

saw·tooth /'sô,tōōTH/ (also **sawtoothed** or **saw-toothed** /-,tōōTHt/) ▶ **adj.** shaped like the teeth of a saw with alternate steep and gentle slopes. ■ Physics (of a waveform) showing a slow linear rise and rapid linear fall or vice versa.

Saw·tooth Range /'sôtōōTH/ a range of the northern Rocky Mountains in south central Idaho, noted for its jagged peaks.

saw-whet owl ▶ **n.** a small North and Central American owl with a call that resembles the sound of a saw blade being sharpened. ● Genus *Aegolius*, family Strigidae: two species, in particular the North American *A. acadicus*.

saw·yer /'sôyər/ ▶ **n.** **1** a person who saws timber for a living.
2 an uprooted tree floating in a river but held fast at one end. [with allusion to the trapped log's movement up and down.]
3 a large longhorn beetle whose larvae bore tunnels in the wood of injured or recently felled trees, producing an audible chewing sound. ● Genus *Monochamus*, family Cerambycidae.
– ORIGIN Middle English (earlier as *sawer*): from the noun **SAW**[1] + **-YER**.

sax /saks/ ▶ **n.** informal a saxophone.
– DERIVATIVES **sax·ist** /-ist/ **n.**
– ORIGIN early 20th cent.: abbreviation.

Sax. ▶ **abbr.** Saxon or Saxony.

sax·a·tile /'saksə,tīl/ ▶ **adj.** living or growing on or among rocks.
– ORIGIN mid 17th cent.: from French *saxatile* or Latin *saxatilis*, from *saxum* 'rock.'

Saxe-Co·burg-Go·tha /'saks 'kōbərg 'gōTHə/ the name of the British royal house 1901–17. The name dates from the accession of Edward VII, whose father, Prince Albert, consort of Queen Victoria, was a prince of the German duchy of Saxe-Coburg and Gotha.

sax·horn /'saks,hôrn/ ▶ **n.** a member of a family of brass instruments with valves and a funnel-shaped mouthpiece, used mainly in military and brass bands.
– ORIGIN from the name of Charles J. *Sax* (1791–1865) and his son Antoine-Joseph "Adolphe" *Sax* (1814–94), Belgian instrument-makers, + **HORN**.

sax·ic·o·line /sak'sikə,līn, -lin/ (also **saxicolous** /-'sikələs/) ▶ **adj.** another term for **SAXATILE**.
– ORIGIN late 19th cent.: from modern Latin *saxicolus* (from *saxum* 'rock' + *colere* 'inhabit') + **-INE**[1].

sax·i·frage /'saksəfrij, -frāj/ ▶ **n.** a low-growing plant of poor soils, bearing small white, yellow, or red flowers and forming rosettes of succulent leaves or hummocks of mossy leaves. Many are grown as alpines in rock gardens. ● Genus *Saxifraga*, family Saxifragaceae.
– ORIGIN late Middle English: from Old French *saxifrage* or late Latin *saxifraga* (*herba*), from Latin *saxum* 'rock' + *frangere* 'break.'

Sax·on /'saksən/ ▶ **n.** **1** a member of a Germanic people that inhabited parts of central and northern Germany from Roman times, many of whom conquered and settled in southern England in the 5th–6th centuries. ■ a native of modern Saxony in Germany.
2 the language of the Saxons, in particular: ■ (**Old Saxon**) the West Germanic language of the ancient Saxons. ■ another term for **OLD ENGLISH**. ■ the Low German dialect of modern Saxony.
▶ **adj.** **1** of or relating to the Anglo-Saxons, their language (Old English), or their period of dominance in England (5th–11th centuries). ■ relating to or denoting the style of early Romanesque architecture preceding the Norman in England.
2 of or relating to Saxony or the continental Saxons or their language.
– DERIVATIVES **Sax·on·ize** /-,nīz/ **v.**
– ORIGIN Middle English: from Old French, from late Latin *Saxones* (plural), of West Germanic origin; related to Old English *Seaxan*, *Seaxe* (plural), perhaps from the base of *sax* 'small ax,' from Old English *seax* 'knife,' of Germanic origin, from an Indo-European root meaning 'cut.'

Sax·o·ny /'saksənē/ a large region and former kingdom in Germany, including the modern states of Saxony, Saxony-Anhalt, and Lower Saxony. German name **SACHSEN**. ■ a state in eastern Germany, on the upper reaches of the Elbe River; capital, Dresden.
– ORIGIN from late Latin *Saxonia*, from Latin *Saxo*, *Saxon-* (see **SAXON**).

sax·o·ny /'saksənē/ ▶ **n.** a fine kind of wool. ■ a fine-quality cloth made from this kind of wool, chiefly used for making coats.
– ORIGIN mid 19th cent.: from **SAXONY**.

Sax·o·ny-An·halt /'änhält/ a state in Germany, on the plains of the Elbe and Saale rivers; capital, Magdeburg. It corresponds to the former duchy of Anhalt and the central part of the former kingdom of Saxony. German name **SACHSEN-ANHALT**.

sax·o·phone /'saksə,fōn/ ▶ **n.** a member of a family of metal wind instruments with a single-reed mouthpiece, used esp. in jazz and dance music.
– DERIVATIVES **sax·o·phon·ic** /,saksə'fänik/ **adj.**, **sax·o·phon·ist** /-,fōnist/ **n.**
– ORIGIN from the name of Adolphe Sax (see **SAXHORN**) + **-PHONE**.

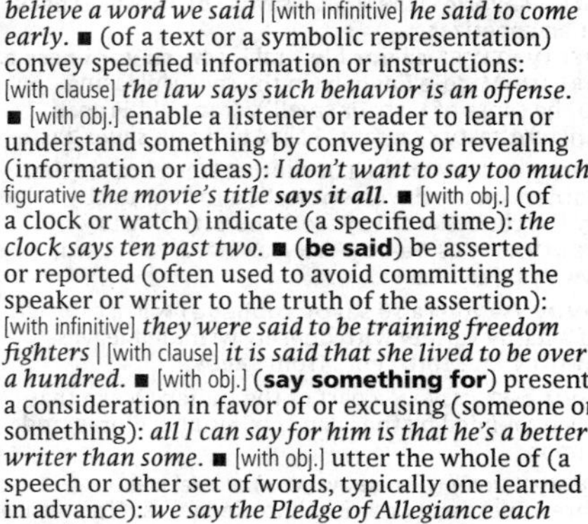
saxophone

say /sā/ ▶ **v.** (**says** /sez/; past and past participle **said** /sed/) **1** [reporting verb] utter words so as to convey information, an opinion, a feeling or intention, or an instruction: [with direct speech] *"Thank you," he said* | [with clause] *he said the fund stood at $100,000* | [with obj.] *our parents wouldn't believe a word we said* | [with infinitive] *he said to come early.* ■ (of a text or a symbolic representation) convey specified information or instructions: [with clause] *the law says such behavior is an offense.* ■ [with obj.] enable a listener or reader to learn or understand something by conveying or revealing (information or ideas): *I don't want to say too much* | figurative *the movie's title says it all.* ■ [with obj.] (of a clock or watch) indicate (a specified time): *the clock says ten past two.* ■ (**be said**) be asserted or reported (often used to avoid committing the speaker or writer to the truth of the assertion): [with infinitive] *they were said to be training freedom fighters* | [with clause] *it is said that she lived to be over a hundred.* ■ [with obj.] (**say something for**) present a consideration in favor of or excusing (someone or something): *all I can say for him is that he's a better writer than some.* ■ [with obj.] utter the whole of (a speech or other set of words, typically one learned in advance): *we say the Pledge of Allegiance each morning.*
2 [with clause] assume something in order to work out what its consequences would be; make a hypothesis: *let's say we pay five thousand dollars in the first year.* ■ used parenthetically to indicate that something is being suggested as possible or likely but not certain: *the form might include, say, a dozen questions.*
▶ **exclam.** informal used to express surprise or to draw attention to a remark or question: *say, did you notice any blood?*
▶ **n.** [in sing.] an opportunity for stating one's opinion or feelings: *the voters are entitled to **have their say** on the treaty.* ■ an opportunity to influence developments and policy: *the assessor will **have a say** in how the money is spent* | *the households concerned would still **have some say** in what happened.*
– PHRASES **go without saying** be obvious: *it goes without saying that teachers must be selected with care.* [translating French (*cela*) *va sans dire.*] **have something to say for oneself** contribute to a conversation or discussion, esp. as an explanation for one's behavior or actions: *haven't you anything to say for yourself?* **how say you?** Law how do you find? (addressed to the jury when requesting its verdict). **I** (or **he**, **she**, etc.) **cannot** (or **could not**) **say** I (or he, she, etc.) do not know. **I'll say** informal used to express emphatic agreement: *"That was a good landing." "I'll say!"* **I must** (or **have to**) **say** I cannot refrain from saying (used to emphasize an opinion): *you have a nerve, I must say!* **I say!** Brit. dated used to express surprise or to draw attention to a remark: *I say, that's a bit much!* **I wouldn't say no** informal used to indicate that one would like something. **not to say** used to introduce a stronger alternative or addition to something already said: *it is easy to become sensitive, not to say paranoid.* **say no more** informal used to indicate that one understands what someone is trying to imply. **says you!** informal used in speech to express disagreement or disbelief: *"He's guilty." "Says you! I think he's innocent."* **say when** informal said when helping someone to food or drink to instruct them to indicate when they have enough. **say the word** give permission or instructions to do something. **that is to say** used to introduce a clarification, interpretation, or correction of something already said. **there is no saying** it is impossible to know. **they say** it is rumored. **to say nothing of** another way of saying **NOT TO MENTION** (see **MENTION**). **to say the least** see **LEAST**. **what do** (or **would**) **you say** used to make a suggestion or offer: *what do you say to a glass of wine?* **when all is said and done** when everything is taken into account (used to indicate that one is making a generalized judgment about a situation). **you can say that again!** informal used in spoken English to express emphatic agreement. **you don't say!** informal used to express amazement or disbelief. **you said it!** informal used to express the feeling that someone's words are true or appropriate.
– DERIVATIVES **say·a·ble** **adj.**, **say·er** **n.** [usu. in combination] *naysayers*.
– ORIGIN Old English *secgan*, of Germanic origin; related to Dutch *zeggen* and German *sagen*.

Say·ers[1] /'sā-ərz, se(ə)rz/, Dorothy L. (1893–1957), English novelist, translator, essayist, and playwright; full name *Dorothy Leigh Sayers*. She is chiefly known for her detective novels that feature amateur detective Lord Peter Wimsey and include *Murder Must Advertise* (1933) and *The Nine Tailors* (1934). She translated the medieval French *La Chanson de Roland* and Dante's *La Divina Commedia*. Her plays include *The Devil to Pay* (1939).

Say·ers[2], Gale (Eugene) (1943–), US football player. Named rookie of the year in 1965, he went on to break touchdown records during his playing career 1965–71 with the Chicago Bears. Football Hall of Fame (1977).

say·ing /'sāiNG/ ▶ **n.** a short, pithy expression that generally contains advice or wisdom. ■ (**sayings**) a collection of such expressions identified with a particular person, esp. a political or religious leader.
– PHRASES **as** (or **so**) **the saying goes** used to introduce or append an expression, drawing attention to its status as a saying or as not part of one's normal language: *I am, as the saying goes, burned out.*

sa·yo·na·ra /,sīə'närə/ ▶ **exclam.** informal goodbye.
– ORIGIN Japanese.

Sayre·ville /'se(ə)rvil/ an industrial and residential borough in eastern New Jersey; pop. 42,208 (est. 2008).

Say's law /sāz/ Economics a law stating that supply creates its own demand.
– ORIGIN 1930s: named after Jean Baptiste *Say* (1767–1832), French economist.

say-so ▶ **n.** [in sing.] informal the power or act of deciding or allowing something: *no new employees come into the organization without his say-so.* ■ (usu. **on someone's say-so**) a person's arbitrary or unauthorized assertion or instruction: *I don't stop on the say-so of anybody's assistant.*

say·yid /'säyid, 'sāyid/ ▶ **n.** a Muslim claiming descent from Muhammad, esp. through Husayn, the prophet's younger grandson. ■ a respectful Muslim form of address.
– ORIGIN Arabic, literally 'lord, prince.'

saz /säz, saz/ ▶ **n.** a long-necked stringed instrument of the lute family, originating in the Ottoman Empire.
– ORIGIN late 19th cent.: from Turkish, from Persian *sāz* 'musical instrument.'

SB ▶ **abbr.** ■ Bachelor of Science. [Latin *Scientiae Baccalaureus*.] ■ simultaneous broadcast. ■ South Britain (England and Wales).

Sb ▶ **symbol** the chemical element antimony.
– ORIGIN from Latin *stibium*.

sb. ▶ **abbr.** substantive.

s.b. ▶ **abbr.** Baseball stolen base; stolen bases.

SBA ▶ **abbr.** Small Business Administration.

S-Bahn /'es ,bän/ ▶ **n.** (in some German cities) a fast urban railroad line or system.
– ORIGIN German, abbreviation of (*Stadt*) *Schnellbahn* '(urban) fast railroad.'

SbE ▶ **abbr.** south by east.

SBS ▶ **abbr.** ■ sick building syndrome. ■ Brit. Special Boat Service.

SbW ▶ **abbr.** south by west.

SC ▶ **abbr.** ■ South Carolina (in official postal use). ■ (in the UK) special constable.

Sc ▶ **symbol** the chemical element scandium.

sc. ▶ **abbr.** that is to say (used to introduce a word to be supplied or an explanation of an ambiguity).
– ORIGIN from SCILICET.

s.c. ▶ **abbr.** small capitals (used as an instruction for a typesetter).

scab /skab/ ▶ **n.** **1** a dry, rough protective crust that forms over a cut or wound during healing.
2 mange or a similar skin disease in animals. ■ [usu. with modifier] any of a number of fungal diseases of plants in which rough patches develop, esp. on apples and potatoes.
3 informal a person or thing regarded with dislike and disgust. ■ derogatory a person who refuses to strike or to join a labor union or who takes over the job responsibilities of a striking worker.
▶ **v.** (**scabs, scabbing, scabbed**) [no obj.] **1** (usu. as adj. **scabbed**) become encrusted or covered with a scab or scabs: *she rested her scabbed fingers on his arm.*
2 act or work as a scab.
– DERIVATIVES **scab·like** /-ˌlīk/ **adj.**
– ORIGIN Middle English (as a noun): from Old Norse *skabb*; related to dialect *shab* (compare with SHABBY). The sense 'contemptible person' (dating from the late 16th cent.) was probably influenced by Middle Dutch *schabbe* 'slut.'

scab·bard /ˈskabərd/ ▶ **n.** a sheath for the blade of a sword or dagger, typically made of leather or metal. ■ a sheath for a gun or other weapon or tool.
– ORIGIN Middle English: from Anglo-Norman French *escalberc*, from a Germanic compound of words meaning 'cut' (related to SHEAR) and 'protect' (related to the second element of HAUBERK).

scab·by /ˈskabē/ ▶ **adj.** (**scabbier, scabbiest**)
1 covered in scabs.
2 informal loathsome; despicable.
– DERIVATIVES **scab·bi·ness n.**

sca·bies /ˈskābēz/ ▶ **n.** a contagious skin disease marked by itching and small raised red spots, caused by the itch mite.
– ORIGIN late Middle English (denoting various skin diseases): from Latin, from *scabere* 'to scratch.' The current sense dates from the early 19th cent.

sca·bi·ous /ˈskābēəs/ ▶ **n.** a plant of the teasel family, with pink, white, or (most commonly) blue pincushion-shaped flowers. ● *Scabiosa, Knautia*, and other genera, family Dipsacaceae: several species.
▶ **adj.** affected with mange; scabby.
– ORIGIN late Middle English: based on Latin *scabiosus* 'rough, scabby'; the noun is from medieval Latin *scabiosa (herba)* 'rough, scabby (plant),' formerly regarded as a cure for skin disease (see SCABIES).

scab·lands /ˈskabˌlandz/ ▶ **plural n.** Geology flat elevated land deeply scarred by channels of glacial or fluvioglacial origin and with poor soil and little vegetation, esp. in the Columbia Plateau of Washington State.

scab·rous /ˈskabrəs/ ▶ **adj.** **1** rough and covered with, or as if with, scabs.
2 indecent; salacious: *scabrous publications.*
– DERIVATIVES **scab·rous·ly adv.**, **scab·rous·ness n.**
– ORIGIN late 16th cent. (first used to describe an author's style as 'harsh, unmusical, unpolished'): from French *scabreux* or late Latin *scabrosus*, from Latin *scaber* 'rough.'

scad /skad/ ▶ **n.** another term for JACK[1] (sense 11) or HORSE MACKEREL.
– ORIGIN early 17th cent.: of unknown origin.

scads /skadz/ ▶ **plural n.** informal a large number or quantity: *they raised scads of children* | [in sing.] *he's installed a scad of microprocessors.*
– ORIGIN mid 19th cent.: of unknown origin.

scaf·fold /ˈskafəld, -ˌfōld/ ▶ **n.** **1** a raised wooden platform used formerly for the public execution of criminals.
2 a structure made using scaffolding.
▶ **v.** [with obj.] attach scaffolding to (a building): (as adj. **scaffolded**) *the soot-black scaffolded structures.*
– DERIVATIVES **scaf·fold·er n.**
– ORIGIN Middle English (denoting a temporary platform from which to repair or erect a building): from Anglo-Norman French, from Old French (*e*)*schaffaut*, from the base of CATAFALQUE.

scaf·fold·ing /ˈskafəldiNG, -ˌfōl-/ ▶ **n.** a temporary structure on the outside of a building, made usually of wooden planks and metal poles, used by workers while building, repairing, or cleaning the building. ■ the materials used in such a structure.

scag /skag/ ▶ **n.** variant spelling of SKAG[1].

scagl·io·la /skalˈyōlə/ ▶ **n.** imitation marble or other stone, made of plaster mixed with glue and dyes, which is then painted or polished.
– ORIGIN mid 18th cent.: from Italian *scagliuola*, diminutive of *scaglia* 'a scale.'

scal·a·ble /ˈskāləbəl/ ▶ **adj.** **1** able to be scaled or climbed.
2 able to be changed in size or scale: *scalable fonts.* ■ (of a computing process) able to be used or produced in a range of capabilities: *it is scalable across a range of systems.*
3 technical able to be measured or graded according to a scale.
– DERIVATIVES **scal·a·bil·i·ty** /ˌskāləˈbilitē/ **n.**

sca·la me·dia /ˈskālə ˈmēdēə/ ▶ **n.** (pl. **scalae mediae** /ˈskālē ˈmēdē-ē/) Anatomy the central duct of the cochlea in the inner ear, containing the sensory cells and separated from the scala tympani and scala vestibuli by membranes.
– ORIGIN late 19th cent.: from Latin, literally 'middle ladder.'

sca·lar /ˈskālər/ Mathematics & Physics ▶ **adj.** (of a quantity) having only magnitude, not direction.
▶ **n.** a scalar quantity. Compare with VECTOR (sense 1 of the noun).
– ORIGIN mid 17th cent.: from Latin *scalaris*, from *scala* 'ladder' (see SCALE[3]).

sca·lar field ▶ **n.** Mathematics a function of a space whose value at each point is a scalar quantity.

sca·lar·i·form /skəˈle(ə)rəˌfôrm/ ▶ **adj.** Botany (esp. of the walls of water-conducting cells) having thickened bands arranged like the rungs of a ladder.
– ORIGIN mid 19th cent.: from Latin *scalaris* 'of a ladder' + -IFORM.

sca·lar prod·uct ▶ **n.** another term for INNER PRODUCT.

sca·la tym·pa·ni /ˈskālə ˈtimpənē/ ▶ **n.** (pl. **scalae tympani** /ˈskālē/) Anatomy the lower bony passage of the cochlea.
– ORIGIN early 18th cent.: from Latin, literally 'ladder of the tympanum.'

sca·la ves·tib·u·li /ˈskālə veˈstibyəlē/ ▶ **n.** (pl. **scalae vestibuli** /ˈskālē/) Anatomy the upper bony passage of the cochlea.
– ORIGIN early 18th cent.: from Latin, literally 'ladder of the vestibule.'

scal·a·wag /ˈskaləˌwag/ (also **scallywag** /ˈskalē-/) ▶ **n.** informal a person who behaves badly but in an amusingly mischievous rather than harmful way; a rascal. ■ historical a white Southerner who collaborated with northern Republicans during Reconstruction, often for personal profit. The term was used derisively by white Southern Democrats who opposed Reconstruction legislation.
– ORIGIN mid 19th cent.: of unknown origin.

scald[1] /skôld/ ▶ **v.** [with obj.] injure with very hot liquid or steam: *the tea scalded his tongue.* ■ heat (milk or other liquid) to near boiling point. ■ immerse (something) briefly in boiling water for various purposes, such as to facilitate the removal of skin from fruit or to preserve meat. ■ cause to feel a searing sensation like that of boiling water on skin: *hot tears scalding her eyes.*
▶ **n.** a burn or other injury caused by hot liquid or steam. ■ any of a number of plant diseases that produce a similar effect to that of scalding, esp. a disease of fruit marked by browning and caused by excessive sunlight, bad storage conditions, or atmospheric pollution. See also SUNSCALD.
– ORIGIN Middle English (as a verb): from Anglo-Norman French *escalder*, from late Latin *excaldare*, from Latin *ex-* 'thoroughly' + *calidus* 'hot.' The noun dates from the early 17th cent.

scald[2] ▶ **n.** variant spelling of SKALD.

scald·ing /ˈskôldiNG/ ▶ **adj.** very hot; burning: *she took a sip of scalding tea* | [as submodifier] *the water was scalding hot.* ■ intense and painful or distressing: *a scalding tirade of abuse.*

scale[1] /skāl/ ▶ **n.** **1** each of the small, thin horny or bony plates protecting the skin of fish and reptiles, typically overlapping one another.
2 something resembling a fish scale in appearance or function, in particular: ■ a thick dry flake of skin. ■ a rudimentary leaf, feather, or bract. ■ each of numerous microscopic tilelike structures covering the wings of butterflies and moths.
3 a flaky deposit, in particular: ■ a white deposit formed in a kettle, boiler, etc., by the evaporation of water containing lime. ■ tartar formed on teeth. ■ a coating of oxide formed on heated metal.
▶ **v.** **1** [with obj.] remove scale or scales from: *he scales the fish and removes the innards.* ■ remove tartar from (teeth) by scraping them.
2 [no obj.] (often as noun **scaling**) (esp. of the skin) form scales: *moisturizers can ease off drying and scaling.* ■ come off in scales or thin pieces; flake off: *the paint was scaling from the brick walls.*
– DERIVATIVES **scaled** /skāld/ **adj.** [often in combination] *a rough-scaled fish*, **scale·less** /ˈskā(l)lis/ **adj.**, **scal·er n.**
– ORIGIN Middle English: shortening of Old French *escale*, from the Germanic base of SCALE[2].

scale[2] ▶ **n.** (usu. **scales**) an instrument for weighing. Scales were originally simple balances (**pairs of scales**) but are now usually devices with an internal weighing mechanism housed under a platform on which the thing to be weighed is placed, with a gauge or electronic display showing the weight. ■ (also **scalepan**) either of the dishes on a simple balance. ■ (**the Scales**) the zodiacal sign or constellation Libra.
▶ **v.** [with obj.] weigh a specified weight: *some men scaled less than ninety pounds.*
– PHRASES **tip the scales** see TIP[2]. **tip the scales at** see TIP[2].
– ORIGIN Middle English (in the sense 'drinking cup,' surviving in South African English): from Old Norse *skál* 'bowl,' of Germanic origin; related to Dutch *schaal*, German *Schale* 'bowl,' also to English dialect *shale* 'dish' Compare with SKOAL.

scale[3] ▶ **n.** **1** a graduated range of values forming a standard system for measuring or grading something: *company employees have hit the top of their pay scales.* ■ the full range of different levels of people or things, from lowest to highest: *two men at opposite ends of the social scale.* ■ a series of marks at regular intervals in a line used in measuring something: *the mean delivery time is plotted against a scale on the right.* ■ a device having such a series of marks: *she read the exact distance off a scale.* ■ a rule determining the distances between such marks: *the vertical axis is given on a logarithmic scale.*
2 [in sing.] the relative size or extent of something: *no one foresaw the scale of the disaster* | *everything in the house is on a grand scale.* ■ [often as modifier] a ratio of size in a map, model, drawing, or plan: *a one-fifth scale model of a seven-story building* | *an Ordnance Survey map on a scale of 1:2500.* ■ (in full **scale of notation**) Mathematics a system of numerical notation in which the value of a digit depends upon its position in the number, successive positions representing successive powers of a fixed base: *the conversion of the number to the binary scale.* ■ Photography the range of exposures over which a photographic material will give an acceptable variation in density.
3 Music an arrangement of the notes in any system of music in ascending or descending order of pitch: *the scale of C major.*
▶ **v.** [with obj.] **1** climb up or over (something high and steep): *thieves scaled an 8-foot fence.*
2 represent in proportional dimensions; reduce or increase in size according to a common scale: (as adj. **scaled**) *scaled plans of the house.* ■ [no obj.] (of a quantity or property) be variable according to a particular scale.
3 estimate the amount of timber that will be produced from (a log or uncut tree).
– PHRASES **play** (or **sing** or **practice**) **scales** Music perform the notes of a scale as an exercise for the fingers or voice. **to scale** with a uniform reduction or enlargement: *it is hard to build models to scale from a drawing.* **in scale** (of a drawing or model) in proportion to the surroundings.
– PHRASAL VERBS **scale something back** reduce something in size, number, or extent, esp. by a constant proportion across the board: *in the short term, even scaling back defense costs money.* **scale something down** (or **scale down**) reduce something (or be reduced) in size, number or extent, esp. by a constant proportion across the board: *manufacturing capacity has been scaled down* | *his whole income scaled down by 20 percent.* **scale something up** (or **scale up**) increase something (or be increased) in size or number: *one cannot suddenly scale up a laboratory procedure by a thousandfold.*
– DERIVATIVES **scal·er n.**
– ORIGIN late Middle English: from Latin *scala* 'ladder' (the verb via Old French *escaler* or medieval Latin *scalare* 'climb'), from the base of Latin *scandere* 'to climb.'

scale ar·mor ▶ **n.** historical armor consisting of small overlapping plates of metal, leather, or horn.

scale in·sect ▶ **n.** a small insect with a protective shieldlike scale. It spends most of its life attached by its mouth to a single plant, sometimes occurring in such large numbers that it becomes a serious pest. ● Superfamily Coccoidea, suborder Homoptera: several families, in particular Coccidae.

scale leaf ▶ **n.** Botany a small modified leaf, esp. a colorless membranous one, such as on a rhizome or forming part of a bulb.

sca·lene /skāˈlēn/ ▶ **adj.** (of a triangle) having sides unequal in length.
▶ **n.** **1** (also **scalene muscle**) Anatomy another term for SCALENUS.
2 a scalene triangle.
– ORIGIN mid 17th cent.: via late Latin from Greek *skalēnos* 'unequal'; related to *skolios* 'bent.'

S

sca·le·nus /skāˈlēnəs/ ▶ **n.** (pl. **scaleni** /-ˈlēnī/) any of several muscles extending from the neck to the first and second ribs.
– ORIGIN early 18th cent.: modern Latin, from late Latin *scalenus* (*musculus*) 'unequal (muscle)' (see SCALENE).

scale of no·ta·tion ▶ **n.** see SCALE³ (sense 2 of the noun).

scale·pan /ˈskālˌpan/ ▶ **n.** see SCALE².

scale·worm /ˈskālˌwərm/ (also **scale worm**) ▶ **n.** a marine bristle worm with scales on the upper surface that have a protective function, and in some species are able to luminesce. ● Family Aphroditidae: *Aphrodite* and other genera. See also SEA MOUSE.

Sca·li·a /skəˈlē(y)ə/, Antonin (1936–), US Supreme Court associate justice 1986– . A conservative and an advocate of judicial restraint, he served in several government posts, taught law at various universities, and served on the US Circuit Court of Appeals in Washington, DC, before being appointed to the Supreme Court by President Reagan.

scal·ing lad·der /ˈskāliNG/ ▶ **n.** historical a ladder used for firefighting or for climbing walls in order to penetrate the defenses of a fortification.

scal·lion /ˈskalyən/ ▶ **n.** a long-necked onion with a small bulb, in particular a shallot or green onion. ● A common scallion is *Allium fistulosum*, family Liliaceae (or Alliaceae).
– ORIGIN late Middle English: from Anglo-Norman French *scaloun*, based on Latin *Ascalonia* (*caepa*) '(onion) of *Ascalon*,' a port in ancient Palestine.

scal·lop /ˈskäləp, ˈskal-/ ▶ **n. 1** an edible bivalve mollusk with a ribbed fan-shaped shell. Scallops swim by rapidly opening and closing the shell valves. ● Family Pectinidae: *Chlamys*, *Pecten*, and other genera. ■ short for SCALLOP SHELL. ■ a small pan or dish shaped like a scallop shell and used for baking or serving food.
2 (usu. **scallops**) each of a series of convex rounded projections forming an ornamental edging cut in material or worked in lace or knitting in imitation of the edge of a scallop shell.
3 another term for ESCALOPE.
▶ **v.** (**scallops**, **scalloping**, **scalloped**) **1** [with obj.] (usu. as adj. **scalloped**) ornament (an edge or material) with scallops: *a scalloped V-shaped neckline.* ■ cut, shape, or arrange in the form of a scallop shell: *he leaned against the scalloped seat of the limousine.*
2 [no obj.] (usu. as noun **scalloping**) gather or dredge for scallops.
3 [with obj.] bake with milk or a sauce: (as adj. **scalloped**) *scalloped potatoes.*
– DERIVATIVES **scal·lop·er** n.
– ORIGIN Middle English: shortening of Old French *escalope*, probably of Germanic origin. The verb dates from the mid 18th cent.

scal·lop shell ▶ **n.** a single valve from the shell of a scallop. ■ historical a representation of this shell worn by a pilgrim as a souvenir of the shrine of St. James at Santiago de Compostela in Spain.

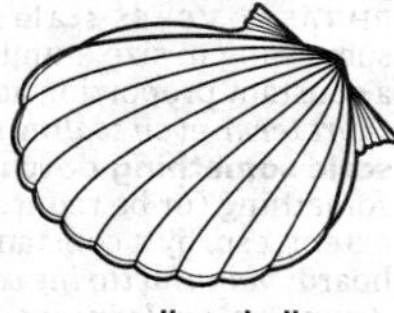
scallop shell

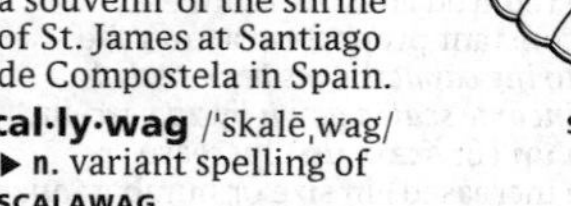

scal·ly·wag /ˈskalēˌwag/ ▶ **n.** variant spelling of SCALAWAG.

sca·lop·pi·ne /ˌskäləˈpēnē, ˌskal-/ (also **scallopini**) ▶ **plural n.** (in Italian cooking) thin, boneless slices of meat, typically veal, sautéed or fried.
– ORIGIN Italian, plural of *scaloppina*, diminutive of *scaloppa* 'envelope.'

scalp /skalp/ ▶ **n.** the skin covering the head, excluding the face. ■ historical the scalp with the hair belonging to it cut or torn away from an enemy's head as a battle trophy, esp. by an American Indian.
▶ **v.** [with obj.] historical take the scalp of (an enemy). ■ informal punish severely: *if I ever heard anybody doing that, I'd scalp them.* ■ informal sell (a ticket) for a popular event at a price higher than the official one: *tickets were scalped for forty times their face value.*
– ORIGIN Middle English (denoting the skull or cranium): probably of Scandinavian origin.

scal·pel /ˈskalpəl/ ▶ **n.** a knife with a small, sharp, sometimes detachable blade, as used by a surgeon.
– ORIGIN mid 18th cent.: from French, or from Latin *scalpellum*, diminutive of *scalprum* 'chisel,' from *scalpere* 'to scratch.'

scalp·er /ˈskalpər/ ▶ **n.** informal a person who resells shares or tickets at a large or quick profit.

scalp lock (also **scalplock**) ▶ **n.** chiefly historical a long lock of hair left on a shaved head, esp. as worn by a North American Indian as a challenge to enemies.

scalpel

scal·y /ˈskālē/ ▶ **adj.** (**scalier**, **scaliest**) covered in scales. ■ (of skin) dry and flaking.
– DERIVATIVES **scal·i·ness** n.

scal·y ant·eat·er ▶ **n.** another term for PANGOLIN.

scam /skam/ ▶ **n.** informal a dishonest scheme; a fraud: *an insurance scam.*
▶ **v.** (**scams**, **scamming**, **scammed**) [with obj.] swindle: *a guy that scams the elderly out of their savings.*
– DERIVATIVES **scam·mer** n.
– ORIGIN 1960s: of unknown origin.

scam·mo·ny /ˈskamənē/ ▶ **n.** a plant of the morning glory family, the dried roots of which yield a strong purgative. ● Two species in the family Convolvulaceae: *Convolvulus scammonia* of Asia, and *Ipomoea orizabensis* of Mexico.
– ORIGIN Old English, from Old French *escamonie* or Latin *scammonia*, from Greek *skammōnia.*

sca·mor·za /skəˈmôrtsə/ ▶ **n.** a mild white Italian cheese made originally from buffalo's milk, but now chiefly from cow's milk, typically produced in a pear shape.
– ORIGIN 1930s: Italian, from *scamozzare*, 'cut off.'

scamp¹ /skamp/ ▶ **n.** informal a person, esp. a child, who is mischievous in a likable or amusing way. ■ a wicked or worthless person; a rogue.
– DERIVATIVES **scamp·ish** adj.
– ORIGIN mid 18th cent. (denoting a highwayman): from obsolete *scamp* 'rob on the highway,' probably from Middle Dutch *schampen* 'slip away,' from Old French *eschamper* 'flee the battlefield,' from *champ* 'field.'

scamp² ▶ **v.** [with obj.] dated do (something) in a perfunctory or inadequate way.
– ORIGIN mid 19th cent.: perhaps the same word as SCAMP¹, but associated in sense with the verb SKIMP.

scamp·er /ˈskampər/ ▶ **v.** [no obj.] (esp. of a small animal or child) run with quick light steps, esp. through fear or excitement: *he scampered in like an overgrown puppy.*
▶ **n.** [in sing.] an act of scampering.
– ORIGIN late 17th cent. (in the sense 'run away'): probably from SCAMP².

scam·pi /ˈskampē/ ▶ **n.** [plural noun] large shrimp or prawns, esp. when prepared or cooked. ■ a dish of shrimp or prawns, typically sautéed in garlic and butter and often topped with bread crumbs.
– ORIGIN Italian.

scan /skan/ ▶ **v.** (**scans**, **scanning**, **scanned**) [with obj.] **1** look at all parts of (something) carefully in order to detect some feature: *he raised his binoculars to scan the coast.* ■ look quickly but not very thoroughly through (a document or other text) in order to identify relevant information: *we scan the papers for news from the trouble spots* | [no obj.] *I scanned through the reference materials.* ■ cause (a surface, object, or part of the body) to be traversed by a detector or an electromagnetic beam: *their brains are scanned so that researchers can monitor the progress of the disease.* ■ cause (a beam) to traverse across a surface or object: *we scanned the beam over a sector of 120°.* ■ resolve (a picture) into its elements of light and shade in a prearranged pattern for the purposes of television transmission. ■ convert (a document or picture) into digital form for storage or processing on a computer: *text and pictures can be scanned into the computer.*
2 analyze the meter of (a line of verse) by reading with the emphasis on its rhythm or by examining the pattern of feet or syllables. ■ [no obj.] (of verse) conform to metrical principles.
▶ **n.** an act of scanning someone or something: *a quick scan of the sports page.* ■ a medical examination using a scanner: *a brain scan.* ■ an image obtained by scanning or with a scanner: *we can't predict anything until we have seen the scan.*
– DERIVATIVES **scan·na·ble** adj.
– ORIGIN late Middle English (as a verb in sense 2 of the verb): from Latin *scandere* 'climb' (in late Latin 'scan (verses)'), by analogy with the raising and lowering of one's foot when marking rhythm. From 'analyze (meter)' arose the senses 'estimate the correctness of' and 'examine minutely,' which led to 'look at searchingly' (late 18th cent).

scan·dal /ˈskandl/ ▶ **n.** an action or event regarded as morally or legally wrong and causing general public outrage: *a bribery scandal involving one of his key supporters.* ■ the outrage or anger caused by such an action or event: *divorce was cause for scandal on the island.* ■ rumor or malicious gossip about such events or actions: *I know that you would want no scandal attached to her name.* ■ [in sing.] a state of affairs regarded as wrong or reprehensible and causing general public outrage or anger: *it's a scandal that many older patients are dismissed as untreatable.*
– ORIGIN Middle English (in the sense 'discredit to religion (by the reprehensible behavior of a religious person)'): from Old French *scandale*, from ecclesiastical Latin *scandalum* 'cause of offense,' from Greek *skandalon* 'snare, stumbling block.'

scan·dal·ize /ˈskandlˌīz/ ▶ **v.** [with obj.] **1** shock or horrify (someone) by a real or imagined violation of propriety or morality: *their lack of manners scandalized their hosts.*
2 Sailing reduce the area of (a fore-and-aft sail) by lowering the head or raising the boom. [mid 19th cent.: alteration of obsolete *scantelize*, from *scantle* 'make small.']
– DERIVATIVES **scan·dal·i·za·tion** /ˌskandl-əˈzāSHən/ n., **scan·dal·iz·er** n.
– ORIGIN late 15th cent. (in the sense 'make a public scandal of'): from French *scandaliser* or ecclesiastical Latin *scandalizare*, from Greek *skandalizein.*

scan·dal·mon·ger /ˈskandlˌməNGgər, -ˌmäNGgər/ ▶ **n.** a person who stirs up public outrage toward someone or their actions by spreading rumors or malicious gossip.
– DERIVATIVES **scan·dal·mon·ger·ing** n.

scan·dal·ous /ˈskandl-əs/ ▶ **adj.** causing general public outrage by a perceived offense against morality or law: *a series of scandalous liaisons* | *a scandalous allegation.* ■ (of a state of affairs) disgracefully bad, typically as a result of someone's negligence or irresponsibility: *a scandalous waste of taxpayers' money.*
– DERIVATIVES **scan·dal·ous·ly** adv., **scan·dal·ous·ness** n.

scan·dal sheet ▶ **n.** derogatory a newspaper or magazine giving prominence to scandalous stories or gossip.

scan·dent /ˈskandənt/ ▶ **adj.** chiefly Paleontology (esp. of a graptolite) having a climbing habit.
– ORIGIN late 17th cent.: from Latin *scandent-* 'climbing,' from the verb *scandere.*

Scan·den·tia /skanˈdenCH(ē)ə/ Zoology a small order of mammals that comprises the tree shrews.
– ORIGIN modern Latin (plural), from Latin *scandent-* 'climbing,' from the verb *scandere.*

Scan·di·na·vi·a /ˌskandəˈnāvēə/ a large peninsula in northwestern Europe, occupied by Norway and Sweden. It is bounded by the Arctic Ocean on the north, the Atlantic Ocean on the west, and the Baltic Sea on the south and the east. ■ a cultural region consisting of the countries of Norway, Sweden, and Denmark and sometimes also of Iceland, Finland, and the Faroe Islands.
– ORIGIN Latin.

Scan·di·na·vi·an /ˌskandəˈnāvēən/ ▶ **adj.** of or relating to Scandinavia, its people, or their languages.
▶ **n. 1** a native or inhabitant of Scandinavia, or a person of Scandinavian descent.
2 the North Germanic languages (Danish, Norwegian, Swedish, Icelandic, Faroese) descended from Old Norse.

scan·di·um /ˈskandēəm/ ▶ **n.** the chemical element of atomic number 21, a soft silvery-white metal resembling the rare earth elements. (Symbol: **Sc**)
– ORIGIN late 19th cent.: modern Latin, from *Scandia*, contraction of *Scandinavia* (where minerals are found containing this element).

scan·ner /ˈskanər/ ▶ **n.** a device for examining, reading, or monitoring something, in particular: ■ Medicine a machine that examines the body through the use of radiation, ultrasound, or magnetic resonance imaging, as a diagnostic aid. ■ Electronics a device that scans documents and converts them into digital data.

scan·ning e·lec·tron mi·cro·scope (abbr.: **SEM**) ▶ **n.** an electron microscope in which the surface of a specimen is scanned by a beam of electrons that are reflected to form an image.

scan·ning tun·nel·ing mi·cro·scope (abbr.: **STM**) ▶ **n.** a high-resolution microscope using neither light nor an electron beam, but with an ultrafine tip able to reveal atomic and molecular details of surfaces.

scan·sion /ˈskanSHən/ ▶ **n.** the action of scanning a line of verse to determine its rhythm. ■ the rhythm of a line of verse.
– ORIGIN mid 17th cent.: from Latin *scansio(n-)*, from *scandere* 'to climb'; compare with SCAN.

scant /skant/ ▶ **adj.** barely sufficient or adequate: *companies with scant regard for the safety of future generations.* ■ [attrib.] barely amounting to a specified number or quantity: *she weighed a scant two pounds.*
▶ **v.** [with obj.] provide grudgingly or in insufficient amounts: *he does not scant his attention to the later writings.* ■ deal with inadequately; neglect: *the press regularly scants a host of issues relating to safety and health.*
– DERIVATIVES **scant·ly** adv., **scant·ness** n.
– ORIGIN Middle English: from Old Norse *skamt*, neuter of *skammr* 'short.'

scant·ling /ˈskantliNG/ ▶ **n. 1** a piece of lumber of small cross section. ■ the size to which a piece of wood or stone is measured and cut.
2 (often **scantlings**) a set of standard dimensions for parts of a structure, esp. in shipbuilding.
3 archaic a specimen, sample, or small amount of something.
– ORIGIN early 16th cent. (denoting prescribed size, or a set of standard dimensions): alteration of obsolete *scantillon* (from Old French *escantillon* 'sample'), by association with the suffix -LING.

scant·y /ˈskantē/ ▶ **adj.** (**scantier, scantiest**) small or insufficient in quantity or amount: *scanty wages.* ■ (of clothing) revealing; skimpy: *the women looked cold in their scanty gowns.*
▶ **plural n.** (**scanties**) brief underpants.
– DERIVATIVES **scant·i·ly** /ˈskantəlē, ˈskantl-ē/ **adv.**, **scant·i·ness n.**
– ORIGIN late 16th cent.: from SCANT + -Y[1].

Sca·pa Flow /skapə, ˈskä-/ a strait in the Orkney Islands, Scotland. It was the site of an important British naval base, esp. during World War I. The German High Seas Fleet was interned there after its surrender and was scuttled in 1919 as an act of defiance against the terms of the Versailles peace settlement.

scape /skāp/ ▶ **n. 1** Botany a long, leafless flower stalk coming directly from a root.
2 Entomology the basal segment of an insect's antenna, esp. when it is enlarged and lengthened (as in a weevil).
– ORIGIN early 19th cent.: via Latin from Greek *skapos* 'rod'; related to SCEPTER.

-scape ▶ **comb. form** denoting a specified type of scene: *moonscape.*
– ORIGIN on the pattern of *(land)scape.*

scape·goat /ˈskāpˌgōt/ ▶ **n.** (in the Bible) a goat sent into the wilderness after the Jewish chief priest had symbolically laid the sins of the people upon it (Lev. 16). ■ a person who is blamed for the wrongdoings, mistakes, or faults of others, esp. for reasons of expediency.
▶ **v.** [with obj.] make a scapegoat of.
– DERIVATIVES **scape·goat·er n.**, **scape·goat·ing n.**, **scape·goat·ism** /-ˌizəm/ **n.**
– ORIGIN mid 16th cent.: from archaic *scape* 'escape' + GOAT.

scape·grace /ˈskāpˌgrās/ ▶ **n.** archaic a mischievous or wayward person, esp. a young person or child; a rascal.
– ORIGIN early 19th cent.: from *scape* (see SCAPEGOAT) + GRACE, literally denoting a person who escapes the grace of God.

scaph·oid /ˈskafˌoid/ ▶ **n.** Anatomy a large carpal bone articulating with the radius below the thumb.
– ORIGIN mid 18th cent. (in the sense 'boat-shaped'): from modern Latin *scaphoides*, from Greek *skaphoeidēs*, from *skaphos* 'boat.'

Sca·phop·o·da /skəˈfäpədə/ Zoology a class of mollusks that comprises the tooth shells.
– DERIVATIVES **scaph·o·pod** /ˈskafəˌpäd/ **n.**
– ORIGIN modern Latin (plural), from Greek *skaphē* 'boat' + *pous, pod-* 'foot.'

scap·u·la /ˈskapyələ/ ▶ **n.** (pl. **scapulae** /-ˌlē/ or **scapulas**) Anatomy technical term for SHOULDER BLADE.
– ORIGIN late 16th cent.: from late Latin, singular of Latin *scapulae* 'shoulder blades.'

scap·u·lar /ˈskapyələr/ ▶ **adj.** Anatomy & Zoology of or relating to the shoulder or shoulder blade.
▶ **n. 1** a short monastic cloak covering the shoulders. ■ a symbol of affiliation to an ecclesiastical order, consisting of two strips of cloth hanging down the breast and back and joined across the shoulders.
2 Medicine a bandage passing over and around the shoulders.
3 Ornithology a scapular feather.
– ORIGIN late 15th cent. (sense 1 of the noun): from late Latin *scapulare*, from *scapula* 'shoulder.' The adjective (late 17th cent.) and the later senses of the noun are from SCAPULA + -AR[1].

scap·u·lar feath·er ▶ **n.** Ornithology a feather covering the shoulder, growing above the region where the wing joins the body.

scap·u·lar·y /ˈskapyəˌlerē/ ▶ **n.** (pl. **scapularies**) another term for SCAPULAR (sense 1 of the noun).
– ORIGIN Middle English: from an Anglo-Norman French variant of Old French *eschapeloyre*, based on late Latin *scapulare* (see SCAPULAR).

scar /skär/ ▶ **n. 1** a mark left on the skin or within body tissue where a wound, burn, or sore has not healed completely and fibrous connective tissue has developed: *a faint scar ran the length of his left cheek.* ■ a lasting effect of grief, fear, or other emotion left on a person's character by a traumatic experience: *the attack has left mental scars on Terry and his family.* ■ a mark left on something following damage of some kind: *Max could see scars of the blast.* ■ a mark left at the point of separation of a leaf, frond, or other part from a plant.
2 a steep high cliff or rock outcrop, esp. of limestone. [Middle English: from Old Norse *sker* 'low reef'; compare with SKERRY.]
▶ **v.** (**scars, scarring, scarred**) [with obj.] mark with a scar or scars: *he is likely to be scarred for life after injuries to his face, arms, and legs* | [as adj., in combination] (**-scarred**) *battle-scarred troops.* ■ [no obj.] form or be marked with a scar.
– DERIVATIVES **scar·less adj.**
– ORIGIN late Middle English: from Old French *escharre*, via late Latin from Greek *eskhara* 'scab.'

scar·ab /ˈskarəb/ ▶ **n.** (also **scarab beetle** or **sacred scarab**) a large dung beetle of the eastern Mediterranean area, regarded as sacred in ancient Egypt. ● *Scarabaeus sacer*, family Scarabaeidae (the **scarab family**). The scarab family also includes the smaller dung beetles and chafers, together with some very large tropical kinds such as Hercules, goliath, and rhinoceros beetles. ■ an ancient Egyptian gem cut in the form of this beetle, sometimes depicted with the wings spread, and engraved with hieroglyphs on the flat underside. ■ any scarabaeid beetle.
– ORIGIN late 16th cent. (originally denoting a beetle of any kind): from Latin *scarabaeus*, from Greek *skarabeios.*

scarab beetle

scar·a·bae·id /ˌskarəˈbē-id/ Entomology ▶ **adj.** of, relating to, or denoting the Scarabaeidae family of beetles.
▶ **n.** a beetle of this family, typically having strong spiky forelegs for burrowing.
– ORIGIN mid 19th cent.: from modern Latin *Scarabaeidae* (plural), from Latin *scarabaeus* (see SCARAB).

scar·a·bae·oid /ˌskarəˈbēˌoid/ ▶ **n.** Entomology a beetle of a large group that includes the scarabaeids, dor beetles, and stag beetles. Scarabaeoids include the largest known beetles, and are distinguished by having platelike terminal segments to the antennae. Formerly called LAMELLICORN. ● Superfamily Scarabaeoidea (formerly Lamellicornia).
– ORIGIN late 19th cent.: from modern Latin *Scarabaeoidea* (plural), from Latin *scarabaeus* (see SCARAB).

scar·a·mouch /ˈskarəˌmo͞osh, -ˌmo͞och/ ▶ **n.** archaic a boastful but cowardly person.
– ORIGIN mid 17th cent.: from Italian *Scaramuccia*, the name of a stock character in Italian farce, from *scaramuccia* 'skirmish,' ultimately from the same Germanic base as SKIRMISH.

scarce /ske(ə)rs/ ▶ **adj.** (esp. of food, money, or some other resource) insufficient for the demand: *as raw materials became scarce, synthetics were developed.* ■ occurring in small numbers or quantities; rare: *the freshwater shrimp becomes scarce in soft water.*
▶ **adv.** archaic scarcely: *a babe scarce two years old.*
– PHRASES **make oneself scarce** informal leave a place, esp. so as to avoid a difficult situation.
– DERIVATIVES **scarce·ness n.**
– ORIGIN Middle English (in the sense 'restricted in quantity or size,' also 'parsimonious'): from a shortening of Anglo-Norman *escars*, from a Romance word meaning 'plucked out, selected.'

scarce·ly /ˈske(ə)rslē/ ▶ **adv.** only just; almost not: *her voice is so low I can scarcely hear what she is saying.* ■ only a very short time before: *she had scarcely dismounted before the door swung open.* ■ used to suggest that something is unlikely to be or certainly not the case: *they could scarcely all be wrong.*

scar·ci·ty /ˈskersitē/ ▶ **n.** (pl. **scarcities**) the state of being scarce or in short supply; shortage: *a time of scarcity* | *the growing scarcity of resources.*

scare /ske(ə)r/ ▶ **v.** [with obj.] cause great fear or nervousness in; frighten: *the rapid questions were designed to scare her into blurting out the truth.* ■ drive or keep (someone) away by frightening them: *the threat of bad weather scared away the crowds.* ■ [no obj.] become scared: *I don't think I scare easily.*
▶ **n.** a sudden attack of fright: *gosh, that gave me a scare!* ■ [usu. with modifier] a general feeling of anxiety or alarm about something: *they were forced to leave the building because of a bomb scare.*
– PHRASAL VERBS **scare something up** informal manage to find or obtain something: *for a price, the box office can usually scare up a pair of tickets.*
– DERIVATIVES **scar·er n.**
– ORIGIN Middle English: from Old Norse *skirra* 'frighten,' from *skjarr* 'timid.'

scare·crow /ˈske(ə)rˌkrō/ ▶ **n.** an object, usually made to resemble a human figure, set up to scare birds away from a field where crops are growing. ■ informal a person who is very badly dressed, odd-looking, or thin. ■ archaic an object of baseless fear.

scared /ske(ə)rd/ ▶ **adj.** fearful; frightened: *she's scared stiff of her dad* | [with clause] *I was scared I was going to kill myself* | [with infinitive] *he's scared to come to you and ask for help.*

scared·y-cat /ˈske(ə)rdē ˌkat/ ▶ **n.** informal a timid person.

scare·mon·ger /ˈske(ə)rˌməNGgər, -ˌmäNGgər/ ▶ **n.** a person who spreads frightening or ominous reports or rumors.
– DERIVATIVES **scare·mon·ger·ing n. & adj.**

scare quotes ▶ **plural n.** quotation marks used around a word or phrase when they are not required, thereby eliciting attention or doubts: *putting the term "global warming" in scare quotes serves to subtly cast doubt on the reality of such a phenomenon.*

scare tac·tics ▶ **plural n.** a strategy intended to influence public reaction by the exploitation of fear.

scarf[1] /skärf/ ▶ **n.** (pl. **scarves** /skärvz/ or **scarfs** /skärfs/) a length or square of fabric worn around the neck or head.
– DERIVATIVES **scarfed** /skärft/ (also **scarved**) **adj.**
– ORIGIN mid 16th cent. (in the sense 'sash (around the waist or over the shoulder)'): probably based on Old Northern French *escarpe*, probably identical with Old French *escharpe* 'pilgrim's bag.'

scarf[2] ▶ **v.** [with obj.] **1** join the ends of (two pieces of timber or metal) by beveling or notching them so that they fit over or into each other.
2 make an incision in the blubber of (a whale).
▶ **n. 1** (also **scarf joint**) a joint connecting two pieces of timber or metal in which the ends are beveled or notched so that they fit over or into each other.
2 an incision made in the blubber of a whale.
– ORIGIN Middle English (as a noun): probably via Old French from Old Norse. The verb dates from the early 17th cent.

scarf[3] ▶ **v.** [with obj.] informal eat or drink (something) hungrily or enthusiastically: *he scarfed down the waffles.*
– ORIGIN 1960s: variant of SCOFF[2].

scarf·skin /ˈskärfˌskin/ ▶ **n.** archaic the thin outer layer of the skin; the epidermis.

scar·i·fi·er /ˈskarəˌfīər/ ▶ **n.** a tool with spikes or prongs used for breaking up matted vegetation in the surface of a lawn. ■ a machine with spikes used for breaking up the surface of a road.

scar·i·fy[1] /ˈskarəˌfī/ ▶ **v.** (**scarifies, scarifying, scarified**) [with obj.] **1** cut and remove debris from (a lawn) with a scarifier. ■ break up the surface of (soil or pavement).
2 make shallow incisions in (the skin), esp. as a medical procedure or traditional cosmetic practice: *she scarified the snakebite with a paring knife.*
3 criticize severely and hurtfully.
– DERIVATIVES **scar·i·fi·ca·tion** /-fiˈkāshən/ **n.**
– ORIGIN late Middle English: from Old French *scarifier*, via late Latin from Greek *skariphasthai* 'scratch an outline,' from *skariphos* 'stylus.'

scar·i·fy[2] /ˈske(ə)rəˌfī/ ▶ **v.** (**scarifies, scarifying, scarified**) (usu. as adj. **scarifying**) informal frighten: *a scarifying mix of extreme violence and absurdist humor.*
– ORIGIN late 18th cent.: formed irregularly from SCARE, perhaps on the pattern of *terrify.*

scar·la·ti·na /ˌskärləˈtēnə/ (also **scarletina**) ▶ **n.** another term for SCARLET FEVER.
– ORIGIN early 19th cent.: modern Latin, from Italian *scarlattina* (feminine), based on *scarlatto* 'scarlet.'

Scar·lat·ti /skärˈlätē/ three Italian composers: **Alessandro** (1660–1725) was an important and prolific composer of operas that carried Italian opera through the baroque period and into the classical. His eldest son, **Pietro Filippo** (1679–1750), was a composer, organist, and choirmaster. Another son, **(Giuseppe) Domenico** (1685–1757), wrote over 550 sonatas for the harpsichord.

scar·let /ˈskärlit/ ▶ **adj. 1** of a brilliant red color: *a mass of scarlet berries.*
2 chiefly dated (of an offense or sin) wicked; heinous. ■ immoral, esp. promiscuous or unchaste.
▶ **n.** a brilliant red color: *papers lettered in scarlet and black.* ■ clothes or material of this color.
– ORIGIN Middle English (originally denoting any brightly colored cloth): shortening of Old French *escarlate*, from medieval Latin *scarlata*, via Arabic and medieval Greek from late Latin *sigillatus*

S

'decorated with small images,' from *sigillum* 'small image.'

scar·let fe·ver ▶ **n.** an infectious bacterial disease affecting esp. children, and causing fever and a scarlet rash. It is caused by streptococci.

scar·le·ti·na ▶ **n.** variant spelling of SCARLATINA.

scar·let pim·per·nel ▶ **n.** a small plant with scarlet flowers that close in rainy or cloudy weather. Native to Europe, it is also widespread throughout much of North America. • *Anagallis arvensis* subsp. *arvensis*, family Primulaceae.

scar·let run·ner (also **scarlet runner bean**) ▶ **n.** a twining bean plant with scarlet flowers and very long flat edible pods. Native to Central and South America, it is widely cultivated in North America. • *Phaseolus coccineus*, family Leguminosae.

scar·let tan·a·ger ▶ **n.** a tanager of eastern North America, the breeding male of which is bright red with black wings and tail. • *Piranga olivacea*, family Emberizidae (subfamily Thraupinae).

scarp /skärp/ ▶ **n.** a very steep bank or slope; an escarpment. ■ the inner wall of a ditch in a fortification. Compare with COUNTERSCARP.
▶ **v.** [with obj.] cut or erode (a slope or hillside) so that it becomes steep, perpendicular, or precipitous. ■ provide (a ditch in a fortification) with a steep scarp and counterscarp.
– ORIGIN late 16th cent. (with reference to fortification): from Italian *scarpa*.

scarp·er /'skärpər/ ▶ **v.** [no obj.] Brit. informal run away: *they left the stuff where it was and scarpered.*
– ORIGIN mid 19th cent.: probably from Italian *scappare* 'to escape,' influenced by rhyming slang *Scapa Flow* 'go.'

Scars·dale /'skärz,dāl/ a residential town in southeastern New York, an affluent suburb of New York City; pop. 17,695 (est. 2008).

scarves /skärvz/ plural form of SCARF[1].

scar·y /'ske(ə)rē/ ▶ **adj.** (**scarier**, **scariest**) informal frightening; causing fear: *a scary movie.* ■ uncannily striking or surprising: *it was scary the way they bonded with each other.*
– DERIVATIVES **scar·i·ly** /-əlē/ **adv.**, **scar·i·ness n.**

scat[1] /skat/ ▶ **v.** (**scats**, **scatting**, **scatted**) [no obj.] informal go away; leave: *Scat! Leave me alone.*
– ORIGIN mid 19th cent.: perhaps an abbreviation of SCATTER, or perhaps from the sound of a hiss (used to drive an animal away) + *-cat*.

scat[2] (also **scat singing**) ▶ **n.** improvised jazz singing in which the voice is used in imitation of an instrument.
▶ **v.** (**scats**, **scatting**, **scatted**) [no obj.] sing in such a way.
– ORIGIN 1920s: probably imitative.

scat[3] ▶ **n.** droppings, esp. those of carnivorous mammals.
– ORIGIN 1950s: from Greek *skōr*, *skat-* 'dung'; compare with SCATOLOGY.

scathe /skāTH/ archaic ▶ **v.** [with obj.] (usu. **be scathed**) harm; injure: *he was barely scathed.* ■ literary damage or destroy by fire or lightning.
▶ **n.** harm; injury.
– ORIGIN Middle English: from Old Norse *skathi* (noun), *skatha* (verb); related to Dutch and German *schaden* (verb).

scath·ing /'skāTHiNG/ ▶ **adj.** witheringly scornful; severely critical: *she launched **a scathing attack** on the governor.*
– DERIVATIVES **scath·ing·ly adv.**

S

sca·tol·o·gy /skə'täləjē/ ▶ **n.** an interest in or preoccupation with excrement and excretion. ■ obscene literature that is concerned with excrement and excretion.
– DERIVATIVES **scat·o·log·i·cal** /'skatl'äjikəl/ **adj.**
– ORIGIN late 19th cent.: from Greek *skōr*, *skat-* 'dung' + -LOGY. Compare with SCAT[3].

scat·ter /'skatər/ ▶ **v.** [with obj.] throw in various random directions: *scatter the coconut over the icing | his family is hoping to scatter his ashes at sea.* ■ (**be scattered**) [usu. with adverbial] occur or be found at intervals rather than all together: *there are many mills scattered throughout the marshlands* | (as adj. **scattered**) *a scattered mountain community.* ■ (of a group of people or animals) separate and move off quickly in different directions: *the roar made the dogs scatter.* ■ cause (a group or people or animals) to act in such a way: *he charged across the foyer, scattering people.* ■ (usu. **be scattered with**) cover (a surface) with objects thrown or spread randomly over it: *sandy beaches scattered with driftwood.* ■ Physics deflect or diffuse (electromagnetic radiation or particles).
▶ **n.** a small, dispersed amount of something: *a scatter of houses on the north shore.* ■ Statistics the degree to which repeated measurements or observations of a quantity differ. ■ Physics the scattering of light, other electromagnetic radiation, or particles.
– DERIVATIVES **scat·ter·a·ble adj.**, **scat·ter·a·tion** /,skatə'rāSHən/ **n.**, **scat·ter·er n.**
– ORIGIN Middle English (as a verb): probably a variant of SHATTER.

scat·ter·brain /'skatər,brān/ ▶ **n.** a person who tends to be disorganized and lacking in concentration.

scat·ter·brained /'skatər,brānd/ ▶ **adj.** (of a person) disorganized and lacking in concentration.

scat·ter di·a·gram ▶ **n.** Statistics a graph in which the values of two variables are plotted along two axes, the pattern of the resulting points revealing any correlation present.

scat·ter·gram /'skatər,gram/ (also **scattergraph**) ▶ **n.** another term for SCATTER DIAGRAM.

scat·ter·gun /'skatər,gən/ ▶ **n.** a shotgun.
▶ **adj.** another term for SCATTERSHOT.

scat·ter·ing /'skatəriNG/ ▶ **n.** [in sing.] an act of scattering something. ■ a small, dispersed amount of something: *the scattering of freckles across her cheeks and forehead.* ■ Physics the process in which electromagnetic radiation or particles are deflected or diffused.

scat·ter·ing an·gle ▶ **n.** Physics the angle through which a scattered particle or beam is deflected.

scat·ter·plot /'skatər,plät/ (also **scatter plot**) ▶ **n.** another term for SCATTER DIAGRAM.

scat·ter rug ▶ **n.** another term for THROW RUG.

scat·ter·shot /'skatər,SHät/ ▶ **adj.** denoting something that is broad but random and haphazard in its range: *a scattershot collection of stories.*

scat·ty /'skatē/ ▶ **adj.** (**scattier**, **scattiest**) informal absentminded and disorganized.
– DERIVATIVES **scat·ti·ly** /-əlē/ **adv.**, **scat·ti·ness n.**
– ORIGIN early 20th cent.: abbreviation of SCATTERBRAINED.

scaup /skôp/ ▶ **n.** a Eurasian, North American, and New Zealand diving duck, the male of which has a black head with a green or purple gloss. • Genus *Aythya*, family Anatidae: three species, in particular the widespread (**greater**) **scaup** (*A. marila*), with a black breast and white sides.
– ORIGIN late 17th cent.: Scots variant of Scots and northern English *scalp* 'mussel bed,' a feeding ground of the duck.

scau·per /'skôpər/ ▶ **n.** variant spelling of SCORPER.

scav·enge /'skavənj/ ▶ **v.** [with obj.] search for and collect (anything usable) from discarded waste: *people sell junk **scavenged from** the garbage* | [no obj.] *the city dump where the squatters scavenge to survive.* ■ (of an animal) search for (carrion) as food. ■ search for discarded items or food in (a place): *the mink is still commonly seen scavenging the beaches of California.* ■ remove (combustion products) from the cylinder of an internal combustion engine on the return stroke of the piston. ■ Chemistry combine with and remove (molecules, radicals, etc.) from a particular medium.
– ORIGIN mid 17th cent. (in the sense 'clean out (dirt)'): back-formation from SCAVENGER.

scav·eng·er /'skavənjər/ ▶ **n.** an animal that feeds on carrion, dead plant material, or refuse. ■ a person who searches for and collects discarded items. ■ Brit. archaic a person employed to clean the streets. ■ Chemistry a substance that reacts with and removes particular molecules, radicals, etc.
– ORIGIN mid 16th cent.: alteration of earlier *scavager*, from Anglo-Norman French *scawager*, from Old Northern French *escauwer* 'inspect,' from Flemish *scauwen* 'to show.' The term originally denoted an officer who collected *scavage*, a toll on foreign merchants' goods offered for sale in a town, later a person who kept the streets clean.

scav·eng·er cell ▶ **n.** another term for PHAGOCYTE.

scav·eng·er hunt ▶ **n.** a game, typically played in an extensive outdoor area, in which participants have to collect a number of miscellaneous objects.

Sc.B. ▶ **abbr.** Bachelor of Science.
– ORIGIN from Latin *Scientiae Baccalaureus*.

SCC ▶ **abbr.** Electronics storage connecting circuit.

ScD ▶ **abbr.** Doctor of Science.
– ORIGIN from Latin *scientiae doctor*.

sce·na /'SHānə/ ▶ **n.** a scene in an opera. ■ an elaborate dramatic solo, usually including recitative.
– ORIGIN Italian, from Latin, 'scene.'

sce·nar·i·o /sə'ne(ə)rē,ō, -'när-/ ▶ **n.** (pl. **scenarios**) a written outline of a movie, novel, or stage work giving details of the plot and individual scenes: *imagine the scenarios for four short stories.* ■ a postulated sequence or development of events: *a possible scenario is that he was attacked after opening the front door.* ■ a setting, in particular for a work of art or literature: *the scenario is World War II.*
– ORIGIN late 19th cent.: from Italian, from Latin *scena* 'scene.'

sce·nar·ist /sə'ne(ə)rist/ ▶ **n.** a screenwriter.

scend /send/ (also **send**) archaic ▶ **n.** the push or surge created by a wave. ■ a pitching or surging movement of a vessel.
▶ **v.** [no obj.] (of a vessel) pitch or surge up in a heavy sea.
– ORIGIN late 15th cent. (as a verb): alteration of SEND[1] or DESCEND. The noun dates from the early 18th cent.

scene /sēn/ ▶ **n. 1** the place where an incident in real life or fiction occurs or occurred: *the emergency team were among the first **on the scene** | relatives left flowers at the scene of the crash.* ■ a place, with the people, objects, and events in it, regarded as having a particular character or making a particular impression: *a scene of carnage.* ■ a landscape: *thick snow had turned the scene outside into a picture postcard.* ■ an incident of a specified nature: *there had already been some scenes of violence.* ■ a place or representation of an incident: *scenes of 1930s America.* ■ [with modifier] a specified area of activity or interest: *the country music scene.* ■ [usu. in sing.] a public display of emotion or anger: *she was loath to **make a scene** in the office.*
2 a sequence of continuous action in a play, movie, opera, or book: *a scene from Brando's first film.* ■ a subdivision of an act of a play in which the time is continuous and the setting fixed and which does not usually involve a change of characters: *beginning at Act One, Scene One.* ■ [usu. as modifier] the pieces of scenery used in a play or opera: *scene changes.*
– PHRASES **behind the scenes** out of sight of the public at a theater or organization. ■ secretly: *diplomatic maneuvers going on behind the scenes.* **change of scene** another way of saying CHANGE OF SCENERY (see SCENERY). **come** (or **appear** or **arrive**) **on the scene** arrive; appear. **hit** (or **make**) **the scene** informal way of saying COME ON THE SCENE above. **not one's scene** informal not something one enjoys or is interested in: *sorry, that witchcraft stuff is not my scene.* **set the scene** describe a place or situation in which something is about to happen. ■ create the conditions for a future event: *the congressman's speech **set the scene for** a bitter debate.*
– ORIGIN mid 16th cent. (denoting a subdivision of a play, or (a piece of) stage scenery): from Latin *scena*, from Greek *skēnē* 'tent, stage.'

scen·er·y /'sēn(ə)rē/ ▶ **n.** the natural features of a landscape considered in terms of their appearance, esp. when picturesque: *spectacular views of mountain scenery.* ■ the painted background used to represent natural features or other surroundings on a theater stage or movie set.
– PHRASES **change of scenery** a move to different surroundings: *we spent the weekend in Seattle just for a change of scenery.*
– PHRASAL VERBS **chew (up) the scenery** (of an actor) overact: *he chews up the courtroom scenery as the unscrupulous attorney.*
– ORIGIN mid 18th cent. (earlier as *scenary*): from Italian *scenario* (see SCENARIO). The change in the ending was due to association with -ERY.

scene-steal·er ▶ **n.** an actor who outshines the rest of the cast, esp. unexpectedly. ■ a person or thing that takes more than their fair share of attention.

scene·ster /'sēnstər/ ▶ **n.** informal a person associated with or immersed in a particular fashionable cultural scene.

sce·nic /'sēnik/ ▶ **adj.** providing or relating to views of impressive or beautiful natural scenery: *the scenic route to Brussels | scenic beauty.* ■ [attrib.] of or relating to theatrical scenery: *a scenic artist from the Metropolitan Opera House.* ■ (of a picture) representing an incident: *the trend to scenic figural work.*
– DERIVATIVES **sce·ni·cal·ly** /-ik(ə)lē/ **adv.**
– ORIGIN early 17th cent. (in the sense 'theatrical'): via Latin from Greek *skēnikos* 'of the stage,' from *skēnē* (see SCENE).

sce·nic rail·way ▶ **n.** an attraction at a fair or in a park consisting of a miniature railroad that runs past natural features and artificial scenery.

sce·nog·ra·phy /sē'nägrəfē/ ▶ **n.** the design and painting of theatrical scenery. ■ (in painting and drawing) the representation of objects in perspective.
– DERIVATIVES **sce·no·graph·ic** /,sēnə'grafik, ,senə-/ **adj.**
– ORIGIN mid 17th cent.: from French *scénographie*, or via Latin from Greek *skēnographia* 'scene-painting,' from *skēnē* (see SCENE).

scent /sent/ ▶ **n. 1** a distinctive smell, esp. one that is pleasant: *the scent of freshly cut hay.* ■ pleasant-smelling liquid worn on the skin; perfume: *she sprayed scent over her body.*
2 a trail indicated by the characteristic smell of an animal and perceptible to hounds or other animals:

the hound followed the scent. ■ a trail of evidence or other signs assisting someone in a search or investigation: *once their interest is aroused, they follow the scent with sleuthlike pertinacity.*
3 archaic the faculty or sense of smell.
▶ **v.** [with obj.] **1** (usu. **be scented with**) impart a pleasant scent to: *a glass of tea scented with lemon balm.*
2 discern by the sense of smell: *a shark can scent blood from well over half a mile away.* ■ sense the presence, existence, or imminence of: *a commander who scented victory.* ■ sniff (the air) for a scent: *the bull advanced, scenting the breeze at every step.*
– PHRASES **on the scent** in possession of a useful clue in a search or investigation; following a trail that will likely lead to the discovery or acquisition of something. **put** (or **throw**) **someone off the scent** mislead someone in the course of a search or investigation.
– DERIVATIVES **scent·less adj.**
– ORIGIN late Middle English (denoting the sense of smell): from Old French *sentir* 'perceive, smell,' from Latin *sentire*. The addition of *-c-* (in the 17th cent.) is unexplained.

scent·ed /ˈsentid/ ▶ **adj.** having a pleasant scent: *scented soap.*

scent gland ▶ **n.** an animal gland that secretes an odorous pheromone or defensive substance, esp. one under the tail of a carnivorous mammal such as a civet or skunk.

scent mark ▶ **n.** (also **scent marking**) an odoriferous substance containing a pheromone that is deposited by a mammal from a scent gland or in the urine or feces, typically on prominent objects in an area.
▶ **v.** (**scent-mark**) [no obj.] (of a mammal) deposit such a substance.

scep·ter /ˈseptər/ (Brit. **sceptre**) ▶ **n.** an ornamented staff carried by rulers on ceremonial occasions as a symbol of sovereignty.
– DERIVATIVES **scep·tered adj.**
– ORIGIN Middle English: from Old French *ceptre*, via Latin from Greek *skēptron*, from *skēptein* (alteration of *skēptesthai*) 'lean on.'

scepter

scep·tic ▶ **n.** British spelling of SKEPTIC.

scep·ti·cal ▶ **adj.** British spelling of SKEPTICAL.

scep·tre ▶ **n.** British spelling of SCEPTER.

sch. ▶ **abbr.** ■ scholar. ■ school. ■ schooner.

scha·den·freu·de /ˈsʜädənˌfroidə/ ▶ **n.** pleasure derived by someone from another person's misfortune.
– ORIGIN German *Schadenfreude*, from *Schaden* 'harm' + *Freude* 'joy.'

Schaum·burg /ˈsʜômˌbərg/ a residential and industrial village in northeastern Illinois, northwest of Chicago; pop. 71,716 (est. 2008).

Schaw·low /ˈsʜôˌlō/, Arthur Leonard (1921–99), US inventor. With Charles H. Townes, he invented the laser. He shared the 1981 Nobel Prize in Physics with Nicolaas Bloembergen (1920–) and Kai M. Siegbahn (1918–2007).

sched·ule /ˈskejo͞ol, -jəl/ ▶ **n.** **1** a plan for carrying out a process or procedure, giving lists of intended events and times: *we have drawn up an engineering schedule.* ■ (usu. **one's schedule**) one's day-to-day plans or timetable: *take a moment out of your busy schedule.* ■ a timetable: *information on airline schedules.*
2 chiefly Law an appendix to a formal document or statute, esp. as a list, table, or inventory.
3 (with reference to an income tax system) any of the forms (named "A," "B," etc.) issued for completion and relating to the various classes into which taxable income is divided.
▶ **v.** [with obj.] arrange or plan (an event) to take place at a particular time: *the release of the single is scheduled for April.* ■ make arrangements for (someone or something) to do something: [with obj. and infinitive] *he is scheduled to be released from prison this spring.*
– PHRASES **ahead of** (or **behind**) **schedule** earlier (or later) than planned or expected. **on** (or **according to**) **schedule** on time; as planned or expected.
– DERIVATIVES **sched·u·lar** /-ər/ **adj.**
– ORIGIN late Middle English (in the sense 'scroll, explanatory note, appendix'): from Old French *cedule*, from late Latin *schedula* 'slip of paper,' diminutive of *scheda*, from Greek *skhedē* 'papyrus leaf.' The verb dates from the mid 19th cent.

sched·uled /ˈskeˌjo͞old, -əld/ ▶ **adj.** included in or planned according to a schedule: *the bus makes one scheduled thirty-minute stop.* ■ (esp. of an airline or flight) relating to or forming part of a regular service rather than specially chartered.

sched·uled caste ▶ **n.** the official name given in India to the lowest caste, considered 'untouchable' in orthodox Hindu scriptures and practice, officially regarded as socially disadvantaged.

USAGE See usage at UNTOUCHABLE.

sched·ul·er /ˈskejo͞olər, ˈskejələr/ ▶ **n.** a person or machine that organizes or maintains schedules. ■ Computing a program that arranges jobs or a computer's operations into an appropriate sequence.

scheel·ite /ˈsʜāˌlīt/ ▶ **n.** a fluorescent mineral, white when pure, that consists of calcium tungstate and is an important ore of tungsten.
– ORIGIN mid 19th cent.: from the name of Carl W. *Scheele* (1742–86), Swedish chemist, + -ITE¹.

schef·fler·a /ˈsʜeflərə, sʜefˈli(ə)rə/ ▶ **n.** an evergreen tropical or subtropical shrub or small tree that is widely grown as a houseplant for its decorative foliage. ● Genus *Schefflera*, family Araliaceae.
– ORIGIN modern Latin, named after J. C. *Scheffler*, 18th-cent. German botanist.

Sche·her·a·za·de /sʜəˌherəˈzäd, -ˈzädə/ the character who narrates the *Arabian Nights*. Her delightful storytelling wins the favor and mercy of her husband, a Persian king.

Scheldt /sʜelt, skelt/ (also **Schelde** /ˈskeldə, ˈsʜel-/) a river in northern Europe. Rising in northern France, it flows 270 miles (432 km) through Belgium and the Netherlands to the North Sea. French name ESCAUT.

sche·ma /ˈskēmə/ ▶ **n.** (pl. **schemata** /-mətə/ or **schemas**) technical a representation of a plan or theory in the form of an outline or model: *a schema of scientific reasoning.* ■ Logic a syllogistic figure. ■ (in Kantian philosophy) a conception of what is common to all members of a class; a general or essential type or form.
– ORIGIN late 18th cent. (as a term in philosophy): from Greek *skhēma* 'form, figure.'

sche·mat·ic /skəˈmatik, skē-/ ▶ **adj.** (of a diagram or other representation) symbolic and simplified. ■ (of thought, ideas, etc.) simplistic or formulaic in character, usually to an extent inappropriate to the complexities of the subject matter: *a highly schematic reading of the play.*
▶ **n.** (in technical contexts) a schematic diagram, in particular of an electric or electronic circuit.
– DERIVATIVES **sche·mat·i·cal·ly** /-ik(ə)lē/ **adv.**

sche·ma·tism /ˈskēməˌtizəm/ ▶ **n.** the arrangement or presentation of something according to a scheme or schema.
– ORIGIN early 17th cent.: from modern Latin *schematismus*, from Greek *skhēmatismos* 'assumption of a certain form,' from *skhēma*, *skhēmat-* 'form.'

sche·ma·tize /ˈskēməˌtīz/ ▶ **v.** [with obj.] arrange or represent in a schematic form.
– DERIVATIVES **sche·ma·ti·za·tion** /ˌskēmətiˈzāsʜən/ **n.**

scheme /skēm/ ▶ **n.** a large-scale systematic plan or arrangement for attaining some particular object or putting a particular idea into effect: *a clever marketing scheme.* ■ a secret or underhanded plan; a plot: *police uncovered a scheme to steal paintings worth more than $250,000.* ■ a particular ordered system or arrangement: *a classical rhyme scheme.*
▶ **v.** [no obj.] make plans, esp. in a devious way or with intent to do something illegal or wrong: [with infinitive] *he schemed to bring about the collapse of the government.*
– PHRASES **the scheme of things** a supposed or apparent overall system, within which everything has a place and in relation to which individual details are ultimately to be assessed: *in the overall scheme of things, we didn't do badly.*
– ORIGIN mid 16th cent. (denoting a figure of speech): from Latin *schema*, from Greek (see SCHEMA). An early sense was 'diagram of the position of celestial objects,' giving rise to 'diagram, outline,' whence the current senses. The unfavorable notion "plot"arose in the mid 18th cent.

schem·er /ˈskēmər/ ▶ **n.** a person who is involved in making secret or underhanded plans.

schem·ing /ˈskēmiNG/ ▶ **adj.** given to or involved in making secret and underhanded plans: *they had mean, scheming little minds.*
▶ **n.** the activity or practice of making such plans.
– DERIVATIVES **schem·ing·ly adv.**

sche·moz·zle ▶ **n.** variant spelling of SHEMOZZLE.

Sche·nec·ta·dy /skəˈnektədē/ an industrial city in eastern New York, northwest of Albany; pop. 61,152 (est. 2008).

Scheng·en a·gree·ment /ˈsʜeNGən/ an intergovernmental agreement on the relaxation of border controls between participating European countries, first signed in Schengen, Luxembourg, in June 1985 by France, West Germany, Belgium, the Netherlands, and Luxembourg. A revised version of the agreement was incorporated into the European Union in 1999 and widened to include non-EU members of a similar Nordic union.

scher·zan·do /skərtˈsändō/ Music ▶ **adv. & adj.** (esp. as a direction) in a playful manner.
– ORIGIN Italian, literally 'joking.'

scher·zo /ˈskertsō/ ▶ **n.** (pl. **scherzos** or **scherzi** /-tsē/) Music a vigorous, light, or playful composition, typically comprising a movement in a symphony or sonata.
– ORIGIN Italian, literally 'jest.'

Schia·pa·rel·li /ˌskyäpəˈrelē, ˌsʜäpə-/, Elsa (1896–1973), French fashion designer, born in Italy.

Schick test /sʜik/ ▶ **n.** Medicine a test for previously acquired immunity to diphtheria, using an intradermal injection of diphtheria toxin.
– ORIGIN early 20th cent.: named after Bela *Schick* (1877–1967), Hungarian-born US pediatrician.

Schil·ler /ˈsʜilər/, (Johann Christoph) Friedrich von (1759–1805), German playwright, poet, historian, and critic. Initially influenced by the *Sturm und Drang* movement, he was later an important figure of the Enlightenment. His historical plays include the trilogy *Wallenstein* (1800), *Mary Stuart* (1800), and *William Tell* (1804).

schil·ling /ˈsʜiliNG/ ▶ **n.** the basic monetary unit of Austria (until replaced by the euro), equal to 100 groschen.
– ORIGIN from German *Schilling*; compare with SHILLING.

Schin·dler /ˈsʜindlər/, Oskar (1908–74), German industrialist. He saved more than 1,200 Jews from concentration camps by employing them first in his enamelware factory in Cracow and then in an armaments factory in Czechoslovakia in 1944. This was dramatized in the movie *Schindler's List* (1993), based on *Schindler's Ark* (1982), a novel by Thomas Keneally.

schip·per·ke /ˈskipərkē/ ▶ **n.** a small black tailless dog of a breed with a ruff of fur around its neck.
– ORIGIN late 19th cent.: from Dutch dialect, literally 'little boatman,' with reference to its use as a watchdog on barges.

schism /ˈs(k)izəm/ ▶ **n.** a split or division between strongly opposed sections or parties, caused by differences in opinion or belief. ■ the formal separation of a church into two churches or the secession of a group owing to doctrinal and other differences. See also GREAT SCHISM.
– ORIGIN late Middle English: from Old French *scisme*, via ecclesiastical Latin from Greek *skhisma* 'cleft,' from *skhizein* 'to split.'

schis·mat·ic /s(k)izˈmatik/ ▶ **adj.** of, characterized by, or favoring schism.
▶ **n.** chiefly historical (esp. in the Christian Church) a person who promotes schism; an adherent of a schismatic group.
– DERIVATIVES **schis·mat·i·cal·ly** /-ik(ə)lē/ **adv.**
– ORIGIN late Middle English: from Old French *scismatique*, via ecclesiastical Latin from ecclesiastical Greek *skhismatikos*, from *skhisma* (see SCHISM).

schist /sʜist/ ▶ **n.** Geology a coarse-grained metamorphic rock that consists of layers of different minerals and can be split into thin irregular plates.
– DERIVATIVES **schis·tous** /-təs/ **adj.**
– ORIGIN late 18th cent.: from French *schiste*, via Latin from Greek *skhistos* 'split,' from the base of *skhizein* 'cleave.'

schis·tose /ˈsʜistōs/ ▶ **adj.** Geology (of metamorphic rock) having a laminar structure like that of schist.
– DERIVATIVES **schis·tos·i·ty** /sʜiˈstäsitē/ **n.**

schis·to·some /ˈsʜistəˌsōm/ ▶ **n.** Zoology & Medicine a parasitic flatworm that needs two hosts to complete its life cycle. The immature form infests freshwater snails, and the adult lives in the blood vessels of birds and mammals, causing bilharzia in humans. Also called BLOOD FLUKE. ● Genus *Schistosoma*, subclass Digenea, class Trematoda.
– ORIGIN early 20th cent.: from modern Latin *Schistosoma*, from Greek *skhistos* 'divided' + *sōma* 'body.'

schis·to·so·mi·a·sis /ˌsʜistōsəˈmīəsis/ ▶ **n.** another term for BILHARZIA (the disease).

PRONUNCIATION KEY ə *ago, up*; ər *over, fur*; a *hat*; ā *ate*; ä *car*; e *let*; ē *see*; i *fit*; ī *by*; NG *sing*; ō *go*; ô *law, for*; oi *toy*; o͝o *good*; o͞o *goo*; ou *out*; TH *thin*; T͟H *then*; ZH *vision*

S

schiz·an·dra /skit'sandrə/ ▶ **n.** a Chinese herb whose berries are credited with various stimulant or medicinal properties. Also called MAGNOLIA VINE. ● *Schisandra chinensis*, family Magnoliaceae.
– ORIGIN mid 19th cent.: modern Latin, *Schisandra*, formed as *schizo-* + Greek *andr-*, *anēr* man, on account of the divided stamens.

schi·zan·thus /ski'zanTHəs/ ▶ **n.** a South American plant of the nightshade family, with irregularly lobed showy flowers marked with one or more contrasting colors. ● Genus *Schizanthus*, family Solanaceae.
– ORIGIN modern Latin, from Greek *skhizein* 'to split' + *anthos* 'flower.'

schiz·o /'skitsō/ informal, offensive ▶ **adj.** (of a person or their behavior) schizophrenic.
▶ **n.** (pl. **schizos**) a schizophrenic.
– ORIGIN 1940s: abbreviation.

schizo- ▶ **comb. form** divided; split: *schizocarp*. ■ relating to schizophrenia: *schizotype*.
– ORIGIN from Greek *skhizein* 'to split.'

schiz·o·af·fec·tive (also **schizoaffective**) ▶ **adj.** (of a person or a mental condition) characterized by symptoms of both schizophrenia and manic-depressive psychosis.

schiz·o·carp /'skitsō,kärp/ ▶ **n.** Botany a dry fruit that splits into single-seeded parts when ripe.

schi·zog·e·nous /ski'zäjənəs, skit'säj-/ ▶ **adj.** Botany (of an intercellular space in a plant) formed by the splitting of the common wall of contiguous cells.
– DERIVATIVES **schiz·o·gen·ic** /,skizəjenik, ,skitsə-/ **adj.**, **schi·zog·e·ny** /ski'zäjənē, skit'säj-/ **n.**

schi·zog·o·ny /ski'zägənē, skit'säg-/ ▶ **n.** Biology asexual reproduction by multiple fission, found in some protozoa, esp. parasitic sporozoans.
– DERIVATIVES **schi·zog·o·nous** /-nəs/ **adj.**
– ORIGIN late 19th cent.: from SCHIZO- 'divided' + Greek *-gonia* 'production.'

schiz·oid /'skit,soid/ ▶ **adj.** Psychiatry denoting or having a personality type characterized by emotional aloofness and solitary habits. ■ informal (in general use) resembling schizophrenia in having inconsistent or contradictory elements; mad or crazy: *it's a frenzied, schizoid place*.
▶ **n.** a schizoid person.

schiz·ont /'skizänt, 'skitsänt/ ▶ **n.** Biology (in certain sporozoan protozoans) a cell that divides by schizogony to form daughter cells.
– ORIGIN early 20th cent.: from SCHIZO- 'divided' + -ONT.

schiz·o·phre·ni·a /,skitsə'frēnēə, -'frenēə/ ▶ **n.** a long-term mental disorder of a type involving a breakdown in the relation between thought, emotion, and behavior, leading to faulty perception, inappropriate actions and feelings, withdrawal from reality and personal relationships into fantasy and delusion, and a sense of mental fragmentation. ■ (in general use) a mentality or approach characterized by inconsistent or contradictory elements.
– DERIVATIVES **schiz·o·phren·ic** /-'frenik/ **adj. & n.**
– ORIGIN early 20th cent.: modern Latin, from Greek *skhizein* 'to split' + *phrēn* 'mind.'

schiz·o·type /'skitsə,tīp/ ▶ **n.** a personality type in which mild symptoms of schizophrenia are present.
– DERIVATIVES **schiz·o·typ·al** /,skitsə'tīpəl/ **adj.**, **schiz·o·typ·y** /,skit'sätəpē/ **n.**

Schle·gel /'SHlāgəl/, August Wilhelm von (1767–1845), German romantic poet and critic, who was among the founders of art history and comparative philology. His brother, **Friedrich von Schlegel** (1772–1829), was a critic, philosopher, and poet who wrote on comparative literature and philology.

schle·miel /SHlə'mēl/ (also **shlemiel**) ▶ **n.** informal a stupid, awkward, or unlucky person.
– ORIGIN late 19th cent.: from Yiddish *shlemiel*.

schlep /SHlep/ (also **schlepp** or **shlep**) informal ▶ **v.** (**schleps, schlepping, schlepped**) [with obj.] haul or carry (something heavy or awkward): *she schlepped her groceries home*. ■ [no obj.] (of a person) go or move reluctantly or with effort: *I would have preferred not to schlep all the way over there to run an errand*.
▶ **n. 1** a tedious or difficult journey.
2 another term for SCHLEPPER.
– ORIGIN early 20th cent. (as a verb): from Yiddish *shlepn* 'drag,' from Middle High German *sleppen*.

schlep·per /'SHlepər/ (also **shlepper**) ▶ **n.** informal an inept or stupid person.
– ORIGIN 1930s: Yiddish, from *shlepn* (see SCHLEP).

Schles·ing·er[1] /'SHlāziNGər, 'SHlesinjər/, Arthur Meier (1888–1965), US historian. He wrote *The Colonial Merchants and the American Revolution, 1763–1776* (1918), *New Viewpoints in American History* (1922), and *The American Reformer* (1950).

Schles·ing·er[2], Arthur Meier, Jr. (1917–2007), US historian; the son of Arthur Meier Schlesinger. A professor at Harvard University 1946–61 and advisor to Presidents Kennedy and Lyndon Johnson, he wrote *The Age of Jackson* (1945), *The Age of Roosevelt* in three volumes (1957–60), *A Thousand Days: John F. Kennedy in the White House* (1965), and *The Imperial Presidency* (1973).

Schles·wig /'SHleswig, 'SHlāsviKH, -vik/ a former Danish duchy, located on the southern part of the Jutland peninsula.

Schles·wig-Hol·stein /'hōl,stīn, -,SHtīn/ a state in northwestern Germany that occupies the southern part of the Jutland peninsula; capital, Kiel. It consists of the former duchies of Schleswig and Holstein.

Schlick /SHlik/, Moritz (1882–1936), German philosopher and physicist; founder of the Vienna Circle.

Schlie·mann /'SHlē,män/, Heinrich (1822–90), German archaeologist. In 1871, he began excavating the mound of Hissarlik in Turkey, where he discovered the remains of nine superimposed cities, one of which he mistakenly identified as Homer's Troy. By 1876, he had undertaken excavations at Mycenae.

schlie·ren /'SHli(ə)rən/ ▶ **plural n.** technical discernible layers in a transparent material that differ from the surrounding material in density or composition. ■ Geology irregular streaks or masses in igneous rock that differ from the surrounding rock in texture or composition.
– ORIGIN late 19th cent.: from German *Schlieren*, plural of *Schliere* 'streak.'

schli·ma·zel /SHlə'mäzəl/ (also **schlemazel**) ▶ **n.** informal a consistently unlucky or accident-prone person.
– ORIGIN Yiddish, from Middle High German, *slim*, 'crooked' + Hebrew, *mazzāl*, 'luck.'

schlock /SHläk/ (also **shlock**) ▶ **n.** informal cheap or inferior goods or material; trash: *they peddle their schlock to willing tourists* | [as modifier] *schlock journalism*.
– DERIVATIVES **schlock·y adj.**
– ORIGIN early 20th cent.: apparently from Yiddish *shlak* 'an apoplectic stroke,' *shlog* 'wretch, untidy person, apoplectic stroke.'

schlock·meis·ter /'SHläk,mīstər/ ▶ **n.** informal a purveyor of cheap or trashy goods.
– ORIGIN early 20th cent.: from SCHLOCK + German *Meister* 'master.'

schlub /SHləb/ (also **shlub**) ▶ **n.** informal a talentless, unattractive, or boorish person.
– ORIGIN 1960s: Yiddish *shlub*, perhaps from Polish *żłób*.

schlump /SHlŏŏmp/ (also **shlump**) ▶ **n.** informal a slow, slovenly, or inept person.
– ORIGIN 1940s: apparently related to Yiddish *shlumperdik* 'dowdy' and German *Schlumpe* 'slattern.'

schmaltz /SHmälts, SHmôlts/ (also **schmalz**) ▶ **n.** informal excessive sentimentality, esp. in music or movies.
– ORIGIN 1930s: from Yiddish *shmaltz*, from German *Schmalz* 'drippings, lard.'

schmaltz·y /'SHmältsē, 'SHmôltsē/ ▶ **adj.** (**schmaltzier, schmaltziest**) informal excessively sentimental: *schmaltzy ballads*.

schmat·te /'SHmätə/ (also **shmatte**) ▶ **n.** informal a rag; a ragged or shabby garment.
– ORIGIN 1970s: Yiddish *shmatte*, from Polish *szmata* 'rag.'

schmear /SHmi(ə)r/ (also **schmeer, shmeer,** or **shmear**) informal ▶ **n. 1** a corrupt or underhanded inducement; a bribe.
2 a smear or spread: *the bagel so perfect with a schmear of low-fat cream cheese*.
▶ **v.** [with obj.] flatter or ingratiate oneself with (someone): *he was constantly buying us drinks and schmearing us up*.
– PHRASES **the whole schmear** everything possible or available; every aspect of the situation: *I'm going for the whole schmear*.
– ORIGIN 1960s: from Yiddish *shmirn* 'flatter, grease.'

Schmidt–Cas·se·grain tel·e·scope /'SHmit 'kasi,grān/ ▶ **n.** a type of catadioptric telescope, using the correcting plate of a Schmidt telescope together with the secondary mirror and rear focus of a Cassegrain telescope.

Schmidt tel·e·scope (also **Schmidt camera**) ▶ **n.** a type of catadioptric telescope used solely for wide-angle astronomical photography, with a thin glass plate at the front to correct for spherical aberration. A curved photographic plate is placed at the prime focus inside the telescope.
– ORIGIN 1930s: named after Bernhard V. *Schmidt* (1879–1935), the German inventor.

Schmitt trig·ger /SHmit/ ▶ **n.** Electronics a bistable circuit in which the output increases to a steady maximum when the input rises above a certain threshold, and decreases almost to zero when the input voltage falls below another threshold.
– ORIGIN 1940s: named after Otto H. *Schmitt* (born 1913), American electronics engineer.

schmo /SHmō/ (also **shmo**) ▶ **n.** (pl. **schmoes**) informal a stupid person. ■ (also **Joe Schmo**) a hypothetical ordinary man.
– ORIGIN 1940s: alteration of SCHMUCK.

schmooze /SHmōōz/ (also **shmooze**) ▶ **v.** [no obj.] talk intimately and cozily; gossip. ■ [with obj.] talk in such a way to (someone), typically in order to manipulate, flatter, or impress them.
▶ **n.** a long and intimate conversation.
– DERIVATIVES **schmooz·er n.**, **schmooz·y adj.**
– ORIGIN late 19th cent. (as a verb): from Yiddish *shmuesn* 'converse, chat.'

schmuck /SHmək/ (also **shmuck**) ▶ **n.** informal a foolish or contemptible person.
– ORIGIN late 19th cent.: from Yiddish *shmok* 'penis.'

schnapps /SHnäps, SHnaps/ ▶ **n.** a strong alcoholic drink resembling gin and often flavored with fruit: *peach schnapps*.
– ORIGIN from German *Schnaps*, literally 'dram of liquor,' from Low German and Dutch *snaps* 'mouthful.'

schnau·zer /'SHnouzər/ ▶ **n.** a medium- or small-sized dog of a German breed with a close wiry coat and heavy whiskers around the muzzle.
– ORIGIN 1920s: from German, from *Schnauze* 'muzzle, snout.'

miniature schnauzer

schnit·zel /'SHnitsəl/ ▶ **n.** a thin slice of veal or other light meat, coated in breadcrumbs and fried.
– ORIGIN from German *Schnitzel*, literally 'slice.'

schnook /SHnŏŏk/ (also **shnook**) ▶ **n.** informal a person easily duped; a fool.
– ORIGIN 1940s: perhaps from German *Schnucke* 'small sheep' or from Yiddish *shnuk* 'snout.'

schnor·rer /'SHnôrər/ (also **shnorrer**) ▶ **n.** informal a beggar or scrounger; a layabout.
– ORIGIN late 19th cent.: from Yiddish *shnorrer*, variant of German *Schnurrer*.

schnoz /SHnäz/ (also **schnozz** or **schnozzola** /SHnä'zōlə/) ▶ **n.** informal a person's nose.
– ORIGIN 1940s: from Yiddish *shnoytz*, from German *Schnauze* 'snout.'

Schoen·berg /'SHə(r)n,bərg, 'SHœn,berk/, Arnold (1874–1951), US composer and music theorist, born in Austria. He introduced atonality into his second string quartet (1907–08), while *Serenade* (1923) is the first example of the technique of serialism.

schol·ar /'skälər/ ▶ **n.** a specialist in a particular branch of study, esp. the humanities; a distinguished academic: *a Hebrew scholar*. ■ chiefly archaic a person who is highly educated or has an aptitude for study: *Mr. Bell declares himself no scholar*. ■ a student holding a scholarship. ■ archaic a student.
– ORIGIN Old English *scol(i)ere* 'schoolchild, student,' from late Latin *scholaris*, from Latin *schola* (see SCHOOL[1]).

schol·ar·ly /'skälərlē/ ▶ **adj.** involving or relating to serious academic study: *scholarly journals* | *a scholarly career*. ■ having or showing knowledge, learning, or devotion to academic pursuits: *a scholarly account of the period* | *an earnest, scholarly man*.
– DERIVATIVES **schol·ar·li·ness n.**

schol·ar·ship /'skälər,SHip/ ▶ **n. 1** academic study or achievement; learning of a high level.
2 a grant or payment made to support a student's education, awarded on the basis of academic or other achievement.

scho·las·tic /skə'lastik/ ▶ **adj. 1** of or concerning schools and education: *scholastic achievement*. ■ of or relating to secondary schools.
2 Philosophy & Theology of, relating to, or characteristic of medieval scholasticism. ■ typical of scholasticism in being pedantic or overly subtle.
▶ **n. 1** Philosophy & Theology, historical an adherent of scholasticism; a schoolman.

S

2 (in the Roman Catholic Church) a member of a religious order, esp. the Society of Jesus, who is between the novitiate and the priesthood.
– DERIVATIVES **scho·las·ti·cal·ly** /-ik(ə)lē/ **adv.**
– ORIGIN late 16th cent. (sense 2 of the adjective): via Latin from Greek *skholastikos* 'studious,' from *skholazein* 'be at leisure to study,' from *skholē* (see SCHOOL¹).

scho·las·ti·cism /skəˈlastiˌsizəm/ ▶ **n.** the system of theology and philosophy taught in medieval European universities, based on Aristotelian logic and the writings of the early Church Fathers and having a strong emphasis on tradition and dogma. ■ narrow-minded insistence on traditional doctrine.

scho·li·ast /ˈskōlēˌast/ ▶ **n.** historical a commentator on ancient or classical literature.
– DERIVATIVES **scho·li·as·tic** /ˌskōlēˈastik/ **adj.**
– ORIGIN late 16th cent.: from medieval Greek *skholiastēs*, from *skholiazein* 'write scholia' (see SCHOLIUM).

scho·li·um /ˈskōlēəm/ ▶ **n.** (pl. **scholia** /-lēə/) historical a marginal note or explanatory comment made by a scholiast.
– ORIGIN mid 16th cent.: modern Latin, from Greek *skholion*, from *skholē* 'learned discussion.'

school¹ /sko͞ol/ ▶ **n. 1** an institution for educating children: *Ryder's children did not go to school at all* | [as modifier] *school supplies.* ■ the buildings used by such an institution: *the cost of building a new school.* ■ [treated as pl.] the students and staff of a school: *the principal was addressing the whole school.* ■ a day's work at school; lessons: *school started at 7 a.m.*
2 any institution at which instruction is given in a particular discipline: *a dancing school.* ■ informal another term for UNIVERSITY. ■ a department or faculty of a college concerned with a particular subject of study: *the School of Dental Medicine.*
3 a group of people, particularly writers, artists, or philosophers, sharing the same or similar ideas, methods, or style: *the Frankfurt school of critical theory.* ■ a style, approach, or method of a specified character: *filmmakers are tired of the skin-deep school of cinema.*
▶ **v.** [with obj.] chiefly formal send to school; educate: *he was schooled in Boston.* ■ train or discipline (someone) in a particular skill or activity: *he schooled her in horsemanship* | *it's important to school yourself to be good at exams.*
– PHRASES **leave school** discontinue one's education: *he left school at 16.* **of** (or **from**) **the old school** see OLD SCHOOL. **the school of hard knocks** see KNOCK. **school of thought** a particular way of thinking, typically one disputed by the speaker: *a school of thought that calls into question the constitutional foundations of this country.*
– ORIGIN Old English *scōl, scolu*, via Latin from Greek *skholē* 'leisure, philosophy, place where lectures are given,' reinforced in Middle English by Old French *escole.*

school² ▶ **n.** a large group of fish or sea mammals.
▶ **v.** [no obj.] (of fish or sea mammals) form a large group.
– ORIGIN late Middle English: from Middle Low German and Middle Dutch *schōle*, of West Germanic origin; related to Old English *scolu* 'troop.' Compare with SHOAL¹.

school age ▶ **n.** the age range of children normally attending school.
– DERIVATIVES **school-age** (or **school-aged**) **adj.**

school board ▶ **n.** a local board or authority responsible for the provision and maintenance of schools.

school·book /ˈsko͞olˌbo͝ok/ ▶ **n.** a textbook used in a school.

school·boy /ˈsko͞olˌboi/ ▶ **n.** a boy attending school. ■ [as modifier] characteristic of or associated with schoolboys, esp. in being immature: *schoolboy humor.*

school bus ▶ **n.** a bus that transports students from home to school, school to home, or to school-sponsored events.

school·child /ˈsko͞olˌCHīld/ ▶ **n.** (pl. **schoolchildren**) a child attending school.

school col·ors ▶ **plural n.** a badge, cap, or other item in the distinctive colors of a particular school, typically awarded to a student who represents the school as a participant in a competitive sport.

school day ▶ **n.** a day on which classes are held in a primary or secondary school.

school·days /ˈsko͞olˌdāz/ ▶ **plural n.** the period in someone's life when they attended school: *a close friend from their schooldays.*

school dis·trict ▶ **n.** a geographical unit for the local administration of schools.

schooled /sko͞old/ ▶ **adj.** [often in combination] educated or trained in a specified activity or in a particular way: *a man well schooled in making money.*

school·er /ˈsko͞olər/ ▶ **n.** [in combination] a student attending a school of the specified kind or being educated in the specified way: *a high-schooler.*

school·fel·low /ˈsko͞olˌfelō/ ▶ **n.** more formal term for SCHOOLMATE.

school·girl /ˈsko͞olˌgərl/ ▶ **n.** a girl attending school. ■ [as modifier] characteristic of or associated with schoolgirls, esp. in being elementary or immature: *schoolgirl French.*

school·house /ˈsko͞olˌhous/ ▶ **n.** a building used as a school, esp. in a small community or village.

school·ing /ˈsko͞oliNG/ ▶ **n.** education or training received, esp. at school: *his parents paid for his schooling.*

school·man /ˈsko͞olmən, -ˌman/ ▶ **n.** (pl. **schoolmen**) historical **1** a teacher in a university in medieval Europe. ■ a scholar or an educator.
2 a scholastic theologian.

school·marm /ˈsko͞olˌmä(r)m/ ▶ **n.** a schoolmistress (typically used with reference to a woman regarded as prim, strict, and brisk in manner).
– DERIVATIVES **school·marm·ish adj.**

school·mas·ter /ˈsko͞olˌmastər/ ▶ **n.** dated a male teacher in a school.
– DERIVATIVES **school·mas·ter·ly adj.**

school·mate /ˈsko͞olˌmāt/ ▶ **n.** informal a person who attends or attended the same school as oneself.

school·mis·tress /ˈsko͞olˌmistris/ ▶ **n.** dated a female teacher in a school.

school night ▶ **n.** a night before a morning on which one must get up for school or (informal) work: *I didn't mean to drink so much red wine on a school night.*

school·room /ˈsko͞olˌro͞om, -ˌro͝om/ ▶ **n.** a room in which a class of students is taught. ■ (**the schoolroom**) used to refer to school as an institution: *I got most of my education outside of the schoolroom.*

school·teach·er /ˈsko͞olˌtēCHər/ ▶ **n.** a person who teaches in a school.
– DERIVATIVES **school·teach·ing** /-ˌtēCHiNG/ **n.**

school vouch·er ▶ **n.** a government-funded voucher redeemable for tuition fees at a school other than the public school that a student could attend free.

school·work /ˈsko͞olˌwərk/ ▶ **n.** work assigned students by their teachers in school: *Brother could do any schoolwork put to him, but he'd answer any spoken question with "I don't know."*

school·yard /ˈsko͞olˌyärd/ ▶ **n.** the grounds of a school, esp. as a place for children to play: *that schoolyard full of kids* | [as modifier] *the schoolyard bully.*

school year ▶ **n.** another term for ACADEMIC YEAR.

schoon·er /ˈsko͞onər/ ▶ **n. 1** a sailing ship with two or more masts, typically with the foremast smaller than the mainmast, and having gaff-rigged lower masts.
2 a tall beer glass.
– ORIGIN early 18th cent.: of unknown origin.

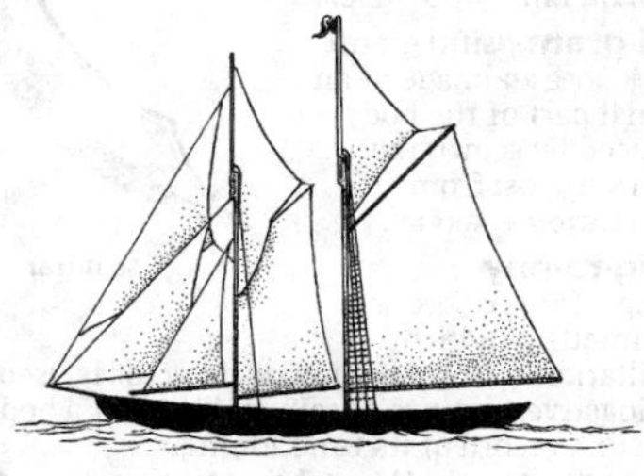

schooner 1

Scho·pen·hau·er /ˈSHōpənˌhou-ər/, Arthur (1788–1860), German philosopher. According to his philosophy, as expressed in *The World as Will and Idea* (1818), the will is identified with ultimate reality and happiness is only achieved by abnegating the will (as desire).

schorl /SHôrl/ ▶ **n.** a black iron-rich variety of tourmaline.
– ORIGIN late 18th cent.: from German *Schörl*, of unknown origin.

schot·tische /ˈSHätiSH/ ▶ **n.** a slow polka.
– ORIGIN mid 19th cent.: from German *der schottische Tanz* 'the Scottish dance.'

Schott·ky bar·ri·er /ˈSHätkē/ ▶ **n.** Electronics an electrostatic depletion layer formed at the junction of a metal and a semiconductor, which causes it to act as an electrical rectifier.
– ORIGIN 1940s: named after Walter *Schottky* (1886–1976), German physicist.

Schrö·der /ˈSHrōdər, ˈSHrā-/, Gerhard (1944–), German statesman; chancellor of Germany 1998–2005.

Schrö·ding·er /ˈSHrādiNGgər, ˈSHrō-/, Erwin (1887–1961), Austrian theoretical physicist, who founded the study of wave mechanics. His general works influenced scientists in many disciplines. Nobel Prize for Physics (1933), shared with Paul Dirac.

Schrö·ding·er e·qua·tion Physics a differential equation that forms the basis of the quantum-mechanical description of matter in terms of the wavelike properties of particles in a field. Its solution is related to the probability density of a particle in space and time.

schtup ▶ **v.** variant spelling of SHTUP.

Schu·bert /ˈSHo͞obərt/, Franz (1797–1828), Austrian composer. His music is associated with the romantic movement for its lyricism and emotional intensity, but it belongs in formal terms to the classical age. He composed more than 500 lieder, including the song cycles *Die Schöne Müllerin* (1823) and *Die Winterreise* (1827).
– DERIVATIVES **Schu·bert·i·an adj.**

Schulz /SHo͝olts/, Charles (1922–2000), US cartoonist. He is remembered as the creator of the widely syndicated "Peanuts" comic strip that featured a range of characters including Charlie Brown and his dog Snoopy. First published in 1950, the comic strip has since appeared in many publications around the world.

Schu·ma·cher /ˈSHo͞oˌmäKHər/, E. F. (1911–77), German economist and conservationist; full name *Ernst Friedrich Schumacher.* His *Small is Beautiful: Economics as if People Mattered* (1973) argues that mass production needs to be replaced by smaller, more energy-efficient enterprises.

Schu·mann /ˈSHo͞omən, -ˌmän/, Robert (Alexander) (1810–56), German composer. A leading romantic composer, he is particularly noted for his songs and piano music, as well as for four symphonies and much chamber music. His wife **Clara Wieck** (1819–96) was a noted pianist and composer.

schuss /SHo͞os, SHo͝os/ ▶ **n.** a straight downhill run on skis.
▶ **v.** [no obj.] make a straight downhill run on skis.
– ORIGIN 1930s: from German *Schuss*, literally 'shot.'

Schuyl·kill Riv·er /ˈsko͞olˌkil, -kəl/ a river that flows for 130 miles (210 km) through eastern Pennsylvania to join the Delaware River at Philadelphia.

schwa /SHwä/ ▶ **n.** Phonetics the unstressed central vowel (as in *a* moment *ago*), represented by the symbol (ə) in the International Phonetic Alphabet.
– ORIGIN late 19th cent.: from German, from Hebrew *šĕwā'.*

Schwa·ben /ˈSHväbən/ German name for SWABIA.

Schwann /SHwän, SHfän/, Theodor Ambrose Hubert (1810–82), German physiologist. He showed that animals (as well as plants) are made up of individual cells and that the egg begins life as a single cell. He also discovered the cells that form the myelin sheaths of nerve fibers (Schwann cells).

Schwar·ze·neg·ger /ˈSHwôrtsəˌnegər, ˈswôrt-/, Arnold (1947–), US actor and politician, born in Austria. He is noted for his action roles in movies such as *Conan the Barbarian* (1982) and *The Terminator* (1984). He also starred in movies such as the comedy *Kindergarten Cop* (1990) and the spy thriller *True Lies* (1994). In 2003, he was elected governor of California.

Schwarz·kopf¹ /ˈSHwôrtsˌkô(p)f, ˈswärtsˌkä(p)f/, Dame Elisabeth (1915–2006), German opera singer; full name *Olga Maria Elisabeth Friederike Schwarzkopf.* She is particularly known for her recitals of German lieder and for her roles in works such as Richard Strauss's *Der Rosenkavalier.*

Schwarz·kopf² /ˈSHwôrtsˌkôpf, ˈSHwärts-, -ˌkäpf/, H. Norman, Jr. (1934–), US army officer; nickname **Stormin' Norman**. He was deputy commander of US forces during the invasion of Grenada 1983. Promoted to full general in 1988 and appointed commander in chief of the US Central Command 1988–91, he led the Allied forces against Iraq in the Persian Gulf War 1991.

Schwarz·schild black hole /ˈSHwôrtsˌCHīld, ˈSHvärtsˌSHilt/ ▶ **n.** Physics a black hole of a kind supposed to result from the complete gravitational collapse of an electrically neutral and nonrotating body, having a physical singularity at the center to which infalling matter inevitably proceeds and at which the curvature of space-time is infinite. A **Schwarzschild radius** is the radius of the boundary of a hole of this type.

– ORIGIN named after Karl *Schwarzschild* (1873–1916), German astronomer.

Schwarz·wald /'sHvärts,vält/ German name for **BLACK FOREST**.

Schweit·zer /'sHwītsər, 'sHfī-/, Albert (1875–1965), German theologian, musician, and medical missionary. He qualified as a doctor in 1913 and went as a missionary to Gabon, where he established a hospital. Nobel Peace Prize (1952).

Schweiz /sHvīts/ German name for **SWITZERLAND**.

Schwe·rin /sHvā'rēn/ a city in northeastern Germany, capital of Mecklenburg-West Pomerania, situated on the southwestern shores of Lake Schwerin; pop. 96,300 (est. 2006).

Schwyz /sHvēts/ a canton in northeastern Switzerland, one of the three original cantons of the Swiss Confederation, to which it gave its name.

sci·ae·nid /sī'ēnid/ ▶ **n.** Zoology a fish of the drum family (Sciaenidae), whose members are mainly marine and important for food or sport.
– ORIGIN early 20th cent.: from modern Latin *Sciaenidae* (plural), from the genus name *Sciaena*, from Greek *skiaina*, denoting a kind of fish.

sci·ag·ra·phy /sī'agrəfē/ ▶ **n.** British spelling of **SKIAGRAPHY**.

sci·am·a·chy /sī'aməkē/ ▶ **n.** archaic sham fighting for exercise or practice. ■ argument or conflict with an imaginary opponent.
– ORIGIN early 17th cent.: from Greek *skiamakhia*, from *skia* 'shadow' + *-makhia* '-fighting.'

sci·at·ic /sī'atik/ ▶ **adj.** of or relating to the hip. ■ of or affecting the sciatic nerve. ■ suffering from or liable to sciatica.
– DERIVATIVES **sci·at·i·cal·ly** /-ik(ə)lē/ **adv.**
– ORIGIN early 16th cent. (as a noun denoting sciatica): from French *sciatique*, via late Latin from Greek *iskhiadikos* 'relating to the hips, subject to sciatica,' from *iskhion* 'hip joint.'

sci·at·i·ca /sī'atikə/ ▶ **n.** pain affecting the back, hip, and outer side of the leg, caused by compression of a spinal nerve root in the lower back, often owing to degeneration of an intervertebral disk.
– ORIGIN late Middle English: from late Latin *sciatica* (*passio*) 'sciatic (affliction),' feminine of *sciaticus*, from Greek *iskhiadikos* (see **SCIATIC**).

sci·at·ic nerve ▶ **n.** Anatomy a major nerve extending from the lower end of the spinal cord down the back of the thigh, and dividing above the knee joint. It is the nerve with the largest diameter in the human body.

SCID ▶ **abbr.** severe combined immune deficiency, a rare genetic disorder in which affected children have no resistance to disease and must be kept isolated from infection from birth.

sci·ence /'sīəns/ ▶ **n.** the intellectual and practical activity encompassing the systematic study of the structure and behavior of the physical and natural world through observation and experiment: *the world of science and technology*. ■ a particular area of this: *veterinary science | the agricultural sciences*. ■ a systematically organized body of knowledge on a particular subject: *the science of criminology*. ■ archaic knowledge of any kind.
– ORIGIN Middle English (denoting knowledge): from Old French, from Latin *scientia*, from *scire* 'know.'

sci·ence fic·tion (abbr.: **SF** or **Sci Fi**) ▶ **n.** fiction based on imagined future scientific or technological advances and major social or environmental changes, frequently portraying space or time travel and life on other planets.

sci·ence park ▶ **n.** an area devoted to scientific research or the development of science-based or technological industries.

sci·en·tial /sī'encHəl/ ▶ **adj.** archaic concerning or having knowledge.
– ORIGIN late Middle English: from late Latin *scientialis*, from *scientia* 'knowledge' (see **SCIENCE**).

sci·en·tif·ic /,sīən'tifik/ ▶ **adj.** based on or characterized by the methods and principles of science: *the scientific study of earthquakes*. ■ relating to or used in science: *scientific instruments*. ■ informal systematic; methodical: *how many people buy food in an organized, scientific way?*
– DERIVATIVES **sci·en·tif·i·cal·ly** /-ik(ə)lē/ **adv.**
– ORIGIN late 16th cent.: from French *scientifique* or late Latin *scientificus* 'producing knowledge,' from *scientia* (see **SCIENCE**). Early use described the liberal arts as opposed to the "mechanic" arts (i.e., arts requiring manual skill).

sci·en·tif·ic man·age·ment ▶ **n.** management of a business, industry, or economy, according to principles of efficiency derived from experiments in methods of work and production, esp. from time-and-motion studies.

sci·en·tif·ic meth·od ▶ **n.** a method of procedure that has characterized natural science since the 17th century, consisting in systematic observation, measurement, and experiment, and the formulation, testing, and modification of hypotheses.

sci·en·tif·ic mis·con·duct ▶ **n.** action that willfully compromises the integrity of scientific research, such as plagiarism or the falsification or fabrication of data.

sci·en·tism /'sīən,tizəm/ ▶ **n.** rare thought or expression regarded as characteristic of scientists. ■ excessive belief in the power of scientific knowledge and techniques.
– DERIVATIVES **sci·en·tis·tic** /,sīən'tistik/ **adj.**

sci·en·tist /'sīəntist/ ▶ **n.** a person who is studying or has expert knowledge of one or more of the natural or physical sciences.

Sci·en·tol·o·gy /,sīən'täləjē/ ▶ **n.** trademark a religious system based on the seeking of self-knowledge and spiritual fulfillment through graded courses of study and training. It was founded by American science-fiction writer **L. Ron Hubbard** (1911–86) in 1955.
– DERIVATIVES **Sci·en·tol·o·gist** /-jist/ **n.**
– ORIGIN from Latin *scientia* 'knowledge' + **-LOGY**.

sci-fi /'sī 'fī/ ▶ **n.** informal short for **SCIENCE FICTION**.

scil·i·cet /'silə,set/ ▶ **adv.** that is to say; namely (introducing a word to be supplied or an explanation of an ambiguity).
– ORIGIN Latin, from *scire licet* 'one is permitted to know.'

scil·la /'silə/ ▶ **n.** a plant of the lily family that typically bears small blue star- or bell-shaped flowers and glossy straplike leaves, native to Eurasia and temperate Africa. ● Genus *Scilla*, family Liliaceae.
– ORIGIN modern Latin, from Latin *scilla* 'sea onion,' from Greek *skilla*.

Scil·ly Isles /'silē/ (also **Isles of Scilly** or **the Scillies**) a group of about 140 small islands (of which 5 are inhabited) off the southwestern tip of England; pop. 2,200 (est. 2006); capital, Hugh Town (on St. Mary's).
– DERIVATIVES **Scil·lo·ni·an** /sə'lōnēən/ **adj. & n.**

scim·i·tar /'simətər, -,tär/ ▶ **n.** a short sword with a curved blade that broadens toward the point, used originally in Eastern countries.
– ORIGIN mid 16th cent.: from French *cimeterre* or Italian *scimitarra*, of unknown origin.

scimitar

scim·i·tar o·ryx (also **scimitar-horned oryx**) ▶ **n.** an oryx with scimitar-shaped horns, now living only along the southern edge of the Sahara. ● *Oryx dammah*, family Bovidae.

scin·ti·gram /'sinti,gram/ ▶ **n.** Medicine an image of an internal part of the body produced by scintigraphy.
– ORIGIN 1950s: from **SCINTILLATION** + **-GRAM**[1].

scin·tig·ra·phy /sin'tigrəfē/ ▶ **n.** Medicine a technique in which a scintillation counter or similar detector is used with a radioactive tracer to obtain an image of a bodily organ or a record of its functioning.
– DERIVATIVES **scin·ti·graph·ic** /,sinti'grafik/ **adj.**
– ORIGIN 1950s: from **SCINTILLATION** + **-GRAPHY**.

scin·til·la /sin'tilə/ ▶ **n.** [in sing.] a tiny trace or spark of a specified quality or feeling: ***a scintilla of doubt***.
– ORIGIN late 17th cent.: from Latin.

scin·til·late /'sin(t)l,āt/ ▶ **v.** [no obj.] emit flashes of light; sparkle. ■ Physics fluoresce momentarily when struck by a photon or charged particle.
– DERIVATIVES **scin·til·lant** /-ənt/ **adj. & n.**
– ORIGIN early 17th cent.: from Latin *scintillat-* 'sparkled,' from the verb *scintillare*, from *scintilla* 'spark.'

scin·til·lat·ing /'sin(t)l,ātiNG/ ▶ **adj.** sparkling or shining brightly: *the scintillating sun*. ■ brilliantly and excitingly clever or skillful: *the audience loved his scintillating wit | the team produced a scintillating second-half performance*.
– DERIVATIVES **scin·til·lat·ing·ly** **adv.**

scin·til·la·tion /,sin(t)l'āsHən/ ▶ **n.** a flash or sparkle of light. ■ the process or state of emitting flashes of light. ■ Physics a small flash of visible or ultraviolet light emitted by fluorescence in a phosphor when struck by a charged particle or high-energy photon. ■ Astronomy the twinkling of the stars, caused by the earth's atmosphere diffracting starlight unevenly.

scin·til·la·tion count·er ▶ **n.** Physics a device for detecting and recording scintillations. Also called **SCINTILLOMETER**.

scin·til·la·tor /'sin(t)l,ātər/ ▶ **n.** Physics a material that fluoresces when struck by a charged particle or high-energy photon. ■ a detector for charged particles and gamma rays in which scintillations produced in a phosphor are detected and amplified by a photomultiplier, giving an electrical output signal.

scin·til·lom·e·ter /,sintl'ämitər/ Another term for **SCINTILLATION COUNTER**.

scin·ti·scan /'sin(t)ə,skan/ ▶ **n.** Medicine another term for **SCINTIGRAM**.
– ORIGIN 1960s: from **SCINTILLATION** + **SCAN**.

sci·o·list /'sīəlist/ ▶ **n.** archaic a person who pretends to be knowledgeable and well informed.
– DERIVATIVES **sci·o·lism** /-,lizəm/ **n.**, **sci·o·lis·tic** /,sīə'listik/ **adj.**
– ORIGIN early 17th cent.: from late Latin *sciolus* (diminutive of Latin *scius* 'knowing,' from *scire* 'know') + **-IST**.

sci·on /'sīən/ ▶ **n. 1** (also **cion**) a young shoot or twig of a plant, esp. one cut for grafting or rooting. **2** a descendant of a notable family: ***he was the scion of a wealthy family***.
– ORIGIN Middle English: from Old French *ciun* 'shoot, twig,' of unknown origin.

Scip·i·o Ae·mil·i·a·nus /'sipē,ō i,milē'ānəs/ (*c.*185–129 BC), Roman general and politician; full name *Publius Cornelius Scipio Aemilianus Africanus Minor*; adoptive grandson of Scipio Africanus. He achieved distinction in the siege of Carthage in 146 during the third Punic War and in his campaign in Spain in 133.

Scip·i·o Af·ri·ca·nus /'sipē,ō ,afri'kānəs/ (236–*c.*184 BC), Roman general and politician; full name *Publius Cornelius Scipio Africanus Major*. He was successful in concluding the second Punic War, by the defeat of the Carthaginians in Spain in 206 and then by the defeat of Hannibal in Africa at Zama in 202.

sci·re fa·ci·as /,sīrē 'fāsHēəs, 'ski(ə)re 'fäkē,äs/ ▶ **n.** Law a writ requiring a person to show why a judgment regarding a record or patent should not be enforced or annulled.
– ORIGIN Latin, literally 'let (the person) know.'

sci·roc·co /sHə'räkō, sə-/ ▶ **n.** variant spelling of **SIROCCO**.

scir·rhus /'s(k)irəs/ ▶ **n.** (pl. **scirrhi** /'s(k)i,rī, 'ski,rē/) Medicine a carcinoma that is hard to the touch.
– DERIVATIVES **scir·rhous** /-əs/ **adj.**
– ORIGIN late Middle English: modern Latin, from Greek *skirros*, from *skiros* 'hard.'

scis·sile /'sisəl, -īl/ ▶ **adj.** chiefly Biochemistry (of a chemical bond) readily undergoing scission.
– ORIGIN early 17th cent.: from Latin *scissilis*, from *sciss-* 'cut, divided,' from the verb *scindere*.

scis·sion /'sizHən, 'sisH-/ ▶ **n.** technical the action or state of cutting or being cut, in particular: ■ chiefly Biochemistry breakage of a chemical bond, esp. one in a long chain molecule so that two smaller chains result. ■ a division or split between people or parties; a schism.
– ORIGIN late Middle English: from Old French, or from late Latin *scissio(n-)*, from *scindere* 'cut, cleave.'

scis·sor /'sizər/ ▶ **v. 1** [with obj.] cut (something) with scissors: *pages scissored out of a magazine*. **2** [with obj.] move (one's legs) back and forth in a way resembling the action of scissors: *he was still hanging on, scissoring his legs uselessly*. ■ [no obj.] (of a person's legs) move in such a way.
▶ **n.** see **SCISSORS**.
– ORIGIN early 17th cent.: from **SCISSORS**.

scis·sor hold (also **scissors hold**) ▶ **n.** Wrestling a hold in which the head or other part of the opponent's body is gripped between the legs, which are then locked by crossing them at the instep or ankles to apply pressure.

scis·sor jack (also **scissors jack**) ▶ **n.** a jack for heavy lifting, operated by a horizontal screw that raises or lowers a frame of hinged, rhombus-shaped linkages.

scis·sor kick (also **scissors kick**) ▶ **n.** (in various sports, particularly swimming and soccer) a kick in which the legs make a sharp snapping movement like the blades of a pair of scissors.
– DERIVATIVES **scis·sor-kick** **v.**

scis·sors /'sizərz/ (also **a pair of scissors**) ▶ **plural n.** an instrument used for cutting cloth, paper, and other thin material, consisting of two blades laid one on top of the other and fastened in the middle so as to allow them to be opened and closed by a thumb and finger inserted through rings on the end

of their handles. ■ (also **scissor**) [often as modifier] an action in which two things cross each other or open and close like the blades of a pair of scissors: *as the fish swims, the tail lobes open and close in a slight scissor action.*
– ORIGIN late Middle English: from Old French *cisoires*, from late Latin *cisoria*, plural of *cisorium* 'cutting instrument,' from *cis-*, variant of *caes-*, stem of *caedere* 'to cut.' The spelling with *sc-* (16th cent.) was by association with the Latin stem *sciss-* 'cut.'

scis·sors and paste ▶ n. & v. another term for CUT AND PASTE.

scis·sor-tailed fly·catch·er ▶ n. (also **scissortail**) a tyrant flycatcher with a very long forked tail, found in the southern US and noted for its spectacular aerial display. ● *Tyrannus forficatus*, family Tyrannidae.

Sci·uro·mor·pha /sī,yŏŏrə'môrfə/ Zoology a major division of the rodents that comprises the squirrels, prairie dogs, and marmots. ● Suborder Sciuromorpha, order Rodentia.
– ORIGIN modern Latin (plural), from Greek *skiouros* (from *skia* 'shadow' + *oura* 'tail') + *morphē* 'form.'

scle·ra /'skli(ə)rə/ ▶ n. Anatomy the white outer layer of the eyeball. At the front of the eye it is continuous with the cornea.
– DERIVATIVES **scle·ral** adj.
– ORIGIN late 19th cent.: modern Latin, from Greek *sklēros* 'hard.'

Scle·rac·tin·i·a /,skli(ə)rak'tinēə/ Zoology an order of coelenterates that comprises the stony corals. Also called MADREPORARIA.
– DERIVATIVES **scle·rac·tin·i·an** n. & adj.
– ORIGIN modern Latin (plural), from Greek *sklēros* 'hard' + *aktis, aktin-* 'ray.'

scle·ren·chy·ma /skli'reNGkəmə/ ▶ n. Botany strengthening tissue in a plant, formed from cells with thickened, typically lignified, walls.
– DERIVATIVES **scle·ren·chym·a·tous** /,skliren'kimətəs/ adj.
– ORIGIN mid 19th cent.: modern Latin, from Greek *sklēros* 'hard' + *enkhuma* 'infusion,' on the pattern of *parenchyma*.

scle·rite /'skli(ə)rīt/ ▶ n. Zoology a component section of an exoskeleton, esp. each of the plates forming the skeleton of an arthropod.
– ORIGIN mid 19th cent.: from Greek *sklēros* 'hard' + -ITE[1].

scle·ri·tis /sklə'rītis/ ▶ n. Medicine inflammation of the sclera.

sclero- ▶ comb. form hard; hardened; hardening: *scleroderma* | *sclerotherapy*.
– ORIGIN from Greek *sklēros* 'hard.'

scle·ro·der·ma /,skli(ə)rə'dərmə, ,skler-/ ▶ n. Medicine a chronic hardening and contraction of the skin and connective tissue, either locally or throughout the body.

scle·roid /'skli(ə)r,oid, 'skler-/ ▶ adj. Botany & Zoology having a hard or hardened texture.
– ORIGIN mid 19th cent.: from Greek *sklēros* 'hard.'

scle·ro·phyll /'skli(ə)rə,fil, 'skler-/ ▶ n. Botany a woody plant with evergreen leaves that are tough and thick in order to reduce water loss.
– DERIVATIVES **scle·ro·phyl·lous** /,skli(ə)rə'filəs, skli'räfələs/ adj.
– ORIGIN early 20th cent.: from Greek *sklēros* 'hard' + *phullon* 'leaf.'

scle·ro·pro·tein /,skli(ə)rō'prōtē(ə)n/ ▶ n. Biochemistry an insoluble structural protein such as keratin, collagen, or elastin.

scle·rosed /skli'rōst, -'rōzd, 'skli(ə)rōst, 'skler-, -ōzd/ ▶ adj. Medicine (esp. of blood vessels) affected by sclerosis.

scle·ro·sing cho·lan·gi·tis /,sklə'rōsiNG ,kōlan'jītis/ ▶ n. Medicine a complication of ulcerative colitis in which the bile ducts become narrow and develop irregularities.
– ORIGIN 1980s: *sclerosing* from the verb *sclerose* (back-formation from SCLEROSED); *cholangitis* from Greek *kholē* 'bile' + *angeion* 'vessel' + -ITIS.

scle·ro·sis /sklə'rōsis/ ▶ n. Medicine **1** abnormal hardening of body tissue. ■ see MULTIPLE SCLEROSIS. **2** excessive resistance to change: *the challenge was to avoid institutional sclerosis.*
– ORIGIN late Middle English (originally denoting a hard external tumor): via medieval Latin from Greek *sklērōsis*, from *sklēroun* 'harden.'

scle·ro·ther·a·py /,skli(ə)rə'THerəpē/ ▶ n. Medicine the treatment of varicose blood vessels by the injection of an irritant that causes inflammation, coagulation of blood, and narrowing of the blood vessel wall.

scle·rot·ic /sklə'rätik/ ▶ adj. **1** Medicine of or having sclerosis. **2** becoming rigid and unresponsive; losing the ability to adapt: *sclerotic management.* **3** Anatomy of or relating to the sclera.
▶ n. another term for SCLERA.

scle·ro·tin /'skli(ə)rətn, 'skler-/ ▶ n. Biochemistry a structural protein that forms the cuticles of insects and is hardened and darkened by a natural tanning process in which protein chains are cross-linked by quinone groups.
– ORIGIN 1940s: from SCLERO- 'hardened,' on the pattern of such words as *keratin*.

scle·ro·ti·um /,sklə'rōSHēəm/ ▶ n. (pl. **sclerotia** /-SHēə/) Botany the hard dark resting body of certain fungi, consisting of a mass of hyphal threads, capable of remaining dormant for long periods.
– ORIGIN mid 19th cent.: modern Latin (former genus name), from Greek *sklēros* 'hard.'

scle·ro·tized /'skli(ə)rə,tizd, 'skler-/ (also **sclerotised**) ▶ adj. Entomology (of an insect's body, or part of one) hardened by conversion into sclerotin.
– DERIVATIVES **scle·ro·ti·za·tion** /,skli(ə)rətə'zāSHən, ,skler-/ n.

scle·ro·tome /'skli(ə)rə,tōm, 'skler-/ ▶ n. Embryology the part of each somite in a vertebrate embryo giving rise to bone or other skeletal tissue. Compare with DERMATOME, MYOTOME.

scle·rous /'skli(ə)rəs, 'skler-/ ▶ adj. (of tissue) hardened or bony.
– ORIGIN mid 19th cent.: from Greek *sklēros* 'hard' + -OUS.

scoff[1] /skôf, skäf/ ▶ v. [no obj.] speak to someone or about something in a scornfully derisive or mocking way: *department officials scoffed at the allegations* | [with direct speech] *"You, a scientist?" he scoffed.*
▶ n. an expression of scornful derision. ■ archaic an object of ridicule: *his army was the scoff of all Europe.*
– DERIVATIVES **scoff·er** n., **scoff·ing·ly** adv.
– ORIGIN Middle English (first used as a noun in the sense 'mockery, scorn'): perhaps of Scandinavian origin.

scoff[2] informal ▶ v. [with obj.] eat (something) quickly and greedily: *she scoffed down several chops* | *a lizard scoffing up insects.* Compare with SCARF[3].
▶ n. food.
– ORIGIN late 18th cent. (as a verb): originally a variant of Scots and dialect *scaff*. The noun is from Afrikaans *schoff*, representing Dutch *schoft* 'quarter of a day,' (by extension) 'meal.'

scoff·law /'skôf,lô, 'skäf-/ ▶ n. informal a person who flouts the law, esp. by failing to comply with a law that is difficult to enforce effectively.

scold /skōld/ ▶ v. [with obj.] remonstrate with or rebuke (someone) angrily: *Mom took Anna away, scolding her for her bad behavior.*
▶ n. a woman who nags or grumbles constantly.
– DERIVATIVES **scold·er** n.
– ORIGIN Middle English (as a noun): probably from Old Norse *skáld* 'skald.'

scold·ing /'skōldiNG/ ▶ n. an angry rebuke or reprimand: *she'd get a scolding from Victoria.*
▶ adj. angrily rebuking or reprimanding: *a scolding glare.*

sco·lex /'skō,leks/ ▶ n. (pl. **scolices** /'skäli,sēz, 'skō-/) Zoology the anterior end of a tapeworm, bearing suckers and hooks for attachment.
– ORIGIN mid 19th cent.: modern Latin, from Greek *skōlēx* 'worm.'

sco·li·o·sis /,skōlē'ōsis/ ▶ n. Medicine abnormal lateral curvature of the spine. Compare with KYPHOSIS and LORDOSIS.
– DERIVATIVES **sco·li·ot·ic** /-'ätik/ adj.
– ORIGIN early 18th cent.: modern Latin, from Greek, from *skolios* 'bent.'

scol·lop /'skäləp, 'skal-/ ▶ n. & v. archaic spelling of SCALLOP.

scom·broid /'skäm,broid/ Zoology ▶ n. a fish of the mackerel family, or one of a larger group that also includes the barracudas and billfishes. ● Family Scombridae or suborder Scombroidei.
▶ adj. of or relating to fish of this family or group.
– ORIGIN mid 19th cent.: from modern Latin *Scombroidea* (superfamily name), from Greek *skombros*, denoting a tuna or mackerel.

sconce[1] /skäns/ ▶ n. **1** a candle holder, or a holder of another light source, that is attached to a wall with an ornamental bracket. **2** a flaming torch or candle secured in such a holder.
– ORIGIN late Middle English (originally denoting a portable lantern with a screen to protect the flame): shortening of Old French *esconse* 'lantern,' or from medieval Latin *sconsa*, from Latin *absconsa (laterna)* 'dark (lantern),' literally 'hidden (lantern)' (i.e., a lantern with a device for concealing the light), from *abscondere* 'to hide.'

sconce[1] 1

sconce[2] ▶ n. archaic a small fort or earthwork defending a ford, pass, or castle gate. ■ a shelter or screen serving as protection from fire or the weather.
– ORIGIN late Middle English: from Dutch *schans* 'brushwood,' from Middle High German *schanze*. The earliest recorded sense 'screen, interior partition' derives perhaps from SCONCE[1]; the later senses date from the late 16th cent.

scone /skōn, skän/ ▶ n. a small unsweetened or lightly sweetened biscuitlike cake made from flour, fat, and milk and sometimes having added fruit.
– ORIGIN early 16th cent. (originally Scots): perhaps from Middle Dutch *schoon(broot)* 'fine (bread).'

scooch /skŏŏCH/ (also **scootch**) ▶ v. [no obj.] informal **1** crouch or squat. **2** move in or pass through a restricted space: *waiters kept trying to scooch by.* ■ [with obj.] move (something or something) a short distance or into a restricted space: *scooch your sleeping bags close together.*
– ORIGIN 19th century: probably alteration of SCROOCH; in sense sense 2 probably influenced by SCOOT.

scoop /skōōp/ ▶ n. **1** a utensil resembling a spoon, with a long handle and a deep bowl, used for removing powdered, granulated, or semisolid substances (such as ice cream) from a container. ■ a short-handled deep shovel used for moving grain, coal, etc. ■ a moving bowl-shaped part of a digging machine, dredger, or other mechanism into which material is gathered. ■ a long-handled spoonlike surgical instrument. ■ a quantity taken up by a scoop: *an apple pie with scoops of ice cream on top.* **2** informal a piece of news published by a newspaper or broadcast by a television or radio station in advance of its rivals. ■ (**the scoop**) the latest information about something.
▶ v. [with obj.] **1** pick up and move (something) with a scoop: *Philip began to scoop grain into his bag.* ■ create (a hollow or hole) with or as if with a scoop: *a hole was scooped out in the floor of the dwelling.* ■ pick up (someone or something) in a swift, fluid movement: *he laughed and scooped her up in his arms.* **2** informal publish a news story before (a rival reporter, newspaper, or radio or television station).
– DERIVATIVES **scoop·er** n., **scoop·ful** n.
– ORIGIN Middle English (originally denoting a utensil for pouring liquids): from Middle Dutch and Middle Low German *schōpe* 'waterwheel bucket'; from a West Germanic base meaning 'draw water'; related to the verb SHAPE.

scoop neck ▶ n. a deeply curved wide neckline on a garment.

scoot /skōōt/ ▶ v. [no obj.] informal go or leave somewhere quickly: *I'd better scoot* | *they scooted off on their bikes.*
– ORIGIN mid 18th cent.: of unknown origin.

scootch /skŏŏCH/ ▶ v. var. of SCOOCH.

scoot·er /'skōōtər/ ▶ n. **1** (also **motor scooter**) a light two-wheeled open motor vehicle on which the driver sits over an enclosed engine with legs together and feet resting on a floorboard. ■ [often with modifier] any small, light, vehicle able to travel quickly across water, ice, or snow. **2** a vehicle typically ridden as a recreation, consisting of a footboard mounted on two wheels and a long steering handle, propelled by resting one foot on the footboard and pushing the other against the ground.
▶ v. [no obj.] travel or ride on a scooter.
– DERIVATIVES **scoot·er·ist** /-ist/ n.

scooter 2

sco·pa /'skōpə/ ▶ n. (pl. **scopae** /-pē/) Zoology a small brushlike tuft of hairs on some insects, esp. that on which pollen collects on the leg of a bee.
– ORIGIN early 19th cent.: from Latin *scopae* (plural) 'twigs, broom.'

scope /skōp/ ▶ n. **1** the extent of the area or subject matter that something deals with or to which it is relevant: *we widened the scope of our investigation* | *such questions go well beyond the scope of this book.* **2** the opportunity or possibility to do or deal with something: *the scope for major change is always limited by political realities.* ■ archaic a purpose, end, or intention: *Plato maintains religion to be the chief aim and scope of human life.*

PRONUNCIATION KEY ə ago, up; ər over, fur; a hat; ā ate; ä car; e let; ē see; i fit; ī by; NG sing; ō go; ô law, for; oi toy; ŏŏ good; ōō goo; ou out; TH thin; TH then; ZH vision

3 informal a telescope, microscope, or other device having a name ending in *-scope*: *infrared night scopes*.
4 Nautical the length of cable extended when a ship rides at anchor.
5 Linguistics & Logic the range of the effect of an operator such as a quantifier or conjunction.
▶ v. [with obj.] 1 assess or investigate (something): *they'd scoped out their market*. ■ set the scope of (a projected undertaking): *it is important that a project is scoped correctly to ensure the budget can be accurately defined*.
2 informal look at carefully; scan: *they watched him scoping the room, looking for Michael*.
– ORIGIN mid 16th cent. (in the sense 'target for shooting at'): from Italian *scopo* 'aim,' from Greek *skopos* 'target,' from *skeptesthai* 'look out.' Sense 3 of the noun is derived from -SCOPE.

-scope ▶ comb. form denoting an instrument for observing, viewing, or examining: *microscope* | *telescope*.
– ORIGIN from modern Latin *-scopium*, from Greek *skopein* 'look at.'

-scopic ▶ comb. form in adjectives corresponding to nouns ending in *-scope* (such as *telescopic* corresponding to *telescope*).

sco·pol·a·mine /skə'pälə,mēn/ ▶ n. Chemistry a poisonous plant alkaloid used as an antiemetic in motion sickness, as a preoperative medication for examination of the eye, and formerly as a sedative and hypnotic. ● Chem. formula: $C_{17}H_{21}NO_4$. It is obtained chiefly from plants of the genus *Scopolia*, family Solanaceae.
– ORIGIN late 19th cent.: from *Scopolia* (genus name of the plants yielding it) + AMINE.

scops owl /skäps/ ▶ n. a small owl with distinctive ear tufts, found in Europe, Africa, and Asia. ● Genus *Otus*, family Strigidae: many species, in particular the widespread **Eurasian scops owl** (*O. scops*).
– ORIGIN early 18th cent.: *scops* from modern Latin *Scops* (former genus name), from Greek *skōps*.

scop·u·la /-lə/ ▶ n. (pl. **scopulae** /'skäpyəlē, 'skäpyəlī/) Zoology a small brushlike structure, esp. on the legs of spiders.
– ORIGIN early 19th cent.: from late Latin, diminutive of Latin *scopa* (see SCOPA).

-scopy ▶ comb. form indicating viewing, observation, or examination, typically with an instrument having a name ending in *-scope*: *endoscopy* | *microscopy*.
– ORIGIN from Greek *skopia* 'observation,' from *skopein* 'examine, look at.'

scor·bu·tic /skôr'byo͞otik/ ▶ adj. relating to or affected with scurvy. See also ANTISCORBUTIC.
– ORIGIN mid 17th cent.: from modern Latin *scorbuticus*, from medieval Latin *scorbutus* 'scurvy,' perhaps from Middle Low German *schorbūk* (from *schoren* 'to break' + *būk* 'belly').

scorch /skôrCH/ ▶ v. 1 [with obj.] burn the surface of (something) with flame or heat: *surrounding houses were scorched by heat from the blast*. ■ [no obj.] become burned when exposed to heat or a flame: *the meat had scorched*. ■ (often as adj. **scorched**) (of the heat of the sun) cause (vegetation or a place) to become dried out and lifeless: *a desolate, scorched landscape*.
2 [no obj.] informal (of a person or vehicle) move very fast: *a sports car scorching along the expressway*.
▶ n. the burning or charring of the surface of something: [as modifier] *a scorch mark*. ■ Botany a form of plant necrosis, typically of fungal origin, marked by browning of leaf margins.
– ORIGIN Middle English (as a verb): perhaps related to Old Norse *skorpna* 'be shriveled.'

S

scorched earth pol·i·cy ▶ n. a military strategy of burning or destroying buildings, crops, or other resources that might be of use to an invading enemy force.

scorch·er /'skôrCHər/ ▶ n. [usu. in sing.] informal 1 a day or period of very hot weather: *next week could be a real scorcher*.
2 a remarkable or extreme example of something, in particular: ■ a very powerfully struck ball: *Winfield hit a scorcher over the left field fence*. ■ a sensational or very good book, film, or song. ■ a heated or violent argument.

scorch·ing /'skôrCHiNG/ ▶ adj. very hot: *the scorching July sun*. ■ (of criticism) harsh; severe. ■ informal very fast: *she set a scorching pace*.
– DERIVATIVES **scorch·ing·ly** adv.

scor·da·tu·ra /,skôrdə'to͝orə/ ▶ n. Music the technique of altering the normal tuning of a stringed instrument to produce particular effects.
– ORIGIN late 19th cent.: Italian, from *scordare* 'be out of tune.'

score /skôr/ ▶ n. 1 the number of points, goals, runs, etc., achieved in a game by a team or an individual: *the final score was 25–16 in favor of Washington*. ■ informal an act of gaining a point, goal, or run in a game. ■ a rating or grade, such as a mark achieved in a test: *an IQ score of 161*. ■ (**the score**) informal the state of affairs; the real facts about the present situation: *"Hey, what's the score here, what's goin' on?"* ■ informal an act of buying illegal drugs. ■ informal the proceeds of a crime.
2 (pl. **same**) a group or set of twenty or about twenty: *a score of men lost their lives in the battle* | *Doyle's success brought imitators* **by the score**. ■ (**scores of**) a large amount or number of something: *he sent scores of enthusiastic letters to friends*.
3 a written representation of a musical composition showing all the vocal and instrumental parts arranged one below the other. ■ the music composed for a movie or play.
4 a notch or line cut or scratched into a surface. ■ historical a running account kept by marks against a customer's name, typically in a tavern.
▶ v. [with obj.] 1 gain (a point, goal, run, etc.) in a competitive game: *Penn State scored two touchdowns in the fourth quarter* | [no obj.] *Martinez scored on Anderson's sacrifice fly*. ■ decide on the score to be awarded to (a competitor): *the judge must score each dog against this standard*. ■ gain (a number of points) for a competitor; be worth: *each correct answer scores ten points*. ■ decide on the scores to be awarded in (a game or competition). ■ [no obj.] record the score during a game; act as scorer. ■ Baseball cause (a teammate) to score: *McNab singled, scoring Reynolds and Diaz*. ■ informal secure (a success or an advantage): *the band scored a hit single*. ■ [no obj.] informal be successful: [with complement] *his new movie scored big*. ■ informal buy or acquire (something, typically illegal drugs): *Sally had scored some acid*. ■ [no obj.] informal succeed in attracting a sexual partner, typically for a casual encounter.
2 orchestrate or arrange (a piece of music), typically for a specified instrument or instruments: *the Quartet Suite was scored for flute, violin, viola da gamba, and continuo*. ■ compose the music for (a movie or play).
3 cut or scratch a notch or line on (a surface): *score the card until you cut through*. ■ historical record (a total owed) by making marks against a customer's name: *a slate on which the old man* **scored up** *vast accounts*. ■ Medicine & Biology examine (experimentally treated cells, bacterial colonies, etc.), making a record of the number showing a particular character.
– PHRASES **keep (the) score** register the score of a game as it proceeds. **know the score** informal be aware of the essential facts about a situation. **on that** (or **this**) **score** so far as that (or this) is concerned: *my priority was to blend new faces into the team, and we have succeeded on that score*. **score points** outdo another person, esp. in an argument. **settle a** (or **the**) **score** 1 take revenge on someone for a past act. 2 dated pay off a debt or other obligation.
– DERIVATIVES **score·less** adj., **scor·er** n.
– ORIGIN late Old English *scoru* 'set of twenty,' from Old Norse *skor* 'notch, tally, twenty,' of Germanic origin; related to SHEAR. The verb (late Middle English) is from Old Norse *skora* 'make an incision.'

score·board /'skôr,bôrd/ ▶ n. a large board on which the score in a game or match is displayed.

score·card /'skôr,kärd/ (also **scoresheet** or **scorebook**) ▶ n. (in sports) a card, sheet, or book in which scores are entered.

score·keep·er /'skôr,kēpər/ ▶ n. a person who keeps the score of a game.

sco·ri·a /'skôrēə/ ▶ n. (pl. **scoriae** /'skôrē-ē/) a cindery, vesicular basaltic lava, typically having a frothy texture. ■ slag separated from molten metal during smelting.
– DERIVATIVES **sco·ri·a·ceous** /,skôrē'āSHəs/ adj.
– ORIGIN late Middle English (denoting slag from molten metal): via Latin from Greek *skōria* 'refuse,' from *skōr* 'dung.' The geological term dates from the late 18th cent.

scor·ing pos·i·tion ▶ n. Baseball a runner's position on second or third base, from which scoring on a base hit is likely.

scorn /skôrn/ ▶ n. the feeling or belief that someone or something is worthless or despicable; contempt: *I do not wish to become the object of scorn* | [in sing.] *a general scorn for human life*. ■ [in sing.] archaic a person viewed with such feeling: *a scandal and a scorn to all who look on thee*. ■ archaic a statement or gesture indicating such feeling.
▶ v. [with obj.] feel or express contempt or derision for: *I was routinely ridiculed and scorned by conservatives and liberals alike*. ■ reject (something) in a contemptuous way: *opponents scorned his offer to negotiate*. ■ [no obj., with infinitive] refuse to do something because one is too proud: *at her lowest ebb, she would have scorned to stoop to such tactics*.
– PHRASES **pour** (or **heap**) **scorn on** speak with contempt or mockery of.
– DERIVATIVES **scorn·er** n. (rare).
– ORIGIN Middle English: shortening of Old French *escarn* (noun), *escharnir* (verb), of Germanic origin.

scorn·ful /'skôrnfəl/ ▶ adj. feeling or expressing contempt or derision: *the justices have been* **scornful of** *the government's conduct* | *scornful laughter*.
– DERIVATIVES **scorn·ful·ly** adv., **scorn·ful·ness** n.

scor·per /'skôrpər/ (also **scauper** /'skôpər/) ▶ n. a sharp chisel-like tool with a curved or squared cutting end, used to scoop out broad lines and areas when engraving wood or metal.

Scor·pi·o /'skôrpē,ō/ Astrology the eighth sign of the zodiac (the Scorpion), which the sun enters about October 23. ■ (**a Scorpio**) (pl. **Scorpios**) a person born when the sun is in this sign.
– DERIVATIVES **Scor·pi·an** /-pēən/ n. & adj.
– ORIGIN Latin.

scor·pi·oid /'skôrpē,oid/ ▶ adj. Zoology of, relating to, or resembling a scorpion. ■ Botany (of a flower cluster) curled up at the end, and uncurling as the flowers develop.
– ORIGIN mid 19th cent.: from Greek from *skorpios* 'scorpion' + -OID.

scor·pi·on /'skôrpēən/ ▶ n. a terrestrial arachnid with lobsterlike pincers and a poisonous sting at the end of its jointed tail, which it can hold curved over the back. Most kinds live in tropical and subtropical areas. ● Order Scorpiones. ■ used in names of other arachnids and insects resembling a scorpion, e.g., **false scorpion, water scorpion**. ■ (**the Scorpion**) the zodiacal sign Scorpio or the constellation Scorpius. ■ (**scorpions**) literary a whip with metal points. [with allusion to 1 Kings 12:11.]
– ORIGIN Middle English: via Old French from Latin *scorpio(n-)*, based on Greek *skorpios* 'scorpion.'

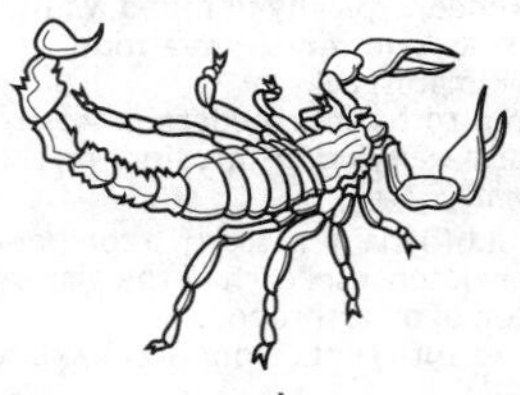
scorpion

scor·pi·on·fish /'skôrpēən,fiSH/ ▶ n. (pl. **same** or **scorpionfishes**) a chiefly bottom-dwelling marine fish that is typically red in color and has spines on the head that are sometimes venomous. ● Family Scorpaenidae: many genera and numerous species, including the redfishes and rockfishes.

scor·pi·on·fly /'skôrpēən,flī/ (also **scorpion fly**) ▶ n. (pl. **scorpionflies**) a slender predatory insect with membranous wings, long legs, and a downward-pointing beak. The terminal swollen section of the male's abdomen is carried curved up like a scorpion's stinger. ● Order Mecoptera: several families, in particular Panorpidae.

Scor·pi·us /'skôrpēəs/ Astronomy a large constellation (the Scorpion). It contains the red giant Antares. ■ (as genitive **Scorpii** /'skôrpē,ī, -,ē/) used with a preceding letter or numeral to designate a star in this constellation: *the star Theta Scorpii*.
– ORIGIN Latin.

Scor·se·se /skôr'sāzē/, Martin (1942–), US movie director. *Mean Streets* (1973) marked the beginning of his long collaboration with Robert De Niro, which continued in *Taxi Driver* (1976), *Raging Bull* (1980), *Goodfellas* (1990), *Cape Fear* (1991), and *Casino* (1995). Other movies include the controversial *The Last Temptation of Christ* (1988).

scor·zo·ne·ra /,skôrzə'ni(ə)rə/ ▶ n. a plant of the daisy family with tapering purple-brown edible roots. Also called BLACK SALSIFY, BLACK OYSTER PLANT. ● *Scorzonera hispanica*, family Compositae. ■ the root of this plant used as a vegetable.
– ORIGIN early 17th cent.: from Italian, from *scorzone*, from an alteration of medieval Latin *curtio(n-)* 'venomous snake' (against whose venom the plant may have been regarded as an antidote).

Scot /skät/ ▶ n. a native of Scotland or a person of Scottish descent. ■ a member of a Gaelic people that migrated from Ireland to Scotland around the late 5th century.
– ORIGIN Old English *Scottas* (plural), from late Latin *Scottus*, of unknown ultimate origin.

USAGE On the different uses of **Scot, Scots, Scottish,** and **Scotch**, see usage at SCOTTISH.

scot /skät/ ▶ n. archaic a payment corresponding to a modern tax, rate, or other assessed contribution.
– ORIGIN late Old English, from Old Norse *skot* 'a shot,' reinforced by Old French *escot*, of Germanic origin; related to SHOT[1].

Scot. ▶ **abbr.** ■ Scotland. ■ Scottish.

Scotch /skäCH/ ▶ **adj.** old-fashioned term for SCOTTISH.
▶ **n. 1** short for SCOTCH WHISKY.
2 (as plural noun **the Scotch**) dated the people of Scotland.
3 dated the form of English spoken in Scotland.
– DERIVATIVES **Scotch·man** n. (dated) (pl. **Scotchmen**), **Scotch·wom·an** n. (dated) (pl. **Scotchwomen**).
– ORIGIN late 16th cent.: contraction of SCOTTISH.

> **USAGE** The use of **Scotch** to mean 'of or relating to Scotland or its people' is disliked by many Scottish people and is now uncommon in modern English. It survives in a number of fixed expressions, such as *Scotch broth* and *Scotch whisky*. For more details, see usage at SCOTTISH.

scotch[1] /skäCH/ ▶ **v. 1** [with obj.] decisively put an end to: *a spokesman has scotched the rumors.* ■ archaic render (something regarded as dangerous) temporarily harmless: *feudal power in France was scotched, though far from killed.*
2 [with obj.] wedge (someone or something) somewhere: *he soon scotched himself against a wall.* ■ archaic prevent (a wheel or other rolling object) from moving or slipping by placing a wedge underneath.
▶ **n.** archaic a wedge placed under a wheel or other rolling object to prevent its moving or slipping.
– ORIGIN early 17th cent. (as a noun): of unknown origin; perhaps related to SKATE[1]. The sense 'render temporarily harmless' is based on an emendation of Shakespeare's *Macbeth* III. ii. 13 as "We have scotch'd the snake, not kill'd it," originally understood as a use of SCOTCH[2]; the sense 'put an end to' (early 19th cent.) results from the influence on this of the notion of wedging or blocking something so as to render it inoperative.

scotch[2] archaic ▶ **v.** [with obj.] cut or score the skin or surface of.
▶ **n.** a cut or score in skin or another surface.
– ORIGIN late Middle English: of unknown origin.

Scotch bon·net (also **Scotch bonnet pepper**) ▶ **n.** another term for HABANERO.

Scotch broth ▶ **n.** a traditional Scottish soup made from beef or mutton stock with pearl barley and vegetables.

Scotch egg ▶ **n.** a hard-boiled egg enclosed in sausage meat, rolled in breadcrumbs, and fried.

Scotch·gard /'skäCH,gärd/ ▶ **n.** trademark a fluorocarbon preparation for giving a waterproof grease- and stain-resistant finish to textiles, leather, and other materials.
▶ **v.** [with obj.] treat with such a substance.

Scotch pine ▶ **n.** a long-lived, medium-sized Eurasian pine tree extensively planted for its timber and other products. It is well established in the northeastern US and the Great Lakes region. ● *Pinus sylvestris*, family Pinaceae.

Scotch tape trademark ▶ **n.** transparent adhesive tape.
▶ **v.** (**Scotch-tape**) [with obj.] stick with transparent adhesive tape.

Scotch whis·ky ▶ **n.** whiskey distilled in Scotland, esp. from malted barley.

> **USAGE** The spelling **Scotch whiskey** is considered improper. For an explanation of when to use the spelling ***whisky*** rather than ***whiskey***, see usage at WHISKEY.

sco·ter /'skōtər/ ▶ **n.** (pl. **same** or **scoters**) a northern diving duck that winters off the coast, the male of which has mainly black plumage. ● Genus *Melanitta*, family Anatidae: three species.
– ORIGIN late 17th cent.: of unknown origin.

scot-free ▶ **adv.** without suffering any punishment or injury: *the people who kidnapped you will **get off scot-free**.*
– ORIGIN from the early sense 'not subject to the payment of scot.'

sco·tia /'skōSHə/ ▶ **n.** (chiefly in classical architecture) a concave molding, esp. at the base of a column.
– ORIGIN mid 16th cent.: via Latin from Greek *skotia*, from *skotos* 'darkness,' with reference to the shadow produced.

Scot·land /'skätlənd/ a country in northern Great Britain and the United Kingdom; pop. 5,169,000 (est. 2008); capital, Edinburgh; languages, English (official) and the Scottish form of Gaelic.

> Scotland was settled by Celtic peoples during the Bronze and early Iron ages. An independent country in the Middle Ages, it was amalgamated with England as a result of the union of the Crowns in 1603 and of the Parliaments in 1707. The distinctive Celtic society of the Highlands, based on clans, was destroyed in the aftermath of the Jacobite uprisings of 1715 and 1745–46. In 1997, the Scots voted to establish a devolved parliament with tax-raising powers. Scotland's economy benefited in the 20th century from the discovery of North Sea oil.

Scot·land Yard the headquarters of the London Metropolitan Police, situated from 1829 to 1890 in Great Scotland Yard off Whitehall, from 1890 until 1967 in New Scotland Yard on the Thames Embankment, and from 1967 in New Scotland Yard, Westminster. ■ used to allude to the Criminal Investigation Department of the London Metropolitan Police force.

sco·to·ma /skə'tōmə/ ▶ **n.** (pl. **scotomas** or **scotomata** /-mətə/) Medicine a partial loss of vision or a blind spot in an otherwise normal visual field.
– DERIVATIVES **sco·tom·a·tous** /-mətəs/ **adj.**
– ORIGIN mid 16th cent. (denoting dizziness and dim vision): via late Latin from Greek *skotōma*, from *skotoun* 'darken,' from *skotos* 'darkness.'

sco·top·ic /skə'tōpik, -'täpik/ ▶ **adj.** Physiology relating to or denoting vision in dim light, believed to involve chiefly the rods of the retina. Often contrasted with PHOTOPIC.
– ORIGIN early 20th cent.: from Greek *skotos* 'darkness' + -OPIA + -IC.

Scots /skäts/ ▶ **adj.** another term for SCOTTISH: *a Scots accent.* [northern variant, originally as *Scottis*.]
▶ **n.** the form of English used in Scotland.

> **USAGE** On the use of **Scots**, **Scot**, **Scottish**, and **Scotch**, see usage at SCOTTISH.

Scots·man /'skätsmən/ ▶ **n.** (pl. **Scotsmen**) a male native or inhabitant of Scotland or a man of Scottish descent.

Scots·wom·an /'skäts,wo͝omən/ ▶ **n.** (pl. **Scotswomen**) a female native or inhabitant of Scotland or a woman of Scottish descent.

Scott[1] /skät/, Dred (*c.* 1795–1858), US slave. He brought suit for his freedom based on the fact that he had lived in free territories for five years, but the US Supreme Court ruled against him in 1857 in a case that became the focus of much heated political controversy. Scott was emancipated later that year and worked as a hotel porter in St. Louis.

Scott[2], Ridley (1939–), English movie director. Notable works: *Alien* (1979), *Blade Runner* (1982), *Thelma and Louise* (1991), and *American Gangster* (2007). His brother **Tony** (1944–) is also a successful movie director, responsible for such works as *Top Gun* (1986) and *True Romance* (1993).

Scott[3], Sir Robert (Falcon) (1868–1912), English explorer and naval officer. During 1910–12, he and four companions made a journey to the South Pole by sled, arriving there in January 1912 to discover that Roald Amundsen had beaten them by a month. Scott and his companions died on the journey back to base.

Scott[4], Sir Walter (1771–1832), Scottish novelist and poet. He established the form of the historical novel in Britain and was influential in his treatment of rural themes and his use of regional speech. Notable novels: *Waverley* (1814), *Ivanhoe* (1819), and *Kenilworth* (1821).

Scott[5], Winfield (1786–1866), US army officer; known as **Old Fuss and Feathers**. A hero of the War of 1812, he became supreme commander of the US Army 1841–61. During the Mexican War, he waged a victorious campaign from Veracruz to Mexico City in 1847. He ran for the office of US president as the Whig candidate in 1852 but was defeated by Democrat Franklin Pierce.

Scot·ti·cism /'skäti,sizəm/ ▶ **n.** a characteristically Scottish phrase, word, or idiom.
– ORIGIN early 18th cent.: from late Latin *Scot(t)icus* + -ISM.

Scot·tie /'skätē/ ▶ **n.** informal (also **Scottie dog**) a Scottish terrier.

Scot·tish /'skätisH/ ▶ **adj.** of or relating to Scotland or its people: *the Scottish Highlands* | *Scottish dancing.*
▶ **n.** (as plural noun **the Scottish**) the people of Scotland. See also SCOTS.
– DERIVATIVES **Scot·tish·ness** n.

> **USAGE** The terms **Scottish**, **Scot**, **Scots**, and **Scotch** are all variants of the same word. They have had different histories, however, and in modern English they have developed different uses and connotations. The normal everyday word used to mean 'of or relating to Scotland or its people' is **Scottish**: *Scottish people*; *Scottish hills*; *Scottish Gaelic*; *she's English, not Scottish*. The normal, neutral word for 'a person from Scotland' is **Scot**, along with **Scotsman**, **Scotswoman**, and the plural form **the Scots** (or, less commonly, **the Scottish**). **Scots** is also used, like **Scottish**, as an adjective meaning 'of or relating to Scotland.' However, it tends to be used in a narrower sense to refer specifically to the form of English used in Scotland: *Scots accent*; *the Scots word for 'night.'* The word **Scotch**, meaning either 'of or relating to Scotland' or 'a person/the people from Scotland,' was widely used in the past by Scottish writers such as Robert Burns and Sir Walter Scott. In the 20th century, it became less common. It is disliked by many Scottish people (as being an 'English' invention) and is now regarded as old-fashioned in most contexts. It survives in certain fixed phrases, as, for example, ***Scotch** broth* and ***Scotch** whisky*.

Scot·tish rite ▶ **n.** a ceremonial rite in a Masonic order.

Scot·tish ter·ri·er ▶ **n.** a small terrier of a rough-haired short-legged breed.

Scotts·dale /'skäts,dāl/ a city in south central Arizona, east of Phoenix; pop. 235,371 (est. 2008).

scoun·drel /'skoundrəl/ ▶ **n.** a dishonest or unscrupulous person; a rogue.
– DERIVATIVES **scoun·drel·ism** /-,lizəm/ **n.**, **scoun·drel·ly adj.**
– ORIGIN late 16th cent.: of unknown origin.

scour[1] /skou(ə)r/ ▶ **v.** [with obj.] **1** clean or brighten the surface of (something) by rubbing it hard, typically with an abrasive or detergent: *he scoured the bathtub.* ■ remove (dirt or unwanted matter) by rubbing in such a way: *use an electric toothbrush to **scour off** plaque* | [no obj.] *I've spent all day mopping and scouring.* ■ (of water or a watercourse) make (a channel or pool) by flowing forcefully over something and removing soil or rock: *a stream came crashing through a narrow cavern to **scour out** a round pool below.*
2 archaic administer a strong purgative to.
▶ **n. 1** the action of scouring or the state of being scoured, esp. by swift-flowing water. ■ [in sing.] an act of rubbing something hard to clean or brighten it: *give the floor a good scour.*
2 (also **scours**) diarrhea in livestock, esp. cattle and pigs.
– DERIVATIVES **scour·er** n.
– ORIGIN Middle English: from Middle Dutch and Middle Low German *schūren*, from Old French *escurer*, from late Latin *excurare* 'clean (off),' from *ex-* 'away' + *curare* 'to clean.'

scour[2] ▶ **v.** [with obj.] subject (a place, text, etc.) to a thorough search in order to locate something: *David **scoured** each newspaper **for** an article on the murder.* ■ [no obj.] move rapidly in a particular direction, esp. in search or pursuit of someone or something: *he scoured up the ladder.*
– ORIGIN late Middle English: related to obsolete *scour* 'moving hastily,' of unknown origin.

scourge /skərj/ ▶ **n. 1** historical a whip used as an instrument of punishment.
2 a person or thing that causes great trouble or suffering: *the scourge of mass unemployment.*
▶ **v.** [with obj.] **1** historical whip (someone) as a punishment.
2 cause great suffering to: *political methods used to scourge and oppress workers.*
– DERIVATIVES **scourg·er** n. (historical).
– ORIGIN Middle English: shortening of Old French *escorge* (noun), *escorgier* (verb), from Latin *ex-* 'thoroughly' + *corrigia* 'thong, whip.'

scour·ing rush ▶ **n.** a horsetail with a very rough, ridged stem, formerly used for scouring and polishing. ● Genus *Equisetum*, family Equisetaceae, in particular *E. hyemale*.

scout[1] /skout/ ▶ **n. 1** a soldier or other person sent out ahead of a main force so as to gather information about the enemy's position, strength, or movements. ■ a ship or other unit employed for reconnaissance, esp. a small fast aircraft. ■ short for TALENT SCOUT. ■ [usu. in sing.] an instance of gathering information, esp. by reconnoitering an area: *I returned from a lengthy scout around the area.*
2 (also **Scout**) a Boy Scout or Girl Scout.
3 informal, dated a man or boy: *I've got nothing against Harrison—he's a **good scout**.*
4 a domestic worker at a college at Oxford University.
▶ **v.** [no obj.] make a search for someone or something in various places: *I was sent to **scout around for** a place to park the camper* | *we **scouted for** clues.* ■ (esp. of a soldier) go ahead of a main force so as to gather information about an enemy's position, strength, or movements. ■ [with obj.] explore or examine (a place or area of business) so as to gather information about it: *American companies are*

keen to scout out business opportunities. ■ look for suitably talented people for recruitment to one's own organization or sports team: *Johnson has been scouting for the Pirates.*
– PHRASES **Scout's honor** the oath taken by a Boy Scout or Girl Scout. ■ informal used to indicate that one has the same honorable standards associated with Scouts and so will stand by a promise or tell the truth.
– DERIVATIVES **scout·er** n.
– ORIGIN late Middle English (as a verb): from Old French *escouter* 'listen,' earlier *ascolter*, from Latin *auscultare*.

scout² ▶ v. [with obj.] rare reject (a proposal or idea) with scorn.
– ORIGIN early 17th cent.: of Scandinavian origin; compare with Old Norse *skúta, skúti* 'a taunt.'

Scout As·so·ci·a·tion (in the UK) a worldwide youth organization founded for boys in 1907 by Lord Baden-Powell with the aim of developing their character by training them in self-sufficiency and survival techniques in the outdoors.

scout car ▶ n. a fast armored vehicle used for military reconnaissance and liaison.

scout·ing /ˈskoutiNG/ ▶ n. **1** the action of gathering information about enemy forces or an area. ■ the activity of a talent scout: [as modifier] *What does the scouting report say about Stoddard's change-up pitch?*
2 (also **Scouting**) the characteristic activity and occupation of a Boy Scout or Girl Scout; the Scout movement.

scout·mas·ter /ˈskout,mastər/ ▶ n. the adult in charge of a group of Boy Scouts.

scow /skou/ ▶ n. a wide-beamed sailing dinghy. ■ a flat-bottomed boat with sloping ends used as a lighter and in dredging and other harbor services.
– ORIGIN mid 17th cent.: from Dutch *schouw* 'ferryboat.'

scowl /skoul/ ▶ n. an angry or bad-tempered expression.
▶ v. [no obj.] frown in an angry or bad-tempered way: *she scowled at him defiantly.*
– DERIVATIVES **scowl·er** n.
– ORIGIN late Middle English (as a verb): probably of Scandinavian origin; compare with Danish *skule* 'scowl.' The noun dates from the early 16th cent.

SCP ▶ abbr. single-cell protein.

SCPO ▶ abbr. Senior Chief Petty Officer.

scrab·ble /ˈskrabəl/ ▶ v. [no obj.] scratch or grope around with one's fingers to find, collect, or hold onto something: *she scrabbled at the grassy slope, desperate for a firm grip.* ■ (of an animal) scratch at something with its claws: *a dog was scrabbling at the door.* ■ [with adverbial of direction] scramble or crawl quickly: *lizards scrabbling across the walls.* ■ make great efforts to get somewhere or achieve something: *I had to scrabble around to find this apartment.*
▶ n. **1** [in sing.] an act of scratching or scrambling for something: *he heard the scrabble of claws behind him.* ■ a struggle to get somewhere or achieve something: *a scrabble among the salesmen to avoid going to the bottom of the heap.*
2 (**Scrabble**) trademark a board game in which players use lettered tiles to create words in a crossword fashion.
– DERIVATIVES **scrab·bler** n.
– ORIGIN mid 16th cent. (in the sense 'make marks at random, scrawl'): from Middle Dutch *schrabbelen*, frequentative of *schrabben* 'to scrape.' The noun sense 'struggle to achieve something' is originally a North American usage dating from the late 18th cent.

S

scrag /skrag/ ▶ v. (**scrags, scragging, scragged**) [with obj.] informal, chiefly Brit. handle roughly; beat up. ■ dated, informal kill, esp. by strangling or hanging.
▶ n. **1** an unattractively thin person or animal.
2 dated, informal a person's neck.
– ORIGIN mid 16th cent. (as a noun): perhaps an alteration of Scots and northern English *crag* 'neck' The verb (mid 18th cent.) developed the sense 'handle roughly' from the early use 'hang, strangle.'

scrag·gly /ˈskrag(ə)lē/ (also **scraggy** /ˈskragē/) ▶ adj. (**scragglier, scraggliest**) (of a person or animal) thin and bony. ■ ragged, thin, or untidy in form or appearance: *a man with a scraggly beard.* ■ (of a plant, tree, or shrubbery) sparsely foliated or having thin, uneven growth: *it was the scraggliest Christmas tree I had ever seen.*
– DERIVATIVES **scrag·gi·ly** /-əlē/ adv., **scrag·gli·ness** (or **scragginess**) n.

scram /skram/ informal ▶ v. (**scrams, scramming, scrammed**) **1** [no obj., usu. in imperative] leave or go away from a place quickly: *get out of here, you miserable wretches—scram!*
2 [with obj.] shut down (a nuclear reactor) in an emergency.
▶ n. the emergency shutdown of a nuclear reactor: *the power plant was cited for its high rate of scrams over the past year.*
– ORIGIN early 20th cent.: probably from the verb SCRAMBLE.

scram·ble /ˈskrambəl/ ▶ v. **1** [no obj.] make one's way quickly or awkwardly up a steep slope or over rough ground by using one's hands as well as one's feet: *we scrambled over the wet boulders.* ■ move hurriedly or clumsily from or into a particular place or position: *she scrambled out of the car | I tried to scramble to my feet.* ■ (**scramble into**) put (clothes) on hurriedly: *Robbie scrambled into jeans and a T-shirt.* ■ [with obj.] informal perform (an action) or achieve (a result) hurriedly, clumsily, or with difficulty. ■ [with infinitive] struggle or compete with others for something in an eager or uncontrolled and undignified way: *firms scrambled to win public-sector contracts.* ■ [with obj.] order (a fighter aircraft or its pilot) to take off immediately in an emergency or for action. ■ (of a fighter aircraft or its pilot) take off in such a way. ■ Football (of a quarterback) run around with the ball behind the line of scrimmage while looking for an open receiver. ■ Football run forward with the ball when unable to pass to an open receiver.
2 [with obj.] make (something) jumbled or muddled: *maybe the alcohol has scrambled his brains.* ■ prepare (eggs) by beating them with a little liquid and then cooking and stirring them gently. ■ make (a broadcast transmission, a telephone message, or electronic data) unintelligible unless received by an appropriate decoding device: (as adj. **scrambled**) *scrambled television signals.*
▶ n. [usu. in sing.] **1** a difficult or hurried clamber up or over something: *an undignified scramble over the wall.* ■ a walk up steep terrain involving the use of one's hands. ■ an eager or uncontrolled and undignified struggle with others to obtain or achieve something: *a **scramble for** high-priced concert seats.* ■ an emergency takeoff by fighter aircraft.
2 a disordered mixture of things: *the program produced a scramble of the letters of the alphabet.*
– DERIVATIVES **scram·bling** /-b(ə)liNG/ n.
– ORIGIN late 16th cent.: imitative; compare with the dialect words *scamble* 'stumble' and *cramble* 'crawl.'

scram·bled eggs /ˈskrambəld/ ▶ n. **1** a dish of eggs prepared by beating them with a little liquid and then cooking and stirring them gently.
2 informal gold braid on a field-grade military officer's cap.

scram·bler /ˈskramb(ə)lər/ ▶ n. **1** a person or thing that scrambles, esp. a device for scrambling a broadcast transmission, a telephone message, or electronic data.
2 a plant with long slender stems supported by other plants.

scram·jet /ˈskram,jet/ ▶ n. Aeronautics a ramjet in which combustion takes place in a stream of gas moving at supersonic speed.
– ORIGIN 1960s: from *s(upersonic)* + *c(ombustion)* + RAMJET.

Scran·ton /ˈskrantn/ an industrial city in northeastern Pennsylvania; pop. 72,233 (est. 2008).
– ORIGIN named after the *Scranton* family, who established a steelworks on the site in 1840, around which the city developed.

scrap¹ /skrap/ ▶ n. **1** a small piece or amount of something, esp. one that is left over after the greater part has been used: *I scribbled her address on **a scrap of** paper | **scraps of** information.* ■ (**scraps**) bits of uneaten food left after a meal, esp. when fed to animals: *he filled Sammy's bowls with fresh water and scraps.* ■ used to emphasize the lack or smallness of something: *there was not **a scrap of** aggression in him | every **scrap of** green land is up for grabs by development.* ■ informal a small person or animal, esp. one regarded with affection or sympathy: *poor little scrap, she's too hot in that coat.* ■ a particularly small thing of its kind: *she was wearing a short black skirt and a tiny scrap of a top.*
2 (also **scrap metal**) discarded metal for reprocessing: *the steamer was eventually sold for scrap.* ■ [often as modifier] any waste articles or discarded material, esp. that which can be put to another purpose: *we're burning scrap lumber.*
▶ v. (**scraps, scrapping, scrapped**) [with obj.] discard or remove from service (a retired, old, or inoperative vehicle, vessel, or machine), esp. so as to convert it to scrap metal: *the decision was made to scrap the entire fleet.* ■ abolish or cancel (something, esp. a plan, policy, or law) that is now regarded as unnecessary, unwanted, or unsuitable: *the station scrapped plans to televise the contest live.*
– ORIGIN late Middle English (as a plural noun denoting fragments of uneaten food): from Old Norse *skrap* 'scraps'; related to *skrapa* 'to scrape.' The verb dates from the late 19th cent.

scrap² informal ▶ n. a fight or quarrel, esp. a minor or spontaneous one.
▶ v. (**scraps, scrapping, scrapped**) [no obj.] engage in such a fight or quarrel. ■ compete fiercely: *the talk-show producers are scrapping for similar audiences.*
– DERIVATIVES **scrap·per** n.
– ORIGIN late 17th cent. (as a noun in the sense 'sinister plot, scheme'): perhaps from the noun SCRAPE.

scrap·book /ˈskrap,bo͝ok/ ▶ n. a book of blank pages for sticking clippings, drawings, or pictures in.
▶ v. [no obj.] (usually as noun **scrapbooking**) create scrapbooks as a hobby: *I scrapbook with the kids nearly every weekend.*

scrape /skrāp/ ▶ v. **1** [with obj.] push or pull a hard or sharp implement across (a surface or object) so as to remove dirt or other matter: *rinse off the carrots and scrape them* | [with obj. and complement] *we scraped the dishes clean.* ■ use a sharp or hard implement to remove (dirt or unwanted matter) from something: *she scraped the mud off her shoes.* ■ apply (a hard or sharp implement) in this way: *he scraped the razor across the stubble on his cheek.* ■ make (a hollow) by scraping away soil or rock: *he found a ditch, scraped a hole, and put the bag in it.*
2 rub or cause to rub by accident against a rough or hard surface, causing damage or injury: [no obj.] *he smashed into the wall and felt his knee **scrape against** the plaster* | [with obj.] *she reversed in a reckless sweep, scraping the left front fender.* ■ [with obj.] draw or move (something) along or over something else, making a harsh noise: *she **scraped back** her chair and stood up.* ■ [no obj.] move with or make such a sound: *she lifted the gate to prevent its scraping along the ground.* ■ [no obj.] humorous play a violin or similar stringed instrument tunelessly: *Katie was scraping away at her cello.* ■ [with obj.] draw one's hair tightly back off the forehead: *her hair was **scraped back** into a ponytail.*
3 [with obj.] just manage to achieve; accomplish with great effort or difficulty: *for some years he **scraped a living** as a tutor.* ■ (**scrape something together/up**) collect or accumulate something with difficulty: *they could hardly scrape up enough money for one ticket, let alone two.* ■ [no obj.] try to save as much money as possible; economize: *they had scrimped and scraped and saved for years.* ■ [no obj.] (**scrape by/along**) manage to live with difficulty: *she has to **scrape by** on Social Security.* ■ [no obj.] narrowly pass by or through something: *there was only just room to **scrape through** between the tree and the edge of the stream.* ■ [no obj.] barely manage to succeed in a particular undertaking: *Clinton **scraped into** office in 1992 | he **scraped through** the entrance exam.*
4 [with obj.] copy (data) from a website using a computer program.
▶ n. **1** an act or sound of scraping: *he heard the scrape of his mother's key in the lock.* ■ an injury or mark caused by scraping: *there was a long, shallow scrape on his shin.* ■ a place where soil has been scraped away, esp. a shallow hollow formed in the ground by a bird during a courtship display or for nesting. ■ Medicine, informal a procedure of dilatation of the cervix and curettage of the uterus, or the result of this. ■ archaic an obsequious bow in which one foot is drawn backward along the ground.
2 informal an embarrassing or difficult predicament caused by one's own unwise behavior: *he'd been in worse scrapes than this before now.*
– PHRASES **scrape acquaintance with** dated contrive to get to know: *aboard the ship, a nice girl scraped acquaintance with me.* **scrape the bottom of the barrel** informal be reduced to using things or people of the poorest quality because there is nothing else available.
– ORIGIN Old English *scrapian* 'scratch with the fingernails,' of Germanic origin, reinforced in Middle English by Old Norse *skrapa* or Middle Dutch *schrapen* 'to scratch.'

scrap·er /ˈskrāpər/ ▶ n. a tool or device used for scraping, esp. for removing dirt, paint, ice, or other unwanted matter from a surface.

scrapheap /ˈskrap,hip/ ▶ n. a pile of discarded materials or articles: *cars on a scrapheap* | figurative *it should be consigned to the scrapheap of technological history.*

scrap·ie /ˈskrāpē/ ▶ n. a disease of sheep involving the central nervous system, characterized by a lack of coordination causing affected animals to rub against trees and other objects for support, and thought to be caused by a viruslike agent such as a prion.
– ORIGIN early 20th cent.: from the verb SCRAPE + -IE.

scrap·ing /ˈskrāpiNG/ ▶ n. the action or sound of something scraping or being scraped: *the scraping of the spoon in the bowl* | [in sing.] *there was a scraping of chairs.* ■ (usu. **scrapings**) a small amount of something that has been obtained by scraping it from a surface: *I got some scrapings from under the girl's fingernails.*

scrap met·al ▶ **n.** another term for **SCRAP**[1] (sense 2 of the noun).

scrap·ple /'skrapəl/ ▶ **n.** scraps of pork or other meat stewed with cornmeal and shaped into loaves for slicing and frying, esp. characteristic of eastern Pennsylavania.
– ORIGIN mid 19th cent.: diminutive of the noun **SCRAP**[1].

scrap·py /'skrapē/ ▶ **adj.** (**scrappier**, **scrappiest**) **1** consisting of disorganized, untidy, or incomplete parts: *scrappy lecture notes piled up unread.* [mid 19th cent.: derivative of **SCRAP**[1].] **2** informal determined, argumentative, or pugnacious: *he played the part of a scrappy detective.* [late 19th cent.: derivative of **SCRAP**[2].]
– DERIVATIVES **scrap·pi·ly** /-əlē/ **adv.**, **scrap·pi·ness n.**

scrap·yard /'skrap,yärd/ ▶ **n.** British term for **JUNKYARD**.

scratch /skracH/ ▶ **v. 1** [with obj.] score or mark the surface of (something) with a sharp or pointed object: *the car's paintwork was battered and scratched* | [no obj.] *he scratched at a stain on his jacket.* ■ make a long, narrow superficial wound in the skin of: *her arms were scratched by the thorns* | *I scratched myself on the tree.* ■ rub (a part of one's body) with one's fingernails to relieve itching: *Jessica lifted her sunglasses and scratched her nose.* ■ make (a mark or hole) by scoring a surface with a sharp or pointed object: *I found two names scratched on one of the windowpanes.* ■ write (something) hurriedly or awkwardly: *pass me my writing things—I'll scratch a few letters before I get up.* ■ remove (something) from something else by pulling a sharp implement over it: *he scratched away the plaster.* ■ [no obj.] make a rasping or grating noise by scraping something over a hard surface: *the dog scratched to be let in* | (as noun **scratching**) *there was a sound of scratching behind the wall.* ■ [no obj.] (often as noun **scratching**) play a record using the scratch technique. (sense 1 of the noun). ■ [no obj.] (of a bird or mammal, esp. a chicken) rake the ground with the beak or claws in search of food. ■ accomplish (something) with great effort or difficulty: *he* ***scratches out a living*** *growing strawberries.* **2** [with obj.] cancel or strike out (writing) with a pen or pencil: *the name of Dr. McNab was* ***scratched out*** *and that of Dr. Daniels substituted.* ■ withdraw (a competitor) from a competition: *Oswald's Zephyr was the second horse to be* ***scratched from*** *a race today.* ■ [no obj.] (of a competitor) withdraw from a competition: *due to a knee injury she was forced to* ***scratch from*** *the race.* ■ cancel or abandon (an undertaking or project): *the original filming schedule has been scratched.*
▶ **n. 1** a mark or wound made by scratching: *the scratches on her arm were throbbing* | [as modifier] *scratch marks on the door.* ■ [in sing.] informal a slight or insignificant wound or injury: *it's nothing—just a scratch.* ■ [in sing.] an act or spell of scratching oneself to relieve itching: *he gave his scalp a good scratch.* ■ a rasping or grating noise produced by something rubbing against a hard surface: *the scratch of a match lighting a cigarette.* ■ a rough hiss, caused by the friction of the stylus in the groove, heard when a record is played. ■ a technique, used esp. in rap music, of stopping a record by hand and moving it back and forth to give a rhythmic scratching effect. **2** the starting point in a handicap for a competitor receiving no odds. [originally denoting a boundary or starting line for sports competitors.] ■ Golf a handicap of zero, indicating that a player is good enough to achieve par on a course. **3** informal money: *he was working to get some scratch together.*
▶ **adj.** [attrib.] **1** assembled or made from whatever is available, and so unlikely to be of the highest quality: *at least two vessels set sail with scratch crews.* **2** (of a sports competitor or event) with no handicap given.
– PHRASES **from scratch** from the very beginning, esp. without utilizing or relying on any previous work for assistance: *he built his own computer company from scratch.* **scratch a —— and find a ——** used to suggest that an investigation of someone or something soon reveals their true nature: *he had been taught to believe "scratch a pious man and find a hypocrite."* **scratch one's head** informal think hard in order to find a solution to something. ■ feel or express bewilderment. **scratch the surface 1** deal with a matter only in the most superficial way: *research has only scratched the surface of the paranormal.* **2** initiate the briefest investigation to discover something concealed: *they have a boring image, but scratch the surface and it's fascinating.* **up to scratch** up to the required standard; satisfactory: *her German was not up to scratch.* **you scratch my back and I'll scratch yours** proverb if you do me a favor, I'll return it.
– DERIVATIVES **scratch·er n.**
– ORIGIN late Middle English: probably a blend of the synonymous dialect words *scrat* and *cratch*, both of uncertain origin; compare with Middle Low German *kratsen* and Old High German *krazzōn*.

scratch·board /'skracH,bôrd/ ▶ **n.** cardboard with a blackened surface that can be scratched or scraped off for making white line drawings.

scratch coat ▶ **n.** a rough coating of plaster scratched before it is quite dry to ensure the adherence of the next coat.

scratch·pad /'skracH,pad/ (also **scratch pad**) ▶ **n.** a notepad. ■ Computing a small, fast memory for the temporary storage of data.

scratch-re·sist·ant ▶ **adj.** (of a surface or hard material) not easily damaged by scratching.

scratch test ▶ **n.** a test for an allergic reaction in which a possible allergen is applied to a scratched area of skin.

scratch·y /'skracHē/ ▶ **adj.** (**scratchier**, **scratchiest**) (esp. of a fabric or garment) having a rough, uncomfortable texture and tending to cause itching or discomfort. ■ (of a voice or sound) rough; grating: *she dropped her voice to a scratchy whisper.* ■ (of a record) making a crackling or rough sound because of scratches on the surface. ■ (of writing or a drawing) done with quick and jagged strokes: *a scratchy ink sketch of a man on horseback.*
– DERIVATIVES **scratch·i·ly** /-əlē/ **adv.**, **scratch·i·ness n.**

scrawl /skrôl/ ▶ **v.** [with obj.] write (something) in a hurried, careless way: *Charlie scrawled his signature* | [no obj.] *he was scrawling on the back of a used envelope.*
▶ **n.** an example of hurried, careless writing: *the page was covered in scrawls and doodles* | *reams of handwritten scrawl.* ■ a note or message written in this way: *Duncan read the scrawl, then passed it to her.*
– DERIVATIVES **scrawl·er n.**, **scrawl·y adj.**
– ORIGIN early 17th cent.: apparently an alteration of the verb **CRAWL**, perhaps influenced by obsolete *scrawl* 'sprawl.'

scrawn·y /'skrônē/ ▶ **adj.** (**scrawnier**, **scrawniest**) (of a person or animal) unattractively thin and bony. ■ (of vegetation) meager or stunted.
– DERIVATIVES **scrawn·i·ness n.**
– ORIGIN mid 19th cent.: variant of dialect *scranny*; compare with archaic *scrannel* 'weak, feeble' (referring to sound).

scream /skrēm/ ▶ **v.** [no obj.] give a long, loud, piercing cry or cries expressing excitement, great emotion, or pain: *they could hear him screaming in pain* | (as adj. **screaming**) *a houseful of barking dogs and screaming children.* ■ [reporting verb] cry something in a high-pitched, frenzied way: [no obj.] *I ran to the house screaming for help* | [with direct speech] *"Get out!" he screamed* | [with obj.] *he screamed abuse into the phone.* ■ urgently and vociferously call attention to one's views or feelings, esp. ones of anger or distress: [with clause] *his supporters scream that he is being done an injustice* | figurative *the creative side of me is screaming out for attention.* ■ make a loud, high-pitched sound: *sirens were screaming from all over the city.* ■ move very rapidly with or as if with such a sound: *a shell screamed overhead.*
▶ **n.** a long, loud, piercing cry expressing extreme emotion or pain: *they were awakened by screams for help.* ■ a high-pitched cry made by an animal: *the screams of the seagulls.* ■ a loud, piercing sound: *the scream of a falling bomb.* ■ [in sing.] informal an irresistibly funny person, thing, or situation: *the movie's a scream.*
– ORIGIN Middle English: origin uncertain; perhaps from Middle Dutch.

scream·er /'skrēmər/ ▶ **n. 1** a person or thing that makes a screaming sound. **2** informal a thing remarkable for speed or impact: *he had a screamer of a lap going in his Penske-Chevy.* ■ an extremely fast ball or shot: *Jones hit a screamer against the right-field wall.* ■ a sensational or very large headline: *his death caused a front-page screamer.* ■ dated a thing that causes screams of laughter. **3** a large gooselike South American waterbird with a short bill, a sharp bony spur on each wing, and a harsh honking call. ● Family Anhimidae: two genera and three species.

scream·ing·ly /'skrēmiNGlē/ ▶ **adv.** [as submodifier] to a very great extent; extremely: *a screamingly dull daily routine.*

scream·ing meem·ies /'mēmēz/ ▶ **plural n.** humorous an attack of panic or anxiety.

scree /skrē/ ▶ **n.** a mass of small loose stones that form or cover a slope on a mountain. ■ a slope covered with such stones.
– ORIGIN early 18th cent.: probably a back-formation from the plural *screes*, from Old Norse *skritha* 'landslide'; related to *skrítha* 'glide.'

screech /skrēcH/ ▶ **v.** [no obj.] (of a person or animal) give a loud, harsh, piercing cry: *she hit her brother, causing him to screech with pain.* ■ make a loud, harsh, squealing sound: (as adj. **screeching**) *she brought the car to a screeching halt.* ■ move rapidly with such a sound: *the van screeched around the corner at top speed.*
▶ **n.** a loud, harsh, piercing cry. ■ a loud, harsh, squealing sound: *a screech of brakes.*
– DERIVATIVES **screech·er n.**, **screech·y adj.** (**screechier**, **screechiest**).
– ORIGIN mid 16th cent.: alteration of archaic *scritch*, of imitative origin.

screech owl ▶ **n.** a small American owl with a screeching call and distinctive ear tufts. ● *Otus asio*, family Strigidae.

screed /skrēd/ ▶ **n. 1** a long speech or piece of writing, typically one regarded as tedious. **2** a leveled layer of material (e.g., cement) applied to a floor or other surface. ■ a strip of plaster or other material placed on a surface as a guide to thickness.
▶ **v.** [with obj.] level (a floor or layer of concrete) with a straight edge using a back and forth motion while moving across the surface.
– ORIGIN Middle English: probably a variant of the noun **SHRED**. The early sense was 'fragment cut from a main piece,' then 'torn strip, tatter,' whence (via the notion of a long roll or list) sense 1 of the noun.

screen /skrēn/ ▶ **n. 1** a fixed or movable upright partition used to divide a room, to give shelter from drafts, heat, or light, or to provide concealment or privacy. ■ a thing providing concealment or protection: *his jeep was discreetly parked behind a screen of trees* | figurative *the article is using science as a screen for unexamined prejudice.* ■ Military a detachment of troops or ships detailed to cover the movements of the main body. ■ [often with modifier] Architecture a partition of carved wood or stone separating the nave of a church from the chancel, choir, or sanctuary. See also **ROOD SCREEN**. ■ a frame with fine wire netting used in a window or doorway to keep out mosquitoes and other flying insects: [as modifier] *a screen door.* ■ a part of an electrical or other instrument that protects it or prevents it from causing electromagnetic interference. ■ Electronics (also **screen grid**) a grid placed between the control grid and the anode of a valve to reduce the capacitance between these electrodes. **2** the surface of a cathode ray tube or similar electronic device, esp. that of a television, VDT, or monitor, on which images and data are displayed. ■ a blank, typically white or silver surface on which a photographic image is projected: *the world's largest movie screen.* ■ (**the screen**) movies or television; the motion-picture industry: *she's a star of the stage as well as the screen.* ■ the data or images displayed on a computer screen: *pressing the F1 key at any time will display a help screen.* ■ Photography a flat piece of ground glass on which the image formed by a camera lens is focused. **3** Printing a transparent, finely ruled plate or film used in halftone reproduction. **4** a large sieve or riddle, esp. one for sorting substances such as grain or coal into different sizes.
▶ **v.** [with obj.] **1** conceal, protect, or shelter (someone or something) with a screen or something forming a screen: *her hair swung across to screen her face* | *a high hedge screened all of the front from passersby.* ■ (**screen something off**) separate something from something else with or as if with a screen: *an area had been screened off as a waiting room.* ■ protect (someone) from something dangerous or unpleasant: *in my country, a man of my rank would be screened completely from any risk of attack.* ■ prevent from causing or protect from electromagnetic interference: *ensure that your microphone leads are properly screened from hum pickup.* **2** show (a movie or video) or broadcast (a television program): *the show is to be screened by HBO later this year.* **3** test (a person or substance) for the presence or absence of a disease or contaminant: *outpatients were* ***screened for*** *cervical cancer.* ■ check on or investigate (someone), typically to ascertain whether they are suitable for or can be trusted in a particular situation or job: *all prospective presidential candidates would have to be screened by the committee.* ■ evaluate or analyze (something) for its suitability for a particular purpose or application: *only one percent of rain forest plants*

S

have been screened for medical use. ■ (**screen someone/something out**) exclude someone or something after such evaluation or investigation: *anti-spam software can screen out large amounts of unwanted e-mail.*
4 pass (a substance such as grain or coal) through a large sieve or screen, esp. so as to sort it into different sizes.
5 Printing project (a photograph or other image) through a transparent ruled plate so as to be able to reproduce it as a halftone.
– DERIVATIVES **screen·a·ble** adj., **screen·er** n., **screen·ful** /-ˌfo͝ol/ n.
– ORIGIN Middle English: shortening of Old Northern French *escren*, of Germanic origin.

screen dump ▶ n. Computing the process or an instance of causing what is displayed on a screen to be printed out. ■ a resulting printout.

screen·ing /ˈskrēniNG/ ▶ n. **1** a showing of a movie, video, or television program.
2 the evaluation or investigation of something as part of a methodical survey, to assess suitability for a particular role or purpose. ■ the testing of a person or group of people for the presence of a disease or other condition: *prenatal screening for Down syndrome.*
3 (**screenings**) refuse separated by sieving grain.

screen pass ▶ n. Football a forward pass to a player protected by a screen of blockers.

screen·play /ˈskrēnˌplā/ ▶ n. the script of a movie, including acting instructions and scene directions.

screen-print ▶ v. [with obj.] (often as adj. **screen-printed**) force ink or metal onto (a surface) through a prepared screen of fine material so as to create a picture or pattern.
▶ n. (**screen print**) a picture or design produced by screen-printing.

screen sav·er (also **screensaver**) ▶ n. Computing a program that, after a set time, replaces an unchanging screen display with a moving image, originally to prevent damage to the phosphor and now mostly for decoration or entertainment.

screen scrap·ing ▶ n. the action of using a computer program to copy data from a website.

screen·shot /ˈskrēnˌSHät/ ▶ n. an image of the display on a computer screen.

screen test ▶ n. a filmed test to ascertain whether an actor is suitable for a movie role.
▶ v. (**screen-test**) [with obj.] give such a test to (an actor).

screen time ▶ n. **1** the time allotted to or occupied by a particular subject, actor, etc., on film or television: *these characters deserve more screen time.*
2 time spent using a device such as a computer, television, or games console.

screen·writ·er /ˈskrēnˌrītər/ ▶ n. a person who writes a screenplay.
– DERIVATIVES **screen·writ·ing** /-ˌrītiNG/ n.

screw /skro͞o/ ▶ n. **1** a short, slender, sharp-pointed metal pin with a raised helical thread running around it and a slotted head, used to join things together by being rotated so that it pierces wood or other material and is held tightly in place. ■ a cylinder with a helical ridge or thread running around the outside (a **male screw**) that can be turned to seal an opening, apply pressure, adjust position, etc., esp. one fitting into a corresponding internally grooved or threaded piece (a **female screw**). ■ (**the screws**) historical an instrument of torture acting in this way. ■ (also **screw propeller**) a ship's or aircraft's propeller (considered as acting like a screw in moving through water or air).
2 an act of turning a screw or other object having a thread. ■ Brit. Billiards another term for DRAW. ■ Brit. a small twisted-up piece of paper, used as a container for a substance such as salt or tobacco.
3 informal a prisoner's derogatory term for a prison guard or warden.
4 [in sing.] vulgar slang an act of sexual intercourse. ■ [with adj.] a sexual partner of a specified ability.
5 [in sing.] Brit. informal, dated an amount of salary or wages: *he's offered me the job with a jolly good screw.*
6 Brit. archaic, informal a mean or miserly person.
7 Brit. informal a worn-out horse.
▶ v. **1** [with obj.] fasten or tighten with a screw or screws: *screw the hinge to your new door.* ■ rotate (something) so as to fit it into or on to a surface or object by means of a spiral thread: *Philip screwed the top on the flask.* ■ [no obj.] (of an object) be attached or removed by being rotated in this way: *a connector that screws on to the gas cylinder.* ■ (**screw something around**) turn one's head or body around sharply: *he screwed his head around to try and find the enemy.*
2 [with obj.] (usu. **be screwed**) informal cheat or swindle (someone), esp. by charging them too much for something: *if you do what they tell you, you're screwed | we ended up getting more money than what they were trying to screw us for.* ■ (**screw something out of**) extort or force something, esp. money, from (someone) by putting them under strong pressure: *your grandmother screwed cash out of him for ten years.*
3 [with obj.] vulgar slang have sexual intercourse with. ■ [no obj.] (of a couple) have sexual intercourse. ■ [in imperative] informal used to express anger or contempt: *Screw him!*
4 [with obj.] Brit. another term for DRAW (sense 8 of the verb).
– PHRASES **have one's head screwed on** (**the right way**) informal have common sense. **have a screw loose** informal be slightly eccentric or mentally disturbed. **put the screws on** informal exert strong psychological pressure on (someone) so as to intimidate them into doing something. **a turn of the screw** informal an additional degree of pressure or hardship added to a situation that is already extremely difficult to bear. **turn** (or **tighten**) **the screw** (or **screws**) informal exert strong pressure on someone.
– PHRASAL VERBS **screw around 1** vulgar slang have many different sexual partners. **2** informal fool around. **screw someone over** informal treat someone unfairly; cheat or swindle someone. **screw up** informal completely mismanage or mishandle a situation: *I'm sorry, Susan, I screwed up.* **screw someone up** informal cause someone to be emotionally or mentally disturbed: *this job can really screw you up.* **screw something up 1** tense the muscles of one's face or around one's eyes, typically so as to register an emotion or because of bright light. **2** informal cause something to fail or go wrong: *why are you trying to screw up your life?* **3** summon up one's courage: *now Stephen had to screw up his courage and confess.*
– DERIVATIVES **screw·a·ble** adj., **screw·er** n.
– ORIGIN late Middle English (as a noun): from Old French *escroue* 'female screw, nut,' from Latin *scrofa*, literally 'sow,' later 'screw.' The early sense of the verb was 'contort (the features), twist around' (late 16th cent).

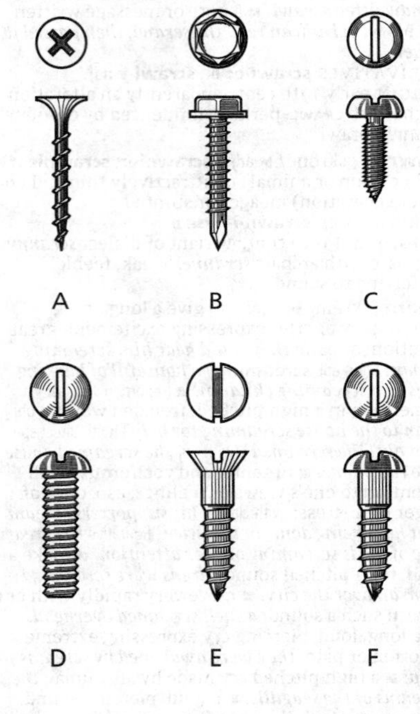

A sheetrock screw, flat head
B self-tapping screw, hex head
C sheet metal screw, pan head
D machine screw, round head
E wood screw, flat head
F wood screw, round head

screws

screw·ball /ˈskro͞oˌbôl/ ▶ n. **1** Baseball a pitched ball that moves in a direction opposite to that of a curveball.
2 informal a crazy or eccentric person.
▶ adj. informal crazy; absurd. ■ relating to or denoting a style of fast-moving comedy film involving eccentric characters or ridiculous situations.
– DERIVATIVES **screw·ball·er** n.

screw cap ▶ n. a round cap or lid with female thread that can be screwed onto a bottle or jar.
– DERIVATIVES **screw-capped** adj.

screw·driv·er /ˈskro͞oˌdrīvər/ ▶ n. **1** a tool with a flattened, cross-shaped, or star-shaped tip that fits into the head of a screw to turn it.
2 a cocktail made from vodka and orange juice.

screwed /skro͞od/ ▶ adj. **1** (of a bolt or other device) having a helical ridge or thread running around the outside.
2 informal in a difficult or hopeless situation; ruined or broken.

screwed-up ▶ adj. informal (of a person) emotionally disturbed; neurotic: *the screwed-up children of wealthy parents.* ■ (of an event or a situation) spoiled by being badly managed or carried out: *that was the most screwed-up audition.*

screw eye ▶ n. a screw with a loop for passing a cord through, instead of a slotted head.

screw jack ▶ n. another term for JACK SCREW.

screw pine ▶ n. another term for PANDANUS.

screw pro·pel·ler ▶ n. see SCREW (sense 1 of the noun).

screw thread ▶ n. see THREAD (sense 4 of the noun).

screw top ▶ n. another term for SCREW CAP.
– DERIVATIVES **screw-topped** adj.

screw·up /ˈskro͞oˌəp/ ▶ n. informal a situation that has been completely mismanaged or mishandled: *a massive bureaucratic screwup.*

screw·worm /ˈskro͞oˌwərm/ ▶ n. a large American blowfly larva that enters the wounds of mammals, developing under the skin and often causing death. The adult fly is called the **screwworm fly**. ● *Cochliomyia* (or *Callitroga*) *hominivorax*, family Calliphoridae.

screw·y /ˈskro͞oē/ ▶ adj. (**screwier**, **screwiest**) informal rather odd or eccentric: *some of the most respected doctors had some of the screwiest ideas.*
– DERIVATIVES **screw·i·ness** n.

Scria·bin /skrēˈäbən/ (also **Skryabin**), Aleksandr (Nikolaevich) (1872–1915), Russian composer and pianist. Much of his later music reflects his interest in mysticism and theosophy, esp. his third symphony. Notable works: *The Divine Poem* (1903) and *Prometheus: The Poem of Fire* (1909–10).

scrib·ble[1] /ˈskribəl/ ▶ v. [with obj.] write or draw (something) carelessly or hurriedly: *he took the clipboard and scribbled something illegible* | (as adj. **scribbled**) *scribbled notes* | [no obj.] *hastily he scribbled in the margin.* ■ [no obj.] informal write for a living or as a hobby: *she spent her last years scribbling and painting.*
▶ n. a piece of writing or a picture produced in this way: *illegible scribbles | he would never be able to decipher your scribble.*
– DERIVATIVES **scrib·bly** /ˈskrib(ə)lē/ adj.
– ORIGIN late Middle English: from medieval Latin *scribillare*, diminutive of Latin *scribere* 'write.'

scrib·ble[2] ▶ v. [with obj.] (often as noun **scribbling**) card (wool, cotton, etc.) coarsely.
– ORIGIN late 17th cent.: probably from Low German; compare with German *schrubbeln* (in the same sense), frequentative of Low German *schrubben* 'to scrub.'

scrib·bler /ˈskrib(ə)lər/ ▶ n. informal a person who writes for a living or as a hobby.

scribe /skrīb/ ▶ n. **1** historical a person who copies out documents, esp. one employed to do this before printing was invented. ■ informal, often humorous a writer, esp. a journalist.
2 (also **Scribe**) Judaism an ancient Jewish record-keeper or, later, a professional theologian and jurist.
3 another term for SCRIBER.
▶ v. [with obj.] **1** chiefly literary write: *he scribed a note that he passed to Dan.*
2 mark with a scriber.
– DERIVATIVES **scrib·al** /-bəl/ adj.
– ORIGIN Middle English (sense 2 of the noun): from Latin *scriba*, from *scribere* 'write.' The verb was first used in the sense 'write down'; in sense 2 of the verb it is perhaps partly a shortening of DESCRIBE.

scrib·er /ˈskrībər/ ▶ n. a pointed instrument used for making marks on wood, bricks, etc., to guide a saw or in sign painting.

scrim /skrim/ ▶ n. strong, coarse fabric, chiefly used for heavy-duty lining or upholstery. ■ Theater a piece of gauze cloth that appears opaque until lit from behind, used as a screen or backdrop. ■ a similar heatproof cloth put over film or television lamps to diffuse the light. ■ a thing that conceals or obscures something: *a thin scrim of fog covered the island.*
– ORIGIN late 18th cent.: of unknown origin.

scrim·mage /ˈskrimij/ ▶ n. **1** a confused struggle or fight.
2 Football the beginning of each down of play, with the ball placed on the ground between the offensive and defensive lines with its longest axis at right angles to the goal line. ■ chiefly Football a session in which teams practice by playing a simulated game.

S

▶ v. [no obj.] chiefly Football engage in a simulated game.
– DERIVATIVES **scrim·mag·er** n.
– ORIGIN late Middle English: alteration of dialect *scrimish*, variant of the noun SKIRMISH.

scrimp /skrimp/ ▶ v. [no obj.] be thrifty or parsimonious; economize: *I have scrimped and saved to give you a good education.*
– ORIGIN mid 18th cent. (in the sense 'keep short of (food)'): from Scots *scrimp* 'meager'; perhaps related to SHRIMP.

scrim·shaw /'skrim,shô/ ▶ v. [with obj.] adorn (whalebone, ivory, shells, or other materials) with carved or colored designs.
▶ n. a piece of work done in such a way.
– ORIGIN early 19th cent.: of unknown origin; perhaps influenced by the surname *Scrimshaw*.

scrip[1] /skrip/ ▶ n. **1** a provisional certificate of money subscribed to a bank or company, entitling the holder to a formal certificate and dividends. ■ such certificates collectively. ■ (also **scrip issue** or **dividend**) Finance an issue of additional shares to shareholders in proportion to the shares already held.
2 (also **land scrip**) a certificate entitling the holder to acquire possession of certain portions of public land.
3 historical paper money in amounts of less than a dollar.
– ORIGIN mid 18th cent.: abbreviation of *subscription receipt*.

scrip[2] ▶ n. historical a small bag or pouch, typically one carried by a pilgrim, shepherd, or beggar.
– ORIGIN Middle English: probably a shortening of Old French *escrepe* 'purse.'

scrip[3] ▶ n. another term for SCRIPT[2].

scri·poph·i·ly /skri'päfəlē/ ▶ n. the collection of old bond and share certificates as a pursuit or hobby. ■ such articles collectively.
– DERIVATIVES **scri·poph·i·list** /-list/ n.
– ORIGIN 1970s: from SCRIP[1] + -PHILY.

script[1] /skript/ ▶ n. **1** handwriting as distinct from print; written characters: *her neat, tidy script.* ■ printed type imitating handwriting. ■ writing using a particular alphabet: *Russian script.*
2 the written text of a play, movie, or broadcast. ■ Computing an automated series of instructions carried out in a specific order. ■ Psychology the social role or behavior appropriate to particular situations that an individual absorbs through cultural influences and association with others.
▶ v. [with obj.] write a script for (a play, movie, or broadcast).
– ORIGIN late Middle English (in the sense 'something written'): shortening of Old French *escript*, from Latin *scriptum*, neuter past participle (used as a noun) of *scribere* 'write.'

script[2] ▶ n. informal a doctor's prescription, esp. one for narcotic drugs.
– ORIGIN 1950s: abbreviation.

Script. ▶ abbr. ■ Scriptural. ■ Scripture.

script kid·die ▶ n. informal, derogatory a person who uses existing computer scripts or code to hack into computers, lacking the expertise to write their own.

scrip·to·ri·um /,skrip'tôrēəm/ ▶ n. (pl. **scriptoria** /-'tôrēə/ or **scriptoriums**) chiefly historical a room set apart for writing, esp. one in a monastery where manuscripts were copied.
– ORIGIN late 18th cent.: from medieval Latin, from Latin *script-* 'written,' from the verb *scribere*.

scrip·tur·al /'skripchərəl/ ▶ adj. of, from, or relating to the Bible: *scriptural quotations from Genesis.*
– DERIVATIVES **scrip·tur·al·ly** adv.
– ORIGIN mid 17th cent.: from late Latin *scripturalis*, from Latin *scriptura* 'writings' (see SCRIPTURE).

scrip·ture /'skripchər/ ▶ n. (often **Scripture** or **Scriptures**) the sacred writings of Christianity contained in the Bible: *passages of scripture* | *the fundamental teachings of the Scriptures.* ■ the sacred writings of another religion.
– ORIGIN Middle English: from Latin *scriptura* 'writings,' from *script-* 'written,' from the verb *scribere*.

script·writ·er /'skript,rītər/ ▶ n. a person who writes a script for a play, movie, or broadcast.
– DERIVATIVES **script·writ·ing** /-,rīting/ n.

scrive·ner /'skriv(ə)nər/ ▶ n. historical a clerk, scribe, or notary.
– ORIGIN Middle English: shortening of Old French *escrivein*, from Latin *scriba* (see SCRIBE).

scrod /skräd/ ▶ n. a young cod, haddock, or similar fish, esp. one prepared for cooking.
– ORIGIN mid 19th cent.: of unknown origin.

scrof·u·la /'skrôfyələ/ ▶ n. chiefly historical a disease with glandular swellings, probably a form of tuberculosis. Also formerly called KING'S EVIL.
– DERIVATIVES **scrof·u·lous** /-ləs/ adj.
– ORIGIN late Middle English: from medieval Latin, diminutive of Latin *scrofa* 'breeding sow' (said to be subject to the disease).

scroll /skrōl/ ▶ n. **1** a roll of parchment or paper for writing or painting on. ■ an ancient book or document on such a roll. ■ an ornamental design or carving resembling a partly unrolled scroll of parchment, e.g., on the capital of a column, or at the end of a stringed instrument. ■ Art & Heraldry a depiction of a narrow ribbon bearing a motto or inscription.
2 [usu. as modifier] the facility that moves a display on a computer screen in order to view new material.
▶ v. **1** [no obj.] move displayed text or graphics in a particular direction on a computer screen in order to view different parts of them: *she scrolled through her file.* ■ (of displayed text or graphics) move up, down, or across a computer screen.
2 [with obj.] cause to move like paper rolling or unrolling: *the wind scrolled back the uppermost layer of loose dust.*
– DERIVATIVES **scroll·a·ble** adj.
– ORIGIN late Middle English: alteration of obsolete *scrow* 'roll,' shortening of ESCROW.

scroll bar (also **scrollbar**) ▶ n. a long thin section at the edge of a computer display by which material can be scrolled using a mouse.

scrolled /skrōld/ ▶ adj. having an ornamental design or carving resembling a scroll of parchment.

scroll·er /'skrōlər/ ▶ n. a computer game in which the background scrolls past at a constant rate.

scroll·ing /'skrōling/ ▶ n. the action of moving displayed text or graphics up, down, or across on a computer screen in order to view different parts of them.
▶ adj. [attrib.] (of an ornamental design or carving) made to resemble a partly unrolled scroll of parchment.

scroll saw ▶ n. a narrow-bladed saw for cutting decorative spiral lines or patterns.

scroll·work /'skrōl,wərk/ ▶ n. decoration consisting of spiral lines or patterns, esp. as cut by a scroll saw.

scrooch /skrōōch/ ▶ v. [no obj.] informal crouch; bend: *he scrooched forward on his chair.*
– ORIGIN mid 19th cent. (originally US): dialect variant of US *scrouge* 'squeeze, crowd,' perhaps reinforced by the verb CROUCH.

Scrooge /skrōōj/, Ebenezer, a miserly curmudgeon in Charles Dickens's novel *A Christmas Carol* (1843). ■ (as noun **a Scrooge**) a person who is miserly.

scro·tum /'skrōtəm/ ▶ n. (pl. **scrota** or **scrotums**) a pouch of skin containing the testicles.
– DERIVATIVES **scro·tal** /'skrōtl/ adj.
– ORIGIN late 16th cent.: from Latin.

scrounge /skrounj/ informal ▶ v. [with obj.] seek to obtain (something, typically food or money) at the expense or through the generosity of others or by stealth: *he had managed to scrounge a free meal* | [no obj.] *we didn't scrounge off the social security.*
▶ n. [in sing.] an act of seeking to obtain something in such a way.
– ORIGIN early 20th cent.: variant of dialect *scrunge* 'steal.'

scroung·er /'skrounjər/ ▶ n. informal a person who borrows from or lives off others. ■ a cleverly resourceful person who finds and procures items for a specific purpose: *no team at camp had a better scrounger than our Eddie.*

scrub[1] /skrəb/ ▶ v. (**scrubs, scrubbing, scrubbed**) [with obj.] rub (someone or something) hard so as to clean them, typically with a brush and water: *he had to scrub the floor* | *she was scrubbing herself down at the sink* | [no obj.] *she scrubbed furiously at the plates.* ■ (**scrub something away/off**) remove dirt by rubbing hard: *it took ages to scrub off the muck.* ■ [no obj.] (**scrub up**) thoroughly clean one's hands and arms, esp. before performing surgery: *the doctor scrubbed up and put on a protective gown.* ■ informal cancel or abandon (something): *they aren't going to want to scrub the mission.* ■ remove impurities from (gas or vapor). ■ [no obj.] (of a rider) rub the arms and legs urgently on a horse's neck and flanks to urge it to move faster.
▶ n. **1** an act of scrubbing something or someone: *give the floor a good scrub.*
2 a semiabrasive cosmetic lotion applied to the face or body in order to cleanse the skin.
3 (**scrubs**) informal term for SCRUB SUIT.
– DERIVATIVES **scrub·ba·ble** adj.
– ORIGIN late 16th cent.: probably from Middle Low German and Middle Dutch *schrobben, schrubben*.

scrub[2] ▶ n. **1** vegetation consisting mainly of brushwood or stunted forest growth. ■ land covered with such vegetation.
2 [as modifier] denoting a shrubby or small form of a plant: *scrub apple trees.* ■ denoting an animal of inferior breed or physique: *a scrub bull.*
3 informal an insignificant or contemptible person. ■ (in sports) a player not among the best or most skilled.
– DERIVATIVES **scrub·by** adj.
– ORIGIN late Middle English (in the sense 'stunted tree'): variant of SHRUB[1].

scrub·ber /'skrəbər/ ▶ n. a brush or other object used to clean something. ■ a person who cleans something. ■ an apparatus using water or a solution for purifying gases or vapors.

scrub brush (Brit. **scrubbing brush**) ▶ n. a hard brush for scrubbing floors, pots and pans, etc.

scrub jay ▶ n. a jay with blue and gray plumage and no crest, found in Mexico, the western US, and central Florida. ● *Aphelocoma coerulescens*, family Corvidae.

scrub·land /'skrəb,land/ ▶ n. (also **scrublands**) land consisting of scrub vegetation.

scrub nurse ▶ n. a nurse who assists a surgeon by performing certain specialized duties during a surgical operation.

scrub oak ▶ n. a shrubby dwarf oak that forms thickets. ● Genus *Quercus*, family Fagaceae: several species, in particular *Q. ilicifolia* of the northeastern Appalachian region.

scrub suit ▶ n. a hygienic outfit worn by surgeons and other surgical staff while performing or assisting at an operation.

scrub ty·phus ▶ n. a rickettsial disease transmitted to humans by mites and found in parts of eastern Asia. Also called TSUTSUGAMUSHI DISEASE.

scrub·wo·man /'skrəb,wŏŏmən/ ▶ n. a woman employed to clean floors, walls, windows, etc.

scruff /skrəf/ ▶ n. the back of a person's or animal's neck: *he grabbed him by the scruff of his neck.*
– ORIGIN late 18th cent.: alteration of dialect *scuff*, of obscure origin.

scruff·y /'skrəfē/ ▶ adj. (**scruffier, scruffiest**) shabby and untidy or dirty: *dressed in scruffy jeans and a baggy T-shirt.*
– DERIVATIVES **scruff·i·ly** /-əlē/ adv., **scruff·i·ness** n.
– ORIGIN mid 17th century (in the sense 'covered with scurf'): from *scruff* 'scurf,' variant of SCURF, + -Y[1]. The sense 'shabby' dates from the late 19th cent.

scrum /skrəm/ ▶ n. Rugby an ordered formation of players, used to restart play, in which the forwards of a team form up with arms interlocked and heads down, and push forward against a similar group from the opposing side. The ball is thrown into the scrum and the players try to gain possession of it by kicking it backward toward their own side. ■ informal, chiefly Brit. a disorderly crowd of people or things: *there was quite a scrum of people at the bar.*
▶ v. (**scrums, scrumming, scrummed**) [no obj.] Rugby form or take part in a scrum.
– ORIGIN late 19th cent.: abbreviation of SCRUMMAGE.

scrum·mage /'skrəmij/ ▶ n. & v. another term for SCRUM.
– DERIVATIVES **scrum·mag·er** n.
– ORIGIN early 19th cent.: variant of SCRIMMAGE.

scrump·tious /'skrəm(p)shəs/ ▶ adj. informal (of food) extremely appetizing or delicious. ■ (of a person) very attractive.
– DERIVATIVES **scrump·tious·ly** adv., **scrump·tious·ness** n.
– ORIGIN mid 19th cent.: of unknown origin.

scrunch /skrənch/ ▶ v. [no obj.] make a loud crunching noise: *crisp yellow leaves scrunched underfoot.* ■ [with obj.] crush or squeeze (something) into a compact mass: *Gloria scrunched the handkerchief into a ball.* ■ become crushed or squeezed in such a way: *their faces scrunch up with concentration.* ■ [with obj.] style (hair) by squeezing or crushing it in the hands to give a tousled look.
▶ n. [in sing.] a loud crunching noise: *Charlotte heard the scrunch of boots on gravel.*
– ORIGIN late 18th cent. (in the sense 'eat or bite noisily'): probably imitative; compare with CRUNCH.

scrunch·ie /'skrənchē/ ▶ n. a circular band of fabric-covered elastic used for fastening the hair.

scru·ple /'skrōōpəl/ ▶ n. **1** (usu. **scruples**) a feeling of doubt or hesitation with regard to the morality or propriety of a course of action: *I had no scruples about eavesdropping* | *without scruple, these politicians use fear as a persuasion weapon.*
2 historical a unit of weight equal to 20 grains, used by apothecaries. ■ archaic a very small amount of something, esp. a quality.
▶ v. [no obj., usu. with negative] hesitate or be reluctant to do something that one thinks may be wrong: *she doesn't scruple to ask her parents for money.*

S

– ORIGIN late Middle English: from French *scrupule* or Latin *scrupulus*, from *scrupus*, literally 'rough pebble,' (figuratively) 'anxiety.'

scru·pu·lous /'skro͞opyələs/ ▶ **adj.** (of a person or process) diligent, thorough, and extremely attentive to details: *the research has been carried out with scrupulous attention to detail.* ■ very concerned to avoid doing wrong: *she's too scrupulous to have an affair with a married man.*
– DERIVATIVES **scru·pu·los·i·ty** /ˌskro͞opyə'läsitē/ **n.**, **scru·pu·lous·ly adv.** [as submodifier] *she was scrupulously polite*, **scru·pu·lous·ness n.**
– ORIGIN late Middle English (in the sense 'troubled with doubts'): from French *scrupuleux* or Latin *scrupulosus*, from *scrupulus* (see SCRUPLE).

scru·ti·nize /'skro͞otnˌīz/ ▶ **v.** [with obj.] examine or inspect closely and thoroughly: *customers were warned to scrutinize the small print.*
– DERIVATIVES **scru·ti·ni·za·tion** /ˌskro͞otn-i'zāsHən/ **n.**, **scru·ti·niz·er n.**

scru·ti·ny /'skro͞otn-ē/ ▶ **n.** (pl. **scrutinies**) critical observation or examination: *every aspect of local government was placed under scrutiny.*
– ORIGIN late Middle English: from Latin *scrutinium*, from *scrutari* 'to search' (originally 'sort trash,' from *scruta* 'trash'). Early use referred to the taking of individual votes in an election procedure.

scry /skrī/ ▶ **v.** (**skries, scrying, skried**) [no obj.] foretell the future using a crystal ball or other reflective object or surface.
– DERIVATIVES **scry·er n.**
– ORIGIN early 16th cent.: shortening of DESCRY.

SCSI /'skəzē/ ▶ **abbr.** Computing small computer system interface, a bus standard for connecting computers and their peripherals.

scu·ba /'sko͞obə/ ▶ **n.** an aqualung. ■ scuba diving.
– ORIGIN 1950s: acronym from *self-contained underwater breathing apparatus.*

scu·ba div·ing ▶ **n.** the sport or pastime of swimming underwater using scuba gear.
– DERIVATIVES **scu·ba dive** (also **scuba-dive**) **v.**, **scu·ba div·er n.**

scud /skəd/ ▶ **v.** (**scuds, scudding, scudded**) [no obj.] move fast in a straight line because or as if driven by the wind: *we lie watching the clouds scudding across the sky | three small ships were scudding before a brisk breeze.*
▶ **n. 1** chiefly literary a formation of vapory clouds driven fast by the wind. ■ a mass of windblown spray. ■ a driving shower of rain or snow; a gust. ■ the action of moving fast in a straight line when driven by the wind: *the scud of the clouds before the wind.*
2 (**Scud**) (also **Scud missile**) a type of long-range surface-to-surface guided missile able to be fired from a mobile launcher.
– ORIGIN mid 16th cent. (as a verb): perhaps an alteration of the noun SCUT[1], thus reflecting the sense 'race like a hare.'

scu·do /'sko͞odō/ ▶ **n.** (pl. **scudi** /-dē/) historical a coin, typically made of silver, formerly used in various Italian states.
– ORIGIN Italian, from Latin *scutum* 'shield.'

scuff /skəf/ ▶ **v.** [with obj.] scrape or brush the surface of (a shoe or other object) against something: *I scuffed the heel of my shoe on a stone.* ■ mark (a surface) by scraping or brushing it, esp. with one's shoes: *the linoleum on the floor was scuffed.* ■ [no obj.] (of an object or surface) become marked by scraping or brushing: *these shoes won't scuff.* ■ drag (one's feet or heels) when walking: *he scuffed his feet boyishly.* ■ [no obj.] walk in such a way: *she scuffed along in her slippers.*
▶ **n.** a mark made by scraping or grazing a surface or object: *dark colors don't show scuffs.*
– ORIGIN early 18th cent.: perhaps of imitative origin.

S

scuf·fle /'skəfəl/ ▶ **n. 1** a short, confused fight or struggle at close quarters: *there were minor scuffles with police.*
2 an act or sound of moving in a hurried, confused, or shuffling manner: *he heard the scuffle of feet.*
▶ **v.** [no obj.] **1** engage in a short, confused fight or struggle at close quarters: *the teacher noticed two students scuffling in the corridor.*
2 [with adverbial of direction] move in a hurried, confused, or awkward way, making a rustling or shuffling sound: *a drenched woman scuffled through the doorway.* ■ [with obj.] (of an animal or person) move (something) in a scrambling or confused manner: *the rabbit struggled free, scuffling his front paws.*
– ORIGIN late 16th cent. (as a verb): probably of Scandinavian origin; compare with Swedish *skuffa* 'to push'; related to SHOVE and SHUFFLE.

scull[1] /skəl/ ▶ **n.** each of a pair of small oars used by a single rower. ■ an oar placed over the stern of a boat to propel it by a side-to-side motion, reversing the blade at each turn. ■ a light, narrow boat propelled with a scull or a pair of sculls. ■ (**sculls**) a race between boats in which each participant uses a pair of oars.
▶ **v.** [no obj.] propel a boat with sculls. ■ [with obj.] transport (someone) in a boat propelled with sculls. ■ (of an aquatic animal) propel itself with fins or flippers.
– ORIGIN Middle English: of unknown origin.

scull[2] ▶ **n.** Canadian a large group of fish that has migrated from the open sea to inshore waters. ■ the season when this happens.
– ORIGIN variant of SCHOOL[2].

scul·ler /'skələr/ ▶ **n.** a person who sculls a boat. ■ a boat propelled with a scull or pair of sculls.

scul·ler·y /'skəl(ə)rē/ ▶ **n.** (pl. **sculleries**) chiefly historical a small kitchen or room at the back of a house used for washing dishes and other dirty household work.
– ORIGIN late Middle English (denoting the department of a household concerned with kitchen utensils): from Old French *escuelerie*, from *escuele* 'dish,' from Latin *scutella* 'salver,' diminutive of *scutra* 'wooden platter.'

scul·lion /'skəlyən/ ▶ **n.** archaic a servant assigned the most menial kitchen tasks.
– ORIGIN late 15th cent.: of unknown origin but perhaps influenced by SCULLERY.

sculp. ▶ **abbr.** ■ sculptor. ■ sculptural. ■ sculpture.

scul·pin /'skəlpən/ ▶ **n.** a chiefly marine fish of the northern hemisphere, with a broad flattened head and spiny scales and fins. ● Cottidae and related families: many genera and numerous species, including the bullheads.
– ORIGIN late 17th cent.: perhaps from obsolete *scorpene*, via Latin from Greek *skorpaina*, denoting a kind of fish.

sculpt /skəlpt/ (also **sculp** /skəlp/) ▶ **v.** [with obj.] create or represent (something) by carving, casting, or other shaping techniques: *sculpting human figures from ivory* | [no obj.] *she was teaching him how to sculpt.*
– ORIGIN mid 19th cent.: from French *sculpter*, from *sculpteur* 'sculptor'; later regarded as a back-formation from SCULPTOR or SCULPTURE.

Sculp·tor /'skəlptər/ Astronomy a faint southern constellation (the Sculptor or Sculptor's Workshop), between Grus and Cetus. ■ (as genitive **Sculptoris** /skəlp'tôris/) used with a preceding letter or numeral to designate a star in this constellation: *the star Delta Sculptoris.*
– ORIGIN Latin.

sculp·tor /'skəlptər/ ▶ **n.** an artist who makes sculptures.
– ORIGIN mid 17th cent.: from Latin, from *sculpt-* 'hollowed out,' from the verb *sculpere.*

sculp·tress /'skəlptrəs/ ▶ **n.** a female artist who makes sculptures.

sculp·tur·al /'skəlpCHərəl/ ▶ **adj.** of, relating to, or resembling sculpture: *sculptural decoration* | *sculptural works.*
– DERIVATIVES **sculp·tur·al·ly adv.**

sculp·ture /'skəlpCHər/ ▶ **n.** the art of making two- or three-dimensional representative or abstract forms, esp. by carving stone or wood or by casting metal or plaster. ■ a work of such a kind: *a bronze sculpture* | *a collection of sculpture.* ■ Zoology & Botany raised or sunken patterns or texture on the surface of a shell, pollen grain, cuticle, or other biological specimen.
▶ **v.** [with obj.] make or represent (a form) by carving, casting, or other shaping techniques: *the choir stalls were each carefully sculptured.* ■ form, shape, or mark as if by sculpture, esp. with strong, smooth curves: (as adj. **sculptured**) *he had an aquiline nose and sculptured lips.*
– ORIGIN late Middle English: from Latin *sculptura*, from *sculpere* 'carve.'

sculp·tur·esque /ˌskəlpCHə'resk/ ▶ **adj.** old-fashioned term for SCULPTURAL.
– DERIVATIVES **sculp·tur·esque·ly adv.**

sculp·tur·ing /'skəlpCHəriNG/ ▶ **n.** the action of forming or shaping something by or as if by sculpture: *the gadget is great for blow-drying, sculpturing, and molding.* ■ the shape produced in such a way: *the mountain's graceful sculpturing.* ■ Zoology & Botany sculpture: *the external sculpturing consists of a series of corrugations.*

scum /skəm/ ▶ **n.** a layer of dirt or froth on the surface of a liquid: *green scum found on stagnant pools.* ■ informal a worthless or contemptible person or group of people: *you drug dealers are the scum of the earth.*
▶ **v.** (**scums, scumming, scummed**) [no obj.] (of a liquid) become covered with a layer of dirt or froth: *the lagoon scummed over.* ■ [with obj.] form a layer of dirt or froth on (a liquid): *litter scummed the surface of the harbor.*
– DERIVATIVES **scum·my adj.** (**scummier, scummiest**).
– ORIGIN Middle English: from Middle Low German and Middle Dutch *schūm*, of Germanic origin.

scum·bag /'skəmˌbag/ ▶ **n.** informal a contemptible or objectionable person.

scum·ble /'skəmbəl/ Art ▶ **v.** [with obj.] modify (a painting or color) by applying a very thin coat of opaque paint to give a softer or duller effect. ■ modify (a drawing) in a similar way with light shading in pencil or charcoal.
▶ **n.** a thin, opaque coat of paint or layer of shading applied to give a softer or duller effect. ■ the effect produced by adding such a coat or layer.
– ORIGIN late 17th cent. (as a verb): perhaps a frequentative of the verb SCUM.

scun·cheon /'skənCHən/ ▶ **n.** the inside face of a doorjamb or window frame.
– ORIGIN Middle English: shortening of Old French *escoinson*, based on *coin* 'corner.'

scun·gil·le /sko͝on'jēlē/ (also **scungile**) ▶ **n.** (pl. **scungilli** /-'jēlē/) a mollusk (esp. with reference to its meat eaten as a delicacy).
– ORIGIN from Italian dialect *scunciglio*, probably an alteration of Italian *conchiglia* 'seashell.'

scun·ner /'skənər/ chiefly Scottish ▶ **n.** a strong dislike: *why have you a scunner against him?* ■ a source of irritation or strong dislike.
▶ **v.** [no obj.] feel disgust or strong dislike.
– ORIGIN late Middle English (first used in the sense 'shrink back with fear'): of unknown origin.

scup /skəp/ ▶ **n.** (pl. **same**) a common porgy with faint dark vertical bars, occurring off the coasts of the northwestern Atlantic. ● *Stenotomus chrysops*, family Sparidae.
– ORIGIN mid 19th cent.: from Narragansett *mishcup.*

scup·per[1] /'skəpər/ ▶ **n.** (usu. **scuppers**) a hole in a ship's side to carry water overboard from the deck. ■ an outlet in the side of a building for draining water.
– ORIGIN late Middle English: perhaps via Anglo-Norman French from Old French *escopir* 'to spit'; compare with German *Speigatt*, literally 'spit hole.'

scup·per[2] ▶ **v.** [with obj.] chiefly Brit. sink (a ship or its crew) deliberately. ■ informal prevent from working or succeeding; thwart: *plans for a casino were scuppered by a public inquiry.*
– ORIGIN late 19th cent. (as military slang in the sense 'kill, esp. in an ambush'): of unknown origin. The sense 'sink' dates from the 1970s.

scup·per·nong /'skəpərˌnäNG, -ˌnôNG/ ▶ **n.** a variety of the muscadine grape native to the basin of the Scuppernong River in North Carolina. ■ (often **scuppernong wine**) wine made from this grape.

scurf /skərf/ ▶ **n.** flakes on the surface of the skin that form as fresh skin develops below, occurring esp. as dandruff. ■ a similar flaky deposit on any surface, esp. one on a plant resulting from a fungal infection.
– DERIVATIVES **scurf·y adj.**
– ORIGIN late Old English *sceorf*, from the base of *sceorfan* 'gnaw,' *sceorfian* 'cut to shreds.'

scur·ril·i·ty /skə'rilitē/ ▶ **n.** (pl. **scurrilities**) the quality of being scurrilous: *a mixture of humor and mild scurrility.*

scur·ril·ous /'skərələs/ ▶ **adj.** making or spreading scandalous claims about someone with the intention of damaging their reputation: *a scurrilous attack on his integrity.* ■ humorously insulting: *a very funny collection of bawdy and scurrilous writings.*
– DERIVATIVES **scur·ril·ous·ly adv.**, **scur·ril·ous·ness n.**
– ORIGIN late 16th cent.: from French *scurrile* or Latin *scurrilus* (from *scurra* 'buffoon') + -OUS.

scur·ry /'skərē/ ▶ **v.** (**scurries, scurrying, scurried**) [no obj.] (of a person or small animal) move hurriedly with short quick steps: *pedestrians scurried for cover.*
▶ **n.** (pl. **scurries**) [in sing.] a situation of hurried and confused movement: *I was in such a scurry.*
– ORIGIN early 19th cent.: abbreviation of *hurry-scurry*, reduplication of HURRY.

scur·vy /'skərvē/ ▶ **n.** a disease caused by a deficiency of vitamin C, characterized by swollen bleeding gums and the opening of previously healed wounds, which particularly affected poorly nourished sailors until the end of the 18th century.
▶ **adj.** (**scurvier, scurviest**) [attrib.] archaic worthless or contemptible: *that was a scurvy trick.*
– DERIVATIVES **scur·vi·ly** /-vəlē/ **adv.**
– ORIGIN late Middle English (as an adjective meaning 'scurfy'): from SCURF + -Y[1]. The noun use (mid 16th cent.) is by association with French *scorbut* (see SCORBUTIC).

scur·vy grass ▶ **n.** a small cresslike European plant with fleshy tar-flavored leaves, growing near the sea. It is rich in vitamin C and was formerly eaten, esp. by sailors, to prevent scurvy. ● Genus *Cochlearia*, family Brassicaceae: several species, in particular *C. officinalis*.

scut[1] /skət/ ▶ **n.** the short tail of a hare, rabbit, or deer.
– ORIGIN late Middle English: of unknown origin; compare with obsolete *scut* 'short,' also 'shorten.'

scut[2] ▶ **n.** informal, chiefly Irish a person perceived as foolish, contemptible, or objectionable.
– ORIGIN late 19th cent.: of unknown origin.

scu·ta /ˈsk(y)o͞otə/ plural form of SCUTUM.

scu·tage /ˈsk(y)o͞otij/ ▶ **n.** (in a feudal society) money paid by a vassal to his lord in lieu of military service.
– ORIGIN late Middle English: from medieval Latin *scutagium*, from Latin *scutum* 'shield.'

Scu·ta·ri /ˈsko͞otərē, -tärē/ a former name for Üsküdar.

scutch /skəCH/ ▶ **v.** [with obj.] dress (fibrous material, esp. retted flax) by beating it.
– DERIVATIVES **scutch·er n.**
– ORIGIN mid 18th cent.: from obsolete French *escoucher*, from Latin *excutere* 'shake out.'

scutch·eon /ˈskəCHən/ ▶ **n.** archaic spelling of ESCUTCHEON.

scute /sk(y)o͞ot/ ▶ **n.** Zoology a thickened horny or bony plate on a turtle's shell or on the back of a crocodile, stegosaurus, etc.
– ORIGIN from Latin *scutum*; see SCUTUM.

scu·tel·lum /sk(y)o͞oˈteləm/ ▶ **n.** (pl. **scutella** /-ˈtelə/) Botany & Zoology a small shieldlike structure, in particular: ■ a modified cotyledon in the embryo of a grass seed. ■ the third dorsal sclerite in each thoracic segment of an insect.
– DERIVATIVES **scu·tel·lar** /-ˈtelər/ **adj.**
– ORIGIN mid 18th cent.: modern Latin, diminutive of Latin *scutum* 'shield.'

scut·ter /ˈskətər/ chiefly Brit. ▶ **v.** [no obj.] (esp. of a small animal) move hurriedly with short steps: *a little dog scuttered up from the cabin.*
▶ **n.** [in sing.] an act or sound of scuttering.
– ORIGIN late 18th cent.: perhaps an alteration of the verb SCUTTLE[2].

scut·tle[1] /ˈskətl/ ▶ **n.** (in full **coal scuttle**) a metal container with a sloping hinged lid and a handle, used to fetch and store coal for a domestic fire. ■ the amount of coal held in such a container: *carrying endless scuttles of coal up from the cellar.*
– ORIGIN late Old English *scutel* 'dish, platter,' from Old Norse *skutill*, from Latin *scutella* 'dish.'

scut·tle[2] ▶ **v.** [no obj.] run hurriedly or furtively with short quick steps: *a mouse scuttled across the floor.*
▶ **n.** [in sing.] an act or sound of scuttling: *I heard the scuttle of rats across the room.*
– ORIGIN late 15th cent.: compare with dialect *scuddle*, frequentative of SCUD.

scut·tle[3] ▶ **v.** [with obj.] sink (one's own ship) deliberately by holing it or opening its seacocks to let water in. ■ deliberately cause (a scheme) to fail: *some of the stockholders are threatening to scuttle the deal.*
▶ **n.** an opening with a lid in a ship's deck or side.
– ORIGIN late 15th cent. (as a noun): perhaps from Old French *escoutille*, from the Spanish diminutive *escotilla* 'hatchway.' The verb dates from the mid 17th cent.

scut·tle·butt /ˈskətl,bət/ ▶ **n.** informal rumor; gossip: *the scuttlebutt has it that he was a spy | the court cautioned against relying on scuttlebutt.*
– ORIGIN early 19th cent. (denoting a water butt on the deck of a ship, providing drinking water): from *scuttled butt.*

Scu·tum /ˈsk(y)o͞otəm/ Astronomy a small constellation (the Shield) near the celestial equator, lying in the Milky Way between Aquila and Serpens. ■ (as genitive **Scuti** /ˈsk(y)o͞otē, -,tī/) used with a preceding letter or numeral to designate a star in this constellation: *the star Beta Scuti.*
– ORIGIN Latin.

scu·tum /ˈsk(y)o͞otəm/ ▶ **n.** (pl. **scuta** /-tə/) Zoology another term for SCUTE. ■ Entomology the second dorsal sclerite in each thoracic segment of an insect.
– ORIGIN late 18th cent.: from Latin, literally 'oblong shield.'

scut work (also **scutwork**) ▶ **n.** informal tedious, menial work.
– ORIGIN 1970s: of unknown origin; compare with SCUT[2].

scuzz /skəz/ ▶ **n.** informal something regarded as disgusting, sordid, or disreputable. ■ a disreputable or unpleasant person.
– DERIVATIVES **scuzz·y adj.**
– ORIGIN 1960s: probably an informal abbreviation of DISGUSTING.

scuzz·ball /ˈskəz,bôl/ (also **scuzzbag** /-,bag/) ▶ **n.** informal a despicable or disgusting person.

Scyl·la /ˈsilə/ Greek Mythology a female sea monster who devoured sailors when they tried to navigate the narrow channel between her cave and the whirlpool Charybdis. In later legend Scylla was a dangerous rock, located on the Italian side of the Strait of Messina.
– PHRASES **between Scylla and Charybdis** /kəˈribdis/ used to refer to a situation involving two dangers in which an attempt to avoid one increases the risk from the other.

scy·phis·to·ma /sīˈfistəmə/ ▶ **n.** (pl. **scyphistomae** /-,mē, -,mī/ or **scyphistomas**) Zoology the fixed polyplike stage in the life cycle of a jellyfish, which reproduces asexually by budding (strobilation).
– ORIGIN late 19th cent.: from Latin *scyphus* 'cup' + Greek *stoma* 'mouth.'

Scy·pho·zo·a /,sīfəˈzōə/ Zoology a class of marine coelenterates that comprises the jellyfishes.
– DERIVATIVES **scy·pho·zo·an n. & adj.**
– ORIGIN modern Latin (plural), from Greek *skuphos* 'drinking cup' + *zōion* 'animal.'

scythe /sīTH/ ▶ **n.** a tool used for cutting crops such as grass or wheat, with a long curved blade at the end of a long pole attached to which are one or two short handles.
▶ **v.** [with obj.] cut with a scythe. ■ [no obj.] move through or penetrate something rapidly and forcefully: *attacking players can scythe through defenses.*
– ORIGIN Old English *sīthe*, of Germanic origin; related to Dutch *zeis* and German *Sense*.

scythe

Scyth·i·a /ˈsiTHēə/ an ancient region in southeastern Europe and Asia. The center of the Scythian empire, which existed between the 8th and 2nd centuries BC, was on the northern shores of the Black Sea and extended from southern Russia to the borders of Persia.
– DERIVATIVES **Scyth·i·an adj. & n.**

SD ▶ **abbr.** South Dakota (in official postal use).

sd. ▶ **abbr.** sound.

s.d. ▶ **abbr.** ■ sine die. ■ Statistics standard deviation.

S.Dak. ▶ **abbr.** South Dakota.

SDR ▶ **abbr.** special drawing right (from the International Monetary Fund).

SDS ▶ **abbr.** Students for a Democratic Society; a left-leaning organization of US college students that formed in 1960. It was active in the Civil Rights movement but is best remembered for its resistance to the VIETNAM WAR.

SE ▶ **abbr.** southeast or southeastern.

Se ▶ **symbol** the chemical element selenium.

se- ▶ **prefix** (in words adopted from Latin) apart; without: *secede | secure.*
– ORIGIN from Latin *se-*, from the earlier preposition and adverb *se.*

sea /sē/ ▶ **n.** (often **the sea**) the expanse of salt water that covers most of the earth's surface and surrounds its landmasses: *a ban on dumping radioactive wastes in the sea | rocky bays lapped by vivid blue sea |* [as modifier] *a sea view.* ■ (often in place names) a roughly definable area of this: *the Black Sea.* ■ (in place names) a large lake: *the Sea of Galilee.* ■ used to refer to waves as opposed to calm sea: *there was still some sea running.* ■ (**seas**) large waves: *the lifeboat met seas of thirty-five feet head-on.* ■ a vast expanse or quantity of something: *she scanned the sea of faces for Stephen.*
– PHRASES **at sea** sailing on the sea. ■ (also **all at sea**) confused or unable to decide what to do: *he feels at sea with economics.* **by sea** by means of a ship or ships: *other army units were sent by sea.* **go to sea** set out on a voyage. ■ become a sailor in a navy or a merchant navy. **on the sea** situated on the coast. **put (out) to sea** leave land on a voyage.
– ORIGIN Old English *sǣ*, of Germanic origin; related to Dutch *zee* and German *See.*

sea an·chor ▶ **n.** an object dragged in the water from the bow of a boat in order to keep the bow pointing into the waves or to lessen leeway.

sea a·nem·o·ne ▶ **n.** a sedentary marine coelenterate with a columnar body that bears a ring of stinging tentacles around the mouth. ● Order Actiniaria, class Anthozoa.

sea-an·gel ▶ **n.** an angel shark.

sea·bag /ˈsē,bag/ ▶ **n.** a sailor's traveling bag or trunk.

sea bass /bas/ ▶ **n.** any of a number of marine fishes that are related to or resemble the common perch, in particular: ● a mainly tropical fish of a large family (Serranidae, the **sea bass family**), esp. one of the genus *Centropristis*, including the **giant sea bass** (*C. stiata*). The sea bass family also includes the groupers. ● (**white sea bass**) a large game fish of the Pacific coast of North America (*Cynoscion nobilis*, family Sciaenidae).

giant sea bass

sea·bed /ˈsē,bed/ ▶ **n.** the ground under the sea; the ocean floor.

Sea·bee /ˈsē,bē/ ▶ **n.** a member of one of the construction battalions of the Civil Engineer Corps of the US Navy.
– ORIGIN representing a pronunciation of the letters *CB* (from *construction battalion.*

sea·bird /ˈsē,bərd/ ▶ **n.** a bird that frequents the sea or coast.

sea bis·cuit ▶ **n. 1** another term for HARDTACK. **2** another term for SAND DOLLAR.

sea·board /ˈsē,bôrd/ ▶ **n.** a region bordering the sea; the coastline: *the eastern seaboard of the U.S.*

sea boat ▶ **n.** [usu. with adj.] a boat or ship considered in terms of its ability to cope with conditions at sea: *she was a surprisingly good sea boat.*

Sea·borg /ˈsē,bôrg/, Glenn (Theodore) (1912–99), US nuclear chemist. During 1940–58, he and his colleagues produced nine of the transuranic elements (plutonium to nobelium) in a cyclotron. He shared the 1951 Nobel Prize for Chemistry with Edwin McMillan (1907–91).

sea·bor·gi·um /sēˈbôrgēəm/ ▶ **n.** the chemical element of atomic number 106, a very unstable element made by high-energy atomic collisions. (Symbol: **Sg**)
– ORIGIN modern Latin, named after G. *Seaborg* (see SEABORG).

sea·borne /ˈsē,bôrn/ ▶ **adj.** transported or traveling by sea: *seaborne trade.*

sea bream ▶ **n.** a deep-bodied marine fish that resembles the freshwater bream, in particular: ● Several genera and species in the family Sparidae (the **sea bream family**), in particular the **red sea bream** (*Pagellus bogaraveo*), which is fished commercially, and the **black sea bream** (*Spondyliosoma cantharus*), a popular angling fish; the sea bream family also includes the porgies. ● a fish of Australasian coastal waters, with a purple back and silver underside (*Seriolella brama*, family Centrolophidae).

sea breeze ▶ **n.** a breeze blowing toward the land from the sea, esp. during the day owing to the relative warmth of the land.

sea buck·thorn ▶ **n.** a bushy Eurasian shrub or small tree that typically grows on sandy coasts. It bears orange berries, and some plants are spiny. ● *Hippophae rhamnoides*, Elaeagnaceae.

sea but·ter·fly ▶ **n.** another term for PTEROPOD.

sea cap·tain ▶ **n.** a person who commands a ship, esp. a merchant ship.

Sea·Cat /ˈsē,kat/ ▶ **n.** trademark a large, high-speed catamaran used as a passenger and car ferry on short sea crossings.

sea change ▶ **n.** a profound or notable transformation.
– ORIGIN from Shakespeare's *Tempest* (I. ii. 403).

sea chant·ey ▶ **n.** see CHANTEY.

sea chest ▶ **n.** a sailor's storage chest.

sea coal ▶ **n.** archaic mineral coal, as distinct from other types of coal such as charcoal.

sea·coast /ˈsē,kōst/ ▶ **n.** the part of the land adjoining or near the sea: *the seacoast of Florida.*

sea·cock /ˈsē,käk/ ▶ **n.** a valve in an opening through a ship's hull below or near the waterline (esp. one connecting a ship's engine-cooling system to the sea).

sea cow ▶ **n.** a sirenian, esp. a manatee.

sea cu·cum·ber ▶ **n.** an echinoderm that has a thick, wormlike body with tentacles around the mouth. They typically have rows of tube feet along the body and breathe by means of a respiratory tree. ● Class Holothuroidea.

S

sea dog ▶ n. **1** informal an old or experienced sailor. **2** Heraldry a mythical beast like a dog with fins, webbed feet, and a scaly tail.

sea duck ▶ n. any of a number of ducks that frequent the sea, esp. the eiders, scoters, and long-tailed duck. ● Tribes Somateriini (and Mergini), family Anatidae: several genera.

sea ea·gle ▶ n. a large Eurasian fish-eating eagle that frequents coasts and wetlands. ● Genus *Haliaetus*, family Accipitridae: several species, in particular the widespread **white-tailed sea eagle** (*H. albicilla*), recently reintroduced to Scotland.

sea egg ▶ n. a sea urchin.

sea el·e·phant ▶ n. another term for ELEPHANT SEAL.

sea fan ▶ n. a horny coral with a vertical treelike or fanlike skeleton, living chiefly in warmer seas. ● *Gorgonis* and other genera, order Gorgonacea.

sea·far·ing /ˈsēˌfe(ə)riNG/ ▶ adj. (of a person) traveling by sea, esp. regularly.
▶ n. the practice of traveling by sea, esp. regularly.
– DERIVATIVES **sea·far·er** /-ˌfe(ə)rər/ n.

seafloor spread·ing ▶ n. Geology the formation of new areas of oceanic crust, which occurs through the upwelling of magma at midocean ridges and its subsequent outward movement on either side.

sea·food /ˈsēˌfo͞od/ ▶ n. shellfish and sea fish, served as food.

sea·front /ˈsēˌfrənt/ ▶ n. another term for BEACHFRONT.

sea-girt ▶ adj. literary surrounded by sea.

sea·go·ing /ˈsēˌgōiNG/ ▶ adj. [attrib.] (of a ship) suitable or designed for voyages on the sea. ■ characterized by or relating to traveling by sea, esp. habitually: *a seagoing life*.

sea goose·ber·ry ▶ n. a common comb jelly with a spherical body bearing two long retractile branching tentacles, typically occurring in swarms. ● *Pleurobrachia pileus*, class Tentaculata.

sea grape ▶ n. a salt-resistant tree of the dock family, bearing grapelike bunches of edible purple fruit and found on the Atlantic coasts of tropical America. ● *Coccoloba uvifera*, family Polygonaceae. ■ the fruit of this tree.

sea·grass /ˈsēˌgras/ ▶ n. a grasslike plant that lives in or close to the sea, esp. eelgrass. ● Genera *Cymodocea* (family Cymodoceaceae), *Zostera* (family Zosteraceae), and others.

sea-green ▶ adj. of a pale bluish green color.

sea·gull /ˈsēˌgəl/ ▶ n. a popular name for a gull.

sea hare ▶ n. a large sea slug that has a minute internal shell and lateral extensions to the foot. Most species can swim, and many secrete distasteful chemicals to deter predators. ● *Aplysia* and other genera, order Anaspidea, class Gastropoda.

sea hol·ly ▶ n. a spiny-leaved plant of the parsley family, with metallic blue teasel-like flowers, growing in sandy places by the sea and native to Europe. ● *Eryngium maritimum*, family Umbelliferae. See also ERYNGIUM.

sea·horse /ˈsēˌhôrs/ (also **sea horse**) ▶ n. **1** a small marine fish with segmented bony armor, an upright posture, a curled prehensile tail, a tubular snout, and a head and neck suggestive of a horse. ● Genus *Hippocampus*, family Syngnathidae: many species, including the European *H. ramulosus* and the American *H. hudsonius*. **2** a mythical creature with a horse's head and fish's tail.

seahorse 1

Sea Is·land cot·ton ▶ n. a fine-quality long-staple cotton grown on islands off the southern US.

Sea Is·lands a chain of islands off the Atlantic coast of northern Florida, Georgia, and South Carolina. They include many resorts and nature preserves and are noted for their African-derived Gullah culture.

sea·kale /ˈsēˌkāl/ ▶ n. a maritime Eurasian plant of the cabbage family, sometimes cultivated for its edible young shoots. ● *Crambe maritima*, family Brassicaceae.

sea·keep·ing /ˈsēˌkēpiNG/ ▶ n. [usu. as modifier] the ability of a vessel to withstand rough conditions at sea.

sea·kind·ly ▶ adj. (of a ship) easy to handle at sea.
– DERIVATIVES **sea·kind·li·ness** n.

sea krait ▶ n. a venomous sea snake with a compressed tail, occurring in tropical coastal waters of the eastern Indian Ocean and western Pacific, coming ashore to bask and breed. ● Genus *Laticauda*, family Elapidae: two species.

SEAL /sēl/ ▶ n. a member of an elite force within the US Navy specializing in guerrilla warfare and counterinsurgency.
– ORIGIN abbreviation of *(se)a (a)ir (l)and* (team).

seal[1] /sēl/ ▶ n. **1** a device or substance that is used to join two things together so as to prevent them from coming apart or to prevent anything from passing between them: *blue smoke from the exhaust suggests worn valve seals*. ■ [in sing.] the state or fact of being joined or rendered impervious by such a substance or device: *many fittings have tapered threads for a better seal*. ■ the water standing in the trap of a drain to prevent sewer gas from backing up through the drain, considered in terms of its depth.
2 a piece of wax, lead, or other material with an individual design stamped into it, attached to a document to show that it has come from the person who claims to have issued it. ■ a design embossed in paper for this purpose. ■ an engraved device used for stamping a design that authenticates a document. ■ a decorative adhesive stamp.
3 a thing regarded as a confirmation or guarantee of something: *the International Monetary Fund is likely to give a seal of approval to the Mexican plan*.
4 (**the seal**) (also **the seal of confession** or **the seal of the confessional**) the obligation on a priest not to divulge anything said during confession: *I was told under the seal*.
▶ v. [with obj.] **1** fasten or close securely: *he folded it, sealed the envelope, and walked to the mailbox*. ■ (**seal something in**) prevent something from escaping by closing a container or opening. ■ (**seal something off**) isolate an area by preventing or monitoring entrance to and exit from it: *the police have sealed off the area in search of the attackers*.
2 apply a nonporous coating to (a surface) to make it impervious: *seal the finish with a satin varnish*.
3 fry (food) briefly in hot fat to prevent it from losing too much of its moisture during subsequent cooking: *heat the oil and seal the lamb on both sides*.
4 conclude, establish, or secure (something) definitively, excluding the possibility of reversal or loss: *to seal the deal he offered Thornton a place on the board of the nascent company*.
5 fix a piece of wax or lead stamped with a design to (a document) to authenticate it.
– PHRASES **my** (or **his**, etc.) **lips are sealed** used to convey that one will not discuss or reveal something. **put** (or **set**) **the seal on** give the final authorization to: *the UN envoy hopes to set the seal on a lasting peace*. ■ provide or constitute the final confirmatory or conclusive factor: *the rain set the seal on his depression*. **seal someone's fate** see FATE. **set** (or **put**) **one's seal to** (or **on**) mark with one's distinctive character: *it was the Stewart dynasty which most markedly set its seal on the place*. **under seal** under legal protection of secrecy: *the judge ordered that the videotape be kept under seal*.
– DERIVATIVES **seal·a·ble** adj.
– ORIGIN Middle English (sense 2 of the noun): from Old French *seel* (noun), *seeler* (verb), from Latin *sigillum* 'small picture,' diminutive of *signum* 'a sign.'

seal[2] ▶ n. a fish-eating aquatic mammal with a streamlined body and feet developed as flippers, returning to land to breed or rest. ● Families Phocidae (the **true seals**) and Otariidae (the **eared seals**, including the fur seals and sea lions). The latter have external ear flaps and are able to sit upright, and the males are much larger than the females. ■ another term for SEALSKIN.
▶ v. [no obj.] (usu. as noun **sealing**) hunt for seals.
– ORIGIN Old English *seolh*, of Germanic origin.

sea lane ▶ n. a route designated for use or regularly used by shipping.

seal·ant /ˈsēlənt/ ▶ n. material used for sealing something so as to make it airtight or watertight.

sea lav·en·der ▶ n. a chiefly maritime plant with small pink or lilac funnel-shaped flowers. Several kinds are cultivated and some are used as everlasting flowers. ● Genus *Limonium* (formerly *Statice*), family Plumbaginaceae.

sea law·yer ▶ n. informal an eloquently and obstinately argumentative person.

seal·coat·ing /ˈsēlˌkōtiNG/ ▶ n. the application of a sealing coat to a paved surface in order to prolong its integrity.
– DERIVATIVES **seal·coat** v.

sealed-beam ▶ adj. denoting a vehicle headlight with a sealed unit consisting of the light source, reflector, and lens.

sealed book ▶ n. archaic term for CLOSED BOOK (see CLOSED).

sealed or·ders ▶ plural n. Military orders that are not to be opened before a specified time.

sea legs ▶ plural n. (**one's sea legs**) a person's ability to keep their balance and not feel seasick when on board a moving ship.

sea lem·on ▶ n. a yellowish sea slug. ● *Archidoris* and other genera, order Nudibranchia, class Gastropoda.

seal·er[1] /ˈsēlər/ ▶ n. **1** a device or substance used to seal something, esp. with a hermetic or an impervious seal.
2 (also **sealer jar**) Canadian a jar with a hermetic seal designed to preserve food such as fruit, pickles, and jams.

seal·er[2] ▶ n. a ship or person engaged in hunting seals.

sea let·tuce ▶ n. an edible seaweed with green fronds that resemble lettuce leaves. ● *Ulva lactuca*, division Chlorophyta.

sea lev·el ▶ n. the level of the sea's surface, used in reckoning the height of geographical features such as hills and as a barometric standard: *it is only 500 feet above sea level*. Compare with MEAN SEA LEVEL.

sea·lift /ˈsēˌlift/ ▶ n. a large-scale transportation of troops, supplies, and equipment by sea.

sea lil·y ▶ n. a sedentary marine echinoderm that has a small body on a long jointed stalk, with featherlike arms to trap food. ● Class Crinoidea.

seal·ing wax ▶ n. a mixture of shellac and rosin with turpentine and pigment, softened by heating and used to make seals.

sea li·on ▶ n. **1** an eared seal occurring mainly on Pacific coasts, the large male of which has a mane on the neck and shoulders. ● Five genera and species in the family Otariidae.
2 Heraldry a mythical beast formed of a lion's head and foreparts and a fish's tail.

sea loch ▶ n. see LOCH.

seal·point /ˈsēlpoint/ ▶ n. a dark brown marking on the fur of the head, tail, and paws of a Siamese cat. ■ a cat with such markings.

seal ring ▶ n. chiefly historical a finger ring with a seal for impressing sealing wax.

seal·skin /ˈsēlˌskin/ ▶ n. [often as modifier] the skin or prepared fur of a seal, esp. when made into a garment.

seal·stone /ˈsēlˌstōn/ ▶ n. a gemstone bearing an engraved device for use as a seal.

seal-top ▶ adj. (of a spoon) having a flat design resembling an embossed seal at the end of its handle.
▶ n. a spoon with such a handle.

Sea·ly·ham /ˈsēlēəm, -lēˌham/ (in full **Sealyham terrier**) ▶ n. a terrier of a wire-haired, short-legged breed.
– ORIGIN late 19th cent.: from *Sealyham*, the name of a village in southwestern Wales, where the dog was first bred.

seam /sēm/ ▶ n. **1** a line along which two pieces of fabric are sewn together in a garment or other article. ■ a line where the edges of two pieces of wood, wallpaper, or another material touch each other. ■ a long thin indentation or scar: *a sun-scorched face fissured with delicate seams*.
2 an underground layer, as of ore or coal.
▶ v. [with obj.] **1** join with a seam: *it can be used for seaming garments*.
2 (usu. as adj. **seamed**) make a long narrow indentation in: *men in middle age have seamed faces*.
– PHRASES **bursting** (or **bulging**) **at the seams** informal (of a place or building) full to overflowing. **come** (or **fall**) **apart at the seams** informal (of a person or system) be in a very poor condition and near to collapse: *the attitude of the airport guard was symptomatic of a system falling apart at the seams*.
– DERIVATIVES **seam·er** n.
– ORIGIN Old English *sēam*, of Germanic origin; related to Dutch *zoom* and German *Saum*.

sea·man /ˈsēmən/ ▶ n. (pl. **seamen**) a person who works as a sailor, esp. one below the rank of officer. ■ a sailor of the lowest rank in the US Navy or Coast Guard, ranking below petty officer. ■ [with adj.] a person regarded in terms of their ability to captain or crew a boat or ship: *he's the best seaman on the coast*.
– DERIVATIVES **sea·man·like** /-ˌlīk/ adj., **sea·man·ly** adj.
– ORIGIN Old English *sǣman* (see SEA, MAN).

sea·man·ship /ˈsēmənˌSHip/ ▶ n. the skill, techniques, or practice of handling a ship or boat at sea.

sea·mark /ˈsēˌmärk/ ▶ n. a conspicuous object distinguishable at sea, serving to guide or warn sailors in navigation.

sea mile ▶ **n.** a unit of distance equal to a minute of arc of a great circle and varying (because the earth is not a perfect sphere) between approximately 2,014 yards (1,842 meters) at the equator and 2,035 yards (1,861 meters) at the pole. Compare with NAUTICAL MILE.

seam·less /ˈsēmlis/ ▶ **adj.** (of a fabric or surface) smooth and without seams or obvious joins: *seamless stockings.* ■ smooth and continuous, with no apparent gaps or spaces between one part and the next: *the seamless integration of footage from different sources.*
– DERIVATIVES **seam·less·ly** adv., **seam·less·ness** n.

sea·moth ▶ **n.** a small fish with bony plates covering the body and large pectoral fins that spread out horizontally like wings. It lives in the warmer waters of the Indo-Pacific. ● Family Pegasidae: several genera and species, including the widely distributed *Eurypegasus draconis*.

sea·mount /ˈsēˌmount/ ▶ **n.** a submarine mountain.

sea mouse ▶ **n.** a large marine bristle-worm with a stout, oval body that bears matted, furlike, iridescent chaetae. ● Genus *Aphrodite*, class Polychaeta.

seam·stress /ˈsēmstris/ ▶ **n.** a woman who sews, esp. one who earns her living by sewing.
– ORIGIN late 16th cent.: from archaic *seamster, sempster* 'tailor, seamstress' + -ESS[1].

seam·y /ˈsēmē/ ▶ **adj.** (**seamier, seamiest**) sordid and disreputable: *a seamy sex scandal.*
– DERIVATIVES **seam·i·ness** n.
– ORIGIN late 16th cent.: from SEAM + -Y[1]. The sense 'disreputable' (early 17th cent.) arose from the notion of 'having the rough edges of seams visible.'

Sean·ad /ˈSHônəd, ˈSHänəTH/ (also **Seanad Éireann** /ˈārən/) the upper house of Parliament in the Republic of Ireland, composed of sixty members, of whom eleven are nominated by the Taoiseach and forty-nine are elected by institutions.
– ORIGIN Irish, 'senate (of Ireland).'

se·ance /ˈsāˌäns/ ▶ **n.** a meeting at which people attempt to make contact with the dead, esp. through the agency of a medium.
– ORIGIN late 18th cent.: French *séance*, from Old French *seoir*, from Latin *sedere* 'sit.'

sea net·tle ▶ **n.** a large, stinging jellyfish. ● *Chrysaora* and other genera, class Scyphozoa: numerous species, including the **East Coast sea nettle** (*C. quinquecirrha*), which is particularly common in Chesapeake Bay during midsummer.

East Coast sea nettle

Sea of A·zov, Sea of Gal·i·lee, etc. see AZOV, SEA OF; GALILEE, SEA OF, etc.

sea ot·ter ▶ **n.** an entirely aquatic marine otter of North Pacific coasts, formerly hunted for its dense fur. It is noted for its habit of floating on its back with a stone balanced on the abdomen, in order to crack open bivalve mollusks. ● *Enhydra lutris*, family Mustelidae.

sea pen ▶ **n.** a marine coelenterate related to the corals, forming a feather-shaped colony with a horny or calcareous skeleton. ● Order Pennatulacea, class Anthozoa.

sea perch ▶ **n.** any of a number of marine fishes that typically have a long-based dorsal fin and that are popular as sporting fish, in particular: ● a fish of the snapper family (Lutjanidae: several genera). ● a surfperch.

sea pink ▶ **n.** another term for THRIFT (sense 2).

sea·plane /ˈsēˌplān/ ▶ **n.** an aircraft with floats instead of wheels, designed to land on and take off from water.

sea·port /ˈsēˌpôrt/ ▶ **n.** a town or city with a harbor for seagoing ships.

sea po·ta·to ▶ **n.** a yellowish-brown European heart urchin. ● *Echinocardium cordatum*, class Echinoidea.

sea pow·er ▶ **n.** a country's naval strength, esp. as a weapon of war.

SEAQ /ˈsēˌak/ ▶ **abbr.** (in the UK) Stock Exchange Automated Quotations (the computer system on which dealers trade shares and seek or provide price quotations on the London Stock Exchange).

sea·quake /ˈsēˌkwāk/ ▶ **n.** a sudden disturbance of the sea caused by a submarine eruption or earthquake.

sear /si(ə)r/ ▶ **v.** [with obj.] burn or scorch the surface of (something) with a sudden, intense heat: *the water got so hot that it seared our lips* | figurative *a sharp pang of disappointment seared her.* ■ [no obj.] (of pain) be experienced as a sudden, burning sensation: *a crushing pain seared through his chest.* ■ brown (food) quickly at a high temperature so that it will retain its juices in subsequent cooking: (as adj. **seared**) *seared chicken livers.* ■ archaic cause to wither. ■ archaic make (someone's conscience, heart, or feelings) insensitive.
▶ **adj.** variant spelling of SERE[1].
– ORIGIN Old English *sēar* (adjective), *sēarian* (verb), of Germanic origin.

search /sərCH/ ▶ **v.** [no obj.] try to find something by looking or otherwise seeking carefully and thoroughly: *I searched among the rocks, but there was nothing* | *Daniel is then able to **search out** the most advantageous mortgage* | *Hugh will be **searching for** the truth.* ■ [with obj.] examine (a place, vehicle, or person) thoroughly in order to find something or someone: *she searched the house from top to bottom* | *the guards searched him for weapons.* ■ [with obj.] look for information or an item of interest in (a computer network or database) by keying words or other characters into a search engine: *I must search the Internet for one of his pictures.*
▶ **n.** an act of searching for someone or something: *the police carried out a thorough search of the premises* | *he plans to go to the Himalayas **in search of** a yeti.* ■ an act of searching a computer database or network: *time-consuming searches of the Internet.* ■ Computing the systematic retrieval of information, or the facility for this. ■ (usu. **searches**) Law an investigation of public records to find if a property is subject to any liabilities or encumbrances.
– PHRASES **search me!** informal I do not know (used for emphasis).
– DERIVATIVES **search·er** n.
– ORIGIN Middle English: from Old French *cerchier* (verb), from late Latin *circare* 'go around,' from Latin *circus* 'circle.'

search·a·ble /ˈsərCHəbəl/ ▶ **adj.** (of a database, website, etc.) capable of being computationally searched: *the archive is fully searchable.* ■ (of an item) able to be located by a computational search: *numbers are not treated as searchable terms.*
– DERIVATIVES **search·a·bil·i·ty** n.

search coil ▶ **n.** Physics a flat coil of insulated wire connected to a galvanometer, used for finding the strength of a magnetic field from the current induced in the coil when it is quickly turned over or withdrawn.

search en·gine ▶ **n.** Computing a program for the retrieval of data from a database or network, esp. the Internet.

search en·gine op·ti·mi·za·tion ▶ **n.** the process of maximizing the number of visitors to a particular website by ensuring that the site appears high on the list of results returned by a search engine.

search·ing /ˈsərCHiNG/ ▶ **adj.** thoroughly scrutinizing, esp. in a disconcerting way: *you have to ask yourselves some searching questions.*
– DERIVATIVES **search·ing·ly** adv.

search·light /ˈsərCHˌlīt/ ▶ **n.** a powerful outdoor electric light with a concentrated beam that can be turned in the required direction.

search par·ty ▶ **n.** a group of people organized to look for someone or something that is lost.

search war·rant ▶ **n.** a legal document authorizing a police officer or other official to enter and search premises.

sear·ing /ˈsi(ə)riNG/ ▶ **adj.** extremely hot or intense: *the searing heat of the sun* | *a searing pain.* ■ severely critical: *a searing indictment of the government's performance.*

sea rob·in ▶ **n.** a gurnard (fish), esp. one of warm seas that has winglike pectoral fins that are brightly colored. ● Family Triglidae: several genera and many species.

sea room ▶ **n.** clear space at sea for a ship to maneuver in.

Sears /si(ə)rz/, Richard Warren (1863–1914), US businessman. He founded his first mail-order business, selling watches, in Minneapolis in 1886, moved to Chicago, and sold the business. He then began a partnership with Alvah Curtis Roebuck (1864–1948), a watch repairman, that became Sears, Roebuck & Co. in 1893.

sea-run ▶ **adj.** (of a migratory fish, esp. a trout or salmon) having returned to the sea after spawning.

sea salt ▶ **n.** salt produced by the evaporation of seawater.

sea·scape /ˈsēˌskāp/ ▶ **n.** a view of an expanse of sea. ■ a picture of such a view.

Sea Scout ▶ **n.** a participant in a program to train Explorer Scouts in seamanship.

sea ser·pent ▶ **n.** a legendary serpentlike sea monster.

sea·shell /ˈsēˌSHel/ ▶ **n.** the shell of a marine mollusk.

sea·shore /ˈsēˌSHôr/ ▶ **n.** (usu. **the seashore**) an area of sandy, stony, or rocky land bordering and level with the sea. ■ Law the land between high- and low-water marks.

sea·sick /ˈsēˌsik/ ▶ **adj.** suffering from sickness or nausea caused by the motion of a ship at sea.
– DERIVATIVES **sea·sick·ness** n.

sea·side /ˈsēˌsīd/ ▶ **n.** (usu. **the seaside**) a place by the sea, esp. a beach area or vacation resort.

sea·side spar·row ▶ **n.** a small sparrow found on the Atlantic coast of North America. ● *Ammodramus maritimus*, family Emberizidae.

sea slat·er ▶ **n.** a common shore-dwelling crustacean that is related to the wood louse. ● *Ligia oceanica*, order Isopoda.

sea slug ▶ **n.** a shell-less marine mollusk that is typically brightly colored, with external gills and a number of appendages on the upper surface. ● Order Nudibranchia, class Gastropoda.

sea snail ▶ **n.** **1** a marine mollusk, esp. one with a spiral shell. ● Subclass Prosobranchia, class Gastropoda.
2 another term for SNAILFISH.

sea snake ▶ **n.** a venomous marine snake with a flattened tail that lives in the warm coastal waters of the Indian and Pacific oceans and does not come onto land. ● Subfamily Hydrophiinae, family Elapidae: several genera and species, including the **yellow-bellied sea snake** (*Pelamis platurus*), the only species found in the open ocean.

sea·son /ˈsēzən/ ▶ **n.** each of the four divisions of the year (spring, summer, autumn, and winter) marked by particular weather patterns and daylight hours, resulting from the earth's changing position with regard to the sun. ■ a period of the year characterized by a particular climatic feature or marked by a particular activity, event, or festivity: *the rainy season* | *the season for gathering pine needles.* ■ a fixed time in the year when a particular sport is played: *basketball season is over.* ■ the time of year when a particular fruit, vegetable, or other food is plentiful and in good condition: *the pies are made with fruit that is **in season*** | *lobster season.* ■ an indefinite or unspecified period of time; a while: *this most beautiful soul, who walked with me for a season in this world.* ■ archaic a proper or suitable time: *to everything there is a season.*
▶ **v.** [with obj.] **1** add salt, herbs, pepper, or other spices to (food): *season the soup to taste with salt and pepper.* ■ add a quality or feature to (something), esp. so as to make it more lively or exciting: *his conversation is seasoned liberally with exclamation points and punch lines.*
2 make (wood) suitable for use as timber by adjusting its moisture content to that of the environment in which it will be used.
– PHRASES **for all seasons** suitable in or appropriate for every kind of weather: *a coat for all seasons.* ■ adaptable to any circumstance: *a singer for all seasons.* **season's greetings** used as an expression of goodwill at Christmas or the New Year.
– ORIGIN Middle English: from Old French *seson*, from Latin *satio(n-)* 'sowing,' later 'time of sowing,' from the root of *serere* 'to sow.'

sea·son·a·ble /ˈsēzənəbəl/ ▶ **adj.** **1** usual for or appropriate to a particular season of the year: *seasonable temperatures.*
2 archaic coming at the right time or meeting the needs of the occasion; opportune.
– DERIVATIVES **sea·son·a·bil·i·ty** /ˌsēzənəˈbilitē/ n., **sea·son·a·ble·ness** n., **sea·son·a·bly** /-blē/ adv.

> **USAGE** Is it seasonable or seasonal? **Seasonable** means 'usual or suitable for the season' or 'opportune': *although seasonable, the weather was not warm enough for a picnic.* **Seasonal** means 'of, depending on, or varying with the season': *seasonal changes in labor requirements draw migrant workers to the area in spring and fall.*

sea·son·al /ˈsēzənəl/ ▶ **adj.** of, relating to, or characteristic of a particular season of the year: *a selection of seasonal fresh fruit.* ■ fluctuating or restricted according to the season or time of year: *there are companies whose markets are seasonal | seasonal rainfall.*
– DERIVATIVES **sea·son·al·i·ty** /ˌsēzəˈnalitē/ **n.**, **sea·son·al·ly adv.**

USAGE See usage at SEASONABLE.

sea·son·al af·fec·tive dis·or·der ▶ **n.** depression associated with late autumn and winter and thought to be caused by a lack of light.

sea·soned /ˈsēzənd/ ▶ **adj. 1** (of food) having had salt, pepper, herbs, or spices added: *seasoned flour.* **2** (of wood) made suitable for use as timber by adjusting its moisture content: *it was made from seasoned, untreated oak.* **3** accustomed to particular conditions; experienced: *she is a seasoned traveler.*

sea·son·ing /ˈsēzəniNG/ ▶ **n. 1** salt, herbs, or spices added to food to enhance the flavor. **2** the process of adjusting the moisture content of wood to make it more suitable for use as timber.

sea·son tick·et ▶ **n.** a ticket for a period of travel or a series of events that costs less than purchasing several separate tickets.

sea spi·der ▶ **n.** a spiderlike marine arachnid that has a narrow segmented body with a minute abdomen and long legs. ● Class Pycnogonida.

sea squill ▶ **n.** see SQUILL (sense 1).

sea squirt ▶ **n.** a marine tunicate that has a baglike body with orifices through which water flows into and out of a central pharynx. ● Class Ascidiacea, subphylum Urochordata.

sea stack ▶ **n.** see STACK (sense 2 of the noun).

sea star ▶ **n.** a starfish.

sea state ▶ **n.** the degree of turbulence at sea, generally measured on a scale of 0 to 9 according to average wave height.

seat /sēt/ ▶ **n. 1** a thing made or used for sitting on, such as a chair or stool. ■ the roughly horizontal part of a chair, on which one's weight rests directly. ■ a sitting place for a passenger in a vehicle or for a member of an audience: *we have a fairly small theater with about 1,300 seats.* ■ a place in an elected legislative or other body: *he lost his seat in the 1998 election.* ■ a site or location of something specified: *Washington, the seat of the federal government.* ■ short for COUNTRY SEAT. ■ short for COUNTY SEAT. ■ a part of a machine that supports or guides another part. **2** a person's buttocks. ■ the part of a garment that covers the buttocks. ■ a manner of sitting on a horse: *he's got the worst seat on a horse of anyone I've ever seen.*
▶ **v.** [with obj.] arrange for (someone) to sit somewhere: *he seated her next to her husband.* ■ (**seat oneself** or **be seated**) sit down: *she invited them to be seated |* (as adj. **seated**) *a dummy in a seated position.* ■ (of a place such as a theater or restaurant) have seats for (a specified number of people): *a large tent that seats 100 to 150 people.* ■ fit in position: *upper boulders were simply seated in the interstices below.*
– PHRASES **by the seat of one's pants** informal by instinct rather than logic or knowledge. **take one's seat** sit down, typically in a seat assigned to one.
– DERIVATIVES **seat·less adj.**
– ORIGIN Middle English (as a noun): from Old Norse *sæti*, from the Germanic base of SIT. The verb dates from the late 16th cent.

S

seat belt (also **seatbelt**) ▶ **n.** a belt or strap securing a person to prevent injury, esp. in a vehicle or aircraft.

-seater ▶ **comb. form** denoting a vehicle, sofa, or building with a specified number of seats: *a six-seater.*

seat·ing /ˈsētiNG/ ▶ **n. 1** the seats with which a building or room is provided: *the restaurant has seating for 80.* **2** an act or time of providing seats, esp. at a restaurant or performance venue: *lunch seatings are from 11 am to 12:30 pm only.*

SEATO /ˈsētō/ ▶ **abbr.** South East Asia Treaty Organization.

sea trout ▶ **n. 1** a troutlike marine fish of the drum family occurring in the western Atlantic. ● Genus *Cynoscion*, family Sciaenidae: several species, including the weakfish. **2** Brit. a European brown trout of a salmonlike migratory race. Also called SALMON TROUT. ● *Salmo trutta trutta*, family Salmonidae.

Se·at·tle¹ /sēˈatl/ a port and industrial city in the state of Washington, on the eastern shores of Puget Sound; pop. 598,541 (est. 2008). First settled in 1852, it is now the largest city in the northwestern US.

Se·at·tle² /sēˈatl/ (also **Seatlh**), Chief (1786–1866), Native American leader of the Suquamish and Duwamish tribes. He signed the Treaty of Port Elliott in 1855, guaranteeing a reservation for his people in what became the state of Washington. The city of Seattle is named for him.

sea tur·tle ▶ **n.** see TURTLE (sense 2).

sea ur·chin ▶ **n.** a marine echinoderm that has a spherical or flattened shell covered in mobile spines, with a mouth on the underside and calcareous jaws. Many species are harvested for food. ● Class Echinoidea: several families and genera, and numerous species, including the **Atlantic purple sea urchin** (*Arbacia punctulata*, family Arbaciidae) and the **green sea urchin** (*Strongylocentrotus drobachiensis*, family Strongylocentrotidae).

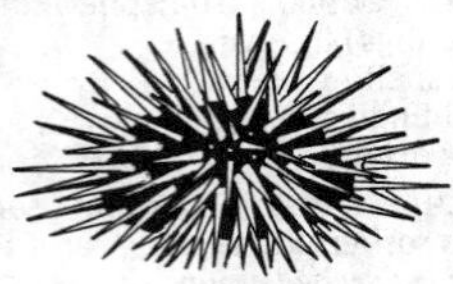
Atlantic purple sea urchin

sea wall ▶ **n.** a wall or embankment erected to prevent the sea from encroaching on or eroding an area of land.

sea·ward /ˈsēwərd/ ▶ **adv.** toward the sea: *after about a mile they turned seaward.*
▶ **adj.** going or pointing toward the sea: *there was a seaward movement of water on the bottom.* ■ nearer or nearest to the sea: *the seaward end of the village.*
▶ **n.** [in sing.] the side that faces or is nearer to the sea: *breakwaters were extended further to seaward.*

sea wasp ▶ **n.** a box jellyfish that can inflict a dangerous sting.

sea·wa·ter /ˈsēˌwôtər, -ˌwätər/ ▶ **n.** water in or taken from the sea.

sea·way /ˈsēˌwā/ ▶ **n. 1** an inland waterway capable of accommodating seagoing ships. ■ (**the Seaway**) see ST. LAWRENCE SEAWAY. ■ a natural channel connecting two areas of sea. ■ a route across the sea used by ships. **2** [in sing.] a stretch of water in which a sea is running: *with the engine mounted amidship, the boat pitches less in a seaway.*

sea·weed /ˈsēˌwēd/ ▶ **n.** large algae growing in the sea or on rocks below the high-water mark.

sea wolf ▶ **n.** another term for WOLFFISH.

sea·wor·thy /ˈsēˌwərT͟Hē/ ▶ **adj.** (of a vessel) in a good enough condition to sail on the sea.
– DERIVATIVES **sea·wor·thi·ness n.**

se·ba·ceous /səˈbāSHəs/ ▶ **adj.** technical of or relating to oil or fat. ■ of or relating to a sebaceous gland or its secretion.
– ORIGIN early 18th cent.: from Latin *sebaceus* (from *sebum* 'tallow') + -OUS.

se·ba·ceous cyst ▶ **n.** a swelling in the skin arising in a sebaceous gland, typically filled with yellowish sebum. Also called WEN¹.

se·ba·ceous gland ▶ **n.** a small gland in the skin which secretes a lubricating oily matter (sebum) into the hair follicles to lubricate the skin and hair.

Se·bas·tian, St. /siˈbasCHən/ (late 3rd century), Roman martyr. According to legend he was a soldier who was shot by archers on the orders of Diocletian. When he recovered, he confronted the emperor and was then clubbed to death. Feast day, January 20.

Se·bas·to·pol /səˈbastəˌpōl, -ˌpôl/ a fortress and naval base in Ukraine, near the southern tip of the Crimea; pop. 339,900 (est. 2009). It was the focal point of military operations during the Crimean War. Ukrainian and Russian name SEVASTOPOL.

SEbE ▶ **abbr.** southeast by east.

seb·or·rhe·a /ˌsebəˈrēə/ (Brit. **seborrhoea**) ▶ **n.** Medicine excessive discharge of sebum from the sebaceous glands.
– DERIVATIVES **seb·or·rhe·ic** /-ˈrē-ik/ **adj.**
– ORIGIN late 19th cent.: from SEBUM + -RRHEA.

Se·bring /ˈsēbriNG/ a city in south central Florida, noted as a car racing center; pop. 10,714 (est. 2008).

SEbS ▶ **abbr.** southeast by south.

se·bum /ˈsēbəm/ ▶ **n.** an oily secretion of the sebaceous glands.
– ORIGIN late 19th cent.: modern Latin, from Latin *sebum* 'grease.'

SEC ▶ **abbr.** Securities and Exchange Commission, a US governmental agency that monitors trading in securities and company takeovers.

sec¹ /sek/ ▶ **abbr.** secant.

sec² ▶ **n.** (**a sec**) informal a second; a very short space of time: *stay put, I'll be back in a sec.*
– ORIGIN late 19th cent.: abbreviation.

sec³ ▶ **adj.** (of wine) dry.
– ORIGIN French, from Latin *siccus.*

Sec. ▶ **abbr.** secretary.

sec. ▶ **abbr.** second(s).

SECAM /ˈsēkam/ ▶ **n.** the television broadcasting system used in France and eastern Europe.
– ORIGIN from French *séquentiel couleur à mémoire* (so named because the color information is transmitted in sequential blocks to a memory in the receiver).

se·cant /ˈsēˌkant, -kənt/ ▶ **n. 1** (abbr.: **sec**) Mathematics the ratio of the hypotenuse to the shorter side adjacent to an acute angle (in a right-angled triangle); the reciprocal of a cosine. **2** Geometry a straight line that cuts a curve in two or more parts.
– ORIGIN late 16th cent.: from French *sécante*, based on Latin *secare* 'to cut.'

sec·a·teurs /ˈsekəˌtərz/ ▶ **plural n.** (also **a pair of secateurs**) chiefly Brit. a pair of pruning clippers for use with one hand.
– ORIGIN mid 19th cent.: plural of French *sécateur* 'cutter,' formed irregularly from Latin *secare* 'to cut.'

Sec·chi disc /ˈsekē/ ▶ **n.** an opaque disk, typically white, used to gauge the transparency of water by measuring the depth (**Secchi depth**) at which the disk ceases to be visible from the surface.
– ORIGIN early 20th cent.: named after Angelo *Secchi* (1818–78), Italian astronomer.

sec·co /ˈsekō/ (also **fresco secco**) ▶ **n.** the technique of painting on dry plaster with pigments mixed in water.
– ORIGIN mid 19th cent.: from Italian, literally 'dry,' from Latin *siccus.*

se·cede /siˈsēd/ ▶ **v.** [no obj.] withdraw formally from membership in a federal union, an alliance, or a political or religious organization: *the kingdom of Belgium seceded from the Netherlands in 1830.*
– DERIVATIVES **se·ced·er n.**
– ORIGIN early 18th cent.: from Latin *secedere*, from *se-* 'apart' + *cedere* 'go.'

Se·cer·nen·te·a /ˌsesərˈnentēə/ Zoology another term for PHASMIDA (sense 2).
– ORIGIN modern Latin (plural), from Latin *secernent-* 'separating,' from the verb *secernere.*

se·ces·sion /səˈseSHən/ ▶ **n.** the action of withdrawing formally from membership of a federation or body, esp. a political state: *the republics want secession from the union.* ■ (**the Secession**) historical the withdrawal of eleven southern states from the Union in 1860, leading to the Civil War. ■ (**the Secession**) variant of SEZESSION.
– DERIVATIVES **se·ces·sion·al** /-SHənl/ **adj.**, **se·ces·sion·ism** /-ˌnizəm/ **n.**, **se·ces·sion·ist** /-ist/ **n.**
– ORIGIN mid 16th cent. (denoting the withdrawal of plebeians from ancient Rome in order to compel the patricians to redress their grievances): from French *sécession* or Latin *secessio(n-)*, from *secedere* 'go apart' (see SECEDE).

Sech·ua·na /seCHˈwänə/ dated ▶ **n. & adj.** variant spelling of SETSWANA.

Seck·el /ˈsekəl/ ▶ **n.** a pear of a small sweet juicy brownish-red variety, grown chiefly in the US.
– ORIGIN early 19th cent.: from the surname of an early grower.

se·clude /siˈklo͞od/ ▶ **v.** [with obj.] keep (someone) away from other people: *I secluded myself up here for a life of study and meditation.*
– ORIGIN late Middle English (in the sense 'obstruct access to'): from Latin *secludere*, from *se-* 'apart' + *claudere* 'to shut.'

se·clud·ed /siˈklo͞odid/ ▶ **adj.** (of a place) not seen or visited by many people; sheltered and private: *the gardens are quiet and secluded.*

se·clu·sion /siˈklo͞oZHən/ ▶ **n.** the state of being private and away from other people: *they enjoyed ten days of peace and seclusion.* ■ archaic a sheltered or private place.
– DERIVATIVES **se·clu·sive** /-siv/ **adj.**
– ORIGIN early 17th cent.: from medieval Latin *seclusio(n-)*, from *secludere* 'shut off' (see SECLUDE).

Sec·o·nal /ˈsekəˌnôl, -ˌnal/ ▶ **n.** trademark a barbiturate drug used as a sedative and hypnotic.
– ORIGIN 1930s: blend of SECONDARY and ALLYL.

sec·ond¹ /ˈsekənd/ ▶ **ordinal number 1** constituting number two in a sequence; coming after the first in time or order; 2nd: *he married for a second time | Herbie was the second of their six children.* ■ secondly (used to introduce a second point or reason): *second, they are lightly regulated; and third, they do business with nonresident clients.* ■ Music an interval spanning two consecutive notes in a diatonic scale. ■ the note that is higher by this interval than the tonic of a diatonic scale or root of a chord. ■ the second in a sequence of a vehicle's gears: *he took the corner in second.* ■ Baseball second

base. ■ the second grade of a school. ■ (**seconds**) informal a second course or second helping of food at a meal. ■ denoting someone or something regarded as comparable to or reminiscent of a better-known predecessor: *a fear that the conflict would turn into a second Vietnam.* ■ an act or instance of seconding.
2 subordinate or inferior in position, rank, or importance: *it was* **second only to** *Copenhagen among Baltic ports | he is a writer first and a scientist second.* ■ additional to that already existing, used, or possessed: *a second home | French as a second language.* ■ the second finisher or position in a race or competition: *he finished second.* ■ Brit. a place in the second-highest grade in an examination, esp. for a degree: *she got a first in moral sciences and a second in history.* ■ Music performing a lower or subordinate of two or more parts for the same instrument or voice: *the second violins.* ■ (**seconds**) goods of an inferior quality. ■ coarse flour, or bread made from it.
3 an assistant, in particular: ■ an attendant assisting a combatant in a duel or boxing match.
▶ **v.** [with obj.] formally support or endorse (a nomination or resolution or its proposer) as a necessary preliminary to adoption or further discussion: *Bertonazzi seconded Birmingham's nomination.* ■ express agreement with: *her view is seconded by most Indian leaders today.* ■ archaic support; back up: *so well was he seconded by the multitude of laborers at his command.*
– PHRASES **every second** see EVERY OTHER at EVERY. **in the second place** as a second consideration or point. **second to none** the best, worst, fastest, etc.
– DERIVATIVES **sec·ond·er n.**
– ORIGIN Middle English: via Old French from Latin *secundus* 'following, second,' from the base of *sequi* 'follow.' The verb dates from the late 16th cent.

sec·ond[2] /ˈsekənd/ ▶ **n. 1** (abbr.: **s**) a sixtieth of a minute of time, which as the SI unit of time is defined in terms of the natural periodicity of the radiation of a cesium-133 atom. (Symbol: **″**) ■ informal a very short time: *his eyes met Charlotte's for a second.*
2 (also **arc second** or **second of arc**) a sixtieth of a minute of angular distance. (Symbol: **″**)
– ORIGIN late Middle English: from medieval Latin *secunda (minuta)* 'second (minute),' feminine (used as a noun) of *secundus*, referring to the "second" operation of dividing an hour by sixty.

sec·ond[3] /siˈkänd/ ▶ **v.** [with obj.] Brit. transfer (a military officer or other official or worker) temporarily to other employment or another position: *I was seconded to a public relations unit.*
– DERIVATIVES **sec·ond·ee** /ˌsekənˈdē/ **n.**
– ORIGIN early 19th cent.: from French *en second* 'in the second rank (of officers).'

sec·ond Ad·am ▶ **n.** (**the second Adam**) (in Christian thought) Jesus Christ.
– ORIGIN with biblical allusion to 1 Cor. 15: 45–47.

Sec·ond A·dar see ADAR.

Sec·ond Ad·vent ▶ **n.** another term for SECOND COMING.

sec·ond·ar·y /ˈsekənˌderē/ ▶ **adj. 1** coming after, less important than, or resulting from someone or something else that is primary: *luck plays a role, but it's ultimately secondary to local knowledge.* ■ [attrib.] of or relating to education for children from the age of eleven to sixteen or eighteen: *a secondary school.* ■ having a reversible chemical reaction and therefore able to store energy. ■ relating to or denoting the output side of a device using electromagnetic induction, esp. in a transformer.
2 (**Secondary**) Geology former term for MESOZOIC.
3 Chemistry (of an organic compound) having its functional group located on a carbon atom that is bonded to two other carbon atoms. ■ (chiefly of amines) derived from ammonia by replacement of two hydrogen atoms by organic groups.
▶ **n.** (pl. **secondaries**) **1** short for. ■ a secondary color. ■ Ornithology a secondary feather. ■ a secondary coil or winding in an electrical transformer.
2 Football the players in the defensive backfield; the area these players cover.
3 (**the Secondary**) Geology, dated the Secondary or Mesozoic era.
– DERIVATIVES **sec·ond·ar·i·ly** /-ˌderəlē/ **adv.**, **sec·ond·ar·i·ness n.**
– ORIGIN late Middle English: from Latin *secundarius* 'of the second quality or class,' from *secundus* (see SECOND[1]).

sec·ond·ar·y ar·tic·u·la·tion ▶ **n.** Phonetics an additional feature in the pronunciation of a consonant (besides the actual place of articulation), such as palatalization or lip-rounding.

sec·ond·ar·y boy·cott ▶ **n.** industrial action by a union against a company on the grounds that does business with another company engaged in a labor dispute.

sec·ond·ar·y col·or ▶ **n.** a color resulting from the mixing of two primary colors.

sec·ond·ar·y ev·i·dence ▶ **n.** Law something, in particular documentation, which confirms the existence of unavailable primary evidence.

sec·ond·ar·y feath·er ▶ **n.** any of the flight feathers growing from the second joint of a bird's wing.

sec·ond·ar·y in·dus·try ▶ **n.** Economics industry that converts the raw materials provided by primary industry into commodities and products for the consumer; manufacturing industry.

sec·ond·ar·y pick·et·ing ▶ **n.** Brit. picketing by strikers of the premises of a firm that trades with their employer but is not otherwise involved in the dispute in question.

sec·ond·ar·y plan·et ▶ **n.** a satellite of a planet.

sec·ond·ar·y proc·ess ▶ **n.** Psychoanalysis a thought process connecting the preconscious and conscious, governed by the reality principle and reflecting the decision-making and problem-solving activity of the ego.

sec·ond·ar·y sec·tor ▶ **n.** Economics the sector of the economy concerned with or relating to primary industry.

sec·ond·ar·y sex·u·al char·ac·ter·is·tics ▶ **plural n.** physical characteristics developed at puberty that distinguish between the sexes but are not involved in reproduction.

sec·ond·ar·y smoke ▶ **n.** British term for SECONDHAND SMOKE.

sec·ond·ar·y smok·ing ▶ **n.** another term for PASSIVE SMOKING.

sec·ond·ar·y stress ▶ **n.** Phonetics (in a system that postulates three levels of stress) the accent on a syllable of a word or breath group that is weaker than the primary stress but stronger than the lack of stress.

sec·ond·ar·y struc·ture ▶ **n.** Biochemistry the local three-dimensional structure of sheets, helices, or other forms adopted by a polynucleotide or polypeptide chain, due to electrostatic attraction between neighboring residues.

sec·ond·ar·y thick·en·ing ▶ **n.** Botany (in the stem or root of a woody plant) the increase in girth resulting from the formation of new woody tissue by the cambium.

sec·ond·ar·y treat·ment ▶ **n.** the further treatment of sewage effluent by biological methods following sedimentation.

sec·ond bal·lot ▶ **n.** a further ballot held to confirm the selection of a candidate where a previous ballot did not yield an absolute majority.

sec·ond best ▶ **adj.** next after the best: *his second-best suit.*
▶ **n.** a less adequate or less desirable alternative: *he would have to settle for second best.*
– PHRASES **come off second best** be defeated in a competition.

sec·ond cause ▶ **n.** Logic a cause that is itself caused.

sec·ond cham·ber ▶ **n.** the upper house of a parliament with two chambers.

sec·ond child·hood ▶ **n.** a period in someone's adult life when they act as a child, either for fun or as a consequence of reduced mental capabilities.

sec·ond class ▶ **n.** [in sing.] a set of people or things grouped together as the second best. ■ the second-best accommodations in an aircraft, train, or ship. ■ Brit. the second-highest division in the results of the examinations for a university degree: *he obtained a second class in modern history.*
▶ **adj. & adv.** (**second-class**) of the second-best quality or in the second division: [as adj.] *until 1914 women were thought of as second-class citizens.* ■ of or relating to the second-best accommodations in an aircraft, train, or ship: [as adj.] *I want second-class tickets* | [as adv.] *they don't fly second-class.* ■ of or relating to a class of mail having lower priority than first-class mail: [as adj.] *second-class postage stamps.* ■ (in North America) denoting a class of mail that includes newspapers and periodicals. ■ [as adj.] Brit. of or relating to the second-highest division in a university examination: *a respectable second-class degree.*

Sec·ond Com·ing ▶ **n.** Christian Theology the prophesied return of Christ to earth at the Last Judgment.

sec·ond cous·in ▶ **n.** see COUSIN.

sec·ond-cut ▶ **adj.** another term for CROSSCUT.

sec·ond-de·gree ▶ **adj.** [attrib.] **1** Medicine denoting burns that cause blistering but not permanent scars.
2 Law denoting a category of a crime, esp. murder, that is less serious than a first-degree crime.

se·conde /səˈkänd/ ▶ **n.** Fencing the second of eight standard parrying positions.
– ORIGIN early 18th cent.: from French, feminine of *second* 'second.'

Sec·ond Em·pire the imperial government in France of Napoleon III, 1852–70. ■ this period in France.

sec·ond floor ▶ **n.** the floor directly above the ground floor. ■ Brit. the floor two levels above the ground floor.

sec·ond-gen·er·a·tion ▶ **adj. 1** denoting the offspring of parents who have immigrated to a particular country: *she was a second-generation American.*
2 of a more advanced stage of technology than previous models or systems.

sec·ond growth ▶ **n. 1** woodland growth that replaces harvested or burned virgin forest: [as modifier] *a thicket of second-growth Ponderosa pine and Douglas fir.*
2 a wine considered to be the second-best in quality compared to the first growth (or PREMIER CRU): [as modifier] *a second-growth wine was added as a bonus for the group.*

sec·ond-guess ▶ **v.** [with obj.] **1** anticipate or predict (someone's actions or thoughts) by guesswork: *he had to second-guess what the environmental regulations would be in five years' time.*
2 judge or criticize (someone) with hindsight: *the prime minister was willing to second-guess senior ministers in public.*
– DERIVATIVES **sec·ond-guess·er n.**

sec·ond·hand /ˈsekən(d)ˈhand/ ▶ **adj. 1** (of goods) having had a previous owner; not new: *a secondhand car.* ■ [attrib.] denoting a store or shop where such goods can be bought: *a secondhand bookstore.*
2 (of information or experience) accepted on another's authority and not from original investigation: *secondhand knowledge of her country.*
▶ **adv. 1** on the basis that something has had a previous owner: *tips on the pitfalls to avoid when buying secondhand.*
2 on the basis of what others have said; indirectly: *I was discounting anything I heard secondhand.*
– PHRASES **at second hand** by hearsay rather than direct observation or experience.

sec·ond hand ▶ **n.** an extra hand in some watches and clocks that moves around to indicate the seconds.

sec·ond·hand smoke ▶ **n.** smoke inhaled involuntarily from tobacco being smoked by others.

sec·ond·hand speech ▶ **n.** conversation on a cellular phone that is overheard by people nearby: *I was alternately amused and annoyed by the secondhand speech in the waiting room.*

sec·ond hon·ey·moon ▶ **n.** a romantic vacation taken by a couple who have been married for some time.

sec·ond-in-com·mand ▶ **n.** the officer next in authority to the commanding or chief officer.

sec·ond in·ten·tion ▶ **n.** Medicine the healing of a wound in which the edges do not meet, and new epithelium must form across granulation tissue: *healing* **by second intention**.

Sec·ond In·ter·na·tion·al see INTERNATIONAL (sense 2 of the noun).

Sec·ond I·sa·iah another name for DEUTERO-ISAIAH.

sec·ond lieu·ten·ant ▶ **n.** a commissioned officer of the lowest rank in the US Army, Air Force, and Marine Corps ranking above chief warrant officer and below first lieutenant.

sec·ond line ▶ **n.** anything used or held in reserve as support, replacement, or reinforcement, in particular: ■ [usu. as modifier] a medical treatment or therapy used in support of another, or as a more drastic measure if the primary treatment is ineffective. ■ a battle line behind the front line to support it and make good its losses. ■ [as modifier] ranking second in strength, effectiveness, ability, or value: *the clutch of second-line U.S. computer manufacturers.*

sec·ond·ly /ˈsekən(d)lē/ ▶ **adv.** in the second place (used to introduce a second point or reason): *he was presented first of all as a hopelessly unqualified candidate and secondly as an extremist.*

sec·ond mate ▶ **n.** an assistant mate on a merchant ship.

sec·ond mes·sen·ger ▶ **n.** Physiology a substance whose release within a cell is promoted by a hormone and that brings about a response by the cell.

sec·ond mort·gage ▶ n. a mortgage taken out on a property that is already mortgaged.

sec·ond name ▶ n. a surname.

sec·ond na·ture ▶ n. a characteristic or habit in someone that appears to be instinctive because that person has behaved in a particular way so often: *deceit was becoming **second nature to her**.*

se·con·do /sə'kändō, -'kôn-/ ▶ n. (pl. **secondi** /-dē/) Music the second or lower part in a duet.
– ORIGIN Italian.

sec·ond of·fi·cer ▶ n. another term for SECOND MATE.

sec·ond per·son ▶ n. see PERSON (sense 2).

sec·ond po·si·tion ▶ n. **1** Ballet a posture in which the feet form a straight line, being turned out to either side with the heels separated by the distance of a small step. ■ a position of the arms in which they are held out to each side of the body, curving forward and slightly upward.
2 Music a position of the left hand on the fingerboard of a stringed instrument nearer to the bridge than the first position, enabling a higher-pitched set of notes to be played.

sec·ond-rate ▶ adj. of mediocre or inferior quality: *a second-rate theater.*
– DERIVATIVES **sec·ond-rat·ed·ness** n., **sec·ond-rat·er** n.

sec·ond read·ing ▶ n. a second presentation of a bill to a legislative assembly, in the US to debate committee reports and in the UK to approve the bill's general principles.

Sec·ond Reich see REICH[1].

Sec·ond Re·pub·lic the republican regime in France from the deposition of King Louis Philippe (1848) to the beginning of the Second Empire (1852).

sec·ond sight ▶ n. the supposed ability to perceive future or distant events; clairvoyance.
– DERIVATIVES **sec·ond-sight·ed** adj.

sec·ond-stor·y man ▶ n. a burglar who enters through an upper-story window.

sec·ond strike ▶ n. a retaliatory attack conducted with weapons designed to withstand an initial nuclear attack (a "first strike").

sec·ond string ▶ n. **1** (in sports) the players who are available to replace or relieve those who start a game: [as modifier] *the second-string quarterback.*
2 an alternative resource or course of action in case another one fails.
– DERIVATIVES **sec·ond-string·er** n.

sec·ond thoughts (also **second thought**) ▶ plural n. a change of opinion or resolve reached after considering something again: ***on second thought**, perhaps he was right.*

sec·ond wind /wind/ ▶ n. [in sing.] a person's ability to breathe freely during exercise, after having been out of breath. ■ a new strength or energy to continue something that is an effort: *she gained a second wind during the campaign and turned the opinion polls around.*

Sec·ond World ▶ n. the former communist block consisting of the Soviet Union and some countries in eastern Europe.

Sec·ond World War another term for WORLD WAR II.

se·cre·cy /'sēkrəsē/ ▶ n. the action of keeping something secret or the state of being kept secret: *the bidding is conducted **in secrecy**.*
– ORIGIN late Middle English: from SECRET, probably on the pattern of *privacy*.

S

se·cret /'sēkrit/ ▶ adj. not known or seen or not meant to be known or seen by others: *how did you guess I had a secret plan? | the resupply effort was probably **kept secret from** Congress.* ■ [attrib.] not meant to be known as such by others: *a secret drinker.* ■ fond of or good at keeping things about oneself unknown: *he can be the most secret man.* ■ (of information or documents) given the security classification above confidential and below top secret.
▶ n. something that is kept or meant to be kept unknown or unseen by others: *a state secret | at first I tried to **keep it a secret from** my wife.* ■ something that is not properly understood; a mystery: *I'm not trying to explain the secrets of the universe in this book.* ■ a valid but not commonly known or recognized method of achieving or maintaining something: *the secret of a happy marriage is compromise.* ■ formerly, the name of a prayer said by the priest in a low voice after the offertory in a Roman Catholic Mass.
– PHRASES **be in on the secret** be among the few people who know something. **in secret** without others knowing. **make no secret of something** make something perfectly clear.
– ORIGIN late Middle English: from Old French, from Latin *secretus* (adjective) 'separate, set apart,' from the verb *secernere*, from *se-* 'apart' + *cernere* 'sift.'

se·cret a·gent ▶ n. a spy acting for a country.

se·cre·ta·gogue /si'krētə,gôg, -,gäg/ ▶ n. Physiology a substance that promotes secretion.
– ORIGIN early 20th cent.: from SECRETE[1] + Greek *agōgos* 'leading.'

sec·re·taire /,sekri'te(ə)r/ ▶ n. a small writing desk; an escritoire.
– ORIGIN late 18th cent.: from French *secrétaire*, literally 'secretary.'

sec·re·tar·i·at /,sekri'te(ə)rēət/ ▶ n. a permanent administrative office or department, esp. a governmental one. ■ [treated as sing. or pl.] the staff working in such an office.
– ORIGIN early 19th cent.: from French *secrétariat*, from medieval Latin *secretariatus*, from *secretarius* (see SECRETARY).

sec·re·tar·y /'sekri,terē/ ▶ n. (pl. **secretaries**) a person employed by an individual or in an office to assist with correspondence, keep records, make appointments, and carry out similar tasks. ■ an official of a society or other organization who conducts its correspondence and keeps its records. ■ an official in charge of a government department: [as title] *Secretary of the Treasury.* ■ a writing desk with shelves on top of it.
– DERIVATIVES **sec·re·tar·i·al** /-'te(ə)rēəl/ adj., **sec·re·tar·y·ship** /-,SHip/ n.
– ORIGIN late Middle English (originally in the sense 'person entrusted with a secret'): from late Latin *secretarius* 'confidential officer,' from Latin *secretum* 'secret,' neuter of *secretus* (see SECRET).

sec·re·tar·y bird ▶ n. a slender, long-legged African bird of prey that feeds on snakes, having a crest likened to a quill pen stuck behind the ear. ● *Sagittarius serpentarius*, the only member of the family Sagittariidae.

sec·re·tar·y gen·er·al ▶ n. (pl. **secretaries general**) a title given to the principal administrator of some organizations, most notably the United Nations.

sec·re·tar·y of state ▶ n. **1** (in the US) the head of the State Department, responsible for foreign affairs.
2 (in the UK) the head of a major government department.
3 (in Canada) a government minister responsible for a specific area within a department.

se·cret bal·lot ▶ n. a ballot in which votes are cast in secret.

se·crete[1] /si'krēt/ ▶ v. [with obj.] (of a cell, gland, or organ) produce and discharge (a substance): *insulin is secreted in response to rising levels of glucose in the blood.*
– DERIVATIVES **se·cre·tor** /-tər/ n., **se·cre·to·ry** /-tərē/ adj.
– ORIGIN early 18th cent.: back-formation from SECRETION.

se·crete[2] ▶ v. [with obj.] conceal; hide: *the assets had been secreted in Swiss bank accounts.*
– ORIGIN mid 18th cent.: alteration of the obsolete verb *secret* 'keep secret.'

se·cre·tin /si'krētn/ ▶ n. Biochemistry a hormone released into the bloodstream by the duodenum (esp. in response to acidity) to stimulate secretion by the liver and pancreas.
– ORIGIN early 20th cent.: from SECRETION + -IN[1].

Se·cret In·tel·li·gence Serv·ice (abbr.: **SIS**) official name for **MI6**.

se·cre·tion /si'krēSHən/ ▶ n. a process by which substances are produced and discharged from a cell, gland, or organ for a particular function in the organism or for excretion. ■ a substance discharged in such a way.
– ORIGIN mid 17th cent.: from French *sécrétion* or Latin *secretio(n-)* 'separation,' from *secret-* 'moved apart,' from the verb *secernere*.

se·cre·tive /'sēkritiv/ ▶ adj. (of a person or an organization) inclined to conceal feelings and intentions or not to disclose information: *she was very secretive about her past.* ■ (of a state or activity) characterized by the concealment of intentions and information: *secretive deals.* ■ (of a person's expression or manner) having an enigmatic or conspiratorial quality: *a secretive smile.*
– DERIVATIVES **se·cre·tive·ly** adv., **se·cre·tive·ness** n.
– ORIGIN mid 19th cent.: back-formation from *secretiveness*, suggested by French *secrétivité*, from *secret* 'secret.'

se·cret·ly /'sēkritlē/ ▶ adv. in a secret way; without others knowing: *the two were secretly married in 1751 | I was embarrassed, but secretly pleased too.*

se·cret po·lice ▶ n. [treated as pl.] a police force working in secret against a government's political opponents.

se·cret sauce ▶ n. a special feature or technique kept secret by an organization and regarded as being the chief factor in its success.

se·cret serv·ice ▶ n. **1** a government department concerned with espionage.
2 (**Secret Service**) (in the US) a branch of the Treasury Department dealing with counterfeiting and providing protection for the president.

se·cret shop·per ▶ n. a person employed by a manufacturer or retailer to pose as a shopper in order to evaluate the quality of customer service. Also called MYSTERY SHOPPER.

se·cret so·ci·e·ty ▶ n. an organization whose members are sworn to secrecy about its activities.

sect /sekt/ ▶ n. a group of people with somewhat different religious beliefs (typically regarded as heretical) from those of a larger group to which they belong. ■ often derogatory a group that has separated from an established church; a nonconformist church. ■ a philosophical or political group, esp. one regarded as extreme or dangerous.
– ORIGIN Middle English: from Old French *secte* or Latin *secta*, literally 'following,' hence 'faction, party,' from the stem of *sequi* 'follow.'

sect. ▶ abbr. section.

sec·tar·i·an /sek'te(ə)rēən/ ▶ adj. denoting or concerning a sect or sects: *ethnic and sectarian differences.* ■ (of an action) carried out on the grounds of membership of a sect, denomination, or other group: *a sectarian attack.* ■ rigidly following the doctrines of a sect or other group.
▶ n. a member of a sect. ■ a person who rigidly follows the doctrines of a sect or other group.
– DERIVATIVES **sec·tar·i·an·ism** /-,nizəm/ n., **sec·tar·i·an·ize** /-,nīz/ v.
– ORIGIN mid 17th cent.: from SECTARY + -AN, reinforced by SECT.

sec·ta·ry /'sektərē/ ▶ n. (pl. **sectaries**) a member of a religious or political sect.
– ORIGIN mid 16th cent.: from modern Latin *sectarius* 'schismatic,' from medieval Latin *sectarius* 'adherent,' from Latin *secta* (see SECT).

sec·tion /'sekSHən/ ▶ n. **1** any of the more or less distinct parts into which something is or may be divided or from which it is made up: *arrange orange sections on a platter.* ■ a relatively distinct part of a book, newspaper, statute, or other document. ■ a measure of land, equal to one square mile. ■ a particular district of a town.
2 a distinct group within a larger body of people or things: *the children's section of the library.* ■ a group of players of a family of instruments within an orchestra: *the brass section.* ■ a small class of students who are part of a larger course but are taught separately: *graduate students lead discussion sections for professors' lecture courses.* ■ [in names] a specified military unit: *a camouflage section was added to the army.* ■ a subdivision of an army platoon. ■ Biology a secondary taxonomic category, esp. a subgenus.
3 the cutting of a solid by or along a plane. ■ the shape resulting from cutting a solid along a plane. ■ a representation of the internal structure of something as if it has been cut through vertically or horizontally. ■ Surgery a separation by cutting. ■ Biology a thin slice of plant or animal tissue prepared for microscopic examination.
▶ v. [with obj.] divide into sections: *she began to section the grapefruit.* ■ (**section something off**) separate an area from a larger one: *parts of the curved balcony had been sectioned off with wrought-iron grilles.* ■ Biology cut (animal or plant tissue) into thin slices for microscopic examination. ■ Surgery divide by cutting: *it is common veterinary practice to section the nerves to the hoof of a limping horse.*
– DERIVATIVES **sec·tioned** adj. [often in combination] *a square-sectioned iron peg.*
– ORIGIN late Middle English (as a noun): from French *section* or Latin *sectio(n-)*, from *secare* 'to cut.' The verb dates from the early 19th cent.

sec·tion·al /'sekSHənl/ ▶ adj. of or relating to a section or subdivision of a larger whole: *a sectional championship.* ■ of or relating to a section or group within a community: *the chairman of the commission looked on sectional interests as a danger to the common good.* ■ of or relating to a view of the structure of an object in section: *sectional drawings.* ■ made or supplied in sections: *sectional sills, made from more than one piece of timber.*
▶ n. a sofa made in sections that can be used separately as chairs.
– DERIVATIVES **sec·tion·al·ize** /-,īz/ v., **sec·tion·al·ly** adv.

sec·tion·al·ism /'sekSHənl,izəm/ ▶ n. restriction of interest to a narrow sphere; undue concern with local interests or petty distinctions at the expense of general well-being.
– DERIVATIVES **sec·tion·al·ist** n. & adj.

sec·tion gang ▶ n. a crew of railroad workers responsible for maintaining a particular section of track.

sec·tion hand ▶ n. a member of a section gang.

sec·tion mark ▶ n. the sign (§) used as a reference mark or to indicate a section of a book.

sec·tor /ˈsektər/ ▶ n. **1** an area or portion that is distinct from others. ■ a distinct part or branch of a nation's economy or society or of a sphere of activity such as education: *the industrial and commercial sector | the business sector of the city*. ■ Military a subdivision of an area for military operations. ■ Computing a subdivision of a track on a magnetic disk.
2 the plane figure enclosed by two radii of a circle or ellipse and the arc between them.
3 a mathematical instrument consisting of two arms hinged at one end and marked with sines, tangents, etc., for making diagrams.
– DERIVATIVES **sec·tor·al** /-rəl/ adj.
– ORIGIN late 16th cent. (in sense 2 and sense 3): from late Latin, a technical use of Latin *sector* 'cutter,' from *sect-* 'cut off,' from the verb *secare*.

sec·to·ri·al /sekˈtôrēəl/ ▶ adj. **1** of or like a sector: *sectorial boundaries*.
2 Zoology denoting a carnassial tooth, or a similar cutting tooth in mammals other than carnivores.

sec·u·lar /ˈsekyələr/ ▶ adj. **1** denoting attitudes, activities, or other things that have no religious or spiritual basis: *secular buildings | secular moral theory*. Contrasted with **SACRED**.
2 Christian Church (of clergy) not subject to or bound by religious rule; not belonging to or living in a monastic or other order. Contrasted with **REGULAR**.
3 Astronomy of or denoting slow changes in the motion of the sun or planets.
4 Economics (of a fluctuation or trend) occurring or persisting over an indefinitely long period: *there is evidence that the slump is not cyclical but secular*.
5 occurring once every century or similarly long period (used esp. in reference to celebratory games in ancient Rome).
▶ n. a secular priest.
– DERIVATIVES **sec·u·lar·ism** /-ˌrizəm/ n., **sec·u·lar·ist** /-rist/ n., **sec·u·lar·i·ty** /ˌsekyəˈlaritē/ n., **sec·u·lar·i·za·tion** /ˌsekyələrəˈzāsʜən/ n., **sec·u·lar·ize** /-ˌrīz/ v., **sec·u·lar·ly** adv.
– ORIGIN Middle English: sense 1 of the adjective and sense 2 of the adjective from Old French *seculer*, from Latin *saecularis*, from *saeculum* 'generation, age,' used in Christian Latin to mean 'the world' (as opposed to the Church); sense 3 of the adjective, sense 4 of the adjective, and sense 5 of the adjective (early 19th cent.) from Latin *saecularis* 'relating to an age or period.'

sec·u·lar arm ▶ n. (**the secular arm**) the legal authority of the civil power as invoked by the church to punish offenders.

sec·u·lar hu·man·ism ▶ n. humanism, with regard in particular to the belief that humanity is capable of morality and self-fulfillment without belief in God.
– DERIVATIVES **sec·u·lar hu·man·ist** n.

se·cund /ˈsēˌkənd, siˈkənd/ ▶ adj. Botany arranged on one side only (such as the flowers of lily of the valley).
– DERIVATIVES **se·cund·ly** adv.
– ORIGIN late 18th cent.: from Latin *secundus* (see **SECOND¹**).

se·cure /siˈkyo͝or/ ▶ adj. fixed or fastened so as not to give way, become loose, or be lost: *check to ensure that all nuts and bolts are secure*. ■ not subject to threat; certain to remain or continue safe and unharmed: *they are working to ensure that their market share remains secure against competition*. ■ protected against attack or other criminal activity: *the official said that no airport could be totally secure*. ■ (of a place of detention) having provisions against the escape of inmates: *a secure unit for youthful offenders*. ■ feeling safe, stable, and free from fear or anxiety: *everyone needs to have a home and to feel secure and wanted*. ■ [predic.] (**secure of**) dated feeling no doubts about attaining; certain to achieve: *she remained poised and complacent, secure of admiration*.
▶ v. [with obj.] fix or attach (something) firmly so that it cannot be moved or lost: *pins secure the handle to the main body*. ■ make (a door or container) hard to open; fasten or lock: *doors are likely to be well secured at night*. ■ protect against threats; make safe: *the government is concerned to secure the economy against too much foreign ownership*. ■ capture (a person or animal): *the suspect is secured and in the back of a patrol car*. ■ succeed in obtaining (something), esp. with difficulty: *the division secured a major contract*. ■ seek to guarantee repayment of (a loan) by having a right to take possession of an asset in the event of nonpayment: *a loan secured on your home*.
– DERIVATIVES **se·cur·a·ble** adj., **se·cure·ly** adv., **se·cure·ment** n.
– ORIGIN mid 16th cent. (in the sense 'feeling no apprehension'): from Latin *securus*, from *se-* 'without' + *cura* 'care.'

se·cure serv·er ▶ n. an Internet server that encrypts confidential information supplied by visitors to web pages, thus protecting the confidentiality.

Se·cu·ri·ta·te /siˌkyo͝oriˈtätā/ the internal security force of Romania, set up in 1948 and officially disbanded during the revolution of December 1989.
– ORIGIN Romanian, 'Security.'

se·cu·ri·tize /səˈkyo͝oriˌtīz/ ▶ v. [with obj.] (often as adj. **securitized**) convert (an asset, esp. a loan) into marketable securities, typically for the purpose of raising cash by selling them to other investors: *the use of securitized debt as a major source of corporate finance*.
– DERIVATIVES **se·cu·ri·ti·za·tion** /-itəˈzāsʜən/ n.

se·cu·ri·ty /siˈkyo͝oritē/ ▶ n. (pl. **securities**) **1** the state of being free from danger or threat: *the system is designed to provide maximum security against toxic spills | job security*. ■ the safety of a state or organization against criminal activity such as terrorism, theft, or espionage: *a matter of national security*. ■ procedures followed or measures taken to ensure such safety: *amid tight security the presidents met in the Colombian resort*. ■ the state of feeling safe, stable, and free from fear or anxiety: *this man could give the emotional security she needed*.
2 a private police force that guards a building, campus, park, etc.
3 a thing deposited or pledged as a guarantee of the fulfillment of an undertaking or the repayment of a loan, to be forfeited in case of default.
4 (often **securities**) a certificate attesting credit, the ownership of stocks or bonds, or the right to ownership connected with tradable derivatives.
– PHRASES **on security of something** using something as a guarantee.
– ORIGIN late Middle English: from Old French *securite* or Latin *securitas*, from *securus* 'free from care' (see **SECURE**).

se·cu·ri·ty blan·ket ▶ n. a blanket or other familiar object that is a comfort to someone, typically a child.

se·cu·ri·ty check ▶ n. a verification of the identity and trustworthiness of someone such as a government employee, in order to maintain security. ■ a search of an area or of a person and their baggage for concealed weapons or bombs.

Se·cu·ri·ty Coun·cil a permanent body of the United Nations seeking to maintain peace and security. It consists of fifteen members, of which five (China, France, Russia, the UK, and the US) are permanent and have the power of veto. The other members are elected for two-year terms.

se·cu·ri·ty guard ▶ n. a person employed to protect something, esp. a building, against intruders or damage.

se·cu·ri·ty patch ▶ n. a software or operating-system patch that is intended to correct a vulnerability to hacking or viral infection: *an e-mail purporting to be a security patch from Microsoft support*.

se·cu·ri·ty risk ▶ n. a person or situation that poses a possible threat to the security of something.

Se·cu·ri·ty Serv·ice official name for **MI5**.

secy. (also **sec'y**) ▶ abbr. secretary.

sed. ▶ abbr. ■ sediment. ■ sedimentation.

se·dan /siˈdan/ ▶ n. **1** (also **sedan chair**) chiefly historical an enclosed chair for conveying one person, carried between horizontal poles by two or more porters.
2 an enclosed automobile for four or more people, having two or four doors.
– ORIGIN perhaps an alteration of an Italian dialect word, based on Latin *sella* 'saddle,' from *sedere* 'sit.'

sedan chair

Se·dan, Bat·tle of a battle fought in 1870 near the town of Sedan in northeastern France, in which the Prussian army defeated a smaller French army under Napoleon III, opening the way for a Prussian advance on Paris and marking the end of the French Second Empire.

se·date¹ /siˈdāt/ ▶ adj. calm, dignified, and unhurried: *in the old days, business was carried on at a rather more sedate pace*. ■ quiet and rather dull: *sedate suburban domesticity*.
– DERIVATIVES **se·date·ly** adv., **se·date·ness** n.
– ORIGIN late Middle English (originally as a medical term meaning 'not sore or painful,' also 'calm, tranquil'): from Latin *sedatus*, past participle of *sedare* 'settle,' from *sedere* 'sit.'

se·date² ▶ v. [with obj.] calm (someone) or make them sleep by administering a sedative drug: *she was heavily sedated*.
– ORIGIN 1960s: back-formation from **SEDATION**.

se·da·tion /siˈdāsʜən/ ▶ n. the administering of a sedative drug to produce a state of calm or sleep: *he was distraught with grief and under sedation*.
– ORIGIN mid 16th cent.: from French *sédation* or Latin *sedatio(n-)*, from *sedare* 'settle' (see **SEDATE¹**).

sed·a·tive /ˈsedətiv/ ▶ adj. promoting calm or inducing sleep: *the seeds have a sedative effect*.
▶ n. a drug taken for its calming or sleep-inducing effect.
– ORIGIN late Middle English: from Old French *sedatif* or medieval Latin *sedativus*, from Latin *sedat-* 'settled,' from the verb *sedare* (see **SEDATE¹**).

sed·en·tar·y /ˈsednˌterē/ ▶ adj. (of a person) tending to spend much time seated; somewhat inactive. ■ (of work or a way of life) characterized by much sitting and little physical exercise. ■ (of a position) sitting; seated. ■ Zoology & Anthropology inhabiting the same locality throughout life; not migratory or nomadic. ■ Zoology (of an animal) sessile.
– DERIVATIVES **sed·en·tar·i·ly** /-ˌte(ə)rəlē/ adv., **sed·en·tar·i·ness** n.
– ORIGIN late 16th cent. (in the sense 'not migratory'): from French *sédentaire* or Latin *sedentarius*, from *sedere* 'sit.'

Se·der /ˈsādər/ ▶ n. a Jewish ritual service and ceremonial dinner for the first night or first two nights of Passover.
– ORIGIN from Hebrew *sēḏer* 'order, procedure.'

sedge /sej/ ▶ n. a grasslike plant with triangular stems and inconspicuous flowers, growing typically in wet ground. Sedges are widely distributed throughout temperate and cold regions. ● Family Cyperaceae: *Carex* and other genera.
– DERIVATIVES **sedg·y** /ˈsejē/ adj.
– ORIGIN Old English *secg*, of Germanic origin, from an Indo-European root shared by Latin *secare* 'to cut.'

Sedge·moor, Bat·tle of a battle fought in 1685 on the plain of Sedgemoor in Somerset, England. The forces of the rebel Duke of Monmouth, who had landed in Dorset as champion of the Protestant cause and pretender to the throne, were decisively defeated by James II's troops.

sedge war·bler ▶ n. a common migratory Eurasian songbird with streaky brown plumage, frequenting marshes and reed beds. ● *Acrocephalus schoenobaenus*, family Sylviidae.

Sedg·wick /ˈsejwik/, Adam (1785–1873), English geologist. He specialized in the fossil record of rocks from North Wales, assigning the oldest of these to a period that he named the Cambrian.

se·dil·i·a /səˈdilēə/ ▶ plural n. (sing. **sedile** /-ˈdīlē/) a group of stone seats for clergy in the south chancel wall of a church, usually three in number and often canopied and decorated.
– ORIGIN late 18th cent.: from Latin, 'seat,' from *sedere* 'sit.'

sed·i·ment /ˈsedəmənt/ ▶ n. matter that settles to the bottom of a liquid; dregs. ■ Geology particulate matter that is carried by water or wind and deposited on the surface of the land or the bottom of a body of water, and may in time become consolidated into rock.
▶ v. [no obj.] settle as sediment. ■ (of a liquid) deposit a sediment. ■ [with obj.] deposit (something) as a sediment: *the DNA was sedimented by centrifugation* | (as adj. **sedimented**) *sedimented waste*.
– DERIVATIVES **sed·i·men·ta·tion** /ˌsedəmənˈtāsʜən/ n.
– ORIGIN mid 16th cent.: from French *sédiment* or Latin *sedimentum* 'settling,' from *sedere* 'sit.'

sed·i·men·ta·ry /ˌsedəˈmentərē/ ▶ adj. of or relating to sediment. ■ Geology (of rock) that has formed from sediment deposited by water or air.

sed·i·men·ta·tion co·ef·fi·cient /ˌsedəmənˈtāsʜən/ (also **sedimentation constant**) ▶ n. Biochemistry a quantity related to the size of a microscopic particle, equal to the terminal outward velocity of the particle when centrifuged in a fluid medium divided by the centrifugal force acting on it, expressed in units of time.

S

se·di·tion /si'disHən/ ▶ **n.** conduct or speech inciting people to rebel against the authority of a state or monarch.
– ORIGIN late Middle English (in the sense 'violent strife'): from Old French, or from Latin *seditio(n-)*, from *sed-* 'apart' + *itio(n-)* 'going' (from the verb *ire*).

se·di·tious /si'disHəs/ ▶ **adj.** inciting or causing people to rebel against the authority of a state or monarch: *the letter was declared seditious.*
– DERIVATIVES **se·di·tious·ly adv.**
– ORIGIN late Middle English: from Old French *seditieux* or Latin *seditiosus*, from *seditio* 'mutinous separation' (see SEDITION).

se·di·tious li·bel ▶ **n.** Law a published statement that is seditious. ■ the action or crime of publishing such a statement.

Sed·na /'sednə/ Astronomy a reddish celestial body about half the size of earth's moon. It is the most distant known object in the solar system and orbits the sun every 10,500 years.

Se·do·na /si'dōnə/ a resort city in north central Arizona, a popular New Age center; pop. 11,599 (est. 2008).

se·duce /si'd(y)o͞os/ ▶ **v.** [with obj.] attract (someone) to a belief or into a course of action that is inadvisable or foolhardy: *they should not be seduced into thinking that their success ruled out the possibility of a relapse.* ■ entice into sexual activity. ■ attract powerfully: *the melody seduces the ear with warm string tones.*
– DERIVATIVES **se·duc·er n., se·duc·i·ble adj.**
– ORIGIN late 15th cent. (originally in the sense 'persuade (someone) to abandon their duty'): from Latin *seducere*, from *se-* 'away, apart' + *ducere* 'to lead.'

se·duc·tion /si'dəksHən/ ▶ **n.** the action of seducing someone: *if seduction doesn't work, she can play on his sympathy* | *she was planning a seduction.* ■ (often **seductions**) a tempting or attractive thing: *the seductions of the mainland.*
– ORIGIN early 16th cent.: from French *séduction* or Latin *seductio(n-)*, from *seducere* 'draw aside' (see SEDUCE).

se·duc·tive /si'dəktiv/ ▶ **adj.** tempting and attractive; enticing: *a seductive voice.*
– DERIVATIVES **se·duc·tive·ly adv., se·duc·tive·ness n.**
– ORIGIN mid 18th cent.: from SEDUCTION, on the pattern of pairs such as *induction, inductive.*

se·duc·tress /si'dəktris/ ▶ **n.** a woman who seduces someone, esp. one who entices a man into sexual activity.
– ORIGIN early 19th cent.: from obsolete *seductor* 'male seducer,' from *seducere* (see SEDUCE).

sed·u·lous /'sejələs/ ▶ **adj.** (of a person or action) showing dedication and diligence: *he watched himself with the most sedulous care.*
– DERIVATIVES **se·du·li·ty** /sə'jo͞olitē/ **n., sed·u·lous·ly adv., sed·u·lous·ness n.**
– ORIGIN mid 16th cent.: from Latin *sedulus* 'zealous' + **-ous**.

se·dum /'sēdəm/ ▶ **n.** a widely distributed fleshy-leaved plant with small star-shaped yellow, pink, or white flowers, grown as an ornamental.
● Genus *Sedum*, family Crassulaceae: many species, including the stonecrops.
– ORIGIN from modern Latin, denoting a houseleek.

see[1] /sē/ ▶ **v.** (**sees, seeing**; past **saw**; past participle **seen**) [with obj.] **1** perceive with the eyes; discern visually: *in the distance she could see the blue sea* | [no obj.] *Andrew couldn't see out of his left eye* | figurative *I can't see into the future.* ■ [with clause] be or become aware of something from observation or from a written or other visual source: *I see from your appraisal report that you have asked for training.* ■ be a spectator of (a film, game, or other entertainment); watch: *I went to see King Lear at the Old Vic.* ■ visit (a place) for the first time: *see Alaska in style.* ■ [in imperative] refer to (a specified source) for further information (used as a direction in a text): *elements are usually classified as metals or non-metals (see chapter 11).* ■ experience or witness (an event or situation): *I shall not live to see it* | [with obj. and complement] *I can't bear to see you so unhappy.* ■ be the time or setting of (something): *the 1970s saw the beginning of a technological revolution.* ■ observe without being able to affect: *they see their rights being taken away.* ■ (**see something in**) find good or attractive qualities in (someone): *I don't know what I see in you.*
2 discern or deduce mentally after reflection or from information; understand: *I can't see any other way to treat it* | [with clause] *I saw that perhaps he was right* | *she could see what Rhoda meant.* ■ [with clause] ascertain after inquiring, considering, or discovering an outcome: *I'll go along to the club and see if I can get a game.* ■ [with obj. and adverbial] regard in a specified way: *he saw himself as a good teacher* | *you and I see things differently.* ■ foresee; view or predict as a possibility: *I can't see him earning any more anywhere else.* ■ used to ascertain or express comprehension, agreement, or continued attention, or to emphasize that an earlier prediction was correct: *it has to be the answer, don't you see?* | *see, I told you I'd come.*
3 meet (someone one knows) socially or by chance: *I went to see Caroline* | *I saw Colin last night.* ■ meet regularly as a boyfriend or girlfriend: *some guy she was seeing was messing her around.* ■ consult (a specialist or professional): *you may need to see a solicitor.* ■ give an interview or consultation to: *the doctor will see you now.*
4 [with obj. and adverbial of direction] escort or conduct (someone) to a specified place: *don't bother seeing me out.* ■ [no obj.] (**see to**) attend to; provide for the wants of: *I'll see to Dad's tea.* ■ [no obj.] ensure: *Lucy saw to it that everyone got enough to eat* | [with clause] *see that no harm comes to him.*
5 (in poker or brag) equal the bet of (an opponent).
– PHRASES **as far as I can see** to the best of my understanding or belief. **as I see it** in my opinion. **be seeing things** see THING. **(I'll) be seeing you** another way of saying SEE YOU. **have seen better days** have declined from former prosperity or good condition: *this part of South London has seen better days.* **have seen it all before** be very worldly or very familiar with a particular situation. **let me see** said as an appeal for time to think before speaking: *Let me see, how old is he now?* **see a man about a dog** humorous said euphemistically when leaving to go to the toilet or keep an undisclosed appointment. **see eye to eye, see fit** see EYE, FIT[1], etc. **see here!** said to give emphasis to a statement or command or to express a protest: *now see here, you're going to get it back for me!* **see one's way clear to do** (or **doing**) **something** find that it is possible or convenient to do something (often used in polite requests). **see someone coming** recognize a person who can be fooled or deceived. **see something coming** foresee or be prepared for an event, typically an unpleasant one. **see someone damned first** Brit. informal said when refusing categorically and with hostility to do what a person wants. **see someone right** Brit. informal make sure that a person is appropriately rewarded or looked after. **see sense** (or **reason**) realize that one is wrong and start acting sensibly. **see the back of** Brit. informal be rid of (an unwanted person or thing): *we were always glad to see the back of her.* **see you** (**later**) informal said when parting from someone. **we'll see about that** said when angrily contradicting or challenging a claim or assertion: *Oh, you think it's funny, do you? We'll see about that!*
– PHRASAL VERBS **see about** attend to; deal with: *he had gone to see about a job he had heard of.* **see after** take care of; look after. **see something of** spend a specified amount of time with (someone) socially: *we saw a lot of the Bakers.* ■ spend some time in (a place): *I want to see something of those countries.* **see someone off 1** accompany a person who is leaving to their point of departure: *they came to the station to see him off.* **2** Brit. repel an invader or intruder: *the dogs saw them off in no time.* ■ informal deal with the threat posed by; get the better of: *they saw off Cambridge in the FA Cup.* **see someone out** Brit. (of an article) last longer than the remainder of someone's life: *no point in fixing the gate, it'll see me out.* **see something out** Brit. come to the end of a period of time or undertaking: *I could well see out my career in Italy.* **see over** Brit. tour and examine (a building or site): *Bridget asked if he'd like to see over the house.* **see through** not be deceived by; detect the true nature of: *he can see through her lies and deceptions.* **see someone through** support a person for the duration of a difficult time. **see something through** persist with an undertaking until it is completed.
– DERIVATIVES **seeable adj.**
– ORIGIN Old English *sēon*, of Germanic origin; related to Dutch *zien* and German *sehen*, perhaps from an Indo-European root shared by Latin *sequi* 'follow.'

see[2] ▶ **n.** the place in which a cathedral church stands, identified as the seat of authority of a bishop or archbishop.
– ORIGIN Middle English: from Anglo-Norman French *sed*, from Latin *sedes* 'seat,' from *sedere* 'sit.'

seed /sēd/ ▶ **n. 1** a flowering plant's unit of reproduction, capable of developing into another such plant. ■ a quantity of these: *grass seed* | *you can grow artichokes from seed.* ■ the cause or latent beginning of a feeling, process, or condition: *the conversation sowed a tiny seed of doubt in his mind.* ■ archaic (chiefly in biblical use) a person's offspring or descendants. ■ a man's semen. ■ (also **seed crystal**) a small crystal introduced into a liquid to act as a nucleus for crystallization. ■ a small container for radioactive material placed in body tissue during radiotherapy.
2 any of a number of stronger competitors in a sports tournament who have been assigned a specified position in an ordered list with the aim of ensuring that they do not play each other in the early rounds: *he knocked the top seed out of the championships.*
▶ **v. 1** [with obj.] sow (land) with seeds: *the shoreline is seeded with a special grass.* ■ sow (a particular kind of seed) on or in the ground. ■ cause (something) to begin to develop or grow: *severance payouts that help seed their new businesses.* ■ place a crystal or crystalline substance in (something) in order to cause crystallization or condensation (esp. in a cloud to produce rain).
2 [no obj.] (of a plant) produce or drop seeds: *mulches encourage many plants to seed freely.* ■ (**seed itself**) (of a plant) reproduce itself by means of its own seeds: *feverfew will seed itself readily.*
3 [with obj.] remove the seeds from (vegetables or fruit): *stem and seed the chilies.*
4 [with obj.] give (a competitor) the status of seed in a tournament: [with complement] *Jeff Tarango, seeded five, was defeated by fellow American Todd Witsken.*
– PHRASES **go** (or **run**) **to seed** (of a plant) cease flowering as the seeds develop. ■ deteriorate in condition, strength, or efficiency: *Mark knows he has allowed himself to go to seed.*
– ORIGIN Old English *sǣd*, of Germanic origin; related to Dutch *zaad*, German *Saat*, also to the verb SOW[1].

seed·bed /'sēd,bed/ ▶ **n.** a bed of fine soil in which seedlings are germinated.

seed cake ▶ **n.** cake containing caraway seeds as flavoring.

seed cap·i·tal ▶ **n.** see SEED MONEY.

seed coat ▶ **n.** Botany the protective outer coat of a seed.

seed corn ▶ **n.** good-quality corn kept for seed.

seed·eat·er /'sēd,ētər/ ▶ **n.** a finch or related songbird that feeds mainly on seeds, in particular: ● a small American bunting (genus *Sporophila*, subfamily Emberizinae, family Emberizidae). ● an African finch related to the canary (genus *Serinus*, family Fringillidae).

seed·ed /'sēdid/ ▶ **adj. 1** [in combination] (of a plant or fruit) having a seed or seeds of a specified kind or number: *a single-seeded fruit.* ■ (of land or an area of ground) having been sown with seed: *seeded lawns.* ■ Heraldry (of a flower) having seeds of a specified tincture.
2 (of a fruit or vegetable) having had the seeds removed: *seeded, chopped tomatoes.*
3 given the status of seed in a sports tournament: *Italy is one of the eight seeded teams.*

seed·er /'sēdər/ ▶ **n. 1** a machine for sowing seed mechanically.
2 a plant that produces seeds in a particular way or under particular conditions: [in combination] *a beautiful, hardy annual self-seeder.*

seed fern ▶ **n.** another term for PTERIDOSPERM.

seed head ▶ **n.** a flower head in seed.

seed leaf ▶ **n.** Botany a cotyledon.

seed·less /'sēdlis/ ▶ **adj.** denoting a fruit that has no seeds: *seedless grapes.*

seed·ling /'sēdliNG/ ▶ **n.** a young plant, esp. one raised from seed and not from a cutting.

seed-lip ▶ **n.** chiefly historical a basket for holding seed, used when sowing by hand.

seed mon·ey ▶ **n.** money allocated to initiate a project.

seed pearl ▶ **n.** a very small pearl.

seed·pod /'sēd,päd/ ▶ **n.** see POD[1] (sense 1 of the noun).

seed po·ta·to ▶ **n.** a potato that is planted and used for the production of seeds.

seeds·man /'sēdzmən/ ▶ **n.** (pl. **seedsmen**) a person who deals in seeds as a profession.

seed-snipe ▶ **n.** a South American bird resembling a small partridge, with mainly brown plumage.
● Family Thinocoridae: two genera and four species.

seed time ▶ **n.** the sowing season.

seed·y /'sēdē/ ▶ **adj.** (**seedier, seediest**) **1** sordid and disreputable: *his seedy affair with a soft-porn starlet.* ■ shabby and squalid: *an increasingly seedy and dilapidated property.*
2 dated unwell: *she felt weak and seedy.*
– DERIVATIVES **seed·i·ly** /'sēdl-ē/ **adv., seed·i·ness n.**

See·ger /'sēgər/, Pete (1919–), US folk musician and songwriter. A prominent figure in the revival of American folk music, he is also noted for his environmental activism, esp. in projects to reclaim the Hudson River. Notable songs: "If I Had a Hammer" (*c.*1949) and "Where Have All the Flowers Gone?" (1956).

see·ing /ˈsē-iNG/ ▶ **conj.** because; since: *seeing as Stuart's an old friend, I thought I might help him out.* ▶ **n.** the action of seeing someone or something. ■ Astronomy the quality of observed images as determined by atmospheric conditions.
– PHRASES **seeing is believing** proverb you need to see something before you can accept that it really exists or occurs.

See·ing Eye dog ▶ **n.** trademark a guide dog trained to lead a blind person.

seek /sēk/ ▶ **v.** (past and past participle **sought** /sôt/) [with obj.] attempt to find (something): *they came here to seek shelter from biting winter winds.* ■ attempt or desire to obtain or achieve (something): *the new regime sought his extradition* | [no obj., with infinitive] *her parents had never sought to interfere with her freedom.* ■ ask for (something) from someone: *he sought help from the police.* ■ (**seek someone/something out**) search for and find someone or something: *it's his job to seek out new customers.* ■ archaic go to (a place): *I sought my bedroom each night to brood over it.*
– PHRASES **seek one's fortune** travel somewhere in the hope of achieving wealth and success. **to seek** archaic lacking; not yet found: *the end she knew, the means were to seek.* ■ (**far to seek**) out of reach; a long way off.
– DERIVATIVES **seek·er n.** [often in combination] *a pleasure-seeker | a job-seeker.*
– ORIGIN Old English *sēcan*, of Germanic origin; related to Dutch *zieken* and German *suchen*, from an Indo-European root shared by Latin *sagire* 'perceive by scent.'

seek time ▶ **n.** Computing the time taken for a disk drive to locate the area on the disk where the data to be read is stored.

seel /sēl/ ▶ **v.** [with obj.] archaic close (a person's eyes); prevent (someone) from seeing: *the wise Gods seel our eyes in our own filth.*
– ORIGIN late 15th cent. (originally a term in falconry meaning 'stitch shut the eyelids of (a hawk)'): from French *ciller*, or medieval Latin *ciliare*, from Latin *cilium* 'eyelid.'

seem /sēm/ ▶ **v.** [no obj.] give the impression or sensation of being something or having a particular quality: [with complement] *Dawn seemed annoyed* | [with infinitive] *there seems to be plenty to eat* | [with clause] *it seemed that he was determined to oppose her.* ■ [with infinitive] used to make a statement or description of one's thoughts, feelings, or actions less assertive or forceful: *I seem to remember giving you very precise instructions.* ■ (**cannot seem to do something**) be unable to do something, despite having tried: *he couldn't seem to remember his lines.* ■ [with clause] (**it seems** or **it would seem**) used to suggest in a cautious, guarded, or polite way that something is true or a fact: *it would seem that he has been fooling us all.*
– ORIGIN Middle English (also in the sense 'suit, befit, be appropriate'): from Old Norse *sœma* 'to honor,' from *sœmr* 'fitting.'

seem·ing /ˈsēmiNG/ ▶ **adj.** appearing to be real or true, but not necessarily being so; apparent: *Ellen's seeming indifference to the woman's fate.* ■ [in combination] giving the impression of having a specified quality: *an angry-seeming man.* ▶ **n.** literary the outward appearance or aspect of someone or something, esp. when considered as deceptive or as distinguished from reality: *that dissidence between inward reality and outward seeming.*

seem·ing·ly /ˈsēmiNGlē/ ▶ **adv.** so as to give the impression of having a certain quality; apparently: *a seemingly competent and well-organized person.* ■ [sentence adverb] according to the facts as one knows them; as far as one knows: *it's touch and go, seemingly, and she's asking for you.*

seem·ly /ˈsēmlē/ ▶ **adj.** conforming to accepted notions of propriety or good taste; decorous: *I felt it was not seemly to observe too closely.*
– DERIVATIVES **seem·li·ness n.**
– ORIGIN Middle English: from Old Norse *sœmiligr*, from *sœmr* 'fitting' (see **SEEM**).

seen /sēn/ past participle of **SEE**[1].

See of Rome ▶ **n.** another term for **HOLY SEE**.

seep /sēp/ ▶ **v.** [no obj.] (of a liquid) flow or leak slowly through porous material or small holes: *water began to seep through the soles of his boots.* ▶ **n.** a place where petroleum or water oozes slowly out of the ground.
– ORIGIN late 18th cent.: perhaps a dialect form of Old English *sīpian* 'to soak.'

seep·age /ˈsēpij/ ▶ **n.** the slow escape of a liquid or gas through porous material or small holes. ■ the quantity of liquid or gas that seeps out.

seer[1] /ˈsēər, si(ə)r/ ▶ **n. 1** a person who is supposed to be able, through supernatural insight, to see what the future holds. ■ an expert who provides forecasts of the economic or political future: *our seers have grown gloomier about prospects for growth.*
2 [usu. in combination] chiefly archaic a person who sees something specified: *a seer of the future | ghost-seers.*
– ORIGIN Middle English: from **SEE**[1] + **-ER**[1].

seer[2] /si(ə)r/ ▶ **n.** (in South Asia) a varying unit of weight (about one kilogram) or liquid measure (about one liter).
– ORIGIN from Hindi *ser.*

seer·suck·er /ˈsi(ə)r,səkər/ ▶ **n.** a printed cotton or synthetic fabric that has a surface consisting of puckered and flat sections, typically in a striped pattern.
– ORIGIN early 18th cent.: from Persian *šir o šakar*, literally 'milk and sugar,' (by transference) 'striped cotton garment.'

see·saw /ˈsē,sô/ ▶ **n.** a long plank balanced in the middle on a fixed support, on each end of which children sit and swing up and down by pushing the ground alternately with their feet. ■ a situation characterized by rapid, repeated changes from one state or condition to another: *the emotional seesaw of a first love affair* | [as modifier] *seesaw interest rates.* ▶ **v.** [no obj.] change rapidly and repeatedly from one position, situation, or condition to another and back again: *the market seesawed as rumors spread of an imminent cabinet reshuffle.* ■ [with obj.] cause (something) to move back and forth or up and down rapidly and repeatedly: *Sybil seesawed the car back and forth.*
– ORIGIN mid 17th cent. (originally used by sawyers as a rhythmical refrain): reduplication of the verb **SAW**[1] (symbolic of the sawing motion).

seethe /sēTH/ ▶ **v.** [no obj.] (of a liquid) bubble up as a result of being boiled: *the brew foamed and seethed.* ■ [with obj.] archaic cook (food) by boiling it in a liquid: *others were cut into joints and seethed in cauldrons made of the animal's own skins.* ■ (of a person) be filled with intense but unexpressed anger: *inwardly he was seething at the slight to his authority.* ■ (of a place) be crowded with people or things moving about in a rapid or hectic way: *the entire cellar was seething with spiders | the village seethed with life.* ■ [with adverbial of direction] (of a crowd of people) move in a rapid or hectic way: *we cascaded down the stairs and seethed across the station* | (as adj. **seething**) *the seething mass of commuters.*
– ORIGIN Old English *sēothan* 'make or keep boiling,' of Germanic origin; related to Dutch *zieden.*

see-through ▶ **adj.** (esp. of clothing) translucent: *this shirt's a bit see-through when it's wet.*

Se·fer /ˈsāfər, ˈsefer/ ▶ **n.** (pl. **Sifrei** /ˈsifrā, siˈfrā/) Judaism a book of Hebrew religious literature. ■ (usu. **Sefer Torah**) a scroll containing the Torah or Pentateuch.
– ORIGIN from Hebrew *sēper tōrāh* 'book of (the) Law.'

seg·ment ▶ **n.** /ˈsegmənt/ **1** each of the parts into which something is or may be divided. ■ a portion of time allocated to a particular broadcast item on radio or television. ■ a separate broadcast item, typically one of a number that make up a particular program. ■ Phonetics the smallest distinct part of a spoken utterance, in particular the vowels and consonants as opposed to stress and intonation. ■ Zoology each of the series of similar anatomical units of which the body and appendages of some animals are composed, such as the visible rings of an earthworm's body.
2 Geometry a part of a figure cut off by a line or plane intersecting it, in particular: ■ the part of a circle enclosed between an arc and a chord. ■ the part of a line included between two points. ■ the part of a sphere cut off by any plane not passing through the center.
▶ **v.** /ˈseg,ment, segˈment/ [with obj.] divide (something) into separate parts or sections: *the unemployed are segmented into two groups.* ■ [no obj.] divide into separate parts or sections: *the market is beginning to segment into a number of well-defined categories.* ■ [no obj.] Embryology (of a cell) undergo cleavage; divide into many cells.
– DERIVATIVES **seg·men·tar·y** /-,terē/ **adj.**, **seg·men·ta·tion** /,segmənˈtāSHən/ **n.**
– ORIGIN late 16th cent. (as a term in geometry): from Latin *segmentum*, from *secare* 'to cut.' The verb dates from the mid 19th cent.

seg·men·tal /segˈmen(t)l/ ▶ **adj. 1** composed of separate parts or sections. ■ Phonetics denoting or relating to the division of speech into segments.
2 Architecture denoting or of the form of an arch the curved part of which forms a shallow arc of a circle, less than a semicircle.
– DERIVATIVES **seg·men·tal·i·za·tion** /-,men(t)liˈzāSHən/ **n.**, **seg·men·tal·ize** /-,īz/ **v.**, **seg·men·tal·ly adv.**

seg·men·ta·tion cav·i·ty ▶ **n.** another term for **BLASTOCOEL**.

seg·men·ted /ˈseg,men(t)id/ ▶ **adj.** consisting of or divided into segments: *segmented labor markets.* ■ Zoology (of an animal's body or appendage) formed of a longitudinal series of similar parts.

se·go /ˈsēgō/ (in full **sego lily**) ▶ **n.** (pl. **segos**) a plant of the lily family, with green and white bell-shaped flowers, native to the western US. Closely related to the **MARIPOSA LILY**. ● *Calochortus nuttalli*, family Liliaceae.
– ORIGIN mid 19th cent. Western Shoshone *sikoo.*

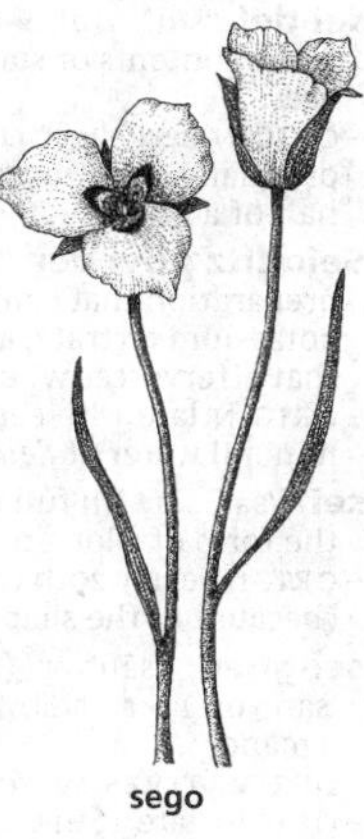
sego

Se·go·vi·a /siˈgōvēə/, Andrés (1893–1987), Spanish guitarist and composer. Largely responsible for the revival of the classical guitar, he elevated its status to that of concert instrument and made a large number of transcriptions of classical music to increase the repertoire of the instrument.

seg·re·gate[1] /ˈsegri,gāt/ ▶ **v.** [with obj.] (usu. **be segregated**) set apart from the rest or from each other; isolate or divide: *hazardous waste needs to be segregated from ordinary trash.* ■ separate or divide (people, activities, or institutions) along racial, sexual, or religious lines: *blacks were segregated in churches, schools, and colleges* | (as adj. **segregated**) *segregated education systems.* ■ [no obj.] Genetics (of pairs of alleles) be separated at meiosis and transmitted independently via separate gametes.
– DERIVATIVES **seg·re·ga·ble** /-gəbəl/ **adj.**, **seg·re·ga·tive** /-,gātiv/ **adj.**
– ORIGIN mid 16th cent.: from Latin *segregat-* 'separated from the flock,' from the verb *segregare*, from *se-* 'apart' + *grex, greg-* 'flock.'

seg·re·gate[2] /ˈsegrəgit, -,gāt/ ▶ **n. 1** Genetics an allele that has undergone segregation.
2 Botany a species within an aggregate.
– ORIGIN late 19th cent.: from Latin *segregatus* 'separate, isolated,' past participle of *segregare* (see **SEGREGATE**[1]).

seg·re·ga·tion /,segriˈgāSHən/ ▶ **n.** the action or state of setting someone or something apart from other people or things or being set apart: *the segregation of pupils with learning difficulties.* ■ the enforced separation of different racial groups in a country, community, or establishment: *an official policy of racial segregation.* ■ Genetics the separation of pairs of alleles at meiosis and their independent transmission via separate gametes.
– DERIVATIVES **seg·re·ga·tion·al** /-SHənl/ **adj.**, **seg·re·ga·tion·ist** /-ist/ **adj. & n.**

se·gue /ˈsegwā, ˈsā-/ ▶ **v.** (**segues, segueing** /ˈsegwā-iNG, ˈsā-/, **segued** /ˈsegwād, ˈsā-/) [no obj.] (in music and film) move without interruption from one song, melody, or scene to another: *allowing one song to segue into the next.*
▶ **n.** an uninterrupted transition from one piece of music or film scene to another.
– ORIGIN Italian, literally 'follows.'

se·gui·dil·la /,segēˈdēə/ ▶ **n.** a Spanish dance in triple time.
– ORIGIN mid 18th cent.: Spanish, from *seguida* 'sequence,' from *seguir* 'follow.'

Se·gur·i·dad /sə,go͝oriˈdäd/ ▶ **n.** the Spanish security service.
– ORIGIN Spanish, literally 'Security.'

Seg·way /ˈseg,wā/ ▶ **n.** trademark a two-wheeled motorized personal vehicle consisting of a platform for the feet mounted above an axle and an upright post surmounted by handles.
– ORIGIN an invented word based on *segue.*

Sehn·sucht /ˈzān,zo͞oKHt/ ▶ **n.** literary yearning; wistful longing.
– ORIGIN German.

sei /sā/ ▶ **n.** another term for **SEI WHALE**.

sei·cen·to /sāˈCHen,tō/ ▶ **n.** [often as modifier] the style of Italian art and literature of the 17th century: *Florentine seicento painting.*
– DERIVATIVES **sei·cen·tist** /-tist/ **n.**
– ORIGIN Italian, '600,' shortened from *mille seicento* '1600,' used with reference to the years 1600–99.

seiche /sāSH/ ▶ **n.** a temporary disturbance or oscillation in the water level of a lake or partially

S

enclosed body of water, esp. one caused by changes in atmospheric pressure.
– ORIGIN mid 19th cent.: from Swiss French, perhaps from German *Seiche* 'sinking (of water).'

sei·del /'sīdl, 'zīdl/ ▶ **n.** dated a beer mug or glass. ■ the contents of such a vessel: *I drank a seidel of beer.*
– ORIGIN early 20th cent.: from German *Seidel*, originally denoting a measure between a third and a half of a liter.

Seid·litz pow·der /'sedlits/ ▶ **n.** a laxative preparation that contains tartaric acid, sodium potassium tartrate, and sodium bicarbonate, and that effervesces when mixed with water.
– ORIGIN late 18th cent.: named with reference to the mineral water of *Seidlitz*, a village in Bohemia.

seif /sāf, sēf/ (in full **seif dune**) ▶ **n.** a sand dune in the form of a long narrow ridge.
– ORIGIN early 20th cent.: from Arabic *sayf* 'sword' (because of the shape).

sei·gneur /sān'yər/ (also **seignior** /sān'yôr, 'sān,yôr/) ▶ **n.** chiefly historical a feudal lord; the lord of a manor.
– DERIVATIVES **sei·gneu·ri·al** /-'yərēəl/ **adj.**
– ORIGIN late 16th cent.: from Old French, from Latin *senior* 'older, elder.'

seign·ior·age /'sānyərij/ (also **seignorage**) ▶ **n.** profit made by a government by issuing currency, esp. the difference between the face value of coins and their production costs. ■ historical the Crown's right to a percentage on bullion brought to a mint for coining. ■ historical a thing claimed by a sovereign or feudal superior as a prerogative.
– ORIGIN late Middle English: from Old French *seignorage*, from *seigneur* (see **SEIGNEUR**).

seign·ior·y /'sānyərē/ (also **seigneury**) ▶ **n.** (pl. **seigniories**) a feudal lordship; the position, authority, or domain of a feudal lord.
– ORIGIN Middle English: from Old French *seignorie*, from *seigneur* (see **SEIGNEUR**).

Seine /sān, sen/ a river in northern France. Rising north of Dijon, it flows northwest for 473 miles (761 km) through the cities of Troyes and Paris to the English Channel near Le Havre.

seine /sān/ ▶ **n.** (also **seine net**) a fishing net that hangs vertically in the water with floats at the top and weights at the bottom edge, the ends being drawn together to encircle the fish.
▶ **v.** [with obj.] fish (an area) with a seine: *the fishermen then seine the weir.* ■ catch (fish) with a seine: *they seine whitefish and salmon.*
– DERIVATIVES **sein·er n.**
– ORIGIN Old English *segne*, via Latin from Greek *sagēnē*; reinforced in Middle English by Old French *saine*.

seise /sēz/ ▶ **v.** see **SEIZE** (sense 3).

sei·sin /'sēzən/ (also **seizin**) ▶ **n.** Law possession of land by freehold. ■ Brit. historical possession, esp. of land: *Richard Fitzhugh did not take seisin of his lands until 1480.*
– ORIGIN Middle English: from Old French *seisine*, from *saisir* 'seize.'

seis·mic /'sīzmik/ ▶ **adj.** of or relating to earthquakes or other vibrations of the earth and its crust. ■ relating to or denoting geological surveying methods involving vibrations produced artificially by explosions. ■ of enormous proportions or effect: *there are seismic pressures threatening American society.*
– DERIVATIVES **seis·mi·cal adj.**, **seis·mi·cal·ly** /-ik(ə)lē/ **adv.**
– ORIGIN mid 19th cent.: from Greek *seismos* 'earthquake' (from *seien* 'to shake') + **-IC**.

seis·mic·i·ty /sīz'misitē/ ▶ **n.** Geology the occurrence or frequency of earthquakes in a region: *the high seismicity of the area.*

seis·mic re·flec·tion ▶ **n.** Geology the reflection of elastic waves at boundaries between bodies of rock of different physical properties, esp. as a technique for prospecting or research.

seis·mic re·frac·tion ▶ **n.** Geology the refraction of elastic waves on passing between bodies of rock having different seismic velocities.

seis·mic ve·loc·i·ty ▶ **n.** Geology the velocity of propagation of elastic waves in a particular rock.

seis·mic wave ▶ **n.** Geology an elastic wave in the earth produced by an earthquake or other means.

seismo- ▶ **comb. form** of an earthquake; relating to earthquakes: *seismograph.*
– ORIGIN from Greek *seismos* 'earthquake.'

seis·mo·gram /'sīzmə,gram/ ▶ **n.** a record produced by a seismograph.

seis·mo·graph /'sīzmə,graf/ ▶ **n.** an instrument that measures and records details of earthquakes, such as force and duration.
– DERIVATIVES **seis·mo·graph·ic** /,sīzmə'grafik/ **adj.**, **seis·mo·graph·i·cal** /,sīzmə'grafikəl/ **adj.**

seis·mol·o·gy /sīz'mäləjē/ ▶ **n.** the branch of science concerned with earthquakes and related phenomena.
– DERIVATIVES **seis·mo·log·i·cal** /,sīzmə'läjikəl/ **adj.**, **seis·mo·log·i·cal·ly** /,sīzmə'läjik(ə)lē/ **adv.**, **seis·mol·o·gist** /-jist/ **n.**

seis·mom·e·ter /sīz'mämitər/ ▶ **n.** another term for **SEISMOGRAPH**.

seis·mo·sau·rus /,sīzmə'sôrəs/ ▶ **n.** a huge late Jurassic dinosaur known from only a few bones, probably the longest ever animal with a length of up to 115–150 feet (35–45 m), and one of the heaviest at up to 110 tons. ● Genus *Seismosaurus*, infraorder Sauropoda, order Saurischia.
– ORIGIN modern Latin, from **SEISMO-** 'of an earthquake' + *sauros* 'lizard.'

sei·tan /'sā,tan/ ▶ **n.** a high-protein vegetarian food made from cooked wheat gluten.
– ORIGIN origin uncertain: perhaps from Japanese *shokubutsusei tanpaku* 'vegetable protein.'

sei whale /sā/ ▶ **n.** a small rorqual with dark steely-gray skin and white grooves on the belly. ● *Balaenoptera borealis*, family Balaenopteridae.
– ORIGIN early 20th cent.: from Norwegian *sejhval*.

sei·za /'sāzə/ ▶ **n.** [in sing.] an upright kneeling position that is traditionally used in Japan in meditation and as part of the preparation in martial arts.
– ORIGIN Japanese, from *sei* 'correct' + *za* 'sitting.'

seize /sēz/ ▶ **v. 1** [with obj.] take hold of suddenly and forcibly: *she jumped up and seized his arm* | *she* ***seized hold of*** *the door handle.* ■ take forcible possession of: *army rebels seized an air force base* | *the current president seized power in a coup.* ■ (of the police or another authority) take possession of (something) by warrant or legal right; confiscate; impound: *police have seized 726 lb of cocaine.* ■ take (an opportunity or initiative) eagerly and decisively: *he seized his chance to attack as Delaney hesitated.* ■ (of a feeling or pain) affect (someone) suddenly or acutely: *he was seized by the most dreadful fear.* ■ strongly appeal to or attract (the imagination or attention): *the story of the king's escape seized the public imagination.* ■ formal understand (something) quickly or clearly: *he always strains to seize the most somber truths.*
2 [no obj.] (of a machine with moving parts or a moving part in a machine) become stuck or jammed: *the engine* ***seized up*** *after only three weeks.*
3 (also **seise**) (**be seized of**) English Law be in legal possession of: *the court is currently seized of custody applications.* ■ historical have or receive freehold possession of (property): *any person who is seized of land has a protected interest in that land.* ■ be aware or informed of: *the judge was fully seized of the point.*
4 Nautical, archaic fasten or attach (someone or something) to something by binding with turns of rope.
– PHRASES **seize the day** make the most of the present moment. [see **CARPE DIEM**.]
– PHRASAL VERBS **seize on/upon** take eager advantage of (something); exploit for one's own purposes: *the government has eagerly seized on the evidence to deny any link between deprivation and crime.*
– DERIVATIVES **seiz·a·ble adj.**, **seiz·er n.**
– ORIGIN Middle English: from Old French *seizir* 'give seisin,' from medieval Latin *sacire*, in the phrase *ad proprium sacire* 'claim as one's own,' from a Germanic base meaning 'procedure.'

sei·zin ▶ **n.** variant spelling of **SEISIN**.

seiz·ing /'sēziNG/ ▶ **n.** Nautical, archaic a length of cord or rope used for fastening or tying.

sei·zure /'sēZHər/ ▶ **n. 1** the action of capturing someone or something using force: *the seizure of the Assembly building* | *another seizure of power by the military.* ■ the action of confiscating or impounding property by warrant of legal right.
2 a sudden attack of illness, esp. a stroke or an epileptic fit: *the patient* ***had a seizure.***

se·jant /'sējənt/ ▶ **adj.** [usu. postpositive] Heraldry (of an animal) sitting upright.
– ORIGIN late 15th cent.: alteration of an Old French variant of *seant* 'sitting,' from the verb *seoir*, from Latin *sedere* 'sit.'

Sejm /sām/ (also **Seym**) ▶ **n.** the lower house of parliament in Poland.
– ORIGIN Polish.

Sekh·met /'sekmet/ Egyptian Mythology a ferocious lioness-goddess, counterpart of the gentle cat-goddess Bastet and wife of Ptah at Memphis.

Sekt /zekt/ ▶ **n.** a German sparkling white wine.
– ORIGIN German.

sel. ▶ **abbr.** ■ select. ■ selected. ■ selection; selections.

se·la·chi·an /sə'lākēən/ Zoology ▶ **n.** an elasmobranch fish of a group that comprises the sharks and dogfishes. ● The former group Selachii, subclass Elasmobranchii: now treated as one, two, or three superorders.
▶ **adj.** of or relating to the selachians.
– ORIGIN mid 19th cent.: from modern Latin *Selachii* (from Greek *selakhos* 'shark') + **-AN**.

se·la·dang /sə'lädäNG/ ▶ **n.** another term for **GAUR**.
– ORIGIN early 19th cent.: from Malay.

se·lag·i·nel·la /sə,lajə'nelə/ ▶ **n.** a creeping mosslike plant of a genus that includes the lesser club mosses. ● Genus *Selaginella*, family Selaginellaceae.
– ORIGIN modern Latin, diminutive of Latin *selago* 'club moss.'

se·lah /'sēlə, 'sel-/ ▶ **exclam.** (in the Bible) occurring frequently at the end of a verse in Psalms and Habakkuk, probably as a musical direction.
– ORIGIN from Hebrew *selāh*.

Sel·craig /'sel,krāg/ see **SELKIRK**.

sel·dom /'seldəm/ ▶ **adv.** not often; rarely: *Islay is seldom visited by tourists* | *he was seldom absent* | [in combination] *an old seldom-used church.*
▶ **adj.** [attrib.] dated not common; infrequent: *a great but seldom pleasure.*
– ORIGIN Old English *seldan*, of Germanic origin; related to Dutch *zelden* and German *selten*, from a base meaning 'strange, wonderful.'

se·lect /sə'lekt/ ▶ **v.** [with obj.] carefully choose as being the best or most suitable: *students must select their own program* | [with obj. and infinitive] *he has been selected to take part* | [no obj.] *you can* ***select from*** *a range of quality products.* ■ [no obj.] (**select for/against**) Biology (in terms of evolution) determine whether (a characteristic or organism) will survive: *a phenotype can be selected against.* ■ use a mouse or keystrokes to mark (something) on a computer screen for a particular operation.
▶ **adj.** (of a group of people or things) carefully chosen from a larger number as being the best or most valuable: *he joined his select team of young Intelligence operatives.* ■ (of a place or group of people) only used by or consisting of a wealthy or sophisticated elite; exclusive: *the opera was seen by a small and highly select audience.*
– DERIVATIVES **se·lect·a·ble adj.**, **se·lect·ness n.**
– ORIGIN mid 16th cent.: from Latin *select-* 'chosen,' from the verb *seligere*, from *se-* 'apart' + *legere* 'choose.'

se·lect com·mit·tee ▶ **n.** a small legislative committee appointed for a special purpose: [in titles] *the House Permanent Select Committee on Intelligence.*

se·lect·ee /sə,lek'tē/ ▶ **n.** a person who is selected. ■ a conscript.

se·lec·tion /sə'leksHən/ ▶ **n. 1** the action or fact of carefully choosing someone or something as being the best or most suitable: *such men decided the selection of candidates* | *they objected to his selection.* ■ a number of carefully chosen things: *the publication of a selection of his poems.* ■ a range of things from which a choice may be made: *the restaurant offers a wide selection of hot and cold dishes.* ■ a horse or horses tipped as worth bets in a race or meeting. ■ data highlighted on a computer screen for a particular operation.
2 Biology a process in which environmental or genetic influences determine which types of organism thrive better than others, regarded as a factor in evolution. See also **NATURAL SELECTION**.
– ORIGIN early 17th cent.: from Latin *selectio(n-)*, from *seligere* 'select by separating off' (see **SELECT**).

se·lec·tion·al /sə'leksHənl/ ▶ **adj.** Linguistics denoting or relating to the process by which only certain words or structures can occur naturally, normally, or correctly in the context of other words.
– DERIVATIVES **se·lec·tion·al·ly adv.**

se·lec·tion pres·sure ▶ **n.** Biology an agent of differential mortality or fertility that tends to make a population change genetically.

se·lec·tion rule ▶ **n.** Physics a rule that describes whether particular quantum transitions in an atom or molecule are allowed or forbidden.

se·lec·tive /sə'lektiv/ ▶ **adj.** relating to or involving the selection of the most suitable or best qualified: *the mini-cow is the result of generations of selective breeding.* ■ (of a person) tending to choose carefully: *he is very selective in his reading.* ■ (of a process or agent) affecting some things and not others: *modern pesticides are more selective in effect.* ■ chiefly Electronics operating at or responding to a particular frequency.
– DERIVATIVES **se·lec·tive·ly adv.**

S

se·lec·tive at·ten·tion ▶ **n.** Psychology the capacity for or process of reacting to certain stimuli selectively when several occur simultaneously.

se·lec·tive·ness /sə'lektivnis/ ▶ **n.** another term for SELECTIVITY.

se·lec·tive serv·ice ▶ **n.** service in the armed forces under conscription.

se·lec·tiv·i·ty /səlek'tivitē/ ▶ **n.** the quality of carefully choosing someone or something as the best or most suitable: *provision is organized on the principle of selectivity.* ■ the property of affecting some things and not others. ■ Electronics the ability of a device to respond to a particular frequency without interference from others.

se·lect·man /sə'lektmən/ ▶ **n.** (pl. **selectmen**) a member of the local government board of a New England town.

se·lec·tor /sə'lektər/ ▶ **n.** a person or thing that selects something, in particular: ■ a device for selecting a particular gear or other setting of a machine or device.

Se·le·ne /sə'lēnē/ Greek Mythology the goddess of the moon who fell in love with Endymion.
– ORIGIN from Greek *selēnē* 'moon.'

se·le·nic ac·id /sə'lenik, -'lē-/ ▶ **n.** Chemistry a crystalline acid analogous to sulfuric acid, made by oxidizing certain selenium compounds. ● Chem. formula: H_2SeO_4.
– DERIVATIVES **sel·e·nate** /'selə,nāt/ **n.**

sel·e·nite /'selə,nīt/ ▶ **n.** a form of gypsum occurring as transparent crystals, sometimes in thin plates.
– ORIGIN mid 17th cent.: via Latin from Greek *selēnitēs lithos* 'moonstone,' from *selēnē* 'moon' + *lithos* 'stone.'

se·le·ni·um /sə'lēnēəm/ ▶ **n.** the chemical element of atomic number 34, a gray crystalline nonmetal with semiconducting properties. (Symbol: **Se**)
– DERIVATIVES **sel·e·nide** /'selə,nīd, -nid/ **n.**
– ORIGIN early 19th cent.: modern Latin, from Greek *selēnē* 'moon.'

se·le·ni·um cell ▶ **n.** a photoelectric device containing a piece of selenium.

seleno- ▶ **comb. form** of, relating to, or shaped like the moon: *selenography.*
– ORIGIN from Greek *selēnē* 'moon.'

se·le·no·dont /sə'lēnə,dänt/ ▶ **adj.** Zoology (of molar teeth) having crescent-shaped ridges on the grinding surfaces, characteristic of the ruminants. ■ (of an ungulate) having such teeth.
– ORIGIN late 19th cent.: from SELENO- 'moon-shaped' + Greek *odous, odont-* 'tooth.'

sel·e·nog·ra·phy /,selə'nägrəfē/ ▶ **n.** the scientific mapping of the moon; lunar geography.
– DERIVATIVES **sel·e·nog·ra·pher** /-fər/ **n.**, **se·le·no·graph·ic** /,selənə'grafik/ **adj.**, **se·le·no·graph·i·cal** /,selənə'grafikəl/ **adj.**

sel·e·nol·o·gy /,selə'näləjē/ ▶ **n.** the scientific study of the moon.
– DERIVATIVES **sel·e·nol·o·gist** /-jist/ **n.**

Sel·es /'seləs/, Monica (1973–), US tennis player, born in Yugoslavia. During 1990–96, she won the women's singles title at three French Open, two US Open, and four Australian Open tournaments.

Se·leu·cid /sə'l(y)o͞osid/ ▶ **adj.** relating to or denoting a dynasty ruling over Syria and a great part of western Asia from 311 to 65 BC. Its capital was at Antioch.
▶ **n.** a member of this dynasty.
– ORIGIN from *Seleucus* Nicator (the name of the founder, one of Alexander the Great's generals) + -ID³.

self /self/ ▶ **n.** (pl. **selves** /selvz/) a person's essential being that distinguishes them from others, esp. considered as the object of introspection or reflexive action: *our alienation from our true selves* | [in sing.] *guilt can be turned against the self* | *language is an aspect of a person's sense of self.* ■ [with adj.] a person's particular nature or personality; the qualities that make a person individual or unique: *by the end of the round he was back to his old self* | *Paula seemed to be her usual cheerful self.* ■ one's own interests or pleasure: *to love in an unpossessive way implies the total surrender of self.*
▶ **pron.** (pl. **selves**) oneself, in particular: ■ [with adj.] (**one's self**) used ironically to refer in specified glowing terms to oneself or someone else: *the only side worth supporting is your own sweet self.*
▶ **adj.** [attrib.] (of a trimming or cover) of the same material and color as the rest of the item: *a dress with self belt.*
▶ **v.** [with obj.] chiefly Botany self-pollinate; self-fertilize: (as noun **selfing**) *the flowers never open and pollination is normally by selfing.* ■ (usu. as adj. **selfed**) Genetics cause (an animal or plant) to breed with or fertilize one of the same hybrid origin or strain: *progeny were derived from selfed crosses.*
– ORIGIN Old English, of Germanic origin; related to Dutch *zelf* and German *selbe.* Early use was emphatic, expressing the sense '(I) myself,' '(he) himself,' etc. The verb dates from the early 20th cent.

self- ▶ **comb. form** of or directed toward oneself or itself: *self-hatred.* ■ by one's own efforts; by its own action: *self-acting.* ■ on, in, for, or relating to oneself or itself: *self-adhesive.*

self-a·ban·don·ment (also **self-abandon**) ▶ **n.** the action of completely surrendering oneself to a desire or impulse.
– DERIVATIVES **self-a·ban·doned adj.**

self-a·base·ment ▶ **n.** the belittling or humiliation of oneself: *he began to apologize with copious tears and self-abasement.*

self-ab·ne·ga·tion ▶ **n.** the denial or abasement of oneself: *she turned the letter into a groveling form of self-abnegation.*

self-ab·sorp·tion ▶ **n. 1** preoccupation with one's own emotions, interests, or situation.
2 Physics the absorption by a body of radiation which it has itself emitted.
– DERIVATIVES **self-ab·sorbed adj.**

self-a·buse /ə'byo͞os/ ▶ **n.** behavior that causes damage or harm to oneself. ■ used euphemistically to refer to masturbation.

self-ac·cu·sa·tion ▶ **n.** the action of accusing oneself, stemming from feelings of guilt.
– DERIVATIVES **self-ac·cu·sa·to·ry adj.**

self-act·ing ▶ **adj.** archaic (of a machine or operation) acting without external influence or control; automatic.

self-ac·tu·al·i·za·tion ▶ **n.** the realization or fulfillment of one's talents and potentialities, esp. considered as a drive or need present in everyone.

self-ad·dressed ▶ **adj.** (esp. of an envelope) bearing one's own address: *enclose a self-addressed stamped envelope.*

self-ad·he·sive ▶ **adj.** coated with a sticky substance; adhering without requiring moistening.

self-ad·just·ing ▶ **adj.** (chiefly of machinery) adjusting itself to meet varying requirements.
– DERIVATIVES **self-ad·just·ment n.**

self-ad·mi·ra·tion ▶ **n.** the admiration of oneself; pride.
– DERIVATIVES **self-ad·mir·ing adj.**

self-ad·vance·ment ▶ **n.** the advancement or promotion of oneself or one's interests: *a positive step in women's self-advancement.*

self-ad·ver·tise·ment ▶ **n.** the active publicization of oneself: *he turned the group into a vehicle for self-advertisement.*
– DERIVATIVES **self-ad·ver·tis·er n.**, **self-advertising adj.**

self-ad·vo·ca·cy ▶ **n.** the action of representing oneself or one's views or interests.

self-af·fir·ma·tion ▶ **n.** the recognition and assertion of the existence and value of one's individual self.

self-ag·gran·dize·ment ▶ **n.** the action or process of promoting oneself as being powerful or important.
– DERIVATIVES **self-ag·gran·diz·ing adj.**

self-al·ien·a·tion ▶ **n.** the process of distancing oneself from one's own feelings or activities, such as may occur in mental illness or as a symptom of emotional distress.

self-a·lign·ing ▶ **adj.** (of a bearing or machine part) capable of aligning itself automatically.

self-a·nal·y·sis ▶ **n.** the analysis of oneself, in particular one's motives and character.
– DERIVATIVES **self-an·a·lyz·ing adj.**

self-an·ni·hi·la·tion ▶ **n.** the annihilation or obliteration of self, esp. as a process of mystical contemplation.

self-ap·point·ed ▶ **adj.** [attrib.] having assumed a position or role without the endorsement of others: *self-appointed experts.*

self-ap·pro·ba·tion ▶ **n.** another term for SELF-APPROVAL.

self-ap·prov·al ▶ **n.** approval or appreciation of oneself.
– DERIVATIVES **self-ap·prov·ing adj.**, **self-ap·prov·ing·ly adv.**

self-as·sem·bly ▶ **n. 1** Biology the spontaneous formation of a ribosome, virus, or other body in a medium containing the appropriate components.
2 Brit. the construction of an object, esp. a piece of furniture, from materials sold in kit form: [as modifier] *self-assembly furniture.*
– DERIVATIVES **self-as·sem·ble v.**

self-as·ser·tion ▶ **n.** the confident and forceful expression or promotion of oneself, one's views, or one's desires.
– DERIVATIVES **self-as·sert·ing adj.** (dated), **self-as·ser·tive adj.**, **self-as·ser·tive·ness n.**

self-as·sess·ment ▶ **n.** assessment or evaluation of oneself or one's actions and attitudes, in particular, of one's performance at a job or learning task considered in relation to an objective standard.

self-as·sur·ance ▶ **n.** confidence in one's own abilities or character.

self-as·sured ▶ **adj.** confident in one's own abilities or character: *a self-assured 16-year-old.*
– DERIVATIVES **self-as·sur·ed·ly adv.**

self-a·ware·ness ▶ **n.** conscious knowledge of one's own character, feelings, motives, and desires: *the process can be painful but it leads to greater self-awareness.*
– DERIVATIVES **self-a·ware adj.**

self-be·tray·al ▶ **n.** the intentional or inadvertent revelation of the truth about one's actions or thoughts.

self-can·cel·ing ▶ **adj. 1** having elements that contradict or negate one another: *some of the speculation had been self-canceling, with newspapers predicting that the government would take quite opposite courses.*
2 (of a mechanical device) designed to stop working automatically when no longer required.

self-cen·sor·ship ▶ **n.** the exercising of control over what one says and does, esp. to avoid castigation: *a climate of self-censorship, fear, and hypocrisy.*

self-cen·tered ▶ **adj.** preoccupied with oneself and one's affairs: *he's far too self-centered to care what you do.*
– DERIVATIVES **self-cen·tered·ly adv.**, **self-cen·tered·ness n.**

self-clean·ing ▶ **adj.** (of an object or apparatus) able to clean itself: *a self-cleaning oven.*

self-clos·ing ▶ **adj.** (esp. of a door or valve) closing automatically.

self-col·ored ▶ **adj.** of a single uniform color: *a self-colored carpet.* ■ of the natural color of something.

self-com·mand ▶ **n.** the ability to control one's emotions; self-control.

self-com·pat·i·ble ▶ **adj.** Botany (of a plant or species) able to be fertilized by its own pollen.

self-con·ceit ▶ **n.** undue pride in oneself.
– DERIVATIVES **self-con·ceit·ed adj.**

self-con·cept ▶ **n.** Psychology an idea of the self constructed from the beliefs one holds about oneself and the responses of others.

self-con·dem·na·tion ▶ **n.** the blaming of oneself: *guilt and self-condemnation were riding her hard.* ■ the inadvertent revelation of one's wrongdoing.
– DERIVATIVES **self-con·demned adj.**, **self-con·demn·ing adj.**

self-con·fessed ▶ **adj.** [attrib.] having openly admitted to being a person with certain characteristics: *a self-confessed chocoholic.*
– DERIVATIVES **self-con·fess·ed·ly** /-'fesidlē/ **adv.**, **self-con·fes·sion n.**, **self-con·fes·sion·al adj.**

self-con·fi·dence ▶ **n.** a feeling of trust in one's abilities, qualities, and judgment.

self-con·fi·dent ▶ **adj.** trusting in one's abilities, qualities, and judgment.
– DERIVATIVES **self-con·fi·dent·ly adv.**

self-con·grat·u·la·tion ▶ **n.** undue complacency or pride regarding one's personal achievements or qualities; self-satisfaction: *a hefty dose of self-congratulation about how noble we are.*
– DERIVATIVES **self-con·grat·u·la·to·ry adj.**

self-con·scious ▶ **adj.** feeling undue awareness of oneself, one's appearance, or one's actions: *I feel a bit self-conscious parking my scruffy old car* | *a self-conscious laugh.* ■ Philosophy & Psychology having knowledge of one's own existence, esp. the knowledge of oneself as a conscious being. ■ (esp. of an action or intention) deliberate and with full awareness, esp. affectedly so: *her self-conscious identification with the upper classes.*
– DERIVATIVES **self-con·scious·ly adv.**, **self-con·scious·ness n.**

self-con·sis·tent ▶ **adj.** not having parts or aspects that are in conflict or contradiction with each other; consistent: *the theory is both rigorous and self-consistent.*
– DERIVATIVES **self-con·sis·ten·cy n.**

self-con·tained ▶ **adj. 1** (of a thing) complete, or having all that is needed, in itself.

2 (of a person) quiet and independent; not depending on or influenced by others.
– DERIVATIVES **self-con·tain·ment** n.

self-con·tempt ▶ n. contempt or loathing for oneself or one's actions: *they expressed self-contempt for having wasted so many hours in front of the idiot box.*
– DERIVATIVES **self-con·temp·tu·ous** adj.

self-con·tra·dic·tion ▶ n. inconsistency between aspects or parts of a whole: *deconstruction is interested in exploring language and revealing self-contradiction and instability* | *a puzzling self-contradiction in masochism.*
– DERIVATIVES **self-con·tra·dict·ing** adj., **self-con·tra·dic·to·ry** adj.

self-con·trol ▶ n. the ability to control oneself, in particular one's emotions and desires or the expression of them in one's behavior, esp. in difficult situations: *Lucy silently struggled for self-control.*
– DERIVATIVES **self-con·trolled** adj.

self-cor·rect·ing ▶ adj. correcting oneself or itself without external help: *the scientific process is self-correcting* | *a self-correcting optical finder.*
– DERIVATIVES **self-cor·rect** v., **self-cor·rec·tion** n.

self-cre·at·ed ▶ adj. created by oneself or itself: *his self-created role as the bad boy of the music scene.*
– DERIVATIVES **self-cre·at·ing** adj., **self-cre·a·tion** n.

self-crit·i·cal ▶ adj. critical of oneself, one's abilities, or one's actions in a self-aware or unduly disapproving manner: *she felt miserably self-critical for her reluctance to go.*
– DERIVATIVES **self-crit·i·cism** n.

self-de·ceit ▶ n. another term for SELF-DECEPTION.

self-de·ceiv·ing ▶ adj. allowing oneself to believe that a false or unvalidated feeling, idea, or situation is true: *I prefer my cynicism to your self-deceiving optimism.*
– DERIVATIVES **self-de·ceiv·er** n.

self-de·cep·tion ▶ n. the action or practice of allowing oneself to believe that a false or unvalidated feeling, idea, or situation is true: *Jane remarked on men's capacity for self-deception.*
– DERIVATIVES **self-de·cep·tive** adj.

self-de·feat·ing ▶ adj. (of an action or policy) unable, because of its inherent qualities, to achieve the end it is designed to bring about.

self-de·fense ▶ n. the defense of one's person or interests, esp. through the use of physical force, which is permitted in certain cases as an answer to a charge of violent crime: *he claimed self-defense in the attempted murder charge* | [as modifier] *self-defense classes.*
– DERIVATIVES **self-de·fen·sive** adj.

self-def·i·ni·tion ▶ n. definition of one's individuality and one's role in life; such definition of a group by its members: *the struggle for national self-definition.*

self-de·light ▶ n. delight in oneself or one's existence.

self-de·lu·sion ▶ n. the action of deluding oneself; failure to recognize reality: *he retreats into a world of fantasy and self-delusion.*

self-de·ni·al ▶ n. the denial of one's own interests and needs; self-sacrifice.
– DERIVATIVES **self-de·ny·ing** adj.

S

self-de·pend·ence ▶ n. reliance on one's own strengths rather than on others; independence.
– DERIVATIVES **self-de·pend·ent** adj.

self-dep·re·cat·ing ▶ adj. modest about or critical of oneself, esp. humorously so: *self-deprecating jokes.*
– DERIVATIVES **self-dep·re·cat·ing·ly** adv., **self-dep·re·ca·tion** n., **self-dep·re·ca·to·ry** adj.

self-de·pre·ci·a·tion ▶ n. another term for SELF-DEPRECATION (see SELF-DEPRECATING).
– DERIVATIVES **self-de·pre·ci·at·ing** adj., **self-de·pre·ci·a·to·ry** adj.

self-de·spair ▶ n. despair or dismay about oneself or one's actions.

self-de·stroy·ing ▶ adj. destroying or capable of destroying oneself or itself; self-destructive.

self-de·struct ▶ v. [no obj.] (of a thing) destroy itself by exploding or disintegrating automatically, having been preset to do so: *the tape would automatically self-destruct after twenty minutes.* ■ [as adj.] denoting a device that enables or causes something to destroy itself in such a way: *the self-destruct button.*
– DERIVATIVES **self-de·struc·tion** n., **self-de·struc·tive** adj., **self-de·struc·tive·ly** adv.

self-de·ter·mi·na·tion ▶ n. the process by which a country determines its own statehood and forms its own allegiances and government: *the changes cannot be made until the country's right to self-determination is recognized.* ■ the process by which a person controls their own life.

self-de·vel·op·ment ▶ n. the process by which a person's character or abilities are gradually developed: *graduates have stressed the value of their courses for self-development.*

self-de·vo·tion ▶ n. the devotion of oneself to a person or cause.

self-di·ag·nose ▶ v. [no obj.] diagnose oneself as having a particular medical condition: *many patients self-diagnose and do not seek medical attention for their symptoms.* ■ [with obj.] diagnose (an illness or other problem) in oneself: *patients will often self-diagnose varicose veins.*
– DERIVATIVES **self-di·ag·no·sis** n.

self-dif·fu·sion ▶ n. Chemistry the migration of constituent atoms or molecules within the bulk of a substance, esp. in a crystalline solid.

self-di·rect·ed ▶ adj. (of an emotion, statement, or activity) directed at oneself: *she grimaces with a bitter self-directed humor.* ■ (of an activity) under one's own control: *self-directed learning.* ■ (of a person) showing initiative and the ability to organize oneself.
– DERIVATIVES **self-di·rec·tion** n.

self-dis·ci·pline ▶ n. the ability to control one's feelings and overcome one's weaknesses; the ability to pursue what one thinks is right despite temptations to abandon it.
– DERIVATIVES **self-dis·ci·plined** adj.

self-dis·cov·er·y ▶ n. the process of acquiring insight into one's own character.

self-dis·gust ▶ n. profound revulsion at one's own character or actions: *his descent into drunkenness filled him with self-disgust.*

self-doubt ▶ n. lack of confidence in oneself and one's abilities: *his later years were plagued by self-doubt.*

self-dram·a·ti·za·tion ▶ n. dramatization of one's own situation or feelings for effect.

self-ed·u·cat·ed ▶ adj. educated largely through one's own efforts, rather than by formal instruction: *he was a self-made and almost self-educated businessman.*
– DERIVATIVES **self-ed·u·ca·tion** n.

self-ef·fac·ing ▶ adj. not claiming attention for oneself; retiring and modest: *his demeanor was self-effacing, gracious, and polite.*
– DERIVATIVES **self-ef·face·ment** n., **self-ef·fac·ing·ly** adv.

self-em·ployed ▶ adj. working for oneself as a freelancer or the owner of a business rather than for an employer: *a self-employed builder.* ■ relating to or designed for people working for themselves: *the rules for self-employed pension plans have been altered.*
– DERIVATIVES **self-em·ploy·ment** n.

self-en·closed ▶ adj. (of a person, community, or system) not choosing to or able to communicate with others or with external systems: *the family is a self-enclosed unit.*

self-es·teem ▶ n. confidence in one's own worth or abilities; self-respect: *assertiveness training for those with low self-esteem.*

self-e·val·u·a·tion ▶ n. another term for SELF-ASSESSMENT.

self-ev·i·dent ▶ adj. not needing to be demonstrated or explained; obvious: *self-evident truths* | [with clause] *it is self-evident that you cannot work 14 hours a day and have time left over for a child.*
– DERIVATIVES **self-ev·i·dence** n., **self-ev·i·dent·ly** adv.

self-ex·am·i·na·tion ▶ n. the study of one's own behavior and motivations: *a period of considerable self-doubt and self-examination.* ■ the action of examining one's own body for signs of illness.

self-ex·cit·ed ▶ adj. Physics relating to or denoting a dynamo-electric machine or analogous system that generates or excites its own magnetic field.

self-ex·ist·ent ▶ adj. existing independently of other beings or causes.

self-ex·plan·a·to·ry ▶ adj. easily understood; not needing explanation: *the film's title is fairly self-explanatory.*

self-ex·pres·sion ▶ n. the expression of one's feelings, thoughts, or ideas, esp. in writing, art, music, or dance.
– DERIVATIVES **self-ex·pres·sive** adj.

self-faced ▶ adj. (of stone) having an undressed surface.

self-feed·er ▶ n. 1 a furnace or machine that renews its own fuel or material automatically. 2 a device for supplying food to farm animals automatically.
– DERIVATIVES **self-feed·ing** adj.

self-fer·tile ▶ adj. Botany (of a plant) capable of self-fertilization.
– DERIVATIVES **self-fer·til·i·ty** n.

self-fer·ti·li·za·tion ▶ n. Biology the fertilization of plants and some invertebrate animals by their own pollen or sperm rather than that of another individual.
– DERIVATIVES **self-fer·ti·lized** adj., **self-fer·ti·liz·ing** adj.

self-fi·nanc·ing ▶ adj. (of an organization or enterprise) having or generating enough income to finance itself.
– DERIVATIVES **self-fi·nanced** adj.

self-flag·el·la·tion ▶ n. the action of flogging oneself, esp. as a form of religious discipline. ■ excessive criticism of oneself.

self-flat·ter·y ▶ n. the holding of an unjustifiably high opinion of oneself or one's actions.
– DERIVATIVES **self-flat·ter·ing** adj.

self-for·get·ful ▶ adj. forgetful of oneself or one's needs.
– DERIVATIVES **self-for·get·ful·ness** n.

self-ful·fill·ing ▶ adj. (of an opinion or prediction) bound to be proved correct or to come true as a result of behavior caused by its being expressed: *expecting something to be bad can turn out to be a self-fulfilling prophecy.*

self-ful·fill·ment (Brit. **self-fulfilment**) ▶ n. the fulfillment of one's hopes and ambitions: *it is the striving for self-fulfillment which guides our lives.*

self-gen·er·at·ing ▶ adj. generated by itself, rather than by some external force: *the strident activity of the industrial scene seems to be self-generating.*

self-glo·ri·fi·ca·tion ▶ n. exaltation of oneself and one's abilities: *they fought not merely for self-glorification but for the common good.*

self-gov·ern·ment ▶ n. 1 government of a country by its own people, esp. after having been a colony. 2 another term for SELF-CONTROL.
– DERIVATIVES **self-gov·erned** adj., **self-gov·ern·ing** adj.

self-grav·i·ta·tion ▶ n. Astronomy the gravitational forces acting among the components of a massive body.

self-guid·ed ▶ adj. (of a walk or visit to a tourist attraction) undertaken without the supervision of a tour guide.

self-ha·tred (also **self-hate**) ▶ n. intense dislike of oneself.

self-heal (also **selfheal**) ▶ n. a purple-flowered plant of the mint family that was formerly widely used for healing wounds. Native to Eurasia, it is now widespread throughout North America. ● *Prunella vulgaris*, family Labiatae.

self-help ▶ n. the use of one's own efforts and resources to achieve things without relying on others: *what government does is not a substitute for what people can do with encouragement and self-help.* ■ [as modifier] designed to assist people in achieving things for themselves: *a self-help group for drug abusers.*

self·hood /ˈselfˌhŏŏd/ ▶ n. the quality that constitutes one's individuality; the state of having an individual identity.

self-i·den·ti·fi·ca·tion ▶ n. the attribution of certain characteristics or qualities to oneself: *self-identification by the old person as sick or inadequate.*

self-i·den·ti·ty ▶ n. the recognition of one's potential and qualities as an individual, esp. in relation to social context: *caring can become the defining characteristic of women's self-identity.*

self-im·age ▶ n. the idea one has of one's abilities, appearance, and personality: *sickness is an affront to one's self-image and dignity.*

self-im·mo·la·tion ▶ n. the offering of oneself as a sacrifice, esp. by burning; such suicidal action in the name of a cause or strongly held belief.

self-im·por·tance ▶ n. an exaggerated sense of one's own value or importance: *he was a big, blustering, opinionated cop, full of self-importance.*
– DERIVATIVES **self-im·por·tant** adj., **self-im·por·tant·ly** adv.

self-im·posed ▶ adj. (of a task or circumstance) imposed on oneself, not by an external force: *he went into self-imposed exile.*

self-im·prove·ment ▶ n. the improvement of one's knowledge, status, or character by one's own efforts.

self-in·com·pat·i·ble ▶ adj. Botany (of a plant or species) unable to be fertilized by its own pollen.
– DERIVATIVES **self-in·com·pat·i·bil·i·ty** n.

self-in·duced ▶ adj. 1 brought about by oneself: *self-induced vomiting.* 2 produced by electrical self-induction.

self-in·duct·ance ▶ n. Physics a measure or coefficient of self-induction in a circuit, usually measured in henries. ■ the property of an electric circuit that permits self-induction.

self-in·duc·tion ▶ n. Physics the induction of an electromotive force in a circuit when the current in that circuit is varied. Compare with MUTUAL INDUCTION.
– DERIVATIVES **self-in·duc·tive** adj.

self-in·dul·gence ▶ n. the quality of being self-indulgent. ■ something done in a self-indulgent way: *Sunday's simpleminded pleasures and self-indulgences.*

self-in·dul·gent ▶ adj. characterized by doing or tending to do exactly what one wants, esp. when this involves pleasure or idleness: *a self-indulgent extra hour of sleep.* ■ (of a creative work) lacking economy and control.
– DERIVATIVES **self-in·dul·gent·ly** adv.

self-in·flict·ed ▶ adj. (of a wound or other harm) inflicted on oneself.

self-in·sur·ance ▶ n. insurance of oneself or one's interests by maintaining a fund to cover possible losses rather than by purchasing an insurance policy.

self-in·ter·est ▶ n. one's personal interest or advantage, esp. when pursued without regard for others.

self-in·ter·est·ed ▶ adj. motivated by one's personal interest or advantage, esp. without regard for others: *many groups pursue self-interested aims.*

self-in·volved ▶ adj. wrapped up in oneself or one's own thoughts.
– DERIVATIVES **self-in·volve·ment** n.

self·ish /ˈselfisн/ ▶ adj. (of a person, action, or motive) lacking consideration for others; concerned chiefly with one's own personal profit or pleasure: *I joined them for selfish reasons.*
– DERIVATIVES **self·ish·ly** adv.

self·ish·ness /ˈselfisнnis/ ▶ n. the quality or condition of being selfish: *an act of pure selfishness.*

self·ism /ˈselfizəm/ ▶ n. concentration on one's own interests; self-centeredness or self-absorption.
– DERIVATIVES **self·ist** n.

self-jus·ti·fi·ca·tion ▶ n. the justification or excusing of oneself or one's actions.
– DERIVATIVES **self-jus·tif·i·ca·to·ry** adj., **self-jus·ti·fy·ing** adj.

self-knowl·edge ▶ n. understanding of oneself or one's own motives or character.
– DERIVATIVES **self-know·ing** adj.

self·less /ˈselfləs/ ▶ adj. concerned more with the needs and wishes of others than with one's own; unselfish: *an act of selfless devotion.*
– DERIVATIVES **self·less·ly** adv., **self·less·ness** n.

self-lim·it·ing ▶ adj. relating to or denoting something that limits itself, in particular: ■ (also **self-limited**) Medicine (of a condition) ultimately resolving itself without treatment. ■ (in psychology) preventing the development or expression of the self.

self-liq·ui·dat·ing ▶ adj. denoting an asset that earns back its original cost out of income over a fixed period. ■ denoting a loan used to finance a project that will bring a sufficient return to pay back the loan and its interest and leave a profit. ■ denoting a sales promotion offer that pays for itself by generating increased sales.

self-load·ing ▶ adj. (esp. of a gun) loading automatically: *a self-loading pistol.*
– DERIVATIVES **self-load·er** n.

self-lock·ing ▶ adj. locking itself shut or in a fixed position: *self-locking screws.*

self-love ▶ n. regard for one's own well-being and happiness (chiefly considered as a desirable rather than narcissistic characteristic).
– DERIVATIVES **self-lov·ing** adj.

self-made ▶ adj. having become successful or rich by one's own efforts: *a self-made millionaire.* ■ made by oneself: *his self-made fortune | a self-made kite.*

self-man·age·ment ▶ n. management of or by oneself; the taking of responsibility for one's own behavior and well-being. ■ the distribution of political control to individual regions of a state, esp. as a form of socialism practiced by its own members.
– DERIVATIVES **self-man·ag·ing** adj.

self-mas·ter·y ▶ n. self-control.

self·mate /ˈself,māt/ ▶ n. Chess a problem in which the solver's task is to force the opponent to deliver checkmate.

self-med·i·cate ▶ v. [no obj.] choose and take medicines oneself, rather than by prescription or on expert advice. ■ take addictive or habituating drugs to relieve stress or other conditions.
– DERIVATIVES **self-med·i·ca·tion** n.

self-mock·ing ▶ adj. mocking oneself: *a wry, self-mocking smile.*
– DERIVATIVES **self-mock·er·y** n., **self-mock·ing·ly** adv.

self-mor·ti·fi·ca·tion ▶ n. the subjugation of appetites or desires by self-denial or self-discipline as an aspect of religious devotion: *voluntary self-mortification such as fasting.*

self-mo·tion ▶ n. movement caused by oneself or itself, not by an external action or agent.
– DERIVATIVES **self-mov·ing** adj.

self-mo·ti·vat·ed ▶ adj. motivated to do or achieve something because of one's own enthusiasm or interest, without needing pressure from others: *she's a very independent, self-motivated individual.*
– DERIVATIVES **self-mo·ti·vat·ing** adj., **self-mo·ti·va·tion** n.

self-mur·der ▶ n. suicide.
– DERIVATIVES **self-mur·der·er** n.

self-mu·ti·la·tion ▶ n. the mutilation of oneself, esp. as a symptom of mental or emotional disturbance.

self-ne·glect ▶ n. neglect of oneself, esp. one's physical well-being.

self·ness /ˈselfnəs/ ▶ n. a person's essential individuality. ■ archaic selfishness; self-regard.

self-ob·sessed ▶ adj. excessively preoccupied with one's own life and circumstances; thinking only about oneself: *even self-obsessed pop stars don't want the rumor mill to overshadow their music.*
– DERIVATIVES **self-ob·ses·sion** n.

self-o·pin·ion·at·ed ▶ adj. having an arrogantly high regard for oneself or one's own opinions: *a pompous, self-opinionated bully.*
– DERIVATIVES **self-o·pin·ion** n.

self-pa·rod·ic ▶ adj. another term for SELF-PARODYING.

self-par·o·dy ▶ n. the intentional or inadvertent parodying or exaggeration of one's usual behavior or speech: *they are soft-spoken and clean-cut to the point of self-parody.*

self-par·o·dy·ing ▶ adj. appearing to parody one's usual behavior or speech, esp. inadvertently: *pathetic, self-parodying former beauty queens propped up by surgery and cosmetics.*

self-per·pet·u·at·ing ▶ adj. perpetuating itself or oneself without external agency or intervention: *the self-perpetuating power of the bureaucracy.*
– DERIVATIVES **self-per·pet·u·a·tion** n.

self-pit·y ▶ n. excessive, self-absorbed unhappiness over one's own troubles.

self-pit·y·ing ▶ adj. characterized by self-pity: *he was in one of his self-pitying moods.*
– DERIVATIVES **self-pit·y·ing·ly** adv.

self-po·lic·ing ▶ n. the process of keeping order or maintaining control within a community without accountability or reference to an external authority. ▶ adj. (of a community) independently responsible for keeping and maintaining order: *as long as the Internet community was relatively small, it could be self-policing.*

self-pol·li·na·tion ▶ n. Botany the pollination of a flower by pollen from the same flower or from another flower on the same plant.
– DERIVATIVES **self-pol·l·inat·ed** adj., **self-pol·li·nat·ing** adj., **self-pol·li·na·tor** n.

self-por·trait ▶ n. a portrait of an artist produced or created by that artist.
– DERIVATIVES **self-por·trai·ture** n.

self-pos·sessed ▶ adj. calm, confident, and in control of one's feelings; composed.

self-pos·ses·sion ▶ n. the state or feeling of being calm, confident, and in control of one's feelings; composure.

self-praise ▶ n. praise of oneself; boasting.

self-pres·er·va·tion ▶ n. the protection of oneself from harm or death, esp. regarded as a basic instinct in human beings and animals.

self-pro·claimed ▶ adj. [attrib.] described as or proclaimed to be such by oneself, without endorsement by others: *exercise books written by self-proclaimed experts.*

self-pro·mo·tion ▶ n. the action of promoting or publicizing oneself or one's activities, esp. in a forceful way: *she's guilty of criminally bad taste and shameless self-promotion.*
– DERIVATIVES **self-pro·mot·er** n., **self-pro·mot·ing** adj.

self-prop·a·gat·ing ▶ adj. (esp. of a plant) able to propagate itself.
– DERIVATIVES **self-prop·a·ga·tion** n.

self-pro·pelled ▶ adj. moving or able to move without external propulsion or agency: *a self-propelled weapon.*
– DERIVATIVES **self-pro·pel·ling** adj.

self-pro·tec·tion ▶ n. protection of oneself or itself.
– DERIVATIVES **self-pro·tec·tive** adj.

self-prov·ing ▶ adj. Law (of a will) accompanied by a witnesses' affidavit for which no oral testimony is needed to be admitted to probate: *we recommend that all wills be self-proving.* ■ of or relating to an affidavit that makes a will self-proving: *attached to the will offered for probate was a self-proving affidavit and certificate executed by the testatrix, the two witnesses to the will, and a notary public.*

self-re·al·i·za·tion ▶ n. fulfillment of one's own potential.

self-ref·er·en·tial ▶ adj. making reference to itself or oneself. ■ (of a literary or other creative work) making reference to itself, its author or creator, or their other work: *self-referential elements in Donne's poems.*
– DERIVATIVES **self-ref·er·ence** n., **self-ref·er·en·ti·al·i·ty** n., **self-ref·er·en·tial·ly** adv.

self-re·flec·tion ▶ n. meditation or serious thought about one's character, actions, and motives.
– DERIVATIVES **self-re·flec·tive** adj.

self-re·flex·ive ▶ adj. containing a reflection or image of itself; self-referential: *sociology's self-reflexive critique.*

self-re·gard ▶ n. regard or consideration for oneself; self-respect. ■ conceit; vanity.
– DERIVATIVES **self-re·gard·ing** adj.

self-reg·u·lat·ing ▶ adj. regulating itself without intervention from external bodies: *advertising is governed by a self-regulating system.*
– DERIVATIVES **self-reg·u·la·tion** n., **self-reg·u·la·to·ry** adj.

self-re·li·ance ▶ n. reliance on one's own powers and resources rather than those of others.

self-re·li·ant ▶ adj. reliant on one's own powers and resources rather than those of others: *a self-reliant little girl.*
– DERIVATIVES **self-re·li·ant·ly** adv.

self-re·new·al ▶ n. the process of renewing oneself or itself.
– DERIVATIVES **self-re·new·ing** adj.

self-re·nun·ci·a·tion ▶ n. renunciation of one's own will; self-sacrifice; unselfishness.

self-re·port ▶ v. [with obj.] provide details about (one's circumstances, typically one's medical or psychological condition): *35% of participants self-reported a history of asthma.*

self-re·proach ▶ n. reproach or blame directed at oneself: *the bitter tears of self-reproach.*
– DERIVATIVES **self-re·proach·ful** adj.

self-re·spect ▶ n. pride and confidence in oneself; a feeling that one is behaving with honor and dignity.

self-re·spect·ing ▶ adj. having self-respect: *proud, self-respecting mountain villagers.* ■ [attrib.] often humorous a person who merits a particular role or name: *no self-respecting editor would run such an article.*

self-re·straint ▶ n. restraint imposed by oneself on one's own actions; self-control.
– DERIVATIVES **self-re·strained** adj.

self-re·veal·ing ▶ adj. revealing one's character or motives, esp. inadvertently: *his most intimate and self-revealing book.*
– DERIVATIVES **self-rev·e·la·tion** n., **self-re·vel·a·to·ry** adj.

self-right·eous ▶ adj. having or characterized by a certainty, esp. an unfounded one, that one is totally correct or morally superior: *self-righteous indignation and complacency.*
– DERIVATIVES **self-right·eous·ly** adv.

self-right·eous·ness ▶ n. the quality or state of being self-righteous.

self-right·ing ▶ adj. (of a boat) designed to right itself when capsized.

self-ris·ing flour ▶ n. flour that has a leavening agent already added.

self-rule ▶ n. another term for SELF-GOVERNMENT (sense 1).

self-sac·ri·fice ▶ n. the giving up of one's own interests or wishes in order to help others or to advance a cause.
– DERIVATIVES **self-sac·ri·fi·cial** adj., **self-sac·ri·fic·ing** adj.

self·same /ˈself,sām/ ▶ adj. [attrib.] (usu. **the selfsame**) exactly the same: *he was standing in the selfsame spot you're filling now.*

PRONUNCIATION KEY ə *ago, up*; ər *over, fur*; a *hat*; ā *ate*; ä *car*; e *let*; ē *see*; i *fit*; ī *by*; NG *sing*; ō *go*; ô *law, for*; oi *toy*; o͝o *good*; o͞o *goo*; ou *out*; TH *thin*; T͟H *then*; ZH *vision*

self-sat·is·fac·tion ▶ n. excessive satisfaction with oneself or one's achievements; smug complacency: *a look of self-satisfaction.*

self-sat·is·fied ▶ adj. excessively and unwarrantedly satisfied with oneself or one's achievements; smugly complacent: *a pompous, self-satisfied fool | a self-satisfied smirk | a self-satisfied air.*

self-seal·ing ▶ adj. sealing itself without the usual process or procedure, in particular: ■ (of a tire, fuel tank, etc.) able to seal small punctures automatically. ■ (of an envelope) self-adhesive.

self-seed ▶ v. [no obj.] (of a plant) propagate itself by seed: (as adj. **self-seeding**) *the early-blooming, self-seeding primula.*
– DERIVATIVES **self-seed·er** n.

self-seek·ing ▶ adj. & n. another term for SELF-SERVING.
– DERIVATIVES **self-seek·er** n.

self-se·lect ▶ v. **1** choose for oneself: [with obj.] *participants were asked to self-select their titles, which were divided into executive and non-executive.*
2 [no obj.] determine one's own status with regard to membership in a group: *the crowd self-selects because this isn't a club for the passing trade.*
▶ adj. allowing users to select: *the chain decided to move condoms from the pharmacy counter to self-select stands.*

self-se·lec·tion ▶ n. the action of putting oneself forward for something.
– DERIVATIVES **self-se·lect·ing** adj.

self-serv·ice ▶ adj. denoting a store, restaurant, or service station where customers select goods for themselves or service their car for themselves and pay a cashier: *a self-service cafeteria.*
▶ n. the system whereby customers select goods for themselves or service their car for themselves and pay a cashier: *providing quick self-service.*

self-serv·ing ▶ adj. having concern for one's own welfare and interests before those of others: *public accountability is replaced by self-serving propaganda.*
▶ n. concern for oneself before others.

self-sim·i·lar ▶ adj. Mathematics (of an object or set of objects) similar to itself at a different time, or to a copy of itself on a different scale.
– DERIVATIVES **self-sim·i·lar·i·ty** n.

self-slaugh·ter ▶ n. literary suicide.

self-sow /ˈsō/ ▶ v. [no obj.] (of a plant) propagate itself by seed: (as adj. **self-sown**) *a batch of self-sown seedlings.*

self-start·er ▶ n. **1** a person who is sufficiently motivated or ambitious to start a new career or business or to pursue further education without the help of others: *he was the self-starter who worked his way up from messenger boy to account executive.*
2 dated the starter of a motor-vehicle engine.
– DERIVATIVES **self-start·ing** adj.

self-ster·ile ▶ adj. Biology incapable of self-fertilization.
– DERIVATIVES **self-ste·ril·i·ty** n.

self-stick ▶ adj. coated with an adhesive on one side for ready application to a surface: *peel off self-stick backing and attach to either side.*

self-stim·u·la·tion ▶ n. **1** used euphemistically to refer to masturbation.
2 Physiology a phenomenon that occurs in the hypothalamus and other areas of the brain, in which the propagation of electrical stimulation has positive reinforcing properties that act to maintain and perpetuate the impulses.

self-stor·age ▶ n. a system whereby individuals rent containers or units of space within a large warehouse to store possessions.

self-styled ▶ adj. [attrib.] using a description or title that one has given oneself: *self-styled experts | the self-styled president of Bougainville.*

self-sub·sist·ent ▶ adj. subsistent without dependence on or support from external agencies: *this colony was virtually self-subsistent, in management methods as in food.*

self-suf·fi·cien·cy ▶ n. the quality or condition of being self-sufficient: *a means of developing economic self-sufficiency.*

self-suf·fi·cient ▶ adj. needing no outside help in satisfying one's basic needs, esp. with regard to the production of food: *I don't think Botswana, due to the climate, could ever be self-sufficient in food.* ■ emotionally and intellectually independent: *their son was a little bit of a loner and very self-sufficient.*
– DERIVATIVES **self-suf·fi·cient·ly** adv.

self-sug·ges·tion ▶ n. another term for AUTOSUGGESTION.

self-sup·port·ing ▶ adj. **1** having the resources to be able to survive without outside assistance.
2 staying up or upright without being supported by something else: *arches were originally self-supporting structures.*
– DERIVATIVES **self-sup·port** n.

self-sur·ren·der ▶ n. the surrender of oneself or one's will to an external influence, an emotion, or another person.

self-sus·tain·ing ▶ adj. able to continue in a healthy state without outside assistance: *his puny farms were years from being self-sustaining.*
– DERIVATIVES **self-sus·tained** adj.

self-sys·tem ▶ n. Psychology the complex of drives and responses relating to the self; the set of potentialities that develop in an individual's character in response to parental and other external influences.

self-tap·ping ▶ adj. (of a screw) able to cut thread in the material into which it is inserted.

self-taught ▶ adj. having acquired knowledge or skill on one's own initiative rather than through formal instruction or training: *a self-taught graphic artist.*

self-tim·er ▶ n. a mechanism in a camera that introduces a delay between the operation of the shutter release and the opening of the shutter, so that the photographer can be included in the photograph.

self-ti·tled ▶ n. (of an album, CD, etc.) having a title that is the same as the performer's name.

self-tor·ture ▶ n. the inflicting of pain, esp. mental pain, on oneself.

self-tran·scend·ence ▶ n. the overcoming of the limits of the individual self and its desires in spiritual contemplation and realization.

self-un·der·stand·ing ▶ n. awareness of and ability to understand one's own actions and reactions.

self-willed ▶ adj. obstinately doing what one wants in spite of the wishes or orders of others: *the child may be very obstinate and self-willed.*
– DERIVATIVES **self-will** n.

self-wind·ing /ˈwīndiNG/ ▶ adj. (chiefly of a watch) wound by some automatic means, such as an electric motor or the movement of the wearer, rather than by hand.

self-worth ▶ n. another term for SELF-ESTEEM.

Sel·juk /selˈjo͞ok, ˈselˌjo͞ok/ ▶ n. a member of any of the Turkish dynasties that ruled Asia Minor in the 11th to 13th centuries, successfully invading the Byzantine Empire and defending the Holy Land against the Crusaders.
▶ adj. of or relating to the Seljuks.
– DERIVATIVES **Sel·juk·i·an** /-ˈjo͞okēən/ adj. & n.
– ORIGIN from Turkish *seljūq*, the name of the reputed ancestor of the dynasty.

sel·kie /ˈselkē/ (also **selky** or **silkie** /ˈsil-/) ▶ n. (pl. **selkies**) Scottish a mythical creature that resembles a seal in the water but assumes human form on land.
– ORIGIN from *selch*, variant of SEAL², + -IE.

Sel·kirk /ˈselˌkərk/, Alexander (1676–1721), Scottish sailor; also called *Alexander Selcraig*. His experiences on one of the uninhabited Juan Fernandez Islands formed the basis of Daniel Defoe's novel *Robinson Crusoe* (1719).

sell /sel/ ▶ v. (past and past participle **sold** /sōld/) [with obj.] **1** give or hand over (something) in exchange for money: *they had sold the car | the family business had been sold off |* [with two objs.] *I was trying to sell him my butterfly collection.* ■ have a stock of (something) available for sale: *the store sells hi-fis, TVs, videos, and other electrical goods.* ■ [no obj.] (of a thing) be purchased: *this magazine of yours won't sell.* ■ (of a publication or recording) attain sales of (a specified number of copies): *the album sold 6 million copies in the U.S.* ■ [no obj.] (**sell for/at**) be available for sale at (a specified price): *these antiques sell for about $375.* ■ [no obj.] (**sell out**) sell all of one's stock of something: *they had nearly sold out of the initial run of 75,000 copies.* ■ [no obj.] (**sell out**) be all sold: *it was clear that the performances would not sell out.* ■ [no obj.] (**sell through**) (of a product) be purchased by a customer from a retail outlet. ■ [no obj.] (**sell up**) sell all of one's property, possessions, or assets: *Ernest sold up and retired.* ■ (**sell oneself**) have sex in exchange for money: *if she was going to sell herself then it would be as well not to come too cheap.* ■ archaic offer (something) dishonorably for money or other reward; make a matter of corrupt bargaining: *do not your lawyers sell all their practice, as your priests their prayers?* ■ (**sell someone out**) betray someone for one's own financial or material benefit: *the clansmen became tenants and the chiefs sold them out.* ■ [no obj.] (**sell out**) abandon one's principles for reasons of expedience: *the prime minister has come under fire for selling out to the U.S.*
2 persuade someone of the merits of: *he sold the idea of making a film about Tchaikovsky | he could get work but he just won't sell himself.* ■ be the reason for (something) being bought: *what sells CDs to most people is convenience.* ■ cause (someone) to become enthusiastic about: (as adj. **sold**) *I'm just not sold on the idea.*
3 archaic trick or deceive (someone): *what we want is to go out of here quiet, and talk this show up, and sell the rest of the town.*
▶ n. informal **1** an act of selling or attempting to sell something: *the excitement of scientific achievement is too subtle a sell to stir the public.*
2 a disappointment, typically one arising from being deceived as to the merits of something: *actually, Hawaii's a bit of a sell.*
– PHRASES **sell someone a bill of goods** see BILL OF GOODS. **sell someone down the river** see RIVER. **sell someone a** (or **the**) **dummy** see DUMMY. **sell someone a pup** see PUP. **sell short** see SHORT. **sell someone/something short** fail to recognize or state the true value of: *don't sell yourself short—you've got what it takes.* **sell one's soul** (**to the devil**) do or be willing to do anything, no matter how wrong it is, in order to achieve one's objective: *universities are selling their souls for commercial success.*
– DERIVATIVES **sell·a·ble** adj.
– ORIGIN Old English *sellan* (verb), of Germanic origin; related to Old Norse *selja* 'give up, sell.' Early use included the sense 'give, hand (something) over voluntarily in response to a request.'

sel·la /ˈselə/ (in full **sella turcica** /ˈtərkikə, -sikə/) ▶ n. (pl. **sellae** /ˈselē, -lī/ or **sellae turcicae** /ˈselē ˈtərsiˌkē, ˈselī ˈtərkiˌkī/) Anatomy a depression in the sphenoid bone, containing the pituitary gland.
– ORIGIN late 17th cent.: from Latin, 'saddle,' (in full) 'Turkish saddle.'

sell-by date ▶ n. a date marked on a perishable product indicating the recommended time by which it should be sold: *milk past its sell-by date.* ■ informal, chiefly Brit. a time after which something or someone is no longer considered desirable or effective: *do broadcasters have a sell-by date?*

sell·down /ˈselˌdoun/ ▶ n. widespread selling of futures, securities, or commodities, triggered by or resulting in falling prices: *a selldown of banking stocks which, in turn, would further depress the market.*

sell·er /ˈselər/ ▶ n. **1** a person who sells something: *street sellers of newspapers, flowers, etc.* ■ (**the seller**) the party in a legal transaction who is selling: *the seller may accept the buyer's offer.*
2 [with adj.] a product that sells in some specified way: *the game will undoubtedly be the biggest seller of the year.*
– PHRASES **seller's** (or **sellers'**) **market** an economic situation in which goods or shares are scarce and sellers can keep prices high.

Sel·lers /ˈselərz/, Peter (1925–80), English comic actor. He established his reputation on *The Goon Show*, a radio series of the 1950s, but he is best known for the "Pink Panther" series of movies of the 1960s and 1970s, in which he played French detective Inspector Clouseau. Other notable movies: *The Lady Killers* (1955) and *Dr. Strangelove* (1964).

sell-in ▶ n. the sale of goods to retail traders prior to public retailing.

sell·ing point ▶ n. a feature of a product for sale that makes it attractive to customers.

sell·ing race ▶ n. a horse race after which the winning horse must be auctioned.

sell-off ▶ n. a sale of assets, typically at a low price, carried out in order to dispose of them rather than as normal trade. ■ a sale of shares, bonds, or commodities, esp. one that causes a fall in price.

sell·out /ˈselˌout/ ▶ n. **1** the selling of an entire stock of something, esp. tickets for an entertainment or sports event. ■ an event for which all tickets are sold: *the game is sure to be a sellout.*
2 a sale of a business or company. ■ a betrayal of one's principles for reasons of expedience: *one of the biggest political sellouts in decades.*

sell-through ▶ n. the ratio of the quantity of goods sold by a retail outlet to the quantity distributed to it wholesale: *the sell-through was amazing, 60 percent.* ■ the retail sale of something, typically a prerecorded videocassette, as opposed to its rental: [as modifier] *the burgeoning sell-through market.*

Sel·ma /ˈselmə/ an industrial city in south central Alabama, on the Alabama River; pop. 18,847 (est. 2008).

selt·zer /ˈseltsər/ (also **seltzer water**) ▶ n. soda water. ■ medicinal mineral water from Niederselters in Germany.
– ORIGIN mid 18th cent.: alteration of German *Selterser*, from (*Nieder*)*selters* (see above).

sel·va /ˈselvə/ ▶ n. a tract of land covered by dense equatorial forest, esp. in the Amazon basin.

–ORIGIN mid 19th cent.: from Spanish or Portuguese, from Latin *silva* 'woods.'

sel·vage /ˈselvij/ ▶ **n.** an edge produced on woven fabric during manufacture that prevents it from unraveling. ■ Geology a zone of altered rock, esp. volcanic glass, at the edge of a rock mass.
–ORIGIN late Middle English: from an alteration of SELF + EDGE, on the pattern of early modern Dutch *selfegghe*. The geological term dates from the 1930s.

selves /selvz/ plural form of SELF.

Sel·ye /ˈselyā/, Hans Hugo Bruno (1907–82), Canadian physician, born in Austria. He showed that environmental stress and anxiety could result in the release of hormones that, over a long period, could produce biochemical and physiological disorders.

Selz·nick /ˈselznik/, David O. (1902–65), US movie producer; full name *David Oliver Selznick*. He made *King Kong* (1933) for RKO and *Anna Karenina* (1935) for MGM before establishing his own production company in 1936, where he produced such screen classics as *Gone with the Wind* (1939) and *Rebecca* (1940).

SEM ▶ **abbr.** scanning electron microscope.

Sem. ▶ **abbr.** ■ seminary. ■ (also **Sem**) Semitic.

sem. ▶ **abbr.** semicolon.

sem·a·code /ˈseməˌkōd/ ▶ **n.** an optical pattern that encodes a URL for recognition by cellular-phone cameras, enabling the user to access a web page by scanning the code with the telephone.

se·man·tic /səˈmantik/ ▶ **adj.** relating to meaning in language or logic.
–DERIVATIVES **se·man·ti·cal·ly** /-ik(ə)lē/ **adv.**
–ORIGIN mid 17th cent.: from French *sémantique*, from Greek *sēmantikos* 'significant,' from *sēmainein* 'signify,' from *sēma* 'sign.'

se·man·tic field ▶ **n.** Linguistics a lexical set of semantically related items, e.g., verbs of perception.

se·man·tic·i·ty /ˌsimanˈtisitē/ ▶ **n.** the quality that a linguistic system has of being able to convey meanings, in particular by reference to the world of physical reality.

se·man·tics /səˈmantiks/ ▶ **plural n.** [usu. treated as sing.] the branch of linguistics and logic concerned with meaning. There are a number of branches and subbranches of semantics, including **formal semantics**, which studies the logical aspects of meaning, such as sense, reference, implication, and logical form, **lexical semantics**, which studies word meanings and word relations, and **conceptual semantics**, which studies the cognitive structure of meaning. ■ the meaning of a word, phrase, sentence, or text: *such quibbling over semantics may seem petty stuff.*
–DERIVATIVES **se·man·ti·cian** /ˌsēmanˈtisHən/ **n.**, **se·man·ti·cist n.**

sem·a·phore /ˈseməˌfôr/ ▶ **n.** **1** a system of sending messages by holding the arms or two flags or poles in certain positions according to an alphabetic code. ■ a signal sent by semaphore.
2 an apparatus for signaling in this way, consisting of an upright with movable parts.
▶ **v.** [with obj.] send (a message) by semaphore or by signals resembling semaphore: *Josh stands facing the rear and semaphoring the driver's intentions.*
–DERIVATIVES **sem·a·phor·ic** /ˌseməˈfôrik/ **adj.**, **sem·a·phor·i·cal·ly** /ˌseməˈfôrik(ə)lē/ **adv.**
–ORIGIN early 19th cent. (denoting a signaling apparatus): from French *sémaphore*, formed irregularly from Greek *sēma* 'sign' + -PHORE.

semaphore 2

Se·ma·rang /səˈmäˌräNG/ a port in Indonesia, on the northern coast of Java; pop. 1,396,000 (est. 2007).

se·ma·si·ol·o·gy /səˌmāsēˈäləjē, -zē-/ ▶ **n.** the branch of knowledge that deals with concepts and the terms that represent them. Compare with ONOMASIOLOGY.
–DERIVATIVES **se·ma·si·o·log·i·cal** /-əˈläjikəl/ **adj.**
–ORIGIN mid 19th cent.: from German *Semasiologie*, from Greek *sēmasia* 'meaning,' from *sēmainein* 'signify.'

sem·bla·ble /ˈsembləbəl/ ▶ **n.** literary a counterpart or equal to someone: *this person is our brother, our semblable, our very self.*
–ORIGIN Middle English (as an adjective meaning 'like, similar'): from Old French, from *sembler* 'seem.'

sem·blance /ˈsembləns/ ▶ **n.** the outward appearance or apparent form of something, esp. when the reality is different: *she tried to force her thoughts back into some **semblance of** order.* ■ archaic resemblance; similarity: *it bears some **semblance to** the thing I have in mind.*
–ORIGIN Middle English: from Old French, from *sembler* 'seem,' from Latin *similare, simulare* 'simulate.'

se·mé /səˈmā/ (also **semée**) ▶ **adj.** Heraldry covered with small bearings of indefinite number (e.g., stars, fleurs-de-lis) arranged all over the field.
–ORIGIN late Middle English: French, literally 'sown,' past participle of *semer*.

Se·mei /ˈsemā/ (also **Semey**) an industrial city and river port in eastern Kazakhstan, on the Irtysh River, close to the border with Russia; pop. 281,800 (est. 2006). Founded in the 18th century, it was known as Semipalatinsk until 1991.

Sem·e·le /ˈseməlē/ Greek Mythology the mother, by Zeus, of Dionysus. The fire of Zeus's thunderbolts killed her but made her child immortal.

se·men /ˈsēmən/ ▶ **n.** the male reproductive fluid, containing spermatozoa in suspension.
–ORIGIN late Middle English: from Latin, literally 'seed,' from *serere* 'to sow.'

se·mes·ter /səˈmestər/ ▶ **n.** a half-year term in a school or college, typically lasting fifteen to eighteen weeks.
–ORIGIN early 19th cent.: from German *Semester*, from Latin *semestris* 'six-monthly,' from *sex* 'six' + *mensis* 'month.'

se·mes·ter·ly /səˈmestərlē/ ▶ **adj.** happening or appearing once per academic semester: *fines may be added onto semesterly expenses.*

Se·mey variant spelling of SEMEI.

sem·i /ˈsemī/ ▶ **n.** (pl. **semis**) informal **1** a tractor-trailer: *she pulled into the path of a semi.*
2 a semifinal: *they defeated them in the semi.*
3 Brit. a semidetached house: *a three-bedroom semi.*
–ORIGIN early 20th cent.: abbreviation.

semi- ▶ **prefix** **1** half: *semicircular.* ■ occurring or appearing twice in a specified period: *semiannual.*
2 partly; in some degree or particular: *semiconscious.* ■ almost: *semidarkness.*
–ORIGIN from Latin; related to Greek *hēmi-*.

sem·i·a·cous·tic /ˌsemēəˈko͞ostik, ˌsemˌī-/ ▶ **adj.** (of a guitar) having both one or more pickups and a hollow body, typically with f-holes.
▶ **n.** a semi-acoustic guitar.

sem·i·an·nu·al /ˌsemēˈanyo͞oəl, ˌsemˌī-/ ▶ **adj.** occurring twice a year; half-yearly: *their semiannual meetings.* ■ (of a plant) living for half a year only.
▶ **n.** a semiannual plant.
–DERIVATIVES **sem·i·an·nu·al·ly adv.**

sem·i·a·quat·ic /ˌsemēəˈkwätik, ˌsemˌī-, -ˈkwatik/ ▶ **adj.** (of an animal) living partly on land and partly in water: *semiaquatic crocodiles.* ■ (of a plant) growing in very wet or waterlogged ground.

sem·i·au·to·bi·o·graph·i·cal /ˌsemiˌôtəˌbīəˈgrafikl ˌ,semī-/ ▶ **adj.** (of a written work) dealing partly with the writer's own life but also containing fictional elements.

sem·i·au·to·mat·ic /ˌsemēˌôtəˈmatik, ˌsemˌī-/ ▶ **adj.** partially automatic: *a semiautomatic climate-control system.* ■ (of a firearm) having a mechanism for self-loading but not for continuous firing: *semiautomatic rifles.*
▶ **n.** a semiautomatic firearm.

sem·i·au·ton·o·mous /ˌsemēôˈtänəməs, ˌsemˌī-/ ▶ **adj.** **1** (of a country, state, or community) having a degree of, but not complete, self-government: *Russia's semiautonomous republics.*
2 acting independently to some degree: *semiautonomous working groups.*

sem·i·base·ment /ˈsemēˌbāsmənt, ˈsemˌī-/ ▶ **n.** a story of a building partly below ground level.

sem·i·bold /ˈsemēˈbōld, ˈsemˌī-/ ▶ **adj.** Printing printed in a typeface with thick strokes but not as thick as bold.

sem·i·breve /ˈsemēˌbrēv, ˈsemˌī-/ ▶ **n.** Music, chiefly Brit. a whole note.

sem·i·cir·cle /ˈsemēˌsərkəl, ˈsemˌī-/ ▶ **n.** a half of a circle or of its circumference. ■ a set of objects arranged in a semicircle: *chairs were in a semicircle around the hearth.*
–DERIVATIVES **sem·i·cir·cu·lar adj.**
–ORIGIN early 16th cent.: from Latin *semicirculus* (see SEMI-, CIRCLE).

sem·i·cir·cu·lar ca·nals ▶ **plural n.** three fluid-filled bony channels in the inner ear. They are situated at right angles to each other and provide information about orientation to the brain to help maintain balance.

sem·i·civ·i·lized /ˌsemēˈsivəˌlīzd, ˌsemˌī-/ ▶ **adj.** partially civilized.

sem·i·clas·si·cal /ˌsemēˈklasikəl, ˌsemˌī-/ ▶ **adj.** **1** (of music) having elements both of classical music and of other more popular genres.
2 Physics (of a theory or method) intermediate between a classical or Newtonian description and one based on quantum mechanics or relativity.

sem·i·co·lon /ˈsemiˌkōlən, ˈsemˌī-/ ▶ **n.** a punctuation mark (;) indicating a pause, typically between two main clauses, that is more pronounced than that indicated by a comma.

sem·i·con·duct·ing /ˈsemēkənˌdəktiNG, ˌsemˌī-/ ▶ **adj.** (of a material or device) having the properties of a semiconductor.

sem·i·con·duc·tor /ˈsemēkənˌdəktər, ˈsemˌī-/ ▶ **n.** a solid substance that has a conductivity between that of an insulator and that of most metals, either due to the addition of an impurity or because of temperature effects. Devices made of semiconductors, notably silicon, are essential components of most electronic circuits.

sem·i·con·scious /ˌsemēˈkänsHəs, ˌsemˌī-/ ▶ **adj.** (of a person) only partially conscious: *he dragged out the semiconscious pilot.* ■ (of a feeling or memory) of which the person experiencing it is only vaguely or partially aware: *semiconscious obsessions.*
–DERIVATIVES **sem·i·con·scious·ness n.**

sem·i·con·serv·a·tive /ˌsemēkənˈsərvətiv, ˌsemˌī-/ ▶ **adj.** Biochemistry relating to or denoting replication of a nucleic acid in which one complete strand of each double helix is directly derived from the parent molecule.
–DERIVATIVES **sem·i·con·serv·a·tive·ly adv.**

sem·i·crys·tal·line /ˌsemēˈkristələn, ˌsemˌī-, -ˌlīn/ ▶ **adj.** Chemistry (of a solid) possessing crystalline character to some degree.

sem·i·cyl·in·der /ˌsemēˈsiləndər, ˌsemˌī-/ ▶ **n.** Geometry half of a cylinder cut longitudinally.
–DERIVATIVES **sem·i·cy·lin·dri·cal** /ˌsemēˌsəˈlindrikəl, ˌsemˌī-/ **adj.**

sem·i·dark·ness /ˌsemēˈdärknəs, ˌsemˌī-/ ▶ **n.** a light level in which it is possible to see, but not clearly.

sem·i·dem·i·sem·i·qua·ver /ˌsemēˌdemēˈsemēˌkwāvər/ ▶ **n.** Music chiefly Brit. another term for HEMIDEMISEMIQUAVER.

sem·i·der·e·lict /ˌsemēˈderəlikt, ˌsemī-/ ▶ **adj.** in a partially derelict state: *a semiderelict farmhouse.*

sem·i·de·tached /ˌsemēdiˈtacHt, ˌsemˌī-/ ▶ **adj.** (of a house) joined to another house on one side only by a common wall.
▶ **n.** Brit. a semidetached house.

sem·i·di·am·e·ter /ˌsemēdīˈamitər, ˌsemˌī-/ ▶ **n.** Astronomy & Geometry half of a diameter; radius.
–ORIGIN late Middle English: from late Latin.

sem·i·doc·u·men·ta·ry /ˌsemēˌdäkyəˈment(ə)rē, ˌsemˌī-/ ▶ **adj.** (of a movie) having a factual background and a fictitious story.
▶ **n.** a semidocumentary movie.

sem·i·dome /ˈsemēˌdōm, ˌsemˌī-/ ▶ **n.** Architecture a half-dome formed by vertical section.

sem·i·dou·ble /ˌsemēˈdəbəl, ˌsemˌī-/ ▶ **adj.** (of a flower) intermediate between single and double in having only the outer stamens converted to petals.

sem·i·el·lip·ti·cal /ˌsemē-iˈliptikəl, ˌsemˌī-/ ▶ **adj.** having the shape of half of an ellipse bisected by one of its diameters, esp. the major axis.

sem·i·ev·er·green /ˌsemēˈevərˌgrēn/ ▶ **adj.** (of a tree or shrub) retaining foliage part way through a season in which the leaves would normally be lost.

sem·i·fi·nal /ˌsemēˈfīnl, ˌsemˌī-/ ▶ **n.** a game or round immediately preceding the final, the winner of which goes on to the final.
–DERIVATIVES **sem·i·fi·nal·ist n.**

sem·i·fin·ished /ˌsemēˈfinisHt, ˌsemˌī-/ ▶ **adj.** prepared for the final stage of manufacture: *crude steel and semifinished metal products.*

sem·i·fit·ted /ˌsemēˈfitid, ˌsemˌī-/ ▶ **adj.** (of a garment) shaped to the body but not closely fitted: *a single-breasted semifitted jacket.*

sem·i·flu·id /ˌsemēˈflo͞o-id, ˌsemˌī-/ ▶ **adj.** having a thick consistency between solid and liquid.
▶ **n.** a semifluid substance.

sem·i·for·mal /ˌsemēˈfôrməl, ˌsemˌī-/ ▶ **adj.** combining formal and informal elements: *in the semiformal atmosphere irritations can be aired.* ■ used to describe clothing that is neither formal nor casual and that is typically worn for a dance, wedding, or other event: *the casino has a semiformal dress code (men must wear a tie and jacket).*

S

▶ n. an event at which semiformal attire is expected: *it had organized its own spring semiformal at a nearby hotel.*

se·mi·fred·do /semēˈfredō/ ▶ n. (pl. **semifreddos**) a partially frozen Italian dessert.
– ORIGIN Italian, from *semi-* **SEMI-** + *freddo* 'cold.'

sem·i·gloss /ˈsemēˌgläs, ˈsemˌī-, -ˌglôs/ ▶ n. a paint that dries to a moderately glossy sheen.

sem·i·in·de·pend·ent ▶ adj. partially free from outside control; not wholly depending on another's authority: *detachments are semi-independent units that are armed differently from their regiment.*

sem·i·in·va·lid /ˌsemēˈinvəlid, ˌsemˌī-/ ▶ n. a partially disabled or somewhat infirm person.

sem·i·le·thal /ˌsemēˈlēTHəl, ˌsemˌī-/ ▶ adj. Genetics relating to or denoting an allele or chromosomal abnormality that impairs the viability of most of the individuals homozygous for it.

sem·i·liq·uid /ˌsemēˈlikwid, ˌsemˌī-/ ▶ adj. & n. another term for **SEMIFLUID**.

sem·i·lit·er·ate /ˌsemēˈlitərit, ˌsemˌī-/ ▶ adj. unable to read or write with ease or fluency; poorly educated: *a high proportion of the population is still relatively poor and semiliterate.* ■ (of a text) poorly written: *the semiliterate glossies.*
▶ n. a person who is poorly educated or unable to read or write with ease or fluency.
– DERIVATIVES **sem·i·lit·er·a·cy** /-əsē/ n.

Sé·mil·lon /sāmē(l)ˈyôN/ ▶ n. a variety of white wine grape grown in France and elsewhere. ■ a white wine made from this grape.
– ORIGIN French dialect, based on Latin *semen* 'seed.'

sem·i·lu·nar /ˌsemēˈlo͞onər, ˌsemˌī-/ ▶ adj. chiefly Anatomy shaped like a half-moon or crescent.
– ORIGIN late Middle English: from medieval Latin *semilunaris* (see **SEMI-**, **LUNAR**).

sem·i·lu·nar bone ▶ n. another term for **LUNATE BONE** (see **LUNATE**).

sem·i·lu·nar car·ti·lage ▶ n. a crescent-shaped cartilage in the knee.

sem·i·lu·nar valve ▶ n. Anatomy each of a pair of valves in the heart, at the bases of the aorta and the pulmonary artery, consisting of three cusps or flaps that prevent the flow of blood back into the heart.

sem·i·ma·jor ax·is /ˈsemēˈmājər, ˈsemˌī-/ ▶ n. Geometry either of the halves of the major axis of an ellipse.

sem·i·mi·nor ax·is /ˈsemēˈmīnər, ˈsemˌī-/ ▶ n. Geometry either of the halves of the minor axis of an ellipse.

sem·i·mon·o·coque /ˌsemēˈmänəˌkōk, -ˌkäk, ˌsemˌī-/ ▶ adj. relating to or denoting aircraft or vehicle structures combining a load-bearing shell with integral frames.

sem·i·month·ly /ˌsemēˈmənTHlē, ˌsemˌī-/ ▶ adj. occurring or published twice a month: *semimonthly paydays.*

sem·i·nal /ˈsemənl/ ▶ adj. **1** (of a work, event, moment, or figure) strongly influencing later developments: *his seminal work on chaos theory.*
2 of, relating to, or denoting semen. ■ Botany of, relating to, or derived from the seed of a plant.
– DERIVATIVES **sem·i·nal·ly** adv.
– ORIGIN late Middle English (sense 2): from Old French *seminal* or Latin *seminalis*, from *semen* 'seed.' Sense 1 dates from the mid 17th cent.

S

sem·i·nal ves·i·cle ▶ n. Anatomy each of a pair of glands that open into the vas deferens near its junction with the urethra and secrete many of the components of semen.

sem·i·nar /ˈseməˌnär/ ▶ n. a conference or other meeting for discussion or training. ■ a class at a college or university in which a topic is discussed by a teacher and a small group of students.
– ORIGIN late 19th cent.: from German *Seminar*, from Latin *seminarium* (see **SEMINARY**).

sem·i·nar·y /ˈseməˌnerē/ ▶ n. (pl. **seminaries**) a college that prepares students to be priests, ministers, or rabbis.
– DERIVATIVES **sem·i·nar·i·an** /ˌseməˈne(ə)rēən/ n., **sem·i·na·rist** /-nərist/ n.
– ORIGIN late Middle English (denoting a seed plot): from Latin *seminarium* 'seed plot,' neuter of *seminarius* 'of seed,' from *semen* 'seed.'

sem·i·nif·er·ous /ˌseməˈnif(ə)rəs/ ▶ adj. producing or conveying semen.
– ORIGIN late 17th cent.: from Latin *semen, semin-* 'seed' + **-FEROUS**.

Sem·i·nole /ˈseməˌnōl/ ▶ n. (pl. **same** or **Seminoles**) **1** a member of an American Indian people of the Creek confederacy and their descendants, noted for resistance in the 19th century to encroachment on their land in Georgia and Florida. Many were resettled in Oklahoma.
2 either of the Muskogean languages, usually Creek, spoken by the Seminole.
▶ adj. of or relating to the Seminole or their language.
– ORIGIN from Creek *simanō·li, simalō·ni*, from American Spanish *cimarrón* 'wild,'(as a noun) 'escaped slave'; compare with **MAROON**.

sem·i·o·chem·i·cal /ˌsemē-ōˈkemikəl, ˌsēmē-/ ▶ n. Biochemistry a pheromone or other chemical that conveys a signal from one organism to another so as to modify the behavior of the recipient organism.

sem·i·of·fi·cial /ˌsemēəˈfisHəl, ˌsemˌī-/ ▶ adj. having some, but not full, official authority or recognition: *a semiofficial visit.*
– DERIVATIVES **sem·i·of·fi·cial·ly** adv.

se·mi·ol·o·gy /ˌsēmēˈäləjē, ˌsemē-, ˌsēmˌī-/ ▶ n. another term for **SEMIOTICS**.
– DERIVATIVES **se·mi·o·log·i·cal** /-əˈläjikəl/ adj., **se·mi·ol·o·gist** /-jist/ n.
– ORIGIN 1920s: from Greek *sēmeion* 'sign' (from *sēma* 'mark') + **-LOGY**.

sem·i·o·paque /ˌsemē-ōˈpāk, ˌsemˌī-/ ▶ adj. not fully clear or transparent.

sem·i·op·er·a /ˌseˌmēˈäp(ə)rə, ˌsemˌī-/ ▶ n. a drama or similar entertainment with a substantial proportion of vocal music in addition to instrumental movements.

sem·i·o·sis /ˌsēmēˈōsis, ˌsemē-, ˌsemˌī-/ ▶ n. Linguistics the process of signification in language or literature.
– ORIGIN early 20th cent.: from Greek *sēmeiosis* '(inference from) a sign.'

se·mi·ot·ics /ˌsēmēˈätiks, ˌsemē-, ˌsemˌī-/ ▶ plural n. [treated as sing.] the study of signs and symbols and their use or interpretation.
– DERIVATIVES **se·mi·ot·ic** adj., **se·mi·ot·i·cal·ly** /-ik(ə)lē/ adv., **se·mi·o·ti·cian** /ˌsemēəˈtisHən, ˌsēmēə-/ n.
– ORIGIN late 19th cent.: from Greek *sēmeiotikos* 'of signs,' from *sēmeioun* 'interpret as a sign.'

Se·mi·pa·la·tinsk /ˌsemipəˈlätinsk, syimipəˈlätyinsk/ former name (until 1991) for **SEMEI**.

sem·i·pal·mat·ed /ˌsemēˈpalˌmātid, -ˈpä(l)-, ˌsemˌī-/ ▶ adj. used in names of wading birds that have toes webbed for part of their length, e.g., **semipalmated sandpiper**.

sem·i·per·ma·nent /ˌsemēˈpərmənənt, ˌsemˌī-/ ▶ adj. less than permanent, but with some stability or endurance: *the company employs him on a semipermanent basis.*
– DERIVATIVES **sem·i·per·ma·nent·ly** adv.

sem·i·per·me·a·ble /ˌsemēˈpərmēəbəl, ˌsemˌī-/ ▶ adj. (of a material or membrane) allowing certain substances to pass through it but not others, esp. allowing the passage of a solvent but not of certain solutes.

sem·i·pre·cious /ˌsemēˈpresHəs, ˌsemˌī-/ ▶ adj. denoting minerals that can be used as gems but are considered to be less valuable than precious stones.

sem·i·pri·vate /ˌsemēˈprīvit, ˌsemˌī-/ ▶ adj. combining public and private elements: *the design gives every unit its own façade and a semiprivate balcony.* ■ (of a hospital room) accommodating two patients.

sem·i·pro ▶ adj. /ˌsemēˈprō, ˌsemī-/ & n. /ˈsemēˌprō, ˈsemī-/ (pl. **semipros**) informal short for **SEMIPROFESSIONAL**.

sem·i·pro·fes·sion·al /ˌsemēprəˈfesHənl, ˌsemˌī-/ ▶ adj. receiving payment for an activity but not relying entirely on it for a living: *a semiprofessional musician.* ■ involving or suitable for people engaged in an activity on such a basis: *training at the semiprofessional level.*
▶ n. a person who is engaged in an activity on such a basis.

sem·i·qua·ver /ˌsemēˈkwāvər/ ▶ n. Music chiefly Brit. a sixteenth note.

Se·mir·a·mis /səˈmirəməs/ Greek Mythology the daughter of an Assyrian goddess who married an Assyrian king. After his death she ruled for many years and became one of the founders of Babylon. She is thought to have been based on the historical queen Sammuramat (*c.*800 BC).

sem·i·re·tired /ˌsemēriˈtī(ə)rd, ˌsemī-/ ▶ adj. having retired or withdrawn from employment or an occupation but continuing to work part-time or occasionally.
– DERIVATIVES **sem·i·re·tire·ment** /-ˈtī(ə)rmənt/ n.

sem·i·rig·id /ˌsemēˈrijid, ˌsemˌī-/ ▶ adj. stiff and solid, but not inflexible: *a semirigid polyethylene hose.* ■ (of an airship) having a stiffened keel attached to a flexible gas container.

sem·i·skilled /ˌsemēˈskild, ˌsemˌī-/ ▶ adj. (of work or a worker) having or needing some, but not extensive, training: *assembly lines of semiskilled workers.*

sem·i·sol·id /ˌsemēˈsälid, ˌsemˌī-/ ▶ adj. highly viscous; slightly thicker than semifluid.

sem·i·sub·mers·i·ble /ˌsemēsəbˈmərsəbəl, ˌsemˌī-/ ▶ adj. denoting an oil or gas drilling platform or barge with submerged pontoons able to be flooded with water when the vessel is anchored on site in order to provide stability.
▶ n. an oil rig of this type.

sem·i·sweet /ˌsemēˈswēt, ˌsemˌī-/ ▶ adj. (of food) slightly sweetened, but less so than normal: *semisweet chocolates.* ■ (of wine) neither dry nor sweet; slightly sweeter than medium dry.

sem·i·syn·thet·ic /ˌsemēsinˈTHetik, ˌsemˌī-/ ▶ adj. Chemistry (of a substance) made by synthesis from a naturally occurring material.

Sem·ite /ˈsemīt/ ▶ n. a member of any of the peoples who speak or spoke a Semitic language, including in particular the Jews and Arabs.
– ORIGIN from modern Latin *Semita*, via late Latin from Greek *Sēm* 'Shem,' son of Noah in the Bible, from whom these people were traditionally supposed to be descended.

Se·mit·ic /səˈmitik/ ▶ adj. **1** relating to or denoting a family of languages that includes Hebrew, Arabic, and Aramaic and certain ancient languages such as Phoenician and Akkadian, constituting the main subgroup of the Afro-Asiatic family.
2 of or relating to the peoples who speak these languages, esp. Hebrew and Arabic.

sem·i·tone /ˈsemēˌtōn, ˈsemˌī-/ ▶ n. Music the smallest interval used in classical Western music, equal to a twelfth of an octave or half a tone; a half step.

sem·i·trail·er /ˈsemēˌtrālər, ˈsemˌī-/ ▶ n. a trailer having wheels at the back but supported at the front by a towing vehicle. ■ a tractor-trailer.

sem·i·trans·par·ent /ˌsemētransˈpe(ə)rənt, ˌsemˌī-, -ˈpar-/ ▶ adj. partially or imperfectly transparent.

sem·i·trop·ics /ˌsemēˈträpiks, ˌsemˌī-/ ▶ plural n. another term for **SUBTROPICS**.
– DERIVATIVES **sem·i·trop·i·cal** /-ˈträpikəl/ adj.

sem·i·vow·el /ˈsemēˌvouəl, ˈsemˌī-/ ▶ n. a speech sound intermediate between a vowel and a consonant, e.g., *w* or *y*.
– ORIGIN mid 16th cent.: from **SEMI-** + **VOWEL**, on the pattern of Latin *semivocalis*.

sem·i·week·ly /ˌsemēˈwēklē, ˌsemˌī-/ ▶ adj. occurring twice a week.

Sem·mel·weis /ˈseməlˌvīs/, Ignaz Philipp (1818–65), Hungarian obstetrician; Hungarian name *Ignác Fülöp Semmelweis*. He discovered the infectious character of puerperal fever and advocated rigorous cleanliness and the use of antiseptics by doctors examining patients.

sem·o·li·na /ˌseməˈlēnə/ ▶ n. the hard grains left after the milling of flour, used in puddings and in pasta.
– ORIGIN late 18th cent.: from Italian *semolino*, diminutive of *semola* 'bran,' from Latin *simila* 'flour.'

sem·per fi·de·lis /ˈsempər fiˈdālis/ (also **semper fi**) ▶ adj. always faithful (the motto of the US Marine Corps).
– ORIGIN Latin.

sem·per·vi·vum /ˌsempərˈvīvəm/ ▶ n. a plant of a genus that includes the houseleek. ● Genus *Sempervivum*, family Crassulaceae.
– ORIGIN modern Latin, from Latin *semper* 'always' + *vivus* 'living.'

sem·pi·ter·nal /ˌsempəˈtərnl/ ▶ adj. eternal and unchanging; everlasting: *his writings have the sempiternal youth of poetry.*
– DERIVATIVES **sem·pi·ter·nal·ly** adv., **sem·pi·ter·ni·ty** /-ˈtərnitē/ n.
– ORIGIN late Middle English: from Old French *sempiternel* or late Latin *sempiternalis*, from Latin *sempiternus*, from *semper* 'always' + *aeternus* 'eternal.'

sem·pli·ce /ˈsempliˌCHā/ ▶ adv. Music (as a direction) in a simple style of performance.
– ORIGIN Italian, literally 'simple.'

sem·pre /ˈsemˌprā/ ▶ adv. Music (in directions) throughout; always: *sempre forte.*
– ORIGIN Italian.

semp·stress /ˈsem(p)stris/ ▶ n. another term for **SEAMSTRESS**.

Sem·tex /ˈsemˌteks/ ▶ n. a very pliable, odorless plastic explosive.
– ORIGIN 1980s: probably a blend of *Semtin* (the name of a village in the Czech Republic near the place of production) and **EXPLOSIVE**.

sen /sen/ ▶ n. (pl. **same**) a monetary unit of Brunei, Cambodia, Indonesia, and Malaysia, equal to one hundredth of a dollar in Brunei, one hundredth of a riel in Cambodia, one hundredth of a rupiah in Indonesia, and one hundredth of a ringgit in Malaysia. [representing **CENT**.] ■ a former monetary unit in Japan, equal to one hundredth of a yen. [Japanese.]

Sen. ▶ **abbr.** ■ Senate. ■ Senator. ■ Senior.

Se·na·na·ya·ke /ˌsänänəˈyäkä/, Don Stephen (1884–1952), Sinhalese statesman; prime minister of Ceylon 1947–52. As prime minister he presided over Ceylon's achievement of full dominion status within the Commonwealth.

se·nar·ius /səˈne(ə)rēəs/ ▶ **n.** (pl. **senarii** /-ˈne(ə)rē,ī, -ˈne(ə)rē,ē/) Prosody a Latin verse of six iambic feet.
– ORIGIN mid 16th cent.: from Latin (see **SENARY**).

sen·a·ry /ˈsenərē/ ▶ **adj.** rare relating to or based on the number six.
– ORIGIN late 16th cent.: from Latin *senarius* 'containing six,' based on *sex* 'six.'

sen·ate /ˈsenit/ ▶ **n.** any of various legislative or governing bodies, in particular: ■ the smaller upper assembly in the US Congress, most US states, France, and other countries. ■ the state council of the ancient Roman republic and empire, which shared legislative power with the popular assemblies, administration with the magistrates, and judicial power with the knights. ■ the governing body of a university or college.
– ORIGIN Middle English: from Old French *senat*, from Latin *senatus*, from *senex* 'old man.'

sen·a·tor /ˈsenitər/ ▶ **n.** a member of a senate.
– DERIVATIVES **sen·a·to·ri·al** /ˌsenəˈtôrēəl/ **adj.**, **sen·a·tor·ship** /-ˌSHip/ **n.**
– ORIGIN Middle English (denoting a member of the ancient Roman senate): from Old French *senateur*, from Latin *senator* (see **SENATE**).

sen·a·tor·i·al cour·tes·y /ˌsenəˈtôrēəl/ ▶ **n.** a custom whereby presidential appointments are confirmed only if there is no objection to them by the senators from the appointee's state, esp. from the senior senator of the president's party from that state.

sen·a·tor·i·al dis·trict ▶ **n.** an electoral division of a state that is represented by a senator in the state's senate.

send¹ /send/ ▶ **v.** (past and past participle **sent** /sent/) **1** [with obj.] cause to go or be taken to a particular destination; arrange for the delivery of, esp. by mail: *we sent a reminder letter but received no reply* | [with two objs.] *he sent her a nice little note.* ■ order or instruct to go to a particular destination or in a particular direction: *Clemons sent me to Bangkok for R&R.* ■ [no obj., with infinitive] send a message or letter: *he sent to invite her to supper.* ■ cause to move sharply or quickly; propel: *the volcano sent clouds of ash up four miles into the air.* ■ (**send someone to**) arrange for someone to go to (an institution) and stay there for a particular purpose: *many parents prefer to send their children to single-sex schools.* **2** [with obj.] informal affect with powerful emotion; put into ecstasy: *it's the spectacle and music that send us, not the words.*
– PHRASES **send someone flying** cause someone to be knocked violently off balance or to the ground. **send someone packing** see **PACK¹**. **send someone to the showers** see **SHOWER**. **send word** send a message: *he sent word that he was busy.*
– PHRASAL VERBS **send away for** order or request that (something) be sent to one: *you can send away for the recipe.* **send someone down** Brit. **1** expel a student from a university. **2** informal sentence someone to imprisonment: *you're going to get sent down for possessing drugs.* **send for** order or instruct (someone) to come to one; summon: *if you don't go I shall send for the police.* ■ order by mail: *send for our mail order catalog.* **send something in** submit material to be considered for a competition or possible publication: *don't forget to send in your entries for our summer competition.* **send off for** another way of saying **SEND AWAY FOR** above. **send someone off** instruct someone to go; arrange for someone's departure: *she sent him off to a lecturing engagement.* ■ (of a referee, esp. in soccer or rugby) order a player to leave the field and take no further part in the game: *the player was sent off for rough play.* **send something off** dispatch something by mail: *please take a moment or two to send off a check to a good cause.* **send something on** transmit mail or luggage to a further destination or in advance of one's own arrival: *I've got your catalog—would you like me to send it on?* **send out for something** order delivery of something: *we sent out for pizza.* **send something out 1** produce or give out something; emit something: *radar signals were sent out in powerful pulses.* **2** dispatch items to a number of people; distribute something widely: *the company sent out written information about the stock.* **send someone up** sentence someone to imprisonment: *he was sent up for arson.* **send someone/something up** informal give an exaggerated imitation of someone or something in order to ridicule them: *the humorist who sent up sacred cows like school spirit.*
– DERIVATIVES **send·a·ble adj.**, **send·er n.**
– ORIGIN Old English *sendan*, of Germanic origin; related to Dutch *zenden* and German *senden*.

send² ▶ **n. & v.** variant spelling of **SCEND**.

Sen·dai /ˈsenˌdī/ a city in Japan, located near the northeastern coast of the island of Honshu; pop. 1,001,387 (2007).

Sen·dai vi·rus /ˈsenˌdī/ ▶ **n.** Biology a parainfluenza virus that causes disease of the upper respiratory tract in mice and is used in the laboratory to produce cell fusion.

Sen·dak /ˈsenˌdak/, Maurice (Bernard) (1928–), US writer and illustrator of children's books. He is best known for his award-winning *Where the Wild Things Are* (1963). He also wrote and illustrated *In the Night Kitchen* (1970) and *Outside Over There* (1981).

sen·dal /ˈsendl/ ▶ **n.** historical a fine, rich silk material, chiefly used to make ceremonial robes and banners.
– ORIGIN Middle English: from Old French *cendal*, ultimately from Greek *sindōn*.

Sen·de·ro Lu·mi·no·so /senˈderō ˌlo͞omiˈnōsō/ Spanish name for **SHINING PATH**.

send·ing /ˈsendiNG/ ▶ **n.** an unpleasant or evil thing or creature supposedly sent by someone with paranormal or magical powers to warn, punish, or take revenge on a person.
– ORIGIN mid 19th cent.: from Old Norse.

send-off ▶ **n.** a celebratory demonstration of goodwill at a person's departure: *I got an affectionate send-off from my colleagues.*

send·up /ˈsendˌəp/ ▶ **n.** informal an act of imitating someone or something in order to ridicule them; a parody: *a delicious sendup of a speech given by a trendy academic.*

se·ne /ˈsānā/ ▶ **n.** (pl. **same** or **senes**) a monetary unit of Samoa, equal to one hundredth of a tala.
– ORIGIN Samoan.

Sen·e·ca¹ /ˈsenəkə/, Lucius Annaeus (*c.*4 BC–AD 65), Roman statesman, philosopher, and playwright; known as **Seneca the Younger**. Son of Seneca the Elder, he became tutor to Nero in 49 and was appointed consul in 57. His *Epistulae Morales* is a notable Stoic work.

Sen·e·ca², Marcus (or Lucius) Annaeus (*c.*55 BC–*c.* AD39), Roman rhetorician, born in Spain; known as **Seneca the Elder**. Father of Seneca the Younger, he is best known for his works on rhetoric, only parts of which survive.

Sen·e·ca³ ▶ **n.** (pl. **same** or **Senecas**) **1** a member of an American Indian people that was one of the Five Nations.
2 the Iroquoian language of this people.
▶ **adj.** of or relating to this people or their language.
– ORIGIN via Dutch from Algonquian.

Sen·e·ca Falls a town in west central New York, west of Cayuga Lake, the site in 1848 of the first women's rights convention in the US; pop. 9,071 (est. 2008).

Sen·e·ca Lake the largest of the Finger Lakes in west central New York, south of Geneva, north of Watkins Glen.

se·ne·ci·o /səˈnēsēō, -SHēō/ ▶ **n.** (pl. **senecios**) a plant of a genus that includes the ragworts and groundsels. Many kinds are cultivated as ornamentals and some are poisonous weeds of grassland. ● Genus *Senecio*, family Compositae.
– ORIGIN modern Latin, from Latin, literally 'old man, groundsel,' with reference to the hairy white fruits.

Sen·e·gal /ˈsenəˌgôl, -ˌgäl/ a country on the coast of West Africa; pop. 13,711,600 (est. 2009); capital, Dakar; languages, French (official), Wolof, and other West African languages.

> Part of the Mali empire in the 14th and 15th centuries, the area was colonized by the French and became part of French West Africa in 1895. Briefly a partner in the Federation of Mali in 1959, Senegal withdrew and became a fully independent republic in 1960. Gambia forms an enclave within Senegal.

– DERIVATIVES **Sen·e·ga·lese** /ˌsenəgəˈlēz, -ˈlēs/ **adj. & n.**

Sen·e·gal Riv·er a river in western Africa that flows for 680 miles (1,088 km) from the Fouta Djallon of northern Guinea, through Mali and then along the Senegal-Mauritania border, to the Atlantic Ocean at St.-Louis in Senegal.

Sen·e·gam·bi·a /ˌseniˈgambēə, -ˈgäm-/ a region in West Africa that consists of the Senegal and Gambia rivers and the area between them. It lies mostly in Senegal and western Mali.

se·nesce /səˈnes/ ▶ **v.** [no obj.] Biology (of a living organism) deteriorate with age.
– ORIGIN mid 17th cent.: from Latin *senescere*, from *senex* 'old.'

se·nes·cence /səˈnesəns/ ▶ **n.** Biology the condition or process of deterioration with age. ■ loss of a cell's power of division and growth.
– DERIVATIVES **se·nes·cent adj.**

sen·e·schal /ˈsenəSHəl/ ▶ **n. 1** historical the steward or major-domo of a medieval great house.
2 chiefly historical a governor or other administrative or judicial officer.
– ORIGIN Middle English: from Old French, from medieval Latin *seniscalus*, from a Germanic compound of words meaning 'old' and 'servant.'

sen·ex /ˈsenˌeks/ ▶ **n.** (pl. **senes** /ˈsenˌēz/) (in literature, esp. comedy) an old man as a stock figure.
– ORIGIN late 19th cent.: from Latin, 'old man.'

se·nhor /sēnˈyôr, sin-/ ▶ **n.** (in Portuguese-speaking regions) a man (often used as a title or polite form of address): *Senhor Emilio Sofia Rosa.*
– ORIGIN Portuguese, from Latin *senior* (see **SENIOR**).

se·nho·ra /sēnˈyôrə, sin-/ ▶ **n.** (in Portuguese-speaking regions) a woman, esp. a married woman (often used as a title or polite form of address): *I look forward to hearing what Senhora Rocha decides.*
– ORIGIN Portuguese, feminine of **SENHOR**.

se·nho·ri·ta /ˌsēnyəˈrētə/ ▶ **n.** (in Portuguese-speaking regions) a young woman, esp. an unmarried one (often used as a title or polite form of address).
– ORIGIN Portuguese, diminutive of **SENHORA**.

se·nile /ˈsēˌnīl, ˈsen-/ ▶ **adj.** (of a person) having or showing the weaknesses or diseases of old age, esp. a loss of mental faculties: *she couldn't cope with her senile husband.* ■ (of a condition) characteristic of or caused by old age: *senile decay.*
▶ **n.** a senile person: *you never know where you stand with these so-called seniles.*
– ORIGIN mid 17th cent.: from French *sénile* or Latin *senilis*, from *senex* 'old man.'

se·nile de·men·tia ▶ **n.** severe mental deterioration in old age, characterized by loss of memory and control of bodily functions.

se·nile plaque ▶ **n.** Medicine a microscopic mass of fragmented and decaying nerve terminals around an amyloid core, numbers of which occur in the brains of people with Alzheimer's disease.

se·nil·i·ty /siˈnilitē/ ▶ **n.** the condition of being senile: *the onset of senility.*

sen·ior /ˈsēnyər/ ▶ **adj. 1** of a more advanced age: *he is 20 years senior to Leonard.* ■ of or for students in the final year of college or high school. ■ relating to or denoting competitors of above a certain age or of the highest status in a particular sport. ■ Brit. of, for, or denoting schoolchildren above a certain age, typically eleven. ■ (often **Senior**) [postpositive] (in names) denoting the elder of two who have the same name in a family, esp. a father as distinct from his son: *Henry James senior.*
2 holding a high and authoritative position: *he is a senior Finance Ministry official.* ■ [predic.] (**senior to**) holding a higher position than: *the people senior to me in my department.*
▶ **n.** a person who is a specified number of years older than someone else: *she was only two years his senior.* ■ an elderly person, esp. one who is retired and living on a pension. ■ a student in the final year of college or high school. ■ Brit. a student in a school for older children, esp. those eleven and over. ■ a competitor of above a certain age or of the highest status in a particular sport: *at fourteen you move up to the seniors.*
– ORIGIN late Middle English: from Latin, literally 'older, older man,' comparative of *senex, sen-* 'old man, old.'

sen·ior chief pet·ty of·fi·cer ▶ **n.** a noncommissioned officer in the US Navy or Coast Guard ranking above chief petty officer and below master chief petty officer.

sen·ior cit·i·zen ▶ **n.** an elderly person, esp. one who is retired and living on a pension.

sen·ior com·mon room ▶ **n.** Brit. a room used for social purposes by fellows, lecturers, and other senior members of a college. ■ [treated as sing. or pl.] the senior members of a college regarded collectively.

sen·ior high school ▶ **n.** a secondary school typically comprising the three highest grades.

sen·ior·i·ty /sēnˈyôritē, -ˈyär-/ ▶ **n. 1** the fact or state of being older or higher in position or status than someone else: *one by one, in order of seniority, employees' names were called.*
2 a privileged position earned by reason of longer service or higher rank: *pay and benefits rise with seniority.*

S

sen·ior mas·ter ser·geant ▶ **n.** a noncommissioned officer in the US Air Force ranking above master sergeant and below chief master sergeant.

sen·ior mo·ment ▶ **n.** informal a temporary mental lapse (humorously attributed to the gradual loss of one's mental faculties as one grows older).

sen·i·ti /ˈsenitē/ ▶ **n.** (pl. **same**) a monetary unit of Tonga, equal to one hundredth of a pa'anga.

sen·na /ˈsenə/ ▶ **n.** the cassia tree. ■ a laxative prepared from the dried pods of this tree.
– ORIGIN mid 16th cent.: from medieval Latin *sena*, from Arabic *sanā*.

Sen·nach·er·ib /səˈnakəˌrib/ (died 681 BC) king of Assyria 705–681; son of Sargon II. In 701, he put down a Jewish rebellion and laid siege to Jerusalem but spared it from destruction (according to 2 Kings 19:35). He also rebuilt the city of Nineveh and made it his capital.

sen·net /ˈsenit/ ▶ **n.** (in the stage directions of Elizabethan plays) a call on a trumpet or cornet to signal the ceremonial entrance or exit of an actor.
– ORIGIN late 16th cent.: perhaps a variant of SIGNET.

Senn·ett /ˈsenit/, Mack (1880–1960), US movie director, producer, and actor; born in Canada; born *Michael Sinnott*. He produced more than 1,000 slapstick comedy shorts and created the Keystone Kops. A special Academy Award in 1938 honored his accomplishments in comedy technique.

sen·night /ˈsenīt/ ▶ **n.** archaic a week.
– ORIGIN Old English *seofon nihta* 'seven nights.'

sen·nit /ˈsenit/ (also **sinnet**) ▶ **n.** plaited straw, hemp, or similar fibrous material used in making hats. ■ Nautical braided cordage in flat, round, or square form, used for making mats, lashings, etc.
– ORIGIN early 17th cent.: of unknown origin.

Se·ñor /sānˈyôr, sen-/ ▶ **n.** (pl. **Señores** /sānˈyôrāz, senˈyôres/ or **Señors**) a title or form of address used of or to a Spanish-speaking man, corresponding to *Mr.* or *sir*: *he is certain his information is correct, señor.*
– ORIGIN Spanish, from Latin *senior* (see SENIOR).

Se·ño·ra /sānˈyôrə, sen-/ ▶ **n.** a title or form of address used of or to a Spanish-speaking woman, corresponding to *Mrs.* or *madam*: *Señora Dolores.*
– ORIGIN Spanish, feminine of SEÑOR.

Se·ño·ri·ta /ˌsānyəˈrētə, ˌsen-/ ▶ **n.** a title or form of address used of or to a Spanish-speaking unmarried woman, corresponding to *Miss*: *a beautiful señorita.*
– ORIGIN Spanish, diminutive of SEÑORA.

Senr. ▶ **abbr.** Senior.

sen·sate /ˈsenˌsāt/ ▶ **adj.** literary perceiving or perceived by the senses: *you are immersed in an illusory, yet sensate, world.*
– ORIGIN mid 17th cent.: from late Latin *sensatus* 'having senses,' from *sensus* (see SENSE).

sen·sa·tion /senˈsāsʜən/ ▶ **n. 1** a physical feeling or perception resulting from something that happens to or comes into contact with the body: *a burning sensation in the middle of the chest.* ■ the capacity to have such feelings or perceptions: *they had lost sensation in one or both forearms.* ■ an inexplicable awareness or impression: [with clause] *she had the eerie sensation that she was being watched.*
2 a widespread reaction of interest and excitement: *his arrest for poisoning caused a sensation.* ■ a person, object, or event that arouses such interest and excitement: *she was a sensation, the talk of the evening.*
– ORIGIN early 17th cent.: from medieval Latin *sensatio(n-)*, from Latin *sensus* (see SENSE).

sen·sa·tion·al /senˈsāsʜənl/ ▶ **adj.** (of an event, a person, or a piece of information) causing great public interest and excitement: *a sensational murder trial.* ■ (of an account or a publication) presenting information in a way that is intended to provoke public interest and excitement, at the expense of accuracy: *cheap sensational periodicals.* ■ informal very good indeed; very impressive or attractive: *you look sensational | a sensational view.*
– DERIVATIVES **sen·sa·tion·al·ly adv.**

sen·sa·tion·al·ism /senˈsāsʜənlˌizəm/ ▶ **n. 1** (esp. in journalism) the use of exciting or shocking stories or language at the expense of accuracy, in order to provoke public interest or excitement: *media sensationalism.*
2 Philosophy another term for PHENOMENALISM.
– DERIVATIVES **sen·sa·tion·al·ist n. & adj.**, **sen·sa·tion·al·is·tic** /senˌsāsʜənlˈistik/ **adj.**

sen·sa·tion·al·ize /senˈsāsʜənlˌīz/ ▶ **v.** [with obj.] (esp. of a newspaper) present information about (something) in a way that provokes public interest and excitement, at the expense of accuracy: *the papers want to sensationalize the tragedy that my family has suffered.*

sense /sens/ ▶ **n. 1** a faculty by which the body perceives an external stimulus; one of the faculties of sight, smell, hearing, taste, and touch: *the bear has a keen sense of smell that enables it to hunt at dusk.*
2 a feeling that something is the case: *she had the sense of being a political outsider.* ■ an awareness or feeling that one is in a specified state: *you can improve your general health and sense of well-being.* ■ (**sense of**) a keen intuitive awareness of or sensitivity to the presence or importance of something: *she had a fine sense of comic timing.*
3 a sane and realistic attitude to situations and problems: *he earned respect by the good sense he showed at meetings.* ■ a reasonable or comprehensible rationale: *I can't see the sense in leaving all the work to you.*
4 a way in which an expression or a situation can be interpreted; a meaning: *it is not clear which sense of the word "characters" is intended in this passage.*
5 chiefly Mathematics & Physics a property, e.g., direction of motion, distinguishing a pair of objects, quantities, effects, etc., that differ only in that each is the reverse of the other. ■ [as modifier] Genetics relating to or denoting a coding sequence of nucleotides, complementary to an antisense sequence.
▶ **v.** [with obj.] perceive by a sense or senses: *with the first frost, they could sense a change in the days.* ■ be aware of: *she could sense her father's anger rising.* ■ [with clause] be aware that something is the case without being able to define exactly how one knows: *he could sense that he wasn't liked.* ■ (of a machine or similar device) detect: *an optical fiber senses a current flowing in a conductor.*
– PHRASES **bring someone to their** (or **come to one's**) **senses** restore someone to (or regain) consciousness. ■ cause someone to (or start to) think and behave reasonably after a period of folly or irrationality. **in a** (or **one**) **sense** used to indicate a particular interpretation of a statement or situation: *in a sense, behavior cannot develop independently of the environment.* **in one's senses** fully aware and in control of one's thoughts and words; sane: *would any man in his senses invent so absurd a story?* **make sense** be intelligible, justifiable, or practicable. **make sense of** find meaning or coherence in: *she must try to make sense of what was going on.* **out of one's senses** in or into a state of insanity. **take leave of one's senses** (in hyperbolic use) go insane.
– ORIGIN late Middle English (as a noun in the sense 'meaning'): from Latin *sensus* 'faculty of feeling, thought, meaning,' from *sentire* 'feel.' The verb dates from the mid 16th cent.

sense da·tum ▶ **n.** Philosophy an immediate object of perception, which is not a material object; a sense impression.

sense-ex·pe·ri·ence ▶ **n.** experience that is derived from the senses.

sen·sei /ˈsenˌsā, senˈsā/ ▶ **n.** (pl. **same**) (in martial arts) a teacher: [as title] *Sensei Ritchie began work.*
– ORIGIN Japanese, from *sen* 'previous' + *sei* 'birth.'

sense·less /ˈsensləs/ ▶ **adj. 1** [often as complement] (of a person) unconscious: *the attack left a policeman beaten senseless.* ■ incapable of sensation: *she knocked the glass from the girl's senseless fingers.*
2 (esp. of violent or wasteful action) without discernible meaning or purpose: *in Vietnam, I saw the senseless waste of human beings.* ■ lacking common sense; wildly foolish: *it was as senseless as crossing Death Valley on foot.*
– DERIVATIVES **sense·less·ly adv.**, **sense·less·ness n.**

sense or·gan ▶ **n.** an organ of the body that responds to external stimuli by conveying impulses to the sensory nervous system.

sen·si·bil·i·ty /ˌsensəˈbilitē/ ▶ **n.** (pl. **sensibilities**) the ability to appreciate and respond to complex emotional or aesthetic influences; sensitivity: *the study of literature leads to a growth of intelligence and sensibility.* ■ (**sensibilities**) a person's delicate sensitivity that makes them readily offended or shocked: *the scale of the poverty revealed by the survey shocked people's sensibilities.* ■ Zoology, dated sensitivity to sensory stimuli.
– ORIGIN late Middle English (denoting the power of sensation): from late Latin *sensibilitas*, from *sensibilis* 'that can be perceived by the senses' (see SENSIBLE).

sen·si·ble /ˈsensəbəl/ ▶ **adj. 1** (of a statement or course of action) chosen in accordance with wisdom or prudence; likely to be of benefit: *I cannot believe that it is sensible to spend so much | a sensible diet.* ■ (of a person) possessing or displaying prudence: *he was a sensible and capable boy.* ■ (of an object) practical and functional rather than decorative: *Mom always made me have sensible shoes.*
2 archaic readily perceived; appreciable: *it will effect a sensible reduction in these figures.* ■ [predic.] (**sensible of/to**) able to notice or appreciate; not unaware of: *we are sensible of the difficulties he faces.*
– DERIVATIVES **sen·si·ble·ness n.**, **sen·si·bly** /-blē/ **adv.**
– ORIGIN late Middle English (also in the sense 'perceptible by the senses'): from Old French, or from Latin *sensibilis*, from *sensus* (see SENSE).

sen·sil·lum /senˈsiləm/ ▶ **n.** (pl. **sensilla** /-ˈsilə/) Zoology (in arthropods and some other invertebrates) a simple sensory receptor consisting of a modified cell or small group of cells of the cuticle or epidermis, typically hair- or rod-shaped.
– ORIGIN early 20th cent.: modern Latin, diminutive of Latin *sensus* 'sense.'

sen·si·tive /ˈsensitiv/ ▶ **adj. 1** quick to detect or respond to slight changes, signals, or influences: *the new method of protein detection was more sensitive than earlier ones | spiders are sensitive to vibrations on their web.* ■ easily damaged, injured, or distressed by slight changes: *the committee called for improved protection of wildlife in environmentally sensitive areas.* ■ (of photographic materials) prepared so as to respond rapidly to the action of light. ■ (of a market) unstable and liable to quick changes of price because of outside influences.
2 (of a person or a person's behavior) having or displaying a quick and delicate appreciation of others' feelings: *I pay tribute to the Minister for his sensitive handling of the bill.* ■ easily offended or upset: *I suppose I shouldn't be so sensitive.*
3 kept secret or with restrictions on disclosure to avoid endangering security: *he was suspected of passing sensitive information to other countries.*
▶ **n.** a person who is believed to respond to occult influences.
– DERIVATIVES **sen·si·tive·ly adv.**, **sen·si·tive·ness n.**
– ORIGIN late Middle English (in the sense 'sensory'): from Old French *sensitif, -ive* or medieval Latin *sensitivus*, formed irregularly from Latin *sentire* 'feel.' The current senses date from the early 19th cent.

sen·si·tive pe·ri·od ▶ **n.** Psychology a time or stage in a person's development when they are more responsive to certain stimuli and quicker to learn particular skills.

sen·si·tive plant ▶ **n. 1** a tropical American plant of the pea family, whose leaflets fold together and leaves bend down when touched. A common weed of sugar cane, it has become naturalized throughout the tropics. ● *Mimosa pudica*, family Leguminosae.
2 informal a delicate or sensitive person.

sen·si·tiv·i·ty /ˌsensiˈtivitē/ ▶ **n.** (pl. **sensitivities**) the quality or condition of being sensitive: *a lack of common decency and sensitivity | he has a sensitivity to cow's milk.* ■ (**sensitivities**) a person's feelings which might be easily offended or hurt; sensibilities: *the rules that matter are practical ones that respect local sensitivities.*

sen·si·tiv·i·ty train·ing ▶ **n.** training intended to sensitize people to their attitudes and behaviors that may unwittingly cause offense to others, esp. members of various minorities.

sen·si·tize /ˈsensiˌtīz/ ▶ **v.** [with obj.] cause (someone or something) to respond to certain stimuli; make sensitive: *the introductory section aims to sensitize students to the methodology of the course.* ■ make (photographic film) sensitive to light: *the kit sensitizes any 35 mm film in hours.* ■ make (an organism) abnormally sensitive to a foreign substance: *the workers had been immunologically sensitized to the enzyme.*
– DERIVATIVES **sen·si·ti·za·tion** /ˌsensitiˈzāsʜən/ **n.**, **sen·si·tiz·er n.**

sen·si·tom·e·ter /ˌsensiˈtämitər/ ▶ **n.** Photography a device for measuring the sensitivity of photographic equipment to light.

sen·sor /ˈsensər/ ▶ **n.** a device that detects or measures a physical property and records, indicates, or otherwise responds to it.
– ORIGIN 1950s: from SENSORY, on the pattern of *motor*.

sen·so·ri·mo·tor /ˌsensərēˈmōtər/ ▶ **adj.** [attrib.] Physiology (of nerves or their actions) having or involving both sensory and motor functions or pathways.

sen·so·ri·neu·ral /ˌsensərēˈn(y)o͝orəl/ ▶ **adj.** Medicine (of hearing loss) caused by a lesion or disease of the inner ear or the auditory nerve.

sen·so·ri·um /senˈsôrēəm/ ▶ **n.** (pl. **sensoria** /-ˈsôrēə/ or **sensoriums**) the sensory apparatus or faculties considered as a whole: *virtual reality technology directed at recreating the human sensorium.*
– DERIVATIVES **sen·so·ri·al** /-ˈsôrēəl/ **adj.**, **sen·so·ri·al·ly** /-ˈsôrēəlē/ **adv.**
– ORIGIN mid 17th cent.: from late Latin, from Latin *sens-* 'perceived,' from the verb *sentire*.

sen·so·ry /ˈsensərē/ ▶ **adj.** of or relating to sensation or the physical senses; transmitted or perceived by the senses: *sensory input.*
– DERIVATIVES **sen·so·ri·ly** /-rəlē/ **adv.**

–ORIGIN mid 18th cent.: from Latin *sens-* 'perceived' (from the verb *sentire*) or from the noun SENSE + -ORY².

sen·so·ry dep·ri·va·tion ▶ n. a process by which someone is deprived of normal external stimuli such as sight and sound for an extended period of time, esp. as an experimental technique in psychology.

sen·su·al /ˈsenSHo͞oəl/ ▶ adj. of or arousing gratification of the senses and physical, esp. sexual, pleasure: *the production of the ballet is sensual and passionate.*
–DERIVATIVES **sen·su·al·ism** /-ˌlizəm/ n., **sen·su·al·ize** /-ˌlīz/ v., **sen·su·al·ly** adv.
–ORIGIN late Middle English (in the sense 'sensory'): from late Latin *sensualis*, from *sensus* (see SENSE).

> USAGE The words **sensual** and **sensuous** are frequently used interchangeably to mean 'gratifying the senses,' especially in a sexual sense. Strictly speaking, this goes against a traditional distinction, by which **sensuous** is a more neutral term, meaning 'relating to the senses rather than the intellect' (*swimming is a beautiful, sensuous experience*), while **sensual** relates to gratification of the senses, especially sexually (*a sensual massage*). In fact, the word **sensuous** is thought to have been invented by John Milton (1641) in a deliberate attempt to avoid the sexual overtones of **sensual**. In practice, the connotations are such that it is difficult to use **sensuous** in Milton's sense. While traditionalists struggle to maintain a distinction, the evidence suggests that the neutral use of **sensuous** is rare in modern English. If a neutral use is intended, it is advisable to use alternative wording.

sen·su·al·ist /ˈsenSHo͞oəlist/ ▶ n. a person devoted to physical, esp. sexual, pleasure: *a dedicated sensualist.*

sen·su·al·i·ty /ˌsenSHo͞oˈalitē/ ▶ n. the enjoyment, expression, or pursuit of physical, esp. sexual, pleasure: *he ate the grapes with surprising sensuality.* ■ the condition of being pleasing or fulfilling to the senses: *life can dazzle with its sensuality, its color.*
–ORIGIN Middle English (denoting the animal side of human nature): from Old French *sensualite*, from late Latin *sensualitas*, from *sensualis* (see SENSUAL).

sen·su la·to /ˈsenso͞o ˈlätō/ ▶ adv. formal in the broad sense.
–ORIGIN Latin.

sen·sum /ˈsensəm/ ▶ n. (pl. **sensa** /-sə/) Philosophy a sense datum.
–ORIGIN mid 19th cent.: modern Latin, 'something sensed,' neuter past participle of Latin *sentire* 'feel.'

sen·su·ous /ˈsenSHo͞oəs/ ▶ adj. **1** relating to or affecting the senses rather than the intellect: *the work showed a deliberate disregard of the more sensuous and immediately appealing aspects of painting.*
2 attractive or gratifying physically, esp. sexually: *her voice was rather deep but very sensuous.*
–DERIVATIVES **sen·su·ous·ly** adv., **sen·su·ous·ness** n.
–ORIGIN mid 17th cent.: from Latin *sensus* 'sense' + -OUS.

> USAGE On the use of the words **sensuous** and **sensual**, see usage at SENSUAL.

sen·su stric·to /ˈsenso͞o ˈstriktō/ ▶ adv. formal strictly speaking; in the narrow sense: *the process was one of substitution rather than change sensu stricto.*
–ORIGIN Latin, 'in the restricted sense.'

sent¹ /sent/ past and past participle of SEND¹.

sent² ▶ n. (pl. **senti** /ˈsentē/) a monetary unit of Estonia, equal to one hundredth of a kroon.
–ORIGIN respelling of CENT.

sen·te /ˈsenˌtē/ ▶ n. (pl. **lisente** /liˈsentē/) a monetary unit of Lesotho, equal to one hundredth of a loti.
–ORIGIN Sesotho.

sen·tence /ˈsentns/ ▶ n. **1** a set of words that is complete in itself, typically containing a subject and predicate, conveying a statement, question, exclamation, or command, and consisting of a main clause and sometimes one or more subordinate clauses. ■ Logic a series of signs or symbols expressing a proposition in an artificial or logical language.
2 the punishment assigned to a defendant found guilty by a court, or fixed by law for a particular offense: *her husband is* **serving** *a three-year sentence for fraud* | *slander of an official carried an eight-year prison sentence.*
▶ v. [with obj.] declare the punishment decided for (an offender): *ten army officers were* **sentenced to** *death.*
–PHRASES **under sentence of** having been condemned to: *he was under sentence of death.*
–ORIGIN Middle English (in the senses 'way of thinking, opinion,' 'court's declaration of punishment,' and 'gist (of a piece of writing)'): via Old French from Latin *sententia* 'opinion,' from *sentire* 'feel, be of the opinion.'

sen·tence ad·verb ▶ n. Grammar an adverb or adverbial phrase that expresses a writer's or speaker's attitude to the content of the sentence in which it occurs (such as *frankly, obviously*), or places the sentence in a particular context (such as *technically, politically*).

> USAGE The traditional definition of an adverb is that it is a word that modifies the meaning of a verb, an adjective, or another adverb, as in, for example, *he shook his head* ***sadly***. However, another important function of some adverbs is to comment on a whole sentence. For example, in the sentence ***sadly***, *he is rather overbearing*, **sadly** expresses the speaker's attitude to what is being stated. Traditionalists take the view that the use of sentence adverbs is inherently suspect and that they should always be paraphrased, using wording such as ***it is sad that*** *he is rather overbearing*. A particular objection is raised to the sentence adverbs **hopefully** and **thankfully**, since they cannot be paraphrased in the usual way (see usage at HOPEFULLY and THANKFULLY). However, there is overwhelming evidence that such usages are well established and widely accepted in everyday speech and writing.

sen·ten·tial /senˈtenCHəl/ ▶ adj. Grammar & Logic of or relating to a sentence: *sentential meaning.*

sen·ten·tious /senˈtenCHəs/ ▶ adj. given to moralizing in a pompous or affected manner: *he tried to encourage his men with sententious rhetoric.*
–DERIVATIVES **sen·ten·tious·ly** adv., **sen·ten·tious·ness** n.
–ORIGIN late Middle English: from Latin *sententiosus*, from *sententia* 'opinion' (see SENTENCE). The original sense was 'full of meaning or wisdom,' later becoming depreciatory.

sen·tient /ˈsenCH(ē)ənt/ ▶ adj. able to perceive or feel things: *she had been instructed from birth in the equality of all sentient life forms.*
–DERIVATIVES **sen·tience** n., **sen·tient·ly** adv.
–ORIGIN early 17th cent.: from Latin *sentient-* 'feeling,' from the verb *sentire*.

sen·ti·ment /ˈsen(t)əmənt/ ▶ n. **1** a view of or attitude toward a situation or event; an opinion: *I agree with your sentiments regarding the road bridge.* ■ general feeling or opinion: *the council sought steps to control the rise of racist sentiment.* ■ archaic the expression of a view or desire esp. as formulated for a toast.
2 a feeling or emotion: *an intense sentiment of horror.* ■ exaggerated and self-indulgent feelings of tenderness, sadness, or nostalgia: *many of the appeals rely on treacly sentiment.*
–ORIGIN late Middle English (in the senses 'personal experience' and 'physical feeling, sensation'): from Old French *sentement*, from medieval Latin *sentimentum*, from Latin *sentire* 'feel.'

sen·ti·men·tal /ˌsen(t)əˈmen(t)l/ ▶ adj. of or prompted by feelings of tenderness, sadness, or nostalgia: *she felt a sentimental attachment to the place creep over her.* ■ (of a work of literature, music, or art) dealing with feelings of tenderness, sadness, or nostalgia, typically in an exaggerated and self-indulgent way: *a sentimental ballad.* ■ (of a person) excessively prone to feelings of tenderness, sadness, or nostalgia: *I'm a sentimental old fool.*
–DERIVATIVES **sen·ti·men·tal·ly** adv.

sen·ti·men·tal·ism /ˌsen(t)əˈmen(t)lˌizəm/ ▶ n. the excessive expression of feelings of tenderness, sadness, or nostalgia in behavior, writing, or speech: *the author blends realism with surrealism, journalism with sentimentalism.*
–DERIVATIVES **sen·ti·men·tal·ist** n.

sen·ti·men·tal·i·ty /ˌsen(t)əmenˈtalitē, -mən-/ ▶ n. (pl. **sentimentalities**) excessive tenderness, sadness, or nostalgia: *there are passages which verge on sentimentality* | *sentimentalities of this kind seem reserved, in her, for people she does not know.*

sen·ti·men·tal·ize /ˌsen(t)əˈmen(t)lˌīz/ ▶ v. [with obj.] treat, regard, or portray (someone or something) with exaggerated and self-indulgent feelings of tenderness, sadness, or nostalgia: (as adj. **sentimentalized**) *the impossibly sentimentalized and saintly ideal of the Virgin Mother.*
–DERIVATIVES **sen·ti·men·tal·i·za·tion** /-ˌmen(t)liˈzāSHən/ n.

sen·ti·men·tal val·ue ▶ n. the value of something to someone because of personal or emotional associations rather than material worth.

sen·ti·nel /ˈsentn-əl/ ▶ n. a soldier or guard whose job is to stand and keep watch. ■ Medicine a thing that acts as an indicator of the presence of disease: [as modifier] *the first national HIV sentinel surveillance program in the developing world.*
▶ v. (**sentinels, sentineling, sentineled**; chiefly Brit. **sentinels, sentinelling, sentinelled**) [with obj.] station a soldier or guard by (a place) to keep watch: *a wide course had been roped off and sentineled with police* | figurative *trees sentineled the trenches.*
–PHRASES **stand sentinel** (of a soldier) keep watch: *soldiers stood sentinel with their muskets* | figurative *a tall round tower standing sentinel over the river.*
–ORIGIN late 16th cent.: from French *sentinelle*, from Italian *sentinella*, of unknown origin.

sen·try /ˈsentrē/ ▶ n. (pl. **sentries**) a soldier stationed to keep guard or to control access to a place.
–PHRASES **stand sentry** keep guard or control access to a place.
–ORIGIN early 17th cent.: perhaps from obsolete *centrinel*, variant of SENTINEL.

sen·try box ▶ n. a structure providing shelter for a standing sentry.

sen·try-go ▶ n. Military the duty of being a sentry.

Se·nu·fo /səˈno͞ofō/ ▶ n. **1** (pl. **same**) a member of a people inhabiting parts of Côte d'Ivoire (Ivory Coast), Mali, and Burkina Faso.
2 the Gur language of this people.
▶ adj. of or relating to this people or their language.
–ORIGIN Akan.

Se·nus·si /səˈno͞osē/ ▶ n. (pl. **same** or **Senussis**) a member of a North African Muslim religious fraternity founded in 1837 by **Sidi Muhammad ibn Ali es-Senussi** (d.1859).

SEO ▶ abbr. Computing search engine optimization.

Seoul /sōl/ the capital of South Korea, located in the northwestern part of the country, on the Han River; pop. 10,456,000 (est. 2008). It was the capital of the Korean Yi dynasty from the late 14th century until 1910, when Korea was annexed by the Japanese. Extensively developed under Japanese rule, it became the capital of South Korea after the partition of 1945.

sep. ▶ abbr. ■ sepal. ■ separable. ■ separate. ■ separated. ■ separation.

se·pal /ˈsēpəl/ ▶ n. Botany each of the parts of the calyx of a flower, enclosing the petals and typically green and leaflike.
–ORIGIN early 19th cent.: from French *sépale*, modern Latin *sepalum*, from Greek *skepē* 'covering,' influenced by French *pétale* 'petal.'

sep·a·ra·ble /ˈsep(ə)rəbəl/ ▶ adj. able to be separated or treated separately: *body and soul are not separable.* ■ Grammar (of a German prefix) separated from the base verb when inflected. ■ Grammar (of a German verb) consisting of a prefix and a base verb that are separated when inflected, e.g., *einführen*. ■ Grammar (of an English phrasal verb) allowing the insertion of the direct object between the base verb and the particle, e.g., *look it over* as opposed to *go over it*.
–DERIVATIVES **sep·a·ra·bil·i·ty** /ˌsep(ə)rəˈbilitē/ n., **sep·a·ra·ble·ness** n., **sep·a·ra·bly** /-blē/ adv.
–ORIGIN late Middle English: from Latin *separabilis*, from *separare* 'disjoin, divide' (see SEPARATE).

sep·a·rate ▶ adj. /ˈsep(ə)rit/ forming or viewed as a unit apart or by itself: *this raises two separate issues* | *he regards the study of literature as quite* **separate from** *life.* ■ not joined or touching physically: *hostels with separate quarters for men and women.* ■ different; distinct: *melt the white and dark chocolate in separate bowls.*
▶ v. /ˈsepəˌrāt/ **1** [with obj.] cause to move or be apart: *police were trying to separate two rioting mobs* | *they were separated by the war.* ■ form a distinction or boundary between (people, places, or things): *only a footpath separated their garden from the shore* | *six years separated the two brothers.* ■ [no obj.] become detached or disconnected: *the second stage of the rocket failed to separate.* ■ [no obj.] leave another person's company: *they separated at the corner, agreeing to meet within two hours.* ■ [no obj.] stop living together as a couple: *after her parents separated, she was brought up by her mother* | (as adj. **separated**) *her parents are separated.* ■ discharge or dismiss (someone) from service or employment: *this year one million veterans will be separated from the service.*
2 divide or cause to divide into constituent or distinct elements: [no obj.] *the milk had* **separated into** *curds and whey* | [with obj.] *separate the eggs and beat the yolks.* ■ [with obj.] extract or remove for use or rejection: *the skins are separated from the juice before fermentation* | figurative *we need to separate fact from speculation.* ■ [with obj.] distinguish between; consider individually: *we cannot separate his thinking from his activity.* ■ (of a factor or quality) distinguish (someone or something) from others: *his position separates him from those who might share his interests.* ■ [with obj.] (**separate something**

S

off) make something form, or view something as, a unit apart or by itself: *the organ loft separating off the choir*.
▶ **n.** (**separates**) things forming units by themselves, in particular: ■ individual items of clothing, such as skirts, jackets, or pants, suitable for wearing in different combinations. ■ the self-contained, freestanding components of a sound-reproduction system. ■ portions into which a soil, sediment, etc., can be sorted according to particle size, mineral composition, or other criteria.
– PHRASES **go one's separate ways** leave in a different direction from someone with whom one has just traveled or spent time. ■ end a romantic, professional, or other relationship. **separate but equal** historical racially segregated but ostensibly ensuring equal opportunities to all races. **separate the men from the boys** see MAN. **separate the sheep from the goats** divide people or things into superior and inferior groups. [with biblical allusion to Matt. 25:33.] **separate the wheat from the chaff** see CHAFF[1].
– DERIVATIVES **sep·a·rate·ness n.**
– ORIGIN late Middle English: from Latin *separat-* 'disjoined, divided,' from the verb *separare*, from *se-* 'apart' + *parare* 'prepare.'

sep·a·rate·ly /'sep(ə)ritlē/ ▶ **adv.** as a separate entity or entities; not together: *they arrived together but left separately* | *I shall consider that figure separately from the prime costs*.

sep·a·rate school ▶ **n.** Canadian a school receiving students from a particular religious group.

sep·a·ra·tion /ˌsepə'rāSHən/ ▶ **n. 1** the action or state of moving or being moved apart: *the damage that might arise from the separation of parents and children*. ■ the state in which a husband and wife remain married but live apart: *legal grounds for divorce or separation* | *she and her husband have agreed to a **trial separation***. See also LEGAL SEPARATION (sense 1).
2 the division of something into constituent or distinct elements: *prose structured into short sentences with meaningful **separation into** paragraphs*. ■ the process of distinguishing between two or more things: *religion involved the separation of the sacred and the profane* | *the constitution imposed a clear **separation between** church and state*. ■ the process of sorting and then extracting or removing a specified substance for use or rejection. ■ short for COLOR SEPARATION. ■ (also **stereo separation**) distinction or difference between the signals carried by the two channels of a stereophonic system. ■ Physics & Aeronautics the generation of a turbulent boundary layer between the surface of a body and a moving fluid, or between two fluids moving at different speeds.
– PHRASES **separation of powers** an act of vesting the legislative, executive, and judicial powers of government in separate bodies.
– ORIGIN late Middle English: via Old French from Latin *separatio(n-)*, from *separare* 'disjoin, divide' (see SEPARATE).

sep·a·ra·tion anx·i·e·ty ▶ **n.** Psychiatry anxiety provoked in a young child by separation or the threat of separation from their mother.

sep·a·ra·tism /'sep(ə)rəˌtizəm/ ▶ **n.** the advocacy or practice of separation of a certain group of people from a larger body on the basis of ethnicity, religion, or gender: *French Canadian separatism*.

sep·a·ra·tist /'sep(ə)rətist/ ▶ **n.** a person who supports the separation of a particular group of people from a larger body on the basis of ethnicity, religion, or gender: *religious separatists*.
▶ **adj.** of or relating to such separation or those supporting it: *a separatist rebellion*.

sep·a·ra·tive /'sep(ə)rətiv/ ▶ **adj.** technical tending to cause division into constituent or individual elements.

sep·a·ra·tor /'sepəˌrātər/ ▶ **n.** a machine or device that separates something into its constituent or distinct elements: *a magnetic separator*. ■ something that keeps two or more things apart: *most mail daemons use commas as separators between addresses*.

sepd. ▶ **abbr.** separated.

Seph·a·dex /'sefəˌdeks/ ▶ **n.** Biochemistry, trademark a preparation of dextran used as a gel in chromatography, electrophoresis, and other separation techniques.
– ORIGIN 1950s: of unknown origin.

Se·phar·di /sə'färdē/ ▶ **n.** (pl. **Sephardim** /-'färdim, -ˌfär'dēm/) a Jew of Spanish or Portuguese descent. They retain their own distinctive customs and rituals, preserving Babylonian Jewish traditions rather than the Palestinian ones of the Ashkenazim. Compare with ASHKENAZI. ■ any Jew of the Middle East or North Africa.
– DERIVATIVES **Se·phar·dic** /-dik/ **adj.**
– ORIGIN modern Hebrew, from *sĕpāraḏ*, a country mentioned in Obad. 20 and taken to be Spain.

Seph·a·rose /'sefəˌrōs, -ˌrōz/ ▶ **n.** Biochemistry, trademark a preparation of agarose used as a gel in chromatography, electrophoresis, and other separation techniques.
– ORIGIN 1960s: of unknown origin.

se·phi·ra /sə'fi(ə)rə/ ▶ **n.** (pl. **sephiroth** /-'fi(ə)rˌōt, -ˌōs/) (in cabalism) each of the ten attributes or emanations surrounding the Infinite and by means of which it relates to the finite. They are represented as spheres on the Tree of Life.
– ORIGIN from Hebrew *sĕpīrāh*.

se·pi·a /'sēpēə/ ▶ **n.** a reddish-brown color associated particularly with monochrome photographs of the 19th and early 20th centuries. ■ a brown pigment prepared from a black fluid secreted by cuttlefish, used in monochrome drawing and in watercolors. ■ a drawing done with this pigment. ■ a blackish fluid secreted by a cuttlefish as a defensive screen.
▶ **adj.** of a reddish-brown color: *old sepia photographs*.
– ORIGIN late Middle English (denoting a cuttlefish): via Latin from Greek *sēpia* 'cuttlefish.' The current senses date from the early 19th cent.

se·poy /'sēˌpoi/ ▶ **n.** historical an Indian soldier serving under British or other European orders. ■ (in South Asia) a police constable.
– ORIGIN from Urdu and Persian *sipāhī* 'soldier,' from *sipāh* 'army.'

Se·poy Mu·ti·ny another term for INDIAN MUTINY.

sep·pu·ku /'sepōōˌkōō, sə'pōōkōō/ ▶ **n.** another term for HARA-KIRI.
– ORIGIN Japanese, from *setsu* 'to cut' + *fuku* 'abdomen.'

seps /seps/ ▶ **n.** an African lizard with a snakelike body and very short or nonexistent legs. ● Genera *Tetradactylus*, family Gerrhosauridae: several species, formerly regarded as skinks.
– ORIGIN mid 16th cent. (denoting a venomous serpent described by classical authors): via Latin from Greek *sēps*, from the base of *sēpein* 'make rotten.'

sep·sis /'sepsis/ ▶ **n.** Medicine the presence in tissues of harmful bacteria and their toxins, typically through infection of a wound.
– ORIGIN late 19th cent.: modern Latin, from Greek *sēpsis*, from *sēpein* 'make rotten.'

sept /sept/ ▶ **n.** a clan, originally one in Ireland.
– ORIGIN early 16th cent.: probably an alteration of SECT.

Sept. ▶ **abbr.** ■ September. ■ Septuagint.

sept- ▶ **comb. form** variant spelling of SEPTI- (as in *septcentenary*).

sep·ta /'septə/ plural form of SEPTUM.

sep·tage /'septij/ ▶ **n.** excrement and other waste material contained in or removed from a septic tank.
– ORIGIN 1970s: from SEPTIC, on the pattern of *sewage*.

sep·tal /'septl/ ▶ **adj.** relating to or acting as a partition, in particular: ■ Anatomy & Biology relating to a septum or septa.

sep·tar·i·um /sep'te(ə)rēəm/ ▶ **n.** (pl. **septaria** /-'te(ə)rēə/) Geology a concretionary nodule, typically of ironstone, having radial cracks filled with calcite or another mineral.
– DERIVATIVES **sep·tar·i·an** /-'te(ə)rēən/ **adj.**
– ORIGIN late 18th cent.: modern Latin, from Latin *septum* 'enclosure.'

sep·tate /'sepˌtāt/ ▶ **adj.** Anatomy & Biology having or partitioned by a septum or septa.
– DERIVATIVES **sep·ta·tion** /sep'tāSHən/ **n.**

sept·cen·ten·ary /ˌsep(t)sen'tenərē, -'sentnˌerē/ ▶ **n.** (pl. **septcentenaries**) the seven-hundredth anniversary of a significant event.
▶ **adj.** of or relating to a seven-hundredth anniversary.

Sep·tem·ber /sep'tembər/ ▶ **n.** the ninth month of the year, in the northern hemisphere usually considered the first month of autumn: *sow the plants in early September* | [as modifier] *a warm September evening*.
– ORIGIN late Old English, from Latin, from *septem* 'seven' (being originally the seventh month of the Roman year).

September 11 (also **9/11**) September 11, 2001. On this date, two hijacked commercial airliners were flown into the World Trade Center in New York City. A third hijacked airliner was crashed into the Pentagon, and a fourth went down in a field in Pennsylvania. The airliners were hijacked by Islamic fundamentalist terrorists believed to be involved with al-Qaeda.

sep·te·nar·i·us /ˌseptə'ne(ə)rēəs/ ▶ **n.** (pl. **septenarii** /-'ne(ə)rēˌī/) Prosody a Latin verse line of seven feet, esp. a trochaic or iambic tetrameter catalectic, used only in comedy.
– ORIGIN early 19th cent.: from Latin, from *septeni* 'in sevens,' from *septem* 'seven.'

sep·te·nar·y /'septəˌnerē/ ▶ **adj.** of, relating to, or divided into seven.
▶ **n.** (pl. **septenaries**) a group or set of seven, in particular: ■ a period of seven years. ■ Music the seven notes of the diatonic scale.
– ORIGIN late Middle English: from Latin *septenarius* (see SEPTENARIUS).

sep·ten·ni·al /sep'tenēəl/ ▶ **adj.** recurring every seven years. ■ lasting for or relating to a period of seven years.
– ORIGIN mid 17th cent.: from late Latin *septennis* (from Latin *septem* 'seven' + *annus* 'year') + -AL.

sep·ten·ni·um /sep'tenēəm/ ▶ **n.** (pl. **septennia** /-'tenēə/ or **septenniums**) rare a specified period of seven years.
– ORIGIN mid 19th cent.: from late Latin, from Latin *septem* 'seven' + *annus* 'year.'

sep·tet /sep'tet/ (also **septette**) ▶ **n.** a group of seven people playing music or singing together. ■ a composition for such a group.
– ORIGIN early 19th cent.: from German *Septett*, from Latin *septem* 'seven.'

septi- (also **sept-**) ▶ **comb. form** seven; having seven: *septivalent*.
– ORIGIN from Latin *septem* 'seven.'

sep·tic /'septik/ ▶ **adj. 1** (chiefly of a wound or a part of the body) infected with bacteria.
2 [attrib.] denoting a drainage system incorporating a septic tank.
▶ **n.** a drainage system incorporating a septic tank.
– DERIVATIVES **sep·ti·cal·ly** /-ik(ə)lē/ **adv.**, **sep·tic·i·ty** /sep'tisitē/ **n.**
– ORIGIN early 17th cent.: via Latin from Greek *sēptikos*, 'rotten.'

sep·ti·ce·mi·a /ˌsepti'sēmēə/ (Brit. **septicaemia**) ▶ **n.** blood poisoning, esp. that caused by bacteria or their toxins.
– DERIVATIVES **sep·ti·ce·mic** /-mik/ **adj.**
– ORIGIN mid 19th cent.: modern Latin, from Greek *sēptikos* + *haima* 'blood.'

sep·tic tank ▶ **n.** a tank, typically underground, in which sewage is collected and allowed to decompose through bacterial activity before draining by means of a leaching field.

sep·til·lion /sep'tilyən/ ▶ **cardinal number** (pl. **septillions** or (with numeral) **same**) a thousand raised to the eighth power (10^{24}).Compare with QUADRILLION. ■ dated, chiefly Brit. a million raised to the seventh power (10^{42}).
– ORIGIN late 17th cent.: from French, from *million*, by substitution of the prefix *septi-* 'seven' (from Latin *septimus* 'seventh') for the initial letters.

sep·ti·mal /'septəməl/ ▶ **adj.** of or relating to the number seven.
– ORIGIN mid 19th cent.: from Latin *septimus* 'seventh' (from *septem* 'seven') + -AL.

sep·time /'sepˌtēm/ ▶ **n.** Fencing the seventh of eight standard parrying positions.
– ORIGIN late 19th cent.: from Latin *septimus* 'seventh.'

sep·ti·va·lent /ˌseptə'vālənt/ ▶ **adj.** Chemistry another term for HEPTAVALENT.

sep·to·ria /sep'tôrēə/ ▶ **n.** a fungus of a genus that includes many kinds that cause diseases in plants. ● Genus *Septoria*, subdivision Deuteromycotina. ■ leaf spot disease caused by such a fungus.
– ORIGIN modern Latin, from Latin *septum* (see SEPTUM).

sep·tu·a·ge·nar·i·an /ˌsepCHōōəjə'ne(ə)rēən/ ▶ **n.** a person who is from 70 to 79 years old.
– ORIGIN late 18th cent.: from Latin *septuagenarius* (based on *septuaginta* 'seventy') + -AN.

Sep·tu·a·ges·i·ma /ˌsepCHōōə'jesəmə/ (also **Septuagesima Sunday**) ▶ **n.** the Sunday before Sexagesima.
– ORIGIN late Middle English: from Latin, 'seventieth (day),' probably named by analogy with QUINQUAGESIMA.

Sep·tu·a·gint /'sepCHōōəˌjint/ ▶ **n.** a Greek version of the Hebrew Bible (or Old Testament), including the Apocrypha, made for Greek-speaking Jews in Egypt in the 3rd and 2nd centuries BC and adopted by the early Christian Churches.
– ORIGIN mid 16th cent. (originally denoting the translators themselves): from Latin *septuaginta* 'seventy,' because of the tradition that it was produced, under divine inspiration, by seventy-two translators working independently.

sep·tum /'septəm/ ▶ **n.** (pl. **septa** /-tə/) chiefly Anatomy & Biology a partition separating two chambers, such as that between the nostrils or the chambers of the heart.
– ORIGIN mid 17th cent.: from Latin *septum*, from *sepire* 'enclose,' from *sepes* 'hedge.'

sep·tu·ple /'septəpəl, sep't(y)ōōpəl, -'təp-/ rare ▶ **adj.** [attrib.] consisting of seven parts or elements. ■ consisting of seven times as much or as many as

usual. ■ (of time in music) having seven beats in a bar.
▶ v. [with obj.] multiply (something) by seven; increase sevenfold.
– ORIGIN early 17th cent. (as a verb): from late Latin *septuplus*, from Latin *septem* 'seven.'

sep·tup·let /sep'təplit, sep't(y)o͞o-/ ▶ n. **1** (usu. **septuplets**) each of seven children born at one birth.
2 Music a group of seven notes to be performed in the time of four or six.
– ORIGIN late 19th cent.: from Latin *septuplus* (see SEPTUPLE), on the pattern of words such as *triplet*.

sep·ul·cher /'sepəlkər/ (Brit. **sepulchre**) ▶ n. a small room or monument, cut in rock or built of stone, in which a dead person is laid or buried.
▶ v. [with obj.] chiefly literary lay or bury in or as if in a sepulcher: *tomes are soon out of print and sepulchered in the dust of libraries*. ■ serve as a burial place for: *when ocean shrouds and sepulchers our dead*.
– ORIGIN Middle English: via Old French from Latin *sepulcrum* 'burial place,' from *sepelire* 'bury.'

se·pul·chral /sə'pəlkrəl/ ▶ adj. of or relating to a tomb or interment: *sepulchral monuments*. ■ gloomy; dismal: *a speech delivered in sepulchral tones*.
– DERIVATIVES **se·pul·chral·ly** adv.
– ORIGIN early 17th cent.: from French *sépulchral* or Latin *sepulchralis*, from *sepulcrum* (see SEPULCHER).

sep·ul·ture /'sepəlCHər/ ▶ n. archaic burial; interment: *the rites of sepulture*.
– ORIGIN Middle English: via Old French from Latin *sepultura*, from *sepelire* 'bury.'

seq. (also **seqq.**) ▶ adv. short for ET SEQ.

se·qua·cious /si'kwāSHəs/ ▶ adj. formal (of a person) lacking independence or originality of thought.
– DERIVATIVES **se·qua·cious·ly** adv., **se·quac·i·ty** /-'kwasitē/ n.
– ORIGIN mid 17th cent.: from Latin *sequax, sequac-* 'following' (from *sequi* 'follow') + -IOUS.

se·quel /'sēkwəl/ ▶ n. a published, broadcast, or recorded work that continues the story or develops the theme of an earlier one. ■ something that takes place after or as a result of an earlier event: *this encouragement to grow potatoes had a disastrous sequel some fifty years later*.
– ORIGIN late Middle English (in the senses 'body of followers,' 'descendants' and 'consequence'): from Old French *sequelle* or Latin *sequella*, from *sequi* 'follow.'

se·que·la /si'kwelə/ ▶ n. (pl. **sequelae** /-'kwelē, -'kwelī/) (usu. **sequelae**) Medicine a condition that is the consequence of a previous disease or injury: *the long-term sequelae of infection*.
– ORIGIN late 18th cent.: from Latin, from *sequi* 'follow.'

se·quence /'sēkwəns/ ▶ n. **1** a particular order in which related events, movements, or things follow each other: *the content of the program should follow a logical sequence*. ■ Music a repetition of a phrase or melody at a higher or lower pitch. ■ Biochemistry the order in which amino acid or nucleotide residues are arranged in a protein, DNA, etc.
2 a set of related events, movements, or things that follow each other in a particular order: *a grueling sequence of exercises | a sonnet sequence*. ■ a set of three or more playing cards of the same suit next to each other in value, for example 10, 9, 8. ■ Mathematics an infinite ordered series of numerical quantities.
3 a part of a film dealing with one particular event or topic: *the famous underwater sequence*.
4 (in the Eucharist) a hymn said or sung after the Gradual or Alleluia that precedes the Gospel.
▶ v. [with obj.] **1** arrange in a particular order: *trainee librarians decide how a set of misfiled cards could be sequenced*. ■ Biochemistry ascertain the sequence of amino acid or nucleotide residues in (a protein, DNA, etc.).
2 play or record (music) with a sequencer.
– PHRASES **in sequence** in a given order.
– ORIGIN late Middle English (sense 4 of the noun): from late Latin *sequentia*, from Latin *sequent-* 'following,' from the verb *sequi* 'follow.'

se·quence danc·ing ▶ n. a type of ballroom dancing in which the couples all perform the same steps and movements simultaneously.

se·quence of ten·ses ▶ n. Grammar the dependence of the tense of a subordinate verb on the tense of the verb in the main clause (e.g., *I think that you* are *wrong; I thought that you* were *wrong*).

se·quenc·er /'sēkwənsər/ ▶ n. **1** a programmable electronic device for storing sequences of musical notes, chords, or rhythms and transmitting them when required to an electronic musical instrument.
2 Biochemistry an apparatus for determining the sequence of amino acids or other monomers in a biological polymer.

se·quent /'sēkwənt/ ▶ adj. archaic following in a sequence or as a logical conclusion.
– DERIVATIVES **se·quent·ly** adv.
– ORIGIN mid 16th cent.: from Old French, or from Latin *sequent-* 'following' (see SEQUENCE).

se·quen·tial /si'kwenCHəl/ ▶ adj. forming or following in a logical order or sequence: *a series of sequential steps*. ■ chiefly Computing performed or used in sequence: *sequential processing of data files*.
– DERIVATIVES **se·quen·ti·al·i·ty** /si,kwenCHē'alitē/ n., **se·quen·tial·ly** adv.
– ORIGIN early 19th cent. (as a medical term in the sense 'following as a secondary condition'): from SEQUENCE, on the pattern of *consequential*.

se·quen·tial ac·cess ▶ n. access to a computer data file that requires the user to read through the file from the beginning in the order in which it is stored. Compare with DIRECT ACCESS.

se·quen·tial cir·cuit ▶ n. Electronics a circuit whose output depends on the order or timing of the inputs. Compare with COMBINATIONAL CIRCUIT.

se·ques·ter /sə'kwestər/ ▶ v. [with obj.] **1** isolate or hide away (someone or something): *Tiberius was sequestered on an island | the jurors had been sequestered since Monday | the artist sequestered himself in his studio for two years*. ■ [no obj.] Chemistry form a chelate or other stable compound with (an ion, atom, or molecule) so that it is no longer available for reactions.
2 take legal possession of (assets) until a debt has been paid or other claims have been met: *the power of courts to sequester the assets of unions*. ■ take forcible possession of (something); confiscate: *rebel property was sequestered and a military government installed*. ■ legally place (the property of a bankrupt) in the hands of a trustee for division among the creditors: (as adj. **sequestered**) *a trustee in a sequestered estate*.
– DERIVATIVES **se·ques·tra·ble** /si'kwestrəbəl/ adj., **se·ques·tra·tor** /'sēkwi,strātər, 'sek-, si'kwes,trātər/ n.
– ORIGIN late Middle English: from Old French *sequestrer* or late Latin *sequestrare* 'commit for safekeeping,' from Latin *sequester* 'trustee.'

se·ques·tered /sə'kwestərd/ ▶ adj. (of a place) isolated and hidden away: *a wild sequestered spot*.

se·ques·trate /'sēkwi,strāt, 'sek-, sə'kwes,trāt/ ▶ v. another term for SEQUESTER.
– ORIGIN late Middle English (in the sense 'separate from general access'): from late Latin *sequestrat-* 'given up for safekeeping,' from the verb *sequestrare* (see SEQUESTER).

se·ques·tra·tion /,sēkwi'strāSHən, ,sek-/ ▶ n. the action of taking legal possession of assets until a debt has been paid or other claims have been met: *if such court injunctions are ignored, sequestration of trade union assets will follow*. ■ the action of taking forcible possession of something; confiscation: *they demanded the sequestration of the incriminating correspondence*. ■ an act of declaring someone bankrupt. ■ the action of making a general cut in government spending: *the measure brings the federal budget closer to sequestration*. ■ Chemistry the action of sequestering a substance.

se·ques·trum /si'kwestrəm/ ▶ n. (pl. **sequestra** /-trə/) Medicine a piece of dead bone tissue occurring within a diseased or injured bone, typically in chronic osteomyelitis.
– DERIVATIVES **se·ques·tral** /-trəl/ adj., **se·ques·trec·to·my** /,sēkwe'strektəmē/ n. (pl. **sequestrectomies**).
– ORIGIN mid 19th cent.: modern Latin, neuter of Latin *sequester* 'standing apart.'

se·quin /'sēkwin/ ▶ n. **1** a small, shiny disk sewn as one of many onto clothing for decoration.
2 historical a Venetian gold coin.
– DERIVATIVES **se·quined** (also **sequinned**) adj.
– ORIGIN late 16th cent. (sense 2): from French, from Italian *zecchino*, from *zecca* 'a mint,' from Arabic *sikka* 'a die for coining.' Sense 1 dates from the late 19th cent.

se·quoi·a /sə'k(w)oi-ə/ ▶ n. a redwood tree, esp. the California redwood.
– ORIGIN from modern Latin *Sequoia* (genus name), from *Sequoya*.

Se·quoi·a Na·tion·al Park a national park in the Sierra Nevada of California, east of Fresno. It was established in 1890 to protect groves of giant sequoia trees, of which the largest, the General Sherman Tree, is thought to be between 3,000 and 4,000 years old.

Se·quoy·a /sə'kwoi-ə/ (also **Sequoyah, Sequoia**) (*c.*1770–1843), Cherokee Indian scholar; Cherokee name *Sogwali*; also known as **George Guess** or **Gist**. He invented a writing system (the Cherokee syllabary) 1809–21 for the Cherokee language and with it taught thousands of Cherokee Indians to read and write. The giant sequoia trees of California are named for him.

ser. ▶ abbr. ■ serial. ■ series. ■ sermon.

se·ra /'si(ə)rə/ plural form of SERUM.

se·rac /sə'rak/ ▶ n. a pinnacle or ridge of ice on the surface of a glacier.
– ORIGIN mid 19th cent.: from Swiss French *sérac*, originally the name of a compact white cheese.

se·ragl·io /sə'rälyō/ ▶ n. (pl. **seraglios**) historical **1** the women's apartments (harem) in a Muslim palace. ■ another term for HAREM (sense 2).
2 historical a Turkish palace, esp. the Sultan's court and government offices at Constantinople.
– ORIGIN late 16th cent.: from Italian *serraglio*, via Turkish from Persian *sarāy* 'palace'; compare with SERAI.

se·ra·i /sə'rī/ ▶ n. another term for CARAVANSARY (sense 1).

Se·raing /sə'raN/ an industrial town in Belgium, on the Meuse River, southwest of Liège; pop. 61,657 (2008).

Se·ram Sea variant spelling of CERAM SEA.

se·ra·pe /sə'räpē/ (also **sarape**) ▶ n. a shawl or blanket worn as a cloak in Latin America.
– ORIGIN Mexican Spanish.

ser·aph /'serəf/ ▶ n. (pl. **seraphim** /'serə,fim/ or **seraphs**) an angelic being, regarded in traditional Christian angelology as belonging to the highest order of the ninefold celestial hierarchy, associated with light, ardor, and purity.
– ORIGIN Old English, back-formation from *seraphim* (plural), via late Latin and Greek from Hebrew *śĕrāpīm*. Compare with CHERUB.

se·raph·ic /sə'rafik/ ▶ adj. characteristic of or resembling a seraph or seraphim: *a seraphic smile*.
– DERIVATIVES **se·raph·i·cal·ly** /-ik(ə)lē/ adv.
– ORIGIN mid 17th cent.: from medieval Latin *seraphicus*, from late Latin *seraphim* (see SERAPH).

Se·raph·ic Doc·tor the nickname of St. Bonaventura.

Se·ra·pis /sə'rāpis/ Egyptian Mythology a god whose cult was developed by Ptolemy I at Memphis as a combination of Apis and Osiris, to unite Greeks and Egyptians in a common worship.

ser·a·skier /,serə'ski(ə)r/ ▶ n. historical the commander in chief and minister of war of the Ottoman Empire.
– ORIGIN Turkish, from Persian *sar'askar* 'head (of the) army.'

Serb /sərb/ ▶ n. a native or inhabitant of Serbia. ■ a person of Serbian descent.
▶ adj. of or relating to Serbia, the Serbs, or their language.
– ORIGIN Serbian *Srb*.

Ser·bi·a /'sərbēə/ a republic in the Balkans; pop. 7,379,300 (est. 2009); official language, Serbian; capital, Belgrade.

> Serbia was conquered by the Turks in the 14th century and regained independence in 1878. Serbian rivalry with the Austro-Hungarian Empire contributed to the outbreak of World War I, after which Serbia was absorbed into the kingdom of Serbs, Croats, and Slovenes (named Yugoslavia from 1929 to 2003). In 1991–92 four out of the six Yugoslav republics seceded; Serbia became involved in armed conflict with neighboring Croatia and in the civil war in Bosnia. On the breakup of Yugoslavia it remained in federation with Montenegro until 2006.

S

Ser·bi·an /'sərbēən/ ▶ n. **1** the Southern Slavic language of the Serbs, almost identical to Croatian but written in the Cyrillic alphabet. See SERBO-CROAT.
2 another term for SERB.
▶ adj. of or relating to Serbia, the Serbs, or their language.

Serbo- ▶ comb. form Serbian; Serbian and ...: *Serbo-Croat*. ■ relating to Serbia.

Ser·bo-Cro·at /,sərbō'krō,ät, 'krōt/ (also **Serbo-Croatian** /krō'āSHən/) ▶ n. a term for the South Slavic language spoken in Serbia, Croatia, and elsewhere in the former Yugoslavia. Serbo-Croat comprises two closely similar forms: Serbian, written in the Cyrillic alphabet, and Croat, written in the Roman alphabet. Since the breakup of Yugoslavia the names of the individual languages have generally been preferred.
▶ adj. of or relating to this language.

Ser·cial /ˈsərsēəl, sərsˈyäl/ ▶ **n.** a variety of wine grape grown chiefly in Madeira. ■ a dry, light Madeira made from this grape.
– ORIGIN Portuguese.

sere[1] /si(ə)r/ (also **sear**) ▶ **adj.** (esp. of vegetation) dry or withered: *small green vineyards encircled by vast sear fields.*
– ORIGIN Old English *sēar*: see SEAR.

sere[2] ▶ **n.** Ecology a natural succession of plant (or animal) communities, esp. a full series from uncolonized habitat to the appropriate climax vegetation. Compare with SUCCESSION.
– ORIGIN early 20th cent.: from Latin *serere* 'join in a series.'

Se·rem·ban /səˈrembən/ a town in southwestern Malaysia; pop. 419,500 (est. 2009).

ser·e·nade /ˌserəˈnād/ ▶ **n.** a piece of music sung or played in the open air, typically by a man at night under the window of his lover. ■ another term for SERENATA.
▶ **v.** [with obj.] entertain (someone) with a serenade: *a strolling guitarist serenades the diners.*
– DERIVATIVES **ser·e·nad·er n.**
– ORIGIN mid 17th cent.: from French *sérénade*, from Italian *serenata*, from *sereno* 'serene.'

ser·e·na·ta /ˌserəˈnätə/ ▶ **n.** Music a cantata with a pastoral subject. ■ a simple form of suite for orchestra or wind band.
– ORIGIN Italian, 'serenade' (see SERENADE).

ser·en·dip·i·tous /ˌserənˈdipitəs/ ▶ **adj.** occurring or discovered by chance in a happy or beneficial way: *a serendipitous encounter.*
– DERIVATIVES **ser·en·dip·i·tous·ly adv.**

ser·en·dip·i·ty /ˌserənˈdipitē/ ▶ **n.** the occurrence and development of events by chance in a happy or beneficial way: *a fortunate stroke of serendipity* | *a series of small serendipities.*
– ORIGIN 1754: coined by Horace Walpole, suggested by *The Three Princes of Serendip*, the title of a fairy tale in which the heroes "were always making discoveries, by accidents and sagacity, of things they were not in quest of."

se·rene /səˈrēn/ ▶ **adj. 1** calm, peaceful, and untroubled; tranquil: *her eyes were closed and she looked very serene* | *serene certainty.*
2 (**Serene**) (in a title) used as a term of respect for members of some European royal families: *His Serene Highness.*
▶ **n.** (usu. **the serene**) archaic an expanse of clear sky or calm sea: *not a cloud obscured the deep serene.*
– DERIVATIVES **se·rene·ly adv.**
– ORIGIN late Middle English (describing the weather or sky as 'clear, fine, and calm'): from Latin *serenus*.

Ser·en·get·i /ˌserənˈgetē/ a vast plain in Tanzania, west of the Great Rift Valley. In 1951 the Serengeti National Park was created to protect the area's large numbers of wildebeest, zebra, and Thomson's gazelle.

Se·re·nis·si·ma /ˌserəˈnisəmə/ ▶ **n.** (**La Serenissima, the Serenissima**) Venice: *the ghost-fleets of the Serenissima's seafaring past.*
– ORIGIN Italian, feminine of *serenissimo* 'most serene.'

se·ren·i·ty /səˈrenitē/ ▶ **n.** (pl. **serenities**) the state of being calm, peaceful, and untroubled: *an oasis of serenity amidst the bustling city.* ■ (**His/Your**, etc., **Serenity**) a title given to a reigning prince or similar dignitary.
– ORIGIN late Middle English: from Old French *serenite*, from Latin *serenitas*, from *serenus* 'clear, fair' (see SERENE).

S

serf /sərf/ ▶ **n.** an agricultural laborer bound under the feudal system to work on his lord's estate.
– DERIVATIVES **serf·age** /-fij/ **n.**, **serf·dom** /-dəm/ **n.**
– ORIGIN late 15th cent. (in the sense 'slave'): from Old French, from Latin *servus* 'slave.'

serge /sərj/ ▶ **n.** a durable twilled woolen or worsted fabric.
– ORIGIN late Middle English: from Old French *sarge*, from a variant of Latin *serica (lana)* 'silken (wool),' from *sericus* (see SILK).

ser·geant /ˈsärjənt/ ▶ **n.** a noncommissioned officer in the armed forces, in particular (in the US Army or Marine Corps) an NCO ranking above corporal and below staff sergeant, or (in the US Air Force) an NCO ranking above airman and below staff sergeant. ■ Brit. a police officer ranking below an inspector. ■ a police officer ranking below a lieutenant.
– DERIVATIVES **ser·gean·cy** /-jənsē/ **n.** (pl. **sergeancies**).
– ORIGIN Middle English: from Old French *sergent*, from Latin *servient-* 'serving,' from the verb *servire*. Early use was as a general term meaning 'attendant, servant' and 'common soldier'; the term was later applied to specific official roles.

ser·geant-at-arms (Brit. **serjeant-at-arms**) ▶ **n.** (pl. **sergeants-at-arms**) an official of a legislative or other assembly whose duty includes maintaining order and security. ■ Brit. historical a knight or armed officer in the service of the monarch or a lord.

Ser·geant Ba·ker ▶ **n.** Austral. a brightly colored edible marine fish with two elongated dorsal fin rays, occurring in warm Australian coastal waters. ● *Aulopus purpurissatus*, family Aulopidae.
– ORIGIN late 19th cent.: of unknown origin.

ser·geant first class ▶ **n.** a noncommissioned officer in the US Army of a rank above staff sergeant and below master sergeant.

ser·geant fish ▶ **n.** another term for COBIA.

ser·geant ma·jor ▶ **n. 1** a noncommissioned officer in the US Army or Marine Corps of the highest rank, above master sergeant and below warrant officer.
2 a warrant officer in the British army.
3 a fish with boldly striped sides that lives in warm seas, typically on coral reefs. ● *Abudefduf saxatilis*, family Pomacentridae.

serg·er /ˈsərjər/ ▶ **n.** a sewing machine used for overcasting to prevent material from fraying at the edge.

Ser·gi·us, St. /ˈsərjēəs/ (1314–92), Russian monastic reformer and mystic; Russian name *Svyatoi Sergi Radonezhsky*. He re-established the monasticism that had been lost through the Tartar invasion and inspired the resistance that saved Russia from the Tartars in 1380. Feast day, September 25.

se·ri·al /ˈsi(ə)rēəl/ ▶ **adj. 1** consisting of, forming part of, or taking place in a series: *a serial publication.* ■ Music using transformations of a fixed series of notes. ■ Computing (of a device) involving the transfer of data as a single sequence of bits. See also SERIAL PORT. ■ Computing (of a processor) running only a single task, as opposed to multitasking. ■ Linguistics (of verbs) used in sequence to form a construction, as in *they wanted, needed, longed for peace.*
2 [attrib.] (of a criminal) repeatedly committing the same offense and typically following a characteristic, predictable behavior pattern: *a suspected serial rapist.* ■ repeatedly following the same behavior pattern: *he was a serial adulterer* | *serial monogamy.*
▶ **n.** a story or play appearing in regular installments on television or radio or in a magazine or newspaper: *a new three-part drama serial.* ■ (usu. **serials**) (in a library) a periodical.
– DERIVATIVES **se·ri·al·i·ty** /ˌsi(ə)rēˈalitē/ **n.**, **se·ri·al·ly adv.**
– ORIGIN mid 19th cent.: from SERIES + -AL, perhaps suggested by French *sérial*.

se·ri·al com·ma ▶ **n.** a comma used after the penultimate item in a list of three or more items, before 'and' or 'or' (e.g., *an Italian painter, sculptor, and architect*). Also called HARVARD COMMA, OXFORD COMMA.

se·ri·al·ism /ˈsi(ə)rēəˌlizəm/ ▶ **n.** Music a compositional technique in which a fixed series of notes, esp. the twelve notes of the chromatic scale, are used to generate the harmonic and melodic basis of a piece and are subject to change only in specific ways. The first fully serial movements appeared in 1923 in works by Arnold Schoenberg. See also TWELVE-TONE.
– DERIVATIVES **se·ri·al·ist adj. & n.**

se·ri·al·ize /ˈsi(ə)rēəˌlīz/ ▶ **v.** [with obj.] **1** publish or broadcast (a story or play) in regular installments: *sections of the book were serialized in The New Yorker.*
2 arrange (something) in a series. ■ Music compose according to the techniques of serialism.
– DERIVATIVES **se·ri·al·i·za·tion** /ˌsi(ə)rēələˈzāsHən/ **n.**

se·ri·al mo·nog·a·my ▶ **n.** the practice of engaging in a succession of monogamous sexual relationships.
– DERIVATIVES **se·ri·al mo·nog·a·mist n.**

se·ri·al num·ber ▶ **n.** a number showing the position of an item in a series, esp. one printed on paper currency or on a manufactured article for the purposes of identification.

se·ri·al port ▶ **n.** Computing a connector by which a device that sends data one bit at a time may be connected to a computer. Compare with PARALLEL PORT.

se·ri·al sec·tion ▶ **n.** Biology each of a series of thin sections through tissue cut in successive parallel planes, esp. for mounting on microscope slides.
– DERIVATIVES **se·ri·al sec·tion·ing n.**

se·ri·ate /ˈsi(ə)rēˌāt/ technical ▶ **adj.** arranged or occurring in one or more series.
▶ **v.** [with obj.] arrange (items) in a sequence according to prescribed criteria.
– DERIVATIVES **se·ri·a·tion** /ˌsi(ə)rēˈāsHən/ **n.**
– ORIGIN mid 19th cent.: back-formation from *seriation*, from SERIES.

se·ri·a·tim /ˌsi(ə)rēˈātəm, -ˈatəm/ ▶ **adv.** formal taking one subject after another in regular order; point by point: *it is proposed to deal with these matters seriatim.*
– ORIGIN late 15th cent.: from medieval Latin, from Latin *series*, on the pattern of Latin *gradatim* and *literatim*.

ser·i·cite /ˈserəˌsīt/ ▶ **n.** a fine-grained fibrous variety of muscovite formed by the alteration of feldspar, found chiefly in schist and in hydrothermally altered rock.
– ORIGIN mid 19th cent.: from Latin *sericum* 'silk' + -ITE[1].

ser·i·cul·ture /ˈseriˌkəlCHər/ ▶ **n.** the production of silk and the rearing of silkworms for this purpose.
– DERIVATIVES **ser·i·cul·tur·al** /ˌseriˈkəlCHərəl/ **adj.**, **ser·i·cul·tur·ist** /ˌseriˈkəlCHərist/ **n.**
– ORIGIN mid 19th cent.: abbreviation of French *sériciculture*, from late Latin *sericum* 'silk' + French *culture* 'cultivation.'

ser·i·e·ma /ˌserēˈēmə, -ˈāmə/ (also **cariama** /ˌkarēˈämə/) ▶ **n.** a large, ground-dwelling South American bird related to the bustards, with a long neck and legs and a crest above the bill. ● Family Cariamidae: two genera and species.
– ORIGIN mid 19th cent.: modern Latin, from Tupi *siriema* 'crested.'

se·ries /ˈsi(ə)rēz/ ▶ **n.** (pl. **same**) **1** a number of things, events, or people of a similar kind or related nature coming one after another: *the explosion was the latest in a series of accidents* | *he gave a series of lectures on modern art.* ■ a set of books, maps, periodicals, or other documents published in a common format or under a common title. ■ a set of games played between two teams, or among any number of individual competitors: *a playoff series against Portland.* See also WORLD SERIES. ■ a set of stamps, banknotes, or coins issued at a particular time or having a common design or theme. ■ a line of products, esp. vehicles or machines, sharing features of design or assembly and marketed with a separate number from other lines: [as modifier] *a series III SWB Land Rover.*
2 a set of related television or radio programs, esp. of a specified kind: *a new drama series.*
3 [as modifier] denoting electrical circuits or components arranged so that the current passes through each successively. The opposite of PARALLEL.
4 Music another term for TONE ROW.
5 Geology (in chronostratigraphy) a range of strata corresponding to an epoch in time, being a subdivision of a system and itself subdivided into stages: *the Pliocene series.*
6 Chemistry a set of elements with common properties or of compounds related in composition or structure: *the metals of the lanthanide series.* Compare with PERIOD (sense 5 of the noun).
7 Mathematics a set of quantities constituting a progression or having the several values determined by a common relation.
8 Phonetics a group of speech sounds having at least one phonetic feature in common but distinguished in other respects.
– PHRASES **in series** (of a set of batteries or electrical components) arranged so that the current passes through each successively.
– ORIGIN early 17th cent.: from Latin, literally 'row, chain,' from *serere* 'join, connect.'

ser·if /ˈserəf/ ▶ **n.** a slight projection finishing off a stroke of a letter, as in T contrasted with T.
– DERIVATIVES **ser·iffed adj.**
– ORIGIN mid 19th cent.: perhaps from Dutch *schreef* 'dash, line,' of Germanic origin.

ser·i·graph /ˈseriˌgraf/ ▶ **n.** a printed design produced by means of a silkscreen.
– DERIVATIVES **se·rig·ra·pher** /səˈrigrəfər/ **n.**, **se·rig·ra·phy** /səˈrigrəfē/ **n.**
– ORIGIN late 19th cent.: formed irregularly from Latin *sericum* 'silk' + -GRAPH.

ser·in /ˈserən/ ▶ **n.** a small Eurasian and North African finch related to the canary, with a short bill and typically streaky plumage. ● Genus *Serinus*, family Fringillidae: several species, in particular the **European serin** (*S. serinus*).
– ORIGIN mid 16th cent. (denoting a canary): from French, 'canary,' of unknown ultimate origin.

ser·ine /ˈserēn, ˈsi(ə)r-, -in/ ▶ **n.** Biochemistry a hydrophilic amino acid that is a constituent of most proteins. ● Chem. formula: $CH_2OHCHNH_2COOH$.
– ORIGIN late 19th cent.: from Latin *sericum* 'silk' + -INE[4].

se·ri·o·com·ic /ˌsi(ə)rē-ōˈkämik/ ▶ **adj.** combining the serious and the comic; serious in intention but jocular in manner or vice versa: *a telling seriocomic critique.*
– DERIVATIVES **se·ri·o·com·i·cal·ly adv.**

se·ri·ous /ˈsi(ə)rēəs/ ▶ **adj. 1** (of a person) solemn or thoughtful in character or manner: *her face grew serious.* ■ (of a subject, state, or activity) demanding careful consideration or application: *marriage is a*

serious matter. ■ (of thought or discussion) careful or profound: *we give serious consideration to safety recommendations.* ■ (of music, literature, or other art forms) requiring deep reflection and inviting a considered response: *he bridges the gap between serious and popular music.*
2 acting or speaking sincerely and in earnest, rather than in a joking or halfhearted manner: *suddenly he wasn't teasing any more—he was deadly serious | actors who are **serious about** their work.*
3 significant or worrying because of possible danger or risk; not slight or negligible: *she escaped serious injury | Haydn was Mozart's only serious rival.*
4 [attrib.] informal substantial in terms of size, number, or quality: *he suddenly had serious money to spend | a serious chocolate cheesecake.*
– ORIGIN late Middle English: from Old French *serieux* or late Latin *seriosus*, from Latin *serius* 'earnest, serious.'

se·ri·ous·ly /'si(ə)rēəslē/ ▶ **adv. 1** in a solemn or considered manner: *the doctor looked seriously at him.*
2 with earnest intent; not lightly or superficially: *I seriously considered canceling my subscription.* ■ really or sincerely (used esp. to indicate a response of surprise or shock): *do you seriously believe that I would jeopardize my career by such acts?* ■ [sentence adverb] used to add sincerity to a statement that is to follow, esp. after a facetious exchange of remarks: ***seriously though**, shortcuts rarely work.* ■ informal used to indicate surprise at what someone has said and to check whether they really meant it: *"I'm dying to know." "Seriously?" "Of course."*
3 to a degree that is significant or worrying because of possible danger or risk: *the amount of fat you eat can seriously affect your health* | [as submodifier] *three men are seriously ill in the hospital.*
4 [as submodifier] informal very: *he was seriously rich | I drove to the station in a seriously bad mood.*
– PHRASES **take someone/something seriously** regard someone or something as important and worthy of attention.

ser·i·ous·ness /'si(ə)rēəsnis/ ▶ **n.** the quality or state of being serious: *we are aware of the seriousness of the situation | she replied with deadly seriousness.*
– PHRASES **in all seriousness** very seriously; not as a joke: *I ask this question in all seriousness.*

ser·jeant-at-arms ▶ **n.** British spelling of SERGEANT-AT-ARMS.

ser·jeant-at-law ▶ **n.** (pl. **serjeants-at-law**) Brit. historical a barrister of the highest rank.

ser·jeant·y /'särjəntē/ ▶ **n.** (pl. **serjeanties**) Brit. historical a form of feudal tenure conditional on rendering some specified personal service to the monarch.

Ser·ling /'sərliNG/, Rod (1924–75), US writer and television producer; full name *Rodman Edward Serling.* He created and hosted the television series *The Twilight Zone* (1959–64) and *Night Gallery* (1970–73). He also wrote many award-winning scripts for television plays such as *Requiem for a Heavyweight* (1957).

ser·mon /'sərmən/ ▶ **n.** a talk on a religious or moral subject, esp. one given during a church service and based on a passage from the Bible. ■ informal a long or tedious piece of admonition or reproof; a lecture.
– DERIVATIVES **ser·mon·ic** /sər'mänik/ **adj.**
– ORIGIN Middle English (also in the sense 'speech, discourse'): from Old French, from Latin *sermo(n-)* 'discourse, talk.'

ser·mon·ette /,sərmə'net/ ▶ **n.** a short sermon.

ser·mon·ize /'sərmə,nīz/ ▶ **v.** [no obj.] compose or deliver a sermon. ■ deliver an opinionated and dogmatic talk to someone: *they confidently sermonize on the fixed nature of identity* | [with obj.] *I just don't like being sermonized.*
– DERIVATIVES **ser·mon·iz·er n.**

Ser·mon on the Mount ▶ **n.** the discourse of Jesus recorded in Matt. 5–7, including the Beatitudes and the Lord's Prayer.

sero- ▶ **comb. form** relating to serum: *serotype.* ■ involving a serous membrane: *serositis.*
– ORIGIN representing SERUM.

se·ro·con·vert /,si(ə)rōkən'vərt/ ▶ **v.** [no obj.] Medicine (of a person) undergo a change from a seronegative to a seropositive condition.
– DERIVATIVES **se·ro·con·ver·sion** /-'vərZHən/ **n.**

se·ro·di·ag·no·sis /,si(ə)rō,dīəg'nōsis/ ▶ **n.** Medicine diagnosis based on the study of blood sera.
– DERIVATIVES **se·ro·di·ag·nos·tic** /-'nästik/ **adj.**

se·rol·o·gy /si'räləjē/ ▶ **n.** the scientific study or diagnostic examination of blood serum, esp. with regard to the response of the immune system to pathogens or introduced substances.
– DERIVATIVES **se·ro·log·ic** /,si(ə)rə'läjik/ **adj.**, **se·ro·log·i·cal adj.**, **se·ro·log·i·cal·ly adv.**, **se·rol·o·gist** /-jist/ **n.**

se·ro·neg·a·tive /,si(ə)rō'negətiv/ ▶ **adj.** Medicine giving a negative result in a test of blood serum, e.g., for the presence of a virus.
– DERIVATIVES **se·ro·neg·a·tiv·i·ty** /-,negə'tivitē/ **n.**

se·ro·pos·i·tive /,si(ə)rō'päzitiv/ ▶ **adj.** Medicine giving a positive result in a test of blood serum, e.g., for the presence of a virus.
– DERIVATIVES **se·ro·pos·i·tiv·i·ty** /-,päzi'tivitē/ **n.**

se·ro·prev·a·lence /,si(ə)rō'prevələns/ ▶ **n.** Medicine the level of a pathogen in a population, as measured in blood serum.

se·ro·sa /sə'rōsə/ ▶ **n.** Physiology the tissue of a serous membrane.
– DERIVATIVES **se·ro·sal adj.**
– ORIGIN modern Latin, feminine of medieval Latin *serosus* 'serous.'

se·ro·si·tis /,sirō'sītis/ ▶ **n.** Medicine inflammation of a serous membrane.

ser·o·tine /'serətin, -,tīn/ ▶ **n.** a medium-sized insectivorous bat found in Eurasia and Africa. ● a chiefly Eurasian bat (genus *Eptesicus*, family Vespertilionidae, in particular the widespread *E. serotinus*). ● an African bat (genus *Pipistrellus*, family Vespertilionidae).
– ORIGIN late 18th cent.: from French *sérotine*, from Latin *serotinus* 'of the evening, late,' from *serus* 'late.'

se·ro·to·ner·gic /,serətō'nərjik/ ▶ **adj.** Biochemistry denoting a nerve ending that releases and is stimulated by serotonin.

ser·o·to·nin /,serə'tōnən, ,si(ə)r-/ ▶ **n.** Biochemistry a compound present in blood platelets and serum that constricts the blood vessels and acts as a neurotransmitter. ● Alternative name: **5-hydroxytryptamine**; chem. formula: $C_{10}H_{12}N_2O$.
– ORIGIN 1940s: from SERUM + TONIC + -IN¹.

se·ro·type /'si(ə)rə,tīp, 'serə-/ Microbiology ▶ **n.** a serologically distinguishable strain of a microorganism.
▶ **v.** [with obj.] assign (a microorganism) to a particular serotype.
– DERIVATIVES **se·ro·typ·ic** /,si(ə)rə'tipik, ,serə-/ **adj.**

se·rous /'si(ə)rəs/ ▶ **adj.** Physiology of, resembling, or producing serum.
– DERIVATIVES **se·ros·i·ty** /si'räsitē/ **n.**
– ORIGIN late Middle English: from French *séreux* or medieval Latin *serosus*, from *serum* (see SERUM).

se·rous mem·brane ▶ **n.** a mesothelial tissue that lines certain internal cavities of the body, forming a smooth, transparent, two-layered membrane lubricated by a fluid derived from serum. The peritoneum, pericardium, and pleura are serous membranes.

se·row /sə'rō, 'serō/ ▶ **n.** a goat-antelope with short sharp horns, long coarse hair, and a beard, native to forested mountain slopes of Southeast Asia, Taiwan, and Japan. ● Genus *Capricornis*, family Bovidae: two species.
– ORIGIN mid 19th cent.: probably from Lepcha *sā-ro.*

Ser·pens /'sərpənz/ Astronomy a large constellation (the Serpent) on the celestial equator, said to represent the snake coiled around Ophiuchus. It is divided into two parts by Ophiuchus, **Serpens Caput** (the "head") and **Serpens Cauda** (the "tail"). ■ (as genitive **Serpentis** /sər'pentis/) used with a preceding letter or numeral to designate a star in this constellation: *the star Beta Serpentis.*
– ORIGIN Latin.

ser·pent /'sərpənt/ ▶ **n. 1** chiefly literary a large snake. ■ **(the Serpent)** a biblical name for Satan (see Gen. 3, Rev. 20). ■ a dragon or other mythical snakelike reptile.
2 a sly or treacherous person, esp. one who exploits a position of trust in order to betray it.
3 historical a bass wind instrument made of leather-covered wood in three U-shaped turns, with a cup-shaped mouthpiece and few keys. It was played in military and church bands from the 17th to 19th centuries.
– ORIGIN Middle English: via Old French from Latin *serpent-* 'creeping,' from the verb *serpere.*

Ser·pen·tes /sər'pentēz/ Zoology another term for OPHIDIA.
– ORIGIN Latin, 'reptiles.'

ser·pen·tine /'sərpən,tēn, -,tīn/ ▶ **adj.** of or like a serpent or snake: *serpentine coils.* ■ winding and twisting like a snake: *serpentine country lanes.* ■ complex, cunning, or treacherous: *his charm was too subtle and serpentine for me.*
▶ **n. 1** a dark green mineral consisting of hydrated magnesium silicate, sometimes mottled or spotted like a snake's skin.
2 a thing in the shape of a winding curve or line, in particular: ■ a riding exercise consisting of a series of half-circles made alternately to right and left.
3 historical a kind of cannon, used esp. in the 15th and 16th centuries.
▶ **v.** [no obj.] move or lie in a winding path or line: *fresh tire tracks serpentined back toward the hopper.*
– ORIGIN late Middle English: via Old French from late Latin *serpentinus* (see SERPENT).

ser·pen·tin·ite /,sərpən'tēnīt, -'tī-/ ▶ **n.** Geology a dark, typically greenish metamorphic rock, consisting largely of serpentine or related minerals, formed when mafic igneous rocks are altered by water.
– ORIGIN 1930s: from SERPENTINE + -ITE¹.

ser·pen·tin·ize /,sərpən'tēnīz/ ▶ **v.** [with obj.] Geology convert into serpentine.
– DERIVATIVES **ser·pen·tin·i·za·tion** /-,tēni'zāSHən/ **n.**

ser·pig·i·nous /sər'pijənəs/ ▶ **adj.** Medicine (of a skin lesion or ulcerated region) having a wavy margin.
– ORIGIN late Middle English: from medieval Latin *serpigo, serpigin-* 'ringworm' (from Latin *serpere* 'to creep') + -OUS.

SERPS /sərps/ ▶ **abbr.** (in the UK) state earnings-related pension scheme.

ser·ra·nid /'serənid/ ▶ **n.** Zoology a fish of the sea bass family (Serranidae), whose members are predatory marine fish with a spiny dorsal fin.
– ORIGIN mid 20th cent.: from modern Latin *Serranidae*, from the genus name *Serranus*, from Latin *serra* 'saw.'

ser·ra·no /sə'ränō/ ▶ **n.** (pl. **serranos**) a small chili of a very hot variety that is used fresh or dried in Mexican cooking.
– ORIGIN from Spanish, literally 'of the mountains, highlander.'

ser·rate /'ser,āt, -it/ ▶ **adj.** chiefly Botany serrated: *serrate leaves.*
– ORIGIN mid 17th cent.: from late Latin *serratus*, from Latin *serra* 'saw.'

ser·rat·ed /'ser,ātid, sə'rātid/ ▶ **adj.** having or denoting a jagged edge; sawlike: *a knife with a serrated edge.*

ser·ra·tion /se'rāSHən/ ▶ **n.** (usu. **serrations**) a tooth or point of a serrated edge or surface: *a heavy-duty knife with sawtooth serrations.*

ser·ried /'serēd/ ▶ **adj.** [attrib.] (of rows of people or things) standing close together: *serried ranks of soldiers | the serried rows of vines.*
– ORIGIN mid 17th cent.: past participle of *serry* 'press close,' probably from French *serré* 'close together,' based on Latin *sera* 'lock.'

ser·tão /sir'touN/ ▶ **n.** (pl. **sertãos**) (in Brazil) an arid region of scrub.
– ORIGIN early 19th cent.: Portuguese.

Ser·to·li cell /sər'tōlē/ ▶ **n.** Anatomy a type of somatic cell around which spermatids develop in the tubules of the testis.
– ORIGIN late 19th cent.: named after Enrico *Sertoli* (1842–1910), Italian histologist.

se·rum /'si(ə)rəm/ ▶ **n.** (pl. **sera** /'si(ə)rə/ or **serums**) an amber-colored, protein-rich liquid that separates out when blood coagulates. ■ the blood serum of an animal, used esp. to provide immunity to a pathogen or toxin by inoculation or as a diagnostic agent.
– ORIGIN late 17th cent.: from Latin, literally 'whey.'

se·rum hep·a·ti·tis ▶ **n.** a viral form of hepatitis transmitted through infected blood products, causing fever, debility, and jaundice.

se·rum sick·ness ▶ **n.** an allergic reaction to an injection of serum, typically mild and characterized by skin rashes, joint stiffness, and fever.

serv. ▶ **abbr.** service.

ser·val /'sərvəl, sər'val/ ▶ **n.** a slender African wildcat with long legs, large ears, and a black-spotted orange-brown coat. ● *Felis serval*, family Felidae.
– ORIGIN late 18th cent.: from French, from Portuguese *cerval* 'deerlike,' from *cervo* 'deer,' from Latin *cervus.*

serv·ant /'sərvənt/ ▶ **n.** a person who performs duties for others, esp. a person employed in a house on domestic duties or as a personal attendant. ■ a person employed in the service of a government. See also CIVIL SERVANT, PUBLIC SERVANT. ■ a devoted and helpful follower or supporter: *a tireless servant of God.*
– DERIVATIVES **serv·ant·hood** /-,ho͝od/ **n.**
– ORIGIN Middle English: from Old French, literally '(person) serving,' present participle (used as a noun) of *servir* 'to serve.'

serve /sərv/ ▶ **v.** [with obj.] **1** perform duties or services for (another person or an organization): *Malcolm has served the church very faithfully.* ■ provide (an area or group of people) with a product or service: *a telecommunications company that serves southern New England.* ■ [no obj.] be employed as a member of the armed forces: *a military engineer who served with the army.* ■ spend (a period) in office, in an apprenticeship, or in prison: *he is serving a ten-year jail sentence.*
2 present (food or drink) to someone: *they serve wine instead of beer | serve white wines chilled.* ■ present (someone) with food or drink: *I'll **serve** you **with** coffee and cake* | [with two objs.] *Peter served them generous portions of soup.* ■ (of food or drink) be enough for: *the recipe serves four people.* ■ attend to (a customer in a store): *she turned to serve the impatient customer.* ■ supply (goods) to a customer. ■ [no obj.] Christian Church act as a server at the celebration of the Eucharist. ■ [with two objs.] archaic play (a trick) on (someone): *I remember the trick you served me.*
3 Law deliver (a document such as a summons or writ) in a formal manner to the person to whom it is addressed: *a warrant was **served on** Jack Sherman.* ■ deliver a document to (someone) in such a way: *they were just about to **serve** him **with** a writ.*
4 be of use in achieving or satisfying: *this book will serve a useful purpose | the union came into existence to serve the interests of musicians.* ■ [no obj.] be of some specified use: *the island's one pub **serves as** a cafe by day* | [with infinitive] *sweat serves to cool down the body.* ■ function for or treat (someone) in a specified way: *the strategy served him well.* ■ (of a male breeding-animal) copulate with (a female).
5 [no obj.] (in tennis and other racket sports) hit the ball or shuttlecock to begin play: *he tossed the ball up to serve* | [with obj.] *serve the ball onto the front wall.*
6 Nautical bind (a rope) with thin cord to protect or strengthen it.
7 Military operate (a gun): *before long Lodge was the only man in his section able to serve the guns.*
▶ **n.** (in tennis and other racket sports) an act or turn of hitting the ball or shuttlecock to start play: *he was let down by an erratic serve.*
– PHRASES **if my memory serves me** if I remember correctly. **serve at table** act as a waiter. **serve someone right** be someone's deserved punishment or misfortune: *it would serve you right if Jeff walked out on you.* **serve one's time** (also **serve out one's time**) hold office for the normal period. ■ (also **serve time**) spend time in office, in an apprenticeship, or in prison. **serve two masters** take orders from two superiors or follow two conflicting or opposing principles or policies at the same time. [with biblical allusion to Matt. 6:24.]
– PHRASAL VERBS **serve out** Tennis win the final game of a set or match while serving: *Fitzgerald then served out for the set.*
– ORIGIN Middle English: from Old French *servir*, from Latin *servire*, from *servus* 'slave.'

serve-and-vol·ley ▶ **adj.** [attrib.] Tennis denoting a style of play in which the server moves close to the net after serving, ready to play an attacking volley off the return.
– DERIVATIVES **serve-and-vol·ley·er n.**

serv·er /'sərvər/ ▶ **n. 1** a person or thing that provides a service or commodity, in particular: ■ a waiter or waitress. ■ Christian Church a person assisting the celebrant at the celebration of the Eucharist. ■ a sideboard or similar piece of furniture, on which food to be served is placed.
2 a computer or computer program that manages access to a centralized resource or service in a network.

serv·er farm ▶ **n.** another term for DATA CENTER.

serv·er·y /'sərvərē/ ▶ **n.** (pl. **serveries**) Brit. a counter, service hatch, or room from which meals are served.

Ser·vi·an[1] /'sərvēən/ ▶ **adj.** of or relating to **Servius Tullius**, the semilegendary sixth king of ancient Rome (*fl.* 6th century BC).

Ser·vi·an[2] ▶ **n. & adj.** archaic variant of SERBIAN.

Ser·vi·an wall a wall encircling the ancient city of Rome, said to have been built by Servius Tullius. See SERVIAN[1].

serv·ice /'sərvis/ ▶ **n. 1** the action of helping or doing work for someone: *millions are involved in voluntary service.* ■ an act of assistance: *he has done us a great service | he volunteered his services as a driver.* ■ assistance or advice given to customers during and after the sale of goods: *they aim to provide better quality of service.* ■ the action or process of serving food and drinks to customers: *they complained of poor bar service.* ■ short for SERVICE CHARGE: *service is included in the final bill.* ■ a period of employment with a company or organization: *he retired after 40 years' service.* ■ employment as a servant: *the pitifully low wages gained from domestic service.* See also IN SERVICE below. ■ the use that can be made of a machine: *the computer should provide good service for years.* ■ a periodic routine inspection and maintenance of a vehicle or other machine: *he took his car in for service | they phoned for service on their air conditioning.* ■ (**the services**) the armed forces: *troops from all branches of the services* | (as modifier **service**) *service personnel.* ■ (**services**) chiefly Brit. an area with parking beside a major road supplying gasoline, refreshments, and other amenities to motorists.
2 a system supplying a public need such as transport, communications, or utilities such as electricity and water: *a regular bus service.* ■ a public department or organization run by the government: *the U.S. Fish and Wildlife Service.*
3 a ceremony of religious worship according to a prescribed form; the prescribed form for such a ceremony: *a funeral service.*
4 [with modifier] a set of matching dishes and utensils used for serving a particular meal: *a dinner service.*
5 (in tennis and other racket sports) the action or right of serving to begin play. ■ a serve.
6 Law the formal delivery of a document such as a writ or summons.
▶ **v.** [with obj.] **1** perform routine maintenance or repair work on (a vehicle or machine): *have your car serviced regularly.* ■ supply and maintain systems for public utilities and transportation and communications in (an area): *the town is small but well serviced.* ■ perform a service or services for (someone): *the state's biggest health maintenance organization servicing the poor.* ■ pay interest on (a debt): *taxpayers are paying $250 million just to service that debt.*
2 (of a male animal) mate with (a female animal). ■ vulgar slang (of a man) have sexual intercourse with (a woman).
– PHRASES **be at someone's service** be ready to assist someone whenever possible. **be of service** be available to assist someone. **in service 1** in or available for use. **2** dated employed as a servant. **out of service** not available for use. **see service** serve in the armed forces: *he saw service in both world wars.* ■ be used: *the building later saw service as a blacksmith's shop.*
– ORIGIN Old English (denoting religious devotion or a form of liturgy), from Old French *servise* or Latin *servitium* 'slavery,' from *servus* 'slave.' The early sense of the verb (mid 19th cent.) was 'be of service to, provide with a service.'

serv·ice·a·ble /'sərvəsəbəl/ ▶ **adj.** fulfilling its function adequately; usable: *an aging but still serviceable water supply system.* ■ functional and durable rather than attractive. ■ in working order: *only twelve aircraft were fully serviceable this morning.*
– DERIVATIVES **serv·ice·a·bil·i·ty** /ˌsərvəsə'bilitē/ **n.**, **serv·ice·a·bly** /-blē/ **adv.**
– ORIGIN Middle English (in the sense 'willing to be of service'): from Old French *servisable*, from *servise* (see SERVICE).

serv·ice ar·e·a ▶ **n. 1** a roadside area where services are available to motorists.
2 the area covered by the signal of a broadcasting station.

serv·ice·ber·ry /'sərvis,berē/ ▶ **n.** (pl. **serviceberries**) **1** the fruit of the service tree.
2 another term for JUNEBERRY.

serv·ice book ▶ **n.** a book of authorized forms of worship used in a church.

serv·ice bu·reau ▶ **n.** Computing an organization providing services such as scanning, prepress, and color printing.

serv·ice cap ▶ **n.** a round, flat-topped cap with a visor that is part of the US Army and US Air Force service uniform.

serv·ice ceil·ing ▶ **n.** the maximum height at which an aircraft can sustain a specified rate of climb dependent on engine type.

serv·ice charge (also **service fee**) ▶ **n.** an extra charge assessed for a service.

serv·ice club ▶ **n.** an association of business or professional people with the aims of promoting community welfare and goodwill.

serv·ice con·tract ▶ **n.** a business agreement between a contractor and customer covering the maintenance and servicing of equipment over a specified period.

serv·ice dress ▶ **n.** Brit. military uniform worn on formal but not ceremonial occasions.

serv·ice e·con·o·my ▶ **n.** an economy or the sector of an economy that is based on trade in services.

serv·ice game ▶ **n.** (in tennis and other racket sports) a game in which a particular player serves. ■ a player's skill or style in serving.

serv·ice in·dus·try ▶ **n.** a business that does work for a customer, and occasionally provides goods, but is not involved in manufacturing.

serv·ice line ▶ **n.** (in tennis, badminton, and other sports) a line on a court marking the limit of the area into which the ball must be served. ■ (esp. in handball and paddleball) a line on a court marking the boundary of the area in which the server must be standing when serving.

serv·ice·man /'sərvəs,mən, -,man/ ▶ **n.** (pl. **servicemen**) **1** a man serving in the armed forces.
2 a person providing maintenance on machinery, esp. domestic machinery.

serv·ice mark ▶ **n.** a legally registered name or designation used in the manner of a trademark to distinguish an organization's services from those of its competitors.

serv·ice mod·ule ▶ **n.** a detachable compartment of a spacecraft carrying fuel and supplies.

serv·ice pack ▶ **n.** (abbr. **SP**) a periodically released update to software from a manufacturer, consisting of requested enhancements and fixes for known bugs.

serv·ice pro·vid·er ▶ **n.** Computing a company that provides its subscribers access to the Internet.

ser·vic·er ▶ **n. 1** a person or organization that services something: *you will have to go to your car servicer for this.*
2 an organization that collects debt payments on behalf of a lender.

serv·ice road ▶ **n.** another term for FRONTAGE ROAD.

ser·vice star ▶ **n.** Military a star awarded to indicate service in a specific battle or campaign.

serv·ice sta·tion ▶ **n.** a gas station, typically one having the facilities to provide automotive repairs and maintenance.

serv·ice stripe ▶ **n.** Military a stripe worn on the left sleeve of an enlisted person's tunic, indicating the number of years in service.

serv·ice tree ▶ **n.** a Eurasian tree of the rose family, closely related to the rowan. ● Genus *Sorbus*, family Rosaceae: the southern European **true service tree** (*S. domestica*), with compound leaves and green-brown fruits that are edible when overripe, and the **wild service tree** (*S. torminalis*), with lobed leaves and brown berries.
– ORIGIN mid 16th cent.: *service* from an alteration of the plural of obsolete *serve*, from Old English *syrfe*, based on Latin *sorbus*.

serv·ice·wom·an /'sərvəs,wo͝omən/ ▶ **n.** (pl. **servicewomen**) a woman serving in the armed forces.

ser·vi·ette /ˌsərvē'et/ ▶ **n.** Brit. & Canadian a table napkin.
– ORIGIN late 15th cent.: from Old French, from *servir* 'to serve.'

ser·vile /'sərvəl, -ˌvīl/ ▶ **adj. 1** having or showing an excessive willingness to serve or please others: *bowing his head in a servile manner.*
2 of or characteristic of a slave or slaves.
– DERIVATIVES **ser·vile·ly adv.**
– ORIGIN late Middle English (in the sense 'suitable for a slave or for the working class'): from Latin *servilis*, from *servus* 'slave.'

ser·vil·i·ty /sər'vilitē/ ▶ **n.** an excessive willingness to serve or please others: *a classic example of media servility.*

serv·ing /'sərviNG/ ▶ **n.** a quantity of food suitable for or served to one person: *a large serving of spaghetti.*

serv·ing·man /'sərviNG,man/ ▶ **n.** (pl. **servingmen**) archaic a male servant or attendant.

Ser·vite /'sər,vīt/ ▶ **n.** a friar or nun of the Catholic religious order of the Servants of Blessed Mary, founded in 1233.
▶ **adj.** of or relating to this order.
– ORIGIN from medieval Latin *Servitae* (plural), from Latin, from *Servi Beatae Mariae*, the formal title of the order (see above).

ser·vi·tor /'sərvitər, -ˌtôr/ ▶ **n.** archaic a person who serves or attends on a social superior. ■ historical an Oxford University undergraduate performing menial duties in exchange for assistance from college funds.
– DERIVATIVES **ser·vi·tor·ship** /-ˌSHip/ **n.**
– ORIGIN Middle English: via Old French from late Latin, from *servit-* 'served,' from the verb *servire* (see SERVE).

ser·vi·tude /'sərvi,t(y)o͞od/ ▶ **n.** the state of being a slave or completely subject to someone more powerful. ■ Law, archaic the subjection of property to an easement.
– ORIGIN late Middle English: via Old French from Latin *servitudo*, from *servus* 'slave.'

serv·let /ˈsərvlit/ ▶ **n.** Computing a small, server-resident program that typically runs automatically in response to user input.

ser·vo /ˈsərvō/ ▶ **n.** (pl. **servos**) short for SERVOMECHANISM or SERVOMOTOR. ■ [as modifier] relating to or involving a servomechanism: *hydraulic and electrical servo systems.*
– ORIGIN late 19th cent.: from Latin *servus* 'slave.'

ser·vo·mech·an·ism /ˈsərvō,mekə,nizəm/ ▶ **n.** a powered mechanism producing motion or forces at a higher level of energy than the input level, e.g., in the brakes and steering of large motor vehicles, esp. where feedback is employed to make the control automatic.

ser·vo·mo·tor /ˈsərvō,mōtər/ ▶ **n.** the motive element in a servomechanism.

SES ▶ **abbr.** socioeconomic status.

ses·a·me /ˈsesəmē/ ▶ **n.** a tall annual herbaceous plant of tropical and subtropical areas of the Old World, cultivated for its oil-rich seeds. ● *Sesamum indicum*, family Pedaliaceae. ■ (**sesame seed**) the edible seeds of this plant, which are used whole or have the oil extracted.
– ORIGIN late Middle English: via Latin from Greek *sēsamon, sēsamē*, probably of Semitic origin; compare with Arabic *simsim.*

ses·a·moid /ˈsesə,moid/ (also **sesamoid bone**) ▶ **n.** a small independent bone or bony nodule developed in a tendon where it passes over an angular structure, typically in the hands and feet. The kneecap is a particularly large sesamoid bone.
– ORIGIN late 17th cent.: from SESAME (with reference to the similarity in shape of a sesame seed) + -OID.

Se·so·tho /səˈsōōtōō/ ▶ **n.** the Sotho language of the Basotho people, an official language in Lesotho and South Africa.
▶ **adj.** of or relating to this language.
– ORIGIN the name in Sesotho.

sesqui- ▶ **comb. form** denoting one and a half: *sesquicentenary.* ■ Chemistry (of a compound) in which a particular element or group is present in a ratio of 3:2 compared with another: *sesquioxide.*
– ORIGIN from Latin *semi-* (see SEMI-) + *-que* 'and.'

ses·qui·al·tera /,seskwiˈaltərə/ ▶ **adj.** [attrib.] Music relating to or denoting a ratio of 3:2, as in an interval of a fifth. ■ denoting a mixture stop in an organ, typically consisting of two ranks of narrow-scaled open flue pipes.
– ORIGIN late Middle English: from Latin, feminine of *sesquialter*, from *sesqui* (see SESQUI-) + *alter* 'second.'

ses·qui·cen·ten·ar·y /,seskwisenˈtenərē/ ▶ **n.** chiefly Brit. (pl. **sesquicentenaries**) a sesquicentennial.
▶ **adj.** of or relating to a sesquicentennial.

ses·qui·cen·ten·ni·al /,seskwisenˈtenēəl/ ▶ **adj.** of or relating to the one-hundred-and-fiftieth anniversary of a significant event.
▶ **n.** a one-hundred-and-fiftieth anniversary.

ses·qui·ox·ide /,seskwēˈäk,sīd/ ▶ **n.** Chemistry an oxide in which oxygen is present in the ratio of three atoms to two of another element.

ses·qui·pe·da·li·an /,seskwəpəˈdālyən/ ▶ **adj.** formal (of a word) polysyllabic; long: *sesquipedalian surnames.* ■ characterized by long words; long-winded: *the sesquipedalian prose of scientific journals.*
– ORIGIN mid 17th cent.: from Latin *sesquipedalis* 'a foot and a half long,' from *sesqui-* (see SESQUI-) + *pes, ped-* 'foot.'

ses·qui·ter·pene /,seskwiˈtər,pēn/ ▶ **n.** Chemistry a terpene with the formula $C_{15}H_{24}$, or a simple derivative of such a compound.

ses·sile /ˈsesəl, -īl/ ▶ **adj.** Biology (of an organism, e.g., a barnacle) fixed in one place; immobile. ■ (of a plant or animal structure) attached directly by its base without a stalk or peduncle: *sporangia may be stalked or sessile.*
– ORIGIN early 18th cent.: from Latin *sessilis*, from *sess-* 'seated,' from the verb *sedere.*

ses·sile oak ▶ **n.** another term for DURMAST OAK.

ses·sion /ˈsesHən/ ▶ **n. 1** a meeting of a deliberative or judicial body to conduct its business. ■ a period during which such meetings are regularly held: *legislation to curb wildcat strikes will be introduced during the coming parliamentary session.* ■ the governing body of a Presbyterian Church.
2 a period devoted to a particular activity: *gym is followed by a training session.* ■ informal a period of heavy or sustained drinking. ■ a period of recording music in a studio, esp. by a session musician: *he did the sessions for a Great Country Hits album.* ■ the period during which a school has classes.
– PHRASES **in session** assembled for or proceeding with business.
– DERIVATIVES **ses·sion·al** /-sHənl/ **adj.**
– ORIGIN late Middle English: from Old French, or from Latin *sessio(n-)*, from *sess-* 'seated' (see SESSILE).

ses·sion clerk ▶ **n.** a chief lay official in the session of a Presbyterian Church.

ses·sion mu·si·cian ▶ **n.** a freelance musician hired to play on recording sessions.

Ses·sions /ˈsesHənz/, Roger (Huntington) (1896–1985), US composer. He composed eight symphonies, as well as operas such as *Montezuma* (1959–63), the cantata "When Lilacs Last in the Dooryard Bloom'd" (1970), and "Concerto for Orchestra" (1981).

ses·terce /ˈsestərs/ (also **sestertius** /seˈstərsH(ē)əs/) ▶ **n.** (pl. **sesterces** /ˈsestərsəz/ or **sestertii** /sesˈtərsHē,ī/) an ancient Roman coin and monetary unit equal to one quarter of a denarius.
– ORIGIN from Latin *sestertius (nummus)* '(coin) that is two and a half (asses).'

ses·tet /sesˈtet/ ▶ **n.** Prosody the last six lines of a sonnet. ■ Music, rare a sextet.
– ORIGIN early 19th cent.: from Italian *sestetto*, from *sesto*, from Latin *sextus* 'a sixth.'

ses·ti·na /seˈstēnə/ ▶ **n.** Prosody a poem with six stanzas of six lines and a final triplet, all stanzas having the same six words at the line-ends in six different sequences that follow a fixed pattern, and with all six words appearing in the closing three-line envoi.
– ORIGIN mid 19th cent.: from Italian, from *sesto* (see SESTET).

Set /set/ variant spelling of SETH.

set[1] /set/ ▶ **v.** (**sets, setting**; past and past participle **set**) **1** [with obj.] put, lay, or stand (something) in a specified place or position: *Dana set the mug of tea down* | *Catherine set a chair by the bed.* ■ (**be set**) be situated or fixed in a specified place or position: *the village was set among olive groves on a hill.* ■ represent (a story, play, movie, or scene) as happening at a specified time or in a specified place: *a spy novel set in Berlin.* ■ mount a precious stone in (something, typically a piece of jewelry): *a bracelet set with emeralds.* ■ mount (a precious stone) in something. ■ Printing arrange (type) as required. ■ Printing arrange the type for (a piece of text): *article headings will be set in Times fourteen point.* ■ prepare (a table) for a meal by placing cutlery, dishes, etc., on it in their proper places. ■ (**set something to**) provide (music) so that a written work can be produced in a musical form: *she set his poem to music.* ■ [no obj.] (of a dancer) acknowledge another dancer, typically one's partner, using the steps prescribed: *the gentleman sets to and turns with the lady on his left hand.* ■ cause (a hen) to sit on eggs. ■ place (eggs) for a hen to sit on. ■ put (a seed or plant) in the ground to grow. ■ give the teeth of (a saw) alternating outward inclinations. ■ Sailing put (a sail) up in position to catch the wind: *a safe distance from shore all sails were set.* See also SET SAIL below.
2 [with obj.] put or bring into a specified state: *plunging oil prices set in motion an economic collapse in Houston* | [with obj. and complement] *the hostages were set free.* ■ cause (someone or something) to start doing something: *the incident set me thinking.* ■ [with obj. and infinitive] instruct (someone) to do something: *he'll set a man to watch you.* ■ give someone (a task): [with two objs.] *the problem we have been set.* ■ devise (a test) and give it to someone to do. ■ establish as (an example) for others to follow, copy, or try to achieve: *the scheme sets a precedent for other companies.* ■ establish (a record): *his time in the 25-meter freestyle set a national record.* ■ decide on: *they set a date for a full hearing at the end of February.* ■ fix (a price, value, or limit) on something: *the unions had set a limit on the size of the temporary workforce.*
3 [with obj.] adjust (a clock or watch), typically to show the right time. ■ adjust (an alarm clock) to sound at the required time. ■ adjust (a device or its controls) so that it performs a particular operation: *you have to be careful not to set the volume too high.* ■ Electronics cause (a binary device) to enter the state representing the numeral 1.
4 [no obj.] harden into a solid or semisolid state: *cook for a further thirty-five minutes until the filling has set.* ■ [with obj.] arrange (the hair) while damp so that it dries in the required style: *she had set her hair on small rollers.* ■ [with obj.] put parts of (a broken or dislocated bone or limb) into the correct position for healing. ■ [with obj.] deal with (a fracture or dislocation) in this way. ■ (of a bone) be restored to its normal condition by knitting together again after being broken: *dogs' bones soon set.* ■ (with reference to a person's face) assume or cause to assume a fixed or rigid expression: *her features never set into a civil parade of attention* | [with obj.] *Travis's face was set as he looked up.* ■ (of the eyes) become fixed in position or in the feeling they are expressing: *his bright eyes set in an expression of mocking amusement.* ■ (of a hunting dog) adopt a rigid attitude indicating the presence of game.
5 [no obj.] (of the sun, moon, or another celestial body) appear to move toward and below the earth's horizon as the earth rotates: *the sun was setting and a warm, red glow filled the sky.*
6 [no obj.] (of a tide or current) take or have a specified direction or course: *a fair tide can be carried well past Lands End before the stream sets to the north.*
7 [with obj.] start (a fire).
8 [with obj.] (of blossom or a tree) develop into or produce (fruit). ■ [no obj.] (of fruit) develop from blossom. ■ (of a plant) produce (seed): *the herb has flowered and started to set seed.*
9 informal, dialect sit: *a perfect lady—just set in her seat and stared.*
– PHRASES **set one's heart** (or **hopes**) **on** have a strong desire for or to do: *she had her heart set on going to college.* **set sail** hoist the sails of a vessel. ■ begin a voyage: *tomorrow we set sail for France.* **set one's teeth** clench one's teeth together. ■ become resolute: *they have set their teeth against a change which would undermine their prospects of forming a government.* **set up shop** see SHOP. **set someone straight** inform someone of the truth of a situation. **set the wheels in motion** do something to begin a process or put a plan into action.
– PHRASAL VERBS **set about 1** start doing something with vigor or determination: *it would be far better to admit the problem openly and set about tackling it.* **2** Brit. informal attack (someone). **set someone against** cause someone to be in opposition or conflict with: *he hadn't meant any harm, but his few words had set her against him.* **set something against** offset something against: *wives' allowances can henceforth be set against investment income.* **set someone apart** give someone an air of unusual superiority: *his blunt views set him apart.* **set something apart** separate something and keep it for a special purpose: *there were books and rooms set apart as libraries.* **set something aside 1** save or keep something, typically money or time, for a particular purpose: *the bank expected to set aside about $700 million for restructuring.* ■ remove land from agricultural production. **2** annul a legal decision or process. **set someone/something back 1** delay or impede the progress of someone or something: *this incident undoubtedly set back research.* **2** informal (of a purchase) cost someone a particular amount of money: *that must have set you back a bit.* **set something by** dated save something for future use. **set someone down** stop and allow someone to alight from a vehicle. **set something down** record something in writing. ■ establish something authoritatively as a rule or principle to be followed: *the Association set down codes of practice for all members to comply with.* **set forth** begin a journey or trip. **set something forth** state or describe something in writing or speech: *the principles and aims set forth in the Charter.* **set forward** archaic start on a journey. **set in** (of something unpleasant or unwelcome) begin and seem likely to continue: *less hardy plants should be brought inside before cold weather sets in.* **set something in** insert something, esp. a sleeve, into a garment. **set off** begin a journey. **set someone off** cause someone to start doing something, esp. laughing or talking: *anything will set him off laughing.* **set something off 1** detonate a bomb. ■ cause an alarm to go off. ■ cause a series of things to occur: *the fear is that this could set off a chain reaction in other financial markets.* **2** serve as decorative embellishment to: *a pink carnation set off nicely by a red bow tie and cream shirt.* **set something off against** another way of saying SET SOMETHING AGAINST above. **set on** (or **upon**) attack (someone) violently. **set someone/something on** (or **upon**) cause or urge a person or animal to attack: *I was asked to leave and threatened with having dogs set upon me.* **set out** begin a journey. ■ aim or intend to do something: *she drew up a plan of what her organization should set out to achieve.* **set something out** arrange or display something in a particular order or position. ■ present information or ideas in a well-ordered way in writing or speech: *this chapter sets out the debate surrounding pluralism.* **set to** begin doing something vigorously: *she set to with bleach and scouring pads to render the vases spotless.* **set someone up 1** establish someone in a particular capacity or role: *his father set him up in business.* ■ informal arrange a meeting between one person and another, with the aim of encouraging a romantic relationship between them: *Todd tried to set her up with one of his friends.* **2** restore or

PRONUNCIATION KEY ə ago, up; ər over, fur; a hat; ā ate; ä car; e let; ē see; i fit; ī by; NG sing; ō go; ô law, for; oi toy; ŏŏ good; ōō goo; ou out; TH thin; TH then; ZH vision

S

enhance the health of someone: *after my operation, the doctor recommended a cruise to set me up again.* **3** informal make an innocent person appear guilty of something: *suppose Zielinski had set him up for Ingram's murder?* **set something up 1** place or erect something in position: *police set up a roadblock on Tenth Street.* **2** establish a business, institution, or other organization. ■ make the arrangements necessary for something: *he asked if I would like him to set up a meeting with the president.* **3** begin making a loud sound. **set oneself up as** establish oneself in (a particular occupation): *he set himself up as an attorney in St. Louis.* ■ claim to be or act like a specified kind of person (used to indicate skepticism as to someone's right or ability to do so): *he set himself up as a crusader for higher press and broadcasting standards.*
– ORIGIN Old English *settan*, of Germanic origin; related to Dutch *zetten*, German *setzen*, also to SIT.

> **USAGE** Set, meaning 'place or put,' is mainly a transitive verb and takes a direct object: *set the flowers on top of the piano.* **Sit**, meaning 'be seated,' is mainly intransitive and does not take a direct object: *sit in this chair while I check the light meter.*

set[2] ▶ **n. 1** a group or collection of things that belong together, resemble one another, or are usually found together: *a set of false teeth* | *a new cell with two sets of chromosomes* | *a spare set of clothes.* ■ a collection of implements, containers, or other objects customarily used together for a specific purpose: *an electric fondue set.* ■ a group of people with common interests or occupations or of similar social status: *it was a fashionable haunt of the literary set.* ■ (in tennis, darts, and other games) a group of games counting as a unit toward a match, only the player or side that wins a defined number or proportion of the games being awarded a point toward the final score: *he took the first set 6-3.* ■ (in jazz or popular music) a sequence of songs or pieces performed together and constituting or forming part of a live show or recording: *a short four-song set.* ■ a group of people making up the required number for a square dance or similar country dance. ■ a fixed number of repetitions of a particular bodybuilding exercise. Compare with REP[5]. ■ Mathematics & Logic a collection of distinct entities regarded as a unit, being either individually specified or (more usually) satisfying specified conditions: *the set of all positive integers.*
2 [in sing.] the way in which something is set, disposed, or positioned: *the shape and set of the eyes.* ■ the posture or attitude of a part of the body, typically in relation to the impression this gives of a person's feelings or intentions: *the determined set of her upper torso.* ■ the flow of a current or tide in a particular direction: *the rudder kept the dinghy straight against the set of the tide.* ■ an arrangement of the hair when damp so that it dries in the required style: *a shampoo and set.* ■ (also **dead set**) a setter's pointing in the presence of game. ■ the alternating outward inclinations of the teeth of a saw. ■ a warp or bend in wood, metal, or another material caused by continued strain or pressure.
3 a radio or television receiver: *a TV set.*
4 a collection of scenery, stage furniture, and other articles used for a particular scene in a play or film. ■ the place or area in which filming is taking place or a play is performed: *the magazine has interviews on set with top directors.*
5 a cutting, young plant, or bulb used in the propagation of new plants. ■ a young fruit that has just formed.
6 the last coat of plaster on a wall.
7 Printing the amount of spacing in type controlling the distance between letters. ■ the width of a piece of type.
8 variant spelling of SETT.
– ORIGIN late Middle English: partly from Old French *sette*, from Latin *secta* 'sect,' partly from SET[1].

S

set[3] ▶ **adj. 1** fixed or arranged in advance: *there is no set procedure.* ■ (of a view or habit) unlikely to change: *I've been on my own a long time and I'm rather set in my ways.* ■ (of a person's expression) held for an unnaturally long time without changing, typically as a reflection of determination. ■ (of a meal or menu in a restaurant) offered at a fixed price with a limited choice of dishes. ■ having a conventional or predetermined wording; formulaic: *witnesses often delivered their testimony according to a set speech.* See also SET PHRASE.
2 [predic.] ready, prepared, or likely to do something: *"All set for tonight?" he asked* | [with infinitive] *water costs look set to increase.* ■ (**set against**) firmly opposed to: *an approach set against tradition and authority.* ■ (**set on**) determined to do (something): *he's set on marrying that girl.*
– ORIGIN late Old English, past participle of SET[1].

se·ta /'sētə/ ▶ **n.** (pl. **setae** /-tē/) chiefly Zoology a stiff hairlike or bristlelike structure, esp. in an invertebrate. ■ Botany (in a moss or liverwort) the stalk supporting the capsule.
– DERIVATIVES **se·ta·ceous** /si'tāsHəs/ **adj.**, **se·tal adj.**
– ORIGIN late 18th cent.: from Latin, 'bristle.'

set-a·side ▶ **n. 1** the policy of taking land out of production to reduce crop surpluses. ■ land taken out of production in this way: *he has fifty acres of set-aside.*
2 a government contract awarded without competition to a minority-owned business.
3 a portion of funds or other resources reserved for a particular purpose: *a set-aside for library services for Native Americans.*

set·back /'set,bak/ ▶ **n. 1** a reversal or check in progress: *a serious setback for the peace process.*
2 Architecture a plain, flat offset in a wall.
3 the distance by which a building or part of a building is set back from the property line.

se-ten·ant /sə 'tenənt, sə tə'nän/ ▶ **adj.** Philately (of stamps of different designs) joined together side by side when printed: *a se-tenant block of four stamps.*
– ORIGIN early 20th cent.: from French, literally 'holding together.'

Seth /seTH/ (also **Set**) Egyptian Mythology an evil god who murdered his brother Osiris and wounded Osiris's son Horus. Seth is represented as having the head of an animal with a long pointed snout.

SETI /'setē/ ▶ **abbr.** Search for Extra-Terrestrial Intelligence, the designation of a series of projects based mainly on attempts to detect artificial radio transmissions from outer space.

set-in ▶ **adj.** [attrib.] (of a sleeve) made separately and inset into a garment.

set list ▶ **n.** a list of the songs that a band or singer intends to perform at a particular concert.

set men·u ▶ **n.** a limited menu offered for a set number of courses, at a fixed price.

set-net ▶ **n.** a fishing net fastened in fixed position.
– DERIVATIVES **set-net·ter n.**

set-off ▶ **n. 1** an item or amount that is or may be set off against another in the settlement of accounts. ■ Law a counterbalancing debt pleaded by the defendant in an action to recover money due. ■ dated a counterbalancing or compensating circumstance or condition: *as a set-off against such discussions there had come an improvement in their pecuniary position.*
2 a step or shoulder at which the thickness of part of a building or machine is reduced.
3 Printing the unwanted transference of ink from one printed sheet or page to another before it has set.

Se·ton /'sētn/, St. Elizabeth Ann (Bayley) (1774–1821), US religious leader, educator, and social reformer. The widowed mother of five children, she converted to Roman Catholicism in 1805. She became a nun in 1809 and by 1813 had founded the Sisters of Charity, a religious order. In 1975, she became the first native-born American to be canonized as a saint.

se·ton /'sētn/ ▶ **n.** Medicine, historical a skein of cotton or other absorbent material passed below the skin and left with the ends protruding, to promote drainage of fluid or to act as a counterirritant.
– ORIGIN late Middle English: from medieval Latin *seto(n-)*, apparently from Latin *seta* 'bristle.'

se·tose /'sē,tōs/ ▶ **adj.** chiefly Zoology bearing bristles or setae; bristly.
– ORIGIN mid 17th cent.: from Latin *seta* 'bristle' + -OSE[1].

set phrase ▶ **n.** an unvarying phrase having a specific meaning, such as "raining cats and dogs," or being the only context in which a word appears, e.g., "aback" in "take aback."

set piece ▶ **n.** a thing that has been carefully or elaborately planned or composed, in particular: ■ a self-contained passage or section of a novel, play, film, or piece of music arranged in an elaborate or conventional pattern for maximum effect: *the film lurches from one comic set piece to another.* ■ a formal and carefully structured speech. ■ a carefully organized and practiced move in a team game by which the ball is returned to play, as at a scrum in rugby or a free kick in soccer. ■ an arrangement of fireworks forming a picture or design.

set play ▶ **n.** Sports a prearranged maneuver carried out from a restart or after a timeout by the team that has the advantage: *the Germans scored the deciding goal on a set play,off a corner kick in the 15th minute.*

set point ▶ **n.** (in tennis and other sports) a point that, if won by a contestant, will also win the set.

set screw ▶ **n.** a screw for adjusting or clamping parts of a machine.

set shot ▶ **n.** Basketball a shot made while standing still.

set square ▶ **n.** a right-angled triangular plate for drawing lines, esp. at 90°, 45°, 60°, or 30°. ■ a form of T-square with an additional arm turning on a pivot for drawing lines at fixed angles to the head.

Sets·wa·na /set'swänə/ ▶ **n.** the Bantu language of the Tswana people, related to the Sotho languages and spoken by over 3 million people in southern Africa.
▶ **adj.** of or relating to this language.
– ORIGIN the name in Setswana.

sett /set/ (also **set**) ▶ **n. 1** the lair or burrow of a badger.
2 the particular pattern of stripes in a tartan.
– ORIGIN Middle English: variant of SET[2], the spelling with *-tt* prevailing in technical senses.

set·tee /se'tē/ ▶ **n.** a long upholstered seat for more than one person, typically with a back and arms.
– ORIGIN early 18th cent.: perhaps a fanciful variant of SETTLE[2].

set·ter /'setər/ ▶ **n. 1** a dog of a large, long-haired breed trained to stand rigid when scenting game. See ENGLISH SETTER, GORDON SETTER, IRISH SETTER.
2 [usu. in combination] a person or thing that sets something: *trend-setters in Hollywood.*

set the·o·ry ▶ **n.** the branch of mathematics that deals with the formal properties of sets as units (without regard to the nature of their individual constituents) and the expression of other branches of mathematics in terms of sets.
– DERIVATIVES **set-the·o·ret·ic adj.**, **set-the·o·ret·i·cal adj.**

set·ting /'setiNG/ ▶ **n. 1** the place or type of surroundings where something is positioned or where an event takes place: *cozy waterfront cottage in a peaceful country setting.* ■ the place and time at which a play, novel, or film is represented as happening: *short stories with a contemporary setting.* ■ a piece of metal in which a precious stone or gem is fixed to form a piece of jewelry. ■ a piece of vocal or choral music composed for particular words: *a setting of Yevtushenko's bleak poem.* ■ short for PLACE SETTING.
2 a speed, height, or temperature at which a machine or device can be adjusted to operate: *if you find the room getting too hot, check the thermostat setting.*

set·ting lo·tion ▶ **n.** lotion applied to damp hair before it is set, enabling it to keep its shape longer.

set·tle[1] /'setl/ ▶ **v. 1** [with obj.] resolve or reach an agreement about (an argument or problem): *every effort was made to settle the dispute.* ■ end (a legal dispute) by mutual agreement: *the matter was settled out of court* | [no obj.] *he sued for libel and then settled out of court.* ■ determine; decide on: *exactly what goes into the legislation has not been settled* | [no obj.] *they had not yet* ***settled on*** *a date for the wedding.* ■ pay (a debt or account): *his bill was settled by charge card* | [no obj.] *I* ***settled up with*** *your brother for my board and lodging.* ■ complete the administration and distribution of a decedent's estate. ■ (**settle something on**) give money or property to (someone) through a deed of settlement or a will. ■ [no obj.] (**settle for**) accept or agree to (something that one considers to be less than satisfactory): *it was too cold for champagne so they settled for a cup of tea.* ■ dated silence (someone considered a nuisance) by some means: *he told me to hold my tongue or he would find a way to settle me.*
2 [no obj.] adopt a more steady or secure style of life, esp. in a permanent job and home: *one day I will settle down and raise a family.* ■ [with adverbial of place] make one's permanent home somewhere: *in 1863 the family settled in London.* ■ begin to feel comfortable or established in a new home, situation, or job: *she* ***settled in*** *happily with a foster family* | *he had* ***settled into*** *his new job.* ■ [with obj.] establish a colony in: *European immigrants settled much of Australia.* ■ (**settle down to**) turn one's attention to; apply oneself to: *Catherine settled down to her studies.* ■ become or make calmer or quieter: [no obj.] *after a few months the controversy settled down* | [with obj.] *try to settle your puppy down before going to bed.*
3 [no obj.] sit or come to rest in a comfortable position: *he settled into an armchair.* ■ [with obj.] make (someone) comfortable in a particular place or position: *she allowed him to settle her in the taxi.* ■ [with obj.] move or adjust (something) so that it rests securely: *she settled her bag on her shoulder.* ■ fall or come down onto a surface: *dust from the mill had settled on the roof.* ■ (of suspended particles) sink slowly in a liquid to form sediment; (of a liquid) become clear or still through this process: *sediment settles near the bottom of the tank* | *he pours a glass and leaves it on the bar to settle.* ■ (of an object or objects) gradually sink down under its or their own weight: *they listened to the soft ticking and creaking as the house settled.* ■ (of a ship or boat) sink gradually.

– PHRASES **settle one's affairs** make any necessary arrangements, such as writing a will, before one's death. **settle someone's hash** see HASH[1].
– DERIVATIVES **set·tle·a·ble** adj., **set·tled·ness** n.
– ORIGIN Old English *setlan* 'to seat, place,' from SETTLE[2].

set·tle[2] ▶ n. a wooden bench with a high back and arms, typically incorporating a box under the seat.
– ORIGIN Old English *setl* 'a place to sit,' of Germanic origin; related to German *Sessel* and Latin *sella* 'seat,' also to SIT.

set·tle·ment /ˈsetlmənt/ ▶ n. **1** an official agreement intended to resolve a dispute or conflict: *unions succeeded in reaching a pay settlement | the settlement of the Sino-Japanese war.* ■ a formal arrangement made between the parties to a lawsuit in order to resolve it, esp. out of court: *the owner reached an out-of-court settlement with the plaintiffs.*
2 a place, typically one that has hitherto been uninhabited, where people establish a community: *the little settlement of Buttermere.* ■ the process of settling in such a place: *the early settlement of Queensland.* ■ the action of allowing or helping people to do this: *he was involved in the sale and settlement of Crown land.*
3 Law an arrangement whereby property passes to a succession of people as dictated by the settlor. ■ the amount or property given.
4 the action or process of settling an account.
5 subsidence of the ground or a structure built on it: *a boundary wall, which has cracked due to settlement, is to be replaced.*

set·tle·ment house ▶ n. an institution in an inner-city area providing educational, recreational, and other social services to the community.

set·tler /ˈsetl-ər, ˈsetlər/ ▶ n. a person who settles in an area, typically one with no or few previous inhabitants.

set·tling time ▶ n. technical the time taken for a measuring or control instrument to get within a certain distance of a new equilibrium value without subsequently deviating from it by that amount.

set·tlor /ˈsetl-ər, ˈsetlər/ ▶ n. Law a person who makes a settlement, esp. of a property.

set-to ▶ n. (pl. **set-tos**) informal a fight or argument: *we had a little set-to about her piano practicing.*

set-top box ▶ n. a box-shaped device that converts a digital television signal to analogue for viewing on a conventional set, or that enables cable or satellite television to be viewed.

set·up /ˈsetˌəp/ ▶ n. [usu. in sing.] informal **1** the way in which something, esp. an organization or equipment, is organized, planned, or arranged: *would you feel comfortable in a team-teaching setup?* ■ an organization or arrangement: *in the present-day family setup, both the parents may be employed.* ■ a set of equipment needed for a particular activity or purpose: *I have a recording setup in my house.* ■ (in a ball game) a pass or play intended to provide an opportunity for another player to score.
2 a scheme or trick intended to incriminate or deceive someone: *"Listen. He didn't die. It was a setup."* ■ a contest with a prearranged outcome.

Seu·rat /səˈrä/, Georges Pierre (1859–91), French painter. The founder of neo-Impressionism, he is chiefly associated with pointillism, which he developed during the 1880s. Among his major paintings using this technique is *Sunday Afternoon on the Island of La Grande Jatte* (1884–86).

Seuss, Dr. /so͞os/, see GEISEL.

Seus·si·an /ˈso͞osiən/ ▶ adj. relating to or characteristic of the Dr. Seuss series of children's books, esp. in being whimsical or fantastical: *the place is clearly recognizable as the remnants of a Gothic cathedral, but with an unreal Seussian quality.*

sev /säv, sev/ ▶ n. an Indian snack consisting of long, thin strands of gram flour, deep-fried and spiced.
– ORIGIN Hindi.

Se·vas·to·pol /səˈvastəˌpōl, ˌsevəˈstōpəl/ Ukrainian and Russian name for SEBASTOPOL.

sev·en /ˈsevən/ ▶ cardinal number equivalent to the sum of three and four; one more than six, or three less than ten; 7: *two sevens are fourteen | the remaining seven were sentenced to terms of imprisonment.* (Roman numeral: **vii, VII**) ■ a group or unit of seven people or things: *animals were offered for sacrifice in sevens.* ■ seven years old: *my mother died when I was seven.* ■ seven o'clock: *the meeting doesn't finish until seven.* ■ a size of garment or other merchandise denoted by seven. ■ a playing card with seven pips.
– ORIGIN Old English *seofon*, of Germanic origin; related to Dutch *zeven* and German *sieben*, from an Indo-European root shared by Latin *septem* and Greek *hepta*.

sev·en dead·ly sins ▶ plural n. (**the seven deadly sins**) (in Christian tradition) the sins of pride, covetousness, lust, anger, gluttony, envy, and sloth.

sev·en·fold /ˈsevənˌfōld/ ▶ adj. seven times as great or as numerous: *stock fund sales were up sevenfold from December.* ■ having seven parts or elements: *the sevenfold purpose of religious education.*
▶ adv. by seven times; to seven times the number or amount: *his rent had gone up sevenfold.*

Sev·en Sag·es seven wise Greeks of the 6th century BC, to each of whom a moral saying is attributed. The seven, named in a traditional list found in Plato, are **Bias**, **Chilon**, **Cleobulus**, **Periander**, **Pittacus**, **Solon**, and **Thales**.

sev·en seas ▶ plural n. (**the seven seas**) all the oceans of the world (conventionally listed as the Arctic, Antarctic, North Pacific, South Pacific, North Atlantic, South Atlantic, and Indian Oceans).

Sev·en Sis·ters (**the Seven Sisters**) **1** Astronomy the star cluster of the Pleiades.
2 a group of women's (or formerly women's) colleges in the eastern US having high academic and social prestige. It includes Barnard, Bryn Mawr, Mount Holyoke, Radcliffe, Smith, Vassar, and Wellesley.

Sev·en Sleep·ers (in early Christian legend) seven noble Christian youths of Ephesus who fell asleep in a cave while fleeing from persecution by the Roman emperor Decius (c.250 AD) and awoke 187 years later.

sev·en·teen /ˌsevənˈtēn, ˈsevənˌtēn/ ▶ cardinal number one more than sixteen, or seven more than ten; 17: *seventeen years later | a list of names, seventeen in all.* (Roman numeral: **xvii, XVII**) ■ seventeen years old: *he joined the Marines at seventeen.* ■ a set or team of seventeen individuals.
– DERIVATIVES **sev·en·teenth** /ˌsevənˈtēnTH, ˈsevənˌtēnTH/ adj. & n.
– ORIGIN Old English *seofontīene*, from the Germanic base of SEVEN.

sev·en·teen-year lo·cust ▶ n. the nymph of the northern species of the periodical cicada. See PERIODICAL CICADA.

sev·enth /ˈsevənTH/ ▶ ordinal number constituting number seven in a sequence; 7th: *his seventh goal of the season | the seventh of June | he was the seventh of eight children.* ■ (**a seventh/one seventh**) each of seven equal parts into which something is or may be divided. ■ the seventh finisher or position in a race or competition: *he finished seventh in the tournament.* ■ seventhly (used to introduce a seventh point or reason). ■ Music an interval spanning seven consecutive notes in a diatonic scale. ■ Music the note that is higher by this interval than the tonic of a diatonic scale or root of a chord. ■ Music a chord in which the seventh note of the scale forms an important component.
– PHRASES **in seventh heaven** see HEAVEN.
– DERIVATIVES **sev·enth·ly** adv.

Sev·enth-day Ad·vent·ist ▶ n. a member of a Protestant sect that preaches the imminent return of Christ to Earth (originally expecting the Second Coming in 1844) and observes Saturday as the sabbath. See also ADVENTIST.

sev·en·ty /ˈsevəntē/ ▶ cardinal number (pl. **seventies**) the number equivalent to the product of seven and ten; ten less than eighty; 70: *about seventy people attended | seventy were arrested.* (Roman numeral: **lxx, LXX**) ■ (**seventies**) the numbers from seventy to seventy-nine, esp. the years of a century or of a person's life: *Dad was now in his seventies.* ■ seventy years old: *she was nearly seventy.* ■ seventy miles an hour: *doing about seventy.*
– DERIVATIVES **sev·en·ti·eth** /-tēəTH/ ordinal number, **sev·en·ty·fold** /-ˌfōld/ adj. & adv.
– ORIGIN Old English *hundseofontig*, from *hund-* (of uncertain origin) + *seofon* 'seven.'

sev·en·ty-eight (usu. **78**) ▶ n. an old phonograph record designed to be played at 78 rpm.

sev·en-up ▶ n. chiefly historical a variety of the card game "all fours" in which the winner is the first to score seven points.

Sev·en Won·ders of the World the seven most spectacular man-made structures of the ancient world.

> Traditionally they comprise (1) the pyramids of Egypt, esp. those at Giza; (2) the Hanging Gardens of Babylon; (3) the Mausoleum of Halicarnassus; (4) the temple of Artemis at Ephesus in Asia Minor; (5) the Colossus of Rhodes; (6) the huge ivory and gold statue of Zeus at Olympia in Peloponnesus, made by Phidias *c.*430 BC; (7) the Pharos of Alexandria (or in some lists, the walls of Babylon).

sev·en-year itch ▶ n. [in sing.] a supposed tendency to infidelity after seven years of marriage.

Sev·en Years War a war (1756–63) that set Britain, Prussia, and Hanover against Austria, France, Russia, Saxony, Sweden, and Spain.

> Its main issues were the struggle between Britain and France for supremacy overseas, and that between Prussia and Austria for the domination of Germany. The British made substantial gains over France abroad, capturing French Canada and undermining French influence in India.
> The war was ended by the Treaties of Paris and Hubertusburg in 1763, leaving Britain the supreme European naval and colonial power and Prussia in an appreciably stronger position than before in central Europe. See also FRENCH AND INDIAN WAR.

sev·er /ˈsevər/ ▶ v. [with obj.] divide by cutting or slicing, esp. suddenly and forcibly: *the head was severed from the body* | (as adj. **severed**) *severed limbs.* ■ put an end to (a connection or relationship); break off: *he severed his relations with Lawrence.*
– DERIVATIVES **sev·er·a·ble** adj.
– ORIGIN Middle English: from Anglo-Norman French *severer*, from Latin *separare* 'disjoin, divide.'

sev·er·al /ˈsev(ə)rəl/ ▶ determiner & pron. more than two but not many: [as determiner] *the author of several books* | [as pronoun] *Van Gogh was just one of several artists who gathered at Auvers | several of his friends attended.*
▶ adj. separate or respective: *the two levels of government sort out their several responsibilities.* ■ Law applied or regarded separately. Often contrasted with JOINT.
– ORIGIN late Middle English: from Anglo-Norman French, from medieval Latin *separalis*, from Latin *separ* 'separate, different.'

> **USAGE** See usage at VARIOUS.

sev·er·al·ly /ˈsev(ə)rəlē/ ▶ adv. separately or individually; each in turn: *the partners are **jointly and severally** liable.*

sev·er·al·ty /ˈsev(ə)rəltē/ ▶ n. archaic the condition of being separate.
– ORIGIN late Middle English: from Anglo-Norman French *severalte*, from *several* (see SEVERAL).

sev·er·ance /ˈsev(ə)rəns/ ▶ n. the action of ending a connection or relationship: *the severance and disestablishment of the Irish Church | a complete severance of links with the Republic.* ■ the state of being separated or cut off: *she works on the feeling of severance, of being deprived of her mother.* ■ dismissal or discharge from employment: [as modifier] *employees were offered severance terms.* ■ short for SEVERANCE PAY.
– ORIGIN late Middle English: from Anglo-Norman French, based on Latin *separare* (see SEVER).

sev·er·ance pay ▶ n. an amount paid to an employee upon dismissal or discharge from employment.

se·vere /səˈvi(ə)r/ ▶ adj. (**severer, severest**) **1** (of something bad or undesirable) very great; intense: *a severe shortage of technicians | a severe attack of asthma | damage is not too severe.* ■ demanding great ability, skill, or resilience: *a severe test of stamina.*
2 strict or harsh: *the charges would have warranted a severe sentence | he is unusually **severe on** what he regards as tendentious pseudo-learning.*
3 very plain in style or appearance: *she wore another severe suit, gray this time.*
– ORIGIN mid 16th cent. (sense 2): from French *sévère* or Latin *severus*.

se·vere·ly /səˈvi(ə)rlē/ ▶ adv. **1** to an undesirably great or intense degree: *our business has been severely affected by the slowdown* | [as submodifier] *severely injured patients.*
2 strictly or harshly: *the culprits will be severely punished.* ■ in a formal and unsmiling way: *"I hope you're not trying to steal my girlfriend," I said severely.*
3 in a very plain style: *her hair was severely pulled back into a bun.*

se·ver·i·ty /səˈveritē/ ▶ n. the fact or condition of being severe: *sentences should reflect the severity of the crime | hay fever symptoms vary in severity.*

Sev·ern /ˈsevərn/ a river of southwestern Britain. Rising in central Wales, it flows northeast and then south in a broad curve for about 180 miles (290 km) to its mouth on the Bristol Channel.

Se·ver·na·ya Zem·lya /ˈsevərnäˌyä ˌzemlēˈä, syivirnäˈyä zemˈlyä/ a group of uninhabited islands in the Arctic Ocean off the northern coast of Russia, to the north of the Taimyr Peninsula.

Se·ve·ro·dvinsk /ˌsevərədˈvinsk, syivyirədˈvyinsk/ a port in northwestern Russia, on the White Sea coast, west of Archangel; pop. 191,400 (est. 2008).

S

Se·ve·rus /sə'vi(ə)rəs/, Septimius (146–211), Roman emperor 193–211; full name *Lucius Septimius Severus Pertinax*. In 208, he led an army to Britain to suppress a rebellion in the north and later died at York.

sev·er·y /'sev(ə)rē/ ▶ n. (pl. **severies**) Architecture a bay or compartment in a vaulted ceiling.
– ORIGIN late Middle English: from Old French *civoire* 'ciborium' (see **CIBORIUM**).

se·vi·che ▶ n. variant spelling of **CEVICHE**.

Se·vier Riv·er /sə'vi(ə)r/ a river that flows for 325 miles (525 km) through central Utah, irrigating the eastern edge of the Great Basin.

Se·ville /sə'vil/ a city in southern Spain, the capital of Andalusia, located on the Guadalquivir River; pop. 699,759 (2008). Spanish name **Sevilla**.

Se·ville or·ange ▶ n. a bitter-tasting orange used for marmalade.

Se·vin /'sevin/ ▶ n. trademark for **CARBARYL**.
– ORIGIN 1950s: of unknown origin.

Sè·vres /'sevrə/ ▶ n. a type of fine porcelain characterized by elaborate decoration on backgrounds of intense color, made at Sèvres in the suburbs of Paris.

sev·ru·ga /sə'vro͞ogə/ ▶ n. a migratory sturgeon found only in the basins of the Caspian and Black Seas, much fished for its caviar. ● *Acipenser stellatus*, family Acipenseridae. ■ caviar obtained from this fish.
– ORIGIN late 16th cent.: from Russian *sevryuga*.

sew /sō/ ▶ v. (past participle **sewn** /sōn/ or **sewed** /sōd/) [with obj.] join, fasten, or repair (something) by making stitches with a needle and thread or a sewing machine: *she sewed the seams and hemmed the border* | [no obj.] *I don't even sew very well*. ■ attach (something) to something else by sewing: *she could sew the veil on properly in the morning*. ■ make (a garment) by sewing.
– PHRASAL VERBS **sew something up** informal bring something to a favorable conclusion: *he sank a 3-pointer to sew up a 120-118 victory*. ■ achieve exclusive control over something: *the U.S. courier market has been more or less sewn up by two companies*.
– ORIGIN Old English *siwan*, of Germanic origin, from an Indo-European root shared by Latin *suere* and Greek *suein*.

sew·age /'so͞oij/ ▶ n. waste water and excrement conveyed in sewers.
– ORIGIN mid 19th cent.: from **SEWER**[1], by substitution of the suffix **-AGE**.

sew·age sludge ▶ n. semiliquid waste obtained from the processing of municipal sewage, often used as a fertilizer.

Sew·ard /'so͞o(w)ərd/, William Henry (1801–72), US statesman and politician. An outspoken anti-slavery politician, he was governor of New York 1839–43, US senator 1849–61, and US secretary of state 1861–69. In 1867, he negotiated the purchase of Alaska from Russia, a purchase that was widely mocked as "Seward's Icebox" and "Seward's Folly."

Sew·ard Pen·in·su·la /'so͞oərd/ a region in northwestern Alaska on the Bering Strait and the Chukchi Sea. Nome lies on its southern coast.

se·wel·lel /sə'weləl/ ▶ n. another term for **MOUNTAIN BEAVER**.
– ORIGIN early 19th cent.: from Chinook Jargon *šwalál* 'robe of mountain-beaver skin.'

S

sew·er[1] /'so͞oər/ ▶ n. an underground conduit for carrying off drainage water and waste matter.
– ORIGIN Middle English (denoting a watercourse to drain marshy land): from Old Northern French *seuwiere* 'channel to drain the overflow from a fishpond,' based on Latin *ex-* 'out of' + *aqua* 'water.'

sew·er[2] /'sōər/ ▶ n. a person who sews.

sew·er·age /'so͞oərij/ ▶ n. the provision of drainage by sewers. ■ another term for **SEWAGE**.

sew·er rat /'so͞oər/ ▶ n. another term for **BROWN RAT**.

sew·ing /'sō-iNG/ ▶ n. the action or activity of sewing. ■ work that is to be or is being sewn: *she put down her sewing*.

sew·ing ma·chine ▶ n. a machine with a mechanically driven needle for sewing or stitching cloth.

sewn /sōn/ past participle of **SEW**.

sex /seks/ ▶ n. **1** (chiefly with reference to people) sexual activity, including specifically sexual intercourse: *he enjoyed talking about sex* | *she didn't want to have sex with him*. ■ [in sing.] euphemistic a person's genitals.
2 either of the two main categories (male and female) into which humans and many other living things are divided on the basis of their reproductive functions: *adults of both sexes*. ■ the fact of belonging to one of these categories: *direct discrimination involves treating someone less favorably on the grounds of their sex*. ■ the group of all members of either of these categories: *she was well known for her efforts to improve the social condition of her sex*.
▶ v. [with obj.] **1** determine the sex of: *sexing chickens*.
2 (**sex something up**) informal present something in a more interesting or lively way: *the department set up a task force to help sex up the concept of conserving water*.
3 (**sex someone up**) informal arouse or attempt to arouse someone sexually.
– DERIVATIVES **sex·er** n.
– ORIGIN late Middle English (denoting the two categories, male and female): from Old French *sexe* or Latin *sexus*.

> **USAGE** On the difference in use between the words sex (in sense 2 above) and **gender**, see usage at **GENDER**.

sex- ▶ comb. form variant spelling of **SEXI-**, shortened before a vowel (as in *sexennial*), or shortened before a consonant (as in *sexfoil*).

sex act ▶ n. any sexual act. ■ (**the sex act**) the act of sexual intercourse.

sex·a·ge·nar·i·an /ˌseksəjə'ne(ə)rēən/ ▶ n. a person who is from 60 to 69 years old.
– ORIGIN mid 18th cent.: from Latin *sexagenarius* (based on *sexaginta* 'sixty') + **-AN**.

Sex·a·ges·i·ma /ˌseksə'jesəmə/ (also **Sexagesima Sunday**) ▶ n. the Sunday before Quinquagesima.
– ORIGIN late Middle English: from ecclesiastical Latin, literally 'sixtieth (day),' probably named by analogy with **QUINQUAGESIMA**.

sex·a·ges·i·mal /ˌseksə'jesəməl/ ▶ adj. **1** of, relating to, or reckoning by sixtieths.
2 of or relating to the number sixty.
▶ n. (also **sexagesimal fraction**) a fraction based on sixtieths (i.e., with a denominator equal to a power of sixty), as in the divisions of the degree and hour.
– DERIVATIVES **sex·a·ges·i·mal·ly** adv.
– ORIGIN late 17th cent.: from Latin *sexagesimus* 'sixtieth' + **-AL**.

sex ap·peal ▶ n. the quality of being attractive in a sexual way: *she just oozes sex appeal*.

sex bomb ▶ n. informal a woman who is very sexually attractive.

sex·ca·pade /'sekskəˌpād/ ▶ n. informal a sexual escapade; an illicit affair.
– ORIGIN 1960s: blend of **SEX** and **ESCAPADE**.

sex·cen·ten·ar·y /ˌseksen'tenərē/ ▶ n. (pl. **sexcentenaries**) the six-hundredth anniversary of a significant event.
▶ adj. of or relating to a six-hundredth anniversary.

sex change ▶ n. a change in a person's physical sexual characteristics, typically by surgery and hormone treatment.

sex chro·ma·tin ▶ n. Biology material found only in the nuclei of female cells (esp. as the Barr body) and believed to represent the inactivated X chromosome.

sex chro·mo·some ▶ n. a chromosome involved with determining the sex of an organism, typically one of two kinds. Also called **HETEROCHROMOSOME**.

> In humans and other mammals females have two similar sex chromosomes (XX) while males have dissimilar ones (XY). In birds and some other animals, females have dissimilar sex chromosomes (ZW) and males similar ones (WW). Some other organisms have a sex chromosome present only in one sex.

sex crime ▶ n. informal a crime involving sexual assault or having a sexual motive.

sex dis·crim·i·na·tion (also **sexual discrimination**) ▶ n. discrimination in employment and opportunity against a person (typically a woman) on grounds of sex.

sex drive ▶ n. the urge to seek satisfaction of sexual needs.

sexed /sekst/ ▶ adj. **1** [with submodifier] having specified sexual appetites: *highly sexed heterosexual males*.
2 [attrib.] having sexual characteristics: *the effects of family and kinship relations on the construction of sexed individuals*.

sex·en·ni·al /sek'senēəl/ ▶ adj. recurring every six years. ■ lasting for or relating to a period of six years.
– ORIGIN mid 17th cent.: from **SEXENNIUM** + **-AL**.

sex·en·ni·um /sek'senēəm/ ▶ n. (pl. **sexennia** /sek'senēə/ or **sexenniums**) rare a specified period of six years.
– ORIGIN 1950s: from Latin, from *sex* 'six' + *annus* 'year.'

sex·foil /'seksˌfoil/ ▶ n. (esp. in architecture) an ornamental design having six leaves or petals radiating from a common center.
– ORIGIN late 17th cent.: from **SEXI-** 'six,' on the pattern of words such as *trefoil*.

sex hor·mone ▶ n. a hormone, such as estrogen or testosterone, affecting sexual development or reproduction.

sexi- (also **sex-** before a vowel) ▶ comb. form six; having six: *sexivalent*.
– ORIGIN from Latin *sex* 'six.'

sex in·dus·try ▶ n. (**the sex industry**) used euphemistically to refer to prostitution.

sex·ism /'sekˌsizəm/ ▶ n. prejudice, stereotyping, or discrimination, typically against women, on the basis of sex.
– DERIVATIVES **sex·ist** adj. & n.

sex·i·va·lent /'seksəˌvālənt/ ▶ adj. Chemistry another term for **HEXAVALENT**.

sex kit·ten ▶ n. informal a young woman who asserts or exploits her sexual attractiveness.

sex·less /'seksləs/ ▶ adj. **1** lacking in sexual desire, interest, activity, or attractiveness: *I've no patience with pious, sexless females*.
2 neither male nor female: *the stylized and sexless falsetto*.
– DERIVATIVES **sex·less·ly** adv., **sex·less·ness** n.

sex life ▶ n. a person's sexual activity and relationships considered as a whole.

sex-linked ▶ adj. chiefly Biology tending to be associated with one sex or the other. ■ (of a gene or heritable characteristic) carried by a sex chromosome.

sex ma·ni·ac ▶ n. informal a person whose need for sexual gratification is excessive or obsessive.

sex ob·ject ▶ n. a person regarded by another only in terms of their sexual attractiveness or availability: *we're now in a period when it is permissible for women to make men into sex objects*.

sex of·fend·er ▶ n. a person who commits a crime involving a sexual act.

sex·ol·o·gy /sek'säləjē/ ▶ n. the study of human sexual life or relationships.
– DERIVATIVES **sex·o·log·i·cal** /ˌseksə'läjikəl/ adj., **sex·ol·o·gist** /-jist/ n.

sex·par·tite /seks'pärˌtīt/ ▶ adj. divided or involving division into six parts: *the sexpartite vault is of 12th-century construction*.
– ORIGIN mid 18th cent.: from **SEXI-** 'six' + **PARTITE**, on the pattern of words such as *bipartite*.

sex·pert /'sekspərt/ ▶ n. informal an expert in sexual matters.

sex·ploi·ta·tion /ˌseksploi'tāsHən/ ▶ n. informal the commercial exploitation of sex, sexual attractiveness, or sexually explicit material.
– ORIGIN 1940s: blend of **SEX** and *exploitation* (see **EXPLOIT**).

sex·pot /'seksˌpät/ ▶ n. informal a sexy person.

sex role ▶ n. the role or behavior learned by a person as appropriate to their sex, determined by the prevailing cultural norms.

sex-starved ▶ adj. lacking and strongly desiring sexual gratification.

sex sym·bol ▶ n. a person widely noted for their sexual attractiveness.

sext /sekst/ ▶ n. a service forming part of the Divine Office of the Western Christian Church, traditionally said (or chanted) at the sixth hour of the day (i.e., noon).
– ORIGIN late Middle English: from Latin *sexta (hora)* 'sixth (hour),' from *sextus* 'sixth.'

Sex·tans /'sekstənz/ Astronomy a faint constellation (the Sextant), lying on the celestial equator between Leo and Hydra. ■ (as genitive **Sextantis** /sek'stantis/) used with a preceding letter or numeral to designate a star in this constellation: *the star Alpha Sextantis*.
– ORIGIN Latin.

sex·tant /'sekstənt/ ▶ n. an instrument with a graduated arc of 60° and a sighting mechanism, used for measuring the angular distances between objects and esp. for taking altitudes in navigation.
– ORIGIN late 16th cent. (denoting the sixth part of a circle): from Latin *sextans, sextant-* 'sixth part,' from *sextus* 'sixth.'

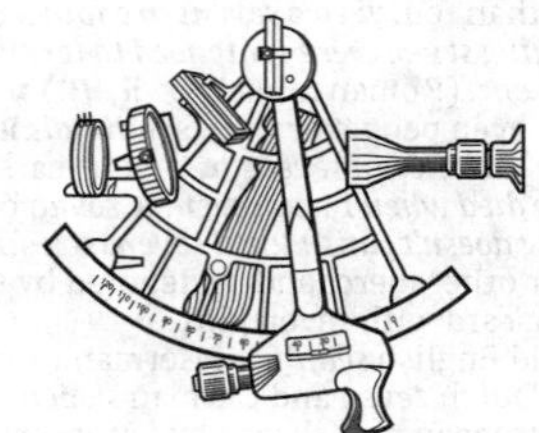

sextant

sex·tet /sek'stet/ (also **sextette**) ▶ **n.** a group of six people playing music or singing together. ■ a composition for such a group. ■ a set of six people or things: *a sextet of new releases.*
–ORIGIN mid 19th cent.: alteration of SESTET, suggested by Latin *sex* 'six.'

sex ther·a·py ▶ **n.** counseling or other therapy that addresses a person's psychological or physical sexual problems.
–DERIVATIVES **sex ther·a·pist** n.

sex·tile /'sek,stīl, -stəl/ ▶ **n.** Astrology an aspect of 60° (one sixth of a circle): *the Jupiter–Saturn cycle is now in sextile to its most difficult period.*
–ORIGIN late Middle English: from Latin *sextilis*, from *sextus* 'sixth.'

sex·til·lion /sek'stilyən/ ▶ **cardinal number** (pl. **sextillions** or (with numeral) **same**) a thousand raised to the seventh power (10^{21}). ■ dated, chiefly Brit. a million raised to the sixth power (10^{36}).
–DERIVATIVES **sex·til·lionth** /sek'stilyənTH/ **ordinal number.**
–ORIGIN late 17th cent.: from French, from *million*, by substitution of the prefix *sexti-* 'six' (from Latin *sextus* 'sixth') for the initial letters.

sex·to·dec·i·mo /,sekstə'desə,mō/ (abbr.: **16mo**) ▶ **n.** (pl. **sextodecimos**) a size of book page that results from folding each printed sheet into sixteen leaves (thirty-two pages). ■ a book of this size.
–ORIGIN late 17th cent.: from Latin *sexto decimo*, ablative of *sextus decimus* 'sixteenth.'

Sex·ton /'sekstən/, Anne (1928–74), US poet; born *Anne Harvey*. Plagued by mental illness, she wrote very emotional poems, many of which are collected in the volumes *To Bedlam and Part Way Back* (1960) and *Live or Die* (1966).

sex·ton /'sekstən/ ▶ **n.** a person who looks after a church and churchyard, sometimes acting as bell-ringer and formerly as a gravedigger.
–ORIGIN Middle English: from Anglo-Norman French *segrestein*, from medieval Latin *sacristanus* (see SACRISTAN).

sex·ton bee·tle ▶ **n.** another term for BURYING BEETLE.

sex tour·ism ▶ **n.** the organization of vacations with the purpose of taking advantage of the lack of restrictions imposed on prostitution and other sexual activities by some foreign countries.
–DERIVATIVES **sex tour** n., **sex tour·ist** n.

sex·tu·ple /sek'st(y)o͞opəl, -'təpəl/ ▶ **adj.** [attrib.] consisting of six parts or things. ■ six times as much or as many.
▶ **n.** a sixfold number or amount.
▶ **v.** [with obj.] multiply by six; increase sixfold.
–DERIVATIVES **sex·tu·ply** /-plē/ adv.
–ORIGIN early 17th cent.: from medieval Latin *sextuplus*, formed irregularly from Latin *sex* 'six,' on the pattern of late Latin *quintuplus* 'quintuple.'

sex·tu·plet /sek'stəplit, -'st(y)o͞oplət/ ▶ **n.** **1** each of six children born at one birth.
2 Music a group of six notes to be performed in the time of four.
–ORIGIN mid 19th cent.: from SEXTUPLE, on the pattern of words such as *triplet*.

sex typ·ing ▶ **n.** **1** Psychology & Sociology the stereotypical categorization of people, or their appearance or behavior, according to conventional perceptions of what is typical of each sex.
2 Biology the process of determining the sex of a person or other organism, esp. in difficult cases where special tests are necessary.
–DERIVATIVES **sex-typed** adj.

sex·u·al /'sekSHo͞oəl/ ▶ **adj.** **1** relating to the instincts, physiological processes, and activities connected with physical attraction or intimate physical contact between individuals: *she had felt the thrill of a sexual attraction.*
2 of or relating to the two sexes or to gender: *sensitivity about sexual stereotypes.* ■ of or characteristic of one sex or the other: *the hormones which control the secondary sexual characteristics.* ■ Biology being of one sex or the other; capable of sexual reproduction.
–DERIVATIVES **sex·u·al·ly** adv.
–ORIGIN mid 17th cent.: from late Latin *sexualis*, from Latin *sexus* 'sex.'

sex·u·al di·mor·phism ▶ **n.** Zoology distinct difference in size or appearance between the sexes of an animal in addition to difference between the sexual organs themselves.

sex·u·al ha·rass·ment ▶ **n.** harassment (typically of a woman) in a workplace, or other professional or social situation, involving the making of unwanted sexual advances or obscene remarks.

sex·u·al in·ter·course ▶ **n.** sexual contact between individuals involving penetration, esp. the insertion of a man's erect penis into a woman's vagina, typically culminating in orgasm and the ejaculation of semen.

sex·u·al in·ver·sion ▶ **n.** see INVERSION (sense 4).

sex·u·al·i·ty /,sekSHo͞o'alitē/ ▶ **n.** (pl. **sexualities**) capacity for sexual feelings: *she began to understand the power of her sexuality.* ■ a person's sexual orientation or preference: *people with proscribed sexualities.* ■ sexual activity.

sex·u·al·ize /'sekSHo͞oə,līz/ ▶ **v.** [with obj.] make sexual; attribute sex or a sex role to: (as adj. **sexualized**) *sexualized images of women.*
–DERIVATIVES **sex·u·al·i·za·tion** /,sekSHo͞oələ'zāSHən/ n.

sex·u·al o·ri·en·ta·tion ▶ **n.** a person's sexual identity in relation to the gender to which they are attracted; the fact of being heterosexual, homosexual, or bisexual.

sex·u·al pol·i·tics ▶ **plural n.** [treated as sing.] the principles determining the relationship of the sexes; relations between the sexes regarded in terms of power.

sex·u·al re·la·tions ▶ **plural n.** sexual behavior between individuals, esp. sexual intercourse.

sex·u·al re·pro·duc·tion ▶ **n.** Biology the production of new living organisms by combining genetic information from two individuals of different types (sexes). In most higher organisms, one sex (male) produces a small motile gamete that travels to fuse with a larger stationary gamete produced by the other (female).

sex·u·al rev·o·lu·tion ▶ **n.** the liberalization of established social and moral attitudes toward sex, particularly that occurring in western countries during the 1960s, as the women's liberation movement and developments in contraception instigated greater experimentation with sex, esp. outside of marriage.

sex·u·al se·lec·tion ▶ **n.** Biology natural selection arising through preference by one sex for certain characteristics in individuals of the other sex.

sex work·er ▶ **n.** used euphemistically to refer to a prostitute.

sex·y /'seksē/ ▶ **adj.** (**sexier, sexiest**) sexually attractive or exciting: *sexy French underwear.* ■ sexually aroused: *neither of them was feeling sexy.* ■ informal exciting; appealing: *I've climbed most of the really sexy west coast mountains.*
–DERIVATIVES **sex·i·ly** /-səlē/ adv., **sex·i·ness** n.

Sey·chelles /sā'SHel(z)/ (also **the Seychelles**) a country that consists of a group of about 90 islands in the Indian Ocean, about 600 miles (1,000 km) northeast of Madagascar; pop. 87,500 (est. 2009); capital, Victoria; languages, French (official), English, and Creole.

> The islands were uninhabited until the mid 18th century, when the French annexed them. The Seychelles were captured by Britain during the Napoleonic Wars and administered from Mauritius before becoming a separate colony in 1903 and an independent republic within the Commonwealth of Nations in 1976.

–DERIVATIVES **Sey·chel·lois** /,sāSHel'wä/ adj. & n. (pl. **same**).

Sey·fert gal·ax·y /'sēfərt/ ▶ **n.** Astronomy a galaxy of a type characterized by a bright compact core that shows strong infrared emission.
–ORIGIN named after Carl K. *Seyfert* (1911–60), US astronomer.

Seym /sām/ ▶ **n.** variant spelling of SEJM.

Sey·mour /'sē,môr/, Jane (*c.*1509–37), third wife of Henry VIII and mother of Edward VI. She married Henry in 1536 and finally provided the king with the male heir he wanted, although she died twelve days afterward.

sez /sez/ ▶ **v.** nonstandard spelling of "says," used in representing uneducated speech: *"Oh Lordy!" sez de man.*

Se·zes·sion /,zet,sesē'ōn/ (also **Secession**) ▶ **n.** (**the Sezession**) a radical movement involving groups of avant-garde German and Austrian artists who, from 1892, organized exhibitions independently of the traditional academies. The **Vienna Secession** founded by Gustav Klimt in 1897 helped to launch the Jugendstil.
–ORIGIN German, literally 'secession.'

SF ▶ **abbr.** ■ science fiction. ■ Sinn Fein. ■ Military Special Forces.

sf ▶ **abbr.** Music sforzando.

SFA ▶ **abbr.** ■ Scottish Football Association. ■ (in the UK) Securities and Futures Authority.

Sfax /sfaks, sfäks/ (also **Safaqis** /sä'fäkis/) a port on the eastern coast of Tunisia; pop. 265,100 (est. 2004).

SFC ▶ **abbr.** Sergeant First Class.

sfor·zan·do /sfôrt'sändō/ (also **sforzato** /sfôrt'sätō/) Music ▶ **adv. & adj.** (esp. as a direction) with sudden emphasis.
▶ **n.** (pl. **sforzandos** or **sforzandi** /-dē/) a sudden or marked emphasis.
–ORIGIN Italian, literally 'using force.'

SFSR ▶ **abbr.** Soviet Federated Socialist Republic.

sfu·ma·to /sfo͞o'mätō/ ▶ **n.** Art the technique of allowing tones and colors to shade gradually into one another, producing softened outlines or hazy forms.
–ORIGIN mid 19th cent.: Italian, literally 'shaded off,' past participle of *sfumare*.

SFX ▶ **abbr.** special effects.
–ORIGIN *FX* representing a pronunciation of *effects*.

sfz ▶ **abbr.** Music sforzando.

SG ▶ **abbr.** ■ Law solicitor general. ■ Physics specific gravity.

Sg ▶ **symbol** the chemical element seaborgium.

sgd ▶ **abbr.** signed.

SGM ▶ **abbr.** sergeant major.

SGML ▶ **abbr.** Computing Standard Generalized Markup Language, an international standard for defining methods of encoding electronic texts to describe layout, structure, syntax, etc., which can then be used for analysis or to display the text in any desired format.

sgraf·fi·to /zgrä'fētō, skrä-/ ▶ **n.** (pl. **sgraffiti** /-tē/) a form of decoration made by scratching through a surface to reveal a lower layer of a contrasting color, typically done in plaster or stucco on walls, or in slip on ceramics before firing.
–ORIGIN mid 18th cent.: Italian, literally 'scratched away,' past participle of *sgraffiare*.

's-Gra·ven·ha·ge /,sKHrävən'häKHə/ Dutch name for HAGUE.

Sgt (also **SGT**) ▶ **abbr.** sergeant.

Sgt. Maj. ▶ **abbr.** Sergeant Major.

sh. ▶ **abbr.** Brit. shilling(s).

Shaan·xi /'SHän'SHē/ (also **Shensi**) a mountainous province in central China; capital, Xian. It is the site of the earliest known settlements of the ancient Chinese civilizations.

Sha·ba /'SHäbə/ a copper-mining region of southeastern Democratic Republic of the Congo (formerly Zaire); capital, Lubumbashi. Former name (until 1972) KATANGA.

Sha·ba·ka /'SHabəkə/ (died 698 BC), Egyptian pharaoh; founder of the 25th dynasty; reigned 712–698 BC; known as **Sabacon**. He promoted the cult of Amun and revived the custom of pyramid burial in his own death arrangements.

Shab·bat /SHä'bät/ ▶ **n.** the Jewish Sabbath.
–ORIGIN from Hebrew *šabbāṯ*.

Shab·bos /'SHäbəs/ (also **Shabbas** or **Shabbes**) ▶ **n.** the Yiddish term for the Jewish Sabbath.
–ORIGIN Yiddish, from Hebrew *šabbāṯ*.

shab·by /'SHabē/ ▶ **adj.** (**shabbier, shabbiest**) in poor condition through long or hard use or lack of care: *a conscript in a shabby uniform saluted the car.* ■ dressed in old or worn clothes. ■ (of behavior) mean and shameful: *shabby, disrespectful treatment.*
–DERIVATIVES **shab·bi·ly** /-əlē/ adv., **shab·bi·ness** n.
–ORIGIN mid 17th cent.: from dialect *shab* 'scab' (from a Germanic base meaning 'itch') + -Y¹.

shab·rack /'SHab,rak/ ▶ **n.** historical a cavalry saddlecloth used in European armies.
–ORIGIN early 19th cent.: from German *Schabracke*, of eastern European origin; compare with Russian *shabrak*.

sha·bu-sha·bu /,SHäbo͞o 'SHäbo͞o/ ▶ **n.** a Japanese dish of pieces of thinly sliced beef or pork cooked quickly with vegetables in boiling water and then dipped in sauce.
–ORIGIN Japanese.

shack /SHak/ ▶ **n.** a roughly built hut or cabin.
▶ **v.** [no obj.] (**shack up**) informal move in or live with someone as a lover.
–ORIGIN late 19th cent.: perhaps from Mexican *jacal*; see JACAL. The early sense of the verb was 'live in a shack' (originally a US usage).

shack·le /'SHakəl/ ▶ **n.** **1** (**shackles**) a pair of fetters connected together by a chain, used to fasten a prisoner's wrists or ankles together. ■ used in reference to something that restrains or impedes: *society is going to throw off the shackles of racism and colonialism.*
2 a metal link, typically U-shaped, closed by a bolt, used to secure a chain or rope to something.

S

PRONUNCIATION KEY ə *ago, up*; ər *over, fur*; a *hat*; ā *ate*; ä *car*; e *let*; ē *see*; i *fit*; ī *by*; NG *sing*; ō *go*; ô *law, for*; oi *toy*; o͝o *good*; o͞o *goo*; ou *out*; TH *thin*; T͟H *then*; ZH *vision*

■ a pivoted link connecting a spring in a vehicle's suspension to the body of the vehicle.
▶ **v.** [with obj.] chain with shackles. ■ restrain; limit: *they seek to shackle the oil and gas companies by imposing new controls.*
– ORIGIN Old English *sc(e)acul* 'fetter,' of Germanic origin; related to Dutch *schakel* 'link, coupling.'

Shack·le·ton /ˈSHakəltən/, Sir Ernest Henry (1874–1922), British explorer. During one of his Antarctic expeditions (1914–16), Shackleton's ship *Endurance* was crushed in the ice. He and his crew eventually reached Elephant Island, from where he and five others made an 800-mile (1,300-km) open-boat voyage to South Georgia to get help.

shack·y /ˈSHakē/ ▶ **adj.** informal (of a building) dilapidated or ramshackle.

shad /SHad/ ▶ **n.** (pl. **same** or **shads**) a herringlike fish that spends much of its life in the sea, typically entering rivers to spawn. It is an important food fish in many regions. ● Genera *Alosa* and *Caspialosa*, family Clupeidae: several species. See TWAITE SHAD.
– ORIGIN Old English *sceadd*, of unknown origin.

shad·blow /ˈSHad,blō/ ▶ **n.** another term for JUNEBERRY.
– ORIGIN mid 19th cent.: from SHAD + BLOW[3] (because its flowering is associated with the presence of spawning shad in the rivers).

shad·bush /ˈSHad,bo͝osh/ (also **shadblow** /-ˌblō/) ▶ **n.** another term for JUNEBERRY.
– ORIGIN early 19th cent.: so named because it flowers at the same time as shad are found in the rivers.

shad·chan ▶ **n.** variant spelling of SHADKHAN.

Shad·dai /SHäˈdī/ ▶ **n.** one of the names given to God in the Hebrew Bible.
– ORIGIN Hebrew, translated as 'Almighty' in English versions of the Bible, but of uncertain meaning.

shad·dock /ˈSHadək/ ▶ **n.** another term for POMELO.
– ORIGIN late 17th cent.: named after Captain *Shaddock*, who introduced it to the West Indies in the 17th cent.

shadd·up /ˌSHətˈəp/ ▶ **exclam.** informal be quiet!: *"Shaddup! If he wants to confess, let him."*
– ORIGIN 1950s: representing a pronunciation of *shut up*.

shade /SHād/ ▶ **n. 1** comparative darkness and coolness caused by shelter from direct sunlight: *sitting in the shade | this area will be* ***in shade*** *for much of the day.* ■ the darker part of a picture. ■ a position of relative inferiority or obscurity: *her elegant pink and black ensemble would* ***put most outfits in the shade.*** ■ (usu. **shades**) literary a shadow or area of darkness: *the shades of evening drew on.* ■ historical a portrait in silhouette.
2 a color, esp. with regard to how light or dark it is or as distinguished from one nearly like it: *various shades of blue | Maria's eyes darkened* ***in shade.*** ■ Art a slight degree of difference between colors. ■ a slightly differing variety of something: *politicians of all shades of opinion.* ■ [in sing.] a slight amount of something: *there is* ***a shade of*** *wistfulness in his rejection.*
3 a lampshade. ■ (often **shades**) a screen or blind on a window. ■ an eyeshade. ■ (**shades**) informal sunglasses.
4 literary a ghost. ■ (**the Shades**) the underworld; Hades.
▶ **v.** [with obj.] **1** screen from direct light: *she shaded her eyes against the sun.* ■ cover, moderate, or exclude the light of: *he shaded the flashlight with his hand.*
2 darken or color (an illustration or diagram) with parallel pencil lines or a block of color: *she* ***shaded in*** *the outline of a chimney.* ■ [no obj.] (of a color or something colored) gradually change into another color: *the sky shaded from turquoise to night blue.*
3 make a slight reduction in the amount, rate, or price of: *banks may shade the margin over base rate they charge customers.*
– PHRASES **a shade ——** a little ——: *he was a shade hung over.* **shades of ——** used to suggest reminiscence of or comparison with someone or something specified: *a long, drawn-out orchestral climax (shades of Wagner or Strauss).*
– DERIVATIVES **shade·less** adj., **shad·er** n.
– ORIGIN Old English *sc(e)adu*, of Germanic origin. Compare with SHADOW.

shad·ing /ˈSHādiNG/ ▶ **n. 1** the darkening or coloring of an illustration or diagram with parallel lines or a block of color. ■ a very slight variation, typically in color or meaning: *the shadings of opinion even among those who are in broad agreement.*
2 a layer of paint or material used to provide shade, esp. for plants: *liquid greenhouse shading.*

shad·khan ▶ **n.** /ˈSHätKHən, SHädˈKHän/ (also **shadchan**) (noun pl. **same**, **shadkhanim** /ˌSHädKHäˈnēm/, or **shadkhans**) a Jewish professional matchmaker or marriage broker.
– ORIGIN from Yiddish *shadkhn*, based on Hebrew *šiddēk* 'negotiate.'

sha·doof /SHäˈdo͞of/ ▶ **n.** a pole with a bucket and counterweight used esp. in Egypt for raising water.
– ORIGIN mid 19th cent.: from Egyptian Arabic *šādūf*.

shadoof

shad·ow /ˈSHadō/ ▶ **n. 1** a dark area or shape produced by a body coming between rays of light and a surface: *trees cast long shadows.* ■ partial or complete darkness, esp. as produced in this way: *the north side of the cathedral was deep in shadow |* (**shadows**) *a stranger slowly approached from the shadows.* ■ the shaded part of a picture. ■ a dark patch or area on a surface: *there are dark shadows beneath your eyes.* ■ a region of opacity on a radiograph: *shadows on his lungs.* ■ short for EYESHADOW.
2 used in reference to proximity, ominous oppressiveness, or sadness and gloom: *the shadow of war fell across Europe | only one shadow lay over Sally's life.* ■ used in reference to something insubstantial or fleeting: *a freedom that was more shadow than substance.* ■ used in reference to a position of relative inferiority or obscurity: *he lived* ***in the shadow of*** *his father.* ■ [with negative] the slightest trace of something: *she knew* ***without a shadow of a doubt*** *that he was lying.* ■ a weak or inferior remnant or version of something: *this fine-looking, commanding man had become* ***a shadow of his former self.*** ■ an expression of perplexity or sadness: *a shadow crossed Maria's face.*
3 an inseparable attendant or companion: *her faithful shadow, a Yorkshire terrier called Heathcliffe.* ■ a person secretly following and observing another. ■ a person who accompanies someone in their daily activities at work in order to gain experience at or insight into a job. ■ [usu. as modifier] Brit. the opposition counterpart of a government minister: *the shadow Chancellor.*
▶ **v.** [with obj.] **1** envelop in shadow; cast a shadow over: *the market is shadowed by St. Margaret's church | a hood shadowed her face.*
2 follow and observe (someone) closely and typically secretly: *he had been up all night shadowing a team of poachers.* ■ Brit. (of an opposition politician) be the counterpart of (a government minister or a ministry). ■ accompany (someone) in their daily activities at work in order to gain experience at or insight into a job.
– PHRASES **be frightened of one's shadow** be very timid or nervous.
– DERIVATIVES **shad·ow·er** n., **shad·ow·less** adj.
– ORIGIN Old English *scead(u)we* (noun), oblique case of *sceadu* (see SHADE), *sceadwian* 'screen or shield from attack,' of Germanic origin; related to Dutch *schaduw* and German *Schatten* (nouns), from an Indo-European root shared by Greek *skotos* 'darkness.'

shad·ow·box /ˈSHadō,bäks/ ▶ **v.** [no obj.] spar with an imaginary opponent as a form of training.
▶ **n.** (**shadow box**) a case with a protective transparent front, used for displaying jewelry, coins, or other small objects.

shad·ow e·con·o·my ▶ **n.** illicit economic activity (such as black market transactions and undeclared work) existing alongside a country's official economy.

shad·ow·graph /ˈSHadō,graf/ ▶ **n.** an image formed by the shadow of an object on a surface. ■ an image formed when light shone through a fluid is refracted differently by regions of different density. ■ a radiograph.

shad·ow·land /ˈSHadō,land/ ▶ **n.** literary a place in shadow. ■ (usu. **shadowlands**) an indeterminate borderland between places or states, typically represented as an abode of ghosts and spirits: *voices laughing in the shadowlands of my recall.*

shad·ow mask ▶ **n.** a perforated metal screen situated directly behind the phosphor screen in certain types of color television tubes, having a pattern of precisely located holes through which the electron beams pass so as to strike the correct dots on the phosphor screen.

shad·ow play ▶ **n.** a display in which the shadows of flat jointed puppets are cast on a screen that is viewed by the audience from the other side. Such shows originated in East Asia, and were popular in London and Paris in the 18th and 19th centuries; they survive in traditional form in Java and Bali.

shad·ow price ▶ **n.** Economics the estimated price of a good or service for which no market price exists.

shad·ow stitch ▶ **n.** a crisscross embroidery stitch used on sheer materials for filling in spaces, worked on the reverse side so as to show through in a shadowy way with an outline resembling a backstitch.

shad·ow work ▶ **n.** embroidery done in shadow stitch.

shad·ow·y /ˈSHadōē/ ▶ **adj.** (**shadowier, shadowiest**) full of shadows: *the shadowy back streets of Stringtown.* ■ of uncertain identity or nature: *a shadowy figure appeared through the mist | the shadowy world of covert operations.* ■ insubstantial; unreal: *they were attacked by a swarm of shadowy, ethereal forms.*
– DERIVATIVES **shad·ow·i·ness** n.

shad·y /ˈSHādē/ ▶ **adj.** (**shadier, shadiest**) situated in or full of shade: *shady woods.* ■ giving shade from sunlight: *they sprawled under a shady carob tree.* ■ informal of doubtful honesty or legality: *he was involved in his grandmother's shady deals.*
– DERIVATIVES **shad·i·ly** adv., **shad·i·ness** n.

shaft /SHaft/ ▶ **n. 1** a long, narrow part or section forming the handle of a tool or club, the body of a spear or arrow, or a similar implement: *the shaft of a golf club | the shaft of a feather.* ■ an arrow or spear. ■ a column, esp. the main part between the base and capital. ■ a long cylindrical rotating rod for the transmission of motive power in a machine. ■ each of the pair of poles between which a horse is harnessed to a vehicle. ■ a ray of light or bolt of lightning: ***a shaft of sunlight.*** ■ a sudden flash of a quality or feeling: ***a shaft of inspiration.*** ■ a remark intended to be witty, wounding, or provoking: *he directs his shafts against her.* ■ vulgar slang a penis. ■ (**the shaft**) informal harsh or unfair treatment: *the executives continue to raise their pay while the workers* ***get the shaft.***
2 a long, narrow, typically vertical hole that gives access to a mine, accommodates an elevator in a building, or provides ventilation.
▶ **v. 1** [no obj.] (of light) shine in beams: *brilliant sunshine shafted through the skylight.*
2 [with obj.] vulgar slang (of a man) have sexual intercourse with (a woman). ■ informal treat (someone) harshly or unfairly: *I suppose she'll get a lawyer and I'll be shafted.*
– DERIVATIVES **shaft·ed** adj. [in combination] *a long-shafted harpoon.*
– ORIGIN Old English *scæft, sceaft* 'handle, pole,' of Germanic origin; related to Dutch *schaft*, German *Schaft*, and perhaps also to SCEPTER. Early senses of the verb (late Middle English) were 'fit with a handle' and 'send out shafts of light.'

shaft drive ▶ **n.** a mechanism in which power is transmitted from an engine by means of a driveshaft, esp. to the wheels of a vehicle or a boat's propeller.
– DERIVATIVES **shaft-driv·en** adj.

Shaftes·bur·y /ˈSHaf(t)s,berē, -b(ə)rē/, Anthony Ashley Cooper, 7th Earl of (1801–85), English philanthropist and social reformer. He inspired much of the legislation designed to improve conditions for the large working class created as a result of the Industrial Revolution.

shaft horse·pow·er ▶ **n.** the power delivered to a propeller or turbine shaft.

shaft·ing /ˈSHaftiNG/ ▶ **n.** a system of connected shafts for transmitting motive power in a machine.

shag[1] /SHag/ ▶ **n. 1** [usu. as modifier] a carpet or rug with a long, rough pile: *wall-to-wall shag carpet.* ■ [as modifier] (of a pile) long and rough: *a shag pile.* ■ cloth with a velvet nap on one side.
2 a thick, tangled hairstyle or mass of hair: *her hair was cut short in a boyish shag* | [as modifier] *a shag cut.*
3 (also **shag tobacco**) a coarse kind of cut tobacco.
– ORIGIN late Old English *sceacga* 'rough matted hair,' of Germanic origin; related to Old Norse *skegg* 'beard' and SHAW.

shag[2] ▶ **n.** a western European and Mediterranean cormorant with greenish-black plumage and a long curly crest in the breeding season. ● *Phalacrocorax aristotelis*, family Phalacrocoracidae. ■ chiefly NZ any cormorant.
– ORIGIN mid 16th cent.: perhaps a use of SHAG[1], with reference to the bird's "shaggy" crest.

shag[3] ▶ **n.** a dance originating in the US in the 1930s and 1940s, characterized by vigorous hopping from one foot to the other.
– ORIGIN of obscure derivation; perhaps from obsolete *shag* 'waggle.'

shag[4] ▶ **v.** [with obj.] Baseball chase or catch (fly balls) for practice.
– ORIGIN early 20th cent.: of unknown origin.

shag[5] Brit. vulgar slang ▶ **v.** (**shags**, **shagging**, **shagged**) [with obj.] have sexual intercourse with (someone). ▶ **n.** an act of sexual intercourse. ■ [with adj.] a sexual partner of a specified ability.
– DERIVATIVES **shag·ga·ble** adj., **shag·ger** n.
– ORIGIN late 18th cent.: of unknown origin.

shag·bark hick·o·ry /'SHag,bärk/ ▶ **n.** see **HICKORY**.

shagged /SHagd/ ▶ **adj.** Brit. informal exhausted: *they were too shagged to do any cleaning.* ■ damaged, ruined, or useless: *I thought my hearing was shagged because I play the drums.*

shag·gy /'SHagē/ ▶ **adj.** (**shaggier**, **shaggiest**) (of hair or fur) long, thick, and unkempt: *the mountain goat has a long, shaggy coat.* ■ having long, thick, unkempt hair or fur: *a huge shaggy English sheepdog.* ■ of or having a covering resembling rough, thick hair.
– PHRASES **shaggy-dog story** a long, rambling story or joke, typically one that is amusing only because it is absurdly inconsequential or pointless. [originally an anecdote of this type, about a shaggy-haired dog (1945).]
– DERIVATIVES **shag·gi·ly** /-əlē/ adv., **shag·gi·ness** n.

shag·gy mane ▶ **n.** a common mushroom that has a tall, narrow white cap covered with shaggy scales, occurring worldwide and edible when young. ● *Coprinus comatus*, family Coprinaceae, class Hymenomycetes.

sha·green /SHə'grēn/ ▶ **n. 1** sharkskin used as a decorative material or, for its natural rough surface of pointed scales, as an abrasive.
2 a kind of untanned leather with a rough granulated surface.
– ORIGIN late 17th cent.: variant of **CHAGRIN** in the literal sense 'rough skin.'

Shah /SHä/, Reza, see **PAHLAVI**[1].

shah /SHä/ ▶ **n.** historical a title of the former monarch of Iran.
– DERIVATIVES **shah·dom** /-dəm/ n.
– ORIGIN mid 16th cent.: from Persian *šāh*, from Old Persian *ḵšāyatiya* 'king.'

sha·ha·da /SHä'hädə/ (also **shahadah**) ▶ **n.** the Muslim profession of faith ("there is no god but Allah, and Muhammad is the messenger of Allah").
– ORIGIN from Arabic *šahāda* 'testimony, evidence.'

sha·hid /SHä'hēd/ (also **shaheed**) ▶ **n.** a Muslim martyr.
– ORIGIN late 19th cent.: from Arabic *šahīd* 'witness, martyr.'

Shahn /SHän/, Ben (1898–1989), US artist and photographer; born in Lithuania; full name *Benjamin Shahn*. His paintings such as "The Passion of Sacco and Vanzetti" (1931–32) are devoted to political and social themes. He was also a photographer for the US Farm Security Administration during the 1930s.

shah·toosh /SHä'tōōSH/ ▶ **n.** high-quality wool from the neck hair of the Himalayan ibex. ■ fabric woven from this.
– ORIGIN mid 19th cent.: via Punjabi from Persian *šāh* 'king' + Kashmiri *tośa* 'fine shawl material.'

shaikh /SHēk, SHāk/ ▶ **n.** variant spelling of **SHEIKH**.

Shai·tan /SHī'tän/ ▶ **n.** (in Muslim countries) the Devil, Satan, or an evil spirit. ■ (**shaitan**) an evilly disposed, vicious, or cunning person or animal.
– ORIGIN from Arabic *šayṭān*.

Shai·va /'SHīvə/ (also **Saiva** /'sīvə/) ▶ **n.** a member of one of the main branches of modern Hinduism, devoted to the worship of the god Shiva as the supreme being. Compare with **VAISHNAVA**.
– DERIVATIVES **Shai·vite** /-vīt/ n. & adj.
– ORIGIN from Sanskrit *śaiva* 'sacred to Shiva.'

Sha·ka /'SHäkə/ (also **Chaka**) (*c.*1787–1828), Zulu chief 1816–28. He reorganized his forces and waged war against the Nguni clans, subjugating them and forming a Zulu empire in southeastern Africa.

shake /SHāk/ ▶ **v.** (past **shook** /SHŏŏk/; past participle **shaken** /'SHākən/) **1** [no obj.] (of a structure or area of land) tremble or vibrate: *buildings shook in Sacramento and tremors were felt in Reno.* ■ [with obj.] cause to tremble or vibrate: *a severe earthquake shook the area.* ■ (of a person, a part of the body, or the voice) tremble uncontrollably from a strong emotion such as fear or anger: *Luke was shaking with rage | her voice shook with passion.*
2 [with obj.] move (an object) up and down or from side to side with rapid, forceful, jerky movements: *she stood in the hall and shook her umbrella.* ■ remove (an object or substance) from something by movements of this kind: *they shook the sand out of their shoes.* ■ informal get rid of or put an end to (something unwanted): *he was unable to shake off the memories of the trenches.* ■ grasp (someone) and move them roughly to and fro, either in anger or to rouse them from sleep: [with obj. and complement] *he gently shook the driver awake and they set off.* ■ brandish in anger or as a warning; make a threatening gesture with: *men shook their fists and shouted.*
3 [with obj.] upset the composure of; shock or astonish: *rumors of a further loss shook the market | the fall shook him up quite badly* | (as adj. **shaken**) *she was visibly shaken and upset when she returned.* ■ cause a change of mood or attitude by shocking or disturbing (someone): *he had to shake himself out of his lethargy.*
▶ **n. 1** an act of shaking: *with a shake of its magnificent antlers the stag charged down the slope | camera shake causes the image to become blurred.* ■ informal an earth tremor. ■ an amount of something that is sprinkled by shaking a container: *add a few shakes of sea salt and black pepper.* ■ short for **MILK SHAKE**. ■ (**the shakes**) informal a fit of trembling or shivering: *I wouldn't go in there, it gives me the shakes.*
2 Music a trill.
– PHRASES **get** (or **give someone**) **a fair shake** informal get (or give someone) just treatment or a fair chance: *I do not believe he gave the industry a fair shake.* **in two shakes** (**of a lamb's tail**) informal very quickly: *I'll be back to you in two shakes.* **more —— than one can shake a stick at** informal used to emphasize the largeness of an amount: *a team with more experience than you can shake a stick at.* **no great shakes** informal not very good or significant: *it is no great shakes as a piece of cinema.* **shake the dust off one's feet** leave indignantly or disdainfully. **shake hands** (**with someone**) (or **shake someone by the hand** or **shake someone's hand**) clasp someone's right hand in one's own at meeting or parting, in reconciliation or congratulation, or as a sign of agreement. **shake one's head** turn one's head from side to side in order to indicate refusal, denial, disapproval, or incredulity: *she shook her head in disbelief.* **shake** (or **quake**) **in one's shoes** (or **boots**) tremble with apprehension. **shake a leg** informal make a start; rouse oneself: *come on, shake a leg.*
– PHRASAL VERBS **shake down** become established in a new place or situation; settle down: *it was disruptive to the industry as it was shaking down after deregulation.* **shake someone down** informal extort money from someone. **shake something down** cause something to fall or settle by shaking. **shake someone off** get away from someone by shaking their grip loose. ■ manage to evade or outmaneuver someone who is following or pestering one: *he thought he had shaken off his pursuer.* ■ (in sports, esp. a race) outdistance another competitor: *in the final lap she looked as though she had shaken off the Dutch girl.* **shake something off** successfully deal with or recover from an illness or injury: *she has shaken off a virus.* **shake on** informal confirm (an agreement) by shaking hands: *they shook on the deal.* **shake out** eventually prove to happen: *we'll see what shakes out.* **shake something out 1** empty something out by shaking a container: *he shook out a handful of painkillers.* **2** spread or open something such as a cloth or garment by shaking it: *she shook out the newspaper.* ■ restore something crumpled to its natural shape by shaking: *she undid her helmet and shook out her frizzled hair.* ■ Sailing unwind or untie a reef to increase the area of a sail. **shake someone up** rouse someone from lethargy, apathy, or complacency: *he had to do something to shake the team up—we lacked spark.* **shake something up 1** mix ingredients by shaking: *use soap flakes shaken up in the water to make bubbles.* **2** make radical changes to the organization or structure of an institution or system: *he presented plans to shake up the legal profession.*
– ORIGIN Old English *sc(e)acan* (verb), of Germanic origin.

shake·down /'SHāk,doun/ ▶ **n.** informal **1** a radical change or restructuring, particularly in a hierarchical organization or group: *the shakedown of the Bank of England in the fall of 1992.* ■ a thorough search of a person or place: *harassment and shakedowns by persons in police uniforms.* ■ a swindle; a piece of extortion: *he wants to eliminate bribery, shakedowns, and bid-rigging in New York City's construction industry.* ■ a test of a new product or model, esp. a vehicle or ship: *the high-orbit shakedown of the lunar module had its merits* | [as modifier] *the software is expected to enter its final shakedown phase by the middle of September.*
2 a makeshift bed.

shak·en /'SHākən/ past participle of **SHAKE**.

sha·ken ba·by syn·drome ▶ **n.** injury to a baby caused by being shaken violently and repeatedly. Shaking can cause swelling of the brain, internal bleeding, detached retinas leading to blindness, mental retardation, and death.

shake·out /'SHāk,out/ ▶ **n.** informal an upheaval or reorganization of a business, market, or organization due to competition and typically involving streamlining and layoffs.

shak·er /'SHākər/ ▶ **n. 1** [with modifier] a container used for mixing ingredients by shaking: *a cocktail shaker.* ■ a container with a pierced top from which a powdered substance such as flour or salt is poured by shaking.
2 (**Shaker**) a member of an American religious sect, the United Society of Believers in Christ's Second Coming, established in England *c.*1750 and living simply in celibate mixed communities. [so named from the wild, ecstatic movements engaged in during worship.] ■ [as modifier] denoting a style of elegantly functional furniture traditionally produced by Shaker communities.
– DERIVATIVES **Shak·er·ism** /-,rizəm/ n. (sense 2).

Shak·er·ess /'SHāk(ə)ris/ ▶ **n.** a female Shaker.

Shak·er Heights /'SHākər/ a city in northeastern Ohio, an affluent suburb east of Cleveland; pop. 26,460 (est. 2008).

Shake·speare /'SHāk,spi(ə)r/, William (1564–1616), English playwright. His plays are written mostly in blank verse and include comedies, historical plays, the Greek and Roman plays, enigmatic comedies, the great tragedies, and the group of tragicomedies with which he ended his career. He also wrote more than 150 sonnets, which were published in 1609, as well as narrative poems.
– DERIVATIVES **Shake·spear·e·an** /SHāk'spi(ə)rēən/ (also **Shakespearian**) n. & adj.

William Shakespeare

Shake·spear·e·an son·net ▶ **n.** another term for **ELIZABETHAN SONNET**.

shake-up (also **shakeup**) ▶ **n.** informal a radical reorganization.

Shakh·ty /'SHäKHtē/ a coal-mining city in southwestern Russia, in the Donets Basin, northeast of Rostov; pop. 244,400 (est. 2008).

shak·o /'SHakō, 'SHā-/ ▶ **n.** (pl. **shakos**) a cylindrical or conical military hat with a brim and a plume or pom-pom.
– ORIGIN early 19th cent.: via French from Hungarian *csákó* (*süveg*) 'peaked (cap),' from *csák* 'peak,' from German *Zacken* 'spike.'

shako

Shak·ti /'SHəktē/ ▶ **n.** Hinduism the female principle of divine energy, esp. when personified as the supreme deity. See also **DEVI** and **PARVATI**.
– ORIGIN from Sanskrit *śakti* 'power, divine energy.'

sha·ku·do /SHä'kōōdō/ ▶ **n.** a Japanese alloy of copper and gold, typically having a blue patina.
– ORIGIN mid 19th cent.: Japanese, from *shaku* 'red' + *dō* 'copper.'

sha·ku·ha·chi /'SHäkōō'häCHē/ ▶ **n.** (pl. **shakuhachis**) a Japanese bamboo flute, held vertically when played.
– ORIGIN late 19th cent.: Japanese, from *shaku*, a measure of length (approx. 0.33 meter) + *hachi* 'eight (tenths).'

shak·y /'SHākē/ ▶ **adj.** (**shakier**, **shakiest**) shaking or trembling: *she managed a shaky laugh.* ■ unstable because of poor construction or heavy use: *a cracked, dangerously shaky table.* ■ not safe or

PRONUNCIATION KEY ə *ago, up*; ər *over, fur*; a *hat*; ā *ate*; ä *car*; e *let*; ē *see*; i *fit*; ī *by*; NG *sing*; ō *go*; ô *law, for*; oi *toy*; ŏŏ *good*; ōō *goo*; ou *out*; TH *thin*; TH *then*; ZH *vision*

S

reliable; liable to fail or falter: *thoroughly shaky evidence | Burns overcame a shaky start to beat the Red Sox.*
– DERIVATIVES **shak·i·ly** /-kilē/ **adv.**, **shak·i·ness n.**

shale /SHāl/ ▶ **n.** soft, finely stratified sedimentary rock that formed from consolidated mud or clay and can be split easily into fragile slabs.
– DERIVATIVES **shal·y** (also **shaley**) **adj.**
– ORIGIN mid 18th cent.: probably from German *Schale*; related to English dialect *shale* 'dish' (see SCALE[2]).

shale oil ▶ **n.** oil obtained from bituminous shale.

shall /SHal/ ▶ **modal v.** (3rd sing. present **shall**) **1** (in the first person) expressing the future tense: *this time next week I shall be in Scotland.* **2** expressing a strong assertion or intention: *they shall succeed | you shall not frighten me out of this.* **3** expressing an instruction or command: *you shall not steal.* **4** used in questions indicating offers or suggestions: *shall I send you the book? | shall we go?*
– ORIGIN Old English *sceal*, of Germanic origin; related to Dutch *zal* and German *soll*, from a base meaning 'owe.'

USAGE There is considerable confusion about when to use **shall** and **will**. The traditional rule in standard English is that **shall** is used with first person pronouns (*I* and *we*) to form the future tense, while **will** is used with second and third persons (*you, he, she, it, they*): ***I shall be late; she will not be there.*** To express a strong determination to do something, these positions are reversed, with **will** being used with the first person and **shall** with the second and third persons: ***I will not tolerate this; you shall go to school.*** In practice, however, **shall** and **will** are today used more or less interchangeably in statements (although not in questions). Given that the forms are frequently contracted (**we'll, she'll,** etc.), there is often no need to make a choice between **shall** and **will**, another factor no doubt instrumental in weakening the distinction. In modern English, the interchangeable use of **shall** and **will** is an acceptable part of standard US and British English.

shal·lop /ˈSHaləp/ ▶ **n.** chiefly historical a light sailboat used mainly for coastal fishing or as a tender. ■ a large heavy boat with one or more masts and carrying fore-and-aft or lug sails and sometimes equipped with guns.
– ORIGIN late 16th cent.: from French *chaloupe*, from Dutch *sloep* 'sloop.'

shal·lot /SHəˈlät, ˈSHalət/ ▶ **n. 1** a small bulb that resembles an onion and is used for pickling or as a substitute for onion. **2** the plant that produces these bulbs, each mature bulb producing a cluster of smaller bulbs. ● *Allium ascalonicum*, family Liliaceae (or Alliaceae).
– ORIGIN mid 17th cent.: shortening of *eschalot*, from French *eschalotte*, alteration of Old French *eschaloigne* (in Anglo-Norman French *scaloun*: see SCALLION).

shal·low /ˈSHalō/ ▶ **adj.** of little depth: *serve the noodles in a shallow bowl | being fairly shallow, the water was warm.* ■ situated at no great depth: *the shallow bed of the North Sea.* ■ varying only slightly from a specified or understood line or direction, esp. the horizontal: *a shallow roof.* ■ not exhibiting, requiring, or capable of serious thought: *a shallow analysis of contemporary society.* ■ (of breathing) taking in little air.
▶ **n.** (**shallows**) an area of the sea, a lake, or a river where the water is not very deep.
▶ **v.** [no obj.] (of the sea, a lake, or a river) become less deep over time or in a particular place: *the boat ground to a halt where the water shallowed.*
– DERIVATIVES **shal·low·ly adv.**, **shal·low·ness n.**
– ORIGIN late Middle English: obscurely related to SHOAL[2].

Shal·ma·ne·ser III /ˌSHalməˈnēzər/ (died 824 BC), king of Assyria 859–824. Most of his reign was devoted to the expansion of his kingdom and the conquest of neighboring lands. According to Assyrian records, he defeated an alliance of Syrian kings and the king of Israel in a battle at Qarqar on the Orontes in 853 BC.
– ORIGIN from *Salmanasar*, the Latin form of the name in the Vulgate (2 Kings 17–19).

sha·lom /SHäˈlōm, SHə-/ ▶ **exclam.** used as salutation by Jews at meeting or parting, meaning "peace." Compare with SALAAM.
– ORIGIN from Hebrew *šālōm*.

shalt /SHalt/ archaic second person singular of SHALL.

shal·war /ˈSHəlˌwär/ ▶ **n.** variant spelling of SALWAR.

sham /SHam/ ▶ **n. 1** a thing that is not what it is purported to be: *the proposed legislation is a farce and a sham.* ■ pretense: *it all turned out to be sham and hypocrisy.* ■ a person who pretends to be someone or something they are not: *he was a sham, totally unqualified for his job as a senior doctor.* **2** short for PILLOW SHAM.
▶ **adj.** bogus; false: *a clergyman who arranged a sham marriage.*
▶ **v.** (**shams, shamming, shammed**) [no obj.] falsely present something as the truth: *was he ill or was he shamming?* ■ [with obj.] pretend to be or to be experiencing: *she shams indifference.*
– DERIVATIVES **sham·mer n.**
– ORIGIN late 17th cent.: perhaps a northern English dialect variant of the noun SHAME.

sha·mal /SHəˈmäl/ ▶ **n.** a hot, dry northwesterly wind blowing across the Persian Gulf in summer, typically causing sandstorms.
– ORIGIN late 17th cent.: from Arabic *šamāl* 'north (wind).'

sha·man /ˈSHämən, ˈSHā-/ ▶ **n.** (pl. **shamans**) a person regarded as having access to, and influence in, the world of good and evil spirits, esp. among some peoples of northern Asia and North America. Typically such people enter a trance state during a ritual, and practice divination and healing.
– DERIVATIVES **sha·man·ic** /SHəˈmanik/ **adj.**, **sha·man·ism** /-ˌnizəm/ **n.**, **sha·man·ist** /-nist/ **n.** & **adj.**, **sha·man·is·tic** /ˌSHäməˈnistik, ˌSHā-/ **adj.**, **sha·man·ize** /-ˌnīz/ **v.**
– ORIGIN late 17th cent.: from German *Schamane* and Russian *shaman*, from Tungus *šaman*.

sha·ma·teur /ˈSHamətər, -ˌtər, -ˌCHŏŏr, -CHər/ ▶ **n.** derogatory a sports player who makes money from sports though classified as amateur.
– DERIVATIVES **sha·ma·teur·ism** /-ˌrizəm/ **n.**
– ORIGIN late 19th cent.: blend of SHAM and AMATEUR.

sham·ba /ˈSHambə/ ▶ **n.** (in East Africa) a cultivated plot of ground; a farm or plantation.
– ORIGIN Kiswahili.

sham·ble /ˈSHambəl/ ▶ **v.** [no obj.] (of a person) move with a slow, shuffling, awkward gait: *he shambled off down the corridor.*
▶ **n.** [in sing.] a slow, shuffling, awkward gait.
– ORIGIN late 16th cent.: probably from dialect *shamble* 'ungainly,' perhaps from the phrase *shamble legs*, with reference to the legs of trestle tables (such as would be used in a meat market: see SHAMBLES).

sham·bles /ˈSHambəlz/ ▶ **plural n.** [treated as sing.] **1** informal a state of total disorder: *my career was in a shambles.* **2** a butcher's slaughterhouse (archaic except in place names). ■ a scene of carnage: *the room was a shambles—their throats had been cut and they lay in a waste of blood.*
– ORIGIN late Middle English (in the sense 'meat market'): plural of earlier *shamble* 'stool, stall,' from Latin *scamellum*, diminutive of *scamnum* 'bench.'

sham·bling /ˈSHamb(ə)liNG/ ▶ **adj.** moving with a slow, shuffling, awkward gait: *a big, shambling, shy man.*

sham·bly /ˈSHamblē/ ▶ **adj.** informal (of a building) ramshackle; rickety. ■ (of a person) awkward; ungainly.

sham·bo·lic /SHamˈbälik/ ▶ **adj.** informal, chiefly Brit. chaotic, disorganized, or mismanaged: *the department's shambolic accounting.*
– ORIGIN 1970s: from SHAMBLES, probably on the pattern of *symbolic*.

shame /SHām/ ▶ **n.** a painful feeling of humiliation or distress caused by the consciousness of wrong or foolish behavior: *she was hot with shame | he felt a pang of shame at telling Alice a lie.* ■ a loss of respect or esteem; dishonor: *the incident had brought shame on his family.* ■ used to reprove someone for something of which they should be ashamed: ***shame on you for hitting a woman | for shame, brother!*** ■ [in sing.] a regrettable or unfortunate situation or action: *it is a shame that they are not better known.* ■ a person, action, or situation that brings a loss of respect or honor: *ignorance of Latin would be a disgrace and a shame to any public man.*
▶ **v.** [with obj.] (of a person, action, or situation) make (someone) feel ashamed: *I tried to shame him into giving some away.* ■ bring shame to: *the entire debacle has shamed our community.* ■ cause (someone) to feel ashamed or inadequate by outdoing or surpassing them: *she shames me with her eighty-year-old energy.*
– PHRASES **put someone to shame** disgrace or embarrass someone by outdoing or surpassing them: *she puts me to shame, she's so capable.*
– ORIGIN Old English *sc(e)amu* (noun), *sc(e)amian* 'feel shame,' of Germanic origin; related to Dutch *schamen* (verb) and German *Scham* (noun), *schämen* (verb).

shame cul·ture ▶ **n.** Anthropology a culture in which conformity of behavior is maintained through the individual's fear of being shamed.

shame·faced /ˈSHāmˌfāst/ ▶ **adj.** feeling or expressing shame or embarrassment: *all the boys looked shamefaced.*
– DERIVATIVES **shame·fac·ed·ly** /-ˌfāsidlē, -ˌfāstlē/ **adv.**, **shame·fac·ed·ness** /-ˌfāsidnis/ **n.**
– ORIGIN mid 16th cent. (in the sense 'modest, shy'): alteration of archaic *shamefast*, by association with FACE.

shame·ful /ˈSHāmfəl/ ▶ **adj.** worthy of or causing shame or disgrace: *a shameful accusation.*
– DERIVATIVES **shame·ful·ly adv.** [as submodifier] *record companies are shamefully slow in fulfilling orders*, **shame·ful·ness n.**
– ORIGIN Old English *sc(e)amful* 'modest, shamefaced' (see SHAME, -FUL).

shame·less /ˈSHāmlis/ ▶ **adj.** (of a person or their conduct) characterized by or showing a lack of shame: *his shameless hypocrisy.*
– DERIVATIVES **shame·less·ly adv.**, **shame·less·ness n.**
– ORIGIN Old English *sc(e)amlēas* (see SHAME, -LESS).

Sha·mir /SHəˈmi(ə)r/, Yitzhak (1915–), Israeli statesman, born in Poland; prime minister 1983–84 and 1986–92; Polish name *Yitzhak Jazernicki*. Under his leadership, Israel did not retaliate when attacked by Iraqi missiles during the Gulf War and possibly averted an escalation of the conflict.

sha·mi·sen /ˈSHamiˌsen/ ▶ **n.** variant spelling of SAMISEN.

sham·mes /ˈSHäməs/ ▶ **n. 1** a sexton in a synagogue. **2** the candle that is used to light the others in a menorah for Hanukkah.

sham·my /ˈSHamē/ (also **shammy leather**) ▶ **n.** (pl. **shammies**) informal term for CHAMOIS (sense 2).
– ORIGIN early 18th cent.: a phonetic spelling.

sham·poo /SHamˈpo͞o/ ▶ **n.** a liquid preparation containing detergent or soap for washing the hair: *he smelt clean, of soap and shampoo | an anti-dandruff shampoo.* ■ a similar substance for cleaning a carpet, soft furnishings, or a car. ■ an act of washing or cleaning something, esp. the hair, with shampoo: *a shampoo and set.*
▶ **v.** (**shampoos, shampooing, shampooed** /-ˈpo͞od/) [with obj.] wash or clean (something, esp. the hair) with shampoo: *Dolly was sitting in the bath shampooing her hair.* ■ (**shampoo something in/out**) wash something in or out of the hair using shampoo: *apply oil to wet hair, otherwise it will be difficult to shampoo it out.*
– ORIGIN mid 18th cent. (in the sense 'massage (as part of a Turkish bath process)'): from Hindi *cāmpo!* 'press!,' imperative of *cāmpnā*.

sham·rock /ˈSHamˌräk/ ▶ **n.** a low-growing, cloverlike plant with three-lobed leaves, used as the national emblem of Ireland. ● The shamrock of legend has been identified with a number of different plants in the family Leguminosae, in particular the lesser yellow trefoil (*Trifolium minus*). ■ a spray or leaf of this plant.
– ORIGIN late 16th cent.: from Irish *seamróg* 'trefoil' (diminutive of *seamar* 'clover').

sha·mus /ˈSHāməs/ ▶ **n.** informal a private detective.
– ORIGIN 1920s: of unknown origin.

Shan /SHan/ ▶ **n.** (pl. **same** or **Shans**) **1** a member of a people living mainly in northern Burma (Myanmar) and adjacent parts of southern China. **2** the Tai language of this people.
▶ **adj.** of or relating to this people or their language.
– ORIGIN Burmese.

Shan·dong /ˈSHänˈdôNG/ (also **Shantung** /-ˈto͝oNG/) a coastal province in eastern China; capital, Jinan. It occupies the Shandong Peninsula that separates southern Bo Hai from the Yellow Sea.

shan·dy /ˈSHandē/ ▶ **n.** (pl. **shandies**) beer mixed with a nonalcoholic drink (typically lemonade).
– ORIGIN late 19th cent.: abbreviation of *shandygaff*, in the same sense, of unknown origin.

Shang /SHANG/ a dynasty that ruled China during part of the 2nd millennium BC, probably the 16th–11th centuries. The period encompassed the invention of Chinese ideographic script and the discovery and development of bronze casting.

Shang·hai /ˈSHANGˈhī/ a city on the eastern coast of China, a port on the estuary of the Yangtze River; pop. 11,283,700 (est. 2006). Until World War II, Shanghai contained areas of British, French, and American settlement. It was the site in 1921 of the founding of the Chinese Communist Party.

shang·hai /ˈSHANGˌhī/ ▶ **v.** (**shanghais, shanghaiing** /-ˌhī-iNG/, **shanghaied** /-ˌhīd/) [with obj.] historical force (someone) to join a ship lacking a full crew by drugging them or using other underhanded means. ■ informal coerce or trick (someone) into a place or position or into doing something: *Brady shanghaied her into his Jaguar and roared off.*
– ORIGIN late 19th cent.: from SHANGHAI.

Shan·go /ˈSHänggō/ ▶ **n.** a religious cult originating in western Nigeria and now practiced chiefly in

parts of the Caribbean. ■ (also **Shangor**) an African god of thunder significant to this cult. ■ a dance associated with this cult.
– ORIGIN 1950s: from Yoruba.

Shan·gri-La /ˌSHANGgri ˈlä/ a Tibetan utopia in **James Hilton's** novel *Lost Horizon* (1933). ■ (as noun **a Shangri-La**) a place regarded as an earthly paradise, esp. when involving a retreat from the pressures of modern civilization.
– ORIGIN from *Shangri* (an invented name) + Tibetan *la* 'mountain pass.'

shank /SHANGK/ ▶ **n. 1** (often **shanks**) a person's leg, esp. the part from the knee to the ankle: *the old man's thin, bony shanks showed through his trousers.* ■ the lower part of an animal's foreleg. ■ this part of an animal's leg as a cut of meat.
2 the shaft or stem of a tool or implement, in particular: ■ a long narrow part of a tool connecting the handle to the operational end. ■ the cylindrical part of a bit by which it is held in a drill. ■ the long stem of a key, spoon, anchor, etc. ■ the straight part of a nail or fishhook.
3 a part or appendage by which something is attached to something else, esp. a wire loop attached to the back of a button. ■ the band of a ring rather than the setting or gemstone.
4 the narrow middle of the sole of a shoe.
▶ **v.** [with obj.] Golf strike (the ball) with the heel of the club: *I shanked a shot and hit a person on a shoulder.*
– DERIVATIVES **shanked adj.** [usu. in combination] *a long-shanked hook.*
– ORIGIN Old English *sceanca*; related to Dutch *schenk* 'leg bone' and High German *Schenkel* 'thigh.' The use of the verb as a golfing term dates from the 1920s.

Shan·kar /ˈSHANGˌkär/, Ravi (1920–), Indian sitar player and composer. From the mid 1950s, he toured Europe and the US giving sitar recitals and doing much to stimulate Western interest in Indian music.

shank·ing /ˈSHANGkiNG/ ▶ **n. 1** Golf the action of striking the ball with the heel of the club.
2 any of a number of plant diseases resulting in the darkening and shriveling of a plant or fruit from the base of a stem or stalk.

shanks' mare (also **shanks' pony**) ▶ **n.** used to refer to one's own legs and the action of walking as a means of conveyance.
– ORIGIN late 18th cent.: first recorded as *shanks-nag* in R. Fergusson's *Poems* (1785).

Shan·non[1] /ˈSHanən/ the longest river in Ireland. It rises in County Leitrim near Lough Allen and flows 240 miles (390 km) south and then west to its estuary on the Atlantic Ocean. ■ an international airport in the Republic of Ireland, situated on the Shannon River west of Limerick.

Shan·non[2], Claude Elwood (1916–2001), US engineer. The pioneer of mathematical communication theory, he also investigated digital circuits and was the first to use the term *bit* to denote a unit of information.

Shan·non's the·o·rem (also **Shannon's information theorem**) a theorem defining the maximum capacity of a communication channel to carry information with no more than an arbitrary error rate, given the bandwidth and signal-to-noise ratio.
– ORIGIN mid 20th cent.: named after C. E. Shannon (see **SHANNON**[2]).

shan·ny /ˈSHanē/ ▶ **n.** (pl. **shannies**) a small, greenish-brown European blenny (fish) of the shoreline and intertidal waters. ● *Blennius pholis*, family Blennidae.
– ORIGIN mid 19th cent.: of unknown origin; compare with earlier *shan*, in the same sense.

shan't /SHant/ ▶ **contraction** chiefly Brit. shall not: *we shan't be gone long.*

shan·ti /ˈSHäntē/ ▶ **n.** Indian peace: [as exclamation] *"Shanti! Shanti! you must not let anger possess you like that."*
– ORIGIN from Sanskrit *śānti* 'peace, tranquility.'

Shan·tou /ˈSHänˈtō/ a port in the province of Guangdong in southeastern China, situated on the South China Sea at the mouth of the Han River; pop. 4,840,500 (est. 2006). It was one of the ports opened up to foreign trade in 1869. Former name **SWATOW**.

shan·tung /SHanˈtəNG/ ▶ **n.** a dress fabric spun from tussore silk with random irregularities in the surface texture.
– ORIGIN late 19th cent.: from **SHANTUNG** (see **SHANDONG**), where it was originally made.

shan·ty[1] /ˈSHantē/ ▶ **n.** (pl. **shanties**) a small, crudely built shack.
– ORIGIN early 19th cent. (originally a North American usage): perhaps from Canadian French *chantier* 'lumberjack's cabin, logging camp.'

shan·ty[2] ▶ **n.** (pl. **shanties**) variant spelling of **CHANTEY**.

shan·ty·man /ˈSHantēˌman/ ▶ **n.** (pl. **shantymen**) a lumberjack.

shan·ty·town /ˈSHantēˌtoun/ ▶ **n.** a deprived area on the outskirts of a town consisting of large numbers of crude dwellings.

Shan·xi /ˈSHänˈSHē/ (also **Shansi** /-ˈsē/) a province in north central China, south of Inner Mongolia; capital, Taiyuan.

SHAPE /SHāp/ ▶ **abbr.** Supreme Headquarters Allied Powers Europe.

shape /SHāp/ ▶ **n. 1** the external form or appearance characteristic of someone or something; the outline of an area or figure: *she liked the shape of his nose* | *houseplants come in all shapes and sizes* | *chest freezers are square or rectangular in shape.* ■ a person or thing that is difficult to see and identify clearly: *he saw a shape through the mist.* ■ a specific form or guise assumed by someone or something: *a fiend in human shape.* ■ a piece of material, paper, etc., made or cut in a particular form: *stick paper shapes on for the puppet's eyes and nose.*
2 [with adj.] the particular condition or state of someone or something: *he was in no shape to drive* | *the building was in poor shape.* ■ the distinctive nature or qualities of something: *the future shape and direction of the country.* ■ definite or orderly arrangement: *check that your structure will give* ***shape to*** *your essay.*
▶ **v.** [with obj.] give a particular shape or form to: *most caves are shaped by the flow of water through limestone* | *shape the dough into two-inch balls.* ■ make (something) fit the form of something else: [with obj. and infinitive] *suits have been shaped to fit so snugly that no curve is undefined.* ■ determine the nature of; have a great influence on: *his childhood was shaped by a loving relationship with his elder brother.* ■ [no obj.] develop in a particular way; progress: *the yacht was shaping well in trials.* ■ form or produce (a sound or words).
– PHRASES **get into shape** (or **get someone into shape**) become (or make someone) physically fitter by exercise: *if you're thinking of getting into shape, take it easy and build up slowly.* **in any (way) shape or form** in any manner or under any circumstances (used for emphasis): *96 percent of the electorate voted against Europeanization in any shape or form.* **in (good) shape** in good physical condition. **in the shape of** represented or embodied by: *retribution arrived in the shape of my irate father.* **whip** (or **knock** or **lick**) **someone/something into shape** act forcefully to bring someone or something into a fitter, more efficient, or better organized state: *a man who whips a chamber orchestra into shape.* **out of shape 1** (of an object) not having its usual or original shape, esp. after being bent or knocked: *check that the pipe end and compression nut are not bent out of shape.* **2** (of a person) in poor physical condition; unfit. **the shape of things to come** the way the future is likely to develop. [the title of a novel by H. G. Wells (1933).] **shape up or ship out** informal used as an ultimatum to someone to improve their performance or behavior or face being made to leave. **take shape** assume a distinct form; develop into something definite or tangible: *the past few months have seen the state's health insurance legislation begin to take shape.*
– PHRASAL VERBS **shape up** develop or happen in a particular way: *it was shaping up to be another bleak year.* ■ informal improve performance or behavior: *we have never been afraid to tell our children to shape up.* ■ become physically fit: *I need to shape up.*
– DERIVATIVES **shap·a·ble** (also **shapeable**) **adj.**, **shaped adj.** [usu. in combination] *egg-shaped* | *X-shaped,* **shap·er n.**
– ORIGIN Old English *gesceap* 'external form,' also 'creation,' *sceppan* 'create,' of Germanic origin.

shaped charge ▶ **n.** an explosive charge with a cavity that focuses the blast into a small area.

shape·less /ˈSHāplis/ ▶ **adj.** (esp. of a garment) lacking a distinctive or attractive shape: *women in shapeless cotton dresses.*
– DERIVATIVES **shape·less·ly adv.**, **shape·less·ness n.**

shape·ly /ˈSHāplē/ ▶ **adj.** (**shapelier**, **shapeliest**) (esp. of a woman or part of her body) having an attractive or well-proportioned shape: *however much she ate made no difference to her shapely figure.*
– DERIVATIVES **shape·li·ness n.**

shape mem·o·ry ▶ **n.** Metallurgy a property exhibited by certain alloys of recovering their initial shape when they are heated after having been plastically deformed.

shape·shift·er /ˈSHāpˌSHiftər/ ▶ **n.** (chiefly in fiction) a person or being with the ability to change their physical form at will.
– DERIVATIVES **shape·shift·ing** /-ˌSHiftiNG/ **n. & adj.**

shape·wear /ˈSHāpˌwe(ə)r/ ▶ **n.** women's tight-fitting underwear intended to control and shape the figure.

Sha·pir·o /SHəˈpi(ə)rō/, Karl (Jay) (1913–2000), US poet. His poems, such as "Elegy for a Dead Soldier" (1944), were collected in volumes such as *V-Letter and Other Poems* (1944), *Adult Book Store* (1976), and *New and Selected Poems 1940–1986* (1987).

shap·ka /ˈSHäpkə/ ▶ **n.** a brimless Russian hat of fur or sheepskin.
– ORIGIN 1940s: Russian, literally 'hat.'

Shap·ley /ˈSHaplē/, Harlow (1885–1972), US astronomer. He carried out an extensive survey of galaxies and used his studies on the distribution of globular star clusters to locate the likely center of the galaxy and to infer its structure and dimensions. He found that the solar system is located on the galaxy's edge and not at its center.

sha·ra·ra /SHəˈrärə/ ▶ **n.** a pair of loose, pleated trousers worn by women from South Asia, typically with a kameez and dupatta.
– ORIGIN from Urdu.

shard /SHärd/ ▶ **n.** a piece of broken ceramic, metal, glass, or rock, typically having sharp edges: *shards of glass flew in all directions.*
– ORIGIN Old English *sceard* 'gap, notch, potsherd,' of Germanic origin: related to Dutch *schaarde* 'notch,' also to **SHEAR**.

share[1] /SHe(ə)r/ ▶ **n.** a part or portion of a larger amount that is divided among a number of people, or to which a number of people contribute: *under the proposals, investors would pay a greater share of the annual fees required* | *we gave them all the chance to have a share in the profits.* ■ one of the equal parts into which a company's capital is divided, entitling the holder to a proportion of the profits: *they bought 33 shares of American Standard.* ■ part proprietorship of property held by joint owners: *Jake had a share in a large seagoing vessel.* ■ [in sing.] the allotted or due amount of something that a person expects to have or to do, or that is expected to be accepted or done by them: *she's done more than her* ***fair share of*** *globe-trotting.*
▶ **v.** [with obj.] have a portion of (something) with another or others: *he* ***shared*** *the pie* ***with*** *her* | *all members of the band equally share the band's profits.* ■ give a portion of (something) to another or others: *money raised will be shared between the two charities.* ■ use, occupy, or enjoy (something) jointly with another or others: *they once shared a house in the Hamptons* | [no obj.] *there weren't enough plates, so we had to share* | (as adj. **shared**) *a shared bottle of wine.* ■ possess (a view or quality) in common with others: *other countries don't share our reluctance to eat goat meat.* ■ [no obj.] (**share in**) (of a number of people or organizations) have a part in (something, esp. an activity): *the companies would share in the development of three oil platforms.* ■ tell someone about (something), esp. something personal: *she had never* ***shared*** *the secret* ***with*** *anyone before.*
– PHRASES **share and share alike** having or receiving an equal share: *their representatives shared the inheritance share and share alike.* **share a moment** see **MOMENT**.
– DERIVATIVES **share·a·ble** (also **sharable**) **adj.**, **shar·er n.**
– ORIGIN Old English *scearu* 'division, part into which something may be divided,' of Germanic origin; related to Dutch *schare* and German *Schar* 'troop, multitude,' also to **SHEAR**. The verb dates from the late 16th cent.

share[2] ▶ **n.** short for **PLOWSHARE**.

share·crop·per /ˈSHe(ə)rˌkräpər/ ▶ **n.** a tenant farmer who gives a part of each crop as rent.
– DERIVATIVES **share·crop v.** (**sharecrops**, **sharecropping**, **sharecropped**).

share·hold·er /ˈSHe(ə)rˌhōldər/ ▶ **n.** an owner of shares in a company.
– DERIVATIVES **share·hold·ing** /-ˌhōldiNG/ **n.**

share op·tion ▶ **n.** British term for **STOCK OPTION**.

share·ware /ˈSHe(ə)rˌwe(ə)r/ ▶ **n.** Computing software that is available free of charge and often distributed informally for evaluation, after which a fee may be requested for continued use.

sha·ri·a /SHäˈrēə/ (also **shariah** or **shariat** /-ät/) ▶ **n.** Islamic canonical law based on the teachings of the Koran and the traditions of the Prophet (Hadith and Sunna), prescribing both religious and secular duties and sometimes retributive penalties for lawbreaking. It has generally been supplemented by legislation adapted to the conditions of the day, though the manner in which it should be applied in modern states is a subject of dispute between Islamic fundamentalists and modernists.

S

–ORIGIN from Arabic *šarī'a*; the variant *shariat* from Urdu and Persian.

sha·rif /SHə'rēf/ (also **shereef** or **sherif**) ▶ **n. 1** a descendant of Muhammad through his daughter Fatima, entitled to wear a green turban or veil. **2** a Muslim ruler, magistrate, or religious leader.

–DERIVATIVES **sha·rif·i·an adj.**

–ORIGIN from Arabic *šarīf* 'noble,' from *šarafa* 'be exalted.'

Shar·jah /'SHärZHə, -jə/ one of the seven member states of the United Arab Emirates; pop. 934,400 (est. 2009). Arabic name **Ash Shariqah**. ■ its capital city, on the Persian Gulf; pop. 845,600 (est. 2009).

shark[1] /SHärk/ ▶ **n. 1** a long-bodied chiefly marine fish with a cartilaginous skeleton, a prominent dorsal fin, and toothlike scales. Most sharks are predatory, although the largest kinds feed on plankton. ● Several orders (or superorders) of the subclass Elasmobranchii: many families. **2** a small Southeast Asian freshwater fish with a sharklike tail, popular in aquariums. ● Two species in the family Cyprinidae: the small **red-tailed black shark** (*Labeo bicolor*), and the larger **black shark** (*Morulius chrysophekadion*). **3** a light grayish-brown European moth, the male of which has pale silvery hind wings. ● Genus *Cucullia*, family Noctuidae: several species, including *C. umbratica*.

–ORIGIN late Middle English: of unknown origin.

shark[2] ▶ **n.** informal **1** a person who unscrupulously exploits or swindles others: *Coleby was a shark, not the sort of man to pay more when he could pay less* | *property sharks want to develop 200 acres around the site*. See also **loan shark**. **2** an expert in a specified field: *a pool shark*.

–ORIGIN late 16th cent.: perhaps from German *Schurke* 'worthless rogue,' influenced by **shark**[1].

shark·skin /'SHärk,skin/ ▶ **n.** the rough scaly skin of a shark, sometimes used as shagreen. ■ a stiff, slightly lustrous synthetic fabric.

shark·suck·er ▶ **n.** a remora, esp. *Echeneis naucrates*, the most abundant remora of warm waters.

sharksucker

Shar·on[1] /'SHarən, 'SHe(ə)r-/ a fertile coastal plain in Israel that lies between the Mediterranean Sea and the hills of Samaria.

Shar·on[2] /SHə'rōn/, Ariel (1928–), Israeli general and Likud statesman, prime minister 2001–06.

shar·on fruit /'SHarən, 'SHe(ə)r-/ ▶ **n.** a persimmon, esp. one of an early fruiting orange variety grown in Israel.

–ORIGIN from **Sharon**[1].

sharp /SHärp/ ▶ **adj. 1** (of an object) having an edge or point that is able to cut or pierce something: *cut the cake with a very sharp knife* | *keep tools sharp*. ■ producing a sudden, piercing physical sensation or effect: *I suddenly felt a sharp pain in my back*. ■ (of a food, taste, or smell) acidic and intense: *sharp goats' milk cheese*. ■ (of a sound) sudden and penetrating: *there was a sharp crack of thunder*. ■ (of words or a speaker) intended or intending to criticize or hurt: *she feared his sharp tongue*. ■ (of an emotion or experience) felt acutely or intensely; painful: *her sharp disappointment was tinged with embarrassment*. **2** tapering to a point or edge: *a sharp pencil* | *her face was thin and her nose sharp*. ■ distinct in outline or detail; clearly defined: *the job was a sharp contrast from her past life* | *the scene was as sharp and clear in his mind as a film*. ■ informal (of clothes or their wearer) neat and stylish: *they were greeted by a young man in a sharp suit*. **3** (of an action or change) sudden and marked: *there was a sharp increase in interest rates* | *he heard her sharp intake of breath*. ■ (of a bend, angle, or turn) making a sudden change of direction: *a sharp turn in the river*. ■ having or showing speed of perception, comprehension, or response: *her sharp eyes missed nothing* | *his old mind was not so sharp as it once was* | *he had a sharp sense of humor*. ■ quick to take advantage, esp. in an unscrupulous or dishonest way: *Paul's a sharp operator*. **4** (of musical sound) above true or normal pitch. ■ [postpositive, in combination] (of a note) a semitone higher than a specified note: *the song sits on E and F-sharp* | *the quartet in C-sharp minor*. ■ (of a key) having a sharp or sharps in the key signature: *recorder players are most comfortable in sharp keys*.

▶ **adv. 1** precisely (used after an expression of time): *the meeting starts at 7:30 sharp*. **2** in a sudden or abrupt way: *the creek bent sharp left* | *he was brought up sharp by Helen's voice*. **3** above the true or normal pitch of musical sound: *he heard him playing a little sharp on the high notes*.

▶ **n. 1** a musical note raised a semitone above natural pitch. ■ the sign (♯) indicating this. **2** a long, sharply pointed needle used for general sewing. ■ (usu. **sharps**) a thing with a sharp edge or point, such as a hypodermic needle, a blade, or a fragment of glass: *the safe disposal of sharps and clinical waste*. **3** informal a swindler or cheat. See also **card sharp**.

▶ **v.** [with obj.] **1** (usu. as adj. **sharped**) Music raise the pitch of (a note). **2** archaic cheat or swindle (someone), esp. at cards: *the fellow is drunk, let's sharp him*. [late 17th cent.: from **sharper**; compare with **shark**[2].]

–PHRASES **sharp as a tack** extremely clever or astute.

–DERIVATIVES **sharp·ly adv.**

–ORIGIN Old English *sc(e)arp*, of Germanic origin; related to Dutch *scherp* and German *scharf*.

Shar-Pei /'SHär 'pā/ (also **shar-pei**) ▶ **n.** (pl. **Shar-Peis**) a compact, squarely built dog of a breed of Chinese origin, with a characteristic wrinkly skin and short bristly coat of a beige, cream, black, or red color.

–ORIGIN 1970s: from Chinese *shā pí*, literally 'sand skin.'

Shar-Pei

sharp·en /'SHärpən/ ▶ **v.** make or become sharp: [with obj.] *she sharpened her pencil* | [no obj.] *her tone sharpened to exasperation*. ■ improve or cause to improve: [no obj.] *they must **sharpen up** or risk losing half their business* | [with obj.] *students will **sharpen up** their reading skills*.

–DERIVATIVES **shar·pen·er n.**

sharp·er /'SHärpər/ ▶ **n.** informal a swindler, esp. at cards.

Sharpe ra·ti·o /SHärp/ ▶ **n.** Finance a measure that indicates the average return minus the risk-free return divided by the standard deviation of return on an investment.

Sharpe·ville mas·sa·cre /'SHärpvəl, -,vil/ the killing of sixty-seven antiapartheid demonstrators by security forces at Sharpeville, a black township south of Johannesburg, on March 21, 1960. Following the massacre, the South African government banned the African National Congress and the Pan-Africanist Congress.

sharp-eyed ▶ **adj.** quick to notice things; observant: *sharp-eyed readers may have already spotted this*.

sharp-fea·tured ▶ **adj.** (of a person) having well-defined facial features.

sharp·ie /'SHärpē/ ▶ **n.** (pl. **sharpies**) **1** a sharp-prowed, flat-bottomed New England sailboat, with one or two masts each rigged with a triangular sail. **2** informal a dishonest and cunning person, esp. a cheat.

sharp·ness /'SHärpnis/ ▶ **n.** the quality or state of being sharp: *the sweet flavor contrasts with the sharpness of the lemon* | *his health and mental sharpness declined*.

sharp prac·tice ▶ **n.** dated dishonest or barely honest dealings.

sharp-set ▶ **adj.** dated very hungry.

sharp·shoot·er /'SHärp,SHōōtər/ ▶ **n.** a person who is very skilled in shooting.

–DERIVATIVES **sharp·shoot·ing** /-,SHōōtiNG/ **n. & adj.**

sharp-tongued ▶ **adj.** (of a person) given to using cutting, harsh, or critical language.

sharp-wit·ted ▶ **adj.** (of a person) quick to notice and understand things.

–DERIVATIVES **sharp-wit·ted·ly adv.**, **sharp-wit·ted·ness n.**

shash·lik /'SHäSH,lik, SHäSH'lik/ ▶ **n.** (pl. **same** or **shashliks**) (in Asia and eastern Europe) a mutton kebab.

–ORIGIN from Russian *shashlyk*, based on Turkish *şiş* 'spit, skewer'; compare with **shish kebab**.

Shas·ta, Mount /'SHastə/ a peak in northern California, the highest point (14,162 feet; 4,317 m) in the Cascade Range within the state. Shasta Lake lies on its south.

Shas·ta dai·sy /'SHästə/ ▶ **n.** a tall, widely cultivated plant of the daisy family that bears large white daisylike flowers. ● *Chrysanthemum superbum* or its hybrids, family Compositae.

–ORIGIN mid 19th cent.: named after Mount *Shasta* in California.

shas·tra /'SHästrə/ (also **sastra**) ▶ **n.** (in Hinduism and some forms of Buddhism) a work of scripture.

–ORIGIN from Sanskrit *śāstra*.

shat /SHat/ past and past participle of **shit**.

Shatt al-A·rab /,SHat al 'arəb, SHät äl 'äräb/ a river in southwestern Asia that is formed by the confluence of the Tigris and Euphrates rivers and flows 120 miles (195 km) through southeastern Iraq to the Persian Gulf. Its lower course forms the border between Iraq and Iran.

–ORIGIN from Arabic, literally 'Arab shore.'

shat·ter /'SHatər/ ▶ **v.** break or cause to break suddenly and violently into pieces: [no obj.] *bullets riddled the bar top, glasses shattered, bottles exploded* | [with obj.] *the window was shattered by a stone*. ■ [with obj.] damage or destroy (something abstract): *the crisis will shatter their confidence*. ■ [with obj.] upset (someone) greatly: *everyone was shattered by the news*.

–DERIVATIVES **shat·ter·er n.**, **shat·ter·proof** /-,prōōf/ **adj.**

–ORIGIN Middle English (in the sense 'scatter, disperse'): perhaps imitative; compare with **scatter**.

shat·ter cone ▶ **n.** Geology a fluted conical structure produced in rock by intense mechanical shock, such as that associated with meteoritic impact.

shat·tered /'SHatərd/ ▶ **adj.** broken into many pieces: *a snaky line of shattered glass*. ■ (of something abstract) damaged or destroyed: *a pale illusion of their shattered dreams*. ■ Brit. informal exhausted: *I usually feel too shattered to do more than crawl into bed*.

shat·ter·ing /'SHatəriNG/ ▶ **adj.** very shocking or upsetting: *he found it a shattering experience*.

–DERIVATIVES **shat·ter·ing·ly adv.**

shau·ri /'SHourē/ ▶ **n.** (pl. **shauris** or **shauries**) (in East Africa) a debate, argument, or problematic issue.

–ORIGIN Kiswahili.

shave /SHāv/ ▶ **v. 1** [no obj.] cut the hair off one's face with a razor: *he washed, shaved, and had breakfast*. ■ [with obj.] cut the hair off (a part of the body) with a razor: *she shaved her legs*. ■ [with obj.] cut the hair off the face or another part of the body of (someone) with a razor: *his wife washed and shaved him*. ■ cut (hair) off with a razor: *professional male swimmers **shave off** their body hair*. **2** [with obj.] cut (a thin slice or slices) from the surface of something: *scrape a large, sharp knife across the surface, **shaving off** rolls of very fine chocolate*. ■ reduce by a small amount: *they shaved profit margins*. ■ remove (a small amount) from something: *she **shaved** 0.5 seconds **off** the record*. **3** [with obj.] pass or send something close to (something else), missing it narrowly: *Scott shaved the post in the 29th minute*.

▶ **n.** an act of shaving hair from the face or a part of the body: *he always needed a shave*.

–ORIGIN Old English *sc(e)afan* 'scrape away the surface of (something) by paring,' of Germanic origin; related to Dutch *schaven* and German *schaben*.

shave·ling /'SHāvliNG/ ▶ **n.** archaic, derogatory a man of the church with a tonsured head.

shav·en /'SHāvən/ ▶ **adj.** shaved: *a boy with a shaven head* | [in combination] *shaven-headed monks*.

shav·er /'SHāvər/ ▶ **n. 1** an electric razor. **2** informal a young lad: *little shavers and their older brothers*.

shave·tail /'SHāv,tāl/ ▶ **n.** military slang, often derogatory a newly commissioned officer, esp. a second lieutenant. ■ informal an inexperienced person: [as modifier] *the shavetail Assistant District Attorney*.

–ORIGIN figuratively, from the early sense 'untrained pack animal' (identified by a shaved tail).

Sha·vi·an /'SHāvēən/ ▶ **adj.** of, relating to, or in the manner of G. B. Shaw, his writings, or ideas.

▶ **n.** an admirer of Shaw or his work.

–ORIGIN from *Shavius* (Latinized form of *Shaw*) + **-an**.

shav·ing /'SHāviNG/ ▶ **n. 1** a thin strip cut off a surface: *she brushed wood shavings from her knees*. **2** the action of shaving.

Sha·vu·oth /SHə'vōō,ōt, ,SHävōō'ōt, SHə'vōōəs/ (also **Shavuot**) ▶ **n.** a major Jewish festival held on the 6th (and usually the 7th) of Sivan, fifty days after the second day of Passover. It was originally a harvest festival, but now also commemorates

S

the giving of the Law (the Torah). Also called PENTECOST, FEAST OF WEEKS.
– ORIGIN from Hebrew *šāḇū'ōṯ* 'weeks,' with reference to the weeks between Passover and Pentecost.

Shaw[1] /SHô/, George Bernard (1856–1950), Irish playwright and writer. His best-known plays combine comedy with a questioning of conventional morality and thought; they include *Candida* (1897), *Man and Superman* (1903), *Major Barbara* (1905), *Pygmalion* (1913), and *St. Joan* (1923). Nobel Prize for Literature (1925).

Shaw[2], Irwin (1913–84), US writer. He wrote the novels *The Young Lions* (1948), *Rich Man, Poor Man* (1970), and *Acceptable Losses* (1982).

shaw /SHô/ ▶ **n.** archaic, chiefly Scottish a small group of trees; a thicket.
– ORIGIN Old English *sceaga*, of Germanic origin; related to SHAG[1].

sha·war·ma /SHə'wärmə/ ▶ **n.** roasted meat, esp. when cooked on a revolving spit and shaved for serving in sandwiches.

shawl /SHôl/ ▶ **n.** a piece of fabric worn by women over the shoulders or head or wrapped around a baby.
– DERIVATIVES **shawled adj.**
– ORIGIN from Urdu and Persian *šāl*, probably from *Shāliāt*, the name of a town in India.

shawl col·lar ▶ **n.** a rounded turned-down collar, without lapel notches, that extends down the front of a garment.

shawm /SHôm/ ▶ **n.** a medieval and Renaissance wind instrument, forerunner of the oboe, with a double reed enclosed in a wooden mouthpiece, and having a penetrating tone.
– ORIGIN Middle English: from Old French *chalemel*, via Latin from Greek *kalamos* 'reed.'

Shaw·nee[1] /SHô'nē/ a city in northeastern Kansas, southwest of Kansas City; pop. 60,954 (est. 2008).

Shaw·nee[2] ▶ **n.** (pl. **same** or **Shawnees**) **1** a member of an American Indian people living formerly in the eastern US and now chiefly in Oklahoma.
2 the Algonquian language of this people.
▶ **adj.** of or relating to the Shawnee or their language.
– ORIGIN Delaware *šā'wanōw* (singular), from the Shawnee self-designation *šā'wanōki* (plural), literally 'southern people.'

shay /SHā/ ▶ **n.** informal term for CHAISE (sense 1).
– ORIGIN early 18th cent.: back-formation from CHAISE, interpreted as plural.

shaykh /SHāk, SHīk/ ▶ **n.** variant spelling of SHEIKH.

sha·zam /SHə'zam/ ▶ **exclam.** used to introduce an extraordinary deed, story, or transformation: *She prayed for his arrival and shazam! There he was.*
– ORIGIN 1940s: an invented word, used by conjurors.

Shcher·ba·kov /'SHerbə,kôf, -,käf, ,SHCHi(ə)rbə'kôf/ former name (1946–57) of RYBINSK.

shchi /'SHCHē/ ▶ **n.** a type of Russian cabbage soup.
– ORIGIN Russian.

she /SHē/ ▶ **pron.** [third person singular] used to refer to a woman, girl, or female animal previously mentioned or easily identified: *my sister told me that she was not happy.* ■ used to refer to a ship, vehicle, country, or other inanimate thing regarded as female: *I was aboard the St. Roch shortly before she sailed for the Northwest Passage.* ■ used to refer to a person or animal of unspecified sex: *only include your child if you know she won't distract you.* ■ any female person: *she who rocks the cradle rules the world.*
▶ **n.** [in sing.] a female; a woman: *society would label him a slut if he were a she.* ■ [in combination] female: *a she-bear | a she-wolf.*
– ORIGIN Middle English: probably a phonetic development of the Old English feminine personal pronoun *hēo, hīe*.

> **USAGE 1** For a discussion of whether to say *I am older than* **she** or *I am older than* **her**, see usage at **PERSONAL PRONOUN** and **THAN**. **2** The use of the pronoun **he** to refer to a person of unspecified sex, once quite acceptable, has become problematic in recent years and is now usually regarded as old-fashioned or sexist. One of the responses to this has been to use **she** in the way that **he** has been used, as in *only include your child if you know* **she** *won't distract you*. In some types of writing, such as books on child care or child psychology, use of **she** has become quite common. In most contexts, however, it is likely to be distracting in the same way that **he** now is, and alternatives such as **he or she** or **they** are preferable. In some contexts where alternation would not distract, writers seeking 'balanced representation' vary the gender of the personal pronoun by using **she** or **her** in one paragraph, and **he** or **him** in the next, and so on. This method should be used with restraint, however, as it may confuse or annoy the reader. See also usage at **HE** and **THEY**.

s/he /'SHē ər 'hē, 'SHē'hē/ ▶ **pron.** a written representation of "he or she" used as a neutral alternative to indicate someone of either sex.

shea /SHē, SHā/ (also **shea tree**) ▶ **n.** a small tropical African tree that bears oily nuts from which shea butter is obtained. ● *Vitellaria paradoxa* (or *Butyrospermum parkii*), family Sapotaceae.
– ORIGIN late 18th cent.: from Mande *sye*.

shea but·ter ▶ **n.** a fatty substance obtained from the nuts of the shea tree, used chiefly in cosmetic skin preparations.

shead·ing /'SHēdiNG/ ▶ **n.** each of the six administrative divisions of the Isle of Man.
– ORIGIN late 16th cent.: variant of *shedding* (see SHED[2]).

sheaf /SHēf/ ▶ **n.** (pl. **sheaves** /SHēvz/) a bundle of grain stalks laid lengthwise and tied together after reaping. ■ a bundle of objects of one kind, esp. papers: *he waved a sheaf of papers in the air.*
▶ **v.** [with obj.] bundle into sheaves.
– ORIGIN Old English *scēaf*, of Germanic origin; related to Dutch *schoof* 'sheaf' and German *Schaub* 'wisp of straw,' also to the verb SHOVE.

sheal·ing /'SHēliNG/ ▶ **n.** variant spelling of SHIELING.

shear /SHi(ə)r/ ▶ **v.** (past participle **shorn** /SHôrn/ or **sheared**) **1** [with obj.] cut the wool off (a sheep or other animal). ■ cut off (something such as hair, wool, or grass), with scissors or shears: *I'll shear off all that fleece.* ■ (**be shorn of**) have something cut off: *they were shorn of their hair* | figurative *the richest man in the U.S. was shorn of nearly $2 billion.*
2 break off or cause to break off, owing to a structural strain: [no obj.] *the derailleur sheared and jammed in the rear wheel* | [with obj.] *the left wing had been almost completely sheared off.*
▶ **n.** a strain in the structure of a substance produced by pressure, when its layers are laterally shifted in relation to each other. See also WIND SHEAR.
– DERIVATIVES **shear·er n.**
– ORIGIN Old English *sceran* (originally in the sense 'cut through with a weapon'), of Germanic origin; related to Dutch and German *scheren*, from a base meaning 'divide, shear, shave.'

> **USAGE** The two verbs **shear** and **sheer** are sometimes confused: see usage at **SHEER[2]**.

Shear·er[1] /'SHi(ə)rər/, Moira (1926–2006), Scottish ballet dancer and actress; full name *Moira Shearer King*. A ballerina with Sadler's Wells from 1942, she is noted for her portrayal of a dedicated ballerina in the movie *The Red Shoes* (1948).

Shear·er[2], Norma (1902–83), US actress; born in Canada; full name Edith Norma Shearer. She made a successful transition from silent to talking movies, appearing in such movies as *A Lady of Chance* (1928), *The Divorcee* (1930), and *Her Cardboard Lover* (1942).

shear·ling /'SHi(ə)rliNG/ ▶ **n.** a sheep that has been shorn once: [as modifier] *a group of shearling rams.* ■ wool or fleece from such a sheep. ■ a coat made from or lined with such wool.

shears /SHi(ə)rz/ (also **a pair of shears**) ▶ **plural n.** a cutting instrument in which two blades move past each other, like scissors but typically larger: *garden shears.*
– ORIGIN Old English *scēara* (plural) 'scissors, cutting instrument,' of Germanic origin; related to Dutch *schaar* and German *Schere*, also to SHEAR.

shear·wa·ter /'SHi(ə)r,wôtər, -,wätər/ ▶ **n. 1** a long-winged seabird related to the petrels, often flying low over the surface of the water far from land. ● Family Procellariidae: three genera, in particular *Puffinus*, and many species.
2 North American term for SKIMMER (sense 2).

sheat·fish /'SHēt,fiSH/ ▶ **n.** (pl. **same** or **sheatfishes**)
– ORIGIN late 16th cent.: from an alteration of SHEATH + FISH[1].

sheath /SHēTH/ ▶ **n.** (pl. **sheaths** /SHēTHz, SHēTHs/) a close-fitting cover for something, esp. something that is elongated in shape, in particular: ■ a cover for the blade of a knife or sword. ■ a structure in living tissue that closely envelops another: *the fatty sheath around nerve fibers.* ■ (also **sheath dress**) a woman's close-fitting dress: *a tight sheath of black and gold lurex.* ■ a protective covering around an electric cable. ■ a condom.
– DERIVATIVES **sheath·less adj.**
– ORIGIN Old English *scǣth, scēath* 'scabbard,' of Germanic origin; related to Dutch *schede*, German *Scheide*, also to the verb SHED[2].

sheath·bill /'SHēTH,bil/ ▶ **n.** a mainly white pigeonlike bird with a horny sheath around the base of the bill, breeding on the coasts of sub-Antarctic islands and feeding by scavenging. ● Family Chionididae and genus *Chionis*: two species.

sheathe /SHēTH/ ▶ **v.** [with obj.] put (a weapon such as a knife or sword) into a sheath. ■ (often **be sheathed in**) encase (something) in a close-fitting or protective covering: *her legs were sheathed in black stockings.*
– ORIGIN late Middle English: from SHEATH.

sheath·ing /'SHēTHiNG/ ▶ **n.** protective casing or covering.

sheath knife ▶ **n.** a short knife similar to a dagger, carried in a sheath.

sheave /SHēv, SHiv/ ▶ **n.** a wheel with a groove for a rope to run on, as in a pulley block.
– ORIGIN Middle English: from a Germanic base meaning 'wheel, pulley.'

sheaves /SHēvz/ plural form of SHEAF.

She·ba /'SHēbə/ the biblical name of Saba in southwestern Arabia. The queen of Sheba visited King Solomon in Jerusalem (1 Kings 10).
– ORIGIN from Hebrew *šĕḇā'*.

she·bang /SHə'baNG/ ▶ **n. 1** [in sing.] informal a matter, operation, or set of circumstances: *the Mafia boss who's running the whole shebang.*
2 archaic a rough hut or shelter.
– ORIGIN mid 19th cent.: of unknown origin.

She·bat /SHə'bät/ ▶ **n.** variant spelling of SHEVAT.

she·been /SHə'bēn/ ▶ **n.** (esp. in Ireland, Scotland, and South Africa) an unlicensed establishment or private house selling alcoholic liquor and typically regarded as slightly disreputable.
– ORIGIN late 18th cent.: from Anglo-Irish *síbín*, from *séibe* 'mugful.'

She·boy·gan /SHi'boigən/ an industrial city in eastern Wisconsin, a port on Lake Michigan; pop. 47,895 (est. 2008).

shed[1] /SHed/ ▶ **n.** a simple roofed structure, typically made of wood or metal, used as a storage space, a shelter for animals, or a workshop. ■ a larger structure, typically with one or more sides open, for storing or maintaining vehicles or other machinery: *a shed is required for the three shunt engines.*
▶ **v.** (**sheds, shedding, shedded**) [with obj.] (usu. **be shedded**) park (a vehicle) in a depot.
– ORIGIN late 15th cent.: apparently a variant of the noun SHADE.

shed[2] ▶ **v.** (**sheds, shedding**; past and past participle **shed**) [with obj.] (of a tree or other plant) allow (leaves or fruit) to fall to the ground: *both varieties shed leaves in winter.* ■ (of a reptile, insect, etc.) allow (its skin or shell) to come off, to be replaced by another one that has grown underneath. ■ (of a mammal) lose (hair) as a result of molting, disease, or age. ■ take off (clothes). ■ discard (something undesirable, superfluous, or outdated): *what they lacked was a willingness to shed the arrogance of the past.* ■ have the property of preventing (something) from being absorbed: *this leather has a superior ability to shed water, sweat, and salt.* ■ eliminate part of (an electrical power load) by disconnecting circuits.
– PHRASES **shed (someone's) blood** be injured or killed (or kill or injure someone). **shed light on** see LIGHT[1]. **shed tears** weep; cry.
– ORIGIN Old English *sc(e)ādan* 'separate out (one selected group), divide,' also 'scatter,' of Germanic origin; related to Dutch and German *scheiden*. Compare with SHEATH.

she'd /SHēd/ ▶ **contraction** she had; she would.

shed·der /'SHedər/ ▶ **n.** a person or thing that sheds something. ■ a female salmon after spawning.

she-dev·il ▶ **n.** a malicious or spiteful woman.

shed·load /'SHed,lōd/ ▶ **n.** Brit. informal a large amount or number: *had she decided to join a rival, she would doubtless be earning a shedload of money.*
– ORIGIN 1990s: from *shed* + *load*; perhaps euphemistic after *shitload*.

Shee·la-na-gig /,SHēlə nə 'gēg/ ▶ **n.** a medieval stone figure of a naked female with the legs wide apart and the hands emphasizing the genitals, found in Britain and Ireland.
– ORIGIN from Irish *Síle na gcíoch* 'Julia of the breasts.'

sheen /SHēn/ ▶ **n.** [in sing.] a soft luster on a surface: *black crushed velvet with a slight sheen* | figurative *he seemed to shine with that unmistakable showbiz sheen.*
▶ **v.** literary shine or cause to shine softly: [with obj.] *men entered with rain sheening their steel helms* | [no obj.] *her black hair sheened in the sun.*
– ORIGIN early 17th cent.: from obsolete *sheen* 'beautiful, resplendent'; apparently related to the verb SHINE.

PRONUNCIATION KEY ə *ago, up*; ər *over, fur*; a *hat*; ā *ate*; ä *car*; e *let*; ē *see*; i *fit*; ī *by*; NG *sing*; ō *go*; ô *law, for*; oi *toy*; o͝o *good*; o͞o *goo*; ou *out*; TH *thin*; TH *then*; ZH *vision*

S

sheen·y[1] /ˈSHēnē/ ▶ **adj.** (**sheenier, sheeniest**) having a sheen; lustrous or shining: *a woman with sheeny hair.*

sheen·y[2] /ˈSHēnē/ ▶ **n.** (pl. **sheenies**) informal, offensive a contemptuous term for a Jewish person.
– ORIGIN early 19th cent.: origin unknown.

sheep /SHēp/ ▶ **n.** (pl. **same**) **1** a domesticated ruminant animal with a thick woolly coat and (typically only in the male) curving horns. It is kept in flocks for its wool or meat, and is proverbial for its tendency to follow others in the flock. ● *Ovis aries*, family Bovidae, descended from the wild mouflon. ■ a wild mammal related to this, such as the argali, bighorn, and urial.
2 a person who is too easily influenced or led: *the party members had become sheep, and she refused to be taken in.*
3 a person regarded as a protected follower of God. [with biblical allusion to Luke 15:6.] ■ informal a member of a minister's congregation.
– PHRASES **count sheep** count imaginary sheep jumping over a fence one by one in an attempt to put oneself to sleep. **make sheep's eyes at** look at (someone) in a foolishly amorous way.
– DERIVATIVES **sheep·like** /-ˌlīk/ **adj.**
– ORIGIN Old English *scēp, scǣp, scēap*; related to Dutch *schaap* and German *Schaf.*

sheep 1

sheep dip ▶ **n.** a liquid preparation for cleansing sheep of parasites or preserving their wool. ■ a place where sheep are dipped in such a preparation.

sheep·dog /ˈSHēpˌdôg, -ˌdäg/ ▶ **n.** a dog trained to guard and herd sheep. ■ a dog of a breed suitable for this.

sheep·dog tri·als ▶ **plural n.** a public competitive display of the skills of sheepdogs.

sheep·fold /ˈSHēpˌfōld/ ▶ **n.** a sheep pen.

sheep·ish /ˈSHēpiSH/ ▶ **adj.** (of a person or expression) showing embarrassment from shame or a lack of self-confidence: *a sheepish grin.*
– DERIVATIVES **sheep·ish·ly adv., sheep·ish·ness n.**

sheep lau·rel ▶ **n.** a North American kalmia that is sometimes cultivated as an ornamental. ● *Kalmia angustifolia*, family Ericaceae.

shee·ple ▶ **plural n.** informal , derogatory people compared to sheep in being docile, foolish, or easily led: *by the time the sheeple wake up and try to change things, it will be too late.*
– ORIGIN 1940s: blend of SHEEP and PEOPLE.

sheep·man /ˈSHēpmən/ ▶ **n.** (pl. **sheepmen**) a sheep rancher.

sheep run (also **sheep station**) ▶ **n.** (esp. in Australia) an extensive tract of land on which sheep are pastured.

S

sheep scab ▶ **n.** an intensely itching skin disease of sheep caused by a parasitic mite. ● The mite is *Psoroptes communis*, family Psoroptidae.

sheep·shank /ˈSHēpˌSHANGk/ ▶ **n.** a kind of knot used to shorten a rope temporarily.

sheeps·head /ˈSHēpsˌhed/ ▶ **n.** (pl. **same**) any of a number of boldly marked edible game fishes that live in warm American waters. ● a black and silver striped porgy of Atlantic coastal and brackish waters (*Archosargus probatocephalus*, family Sparidae). ● (**California sheepshead**) a black and red wrasse of Californian coastal waters (*Semicossyphus pulcher*, family Labridae).

sheep·skin /ˈSHēpˌskin/ ▶ **n.** a sheep's skin with the wool on, esp. when made into a garment or rug: [as modifier] *a sheepskin coat.* ■ leather from a sheep's skin used in bookbinding. ■ informal a diploma.

sheep sor·rel ▶ **n.** a sorrel that is common on acid soils in north temperate regions. ● *Rumex acetosella*, family Polygonaceae.

sheep tick ▶ **n.** a large tick that infests many mammals, including humans, and frequently transmits diseases. ● *Ixodes ricinus*, family Ixodidae.

sheep walk ▶ **n.** Brit. a tract of land on which sheep are pastured.

sheer[1] /SHi(ə)r/ ▶ **adj. 1** [attrib.] nothing other than; unmitigated (used for emphasis): *she giggled with sheer delight | marriage is sheer hard work.*
2 (esp. of a cliff or wall) perpendicular or nearly so: *the sheer ice walls.*
3 (of a fabric) very thin; diaphanous: *sheer white silk chiffon.*
▶ **adv. 1** perpendicularly: *the ridge fell sheer, in steep crags.*
2 archaic completely; right: *she went sheer forward when the door was open.*
▶ **n.** a very fine or diaphanous fabric or article.
– DERIVATIVES **sheer·ly adv., sheer·ness n.**
– ORIGIN Middle English (in the sense 'exempt, cleared'): probably an alteration of dialect *shire* 'pure, clear,' from the Germanic base of the verb SHINE. In the mid 16th cent. the word was used to describe clear, pure water, and also sense 3 of the adjective.

sheer[2] ▶ **v.** [no obj.] (typically of a boat or ship) swerve or change course quickly: *the boat sheered off to beach further up the coast.* ■ avoid or move away from an unpleasant topic: *her mind* **sheered away** *from images she didn't want to dwell on.*
▶ **n.** a sudden deviation from a course, esp. by a boat.
– ORIGIN early 17th cent.: perhaps from Middle Low German *scheren* 'to shear.'

USAGE The two verbs **sheer** and **shear** have a similar origin but do not have identical meanings. **Sheer**, the less common verb, means 'swerve or change course quickly': *the boat sheers off the bank.* **Shear**, on the other hand, usually means 'cut the wool off (a sheep)' and can also mean 'break off (usually as a result of structural strain)': *the pins broke and the wing part sheared off.*

sheer[3] ▶ **n.** the upward slope of a ship's lines toward the bow and stern.
– ORIGIN late 17th cent.: probably from the noun SHEAR.

sheer·legs /ˈSHi(ə)rˌlegz/ ▶ **plural n.** [treated as sing.] a hoisting apparatus made from poles joined at or near the top and separated at the bottom, used for masting ships, installing engines, and lifting other heavy objects.

sheesh /SHēSH/ ▶ **exclam.** used to express disbelief or exasperation: *sheesh! what fun is it to mock people when they don't even get it?*

sheet[1] /SHēt/ ▶ **n. 1** a large rectangular piece of cotton or other fabric, used on a bed to cover the mattress and as a layer beneath blankets when these are used. ■ used in comparisons to describe the pallor of a person who is ill or has had a shock: *Are you OK? You're* **as white as a sheet.** ■ a broad flat piece of material such as metal or glass: *the small pipe has been formed from a flat sheet of bronze.*
2 a rectangular piece of paper, esp. one of a standard size produced commercially and used for writing and printing on: *a* **sheet of** *unmarked* **paper.** ■ a quantity of text or other information contained on such a piece of paper: *he produced yet another* **sheet of figures.** ■ a flat piece of paper as opposed to a reel of continuous paper, the bound pages of a book, or a folded map. ■ all the postage stamps printed on one piece of paper: *a sheet of stamps.* ■ a map, esp. one part of a series covering a larger area.
3 an extensive unbroken surface area of something: **a sheet of ice.** ■ a broad moving mass of flames or water: *the rain was still falling in sheets.*
▶ **v. 1** [with obj.] cover with or wrap in a sheet or sheets: *we sheeted a narrow bed.*
2 [no obj.] (of rain) fall in large quantities: *rain sheeted down.*
– ORIGIN Old English *scēte, scīete*, of Germanic origin; related to the verb SHOOT in its primary sense 'to project.'

sheet[2] Nautical ▶ **n. 1** a rope attached to the lower corner of a sail for securing or extending the sail or for altering its direction.
2 (**sheets**) the space at the bow or stern of an open boat.
▶ **v.** [with obj.] (**sheet something in/out**) make a sail more or less taut. ■ (**sheet something home**) extend a sail by tightening the sheets so that the sail is set as flat as possible.
– PHRASES **two** (or **three**) **sheets to the wind** informal drunk.
– ORIGIN Old English *scēata* 'lower corner of a sail,' of Germanic origin; related to Old Norse *skauti* 'kerchief' (see also SHEET[1]).

sheet an·chor ▶ **n.** a person or thing that is very dependable and relied upon in the last resort.
– ORIGIN late 15th cent. (denoting an additional anchor for use in emergencies): perhaps related to obsolete *shot*, denoting two cables spliced together, later influenced by SHEET[2].

sheet bend ▶ **n.** a knot used for temporarily fastening one rope through the loop of another.

sheet·ed /ˈSHētid/ ▶ **adj. 1** covered with or enveloped in a sheet of cloth: *the sheeted body.*
2 Geology (of rock) fissured or divided into layers, esp. by faulting.

sheet·ing /ˈSHētiNG/ ▶ **n.** material formed into or used as a sheet: *a window covered with plastic sheeting.*

sheet·let /ˈSHētlit/ ▶ **n.** a small unseparated sheet of postage stamps.

sheet light·ning ▶ **n.** lightning with its brightness diffused by reflection within clouds.

sheet met·al ▶ **n.** metal formed into thin sheets, typically by rolling or hammering.

sheet mu·sic ▶ **n.** printed music, as opposed to performed or recorded music. ■ music published in single or interleaved sheets, not bound.

sheet pile ▶ **n.** a pile that is pressed or molded from sheet metal or vinyl so as to interlock with other such piles to form a retaining wall or other piling installation.
– DERIVATIVES **sheet-piling n.**

Sheet·rock /ˈSHētˌräk/ ▶ **n.** trademark a plasterboard made of gypsum layered between sheets of heavy paper.

Shef·field /ˈSHefēld/ an industrial city in northern England; pop. 417,700 (est. 2009). It is noted for the manufacture of cutlery and silverware and for the production of steel.

Shef·field plate ▶ **n.** copper plated with silver by rolling and edging with silver film and ribbon, esp. as produced in Sheffield, England, between 1760 and 1840.

sheikh /SHēk, SHāk/ (also **sheik, shaikh,** or **shaykh**) ▶ **n. 1** an Arab leader, in particular the chief or head of an Arab tribe, family, or village.
2 a leader in a Muslim community or organization.
– DERIVATIVES **sheikh·dom** /-dəm/ **n.**
– ORIGIN late 16th cent.: based on Arabic *šayḵ* 'old man, sheikh,' from *šāḵa* 'be or grow old.'

shei·tel /ˈSHātl, ˈSHītl/ ▶ **n.** (among Orthodox Ashkenazic Jews) a wig worn by a married woman.
– ORIGIN late 19th cent.: from Yiddish *sheytl*, from a Germanic base meaning 'crown of the head.'

shek·el /ˈSHekəl/ ▶ **n.** the basic monetary unit of modern Israel, equal to 100 agorot. ■ historical a silver coin and unit of weight used in ancient Israel and the Middle East. ■ (**shekels**) informal money; wealth.
– ORIGIN from Hebrew *šeqel*, from *šāqal* 'weigh.'

She·ki·nah /SHəKHēˈnä, -ˈKHēnə, SHiˈkēnə, -ˈkī-/ (also **Shekhinah**) ▶ **n.** (in Jewish and Christian theology) the glory of the divine presence, conventionally represented as light or interpreted symbolically (in Kabbalism as a divine feminine aspect).
– ORIGIN mid 17th cent.: from late Hebrew, from *šākan* 'dwell, rest.'

shel·duck /ˈSHelˌdək/ (male also **sheldrake** /ˈSHelˌdrāk/) ▶ **n.** (pl. **same** or **shelducks**) a large gooselike Old World duck with brightly colored plumage, typically showing black and white wings in flight. ● Genus *Tadorna*, family Anatidae: several species, in particular *T. tadorna* of Eurasian coasts, with white, greenish-black, and chestnut plumage.
– ORIGIN early 18th cent.: probably from dialect *sheld* 'pied' (related to Middle Dutch *schillede* 'variegated') + DUCK[1].

shelf /SHelf/ ▶ **n.** (pl. **shelves** /SHelvz/) a flat length of wood or rigid material, attached to a wall or forming part of a piece of furniture, that provides a surface for the storage or display of objects. ■ a ledge of rock or protruding strip of land. ■ a submarine bank, or a part of the continental shelf.
– PHRASES **off the shelf** not designed or made to order but taken from existing stock or supplies: *off-the-shelf software packages.* **on the shelf** (of people or things) no longer useful or desirable: *an injury that has kept him on the shelf.*
– DERIVATIVES **shelf·ful** /-ˌfo͝ol/ **n.** (pl. **shelffuls**), **shelf·like** /-ˌlīk/ **adj.**
– ORIGIN Middle English: from Middle Low German *schelf*; related to Old English *scylfe* 'partition,' *scylf* 'crag.'

shelf life ▶ **n.** the length of time for which an item remains usable, fit for consumption, or saleable.

shelf mark ▶ **n.** a notation on a book showing its place in a library.

shelf space ▶ **n.** the amount of available space on a shelf.

shelf-sta·ble ▶ **adj.** able to survive long periods on store or home shelves without spoiling: *a growing number of dairy-based beverages are shelf-stable and can be stored in the pantry rather than the refrigerator.*

shell /SHel/ ▶ **n. 1** the hard protective outer case of a mollusk or crustacean: *cowrie shells | the technique of carving shell.* ■ the thin outer covering of an animal's egg, which is hard and fragile in that of a bird but leathery in that of a reptile. ■ the outer case of a nut kernel or seed. ■ the carapace of a tortoise, turtle, or terrapin. ■ the wing cases of

a beetle. ■ the integument of an insect pupa or chrysalis. ■ (**one's shell**) used with reference to a state of shyness or introversion: *she'll soon come out of her shell with the right encouragement.*
2 something resembling or likened to a shell because of its shape or its function as an outer case: *pasta shells | baked pastry shells filled with cheese.* ■ the walls of an unfinished or gutted building or other structure: *the hotel was a shell, the roof having collapsed completely.* ■ an outer form without substance: *he was a shell of the man he had been previously.* ■ a light racing boat used in the sport of crew. ■ the metal framework of a vehicle body. ■ an inner or roughly made coffin. ■ the hand guard of a sword. ■ Physics each of a set of orbitals around the nucleus of an atom, occupied or able to be occupied by electrons of similar energies.
3 an explosive artillery projectile or bomb: *the sound of the shell passing over, followed by the explosion* | [as modifier] *shell holes.* ■ a hollow metal or paper case used as a container for fireworks, explosives, or cartridges. ■ a cartridge.
4 Computing short for SHELL PROGRAM.
▶ **v. 1** [with obj.] bombard with shells: *the guns started shelling their positions.*
2 [with obj.] remove the shell or pod from (a nut or seed): *they were shelling peas* | (as adj. **shelled**) *shelled Brazil nuts.*
3 [no obj.] gather seashells: *there was nothing to do except swim or go shelling on the beaches.*
– PHRASAL VERBS **shell something out** (or **shell out**) informal pay a specified amount of money, esp. an amount that is resented as being excessive: *it doesn't make sense to shell out $8.50 for an elevator ride.*
– DERIVATIVES **shelled adj.** [in combination:] *a soft-shelled clam*, **shell-less adj.**, **shell-like** /-ˌlīk/ **adj.**, **shell·y** /ˈSHelē/ **adj.**
– ORIGIN Old English *scell* (noun), of Germanic origin; related to Dutch *schel* 'scale, shell,' also to SCALE[1]. The verb dates from the mid 16th cent. in sense 2 of the verb.

she'll /SHēl/ ▶ **contraction** she shall; she will.

shel·lac /SHəˈlak/ ▶ **n.** lac resin melted into thin flakes, used for making varnish.
▶ **v. (shellacs, shellacking** /-ˈlakiNG/, **shellacked** /-ˈlakt/) [with obj.] **1** (often as adj. **shellacked**) varnish (something) with shellac.
2 (usu. **be shellacked**) informal defeat or beat (someone) decisively: *they were shellacked in the 1982 election.*
– ORIGIN mid 17th cent.: from SHELL + LAC[1], translating French *laque en écailles* 'lac in thin plates.'

shell·back /ˈSHelˌbak/ ▶ **n.** informal an old or experienced sailor, esp. one who has crossed the equator.

shell bit ▶ **n.** a gouge-shaped boring bit.

shell com·pa·ny ▶ **n.** an inactive company used as a vehicle for various financial maneuvers or kept dormant for future use in some other capacity.

Shel·ley[1] /ˈSHelē/, Mary (Wollstonecraft) (1797–1851), English writer; daughter of William Godwin and Mary Wollstonecraft. She eloped with Percy Bysshe Shelley in 1814 and married him in 1816. She is chiefly remembered as the author of the Gothic novel *Frankenstein, or the Modern Prometheus* (1818).

Shel·ley[2], Percy Bysshe (1792–1822), English poet. A leading figure of the romantic movement with radical political views, his works include *Queen Mab* (1813), *Prometheus Unbound* (1820), and *Adonais* (1821), an elegy on the death of Keats. He was the husband of Mary Shelley.

shell·fire /ˈSHelˌfīr/ ▶ **n.** bombardment by artillery shells.

shell·fish /ˈSHelˌfiSH/ ▶ **n.** (pl. **same**) an aquatic shelled mollusk (e.g., an oyster or cockle) or a crustacean (e.g., a crab or shrimp), esp. one that is edible. ■ such mollusks or crustaceans as food.

shell game ▶ **n.** a game involving sleight of hand, in which three inverted cups or nutshells are moved about, and contestants must spot which is the one with a pea or other object underneath. ■ a deceptive and evasive action or ploy, esp. a political one: *officials played a shell game by loading prisoners onto buses during population counts at the jail.*

shell jack·et ▶ **n.** an army officer's tight-fitting undress jacket reaching to the waist.

shell lime ▶ **n.** fine-quality lime produced by roasting seashells.

shell pink ▶ **n.** a delicate pale pink.

shell pro·gram ▶ **n.** Computing a program that provides an interface between the user and the operating system.

shell shock ▶ **n.** psychological disturbance caused by prolonged exposure to active warfare, esp. being under bombardment. Also called COMBAT FATIGUE.
– ORIGIN World War I: with reference to exposure to shellfire.

shell-shocked ▶ **adj.** suffering from shell shock. ■ shocked or confused because of a sudden alarming experience: *he told shell-shocked investors that the company needed still more money to survive the year.*

shell·work /ˈSHelˌwərk/ ▶ **n.** ornamentation consisting of shells cemented onto a surface.

Shel·ta /ˈSHeltə/ ▶ **n.** an ancient secret language used by Irish and Welsh gypsies, based largely on altered Irish or Gaelic words.
– ORIGIN late 19th cent.: of unknown origin.

shel·ter /ˈSHeltər/ ▶ **n.** a place giving temporary protection from bad weather or danger. ■ a place providing food and accommodations for the homeless. ■ an animal sanctuary. ■ a shielded or safe condition; protection: *he hung back in the shelter of a rock | you're welcome to take shelter from the storm.*
▶ **v.** [with obj.] protect or shield from something harmful, esp. bad weather: *the hut sheltered him from the cold wind.* ■ [no obj.] find refuge or take cover from bad weather or danger: *people were sheltering under store canopies and trees.* ■ prevent (someone) from having to do or face something difficult or unpleasant. ■ protect (income) from taxation: *only your rental income can be sheltered.*
– DERIVATIVES **shel·ter·er n.**, **shel·ter·less adj.**
– ORIGIN late 16th cent.: perhaps an alteration of obsolete *sheltron* 'phalanx,' from Old English *scieldtruma*, literally 'shield troop.'

shel·ter belt ▶ **n.** a line of trees or shrubs planted to protect an area, esp. a farm field, from strong winds and the erosion they cause.

shel·tered /ˈSHeltərd/ ▶ **adj.** (of a place) protected from bad weather: *the plants need a shady, sheltered spot in the garden.* ■ protected from difficulties or unpleasant realities: *she led a sheltered life until her mother and father went through a bitter divorce | a sheltered childhood.*

shel·tered work·shop ▶ **n.** a supervised workplace for physically disabled or mentally handicapped adults.

shel·ter·wood /ˈSHeltərˌwo͝od/ ▶ **n.** mature trees left standing to provide shelter in which saplings can grow.

shel·tie /ˈSHeltē/ (also **shelty**) ▶ **n.** (pl. **shelties**) a Shetland pony or sheepdog.
– ORIGIN early 17th cent.: probably representing an Orkney pronunciation of Old Norse *Hjalti* 'Shetlander.'

shelve[1] /SHelv/ ▶ **v.** [with obj.] **1** place or arrange (items, esp. books) on a shelf.
2 decide not to proceed with (a project or plan), either temporarily or permanently: *plans to reopen the school have been shelved.*
3 fit with shelves: *one whole long wall was shelved.*
– DERIVATIVES **shelv·er n.**
– ORIGIN late 16th cent. (in the sense 'project like a shelf' (Shakespearean usage)): from *shelves*, plural of SHELF.

shelve[2] ▶ **v.** [no obj.] (of ground) slope downward in a specified manner or direction: *the ground shelved gently down to the water.*
– ORIGIN late Middle English: origin uncertain; perhaps from SHELF.

shelves /SHelvz/ plural form of SHELF.

shelv·ing /ˈSHelviNG/ ▶ **n.** shelves collectively: *a lack of shelving and cupboards.* ■ the action of shelving something.

Shem /SHem/ (in the Bible) a son of Noah (Gen. 10:21), traditional ancestor of the Semites.

She·ma /SHəˈmä/ a Hebrew text consisting of three passages from the Pentateuch and beginning "Hear, O Israel, the Lord is our God, the Lord is one." It forms an important part of Jewish evening and morning prayer and is used as a Jewish confession of faith.
– ORIGIN Hebrew, literally 'hear,' the first word of Deut. 6:4.

she-male (also **shemale**) ▶ **n.** informal a transvestite. ■ a passive male homosexual. ■ a hermaphrodite.

she·moz·zle /SHəˈmäzəl/ (also **schemozzle**) ▶ **n.** informal a state of chaos and confusion; a muddle.
– ORIGIN late 19th cent.: Yiddish, suggested by late Hebrew *šel-lō'-mazzāl* 'of no luck.'

shen /SHen/ ▶ **n.** (pl. **same**) (in Chinese thought) the spiritual element of a person's psyche.
– ORIGIN from Chinese *shén*.

Shen·an·do·ah /ˌSHenənˈdōə/ a river in Virginia. Rising in two headstreams, one on each side of the Blue Ridge Mountains, it flows about 150 miles (240 km) north to join the Potomac River at Harpers Ferry.

Shen·an·do·ah Na·tion·al Park a national park in the Blue Ridge Mountains of northern Virginia, southeast of the Shenandoah River. It was established in 1935.

she·nan·i·gans /SHəˈnanəgənz/ ▶ **plural n.** informal secret or dishonest activity or maneuvering: *widespread financial shenanigans had ruined the fortunes of many.* ■ silly or high-spirited behavior; mischief.
– ORIGIN mid 19th cent.: of unknown origin.

Shen·yang /ˈSHenˈyaNG, ˈSHənˈyäNG/ a city in northeastern China; pop. 4,101,200 (est. 2006). It is the capital of the province of Liaoning. Former name MUKDEN.

Shen·zhen /ˈSHenˈZHen, -ˈzen, ˈSHənˈjən/ an industrial city in southern China, north of Hong Kong; pop. 1,819,300 (est. 2006).

She·ol /ˈSHēˌōl, SHēˈōl/ the Hebrew underworld, abode of the dead.
– ORIGIN Hebrew.

shep·herd /ˈSHepərd/ ▶ **n.** a person who tends and rears sheep. ■ a member of the clergy who provides spiritual care and guidance for a congregation. ■ short for GERMAN SHEPHERD.
▶ **v.** [with obj.] **1** (usu. as noun **shepherding**) tend (sheep) as a shepherd. ■ give guidance to (someone), esp. on spiritual matters: *she had to submit the control of her career and money to a group who shepherded her.*
2 guide or direct in a particular direction: *we were shepherded around with great ceremony.*
– ORIGIN Old English *scēaphierde*, from *scēap* 'sheep' + *hierde* 'herder;' see SHEEP and HERD.

shep·herd dog ▶ **n.** a sheepdog.

shep·herd·ess /ˈSHepərdis/ ▶ **n.** a female shepherd. ■ an idealized or romanticized rustic maiden in pastoral literature.

shep·herd sat·el·lite (also **shepherd moon**) ▶ **n.** Astronomy a small moon orbiting close to a planetary ring, esp. of Saturn, and whose gravitational field confines the ring within a narrow band.

shep·herd's crook ▶ **n.** a staff with a hook at one end used by shepherds.

shep·herd's nee·dle ▶ **n.** a white-flowered Eurasian plant of the parsley family, with long, needle-shaped fruit. ● *Scandix pecten-veneris*, family Umbelliferae.

shep·herd's pie ▶ **n.** a dish of ground meat under a layer of mashed potato.

shep·herd's plaid (also **shepherd's check**) ▶ **n.** a small black-and-white check pattern. ■ woolen cloth with this pattern.

shep·herd's purse ▶ **n.** a widely distributed white-flowered weed of the cabbage family, with triangular or heart-shaped seedpods. ● *Capsella bursa-pastoris*, family Brassicaceae.

sher·ard·ize /ˈSHerərˌdīz/ ▶ **v.** [with obj.] coat (iron or steel) with zinc by heating it in contact with zinc dust.
– ORIGIN early 20th cent.: from the name of *Sherard* Cowper-Coles (1867–1936), English inventor, + -IZE.

Sher·a·ton /ˈSHerətn/ ▶ **adj.** [attrib.] (of furniture) designed, made by, or in the simple, delicate, and graceful style of the English furniture maker Thomas Sheraton (1751–1806).

sher·bet /ˈSHərbit/ ▶ **n.** a frozen dessert made with fruit juice added to milk or cream, egg white, or gelatin. ■ a frozen fruit juice and sugar mixture served as a dessert or between courses of a meal to cleanse the palate. ■ (esp. in Arab countries) a cooling drink of sweet diluted fruit juices. ■ Brit. a flavored sweet effervescent powder eaten alone or made into a drink.
– ORIGIN early 17th cent.: from Turkish *şerbet*, Persian *šerbet*, from Arabic *šarba* 'drink,' from *šariba* 'to drink.' Compare with SYRUP.

> **USAGE** The tendency to insert an **r** into the second syllable of **sherbet** is common; the misspelling **sherbert** accounts for around a quarter of the citations for the word in the Oxford English Corpus.

sherd /SHərd/ ▶ **n.** another term for POTSHERD.

she·reef /SHəˈrēf/ (also **sherif**) ▶ **n.** variant spelling of SHARIF.

Sher·i·dan[1] /ˈSHeridn/, Philip Henry (1831–88) US army officer. A severe and effective Union cavalry commander in the Civil War, he was noted for his decisive victories and plundering raids. In April 1865, he cut off the Confederate retreat at Appomattox, forcing the surrender of General Lee.

S

In 1884, he became commander in chief of the US army.

Sher·i·dan[2], Richard Brinsley (1751–1816), Irish playwright and politician. His plays are comedies of manners and include *The Rivals* (1775) and *The School for Scandal* (1777). In 1780, he entered Parliament, became a celebrated orator, and held senior government posts.

sher·iff /ˈsHerif/ ▶ **n.** (in the US) an elected officer in a county who is responsible for keeping the peace. ■ (also **high sheriff**) (in England and Wales) the chief executive officer of the Crown in a county, having various administrative and judicial functions. ■ an honorary officer elected annually in some English towns. ■ (in Scotland) a judge.
– DERIVATIVES **sher·iff·dom** /-dəm/ **n.**
– ORIGIN Old English *scīrgerēfa* (see SHIRE, REEVE[1]).

sher·iff clerk ▶ **n.** (in Scotland) the clerk of a sheriff's court.

Sher·lock /ˈsHərˌläk/ ▶ **n.** informal a person who investigates mysteries or shows great perceptiveness: *it doesn't take a Sherlock to figure out that she's lying to me.*
– ORIGIN early 20th cent.: from *Sherlock* Holmes (see HOLMES[2]).

Sher·man[1], Roger (1721–93), American politician. A Connecticut legislator and jurist, he was an avid proponent of American independence. He held the distinction of having signed all of the following: the Articles of Association 1774, the Declaration of Independence 1776, the Articles of Confederation 1777, and the Constitution 1787. He served as a US senator 1791–93.

Sher·man[2], William Tecumseh (1820–91), US general. In 1864, during the Civil War, he was appointed commander of Union forces in the West. He set out with 60,000 men on a "March to the Sea" through Georgia, during which he crushed Confederate forces and broke civilian morale by his policy of deliberate destruction of the territory through which he passed. He served as commander of the army 1869–84.

William Tecumseh Sherman

Sher·man tank ▶ **n.** an American type of medium tank, used in large numbers during World War II.

Sher·pa /ˈsHərpə/ ▶ **n.** (pl. **same** or **Sherpas**) a member of a Himalayan people living on the borders of Nepal and Tibet, renowned for their skill in mountaineering. ■ a civil servant or diplomat who undertakes preparatory political work prior to a summit conference.
– ORIGIN from Tibetan *sharpa* 'inhabitant of an eastern country.'

S

Sher·ring·ton /ˈsHəriNGtən/, Sir Charles Scott (1857–1952), English physiologist. He contributed greatly to the understanding of the nervous system and introduced the concept of reflex actions and the reflex arc. Nobel Prize for Physiology or Medicine (1932).

sher·ry /ˈsHerē/ ▶ **n.** (pl. **sherries**) a fortified wine originally and mainly from southern Spain, often drunk as an aperitif.
– DERIVATIVES **sher·ried adj.**
– ORIGIN late 16th cent.: alteration of archaic *sherris*, interpreted as plural, from Spanish (*vino de*) *Xeres* 'Xeres (wine)' (Xeres being the former name of JEREZ).

sher·wa·ni /sHərˈwänē/ ▶ **n.** (pl. **sherwanis**) a knee-length coat buttoning to the neck, worn by men from South Asia.
– ORIGIN from Urdu and Persian *šīrwānī* 'from Shirvan' (referring to a town in northeastern Persia).

she's /sHēz/ ▶ **contraction** she is; she has.

Shet·land Is·lands /ˈsHetlənd/ (also **Shetland** or **the Shetlands**) a group of about 100 islands off the north coast of Scotland, northeast of the Orkneys, that constitute the administrative region of Shetland; pop. 21,800 (est. 2009); chief town, Lerwick. Together with the Orkney Islands, the Shetland Islands became a part of Scotland in 1472.
– DERIVATIVES **Shet·land·er n.**

Shet·land po·ny ▶ **n.** a pony of a small, hardy, rough-coated breed.

Shet·land sheep ▶ **n.** a sheep of a hardy, short-tailed breed native to Shetland and bred esp. for its fine wool.

Shet·land sheep·dog ▶ **n.** a small dog of a collielike breed.

Shet·land wool ▶ **n.** a type of fine loosely twisted wool from Shetland sheep.

Shev·ard·na·dze /ˌsHevərdˈnädzə/, Eduard (Amvrosievich) (1928–), Soviet statesman, and head of state of Georgia 1995–2003. He was minister of foreign affairs 1985–90 under President Gorbachev before becoming head of state of his native Georgia.

She·vat /sHəˈvät/ (also **Shebat**) ▶ **n.** (in the Jewish calendar) the fifth month of the civil and eleventh of the religious year, usually coinciding with parts of January and February.
– ORIGIN from Hebrew *šᵉbaṭ*.

shew /sHō/ ▶ **v.** old-fashioned variant spelling of SHOW.

shew·bread (also **showbread** /ˈsHōˌbred/) ▶ **n.** twelve loaves placed every Sabbath in the Jewish Temple and eaten by the priests at the end of the week.
– ORIGIN mid 16th cent.: suggested by German *Schaubrot*, representing Hebrew *leḥem pānīm*, literally 'bread of the face (of God).'

shf (also **SHF**) ▶ **abbr.** superhigh frequency.

shh /sH/ (also **sh**) ▶ **exclam.** used to call for silence: *"Shh! Keep your voice down!"*
– ORIGIN mid 19th cent.: variant of HUSH.

Shi·a /ˈsHēˌä/ (also **Shi'a**) ▶ **n.** (pl. **same** or **Shias**) one of the two main branches of Islam, followed esp. in Iran, that rejects the first three Sunni caliphs and regards Ali, the fourth caliph, as Muhammad's first true successor. Compare with SUNNI. ■ a Muslim who adheres to this branch of Islam.
– ORIGIN from Arabic *šī'a* 'party (of Ali).'

shi·at·su /sHēˈätso͞o/ ▶ **n.** a form of therapy of Japanese origin based on the same principles as acupuncture, in which pressure is applied to certain points on the body using the hands.
– ORIGIN 1960s: Japanese, literally 'finger pressure.'

shib·bo·leth /ˈsHibəliTH, -ˌleTH/ ▶ **n.** a custom, principle, or belief distinguishing a particular class or group of people, esp. a long-standing one regarded as outmoded or no longer important: *the party began to break with the shibboleths of the left.*
– ORIGIN mid 17th cent.: from Hebrew *šibbōlet* 'ear of corn,' used as a test of nationality by its difficult pronunciation (Judg. 12:6).

shick·er /ˈsHikər/ (also **shikker**) informal ▶ **adj.** (also **shickered** /-ərd/, **shikkered**) [predic.] drunk: *they got shickered, talked cars and deals.*
▶ **n.** a drunk.
– ORIGIN late 19th cent.: from Yiddish *shiker*, from Hebrew *šikkōr*, from *šākar* 'be drunk.'

shid·duch /ˈsHidəKH, sHiˈdo͝oKH/ ▶ **n.** (pl. **shidduchim** /ˌsHido͝oˈKHēm/) a Jewish arranged marriage.
– ORIGIN late 19th cent.: Yiddish, from Hebrew *šiddūḵ* 'negotiation (of a marriage).'

shied /sHīd/ past and past participle of SHY[2].

shield /sHēld/ ▶ **n. 1** a broad piece of metal or another suitable material, held by straps or a handle attached on one side, used as a protection against blows or missiles.
2 something shaped like a shield, in particular: ■ a police officer's badge. ■ Heraldry a stylized representation of a shield used for displaying a coat of arms. ■ Geology a large rigid area of the earth's crust, typically of Precambrian rock, that has been unaffected by later orogenic episodes, e.g., the Canadian Shield.
3 a person or thing providing protection: *a protective coating of grease provides a shield against abrasive dirt.* ■ a protective plate or screen on machinery or equipment. ■ a device or material that prevents or reduces the emission of light or other radiation. ■ short for DRESS SHIELD. ■ a hard flat or convex part of an animal, esp. a shell.
▶ **v.** [with obj.] protect (someone or something) from a danger, risk, or unpleasant experience: *he pulled the cap lower to shield his eyes from the glare | these people have been completely shielded from economic forces.* ■ prevent from being seen: *the rocks she sat behind shielded her from the lodge.* ■ enclose or screen (a piece of machinery) to protect the user. ■ prevent or reduce the escape of sound, light, or other radiation from (something): *uranium shutters shield the cobalt radioactive source.*
– DERIVATIVES **shield·less adj.**
– ORIGIN Old English *scild* (noun), *scildan* (verb), of Germanic origin; related to Dutch *schild* and German *Schild*, from a base meaning 'divide, separate.'

shield bug ▶ **n.** another term for STINK BUG.

shield fern ▶ **n.** any of a number of ferns that have circular shieldlike scales protecting the spore cases. ● a European fern of damp woodland (genus *Polystichum*, family Dryopteridaceae). ● an evergreen fern (genus *Thelypteris*, family Thelypteridaceae). ■ Austral. a fern of forested country (family Aspidiaceae).

shield law ▶ **n.** a law that protects witnesses from revealing certain information, esp. in court. ■ a law that protects journalists from having to reveal confidential sources. ■ a law that protects rape victims from having to reveal details of their sexual history.

shield·tail snake /ˈsHēl(d)ˌtā/ (also **shield-tailed snake**) ▶ **n.** a burrowing snake that has a flat disk formed from an enlarged scale on the upper surface of the tail, native to the rain forests of southern India and Sri Lanka. ● *Rhinophis*, *Uropeltis*, and other genera, family Uropeltidae: numerous species.

shield vol·ca·no ▶ **n.** Geology a broad, domed volcano with gently sloping sides, characteristic of the eruption of fluid, basaltic lava.

shiel·ing /ˈsHēliNG/ (also **shealing**) ▶ **n.** Scottish a roughly constructed hut used while pasturing animals. ■ an area of pasture.
– ORIGIN mid 16th cent.: from Scots *shiel* 'hut' (of unknown origin) + -ING[1].

shift /sHift/ ▶ **v.** move or cause to move from one place to another, esp. over a small distance: [with obj.] *I shift the weight back to the other leg* | [no obj.] *the roof cracked and shifted.* ■ [no obj.] change the position of one's body, esp. because one is nervous or uncomfortable: *he shifted a little in his chair.* ■ [with obj.] change the emphasis, direction, or focus of: *she's shifting the blame onto me.* ■ [no obj.] change in emphasis, direction, or focus: *the wind had shifted to the east | the balance of power shifted abruptly.* ■ [with obj.] Computing move (data) one or more places to the right or left in a register: *the partial remainder is shifted left.* ■ [no obj.] press the shift key on a typewriter or computer keyboard. ■ [with obj.] informal sell (something): *a lot of high-priced product you simply don't know how to shift.* ■ [no obj.] change gear in a vehicle: *she shifted down to fourth.* ■ [no obj.] archaic be evasive or indirect: *they know not how to shift and rob as the old ones do.*
▶ **n. 1** a slight change in position, direction, or tendency: *a shift of wind took us by surprise | a shift in public opinion.* ■ Astronomy the displacement of spectral lines. See also REDSHIFT. ■ (also **shift key**) a key on a typewriter or computer keyboard used to switch between two sets of characters or functions, principally between lower- and upper-case letters. ■ short for SOUND SHIFT. ■ the gearshift or gear-changing mechanism in a motor vehicle. ■ Building the positioning of successive rows of bricks so that their ends do not coincide. ■ Computing a movement of the digits of a word in a register one or more places to left or right, equivalent to multiplying or dividing the corresponding number by a power of whatever number is the base. ■ Football a change of position by two or more players before the ball is put into play.
2 one of two or more recurring periods in which different groups of workers do the same jobs in relay: *the night shift.* ■ a group of workers who work in this way.
3 (also **shift dress**) a woman's straight, unwaisted dress. ■ historical a long, loose-fitting undergarment.
4 archaic an ingenious or devious device or stratagem: *the thousand shifts and devices of which Hannibal was a master.*
– PHRASES **make shift** do what one wants to do in spite of not having ideal conditions. **shift for oneself** manage as best one can without help. **shift one's ground** say or write something that contradicts something one has previously written or said. **shifting sands** something that is constantly changing, esp. unpredictably: *whether something is accepted depends upon the shifting sands of taste.*
– DERIVATIVES **shift·a·ble** /ˈsHiftəbəl/ **adj.**
– ORIGIN Old English *sciftan* 'arrange, divide, apportion,' of Germanic origin; related to German *schichten* 'to layer, stratify.' A common Middle English sense 'change, replace' gave rise to the noun sense 3 of the noun (via the notion of changing one's clothes) and sense 2 of the noun (via the concept of relays of workers).

shift·er /ˈsHiftər/ ▶ **n.** [usu. in combination] a person or thing that shifts something: *each morning the rock-shifters travel by donkey cart to start work.* ■ a gearbox of a motor vehicle or a set of gear levers on a bicycle: *a new, improved five-speed shifter.*

shift·ing cul·ti·va·tion (also **shifting agriculture**) ▶ n. a form of agriculture, used esp. in tropical Africa, in which an area of ground is cleared of vegetation and cultivated for a few years and then abandoned for a new area until its fertility has been naturally restored.

shift·less /ˈSHiftlis/ ▶ adj. (of a person or action) characterized by laziness, indolence, and a lack of ambition: *a shiftless lot of good-for-nothings.*
– DERIVATIVES **shift·less·ly** adv., **shift·less·ness** n.

shift lev·er ▶ n. another term for GEARSHIFT.

shift reg·is·ter ▶ n. Computing a register that is designed to allow the bits of its contents to be moved to left or right.

shift work ▶ n. work comprising recurring periods in which different groups of workers do the same jobs in rotation.

shift·y /ˈSHiftē/ ▶ adj. (**shiftier, shiftiest**) informal (of a person or their manner) appearing deceitful or evasive: *a shifty, fast-talking lawyer.*
– DERIVATIVES **shift·i·ly** /-əlē/ adv., **shift·i·ness** n.

Shi·ga tox·in /ˈSHēgə/ ▶ n. a toxin produced by certain strains of the bacterium *E. coli* that is pathogenic in humans: *during infection there are changes of cytokine levels that can be ascribed to an effect of Shiga toxin on different cell types.*
– ORIGIN c. 2000: the name arose when it was discovered that the toxin was virtually indistinguishable in both structure and function from the toxin produced by *Shigella dysenteriae*, which was in turn named for Kiyoshi *Shiga*; see SHIGELLA.

shi·gel·la /SHəˈgelə/ ▶ n. a bacterium that is an intestinal pathogen of humans and other primates, some kinds of which cause dysentery. ● Genus *Shigella*; Gram-negative rods.
– ORIGIN modern Latin, from the name of Kiyoshi *Shiga* (1870–1957), Japanese bacteriologist, + the diminutive suffix *-ella*.

Shih Tzu /ˈSHē ˈdzo͞o/ ▶ n. a dog of a breed with long, silky, erect hair and short legs.
– ORIGIN 1920s: from Chinese *shizi* 'lion.'

shi·i·ta·ke /SHēˈtäkē, SHē-ēˈtäke/ (also **shiitake mushroom**) ▶ n. an edible mushroom that grows on fallen timber, cultivated in Japan and China. ● *Lentinus edodes*, family Pleurotaceae, class Hymenomycetes.
– ORIGIN late 19th cent.: from Japanese, from *shii*, denoting a kind of oak, + *take* 'mushroom.'

Shi·ite /ˈSHēˌīt/ (also **Shi'ite**) ▶ n. an adherent of the Shia branch of Islam.
▶ adj. of or relating to Shia.
– DERIVATIVES **Shi·ism** /ˈSHēˌizəm/ (also **Shi'ism**) n.

Shi·jia·zhuang /ˈSHœˈjyäˈjwäNG/ a city in northeast central China, capital of Hebei province; pop. 2,241,500 (est. 2006).

shi·kar /SHiˈkär/ ▶ n. Indian hunting as a sport.
– ORIGIN from Urdu and Persian *šikār*.

shi·ka·ra /SHiˈkärə/ ▶ n. Indian (in Kashmir) a houseboat. ■ variant spelling of SHIKARI (sense 2).
– ORIGIN via Kashmiri from Persian *šikārī* 'of hunting.'

shi·ka·ri /SHiˈkärē/ ▶ n. (pl. **shikaris**) Indian **1** a hunter. ■ a guide on hunting expeditions.
2 (also **shikara**) (in Kashmir) a light, flat-bottomed boat.
– ORIGIN via Urdu from Persian *šikārī* 'of hunting.'

shik·ker /ˈSHikər/ ▶ adj. & n. variant spelling of SHICKER.

Shi·ko·ku /SHiˈkōˌko͞o/ the smallest of the four main islands of Japan, an administrative region; pop. 4,142,000 (est. 2005); capital, Matsuyama. The Inland Sea separates it from Kyushu on the west and Honshu on the north.

shik·ra /ˈSHikrə/ ▶ n. a small, stocky sparrow hawk found in Africa and central and southern Asia. ● Genus *Accipiter*, family Accipitridae: two species, in particular the widespread *A. badius*.
– ORIGIN mid 19th cent.: from Persian and Urdu *šikara*.

shik·sa /ˈSHiksə/ ▶ n. often derogatory (used esp. by Jews) a gentile girl or woman.
– ORIGIN late 19th cent.: from Yiddish *shikse*, from Hebrew *šiqṣāh* (from *šeqeṣ* 'detested thing' + the feminine suffix *-āh*).

shill /SHil/ informal ▶ n. an accomplice of a hawker, gambler, or swindler who acts as an enthusiastic customer to entice or encourage others.
▶ v. [no obj.] act or work as such a person.
– ORIGIN early 20th cent.: probably from earlier *shillaber*, of unknown origin.

shil·le·lagh /SHəˈlālē/ ▶ n. a thick stick of blackthorn or oak used in Ireland, typically as a weapon.
– ORIGIN late 18th cent.: from the name of the town *Shillelagh*, in County Wicklow, Ireland.

shil·ling /ˈSHiliNG/ ▶ n. **1** a former British coin and monetary unit equal to one twentieth of a pound or twelve pence.
2 the basic monetary unit in Kenya, Tanzania, and Uganda, equal to 100 cents.
– ORIGIN Old English *scilling*, of Germanic origin; related to Dutch *schelling* and German *Schilling*.

Shil·long /SHiˈlôNG/ a city in northeastern India, capital of the state of Meghalaya; pop. 141,700 (est. 2009).

Shil·luk /SHəˈlo͝ok/ ▶ n. (pl. **same** or **Shilluks**) **1** a member of a Sudanese people living mainly on the west bank of the Nile.
2 the Nilotic language of this people.
▶ adj. of or relating to this people or their language.
– ORIGIN the name in Shilluk.

shil·ly-shal·ly /ˈSHilē ˌSHalē/ ▶ v. (**shilly-shallies, shilly-shallying, shilly-shallied**) [no obj.] fail to act resolutely or decisively: *the government shilly-shallied about the matter.*
▶ n. indecisive behavior.
– DERIVATIVES **shil·ly-shal·ly·er** /ˌSHalēər/ (also **-shallier**) n.
– ORIGIN mid 18th cent.: originally as *shill I, shall I*, reduplication of *shall I?*

Shi·loh /ˈSHīlō/ a historic site in southwestern Tennessee, near Pittsburg Landing on the Tennessee River, site of a major Civil War battle in April 1862.

shim /SHim/ ▶ n. a washer or thin strip of material used to align parts, make them fit, or reduce wear.
▶ v. (**shims, shimming, shimmed**) [with obj.] wedge (something) or fill up (a space) with a shim.
– ORIGIN early 18th cent.: of unknown origin.

Shim·la /ˈSHimlə/ (also **Simla**) a city in northeastern India, capital of the state of Himachal Pradesh; pop. 208,600 (est. 2009).

shim·mer /ˈSHimər/ ▶ v. [no obj.] shine with a soft tremulous light: *the sea shimmered in the sunlight.*
▶ n. [in sing.] a light with such qualities: *a pale shimmer of moonlight.*
– DERIVATIVES **shim·mer·ing·ly** adv., **shim·mer·y** adj.
– ORIGIN late Old English *scymrian*, of Germanic origin; related to German *schimmern*, also to SHINE. The noun dates from the early 19th cent.

shim·my /ˈSHimē/ ▶ n. (pl. **shimmies**) **1** a kind of ragtime dance in which the whole body shakes or sways. ■ shaking, esp. abnormal vibration of the wheels of a motor vehicle: *steering stabilizers reduce shimmy even from oversized tires.*
2 archaic informal term for CHEMISE.
▶ v. (**shimmies, shimmying, shimmied**) [no obj.] dance the shimmy. ■ shake or vibrate abnormally: *he braked hard and felt the car shimmy dangerously.* ■ move effortlessly or with a graceful swaying motion: *her hair swung in waves as she shimmied down the catwalk | he shimmied right to the top of one of the chimneys.*
– ORIGIN early 20th cent.: of unknown origin.

shin /SHin/ ▶ n. the front of the leg below the knee. ■ a cut of beef from the lower part of a cow's leg.
▶ v. (**shins, shinning, shinned**) [no obj.] (**shin up/down**) climb quickly up or down by gripping with one's arms and legs: *he shinned up a tree.*
– ORIGIN Old English *scinu*, probably from a Germanic base meaning 'narrow or thin piece'; related to German *Schiene* 'thin plate' and Dutch *scheen*. The verb was originally in nautical use (early 19th cent).

Shin Bet /ˌSHin ˌbet/ (also **Shin Beth**) the principal security service of Israel, concerned primarily with counter-espionage.
– ORIGIN modern Hebrew, the initial letters of the first two words of *šērūṯ biṭṭāhōn kĕlālī* '(general) security service.'

shin·bone /ˈSHinˌbōn/ ▶ n. the tibia.

shin·dig /ˈSHinˌdig/ ▶ n. informal a large, lively party, esp. one celebrating something.
– ORIGIN mid 19th cent.: probably from the nouns SHIN and DIG, influenced later by SHINDY.

shin·dy /ˈSHindē/ ▶ n. (pl. **shindies**) informal a noisy disturbance or quarrel: *there were plenty of gulls kicking up a shindy.* ■ a large, lively party.
– ORIGIN early 19th cent.: perhaps an alteration of SHINTY.

shine /SHīn/ ▶ v. (past and past participle **shone** /SHōn/ or **shined**) [no obj.] **1** (of the sun or another source of light) give out a bright light: *the sun shone through the window.* ■ glow or be bright with reflected light: *I could see his eyes shining in the light of the fire.* ■ [with obj.] direct (a flashlight or other light) somewhere in order to see something in the dark: *an usher shines his flashlight into the boys' faces.* ■ (of a person's eyes) be bright with the expression of a particular emotion: *his eyes shone with excitement.*
2 be very talented or perform very well: *she shines at comedy.*
3 (past **shined**) [with obj.] make (an object made of leather, metal, or wood) bright by rubbing it; polish: *his shoes were shined to perfection.*
▶ n. [in sing.] a quality of brightness, esp. from reflected light: *use shoe polish to try and get a shine | my hair has lost its shine.* ■ an act of rubbing something to give it a shiny surface: *Tom's shoes got a quick shine from a boy with a buffing cloth.* ■ offensive a contemptuous term for a black or dark-skinned person.
– PHRASES **take the shine off** spoil the brilliance or excitement of: *the absence of new jobs has taken some of the shine off his stellar popularity ratings.* **take a shine to** informal develop a liking for.
– PHRASAL VERBS **shine through** (of a good quality or skill) be clearly evident: *at Regis his talent shone through.*
– ORIGIN Old English *scīnan*, of Germanic origin; related to Dutch *schijnen* and German *scheinen*.

shin·er /ˈSHīnər/ ▶ n. **1** a thing that shines or reflects light: *moonlight blanked the weakest shiners, but the more powerful stars were gleaming.* ■ [in combination] a person or thing that polishes something: *shoeshiners.*
2 informal a black eye.
3 a small silvery North American freshwater fish of the minnow family that typically has colorful markings. ● *Notropis* and other genera, family Cyprinidae: several species.

shin·gle[1] /ˈSHiNGgəl/ ▶ n. a mass of small rounded pebbles, esp. on a seashore.
– DERIVATIVES **shin·gly** /-g(ə)lē/ adj.
– ORIGIN late Middle English: of unknown origin.

shin·gle[2] ▶ n. **1** a rectangular tile of asphalt composite, wood, metal, or slate used on walls or roofs.
2 dated a woman's short haircut in which the hair tapers from the back of the head to the nape of the neck. [so named because of the layering.]
3 a small signboard, esp. one found outside a doctor's or lawyer's office.
▶ v. [with obj.] **1** roof or clad with shingles: (as adj. **shingled**) *a tower surmounted by a shingled spire.*
2 dated cut (a woman's hair) in a shingle.
– PHRASES **hang out one's shingle** begin to practice a profession.
– ORIGIN Middle English (as a noun): apparently from Latin *scindula*, earlier *scandula* 'a split piece of wood.'

shin·gle·back /ˈSHiNGgəlˌbak/ (also **shingleback lizard**) ▶ n. a slow-moving, heavily built lizard with scales resembling those of pine cones, occurring in arid regions of Australia. ● *Trachydosaurus rugosus*, family Scincidae.

shin·gles /ˈSHiNGgəlz/ ▶ plural n. [treated as sing.] Medicine an acute, painful inflammation of the nerve ganglia, with a skin eruption often forming a girdle around the middle of the body. It is caused by the same virus as chickenpox. Also called HERPES ZOSTER.
– ORIGIN late Middle English: representing medieval Latin *cingulus*, variant of Latin *cingulum* 'girdle,' from *cingere* 'gird.'

shin guard ▶ n. a pad worn to protect the shins when playing soccer, hockey, and other sports.

shin·ing /ˈSHīniNG/ ▶ adj. **1** giving out or reflecting bright light: *a shining expanse of water.*
2 brilliant or excellent at something: *he has set a shining example with his model behavior.*
– DERIVATIVES **shin·ing·ly** /-niNGlē/ adv.

Shin·ing Path a Peruvian Maoist revolutionary movement and terrorist organization, founded in 1970 and led by **Abimael Guzmán** (1934–) until his capture and imprisonment in 1992. At first the movement operated in rural areas, but in the 1980s it began to launch terrorist attacks in Peruvian towns and cities.
– ORIGIN translating Spanish SENDERO LUMINOSO.

Shin·kan·sen /ˈSHinkänˌsen/ ▶ n. (pl. **same**) (in Japan) a railroad system carrying high-speed passenger trains. ■ (also **shinkansen**) a train operating on such a system.
– ORIGIN Japanese, from *shin* 'new' + *kansen* 'main line.'

shin·ny[1] /ˈSHinē/ ▶ v. (**shinnies, shinnying, shinnied**) another term for SHIN: *he loved to shinny up that tree.*
– ORIGIN late 19th cent.: from the noun SHIN + -Y[2].

shin·ny[2] (also **shinny hockey**) ▶ n. an informal form of ice hockey played esp. by children, on the street or on ice: *we used to play shinny on the canal with tin cans.*
– ORIGIN variant of SHINTY.

PRONUNCIATION KEY ə *ago, up*; ər *over, fur*; a *hat*; ā *ate*; ä *car*; e *let*; ē *see*; i *fit*; ī *by*; NG *sing*; ō *go*; ô *law, for*; oi *toy*; o͝o *good*; o͞o *goo*; ou *out*; TH *thin*; T̲H̲ *then*; ZH *vision*

S

Shi·no·la /SHī'nōlə/ ▶ **n.** trademark a brand of boot polish. ■ informal used as a euphemism for "shit": *there'll be the same old Shinola on television.*
– PHRASES **not know shit from Shinola** vulgar slang used to indicate that someone is ignorant or innocent.
– ORIGIN early 20th cent.: from SHINE + *-ola.*

shin pad ▶ **n.** another term for SHIN GUARD.

shin·plas·ter /'SHin,plastər/ ▶ **n.** informal historical **1** a piece of paper currency or a promissory note regarded as having little or no value.
2 Canadian a twenty-five cent bill.
– ORIGIN so named because of the resemblance to a square piece of paper soaked in vinegar and used to bandage the shin.

shin splints ▶ **plural n.** [treated as sing. or pl.] acute pain in the shin and lower leg caused by prolonged running, typically on hard surfaces.

Shin·to /'SHin,tō/ ▶ **n.** a Japanese religion dating from the early 8th century and incorporating the worship of ancestors and nature spirits and a belief in sacred power (**kami**) in both animate and inanimate things. It was the state religion of Japan until 1945. See also AMATERASU.
– DERIVATIVES **Shin·to·ism** /-izəm/ **n.**, **Shin·to·ist** /-ist/ **n.**
– ORIGIN Japanese, from Chinese *shen dao* 'way of the gods.'

shin·ty /'SHin(t)ē/ ▶ **n.** (pl. **shinties**) a Scottish game resembling field hockey, played by two teams of twelve with curved sticks and a leather-covered cork ball.
– ORIGIN mid 18th cent. (earlier as *shinny*): apparently from the cry *shin ye, shin you, shin t' ye,* used in the game, of unknown origin.

shin·y /'SHīnē/ ▶ **adj.** (**shinier**, **shiniest**) (of a smooth surface) reflecting light, typically because very clean or polished: *shiny hair | shiny black shoes.*
– DERIVATIVES **shin·i·ly** /-əlē/ **adv.**, **shin·i·ness n.**

ship /SHip/ ▶ **n.** a vessel larger than a boat for transporting people or goods by sea. ■ a sailing vessel with a bowsprit and three or more square-rigged masts. ■ informal any boat, esp. a racing boat. ■ a spaceship. ■ an aircraft.
▶ **v.** (**ships**, **shipping**, **shipped**) [with obj.] **1** transport (goods or people) on a ship: *the wounded soldiers were shipped home.* ■ send by some other means of transport or by mail: *the freight would be shipped by rail | spare parts were quickly shipped out.* ■ [no obj.] (of a product) be made available for purchase: *the cellular phone is expected to ship at about $500 sometime this summer.* ■ [no obj.] (**ship out**) (of a naval force) go to sea from a home port: *Bob got sick a week before we shipped out.* ■ [no obj.] dated embark on a ship: *people wishing to get from London to New York ship at Liverpool.* ■ [no obj.] (of a sailor) serve on a ship: *Jack, you shipped with the Admiral once, didn't you?*
2 (of a boat) take in (water) over the side.
3 take (oars) from the oarlocks and lay them inside a boat. ■ fix (something such as a rudder or mast) in its place on a ship.
– PHRASES **a sinking ship** used in various phrases to describe an organization or endeavor that is failing, usually in the context of criticizing someone for leaving it: *they have fled like rats from a sinking ship.* **take ship** set off on a voyage by ship; embark: *finally, he took ship for Boston.* **when one's ship comes in** when one's fortune is made.
– PHRASAL VERBS **ship out ship something out** send (goods) to a distributor or customer, esp. by ship.
– DERIVATIVES **ship·less adj.**, **ship·pa·ble adj.**
– ORIGIN Old English *scip* (noun), late Old English *scipian* (verb), of Germanic origin; related to Dutch *schip* and German *Schiff.*

-ship ▶ **suffix** forming nouns: **1** denoting a quality or condition: *companionship | friendship.*
2 denoting status, office, or honor: *ambassadorship | citizenship.* ■ denoting a tenure of office: *chairmanship.*
3 denoting a skill in a certain capacity: *entrepreneurship.*
4 denoting the collective individuals of a group: *membership.*
– ORIGIN Old English *-scipe, scype,* of Germanic origin.

ship·board /'SHip,bôrd/ ▶ **n.** [as modifier] used or occurring on board a ship: *playing in a shipboard jazz orchestra.*
– PHRASES **on shipboard** on board a ship.

ship·break·er /'SHip,brākər/ ▶ **n.** a contractor who breaks up old ships for scrap.

ship·bro·ker /'SHip,brōkər/ ▶ **n.** a broker who specializes in arranging charters, cargo space, and passenger bookings on ships.

ship·build·er /'SHip,bildər/ ▶ **n.** a person or company whose job or business is the design and construction of ships.
– DERIVATIVES **ship·build·ing** /-,bildiNG/ **n.**

ship ca·nal ▶ **n.** a canal wide and deep enough for ships to transit it.

ship chan·dler ▶ **n.** see CHANDLER.

ship·fe·ver ▶ **n.** typhus.

ship fit·ter ▶ **n.** a person employed to manufacture or assemble the structural parts of a ship.

ship·lap /'SHip,lap/ ▶ **v.** [with obj.] fit (boards) together by halving so that each overlaps the one below: (as adj. **shiplapped**) *shiplapped pine used as facing for the first floor.*
▶ **n.** boards that have been fitted together in this way, typically used for cladding. ■ [usu. as modifier] a joint between boards made by halving: *a shiplap joint.*

ship·load /'SHip,lōd/ ▶ **n.** as much cargo or as many people as a ship can carry.

ship·mas·ter /'SHip,mastər/ ▶ **n.** a ship's captain.

ship·mate /'SHip,māt/ ▶ **n.** a fellow member of a ship's crew.

ship·ment /'SHipmənt/ ▶ **n.** the action of shipping goods: *logs waiting for shipment | shipments begin this month.* ■ a quantity of goods shipped; a consignment: *coal and oil shipments.*

ship of the des·ert ▶ **n.** literary a camel.

ship of the line ▶ **n.** historical a sailing warship of the largest size, used in the line of battle.

ship·own·er /'SHip,ōnər/ ▶ **n.** a person or company owning a ship or a share in a ship.

ship·per /'SHipər/ ▶ **n.** a person or company that sends or transports goods by sea, land, or air.
– ORIGIN late Old English *scipere* 'sailor' Current senses date from the mid 18th cent.

ship·ping /'SHipiNG/ ▶ **n.** ships considered collectively, esp. those in a particular area or belonging to a particular country: *the volume of shipping using these ports.* ■ the transport of goods by sea or some other means. ■ a charge imposed by a retail company to send merchandise to a customer: *statues were available at $20 plus $4 for shipping and handling.*

ship·ping a·gent ▶ **n.** a licensed agent in a port who transacts or supervises a ship's business, such as customs and immigration procedures, insurance, or documentation, on behalf of the owner.

ship-rigged ▶ **adj.** (of a sailing ship) square-rigged.

Ship·rock /'SHip,räk/ an eroded volcanic feature that stands above the desert in northwestern New Mexico near the Four Corners. Sacred to the Navajo, it served as a landmark for travelers.

ship's bis·cuit ▶ **n.** British term for HARDTACK.

ship's boat ▶ **n.** a small boat carried on board a ship.

ship's com·pa·ny ▶ **n.** the crew of a ship.

ship·shape /'SHip,SHāp/ ▶ **adj.** in good order; trim and neat: *he checked that everything was shipshape.*

ship's hus·band ▶ **n.** an agent who is responsible for providing maintenance and supplies for a ship in port.
– DERIVATIVES **ship's hus·band·ry n.**

ship's pa·pers ▶ **plural n.** documents establishing the details of a ship, including ownership, nationality, and the nature of the cargo.

ship-to-shore ▶ **adj.** from a ship to land: *ship-to-shore phone calls.*
▶ **n.** a radiotelephone connecting a ship to land, or connecting a train or other vehicle to a control center.

ship·way /'SHip,wā/ ▶ **n.** a slope on which a ship is built and down which it slides to be launched.

ship·worm /'SHip,wərm/ ▶ **n.** another term for TEREDO.

ship·wreck /'SHip,rek/ ▶ **n.** the destruction of a ship at sea by sinking or breaking up, e.g., in a storm or after running aground. ■ a ship so destroyed: *the detritus of a forgotten shipwreck in an Arctic sea.*
▶ **v.** (**be shipwrecked**) (of a person or ship) suffer a shipwreck: *he was shipwrecked off the coast of Sardinia and nearly drowned | figurative her right to a fair trial might be shipwrecked by prosecutorial misconduct.*

ship·wright /'SHip,rīt/ ▶ **n.** a shipbuilder.

ship·yard /'SHip,yärd/ ▶ **n.** a place where ships are built and repaired.

Shi·ras /'SHīrəs/, George, Jr. (1832–1924), US Supreme Court associate justice 1892–1903. He was appointed to the Court by President Benjamin Harrison.

Shi·raz¹ /SHi'räz/ a city in southwest central Iran; pop. 1,227,331 (2006).

Shi·raz² /SH(i)ə'räz/ ▶ **n.** a variety of black wine grape. ■ a red wine made from this grape.
– ORIGIN from SHIRAZ¹, apparently an alteration of French *syrah,* influenced by the belief that the vine was brought from Iran by the Crusades.

shire /SHī(ə)r/ ▶ **n.** Brit. a county, esp. in England. ■ (**the Shires**) used in reference to parts of England regarded as strongholds of traditional rural culture, esp. the rural Midlands.
– ORIGIN Old English *scir* 'care, official charge, county,' of Germanic origin.

-shire ▶ **comb. form** forming the names of counties: *Oxfordshire | Yorkshire.*

shire coun·ty ▶ **n.** (in the UK) a nonmetropolitan county (in existence since 1974).

shire horse ▶ **n.** a heavy powerful horse of a draft breed, originally from the English Midlands.

shirk /SHərk/ ▶ **v.** [with obj.] avoid or neglect (a duty or responsibility): *their sole motive is to shirk responsibility and rip off the company.* ■ [no obj.] [usu. with negative] (**shirk from**) be unwilling to do (something difficult): *we will not shirk from closing a school if the evidence should justify it.*
▶ **n.** archaic a person who shirks.
– DERIVATIVES **shirk·er n.**
– ORIGIN mid 17th cent. (in the sense 'practice fraud or trickery'): from obsolete *shirk* 'sponger,' perhaps from German *Schurke* 'scoundrel.'

shirr /SHər/ ▶ **v.** [with obj.] **1** gather (an area of fabric or part of a garment) by means of drawn or elasticized threads in parallel rows: (as adj. **shirred**) *a swimsuit with a shirred front* | (as noun **shirring**) *shirring is flattering to all figure types.*
2 bake (an egg without its shell).
– ORIGIN mid 19th cent.: of unknown origin.

shirt /SHərt/ ▶ **n.** a garment for the upper body made of cotton or a similar fabric, with a collar, sleeves, and buttons down the front. ■ [usu. with modifier] a similar garment of stretchable material with few or no buttons, typically worn as casual wear or for sports: *a rugby shirt.*
– PHRASES **keep your shirt on** informal don't lose your temper; stay calm. **lose one's shirt** informal lose all one's possessions. **the shirt off one's back** informal one's last remaining possessions: *we share things—we'd give our shirt off our back to another.*
– DERIVATIVES **shirt·ed adj.** [often in combination] *the black-shirted balladeer,* **shirt·less adj.**
– ORIGIN Old English *scyrte,* of Germanic origin; related to Old Norse *skyrta* (compare with SKIRT), Dutch *schort,* German *Schürze* 'apron,' also to SHORT; probably from a base meaning 'short garment.'

shirt·dress /'SHərt,dres/ ▶ **n.** a dress with a collar and buttons in the style of a shirt, typically cut without a seam at the waist.

shirt·front /'SHərt,frənt/ ▶ **n.** the breast of a shirt, in particular the part that shows when a suit is worn.

shirt·ing /'SHərtiNG/ ▶ **n.** a material for making shirts, esp. a fine cotton in plain colors or incorporating a traditional woven stripe.

shirt·sleeve /'SHərt,slēv/ ▶ **n.** (usu. **shirtsleeves**) the sleeve of a shirt: *he rolled up his shirtsleeves.*
▶ **adj.** (of weather) warm enough to wear a shirt with no jacket: *the shirtsleeve November days before the hard cold set in.*
– PHRASES **in (one's) shirtsleeves** wearing a shirt with nothing over it.
– DERIVATIVES **shirt·sleeved adj.**

shirt·tail /'SHər,tāl/ ▶ **n.** (also **shirttails**) the lower, typically curved, part of a shirt that comes below the waist.
▶ **adj.** (of relatives) distantly related: *if you checked back far enough, they were shirttail cousins of Curly's parents.*

shirt·waist /'SHərt,wāst/ ▶ **n.** a woman's blouse that resembles a shirt. ■ (also **shirtwaist dress** or **shirtwaister**) a woman's dress with a seam at the waist, its bodice incorporating a collar and buttons in the style of a shirt.

shirt·y /'SHərtē/ ▶ **adj.** (**shirtier**, **shirtiest**) informal irritable; querulous: *don't get annoyed or shirty on the phone.*
– DERIVATIVES **shirt·i·ly** /-əlē/ **adv.**, **shirt·i·ness n.**

shish ke·bab /'SHiSH kə,bäb/ ▶ **n.** a dish of pieces of marinated meat and vegetables cooked and served on skewers.
– ORIGIN from Turkish *şiş kebap,* from *şiş* 'skewer' + *kebāp* 'roast meat.'

shi·so /'SHēsō/ ▶ **n.** an Asian plant of the mint family used as a culinary herb.
– ORIGIN Japanese.

shit /SHit/ vulgar slang ▶ **n. 1** feces. ■ [in sing.] an act of defecating.
2 a contemptible or worthless person.
3 something worthless; garbage; nonsense. ■ unpleasant experiences or treatment.
4 personal belongings; stuff.
5 any psychoactive drug, esp. marijuana.
▶ **v.** (**shits**, **shitting**; past and past participle **shitted** or **shit** or **shat** /SHat/) **1** [no obj.] expel feces from the body. ■ (**shit oneself**) soil one's clothes as a result

of expelling feces accidentally. ■ (**shit oneself**) be very frightened.
2 [with obj.] tease or try to deceive (someone): *I shit you not.*
▶ **exclam.** an exclamation of disgust, anger, or annoyance.
– PHRASES **beat the shit out of** see **BEAT**. **be shitting bricks** be extremely nervous or frightened. **eat shit** an exclamation expressing anger or contempt for, or rejection of, someone. **get one's shit together** organize oneself so as to be able to deal with or achieve something. **in deep shit** (or **in the shit**) in trouble; in a difficult situation. **no shit** used to seek confirmation of the truth of a statement or to confirm the truth of a statement. **not give a shit** not care at all. **not know shit** not know anything. **not worth a shit** worthless. **shit for brains** a stupid person. **shit on someone** show contempt or disregard for someone. **be up shit** (or **shit's**) **creek** (**without a paddle**) be in an awkward predicament. **when the shit hits the fan** when the disastrous consequences of something become public.
– ORIGIN Old English *scitte* 'diarrhea,' of Germanic origin; related to Dutch *schijten*, German *scheissen* (verb). The term was originally neutral and used without vulgar connotation.

shit·bag /'SHit,bag/ ▶ **n.** vulgar slang a contemptible or worthless person.

shit·can /'SHit,kan/ ▶ **v.** (**shitcans, shitcanning, shitcanned**) [with obj.] vulgar slang throw (something) away: *rip up those pictures and shitcan the negatives.* ■ discard or reject (someone or something): *it's hard to shitcan someone who keeps winning writing awards.*

shite /SHīt/ ▶ **n. & exclam.** Brit. vulgar slang another term for **SHIT**.

shit-eat·ing ▶ **adj.** vulgar slang smug; self-satisfied.

shite·poke /'SHīt,pōk/ ▶ **n.** informal any of a number of birds of the heron family. ● Several species in the family Ardeidae, in particular the green-backed *Butorides striatus*.
– ORIGIN late 18th cent.: from **SHITE** (because of the bird's habit of defecating when disturbed) + the noun **POKE**[1].

shit·face /'SHit,fās/ ▶ **n.** vulgar slang an obnoxious person.

shit-faced (also **shitfaced**) ▶ **adj.** [predic.] vulgar slang drunk or under the influence of drugs.

shit·head /'SHit,hed/ ▶ **n.** vulgar slang a contemptible person.

shit·hole /'SHit,hōl/ ▶ **n.** vulgar slang an extremely dirty, shabby, or otherwise unpleasant place.

shit·house /'SHit,hous/ ▶ **n.** vulgar slang a toilet. ■ an extremely unpleasant place.
– PHRASES **be built like a brick shithouse 1** (of a person) having a very solid physique. **2** (of a woman) having a very attractive figure.

shit·kick·er /'SHit,kikər/ ▶ **n.** vulgar slang **1** an unsophisticated or oafish person, esp. one from a rural area.
2 a person who listens to or performs country music.
3 (**shitkickers**) substantially made boots with thick soles and typically with reinforced toes.
– DERIVATIVES **shit·kick·ing** /-,kiking/ **adj.**

shit·less /'SHitlis/ ▶ **adj.** (in phrase **be scared** (or **bored**) **shitless**) vulgar slang be extremely frightened (or bored).

shit list (also **shitlist**) ▶ **n.** vulgar slang a list of those whom one dislikes or plans to harm.

shit·load /'SHit,lōd/ ▶ **n.** vulgar slang a large amount or number: *I have a shitload of work to do this week.*
– ORIGIN 1960s: from *shit* + *load*.

shit-scared ▶ **adj.** vulgar slang terrified.

shit stir·rer ▶ **n.** vulgar slang a person who takes pleasure in causing trouble or discord.
– DERIVATIVES **shit stir·ring n.**

shit·storm /'SHit,stôrm/ ▶ **n.** vulgar slang a situation marked by violent controversy.

shit·ty /'SHitē/ ▶ **adj.** (**shittier, shittiest**) vulgar slang **1** (of a person or action) contemptible; worthless. ■ (of an experience or situation) unpleasant; awful.
2 covered with excrement.

shit·work /'SHit,wərk/ ▶ **n.** vulgar slang work considered to be menial or routine.

shi·ur /SHē'o͝or/ ▶ **n.** (pl. **shiurim** /SHē'o͝orim, SHēo͝o'rēm/) Judaism a Talmudic study session, usually led by a rabbi.

shiv /SHiv/ ▶ **n.** informal a knife or razor used as a weapon.
– ORIGIN probably from Romany *chiv* 'blade.'

Shi·va /'SHēvə/ (also **Siva**) (in Indian religion) a god associated with the powers of reproduction and dissolution.

Shiva is regarded by some as the supreme being and by others as forming a triad with Brahma and Vishnu. He is worshiped in many aspects: as destroyer, ascetic, lord of the cosmic dance, and lord of beasts, and through the symbolic lingam. His wife is Parvati.

– ORIGIN from Sanskrit *Śiva*, literally 'the auspicious one.'

Shiva

shi·va /'SHivə/ (also **shivah**) ▶ **n.** Judaism a period of seven days' formal mourning for the dead, beginning immediately after the funeral: *she went to her sister's funeral and sat shiva.*
– ORIGIN from Hebrew *šib'āh* 'seven.'

Shi·va·ji /'SHivəjē/ (also **Sivaji**) (1627–80), Indian raja of the Marathas 1674–80. He raised a successful Hindu revolt against Muslim rule in 1659 and expanded Maratha territory.

shiv·a·ree ▶ **n.** variant spelling of **CHARIVARI**.

shive /SHīv/ ▶ **n.** a broad plug hammered into a hole in the top of a cask when the cask has been filled.
– ORIGIN Middle English: related to **SHEAVE**. The original sense was 'slice (of bread),' later 'piece of split wood'; the current sense dates from the mid 19th cent.

shiv·er[1] /'SHivər/ ▶ **v.** [no obj.] (of a person or animal) shake slightly and uncontrollably as a result of being cold, frightened, or excited: *they shivered in the damp foggy cold.*
▶ **n.** a momentary trembling movement: *she gave a little shiver as the wind flicked at her bare arms | the way he looked at her sent shivers down her spine.* ■ (**the shivers**) a spell or an attack of trembling, typically as a result of fear or horror: *a look that gave him the shivers.*
– DERIVATIVES **shiv·er·er n., shiv·er·ing·ly adv.**
– ORIGIN Middle English *chivere*, perhaps an alteration of dialect *chavele* 'to chatter,' from Old English *ceafl* 'jaw.'

shiv·er[2] ▶ **n.** (usu. **shivers**) each of the small fragments into which something such as glass is shattered when broken; a splinter.
▶ **v.** [no obj.] rare break into such splinters or fragments: *the world seemed to shiver into a million splinters of prismatic color.*
– PHRASES **shiver my** (or **me**) **timbers** a mock oath attributed to sailors.
– ORIGIN Middle English: from a Germanic base meaning 'to split'; related to German *Schiefer* 'slate.'

shiv·er·y /'SHiv(ə)rē/ ▶ **adj.** shaking or trembling as a result of cold, illness, fear, or excitement: *he felt cold and shivery.*

Shiv Se·na /SHiv 'sānə/ ▶ **n.** a Hindu nationalist organization centered in Maharashtra.
– ORIGIN from Sanskrit *śiva* 'auspicious' + *sena* 'army.'

Shi·zu·o·ka /,SHēzo͞o'ōkä/ a port on the southern coast of the island of Honshu in Japan; pop. 711,882 (2007).

shle·miel /SHlə'mēl/ ▶ **n.** variant spelling of **SCHLEMIEL**.

shlep ▶ **v.** variant spelling of **SCHLEP**.

shlock ▶ **n.** variant spelling of **SCHLOCK**.

shlub /SHləb/ ▶ **n.** variant spelling of **SCHLUB**.

shm ▶ **abbr.** simple harmonic motion.

shmat·te /'SHmätə/ ▶ **n.** variant spelling of **SCHMATTE**.

shmear /SHmi(ə)r/ (also **shmeer**) ▶ **n. & v.** variant spelling of **SCHMEAR**.

shmo /SHmō/ ▶ **n.** (pl. **shmoes**) variant spelling of **SCHMO**.

shmuck ▶ **n.** variant spelling of **SCHMUCK**.

sho /SHō/ ▶ **adv.** nonstandard spelling of **SURE**, representing its pronunciation in the southern US: *I sho is glad to see ya.*
– PHRASES **sho nuff** nonstandard spelling of **SHO** (see **SURE**): *you sho nuff got some foxes in this here town!*

Sho·ah /'SHōə, SHō'ä/ ▶ **n.** (**the Shoah**) another term for **THE HOLOCAUST** (see **HOLOCAUST** (sense 1)).
– ORIGIN modern Hebrew, literally 'catastrophe.'

shoal[1] /SHōl/ ▶ **n.** a large number of fish swimming together: *a shoal of bream.* Compare with **SCHOOL**[2]. ■ informal a large number of people: *a rock star's entrance, first proceeding with his shoal of attendants.*
▶ **v.** [no obj.] (of fish) form shoals.
– ORIGIN late 16th cent.: probably from Middle Dutch *schōle* 'troop.' Compare with **SCHOOL**[2].

shoal[2] ▶ **n.** an area of shallow water, esp. as a navigational hazard. ■ a submerged sandbank visible at low water. ■ (usu. **shoals**) a hidden danger or difficulty: *he alone could safely guide them through Hollywood's treacherous shoals.*
▶ **v.** [no obj.] (of water) become shallower.
▶ **adj.** (of water) shallow.
– DERIVATIVES **shoal·y adj.**
– ORIGIN Old English *sceald* (adjective), of Germanic origin; related to **SHALLOW**.

shoat /SHōt/ (also **shote**) ▶ **n.** a young pig, esp. one that is newly weaned.
– ORIGIN late Middle English: of unknown origin; compare with West Flemish *schote*.

sho·chet /'SHōKHāt, -KHit, 'SHoi-, SHō'KHet/ ▶ **n.** (pl. **shochetim** /SHōKH'tēm/) a person officially certified as competent to kill cattle and poultry in the manner prescribed by Jewish law.
– ORIGIN late 19th cent.: from Hebrew *šōḥēṭ* 'slaughtering.'

sho·chu /'SHōCHo͞o/ ▶ **n.** a rough Japanese liquor distilled from any of various ingredients, including sake dregs.
– ORIGIN from Japanese *shōchū*.

shock[1] /SHäk/ ▶ **n. 1** a sudden upsetting or surprising event or experience: *it was a shock to face such hostile attitudes when I arrived.* ■ a feeling of disturbed surprise resulting from such an event: *her death gave us all a terrible shock | her eyes opened wide in shock.* ■ an acute medical condition associated with a fall in blood pressure, caused by such events as loss of blood, severe burns, bacterial infection, allergic reaction, or sudden emotional stress, and marked by cold, pallid skin, irregular breathing, rapid pulse, and dilated pupils: *he died of shock due to massive abdominal hemorrhage.* ■ a disturbance causing instability in an economy: *trading imbalances caused by the two oil shocks.* ■ short for **ELECTRIC SHOCK**.
2 a violent shaking movement caused by an impact, explosion, or tremor: *earthquake shocks | rackets today don't bend or absorb shock the way wooden rackets do.* ■ short for **SHOCK ABSORBER**.
▶ **v. 1** [with obj.] cause (someone) to feel surprised and upset: *she was shocked at the state of his injuries.* ■ offend the moral feelings of; outrage: *the revelations shocked the nation.* ■ [no obj.] experience such feelings: *he shocked so easily.* ■ (usu. **be shocked**) affect with physiological shock, or with an electric shock.
2 [no obj.] archaic collide violently: *carriage after carriage shocked fiercely against the engine.*
– DERIVATIVES **shock·a·bil·i·ty** /-ə'bilitē/ **n., shock·a·ble adj.**
– ORIGIN mid 16th cent.: from French *choc* (noun), *choquer* (verb), of unknown origin. The original senses were 'throw (troops) into confusion by charging at them' and 'an encounter between charging forces,' giving rise to the notion of 'sudden violent blow or impact.'

shock[2] ▶ **n.** a group of twelve sheaves of grain placed upright and supporting each other to allow the grain to dry and ripen.
▶ **v.** [with obj.] arrange (sheaves of grain) in such a group.
– ORIGIN Middle English: perhaps from Middle Dutch and Middle Low German *schok*, of unknown origin.

shock[3] ▶ **n.** an unkempt or thick mass of hair: *a slender man with an untamable shock of black hair.*
– ORIGIN mid 17th cent.: origin uncertain; compare with obsolete *shough*, denoting a breed of lapdog. The word originally denoted a dog with long shaggy hair, and was then used as an adjective meaning 'unkempt, shaggy.' The current sense dates from the early 19th cent.

shock ab·sorb·er ▶ **n.** a device for absorbing jolts and vibrations, esp. on a motor vehicle.

shock cord ▶ **n.** heavy elasticized cord; bungee cord.

shock·er /'SHäkər/ ▶ **n.** informal **1** something that shocks, esp. through being unacceptable or sensational: *the play's penultimate sequence is a shocker.* ■ a person who behaves badly or acts in a sensational manner: *I was a shocker when I was younger.*
2 Brit. a shock absorber.

S

shock·head·ed /ˈSHäkˌhedid/ ▸ **adj.** having thick, shaggy, and unkempt hair.

shock·ing /ˈSHäkiNG/ ▸ **adj.** causing indignation or disgust; offensive: *shocking behavior.* ■ causing a feeling of surprise and dismay: *she brought shocking news.*
– DERIVATIVES **shock·ing·ly adv., shock·ing·ness n.**

shock·ing pink ▸ **n.** a vibrant shade of pink.

shock jock ▸ **n.** a disc jockey on a talk-radio show who expresses opinions in a deliberately offensive or provocative way.

Shock·ley /ˈSHäklē/, William (Bradford) (1910–89), US physicist, born in Britain. Shockley and his researchers at Bell Laboratories developed the transistor in 1948. He later became a controversial figure because of his views on race and intelligence. Nobel Prize for Physics (1956), shared with John Bardeen and Walter Brattain.

shock·proof /ˈSHäkˌpro͞of/ ▸ **adj. 1** designed to resist damage when dropped or knocked: *a shockproof watch.*
2 not easily shocked: *the teacher puts them at ease by her shockproof attitude toward ignorance.*

shock stall ▸ **n.** a marked increase in drag and a loss of lift and control on an aircraft approaching the speed of sound.

shock tac·tics ▸ **plural n.** a strategy using sudden violent or extreme action to shock someone into doing something.

shock ther·a·py (also **shock treatment**) ▸ **n.** treatment of chronic mental conditions by electroconvulsive therapy or by inducing physiological shock. ■ sudden and drastic measures taken to solve an intractable problem.

shock troops ▸ **plural n.** a group of soldiers trained specially for carrying out a sudden assault.

shock wave ▸ **n.** a sharp change of pressure in a narrow region traveling through a medium, esp. air, caused by explosion or by a body moving faster than sound. ■ (usu. **shock waves**) a widespread feeling of shock caused by an unexpected event: *the oil embargo sent shock waves through the American economy.*

shock work·er ▸ **n.** (in the former Soviet Union) a worker whose group exceeded production quotas and was assigned to a particularly urgent or arduous task.

shod /SHäd/ past and past participle of **SHOE**.

shod·dy /ˈSHädē/ ▸ **adj.** (**shoddier, shoddiest**) badly made or done: *we're not paying good money for shoddy goods.* ■ lacking moral principle; sordid: *a shoddy misuse of the honor system.*
▸ **n.** an inferior quality yarn or fabric made from the shredded fiber of waste woolen cloth or clippings.
– DERIVATIVES **shod·di·ly** /-əlē/ **adv., shod·di·ness n.**
– ORIGIN mid 19th cent.: of unknown origin.

shoe /SHo͞o/ ▸ **n. 1** a covering for the foot, typically made of leather, with a sturdy sole and not reaching above the ankle. ■ a horseshoe.
2 something resembling a shoe in shape or use, in particular: ■ a drag for a wheel. ■ short for **BRAKE SHOE**. ■ a socket, esp. on a camera, for fitting a flash unit or other accessory. ■ a metal rim or ferrule, esp. on the runner of a sled. ■ a box from which cards are dealt in casinos at baccarat or some other card games.
▸ **v.** (**shoes, shoeing** /ˈSHo͞oiNG/; past and past participle **shod** /SHäd/) [with obj.] fit (a horse) with a shoe or shoes. ■ (**be shod**) [with adverbial] (of a person) be wearing shoes of a specified kind: *his large feet were shod in sneakers.* ■ protect (the end of an object such as a pole) with a metal shoe: *the four wooden balks were each shod with heavy iron heads.* ■ fit a tire to (a wheel).
– PHRASES **be** (or **put oneself**) **in another person's shoes** be (or put oneself) in another person's situation or predicament: *if I'd been in your shoes I'd have walked out on him.* **dead men's shoes** property or a position coveted by a prospective successor but available only on a person's death. **if the shoe fits, wear it** used as a way of suggesting that someone should accept a generalized remark or criticism as applying to themselves. **the shoe** (or Brit. **boot**) **is on the other foot** the situation, in particular the holding of advantage, has reversed. **shoe leather** informal used in reference to the wear on shoes through walking: *you can save on shoe leather by giving us your instructions over the telephone.* **wait for the other shoe to drop** informal be prepared for a further or consequential event or complication to occur.
– DERIVATIVES **shoe·less adj.**
– ORIGIN Old English *scōh* (noun), *scōg(e)an* (verb), of Germanic origin; related to Dutch *schoen* and German *Schuh*.

shoe·bill /ˈSHo͞oˌbil/ ▸ **n.** an African stork with gray plumage and a very large bill shaped like a wooden shoe. ● *Balaeniceps rex*, the only member of the family Balaenicipitidae.

shoe·black /ˈSHo͞oˌblak/ ▸ **n.** dated, chiefly Brit. a person who shines the shoes of passersby for payment.

shoe·box /ˈSHo͞oˌbäks/ ▸ **n.** a box in which a pair of shoes is delivered or sold. ■ used in references to small or uniform rooms or spaces: *a shoebox of a room.*

shoe·gaz·ing /ˈSHo͞oˌgāziNG/ ▸ **n.** a style of rock music characterized by a sound in which the distinctions between separate instruments and vocals are blurred.
– ORIGIN 1990s: from the supposed tendency of the performers to look down, rather than at the audience.

shoe·horn /ˈSHo͞oˌhôrn/ ▸ **n.** a curved instrument used to ease one's heel into a shoe.
▸ **v.** [with obj.] force into an inadequate space: *people were shoehorned into cramped corners.*

shoe·lace /ˈSHo͞oˌlās/ ▸ **n.** a cord or leather strip passed through eyelets or hooks on opposite sides of a shoe and pulled tight and fastened.

Shoe·mak·er /ˈSHo͞oˌmākər/, Willie (1931–2003), US jockey; full name *William Lee Shoemaker*. He held the record in horse racing for all-time career wins (8,833) from 1970 until 1999. He won the Kentucky Derby four times (1955, 1959, 1965, 1986), the Belmont Stakes five times (1957, 1959, 1962, 1967, 1975), and the Preakness twice (1963, 1967).

shoe·mak·er /ˈSHo͞oˌmākər/ ▸ **n.** a person who makes shoes and other footwear as a profession.
– DERIVATIVES **shoe·mak·ing** /-ˌmākiNG/ **n.**

Shoe·mak·er–Le·vy 9 /ˈSHo͞oˌmākər ˈlēvē ˈnīn/ a comet discovered in March 1993, when it had just broken up as a result of passing very close to Jupiter. In July 1994 more than twenty separate fragments impacted successively on Jupiter, causing large explosions in its atmosphere.
– ORIGIN named after Carolyn (1929–) and Eugene *Shoemaker* (1928–97), US astronomers, and David *Levy* (1948–), Canadian astronomer, discoverers of the comet.

shoe·pac /ˈSHo͞oˌpak/ (also **shoepack**) ▸ **n.** a commercially manufactured oiled leather boot, typically having a rubber sole.
– ORIGIN mid 18th cent.: from Delaware (Unami) *sippack* 'shoes,' from *čipahkpo* 'moccasins,' later assimilated to **SHOE**.

shoe·shine /ˈSHo͞oˌSHīn/ ▸ **n.** an act of polishing someone's shoes, esp. for payment: [as modifier] *a shoeshine boy.*
– DERIVATIVES **shoe·shin·er n.**

shoe·string /ˈSHo͞oˌstriNG/ ▸ **n. 1** informal a small or inadequate budget: *they proved capable of producing high-quality material **on a shoestring*** | [as modifier] *a shoestring budget.*
2 a shoelace.
▸ **adj.** [attrib.] (of a save or tackle in sports) near or around the ankles or feet, or just above the ground.

shoe·string po·ta·toes ▸ **plural n.** potatoes cut into long thin strips and deep-fried.

shoe tree ▸ **n.** a shaped block inserted into a shoe when it is not being worn, to keep the shoe in shape.

sho·far /ˈSHōfər, SHōˈfär/ ▸ **n.** (pl. **shofars** or **shofroth** /SHōˈfrōt, -ˈfrōs/) a ram's-horn trumpet used by ancient Jews in religious ceremonies and as a battle signal, now sounded at Rosh Hashanah and Yom Kippur.
– ORIGIN from Hebrew *šōpār*, (plural) *šōpārōṯ*.

sho·gun /ˈSHōgən/ ▸ **n.** a hereditary commander-in-chief in feudal Japan. Because of the military power concentrated in his hands and the consequent weakness of the nominal head of state (the mikado or emperor), the shogun was generally the real ruler of the country until feudalism was abolished in 1867.
– DERIVATIVES **sho·gun·ate** /-gənit, -gəˌnāt/ **n.**
– ORIGIN Japanese, from Chinese *jiāng jūn* 'general.'

sho·ji /ˈSHōjē/ (also **shoji screen**) ▸ **n.** (pl. **same** or **shojis**) (in Japan) a sliding outer or inner door made of a latticed screen covered with white paper.
– ORIGIN from Japanese *shōji*.

sho·jo /ˈSHōˌjō/ ▸ **n.** manga intended for a primarily female audience.
– ORIGIN from Japanese *shojo manga* 'girls' comics.'

Sho·la·pur variant spelling of **SOLAPUR**.

Sho·lom A·leich·em /ˈSHōləm əˈlākəm/ (1859–1916), US Yiddish writer; born in Ukraine; born *Solomon J. Rabinowitz*. He wrote about common Russian Jews who lived in small towns. His stories, esp. *Tevye's Daughters* (1894) formed the basis for the musical *Fiddler on the Roof* (1964).

Sho·na /ˈSHōnə/ ▸ **n.** (pl. **same** or **Shonas**) **1** a member of a group of peoples inhabiting parts of southern Africa. See also **MASHONA**.
2 any of the Bantu languages spoken by these peoples.
▸ **adj.** of or relating to the Shona or their languages.
– ORIGIN a local name.

shone /SHōn/ past and past participle of **SHINE**.

shoo /SHo͞o/ ▸ **exclam.** a word said to frighten or drive away a person or animal.
▸ **v.** (**shoos, shooing, shooed** /SHo͞od/) [with obj.] make (a person or animal) go away by waving one's arms at them, saying "shoo," or otherwise acting in a discouraging manner: *I went to comfort her but she shooed me away.*
– ORIGIN a natural exclamation: first recorded in late Middle English. The verb use dates from the early 17th cent.

shoo-fly pie (also **shoofly pie**) ▸ **n.** a rich pie made with molasses and topped with crumbs.
– ORIGIN from the US interjection *shoo-fly* (referring to the need to wave flies away from the sweet treacle).

shoo-in ▸ **n.** a person or thing that is certain to succeed, esp. someone who is certain to win a competition: *he was a shoo-in for re-election.*
– ORIGIN 1930s: from the earlier use of the term denoting the winner of a rigged horse race.

shook[1] /SHo͝ok/ past of **SHAKE** ▸ **adj.** [predic.] (**shook up**) informal emotionally or physically disturbed; upset: *she looks pretty shook up from the letter.*

shook[2] ▸ **n.** a set of components ready for assembly into a box or cask.
– ORIGIN late 18th cent.: of unknown origin.

shoot /SHo͞ot/ ▸ **v.** (past and past participle **shot** /SHät/)
1 [with obj.] kill or wound (a person or animal) with a bullet or arrow: *he was shot in the leg during an armed robbery* | [with obj. and complement] *troops shot dead 29 people.* ■ [no obj.] fire a bullet from a gun or discharge an arrow from a bow: *he shot at me twice* | *the troops were ordered to **shoot to kill*** | [with obj.] *they shot a volley of arrows into the village.* ■ cause (a gun) to fire. ■ damage or remove (something) with a bullet or missile: *Guy, shoot their hats off.* ■ [no obj.] hunt game with a gun: *we go to Scotland to shoot every autumn.* ■ [no obj.] (**shoot over**) shoot game over (an estate or other area of countryside). ■ shoot game in or on (an estate, cover, etc.).
2 [no obj.] move suddenly and rapidly in a particular direction: *the car shot forward* | *Ward's hand shot out, grabbing his arm.* ■ [with obj.] cause to move suddenly and rapidly in a particular direction: *he would have fallen if Marc hadn't shot out a hand to stop him* | *Beauchamp shot United into the lead.* ■ [with obj.] direct (a glance, question, or remark) at someone: [with two objs.] *Luke shot her a quick glance* | [with direct speech] *"I can't believe what I'm hearing," she shot back.* ■ used to invite a comment or question: *"May I just ask you one more question?" "Shoot."* ■ (of a pain) move with a sharp stabbing sensation: *Claudia felt a shaft of pain shoot through her chest* | figurative *a pang of regret shot through her.* ■ [with obj.] (of a boat) sweep swiftly down or under (rapids, a waterfall, or a bridge). ■ [with obj.] informal (of a motor vehicle) pass (a traffic light at red). ■ extend sharply in a particular direction: *a road that seemed to just shoot upward at a terrifying angle.* ■ [with obj.] move (a door bolt) to fasten or unfasten a door.
3 [no obj.] (in soccer, hockey, basketball, etc.) kick, hit, or throw the ball or puck in an attempt to score a goal: *Williams twice shot wide* | [with obj.] *after school, we'd go straight out in the alley to shoot baskets.* ■ [with obj.] informal make (a specified score) for a round of golf: *in the second round he shot a 65.* ■ [with obj.] informal play a game of (pool or dice).
4 [with obj.] film or photograph (a scene, film, etc.): *she has just been commissioned to shoot a video* | [no obj.] *point the camera and just shoot—nothing could be easier.*
5 [no obj.] (of a plant or seed) send out buds or shoots; germinate. ■ (of a bud or shoot) appear; sprout.
6 [with obj.] informal inject oneself or another person with (a narcotic drug): *he shot dope into his arm.*
7 [with obj.] plane (the edge of a board) accurately.
▸ **n. 1** a young branch or sucker springing from the main stock of a tree or other plant: *he nipped off the new shoots that grew where the leaves joined the stems.*
2 an occasion when a group of people hunt and shoot game for sport: *a grouse shoot.* ■ Brit. land used for shooting game. ■ a shooting match or contest: *activities include a weekly rifle shoot.*
3 an occasion when a professional photographer takes photographs or when a film or video is being made: *a photo shoot* | *a fashion shoot.*
4 variant spelling of **CHUTE**[1].
5 a rapid in a stream: *follow the portages that skirt all nine shoots of whitewater.*
▸ **exclam.** informal used as a euphemism for 'shit': *shoot, it was a great day to be alive.*
– PHRASES **have shot one's bolt** see **BOLT**[1]. **shoot the breeze** (or **the bull**) informal have a casual

conversation. **shoot one's cuffs** pull one's shirt cuffs out to project beyond the cuffs of one's jacket or coat. **shoot from the hip** informal react suddenly or without careful consideration of one's words or actions. **shoot oneself in the foot** informal inadvertently make a situation worse for oneself. **shoot it out** informal engage in a decisive confrontation, typically a gun battle. **shoot a line** Brit. informal describe something in an exaggerated, untruthful, or boastful way: *he never shot a line about his escapades.* **shoot one's mouth off** informal talk boastfully or indiscreetly.

– PHRASAL VERBS **shoot someone/something down** bring down an aircraft or missile by shooting at it: *their helicopter was shot down by an air-to-air missile.* ■ kill or wound someone by shooting them, esp. in a ruthless way: *troops shot down 28 demonstrators.* ■ crush someone or their opinions by forceful criticism or argument: *she tried to argue and got shot down in flames for her trouble.* **shoot through** Austral./NZ informal leave, typically to escape from or avoid someone or something: *me wife's shot through and I can't pay the rent.* [1940s: from *shoot through like a Bondi tram* (Bondi being the name of a Sydney suburb).] **shoot up 1** (esp. of a child) grow taller rapidly: *when she hit thirteen she shot up to a startling 5 foot 9.* ■ (of a price or amount) rise suddenly. **2** see SHOOT SOMEONE/SOMETHING UP below. **shoot someone/something up 1** cause great damage to something by shooting; kill or wound someone by shooting: *the police shot up our building.* **2** (also **shoot up**) informal inject a narcotic drug; inject someone with a narcotic drug: *she went home and shot up alone in her room | I was shooting up cocaine.*

– DERIVATIVES **shoot·a·ble** adj.

– ORIGIN Old English *scēotan*, of Germanic origin; related to Dutch *schieten* and German *schiessen*, also to SHEET[1], SHOT[1], and SHUT.

shoot-down ▶ n. an act or instance of bringing down an aircraft by shooting at it.

shoot-'em-up ▶ n. informal a fast-moving story or movie, of which gunfire is a dominant feature. ■ a simple computer game in which the sole objective is to kill as many enemies as possible to achieve a high score.

shoot·er /ˈSHo͞otər/ ▶ n. **1** a person who uses a gun either regularly or on a particular occasion. ■ informal a gun.
2 a member of a team in games such as basketball whose role is to attempt to score goals. ■ a person who throws a die or dice.
3 a marble used to shoot at other marbles.
4 informal a small alcoholic drink, esp. of distilled liquor: *geez, he could use a shooter of whiskey.*

shoot·ing /ˈSHo͞otiNG/ ▶ n. the action or practice of shooting: *the unprovoked shooting of civilians by soldiers | 20,000 fatal shootings a year.* ■ the sport or pastime of shooting with a gun. ■ the right of shooting game over an area of land. ■ an estate or other area rented to shoot over.
▶ adj. moving or growing quickly: *shooting beams of light played over the sea.* ■ (of a pain) sudden and piercing.

– PHRASES **the whole shooting match** informal everything: *the whole shooting match is being computerized.*

shoot·ing board ▶ n. a board with a step-shaped profile used to guide the motion of a plane relative to a workpiece to ensure accurate planing.

shoot·ing brake ▶ n. Brit. dated a station wagon.

shoot·ing coat ▶ n. a padded waterproof coat with large pockets, worn when shooting game. ■ archaic term for MORNING COAT.

shoot·ing gal·ler·y ▶ n. a room or fairground booth used for recreational shooting at targets with guns or air guns. ■ informal a place used for taking drugs, esp. injecting heroin.

shoot·ing i·ron ▶ n. informal a firearm.

shoot·ing range ▶ n. an area provided with targets for the controlled practice of shooting.

shoot·ing script ▶ n. a final movie or television script with scenes arranged in the order in which they will be filmed.

shoot·ing star[1] ▶ n. a small, rapidly moving meteor burning up on entering the earth's atmosphere.

shoot·ing star[2] ▶ n. a North American plant of the primrose family, with white, pink, or purple hanging flowers with backward curving petals. The flowers are carried above the leaves on slender stems and turn to face up following fertilization. ● Genus *Dodecatheon*, family Primulaceae: several species, esp. *D. meadia*.

shooting star[2]

shoot·ing stick ▶ n. a walking stick with a handle that unfolds to form a seat and a sharpened end that can be stuck firmly in the ground.

shoot·ing war ▶ n. a war in which there is armed conflict, as opposed to mere threats, propaganda, or sanctions.

shoot·ist /ˈSHo͞otist/ ▶ n. informal a person who shoots, esp. one skilled in shooting, as a marksman.
– ORIGIN mid 19th cent.: from *shoot* + *-ist*.

shoot-out ▶ n. informal a decisive gun battle. ■ (also **penalty shoot-out**) Soccer a tiebreaker decided by each side taking a specified number of penalty kicks.

shoot-the-chute (also **shoot-the-chutes**) ▶ n. another term for CHUTE-THE-CHUTE.
▶ v. (**shoot the chute** or **shoot the chutes**) another term for CHUTE THE CHUTE (see CHUTE-THE-CHUTE).

shop /SHäp/ ▶ n. **1** a building or part of a building where goods or services are sold; a store: *a card shop | a barber shop.* ■ [in sing.] informal an act of going shopping: *she slogged her way around the supermarket doing the weekly shop.*
2 [usu. with modifier] a place where things are manufactured or repaired; a workshop: *an auto repair shop.* ■ a room or department in a factory where a particular stage of production is carried out: *the machine shop.* ■ short for SHOP CLASS: *I got an A in shop last year.*
▶ v. (**shops, shopping, shopped**) **1** [no obj.] go to a store or stores to buy goods: *she shopped for groceries twice a week.* ■ (**shop around**) look for the best available price or rate for something: *they shopped around for cheaper food.* ■ short for WINDOW-SHOP.
2 [with obj.] informal, chiefly Brit. inform on (someone): *a concerned member of the public had shopped him—wrongly—for accepting monetary reward.*

– PHRASES **close** (or **shut**) **up shop** cease business or operation, either temporarily or permanently: *the cafes must shut up shop by July 22.* ■ informal stop some activity: *rather than close up shop, the team has returned to fighting trim.* **set up shop** establish oneself in a business: *he set up shop as a hairdresser in Soho.* **talk shop** discuss matters concerning one's work, esp. at a social occasion when this is inappropriate.

– ORIGIN Middle English: shortening of Old French *eschoppe* 'lean-to booth,' of West Germanic origin; related to German *Schopf* 'porch' and English dialect *shippon* 'cattle shed.' The verb is first recorded (mid 16th cent.) in the sense 'imprison' (from an obsolete slang use of the noun for 'prison'), hence sense 2 of the verb.

shop·a·hol·ic /ˌSHäpəˈhôlik, -ˈhälik/ ▶ n. informal a compulsive shopper.
– ORIGIN 1980s: blend of SHOP and ALCOHOLIC.

shop class ▶ n. a class in which practical skills such as carpentry or engineering are taught: *back in high school I made a wooden dummy in shop class.*

shop floor ▶ n. [in sing.] the part of a workshop or factory where production as distinct from administrative work is carried out: *working conditions on the shop floor.*

shop·front /ˈSHäpˌfrənt/ ▶ n. chiefly Brit. another term for STOREFRONT (sense 1).

shop·girl (also **shop girl**) ▶ n. dated a female salesclerk.

shop·house /ˈSHäpˌhous/ ▶ n. (in Southeast Asia) a store opening onto the sidewalk and also used as the owner's residence.

shop·keep·er /ˈSHäpˌkēpər/ ▶ n. the owner and manager of a shop.
– DERIVATIVES **shop·keep·ing** /-ˌkēpiNG/ n.

shop·lift·ing /ˈSHäpˌliftiNG/ ▶ n. the criminal action of stealing goods from a shop while pretending to be a customer.
– DERIVATIVES **shop·lift** v., **shop·lift·er** /-ˌliftər/ n.

shop·man /ˈSHäpmən/ ▶ n. (pl. **shopmen**) Brit. dated a male salesclerk or shopkeeper.

shoppe ▶ n. a deliberately archaic spelling of SHOP, used in the hopes of imbuing a store with old-fashioned charm or quaintness: *the mishmash of the usual Tourist Gift Shoppe.*

shop·per /ˈSHäpər/ ▶ n. a person who is shopping.

shop·ping /ˈSHäpiNG/ ▶ n. [often as modifier] the purchasing of goods from stores: *a busy shopping area.* ■ goods bought from stores, esp. food and household goods: *I unloaded all the shopping.*

shop·ping cart ▶ n. a bag or basket on wheels for carrying shopping purchases, in particular one on wheels provided for the use of supermarket customers.

shop·ping cen·ter ▶ n. an area or complex of stores with adjacent parking.

shop·ping list ▶ n. a list of purchases to be made. ■ a list of items to be considered or acted on: *a lengthy shopping list of detailed proposals.*

shop·ping mall ▶ n. see MALL (sense 1).

shop·ping trol·ley ▶ n. British term for SHOPPING CART.

shop-soiled ▶ adj. British term for SHOPWORN.

shop stew·ard ▶ n. a person elected by workers, for example in a factory, to represent them in dealings with management.

shop·talk /ˈSHäpˌtôk/ (also **shop talk**) ▶ n. conversation about one's occupation or business at an informal or social occasion.

shop·walk·er /ˈSHäpˌwôkər/ ▶ n. British term for FLOORWALKER.

shop win·dow (also **shopwindow**) ▶ n. a window of a store, in which goods are displayed.

shop·worn /ˈSHäpˌwôrn/ ▶ adj. (of an article) made dirty or imperfect by being displayed or handled in a store: *he brought out some shopworn lettuce |* figurative *he appraised his brown but slightly shopworn body in the mirror.*

shore[1] /SHôr/ ▶ n. the land along the edge of a sea, lake, or other large body of water: *I took the tiller and made for the shore.* ■ Law the land between ordinary high- and low-water marks. ■ (usu. **shores**) a country or other geographic area bounded by a coast: *the shores of the New World.*
– PHRASES **on shore** ashore; on land: *are any of the crew left on shore?*
– DERIVATIVES **shore·less** adj., **shore·ward** /-wərd/ adj. & adv., **shore·wards** /-wərdz/ adv.
– ORIGIN Middle English: from Middle Dutch and Middle Low German *schōre*; perhaps related to the verb SHEAR.

shore[2] ▶ n. a prop or beam set obliquely against something weak or unstable as a support.
– PHRASAL VERBS **shore something up** support or hold up something with props or beams: *rescue workers had to shore up the building, which was in danger of collapse.* ■ support or assist something that would otherwise fail or decline: *Congress approved a $700 billion plan to shore up the financial industry.*
– ORIGIN Middle English: from Middle Dutch and Middle Low German *schore* 'prop,' of unknown origin.

shore[3] archaic past of SHEAR.

shore-based ▶ adj. operating from or based on a shore: *shore-based guns.*

shore·bird /ˈSHôrˌbərd/ ▶ n. a wader of the order Charadriiformes, such as a sandpiper. ■ any bird that frequents the shore.

shore crab ▶ n. a crab that inhabits the seashore and shallow waters. ● Several species, in particular the dark green **common shore crab** (*Carcinus maenas*, family Carcinidae) of Europe.

shore·lark /ˈSHôrˌlärk/ ▶ n. British term for HORNED LARK.

shore leave ▶ n. leisure time spent ashore by a sailor: *the hall was full of sailors on shore leave.*

Shore·line /ˈSHôrˌlīn/ a city in northwestern Washington, north of Seattle; pop. 52,005 (est. 2008).

shore·line /ˈSHôrˌlīn/ ▶ n. the line along which a large body of water meets the land: *he walked along the shoreline.*

shore·side /ˈSHôrˌsīd/ ▶ n. the edge of a shore: [as modifier] *a shoreside restaurant.*

shor·ing /ˈSHôriNG/ ▶ n. shores or props used to support or hold up something weak or unstable.

shorn /SHôrn/ past participle of SHEAR.

short /SHôrt/ ▶ adj. **1** measuring a small distance from end to end: *short, dark hair | a short flight of steps | the bed was too short for him.* ■ (of a journey) covering a small distance: *the hotel is a short walk from the sea.* ■ (of a garment or sleeves on a garment) only covering the top part of a person's arms or legs: *a short skirt.* ■ (of a person) small in height: *he is short and tubby.* ■ (of a ball in cricket, a shot in tennis, etc.) traveling only a small distance before bouncing: *he uses his opportunities to attack every short ball.* ■ short for SHORTSTOP.
2 lasting or taking a small amount of time: *visiting London for a short break | a short conversation.* ■ [attrib.] seeming to last less time than is the case;

passing quickly: *in 10 short years all this changed.* ■ (of a person's memory) retaining things for only a small amount of time: *he has a short memory for past misdeeds.* ■ Stock Market (of stocks or other securities or commodities) sold in advance of being acquired, with reliance on the price falling so that a profit can be made. ■ Stock Market (of a broker, position in the market, etc.) buying or based on such stocks or other securities or commodities. ■ denoting or having a relatively early date for the maturing of a bill of exchange.
3 relatively small in extent: *a short speech | he wrote a short book.* ■ [predic.] (**short of/on**) not having enough of (something); lacking or deficient in: *they were short of provisions | I know you're short on cash.* ■ [predic.] in insufficient supply: *food is short.* ■ [predic.] (of a person) terse; uncivil: *he was often sharp and rather* ***short with*** *her.*
4 Phonetics (of a vowel) categorized as short with regard to quality and length (e.g., in standard British English the vowel in *good* is short as distinct from the long vowel in *food*). ■ Prosody (of a vowel or syllable) having the lesser of the two recognized durations.
5 (of odds or a chance) reflecting or representing a high level of probability: *they have been backed at short odds to win thousands.*
6 (of pastry) containing a high proportion of fat to flour and therefore crumbly. ■ (of clay) having poor plasticity.
▶ **adv.** (chiefly in sports) at, to, or over a relatively small distance: *you go deep and you go short.* ■ not as far as the point aimed at; not far enough: *all too often you pitch the ball short.*
▶ **n. 1** Brit. a drink of spirits served in a small measure.
2 a short film as opposed to a feature film. ■ a short sound such as a short signal in Morse code or a short vowel or syllable: *her call was two longs and a short.* ■ a short circuit.
3 Stock Market a person who sells short. ■ (**shorts**) Stock Market short-dated stocks.
4 (**shorts**) a mixture of bran and coarse flour.
▶ **v. 1** short-circuit or cause to short-circuit: [no obj.] *the electrical circuit had* ***shorted out*** | [with obj.] *if the contact terminals are shorted, the battery quickly overheats.* [early 20th cent.: abbreviation.]
2 ■ [with obj.] Stock Market sell (stocks or other securities or commodities) in advance of acquiring them, with the aim of making a profit when the price falls.
– PHRASES **be caught** (or Brit. **taken**) **short** be put at a disadvantage: *the troubled company has been caught short by price competition in a recession-stricken market.* ■ Brit. informal urgently need to urinate or defecate. **two bricks short of a load, (an oar short of a pair,** etc.) informal (of a person) stupid; crazy: *she's two bricks short of a load.* **bring** (or **pull**) **someone up short** make someone check or pause abruptly: *he was entering the office when he was brought up short by the sight of John.* **come short** fail to reach a goal or standard: *we're so close to getting the job done, but we keep* ***coming up*** *short.* ■ S. African get into trouble: *if you try to trick him you'll come short.* **for short** as an abbreviation or nickname: *the File Transfer Protocol, or ftp for short.* **get** (or **have**) **someone by the short hairs** (or Brit. **short and curlies**) informal have complete control of a person. [from military slang, referring to pubic hair.] **go short** not have enough of something, esp. food: *you won't go short when I die.* **in short** to sum up; briefly: *different plants, different animals, different weather—in short, a whole different ecosystem.* **in short order** immediately; rapidly: *after the killing the camp had been shut down in short order.* **in the short run** in the near future. **in short supply** scarce. **in the short term** in the near future. **little** (or **nothing**) **short of** almost (or equal to); little (or nothing) less than: *he regarded the cost of living as little short of scandalous.* **make short work of** accomplish, consume, or destroy quickly: *we made short work of our huge portions.* **sell short** Stock Exchange sell stock or other securities or commodities that one does not own at the time, in the hope of buying at a lower price before the delivery time. **short and sweet** brief and pleasant: *his comments were short and sweet.* **the short end of the stick** an outcome in which one has less advantage than others. **short for** an abbreviation or nickname for: *I'm Robbie—short for Roberta.* **short of** less than: *he died at sixty-one, four years short of his pensionable age.* ■ not reaching as far as: *a rocket failure left a satellite tumbling in an orbit far short of its proper position.* ■ without going so far as (some extreme action): *short of putting out an all-persons alert, there's little else we can do.* **short of breath** panting; short-winded. **short, sharp shock** see **SHOCK**[1]. **stop short** stop suddenly or abruptly. **stop short of** not go as far as (some extreme action): *the measures stopped short of establishing direct trade links.*
– DERIVATIVES **short·ish** adj., **short·ness** n.
– ORIGIN Old English *sceort*, of Germanic origin; related to **SHIRT** and **SKIRT**.

short-act·ing ▶ **adj.** (chiefly of a drug) having effects that only last for a short time.

short·age /ˈSHôrtij/ ▶ **n.** a state or situation in which something needed cannot be obtained in sufficient amounts: ***a shortage of*** *hard cash | food shortages.*

short-arm ▶ **adj.** denoting a blow or throw executed with the arm not fully extended or with motion from the elbow only.

short·bread /ˈSHôrtˌbred/ ▶ **n.** a crisp, rich, crumbly type of cookie made with butter, flour, and sugar.
– ORIGIN early 19th cent.: *short* from **SHORT** in the sense 'easily crumbled.'

short·cake /ˈSHôrtˌkāk/ ▶ **n. 1** a small cake made of biscuit dough and typically served with fruit and whipped cream as a dessert.
2 a dessert made from shortcake topped with fruit, typically strawberries, and whipped cream.
– ORIGIN late 16th cent.: see **SHORTBREAD**.

short·change /ˈSHôrtˈCHānj/ ▶ **v.** [with obj.] cheat (someone) by giving insufficient money as change: *I'm sure I was shortchanged at the bar.* ■ treat unfairly by withholding something of value: *residents perennially complain about their own children's needs being shortchanged.*

short cir·cuit ▶ **n.** in a device, an electrical circuit of lower resistance than that of a normal circuit, typically resulting from the unintended contact of components and consequent accidental diversion of the current.
▶ **v.** (**short-circuit**) (with reference to an electrical device) malfunction or fail, or cause to do this, as a result of a short circuit across it: [no obj.] *the birds caused the electricity supply to short-circuit* | [with obj.] *water had leaked into the washing machine's motor, short-circuiting it.* ■ [with obj.] shorten (a process or activity) by using a more direct (but often improper) method: *the normal processes of a democracy should not be short-circuited.*

short·com·ing /ˈSHôrtˌkəmiNG/ ▶ **n.** (usu. **shortcomings**) a fault or failure to meet a certain standard, typically in a person's character, a plan, or a system: *he is so forthright about his shortcomings, it's hard to chastise him.*

short com·mons ▶ **plural n.** see **COMMONS**.

short cov·er·ing ▶ **n.** the buying in of stocks or other securities or commodities that have been sold short, typically to avoid loss when prices move upward.

short·cut /ˈSHôrtˌkət/ ▶ **n.** an shorter alternative route. ■ an accelerated way of doing or achieving something: *the promise of* ***a shortcut to*** *optimum health and fitness is a tantalizing one.* ■ Computing a record of the address of a file, website, or other data made to enable quick access.

short-dat·ed ▶ **adj.** (of a stock or bond) due for early payment or redemption.

short-day ▶ **adj.** [attrib.] (of a plant) needing a daily period of darkness of more than a certain length to initiate flowering, which therefore happens naturally as the days shorten in the autumn.

short di·vi·sion ▶ **n.** arithmetical division in which the quotient is written directly without a succession of intermediate calculations.

short-eared owl ▶ **n.** a migratory day-flying owl that frequents open country, found in northern Eurasia and North and South America. ● *Asio flammeus*, family Strigidae.

short·en /ˈSHôrtn/ ▶ **v.** make or become shorter: [with obj.] *he shortened his stride* | [no obj.] *around mid-September, days shorten and temperatures dip.* ■ [with obj.] Sailing reduce the amount of (sail) exposed to the wind. ■ (with reference to gambling odds) make or become shorter; decrease: [no obj.] *the odds had shortened to 14-1.* ■ [with obj.] Prosody & Phonetics make (a vowel or syllable) short.

short·en·ing /ˈSHôrtniNG, ˈSHôrtn-iNG/ ▶ **n.** butter or other fat used for making pastry or bread.

short·fall /ˈSHôrtˌfôl/ ▶ **n.** a deficit of something required or expected: *they are facing an expected $10 billion* ***shortfall in*** *revenue.*

short-fused ▶ **adj.** informal likely to lose one's temper.

short game ▶ **n.** the part of golf concerned with approach shots and putting: *two tips to improve your short game.*

short·hair /ˈSHôrtˌhe(ə)r/ ▶ **n.** a cat of a short-haired breed.

short·hand /ˈSHôrtˌhand/ ▶ **n.** a method of rapid writing by means of abbreviations and symbols, used esp. for taking dictation. The major systems of shorthand are those devised in 1837 by Sir Isaac Pitman and in 1888 by John R. Gregg (1867–1948). ■ [in sing.] a short and simple way of expressing or referring to something: *poetry for him is simply a* ***shorthand for*** *literature that has aesthetic value.*

short-hand·ed ▶ **adj. 1** not having enough or the usual number of staff or crew: *the kitchen was a bit short-handed* | [as adv.] *because two cashiers were out with the flu, we worked short-handed.*
2 Ice Hockey (of a goal) scored by a team playing with fewer players on the ice than their opponent. ■ (of a situation) occurring while or because a team has fewer than six players on the ice.

short haul ▶ **n.** a relatively short distance in terms of travel or the transport of goods: *it is only a short haul over the mountains to Los Angeles* | [as modifier] *short-haul routes.*

short hop ▶ **n.** Baseball a batted or thrown ball that hits the ground and is caught low just as it makes a bounce: *he got that one* ***on the short hop.***
▶ **v.** [with obj.] (**short-hop**) (of a fielder) catch a ball just as it bounces from the ground: *Boggs short-hopped it and threw to first.*

short·horn /ˈSHôrtˌhôrn/ ▶ **n.** an animal of a breed of cattle with short horns.

short hun·dred·weight ▶ **n.** see **HUNDREDWEIGHT**.

short·ie /ˈSHôrtē/ ▶ **n.** variant spelling of **SHORTY**.

short list (also **shortlist**) ▶ **n.** a list of selected candidates from which a final choice is made: *a short list of four companies.*
▶ **v.** [with obj.] (**short-list**) put (someone or something) on a short list: *the novel was* ***short-listed for*** *the Booker Prize.*

short-lived /ˈlivd, ˈlīvd/ ▶ **adj.** lasting only a short time: *a short-lived romance | these benefits are likely to be short-lived.*

short·ly /ˈSHôrtlē/ ▶ **adv. 1** in a short time; soon: *the new database will shortly be available for consultation | the flight was hijacked* ***shortly after*** *takeoff.*
2 in a few words; briefly: *they received a letter shortly outlining the proposals.* ■ abruptly, sharply, or curtly: *"Do you like football?" "I do not," she said shortly.*
– ORIGIN Old English *scortlīce* (see **SHORT**, **-LY**[2]).

short or·der ▶ **n.** an order or dish of food that can be quickly prepared and served: *a short order of souvlaki* | [as modifier] *I'm a short-order cook.*
– PHRASES **in short order** see **SHORT**.

short-range ▶ **adj.** [attrib.] **1** (esp. of a vehicle or missile) only able to be used or be effective over short distances: *short-range nuclear weapons.*
2 of or over a short period of future time: *short-range forecasting.*

short ribs ▶ **n.** a narrow cut of beef containing the ends of the ribs near the breastbone.

short-run ▶ **adj.** taken or considered over a short time period; short-term: *the short-run impact appears to be positive.* ■ Printing produced in or relating to a print run of relatively few copies.

shorts /SHôrts/ ▶ **plural n.** short pants that reach only to the thighs or knees: *cycling shorts.* ■ men's underpants.

short score ▶ **n.** Music a score in which the parts are condensed onto a small number of staves.

short-sheet ▶ **v.** [with obj.] fold and arrange the sheet on (a bed) in such a way that anyone getting into the bed will be unable to stretch their legs out beyond the middle of the bed, as a practical joke.

short shrift ▶ **n.** rapid and unsympathetic dismissal; curt treatment: *the judge gave short shrift to an argument based on the right to free speech.* ■ archaic little time between condemnation and execution or punishment.

short·sight·ed /ˈSHôrtˈsītid/ ▶ **adj.** British term for **NEARSIGHTED**. ■ lacking imagination or foresight: *expedient, shortsighted solutions to problems.*
– DERIVATIVES **short·sight·ed·ly** adv., **short·sight·ed·ness** n.

short-sleeved ▶ **adj.** having sleeves that do not reach below the elbow: *a short-sleeved silk top.*

short-staffed ▶ **adj.** having too few or fewer than the usual number of staff: *we're rather short-staffed what with Christmas and everything.*

short-stay ▶ **adj.** [attrib.] denoting a place in which someone or something stays or remains for only a short period: *short-stay accommodations.* ■ denoting a person staying somewhere for only a short period of time: *short-stay patients.*

short·stop /ˈSHôrtˌstäp/ ▶ **n.** Baseball a fielder positioned in the infield between second and third base, or the position itself.

short sto·ry ▶ **n.** a story with a fully developed theme but significantly shorter and less elaborate than a novel.

short sub·ject ▶ **n.** a short movie, typically one shown before the screening of a feature film.

short suit ▶ **n.** (in bridge or whist) a holding of only one or two cards of one suit in a hand.

short-tailed wea·sel ▶ **n.** another term for STOAT.

short tem·per ▶ **n.** a tendency to lose one's temper quickly.

short-tem·pered ▶ **adj.** quick to lose one's temper.

short ten·nis ▶ **n.** tennis played on a small court with a small racket and a soft ball, used esp. as an introduction to the game for children.

short-term ▶ **adj.** occurring in or relating to a relatively short period of time: *it might be a wise short-term investment.*

short-term·ism /ˈtərmizəm/ ▶ **n.** concentration on short-term projects or objectives for immediate profit at the expense of long-term security.

short-tim·er ▶ **n.** military slang a person nearing the end of their period of military service.

short ti·tle ▶ **n.** an abbreviated form of a title of a book or document.

short ton ▶ **n.** see TON[1].

short waist ▶ **n. 1** a short upper body, with a high waist.
2 archaic a woman's dress with a high waist.

short·wave /ˈSHôrtˈwāv/ ▶ **n.** a radio wave of a wavelength between about 10 and 100 m (and a frequency of about 3 to 30 MHz): [as modifier] *a shortwave transmitter.* ■ broadcasting using radio waves of this wavelength: [as modifier] *shortwave radio.*

short weight ▶ **n.** weight that is less than that declared: *unscrupulous retailers give short weight by including an excessive amount of packaging.*

short-wind·ed /ˈwindid/ ▶ **adj.** (of a person) out of breath or quickly becoming so.

short·y /ˈSHôrtē/ (also **shortie**) ▶ **n.** (pl. **shorties**) informal a person who is shorter than average (often used as a nickname). ■ [often as modifier] a short garment, esp. a short dress or nightgown: *she pulled on a shorty nightshirt.*

Sho·sho·ne /SHōˈSHōnē/ ▶ **n.** (pl. **same** or **Shoshones**) **1** a member of an American Indian people living chiefly in Wyoming, Idaho, and Nevada.
2 the Uto-Aztecan language of this people.
▶ **adj.** of or relating to the Shoshone or their language.
– ORIGIN of unknown origin.

Sho·sta·ko·vich /ˌSHästəˈkōviCH, ˌSHôstəˈkôviCH/, Dmitri (Dmitrievich) (1906–75), Russian composer. Although he experimented with atonality and 12-note techniques, his music always returned to a basic tonality.

shot[1] /SHät/ ▶ **n. 1** the firing of a gun or cannon: *he brought down a caribou with a single shot to the neck* | figurative *the opening shots have been fired in a legal battle over repairs.* ■ an attempt to hit a target by shooting: *he asked me if I would like to* ***have a shot*** *at a pheasant.* ■ [with modifier] the range of a gun or cannon: *six more desperadoes came galloping up and halted just out of rifle shot.* ■ a critical or aggressive remark: *Paul tried one last shot—"You realize what you want will cost more money?"* ■ [with adj.] a person with a specified level of ability in shooting: *he was an excellent shot at short and long distances.*
2 a hit, stroke, or kick of the ball in sports such as basketball, tennis, or golf: *his partner pulled off a winning backhand shot.* ■ an attempt to drive a ball into a goal; an attempt to score: *he took a shot that the goalie stopped.* ■ informal an attempt to do something: *several of the competitors will* ***have a shot*** *at the title.*
3 (pl. **same**) a ball of stone or metal used as a missile fired from a large gun or cannon. ■ (also **lead shot**) tiny lead pellets used in quantity in a single charge or cartridge in a shotgun. ■ a heavy ball thrown by a shot-putter.
4 a photograph: *she* ***took a shot*** *of me holding a lamp near my face.* ■ a film sequence photographed continuously by one camera: *the movie's opening shot is of a character walking across a featureless landscape.* ■ the range of a camera's view: *a prop man was standing just* ***out of shot.***
5 informal a small drink, esp. of distilled liquor: *he took a shot of whiskey.* ■ an injection of a drug or vaccine: *Jerry gave the monkey a shot of a sedative.*
6 [usu. with modifier] the launch of a space rocket: *a moon shot.*
– PHRASES **give it one's best shot** informal do the best that one can. **like a shot** informal without hesitation; willingly: *"Would you go back?" "Like a shot."* **a shot across the bows** see BOW[3]. **a shot in the arm** informal an encouraging stimulus: *the movie was a real shot in the arm for our crew.* **a shot in the dark** see DARK.
– ORIGIN Old English *sc(e)ot, gesc(e)ot,* of Germanic origin; related to German *Geschoss,* from the base of the verb SHOOT.

shot[2] past and past participle of SHOOT ▶ **adj. 1** (of colored cloth) woven with a warp and weft of different colors, giving a contrasting iridescent effect when looked at from different angles: *a dress of shot silk.* ■ interspersed with a different color: *dark hair shot with silver.*
2 informal ruined or worn out: *a completely shot engine will put you out of the race* | *my nerves are shot.* ■ [predic.] drunk.
– PHRASES **get** (or **be**) **shot of** Brit. informal get (or be) rid of. **shot through with** suffused with (a particular feature or quality): *the mist was shot through with orange spokes of light.* **shot to pieces** (or **to hell**) informal ruined.

shot-blast ▶ **v.** [with obj.] clean or strip (a metal or other surface) by directing a high-speed stream of steel particles at it.

shot·crete /ˈSHätkrēt/ ▶ **n.** another term for GUNITE.
– ORIGIN 1950s: from SHOT[2] + CONCRETE.

shote /SHōt/ ▶ **n.** variant spelling of SHOAT.

shot glass ▶ **n.** a small glass used for serving liquor.

shot·gun /ˈSHätˌgən/ ▶ **n. 1** a smoothbore gun for firing small shot at short range.
2 (also **shotgun formation**) Football an offensive formation in which the quarterback receives the snap while standing several yards behind the line of scrimmage.
▶ **adj. 1** aimed at a wide range of things; with no specific target: *many companies use the shotgun approach, aiming advertising at the widest possible audience.*
2 (of a house or other structure) with the rooms lined up one behind another, forming a long narrow whole: *his family lived in a shotgun shack in South Memphis.*
▶ **v. 1** shoot at or kill with a shotgun.
2 consume (a canned beverage) in one go by punching a hole near the can's base and upturning it over one's mouth: *shotgunning beers.* ■ consume (any beverage) in one go: *I shotgunned two tumblers of Jack D and chased it with a Mickey's.*
– PHRASES **ride shotgun** see RIDE.

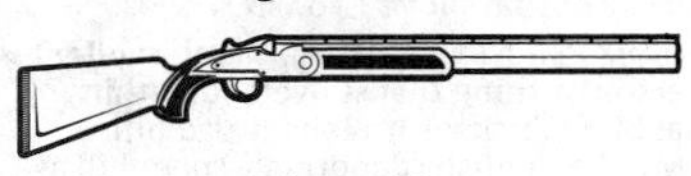

shotgun 1

shot·gun mar·riage (also **shotgun wedding**) ▶ **n.** informal an enforced or hurried wedding, esp. because the bride is pregnant.

shot·gun mi·cro·phone ▶ **n.** another term for GUN MICROPHONE.

shot hole ▶ **n. 1** a hole made by the passage of a shot.
2 a hole bored in rock for the insertion of a blasting charge.
3 a small round hole made in a leaf by a fungus or bacterium, esp. in a fruit tree following an attack of leaf spot. ■ a small hole made in wood by a boring beetle.

shot·mak·ing /ˈSHätˌmākiNG/ ▶ **n.** the playing of aggressive or decisive strokes in tennis, golf, and other games.
– DERIVATIVES **shot·mak·er** /-ˌmākər/ **n.**

Sho·to·kan /SHōˈtōkən/ ▶ **n.** [usu. as modifier] a style of karate that is popular in many countries.
– ORIGIN Japanese, from *shō* 'right, true' + *to* 'way' + *kan* 'mansion.'

shot-peen ▶ **v.** [with obj.] shape (sheet metal) by bombarding it with a stream of metal shot.

shot put ▶ **n.** an athletic contest in which a very heavy round ball is thrown as far as possible.
– DERIVATIVES **shot-put·ter n., shot-put·ting n.**

shot·ted /ˈSHätid/ ▶ **adj.** filled or weighted with shot.

shot·ten her·ring /ˈSHätn/ ▶ **n.** a herring that has spawned. ■ archaic a weakened or dispirited person.
– ORIGIN Middle English: *shotten,* archaic past participle of SHOOT, in the specialized sense 'discharge (spawn).'

shot tow·er ▶ **n.** historical a tower in which shot was made from molten lead poured through sieves at the top and falling into water at the bottom.

should /SHo͝od/ ▶ **modal v.** (3rd sing. **should**) **1** used to indicate obligation, duty, or correctness, typically when criticizing someone's actions: *he should have been careful* | *I think we should trust our people more* | *you shouldn't have gone.* ■ indicating a desirable or expected state: *by now students should be able to read with a large degree of independence.* ■ used to give or ask advice or suggestions: *you should go back to bed* | *what should I wear?* ■ (**I should**) used to give advice: *I should hold out if I were you.*
2 used to indicate what is probable: *$348 million should be enough to buy him out* | *the bus should arrive in a few minutes.*
3 formal expressing the conditional mood. ■ (in the first person) indicating the consequence of an imagined event: *if I were to obey my first impulse, I should spend my days writing letters.* ■ referring to a possible event or situation: *if you should change your mind, I'll be at the hotel* | *should anyone arrive late, admission is likely to be refused.*
4 used in a clause with "that" after a main clause describing feelings: *it is astonishing that we should find violence here.*
5 used in a clause with "that" expressing purpose: *in order that training should be effective it must be planned systematically.*
6 (in the first person) expressing a polite request or acceptance: *we should be grateful for your advice.*
7 (in the first person) expressing a conjecture or hope: *he'll have a sore head, I should imagine* | *"It won't happen again." "I should hope not."*
8 used to emphasize to a listener how striking an event is or was: *you should have seen Marge's face.* ■ (**who/what should —— but**) emphasizing how surprising an event was: *I was in this store when who should I see across the street but Toby.*
– ORIGIN Old English *sceolde:* past of SHALL.

USAGE As with **shall** and **will**, there is confusion about when to use **should** and **would**. The traditional rule is that **should** is used with first person pronouns (*I* and *we*), as in *I said* ***I should*** *be late,* and **would** is used with second and third persons (*you, he, she, it, they*), as in *you didn't say you* ***would*** *be late.* In practice, however, **would** is normally used instead of **should** in reported speech and conditional clauses: *I said* ***I would*** *be late; if we had known,* ***we would*** *have invited her.* In spoken and informal contexts, the issue rarely arises, since the distinction is obscured by the use of the contracted forms **I'd, we'd**, etc. In modern English, uses of **should** are dominated by the senses relating to obligation (for which **would** cannot be substituted), as in *you* ***should*** *go out more often,* and for related emphatic uses, as in *you* ***should*** *have seen her face!*

shoul·der /ˈSHōldər/ ▶ **n. 1** the upper joint of the human arm and the part of the body between this and the neck. ■ (in quadrupeds) the joint of the upper forelimb and the adjacent part of the back. ■ the part of a bird or insect at which the wing is attached. ■ a large cut of meat from the upper foreleg and shoulder blade of an animal: *a shoulder of lamb.* ■ a part of a garment covering the shoulder: *a jacket with padded shoulders.* ■ (**shoulders**) the upper part of the back and arms: *a tall youth with broad shoulders.* ■ (**shoulders**) this part of the body regarded as bearing responsibility or hardship or providing strength: *all accounts place the blame squarely on his shoulders.*
2 a part of something resembling a shoulder in shape, position, or function: *the shoulder of a pulley.* ■ a point at which a steep slope descends from a plateau or highland area: *the shoulder of the hill sloped down.*
3 a paved strip alongside a road for stopping on in an emergency.
▶ **v. 1** [with obj.] put (something heavy) over one's shoulder or shoulders to carry: *we shouldered our crippling backpacks and set off slowly up the hill.* ■ take on (a burden or responsibility): *she shouldered the blame for the incident.*
2 [with obj.] push (someone or something) out of one's way with one's shoulder: *she shouldered him brusquely aside.* ■ [no obj.] move in this way: *he shouldered past a woman with a baby* | *he* ***shouldered his way*** *through the seething mass of children.*
– PHRASES **be looking over one's shoulder** be anxious or insecure about a possible danger: *takeovers are the thing that keeps suppliers looking over their shoulders.* **put one's shoulder to the wheel** set to work vigorously. **shoulder arms** hold a rifle against the side of the body, barrel upward. **a shoulder to cry on** someone who listens sympathetically to one's problems. **shoulder to shoulder** side by side: *everyone is bunched together shoulder to shoulder.* ■ acting together toward a common aim; with united effort: *we fought shoulder to shoulder with the rest of the country.*
– DERIVATIVES **shoul·dered** /ˈSHōldərd/ **adj.** [in combination] *broad-shouldered.*
– ORIGIN Old English *sculdor;* related to Dutch *schouder* and German *Schulter.*

shoul·der bag ▶ **n.** a bag with a long strap that is hung over the shoulder.

shoul·der belt ▶ **n.** a seat belt that passes over the shoulder and across the chest. ■ a bandolier or

PRONUNCIATION KEY ə *ago, up;* ər *over, fur;* a *hat;* ā *ate;* ä *car;* e *let;* ē *see;* i *fit;* ī *by;* NG *sing;* ō *go;* ô *law, for;* oi *toy;* o͝o *good;* o͞o *goo;* ou *out;* TH *thin;* T͟H *then;* ZH *vision*

other strap passing over one shoulder and under the opposite arm.

shoul·der blade ▶ n. either of the large, flat, triangular bones that lie against the ribs in the upper back and provide attachments for the bone and muscles of the upper arm. Also called SCAPULA.

should·er har·ness ▶ n. a strap worn around or across the shoulder, specifically. ■ the part of a seat belt that lies diagonally across the chest. ■ (also **shoulder holster**) a strap worn around the shoulder and under one arm with a holster for carrying a firearm.

shoul·der-high ▶ adj. & adv. up to or at the height of the shoulders: [as adj.] *a glade of shoulder-high grass* | [as adv.] *he was lifted shoulder-high.*

shoul·der hol·ster ▶ n. a gun holster worn under the armpit.

shoul·der-in ▶ n. (in dressage) a movement in which the horse moves parallel to the side of the arena, with its hindquarters carried closer to the wall than its shoulders and its body curved toward the center.

shoul·der joint ▶ n. the joint connecting an upper limb or forelimb to the body. It is a ball-and-socket joint in which the head of the humerus fits into the socket of the scapula.

shoul·der knot ▶ n. a knot of ribbon, metal, or lace worn as part of ceremonial dress.

shoul·der-length ▶ adj. (of hair) reaching down to the shoulders.

shoul·der pad ▶ n. a spongy, shaped pad sewn into the shoulder of a garment to provide bulk and shape. ■ a hard protective pad for the shoulders used in certain sports, such as ice hockey and football.

shoul·der sea·son (also **shoulder period**) ▶ n. a travel period between peak and off-peak seasons.

shoul·der stand ▶ n. a gymnastic movement in which, starting from a supine position, the torso and legs are raised vertically over the head and supported on the shoulders and arms.

shoul·der strap ▶ n. a narrow strip of material going over the shoulder from the front to the back of a garment. ■ a long strap attached to a bag for carrying it over the shoulder. ■ a strip of cloth from shoulder to collar on a military uniform bearing a symbol of rank. ■ a similar strip on a raincoat.

shoul·der-surf·ing ▶ n. the practice of spying on the user of an ATM, computer, or other electronic device in order to obtain their personal access information.
– DERIVATIVES **shoul·der-surf·er** n.

should·n't /ˈSHo͝odnt/ ▶ contraction should not.

shout /SHout/ ▶ v. **1** [no obj.] (of a person) utter a loud call or cry, typically as an expression of a strong emotion: *she shouted for joy.* ■ [reporting verb] say something very loudly; call out: [with obj.] *he leaned out of his window and shouted abuse at them* | *I shouted out a warning* | [with direct speech] *"Come back!" she shouted.* ■ (**shout at**) speak loudly and angrily to; insult or scold loudly: *he apologized because he had shouted at her in front of them all.* ■ [with obj.] (**shout someone down**) prevent someone from speaking or being heard by shouting: *he was shouted down as he tried to explain the decision.* ■ [with obj.] indicate or express (a particular quality or characteristic) unequivocally or powerfully: *from crocodile handbag to gold-trimmed shoes, she shouted money.*
2 [with two objs.] Austral./NZ informal treat (someone) to (something, esp. a drink): *I'll shout you a beer.* ■ [no obj.] buy a round of drinks: *anyone shooting a hole in one must shout for all players present on the course.*
▶ n. **1** a loud cry expressing a strong emotion or calling attention: *his words were interrupted by warning shouts.*
2 (**one's shout**) Brit. informal one's turn to buy a round of drinks: *"Do you want another drink? My shout."*
– PHRASES **give someone a shout** informal call for someone's attention. ■ call on or get in touch with someone. **in with a shout** Brit. informal having a good chance: *they were definitely in with a shout of bringing off a victory.* **shout something from the rooftops** talk about something openly and jubilantly, esp. something that is personal or has previously been kept secret. **shout the odds** chiefly Brit. talk in a loud and opinionated way.
– DERIVATIVES **shout·er** n., **shout·y** adj. (informal).
– ORIGIN late Middle English: perhaps related to SHOOT; compare with Old Norse *skúta* 'a taunt,' also with the verb SCOUT[2].

shout·ing match ▶ n. a loud quarrel.

shout-out ▶ n. informal a message of congratulation, support, or appreciation: *a special shout-out to Marlon Brando, Al Pacino, James Gandolfini, and Robert DeNiro for being such kick-ass cinematic mobsters.*

shove /SHəv/ ▶ v. [with obj.] push (someone or something) roughly: *police started pushing and shoving people down the street* | [no obj.] *kids pushed, kicked, and shoved.* ■ [no obj.] make one's way by pushing someone or something: *Woody shoved past him.* ■ put (something) somewhere carelessly or roughly: *she shoved the books into her briefcase.* ■ (**shove it**) informal used to express angry dismissal of something: *I should have told the boss to shove it.*
▶ n. [usu. in sing.] a strong push: *she gave him a hefty shove and he nearly fell.*
– PHRASAL VERBS **shove off 1** [usu. in imperative] informal go away: *shove off—you're bothering the customers.* **2** push away from the shore or another vessel in a boat.
– ORIGIN Old English *scūfan* (verb), of Germanic origin; related to Dutch *schuiven* and German *schieben*, also to SHUFFLE.

shove-half·pen·ny /ˈSHəv ˈhāp(ə)nē/ ▶ n. a game in which coins are struck so that they slide across a marked board on a table.

shov·el /ˈSHəvəl/ ▶ n. a tool with a broad flat blade and typically upturned sides, used for moving coal, earth, snow or other material. ■ a machine or part of a machine having a similar shape or function. ■ an amount of something carried or moved with shovel: *a few shovels of earth.*
▶ v. (**shoveled**, **shoveling**; Brit. **shovelled**, **shovelling**) [with obj.] move (coal, earth, snow, or similar material) with a shovel: *she shoveled coal on the fire.* ■ remove snow from (an area) with a shovel: *I'll clean the basement and shovel the walk.* ■ informal put or push (something, typically food) somewhere quickly and in large quantities: *Dave was shoveling pasta into his mouth.*
– DERIVATIVES **shov·el·ful** /-ˌfo͝ol/ n. (pl. **shovelfuls**).
– ORIGIN Old English *scofl*, of Germanic origin; related to Dutch *schoffel*, German *Schaufel*, also to the verb SHOVE.

shov·el·board /ˈSHəvəlˌbôrd/ ▶ n. British term for SHUFFLEBOARD.
– ORIGIN mid 16th cent.: alteration of obsolete *shoveboard*, from SHOVE + BOARD.

shov·el·er /ˈSHəv(ə)lər/ (chiefly Brit. **shoveller**) ▶ n.
1 a person or thing that shovels something.
2 a dabbling duck with a long broad bill. [late Middle English (denoting a spoonbill): alteration of earlier *shovelard*, from SHOVEL, perhaps influenced by *mallard*.] ● Genus *Anas*, family Anatidae: four species, in particular *A. clypeata* of Eurasia and North America.

shov·el hat ▶ n. a black felt hat with a low round crown and a broad brim turned up at the sides, formerly worn esp. by clergymen.

shov·el·ware /ˈSHəvəlˌwe(ə)r/ ▶ n. Computing software or online content that has been added to a CD or placed on the Internet without having been altered so as to suit the new medium.
– ORIGIN 1980s: from the notion of 'shoveling' the information onto a CD or the Internet indiscriminately.

show /SHō/ ▶ v. (past participle **shown** /SHōn/ or **showed**) **1** be or allow or cause to be visible: [no obj.] *wrinkles were starting to show on her face* | [no obj., with complement] *the muscles of her jaws showed white through the skin* | [with obj.] *a white blouse will show the blood.* ■ [with obj.] offer, exhibit, or produce (something) for scrutiny or inspection: *an alarm salesperson should show an ID card* | [with two objs.] *he wants to show you all his woodwork stuff.* ■ [with obj.] put on display in an exhibition or competition: *he ceased early in his career to show his work* | [no obj.] *other artists who showed there included Robert Motherwell.* ■ [with obj.] present (a movie or television program) on a screen for public viewing. ■ [no obj.] (of a movie) be presented in this way: *a movie showing at the Venice Film Festival.* ■ [with obj.] indicate (a particular time, measurement, etc.): *a travel clock showing the time in different cities.* ■ [with obj.] represent or depict in art: *a postcard showing the Wicklow Mountains.* ■ (**show oneself**) allow oneself to be seen; appear in public: *he was amazed that she would have the gall to show herself.* ■ [no obj.] informal arrive or turn up for an appointment or at a gathering: *her date failed to show.* ■ [no obj.] finish third or in the first three in a race. ■ [no obj.] informal (of a woman) be visibly pregnant: *Shirley was four months pregnant and just starting to show.*
2 [with obj.] display or allow to be perceived (a quality, emotion, or characteristic): *it was Frank's turn to show his frustration* | *his sangfroid showed signs of cracking.* ■ accord or treat someone with (a specified quality): *he urged his soldiers to fight them and show no mercy* | [with two objs.] *he has learned to show women some respect.* ■ [no obj.] (of an emotion) be noticeable: *he tried not to let his relief show.*
3 [with obj.] demonstrate or prove: *experts say this shows the benefit of regular inspections* | [with clause] *the figures show that the underlying rate of inflation continues to fall.* ■ (**show oneself**) prove or demonstrate oneself to be: [with infinitive] *she showed herself to be a harsh critic* | [with complement] *he showed himself to be an old-fashioned Baptist separatist.* ■ cause to understand or be capable of doing something by explanation or demonstration: *he showed the boy how to operate the machine.* ■ [with obj.] conduct or lead: *show them in, please.*
▶ n. **1** a spectacle or display of something, typically an impressive one: *spectacular shows of bluebells.*
2 a public entertainment, in particular: ■ a play or other stage performance, esp. a musical. ■ a program on television or radio. ■ [usu. with adj. or noun modifier] an event or competition involving the public display or exhibition of animals, plants, or products: *the annual agricultural show.* ■ informal an undertaking, project, or organization: *I man a desk in a little office. I don't run the show.* ■ informal an opportunity for doing something; a chance: *I didn't have a show.*
3 an outward appearance or display of a quality or feeling: *Joanie was frightened of any show of affection.* ■ an outward display intended to give a particular, false impression: *Drew made a show of looking around for firewood* | *they are all show and no go.*
4 Medicine a discharge of blood and mucus from the vagina at the onset of labor or menstruation.
– PHRASES **for show** for the sake of appearance rather than for use. **get** (or **keep**) **the show on the road** informal begin (or succeed in continuing with) an undertaking or enterprise: *"Let's get this show on the road—we're late already."* **good** (or **bad** or **poor**) **show!** Brit. informal, dated used to express approval (or disapproval or dissatisfaction). **have something** (or **nothing**) **to show for** have a (or no) visible result of (one's work or experience): *a year later, he had nothing to show for his efforts.* **on show** being exhibited. **show one's cards** another way of saying SHOW ONE'S HAND below. **show cause** Law produce satisfactory grounds for application of (or exemption from) a procedure or penalty. **show someone the door** dismiss or eject someone from a place. **show one's face** appear in public: *she had been up in court and was so ashamed she could hardly show her face.* **show the flag** see FLAG[1]. **show one's hand** (in a card game) reveal one's cards. ■ disclose one's plans: *he needed hard evidence, and to get it he would have to show his hand.* **show of force** a demonstration of the forces at one's command and of one's readiness to use them. **show of hands** the raising of hands among a group of people to indicate a vote for or against something, with numbers typically being estimated rather than counted. **show the way** indicate the direction to be followed to a particular place. ■ indicate what can or should be done by doing it first: *Morgan showed the way by becoming Deputy Governor of Jamaica.*
– PHRASAL VERBS **show something forth** archaic exhibit: *the heavens show forth the glory of God.* **show off** informal make a deliberate or pretentious display of one's abilities or accomplishments. **show someone/something off** display or cause others to take notice of someone or something that is a source of pride: *his jeans were tight-fitting, showing off his compact figure.* **show out** Bridge reveal that one has no cards of a particular suit. **show someone around** act as a guide for someone to points of interest in a place or building. **show through** (of one's real feelings) be revealed inadvertently. **show up 1** be conspicuous or clearly visible. **2** informal arrive or turn up for an appointment or gathering. **show someone/something up** make someone or something conspicuous or clearly visible: *a rising moon showed up the wild seascape.* ■ expose someone or something as being bad or faulty in some way: *it's a pity they haven't showed up the authorities for what they are.* ■ (**show someone up**) informal embarrass or humiliate someone: *she says I showed her up in front of her friends.*
– ORIGIN Old English *scēawian* 'look at, inspect,' from a West Germanic base meaning 'look'; related to Dutch *schouwen* and German *schauen*.

Sho·wa /ˈSHōwä/ ▶ n. [usu. as modifier] the period when Japan was ruled by the emperor Hirohito.
– ORIGIN Japanese, from *shō* 'bright, clear' + *wa* 'harmony.'

show-and-tell ▶ n. a teaching method, used esp. in teaching young children, in which students are encouraged to bring items they have selected to class and describe them to their classmates.

show band ▶ n. a band that plays cover versions of popular songs. ■ a band, esp. a jazz band, that performs with theatrical extravagance.

show bill ▶ n. an advertising poster, esp. for a theater performance. ■ a listing of events at a horse show: *Horse & Pony Association show bill.*

show biz ▶ n. informal term for SHOW BUSINESS.
– DERIVATIVES **show·biz·zy** /ˈSHōˌbizē/ adj.

S

show·boat /ˈSHōˌbōt/ ▶ **n.** a river steamboat on which theatrical performances are given. ■ informal a show-off; an exhibitionist.
▶ **v.** [no obj.] informal show off: (as adj. **showboating**) *a lot of showboating politicians.*
– DERIVATIVES **show·boat·er n.**

show busi·ness ▶ **n.** the theater, movies, television, and pop music as a profession or industry.

show·card /ˈSHōˌkärd/ ▶ **n.** a large card bearing a conspicuous design, used esp. in advertising, market research, and teaching.

show·case /ˈSHōˌkās/ ▶ **n.** a glass case used for displaying articles in a store or museum. ■ a place or occasion for presenting something favorably to general attention: *the gallery will provide **a showcase for** Atlanta's young photographers.*
▶ **v.** [with obj.] exhibit; display: *the albums showcase his production skills.*

show·down /ˈSHōˌdoun/ ▶ **n.** a final test or confrontation intended to settle a dispute. ■ (in poker) the requirement at the end of a round that the players who remain in must show their cards to determine which is the strongest hand.

show·er /ˈSHou(-ə)r/ ▶ **n. 1** a brief and usually light fall of rain, hail, sleet, or snow. ■ a mass of small things falling or moving at the same time: ***a shower of** dust sprinkled his face.* ■ a large number of things happening or given to someone at the same time: *he was pleased by the shower of awards.* ■ a group of particles produced by a cosmic-ray particle in the earth's atmosphere.
2 an enclosure in which a person stands under a spray of water to wash. ■ the apparatus that produces such a spray of water. ■ (also **shower bath**) an act of washing oneself in a shower.
3 [often with modifier] a party at which presents are given to someone, typically a woman who is about to get married or have a baby: *she loved going to baby showers.*
▶ **v. 1** [no obj.] (of a mass of small things) fall or be thrown in a shower: *bits of broken glass showered over me.* ■ [with obj.] cause (a mass of small things) to fall in a shower: *his hooves showered sparks across the concrete floor.* ■ [with obj.] (**shower someone with**) throw (a number of small things) all at once toward someone: *hooligans showered him with rotten eggs.* ■ [with obj.] (**shower someone with**) give someone a great number of (things): *he showered her with kisses.* ■ [with obj.] (**shower something on/upon**) give a great number of things to (someone): *senior officers showered praise on their young cadet.*
2 [no obj.] wash oneself in a shower.
– PHRASES **send someone to the showers** informal send off or eject someone from a match, race, or contest.
– ORIGIN Old English *scūr* 'light fall of rain, hail, etc.,' of Germanic origin; related to Dutch *schoer* and German *Schauer.*

show·er·proof /ˈSHou(-ə)rˌpro͞of/ ▶ **adj.** (of a garment) resistant to light rain.
▶ **v.** [with obj.] make showerproof.

show·er·y /ˈSHou(-ə)rē/ ▶ **adj.** (of weather or a period of time) characterized by frequent showers of rain.

show·girl /ˈSHōˌgərl/ ▶ **n.** an actress who sings and dances in musicals, variety acts, and similar shows.

show house (also **show home**) ▶ **n.** British term for MODEL HOME.

show·ing /ˈSHō-iNG/ ▶ **n.** the action of showing something or the fact of being shown: *German shepherd, championship quality, excellent results in showing.* ■ a presentation of a movie or television program: *another showing of the three-part series.* ■ a performance of a specified quality: *a strong second-place showing in a recent Florida straw poll.*
– ORIGIN Old English *scēawung.*

show jump·ing ▶ **n.** the competitive sport of riding horses over a course of fences and other obstacles in an arena, with penalty points for errors.
– DERIVATIVES **show jump n., show jumper n.**

show·man /ˈSHōmən/ ▶ **n.** (pl. **showmen**) a person who produces or presents shows as a profession, esp. the proprietor, manager, or MC of a circus, fair, or other variety show. ■ a person skilled in dramatic or entertaining presentation, performance, or publicity.
– DERIVATIVES **show·man·ship** /-ˌSHip/ **n.**

Show Me State a nickname for the state of MISSOURI.

shown /SHōn/ past participle of SHOW.

show-off ▶ **n.** informal a person who acts pretentiously or who publicly parades themselves, their possessions, or their accomplishments.

show·piece /ˈSHōˌpēs/ ▶ **n.** something that attracts attention or admiration as an outstanding example of its type: *the factory has expanded and become a showpiece of American industry.* ■ something that offers a particular opportunity for a display of skill: *the serenade was a showpiece for the wind section.* ■ an item of work presented for exhibition or display.

show·place /ˈSHōˌplās/ ▶ **n.** a place of beauty or interest attracting many visitors.

show·reel /ˈSHōˌrēl/ ▶ **n.** a short videotape containing examples of an actor's or director's work for showing to potential employers.

show·room /ˈSHōˌro͞om, -ˌro͝om/ ▶ **n.** a room used to display goods for sale, such as appliances, cars, or furniture.

show-stop·per ▶ **n.** informal a performance or item receiving prolonged applause. ■ something that is striking or has great popular appeal: *a show-stopper of a smile.*
– DERIVATIVES **show-stop·ping adj.**

show tri·al ▶ **n.** a judicial trial held in public with the intention of influencing or satisfying public opinion, rather than of ensuring justice.

show tune ▶ **n.** a song from a musical that has become popular in its own right.

show win·dow ▶ **n.** a store window looking onto a street, used for exhibiting goods.

show·y /ˈSHō-ē/ ▶ **adj.** (**showier, showiest**) having a striking appearance or style, typically by being excessively bright, colorful, or ostentatious: *showy flowers | she wore a great deal of showy costume jewelry.*
– DERIVATIVES **show·i·ly** /-əlē/ **adv., show·i·ness n.**

sho·yu /ˈSHōyo͞o/ ▶ **n.** a type of Japanese soy sauce.
– ORIGIN from Japanese *shōyu.*

s.h.p. ▶ **abbr.** shaft horsepower.

shpt. ▶ **abbr.** shipment.

shr. ▶ **abbr.** share; shares.

shrank /SHraNGk/ past of SHRINK.

shrap·nel /ˈSHrapnəl/ ▶ **n.** fragments of a bomb, shell, or other object thrown out by an explosion.
– ORIGIN early 19th cent.: named after General Henry *Shrapnel* (1761–1842), the British soldier who invented the shell.

shred /SHred/ ▶ **n.** (usu. **shreds**) a strip of some material, such as paper, cloth, or food, that has been torn, cut, or scraped from something larger: *her beautiful dress was **torn to shreds.*** ■ [often with negative] a very small amount: *there was not **a shred of** evidence that linked him to the fire.*
▶ **v.** (**shreds, shredding, shredded**) [with obj.] tear or cut into shreds: (as adj. **shredded**) *shredded cabbage.*
– PHRASES **in shreds** very badly damaged; destroyed or ruined: *my reputation will be in shreds.* **tear someone/something to shreds** informal criticize someone or something forcefully or aggressively: *a defense counsel would tear his evidence to shreds.*
– ORIGIN late Old English *scrēad* 'piece cut off,' *scrēadian* 'trim, prune'; related to SHROUD.

shred·ded wheat ▶ **n.** a breakfast cereal made of cooked wheat in long brittle shreds that are pressed into compact pieces.

shred·der /ˈSHredər/ ▶ **n. 1** a machine or other device for shredding something, esp. documents.
2 informal a snowboarder. [from the notion that snowboarders tear up snow, making it bad for skiing.]

Shreve·port /ˈSHrēvˌpôrt/ an industrial city in northwestern Louisiana, on the Red River, near the border with Texas; pop. 199,729 (est. 2008).

shrew /SHro͞o/ ▶ **n. 1** a small mouselike insectivorous mammal with a long pointed snout and tiny eyes. ● Family Soricidae: many genera, in particular *Sorex* and *Crocidura,* and numerous species.
2 a bad-tempered or aggressively assertive woman.
– ORIGIN Old English *scrēawa, scrǣwa,* of Germanic origin; related words in Germanic languages have senses such as 'dwarf,' 'devil,' or 'fox.'

shrewd /SHro͞od/ ▶ **adj. 1** having or showing sharp powers of judgment; astute: *she was shrewd enough to guess the motive behind his gesture | a shrewd career move.*
2 archaic (esp. of weather) piercingly cold: *a shrewd east wind.* ■ (of a blow) severe: *a bayonet's shrewd thrust.* ■ mischievous; malicious.
– DERIVATIVES **shrewd·ly adv., shrewd·ness n.**
– ORIGIN Middle English (in the sense 'evil in nature or character'): from SHREW in the sense 'evil person or thing,' or as the past participle of obsolete *shrew* 'to curse.' The word developed the sense 'cunning,' and gradually gained a favorable connotation during the 17th cent.

shrew·ish /ˈSHro͞o-iSH/ ▶ **adj.** (of a woman) bad-tempered or aggressively assertive: *his shrewish wife.*
– DERIVATIVES **shrew·ish·ly adv., shrew·ish·ness n.**

shrew-mole ▶ **n.** a small shrewlike mole with a long tail, native to Asia and North America. ● *Neurotrichus* and other genera, family Talpidae: five species, including *N. gibbsii* of the western US.

Shri /SHrē/ ▶ **n.** Indian variant spelling of SRI.

shriek /SHrēk/ ▶ **v.** [no obj.] utter a high-pitched piercing sound or words, esp. as an expression of terror, pain, or excitement: *the audience **shrieked with laughter*** | [with direct speech] *"There it is!" she shrieked* | [with obj.] *she was shrieking abuse at a taxi driver.* ■ (of something inanimate) make a high-pitched screeching sound: *the wheels shrieked as the car sped away.* ■ be very obvious or strikingly discordant: *the patterned carpets shrieked at Betsy from the shabby store.*
▶ **n.** a high-pitched piercing cry or sound; a scream: *shrieks of laughter.*
– DERIVATIVES **shriek·er n.**
– ORIGIN late 15th cent. (as a verb): imitative; compare with dialect *screak,* Old Norse *skrækja,* also with SCREECH.

shriev·al /ˈSHrēvəl/ ▶ **adj.** chiefly historical of or relating to a sheriff.
– ORIGIN late 17th cent.: from *shrieve,* obsolete variant of SHERIFF.

shriev·al·ty /ˈSHrēvəltē/ ▶ **n.** (pl. **shrievalties**) chiefly historical the office, jurisdiction, or tenure of a sheriff.

shrift /SHrift/ ▶ **n.** archaic confession, esp. to a priest: *go to shrift.* See also SHORT SHRIFT. ■ absolution by a priest.
– ORIGIN Old English *scrift* 'penance imposed after confession,' from SHRIVE.

shrike /SHrīk/ ▶ **n.** a songbird with a strong sharply hooked bill, often impaling its prey of small birds, lizards, and insects on thorns. Also called BUTCHERBIRD. ● Family Laniidae: several genera and numerous species, esp. in Africa, e.g., the **northern shrike** (*Lanius excubitor*), of both Eurasia and North America. ■ used in names of similar birds of other families, e.g., **peppershrike.**
– ORIGIN mid 16th cent.: perhaps related to Old English *scrīc* 'thrush' and Middle Low German *schrīk* 'corncrake,' of imitative origin.

shrill /SHril/ ▶ **adj.** (of a voice or sound) high-pitched and piercing: *a shrill laugh.* ■ derogatory (esp. of a complaint or demand) loud and forceful: *a concession to their shrill demands.*
▶ **v.** [no obj.] make a shrill noise: *a piercing whistle shrilled through the night air.* ■ speak or cry with a shrill voice: [with direct speech] *"For God's sake!" shrilled Jan.*
▶ **n.** [in sing.] a shrill sound or cry: *the rising shrill of women's voices.*
– DERIVATIVES **shrill·ness n., shril·ly** /ˈSHri(l)lē/ **adv.**
– ORIGIN late Middle English: of Germanic origin; related to Low German *schrell* 'sharp in tone or taste.'

shrimp /SHrimp/ ▶ **n.** (pl. **same** or **shrimps**) a small free-swimming crustacean with an elongated body, typically marine and frequently harvested for food. ● *Pandalus, Penaeus, Crangon,* and other genera, order Decapoda: numerous species, including the commercially important **pink shrimp** (*Penaeus duorarum*). ■ informal, derogatory a small, physically weak person.
▶ **v.** [no obj.] fish for shrimp: (as adj. **shrimping**) *a shrimping net.*
– DERIVATIVES **shrimp·y adj.**
– ORIGIN Middle English: probably related to Middle Low German *schrempen* 'to wrinkle,' Middle High German *schrimpfen* 'to contract,' also to SCRIMP.

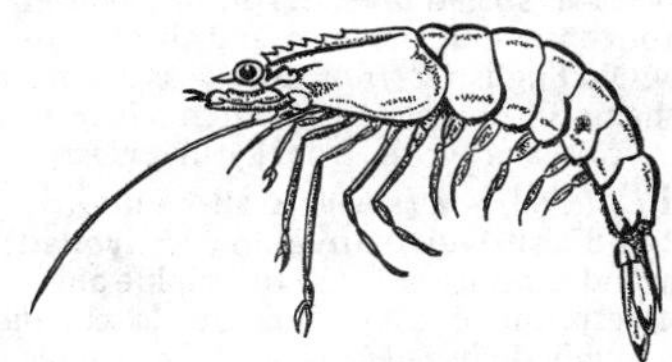

pink shrimp

shrimp·er /ˈSHrimpər/ ▶ **n. 1** a boat designed or used for catching shrimp.
2 a person who fishes for shrimp.

shrimp plant ▶ **n.** an evergreen Mexican shrub with clusters of small flowers in pinkish-brown or pale yellow bracts that are said to resemble shrimp, widely grown as a houseplant. ● *Justicia brandegeana,* family Acanthaceae.

shrine /SHrīn/ ▶ **n.** a place regarded as holy because of its associations with a divinity or a sacred

S

person or relic, typically marked by a building or other construction. ■ a place associated with or containing memorabilia of a particular revered person or thing: *her grave has become a shrine for fans from all over the world.* ■ a casket containing sacred relics; a reliquary. ■ a niche or enclosure containing a religious statue or other object.
▶ v. [with obj.] literary enshrine.
– ORIGIN Old English *scrīn* 'cabinet, chest, reliquary,' of Germanic origin; related to Dutch *schrijn* and German *Schrein*, from Latin *scrinium* 'chest for books.'

Shrin·er /ˈSHrīnər/ ▶ n. a member of the Ancient Arabic Order of Nobles of the Mystic Shrine, a charitable society founded in the US in 1872.

shrink /SHriNGk/ ▶ v. (past **shrank** /SHraNGk/; past participle **shrunk** /SHrəNGk/ or (esp. as adj.) **shrunken** /ˈSHrəNGkən/) **1** become or make smaller in size or amount; contract or cause to contract: [no obj.] *the workforce has shrunk to less than a thousand* | [with obj.] *the summer sun had shrunk and dried the wood* | (as adj **shrinking**) *the shrinking market has provoked a massive price war.* ■ [no obj.] (of clothes or material) become smaller as a result of being immersed in water. ■ (as adj. **shrunken**) (esp. of a person's face or other part of the body) withered, wrinkled, or shriveled through old age or illness: *a tiny shrunken face and enormous eyes.* ■ [no obj.] (**shrink into oneself**) become withdrawn. ■ [with obj.] (**shrink something on**) slip a metal tire or other fitting onto (something) while it is expanded with heat and allow it to tighten in place: *the metal is unsuitable for shrinking onto wooden staves.*
2 [no obj.] move back or away, esp. because of fear or disgust: *she shrank away from him, covering her face* | *he shrank back against the wall.* ■ [often with negative] (**shrink from**) be averse to or unwilling to do (something difficult or unappealing): *I don't shrink from my responsibilities.*
▶ n. informal a clinical psychologist, psychiatrist, or psychotherapist: *you should see a shrink.* [from *headshrinker.*]
– DERIVATIVES **shrink·a·ble** adj., **shrink·er** n., **shrink·ing·ly** adv.
– ORIGIN Old English *scrincan*, of Germanic origin; related to Swedish *skrynka* 'to wrinkle.'

shrink·age /ˈSHriNGkij/ ▶ n. the process, fact, or amount of shrinking: *give long curtains good hems to allow for shrinkage.* ■ an allowance made for reduction in the earnings of a business due to wastage or theft.

shrink-fit ▶ adj. designed to fit perfectly after anticipated shrinkage: *a shrink-fit chuck.*
▶ n. a system that uses shrink-fit parts or fittings.

shrink·ing vi·o·let ▶ n. informal an exaggeratedly shy person: *Dorothy is no shrinking violet when it comes to expressing her views.*

shrink-re·sist·ant ▶ adj. (of textiles or garments) resistant to shrinkage.

shrink-wrap ▶ v. [with obj.] package (an article) by enclosing it in clinging transparent plastic film that shrinks tightly onto it: (as adj. **shrink-wrapped**) *shrink-wrapped blocks of cheese.* ■ (as adj. **shrink-wrapped**) Computing (of a product) sold commercially as a ready-made software package.
▶ n. clinging transparent plastic film used to enclose an article as packaging.

shrive /SHrīv/ ▶ v. (past **shrove** /SHrōv/; past participle **shriven** /ˈSHrivən/) [with obj.] archaic (of a priest) hear the confession of, assign penance to, and absolve (someone). ■ (**shrive oneself**) present oneself to a priest for confession, penance, and absolution.
– ORIGIN Old English *scrīfan* 'impose as a penance,' of Germanic origin; related to Dutch *schrijven* and German *schreiben* 'write,' from Latin *scribere* 'write.'

shriv·el /ˈSHrivəl/ ▶ v. (**shrivels, shriveling, shriveled**; Brit. **shrivels, shrivelling, shrivelled**) wrinkle and contract or cause to wrinkle and contract, esp. due to loss of moisture: [no obj.] *the flowers simply shriveled up* | [with obj.] *a heat wave so intense that it shriveled the grapes in every vineyard.* ■ [no obj.] lose momentum, will, or desire; become insignificant or ineffectual: *his spirit shriveled and his talent atrophied.* ■ [with obj.] cause to feel worthless or insignificant: *she shriveled him with one glance.*
– ORIGIN mid 16th cent.: perhaps of Scandinavian origin; compare with Swedish dialect *skryvla* 'to wrinkle.'

shriv·eled /ˈSHrivəld/ (Brit. **shrivelled**) ▶ adj. wrinkled and contracted, esp. due to loss of moisture or old age: *her long, shriveled hand.*

shriv·en /ˈSHrivən/ past participle of **SHRIVE**.

shroom /SHro͞om/ ▶ n. informal a mushroom, esp. one with hallucinogenic properties.
– DERIVATIVES **shroom·er** n.
– ORIGIN 1970s: shortening of **MUSHROOM**.

shroud /SHroud/ ▶ n. **1** a length of cloth or an enveloping garment in which a dead person is wrapped for burial: *he was buried in a linen shroud.* ■ technical a protective casing or cover.
2 a thing that envelops or obscures something: *a shroud of mist* | *they operate behind a shroud of secrecy.*
3 (**shrouds**) a set of ropes forming part of the standing rigging of a sailing vessel and supporting the mast from the sides. ■ (also **shroud line**) each of the lines joining the canopy of a parachute to the harness.
▶ v. [with obj.] **1** wrap or dress (a body) in a shroud for burial.
2 cover or envelop so as to conceal from view: *mountains shrouded by cloud* | *the mystery that shrouds the origins of the universe.*
– ORIGIN late Old English *scrūd* 'garment, clothing,' of Germanic origin, from a base meaning 'cut'; related to **SHRED**. An early sense of the verb (Middle English) was 'cover so as to protect.'

shroud-laid ▶ adj. (of rope) made of four strands laid right-handed, typically around a core, used esp. on yachts.

shrove /SHrōv/ past of **SHRIVE**.

Shrove·tide /ˈSHrōvˌtīd/ ▶ n. Shrove Tuesday and the two days preceding it, when it was formerly customary to attend confession.
– ORIGIN late Middle English: of obscure origin; the first element related to **SHRIVE**.

Shrove Tues·day /SHrōv/ ▶ n. the day before Ash Wednesday. Though named for its former religious significance, it is chiefly marked by feasting and celebration, which traditionally preceded the observance of the Lenten fast. Compare with **MARDI GRAS**.

shrub[1] /SHrəb/ ▶ n. a woody plant that is smaller than a tree and has several main stems arising at or near the ground.
– DERIVATIVES **shrub·by** adj.
– ORIGIN Old English *scrubb*, *scrybb* 'shrubbery'; compare with West Flemish *schrobbe* 'vetch,' Norwegian *skrubba* 'dwarf cornel,' also with **SCRUB**[2].

shrub[2] ▶ n. **1** a drink made of sweetened fruit juice and liquor, typically rum or brandy.
2 a slightly acid cordial made from fruit juice and water.
– ORIGIN early 18th cent.: from Arabic *šurb*, *šarāb*, from *šariba* 'to drink'; compare with **SHERBET** and **SYRUP**.

shrub·ber·y /ˈSHrəb(ə)rē/ ▶ n. (pl. **shrubberies**) shrubs collectively. ■ an area planted with shrubs.

shrug /SHrəg/ ▶ v. (**shrugs, shrugging, shrugged**) [with obj.] raise (one's shoulders) slightly and momentarily to express doubt, ignorance, or indifference: *Jimmy looked inquiringly at Pete, who shrugged his shoulders* | [no obj.] *he just shrugged and didn't look interested.* ■ (**shrug something off**) dismiss something as unimportant: *the managing director shrugged off the criticism.*
▶ n. **1** an act or instance of shrugging one's shoulders: *she gave him a dismissive shrug.*
2 a woman's close-fitting cardigan or jacket, cut short at the front and back so that only the arms and shoulders are covered.
– ORIGIN late Middle English (in the sense 'fidget'): of unknown origin.

shrunk /SHrəNGk/ (also **shrunken**) past participle of **SHRINK**.

shtetl /ˈSHtetl, ˈSHtātl/ ▶ n. (pl. **shtetlach** /ˈSHtetläKH, ˈSHtätläKH/ or **shtetls**) historical a small Jewish town or village in eastern Europe.
– ORIGIN 1940s: Yiddish, 'little town.'

shtick /SHtik/ ▶ n. informal an attention-getting or theatrical routine, gimmick, or talent.
– ORIGIN 1960s: Yiddish, from German *Stück* 'piece.'

shtup /SHto͝op/ (also **schtup**) vulgar slang ▶ v. (**shtups, shtupping, shtupped**) [with obj.] have sexual intercourse with (someone).
▶ n. an act of sexual intercourse.
– ORIGIN 1960s: Yiddish.

shu·bun·kin /SHo͞oˈbəNGkin, ˈSHo͞obənˌkin/ ▶ n. a goldfish of an ornamental variety, having black spots, red patches, and long fins and tail.
– ORIGIN early 20th cent.: from Japanese.

shuck /SHək/ ▶ n. **1** an outer covering such as a husk or pod, esp. the husk of an ear of corn. ■ the shell of an oyster or clam. ■ the integument of certain insect pupae or larvae.
2 informal a person or thing regarded as worthless or contemptible: *William didn't dig the idea at all and said it was a shuck.*
▶ exclam. (**shucks**) informal used to express surprise, regret, irritation, or, in response to praise, self-deprecation: *"Thank you for getting it." "Oh, shucks, it was nothing."* See also **AW-SHUCKS**.
▶ v. [with obj.] **1** remove the shucks from corn or shellfish: *shuck and drain the oysters.* ■ informal take off (a garment): *she shucked off her nightdress and started dressing.* ■ informal abandon; get rid of: *the regime's ability to shuck off its totalitarian characteristics.*
2 informal cause (someone) to believe something that is not true; fool or tease.
– DERIVATIVES **shuck·er** n.
– ORIGIN late 17th cent.: of unknown origin.

shud·der /ˈSHədər/ ▶ v. [no obj.] (of a person) tremble convulsively, typically as a result of fear or revulsion: *I shuddered with horror.* ■ (esp. of a vehicle, machine, or building) shake or vibrate deeply: *the train shuddered and edged forward.* ■ (usu. as adj. **shuddering**) (of a person's breathing) be unsteady, esp. as a result of emotional disturbance: *he drew a deep, shuddering breath.*
▶ n. an act of shuddering: *the elevator rose with a shudder* | figurative *the peso's devaluation sent shudders through the market.*
– PHRASES **give someone the shudders** informal cause someone to feel repugnance or fear: *it gives me the shudders to hear you use words like that.* **I shudder to think** used to convey that something is too unpleasant to contemplate: *I shudder to think what might have happened if he hadn't woken you up.*
– DERIVATIVES **shud·der·ing·ly** adv., **shud·der·y** adj.
– ORIGIN Middle English (as a verb): from Middle Dutch *schūderen*, from a Germanic base meaning 'shake.'

Shu·dra (also **Sudra** /ˈso͞odrə/) ▶ n. a member of the worker caste, lowest of the four Hindu castes.
– ORIGIN from Sanskrit *śūdra*.

shuf·fle /ˈSHəfəl/ ▶ v. **1** [no obj.] walk by dragging one's feet along or without lifting them fully from the ground: *I stepped into my skis and shuffled to the edge of the steep slope* | (as adj. **shuffling**) *she heard Grandma's shuffling steps.* ■ shift one's position while sitting or move one's feet while standing, typically because of boredom, nervousness, or embarrassment: *Christine shuffled uneasily in her chair* | [with obj.] *Ben shuffled his feet in the awkward silence.*
2 [with obj.] rearrange (a deck of cards) by sliding the cards over each other quickly. ■ move (people or things) around so as to occupy different positions or to be in a different order: *she shuffled her papers into a neat pile.* ■ [no obj.] (**shuffle through**) sort or look through (a number of things) hurriedly: *he shuffled through the papers on his desk.*
3 [with obj.] (**shuffle something into**) put part of one's body into (an item of clothing), typically in a clumsy way: *shuffling her feet into a pair of shoes, she tiptoed out of the room.* ■ (**shuffle something off**) get out of or avoid a responsibility or obligation: *some hospitals can shuffle off their responsibilities by claiming to have no suitable facilities.* ■ [no obj.] archaic behave in a shifty or evasive manner: *Mr. Mills did not frankly own it, but seemed to shuffle about it.* ■ [no obj.] (**shuffle out of**) archaic get out of (a difficult situation) in an underhanded or evasive manner: *he shuffles out of the consequences by vague charges of undue influence.*
▶ n. **1** [in sing.] a shuffling movement, walk, or sound: *there was a shuffle of approaching feet.* ■ a quick dragging or scraping movement of the feet in dancing. ■ a dance performed with such steps. ■ a piece of music for or in the style of such a dance. ■ a rhythmic motif based on such a dance step and typical of early jazz, consisting of alternating quarter notes and eighth notes in a triplet pattern.
2 an act of shuffling a deck of cards. ■ a change of order or relative positions; a reshuffle: *the president will deliver a speech short on economic details Cabinet shuffles but long on fight.* ■ a facility on a CD player for playing tracks in an arbitrary order: [as modifier] *a fully programmable CD changer with shuffle play.*
3 archaic a piece of equivocation or subterfuge.
– PHRASES **be** (or **get**) **lost in the shuffle** informal be overlooked or missed in a confused or crowded situation. **shuffle off this mortal coil** see **COIL**[2].
– DERIVATIVES **shuf·fler** /ˈSHəf(ə)lər/ n.
– ORIGIN mid 16th cent.: perhaps from Low German *schuffeln* 'walk clumsily,' also 'deal dishonestly, shuffle (cards),' of Germanic origin; related to **SHOVE** and **SCUFFLE**.

shuf·fle·board /ˈSHəfəlˌbôrd/ ▶ n. a game played by pushing disks with a long-handled cue over a marked surface.
– ORIGIN see **SHOVELBOARD**.

shuf·ti /ˈSHo͝oftē/ ▶ n. (pl. **shuftis** /-tēz/) Brit. informal a look or reconnoiter, esp. a quick one: *I'll take a shufti round the wood while I'm about it.*
– ORIGIN 1940s (originally military slang): from Arabic *šāfa* 'try to see.'

shul /SHo͞ol, SHo͝ol/ ▶ n. a synagogue: *on High Holidays he attended shul.*
– ORIGIN late 19th cent.: Yiddish, from German *Schule* 'school.'

Shu·la /ˈSHo͞olə/, Don (1930–), US football coach and player; full name *Donald Francis Shula*. After seven seasons of playing professional football, he coached the Baltimore Colts 1963–69 and then the Miami Dolphins 1970–95. Upon his retirement in 1995, he had achieved a record 347 regular season and playoff games won. Football Hall of Fame (1997).

shu·mai /ˈSHo͞oˌmī/ ▶ **plural n.** small steamed dumplings, typically stuffed with seafood and vegetables.
– ORIGIN Japanese, ultimately from Chinese.

Shu·men /ˈSHo͞oˌmen/ an industrial city in northeastern Bulgaria; pop. 86,978 (2008).

shun /SHən/ ▶ **v.** (**shuns, shunning, shunned**) [with obj.] persistently avoid, ignore, or reject (someone or something) through antipathy or caution: *he shunned fashionable society*.
– ORIGIN Old English *scunian* 'abhor, shrink back with fear, seek safety from an enemy,' of unknown origin.

shunt /SHənt/ ▶ **v. 1** [with obj.] push or pull (a train or part of a train) from the main line to a siding or from one track to another: *their train had been shunted into a siding*. ■ (usu. **be shunted**) push or shove (someone or something): *chairs were being shunted back and forth*. ■ direct or divert (someone or something) to a less important place or position: *amateurs were gradually being shunted to filing jobs*.
2 [with obj.] provide (an electrical current) with a conductor joining two points of a circuit, through which more or less of the current may be diverted.
▶ **n. 1** an act of pushing or shoving something.
2 an electrical conductor joining two points of a circuit, through which more or less of a current may be diverted. ■ Surgery an alternative path for the passage of the blood or other body fluid: [as modifier] *shunt surgery*.
– ORIGIN Middle English (in the sense 'move suddenly aside'): perhaps from SHUN.

shunt·er /ˈSHəntər/ ▶ **n.** a small locomotive used for shunting. ■ a railroad worker engaged in such work, esp. to couple and uncouple wagons.

shun·ya·ta /ˈSHo͞onyəˌtä/ (also **sunyata**) ▶ **n.** Buddhism the doctrine that phenomena are devoid of an immutable or determinate intrinsic nature. Compare with TATHATA.
– ORIGIN from Sanskrit *śūnyatā* 'emptiness.'

shu·ra /ˈSHo͝orə/ ▶ **n.** Islam the principle of consultation, in particular as applied to government. ■ a consultative council.
– ORIGIN from Arabic *šūrā* 'consultation.'

shu·ri·ken /ˈSHo͝oriˌken/ ▶ **n.** a weapon in the form of a star with projecting blades or points, used as a missile in some martial arts.
– ORIGIN Japanese, literally 'dagger in the hand.'

shush /SHo͝oSH, SHəSH/ ▶ **exclam.** be quiet: *"Shush! Do you want to wake everyone?"*
▶ **n. 1** an utterance of "shush": *the thumps were followed by shushes from the aunts*.
2 chiefly Brit. a soft swishing or rustling sound.
▶ **v. 1** [with obj.] tell or signal (someone) to be silent: *she shushed him with a wave*. ■ [no obj.] become or remain silent: *Beth told her to shush*.
2 [no obj.] chiefly Brit. move with or make a soft swishing or rustling sound: *I stood to watch a big liner shushing slowly past* | (as noun **shushing**) *she could hear the gentle shushing of the waves*.
– ORIGIN 1920s: imitative.

Shu·swap /ˈSHo͞oˌswäp/ ▶ **n.** (pl. **same** or **Shuswaps**) **1** a member of an American Indian people of southern British Columbia.
2 the Salishan language of this people.
▶ **adj.** of or relating to this people or their language.
– ORIGIN from the Shuswap self-designation *sexwépemc*.

shut /SHət/ ▶ **v.** (**shuts, shutting**; past and past participle **shut**) [with obj.] move (something) into position so that it blocks an opening: *shut the window, please* | *she shut her lips tight* | (as adj. **shut**) *she slammed the door shut*. ■ [no obj.] (of something that can block an opening) move or be moved into position: *the door shut behind him*. ■ block an opening into (something) by moving something into position: *he shut the box and locked it*. ■ (**shut it**) [in imperative] Brit. informal stop talking; be quiet. ■ keep (someone or something) in a place by closing something such as a door: *it was his own dog that he had accidentally shut outside*. ■ fold or bring together the sides of (something) so as to close it: *he shut his book*. ■ prevent access to or along: *they ought to shut the path up to that terrible cliff*. ■ make or become unavailable for business or service, either permanently or until due to be open again; close: *we shut the shop for lunch* | [no obj.] *the accident and emergency departments will shut*.
– PHRASES **be** (or **get**) **shut of** informal be (or get) rid of: *I'd be glad to be shut of him*. **shut the door on** (or **to**) see DOOR. **shut one's eyes to** see EYE. **shut one's mind to** see MIND. **shut the stable door after the horse has bolted** try to avoid or prevent something bad or unwelcome when it is already too late to do so. **shut up shop** see SHOP. **shut your face** (or **mouth** or **trap**)! informal used as a rude or angry way of telling someone to be quiet.
– PHRASAL VERBS **shut down** (or **shut something down**) cease (or cause something to cease) business or operation: *the plant's operators decided to shut down the reactor*. **shut someone/something in** keep someone or something inside a place by closing something such as a door: *her parents shut her in an upstairs room*. ■ enclose or surround a place: *the village is shut in by the mountains on either side*. ■ trap something by shutting a door or drawer on it: *you shut your finger in the door*. **shut off** (or **shut something off**) (used esp. in relation to water, electricity, or gas) stop (or cause something to stop) flowing: *he was about to shut off the power*. ■ stop (or cause something to stop) working: *the engines shut off automatically*. ■ (**shut something off**) block the entrances and exits of something: *the six compartments were being shut off from each other*. **shut oneself off** isolate oneself from other people. **shut someone/something out** keep someone or something out of a place or situation: *the door swung closed behind them, shutting out some of the noise*. ■ prevent an opponent from scoring in a game. ■ screen someone or something from view: *clouds shut out the stars*. ■ prevent something from occurring: *there was a high-mindedness that shut out any consideration of alternatives*. ■ block something such as a painful memory from the mind: *anything he didn't like he shut out*. **shut up** (or **shut someone up**) [often in imperative] informal stop (or cause someone to stop) talking: *just shut up and listen* | *I lifted a finger slightly to shut him up*. **shut something up** close all doors and windows of a building or room, typically because it will be unoccupied for some time.
– ORIGIN Old English *scyttan* 'put (a bolt) in position to hold fast'; related to Dutch *schutten* 'shut up, obstruct,' also to SHOOT.

shut·down /ˈSHətˌdoun/ ▶ **n.** a closure of a factory or system, typically a temporary closure due to a malfunction or for maintenance. ■ a turning off of a computer or computer system.

Shute /SHo͞ot/, Nevil (1899–1960), English novelist; pseudonym of *Nevil Shute Norway*. After World War II he settled in Australia, which provides the setting for his later novels. Notable works: *A Town Like Alice* (1950) and *On the Beach* (1957).

shut-eye ▶ **n.** informal sleep: *we'd better get some shut-eye*.

shut-in ▶ **n. 1** a person confined indoors, esp. as a result of physical or mental disability.
2 a state or period in which an oil or gas well has available but unused capacity.

shut·off ▶ **n.** [usu. as modifier] a device used for stopping a supply or operation: *a shutoff valve*. ■ the cessation of flow, supply, or activity.

shut·out /ˈSHətˌout/ ▶ **n.** a competition or game in which the losing side fails to score.

shut·out bid ▶ **n.** Bridge a high bid intended to end the auction; a preemptive bid.

shut·ter /ˈSHətər/ ▶ **n. 1** each of a pair of hinged panels, often louvered, fixed inside or outside a window that can be closed for security or privacy or to keep out light.
2 Photography a device that opens and closes to expose the film in a camera.
3 Music the blind enclosing the swell box in an organ, used for controlling the volume of sound.
▶ **v.** [with obj.] close the shutters of (a window or building): *the windows were shuttered against the afternoon heat* | (as adj. **shuttered**) *barred and shuttered stores*. ■ close (a business): *the city was gripped by economic forces that were squeezing its tax base and shuttering its factories*.
– DERIVATIVES **shut·ter·less** adj.

shut·ter·bug /ˈSHətərˌbəg/ ▶ **n.** informal an enthusiastic amateur photographer.

shut·ter·ing /ˈSHətəriNG/ ▶ **n.** wood in planks or strips used as a temporary structure for fencing to contain setting concrete, to support the sides of dirt trenches, or for similar purposes. ■ a temporary structure of this kind.

shut·ter pri·or·i·ty ▶ **n.** Photography a system used in some automatic cameras in which the shutter speed is selected by the user and the appropriate aperture is then set by the camera. Compare with APERTURE PRIORITY.

shut·ter re·lease ▶ **n.** the button on a camera that is pressed to make the shutter open.

shut·ter speed ▶ **n.** Photography the time for which a shutter is open at a given setting.

shut·tle /ˈSHətl/ ▶ **n. 1** a form of transportation that travels regularly between two places: *the nine o'clock shuttle from Boston* | [as modifier] *a shuttle bus service from the city center*. ■ short for SPACE SHUTTLE.
2 a wooden device with two pointed ends holding a bobbin, used for carrying the weft thread between the warp threads in weaving. ■ a bobbin carrying the lower thread in a sewing machine.
3 short for SHUTTLECOCK.
▶ **v.** [no obj.] travel regularly between two or more places: *he shuttled between Manhattan and Silicon Valley*. ■ [with obj.] transport in a shuttle: *the river taxi shuttled employees between the newspaper's offices and the capital*.
– ORIGIN Old English *scytel* 'dart, missile,' of Germanic origin; compare with Old Norse *skutill* 'harpoon'; related to SHOOT. Sense 1 and the verb are from the movement of the bobbin from one side of the loom to the other and back.

shut·tle·cock /ˈSHətlˌkäk/ ▶ **n.** a cork to which feathers are attached to form a cone shape, or a similar object of plastic, struck with rackets in the games of badminton and battledore.

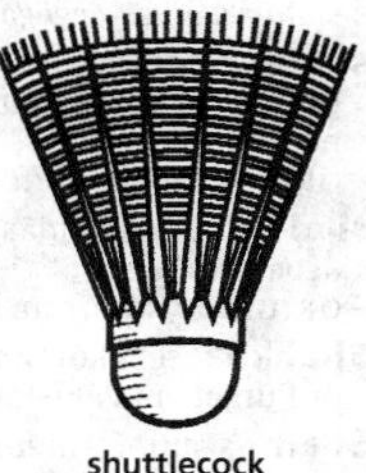
shuttlecock

shut·tle·craft /ˈSHətlˌkraft/ ▶ **n.** (in science fiction) a space shuttle, typically one used for traveling between a larger spaceship and a planet or between planets in a solar system.

shut·tle di·plo·ma·cy ▶ **n.** negotiations conducted by a mediator who travels between two or more parties that are reluctant to hold direct discussions.

shy[1] /SHī/ ▶ **adj.** (**shyer, shyest**) **1** being reserved or having or showing nervousness or timidity in the company of other people: *I was pretty shy at school* | *a shy smile*. ■ [predic.] (**shy about**) slow or reluctant to do (something): *she has never been shy about discussing her efforts to raise aesthetic standards*. ■ [in combination] having a dislike of or aversion to a specified thing: *they were a little camera-shy*. ■ (of a wild mammal or bird) reluctant to remain in sight of humans.
2 [predic.] (**shy of**) informal less than; short of: *he won the championship with a score three points shy of a world record*. ■ before: *he left school just shy of his fourteenth birthday*.
3 (of a plant) not bearing flowers or fruit well or prolifically.
▶ **v.** (**shies, shying, shied**) [no obj.] (esp. of a horse) start suddenly aside in fright at an object, noise, or movement. ■ (**shy from**) avoid doing or becoming involved in (something) due to nervousness or a lack of confidence: *don't shy away from saying what you think*.
▶ **n.** a sudden startled movement, esp. of a frightened horse.
– DERIVATIVES **shy·er** /ˈSHī(ə)r/ **n.**, **shy·ly** adv.
– ORIGIN Old English *scēoh* '(of a horse) easily frightened,' of Germanic origin; related to German *scheuen* 'shun,' *scheuchen* 'scare'; compare with ESCHEW. The verb dates from the mid 17th cent.

shy[2] dated ▶ **v.** (**shies, shying, shied**) [with obj.] fling or throw (something) at a target: *he tore the glasses off and shied them at her*.
▶ **n.** (pl. **shies**) an act of flinging or throwing something at a target.
– PHRASES **have a shy at** try to hit something, esp. with a ball or stone. ■ archaic attempt to do or obtain something. ■ archaic jeer at: *you are always having a shy at Lady Ann and her relations*.
– ORIGIN late 18th cent.: of unknown origin.

Shy·lock /ˈSHīˌläk/ a Jewish moneylender in Shakespeare's *Merchant of Venice*, who lends money to Antonio but demands in return a pound of Antonio's own flesh should the debt not be repaid on time. ■ (as noun **a Shylock**) a moneylender who charges extremely high rates of interest.

shy·ness /ˈSHīnis/ ▶ **n.** the quality or state of being shy: *gradually he overcame his natural shyness*.

shy·ster /ˈSHīstər/ ▶ **n.** informal a person, esp. a lawyer, who uses unscrupulous, fraudulent, or deceptive methods in business.
– ORIGIN mid 19th cent.: origin uncertain; perhaps related to German *Scheisser* 'worthless person.'

SI ▶ **abbr.** ■ the international system of units of measurement. [from French *Système International*.] ■ Law statutory instrument.

Si ▶ **symbol** the chemical element silicon.

si /sē/ ▶ **n.** Music another term for TI.
– ORIGIN early 18th cent.: from the initial letters of *Sancte Iohannes*, the closing words of a Latin hymn (see SOLMIZATION).

PRONUNCIATION KEY ə *ago, up*; ər *over, fur*; a *hat*; ā *ate*; ä *car*; e *let*; ē *see*; i *fit*; ī *by*; NG *sing*; ō *go*; ô *law, for*; oi *toy*; o͝o *good*; o͞o *goo*; ou *out*; TH *thin*; T͟H *then*; ZH *vision*

S

Sia·chen Glac·ier /'syäCHən/ a glacier in the Karakoram mountains in northwestern India, at an altitude of about 17,800 feet (5,500 m). Extending over 44 miles (70 km), it is one of the world's longest glaciers.

si·al /'sī,al/ ▶ **n.** Geology the material of the upper or continental part of the earth's crust, characterized as being of relatively low density and rich in silica and alumina. Contrasted with **SIMA**.
– ORIGIN 1920s: from the initial letters of **SILICA** and **ALUMINA**.

si·al·a·gogue /sī'alə,gäg/ ▶ **n.** Medicine a drug that promotes the secretion of saliva.
– ORIGIN late 18th cent.: from French, from Greek *sialon* 'saliva' + *agōgos* 'leading.'

si·al·ic ac·id /sī'alik/ ▶ **n.** Biochemistry a substance present in saliva that consists of acyl derivatives of neuraminic acid.
– ORIGIN 1950s: *sialic* from Greek *sialon* 'saliva' + **-IC**.

si·al·i·dase /sī'alidās/ ▶ **n.** another term for **NEURAMINIDASE**.
– ORIGIN 1950s: from Greek *sialon* 'saliva' + **-IDE** + **-ASE**.

Si·al·kot /sē'älkōt/ an industrial city in the province of Punjab, in Pakistan; pop. 502,700 (est. 2009).

Si·am /sī'am/ former name (until 1939) of **THAILAND**.

Si·am, Gulf of former name of the Gulf of Thailand (see **THAILAND, GULF OF**).

si·a·mang /'sēə,mäNG/ ▶ **n.** a large black gibbon native to Sumatra and the Malay peninsula. ● *Hylobates syndactylus*, family Hylobatidae.
– ORIGIN early 19th cent.: from Malay.

Si·a·mese /,sīə'mēz/ ▶ **n.** (pl. **same**) **1** dated a native of Siam (now Thailand).
2 old-fashioned term for **THAI** (the language).
3 (also **Siamese cat**) a cat of a lightly built short-haired breed characterized by slanting blue eyes and typically pale fur with darker points.
▶ **adj.** dated of or concerning Siam, its people, or language.

Si·a·mese fight·ing fish ▶ **n.** see **FIGHTING FISH**.

Si·a·mese twin ▶ **plural n.** dated term for **CONJOINED TWIN**.
– ORIGIN with reference to the *Siamese* men Chang and Eng (1811–74), who, despite being joined at the waist, led an active life.

SIB ▶ **abbr.** Brit. Securities and Investment Board, a regulatory body that oversees London's financial markets.

sib /sib/ ▶ **n. 1** chiefly Zoology a brother or sister; a sibling.
2 Anthropology a group of people recognized by an individual as his or her kindred.
– ORIGIN Old English, 'related by birth or descent,' of unknown origin. Sense 1 dates from the early 20th cent.

Si·be·li·us /si'bālēəs/, Jean (1865–1957), Finnish composer; born *Johan Julius Christian Sibelius*. His affinity for his country's landscape and legends, esp. the epic *Kalevala*, is expressed in a series of symphonic poems including *The Swan of Tuonela* (1893), *Finlandia* (1899), and *Tapiola* (1925).

Ši·be·nik /SHē'benik/ an industrial city and port in Croatia, on the Adriatic coast; pop. 37,200 (est. 2009).

Si·be·ri·a /sī'bi(ə)rēə/ a vast region of Russia that extends from the Ural Mountains to the Pacific Ocean and from the Arctic coast to the northern borders of Kazakhstan, Mongolia, and China. Noted for the severity of its winters, it was traditionally used as a place of exile; it is now a major source of minerals and hydroelectric power.
– DERIVATIVES **Si·be·ri·an adj. & n.**

Si·be·ri·an ti·ger ▶ **n.** a tiger of a large and threatened race with a long thick coat, found in southeastern Siberia and northeastern China.

sib·i·lant /'sibələnt/ ▶ **adj.** Phonetics (of a speech sound) sounded with a hissing effect, for example *s*, *sh*. ■ making or characterized by a hissing sound: *his sibilant whisper*.
▶ **n.** Phonetics a sibilant speech sound.
– DERIVATIVES **sib·i·lance n.**
– ORIGIN mid 17th cent.: from Latin *sibilant-* 'hissing,' from the verb *sibilare*.

sib·i·late /'sibə,lāt/ ▶ **v.** [with obj.] utter with a hissing sound.
– DERIVATIVES **sib·i·la·tion** /,sibə'lāSHən/ **n.**
– ORIGIN mid 17th cent.: from Latin *sibilat-* 'hissed, whistled,' from the verb *sibilare*.

Si·biu /sē'byōō/ an industrial city in central Romania; pop. 154,452 (2006).

sib·li·cide /'sibli,sīd/ ▶ **n.** Zoology the killing of a sibling or siblings, as a behavior pattern typical in various animal groups.

sib·ling /'sibliNG/ ▶ **n.** each of two or more children or offspring having one or both parents in common; a brother or sister.
– ORIGIN Old English in the sense 'relative' (see **SIB**, **-LING**). The current sense dates from the early 20th cent.

sib·ship /'sibSHip/ ▶ **n.** chiefly Zoology a group of offspring having the same two parents. ■ Anthropology the state of belonging to a sib or the same sib.

sib·yl /'sibəl/ ▶ **n.** a woman in ancient times supposed to utter the oracles and prophecies of a god. ■ literary a woman able to foretell the future.
– DERIVATIVES **sib·yl·line** /'sibə,lin, -,lēn/ **adj.**
– ORIGIN from Old French *Sibile* or medieval Latin *Sibilla*, via Latin from Greek *Sibulla*.

sic[1] /sik/ ▶ **adv.** used in brackets after a copied or quoted word that appears odd or erroneous to show that the word is quoted exactly as it stands in the original, as in *a story must hold a child's interest and "enrich his* [sic] *life."*
– ORIGIN Latin, literally 'so, thus.'

sic[2] (also **sick**) ▶ **v.** (**sics, siccing, sicced** or **sics, sicking, sicked**) [with obj.] (**sic something on**) set a dog or other animal on (someone): *the plan was to surprise the heck out of the grizzly by sicking the dog on him*. ■ (**sic someone on**) informal set someone to pursue, keep watch on, or accompany (another).
– ORIGIN mid 19th cent.: dialect variant of **SEEK**.

Sic. ▶ **abbr.** ■ Sicilian. ■ Sicily.

sic·ca·tive /'sikətiv/ ▶ **n.** a drying agent used as a component of paint.
– ORIGIN late Middle English: from late Latin *siccativus*, from *siccare* 'to dry.'

Si·chuan /'sicH'wän, 'sœcH-/ (also **Szechuan** or **Szechwan** /'secH-/) a province in west central China; capital, Chengdu.

Si·ci·lia /si'silyə, sē'CHēlyä/ Italian name for **SICILY**.

si·cil·i·a·no /sə,silē'änō/ (also **siciliana**) ▶ **n.** (pl. **sicilianos**) a dance, song, or instrumental piece in 6/8 or 12/8 time and evoking a pastoral mood.
– ORIGIN Italian, literally 'Sicilian.'

Si·cil·ian Ves·pers /sə'silēən, -yən 'vespərz/ a massacre of French inhabitants of Sicily that began near Palermo at the time of vespers on Easter Monday in 1282. The ensuing war resulted in the replacement of the unpopular French Angevin dynasty by the Spanish House of Aragon.

Sic·i·ly /'sisəlē/ a large Italian island in the Mediterranean Sea, off the southwestern tip of Italy; capital, Palermo. It is separated from the Italian mainland by the Strait of Messina. Its highest point is Mount Etna. Italian name **SICILIA**.
– DERIVATIVES **Si·cil·ian** /si'silyən/ **adj. & n.**

sick[1] /sik/ ▶ **adj. 1** affected by physical or mental illness: *nursing very sick children* | *we were sick with bronchitis* | (as plural noun **the sick**) *visiting the sick and the elderly*. ■ of or relating to those who are ill: *the company organized a sick fund for its workers*. ■ (of an organization, system, or society) suffering from serious problems, esp. of a financial nature: *their economy remains sick*. ■ archaic pining or longing for someone or something: *he was sick for a sight of her*.
2 [predic.] feeling nauseous and wanting to vomit: *he was starting to feel sick* | *Mark felt sick with fear*. ■ [attrib.] (of an emotion) so intense as to cause one to feel unwell or nauseous: *he had a sick fear of returning*. ■ informal disappointed, mortified, or miserable: *he looked pretty sick at that, but he eventually agreed*.
3 [predic.] (**sick of**) intensely annoyed with or bored by (someone or something) as a result of having had too much of them: *I'm absolutely sick of your moods*.
4 informal (esp. of humor) having something unpleasant such as death, illness, or misfortune as its subject and dealing with it in an offensive way: *this was someone's idea of a sick joke*. ■ (of a person) having abnormal or unnatural tendencies; perverted: *he is a deeply sick man from whom society needs to be protected*.
5 informal excellent.
▶ **n.** Brit. informal vomit.
▶ **v.** [with obj.] (**sick something up**) Brit. informal bring something up by vomiting.
– PHRASES **be sick 1** be ill. **2** vomit. **fall** (or **take**) **sick** become ill. **get sick 1** become ill. **2** vomit. **make someone sick** cause someone to vomit or feel nauseous or unwell: *sherry makes me sick and so do cigars*. ■ cause someone to feel intense annoyance or disgust: *you're so damned self-righteous you make me sick!* **—— oneself sick** do something to such an extent that one feels nauseous or unwell (often used for emphasis): ***she was worrying herself sick about Mike***. **sick and tired of** informal annoyed about or bored with (something) and unwilling to put up with it any longer: *I am sick and tired of all the criticism*. **(as) sick as a dog** informal extremely ill. **(as) sick as a parrot** Brit. informal extremely disappointed. **the sick man of ——** a country that is politically or economically unsound, esp. in comparison with its neighbors in the region specified: *the country had been the sick man of Europe for too long*. [from a use of *sick man*, frequently applied in the late 19th cent. to the Sultan of Turkey, later extended to Turkey and other countries.] **sick to death of** informal another way of saying **SICK AND TIRED OF** above. **sick to one's stomach** nauseous. ■ disgusted.
– DERIVATIVES **sick·ish adj.**
– ORIGIN Old English *sēoc* 'affected by illness,' of Germanic origin; related to Dutch *ziek* and German *siech*.

> **WORD TRENDS** A common trick of slang is to invert meanings, so that seemingly negative words are used as terms of approval—**bad** and **wicked** are two established examples, with positive uses dating back to 1897 and 1920, respectively. **Sick** is a more recent arrival, first seen as a synonym for 'excellent' or 'very impressive' in 1983: *it was a sick party and there were tons of cool people there*. It is particularly common in skateboard and snowboard culture, where it can be used to imply an element of risk and danger: *Shawn is a badass skater. He busts some sick tricks.*

sick[2] ▶ **v.** variant of **SIC**[2].

sick·bay /'sik,bā/ (also **sick bay**) ▶ **n.** a room or building set aside for the treatment or accommodation of the sick, esp. within a military base or on board a ship.

sick·bed /'sik,bed/ ▶ **n.** an invalid's bed (often used to refer to the state or condition of being an invalid): *he had climbed from his sickbed to help the club*.

sick build·ing syn·drome ▶ **n.** a condition affecting office workers, typically marked by headaches and respiratory problems, attributed to unhealthy or stressful factors in the working environment such as poor ventilation.

sick call ▶ **n. 1** a visit to a sick person, typically one made by a doctor or priest.
2 Military a summons for those reporting sick to attend for treatment.

sick day ▶ **n.** a day taken off from work because of illness.

sick·en /'sikən/ ▶ **v. 1** [with obj.] make (someone) feel disgusted or appalled: *she was sickened by the bomb attack*. ■ [no obj.] archaic feel disgust or horror: *he sickened at the thought*.
2 [no obj.] become ill: *Dawson sickened unexpectedly and died in 1916*.

sick·en·er /'sikənər/ ▶ **n. 1** informal something that causes disgust or severe disappointment.
2 (**the sickener**) a poisonous toadstool with a red cap and a white or cream-colored stem and gills, found commonly in both Eurasia and North America. ● Genus *Russula*, family Russulaceae, class Hymenomycetes, in particular *R. emetica*.

sick·en·ing /'sikəniNG/ ▶ **adj.** causing or liable to cause a feeling of nausea or disgust: *a sickening stench of blood* | *she hit the ground with a sickening thud*. ■ informal causing irritation or annoyance.
– DERIVATIVES **sick·en·ing·ly adv.**

sick head·ache ▶ **n.** a headache accompanied by nausea, particularly a migraine.

sick·ie /'sikē/ ▶ **n.** informal another term for **SICKO**.

sick·le /'sikəl/ ▶ **n.** a short-handled farming tool with a semicircular blade, used for cutting grain, lopping, or trimming.
– ORIGIN Old English *sicol*, *sicel*, of Germanic origin; related to Dutch *sikkel* and German *Sichel*, based on Latin *secula*, from *secare* 'to cut.'

sickle

sick leave ▶ **n.** leave of absence granted because of illness.

sick·le·bill /'sikəl,bil/ ▶ **n.** any of a number of birds with a long narrow down-curved bill. ● a tropical American hummingbird (genus *Eutoxeres*, family Trochilidae: two species). ● a New Guinea bird of paradise (two genera in the family Paradisaeidae).

sick·le cell a·ne·mi·a /'sikəl sel ə'nēmēə/ (also **sickle cell disease**) ▶ **n.** a severe hereditary form of anemia in which a mutated form of hemoglobin distorts the red blood cells into a crescent shape at low oxygen levels. It is most common among those of African descent.

sick·le cell trait ▶ **n.** a relatively mild condition caused by the presence of a single gene for sickle cell anemia, producing a smaller amount of abnormal hemoglobin and conferring some resistance to malaria.

sick·le feath·er ▶ n. each of the long middle feathers of a rooster's tail.

sick list ▶ n. a list, esp. in the military, of people who are ill and unable to work.

sick·ly /ˈsiklē/ ▶ adj. (**sicklier, sickliest**) **1** often ill; in poor health: *she was a thin, sickly child.* ■ (of a person's complexion or expression) indicative of poor health: *his usual sickly pallor.* ■ literary (of a place, climate, or time) causing or characterized by unhealthiness: *a deep sickly vaporous swamp.*
2 (of a flavor, smell, color, or light) so unpleasant as to induce discomfort or nausea: *the walls were painted a sickly green | she liked her coffee sweet and sickly.* ■ excessively sentimental or mawkish: *a sickly fable of delicate young lovers.*
– DERIVATIVES **sick·li·ness** n.
– ORIGIN late Middle English: probably suggested by Old Norse *sjúkligr.*

sick-mak·ing ▶ adj. informal nauseatingly unpleasant or shocking: *a sick-making stench.* ■ overly sentimental, coy, or trite.

sick·ness /ˈsiknis/ ▶ n. **1** the state of being ill: *she was absent through sickness.* ■ [often with adj. or noun modifier] a particular type of illness or disease: *botulism causes fodder sickness of horses | a woman suffering an incurable sickness.*
2 the feeling or fact of being affected with nausea or vomiting: *she felt a wave of sickness wash over her | travel sickness.*
– ORIGIN Old English *sēocnesse* (see SICK¹, -NESS).

sick·o /ˈsikō/ ▶ n. (pl. **sickos**) informal a mentally ill or perverted person, esp. one who is sadistic.

sick·out /ˈsik ˌout/ ▶ n. informal an organized period of unwarranted sick leave taken as a form of group protest, usually as a measure to avoid a formal strike.

sick·room /ˈsikˌro͞om/ ▶ n. a room in a school or place of work occupied by or set apart for people who are unwell.

sick tick·et ▶ n. humorous a person with an affinity for sick humor: *you'd have to be a sick ticket to eat candy called "gummy rats."*

si·dal·cea /siˈdalsHēə/ ▶ n. a herbaceous North American plant of the mallow family, several kinds of which are cultivated as ornamentals. ● Genus *Sidalcea*, family Malvaceae.
– ORIGIN modern Latin, from *Sida* + *Alcea*, names of related genera.

sid·dha /ˈsidə/ ▶ n. Hinduism one who has achieved spiritual realization and supernatural power.
– ORIGIN Sanskrit.

Sid·dhar·tha Gau·ta·ma /siˈdärtə ˈgôtəmə, siˈdärTHə-/ see BUDDHA.

sid·dhi /ˈsidē/ ▶ n. Hinduism & Buddhism **1** complete understanding and enlightenment possessed by a siddha.
2 (pl. **siddhis**) a paranormal power possessed by a siddha.
– ORIGIN Sanskrit.

side /sīd/ ▶ n. **1** a position to the left or right of an object, place, or central point: *a town on the other side of the river | on either side of the entrance was a garden | Rachel tilted her head to one side.* ■ either of the two halves of an object, surface, or place regarded as divided by an imaginary central line: *she lay on her side of the bed | the left side of the brain.* ■ the right or the left part of a person's or animal's body, esp. of the human torso: *he has been paralyzed on his right side since birth.* ■ [in sing.] a place or position closely adjacent to someone: *his wife stood at his side.* ■ either of the lateral halves of the body of a butchered animal, or an animal or fish prepared for eating: *a side of beef.*
2 an upright or sloping surface of a structure or object that is not the top or bottom and generally not the front or back: *a car crashed into the side of the house | line the sides of the cake pan |* [as modifier] *a side entrance.* ■ each of the flat surfaces of a solid object. ■ either of the two surfaces of something flat and thin, such as paper or cloth. ■ the amount of writing needed to fill one side of a sheet of paper: *she told us not to write more than three sides.* ■ either of the two faces of a record or of the two separate tracks on a length of recording tape.
3 a part or region near the edge and away from the middle of something: *a minivan was parked at the side of the road | cabins on the south side of the clearing.* ■ [as modifier] subsidiary to or less important than something: *a side dish of fresh vegetables.* ■ a dish served as subsidiary to the main one: *sides of German potato salad and red cabbage.* ■ each of the lines forming the boundary of a plane rectilinear figure: *the farm buildings formed three sides of a square.*
4 a person or group opposing another or others in a dispute, contest, or debate: *the two sides agreed to resume border trade | whose side are you on?* ■ chiefly Brit. a sports team. ■ the position, interests, or attitude of one person or group, esp. when regarded as being in opposition to another or others: *Mrs. Burt hasn't kept her side of the bargain | the conservationists are on the city's side of the case.* ■ a particular aspect of something, esp. a situation or a person's character: *her ability to put up with his disagreeable side.* ■ a person's kinship or line of descent as traced through either their father or mother: *Richard was of French descent on his mother's side.*
5 (also **sidespin**) horizontal spinning motion given to a ball. ■ Billiards another term for ENGLISH (sense 3 of the noun).
▶ v. **1** [no obj.] (**side with/against**) support or oppose in a conflict, dispute, or debate: *he felt that Max had betrayed him by siding with Beatrice.*
2 [with obj.] provide with a side or sides; form the side of: *the hills that side a long valley.*
– PHRASES **by** (or **at**) **someone's side** close to someone, esp. so as to give them comfort or moral support: *a stepson who stayed by your side when your own son deserted you.* **by the side of** close to: *a house by the side of the road.* **from side to side 1** alternately left and right from a central point: *I shook my head frantically from side to side.* **2** across the entire width; right across: *the fleet stretched four miles from side to side.* **have something on one's side** (or **something is on one's side**) something is operating to one's advantage: *now that he had time on his side, Tom relaxed a little.* **on** (or **to**) **one side** out of one's way; aside. ■ to be dealt with or considered later, esp. because tending to distract one from something more important: *before the kickoff a player has to set his disappointments and frustrations to one side.* **on the —— side** tending toward being ——; rather —— (used to qualify an adjective): *these shoes are a bit on the tight side.* **on the side 1** in addition to one's regular job or as a subsidiary source of income: *no one lived in the property, but the caretaker made a little on the side by renting rooms out.* **2** secretly, esp. with regard to a relationship in addition to one's legal or regular partner: *Brian had a mistress on the side.* **3** served separately from the main dish: *a club sandwich with french fries on the side.* **side by side** (of two or more people or things) close together and facing the same way: *on we jogged, side by side, for a mile.* ■ together: *we have been using both systems, side by side, for two years.* ■ (of people or groups) supporting each other; in cooperation: *the two institutions worked side by side in complete harmony.* **side of the fence** see FENCE. **take sides** support one person or cause against another or others in a dispute, conflict, or contest: *I do not want to take sides in this matter.* **take** (or **draw**) **someone to one side** speak to someone in private, esp. so as to advise or warn them about something. **this side of 1** before (a particular time, date, or event): *this side of midnight.* ■ yet to reach (a particular age): *I'm this side of forty-five.* **2** informal used in superlative expressions to denote that something is comparable with a paragon or model of its kind: *the finest coffee this side of Brazil.*
– DERIVATIVES **side·less** adj.
– ORIGIN Old English *side* 'left or right part of the body,' of Germanic origin; related to Dutch *zijde* and German *Seite*, probably from a base meaning 'extending lengthwise.'

side·arm¹ /ˈsīdˌärm/ ▶ adj. (of a throw, pitch, or cast) performed or delivered with a sweeping motion of the arm at or below shoulder level. ■ (of a person, typically a baseball pitcher) using such a sweeping motion of the arm.
▶ adv. in a sidearm manner: *I could throw sidearm.*
▶ v. [with obj.] chiefly Baseball throw or pitch a ball to (someone) with such a motion of the arm. ■ throw or pitch (a ball or other object) in this way.
– DERIVATIVES **side·arm·er** n.

side·arm² (also **side arm**) ▶ n. a weapon worn at a person's side, such as a pistol or other small firearm (or, formerly, a sword or bayonet).

side·band /ˈsīdˌband/ ▶ n. Telecommunications one of two frequency bands on either side of the carrier wave, containing the modulated signal.

side·bar /ˈsīdˌbär/ ▶ n. a short article in a newspaper or magazine, typically boxed, placed alongside a main article, and containing additional or explanatory material. ■ a secondary, additional, or incidental thing; a side issue. ■ (also **sidebar conference**) (in a court of law) a discussion between the lawyers and the judge held out of earshot of the jury.

side bet ▶ n. a bet over and above the main bet, esp. on a subsidiary issue.

side·board /ˈsīdˌbôrd/ ▶ n. **1** a flat-topped piece of furniture with cupboards and drawers, placed along a wall and used for storing dishes, glasses, and table linen.
2 (usu. **sideboards**) Brit. sideburns.
3 a board forming the side, or a part of the side, of a structure, esp. a removable board at the side of a truck or trailer.

side·burn /ˈsīdˌbərn/ ▶ n. (usu. **sideburns**) a strip of hair grown by a man down each side of the face in front of his ears.
– ORIGIN late 19th cent.: originally *burnside*, from the name of General *Burnside* (1824–81), who affected this style.

side·car /ˈsīdˌkär/ ▶ n. **1** a small, low vehicle attached to the side of a motorcycle for carrying passengers.
2 a cocktail of brandy and lemon juice with orange liqueur.

side chain ▶ n. Chemistry a group of atoms attached to the main part of a molecule and having a ring or chain structure.

side chair ▶ n. an upright wooden chair without arms.

side chap·el ▶ n. a subsidiary chapel opening off the side aisle in a large church.

side·cut /ˈsīdˌkət/ ▶ n. a curve in the side of a ski or snowboard that allows it to turn more smoothly.

sid·ed /ˈsīdid/ ▶ adj. [in combination] having sides of a specified number or type: *narrow, steep-sided canyons.*
– DERIVATIVES **sid·ed·ly** adv. [in combination], **sid·ed·ness** n.

side dish ▶ n. a dish served as subsidiary to the main one: *both were served with an excellent side dish of fresh vegetables.*

side door ▶ n. a door in or at the side of a building.

side drum ▶ n. another term for SNARE DRUM.
– ORIGIN late 18th cent.: so named because it was originally played, suspended from the drummer's side.

side ef·fect ▶ n. a secondary, typically undesirable effect of a drug or medical treatment: *many anticancer drugs now in use have toxic side effects.*

side glance ▶ n. a sideways or brief glance.

side·grade /ˈsīd ˌgrād/ ▶ n. a marketing incentive aimed at persuading a consumer to switch to a competitor's product: *a competitive sidegrade to Canvas or CorelDraw.*
▶ v. switch to a competitive product: *I'd prefer to sidegrade to Windows Media Player 10 at some point.*

side·hill /ˈsīdˌhil/ ▶ n. a hillside.

side is·sue ▶ n. a point or topic connected to or raised by some other issue, but not as important, esp. one that distracts attention from the more important issue.

side·kick /ˈsīdˌkik/ ▶ n. informal a person's assistant or close associate, esp. one who has less authority than that person.

side·light /ˈsīdˌlīt/ ▶ n. **1** a light placed at the side of something. ■ (**sidelights**) a ship's port (red) and starboard (green) navigation lights. ■ natural light coming from the side.
2 a narrow window or pane of glass set alongside a door or larger window.
3 a piece of incidental information that helps to clarify or enliven a subject.

side·line /ˈsīdˌlīn/ ▶ n. **1** an activity done in addition to one's main job, esp. to earn extra income: [as modifier] *a sideline career as a stand-up comic.* ■ an auxiliary line of goods or business: *electronic handbooks are a lucrative sideline for the firm.*
2 (usu. **sidelines**) either of the two lines bounding the longer sides of a football field, basketball court, tennis court, or similar playing area. ■ the area immediately outside such lines as a place for nonplayers, substitutes, or spectators: *his son watched from the sidelines.* See also ON THE SIDELINES below.
▶ v. [with obj.] cause (a player) to be unable to play on a team or in a game: *he has been sidelined for the last six weeks with a fractured wrist.* ■ remove from the center of activity or attention; place in a less influential position: *a respected lawyer will be sidelined by alcohol abuse.*
– PHRASES **on** (or **from**) **the sidelines** in (or from) a position where one is observing a situation but is unable or unwilling to be directly involved in it.

side·long /ˈsīdˌlôNG/ ▶ adj. & adv. directed to or from one side; sideways: [as adj.] *Steve gave her a sidelong glance |* [as adv.] *he looked sidelong at her with a quick smile.*
– ORIGIN late Middle English: alteration of earlier *sideling*, from SIDE + the adverbial suffix *-ling*.

side·man /ˈsīdˌman/ ▶ **n.** (pl. **sidemen**) a supporting musician in a jazz band or rock group.

side·meat /ˈsīdˌmēt/ ▶ **n.** salt pork or bacon, typically cut from the side of the pig.

side-necked tur·tle ▶ **n.** a freshwater turtle with a relatively long head and neck that is retracted sideways into the shell for defense. ● Suborder Pleurodira: families Chelidae (South America and Australasia) and Pelomedusidae (South America and southern Africa), and several genera.

side note ▶ **n.** a marginal note in a text.

side-on ▶ **adv.** with the side of someone or something toward something else: *the ship was wallowing side-on to the swell.*
▶ **adj.** directed from or toward a side: *a shot of the crowd from the side-on camera.* ■ (of a collision) involving the side of a vehicle.

side plate ▶ **n.** a plate smaller than a dinner plate, used for bread or other accompaniments to a meal.

si·de·re·al /sīˈdi(ə)rēəl/ ▶ **adj.** of or with respect to the distant stars (i.e., the constellations or fixed stars, not the sun or planets).
– ORIGIN mid 17th cent.: from Latin *sidereus* (from *sidus, sider-* 'star') + **-AL**.

si·de·re·al clock ▶ **n.** Astronomy a clock measuring sidereal time in terms of 24 equal divisions of a sidereal day.

si·de·re·al day ▶ **n.** Astronomy the time between two consecutive transits of the First Point of Aries. It represents the time taken by the earth to rotate on its axis relative to the stars, and is almost four minutes shorter than the solar day because of the earth's orbital motion.

si·de·re·al month ▶ **n.** Astronomy the time it takes the moon to orbit once around the earth with respect to the stars (approximately 27 $^{1}/_{4}$ days).

si·de·re·al pe·ri·od ▶ **n.** Astronomy the period of revolution of one body around another with respect to the distant stars.

si·de·re·al time ▶ **n.** Astronomy time reckoned from the motion of the earth (or a planet) relative to the distant stars (rather than with respect to the sun).

si·de·re·al year ▶ **n.** Astronomy the orbital period of the earth around the sun, taking the stars as a reference frame, being 20 minutes longer than the tropical year because of precession.

sid·er·ite /ˈsidəˌrīt/ ▶ **n. 1** a brown mineral consisting of ferrous carbonate, occurring as the main component of some kinds of ironstone or as rhombohedral crystals in mineral veins.
2 a meteorite consisting mainly of nickel and iron.
– DERIVATIVES **sid·er·it·ic** /ˌsidəˈritik/ **adj.**
– ORIGIN late 16th cent. (denoting lodestone): from Greek *sidēros* 'iron' + **-ITE**[1].

sidero-[1] ▶ **comb. form** of or relating to the stars: *siderostat.*
– ORIGIN from Latin *sidus, sider-* 'star.'

sidero-[2] ▶ **comb. form** of or relating to iron: *siderophore.*
– ORIGIN from Greek *sidēros* 'iron.'

side road ▶ **n.** a minor or subsidiary road, esp. one joining or diverging from a main road.

sid·er·o·phore /ˈsidərəˌfôr/ ▶ **n.** Biochemistry a molecule that binds and transports iron in microorganisms.

sid·er·o·stat /ˈsidərəˌstat/ ▶ **n.** Astronomy an instrument used for keeping the image of a celestial object in a fixed position.

side·sad·dle /ˈsīdˌsadl/ ▶ **n.** a saddle in which the rider has both feet on the same side of the horse. It is typically used by a woman rider wearing a skirt.
▶ **adv.** sitting in this position on a horse.

side shoot ▶ **n.** a shoot growing from the side of a plant's stem.

side·show /ˈsīdˌSHō/ ▶ **n.** a small show or stall at an exhibition, fair, or circus. ■ a minor or diverting incident or issue, esp. one that distracts attention from something more important.

side·slip /ˈsīdˌslip/ ▶ **n.** a sideways skid or slip. ■ Aeronautics a sideways movement of an aircraft, esp. downward toward the inside of a turn. ■ (in skiing and surfing) an act of traveling down a slope or wave in a direction not in line with one's skis or board.
▶ **v.** [no obj.] skid or slip sideways: *the weight counteracts the tire's tendency to sideslip.* ■ Aeronautics move in a sideslip. ■ (in skiing and surfing) travel sideways or in any direction not in line with one's skis or board.

side·spin /ˈsīdˌspin/ ▶ **n.** see **SIDE** (sense 5 of the noun).

side split ▶ **n.** Canadian a split-level house with fewer stories on one side than the other.

side·split·ting /ˈsīdˌspliting/ ▶ **adj.** informal extremely amusing; causing violent laughter: *sidesplitting anecdotes.*

side·step /ˈsīdˌstep/ ▶ **v.** (**sidesteps, sidestepping, sidestepped**) [with obj.] avoid (someone or something) by stepping sideways: *as she walked she sidestepped the many cracks in the pavement.* ■ avoid dealing with or discussing (something problematic or disagreeable): *he neatly sidestepped the questions about riots.* ■ [no obj.] Skiing climb or descend by lifting alternate skis while sideways on the slope.
▶ **n.** a step taken sideways, typically to avoid someone or something.
– DERIVATIVES **side·step·per n.**

side·stream smoke /ˈsīdˌstrēm/ ▶ **n.** smoke that passes from a cigarette into the surrounding air, rather than into the smoker's lungs.

side street ▶ **n.** a minor or subsidiary street.

side·stroke /ˈsīdˌstrōk/ ▶ **n.** [in sing.] a swimming stroke similar to the breaststroke in which the swimmer lies on their side.

side suit ▶ **n.** Bridge a suit other than the trump suit.

side·swipe /ˈsīdˌswīp/ ▶ **n. 1** a glancing blow from or on the side of something, esp. a motor vehicle.
2 a passing critical remark about someone or something.
▶ **v.** [with obj.] strike (someone or something) with or as if with a glancing blow: *Curtis jerked the wheel hard over and sideswiped the other car.*

side ta·ble ▶ **n.** a table placed at the side of a room or apart from the main table.

side tone ▶ **n.** feedback in a telephone receiver, in particular the reproduction of the user's own voice.

side·track /ˈsīdˌtrak/ ▶ **v.** [with obj.] (usu. **be/get sidetracked**) **1** cause (someone) to be distracted from an immediate or important issue: *he does not let himself get sidetracked by fads and trends.* ■ divert (a project or debate) away from a central issue or previously determined plan: *the effort at reform has been sidetracked for years.*
2 direct (a train) onto a branch line or siding. ■ divert (a well or borehole) to reach a productive deposit or to avoid an obstruction.
▶ **n.** a minor path or track. ■ a railroad branch line or siding. ■ a well or borehole that runs partly to one side of the original line of drilling.

side trip ▶ **n.** a minor excursion during a voyage or trip.

side view ▶ **n.** a view from the side.

side·walk /ˈsīdˌwôlk/ ▶ **n.** a paved path for pedestrians at the side of a road.

side·wall /ˈsīdˌwôl/ ▶ **n. 1** (often **side wall**) a wall forming the side of a structure or room.
2 the side of a tire, typically marked or colored distinctively.

side·ward /ˈsīdwərd/ ▶ **adj.** another term for **SIDEWAYS**.
▶ **adv.** (also **sidewards** /-wərdz/) another term for **SIDEWAYS**.

side·ways /ˈsīdˌwāz/ ▶ **adv. & adj.** to, toward, or from the side: [as adv.] *she tilted her body sideways* | [as adj.] *he hurried toward his office without a sideways glance.* ■ [as adv.] with one side facing forward: *the truck slid sideways across the road.* ■ so as to occupy a job or position at the same level as one previously held rather than be promoted or demoted: [as adj.] *after the reshuffle there were sideways moves for managers.* ■ by an indirect way: [as adv.] *he came into politics sideways, as campaign manager for the president.* ■ [as adj.] from an unconventional or unorthodox viewpoint: *take a sideways look at daily life.*
– PHRASES **knock someone sideways** see **KNOCK**.

side·wheel·er ▶ **n.** a steamboat with paddle wheels on either side.
– DERIVATIVES **side-wheel adj.**

side whisk·ers ▶ **plural n.** whiskers or sideburns on a man's cheeks.

side·wind /ˈsīdˌwīnd/ ▶ **v.** [no obj.] (often as noun **sidewinding**) (of a sidewinder or other snake) move sideways in a series of S-shaped curves.

side wind /sīd wind/ ▶ **n.** a wind blowing predominantly from one side.

side·wind·er[1] /ˈsīdˌwīndər/ ▶ **n.** a pale-colored, nocturnal, burrowing rattlesnake that moves sideways over sand by throwing its body into S-shaped curves. It is found in the deserts of North America. ● *Crotalus cerastes*, family Viperidae.

side·wind·er[2] ▶ **n.** a heavy blow with the fist delivered from or on the side.

side·wise /ˈsīdˌwīz/ ▶ **adv. & adj.** another term for **SIDEWAYS**.

Sidhe /SHē/ ▶ **plural n.** the fairy people of Irish folklore, said to live beneath the hills and often identified as the remnant of the ancient Tuatha Dé Danann.
– ORIGIN from Irish *aos sidhe* 'people of the fairy mound.'

Si·di bel Ab·bès /ˈsēdē bel əˈbes/ a town in northern Algeria, south of Oran; pop. 197,600 (est. 2009).

sid·ing /ˈsīdiNG/ ▶ **n. 1** a short track at the side of and opening onto a railroad line, used chiefly for shunting or stabling trains. ■ a loop line.
2 cladding material for the outside of a building.

si·dle /ˈsīdl/ ▶ **v.** [no obj.] walk in a furtive, unobtrusive, or timid manner, esp. sideways or obliquely: *I sidled up to her.*
▶ **n.** [in sing.] an instance of walking in this way.
– ORIGIN late 17th cent.: back-formation from *sideling* (see **SIDELONG**).

Si·don /ˈsīdn/ a city in Lebanon, on the Mediterranean coast, south of Beirut; pop. 58,400 (est. 2009). Founded in the 3rd millennium BC, it was a Phoenician seaport and city state. Arabic name **SAIDA**.

Sid·ra, Gulf of /ˈsidrə/ (also **Gulf of Sirte**) a broad inlet of the Mediterranean Sea on the coast of Libya, between the towns of Benghazi and Misratah.

SIDS /sidz/ ▶ **abbr.** sudden infant death syndrome.

Sie·ben·ge·bir·ge /ˈzēbəngəˌbirgə/ a range of hills in western Germany, on the right bank of the Rhine River, southeast of Bonn.

siege /sēj/ ▶ **n.** a military operation in which enemy forces surround a town or building, cutting off essential supplies, with the aim of compelling the surrender of those inside: *Verdun had withstood a siege of ten weeks* | [as modifier] *siege warfare.* ■ a similar operation by a police or other force to compel the surrender of an armed person. ■ a prolonged period of misfortune: *I've been having a siege of headaches.*
– PHRASES **lay siege to** conduct a siege of (a place): *government forces laid siege to the building* | figurative *the press laid siege to her apartment.* **under siege** (of a place) undergoing a siege: *the fort had been under siege by guerrillas since June* | figurative *we are under siege from budget cuts.*
– ORIGIN Middle English: from Old French *sege*, from *asegier* 'besiege.'

siege e·con·o·my ▶ **n.** an economy in which import controls are imposed and the export of capital is curtailed.

siege gun ▶ **n.** a heavy gun used in attacking a place under siege.

siege men·tal·i·ty ▶ **n.** a defensive or paranoid attitude based on the belief that others are hostile toward one.

Sieg·fried /ˈsēgˌfrēd/ the hero of the first part of the Nibelungenlied. A prince of the Netherlands, Siegfried obtains a hoard of treasure by killing the dragon Fafner. He marries Kriemhild, and helps Gunther to win Brunhild before being killed by Hagen.

Sieg·fried Line /ˈsēgˌfrēd/ the line of defense constructed by the Germans along the western frontier of Germany before World War II. ■ another term for **HINDENBURG LINE**.

Sieg Heil /ˌsēg ˈhīl/ ▶ **exclam.** a victory salute used originally by Nazis at political rallies.
– DERIVATIVES **Sieg-Heil·ing adj.**
– ORIGIN German, literally 'hail victory!'

Sie·mens /ˈzēmənz, ˈsē-/ a German family of scientific entrepreneurs and engineers. **Ernst Werner von Siemens** (1816–92) was an electrical engineer who developed the process of electroplating, devised an electric generator that used an electromagnet, and pioneered electrical traction. His brother **Karl Wilhelm** (1823–83) (also known as *Sir Charles William Siemens*) moved to England, where he developed the open-hearth steel furnace and designed the cable-laying steamship *Faraday*. Their brother **Friedrich** (1826–1904) applied the principles of the open-hearth furnace to glassmaking.

sie·mens /ˈsēmənz/ (abbr.: **S**) ▶ **n.** Physics the SI unit of conductance, equal to one reciprocal ohm.
– ORIGIN 1930s: named after K. W. von **SIEMENS**.

Si·e·na /sēˈenə/ a city in west central Italy, in Tuscany; pop. 54,159 (2008). In the 13th and 14th centuries, it was the center of a flourishing school of art.
– DERIVATIVES **Si·en·ese** /ˌsēəˈnēz, -ˈnēs/ **adj. & n.**

si·en·na /sēˈenə/ ▶ **n.** a kind of ferruginous earth used as a pigment in painting, normally yellowish-brown in color (**raw sienna**) or deep reddish-brown when roasted (**burnt sienna**). ■ the color of this pigment.
– ORIGIN late 18th cent.: from Italian (*terra di*) *Sienna* '(earth of) Siena.'

S

Sier·pin·ski tri·an·gle /sHi(ə)r'pinskē/ (also **Sierpinski gasket**) ▶ **n.** Mathematics a fractal based on a triangle with four equal triangles inscribed in it. The central triangle is removed and each of the other three treated as the original was, and so on, creating an infinite regression in a finite space.
– ORIGIN 1970s: named after Waclaw *Sierpiński* (1882–1969), Polish mathematician.

si·er·ra /sē'erə/ ▶ **n.** **1** a long jagged mountain chain. **2** a code word representing the letter S, used in radio communication.
– ORIGIN mid 16th cent.: Spanish, from Latin *serra* 'saw.'

Si·er·ra Le·one /sē,erə lē'ōn/ a country on the coast of West Africa; pop. 5,132,100 (est. 2009); capital, Freetown; languages, English (official), English Creole, Temne, and other West African languages.

An area of British influence from the late 18th century, the district around Freetown on the coast became a colony in 1807, serving as a center for operations against slave traders. The large inland territory was not declared a protectorate until 1896. Sierra Leone achieved independence within the Commonwealth of Nations in 1961 but was suspended from the organization in 1997 following military coups in 1992 and 1997. National elections were held in 2002, and UN peacekeepers withdrew in 2004, but the situation remained unstable.

– DERIVATIVES **Si·er·ra Le·o·ne·an** /lē'ōnēən/ **adj. & n.**

Si·er·ra Ma·dre /'mä,drā/ a mountain system in Mexico that extends from the border with the US on the north to the southern border with Guatemala.

Si·er·ra Ne·va·da **1** a mountain range in southern Spain, in Andalusia, southeast of Granada. **2** a mountain range in eastern California. Rising sharply from the Great Basin on the east, it descends more gently to California's Central Valley on the west.

Si·er·ra Vis·ta /sē'erə 'vistə/ a city in the southeastern corner of Arizona, just north of the Mexican border; pop. 43,320 (est. 2008).

si·es·ta /sē'estə/ ▶ **n.** an afternoon rest or nap, esp. one taken during the hottest hours of the day in a hot climate.
– ORIGIN mid 17th cent.: Spanish, from Latin *sexta* (*hora*) 'sixth hour.'

sieve /siv/ ▶ **n.** a utensil consisting of a wire or plastic mesh held in a frame, used for straining solids from liquids, for separating coarser from finer particles, or for reducing soft solids to a pulp. ■ used figuratively with reference to the fact that a sieve does not hold all its contents: *she's forgotten all the details already—she's got* ***a mind like a sieve.***
▶ **v.** [with obj.] put (a food substance or other material) through a sieve. ■ (usu. **sieve something out**) remove (unwanted items): *filters sieve large particles out of the water to prevent them from harming the pumps.* ■ [no obj.] (**sieve through**) examine in detail: *lawyers had sieved through her contract.*
– DERIVATIVES **sieve·like** /-,līk/ **adj.**
– ORIGIN Old English *sife* (noun); related to Dutch *zeef* and German *Sieb.*

sieve cell ▶ **n.** Botany a sieve element of a primitive type present in ferns and gymnosperms, with narrow pores and no sieve plate.

sieve el·e·ment ▶ **n.** Botany an elongated cell in the phloem of a vascular plant, in which the primary wall is perforated by pores through which water is conducted.

sieve plate ▶ **n.** Botany an area of relatively large pores present in the common end walls of sieve tube elements. ■ Zoology a perforated plate in the integument of an invertebrate, esp. the madreporite of an echinoderm.

sie·vert /'sēvərt/ (abbr.: **Sv**) ▶ **n.** Physics the SI unit of dose equivalent (the biological effect of ionizing radiation), equal to an effective dose of a joule of energy per kilogram of recipient mass.
– ORIGIN 1940s: named after Rolf M. *Sievert* (1896–1966), Swedish radiologist.

sieve tube ▶ **n.** Botany a series of sieve tube elements placed end to end to form a continuous tube.

sieve tube el·e·ment (also **sieve tube member**) ▶ **n.** Botany a sieve element of a type present in angiosperms, a series of which are joined end to end to form sieve tubes, with sieve plates between the elements.

si·fa·ka /sHə'fakə, -'fäkə, sə-/ ▶ **n.** a large gregarious lemur that leaps from tree to tree in an upright position. ● Genus *Propithecus,* family Indriidae: two species.
– ORIGIN mid 19th cent.: from Malagasy.

sift /sift/ ▶ **v.** [with obj.] **1** put (a fine, loose, or powdery substance) through a sieve so as to remove lumps or large particles: *sift the flour into a large bowl.* ■ cause to flow or pass as through a sieve: *Melanie sifted the warm sand through her fingers.* ■ [no obj.] (of snow, ash, etc.) descend or float down lightly or sparsely as if sprinkled from a sieve: *ash began to sift down around them.*
2 examine (something) thoroughly so as to isolate that which is most important or useful: *until we sift the evidence ourselves, we can't comment objectively* | [no obj.] *the fourth stage involves* ***sifting through*** *the data and evaluating it.* ■ (**sift something out**) separate something, esp. something to be discarded, from something else: *he asked for streamlined procedures to sift out frivolous applications.*
▶ **n.** [usu. in sing.] an act of sifting something, esp. so as to isolate that which is most important or useful: *a careful archaeological sift must be made through the debris.* ■ an amount of sifted material: *the floor was dusted with a fine sift of flour.*
– DERIVATIVES **sift·er n.**
– ORIGIN Old English *siftan*; related to Dutch *ziften,* also to SIEVE.

SIG /sig/ ▶ **abbr.** Computing special interest group.

sig /sig/ ▶ **n.** Computing, informal a short personalized message at the end of an e-mail.
– ORIGIN 1990s: abbreviation of SIGNATURE.

Sig. ▶ **abbr.** Signor.

Sig·a·to·ka /,sigə'tōkə/ ▶ **n.** a fungal disease of banana plants characterized by elongated spots on the leaves, which then rot completely. ● The fungus is *Mycosphaerella musicola,* subdivision Ascomycotina.
– ORIGIN 1920s: named after a district in Fiji.

sigh /sī/ ▶ **v.** [no obj.] emit a long, deep, audible breath expressing sadness, relief, tiredness, or a similar feeling: *Harry sank into a chair and sighed with relief* | [with direct speech] *"I'm in a bit of a mess," Elaine sighed.* ■ (of the wind or something through which the wind blows) make a sound resembling this: *a breeze made the treetops sigh.* ■ (**sigh for**) literary feel a deep yearning for (someone or something lost, unattainable, or distant): *he sighed for days gone by.*
▶ **n.** a long, deep, audible exhalation expressing sadness, relief, tiredness, or a similar feeling: *she let out a long sigh of despair* | figurative *when the aircraft touched down I* ***breathed a sigh of relief.*** ■ a gentle sound resembling this, esp. one made by the wind.
– ORIGIN Middle English (as a verb): probably a back-formation from *sighte,* past tense of *siche, sike,* from Old English *sīcan.*

sight /sīt/ ▶ **n.** **1** the faculty or power of seeing: *Joseph lost his sight as a baby* | [as modifier] *a sight test.* ■ the action or fact of seeing someone or something: *I've always been scared of the sight of blood.* ■ the area or distance within which someone can see or something can be seen: *he now refused to let Rose out of his sight.* ■ dated a person's view or consideration: *we are all equal* ***in the sight of God.***
2 a thing that one sees or that can be seen: *John was a familiar sight in the bar for many years* | *he was getting used to seeing unpleasant sights.* ■ (**sights**) places of interest to tourists and visitors in a city, town, or other place: *she offered to show me the sights.* ■ (**a sight**) informal a person or thing having a ridiculous, repulsive, or disheveled appearance: *"I must look a frightful sight," she said.*
3 (usu. **sights**) a device on a gun or optical instrument used for assisting a person's precise aim or observation.
▶ **v.** **1** [with obj.] manage to see or observe (someone or something); catch an initial glimpse of: *tell me when you sight London Bridge* | (as noun **sighting**) *the unseasonal sighting of a cuckoo.*
2 [no obj.] take aim by looking through the sights of a gun: *she sighted down the barrel.* ■ take a detailed visual measurement of something with or as with a sight. ■ [with obj.] adjust the sight of (a firearm or optical instrument).
– PHRASES **at first sight** on first seeing or meeting someone: *it was* ***love at first sight.*** ■ after an initial impression (which is then found to be different from what is actually the case): *the debate is more complex than it seems at first sight.* **catch** (or **get a**) **sight of** glimpse for a moment; suddenly notice: *when she caught sight of him she smiled.* **in sight** visible: *no other vehicle was in sight.* ■ near at hand; close to being achieved or realized: *the minister insisted that agreement was in sight.* **in** (or **within**) **sight of** so as to see or be seen from: *I climbed the hill and came in sight of the house.* ■ within reach of; close to attaining: *he was safe for the moment and in sight of victory.* **in** (or **within**) **one's sights** visible, esp. through the sights of one's gun. ■ within the scope of one's ambitions or expectations: *he had the prize firmly in his sights.* **lose sight of** be no longer able to see. ■ fail to consider, be aware of, or remember: *we should not lose sight of the fact that the issues involved are moral ones.* **not a pretty sight** informal not a pleasant spectacle or situation. **on** (or **at**) **sight** as soon as someone or something has been seen: *in Africa, paramilitary game wardens shoot poachers on sight.* **out of sight 1** not visible: *she saw them off, waving until the car was out of sight.* **2** (also **outasight**) [often as exclamation] informal extremely good; excellent: [as adj.] *these stereophones are an out-of-sight choice.* **out of sight, out of mind** proverb you soon forget people or things that are no longer visible or present. (**get**) **out of my sight!** go away at once! **raise** (or **lower**) **one's sights** become more (or less) ambitious; increase (or lower) one's expectations. **set one's sights on** have as an ambition; hope strongly to achieve or reach: *Katherine set her sights on college.* **a sight ——** informal or dialect used to indicate that something is so described to a considerable extent: *the old lady is a sight cleverer than Sarah* | *he's a sight too full of himself.* **a sight for sore eyes** informal a person or thing that one is extremely pleased or relieved to see. **a sight to behold** a person or thing that is particularly impressive or worth seeing.
– DERIVATIVES **sight·er n.**
– ORIGIN Old English (*ge*)*sihth* 'something seen'; related to Dutch *zicht* and German *Gesicht* 'sight, face, appearance.' The verb dates from the mid 16th cent. (sense 2 of the verb).

sight de·pos·it ▶ **n.** Finance a bank deposit that can be withdrawn immediately without notice or penalty.

sight·ed /'sītid/ ▶ **adj.** (of a person) having the ability to see; not blind: *a sighted guide is needed* | (as plural noun **the sighted**) *for the sighted, it is hard to imagine a world without vision.* ■ [in combination] having a specified kind of sight: *the keen-sighted watcher may catch a glimpse.*

sight gag ▶ **n.** informal a visual joke.

sight glass ▶ **n.** a transparent tube or window through which the level of liquid in a reservoir or supply line can be checked visually.

sight·hound /'sīt,hound/ ▶ **n.** a hound originally bred to hunt independently from humans, such as a greyhound or a whippet.

sight·ing shot ▶ **n.** an experimental shot to guide shooters in adjusting their sights.

sight·less /'sītlis/ ▶ **adj.** unable to see; blind: *blank, sightless eyes.* ■ literary invisible.
– DERIVATIVES **sight·less·ly adv., sight·less·ness n.**

sight line (also **sightline**) ▶ **n.** a hypothetical line from someone's eye to what is seen (used esp. with reference to good or bad visibility): *the theater has great acoustics and splendid sight lines* | *the authorities require good sight lines at road junctions.*

sight·ly /'sītlē/ ▶ **adj.** pleasing to the eye: *metal guards can also be used but are less sightly.*
– DERIVATIVES **sight·li·ness n.**

sight-read ▶ **v.** [with obj.] read and perform (music) at sight, without preparation.
– DERIVATIVES **sight-read·er n., sight-read·ing n.**

sight rhyme ▶ **n.** another term for EYE RHYME.

sight·see·ing /'sīt,sēiNG/ ▶ **n.** the activity of visiting places of interest in a particular location: *our two-week trip combines spectacular sightseeing and superb hospitality.*
– DERIVATIVES **sight·see v.**

sight·se·er /'sīt,siər/ ▶ **n.** a person who goes sightseeing: *hordes of sightseers.*

sight-sing ▶ **v.** [with obj.] sing (music) at sight, without preparation.

sight un·seen ▶ **adv.** without the opportunity to look at the object in question beforehand: *they bought their computers sight unseen through the mail.* ■ without being seen: *what other treasures remain sight unseen?*

S

sight·wor·thy /'sīt,wərT͟Hē/ ▶ **adj.** rare worth seeing or visiting.

sig·il /'sijəl/ ▶ **n.** an inscribed or painted symbol considered to have magical power. ■ archaic a seal: *the supply wains bore the High King's sigil.* ■ literary a sign or symbol.
– ORIGIN late Middle English: from late Latin *sigillum* 'sign.'

SIGINT /'sigint/ ▶ **abbr.** signals intelligence.

sig·lum /'sigləm/ ▶ **n.** (pl. **sigla** /'siglə/) a letter (esp. an initial) or other symbol used to denote a word in a book, esp. to refer to a particular text.
– ORIGIN early 18th cent.: from late Latin *sigla* (plural), perhaps from *singula,* neuter plural of *singulus* 'single.'

sig·ma /'sigmə/ ▶ **n.** **1** the eighteenth letter of the Greek alphabet (Σ, σ), transliterated as 's.' ● The form ς is used instead of σ at the end of a

PRONUNCIATION KEY ə *ago, up;* ər *over, fur;* a *hat;* ā *ate;* ä *car;* e *let;* ē *see;* i *fit;* ī *by;* NG *sing;* ō *go;* ô *law, for;* oi *toy;* o͝o *good;* o͞o *goo;* ou *out;* TH *thin;* T͟H *then;* ZH *vision*

word. The uncial form, called **lunate sigma** and resembling the letter C, is also sometimes used.
2 (**Sigma**) [followed by Latin genitive] Astronomy the eighteenth star in a constellation: *Sigma Octantis*.
3 Chemistry & Physics relating to or denoting an electron or orbital with zero angular momentum around an internuclear axis. ▶ **symbol** ■ (Σ) mathematical sum. ■ (σ) standard deviation.

sig·mate /ˈsigmāt, -mit/ ▶ **adj.** having the shape of a Σ or a letter S.

sig·moid /ˈsigmoid/ ▶ **adj. 1** curved like the uncial sigma (C); crescent-shaped.
2 S-shaped.
▶ **n.** Anatomy short for SIGMOID COLON.
– DERIVATIVES **sig·moi·dal** /sigˈmoidəl/ **adj.**
– ORIGIN late 17th cent.: from Greek *sigmoeidēs*, from *sigma* (see SIGMA).

sig·moid co·lon ▶ **n.** Anatomy the S-shaped last part of the large intestine, leading into the rectum.

sig·moid·os·co·py /ˌsigmoiˈdäskəpē/ ▶ **n.** examination of the sigmoid colon by means of a flexible tube inserted through the anus.
– DERIVATIVES **sig·moid·o·scope** /sigˈmoidəˌskōp/ **n.**, **sig·moid·o·scop·ic** /sigˌmoidəˈskäpik/ **adj.**

sign /sīn/ ▶ **n. 1** an object, quality, or event whose presence or occurrence indicates the probable presence or occurrence of something else: *flowers are often given as a sign of affection* | [with clause] *the stores are full, which is a sign that the recession is past its worst.* ■ something regarded as an indication or evidence of what is happening or going to happen: ***the signs are*** *that counterfeiting is growing at an alarming rate.* ■ [with negative] used to indicate that someone or something is not present where they should be or are expected to be: *there was still no sign of her.* ■ Medicine an indication of a disease detectable by a medical practitioner even if not apparent to the patient. Compare with SYMPTOM. ■ a miracle regarded as evidence of supernatural power (chiefly in biblical and literary use). ■ any trace of a wild animal, esp. its tracks or droppings: *wolverine sign.*
2 a gesture or action used to convey information or instructions: *she gave him the thumbs-up sign.* ■ a notice that is publicly displayed giving information or instructions in a written or symbolic form: *I didn't see the stop sign.* ■ an action or reaction that conveys something about someone's state or experiences: *she gave no sign of having seen him.* ■ a gesture used in a system of sign language. ■ short for SIGN LANGUAGE. ■ a symbol or word used to represent an operation, instruction, concept, or object in algebra, music, or other subjects. ■ a word or gesture given according to prior arrangement as a means of identification; a password.
3 (also **zodiacal sign**) Astrology each of the twelve equal sections into which the zodiac is divided, named from the constellations formerly situated in each, and associated with successive periods of the year according to the position of the sun on the ecliptic: *a person born* ***under the sign of*** *Virgo.*
4 Mathematics the positiveness or negativeness of a quantity.
▶ **v. 1** [with obj.] write one's name on (a letter, card, or similar item) to identify oneself as the writer or sender: *the card was signed by the whole class.* ■ indicate agreement with or authorization of the contents of (a document or other written or printed material) by attaching a signature: *the two countries signed a nonaggression treaty.* ■ write (one's name) for purposes of identification or authorization: *she signed her name in the book* | [with obj. and complement] *she* ***signed herself*** *Ingrid* | [no obj.] *he signed on the dotted line.* ■ engage (someone, typically a sports player or a musician) to work for one by signing a contract with them: *the company signed 30 bands.* ■ [no obj.] sign a contract committing oneself to work for a particular person or organization: *Sherman has* ***signed for*** *another two seasons.*
2 [no obj.] use gestures to convey information or instructions: [with infinitive] *she signed to her husband to leave the room.* ■ communicate in sign language: *she was learning to sign.* ■ [with obj.] express or perform (something) in sign language: (as adj. **signed**) *the theater routinely puts on signed performances.* ■ [with obj.] archaic mark or consecrate with the sign of the cross.
– PHRASES **sign of the cross** a Christian sign made in blessing or prayer by tracing a cross from the forehead to the chest and to each shoulder, or in the air. **sign of the times** something judged to exemplify or indicate the nature or quality of a particular period, typically something unwelcome or unpleasant: *the theft was a sign of the times.* **signed, sealed, and delivered** (or **signed and sealed**) formally and officially agreed and in effect.
– PHRASAL VERBS **sign something away/over** officially relinquish rights or property by signing a deed: *I have no intention of signing away my inheritance.* **sign for** sign a receipt to confirm that one has received (something delivered or handed over). **sign in** sign a register on arrival, typically in a hotel. **sign someone in** record someone's arrival in a register. **sign off** conclude a letter, broadcast, or other message: *he signed off with a few words of advice.* ■ sign to record that one is leaving work for the day. ■ Bridge indicate by a conventional bid that one is seeking to end the bidding. **sign someone off** record that someone is entitled to miss work, typically because of illness. **sign off on** informal assent or give one's approval to: *it was hard to get celebrities to sign off on those issues.* **sign on** chiefly Brit. commit oneself to employment, membership in a society, or some other undertaking: *I'll* ***sign on with*** *an advertising agency.* **sign someone on** take someone into one's employment. **sign out** sign a register to record one's departure, typically from a hotel. **sign someone out** authorize someone's release or record their departure by signing a register. **sign something out** sign to indicate that one has borrowed or hired something: *I signed out the keys.* **sign up** commit oneself to a period of employment or education or to some other undertaking: *he* ***signed up for*** *a ten-week course.* ■ enlist in the armed forces. ■ (also **sign something up**) conclude a business deal: *the company has already signed up a few orders.* **sign someone up** formally engage someone in employment.
– DERIVATIVES **sign·er** **n.**
– ORIGIN Middle English: from Old French *signe* (noun), *signer* (verb), from Latin *signum* 'mark, token.'

Si·gnac /sēˈnyäk/, Paul (1863–1935), French neo-Impressionist painter. A pointillist painter, his technique was characterized by the use of small dashes and patches of pure color rather than dots.

sign·age /ˈsīnij/ ▶ **n.** signs collectively, esp. commercial or public display signs.

sig·nal[1] /ˈsignəl/ ▶ **n. 1** a gesture, action, or sound that is used to convey information or instructions, typically by prearrangement between the parties concerned: *the firing of the gun was the* ***signal for*** *a chain of beacons to be lit* | [with infinitive] *the policeman raised his hand as a signal to stop.* ■ an indication of a state of affairs: *the markets are waiting for a clear signal about the direction of policy.* ■ an event or statement that provides the impulse or occasion for something specified to happen: *the champion's announcement that he was retiring was the* ***signal for*** *scores of journalists to gather at his last match.* ■ an apparatus on a railroad, typically a colored light or a semaphore, giving indications to train engineers of whether or not the line is clear. ■ Bridge a prearranged convention of bidding or play intended to convey information to one's partner.
2 an electrical impulse or radio wave transmitted or received: *equipment for receiving TV signals.*
▶ **v.** (**signals, signaling, signaled**; chiefly Brit. **signals, signalling, signalled**) [no obj.] transmit information or instructions by means of a gesture, action, or sound: *hold your fire until I signal.* ■ [with obj. and infinitive] instruct (someone) to do something by means of gestures or signs rather than explicit orders: *she signaled Charlotte to be silent.* ■ (of a cyclist, motorist, or vehicle) indicate an intention to turn in a specified direction using an extended arm or flashing indicator: [with complement] *Stone signaled right* | [with infinitive] *the truck signaled to turn left.* ■ indicate the existence or occurrence of (something) by actions or sounds: [with obj.] *they could signal displeasure by refusing to cooperate* | [with clause] *she gave a glance that signaled that her father was being secretive.*
– DERIVATIVES **sig·nal·er** **n.**
– ORIGIN late Middle English: from Old French, from medieval Latin *signale*, neuter of late Latin *signalis*, from Latin *signum* 'mark, token' (see SIGN). The verb dates from the early 19th cent.

sig·nal[2] ▶ **adj.** [attrib.] striking in extent, seriousness, or importance; outstanding: *he attacked the administration for its signal failure of leadership.*
– DERIVATIVES **sig·nal·ly** **adv.**
– ORIGIN early 17th cent.: from French *signalé*, from the Italian past participle *segnalato* 'distinguished, made illustrious,' from *segnale* 'a signal.'

sig·nal box (also **signal tower**) ▶ **n.** Brit. a building beside a railroad track from which signals, switches, and other equipment are controlled.

sig·nal-call·er ▶ **n.** Football a player who signals the next play or formation to team members.

sig·nal·ize /ˈsignəˌlīz/ ▶ **v.** [with obj.] **1** mark or indicate (something), esp. in a striking or conspicuous manner: *people seek to change their name to signalize a change in status that has taken place.* ■ archaic make (something) noteworthy or remarkable: *a little flower with not much to signalize it.*
2 provide (an intersection) with traffic signals.

sig·nal·man /ˈsignəlmən/ ▶ **n.** (pl. **signalmen**) a person responsible for sending and receiving naval or military signals. ■ another term for SWITCHMAN.

sig·nals in·tel·li·gence ▶ **n.** the branch of military intelligence concerned with the monitoring, interception, and interpretation of radio signals, radar signals, and telemetry.

sig·nal-to-noise ra·tio ▶ **n.** the ratio of the strength of an electrical or other signal carrying information to that of interference, generally expressed in decibels. ■ informal a measure of how much useful information there is in a system, such as the Internet, as a proportion of the entire contents.

sig·na·to·ry /ˈsignəˌtôrē/ ▶ **n.** (pl. **signatories**) a party that has signed an agreement, esp. a country that has signed a treaty: *Bulgaria is a* ***signatory to*** *a variety of international human rights conventions* | [as modifier] *the signatory states.*
– ORIGIN late 19th cent.: from Latin *signatorius* 'of sealing,' from *signat-* 'marked (with a cross),' from the verb *signare*.

sig·na·ture /ˈsignəCHər, -ˌCHo͝or/ ▶ **n. 1** a person's name written in a distinctive way as a form of identification in authorizing a check or document or concluding a letter. ■ the action of signing a document: *the license was sent to the customer for signature.* ■ a distinctive pattern, product, or characteristic by which someone or something can be identified: *the chef produced the pâté that was his signature* | [as modifier] *his signature dish.*
2 Music short for KEY SIGNATURE or TIME SIGNATURE.
3 Printing a letter or figure printed at the foot of one or more pages of each sheet of a book as a guide in binding. ■ a printed sheet after being folded to form a group of pages.
4 the part of a medical prescription that gives instructions about the use of the medicine or drug prescribed.
– ORIGIN mid 16th cent. from medieval Latin *signatura* 'signature of a sovereign on an official document,' from Latin *signare* 'to sign, mark.'

sig·na·ture tune ▶ **n.** chiefly Brit. a distinctive piece of music associated with a particular program or performer on television or radio; a theme song.

sign·board /ˈsīnˌbôrd/ ▶ **n.** a board displaying the name or logo of a business or product. ■ a board displaying a sign to direct traffic or travelers.

sign·ee /sīˈnē, ˈsīnē/ ▶ **n.** a person who has signed a contract or other official document.

sig·net /ˈsignit/ ▶ **n.** historical a small seal, esp. one set in a ring, used instead of or with a signature to give authentication to an official document.
– ORIGIN late Middle English: from Old French, or from medieval Latin *signetum*, diminutive of *signum* 'token, seal.'

sig·net ring ▶ **n.** a ring with letters, usually one's initials, or a design carved into it.

si·gni·fiant /ˈsignəˌfīənt/ ▶ **n.** another term for SIGNIFIER.

sig·nif·i·cance /sigˈnifikəns/ ▶ **n. 1** the quality of being worthy of attention; importance: *adolescent education was felt to be a social issue of some significance.*
2 the meaning to be found in words or events: *the significance of what was happening was clearer to me than to her.*
3 (also **statistical significance**) the extent to which a result deviates from that expected to arise simply from random variation or errors in sampling.
– ORIGIN late Middle English (denoting unstated meaning): from Old French, or from Latin *significantia*, from *significare* 'indicate, portend.'

sig·nif·i·cant /sigˈnifikənt/ ▶ **adj. 1** sufficiently great or important to be worthy of attention; noteworthy: *a significant increase in sales.*
2 having a particular meaning; indicative of something: *in times of stress her dreams seemed to her especially significant.* ■ suggesting a meaning or message that is not explicitly stated: *she gave him a significant look.*
3 Statistics of, relating to, or having significance.
– ORIGIN late 16th cent. (sense 2): from Latin *significant-* 'indicating,' from the verb *significare* (see SIGNIFY).

sig·nif·i·cant fig·ure (also **significant digit**) ▶ **n.** Mathematics each of the digits of a number that are used to express it to the required degree of accuracy, starting from the first nonzero digit: *this text will round numbers to three significant figures.*

sig·nif·i·cant·ly /sigˈnifikəntlē/ ▶ **adv. 1** in a sufficiently great or important way as to be worthy of attention: *energy bills have increased significantly this year* | [as submodifier] *their situation is significantly different from ours.*
2 in a way that has a particular meaning: [as sentence adverb] *significantly, he has refused to give a straight answer to this question.* ■ in a manner that suggests

a meaning or message that is not explicitly stated: *he paused significantly.*

sig·nif·i·cant oth·er ▶ **n.** a person with whom someone has an established romantic or sexual relationship.

sig·ni·fi·ca·tion /ˌsignəfiˈkāSHən/ ▶ **n.** the representation or conveying of meaning. ■ an exact meaning or sense.
– ORIGIN Middle English: via Old French from Latin *significatio(n-)*, from *significare* 'indicate' (see **SIGNIFY**).

sig·nif·i·ca·tive /sigˈnifikātiv/ ▶ **adj.** rare being a symbol or sign of something; having a meaning.

sig·nif·i·ca·tor /sigˈnifikātər/ ▶ **n.** Astrology (in a horary chart) the planet that signifies the inquirer, or the subject of the question. ■ a card chosen to represent the inquirer in a tarot reading.

sig·ni·fied /ˈsignəˌfīd/ ▶ **n.** Linguistics the meaning or idea expressed by a sign, as distinct from the physical form in which it is expressed. Compare with **SIGNIFIER**.

sig·ni·fi·er /ˈsignəˌfīər/ ▶ **n.** Linguistics a sign's physical form (such as a sound, printed word, or image) as distinct from its meaning. Compare with **SIGNIFIED**.

sig·ni·fy /ˈsignəˌfī/ ▶ **v.** (**signifies, signifying, signified**) **1** [with obj.] be an indication of: *this decision signified a fundamental change in their priorities.* ■ be a symbol of; have as meaning: *the church used this image to signify the Holy Trinity.* ■ (of a person) indicate or declare (a feeling or intention): *signify your agreement by signing the letter below.* ■ [no obj. with negative] be of importance: *the locked door doesn't necessarily signify.*
2 [no obj.] informal (among black Americans) exchange boasts or insults as a game or ritual.
– ORIGIN Middle English: from Old French *signifier*, from Latin *significare* 'indicate, portend,' from *signum* 'token.'

sign·ing /ˈsīniNG/ ▶ **n. 1** the action of writing one's signature on an official document: *he plans to oversee the signing of modest agreements on energy, education, and the environment.* ■ the action of recruiting someone, esp. to a professional sports team or record company: *the signing of overseas players* | [as modifier] *a signing bonus.* ■ Brit. a person who has recently been recruited, esp. to join a professional sports team or record company: *Manchester United's latest signing.* ■ an event in a bookstore or other place at which an author signs a number of books to gain publicity and sales.
2 sign language.
3 the provision of signs in a street or other place.

sign lan·guage ▶ **n.** a system of communication using visual gestures and signs, as used by deaf people.

sign-off ▶ **n. 1** the conclusion of a letter, broadcast, or other message: *that was their daily sign-off on the TV show.*
2 Bridge a bid indicating that the bidder wishes to end bidding.

Si·gnor /sēnˈyôr/ (also **Signore**) ▶ **n.** (pl. **Signori** /sēnˈyôrē/) a title or form of address used of or to an Italian-speaking man, corresponding to *Mr.* or *sir*: *Signor Ugolotti* | *I am a man of honor, Signor.*
– ORIGIN Italian, from Latin *senior* (see **SENIOR**).

Si·gno·ra /sēnˈyôrə/ ▶ **n.** a title or form of address used of or to an Italian-speaking married woman, corresponding to *Mrs.* or *madam*: *good night, Signora.*
– ORIGIN Italian, feminine of *signor* (see **SIGNOR**).

Si·gno·ri·na /ˌsēnyəˈrēnə/ ▶ **n.** a title or form of address used of or to an Italian-speaking unmarried woman, corresponding to *Miss*: *Signorina Rosalba.*
– ORIGIN Italian, diminutive of *signora* (see **SIGNORA**).

sig·no·ry /ˈsēnyərē/ ▶ **n.** (pl. **signories**) another term for **SEIGNIORY**.

sign·post /ˈsīnˌpōst/ ▶ **n.** a sign giving information such as the direction and distance to a nearby town, typically found at a crossroads. ■ something that acts as guidance or a clue to an unclear or complicated issue: *there are few unambiguous signposts for doctors facing ethical issues.*
▶ **v.** [with obj.] provide (an area) with a signpost or signposts: *most of the walks were well signposted.* ■ chiefly Brit. indicate (a place or feature) with a signpost: *Battle is clearly signposted off all the main roads.*

sign-up ▶ **n.** [usu. as modifier] the action of enrolling for something or of enrolling or employing someone: *a sign-up fee of $29.95.*

Sig·urd /ˈsigərd/ (in Norse legend) the Norse equivalent of Siegfried, husband of Gudrun.

Si·ha·nouk /ˈsēəˌno͝ok/, Norodom (1922–), Cambodian king 1941–55 and 1993–2004; prime minister 1955–60; head of state 1960–70 and 1975–76.

si·ka /ˈsēkə/ (also **sika deer**) ▶ **n.** a forest-dwelling deer with a grayish winter coat that turns yellowish-brown with white spots in summer. It is native to Japan and Southeast Asia and naturalized elsewhere. ● *Cervus nippon*, family Cervidae.
– ORIGIN late 19th cent.: from Japanese *shika.*

Sikh /sēk/ ▶ **n.** an adherent of Sikhism.
▶ **adj.** of or relating to Sikhs or Sikhism.
– ORIGIN from Punjabi, 'disciple,' from Sanskrit *śiṣya.*

Sikh·ism /ˈsēkizəm/ ▶ **n.** a monotheistic religion founded in Punjab in the 15th century by Guru Nanak.

> Sikh teaching centers on spiritual liberation and social justice and harmony, though the community took on a militant aspect during early conflicts. The last guru, Gobind Singh (1666–1708), passed his authority to the scripture, the Adi Granth, and to the Khalsa, the body of initiated Sikhs.

Si·king /ˈSHēˈjiNG/ former name of **XIAN**.

Sik·kim /ˈsikim/ a state in northeastern India, in the eastern Himalayas, between Bhutan and Nepal, on the border with Tibet; capital, Gangtok. After British rule, it became an Indian protectorate and then, in 1975, a state of India.
– DERIVATIVES **Sik·kim·ese** /ˌsikiˈmēz, -ˈmēs/ **adj. & n.**

Si·kor·sky /siˈkôrskē/, Igor (Ivanovich) (1889–1972), US aircraft designer, born in Russia. He built the Grand, the first large four-engined aircraft, in 1913. He went on to establish the Sikorsky company in the US and, in 1939, developed the first mass-produced helicopter.

si·lage /ˈsīlij/ ▶ **n.** grass or other green fodder compacted and stored in airtight conditions, typically in a silo, without first being dried, and used as animal feed in the winter.
▶ **v.** [no obj.] (often as noun **silaging**) make silage. ■ [with obj.] preserve (grass and other green fodder) as silage.
– ORIGIN late 19th cent.: alteration of **ENSILAGE**, influenced by **SILO**.

sil·ane /ˈsilān/ ▶ **n.** Chemistry a colorless gaseous compound of silicon and hydrogen that has strong reducing properties and is spontaneously flammable in air. ● Chem. formula: SiH_4. ■ any of the large class of hydrides of silicon analogous to the alkanes.
– ORIGIN early 20th cent.: from **SILICON** + **-ANE**[2].

si·las·tic /siˈlastik/ ▶ **n.** trademark silicone rubber.
– ORIGIN 1940s: blend of **SILICON** and **ELASTIC**.

Si·lat /siˈlat/ ▶ **n.** the Malay art of self-defense, practiced as a martial art or accompanied by drums as a ceremonial display or dance.
– ORIGIN Malay.

sild /sild/ ▶ **n.** (pl. **same**) a small immature herring, esp. one caught in northern European seas.
– ORIGIN 1920s: from Danish and Norwegian.

sil·den·a·fil cit·rate /silˈdenəˌfil/ ▶ **n.** a crystalline compound that works by inhibiting the breakdown of enzymes that leads to loss of erection. Also called **VIAGRA** (trademark). ● Chem. formula: $C_{22}H_{30}N_6O_4S$.

si·lence /ˈsīləns/ ▶ **n.** complete absence of sound: *sirens pierce the silence of the night* | *an eerie silence descended over the house.* ■ the fact or state of abstaining from speech: *Karen had withdrawn into sullen silence* | *she was* ***reduced to silence*** *for a moment.* ■ the avoidance of mentioning or discussing something: *politicians keep their silence on the big questions.* ■ the state of standing still and not speaking as a sign of respect for someone deceased or in an opportunity for prayer: ***a moment of silence*** *presided over by a local minister.*
▶ **v.** [with obj.] cause to become silent; prohibit or prevent from speaking: *the team's performance silenced their critics* | *freedom of the press cannot be silenced by tanks.* ■ (usu. as adj. **silenced**) fit (a gun or other loud mechanism) with a silencer: *a silenced .22 rifle.*
– PHRASES **in silence** without speech or other sound: *we finished our meal in silence.*
– ORIGIN Middle English: from Old French, from Latin *silentium*, from *silere* 'be silent.'

si·lenc·er /ˈsīlənsər/ ▶ **n.** a device for reducing the noise emitted by a gun or other loud mechanism. ■ British term for **MUFFLER** (sense 2).

si·lent /ˈsīlənt/ ▶ **adj.** not making or accompanied by any sound: *the woods were still and silent.* ■ (of a person) not speaking: *she fell silent for a moment.* ■ not expressed aloud: *a silent prayer.* ■ (of a letter) written but not pronounced, e.g., *b* in *doubt.* ■ (of a movie) without an accompanying soundtrack. ■ saying or recording nothing on a particular subject: *the poems are silent on the question of marriage.* ■ (of a person) not prone to speak much; taciturn: *I'm the strong, silent type.*
– PHRASES **(as) silent as the grave** see **GRAVE**[1]. **the silent majority** the majority of people, regarded as holding moderate opinions but rarely expressing them. **the silent treatment** a stubborn refusal to talk to someone, esp. after a recent argument or disagreement.
– DERIVATIVES **si·lent·ly adv.**
– ORIGIN late 15th cent. (in the sense 'not speaking'): from Latin *silent-* 'being silent,' from the verb *silere.*

si·lent but·ler ▶ **n.** a container with a handle and a hinged cover, used for collecting table crumbs or emptying ashtrays.

si·lent com·merce ▶ **n.** a group of technologies based on wireless communications and sensing devices that permit various business and marketing activities to proceed without direct human intervention, on the basis of communications between tagged products and controlling software.

si·lent part·ner ▶ **n.** a partner not sharing in the actual work of a firm.

Si·le·nus /sīˈlēnəs/ Greek Mythology an aged woodland deity, one of the sileni, who was entrusted with the education of Dionysus. He is depicted either as dignified and musical, or as an old drunkard. ■ (as noun **a silenus**) (pl. **sileni** /-ˈlēˌnī/) a woodland spirit, usually depicted in art as old and having ears like those of a horse.

Si·le·sia /sīˈlēZHə, -SHə/ a region of central Europe that is centered on the upper Oder valley, now largely in southwestern Poland. It was partitioned at various times among the states of Prussia, Austria–Hungary, Poland, and Czechoslovakia.
– DERIVATIVES **Si·le·sian adj. & n.**

si·lex /ˈsīleks/ ▶ **n.** silica, esp. quartz or flint.
– ORIGIN late 16th cent.: from Latin, 'flint.'

sil·hou·ette /ˌsilo͞oˈet/ ▶ **n.** the dark shape and outline of someone or something visible against a lighter background, esp. in dim light. ■ a representation of someone or something showing the shape and outline only, typically colored in solid black.
▶ **v.** [with obj.] (usu. **be silhouetted**) cast or show (someone or something) as a dark shape and outline against a lighter background: *the castle* ***was silhouetted against*** *the sky.*

silhouette

– PHRASES **in silhouette** seen or placed as a silhouette.
– ORIGIN late 18th cent.: named (although the reason remains obscure) after Étienne de *Silhouette* (1709–67), French author and politician.

sil·i·ca /ˈsilikə/ ▶ **n.** a hard, unreactive, colorless compound that occurs as the mineral quartz and as a principal constituent of sandstone and other rocks. ● Alternative name: **silicon dioxide**; chem. formula: SiO_2.
– DERIVATIVES **si·li·ceous** /səˈliSHəs/ (also **silicious**) **adj.**
– ORIGIN early 19th cent.: from Latin *silex, silic-* 'flint,' on the pattern of words such as *alumina.*

sil·i·ca gel ▶ **n.** hydrated silica in a hard granular hygroscopic form used as a desiccant.

sil·i·cate /ˈsiləˌkāt, -kit/ ▶ **n.** Chemistry a salt in which the anion contains both silicon and oxygen, esp. one of the anion SiO_4^{2-}. ■ any of the many minerals consisting primarily of SiO_4^{2-} combined with metal ions, forming a major component of the rocks of the earth's crust.

si·lic·ic /səˈlisik/ ▶ **adj.** Geology (of rocks) rich in silica.

si·lic·ic ac·id ▶ **n.** Chemistry a weakly acidic colloidal hydrated form of silica made by acidifying solutions of alkali metal silicates.

si·lic·i·clas·tic /siˌlisəˈklastik/ ▶ **adj.** Geology relating to or denoting clastic rocks consisting largely of silica or silicates.

sil·i·cide /ˈsiləˌsīd/ ▶ **n.** Chemistry a binary compound of silicon with another element or group.

si·lic·i·fy /səˈlisəˌfī/ ▶ **v.** (**silicifies, silicifying, silicified**) [with obj.] (usu. **be silicified**) convert into or impregnate with silica.
– DERIVATIVES **si·lic·i·fi·ca·tion** /səˌlisəfiˈkāSHən/ **n.**

si·li·co·fla·gel·late /ˌsilәkōˈflajəˌlāt/ ▶ **n.** Zoology a marine flagellate of the order Silicoflagellida, distinguished by a siliceous skeleton and radiating spines.

sil·i·con /ˈsiləˌkän, -kən/ ▶ **n.** the chemical element of atomic number 14, a nonmetal with semiconducting properties, used in making electronic circuits. Pure

S

silicon exists in a shiny dark gray crystalline form and as an amorphous powder. (Symbol: **Si**)
– ORIGIN early 19th cent.: alteration of earlier *silicium*, from Latin *silex*, *silic-* 'flint,' on the pattern of *carbon* and *boron*.

sil·i·con car·bide ▶ n. a hard refractory crystalline compound of silicon and carbon; carborundum. ● Chem. formula: SiC.

sil·i·con chip ▶ n. a microchip.

sil·i·cone /ˈsiləˌkōn/ ▶ n. any of a class of synthetic materials that are polymers with a chemical structure based on chains of alternate silicon and oxygen atoms, with organic groups attached to the silicon atoms. Such compounds are typically resistant to chemical attack and insensitive to temperature changes and are used to make rubber, plastics, polishes, and lubricants.
▶ v. [with obj.] (usu. **be siliconed**) join or otherwise treat (something) with a silicone.

sil·i·con·ize /ˈsilikəˌnīz/ ▶ v. [with obj.] (often as adj. **siliconized**) coat or otherwise treat (something) with silicone.

Sil·i·con Val·ley a name given to an area between San Jose and Palo Alto in Santa Clara County, California, noted for its computing and electronics industries.

sil·i·co·sis /ˌsiləˈkōsis/ ▶ n. Medicine lung fibrosis caused by the inhalation of dust containing silica.
– DERIVATIVES **sil·i·cot·ic** /ˌsiləˈkätik/ adj.

sil·i·qua /ˈsilikwə/ (also **silique** /səˈlēk/) ▶ n. (pl. **siliquae** /ˈsiləˌkwē/ or **siliques** /səˈlēks, ˈsiliks/) Botany the long, narrow seedpod of many plants of the cabbage family, splitting open when mature.
– DERIVATIVES **sil·i·quose** /-ˌkwōs/ adj.
– ORIGIN Latin, literally 'pod.'

silk /silk/ ▶ n. a fine, strong, soft, lustrous fiber produced by silkworms in making cocoons and collected to make thread and fabric. ■ [often as modifier] thread or fabric made from the fiber produced by the silkworm: *a silk shirt*. ■ (**silks**) garments made from such fabric, esp. as worn by a jockey in the colors of a particular horse owner. ■ Riding a cover worn over a riding hat made from a silklike fabric. ■ Brit. informal a Queen's (or King's) Counsel. [so named because of the right accorded to wear a gown made of this cloth.] ■ any silklike threads that grow in plants, such as at the end of an ear of corn or in a milkweed pod.
– DERIVATIVES **silk·like** /ˈsilkˌlīk/ adj.
– ORIGIN Old English *sioloc*, *seolec*, from late Latin *sericum*, neuter of Latin *sericus*, based on Greek *Sēres*, the name given to the inhabitants of the Far Eastern countries from which silk first came overland to Europe.

silk cot·ton ▶ n. another term for KAPOK.

silk-cot·ton tree ▶ n. a tree that produces silk cotton (kapok). ● Two species in the family Bombacaceae: the **Indian silk-cotton tree** (*Bombax ceiba*) and the ceiba.

silk du·pi·on ▶ n. see DUPION.

silk·en /ˈsilkən/ ▶ adj. made of silk: *a silken ribbon*. ■ soft or lustrous like silk: *silken hair*.
– ORIGIN Old English *seolcen* (see SILK, -EN²).

silk gland ▶ n. a gland in a silkworm, spider, or other arthropod that secretes the substance that hardens as threads of silk or web.

S

silk hat ▶ n. a man's tall, cylindrical hat covered with black silk plush.

sil·kie /ˈsilkē/ ▶ n. (pl. **silkies**) **1** a small chicken of a breed characterized by long soft plumage.
2 variant spelling of SELKIE.

silk moth ▶ n. see SILKWORM MOTH.

silk oak (also **silky oak**) ▶ n. a tall Australian tree that yields silky-textured timber similar to oak. ● Several species in the family Proteaceae, in particular *Cardwellia sublimis* and the frequently cultivated *Grevillea robusta*.

Silk Road (also **Silk Route**) an ancient caravan route that linked Xian in central China with the eastern Mediterranean. It was established during the period of Roman rule in Europe and took its name from the silk that was brought to the west from China.

silk·screen /ˈsilkˌskrēn/ (also **silk screen**) ▶ n. a screen of fine mesh used in screen-printing. ■ a print made by screen-printing.
▶ v. [with obj.] print, decorate, or reproduce using a silkscreen.

silk-stock·ing ▶ adj. wealthy; aristocratic: *a silk-stocking crowd*.

silk tree ▶ n. an ornamental tree of the pea family with fernlike leaves and showy pink plumelike flowers that open in midsummer. It is naturalized in most of the eastern US. ● *Albizia julibrissin*, family Fabaceae.

silk·worm /ˈsilkˌwərm/ ▶ n. the commercially bred caterpillar of the domesticated silkworm moth (*Bombyx mori*), which spins a silk cocoon that is processed to yield silk fiber. ■ a commercial silk-yielding caterpillar of a saturniid moth. See TUSSORE, TUSSORE MOTH.
– ORIGIN Old English *seolcwyrm* (see SILK, WORM).

silk·worm moth ▶ n. a large moth with a caterpillar that spins a protective silken cocoon. ● (also **the silk moth**) a domesticated Asian moth whose larva is the chief commercial silkworm (*Bombyx mori*, family Bombycidae). ● (also **giant silk moth**) a saturniid moth.

silk·y /ˈsilkē/ ▶ adj. (**silkier**, **silkiest**) of or resembling silk, esp. in being soft, fine, and lustrous: *the fur felt silky and soft*. ■ (of a person or their speech or manner) suave and smooth, esp. in a way intended to be persuasive: *a silky, seductive voice*.
– DERIVATIVES **silk·i·ly** /ˈsilkəlē/ adv., **silk·i·ness** n.

sill /sil/ ▶ n. a shelf or slab of stone, wood, or metal at the foot of a window or doorway. ■ a strong horizontal member at the base of any structure, e.g., in the frame of a motor or rail vehicle. ■ Geology a tabular sheet of igneous rock intruded between and parallel with the existing strata. Compare with DIKE¹. ■ an underwater ridge or rock ledge extending across the bed of a body of water.
– ORIGIN Old English *syll*, *sylle* 'horizontal beam forming a foundation,' of Germanic origin; related to German *Schwelle* 'threshold.'

sil·la·bub ▶ n. archaic spelling of SYLLABUB.

sil·li·man·ite /ˈsiləməˌnīt/ ▶ n. an aluminosilicate mineral typically occurring as fibrous masses, commonly in schist or gneiss.
– ORIGIN mid 19th cent.: from the name of Benjamin *Silliman* (1779–1864), US chemist + -ITE¹.

Sil·li·toe /ˈsiləˌtō/, Alan (1928–), English writer. He is noted for his novels about working-class provincial life. Notable works: *Saturday Night and Sunday Morning* (1958) and *The Loneliness of the Long-Distance Runner* (1959).

Sills /silz/, Beverly (1929–2007), US opera singer; born *Belle Miriam Silverman*. Her association with the New York City Opera included a career as a soprano 1955–80 and the positions of general director 1979–88 and president 1989–90. In 1993, she became the first woman chairperson of the Lincoln Center for the Performing Arts.

sil·ly /ˈsilē/ ▶ adj. (**sillier**, **silliest**) having or showing a lack of common sense or judgment; absurd and foolish: *another of his silly jokes* | *"Don't be silly!" she said*. ■ ridiculously trivial or frivolous: *he would brood about silly things*. ■ [as complement] used to convey that an activity or process has been engaged in to such a degree that someone is no longer capable of thinking or acting sensibly: *he often drank himself silly* | *his mother worried herself silly over him*. ■ archaic (esp. of a woman, child, or animal) helpless; defenseless.
▶ n. (pl. **sillies**) informal a foolish person (often used as a form of address): *Come on, silly*.
– PHRASES **the silly season** high summer, regarded as the season when newspapers often publish trivial material because of a lack of important news.
– DERIVATIVES **sil·li·ly** /ˈsiləlē/ adv., **sil·li·ness** n.
– ORIGIN late Middle English (in the sense 'deserving of pity or sympathy'): alteration of dialect *seely* 'happy,' later 'innocent, feeble,' from a West Germanic base meaning 'luck, happiness.' The sense 'foolish' developed via the stages 'feeble' and 'unsophisticated, ignorant.'

sil·ly bil·ly ▶ n. informal, chiefly Brit. a stupid or foolish person.

Sil·ly Put·ty ▶ n. trademark a moldable silicone-based substance, sold chiefly as a toy, with remarkable properties of stretching and bouncing.

si·lo /ˈsīlō/ ▶ n. (pl. **silos**) **1** a tower or pit on a farm used to store grain. ■ a pit or other airtight structure in which green crops are compressed and stored as silage.
2 an underground chamber in which a guided missile is kept ready for firing.
3 a system, process, department, etc. that operates in isolation from others: *it's vital that team members step out of their silos and start working together*.
– ORIGIN mid 19th cent.: from Spanish, via Latin from Greek *siros* 'cornpit.'

silo 1

Si·lo·am /sīˈlōəm, si-/ (in the New Testament) a spring and pool of water near Jerusalem, where a man born blind was told by Jesus to wash, thereby gaining sight.

si·lox·ane /siˈläksān/ ▶ n. Chemistry a compound having a molecular structure based on a chain of alternate silicon and oxygen atoms, esp. (as in silicone) with organic groups attached to the silicon atoms.
– ORIGIN early 20th cent.: blend of SILICON and OXYGEN + -ANE².

silt /silt/ ▶ n. fine sand, clay, or other material carried by running water and deposited as a sediment, esp. in a channel or harbor. ■ a bed or layer of such material. ■ technical sediment whose particles are between clay and sand in size (typically 0.002–0.06 mm).
▶ v. [no obj.] become filled or blocked with silt: *the river's mouth had silted up* | (as noun **silting**) *the silting of the river estuary*. ■ [with obj.] fill or block with silt.
– DERIVATIVES **sil·ta·tion** /silˈtāSHən/ n., **silt·y** adj.
– ORIGIN late Middle English: probably originally denoting a salty deposit and of Scandinavian origin, related to Danish and Norwegian *sylt* 'salt marsh,' also to SALT.

silt·stone /ˈsiltˌstōn/ ▶ n. Geology fine-grained sedimentary rock consisting of consolidated silt.

Si·lu·ri·an /siˈlo͝orēən, sī-/ ▶ adj. Geology of, relating to, or denoting the third period of the Paleozoic era, between the Ordovician and Devonian periods. ■ (as noun **the Silurian**) the Silurian period or the system of rocks deposited during it.

> The Silurian lasted from about 439 million to 409 million years ago. The first true fish and land plants appeared during the period, and the end of the period is marked by the climax of the Caledonian orogeny.

– ORIGIN early 18th cent.: from Latin *Silures* (denoting a people of ancient southeastern Wales) + -IAN.

sil·van ▶ adj. variant spelling of SYLVAN.

Sil·va·nus /silˈvānəs/ Roman Mythology an Italian woodland deity identified with Pan.

sil·ver /ˈsilvər/ ▶ n. **1** a precious shiny grayish-white metal, the chemical element of atomic number 47. (Symbol: **Ag**)

> A transition metal, silver is found in nature as the native metal as well as in combined form in ore minerals. It is valued for use in jewelry and other ornaments and formerly in coins, and the decomposition of silver salts by the action of light (depositing metallic silver) is the basis of photography.

2 a shiny gray-white color or appearance like that of silver: *the dark hair was now highlighted with silver*.
3 silver dishes, containers, or cutlery: *thieves stole $5,000 worth of silver* | *the family silver*. ■ household cutlery of any material: *it is important to wash table silver in hot soapy water immediately after each meal*.
4 coins made from silver or from a metal that resembles silver. ■ chiefly Scottish money.
5 short for SILVER MEDAL.
▶ adj. [attrib.] denoting a twenty-fifth anniversary.
▶ v. [with obj.] (often as adj. **silvered**) coat or plate with silver: *large silvered candlesticks*. ■ provide (mirror glass) with a backing of a silver-colored material in order to make it reflective. ■ literary (esp. of the moon) give a silvery appearance to: *the brilliant moon silvered the turf*. ■ turn (a person's hair) gray or white. ■ [no obj.] (of a person's hair) turn gray or white.
– PHRASES **be born with a silver spoon in one's mouth** be born into a wealthy family of high social standing. **every cloud has a silver lining** proverb every difficult or sad situation has a comforting or more hopeful aspect even though this may not be immediately apparent. **the silver screen** the movie industry; movies collectively: *stars of the silver screen*.
– ORIGIN Old English *seolfor*, of Germanic origin; related to Dutch *zilver* and German *Silber*.

sil·ver age ▶ n. a period regarded as notable but inferior to a golden age: *the age may in hindsight be seen as not entirely contemptible, perhaps even as a silver age*.

sil·ver·back /ˈsilvərˌbak/ ▶ n. a mature male mountain gorilla, distinguished by an area of white or silvery hair across the back and acting as the dominant member of its social group.

sil·ver·ber·ry /ˈsilvərˌberē/ ▶ n. (pl. **silverberries**) a North American shrub related to the oleaster, with red-brown stems and silvery leaves, flowers, and berries. ● *Elaeagnus commutata*, family Elaeagnaceae.

sil·ver birch ▶ **n.** a European birch with silver-gray bark, common on poorer soils to the northern limit of tree growth. ● *Betula pendula*, family Betulaceae. ■ another term for **PAPER BIRCH**.

sil·ver bul·let ▶ **n.** a bullet made of silver, used in fiction as a supposedly magical method of killing werewolves. ■ a simple and seemingly magical solution to a complicated problem: *the Internet, like TQM and Re-engineering, proved to be no silver bullet.*

sil·ver chlo·ride ▶ **n.** a white insoluble powder that darkens on exposure to light, owing to the production of metallic silver. It is used in making photographic emulsions and papers.

sil·ver·eye /ˈsilvərˌī/ ▶ **n.** an Australasian songbird of the white-eye family, with mainly greenish plumage and a white ring around the eye. ● Genus *Zosterops*, family Zosteropidae: two or three species.

sil·ver fir ▶ **n.** a fir tree with foliage that appears silvery or bluish because of whitish lines on the undersides of the needles. ● Genus *Abies*, family Pinaceae: several species, in particular the European *A. alba* and the North American *A. amabilis*, a coastal tree found from southern Alaska to northern California.

sil·ver·fish /ˈsilvərˌfisн/ ▶ **n.** (pl. **same** or **silverfishes**) **1** a chiefly nocturnal silvery bristletail that frequents houses and other buildings, feeding on starchy materials. ● *Lepisma saccharina*, family Lepismatidae.
2 a silver-colored fish, esp. a variety of goldfish.

sil·ver fox ▶ **n.** a red fox of a North American variety that has black fur with white tips. ■ the fur of this animal.

sil·ver gilt ▶ **n.** gilded silver. ■ an imitation gilding of yellow lacquer over silver leaf.

sil·ver·ing /ˈsilvəriNG/ ▶ **n.** silver-colored material used to coat glass in order to make it reflective.

sil·ver i·o·dide ▶ **n.** a yellow insoluble powder that darkens on exposure to light. It is used in photography and artificial rainmaking. ● Chem. formula: AgI.

sil·ver ju·bi·lee ▶ **n.** the twenty-fifth anniversary of a significant event.

sil·ver leaf ▶ **n.** **1** a fungal disease of ornamental and fruit trees, esp. plum trees, resulting in silvery discoloration of the leaves. ● The fungus is *Chondrostereum purpureum*, family Stereaceae, class Hymenomycetes.
2 silver that has been beaten into a very thin sheet, suitable for applying to surfaces as a decoration.

sil·ver ma·ple ▶ **n.** a maple of eastern North America with leaves that are silvery underneath. ● *Acer saccharinum*, family Aceraceae.

sil·ver med·al ▶ **n.** a medal made of or colored silver, customarily awarded for second place in a race or other competition.

sil·vern /ˈsilvərn/ ▶ **adj.** archaic term for **SILVER**.
– ORIGIN Old English *seolfren, silfren* (see **SILVER**, **-N**[1]).

sil·ver ni·trate ▶ **n.** a colorless solid, soluble in water, formerly used in photography. ● Chem. formula: $AgNO_3$.

sil·ver pa·per ▶ **n.** **1** chiefly Brit. foil made of aluminum or other silver-colored metal.
2 archaic fine white tissue paper.

sil·ver plate ▶ **n.** a thin layer of silver electroplated or otherwise applied as a coating to another metal. ■ objects coated with silver. ■ plates, dishes, etc., made of silver.
▶ **v.** (**silver-plate**) [with obj.] cover (something) with a thin layer of silver.

sil·ver·point /ˈsilvərˌpoint/ ▶ **n.** the art of drawing with a silver-pointed instrument on paper prepared with a coating of powdered bone or zinc white, creating a fine durable line composed of metal fragments.

sil·ver salm·on ▶ **n.** another term for **COHO**.

sil·ver serv·ice ▶ **n.** a style of serving food at formal meals in which the server uses a silver spoon and fork in one hand to serve the food item by item onto the diner's plate.

sil·ver·side /ˈsilvərˌsīd/ ▶ **n.** **1** (also **silversides**) a small, slender, chiefly marine fish with a bright silver line along its sides. ● Family Atherinidae: several genera and species.
2 Brit. the upper side of a round of beef from the outside of the leg.

sil·ver·smith /ˈsilvərˌsmiтн/ ▶ **n.** a person who makes silver articles.
– DERIVATIVES **sil·ver·smith·ing n.**

sil·ver sol·der ▶ **n.** a brazing alloy consisting largely of copper and silver.

Sil·ver Spring a residential and commercial suburb in central Maryland, just north of Washington, DC; pop. 76,540 (2000).

sil·ver stand·ard ▶ **n.** historical a system by which the value of a currency is defined in terms of silver, for which the currency may be exchanged. Compare with **GOLD STANDARD**.

Sil·ver Star ▶ **n.** a decoration bestowed by the US Army upon a soldier for gallantry in action.

Sil·ver State a nickname for the state of **NEVADA**.

Sil·ver·stein /ˈsilvərˌstin, -ˌstēn/, Shel (1932–99), US poet, writer, and cartoonist; full name *Sheldon Alan Silverstein*; also known as **Uncle Shelby**. He is best known for his children's stories and poetry such as in *The Giving Tree* (1964), *Where the Sidewalk Ends* (1974), *The Light in the Attic* (1981), and *Falling Up* (1996).

sil·ver surf·er ▶ **n.** informal an elderly person who is a regular or enthusiastic Internet user.

sil·ver·sword /ˈsilvərˌsôrd/ ▶ **n.** a Hawaiian plant of the daisy family that has long narrow leaves with silvery hairs and clusters of purplish flowers. ● Genus *Argyroxiphium*, family Compositae.

sil·ver thaw ▶ **n.** a glassy coating of ice formed on the ground or an exposed surface by freezing rain or the refreezing of thawed ice.

sil·ver tongue ▶ **n.** a tendency to be eloquent and persuasive in speaking.
– DERIVATIVES **sil·ver-tongued adj.**

sil·ver·ware /ˈsilvərˌwer/ ▶ **n.** dishes, containers, or cutlery made of or coated with silver. ■ eating and serving utensils made of any material.

sil·ver wed·ding (also **silver wedding anniversary**) ▶ **n.** the twenty-fifth anniversary of a wedding.

sil·ver·weed /ˈsilvərˌwēd/ ▶ **n.** a yellow-flowered herbaceous potentilla with silvery compound leaves, a common grassland weed of north temperate regions. ● *Potentilla anserina*, family Rosaceae.

sil·ver·y /ˈsilvərē/ ▶ **adj.** like silver in color or appearance; shiny and gray-white: *shoals of silvery fish.* ■ (of a person's hair) gray-white and lustrous. ■ (of a sound) gentle, clear, and melodious: *a little silvery laugh.*
– DERIVATIVES **sil·ver·i·ness n.**

sil·vi·cul·ture /ˈsilviˌkəlcнər/ ▶ **n.** the growing and cultivation of trees.
– DERIVATIVES **sil·vi·cul·tur·al** /ˌsilviˈkəlcнərəl/ **adj.**, **sil·vi·cul·tur·ist** /ˌsilviˈkəlcнərist/ **n.**
– ORIGIN late 19th cent.: from French *sylviculture*, from Latin *silva* 'wood' + French *culture* 'cultivation.'

s'il vous plaît /ˌsēl vo͞o ˈple/ ▶ **adv.** French for **PLEASE**.
– ORIGIN French, literally 'if it pleases you.'

SIM /sim/ (also **SIM card**) ▶ **n.** a smart card inside a cellular phone, carrying an identification number unique to the owner, storing personal data, and preventing operation if removed.
– ORIGIN 1980s: acronym from *subscriber identification module.*

sim /sim/ ▶ **n.** informal a video game that simulates an activity such as flying an aircraft or playing a sport.
– ORIGIN late 20th cent.: abbreviation of *simulation* (see **SIMULATE**).

si·ma /ˈsīmə/ ▶ **n.** Geology the material of the lower part of the earth's crust, underlying both the ocean and the continents, characterized as relatively dense and rich in silica and magnesia. Contrasted with **SIAL**.
– ORIGIN early 20th cent.: blend of **SILICA** + **MAGNESIUM**.

si·ma·zine /ˈsīməˌzēn/ ▶ **n.** a synthetic compound derived from triazine and used as a herbicide, esp. to kill broadleaved weeds and grasses before they emerge.
– ORIGIN 1950s: blend of **SYMMETRICAL** and **TRIAZINE**.

Sim·birsk /s(y)imˈb(y)irsk/ a city in western Russia, a port on the Volga River, southeast of Nizhni Novgorod; pop. 607,000 (est. 2008). Between 1924 and 1992 it was called Ulyanovsk, in honor of Vladimir Ilich Ulyanov Lenin, who was born here in 1870.

sim·cha /ˈsimcнə/ ▶ **n.** a Jewish private party or celebration.
– ORIGIN from Hebrew *śimḥāh* 'rejoicing.'

Si·me·non /ˌsēməˈnôN/, Georges (Joseph Christian) (1903–89), French novelist, born in Belgium. He is best known for his series of detective novels that feature Commissaire Maigret.

Sim·e·on /ˈsimēən/ (in the Bible) a Hebrew patriarch, second son of Jacob and Leah. ■ the tribe of Israel traditionally descended from him.

Sim·fe·ro·pol /s(y)imfiˈrôpəl/ a city in the Crimea, Ukraine; pop. 337,100 (est. 2009). It was settled by the Tartars in the 16th century, when it was known as Ak-Mechet, and was seized in 1736 by the Russians.

sim·i·an /ˈsimēən/ ▶ **adj.** relating to, resembling, or affecting apes or monkeys: *simian immunodeficiency virus*. Compare with **PROSIMIAN**.
▶ **n.** an ape or monkey.
– ORIGIN early 17th cent.: from Latin *simia* 'ape,' perhaps via Latin from Greek *simos* 'flat-nosed.'

sim·i·lar /ˈsimələr/ ▶ **adj.** resembling without being identical: *a soft cheese similar to Brie | northern India and similar areas.* ■ Geometry (of geometric figures) having the same shape, with the same angles and proportions, though not necessarily of the same size.
▶ **n.** chiefly archaic a person or thing similar to another. ■ (usu. **similars**) a substance that produces effects resembling the symptoms of particular diseases (the basis of homeopathic treatment): *the principle of treatment by similars.*
– ORIGIN late 16th cent. (also as a term in anatomy meaning 'homogeneous'): from French *similaire* or medieval Latin *similaris*, from Latin *similis* 'like.'

sim·i·lar·i·ty /ˌsiməˈlaritē/ ▶ **n.** (pl. **similarities**) the state or fact of being similar: *the similarity of symptoms makes them hard to diagnose.* ■ (usu. **similarities**) a similar feature or aspect: *the similarities between people of different nationalities.*

sim·i·lar·ly /ˈsimələrlē/ ▶ **adv.** [usu. as submodifier] in a similar way: *a similarly priced property.* ■ [sentence adverb] used to indicate a similarity between two facts or events: *The diaries of politicians tend to be self-justifying. Similarly, autobiographies may be idealized.*

sim·i·le /ˈsiməlē/ ▶ **n.** a figure of speech involving the comparison of one thing with another thing of a different kind, used to make a description more emphatic or vivid (e.g., *as brave as a lion, crazy like a fox*). ■ the use of such a method of comparison.
– ORIGIN late Middle English: from Latin, neuter of *similis* 'like.'

si·mil·i·tude /siˈmiləˌt(y)o͞od/ ▶ **n.** the quality or state of being similar to something. ■ archaic a comparison between two things. ■ archaic a person or thing resembling someone or something else.
– ORIGIN late Middle English: from Old French, from Latin *similitudo*, from *similis* 'like.'

Si·mi Val·ley /ˈsēmē, siˌmē/ a city in southwestern California, northwest of Los Angeles; pop. 120,543 (est. 2008).

Sim·la /ˈsimlə/ variant spelling of **SHIMLA**.

SIMM /sim/ ▶ **abbr.** Computing single in-line memory module, containing RAM chips.

Sim·men·tal /ˈzimənˌtäl/ ▶ **n.** an animal of a red and white breed of cattle farmed for both meat and milk.
– ORIGIN 1950s: named after a valley in central Switzerland.

sim·mer /ˈsimər/ ▶ **v.** [no obj.] (of water or food) stay just below the boiling point while being heated: *the goulash was simmering slowly in the oven* | figurative *the disagreement simmered for years and eventually boiled over.* ■ [with obj.] keep (something) at such a point when cooking or heating it: *simmer the sauce gently until thickened.* ■ be in a state of suppressed anger or excitement: *she was simmering with resentment.* ■ (**simmer down**) become calmer and quieter.
▶ **n.** [in sing.] a state or temperature just below the boiling point: *bring the water to a simmer.*
– ORIGIN mid 17th cent.: alteration of dialect *simper* (in the same sense), perhaps imitative.

S

sim·nel cake /ˈsimnəl/ ▶ **n.** chiefly Brit. a rich fruitcake, typically with a marzipan covering and decoration, eaten esp. at Easter or during Lent.
– ORIGIN mid 17th cent.: *simnel* from Old French *simenel*, based on Latin *simila* or Greek *semidalis* 'fine flour.'

si·mo·le·on /səˈmōlēən/ ▶ **n.** informal a dollar.
– ORIGIN late 19th cent.: perhaps on the pattern of *napoleon*.

Si·mon, Neil (1927–), US playwright; full name *Marvin Neil Simon*. Most of his plays are wry comedies that portray aspects of middle-class life. They include *Barefoot in the Park* (1963), *The Odd Couple* (1965), and *Lost in Yonkers* (1991). Many of his plays were made into movies.

Si·mon, St., an apostle; known as **Simon the Zealot**. According to one tradition, he preached and was martyred in Persia along with St. Jude. Feast day (with St. Jude), October 28.

Si·mon·i·des /sīˈmänədˌēz/ (*c.*556–468 BC), Greek lyric poet. Much of his poetry celebrates the heroes of the Persian Wars.

si·mon·ize /ˈsīməˌnīz/ ▶ **v.** [with obj.] polish (a motor vehicle).
– ORIGIN 1930s: from the proprietary name *Simoniz* + **-IZE**.

si·mon-pure /ˈsīmən ˌpyo͝or/ ▶ **adj.** completely genuine, authentic, or honest.
– ORIGIN late 18th cent.: from (*the real*) *Simon Pure*, a character in Centlivre's *Bold Stroke for a Wife* (1717), who for part of the play is impersonated by another character.

Si·mon Says /ˈsīmən sez/ ▶ **n.** a children's game in which players must obey the leader's instructions if (and only if) they are prefaced with the words "Simon says."

si·mo·ny /ˈsīmənē, ˈsi-/ ▶ **n.** chiefly historical the buying or selling of ecclesiastical privileges, for example pardons or benefices.
– DERIVATIVES **si·mo·ni·ac** /sīˈmōnēˌak, si-/ **adj. & n.**, **si·mo·ni·a·cal** /ˌsīməˈnīəkəl, si-/ **adj.**
– ORIGIN Middle English: from Old French *simonie*, from late Latin *simonia*, from *Simon* Magus (Acts 8:18).

si·moom /siˈmo͞om/ (also **simoon** /-ˈmo͞on/) ▶ **n.** a hot, dry, dust-laden wind blowing in the desert, esp. in Arabia.
– ORIGIN late 18th cent.: from Arabic *samūm*, from *samma* 'to poison.'

simp /simp/ ▶ **n.** informal a silly or foolish person.
– ORIGIN early 20th cent.: abbreviation of **SIMPLETON**.

sim·pa·ti·co /simˈpatiˌkō/ ▶ **adj.** (of a person) likable and easy to get along with. ■ having or characterized by shared attributes or interests; compatible: *a simpatico relationship*.
– ORIGIN Italian and Spanish, 'sympathetic.'

sim·per /ˈsimpər/ ▶ **v.** [no obj.] smile or gesture in an affectedly coquettish, coy, or ingratiating manner: *she simpered, looking pleased with herself*.
▶ **n.** [usu. in sing.] an affectedly coquettish, coy, or ingratiating smile or gesture: *an exaggerated simper*.
– DERIVATIVES **sim·per·ing·ly adv.**
– ORIGIN mid 16th cent.: of unknown origin; compare with German *zimpfer* 'elegant, delicate.'

sim·ple /ˈsimpəl/ ▶ **adj.** (**simpler, simplest**) **1** easily understood or done; presenting no difficulty: *a simple solution* | *camcorders are now so simple to operate*. ■ plain, basic, or uncomplicated in form, nature, or design; without much decoration or ornamentation: *a simple white blouse* | *the house is furnished in a simple country style*. ■ [attrib.] used to emphasize the fundamental and straightforward nature of something: *the simple truth*.
2 composed of a single element; not compound. ■ Mathematics denoting a group that has no proper normal subgroup. ■ Botany (of a leaf or stem) not divided or branched. ■ (of a lens, microscope, etc.) consisting of a single lens or component. ■ (in English grammar) denoting a tense formed without an auxiliary, e.g., *sang* as opposed to *was singing*. ■ (of interest) payable on the sum loaned only. Compare with **COMPOUND**[1].
3 of or characteristic of low rank or status; humble and unpretentious: *a simple Buddhist monk*.
4 of low or abnormally low intelligence.
▶ **n.** chiefly historical a medicinal herb, or a medicine made from one: *the gatherers of simples*.
– DERIVATIVES **sim·ple·ness n.**
– ORIGIN Middle English: from Old French, from Latin *simplus*. The noun sense (mid 16th cent.) originally referred to a medicine made from one constituent, esp. from one plant.

sim·ple eye ▶ **n.** a small eye of an insect or other arthropod that has only one lens, typically present in one or more pairs. Also called **OCELLUS**. Contrasted with **COMPOUND EYE**.

sim·ple frac·ture ▶ **n.** a fracture of the bone only, without damage to the surrounding tissues or breaking of the skin. Compare with **COMPOUND FRACTURE**.

sim·ple har·mon·ic mo·tion ▶ **n.** Physics oscillatory motion under a retarding force proportional to the amount of displacement from an equilibrium position.

sim·ple in·ter·val ▶ **n.** Music an interval of one octave or less.

sim·ple ma·chine ▶ **n.** Mechanics any of the basic mechanical devices for applying a force, such as an inclined plane, wedge, or lever.

sim·ple ma·jor·i·ty ▶ **n.** a majority in which the highest number of votes cast for any one candidate, issue, or item exceeds the second-highest number, while not constituting an absolute majority.

sim·ple·mind·ed /ˈsimpəlˈmīndid/ ▶ **adj.** having or showing very little intelligence or judgment.
– DERIVATIVES **sim·ple·mind·ed·ly adv.**, **sim·ple·mind·ed·ness n.**

sim·ple sen·tence ▶ **n.** a sentence consisting of only one clause, with a single subject and predicate.

Sim·ple Si·mon ▶ **n.** a foolish or gullible person.
– ORIGIN probably from the name of a character who is featured in various nursery rhymes.

sim·ple time ▶ **n.** musical rhythm or meter in which each beat in a measure can be subdivided simply into halves or quarters. Compare with **COMPOUND TIME**.

sim·ple·ton /ˈsimpəltən/ ▶ **n.** a foolish or gullible person.
– ORIGIN mid 17th cent.: from **SIMPLE**, on the pattern of surnames derived from place names ending in *-ton*.

sim·plex /ˈsimpleks/ ▶ **adj.** technical composed of or characterized by a single part or structure. ■ (of a communications system, computer circuit, etc.) only allowing transmission of signals in one direction at a time.
▶ **n.** a simple or uncompounded word.
– ORIGIN late 16th cent.: from Latin, literally 'single,' variant of *simplus* 'simple.'

sim·plex meth·od ▶ **n.** Mathematics a standard method of maximizing a linear function of several variables under several constraints on other linear functions.

sim·plic·i·ty /simˈplisitē/ ▶ **n.** the quality or condition of being easy to understand or do: *for the sake of simplicity, this chapter will concentrate on one theory*. ■ the quality or condition of being plain or natural: *the grandeur and simplicity of Roman architecture*. ■ a thing that is plain, natural, or easy to understand: *the simplicities of pastoral living*.
– PHRASES **be simplicity itself** be extremely easy.
– ORIGIN late Middle English: from Old French *simplicite* or Latin *simplicitas*, from *simplex* (see **SIMPLEX**).

sim·pli·fy /ˈsimpləˌfī/ ▶ **v.** (**simplifies, simplifying, simplified**) [with obj.] make (something) simpler or easier to do or understand: *an overhaul of court procedure to simplify litigation*.
– DERIVATIVES **sim·pli·fi·ca·tion** /ˌsimpləfiˈkāsʜən/ **n.**
– ORIGIN mid 17th cent.: from French *simplifier*, from medieval Latin *simplificare*, from Latin *simplus* (see **SIMPLE**).

sim·plism /ˈsimplizəm/ ▶ **n.** rare the oversimplification of an issue.

sim·plis·tic /simˈplistik/ ▶ **adj.** treating complex issues and problems as if they were much simpler than they really are: *simplistic solutions*.
– DERIVATIVES **sim·plis·ti·cal·ly adv.**

sim·ply /ˈsimplē/ ▶ **adv. 1** in a straightforward or plain manner: *speaking simply and from the heart*.
2 merely; just: *simply complete the application form*. ■ [as submodifier] absolutely; completely (used for emphasis): *it makes Terry simply furious*. ■ [sentence adverb] used to introduce a short summary of a situation: *quite simply, some things have to be taught*.

Simp·son[1] /ˈsim(p)sən/, Sir James Young (1811–71), Scottish surgeon and obstetrician. He discovered the usefulness of chloroform as an anesthetic.

Simp·son[2], O. J. (1947–), US football player and actor; full name *Orenthal James Simpson*. Following a successful career as a running back for the Buffalo Bills 1969–77 and the San Francisco 49ers 1978–79, he became a television sports commentator. He was arrested in 1994, accused of murdering his ex-wife Nicole Brown Simpson (1959–94) and Ronald Goldman (1968–94). He was acquitted after a lengthy, high-profile trial, but in a 1997 civil court, he was found liable for both wrongful deaths.

Simp·son[3], Wallis (1896–1986), wife of Edward, Duke of Windsor (Edward VIII); born *Wallis Warfield*. Her relationship with the king caused a scandal in view of her status as an American divorcee and forced his abdication in 1936.

Simp·son's rule /ˈsimpsənz/ Mathematics an arithmetical rule for estimating the area under a curve where the values of an odd number of ordinates, including those at each end, are known.
– ORIGIN late 19th cent.: named after Thomas *Simpson* (1710–61), English mathematician.

sim·ul /ˈsiməl/ ▶ **n.** Chess a display in which a player plays a number of games simultaneously against different opponents.
– ORIGIN 1960s: abbreviation of **SIMULTANEOUS**.

sim·u·la·crum /ˌsimyəˈlākrəm, -ˈlak-/ ▶ **n.** (pl. **simulacra** /-ˈlākrə, -ˈlakrə/ or **simulacrums**) an image or representation of someone or something: *a small-scale simulacrum of a skyscraper*. ■ an unsatisfactory imitation or substitute: *a bland simulacrum of American soul music*.
– ORIGIN late 16th cent.: from Latin, from *simulare* (see **SIMULATE**).

sim·u·lant /ˈsimyələnt/ ▶ **n.** a thing that simulates or resembles something else: *jade simulants*.
– ORIGIN mid 18th cent.: from Latin *simulant-* 'copying, representing,' from the verb *simulare*.

sim·u·late /ˈsimyəˌlāt/ ▶ **v.** [with obj.] imitate the appearance or character of: *red ocher intended to simulate blood*. ■ pretend to have or feel (an emotion): *it was impossible to force a smile, to simulate pleasure*. ■ produce a computer model of: *future population changes were simulated by computer*.
– DERIVATIVES **sim·u·la·tion** /ˌsimyəˈlāsʜən/ **n.**, **sim·u·la·tive** /-ˌlātiv/ **adj.**
– ORIGIN mid 17th cent.: from Latin *simulat-* 'copied, represented,' from the verb *simulare*, from *similis* 'like.'

sim·u·lat·ed /ˈsimyəˌlātid/ ▶ **adj.** manufactured in imitation of some other material: *a simulated leather handbag*. ■ (of an emotion) pretended or feigned: *she howled in simulated anguish*. ■ imitating the conditions of something, esp. as a training exercise: *a simulated terrorist attack*.

sim·u·la·tor /ˈsimyəˌlātər/ ▶ **n.** a machine with a similar set of controls designed to provide a realistic imitation of the operation of a vehicle, aircraft, or other complex system, used for training purposes. ■ (also **simulator program**) a program enabling a computer to execute programs written for a different operating system.

si·mul·cast /ˈsīməlˌkast/ ▶ **n.** a simultaneous transmission of the same program on radio and television, or on two or more channels. ■ a live transmission of a public celebration or sports event: *simulcasts of live races*.
▶ **v.** (past and past participle **simulcast**) [with obj.] broadcast (a simulcast transmission): *the show will be simulcast live to 201 countries*.
– ORIGIN 1940s: blend of **SIMULTANEOUS** and **BROADCAST**.

si·mul·ta·ne·ous /ˌsīməlˈtānēəs/ ▶ **adj.** occurring, operating, or done at the same time: *a simultaneous withdrawal of all troops* | *simultaneous translation*.
– DERIVATIVES **si·mul·ta·ne·i·ty** /ˌsīməltəˈnēitē/ **n.**, **si·mul·ta·ne·ous·ness n.**
– ORIGIN mid 17th cent.: based on Latin *simul* 'at the same time,' probably influenced by late Latin *momentaneus*.

si·mul·ta·ne·ous e·qua·tions ▶ **plural n.** equations involving two or more unknowns that are to have the same values in each equation.

si·mul·ta·ne·ous·ly /ˌsīməlˈtānēəslē/ ▶ **adv.** at the same time: *the telethon was broadcast simultaneously on 31 US networks*.

si·murg /siˈmərg/ ▶ **n.** (in Persian mythology) a large mythical bird of great age, believed to have the power of reasoning and speech.
– ORIGIN from Persian *sīmurġ*, from Pahlavi *sēn* 'eagle' + *murġ* 'bird.'

sin[1] /sin/ ▶ **n.** an immoral act considered to be a transgression against divine law: *a sin in the eyes of God* | *the human capacity for sin*. ■ an act regarded as a serious or regrettable fault, offense, or omission: *he committed the unforgivable sin of refusing to give interviews* | humorous *with air like this, it's a sin not to go out*.
▶ **v.** (**sins, sinning, sinned**) [no obj.] commit a sin: *I sinned and brought shame down on us*. ■ (**sin against**) offend against (God, a person, or a principle): *I had sinned against my master*.
– PHRASES **(as) —— as sin** informal having a particular undesirable quality to a high degree: *as ugly as sin*. **live in sin** informal, dated live together as though married. **sin of commission** a sinful action. **sin of omission** a sinful failure to perform an action.
– ORIGIN Old English *synn* (noun), *syngian* (verb); probably related to Latin *sons, sont-* 'guilty.'

sin[2] /sīn/ ▶ **abbr.** sine.

Si·nai /ˈsīˌnī/ an arid mountainous peninsula in northeastern Egypt that extends into the Red Sea between the Gulf of Suez and the Gulf of Aqaba. It was occupied by Israel between 1967 and 1982. In the south is Mount Sinai, where, according to the Bible, Moses received the Ten Commandments (Exod. 19–34).

Si·na·it·ic /ˌsinēˈitik/ ▶ **adj.** of or relating to Mount Sinai or the Sinai peninsula.

Si·na·lo·a /ˌsēnəˈlōə/ a state on the Pacific coast of Mexico; capital, Culiacán Rosales.

Si·nan·thro·pus /sinˈanᴛʜrəpəs, sī-/ ▶ **n.** a former genus name applied to some fossilized hominids found in China in 1926. See **PEKING MAN**.
– ORIGIN modern Latin, from **SINO-** 'Chinese' (because remains were found near Beijing) + Greek *anthrōpos* 'man.'

Si·na·tra /səˈnätrə/, Frank (1915–98), US singer and actor; full name *Francis Albert Sinatra*. He became a star in the 1940s with a large teenage following. His many hits included "Night and Day," "My Way," and

S

"New York, New York." Notable movies: *From Here to Eternity* (1953), *Ocean's Eleven* (1960), and *The Detective* (1968).

Frank Sinatra

Sin·bad the Sail·or /ˈsinˌbad/ (also **Sindbad** /ˈsindˌbad/) the hero of one of the tales in the *Arabian Nights*, who relates the fantastic adventures he meets with in his voyages.

since /sins/ ▶ **prep., conj., & adv. 1** in the intervening period between (the time mentioned) and the time under consideration, typically the present: [as prep.] *she has suffered from cystic fibrosis since 1984* | *the worst property slump since the war* | [as conjunction] *I've felt better since I've been here* | [as adv.] *she ran away on Friday and we haven't seen her since.*
2 [conjunction] for the reason that: because: *delegates were delighted, since better protection of rhino reserves will help protect other rare species.*
3 [adv.] ago: *the settlement had vanished* ***long since.***
– ORIGIN late Middle English: contraction of obsolete *sithence*, or from dialect *sin* (both from dialect *sithen* 'thereupon, afterward, ever since').

> **USAGE** When using **since** as a causal conjunction to mean 'because' or 'given that,' be aware that in some contexts or constructions the word may be construed as referring to time. For example, in the sentence, *Since Mrs. Jefferson moved to Baltimore in the 1990s, she was not aware of the underlying complexities*, it is not clear, especially at the beginning, whether **since** means 'because' or 'from the time when.' It is often better to simply say 'because,' if that is the intended meaning.

sin·cere /sinˈsi(ə)r/ ▶ **adj.** (**sincerer**, **sincerest**) free from pretense or deceit; proceeding from genuine feelings: *they offer their sincere thanks to Paul.* ■ (of a person) saying what they genuinely feel or believe; not dishonest or hypocritical.
– DERIVATIVES **sin·cere·ness** n.
– ORIGIN mid 16th cent. (also in the sense 'not falsified, unadulterated'): from Latin *sincerus* 'clean, pure.'

sin·cere·ly /sinˈsi(ə)rlē/ ▶ **adv.** in a sincere or genuine way: *I sincerely hope that we shall have a change of government* | [as submodifier] *sincerely held differences of belief.* ■ (also **sincerely yours** or **yours sincerely**) a formula used to end a letter, typically a formal one in which the recipient is addressed by name.

sin·cer·i·ty /sinˈseritē/ ▶ **n.** the quality of being free from pretense, deceit, or hypocrisy: *the sincerity of his beliefs is unquestionable.*

sin·ci·put /ˈsinsəpət/ ▶ **n.** Anatomy the front of the skull from the forehead to the crown.
– DERIVATIVES **sin·cip·i·tal** /sinˈsipitl/ **adj.**
– ORIGIN late 16th cent.: from Latin, from *semi-* 'half' + *caput* 'head.'

Sin·clair /sinˈkle(ə)r/, Upton (Beall) (1878–1968), US novelist and social reformer. He agitated for social justice in 79 books, including *The Jungle* (1906) and the 11-volume "Lanny Budd" series (1940–53).

Sind /sind/ a province of southeastern Pakistan, traversed by the lower reaches of the Indus River; capital, Karachi.

Sind·hi /ˈsindē/ ▶ **n.** (pl. **Sindhis**) **1** a native or inhabitant of Sind.
2 the Indic language of Sind, used also in western India.
▶ **adj.** of or relating to the province of Sind or its people, or the Sindhi language.
– ORIGIN from Persian and Urdu *sindi*, from Sanskrit *sindhu* 'river' (specifically the Indus). See **HINDI**, **INDUS**[1].

sine /sīn/ ▶ **n.** Mathematics the trigonometric function that is equal to the ratio of the side opposite a given angle (in a right triangle) to the hypotenuse.
– ORIGIN late 16th cent.: from Latin *sinus* 'curve,' used in medieval Latin as a translation of Arabic *jayb* 'pocket, sine.'

si·ne·cure /ˈsīnəˌkyo͝or, ˈsi-/ ▶ **n.** a position requiring little or no work but giving the holder status or financial benefit.
– DERIVATIVES **si·ne·cur·ism** /ˈsīnəkyo͝orizəm, si-/ **n.**, **si·ne·cur·ist** /ˈsīnəˌkyo͝orist, si-/ **n.**
– ORIGIN mid 17th cent.: from Latin *sine cura* 'without care.'

sine curve /sīn/ (also **sine wave**) ▶ **n.** a curve representing periodic oscillations of constant amplitude as given by a sine function. Also called **SINUSOID**.

si·ne di·e /ˈsīnə ˈdīē, ˈsēnā ˈdēā/ ▶ **adv.** (with reference to business or proceedings that have been adjourned) with no appointed date for resumption: *the case was adjourned sine die.*
– ORIGIN Latin, literally 'without a day.'

si·ne qua non /ˌsini ˌkwä ˈnōn, ˌsini ˌkwä ˈnän/ ▶ **n.** an essential condition; a thing that is absolutely necessary: *grammar and usage are the sine qua non of language teaching and learning.*
– ORIGIN Latin, literally '(cause) without which not.'

sin·ew /ˈsinyo͞o/ ▶ **n.** a piece of tough fibrous tissue uniting muscle to bone or bone to bone; a tendon or ligament. ■ (usu. **sinews**) the parts of a structure, system, or thing that give it strength or bind it together: *the sinews of government.*
▶ **v.** [with obj.] (usu. as adj. **sinewed**) literary strengthen with or as if with sinews: *the sinewed shape of his back.*
– DERIVATIVES **sin·ew·less adj.**
– ORIGIN Old English *sin(e)we* 'tendon,' of Germanic origin; related to Dutch *zeen* and German *Sehne.*

sin·ew·y /ˈsinyo͞owē/ ▶ **adj.** consisting of or resembling sinews. ■ (of a person or animal) lean and muscular: *a short, sinewy, sunburnt man* | figurative *the language is spare and sinewy.*

sin·fo·ni·a /ˌsinfəˈnēə/ ▶ **n.** Music a symphony. ■ (in the 17th and 18th centuries) an orchestral piece used as an introduction, interlude, or postlude to an opera, oratorio, cantata, or suite.
– ORIGIN Italian.

sin·fo·ni·a con·cer·tan·te /ˌsinfəˈnēə ˌkänsərˈtäntā/ ▶ **n.** a piece of music for orchestra with more than one soloist, typically from the 18th century.
– ORIGIN Italian, literally 'harmonizing symphony.'

sin·fo·niet·ta /ˌsinfənˈyetə/ ▶ **n.** Music a short or simple symphony. ■ a small symphony orchestra.
– ORIGIN Italian, diminutive of *sinfonia* (see **SINFONIA**).

sin·ful /ˈsinfəl/ ▶ **adj.** wicked and immoral; committing or characterized by the committing of sins: *sinful men* | *a sinful way of life.* ■ highly reprehensible: *a sinful waste.*
– DERIVATIVES **sin·ful·ly adv.**, **sin·ful·ness n.**
– ORIGIN Old English *synfull* (see **SIN**[1], **-FUL**).

sing /siNG/ ▶ **v.** (past **sang** /saNG/; past participle **sung** /səNG/) **1** [no obj.] make musical sounds with the voice, esp. words with a set tune: *Bella sang to the baby.* ■ [with obj.] perform (a song, words, or tune) in this way: *someone started singing "God Bless America"* | (as noun **singing**) *the singing of hymns in Latin.* ■ (**sing along**) sing in accompaniment to a song or piece of music. ■ (**sing something out**) call something out loudly; shout: *he sang out a greeting.* ■ (of a bird) make characteristic melodious whistling and twittering sounds: *the birds were singing in the chestnut trees.*
2 [no obj.] make a high-pitched whistling or buzzing sound: *the kettle was beginning to sing.* ■ (of a person's ear) be affected with a continuous buzzing sound, esp. as the aftereffect of a blow or loud noise: *a stinging slap that made my ear sing.*
3 [no obj.] informal act as an informer to the police: *as soon as he got put under pressure, he* ***sang like a canary.***
4 [with obj.] recount or celebrate in a work of literature, esp. poetry: *poetry should sing the strangeness and variety of the human race* | [no obj.] *these poets* ***sing of*** *the North American experience.* ■ archaic compose poetry.
▶ **n.** [in sing.] informal an act or spell of singing. ■ a meeting for amateur singing.
– PHRASES **sing a different tune** change one's opinion about or attitude toward someone or something. **sing for one's supper** see **SUPPER**. **sing the praises of** see **PRAISE**. **sing someone to sleep** cause someone to fall asleep by singing gently to them.
– DERIVATIVES **sing·a·ble adj.**, **sing·ing·ly adv.**
– ORIGIN Old English *singan* (verb), of Germanic origin; related to Dutch *zingen* and German *singen.*

sing. ▶ **abbr.** singular.

sing-a-long (also **singalong**) ▶ **n.** an informal occasion when people sing together in a group. ■ [usu. as modifier] a light popular song or tune to which one can easily sing along in accompaniment: *an album featuring simple, sing-along tunes.*

Sin·ga·pore /ˈsiNGəˌpôr/ a country in Southeast Asia that consists of the island of Singapore (linked by a causeway to the southern tip of the Malay Peninsula) and about 54 smaller islands; pop. 4,657,500 (est. 2009); capital, Singapore City; official languages, Malay, Chinese, Tamil, and English.

> Established as a trading post under the East India Company in 1819, Singapore came under British colonial rule in 1867. Singapore rapidly grew to become the most important commercial center and naval base in Southeast Asia. After World War II, it became first a British Crown Colony in 1946 and then a self-governing state within the Commonwealth of Nations in 1959. Federated with Malaysia in 1963, it declared full independence two years later. In terms of tonnage handled, Singapore's port is the world's busiest.

– DERIVATIVES **Sin·ga·po·re·an** /ˌsiNGəˈpôrēən/ **adj. & n.**

Sin·ga·pore sling ▶ **n.** a cocktail made from gin and cherry brandy.

singe /sinj/ ▶ **v.** (**singes**, **singeing**, **singed**) [with obj.] burn (something) superficially or lightly: *the fire had singed his eyebrows* | (as adj. **singed**) *a smell of singed feathers.* ■ [no obj.] be burned in this way: *the heat was so intense I could feel the hairs on my hands singe.* ■ burn the bristles or down off (the carcass of a pig or fowl) to prepare it for cooking.
▶ **n.** a superficial burn.
– ORIGIN Old English *sencgan*; related to Dutch *zengen.*

Sing·er[1] /ˈsiNGər/, Isaac Bashevis (1904–91), US novelist and short-story writer, born in Poland. His work blends realistic detail and elements of fantasy, mysticism, and magic to portray the lives of Polish Jews during many periods. Notable works: *The Magician of Lublin* (1955), *The Slave* (1962), and *Collected Stories* (1982). Nobel Prize for Literature (1978).

Sing·er[2], Isaac Merrit (1811–75), US inventor. He designed and built the first commercially successful sewing machine in 1852. Singer's company became the world's largest sewing machine manufacturer.

sing·er /ˈsiNGər/ ▶ **n.** a person who sings, esp. professionally: *a pop singer.*

sing·er-song·writ·er ▶ **n.** a person who sings and writes popular songs, esp. professionally.

Singh /siNG/ ▶ **n.** a title or surname adopted by certain warrior castes of northern India, esp. by male members of the Sikh Khalsa.
– ORIGIN from Punjabi *sińgh* 'lion,' from Sanskrit *siṃha* 'lion.'

Sin·gha·lese /ˌsiNGgəˈlēz, -ˈlēs/ ▶ **n. & adj.** variant spelling of **SINHALESE**.

sin·gle /ˈsiNGgəl/ ▶ **adj. 1** [attrib.] only one; not one of several: *a single red rose* | *the kingdom was ruled over by a single family.* ■ regarded separately or as distinct from each other or others in a group: *she wrote down every single word* | *it's our single most popular beach.* ■ [with negative] even one (used for emphasis): *they didn't receive a single reply.* ■ designed or suitable for one person: *a single bed.* ■ archaic not accompanied or supported by others; alone.
2 unmarried or not involved in a stable sexual relationship: *a single mother.*
3 [attrib.] consisting of one part: *the studio was a single large room.* ■ Brit. (of a ticket) not valid for the return trip; one-way. ■ (of a flower) having only one whorl of petals. ■ denoting an alcoholic drink that consists of one measure of liquor: *a single whiskey.*
4 archaic free from duplicity or deceit; ingenuous: *a pure and single heart.*
▶ **n. 1** an individual person or thing rather than part of a pair or a group. ■ a short record or CD featuring one main one song or track. ■ (**singles**) people who are unmarried or not involved in a stable sexual relationship: [as modifier] *a singles bar.* ■ Brit. a one-way ticket. ■ a bedroom, esp. in a hotel, that is suitable for one person. ■ a single measure of liquor. ■ informal a one-dollar bill.
2 Baseball a hit that allows the batter to reach first base safely.
3 (**singles**) (esp. in tennis and badminton) a game or competition for individual players, not pairs or teams.
▶ **v.** [with obj.] **1** (**single someone/something out**) choose someone or something from a group for special treatment: *one newspaper was* ***singled out*** *for criticism.*
2 [no obj.] Baseball hit a single: *Aaron singled to center.* ■ (**single in**) [with obj.] cause (a run) to be scored by

S

hitting a single: *they each singled in a run.* ■ [with obj.] advance (a runner) by hitting a single.
– DERIVATIVES **sin·gle·ness** n.
– ORIGIN Middle English: via Old French from Latin *singulus*, related to *simplus* 'simple.'

sin·gle-act·ing ▶ adj. (of an engine) having pressure applied only to one side of the piston.

sin·gle-ac·tion ▶ adj. (of a gun) needing to be cocked by hand before it can be fired.

sin·gle-blind ▶ adj. [attrib.] denoting a test or experiment in which information that may bias the results is concealed from either tester or subject. Compare with **DOUBLE-BLIND**.

sin·gle bond ▶ n. a chemical bond in which one pair of electrons is shared between two atoms.

sin·gle-breast·ed ▶ adj. (of a jacket or coat) showing only one row of buttons at the front when fastened.

sin·gle com·bat ▶ n. fighting between two people: *these two have been engaging in single combat for years.*

sin·gle-cop·y ▶ adj. Genetics (of a gene or genetic sequence) present in a genome in only one copy.

sin·gle cur·ren·cy ▶ n. a currency used by all the members of an economic federation. ■ (also **single European currency**) the currency (the euro) that replaced the national currencies of twelve member states of the European Union in 2002.

sin·gle-cut ▶ adj. (of a file) having grooves cut in one direction only, not crossing each other.

sin·gle-end·ed ▶ adj. (of an electronic device) designed for use with unbalanced signals and therefore having one input and one output terminal grounded.

sin·gle-en·try ▶ adj. denoting a system of bookkeeping in which each transaction is entered in one account only.

sin·gle file ▶ n. [in sing.] a line of people or things arranged one behind another: *we trooped along in single file* | [as modifier] *a single-file column.*
▶ adv. one behind another: *we walked single file.*

sin·gle-foot ▶ v. [no obj.] (of a horse) walk by moving both legs on each side in alternation, each foot falling separately.

sin·gle-hand·ed (also **singlehanded** /ˌsiNGgəlˈhandid/) ▶ adv. & adj. **1** done without help from anyone else: [as adv.] *sailing single-handed around the world* | [as adj.] *a single-handed crusade.* **2** done or designed to be used with one hand: [as adv.] *the tool is easy to use single-handed* | [as adj.] *a single-handed ax.*
– DERIVATIVES **sin·gle-hand·ed·ly** (or **singlehandedly**) adv., **sin·gle-hand·ed·ness** (or **singlehandedness**) n.

sin·gle-hand·er ▶ n. a boat or other craft that can be sailed single-handed. ■ a person who sails a boat or yacht single-handed.

sin·gle-lens re·flex ▶ adj. denoting a reflex camera in which the lens that forms the image on the film also provides the image in the viewfinder.

sin·gle malt (also **single-malt whiskey**) ▶ n. whiskey unblended with any other malt.

sin·gle mar·ket ▶ n. an association of countries trading with each other without restrictions or tariffs. The European single market came into effect on January 1, 1993.

sin·gle-mind·ed (also **singleminded** /ˌsiNGgəlˈmīndid/) ▶ adj. having or concentrating on only one aim or purpose: *the single-minded pursuit of profit.*
– DERIVATIVES **sin·gle-mind·ed·ly** (or **singlemindedly**) adv., **sin·gle-mind·ed·ness** (or **singlemindedness**) n.

sin·gle nu·cle·o·tide pol·y·mor·phism ▶ n. (abbr. **SNP**) a variation in a single base pair in a DNA sequence.

sin·gle par·ent ▶ n. a person bringing up a child or children without a partner.

sin·gles bar ▶ n. a bar for single people seeking company.

sin·gle-seat·er ▶ n. a vehicle or aircraft for one person.

sin·gle-source ▶ v. [with obj.] give a franchise to a single supplier for (a particular product).

sin·gle·stick /ˈsiNGgəlˌstik/ ▶ n. Fencing a wooden stick of about a sword's length. ■ fencing with such a stick.

sin·glet /ˈsiNGglit/ ▶ n. **1** chiefly Brit. a sleeveless garment worn under or instead of a shirt.
2 Physics a single unresolvable line in a spectrum, not part of a multiplet. ■ a state or energy level with zero spin, giving a single value for a particular quantum number. ■ Chemistry an atomic or molecular state in which all electron spins are paired.
– ORIGIN mid 18th cent. (originally denoting a man's short jacket): from **SINGLE** (because the garment was unlined) + **-ET**[1], on the pattern of *doublet.*

sin·gle·ton /ˈsiNGgəltən/ ▶ n. a single person or thing of the kind under consideration: *splitting the clumps of plants into singletons.* ■ [often as modifier] a child or animal born singly, rather than one of a multiple birth: *singleton boys.* ■ (in card games, esp. bridge) a card that is the only one of its suit in a hand. ■ Mathematics & Logic a set that contains exactly one element.
– ORIGIN late 19th cent.: from **SINGLE**, on the pattern of *simpleton.*

sin·gle·tree /ˈsiNGgəlˌtrē/ ▶ n. a crossbar pivoted in the middle, to which the traces are attached in a horse-drawn wagon or plow.

sin·gly /ˈsiNGglē/ ▶ adv. one at a time; separately or individually: *he talked to the players singly and in groups.*

Sing Sing /siNG siNG/ a New York State prison, built in 1825–28 in the town of Ossining (formerly Sing Sing) on the Hudson River, and once notorious for its severe discipline.

sing·song /ˈsiNGˌsôNG/ ▶ adj. (of a person's voice) having a repeated rising and falling rhythm: *the singsong voices of children reciting tables.*
▶ n. **1** informal, chiefly Brit. an informal gathering for singing.
2 [in sing.] a singsong way of speaking.
▶ v. (**singsongs, singsonging, singsonged**) [no obj.] speak or recite something in a singsong manner.

sing·song girl /ˈsiNGˌsôNG/ ▶ n. (in China) a female entertainer.

sing·spiel /ˈsiNGˌspēl, ˈziNGˌSHpēl/ ▶ n. (pl. **singspiele** /-ˌspēlə, -ˌSHpēlə/) a form of German light opera, typically with spoken dialogue, popular esp. in the late 18th century.
– ORIGIN from German *singen* 'sing' + *Spiel* 'play.'

sin·gu·lar /ˈsiNGgyələr/ ▶ adj. **1** exceptionally good or great; remarkable: *the singular beauty of the desert.* ■ strange or eccentric in some respect: *no explanation accompanied this rather singular statement.* ■ Mathematics (of a square matrix) having a zero determinant. ■ Mathematics denoting a point that is a singularity.
2 Grammar (of a word or form) denoting or referring to just one person or thing.
3 single; unique: *she always thought of herself as singular, as his only daughter.*
▶ n. (usu. **the singular**) Grammar the singular form of a word: *the first person singular.*
– ORIGIN Middle English (in the sense 'solitary, single,' also 'beyond the average'): from Old French *singuler*, from Latin *singularis*, from *singulus* (see **SINGLE**).

sin·gu·lar·i·ty /ˌsiNGgyəˈlaritē/ ▶ n. (pl. **singularities**) **1** the state, fact, quality, or condition of being singular: *he believed in the singularity of all cultures.* ■ a peculiarity or odd trait.
2 Physics & Mathematics a point at which a function takes an infinite value, esp. in space-time when matter is infinitely dense, as at the center of a black hole.
– ORIGIN Middle English: from Old French *singularite*, from late Latin *singularitas*, from *singularis* 'unique' (see **SINGULAR**).

sin·gu·lar·ize /ˈsiNGgyələˌrīz/ ▶ v. [with obj.] rare
1 make distinct or conspicuous.
2 give a singular form to (a word).
– DERIVATIVES **sin·gu·lar·i·za·tion** /ˌsiNGgyələrəˈzāSHən, ˌsiNGgyələˌrīˈzāSHən, ˌsiNGgyəˌle(ə)rəˈzāSHən/ n.

sin·gu·lar·ly /ˈsiNGgyələrlē/ ▶ adv. in a remarkable or noticeable way: *you have singularly failed to live up to your promises* | [as submodifier] *a singularly unattractive color.* ■ in a strange or eccentric way: *Charlotte thought her very singularly dressed.*

sinh /sīn, ˌsīnˈāCH, sinCH/ ▶ abbr. Mathematics hyperbolic sine.
– ORIGIN late 19th cent.: from *sin(e)* + *h(yperbolic).*

Sin·ha·lese /ˌsinhəˈlēz, -ˈlēs/ (also **Singhalese** /ˌsiNGgə-/, **Sinhala** /sinˈhälə/) ▶ n. (pl. **same**) **1** a member of a people originally from northern India, now forming the majority of the population of Sri Lanka.
2 the Indic language of this people.
▶ adj. of or relating to this people or language.
– ORIGIN from Sanskrit *Siṁhala* 'Sri Lanka' + **-ESE**.

sin·is·ter /ˈsinistər/ ▶ adj. **1** giving the impression that something harmful or evil is happening or will happen: *there was something sinister about that murmuring voice.* ■ evil or criminal: *there might be a more sinister motive behind the government's actions.*
2 [attrib.] archaic & Heraldry of, on, or toward the left-hand side (in a coat of arms, from the bearer's point of view, i.e., the right as it is depicted). The opposite of **DEXTER**[1].
– DERIVATIVES **sin·is·ter·ly** adv., **sin·is·ter·ness** n.
– ORIGIN late Middle English (in the sense 'malicious, underhanded'): from Old French *sinistre* or Latin *sinister* 'left.'

sin·is·tral /ˈsinəstrəl/ ▶ adj. of or on the left side or the left hand (the opposite of **DEXTRAL**), in particular: ■ left-handed. ■ Geology relating to or denoting a strike-slip fault in which the motion of the block on the opposite side of the fault from an observer is toward the left. ■ Zoology (of a spiral mollusk shell) with whorls rising to the left and coiling in a clockwise direction.
– DERIVATIVES **sin·is·tral·i·ty** /ˌsinəˈstralitē/ n., **sin·is·tral·ly** adv.

sin·is·trorse /ˈsinəˌstrôrs/ ▶ adj. rising toward the left, esp. of the spiral stem of a plant.
– ORIGIN mid 19th cent.: from Latin *sinistrorsus*, from *sinister* 'left' + *vertere* 'turn.'

Si·nit·ic /siˈnitik/ ▶ adj. of, relating to, or denoting the division of the Sino-Tibetan language family that includes the many forms of spoken Chinese.

sink[1] /siNGk/ ▶ v. (past **sank** /saNGk/ or **sunk** /səNGk/; past participle **sunk** /səNGk/) **1** [no obj.] go down below the surface of something, esp. of a liquid; become submerged: *he saw the coffin sink below the surface of the waves.* ■ (of a ship) go to the bottom of the sea or some other body of water because of damage or a collision: *the trawler sank with the loss of all six crew members.* ■ disappear and not be seen or heard of again: *the film sank virtually without trace.* ■ [with obj.] cause (a ship) to go to the bottom of the sea or other body of water: *a freak wave sank their boat near the shore.* ■ [with obj.] cause to fail: *she apparently wishes to sink the company.* ■ [with obj.] conceal, keep in the background, or ignore: *they agreed to sink their differences.*
2 [no obj.] descend; drop: *Sam felt the ground sinking beneath his feet* | *you can relax on the veranda as the sun sinks.* ■ (of a person) lower oneself or drop gently: *she sank back onto her pillow.* ■ [with adverbial of direction] gradually penetrate the surface of something: *her feet sank into the thick pile of the carpet.* ■ [with obj.] (**sink something into**) cause something sharp to penetrate (a surface): *the dog sank its teeth into her arm.*
3 [no obj.] gradually decrease or decline in value, amount, quality, or intensity: *their output sank to a third of the prewar figure* | *the reputation of the mayor sank to a very low level.* ■ lapse or fall into a particular state or condition, typically one that is unwelcome or unpleasant: *he **sank into a coma** after suffering a brain hemorrhage.* ■ approach death: *the doctor concluded that Sanders was sinking fast.*
4 [with obj.] insert beneath a surface by digging or hollowing out: *rails attached with screws sunk below the surface of the wood.* ■ excavate (a well) or bore (a shaft) more or less vertically downward: *they planned to sink a gold mine in Oklahoma.* ■ hit (a ball) into a hole in golf or billiards. ■ insert into something: *Kelly stood watching, her hands sunk deep into her pockets.*
– PHRASES **a** (or **that**) **sinking feeling** an unpleasant feeling caused by the realization that something unpleasant or undesirable has happened or is about to happen. **sink or swim** fail or succeed entirely by one's own efforts.
– PHRASAL VERBS **sink in** (of words or facts) be fully understood or realized: *Peter read the letter twice before its meaning sank in.* **sink something into** put money or energy into (something); invest something in: *many investors sank their life savings into the company.*
– DERIVATIVES **sink·a·ble** adj., **sink·age** /ˈsiNGkij/ n.
– ORIGIN Old English *sincan*, of Germanic origin; related to Dutch *zinken* and German *sinken.*

> **USAGE** Historically, the past tense of **sink** has been both **sank** and **sunk** (*the boat sank*; *the boat sunk*), and the past participle has been both **sunk** and **sunken** (*the boat had already sunk*; *the boat had already sunken*). In modern English, the past is generally **sank** and the past participle is **sunk**, with the form **sunken** now surviving only as an adjective, as in *a sunken garden* or *sunken cheeks.*

sink[2] ▶ n. **1** a fixed basin with a water supply and a drain.
2 a pool or marsh in which a river's water disappears by evaporation or percolation. ■ technical a body or process that acts to absorb or remove energy or a particular component from a system: *a heat sink* | *the oceans can act as a sink for CO_2.* The opposite of **SOURCE**.
3 short for **SINKHOLE**.
4 a place of vice or corruption: *moralizers complain that the Net is simply a festering sink of iniquity.*
– ORIGIN Middle English: from **SINK**[1].

sink·er /ˈsiNGkər/ ▶ n. **1** a weight used to sink a fishing line or sounding line.
2 (also **sinker ball**) Baseball a pitch that drops markedly as it nears home plate.

3 a type of windsurfing board of insufficient buoyancy to support a person unless moving fast. **4** a doughnut.

sink·hole /ˈsiNGkˌhōl/ ▶ **n.** a cavity in the ground, esp. in limestone bedrock, caused by water erosion and providing a route for surface water to disappear underground.

sink·ing fund ▶ **n.** a fund formed by periodically setting aside money for the gradual repayment of a debt or replacement of a wasting asset.

sin·less /ˈsinlis/ ▶ **adj.** free from sin: *the sinless life of Christ.*
– DERIVATIVES **sin·less·ly adv., sin·less·ness n.**

sin·ner /ˈsinər/ ▶ **n.** a person who transgresses against divine law by committing an immoral act or acts.

sin·net /ˈsinit/ variant spelling of **SENNIT.**

Sinn Fein /ˈSHin ˈfān/ a political movement and party seeking a united republican Ireland.

> Founded in 1905, Sinn Fein became increasingly committed to Republicanism after the failure of the Home Rule movement. Having won a majority of Irish seats in the 1918 general election, its members refused to go to Westminster and set up their own parliament in Ireland in 1919. After a split in the 1920s, when many of its members joined Fianna Fáil, the party began to function as the political wing of the IRA. It now sends representatives to the Northern Ireland Assembly and the Irish Dáil; Sinn Fein MPs elected to the British House of Commons do not take up their seats.

– DERIVATIVES **Sinn Fein·er n.**
– ORIGIN from Irish *sinn féin* 'we ourselves.'

Sino- /ˈsīnō/ ▶ **comb. form** Chinese; Chinese and ...: *Sino-American.* ■ relating to China.

si·no·a·tri·al node /ˌsīnōˈātrēəl/ ▶ **n.** Anatomy a small body of specialized muscle tissue in the wall of the right atrium of the heart that acts as a pacemaker by producing a contractile signal at regular intervals.
– ORIGIN early 20th cent.: from **SINUS** + *atrial* (see **ATRIUM**).

sin of·fer·ing ▶ **n.** (in traditional or ancient Judaism) an offering made as an atonement for sin.

Si·no-Jap·a·nese Wars two wars (1894–95, 1937–45) fought between China and Japan.

> The first war, caused by rivalry over Korea, was ended by a treaty in Japan's favor and led to the eventual overthrow of the Manchus in 1912. In the second war, Japanese expansionism led to trouble in Manchuria in 1931 and to the establishment of a Japanese puppet state (Manchukuo) a year later.

Si·nol·o·gy /sīˈnäləjē/ ▶ **n.** the study of Chinese language, history, customs, and politics.
– DERIVATIVES **Si·no·log·i·cal** /ˌsinlˈäjikəl, ˌsin-/ **adj.**, **Si·nol·o·gist** /-jist/ **n.**

Si·no-Ti·bet·an ▶ **adj.** of, relating to, or denoting a large language family of eastern Asia whose branches include Sinitic (Chinese), Tibeto-Burman (Burmese and Tibetan), and, in some classifications, Tai (Thai and Lao). They are tonal languages, but the exact relationships among them are unclear.
▶ **n.** this language family.

sin·se·mil·la /ˌsinsəˈmēyə/ ▶ **n.** marijuana of a variety that has a particularly high concentration of psychoactive agents.
– ORIGIN 1970s: from American Spanish, literally 'without seed.'

sin tax ▶ **n.** informal a tax on items considered undesirable or harmful, such as alcohol or tobacco.

sin·ter /ˈsin(t)ər/ ▶ **n. 1** Geology a hard siliceous or calcareous deposit precipitated from mineral springs.
2 solid material that has been sintered, esp. a mixture of iron ore and other materials prepared for smelting.
▶ **v.** [with obj.] make (a powdered material) coalesce into a solid or porous mass by heating it (and usually also compressing it) without liquefaction. ■ [no obj.] coalesce in this way.
– ORIGIN late 18th cent. (as a noun): from German *Sinter*; compare with **CINDER.**

Sint Maar·ten /sint ˈmärtin/ Dutch name for **ST. MARTIN.**

sin·u·ate /ˈsinyo͞oˌāt, -it/ ▶ **adj.** Botany & Zoology having a wavy or sinuous margin; with alternate rounded notches and lobes.
– ORIGIN late 17th cent.: from Latin *sinuatus*, past participle of *sinuare* 'to bend.'

Sin·ui·ju /ˈSHinˈwēˈjo͞o/ a city and port in North Korea, on the Yalu River near its mouth on the Yellow Sea; pop. 383,200 (est. 2003).

sin·u·os·i·ty /ˌsinyo͞oˈäsitē/ ▶ **n.** (pl. **sinuosities**) the ability to curve or bend easily and flexibly. ■ a bend, esp. in a stream or road.
– ORIGIN late 16th cent.: from French *sinuosité* or medieval Latin *sinuositas*, from *sinuosus* (see **SINUOUS**).

sin·u·ous /ˈsinyo͞oəs/ ▶ **adj.** having many curves and turns: *the river follows a sinuous trail through the forest.* ■ lithe and supple: *the sinuous grace of a cat.*
– DERIVATIVES **sin·u·ous·ly adv., sin·u·ous·ness n.**
– ORIGIN late 16th cent.: from French *sinueux* or Latin *sinuosus*, from *sinus* 'a bend.'

si·nus /ˈsīnəs/ ▶ **n. 1** (often **sinuses**) Anatomy & Zoology a cavity within a bone or other tissue, esp. one in the bones of the face or skull connecting with the nasal cavities. ■ an irregular venous or lymphatic cavity, reservoir, or dilated vessel. ■ Medicine an infected tract leading from a deep-seated infection and discharging pus to the surface. ■ Botany a rounded notch between two lobes on the margin of a leaf or petal.
2 [as modifier] Physiology relating to or denoting the sinoatrial node of the heart or its function as a pacemaker: *sinus rhythm* | *sinus tachycardia.*
– ORIGIN late Middle English (in the medical sense): from Latin, literally 'a recess, bend, bay.'

si·nus·i·tis /ˌsīnəˈsītis/ ▶ **n.** Medicine inflammation of a nasal sinus.

si·nus·oid /ˈsīnəˌsoid/ ▶ **n. 1** a curve having the form of a sine wave.
2 Anatomy a small irregularly shaped blood vessel found in certain organs, esp. the liver.
– DERIVATIVES **si·nus·oi·dal** /ˌsīnəˈsoidl/ **adj.**, **si·nus·oi·dal·ly** /ˌsīnəˈsoidəlē/ **adv.**
– ORIGIN early 19th cent.: from French *sinusoïde*, from Latin *sinus* (see **SINUS**).

si·nus ve·no·sus /vēˈnōsəs/ ▶ **n.** Zoology the first chamber of the heart in fish, amphibians, and reptiles, emptying into the right atrium.
– ORIGIN early 19th cent.: modern Latin, literally 'venous cavity.'

Sion /ˈsīən/ ▶ **n.** variant spelling of **ZION.**

-sion ▶ **suffix** forming nouns such as *mansion, persuasion.*
– ORIGIN from Latin participial stems ending in *-s* + **-ION.**

Siou·an /ˈso͞oən/ ▶ **n.** a family of North American Indian languages spoken by the Sioux and related peoples, including Crow, Dakota, Hidatsa, Lakota, Mandan, Omaha, and Yankton.
▶ **adj.** of, relating to, or denoting this language family.

Sioux /so͞o/ ▶ **n.** (pl. **same**) another term for the Dakota people or their language. See **DAKOTA**[2].
▶ **adj.** of or relating to this people or their language.
– ORIGIN North American French, from *Nadouessioux*, from Ojibwa (Ottawa dialect) *nātowēssiwak*, by substitution of the French plural ending *-x* for the Ojibwa plural *-ak.*

Sioux Cit·y a commercial and industrial city in northwestern Iowa, on the Missouri and Big Sioux rivers; pop. 82,807 (est. 2008).

Sioux Falls the largest city in South Dakota, a commercial and industrial center in the southeastern part of the state, on the Big Sioux River; pop. 154,997 (est. 2008).

Sioux State a nickname for the state of **NORTH DAKOTA.**

sip /sip/ ▶ **v.** (**sips, sipping, sipped**) [with obj.] drink (something) by taking small mouthfuls: *I sat sipping coffee* | [no obj.] *she sipped at her tea.*
▶ **n.** a small mouthful of liquid: *she took **a sip of** the red wine.*
– DERIVATIVES **sip·per n.**
– ORIGIN late Middle English: perhaps a modification of **SUP**[1], as symbolic of a less vigorous action.

SIPC ▶ **abbr.** ■ Securities Investor Protection Corporation. ■ Simply Interactive Personal Computer.

sipe /sīp/ ▶ **n.** a groove or channel in the tread of a tire to improve its grip.
– ORIGIN 1950s: from dialect *sipe* 'oozing, trickling,' of unknown origin.

si·phon /ˈsīfən/ (also **syphon**) ▶ **n.** a pipe or tube used to convey liquid upward from a reservoir and then down to a lower level of its own accord. Once the liquid has been forced into the tube, typically by suction or immersion, flow continues unaided. ■ Zoology a tubular organ in an aquatic animal, esp. a mollusk, through which water is drawn in or expelled.
▶ **v.** [with obj.] draw off or convey (liquid) by means of a siphon. ■ draw off or transfer over a period of time, esp. illegally or unfairly: *he's been **siphoning** money **off** the firm.*
– DERIVATIVES **si·phon·age** /-nij/ **n.**, **si·phon·al** /-nəl/ **adj.** (Zoology), **si·phon·ic** /sīˈfänik/ **adj.**
– ORIGIN late Middle English: from French, or via Latin from Greek *siphōn* 'pipe.' The verb dates from the mid 19th cent.

Si·phon·ap·ter·a /ˌsīfəˈnaptərə/ Entomology an order of insects that comprises the fleas.
– DERIVATIVES **si·pho·nap·ter·an** /-rən/ **n. & adj.**
– ORIGIN modern Latin (plural), from Greek *siphōn* 'tube' + *apteros* 'wingless.'

Si·pho·noph·o·ra /ˌsīfəˈnäfərə/ Zoology an order of colonial marine coelenterates that includes the Portuguese man-of-war, having a float or swimming bell for drifting or swimming on the open sea.
– ORIGIN modern Latin (plural), from Greek *siphōn* 'tube' + *pherein* 'to bear.'

si·pho·no·phore /ˈsīfənəˌfôr, sīˈfänə-/ ▶ **n.** Zoology a colonial marine coelenterate of the order Siphonophora, such as a Portuguese man-of-war.

si·phon·o·stele /ˈsīfənəˌstēl, sīˈfänəˌstēl/ ▶ **n.** Botany a stele consisting of a core of pith surrounded by concentric layers of xylem and phloem.

si·phun·cle /ˈsīfəNGkəl/ ▶ **n.** Zoology (in shelled cephalopods such as nautiloids and ammonoids) a calcareous tube containing living tissue running through all the shell chambers, serving to pump fluid out of vacant chambers in order to adjust buoyancy.
– ORIGIN mid 18th cent.: from Latin *siphunculus* 'small tube.'

Si·phun·cu·la·ta /sīˌfəNGkyəˈlätə/ Entomology another term for **ANOPLURA.**
– ORIGIN modern Latin (plural), from Latin *siphunculus* 'little pipe.'

sip·pet /ˈsipit/ ▶ **n.** a small piece of bread or toast, used to dip into soup or sauce or as a garnish.
– ORIGIN mid 16th cent.: apparently a diminutive of **SOP.**

sip·py cup ▶ **n.** a small beaker with a lid and a spout, for an infant or young child to drink from.

Si·pun·cu·la /sīˈpəNGkyələ/ Zoology a small phylum that comprises the peanut worms.
– DERIVATIVES **si·pun·cu·lan** /-lən/ **n. & adj.**, **si·pun·cu·lid** /sīˈpəNGkyəlid/ **n. & adj.**
– ORIGIN modern Latin (plural), from *Sipunculus* (genus name), based on a variant of Latin *siphunculus* 'small tube.'

sir /sər/ (also **Sir**) ▶ **n.** used as a polite or respectful way of addressing a man, esp. one in a position of authority: *excuse me, sir.* ■ used to address a man at the beginning of a formal or business letter: *Dear Sir.* ■ (in Britain) used as a title before the given name of a knight or baronet. ■ another expression for **SIREE.**
– ORIGIN Middle English: reduced form of **SIRE.**

Sir. ▶ **abbr.** (in biblical references) Sirach (Apocrypha).

Si·ra·cu·sa /ˌsērăˈko͞ozä/ Italian name for **SYRACUSE** (sense 1).

sir·dar ▶ **n.** variant spelling of **SARDAR.**

Sir·dar·yo /sirˈdäryə, ˌsirdärˈyä/ a river in central Asia. Rising in two headstreams in the Tien Shan mountains in eastern Uzbekistan, it flows for about 1,380 miles (2,220 km) west and northwest through southern Kazakhstan to the Aral Sea.

sire /sīr/ ▶ **n. 1** the male parent of an animal, esp. a stallion or bull kept for breeding.
2 archaic a respectful form of address for someone of high social status, esp. a king. ■ a father or other male forebear.
▶ **v.** [with obj.] be the male parent of (an animal). ■ literary (of a person) be the father of.
– ORIGIN Middle English (sense 2 of the noun): from Old French, from an alteration of Latin *senior* (see **SENIOR**). Sense 1 of the noun dates from the early 16th cent.

sir·ee /səˈrē/ (also **sirree**) ▶ **exclam.** informal used for emphasis, esp. after *yes* and *no*: *he's not the type to treat young employees like mud, no siree.*
– ORIGIN early 19th cent.: from **SIR** + the emphatic suffix *-ee.*

si·ren /ˈsīrən/ ▶ **n. 1** a device that makes a loud prolonged sound as a signal or warning: *ambulance sirens.*
2 Greek Mythology each of a number of women or winged creatures whose singing lured unwary sailors onto rocks. ■ a woman who is considered to be alluring or fascinating but also dangerous in some way.
3 an eel-like American amphibian with tiny forelimbs, no hind limbs, small eyes, and external gills, typically living in muddy pools. ● Family Sirenidae: genera *Siren* and *Pseudobranchus,*

S

and three species, including the **greater siren** (*S. lacertina*).
– ORIGIN Middle English (denoting an imaginary type of snake): from Old French *sirene*, from late Latin *Sirena*, feminine of Latin *Siren*, from Greek *Seirēn*.

Si·re·ni·a /sīˈrēnēə/ Zoology an order of large aquatic plant-eating mammals that includes the manatees and dugong. They live chiefly in tropical coastal waters and are distinguished by paddlelike forelimbs and a tail flipper replacing hind limbs. ● Order Sirenia: two families and four living species.
– ORIGIN modern Latin (see **SIREN**).

si·re·ni·an /sīˈrēnēən/ Zoology ▶ n. a large aquatic plant-eating mammal of the order Sirenia, such as a manatee or dugong.
▶ adj. relating to or denoting sirenians.

Sir Ga·la·had ▶ n. see **GALAHAD**.

Sir·i·us /ˈsi(ə)rēəs/ Astronomy the brightest star in the sky, south of the celestial equator in the constellation Canis Major. It is a binary star with a dim companion, which is a white dwarf. Also called **DOG STAR**.
– ORIGIN Latin, from Greek *seirios astēr* 'scorching star,' because it rose with the sun in the heat of summer. See **DOG DAYS**.

sir·loin /ˈsərloin/ ▶ n. the choicer part of a loin of beef: [as modifier] *fresh sirloin steaks*.
– ORIGIN late Middle English: from Old French (see **SUR-**[1], **LOIN**).

si·roc·co /səˈräkō/ (also **scirocco** /SHəˈräkō, sə-/) ▶ n. (pl. **siroccos**) a hot wind, often dusty or rainy, blowing from North Africa across the Mediterranean to southern Europe.
– ORIGIN early 17th cent.: from Italian *scirocco*, from Arabic *šarḳ* 'east wind.'

sir·rah /ˈsirə/ ▶ n. archaic used as a term of address for a man or boy, esp. one younger or of lower status than the speaker.
– ORIGIN early 16th cent.: probably from **SIRE**, when still two syllables in Middle English, with the second syllable assimilated to **AH**.

sir·ta·ki ▶ n. variant spelling of **SYRTAKI**.

sir·up ▶ n. variant spelling of **SYRUP**.

sir·up·y ▶ adj. variant spelling of **SYRUPY**.

SIS ▶ abbr. (in the UK) Secret Intelligence Service. See **MI6**.

sis /sis/ ▶ n. informal a person's sister (often used as a form of address): *where are you going, sis?*
– ORIGIN mid 17th cent.: abbreviation.

si·sal /ˈsīsəl, ˈsī-/ ▶ n. a Mexican agave with large fleshy leaves, cultivated for fiber production. ● *Agave sisalana*, family Agavaceae. ■ the fiber made from this plant, used esp. for ropes or matting.
– ORIGIN mid 19th cent.: from *Sisal*, the name of a port in Yucatán, Mexico.

sis·kin /ˈsiskin/ ▶ n. a small songbird related to the goldfinch. ● Genus *Carduelis* (and *Serinus*), family Fringillidae: several species, including the **pine siskin** (*C. pinus*) of North America, with dark-streaked plumage, notched tail, and touches of yellow on wings and tail.
– ORIGIN mid 16th cent.: from Middle Dutch *siseken*, a diminutive related to German *Zeisig*, of Slavic origin.

S

Sis·ki·you Moun·tains /ˈsiskē,(y)o͞o/ a forested range of the Klamath Mountains, in northwestern California and southwestern Oregon.

Sis·ley /sēˈslā, ˈsizlē/, Alfred (1839–99), French painter, of English descent. He is chiefly remembered for his Impressionist paintings of the countryside around Paris in the 1870s.

sis·sy /ˈsisē/ informal ▶ n. (pl. **sissies**) a person regarded as effeminate or cowardly.
▶ adj. (**sissier, sissiest**) feeble and cowardly.
– DERIVATIVES **sis·si·fied** /ˈsisə,fīd/ adj., **sis·si·ness** n., **sis·sy·ish** adj.
– ORIGIN mid 19th cent. (in the sense 'sister'): from **SIS** + **-Y**[2].

sis·ter /ˈsistər/ ▶ n. **1** a woman or girl in relation to other daughters and sons of her parents. ■ a sister-in-law. ■ a close female friend or associate, esp. a female fellow member of a labor union or other organization. ■ (often **Sister**) a member of a religious order or congregation of women. ■ a fellow woman seen in relation to feminist issues. ■ informal a black woman (chiefly used as a term of address by other black people). ■ [usu. as modifier] a thing, esp. an organization, that bears a relationship to another of common origin or allegiance or mutual association: *Eastern's sister airline, Continental* | *a sister ship*.
2 (often **Sister**) Brit. a senior female nurse, typically in charge of a ward.
– DERIVATIVES **sis·ter·li·ness** n., **sis·ter·ly** adj.
– ORIGIN Old English, of Germanic origin; related to Dutch *zuster* and German *Schwester*, from an Indo-European root shared by Latin *soror*.

sis·ter cit·y ▶ n. a city that is linked to another, usually for the purposes of cultural exchange.

sis·ter·hood /ˈsistər,ho͝od/ ▶ n. **1** the relationship between sisters. ■ the feeling of kinship with and closeness to a group of women or all women.
2 (often **Sisterhood**) an association, society, or community of women linked by a common interest, religion, or trade.

sis·ter-in-law ▶ n. (pl. **sisters-in-law**) the sister of one's wife or husband. ■ the wife of one's brother or brother-in-law.

Sis·ter of Mer·cy ▶ n. a member of a Roman Catholic congregation of women founded for educational or charitable purposes, esp. that founded in Dublin in 1827.

Sis·tine /ˈsistēn/ ▶ adj. of or relating to any of the popes called Sixtus, esp. Sixtus IV.
– ORIGIN from Italian *Sistino*, from *Sisto* 'Sixtus.'

Sis·tine Chap·el a chapel in the Vatican, built in the late 15th century by Pope Sixtus IV, containing a painted ceiling and fresco of the Last Judgment by Michelangelo and also frescoes by Botticelli.

sis·trum /ˈsistrəm/ ▶ n. (pl. **sistra** /ˈsistrə/ or **sistrums**) a musical instrument of ancient Egypt consisting of a metal frame with transverse metal rods that rattled when the instrument was shaken.
– ORIGIN late Middle English: via Latin from Greek *seistron*, from *seiein* 'to shake.'

sistrum

Sis·y·phe·an /,sisəˈfēən/ ▶ adj. (of a task) such that it can never be completed.
– ORIGIN late 16th cent.: from Latin *Sisypheius* (based on Greek *Sisuphos*: see **SISYPHUS**) + **-AN**.

Sis·y·phus /ˈsisəfəs/ Greek Mythology the son of Aeolus, punished in Hades for his misdeeds in life by being condemned to the eternal task of rolling a large stone to the top of a hill, from which it always rolled down again.

sit /sit/ ▶ v. (**sits, sitting**; past and past participle **sat** /sat/) **1** [no obj.] adopt or be in a position in which one's weight is supported by one's buttocks rather than one's feet and one's back is upright: *you'd better sit down* | *I sat next to him at dinner*. ■ [with obj.] cause to adopt or be in such a position: ***sit yourself down*** *and I'll bring you some coffee*. ■ (of an animal) rest with the hind legs bent and the body close to the ground: *it is important for a dog to sit when instructed*. ■ (of a bird) rest on a branch; perch. ■ (of a bird) remain on its nest to incubate its egg: (as adj. **sitting**) *a sitting hen*. ■ [with obj.] ride or keep one's seat on (a horse). ■ [with obj.] not use (a player) in a game: *the manager must decide who to sit in the World Series*. ■ [with obj.] (of a table, room, or building) be large enough for (a specified number of seated people): *the cathedral sat about 3,000 people*. ■ (**sit for**) pose, typically in a seated position, for (an artist or photographer): *Walter Deverell asked her to sit for him*. ■ be or remain in a particular position or state: *the fridge was sitting in a pool of water*. ■ [with adverbial] (of an item of clothing) fit a person well or badly as specified: *the blue uniform sat well on his big frame*. ■ (**sit with**) be harmonious with: *his shyness doesn't sit easily with Hollywood tradition*.
2 [no obj.] (of a legislature, committee, court of law, etc.) be engaged in its business: *Congress continued sitting until March 16*. ■ serve as a member of a council, jury, or other official body: *they were determined that women jurists should sit on the tribunal*.
3 [with obj.] chiefly Brit. take (an examination): *pupils are required to sit nine subjects at GCSE* | [no obj.] *he was about to sit for his Cambridge entrance exam*.
4 [no obj., usu. in combination] stay in someone's house while they are away and look after their house or pet: *Kelly had been cat-sitting for me*. ■ babysit.
▶ n. [in sing.] **1** a period of sitting: *a sit in the shade*.
2 archaic the way in which an item of clothing fits someone: *the sit of her gown*.
– PHRASES **sit at someone's feet** be someone's student or follower. **sit in judgment** see **JUDGMENT**. **sit on the fence** see **FENCE**. **sit on one's ass** vulgar slang do nothing; fail to take action. **sit on one's hands** take no action. **sit** (**heavy**) **on the stomach** (of food) take a long time to be digested. **sit tight** informal remain firmly in one's place. ■ refrain from taking action or changing one's mind: *we're advising our clients to sit tight and neither to buy nor sell*. **sit up** (**and take notice**) informal suddenly start paying attention or have one's interest aroused.
– PHRASAL VERBS **sit back** relax: *sit back and enjoy the music*. ■ take no action; choose not to become involved: *I can't just sit back and let Betsy do all the work*. **sit by** take no action in order to prevent something undesirable from occurring: *I'm not going to sit by and let an innocent man go to jail*. **sit down** archaic encamp outside a city in order to besiege it: *with a large force he sat down before Ravenna*. **sit in 1** (of a group of people) occupy a place as a form of protest. **2** attend a meeting or discussion without taking an active part in it: *I sat in on a training session for therapists*. **sit in for** temporarily carry out the duties of (another person). **sit on** informal **1** fail to deal with: *she sat on the article until a deadline galvanized her into putting words to paper*. **2** subdue (someone), typically by saying something intended to discomfit or embarrass them. ■ suppress (something): *tell them to sit on this story until we hear from Quinlan*. **sit something out** not take part in a particular event or activity: *he had to sit out the first playoff game*. ■ wait without moving or taking action until a particular unwelcome situation or process is over: *most of the workers seem to be sitting the crisis out, waiting to see what will happen*. **sit through** stay until the end of (a tedious or lengthy meeting or performance). **sit up** (or **sit someone up**) **1** move (or cause someone to move) from a lying or slouching to a sitting position: *Amy sat up and rubbed her eyes* | *I'll sit you up on the pillows*. **2** refrain from going to bed until a later time than usual: *we sat up late to watch a horror film*.
– ORIGIN Old English *sittan*, of Germanic origin; related to Dutch *zitten*, German *sitzen*, from an Indo-European root shared by Latin *sedere* and Greek *hezesthai*.

USAGE For guidance on the differences between sit and set, see usage at **SET**[1].

Si·ta /ˈsē,tä/ (in the Ramayana) the wife of Rama. She is the Hindu model of the ideal woman, an incarnation of Lakshmi.
– ORIGIN from Sanskrit *Sītā*, literally 'furrow.'

si·tar /siˈtär/ ▶ n. a large, long-necked Indian lute with movable frets, played with a wire pick.
– DERIVATIVES **si·tar·ist** /-ist/ n.
– ORIGIN via Urdu from Persian *sitār*, from *sih* 'three' + *tār* 'string.'

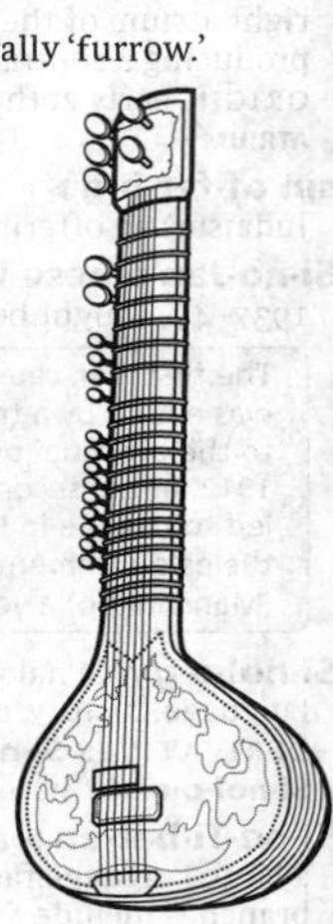
sitar

sit·a·tun·ga /,sitəˈto͝oNGgə/ ▶ n. a brown or grayish antelope with splayed hoofs and, in the male, spiral horns, inhabiting swampy areas in central and East Africa. ● *Tragelaphus spekii*, family Bovidae.
– ORIGIN late 19th cent.: from Kiswahili.

sit·com /ˈsit,käm/ ▶ n. informal a situation comedy.
– ORIGIN 1960s: abbreviation.

sit-down ▶ adj. [attrib.] (of a meal) eaten sitting at a table. ■ (of a protest) in which demonstrators occupy their workplace or sit down on the ground in a public place, refusing to leave until their demands are met.
▶ n. a period of sitting down; a short rest. ■ a sit-down protest.

site /sīt/ ▶ n. an area of ground on which a town, building, or monument is constructed: *the proposed site of a hydroelectric dam*. ■ a place where a particular event or activity is occurring or has occurred: *the site of the Battle of Antietam* | *materials for repairs are always on site*. ■ short for **BUILDING SITE**. ■ short for **WEBSITE**.
▶ v. [with obj.] (usu. **be sited**) fix or build (something) in a particular place: *the rectory is sited behind the church* | (as noun **siting**) *decisions concerning the siting of nuclear power plants*.
– ORIGIN late Middle English (as a noun): from Anglo-Norman French, or from Latin *situs* 'local position.' The verb dates from the late 16th cent.

sit-in ▶ n. a form of protest in which demonstrators occupy a place, refusing to leave until their demands are met.

Sit·ka /ˈsitkə/ a city in the panhandle of southwestern Alaska, on Baranof Island; pop. 8,889 (est. 2008).

Sit·ka spruce /ˈsitkə spro͞os/ ▶ n. a fast-growing spruce tree of the northern Pacific coast of North America, widely cultivated in Britain for its strong lightweight timber. ● *Picea sitchensis*, family Pinaceae.

–ORIGIN late 19th cent.: named after *Sitka*, a town in Alaska.

sit·rep /ˈsitˌrep/ ▶ **n.** informal a report on the current military situation in a particular area.
–ORIGIN 1940s: from *sit(uation) rep(ort)*.

Sit·tang /ˈsiˌtäNG/ a river in southern Burma (Myanmar). Rising in the Pegu mountains, it flows about 350 miles (560 km) south into the Bay of Bengal at the Gulf of Martaban.

sit·ter /ˈsitər/ ▶ **n. 1** a person who sits, esp. for a portrait. ■ a hen sitting on eggs.
2 [usu. in combination] a person who looks after children, pets, or a house while the parents or owners are away: *a house-sitter.* ■ a person who provides care and companionship for people who are ill.

sit·ting /ˈsitiNG/ ▶ **n.** a continuous period of being seated, esp. when engaged in a particular activity: *the whole roast was eaten at one sitting.* ■ a period of time spent as a model for an artist or photographer. ■ a scheduled period of time when a group of people are served a meal, esp. in a restaurant: *there will be two sittings for Christmas lunch.* ■ a period of time during which a committee or legislature is engaged in its normal business. ■ Brit. Law a period of time when a court of law holds sessions.
▶ **adj.** [attrib.] **1** denoting a person who has sat down or the position of such a person: *a sitting position.* ■ (of an animal or bird) not running or flying.
2 (of an elected representative) current; present: *the resignation of the sitting congressman.*
3 (of a hen or other bird) settled on eggs for the purpose of incubating them.

Sit·ting Bull (*c.*1831–90), Sioux chief; Sioux name *Tatanka Iyotake*. He led the Sioux in the fight to retain their lands; this resulted in the massacre of Lt. Col. Custer and his men at Little Bighorn. He was killed by reservation police during the Ghost Dance turmoil.

Sitting Bull

sit·ting duck (also **sitting target**) ▶ **n.** informal a person or thing with no protection against an attack or other source of danger.

sit·ting room ▶ **n.** a room in a house or hotel in which people can sit down and relax.

sit·ting trot ▶ **n.** a style of riding in which a rider remains seated while a horse is trotting, rather than rising from the saddle on alternate strides.

sit·u·ate ▶ **v.** /ˈsiCHo͞oˌāt/ [with obj.] (usu. **be situated**) fix or build (something) in a certain place or position: *the pilot light is usually situated at the front of the boiler* | (as adj. with submodifier **situated**) *a conveniently situated hotel.* ■ put in context; describe the circumstances surrounding (something): *it is necessary to situate these ideas in the wider context of the economy.* ■ (**be situated**) [with adverbial] be in a specified financial or marital position: *Amy is now comfortably situated.*
▶ **adj.** /ˈsiCHo͞oit/ Law or archaic situated.
–ORIGIN late Middle English: from medieval Latin *situat-* 'placed,' from the verb *situare*, from Latin *situs* 'site.'

sit·u·a·tion /ˌsiCHo͞oˈāSHən/ ▶ **n. 1** a set of circumstances in which one finds oneself; a state of affairs: *the situation between her and Jake had come to a head* | *the political situation in Russia.*
2 the location and surroundings of a place: *the situation of the town is pleasant.*
3 formal a position of employment; a job.
–DERIVATIVES **sit·u·a·tion·al** /–SHənl/ **adj.**, **sit·u·a·tion·al·ly adv.**
–ORIGIN late Middle English (sense 2): from French, or from medieval Latin *situatio(n-)*, from *situare* 'to place' (see SITUATE). Sense 1 dates from the early 18th cent.

sit·u·a·tion com·e·dy ▶ **n.** a television or radio series in which the same set of characters are involved in various amusing situations.

sit·u·a·tion eth·ics (also **situational ethics**) ▶ **plural n.** [treated as sing.] Philosophy the doctrine of flexibility in the application of moral laws according to circumstances.

sit·u·a·tion·ism /ˌsiCHo͞oˈāSHəˌnizəm/ ▶ **n.** the theory that human behavior is determined by surrounding circumstances rather than by personal qualities.
–DERIVATIVES **sit·u·a·tion·ist n. & adj.**

sit-up ▶ **n.** a physical exercise designed to strengthen the abdominal muscles, in which a person sits up from a supine position without using the arms for leverage.

sit-up·on ▶ **n.** informal, humorous a person's buttocks.

si·tus /ˈsītəs, ˈsē-/ ▶ **n.** Law the place to which, for purposes of legal jurisdiction or taxation, a property belongs.

si·tus in·ver·sus /ˈsītəs inˈvərsəs, ˈsē-/ ▶ **n.** Medicine an uncommon condition in which the heart and other organs of the body are transposed through the sagittal plane to lie on the opposite (left or right) side from the usual.
–ORIGIN late 19th cent.: from Latin *situs inversus viscerum* 'inverted placing of the internal organs.'

Sit·well /ˈsitwəl, -ˌwel/, Dame Edith (Louisa) (1887–1964), English poet and critic. Her early verse, with that of her brothers **Osbert** (1892–1969) and **Sacheverell** (1897–1988), marked a revolt against the prevailing Georgian style of the day.

sitz bath /sits/ ▶ **n.** a bath in which only the buttocks and hips are immersed in water.
–ORIGIN mid 19th cent.: partial translation of German *Sitzbad*, from *sitzen* 'sit' + *Bad* 'bath.'

sitz·fleisch /ˈsitsˌflīSH/ ▶ **n.** informal a person's buttocks. ■ power to endure or to persevere in an activity; staying power.
–ORIGIN from German, from *sitzen* 'sit' + *Fleisch* 'flesh.'

sitz·krieg /ˈsitsˌkrēg/ ▶ **n.** a war, or a phase of a war, in which there is little or no active warfare.
–ORIGIN 1940s: suggested by BLITZKRIEG, from German *sitzen* 'sit.'

sitz·mark /ˈsitsˌmärk/ ▶ **n.** an impression made in the snow by a skier falling backward.
–ORIGIN 1930s: from German *sitzen* 'sit' + the noun MARK[1].

Si·va /ˈSHēvə, ˈsē-/ variant spelling of SHIVA.

Si·va·ji variant spelling of SHIVAJI.

Si·van /ˈsivən/ ▶ **n.** (in the Jewish calendar) the ninth month of the civil and third of the religious year, usually coinciding with parts of May and June.
–ORIGIN from Hebrew *sīwān*.

Si·wa·lik Hills /siˈwälik/ a range of foothills in the southern Himalayas that extend from northeastern India across Nepal to Sikkim.

Si·wash /ˈsīwäSH, -wôSH/ ▶ **n.** derogatory **1** an American Indian of the northern Pacific coast.
2 another term for CHINOOK JARGON.
▶ **adj.** derogatory of or relating to American Indians of the northern Pacific coast.
▶ **v.** [no obj.] camp without a tent.
–ORIGIN Chinook Jargon, from Canadian French *sauvage* 'wild.'

six /siks/ ▶ **cardinal number** equivalent to the product of two and three; one more than five, or four less than ten; 6: *she's lived here six months* | *six of the people arrested have been charged* | *a six-week tour.* (Roman numeral: **vi, VI**) ■ a group or unit of six people or things. ■ six years old: *a child of six.* ■ six o'clock: *it's half past six.* ■ a size of garment or other merchandise denoted by six. ■ a playing card or domino with six pips.
–PHRASES **at sixes and sevens** in a state of total confusion or disarray. **knock** (or **hit**) **someone for six** Brit. informal utterly surprise or overcome someone. [alluding to the highest-scoring hit in cricket.] **six feet under** informal dead and buried. **six of one and half a dozen of the other** (Brit. **six and two threes**) used to convey that there is little real difference between two alternatives.
–ORIGIN Old English *siex, six, syx*, of Germanic origin; related to Dutch *zes* and German *sechs*, from an Indo-European root shared by Latin *sex* and Greek *hex*.

Six, Les see LES SIX.

Six Day War a war, June 5–10, 1967, in which Israel occupied Sinai, the Old City of Jerusalem, the West Bank, and the Golan Heights and defeated an Egyptian, Jordanian, and Syrian alliance. Arab name JUNE WAR.

six·fold /ˈsiksˌfōld/ ▶ **adj.** six times as great or as numerous: *a sixfold increase in their overheads.* ■ having six parts or elements: *a sixfold plan of action.*
▶ **adv.** by six times; to six times the number or amount: *coal prices have risen sixfold.*

six-gun ▶ **n.** another term for SIX-SHOOTER.

Six Na·tions ▶ **plural n.** (**the Six Nations**) the Five Nations of the original Iroquois confederacy after the Tuscarora joined them in 1722.

six-pack ▶ **n. 1** a pack of six cans of beer or soft drinks typically held together with a plastic fastener.
2 informal a set of well-developed abdominal muscles: [as modifier] *six-pack abs.*

six·pence /ˈsiksˌpens, -pəns/ ▶ **n.** Brit. a coin worth six old pence, withdrawn in 1980. ■ the sum of six pence, esp. before decimalization (1971).

six·pen·ny /ˈsiksˌpenē, -pənē/ ▶ **adj.** [attrib.] Brit. costing or worth six pence, esp. before decimalization (1971).

six-shoot·er ▶ **n.** a revolver with six chambers.

sixte /sikst/ ▶ **n.** Fencing the sixth of eight standard parrying positions.
–ORIGIN late 19th cent.: French, from Latin *sextus* 'sixth.'

six·teen /sikˈstēn, ˈsikˌstēn/ ▶ **cardinal number** equivalent to the product of four and four; one more than fifteen, or six more than ten; 16: *sixteen miles east of Detroit* | *sixteen of our eighteen patients.* (Roman numeral: **xvi, XVI**) ■ a size of garment or other merchandise denoted by sixteen. ■ sixteen years old: *a daughter of sixteen.*
–DERIVATIVES **six·teenth** /sikˈstēnTH, ˈsikˌstēnTH/ **ordinal number.**
–ORIGIN Old English *siextiene* (see SIX, -TEEN).

six·teen·mo /ˌsiksˈtēnmō/ ▶ **n.** (pl. **sixteenmos**) another term for SEXTODECIMO.

six·teenth note /ˌsiksˈtēnTH/ ▶ **n.** Music a note having the time value of a sixteenth of a whole note or half an eighth note, represented by a large dot with a two-hooked stem. Also called SEMIQUAVER.

sixth /siksTH/ ▶ **ordinal number** constituting number six in a sequence; 6th: *her sixth novel* | *the sixth of the month* | *to the original five categories we add a sixth.* ■ (**a sixth/one sixth**) each of six equal parts into which something is or may be divided: *a sixth of the total population.* ■ the sixth finisher or position in a race or other competition: *he could only finish sixth.* ■ sixthly (used to introduce a sixth point or reason): *sixth, given all the facts there is no logical reason why we can't make a decision.* ■ Music an interval spanning six consecutive notes in a diatonic major or minor scale, e.g., C to A (**major sixth**) or A to F (**minor sixth**). ■ Music the note that is higher by this interval than the tonic of a scale or root of a chord.
–DERIVATIVES **sixth·ly adv.**

sixth sense ▶ **n.** [in sing.] a supposed intuitive faculty giving awareness not explicable in terms of normal perception: *some sixth sense told him he was not alone.*

six·ty /ˈsikstē/ ▶ **cardinal number** (pl. **sixties**) the number equivalent to the product of six and ten; ten more than fifty; 60: *a crew of sixty* | *sixty bedrooms* | *sixty percent of the children.* (Roman numeral: **lx, LX**) ■ (**sixties**) the numbers from sixty to sixty-nine, esp. the years of a century or of a person's life: *Morris was in his early sixties* | *the flower children of the sixties.* ■ sixty miles an hour: *they were doing sixty.* ■ sixty years old: *he retired at sixty.*
–DERIVATIVES **six·ti·eth** /-iTH/ **ordinal number, six·ty·fold** /-ˈfōld/ **adj. & adv.**
–ORIGIN Old English *siextig* (see SIX, -TY[2]).

six·ty-four·mo /ˌsikstē ˈfôrmō/ ▶ **n.** (pl. **sixty-fourmos**) a size of book in which each leaf is one sixty-fourth the size of a printing sheet. ■ a book of this size.

six·ty-fourth note ▶ **n.** Music a note with the time value of half a thirty-second note, represented by a large dot with a four-flagged stem.

six·ty-four thou·sand dol·lar ques·tion ▶ **n.** informal something that is not known and on which a great deal depends.
–ORIGIN 1950s: from a question posed for the top prize in a television quiz show of the same name.

six·ty-nine ▶ **n.** informal sexual activity between two people involving mutual oral stimulation of their genitals.
–ORIGIN from the position of the couple.

siz·a·ble /ˈsīzəbəl/ (also **sizeable**) ▶ **adj.** fairly large: *a sizable proportion of the population* | *a sizable apartment.*
–DERIVATIVES **siz·a·bly** /-blē/ **adv.**

siz·ar /ˈsīzər/ ▶ **n.** an undergraduate at Cambridge University or at Trinity College, Dublin, receiving financial help from the college and formerly having certain menial duties.

S

PRONUNCIATION KEY ə *ago, up*; ər *over, fur*; a *hat*; ā *ate*; ä *car*; e *let*; ē *see*; i *fit*; ī *by*; NG *sing*; ō *go*; ô *law, for*; oi *toy*; o͝o *good*; o͞o *goo*; ou *out*; TH *thin*; T͟H *then*; ZH *vision*

– DERIVATIVES **siz·ar·ship** /-,SHip/ **n.**
– ORIGIN late 16th cent.: from obsolete *size* 'ration of bread, beer, etc' + -**AR**[2].

size[1] /sīz/ ▶ **n. 1** the relative extent of something; a thing's overall dimensions or magnitude; how big something is: *the schools varied in size* | *a forest the size of Connecticut* | *houses of all sizes.* ■ extensive dimensions or magnitude: *she seemed slightly awed by the size of the building.*
2 each of the classes, typically numbered, into which garments or other articles are divided according to how large they are: *I can never find anything in my size.* ■ a person or garment corresponding to such a numbered class: *she's a size 10.*
▶ **v.** [with obj.] alter or sort in terms of size or according to size: *some drills are sized in millimeters.* ■ (**size something up**) estimate or measure something's dimensions: *she was trying to size up a room with a tape measure.* ■ (**size someone/something up**) informal form an estimate or rough judgment of someone or something: *the two men sized each other up.*
▶ **adj.** [in combination] having a specified size; sized: *marble-size chunks of hail.*
– PHRASES **of a size** (of two or more people or things) having the same dimensions. **of some size** fairly large. **that's about the size of it** informal said to confirm someone's assessment of a situation, esp. of one regarded as bad. **to size** to the dimensions wanted: *the PVC sheet is easily cut to size.*
– DERIVATIVES **siz·er n.**
– ORIGIN Middle English (also in the sense 'assize, ordinance fixing a rate of payment'): from Old French *sise*, from *assise* 'ordinance,' or a shortening of **ASSIZE**.

size[2] ▶ **n.** a gelatinous solution used in gilding paper, stiffening textiles, and preparing plastered walls for decoration.
▶ **v.** [with obj.] treat with size to glaze or stiffen.
– ORIGIN Middle English: perhaps the same word as **SIZE**[1].

size·a·ble ▶ **adj.** variant spelling of **SIZABLE**.

sized /sīzd/ ▶ **adj.** [in combination or with submodifier] having a specified size: *sparrow-sized birds* | *comfortably sized rooms.*

size·ism /ˈsīz,izəm/ (also **sizism**) ▶ **n.** prejudice or discrimination on the grounds of a person's size: *requiring large passengers to buy two seats is pure sizeism.*
– DERIVATIVES **size·ist** (also **sizist**) **adj. & n.**
– ORIGIN from *size* + *-ism* 'basis for prejudice.'

size ze·ro ▶ **n.** a very small size of women's clothing.

siz·zle /ˈsizəl/ ▶ **v.** [no obj.] (of food) make a hissing sound when frying or cooking: *the bacon began to sizzle in the pan.* ■ informal be very hot: *we sizzled in blazing sunshine this week.* ■ informal be very exciting or passionate, esp. sexually: *they simply sizzle as their affair develops.*
▶ **n.** [in sing.] a hissing sound, as of food frying or cooking: *the sizzle of hot dogs.* ■ informal a state or quality of great excitement or passion: *a dance routine with lots of sizzle.*
– DERIVATIVES **siz·zler** /ˈsiz(ə)lər/ **n.**
– ORIGIN early 17th cent.: imitative.

siz·zling /ˈsiz(ə)liNG/ ▶ **adj.** informal very hot: *the sizzling summer temperatures.* ■ very exciting or passionate, esp. sexually: *that was the start of a sizzling affair.*

SJ ▶ **abbr.** Society of Jesus.

Sjæl·land /ˈSHelän/ Danish name for **ZEALAND**.

sjam·bok /SHamˈbäk, -ˈbək, ˈSHambäk, -bək/ ▶ **n.** (in South Africa) a long, stiff whip, originally made of rhinoceros hide.
▶ **v.** (**sjamboks, sjambokking, sjambokked**) [with obj.] flog with a sjambok.
– ORIGIN from South African Dutch *tjambok*, via Malay from Urdu *chābuk*.

SJC ▶ **abbr.** (in the US) Supreme Judicial Court.

SJD ▶ **abbr.** Doctor of Juridical Science.
– ORIGIN Latin *Scientiae Juridicae Doctor*.

Sjö·gren's syn·drome /ˈSHəgrənz/ (also **Sjögren's disease**) ▶ **n.** Medicine a chronic autoimmune condition characterized by degeneration of the salivary and lachrymal glands, causing dryness of the mouth and eyes.
– ORIGIN 1930s: named after Henrik S. C. Sjögren (1899–1986), Swedish physician.

SK ▶ **abbr.** Saskatchewan (in official postal use).

sk. ▶ **abbr.** sack.

ska /skä/ ▶ **n.** a style of fast popular music having a strong offbeat and originating in Jamaica in the 1960s, a forerunner of reggae.
– ORIGIN 1960s: of unknown origin.

skag[1] /skag/ (also **scag**) ▶ **n.** informal **1** heroin.
2 an unattractive woman.
– ORIGIN early 20th cent. (in sense 'cigarette'): of unknown origin.

skag[2] ▶ **n.** variant spelling of **SKEG**.

Skag·er·rak /ˈskagə,rak, ˈskägə,räk/ (**the Skagerrak**) a strait that separates southern Norway from the northwest coast of Denmark.

Skag·way /ˈskag,wā/ a city in southwestern Alaska, in the panhandle; pop. 862 (est. 2000). A cruise ship port, it was a gateway to the 1897–98 Klondike gold rush.

skald /skôld, skäld/ (also **scald**) ▶ **n.** historical (in ancient Scandinavia) a composer and reciter of poems honoring heroes and their deeds.
– DERIVATIVES **skald·ic** /-ik/ **adj.**
– ORIGIN from Old Norse *skáld*, of unknown origin.

Skan·da /ˈskəndə/ Hinduism the Hindu war god, first son of Shiva and Parvati and brother of Ganesha. He is depicted as a boy or youth, sometimes with six heads and often with his mount, a peacock.

skank /skaNGk/ ▶ **n. 1** informal a sleazy or unpleasant person. ■ derogatory a promiscuous woman: *the office skank.*
2 a steady-paced dance performed to reggae music, characterized by rhythmically bending forward, raising the knees, and extending the hands palms-downward. ■ reggae music suitable for such dancing.
▶ **v. 1** [with obj.] swindle or deceive: *they made a tidy sum skanking the tourists.* ■ obtain by deception or theft: *I skanked the poster off some wall.*
2 [no obj.] (often as adj. **skanking**) play reggae music or dance in this style.
– ORIGIN 1970s: of unknown origin.

skank·y /ˈskaNGkē/ ▶ **adj.** informal (esp. of a person) dirty and unpleasant: *the skanky folk who populate L.A.'s film scene.*

skarn /skärn/ ▶ **n.** Geology lime-bearing siliceous rock produced by the metamorphic alteration of limestone or dolomite.
– ORIGIN early 20th cent.: from Swedish, literally 'dung, filth.'

skat /skat/ ▶ **n.** a three-handed trick-taking card game with bidding, played with 32 cards.
– ORIGIN mid 19th cent.: from German, from Italian *scarto* 'a discard,' from *scartare* 'discard.'

skate[1] /skāt/ ▶ **n.** an ice skate or roller skate. ■ a device, typically with wheels on the underside, used to move a heavy or unwieldy object.
▶ **v.** [no obj.] **1** move on ice skates or roller skates in a gliding fashion: *the boys were skating on the ice.* ■ [with obj.] perform (a specified figure) on skates: *figure eights skated entirely on one foot.* ■ ride on a skateboard.
2 (**skate over/around**) pass over or refer only fleetingly to (a subject or problem): *she seemed to skate over the next part of her story.*
3 (**skate through**) make quick and easy progress through: *he admits he had expected to skate through the system.*
– DERIVATIVES **skat·er n.**
– ORIGIN mid 17th cent. (originally as the plural *scates*): from Dutch *schaats* (singular but interpreted as plural), from Old French *eschasse* 'stilt.'

skate[2] ▶ **n.** (pl. **same** or **skates**) a typically large marine fish of the ray family with a cartilaginous skeleton and a flattened diamond-shaped body. ● Family Rajidae: numerous species, in particular the commercially valuable *Raja batis*. ■ the flesh of a skate or thornback used as food.
– ORIGIN Middle English: from Old Norse *skata*.

skate·board /ˈskāt,bôrd/ ▶ **n.** a short narrow board with two small wheels fixed to the bottom of either end, on which (as a recreation or sport) a person can ride in a standing or crouching position, propelling themselves by occasionally pushing one foot against the ground.
▶ **v.** [no obj.] (often as noun **skateboarding**) ride on a skateboard.
– DERIVATIVES **skate·board·er n.**

skate·park /ˈskāt,pärk/ ▶ **n.** an area designated and equipped for skateboarding.

skat·ing /ˈskātiNG/ ▶ **n.** the action or activity of skating on ice skates, roller skates, or a skateboard as a sport or pastime.

skat·ing rink ▶ **n.** an expanse of ice artificially made for skating, or a floor used for roller skating.

skean dhu /,skē(ə)n ˈT͟Hōō, ˈdōō/ ▶ **n.** a dagger worn in the stocking as part of Highland dress.
– ORIGIN early 19th cent.: from Irish and Scottish Gaelic *sgian* 'knife' + Scottish Gaelic *dubh* 'black.'

sked /sked/ informal ▶ **n.** short for **SCHEDULE**.

ske·dad·dle /skiˈdadl/ ▶ **v.** [no obj.] informal depart quickly or hurriedly; run away: *when he saw us, he skedaddled.*
▶ **n.** a hurried departure or flight.
– ORIGIN mid 19th cent.: of unknown origin.

skeet /skēt/ (also **skeet shooting**) ▶ **n.** a shooting sport in which a clay target is thrown from a trap to simulate the flight of a bird.
– DERIVATIVES **skeet shoot·er n.**
– ORIGIN 1920s: apparently a pseudoarchaic alteration of the verb **SHOOT**.

skee·ter /ˈskētər/ ▶ **n.** informal a mosquito.
– ORIGIN mid 19th cent.: shortened form, representing a casual pronunciation.

skee·vy /ˈskēvē/ ▶ **adj.** informal unpleasant, squalid, or distasteful: *a skeevy Vegas motel.*
– ORIGIN 1970s: from Italian *schifo* 'repugnance, disgust.'

skeg /skeg/ (also **skag**) ▶ **n.** a tapering or projecting stern section of a vessel's keel, which protects the propeller and supports the rudder. ■ a fin underneath the rear of a surfboard.
– ORIGIN early 17th cent.: from Old Norse *skegg* 'beard,' perhaps from Dutch *scheg*.

skein /skān/ ▶ **n.** a length of thread or yarn, loosely coiled and knotted. ■ a tangled or complicated arrangement, state, or situation: ***the skeins of her long hair*** | figurative ***a skein of lies.*** ■ a flock of wild geese or swans in flight, typically in a V-shaped formation.
– ORIGIN Middle English: shortening of Old French *escaigne*, of unknown origin.

skel·e·tal /ˈskelətl/ ▶ **adj.** of, relating to, or functioning as a skeleton: *the skeletal remains of aquatic organisms.* ■ very thin; emaciated: *a small, skeletal boy clothed in rags.* ■ existing only in outline or as a framework of something: *a skeletal plot for a novel* | *the skeletal leaves of long-faded roses.*
– DERIVATIVES **skel·e·tal·ly adv.**

skel·e·tal mus·cle ▶ **n.** a muscle that is connected to the skeleton to form part of the mechanical system that moves the limbs and other parts of the body. ■ another term for **STRIATED MUSCLE**.

skel·e·ton /ˈskelitn/ ▶ **n.** an internal or external framework of bone, cartilage, or other rigid material supporting or containing the body of an animal or plant. ■ used in exaggerated reference to a very thin or emaciated person or animal: *she was no more than a skeleton at the end.* ■ the remaining part of something after its life or usefulness is gone: *the chapel was stripped to a skeleton of its former self.* ■ the supporting framework, basic structure, or essential part of something: *the concrete skeleton of an unfinished building* | *the skeleton of a report.* ■ [as modifier] denoting the essential or minimum number of people, things, or parts necessary for something: *there was only a skeleton staff on duty.*
– PHRASES **skeleton in the closet** a discreditable or embarrassing fact that someone wishes to keep secret.
– DERIVATIVES **skel·e·ton·ize** /-,īz/ **v.**
– ORIGIN late 16th cent.: modern Latin, from Greek, neuter of *skeletos* 'dried up,' from *skellein* 'dry up.'

Skel·e·ton Coast an arid coastal area in Namibia. Comprised of the northern part of the Namib desert, it extends from Walvis Bay in the south to the border with Angola.

skel·e·ton key ▶ **n.** a key designed to fit many locks by having the interior of the bit hollowed.

skell /skel/ ▶ **n.** informal (in New York) a tramp or homeless person.
– ORIGIN 1980s: perhaps a shortening of *skeleton*.

Skel·ton /ˈskeltn/, Red (1913–97), US comedian; born *Richard Bernard Skelton*. A stage, circus, and movie performer, he starred in the television series *The Red Skelton Show* (1951–71) and brought to life characters such as Clem Kadiddlehopper, Freddie the Freeloader, and Mean Widdle Kid.

skep /skep/ ▶ **n.** a straw or wicker beehive. ■ archaic a wooden or wicker basket.
– ORIGIN late Old English *sceppe* 'basket,' from Old Norse *skeppa* 'basket, bushel.'

skep·tic /ˈskeptik/ (Brit. **sceptic**) ▶ **n. 1** a person inclined to question or doubt all accepted opinions. ■ a person who doubts the truth of Christianity and other religions; an atheist or agnostic.
2 Philosophy an ancient or modern philosopher who denies the possibility of knowledge, or even rational belief, in some sphere.

> The leading ancient skeptic was Pyrrho, whose followers at the Academy vigorously opposed Stoicism. Modern skeptics have held diverse views: the most extreme have doubted whether any knowledge at all of the external world is possible (see **SOLIPSISM**), while others have questioned the existence of objects beyond our experience of them.

▶ **adj.** another term for **SKEPTICAL**.
– ORIGIN late 16th cent. (sense 2 of the noun): from French *sceptique*, or via Latin from Greek *skeptikos*, from *skepsis* 'inquiry, doubt.'

skep·ti·cal /ˈskeptikəl/ (Brit. **sceptical**) ▶ **adj. 1** not easily convinced; having doubts or reservations: *the public were deeply skeptical about some of the proposals*.
2 Philosophy relating to the theory that certain knowledge is impossible.
– DERIVATIVES **skep·ti·cal·ly** /-ik(ə)lē/ (Brit. **sceptically**) **adv.**

skep·ti·cism /ˈskeptəˌsizəm/ (Brit. **scepticism**) ▶ **n. 1** a skeptical attitude; doubt as to the truth of something: *these claims were treated with skepticism*.
2 Philosophy the theory that certain knowledge is impossible.

sker·ry /ˈskerē/ ▶ **n.** (pl. **skerries**) Scottish a reef or rocky island.
– ORIGIN early 17th cent.: Orkney dialect, from Old Norse *sker*. Compare with **SCAR**.

sketch /skeCH/ ▶ **n. 1** a rough or unfinished drawing or painting, often made to assist in making a more finished picture: *a charcoal sketch*. ■ a brief written or spoken account or description of someone or something, giving only basic details: *a biographical sketch of Ernest Hemingway*. ■ a rough or unfinished version of any creative work.
2 a short humorous play or performance, consisting typically of one scene in a comedy program.
3 informal a comical or amusing person or thing.
▶ **v.** [with obj.] make a rough drawing of: *as they talked, Modigliani began to sketch her* | [no obj.] *Jeanne sketched and painted whenever she had the time*. ■ give a brief account or general outline of: *they sketched out the prosecution case*. ■ perform (a gesture) with one's hands or body: *he sketched a graceful bow in her direction*.
– DERIVATIVES **sketch·er** **n.**
– ORIGIN mid 17th cent.: from Dutch *schets* or German *Skizze*, from Italian *schizzo*, from *schizzare* 'make a sketch,' based on Greek *skhedios* 'done extempore.'

sketch·book /ˈskeCHˌbo͝ok/ ▶ **n.** (also **sketchpad** /-ˌpad/) a pad or book of drawing paper for sketching on. ■ a book of drawings or literary sketches.

sketch·y /ˈskeCHē/ ▶ **adj.** (**sketchier**, **sketchiest**) not thorough or detailed: *the information they had was sketchy*. ■ (of a picture) resembling a sketch; consisting of outline without much detail.
– DERIVATIVES **sketch·i·ly** /ˈskeCHəlē/ **adv.**, **sketch·i·ness** **n.**

skew /skyo͞o/ ▶ **adj. 1** neither parallel nor at right angles to a specified or implied line; askew; crooked: *his hat looked slightly skew* | *a skew angle*. ■ Statistics (of a statistical distribution) not symmetrical.
2 Mathematics (of a pair of lines) neither parallel nor intersecting. ■ (of a curve) not lying in a plane.
▶ **n.** an oblique angle; a slant. ■ a bias toward one particular group or subject: *the paper had a working-class skew*. ■ Statistics the state of not being symmetrical.
▶ **v.** [no obj.] suddenly change direction or position: *the car had skewed across the track*. ■ twist or turn or cause to do this: *he skewed around in his saddle* | [with obj.] *his leg was skewed in and pushed against the other one*. ■ [with obj.] make biased or distorted in a way that is regarded as inaccurate, unfair, or misleading: *the curriculum is skewed toward the practical subjects*. ■ [with obj.] Statistics cause (a distribution) to be asymmetrical.
– DERIVATIVES **skew·ness** **n.**
– ORIGIN late Middle English (as a verb in the sense 'move obliquely'): shortening of Old Northern French *eskiuwer*, variant of Old French *eschiver* 'eschew.' The adjective and noun (early 17th cent.) are from the verb.

skew arch (also **skew bridge**) ▶ **n.** an arch (or bridge) with the line of the arch not at right angles to the abutment.

skew·back /ˈskyo͞oˌbak/ ▶ **n.** the sloping face of the abutment on which an extremity of an arch rests.

skew·bald /ˈskyo͞oˌbôld/ ▶ **adj.** (of an animal) with irregular patches of white and another color (properly not black). Compare with **PIEBALD**.
▶ **n.** a skewbald animal, esp. a horse.
– ORIGIN mid 17th cent.: from obsolete *skewed* 'skewbald' (of uncertain origin), on the pattern of *piebald*.

skew·er /ˈskyo͞oər/ ▶ **n.** a long piece of wood or metal used for holding pieces of food, typically meat, together during cooking.
▶ **v.** [with obj.] fasten together or pierce with a pin or skewer: (as adj. **skewered**) *skewered meat and fish*. ■ informal criticize (someone) sharply.
– ORIGIN late Middle English: of unknown origin.

skew-sym·met·ric ▶ **adj.** Mathematics (of a matrix) having all the elements of the principal diagonal equal to zero, and each of the remaining elements equal to the negative of the element in the corresponding position on the other side of the diagonal.

ski /skē/ ▶ **n.** (pl. **skis**) each of a pair of long narrow pieces of hard flexible material, typically pointed and turned up at the front, fastened under the feet for gliding over snow. ■ a similar device attached beneath a vehicle or aircraft. ■ [as modifier] of, relating to, or used for skiing: *a ski instructor* | *ski boots*. ■ another term for **WATERSKI**.
▶ **v.** (**skis**, **skied** /skēd/, **skiing** /ˈskē-iNG/) [no obj.] travel over snow on skis; take part in the sport or recreation of skiing: *they skied down the mountain*. ■ [with obj.] ski on (a particular ski run or type of snow): *spring snow is not always easy to ski*.
– DERIVATIVES **ski·a·ble** **adj.**
– ORIGIN mid 18th cent.: from Norwegian, from Old Norse *skíth* 'stick of wood, snowshoe.'

ski·ag·ra·phy /skīˈagrəfē/ (Brit. **sciagraphy**) ▶ **n.** the use of shading and the projection of shadows to show perspective in architectural or technical drawing.
– DERIVATIVES **ski·a·gram** /ˈskīəˌgram/ **n.**, **ski·a·graph** /ˈskīəˌgraf/ **n. & v.**, **ski·a·graph·ic** /ˌskīəˈgrafik/ **adj.**
– ORIGIN late 16th cent.: from French *sciagraphie*, via Latin from Greek *skiagraphia*, from *skia* 'shadow.'

Skia·thos /ˈskīəˌTHäs, ˈskēəˌTHôs/ a Greek island in the Aegean Sea, part of the Northern Sporades group. Greek name **Skíathos**.

ski-bob /ˈskē ˌbäb/ ▶ **n.** a device resembling a bicycle with skis instead of wheels, used for sliding down snow-covered slopes.
▶ **v.** (**ski-bobs**, **ski-bobbing**, **ski-bobbed**) [no obj.] ride a ski-bob.
– DERIVATIVES **ski-bob·ber** **n.**

skid /skid/ ▶ **v.** (**skids**, **skidding**, **skidded**) **1** [no obj.] (of a vehicle) slide, typically sideways or obliquely, on slippery ground or as a result of stopping or turning too quickly: *the taxicab skidded to a halt*. ■ slip; slide: *Barbara's foot skidded, and she fell to the floor*. ■ [with obj.] cause to skid: *he skidded his car*. ■ [with obj.] move a heavy object on skids: *they skidded the logs down the hill to the waterfront*. ■ decline; deteriorate: *its shares have skidded 29% since March*.
2 [with obj.] fasten a skid to (a wheel) as a brake.
▶ **n. 1** an act of skidding or sliding: *the Volvo went into a skid*.
2 a runner attached to the underside of an aircraft for use when landing on snow or grass. ■ each of a set of wooden rollers used for moving a log or other heavy object.
3 a braking device consisting of a wooden or metal shoe preventing a wheel from revolving.
4 a beam or plank used to support a ship under construction or repair.
– PHRASES **hit the skids** informal begin a rapid decline or deterioration. **on the skids** informal (of a person or their career) in a bad state; failing. **put the skids under** informal hasten the decline or failure of.
– ORIGIN late 17th cent. (as a noun in the sense 'supporting beam'): perhaps related to Old Norse *skíth* (see **SKI**).

skid·doo /skəˈdo͞o/ (also **skidoo**) ▶ **v.** (**skiddoos**, **skiddooing**, **skiddooed**) [no obj.] informal, dated leave somewhere quickly.
– PHRASES **twenty-three skiddoo** a hasty departure. [the origin of *twenty-three* is unknown.]
– ORIGIN early 20th cent.: perhaps from **SKEDADDLE**. The term is said to have been used originally in reference to male onlookers chased by police from the Flatiron Building, 23rd Street, New York, where the skirts of female passersby were raised by winds intensified by the building's design.

skid·pad /ˈskidˌpad/ ▶ **n.** a road surface used for testing the ability of automobiles to withstand lateral acceleration.

skid road ▶ **n.** a road along which logs are hauled. ■ historical a part of a town frequented by loggers. ■ another term for **SKID ROW**.

skid row /rō/ ▶ **n.** informal a run-down part of a town frequented by vagrants, alcoholics, and drug addicts. ■ a desperately unfortunate or difficult situation: *I don't want to end up on skid row*.
– ORIGIN 1930s: alteration of **SKID ROAD**.

ski·er /ˈskēər/ ▶ **n.** a person who skis.

skiff /skif/ ▶ **n.** a shallow, flat-bottomed open boat with sharp bow and square stern.
– ORIGIN late 15th cent.: from French *esquif*, from Italian *schifo*, of Germanic origin; related to **SHIP**.

skif·fle /ˈskifəl/ ▶ **n. 1** (in the US) a style of 1920s and 1930s jazz deriving from blues, ragtime, and folk music, using both improvised and conventional instruments.
2 Brit. a kind of folk music with a blues or jazz flavor that was popular in the 1950s, played by a small group and often incorporating improvised instruments such as washboards.
– ORIGIN 1920s: perhaps imitative.

ski-fly·ing ▶ **n.** a form of ski jumping incorporating aerodynamic principles to lengthen the jump.

ski·ing /ˈskēiNG/ ▶ **n.** the action of traveling over snow on skis, esp. as a sport or recreation. Competitive skiing falls into two categories: **Nordic** (cross-country racing, jumping, and biathlon) and **Alpine** (downhill or straight racing, and slalom racing around a series of markers).

ski·jor·ing /ˌskēˈjôriNG, ˈskēˌjôriNG/ ▶ **n.** the action of being pulled over snow or ice on skis by a horse or dog or a motor vehicle, as a sport or recreation activity.
– DERIVATIVES **ski·jor·er** /-rər/ **n.**
– ORIGIN 1920s: from Norwegian *skikjøring*, from *ski* 'ski' + *kjøre* 'drive.'

ski jump ▶ **n.** a steep slope leveling off before a drop to a lower slope, used in Nordic skiing to perform jumps. ■ a leap made from such a slope.
– DERIVATIVES **ski jump·er** **n.**, **ski jump·ing** **n.**

skil·full ▶ **adj.** chiefly Brit. variant spelling of **SKILLFUL**.

ski lift ▶ **n.** a system used to transport skiers up a slope to the top of a run, typically consisting of moving seats attached to an overhead cable.

skill /skil/ ▶ **n.** the ability to do something well; expertise: *difficult work, taking great skill*. ■ a particular ability: *the basic skills of cooking*.
– DERIVATIVES **skill-less** **adj.** (archaic).
– ORIGIN late Old English *scele* 'knowledge,' from Old Norse *skil* 'discernment, knowledge.'

skilled /skild/ ▶ **adj.** having or showing the knowledge, ability, or training to perform a certain activity or task well: *a lab technician skilled in electronics* | *skilled draftsmen*. ■ based on such training or experience; showing expertise: *skilled legal advice*. ■ (of work) requiring special abilities or training: *a highly skilled job*.

skil·let /ˈskilit/ ▶ **n.** a frying pan. ■ historical a small metal cooking pot with a long handle, typically having legs.
– ORIGIN Middle English: perhaps from Old French *escuelete*, diminutive of *escuele* 'platter,' from late Latin *scutella*.

skill·ful /ˈskilfəl/ (also chiefly Brit. **skilful**) ▶ **adj.** having or showing skill: *a skillful infielder* | *his skillful use of propaganda*.
– DERIVATIVES **skill·ful·ly** **adv.**, **skill·ful·ness** **n.**

skill set ▶ **n.** a person's range of skills or abilities.

skim /skim/ ▶ **v.** (**skims**, **skimming**, **skimmed**) **1** [with obj.] remove (a substance) from the surface of a liquid: *as the scum rises, skim it off*. ■ remove a substance from the surface of (a liquid): *bring to the boil, then skim it to remove any foam*. ■ informal steal or embezzle (money), esp. in small amounts over a period of time: *she was skimming money from the household kitty*. ■ (often as noun **skimming**) fraudulently copy (credit or debit card details) with a card swipe or other device.
2 [no obj., with adverbial of direction] go or move quickly and lightly over or on a surface or through the air: *he let his fingers skim across her shoulders*. ■ [with obj.] pass over (a surface), nearly or lightly touching it in the process: *we stood on the bridge, watching swallows skimming the water*. ■ [with obj.] throw (a flat stone) low over an expanse of water so that it bounces on the surface several times. ■ [with obj.] read (something) quickly or cursorily so as to note only the important points: *he sat down and skimmed the report* | [no obj.] *she skimmed through the newspaper*. ■ (**skim over**) deal with or treat (a subject) briefly or superficially.
▶ **n. 1** a thin layer of a substance on the surface of a liquid: *a skim of ice*.
2 an act of reading something quickly or superficially: *a quick skim through the pamphlet*.
– ORIGIN Middle English (in the sense 'remove scum from (a liquid)'): back-formation from **SKIMMER**, or from Old French *escumer*, from *escume* 'scum, foam.'

ski mask ▶ **n.** a protective covering for the head and face, with holes for the eyes, nose, and mouth.

skim·board /ˈskimˌbôrd/ ▶ **n.** a type of surfboard, typically round or short, used for riding shallow water.

skim·mer /ˈskimər/ ▶ **n. 1** a person or thing that skims, in particular: ■ a utensil or device for removing a substance from the surface of a liquid. ■ a device or craft designed to collect oil spilled on water. ■ a hydroplane, hydrofoil, hovercraft, or other vessel that has little or no displacement when traveling.
2 a long-winged seabird related to the terns, feeding by flying low over the water surface with

S

its knifelike extended lower mandible immersed. ● Genus *Rynchops*, family Rynchopidae (or Laridae): three species, one each in Africa, Asia, and America.
3 a flat, broad-brimmed straw hat. ■ informal a close-fitting dress.
4 a broad-bodied dragonfly commonly found at ponds and swamps. It can rest for long periods on a perch, from which it darts out to grab prey. ● Libellulidae and related families: several genera and numerous species, including the **twelve-spotted skimmer** (*Libellula pulchella*).
– ORIGIN Middle English: from Old French *escumoir*, from *escumer* 'skim,' from *escume* 'scum.'

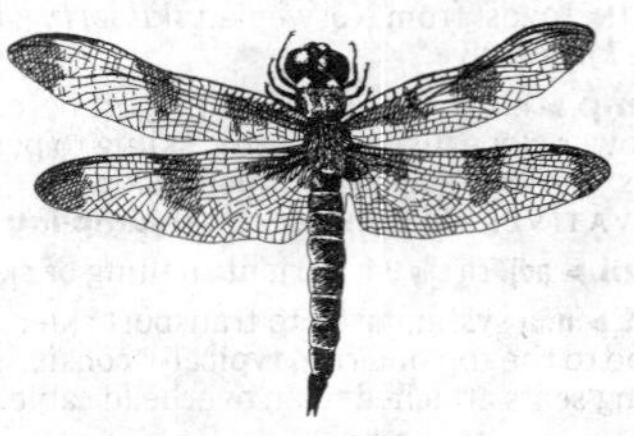
twelve-spotted skimmer

skim milk (also **skimmed milk**) ▶ n. milk from which the cream has been removed.

skim·ming·ton /'skimiNGtən/ ▶ n. historical a procession made through a village intended to bring ridicule on and make an example of a nagging wife or an unfaithful husband.
– PHRASES **ride skimmington** hold such a procession.
– ORIGIN early 17th cent.: perhaps from *skimming-ladle*, used as a thrashing instrument during the procession.

ski·mo·bile /'skēmō,bēl/ ▶ n. a snowmobile.

skimp /skimp/ ▶ v. [no obj.] expend or use less time, money, or material on something than is necessary in an attempt to economize: *don't skimp on insurance when you travel overseas.*
– ORIGIN late 18th cent.: of unknown origin; compare with SCAMP² and SCRIMP.

skimp·y /'skimpē/ ▶ adj. (**skimpier, skimpiest**) (of clothes) short and revealing: *a skimpy dress.* ■ providing or consisting of less than is needed; meager: *my knowledge of music is extremely skimpy.*
– DERIVATIVES **skimp·i·ly** /'skimpəlē/ adv., **skimp·i·ness** n.

skin /skin/ ▶ n. **1** the thin layer of tissue forming the natural outer covering of the body of a person or animal: *I use body lotion to keep my skin soft | a flap of skin.* ■ the skin of a dead animal with or without the fur, used as material for clothing or other items: *is this real crocodile skin?* ■ a container made from the skin of an animal such as a goat, used for holding liquids.
2 an outer layer or covering, in particular: ■ the peel or outer layer of certain fruits or vegetables. ■ the thin outer covering of a sausage. ■ a thin layer forming on the surface of certain hot liquids, such as milk, as they cool. ■ the outermost layer of a structure such as a building or aircraft. ■ Computing a customized graphic user interface for an application or operating system: *music, reviews, and attitude all wrapped up in the skin of a catalog.* ■ (usu. **skins**) a strip of sealskin or other material attached to the underside of a ski to prevent a skier from slipping backward while climbing.
3 informal a skinhead.
4 (usu. **skins**) informal (esp. in jazz) a drum or drum head.
5 [as modifier] informal relating to or denoting pornographic literature or films: *the skin trade.*
▶ v. (**skins, skinning, skinned**) **1** [with obj.] remove the skin from (an animal or a fruit or vegetable). ■ (in hyperbolic use) punish severely: *Dad would skin me alive if I forgot it.* ■ scratch or scrape the skin off (a part of one's body): *he scrambled down from the tree with such haste that he skinned his knees.* ■ informal take money from or swindle (someone).
2 [with obj.] archaic cover with skin: *the wound was skinned, but the strength of his leg was not restored.* ■ [no obj.] (of a wound) form new skin: *the hole in his skull skinned over.*
– PHRASES **be skin and bones** (of a person or animal) be very thin. **by the skin of one's teeth** by a very narrow margin; barely: *I only got away by the skin of my teeth.* [from a misquotation of Job 19:20: "I am escaped with the skin of my teeth" (i.e., and nothing else). Current use reflects a different sense.] **get under someone's skin** informal **1** annoy or irritate someone intensely: *it was the sheer effrontery of them that got under my skin.* **2** fill someone's mind in a compelling and persistent way. **3** reach or display a deep understanding of someone: *movies that get under the skin of our national character.* **give someone (some) skin** informal shake or slap hands together as a gesture or friendship or solidarity. **have a thick** (or **thin**) **skin** be insensitive (or oversensitive) to criticism or insults. **have skin in the game** informal have a personal investment in an organization or undertaking, and therefore a vested interest in its success. **it's no skin off my nose** (or **off my back**) informal (usually spoken with emphasis on "my") used to indicate that one is not offended or adversely affected by something: *it's no skin off my nose if you don't want dessert.* **keep** (or **sleep in**) **a whole skin** archaic escape being wounded or injured. **make someone's skin** (or **flesh**) **crawl** (or **creep**) cause someone to feel fear, horror, or disgust: *a person dying in a fire—doesn't it make your skin crawl?* **save someone's skin** see SAVE¹. **there's more than one way to skin a cat** proverb there's more than one way of achieving one's aim. **under the skin** in reality, as opposed to superficial appearances: *he still believes that all women are goddesses under the skin.*
– DERIVATIVES **skin·less** adj.
– ORIGIN late Old English *scinn*, from Old Norse *skinn*; related to Dutch *schinden* 'flay, peel' and German *schinden*.

skin-deep ▶ adj. not deep or lasting; superficial: *their left-wing attitudes were only skin-deep.*

skin div·ing ▶ n. the action or sport of swimming under water without a diving suit, typically in deep water using an aqualung and flippers.
– DERIVATIVES **skin-dive** v., **skin div·er** n.

skin ef·fect ▶ n. Physics the tendency of a high-frequency alternating current to flow through only the outer layer of a conductor.

skin flick (also **skinflick**) ▶ n. informal a pornographic film.

skin·flint /'skin,flint/ ▶ n. informal a person who spends as little money as possible; a miser.

skin fold ▶ n. a fold of skin and underlying fat formed by pinching, the thickness of which is a measure of nutritional status.

skin·ful /'skinfo͝ol/ ▶ n. [in sing.] informal enough alcoholic drink to make one drunk: *he had a skinful on New Year's Eve.*

skin game ▶ n. informal a rigged gambling game; a swindle.

skin graft ▶ n. a surgical operation in which a piece of healthy skin is transplanted to a new site on the body. ■ a piece of skin transferred in this way.

skin·head /'skin,hed/ ▶ n. a young man of a subculture characterized by close-cropped hair and heavy boots, often perceived as aggressive.

skink /skiNGk/ ▶ n. a smooth-bodied lizard with short or absent limbs, typically burrowing in sandy ground, and occurring throughout tropical and temperate regions. ● Family Scincidae: numerous genera and species.
– ORIGIN late 16th cent.: from French *scinc* or Latin *scincus*, from Greek *skinkos*.

skinned /skind/ ▶ adj. [in combination] having a skin of a specified type: *a fair-skinned woman.*
– PHRASES **be thin-skinned** (or **thick-skinned**) be sensitive (or insensitive) to criticism or insults.

Skin·ner /'skinər/, B. F. (1904–90), US behaviorist psychologist; full name *Burrhus Frederic Skinner*. He promoted the view that the proper aim of psychology should be to predict behavior and hence be able to control it. He applied the results of his studies to the development of programmed learning and to educational practice.

skin·ner /'skinər/ ▶ n. a person who skins animals or prepares skins. ■ a person who deals in animal skins; a furrier.

Skin·ner box /'skinər/ ▶ n. Psychology an apparatus for studying instrumental conditioning in animals (typically rats or pigeons) in which the animal is isolated and provided with a lever or switch that it learns to use to obtain a reward, such as a food pellet, or to avoid a punishment, such as an electric shock.
– ORIGIN 1940s: named after B. F. SKINNER.

skin·ny /'skinē/ ▶ adj. (**skinnier, skinniest**) **1** (of a person or part of their body) very thin: *his skinny arms.*
2 ■ (of an article of clothing) tight-fitting: *a skinny black dress.*
3 informal (of coffee) made with skimmed or semi-skimmed milk: *one skinny latte to go, please.*
▶ n. informal **1** (pl. **skinnies**) a skinny person.
2 (**the skinny**) confidential information on a particular person or topic: *the inside skinny is that he didn't know the deal was in the works.*
– DERIVATIVES **skin·ni·ness** n.

skin·ny-dip ▶ v. [no obj.] informal swim naked.
▶ n. a naked swim.

skin-pop informal ▶ v. [with obj.] inject (a drug, typically a narcotic) subcutaneously.
▶ n. a subcutaneous injection of a drug, typically a narcotic.
– DERIVATIVES **skin-pop·per** n.

skins game ▶ n. a game of competitive golf in which players make wagers on each hole, the pot carrying over to the next hole whenever two players tie.

skint /skint/ ▶ adj. Brit. informal (of a person) having little or no money available: *I'm a bit skint just now.*
– ORIGIN 1920s: variant of colloquial *skinned*, in the same sense, past participle of SKIN.

skin test ▶ n. a test for an immune reaction performed by applying a substance topically or injecting it into the skin.
▶ v. (**skin-test**) [with obj.] (usu. as noun **skin-testing**) perform such a test on (someone).

skin-tight /'skin'tīt/ ▶ adj. (of a garment) very close-fitting.

skip¹ /skip/ ▶ v. (**skips, skipping, skipped**) [no obj.] move along lightly, stepping from one foot to the other with a hop or bounce: *she began to skip down the path.* ■ jump over a rope that is held at both ends by oneself or two other people and turned repeatedly over the head and under the feet, as a game or for exercise. ■ [with obj.] jump over (a rope) in such a way: *the girls had been skipping rope.* ■ [with obj.] jump lightly over: *the children used to skip the puddles.* ■ [with obj.] omit (part of a book that one is reading, or a stage in a sequence that one is following): *the video manual allows the viewer to skip sections he's not interested in* | [no obj.] *she disliked him so much that she skipped over any articles that mentioned him.* ■ [with obj.] fail to attend or deal with as appropriate; miss: *I wanted to skip my English lesson to visit my mother | try not to skip breakfast.* ■ move quickly and in an unmethodical way from one point or subject to another: *Marian skipped halfheartedly through the book.* ■ [with obj.] informal depart quickly and secretly from: *she skipped her home amid rumors of a romance.* ■ informal run away; disappear: *I'm not giving them a chance to skip off again.* ■ (**skip it**) informal abandon an undertaking, conversation, or activity: *after several wrong turns in our journey, we almost decided to skip it.* ■ [with obj.] throw (a stone) so that it ricochets off the surface of water.
▶ n. a light, bouncing step; a skipping movement: *he moved with a strange, dancing skip.* ■ Computing an act of passing over part of a sequence of data or instructions. ■ informal a person who defaults or absconds.
– ORIGIN Middle English: probably of Scandinavian origin.

skip² ▶ n. Brit. a dumpster.

skip³ ▶ n. the captain or director of a team in lawn bowling or curling.
▶ v. (**skips, skipping, skipped**) [with obj.] act as skip of (a side).
– ORIGIN early 19th cent. (originally Scots): abbreviation of SKIPPER¹.

ski pants ▶ plural n. trousers worn for skiing. ■ women's trousers imitating a style of these, made of stretchy fabric with tapering legs and an elastic stirrup under each foot.

skip·jack /'skip,jak/ ▶ n. **1** (also **skipjack tuna**) a small tuna with dark horizontal stripes, widely distributed throughout tropical and temperate seas. Also called BONITO or OCEAN BONITO. ● *Katsuwonus* (or *Euthynnus*) *pelamis*, family Scombridae.
2 another term for CLICK BEETLE.
3 a sloop-rigged sailboat with vertical sides and a flat V-shaped bottom, used chiefly on the east coast of the US.
– ORIGIN early 18th cent.: from the verb SKIP¹ + JACK¹. Sense 1 is from the fish's habit of jumping out of the water; sense 2 and sense 3 arose in the 19th cent.

ski-plane ▶ n. an airplane fitted with skis for landing on snow or ice.

ski pole ▶ n. either of two lightweight poles held by a skier to assist in balance or propulsion.

skip·per¹ /'skipər/ informal ▶ n. the captain of a ship or boat. ■ the captain of a team in a game or sport. ■ the captain of an aircraft.
▶ v. [with obj.] act as captain of.
– ORIGIN late Middle English: from Middle Dutch and Middle Low German *schipper*, from *schip* 'ship.'

skip·per² ▶ n. **1** a person or thing that skips. ■ used in names of small insects and crustaceans that skip or hop.
2 a small brownish mothlike butterfly with rapid darting flight. ● Family Hesperiidae: numerous genera.
3 the Atlantic saury (see SAURY).

skip·pet /'skipit/ ▶ n. chiefly historical a small round wooden box used to preserve documents and seals.
– ORIGIN late Middle English: of unknown origin.

skirl /skərl/ ▶ n. a shrill sound, esp. that of bagpipes.

S

▶ **v.** [no obj.] (of bagpipes) make such a sound.
– ORIGIN late Middle English (as a verb): probably of Scandinavian origin; ultimately imitative.

skir·mish /ˈskərmisн/ ▶ **n.** an episode of irregular or unpremeditated fighting, esp. between small or outlying parts of armies or fleets. ■ a short argument: *there was a skirmish over the budget.*
▶ **v.** [no obj.] (often as noun **skirmishing**) engage in a skirmish: *reports of skirmishing along the border.*
– DERIVATIVES **skir·mish·er** n.
– ORIGIN Middle English (as a verb): from Old French *eskirmiss-*, lengthened stem of *eskirmir*, from a Germanic verb meaning 'defend;' related to SCRIMMAGE.

skirr /skər/ ▶ **v.** [no obj.] rare move rapidly, esp. with a whirring sound: *five dark birds rose skirring away.*
– ORIGIN mid 16th cent.: perhaps related to SCOUR[1] or SCOUR[2].

skirt /skərt/ ▶ **n.** a woman's outer garment fastened around the waist and hanging down around the legs. ■ the part of a coat or dress that hangs below the waist. ■ informal a woman or women regarded as objects of sexual desire: *so, Al, off to chase some skirt?* ■ the curtain that hangs around the base of a hovercraft to contain the air cushion. ■ a surface that conceals or protects the wheels or underside of a vehicle or aircraft. ■ a small flap on a saddle, covering the bar from which the stirrup leather hangs. ■ archaic an edge, border, or extreme part. Compare with OUTSKIRTS.
▶ **v.** [with obj.] go around or past the edge of: *he did not go through the city but skirted it.* ■ be situated along or around the edge of: *the fields that skirted the highway were full of cattle.* ■ [no obj.] (**skirt along/around**) go along or around (something) rather than directly through or across it: *the river valley skirts along the northern slopes of the hills.* ■ attempt to ignore; avoid dealing with: *there was a subject she was always skirting* | [no obj.] *the treaty skirted around the question of political cooperation.*
– DERIVATIVES **skirt·ed** adj. [in combination] *a full-skirted dress.*
– ORIGIN Middle English: from Old Norse *skyrta* 'shirt'; compare with synonymous Old English *scyrte*, also with SHORT. The verb dates from the early 17th cent.

skirt-chas·er ▶ **n.** informal a man who pursues women amorously and is casual in his affections; a womanizer.

skirt·ing /ˈskərtiNG/ (also **skirting board**) ▶ **n.** chiefly Brit. a baseboard.

skirt steak ▶ **n.** a beefsteak cut from the diaphragm muscle.

ski run ▶ **n.** a track on a slope for skiing.

skit /skit/ ▶ **n.** a short comedy sketch or piece of humorous writing, esp. a parody: *a skit on daytime magazine programs.*
– ORIGIN early 18th cent. (in the sense 'satirical comment or attack'): related to the rare verb *skit* 'move lightly and rapidly,' perhaps from Old Norse (compare with *skjóta* 'shoot').

ski tour·ing ▶ **n.** chiefly Brit. cross-country skiing.
– DERIVATIVES **ski tour** n., **ski tour·er** n.

ski tow ▶ **n.** **1** a type of ski lift, with a moving rope or with bars suspended from a moving overhead cable.
2 a tow rope for waterskiers.

skit·ter /ˈskitər/ ▶ **v.** [no obj.] **1** move lightly and quickly or hurriedly: *the girls skittered up the stairs* | figurative *her mind skittered back to that day at the office.*
2 [with obj.] draw (bait) jerkily across the surface of the water as a technique in fishing.
– ORIGIN mid 19th cent.: apparently a frequentative of *skite* 'move rapidly,' perhaps of Norse origin.

skit·ter·y /ˈskitərē/ ▶ **adj.** restless; skittish: *a skittery horse.*

skit·tish /ˈskitisн/ ▶ **adj.** (of an animal, esp. of a horse) excitable or easily scared: *a skittish chestnut mare* | figurative *skittish investors withdrew their money from equity markets.* ■ (of a person) playfully frivolous or unpredictable: *my skittish and immature mother.*
– DERIVATIVES **skit·tish·ly** adv., **skit·tish·ness** n.
– ORIGIN late Middle English: perhaps from the rare verb *skit* 'move lightly and rapidly.'

skit·tle /ˈskitl/ ▶ **n.** **1** (**skittles**) [treated as sing.] a game played, chiefly in Britain, with wooden pins, typically nine in number, set up at the end of an alley to be bowled down with a wooden ball or disk.
2 a pin used in the game of skittles.
– ORIGIN mid 17th cent.: of unknown origin. The word *skyttel* exists in Danish and Swedish in the sense 'shuttle, child's marble,' but there is no evidence to connect this with the game of skittles.

skive[1] /skīv/ Brit. informal ▶ **v.** [no obj.] avoid work or a duty by staying away or leaving early; shirk: *I skived off school* | [with obj.] *she used to skive lessons.*
▶ **n.** [in sing.] an instance of avoiding work or a duty in this way. ■ an easy option.
– DERIVATIVES **skiv·er** n.
– ORIGIN early 20th cent.: perhaps from French *esquiver* 'slink away.'

skive[2] ▶ **v.** [with obj.] technical pare (the edge of a piece of leather or other material) so as to reduce its thickness.
– ORIGIN early 19th cent.: from Old Norse *skífa*; related to SHIVE.

skiv·vy /ˈskivē/ ▶ **n.** (pl. **skivvies**) **1** (**skivvies**) trademark underwear, esp. a set consisting of undershirt and underpants, or just the underpants. [originally a US Navy term.]
2 (also **skivvy shirt**) a lightweight high-necked, long-sleeved garment. ■ an undershirt or T-shirt.
3 Brit. informal a low-ranking female domestic servant. ■ a person doing work that is poorly paid and considered menial.
▶ **v.** (**skivvies, skivvying, skivvied**) [no obj.] informal do menial household tasks; work as a skivvy.
– ORIGIN early 20th cent.: of unknown origin.

ski·wear /ˈskē,we(ə)r/ ▶ **n.** clothing designed or suitable for skiing.

skoal /skōl/ (also **skol**) ▶ **exclam.** used to express friendly feelings toward one's companions before drinking.
– ORIGIN early 17th cent. (a Scots use): from Danish and Norwegian *skaal*, Swedish *skål*, from Old Norse *skál* 'bowl'; perhaps introduced through the visit of James VI to Denmark in 1589. Compare with SCALE[2].

Sko·kie /ˈskōkē/ a residential and industrial village in northeastern Illinois, northwest of Chicago; pop. 66,620 (est. 2008).

skoosh /sko͝osн/ (also **scoosh**) ▶ **v.** Scottish squirt or splash (liquid).
▶ **n.** a splash or squirt of liquid.
– ORIGIN imitative.

Skop·je /ˈskôpye/ the capital of the republic of Macedonia, located in the northern part of the country, on the Vardar River; pop. 522,200 (est. 2006).

skort /skôrt/ ▶ **n.** shorts with full legs and a central flap in front.
– ORIGIN blend of SKIRT and *short* (see SHORTS).

skosh /skōsн/ ▶ **n.** informal a small amount; a little.
– PHRASES **a skosh** somewhat; slightly: *it's a skosh more formal than one might like.*
– ORIGIN 1950s: from Japanese *sukoshi.*

Skr. ▶ **abbr.** Sanskrit.

Skrya·bin /skrēˈäbən/ variant spelling of SCRIABIN.

Skt. ▶ **abbr.** Sanskrit.

SKU /skyo͞o/ ▶ **abbr.** stock-keeping unit.

sku·a /ˈskyo͞oə/ ▶ **n.** a large brownish predatory seabird related to the gulls, pursuing other birds to make them disgorge fish they have caught. ● Family Stercorariidae: genera *Catharacta* (four larger species) and *Stercorarius* (three smaller species). See also JAEGER.
– ORIGIN late 17th cent.: modern Latin, from Faroese *skúvur*, from Old Norse *skúfr* (apparently imitative).

skul·dug·ger·y /skəlˈdəgərē/ (also **skullduggery**) ▶ **n.** underhanded or unscrupulous behavior; trickery: *a firm that investigates commercial skulduggery.*
– ORIGIN mid 19th cent.: alteration of Scots *sculduddery*, of unknown origin.

skulk /skəlk/ ▶ **v.** [no obj.] keep out of sight, typically with a sinister or cowardly motive: *don't skulk outside the door like a spy!* ■ [with adverbial of direction] move stealthily or furtively: *he spent most of his time skulking about the corridors.* ■ shirk duty.
▶ **n.** a group of foxes.
– DERIVATIVES **skulk·er** n.
– ORIGIN Middle English: of Scandinavian origin; compare with Norwegian *skulka* 'lurk,' and Danish *skulke*, Swedish *skolka* 'shirk.'

skull /skəl/ ▶ **n.** a framework of bone or cartilage enclosing the brain of a vertebrate; the skeleton of a person's or animal's head. ■ informal a person's head or brain: *a skull crammed with too many thoughts.*
▶ **v.** [with obj.] hit (someone) on the head.
– PHRASES **out of one's skull** informal **1** out of one's mind; crazy. **2** very drunk. **skull and crossbones** a representation of a skull with two thigh bones crossed below it as an emblem of piracy or death.
– DERIVATIVES **skulled** adj. [in combination] *long-skulled.*
– ORIGIN Middle English *scolle*; of unknown origin; compare with Old Norse *skoltr.*

skull·cap /ˈskəl,kap/ ▶ **n.** **1** a small close-fitting cap without a brim.
2 the top part of the skull.
3 a widely distributed plant of the mint family, whose tubular flowers have a helmet-shaped cup at the base. ● Genus *Scutellaria*, family Labiatae.

skullcap 1

skull ses·sion ▶ **n.** informal a discussion or conference, esp. to discuss policies, tactics, and maneuvers.

skunk /skəNGk/ ▶ **n.** a cat-sized American mammal of the weasel family, with distinctive black-and-white-striped fur. When threatened it squirts a fine spray of foul-smelling irritant liquid from its anal glands toward its attacker. ● *Mephitis* and other genera, family Mustelidae: several species, in particular the **striped skunk** (*M. mephitis*). ■ the fur of the skunk. ■ informal a contemptible person.
▶ **v.** [with obj.] informal **1** defeat (someone) overwhelmingly in a game or contest, esp. by preventing them from scoring at all.
2 dated fail to pay (a bill or creditor).
– ORIGIN mid 17th cent.: from Massachusett *squunck*; cognate forms occur in many other American Indian languages.

skunk cab·bage ▶ **n.** a North American plant of the arum family, the flower of which has a distinctive unpleasant smell. ● Two species in the family Araceae: the western **yellow skunk cabbage** (*Lysichitum americanum*), with a stalked yellow flower, and the eastern *Symplocarpus foetidus*, with a greenish purple flower.

skunk cabbage

skunk·works /ˈskəNGk,wərks/ (also **skunk works**) ▶ **plural n.** [usu. treated as sing.] informal an experimental laboratory or department of a company or institution, typically smaller than and independent of its main research division.
– ORIGIN 1970s: allegedly from an association with the *Skonk Works*, an illegal still in the Li'l Abner comic strip.

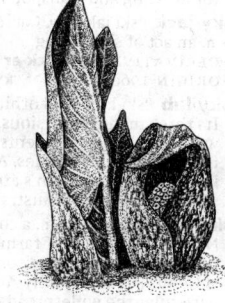

skunk·y ▶ **adj.** **1** like a skunk.
2 disagreeably tainted: *skunky beer.*

skut·te·rud·ite /ˈskətə,rədīt/ ▶ **n.** a metallic-gray mineral, typically forming cubic or octahedral crystals, consisting chiefly of an arsenide of cobalt and nickel.
– ORIGIN mid 19th cent.: from *Skutterud* (now Skotterud), a village in southeastern Norway, + -ITE[1].

sky /skī/ ▶ **n.** (pl. **skies**) (often **the sky**) the region of the atmosphere and outer space seen from the earth: *hundreds of stars shining in the sky* | *Jillson had never seen so much sky.* ■ literary heaven; heavenly power: *the just vengeance of incensed skies.*
▶ **v.** (**skies, skying, skied**) [with obj.] informal hit (a ball) high into the air: *he skied his tee shot.* ■ hang (a picture) very high on a wall, esp. in an exhibition.
– PHRASES **out of a clear blue sky** see BLUE. **the sky's the limit** informal there is practically no limit (to something such as a price that can be charged or the opportunities afforded to someone). **to the skies** very highly; enthusiastically: *he wrote to his sister praising Lizzie to the skies.*
– DERIVATIVES **sky·ey** /ˈskīē/ adj., **sky·less** adj.
– ORIGIN Middle English (also in the plural denoting clouds): from Old Norse *ský* 'cloud.' The verb dates from the early 19th cent.

sky blue ▶ **n.** a bright clear blue.

sky·box /ˈskī,bäks/ ▶ **n.** a luxurious enclosed seating area located high in a sports arena.

sky·bridge /ˈskī,brij/ ▶ **n.** another term for SKYWALK.

sky bur·i·al ▶ **n.** a Tibetan funeral ritual involving the exposure of a dismembered corpse to sacred vultures.

sky·cap /ˈskī,kap/ ▶ **n.** a porter at an airport.

sky-clad ▶ **adj.** naked (used esp. in connection with modern pagan ritual).
– ORIGIN early 20th cent.: probably a translation of Sanskrit *Digāmbara*, denoting a Jain sect.

sky·div·ing /ˈskī,dīviNG/ ▶ **n.** the sport of jumping from an aircraft and performing acrobatic maneuvers in the air during free fall before landing by parachute.
– DERIVATIVES **sky·dive** v., **sky·div·er** n.

PRONUNCIATION KEY ə *ago, up*; ər *over, fur*; a *hat*; ā *ate*; ä *car*; e *let*; ē *see*; i *fit*; ī *by*; NG *sing*; ō *go*; ô *law, for*; oi *toy*; o͝o *good*; o͞o *goo*; ou *out*; TH *thin*; TH *then*; ZH *vision*

Skye /skī/ a mountainous island in the Inner Hebrides, linked to the west coast of Scotland by a bridge; chief town, Portree.

Skye ter·ri·er ▶ **n.** a small long-haired terrier of a slate-colored or beige-colored Scottish breed.

sky·flow·er /ˈskīˌflou(-ə)r/ ▶ **n.** a shrub of the verbena family, with clusters of lilac flowers and yellow berries, native to Central and South America. ● *Duranta erecta*, family Verbenaceae.

sky·glow /ˈskīˌglō/ ▶ **n.** brightness of the night sky in a built-up area as a result of light pollution.

sky-high ▶ **adv. & adj.** as if reaching the sky; very high: [as adv.] *they saved a president from being blown sky-high.* ■ at or to a very high level; very great: [as adj.] *sky-high premiums.*

sky·hook /ˈskīˌho͝ok/ ▶ **n. 1** dated an imaginary or fanciful device by which something could be suspended in the air. ■ a proposed cable or other structure reaching from the earth's surface to a satellite, which could be used for transporting spacecraft or other items into space.
2 Climbing a small flattened hook, with an eye for attaching a rope, fixed temporarily into a rock face.
3 Basketball a very high-arcing hook shot.
4 a helicopter equipped with a steel line and hook for hoisting and transporting heavy objects.

sky·jack /ˈskīˌjak/ ▶ **v.** [with obj.] hijack (an aircraft).
▶ **n.** an act of skyjacking.
– DERIVATIVES **sky·jack·er n.**
– ORIGIN 1960s: blend of **SKY** and **HIJACK**.

Sky·lab /ˈskīˌlab/ a US orbiting space laboratory. Its three manned missions, all launched in 1973, were used for experiments in zero gravity and for astrophysical studies. Abandoned in 1974, it re-entered the earth's atmosphere in 1979, scattering debris in Australia and the Indian Ocean.

sky·lark /ˈskīˌlärk/ ▶ **n.** a common Eurasian and North African lark of farmland and open country, noted for its prolonged song during hovering flight. ● Genus *Alauda*, family Alaudidae: two species, in particular the widespread *A. arvensis*.
▶ **v.** [no obj.] pass time by playing tricks or practical jokes; indulge in horseplay: *he was skylarking with a friend when he fell into a pile of boxes.* [late 17th cent. (originally in nautical use): by association with the verb **LARK**[2].]

sky·light /ˈskīˌlīt/ ▶ **n.** a window installed in a roof or ceiling.

sky·light·ed /ˈskīˌlītid/ (also **skylit** /ˈskīˌlit/) ▶ **adj.** fitted with or lit by a skylight or skylights: *skylighted rooms | hunters who sit at the crest of a hill allow the turkey to see them skylighted against the horizon.*

sky·line /ˈskīˌlīn/ ▶ **n.** an outline of land and buildings defined against the sky: *the skyline of the city.*

sky pi·lot ▶ **n.** informal a member of the clergy, esp. a military chaplain.

skyr /ski(ə)r/ ▶ **n.** an Icelandic dish consisting of curdled milk.
– ORIGIN Icelandic.

sky·rock·et /ˈskīˌräkit/ ▶ **n.** a rocket designed to explode high in the air as a signal or firework.
▶ **v.** (**skyrockets, skyrocketing, skyrocketed**) [no obj.] informal (of a price, rate, or amount) increase very steeply or rapidly: *the cost of housing has skyrocketed.*

S

sky·sail /ˈskīˌsāl/ ▶ **n.** a light sail above the royal.

sky·scrap·er /ˈskīˌskrāpər/ ▶ **n. 1** a very tall building of many stories.
2 another term for **SKYSAIL**.

sky·surf·ing /ˈskīˌsərfiNG/ ▶ **n.** the sport of jumping from an aircraft and surfing through the air on a board before landing by parachute.

sky·walk /ˈskīˌwôk/ ▶ **n.** an enclosed overhead walkway between buildings.

sky·ward /ˈskīwərd/ ▶ **adv.** (also **skywards**) toward the sky: *flames were now shooting skyward.*
▶ **adj.** moving or directed toward the sky: *the city was heavily guarded by skyward laser batteries.*

sky·watch /ˈskīˌwäCH/ ▶ **v.** [no obj.] informal observe or monitor the sky, esp. for heavenly bodies or aircraft.
– DERIVATIVES **sky·watch·er n.**

sky wave ▶ **n.** a radio wave reflected from the ionosphere.

sky·way /ˈskīˌwā/ ▶ **n. 1** a recognized route followed by aircraft.
2 another term for **SKYWALK**.
3 an elevated highway.

sky·writ·ing /ˈskīˌrītiNG/ ▶ **n.** words in the form of smoke trails made by an airplane, esp. for advertising.
– DERIVATIVES **sky·writ·er** /-tər/ **n.**

SL ▶ **abbr.** source language.

s.l. ▶ **abbr.** ■ salvage loss. ■ (also **sl.**) (in a bibliography) without place (of publication noted). [from Latin *sine loco*.]

slab /slab/ ▶ **n.** a large, thick, flat piece of stone, concrete, or wood, typically rectangular: *paving slabs | she settled on a slab of rock.* ■ a large, thick slice or piece of cake, bread, chocolate, etc.: *a slab of bread and cheese.* ■ Climbing a large, smooth, steep body of rock. ■ an outer piece of timber sawn from a log. ■ a table used for laying a body on in a morgue.
▶ **v.** (**slabs, slabbing, slabbed**) [with obj.] (often as noun **slabbing**) remove slabs from (a log or tree) to prepare it for sawing into planks.
– DERIVATIVES **slabbed adj., slab·by adj.**
– ORIGIN Middle English: of unknown origin.

slab av·a·lanche ▶ **n.** an avalanche formed by a sheet of snow breaking loose.

slab·ber /ˈslabər/ chiefly Scottish Irish ▶ **v.** [no obj.] dribble at the mouth; slaver: *he was slabbering like a child.*
– ORIGIN mid 16th cent. (in the sense 'dribble on'): related to dialect *slab* 'muddy place, puddle.'

slack[1] /slak/ ▶ **adj. 1** not taut or held tightly in position; loose: *a slack rope | her mouth went slack.*
2 (of business) characterized by a lack of work or activity; quiet: *business was rather slack.* ■ slow or sluggish: *they were working at a slack pace.* ■ having or showing laziness or negligence: *slack accounting procedures.*
3 (of a tide) neither ebbing nor flowing: *soon the water will become slack, and the tide will turn.*
▶ **n. 1** the part of a rope or line that is not held taut; the loose or unused part: *I picked up the rod and wound in the slack.*
2 (**slacks**) casual trousers.
3 informal a spell of inactivity or laziness: *he slept deeply, refreshed by a little slack in the daily routine.*
▶ **v.** [with obj.] **1** loosen (something, esp. a rope). ■ reduce the intensity or speed of (something); slacken: *the horse slacked his pace.* ■ [no obj.] (**slack off**) decrease in quantity or intensity: *the flow of blood slacked off.* ■ [no obj.] informal work slowly or lazily: *she reprimanded her girls if they were slacking.* ■ [no obj.] (**slack up**) slow down: *the animal doesn't slack up until he reaches the trees.*
2 slake (lime).
▶ **adv.** loosely: *their heads were hanging slack in attitudes of despair.*
– PHRASES **cut someone some slack** informal allow someone some leeway in their conduct. **take** (or **pick**) **up the slack 1** use up a surplus or improve the use of resources to avoid an undesirable lull in business: *as domestic demand starts to flag, foreign demand will help pick up the slack.* **2** pull on the loose end or part of a rope in order to make it taut.
– DERIVATIVES **slack·ly adv., slack·ness n.**
– ORIGIN Old English *slæc* 'inclined to be lazy, unhurried,' of Germanic origin; related to Latin *laxus* 'loose.'

slack[2] ▶ **n.** coal dust or small pieces of coal.
– ORIGIN late Middle English: probably from Low German or Dutch.

slack·en /ˈslakən/ ▶ **v.** make or become slack: [with obj.] *he slackened his grip | the joints can be tightened and slackened off again* | [no obj.] *the pace never slackens.*

slack·er /ˈslakər/ ▶ **n.** informal a person who avoids work or effort. ■ a person who evades military service. ■ a young person (esp. in the 1990s) of a subculture characterized by apathy and aimlessness.

slack wa·ter ▶ **n.** the state of the tide when it is turning, esp. at low tide.

slag /slag/ ▶ **n. 1** stony waste matter separated from metals during the smelting or refining of ore. ■ similar material produced by a volcano; scoria.
2 Brit. informal, derogatory a promiscuous woman.
▶ **v.** (**slags, slagging, slagged**) [no obj.] (usu. as noun **slagging**) produce deposits of slag.
– DERIVATIVES **slag·gy adj.** (**slaggier, slaggiest**).
– ORIGIN mid 16th cent.: from Middle Low German *slagge*, perhaps from *slagen* 'strike,' with reference to fragments formed by hammering.

slag heap ▶ **n.** a hill or area of refuse from a mine or industrial site.

slain /slān/ past participle of **SLAY**[1].

slake /slāk/ ▶ **v.** [with obj.] **1** quench or satisfy (one's thirst): *slake your thirst with some lemonade.* ■ satisfy (desires): *restaurants worked to slake the Italian obsession with food.*
2 combine (quicklime) with water to produce calcium hydroxide.
– ORIGIN Old English *slacian* 'become less eager,' also 'slacken,' from the adjective *slæc* 'slack'; compare with Dutch *slaken* 'diminish, relax.'

slaked lime ▶ **n.** see **LIME**[1].

sla·lom /ˈsläləm/ ▶ **n.** a ski race down a winding course marked by flags or poles. ■ a sporting event on water with a winding course marked by obstacles, typically a canoe or sailing race.
▶ **v.** [no obj.] move or race in a winding path, avoiding obstacles: *she drove with reckless speed, slaloming in and out of the stalled cars.*
– DERIVATIVES **sla·lom·er n.**
– ORIGIN 1920s: from Norwegian *slalåm*, literally 'sloping track.'

slam[1] /slam/ ▶ **v.** (**slams, slamming, slammed**) [with obj.] shut (a door, window, or lid) forcefully and loudly: *he slams the door behind him as he leaves.* ■ [no obj.] be closed forcefully and loudly: *she heard a car door slam.* ■ push or put somewhere with great force: *Charlie slammed down the phone.* ■ [no obj.] (**slam into**) crash into; collide heavily with: *the car mounted the sidewalk, slamming into a lamppost.* ■ informal hit (something) with great force in a particular direction: *he slammed a shot into the net.* ■ put (something) into action suddenly or forcefully: *I slammed on the brakes.* ■ [no obj.] move violently or loudly: *he slammed out of the room.* ■ (usu. **be slammed**) informal criticize severely: *his efforts to slam the president destroyed his own campaign.* ■ informal score points against or gain a victory over (someone) easily: *the Blue Devils slammed Kansas to win the title.* ■ (often as noun **slamming**) (of a telephone company) take over the account of (a telephone customer) without their permission.
▶ **n. 1** [usu. in sing.] a loud bang caused by the forceful shutting of something such as a door: *the back door closed with a slam.*
2 (usu. **the slam**) informal prison. [abbr. of **SLAMMER**.]
3 a poetry contest in which competitors recite their entries and are judged by members of the audience,

Great Pyramid at Giza, Egypt
481 feet
2570 BC

Chartres Cathedral, France
378 / 350 feet
1230

Leaning Tower of Pisa, Italy
181 feet
1372

Statue of Liberty, New York Harbor
301 feet
1884

Washington Monument, Washington, DC
555 feet
1884

Eiffel Tower, Paris
984 feet
1889

Empire State Building, New Yo
1,250 feet
1931

skyscrapers and other tall structures

the winner being elected after several elimination rounds. [of unknown origin.]
– ORIGIN late 17th cent.: probably of Scandinavian origin; compare with Old Norse *slam(b)ra*.

slam² ▶ **n.** Bridge a grand slam (all thirteen tricks) or small slam (twelve tricks), for which bonus points are scored if bid and made.
– ORIGIN early 17th cent. (originally the name of a card game): perhaps from obsolete *slampant* 'trickery.'

slam-bang informal ▶ **adj.** exciting and energetic: *a slam-bang action cartoon.* ■ with no niceties, subtleties, or restraints; direct and forceful: *the slam-bang world of daily journalism.*
▶ **adv.** suddenly and forcefully or violently: *I walked slam-bang into this character.*

slam-danc·ing ▶ **n.** a form of dancing to rock music in which the dancers deliberately collide with one another.
– DERIVATIVES **slam-dance v.**, **slam danc·er n.**

slam dunk ▶ **n.** Basketball a shot in which a player thrusts the ball forcefully down through the basket. ■ [usu. as modifier] informal something reliable or unfailing; a foregone conclusion or certainty: *a movie predicted to be the season's one slam-dunk hit.*
▶ **v. (slam-dunk)** [with obj.] thrust (the ball) forcefully down through the basket. ■ informal defeat or dismiss decisively: *they continue to slam-dunk every proposal we make.*

slam·mer /'slamər/ ▶ **n. 1** (usu. **the slammer**) informal prison.
2 a person who deliberately collides with others when slam-dancing.

s.l.a.n. ▶ **abbr.** without place, year, or name of publication. [from Latin *sine loco, anno, vel nomine*.]

slan·der /'slandər/ ▶ **n.** Law the action or crime of making a false spoken statement damaging to a person's reputation: *he is suing the TV network for slander*. Compare with LIBEL. ■ a false and malicious spoken statement: *I've had just about all I can stomach of your slanders.*
▶ **v.** [with obj.] make false and damaging statements about (someone): *they were accused of slandering the head of state.*
– DERIVATIVES **slan·der·er n.**
– ORIGIN Middle English: from Old French *esclandre*, alteration of *escandle*, from late Latin *scandalum* (see SCANDAL).

slan·der·ous /'slandərəs/ ▶ **adj.** (of a spoken statement) false and malicious: *slanderous allegations.*
– DERIVATIVES **slan·der·ous·ly** /-rəslē/ **adv.**

slang /slaNG/ ▶ **n.** a type of language that consists of words and phrases that are regarded as very informal, are more common in speech than writing, and are typically restricted to a particular context or group of people: *grass is slang for marijuana | army slang.*
▶ **v.** [with obj.] informal attack (someone) using abusive language: *he watched ideological groups slanging one another.*
– ORIGIN mid 18th cent.: of unknown origin.

slang·y /'slaNGē/ ▶ **adj.** (**slangier**, **slangiest**) using or denoting slang: *the style is so slangy as to be incomprehensible | a slangy, stand-up comedian.*
– DERIVATIVES **slang·i·ly** /'slaNGgəlē/ **adv.**, **slang·i·ness n.**

slant /slant/ ▶ **v.** slope or lean in a particular direction; diverge or cause to diverge from the vertical or horizontal: [no obj.] *a plowed field slanted up to the skyline* | [with obj.] *slant your skis as you turn to send up a curtain of water.* ■ (esp. of light or shadow) fall in an oblique direction: *the early sun slanted across the mountains.* ■ [with obj.] (often as adj. **slanted**) present or view (information) from a particular angle, esp. in a biased or unfair way: *slanted news coverage.*
▶ **n. 1** [in sing.] a sloping position: *the hedge grew at a* **slant** | *cut flower stems* **on the slant**.
2 a particular point of view from which something is seen or presented: *a new* **slant on** *science.*
▶ **adj.** [attrib.] sloping: *slant pockets.*
– ORIGIN late Middle English: variant of dialect *slent*, of Scandinavian origin, probably influenced by ASLANT.

slant·ing /'slantiNG/ ▶ **adj.** positioned or directed in a sloping or oblique direction: *the slanting beams of the roof | the slanting rays of the evening sun.*

slant·wise /'slant,wīz/ ▶ **adj. & adv.** at an angle or in a sloping direction: [as adj.] *a slantwise glance* | [as adv.] *the bird veers and drops slantwise toward the tree.*

slap /slap/ ▶ **v.** (**slaps**, **slapping**, **slapped**) [with obj.] hit (someone or something) with the palm of one's hand or a flat object: *my sister slapped my face.* ■ [no obj.] hit against or into something with the sound of such an action: *water* **slapped against** *the boat.* ■ (**slap someone down**) informal reprimand someone forcefully. ■ put or apply (something) somewhere quickly, carelessly, or forcefully: *slap on a bit of makeup.* ■ (**slap something on**) informal impose a fine or other penalty on: *the government had slapped an embargo on imports.*
▶ **n.** a blow with the palm of the hand or a flat object: *he gave her a slap across her cheek.* ■ a sound made or as if made by such an action: *she heard the slap of water against the harbor wall.*
▶ **adv.** informal suddenly and directly, esp. with great force: *storming out of her room, she ran slap into Luke.* ■ exactly; right: *we passed slap through the middle of an enemy armored unit.*
– PHRASES **slap in the face** an unexpected rejection or affront. **slap someone around** beat or hit someone repeatedly: *The teachers knew to watch out to make sure none of the other kids got slapped around | The people responsible need to be slapped around a little and forced to correct things.* **slap on the back** congratulations or commendations: *they deserve a hearty slap on the back for their efforts.* **slap someone on the back** congratulate someone. **slap on the wrist** a mild reprimand or punishment.
– ORIGIN late Middle English (as a verb): probably imitative. The noun dates from the mid 17th cent.

slap and tick·le ▶ **n.** Brit. informal physical amorous play.

slap bass /bās/ ▶ **n.** a style of playing double bass or bass guitar by pulling and releasing the strings sharply against the fingerboard, used for effect in jazz or popular music.
– DERIVATIVES **slap bass·ist** /-ist/ **n.**

slap·dash /'slap,dasH/ ▶ **adj.** done too hurriedly and carelessly: *he gave a slapdash performance.*
▶ **adv.** dated hurriedly and carelessly.

slap·hap·py /'slap,hapē/ ▶ **adj.** informal **1** casual or flippant in a cheerful and often irresponsible way: *he possessed slaphappy courage.* ■ (of an action or operation) unmethodical; poorly thought out: *slaphappy surveying methods.*
2 dazed or stupefied from happiness or relief: *she's a bit slaphappy after such a narrow escape.*

slap·jack /'slap,jak/ ▶ **n.** a pancake.

slap shot ▶ **n.** Ice Hockey a hard shot made by raising the stick about waist-high before striking the puck with a sharp slapping motion.

slap·stick /'slap,stik/ ▶ **n.** comedy based on deliberately clumsy actions and humorously embarrassing events: [as modifier] *slapstick humor.* ■ a device consisting of two flexible pieces of wood joined together at one end, used by clowns and in pantomime to produce a loud slapping noise.

slap-up ▶ **adj.** [attrib.] informal, chiefly Brit. (of a meal or celebration) large and sumptuous: *a slap-up dinner.*

slash¹ /slasH/ ▶ **v.** [with obj.] cut (something) with a violent sweeping movement, typically using a knife or sword: *a tire was slashed on my car | they cut and* **slashed their way** *to the river* | [no obj.] *the man* **slashed at** *him with a sword.* ■ informal reduce (a price, quantity, etc.) greatly: *the workforce has been slashed by 2,000.* ■ archaic lash, whip, or thrash severely. ■ archaic crack (a whip). ■ archaic criticize (someone or something) severely.
▶ **n. 1** a cut made with a wide, sweeping stroke: *the man took a mighty slash at his head with a large sword.* ■ a wound or gash made by such an action: *he staggered over with a crimson slash across his temple.* ■ a bright patch or flash of color or light: *yellow and gold foliage, with the odd* **slash of** *red.*
2 an oblique stroke (/) in print or writing, used between alternatives (e.g., *and/or*), in fractions (e.g., *3/4*), in ratios (e.g., *miles/day*), or between separate elements of a text. ■ [as modifier] denoting or belonging to a genre of fiction, chiefly published in fanzines, in which any of various male pairings from the popular media is portrayed as having a homosexual relationship. [1980s: from the use of an oblique stroke to link adjoining names or initials (as in *Kirk/Spock* and *K/S*.]
3 debris resulting from the felling or destruction of trees.
– ORIGIN late Middle English: perhaps imitative, or from Old French *esclachier* 'break in pieces.' The noun dates from the late 16th cent.

slash² ▶ **n.** a tract of swampy ground, esp. in a coastal region.
– ORIGIN mid 17th cent.: of uncertain origin.

slash-and-burn ▶ **adj.** [attrib.] of, relating to, or denoting a method of agriculture in which existing vegetation is cut down and burned off before new seeds are sown, typically used as a method for clearing forest land for farming. ■ aggressive and merciless: *her slash-and-burn campaigning style.*

slash·er /'slasHər/ ▶ **n.** informal **1** a person or thing that slashes.
2 (also **slasher film** or **slasher movie**, etc.) a horror movie, esp. one in which victims (typically women or teenagers) are slashed with knives and razors.

slash·ing /'slasHiNG/ ▶ **adj.** [attrib.] informal vigorously incisive or effective: *a slashing magazine attack on her.*

slash pine ▶ **n.** a fast-growing, long-needled pine found in low-lying coastal areas (slashes) of the southeastern US, commonly harvested for timber.
● *Pinus elliottii*, family Pinaceae.

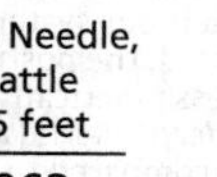
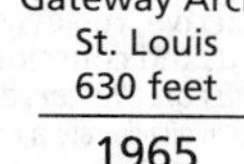
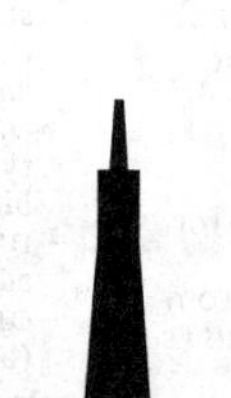
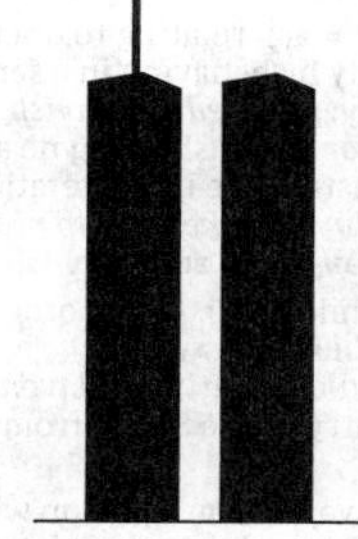
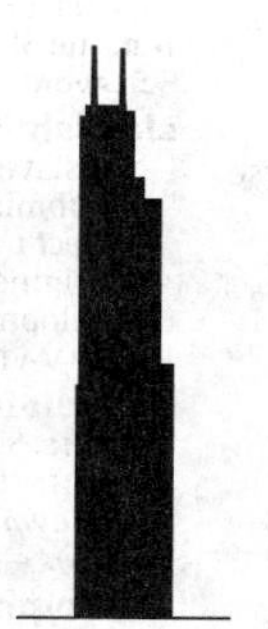

Space Needle, Seattle 605 feet 1962

Gateway Arch, St. Louis 630 feet 1965

Transamerica Pyramid, San Francisco 853 feet 1972

Former World Trade Center, New York 1,368 / 1,362 feet 1972

Sears Tower, Chicago 1,454 feet 1974

CN Tower, Toronto 1,815 feet 1976

Petronas Towers, Kuala Lumpur 1,482 feet 1997

skyscrapers and other tall structures

slash pock·et ▶ **n.** a pocket set in a garment with a slit for the opening.

slat /slat/ ▶ **n.** a thin, narrow piece of wood, plastic, or metal, esp. one of a series that overlap or fit into each other, as in a fence or a Venetian blind.
– DERIVATIVES **slat·ted adj.**
– ORIGIN late Middle English (in the sense 'roofing slate'): shortening of Old French *esclat* 'splinter,' from *esclater* 'to split;' related to ÉCLAT, SLATE. The current sense dates from the mid 18th cent.

slate /slāt/ ▶ **n. 1** a fine-grained gray, green, or bluish metamorphic rock easily split into smooth, flat pieces. ■ a flat piece of such rock used as roofing material.
2 a flat piece of slate used for writing on, typically framed in wood, formerly used in schools. ■ a list of candidates for election to a post or office, typically a group sharing a set of political views: *another slate of candidates will be picked for the state convention.* ■ a range of something offered: *the company has revealed details of a $60 million slate of film productions.* ■ a board showing the identifying details of a take of a motion picture, which is held in front of the camera at its beginning and end.
3 [usu. as modifier] a bluish-gray color: *suits of slate gray.*
▶ **v.** [with obj.] **1** cover (something, esp. a roof) with slates.
2 Brit. informal criticize severely: *his work was slated by the critics.*
3 (usu. **be slated**) schedule; plan: *renovations are slated for late June* | [with obj.] *construction is slated to begin late next year.* ■ (usu. **be slated**) nominate (someone) as a candidate for an office or post: *I understand that I am being slated for promotion.*
4 identify (a movie take) using a slate.
– PHRASES **wipe the slate clean** see WIPE.
– DERIVATIVES **slat·y adj.**
– ORIGIN Middle English *sclate, sklate*, shortening of Old French *esclate*, feminine, synonymous with *esclat* 'piece broken off' (see SLAT). Sense 3 of the verb of the verb arose from the practice of noting a name on a writing slate.

Sla·ter /'slātər/, Samuel (1768–1835), US inventor and industrialist; born in England. He emigrated from England and, after building a technologically advanced spinning mill from memory in Rhode Island in 1793, he set up his own mills in New England.

slat·er /'slātər/ ▶ **n. 1** a person who slates roofs for a living.
2 a wood louse or similar isopod. ● Several species in the order Isopoda. See also SEA SLATER.

slath·er /'slaT͟Hər/ ▶ **v.** [with obj.] informal spread or smear (a substance) thickly or liberally: *slather on some tanning lotion* | *biscuits slathered with butter.*
▶ **n.** (often **slathers**) informal a large amount of something: *slathers of cream.*
– ORIGIN early 19th cent.: of unknown origin.

slat·tern /'slatərn/ ▶ **n.** dated a dirty, untidy woman.
– ORIGIN mid 17th cent.: related to *slattering* 'slovenly,' from dialect *slatter* 'to spill, slop,' frequentative of *slat* 'strike,' of unknown origin.

slat·tern·ly /'slatərnlē/ ▶ **adj.** dated (of a woman or her appearance) dirty and untidy.
– DERIVATIVES **slat·tern·li·ness n.**

slaugh·ter /'slôtər/ ▶ **n.** the killing of animals for food. ■ the killing of a large number of people or animals in a cruel or violent way; massacre: *the slaughter of 20 peaceful demonstrators.* ■ informal a thorough defeat: *an absolute slaughter by the Red Sox.*
▶ **v.** [with obj.] kill (animals) for food. ■ kill (people or animals) in a cruel or violent way, typically in large numbers: *innocent civilians are being slaughtered.* ■ informal defeat (an opponent) thoroughly: *our team was slaughtered in the finals.*
– DERIVATIVES **slaugh·ter·er n., slaugh·ter·ous** /-rəs/ **adj.**
– ORIGIN Middle English (as a noun): from Old Norse *slátr* 'butcher's meat'; related to SLAY¹. The verb dates from the mid 16th cent.

slaugh·ter·house /'slôtər,hous/ ▶ **n.** a place where animals are slaughtered for food.

Slav /släv/ ▶ **n.** a member of a group of peoples in central and eastern Europe speaking Slavic languages.
▶ **adj.** another term for SLAVIC.
– DERIVATIVES **Slav·ist n.**
– ORIGIN from medieval Latin *Sclavus*, late Greek *Sklabos*, later also from medieval Latin *Slavus*.

slave /slāv/ ▶ **n.** chiefly historical a person who is the legal property of another and is forced to obey them. ■ a person who works very hard without proper remuneration or appreciation: *by the time I was ten, I had become her slave, doing all the housework.* ■ a person who is excessively dependent upon or controlled by something: *the poorest people of the world are slaves to the banks* | *she was no slave to fashion.* ■ a device, or part of one, directly controlled by another: [as modifier] *a slave cassette deck.* Compare with MASTER¹. ■ an ant captured in its pupal state by an ant of another species, for which it becomes a worker.
▶ **v.** [no obj.] work excessively hard: *after slaving away for fourteen years, all he gets is two thousand.* ■ [with obj.] subject (a device) to control by another: *should the need arise, the two channels can be slaved together.*
– ORIGIN Middle English: shortening of Old French *esclave*, equivalent of medieval Latin *sclava* (feminine) 'Slavic (captive)': some South Slavic peoples had been reduced to a servile state by conquest in the 9th cent.

Slave Coast a part of the west coast of Africa, between the Volta River and Mount Cameroon, from which slaves were exported in the 16th–19th centuries.

slave driv·er ▶ **n.** a person who oversees and urges on slaves at work. ■ a person who works others very hard.
– DERIVATIVES **slave-drive v.**

slave·hold·er /'slāv,hōldər/ ▶ **n.** an owner of slaves.
– DERIVATIVES **slave·hold·ing n.**

slave la·bor ▶ **n.** labor that is coerced and inadequately rewarded, or the people who perform such labor: *most of production is carried out by slave labor* | *they treat us like slave labor.*

slave-mak·ing ant (also **slave-maker ant**) ▶ **n.** an ant that raids the nests of other ant species and steals the pupae, which later become workers in the new colony. ● Several species in the family Formicidae, in particular the European *Formica sanguinea*. See also AMAZON ANT.

slav·er¹ /'slāvər/ ▶ **n.** chiefly historical a person dealing in or owning slaves. ■ a ship used for transporting slaves.

slav·er² /'slavər/ ▶ **n. 1** saliva running from the mouth.
2 archaic excessive or obsequious flattery.
▶ **v.** [no obj.] let saliva run from the mouth: *the Labrador was slavering at the mouth.* ■ show excessive desire: *suburbanites slavering over drop-dead models.*
– ORIGIN Middle English: probably from Low German; compare with SLOBBER.

slav·er·y /'slāvərē/ ▶ **n.** the state of being a slave: *thousands had been sold into slavery.* ■ the practice or system of owning slaves. ■ a condition compared to that of a slave in respect of exhausting labor or restricted freedom: *female domestic slavery.* ■ excessive dependence on or devotion to something: *slavery to tradition.*

slave ship ▶ **n.** historical a ship transporting slaves, esp. one carrying slaves from Africa.

Slave State (also **slave state**) ▶ **n.** historical any of the southern states of the US in which slavery was legal before the Civil War.

slave trade ▶ **n.** chiefly historical the procuring, transporting, and selling of human beings as slaves, in particular the former trade in African blacks as slaves by European countries and North America.
– DERIVATIVES **slave trad·er n.**

slav·ey /'slāvē/ ▶ **n.** (pl. **slaveys**) Brit. informal, dated a maidservant, esp. a hard-worked one.

Slav·ic /'slävik/ ▶ **adj.** of, relating to, or denoting the branch of the Indo-European language family that includes Russian, Ukrainian, and Belorussian (**East Slavic**), Polish, Czech, Slovak, and Sorbian (**West Slavic**), and Bulgarian, Serbian, Croatian, Macedonian, and Slovene (**South Slavic**). ■ of, relating to, or denoting the peoples of central and eastern Europe who speak any of these languages.
▶ **n.** the Slavic languages collectively. See also SLAVONIC.

slav·ish /'slāviSH/ ▶ **adj.** relating to or characteristic of a slave, typically by behaving in a servile or submissive way: *he noted the slavish, feudal respect they had for her.* ■ showing no attempt at originality, constructive interpretation, or development: *a slavish adherence to protocol.*
– DERIVATIVES **slav·ish·ly adv., slav·ish·ness n.**

Sla·von·ic /slə'vänik/ ▶ **adj. & n.** another term for SLAVIC. See also CHURCH SLAVIC.
– ORIGIN from medieval Latin *S(c)lavonicus*, from *S(c)lavonia* 'country of the Slavs,' from *Sclavus* (see SLAV).

Slav·o·phile /'slavə,fīl/ ▶ **n.** a person who greatly admires the Slavic peoples or their languages.

slaw /slô/ ▶ **n.** coleslaw.
– ORIGIN late 18th cent.: from Dutch *sla*, shortened from *salade* 'salad.'

slay¹ /slā/ ▶ **v.** (past **slew** /slo͞o/; past participle **slain** /slān/) [with obj.] archaic, literary kill (a person or animal) in a violent way: *St. George slew the dragon.* ■ murder (someone) (used chiefly in journalism): *a man was slain with a shotgun.* ■ informal greatly impress or amuse (someone): *you slay me, you really do.*
– DERIVATIVES **slay·er n.**
– ORIGIN Old English *slēan* 'strike, kill,' of Germanic origin; related to Dutch *slaan* and German *schlagen*.

slay² ▶ **n.** variant spelling of SLEY.

slay·ing /'slāiNG/ ▶ **n.** archaic, literary the killing of a person or animal: *the slaying of a dragon.* ■ the murder of someone (used chiefly in journalism): *a gangland slaying.*

SLBM ▶ **abbr.** submarine-launched ballistic missile.

SLCM ▶ **abbr.** sea-launched cruise missile.

sld. ▶ **abbr.** ■ sailed. ■ sealed.

SLE ▶ **abbr.** systemic lupus erythematosus.

sleaze /slēz/ ▶ **n.** immoral, sordid, and corrupt behavior or material, esp. in business or politics: *political campaigns that are long on sleaze and short on substance.* ■ informal a sordid, corrupt, or immoral person.
▶ **v.** [no obj.] informal behave in an immoral, corrupt, or sordid way: *you're the last person who has to sleaze around bars.*
– ORIGIN 1960s: back-formation from SLEAZY.

sleaze·ball /'slēz,bôl/ (also **sleazebag** /-,bag/) ▶ **n.** informal a disreputable, disgusting, or despicable person (also used as a general term of abuse).

slea·zoid /'slē,zoid/ (also **sleazo** /-,zō/) informal ▶ **adj.** sleazy, sordid, or despicable: *a sleazoid lawyer.*
▶ **n.** a sleazy, sordid, or despicable person.

slea·zy /'slēzē/ ▶ **adj.** (**sleazier, sleaziest**) **1** (of a person or situation) sordid, corrupt, or immoral. ■ (of a place) squalid and seedy: *a sleazy all-night cafe.*
2 dated (of textiles and clothing) flimsy.
– DERIVATIVES **slea·zi·ly** /'slēzəlē/ **adv., slea·zi·ness n.**
– ORIGIN mid 17th cent.: of unknown origin.

sled /sled/ ▶ **n.** a vehicle on runners for traveling over snow or ice, either pushed or pulled, drawn by horses, dogs, or a motor vehicle, or allowed to slide downhill. ■ another term for SLEDGE¹. ■ another term for SNOWMOBILE.
▶ **v.** (**sleds, sledding, sledded**) [no obj.] ride on a sled: *they sledded down the slopes in the frozen snow* | (as noun **sledding**) *the sledding has been excellent this year.*
– ORIGIN Middle English: from Middle Low German *sledde*; related to the verb SLIDE.

sled dog ▶ **n.** a dog trained to pull a sled, esp. as one of a team.

sledge¹ /slej/ ▶ **n.** a vehicle on runners for conveying loads or passengers esp. over snow or ice, often pulled by draft animals. ■ British term for SLED.
▶ **v.** [with obj.] carry (a load or passengers) on a sledge: *the task of sledging lifeboats across tundra.*
– ORIGIN late 16th cent. (as a noun): from Middle Dutch *sleedse*; related to SLED. The verb dates from the early 18th cent.

sledge² ▶ **n.** a sledgehammer.
– ORIGIN Old English *slecg*, from a Germanic base meaning 'to strike,' related to SLAY¹.

sledge·ham·mer /'slej,hamər/ ▶ **n.** a large, heavy hammer used for such jobs as breaking rocks and driving in fence posts. ■ [as modifier] powerful; forceful: *sledgehammer blows.* ■ [as modifier] ruthless, insensitive, or using unnecessary force: *under his sledgehammer direction, anything of subtlety is swamped.*
▶ **v.** [with obj.] hit with a sledgehammer.

sleek /slēk/ ▶ **adj.** (of hair, fur, or skin) smooth and glossy: *he was tall, with sleek, dark hair.* ■ (of a person or animal) having smooth, glossy skin, hair, or fur, often taken as a sign of physical fitness: *a sleek black cat.* ■ (of a person) having a wealthy and well-groomed appearance: *his sleek and elegant sisters.* ■ (of an object) having an elegant, streamlined shape or design: *his sleek black car slid through the traffic.* ■ ingratiating; unctuous: *she gave Guy a sleek smile to underline her words.*
▶ **v.** [with obj.] make (the hair) smooth and glossy, typically by applying pressure or moisture to it: *her black hair was sleeked down.*
– DERIVATIVES **sleek·ly adv., sleek·ness n., sleek·y adj.**
– ORIGIN late Middle English: a later variant of SLICK (adjective and verb).

sleep /slēp/ ▶ **n. 1** a condition of body and mind such as that which typically recurs for several hours every night, in which the nervous system is relatively inactive, the eyes closed, the postural muscles relaxed, and consciousness practically suspended: *I was on the verge of sleep* | [in sing.] *a good night's sleep.* ■ chiefly literary a state compared to or resembling this, such as death or complete silence or stillness: *a photograph of the poet in his last sleep.*

S

2 a gummy or gritty secretion found in the corners of the eyes after sleep: *she sat up, rubbing the sleep from her eyes.*
▶ **v.** (past and past participle **slept** /slept/) [no obj.] **1** rest in such a condition; be asleep: *she slept for half an hour* | (as adj. **sleeping**) *he looked at the sleeping child.* ■ be inactive or dormant: *Copenhagen likes to be known as the city that never sleeps.* ■ literary be at peace in death; lie buried: *he sleeps beneath the silver birches.*
2 [with obj.] provide (a specified number of people) with beds, rooms, or places to stay the night: *studios sleeping two people cost $70 a night.*
3 [with adverbial] have sexual intercourse or be involved in a sexual relationship: *I won't sleep with a man who doesn't respect me.*
– PHRASES **one could do something in one's sleep** informal one regards something as so easy that it will require no effort or conscious thought to accomplish: *she knew the music perfectly, could sing it in her sleep.* **get to sleep** manage to fall asleep. **go to sleep** fall asleep. ■ (of a limb) become numb as a result of prolonged pressure. **let sleeping dogs lie** proverb avoid interfering in a situation that is currently causing no problems but might do so as a result of such interference. **lose sleep** see LOSE. **put someone to sleep** make someone unconscious by the use of drugs, alcohol, or an anesthetic. ■ (also **send someone to sleep**) bore someone greatly. **put something to sleep** kill an animal, esp. an old, sick, or badly injured one, painlessly (used euphemistically). ■ Computing put a computer on standby while it is not being used, esp. in order to reduce power consumption. **sleep easy** see EASY. **sleep like a log** (or **top**) sleep very soundly. **sleep on it** informal delay making a decision on something until the following day so as to have more time to consider it. **the sleep of the just** a deep, untroubled sleep. **sleep rough** see ROUGH. **sleep tight** [usu. in imperative] sleep well (said to someone when parting from them at night). **sleep with one eye open** sleep very lightly, aware of what is happening around one.
– PHRASAL VERBS **sleep around** informal have many casual sexual partners. **sleep in** remain asleep or in bed later than usual in the morning. ■ sleep by night at one's place of work. **sleep something off/away** dispel the effects of or recover from something by going to sleep: *she thought it wise to let him sleep off his hangover.* **sleep out** sleep outdoors. **sleep over** spend the night at a place other than one's own home: *Katie was asked to sleep over with Jenny.*
– ORIGIN Old English *slēp, slǣp* (noun), *slēpan, slǣpan* (verb), of Germanic origin; related to Dutch *slapen* and German *schlafen.*

sleep·er /ˈslēpər/ ▶ **n. 1** [with adj.] a person or animal who is asleep or who sleeps in a specified way: *he was a light sleeper, for long periods an insomniac.*
2 a thing used for or connected with sleeping, in particular: ■ a train carrying sleeping cars. ■ a sleeping car, or a berth in one. ■ (often **sleepers**) one-piece coverall pajamas for a baby or small child. ■ a sofa or chair that converts into a bed.
3 a movie, book, play, etc., that achieves sudden unexpected success after initially attracting little attention, typically one that proves popular without much promotion or expenditure. ■ an antique whose true value goes unrecognized for some time. ■ (also **sleeper agent**) a secret agent who remains inactive for a long period while establishing a secure position.
4 Brit. a railroad tie.
5 a stocky fish with mottled coloration that occurs widely in warm seas and fresh water. ● *Dormitator* and other genera, family Gobiidae (or Eleotridae): many species.

sleep·er cell ▶ **n.** a secretive group of spies or terrorist agents that remain inactive within a target population until ordered to act.

sleep-in ▶ **adj.** [attrib.] (of a domestic employee) resident in an employer's house: *a sleep-in babysitter.*
▶ **n.** a form of protest in which the participants sleep overnight in premises that they have occupied: *a student sleep-in began last night.*

sleep·i·ness /ˈslēpēnis/ ▶ **n.** the state of being sleepy: *long road trips cause fatigue and sleepiness.*

sleep·ing bag ▶ **n.** a warm lined padded bag to sleep in, esp. when camping.

sleep·ing car ▶ **n.** a railroad car provided with beds or berths.

sleep·ing part·ner ▶ **n.** British term for SILENT PARTNER.

sleep·ing pill ▶ **n.** a tablet of a drug that helps to induce sleep.

sleep·ing sick·ness ▶ **n. 1** a tropical disease caused by a parasitic protozoan (trypanosome) that is transmitted by the bite of the tsetse fly. It causes fever, chills, pain in the limbs, and anemia, and eventually affects the nervous system causing extreme lethargy and death. See also TRYPANOSOMIASIS.
2 another term for ENCEPHALITIS LETHARGICA.

sleep-learn·ing ▶ **n.** learning by hearing while asleep, typically by playing a tape recording of what is to be learned.

sleep·less /ˈslēplis/ ▶ **adj.** characterized by or experiencing lack of sleep: *another sleepless night* | *Lisa lay sleepless.* ■ chiefly literary continually active or moving: *the sleepless river.*
– DERIVATIVES **sleep·less·ly adv., sleep·less·ness n.**

sleep mode ▶ **n.** Electronics a power-saving mode of operation in which devices or parts of devices are switched off until needed.

sleep-out ▶ **n.** an occasion of sleeping outdoors.

sleep·o·ver /ˈslēpˌōvər/ ▶ **n.** an occasion of spending the night away from home, or of having a guest or guests spend the night in one's home, esp. as a party for children.

sleep·walk /ˈslēpˌwôk/ ▶ **v.** [no obj.] walk around and sometimes perform other actions while asleep.
▶ **n.** an instance of such activity.
– DERIVATIVES **sleep·walk·er n.**

sleep·wear /ˈslēpˌwe(ə)r/ ▶ **n.** pajamas or other clothing suitable for wearing in bed.

sleep·y /ˈslēpē/ ▶ **adj.** (**sleepier, sleepiest**) needing or ready for sleep: *the wine had made her sleepy.* ■ showing the effects of sleep: *she rubbed her sleepy eyes.* ■ inducing sleep; soporific: *the sleepy heat of the afternoon.* ■ (of a place) without much activity: *he turned off the road into a sleepy little town.* ■ (of a business, organization, or industry) lacking the ability or will to respond to change; not dynamic: *it was once a sleepy subsidiary of Foster & Sykes.*
– DERIVATIVES **sleep·i·ly** /ˈslēpəlē/ **adv.**

sleep·y·head /ˈslēpēˌhed/ ▶ **n.** a sleepy or inattentive person (usually as a form of address): *come on, sleepyhead, time to get up.*

Sleep·y Hol·low a town in southeastern New York, east of the Hudson River and north of Tarrytown. It is associated with the writings of Washington Irving.

sleet /slēt/ ▶ **n.** a form of precipitation consisting of ice pellets, often mixed with rain or snow. ■ a thin coating of ice formed by sleet or rain freezing on contact with a cold surface.
▶ **v.** [no obj.] (**it sleets, it is sleeting,** etc.) sleet falls: *it was sleeting so hard we could barely see.*
– DERIVATIVES **sleet·y adj.**
– ORIGIN Middle English: of Germanic origin; probably related to Middle Low German *slōten* (plural) 'hail' and German *Schlosse* 'hailstone.'

sleeve /slēv/ ▶ **n.** the part of a garment that wholly or partly covers a person's arm: *a shirt with the sleeves rolled up.* ■ a protective paper or cardboard cover for a record, CD, or DVD. ■ a protective or connecting tube fitting over or enclosing a rod, spindle, or smaller tube.
– PHRASES **up one's sleeve** (of a strategy, idea, or resource) kept secret and in reserve for use when needed: *he was new to the game but had a few tricks up his sleeve.* **wear one's heart on one's sleeve** see HEART.
– DERIVATIVES **sleeved adj.** [often in combination] *a cap-sleeved shirt*, **sleeve·less adj.**
– ORIGIN Old English *slēfe, slīef(e), slȳf*; related to Middle Dutch *sloove* 'covering.'

sleeve board (also **sleeveboard**) ▶ **n.** a small ironing board over which a sleeve is pulled for pressing.

sleeve valve ▶ **n.** a valve in the form of a cylinder that slides to cover and uncover an inlet or outlet.

sleigh /slā/ ▶ **n.** a sled drawn by horses or reindeer, esp. one used for passengers.
▶ **v.** [no obj.] (usu. as noun **sleighing**) ride on a sleigh.
– ORIGIN early 17th cent. (originally a North American usage): from Dutch *slee*; related to SLED.

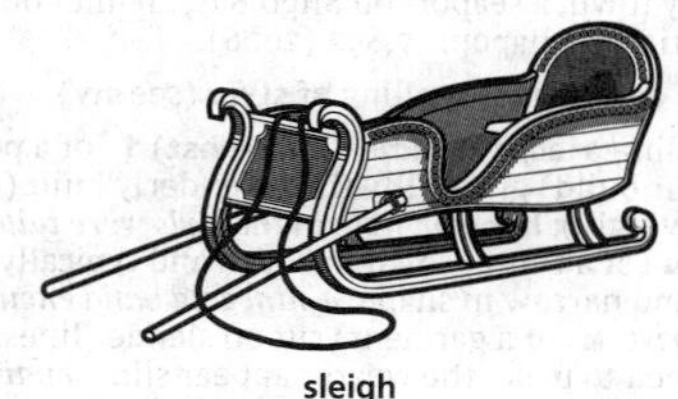
sleigh

sleigh bed ▶ **n.** a bed resembling a sleigh, with an outward curving headboard and footboard.

sleigh bell ▶ **n.** a tinkling bell attached to the harness of a sleigh horse.

sleight /slīt/ ▶ **n.** literary the use of dexterity or cunning, esp. so as to deceive: *except by sleight of logic, the two positions cannot be harmonized.*
– PHRASES **sleight of hand** manual dexterity, typically in performing tricks: *a nifty bit of sleight of hand got the ashtray into the correct position.* ■ skillful deception: *this is financial sleight of hand of the worst sort.*
– ORIGIN Middle English *sleghth* 'cunning, skill,' from Old Norse *slœgth*, from *slœgr* 'sly.'

slen·der /ˈslendər/ ▶ **adj.** (**slenderer, slenderest**) **1** (of a person or part of the body) gracefully thin: *her slender neck.* ■ (esp. of a rod or stem) of small girth or breadth: *slender iron railings.*
2 (of something abstract) barely sufficient in amount or basis: *a slender majority of four.*
– DERIVATIVES **slen·der·ly adv., slen·der·ness n.**
– ORIGIN late Middle English: of unknown origin.

slen·der·ize /ˈslendəˌrīz/ ▶ **v.** [with obj.] (usu. as adj. **slenderizing**) make (a person or a part of their body) appear more slender: *my mother has always held that dark colors are slenderizing.* ■ [no obj.] (of a person) lose weight; become slim. ■ reduce the size of (something): *a campaign promise that he would slenderize the executive branch.*

slen·der lo·ris ▶ **n.** see LORIS.

slept /slept/ past and past participle of SLEEP.

sleuth /slo͞oth/ informal ▶ **n.** a detective.
▶ **v.** [no obj.] (often as noun **sleuthing**) carry out a search or investigation in the manner of a detective: *scientists began their genetic sleuthing for honey mushrooms four years ago.* ■ [with obj.] dated investigate (someone or something).
– ORIGIN Middle English (originally in the sense 'track,' in SLEUTH-HOUND): from Old Norse *slóth*; compare with SLOT[2]. Current senses date from the late 19th cent.

sleuth-hound ▶ **n.** dated a bloodhound. ■ informal an eager investigator; a detective.

S lev·el ▶ **n.** (in the UK except Scotland) an examination, or a pass of one, typically taken together with an A level in the same subject, but having a more advanced syllabus.
– ORIGIN abbreviation of *Special level* or (formerly) *Scholarship level.*

slew[1] /slo͞o/ (also **slue**) ▶ **v. 1** turn or slide violently or uncontrollably in a particular direction: [no obj.] *the Chevy slewed from side to side in the snow* | [with obj.] *he managed to slew the aircraft around before it settled on the runway.*
2 [no obj.] (of an electronic device) undergo slewing.
▶ **n.** [in sing.] a violent or uncontrollable sliding movement: *I was assaulted by the thump and slew of the van.*
– ORIGIN mid 18th cent. (originally in nautical use): of unknown origin.

slew[2] past of SLAY[1].

slew[3] ▶ **n.** informal a large number or quantity of something: *he asked me a slew of questions.*
– ORIGIN mid 19th cent.: from Irish *sluagh.*

slew·ing /ˈslo͞oiNG/ ▶ **n.** Electronics the response of an electronic device to a sudden large increase in input, esp. one that causes the device to respond at its maximum rate.

slew rate ▶ **n.** Electronics the maximum rate at which an amplifier can respond to an abrupt change of input level.

sley /slā/ (also **slay**) ▶ **n.** a tool used in weaving to force the weft into place.
– ORIGIN Old English *slege*; related to SLAY[1].

slice /slīs/ ▶ **n. 1** a thin, broad piece of food, such as bread, meat, or cake, cut from a larger portion: *four slices of bread* | *potato slices.* ■ a portion or share of something: *local authorities control a huge slice of public spending.*
2 Golf a stroke that makes the ball curve away to the right (for a left-handed player, the left), typically inadvertently. Compare with HOOK. ■ (in other sports) a shot or stroke made with glancing contact to impart spin.
3 a utensil with a broad, flat blade for lifting foods such as cake and fish.
▶ **v.** [with obj.] **1** cut (something, esp. food) into slices: *slice the onion into rings* | (as adj. **sliced**) *a sliced loaf.* ■ (**slice something off/from**) cut something or a piece of something off or from (something larger), typically with one clean cut: *he sliced a corner from a fried egg* | figurative *he sliced 70 seconds off the record.* ■ cut with or as if with a sharp implement: *the bomber's wings were slicing the air with some efficiency* | [no obj.] *the blade sliced into his palm.*

PRONUNCIATION KEY ə *ago, up*; ər *over, fur*; a *hat*; ā *ate*; ä *car*; e *let*; ē *see*; i *fit*; ī *by*; NG *sing*; ō *go*; ô *law, for*; oi *toy*; o͝o *good*; o͞o *goo*; ou *out*; TH *thin*; T͟H *then*; ZH *vision*

■ [no obj.] move easily and quickly: *Senna then sliced past Berger to take third place.*
2 Golf strike (the ball) or play (a stroke) so that the ball curves away to the right (for a left-handed player, the left), typically inadvertently. ■ (in other sports) propel (the ball) with a glancing contact to impart spin: *Evans went and sliced a corner into his own net.*
– PHRASES **slice and dice** divide a quantity of information up into smaller parts, esp. in order to analyze it more closely or in different ways: *each network has analysis teams that slice and dice the exit poll information to find a conclusion.* **slice of life** a realistic representation of everyday experience in a movie, play, or book.
– DERIVATIVES **slice·a·ble** adj., **slic·er** n. [often in combination] *a cheese-slicer.*
– ORIGIN Middle English (in the sense 'fragment, splinter'): shortening of Old French *esclice* 'splinter,' from the verb *esclicier*, of Germanic origin; related to German *schleissen* 'to slice,' also to SLIT.

slick /slik/ ▶ adj. **1** (of an action or thing) done or operating in an impressively smooth, efficient, and apparently effortless way: *a slick piece of software.* ■ smooth and superficially impressive but insincere or shallow: *the brands are backed by slick advertising | he's a slick con man.*
2 (of skin or hair) smooth and glossy: *a dandy-looking dude with a slick black ponytail.* ■ (of a surface) smooth, wet, and slippery: *she tumbled back against the slick, damp wall.*
▶ n. **1** an oil slick. ■ a small smear or patch of a glossy or wet substance, esp. a cosmetic: *a slick of lip balm.*
2 (usu. **slicks**) a race car or bicycle tire without a tread, for use in dry weather conditions.
3 informal a glossy magazine.
▶ v. **1** [with obj.] make (one's hair) flat, smooth, and glossy by applying water, oil, or cream to it: *his damp hair was slicked back* | [as adj. in combination] (**slicked**) *his slicked-down hair.* ■ cover with a film of liquid; make wet or slippery: *she woke to find her body slicked with sweat* | [as adj. in combination] (**-slicked**) *a rain-slicked road.*
2 (**slick someone/something up**) make someone or something smart, tidy, or stylish.
– DERIVATIVES **slick·ly** adv., **slick·ness** n.
– ORIGIN Middle English (in the senses 'glossy' and 'make smooth or glossy'): probably from Old English and related to Old Norse *slíkr* 'smooth'; compare with SLEEK.

slick·en·side /'slikən,sīd/ ▶ n. (usu. **slickensides**) Geology a polished and striated rock surface that results from friction along a fault or bedding plane.
– ORIGIN mid 18th cent.: from a dialect variant of the adjective SLICK + SIDE.

slick·er /'slikər/ ▶ n. **1** informal a crook or swindler. ■ short for CITY SLICKER.
2 a raincoat made of smooth material.

slide /slīd/ ▶ v. (past and past participle **slid** /slid/) [no obj.] move along a smooth surface while maintaining continuous contact with it: *she slid down the bank into the water* | (as adj. **sliding**) *the tank should have a sliding glass cover.* ■ [with obj.] move (something) along a surface in such a way: *she slid the keys over the table.* ■ move smoothly, quickly, or unobtrusively: [no obj.] *I quickly slid into a seat at the back of the hall* | [with obj.] *she slid the bottle into her pocket.* ■ change gradually to a worse condition or lower level: *the country faces the prospect of sliding from recession into slump.*
▶ n. **1** a structure with a smooth sloping surface for children to slide down. ■ a smooth stretch or slope of ice or packed snow for sledding on. ■ an act of moving along a smooth surface while maintaining continuous contact with it: *use an ice ax to halt a slide on ice and snow.* ■ Baseball a sliding approach to a base along the ground. ■ a decline in value or quality: *the current slide in house prices.*
2 a part of a machine or musical instrument that slides. ■ the place on a machine or instrument where a sliding part operates. ■ slide guitar: *I'd been playing slide for years.*
3 (also **microscope slide**) a rectangular piece of glass on which an object is mounted or placed for examination under a microscope. ■ a mounted transparency, typically one placed in a projector for viewing on a screen: [as modifier] *a slide show.*
4 a sandal or light shoe without a back.
– PHRASES **let something slide** negligently allow something to deteriorate: *Papa had let the business slide after Mama's death.*
– DERIVATIVES **slid·a·ble** adj.
– ORIGIN Old English *slīdan* (verb); related to SLED and SLEDGE¹. The noun, first in the sense 'act of sliding,' is recorded from the late 16th cent.

slide fas·ten·er ▶ n. dated a zipper.

slide gui·tar ▶ n. a style of guitar playing in which a glissando effect is produced by moving a bottleneck or similar device over the strings, used esp. in blues.

slide pro·jec·tor ▶ n. a piece of equipment used for displaying photographic slides on a screen.

slid·er /'slīdər/ ▶ n. **1** a North American freshwater turtle with a red or yellow patch on the side of the head. ● Genus *Trachemys* (or *Pseudemys*), family Emydidae: several species, in particular the **red-eared** (or **pond**) **slider** (*T. scripta*).
2 Baseball a pitch that moves laterally as it nears home plate.
3 (usu. **sliders**) a sliding door, esp. one with a glass panel.
4 Electronics a knob or lever that is moved horizontally or vertically to control a variable, such as the volume of a radio.

red-eared slider

slide rule ▶ n. a ruler with a sliding central strip, marked with logarithmic scales and used for making rapid calculations, esp. multiplication and division.

slide show ▶ n. a presentation supplemented by or based on a series of projected images or photographic slides.

slide valve ▶ n. a piece that opens and closes an aperture by sliding across it.

slid·ing door ▶ n. a door drawn across an aperture on a groove or suspended from a track, rather than turning on hinges.

slid·ing scale ▶ n. a scale of fees, taxes, wages, etc., that varies in accordance with variation of some standard.

slid·ing seat ▶ n. a seat able to slide back and forth on runners, esp. one in a racing rowboat used to adjust the length of a stroke.

slight /slīt/ ▶ adj. **1** small in degree; inconsiderable: *a slight increase | a slight ankle injury | the chance of success is very slight.* ■ (esp. of a creative work) not profound or substantial; somewhat trivial or superficial: *a slight plot.*
2 (of a person or their build) not sturdy and strongly built: *she was slight and delicate-looking.*
▶ v. [with obj.] **1** insult (someone) by treating or speaking of them without proper respect or attention: *he was careful not to slight a guest.*
2 archaic raze or destroy (a fortification).
▶ n. an insult caused by a failure to show someone proper respect or attention: *an unintended slight can create grudges | he was seething at the slight to his authority.*
– PHRASES **not in the slightest** not at all: *he didn't mind in the slightest.* **the slightest ——** [usu. with negative] any —— whatsoever: *I don't have the slightest idea.*
– DERIVATIVES **slight·ish** adj., **slight·ness** n.
– ORIGIN Middle English; the adjective from Old Norse *sléttr* 'smooth' (an early sense in English), of Germanic origin; related to Dutch *slechts* 'merely' and German *schlicht* 'simple,' *schlecht* 'bad'; the verb (originally in the sense 'make smooth or level'), from Old Norse *slétta*. The sense 'treat with disrespect' dates from the late 16th cent.

slight·ing /'slīting/ ▶ adj. showing a lack of respect; insulting or disparaging: *slighting references to Irish Catholics.*
– DERIVATIVES **slight·ing·ly** adv.

slight·ly /'slītlē/ ▶ adv. **1** to a small degree; not considerably: *he lowered his voice slightly* | [as submodifier] *they are all slightly different.*
2 (with reference to a person's build) in a slender way: *a slightly built girl.*

Sli·go /'slīgō/ a county in the Republic of Ireland, in the western part of the province of Connacht. ■ its county town, a seaport on Sligo Bay, an inlet of the Atlantic Ocean; pop. 17,892 (2006).

sli·ly ▶ adv. variant spelling of SLYLY (see SLY).

slim /slim/ ▶ adj. (**slimmer**, **slimmest**) **1** (of a person or their build) gracefully thin; slenderly built (used approvingly): *her slim figure | the girls were tall and slim.* ■ (of a thing) small in width and typically long and narrow in shape: *a slim gold band encircled her wrist.* ■ (of a garment) cut on slender lines; designed to make the wearer appear slim: *a pair of slim, immaculately cut slacks.* ■ (of a business or other organization) reduced to a smaller size in the hope that it will become more efficient.
2 (of something abstract, esp. a chance or margin) very small: *there was just a slim chance of success | the evidence is slim.*
▶ v. (**slims**, **slimming**, **slimmed**) [no obj.] make oneself thinner by dieting and sometimes exercising: *I need to slim down a bit* | (as noun **slimming**) *an aid to slimming.* ■ [with obj.] make (a person or a bodily part) thinner in such a way: *how can I slim down my hips?* ■ [with obj.] reduce (a business or other organization) to a smaller size in the hope of making it more efficient: *restructuring and slimming down the organization.*
▶ n. (also **slim disease**) African term for AIDS.
– DERIVATIVES **slim·ly** adv., **slim·ness** n.
– ORIGIN mid 17th cent.: from Low German or Dutch (from a base meaning 'slanting, cross, bad'), of Germanic origin. The pejorative sense found in Dutch and German existed originally in the English noun *slim* 'lazy or worthless person.'

slime /slīm/ ▶ n. a moist, soft, and slippery substance, typically regarded as repulsive: *the cold stone was wet with slime.*
▶ v. [with obj.] cover with slime: *what grass remained was slimed over with pale brown mud.*
– ORIGIN Old English *slīm*, of Germanic origin; related to Dutch *slijm* and German *Schleim* 'mucus, slime,' Latin *limus* 'mud,' and Greek *limnē* 'marsh.'

slime·ball /'slīm,bôl/ ▶ n. informal a repulsive or despicable person.

slime mold ▶ n. a simple organism that consists of an acellular mass of creeping jellylike protoplasm containing nuclei, or a mass of ameboid cells. When it reaches a certain size it forms a large number of spore cases. ● Division Myxomycota, kingdom Fungi, in particular the class Myxomycetes; also treated as protozoan (phylum Gymnomyxa, kingdom Protista).

slim jim ▶ n. informal a very slim person or thing, in particular: ■ (**slim jims**) a pair of long narrow trousers. ■ (also **Slim Jim**) trademark a long thin variety of smoked sausage. ■ a long flexible metal strip with a hooked end, used by car thieves and others for entering a locked vehicle.

slim·line /'slim,līn/ ▶ adj. (of a person or article) slender in design or build: *a slimline phone.*

slim vol·ume ▶ n. a book, typically of verse, by a little-known author.

slim·y /'slīmē/ ▶ adj. (**slimier**, **slimiest**) covered by or having the feel or consistency of slime: *the thick, slimy mud | the walls were slimy with lichens.* ■ informal disgustingly immoral, dishonest, or obsequious: *he was a slimy people-pleaser.*
– DERIVATIVES **slim·i·ly** /-məlē/ adv., **slim·i·ness** n.

sling¹ /sliNG/ ▶ n. **1** a flexible strap or belt used in the form of a loop to support or raise a weight: *the horse had to be supported by a sling fixed to the roof.* ■ a bandage or soft strap looped around the neck to support an injured arm: *she had her arm in a sling.* ■ a pouch or frame for carrying a baby, supported by a strap around the neck or shoulders. ■ a short length of rope used to provide additional support for the body in rappelling or climbing.
2 a simple weapon in the form of a strap or loop, used to hurl stones or other small missiles.
▶ v. (past and past participle **slung** /sləNG/) **1** [with obj.] suspend or arrange (something), esp. with a strap or straps, so that it hangs loosely in a particular position: *a hammock was slung between two trees.* ■ carry (something, esp. a garment) loosely and casually: *he had his jacket **slung over** one shoulder.*
2 [with obj.] informal throw; fling (often used to express the speaker's casual attitude): *sling a few things into your knapsack.* ■ hurl (a stone or other missile) from a sling or similar weapon. ■ hoist or transfer (something) with a sling: *horse after horse was slung up from the barges.*
– PHRASES **put someone's** (or **have one's**) **ass in a sling** vulgar slang cause someone to be (or be) in trouble. **sling hash** informal serve food in a cafe or diner. **slings and arrows** used with reference to adverse factors or circumstances: *the slings and arrows of outrageous critics.* [with reference to Shakespeare's *Hamlet* III. i. 58.]
– DERIVATIVES **sling·er** n.
– ORIGIN Middle English: probably from Low German, of symbolic origin; compare with German *Schlinge* 'noose, snare.' Sense 2 of the verb is from Old Norse *slyngva*.

sling² ▶ n. a sweetened drink of liquor, esp. gin, and water. See also SINGAPORE SLING.
– ORIGIN mid 18th cent.: of unknown origin.

slingback /'sliNGbak/ ▶ n. a shoe held in place by a strap around the back of the ankle: [as modifier] *a pair of red slingback pumps.*

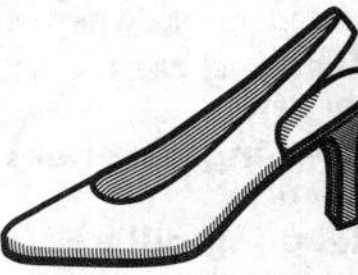
sling-back

sling·shot /'sliNG,SHät/ ▶ n. a forked stick, to which an elastic strap (or a pair of elastic bands connected by a small sling) is fastened to the two prongs, typically used

for shooting small stones. ■ [often as modifier] the effect of the gravitational pull of a celestial body in accelerating and changing the course of another body or a spacecraft.
▶ **v.** (**slingshots, slingshotting**; past and past participle **slingshot** or **slingshotted**) forcefully accelerate or cause to accelerate through use of gravity: [no obj.] *the car would hit the first dip, then slingshot off the second rise* | [with obj.] *Jupiter's gravity slingshots the fragments toward Earth.*

slingshot

slink /sliNGk/ ▶ **v.** (past and past participle **slunk** /slәNGk/) [no obj.] move smoothly and quietly with gliding steps, in a stealthy or sensuous manner: *the fox came slinking through the woods.* ■ come or go unobtrusively or furtively: *all his so-called friends have slunk off.*
▶ **n.** [in sing.] an act of moving in this way: *she moved with a sensuous slink.*
– ORIGIN Old English *slincan* 'crawl, creep'; compare with Middle Dutch and Middle Low German *slinken* 'subside, sink.'

slink·y /ˈsliNGkē/ ▶ **adj.** (**slinkier, slinkiest**) informal graceful and sinuous in movement, line, or figure: *a slinky black evening dress.*
▶ **n.** (**Slinky**) trademark a toy consisting of a flexible helical spring that can be made to somersault down steps.
– DERIVATIVES **slink·i·ly** /ˈsliNGkәlē/ **adv.**, **slink·i·ness n.**

slip[1] /slip/ ▶ **v.** (**slips, slipping, slipped**) **1** [no obj.] (of a person or animal) slide unintentionally for a short distance, typically losing one's balance or footing: *I slipped on the ice* | *he kept slipping in the mud.* ■ [with adverbial of direction] (of a thing) accidentally slide or move out of position or from someone's grasp: *the envelope slipped through Luke's fingers* | *a wisp of hair had slipped down over her face.* ■ fail to grip or make proper contact with a surface: *the front wheels began to slip* | (as adj. **slipping**) *a badly slipping clutch.* ■ [with adverbial of direction] go or move quietly or quickly, without attracting notice: *we slipped out by a back door.* ■ pass or change to a lower, worse, or different condition, typically in a gradual or imperceptible way: *many people feel standards have slipped* | [with complement] *profits slipped 31 percent.* ■ (**be slipping**) informal be behaving in a way that is not up to one's usual level of performance: *you're slipping, Joe—you need a vacation.* ■ (**slip away/by**) (of time) elapse: *the night was slipping away.* ■ [with obj.] put (something) in a particular place or position quietly, quickly, or stealthily: *she slipped the map into her pocket* | [with two objs.] *I slipped him a ten-spot to keep quiet.* ■ (**slip into/out of**) put on or take off (a garment) quickly and easily. ■ (**slip something in**) insert a remark smoothly or adroitly into a conversation.
2 [with obj.] escape or get loose from (a means of restraint): *the giant balloon slipped its moorings.* ■ [no obj.] (**slip out**) (of a remark) be uttered inadvertently. ■ (of a thought or fact) fail to be remembered by (one's mind or memory); elude (one's notice): *a beautiful woman's address was never likely to slip his mind.* ■ release (an animal, typically a hunting dog) from restraint. ■ Knitting move (a stitch) to the other needle without knitting it. ■ release (the clutch of a motor vehicle) slightly or for a moment. ■ (of an animal) produce (dead young) prematurely; abort.
▶ **n. 1** an act of sliding unintentionally for a short distance: *a single slip could send them plummeting down the mountainside.* ■ a fall to a lower level or standard: *a continued slip in house prices.* ■ relative movement of an object or surface and a solid surface in contact with it. ■ a reduction in the movement of a pulley or other mechanism due to slipping of the belt, rope, etc. ■ a sideways movement of an aircraft in flight, typically downward toward the center of curvature of a turn. ■ Geology the extent of relative horizontal displacement of corresponding points on either side of a fault plane.
2 a minor or careless mistake: *the judge made a slip in his summing up.*
3 a woman's loose-fitting, dress- or skirt-length undergarment, suspended by shoulder straps (**full slip**) or by an elasticized waistband (**half slip**): *a silk slip.*
4 a slope built leading into water, used for launching and landing boats and ships or for building and repairing them. ■ a space in which to dock a boat or ship, esp. between two wharves or piers.
5 (also **slip leash**) a leash that enables a dog to be released quickly.
6 Knitting short for SLIP STITCH: *one color at a time should be knitted in striped slip.*
– PHRASES **give someone the slip** informal evade or escape from someone. **let something slip 1** reveal something inadvertently in the course of a conversation: [with clause] *Alex had let slip he was married.* **2** archaic release a hound from the leash so as to begin the chase: *let slip the dogs of war.* **let something slip through one's fingers** (or **grasp**) lose hold or possession of something. **slip of the pen** (or **the tongue**) a minor mistake in writing (or speech). **there's many a slip 'twixt cup and lip** proverb many things can go wrong between the start of a project and its completion; nothing is certain until it has happened.
– PHRASAL VERBS **slip away** depart without saying goodbye; leave quietly or surreptitiously. ■ slowly disappear; recede or dwindle: *his ability to concentrate is slipping away.* ■ die peacefully (used euphemistically): *he lay there and quietly slipped away.* **slip something over on** informal take advantage of (someone) by trickery. **slip up** informal make a careless error: *they often slipped up when it came to spelling.*
– ORIGIN Middle English (in the sense 'move quickly and softly'): probably from Middle Low German *slippen* (verb); compare with SLIPPERY.

slip[2] ▶ **n. 1** a small piece of paper, typically a form for writing on or one giving printed information: *his monthly salary slip* | *complete the tear-off slip below.* ■ a long, narrow strip of a thin material such as wood.
2 a cutting taken from a plant for grafting or planting; a scion.
– PHRASES **a slip of a ——** used to denote a small, slim person: *you are little more than a slip of a girl.*
– ORIGIN late Middle English: probably from Middle Dutch and Middle Low German *slippe* 'cut, strip.'

slip[3] ▶ **n.** a creamy mixture of clay, water, and typically a pigment, used esp. for decorating earthenware.
– ORIGIN mid 17th cent.: of obscure origin; compare with Norwegian *slip(a)* 'slime.'

slip·case /ˈslipˌkās/ ▶ **n.** a close-fitting case open at one side or end for an object such as a book.

slip cast·ing ▶ **n.** the manufacture of ceramics by allowing slip to solidify in a mold.
– DERIVATIVES **slip-cast adj.**

slip·cov·er /ˈslipˌkәvәr/ ▶ **n.** a removable fitted cloth cover for a chair or sofa. ■ a jacket or slipcase for a book.

slip·form /ˈslipˌfôrm/ ▶ **n.** a mold in which a concrete structure of uniform cross section is cast by filling the mold with liquid concrete and then continuously moving and refilling it at a sufficiently slow rate for the emerging part to have partially set.

slip-joint pli·ers ▶ **plural n.** pliers with a slot in one jaw through which the other jaw slides, permitting an adjustable span.

slip knot ▶ **n. 1** a knot that can be undone by a pull. **2** a running knot.

slip-on ▶ **adj.** (esp. of shoes or clothes) having no (or few) fasteners and therefore able to be put on and taken off quickly.
▶ **n.** a shoe or garment that can be easily slipped on and off.

slip·o·ver /ˈslipˌōvәr/ ▶ **n.** a pullover, typically one without sleeves.
▶ **adj.** [attrib.] (of a garment) designed to be put on over the head: *a slipover sweater.*

slip·page /ˈslipij/ ▶ **n.** the action or process of something slipping or subsiding; the amount or extent of this: *$16 million has been spent on cracks and slippage.* ■ failure to meet a standard or deadline: the extent of this: *slippage on any job will entail slippage on the overall project.*

slipped /slipt/ ▶ **adj.** Heraldry (of a flower or leaf) depicted with a stalk.

slipped disc (also **slipped disk**) ▶ **n.** a vertebral disc that is displaced or partly protruding, pressing on nearby nerves and causing back pain or sciatica. See DISK (sense 3 of the noun).

slip·per /ˈslipәr/ ▶ **n.** a comfortable slip-on shoe that is worn indoors. ■ a light slip-on shoe, esp. one used for dancing.
– DERIVATIVES **slip·pered adj.**

slip·per·ette /ˌslipәˈret/ ▶ **n.** trademark a disposable slipper or similar foot covering, esp. of a kind distributed to airline passengers.

slip·per·i·ness /ˈslipәrēnis/ ▶ **n.** the quality or state of being slippery: *a play about the slipperiness of language.*

slip·per sock ▶ **n.** a thick sock, typically with a leather or vinyl sole, for use as a slipper.

slip·per·y /ˈslipәrē/ ▶ **adj.** (of a surface or object) difficult to hold firmly or stand on because it is smooth, wet, or slimy: *slippery ice* | *her hand was slippery with sweat.* ■ (of a person) evasive and unpredictable; not to be relied on: *Martin's a slippery customer.* ■ (of a word or concept) elusive in meaning because changing according to one's point of view: *the word "intended" is a decidedly slippery one.*
– PHRASES **slippery slope** an idea or course of action which will lead to something unacceptable, wrong, or disastrous: *he is on the slippery slope toward a life of crime.*
– DERIVATIVES **slip·per·i·ly** /ˈslipәrәlē/ **adv.**
– ORIGIN late 15th cent.: from dialect *slipper* 'slippery.'

slip·per·y elm ▶ **n.** a North American elm with coarsely textured leaves and rough outer bark. The mucilaginous inner bark of this tree has long been used medicinally. ● *Ulmus rubra* (or *fulva*), family Ulmaceae.

slip·py /ˈslipē/ ▶ **adj.** (**slippier, slippiest**) informal slippery: *the path was slippy with mud* | *slippy tires.*
– DERIVATIVES **slip·pi·ness n.**

slip ring ▶ **n.** a ring in a dynamo or electric motor that is attached to and rotates with the shaft, passing an electric current to a circuit via a fixed brush pressing against it.

slip·sheet /ˈslipˌSHēt/ ▶ **n.** Printing a sheet of paper placed between newly printed sheets to prevent offset or smudging.

slip·shod /ˈslipˌSHäd/ ▶ **adj.** (typically of a person or method of work) characterized by a lack of care, thought, or organization: *he'd caused many problems with his slipshod management.* ■ archaic (of shoes) worn down at the heel.
– ORIGIN late 16th cent. (originally in the sense 'wearing slippers or loose shoes'): from the verb SLIP[1] + SHOD.

slip stitch ▶ **n. 1** (in sewing) a loose stitch joining layers of fabric and not visible externally.
2 [often as modifier] Knitting a type of stitch in which the stitches are moved from one needle to the other without being knitted: *a slip-stitch pattern.*
▶ **v.** (**slip-stitch**) [with obj.] sew or knit with such stitches.

slip·stone /ˈslipˌstōn/ (also **slip stone**) ▶ **n.** a small rounded or tapered whetstone used to sharpen woodworking tools.

slip·stream /ˈslipˌstrēm/ ▶ **n. 1** a current of air or water driven back by a revolving propeller or jet engine. ■ the partial vacuum created in the wake of a moving vehicle, often used by other vehicles in a race to assist in passing.
2 an assisting force regarded as drawing something along behind something else: *when the U.S. economy booms, the rest of the world is pulled along in the slipstream.*
▶ **v.** [no obj.] (esp. in auto racing) another term for DRAFT (sense 4 of the verb). ■ [with obj.] travel in the slipstream of (someone), esp. in order to overtake them.

slip-up ▶ **n.** informal a mistake or blunder.

slip·ware /ˈslipˌwe(ә)r/ ▶ **n.** pottery decorated with slip (see SLIP[3]).

slip·way /ˈslipˌwā/ ▶ **n.** another term for SLIP[1] (sense 4 of the noun).

slit /slit/ ▶ **n.** a long, narrow cut or opening: *make a slit in the stem under a bud* | *arrow slits.*
▶ **v.** (**slits, slitting, slit**) [with obj.] make a long, narrow cut in (something): *give me the truth or I will slit your throat* | [with obj. and complement] *he slit open the envelope.* ■ cut (something) into strips: *a wide recording head magnetizes the tape before it is slit to domestic size.* ■ (past **slitted**) form (one's eyes) into slits; squint.
– DERIVATIVES **slit·ter n.**
– ORIGIN late Old English *slite* (noun); related to Old English *slitan* 'split, rend' (of Germanic origin).

slith·er /ˈsliT͟Hәr/ ▶ **v.** [no obj.] move smoothly over a surface with a twisting or oscillating motion: *I spied a baby adder slithering away.* ■ slide or slip unsteadily on a loose or slippery surface: *we slithered down a snowy mountain track.*
▶ **n.** [in sing.] a movement in such a manner: *a snakelike slither across the grass.*
– DERIVATIVES **slith·er·y adj.**
– ORIGIN Middle English: alteration of the dialect verb *slidder*, frequentative from the base of SLIDE.

slit lamp ▶ **n.** Medicine a lamp that emits a narrow but intense beam of light, used for examining the interior of the eye.

slit trench ▶ **n.** a narrow trench for a soldier or a small group of soldiers and their equipment.

Sli·ven /ˈslivәn/ a commercial city in east central Bulgaria, in the foothills of the Balkan Mountains; pop. 94,456 (2008).

S

sliv·er /ˈslivər/ ▶ **n.** a small, thin, narrow piece of something cut or split off a larger piece: *a sliver of cheese* | figurative *there was a sliver of light under his door.* ■ a strip of loose untwisted textile fibers produced by carding.
▶ **v.** [with obj.] (usu. as adj. **slivered**) cut or break (something) into small, thin, narrow pieces: *slivered almonds.* ■ convert (textile fibers) into slivers.
– ORIGIN late Middle English: from dialect *slive* 'cleave.'

sliv·o·vitz /ˈslivəˌvits/ ▶ **n.** a type of plum brandy made chiefly in eastern Europe.
– ORIGIN Croatian *šljivovica*, from *šljiva* 'plum;' compare with SLOE.

Sloan /slōn/, John French (1871–1951), US artist. A member of the Ashcan School, he painted scenes of New York City such as in "Backyards, Greenwich Village" (1914).

slob /släb/ ▶ **n.** informal a lazy and slovenly person.
– DERIVATIVES **slob·bish** adj., **slob·by** adj.
– ORIGIN late 18th cent.: from Irish *slab* 'mud,' from Anglo-Irish *slab* 'ooze, sludge,' probably of Scandinavian origin.

slob·ber /ˈsläbər/ ▶ **v.** [no obj.] have saliva dripping copiously from the mouth: *Fido tended to slobber* | (as adj. **slobbering**) *big slobbering kisses.* ■ (**slobber over**) be excessively sentimental; show excessive enthusiasm for: *news executives slobbered over him for autographs* | *they took turns slobbering all over the new baby.*
▶ **n.** saliva dripping copiously from the mouth.
– DERIVATIVES **slob·ber·y** adj.
– ORIGIN late Middle English: probably from Middle Dutch *slobberen* 'walk through mud,' also 'feed noisily,' of imitative origin.

sloe /slō/ ▶ **n.** another term for BLACKTHORN. ■ the small bluish-black fruit of the blackthorn, with a sharp sour taste.
– ORIGIN Old English *slā(h)*, of Germanic origin; related to Dutch *slee* and German *Schlehe*, from an Indo-European root probably shared by Latin *livere* 'be blue' and Croatian *šljiva* 'plum;' compare with SLIVOVITZ.

sloe-eyed ▶ **adj.** having attractive dark, typically almond-shaped eyes.

sloe gin ▶ **n.** a liqueur made by steeping sloes in gin.

slog /släg/ informal ▶ **v.** (**slogs, slogging, slogged**) **1** [no obj.] work hard over a period of time: *they were slogging away to meet a deadline.* ■ [with adverbial of direction] walk or move with difficulty or effort: *he slogged home through the gray slush.*
2 [no obj.] hit forcefully and typically wildly, esp. in boxing: *the fighters were slogging away.* ■ (**slog it out**) fight or compete at length or fiercely.
▶ **n.** [usu. in sing.] a spell of difficult, tiring work or traveling: *it would be **a hard slog** back to the camp.*
– DERIVATIVES **slog·ger** n.
– ORIGIN early 19th cent.: of unknown origin; compare with SLUG[2].

slo·gan /ˈslōgən/ ▶ **n.** a short and striking or memorable phrase used in advertising. ■ a motto associated with a political party or movement or other group. ■ historical a Scottish Highland war cry.
– ORIGIN early 16th cent.: from Scottish Gaelic *sluagh-ghairm*, from *sluagh* 'army' + *gairm* 'shout.'

slo·gan·eer /ˌslōgəˈnir/ ▶ **v.** (usu. as noun **sloganeering**) [no obj.] employ or invent slogans, typically in a political context.
▶ **n.** a person who does this: *as the sloganeers put it: "peace through strength."*

S

slo·ka /ˈslōkə/ ▶ **n.** a couplet of Sanskrit verse, esp. one in which each line contains sixteen syllables.
– ORIGIN from Sanskrit *śloka* 'noise, praise.'

slo-mo /ˈslō ˈmō/ (also **slomo**) ▶ **n.** informal short for SLOW MOTION.

sloop /slo͞op/ ▶ **n.** a one-masted sailboat with a fore-and-aft mainsail and a jib. ■ (also **sloop of war**) historical a small square-rigged sailing warship with two or three masts. ■ historical a small antisubmarine warship used for convoy escort in World War II.
– ORIGIN early 17th cent.: from Dutch *sloep(e)*, of unknown origin.

sloop-rigged ▶ **adj.** rigged as a sloop.

slop[1] /släp/ ▶ **v.** (**slops, slopping, slopped**) **1** [no obj.] (of a liquid) spill or flow over the edge of a container, typically as a result of careless handling: *water slopped over the edge of the sink.* ■ [with obj.] cause (a liquid) to spill or overflow in such a way: *in spite of his care he slopped some water.* ■ [with obj.] apply or put (something) somewhere in a casual or careless manner: *they spent their weekend slopping on paint.* ■ (**slop through**) wade through (a wet or muddy area): *they were slopping through paddy fields.*
2 [with obj.] feed slops to (an animal, esp. a pig).
3 [no obj.] speak or write in a sentimentally effusive manner; gush: *she **slopped over** her dog.*
▶ **n. 1** (usu. **slops**) waste water from a kitchen, bathroom, or chamber pot that has to be emptied by hand: *sink slops.* ■ (usu. **slops**) semiliquid kitchen refuse, often used as animal food. ■ unappetizing weak, semiliquid food: *they fed us some slop in a bowl.*
2 sentimental language or material: *country music is not all commercial slop.*
– ORIGIN mid 16th cent. (in the sense 'to spill, splash'): probably related to SLIP[3]. Early use of the noun denoted watery mud, the first of the current senses ('unappetizing food') dating from the mid 17th cent.

slop[2] ▶ **n.** archaic **1** a workman's loose outer garment.
2 (**slops**) wide, baggy pants common in the 16th and early 17th centuries, esp. as worn by sailors. ■ clothes and bedding supplied to sailors by the navy.
– ORIGIN late Middle English (sense 1): from the second element of Old English *oferslop* 'surplice,' literally '(something) slipped over.'

slope /slōp/ ▶ **n. 1** a surface of which one end or side is at a higher level than another; a rising or falling surface: *he slithered helplessly down the slope.* ■ a difference in level or sideways position between the two ends or sides of a thing: *the roof should have a slope sufficient for proper drainage* | *the backward slope of the chair.* ■ (often **slopes**) a part of the side of a hill or mountain, esp. as a place for skiing: *a ten-minute cable-car ride delivers you to the slopes.* ■ the gradient of a graph at any point. ■ Electronics the transconductance of a valve, numerically equal to the gradient of one of the characteristic curves of the valve.
2 informal, offensive a person from Asia, esp. Vietnam or elsewhere in Southeast Asia.
▶ **v.** [no obj.] (of a surface or line) be inclined from a horizontal or vertical line; slant up or down: *the garden **sloped down** to a stream* | *the ceiling sloped.* ■ [with obj.] place or arrange in such a position or inclination: *Poole sloped his shoulders* | (as adj. **sloped**) *a sloped leather writing surface.*
– ORIGIN late 16th cent. (as a verb): from the obsolete adverb *slope*, a shortening of ASLOPE.

slop·ing /ˈslōpiNG/ ▶ **adj.** inclined from a horizontal or vertical line: *a sloping floor.*

slop·py /ˈsläpē/ ▶ **adj.** (**sloppier, sloppiest**) **1** (of semifluid matter) containing too much liquid; watery: *do not make the concrete too sloppy.*
2 careless and unsystematic; excessively casual: *your speech has always been sloppy.*
3 (of a garment) casual and loose-fitting: *she wore a sloppy sweater and jeans.*
4 informal (of literature or behavior) weakly or foolishly sentimental: *lovers of sloppy romance.*
– DERIVATIVES **slop·pi·ly** /ˈsläpəlē/ adv., **slop·pi·ness** n.

slop·py joe ▶ **n.** informal a sandwich with a filling of ground beef that has been seasoned with a sauce of tomatoes and spices.

slosh /släsH/ ▶ **v.** [no obj.] (of liquid in a container) move irregularly with a splashing sound: *water in the boat sloshed around under our feet* | figurative *there is so much money now **sloshing around** in professional tennis.* ■ (of a person) move through liquid with a splashing sound: *they sloshed up the tracks in the dank woods.* ■ [with obj.] pour (liquid) clumsily: *she sloshed coffee into a cracked cup.*
▶ **n.** an act or sound of splashing: *the distant slosh of the washing machine in the basement.*
– ORIGIN early 19th cent.: variant of the noun SLUSH.

sloshed /släsHt/ ▶ **adj.** informal drunk: *I drank a lot of wine and got sloshed.*

slosh·y /ˈsläsHē/ ▶ **adj.** (**sloshier, sloshiest**)
1 wet and sticky; slushy: *the hoofprints are sloshy depressions.*
2 informal excessively sentimental; sloppy: *the program is a sloshy and patronizing affair.*

Slot /slät/ (**the Slot**) name given in World War II by US forces to New Georgia Sound, in the central Solomon Islands. Japanese forces trying to defend Guadalcanal were seen as coming consistently down this passage from the northwest.

slot[1] /slät/ ▶ **n. 1** a long, narrow aperture or slit in a machine for something to be inserted: *he slid a coin into the slot of the jukebox.* ■ a groove or channel into which something fits or in which something works, such as one in the head of a screw.
2 an allotted place in an arrangement or plan such as a broadcasting schedule: *a late-night television slot* | *landing slots at O'Hare.*
▶ **v.** (**slots, slotting, slotted**) [with obj.] place (something) into a long, narrow aperture: *he slotted a cassette into the tape machine* | *the plates come in sections that can be **slotted together**.* ■ [no obj.] be placed or able to be placed into such an aperture: *the processors will slot into a personal computer.*
– DERIVATIVES **slot·ted** adj.
– ORIGIN late Middle English (in the sense 'slight depression running down the middle of the chest,' surviving as a Scots term): from Old French *esclot*, of obscure origin.

slot[2] ▶ **n.** (usu. **slots**) the track of a deer, visible as slotted footprints in soft ground.
– ORIGIN late 16th cent.: from Old French *esclot* 'hoofprint of a horse,' probably from Old Norse *slóth* 'trail'; compare with SLEUTH.

slot·back /ˈslätˌbak/ ▶ **n.** Football an offensive back who is positioned between the tackle and the split end.

slot car ▶ **n.** an electrically driven miniature race car that travels in a slot in a track.

sloth /slôTH, släTH, slōTH/ ▶ **n. 1** reluctance to work or make an effort; laziness: *he should overcome his natural sloth and complacency.*
2 a slow-moving tropical American mammal that hangs upside down from the branches of trees using its long limbs and hooked claws. ● Families Bradypodidae (three species of **three-toed sloth** in genus *Bradypus*) and Megalonychidae (two species of **two-toed sloth** in genus *Choloepus*), order Xenarthra (or Edentata).
– ORIGIN Old English: from SLOW + -TH[2].

three-toed sloth

sloth bear ▶ **n.** a shaggy-coated nocturnal Indian bear that uses its long curved claws for hanging upside down like a sloth and for opening termite mounds to feed on the insects. ● *Melursus ursinus*, family Ursidae.

sloth·ful /ˈslôTHfəl, släTH-, ˈslōTH-/ ▶ **adj.** lazy: *fatigue made him slothful.*
– DERIVATIVES **sloth·ful·ly** adv., **sloth·ful·ness** n.

slot ma·chine ▶ **n.** a machine worked by the insertion of a coin, in particular: ■ a gaming machine that generates random combinations of symbols on a dial, certain combinations winning varying amounts of money for the player. ■ chiefly Brit. a vending machine selling small items.

slot·ted spoon ▶ **n.** a large spoon with slots or holes for draining liquid from food.

slouch /slouCH/ ▶ **v. 1** [no obj.] stand, move, or sit in a lazy, drooping way: *he slouched against the wall* | (**be slouched**) *he was slouched in his chair.*
2 [with obj.] dated bend one side of the brim of (a hat) downward.
▶ **n.** [in sing.] **1** a lazy, drooping posture or movement: *his stance was a round-shouldered slouch.*
2 [usu. with negative] informal an incompetent person: *my brother was no slouch at making a buck.*
3 a downward bend of a hat brim.
– DERIVATIVES **slouch·y** adj.
– ORIGIN early 16th cent. (in the sense 'lazy, slovenly person'): of unknown origin. *Slouching* was used to mean 'hanging down, drooping' (specifically describing a hat with a brim hanging over the face), and 'having an awkward posture' from the 17th cent.

slouch hat ▶ **n.** a hat with a wide flexible brim.

slough[1] /slou, slo͞o/ ▶ **n. 1** a swamp. ■ a muddy side channel or inlet.
2 a situation characterized by lack of progress or activity: *the economic slough of the interwar years.*
– DERIVATIVES **slough·y** adj.
– ORIGIN Old English *slōh, slō(g)*, of unknown origin.

slough[2] /sləf/ ▶ **v.** [with obj.] (usu. **slough something off**) shed or remove (a layer of dead skin): *a snake sloughs off its old skin* | *exfoliate once a week to slough off any dry skin.* ■ get rid of (something undesirable or no longer required): *he is concerned to slough off the country's bad environmental image.* ■ [no obj.] (**slough off**) (of dead skin) drop off; be shed. ■ [no obj.] (**slough away/down**) (of soil or rock) collapse or slide into a hole or depression.
▶ **n.** the dropping off of dead tissue from living flesh: *the drugs can cause blistering and slough.*
– DERIVATIVES **slough·y** adj.
– ORIGIN Middle English (as a noun denoting a skin, esp. the outer skin shed by a snake): perhaps related to Low German *slu(we)* 'husk, peel.' The verb dates from the early 18th cent.

Slough of De·spond (also **slough of despond** /ˈslou əv dəˈspänd/) ▶ **n.** a state of hopeless depression: *while everyone is having a blast I am sinking into the Slough of Despond.*
– ORIGIN the name of a deep boggy place in John Bunyan's *The Pilgrim's Progress* between the City of Destruction and the gate at the beginning of Christian's journey.

Slo·vak /ˈslōväk, -vak/ ▶ **n. 1** a native or inhabitant of Slovakia, or a person of Slovak descent.
2 the West Slavic language of Slovakia, closely related to Czech.
▶ **adj.** of or relating to this people or their language.
– ORIGIN the name in Slovak, from a Slavic root shared with SLOVENE and perhaps related to *slovo* 'word.'

Slo·va·ki·a /slōˈväkēə/ a country in central Europe; pop. 5,463,000 (est. 2009); capital, Bratislava; languages, Slovak (official) and Hungarian.

Slovakia was dominated by Hungary until it declared independence in 1918 and united with the Czech-speaking areas of Bohemia and Moravia to form Czechoslovakia. The eastern of the two constituent republics of Czechoslovakia, Slovakia became independent on the partition of that country on January 1, 1993. It joined NATO and the EU in 2004.

– DERIVATIVES **Slo·va·ki·an** adj. & n.

slov·en /ˈsləvən/ ▶ **n.** dated a person who is habitually messy or careless.
– ORIGIN late 15th cent. (in the sense 'person with base manners'): perhaps from Flemish *sloef* 'dirty' or Dutch *slof* 'careless, negligent.'

Slo·vene /ˈslōvēn/ ▶ **n. 1** a native or inhabitant of Slovenia, or a person of Slovene descent.
2 the South Slavic language of this people.
▶ **adj.** of or relating to Slovenia, its people, or their language.
– ORIGIN from Slovene *Slovenec*, from a Slavic root shared with SLOVAK and perhaps related to *slovo* 'word.'

Slo·ve·ni·a /slōˈvēnēə/ a country in southeastern Europe; pop. 2,005,700 (est. 2009); capital, Ljubljana; official language, Slovene.

Slovenia formed part of the Austrian empire and in 1919 was ceded to the kingdom of Serbs, Croats, and Slovenes (named Yugoslavia from 1929) of which it remained a constituent republic until it declared its independence in 1991. It joined NATO and the EU in 2004.

Slo·ve·ni·an /slōˈvēnēən/ ▶ **n. & adj.** another term for SLOVENE.

slov·en·ly /ˈsləvənlē, ˈslä-/ ▶ **adj.** (esp. of a person or their appearance) messy and dirty: *he was upbraided for his slovenly appearance.* ■ (esp. of a person or action) careless; excessively casual: *slovenly speech.*
– DERIVATIVES **slov·en·li·ness** n.

slow /slō/ ▶ **adj. 1** moving or operating, or designed to do so, only at a low speed; not quick or fast: *a time when diesel cars were slow and noisy* | *a slow dot-matrix printer.* ■ taking a long time to perform a specified action: *she was a slow reader* | [with infinitive] *large organizations can be slow to change.* ■ lasting or taking a long time: *a slow process* | *the journey home was slow.* ■ [attrib.] not allowing or intended for fast travel: *the slow lane.* ■ (of a playing field) likely to make the ball bounce or run slowly or to prevent competitors from traveling fast.
2 [predic. or as complement] (of a clock or watch) showing a time earlier than the correct time: *the clock was five minutes slow.*
3 not prompt to understand, think, or learn: *he's so slow, so unimaginative.*
4 uneventful and rather dull: *a slow and mostly aimless narrative.* ■ (of business) with little activity; slack: *sales were slow.*
5 Photography (of a film) needing long exposure. ■ (of a lens) having a small aperture.
6 (of a fire or oven) burning or giving off heat gently: *bake the dish in a preheated slow oven.*
▶ **adv.** at a slow pace; slowly: *the train went slower and slower* | [in combination] *a slow-moving river.*
▶ **v.** [no obj.] reduce one's speed or the speed of a vehicle or process: *the train slowed to a halt* | *investment has slowed down* | [with obj.] *he slowed the car.* ■ (**slow down/up**) live or work less actively or intensely: *I wasn't feeling well and had to slow down.*
– PHRASES **slow but sure** not quick but achieving the required result eventually: *a slow but sure increase in the price of gold.*
– DERIVATIVES **slow·ish** adj., **slow·ness** n.
– ORIGIN Old English *slāw* 'slow-witted, sluggish,' of Germanic origin.

USAGE The word **slow** is normally used as an adjective (*a slow learner; the journey was slow*). It is also used as an adverb in certain specific contexts, including compounds such as *slow-acting* and *slow-moving* and in the expression *go slow*. Other adverbial use is informal and usually regarded as nonstandard, as in *he drives too slow* and *go as slow as you can*. In such contexts, standard English uses **slowly** instead. The use of **slow** and **slowly** in this respect contrasts with the use of **fast**, which is completely standard in use as both an adjective and an adverb; there is no word '*fastly*'.

slow·coach /ˈslōˌkōCH/ ▶ **n.** informal British term for SLOWPOKE.

slow cook·er ▶ **n.** a large electric pot used for cooking food, esp. stews, very slowly.

slow·down /ˈslōˌdoun/ ▶ **n.** an act of slowing down: *a traffic slowdown in the passing lane.* ■ a decline in economic activity.

slow drag ▶ **n.** a slow blues rhythm or piece of music.
▶ **v.** (**slow-drag**) [no obj.] dance to such a rhythm.

slow lo·ris ▶ **n.** see LORIS.

slow·ly /ˈslōlē/ ▶ **adv.** at a slow speed; not quickly: *they moved forward slowly.*
– PHRASES **slowly but surely** achieving the desired results gradually and reliably rather than quickly and spectacularly: *the new church began, slowly but surely, to grow.*

USAGE See usage at SLOW.

slow march ▶ **n.** [in sing.] a military marching pace approximately half the speed of the quick march.

slow match ▶ **n.** historical a slow-burning wick or cord for lighting explosives.

slow mo·tion ▶ **n.** the action of showing film or playing back video more slowly than it was made or recorded, so that the action appears slower than in real life: *the scene was shown in slow motion* | [as modifier] *a slow-motion sequence.*

slow neu·tron ▶ **n.** a neutron with low kinetic energy, esp. after moderation.

slow·poke /ˈslōˌpōk/ ▶ **n.** informal a person who acts or moves slowly: *we were yelling for the slowpokes to catch up.*

slow-scan ▶ **adj.** [attrib.] Telecommunications scanning at a much slower rate than usual, so that the resulting signal has a much smaller bandwidth: *a slow-scan transmission.*

slow track ▶ **n.** a route or method that results in slow progress: *a slow track to economic and monetary union.* Compare with FAST TRACK.

slow-twitch ▶ **adj.** [attrib.] Physiology (of a muscle fiber) contracting slowly, providing endurance rather than strength.

slow vi·rus ▶ **n.** a virus or viruslike organism that multiplies slowly in the host organism and has a long incubation period.

slow-wit·ted ▶ **adj.** slow to understand, think, or learn; stupid: *the slow-witted interviewer failed to pounce on his remarks.*

slow-worm ▶ **n.** a small snakelike Eurasian legless lizard that is typically brownish or copper-colored and that gives birth to live young. Also called BLINDWORM. ● *Anguis fragilis*, family Anguidae.
– ORIGIN Old English *slāwyrm*, from *slā-* (of uncertain origin) + *wyrm* 'snake.'

SLR ▶ **abbr.** ■ self-loading rifle. ■ single-lens reflex.

slub[1] /sləb/ ▶ **n.** a lump or thick place in yarn or thread. ■ fabric woven from yarn with such a texture.
▶ **adj.** [attrib.] (of fabric) having an irregular appearance caused by uneven thickness of the warp.
– DERIVATIVES **slubbed** adj.
– ORIGIN early 19th cent.: of unknown origin.

slub[2] ▶ **n.** wool that has been slightly twisted in preparation for spinning.
▶ **v.** (**slubs, slubbing, slubbed**) [with obj.] twist (wool) in this way.
– ORIGIN mid 19th cent.: of unknown origin.

sludge /sləj/ ▶ **n.** thick, soft, wet mud or a similar viscous mixture of liquid and solid components, esp. the product of an industrial or refining process. ■ dirty oil, esp. in the sump of an internal combustion engine. ■ sea ice newly formed in small pieces.
– DERIVATIVES **sludg·y** adj.
– ORIGIN early 17th cent.: of uncertain origin; compare with SLUSH.

slue ▶ **v. & n.** variant spelling of SLEW[1].

slug[1] /sləg/ ▶ **n. 1** a tough-skinned terrestrial mollusk that typically lacks a shell and secretes a film of mucus for protection. It can be a serious plant pest. See also SEA SLUG. ● Order Stylommatophora, class Gastropoda.
2 a slow, lazy person; a sluggard.
3 an amount of an alcoholic drink, typically liquor, that is gulped or poured: *he took a slug of whiskey.* [mid 18th cent.: figuratively from sense 4 of the noun.]
4 an elongated, typically rounded piece or metal: *the reactor uses embedded slugs of uranium.* ■ a counterfeit coin; a token. ■ a bullet, esp. one of lead. ■ a missile for an air gun. ■ a line of type in Linotype printing. ■ Printing a metal bar used in spacing.
▶ **v.** (**slugs, slugging, slugged**) [with obj.] drink (something, typically alcohol) in a large draft; swig: *she picked up her drink and slugged it straight back.*
– ORIGIN late Middle English (sense 2 of the noun): probably of Scandinavian origin; compare with Norwegian dialect *slugg* 'large heavy body.' Sense 1 dates from the early 18th cent.

slug[2] informal ▶ **v.** (**slugs, slugging, slugged**) [with obj.] strike (someone) with a hard blow: *he was the one who'd get slugged.* ■ (**slug it out**) settle a dispute or contest by fighting or competing fiercely: *they went outside to slug it out.*
▶ **n.** a hard blow.
– ORIGIN mid 19th cent.: of unknown origin; compare with the verb SLOG.

slug·a·bed /ˈsləgəˌbed/ ▶ **n.** a lazy person who stays in bed late.
– ORIGIN late 16th cent.: from the rare verb *slug* 'be lazy or slow' + ABED.

slug·fest /ˈsləgˌfest/ ▶ **n.** informal a tough and challenging contest, esp. in sports such as boxing and baseball.
– ORIGIN early 20th cent.: from SLUG[2] + -FEST.

slug·gard /ˈsləgərd/ ▶ **n.** a lazy, sluggish person.
– DERIVATIVES **slug·gard·li·ness** n., **slug·gard·ly** adj.
– ORIGIN Middle English: from the rare verb *slug* 'be lazy or slow' + -ARD.

slug·ger /ˈsləgər/ ▶ **n.** person who throws hard punches. ■ Baseball a player who consistently hits for power, esp. home runs and doubles.

slug·gish /ˈsləgiSH/ ▶ **adj.** slow-moving or inactive: *a sluggish stream.* ■ lacking energy or alertness: *Alex woke late feeling tired and sluggish.* ■ slow to respond or make progress: *the car had been sluggish all morning.*
– DERIVATIVES **slug·gish·ly** adv., **slug·gish·ness** n.
– ORIGIN late Middle English: from the noun SLUG[1] or the verb *slug* (see SLUGGARD) + -ISH[1].

sluice /slo͞os/ ▶ **n. 1** (also **sluice gate**) a sliding gate or other device for controlling the flow of water, esp. one in a lock gate. ■ (also **sluiceway**) an artificial water channel for carrying off overflow or surplus water. ■ (in gold mining) a channel or trough constructed with grooves into which a current of water is directed in order to separate gold from the sand or gravel containing it.
2 an act of rinsing or showering with water: *a sluice with cold water.*
▶ **v.** [with obj.] wash or rinse freely with a stream or shower of water: *she sluiced her face in cold water* | *crews sluiced down the decks of their ship.* ■ [no obj.] (of water) pour, flow, or shower freely: *the waves sluiced over them.*
– ORIGIN Middle English (as a noun): from Old French *escluse* 'sluice gate,' based on Latin *excludere* 'exclude.' The verb dates from the late 16th cent.

slum /sləm/ ▶ **n.** a squalid and overcrowded urban street or district inhabited by very poor people. ■ a house or building unfit for human habitation.
▶ **v.** (**slums, slumming, slummed**) [no obj.] informal spend time at a lower social level than one's own through curiosity or for charitable purposes: *rich tourists slumming among the quaintly dangerous natives.* ■ (**slum it**) put up with conditions that are less comfortable or of a lower quality than one is used to: *businessmen are having to slum it in aircraft economy class seats.*
– DERIVATIVES **slum·mer** n.
– ORIGIN early 19th cent. (originally slang, in the sense 'room'): of unknown origin.

slum·ber /ˈsləmbər/ literary ▶ **v.** [no obj.] sleep: *Sleeping Beauty slumbered in her forest castle* | figurative *the village street slumbered under the afternoon sun.*
▶ **n.** (often **slumbers**) a sleep: *scaring folk from their slumbers.*
– DERIVATIVES **slum·ber·er** n., **slum·brous** /-brəs/ (also **slumberous** /-bərəs/) adj.
– ORIGIN Middle English: alteration of Scots and northern English *sloom*, in the same sense. The *-b-* was added for ease of pronunciation.

slum·ber·land /ˈsləmbərˌland/ ▶ **n.** literary or humorous the state of being asleep.

S

slum·ber par·ty ▶ **n.** a party, typically for preteen or teenage girls, in which all the guests spend the night at the house where the party is held.

slum·gul·lion /ˌsləmˈgəlyən/ ▶ **n.** informal cheap or insubstantial stew.

slum·lord /ˈsləmˌlôrd/ ▶ **n.** informal a landlord of slum property, esp. one who profiteers.

slum·my /ˈsləmē/ ▶ **adj.** (**slummier**, **slummiest**) full of slums, or resembling a slum: *a slummy neighborhood.*
– DERIVATIVES **slum·mi·ness n.**

slump /sləmp/ ▶ **v.** [no obj.] **1** [with adverbial] sit, lean, or fall heavily and limply, esp. with a bent back: *she slumped against the cushions* | (**be slumped**) *Denis was slumped in his seat.*
2 undergo a sudden severe or prolonged fall in price, value, or amount: *land prices slumped.* ■ fail or decline substantially: *the Giants* ***slumped to an*** *8–8 record.*
▶ **n.** a sudden severe or prolonged fall in the price, value, or amount of something: *a slump in annual profits.* ■ a prolonged period of abnormally low economic activity, typically bringing widespread unemployment. ■ a period of substantial failure or decline: *the organization's recent slump.*
– DERIVATIVES **slump·y adj.**
– ORIGIN late 17th cent. (in the sense 'fall into a bog'): probably imitative and related to Norwegian *slumpe* 'to fall.'

slung /sləNG/ past and past participle of SLING[1].

slung shot ▶ **n.** a hard object, such as a metal ball, attached by a strap or thong to the wrist and used as a weapon.

slunk /sləNGk/ past and past participle of SLINK.

slur /slər/ ▶ **v.** (**slurs**, **slurring**, **slurred**) [with obj.] **1** speak (words or speech) indistinctly so that the sounds run into one another: *he was slurring his words like a drunk.* ■ [no obj.] (of words or speech) be spoken in this way: *his speech was beginning to slur.* ■ pass over (a fact or aspect) so as to conceal or minimize it: *essential attributes are being slurred over or ignored.*
2 Music perform (a group of two or more notes) legato: (as adj. **slurred**) *a group of slurred notes.* ■ mark (notes) with a slur.
3 make damaging or insulting insinuations or allegations about: *try and slur the integrity of the police to secure an acquittal.*
▶ **n. 1** an insinuation or allegation about someone that is likely to insult them or damage their reputation: *the comments were* ***a slur on*** *the staff* | *a racial slur.*
2 an act of speaking indistinctly so that sounds or words run into one another or a tendency to speak in such a way: *there was a mean slur in his voice.*
3 Music a curved line used to show that a group of two or more notes is to be sung to one syllable or played or sung legato.
– ORIGIN early 17th cent.: of unknown origin. The Middle English noun *slur* 'thin, fluid mud' gave rise to the early verb senses 'smear, smirch' and 'disparage (a person),' later 'gloss over (a fault),' whence current usage.

slurp /slərp/ ▶ **v.** [with obj.] eat or drink (something) with a loud sloppy sucking noise: *she slurped her coffee* | [no obj.] *he slurped noisily from a wine cup.*
▶ **n.** a loud sucking sound made while eating or drinking: *she drank it down with a loud slurp.*
– DERIVATIVES **slurp·y adj.**
– ORIGIN mid 17th cent.: from Dutch *slurpen.*

S

slur·ry /ˈslərē/ ▶ **n.** (pl. **slurries**) a semiliquid mixture, typically of fine particles of manure, cement, or coal suspended in water.
– ORIGIN late Middle English: related to dialect *slur* 'thin mud,' of unknown origin.

slush /sləSH/ ▶ **n. 1** partially melted snow or ice: *the snow was turning into brown slush in the gutters.* ■ watery mud.
2 informal excessive sentiment: *the slush of Hollywood's romantic fifties films.*
▶ **v.** [no obj.] make a squelching or splashing sound: *there was water slushing around in the galley.*
– ORIGIN mid 17th cent.: probably imitative; compare with SLOSH.

slush fund ▶ **n.** a reserve of money used for illicit purposes, esp. political bribery.
– ORIGIN mid 19th cent.: originally nautical slang denoting money collected to buy luxuries, from the sale of *slush*, the refuse grease from the meat cooked aboard ship.

slush pile ▶ **n.** informal a stack of unsolicited manuscripts that have been sent to a publishing company for consideration.

slush·y /ˈsləSHē/ ▶ **adj.** (**slushier**, **slushiest**) **1** resembling, consisting of, or covered with slush: *slushy snow.*
2 informal excessively sentimental: *slushy novels.*
– DERIVATIVES **slush·i·ness n.**

slut /slət/ ▶ **n.** a slovenly or promiscuous woman.
– DERIVATIVES **slut·tish adj.**, **slut·tish·ness n.**
– ORIGIN Middle English: of unknown origin.

SLV ▶ **abbr.** standard launch vehicle.

sly /slī/ ▶ **adj.** (**slyer**, **slyest**) having or showing a cunning and deceitful nature: *she had a sly personality.* ■ (of a remark, glance, or facial expression) showing in an insinuating way that one has some secret knowledge that may be harmful or embarrassing: *he gave a sly grin.* ■ (of an action) surreptitious: *a sly sip of water.*
– PHRASES **on the sly** in a secretive fashion: *she was drinking on the sly.*
– DERIVATIVES **sly·ly** (also **slily**) **adv.**, **sly·ness n.**
– ORIGIN Middle English (also in the sense 'dexterous'): from Old Norse *slœgr* 'cunning,' originally 'able to strike,' from the verb *slá*; compare with SLEIGHT.

sly·boots /ˈslīˌbo͞ots/ ▶ **n.** informal a sly person.

slype /slīp/ ▶ **n.** a covered way or passage between a cathedral transept and the chapter house or deanery.
– ORIGIN mid 19th cent.: perhaps a variant of dialect *slipe* 'long narrow piece of ground.'

SM ▶ **abbr.** ■ service mark. ■ sadomasochism. ■ sergeant major. ■ short meter.

Sm ▶ **symbol** the chemical element samarium.

sm. ▶ **abbr.** small.

S-M (also **s-m**, **S/M**, **s/m**) ▶ **abbr.** ■ (also **S&M**) sadomasochism. ■ sadomasochistic.

SMA ▶ **abbr.** Surplus Marketing Administration.

smack[1] /smak/ ▶ **n.** a sharp slap or blow, typically one given with the palm of the hand: *she gave Mark a smack across the face.* ■ a loud, sharp sound made by such a blow or a similar action: *she closed the ledger with a smack.* ■ a loud kiss: *I was saluted with two hearty smacks on my cheeks.*
▶ **v.** [with obj.] strike (someone or something), typically with the palm of the hand and as a punishment: *Jessica smacked his face quite hard.* ■ smash, drive, or put forcefully into or onto something: *he smacked a fist into the palm of a black-gloved hand.* ■ part (one's lips) noisily in eager anticipation or enjoyment of food, drink, or other pleasures. ■ archaic crack (a whip).
▶ **adv.** informal **1** in a sudden and violent way: *I ran smack into the back of a parked truck.*
2 exactly; precisely: *our mother's house was smack in the middle of the city.*
– ORIGIN mid 16th cent. (in the sense 'part (one's lips) noisily'): from Middle Dutch *smacken*, of imitative origin; compare with German *schmatzen* 'eat or kiss noisily.'

smack[2] ▶ **v.** [no obj.] (**smack of**) have a flavor of; taste of: *the tea smacked of peppermint.* ■ suggest the presence or effects of (something wrong or unpleasant): *the whole thing smacks of a cover-up.*
▶ **n.** (**a smack of**) a flavor or taste of: *anything with even a modest smack of hops dries the palate.* ■ a trace or suggestion of: *I hear the smack of collusion between them.*
– ORIGIN Old English *smæc* 'flavor, smell,' of Germanic origin; related to Dutch *smaak* and German *Geschmack.*

smack[3] ▶ **n.** a fishing boat, often one equipped with a well for keeping the caught fish alive. ■ chiefly Brit. a single-masted sailboat used for fishing or coastal commerce.
– ORIGIN early 17th cent.: from Dutch *smak*, of unknown ultimate origin.

smack[4] ▶ **n.** informal heroin.
– ORIGIN 1940s: probably an alteration of Yiddish *shmek* 'a sniff.'

smack dab ▶ **adv.** informal exactly; precisely: *here I am in Bolivia, smack dab in the heart of South America.*

smack·down /ˈsmakˌdoun/ ▶ **n.** informal **1** a bitter contest or confrontation: *the age-old man versus Nature smackdown.*
2 a decisive or humiliating defeat or setback.
– ORIGIN 1990s: from SMACK[1].

smack·er /ˈsmakər/ (also **smackeroo** /ˌsmakəˈro͞o/) ▶ **n.** informal **1** a dollar: *it set me back fifteen smackers.*
2 a loud kiss.

small /smôl/ ▶ **adj.** of a size that is less than normal or usual: *the room was small and quiet* | *the small hill that sheltered the house.* ■ not great in amount, number, strength, or power: *a small amount of money.* ■ not fully grown or developed; young: *as a small boy, he spent his days either reading or watching TV.* ■ used as the first letter of a word that has both a general and a specific use to show that in this case the general use is intended: *I meant "catholic" with a small c.* ■ insignificant; unimportant: *these are small points.* ■ (of a voice) lacking strength and confidence: *"I'm scared," she said in a small voice.* ■ [attrib.] little; hardly any: *the captain had been paying small attention.* ■ [attrib.] (of a business or its owner) operating on a modest scale: *a small farmer.* ■ archaic low or inferior in rank or position; socially undistinguished: *at dinner, some of the smaller neighbors were invited.*
▶ **n.** (**smalls**) Brit. informal small items of clothing, esp. underwear.
▶ **adv.** into small pieces: *the okra cut up small.* ■ in a small size: *you shouldn't write so small.*
– PHRASES **feel** (or **look**) **small** feel (or look) contemptibly weak or insignificant. **it's a small world** used to express surprise at meeting an acquaintance or discovering a personal connection in a distant place or an unexpected context. **no small ——** a good deal of ——: *a matter of no small consequence.* **the small of the back** the part of a person's back where the spine curves in at the level of the waist. **small potatoes** informal something insignificant or unimportant: *her business was small potatoes.* **small wonder** not very surprising: *it's small wonder that her emotions had seesawed.*
– DERIVATIVES **small·ish adj.**, **small·ness n.**
– ORIGIN Old English *smæl*, of Germanic origin; related to Dutch *smal* and German *schmal.*

small arms ▶ **plural n.** portable firearms, esp. rifles, pistols, and light machine guns.

small beer ▶ **n. 1** chiefly Brit. a thing that is considered unimportant: *even with $10,000 to invest, you are still small beer for most stockbrokers.*
2 archaic weak beer.

small-bore ▶ **adj.** denoting a firearm with a narrow bore, in international and Olympic shooting generally .22 inch caliber. ■ informal trivial; unimportant: *small-bore economic issues.*

small cal·o·rie ▶ **n.** see CALORIE.

small-cap ▶ **adj.** [attrib.] Finance denoting or relating to the stock of a company with a small capitalization.

small cap·i·tal ▶ **n.** a capital letter that is of the same height as a lowercase x in the same typeface, as THIS.

small change ▶ **n.** coins of low value. ■ a thing that is considered trivial: *his wrongdoings were small change compared to a lot of happenings in the city.*

small claims court ▶ **n.** a local court in which claims for small sums of money can be heard and decided quickly and cheaply, without legal representation.

small craft ▶ **n.** a small boat or fishing vessel.

small for·ward ▶ **n.** Basketball a forward who is typically smaller than a power forward, and is often more agile and a better shot.

small fry ▶ **plural n.** young fish, animals, or children. ■ insignificant people or things: *high-ranking officials escaped prosecution while numerous small fry were imprisoned.*

small·hold·ing ▶ **n.** chiefly Brit. an agricultural holding smaller than a farm. ■ the practice of farming such a piece of land: *cooperation with neighbors is the key to successful smallholding.*
– DERIVATIVES **small·hold·er n.**

small hours ▶ **plural n.** (**the small hours**) another way of saying THE WEE HOURS (see WEE).

small in·tes·tine ▶ **n.** the part of the intestine that runs between the stomach and the large intestine; the duodenum, jejunum, and ileum collectively.

small let·ter ▶ **n.** a lowercase letter, as distinct from a capital letter.

small-mind·ed ▶ **adj.** having or showing rigid opinions or a narrow outlook; petty.
– DERIVATIVES **small-mind·ed·ly adv.**, **small-mind·ed·ness n.**

small·mouth /ˈsmôlˌmouTH/ ▶ **n.** the smallmouth bass. See BLACK BASS.

small·pox /ˈsmôlˌpäks/ ▶ **n.** an acute contagious viral disease, with fever and pustules usually leaving permanent scars. It was effectively eradicated through vaccination by 1979. Also called VARIOLA.

small print ▶ **n.** another term for FINE PRINT.

small-scale ▶ **adj.** of limited size or extent: *a small-scale research project* | *small-scale manufacturing.*

small screen ▶ **n.** (**the small screen**) television as a medium: *transplanting the timeless values of good literature to the small screen.*

small slam ▶ **n.** Bridge the bidding and winning of twelve of the thirteen tricks.

small-sword ▶ **n.** chiefly historical a light, tapering thrusting sword used for fencing or dueling.

small talk ▶ **n.** polite conversation about unimportant or uncontroversial matters, esp. as engaged in on social occasions: *propriety required that he face these people and make small talk.*

small-time ▶ **adj.** informal unimportant; minor: *a small-time gangster.*
– DERIVATIVES **small-tim·er n.**

small-town ▶ adj. of, relating to, or characteristic of a small town, esp. as considered to be unsophisticated or petty: *small-town gossip*.

smalt /smôlt/ ▶ n. chiefly historical glass colored blue with cobalt oxide. ■ a pigment made by pulverizing such glass.
– ORIGIN mid 16th cent.: from French, from Italian *smalto*, of Germanic origin; related to SMELT[1].

smalt·ite /ˈsmôlˌtīt/ ▶ n. a metallic-gray mineral consisting chiefly of cobalt arsenide, typically occurring as cubic or octahedral crystals.
– ORIGIN mid 19th cent.: from *smaltine* (a rare word with the same sense) + -ITE[1].

smarm /smärm/ informal ▶ v. **1** [no obj.] chiefly Brit. behave in an ingratiating way in order to gain favor: *I **smarmed my way** into the air force*.
2 [with obj.] smooth down (one's hair), esp. with water, oil, or gel: *he had **smarmed** his hair **down***.
▶ n. ingratiating behavior: *it takes a combination of smarm and confidence to persuade them*.
– ORIGIN mid 19th cent. (originally dialect in the sense 'smear, bedaub'): of unknown origin.

smarm·y /ˈsmärmē/ ▶ adj. (**smarmier**, **smarmiest**) informal ingratiating and wheedling in a way that is perceived as insincere or excessive: *a smarmy, unctuous reply*.
– DERIVATIVES **smarm·i·ly** /-məlē/ adv., **smarm·i·ness** n.

smart /smärt/ ▶ adj. **1** informal having or showing a quick-witted intelligence: *if he was that smart he would never have been tricked*. ■ (of a device) programmed so as to be capable of some independent action: *hi-tech smart weapons*. ■ showing impertinence by making clever or sarcastic remarks: *don't get smart or I'll whack you one*.
2 (of a person) clean, neat, and well-dressed: *you look very smart*. ■ (of clothes) attractively neat and stylish: *a smart blue skirt*. ■ (of a thing) bright and fresh in appearance: *a smart green van*. ■ (of a person or place) fashionable and upscale: *a smart restaurant*.
3 quick; brisk: *I gave him a smart salute*. ■ painfully severe: *a dog that snaps is given a smart blow*.
▶ v. [no obj.] (of a wound or part of the body) cause a sharp, stinging pain: *the wound was smarting* | (as adj. **smarting**) *Susan rubbed her smarting eyes*. ■ (of a person) feel upset and annoyed: *chiefs of staff are still smarting from the government's cuts*.
▶ n. **1** (**smarts**) informal intelligence; acumen: *I don't think I have the smarts for it*.
2 sharp stinging pain: *the smart of the recent blood-raw cuts*. ■ archaic mental pain or suffering: *sorrow is the effect of smart, and smart the effect of faith*.
– DERIVATIVES **smart·ly** adv., **smart·ness** n.
– ORIGIN Old English *smeortan* (verb); related to German *schmerzen*; the adjective is related to the verb, the original sense (late Old English) being 'causing sharp pain'; from this arose 'keen, brisk,' whence the current senses of 'mentally sharp' and 'neat in a brisk, sharp style.'

> **WORD TRENDS** It may be time to worry when your refrigerator has a higher IQ than you do. The use of **smart** to refer to devices capable of seemingly intelligent and independent action was first seen in 1972, with *smart bomb* one of the earliest combinations. *Smart cards* followed in 1980, and have become such a part of modern life that, after *people*, *card* is the word most often modified by **smart**, according to the Oxford English Corpus. In recent years, even the most everyday objects have become **smart**: there are *smart dryers* that know when your clothes are dry, and *smart refrigerators* that tell you when your milk is about to go bad. **Smart** now also refers to things done efficiently and with careful planning: *understanding how organizations create smart strategies for change* | *unless the city council develops a land use plan to ensure smart growth, urban sprawl could cripple the city*.

smart al·eck (also **smart alec**) informal ▶ n. a person who is irritating because they behave as if they know everything.
▶ adj. irritating as a result of behaving as if one knows everything: *a smart-aleck answer*.
– DERIVATIVES **smart-al·eck·y** adj.
– ORIGIN mid 19th cent.: from SMART + *Aleck*, diminutive of the given name *Alexander*.

smart-ass ▶ n. informal another term for SMART ALECK.

smart bomb ▶ n. a radio-controlled or laser-guided bomb, often with a built-in computer.

smart card ▶ n. a plastic card with a built-in microprocessor, used typically for electronic processes such as financial transactions and personal identification.

smart dust ▶ n. a collection of microelectromechanical systems forming a simple computer in a container light enough to remain suspended in air, used mainly for information gathering in environments that are hostile to life.

smart·en /ˈsmärtn/ ▶ v. [with obj.] make (something) smarter in appearance: *he spent part of the proceeds on **smartening up** his office*. ■ [no obj.] (**smarten up**) acquire more common sense; behave more wisely: *if you don't smarten up soon, you'll find yourself out on the street*. ■ [no obj.] (**smarten up**) make one's appearance smarter: *I'd like to smarten up and shave*.

smart growth ▶ n. planned economic and community development that attempts to curb urban sprawl and worsening environmental conditions.

smart mob ▶ n. a group of people who assemble, move, or act collectively by using cellular phones or other wireless devices to communicate.

smart mon·ey ▶ n. money bet or invested by people with expert knowledge: *the smart money in entertainment is invested in copyright*. ■ knowledgeable people collectively: *the smart money in music programming is abandoning pop*.

smart mouth informal ▶ n. an ability or tendency to make impertinent retorts; impudence: *why do you hide behind that smart mouth all the time?*
▶ v. (**smart-mouth**) [no obj.] make impudent remarks to someone.
– DERIVATIVES **smart-mouthed** adj.

smart·phone /ˈsmärtˌfōn/ ▶ n. a cellular phone that incorporates a palmtop computer or PDA.

smart quotes ▶ plural n. Computing quotation marks that, although all keyed the same, are automatically interpreted and set as opening or closing marks rather than vertical lines.

smart set ▶ n. (**the smart set**) fashionable people considered as a group.

smart·weed /ˈsmärtˌwēd/ ▶ n. a plant of the dock family, typically having slender leaves and a short spike of tiny compact flowers. ● Genus *Polygonum*, family Polygonaceae: several species.

smart·y /ˈsmärtē/ ▶ n. (pl. **smarties**) informal **1** a know-it-all or a smart aleck.
2 dated a smartly dressed person; a member of the smart set.

smart·y-pants ▶ n. another term for SMARTY (sense 1).

smash /smaSH/ ▶ v. **1** [with obj.] violently break (something) into pieces: *the thief smashed a window to get into the car* | *gone are the days when he **smashed up** hotels*. ■ [no obj.] be violently broken into pieces; shatter: *the glass ball smashed instantly on the pavement*. ■ violently knock down or crush inward: *soldiers **smashed down** doors*. ■ crash and severely damage (a vehicle): *my Volvo's been **smashed up***. ■ hit or attack (someone) very violently: *Donald smashed him over the head*. ■ easily or comprehensively beat (a record): *he smashed the course record*. ■ completely defeat, destroy, or foil (something regarded as hostile or dangerous): *a deliberate attempt to smash the union movement*.
2 [no obj.] move so as to hit or collide with something with great force and impact: *their plane smashed into a mountainside*. ■ [with obj.] (in sports) strike (the ball) or score (a goal, run, etc.) with great force: *he smashed that one into the bleachers for another two-run homer*. ■ [with obj.] (in tennis, badminton, and similar sports) strike (the ball or shuttlecock) downward with a hard overhand stroke.
▶ n. **1** an act or sound of something smashing: *he heard the smash of glass*. ■ a violent collision or impact between vehicles: *a car smash*. ■ a violent blow: *a forearm smash*. ■ a stroke in tennis, badminton, and similar sports in which the ball is hit downward with a hard overhand volley. ■ informal, dated a bankruptcy or financial failure.
2 (also **smash hit**) informal a very successful song, film, show, or performer: *a box-office smash*.
3 a mixture of liquors (typically brandy) with flavored water and ice.
– ORIGIN early 18th cent. (as a noun): probably imitative, representing a blend of words such as *smack, smite* with *bash, mash*, etc.

smashed /smaSHt/ ▶ adj. **1** violently or badly broken or shattered: *a smashed collarbone*.
2 [predic.] informal very drunk: *when they go back to the barracks, the single men get smashed*.

smash·er /ˈsmaSHər/ ▶ n. **1** Brit. informal a very attractive or impressive person or thing: *his wife is a smasher*.
2 [usu. in combination] a person or device that breaks something up: *riot police had clashed with window smashers*.

smash·ing /ˈsmaSHiNG/ ▶ adj. informal, chiefly Brit. excellent; wonderful: *you look smashing!*
– DERIVATIVES **smash·ing·ly** adv.

smash-mouth ▶ adj. & adv. Sports (of a style of play) aggressive and confrontational: *we're coming into this game ready to play smash-mouth because we know that's the type of game it's going to be*.

smash-up ▶ n. informal a violent collision, esp. of cars.

smat·ter·ing /ˈsmatəriNG/ (also **smatter**) ▶ n. a slight superficial knowledge of a language or subject: *Edward had only **a smattering of** Spanish*. ■ a small amount of something: ***a smattering of** snow*.
– ORIGIN mid 16th cent.: from *smatter* 'talk ignorantly, prate' (surviving in Scots), of unknown origin.

smaze /smāz/ ▶ n. a mixture of smoke and haze.

SME ▶ abbr. small to medium-sized enterprise, a company with no more than 500 employees.

smear /smi(ə)r/ ▶ v. [with obj.] **1** coat or mark (something) messily or carelessly with a greasy or sticky substance: *his face was **smeared with** dirt*. ■ spread (a greasy, oily, or sticky substance) over something: *Barbara smeared peanut butter on a slice of bread*. ■ messily blur the outline of (something such as writing or paint); smudge: *her lipstick was smeared*.
2 damage the reputation of (someone) by false accusations; slander: *someone was trying to smear her by faking letters*.
▶ n. **1** a mark or streak of a greasy or sticky substance: *there was an oil smear on his jacket*.
2 a sample of material spread thinly on a microscope slide for examination, typically for medical diagnosis: *the smears were stained for cryptosporidium*.
3 a false accusation intended to damage someone's reputation: *the media were indulging in unwarranted smears*.
4 Climbing an insecure foothold.
– DERIVATIVES **smear·y** adj., **smear·er** n.
– ORIGIN Old English *smierwan* (verb), *smeoru* 'ointment, grease,' of Germanic origin; related to German *schmieren* (verb), *Schmer* (noun).

smear cam·paign ▶ n. a plan to discredit a public figure by making false or dubious accusations.

smec·tic /ˈsmektik/ ▶ adj. denoting or involving a state of a liquid crystal in which the molecules are oriented in parallel and arranged in well-defined planes. Compare with NEMATIC.
▶ n. a substance of this type.
– ORIGIN late 17th cent.: via Latin from Greek *smēktikos* 'cleansing' (because of the soaplike consistency).

smec·tite /ˈsmekˌtīt/ ▶ n. a type of clay mineral (e.g., montmorillonite) that undergoes reversible expansion on absorbing water.
– ORIGIN early 19th cent.: from Greek *smēktis* 'fuller's earth' + -ITE[1].

smeg·ma /ˈsmegmə/ ▶ n. a sebaceous secretion in the folds of the skin, esp. under a man's foreskin.
– ORIGIN early 19th cent.: via Latin from Greek *smēgma* 'soap,' from *smēkhein* 'cleanse.'

smell /smel/ ▶ n. the faculty or power of perceiving odors or scents by means of the organs in the nose: *a highly developed sense of smell* | *dogs locate the bait by smell*. ■ a quality in something that is perceived by this faculty; an odor or scent: *lingering kitchen smells* | *a smell of coffee*. ■ an unpleasant odor: *twenty-seven cats lived there—you can imagine the smell!* ■ [in sing.] an act of inhaling in order to ascertain an odor or scent: *have a smell of this*.
▶ v. (past and past participle **smelt** /smelt/ or **smelled**) **1** [with obj.] perceive or detect the odor or scent of (something): *I think I can smell something burning*. ■ sniff at (something) in order to perceive or detect its odor or scent: *the dogs smell each other*. ■ (**smell something out**) detect or discover something by the faculty of smell: *his nose can smell out an animal from ten miles away*. ■ detect or suspect (something) by means of instinct or intuition: *he can smell trouble long before it gets serious* | *he can **smell out** weakness in others*.
2 [no obj.] emit an odor or scent of a specified kind: *it **smelled like** cough medicine* | [with complement] *the food smelled and tasted good* | [as adj., in combination] (**-smelling**) *pungent-smelling food*. ■ have a strong or unpleasant odor: *if I don't get a bath soon I'll start to smell* | ***it smells in here***. ■ appear in a certain way; be suggestive of something: ***it smells like** a hoax to me*.
– PHRASES **smell blood** discern weakness or vulnerability in an opponent. **smell a rat** informal suspect trickery or deception. **smell the roses** informal enjoy or appreciate what is often ignored.

S

smell something up permeate an area with a bad smell: *he smelled up the whole house.*
– DERIVATIVES **smell·a·ble** adj., **smell·er** n.
– ORIGIN Middle English: of unknown origin.

smell·ing salts ▶ plural n. chiefly historical a pungent substance sniffed as a restorative in cases of faintness or headache, typically consisting of ammonium carbonate mixed with perfume.

smell·y /ˈsmelē/ ▶ adj. (**smellier, smelliest**) having a strong or unpleasant smell: *smelly feet.*
– DERIVATIVES **smell·i·ness** n.

smelt[1] /smelt/ ▶ v. [with obj.] (often as noun **smelting**) extract (metal) from its ore by a process involving heating and melting: *tin smelting.* ■ extract a metal from (ore) in this way.
– ORIGIN mid 16th cent.: from Middle Dutch and Middle Low German *smelten*; related to the verb MELT.

smelt[2] past and past participle of SMELL.

smelt[3] ▶ n. (pl. **same** or **smelts** /smelts/) a small silvery fish that lives in both marine and fresh water and is sometimes fished commercially, in particular: ● a fish of the northern hemisphere (family Osmeridae: *Osmerus* and other genera). ● a fish of Australasian waters (family Retropinnidae: several genera).
– ORIGIN Old English; obscurely related to various European names of fish; compare with SMOLT.

smelt·er /ˈsmeltər/ ▶ n. an installation or factory for smelting a metal from its ore. ■ a person engaged in the business of smelting.

Smersh /smərsн/ the popular name for the Russian counterespionage organization responsible for maintaining security within the Soviet armed and intelligence services.
– ORIGIN abbreviation of Russian *Smert' shpionam*, literally 'death to spies.'

Sme·ta·na /ˈsmetn-ə/, Bedřich (1824–84), Czech composer. He was dedicated to the cause of Czech nationalism, as is apparent in his operas such as *The Bartered Bride* (1866), and in his cycle of symphonic poems *Ma Vlast* (*"My Country"* 1874–79).

sme·ta·na /ˈsmetn-ə/ ▶ n. sour cream.
– ORIGIN Russian, from *smetat'* 'sweep off.'

smew /smyo͞o/ ▶ n. a small migratory merganser of northern Eurasia, the male of which has white plumage with a crest and fine black markings. ● *Mergus albellus*, family Anatidae.
– ORIGIN late 17th cent.: obscurely related to Dutch *smient* 'wigeon' and German *Schmeiente* 'small wild duck.'

smidge /smij/ ▶ n. informal another term for SMIDGEN: *a smidge over five foot two.*

smid·gen /ˈsmijin/ (also **smidgeon** or **smidgin**) ▶ n. informal a small amount of something: *add a smidgen of cayenne.*
– ORIGIN mid 19th cent.: perhaps from Scots *smitch* in the same sense.

smi·lax /ˈsmīlaks/ ▶ n. **1** a widely distributed climbing shrub with hooks and tendrils. Several South American species yield sarsaparilla from their roots, and some are cultivated as ornamentals. ● Genus *Smilax*, family Liliaceae.
2 a climbing asparagus, the decorative foliage of which is used by florists. ● *Asparagus* (or *Myrsiphyllum*) *asparagoides*, family Liliaceae.
– ORIGIN late 16th cent.: via Latin from Greek.

S

smile /smīl/ ▶ v. [no obj.] form one's features into a pleased, kind, or amused expression, typically with the corners of the mouth turned up and the front teeth exposed: *she was smiling | he smiled at Shelley |* (as adj. **smiling**) *smiling faces.* ■ [with obj.] express (a feeling) with such an expression: *he smiled his admiration of the great stone circle.* ■ (**smile at/on/upon**) regard favorably or indulgently: *at first fortune smiled on him.* ■ (often as adj. **smiling**) literary (esp. of a landscape) have a bright or pleasing aspect: *smiling groves and terraces.*
▶ n. a pleased, kind, or amused facial expression, typically with the corners of the mouth turned up and the front teeth exposed: *he flashed his most winning smile | she greeted us all with a smile.*
– PHRASES **be all smiles** informal (of a person) look very cheerful and pleased, esp. in contrast to a previous mood. **come up smiling** informal recover from adversity and cheerfully face what is to come.
– DERIVATIVES **smil·er** n., **smil·ing·ly** adv.
– ORIGIN Middle English: perhaps of Scandinavian origin; related to SMIRK.

Smi·ley /ˈsmīlē/, Jane Graves (1949–), US writer. She wrote the award-winning novel *A Thousand Acres* (Pulitzer Prize, 1991), as well as *Moo* (1995), *The All-True Travels and Adventures of Lidie Newton* (1998), and *Horse Heaven* (2000).

smil·ey /ˈsmīlē/ ▶ adj. informal smiling; cheerful: *he drew a smiley face.*
▶ n. (in electronic communications) a symbol that represents a smiling face, typically formed by the characters :-) and used to indicate that the writer is pleased or joking.

smirch /smərcн/ ▶ v. [with obj.] make (something) dirty; soil: *the window was smirched by heat and smoke.* ■ discredit (a person or their reputation); taint: *I am not accustomed to having my honor smirched.*
▶ n. a dirty mark or stain. ■ a blot on someone's character; a flaw.
– ORIGIN late 15th cent.

smirk /smərk/ ▶ v. [no obj.] smile in an irritatingly smug, conceited, or silly way: *he smirked in triumph.*
▶ n. a smug, conceited, or silly smile: *Gloria pursed her mouth in a self-satisfied smirk.*
– DERIVATIVES **smirk·er** n., **smirk·i·ly** /-kəlē/ adv., **smirk·ing·ly** adv., **smirk·y** adj.
– ORIGIN Old English *sme(a)rcian*, from a base shared by SMILE. The early sense was 'to smile'; it later gained a notion of smugness or silliness.

smit /smit/ archaic past participle of SMITE.

smite /smīt/ ▶ v. (past **smote** /smōt/; past participle **smitten** /ˈsmitn/) **1** [with obj.] literary strike with a firm blow: *he smites the water with his sword.* ■ archaic defeat or conquer (a people or land): *he may smite our enemies.* ■ (usu. **be smitten**) (esp. of disease) attack or affect severely: *various people had been smitten with untimely summer flu.*
2 (**be smitten**) be strongly attracted to someone or something: *she was so smitten with the boy.*
▶ n. archaic a heavy blow or stroke with a weapon or the hand.
– DERIVATIVES **smit·er** n.
– ORIGIN Old English *smītan* 'to smear, blemish,' of Germanic origin; related to Dutch *smijten* and German *schmeissen* 'to fling.'

Smith[1] /smiтн/, Adam (1723–90), Scottish economist and philosopher. Often regarded as the founder of modern economics, he advocated minimal state interference in economic matters and discredited mercantilism. His works include *Inquiry into the Nature and Causes of the Wealth of Nations* (1776).

Smith[2], Bessie (1894–1937), US blues singer. She became a leading artist in the 1920s and made over 150 recordings, including some with Benny Goodman and Louis Armstrong. She was involved in a car accident and died after being refused admission to a "whites only" hospital.

Smith[3], David (Roland) (1906–65), US sculptor. His early works were marked by recurring motifs of human violence and greed. These later gave way to a calmer, more monumental style, as in the *Cubi* series.

Smith[4], John (c.1580–1631), American colonist; born in England. One of the leading promoters of English colonization in America, he helped to found the colony of Jamestown in 1607 and served as its president 1608–09. When captured by Indians from Powhatan's tribe, he was rescued by Pocahontas, Powhatan's daughter.

Smith[5], Joseph (1805–44), US religious leader and founder of the Church of Jesus Christ of Latter-Day Saints (the Mormons). In 1827, according to his own account, he was led by divine revelation to find the sacred texts written by the prophet **Mormon**, which he published as *The Book of Mormon* in 1830. He founded the Mormon Church in the same year and later established a large community in Illinois, where he was arrested and murdered by a mob.

Smith[6], Kate (1909–86), US singer; full name *Kathryn Elizabeth Smith*. She began *The Kate Smith Show* on radio in 1931 with her theme song "When the Moon Comes Over the Mountain." In 1938, she introduced Irving Berlin's "God Bless America," which also became her trademark song.

Smith[7], Margaret Chase (1897–1995), US politician. A Republican from Maine, she was a member of the US House of Representatives 1940–1949 and a US senator 1949–73, making her the first woman to serve in both houses of Congress.

smith /smiтн/ ▶ n. a worker in metal. ■ short for BLACKSMITH.
▶ v. [with obj.] treat (metal) by heating, hammering, and forging it: *tin-bronze was cast into ingots before being smithed into bracelets.*
– ORIGIN Old English, of Germanic origin; related to Dutch *smid* and German *Schmied*.

-smith ▶ comb. form denoting a person skilled in creating something with a specified material: *goldsmith | wordsmith.*

Smith & Wes·son /smiтн and ˈwesən/ ▶ n. trademark a type of firearm, in particular a type of revolver.
– ORIGIN mid 19th cent.: named after Horace *Smith* (1808–93) and Daniel B. *Wesson* (1825–1906), founders of an US firm of gunsmiths.

smith·er·eens /ˌsmiтнəˈrēnz/ ▶ plural n. informal small pieces: *a grenade blew him to smithereens.*
– ORIGIN early 19th cent.: probably from Irish *smidirín*.

smith·er·y /ˈsmiтнərē/ ▶ n. the work of or goods made by a smith.

Smith·field /ˈsmiтнˌfēld/ a town in southern Virginia, in the Tidewater, known for its production of ham; pop. 7,034 (est. 2008).

Smith·so·ni·an In·sti·tu·tion /ˌsmiтнˈsōnēən/ a foundation for scientific research, established in 1836 and based in Washington, DC. It operates more than a dozen museums and institutes in Washington and other cities. It originated with a bequest in the will of English chemist and mineralogist James Smithson (1765–1829).

smith·son·ite /ˈsmiтнsəˌnīt/ ▶ n. a yellow, gray, or green mineral consisting of zinc carbonate typically occurring as crusts or rounded masses.
– ORIGIN mid 19th cent.: from the name *Smithson* (see SMITHSONIAN INSTITUTION) + -ITE[1].

Smith·town /ˈsmiтнˌtoun/ a residential town on the northern shore of Long Island in New York; pop. 121,162 (est. 2008).

smith·y /ˈsmiтнē/ ▶ n. (pl. **smithies**) a blacksmith's workshop; a forge. ■ a blacksmith.
– ORIGIN Middle English, from Old Norse *smithja*.

smit·ten /ˈsmitn/ past participle of SMITE.

SMN ▶ abbr. seaman.

smock /smäk/ ▶ n. a loose dress or blouse, with the upper part closely gathered in smocking. ■ a loose garment worn over one's clothes to protect them: *an artist's smock.* ■ (also **smock-frock**) historical a smocked linen overgarment worn by an agricultural worker.
▶ v. [with obj.] (usu. as adj. **smocked**) decorate (something) with smocking: *smocked dresses.*
– ORIGIN Old English *smoc* 'woman's loose-fitting undergarment'; probably related to Old English *smūgan* 'to creep' and Old Norse *smjúga* 'put on a garment, creep into.' The use of the verb as a needlework term dates from the late 19th cent.

smock·ing /ˈsmäkiNG/ ▶ n. decoration on a garment created by gathering a section of the material into tight pleats and holding them together with parallel stitches in an ornamental pattern.

smog /smäg/ ▶ n. fog or haze combined with smoke and other atmospheric pollutants.
– DERIVATIVES **smog·gy** adj.
– ORIGIN early 20th cent.: blend of SMOKE and FOG[1].

smoke /smōk/ ▶ n. a visible suspension of carbon or other particles in air, typically one emitted from a burning substance: *bonfire smoke.* ■ an act of smoking tobacco: *I'm dying for a smoke.* ■ informal a cigarette or cigar.
▶ v. **1** [no obj.] emit smoke or visible vapor: *heat the oil until it just smokes |* (as adj. **smoking**) *they huddled around his smoking fire in the winter damp.* ■ inhale and exhale the smoke of tobacco or a drug: *Janine was sitting at the kitchen table smoking |* (as noun **smoking**) *the effect of smoking on health |* [with obj.] *he smoked forty cigarettes a day.*
2 [with obj.] (often as adj. **smoked**) cure or preserve (meat or fish) by exposure to smoke: *smoked salmon.* ■ treat (glass) so as to darken it: *the smoked glass of his lenses.* ■ fumigate, cleanse, or purify by exposure to smoke. ■ subdue (insects, esp. bees) by exposing them to smoke. ■ (**smoke someone/something out**) drive someone or something out of a place by using smoke: *we will fire the roof and smoke him out.* ■ (**smoke someone out**) force someone to make something known: *as the press smokes him out on other human rights issues, he will be revealed as a social conservative.*
3 [with obj.] informal kill (someone) by shooting. ■ defeat overwhelmingly in a fight or contest.
4 [with obj.] archaic make fun of (someone): *we baited her and smoked her.*
– PHRASES **blow smoke** try to mislead or threaten someone by giving false or exaggerated information: *the coach has been blowing smoke for the past three years about our program.* **go up in smoke** informal be destroyed by fire. ■ (of a plan) come to nothing: *more than one dream is about to go up in smoke.* **where there's smoke there's fire** proverb there's always some reason for a rumor. **smoke and mirrors** the obscuring or embellishing of the truth of a situation with misleading or irrelevant information: *the budget process is an exercise in smoke and mirrors.* [with reference to illusion created by magic tricks.] **smoke like a chimney** smoke tobacco incessantly.
– DERIVATIVES **smok·a·ble** (also **smokeable**) adj.
– ORIGIN Old English *smoca* (noun), *smocian* (verb), from the Germanic base of *smēocan* 'emit smoke'; related to Dutch *smook* and German *Schmauch*.

smoke bomb ▶ n. a bomb that emits dense smoke as it explodes, used to produce a smoke screen.

smoke·box /ˈsmōkˌbäks/ ▸ **n.** a device for catching or producing and containing smoke, in particular: ■ an oven for smoking food. ■ the chamber in a steam engine or boiler between the flues and the funnel or chimney stack. ■ another term for **SMOKER** (sense 4).

smoke·bush /ˈsmōkˌbo͝osн/ (also **smoke bush**) ▸ **n.** another term for **SMOKE TREE**.

smoke de·tec·tor (also **smoke alarm**) ▸ **n.** a fire-protection device that automatically detects and gives a warning of the presence of smoke.

smoke-dry ▸ **v.** [with obj.] cure (meat or fish) by exposing it to smoke.

smoke-free ▸ **adj.** without smoke: *a smoke-free environment.* ■ where smoking is not permitted: *a smoke-free train.*

smoke·house /ˈsmōkˌhous/ ▸ **n.** a shed or room for curing food by exposure to smoke.

smoke·jump·er /ˈsmōkˌjəmpər/ (also **smoke jumper**) ▸ **n.** a firefighter who parachutes in to the site of a forest fire.

smoke·less /ˈsmōkləs/ ▸ **adj.** producing or emitting little or no smoke: *smokeless fuel.*

smoke·less to·bac·co ▸ **n.** tobacco that is chewed or snuffed rather than smoked by the user.

smok·er /ˈsmōkər/ ▸ **n. 1** a person who smokes tobacco regularly. ■ (also **smoking car**) a train compartment in which smoking is allowed.
2 a person or device that smokes fish or meat.
3 dated an informal social gathering for men.
4 a device that emits smoke for subduing bees in a hive.

smoke ring ▸ **n.** a ring-shaped puff of smoke exhaled by a smoker.

smok·er's cough ▸ **n.** a persistent cough caused by smoking.

smoke screen (also **smokescreen**) ▸ **n.** a cloud of smoke created to conceal military operations. ■ a ruse designed to disguise someone's real intentions or activities: *he tried to create a smokescreen by quibbling about the statistics.*

smoke shop ▸ **n.** a store selling tobacco products and smoking equipment.

smoke sig·nal ▸ **n.** a column of smoke used as a way of conveying a message to a distant person. ■ an indication of someone's intentions or views: *the Iowa caucuses might have given a small smoke signal of the Democrats' likely choice.*

smoke·stack /ˈsmōkˌstak/ ▸ **n.** a chimney or funnel for discharging smoke from a locomotive, ship, factory, etc. and helping to induce a draft. ■ [as modifier] pertaining to heavy industry: *America's smokestack cities and blue-collar suburbs.*

smoke tree ▸ **n.** a shrub or small tree of the cashew family that bears long feathery plumes of flowers, giving it a smoky appearance. ● Genus *Cotinus*, family Anacardiaceae: two species, the European *C. coggygria*, grown in North America as an ornamental, and the rare American *C. obovatus.*

smok·ie /ˈsmōkē/ ▸ **n.** Scottish a smoked haddock.

smok·ing gun ▸ **n.** a piece of incontrovertible incriminating evidence.

smok·ing jack·et ▸ **n.** a man's comfortable jacket, typically made of velvet, formerly worn while smoking after dinner.

smok·ing room ▸ **n.** a room set aside for smoking in a hotel or other public building.

smok·o /ˈsmōkō/ (also **smoke-ho**) ▸ **n.** (pl. **smokos**) Austral./NZ informal a rest from work for a smoke; a tea break.

smok·y /ˈsmōkē/ ▸ **adj.** (**smokier, smokiest**) filled with or smelling of smoke: *a smoky office.* ■ producing or obscured by a great deal of smoke: *smoky factory chimneys.* ■ having the taste or aroma of smoked food: *smoky bacon.* ■ like smoke in color or appearance: *smoky eyes.*
– DERIVATIVES **smok·i·ly** /-kəlē/ **adv.**, **smok·i·ness n.**

Smok·y Hill Riv·er a river that flows for 540 miles (870 km) from Colorado across Kansas.

smok·y quartz ▸ **n.** a semiprecious variety of quartz ranging in color from light grayish-brown to nearly black.

smol·der /ˈsmōldər/ ▸ **v.** [no obj.] burn slowly with smoke but no flame: *the bonfire still smoldered, the smoke drifting over the paddock.* ■ show or feel barely suppressed anger, hatred, or another powerful emotion: *Anna smoldered with indignation* | (as adj. **smoldering**) *he met her smoldering eyes.* ■ exist in a suppressed or concealed state: *the controversy smoldered on for several years* | (as adj. **smoldering**) *smoldering rage.*
▸ **n.** smoke coming from a fire that is burning slowly without a flame: *the last acrid smolder of his cigarette.*
– DERIVATIVES **smol·der·ing·ly adv.**
– ORIGIN late Middle English: related to Dutch *smeulen.*

Smo·lensk /smōˈlensk, smәˈlyensk/ a city in western Russia, on the Dnieper River, close to the border with Belarus; pop. 316,500 (est. 2008).

smolt /smōlt/ ▸ **n.** a young salmon (or trout) after the parr stage, when it becomes silvery and migrates to the sea for the first time.
– ORIGIN late Middle English (originally Scots and northern English): of unknown origin; compare with **SMELT**[3].

smooch /smo͞ocн/ informal ▸ **v.** [no obj.] kiss and cuddle amorously: *the young lovers smooched in their car.* ■ Brit. dance slowly in a close embrace.
▸ **n.** a kiss or a spell of amorous kissing and cuddling: *a slurpy smooch on the ear.* ■ Brit. a period of slow dancing in a close embrace: *they suggest a dance but it turns into a smooch.*
– DERIVATIVES **smooch·er n.**, **smooch·y adj.** (**smoochier, smoochiest**).
– ORIGIN 1930s: from dialect *smouch*, of imitative origin.

smoosh /smo͞osн/ ▸ **v.** [with obj.] informal squash, crush, or flatten: *use a sharp knife so as not to smoosh the broccoli.*
– ORIGIN mid 20th cent.: origin unknown.

Smoot /smo͞ot/, George (1945–), US astrophysicist; full name *George Fitzgerald Smoot III.* His work with John C. Mather on the COBE project advanced the study of the Big Bang theory. Nobel Prize for Physics (2006), shared with Mather.

smooth /smo͞oth/ ▸ **adj. 1** having an even and regular surface or consistency; free from perceptible projections, lumps, or indentations: *smooth flat rocks* | *a smooth skin tans more easily.* ■ (of a liquid) with an even consistency; without lumps: *cook gently until the sauce is smooth.* ■ (of the sea or another body of water) without heavy waves; calm: *the smooth summer sea.* ■ (of movement) without jerks: *the trucks gave a smooth ride* | *graphics are excellent, with fast, smooth scrolling.* ■ (of an action, event, or process) without problems or difficulties: *the group's expansion into the U.S. market was not quite so smooth.* ■ denoting the face of a tennis or squash racket without the projecting loops from the stringing process (used as a call when the racket is spun to decide the right to serve first or to choose ends); the opposite of **ROUGH**.
2 (of food or drink) without harshness or bitterness: *a lovely, smooth, very fruity wine.* ■ (of a person or their manner, actions, or words) suavely charming in a way considered to be unctuous: *his voice was infuriatingly smooth.*
▸ **v.** [with obj.] give (something) a flat, regular surface or appearance by running one's hand over it: *she* ***smoothed out*** *the newspaper.* ■ rub off the rough edges of (something): *you can use sandpaper to smooth the joint.* ■ deal successfully with (a problem, difficulty, or perceived fault): *these doctrinal disputes were* ***smoothed over.*** ■ free (a course of action) from difficulties or problems: *a conference would be held to smooth the way for the establishment of the provisional government.* ■ modify (a graph, curve, etc.) so as to lessen irregularities: *values are collected over a long period of time so that fluctuations are* ***smoothed out.***
▸ **adv.** archaic in a way that is without difficulties: *the course of true love never did run smooth.*
– PHRASES **smooth someone's ruffled feathers** see **RUFFLE**.
– DERIVATIVES **smooth·a·ble adj.**, **smooth·er n.**, **smooth·ish adj.**
– ORIGIN Old English *smōth*, probably of Germanic origin, though no cognates are known. The verb dates from Middle English.

smooth·bore /ˈsmo͞othˌbôr/ ▸ **n.** [often as modifier] a gun with an unrifled barrel: *smoothbore muskets.*

smooth breath·ing ▸ **n.** see **BREATHING** (sense 2).

smooth-faced ▸ **adj. 1** concealing one's true feelings by a show of friendliness.
2 clean-shaven.

smooth hound ▸ **n.** a small European shark that typically lives close to the bottom in shallow waters. ● Genus *Mustelus*, family Triakidae: two species.

smooth·ie /ˈsmo͞othē/ ▸ **n. 1** informal a man with a smooth, suave manner: *a smoothie with an eye for a pretty girl.*
2 a thick, smooth drink of fresh fruit puréed with milk, yogurt, or ice cream.

smooth·ly /ˈsmo͞othlē/ ▸ **adv. 1** in a smooth way: *the bust is smoothly carved in white marble* | *traffic was soon flowing smoothly again.*
2 without problems or difficulties: *everything seemed to be* ***going smoothly.***

smooth mus·cle ▸ **n.** Physiology muscle tissue in which the contractile fibrils are not highly ordered, occurring in the gut and other internal organs and not under voluntary control. Often contrasted with **STRIATED MUSCLE**.

smooth·ness /ˈsmo͞othnis/ ▸ **n.** the quality or state of being smooth: *the smoothness of her skin* | *the evacuation went off with remarkable smoothness.*

smooth newt ▸ **n.** a small yellowish-brown smooth-skinned newt that is widely distributed throughout Europe and western Asia. ● *Triturus vulgaris*, family Salamandridae.

smooth snake ▸ **n.** a harmless Eurasian snake that is gray to reddish in color, typically living in heathy country where it feeds on lizards. ● *Coronella austriaca*, family Colubridae.

smooth talk ▸ **n.** charming or flattering language, esp. when used to persuade someone to do something.
▸ **v.** (**smooth-talk**) [with obj.] use such language to (someone), esp. to persuade them to do something: *don't try to smooth-talk me.*
– DERIVATIVES **smooth talk·er n.**

smooth-talk·ing ▸ **adj.** using charming or flattering language, esp. to persuade someone to do something: *a smooth-talking salesman.*

smooth tongue ▸ **n.** [in sing.] the ability or tendency to use insincere flattery or persuasion: *your smooth tongue could even turn your mistakes to your advantage.*
– DERIVATIVES **smooth-tongued adj.**

s'more /smôr/ (also **smore**) ▸ **n.** a sweet snack consisting of a chocolate bar and toasted marshmallows sandwiched between graham crackers.
– ORIGIN 1930s: contraction of *some more.*

smor·gas·bord /ˈsmôrgəsˌbôrd/ ▸ **n.** a buffet offering a variety of hot and cold meats, salads, hors d'oeuvres, etc. ■ a wide range of something; a variety: *the album is a smorgasbord of different musical styles.*
– ORIGIN Swedish, from *smörgås* '(slice of) bread and butter' (from *smör* 'butter' + *gås* 'goose, lump of butter') + *bord* 'table.'

smor·zan·do /smôrtˈsändō/ Music ▸ **adv. & adj.** (esp. as a direction) dying away.
– ORIGIN Italian, literally 'extinguishing.'

smote /smōt/ past of **SMITE**.

smoth·er /ˈsməthər/ ▸ **v.** [with obj.] kill (someone) by covering their nose and mouth so that they suffocate. ■ extinguish (a fire) by covering it. ■ (**smother someone/something in/with**) cover someone or something entirely with: *rich orange sorbets smothered in fluffy whipped cream* | figurative *he smothered her with kisses.* ■ make (someone) feel trapped and oppressed by acting in an overly protective manner toward them: *it's time for you to leave the house—she'll smother you if you remain.* ■ suppress (a feeling or an action): *she smothered a sigh.* ■ (in sports) stop the motion of (the ball or a shot) by falling on it and covering it: *the goalkeeper was able to smother the ball.* ■ cook in a covered container, typically with a sauce and vegetables on top: (as adj. **smothered**) *smothered fried chicken.*
▸ **n.** a mass of something that stifles or obscures: *all this vanished in a smother of foam.*
– DERIVATIVES **smoth·er·y adj.**
– ORIGIN Middle English (as a noun in the sense 'stifling smoke'): from the base of Old English *smorian* 'suffocate.'

smoth·ered mate ▸ **n.** Chess checkmate in which the king has no vacant square to move to and is checkmated by a knight.

smoul·der /ˈsmōldər/ ▸ **v.** British spelling of **SMOLDER**.

SMPTE ▸ **abbr.** Society of Television and Motion Picture Engineers (used to denote a time coding system for synchronizing video and audiotapes).

smrit·i /ˈsmritē/ ▸ **n.** (pl. **smritis**) a Hindu religious text containing traditional teachings on religion, such as the Mahabharata.
– ORIGIN from Sanskrit *smṛti* 'remembrance.'

SMS ▸ **abbr.** short message (or messaging) service, a system that enables cellular phone users to send and receive text messages.
▸ **n.** (pl. **SMSs**) a text message that is sent or received using SMS.
▸ **v.** (**SMSs, SMSing, SMSed**) [no obj.] send someone a text message using SMS: *I'm SMSing more than speaking on my phone these days* | [with obj.] *SMS me or send me an e-mail.*

SMSA ▸ **abbr.** Standard Metropolitan Statistical Area.

SMSgt (also **SMSGT**) ▸ **abbr.** senior master sergeant.

SMTP ▸ abbr. Computing simple mail transfer protocol, a data transmission format used to send and receive e-mail.

smudge[1] /sməj/ ▸ n. a blurred or smeared mark on the surface of something: *a smudge of blood on the floor.* ■ an indistinct or blurred view or image: *the low smudge of hills on the horizon.*
▸ v. [with obj.] cause (something) to become messily smeared by rubbing it: *she dabbed her eyes, careful not to smudge her makeup.* ■ [no obj.] become smeared when rubbed: *mascaras that smudge or flake around the eyes.* ■ make blurred or indistinct: *the photograph had been smudged by the photocopier and was by no means as clear as the original.*
– DERIVATIVES **smudge·less** adj.
– ORIGIN late Middle English (as a verb in the sense 'soil, stain'): of unknown origin. The noun dates from the late 18th cent.

smudge[2] ▸ n. a smoky outdoor fire that is lit to keep off insects or protect plants against frost.
– ORIGIN mid 18th cent. (in the sense 'suffocating smoke'): of unknown origin; related to obsolete *smudge* 'cure herring by smoking,' of obscure origin.

smudge pot ▸ n. a container for a smudge (see SMUDGE[2]).

smudg·y /'sməjē/ ▸ adj. (**smudgier, smudgiest**) smeared or blurred from being smudged: *a smudgy photograph.*
– DERIVATIVES **smudg·i·ly** /-jəlē/ adv., **smudg·i·ness** n.

smug /sməg/ ▸ adj. (**smugger, smuggest**) having or showing an excessive pride in oneself or one's achievements: *he was feeling smug after his win.*
– DERIVATIVES **smug·ly** adv., **smug·ness** n.
– ORIGIN mid 16th cent. (originally in the sense 'neat, spruce'): from Low German *smuk* 'pretty.'

smug·gle /'sməgəl/ ▸ v. [with obj.] move (goods) illegally into or out of a country: *he's been smuggling cigarettes from Gibraltar into Spain* | (as noun **smuggling**) *cocaine smuggling has increased alarmingly.* ■ convey (someone or something) somewhere secretly and illicitly: *he smuggled out a message.*
– ORIGIN late 17th cent.: from Low German *smuggelen*, of unknown ultimate origin.

smug·gler /'sməg(ə)lər/ ▸ n. a person who smuggles goods: *drug smugglers.*

smush /sməsʜ, smo͝osʜ/ ▸ v. [with obj.] informal crush; smash: *they smushed marshmallows in their mouths.*
– ORIGIN early 19th cent.: alteration of MUSH[1].

smut /smət/ ▸ n. **1** a small flake of soot or other dirt: *all those black smuts from the engine.*
2 a fungal disease of grains in which parts of the ear change to black powder. ● The fungi belong to *Ustilago* and other genera, order Ustilaginales, class Teliomycetes.
3 obscene or lascivious talk, writing, or pictures: *porn, in this view, is far from being harmless smut.*
▸ v. (**smuts, smutting, smutted**) [with obj.] (often as adj. **smutted**) **1** mark with flakes or soot or other dirt: *the smutted sky.*
2 infect (a plant) with smut: *smutted wheat.*
– ORIGIN late Middle English (in the sense 'defile, corrupt, make obscene'): related to German *schmutzen*; compare with SMUDGE[1]. The noun dates from the mid 17th cent.

Smuts /sməts, smʏts/, Jan (Christiaan) (1870–1950), South African statesman and soldier; prime minister 1919–24 and 1939–48. He led Boer forces during the Second Boer War and later commanded Allied troops against German East Africa in 1916. He helped to found the League of Nations.

smut·ty /'smətē/ ▸ adj. (**smuttier, smuttiest**) (of talk, writing, or pictures) obscene or lascivious: *smutty jokes.*
– DERIVATIVES **smut·ti·ly** /-təlē/ adv., **smut·ti·ness** n.

SMV ▸ abbr. slow-moving vehicle.

Smyr·na /'smərnə/ **1** an ancient city on the western coast of Asia Minor, on the site of modern Izmir in Turkey.
2 a city in northwestern Georgia, northwest of Atlanta; pop. 49,854 (est. 2008).

Sn ▸ symbol the chemical element tin.
– ORIGIN from late Latin *stannum* 'tin.'

s.n. ▸ abbr. without name. [from Latin *sine nomine.*]

snack /snak/ ▸ n. a small amount of food eaten between meals. ■ a light meal that is eaten in a hurry or in a casual manner.
▸ v. [no obj.] eat a snack: *she likes to snack on yogurt.*
– ORIGIN Middle English (originally in the sense 'snap, bite'): from Middle Dutch *snac(k)*, from *snacken* 'to bite,' variant of *snappen.* Senses relating to food date from the late 17th cent.

snack bar ▸ n. a place where snacks are sold.

snack·ette /ˌsna'ket/ ▸ n. W. Indian a small store selling snacks, cigarettes, and minor groceries.

snaf·fle /'snafəl/ ▸ n. (also **snaffle bit**) (on a bridle) a simple bit, typically a jointed one, used with a single set of reins. ■ (also **snaffle bridle**) a bridle with such a bit.
▸ v. [with obj.] informal, chiefly Brit. take (something) for oneself, typically quickly or without permission: *shall we snaffle some of Bernard's sherry?*
– ORIGIN mid 16th cent. (denoting a bridle bit): probably from Low German or Dutch; compare with Middle Low German and Middle Dutch *snavel* 'beak, mouth.' The verb (mid 19th cent.) is perhaps a different word.

sna·fu /sna'fo͞o/ informal ▸ n. a confused or chaotic state; a mess: *an enormous amount of my time was devoted to untangling snafus.*
▸ adj. in utter confusion or chaos: *our refrigeration plant is snafu.*
▸ v. [with obj.] throw (a situation) into chaos: *you ignored his orders and snafued everything.*
– ORIGIN 1940s: acronym from *situation normal: all fouled* (or *fucked*) *up.*

snag /snag/ ▸ n. **1** an unexpected or hidden obstacle or drawback: *the picture's U.S. release* ***hit a snag.***
2 a sharp, angular, or jagged projection: *keep an emery board handy in case of nail snags.* ■ a rent or tear in fabric caused by such a projection.
3 a dead tree.
▸ v. (**snags, snagging, snagged**) [with obj.] catch or tear (something) on a projection: *thorns snagged his sweater.* ■ [no obj.] become caught on a projection: *radio aerials* ***snagged on*** *bushes and branches.* ■ informal catch or obtain (someone or something): *it's the first time they've snagged the star for a photo.*
– DERIVATIVES **snag·gy** adj. (sense 2 of the noun).
– ORIGIN late 16th cent. (sense 2 of the noun): probably of Scandinavian origin. The early sense 'stump sticking out from a tree trunk' gave rise to a US sense 'submerged piece of timber obstructing navigation,' of which sense 1 is originally a figurative use. Current verb senses arose in the 19th cent.

snag·gle /'snagəl/ ▸ n. a tangled or knotted mass: figurative *a snaggle of import restrictions.*
▸ v. [no obj.] become knotted or tangled: *the column of smoke snaggled for a moment.*
– ORIGIN early 20th cent.: from the noun SNAG + -LE[2].

snag·gle·tooth /'snagəlˌto͞otʜ/ ▸ n. **1** (pl. **snaggleteeth** /-ˌtētʜ/) an irregular or projecting tooth.
2 (pl. **snaggletooths**) a small deep-sea fish with large fangs at the front of the jaws and a number of light organs on the body. ● Family Astronesthidae: several genera and species.
– DERIVATIVES **snag·gle·toothed** adj.

snail /snāl/ ▸ n. a mollusk with a single spiral shell into which the whole body can be withdrawn. ● Most orders in the class Gastropoda. ■ (in metaphorical use) any person or thing that moves exceedingly slowly: *a tedious and complicated process enough to exasperate a snail.*
– DERIVATIVES **snail·like** /-ˌlīk/ adj.
– ORIGIN Old English *snæg(e)l*, of Germanic origin; related to German *Schnecke.*

snail

snail dart·er ▸ n. a small percoid freshwater fish of a type found in US rivers, now nearly extinct.

snail·fish /'snālˌfisʜ/ ▸ n. (pl. **same** or **snailfishes**) a small fish of cool or cold seas, with loose jellylike skin and typically a ventral sucker. Also called SEA SNAIL. ● *Liparis* and other genera, family Cyclopteridae: several species, including *L. liparis* of the North Atlantic.

snail mail ▸ n. informal the ordinary postal system as opposed to e-mail.

snail's pace ▸ n. [in sing.] an extremely slow speed: *he drove at a snail's pace.*
– DERIVATIVES **snail-paced** adj.

snake /snāk/ ▸ n. **1** a long limbless reptile that has no eyelids, a short tail, and jaws that are capable of considerable extension. Some snakes have a venomous bite. ● Suborder Ophidia (or Serpentes), order Squamata: many families. ■ (in general use) a limbless lizard or amphibian.
2 (also **snake in the grass**) a treacherous or deceitful person: *that man is a cold-blooded snake.*
3 (in full **plumber's snake**) a long flexible wire for clearing obstacles in piping.
4 (**the snake**) a former system of interconnected exchange rates for the currencies of EC countries.
▸ v. [no obj.] move or extend with the twisting motion of a snake: *a rope snaked down.*
– DERIVATIVES **snake·like** /-ˌlīk/ adj.
– ORIGIN Old English *snaca*, of Germanic origin.

snake·bark ma·ple /'snākˌbärk/ ▸ n. a maple tree with longitudinal pale stripes on the bark. ● Genus *Acer*, family Aceraceae: several species, in particular *A. davidii* of eastern Asia and the striped maple of North America.

snake·bird /'snākˌbərd/ ▸ n. another term for ANHINGA.

snake·bite /'snākˌbīt/ ▸ n. **1** the bite of a snake, esp. a venomous one.
2 Brit. a drink consisting of draft cider and lager in equal proportions.

snake·bit·ten /'snākˌbitn/ ▸ adj. informal doomed to misfortune; unlucky: *the snakebitten space shuttle chalked up a fourth launch delay.*

Snake·board /'snākˌbôrd/ ▸ n. trademark a type of skateboard consisting of two footplates joined by a bar, allowing for greater speed and maneuverability than with a standard skateboard.
– DERIVATIVES **snake·board·er** n., **snake·board·ing** n.
– ORIGIN 1990s: blend of *snake* and *skateboard.*

snake charm·er ▸ n. an entertainer who appears to make snakes move by playing music.

snake dance ▸ n. a dance in which the performers handle live snakes, imitate the motions of snakes, or form a line that moves in a zigzag fashion, in particular a ritual dance of the Hopi Indians involving the handling of live rattlesnakes.
▸ v. (**snake-dance**) [no obj.] dance in any of these ways.

snake eyes ▸ plural n. [treated as sing.] informal a throw of two ones with a pair of dice. ■ the worst possible result; a complete lack of success: *his elegant, amusing book sadly came up snake eyes.*

snake fence (also **snake-rail fence**) ▸ n. a fence made of roughly split rails or poles joined in a zigzag pattern with their ends crossing.

snake·fish /'snākˌfisʜ/ ▸ n. (pl. **same** or **snakefishes**) see CUTLASSFISH, LIZARDFISH.

snake fly ▸ n. a slender woodland insect with transparent wings and a long "neck" that allows the head to be raised above the body. ● Family Raphidiidae, order Neuroptera: *Raphidia* and other genera.

snake·head /'snākˌhed/ ▸ n. a freshwater fish with a broad, heavily scaled head and a long cylindrical body, native to tropical Africa and Asia. ● Family Channidae: several genera and species.

snake mack·er·el ▸ n. another term for ESCOLAR.

snake oil ▸ n. informal a substance with no real medicinal value sold as a remedy for all diseases. ■ a product, policy, etc. of little real worth or value that is promoted as the solution to a problem: *the new tax plan was denounced as snake oil.*

snake pit ▸ n. a pit containing poisonous snakes. ■ a scene of vicious behavior or ruthless competition: *the literary snake pits of New York.* ■ a place of overcrowded squalor, esp. a poorly run mental hospital: *the clinic opened in 1949, when most drug and alcohol sanitariums were still snake pits.* [1946: from the title of a novel by Mary Jane Ward.]

snake-rail fence ▸ n. another term for SNAKE FENCE.

Snake Riv·er a river in northwestern US. Rising in Yellowstone National Park in Wyoming, it flows for 1,038 miles (1,670 km) through Idaho into the state of Washington, where it joins the Columbia River.

snake·root /'snakˌro͞ot, -ˌro͝ot/ ▸ n. **1** any of a number of North American plants reputed to contain an antidote to snake poison, in particular: ● (**Virginia snakeroot**) a birthwort with long heart-shaped leaves and curved tubular flowers (*Aristolochia serpentaria*, family Aristolochiaceae). ● (**white snakeroot**) a poisonous plant that causes milk sickness in livestock (*Eupatorium rugosum*, family Compositae).
2 any of a number of plants thought to resemble a snake in shape, in particular **Indian snakeroot** (see RAUWOLFIA).

snake·skin /'snākˌskin/ ▸ n. [often as modifier] the skin of a snake: *snakeskin boots.*

snake·weed /'snākˌwēd/ ▸ n. **1** another term for SNAKEROOT.
2 old-fashioned term for BISTORT.

snake·wood /'snākˌwo͝od/ ▸ n. **1** a tree or shrub that has wood from which a snakebite antidote or other medicinal extract is obtained. ● Several species, in particular the tree *Strychnos minor* (or *colubrina*) (family Loganiaceae), of the Indian subcontinent.
2 a tropical American tree that has timber with a snakeskin pattern, used for decorative work. ● *Brosimum rubescens*, family Moraceae.

snak·y /ˈsnākē/ ▶ **adj.** (**snakier**, **snakiest**) like a snake in appearance; long and sinuous: *a long snaky whip.* ■ of the supposed nature of a snake in showing coldness, venom, or cunning: *a snaky friend.*
–DERIVATIVES **snak·i·ly** /-kəlē/ **adv.**, **snak·i·ness n.**

snap /snap/ ▶ **v.** (**snaps**, **snapping**, **snapped**) **1** break or cause to break suddenly and completely, typically with a sharp cracking sound: [no obj.] *guitar strings kept snapping* | [with obj.] *dead twigs can be* **snapped off**. ■ [no obj.] emit a sudden, sharp cracking sound: *banners snapping in the breeze.* ■ [no obj.] (of an animal) make a sudden audible bite: *a dog was* **snapping at** *his heels.* ■ [with obj. or adverbial] cause to move or alter in a specified way with a brisk movement and typically a sharp sound: *Rosa snapped her bag shut.* ■ [no obj.] move or alter in this way: *his mouth snapped into a tight, straight line.* ■ [no obj.] suddenly lose one's self-control: *she claims she snapped after years of violence.* ■ [reporting verb] say something quickly and irritably to someone: [no obj.] *McIllvanney* **snapped at** *her* | [with direct speech] *"I really don't much care," she snapped.*
2 [with obj.] take a snapshot of: *he planned to spend the time snapping rare wildlife* | [no obj.] *photographers were* **snapping away** *at her.*
3 [with obj.] Football put (the ball) into play by a quick backward movement from the ground.
4 [with obj.] fasten with snaps: *he pulled a white rubber swim hat over his head and snapped it under his chin.*
▶ **n. 1** a sudden, sharp cracking sound or movement: *she closed her purse with a snap.* ■ [in sing.] a hurried, irritable tone or manner: *"I'm still waiting," he said with a snap.* ■ vigor or liveliness of style or action; zest: *the snap of the dialogue.*
2 (usu. **snaps**) a small fastener on clothing, engaged by pressing its two halves together.
3 [in sing.] informal an easy task: *a control panel that makes operation a snap.*
4 Football a quick backward movement of the ball from the ground that begins a play.
5 a snapshot.
6 Brit. a card game in which cards from two piles are turned over simultaneously and players call "snap" as quickly as possible when two similar cards are exposed.
▶ **adj.** [attrib.] done or taken on the spur of the moment, unexpectedly, or without notice: *a snap judgment* | *he could call a snap election.*
–PHRASES **in a snap** informal in a moment; almost immediately: *gourmet-quality meals are ready in a snap.* **snap one's fingers** make a sharp clicking sound by bending the last joint of the middle finger against the thumb and suddenly releasing it, typically in order to attract attention in a peremptory way or to accompany the beat of music. **snap someone's head off** see HEAD.
–PHRASAL VERBS **snap back** recover quickly and easily from an illness or period of difficulty: *our bodies can snap back pretty well from short-term bouts of stress.* **snap out of** [often in imperative] informal get out of (a bad or unhappy mood) by a sudden effort: *come on, Fran—snap out of it!* **snap something up** quickly and eagerly buy or secure something that is in short supply or being sold cheaply: *all the tickets have been snapped up.*
–DERIVATIVES **snap·ping·ly adv.**
–ORIGIN late 15th cent. (in the senses 'make a sudden audible bite' and 'quick sharp biting sound'): probably from Middle Dutch or Middle Low German *snappen* 'seize'; partly imitative.

snap-ac·tion ▶ **adj.** [attrib.] **1** denoting a switch or relay that makes and breaks contact rapidly, whatever the speed of the activating mechanism.
2 denoting a gun whose hinged barrel is secured by a spring catch.
▶ **n.** (**snap action**) the operation of such a switch, relay, or gun.

snap bean ▶ **n.** a bean of a variety grown for its edible pods.
–ORIGIN late 18th cent.: so named because the pods are broken into pieces to be eaten.

snap-brim ▶ **adj.** (of a hat) with a brim that can be turned up and down at opposite sides.

snap·drag·on /ˈsnapˌdragən/ ▶ **n.** a plant of the figwort family, bearing spikes of brightly colored two-lobed flowers that gape like a mouth when a bee lands on the curved lip. ● Genus *Antirrhinum*, family Scrophulariaceae: several species, in particular the widely cultivated *A. majus*.

snap hook ▶ **n.** a hook with a spring allowing the entrance but preventing the escape of a cord, key ring, etc.

snap lock ▶ **n.** a feature of a device or component that allows it to be fastened automatically when pushed into position: [as modifier] *the top is secured by snap-lock buckles.*

snap-on (also **snap-in**) ▶ **adj.** [attrib.] denoting a cover or attachment that is attached or secured with a snap.

snap pea ▶ **n.** another term for SUGAR SNAP.

snap·per /ˈsnapər/ ▶ **n. 1** a marine fish that is typically reddish and is valued as food. ● a fish of a widespread tropical family (Lutjanidae, the **snapper family**) that snaps its toothed jaws. See also RED SNAPPER.
2 another term for SNAPPING TURTLE.
3 chiefly Brit. a paper cracker, or the part of a cracker that makes a bang.
4 Brit. informal a photographer.

snap·ping tur·tle ▶ **n.** a large American freshwater turtle with a long neck and strong hooked jaws. ● Family Chelydridae: two North American species, the **common snapping turtle** (*Chelydra serpentina*) and the larger **alligator snapping turtle** (*Macroclemys temminckii*).

common snapping turtle

snap·pish /ˈsnapiSH/ ▶ **adj.** (of a dog) irritable and inclined to bite. ■ irritable and curt: *she was often snappish with the children.*
–DERIVATIVES **snap·pish·ly adv.**, **snap·pish·ness n.**

snap·py /ˈsnapē/ ▶ **adj.** (**snappier**, **snappiest**) informal **1** irritable and inclined to speak sharply; snappish: *anything unusual made her snappy and nervous.*
2 cleverly concise; neat: *snappy catchphrases.* ■ neat and elegant: *a snappy dresser.*
–PHRASES **make it snappy** be quick about it: *into bed and make it snappy!*
–DERIVATIVES **snap·pi·ly** /-pəlē/ **adv.**, **snap·pi·ness n.**

snap roll ▶ **n.** a maneuver in which an aircraft makes a single quick revolution about its longitudinal axis while flying horizontally.

snap·shot /ˈsnapˌSHät/ ▶ **n. 1** an informal photograph taken quickly, typically with a small handheld camera. ■ a brief look or summary: *this excellent book can only be a snapshot of a complex industry.* ■ Computing a record of the contents of a storage location or data file at a given time.
2 (**snap shot**) a shot taken quickly by a hunter.

snare /sne(ə)r/ ▶ **n. 1** a trap for catching birds or animals, typically one having a noose of wire or cord. ■ a thing likely to lure or tempt someone into harm or error: *the wickedness and snares of the Devil.*
2 a length of wire, gut, or hide stretched across a drumhead to produce a rattling sound. ■ short for SNARE DRUM.
3 Surgery a wire loop for severing polyps or other growths.
▶ **v.** [with obj.] catch (a bird or mammal) in a snare. ■ catch or trap (someone): *I snared a passing waiter.*
–DERIVATIVES **snar·er n.**
–ORIGIN late Old English *sneare*, from Old Norse *snara*.

snare drum ▶ **n.** a small drum in the form of a short cylinder with a membrane at each end, the upper one being struck with hard sticks and the lower one fitted with snares. It originated in military use.
–ORIGIN probably from Middle Low German and Middle Dutch *snare* 'harp string.'

snarf /snärf/ ▶ **v.** [with obj.] informal eat or drink quickly or greedily: *they* **snarfed up** *frozen yogurt.*
–ORIGIN 1950s: perhaps imitative.

snark /snärk/ ▶ **n.** an imaginary animal (used to refer to someone or something that is difficult to track down).
–ORIGIN 1876: nonsense word coined by Lewis Carroll in *The Hunting of the Snark.*

snark·y /ˈsnärkē/ ▶ **adj.** (**snarkier**, **snarkiest**) informal (of a person, words, or a mood) sharply critical; cutting; snide: *the kid who makes snarky remarks in class.* ■ cranky; irritable: *Bobby's always a bit snarky before his nap.*

snarl[1] /snärl/ ▶ **v.** [no obj.] (of an animal such as a dog) make an aggressive growl with bared teeth: (as adj. **snarling**) *snarling Dobermans.* ■ [reporting verb] (of a person) say something in an angry, bad-tempered voice: *I used to* **snarl at** *anyone I disliked* | [with direct speech] *"Shut your mouth!" he snarled* | [with obj.] *he snarled a few choice remarks at them.*
▶ **n.** an act or sound of snarling: *the cat drew its mouth back in a snarl.*
–DERIVATIVES **snarl·er n.**, **snarl·ing·ly adv.**, **snarl·y adj.**
–ORIGIN late 16th cent.: extension of obsolete *snar*, of Germanic origin; related to German *schnarren* 'rattle, snarl,' probably imitative.

snarl[2] ▶ **v.** [with obj.] **1** entangle or impede (something): *the bus got* **snarled up** *in the downtown traffic.*
2 decorate (metalwork) with raised shapes by hammering the underside.
▶ **n.** a knot or tangle: *snarls of wild raspberry plants* | *our hair hung in damp snarls.*
–ORIGIN late Middle English (in the senses 'snare, noose' and 'catch in a snare'): from SNARE.

snarl-up ▶ **n.** informal a traffic jam. ■ a muddle or mistake: *there's a snarl-up in editing.*

snatch /snaCH/ ▶ **v.** [with obj.] quickly seize (something) in a rude or eager way: *she snatched a cookie from the plate* | figurative *a victory snatched from the jaws of defeat.* ■ informal steal (something) or kidnap (someone), typically by seizing or grabbing suddenly: *a mission to snatch Winston Churchill.* ■ [no obj.] (**snatch at**) hastily or ineffectually attempt to seize (something): *she snatched at the handle.* ■ quickly secure or obtain (something) when a chance presents itself: *we snatched a few hours' sleep.* ■ [no obj.] (**snatch at**) eagerly take or accept (an offer or opportunity): *I snatched at the chance.*
▶ **n. 1** an act of snatching or quickly seizing something: *a quick snatch of breath.* ■ a short spell of doing something: *brief snatches of sleep.* ■ a fragment of song or talk: *picking up snatches of conversation.* ■ informal a kidnapping or theft.
2 Weightlifting the rapid raising of a weight from the floor to above the head in one movement.
3 vulgar slang a woman's genitals.
–DERIVATIVES **snatch·er n.**, **snatch·y adj.**
–ORIGIN Middle English *sna(c)che* (verb) 'suddenly snap at,' (noun) 'a snare'; perhaps related to SNACK.

snaz·zy /ˈsnazē/ ▶ **adj.** (**snazzier**, **snazziest**) informal stylish and attractive: *snazzy little silk dresses.*
–DERIVATIVES **snaz·zi·ly** /-zəlē/ **adv.**, **snaz·zi·ness n.**
–ORIGIN 1960s: of unknown origin.

SNCC ▶ **abbr.** Student Nonviolent Coordinating Committee, a US civil-rights student organization active in the 1960s.

Snead /snēd/, Sam (1912–2002), US golfer; full name *Samuel Jackson Snead*; nickname **Slammin' Sammy**. He won a record 81 tournaments of the PGA Tour, including the Masters (1949, 1952, 1954), the PGA (1942, 1949, 1951), and the British Open (1946).

sneak /snēk/ ▶ **v.** (past **sneaked** or informal **snuck** /ˈsnək/) [no obj.] move or go in a furtive or stealthy manner: *I sneaked out by the back exit.* ■ [with obj.] convey (someone or something) in such a way: *someone sneaked a camera inside.* ■ [with obj.] do or obtain (something) in a stealthy or furtive way: *she sneaked a glance at her watch.* ■ (**sneak up on**) creep up on (someone) without being detected: *he sneaks up on us slyly.*
▶ **n.** informal **1** a furtive and contemptible person: *he was branded a prying sneak for eavesdropping on intimate conversation.*
2 (usu. **sneaks**) short for SNEAKER.
▶ **adj.** [attrib.] acting or done surreptitiously, unofficially, or without warning: *a sneak thief* | *a sneak preview.*
–ORIGIN late 16th cent.: probably dialect; perhaps related to obsolete *snike* 'to creep.'

> **USAGE** The traditional standard past form of **sneak** is **sneaked** (*she* **sneaked** *around the corner*). An alternative past form, **snuck** (*she* **snuck** *past me*), arose in the US in the 19th century. Until very recently, **snuck** was confined to US dialect use and was regarded as nonstandard. However, in the last few decades, its use has spread in the US, where it is now regarded as a standard alternative to **sneaked** in all but the most formal contexts. In the Oxford English Corpus, there are now more US citations for **snuck** than there are for **sneaked**, and there is evidence of **snuck** gaining ground in British English as well.

sneak·box /ˈsnēkˌbäks/ ▶ **n.** a small, flat boat masked with brush or weeds, used in wildfowl hunting.

sneak·er /ˈsnēkər/ ▶ **n.** a soft shoe with a rubber sole worn for sports or casual occasions.

sneak·ing /ˈsnēkiNG/ ▶ **adj.** [attrib.] **1** (of a feeling) persistent in one's mind but reluctantly held or not

S

fully recognized; nagging: *I've a sneaking suspicion they'll do well.*
2 informal furtive and contemptible: *an unpleasant, sneaking habit.*
– DERIVATIVES **sneak·ing·ly** adv.

sneak·y /ˈsnēkē/ ▶ adj. (**sneakier, sneakiest**) furtive; sly: *sneaky, underhanded tactics.* ■ (of a feeling) secret; reluctant: *I developed a sneaky fondness for the old lady.*
– DERIVATIVES **sneak·i·ly** /-kəlē/ adv., **sneak·i·ness** n.

sneck /snek/ Scottish N. English ▶ n. Scottish & N. English a latch on a door or window.
▶ v. [with obj.] Scottish & N. English close or fasten (a door or window) with a latch.
– ORIGIN Middle English: obscurely related to SNATCH.

sneer /sni(ə)r/ ▶ n. a contemptuous or mocking smile, remark, or tone: *he acknowledged their presence with a condescending sneer.*
▶ v. [no obj.] smile or speak in a contemptuous or mocking manner: *she had sneered at their bad taste* | [with direct speech] *"I see you're conservative in your ways," David sneered.*
– DERIVATIVES **sneer·er** n., **sneer·ing·ly** adv.
– ORIGIN late Middle English: probably of imitative origin.

sneeze /snēz/ ▶ v. [no obj.] make a sudden involuntary expulsion of air from the nose and mouth due to irritation of one's nostrils: *the smoke made her sneeze.*
▶ n. an act or the sound of expelling air from the nose in such a way: *he stopped a sudden sneeze.*
– PHRASES **not to be sneezed at** informal not to be rejected without careful consideration; worth having or taking into account: *a saving of $550 was not to be sneezed at.*
– DERIVATIVES **sneez·er** n., **sneez·y** adj.
– ORIGIN Middle English: apparently an alteration of Middle English *fnese* due to misreading or misprinting (after initial *fn-* had become unfamiliar), later adopted because it sounded appropriate.

sneeze·weed /ˈsnēz,wēd/ ▶ n. a yellow-flowered North American plant of the daisy family, with turned-back rays and a globular disk. Some kinds are toxic to grazing animals and some are used medicinally, esp. by American Indians, in the treatment of colds. ● Genus *Helenium*, family Compositae: several species, including *H. autumnale.*

sneeze·wort /ˈsnēzwərt, -wôrt/ (also **sneezewort yarrow**) ▶ n. a Eurasian yarrow, naturalized in North America, whose dried leaves induce sneezing. ● *Achillea ptarmica*, family Compositae.

snell /snel/ ▶ n. a short line of gut or horsehair by which a fishhook is attached to a longer line.
▶ v. [with obj.] tie or fasten (a hook) to a line: (as adj. **snelled**) *a snelled or long-shanked hook.*
– ORIGIN mid 19th cent.: of unknown origin.

Snel·len test /ˈsnelən/ ▶ n. a test of visual acuity using rows of letters printed in successively decreasing sizes (the **Snellen scale**).
– ORIGIN mid 19th cent.: named after Hermann *Snellen* (1834–1908), Dutch ophthalmologist.

Snell's law /snelz/ Physics a law stating that the ratio of the sines of the angles of incidence and refraction of a wave are constant when it passes between two given media.
– ORIGIN late 19th cent.: named after Willebrord Van Roijen *Snell* (1591–1626), Dutch mathematician.

SNG ▶ abbr. synthetic natural gas.

snick /snik/ ▶ v. [with obj.] **1** cut a small notch or incision in (something): *the stem can be carefully snicked to allow the bud to swell.*
2 cause (something) to make a sharp clicking sound: [with obj. and complement] *he placed the pen in the briefcase and snicked it shut.* ■ [no obj.] make such a sound: *the bolt snicked into place.*
▶ n. **1** a small notch or cut: *he had several shaving snicks.*
2 a sharp click: *he heard the snick of the latch.*
– ORIGIN late 17th cent.: probably from obsolete *snick or snee* 'fight with knives.'

snick·er /ˈsnikər/ ▶ v. [no obj.] give a smothered or half-suppressed laugh; snigger. ■ (of a horse) whinny.
▶ n. a smothered laugh; a snigger. ■ a whinny.
– DERIVATIVES **snick·er·ing·ly** adv.
– ORIGIN late 17th cent.: imitative.

snide /snīd/ ▶ adj. **1** derogatory or mocking in an indirect way: *snide remarks about my mother.* ■ (of a person) devious and underhanded: *a snide divorce lawyer.*
2 chiefly Brit. counterfeit; inferior: *snide Rolex watches.*
▶ n. an unpleasant or underhanded person or remark.
– DERIVATIVES **snide·ly** adv., **snide·ness** n., **snide·y** adj.
– ORIGIN mid 19th cent. (originally slang in sense 2 of the adjective): of unknown origin.

sniff /snif/ ▶ v. [no obj.] draw in air audibly through the nose to detect a smell, to stop it from running, or to express contempt: *his dog sniffed at my trousers* | [with direct speech] *"You're behaving in an unladylike fashion," sniffed Mother.* ■ [with obj.] draw in (a scent, substance, or air) through the nose. ■ [usu. with negative] (**sniff at**) show contempt or dislike for: *the price is not to be sniffed at.* ■ (**sniff around**) informal investigate covertly, esp. to find out confidential or incriminating information about someone. ■ [with obj.] (**sniff something out**) informal discover something by investigation: *he made millions upon millions sniffing out tax loopholes for companies.*
▶ n. an act or sound of drawing air through the nose: *he gave a sniff of disapproval.* ■ an amount of air or other substance taken up in such a way: *his drug use was confined to a sniff of amyl nitrite.* ■ [in sing.] informal a trace, hint, or small amount: *they're off at the first sniff of trouble.* ■ [in sing.] Brit. informal a small chance: *the Olympic hosts will at least get a sniff at a medal.*
– ORIGIN Middle English: imitative.

sniff·er /ˈsnifər/ ▶ n. **1** a person who sniffs, esp. one who sniffs a drug or toxic substance: [with adj.] *a glue sniffer.* ■ informal a device for detecting an invisible and dangerous substance, such as gas or radiation: *electronic sniffers are used to detect the presence of a nuclear mass.*
2 informal a person's nose.
3 (also **sniffer program**) a computer program that detects and records a variety of restricted information, esp. the secret passwords needed to gain access to files or networks.

sniff·er dog ▶ n. informal a dog trained to find drugs or explosives by smell.

snif·fle /ˈsnifəl/ ▶ v. [no obj.] sniff slightly or repeatedly, typically because of a cold or fit of crying.
▶ n. an act of sniffing in such a way: *he was restraining his sniffles rather well.* ■ a head cold causing a running nose and sniffing: *she had a slight cough and a sniffle* | *they may get damp and catch the sniffles.*
– DERIVATIVES **snif·fler** /ˈsnif(ə)lər/ n., **snif·fly** /ˈsnif(ə)lē/ adj.
– ORIGIN mid 17th cent.: imitative; compare with SNIVEL.

snif·fy /ˈsnifē/ ▶ adj. (**sniffier, sniffiest**) informal scornful; contemptuous: *some people are sniffy about tea bags.*
– DERIVATIVES **sniff·i·ly** /-fəlē/ adv., **sniff·i·ness** n.

snif·ter /ˈsniftər/ ▶ n. a footed glass that is wide at the bottom and tapers to the top, used for brandy and other drinks. ■ informal a small quantity of an alcoholic drink: *care to join me for a snifter?*
– ORIGIN mid 19th cent.: imitative; compare with dialect *snift* 'to snort.'

snifter

snig·ger /ˈsnigər/ ▶ n. a smothered or half-suppressed laugh.
▶ v. [no obj.] give such a laugh: *the boys at school were sure to snigger at him behind his back* | [with direct speech] *"Doesn't he look like a fool?" they sniggered.*
– DERIVATIVES **snig·ger·er** n., **snig·ger·ing·ly** adv.
– ORIGIN early 18th cent.: later variant of SNICKER.

snig·ger·y /ˈsnigərē/ ▶ adj. informal characterized by or liable to cause sniggering: *sniggery jokes.*

snig·gle /ˈsnigəl/ ▶ v. [no obj.] fish for eels by pushing a baited hook into holes in which they are hiding.
– ORIGIN mid 17th cent.: frequentative, based on earlier *snig* 'small eel,' of unknown origin.

snip /snip/ ▶ v. (**snips, snipping, snipped**) [with obj.] cut (something) with scissors or shears, typically with small quick strokes: *she snipped layers into the hair around her face* | [no obj.] *she inspected the embroidery, snipping at loose threads.*
▶ n. **1** an act of cutting something in such a way: *he took a snip at a dandelion on the grass.* ■ a small piece of something that has been cut off: *the collage consists of snips of wallpaper.*
2 informal a small or insignificant person: *imagine that little snip telling me I was wrong!*
3 (**snips**) hand shears, esp. for cutting metal: *use tin snips.*
4 [in sing.] Brit. informal a surprisingly cheap item; a bargain: *the wine is a snip at £2.65.* ■ dated a thing that is easily achieved.
– ORIGIN mid 16th cent. (in the sense 'a shred'): from Low German *snip* 'small piece,' of imitative origin.

snipe /snīp/ ▶ n. (pl. **same** or **snipes**) a wading bird of marshes and wet meadows, with brown camouflaged plumage, a long straight bill, and typically a drumming display flight. See also PAINTED SNIPE, SEED-SNIPE. ● *Gallinago* and other genera, family Scolopacidae: several species, e.g., the **common snipe** (*G. gallinago*).
▶ v. [no obj.] shoot at someone from a hiding place, esp. accurately and at long range: *the soldiers in the trench sniped at us.* ■ make a sly or petty verbal attack: *the state governor constantly sniped at the president* | (as noun **sniping**) *there has been some sniping about inept leadership.*
– DERIVATIVES **snip·er** n.
– ORIGIN Middle English: probably of Scandinavian origin; compare with Icelandic *mýrisnípa*; obscurely related to Dutch *snip* and German *Schnepfe*.

snipe eel ▶ n. a slender marine eel with a long, thin, beaklike snout, typically occurring in deep water. ● Family Nemichthyidae: several genera and species.

snipe fly ▶ n. a slender, long-legged predatory fly. ● Family Rhagionidae: many genera and species.

snip·pet /ˈsnipit/ ▶ n. a small piece or brief extract: *snippets of information about the war.*
– DERIVATIVES **snip·pet·y** adj.

snip·py /ˈsnipē/ ▶ adj. (**snippier, snippiest**) informal curt or sharp, esp. in a condescending way: *a snippy note from our landlord.*
– DERIVATIVES **snip·pi·ly** /-pəlē/ adv., **snip·pi·ness** n.

snit /snit/ ▶ n. informal a fit of irritation; a sulk: *the ambassador and delegation had withdrawn in a snit.*
– ORIGIN 1930s: of unknown origin.

snitch /sniCH/ informal ▶ v. **1** [with obj.] steal.
2 [no obj.] inform on someone: *she wouldn't tell who snitched on me.*
▶ n. an informer.
– ORIGIN late 17th cent.: of unknown origin.

sniv·el /ˈsnivəl/ ▶ v. (**snivels, sniveling, sniveled**; Brit. **snivels, snivelling, snivelled**) [no obj.] cry and sniffle: *Kate started to snivel, looking sad and stunned.* ■ complain in a whining or tearful way: *he shouldn't snivel about his punishment* | (as adj. **sniveling**) *you sniveling little brat!*
▶ n. a slight sniff indicating suppressed emotion or crying: *Lucy's torrent of howls weakened to a snivel.*
– DERIVATIVES **sniv·el·er** n., **sniv·el·ing·ly** adv.
– ORIGIN late Old English (recorded only in the verbal noun *snyflung* 'mucus'), from *snofl*, in the same sense; compare with SNUFFLE.

sniv·el gear ▶ n. the items carried by a soldier for personal comfort in inclement weather.

snob /snäb/ ▶ n. a person with an exaggerated respect for high social position or wealth who seeks to associate with social superiors and dislikes people or activities regarded as lower-class. ■ [with adj. or noun modifier] a person who believes that their tastes in a particular area are superior to those of other people: *a musical snob.*
– DERIVATIVES **snob·bism** /-ˌbizəm/ n., **snob·by** adj. (**snobbier, snobbiest**).
– ORIGIN late 18th cent. (originally dialect in the sense 'cobbler'): of unknown origin; early senses conveyed a notion of 'lower status or rank,' later denoting a person seeking to imitate those of superior social standing or wealth. Folk etymology connects the word with Latin *sine nobilitate* 'without nobility' but the earliest recorded sense has no connection with this.

snob·ber·y /ˈsnäbərē/ ▶ n. (pl. **snobberies**) the character or quality of being a snob: *the worst aspects of English class snobbery.*

snob·bish /ˈsnäbiSH/ ▶ adj. of, characteristic of, or like a snob: *the writer takes a rather snobbish tone.*
– DERIVATIVES **snob·bish·ly** adv., **snob·bish·ness** n.

SNOBOL /ˈsnō,bôl/ ▶ n. a high-level computer programming language used esp. in manipulating textual data.
– ORIGIN 1960s: formed from letters taken from *string-oriented symbolic language*, on the pattern of *COBOL*.

snob val·ue ▶ n. value attached to something for its power to indicate supposed social superiority; cachet: *the coffin was more expensive and carried snob value.*

sno-cone ▶ n. variant spelling of SNOW CONE.

snog /snäg/ Brit. informal ▶ v. (**snogs, snogging, snogged**) [with obj.] kiss and caress amorously.
▶ n. an act or spell of amorous kissing and caressing.
– DERIVATIVES **snog·ger** n.
– ORIGIN 1940s: of unknown origin.

snood /sno͝od/ ▶ n. **1** an ornamental hairnet or fabric bag worn over the hair at the back of a woman's head. ■ historical a ribbon or band worn by unmarried women in Scotland to confine their hair.
2 a wide ring of knitted material worn as a hood or scarf.
3 a short line attaching a hook to a main line in sea fishing.
– ORIGIN Old English *snōd*, of unknown origin.

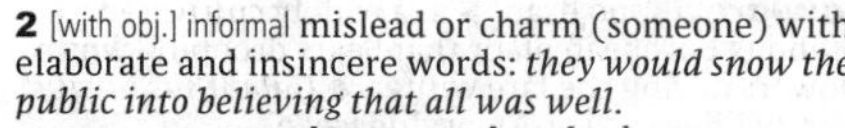

snook[1] /sno͝ok/ ▶ **n.** a large edible game fish of the Caribbean that is sometimes found in brackish water. ● *Centropomus undecimalis*, family Centropomidae.
– ORIGIN late 17th cent.: from Dutch *snoek* 'pike.'

snook[2] ▶ **n.** (in phrase **cock a snook**) informal, chiefly Brit. place one's hand so that the thumb touches one's nose and the fingers are spread out, in order to express contempt: *you wouldn't be so quick to cock a snook if she were actually looking at you.* ■ openly show contempt or a lack of respect for someone or something; thumb one's nose: *he spent a lifetime cocking a snook at the art world.*
– ORIGIN late 18th cent.: of unknown origin.

snook·er /ˈsno͝okər/ ▶ **n.** a game played with cues on a billiard table in which the players use a cue ball (white) to pocket the other balls (fifteen red and six colored) in a set order. ■ a position in a game of snooker or pool in which a player cannot make a direct shot at any permitted ball; a shot placing an opponent in such a position: *he needed a snooker to have a chance of winning the frame.*
▶ **v.** [with obj.] subject (oneself or one's opponent) to a snooker. ■ trick, entice, or trap: *they were snookered into buying books at prices that were too high.* ■ Brit. leave (someone) in a difficult position; thwart: *I managed to lose my car keys—that was me snookered.*
– ORIGIN late 19th cent.: of unknown origin.

snoop /sno͞op/ informal ▶ **v.** [no obj.] investigate or look around furtively in an attempt to find out something, esp. information about someone's private affairs: *your sister might find the ring if she goes snooping around* | (as adj. **snooping**) *snooping neighbors.*
▶ **n.** [in sing.] an act of looking around in such a way: *I could go back to her cottage and have another snoop.* ■ a person who investigates in such a way.
– DERIVATIVES **snoop·er n.**, **snoop·y adj.**
– ORIGIN mid 19th cent.: from Dutch *snoepen* 'eat on the sly.'

snoop·er·scope /ˈsno͞opərˌskōp/ ▶ **n.** a device that converts infrared radiation into a visible image, used for seeing in the dark.

snoot /sno͞ot/ ▶ **n. 1** informal a person's nose.
2 informal a person who shows contempt for those considered to be of a lower social class: *the snoots complain that the paper has lowered its standards.*
3 a tubular or conical attachment used to produce a narrow beam from a spotlight.
– ORIGIN mid 19th cent.: variant of **SNOUT**.

snoot·ful /ˈsno͞otˌfo͝ol/ ▶ **n.** enough alcoholic drink to make one drunk: *they're tongue-tied until they've had a snootful.* ■ as much as one can take of something: *he decided he'd had a snootful of playing the role.*

snoot·y /ˈsno͞otē/ ▶ **adj.** (**snootier, snootiest**) informal showing disapproval or contempt toward others, esp. those considered to belong to a lower social class: *snooty neighbors.*
– DERIVATIVES **snoot·i·ly** /-tl-ē/ **adv.**, **snoot·i·ness n.**
– ORIGIN early 20th cent.: from **SNOOT** + **-Y**[1]; compare with **SNOTTY**.

snooze /sno͞oz/ informal ▶ **n.** a short, light sleep, esp. during the day: *he settled in the grass for a snooze.* ■ a boring event or person: *months go by and the job's a snooze.*
▶ **v.** [no obj.] have a short, light sleep: *the children play beach games while the adults snooze in the sun.*
– DERIVATIVES **snooz·er** /ˈsno͞ozər/ **n.**, **snooz·y** /ˈsno͞ozē/ **adj.** (**snoozier, snooziest**).
– ORIGIN late 18th cent.: of unknown origin.

snooze but·ton ▶ **n.** a control on a clock that sets an alarm to repeat after a short interval, allowing time for a little more sleep.

snore /snôr/ ▶ **n.** a snorting or grunting sound in a person's breathing while asleep: *she lay on the mattress listening to Sally's snores.* ■ informal a thing that is extremely boring: *she sings a version of "Passionate Kisses" that's a certified snore.*
▶ **v.** [no obj.] breathe with a snorting or grunting sound while asleep: *he was snoring loudly* | (as noun **snoring**) *you keep me awake all night with your snoring.*
– DERIVATIVES **snor·er n.**
– ORIGIN Middle English (in the sense 'a snort, snorting'): probably imitative; compare with **SNORT**.

snor·kel /ˈsnôrkəl/ ▶ **n. 1** a short curved tube for a swimmer to breathe through while keeping the face under water. ■ a tube used by a submarine just below the surface as a fresh-air intake.
2 (**Snorkel**) trademark a type of hydraulically elevated platform for firefighting.
▶ **v.** (**snorkels, snorkeling, snorkeled**; Brit. **snorkels, snorkelling, snorkelled**) [no obj.] (often as noun **snorkeling**) swim using a snorkel: *the sea is incredibly clear, which is ideal for snorkeling* | *snorkel around the unspoiled coral reefs.*
– DERIVATIVES **snor·kel·er n.**
– ORIGIN 1940s: from German *Schnorchel.*

snorkel 1

Snor·ri Stur·lu·son /ˈsnôrē ˈstərləsən/ (1178–1241), Icelandic historian and poet. A leading figure of medieval Icelandic literature, he wrote the *Younger Edda* or *Prose Edda* and the *Heimskringla*, a history of the kings of Norway from mythical times to 1177.

snort /snôrt/ ▶ **n.** an explosive sound made by the sudden forcing of breath through one's nose, used to express indignation, derision, or incredulity: *he gave a snort of disgust.* ■ a similar sound made by an animal, typically when excited or frightened. ■ informal a quantity of an illegal drug, esp. cocaine, inhaled in powdered form through the nose: *they were high on a few snorts.* ■ informal a measure of an alcoholic drink: *a bottle of rum was opened and they took a good long snort.*
▶ **v.** [no obj.] make a sudden sound through one's nose, esp. to express indignation or derision: *she snorted with laughter* | [with direct speech] *"How perfectly ridiculous!" he snorted.* ■ (of an animal) make such a sound, esp. when excited or frightened. ■ [with obj.] informal inhale (the powdered form of an illegal drug, esp. cocaine) through the nosei.
– ORIGIN late Middle English (as a verb, also in the sense 'snore'): probably imitative; compare with **SNORE**. The noun dates from the early 19th cent.

snort·er /ˈsnôrtər/ ▶ **n.** informal **1** a person or thing that snorts, esp. someone who inhales cocaine.
2 Brit. dated a thing that is an extreme or remarkable example of its kind, esp. for its strength or severity: *the opening batsman fended off a snorter.*

snot /snät/ ▶ **n.** informal nasal mucus. ■ an arrogant or conceited person. ■ a contemptible or worthless person.
– ORIGIN late Middle English: probably from Middle Dutch and Middle Low German; related to **SNOUT**.

snot-nosed ▶ **adj.** informal childish and inexperienced (used as a general term of abuse): *a boy at thirteen is a snot-nosed kid.* ■ (of a person) considering oneself superior; conceited: *a snot-nosed snob.*

snot rag ▶ **n.** informal a handkerchief.

snot·ter /ˈsnätər/ ▶ **n.** Nautical a fitting that holds the heel of a sprit close to the mast. ■ a length of rope with an eye spliced in each end.
– ORIGIN mid 18th cent.: of unknown origin.

snot·ty /ˈsnätē/ ▶ **adj.** (**snottier, snottiest**) informal
1 full of or covered with nasal mucus: *a snotty nose.*
2 having or showing a superior or conceited attitude: *a snotty letter.*
– DERIVATIVES **snot·ti·ly** /-tl-ē/ **adv.**, **snot·ti·ness n.**

snot·ty-nosed ▶ **adj.** informal another term for **SNOT-NOSED**.

snout /snout/ ▶ **n. 1** the projecting nose and mouth of an animal, esp. a mammal. ■ derogatory a person's nose. ■ the projecting front or end of something such as a pistol.
2 Brit. informal a cigarette. ■ tobacco. [late 19th cent.: of unknown origin.]
3 Brit. informal a police informer.
– DERIVATIVES **snout·ed adj.** [often in combination] *long-snouted baboons*, **snout·y adj.**
– ORIGIN Middle English: from Middle Dutch and Middle Low German *snūt*; related to **SNOT**.

snout bee·tle ▶ **n.** another term for **WEEVIL**.

Snow /snō/, C. P., 1st Baron Snow of Leicester (1905–80), English novelist and scientist; full name *Charles Percy Snow.* He is best known for his sequence of 11 novels, starting with *Strangers and Brothers* (1940), that deals with moral dilemmas in the academic world and for his lecture *Two Cultures* (1959).

snow /snō/ ▶ **n. 1** atmospheric water vapor frozen into ice crystals and falling in light white flakes or lying on the ground as a white layer: *we were trudging through deep snow* | *the first snow of the season.*
2 something that resembles snow in color or texture, in particular: ■ a mass of flickering white spots on a television or radar screen, caused by interference or a poor signal. ■ informal cocaine. ■ a dessert or other dish resembling snow: *vanilla snow.* ■ [with modifier] a frozen gas resembling snow: *carbon dioxide snow.*
▶ **v. 1** [no obj.] (**it snows, it is snowing**, etc.) snow falls: *it's not snowing so heavily now.* ■ (**be snowed in**) be confined or blocked by a large quantity of snow: *I was snowed in for a week.*
2 [with obj.] informal mislead or charm (someone) with elaborate and insincere words: *they would snow the public into believing that all was well.*
– PHRASAL VERBS **be snowed under** be overwhelmed with a large quantity of something, esp. work: *he's been snowed under with urgent cases.*
– DERIVATIVES **snow·less adj.**, **snow·like** /-ˌlīk/ **adj.**
– ORIGIN Old English *snāw*, of Germanic origin; related to Dutch *sneeuw* and German *Schnee*, from an Indo-European root shared by Latin *nix, niv-* and Greek *nipha.*

snow·ball /ˈsnōˌbôl/ ▶ **n. 1** a ball of packed snow, esp. one made for throwing at other people for fun. ■ a thing that grows rapidly in intensity or importance: *a public-debt snowball* | [as modifier] *the closures are expected to have a snowball effect, impacting jobs and tax revenues.*
2 a dessert resembling a ball of snow, esp. one containing or covered in ice cream.
3 a cocktail containing gin, anisette, and cream.
▶ **v. 1** [with obj.] throw snowballs at: *I made sure the other kids stopped snowballing Celia.*
2 [no obj.] increase rapidly in size, intensity, or importance: *the campaign was snowballing.*
– PHRASES **a snowball's chance (in hell)** informal no chance at all: *the plan has a snowball's chance in hell of being accepted.*

snow·ball bush (also **snowball tree**) ▶ **n.** a guelder rose, esp. one of a sterile variety that produces large globular white flower heads.

snow·bell /ˈsnōˌbel/ ▶ **n.** an Asian tree related to the storax, bearing clusters of fragrant white hanging flowers at midsummer, widely cultivated as an ornamental. ● *Styrax japonica*, family Styracaceae.

snow·ber·ry /ˈsnōˌberē/ ▶ **n.** (pl. **snowberries**) a North American shrub of the honeysuckle family, bearing white berries and often cultivated as an ornamental or for hedging. ● *Symphoricarpos albus*, family Caprifoliaceae.

snow·bird /ˈsnōˌbərd/ ▶ **n. 1** informal a northerner who moves to a warmer southern state in the winter.
2 a widespread and variable junco with gray or brown upper parts and a white belly. ● *Junco hyemalis*, family Emberizidae (subfamily Emberizinae). Alternative names: **northern junco, dark-eyed junco, slate-colored junco.** ■ the snow bunting.

snow-blind ▶ **adj.** temporarily blinded by the glare of light reflected by a large expanse of snow.
– DERIVATIVES **snow blind·ness n.**

snow·blink /ˈsnōˌbliNGk/ ▶ **n.** a white reflection in the sky of snow or ice on the ground.

snow·blow·er /ˈsnōˌblōər/ ▶ **n.** a machine that clears fallen snow by blowing it to the side.

snow·board /ˈsnōˌbôrd/ ▶ **n.** a board resembling a short, broad ski, used for sliding downhill on snow.
▶ **v.** [no obj.] slide downhill on such a board: (as noun **snowboarding**) *the thrills of snowboarding.*
– DERIVATIVES **snow·board·er n.**

snow boot ▶ **n.** a warm waterproof boot worn in the snow.

snow·bound /ˈsnōˌbound/ ▶ **adj.** prevented from traveling or going out by snow or snowy weather: *he was snowbound in the nearby mountains.* ■ covered in snow or inaccessible because of it: *a snowbound Alpine village.*

snow bunt·ing ▶ **n.** a northern bunting that breeds mainly in the Arctic, the male having white plumage with a black back in the breeding season. ● *Plectrophenax nivalis*, family Emberizidae (subfamily Emberizinae).

snow·cap /ˈsnōˌkap/ ▶ **n. 1** a covering of snow on the top of a mountain.
2 a small Central American hummingbird with mainly purple plumage and a white crown. ● *Microchera albocoronata*, family Trochilidae.
– DERIVATIVES **snow-capped adj.** (sense 1).

snow·cat /ˈsnōˌkat/ ▶ **n.** another term for **SNOWMOBILE**.
– ORIGIN 1940s: from **SNOW** + **CATERPILLAR**.

snow chains ▶ **plural n.** a pair or set of meshes of metal chain, fitted around a vehicle's tires to give extra traction in snow.

snow cone (also **sno-cone**) ▶ **n.** a paper cup filled with fruit-flavored crushed ice.

snow crab ▶ **n.** an edible spider crab found off the eastern seaboard of Canada. ● *Chionoecetes opilio*, section Oxyrhyncha.

snow·drift /ˈsnōˌdrift/ ▶ **n.** a bank of deep snow heaped up by the wind.

S

snow·drop /ˈsnōˌdräp/ ▶ **n.** a widely cultivated bulbous European plant that bears drooping white flowers during the late winter. ● *Galanthus nivalis*, family Liliaceae (or Amaryllidaceae).

snow·fall /ˈsnōˌfôl/ ▶ **n.** a fall of snow: *heavy snowfalls made travel absolutely impossible.* ■ the quantity of snow falling within a given area in a given time: *winters with above-average snowfall.*

snow fence ▶ **n.** a fence erected to prevent hazardous snowdrifts, typically by the side of a road.

snow·field /ˈsnōˌfēld/ ▶ **n.** a permanent wide expanse of snow in mountainous or polar regions.

snow·flake /ˈsnōˌflāk/ ▶ **n. 1** a flake of snow, esp. a feathery ice crystal, typically displaying delicate sixfold symmetry.
2 a white-flowered Eurasian plant related to and resembling the snowdrop, typically blooming in the summer or autumn. ● Genus *Leucojum*, family Liliaceae (or Amaryllidaceae).

snow flea ▶ **n.** either of two small insects that appear on or near snow in northern regions or on mountains. ● a springtail that often swarms on snow, making it appear black (family Isotomidae, including the Alpine *Isotoma saltans* and the North American *Hypogastrura nivicola*). ● a small flightless scorpionfly that feeds on mosses (family Boreidae, including the Eurasian *Boreus hyemalis*).

snow globe ▶ **n.** a toy or ornament consisting of a model of a scene in a liquid containing white particles that, when shaken, mimic a snowstorm.

snow goose ▶ **n.** a gregarious goose that breeds in Arctic Canada and Greenland, typically having white plumage with black wing tips. ● *Anser caerulescens*, family Anatidae.

snow gun ▶ **n.** a machine that makes artificial snow and blows it onto ski slopes.

snow job ▶ **n.** informal a deception or concealment of one's real motive in an attempt to flatter or persuade: *we need to* ***do a snow job on*** *him.*

snow leop·ard ▶ **n.** a rare large cat that has pale gray fur patterned with dark blotches and rings, living in the Altai mountains, Hindu Kush, and Himalayas. Also called OUNCE². ● *Panthera uncia*, family Felidae.

snow line ▶ **n.** (usu. **the snow line**) the altitude above which some snow remains on the ground in a particular place throughout the year. ■ the altitude above which there is snow on the ground in a particular place at a given time.

snow ma·chine ▶ **n.** another term for SNOWMOBILE.

snow·making /ˈsnōˌmākiNG/ ▶ **n.** [often as modifier] the production of artificial snow, esp. for ski slopes: *snowmaking machines.*

snow·man /ˈsnōˌman/ ▶ **n.** (pl. **snowmen**) a representation of a human figure created with compressed snow.

snow·melt /ˈsnōˌmelt/ ▶ **n.** the melting of fallen snow: *heavy rains combine with rapid snowmelt.* ■ water that results from this: *the day was springlike and the snowmelt shone in blue and gold.*

snow·mo·bile /ˈsnōmōˌbēl/ ▶ **n.** a motor vehicle, esp. one with runners in the front and caterpillar tracks in the rear, for traveling over snow.
▶ **v.** [no obj.] travel by snowmobile: (as noun **snowmobiling**) *the county offers snowmobiling, ice fishing, kayaking, and rafting.*
– DERIVATIVES **snow·mo·bil·er** **n.**

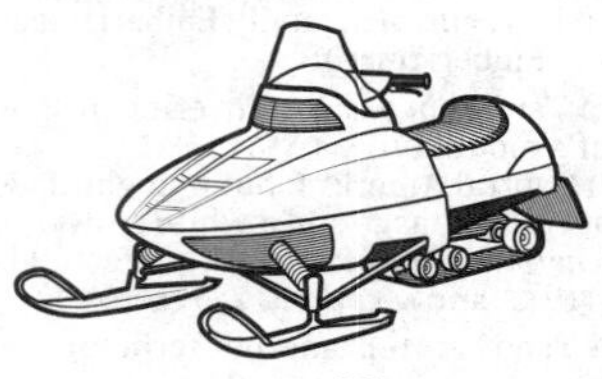
snowmobile

snow·pack /ˈsnōˌpak/ ▶ **n.** a mass of snow on the ground that is compressed and hardened by its own weight.

snow pea ▶ **n.** a pea of a variety with an edible pod, eaten when the pod is young and flat. Compare with SUGAR SNAP.

snow·plow /ˈsnōˌplou/ (Brit. **snowplough**) ▶ **n. 1** an implement or vehicle for clearing roads of snow by pushing it aside.
2 Skiing an act of turning the points of one's skis inward in order to slow down or turn.
▶ **v.** [no obj.] ski with the tips of one's skis pointing inward in order to slow down or turn.

snow·scape /ˈsnōˌskāp/ ▶ **n.** a landscape covered in snow. ■ a picture of such a landscape.

snow·shoe /ˈsnōˌSHo͞o/ ▶ **n.** a flat device resembling a racket that is attached to the sole of a boot and used for walking on snow.
▶ **v.** [no obj.] travel wearing snowshoes: *we snowshoed down into the next valley.*
– DERIVATIVES **snow·sho·er** /-ər/ **n.**, **snow·shoe·ing** /-iNG/ **n.**

snow·shoe hare (also **snowshoe rabbit**) ▶ **n.** a North American hare with large hairy hind feet, fairly small ears, and a white winter coat. ● *Lepus americanus*, family Leporidae.

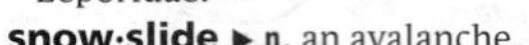
snowshoes

snow·slide ▶ **n.** an avalanche.

snow·storm /ˈsnōˌstôrm/ ▶ **n.** a heavy fall of snow, esp. with a high wind. ■ a shower or large quantity of something: *it swam away in a flurry of wings and flippers, raising a snowstorm of foam.* ■ SNOW GLOBE.

snow·suit /ˈsnōˌso͞ot/ ▶ **n.** a child's one- or two-piece coverall with a warm lining for protection against cold and often with a water-repellent outer material.

snow throw·er ▶ **n.** another term for SNOWBLOWER.

snow tire ▶ **n.** a tire with a tread that gives extra traction on snow or ice.

snow-white ▶ **adj.** of a pure white color: *perfect spotless utensils on a snow-white tablecloth.*

snow·y /ˈsnōē/ ▶ **adj.** (**snowier**, **snowiest**) covered with snow: *snowy mountains.* ■ (of weather or a period of time) characterized by snowfall: *a snowy January day.* ■ of or like snow, esp. in being pure white: *snowy hair.*
– DERIVATIVES **snow·i·ly** /ˈsnōəlē/ **adv.**, **snow·i·ness** **n.**

snow·y e·gret ▶ **n.** a North American egret with all-white plumage, black legs, and yellow feet. ● *Egretta thula*, family Ardeidae.

snow·y owl ▶ **n.** a large northern owl that breeds mainly in the Arctic tundra, the male being entirely white and the female having darker markings. ● *Nyctea scandiaca*, family Strigidae.

snow·y plov·er ▶ **n.** a small white-breasted plover related to the ringed plover, found on most continents. ● *Charadrius alexandrinus*, family Charadriidae.

SNP /snip/ ▶ **abbr.** single nucleotide polymorphism.

Snr. ▶ **abbr.** chiefly Brit. Senior: *John Hammond Snr.*

snub /snəb/ ▶ **v.** (**snubs**, **snubbing**, **snubbed**) [with obj.] **1** rebuff, ignore, or spurn disdainfully: *he snubbed faculty members and students alike | he snubbed her request to wind up the debate.*
2 check the movement of (a horse or boat), esp. by a rope wound around a post: *a horse snubbed to a tree.*
▶ **n.** an act of showing disdain or a lack of cordiality by rebuffing or ignoring someone or something: *he couldn't help thinking that the whole thing was meant to be taken as a snub.*
▶ **adj.** (of a person's or animal's nose) short and turned up at the end: [in combination] *snub-nosed.*
– ORIGIN Middle English (as a verb, originally in the sense 'rebuke with sharp words'): from Old Norse *snubba* 'chide, check the growth of.' The adjective dates from the early 18th cent.

snub·ber /ˈsnəbər/ ▶ **n. 1** a simple kind of shock absorber.
2 an electric circuit intended to suppress voltage spikes.

snuck /snək/ informal past and past participle of SNEAK.

snuff¹ /snəf/ ▶ **v.** [with obj.] extinguish (a candle): *a breeze* ***snuffed out*** *the candle.* ■ dated trim the charred wick from (a candle). ■ informal kill or put an end to in an abrupt or sudden manner: *his life* ***was snuffed out*** *by a sniper's bullet.* ■ (**snuff it**) Brit. informal die.
▶ **n.** the charred part of a candle wick.
– ORIGIN late Middle English: of unknown origin.

snuff² ▶ **n.** powdered tobacco that is sniffed up the nostril rather than smoked: *a pinch of snuff.*
▶ **v.** [with obj.] inhale or sniff at (something): *they stood* ***snuffing up*** *the keen cold air.* ■ [no obj.] archaic sniff up powdered tobacco.
– PHRASES **up to snuff** informal **1** meeting the required standard: *they need a million dollars to get their facilities up to snuff.* ■ in good health: *he hadn't felt up to snuff all summer.* **2** Brit. archaic not easily deceived; knowing: *an up-to-snuff old vagabond.*
– ORIGIN late Middle English (as a verb): from Middle Dutch *snuffen* 'to snuffle.' The noun dates from the late 17th cent. and is probably an abbreviation of Dutch *snuftabak.*

snuff·box /ˈsnəfˌbäks/ ▶ **n.** a small ornamental box for holding snuff.

snuff·er /ˈsnəfər/ (also **candlesnuffer**) ▶ **n.** a small hollow metal cone on the end of a handle, used to extinguish a candle by smothering the flame. ■ (usu. **snuffers** or **candlesnuffers**) an implement resembling scissors with an inverted metal cup attached to one blade, used to extinguish a candle or trim its wick.

snuff film (also **snuff movie**) ▶ **n.** informal a pornographic movie of an actual murder.

snuf·fle /ˈsnəfəl/ ▶ **v.** [no obj.] breathe noisily through the nose due to a cold or crying: *Alice was weeping quietly, snuffling a little.* ■ (esp. of an animal) make repeated sniffing sounds as though smelling at something: *the collie snuffled around his boots* | (as noun **snuffling**) *she heard a strange, persistent snuffling.*
▶ **n.** a sniff or sniffing sound: *a silence broken only by the faint snuffles of the dogs.* ■ (usu. **the snuffles**) informal a cold or other infection that causes sniffing: *he went down with the snuffles.*
– DERIVATIVES **snuf·fler** **n.**, **snuf·fly** **adj.**
– ORIGIN late 16th cent.: probably from Low German and Dutch *snuffelen*; compare with SNUFF² and SNIVEL.

snuff·y¹ /ˈsnəfē/ ▶ **adj.** (**snuffier**, **snuffiest**) archaic supercilious or contemptuous: *some snuffy old stockbroker.* ■ easily offended; annoyed.

snuff·y² ▶ **adj.** archaic resembling powdered tobacco in color or substance.

snug /snəg/ ▶ **adj.** (**snugger**, **snuggest**) **1** comfortable, warm, and cozy; well protected from the weather or cold: *she was safe and snug in Ruth's arms | a snug cottage.* ■ archaic (of an income or employment) allowing one to live in comfort and comparative ease.
2 (esp. of clothing) very tight or close-fitting: *a well-shaped hood for a snug fit.*
▶ **n.** Brit. a small, comfortable public room in a pub or inn.
▶ **v.** (**snugs**, **snugging**, **snugged**) [with obj.] place (something) safely or cozily: *she tucks him in, snugging the blanket up to his chin.* ■ [no obj.] settle comfortably and cozily: *the passengers snugged down among the cargo.*
– PHRASES **snug as a bug** (**in a rug**) humorous in an extremely comfortable position or situation.
– DERIVATIVES **snug·ly** **adv.**, **snug·ness** **n.**
– ORIGIN late 16th cent. (originally in nautical use in the sense 'shipshape, compact, prepared for bad weather'): probably of Low German or Dutch origin.

snug·ger·y /ˈsnəgərē/ ▶ **n.** (pl. **snuggeries**) a cozy or comfortable place, esp. someone's private room or den. ■ Brit. archaic another term for SNUG.

snug·gle /ˈsnəgəl/ ▶ **v.** settle or move into a warm, comfortable position: [no obj.] ***I snuggled down*** *in my sleeping bag* | [with obj.] *she snuggled her head into his shoulder.*
– ORIGIN late 17th cent.: frequentative of the verb SNUG.

so¹ /sō/ ▶ **adv. 1** [as submodifier] to such a great extent: *the words tumbled out so fast* ***that*** *I could barely hear them | don't look so worried | I'm not* ***so*** *foolish* ***as*** *to say that.* ■ extremely; very much (used for emphasis): *she looked so pretty | I do love it so.* ■ informal used to emphasize a clause or negative statement: *that's so not fair | you are so going to regret this.* ■ informal used with a gesture to indicate size: *the bird was about so long.*
2 [as submodifier with negative] to the same extent (used in comparisons): *he isn't so bad as you'd think | without his parents' support, he would not have done so well.*
3 referring back to something previously mentioned. ■ that is the case: *"Is it going to rain?" "I think so." | if she notices, she never says so.* ■ the truth: *I hear that you're a writer—is that so?* ■ similarly; and also: *times have changed and so have I.* ■ expressing agreement: *"It's cold in here." "So it is."* ■ informal used to emphatically contradict a negative statement: *it is so!*
4 in the way described or demonstrated; thus: *hold your arms so |* ***so it was that*** *he was still a bachelor.*
▶ **conj. 1** and for this reason; therefore: *it was still painful, so I went to see a specialist | you know I'm telling the truth, so don't interrupt.* ■ (**so that**) with the result that: *it was overgrown with brambles, so that I had difficulty making any progress.*
2 (**so that**) with the aim that; in order that: *they whisper to each other so that no one else can hear.*
3 and then; as the next step: *and so to the finals.*
4 introducing a question: *so, what did you do today?* ■ introducing a question following on from what was said previously: *so what did he do about it?* ■ (also **so what?**) informal why should that be considered significant?: *"Marv is wearing a suit." "So?" | so what if he failed?*

5 introducing a statement that is followed by a defensive comment: *so I like anchovies—what's wrong with that?*
6 introducing a concluding statement: *so that's that.*
7 in the same way; correspondingly: *just as bad money drives out good, so does bad art drive out the good.*
– PHRASES **and so on** (or **forth**) and similar things; et cetera: *these snacks include cheeses, cold meats, and so on.* **just so much** chiefly derogatory emphasizing a large amount of something: *it's just so much ideological cant.* **not so much —— as ——** not —— but rather ——: *the novel was not so much unfinished as unfinishable.* **only so much** a limited amount: *there is only so much you can do to protect yourself.* **or so** see OR[1]. **so as to do something** in order to do something: *she had put her hair up so as to look older.* **so be it** an expression of acceptance or resignation. **so far** see FAR. **so far, so good** see FAR. **so long!** informal goodbye until we meet again. **so long as** see LONG[1]. **so many** (or **much**) indicating a particular but unspecified quantity: *so many hours at such-and-such a speed.* **so much as** [with negative] even: *he sat down without so much as a word to anyone.* **so much for 1** indicating that one has finished talking about something: *So much for the melodic line. We now turn our attention to the accompaniment.* **2** suggesting that something has not been successful or useful: *so much for that idea!* **so much so that** to such an extent that: *I was fascinated by the company, so much so that I wrote a book about it.* **so to speak** (or **say**) used to highlight the fact that one is describing something in an unusual or metaphorical way: *delving into the body's secrets, I looked death in the face, so to speak.*
– ORIGIN Old English *swā*, of Germanic origin; related to Dutch *zo* and German *so*.

so[2] ▶ **n.** alternate spelling of SOL[1].

So. ▶ **abbr.** South.

s.o. ▶ **abbr.** ■ seller's option. ■ shipping order.

-so ▶ **comb. form** equivalent to -SOEVER.

soak /sōk/ ▶ **v.** [with obj.] **1** make or allow (something) to become thoroughly wet by immersing it in liquid: *soak the beans overnight in water.* ■ [no obj.] be immersed in water or another liquid: *she spent some time soaking in a hot bath.* ■ (of a liquid) cause (something or someone) to become extremely wet: *the rain poured down, soaking their hair.* ■ [no obj.] (of a liquid) penetrate or permeate completely: *cold water was soaking into my shoes.* ■ **(soak something off/out)** remove something by immersing it in water for a period of time: *don't disturb the wound—soak the dressing off if necessary.* **2** informal impose heavy charges or taxation on: *few of us common people care how much tax Congress soaks on racing motorboats.*
3 [no obj.] archaic, informal drink heavily: *you keep soaking in taverns.*
▶ **n. 1** [in sing.] an act of immersing someone or something in liquid for a period of time: *I'm looking forward to a long soak in the tub.*
2 informal a heavy drinker: *his daughter stayed up to put the old soak to bed.*
– PHRASAL VERBS **soak oneself in** immerse oneself in (a particular experience, activity, or interest): *he soaked himself in the music of Mozart.* **soak something up** absorb a liquid: *use clean tissues to soak up any droplets of water.* ■ expose oneself to or experience (something beneficial or enjoyable): *lie back and soak up the Mediterranean sun | he spends his time painting and soaking up the culture.* ■ informal cost or use up money: *the project had soaked up over $1 billion.*
– DERIVATIVES **soak·age** /ˈsōkij/ **n.**, **soak·er n.**
– ORIGIN Old English *socian* 'become saturated with a liquid by immersion'; related to *sūcan* 'to suck.'

soaked /sōkt/ ▶ **adj.** extremely wet; saturated: *my shirt is soaked through | she was soaked to the skin |* [in combination] figurative *a sun-soaked beach.*

soak·ing /ˈsōkiNG/ ▶ **adj.** extremely wet; wet through: *his jacket was soaking.*
▶ **n.** an act of wetting something thoroughly: *in spring, give the soil a good soaking.*

so-and-so ▶ **n.** (pl. **so-and-sos**) a person or thing whose name the speaker does not need to specify or does not know or remember. ■ informal a person who is disliked or is considered to have a particular characteristic, typically an unfavorable one: *nosy old so-and-so!*

soap /sōp/ ▶ **n. 1** a substance used with water for washing and cleaning, made of a compound of natural oils or fats with sodium hydroxide or another strong alkali, and typically having perfume and coloring added: *a bar of soap.*
2 informal a soap opera: *the soaps are at the top of the ratings.*
▶ **v.** [with obj.] wash with soap: *she soaped her face.*
– PHRASES **no soap** informal used to convey that there is no chance of something happening or occurring: *They needed a writer with some enthusiasm. No soap.*
– DERIVATIVES **soap·less adj.**
– ORIGIN Old English *sāpe*; related to Dutch *zeep* and German *Seife*. The verb dates from the mid 16th cent.

soap·ber·ry /ˈsōp,berē/ ▶ **n.** (pl. **soapberries**) a tree or shrub with berries that produce a soapy froth when crushed, in particular: ● a plant with saponin-rich berries that are used as a soap substitute (genus *Sapindus*, family Sapindaceae). ● another term for BUFFALO BERRY. ■ the berry of any of these plants.

soap·box /ˈsōp,bäks/ ▶ **n.** a box or crate used as a makeshift stand by a public speaker: [as modifier] *a soapbox orator.* ■ a thing that provides an opportunity for someone to air their views publicly: *fanzines are soapboxes for critical sports fans.*

soap·box der·by (also **Soap Box Derby** trademark) ▶ **n.** a race for children driving motorless, improvised vehicles made from crates and crudely resembling race cars.

soap bub·ble ▶ **n.** an iridescent bubble consisting of air in a thin film of soapy water.

soap·fish /ˈsōp,fisH/ ▶ **n.** (pl. **same** or **soapfishes**) a stout-bodied fish of tropical seas that produces large amounts of toxic mucus from the skin, giving it a soapy feel when handled. ● Family Grammistidae, several genera and species.

soap flakes ▶ **plural n.** dated soap in the form of thin flakes, typically used for washing clothes.

soap op·er·a ▶ **n.** a television or radio drama series dealing typically with daily events in the lives of the same group of characters.
– ORIGIN 1930s: so named because such serials were originally sponsored by soap manufacturers.

soap plant ▶ **n.** a plant of the lily family with white flowers, found in dry habitats of California. The fiber-covered bulbs were used as soap by American Indians. ● Genus *Chlorogalum*, family Liliaceae: two species, the wavy-leaved *C. pomeridianum* and the narrow-leaved *C. angustifolium*.

soap pow·der ▶ **n.** detergent in the form of a powder, typically used for washing clothes.

soap·stone /ˈsōp,stōn/ ▶ **n.** a soft rock consisting largely of talc. Compare with STEATITE.

soap·suds /ˈsōp,sədz/ ▶ **plural n.** froth made from soap and water.

soap·wort /ˈsōpwərt, -,wôrt/ ▶ **n.** a plant of the pink family, with fragrant pink or white flowers and leaves that were formerly used to make soap. ● *Saponaria officinalis*, family Caryophyllaceae.

soap·y /ˈsōpē/ ▶ **adj.** (**soapier, soapiest**)
1 containing or covered with soap: *hot soapy water.* ■ of or like soap: *his hands smelled soapy.* ■ (of a person or behavior) unpleasantly flattering and ingratiating: *a soapy, fawning look.*
2 informal characteristic of a soap opera: *soapy little turns of plot.*
– DERIVATIVES **soap·i·ly** /-pəlē/ **adv.**, **soap·i·ness n.**

soar /sôr/ ▶ **v.** [no obj.] fly or rise high in the air: *the bird spread its wings and soared into the air |* figurative *when she heard his voice, her spirits soared.* ■ maintain height in the air without flapping wings or using engine power: *the gulls soared on the summery winds.* ■ increase rapidly above the usual level: *the cost of living continued to soar |* (as adj. **soaring**) *the soaring crime rate.*
– DERIVATIVES **soar·er n.**, **soar·ing·ly adv.**
– ORIGIN late Middle English: shortening of Old French *essorer*, based on Latin *ex-* 'out of' + *aura* 'breeze.'

soar·a·way /ˈsôrə,wā/ ▶ **adj.** [attrib.] Brit. informal making or characterized by rapid or impressive progress: *a soaraway success.*

So·a·ve /ˈswävā/ ▶ **n.** a dry white wine produced in the region of northern Italy around Soave.

SOB ▶ **abbr.** informal son of a bitch.

sob /säb/ ▶ **v.** (**sobs, sobbing, sobbed**) [no obj.] cry noisily, making loud, convulsive gasps: *he broke down and sobbed like a child |* [with obj.] *he sobbed himself to sleep.* ■ [with obj.] say while crying noisily: [with direct speech] *"I thought they'd killed you," he sobbed weakly.*
▶ **n.** an act or sound of sobbing: *with a sob of despair she threw herself onto the bed.*
– DERIVATIVES **sob·bing·ly adv.**
– ORIGIN Middle English: perhaps of Dutch or Low German origin; compare with Dutch dialect *sabben* 'to suck.'

so·ba /ˈsōbə/ ▶ **n.** Japanese noodles made from buckwheat flour.
– ORIGIN Japanese.

so·ber /ˈsōbər/ ▶ **adj.** (**soberer, soberest**) not affected by alcohol; not drunk. ■ serious, sensible, and solemn: *a sober view of life | his expression became sober.* ■ free from alcoholism; not habitually drinking alcohol: *I've been clean and sober for five years.* ■ muted in color: *a sober gray suit.*
▶ **v.** make or become sober after drinking alcohol: [with obj.] *that coffee* **sobered him up** | [no obj.] *I ought* **to sober up** *a bit.* ■ make or become more serious, sensible, and solemn: [no obj.] *his expression sobered her |* (as adj. **sobering**) *a sobering thought.*
– DERIVATIVES **so·ber·ing·ly adv.**, **so·ber·ly adv.**
– ORIGIN Middle English: from Old French *sobre*, from Latin *sobrius*.

so·ber·sides /ˈsōbər,sīdz/ ▶ **n.** informal a sedate and serious person.
– DERIVATIVES **so·ber·sid·ed** /-ˈsīdid/ **adj.**

So·bies·ki /sôbˈyäskē/, John, see JOHN III.

so·bri·e·ty /səˈbrīətē, sō-/ ▶ **n.** the state of being sober: *the price of beer compelled me to maintain a certain level of sobriety.* ■ the quality of being staid or solemn.
– ORIGIN late Middle English: from Old French *sobriete* or Latin *sobrietas*, from *sobrius* (see SOBER).

so·bri·quet /ˈsōbri,kā, -,ket/ (also **soubriquet** /ˈsōōbri-/) ▶ **n.** a person's nickname.
– ORIGIN mid 17th cent.: French, originally in the sense 'tap under the chin,' of unknown origin.

sob sis·ter ▶ **n.** informal a female journalist who writes articles with sentimental appeal or answers readers' problems. ■ an overly sentimental woman.

sob sto·ry ▶ **n.** informal a story or explanation intended to make someone feel sympathy for the person relating it.

soc /sōsH/ ▶ **n.** informal (esp. among academics) sociology: [as modifier] *she's a soc major.*

Soc. ▶ **abbr.** ■ Socialist. ■ Society.

so·ca /ˈsōkə/ ▶ **n.** calypso music with elements of soul, originally from Trinidad.
– ORIGIN 1970s: blend of SOUL and CALYPSO.

soc·age /ˈsäkij/ (also **soccage**) ▶ **n.** historical a feudal tenure of land involving payment of rent or other nonmilitary service to a superior.
– ORIGIN Middle English: from Anglo-Norman French, from *soc*, variant of SOKE.

so-called ▶ **adj.** [attrib.] used to show that something or someone is commonly designated by the name or term specified: *next on the list are so-called "soft" chemicals like phosphorous acid.* ■ used to express one's view that such a name or term is inappropriate: *she could trust him more than any of her so-called friends.*

soc·cer /ˈsäkər/ ▶ **n.** a game played by two teams of eleven players with a round ball that may not be touched with the hands or arms during play except by the goalkeepers. The object of the game is to score goals by kicking or heading the ball into the opponents' goal.
– ORIGIN late 19th cent.: from a shortening of ASSOCIATION FOOTBALL + an extended use of -ER[1].

soc·cer mom ▶ **n.** informal a middle-class suburban mother who spends a great deal of time taking her children to play soccer or engage in other activities.

So·chi /ˈsōCHē/ a port and resort in southwestern Russia, located in the western foothills of the Caucasus, on the Black Sea coast, close to the border with Georgia; pop. 334,300 (est. 2008).

so·cia·bil·i·ty /,sōsHəˈbilitē/ ▶ **n.** the quality of being sociable: *for all his sociability, he never really connects with people.*

so·cia·ble /ˈsōsHəbəl/ ▶ **adj.** willing to talk and engage in activities with other people; friendly: *being a sociable person, Eva loved entertaining.* ■ (of a place, occasion, or activity) marked by friendliness: *a very sociable little village.*
▶ **n. 1** historical an open carriage with facing side seats.
2 dated an informal social gathering: *a church sociable.*
– DERIVATIVES **so·cia·ble·ness n.**, **so·cia·bly** /-blē/ **adv.**
– ORIGIN mid 16th cent.: from French, or from Latin *sociabilis*, from *sociare* 'unite,' from *socius* 'companion.'

so·cial /ˈsōsHəl/ ▶ **adj. 1** [attrib.] of or relating to society or its organization: *alcoholism is recognized as a major social problem | a traditional Japanese social structure.* ■ of or relating to rank and status in society: *a recent analysis of social class in Britain | her mother is a lady of the highest social standing.* ■ needing companionship and therefore best suited to living in communities: *we are social beings as well as individuals.* ■ relating to or designed for activities in which people meet each other for pleasure: *Guy led a full social life.*

S

2 Zoology (of a bird) gregarious; breeding or nesting in colonies. ■ (of an insect) living together in organized communities, typically with different castes, as ants, bees, wasps, and termites do. ■ (of a mammal) living together in groups, typically in a hierarchical system with complex communication.
▶ **n.** an informal social gathering, esp. one organized by the members of a particular club or group: *a church social.*
– DERIVATIVES **so·ci·al·i·ty** /ˌsōSHēˈalədē/ **n.**, **so·cial·ly** /ˈsōSHəlē/ **adv.** *families who are socially disadvantaged.*
– ORIGIN late Middle English: from Old French, or from Latin *socialis* 'allied,' from *socius* 'friend.'

so·cial an·thro·pol·o·gy ▶ **n.** see ANTHROPOLOGY.

so·cial as·sis·tance ▶ **n.** Canadian term for SOCIAL SECURITY.

so·cial ben·e·fit ▶ **n.** a benefit payable under a social security system.

so·cial cap·i·tal ▶ **n.** the networks of relationships among people who live and work in a particular society, enabling that society to function effectively.

so·cial climb·er ▶ **n.** derogatory a person who is eager to gain a higher social status. Also called CLIMBER.
– DERIVATIVES **so·cial climb·ing n.**

so·cial con·science ▶ **n.** a sense of responsibility or concern for the problems and injustices of society.

so·cial con·tract (also **social compact**) ▶ **n.** an implicit agreement among the members of a society to cooperate for social benefits, for example by sacrificing some individual freedom for state protection. Theories of a social contract became popular in the 16th, 17th, and 18th centuries among theorists such as Thomas Hobbes, John Locke, and Jean-Jacques Rousseau, as a means of explaining the origin of government and the obligations of subjects.

so·cial cred·it ▶ **n.** the economic theory that consumer purchasing power should be increased either by subsidizing producers so that they can lower prices or by distributing the profits of industry to consumers.

so·cial Dar·win·ism ▶ **n.** the theory that individuals, groups, and peoples are subject to the same Darwinian laws of natural selection as plants and animals. Now largely discredited, social Darwinism was advocated by Herbert Spencer and others in the late 19th and early 20th centuries and was used to justify political conservatism, imperialism, and racism and to discourage intervention and reform.

so·cial de·moc·ra·cy ▶ **n.** a socialist system of government achieved by democratic means.
– DERIVATIVES **so·cial dem·o·crat n.**

so·cial dis·ease ▶ **n.** informal a venereal disease.

so·cial dis·tance ▶ **n.** the perceived or desired degree of remoteness between a member of one social group and the members of another, as evidenced in the level of intimacy tolerated between them.

so·cial drink·er ▶ **n.** a person who drinks alcohol chiefly on social occasions and only in moderate quantities.
– DERIVATIVES **so·cial drink·ing n.**

so·cial en·gi·neer·ing ▶ **n.** the application of sociological principles to specific social problems.
– DERIVATIVES **so·cial en·gi·neer n.**

S

so·cial fact ▶ **n.** a thing originating in the institutions or culture of a society that affects the behavior or attitudes of an individual member of that society.

so·cial ge·og·ra·phy ▶ **n.** the study of people and their environment with particular emphasis on social factors.

so·cial gos·pel ▶ **n.** Christian faith practiced as a call not just to personal conversion but to social reform.
– DERIVATIVES **so·cial gos·pel·er n.**

so·cial in·sur·ance ▶ **n.** a system of compulsory contribution to provide government assistance in sickness, unemployment, etc.

so·cial·ism /ˈsōSHəˌlizəm/ ▶ **n.** a political and economic theory of social organization that advocates that the means of production, distribution, and exchange should be owned or regulated by the community as a whole. ■ policy or practice based on this theory. ■ (in Marxist theory) a transitional social state between the overthrow of capitalism and the realization of communism.

> The term "socialism" has been used to describe positions as far apart as anarchism, Soviet state communism, and social democracy; however, it necessarily implies an opposition to the untrammeled workings of the economic market. The socialist parties that have arisen in most European countries from the late 19th century have generally tended toward social democracy.

– ORIGIN early 19th cent.: from French *socialisme*, from *social* (see SOCIAL).

so·cial·ist /ˈsōSHəˌlist/ ▶ **n.** a person who advocates or practices socialism.
▶ **adj.** adhering to or based on the principles of socialism: *the history of socialist movement.*
– DERIVATIVES **so·cial·is·tic** /ˌsōSHəˈlistik/ **adj.**, **so·cial·is·ti·cal·ly** /ˌsōSHəˈlistik(ə)lē/ **adv.**

so·cial·ist re·al·ism ▶ **n.** the theory of art, literature, and music officially sanctioned by the state in some communist countries (esp. in the Soviet Union under Stalin), by which artistic work was supposed to reflect and promote the ideals of a socialist society.

so·cial·ite /ˈsōSHəˌlīt/ ▶ **n.** a person who is well known in fashionable society and is fond of social activities and entertainment.

so·cial·ize /ˈsōSHəˌlīz/ ▶ **v. 1** [no obj.] mix socially with others: *he didn't mind* **socializing with** *his staff.*
2 [with obj.] make (someone) behave in a way that is acceptable to their society: *newcomers are* **socialized into** *orthodox ways* | (as adj. **socializing**) *a socializing effect.*
3 [with obj.] organize according to the principles of socialism: (as adj. **socialized**) *socialized economies.*
– DERIVATIVES **so·cial·i·za·tion** /ˌsōSHəliˈzāSHən/ **n.** (sense 2 and sense 3).

so·cial·ized med·i·cine ▶ **n.** the provision of medical and hospital care for all by means of public funds.

so·cial lad·der (also **social scale**) ▶ **n.** (usu. **the social ladder**) the hierarchical structure of society or of a society: *it would be a step up the social ladder for him when the marriage came off.*

so·cial mar·ket e·con·o·my (also **social market**) ▶ **n.** an economic system based on a free market operated in conjunction with state provision for those unable to sell their labor, such as people who are elderly or unemployed.

so·cial me·di·a ▶ **n.** [treated as sing. or pl.] websites and applications used for social networking.

so·cial net·work ▶ **n.1** a network of social interactions and personal relationships.
2 a dedicated website or other application that enables users to communicate with each other by posting information, comments, messages, images, etc.

so·cial net·work·ing ▶ **n.** the use of dedicated websites and applications to communicate informally with other users, or to find people with similar interests to oneself.

so·cial proc·ess ▶ **n.** the pattern of growth and change in a society over the years.

so·cial pro·mot·ion ▶ **n.** the practice promoting a child to the next grade level regardless of skill mastery in the belief that it will promote self-esteem.

so·cial psy·chol·o·gy ▶ **n.** the branch of psychology that deals with social interactions, including their origins and their effects on the individual.
– DERIVATIVES **so·cial psy·chol·o·gist n.**

so·cial re·al·ism ▶ **n.** the realistic depiction in art of contemporary life, as a means of social or political comment.

so·cial scale ▶ **n.** another term for SOCIAL LADDER.

so·cial sci·ence ▶ **n.** the scientific study of human society and social relationships. ■ a subject within this field, such as economics or politics.
– DERIVATIVES **so·cial sci·en·tist n.**

so·cial sec·re·tar·y ▶ **n.** a person who arranges the social activities of a person or organization.

so·cial se·cu·ri·ty ▶ **n.** any government system that provides monetary assistance to people with an inadequate or no income. ■ (**Social Security**) (in the US) a federal insurance program that provides benefits to retired people and those who are unemployed or disabled.

So·cial Se·cur·i·ty num·ber (abbr.: **SSN**) ▶ **n.** (in the US) a number in the format 000-00-0000, unique for each individual, used to track Social Security benefits and for other identification purposes.

so·cial serv·ice ▶ **n.** (**social services**) government services provided for the benefit of the community, such as education, medical care, and housing. ■ activity aiming to promote the welfare of others.

so·cial soft·ware ▶ **n.** computer software that enables users to interact and share data.

so·cial stud·ies ▶ **plural n.** [treated as sing.] various aspects or branches of the study of human society, considered as an educational discipline.

so·cial u·nit ▶ **n.** an individual, or a group or community, considered as a discrete constituent of a society or larger group.

so·cial work ▶ **n.** work carried out by trained personnel with the aim of alleviating the conditions of those in need of help or welfare.
– DERIVATIVES **so·cial work·er n.**

so·ci·e·tal /səˈsīitl/ ▶ **adj.** of or relating to society or social relations: *societal change.*
– DERIVATIVES **so·ci·e·tal·ly adv.**

so·ci·e·ty /səˈsīətē/ ▶ **n.** (pl. **societies**) **1** the aggregate of people living together in a more or less ordered community: *drugs, crime, and other dangers to society.* ■ the community of people living in a particular country or region and having shared customs, laws, and organizations: *the high incidence of violence in American society* | *modern industrial societies.* ■ [with adj.] a specified section of such a community: *no one in polite society uttered the word.* ■ (also **high society**) the aggregate of people who are fashionable, wealthy, and influential, regarded as forming a distinct group in a community: [as modifier] *a society wedding.* ■ a plant or animal community.
2 an organization or club formed for a particular purpose or activity: [in names] *the American Society for the Prevention of Cruelty to Animals.*
3 the situation of being in the company of other people: *she shunned the society of others.*
– ORIGIN mid 16th cent. (in the sense 'companionship, friendly association with others'): from French *société*, from Latin *societas*, from *socius* 'companion.'

So·ci·e·ty Is·lands a group of islands in the South Pacific Ocean that form part of French Polynesia.
– ORIGIN named in honor of the Royal Society by Captain Cook, who visited the islands in 1769.

So·ci·e·ty of Je·sus official name of the Jesuits (see JESUIT).

socio- ▶ **comb. form 1** relating to society; society and ...: *socioeconomic.*
2 relating to sociology; sociology and ...: *sociolinguistics.*
– ORIGIN from Latin *socius* 'companion.'

so·ci·o·bi·ol·o·gy /ˌsōsēōˌbīˈäləjē/ ▶ **n.** the scientific study of the biological (esp. ecological and evolutionary) aspects of social behavior in animals and humans.
– DERIVATIVES **so·ci·o·bi·o·log·i·cal** /-ˌbīəˈläjikəl/ **adj.**, **so·ci·o·bi·o·log·i·cal·ly** /-ˌbīəˈläjik(ə)lē/ **adv.**, **so·ci·o·bi·ol·o·gist** /-jist/ **n.**

so·ci·o·cul·tur·al /ˌsōsēōˈkəlCHərəl/ ▶ **adj.** combining social and cultural factors.
– DERIVATIVES **so·ci·o·cul·tur·al·ly adv.**

so·ci·o·e·col·o·gy /ˌsōsēōˌēˈkäləjē, -ˈekä-/ ▶ **n.** the branch of science that deals with the interactions among the members of a species, and between them and the environment.
– DERIVATIVES **so·ci·o·ec·o·log·i·cal** /-kəˈlsHjikəl/ **adj.**, **so·ci·o·e·col·o·gist** /-jist/ **n.**

so·ci·o·ec·o·nom·ic /ˌsōsēōˌēkəˈnämik, -ˌekə-/ ▶ **adj.** relating to or concerned with the interaction of social and economic factors.
– DERIVATIVES **so·ci·o·ec·o·nom·i·cal·ly adv.**

so·ci·o·ge·no·mics /ˌsōsēōjēˈnämiks, -ji-, -ˈnōmiks/ ▶ **plural n.** [treated as singular] a scientific discipline that attempts to find the genetic basis of social behavior and its evolution.

so·ci·o·lect /ˈsōsēōˌlekt/ ▶ **n.** the dialect of a particular social class.
– ORIGIN 1970s: from SOCIO- + *-lect* as in DIALECT.

so·ci·o·lin·guis·tics /ˌsōsēōliNGˈgwistiks/ ▶ **plural n.** [treated as sing.] the study of language in relation to social factors, including differences of regional, class, and occupational dialect, gender differences, and bilingualism.
– DERIVATIVES **so·ci·o·lin·guist** /-ˈliNGgwist/ **n.**, **so·ci·o·lin·guis·tic adj.**, **so·ci·o·lin·guis·ti·cal·ly** /-ik(ə)lē/ **adv.**

so·ci·ol·o·gy /ˌsōsēˈäləjē/ ▶ **n.** the study of the development, structure, and functioning of human society. ■ the study of social problems.
– DERIVATIVES **so·ci·o·log·i·cal** /ˌsōsēōˈläjikəl/ **adj.**, **so·ci·o·log·i·cal·ly** /ˌsōsēōˈläjik(ə)lē/ **adv.**, **so·ci·ol·o·gist** /-jist/ **n.**
– ORIGIN mid 19th cent.: from French *sociologie* (see SOCIO-, -LOGY).

so·ci·om·e·try /ˌsōsēˈämətrē/ ▶ **n.** the quantitative study and measurement of relationships within a group of people.
– DERIVATIVES **so·ci·o·met·ric** /ˌsōsēōˈmetrik/ **adj.**, **so·ci·o·met·ri·cal·ly** /ˌsōsēōˈmetrik(ə)lē/ **adv.**, **so·ci·om·e·trist** /-trist/ **n.**

so·ci·o·path /ˈsōsēōˌpaTH/ ▶ **n.** a person with a personality disorder manifesting itself in extreme antisocial attitudes and behavior and a lack of conscience.
– DERIVATIVES **so·ci·o·path·ic** /ˌsōsēōˈpaTHik/ **adj.**, **so·ci·op·a·thy** /ˌsōsēˈäpəTHē/ **n.**

so·ci·o·po·lit·i·cal /ˌsōsēōpəˈlitikəl/ ▶ **adj.** combining social and political factors.

sock /säk/ ▶ **n. 1** a garment for the foot and lower part of the leg, typically knitted from wool, cotton, or nylon. ■ a removable inner sole placed inside a shoe or boot for added warmth or to improve the fit.

■ a white marking on the lower part of a horse's leg, not extending as far as the knee or hock. Compare with **stocking**.
2 informal a hard blow: *a sock on the jaw.* ■ force or emphasis: *we have enough speed and sock in our lineup to score runs.*
▶ **v.** [with obj.] informal hit forcefully: *Jess socked his father across the face.* ■ (often **be socked with**) affect disadvantageously: *consumers have been socked with huge price increases.*
– PHRASES **knock** (or **blow**) **someone's socks off** informal amaze or impress someone. **knock the socks off** informal surpass or beat: *it will knock the socks off the opposition.* **—— one's socks off** informal do something with great energy and enthusiasm: *she acted her socks off.* **put a sock in it** [usu. in imperative] Brit. informal stop talking. **sock and buskin** archaic the theatrical profession; drama. **sock it to someone** informal attack or make a forceful impression on someone.
– PHRASAL VERBS **sock something away** put money aside as savings: *you'll need to sock away about $900 a month.* **sock something in** (or **sock in**) (of weather) envelop: *the beach was socked in with fog.*
– ORIGIN Old English *socc* 'light shoe,' of Germanic origin, from Latin *soccus* 'comic actor's shoe, light low-heeled slipper,' from Greek *sukkhos*.

sock·et /ˈsäkit/ ▶ **n. 1** a natural or artificial hollow into which something fits or in which something revolves: *the eye socket.* ■ the part of the head of a golf club into which the shaft is fitted.
2 an electrical device receiving a plug or light bulb to make a connection.
▶ **v.** (**sockets, socketing, socketed**) [with obj.] **1** place in or fit with a socket.
2 Golf old-fashioned term for **shank**.
– ORIGIN Middle English (in the sense 'head of a spear, resembling a plowshare'): from an Anglo-Norman French diminutive of Old French *soc* 'plowshare,' probably of Celtic origin.

sock·et set ▶ **n.** a number of detachable sockets of different sizes for use with a socket wrench.

sock·et wrench ▶ **n.** a ratchet tool with a series of detachable sockets for tightening and loosening nuts of different sizes.

sock·eye /ˈsäk,ī/ (also **sockeye salmon**) ▶ **n.** a commercially valuable salmon of the North Pacific and rivers draining into it. Also called **red salmon**. ● *Oncorhynchus nerka*, family Salmonidae. See also **kokanee**.
– ORIGIN late 19th cent.: by folk etymology from Salish *sukai*, literally 'fish of fishes.'

sock hop ▶ **n.** dated a dance for young teenagers at which they may dance in stocking feet.

sock·ing /ˈsäkiNG/ ▶ **adv.** [as submodifier] Brit. informal used for emphasis: *a brooch with a socking great diamond in the middle.*

sock·o /ˈsäkō/ ▶ **adj.** informal stunningly effective or successful: *a sellout, socko performance.*
– ORIGIN 1920s: from **sock** in the sense 'forceful blow' + **-o**.

so·cle /ˈsäkəl/ ▶ **n.** Architecture a plain low block or plinth serving as a support for a column, urn, statue, etc., or as the foundation of a wall.
– ORIGIN early 18th cent.: from French, from Italian *zoccolo*, literally 'wooden shoe,' from Latin *socculus*, from *soccus* (see **sock**).

Soc·ra·tes /ˈsäkrə,tēz/ (469–399 BC), ancient Athenian philosopher. As represented in the writings of his disciple Plato, he engaged in dialogue with others in an attempt to reach understanding and ethical concepts by exposing and dispelling error (the **Socratic method**). Charged with introducing strange gods and corrupting the young, he committed suicide as required.

So·crat·ic /səˈkratik/ ▶ **adj.** of or relating to Socrates or his philosophy.
▶ **n.** a follower of Socrates.
– DERIVATIVES **So·crat·i·cal·ly** /-ik(ə)lē/ **adv.**

So·crat·ic e·len·chus /səˈkratik iˈleNGkəs/ ▶ **n.** see **elenchus**.

So·crat·ic i·ro·ny ▶ **n.** a pose of ignorance assumed in order to entice others into making statements that can then be challenged.

sod[1] /säd/ ▶ **n.** (**the sod**) the surface of the ground, with the grass growing on it. ■ a piece of this, usually sold in rolls and used to start a new lawn, athletic field, etc.
▶ **v.** (**sods, sodding, sodded**) [with obj.] cover with sod or pieces of turf: *the stadium has been sodded.*
– PHRASES **the old sod** one's native country. **under the sod** dead and buried in a grave.
– ORIGIN late Middle English: from Middle Dutch and Middle Low German *sode*, of unknown ultimate origin.

sod[2] chiefly Brit. vulgar slang ▶ **n.** an unpleasant or obnoxious person. ■ a person of a specified kind. ■ something that is difficult or causes problems.
▶ **v.** (**sods, sodding, sodded**) [with obj.] used to express one's anger or annoyance at someone or something. ■ [no obj.] (**sod off**) [in imperative] go away. ■ (as adj. **sodding**) used as a general term of contempt.
– PHRASES **sod all** absolutely nothing.
– ORIGIN early 19th cent.: abbreviation of **sodomite**.

so·da /ˈsōdə/ ▶ **n. 1** (also **soda water** or **club soda**) carbonated water (originally made with sodium bicarbonate) drunk alone or with liquor or wine: *a whiskey and soda.* ■ (also **soda pop**) a carbonated soft drink: *a can of soda.*
2 sodium carbonate, esp. as a natural mineral or as an industrial chemical. ■ sodium in chemical combination: *nitrate of soda.*
– ORIGIN late Middle English (sense 2): from medieval Latin, from Arabic *suwwad* 'saltwort.'

so·da ash ▶ **n.** commercially manufactured anhydrous sodium carbonate.

so·da bread ▶ **n.** bread leavened with baking soda.

so·da crack·er ▶ **n.** a thin, crisp cracker leavened with baking soda.

so·da foun·tain ▶ **n.** a device that dispenses soda water or soft drinks. ■ a shop or counter selling drinks from such a device.

so·da jerk (also **soda jerker**) ▶ **n.** informal, dated a person who serves and sells soft drinks and ice cream at a soda fountain.

so·da lake ▶ **n.** a salt lake with a high content of sodium salts.

so·da lime ▶ **n.** a mixture of calcium oxide and sodium hydroxide.

so·da·lite /ˈsōdl,īt/ ▶ **n.** a blue mineral consisting mainly of an aluminosilicate and chloride of sodium, occurring chiefly in alkaline igneous rocks.
– ORIGIN early 19th cent.: from **soda** + **-lite**.

so·dal·i·ty /sōˈdalitē/ ▶ **n.** (pl. **sodalities**) a confraternity or association, esp. a Roman Catholic religious guild or brotherhood.
– ORIGIN early 17th cent.: from French *sodalité* or Latin *sodalitas*, from *sodalis* 'comrade.'

so·da pop ▶ **n.** see **soda** (sense 1).

so·da wa·ter ▶ **n.** see **soda** (sense 1).

sod·bust·er /ˈsäd,bəstər/ ▶ **n.** informal a farmer or farm worker who plows the land.

sod·den /ˈsädn/ ▶ **adj.** saturated with liquid, esp. water; soaked through: *his clothes were sodden.* ■ [in combination] having drunk an excessive amount of a particular alcoholic drink: *a whiskey-sodden criminal.*
▶ **v.** [with obj.] archaic saturate (something) with water.
– DERIVATIVES **sod·den·ly adv.**, **sod·den·ness n.**
– ORIGIN Middle English (in the sense 'boiled, cooked by boiling'): archaic past participle of **seethe**.

Sod·dy /ˈsädē/, Frederick (1877–1956), English physicist. He assisted William Ramsay in the discovery of helium, formulated a theory of isotopes, and coined the word *isotope* in 1913 after working on radioactive decay. Nobel Prize for Chemistry (1921).

so·dger /ˈsōjər/ ▶ **n.** nonstandard spelling of **soldier**, used to represent regional pronunciation.

so·dic /ˈsōdik/ ▶ **adj.** of or containing sodium. ■ Mineralogy (of mineral, rock, or soil) containing a higher proportion of sodium than usual.

so·di·um /ˈsōdēəm/ ▶ **n.** the chemical element of atomic number 11, a soft silver-white reactive metal of the alkali metal group. (Symbol: **Na**)
– ORIGIN early 19th cent.: from **soda** + **-ium**.

so·di·um am·y·tal ▶ **n.** see **Amytal**.

so·di·um bi·car·bon·ate ▶ **n.** a soluble white powder used in fire extinguishers and effervescent drinks and as a leavening agent in baking. Also called **baking soda**. ● Chem. formula: $NaHCO_3$.

so·di·um car·bon·ate ▶ **n.** a white alkaline compound with many commercial applications including the manufacture of soap and glass. Also called **washing soda**. ● Chem. formula: Na_2CO_3.

so·di·um chlo·ride ▶ **n.** a colorless crystalline compound occurring naturally in seawater and halite; common salt. ● Chem. formula: NaCl.

so·di·um cy·a·nide ▶ **n.** a white odorless crystalline soluble compound that has, when damp, an odor of hydrogen cyanide. It is used for extracting gold and silver from their ores and for case-hardening steel. ● Chem. formula: NaCN.

so·di·um hy·drox·ide ▶ **n.** a strongly alkaline white deliquescent compound used in many industrial processes, e.g., the manufacture of soap and paper. ● Chem. formula: NaOH.

so·di·um ni·trate ▶ **n.** a white powdery compound used mainly in the manufacture of fertilizers. ● Chem. formula: $NaNO_3$.

so·di·um thi·o·sul·phate /,THīōˈsəlfāt/ ▶ **n.** a white soluble compound used in photography as a fixer to dissolve unchanged silver halides. Also called **hypo**[1]. ● Chem. formula: $Na_2S_2O_3$.

so·di·um-va·por lamp (also **sodium lamp**) ▶ **n.** a lamp in which an electrical discharge in sodium vapor gives a yellow light, typically used in street lighting.

Sod·om /ˈsädəm/ a town in ancient Palestine, probably south of the Dead Sea. According to Genesis, it was destroyed by fire from heaven, together with Gomorrah, for the wickedness of its inhabitants. ■ (as noun **a Sodom**) a wicked or depraved place.

sod·om·ite /ˈsädə,mīt/ ▶ **n.** a person who engages in sodomy.
– DERIVATIVES **sod·o·mit·ic** /,sädəˈmitik/ **adj.**, **sod·o·mit·i·cal** /,sädəˈmitikəl/ **adj.**
– ORIGIN Middle English (in the sense 'sodomy'): via Old French from late Latin *Sodomita*, from Greek *Sodomitēs* 'inhabitant of Sodom.'

sod·om·y /ˈsädəmē/ ▶ **n.** sexual intercourse involving anal or oral copulation.
– DERIVATIVES **sod·om·ize** /ˈsädə,mīz/ **v.**
– ORIGIN Middle English: from medieval Latin *sodomia*, from late Latin *peccatum Sodomiticum* 'sin of Sodom' (after Gen. 19:5, which implies that the men of Sodom practiced homosexual rape) (see **Sodom**).

Sod's Law /sädz/ another name for **Murphy's Law**.

SOE ▶ **abbr.** Special Operations Executive.

so·ev·er /sōˈevər/ ▶ **adv.** archaic or literary of any kind; to any extent: *how great soever the assurance is.*

-soever ▶ **comb. form** of any kind; to any extent: *whatsoever* | *whosoever.*
– ORIGIN Middle English: originally as the phrase *so ever.*

so·fa /ˈsōfə/ ▶ **n.** a long upholstered seat with a back and arms, for two or more people.
– ORIGIN early 17th cent.: from French, based on Arabic *ṣuffa.*

so·fa bed ▶ **n.** a sofa that can be converted into a bed, typically for occasional use.

SOFAR /ˈsōfär/ (also **sofar**) ▶ **n.** a system in which the sound waves from an underwater explosion are detected and located by three or more listening stations, useful in determining the position at sea of survivors of a disaster.
– ORIGIN 1940s: from *So(und) f(ixing) a(nd) r(anging).*

sof·fit /ˈsäfit/ ▶ **n.** the underside of an architectural structure such as an arch, a balcony, or overhanging eaves.
– ORIGIN early 17th cent.: from French *soffite* or Italian *soffitto*, based on Latin *suffixus* 'fastened below.'

So·fi·a /sōˈfēə, ˈsōfēə/ the capital of Bulgaria, in the western part of the country; pop. 1,162,898 (2008).

so·fri·to /sōˈfrētō/ ▶ **n.** a Caribbean and Latin American sauce of tomatoes, onions, peppers, garlic, and herbs.
– ORIGIN American Spanish, from past participle of Spanish *sofreír* 'to fry.'

S. of S. ▶ **abbr.** Bible Song of Songs (or Song of Solomon).

S. of Sol. ▶ **abbr.** Bible Song of Solomon.

soft /sôft/ ▶ **adj. 1** easy to mold, cut, compress, or fold; not hard or firm to the touch: *soft margarine* | *the ground was soft beneath their feet.* ■ having a smooth surface or texture that is pleasant to touch; not rough or coarse: *soft crushed velvet* | *her hair felt very soft.* ■ rounded; not angular: *the soft edges of their adobe home.*
2 having a pleasing quality involving a subtle effect or contrast rather than sharp definition: *the soft glow of the lamps* | *the moon's pale light cast soft shadows.* ■ (of a voice or sound) quiet and gentle: *they spoke in soft whispers.* ■ (of rain, wind, or other natural force) not strong or violent: *a soft breeze rustled the trees.* ■ (of a consonant) pronounced as a fricative (as *c* in *ice*). ■ (of a market, currency, or commodity) falling or likely to fall in value.
3 sympathetic, lenient, or compassionate, esp. to a degree perceived as excessive; not strict or sufficiently strict: *the administration is not becoming soft on crime* | *Julia's soft heart was touched by his grief.* ■ (of words or language) not harsh or angry; conciliatory; soothing: *he was no good with soft words, gentle phrases.* ■ not strong or robust: *soft, out-of-shape executives in a computer company.* ■ informal (of a job or way of life) requiring little effort. ■ (of news or other journalism) regarded more as entertainment than as basic news: *fashion*

is regarded as soft news. ■ willing to compromise in political matters; moderate: *candidates ranging from far right to soft left.* ■ informal foolish; silly: *he must be going soft in the head.* ■ [predic.] (**soft on**) informal infatuated with: *was Brendan soft on her?*
4 (of a drink) not alcoholic: *all they had was ginger ale and a few other soft drinks.* ■ (of a drug) not likely to cause addiction. ■ (of water) free from mineral salts that make lathering difficult. ■ (of radiation) having little penetrating power. ■ (of a detergent) biodegradable. ■ (also **soft-core**) (of pornography) suggestive or erotic but not explicit.
▶ **adv.** softly: *I can just speak soft and she'll hear me.* ■ in a weak or foolish way: *don't talk soft.*
– PHRASES **have a soft spot for** be fond of or affectionate toward. **soft option** an easier alternative: *probation should in no sense be seen as a soft option by the judiciary.* **soft touch** (also **easy touch**) informal a person who readily gives or does something if asked.
– DERIVATIVES **soft·ish** adj., **soft·ness** n.
– ORIGIN Old English *sōfte* 'agreeable, calm, gentle'; related to Dutch *zacht* and German *sanft*.

sof·ta /'sôftə/ ▶ **n.** a Muslim student of sacred law and theology.
– ORIGIN Turkish, from Persian *sūḵta* 'burned, on fire.'

soft·ball /'sôf(t),bôl/ ▶ **n.** a modified form of baseball played on a smaller field with a larger ball, seven rather than nine innings, and underarm pitching. The game evolved during the late 19th century from a form of indoor baseball. ■ the ball used in this game.

soft-boiled ▶ **adj.** (of an egg) boiled for a short time, leaving the yolk soft or liquid.

soft chan·cre /'SHANGkər/ ▶ **n.** another term for CHANCROID.

soft clam ▶ **n.** another term for SOFT-SHELL CLAM.

soft coal ▶ **n.** bituminous coal.

soft cop·y ▶ **n.** Computing a legible version of a piece of data that is not printed on a physical medium, esp. as stored or displayed on a computer.

soft cor·al ▶ **n.** see CORAL (sense 2).

soft-core ▶ **adj.** another term for SOFT (sense 4 of the adjective).

soft·cov·er /'sôf(t),kəvər/ ▶ **adj. & n.** another term for PAPERBACK.

soft crab ▶ **n.** another term for SOFT-SHELL CRAB.

soft drink ▶ **n.** a nonalcoholic drink, esp. one that is carbonated.

soft·en /'sôfən/ ▶ **v. 1** make or become less hard: [with obj.] *plant extracts to soften and moisturize the skin* | [no obj.] *let the vegetables soften over a low heat.* ■ [no obj.] (of a market, currency, or commodity) fall in value: *the share price has softened recently.*
2 make or become less severe: [with obj.] *some Democrats tried to* ***soften the blow*** *by substituting a smaller cut in the property tax rate* | [no obj.] *her expression softened at the sight of Diane's white face.* ■ [with obj.] undermine the resistance of (someone): *the blockade appears a better weapon with which to* ***soften them up*** *for eventual surrender.*
3 [with obj.] remove mineral salts from (water).

soft·en·er /'sôf(ə)nər/ ▶ **n.** a substance or device that softens something, esp. a fabric softener.

soft·en·ing of the brain ▶ **n.** informal or archaic mental deterioration, esp. senile dementia, supposedly resulting from degeneration of the brain tissue.

soft fo·cus ▶ **n.** deliberate slight blurring or lack of definition in a photograph or movie.
▶ **adj.** (**soft-focus**) characterized by or producing such a lack of definition. ■ denoting a point of view or style of presentation that obscures or avoids sharp definition in order to be more widely acceptable: *soft-focus, nonpolitical essays about American life.*

soft fruit ▶ **n.** Brit. a small stoneless fruit, such as a strawberry or a black currant.

soft goods ▶ **plural n.** textiles.

soft-head·ed (also **softheaded**) ▶ **adj.** lacking wisdom or intelligence.
– DERIVATIVES **soft-head·ed·ness** n.

soft·heart·ed /'sôft'härtid/ ▶ **adj.** kind and compassionate.
– DERIVATIVES **soft·heart·ed·ness** n.

soft hy·phen ▶ **n.** a hyphen inserted into a word not otherwise hyphenated, to be displayed or typeset only if it falls at the end of a line of text.

soft·ie /'sôftē/ (also **softy**) ▶ **n.** (pl. **softies**) informal a softhearted, weak, or sentimental person.

soft i·ron ▶ **n.** iron that has a low carbon content and is easily magnetized and demagnetized, used to make the cores of solenoids and other electrical equipment.

soft land·ing ▶ **n.** a controlled landing of a spacecraft during which no serious damage is incurred.
– DERIVATIVES **soft-land** v.

soft line ▶ **n.** a flexible and moderate attitude or policy: *the chancellor is taking a soft line on inflation.*

soft loan ▶ **n.** a loan, typically one to a developing country, made on terms very favorable to the borrower.

soft·ly /'sôf(t)lē/ ▶ **adv.** in a quiet voice or manner: *"Can't you sleep?" she asked softly* | *the door opened softly.* ■ with a gentle or slow movement: *he touched her cheek softly.* ■ in a pleasantly subdued manner: *the room was softly lit by a lamp.*

soft mon·ey ▶ **n.** a contribution to a political party that is not accounted as going to a particular candidate, thus avoiding various legal limitations.

soft-nosed ▶ **adj.** (of a bullet) expanding on impact.

soft pal·ate /'palit/ ▶ **n.** the fleshy, flexible part toward the back of the roof of the mouth.

soft-paste ▶ **adj.** denoting artificial porcelain, typically made with white clay and ground glass and fired at a comparatively low temperature.

soft ped·al ▶ **n.** a pedal on a piano that can be pressed to make the tone softer. See also UNA CORDA.
▶ **v.** (**soft-pedal**) [with obj.] Music play with the soft pedal down. ■ refrain from emphasizing the more unpleasant aspects of; play down: *the administration's decision to soft-pedal the missile program.*

soft·phone /'säft,fōn/ ▶ **n.** a piece of software that allows the user to make telephone calls over the Internet via a computer.

soft pow·er ▶ **n.** a persuasive approach to international relations, typically involving the use of economic or cultural influence. Compare with HARD POWER.

soft rock ▶ **n.** rock music with a less persistent beat and more emphasis on lyrics and melody than hard rock has.

soft roe ▶ **n.** see ROE[1].

soft rot ▶ **n.** any of a number of bacterial and fungal diseases of fruit and vegetables in which the tissue becomes soft and slimy. ■ any of a number of fungal conditions affecting timber, which becomes soft and friable.

soft sell ▶ **n.** [in sing.] subtly persuasive selling.
▶ **v.** (**soft-sell**) [with obj.] sell (something) by using such a method.

soft-shell clam (also **softshell clam**) ▶ **n.** a marine bivalve mollusk with a thin shell and a long siphon, valued as food on the east coast of North America. Also called SOFT CLAM, STEAMER. ● Genus *Mya*, family Myidae, esp. *M. arenaria*.

soft-shell crab (also **softshell crab**) ▶ **n.** a crab, esp. a blue crab, that has recently molted and has a new shell that is still soft and edible. Also called SOFT CRAB.

soft-shelled tur·tle (also **soft-shell turtle**) ▶ **n.** a freshwater turtle with a flattened leathery shell, native to Asia, Africa, and North America. ● Family Trionychidae: several genera and many species, including the **spiny soft-shelled turtle** *Apalone* (or (Trionyx) spinifera) of North America.

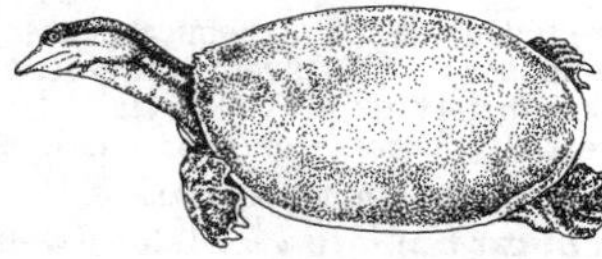

spiny soft-shelled turtle

soft-shoe ▶ **n.** a kind of tap dance performed in soft-soled shoes: *he could dance a jig or a soft-shoe* | [as modifier] *a soft-shoe shuffle.*
▶ **v.** [no obj.] perform a dance of this kind. ■ move quietly and carefully so as not to draw attention to oneself: *I soft-shoed after him* | figurative *he soft-shoed into a safer topic of conversation.*

soft shoul·der ▶ **n.** an unpaved strip of land at the side of a road.

soft skills ▶ **plural n.** personal attributes that enable someone to interact effectively and harmoniously with other people.

soft soap ▶ **n. 1** a semifluid soap, esp. one made with potassium rather than sodium salts.
2 informal persuasive flattery.
▶ **v.** (**soft-soap**) [with obj.] informal use flattery in order to persuade or cajole (someone) to do something.

soft-spo·ken ▶ **adj.** speaking or said with a gentle, quiet voice.

soft tar·get ▶ **n.** a person or thing that is relatively unprotected or vulnerable, esp. to military or terrorist attack.

soft-top ▶ **n.** another term for CONVERTIBLE (sense 1 of the noun). ■ (**soft top**) the roof of a convertible.

soft·ware /'sôft,we(ə)r/ ▶ **n.** the programs and other operating information used by a computer. Compare with HARDWARE.

soft·ware li·brar·y ▶ **n.** see LIBRARY.

soft wheat ▶ **n.** wheat of a variety having a soft grain rich in starch.

soft·wood /'sôft,wo͝od/ ▶ **n. 1** the wood from a conifer (such as pine, fir, or spruce) as distinguished from that of broadleaved trees. ■ a tree producing such wood.
2 (in gardening) young pliable growth on shrubs and other plants from which cuttings can be taken.

soft·y ▶ **n.** variant spelling of SOFTIE.

SOG ▶ **abbr.** Special Operations Group.

sog·gy /'sägē/ ▶ **adj.** (**soggier**, **soggiest**) wet and soft: *the sandbags were soggy and split open* | figurative *the chorus sings powerfully but the interpretation is ultimately soggy.*
– DERIVATIVES **sog·gi·ly** /'sägəlē/ adv., **sog·gi·ness** n.
– ORIGIN early 18th cent. (in the sense 'boggy'): from dialect *sog* 'a swamp' + -Y[1].

Sogne Fiord /'sôNGnə/ a fiord on the western coast of Norway. The longest and deepest fiord in the country, it extends inland for about 125 miles (200 km), with a maximum depth of 4,291 feet (1,308 m). Norwegian name **Sognafjorden**.

so·go sho·sha /'sōgō 'SHōSHə/ ▶ **n.** (pl. **same**) a very large Japanese company that trades internationally in a wide range of goods and services.
– ORIGIN Japanese, from *sōgō* 'comprehensive' + *shōsha* 'mercantile society.'

SOHO /'sō,hō/ ▶ **adj.** relating to a market for relatively inexpensive consumer electronics used by individuals and small companies.
– ORIGIN 1990s: acronym from *small office home office*.

So·Ho /'sō,hō/ a district in southern Manhattan in New York City, known for its artist-occupied industrial lofts and galleries. Its name is derived from *South* of *Houston* Street.

soi-di·sant /,swä dē'zän(t)/ ▶ **adj.** self-styled; so-called: *a soi-disant novelist.*
– ORIGIN French, from *soi* 'oneself' + *disant* 'saying.'

soi·gné /swän'yā/ ▶ **adj.** (fem. **soignée** pronunc. **same**) dressed very elegantly; well groomed: *she was dark, petite, and soignée.*
– ORIGIN past participle of French *soigner* 'take care of,' from *soin* 'care.'

soil[1] /soil/ ▶ **n.** the upper layer of earth in which plants grow, a black or dark brown material typically consisting of a mixture of organic remains, clay, and rock particles: *blueberries need very acid soil* | figurative *the Garden State has provided fertile soil for the specialty beer market.* ■ the territory of a particular nation: *the stationing of U.S. troops on Japanese soil.*
– DERIVATIVES **soil·less** adj.
– ORIGIN late Middle English: from Anglo-Norman French, perhaps representing Latin *solium* 'seat,' by association with *solum* 'ground.'

soil[2] ▶ **v.** [with obj.] make dirty: *he might soil his expensive suit* | (as adj. **soiled**) *a soiled T-shirt.* ■ (esp. of a child, patient, or pet) make (something) dirty by defecating in or on it. ■ bring discredit to; tarnish: *what good is there in soiling your daughter's reputation?*
▶ **n.** waste matter, esp. sewage containing excrement. See also NIGHT SOIL. ■ archaic a stain or discoloring mark.
– ORIGIN Middle English (as a verb): from Old French *soiller*, based on Latin *sucula*, diminutive of *sus* 'pig.' The earliest use of the noun (late Middle English) was 'muddy wallow for wild boar'; current noun senses date from the early 16th cent.

soil[3] ▶ **v.** [with obj.] rare feed (cattle) on fresh-cut green fodder (originally for the purpose of purging them).
– ORIGIN early 17th cent.: perhaps from SOIL[2].

soil me·chan·ics ▶ **plural n.** [usu. treated as sing.] the branch of science concerned with the properties and behavior of soil as they affect its use in civil engineering.

soil pipe ▶ **n.** a sewage or waste water pipe.

soil sci·ence ▶ **n.** the branch of science concerned with the formation, nature, ecology, and classification of soils.

soil stack ▶ **n.** the pipe that takes all the waste water from the upstairs plumbing system of a building.

soi·rée /swä'rā/ ▶ **n.** an evening party or gathering, typically in a private house, for conversation or music.
– ORIGIN French, from *soir* 'evening.'

soi·xante-neuf /,swäsän(t) 'nəf, -zän(t)-/ ▶ **n.** another term for SIXTY-NINE.

S

– ORIGIN French, literally 'sixty-nine,' from the position of the couple.

so·journ /'sōjərn/ formal ▶ **n.** a temporary stay: *her sojourn in Rome.*
▶ **v.** [no obj.] stay somewhere temporarily: *she had sojourned once in Egypt.*
– DERIVATIVES **so·journ·er** **n.**
– ORIGIN Middle English: from Old French *sojourner*, based on Latin *sub-* 'under' + late Latin *diurnum* 'day.'

So·ka Gak·kai /ˌsōkə 'gäkī/ a political and lay religious organization founded in Japan in 1930, based on the teachings of the Nichiren Buddhist sect.
– ORIGIN Japanese, from *sō* 'create' + *ka* 'value' + *gakkai* '(learned) society.'

so·kai·ya /ˌsō'kīyə/ ▶ **n.** (pl. **same**) a holder of shares in a Japanese company who tries to extort money from it by threatening to cause trouble for executives at a general meeting of the shareholders.
– ORIGIN Japanese, from *sōkai* 'general meeting' + *-ya* 'dealer.'

soke /sōk/ ▶ **n.** Brit. historical a right of local jurisdiction. ■ a district under a particular jurisdiction; a minor administrative district.
– ORIGIN late Old English, back-formation from obsolete *soken* 'habitual visiting of a place.'

So·kol /'säkäl/ ▶ **n.** a Slavic gymnastic society aiming to promote a communal spirit and physical fitness, originating in Prague in 1862.
– ORIGIN Czech, literally 'falcon' (the emblem of the society).

SOL ▶ **abbr.** vulgar slang shit out of luck.

Sol /säl, sōl/ Roman Mythology the sun, esp. when personified as a god.
– ORIGIN Latin.

sol[1] /sōl/ (also **so**) ▶ **n.** Music (in solmization) the fifth note of a major scale. ■ the note G in the fixed-do system.
– ORIGIN Middle English *sol*: representing (as an arbitrary name for the note) the first syllable of *solve*, taken from a Latin hymn (see SOLMIZATION).

sol[2] /säl, sôl/ ▶ **n.** Chemistry a fluid suspension of a colloidal solid in a liquid.
– ORIGIN late 19th cent.: abbreviation of SOLUTION.

sol[3] /sōl, sôl/ (also **nuevo sol** /'nwāvō/) ▶ **n.** (pl. **soles** /'sōlāz, 'sôles/) the basic monetary unit of Peru, equal to 100 centavos. It replaced the inti in 1991.
– ORIGIN Spanish, literally 'sun.'

sol. ▶ **abbr.** ■ soluble. ■ solution.

-sol ▶ **comb. form** in nouns denoting different kinds and states of soil: *histosol* | *vertisol.*
– ORIGIN from Latin *solum* 'soil.'

so·la[1] /'sōlə/ ▶ **n.** an Indian swamp plant of the pea family, with stems that yield the pith that is used to make sola topis. ● *Aeschynomene indica*, family Leguminosae.
– ORIGIN mid 19th cent.: from Bengali *solā*, Hindi *śolā*.

so·la[2] ▶ **n.** feminine form of SOLUS.

sol·ace /'sälis/ ▶ **n.** comfort or consolation in a time of distress or sadness: *she sought solace in her religion.*
▶ **v.** [with obj.] give solace to.
– ORIGIN Middle English: from Old French *solas* (noun), *solacier* (verb), based on Latin *solari* 'to console.'

so·lan /'sōlən/ (also **solan goose**) ▶ **n.** the northern gannet. See GANNET (sense 1).
– ORIGIN late Middle English: probably from Old Norse *súla* 'gannet' + *and-* 'duck.'

sol·a·na·ceous /ˌsälə'nāsнəs/ ▶ **adj.** Botany of, relating to, or denoting plants of the nightshade family (Solanaceae).
– ORIGIN early 19th cent.: from modern Latin *Solanaceae* (plural), based on Latin *solanum* 'nightshade,' + -OUS.

so·lan·der /sə'landər/ (also **solander box**) ▶ **n.** a protective box made in the form of a book, for holding such items as botanical specimens, maps, and color plates.
– ORIGIN late 18th cent.: named after Daniel C. *Solander* (1736–82), Swedish botanist.

so·la·nine /'sōləˌnēn, -nin/ ▶ **n.** Chemistry a poisonous compound that is present in green potatoes and in related plants. It is a steroid glycoside of the saponin group.
– ORIGIN mid 19th cent.: from French, from the genus name *Solanum* + -INE[4].

so·la·num /sō'lānəm/ ▶ **n.** a plant of a genus that includes the potato and woody nightshade. ● Genus *Solanum*, family Solanaceae.
– ORIGIN Latin.

So·la·pur /'sнōləˌpo͝or/ (also **Sholapur**) a city in western India, on the Deccan plateau in the state of Maharashtra; pop. 1,128,900 (est. 2009).

so·lar[1] /'sōlər/ ▶ **adj.** of, relating to, or determined by the sun: *solar radiation.* ■ relating to or denoting energy derived from the sun's rays: *solar heating.*
– ORIGIN late Middle English: from Latin *solaris*, from *sol* 'sun.'

so·lar[2] ▶ **n.** Brit. an upper chamber in a medieval house.
– ORIGIN Middle English: from Anglo-Norman French *soler*, from Latin *solarium* 'gallery, terrace.'

so·lar bat·ter·y (also **solar cell**) ▶ **n.** a device converting solar radiation into electricity.

so·lar con·stant ▶ **n.** Physics the rate at which energy reaches the earth's surface from the sun, usually taken to be 1,388 watts per square meter.

so·lar day ▶ **n.** the time between successive meridian transits of the sun at a particular place.

so·lar e·clipse ▶ **n.** an eclipse in which the sun is obscured by the moon.

so·lar en·er·gy ▶ **n.** radiant energy emitted by the sun. ■ another term for SOLAR POWER.

so·lar flare ▶ **n.** Astronomy a brief eruption of intense high-energy radiation from the sun's surface, associated with sunspots and causing electromagnetic disturbances on the earth, as with radio frequency communications and power line transmissions.

so·lar·i·um /sə'le(ə)rēəm, sō-/ ▶ **n.** (pl. **solariums** or **solaria** /-'le(ə)rēə/) a room fitted with extensive areas of glass to admit sunlight. ■ a room equipped with sunlamps or tanning beds that can be used to acquire an artificial suntan.
– ORIGIN mid 19th cent.: from Latin, literally 'sundial, place for sunning oneself,' from *sol* 'sun.'

so·lar·ize /'sōləˌrīz/ ▶ **v.** [with obj.] Photography change the relative darkness of (a part of an image) by overexposure to light.
– DERIVATIVES **so·lar·i·za·tion** /ˌsōləri'zāsнən/ **n.**

so·lar mass ▶ **n.** Astronomy the mass of the sun used as a unit of mass, equal to 1.989×10^{30} kg.

so·lar myth ▶ **n.** a myth ascribing the sun's course or attributes to a particular god or hero.

so·lar neu·tri·no u·nit /n(y)o͞o'trēnō/ (abbr.: **SNU**) ▶ **n.** Astronomy a unit used in expressing the detected flux of neutrinos from the sun, equal to 10^{-36} neutrino captures per target atom per second.

so·lar pan·el ▶ **n.** a panel designed to absorb the sun's rays as a source of energy for generating electricity or heating.

so·lar plex·us /'pleksəs/ ▶ **n.** a complex of ganglia and radiating nerves of the sympathetic system at the pit of the stomach.

so·lar pond ▶ **n.** a pool of very salty water in which convection is inhibited, allowing accumulation of energy from solar radiation in the lower layers.

so·lar pow·er ▶ **n.** power obtained by harnessing the energy of the sun's rays.

so·lar sys·tem ▶ **n.** Astronomy the collection of eight planets and their moons in orbit around the sun, together with smaller bodies in the form of asteroids, meteoroids, and comets.

so·lar wind ▶ **n.** the continuous flow of charged particles from the sun that permeates the solar system.

so·lar year ▶ **n.** see YEAR (sense 1).

SOLAS /'sōləs/ ▶ **n.** [usu. as modifier] the provisions made during a series of international conventions governing maritime safety.
– ORIGIN 1960s: acronym from *safety of life at sea.*

so·la·ti·um /sə'lāsнēəm/ ▶ **n.** (pl. **solatia** /-sнēə/) informal a thing given to someone as a compensation or consolation: *a suitable solatium in the form of an apology was offered to him.*
– ORIGIN early 19th cent.: from Latin, literally 'solace.'

so·la to·pi /'sōlə 'tōpē/ ▶ **n.** (pl. **sola topis**) an Indian sun hat made from the pith of the stems of sola plants.

sold /sōld/ past and past participle of SELL.

sol·der /'sädər/ ▶ **n.** a low-melting alloy, esp. one based on lead and tin or (for higher temperatures) on brass or silver, used for joining less fusible metals.
▶ **v.** [with obj.] join with solder.
– DERIVATIVES **sol·der·a·ble** **adj.**, **sol·der·er** **n.**
– ORIGIN Middle English: from Old French *soudure*, from the verb *souder*, from Latin *solidare* 'fasten together,' from *solidus* 'solid.'

sol·der·ing i·ron ▶ **n.** a tool used for melting solder and applying it to metals that are to be joined.

sol·di /'säldē/ plural form of SOLDO.

sol·dier /'sōljər/ ▶ **n.** **1** a person who serves in an army. ■ (also **common soldier** or **private soldier**) a private in an army.
2 Entomology a wingless caste of ant or termite with a large specially modified head and jaws, involved chiefly in defense.
3 Brit. informal a strip of bread or toast, used for dipping into a soft-boiled egg. ■ [usu. as modifier] an upright brick, timber, or other building element.
▶ **v.** [no obj.] serve as a soldier: (as noun **soldiering**) *soldiering was what the colonel understood.*
■ (**soldier on**) informal carry on doggedly; persevere: *Gary wasn't enjoying this, but he soldiered on.*
■ informal work more slowly than one's capacity; loaf or malinger: *is it the reason you've been soldiering on the job?*
– DERIVATIVES **sol·dier·ly** **adj.**, **sol·dier·ship** /-ˌsнip/ **n.** (archaic).
– ORIGIN Middle English: from Old French *soldier*, from *soulde* '(soldier's) pay,' from Latin *solidus* (see SOLIDUS). The verb dates from the early 17th cent.

sol·dier bee·tle ▶ **n.** an elongated flying beetle with soft downy wing cases, typically found on flowers where it hunts other insects. ● Family Cantharidae: several genera.

sol·dier·fish /'sōljərˌfisн/ ▶ **n.** (pl. **same** or **soldierfishes**) a squirrelfish that is typically bright red in color. ● Several genera and species in the family Holocentridae.

sol·dier fly ▶ **n.** a bright metallic fly with a flattened body, frequently basking in the sun with its wings folded flat over the body. ● Family Stratiomyidae: many genera.

sol·dier of for·tune ▶ **n.** a person who works as a soldier for any country or group that will pay them; a mercenary.

sol·dier·y /'sōljərē/ ▶ **n.** (pl. **soldieries**) soldiers collectively: *the town was filled with disbanded soldiery.* ■ military training or knowledge: *the arts of soldiery.*

sol·do /'säldō/ ▶ **n.** (pl. **soldi** /'säldē/) a former Italian coin and monetary unit worth the twentieth part of a lira.
– ORIGIN Italian, from Latin *solidus* (see SOLIDUS).

sole[1] /sōl/ ▶ **n.** the undersurface of a person's foot: *the soles of their feet were nearly black with dirt.* ■ the section forming the underside of a piece of footwear (typically excluding the heel when this forms a distinct part). ■ the part of the undersurface of a person's foot between the toes and the instep. ■ the undersurface of a tool or implement such as a plane or the head of a golf club. ■ the floor of a ship's cabin or cockpit.
▶ **v.** [with obj.] (usu. **be soled**) put a new sole onto (a shoe).
– DERIVATIVES **soled** **adj.** [in combination] *rubber-soled shoes.*
– ORIGIN Middle English: from Old French, from Latin *solea* 'sandal, sill,' from *solum* 'bottom, pavement, sole'; compare with Dutch *zool* and German *Sohle.*

sole[2] ▶ **n.** a marine flatfish of almost worldwide distribution, important as a food fish. ● Several species in the families Soleidae, Pleuronectidae, and Bothidae. See DOVER SOLE, LEMON SOLE.
– ORIGIN Middle English: from Old French, from Provençal *sola*, from Latin *solea* (see SOLE[1]), named from its shape.

sole[3] ▶ **adj.** [attrib.] one and only: *my sole aim was to contribute to the national team.* ■ belonging or restricted to one person or group of people: *loans can be in sole or joint names* | *the health club is for the sole use of our guests.* ■ archaic (esp. of a woman) unmarried. ■ archaic alone; unaccompanied.
– ORIGIN late Middle English (also in the senses 'secluded' and 'unrivaled'): from Old French *soule*, from Latin *sola*, feminine of *solus* 'alone.'

sol·e·cism /'sāləˌsizəm, 'sō-/ ▶ **n.** a grammatical mistake in speech or writing. ■ a breach of good manners; a piece of incorrect behavior.
– DERIVATIVES **sol·e·cis·tic** /ˌsälə'sistik, ˌsō-/ **adj.**
– ORIGIN mid 16th cent.: from French *solécisme*, or via Latin from Greek *soloikismos*, from *soloikos* 'speaking incorrectly.'

So·le·dad /'sōliˌdad/ a city in the Salinas Valley of west central California, home to a well-known state prison; pop. 28,124 (est. 2008).

sole·ly /'sōl(l)ē/ ▶ **adv.** not involving anyone or anything else; only: *he is solely responsible for any debts the company may incur* | *people are appointed solely on the basis of merit.*

sol·emn /'säləm/ ▶ **adj.** formal and dignified: *a solemn procession.* ■ not cheerful or smiling; serious: *Tim looked very solemn.* ■ characterized by deep sincerity: *he swore a solemn oath to keep faith.*

S

– DERIVATIVES **sol·emn·ly** adv., **sol·emn·ness** n.
– ORIGIN Middle English (in the sense 'associated with religious rites'): from Old French *solemne*, from Latin *sollemnis* 'customary, celebrated at a fixed date,' from *sollus* 'entire.'

so·lem·ni·ty /sə'lemnitē/ ▶ n. (pl. **solemnities**) the state or quality of being serious and dignified: *his ashes were laid to rest with great solemnity.* ■ (usu. **solemnities**) a formal, dignified rite or ceremony: *the ritual of the church was observed in all its solemnities.*
– ORIGIN Middle English (in the sense 'observance of formality and ceremony,' frequently in the phrases *in solemnity, with solemnity*): from Old French *solemnite*, from Latin *sollemnitas*, from *sollemnis* (see SOLEMN).

sol·em·nize /'säləm,nīz/ ▶ v. [with obj.] duly perform (a ceremony, esp. that of marriage). ■ mark with a formal ceremony.
– DERIVATIVES **sol·em·ni·za·tion** /,säləmni'zāsʜən/ n.
– ORIGIN late Middle English: from Old French *solemniser*, from medieval Latin *solemnizare*, from Latin *sollemnis* (see SOLEMN).

Sol·emn League and Cov·e·nant an agreement made in 1643 between the English Parliament and the Scottish Covenanters during the English Civil War, by which the Scots would provide military aid in return for the establishment of a Presbyterian system in England, Scotland, and Ireland. Although the Scottish support proved crucial in the Parliamentary victory, the principal Presbyterian leaders were expelled from Parliament in 1647 and the covenant was never honored.

Sol·emn Mass ▶ n. another term for HIGH MASS.

so·le·no·don /sə'lēnə,dän, -'lenə-/ ▶ n. a forest-dwelling mammal with a long flexible snout and a stiff muscular tail, occurring only in Cuba and Hispaniola. ● Family Solenodontidae and genus *Solenodon*: two species.
– ORIGIN modern Latin, from Greek *sōlēn* 'channel, pipe' + *odō* (variant of *odous, odont-*) 'tooth.'

so·le·noid /'sōlə,noid/ ▶ n. a cylindrical coil of wire acting as a magnet when carrying electric current.
– DERIVATIVES **so·le·noi·dal** /,sōlə'noidl/ adj.
– ORIGIN early 19th cent.: from French *solénoïde*, from Greek *sōlēn* 'channel, pipe.'

So·lent /'sōlənt/ (**the Solent**) a channel between the northwestern coast of the Isle of Wight and the mainland of southern England.

sole·plate /'sōl,plāt/ ▶ n. **1** a metal plate forming the base of an electric iron, machine saw, or other machine.
2 a horizontal timber at the base of a wall frame.

so·le·ra /sə'le(ə)rə/ ▶ n. (also **solera system**) a Spanish method of producing wine, esp. sherry and Madeira, whereby small amounts of younger wines stored in an upper tier of casks are systematically blended with the more mature wine in the casks below. ■ (also **solera wine**) a blend of sherry or Malaga wine produced by the solera system. ■ a wine cask, typically one with a capacity of four hogsheads, on the bottom tier of the solera system and containing the oldest wine.
– ORIGIN Spanish, literally 'crossbeam, stone base.'

So·leure /sô'lœr/ French name for SOLOTHURN.

so·le·us /'sōlēəs/ (also **soleus muscle**) ▶ n. Anatomy a broad muscle in the lower calf, below the gastrocnemius, that flexes the foot to point the toes downward.
– ORIGIN late 17th cent.: modern Latin, from Latin *solea* 'sole.'

S

sol-fa /,sōl 'fä/ ▶ n. short for TONIC SOL-FA.
▶ v. (**sol-fas, sol-faing, sol-faed** /-'fäd/) [with obj.] sing using the sol-fa syllables.

sol·fa·ta·ra /,sälfə'tärə, ,sōl-/ ▶ n. Geology a volcanic crater emitting only sulfurous and other gases.
– ORIGIN late 18th cent.: from the name of a volcano near Naples, from Italian *solfo* 'sulfur.'

sol·fège /säl'fezʜ/ ▶ n. Music **1** solmization. ■ an exercise in singing using solmization syllables.
2 the study of singing and musicianship using solmization syllables.
– ORIGIN early 20th cent.: French, from Italian *solfeggio*.

sol·feg·gio /säl'fejē,ō/ ▶ n. (pl. **solfeggi** /-jē/) another term for SOLFÈGE (sense 1).
– ORIGIN late 18th cent.: Italian.

so·li /'sōlē/ plural form of SOLO.

so·lic·it /sə'lisit/ ▶ v. (**solicits, soliciting, solicited**) [with obj.] ask for or try to obtain (something) from someone: *he called a meeting to solicit their views.* ■ ask (someone) for something: *historians and critics are solicited for opinions by the auction houses.* ■ [no obj.] accost someone and offer one's or someone else's services as a prostitute: (as noun **soliciting**) *although prostitution was not itself an offense, soliciting was.*
– DERIVATIVES **so·lic·i·ta·tion** /sə,lisə'tāsʜən/ n.
– ORIGIN late Middle English: from Old French *solliciter*, from Latin *sollicitare* 'agitate,' from *sollicitus* 'anxious,' from *sollus* 'entire' + *citus* (past participle of *ciere* 'set in motion').

so·lic·i·tor /sə'lisitər/ ▶ n. **1** a person who tries to obtain business orders, advertising, etc.; a canvasser.
2 the chief law officer of a city, town, or government department. ■ Brit. a member of the legal profession qualified to deal with conveyancing, the drawing up of wills, and other legal matters.
– ORIGIN late Middle English (denoting an agent or deputy): from Old French *solliciteur*, from *solliciter* (see SOLICIT).

so·lic·i·tor gen·er·al ▶ n. (pl. **solicitors general**) the law officer directly below the attorney general in the US Department of Justice, responsible for arguing cases before the US Supreme Court. ■ a similar position in some US states.

so·lic·i·tous /sə'lisitəs/ ▶ adj. characterized by or showing interest or concern: *she was always solicitous about the welfare of her students | a solicitous inquiry.* ■ archaic eager or anxious to do something: *he was solicitous to cultivate her mamma's good opinion.*
– DERIVATIVES **so·lic·i·tous·ly** adv., **so·lic·i·tous·ness** n.
– ORIGIN mid 16th cent.: from Latin *sollicitus* (see SOLICIT) + -OUS.

so·lic·i·tude /sə'lisi,t(y)o͞od/ ▶ n. care or concern for someone or something: *I was touched by his solicitude.*
– ORIGIN late Middle English: from Old French *sollicitude*, from Latin *sollicitudo*, from *sollicitus* (see SOLICITOUS).

sol·id /'sälid/ ▶ adj. (**solider, solidest**) **1** firm and stable in shape; not liquid or fluid: *the stream was frozen solid | solid fuels.* ■ strongly built or made of strong materials; not flimsy or slender: *a solid door with good, secure locks.* ■ having three dimensions: *a solid figure with six plane faces.* ■ [attrib.] concerned with objects having three dimensions: *solid geometry.*
2 not hollow or containing spaces or gaps: *a sculpture made out of solid rock | a solid mass of flowers | the stores were packed solid.* ■ consisting of the same substance throughout: *solid silver cutlery.* ■ (of typesetting) without extra space between the lines of characters. ■ (of a line or surface) without spaces; unbroken: *the solid outline encloses the area within which we measured.* ■ (of time) uninterrupted; continuous: *a solid day of meetings | [postpositive] it poured for two hours solid.*
3 dependable; reliable: *the defense is solid | there is solid evidence of lower inflation.* ■ sound but without any special qualities or flair: *the rest of the acting is solid.* ■ unanimous or undivided: *they received solid support from their teammates.* ■ financially sound: *the company is very solid and will come through the current recession.* ■ [predic.] (**solid with**) informal on good terms with: *he thought he could put himself **in solid with** you by criticizing her.*
▶ n. a substance or object that is solid rather than liquid or fluid. ■ (**solids**) food that is not liquid: *she drinks only milk and rarely eats solids.* ■ Geometry a body or geometric figure having three dimensions.
– DERIVATIVES **sol·id·ly** adv., **sol·id·ness** n.
– ORIGIN late Middle English: from Latin *solidus*; related to *salvus* 'safe' and *sollus* 'entire.'

sol·i·da·go /,sälə'dāgō/ ▶ n. (pl. **solidagos**) a plant of the genus *Solidago* in the daisy family, esp. (in gardening) goldenrod.
– ORIGIN modern Latin, from a medieval Latin alteration of late Latin *consolida* 'comfrey.'

sol·id an·gle ▶ n. a three-dimensional analog of an angle, such as that subtended by a cone or formed by planes meeting at a point. It is measured in steradians.

sol·i·dar·i·ty /,sälə'de(ə)ritē/ ▶ n. **1** unity or agreement of feeling or action, esp. among individuals with a common interest; mutual support within a group: *factory workers voiced solidarity with the striking students.*
2 (**Solidarity**) an independent trade union movement in Poland that developed into a mass campaign for political change and inspired popular opposition to communist regimes across eastern Europe during the 1980s. [translating Polish *Solidarność*.]
– ORIGIN mid 19th cent.: from French *solidarité*, from *solidaire* 'solidary.'

sol·i·dar·y /'sälə,derē/ ▶ adj. (of a group or community) characterized by solidarity or coincidence of interests.
– ORIGIN early 19th cent.: from French *solidaire*, from *solide* 'solid.'

sol·id-bod·y ▶ adj. denoting or relating to an electric guitar without a sound box, the strings being mounted on a solid shaped block forming the guitar body.

sol·id-drawn ▶ adj. (of a tube) pressed or drawn out from a solid bar of metal.

sol·i·di /'säli,dī/ plural form of SOLIDUS.

so·lid·i·fy /sə'lidə,fī/ ▶ v. (**solidifies, solidifying, solidified**) make or become hard or solid: [no obj.] *the magma slowly solidifies and forms crystals.* ■ [with obj.] make stronger; reinforce: *social and political pressures helped to solidify national identities.*
– DERIVATIVES **so·lid·i·fi·ca·tion** /sə,lidəfi'kāsʜən/ n., **so·lid·i·fi·er** /-ər/ n.

so·lid·i·ty /sə'liditē/ ▶ n. the quality or state of being firm or strong in structure: *the sheer strength and solidity of Romanesque architecture.* ■ the quality of being substantial or reliable in character: *he exuded an aura of reassuring solidity.*

sol·id so·lu·tion ▶ n. Chemistry a solid mixture containing a minor component uniformly distributed within the crystal lattice of the major component.

sol·id South ▶ n. (**the solid South**) chiefly historical the politically united southern states of the US, traditionally regarded as giving unanimous electoral support to the Democratic Party.

sol·id state ▶ n. the state of matter in which materials are not fluid but retain their boundaries without support, the atoms or molecules occupying fixed positions with respect to one another and unable to move freely.
▶ adj. (**solid-state**) (of a device) making use of the electronic properties of solid semiconductors (as opposed to electron tubes).

sol·i·dus /'sälidəs/ ▶ n. (pl. **solidi** /-,dī/) **1** another term for SLASH¹ (sense 2 of the noun).
2 (also **solidus curve**) Chemistry a curve in a graph of the temperature and composition of a mixture, below which the substance is entirely solid.
3 historical a gold coin of the later Roman Empire. [from Latin *solidus* (*nummus*).]
– ORIGIN Latin, literally 'solid.'

so·li·fluc·tion /,sälə'fləksʜən, ,sō-/ ▶ n. Geology the gradual movement of wet soil or other material down a slope, esp. where frozen subsoil acts as a barrier to the percolation of water.
– ORIGIN early 20th cent.: from Latin *solum* 'soil' + *fluctio(n-)* 'flowing,' from the verb *fluere*.

so·lil·o·quy /sə'liləkwē/ ▶ n. (pl. **soliloquies**) an act of speaking one's thoughts aloud when by oneself or regardless of any hearers, esp. by a character in a play. ■ a part of a play involving such an act.
– DERIVATIVES **so·lil·o·quist** /-kwist/ n., **so·lil·o·quize** /-,kwīz/ v.
– ORIGIN Middle English: from late Latin *soliloquium*, from Latin *solus* 'alone' + *loqui* 'speak.'

sol·ip·sism /'sälip,sizəm/ ▶ n. the view or theory that the self is all that can be known to exist.
– DERIVATIVES **sol·ip·sist** n., **sol·ip·sis·tic** /,sälip'sistik/ adj., **sol·ip·sis·ti·cal·ly** /,sälip'sistik(ə)lē/ adv.
– ORIGIN late 19th cent.: from Latin *solus* 'alone' + *ipse* 'self' + -ISM.

sol·i·taire /'sälə,te(ə)r/ ▶ n. **1** any of various card games played by one person, the object of which is to use up all one's cards by forming particular arrangements and sequences.
2 a diamond or other gem set in a piece of jewelry by itself. ■ a ring set with such a gem.
3 either of two large extinct flightless birds related to the dodo, found on two of the Mascarene Islands until they were exterminated in the 18th century. ● Family Raphidae: the **Rodriguez solitaire** (*Pezophaps solitaria*), and the poorly known **Réunion solitaire** (*Ornithaptera solitaria*).
4 a large American thrush with mainly gray plumage and a short bill. ● Genus *Myadestes*, subfamily Turdinae, family Muscicapidae: several species.
– ORIGIN early 18th cent.: from French, from Latin *solitarius* (see SOLITARY).

sol·i·tar·y /'sälə,terē/ ▶ adj. done or existing alone: *I live a pretty solitary life | tigers are essentially solitary.* ■ (of a place) secluded or isolated: *solitary farmsteads.* ■ [attrib. often with negative] single; only: *we have not a solitary shred of evidence to go on.* ■ (of a bird, mammal, or insect) living alone or in pairs, esp. in contrast to related social forms: *a solitary wasp.* ■ (of a flower or other part) borne singly.
▶ n. (pl. **solitaries**) **1** a recluse or hermit.
2 informal short for SOLITARY CONFINEMENT.
– DERIVATIVES **sol·i·tar·i·ly** /-rəlē/ adv., **sol·i·tar·i·ness** n.
– ORIGIN Middle English: from Latin *solitarius*, from *solus* 'alone.'

sol·i·tar·y con·fine·ment ▶ n. the isolation of a prisoner in a separate cell as a punishment.

sol·i·tar·y wave ▶ n. another term for SOLITON.

sol·i·ton /ˈsäliˌtän/ ▶ **n.** Physics a quantum or quasiparticle propagated as a traveling nondissipative wave that is neither preceded nor followed by another such disturbance.
– ORIGIN 1960s: from **SOLITARY** + **-ON**.

sol·i·tude /ˈsäləˌt(y)o͞od/ ▶ **n.** the state or situation of being alone: *she savored her few hours of freedom and solitude.* ■ a lonely or uninhabited place.
– ORIGIN Middle English: from Old French, or from Latin *solitudo*, from *solus* 'alone.'

sol·mi·za·tion /ˌsälmiˈzāsʜən, sōl-/ ▶ **n.** Music a system of associating each note of a scale with a particular syllable, esp. to teach singing.

> The commonest European system, still in use, originally named the notes *ut, re, mi, fa, sol, la* in groups of six (hexachords) beginning on G, C, or F, using syllables from a Latin hymn for St. John the Baptist's Day in which each phrase begins on the next note in the scale: "*Ut* queant laxis *re*sonare fibris *Mi*ra gestorum *fa*muli tuorum, *Sol*ve polluti *la*bili reatum, Sancte Iohannes." A seventh note *si* was added later (from the initials of Sancte Iohannes). Modern systems typically use the sequence as arbitrarily adapted in the 19th century: *do, re, mi, fa, sol, la, ti*, with do being C in the fixed-do system and the keynote in the movable-do or tonic sol-fa system.

– ORIGIN mid 18th cent.: from French *solmisation*, based on *sol* 'sol' + *mi*.

soln. ▶ **abbr.** solution.

Soln·ho·fen /ˈzōlnˈhōfən/ a village in Bavaria, Germany, near which there are extensive, thinly stratified beds of lithographic limestone dating from the Upper Jurassic period. These beds are noted as the chief source of archaeopteryx fossils.

so·lo /ˈsōlō/ ▶ **n.** (pl. **solos**) **1** a thing done by one person unaccompanied, in particular: ■ (pl. **solos** or **soli** /ˈsōlē/) a piece of vocal or instrumental music or a dance, or a part or passage in one, for one performer. ■ an unaccompanied flight by a pilot in an aircraft.
2 a card game in which one player plays against the others in an attempt to win a specified number of tricks.
▶ **adj. & adv.** for or done by one person alone; unaccompanied: [as adj.] *a solo album* | [as adv.] *she'd spent most of her life flying solo.*
▶ **v.** (**soloes, soloing, soloed**) [no obj.] perform something unaccompanied, in particular: ■ perform an unaccompanied piece of music or a part or passage in one. ■ fly an aircraft unaccompanied. ■ undertake solo climbing.
– ORIGIN late 17th cent. (as a musical term): from Italian, from Latin *solus* 'alone.'

so·lo climb·ing ▶ **n.** the sport of climbing unaided by ropes and other equipment, and without the assistance of other people.
– DERIVATIVES **so·lo climb·er n.**

so·lo·ist /ˈsōlōist/ ▶ **n.** a singer or other musician who performs a solo.

Sol·o·mon /ˈsäləmən/, son of David; king of Israel *c.*970–*c.*930 BC. In the Bible he is traditionally associated with the Song of Songs, Ecclesiastes, and Proverbs, while his wisdom is illustrated by the Judgment of Solomon. ■ (as noun, usu. **a Solomon**) a very wise person.
– DERIVATIVES **Sol·o·mon·ic** /ˌsäləˈmänik/ **adj.**

Sol·o·mon Is·lands (also **the Solomons**) a country that consists of a group of islands in the southwestern Pacific, to the east of New Guinea; pop. 595,600 (est. 2009); capital, Honiara; languages, English (official), Pidgin, and local Austronesian languages.

> The islands were divided between Britain and Germany in the late 19th century; the southern islands became a British protectorate in 1893 while the north remained German until mandated to Australia in 1920. With the exception of the northern part of the chain (now part of Papua New Guinea), the Solomons became self-governing in 1976 and fully independent within the Commonwealth of Nations two years later.

– DERIVATIVES **Sol·o·mon Is·land·er n.**

Sol·o·mon's seal ▶ **n. 1** a figure similar to the Star of David.
2 a widely distributed plant of the lily family, having arching stems that bear a double row of broad leaves with drooping flowers in their axils. ● Genus *Polygonatum*, family Liliaceae: many species, including *P. biflorum*, which has greenish-yellow paired flowers and is common in the woods of the eastern US.

Solomon's seal 1

So·lon /ˈsōlən, ˈsōˌlän/ (*c.*630–*c.*560 BC), Athenian statesman and lawgiver. One of the Seven Sages, he revised the code of laws established by Draco. His division of the citizens into four classes based on wealth rather than birth was the basis for Athenian democracy.

So·lo·thurn /ˈzôləˌtərn/ a canton in northwestern Switzerland, in the Jura mountains. French name **SOLEURE**. ■ its capital, a town on the Aare River; pop. 15,364 (2007).

sol·stice /ˈsōlstis/ ▶ **n.** either of the two times in the year, the **summer solstice** and the **winter solstice**, when the sun reaches its highest or lowest point in the sky at noon, marked by the longest and shortest days.
– DERIVATIVES **sol·sti·tial** /sōlˈstisʜəl/ **adj.**
– ORIGIN Middle English: from Old French, from Latin *solstitium*, from *sol* 'sun' + *stit-* 'stopped, stationary' (from the verb *sistere*).

Sol·ti /ˈsʜōltē/, Sir Georg (1912–97), British conductor, born in Hungary. He was conductor of the Chicago Symphony Orchestra 1969–91 and the London Philharmonic Orchestra 1979–83.

sol·u·bi·lize /ˈsälyəbəˌlīz/ ▶ **v.** [with obj.] technical make (a substance) soluble or more soluble.
– DERIVATIVES **sol·u·bi·li·za·tion** /ˌsälyəbəliˈzāsʜən/ **n.**

sol·u·ble /ˈsälyəbəl/ ▶ **adj. 1** (of a substance) able to be dissolved, esp. in water: *the poison is soluble in alcohol.*
2 (of a problem) able to be solved.
– DERIVATIVES **sol·u·bil·i·ty** /ˌsälyəˈbilitē/ **n.**
– ORIGIN late Middle English: from Old French, from late Latin *solubilis*, from *solvere* (see **SOLVE**).

sol·u·ble glass ▶ **n.** another term for **WATER GLASS** (sense 1).

so·lu·nar /sōˈlo͞onər/ ▶ **adj.** of or relating to the combined influence or conjunction of the sun and moon.
– ORIGIN late 18th cent.: blend of **SOL** and **LUNAR**.

so·lus /ˈsōləs/ ▶ **adj.** (fem. **sola** /ˈsōlə/) alone or unaccompanied (used esp. as a stage direction).
– ORIGIN Latin.

sol·ute /ˈsälˌyo͞ot/ ▶ **n.** the minor component in a solution, dissolved in the solvent.
– ORIGIN late 19th cent.: from Latin *solutum*, neuter of *solutus* 'loosened,' past participle of the verb *solvere*.

so·lu·tion /səˈlo͞osʜən/ ▶ **n. 1** a means of solving a problem or dealing with a difficult situation: *there are no easy solutions to financial and marital problems.* ■ the correct answer to a puzzle: *the solution to this month's crossword.* ■ (**solutions**) products or services designed to meet a particular need: *we are an Internet marketing firm specializing in e-commerce solutions.*
2 a liquid mixture in which the minor component (the solute) is uniformly distributed within the major component (the solvent). ■ the process or state of being dissolved in a solvent.
3 archaic the action of separating or breaking down; dissolution: *the solution of British supremacy in South Africa.*
– ORIGIN late Middle English: from Old French, from Latin *solutio(n-)*, from *solvere* 'loosen' (see **SOLVE**).

> **WORD TRENDS** Everyone is familiar with advertisements offering all manner of **solutions**: *high-end storage solutions* | *a leading provider of payment solutions*. The usage began during the 1990s in the computer industry, where **solutions** were packages of software and hardware put together by IT companies to do a particular job for their customers. It is now an all-purpose word in commercial language for products, services, or companies, and is sometimes almost meaningless: *frozen meal solutions* are just frozen meals, after all. The term's overuse perhaps implies a stressed, anxious society, where everyday needs are marketed as problems that require solving. See also **ISSUE**.

so·lu·tion set ▶ **n.** Mathematics the set of all the solutions of an equation or condition.

So·lu·tre·an /səˈlo͞otrēən/ ▶ **adj.** Archaeology of, relating to, or denoting an Upper Paleolithic culture of central and southwestern France and parts of Iberia. It is dated to about 21,000–18,000 years ago, following the Aurignacian and preceding the Magdalenian. ■ (as noun **the Solutrean**) the Solutrean culture or period.
– ORIGIN late 19th cent.: from *Solutré*, the site of a cave in eastern France, where objects from this culture were found, + **-AN**.

solv·ate /ˈsälvāt/ ▶ **v.** [with obj.] Chemistry (of a solvent) enter into reversible chemical combination with (a dissolved molecule, ion, etc.).
▶ **n.** a more or less loosely bonded complex formed between a solvent and a dissolved species.
– DERIVATIVES **solv·a·tion** /sälˈvāsʜən/ **n.**
– ORIGIN early 20th cent.: formed irregularly from **SOLVE** + **-ATE**[1].

Sol·vay pro·cess /ˈsälvā/ ▶ **n.** Chemistry an industrial process for obtaining sodium carbonate from limestone, ammonia, and brine.
– ORIGIN late 19th cent.: named after Ernest *Solvay* (1838–1922), Belgian chemist.

solve /sälv, sôlv/ ▶ **v.** [with obj.] find an answer to, explanation for, or means of effectively dealing with (a problem or mystery): *the policy could solve the town's housing crisis* | *a murder investigation that has never been solved.*
– DERIVATIVES **solv·a·ble adj.**, **solv·er n.**
– ORIGIN late Middle English (in the sense 'loosen, dissolve, untie'): from Latin *solvere* 'loosen, unfasten.'

sol·vent /ˈsälvənt/ ▶ **adj. 1** having assets in excess of liabilities; able to pay one's debts: *interest rate rises have very severe effects on normally solvent companies.*
2 [attrib.] able to dissolve other substances: *osmotic, chemical, or solvent action.*
▶ **n.** the liquid in which a solute is dissolved to form a solution. ■ a liquid, typically one other than water, used for dissolving other substances. ■ something that acts to weaken or dispel a particular attitude or situation: *an unrivaled solvent of social prejudices.*
– DERIVATIVES **sol·ven·cy n.**
– ORIGIN mid 17th cent.: from Latin *solvent-* 'loosening, unfastening, paying,' from the verb *solvere*.

sol·vent a·buse ▶ **n.** the use of certain volatile organic solvents as intoxicants by inhalation, e.g., glue sniffing.

Sol·way Firth /ˌsôlwā/ an inlet of the Irish Sea that separates northwestern England from Dumfries and Galloway in Scotland.

Sol·zhe·ni·tsyn /ˌsōlzʜəˈnētsən, ˌsôl-/, Alexander (1918–2008), Russian novelist; Russian name *Aleksandr Isaevich Solzhenitsyn.* After spending eight years in a labor camp, he began writing. He was exiled in 1974 and eventually returned in 1994. Notable works: *One Day in the Life of Ivan Denisovich* (1962), *Cancer Ward* (1968), and *The Gulag Archipelago* (1973). Nobel Prize for Literature (1970).

som /sōm/ ▶ **n.** (pl. **same**) the basic monetary unit of Kyrgyzstan, equal to 100 tiyin.

so·ma[1] /ˈsōmə/ ▶ **n.** [usu. in sing.] Biology the parts of an organism other than the reproductive cells. ■ the body as distinct from the soul, mind, or psyche.
– ORIGIN late 19th cent.: from Greek *sōma* 'body.'

so·ma[2] ▶ **n.** Hinduism an intoxicating drink prepared from a plant and used in Vedic ritual, believed to be the drink of the gods. ■ (also **soma plant**) the plant from which this drink is prepared. See **HOM**. ■ (in Aldous Huxley's novel *Brave New World*) a narcotic drug which produces euphoria and hallucination, distributed by the state in order to promote content and social harmony.
– ORIGIN Sanskrit *sōma*.

som·aes·thet·ic ▶ **adj.** British spelling of **SOMESTHETIC**.

So·ma·li /səˈmälē, sō-/ ▶ **n.** (pl. **same** or **Somalis**) a member of a mainly Muslim people of Somalia. ■ the Cushitic language that is the official language of Somalia, also spoken in Djibouti and parts of Kenya and Ethiopia. ■ a native or inhabitant of Somalia.
▶ **adj.** of or relating to Somalia, the Somalis, or their language.
– DERIVATIVES **So·ma·li·an** /-lēən/ **adj. & n.**
– ORIGIN the name in Somali.

So·ma·li·a /səˈmälēə, sōˈmälyə/ a country in northeastern Africa, on the peninsula known as the Horn of Africa; pop. 9,832,000 (est. 2009); capital, Mogadishu; languages, Somali and Arabic (both official).

> The area of the Horn of Africa was divided between British and Italian spheres of influence in the late 19th century, and the modern republic of Somalia became independent in 1960 following the unification of the former British Somaliland and Italian Somalia. Civil war broke out in Somalia in 1988 and led to the overthrow of the government in 1991; in that year northern Somalia declared independence as the Somaliland Republic, and central government in the country remains weak.

So·ma·li Pen·in·su·la another name for **HORN OF AFRICA**.

so·man /ˈsōmən/ (also **Soman**) ▶ **n.** a lethal organophosphorus nerve gas, developed in Germany during World War II.
– ORIGIN 1950s: from German, of unknown origin.

so·mat·ic /səˈmatik, sō-/ ▶ **adj.** of or relating to the body, esp. as distinct from the mind. ■ Biology of or relating to the soma.
– DERIVATIVES **so·mat·i·cal·ly adv.**
– ORIGIN late 18th cent.: from Greek *sōmatikos*, from *sōma* 'body.'

so·mat·ic cell ▶ **n.** Biology any cell of a living organism other than the reproductive cells.

so·mat·i·za·tion /səˌmatəˈzāSHən, ˈsōmə-/ ▶ **n.** Psychiatry the production of recurrent and multiple medical symptoms with no discernible organic cause.

somato- ▶ **comb. form** of or relating to the human or animal body: *somatotype*.
– ORIGIN from Greek *sōma*, *sōmat-* 'body.'

so·mat·o·me·din /səˌmatəˈmēdn, ˌsōmə-/ ▶ **n.** Biochemistry a hormone that acts as an intermediate in the stimulation of tissue growth by growth hormone.
– ORIGIN 1970s: from **SOMATO-** 'of the body' + (*inter*) *med*(*iary*) + **-IN**[1].

so·mat·o·pleure /səˈmatəˌplo͝o(ə)r, ˈsōmətə-/ ▶ **n.** Embryology a layer of tissue in a vertebrate embryo comprising the ectoderm and the outer layer of mesoderm, and giving rise to the amnion, the chorion, and part of the body wall. Often contrasted with **SPLANCHNOPLEURE**.
– ORIGIN late 19th cent.: from **SOMATO-** 'of the body' + Greek *pleura* 'side.'

so·mat·o·sen·so·ry /səˌmatəˈsensərē, ˌsōmətə-/ ▶ **adj.** Physiology relating to or denoting a sensation (such as pressure, pain, or warmth) that can occur anywhere in the body, in contrast to one localized at a sense organ (such as sight, balance, or taste). Also called **SOMESTHETIC**.

so·mat·o·stat·in /səˌmatəˈstatn, ˌsōmə-/ ▶ **n.** Biochemistry a hormone secreted in the pancreas and pituitary gland that inhibits gastric secretion and somatotropin release.

so·mat·o·tro·pin /səˌmatəˈtrōpən/ (also **somatotrophin**) ▶ **n.** Biochemistry a growth hormone secreted by the anterior pituitary gland.

so·mat·o·type /səˈmatəˌtīp, ˌsōmə-/ ▶ **n.** a category to which people are assigned according to the extent to which their bodily physique conforms to a basic type (usually endomorphic, mesomorphic, or ectomorphic).
– DERIVATIVES **so·mat·o·typ·ing n.**
– ORIGIN 1940s: coined by W. H. Sheldon in *Varieties of Human Physique*.

som·ber /ˈsämbər/ (Brit. also **sombre**) ▶ **adj.** dark or dull in color or tone; gloomy: *the night skies were somber and starless.* ■ oppressively solemn or sober in mood; grave: *he looked at her with a somber expression.*
– DERIVATIVES **som·ber·ly adv.**, **som·ber·ness n.**
– ORIGIN mid 18th cent.: from French, based on Latin *sub* 'under' + *umbra* 'shade.'

som·bre·ro /sämˈbre(ə)rō/ ▶ **n.** (pl. **sombreros**) a broad-brimmed felt or straw hat, typically worn in Mexico and the southwestern US.
– ORIGIN Spanish, from *sombra* 'shade' (see **SOMBER**).

S

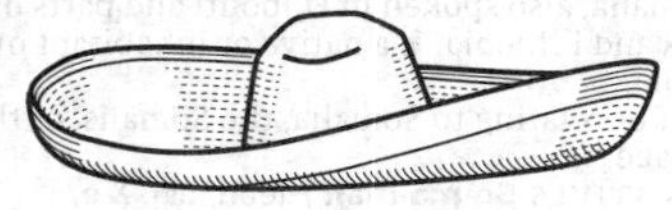

sombrero

some /səm/ ▶ **determiner 1** an unspecified amount or number of: *I made some money running errands | he played some records for me.*
2 used to refer to someone or something that is unknown or unspecified: *she married some newspaper magnate twice her age | there must be some mistake | he's in* **some kind of** *trouble.*
3 (used with a number) approximately: *some thirty different languages are spoken.*
4 a considerable amount or number of: *he went to some trouble | I've known you for some years now.*
5 at least a small amount or number of: *he liked some music but generally wasn't musical.*
6 expressing admiration of something notable: *that was some goal.* ■ used ironically to express disapproval or disbelief: *Mr. Power gave his stock reply. Some help.*
▶ **pron. 1** an unspecified number or amount of people or things: *here are some of our suggestions | if you want whiskey I'll give you some.*
2 at least a small amount or number of people or things: *surely some have noticed.*
▶ **adv.** informal to some extent; somewhat: *when you get to the majors, the rules change some.*
– PHRASES **and then some** informal and plenty more than that: *we got our money's worth and then some.* **some few** see **FEW**. **some little** a considerable amount of: *we are going to be working together for some little time yet.*
– ORIGIN Old English *sum*, of Germanic origin, from an Indo-European root shared by Greek *hamōs* 'somehow' and Sanskrit *sama* 'any, every.'

-some[1] ▶ **suffix** [forming adjectives meaning:] **1** productive of: *loathsome.*
2 characterized by being: *wholesome.* ■ apt to: *tiresome.*
– ORIGIN Old English *-sum*.

-some[2] ▶ **suffix** (forming nouns) denoting a group of a specified number: *foursome.*
– ORIGIN Old English *sum* 'some.'

-some[3] ▶ **comb. form** denoting a portion of a body, esp. a particle of a cell: *chromosome.*
– ORIGIN from Greek *sōma* 'body.'

some·bod·y /ˈsəmˌbädē/ ▶ **pron. 1** some person; someone.
2 a person of importance or authority: *I'd like to be somebody |* [as noun] *nobodies who want to become somebodies.*

some·day /ˈsəmˌdā/ ▶ **adv.** at some time in the future: *I know someday my whole family will be together and happy.*

some·how /ˈsəmˌhou/ ▶ **adv.** in some way; by some means: *somehow I managed to get the job done.* ■ for a reason that is not known or specified: *he looked different somehow.*

some·one /ˈsəmˌwən/ ▶ **pron. 1** an unknown or unspecified person; some person: *there's someone at the door | someone from the audience shouted out.*
2 a person of importance or authority: *a small-time lawyer keen to be someone.*

some·place /ˈsəmˌplās/ ▶ **adv. & pron.** informal another term for **SOMEWHERE**.

som·er·sault /ˈsəmərˌsôlt/ ▶ **n.** an acrobatic movement in which a person turns head over heels in the air or on the ground and lands or finishes on their feet: *a backward somersault |* figurative *Paula's stomach turned a somersault.*
▶ **v.** [no obj.] perform such an acrobatic feat, or make a similar movement accidentally: *his car somersaulted into a ditch.*
– ORIGIN mid 16th cent. (as a noun): from Old French *sombresault*, from Provençal *sobresaut*, from *sobre* 'above' + *saut* 'leap.'

Som·er·ville /ˈsəmərˌvil/ an industrial and residential city in eastern Massachusetts, northwest of Boston; pop. 75,662 (est. 2008).

som·es·thet·ic /ˌsōmesˈTHetik/ (Brit. **somaesthetic**) ▶ **adj.** another term for **SOMATOSENSORY**.
– ORIGIN late 19th cent.: from Greek *sōma* 'body' + **AESTHETIC**.

some·thing /ˈsəmˌTHiNG/ ▶ **pron. 1** a thing that is unspecified or unknown: *we stopped for something to eat | I knew something terrible had happened | something about her frightened me.*
2 used in various expressions indicating that a description or amount being stated is not exact: *a wry look,* **something between** *amusement and regret | grassland totaling* **something over** *three hundred acres | there were* **something like** *fifty applications.*
▶ **adv.** [as submodifier] **1** informal used for emphasis with a following adjective functioning as an adverb: *my back hurts something terrible.*
2 archaic or dialect to some extent; somewhat: *the people were something scared.*
– PHRASES **or something** informal added as a reference to an unspecified alternative similar to the thing mentioned: *you look like you just climbed a mountain or something.* **really** (or **quite**) **something** informal something considered impressive or notable: *Want to see the library? It's really something.* **something else** informal an exceptional person or thing: *the reaction from the crowd was something else.* **something of** to some degree: *Richard was something of an expert at the game.* **something or other** see **OTHER**. **there is something in/to ——** —— is worth considering; there is some truth in ——: *perhaps there is something to his theory | I think there's something in this alien business.* **thirty-something** (**forty-something**, etc.) informal an unspecified age between thirty and forty (forty and fifty, etc.): *I'm guessing she's forty-something |* [as noun] *she writes a column geared to twenty- and thirty-somethings.*
– ORIGIN Old English *sum thing* (see **SOME, THING**).

some·time /ˈsəmˌtīm/ ▶ **adv.** at some unspecified or unknown time: *you must come and have supper sometime | sometime after six everybody left.* ■ archaic at one time; formerly: *the Emperor Constantine used this speech sometime unto his bishops.*
▶ **adj. 1** former: *the sometime editor of the paper.*
2 occasional: *a sometime contributor.*

some·times /ˈsəmˌtīmz/ ▶ **adv.** occasionally, rather than all of the time: *sometimes I want to do things on my own.*

some·way /ˈsəmˌwā/ ▶ **adv.** (often **someways**) informal in some way or manner; by some means: *we've got to make money someway.*

some·what /ˈsəmˌ(h)wät/ ▶ **adv.** to a moderate extent or by a moderate amount: *matters have improved somewhat since then |* [as submodifier] *a somewhat thicker book.*
– PHRASES **somewhat of** something of: *it was somewhat of a disappointment.*

some·when /ˈsəmˌ(h)wen/ ▶ **adv.** informal at some time: *somewhen between 1918 and 1930.*

some·where /ˈsəmˌ(h)we(ə)r/ ▶ **adv.** in or to some place: *I've seen you somewhere before | can we go somewhere warm?* ■ used to indicate an approximate amount: *it cost* **somewhere around** *two thousand dollars.*
▶ **pron.** some unspecified place: *in search of somewhere to live.*
– PHRASES **get somewhere** informal make progress; achieve success.

so·mite /ˈsōmīt/ ▶ **n.** Zoology each of a number of body segments containing the same internal structures, clearly visible in invertebrates such as earthworms but also present in the embryonic stages of vertebrates. Also called **METAMERE**.
– ORIGIN mid 19th cent.: from Greek *sōma* 'body' + **-ITE**[1].

Somme /sôm, säm/ a river in northern France. Rising east of Saint-Quentin, it flows 153 miles (245 km) through Amiens to the English Channel northeast of the port of Dieppe. The area around it was the scene of heavy fighting in World War I.

Somme, Battle of the a major battle of World War I between the British and the Germans, on the Western Front in northern France July–November 1916. More than a million men on both sides were killed or wounded.

som·me·lier /ˌsəməlˈyā/ ▶ **n.** a wine steward.
– ORIGIN early 19th cent.: French, literally 'butler.'

som·nam·bu·lism /sämˈnambyəˌlizəm/ ▶ **n.** sleepwalking.
– DERIVATIVES **som·nam·bu·lant** /-lənt/ **adj.**, **som·nam·bu·lant·ly** /-ləntlē/ **adv.**, **som·nam·bu·list n.**, **som·nam·bu·lis·tic** /-ˌnambyəˈlistik/ **adj.**, **som·nam·bu·lis·ti·cal·ly** /-ˌnambyəˈlistik(ə)lē/ **adv.**
– ORIGIN late 18th cent.: from French *somnambulisme*, from Latin *somnus* 'sleep' + *ambulare* 'to walk.'

som·nif·er·ous /sämˈnifərəs/ ▶ **adj.** tending to induce sleep; soporific.
– ORIGIN early 17th cent.: from Latin *somnifer* (from *somnium* 'dream') + **-OUS**.

som·no·lent /ˈsämnələnt/ ▶ **adj.** sleepy; drowsy. ■ causing or suggestive of drowsiness: *a somnolent summer day.* ■ Medicine abnormally drowsy.
– DERIVATIVES **som·no·lence n.**, **som·no·len·cy n.**, **som·no·lent·ly adv.**
– ORIGIN late Middle English (in the sense 'causing sleepiness'): from Old French *sompnolent* or Latin *somnolentus*, from *somnus* 'sleep.'

So·mo·za /səˈmōsə, -zə/ the name of a family of Nicaraguan statesmen. ■ **Anastasio** (1896–1956), president 1937–47 and 1951–56; full name *Anastasio Somoza García*. He took presidential office following a military coup in 1936 and ruled Nicaragua as a virtual dictator. ■ **Luis** (1922–67), president 1957–63; son of Anastasio; full name *Luis Somoza Debayle*. ■ **Anastasio** (1925–80), president 1967–79; younger brother of Luis; full name *Anastasio Somoza Debayle*. His dictatorial regime was overthrown by the Sandinistas, and he was assassinated while in exile in Paraguay.

son /sən/ ▶ **n.** a boy or man in relation to either or both of his parents. ■ a male offspring of an animal. ■ a male descendant: *the sons of Adam.* ■ (**the Son**) (in Christian belief) the second person of the Trinity; Christ. ■ a man considered in relation to his native country or area: *one of Nevada's most famous sons.* ■ a man regarded as the product of a particular person, influence, or environment: *sons of the French Revolution.* ■ (also **my son**) used by an elder person as a form of address for a boy or young man: *"You're on private land, son."*
– PHRASES **son of a bitch** (pl. **sons of bitches**) informal used as a general term of contempt or abuse. **son of a gun** (pl. **sons of guns**) informal a jocular or affectionate way of addressing or referring to someone: *he's a pretentious son of a gun, but he's got a heart of gold.* [with reference to the guns carried aboard ships: the epithet is said to have been applied originally to babies born at sea to women allowed to accompany their husbands.]
– DERIVATIVES **son·ship** /ˈsənˌSHip/ **n.**

–ORIGIN Old English *sunu*, of Germanic origin; related to Dutch *zoon* and German *Sohn*, from an Indo-European root shared by Greek *huios*.

so·nar /ˈsōˌnär/ ▶ **n.** a system for the detection of objects under water and for measuring the water's depth by emitting sound pulses and detecting or measuring their return after being reflected. ■ an apparatus used in this system. ■ the method of echolocation used in air or water by animals such as whales and bats.
–ORIGIN 1940s: from *so(und) na(vigation and) r(anging)*, on the pattern of *radar*.

so·na·ta /səˈnätə/ ▶ **n.** a composition for an instrumental soloist, often with a piano accompaniment, typically in several movements with one or more in sonata form.
–ORIGIN late 17th cent.: Italian, literally 'sounded' (originally as distinct from 'sung'), feminine past participle of *sonare*.

so·na·ta form (also **sonata-allegro form**) ▶ **n.** Music a type of composition in three sections (exposition, development, and recapitulation) in which two themes or subjects are explored according to set key relationships. It forms the basis for much classical music, including the sonata, symphony, and concerto.

son·a·ti·na /ˌsänəˈtēnə/ ▶ **n.** a simple or short sonata.
–ORIGIN mid 18th cent.: Italian, diminutive of **SONATA**.

sonde /sänd/ ▶ **n.** an instrument probe that automatically transmits information about its surroundings underground, under water, in the atmosphere, etc.
–ORIGIN early 20th cent.: from French, literally 'sounding (line).'

Sond·heim /ˈsändˌhīm/, Stephen (Joshua) (1930–), US composer and lyricist. He became known for his lyrics for *West Side Story* (1957) and has since written a number of musicals, including *A Little Night Music* (1973), *Sweeney Todd* (1979), and *Sunday in the Park with George* (1984).

sone /sōn/ ▶ **n.** a unit of subjective loudness, equal to 40 phons.
–ORIGIN 1930s: from Latin *sonus* 'a sound.'

son et lu·mière /ˈsôn nā lo͞omˈyer, lʏˈmyer/ ▶ **n.** an entertainment held by night at a historic monument or building, telling its history by the use of lighting effects and recorded sound.
–ORIGIN French, literally 'sound and light.'

Song variant spelling of **SUNG**.

song /sôNG/ ▶ **n.** a short poem or other set of words set to music or meant to be sung. ■ singing or vocal music: *the young airmen* ***broke into song****.* ■ a musical composition suggestive of a song. ■ the musical phrases uttered by some birds, whales, and insects, typically forming a recognizable and repeated sequence and used chiefly for territorial defense or for attracting mates. ■ a poem, esp. one in rhymed stanzas: *The Song of Hiawatha.* ■ archaic poetry.
–PHRASES **for a song** informal very cheaply: *the place was going for a song.* **on song** Brit. informal performing well: *when he is on song, no one can stop him.* **a song and dance** informal a long explanation that is pointless or deliberately evasive: *Don't give me a song and dance, Sandy. Yes or no?* ■ chiefly Brit. a fuss or commotion: *she would be sure to* ***make a song and dance about*** *her aching feet.*
–ORIGIN Old English *sang*, of Germanic origin; related to Dutch *zang* and German *Sang*, also to **SING**.

song·bird /ˈsôNGˌbərd/ ▶ **n. 1** a bird with a musical song.
2 Ornithology a perching bird of an advanced group distinguished by having the muscles of the syrinx attached to the bronchial semirings; an oscine passerine. ● Suborder Oscines, order Passeriformes; in Europe 'songbird' is effectively synonymous with 'passerine' or 'perching bird.'.
3 informal a female singer: *the title track is the kind of tune any Nashville songbird could do.*

song·book /ˈsôNGˌbo͝ok/ ▶ **n.** a book containing a collection of songs with music.

song·craft /ˈsäNGˌkraft/ ▶ **n.** the art or skill of writing or composing songs.

song cy·cle ▶ **n.** a set of related songs, often on a romantic theme, intended to form a single musical entity.

song form ▶ **n.** a form used in the composition of a song, in particular a simple melody and accompaniment or a three-part work in which the third part is a repetition of the first.

Son·ghai /säNGˈgī/ ▶ **n.** (pl. **same** or **Songhais**) **1** a member of a people living mainly in Niger and Mali.
2 the Nilo-Saharan language of this people.
▶ **adj.** of or relating to this people or their language.
–ORIGIN the name in Songhai.

Song Hong Vietnamese name for **RED RIVER** (sense 1).

Song·kran /ˈsäNGˌkrän/ ▶ **n.** a festival celebrating the traditional Thai New Year, held in April and marked by the throwing and sprinkling of water.
–ORIGIN Thai.

Song·nam /ˈsəNGˈnäm/ a city in northwestern South Korea, southeast of Seoul; pop. 958,300 (est. 2008).

Song of Songs (also **Song of Solomon**) a book of the Bible containing an anthology of Hebrew love poems traditionally ascribed to Solomon but in fact dating from a much later period. Jewish and Christian writers have interpreted the book allegorically as representing God's relationship with his people, or with the soul.

song·smith /ˈsôNGˌsmiTH/ ▶ **n.** informal a person who writes popular songs.

song spar·row ▶ **n.** a sparrowlike North American bird related to the buntings, noted for its constant and characteristic song. ● *Melospiza melodia*, family Emberizidae (subfamily Emberizinae).

song·ster /ˈsôNGstər/ ▶ **n.** a person who sings, esp. fluently and skillfully. ■ a person who writes songs or verse. ■ a songbird.
–ORIGIN Old English *sangestre* (see **SONG**, **-STER**).

song·stress /ˈsôNGstris/ ▶ **n.** a female songster.

song thrush ▶ **n.** a common European and central Asian thrush with a buff spotted breast, having a loud song in which each phrase is repeated two or three times. ● *Turdus philomelos*, subfamily Turdinae, family Muscicapidae.

song·writ·er /ˈsôNGˌrītər/ ▶ **n.** a person who writes popular songs or the music for them.
–DERIVATIVES **song·writ·ing n.**

son·ic /ˈsänik/ ▶ **adj.** relating to or using sound waves. ■ denoting or having a speed equal to that of sound.
–DERIVATIVES **son·i·cal·ly** /-ik(ə)lē/ **adv.**
–ORIGIN 1920s: from Latin *sonus* 'sound' + **-IC**.

son·i·cate /ˈsänikāt/ Biochemistry ▶ **v.** [with obj.] (usu. **be sonicated**) subject (a biological sample) to ultrasonic vibration so as to fragment the cells, macromolecules, and membranes.
▶ **n.** a biological sample that has been subjected to such treatment.
–ORIGIN 1950s: from **SONIC** + **-ATE**[2].

son·ic bar·ri·er ▶ **n.** another term for **SOUND BARRIER**.

son·ic boom ▶ **n.** a loud explosive noise caused by the shock wave from an aircraft traveling faster than the speed of sound.

son·ics /ˈsäniks/ ▶ **plural n.** musical sounds artificially produced or reproduced.

So·nin·ke /säˈnēNGkā/ ▶ **n.** (pl. **same** or **Soninkes**) **1** a member of a people living in Mali and Senegal.
2 the Mande language of this people.
▶ **adj.** of or relating to this people or their language.
–ORIGIN the name in Soninke.

son-in-law ▶ **n.** (pl. **sons-in-law**) the husband of one's daughter.

son·net /ˈsänit/ ▶ **n.** a poem of fourteen lines using any of a number of formal rhyme schemes, in English typically having ten syllables per line.
▶ **v.** (**sonnets, sonneting, sonneted**) [no obj.] archaic compose sonnets. ■ [with obj.] celebrate in a sonnet.
–ORIGIN mid 16th cent.: from French, or from Italian *sonetto*, diminutive of *suono* 'a sound.'

son·net·eer /ˌsäniˈti(ə)r/ ▶ **n.** a writer of sonnets.

son·ny /ˈsənē/ ▶ **n.** informal used by an older person as a familiar form of address to a young boy. ■ (Brit. also **Sonny Jim**) used as a humorous or patronizing way of addressing a man: *look, sonny, that's all I can tell you.*

sono- ▶ **comb. form** of or relating to sound: *sonometer.*
–ORIGIN from Latin *sonus* 'sound.'

son·o·bu·oy /ˈsänəˌbo͞oē, -ˌboi/ ▶ **n.** a buoy equipped to detect underwater sounds and transmit them by radio.

son·o·gram /ˈsänəˌgram/ ▶ **n. 1** a graph representing a sound, showing the distribution of energy at different frequencies.
2 a visual image produced from an ultrasound examination.

so·nog·ra·phy /səˈnägrəfē/ ▶ **n. 1** the analysis of sound using an instrument that produces a graphical representation of its component frequencies.
2 another term for **ULTRASONOGRAPHY**.
–DERIVATIVES **son·o·graph** /ˈsänəˌgraf/ **n.**, **son·o·graph·ic** /ˌsänəˈgrafik/ **adj.**

son·o·lu·mi·nes·cence /ˌsänōˌlo͞oməˈnesəns/ ▶ **n.** Physics luminescence excited in a substance by the passage of sound waves through it.
–DERIVATIVES **son·o·lu·mi·nes·cent adj.**

So·no·ma Coun·ty /səˈnōmə/ a county in northwestern California, known for its wineries; pop. 466,741 (est. 2008).

So·no·ra /səˈnôrə/ a state of northwestern Mexico, on the Gulf of California; capital, Hermosillo.

So·no·ra Des·ert an arid region in North America, in southeastern California and southwestern Arizona in the US and much of Baja California and the western part of Sonora in Mexico.

So·no·ran /səˈnôrən/ ▶ **adj.** relating to, denoting, or characteristic of a biogeographical region including desert areas of the southwestern US and central Mexico.
–ORIGIN late 19th cent.: from **SONORA** + **-AN**.

so·no·rant /ˈsänərənt/ ▶ **n.** Phonetics a sound produced with the vocal cords so positioned that spontaneous voicing is possible; a vowel, a glide, or a liquid or nasal consonant.
–ORIGIN 1930s: from **SONOROUS** + **-ANT**.

so·nor·i·ty /səˈnôritē/ ▶ **n.** the quality or fact of being sonorous. ■ Phonetics the relative loudness of a speech sound.

so·no·rous /ˈsänərəs/ ▶ **adj.** (of a person's voice or other sound) imposingly deep and full. ■ capable of producing a deep or ringing sound: *the alloy is sonorous and useful in making bells.* ■ (of a speech or style) using imposing language: *they had expected the lawyers to deliver sonorous lamentations.*
–DERIVATIVES **so·no·rous·ly adv.**, **so·no·rous·ness n.**
–ORIGIN early 17th cent.: from Latin *sonorus* (from *sonor* 'sound') + **-OUS**.

son·sy /ˈsänsē/ (also **sonsie**) ▶ **adj.** (**sonsier, sonsiest**) Scottish literary having an attractive and healthy appearance.
–ORIGIN mid 16th cent. (also in the sense 'lucky'): from Irish and Scottish Gaelic *sonas* 'good fortune' (from *sona* 'fortunate') + **-Y**[1].

Son·tag /ˈsänˌtag/, Susan (1933–2004), US writer and critic. She established her reputation as a radical intellectual with *Against Interpretation* (essays, 1966). Other notable works: *On Photography* (1976) and *Illness as Metaphor* (1979).

sook[1] /so͞ok, sək/ ▶ **n.** a female crab.
–ORIGIN 1950s: of unknown origin.

sook[2] ▶ **n.** informal, chiefly Austral./NZ & Canadian **1** a person lacking spirit or self-confidence; a coward.
2 a hand-reared calf.
–ORIGIN mid 19th cent.: dialect variant of the noun **SUCK**.

soon /so͞on/ ▶ **adv. 1** in or after a short time: *everyone will soon know the truth | he'll be home soon | they arrived soon after 7:30.* ■ early: *it's a pity you have to leave so soon | I wish you'd told me sooner | it was too soon to know.*
2 used to indicate one's preference in a particular matter: ***I'd just as soon*** *Tim did it | I would sooner resign than transfer to Toronto.*
–PHRASES **no sooner —— than** used to convey that the second event mentioned happens immediately after the first: *she had no sooner spoken than the telephone rang.* **sooner or later** at some future time; eventually: *you'll have to tell him sooner or later.*
–DERIVATIVES **soon·ish adv.**
–ORIGIN Old English *sōna* 'immediately.'

> **USAGE** In standard English, the phrase **no sooner** is followed by **than**, as in *we had no sooner arrived* **than** *we had to leave.* This is because **sooner** is a comparative, and comparatives are followed by **than** (*earlier than; better than*, etc.). It is incorrect to follow **no sooner** with **when** rather than **than**, as in *we had no sooner arrived* **when** *we had to leave.*

Soon·er State /ˈso͞onər/ a nickname for the state of **OKLAHOMA**.
–ORIGIN *Sooner* in the sense "one who acts prematurely," i.e., a person who tried to get into the frontier territory of Oklahoma before the US government opened it to settlers in 1889.

soot /so͝ot/ ▶ **n.** a black powdery or flaky substance consisting largely of amorphous carbon, produced by the incomplete burning of organic matter.
▶ **v.** [with obj.] cover or clog (something) with soot.
–PHRASES (**as**) **black as soot** intensely black.
–ORIGIN Old English *sōt*, of Germanic origin; related to German dialect *Sott*, from an Indo-European root shared by the verb **SIT**.

sooth /so͞oTH/ ▶ **n.** archaic truth.
–PHRASES **in sooth** in truth; really.
–ORIGIN Old English *sōth* (originally as an adjective in the sense 'genuine, true'), of Germanic origin.

soothe /so͞oT͟H/ ▶ **v.** [with obj.] gently calm (a person or their feelings): *a shot of brandy might soothe his nerves.* ■ reduce pain or discomfort in (a part of the body): *to soothe the skin try chamomile or thyme.*

■ relieve or ease (pain): *it contains a mild anesthetic to soothe the pain.*
– DERIVATIVES **sooth·er** n.
– ORIGIN Old English *sōthian* 'verify, show to be true,' from *sōth* 'true' (see SOOTH). In the 16th cent. the verb passed through the senses 'corroborate (a statement),' 'humor (a person) by expressing assent' and 'flatter by one's assent,' whence 'mollify, appease' (late 17th cent).

sooth·ing /'so͞oᴛʜiɴɢ/ ▶ adj. having a gently calming effect: *she put on some soothing music.* ■ reducing pain or discomfort: *almond oil is renowned for its soothing properties.*
– DERIVATIVES **sooth·ing·ly** adv.

sooth·say·er /'so͞oᴛʜ,sāər/ ▶ n. a person supposed to be able to foresee the future.
– DERIVATIVES **sooth·say·ing** n.
– ORIGIN Middle English (in the sense 'person who speaks the truth'): see SOOTH.

soot·y /'so͝otē/ ▶ adj. (**sootier**, **sootiest**) covered with or colored like soot: *the front of the fireplace was blackened and sooty | his olive skin and sooty eyes.* ■ used in names of birds and other animals that are mainly blackish or brownish black, e.g., **sooty tern**.
– DERIVATIVES **soot·i·ly** /'so͝otəlē/ adv., **soot·i·ness** n.

soot·y mold ▶ n. a black velvety mold that grows on the surfaces of leaves and stems affected by honeydew. ● Family Capnodiaceae, subdivision Ascomycotina.

soot·y tern ▶ n. a large oceanic tern that is blackish above and white below, and breeds throughout the tropical oceans. ● *Sterna fuscata.*

SOP ▶ abbr. Standard Operating Procedure.

sop /säp/ ▶ n. **1** a thing given or done as a concession of no great value to appease someone whose main concerns or demands are not being met: *my agent telephones as a sop but never finds me work.*
2 a piece of bread dipped in gravy, soup, or sauce.
▶ v. (**sops**, **sopping**, **sopped**) [with obj.] **1** (**sop something up**) soak up liquid using an absorbent substance: *he used some bread to sop up the sauce.*
2 wet thoroughly; soak.
– ORIGIN Old English *soppian* 'dip (bread) in liquid,' *sopp* (noun), probably from the base of Old English *sūpan* 'sup.' Sense 1 (mid 17th cent.) alludes to the sop used by Aeneas on his visit to Hades to appease Cerberus.

sop. ▶ abbr. soprano.

so·pai·pil·la /,sōpī'pēyə/ (also **sopapilla** /,sōpə-/) ▶ n. (esp. in New Mexico) a deep-fried pastry, typically square, eaten with honey or sugar or as a bread.
– ORIGIN American Spanish.

soph säf ▶ n. informal sophomore: *the sophs get their assignments tomorrow.*

soph. ▶ abbr. sophomore.

soph·ism /'säfizəm/ ▶ n. a fallacious argument, esp. one used deliberately to deceive.
– ORIGIN late Middle English: from Old French *sophime*, via Latin from Greek *sophisma* 'clever device,' from *sophizesthai* 'become wise' (see SOPHIST).

soph·ist /'säfist/ ▶ n. a paid teacher of philosophy and rhetoric in ancient Greece, associated in popular thought with moral skepticism and specious reasoning. ■ a person who reasons with clever but fallacious arguments.
– DERIVATIVES **so·phis·tic** /sə'fistik/ adj., **so·phis·ti·cal** /sə'fistikəl/ adj., **so·phis·ti·cal·ly** /sə'fistik(ə)lē/ adv.
– ORIGIN mid 16th cent.: via Latin from Greek *sophistēs*, from *sophizesthai* 'devise, become wise,' from *sophos* 'wise.'

S

so·phis·ti·cate ▶ v. /sə'fistə,kāt/ [with obj.] make (someone or something) more sophisticated: *readers who have been sophisticated by modern literary practice | functions that other software applications have sophisticated.* ■ [no obj.] archaic talk or reason in an impressively complex and educated manner. ■ archaic mislead or corrupt (a person, an argument, the mind, etc.) by sophistry: *books of casuistry, which sophisticate the understanding and defile the heart.*
▶ adj. /sə'fistə,kāt, -kit/ archaic sophisticated.
▶ n. /sə'fistə,kāt, -kit/ a person with much worldly experience and knowledge of fashion and culture: *he is still the butt of jokes made by New York sophisticates.*
– ORIGIN late Middle English (as an adjective in the sense 'adulterated,' and as a verb in the sense 'mix with a foreign substance'): from medieval Latin *sophisticatus* 'tampered with,' past participle of the verb *sophisticare*, from *sophisticus* 'sophistic.' The shift of sense probably occurred first in the adjective *unsophisticated*, from 'uncorrupted' via 'innocent' to 'inexperienced, uncultured.' The noun dates from the early 20th cent.

so·phis·ti·cat·ed /sə'fisti,kātid/ ▶ adj. (of a machine, system, or technique) developed to a high degree of complexity: *highly sophisticated computer systems.* ■ (of a person or their thoughts, reactions, and understanding) aware of and able to interpret complex issues; subtle: *discussion and reflection are necessary for a sophisticated response to a text.* ■ having, revealing, or proceeding from a great deal of worldly experience and knowledge of fashion and culture: *a chic, sophisticated woman | a young man with sophisticated tastes.* ■ appealing to people with such knowledge of experience: *a sophisticated restaurant.*
– DERIVATIVES **so·phis·ti·cat·ed·ly** adv.

so·phis·ti·ca·tion /sə,fisti'kāsʜən/ ▶ n. the quality of being sophisticated: *her air of sophistication and confidence | the technological sophistication of their products.*

soph·ist·ry /'säfəstrē/ ▶ n. (pl. **sophistries**) the use of fallacious arguments, esp. with the intention of deceiving. ■ a fallacious argument.

Soph·o·cles /'säfə,klēz/ (c.496–406 BC), Greek playwright. His seven surviving plays are notable for their complexity of plot and depth of characterization and for their examination of the relationship between mortals and the divine order. Notable plays: *Antigone* and *Oedipus Rex* (also called *Oedipus Tyrannus*).

soph·o·more /'säf(ə),môr/ ▶ n. a second-year college or high school student.
– ORIGIN mid 17th cent.: perhaps from earlier *sophumer*, from *sophum*, *sophom* (obsolete variants of SOPHISM) + -ER¹.

soph·o·mor·ic /,säf(ə)'môrik/ ▶ adj. of, relating to, or characteristic of a sophomore: *my sophomoric years.* ■ pretentious or juvenile: *sophomoric double entendres.*

So·phy /'sōfē, 'sä-/ ▶ n. (pl. **Sophies**) historical a former title for the ruler of Persia associated esp. with the Safavid dynasty.
– ORIGIN from Arabic *Ṣafī-al-dīn* 'pure of religion.'

sop·o·rif·ic /,säpə'rifik/ ▶ adj. tending to induce drowsiness or sleep: *the motion of the train had a somewhat soporific effect.* ■ sleepy or drowsy: *some medicine made her soporific.* ■ tediously boring or monotonous: *a libel trial is in large parts intensely soporific.*
▶ n. a drug or other agent of this kind.
– DERIVATIVES **sop·o·rif·i·cal·ly** /-ik(ə)lē/ adv.
– ORIGIN mid 17th cent.: from Latin *sopor* 'sleep' + -IFIC.

sop·ping /'säpiɴɢ/ ▶ adj. saturated with liquid; wet through: *get those sopping clothes off* | [as submodifier] *the handkerchief was sopping wet.*
– ORIGIN mid 19th cent.: present participle of SOP.

sop·py /'säpē/ ▶ adj. (**soppier**, **soppiest**) informal self-indulgently sentimental: *I look at babies with a soppy smile on my face | an enjoyably soppy story.* ■ Brit. lacking spirit and common sense; feeble: *my little sisters were too soppy for our adventurous games.*
– DERIVATIVES **sop·pi·ly** /'säpəlē/ adv., **sop·pi·ness** n.
– ORIGIN early 19th cent. (in the sense 'soaked with water'): from SOP + -Y¹.

so·pra·ni·no /,säprə'nēnō/ ▶ n. Music (pl. **sopraninos**) an instrument, esp. a recorder or saxophone, higher than soprano.
– ORIGIN early 20th cent.: Italian, diminutive of SOPRANO.

so·pran·o /sə'pranō/ ▶ n. (pl. **sopranos**) the highest of the four standard singing voices: *a piece composed for soprano, flute, and continuo* | [as modifier] *a good soprano voice.* ■ a female or boy singer with such a voice. ■ a part written for such a voice. ■ [usu. as modifier] an instrument of a high or the highest pitch in its family: *a soprano saxophone.*
– ORIGIN mid 18th cent.: Italian, from *sopra* 'above,' from Latin *supra.*

so·pran·o clef /klef/ ▶ n. Music an obsolete clef placing middle C on the lowest line of the staff.

so·pran·o re·cord·er ▶ n. Music the most common size of recorder, with a range of two octaves from the C above middle C upward.

so·ra /'sôrə/ (also **sora crake** or **rail**) ▶ n. a common small brown and gray American rail, frequenting marshes. ● *Porzana carolina*, family Rallidae.
– ORIGIN early 18th cent.: probably from an American Indian language.

Sorb /sôrb/ ▶ n. a member of a Slavic people living in parts of southeastern Brandenburg and eastern Saxony. Also called WEND.
– ORIGIN from German *Sorbe.*

sorb /sôrb/ ▶ n. the fruit of the true service tree.
– ORIGIN early 16th cent.: from French *sorbe* or Latin *sorbus* 'service tree,' *sorbum* 'serviceberry.'

sor·bent /'sôrbənt/ ▶ n. Chemistry a substance that has the property of collecting molecules of another substance by sorption.
– ORIGIN early 20th cent.: from *sorb* 'take up by sorption,' on the pattern of *absorbent.*

sor·bet /sôr'bā, 'sôrbit/ ▶ n. a dessert consisting of frozen fruit juice or flavored water and sugar. ■ archaic an Arabian sherbet.
– ORIGIN late 16th cent.: from French, from Italian *sorbetto*, from Turkish *şerbet*, based on Arabic *šariba* 'to drink'; compare with SHERBET.

Sorb·i·an /'sôrbēən/ ▶ adj. of or relating to the Sorbs or their language.
▶ n. the West Slavic language of the Sorbs, which has been revived from near extinction and has around 70,000 speakers. Also called WENDISH or LUSATIAN.

sor·bi·tan /'sôrbə,tan/ ▶ n. [usu. as modifier] Chemistry any of a group of compounds that are cyclic ethers derived from sorbitol or its derivatives.
– ORIGIN 1930s: blend of SORBITOL and ANHYDRIDE.

sor·bi·tol /'sôrbi,tôl, -,täl/ ▶ n. Chemistry a sweet-tasting crystalline compound found in some fruit. ● A hexahydric alcohol; chem. formula: $CH_2OH(CHOH)_4CH_2OH$.
– ORIGIN late 19th cent.: from SORB + -ITE¹ + -OL.

Sor·bonne /sôr'bən/ the seat of the faculties of science and literature of the University of Paris.
– ORIGIN originally a theological college founded by Robert de *Sorbon*, chaplain to Louis IX, c.1257.

sor·cer·er /'sôrsərər/ ▶ n. a person who claims or is believed to have magic powers; a wizard.
– ORIGIN late Middle English: from *sorser* (from Old French *sorcier*, based on Latin *sors, sort-* 'lot') + -ER¹.

sor·cer·er's ap·pren·tice ▶ n. a person who instigates a process or project which they are then unable to control.
– ORIGIN translating French *l'apprenti sorcier*, a symphonic poem (1897) by Paul Dukas, suggested by German *der Zauberlehrling* (1797), a poem by Goethe.

sor·cer·ess /'sôrsəris/ ▶ n. a female sorcerer; a witch.

sor·cer·y /'sôrsərē/ ▶ n. the use of magic, esp. black magic.
– DERIVATIVES **sor·cer·ous** /-rəs/ adj.

sor·did /'sôrdid/ ▶ adj. involving ignoble actions and motives; arousing moral distaste and contempt: *the story paints a sordid picture of bribes and scams.* ■ dirty or squalid: *the overcrowded housing conditions were sordid and degrading.*
– DERIVATIVES **sor·did·ly** adv., **sor·did·ness** n.
– ORIGIN late Middle English (as a medical term in the sense 'purulent'): from French *sordide* or Latin *sordidus*, from *sordere* 'be dirty.' The current senses date from the early 17th cent.

sor·di·no /sôr'dēnō/ ▶ n. (pl. **sordini** /-nē/) Music a mute. ■ (**sordini**) (on a piano) the dampers.
– ORIGIN late 16th cent.: from Italian, from *sordo* 'mute,' from Latin *surdus.*

sor·dor /'sôrdər/ ▶ n. chiefly literary physical or moral sordidness.
– ORIGIN early 19th cent.: from SORDID, on the pattern of the pair *squalid, squalor.*

sore /sôr/ ▶ adj. (of a part of one's body) painful or aching: *my feet were sore and my head ached.* ■ [predic.] suffering pain from a part of one's body: *he was sore from the long ride.* ■ [predic.] informal upset and angry: *I didn't even know they were sore at us.* ■ [attrib.] severe; urgent: *we're in sore need of him.*
▶ n. a raw or painful place on the body: *we had sores on our hands.* ■ a cause or source of distress or annoyance: *there's no point raking over the past and opening old sores.*
▶ adv. archaic extremely; severely: *they were sore afraid.*
– PHRASES **sore point** a subject or issue about which someone feels distressed or annoyed: *the glamorous image of their paramilitary rivals was always a sore point with the police.* **stand** (or **stick**) **out like a sore thumb** be obviously different from the surrounding people or things.
– DERIVATIVES **sore·ness** n.
– ORIGIN Old English *sār* (noun and adjective), *sāre* (adverb), of Germanic origin; related to Dutch *zeer* 'sore' and German *sehr* 'very.' The original sense was 'causing intense pain, grievous,' whence the adverbial use.

sore·head /'sôr,hed/ ▶ n. informal a person who is in a bad temper or easily irritated.

sore·ly /'sôrlē/ ▶ adv. to a very high degree or level of intensity (esp. of an unwelcome or unpleasant state or emotion): *she would sorely miss his company | help was sorely needed.*
– ORIGIN Old English *sārlīce* (see SORE, -LY²).

sor·ghum /'sôrgəm/ ▶ n. a widely cultivated cereal native to warm regions of the Old World. It is a major source of grain and of feed for livestock. ● Genus *Sorghum*, family Gramineae: many species, in particular *S. bicolor* and its cultivars. ■ a syrupy sweetener made from a type of this cereal.
– ORIGIN late 16th cent.: modern Latin, from Italian *sorgo*, perhaps based on a variant of Latin *syricum* 'Syrian.'

so·ri /ˈsôˌrī/ plural form of **SORUS**.

so·ro·ral /səˈrôrəl/ ▶ **adj.** formal of or like a sister or sisters.
– ORIGIN mid 17th cent.: from Latin *soror* 'sister' + **-AL**.

so·ror·i·ty /səˈrôritē, -ˈrä-/ ▶ **n.** (pl. **sororities**) a society for female students in a university or college, typically for social purposes.
– ORIGIN mid 16th cent.: from medieval Latin *sororitas*, or from Latin *soror* 'sister' (on the pattern of *fraternity*).

so·ro·sis /səˈrōsis/ ▶ **n.** (pl. **soroses** /-ˌsēz/) Botany a fleshy multiple fruit, e.g., a pineapple or mulberry, derived from the ovaries of several flowers.
– ORIGIN mid 19th cent.: modern Latin, from Greek *sōros* 'heap.'

sorp·tion /ˈsôrpSHən/ ▶ **n.** Chemistry absorption and adsorption considered as a single process.
– ORIGIN early 20th cent.: back-formation from **ABSORPTION** and **ADSORPTION** (see **ADSORB**).

sor·rel[1] /ˈsôrəl/ ▶ **n.** a European plant of the dock family, with arrow-shaped leaves that are used in salads and cooking for their acidic flavor. See also **WOOD SORREL**. ● Genus *Rumex*, family Polygonaceae: several species, including the **English sorrel** (*R. acetosa*) and the more slender-leaved **French sorrel** (*R. scutatus*).
– ORIGIN late Middle English: from Old French *sorele*, of Germanic origin; related to **SOUR**.

sor·rel[2] ▶ **n.** a horse with a light reddish-brown coat. ■ [usu. as modifier] a light reddish-brown color: *a sorrel mare with four white socks*.
– ORIGIN Middle English: from Old French *sorel*, from *sor* 'yellowish,' from a Germanic adjective meaning 'dry.'

sor·rel tree ▶ **n.** another term for **SOURWOOD**.

sor·row /ˈsärō/ ▶ **n.** a feeling of deep distress caused by loss, disappointment, or other misfortune suffered by oneself or others: *he understood the sorrow and discontent underlying his brother's sigh*. ■ an event or circumstance that causes such a feeling: *it was a great sorrow to her when they separated*. ■ the outward expression of grief; lamentation.
▶ **v.** [no obj.] feel or display deep distress: (as adj. **sorrowing**) *the sorrowing widower found it hard to relate to his sons*.
– ORIGIN Old English *sorh*, *sorg* (noun), *sorgian* (verb), of Germanic origin; related to Dutch *zorg* and German *Sorge*.

sor·row·ful /ˈsärəfəl/ ▶ **adj.** feeling or showing grief: *she looked at him with sorrowful eyes*. ■ causing grief: *the sorrowful news of his father's death*.
– DERIVATIVES **sor·row·ful·ly** adv., **sor·row·ful·ness** n.
– ORIGIN Old English *sorhful* (see **SORROW**, **-FUL**).

sor·ry /ˈsärē, ˈsô-/ ▶ **adj.** (**sorrier**, **sorriest**) **1** [predic.] feeling distress, esp. through sympathy with someone else's misfortune: *I was sorry to hear about what happened to your family*. ■ (**sorry for**) filled with compassion for: *he couldn't help feeling sorry for her when he heard how she'd been treated*. ■ feeling regret or penitence: *he said he was sorry he had upset me* | *I'm sorry if I was a bit brusque*. ■ used as an expression of apology: *sorry—I was trying not to make a noise*. ■ used as a polite request that someone should repeat something that one has failed to hear or understand: *Sorry? In case I what?* **2** [attrib.] in a poor or pitiful state or condition: *he looks a sorry sight with his broken jaw*. ■ unpleasant and regrettable, esp. on account of incompetence or misbehavior: *we feel so ashamed that we keep quiet about the whole sorry business*.
– PHRASES **sorry for oneself** sad and self-pitying.
– DERIVATIVES **sor·ri·ly** /ˈsärəlē, ˈsô-/ adv., **sor·ri·ness** n.
– ORIGIN Old English *sārig* 'pained, distressed,' from the base of the noun **SORE**. The shortening of the root vowel has given the word an apparent connection with the unrelated **SORROW**.

sort /sôrt/ ▶ **n. 1** a category of things or people having some common feature; a type: *if only we knew the sort of people she was mixing with* | *a radical change poses **all sorts of** questions*. ■ [with adj.] informal a person of a specified character or nature: *Frank was a genuinely friendly sort*. ■ archaic a manner or way: *in law also the judge is **in a sort** superior to his king*. **2** Computing the arrangement of data in a prescribed sequence. **3** Printing a letter or piece in a font of type.
▶ **v.** [with obj.] **1** arrange systematically in groups; separate according to type, class, etc.: *she **sorted out** the clothes, some to be kept, some to be thrown away*. ■ (**sort through**) look at (a group of things) one after another in order to classify them or make a selection: *she sat down and sorted through her mail*. **2** resolve (a problem or difficulty): *the teacher helps the children to **sort out** their problems*. ■ resolve the problems or difficulties of (oneself): *I need time to sort myself out*.
– PHRASES **after a sort** dated after a fashion. **in some sort** to a certain extent: *I am in some sort indebted to you*. **nothing of the sort** used as an emphatic way of denying permission or refuting an earlier statement or assumption: *"I'll pay." "You'll do nothing of the sort."* **of a sort** (or **of sorts**) informal of an atypical and typically inferior type: *the training camp actually became a tourist attraction of sorts*. **out of sorts** slightly unwell: *feeling nauseous and generally out of sorts*. ■ in low spirits; irritable: *the trying events of the day had put him out of sorts*. **sort of** informal to some extent; in some way or other (used to convey inexactness or vagueness): *"Do you see what I mean?" "Sort of," answered Jean cautiously*. **the —— sort** the kind of person likely to do or be involved with the thing specified: *she'd never imagined Steve to be the marrying sort*.
– PHRASAL VERBS **sort someone out** informal deal with someone who is causing trouble, typically by restraining, reprimanding, or punishing them: *if he can't pay you, I'll sort him out*. **sort something out 1** separate something from a mixed group: *she started **sorting out** the lettuce **from** the spinach*. **2** arrange or organize something: *they are anxious to sort out traveling arrangements*.
– DERIVATIVES **sort·a·ble** adj., **sort·er** n.
– ORIGIN late Middle English: from Old French *sorte*, from an alteration of Latin *sors*, *sort-* 'lot, condition.'

> **USAGE** The construction **these sort of**, as in *I don't want to answer **these sort of** questions*, is technically ungrammatical because **these** is plural and needs to agree with a plural noun (**sorts**). The construction is undoubtedly common, however, and has been used for hundreds of years. There are some grammarians who analyze the construction differently, seeing the words "these sort of" as a single invariable unit. For more details, see usage at **KIND**[1].

sort·a /ˈsôrtə/ informal ▶ **contraction** sort of: *I did sorta like the movie*.

sor·tal /ˈsôrtl/ Linguistics & Philosophy ▶ **adj.** denoting or relating to a term representing a semantic feature that applies to an entity, classifying it as being of a particular kind.
▶ **n.** a term of this kind, for example *human* as opposed to *engineer*.

sor·ta·tion /sôrˈtāSHən/ ▶ **n.** (esp. in data processing) the process of sorting or its result.
– ORIGIN mid 19th cent.: from *sort* (verb) + *-ation*.

sort·ed /ˈsôrtid/ ▶ **adj.** Brit. informal organized; arranged; fixed up: *"And your social commitments?" "They're well sorted."* ■ (of a person) confident, organized, and emotionally well balanced: *a pretty sorted kind of fellow*.

sor·tes /ˈsôrˌtēz, -ˌtāz/ ▶ **plural n.** [treated as sing.] divination, or the seeking of guidance, by chance selection of a passage in the Bible or another text regarded as authoritative.
– ORIGIN Latin, 'chance selections (of the Bible).'

sort·ie /ˌsôrˈtē, ˈsôrtē/ ▶ **n.** an attack made by troops coming out from a position of defense. ■ an operational flight by a single military aircraft. ■ a short trip or journey: *an early-morning sortie into the garden of our hotel*. ■ an attempt to participate in a new activity or sphere: *this latest book is the author's first sortie into non-fiction*.
▶ **v.** (**sorties**, **sortieing**, **sortied**) [no obj.] come out from a defensive position to make an attack.
– ORIGIN late 18th cent.: from French, feminine past participle of *sortir* 'go out.'

sor·ti·lege /ˈsôrdl-ij/ ▶ **n.** chiefly historical the practice of foretelling the future from a card or other item drawn at random from a collection.
– ORIGIN late Middle English: via Old French from medieval Latin *sortilegium* 'sorcery,' from Latin *sortilegus* 'sorcerer,' from *sors*, *sort-* 'lot, chance' + *legere* 'choose.'

sor·ti·tion /sôrˈtiSHən/ ▶ **n.** the action of selecting or determining something by the casting or drawing of lots.
– ORIGIN late 16th cent.: from Latin *sortitio(n-)*, from *sortire* 'divide or obtain by lot.'

so·rus /ˈsôrəs/ ▶ **n.** (pl. **sori** /ˈsôrī/) Botany a cluster of spore-producing receptacles on the underside of a fern frond. ■ a gamete-producing or fruiting body in certain algae and fungi.
– ORIGIN mid 19th cent.: modern Latin, from Greek *sōros* 'heap.'

SOS ▶ **n.** (pl. **SOSs**) an international code signal of extreme distress, used esp. by ships at sea. ■ an urgent appeal for help. ■ Brit. a message broadcast to an untraceable person in an emergency: *here is an SOS message for Mr. Arthur Brown about his brother, who is dangerously ill*.
– ORIGIN early 20th cent.: letters chosen as being easily transmitted and recognized in Morse code; by folk etymology an abbreviation of *save our souls*.

Sos·no·wiec /sôsˈnôvyets/ an industrial mining town in southwestern Poland, west of Cracow; pop. 223,284 (2007).

so-so ▶ **adj.** neither very good nor very bad: *a happy ending to a so-so season* | *"How are you?" "So-so."*

sos·te·nu·to /ˌsästəˈnōōtō/ Music ▶ **adj.** (of a passage of music) to be played in a sustained or prolonged manner.
▶ **n.** (pl. **sostenutos**) a passage to be played in a sustained and prolonged manner. ■ performance in this manner.
– ORIGIN Italian, 'sustained.'

sot /sät/ ▶ **n.** a habitual drunkard.
▶ **v.** (**sots**, **sotting**, **sotted**) [no obj.] archaic drink habitually.
– DERIVATIVES **sot·tish** adj.
– ORIGIN late Old English *sott* 'foolish person,' from medieval Latin *sottus*, reinforced by Old French *sot* 'foolish.' The current sense of the noun dates from the late 16th cent.

so·te·ri·ol·o·gy /səˌti(ə)rēˈäləjē/ ▶ **n.** Theology the doctrine of salvation.
– DERIVATIVES **so·te·ri·o·log·i·cal** /-ēəˈläjikəl/ adj.
– ORIGIN mid 19th cent.: from Greek *sōtēria* 'salvation' + **-LOGY**.

So·thic /ˈsōTHik, ˈsä-/ ▶ **adj.** of or relating to Sirius (the Dog Star), esp. with reference to the ancient Egyptian year fixed by its heliacal rising.
– ORIGIN early 19th cent.: from Greek *Sōthis* (from an Egyptian name of the Dog Star) + **-IC**.

So·tho /ˈsōtō/ ▶ **n.** (pl. **same** or **Sothos**) **1** a member of a group of peoples living chiefly in Botswana, Lesotho, and northern South Africa. **2** the group of Bantu languages spoken by these peoples.
▶ **adj.** of or relating to this people or their languages.
– ORIGIN the stem of **BASOTHO** and **SESOTHO**.

so·tol /ˈsōˌtōl/ ▶ **n.** a North American desert plant of the agave family, with spiny-edged leaves and small white flowers. ● Genus *Dasylirion*, family Agavaceae: several species, including **smooth-leaf sotol** (*D. leiophyllum*). ■ an alcoholic drink made from the sap of this plant.
– ORIGIN late 19th cent.: via American Spanish from Nahuatl *tzotolli*.

So·to·ma·yor /sōtəˈmīyôr/, Sonia Maria (1954–), US Supreme Court associate justice 2009–. The Court's first Hispanic justice, she was appointed by President Obama.

sot·to vo·ce /ˈsätō ˈvōCHē/ ▶ **adv. & adj.** (of singing or a spoken remark) in a quiet voice, as if not to be overheard: [as adv.] *"It won't be cheap," he added sotto voce* | [as adj.] *a sotto voce remark*.
– ORIGIN from Italian *sotto* 'under' + *voce* 'voice.'

sou /sōō/ ▶ **n.** historical a former French coin of low value. ■ [usu. with negative] informal a very small amount of money: *he didn't have a sou*.
– ORIGIN French, originally as *sous* (plural), from Old French *sout*, from Latin *solidus* (see **SOLIDUS**).

sou' /sou/ ▶ **abbr.** (esp. in compounds) south: *the sou'west wind was quite a gale at times*.

sou·bise /sōōˈbēz/ ▶ **n.** a thick white sauce made with onion purée and often served with fish or eggs.
– ORIGIN named after Charles de Rohan *Soubise* (1715–87), French general and courtier.

sou·bre·saut /ˌsōōbrəˈsō/ ▶ **n.** (pl. pronunc. **same**) Ballet a straight-legged jump from both feet with the toes pointed and feet together, one behind the other.
– ORIGIN French.

sou·brette /sōōˈbret/ ▶ **n.** a minor female role in a comedy, typically that of a pert maidservant.
– ORIGIN mid 18th cent.: French, from Provençal *soubreto*, feminine of *soubret* 'coy,' from *sobrar*, from Latin *superare* 'be above.'

sou·bri·quet ▶ **n.** variant spelling of **SOBRIQUET**.

sou·chong /ˈsōōˈCHÔNG, ˈSHÔNG/ ▶ **n.** a fine black variety of China tea.
– ORIGIN mid 18th cent.: from Chinese *siú* 'small' + *chúng* 'sort.'

sou·cou·yant /ˌsōōkōōˈyän(t)/ ▶ **n.** (in eastern Caribbean folklore) a malignant witch believed to shed her skin by night and suck the blood of her victims.
– ORIGIN West Indian Creole.

souf·fle /ˈsōōfəl/ ▶ **n.** Medicine a low murmuring or blowing sound heard through a stethoscope.
– ORIGIN late 19th cent.: from French, from *souffler* 'to blow,' from Latin *sufflare*.

PRONUNCIATION KEY ə *ago*, *up*; ər *over*, *fur*; a *hat*; ā *ate*; ä *car*; e *let*; ē *see*; i *fit*; ī *by*; NG *sing*; ō *go*; ô *law*, *for*; oi *toy*; ŏŏ *good*; ōō *goo*; ou *out*; TH *thin*; TH *then*; ZH *vision*

souf·flé /so͞oˈflā/ ▶ **n.** a light, spongy baked dish made typically by adding flavored egg yolks to stiffly beaten egg whites. ■ any of various light dishes made with beaten egg whites.
– ORIGIN French, literally 'blown,' past participle of *souffler* (see SOUFFLE).

Sou·fri·ère /so͞oˈfrēer/ **1** a dormant volcano on the French island of Guadeloupe in the Caribbean Sea. Rising to 4,813 feet (1,468 m), it is the highest peak in the Lesser Antilles.
2 an active volcanic peak on the island of St. Vincent in the Caribbean. It rises to a height of 4,006 feet (1,234 m).
– ORIGIN French, from *soufre* 'sulfur.'

sough /səf, sou/ ▶ **v.** [no obj.] (of the wind in trees, the sea, etc.) make a moaning, whistling, or rushing sound.
▶ **n.** [in sing.] a sound of this type.
– ORIGIN Old English *swōgan*, of Germanic origin.

sought /sôt/ past and past participle of SEEK.

sought af·ter ▶ **adj.** in demand; generally desired: *this print will be much sought after by collectors | the most expensive and sought-after perfume.*

souk /so͞ok/ (also **suk**, **sukh**, or **suq**) ▶ **n.** an Arab market or marketplace; a bazaar.
– ORIGIN from Arabic *sūḳ*.

sou·kous /ˈso͞oˌko͞os/ ▶ **n.** a style of African popular music characterized by syncopated rhythms and intricate contrasting guitar melodies, originating in the Democratic Republic of the Congo (formerly Zaire).
– ORIGIN perhaps from French *secouer* 'to shake.'

soul /sōl/ ▶ **n. 1** the spiritual or immaterial part of a human being or animal, regarded as immortal. ■ a person's moral or emotional nature or sense of identity: *in the depths of her soul, she knew he would betray her.* ■ emotional or intellectual energy or intensity, esp. as revealed in a work of art or an artistic performance: *their interpretation lacked soul.*
2 the essence or embodiment of a specified quality: *he was* ***the soul of*** *discretion | brevity is the soul of wit.* ■ an individual person: *I'll never tell a soul.* ■ a person regarded with affection or pity: *she's a nice old soul.*
3 African-American culture or ethnic pride. ■ short for SOUL MUSIC.
– PHRASES **bare one's soul** see BARE. **the life and soul of the party** see LIFE. **lost soul** a soul that is damned. ■ chiefly humorous a person who seems unable to cope with everyday life. **sell one's soul (to the devil)** see SELL. **upon my soul** dated an exclamation of surprise.
– DERIVATIVES **souled** **adj.** [in combination] *she was a great-souled character.*
– ORIGIN Old English *sāwol*, *sāw(e)l*, of Germanic origin; related to Dutch *ziel* and German *Seele*.

soul broth·er ▶ **n.** US informal used as a term of address or reference between African-American men. ■ a man whose thoughts, feelings, and attitudes closely match those of another; a kindred spirit.

soul food ▶ **n.** traditional southern African-American food.

soul·ful /ˈsōlfəl/ ▶ **adj.** expressing or appearing to express deep and often sorrowful feeling: *she gave him a soulful glance.*
– DERIVATIVES **soul·ful·ly** **adv.**, **soul·ful·ness** **n.**

S

soul kiss ▶ **n.** another term for FRENCH KISS.

soul·less /ˈsōlˌlis/ ▶ **adj.** (of a building, room, or other place) lacking character and individuality: *she found the apartment beautiful but soulless.* ■ (of an activity) tedious and uninspiring: *soulless, nonproductive work.* ■ lacking or suggesting the lack of human feelings and qualities: *two soulless black eyes were watching her.*
– DERIVATIVES **soul·less·ly** **adv.**, **soul·less·ness** **n.**

soul mate (also **soulmate**) ▶ **n.** a person ideally suited to another as a close friend or romantic partner.

soul mu·sic ▶ **n.** a kind of music incorporating elements of rhythm and blues and gospel music, popularized by African-Americans. Characterized by an emphasis on vocals and an impassioned improvisatory delivery, it is associated with performers such as Marvin Gaye, Aretha Franklin, James Brown, and Otis Redding.

soul-search·ing ▶ **n.** deep and anxious consideration of one's emotions and motives or of the correctness of a course of action.
▶ **adj.** involving or expressing such consideration: *long, soul-searching conversations about religion.*

soul sis·ter ▶ **n.** US informal used as a term of address or reference between African-American women. ■ a woman whose thoughts, feelings, and attitudes closely match those of another; a kindred spirit.

soul·ster /ˈsōlstər/ ▶ **n.** informal a singer of soul music.

Sound /sound/ (**the Sound**) another name for ØRESUND.

sound[1] /sound/ ▶ **n. 1** vibrations that travel through the air or another medium and can be heard when they reach a person's or animal's ear: *light travels faster than sound.* ■ a group of vibrations of this kind; a thing that can be heard: *she heard the sound of voices in the hall | don't make a sound.* ■ the area or distance within which something can be heard: *we were always* ***within sound of*** *the train whistles.*
2 (also **musical sound**) sound produced by continuous and regular vibrations, as opposed to noise. ■ short for SPEECH SOUND.
3 music, speech, and sound effects when recorded, used to accompany a film or video production, or broadcast: [as modifier] *a sound studio.* ■ broadcasting by radio as distinct from television. ■ the distinctive quality of the music of a particular composer or performer or of the sound produced by a particular musical instrument: *the sound of the Beatles.* ■ (**sounds**) informal music, esp. popular music: *sounds of the sixties.*
4 the ideas or impressions conveyed by words: *you've had a hard day,* ***by the sound of it.***
▶ **v. 1** emit or cause to emit sound: [no obj.] *a loud buzzer sounded* | [with obj.] *she sounded the horn.* ■ [with obj.] give an audible signal to indicate (something): *a different bell begins to sound midnight.* ■ [with obj.] express or convey (a warning): *pharmaceutical companies are* ***sounding the alarm*** *about counterfeit drugs.* ■ [with obj.] test (the lungs or another body cavity) by noting the sound they produce: *the doctor sounded her chest.*
2 [no obj.] convey a specified impression when heard: [with complement] *he sounded worried.* ■ (of something or someone that has been described to one) convey a specified impression: ***it sounds as though*** *you really do believe that* | [with complement] *the house sounds lovely.*
– PHRASAL VERBS **sound off** express one's opinions in a loud or forceful manner.
– DERIVATIVES **sound·less** **adj.**, **sound·less·ly** **adv.**, **sound·less·ness** **n.**
– ORIGIN Middle English *soun*, from Anglo-Norman French *soun* (noun), *suner* (verb), from Latin *sonus*. The form with *-d* was established in the 16th cent.

sound[2] ▶ **adj. 1** in good condition; not damaged, injured, or diseased: *they returned* ***safe and sound*** | *he was not of sound mind.* ■ based on reason, sense, or judgment: *sound advice for healthy living | the scientific content is sound.* ■ competent, reliable, or holding acceptable views: *he's a bit stuffy, but he's very sound on his law.* ■ financially secure: *she could get her business on a sound footing for the first time.*
2 (of sleep) deep and undisturbed. ■ (of a person) tending to sleep deeply: *I am a sound sleeper.*
3 severe: *such people should be given a sound thrashing.*
▶ **adv.** soundly: *he was sound asleep.*
– PHRASES **(as) sound as a bell** in perfect condition.
– DERIVATIVES **sound·ly** **adv.**, **sound·ness** **n.**
– ORIGIN Middle English: from Old English *gesund*; related to Dutch *gezond* and German *gesund*.

sound[3] ▶ **v. 1** [with obj.] ascertain (the depth of water), typically by means of a line or pole or using sound echoes. ■ Medicine examine (a person's bladder or other internal cavity) with a long surgical probe.
2 [with obj.] question (someone), typically in a cautious or discreet way, as to their opinions or feelings on a subject: *we'll* ***sound out*** *our representatives first.* ■ inquire into (someone's opinions of feelings) in this way: *officials arrived to* ***sound out*** *public opinion at meetings in factories.*
3 [no obj.] (esp. of a whale) dive down steeply to a great depth.
▶ **n.** a long surgical probe, typically with a curved, blunt end.
– DERIVATIVES **sound·er** **n.**
– ORIGIN late Middle English: from Old French *sonder*, based on Latin *sub-* 'below' + *unda* 'wave.'

sound[4] ▶ **n.** a narrow stretch of water forming an inlet or connecting two wider areas of water such as two seas or a sea and a lake.
– ORIGIN Middle English: from Old Norse *sund* 'swimming, strait'; related to SWIM.

sound·a·like /ˈsoundəˌlīk/ ▶ **n.** a person or thing that closely resembles another in sound, esp. someone whose voice or style of speaking or singing is very similar to that of a famous person.

sound bar·ri·er ▶ **n.** (**the sound barrier**) the increased drag, reduced controllability, and other effects that occur when an aircraft approaches the speed of sound, formerly regarded as an obstacle to supersonic flight.

sound bite ▶ **n.** a short extract from a recorded interview, chosen for its pungency or appropriateness.

sound·board /ˈsoun(d)ˌbôrd/ (also **sounding board**) ▶ **n.** a thin sheet of wood over which the strings of a piano or similar instrument are positioned to increase the sound produced.

sound box (also **soundbox** /ˈsoun(d)ˌbäks/) ▶ **n.** the hollow chamber that forms the body of a stringed musical instrument and provides resonance.

sound card ▶ **n.** a device that can be slotted into a computer to allow the use of audio components for multimedia applications.

sound check (also **soundcheck** /ˈsoun(d)ˌCHek/) ▶ **n.** a test of sound equipment before a musical performance or recording to check that the desired sound is being produced.

sound con·di·tion·er ▶ **n.** a device designed to mask or block out undesirable sounds by generating white noise or some other continuous, unobtrusive sound.

sound ef·fect ▶ **n.** a sound other than speech or music made artificially for use in a play, movie, or other broadcast production: *the play used sound effects of galley oars and blood-curdling yells.*

sound en·gi·neer ▶ **n.** a technician dealing with acoustics for a broadcast or musical performance.

Sound·ex /ˈsoundeks/ ▶ **n.** Computing a phonetic coding system intended to suppress spelling variations, used esp. to encode surnames for the linkage of medical and other records.
– ORIGIN 1950s: from SOUND[1] + the arbitrary ending *-ex*.

sound hole ▶ **n.** an aperture in the belly of a stringed instrument.

sound·ing[1] /ˈsoundiNG/ ▶ **n. 1** the action or process of measuring the depth of the sea or other body of water. ■ a measurement taken by sounding. ■ the determination of any physical property at a depth in the sea or at a height in the atmosphere. ■ (**soundings**) archaic the area of sea close to the shore that is shallow enough for the bottom to be reached by means of a sounding line.
2 (**soundings**) information or evidence ascertained as a preliminary step before deciding on a course of action: *he's been* ***taking soundings*** *about the possibility of moving his offices.*

sound·ing[2] ▶ **adj.** [attrib.] archaic giving forth sound, esp. loud or resonant sound: *he went in with a sounding plunge.* ■ having an imposing sound but little substance: *the orator has been apt to deal in sounding commonplaces.*

sound·ing board ▶ **n. 1** a board or screen placed over or behind a pulpit or stage to reflect a speaker's voice forward. ■ another term for SOUNDBOARD.
2 a person or group whose reactions to suggested ideas are used as a test of their validity or likely success before they are made public: *I considered him mainly as a sounding board for my impressions.* ■ a channel through which ideas are disseminated.

sound·ing line ▶ **n.** a weighted line with distances marked off at regular intervals, used to measure the depth of water under a boat.

sound·ing rod ▶ **n.** a rod used to measure the depth of water under a boat or in a ship's hold or other container.

sound post ▶ **n.** a small wooden rod wedged between the front and back surfaces of a violin or similar instrument and modifying its vibrations.

sound pres·sure ▶ **n.** Physics the difference between the instantaneous pressure at a point in the presence of a sound wave and the static pressure of the medium.

sound·proof /ˈsoun(d)ˌpro͞of/ ▶ **adj.** preventing, or constructed of material that prevents, the passage of sound: *there was a soundproof, state-of-the-art recording studio.*
▶ **v.** [with obj.] make (a room or building) resistant to the passage of sound.
– DERIVATIVES **sound·proof·ing** **n.**

sound·scape /ˈsoun(d)ˌskāp/ ▶ **n.** a piece of music considered in terms of its component sounds: *his lush keyboard soundscapes.* ■ the sounds heard in a particular location, considered as a whole: *institutions concerned with the world soundscape as an ecologically balanced entity.*

sound shift ▶ **n.** Linguistics a systematic change in the pronunciation of a set of speech sounds as a language evolves.

sound spec·tro·graph ▶ **n.** an instrument for analyzing sound into its frequency components.

sound·stage /ˈsoun(d)ˌstāj/ (also **sound stage**) ▶ **n.** an area of a movie studio with acoustic properties suitable for the recording of sound, typically used to record dialogue.

sound sym·bol·ism ▶ **n.** the partial representation of the sense of a word by its sound, as in *bang*, *fizz*, and *slide*. See also ONOMATOPOEIA.

sound sys·tem ▶ **n.** a set of equipment for the reproduction and amplification of sound.

sound·track /ˈsoun(d)ˌtrak/ ▶ **n.** a recording of the musical accompaniment to a movie: *she has requested a collaboration for the soundtrack to her forthcoming movie.* ■ a strip on the edge of a film on which the sound component is recorded.
▶ **v.** [with obj.] provide (a movie) with a soundtrack: *it is soundtracked by the great Ennio Morricone.*

sound wave ▶ **n.** Physics a wave of compression and rarefaction, by which sound is propagated in an elastic medium such as air.

soup /so͞op/ ▶ **n. 1** a liquid dish, typically made by boiling meat, fish, or vegetables, etc., in stock or water: *a bowl of tomato soup.*
2 a substance or mixture perceived to resemble soup in appearance or consistency: *the waves and the water beyond have become a thick brown soup.* ■ informal the chemicals in which film is developed.
3 informal nitroglycerine or gelignite, esp. as used for safecracking.
– PHRASES **from soup to nuts** informal from beginning to end; completely: *I know all about that game from soup to nuts.* [from the courses of a dinner.] **in the soup** informal in trouble.
– PHRASAL VERBS **soup something up** informal increase the power and efficiency of an engine or other machine. ■ make something more elaborate or impressive: *we had to soup up the show for the new venue.* [1930s, perhaps influenced by SUPER-.]
– DERIVATIVES **soup·like** adj.
– ORIGIN Middle English: from Old French *soupe* 'sop, broth (poured on slices of bread),' from late Latin *suppa*, of Germanic origin.

soup and fish ▶ **n.** Brit. informal, dated men's evening dress.
– ORIGIN so named from the traditional first two courses of a formal dinner.

soup·çon /so͞opˈsôN/ ▶ **n.** [in sing.] a very small quantity of something: *a soupçon of mustard.*
– ORIGIN mid 18th cent.: French, from Old French *souspeçon*, from medieval Latin *suspectio* (see SUSPICION).

soup kitch·en ▶ **n.** a place where free food is served to those who are homeless or destitute.

soup plate ▶ **n.** a deep, wide-rimmed plate in which soup is served.

soup·spoon /ˈso͞opˌspo͞on/ (also **soup spoon**) ▶ **n.** a large spoon with a round bowl, used for eating soup.

soup·y /ˈso͞opē/ ▶ **adj.** (**soupier**, **soupiest**) having the appearance or consistency of soup: *a soupy stew.* ■ (of the air or climate) humid. ■ informal mawkishly sentimental: *soupy nostalgia.*
– DERIVATIVES **soup·i·ly** /ˈso͞opəlē/ adv., **soup·i·ness** n.

sour /ˈsou(ə)r/ ▶ **adj. 1** having an acid taste like lemon or vinegar: *she sampled the wine and found it was sour.* ■ (of food, esp. milk) spoiled because of fermentation. ■ having a rancid smell: *her breath was always sour.*
2 feeling or expressing resentment, disappointment, or anger: *she was quite a different woman from the sour, bored creature I had known.*
3 (of soil) deficient in lime and usually dank.
4 (of petroleum or natural gas) containing a relatively high sulfur content.
▶ **n.** [with modifier] a drink made by mixing an alcoholic beverage with lemon juice or lime juice: *a rum sour.*
▶ **v.** make or become sour: [with obj.] *water soured with tamarind* | (as adj. **soured**) *soured cream* | [no obj.] *a bowl of milk was souring in the sun.* ■ make or become unpleasant, acrimonious, or difficult: [with obj.] *a dispute soured relations between the two countries for over a year* | [no obj.] *many friendships have soured over borrowed money.*
– PHRASES **go** (or **turn**) **sour** become less pleasant or attractive; turn out badly: *the case concerns a property deal that turned sour.* **sour grapes** used to refer to an attitude in which someone adopts a negative attitude to something because they cannot have it themselves: *government officials dismissed many of the complaints as sour grapes.* [with allusion to Aesop's fable *The Fox and the Grapes*.]
– DERIVATIVES **sour·ish** adj., **sour·ly** adv., **sour·ness** n.
– ORIGIN Old English *sūr*, of Germanic origin; related to Dutch *zuur* and German *sauer*.

sour ball ▶ **n.** a hard candy, esp. a jawbreaker, with a sour flavor.

source /sôrs/ ▶ **n.** a place, person, or thing from which something comes or can be obtained: *mackerel is a good source of fish oil.* ■ a spring or fountainhead from which a river or stream issues: *the source of the Nile.* ■ a person who provides information: *military sources announced a reduction in strategic nuclear weapons.* ■ a book or document used to provide evidence in research. ■ technical a body or process by which energy or a particular component enters a system. The opposite of SINK[2]. ■ Electronics a part of a field-effect transistor from which carriers flow into the inter-electrode channel.
▶ **v.** [with obj.] obtain from a particular source: *each type of coffee is sourced from one country.* ■ find out where (something) can be obtained: *she was called upon to source a supply of carpet.*
– PHRASES **at source** chiefly Brit. at the point of origin or issue: *reduction of pollution at source.* ■ used to show that an amount is deducted from earnings or other payments before they are made: *your pension contribution will be deducted at source.*
– DERIVATIVES **source·less** adj.
– ORIGIN late Middle English: from Old French *sours(e)*, past participle of *sourdre* 'to rise,' from Latin *surgere*.

source·book /ˈsôrsˌbo͝ok/ ▶ **n.** a collection of writings and articles on a particular subject, esp. one used as a basic introduction to that subject.

source code ▶ **n.** Computing a text listing of commands to be compiled or assembled into an executable computer program.

source crit·i·cism ▶ **n.** the analysis and study of the sources used by biblical authors.

source pro·gram ▶ **n.** Computing a program written in a language other than machine code, typically a high-level language.

source rock ▶ **n.** Geology a rock from which later sediments are derived or in which a particular mineral originates. ■ a sediment containing sufficient organic matter to be a future source of hydrocarbons.

sour cher·ry ▶ **n.** a jawbreaker candy with a sour flavor.
▶ **n.** another term for MORELLO.

sour cream ▶ **n.** cream that has been deliberately fermented by the addition of certain bacteria.

sour·dough /ˈsou(ə)rˌdō/ ▶ **n. 1** leaven for making bread, consisting of fermenting dough, typically that left over from a previous batch. ■ bread made using such leaven.
2 an experienced prospector in the western US or Canada; an old-timer.

Sour·dough State a nickname for the state of ALASKA.

sour·gum /ˈsou(ə)rˌgəm/ (also **sour gum**) ▶ **n.** a tupelo of eastern North America, with dark bark that has a deeply checkered pattern. Its bitter blue fruits are eaten by black bears and numerous species of birds. Also called BLACK GUM, BLACK TUPELO, PEPPERIDGE. ● *Nyssa sylvatica*, family Nyssaceae.

sour mash ▶ **n.** a mash used in distilling certain malt whiskeys. ■ whiskey distilled from this.

sour·puss /ˈsou(ə)rˌpo͝os/ ▶ **n.** informal a bad-tempered or habitually sullen person.
– ORIGIN 1930s (originally US): from SOUR + PUSS[2].

sour·sop /ˈsou(ə)rˌsäp/ ▶ **n. 1** a large acidic fruit with white fibrous flesh.
2 the evergreen tropical American tree that bears this fruit. ● *Annona muricata*, family Annonaceae.

sour·wood /ˈsou(ə)rˌwo͝od/ ▶ **n.** a North American tree of the heath family with sour-tasting leaves. Most common in the southeastern US, it has drooping clusters of white bell-like flowers in early summer and bright red foliage in autumn. Also called SORREL TREE. ● *Oxydendrum arboreum*, family Ericaceae.

sous- ▶ **prefix** (in words adopted from French) subordinate: *sous-chef.*
– ORIGIN from French *sous* 'under.'

Sou·sa /ˈso͞ozə/, John Philip (1854–1932), US composer and conductor; known as the *March King*. His works include more than a hundred marches, for example *The Stars and Stripes Forever*, *King Cotton*, and *Hands Across the Sea*. The sousaphone, invented in 1898, was named in his honor.

sou·sa·phone /ˈso͞ozəˌfōn/ ▶ **n.** a form of tuba with a wide bell pointing forward above the player's head and circular coils resting on the player's left shoulder and right hip, used in marching bands.
– DERIVATIVES **sou·sa·phon·ist** /-ist/ n.
– ORIGIN 1920s: named after J. P. SOUSA, on the pattern of *saxophone*.

souse /sous/ ▶ **v.** [with obj.] soak in or drench with liquid: *souse the quilts in warm suds until thoroughly clean.*
▶ **n. 1** liquid, typically salted, used for pickling. ■ pickled food, esp. a pig's head.
2 informal a drunkard. ■ dated a drinking bout.
– ORIGIN late Middle English (as a noun denoting pickled meat): from Old French *sous* 'pickle,' of Germanic origin; related to SALT.

soused /soust/ ▶ **adj. 1** (of food, esp. fish) preserved in a pickling solution or a marinade: *soused herring.*
2 informal drunk: *I was soused to the eyeballs.*

sous·lik /ˈso͞oslik/ (also **suslik** /ˈsəsˌlik/) ▶ **n.** a short-tailed ground squirrel native to Eurasia and the Arctic. ● Genus *Spermophilus*, family Sciuridae: several species, in particular the **European souslik** (*S. citellus*).
– ORIGIN late 18th cent.: from Russian.

Sousse /so͞os/ (also **Susah**, **Susa** /ˈso͞ozə/) a port and resort on the east coast of Tunisia; pop. 173,000 (est. 2004).

sous vide /so͞o ˈvēd/ ▶ **n.** a method of treating food by partial cooking followed by vacuum-sealing and chilling.
▶ **adj. & adv.** (of food or cooking) involving such preparation: [as adj.] *a convection oven can be used in sous vide operations* | [as adv.] *cooking cuisine sous vide.*
– ORIGIN French, literally 'under vacuum.'

sou·tache /so͞oˈtaSH/ ▶ **n.** a narrow, flat, ornamental braid used to trim garments.
– ORIGIN mid 19th cent.: from French, from Hungarian *sujtás*.

sou·tane /so͞oˈtän/ ▶ **n.** a type of cassock worn by Roman Catholic priests.
– ORIGIN mid 19th cent.: from French, from Italian *sottana*, from *sotto* 'under,' from Latin *subtus*.

sou·te·neur /ˌso͞otnˈər/ ▶ **n.** a pimp.
– ORIGIN French, literally 'protector.'

Sou·ter /ˈso͞otər/, David (Hackett) (1939–), US Supreme Court associate justice 1990–2009. Considered a moderate conservative, he worked for the justice system in New Hampshire 1971–90 before being appointed to the Supreme Court by President George H. W. Bush.

sou·ter /ˈso͞otər/ (also **soutar**) ▶ **n.** Scottish & N. English a shoemaker.
– ORIGIN Old English *sūtere*, from Latin *sutor*, from *suere* 'sew.'

South /souTH/ (**the South**) in the US, a term with several definitions, most commonly the 11 states of the 1861–65 Confederacy: Alabama, Arkansas, Florida, Georgia, Louisiana, Mississippi, North Carolina, South Carolina, Tennessee, Texas, and Virginia.
– DERIVATIVES **South·ern** adj.

south /souTH/ ▶ **n.** (usu. **the south**) **1** the direction toward the point of the horizon 90° clockwise from east, or the point on the horizon itself: *the breeze came from the south* | *they trade with the countries to the south.* ■ the compass point corresponding to this.
2 the southern part of the world or of a specified country, region, or town: *he was staying in the south of France.* ■ (usu. **the South**) the southern states of the US.
3 [as name] (**South**) Bridge the player sitting opposite and partnering North.
▶ **adj.** [attrib.] **1** lying toward, near, or facing the south: *the south coast.* ■ (of a wind) blowing from the south.
2 of or denoting the southern part of a specified area, city, or country or its inhabitants: *Telegraph Hill in South Boston.*
▶ **adv. 1** to or toward the south: *they journeyed south along the valley* | *it is handily located ten miles south of Baltimore.*
2 (**south of**) below (a particular amount, cost, etc.): *media spending last year was south of $1 million.*
▶ **v.** [no obj.] move toward the south: *the wind southed a point or two.* ■ (of a celestial body) cross the meridian.
– PHRASES **down south** informal to or in the south of a country. **go south** informal fall in value, deteriorate, or fail. **south by east** (or **west**) between south and south-southeast (or south-southwest).
– ORIGIN Old English *sūth*, of Germanic origin; related to Low German *sud*.

South Af·ri·ca a country that occupies the most southern part of Africa; pop. 49,052,500 (est. 2009); administrative capital, Pretoria; legislative capital, Cape Town; judicial capital, Bloemfontein; languages, English, Afrikaans, Zulu, Xhosa, and others.

> Settled by the Dutch in the 17th century, the area of the cape came under British administration in 1806. There followed inland expansion and British dominance of local populations, culminating in victory in the Zulu and Boer Wars at the end of the 19th century. The colonies of Natal, the Cape, Transvaal, and Orange Free State joined to form the self-governing Union of South Africa in 1910. In 1961 South Africa became a republic and left the Commonwealth of Nations. From 1948, it pursued a policy of white minority rule (apartheid), which led to international diplomatic isolation. A gradual dismantling of apartheid began in 1990 following the release of the African National Congress leader Nelson Mandela. Majority rule was achieved after the country's first

S

democratic elections in April 1994, won by the ANC. South Africa rejoined the Commonwealth in 1994.

– DERIVATIVES **South Af·ri·can** adj. & n.

South Af·ri·can Dutch ▶ n. the Afrikaans language from the 17th to the 19th centuries, during its development from Dutch.

South A·mer·i·ca a continent that comprises the southern half of the American landmass, connected to North America by the Isthmus of Panama. It includes the Falkland Islands, the Galapagos Islands, and Tierra del Fuego. See also AMERICA.

– DERIVATIVES **South A·mer·i·can** adj. & n.

South·amp·ton /souTH'(h)am(p)tən/ **1** an industrial city and seaport on the southern coast of England; pop. 234,800 (est. 2009).
2 a resort and residential town in southeastern New York, at the eastern end of Long Island; pop. 61,290 (est. 2008).

South A·sia the southern part of Asia, in particular India, Pakistan, Bangladesh, Nepal, and Sri Lanka.

– DERIVATIVES **South A·sian** adj. & n.

South At·lan·tic O·cean see ATLANTIC OCEAN.

South Aus·tral·ia a state in south central Australia; capital, Adelaide.

South·a·ven /'sou,THāvən/ a city in northeastern Mississippi, just south of the Tennessee border and of Memphis in Tennessee; pop. 44,076 (est. 2008).

South Bend an industrial city in northern Indiana; pop. 103,807 (est. 2008). The University of Notre Dame is nearby to the north.

South Bos·ton a residential district of eastern Boston in Massachusetts, noted for its Irish working-class community. Familiarly, ***Southie***.

south·bound /'souTH,bound/ ▶ adj. traveling or leading toward the south: *southbound traffic | the southbound two-lane road.*

South Car·o·li·na /,karə'līnə/ a state in the southeastern US, on the coast of the Atlantic Ocean; pop. 4,479,800 (est. 2008); capital, Columbia; statehood, May 23, 1788 (8). The region was permanently settled by the English from 1663. Separated from North Carolina in 1729, it became one of the original thirteen states. In 1860, it was the first state to secede from the Union, precipitating the Civil War.

– DERIVATIVES **South Car·o·lin·i·an** n. & adj.

South Chi·na Sea see CHINA SEA.

South Da·ko·ta a state in the northern central US; pop. 804,194 (est. 2008); capital, Pierre; statehood, Nov. 2, 1889 (40). Acquired partly by the Louisiana Purchase in 1803, it became a part of the former Dakota Territory in 1861. The scene of a gold rush in 1874, it separated from North Dakota in 1889.

– DERIVATIVES **South Da·ko·tan** n. & adj.

South·down /'souTH,doun/ ▶ n. a sheep of a breed raised esp. for mutton, originally on the South Downs of southern England.

south·east /,souTH'ēst/ ▶ n. **1** (usu. **the southeast**) the direction toward the point of the horizon midway between south and east, or the point on the horizon itself: *a ship was coming in from the southeast.* ■ the compass point corresponding to this.
2 (also **the Southeast**) the southeastern part of a country, region, or town: *most "Mexican" foods in the southeast are actually Texan.*
▶ adj. [attrib.] **1** lying toward, near, or facing the southeast: *a table stood in the southeast corner.* ■ (of a wind) blowing from the southeast.
2 of or denoting the southeastern part of a specified country, region, or town or its inhabitants: *Southeast Asia.*
▶ adv. to or toward the southeast: *turn southeast to return to your starting point.*

– DERIVATIVES **south·east·ern** /-ərn/ adj.

South·east A·sia the part of southeastern Asia that includes the countries of Cambodia, Indonesia, Laos, Malaysia, Burma (Myanmar), Philippines, Singapore, Thailand, and Vietnam.

South East A·sia Trea·ty Or·gan·i·za·tion (abbr.: **SEATO**) a defense alliance that existed between 1954 and 1977 for countries of Southeast Asia and part of the southwestern Pacific, to further a US policy of containing communism. Its members were Australia, Britain, France, New Zealand, Pakistan, the Philippines, Thailand, and the US.

south·east·er /,souTH'ēstər/ ▶ n. a wind blowing from the southeast.

south·east·er·ly /,souTH'ēstərlē/ ▶ adj. & adv. another term for SOUTHEAST: [as adj.] *southeasterly winds* | [as adv.] *the route turns southeasterly.*
▶ n. another term for SOUTHEASTER.

south·east·ward /,souTH'ēstwərd/ ▶ adv. (also **southeastwards**) toward the southeast: *he walked southeastward from the river.*
▶ adj. situated in, directed toward, or facing the southeast.

South E·qua·to·ri·al Cur·rent an ocean current that flows west across the Pacific Ocean just south of the equator.

south·er·ly /'səTHərlē/ ▶ adj. & adv. in a southward position or direction: [as adj.] *the most southerly of the Greek islands* | [as adv.] *they made off southerly.* ■ (of a wind) blowing from the south: [as adj.] *a southerly gale* | [as adv.] *the wind had backed southerly.*
▶ n. (often **southerlies**) a wind blowing from the south.

south·ern /'səTHərn/ ▶ adj. **1** [attrib.] situated in the south or directed toward or facing the south: *the southern hemisphere.* ■ (of a wind) blowing from the south.
2 living in or originating from the south: *the southern rural poor.* ■ of, relating to, or characteristic of the south or its inhabitants: *a faintly southern accent.*

– DERIVATIVES **south·ern·most** /-,mōst/ adj.

– ORIGIN Old English *sūtherne* (see SOUTH, -ERN).

South·ern Alps a mountain range on South Island, New Zealand. Running roughly parallel to the west coast, it extends for almost the entire length of the island. Mount Cook, its highest peak, rises to 12,349 feet (3,764 m).

South·ern Bap·tist ▶ n. a member of a large convention of Baptist churches established in the US in 1845, typically having a fundamentalist and evangelistic approach to Christianity.

South·ern blot ▶ n. Biology a procedure for identifying specific sequences of DNA, in which fragments separated on a gel are transferred directly to a second medium on which detection by hybridization may be carried out.

– ORIGIN late 20th cent.: named after Edwin M. *Southern* (born 1938), British biochemist.

South·ern Cone ▶ n. the region of South America comprising the countries of Brazil, Paraguay, Uruguay, Argentina, and Chile.

South·ern Cross Astronomy the smallest constellation (the Crux or Cross), but the most familiar one to observers in the southern hemisphere. It contains the bright star Acrux, the "Jewel Box" star cluster, and most of the Coalsack nebula.

south·ern·er /'səTHərnər/ (also **Southerner**) ▶ n. a native or inhabitant of the south, esp. of the southern US.

south·ern-fried ▶ adj. (of food, esp. chicken) coated in flour, egg, and breadcrumbs and then deep-fried.

south·ern hem·i·sphere the half of the earth that is south of the equator.

South·ern Lights another name for the aurora australis. See AURORA.

South·ern O·cean the sea surrounding Antarctica. It consists of parts of the southern Atlantic, Pacific, and Indian oceans. Also called ANTARCTIC OCEAN.

South·ern Pines a resort town in south central North Carolina, noted for its golf courses; pop. 12,675 (est. 2008).

South·ern Rho·de·sia see ZIMBABWE.

south·ern·wood /'səTHərn,wo͝od/ ▶ n. a bushy artemisia native to southern Europe. Also called LAD'S LOVE, OLD MAN. ● *Artemisia abrotanum*, family Compositae.

Sou·they /'souTHē, 'səTHē/, Robert (1774–1843), English poet. Associated with the Lake Poets, he was best known for his shorter poems, such as the "Battle of Blenheim" (1798). He was made England's poet laureate in 1813.

South·field /'souTH'fēld/ a residential and industrial city in southeastern Michigan, northwest of Detroit; pop. 75,392 (est. 2008).

South Gate an industrial city in southwestern California, southeast of Los Angeles; pop. 96,640 (est. 2008).

South Geor·gia a British overseas territory in the South Atlantic Ocean, a barren island situated 700 miles (1,120 km) east of the Falkland Islands. It was first explored in 1775 by Captain James Cook, who named the island after George III.

South Had·ley /'hadlē/ a town in western Massachusetts, on the Connecticut River, north of Springfield, home to Mount Holyoke College; pop. 17,241 (est. 2008).

south·ing /'souTHiNG/ ▶ n. distance traveled or measured southward, esp. at sea. ■ a figure or line representing southward distance on a map. ■ Astronomy the transit of a celestial object, esp. the sun, across the meridian due south of the observer. ■ Astronomy the angular distance of a star or other object south of the celestial equator.

South Is·land the larger and more southern of the two main islands of New Zealand, separated from North Island by Cook Strait.

South Jor·dan a city in northern Utah, a southern suburb of Salt Lake City; pop. 51,131 (est. 2008).

South Kings·town /'kiNGstən, 'kiNGz,toun/ a town in southern Rhode Island; pop. 29,082 (est. 2008).

South Ko·re·a a country in East Asia, occupying the southern part of the peninsula of Korea; pop. 48,509,000 (est. 2009); official language, Korean; capital, Seoul. Official name KOREA, REPUBLIC OF.

South Korea was formed in 1948 when Korea was partitioned along the 38th parallel; the Korean War (1950–53) was followed by decades of hostility between North and South Korea, but a summit meeting of the two leaders was held in 2000. An emerging industrial power, South Korea has had one of the world's fastest-growing economies since the 1960s.

– DERIVATIVES **South Ko·re·an** adj. & n.

South Ork·ney Is·lands a group of uninhabited islands in the South Atlantic Ocean, northeast of the Antarctic Peninsula. Discovered in 1821, they are administered as part of the British Antarctic Territory.

South Os·se·ti·a an autonomous region of Georgia, situated in the Caucasus on the border with Russia; capital, Tskhinvali. See also OSSETIA.

South Pass a valley in the Wind River Mountains of southwestern Wyoming that was a major route for settlers moving west through the Rocky Mountains during the 19th century.

south·paw /'souTH,pô/ ▶ n. a left-handed person, esp. a boxer who leads with the right hand or a baseball pitcher.

– ORIGIN mid 19th cent. (denoting the left hand or a punch with the left hand): the usage in baseball is perhaps from the orientation of early baseball fields to the same points of the compass, such that the pitcher's left arm was on the "south" side of his body.

South Platte Riv·er a river that flows for 425 miles (685 km) from the Rocky Mountains in Colorado through Denver and across Colorado to Nebraska, where it joins the North Platte River to form the Platte River.

South Pole ▶ n. see POLE[2].

South Port·land a city in southern Maine, a southwestern suburb of Portland; pop. 23,803 (est. 2008).

South Sand·wich Is·lands a group of uninhabited volcanic islands in the South Atlantic Ocean, 300 miles (480 km) southeast of South Georgia. They are administered from the Falkland Islands.

South Sea (also **South Seas**) archaic the southern Pacific Ocean.

South Sea Bub·ble a speculative boom in the shares of the South Sea Company in 1720 that ended with the failure of the company and a general financial collapse.

South Shet·land Is·lands a group of uninhabited islands in the South Atlantic Ocean, north of the Antarctic Peninsula. Discovered in 1819, they are administered as part of the British Antarctic Territory.

south-south·east ▶ n. the compass point or direction midway between south and southeast.

south-south·west ▶ n. the compass point or direction midway between south and southwest.

South Uist see UIST.

south·ward /'souTHwərd/ ▶ adj. in a southerly direction: *employment and people began a southward drift.*
▶ adv. (also **southwards**) toward the south: *he took a train that carried him southward.*
▶ n. (**the southward**) the direction or region to the south: *cool air from the ocean to the southward.*

– DERIVATIVES **south·ward·ly** adv.

south·west /,souTH'west/ ▶ n. **1** (usu. **the southwest**) the direction toward the point of the horizon midway between south and west, or the point of the horizon itself: *clouds uncoiled from the southwest.* ■ the compass point corresponding to this.
2 the southwestern part of a country, region, or town: *the beach is in the southwest of the island.* ■ (usu. **the Southwest**) the southwestern part of the US: *the desert turtle population in the Southwest.*
▶ adj. [attrib.] **1** lying toward, near, or facing the southwest: *the southwest tower collapsed in a storm.* ■ (of a wind) blowing from the southwest.

2 of or denoting the southwestern part of a specified country, region, or town or its inhabitants: *fishing in southwest Alaska's Bristol Bay area.*
▶ **adv.** to or toward the southwest: *they drove directly southwest.*
– DERIVATIVES **south·west·ern** /-ərn/ **adj.**

South West Af·ri·ca former name of **NAMIBIA.**

South West Af·ri·ca Peo·ple's Or·gan·i·za·tion (abbr.: **SWAPO**) a nationalist organization formed in Namibia in 1964–66 to oppose the illegitimate South African rule over the region. It waged a guerrilla campaign, operating largely from Angola; it eventually gained UN recognition, and won elections in 1989.

south·west·er /ˌsouTH'westər/ ▶ **n.** a wind blowing from the southwest.

south·west·er·ly /ˌsouTH'westərlē/ ▶ **adj. & adv.** another term for **SOUTHWEST.**
▶ **n.** another term for **SOUTHWESTER.**

south·west·ward /ˌsouTH'westwərd/ ▶ **adv.** (also **southwestwards**) toward the southwest: *the governor sent two companies of foot soldiers southwestward.*
▶ **adj.** situated in, directed toward, or facing the southwest: *the southwestward extension of the valley.*

Sou·tine /sōō'tēn/, Chaim (1893–1943), French painter, born in Lithuania. A major exponent of expressionism, his early pictures were of grotesque figures, while his later pictures tended to be still lifes.

sou·ve·nir /ˌsōōvə'ni(ə)r/ ▶ **n.** a thing that is kept as a reminder of a person, place, or event.
▶ **v.** [with obj.] informal take as a memento: *many parts of the aircraft have been souvenired.*
– ORIGIN late 18th cent.: from French, from *souvenir* 'remember,' from Latin *subvenire* 'occur to the mind.'

souv·la·ki /sōōv'läkē/ ▶ **n.** (pl. **souvlakia** /-'läkyä/ or **souvlakis**) a Greek dish of pieces of meat grilled on a skewer: *a generous plate of souvlaki | souvlakia in pita.*
– ORIGIN modern Greek.

sou'·west·er /ˌsou'westər/ ▶ **n.** a waterproof hat with a broad flap covering the neck.

sou'wester

sov·er·eign /'säv(ə)rən/ ▶ **n. 1** a supreme ruler, esp. a monarch.
2 a former British gold coin worth one pound sterling, now only minted for commemorative purposes.
▶ **adj.** possessing supreme or ultimate power: *in modern democracies the people's will is in theory sovereign.* ■ [attrib.] (of a nation or its affairs) acting or done independently and without outside interference: *a sovereign, democratic republic | accusations of interference in sovereign affairs.* ■ [attrib.] archaic or literary possessing royal power and status: *our most sovereign lord the King.* ■ [attrib.] dated very good or effective: *a sovereign remedy for all ills.*
– DERIVATIVES **sov·er·eign·ly** adv.
– ORIGIN Middle English: from Old French *soverain,* based on Latin *super* 'above.' The change in the ending was due to association with **REIGN.**

sov·er·eign pon·tiff ▶ **n.** see **PONTIFF.**

sov·er·eign·tist /'säv(ə)rənˌtist/ ▶ **n.** Canadian a person who supports Quebec's right to self-government or full independence.

sov·er·eign·ty /'säv(ə)rəntē/ ▶ **n.** (pl. **sovereignties**) supreme power or authority: *how can we hope to wrest sovereignty away from the oligarchy and back to the people?* ■ the authority of a state to govern itself or another state: *national sovereignty.* ■ a self-governing state.
– ORIGIN late Middle English: from Old French *sovereinete,* from *soverain* (see **SOVEREIGN**).

sov·er·eign wealth fund (abbr.: **SWF**) ▶ **n.** a government-owned investment fund.

so·vi·et /'sōvēit, -ˌet/ ▶ **n. 1** an elected local, district, or national council in the former Soviet Union. ■ a revolutionary council of workers or peasants in Russia before 1917.
2 (**Soviet**) a citizen of the former Soviet Union.
▶ **adj.** (**Soviet**) of or concerning the former Soviet Union.
– DERIVATIVES **So·vi·et·i·za·tion** /ˌsōvēiti'zāSHən/ **n.,** **So·vi·et·ize** /-ˌtīz/ **v.**
– ORIGIN early 20th cent.: from Russian *sovet* 'council.'

So·vi·et·ol·o·gist /ˌsōvēi'täləjist/ ▶ **n.** a person who studies the former Soviet Union.
– DERIVATIVES **So·vi·et·o·log·i·cal** /-tə'läjikəl/ **adj.,** **So·vi·et·ol·o·gy** /-jē/ **n.**

So·vi·et Un·ion a former federation of communist republics that occupied the northern half of Asia and part of eastern Europe; capital, Moscow. Created from the Russian empire in the aftermath of the 1917 Russian Revolution, the Soviet Union was the largest country in the world. After World War II, it emerged as a superpower that rivaled the US and led to the Cold War. After decades of repression and economic failure, the Soviet Union was formally dissolved in 1991. Some of its constituents joined a looser confederation, the Commonwealth of Independent States. Full name **UNION OF SOVIET SOCIALIST REPUBLICS.**

sov·khoz /'sävˌkôz/ ▶ **n.** (pl. **same, sovkhozes,** or **sovkhozy** /-ˌkôzē/) a state-owned farm in the former Soviet Union.
– ORIGIN Russian, from *sov(etskoe) khoz(yaĭstvo)* 'Soviet farm.'

sow¹ /sō/ ▶ **v.** (past **sowed**; past participle **sown** /sōn/ or **sowed**) [with obj.] plant (seed) by scattering it on or in the earth: *sow a thin layer of seeds on top.* ■ plant the seeds of (a plant or crop): *the corn had just been sown.* ■ plant (a piece of land) with seed: *the field used to be sown with oats.* ■ (**be sown with**) be thickly covered with: *we walked through a valley sown with boulders.* ■ cause to appear or spread: *the new policy has sown confusion and doubt.*
– PHRASES **sow the seeds** (or **seed**) **of** do something that will eventually bring about (a particular result, esp. a disastrous one): *the seeds of dissension had been sown.*
– DERIVATIVES **sow·er n.**
– ORIGIN Old English *sāwan,* of Germanic origin; related to Dutch *zaaien* and German *säen.*

sow² /sou/ ▶ **n. 1** an adult female pig, esp. one that has farrowed. ■ the female of certain other mammals, e.g., the guinea pig.
2 a large block of metal (larger than a "pig") made by smelting.
– ORIGIN Old English *sugu;* related to Dutch *zeug,* German *Sau,* from an Indo-European root shared by Latin *sus* and Greek *hus* 'pig.'

sow·back /'souˌbak/ ▶ **n.** a low ridge of sand.

sow·bug /'souˌbəg/ (also **sow bug**) ▶ **n.** another term for **WOOD LOUSE.**

So·we·to /sə'wetō, -'wātō/ a large urban area, consisting of several townships, in South Africa, southwest of Johannesburg. In 1976, demonstrations against the compulsory use of Afrikaans in schools resulted in violent police activity and the deaths of hundreds of people.
– DERIVATIVES **So·we·tan** /-'wetn, -'wātn/ **n. & adj.**
– ORIGIN from *So(uth) We(stern) To(wnships).*

sown /sōn/ past participle of **SOW¹.**

sow this·tle /'sou ˌTHisəl/ ▶ **n.** a Eurasian plant with yellow flowers, thistlelike leaves, and milky sap. Also called **MILK THISTLE.** ● Genus *Sonchus,* family Compositae.

sox /säks/ ▶ **n.** nonstandard plural spelling of **SOCK** (sense 1 of the noun).

Soxh·let /'säkslət/ ▶ **n.** [as modifier] Chemistry denoting a form of condensing apparatus used for the continuous solvent extraction of a solid.
– ORIGIN late 19th cent.: named after Franz *Soxhlet* (1848–1926), Belgian chemist.

soy /soi/ ▶ **n.** another term for **SOYBEAN.**
– ORIGIN from Japanese *shō-yu,* from Chinese *shi-yu,* from *shi* 'salted beans' + *yu* 'oil.'

soy·a /'soiə/ (also **soya bean**) ▶ **n.** British term for **SOY** or **SOYBEAN.**
– ORIGIN late 17th cent.: from Dutch *soja,* from Malay *soi* (see **SOY**).

soy·bean /'soiˌbēn/ ▶ **n.** a leguminous plant native to Asia, *Glycine max,* widely cultivated for its edible seeds. ■ the fruit of this plant, used in a variety of foods and fodder, esp. as a replacement for animal protein.

So·yin·ka /soi'iNGkə/, Wole (1934–), Nigerian playwright, novelist, and critic; full name *Akinwande Oluwole Soyinka.* His writing often uses satire to explore the contrast between traditional and modern society in Africa. Notable works: *The Lion and the Jewel* (1959) and *The Interpreters* (1965). Nobel Prize for Literature (1986).

soy·meal /'soiˌmēl/ ▶ **n.** a high-protein foodstuff made by cracking, heating, flaking, cooking, and grinding soybeans. It is used in livestock feeds and as a raw ingredient in some processed foods. Also called **soybean meal.**

soy milk (also **soybean milk**) ▶ **n.** the liquid obtained by suspending soybean flour in water, used as a fat-free substitute for milk, particularly by vegans and by those unable to tolerate milk products.

soy sauce (also chiefly Brit. **soya sauce**) ▶ **n.** a sauce made with fermented soybeans, used in Chinese and Japanese cooking.

So·yuz /'sôˌyōōz/ a series of manned Soviet orbiting spacecraft, used to investigate the operation of orbiting space stations.
– ORIGIN from Russian *Soyúz,* literally 'union.'

soz·zled /'säzəld/ ▶ **adj.** informal very drunk: *Uncle Brian's sozzled!*
– ORIGIN late 19th cent.: past participle of dialect *sozzle* 'mix sloppily,' probably of imitative origin.

SP ▶ **abbr.** ■ starting price. ■ service pack (usually followed by a number): *Windows 2000 SP3 and SP4.*

Sp. ▶ **abbr.** ■ Spain. ■ Spaniard. ■ (also **Sp**) Spanish.

sp. ▶ **abbr.** species (usually singular).

s.p. ▶ **abbr.** without issue; childless. [from Latin *sine prole.*]

Spa /spä/ a small town in eastern Belgium, southeast of Liège; pop. 10,549 (2008). It has been celebrated since medieval times for the curative properties of its mineral springs.

spa /spä/ ▶ **n.** a mineral spring considered to have health-giving properties. ■ a place or resort with such a spring. ■ a commercial establishment offering health and beauty treatment through such means as steam baths, exercise equipment, and massage. ■ a bath or small pool containing hot aerated water.
– ORIGIN early 17th cent.: from **SPA.**

Spaatz /späts/, Carl (1891–1974), US Air Force officer; born *Carl Andrew Spatz.* He directed the US bombing force in Germany in 1944 and in Japan in 1945, including the dropping of atomic bombs on Hiroshima and Nagasaki. In 1947–48, he served as the first chief of staff of the newly independent US Air Force.

space /spās/ ▶ **n. 1** a continuous area or expanse that is free, available, or unoccupied: *a table took up much of the space | we shall all be living together in a small space | the space between a wall and a utility pipe | he backed out of the parking space.* ■ an area of land that is not occupied by buildings: *she had a love of open spaces.* ■ a blank between printed, typed, or written words, characters, numbers, etc. ■ Music each of the four gaps between the five lines of a staff. ■ an interval of time (often used to suggest that the time is short, considering what has happened or been achieved in it): *both their cars were stolen in the space of three days.* ■ pages in a newspaper, or time between television or radio programs, available for advertising. ■ (also **commercial space**) an area rented or sold as business premises. ■ the amount of paper used or needed to write about a subject: *there is no space to give further details.* ■ the freedom and scope to live, think, and develop in a way that suits one: *a teenager needing her own space.* ■ Telecommunications one of two possible states of a signal in certain systems. The opposite of **MARK¹** (sense 2 of the noun).
2 the dimensions of height, depth, and width within which all things exist and move: *the work gives the sense of a journey in space and time.* ■ (also **outer space**) the physical universe beyond the earth's atmosphere. ■ the near vacuum extending between the planets and stars, containing small amounts of gas and dust. ■ Mathematics a mathematical concept generally regarded as a set of points having some specified structure.
▶ **v. 1** [with obj.] (usu. **be spaced**) position (two or more items) at a distance from one another: *the houses are spaced out.* ■ (in printing or writing) put blanks between (words, letters, or lines): (as noun **spacing**) *the default setting is single line spacing.*
2 (usu. **be spaced out** or **space out**) informal be or become distracted, euphoric, or disoriented, esp. from taking drugs; cease to be aware of one's surroundings: *I was so tired that I began to feel totally spaced out | I kind of space out for a few minutes.*
– PHRASES **watch this space** informal further developments are expected and more information will be given later.
– DERIVATIVES **spac·er n.**
– ORIGIN Middle English: shortening of Old French *espace,* from Latin *spatium.* Current verb senses date from the late 17th cent.

space age ▶ **n.** (**the space age** or **the Space Age**) the era starting when the exploration of space became possible: *as the Space Age evolved, massive amounts of data gushed in.*
▶ **adj.** (**space-age**) very modern; technologically advanced: *a space-age control room.*

space bar ▶ **n.** a long key on a typewriter or computer keyboard for making a space between words.

S

space blan·ket ▶ **n.** a light metal-coated sheet designed to retain heat.

space ca·det ▶ **n.** a trainee astronaut. ■ an enthusiast for space travel, typically a young person. ■ informal a person perceived as out of touch with reality, as though high on drugs.

space cap·sule ▶ **n.** a small spacecraft or the part of a larger one that contains the instruments or crew.

space charge ▶ **n.** Physics a collection of particles with a net electric charge occupying a region, either in free space or in a device.

space·craft /ˈspāsˌkraft/ ▶ **n.** (pl. **same** or **spacecrafts**) a vehicle used for traveling in space.

space den·si·ty ▶ **n.** Astronomy the frequency of occurrence of stars, particles, or other heavenly bodies, per specified volume of space.

space·far·ing /ˈspāsˌfe(ə)riNG/ ▶ **n.** the action or activity of traveling in space: *the complications in spacefaring* | [as modifier] *spacefaring nations are racing to develop new technologies.*
– DERIVATIVES **space·far·er** /-rer/ **n.**

space flight ▶ **n.** a journey through space: *the 30th anniversary of the first space flight.* ■ space travel: *the stresses involved in space flight.*

space frame ▶ **n.** a three-dimensional structural framework that is designed to behave as an integral unit and to withstand loads applied at any point.

space heat·er ▶ **n.** a self-contained appliance, usually electric, for heating an enclosed room.
– DERIVATIVES **space-heat·ed adj.**, **space heat·ing n.**

space lat·tice /ˈlatis/ ▶ **n.** Crystallography a regular, indefinitely repeated array of points in three dimensions in which the points lie at the intersections of three sets of parallel equidistant planes.

space·man /ˈspāsˌman, -mən/ ▶ **n.** (pl. **spacemen**) a male astronaut.

space op·er·a ▶ **n.** informal a novel, movie, or television program set in outer space, typically of a simplistic and melodramatic nature.

space·plane /ˈspāsˌplān/ ▶ **n.** an aircraft that takes off and lands conventionally but is capable of entry into orbit or travel through space.

space·port /ˈspāsˌpôrt/ ▶ **n.** a base from which spacecraft are launched.

space probe ▶ **n.** see **PROBE**.

space race ▶ **n.** (**the space race**) the competition between nations regarding achievements in the field of space exploration.

space rock·et ▶ **n.** a rocket designed to travel through space or to launch a spacecraft.

space-sav·ing ▶ **adj.** occupying little space; enabling the available space to be used economically: *a space-saving flat LCD screen.*

space·ship /ˈspā(s)ˌSHip/ ▶ **n.** a spacecraft, esp. one controlled by a crew.

Space·ship Earth ▶ **n.** [in sing.] the world considered as possessing finite resources common to all humankind.
– ORIGIN 1966: first appeared in the title of a work by B. Ward.

space shot ▶ **n.** the launch of a spacecraft and its subsequent progress in space.

space shut·tle ▶ **n.** a rocket-launched spacecraft, able to land like an unpowered aircraft, used to make repeated journeys between the earth and earth orbit.

S

space sta·tion ▶ **n.** a large artificial satellite used as a long-term base for manned operations in space.

space·suit /ˈspāsˌso͞ot/ ▶ **n.** a garment designed to allow an astronaut to survive in space.

space tel·e·scope ▶ **n.** an astronomical telescope that operates in space by remote control, to avoid interference by the earth's atmosphere.

space-time ▶ **n.** Physics the concepts of time and three-dimensional space regarded as fused in a four-dimensional continuum.

space trav·el ▶ **n.** travel through outer space.
– DERIVATIVES **space trav·el·er n.**

space ve·hi·cle ▶ **n.** a spacecraft.

space·walk /ˈspāsˌwôk/ ▶ **n.** a period of physical activity engaged in by an astronaut in space outside a spacecraft.
– DERIVATIVES **space·walk·er n.**

space warp ▶ **n.** an imaginary or hypothetical distortion of space-time that enables space travelers to travel faster than light or otherwise make journeys contrary to the commonly accepted laws of physics.

space weath·er ▶ **n.** natural processes in space that can affect the near-earth environment, satellites, and space travel, such as magnetospheric disturbances solar coronal events.

space·wom·an /ˈspāsˌwo͝omən/ ▶ **n.** (pl. **spacewomen**) a female astronaut.

spac·ey /ˈspāsē/ (also **spacy**) ▶ **adj.** (**spacier**, **spaciest**) informal out of touch with reality, as though high on drugs: *I remember babbling, high and spacey.* ■ (of popular, esp. electronic music) drifting and ethereal.

spa·cial ▶ **adj.** variant spelling of **SPATIAL**.

spa·cious /ˈspāSHəs/ ▶ **adj.** (esp. of a room or building) having ample space.
– DERIVATIVES **spa·cious·ly adv.**, **spa·cious·ness n.**
– ORIGIN late Middle English: from Old French *spacios* or Latin *spatiosus*, from *spatium* (see **SPACE**).

spack·le /ˈspakəl/ ▶ **n.** US trademark a compound used to fill cracks in plaster and produce a smooth surface.
▶ **v.** [with obj.] repair (a surface) or fill (a hole or crack) with Spackle.
– ORIGIN 1920s: perhaps a blend of **SPARKLE** and German *Spachtel* 'putty knife, mastic.'

spade¹ /spād/ ▶ **n.** a tool with a sharp-edged, typically rectangular, metal blade and a long handle, used for digging or cutting earth, sand, turf, etc. ■ a tool of a similar shape for another purpose, esp. one for removing the blubber from a whale.
▶ **v.** [with obj.] dig in (ground) with a spade: *while spading the soil, I think of the flowers.* ■ move (soil) with a spade: *earth is spaded into the grave.*
– PHRASES **call a spade a spade** speak plainly without avoiding unpleasant or embarrassing issues.
– DERIVATIVES **spade·ful** /-ˌfo͝ol/ **n.** (pl. **spadefuls**).
– ORIGIN Old English *spadu*, *spada*, of Germanic origin; related to Dutch *spade*, German *Spaten*, also to Greek *spathē* 'blade, paddle.'

spade² ▶ **n.** **1** (**spades**) one of the four suits in a conventional deck of playing cards, denoted by a black inverted heart-shaped figure with a small stalk. ■ (**a spade**) a card of this suit.
2 informal, offensive a black person.
– PHRASES **in spades** informal to a very high degree: *he got his revenge now in spades.*
– ORIGIN late 16th cent.: from Italian *spade*, plural of *spada* 'sword,' via Latin from Greek *spathē*; compare with **SPADE¹**.

spade·fish /ˈspādˌfiSH/ ▶ **n.** (pl. **same** or **spadefishes**) a marine fish with an almost disk-shaped body. It lives in tropical inshore waters, where it often forms schools. ● *Chaetodipterus* and other genera, family Ephippidae: several species, including the western Atlantic *C. faber*.

spade foot ▶ **n.** a square enlargement at the end of a chair leg.

spade·foot toad /ˈspādˌfo͝ot/ ▶ **n.** a plump, short-legged burrowing toad with a prominent sharp-edged tubercle on the hind feet, native to North America and Europe. ● Family Pelobatidae: several genera, including *Scaphiophus* (of America) and *Pelobates* (of Europe), and several species, in particular *P. fuscus*.

spade·work /ˈspādˌwərk/ ▶ **n.** routine or difficult preparatory work.

spa·dille /spəˈdil/ ▶ **n.** (in the card games ombre and quadrille) the ace of spades.
– ORIGIN late 17th cent.: from French, from Spanish *espadilla*, diminutive of *espada* 'sword' (see **SPADE²**).

spa·dix /ˈspādiks/ ▶ **n.** (pl. **spadices** /-dəsēz/) **1** Botany a spike of minute flowers closely arranged around a fleshy axis and typically enclosed in a spathe, characteristic of the arums.
2 Zoology (in certain invertebrates) a part or organ that is more or less conical in shape, e.g., a group of connected tentacles in a nautiloid.
– ORIGIN mid 18th cent.: via Latin from Greek, literally 'palm branch.'

spaetz·le /ˈSHpetslə, -səl, -slē/ (also **spätzle**) ▶ **plural n.** [treated as sing. or pl.] small dumplings of a type made in southern Germany and Alsace, consisting of seasoned dough poached in boiling water.
– ORIGIN from German dialect *Spätzle*, literally 'little sparrows.'

spag bol /ˈspag ˈbōl/ ▶ **abbr.** informal, chiefly Brit. spaghetti bolognese.

spa·ghet·ti /spəˈgetē/ ▶ **n.** pasta made in long, slender, solid strings. ■ an Italian dish consisting largely of this, typically with a sauce. ■ Electronics a type of narrow tubing that encases and insulates wire. ■ a tangle of stringlike objects, resembling a plate of cooked spaghetti: *a clumsy spaghetti of coils and wires.*
– ORIGIN Italian, plural of the diminutive of *spago* 'string.'

spa·ghet·ti bo·lo·gnese /ˌbōlənˈyēz, -ˈyāz/ ▶ **n.** spaghetti served with a sauce of ground beef, tomato, onion, and herbs.
– ORIGIN Italian, literally 'spaghetti of Bologna.'

spa·ghet·ti·ni /ˌspagəˈtēnē/ ▶ **n.** pasta in the form of strings of thin spaghetti.
– ORIGIN Italian, diminutive of *spaghetti* 'little strings' (see **SPAGHETTI**).

spa·ghet·ti squash ▶ **n.** an edible squash of a variety with slightly stringy flesh which when cooked has a texture and appearance like that of spaghetti. Also called **VEGETABLE SPAGHETTI**.

spa·ghet·ti strap ▶ **n.** a thin shoulder strap on an item of women's clothing.

spa·ghet·ti west·ern ▶ **n.** informal a movie about the American Old West made cheaply in Europe, typically by an Italian producer and director.

spa·hi /ˈspähē/ ▶ **n.** historical **1** a member of the Turkish irregular cavalry.
2 a member of the Algerian cavalry in French service.
– ORIGIN mid 16th cent.: from Turkish *sipahi*, from Persian *sipāhī* (see **SEPOY**).

Spahn /spän/, Warren (Edward) (1921–2003), US baseball player. He played for the Boston (later Milwaukee) Braves 1942–65 and held the record for the most games won (363) by a left-handed pitcher. Baseball Hall of Fame (1973).

Spain /spān/ a country in southwestern Europe that occupies the greater part of the Iberian peninsula; pop. 40,525,000 (est. 2009); capital, Madrid; languages, Spanish (official) and Catalan. Spanish name **ESPAÑA**.

> Spain was dominated by the Moors between 711 and 718 until the rise of independent Christian kingdoms, notably Aragon and Castile, in the medieval period; the last Moorish stronghold, Granada, was won back in the late 15th century. Under the Habsburg kings of the 16th century, Spain became the dominant European power, building up a huge empire in America and elsewhere; most of this was lost in the early 19th century. The Spanish Civil War (1936–39) was followed by the establishment of a Fascist dictatorship under General Franco; after his death in 1975 a constitutional monarchy was re-established. Spain became a member of the EC (now the EU) in 1986.

spake /spāk/ archaic literary past of **SPEAK**.

spall /spôl/ ▶ **v.** [with obj.] break (ore, rock, stone, or concrete) into smaller pieces, esp. in preparation for sorting. ■ [no obj.] (of ore, rock, or stone) break off in fragments: *cracks below the surface cause slabs of material to spall off.*
▶ **n.** a splinter or chip, esp. of rock.
– ORIGIN late Middle English (as a noun): of unknown origin. The verb dates from the mid 18th cent.

spall·a·tion /spôˈlāSHən/ ▶ **n.** **1** Physics the breakup of a bombarded nucleus into several parts.
2 Geology separation of fragments from the surface of a rock, esp. by interaction with a compression wave.

spal·peen /spalˈpēn/ ▶ **n.** Irish a rascal.
– ORIGIN late 18th cent. (denoting a migratory farm worker): from Irish *spailpín*, of unknown origin.

spalt·ed /ˈspôltid/ ▶ **adj.** (of wood) containing blackish irregular lines as a result of fungal decay, and sometimes used to produce a decorative surface.
– ORIGIN 1970s: from dialect *spalt* 'to split, splinter' + **-ED¹**.

spam /spam/ ▶ **n.** **1** (**Spam**) trademark a canned meat product made mainly from ham.
2 irrelevant or inappropriate messages sent on the Internet to a large number of recipients.
▶ **v.** [with obj.] send the same message indiscriminately to (large numbers of recipients) on the Internet.
– DERIVATIVES **spam·mer n.**
– ORIGIN 1930s: apparently from *sp(iced h)am*.

span¹ /span/ ▶ **n.** the full extent of something from end to end; the amount of space that something covers: *a warehouse with a clear span of 28 feet.* ■ the length of time for which something lasts: *a short concentration span.* ■ the wingspan of an aircraft or a bird. ■ an arch or part of a bridge between piers or supports. ■ the maximum distance between the tips of the thumb and little finger, taken as the basis of a measurement equal to 9 inches. ■ archaic a short distance or time.
▶ **v.** (**spans, spanning, spanned**) [with obj.] (of a bridge, arch, etc.) extend from side to side of: *the stream was spanned by a narrow bridge.* ■ extend across (a period of time or a range of subjects): *their interests span almost all the conventional disciplines.* ■ cover or enclose with the length of one's hand: *her waist was slender enough for him to span with his hands.*
– ORIGIN Old English, 'distance between the tips of the thumb and little finger,' of Germanic origin; reinforced in Middle English by Old French *espan*.

span² ▶ **n. 1** Nautical a rope with its ends fastened at different points to a spar or other object in order to provide a purchase.
2 a team of people or animals, in particular: ■ a matched pair of horses, mules, or oxen.
– ORIGIN mid 16th cent. (as a verb meaning 'harness or yoke (an animal)'): from Dutch or Low German *spannen*. The noun (originally in nautical use) dates from the mid 18th cent.

span³ ▶ **adj.** see SPICK AND SPAN.

span⁴ chiefly archaic past of SPIN.

Span. ▶ **abbr.** ■ Spaniard. ■ Spanish.

spa·na·ko·pi·ta /ˌspanəˈkäpitə/ ▶ **n.** (in Greek cooking) a phyllo pastry stuffed with spinach and feta cheese.
– ORIGIN modern Greek, literally 'spinach pie.'

span·dex /ˈspandeks/ ▶ **n.** a type of stretchy polyurethane fabric.
– ORIGIN 1950s: an arbitrary formation from EXPAND.

span·drel /ˈspandrəl/ ▶ **n.** Architecture the almost triangular space between one side of the outer curve of an arch, a wall, and the ceiling or framework. ■ the space between the shoulders of adjoining arches and the ceiling or molding above.
– ORIGIN late Middle English: perhaps from Anglo-Norman French *spaund(e)re*, or from *espaundre* 'expand.'

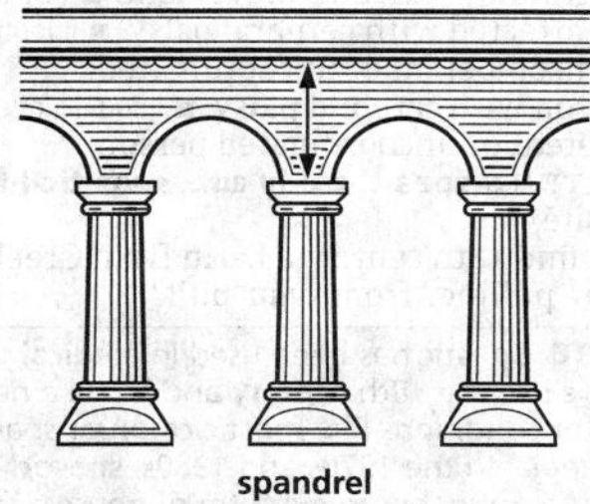
spandrel

span·drel wall ▶ **n.** a wall built on the curve of an arch, filling in the spandrel.

spang /spaNG/ ▶ **adv.** informal directly; completely: *looking the general right spang in the eye*.
– ORIGIN mid 19th cent.: of unknown origin.

span·gle /ˈspaNGgəl/ ▶ **n.** a small thin piece of glittering material, typically used in quantity to ornament a dress; a sequin. ■ a small sparkling object; a spot of bright color or light.
▶ **v.** [with obj.] (usu. as adj. **spangled**) cover with spangles or other small sparkling objects: *a spangled Christmas doll*.
– DERIVATIVES **span·gly** adj.
– ORIGIN late Middle English: diminutive from obsolete *spang* 'glittering ornament,' from Middle Dutch *spange* 'buckle.'

span·gle gall ▶ **n.** a reddish disk-shaped gall that forms on the undersides of oak leaves in response to the developing larva of a gall wasp. It results from eggs laid in the summer and alternates with the currant gall.

Spang·lish /ˈspaNGglisH/ ▶ **n.** a hybrid language combining words and idioms from both Spanish and English, esp. Spanish speech that uses many English words and expressions.

span·iel /ˈspanyəl/ ▶ **n.** a dog of a breed with a long silky coat and drooping ears. ■ used in similes and metaphors as a symbol of devotion or obsequiousness: *I followed my uncles around as faithfully as any spaniel*.
– ORIGIN Middle English: from Old French *espaigneul* 'Spanish (dog),' from Latin *Hispaniolus* 'Spanish.'

Span·ish /ˈspanisH/ ▶ **adj.** of or relating to Spain, its people, or its language.
▶ **n. 1** (as plural noun **the Spanish**) the people of Spain.
2 the Romance language of most of Spain and of much of Central and South America and several other countries.
– DERIVATIVES **Span·ish·ness** n.
– ORIGIN Middle English: from SPAIN + -ISH¹, with later shortening of the first vowel.

Span·ish A·mer·i·ca the parts of America once colonized by Spaniards and in which Spanish is still generally spoken. This includes most of Central and South America (except Brazil) and part of the Caribbean.

Span·ish-A·mer·i·can War a war between Spain and the US in the Caribbean and the Philippines in 1898. American public opinion having been aroused by Spanish atrocities in Cuba and the destruction of the warship *Maine* in Santiago harbor, the US declared war and successfully invaded Cuba, Puerto Rico, and the Philippines, all of which Spain gave up by the Treaty of Paris (1898).

Span·ish Ar·ma·da see ARMADA.

Span·ish bay·o·net (also **Spanish dagger**) ▶ **n.** a yucca native to the southern US and the American tropics. ● Genus *Yucca*, family Agavaceae: several species, in particular *Y. aloifolia*.

Span·ish broom ▶ **n.** a Mediterranean broom with fragrant yellow flowers and almost leafless stems that were formerly used in basketry. ● *Spartium junceum*, family Leguminosae.

Span·ish chest·nut ▶ **n.** see CHESTNUT (sense 2).

Span·ish Civ·il War the conflict (1936–39) between Nationalist forces (including monarchists and members of the Falange Party) and Republicans (including socialists, communists, and Catalan and Basque separatists) in Spain.

> It began with a military uprising against the leftist, Republican Popular Front government in July 1936. In bitter fighting the Nationalists, led by General Franco, gradually gained control of the countryside but failed to capture the capital, Madrid. After periods of prolonged stalemate, Franco finally succeeded in capturing Barcelona and Madrid in early 1939. He established a Fascist dictatorship that lasted until his death in 1975.

Span·ish-Co·lo·ni·al ▶ **adj.** denoting a style of architecture characteristic of Spanish America.

Span·ish flu (also **Spanish influenza**) ▶ **n.** influenza caused by an influenza virus of type A, in particular that of the pandemic that began in 1918.

Span·ish fly ▶ **n.** a bright green European blister beetle with a mousy smell. ● *Lytta vesicatoria*, family Meloidae. ■ a toxic preparation of the dried bodies of these beetles, formerly used in medicine as a counterirritant and sometimes taken as an aphrodisiac. Also called CANTHARIDES.

Span·ish gui·tar ▶ **n.** the standard six-stringed acoustic guitar, used esp. for classical and folk music.

Span·ish i·bex (also **Spanish goat**) ▶ **n.** see IBEX.

Span·ish In·qui·si·tion /ˌiNGkwiˈzisHən/ an ecclesiastical court established in Roman Catholic Spain in 1478 and directed originally against converts from Judaism and Islam but later also against Protestants. It operated with great severity until suppressed in the early 19th century.

Span·ish mack·er·el ▶ **n.** a large edible game fish related to the mackerel. ● Genus *Scomberomorus*, family Scombridae: several species, in particular *S. maculatus* of the tropical Atlantic, and *S. commerson* of the Indo-Pacific.

Span·ish Main /mān/ the former name for the north coast of South America between the Orinoco River and Panama and adjoining parts of the Caribbean Sea when they were under Spanish control.

Span·ish Mis·sion ▶ **n.** [as modifier] denoting a style of architecture characteristic of the Catholic missions in Spanish America.

Span·ish moss ▶ **n.** a tropical American plant that grows as silvery-green festoons on trees, obtaining water and nutrients directly through its surface. ● *Tillandsia usneoides*, family Bromeliaceae. See also AIR PLANT.

Span·ish nee·dles ▶ **n.** an American beggar ticks with rayless flowers that develop into a cluster of barbed achenes. ● *Bidens bipinnata*, family Compositae.

Span·ish om·e·let ▶ **n.** an omelet containing chopped vegetables, often served open rather than folded.

Span·ish on·ion ▶ **n.** a large cultivated onion with a mild flavor.

Span·ish rice ▶ **n.** a dish of rice with onions, peppers, tomatoes, and other vegetables, often colored and flavored with saffron.

Span·ish Sa·har·a former name (1958–75) of WESTERN SAHARA.

Span·ish Suc·ces·sion, War of the a European war (1701–14), provoked by the death of the Spanish king Charles II without issue. The Grand Alliance of Britain, the Netherlands, and the Holy Roman Emperor threw back a French invasion of the Low Countries and prevented Spain and France from being united under one crown.

Span·ish Town a town in Jamaica, west of Kingston, the second largest town in Jamaica, a former capital; pop. 148,800 (est. 2006).

Span·ish wind·lass ▶ **n.** a device for tightening a rope or cable by twisting it using a stick as a lever.

spank /spaNGk/ ▶ **v.** [with obj.] slap with one's open hand or a flat object, esp. on the buttocks as a punishment: *she was spanked for spilling ink on the carpet*.
▶ **n.** a slap of this type.
– ORIGIN early 18th cent.: perhaps imitative.

spank·er /ˈspaNGkər/ ▶ **n. 1** a fore-and-aft sail set on the after side of a ship's mast, esp. the mizzenmast.
2 informal, dated a very fine person or thing.

spank·ing /ˈspaNGkiNG/ ▶ **adj. 1** (esp. of a horse or its gait) lively; brisk: *a spanking trot*.
2 informal very good: *we had a spanking time*. ■ fine and impressive: *a spanking white Rolls Royce* | [as submodifier] *a spanking new conference center*.
▶ **n.** [in sing.] an act of slapping, esp. on the buttocks as a punishment for children: *you deserve a good spanking*.

span·ner /ˈspanər/ ▶ **n.** chiefly Brit. a wrench.
– ORIGIN late 18th cent.: from German *spannen* 'draw tight' + -ER¹.

span of con·trol ▶ **n.** the area of activity or number of functions, people, or things for which an individual or organization is responsible.

span·sule /ˈspansōōl/ ▶ **n.** trademark a capsule that when swallowed releases one or more medicinal drugs over a set period.
– ORIGIN mid 20th cent.: blend of the noun SPAN¹ and CAPSULE.

span·worm /ˈspanˌwərm/ ▶ **n.** another term for INCHWORM.

spar¹ /spär/ ▶ **n.** a thick, strong pole such as is used for a mast or yard on a ship. ■ the main longitudinal beam of an airplane wing.
– ORIGIN Middle English: shortening of Old French *esparre*, or from Old Norse *sperra*; related to Dutch *spar* and German *Sparren*.

spar² ▶ **v.** (**spars, sparring, sparred**) [no obj.] make the motions of boxing without landing heavy blows, as a form of training: *one contestant broke his nose while sparring*. ■ engage in argument, typically of a kind that is prolonged or repeated but not violent: *mother and daughter spar regularly over drink, drugs, and career*. ■ (of a gamecock) fight with the feet or spurs.
▶ **n. 1** a period or bout of sparring.
2 informal, chiefly Brit. a close friend.
– ORIGIN Old English *sperran, spyrran* 'strike out,' of unknown origin; compare with Old Norse *sperrask* 'kick out.'

spar³ ▶ **n.** [usu. in combination or with modifier] a crystalline, easily cleavable, light-colored mineral.
– DERIVATIVES **spar·ry** adj.
– ORIGIN late 16th cent.: from Middle Low German; related to Old English *spærstān* 'gypsum.'

spar·a·ble /ˈsparəbəl/ ▶ **n.** a headless nail used for the soles and heels of shoes.
– ORIGIN early 17th cent.: contraction of *sparrow-bill*, in the same sense.

spar bu·oy ▶ **n.** a buoy made of a spar with one end moored so that the other stands up.

spar deck ▶ **n.** an upper deck of a ship or other vessel.

spare /spe(ə)r/ ▶ **adj. 1** additional to what is required for ordinary use: *few people had spare cash for inessentials*. ■ not currently in use or occupied: *the spare bedroom*.
2 with no excess fat; thin: *a spare, bearded figure*. ■ elegantly simple: *her clothes are smart and spare in style*. ■ meager; nearly inadequate: *the furnishings were spare and unadorned*.
▶ **n. 1** an item kept in case another item of the same type is lost, broken, or worn out. ■ a spare tire: *make sure there are no problems with any of the tires, including the spare*.
2 (in tenpin bowling) an act of knocking down all the pins with two consecutive rolls of the ball.
▶ **v. 1** [with two objs.] give (something of which one has enough) to (someone); afford to give to: *she asked if I could spare her a dollar or two*. ■ make free or available: *I'm sure you can spare me a moment*. ■ [no obj.] archaic be frugal: *but some will spend, and some will spare*.
2 [with obj.] refrain from killing, injuring, or distressing: *there was no way the men would spare her*. ■ [with two objs.] refrain from inflicting (something) on (someone): *the country had until now been spared the violence occurring elsewhere*. ■ (**spare oneself**) [with negative] try to ensure or satisfy one's own comfort or needs: *in her concern to help others, she has never spared herself*.
– PHRASES **go spare** Brit. informal **1** become extremely angry or distraught: *he'd go spare if he lost the money*. **2** be unwanted or not needed and therefore available for use: *I didn't have much money going spare*. **spare no effort** do everything one possibly can in order to achieve something: *we will spare no effort to secure the release of the captives*. **spare no expense** (or **no expense spared**) pay any amount in order to achieve something. **spare the rod and**

spoil the child see **rod**. **spare a thought for** chiefly Brit. remember: *spare a thought for our volunteer group at Christmas*. **to spare** left over: *that turkey will feed ten people with some to spare*.
– DERIVATIVES **spare·ly** adv., **spare·ness** n., **spar·er** n. (rare).
– ORIGIN Old English *spær* 'not plentiful, meager,' *sparian* 'refrain from injuring,' 'refrain from using,' of Germanic origin; related to Dutch and German *sparen* 'to spare.'

spare part ▶ n. a duplicate part to replace a lost or damaged part of a machine.

spare·ribs /ˈspe(ə)rˌribz/ (also **spare ribs**) ▶ plural n. closely trimmed ribs of pork or sometimes beef.
– ORIGIN late 16th cent.: probably from Middle Low German *ribbesper* (by transposition of the syllables), and associated with the adjective **spare**.

spare time ▶ n. time that is not taken up by one's usual activities; leisure time.

spare tire ▶ n. an extra tire carried in a motor vehicle for emergencies. ■ informal a roll of fat around a person's waist.

sparge /spärj/ chiefly technical ▶ v. [with obj.] moisten by sprinkling, esp. with water in brewing.
▶ n. the action of sprinkling or splashing. ■ a spray of hot water, esp. water sprinkled over malt when brewing.
– DERIVATIVES **sparg·er** n.
– ORIGIN late 16th cent. (as a verb in the sense 'sprinkle (water) around'): apparently from Latin *spargere* 'to sprinkle.' The current senses date from the early 19th cent.

spar·id /ˈsparid/ ▶ n. Zoology a fish of the sea bream family (Sparidae), whose members are marine and have deep bodies with long spiny dorsal fins.
– ORIGIN 1960s: from modern Latin *Sparidae* (plural), via Latin from Greek *sparos* 'sea bream.'

spar·ing /ˈspe(ə)riNG/ ▶ adj. moderate; economical: *physicians advised sparing use of the ointment*.
– DERIVATIVES **spar·ing·ly** adv., **spar·ing·ness** n.

Spark /spärk/, Dame Muriel (1918–2006), Scottish novelist. Notable works: *The Prime of Miss Jean Brodie* (1961), *The Mandelbaum Gate* (1965), and *Symposium* (1990).

spark[1] /spärk/ ▶ n. **1** a small fiery particle thrown off from a fire, alight in ashes, or produced by striking together two hard surfaces such as stone or metal. ■ a light produced by a sudden disruptive electrical discharge through the air. ■ a discharge such as this serving to ignite the explosive mixture in an internal combustion engine. ■ a small bright object or point: *there was a spark of light*.
2 a trace of a specified quality or intense feeling: *a tiny spark of anger flared within her*. ■ a sense of liveliness and excitement: *there was a spark between them at their first meeting*.
▶ v. **1** [no obj.] emit sparks of fire or electricity: *the ignition sparks as soon as the gas is turned on*. ■ produce sparks at the point where an electric circuit is interrupted.
2 [with obj.] ignite: *the explosion sparked a fire*. ■ provide the stimulus for (a dramatic event or process): *the severity of the plan **sparked off** street protests*.
– PHRASES **spark out** Brit. informal completely unconscious: *I think he would knock Bowe spark out*. **sparks fly** an encounter becomes heated or lively: *sparks always fly when you two get together*.
– DERIVATIVES **spark·er** n., **spark·less** adj., **spark·y** adj.
– ORIGIN Old English *spærca*, *spearca*, of unknown origin.

spark[2] archaic ▶ n. a lively young fellow.
▶ v. [no obj.] engage in courtship.
– DERIVATIVES **spark·ish** adj.
– ORIGIN early 16th cent.: probably a figurative use of **spark**[1].

spark cham·ber ▶ n. Physics an apparatus designed to show ionizing particles.

spark gap ▶ n. a space between electrical terminals across which a transient discharge passes.

spark·ing plug ▶ n. Brit. another term for **spark plug**.

spar·kle /ˈspärkəl/ ▶ v. [no obj.] **1** shine brightly with flashes of light: *her earrings sparkled as she turned her head*.
2 be vivacious and witty: *after a glass of wine, she began to sparkle*.
▶ n. **1** a glittering flash of light: *there was a sparkle in his eyes*.
2 vivacity and wit: *she's got a kind of sparkle*.
– DERIVATIVES **spar·kly** adj.
– ORIGIN Middle English: frequentative (verb) or diminutive (noun) of **spark**[1].

spar·kler /ˈspärk(ə)lər/ ▶ n. **1** a thing that sparkles, in particular: ■ a handheld firework that emits sparks. ■ informal a gemstone, esp. a diamond. ■ informal a sparkling wine.
2 a nozzle attached to the spout on a beer pump to give the beer a frothy head.

spar·kling /ˈspärk(ə)liNG/ ▶ adj. **1** shining brightly with flashes of light: *her sparkling blue eyes*. ■ lively and witty: *sparkling dialogue*.
2 (of a drink) effervescent: *sparkling wine*. Compare with **still**[1].
– DERIVATIVES **spar·kling·ly** adv.

spark plug ▶ n. a device for firing the explosive mixture in an internal combustion engine.

Sparks /spärks/ a city in western Nevada, just east of Reno; pop. 88,602 (est. 2008).

spar·ling /ˈspärliNG/ ▶ n. an edible European smelt (fish) that migrates into fresh water to spawn. ● *Osmerus eperlanus*, family Osmeridae.
– ORIGIN Middle English: shortening of Old French *esperlinge*, of Germanic origin.

spar·ring part·ner ▶ n. a boxer employed to engage in sparring with another as training. ■ a person with whom one continually argues or contends.

spar·row /ˈsparō/ ▶ n. **1** a small finchlike Old World bird related to the weaverbirds, typically with brown and gray plumage. ● Family Passeridae (or Ploceidae): four genera, in particular *Passer*, and many species, e.g., the cosmopolitan **house sparrow** (*P. domesticus*).
2 any of a number of birds that resemble true sparrows in size or color. ● an American bunting (many genera in the subfamily Emberizinae, family Emberizidae). ● a waxbill, in particular the Java sparrow.
– ORIGIN Old English *spearwa*, of Germanic origin.

spar·row·grass /ˈsparōˌgras/ ▶ n. dialect term for **asparagus**.
– ORIGIN mid 17th cent.: corruption (by folk etymology) of obsolete *sparagus* 'asparagus.'

spar·row hawk ▶ n. a small Old World woodland hawk that preys on small birds. ● Genus *Accipiter*, family Accipitridae: many species, in particular the widespread **northern sparrow hawk** (*A. nisus*). ■ the American kestrel (see **kestrel**).

sparse /spärs/ ▶ adj. thinly dispersed or scattered: *areas of sparse population*. ■ austere; meager: *an elegantly sparse chamber*.
– DERIVATIVES **sparse·ly** adv., **sparse·ness** n., **spar·si·ty** /ˈspärsitē/ n.
– ORIGIN early 18th cent. (used to describe writing in the sense 'widely spaced'): from Latin *sparsus*, past participle of *spargere* 'scatter.'

Spar·ta /ˈspärtə/ a city in the southern Peloponnese in Greece, capital of the department of Laconia; pop. 14,400 (est. 2009). It was a powerful city state in the 5th century BC and defeated its rival Athens in the Peloponnesian War to become the leading city of Greece.

Spar·ta·cist /ˈspärtəsist/ ▶ n. a member of the Spartacus League.

Spar·ta·cus /ˈspärtəkəs/ (died *c.*71 BC), Thracian slave and gladiator. He led a revolt against Rome in 73, but eventually was defeated by Crassus in 71 and crucified.

Spar·ta·cus League a German revolutionary socialist group founded in 1916 by Rosa Luxemburg and **Karl Liebknecht** (1871–1919). At the end of 1918 the group became the German Communist Party, which in 1919 organized an uprising in Berlin that was brutally crushed.
– ORIGIN *Spartacus* was adopted as a pseudonym by Karl Liebknecht.

Spar·tan /ˈspärtn/ ▶ adj. of or relating to Sparta in ancient Greece. ■ (usu. **spartan**) showing the indifference to comfort or luxury traditionally associated with ancient Sparta: *spartan but adequate rooms*.
▶ n. a citizen of Sparta.

Spar·tan·burg /ˈspärtnˌbərg/ an industrial and commercial city in northwestern South Carolina; pop. 39,584 (est. 2008).

spar·ti·na /ˈspärtn-ə/ (also **spartina grass**) ▶ n. a plant of a genus that comprises the cordgrasses. ● Genus *Spartina*, family Gramineae.
– ORIGIN modern Latin, from Greek *spartinē* 'rope.'

spar tree ▶ n. Forestry a tree or other tall structure to which cables are attached for hauling logs.

spasm /ˈspazəm/ ▶ n. a sudden involuntary muscular contraction or convulsive movement. ■ a sudden and brief spell of an activity or sensation: *a spasm of coughing woke him*. ■ prolonged involuntary muscle contraction: *the airways in the lungs **go into spasm***.
– ORIGIN late Middle English: from Old French *spasme*, or via Latin from Greek *spasmos*, *spasma*, from *span* 'pull.'

spas·mod·ic /spazˈmädik/ ▶ adj. occurring or done in brief, irregular bursts: *spasmodic fighting continued*. ■ caused by, subject to, or in the nature of a spasm or spasms: *a spasmodic cough*.
– DERIVATIVES **spas·mod·i·cal·ly** /-ik(ə)lē/ adv.
– ORIGIN late 17th cent.: from modern Latin *spasmodicus*, from Greek *spasmōdēs*, from *spasma* (see **spasm**).

spas·mo·lyt·ic /ˌspazməˈlitik/ Medicine ▶ adj. (of a drug or treatment) able to relieve spasm of smooth muscle.
▶ n. a drug of this kind.

spas·mo·phil·i·a /ˌspazməˈfilēə/ ▶ n. Medicine undue tendency of the muscles to contract, caused by ionic imbalance in the blood, or associated with anxiety disorders.
– DERIVATIVES **spas·mo·phile** /ˈspazməˌfil/ n.

Spas·sky /ˈspaskē, ˈspäs-/, Boris (Vasilevich) (1937–), Russian chess player; world champion 1969–72. He was defeated by Bobby Fischer in 1972 and moved to Paris in 1975. In 1992, he had a rematch with Fischer, played in Montenegro and Serbia; Fischer won again.

spas·tic /ˈspastik/ ▶ adj. relating to or affected by muscle spasm. ■ relating to or denoting a form of muscular weakness (**spastic paralysis**) typical of cerebral palsy, caused by damage to the brain or spinal cord and involving reflex resistance to passive movement of the limbs and difficulty in initiating and controlling muscular movement. ■ (of a person) affected with cerebral palsy. ■ informal, offensive incompetent or uncoordinated.
▶ n. a person with cerebral palsy. ■ informal, offensive an incompetent or uncoordinated person.
– DERIVATIVES **spas·ti·cal·ly** adv., **spas·tic·i·ty** /spaˈstisitē/ n.
– ORIGIN mid 18th cent.: via Latin from Greek *spastikos* 'pulling,' from *span* 'pull.'

> **USAGE** Spastic has been used in medical senses since the 18th century and is still a neutral term for conditions like *spastic colon* or *spastic paraplegia*. In the 1970s and 1980s, **spastic**, usually used as a noun, became a term of abuse and was directed toward anyone regarded as incompetent or physically uncoordinated. Nowadays, this latter use of **spastic**, whether as a noun or as an adjective, is likely to cause offense, and it is preferable to use phrasing such as *person with cerebral palsy* instead of the noun **spastic**.

spat[1] /spat/ past and past participle of **spit**[1].

spat[2] ▶ n. **1** (usu. **spats**) historical a short cloth gaiter covering the instep and ankle.
2 a cover for the upper part of an aircraft wheel.
– ORIGIN early 19th cent.: abbreviation of **spatterdash**.

spat[2] 1

spat[3] informal ▶ n. a petty quarrel.
▶ v. (**spats, spatting, spatted**) [no obj.] quarrel pettily. ■ [with obj.] slap lightly: *I spatted your hands when you were naughty*.
– ORIGIN early 19th cent. (originally a US colloquial usage): probably imitative.

spat[4] ▶ n. the spawn or larvae of shellfish, esp. oysters.
– ORIGIN mid 17th cent.: from Anglo-Norman French, of unknown ultimate origin.

spatch·cock /ˈspaCHˌkäk/ ▶ n. a chicken or game bird split open and grilled.
▶ v. [with obj.] split open (a poultry or game bird) to prepare it for grilling. ■ informal, chiefly Brit. add (a phrase, sentence, clause, etc.) in a context where it is inappropriate: *a new clause has been spatchcocked into the bill*.
– ORIGIN late 18th cent. (originally an Irish usage): perhaps related to the noun **dispatch** + **cock**[1], but compare with **spitchcock**.

spate /spāt/ ▶ n. **1** [usu. in sing.] a large number of similar things or events appearing or occurring in quick succession: *a spate of attacks on travelers*.
2 chiefly Brit. a sudden flood in a river, esp. one caused by heavy rains or melting snow.
– PHRASES **in (full) spate** (of a river) overflowing due to a sudden flood. ■ (of a person or action) at the height of activity: *work was in full spate*.
– ORIGIN late Middle English (originally Scots and northern English in the sense 'flood, inundation'): of unknown origin.

spathe /spāTH/ ▶ n. Botany a large sheathing bract enclosing the flower cluster of certain plants, esp. the spadix of arums and palms.
– ORIGIN late 18th cent.: via Latin from Greek *spathē* 'broad blade.'

spath·u·late /ˈspaTHyəlit, -ˌlāt/ ▶ adj. Botany & Zoology variant spelling of **spatulate**.

spa·tial /ˈspāsнəl/ (also **spacial**) ▶ **adj.** of or relating to space: *the spatial distribution of population* | *a mouse's spatial memory.*
– DERIVATIVES **spa·ti·al·i·ty** /ˌspāsнēˈalitē/ **n.**, **spa·tial·i·za·tion** /ˌspāsнələˈzāsнən/ **n.**, **spa·tial·ize** /ˈspāsнəˌlīz/ **v.**, **spa·tial·ly adv.**
– ORIGIN mid 19th cent.: from Latin *spatium* 'space' + -AL.

spa·ti·o·tem·po·ral /ˌspāsнēōˈtempərəl/ ▶ **adj.** Physics & Philosophy belonging to both space and time or to space-time.
– DERIVATIVES **spa·ti·o·tem·po·ral·ly adv.**

Spät·le·se /ˈsнpātˌlāzə/ ▶ **n.** (pl. **Spätleses** or **Spätlesen** /-zən/,) a white wine of German origin or style made from grapes harvested late in the season.
– ORIGIN from German, from *spät* 'late' + *Lese* 'picking, vintage.'

spat·ter /ˈspatər/ ▶ **v.** [with obj.] cover with drops or spots of something: *passing vehicles **spattered** his shoes and pants **with** mud.* ■ scatter or splash (liquid, mud, etc.) over a surface: *he spatters grease all over the stove.* ■ [no obj.] fall so as to be scattered over an area: *she watched the raindrops spatter down.*
▶ **n.** a spray or splash of something. ■ a sprinkling: *there was a spatter of freckles over her nose.* ■ a short outburst of sound: *the sharp spatter of shots.*
– ORIGIN mid 16th cent. (in the sense 'splutter while speaking'): frequentative, from a base shared by Dutch and Low German *spatten* 'burst, spout.'

spat·ter·dash /ˈspatərˌdasн/ ▶ **n.** (usu. **spatterdashes**) historical a long gaiter or legging worn to keep stockings or pants clean, esp. when riding.

spat·ter·dock /ˈspatərˌdäk/ ▶ **n.** a yellow-flowered water lily. ● Genus *Nuphar*, family Nymphaeaceae: several species, in particular *N. advena.*

spat·ter·ware /ˈspatərˌwer/ ▶ **n.** pottery decorated by sponging with color; sponged ware.

spat·u·la /ˈspacнələ/ ▶ **n.** an implement with a broad, flat, blunt blade, used for mixing and spreading things, esp. in cooking and painting. ■ British term for TONGUE DEPRESSOR.
– ORIGIN early 16th cent.: from Latin, variant of *spathula*, diminutive of *spatha* (see SPATHE).

spat·u·late /ˈspacнələt/ ▶ **adj.** having a broad, rounded end: *his thick, spatulate fingers.* ■ (also **spathulate**) Botany & Zoology broad at the apex and tapered to the base: *large spatulate leaves.*

spätz·le ▶ **plural n.** variant spelling of SPAETZLE.

spav·in /ˈspavin/ ▶ **n.** a disorder of a horse's hock. See BONE SPAVIN.
– DERIVATIVES **spav·ined adj.**
– ORIGIN late Middle English: shortening of Old French *espavin*, variant of *esparvain*, of Germanic origin.

spawn /spôn/ ▶ **v. 1** [no obj.] (of a fish, frog, mollusk, crustacean, etc.) release or deposit eggs: *the fish spawn among fine-leaved plants* | [with obj.] *a large brood is spawned.* ■ (**be spawned**) (of a fish, frog, etc.) be laid as eggs.
2 [with obj.] often derogatory (of a person) produce (offspring): *why had she married a man who could spawn a boy like that?* ■ [with obj.] produce or generate, esp. in large numbers: *the decade spawned a bewildering variety of books on the forces.* ■ [with obj.] Computing generate (a dependent or subordinate computer process).
▶ **n. 1** the eggs of fish, frogs, etc.: *the fish covers its spawn with gravel.* ■ the process of producing spawn.
2 the product or offspring of a person or place (used to express distaste or disgust): *the spawn of chaos: demons and sorcerers.*
3 the mycelium of a fungus, esp. a cultivated mushroom.
– DERIVATIVES **spawn·er n.**
– ORIGIN late Middle English: shortening of Anglo-Norman French *espaundre* 'to shed roe,' variant of Old French *espandre* 'pour out,' from Latin *expandere* 'expand.'

spay /spā/ ▶ **v.** [with obj.] (usu. **be spayed**) sterilize (a female animal) by removing the ovaries: *the animals must be spayed or neutered before they are given up for adoption.*
– ORIGIN late Middle English: shortening of Old French *espeer* 'cut with a sword,' from *espee* 'sword,' from Latin *spatha* (see SPATHE).

spaz /spaz/ (also **spazz**) informal ▶ **n.** (pl. **spazzes**) offensive short for SPASTIC.
▶ **v.** [no obj.] (**spaz out**) lose physical or emotional control: *he offered a post-game assessment: "I spazzed out real bad."*
– ORIGIN 1960s: abbreviation of SPASTIC.

SPCA ▶ **abbr.** Society for the Prevention of Cruelty to Animals.

SPCC ▶ **abbr.** Society for the Prevention of Cruelty to Children.

SPCK ▶ **abbr.** Society for Promoting Christian Knowledge.

speak /spēk/ ▶ **v.** (past **spoke** /spōk/; past participle **spoken** /ˈspōkən/) [no obj.] **1** say something in order to convey information, an opinion, or a feeling: *in his agitation he was unable to speak* | *she refused to speak about the incident.* ■ have a conversation: *I wish to **speak** privately **with** you* | *I'll **speak to** him if he calls.* ■ [with obj.] utter (a word, message, speech, etc.): *patients copy words spoken by the therapist.* ■ [with obj.] communicate in or be able to communicate in (a specified language): *my mother spoke Russian.* ■ make a speech before an audience, or make a contribution to a debate: *twenty thousand people attended to hear him speak.* ■ (**speak for**) express the views or position of (another person or group): *he claimed to speak for the majority of local people.* ■ convey one's views or position indirectly: ***speaking through** his attorney, he refused to join the debate.* ■ (**speak of**) mention or discuss in speech or writing: *the books speak of betrayal.* ■ (of behavior, a quality, an event, etc.) serve as evidence for something: *her harping on him **spoke** strongly **of** a crush* | [with obj.] *his frame spoke tiredness.* ■ (of an object that typically makes a sound when it functions) make a characteristic sound: *the gun spoke again.* ■ [with obj. or adverbial] archaic show or manifest (someone or something) to be in a particular state or to possess a certain quality: *she had seen nothing that spoke him of immoral habits.* ■ (of an organ pipe or other musical instrument) make a sound: *insufficient air circulates for the pipes to speak.* ■ (of a dog) bark. ■ [with obj.] Nautical, archaic hail and hold communication with (a ship) at sea.
2 (**speak to**) talk to in order to reprove or advise: *she tried to speak to Seth about his drinking.* ■ talk to in order to give or extract information: *he had spoken to the police.* ■ discuss or comment on formally: *the Church wants to speak to real issues.* ■ appeal or relate to: *the story spoke to him directly.*
– PHRASES **not to speak of** used in introducing a further factor to be considered: *the rent had to be paid, not to speak of school tuition.* **nothing** (or **no ——** or **none**) **to speak of** used to indicate that there is some but very little of something: *I've no capital—well, none to speak of.* **so to speak** see SO[1]. **something speaks for itself** something's implications are so clear that it needs no supporting evidence or comments: *the figures speak for themselves.* **speak for oneself** give one's own opinions. ■ [in imperative] used to tell someone that what they have said may apply to them but does not apply to others: *"This is such a boring place." "Speak for yourself—I like it."* **speak in tongues** see TONGUE. **speaking of** used to introduce a statement or question about a topic recently alluded to: *speaking of cost, can I afford to buy it?* **speak one's mind** express one's feelings or opinions frankly. **speak volumes** (of a gesture, circumstance, or object) convey a great deal: *a look that spoke volumes.* ■ be good evidence for: *his record **speaks volumes for** his determination.* **speak well** (or **ill**) **of** praise (or criticize).
– PHRASAL VERBS **speak out** (or **up**) express one's feelings or opinions frankly and publicly: *the administration will be forthright in speaking out against human rights abuses.* **speak up** speak more loudly: *We can't hear you. Speak up!* **speak up for** speak in defense or support of: *there was no independent body to speak up for press freedoms.*
– DERIVATIVES **speak·a·ble adj.**
– ORIGIN Old English *sprecan*, later *specan*; related to Dutch *spreken* and German *sprechen*.

-speak ▶ **comb. form** forming nouns denoting a manner of speaking, characteristic of a specified field or group: *technospeak.*
– ORIGIN on the pattern of (*New*)*speak*.

speak·eas·y /ˈspēkˌēzē/ ▶ **n.** (pl. **speakeasies**) informal (during Prohibition) an illicit liquor store or nightclub.

speak·er /ˈspēkər/ ▶ **n. 1** a person who speaks. ■ a person who delivers a speech or lecture. ■ [usu. with modifier or in combination] a person who speaks a specified language: *he is a fluent English and French speaker.*
2 (**Speaker**) the presiding officer in a legislative assembly, esp. the House of Representatives.
3 short for LOUDSPEAKER: *a cassette player with two speakers.*
– DERIVATIVES **speak·er·ship** /-ˌsнip/ **n.** (sense 2).

speak·er·phone /ˈspēkərˌfōn/ ▶ **n.** a telephone with a loudspeaker and microphone, allowing it to be used without picking up the handset.

speak·ing /ˈspēkiɴɢ/ ▶ **n.** the action of conveying information or expressing one's thoughts and feelings in spoken language. ■ the activity of delivering speeches or lectures: *public speaking.*
▶ **adj.** [attrib.] used for or engaged in speech: *you have a clear speaking voice.* ■ conveying meaning as though in words: *she gave him a speaking look.* ■ (of a portrait) so like the subject as to seem to be alive and capable of speech: *a speaking likeness.* ■ [in combination] able to communicate in a specified language: *an English-speaking guide.*
– PHRASES **on speaking terms 1** slightly acquainted. **2** sufficiently friendly to talk to each other: *she parted from her mother barely on speaking terms.* **—— speaking** used to indicate the degree of accuracy intended in a statement or the point of view from which it is made: *broadly speaking, there are three major models for local-central relations.* **speaking in tongues** another term for GLOSSOLALIA.

speak·ing trum·pet ▶ **n.** historical an instrument for making the voice carry, esp. at sea.

speak·ing tube ▶ **n.** a pipe for conveying a person's voice from one room or building to another.

spear /spi(ə)r/ ▶ **n.** a weapon with a long shaft and a pointed tip, typically of metal, used for thrusting or throwing. ■ a similar barbed instrument used for catching fish. ■ archaic a spearman. ■ a plant shoot, esp. a pointed stem of asparagus or broccoli.
▶ **v.** [with obj.] pierce or strike with a spear or other pointed object: *she speared her last French fry with her fork.* ■ quickly extend the arm to catch (a fast-moving ball or other object): *he hit a line drive that Bogar speared backhanded.*
– ORIGIN Old English *spere*, of Germanic origin; compare with Dutch *speer* and German *Speer*.

spear car·ri·er ▶ **n.** an actor with a walk-on part. ■ an unimportant participant in something.

spear·fish /ˈspi(ə)rˌfisн/ ▶ **n.** (pl. **same** or **spearfishes**) a billfish that resembles the marlin. ● Genus *Tetrapturus*, family Istiophoridae: several species.
▶ **v.** [no obj.] fish using a spear: *resort owners do not allow tourists to spearfish* | (as noun **spearfishing**) *spearfishing is strictly illegal in the marine parks.*

spear grass (also **speargrass**) ▶ **n.** any of a number of grasses with hard pointed seed heads, some of which are sharp enough to harm livestock. ● *Heteropogon, Stipa*, and other genera, family Gramineae.

spear·gun /ˈspi(ə)rˌgən/ ▶ **n.** a gun used to propel a spear in underwater fishing.

spear·head /ˈspi(ə)rˌhed/ ▶ **n.** the point of a spear. ■ an individual or group chosen to lead an attack or movement: *she became the **spearhead of** a health education program.*
▶ **v.** [with obj.] lead (an attack or movement): *he's spearheading a campaign to reduce the number of accidents at work.*

spear·man /ˈspi(ə)rmən/ ▶ **n.** (pl. **spearmen**) chiefly historical a man, esp. a soldier, who uses a spear.

spear·mint /ˈspi(ə)rˌmint/ ▶ **n.** the common garden mint, used as a culinary herb and to flavor candy, chewing gum, etc. ● *Mentha spicata*, family Labiatae.

spear side ▶ **n.** the male side or members of a family. The opposite of DISTAFF SIDE.

spear·wort /ˈspi(ə)rwərt, -ˌwôrt/ ▶ **n.** a plant of the buttercup family that grows in marshes and ditches, with thick hollow stems and long narrow spear-shaped leaves. ● Genus *Ranunculus*, family Rununculaceae: the **lesser spearwort** (*R. flammula*) and the less common **greater spearwort** (*R. lingua*).

spec[1] /spek/ ▶ **n.** (in phrase **on spec**) informal in the hope of success but without any specific commission or instructions: *he built the factory on spec and hoped someone would buy it.*
– ORIGIN late 18th cent.: abbreviation of SPECULATION.

spec[2] ▶ **n.** informal a detailed working description: *I'll have to look at the specs on the equipment* | [as modifier] *our spec chart indicates a transmission speed of 9 seconds.*
– ORIGIN 1950s: abbreviation of SPECIFICATION.

spe·cial /ˈspesнəl/ ▶ **adj.** better, greater, or otherwise different from what is usual: *they always made a special effort at Christmas.* ■ exceptionally good or precious: *she's a very special person.* ■ belonging specifically to a particular person or place: *we want to preserve our town's special character.* ■ designed or organized for a particular person, purpose, or occasion: *we will return by special coaches.* ■ (of a subject) studied in particular depth. ■ used to denote education for children with particular needs, esp. those with learning difficulties. ■ Mathematics denoting a group consisting of matrices of unit determinant.
▶ **n.** a thing, such as an event, product, or broadcast, that is designed or organized for a particular occasion or purpose: *television's election night*

S

PRONUNCIATION KEY ə ago, up; ər over, fur; a hat; ā ate; ä car; e let; ē see; i fit; ī by; NG sing; ō go; ô law, for; oi toy; o͝o good; o͞o goo; ou out; TH thin; T̲H̲ then; ZH vision

specials. ■ a dish not on the regular menu at a restaurant but served on a particular day. ■ informal a product or service offered at a temporarily reduced price.
– PHRASES **on special** available for sale at a reduced price: *they have hamburger buns on special today.*
– DERIVATIVES **spe·cial·ness** n.
– ORIGIN Middle English: shortening of Old French *especial* 'especial' or Latin *specialis*, from *species* 'appearance' (see SPECIES).

Spe·cial Branch (in the UK) the police department dealing with political security.

spe·cial case ▶ n. **1** a situation or person that has unusual qualities or needs.
2 Law a written statement of fact presented by litigants to a court.

spe·cial cor·re·spond·ent ▶ n. a journalist writing for a newspaper on special events or a special area of interest.

spe·cial de·liv·er·y ▶ n. a former express mail service of the US Postal Service that involved expedited delivery of mail, often by special courier. ■ any mail service that involves special handling or expedited delivery. ■ a letter or parcel sent by a special-delivery service.

spe·cial draw·ing rights (abbr.: **SDR**) ▶ plural n. a form of international money, created by the International Monetary Fund, and defined as a weighted average of various convertible currencies.

spe·cial e·di·tion ▶ n. an edition of a newspaper, magazine, television program, etc., that differs from the usual format, esp. in concentrating on one particularly important story.

spe·cial ef·fect ▶ n. an illusion created for movies and television by props, camerawork, computer graphics, etc.: *a non-stop action rollercoaster filled with amazing stunts and spectacular special effects.*

Spe·cial For·ces ▶ n. an elite force within the US Army specializing in guerrilla warfare and counterinsurgency.

spe·cial in·ten·tion ▶ n. (in the Roman Catholic Church) a special aim or purpose for which a Mass is celebrated or prayers are said.

spe·cial in·ter·est (also **special interest group**) ▶ n. a group of people or an organization seeking or receiving special advantages, typically through political lobbying.

spe·cial·ist /ˈspeSHəlist/ ▶ n. a person who concentrates primarily on a particular subject or activity; a person highly skilled in a specific and restricted field. ■ a physician highly trained in a particular branch of medicine. ■ (in the US Army) an enlisted person of one of four grades (**specialist 4**, equivalent to the rank of corporal, being the most junior, **specialist 7**, equivalent to sergeant first class, being the most senior) who has technical or administrative duties but does not exercise command.
▶ adj. possessing or involving detailed knowledge or study of a restricted topic: *the project may involve people with specialist knowledge.* ■ [attrib.] concentrating on a restricted field, market, or area of activity: *a specialist electrical shop.*
– DERIVATIVES **spe·cial·ism** /-ˌlizəm/ n.

spe·ci·al·i·ty /ˌspeSHēˈalitē/ ▶ n. (pl. **specialities**) British term for SPECIALTY.
– ORIGIN late Middle English (denoting the quality of being special or distinctive): from Old French *especialite* or late Latin *specialitas*, from Latin *specialis* (see SPECIAL).

S

spe·cial·ize /ˈspeSHəˌlīz/ ▶ v. [no obj.] concentrate on and become expert in a particular subject or skill: *he could specialize in tropical medicine.* ■ confine oneself to providing a particular product or service: *the company specialized in commercial brochures.* ■ make a habit of engaging in a particular activity: *a group of writers has specialized in attacking the society they live in.* ■ [with obj.] Biology adapt or set apart (an organ or part) to serve a special function or to suit a particular way of life: *zooids specialized for different functions.*
– DERIVATIVES **spe·cial·i·za·tion** /ˌspeSHəliˈzāSHən/ n.
– ORIGIN early 17th cent.: from French *spécialiser*, from *spécial* 'special.'

spe·cial·ized /ˈspeSHəˌlīzd/ ▶ adj. requiring or involving detailed and specific knowledge or training: *skilled treatment for these patients is very specialized.* ■ concentrating on a small area of a subject: *periodicals have become more and more specialized.* ■ designed for a particular purpose: *specialized software.*

spe·cial·ly /ˈspeSHəlē/ ▶ adv. for a special purpose: *they have been fabricated specially for this boat* | [as submodifier] *a specially commissioned report.*

USAGE On the differences between **specially** and **especially**, see usage at ESPECIALLY.

spe·cial needs ▶ plural n. (in the context of children at school) particular educational requirements resulting from learning difficulties, physical disability, or emotional and behavioral difficulties.

Spe·cial O·lym·pics ▶ n. an international competition, modeled on the Olympic Games, in which mentally and physically handicapped athletes compete.

Spe·cial Op·er·a·tions Ex·ec·u·tive (abbr.: **SOE**) a secret British military service during World War II, set up in 1940 to carry out clandestine operations and coordinate with resistance movements in Europe and later East Asia.

spe·cial plead·ing ▶ n. argument in which the speaker deliberately ignores aspects that are unfavorable to their point of view. ■ appeals to give a particular interest group special treatment: *we heard his special pleading for his constituency.*

spe·cial sort ▶ n. Printing a character, such as an accented letter or a symbol, that is not normally included in any font.

spe·cial team ▶ n. Football a squad that is used for kickoffs, punts, or other special plays.

spe·cial·ty /ˈspeSHəltē/ (Brit. also **speciality** /ˌspeSHēˈalitē/) ▶ n. (pl. **specialties**) **1** a pursuit, area of study, or skill to which someone has devoted much time and effort and in which they are expert: *his specialty was watercolors.* ■ a particular branch of medicine or surgery. ■ a product, esp. a type of food, that a person or region is famous for making well: *the local specialties are all seafood.* ■ [as modifier] meeting particular tastes or needs: *specialty potatoes for salads.*
2 Law a contract under seal.
– ORIGIN Middle English (denoting special affection or attachment): shortening of Old French *especialte*, from *especial* (see SPECIAL).

spe·cial ver·dict ▶ n. Law a verdict that requires an answer to a specific detailed question. ■ a verdict that an accused is not guilty by reason of insanity.

spe·ci·a·tion /ˌspēSHēˈāSHən, ˌspēsē-/ ▶ n. Biology the formation of new and distinct species in the course of evolution.
– DERIVATIVES **spe·ci·ate** /ˈspēSHēˌāt, spēsē-/ v.

spe·cie /ˈspēSHē, -sē/ ▶ n. money in the form of coins rather than notes.
– PHRASES **in specie 1** in coin. **2** Law in the real, precise, or actual form specified: *the plaintiff could not be sure of recovering his goods in specie.*
– ORIGIN mid 16th cent.: from Latin, ablative of *species* 'form, kind,' in the phrase *in specie* 'in the actual form.'

spe·cies /ˈspēsēz, -SHēz/ ▶ n. (pl. **same**) **1** (abbr.: **sp., spp.**) Biology a group of living organisms consisting of similar individuals capable of exchanging genes or interbreeding. The species is the principal natural taxonomic unit, ranking below a genus and denoted by a Latin binomial, e.g., *Homo sapiens.* ■ Logic a group subordinate to a genus and containing individuals agreeing in some common attributes and called by a common name. ■ a kind or sort: *a species of invective at once tough and suave.* ■ used humorously to refer to people who share a characteristic or occupation: *a political species that is becoming more common, the environmental statesman.* ■ Chemistry & Physics a particular kind of atom, molecule, ion, or particle: *a new molecular species.*
2 Christian Church the visible form of each of the elements of consecrated bread and wine in the Eucharist.
– ORIGIN late Middle English: from Latin, literally 'appearance, form, beauty,' from *specere* 'to look.'

spe·cies bar·ri·er ▶ n. the natural mechanisms that prevent a virus or disease from spreading from one species to another.

spe·cies·ism /ˈspēSHēˌzizəm, spēsē-/ ▶ n. the assumption of human superiority leading to the exploitation of animals.
– DERIVATIVES **spe·cies·ist** adj. & n.

spe·cies rose ▶ n. a rose belonging to a distinct species and not to one of the many varieties produced by hybridization.

specif. ▶ abbr. specific; specifically.

spe·cif·ic /spəˈsifik/ ▶ adj. **1** clearly defined or identified: *increasing the electricity supply only until it met specific development needs.* ■ precise and clear in making statements or issuing instructions: *when ordering goods be specific.* ■ belonging or relating uniquely to a particular subject: *information needs are often very specific to companies and individuals.*
2 Biology of, relating to, or connected with species or a species.
3 (of a duty or a tax) levied at a fixed rate per physical unit of the thing taxed, regardless of its price.
4 Physics of or denoting a number equal to the ratio of the value of some property of a given substance to the value of the same property of some other substance used as a reference, such as water, or of a vacuum, under equivalent conditions. ■ of or denoting a physical quantity expressed in terms of a unit mass, volume, or other measure, in order to give a value independent of the properties or scale of the particular system studied.
▶ n. **1** dated a medicine or remedy effective in treating a particular disease or part of the body.
2 (usu. **specifics**) a precise detail: *he worked through the specifics of the contract.*
– DERIVATIVES **spe·cif·i·cal·ly** adv., **spec·i·fic·i·ty** /ˌspesəˈfisitē/ n.
– ORIGIN mid 17th cent. (originally in the sense 'having a special determining quality'): from late Latin *specificus*, from Latin *species* (see SPECIES).

spe·cif·ic ac·tiv·i·ty ▶ n. Physics the activity of a given radioisotope per unit mass.

spec·i·fi·ca·tion /ˌspesəfiˈkāSHən/ ▶ n. an act of describing or identifying something precisely or of stating a precise requirement: *give a full specification of the job advertised* | *there was no clear specification of objectives.* ■ (usu. **specifications**) a detailed description of the design and materials used to make something. ■ a standard of workmanship, materials, etc., required to be met in a piece of work: *everything was built to a higher specification.* ■ a description of an invention accompanying an application for a patent.
– ORIGIN late 16th cent.: from medieval Latin *specificatio(n-)*, from late Latin *specificare* (see SPECIFY).

spe·cif·ic charge ▶ n. Physics the ratio of the charge of an ion or subatomic particle to its mass.

spe·cif·ic dis·ease ▶ n. a disease caused by a particular and characteristic organism.

spe·cif·ic ep·i·thet /spəˈsifik ˈepəˌTHet/ ▶ n. chiefly Botany & Microbiology the second element in the Latin binomial name of a species, which follows the generic name and distinguishes the species from others in the same genus. Compare with SPECIFIC NAME, TRIVIAL NAME.

spe·cif·ic grav·i·ty ▶ n. Chemistry the ratio of the density of a substance to the density of a standard, usually water for a liquid or solid, and air for a gas.

spe·cif·ic heat ▶ n. Physics the heat required to raise the temperature of the unit mass of a given substance by a given amount (usually one degree).

spe·cif·ic name ▶ n. chiefly Botany & Microbiology the Latin binomial name of a species, consisting of the generic name followed by the specific epithet. ■ chiefly Zoology another term for SPECIFIC EPITHET.

spe·cif·ic per·for·mance ▶ n. Law the performance of a contractual duty, as ordered in cases where damages would not be adequate remedy.

spec·i·fy /ˈspesəˌfī/ ▶ v. (**specifies, specifying, specified**) [with obj.] identify clearly and definitely: *the coup leader promised an election but did not specify a date.* ■ [with clause] state a fact or requirement clearly and precisely: *the agency failed to* **specify** *that the workers were not their employees.* ■ include in an architect's or engineer's specifications: *naval architects specified circular portholes.*
– DERIVATIVES **spec·i·fi·a·ble** /ˌspesəˈfīəbəl/ adj., **spec·i·fi·er** n.
– ORIGIN Middle English: from Old French *specifier* or late Latin *specificare* (see SPECIFIC).

spec·i·men /ˈspesəmən/ ▶ n. an individual animal, plant, piece of a mineral, etc., used as an example of its species or type for scientific study or display. ■ an example of something such as a product or piece of work, regarded as typical of its class or group. ■ a sample for medical testing, esp. of urine. ■ informal used to refer humorously to a person or animal: *in her he found himself confronted by a sorrier specimen than himself.*
– ORIGIN early 17th cent. (in the sense 'pattern, model'): from Latin, from *specere* 'to look.'

spec·i·men plant ▶ n. an unusual or impressive plant grown as a focus of interest in a garden.

spe·cious /ˈspēSHəs/ ▶ adj. superficially plausible, but actually wrong: *a specious argument.* ■ misleading in appearance, esp. misleadingly attractive: *the music trade gives Golden Oldies a specious appearance of novelty.*
– DERIVATIVES **spe·cious·ly** adv., **spe·cious·ness** n.
– ORIGIN late Middle English (in the sense 'beautiful'): from Latin *speciosus* 'fair,' from *species* (see SPECIES).

speck /spek/ ▶ n. a tiny spot: *the figure in the distance had become a mere speck.* ■ a small particle of a substance: *specks of dust.*

▶ **v.** [with obj.] (usu. **be specked**) mark with small spots: *their skin was specked with goose pimples.*
– DERIVATIVES **speck·less** **adj.**
– ORIGIN Old English *specca*; compare with the noun SPECKLE.

speck·le /ˈspekəl/ ▶ **n.** (usu. **speckles**) a small spot or patch of color.
▶ **v.** [with obj.] mark with a large number of small spots or patches of color: *stars speckled the sky.*
– ORIGIN late Middle English (as a noun): from Middle Dutch *spekkel*; the verb (late 16th cent.) from the noun or a back-formation from *speckled*.

speck·led /ˈspekəld/ ▶ **adj.** covered or marked with a large number of small spots or patches of color: *a large speckled brown egg | its body is gray speckled with dark spots.*

speck·led trout ▶ **n.** the brook trout. See CHAR[1].

speck·led wood ▶ **n.** a brown Eurasian butterfly with cream or orange markings, favoring light woodland habitats. ● *Pararge aegeria*, subfamily Satyrinae, family Nymphalidae.

specs /speks/ ▶ **plural n.** informal **1** a pair of spectacles. **2** plural form of SPEC[2].
– ORIGIN early 19th cent.: abbreviation.

spect /spekt/ ▶ **v.** nonstandard form of EXPECT: *I spect they've been to a party.*

spec·ta·cle /ˈspektəkəl/ ▶ **n.** a visually striking performance or display: *the acrobatic feats make a good spectacle | the show is pure spectacle.* ■ an event or scene regarded in terms of its visual impact: *the spectacle of a city's mass grief.*
– PHRASES **make a spectacle of oneself** draw attention to oneself by behaving in a ridiculous way in public.
– ORIGIN Middle English: via Old French from Latin *spectaculum* 'public show,' from *spectare*, frequentative of *specere* 'to look.'

spec·ta·cled /ˈspektəkəld/ ▶ **adj.** wearing spectacles. ■ used in names of animals with markings that resemble spectacles.

spec·ta·cled bear ▶ **n.** a South American bear with a black or dark brown coat and white markings around the eyes. ● *Tremarctos ornatus*, family Ursidae.

spec·ta·cled cai·man /ˈkāmən/ ▶ **n.** a small South American caiman with a bony ridge between the eyes that gives the appearance of spectacles. ● *Caiman sclerops*, family Alligatoridae.

spec·ta·cled co·bra ▶ **n.** an Asian cobra with a marking on the hood that resembles spectacles. Also called INDIAN COBRA, ASIAN COBRA. ● *Naja naja*, family Elapidae.

spectacled cobra

spec·ta·cles /ˈspektəkəlz/ ▶ **plural n.** another term for GLASSES.

spec·tac·u·lar /spekˈtakyələr/ ▶ **adj.** beautiful in a dramatic and eye-catching way: *spectacular mountain scenery.* ■ strikingly large or obvious: *the party suffered a spectacular loss in the election.*
▶ **n.** an event such as a pageant or musical, produced on a large scale and with striking effects.
– DERIVATIVES **spec·tac·u·lar·ly** **adv.**
– ORIGIN late 17th cent.: from SPECTACLE, on the pattern of words such as *oracular.*

spec·tate /spekˈtāt/ ▶ **v.** [no obj.] be a spectator, esp. at a sporting event: *an entire defense starts to spectate like fans in the stands.*
– ORIGIN early 18th cent.: back-formation from SPECTATOR.

spec·ta·tor /ˈspekˌtātər/ ▶ **n.** a person who watches at a show, game, or other event.
– DERIVATIVES **spec·ta·to·ri·al** /ˌspektəˈtôrēəl/ **adj.** (rare).
– ORIGIN late 16th cent.: from French *spectateur* or Latin *spectator*, from *spectare* 'gaze at, observe' (see SPECTACLE).

spec·ta·tor sport ▶ **n.** a sport that many people find entertaining to watch.

spec·ter /ˈspektər/ (Brit. **spectre**) ▶ **n.** a ghost. ■ something widely feared as a possible unpleasant or dangerous occurrence: *the specter of nuclear holocaust.*
– ORIGIN early 17th cent.: from French *spectre* or Latin *spectrum* (see SPECTRUM).

spec·ti·no·my·cin /ˌspektənəˈmīsin/ ▶ **n.** Medicine a bacterial antibiotic used as an alternative to penicillin. ● The drug is obtained from the bacterium *Streptomyces spectabilis.*
– ORIGIN 1960s: from the specific epithet *spectabilis* (see above), literally 'visible, remarkable' + -MYCIN.

Spec·tor /ˈspektər/, Phil (1940–), US record producer and songwriter; full name *Harvey Phillip Spector*. He pioneered a "wall of sound" style, using echo and tape loops, and had a succession of hit recordings in the 1960s with groups such as the Ronettes and the Crystals. In 2009, he was convicted of murdering actress Lana Clarkson (1962–2003).

spec·tra /ˈspektrə/ plural form of SPECTRUM.

spec·tral /ˈspektrəl/ ▶ **adj.** **1** of or like a ghost. [early 18th cent.: from SPECTER + -AL.]
2 of or concerning spectra or the spectrum. [mid 19th cent.: from SPECTRUM + -AL.]
– DERIVATIVES **spec·tral·ly** **adv.**

spec·tral in·dex ▶ **n.** an exponential factor relating the flux density of a radio source to its frequency.

spec·tral tar·si·er /ˈtärsēər/ ▶ **n.** a tarsier that has a tail with a long bushy tuft and a scaly base, native to Sulawesi. ● *Tarsius spectrum*, family Tarsiidae.

spec·tral type (also **spectral class**) ▶ **n.** Astronomy the group in which a star is classified according to its spectrum, esp. using the Harvard classification.

spec·tre ▶ **n.** British spelling of SPECTER.

spectro- ▶ **comb. form** representing SPECTRUM.

spec·tro·gram /ˈspektrəˌgram/ ▶ **n.** a photographic or other visual or electronic representation of a spectrum.

spec·tro·graph /ˈspektrəˌgraf/ ▶ **n.** an apparatus for photographing or otherwise recording spectra.
– DERIVATIVES **spec·tro·graph·ic** /ˌspektrəˈgrafik/ **adj.**, **spec·tro·graph·i·cal·ly** /ˌspektrəˈgrafik(ə)lē/ **adv.**, **spec·trog·ra·phy** /spekˈträgrəfē/ **n.**

spec·tro·he·li·o·graph /ˌspektrōˈhēlēəˌgraf/ ▶ **n.** an instrument for taking photographs of the sun in light of one wavelength only.

spec·tro·he·li·o·scope /ˌspektrōˈhēlēəˌskōp/ ▶ **n.** a device similar to a spectroheliograph that produces a directly observable monochromatic image of the sun.

spec·trom·e·ter /spekˈträmitər/ ▶ **n.** an apparatus used for recording and measuring spectra, esp. as a method of analysis.
– DERIVATIVES **spec·tro·met·ric** /ˌspektrəˈmetrik/ **adj.**, **spec·trom·e·try** /spekˈträmətrē/ **n.**

spec·tro·pho·tom·e·ter /ˌspektrōfōˈtämitər/ ▶ **n.** an apparatus for measuring the intensity of light in a part of the spectrum, esp. as transmitted or emitted by particular substances.
– DERIVATIVES **spec·tro·pho·to·met·ric** /ˌspektrəˌfōtəˈmetrik/ **adj.**, **spec·tro·pho·to·met·ri·cal·ly** /ˌspektrəˌfōtəˈmetrik(ə)lē/ **adv.**, **spec·tro·pho·tom·e·try** /-mətrē/ **n.**

spec·tro·scope /ˈspektrəˌskōp/ ▶ **n.** an apparatus for producing and recording spectra for examination.

spec·tros·co·py /spekˈträskəpē/ ▶ **n.** the branch of science concerned with the investigation and measurement of spectra produced when matter interacts with or emits electromagnetic radiation.
– DERIVATIVES **spec·tro·scop·ic** /ˌspektrəˈskäpik/ **adj.**, **spec·tro·scop·i·cal·ly** /ˌspektrəˈskäpik(ə)lē/ **adv.**, **spec·tros·co·pist** /-pist/ **n.**

spec·trum /ˈspektrəm/ ▶ **n.** (pl. **spectra** /-trə/) **1** a band of colors, as seen in a rainbow, produced by separation of the components of light by their different degrees of refraction according to wavelength. ■ (**the spectrum**) the entire range of wavelengths of electromagnetic radiation. ■ an image or distribution of components of any electromagnetic radiation arranged in a progressive series according to wavelength. ■ a similar image or distribution of components of sound, particles, etc., arranged according to such characteristics as frequency, charge, and energy.
2 used to classify something, or suggest that it can be classified, in terms of its position on a scale between two extreme or opposite points: *the left or the right of the political spectrum.* ■ a wide range: *self-help books are covering a broader and broader spectrum.*
– ORIGIN early 17th cent. (in the sense 'specter'): from Latin, literally 'image, apparition,' from *specere* 'to look.'

spec·trum an·a·lyz·er ▶ **n.** a device for analyzing a system of oscillations, esp. sound, into its separate components.

spec·u·la /ˈspəkyələ/ plural form of SPECULUM.

spec·u·lar /ˈspekyələr/ ▶ **adj.** of, relating to, or having the properties of a mirror.
– ORIGIN late 16th cent. (in *specular stone*, a substance formerly used as glass): from Latin *specularis*, from *speculum* (see SPECULUM).

spec·u·lar i·ron ore ▶ **n.** hematite with a metallic luster.

spec·u·late /ˈspekyəˌlāt/ ▶ **v.** [no obj.] **1** form a theory or conjecture about a subject without firm evidence: *my colleagues speculate about my private life* | [with clause] *observers* **speculated that** *the authorities wished to improve their image.*
2 invest in stocks, property, or other ventures in the hope of gain but with the risk of loss: *he didn't look as though he had the money to* **speculate in** *stocks.*
– DERIVATIVES **spec·u·la·tor** /-ˌlātər/ **n.**
– ORIGIN late 16th cent.: from Latin *speculat-* 'observed from a vantage point,' from the verb *speculari*, from *specula* 'watchtower,' from *specere* 'to look.'

spec·u·la·tion /ˌspekyəˈlāsHən/ ▶ **n.** **1** the forming of a theory or conjecture without firm evidence: *there has been widespread speculation that he plans to quit | these are only speculations.*
2 investment in stocks, property, or other ventures in the hope of gain but with the risk of loss: *the company's move into property speculation.*

spec·u·la·tive /ˈspekyəˌlātiv, -lətiv/ ▶ **adj.** **1** engaged in, expressing, or based on conjecture rather than knowledge: *discussion of the question is largely speculative.*
2 (of an investment) involving a high risk of loss. ■ (of a business venture) undertaken on the chance of success, without a preexisting contract.
– DERIVATIVES **spec·u·la·tive·ly** **adv.**, **spec·u·la·tive·ness** **n.**

spec·u·la·tive build·er ▶ **n.** a person who has houses constructed without securing buyers in advance.

spec·u·lum /ˈspekyələm/ ▶ **n.** (pl. **specula** /-lə/) **1** Medicine a metal or plastic instrument that is used to dilate an orifice or canal in the body to allow inspection.
2 Ornithology a bright patch of plumage on the wings of certain birds, esp. a strip of metallic sheen on the secondary flight feathers of many ducks.
3 a mirror or reflector of glass or metal, esp. (formerly) a metallic mirror in a reflecting telescope. ■ short for SPECULUM METAL.
– ORIGIN late Middle English: from Latin, literally 'mirror,' from *specere* 'to look.'

spec·u·lum met·al ▶ **n.** an alloy of copper and tin used to make mirrors, esp. formerly for telescopes.

sped /sped/ past and past participle of SPEED.

speech /spēcH/ ▶ **n.** **1** the expression of or the ability to express thoughts and feelings by articulate sounds: *he was born deaf and without the power of speech.* ■ a person's style of speaking: *she wouldn't accept his correction of her speech.* ■ the language of a nation, region, or group: *the distinctive rhythms of their speech.*
2 a formal address or discourse delivered to an audience: *the headmistress made a speech about how much they would miss her.* ■ a sequence of lines written for one character in a play.
– ORIGIN Old English *sprǣc*, *sprēc*, later *spēc*: related to Dutch *spraak*, German *Sprache*, also to SPEAK.

speech act ▶ **n.** Linguistics & Philosophy an utterance considered as an action, particularly with regard to its intention, purpose, or effect.

speech cen·ter (also **speech area**) ▶ **n.** a region of the brain involved in the comprehension or production of speech.

speech com·mu·ni·ty ▶ **n.** a group of people sharing a common language or dialect.

speech·i·fy /ˈspēcHəˌfī/ ▶ **v.** (**speechifies, speechifying, speechified**) [no obj.] deliver a speech, esp. in a tedious or pompous way: *writers should write, not speechify* | (as noun **speechifying**) *the after-dinner speechifying begins.*
– DERIVATIVES **speech·i·fi·ca·tion** /ˌspēcHəfiˈkāsHən/ **n.**, **speech·i·fi·er** **n.**

speech·less /ˈspēcHlis/ ▶ **adj.** unable to speak, esp. as the temporary result of shock or some strong emotion: *he was speechless with rage.* ■ unable to be expressed in words: *surges of speechless passion.*
– DERIVATIVES **speech·less·ly** **adv.**, **speech·less·ness** **n.**
– ORIGIN Old English *spǣclēas* (see SPEECH, -LESS).

speech pa·thol·o·gy /pəˈTHäləjē/ ▶ **n.** the study and treatment of speech and language problems.
– DERIVATIVES **speech pa·thol·o·gist** /-jist/ **n.**

PRONUNCIATION KEY ə *ago, up*; ər *over, fur*; a *hat*; ā *ate*; ä *car*; e *let*; ē *see*; i *fit*; ī *by*; NG *sing*; ō *go*; ô *law, for*; oi *toy*; o͝o *good*; o͞o *goo*; ou *out*; TH *thin*; T͟H *then*; ZH *vision*

speech·read·ing /ˈspēCH,rēdiNG/ ▶ **n.** lip-reading.

speech rec·og·ni·tion ▶ **n.** Computing the ability of a computer to identify and respond to the sounds produced in human speech: [as modifier] *speech recognition technologies*.

speech sound ▶ **n.** a phonetically distinct unit of speech.

speech syn·the·siz·er /ˈsinTHə,sīzər/ ▶ **n.** a machine that generates spoken language on the basis of written input.
– DERIVATIVES **speech syn·the·sis** /ˈsinTHəsis/ **n.**

speech ther·a·py ▶ **n.** training to help people with speech and language problems to speak more clearly.
– DERIVATIVES **speech ther·a·pist n.**

speech·writ·er /ˈspēCH,rītər/ ▶ **n.** a person employed to write speeches for others to deliver.

speed /spēd/ ▶ **n. 1** the rate at which someone or something is able to move or operate: *we turned onto the runway and began to **gather speed** | an engine running at full speed | the car has a top speed of 147 mph.* rapidity of movement or action: *the accident was due to excessive speed.* ■ the rate at which something happens or is done: *they were bemused by the speed of events | the course is delivered on CDROM so students can progress at their own speed.*
2 each of the possible gear ratios of a bicycle or motor vehicle.
3 the light-gathering power or f-number of a camera lens. ■ the duration of a photographic exposure. ■ the sensitivity of photographic film to light.
4 informal an amphetamine drug, esp. methamphetamine.
5 informal something that matches one's tastes or inclinations: *oak tables and chairs are more his speed.*
6 archaic success; prosperity: *wish me good speed.*
▶ **v.** (past **sped** /sped/ or **speeded**) **1** [no obj.] move quickly: *I got into the car and home we sped.* ■ (of a motorist) travel at a speed that is greater than the legal limit: *the car that crashed was speeding.* ■ **(speed up)** move or work more quickly: *you force yourself to speed up because you don't want to keep others waiting.* ■ [with obj.] cause to move, act, or happen more quickly: *recent initiatives have sought to **speed up** decision-making.*
2 [with obj.] archaic make prosperous or successful: *may God speed you.*
3 [no obj.] informal take or be under the influence of an amphetamine drug: *more kids than ever are speeding, tripping, and getting stoned.*
– PHRASES **at speed** quickly: *a car flashed past them at speed.* **up to speed** operating at full speed. ■ (of a person or company) performing at an anticipated rate or level. ■ (of a person) fully informed or up to date: *that reminds me to bring you up to speed on the soap opera.*
– DERIVATIVES **speed·er n.**
– ORIGIN Old English *spēd* (noun), *spēdan* (verb), from the Germanic base of Old English *spōwan* 'prosper, succeed,' a sense reflected in early usage.

speed bag ▶ **n.** a small punching bag used by boxers for practicing quick punches.

speed·ball /ˈspēd,bôl/ ▶ **n.** informal a mixture of cocaine and heroin.

speed·boat /ˈspēd,bōt/ ▶ **n.** a motorboat designed for high speed.
– DERIVATIVES **speed·boat·ing n.**

S

speed bump (Brit. also **speed hump**) ▶ **n.** a ridge set in a road surface, typically at intervals, to control the speed of vehicles.

speed dat·ing (trademark **SpeedDating**) ▶ **n.** an organized social activity in which people seeking romantic relationships have a series of short conversations with potential partners in order to determine whether there is mutual interest.

speed di·al ▶ **n.** a function on some telephones that allows numbers to be entered into a memory and dialed using fewer buttons.
▶ **v. (speed-dial)** [with obj.] dial (a telephone number) by using the speed dial function.

speed·i·ly /ˈspēdəlē/ ▶ **adv.** quickly or promptly: *your claim will be dealt with as speedily as possible.*

speed lim·it ▶ **n.** the maximum speed at which a vehicle may legally travel on a particular stretch of road.

speed lim·it·er another term for **LIMITER**.

speed mer·chant ▶ **n.** informal **1** a motorist who enjoys driving fast.
2 Baseball a player noted for speed, such as a very fast base runner or a fastball pitcher.

speed·o /ˈspēdō/ ▶ **n.** (pl. **speedos**) **1** informal short for **SPEEDOMETER**.
2 (Speedos) trademark men's brief, tight swimming trunks.

speed·om·e·ter /spəˈdämitər/ ▶ **n.** an instrument on a vehicle's dashboard indicating its speed.

speed-read /rēd/ ▶ **v.** read rapidly by assimilating several phrases or sentences at once.
– DERIVATIVES **speed-read·er n.**

speed skat·ing ▶ **n.** the sport of competitive racing on specially designed skates, typically around an oval track.

speed·ster /ˈspēdstər/ ▶ **n.** informal a person or thing that operates well at high speed, for example a fast car.

speed trap ▶ **n.** an area of road in which hidden police detect vehicles exceeding a speed limit, typically by radar.

speed-up ▶ **n.** an increase in speed, esp. in a person's or machine's rate of working.

speed·way /ˈspēd,wā/ ▶ **n.** a stadium or track used for automobile or motorcycle racing. ■ a highway for fast motor traffic. ■ Brit. a form of motorcycle racing on an oval dirt track, typically in a stadium.

speed·well /ˈspēd,wel/ ▶ **n.** a small creeping herbaceous plant of north temperate regions, with small blue or pink flowers. ● Genus *Veronica*, family Scrophulariaceae: several species, including the **germander speedwell**.

speed·writ·ing /ˈspēd,rītiNG/ ▶ **n.** trademark a form of shorthand using the letters of the alphabet.
– DERIVATIVES **speed·writ·er** /-tər/ **n.**

speed·y /ˈspēdē/ ▶ **adj.** (**speedier, speediest**)
1 done or occurring quickly: *a speedy recovery.*
2 moving quickly: *a speedy center fielder.*
– DERIVATIVES **speed·i·ness n.**

speed·y tri·al ▶ **n.** chiefly Law a criminal trial held after minimal delay, as considered to be a citizen's constitutional right.

Speer /spi(ə)r/, Albert (1905–81), German architect and Nazi government official; designer of the Nuremberg stadium for the 1934 Nazi Party congress. He was also minister for armaments and munitions. Following the Nuremberg trials, he served 20 years in Spandau prison.

speiss /spīs/ ▶ **n.** a mixture of impure arsenides and antimonides of nickel, cobalt, iron, and other metals, produced in the smelting of cobalt and other ores.
– ORIGIN late 18th cent.: from German *Speise* 'food, amalgam.'

Speke /spēk/, John Hanning (1827–64), English explorer. With Sir Richard Burton, he was the first European to visit Lake Tanganyika (1858). He also explored Lake Victoria, naming it in honor of the queen.

spe·le·ol·o·gy /,spēlēˈäləjē/ ▶ **n.** the study or exploration of caves.
– DERIVATIVES **spe·le·o·log·i·cal** /,spēlēəˈläjikəl/ **adj.**, **spe·le·ol·o·gist** /-jist/ **n.**
– ORIGIN late 19th cent.: from French *spéléologie*, via Latin from Greek *spēlaion* 'cave.'

spe·le·o·them /ˈspēlēə,THem/ ▶ **n.** Geology a structure formed in a cave by the deposition of minerals from water, e.g., a stalactite or stalagmite.
– ORIGIN 1950s: from Greek *spēlaion* 'cave' + *thema* 'deposit.'

spell[1] /spel/ ▶ **v.** (past and past participle **spelled** /speld/ or chiefly Brit. **spelt** /spelt/) [with obj.] write or name the letters that form (a word) in correct sequence: *Dolly spelled her name* | [no obj.] *journals have a house style about how to spell.* ■ (of letters) make up or form (a word): *the letters spell the word "how."* ■ be recognizable as a sign or characteristic of: *she had the chic, efficient look that spells Milan.* ■ lead to: *the plans would spell disaster for the economy.*
– PHRASAL VERBS **spell something out** speak the letters that form a word in sequence. ■ explain something in detail: *I'll spell out the problem again.*
– ORIGIN Middle English: shortening of Old French *espeller*, from the Germanic base of **SPELL**[2].

spell[2] ▶ **n.** a form of words used as a magical charm or incantation. ■ a state of enchantment caused by such a form of words: *the magician may **cast a spell on** himself.* ■ an ability to control or influence people as though one had magical power over them: *she is afraid that you are waking from her spell.*
– PHRASES **under a spell** not fully in control of one's thoughts and actions, as though in a state of enchantment. **under someone's spell** so devoted to someone that they seem to have magic power over one.
– ORIGIN Old English *spel(l)* 'narration,' of Germanic origin.

spell[3] ▶ **n.** a short period: *I want to get away from racing for a spell.* ■ a period spent in an activity: *a spell of greenhouse work.* ■ a period of a specified kind of weather: *an early cold spell in autumn.* ■ a period of suffering from a specified kind of illness: *she plunges off a yacht and suffers a spell of amnesia.* ■ Austral. a period of rest from work.
▶ **v.** [with obj.] allow (someone) to rest briefly by taking their place in some activity: *I got sleepy and needed her to spell me for a while at the wheel.* ■ [no obj.] Austral. take a brief rest: *I'll spell for a bit.*
– ORIGIN late 16th cent.: variant of dialect *spele* 'take the place of,' of unknown origin. The early sense of the noun was 'shift of relief workers.'

spell·bind /ˈspel,bīnd/ ▶ **v.** (past and past participle **spellbound**) [with obj.] hold the complete attention of (someone) as though by magic; fascinate: (as adj. **spellbound**) *the killer whale gave the spellbound audience a good soaking.*
– DERIVATIVES **spell·bind·er n.**

spell·bind·ing /ˈspel,bīndiNG/ ▶ **adj.** holding one's attention completely as though by magic; fascinating: *she told the spellbinding story of her life.*
– DERIVATIVES **spell·bind·ing·ly adv.**

spell·check /ˈspel,CHek/ ▶ **v.** [with obj.] check the spelling in (a text) using a spellchecker.
▶ **n.** a check of the spelling in a file of text using a spellchecker. ■ a spellchecker.

spell·check·er /ˈspel,CHeker/ ▶ **n.** a computer program that checks the spelling of words in files of text, typically by comparison with a stored list of words.

spell·er /ˈspelər/ ▶ **n.** [with adj.] a person who spells with a specified ability: *a very weak speller.* ■ a book for teaching spelling. ■ another term for **SPELLCHECKER**.

spell·ing /ˈspeliNG/ ▶ **n.** the process or activity of writing or naming the letters of a word. ■ the way a word is spelled: *the spelling of his name was influenced by French.* ■ a person's ability to spell words: *her spelling was deplorable.*

spell·ing bee ▶ **n.** a spelling competition.

spell·ing check·er ▶ **n.** another term for **SPELLCHECKER**.

spelt[1] chiefly Brit. past and past participle of **SPELL**[1].

spelt[2] /spelt/ ▶ **n.** an old kind of wheat with bearded ears and spikelets that each contain two narrow grains, not widely grown but favored as a health food. Compare with **EINKORN, EMMER**. ● *Triticum spelta*, family Gramineae.
– ORIGIN late Old English, from Old Saxon *spelta*. The word was rare until the 16th cent., when it was readopted from Middle Dutch.

spel·ter /ˈspeltər/ ▶ **n.** commercial crude smelted zinc. ■ a solder or other alloy in which zinc is the main constituent.
– ORIGIN mid 17th cent.: compare with Old French *espeautre*, Middle Dutch *speauter*; related to **PEWTER**.

spe·lunk·ing /spiˈləNGkiNG/ ▶ **n.** the exploration of caves, esp. as a hobby.
– DERIVATIVES **spe·lunk·er** /-kər/ **n.**
– ORIGIN 1940s: from obsolete *spelunk* 'cave' (from Latin *spelunca*) + **-ING**[1].

spence /spens/ ▶ **n.** archaic a larder.
– ORIGIN late Middle English: shortening of Old French *despense*, from Latin *dispensa*, feminine past participle of *dispendere* (see **DISPENSE**).

Spen·cer /ˈspensər/, Herbert (1820–1903), English philosopher and sociologist. He sought to apply the theory of natural selection to human societies, developing social Darwinism and coining the phrase "survival of the fittest" in 1864.

spen·cer[1] /ˈspensər/ ▶ **n.** a short, close-fitting jacket, worn by women and children in the early 19th century. ■ a thin woolen vest, worn by women for extra warmth in winter.
– ORIGIN probably named after the second Earl *Spencer* (1758–1834), English politician.

spen·cer[2] ▶ **n.** Sailing a boomless gaff sail on a square-rigged ship's foremast or mainmast (replaced in the mid 19th cent. by staysails).
– ORIGIN mid 19th cent.: of unknown origin.

Spen·ce·ri·an /spenˈsi(ə)rēən/ ▶ **adj.** of or relating to a style of sloping handwriting widely taught in American schools from around 1850.
– ORIGIN mid 19th cent.: named after the US calligrapher Platt Rogers *Spencer* (1800–64) who developed it.

spend /spend/ ▶ **v.** (past and past participle **spent** /spent/) [with obj.] pay out (money) in buying or hiring goods or services: *the firm has spent $100,000 on hardware and software.* ■ pay out (money) for a particular person's benefit or for the improvement of something: *the college **spent** $140 **on** each of its students.* ■ used to show the activity in which someone is engaged or the place where they are living over a period of time: *she spent a lot of time traveling.* ■ use or give out the whole of; exhaust: *she couldn't buy any more because she had already spent her money | the initial surge of interest had **spent itself**.*
▶ **n.** informal an amount of money paid for a particular purpose or over a particular period of time: *the average spend at the cafe is about $10 a head.*

–PHRASES **spend a penny** Brit. informal urinate (used euphemistically). [with reference to the coin-operated locks of public toilets.]
–DERIVATIVES **spend·a·ble** adj., **spend·er** n.
–ORIGIN Old English *spendan*, from Latin *expendere* 'pay out'; partly also a shortening of obsolete *dispend*, from Latin *dispendere* 'pay out.'

Spen·der /'spendər/, Sir Stephen (1909–95), English poet and critic. In his critical work *The Destructive Element* (1935) he defended the importance of political subject matter in literature.

spend·ing mon·ey ▶ n. money available to be spent on pleasures and entertainment.

spend·thrift /'spen(d),THrift/ ▶ n. a person who spends money in an extravagant, irresponsible way.

spend·y /'spendē/ ▶ adj. informal costing a great deal; expensive. ■ spending a great deal of money; extravagant: *that's not a real spendy crowd—they eat fast food.*

Speng·ler /'speNGglər, 'SHpeNG-/, Oswald (1880–1936), German philosopher. In his book *The Decline of the West* (1918–22) he argued that civilizations undergo a seasonal cycle of a thousand years and are subject to growth and decay analogous to biological species.

Spen·ser /'spensər/, Edmund (*c.*1552–99), English poet. He is best known for his allegorical romance *The Faerie Queene* (1590; 1596) that celebrated Queen Elizabeth I and was written in the Spenserian stanza.
–DERIVATIVES **Spen·se·ri·an** /spen'si(ə)rēən/ adj.

Spen·se·ri·an stan·za ▶ n. the stanza used by Spenser in *The Faerie Queene*, consisting of eight iambic pentameters and an alexandrine, with the rhyming scheme *ababbcbcc*.

spent /spent/ past and past participle of SPEND.
▶ adj. having been used and unable to be used again: *a spent matchstick.* ■ having no power or energy left: *the movement has become a spent force.*

spent tan ▶ n. see TAN[1] (sense 2 of the noun).

sperm /spərm/ ▶ n. (pl. **same** or **sperms**) **1** short for SPERMATOZOON. ■ informal semen. [late Middle English: via late Latin from Greek *sperma* 'seed,' from *speirein* 'to sow.']
2 short for SPERM WHALE. ■ short for SPERMACETI or SPERM OIL.

sper·ma·cet·i /,spərmə'setē/ ▶ n. a white waxy substance produced by the sperm whale, formerly used in candles and ointments. It is present in a rounded organ in the head, where it focuses acoustic signals and aids in the control of buoyancy.
–ORIGIN late 15th cent.: from medieval Latin, from late Latin *sperma* 'sperm' + *ceti* 'of a whale' (genitive of *cetus*, from Greek *kētos* 'whale'), from the belief that it was whale spawn.

sper·ma·the·ca /,spərmə'THēkə/ ▶ n. (pl. **spermathecae** /-kē/) Zoology (in a female or hermaphrodite invertebrate) a receptacle in which sperm is stored after mating.
–ORIGIN early 19th cent.: from late Latin *sperma* 'sperm' + THECA.

sper·mat·ic /spər'matik/ ▶ adj. [attrib.] of or relating to sperm or semen.
–DERIVATIVES **sper·mat·i·cal·ly** adv.
–ORIGIN late Middle English: via late Latin from Greek *spermatikos*, from *sperma* (see SPERM).

sper·mat·ic cord ▶ n. a bundle of nerves, ducts, and blood vessels connecting the testicles to the abdominal cavity.

sper·ma·tid /'spərmə,tid/ ▶ n. Biology an immature male sex cell formed from a spermatocyte that can develop into a spermatozoon without further division.
–DERIVATIVES **sper·ma·ti·dal** /,spərmə'tīdl/ adj.

spermato- ▶ comb. form Biology relating to sperm or seeds: *spermatophore* | *spermatozoid.*
–ORIGIN from Greek *sperma, spermat-* 'sperm.'

sper·mat·o·cyte /spər'matə,sīt/ ▶ n. Biology a cell produced at the second stage in the formation of spermatozoa, formed from a spermatogonium and dividing by meiosis into spermatids.

sper·mat·o·gen·e·sis /,spərmətə'jenəsis, spər,ma-/ ▶ n. Biology the production or development of mature spermatozoa.

sper·mat·o·go·ni·um /spər,matə'gōnēəm, ,spərmə-/ ▶ n. (pl. **spermatogonia** /-'gōnēə/) Biology a cell produced at an early stage in the formation of spermatozoa, formed in the wall of a seminiferous tubule and giving rise by mitosis to spermatocytes.
–DERIVATIVES **sper·mat·o·go·ni·al** /-nēəl/ adj.
–ORIGIN late 19th cent.: from SPERM + modern Latin *gonium* (from Greek *gonos* 'offspring, seed').

sper·mat·o·phore /spər'matə,fôr/ ▶ n. Zoology a protein capsule containing a mass of spermatozoa, transferred during mating in various insects, arthropods, cephalopod mollusks, etc.

sper·mat·o·phyte /spər'matə,fīt/ ▶ n. Botany a plant of a large division that comprises those that bear seeds, including the gymnosperms and angiosperms. ● Division Spermatophyta.

sper·ma·to·zo·id /,spərmətə'zoid, spər,ma-/ ▶ n. Botany a motile male gamete produced by a lower plant or a gymnosperm. Also called ANTHEROZOID.

sper·ma·to·zo·on /,spərmətə'zōən, spər,ma-/ ▶ n. (pl. **spermatozoa** /-'zōə/) Biology the mature motile male sex cell of an animal, by which the ovum is fertilized, typically having a compact head and one or more long flagella for swimming.
–DERIVATIVES **sper·ma·to·zo·al** /-zōəl/ adj., **sper·ma·to·zo·an** /-'zōən/ adj.
–ORIGIN mid 19th cent.: from Greek *sperma, spermat-* 'seed' + *zōion* 'animal.'

sperm bank ▶ n. a place where semen is kept in cold storage for use in artificial insemination.

sperm count ▶ n. a measure of the number of spermatozoa per ejaculation or per measured amount of semen, used as an indication of a man's fertility.

sper·mi·cide /'spərmə,sīd/ ▶ n. a substance that kills spermatozoa, used as a contraceptive.
–DERIVATIVES **sper·mi·cid·al** /,spərmə'sīdl/ adj.

sper·mi·dine /'spərmə,dēn/ ▶ n. Biochemistry a colorless compound with a similar distribution and effect to spermine. ● A polyamine; chem. formula: $H_2N(CH_2)_3NH(CH_2)_4NH_2$.
–ORIGIN 1920s: from SPERM + -IDE + -INE[4].

sper·mine /'spər,mēn/ ▶ n. Biochemistry a deliquescent compound that acts to stabilize various components of living cells and is widely distributed in living and decaying tissues. ● A polyamine; chem. formula: $(H_2N(CH_2)_3NH(CH_2)_2)_2$.
–ORIGIN so called because first found in sperm.

spermo- ▶ comb. form equivalent to SPERMATO-.

sperm oil ▶ n. an oil found with spermaceti in the head of the sperm whale, used formerly as a lubricant.

sperm whale ▶ n. a toothed whale with a massive head, typically feeding at great depths on squid, formerly valued for the spermaceti and sperm oil in its head and the ambergris in its intestines. ● Family Physeteridae: two genera and three species, in particular the very large *Physeter macrocephalus* (also called CACHALOT).
–ORIGIN mid 19th cent.: *sperm*, abbreviation of SPERMACETI.

spes·sart·ine /'spesər,tēn/ ▶ n. a form of garnet containing manganese and aluminum, occurring as orange-red to dark brown crystals.
–ORIGIN mid 19th cent.: from French, from *Spessart*, the name of a district in northwestern Bavaria, Germany, + -INE[4].

spew /spyo͞o/ ▶ v. [with obj.] expel large quantities of (something) rapidly and forcibly: *buses were spewing out black clouds of exhaust.* ■ [no obj.] be poured or forced out in large quantities: *oil spewed out of the damaged tanker.* ■ [no obj.] informal vomit.
–DERIVATIVES **spew·er** n.
–ORIGIN Old English *spīwan, spēowan*, of Germanic origin; related to German *speien*.

Spey /spā/ a river in east central Scotland. Rising in the Grampian Mountains east of the Great Glen, it flows 108 mi. (171 km.) northeast to the North Sea.

SPF ▶ abbr. sun protection factor (indicating the effectiveness of protective skin preparations).

sphag·num /'sfagnəm, 'spag-/ ▶ n. a plant of a genus that comprises the peat mosses. ● Genus *Sphagnum*, family Sphagnaceae.
–ORIGIN mid 18th cent.: modern Latin, from Greek *sphagnos*, denoting a kind of moss.

sphal·er·ite /'sfalə,rīt/ ▶ n. a shiny mineral, yellow to dark brown or black in color, consisting of zinc sulfide.
–ORIGIN mid 19th cent.: from Greek *sphaleros* 'deceptive' + -ITE[1]. Compare with BLENDE.

sphene /sfēn/ ▶ n. a greenish-yellow or brown mineral consisting of a silicate of calcium and titanium, occurring in granitic and metamorphic rocks in wedge-shaped crystals.
–ORIGIN early 19th cent.: from French *sphène*, from Greek *sphēn* 'wedge.'

sphe·noid /'sfēnoid/ Anatomy ▶ n. (also **sphenoid bone**) a compound bone that forms the base of the cranium, behind the eye and below the front part of the brain. It has two pairs of broad lateral "wings" and a number of other projections, and contains two air-filled sinuses.
▶ adj. of or relating to this bone.
–DERIVATIVES **sphe·noi·dal** /sfē'noidl/ adj.
–ORIGIN mid 18th cent.: from modern Latin *sphenoides*, from Greek *sphēnoeidēs*, from *sphēn* 'wedge.'

Sphe·nop·si·da /sfi'näpsidə/ Botany a class of pteridophyte plants that comprises the horsetails and their extinct relatives.
–DERIVATIVES **sphe·nop·sid** /-sid/ n. & adj.
–ORIGIN modern Latin (plural), from Greek *sphēn* 'wedge' + *opsis* 'appearance.'

sphere /sfi(ə)r/ ▶ n. **1** a round solid figure, or its surface, with every point on its surface equidistant from its center. ■ an object having this shape; a ball or globe. ■ a globe representing the earth. ■ chiefly literary a celestial body. ■ literary the sky perceived as a vault upon or in which celestial bodies are represented as lying. ■ each of a series of revolving concentrically arranged spherical shells in which celestial bodies were formerly thought to be set in a fixed relationship.
2 ;an area of activity, interest, or expertise; a section of society or an aspect of life distinguished and unified by a particular characteristic: *political reforms to match those in the economic sphere* | *his new wife's skill in the domestic sphere.*
▶ v. [with obj.] archaic enclose in or as if in a sphere. ■ form into a rounded or perfect whole.
–PHRASES **music** (or **harmony**) **of the spheres** the natural harmonic tones supposedly produced by the movement of the celestial spheres or the bodies fixed in them. **sphere of influence** (or **interest**) a country or area in which another country has power to affect developments although it has no formal authority. ■ a field or area in which an individual or organization has power to affect events and developments.
–DERIVATIVES **spher·al** /-əl/ adj. (archaic).
–ORIGIN Middle English: from Old French *espere*, from late Latin *sphera*, earlier *sphaera*, from Greek *sphaira* 'ball.'

-sphere ▶ comb. form denoting a structure or region of spherical form, esp. a region around the earth: *ionosphere.*
–ORIGIN from SPHERE, on the pattern of (*atmo*)*sphere*.

spher·ic /'sfi(ə)rik, 'sfer-/ ▶ adj. spherical.
–DERIVATIVES **sphe·ric·i·ty** /sfi'risitē/ n.

spher·i·cal /'sfi(ə)rikəl, 'sfer-/ ▶ adj. shaped like a sphere. ■ of or relating to the properties of spheres. ■ formed inside or on the surface of a sphere.
–DERIVATIVES **spher·i·cal·ly** adv.
–ORIGIN late 15th cent.: via late Latin from Greek *sphairikos*, from *sphaira* (see SPHERE).

spher·i·cal ab·er·ra·tion /,abə'rāSHən/ ▶ n. a loss of definition in the image arising from the surface geometry of a spherical mirror or lens.

spher·i·cal an·gle ▶ n. an angle formed by the intersection of two great circles of a sphere.

spher·i·cal co·or·di·nates (also **spherical polar coordinates**) ▶ plural n. three coordinates that define the location of a point in three-dimensional space. They are the length of its radius vector *r*, the angle θ between the vertical plane containing this vector and the *x*-axis, and the angle φ between this vector and the horizontal *x–y* plane. ● Usually written (*r*, θ, φ).

spher·i·cal tri·an·gle ▶ n. a triangle formed by three arcs of great circles on a sphere.

spher·i·cal trig·o·nom·e·try ▶ n. the branch of trigonometry concerned with the measurement of the angles and sides of spherical triangles.

sphe·roid /'sfi(ə)r,oid/ ▶ n. a spherelike but not perfectly spherical body. ■ a solid generated by a half-revolution of an ellipse about its major axis (**prolate spheroid**) or minor axis (**oblate spheroid**).
–DERIVATIVES **sphe·roi·dal** /sfi'roidl/ adj., **sphe·roi·dic·i·ty** /,sfi(ə)roi'disitē/ n.

sphe·ro·plast /'sfi(ə)rə,plast, 'sfer-/ ▶ n. Biology a bacterium or plant cell bound by its plasma membrane, the cell wall being deficient or lacking and the whole having a spherical form.

spher·ule /'sfi(ə)r(y)o͞ol, 'sfer-/ ▶ n. a small sphere.
–DERIVATIVES **spher·u·lar** /-yo͝olər/ adj.
–ORIGIN mid 17th cent.: from late Latin *sphaerula*, diminutive of Latin *sphaera* (see SPHERE).

spher·u·lite /'sfi(ə)r(y)ə,līt, 'sfer-/ ▶ n. chiefly Geology a small spheroidal mass of crystals (esp. of a mineral) grouped radially around a point.
–DERIVATIVES **spher·u·lit·ic** /,sfi(ə)r(y)ə'litik, ,sfer-/ adj.
–ORIGIN early 19th cent.: from SPHERULE + -ITE[1].

sphinc·ter /'sfiNGktər/ ▶ n. Anatomy a ring of muscle surrounding and serving to guard or close an opening or tube, such as the anus or the openings of the stomach.

S

– DERIVATIVES **sphinc·ter·al** /-əl/ **adj.**, **sphinc·ter·ic** /ˌsfiNGk'terik/ **adj.**
– ORIGIN late 16th cent.: via Latin from Greek *sphinktēr*, from *sphingein* 'bind tight.'

sphin·gid /'sfinjid/ ▶ **n.** Entomology a moth of the hawk moth family (Sphingidae).
– ORIGIN early 20th cent.: from modern Latin *Sphingidae* (plural), from Greek *Sphinx* (see SPHINX).

sphingo- ▶ **comb. form** used in the names of various related compounds isolated from the brain and nervous tissue: *sphingomyelin.*
– ORIGIN from Greek *Sphinx, Sphing-* 'Sphinx,' originally in *sphingosine*, with reference to the enigmatic nature of the compound.

sphin·go·lip·id /ˌsfiNGgō'lipid/ ▶ **n.** Biochemistry any of a class of compounds that are fatty acid derivatives of sphingosine and occur chiefly in the cell membranes of the brain and nervous tissue.

sphin·go·my·e·lin /ˌsfiNGgō'mīəlin/ ▶ **n.** Biochemistry a substance that occurs widely in brain and nervous tissue, consisting of complex phosphoryl derivatives of sphingosine and choline.

sphin·go·sine /'sfiNGgəˌsēn/ ▶ **n.** Biochemistry a basic compound that is a constituent of a number of substances important in the metabolism of nerve cells, esp. sphingomyelins. ● A crystalline alcohol; chem. formula: $C_{18}H_{37}NO_2$.

sphinx /sfiNGks/ ▶ **n. 1** (**Sphinx**) Greek Mythology a winged monster of Thebes, having a woman's head and a lion's body. It propounded a riddle about the three ages of man, killing those who failed to solve it, until Oedipus was successful, whereupon the Sphinx committed suicide. ■ (**the Sphinx**) an ancient Egyptian stone figure having a lion's body and a human or animal head, esp. the huge statue near the Pyramids at Giza. ■ (usu. **sphinx**) an enigmatic or inscrutable person.
2 (also **sphinx moth**) another term for HAWK MOTH.
– ORIGIN late Middle English: via Latin from Greek *Sphinx*, apparently from *sphingein* 'draw tight.'

the Sphinx at Giza

sp ht ▶ **abbr.** specific heat.

sphygmo- ▶ **comb. form** Physiology of or relating to the pulse or pulsation: *sphygmograph.*
– ORIGIN from Greek *sphugmos* 'pulse.'

sphyg·mo·graph /'sfigməˌgraf/ ▶ **n.** an instrument that produces a line recording the strength and rate of a person's pulse.

sphyg·mo·ma·nom·e·ter /ˌsfigmōmə'nämitər/ ▶ **n.** an instrument for measuring blood pressure, typically consisting of an inflatable rubber cuff that is applied to the arm and connected to a column of mercury next to a graduated scale, enabling the determination of systolic and diastolic blood pressure by increasing and gradually releasing the pressure in the cuff.
– DERIVATIVES **sphyg·mo·ma·nom·e·try** /-mətrē/ **n.**

Sphynx /sfinNGsk/ ▶ **n.** a cat of a hairless breed, originally from North America.

spic /spik/ ▶ **n.** informal, offensive a contemptuous term for a Spanish-speaking person from Central or South America or the Caribbean.
– ORIGIN early 20th cent.: abbreviation of US slang *spiggoty*, in the same sense, of uncertain origin: perhaps an alteration of *speak the* in 'no speak the English.'

Spi·ca /'spīkə/ Astronomy the brightest star in the constellation Virgo.
– ORIGIN Latin, literally 'ear of wheat (in the hand of the goddess).'

spi·ca /'spīkə/ ▶ **n.** Medicine a bandage folded into a spiral arrangement resembling an ear of wheat or barley.
– ORIGIN late 17th cent.: from Latin, literally 'spike, ear of corn'; related to *spina* 'spine.' The current sense is influenced by Greek *stakhus* 'ear of wheat.'

spic and span ▶ **adj.** variant spelling of SPICK AND SPAN.

spic·ca·to /spi'kätō/ Music ▶ **n.** a style of staccato playing on stringed instruments involving bouncing the bow on the strings.
▶ **adj. & adv.** to be performed in this style.
– ORIGIN Italian, literally 'detailed, distinct.'

spice /spīs/ ▶ **n. 1** an aromatic or pungent vegetable substance used to flavor food, e.g., cloves, pepper, or mace: *enjoy the taste and aroma of freshly ground spices.* ■ an element providing interest and excitement: *healthy rivalry adds spice to the game.*
2 a russet color.
▶ **v.** [with obj.] (often as adj. **spiced**) flavor with spice: *turbot with a spiced sauce.* ■ add an interesting or piquant quality to; make more exciting: *she was probably adding details to spice up the story.*
– ORIGIN Middle English: shortening of Old French *espice*, from Latin *species* 'sort, kind,' in late Latin 'wares.'

spice·bush /'spīsˌbo͝osH/ ▶ **n.** a North American shrub with aromatic leaves, bark, and fruit. The leaves were formerly used for a tea and the fruit as an allspice substitute. ● *Lindera benzoin*, family Lauraceae.

Spice Is·lands former name of **Molucca Islands**.

spick and span /ˌspik ən 'span/ (also **spic and span**) ▶ **adj.** spotlessly clean and well looked after: *I have to get my apartment spick and span.*
– ORIGIN late 16th cent. (in the sense 'brand new'): from *spick and span new*, emphatic extension of dialect *span new*, from Old Norse *spán-nýr*, from *spánn* 'chip' + *nýr* 'new'; *spick* influenced by Dutch *spiksplinternieuw*, literally 'splinter new.'

spic·ule /'spikˌyo͞ol/ ▶ **n. 1** technical a minute sharp-pointed object or structure that is typically present in large numbers, such as a fine particle of ice. ■ Zoology each of the small needlelike or sharp-pointed structures of calcite or silica that make up the skeleton of a sponge.
2 Astronomy a short-lived, relatively small radial jet of gas in the chromosphere or lower corona of the sun.
– DERIVATIVES **spic·u·lar** /-yələr/ **adj.**, **spic·u·late** /-yəlit, -yəˌlāt/ **adj.**, **spic·u·la·tion n.**
– ORIGIN late 18th cent.: from modern Latin *spicula, spiculum*, diminutives of *spica* 'ear of grain.'

spic·y /'spīsē/ ▶ **adj.** (**spicier, spiciest**) flavored with or fragrant with spice: *pasta in a spicy tomato sauce.*

spi·der /'spīdər/ ▶ **n.** an eight-legged predatory arachnid with an unsegmented body consisting of a fused head and thorax and a rounded abdomen. Spiders have fangs that inject poison into their prey, and most kinds spin webs in which to capture insects. ● Order Araneae, class Arachnida. ■ used in names of similar or related arachnids, e.g., **sea spider, sun spider**. ■ any object resembling a spider, esp. one having numerous or prominent legs or radiating spokes. ■ a cast-iron iron frying pan, originally made with legs for cooking on coals in a hearth. ■ a long-legged rest for a billiard cue that can be placed over a ball without touching it.
▶ **v.** [no obj.] move in a scuttling manner suggestive of a spider: *a treecreeper spidered head first down the tree trunk.* ■ form a pattern suggestive of a spider or its web.
– DERIVATIVES **spi·der·ish adj.**
– ORIGIN late Old English *spīthra*, from *spinnan* (see SPIN).

spi·der crab ▶ **n.** a crab with long thin legs and a compact pear-shaped body, which is camouflaged in some kinds by attached sponges and seaweed. ● Majidae and other families, order Decapoda: *Macropodia* and other genera.

spi·der flow·er ▶ **n.** a plant with clusters of flowers that have long protruding stamens or styles, giving the flower head a spiderlike appearance. ● a South American plant (genus *Cleome*, family Capparidaceae, in particular *C. hassleriana*). ● an Australian grevillea.

spi·der hole ▶ **n.** a trench or indentation used by a spider for rest or ambush. ■ a small, rough excavation for concealing a person, as from an enemy.

spi·der lil·y ▶ **n.** a lily that typically has long slender petals or elongated petallike parts around the flower. ● *Hymenocallis* and other genera, family Liliaceae (or Amaryllidaceae).

spi·der·ling /'spīdərliNG/ ▶ **n.** a young spider.

spi·der·man /'spīdərˌman/ ▶ **n.** (pl. **spidermen**) Brit. informal a person who works at great heights in building work.

spi·der mite ▶ **n.** an active plant-eating mite that resembles a minute spider and is frequently a serious garden and greenhouse pest. ● Family Tetranychidae: many species, in particular the **red spider mite** (*Tetranychus urticae*).

spi·der mon·key ▶ **n.** a South American monkey with very long limbs and a long prehensile tail. ● Genus *Ateles*, family Cebidae: four species.

spi·der ne·vus /'nēvəs/ ▶ **n.** a cluster of minute red blood vessels visible under the skin, occurring typically during pregnancy or as a symptom of certain diseases (e.g., cirrhosis or acne rosacea).

spi·der plant ▶ **n.** a plant of the lily family that has long narrow leaves with a central yellow or white stripe, native to southern Africa and popular as a houseplant. ● *Chlorophytum comosum*, family Liliaceae.

spider plant

spi·der veins ▶ **plural n.** dilated capillaries on the skin, resembling spider legs, and common among children and pregnant women.

spi·der·web /'spīdərweb/ ▶ **n.** a web made by a spider. ■ a thing resembling such a web: *the spiderweb of overhead transmission lines.* ■ a type of turquoise crisscrossed with fine dark lines.
▶ **v.** (**spiderwebs, spiderwebbing, spiderwebbed**) [with obj.] cover with a pattern resembling a spiderweb: *a glass block spiderwebbed with cracks.*

spi·der·wort /'spīdərwərt, -wôrt/ ▶ **n.** an American plant whose flowers bear long hairy stamens. ● Genus *Tradescantia*, family Commelinaceae: several species, including the blue-flowered North American *T. virginiana*, from which many cultivars have been derived.

spi·der·y /'spīdərē/ ▶ **adj.** resembling a spider, esp. having long, thin, angular lines like a spider's legs: *the letters were written in a spidery hand.*

spie·gel·ei·sen /'spēgəˌlīzən/ ▶ **n.** an alloy of iron and manganese, used in steelmaking.
– ORIGIN mid 19th cent.: from German, from *Spiegel* 'mirror' + *Eisen* 'iron.'

spiel /spēl, sHpēl/ informal ▶ **n.** a long or fast speech or story, typically one intended as a means of persuasion or as an excuse but regarded with skepticism or contempt by those who hear it: *he delivers a breathless and effortless spiel in promotion of his new novel.*
▶ **v.** [with obj.] reel off; recite: *he solemnly spieled all he knew.* ■ [no obj.] speak glibly or at length.
– ORIGIN late 19th cent.: from German *Spiel* 'a game.'

Spiel·berg /'spēlˌbərg/, Steven (1947–), US movie director and producer. His science-fiction and adventure movies such as *ET* (1982), *Jaws* (1985), *Jurassic Park* (1992), and *Saving Private Ryan* (1998) broke box-office records, while *Schindler's List* (1993) won seven Academy Awards.

spiel·er /'spēlər/ informal ▶ **n. 1** a glib or voluble speaker.
2 Austral./NZ a gambler or swindler.
3 chiefly Brit. a gambling club.
– ORIGIN mid 19th cent.: from German *Spieler* 'player' (see SPIEL).

spiff /spif/ ▶ **v.** [with obj.] (**spiff someone/something up**) informal make someone or something attractive, tidy, or stylish: *he arrived all spiffed up in a dinner jacket.*
– ORIGIN late 19th cent.: perhaps from dialect *spiff* 'well-dressed.'

spif·fing /'spifiNG/ ▶ **adj.** Brit. informal, dated excellent; splendid: *how spiffing you look!*
– ORIGIN late 19th cent.: of unknown origin.

spif·fli·cate /'spifliˌkāt/ (also **spiflicate**) ▶ **v.** [with obj.] informal, humorous treat roughly or severely; destroy: *the mosquito was spifflicated.*
– DERIVATIVES **spif·fli·ca·tion** /ˌspifli'kāsHən/ **n.**
– ORIGIN mid 18th cent.: a fanciful formation.

spiff·y /'spifē/ ▶ **adj.** (**spiffier, spiffiest**) informal smart in appearance: *a spiffy new outfit.*
– DERIVATIVES **spif·fi·ly** /'spifəlē/ **adv.**
– ORIGIN mid 19th cent.: of unknown origin.

spig·ot /'spigət/ ▶ **n. 1** a small peg or plug, esp. for insertion into the vent of a cask.
2 a faucet. ■ a device for controlling the flow of liquid in a faucet.
3 the plain end of a section of a pipe fitting into the socket of the next one.
– ORIGIN Middle English: perhaps an alteration of Provençal *espigou(n)*, from Latin *spiculum*, diminutive of *spicum*, variant of *spica* (see SPICA).

spike[1] /spīk/ ▶ **n. 1** a thin, pointed piece of metal, wood, or another rigid material. ■ a large stout nail, esp. one used to fasten a rail to a railroad tie. ■ each of several metal points set into the sole of an athletic shoe to prevent slipping. ■ (**spikes**) a pair of athletic shoes with such metal points. ■ short for SPIKE HEEL. ■ informal a hypodermic needle.

2 a sharp increase in the magnitude or concentration of something: *the oil price spike.* ■ Electronics a pulse of very short duration in which a rapid increase in voltage is followed by a rapid decrease.
▶ **v.** [with obj.] **1** impale on or pierce with a sharp point: *she spiked another oyster.* ■ Baseball injure (a player) with the spikes on one's shoes. ■ (of a newspaper editor) reject (a story) by or as if by filing it on a spike: *the editors deemed the article in bad taste and spiked it.* ■ stop the progress of (a plan or undertaking); put an end to: *he doubted they would spike the entire effort over this one negotiation.* ■ historical render (a gun) useless by plugging up the vent with a spike.
2 form into or cover with sharp points: *his hair was matted and spiked with blood.* ■ [no obj.] take on a sharp, pointed shape: *lightning spiked across the sky.* ■ [no obj.] increase and then decrease sharply; reach a peak: *oil prices would spike and fall again.*
3 informal add alcohol or a drug to contaminate (drink or food) surreptitiously: *she bought me an orange juice and spiked it with vodka.* ■ add sharp or pungent flavoring to (food or drink): *spike the liquid with lime or lemon juice.* ■ enrich (a nuclear reactor or its fuel) with a particular isotope.
4 (in volleyball) hit (the ball) forcefully from a position near the net so that it moves downward into the opposite court. ■ Football fling (the ball) forcefully to the ground, typically in celebration of a touchdown.
– ORIGIN Middle English: perhaps from Middle Low German and Middle Dutch *spiker*, related to SPOKE[1]. The verb dates from the early 17th cent.

spike[2] ▶ **n.** Botany a flower cluster formed of many flower heads attached directly to a long stem. Compare with CYME, RACEME.
– ORIGIN late Middle English (denoting an ear of corn): from Latin *spica* (see SPICA).

spike heel ▶ **n.** a high tapering heel on a woman's shoe.

spike·let /'spīklit/ ▶ **n.** Botany the basic unit of a grass flower, consisting of two glumes or outer bracts at the base and one or more florets above.

spike·nard /'spīk,närd/ ▶ **n. 1** historical a costly perfumed ointment much valued in ancient times.
2 the Himalayan plant of the valerian family that produces the rhizome from which this ointment was prepared. ● *Nardostachys grandiflora*, family Valerianaceae. ■ a plant resembling spikenard in fragrance.
– ORIGIN Middle English: from medieval Latin *spica nardi* (see SPIKE[2], NARD), translating Greek *nardostakhus*.

spik·y /'spīkē/ ▶ **adj.** (**spikier**, **spikiest**) like a spike or spikes or having many spikes: *he has short spiky hair.* ■ informal easily offended or annoyed.
– DERIVATIVES **spik·i·ly** /-kəlē/ **adv.**, **spik·i·ness n.**

spile /spīl/ ▶ **n. 1** a small wooden peg or spigot for stopping a cask. ■ a small wooden or metal spout for tapping the sap from a sugar maple.
2 a large, heavy timber driven into the ground to support a superstructure.
▶ **v.** [with obj.] broach (a cask) with a peg in order to draw off liquid.
– ORIGIN early 16th cent.: from Middle Dutch and Middle Low German, 'wooden peg'; sense 2 of the noun apparently an alteration of PILE[2].

spi·lite /'spī,līt/ ▶ **n.** Geology an altered form of basalt, rich in albite and commonly amygdaloidal in texture, typical of basaltic lava solidified under water.
– DERIVATIVES **spi·lit·ic** /spī'litik/ **adj.**
– ORIGIN mid 19th cent.: from French *spillite*, from Greek *spilos* 'spot, stain.'

spill[1] /spil/ ▶ **v.** (past and past participle **spilt** /spilt/ or **spilled**) [with obj.] cause or allow (liquid) to flow over the edge of its container, esp. unintentionally: *you'll spill that coffee if you're not careful* | figurative *azaleas spilled cascades of flowers over the pathways.* ■ [no obj.] (of liquid) flow over the edge of its container: *some of the wine spilled onto the floor* | figurative *light spilled into the room from the landing.* ■ (with reference to the contents of something) empty out or be emptied out onto a surface: [no obj.] *passengers' baggage had **spilled out** of the hold* | [with obj.] *injured cells tend to swell up and burst, spilling their contents.* ■ [no obj.] (of a number of people) move out of somewhere quickly: *students began to spill out of the building.* ■ informal reveal (confidential information) to someone: *he was reluctant to spill her address.* ■ cause (someone) to fall off a horse or bicycle: *the horse was wrenched off course, spilling his rider.* ■ Sailing let (wind) out of a sail, typically by slackening the sheets. ■ Brit. (in the context of ball games) drop (the ball).
▶ **n. 1** a quantity of liquid that has spilled or been spilled: *a 25-ton oil spill* | *wipe up spills immediately* | figurative *their shifting spill of lantern-light.* ■ an instance of a liquid spilling or being spilled: *he was absolved from any blame for the oil spill.*
2 a fall from a horse or bicycle: *Granddad took a spill while riding the bay mare.*
– PHRASES **spill the beans** informal reveal secret information unintentionally or indiscreetly. **spill (someone's) blood** kill or wound people. **spill one's guts** informal reveal copious information to someone in an uninhibited way.
– PHRASAL VERBS **spill over** (of a bad situation or strong emotion) reach a point at which it can no longer be controlled or contained: *years of frustration **spilled over into** violence.*
– DERIVATIVES **spill·er n.**
– ORIGIN Old English *spillan* 'kill, destroy, waste, shed (blood)'; of unknown origin.

spill[2] ▶ **n.** a thin strip of wood or paper used for lighting a fire, candle, pipe, etc.
– ORIGIN Middle English (in the sense 'sharp fragment of wood'): obscurely related to SPILE. The current sense dates from the early 19th cent.

spill·age /'spilij/ ▶ **n.** the action of causing or allowing a liquid to spill, or liquid spilled in this way: *accidents involving chemical spillage* | *oil spillages at sea.*

Spil·lane /spə'lān/, Mickey (1918–2006), US writer; pseudonym of *Frank Morrison Spillane.* His popular detective novels, many of which feature private detective Mike Hammer, include *My Gun Is Quick* (1950) and *The Big Kill* (1951).

spil·li·kin /'spilikin/ ▶ **n. 1** (**spillikins**) another term for JACKSTRAWS.
2 a splinter or fragment.
– ORIGIN mid 18th cent.: from SPILL[2] + -KIN.

spill·o·ver /'spil,ōvər/ ▶ **n.** an instance of overflowing or spreading into another area: *there has been a spillover into public schools of the ethos of private schools.* ■ a thing that spreads or has spread into another area: *the village was a spillover from a neighboring, larger village.* ■ [usu. as modifier] an unexpected consequence, repercussion, or byproduct: *the spillover effect of the quarrel.*

spill·way /'spil,wā/ ▶ **n.** a passage for surplus water from a dam. ■ a natural drainage channel cut by water from melting glaciers or ice fields.

spilt /spilt/ past and past participle of SPILL[1].

spilth /spilTH/ ▶ **n.** archaic the action of spilling; material that is spilled.

spin /spin/ ▶ **v.** (**spins**, **spinning**, **spun** /spən/)
1 turn or cause to turn or whirl around quickly: [no obj.] *the girl **spun around** in alarm* | *the rear wheels spun violently* | [with obj.] *he fiddled with the radio, spinning the dial.* ■ [no obj.] (of a person's head) give a sensation of dizziness: *the figures were enough to make her head spin.* ■ [with obj.] chiefly Cricket impart a revolving motion to (a ball) when bowling. ■ [no obj.] (of a ball) move through the air with such a revolving motion. ■ [with obj.] give (a news story or other information) a particular interpretation, esp. a favorable one. ■ [with obj.] shape (sheet metal) by pressure applied during rotation on a lathe: (as adj. **spun**) *spun metal components.*
2 [with obj.] draw out (wool, cotton, or other material) and convert it into threads, either by hand or with machinery: *they **spin** wool **into** the yarn for weaving* | (as adj. **spun**) *spun glass.* ■ make (threads) in this way: *this method is used to spin filaments from syrups.* ■ (of a spider or a silkworm or other insect) produce (gossamer or silk) or construct (a web or cocoon) by extruding a fine viscous thread from a special gland.
3 [no obj.] fish with a spinner: *they were spinning for salmon in the lake.*
▶ **n. 1** a rapid turning or whirling motion: *he concluded the dance with a double spin.* ■ revolving motion imparted to a ball in a game such as baseball, cricket, tennis, or billiards: *this racket enables the player to impart more spin to the ball.* ■ [in sing.] a particular bias, interpretation, or point of view, intended to create a favorable (or sometimes, unfavorable) impression when presented to the public: *he tried to put a positive spin on the president's campaign.* ■ [usu. in sing.] an uncontrolled fast revolving descent of an aircraft, resulting from a stall: *he tried to stop the plane from **going into a spin**.* ■ Physics the intrinsic angular momentum of a subatomic particle.
2 [in sing.] informal a brief trip in a vehicle for pleasure: *a spin around town.*
– PHRASES **spin one's wheels** informal waste one's time or efforts. **spin a yarn** tell a long, far-fetched story.
– PHRASAL VERBS **spin something off** (of a parent company) turn a subsidiary into a new and separate company. **spin out** (of a driver or car) lose control, esp. in a skid. **spin something out** make something last as long as possible: *they seem keen to spin out the debate through their speeches and interventions.* ■ spend or occupy time aimlessly or without profit: *Shane and Mary played games to spin out the afternoon.*
– ORIGIN Old English *spinnan* 'draw out and twist (fiber)'; related to German *spinnen*. The noun dates from the mid 19th cent.

spi·na bif·i·da /'spīnə 'bifidə/ ▶ **n.** a congenital defect of the spine in which part of the spinal cord and its meninges are exposed through a gap in the backbone. It often causes paralysis of the lower limbs, and sometimes mental handicap.
– ORIGIN early 18th cent.: modern Latin (see SPINE, BIFID).

spin·ach /'spiniCH/ ▶ **n.** a widely cultivated edible Asian plant of the goosefoot family, with large, dark green leaves that are eaten raw or cooked as a vegetable. ● *Spinacia oleracea*, family Chenopodiaceae.
– DERIVATIVES **spin·ach·y adj.**
– ORIGIN Middle English: probably from Old French *espinache*, via Arabic from Persian *aspānāk*.

spi·nal /'spīnl/ ▶ **adj.** of or relating to the spine: *spinal injuries.* ■ relating to or forming the central axis or backbone of something: *the building of a new spinal road.*
– DERIVATIVES **spi·nal·ly adv.**
– ORIGIN late 16th cent.: from late Latin *spinalis*, from Latin *spina* (see SPINE).

spi·nal ca·nal ▶ **n.** a cavity that runs successively through each of the vertebrae and contains the spinal cord.

spi·nal col·umn ▶ **n.** the spine; the backbone.

spi·nal cord ▶ **n.** the cylindrical bundle of nerve fibers and associated tissue that is enclosed in the spine and connects nearly all parts of the body to the brain, with which it forms the central nervous system.

spi·nal tap ▶ **n.** another term for LUMBAR PUNCTURE.

spin·dle /'spindl/ ▶ **n. 1** a slender rounded rod with tapered ends used in hand spinning to twist and wind thread from a mass of wool or flax held on a distaff. ■ a pin or rod used on a spinning wheel to twist and wind the thread. ■ a pin bearing the bobbin of a spinning machine. ■ a measure of length for yarn, equal to 15,120 yards (13,826 m) for cotton or 14,400 yards (13,167 m) for linen. ■ a pointed metal rod on a base, used to impale paper items for temporary filing. ■ a turned piece of wood used as a banister or chair leg.
2 a rod or pin serving as an axis that revolves or on which something revolves. ■ the vertical rod at the center of a record turntable that keeps the record in place during play.
3 Biology a slender mass of microtubules formed when a cell divides. At metaphase, the chromosomes become attached to it by their centromeres before being pulled toward its ends.
4 (also **spindle tree**) a shrub or small tree with slender toothed leaves and pink capsules containing bright orange seeds. The hard timber was formerly used for making spindles. ● Genus *Euonymus*, family Celastraceae: several species, in particular the Eurasian *E. europaeus*.
▶ **v.** [with obj.] impale (a piece of paper) on a metal spindle for temporary filing purposes: *do not fold, spindle, or mutilate.*
– ORIGIN Old English *spinel*, from the base of the verb SPIN.

spin·dle cell ▶ **n.** a narrow, elongated cell, in particular: ■ Medicine a cell of this shape indicating the presence of a type of sarcoma. ■ Zoology a cell of this shape present in the blood of most nonmammalian vertebrates, functioning as a platelet.

spin·dle legs (also **spindleshanks** /'spindl,SHANGks/) ▶ **plural n.** long thin legs. ■ [treated as sing.] a person with long thin legs.
– DERIVATIVES **spin·dle-leg·ged adj.**

spin·dle-shaped ▶ **adj.** having a circular cross section and tapering toward each end.

spin·dle tree ▶ **n.** see SPINDLE (sense 4 of the noun).

spin·dly /'spin(d)lē/ ▶ **adj.** (of a person or limb) long or tall and thin: *spindly arms and legs.* ■ (of a thing) thin and weak or insubstantial in construction: *spindly chairs.*

spin doc·tor ▶ **n.** informal a spokesperson employed to give a favorable interpretation of events to the media, esp. on behalf of a political party.

spin-down ▶ **n.** a decrease in the speed of rotation of a spinning object, in particular a heavenly body or a computer disk.

spin·drift /'spin,drift/ ▶ **n.** spray blown from the crests of waves by the wind. ■ driving snow or sand.

–ORIGIN early 17th cent. (originally Scots): variant of *spoondrift*, from archaic *spoon* 'run before wind or sea' + the noun DRIFT.

spin dry·er ▶ n. a machine for drying wet clothes by spinning them in a revolving perforated drum.
–DERIVATIVES **spin-dry** v.

spine /spīn/ ▶ n. **1** a series of vertebrae extending from the skull to the small of the back, enclosing the spinal cord and providing support for the thorax and abdomen; the backbone. ■ a thing's central feature or main source of strength: *players who will form the spine of our team.* ■ resolution or strength of character. ■ the part of a book's jacket or cover that encloses the inner edges of the pages, facing outward when the book is on a shelf and typically bearing the title and the author's name.
2 Zoology & Botany any hard pointed defensive projection or structure, such as a prickle of a hedgehog, a spikelike projection on a sea urchin, a sharp ray in a fish's fin, or a spike on the stem of a plant. ■ Geology a tall mass of viscous lava extruded from a volcano.
–DERIVATIVES **spined** adj. [in combination] *broken-spined paperbacks.*
–ORIGIN late Middle English: shortening of Old French *espine*, or from Latin *spina* 'thorn, prickle, backbone.'

spine-chill·er ▶ n. a story or movie that inspires terror and excitement.

spine-chill·ing ▶ adj. inspiring terror or terrified excitement: *a spine-chilling silence.*

spi·nel /spi'nel/ ▶ n. a hard glassy mineral occurring as octahedral crystals of variable color and consisting chiefly of magnesium and aluminum oxides. ■ Chemistry any of a class of oxides including this, containing aluminum and another metal and having the general formula MAl_2O_4.
–ORIGIN early 16th cent.: from French *spinelle*, from Italian *spinella*, diminutive of *spina* 'thorn.'

spine·less /'spīnlis/ ▶ adj. **1** having no spine or backbone; invertebrate.
2 lacking resolution; weak and purposeless: *a spineless coward.*
3 (of an animal or plant) lacking spines: *spineless forms of prickly pear have been selected.*
–DERIVATIVES **spine·less·ly** adv., **spine·less·ness** n.

spi·nel ru·by ▶ n. a deep red variety of spinel, often of gem quality.

spin·et /'spinit/ ▶ n. **1** historical a small harpsichord with the strings set obliquely to the keyboard, popular in the 18th century.
2 a type of small upright piano.
–ORIGIN mid 17th cent.: shortening of obsolete French *espinette*, from Italian *spinetta* 'virginal, spinet,' diminutive of *spina* 'thorn' (see SPINE), the strings being plucked by quills.

spine-tin·gling ▶ adj. informal thrilling or pleasurably frightening: *a spine-tingling adventure.*

Spin·garn /'spin,gärn/, Joel Elias (1875–1939), US writer, critic, and social reformer. A founder of the National Association for the Advancement of Colored People (NAACP) in 1909, he established the Spingarn Medal, given annually to an African American for exceptional achievement, in 1913. He was also a founder of Harcourt, Brace & Co. in 1919 and worked as its literary adviser until 1924.

S

spin·mei·ster /'spin,mīstər/ ▶ n. informal another term for SPIN DOCTOR.
–ORIGIN 1990s: from *spin* + *-meister.*

spin·na·ker /'spinəkər/ ▶ n. a large three-cornered sail, typically bulging when full, set forward of the mainsail of a yacht when running before the wind.
–ORIGIN mid 19th cent.: apparently a fanciful formation from *Sphinx*, the name of the yacht first using it, perhaps influenced by SPANKER.

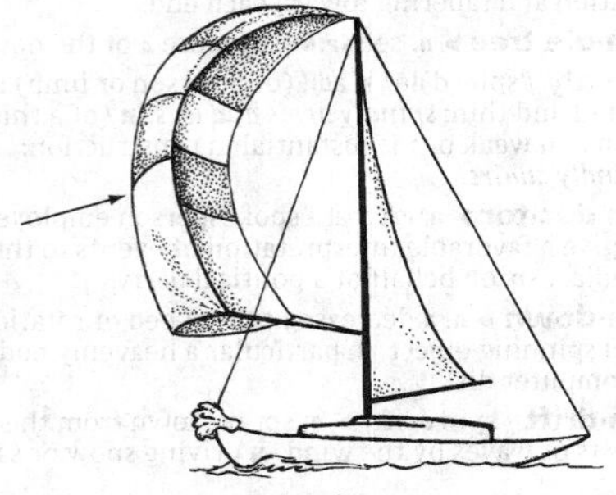
spinnaker

spin·ner /'spinər/ ▶ n. **1** a person occupied in making thread by spinning.
2 a person or thing that spins.
3 (also **spinnerbait**) Fishing a lure designed to revolve when pulled through the water. ■ a type of fishing fly, used chiefly for trout.
4 a metal fairing that is attached to and revolves with the propeller boss of an aircraft in order to streamline it.

spin·ner dol·phin ▶ n. a dolphin of warm seas that has a long slender beak and is noted for rotating several times while leaping into the air. ● Genus *Stenella*, family Delphinidae: two species, in particular *S. longirostris.*

spin·ner·et /,spinə'ret/ ▶ n. Zoology any of a number of different organs through which the silk, gossamer, or thread of spiders, silkworms, and certain other insects is produced. ■ (in the production of man-made fibers) a cap or plate with a number of small holes through which a fiber-forming solution is forced.

spin·ney /'spinē/ ▶ n. (pl. **spinneys**) Brit. a small area of trees and bushes.
–ORIGIN late 16th cent.: shortening of Old French *espinei*, from an alteration of Latin *spinetum* 'thicket,' from *spina* 'thorn.'

spin·ning[1] /'spiNiNG/ ▶ n. the action or process of converting fibers into thread or yarn.

spin·ning[2] ▶ n. trademark an intense form of aerobic exercise performed on stationary exercise bikes and led by an instructor who sets the constantly varying pace.

spin·ning jen·ny ▶ n. historical a machine for spinning with more than one spindle at a time, patented by James Hargreaves in 1770.

spin·ning mule ▶ n. see MULE[1] (sense 3).

spin·ning top ▶ n. see TOP[2].

spin·ning wheel ▶ n. an apparatus for spinning yarn or thread, with a spindle driven by a wheel attached to a crank or treadle.

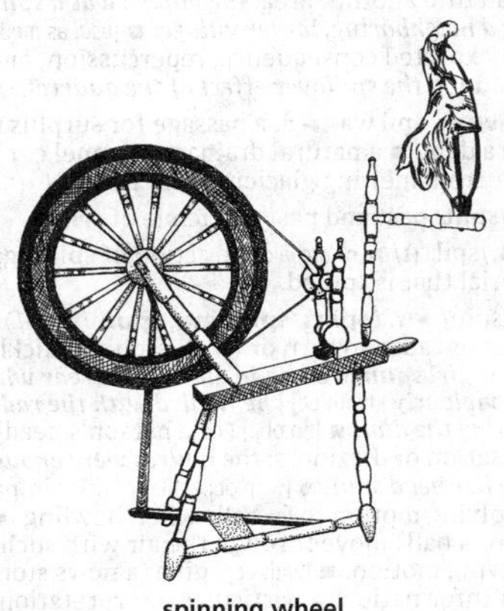
spinning wheel

spin·ny /'spinē/ ▶ adj. Canadian informal insane; crazy.

spin-off (also **spinoff**) ▶ n. a byproduct or incidental result of a larger project: *the commercial spin-off from defense research.* ■ a product marketed by its association with a popular television program, movie, personality, etc.: [as modifier] *spin-off merchandising.* ■ a subsidiary of a parent company that has been sold off, creating a new company.

Spi·no·ne /spi'nōnē/ ▶ n. (pl. **Spinoni** pronunc. **same**) a wire-haired gun dog of an Italian breed, typically white with brown markings, drooping ears, and a docked tail.
–ORIGIN 1940s: Italian.

spi·nose /'spīnōs/ (also **spinous** /-nəs/) ▶ adj. chiefly Botany, Zoology having spines; spiny: *spinose forms will need care in collecting.*

spin-out ▶ n. informal **1** another term for SPIN-OFF.
2 a skidding spin by a vehicle out of control.

Spi·no·za /spi'nōzə/, Baruch (or Benedict) de (1632–77), Dutch philosopher. Spinoza espoused a pantheistic system, seeing "God or nature" as a single infinite substance, with mind and matter being two incommensurable ways of conceiving the one reality.
–DERIVATIVES **Spi·no·zism** /-,zizəm/ n., **Spi·no·zist** /-zist/ n. & adj., **Spi·no·zis·tic** /,spinə'zistik/ adj.

spin-sta·bi·lized ▶ adj. (of a satellite or spacecraft) stabilized in a desired orientation by being made to rotate about an axis.
–DERIVATIVES **spin-sta·bi·li·za·tion** n.

spin·ster /'spinstər/ ▶ n. derogatory an unmarried woman, typically an older woman beyond the usual age for marriage.
–DERIVATIVES **spin·ster·hood** /-,ho͝od/ n., **spin·ster·ish** adj.
–ORIGIN late Middle English (in the sense 'woman who spins'): from the verb SPIN + -STER; in early use the term was appended to names of women to denote their occupation. The current sense dates from the early 18th cent.

> **USAGE** The development of the word **spinster** is a good example of the way in which a word acquires strong connotations to the extent that it can no longer be used in a neutral sense. From the 17th century, the word was appended to names as the official legal description of an unmarried woman: *Elizabeth Harris of Boston, Spinster*. This type of use survives today only in some legal and religious contexts. In modern everyday English, however, **spinster** cannot be used to mean simply 'unmarried woman'; as such, it is a derogatory term, referring or alluding to a stereotype of an older woman who is unmarried, childless, prissy, and repressed.

spin·thar·i·scope /spin'THarə,skōp/ ▶ n. Physics an instrument that shows the incidence of alpha particles by flashes on a fluorescent screen.
–ORIGIN early 20th cent.: formed irregularly from Greek *spintharis* 'spark' + -SCOPE.

spin-the-bot·tle ▶ n. a party game in which players take turns spinning a bottle lying flat, and then kiss the person to whom the bottle neck points on stopping.

spin·to /'spintō/ ▶ n. (pl. **spintos**) a lyric soprano or tenor voice of powerful dramatic quality. ■ a singer with such a voice.
–ORIGIN 1950s: Italian, literally 'pushed,' past participle of *spingere* 'push.'

spin·tron·ics /,spin'träniks/ ▶ plural n. [treated as sing.] a field of electronics in which electron spin is manipulated to yield a desired outcome.
–DERIVATIVES **spin·tron·ic** adj. *a spintronic transistor that could play a major role in the quest for quantum computing.*

spin·u·lose /'spīnyə,lōs/ ▶ adj. Botany & Zoology having small spines.
–ORIGIN early 19th cent.: from modern Latin *spinulosus*, from *spinula*, diminutive of *spina* 'thorn, spine.'

spin·y /'spīnē/ ▶ adj. (**spinier, spiniest**) full of or covered with prickles: *a spiny cactus.* ■ informal difficult to understand or handle: *a spiny problem.*
–DERIVATIVES **spin·i·ness** n.

spin·y ant·eat·er ▶ n. another term for ECHIDNA.

spin·y dog·fish ▶ n. a large white-spotted gray dogfish with venomous spines in front of the dorsal fins. It occurs in the North Atlantic and the Mediterranean, often in large shoals. ● *Squalus acanthias*, family Squalidae.

spin·y lob·ster ▶ n. a large edible crustacean with a spiny shell and long heavy antennae, but lacking the large claws of true lobsters. ● Family Palinuridae: several genera and species, in particular *Palinuris vulgaris* of European waters, and the **California spiny lobster** (*Panulirus interruptus*).

spin·y mouse ▶ n. a mouse that has spines mixed with the hair on its back, native to Africa and southwestern Asia. ● Genus *Acomys*, family Muridae: several species.

spi·ra·cle /'spirəkəl, 'spī-/ ▶ n. Zoology an external respiratory opening, esp. each of a number of pores on the body of an insect, or each of a pair of vestigial gill slits behind the eye of a cartilaginous fish.
–DERIVATIVES **spi·rac·u·lar** /spi'rakyələr, spī-/ adj.
–ORIGIN late 18th cent.: from Latin *spiraculum*, from *spirare* 'breathe.'

spi·rae·a ▶ n. variant spelling of SPIREA.

spi·ral /'spīrəl/ ▶ adj. winding in a continuous and gradually widening (or tightening) curve, either around a central point on a flat plane or about an axis so as to form a cone: *a spiral pattern.* ■ winding in a continuous curve of constant diameter about a central axis, as though along a cylinder; helical. ■ (of a staircase) constantly turning in one direction as it rises, around a solid or open center. ■ Medicine (of a fracture) curving around a long bone lengthwise. ■ short for SPIRAL-BOUND: *a spiral notebook.*
▶ n. **1** a spiral curve, shape, or pattern: *he spotted a spiral of smoke.* ■ a spiral spring. ■ Astronomy short for SPIRAL GALAXY.
2 a progressive rise or fall of prices, wages, etc., each responding to an upward or downward stimulus provided by a previous one: *an inflationary spiral.* ■ a process of deterioration through the continuous increase or decrease of a specified feature: *a downward spiral of sex and drink.*
3 Football a pass or kick that moves smoothly through the air while spinning on its long axis.
▶ v. (**spirals, spiraling, spiraled**; Brit. **spirals, spiralling, spiralled**) **1** [no obj.] move in a spiral course: *a wisp of smoke spiraled up from the trees.* ■ [with obj.] cause to have a spiral shape or follow a

spiral course: *spiral the bandage around the injured limb.*
2 [no obj.] show a continuous and dramatic increase: *inflation continued to spiral* | (as adj. **spiraling**) *he needed to relax after the spiraling tensions of the day.* ■ (**spiral down/downward**) decrease or deteriorate continuously: *he expects the figures to spiral down further.*
–DERIVATIVES **spi·ral·ly** adv.
–ORIGIN mid 16th cent. (as an adjective): from medieval Latin *spiralis*, from Latin *spira* 'coil' (see SPIRE²).

spi·ral-bound ▶ adj. (of a book or notepad) bound with a wire or plastic spiral threaded through a row of holes along one edge.

spi·ral gal·ax·y ▶ n. a galaxy in which the stars and gas clouds are concentrated mainly in one or more spiral arms.

spi·rant /ˈspīrənt/ ▶ adj. Phonetics (of a consonant) uttered with a continuous expulsion of breath.
▶ n. such a consonant; a fricative.
–DERIVATIVES **spi·rant·i·za·tion** /ˌspīrəntəˈzāSHən/ n., **spi·rant·ize** /-ˌtīz/ v.
–ORIGIN mid 19th cent.: from Latin *spirant-* 'breathing,' from the verb *spirare*.

spire¹ /spī(ə)r/ ▶ n. a tapering conical or pyramidal structure on the top of a building, typically a church tower. ■ the continuation of a tree trunk above the point where branching begins, esp. in a tree of a tapering form. ■ a long tapering object: *spires of delphiniums.*
–DERIVATIVES **spired** adj., **spir·y** adj.
–ORIGIN Old English *spīr* 'tall slender stem of a plant'; related to German *Spier* 'tip of a blade of grass.'

spire¹

spire² ▶ n. Zoology the upper tapering part of the spiral shell of a gastropod mollusk, comprising all but the whorl containing the body.
–ORIGIN mid 16th cent. (in the general sense 'a spiral'): from French, or via Latin from Greek *speira* 'a coil.'

spi·re·a /spīˈrēə/ (also **spiraea**) ▶ n. a shrub of the rose family, with clusters of small white or pink flowers. Found throughout the northern hemisphere, it is widely cultivated as a garden ornamental. ● Genus *Spiraea*, family Rosaceae.
–ORIGIN modern Latin, from Greek *speiraia*, from *speira* 'a coil.'

spi·reme (also **spirem**) ▶ n. Biochemistry, dated the tangled strands of chromosomal material seen in the early stages of cell division, formerly believed to be a single continuous strand (or two in a diploid cell, etc.).
–ORIGIN from German *spirem*, from Greek 'coil,' 'convolution.'

spire shell ▶ n. a marine or freshwater mollusk with a long conical spiral shell. ● Hydrobiidae and related families, class Gastropoda.

spi·ril·lum /spīˈriləm/ ▶ n. (pl. **spirilla** /-lə/) a bacterium with a rigid spiral structure, found in stagnant water and sometimes causing disease. ● Genus *Spirillum*; Gram-negative.
–ORIGIN modern Latin, irregular diminutive of Latin *spira* 'a coil.'

spir·it /ˈspirit/ ▶ n. **1** the nonphysical part of a person that is the seat of emotions and character; the soul: *we seek a harmony between body and spirit.* ■ such a part regarded as a person's true self and as capable of surviving physical death or separation: *a year after he left, his spirit is still present.* ■ such a part manifested as an apparition after their death; a ghost. ■ a supernatural being: *shrines to nature spirits.* ■ (**the Spirit**) short for HOLY SPIRIT. ■ archaic a highly refined substance or fluid thought to govern vital phenomena.
2 [in sing.] those qualities regarded as forming the definitive or typical elements in the character of a person, nation, or group or in the thought and attitudes of a particular period: *the university is a symbol of the nation's egalitarian spirit.* ■ [with adj.] a person identified with their most prominent mental or moral characteristics or with their role in a group or movement: *he was a leading spirit in the conference.* ■ a specified emotion or mood, esp. one prevailing at a particular time: *I hope the team will build on this spirit of confidence.* ■ (**spirits**) a person's mood: *the warm weather lifted everyone's spirits after the winter.* ■ the quality of courage, energy, and determination or assertiveness: *his visitors admired his spirit and good temper.* ■ the attitude or intentions with which someone undertakes or regards something: *he confessed in a spirit of self-respect, not defiance.* ■ the real meaning or the intention behind something as opposed to its strict verbal interpretation: *the rule had been broken in spirit if not in letter.*
3 (usu. **spirits**) strong distilled liquor such as brandy, whiskey, gin, or rum. ■ [with modifier] a volatile liquid, esp. a fuel, prepared by distillation: *aviation spirit.* ■ archaic a solution of volatile components extracted from something, typically by distillation or by solution in alcohol: *spirits of turpentine.*
▶ v. (**spirits, spiriting, spirited**) [with obj.] convey rapidly and secretly: *stolen cows were spirited away some distance to prevent detection.*
–PHRASES **enter into the spirit** join wholeheartedly in an event, esp. one of celebration and festivity: *he entered into the spirit of the occasion by dressing as a Pierrot.* **in** (or **in the**) **spirit** in thought or intention though not physically: *he couldn't be here in person, but he is with us in spirit.* **out of spirits** sad; discouraged: *I was too tired and out of spirits to eat or drink much.* **the spirit is willing but the flesh is weak** proverb someone has good intentions but fails to live up to them. [with biblical allusion to Matt. 26:41.] **when the spirit moves someone** when someone feels inclined to do something: *he can be quite candid when the spirit moves him.* [a phrase originally in Quaker use, with reference to the Holy Spirit.] **the spirit world** (in animistic and occult belief) the nonphysical realm in which disembodied spirits have their existence.
–PHRASAL VERBS **spirit someone up** archaic stimulate, animate, or cheer up someone.
–ORIGIN Middle English: from Anglo-Norman French, from Latin *spiritus* 'breath, spirit,' from *spirare* 'breathe.'

spir·it·ed /ˈspiritid/ ▶ adj. **1** full of energy, enthusiasm, and determination: *a spirited campaigner for women's rights.*
2 [in combination] having a specified character, outlook on life, or mood: *he was a warmhearted, generous-spirited man.*
–DERIVATIVES **spir·it·ed·ly** adv., **spir·it·ed·ness** n.

spir·it gum ▶ n. a quick-drying solution of gum, chiefly used by actors to attach false hair to their faces.

spir·it·ism /ˈspiriˌtizəm/ ▶ n. another term for SPIRITUALISM (sense 1).
–DERIVATIVES **spir·it·ist** /ˈspiritist/ adj. & n., **spir·it·is·tic** /ˌspiriˈtistik/ adj.

spir·it lamp ▶ n. a lamp burning volatile spirits, esp. methylated spirits, instead of oil.

spir·it·less /ˈspiritlis/ ▶ adj. lacking courage, vigor, or vivacity: *Ruth and I played a spiritless game of Scrabble.* ■ depressed, downcast, or melancholy: *over the course of just one summer, our irrepressible Michael had become dark and spiritless.*
–DERIVATIVES **spir·it·less·ly** adv., **spir·it·less·ness** n.

spir·it lev·el ▶ n. another term for LEVEL (sense 3 of the noun).

spir·it of harts·horn /ˈhärtsˌhôrn/ ▶ n. see HARTSHORN.

spir·it of wine (also **spirits of wine**) ▶ n. archaic purified alcohol.

spir·i·tous /ˈspiritəs/ ▶ adj. another term for SPIRITUOUS.

spir·its of salt ▶ n. archaic term for HYDROCHLORIC ACID.

spir·it·u·al /ˈspiriCHo͞oəl/ ▶ adj. **1** of, relating to, or affecting the human spirit or soul as opposed to material or physical things: *I'm responsible for his spiritual welfare* | *the spiritual values of life.* ■ (of a person) not concerned with material values or pursuits.
2 of or relating to religion or religious belief: *the tribe's spiritual leader.*
▶ n. (also **Negro spiritual**) a religious song of a kind associated with black Christians of the southern US, and thought to derive from the combination of European hymns and African musical elements by black slaves.
–PHRASES **one's spiritual home** a place in which one feels a profound sense of belonging: *I had always thought of Italy as my spiritual home.*
–DERIVATIVES **spir·it·u·al·i·ty** /ˌspiriCHo͞oˈalitē/ n., **spir·it·u·al·ly** adv.
–ORIGIN Middle English: from Old French *spirituel*, from Latin *spiritualis*, from *spiritus* (see SPIRIT).

spir·it·u·al·ism /ˈspiriCHo͞oəˌlizəm/ ▶ n. **1** a system of belief or religious practice based on supposed communication with the spirits of the dead, esp. through mediums.
2 Philosophy the doctrine that the spirit exists as distinct from matter, or that spirit is the only reality.
–DERIVATIVES **spir·it·u·al·ist** n., **spir·it·u·al·is·tic** /ˌspiriCHo͞oəˈlistik/ adj.

spir·it·u·al·ize /ˈspiriCHo͞oəˌlīz/ ▶ v. [with obj.] elevate to a spiritual level.
–DERIVATIVES **spir·it·u·al·i·za·tion** /ˌspiriCHo͞oələˈzāSHən/ n.

spir·it·u·ous /ˈspiriCHo͞oəs/ ▶ adj. formal or archaic containing much alcohol; distilled: *spirituous beverages.*
–ORIGIN late 16th cent. (in the sense 'spirited, lively'): from Latin *spiritus* 'spirit' + -OUS, or from French *spiritueux*.

spir·i·tus /ˈspiritəs/ ▶ n. Latin term for BREATH, often used figuratively to mean spirit.

spir·i·tus rec·tor /ˈspiritus ˈrektər/ ▶ n. a ruling or directing spirit.
–ORIGIN Latin.

spiro-¹ ▶ comb. form **1** spiral; in a spiral: *spirochete.*
2 Chemistry denoting a molecule with two rings with one atom common to both: *spironolactone.*
–ORIGIN from Latin *spira*, Greek *speira* 'a coil.'

spiro-² ▶ comb. form relating to breathing: *spirometer.*
–ORIGIN formed irregularly from Latin *spirare* 'breathe.'

spi·ro·chete /ˈspīrəˌkēt/ (Brit. **spirochaete**) ▶ n. a flexible spirally twisted bacterium, esp. one that causes syphilis. ● *Treponema* and other genera, order Spirochaetales; Gram-negative.
–ORIGIN late 19th cent.: from SPIRO-¹ 'in a spiral' + Greek *khaitē* 'long hair.'

spi·ro·graph /ˈspīrəˌgraf/ ▶ n. an instrument for recording breathing movements.
–DERIVATIVES **spi·ro·graph·ic** /ˌspīrəˈgrafik/ adj.

spi·ro·gy·ra /ˌspīrəˈjīrə/ ▶ n. Botany a filamentous freshwater green alga containing spiral bands of chloroplasts. ● Genus *Spirogyra*, division Chlorophyta.
–ORIGIN modern Latin, from SPIRO-¹ 'spiral' + Greek *guros, gura* 'round.'

spi·rom·e·ter /spīˈrämitər/ ▶ n. an instrument for measuring the air capacity of the lungs.
–DERIVATIVES **spi·rom·e·try** /-mitrē/ n.

spi·ro·no·lac·tone /ˌspīrənōˈlaktōn/ ▶ n. Medicine a steroid derivative that is an aldosterone antagonist, which promotes sodium excretion and is used in the treatment of certain types of edema and hypertension. ● Chem. formula: $C_{24}H_{32}O_4S$.
–ORIGIN 1960s: from SPIRO-¹ (sense 2) + LACTONE, with the insertion of -ONE.

spirt /spərt/ ▶ v. & n. old-fashioned spelling of SPURT.

spi·ru·li·na /ˌspīrəˈlīnə/ ▶ n. filamentous cyanobacteria that form tangled masses in warm alkaline lakes in Africa and Central and South America. ● Genus *Spirulina*, division Cyanobacteria. ■ (usu. **Spirulina**) the substance of such growths dried and prepared as a food or food additive, which is a rich source of many vitamins and minerals.
–ORIGIN modern Latin, from *spirula* 'small spiral (shell).'

spit¹ /spit/ ▶ v. (**spits, spitting**; past and past participle **spat** /spat/ or **spit**) [no obj.] **1** eject saliva forcibly from one's mouth, sometimes as a gesture of contempt or anger: *Todd spit in Hugh's face.* ■ [with obj.] forcibly eject (food or liquid) from one's mouth: *he spits out his piece of coconut* | figurative *ATMs that spit out $20 bills.* ■ (**spit up**) (esp. of a baby) vomit or regurgitate food. ■ [with obj.] utter in a hostile or aggressive way: *she spat abuse at the jury* | [with direct speech] *"Go to hell!" she spat.* ■ be extremely angry or frustrated: *he was spitting with sudden fury.* ■ (of a fire or something being cooked) emit small bursts of sparks or hot fat with a series of short, explosive noises. ■ (of a cat) make a hissing noise as a sign of anger or hostility.
2 (**it spits, it is spitting**, etc.) Brit. light rain falls: *it began to spit.*
▶ n. **1** saliva, typically that which has been ejected from a person's mouth. ■ short for CUCKOO SPIT.
2 an act of spitting.
–PHRASES **spit in the eye** (or **face**) **of** show contempt or scorn for. **spit it out** informal used to urge someone to say or confess something quickly: *spit it out, man, I haven't got all day.*
–ORIGIN Old English *spittan*, of imitative origin.

spit² ▶ n. **1** a long, thin metal rod pushed through meat in order to hold and turn it while it is roasted over an open fire: *chicken cooked on a spit.*
2 a narrow point of land projecting into the sea: *a narrow spit of land shelters the bay.*
▶ v. (**spits, spitting, spitted**) [with obj.] put a spit through (meat) in order to roast it over an open fire: *I spitted the squirrel meat and turned it over the flames.*

S

– ORIGIN Old English *spitu*; related to Dutch *spit* and German *Spiess*.

spit³ ▶ **n.** (pl. **same** or **spits**) a layer of earth whose depth is equal to the length of the blade of a spade: *break up the top spit with a fork.*
– ORIGIN early 16th cent.: from Middle Dutch and Middle Low German; probably related to SPIT².

spit and pol·ish ▶ **n.** thorough or exaggerated cleaning and polishing, esp. by a soldier: *they gave the dining room some extra spit and polish.*

spit·ball /ˈspitˌbôl/ ▶ **n. 1** a piece of paper that has been chewed and shaped into a ball for use as a missile.
2 Baseball an illegal pitch made with a ball moistened with saliva or another substance to make it move erratically.
▶ **v.** [with obj.] informal throw out (a suggestion) for discussion: *I'm just spitballing a few ideas.*
– DERIVATIVES **spit·ball·er n.**

spitch·cock /ˈspiCHˌkäk/ ▶ **n.** an eel that has been split and grilled or fried.
▶ **v.** [no obj.] prepare (an eel or other fish) in this way.
– ORIGIN late 15th cent.: of unknown origin; compare with SPATCHCOCK.

spit curl ▶ **n.** a small curl of hair trained to lie flat on the forehead, at the nape of the neck, or in front of the ear.

spite /spīt/ ▶ **n.** a desire to hurt, annoy, or offend someone: *he'd think I was saying it out of spite.* ■ archaic an instance of such a desire; a grudge: *it seemed as if the wind had a spite at her.*
▶ **v.** [with obj.] deliberately hurt, annoy, or offend (someone): *he put the house up for sale to spite his family.*
– PHRASES **in spite of** without being affected by the particular factor mentioned: *he was suddenly cold in spite of the sun.* **in spite of oneself** although one did not want or expect to do so: *Oliver smiled in spite of himself.*
– ORIGIN Middle English: shortening of Old French *despit* 'contempt,' *despiter* 'show contempt for.'

spite·ful /ˈspītfəl/ ▶ **adj.** showing or caused by malice: *the teachers made spiteful little jokes about me.*
– DERIVATIVES **spite·ful·ly adv.**, **spite·ful·ness n.**

spit·fire /ˈspitˌfīr/ ▶ **n.** a person with a fierce temper.

Spit·head /ˌspitˈhed/ a channel between the northeastern coast of the Isle of Wight and the mainland of southern England. It offers sheltered access to Southampton Water and deep anchorage.

spit-roast ▶ **v.** [with obj.] (usu. as adj. **spit-roasted**) cook (a piece of meat) on a spit: *spit-roasted lamb.*

Spits·ber·gen /ˈspitsˌbərgən/ a Norwegian island in the Svalbard archipelago, in the Arctic Ocean north of Norway; principal settlement, Longyearbyen.

spit·ter /ˈspitər/ ▶ **n. 1** a person who spits.
2 another term for SPITBALL (sense 2 of the noun).

spit·ting co·bra ▶ **n.** an African cobra that defends itself by spitting venom from the fangs, typically at the aggressor's eyes. ● Genera *Naja* and *Hemachatus*, family Elapidae: three species, in particular the **black-necked spitting cobra** (*N. nigricollis*).

spitting distance ▶ **n.** a very short distance: *the hotel is within spitting distance of the beach.* ■ (of an outcome) expected to happen with near certainty: *whoever takes Pennsylvania in the primary will be in spitting distance of winning.*

spit·ting im·age ▶ **n.** (**the spitting image of**) informal the exact double of (another person or thing): *she's the spitting image of her mother.*
– ORIGIN late 19th cent.: originally as *the spit of* or *the spit and image of*; perhaps from the idea of a person apparently being formed from the spit of another, so great is the similarity between them.

spit·tle /ˈspitl/ ▶ **n.** saliva, esp. as ejected from the mouth.
– DERIVATIVES **spit·tly adj.**
– ORIGIN late 15th cent.: alteration of dialect *spattle*, by association with SPIT¹.

spit·tle·bug /ˈspitlˌbəg/ ▶ **n.** another term for FROGHOPPER.

spit·toon /spiˈto͞on/ ▶ **n.** a metal or earthenware pot typically having a funnel-shaped top, used for spitting into.

Spitz /spits/, Mark (Andrew) (1950–), US swimmer. He won 7 gold medals in the 1972 Olympic Games at Munich and set 27 world records for freestyle and butterfly between 1967 and 1972.

spitz /spits/ ▶ **n.** a dog of a small breed with a pointed muzzle, esp. a Pomeranian.
– ORIGIN mid 19th cent.: from German *Spitz(hund)*, from *spitz* 'pointed' + *Hund* 'dog.'

spiv /spiv/ ▶ **n.** Brit. informal a man, typically characterized by flashy dress, who makes a living by disreputable dealings.
– DERIVATIVES **spiv·vish adj.**, **spiv·vy adj.**
– ORIGIN 1930s: perhaps related to SPIFFY.

splake /splāk/ ▶ **n.** a hybrid trout of North American lakes. ● Produced by crossing the speckled trout (*Salvelinus fontinalis*) with the lake trout (*S. namaycush*).
– ORIGIN 1950s: blend of *speckled* and LAKE¹.

splanch·nic /ˈsplaNGknik/ ▶ **adj.** of or relating to the viscera or internal organs, esp. those of the abdomen.
– ORIGIN late 17th cent.: from modern Latin *splanchnicus*, from Greek *splankhnikos*, from *splankhna* 'entrails.'

splanch·no·pleure /ˈsplaNGknəˌplo͝or/ ▶ **n.** Embryology a layer of tissue in a vertebrate embryo comprising the endoderm and the inner layer of mesoderm, and giving rise to the gut, lungs, and yolk sac. Often contrasted with SOMATOPLEURE.
– ORIGIN late 19th cent.: from Greek *splankhna* 'entrails' + *pleura* 'side.'

splash /splaSH/ ▶ **n.** a sound made by something striking or falling into liquid: *we hit the water with a mighty splash.* ■ a spell of moving about in water energetically: *the girls joined them for a final splash in the pool.* ■ a small quantity of liquid that has fallen or been dashed against a surface: ***a splash of** gravy.* ■ a small quantity of liquid added to a drink: ***a splash of** lemonade.* ■ a bright patch of color: *add a red scarf to give **a splash of** color.* ■ informal a prominent or sensational news feature or story: *a front-page splash.* ■ informal a striking, ostentatious, or exciting effect or event: *there's going to be a big splash when Mike returns to the ring.*
▶ **v.** [with obj.] cause (liquid) to strike or fall on something in irregular drops: *she splashed cold water onto her face.* ■ make wet by doing this: *they splashed each other with water.* ■ [no obj.] (of a liquid) fall or be scattered in irregular drops: *a tear fell and splashed onto the pillow.* ■ [no obj.] strike or move around in a body of water, causing it to fly about noisily: *some stones splashed into the water | wheels splashed through a puddle.* ■ (**be splashed with**) be decorated with scattered patches of: *a field splashed with purple clover.* ■ print (a story or photograph, esp. a sensational one) in a prominent place in a newspaper or magazine: *the story was splashed across the front pages.*
– PHRASES **make a splash** informal attract a great deal of attention.
– PHRASAL VERBS **splash down** (of a spacecraft) land on water. **splash out** (or **splash money out**) Brit. informal spend money freely: *she splashed out on a Mercedes.*
– ORIGIN early 18th cent. (as a verb): alteration of PLASH¹.

splash·board /ˈsplaSHˌbôrd/ ▶ **n.** a screen designed to protect the passengers of a vehicle or boat from splashes.

splash·down /ˈsplaSHˌdoun/ ▶ **n.** the alighting of a returning spacecraft on the sea, with the assistance of parachutes.

splash·y /ˈsplaSHē/ ▶ **adj.** (**splashier**, **splashiest**)
1 characterized by water flying about noisily in irregular drops: *a splashy waterfall.* ■ characterized by irregular patches of bright color: *splashy floral silks.*
2 informal attracting a great deal of attention; elaborately or ostentatiously impressive: *I don't care for splashy Hollywood parties.*

splat¹ /splat/ ▶ **n.** a piece of thin wood in the center of a chair back.
– ORIGIN mid 19th cent.: from obsolete *splat* 'split up'; related to SPLIT.

splat² informal ▶ **n.** a sound of something soft and wet or heavy striking a surface: *the goblin makes a huge splat as he hits the ground.*
▶ **adv.** with a sound of this type: *he lands splat on his right elbow.*
▶ **v.** (**splats**, **splatting**, **splatted**) [with obj.] crush or squash (something) with a sound of this type: *he was splatting a bug.* ■ [no obj.] land or be squashed with a sound of this type.
– ORIGIN late 19th cent.: abbreviation of SPLATTER.

splat·ter /ˈsplatər/ ▶ **v.** [with obj.] splash with a sticky or viscous liquid: *a passing cart rolled by, splattering him with mud.* ■ splash (such a liquid) over a surface or object. ■ [no obj.] (of such a liquid) splash: *heavy droplets of rain splatter onto the windshield.* ■ informal prominently or sensationally publish (a story) in a newspaper: *the story is splattered over pages two and three.*
▶ **n. 1** a spot or trail of a sticky or viscous liquid splashed over a surface or object: *each puddle we crossed threw **a splatter of** mud on the windshield.*
2 [as modifier] informal denoting or referring to films featuring many violent and gruesome deaths: *a splatter movie.*
– ORIGIN late 18th cent.: imitative.

splat·ter·punk /ˈsplatərˌpəNGk/ ▶ **n.** informal a literary genre characterized by the explicit description of horrific, violent, and often pornographic scenes.

splay /splā/ ▶ **v.** [with obj.] thrust or spread (things, esp. limbs or fingers) out and apart: *her hands were splayed across his broad shoulders | he stood with his legs and arms **splayed out**.* ■ [no obj.] (esp. of limbs or fingers) be thrust or spread out and apart: *his legs **splayed out** in front of him.* ■ [no obj.] (of a thing) diverge in shape or position; become wider or more separated: *the river **splayed out**, deepening to become an estuary.* ■ (usu. as adj. **splayed**) construct (a window, doorway, or aperture) so that it diverges or is wider at one side of the wall than the other: *the walls are pierced by splayed window openings.*
▶ **n. 1** a widening or outward tapering of something, in particular: ■ a tapered widening of a road at an intersection to increase visibility. ■ a splayed window aperture or other opening.
2 a surface making an oblique angle with another, such as the splayed side of a window or embrasure. ■ the degree of bevel or slant of a surface.
▶ **adj.** [usu. in combination] turned outward or widened: *the girls were sitting splay-legged.*
– ORIGIN Middle English (in the sense 'unfold to view, display'): shortening of the verb DISPLAY.

splay-foot ▶ **n.** a broad flat foot turned outward.
– DERIVATIVES **splay-foot·ed adj.**

spleen /splēn/ ▶ **n. 1** Anatomy an abdominal organ involved in the production and removal of blood cells in most vertebrates and forming part of the immune system.
2 bad temper; spite: *he could **vent his spleen** on the institutions that had duped him.* [from the earlier belief that the spleen was the seat of such emotions.]
– DERIVATIVES **spleen·ful** /-fəl/ **adj.** (sense 2).
– ORIGIN Middle English: shortening of Old French *esplen*, via Latin from Greek *splēn*.

spleen·wort /ˈsplēnwərt, -ˌwôrt/ ▶ **n.** a small fern that grows in rosettes on rocks and walls, typically with rounded or triangular lobes on a slender stem and formerly used as a remedy for disorders of the spleen. ● Genus *Asplenium*, family Aspleniaceae.

splen- ▶ **comb. form** Anatomy of or relating to the spleen: *splenectomy.*
– ORIGIN from Greek *splēn* 'spleen.'

Splen·da /ˈsplendə/ ▶ **n.** trademark an artificial sweetener used as a calorie-free sugar substitute.

splen·dent /ˈsplendənt/ ▶ **adj.** archaic shining brightly. ■ illustrious; great.
– ORIGIN late 15th cent.: from Latin *splendent-* 'shining,' from the verb *splendere*.

splen·did /ˈsplendid/ ▶ **adj.** magnificent; very impressive: *a splendid view of Windsor Castle | his robes were splendid.* ■ informal excellent; very good: *a splendid fellow* | [as exclamation] *"Is your family well? Splendid!"*
– PHRASES **splendid isolation** used to emphasize the isolation of a person or thing: *the stone stands **in splendid isolation** near the moorland road.* [1896: first applied to the period from 1890 to 1907 when Britain pursued a policy of diplomatic and commercial noninvolvement.]
– DERIVATIVES **splen·did·ly adv.** [as submodifier] *a splendidly ornate style*, **splen·did·ness n.**
– ORIGIN early 17th cent.: from French *splendide* or Latin *splendidus*, from *splendere* 'shine, be bright.'

splen·dif·er·ous /splenˈdifərəs/ ▶ **adj.** informal, humorous splendid: *a splendiferous Sunday dinner.*
– DERIVATIVES **splen·dif·er·ous·ly adv.**, **splen·dif·er·ous·ness n.**
– ORIGIN mid 19th cent.: formed irregularly from SPLENDOR.

splen·dor /ˈsplendər/ (Brit. **splendour**) ▶ **n.** magnificent and splendid appearance; grandeur: *the splendor of the Florida Keys.* ■ (**splendors**) magnificent features or qualities: *the splendors of the imperial court.*
– ORIGIN late Middle English: from Anglo-Norman French *splendur* or Latin *splendor*, from *splendere* 'shine, be bright.'

sple·nec·to·my /spləˈnektəmē/ ▶ **n.** (pl. **splenectomies**) a surgical operation involving removal of the spleen.

sple·net·ic /spləˈnetik/ ▶ **adj. 1** bad-tempered; spiteful: *a splenetic outburst.*
2 archaic term for SPLENIC.
– DERIVATIVES **sple·net·i·cal·ly adv.** (sense 1).
– ORIGIN late Middle English (as a noun denoting a person with a diseased spleen): from late Latin *spleneticus*, from Greek *splēn* (see SPLEEN).

splen·ic /ˈsplēnik, ˈsple-/ ▶ **adj.** of or relating to the spleen: *the splenic artery.*

–ORIGIN early 17th cent.: from French *splénique*, or via Latin from Greek *splēnikos*, from *splēn* (see SPLEEN).

sple·ni·tis /splēˈnītis, sple-/ ▶ **n.** Medicine inflammation of the spleen.

sple·ni·um /ˈsplēnēəm/ ▶ **n.** Anatomy the thick posterior part of the corpus callosum of the brain.
–DERIVATIVES **sple·ni·al** /ˈsplēnēəl/ **adj.**
–ORIGIN mid 19th cent.: from Latin.

sple·ni·us /ˈsplēnēəs/ (also **splenius muscle**) ▶ **n.** (pl. **splenii** /-nēˌī/) Anatomy any of two pairs of muscles attached to the vertebrae in the neck and upper back that draw back the head.
–ORIGIN mid 18th cent.: modern Latin, from Greek *splēnion* 'bandage.'

sple·no·meg·a·ly /ˌsplēnəˈmegəlē, ˌsple-/ ▶ **n.** abnormal enlargement of the spleen.
–ORIGIN early 20th cent.: from SPLEN- 'spleen' + Greek *megas, megal-* 'great.'

splice /splīs/ ▶ **v.** [with obj.] join or connect (a rope or ropes) by interweaving the strands: *we learned how to weave and splice ropes* | *a cord was* **spliced on** | figurative *the work splices detail and generalization.* ■ join (pieces of timber, film, or tape) at the ends: *commercials can be spliced in later* | *I was splicing* **together** *a video from the footage on opium-growing.* ■ Genetics join or insert (a gene or gene fragment).
▶ **n.** a union of two ropes, pieces of timber, or similar materials spliced together at the ends.
–DERIVATIVES **splic·er** **n.**
–ORIGIN early 16th cent.: probably from Middle Dutch *splissen*, of unknown origin.

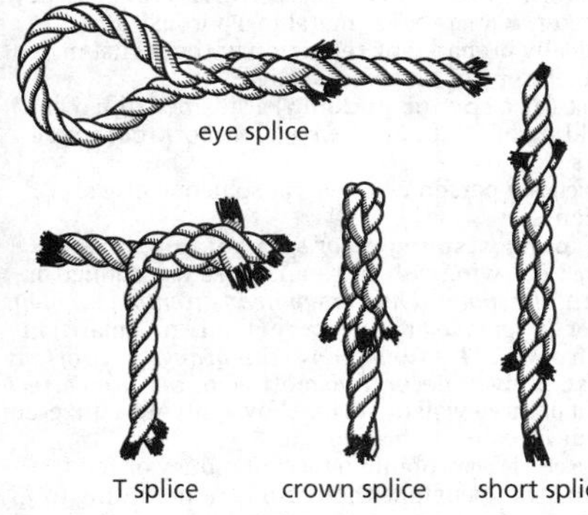

rope splices

spliff /splif/ ▶ **n.** Brit. informal a marijuana cigarette.
–ORIGIN 1930s: of unknown origin.

spline /splīn/ ▶ **n.** **1** a rectangular key fitting into grooves in the hub and shaft of a wheel, esp. one formed integrally with the shaft that allows movement of the wheel on the shaft. ■ a corresponding groove in a hub along which the key may slide.
2 a slat. ■ a flexible wood or rubber strip used esp. in drawing large curves.
3 (also **spline curve**) Mathematics a continuous curve constructed so as to pass through a given set of points and have a certain number of continuous derivatives.
▶ **v.** [with obj.] secure (a part) by means of a spline. ■ (usu. as adj. **splined**) fit with a spline: *splined freewheels.*
–ORIGIN mid 18th cent. (originally East Anglian dialect): perhaps related to SPLINTER.

splint /splint/ ▶ **n.** **1** a strip of rigid material used for supporting and immobilizing a broken bone when it has been set: *she had to wear splints on her legs.*
2 a long, thin strip of wood used to light a fire. ■ a rigid or flexible strip, esp. of wood, used in basketwork.
3 a bony enlargement on the inside of a horse's leg, on the splint bone.
▶ **v.** [with obj.] secure (a broken limb) with a splint or splints: *his leg was splinted.*
–ORIGIN Middle English (sense 2 of the noun): from Middle Dutch and Middle Low German *splinte* 'metal plate or pin'; related to SPLINTER.

splint bone ▶ **n.** either of two small bones in the foreleg of a horse or other large quadruped, lying behind and close to the cannon bone.

splin·ter /ˈsplin(t)ər/ ▶ **n.** a small, thin, sharp piece of wood, glass, or similar material broken off from a larger piece: *a splinter of ice.*
▶ **v.** break or cause to break into small sharp fragments: [no obj.] *the soap box splintered* | [with obj.] *he crashed into a fence, splintering the wooden barricade.* ■ (of a group or organization) separate into smaller units, typically as a result of disagreement: *the party had begun to splinter into factions.*
–DERIVATIVES **splin·ter·y** **adj.**
–ORIGIN Middle English: from Middle Dutch *splinter, splenter*; related to SPLINT.

splin·ter group (also **splinter party**) ▶ **n.** a small organization, typically a political party, that has broken away from a larger one.

splin·ter-proof ▶ **adj.** **1** capable of withstanding splinters from bursting shells or bombs: *splinter-proof shutters.*
2 not producing splinters when broken: *splinter-proof glass.*

Split /split/ a seaport on the coast of southern Croatia; pop. 177,500 (est. 2009). It contains the ruins of the palace of the emperor Diocletian, built in about AD 300.

split /split/ ▶ **v.** (**splits, splitting, split**) **1** break or cause to break forcibly into parts, esp. into halves or along the grain: [no obj.] *the ice cracked and heaved and split* | [with obj.] *split and toast the muffins.* ■ remove or be removed by breaking, separating, or dividing: [with obj.] *the point was pressed against the edge of the flint to* **split off** *flakes* | [no obj.] *an incentive for regions to* **split away** *from countries.* ■ divide or cause to divide into parts or elements: [no obj.] *the river had* **split into** *a number of channels* | [with obj.] *splitting water into oxygen and hydrogen.* ■ [with obj.] divide and share (something, esp. resources or responsibilities): *they met up and split the booty.* ■ [with obj.] cause the fission of (an atom). ■ [with obj.] issue new shares of (stock) to existing stockholders in proportion to their current holdings.
2 (with reference to a group of people) divide into two or more groups: [no obj.] *let's* **split up** *and find the other two* | [with obj.] *once again the family was* **split up**. ■ [no obj.] end a marriage or an emotional or working relationship: *I* **split up with** *my boyfriend a year ago.* ■ [with obj.] (of an issue) cause (a group) to be divided because of opposing views: *the party was deeply* **split over** *its future direction.*
3 [no obj.] informal (of one's head) suffer great pain from a headache: *my head is splitting* | (as adj. **splitting**) *a splitting headache.*
4 [no obj.] informal leave a place, esp. suddenly: *"Let's split," Harvey said.*
5 [no obj.] Brit. informal betray the secrets of or inform on someone: *I told him I wouldn't* **split on** *him.*
▶ **n.** **1** a tear, crack, or fissure in something, esp. down the middle or along the grain: *light squeezed through a small split in the curtain.* ■ an instance or act of splitting or being split; a division: *the split between the rich and the poor.* ■ a separation into parties or within a party; a schism: *the accusations caused a split in the party.* ■ an ending of a marriage or an emotional or working relationship: *a much-publicized split with his wife.* ■ short for STOCK SPLIT.
2 (**a split** or **the splits**) (in gymnastics and dance) an act of leaping in the air or sitting down with the legs straight and at right angles to the upright body, one in front and the other behind, or one at each side: *I could never* **do a split** *before.*
3 a thing that is divided or split, in particular: ■ a bun, roll, or cake that is split or cut in half. ■ a split osier used in basketwork. ■ each strip of steel or cane that makes up the reed in a loom. ■ half a bottle or glass of champagne or other liquor. ■ a single thickness of split hide. ■ (in bowling) a formation of standing pins after the first ball in which there is a gap between two pins or groups of pins, making a spare unlikely. ■ a drawn game or series. ■ a split-level house.
4 the time taken to complete a recognized part of a race, or the point in the race where such a time is measured.
–PHRASES **split the difference** take the average of two proposed amounts. **split hairs** see HAIR. **split one's sides** (also **split a gut**) informal be convulsed with laughter: *the dynamic comedy duo will have you splitting your sides with laughter.* **split the ticket** (or **one's vote**) vote for candidates of more than one party. **split the vote** (of a candidate or minority party) attract votes from another candidate or party with the result that both are defeated by a third.
–ORIGIN late 16th cent. (originally in the sense 'break up (a ship),' describing the force of a storm or rock): from Middle Dutch *splitten*, of unknown ultimate origin.

split-brain ▶ **adj.** [attrib.] Psychiatry (of a person or animal) having the corpus callosum severed or absent, so as to eliminate the main connection between the two hemispheres of the brain.

split de·ci·sion ▶ **n.** a decision based on a majority verdict rather than on a unanimous one, esp. on a court panel or among referees judging the winner of a boxing match.

split end ▶ **n.** **1** (usu. **split ends**) a tip of a person's hair that has split from dryness or ill-treatment.
2 Football an offensive end positioned on the line of scrimmage but several yards away from the other linemen.

split-half ▶ **adj.** [attrib.] Statistics relating to or denoting a technique of splitting a body of supposedly homogeneous data into two halves and calculating the results separately for each to assess their reliability.

split im·age ▶ **n.** an image in a rangefinder or camera focusing system that has been bisected by optical means, the halves being aligned only when the system is in focus.

split in·fin·i·tive ▶ **n.** a construction consisting of an infinitive with an adverb or other word inserted between *to* and the verb, e.g., *she seems to really like it.*

USAGE Is it wrong to use a **split infinitive**, separating the infinitive marker *to* from the verb? If so, then these statements are grammatically incorrect: *you have* **to** *really* **watch** *him;* **to** *boldly* **go** *where no one has gone before.* Writers who long ago insisted that English could be modeled on Latin created the "rule" that the English infinitive must not be split: *to clearly state* violates this rule; one must say *to state clearly.* But the Latin infinitive is one word (e.g., *amare*, 'to love') and cannot be split, so the rule is not firmly grounded, and treating two English words as one can lead to awkward, stilted sentences. In particular, the placing of an adverb in English is extremely important in giving the appropriate emphasis. Consider, for example, the "corrected" forms of the previous examples: *you really have* **to watch** *him;* **to go** *boldly where no one has gone before.* The original, intended emphasis of each statement has been changed, and for no other reason than to satisfy an essentially unreasonable rule. Some traditionalists may continue to hold up the split infinitive as an error, but in standard English, the principle of allowing split infinitives is broadly accepted as both normal and useful.

split-lev·el ▶ **adj.** (of a building) having a room or rooms higher than others by less than a whole story: *a large split-level house.* ■ (of a room) having its floor on two levels.
▶ **n.** a split-level building.

split pea ▶ **n.** a pea dried and split in half for cooking.

split per·son·al·i·ty ▶ **n.** less common term for MULTIPLE PERSONALITY. ■ archaic term for SCHIZOPHRENIA.

split-phase ▶ **adj.** denoting or relating to an induction motor or other device utilizing two or more voltages at different phases produced from a single-phase supply.

split-rail ▶ **adj.** denoting a fence or enclosure made from pieces of wood split lengthwise from a log.

split run ▶ **n.** a print run of a newspaper during which some articles or advertisements are changed so as to produce different editions.

split screen ▶ **n.** a movie, television, or computer screen on which two or more separate images are displayed.

split sec·ond ▶ **n.** a very brief moment of time: *for a split second, I hesitated.*
▶ **adj.** very rapid or accurate: *split-second timing is crucial.*

split shift ▶ **n.** a working shift comprising two or more separate periods of duty in a day.

split shot ▶ **n.** **1** (also **split-shot**) small pellets used to weight a fishing line.
2 Croquet a stroke driving two touching balls in different directions.

splits·ville /ˈsplitsˌvil/ ▶ **n.** informal the termination of a relationship, esp. a romantic one: *it's splitsville for Steve and Nikki.*
–ORIGIN 1980s: from SPLIT + *-s-* + -VILLE.

split·ter /ˈsplitər/ ▶ **n.** a person or thing occupied in or designed for splitting something: *a log splitter.* ■ a person, esp. a taxonomist, who attaches more importance to differences than to similarities in classification. Contrasted with LUMPER.

split·tism /ˈsplitizəm/ ▶ **n.** (among communists, or in communist countries) the pursuance of factional interests in opposition to official Communist Party policy.
–DERIVATIVES **split·tist** **n.**

splodge /spläj/ ▶ **n. & v.** Brit. another term for SPLOTCH.
–DERIVATIVES **splodgy** **adj.**

splosh /spläsH/ informal ▶ **v.** [no obj.] make a soft splashing sound as one moves: *he sploshed across the road.*

PRONUNCIATION KEY ə *ago, up*; ər *over, fur*; a *hat*; ā *ate*; ä *car*; e *let*; ē *see*; i *fit*; ī *by*; NG *sing*; ō *go*; ô *law, for*; oi *toy*; o͝o *good*; o͞o *goo*; ou *out*; TH *thin*; T͟H *then*; ZH *vision*

S

▶ **n.** a soft splashing sound: *a quiet splosh*. ■ a splash of liquid: *sploshes of wine*.
– ORIGIN mid 19th cent.: imitative.

splotch /spläCH/ informal ▶ **n.** a daub, blot, or smear of something, typically a liquid: *a splotch of red in a larger area of yellow*.
▶ **v.** [with obj.] (usu. **be splotched**) make such a daub, blot, or smear on: *a rag splotched with grease*.
– DERIVATIVES **splotch·y adj.**
– ORIGIN early 17th cent.: perhaps a blend of SPOT and obsolete *plotch* 'blotch.'

splurge /splərj/ informal ▶ **n.** an act of spending money freely or extravagantly: *the annual pre-Christmas splurge*. ■ a large or excessive amount of something: *there has recently been a splurge of teach-yourself books*.
▶ **v.** [with obj.] spend (money) freely or extravagantly: *I'd splurged about $2,500 on clothes* | [no obj.] *we splurged on T-bone steaks*.
– ORIGIN early 19th cent. (originally US): probably imitative.

splurt /splərt/ informal ▶ **n.** a sudden gush, esp. of saliva. ■ a sudden brief outburst of something: *I let out a splurt of laughter*.
▶ **v.** [with obj.] push out with force; spit out: *the rear wheels splurted gravel*.
– ORIGIN late 18th cent.: imitative.

splut·ter /'splətər/ ▶ **v.** [no obj.] make a series of short explosive spitting or choking sounds: *she coughed and spluttered, tears coursing down her face*. ■ [reporting verb] say something rapidly, indistinctly, and with a spitting sound, as a result of anger, embarrassment, or another strong emotion: [with obj.] *he began to splutter excuses* | [with direct speech] *"How dare you?" she spluttered*. ■ [with obj.] spit (something) out from one's mouth noisily and in small splashes: *spluttering brackish water, he struggled to regain his feet*.
▶ **n.** a short explosive spitting or choking noise.
– DERIVATIVES **splut·ter·er n.**, **splut·ter·ing·ly adv.**
– ORIGIN late 17th cent.: imitative; compare with SPUTTER.

Spock /späk/, Benjamin McLane (1903–98), US pediatrician and writer; known as **Dr. Spock**. His influential manual *The Common Sense Book of Baby and Child Care*, first published in 1946, challenged traditional ideas in child-rearing in favor of a psychological approach.

Benjamin Spock

Spode /spōd/ ▶ **n.** trademark fine pottery or porcelain made at the factories of the English potter Josiah Spode (1755–1827) or his successors, characteristically consisting of ornately decorated and gilded services and large vases.

spod·o·sol /'spädəˌsäl, -ˌsôl/ ▶ **n.** Soil Science a soil of an order rich in aluminum oxide and organic matter, typically characterized by low fertility, and including most podzols.
– ORIGIN 1960s: from Greek *spodos* 'ashes, embers' + -SOL + Latin *solum* 'soil.'

spod·u·mene /'späjo͞oˌmēn/ ▶ **n.** a translucent, typically grayish-white aluminosilicate mineral that is an important source of lithium.
– ORIGIN early 19th cent.: from French *spodumène*, from Greek *spodoumenos* 'burning to ashes,' present participle of *spodousthai*, from *spodos* 'ashes.'

spoil /spoil/ ▶ **v.** (past and past participle **spoiled** or chiefly Brit. **spoilt** /spoilt/) [with obj.] **1** diminish or destroy the value or quality of: *I wouldn't want to spoil your fun* | *a series of political blunders spoiled their chances of being re-elected*. ■ prevent someone from enjoying (an occasion or event): *she was afraid of spoiling Christmas for the rest of the family*. ■ [no obj.] (of food) become unfit for eating: *I've got some ham that'll spoil if we don't eat it tonight*.
2 harm the character of (a child) by being too lenient or indulgent: *the last thing I want to do is spoil Thomas* | (as adj. **spoiled**) *a spoiled child*. ■ treat with great or excessive kindness, consideration, or generosity: *breakfast in bed—you're spoiling me!*
3 [no obj.] (**be spoiling for**) be extremely or aggressively eager for: *Cooper was spoiling for a fight*.
4 archaic rob (a person or a place) of goods or possessions by force or violence.
▶ **n. 1** (usu. **spoils**) goods stolen or taken forcibly from a person or place: *the looters carried their spoils away*.
2 waste material brought up during the course of an excavation or a dredging or mining operation.
– ORIGIN Middle English (in the sense 'to plunder'): shortening of Old French *espoille* (noun), *espoillier* (verb), from Latin *spoliare*, from *spolium* 'plunder, skin stripped from an animal,' or a shortening of DESPOIL.

spoil·age /'spoilij/ ▶ **n. 1** the action of spoiling, esp. the deterioration of food and perishable goods.
2 waste produced by material being spoiled, esp. paper that is spoiled in printing.

spoil·er /'spoilər/ ▶ **n. 1** a person or thing that spoils something. ■ (esp. in a political context) a person who obstructs or prevents an opponent's success while having no chance of winning a contest themselves. ■ a description of an important plot development in a television show, movie, etc., before it is shown to the public. ■ a news story published to divert attention from and reduce the impact of a similar item published elsewhere.
2 a flap on the wing of an aircraft or glider that can be projected in order to create drag and so reduce speed. ■ a similar device on a motor vehicle intended to prevent it from being lifted off the road when traveling at very high speeds.
3 an electronic device for preventing unauthorized copying of sound recordings by means of a disruptive signal inaudible on the original.

spoils·man /'spoilzmən/ ▶ **n.** (pl. **spoilsmen**) a person who seeks to profit by the spoils system; a person who supports this system.

spoil·sport /'spoilˌspôrt/ ▶ **n.** a person who behaves in a way that spoils others' pleasure, esp. by not joining in an activity.

spoils sys·tem ▶ **n.** the practice of a successful political party giving public office to its supporters.

spoilt /spoilt/ chiefly Brit. past and past participle of SPOIL.

Spo·kane /spō'kan/ a city in eastern Washington, at the falls of the Spokane River, near the border with Idaho; pop. 202,319 (est. 2008).

spoke[1] /spōk/ ▶ **n.** each of the bars or wire rods connecting the center of a wheel to its outer edge. ■ each of a set of radial handles projecting from a ship's wheel. ■ each of the metal rods in an umbrella to which the material is attached.
– DERIVATIVES **spoked adj.** [in combination] *a wire-spoked wheel*.
– ORIGIN Old English *spāca*; related to Dutch *speek*, German *Speiche*, from the base of SPIKE[1].

spoke[2] past of SPEAK.

spo·ken /'spōkən/ past participle of SPEAK.
▶ **adj.** [in combination] speaking in a specified way: *a blunt-spoken man*.
– PHRASES **be spoken for** be already claimed, owned, or reserved. ■ (of a person) already have a romantic commitment: *he knows Claudine is spoken for*.

spoke·shave /'spōkˌSHāv/ ▶ **n.** a small plane with a handle on each side of its blade, used for shaping curved surfaces (originally wheel spokes).
▶ **v.** [with obj.] shape with a plane of this type.

spokes·man /'spōksmən/ ▶ **n.** (pl. **spokesmen**) a person, esp. a man, who makes statements on behalf of another individual or a group: *a spokesman for Greenpeace*.
– ORIGIN early 16th cent.: formed irregularly from SPOKE[2], on the pattern of words such as *craftsman*.

spokes·mod·el /'spōksˌmädl/ ▶ **n.** informal an attractive and stylishly dressed person, esp. a young woman, who advertises or promotes something.

spokes·per·son /'spōksˌpərsən/ ▶ **n.** (pl. **spokespersons** or **spokespeople** /-ˌpēpəl/) a spokesman or spokeswoman (used as a neutral alternative).

spokes·wom·an /'spōksˌwo͝omən/ ▶ **n.** (pl. **spokeswomen**) a woman who makes statements on behalf of another individual or a group.

spo·li·a·tion /ˌspōlē'āSHən/ ▶ **n. 1** the action of ruining or destroying something: *the spoliation of the countryside*.
2 the action of taking goods or property from somewhere by illegal or unethical means: *the spoliation of the Church*.
– DERIVATIVES **spo·li·a·tor** /'spōlēˌātər/ **n.**
– ORIGIN late Middle English (denoting pillaging): from Latin *spoliatio(n-)*, from the verb *spoliare* 'strip, deprive' (see SPOIL).

spon·da·ic /spän'dāik/ ▶ **adj.** Prosody of or concerning spondees. ■ (of a hexameter) having a spondee as its fifth foot.
– ORIGIN late 16th cent.: via French or late Latin from Greek *spondeiakos*, from *spondeios* (see SPONDEE).

spon·dee /'spändē/ ▶ **n.** Prosody a foot consisting of two long (or stressed) syllables.
– ORIGIN late Middle English: from Old French, or via Latin from Greek *spondeios* (*pous*) '(foot) of a libation,' from *spondē* 'libation' (being characteristic of music accompanying libations).

spon·dy·li·tis /ˌspändə'lītis/ ▶ **n.** Medicine inflammation of the joints of the backbone. See also ANKYLOSING SPONDYLITIS.
– ORIGIN mid 19th cent.: from Latin *spondylus* 'vertebra' (from Greek *spondulos*) + -ITIS.

spon·dy·lo·sis /ˌspändə'lōsis/ ▶ **n.** Medicine a painful condition of the spine resulting from the degeneration of the intervertebral disks.
– ORIGIN early 20th cent.: from Greek *spondulos* 'vertebra' + -OSIS.

sponge /spənj/ ▶ **n. 1** a primitive sedentary aquatic invertebrate with a soft porous body that is typically supported by a framework of fibers or calcareous or glassy spicules. Sponges draw in a current of water to extract nutrients and oxygen. ● Phylum Porifera: several classes.
2 a piece of a soft, light, porous substance originally consisting of the fibrous skeleton of such an invertebrate but now usually made of synthetic material. Sponges absorb liquid and are used for washing and cleaning. ■ [in sing.] an act of wiping or cleaning with a sponge: *they gave him a quick sponge down*. ■ such a substance used as padding or insulating material: *the headguard is padded with sponge*. ■ a piece of such a substance impregnated with spermicide and inserted into a woman's vagina as a form of barrier contraceptive. ■ informal a heavy drinker. ■ [with modifier] metal in a porous form, typically prepared by reduction without fusion or by electrolysis: *platinum sponge*.
3 Brit. (also **sponge pudding**) a steamed or baked pudding of fat, flour, and eggs. ■ short for SPONGE CAKE.
4 informal a person who lives at someone else's expense.
▶ **v.** (**sponges, sponging** or **spongeing, sponged**)
1 [with obj.] wipe, rub, or clean with a wet sponge or cloth: *she sponged him down in an attempt to cool his fever*. ■ remove or wipe away (liquid or a mark) in such a way: *I'll go and sponge this orange juice off my dress*. ■ give a decorative mottled or textured effect to (a painted wall or surface) by applying a different shade of paint with a sponge.
2 [no obj.] informal obtain or accept money or food from other people without doing or intending to do anything in return: *they found they could earn a perfectly good living by sponging off others*. ■ [with obj.] obtain (something) in such a way: *he edged closer, clearly intending to sponge money from her*.
– DERIVATIVES **sponge·a·ble adj.**, **sponge·like** /'spənjˌlīk/ **adj.**
– ORIGIN Old English (sense 2 of the noun), via Latin from Greek *spongia*, later form of *spongos*, reinforced in Middle English by Old French *esponge*.

sponge bath ▶ **n.** an all-over washing, as given to a person confined to bed, done with a wet sponge or washcloth rather than in a tub or shower.

sponge cake /'spənj ˌkāk/ ▶ **n.** a very light sweet cake of spongelike consistency, made with little or no fat.

sponge cloth ▶ **n.** soft, lightly woven cloth with a slightly wrinkled surface.

sponge pud·ding ▶ **n.** see SPONGE (sense 3 of the noun).

spong·er /'spənjər/ ▶ **n. 1** informal a person who lives at others' expense.
2 a person who applies paint to pottery using a sponge.

sponge rub·ber ▶ **n.** rubber latex processed into a spongelike substance.

sponge tree ▶ **n.** another term for HUISACHE.

spon·gi·form /'spənjiˌfôrm/ ▶ **adj.** chiefly Veterinary Medicine having, relating to, or denoting a porous structure or consistency resembling that of a sponge.

spon·gin /'spənjin/ ▶ **n.** Biochemistry the horny or fibrous substance found in the skeleton of many sponges.

spon·gy /'spənjē/ ▶ **adj.** (**spongier, spongiest**) like a sponge, esp. in being porous, compressible, elastic, or absorbent: *a soft, spongy blanket of moss*. ■ (of metal) having an open, porous structure: *spongy platinum*. ■ (chiefly of a motor vehicle's braking system) lacking firmness.
– DERIVATIVES **spon·gi·ly** /'spənjəlē/ **adv.**, **spon·gi·ness n.**

spon·son /'spänsən/ ▶ **n.** a projection on the side of a boat, ship, or seaplane. ■ a gun platform standing out from a warship's side. ■ a short subsidiary wing that serves to stabilize a seaplane. ■ a buoyancy chamber fitted to a boat's hull, esp. on a canoe.

■ a triangular platform supporting the wheel on a paddle steamer.
– ORIGIN mid 19th cent.: of unknown origin.

spon·sor /ˈspänsər/ ▶ **n.** **1** a person or organization that provides funds for a project or activity carried out by another, in particular: ■ an individual or organization that pays some or all of the costs involved in staging a sporting or artistic event in return for advertising. ■ a person who pledges to donate a certain amount of money to another person after they have participated in a fund-raising event organized on behalf of a charity. ■ a business or organization that pays for or contributes to the costs of a radio or television program in return for advertising.
2 a person who introduces and supports a proposal for legislation: *a leading sponsor of the bill.* ■ a person taking official responsibility for the actions of another: *they act as informants, sponsors, and contacts for new immigrants.* ■ a godparent at a child's baptism. ■ (esp. in the Roman Catholic Church) a person presenting a candidate for confirmation.
▶ **v.** [with obj.] **1** provide funds for (a project or activity or the person carrying it out): *Joe is being sponsored by his church.* ■ pay some or all of the costs involved in staging (a sporting or artistic event) in return for advertising. ■ pledge to donate a certain sum of money to (someone) after they have participated in a fund-raising event organized on behalf of a charity. ■ (often as adj. **sponsored**) pledge to donate money because someone is taking part in (such an event): *they raised $70 by a sponsored walk.*
2 introduce and support (a proposal) in a legislative assembly: *Senator Hardin sponsored the bill.* ■ propose and organize (negotiations or talks) between other people or groups: *the U.S. sponsored negotiations between the two sides.*
– ORIGIN mid 17th cent. (as a noun): from Latin, from *spondere* 'promise solemnly.' The verb dates from the late 19th cent.

spon·sor·ship /ˈspänsərˌSHip/ ▶ **n.** the position of being a sponsor: *the company's sponsorship of the tournament.* ■ financial support received from a sponsor: *he has attracted more than $50,000 in sponsorship.*

spon·ta·ne·i·ty /ˌspäntəˈnēitē, -ˈnā-/ ▶ **n.** the condition of being spontaneous; spontaneous behavior or action: *she occasionally tore up her usual schedule in favor of spontaneity.*

spon·ta·ne·ous /spänˈtānēəs/ ▶ **adj.** performed or occurring as a result of a sudden inner impulse or inclination and without premeditation or external stimulus: *the audience broke into spontaneous applause | a spontaneous display of affection.* ■ (of a person) having an open, natural, and uninhibited manner. ■ (of a process or event) occurring without apparent external cause: *spontaneous miscarriages.* ■ archaic (of a plant) growing naturally and without being tended or cultivated. ■ Biology (of movement or activity in an organism) instinctive or involuntary: *the spontaneous mechanical activity of circular smooth muscle.*
– DERIVATIVES **spon·ta·ne·ous·ly** **adv.**
– ORIGIN mid 17th cent.: from late Latin *spontaneus* (from (*sua*) *sponte* 'of (one's) own accord') + **-ous**.

spon·ta·ne·ous com·bus·tion ▶ **n.** the ignition of organic matter (e.g., hay or coal) without apparent cause, typically through heat generated internally by rapid oxidation.

spon·ta·ne·ous gen·er·a·tion ▶ **n.** historical the supposed production of living organisms from nonliving matter, as inferred from the apparent appearance of life in some infusions.

spoof /spo͞of/ informal ▶ **n.** **1** a humorous imitation of something, typically a film or a particular genre of film, in which its characteristic features are exaggerated for comic effect: *a Robin Hood spoof.*
2 a trick played on someone as a joke.
▶ **v.** [with obj.] **1** imitate (something) while exaggerating its characteristic features for comic effect: *it is a movie that spoofs other movies.*
2 hoax or trick (someone): *they proceeded to spoof Western intelligence with false information.* ■ interfere with (radio or radar signals) so as to make them useless.
– DERIVATIVES **spoof·er** **n.**, **spoof·er·y** /ˈspo͞ofərē/ **n.**
– ORIGIN late 19th cent.: coined by Arthur Roberts (1852–1933), English comedian.

spook /spo͝ok/ informal ▶ **n.** **1** a ghost.
2 a spy: *a CIA spook.*
3 dated, offensive a contemptuous term for a black person.
▶ **v.** [with obj.] frighten; unnerve: *they spooked a couple of grizzly bears.* ■ [no obj.] (esp. of an animal) take fright suddenly: *he'll spook if we make any noise.*
– ORIGIN early 19th cent.: from Dutch, of unknown origin.

spook·y /ˈspo͝okē/ ▶ **adj.** (**spookier**, **spookiest**) informal **1** sinister or ghostly in a way that causes fear and unease: *I bet this place is really spooky late at night.*
2 (of a person or animal) easily frightened; nervous.
– DERIVATIVES **spook·i·ly** /ˈspo͝okəlē/ **adv.**, **spook·i·ness** **n.**

spool[1] /spo͞ol/ ▶ **n.** a cylindrical device on which film, magnetic tape, thread, or other flexible materials can be wound; a reel: *spools of electrical cable.* ■ a cylindrical device attached to a fishing rod and used for winding and unwinding the line as required. ■ [as modifier] denoting furniture of a style popular in England in the 17th century and North America in the 19th century, typically ornamented with a series of small knobs resembling spools: *a narrow spool bed.*
▶ **v.** **1** [with obj.] wind (magnetic tape or thread) onto a spool: *he was trying to spool his tapes back into the cassettes with a pencil eraser.* ■ [no obj.] be wound on or off a spool: *the plastic reel allows the line to run free as it spools out.*
2 [no obj.] (of an engine) increase its speed of rotation, typically to that required for operation: *a jet engine can take up to six seconds to spool up.*
– ORIGIN Middle English (denoting a cylinder onto which spun thread is wound): shortening of Old French *espole* or from Middle Low German *spôle*, of West Germanic origin; related to Dutch *spoel* and German *Spule*. The verb dates from the early 17th cent.

spool[2] ▶ **v.** [with obj.] Computing send (data that is intended for printing or processing on a peripheral device) to an intermediate store: *users can set which folder they wish to spool files to.*
– ORIGIN acronym from *simultaneous peripheral operation online*.

spoon /spo͞on/ ▶ **n.** **1** an implement consisting of a small, shallow oval or round bowl on a long handle, used for eating, stirring, and serving food. ■ the contents of such an implement: *three spoons of sugar.* ■ (**spoons**) a pair of spoons held in the hand and beaten together rhythmically as a percussion instrument.
2 a thing resembling a spoon in shape, in particular: ■ (also **spoon bait**) a fishing lure designed to wobble when pulled through the water. ■ an oar with a broad curved blade. ■ Golf, dated a club with a slightly concave wooden head.
▶ **v.** **1** [with obj.] convey (food) somewhere by using a spoon: *Rosie spooned sugar into her mug.* ■ hit (a ball) up into the air with a soft or weak stroke: *he spooned his shot high over the bar.*
2 [no obj.] informal, dated (of two people) behave in an amorous way; kiss and cuddle: *I saw them spooning on the beach.* ■ (of two people) lie close together sideways and front to back with bent knees, so as to fit together like spoons.
– DERIVATIVES **spoon·er** **n.** (sense 2 of the verb), **spoon·ful** /-ˌfo͝ol/ **n.** (pl. **spoonfuls** /-ˌfo͝olz/).
– ORIGIN Old English *spōn* 'chip of wood,' of Germanic origin; related to German *Span* 'shaving.' Sense 1 of the noun is of Scandinavian origin. The verb dates from the early 18th cent.

spoon·bill /ˈspo͞onˌbil/ ▶ **n.** a tall mainly white or pinkish wading bird related to ibises, having a long bill with a very broad flat tip. ● Genera *Platalea* and *Ajaia*, family Threskiornithidae: several species.

spoon bread ▶ **n.** soft cornbread served with a spoon.

spoon·er·ism /ˈspo͞onəˌrizəm/ ▶ **n.** a verbal error in which a speaker accidentally transposes the initial sounds or letters of two or more words, often to humorous effect, as in the sentence *you have hissed the mystery lectures*, accidentally spoken instead of the intended sentence *you have missed the history lectures*.
– ORIGIN early 20th cent.: named after the Rev. W. A. *Spooner* (1844–1930), an English scholar who reputedly made such errors in speaking.

spoon-feed ▶ **v.** [with obj.] feed (someone) by using a spoon. ■ provide (someone) with so much help or information that they do not need to think for themselves.

Spoon Riv·er a river that flows for 160 miles (260 km) through central Illinois, associated with the verse of Edgar Lee Masters.

spoon·worm /ˈspo͞onˌwərm/ ▶ **n.** an unsegmented wormlike marine invertebrate that lives in burrows, crevices, or discarded shells. Spoonworms typically have a sausage-shaped body with a long proboscis that can be extended over the seabed. ● Phylum Echiura.

spoon·y /ˈspo͞onē/ informal ▶ **adj.** (**spoonier**, **spooniest**) dated sentimentally or foolishly amorous: *I was spoony over Miss Talmadge to the point of idolatry.* ■ archaic foolish; silly.
▶ **n.** (pl. **spoonies**) archaic a simple, silly, or foolish person.
– DERIVATIVES **spoon·i·ly** /ˈspo͞onəlē/ **adv.**, **spoon·i·ness** **n.**

spoor /spo͝or, spô(ə)r/ ▶ **n.** the track or scent of an animal: *they searched around the hut for a spoor | the trail is marked by wolf spoor.*
▶ **v.** [with obj.] follow the track or scent of (an animal or person): *taking the spear, he set off to spoor the man.*
– DERIVATIVES **spoor·er** **n.**
– ORIGIN early 19th cent.: from Afrikaans, from Middle Dutch *spor*, of Germanic origin.

Spor·a·des /ˈspôrəˌdēz/ two groups of Greek islands in the Aegean Sea. The **Northern Sporades**, which lie close to the eastern coast of mainland Greece, include the islands of Euboea, Skiros, Skiathos, and Skopelos. The **Southern Sporades**, situated off the western coast of Turkey, include Rhodes and the other islands of the Dodecanese.

spo·rad·ic /spəˈradik/ ▶ **adj.** occurring at irregular intervals or only in a few places; scattered or isolated: *sporadic fighting broke out.*
– DERIVATIVES **spo·rad·i·cal·ly** /-ik(ə)lē/ **adv.**
– ORIGIN late 17th cent.: via medieval Latin from Greek *sporadikos*, from *sporas*, *sporad-* 'scattered'; related to *speirein* 'to sow.'

spo·ran·gi·o·phore /spəˈranjēəˌfôr/ ▶ **n.** Botany (in a fungus) a specialized hypha bearing sporangia.

spo·ran·gi·um /spəˈranjēəm/ ▶ **n.** (pl. **sporangia** /-jēə/) Botany (in ferns and lower plants) a receptacle in which asexual spores are formed.
– DERIVATIVES **spo·ran·gi·al** /-jēəl/ **adj.**
– ORIGIN early 19th cent.: modern Latin, from Greek *spora* 'spore' + *angeion* 'vessel.'

spore /spôr/ ▶ **n.** Biology a minute, typically one-celled, reproductive unit capable of giving rise to a new individual without sexual fusion, characteristic of lower plants, fungi, and protozoans. ■ Botany (in a plant exhibiting alternation of generations) a haploid reproductive cell that gives rise to a gametophyte. ■ Microbiology (in bacteria) a rounded resistant form adopted by a bacterial cell in adverse conditions.
– ORIGIN mid 19th cent.: from modern Latin *spora*, from Greek *spora* 'sowing, seed,' from *speirein* 'to sow.'

spork /spôrk/ ▶ **n.** a spoon-shaped eating utensil with short tines at the tip.
– ORIGIN early 20th cent.: blend of *spoon* and *fork*.

sporo- ▶ **comb. form** Biology of or relating to spores: *sporogenesis*.
– ORIGIN from Greek *spora* 'spore.'

spo·ro·cyst /ˈspôrəˌsist/ ▶ **n.** Zoology a parasitic fluke in the initial stage of infection in a snail host, developed from a miracidium. ■ (in parasitic sporozoans) an encysted zygote in an invertebrate host.

spo·ro·gen·e·sis /ˌspôrəˈjenəsis/ ▶ **n.** chiefly Botany the process of spore formation.

spo·rog·e·nous /spəˈräjənəs/ ▶ **adj.** chiefly Botany (of an organism or tissue) producing spores.

spo·rog·o·ny /spəˈrägənē/ ▶ **n.** Zoology the asexual process of spore formation in parasitic sporozoans.

spo·ro·phore /ˈspôrəˌfôr/ ▶ **n.** Botany the spore-bearing structure of a fungus.

spo·ro·phyte /ˈspôrəˌfīt/ ▶ **n.** Botany (in the life cycle of plants with alternating generations) the asexual and usually diploid phase, producing spores from which the gametophyte arises. It is the dominant form in vascular plants, e.g., the frond of a fern.
– DERIVATIVES **spo·ro·phyt·ic** /ˌspôrəˈfitik/ **adj.**

spo·ro·tri·cho·sis /ˌspôrətriˈkōsis/ ▶ **n.** Medicine a chronic fungal infection producing nodules and ulcers in the lymph nodes and skin. ● The disease is caused by the fungus *Sporothrix schenckii*.

Spo·ro·zo·a /ˌspôrəˈzōə/ Zoology & Medicine a phylum of mainly parasitic spore-forming protozoans that have a complex life cycle with sexual and asexual generations. They include the organisms that cause malaria, babesiosis, coccidiosis, and toxoplasmosis. Also called **APICOMPLEXA**.
– ORIGIN modern Latin (plural), from **SPORE** + Greek *zōia* 'animals.'

spo·ro·zo·an /ˌspôrəˈzōən/ Zoology & Medicine ▶ **n.** a protozoan of the phylum Sporozoa.
▶ **adj.** relating to or denoting sporozoans.

spo·ro·zo·ite /ˌspôrəˈzōˌīt/ ▶ **n.** Zoology & Medicine a motile sporelike stage in the life cycle of some parasitic sporozoans (e.g., the malaria organism) that is typically the infective agent introduced into a host.
– ORIGIN late 19th cent.: from **SPORO-** 'relating to spores' + Greek *zōion* 'animal' + **-ITE**.

spor·ran /ˈspärən/ ▶ **n.** a small pouch worn around the waist so as to hang in front of the kilt as part of men's Scottish Highland dress.
– ORIGIN mid 18th cent.: from Scottish Gaelic *sporan*.

sport /spôrt/ ▶ **n.** **1** an activity involving physical exertion and skill in which an individual or team competes against another or others for entertainment: *team sports such as baseball and soccer* | (as modifier **sports**) *a sports center*. ■ dated entertainment; fun: *it was considered great sport to trip him up*. ■ archaic a source of amusement or entertainment: *I do not wish to show myself the sport of a man like Williams*.
2 informal a person who behaves in a good or specified way in response to teasing, defeat, or a similarly trying situation: *go on, be a sport!* | *Angela's a bad sport*.
3 Biology an animal or plant showing abnormal or striking variation from the parent type, esp. in form or color, as a result of spontaneous mutation.
▶ **v.** **1** [with obj.] wear or display (a distinctive or noticeable item): *he was sporting a huge handlebar mustache*.
2 [no obj.] amuse oneself or play in a lively, energetic way: *the children sported in the water*.
– PHRASES **in sport** for fun: *I have assumed the name was given more or less in sport*. **make sport of** dated make fun of. **the sport of kings** horse racing.
– DERIVATIVES **sport·er n.**
– ORIGIN late Middle English (in the sense 'pastime, entertainment'): shortening of DISPORT.

sport coat (also **sports coat** or **sport jacket** or **sports jacket**) ▶ **n.** a man's jacket resembling a suit jacket, for informal wear.

spor·tif /spôrˈtēf/ ▶ **adj.** (of a person) active or interested in athletic sports: *he was sportif and ready for action*. ■ (of an action or event) intended in fun or as a joke. ■ (of a garment or style of dress) suitable for sport or informal wear; casual.
▶ **n.** a person who is active or interested in sport.
– ORIGIN French.

sport·ing /ˈspôrtiNG/ ▶ **adj.** **1** [attrib.] connected with or interested in sports: *a major sporting event*.
2 fair and generous in one's behavior or treatment of others, esp. in a game or contest: *it was not very sporting of Smith to hit Gonzales with that pitch*.
– DERIVATIVES **sport·ing·ly adv.** (sense 2).

sport·ing chance ▶ **n.** [in sing.] a reasonable chance of winning or succeeding: *I'll give you a sporting chance*.

spor·tive /ˈspôrtiv/ ▶ **adj.** playful; lighthearted. ■ archaic amorous or lustful.
– DERIVATIVES **spor·tive·ly adv.**, **spor·tive·ness n.**

sports bar ▶ **n.** a bar where televised sporting events are shown continuously.

sports car ▶ **n.** a low-built car designed for performance at high speeds.

sports·cast /ˈspôrtsˌkast/ ▶ **n.** a broadcast of sports news or a sports event.
– DERIVATIVES **sports·cast·er n.**, **sports·cast·ing n.**

sports·man /ˈspôrtsmən/ ▶ **n.** (pl. **sportsmen**) a man who takes part in a sport, esp. as a professional. ■ a person who behaves sportingly. ■ dated a man who hunts or shoots wild animals as a pastime.
– DERIVATIVES **sports·man·like** /-ˌlīk/ **adj.**, **sports·man·ship** /-ˌSHip/ **n.**

sports·per·son /ˈspôrtsˌpərsən/ ▶ **n.** (pl. **sportspersons** or **sportspeople** /-ˌpēpəl/) a sportsman or sportswoman (used as a neutral alternative).

sport·ster /ˈspôrtstər/ ▶ **n.** informal a sports car.

sports·wear /ˈspôrtsˌwe(ə)r/ ▶ **n.** clothes worn for casual outdoor use or for such sports activities as jogging, cycling, tennis, sailing, etc.

sports·wom·an /ˈspôrtsˌwo͝omən/ ▶ **n.** (pl. **sportswomen**) a woman who takes part in sports, esp. professionally.
– DERIVATIVES **sports·wom·an·ship** /-ˌSHip/ **n.**

sports·writ·er /ˈspôrtsˌrītər/ ▶ **n.** a journalist who writes about sports.
– DERIVATIVES **sports·writ·ing** /-tiNG/ **n.**

sport u·til·i·ty ve·hi·cle (abbr.: **SUV**) ▶ **n.** a high-performance four-wheel-drive vehicle.

sport·y /ˈspôrtē/ ▶ **adj.** (**sportier**, **sportiest**) informal flashy or showy in dress or behavior. ■ (of clothing) casual yet attractively stylish: *a sporty outfit*. ■ (of a car) compact and with fast acceleration: *a sporty red coupe*. ■ fond of or good at sports.
– DERIVATIVES **sport·i·ly** /ˈspôrtəlē/ **adv.**, **sport·i·ness n.**

spor·u·late /ˈspôryəˌlāt/ ▶ **v.** [no obj.] Biology produce or form a spore or spores.
– DERIVATIVES **spor·u·la·tion** /ˌspôryəˈlāSHən/ **n.**

spor·ule /ˈspôryo͞ol/ ▶ **n.** Biology a small spore.
– DERIVATIVES **spor·u·lar** /-yələr/ **adj.**

S

s'pose /s(ə)ˈpōz/ ▶ **v.** nonstandard spelling of SUPPOSE, representing informal speech.

spot /spät/ ▶ **n.** **1** a small round or roundish mark, differing in color or texture from the surface around it: *ladybugs have black spots on their red wing covers*. ■ a small mark or stain: *a spot of mildew on the wall*. ■ a pimple. ■ archaic a moral blemish or stain. ■ a pip on a domino, playing card, or die. ■ [in combination] informal a banknote of a specified value: *a ten-spot*.
2 a particular place or point: *a nice secluded spot* | *an ideal picnic spot*. ■ [with adj.] a small feature or part of something with a particular quality: *his bald spot* | *there was one bright spot in a night of dismal failure*. ■ a position within a listing; a ranking: *the runner-up spot*. ■ Sports an advantage allowed to a player as a handicap. ■ a place for an individual item within a show: *she couldn't do her usual singing spot in the club*.
3 informal, chiefly Brit. a small amount of something: *a spot of rain*.
4 [as modifier] denoting a system of trading in which commodities or currencies are delivered and paid for immediately after a sale: *trading in the spot markets* | *the current spot price*.
5 short for SPOTLIGHT.
▶ **v.** (**spots**, **spotting**, **spotted**) **1** [with obj.] see, notice, or recognize (someone or something) that is difficult to detect or that one is searching for: *Andrew spotted the ad in the paper* | *the men were spotted by police*. ■ (usu. **be spotted**) recognize that (someone) has a particular talent, esp. for sports or show business: *we were spotted by a talent scout*. ■ [no obj.] Military locate an enemy's position, typically from the air: *they were spotting for enemy aircraft*.
2 [with obj.] (usu. **be spotted**) mark with spots: *the velvet was spotted with stains*. ■ [no obj.] become marked with spots: *a damp atmosphere causes the flowers to spot*. ■ cover (a surface or area) thinly: *thorn trees spotted the land*. ■ archaic stain or sully the moral character or qualities of.
3 [with obj.] place (a billiard ball or football) on its designated starting point.
4 [with two objs.] informal give or lend (money) to (someone): *I'll spot you $300*. ■ allow (an advantage) to (someone) in a game or sport: *the higher-rated team spots the lower-rated team the difference in their handicaps*.
5 [with obj.] observe or assist (a gymnast) during a performance in order to minimize the chance of injury to the gymnast.
– PHRASES **hit the spot** informal be exactly what is required: *the cup of coffee hit the spot*. **in a spot** informal in a difficult situation. **on the spot** **1** without any delay; immediately: *he offered me the job on the spot*. **2** at the scene of an action or event: *journalists on the spot reported no progress*. **put someone on the spot** informal force someone into a situation in which they must make a difficult decision or answer a difficult question.
– ORIGIN Middle English: perhaps from Middle Dutch *spotte*. The sense 'notice, recognize' arose from the early 19th-cent. slang use 'note as a suspect or criminal.'

spot-buy ▶ **v.** [with obj.] Stock Market pay for (a currency or commodity) immediately after a sale is made.

spot check ▶ **n.** a test made without warning on a randomly selected subject.
▶ **v.** (**spot-check**) [with obj.] subject (someone or something) to such a test.

spot·less /ˈspätlis/ ▶ **adj.** absolutely clean or pure; immaculate: *a spotless white apron*.
– DERIVATIVES **spot·less·ly adv.**, **spot·less·ness n.**

spot·light /ˈspätˌlīt/ ▶ **n.** a lamp projecting a narrow, intense beam of light directly onto a place or person, esp. a performer on stage. ■ a beam of light from a lamp of this kind: *the knife flashed in the spotlight*. ■ (**the spotlight**) intense scrutiny or public attention: *she was constantly in the media spotlight*.
▶ **v.** (past and past participle **spotlighted** or **spotlit** /-lit/) [with obj.] illuminate with a spotlight: *the dancers are spotlighted from time to time throughout the evening*. ■ direct attention to (a particular problem or situation): *the protest spotlighted the overcrowding in federal prisons*.

spot me·ter ▶ **n.** Photography a photometer that measures the intensity of light received within a cone of small angle, usually 2° or less.

spot news ▶ **n.** news reported of events as they occur.

Spot·syl·va·nia Coun·ty /ˌspätsəlˈvānēə/ a rural county in northeastern Virginia, site of Civil War battles including those at Fredericksburg and Spotsylvania Court House; pop. 120,031 (est. 2008).

spot·ted /ˈspätid/ ▶ **adj.** marked or decorated with spots.
– DERIVATIVES **spot·ted·ness n.**

spot·ted ca·vy ▶ **n.** another term for PACA.

spot·ted deer ▶ **n.** another term for AXIS DEER.

spot·ted dick ▶ **n.** Brit. a suet pudding containing currants.

spot·ted fe·ver ▶ **n.** any of a number of diseases characterized by fever and skin spots. ■ cerebrospinal meningitis. ■ typhus. ■ see ROCKY MOUNTAIN SPOTTED FEVER.

spot·ted hy·e·na /hīˈēnə/ ▶ **n.** a southern African hyena that has a grayish-yellow to reddish coat with irregular dark spots, and a loud laughing call. Also called LAUGHING HYENA. ● *Crocuta crocuta*, family Hyaenidae.

spotted hyena

spot·ted knap·weed ▶ **n.** a biennial herb of European origin with pink flowers on prickly stems. It is established across most of North America and is regarded as a noxious weed nearly everywhere. ● *Centaurea biebersteinii*, family Compositae.

spot·ted tur·tle ▶ **n.** a North American freshwater turtle with few or numerous yellow spots on the carapace. Once abundant, esp. along the east coast of the US, the spotted turtle is protected in many areas. ● *Clemmys guttata*, family Emydidae.

spotted turtle

spot·ter /ˈspätər/ ▶ **n.** informal a person employed by a company or business to keep watch on employees or customers. ■ an aviator or aircraft employed in locating or observing enemy positions: [as modifier] *spotter planes*. ■ a person who observes or assists a gymnast or weightlifter during a performance or practice in order to minimize the chance of injury to the gymnast or weightlifter.

spot·ty /ˈspätē/ ▶ **adj.** (**spottier**, **spottiest**) marked with spots: *a spotty purple flower*. ■ of uneven quality; patchy: *his spotty record on the environment*.
– DERIVATIVES **spot·ti·ly** /ˈspätəlē/ **adv.**, **spot·ti·ness n.**

spot-weld ▶ **v.** [with obj.] join by welding at a number of separate points: *the wire was spot-welded in place*.
▶ **n.** (**spot weld**) each of the welds so made.
– DERIVATIVES **spot weld·er n.**, **spot weld·ing n.**

spous·al /ˈspouzəl/ ▶ **adj.** [attrib.] Law of or relating to marriage or to a husband or wife: *the spousal benefits of married couples*.

spouse /spous/ ▶ **n.** a husband or wife, considered in relation to their partner.
– ORIGIN Middle English: from Old French *spous(e)*, variant of *espous(e)*, from Latin *sponsus* (masculine), *sponsa* (feminine), past participles of *spondere* 'betroth.'

spout /spout/ ▶ **n.** **1** a tube or lip projecting from a container, through which liquid can be poured: *a teapot with a chipped spout*. ■ a pipe or trough through which water may be carried away or from which it can flow out. ■ a sloping trough for conveying something to a lower level; a chute. ■ historical a lift in a pawnshop used to convey pawned items up for storage.
2 a stream of liquid issuing from somewhere with great force: *the tall spouts of geysers*. ■ the plume of water vapor ejected from the blowhole of a whale: *the spout of an occasional whale*.
▶ **v.** [with obj.] **1** send out (liquid) forcibly in a stream: *volcanoes spouted ash and lava*. ■ [no obj.] (of a liquid) flow out of somewhere in such a way: *blood was spouting from the cuts on my hand*. ■ (of a whale or dolphin) eject (water vapor and air) through its blowhole.

2 express (one's views or ideas) in a lengthy, declamatory, and unreflecting way: *he was spouting platitudes about animal rights* | [no obj.] *they like to spout off at each other.*
– PHRASES **up the spout** Brit. informal **1** no longer working, or unlikely to be useful or successful. **2** (of a woman) pregnant. **3** pawned: *by Friday, half his belongings were up the spout.*
– DERIVATIVES **spout·ed** adj., **spout·er** n., **spout·less** adj.
– ORIGIN Middle English (as a verb): from Middle Dutch *spouten*, from an imitative base shared by Old Norse *spýta* 'to spit.'

spp. ▶ abbr. species (plural).

SPQR ▶ abbr. historical the Senate and people of Rome.
– ORIGIN from Latin *Senatus Populusque Romanus*.

spr. ▶ abbr. spring.

Sprach·ge·fühl /'sнpräkgə,fo͝ol/ ▶ n. intuitive feeling for the natural idiom of a language. ■ the essential character of a language.
– ORIGIN German, from *Sprache* 'speech, a language' + *Gefühl* 'feeling.'

sprad·dle /'spradl/ ▶ v. [with obj.] (usu. as adj. **spraddled**) spread (one's legs) far apart: *the cat's spraddled hind legs.*
– ORIGIN mid 17th cent. (in the sense 'sprawl'): probably from *sprad*, dialect past participle of SPREAD.

sprag /sprag/ ▶ n. **1** a simple brake on a vehicle, esp. a stout stick or bar inserted between the spokes of a wheel to check its motion. ■ a one-way clutch that keeps a vehicle from rolling backwards.
2 Mining a prop used to support a roof, wall, or seam.
– ORIGIN mid 19th cent: of unknown origin.

sprain /sprān/ ▶ v. [with obj.] wrench or twist the ligaments of (an ankle, wrist, or other joint) violently so as to cause pain and swelling but not dislocation: *he left in a wheelchair after spraining an ankle.*
▶ n. the result of such a wrench or twist of a joint.
– ORIGIN early 17th cent.: of unknown origin.

sprang /spraNG/ past of SPRING.

USAGE See usage at SPRING.

sprat /sprat/ ▶ n. a small marine fish of the herring family, widely caught for food and fish products.
● *Sprattus* and other genera, family Clupeidae: several species, in particular *S. sprattus* of European inshore waters. ■ any of a number of small fishes that resemble the true sprats, e.g., the sand eel.
– ORIGIN late 16th cent.: variant of Old English *sprot*, of unknown origin.

Sprat·ly Is·lands /'spratlē/ a group of small islands and coral reefs in the South China Sea, between Vietnam and Borneo. Dispersed over a distance of about 600 miles (965 km), the islands are variously claimed by China, Taiwan, Vietnam, the Philippines, and Malaysia.

sprawl /sprôl/ ▶ v. [no obj.] sit, lie, or fall with one's arms and legs spread out in an ungainly or awkward way: *the door shot open, sending him sprawling across the pavement* | *she lay sprawled on the bed.* ■ spread out over a large area in an untidy or irregular way: *the town sprawled along several miles of cliff top* | (as adj. **sprawling**) *the sprawling suburbs.*
▶ n. [usu. in sing.] an ungainly or carelessly relaxed position in which one's arms and legs are spread out: *she fell into a sort of luxurious sprawl.* ■ a group or mass of something that has spread out in an untidy or irregular way: *a sprawl of buildings.* ■ the expansion of an urban or industrial area into the adjoining countryside in a way perceived to be disorganized and unattractive: *the growth of urban sprawl.*
– DERIVATIVES **sprawl·ing·ly** adv.
– ORIGIN Old English *spreawlian* 'move the limbs convulsively'; related to Danish *sprælle* 'kick or splash around.' The noun dates from the early 18th cent.

spray¹ /sprā/ ▶ n. liquid that is blown or driven through the air in the form of tiny drops: *a torrent of white foam and spray* | *a fine spray of mud.* ■ a liquid preparation that can be forced out of a can or other container in such a form: *a can of insect spray.* ■ a can or container holding such a preparation. ■ an act of applying such a preparation: *refresh your flowers with a quick spray.*
▶ v. [with obj.] apply (liquid) to someone or something in the form of a shower of tiny drops: *the product can be sprayed onto wet or dry hair.* ■ sprinkle or cover (someone or something) with a shower of tiny drops of liquid: *she sprayed herself with perfume.* ■ [no obj.] (of liquid) be driven through the air or forced out of something in such a form: *water sprayed into the air.* ■ treat (a plant) with insecticide or herbicide in such a way: *avoid spraying your plants with pesticides.* ■ scatter (something) somewhere with great force: *the truck shuddered to a halt, spraying gravel from under its wheels.* ■ fire a rapid succession of bullets at: *enemy gunners sprayed the decks of the warships.* ■ (of a male cat) direct a stream of urine over (an object or area) to mark a territory. ■ (in a sporting context) kick, hit, or throw (the ball) in an unpredictable or inaccurate direction: *he began his round by spraying his fairway shots.*
– DERIVATIVES **spray·a·ble** adj., **spray·er** n.
– ORIGIN early 17th cent. (earlier as *spry*): related to Middle Dutch *spra(e)yen* 'sprinkle.'

spray² ▶ n. a stem or small branch of a tree or plant, bearing flowers and foliage: *a spray of honeysuckle.* ■ a bunch of cut flowers arranged in an attractive way. ■ a brooch in the form of a bouquet of flowers.
– ORIGIN Middle English: representing late Old English *(e)sprei*, recorded in personal and place names, of unknown origin.

spray·deck /'sprā,dek/ ▶ n. a flexible cover that is fitted to the opening in the top of a kayak to form a waterproof seal around the kayaker's body.

spray-dry ▶ v. [with obj.] dry (a foodstuff or a ceramic material) by spraying particles of it into a current of hot air, the water in the particles being rapidly evaporated.
– DERIVATIVES **spray dry·er** n.

spray gun ▶ n. a device resembling a gun that is used to spray a liquid such as paint or pesticide under pressure.

spray-paint ▶ v. [with obj.] paint (an image or message) onto a surface with a spray. ■ paint (a surface) with a spray: *they were spray-painting the chairs.*
▶ n. (**spray paint**) paint that is contained in an aerosol can for the purpose of spraying onto a surface.

spray·skirt /'sprā,skərt/ ▶ n. another term for SPRAYDECK.

spread /spred/ ▶ v. (past and past participle **spread**)
1 [with obj.] open out (something) so as to extend its surface area, width, or length: *I spread a towel on the sand and sat down* | *she helped Chris to **spread out** the map.* ■ stretch out (arms, legs, hands, fingers, or wings) so that they are far apart: *the swan spread its wings.*
2 [no obj., with adverbial] extend over a large or increasing area: *she stood at the window looking at the town spread out below.* ■ (**spread out**) (of a group of people) move apart so as to cover a wider area: *the Marines spread out across the docks.* ■ [with obj. and adverbial] distribute or disperse (something) over a certain area: *volcanic eruptions spread dust high into the stratosphere.* ■ gradually reach or cause to reach a larger and larger area or more and more people: [no obj.] *the violence spread from the city to the suburbs* | [with obj.] *she's always spreading rumors about other people.* ■ (of people, animals, or plants) become distributed over a large or larger area: *the owls have spread as far north as Yellowknife.* ■ [with obj. and adverbial] distribute (something) in a specified way: *you can **spread** the payments **over** as long a period as you like.*
3 [with obj. and adverbial] apply (a substance) to an object or surface in an even layer: *he sighed, spreading jam on a croissant.* ■ cover (a surface) with a substance in such a way: *spread each slice thinly with mayonnaise.* ■ [no obj., with adverbial] be able to be applied in such a way: *the whipped butter spreads easily.*
4 [with obj.] archaic lay (a table) for a meal.
▶ n. **1** the fact or process of spreading over an area: *the spread of AIDS* | *the spread of the urban population into rural areas.*
2 the extent, width, or area covered by something: *the male's antlers can attain a spread of six feet.* ■ the wingspan of a bird. ■ an expanse or amount of something: *the green spread of the park.* ■ a large farm or ranch.
3 the range or variety of something: *a wide spread of ages.* ■ the difference between two rates or prices: *the very narrow spread between borrowing and deposit rates.* ■ short for POINT SPREAD.
4 a soft paste that can be applied in a layer to bread or other food.
5 an article or advertisement covering several columns or pages of a newspaper or magazine, esp. one on two facing pages: *a double-page spread.* ■ a bedspread.
6 informal a large and impressively elaborate meal.
– PHRASES **spread like wildfire** see WILDFIRE. **spread oneself too thin** be involved in so many different activities or projects that one's time and energy are not used to good effect. **spread one's wings** see WING.
– DERIVATIVES **spread·a·ble** adj.
– ORIGIN Old English *-sprǣdan* (used in combinations); related to Dutch *spreiden* and German *spreiten*.

spread-ea·gle ▶ v. [with obj.] (usu. **be spread-eagled**) stretch (someone) out with their arms and legs extended: *he lay spread-eagled in the road.* ■ [no obj.] Skating perform a spread eagle.
▶ n. (**spread eagle**) an emblematic representation of an eagle with its legs and wings extended. ■ Figure Skating a straight glide made with the feet in a line, with the heels touching, and the arms stretched out to either side.
▶ adj. **1** stretched out with one's arms and legs extended: *prisoners are chained to their beds, spread-eagle, for days at a time.*
2 loudly or aggressively patriotic about the US: *spread-eagle oratory.*

spread·er /'spredər/ ▶ n. a device used for spreading or scattering a substance over a wide area. ■ a person who spreads or disseminates something: *children are major spreaders of influenza in schools.* ■ [often in combination] a device that spreads apart one thing from another: *rubber toe-spreaders used for pedicures.* ■ a bar attached to the mast of a yacht in order to spread the angle of the upper shrouds.

spread·sheet /'spred,sнēt/ ▶ n. a computer program in which figures arranged in the rows and columns of a grid can be manipulated and used in calculations.
▶ v. [no obj.] (usu. as noun **spreadsheeting**) use such a computer program.

Sprech·ge·sang /'sнprekgə,zäNG/ (also **sprechgesang**) ▶ n. Music a style of dramatic vocalization intermediate between speech and song.
– ORIGIN German, literally 'speech song.'

Sprech·stim·me /'sнprek,sнtimə/ (also **sprechstimme**) ▶ n. Music another term for SPRECHGESANG. ■ the kind of voice used in Sprechgesang.
– ORIGIN German, literally 'speech voice.'

spree /sprē/ ▶ n. a spell or sustained period of unrestrained activity of a particular kind: *he went on a six-month crime spree* | *a shopping spree.* ■ a spell of unrestrained drinking.
▶ v. (**sprees, spreeing, spreed**) [no obj.] dated take part in a spree.
– ORIGIN late 18th cent.: of unknown origin.

sprei·te /sprīt, 'sнprītə/ ▶ n. (pl. **spreiten** /'sprītn, 'sнprī-/ or **spreites**) Paleontology a banded pattern of uncertain origin found in the infill of the burrows of certain fossil invertebrates.
– ORIGIN 1960s: from German *Spreite* 'layer, lamina.'

sprez·za·tu·ra /,spretsə't(y)o͝orə/ ▶ n. studied carelessness, esp. as a characteristic quality or style of art or literature.
– ORIGIN Italian.

sprig¹ /sprig/ ▶ n. a small stem bearing leaves or flowers, taken from a bush or plant: *a sprig of holly.* ■ a descendant or younger member of a family or social class: *a sprig of the French nobility.* ■ archaic, chiefly derogatory a young man. ■ a small molded decoration applied to a piece of pottery before firing.
▶ v. [with obj.] decorate (pottery) with small, separately molded designs.
– DERIVATIVES **sprig·gy** adj.
– ORIGIN Middle English: from or related to Low German *sprick*.

sprig² ▶ n. another term for GLAZIER'S POINT.
– ORIGIN Middle English: of unknown origin.

sprigged /sprigd/ ▶ adj. (chiefly of fabric or paper) decorated with a design of sprigs of leaves or flowers.

spright·ly /'sprītlē/ (also **spritely**) ▶ adj. (**sprightlier, sprightliest**) (esp. of an old person) lively; full of energy: *she was quite sprightly for her age.*
– DERIVATIVES **spright·li·ness** n.
– ORIGIN late 16th cent.: from *spright* (rare variant of SPRITE) + -LY¹.

spring /spriNG/ ▶ v. (past **sprang** /spraNG/ or **sprung** /sprəNG/; past participle **sprung**) **1** [no obj.] move or jump suddenly or rapidly upward or forward: *I sprang out of bed* | figurative *they sprang to her defense.* ■ move rapidly or suddenly from a constrained position by or as if by the action of a spring: *the drawer sprang open.* ■ operate suddenly by means of a mechanism: [no obj.] *the engine sprang into life.* ■ [with obj.] cause (a game bird) to rise from cover. ■ [with obj.] informal bring about the escape or release of (a prisoner): *the president sought to spring the hostages.*
2 [no obj.] (**spring from**) originate or arise from: *madness and creativity could spring from the same source.* ■ appear suddenly or unexpectedly from:

S

tears sprang from his eyes. ■ (**spring up**) suddenly develop or appear: *a terrible storm sprang up.* ■ [with obj.] (**spring something on**) present or propose something suddenly or unexpectedly to (someone): *we decided to spring a surprise on them.*
3 [with obj.] (usu. as adj. **sprung**) cushion or fit (a vehicle or item of furniture) with springs: *a fully sprung mattress.*
4 [no obj.] (esp. of wood) become warped or split. ■ [with obj.] (of a boat) suffer splitting of (a mast or other part).
5 [no obj.] (**spring for**) informal pay for, esp. as a treat for someone else: *he's never offered to spring for dinner.* ■ [with obj.] archaic spend (money): *he might spring a few pennies more.*
▶ **n. 1** the season after winter and before summer, in which vegetation begins to appear, in the northern hemisphere from March to May and in the southern hemisphere from September to November: *in spring the garden is a feast of blossom* | [as modifier] *spring rain* | figurative *he was in the spring of his years.* ■ Astronomy the period from the vernal equinox to the summer solstice. ■ short for SPRING TIDE.
2 a resilient device, typically a helical metal coil, that can be pressed or pulled but returns to its former shape when released, used chiefly to exert constant tension or absorb movement. ■ the ability to spring back strongly; elasticity: *the mattress has lost its spring.*
3 [in sing.] a sudden jump upward or forward: *with a sudden spring, he leapt onto the table.* ■ informal, dated an escape or release from prison.
4 a place where water or oil wells up from an underground source, or the basin or flow formed in such a way: [as modifier] *spring water.* ■ the origin or a source of something: *the place was a spring of musical talent.*
5 an upward curvature of a ship's deck planking from the horizontal. ■ a split in a wooden plank or spar under strain.
– PHRASES **spring a leak** (of a boat or container) develop a leak. [originally a phrase in nautical use, referring to timbers springing out of position.]
spring a trap cause a trap for catching animals to close suddenly. ■ trick someone into doing something: *she decided to spring the trap after noticing that her husband was behaving erratically.*
– DERIVATIVES **spring·less adj.**, **spring·like** /-ˌlīk/ **adj.**
– ORIGIN Old English *spring* (noun), *springan* (verb), of Germanic origin; related to Dutch and German *springen.* Early use in the senses 'head of a well' and 'rush out in a stream' gave rise to the figurative use 'originate.'

USAGE In British English the standard past tense is **sprang** (*she sprang forward*), while in US English the past can be either **sprang** or **sprung** (*I sprung out of bed*). In both British and US English, the past participle is always **sprung** (*by late afternoon, the boat had sprung another leak*).

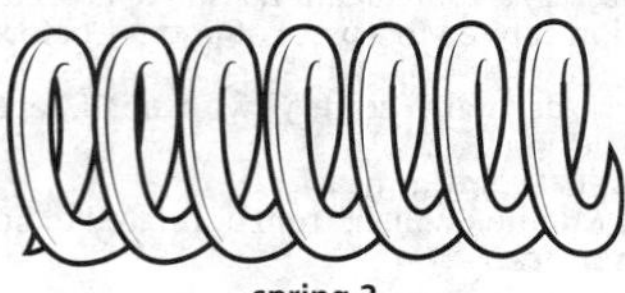
spring 2

spring beau·ty ▶ **n.** a spring-flowering succulent plant of the purslane family. ● Genus *Claytonia*, family Portulacaceae: several species, in particular the white- or pink-flowered *C. virginica*, found in moist woods in North America.

spring·board /ˈspriNGˌbôrd/ ▶ **n.** a strong, flexible board from which someone can jump in order to gain added impetus when performing a dive or a gymnastic movement. ■ a thing that lends impetus or assistance to a particular action, enterprise, or development: *an economic plan that may be the springboard for recovery.*

spring·bok /ˈspriNGˌbäk/ ▶ **n.** a gazelle with a characteristic habit of leaping (pronking) when disturbed, forming large herds on arid plains in southern Africa. ● *Antidorcas marsupialis*, family Bovidae.
– ORIGIN late 18th cent.: from Afrikaans, from Dutch *springen* 'to spring' + *bok* 'antelope.'

spring chick·en ▶ **n. 1** [usu. with negative] informal a young person: *you're no spring chicken yourself anymore.*
2 a young chicken for eating (originally available only in spring).

spring clean·ing ▶ **n.** a thorough cleaning of a house or room, typically undertaken in spring.
▶ **v.** (**spring-clean**) [with obj.] clean (a home or room) thoroughly: *it was Veronica who spring-cleaned the apartment.*

Spring·dale /ˈspriNGˌdāl/ a commercial and agricultural city in northwestern Arkansas; pop. 68,180 (est. 2008).

springe /sprinj/ ▶ **n.** a noose or snare for catching small game.
– ORIGIN Middle English: from the base of SPRING.

spring e·qui·nox ▶ **n.** another term for VERNAL EQUINOX.

spring·er /ˈspriNGər/ ▶ **n. 1** (usu. **springer spaniel**) a small spaniel of a breed originally used to spring game. There are two main breeds, the **English springer spaniel**, typically black and white or brown and white, and the less common red and white **Welsh springer spaniel**.
2 Architecture the lowest stone in an arch, where the curve begins.
3 a cow or heifer near to calving.

spring·er·le /SHpriNGərlə/ ▶ **n.** (pl. **same** or **springerles**) a German anise-flavored Christmas cookie with an embossed design on top made with a special rolling pin.
– ORIGIN German dialect *Springerle*, literally 'little jumping horses.'

spring fe·ver ▶ **n.** a feeling of restlessness and excitement felt at the beginning of spring.

Spring·field /ˈspriNGˌfēld/ **1** the state capital of Illinois; pop. 117,352 (est. 2008). It was the home and burial place of Abraham Lincoln.
2 a city in southwestern Massachusetts, on the Connecticut River; pop. 150,640 (est. 2008). It was first settled in 1636.
3 a city in southwestern Missouri, on the northern edge of the Ozark Mountains; pop. 156,206 (est. 2008).
4 a city in west central Ohio, west of Columbus and northeast of Dayton; pop. 62,269 (est. 2008).
5 a city in western Oregon, on the Willamette River, an eastern suburb of Eugene; pop. 57,224 (est. 2008).

spring·form pan /ˈspriNGˌfôrm/ ▶ **n.** a round cake pan with a removable bottom that is held in place by a sprung collar forming the sides.

spring·hare /ˈspriNGˌhe(ə)r/ (also **springhaas** /ˈspriNGˌhäs/) ▶ **n.** (pl. **springhares** also **springhaas**) a large nocturnal burrowing rodent resembling a miniature kangaroo, with a rabbitlike head, a long bushy tail, and long hind limbs, native to southern Africa. ● *Pedetes capensis*, the only member of the family Pedetidae.

spring line ▶ **n.** a hawser laid out diagonally aft from a ship's bow or forward from a ship's stern and secured to a fixed point in order to prevent movement or assist maneuvering.

spring-load·ed ▶ **adj.** containing a compressed or stretched spring pressing one part against another: *a spring-loaded clothespin.*

spring lock ▶ **n.** a type of lock with a spring-loaded bolt that requires a key to open it, as distinct from a deadbolt.

spring on·ion ▶ **n.** British term for GREEN ONION.

spring peep·er ▶ **n.** see PEEPER[2].

spring roll ▶ **n.** an Asian snack consisting of rice paper filled with minced vegetables and usually meat, rolled into a cylinder and fried.

Spring·steen /ˈspriNGˌstēn/, Bruce (Frederick Joseph) (1949–), US rock singer, songwriter, and guitarist; noted for his songs about working-class life in the US. Notable albums: *Born to Run* (1975) and *Born in the U.S.A.* (1984).

spring·tail /ˈspriNGˌtāl/ ▶ **n.** a minute primitive wingless insect that has a springlike organ under the abdomen that enables it to leap when disturbed. Springtails are abundant in the soil and leaf litter. ● Order Collembola: many families.

spring·tide ▶ **n.** literary term for SPRINGTIME.

spring tide /ˈspriNG ˌtīd/ ▶ **n.** a tide just after a new or full moon, when there is the greatest difference between high and low water.

spring·time /ˈspriNGˌtīm/ ▶ **n.** the season of spring. ■ literary the early part or first stage of something: *the springtime of their marriage.*

spring train·ing ▶ **n.** Baseball the preseason period, esp. in February and March, when baseball players prepare for the upcoming season.

spring wa·ter ▶ **n.** water from a spring, as opposed to river water or rainwater.

spring·y /ˈspriNGē/ ▶ **adj.** (**springier**, **springiest**) springing back quickly when squeezed or stretched; elastic: *the springy turf.* ■ (of movements) light and confident: *he left the room with a springy step.*
– DERIVATIVES **spring·i·ly** /ˈspriNGəlē/ **adv.**, **spring·i·ness n.**

sprin·kle /ˈspriNGkəl/ ▶ **v. 1** [with obj.] scatter or pour small drops or particles of a substance over (an object or surface): *I sprinkled the floor with water.* ■ scatter or pour (small drops or particles of a substance) over an object or surface: *sprinkle sesame seeds over the top.* ■ distribute or disperse something randomly or irregularly throughout (something): *he sprinkled his conversation with quotations.* ■ place or attach (a number of things) at irregularly spaced intervals: *a dress with little daisies sprinkled all over it.*
2 [no obj.] (**it sprinkles, it is sprinkling**, etc.) rain very lightly: *it began to sprinkle.*
▶ **n. 1** a small quantity or amount of something scattered over an object or surface: *a generous sprinkle of pepper* | figurative *fiction with a sprinkle of fact.*
2 [in sing.] a light rain.
3 (**sprinkles**) tiny sugar shapes, typically strands and balls, used for decorating cakes and desserts.
– ORIGIN late Middle English: perhaps from Middle Dutch *sprenkelen.*

sprin·kler /ˈspriNGk(ə)lər/ ▶ **n.** a device that sprays water. ■ a device used for watering lawns. ■ an automatic fire extinguisher installed in the ceilings of a building.

sprin·kling /ˈspriNGk(ə)liNG/ ▶ **n.** a small thinly distributed amount of something: ***a sprinkling of gray in his hair.***

sprint /sprint/ ▶ **v.** [no obj.] run at full speed over a short distance: *I saw Charlie sprinting through the traffic toward me.*
▶ **n.** an act or short spell of running at full speed. ■ a short, fast race in which the competitors run a distance of 400 meters or less: *the 100 meters sprint.* ■ a short, fast race or exercise in cycling, swimming, horse racing, etc.
– DERIVATIVES **sprint·er n.**
– ORIGIN late 18th cent. (as a dialect term meaning 'a bound or spring'): related to Swedish *spritta.*

sprint·ing /ˈsprintiNG/ ▶ **n.** the competitive athletic sport of running distances of 400 meters or less.

sprit /sprit/ ▶ **n.** Sailing a small spar reaching diagonally from low on a mast to the upper outer corner of a sail.
– ORIGIN Old English *sprēot* '(punting) pole'; related to SPROUT.

sprite /sprīt/ ▶ **n. 1** an elf or fairy.
2 a computer graphic that may be moved on-screen and otherwise manipulated as a single entity.
3 a faint flash, typically red, sometimes emitted in the upper atmosphere over a thunderstorm owing to the collision of high-energy electrons with air molecules.
– ORIGIN Middle English: alteration of *sprit*, a contraction of SPIRIT.

sprite·ly ▶ **adj.** variant spelling of SPRIGHTLY.

sprit·sail /ˈspritˌsāl, -səl/ ▶ **n.** a sail extended by a sprit. ■ historical a sail extended by a yard set under a ship's bowsprit.

spritz /sprits/ ▶ **v.** [with obj.] squirt or spray something at or onto (something) in quick short bursts: *she spritzed her neck with cologne.* ■ spray (a liquid) in this way: *she spritzed some perfume behind her ears.*
▶ **n.** an act or an instance of squirting or spraying in quick short bursts.
– ORIGIN early 20th cent.: from German *spritzen* 'to squirt.'

spritz·er /ˈspritsər/ ▶ **n.** a mixture of wine and soda water.
– ORIGIN 1960s: from German *Spritzer* 'a splash.'

sprock·et /ˈspräkit/ ▶ **n.** each of several projections on the rim of a wheel that engage with the links of a chain or with holes in film, tape, or paper. ■ (also **sprocket wheel**) a wheel with teeth of this kind.
– ORIGIN mid 16th cent. (denoting a triangular piece of timber used in a roof): of unknown origin.

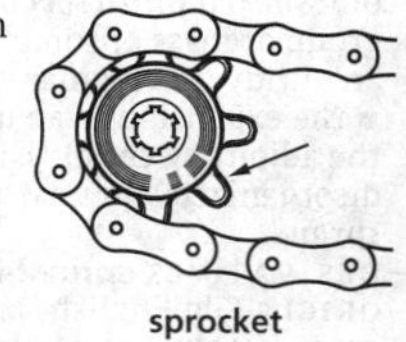
sprocket

sprout /sprout/ ▶ **v.** [no obj.] (of a plant) put forth shoots: *the weeds begin to sprout.* ■ [with obj.] grow (plant shoots or hair): *many black cats sprout a few white hairs.* ■ [no obj.] (of a plant, flower, or hair) start to grow; spring up: *crocuses sprouted up from the grass.* ■ [no obj.] appear or develop suddenly and in large numbers: *plush new hotels are **sprouting up** everywhere.*
▶ **n. 1** a shoot of a plant. ■ (**sprouts**) young shoots eaten as a vegetable, esp. the shoots of alfalfa, mung beans, or soybeans.
2 short for BRUSSELS SPROUT.
– ORIGIN Middle English: related to Dutch *spruiten* and German *spriessen.*

Spru·ance /ˈsprōōəns/, Raymond Ames (1886–1969), US admiral. After commanding in various areas in the Pacific during World War II, he was made commander in chief of the US Pacific fleet 1945–46.

S

He later served as the US ambassador to the Philippines 1952–55.

spruce[1] /spro͞os/ ▶ **n.** a widespread coniferous tree that has a distinctive conical shape and hanging cones, widely grown for timber, pulp, and Christmas trees. ● Genus *Picea*, family Pinaceae: many species.
– ORIGIN late Middle English (denoting Prussia or something originating in Prussia): alteration of obsolete *Pruce* 'Prussia.' The application to the tree dates from the early 17th cent.

spruce[2] ▶ **adj.** neat in dress and appearance: *he looked as spruce as if he were getting married.*
▶ **v.** [with obj.] (**spruce someone/something up**) make a person or place smarter or tidier: *the fund will be used to spruce up historic buildings.*
– DERIVATIVES **spruce·ly adv.**, **spruce·ness n.**
– ORIGIN late 16th cent.: perhaps from SPRUCE[1] in the obsolete sense 'Prussian,' in the phrase *spruce (leather) jerkin.*

spruce beer ▶ **n.** a fermented drink using spruce twigs and needles as flavoring.

spruce bud·worm ▶ **n.** the brown caterpillar of a small North American moth that is a serious pest of spruce and other conifers. ● *Choristoneura fumiferana*, family Tortricidae.

sprue[1] /spro͞o/ ▶ **n.** a channel through which metal or plastic is poured into a mold. ■ a piece of metal or plastic that has solidified in a sprue, esp. one joining a number of small molded plastic items.
– ORIGIN early 19th cent.: of unknown origin.

sprue[2] ▶ **n.** disease of the small intestine causing malabsorption of food, in particular: ■ (also **tropical sprue**) a disease characterized by ulceration of the mouth and chronic enteritis, suffered by visitors to tropical regions from temperate countries. ■ (also **nontropical sprue**) another term for CELIAC DISEASE.
– ORIGIN late 19th cent.: from Dutch *spruw* 'thrush'; perhaps related to Flemish *spruwen* 'sprinkle.'

sprung /sprəNG/ past and past participle of SPRING.

USAGE See usage at SPRING.

sprung rhythm ▶ **n.** a poetic meter approximating speech, each foot having one stressed syllable followed by a varying number of unstressed ones.
– ORIGIN late 19th cent.: coined by G. M. Hopkins, who used the meter.

spry /sprī/ ▶ **adj.** (**spryer**, **spryest** or **sprier**, **spriest**) (esp. of an old person) active; lively: *he continued to look spry and active well into his eighties.*
– DERIVATIVES **spry·ly adv.**, **spry·ness n.**
– ORIGIN mid 18th cent.: of unknown origin.

s.p.s. ▶ **abbr.** without surviving issue. [from Latin *sine prole superstite*.]

spt. ▶ **abbr.** seaport.

spud /spəd/ ▶ **n.** **1** informal a potato.
2 a small, narrow spade for cutting the roots of plants, esp. weeds.
3 [often as modifier] a short length of pipe that is used to connect two components or that takes the form of a projection from a fitting to which a pipe may be screwed: *a spud washer.*
4 a chisel-like tool, as for removing bark or digging into ice.
▶ **v.** (**spuds**, **spudding**, **spudded**) [with obj.] **1** dig up or cut (plants, esp. weeds) with a spud.
2 make the initial drilling for (an oil well).
– ORIGIN late Middle English (denoting a short knife): of unknown origin. The sense 'potato' (dating from the mid 19th cent.) was originally slang and dialect.

spud wrench ▶ **n.** a long bar with a socket on the end for tightening bolts.

spue /spyo͞o/ ▶ **v.** archaic spelling of SPEW.

spu·man·te /spəˈmäntē, spyə-/ ▶ **n.** an Italian sparkling white wine.
– ORIGIN Italian, literally 'sparkling.'

spume /spyo͞om/ literary ▶ **n.** froth or foam, esp. that found on waves.
▶ **v.** [no obj.] form or produce a mass of froth or foam: *water was spuming under the mill.*
– DERIVATIVES **spu·mous** /-məs/ **adj.**, **spum·y adj.**
– ORIGIN late Middle English: from Old French *(e)spume* or Latin *spuma.*

spu·mo·ni /spo͞oˈmōnē/ (also **spumone**) ▶ **n.** a kind of ice cream with different colors and flavors in layers, and often made with bits of fruit and nuts.
– ORIGIN from Italian *spumone*, from *spuma* 'foam.'

spun /spən/ past and past participle of SPIN.

spunk /spəNGk/ ▶ **n.** **1** informal courage and determination.
2 tinder; touchwood.
3 Brit. vulgar slang semen.
– ORIGIN mid 16th cent. (in the sense 'a spark, vestige'): of unknown origin; perhaps a blend of SPARK[1] and obsolete *funk* 'spark.'

spunk·y /ˈspəNGkē/ ▶ **adj.** (**spunkier**, **spunkiest**) informal courageous and determined: *a spunky performance.*
– DERIVATIVES **spunk·i·ly** /ˈspəNGkəlē/ **adv.**, **spunk·i·ness n.**

spun silk ▶ **n.** yarn made of short-fibered and waste silk. ■ fabric made from this yarn.

spun sug·ar ▶ **n.** hardened sugar syrup drawn out into long filaments and used to make cotton candy or as a decoration for sweet dishes.

spun yarn ▶ **n.** Nautical cord made by twisting together from two to four untwisted yarns of tarred hemp.

spur /spər/ ▶ **n.** **1** a device with a small spike or a spiked wheel that is worn on a rider's heel and used for urging a horse forward. ■ a hard spike on the back of the leg of a cock or male game bird, used in fighting. ■ a steel point fastened to the leg of a gamecock.
2 a thing that prompts or encourages someone; an incentive: *profit was both the spur and the reward of enterprise.*
3 a thing that projects or branches off from a main body, in particular: ■ a projection from a mountain or mountain range. ■ a short branch road or rail line. ■ Botany a slender tubular projection from the base of a flower, e.g., a honeysuckle or orchid, typically containing nectar. ■ a short fruit-bearing side shoot. ■ Medicine a short pointed growth or process on a part of the body.
▶ **v.** (**spurs**, **spurring**, **spurred**) [with obj.] urge (a horse) forward by digging one's spurs into its sides: *she spurred her horse toward the hedge.* ■ give an incentive or encouragement to (someone): *her sons' passion for computer games spurred her on to set up a software store.* ■ cause or promote the development of; stimulate: *governments cut interest rates to spur demand.*
– PHRASES **on the spur of the moment** on impulse; without planning in advance: *I don't generally do things on the spur of the moment* | [as adj.] *a spur-of-the-moment decision.*
– DERIVATIVES **spur·less adj.**, **spurred adj.**
– ORIGIN Old English *spora, spura*, of Germanic origin; related to Dutch *spoor* and German *Sporn*, also to SPURN.

spur 1

spurge /spərj/ ▶ **n.** a herbaceous plant or shrub with milky latex and very small typically greenish flowers. Many kinds are cultivated as ornamentals and some are of commercial importance. ● Genus *Euphorbia*, family Euphorbiaceae: numerous species.
– ORIGIN late Middle English: shortening of Old French *espurge*, from *espurgier*, from Latin *expurgare* 'cleanse' (because of the purgative properties of the milky latex).

spur gear ▶ **n.** a gearwheel with teeth projecting parallel to the wheel's axis.

spurge lau·rel ▶ **n.** a low-growing evergreen Eurasian shrub with leathery leaves, small green flowers, and black poisonous berries. ● *Daphne laureola*, family Thymelaeaceae.

spu·ri·ous /ˈspyo͝orēəs/ ▶ **adj.** not being what it purports to be; false or fake: *separating authentic and spurious claims.* ■ (of a line of reasoning) apparently but not actually valid: *this spurious reasoning results in nonsense.* ■ archaic (of offspring) illegitimate.
– DERIVATIVES **spu·ri·ous·ly adv.**, **spu·ri·ous·ness n.**
– ORIGIN late 16th cent. (in the sense 'born out of wedlock'): from Latin *spurius* 'false' + **-ous**.

spurn /spərn/ ▶ **v.** [with obj.] reject with disdain or contempt: *he spoke gruffly, as if afraid that his invitation would be spurned.* ■ archaic strike, tread, or push away with the foot: *with one touch of my feet, I spurn the solid Earth.*
▶ **n.** archaic an act of spurning.
– DERIVATIVES **spurn·er n.**
– ORIGIN Old English *spurnan, spornan*; related to Latin *spernere* 'to scorn'; compare with SPUR.

spur·rey /ˈspərē, ˈspə-rē/ (also **spurry**) ▶ **n.** (pl. **spurreys** or **spurries**) a small widely distributed plant of the pink family, with pink or white flowers. ● Genera *Spergula* and *Spergularia*, family Caryophyllaceae: several species, in particular **corn spurrey** (*Spergula arvensis*), a spindly weed of cornfields, and **sand spurrey** (*Spergularia rubra*), of sandy and gravelly soils.
– ORIGIN late 16th cent.: from Dutch *spurrie*; probably related to medieval Latin *spergula.*

spur·ri·er /ˈspərēər/ ▶ **n.** rare a person who makes spurs.

spurt /spərt/ ▶ **v.** [no obj.] gush out in a sudden and forceful stream: *he cut his finger, and blood spurted over the sliced potatoes.* ■ [with obj.] cause to gush out suddenly: *the kettle boiled and spurted scalding water everywhere.* ■ move with a sudden burst of speed: *the other car had spurted to the top of the ramp* | figurative *automobile sales spurted 2.1 percent in May.*
▶ **n.** a sudden gushing stream: *a sudden spurt of blood gushed into her eyes.* ■ a sudden marked burst or increase of activity or speed: *late in the race he put on a spurt and reached second place* | *a growth spurt.*
– ORIGIN mid 16th cent.: of unknown origin.

spur wheel ▶ **n.** another term for SPUR GEAR.

Sput·nik /ˈspətnik, ˈspo͝ot-/ ▶ **n.** each of a series of Soviet artificial satellites, the first of which (launched on October 4, 1957) was the first satellite to be placed in orbit.
– ORIGIN Russian, literally 'fellow-traveler.'

sput·ter /ˈspətər/ ▶ **v.** **1** [no obj.] make a series of soft explosive sounds, typically when being heated or as a symptom of a fault: *the engine sputtered and stopped.* ■ [reporting verb] speak in a series of incoherent bursts as a result of indignation or some other strong emotion: [with direct speech] *"But ... but ..." she sputtered.* ■ [with obj.] emit with a spitting sound: *the goose is in the oven, sputtering fat.* ■ [with adverbial] proceed or develop in a spasmodic and feeble way: *strikes in the public services sputtered on.*
2 [with obj.] Physics deposit (metal) on a surface by using fast ions to eject particles of it from a target. ■ cover (a surface) with metal by this method.
▶ **n.** a series of soft explosive sounds, typically produced by an engine or by something heating or burning: *the sputter of the motor died away.*
– DERIVATIVES **sput·ter·er n.**
– ORIGIN late 16th cent. (as a verb): from Dutch *sputteren*, of imitative origin.

spu·tum /ˈspyo͞otəm/ ▶ **n.** a mixture of saliva and mucus coughed up from the respiratory tract, typically as a result of infection or other disease and often examined microscopically to aid medical diagnosis.
– ORIGIN late 17th cent.: from Latin, neuter past participle of *spuere* 'to spit.'

spy /spī/ ▶ **n.** (pl. **spies**) a person who secretly collects and reports information on the activities, movements, and plans of an enemy or competitor. ■ a person who keeps watch on others secretly: [as modifier] *a spy camera.*
▶ **v.** (**spies**, **spied**, **spying**) [no obj.] work for a government or other organization by secretly collecting information about enemies or competitors: *he agreed to spy for the West.* ■ (**spy on**) observe (someone) furtively: *the couple were spied on by reporters.* ■ [with obj.] discern or make out, esp. by careful observation: *he could spy a figure in the distance.* ■ [with obj.] (**spy something out**) collect information about something to use in deciding how to act: *he would go and spy out the land.*
– DERIVATIVES **spy·ing n.**
– ORIGIN Middle English: shortening of Old French *espie* 'espying,' *espier* 'espy,' of Germanic origin, from an Indo-European root shared by Latin *specere* 'behold, look.'

spy·glass /ˈspīˌglas/ ▶ **n.** a small handheld telescope.

spyglass

spy·mas·ter /ˈspīˌmastər/ ▶ **n.** the head of an organization of spies.

spy·ware /ˈspīˌwe(ə)r/ ▶ **n.** software that enables a user to obtain covert information about another's computer activities by transmitting data covertly from their hard drive.

sq ▶ **abbr.** square: *51,100 sq km.*

SQL ▶ **abbr.** Computing Structured Query Language, an international standard for database manipulation.

squab /skwäb/ ▶ **n.** **1** a young unfledged pigeon. ■ the flesh of such a bird as food: *roast squab.*
2 a thick stuffed cushion, esp. one covering the seat of a chair or sofa.
▶ **adj.** archaic (of a person) short and fat.
– ORIGIN mid 17th cent. (in the sense 'inexperienced person'): of unknown origin; compare with obsolete *quab* 'shapeless thing' and Swedish dialect *skvabba* 'fat woman.'

squab·ble /ˈskwäbəl/ ▶ **n.** a noisy quarrel about something petty or trivial: *family squabbles.*

▶ v. [no obj.] quarrel noisily over a trivial matter: *the boys were squabbling over a ball.*
– DERIVATIVES **squab·bler** /ˈskwäb(ə)lər/ n.
– ORIGIN early 17th cent.: probably imitative; compare with Swedish dialect *skvabbel* 'a dispute.'

squad /skwäd/ ▶ n. [treated as sing. or pl.] a small group of people having a particular task: *an assassination squad.* ■ a small number of soldiers assembled for drill or assigned to some special task, esp. an infantry unit forming part of a platoon. ■ a group of sports players or competitors from which a team is chosen: *eleven first-string players on the Nebraska squad.* ■ a division of a police force dealing with a particular crime or type of crime: *the narcotics crime squad.*
– ORIGIN mid 17th cent.: shortening of French *escouade*, variant of *escadre*, from Italian *squadra* 'square.'

squad car ▶ n. a police patrol car.

squad·ron /ˈskwädrən/ ▶ n. an operational unit in an air force consisting of two or more flights of aircraft and the personnel required to fly them. ■ a principal division of an armored or cavalry regiment, consisting of two or more troops. ■ a group of warships detached on a particular duty or under the command of a flag officer. ■ informal a large group of people or things: *he immediately commissioned a squadron of architects.*
– ORIGIN mid 16th cent. (originally denoting a group of soldiers in square formation): from Italian *squadrone*, from *squadra* 'square.'

squal·a·mine /ˈskwälə,mēn/ ▶ n. Biochemistry a compound of the steroid type that is found in sharks and that has antibiotic properties.
– ORIGIN late 20th cent.: from Latin *squalus* (denoting a kind of marine fish and used as a rare term in English for 'shark') + AMINE.

squa·lene /ˈskwālēn/ ▶ n. Biochemistry an oily liquid hydrocarbon that occurs in shark liver oil and human sebum, and is a metabolic precursor of sterols. ● A triterpenoid; chem. formula: $C_{30}H_{50}$.
– ORIGIN early 20th cent.: from Latin *squalus* (see SQUALAMINE) + -ENE.

squal·id /ˈskwälid/ ▶ adj. (of a place) extremely dirty and unpleasant, esp. as a result of poverty or neglect: *the squalid, overcrowded prison.* ■ showing or involving a contemptible lack of moral standards: *a squalid attempt to save themselves from electoral embarrassment.*
– DERIVATIVES **squal·id·ly** adv., **squal·id·ness** n.
– ORIGIN late 16th cent.: from Latin *squalidus*, from *squalere* 'be rough or dirty.'

squall /skwôl/ ▶ n. a sudden violent gust of wind or a localized storm, esp. one bringing rain, snow, or sleet: *low clouds and squalls of driving rain.* ■ a loud cry: *he emitted a short mournful squall.*
▶ v. [no obj.] (of a baby or small child) cry noisily and continuously: *Sarah was squalling in her crib.*
– ORIGIN mid 17th cent.: probably an alteration of SQUEAL, influenced by BAWL.

squall line ▶ n. Meteorology a narrow band of high winds and storms associated with a cold front.

squall·y /ˈskwôlē/ ▶ adj. (**squallier**, **squalliest**) (of weather) characterized by squalls: *squally showers.*

squal·or /ˈskwälər/ ▶ n. a state of being extremely dirty and unpleasant, esp. as a result of poverty or neglect: *they lived in squalor and disease.*
– ORIGIN early 17th cent.: from Latin, from *squalere* 'be dirty.'

S

Squa·ma·ta /skwāˈmätə/ Zoology a large order of reptiles that comprises the snakes, lizards, and worm lizards.
– ORIGIN modern Latin (plural), from Latin *squama* 'scale.'

squa·mate /ˈskwāmāt/ Zoology ▶ n. a reptile of the large order Squamata; a snake, lizard, or worm lizard.
▶ adj. relating to or denoting squamates.

Squa·mish /ˈskwämisн/ ▶ n. (pl. **same**) **1** a member of an American Indian people of southwestern British Columbia.
2 the Salishan language of this people.
▶ adj. of or relating to this people or their language.
– ORIGIN alteration of the Squamish name.

squa·mo·sal /skwəˈmōsəl/ ▶ n. Zoology the squamous portion of the temporal bone, esp. when this forms a separate bone that, in mammals, articulates with the lower jaw.
– ORIGIN mid 19th cent.: from Latin *squamosus* (from *squama* 'scale') + -AL.

squa·mous /ˈskwāməs/ (also **squamose**) ▶ adj. covered with or characterized by scales: *a squamous black hide.* ■ Anatomy relating to, consisting of, or denoting a layer of epithelium that consists of very thin flattened cells: *squamous cell carcinoma.* ■ [attrib.] Anatomy denoting the flat portion of the temporal bone that forms part of the side of the skull.
– ORIGIN late Middle English: from Latin *squamosus*, from *squama* 'scale.'

squan·der /ˈskwändər/ ▶ v. [with obj.] waste (something, esp. money or time) in a reckless and foolish manner: *entrepreneurs squander their profits on expensive cars.* ■ allow (an opportunity) to pass or be lost: *the team squandered several good scoring chances.*
– DERIVATIVES **squand·er·er** n.
– ORIGIN late 16th cent.: of unknown origin.

Squan·to /ˈskwäntō/ (c.1585–1622), Pawtuxet Indian, later of the Wampanoag tribe in what is now Massachusetts. He was captured by an English sea captain and taken to Spain to be sold into slavery. He escaped, made his way to England, and from there returned to North America. He befriended the Pilgrims in Plymouth Colony in 1621 and acted as their interpreter and adviser on planting and fishing.

square /skwe(ə)r/ ▶ n. **1** a plane figure with four equal straight sides and four right angles. ■ a thing having such a shape or approximately such a shape: *she tore a bit of cloth into a four-inch square.* ■ a thing having the shape or approximate shape of a cube: *a small square of chocolate.* ■ an open (typically four-sided) area surrounded by buildings in a town, village, or city: *a market square* | [in place names] *Herald Square.* ■ an open area at the meeting of streets. ■ a small square area on the board used in a game. ■ a block of buildings bounded by four streets. ■ historical a body of infantry drawn up in rectangular form. ■ a unit of 100 square ft. used as a measure of flooring, roofing, etc.
2 the product of a number multiplied by itself: *a circle's area is proportional to the square of its radius.*
3 an L-shaped or T-shaped instrument used for obtaining or testing right angles: *a carpenter's square.* ■ Astrology an aspect of 90° (one quarter of a circle): *Venus* ***in square to*** *Jupiter.*
4 informal a person considered to be old-fashioned or boringly conventional in attitude or behavior.
5 informal a square meal: *three squares a day.*
▶ adj. **1** having the shape or approximate shape of a square: *a square table.* ■ having the shape or approximate shape of a cube: *a square box.* ■ having or in the form of two right angles: *a suitable length of wood with square ends.* ■ having an outline resembling two corners of a square: *his square jaw.* ■ broad and solid in shape: *he was short and square.*
2 denoting a unit of measurement equal to the area of a square whose side is of the unit specified: *30,000 square feet of new gallery space.* ■ [postpositive] denoting the length of each side of a square shape or object: *the office was fifteen feet square.*
3 at right angles; perpendicular: *these lines must be* ***square to*** *the top and bottom marked edges.* ■ Astrology having or denoting an aspect of 90°: *Jupiter is square to the Sun.*
4 level or parallel: *place one piece of wood on top of the other, ensuring that they are exactly square.* ■ properly arranged; in good order: *we should get everything square before we leave.* ■ compatible or in agreement: *he wanted to make sure we were* ***square with*** *the court's decision and not subject to a lawsuit.* ■ fair and honest: *she'd been as square with him as anybody could be.*
5 (of two people) owing nothing to each other: *an acknowledgment that we are square.* ■ with both players or sides having equal scores in a game: *the goal brought the match* ***all square*** *once again.*
6 informal old-fashioned or boringly conventional: *Elvis was anything but square.*
7 (of rhythm) simple and straightforward.
▶ adv. directly; straight: *it hit me square in the forehead.* ■ informal fairly; honestly: *I'd acted square and on the level with him.*
▶ v. [with obj.] **1** make square or rectangular; give a square or rectangular cross section to: *you can* ***square off*** *the other edge.* ■ (usu. as adj. **squared**) mark out in squares.
2 multiply (a number) by itself: *5 squared equals 25.* ■ [usu. as postpositive adj.] (**squared**) convert (a linear unit of measurement) to a unit of area equal to a square whose side is of the unit specified: *there were only three people per kilometer squared.*
3 make compatible; reconcile: *I'm able to* ***square*** *my profession* ***with*** *my religious beliefs.* ■ [no obj.] be compatible: *do those announcements really* ***square with*** *the facts?*
4 balance (an account): *they're anxious to square their books before the audit.* ■ make the score of (a match or game) even: [with obj. and complement] *his goal squared the match 1-1.* ■ informal secure the help, acquiescence, or silence of (someone), esp. by offering an inducement: *trying to square the press.*
5 bring (one's shoulders) into a position in which they appear square and broad, typically to prepare oneself for a difficult task or event: *chin up, shoulders squared, she stepped into the room.* ■ (**square oneself**) adopt a posture of defense.
6 Sailing set (a yard or other part of a ship) approximately at right angles to the keel or other point of reference.
7 Astrology (of a planet) have a square aspect with (another planet or position): *Saturn squares the Sun on the 17th.*
– PHRASES **back to** (or **at**) **square one** informal back to where one started, with no progress having been made. **on the square 1** informal honest; straightforward. **2** informal honestly; fairly. **3** at right angles. **out of square** not at right angles. **square accounts with** see ACCOUNT. **square the circle** construct a square equal in area to a given circle (a problem incapable of a purely geometric solution). ■ do something that is considered to be impossible. **a square peg in a round hole** see PEG.
– PHRASAL VERBS **square something away** arrange or deal with something in a satisfactory way: *don't you worry, we'll get things squared away.* **square off** assume the attitude of a person about to fight: *the two men squared off* | figurative *a debate gives the candidates an opportunity to square off.* **square up** settle or pay an account: *would you square up the bill?* ■ settle a dispute or misunderstanding: *I want to square up whatever's wrong between us.*
– DERIVATIVES **square·ness** n., **squar·er** n., **squar·ish** adj.
– ORIGIN Middle English: shortening of Old French *esquare* (noun), *esquarre* (past participle, used as an adjective), *esquarrer* (verb), based on Latin *quadra* 'square.'

square brack·et ▶ n. another term for SCUNCHEON.

square dance ▶ n. a country dance that starts with four couples facing one another in a square, with the steps and movements shouted out by a caller.
▶ v. (**square dance**) [no obj.] (often as noun **square dancing**) participate in a square dance.
– DERIVATIVES **square danc·er** n.

square deal ▶ n. [usu. in sing.] a fair bargain or treatment: *the workers feel they are not getting a square deal.*

square·head /ˈskwe(ə)r,hed/ ▶ n. informal **1** a stupid or inept person.
2 offensive a person of German, Dutch, or Scandinavian, esp. Swedish, origin.

square knot ▶ n. a type of double knot that is made symmetrically to hold securely and to be easy to untie.

square law ▶ n. Physics a law relating two variables, one of which varies (directly or inversely) as the square of the other. See also INVERSE SQUARE LAW.

square·ly /ˈskwe(ə)rlē/ ▶ adv. directly, without deviating to one side: *Ashley looked at him squarely.* ■ in a direct and uncompromising manner; without equivocation: *they placed the blame squarely on the president.*

square meal ▶ n. a substantial, satisfying, and balanced meal: *three square meals a day.*
– ORIGIN said to derive from nautical use, with reference to the square platters on which meals were served on board ship.

square meas·ure ▶ n. a unit of measurement relating to area.

square-rigged ▶ adj. (of a sailing ship) having the principal sails at right angles to the length of the ship, supported by horizontal yards attached to the mast or masts.

square-rig·ger ▶ n. a square-rigged sailing ship.

square rod ▶ n. see ROD (sense 3).

square root ▶ n. a number that produces a specified quantity when multiplied by itself: *7 is a square root of 49.*

square sail ▶ n. a four-cornered sail supported by a yard attached to a mast.

square-should·ered ▶ adj. (of a person) having broad shoulders that do not slope.

square·tail /ˈskwe(ə)r,tāl/ ▶ n. a fish of warm seas that has a slender cylindrical body and long tail, the base of which is square in cross section. ● Family Tetragonuridae and genus *Tetragonurus*: several species.

square-toed ▶ adj. (of shoes or boots) having broad, square toes. ■ archaic old-fashioned or formal.

square wave ▶ n. Electronics a periodic wave that varies abruptly in amplitude between two fixed values, spending equal times at each.

squark /skwärk/ ▶ n. Physics the supersymmetric counterpart of a quark, with spin 0 instead of $^1/_2$.
– ORIGIN 1980s: from *s(uper)* + QUARK[1].

squash[1] /skwäsн, skwôsн/ ▶ v. [with obj.] crush or squeeze (something) with force so that it becomes flat, soft, or out of shape: *wash and squash the cans for the recycling bin* | (as adj. **squashed**) *a squashed banana.* ■ squeeze or force (someone or something)

into a small or restricted space: *she squashed some of her clothes inside the bag.* ■ [no obj.] make one's way into a small or restricted space: *I squashed into the middle of the crowd.* ■ suppress, stifle, or subdue (a feeling, conjecture, or action): *the mournful sound did nothing to squash her high spirits.* ■ firmly reject (an idea or suggestion): *the proposal was immediately squashed by the Historical Society.*
▶ **n. 1** [in sing.] a state of being squeezed or forced into a small or restricted space: *it was a tight squash but he didn't seem to mind.*
2 chiefly Brit. a concentrated liquid made from fruit juice and sugar, which is diluted to make a drink: *orange squash.*
3 (also **squash racquets**) a game in which two players use rackets to hit a small, soft rubber ball against the walls of a closed court.
4 Biology a preparation of softened tissue that has been made thin for microscopic examination by gently compressing or tapping it.
– ORIGIN mid 16th cent. (as a verb): alteration of QUASH.

squash² ▶ **n.** (pl. **same** or **squashes**) **1** an edible gourd, the flesh of which may be cooked and eaten as a vegetable.
2 the trailing plant of the gourd family that produces this fruit. ● Genus *Cucurbita*, family Cucurbitaceae: many species and varieties, including the **winter squashes** and **summer squashes**.
– ORIGIN mid 17th cent.: abbreviation of Narragansett *asquutasquash.*

squash·ber·ry /ˈskwäsh,berē, ˈskwôsh-/ ▶ **n.** (pl. **squashberries**) a North American viburnum which bears edible berries. ● *Viburnum edule*, family Caprifoliaceae.

squash blos·som ▶ **n.** [as modifier] denoting a type of silver jewelry made by Navajos characterized by designs resembling the flower of the squash plant.

squash bug ▶ **n.** a dark-colored bug with forewings marked by many veins. ● Family Coreidae, suborder Heteroptera: many species, in particular the North American *Anasa tristis*, a serious pest of squashes and similar fruit.

squash·y /ˈskwäshē, ˈskwôshē/ ▶ **adj.** (**squashier, squashiest**) easily crushed or squeezed into a different shape; having a soft consistency: *a big, squashy leather chair.*
– DERIVATIVES **squash·i·ly** /ˈskwäshəlē, ˈskwôshəlē/ **adv.**, **squash·i·ness n.**

squat /skwät/ ▶ **v.** (**squats, squatting, squatted**) **1** [no obj.] crouch or sit with one's knees bent and one's heels close to or touching one's buttocks or the back of one's thighs: *I squatted down in front of him.* ■ [with obj.] Weightlifting crouch down in such a way and rise again while holding (a specified weight) at one's shoulders: *he can squat 850 pounds.*
2 [no obj.] unlawfully occupy an uninhabited building or settle on a piece of land: *eight families are squatting in the house.* ■ [with obj.] occupy (an uninhabited building) in such a way.
▶ **adj.** (**squatter, squattest**) short and thickset; disproportionately broad or wide: *he was muscular and squat | a squat gray house.*
▶ **n. 1** [in sing.] a position in which one's knees are bent and one's heels are close to or touching one's buttocks or the back of one's thighs. ■ Weightlifting an exercise in which a person squats down and rises again while holding a barbell at shoulder level. ■ (in gymnastics) an exercise involving a squatting movement or action.
2 informal short for DIDDLY-SQUAT: *I didn't know squat about writing plays.*
3 chiefly Brit. a building occupied by people living in it without the legal right to do so. ■ an unlawful occupation of an uninhabited building.
– DERIVATIVES **squat·ly adv.**, **squat·ness n.**
– ORIGIN Middle English (in the sense 'thrust down with force'): from Old French *esquatir* 'flatten,' based on Latin *coactus*, past participle of *cogere* 'compel' (see COGENT). The current sense of the adjective dates from the mid 17th cent.

squat·ter /ˈskwätər/ ▶ **n.** a person who unlawfully occupies an uninhabited building or unused land. ■ historical a settler with no legal title to the land occupied, typically one on land not yet allocated by a government.

squat thrust ▶ **n.** an exercise in which the legs are thrust backward to their full extent from a squatting position with the hands on the floor.

squaw /skwô/ ▶ **n.** offensive an American Indian woman or wife. ■ a woman or wife.
– ORIGIN mid 17th cent.: from Narragansett *squaws* 'woman,' with related forms in many Algonquian dialects.

USAGE Until relatively recently, the word **squaw**, derived from an Algonquian language, was used neutrally in anthropological and other contexts to mean 'an American Indian woman or wife.' With changes in the political climate in the second half of the 20th century, however, the derogatory attitudes of the past toward American Indian women have meant that the word cannot now be used in any sense without being offensive.

squaw·fish /ˈskwô,fish/ ▶ **n.** (pl. **same** or **squawfishes**) a large predatory freshwater fish of the minnow family, with a slender body and large mouth, found in western North America. ● Genus *Ptychocheilus*, family Cyprinidae: several species, in particular the **northern squawfish** (*P. oregonensis*).
– ORIGIN late 19th cent.: the word derives from the former importance to American Indians of such fish, as food.

squawk /skwôk/ ▶ **v.** [no obj.] (of a bird) make a loud, harsh noise: *the geese flew upriver, squawking.* ■ [with direct speech] (of a person) say something in a loud, discordant tone: *"What are you doing?" she squawked.* ■ complain or protest about something.
▶ **n.** a loud, harsh or discordant noise made by a bird or a person. ■ a complaint or protest: *her plan provoked a loud squawk from her friends.*
– DERIVATIVES **squawk·er n.**
– ORIGIN early 19th cent.: imitative.

squawk box ▶ **n.** informal a loudspeaker, in particular one that is part of an intercom system.

squaw man ▶ **n.** offensive a white or black man married to an American Indian woman.

squaw·root /ˈskwô,ro͞ot/ ▶ **n.** either of two North American plants. ● a yellow-brown parasitic plant related to the broomrape (*Conopholis americana*, family Orobanchaceae). ● the blue cohosh. See COHOSH.

Squaw Val·ley /skwô/ a resort in northeastern California, on Lake Tahoe, site of the 1960 Winter Olympic games.

squeak /skwēk/ ▶ **n.** a short, high-pitched sound or cry: *the door opened with a slight squeak.* ■ [with negative] a single remark, statement, or communication: *I didn't hear a squeak from him for months.*
▶ **v.** [no obj.] **1** make a high-pitched sound or cry: *he oiled the hinges to stop them from squeaking.* ■ [with direct speech] say something in a nervous or excited high-pitched tone: *"You're scaring me," she squeaked.* ■ informal inform on someone.
2 [with adverbial] informal succeed in achieving something by a very narrow margin: *the bill squeaked through with just six votes to spare.* ■ (**squeak by**) make or have just enough money for basic necessities: *she was squeaking by on her minimum-wage job.*
– ORIGIN late Middle English (as a verb): imitative; compare with Swedish *skväka* 'croak,' also with SQUEAL and SHRIEK. The noun dates from the early 17th cent.

squeak·er /ˈskwēkər/ ▶ **n.** a person or thing that squeaks. ■ informal a competition or election won or likely to be won by a narrow margin.

squeak·y /ˈskwēkē/ ▶ **adj.** (**squeakier, squeakiest**) having or making a high-pitched sound or cry: *a high, squeaky voice.*
– DERIVATIVES **squeak·i·ly** /-kəlē/ **adv.**, **squeak·i·ness n.**

squeak·y clean ▶ **adj.** informal completely clean: *squeaky clean restrooms.* ■ beyond reproach; without vice: *politicians who are less than squeaky clean.*

squeal /skwēl/ ▶ **n.** a long, high-pitched cry or noise: *we heard a splash and a squeal.*
▶ **v.** [no obj.] **1** make such a cry or noise: *the girls squealed with delight.* ■ [with direct speech] say something in a high-pitched, excited tone: *"Don't you dare!" she squealed.* ■ informal complain or protest about something: *the bookies only squealed because we beat them.*
2 informal inform on someone to the police or a person in authority: *she feared they would victimize her for squealing on their pals.*
– DERIVATIVES **squeal·er n.** (sense 2 of the verb).
– ORIGIN Middle English (as a verb): imitative. The noun dates from the mid 18th cent.

squeam·ish /ˈskwēmish/ ▶ **adj.** (of a person) easily made to feel sick, faint, or disgusted, esp. by unpleasant images, such as the sight of blood: *he was a bit squeamish at the sight of the giant needles.* ■ (of a person) having strong moral views; scrupulous: *she was not squeamish about using her social influence in support of her son.*
– DERIVATIVES **squeam·ish·ly adv.**, **squeam·ish·ness n.**
– ORIGIN late Middle English: alteration of dialect *squeamous*, from Anglo-Norman French *escoymos*, of unknown origin.

squee·gee /ˈskwē,jē/ ▶ **n.** a scraping implement with a rubber-edged blade set on a handle, typically used for cleaning windows. ■ a similar small instrument or roller used esp. in photography for squeezing water out of prints. ■ [usu. as modifier] informal a person who cleans the windshield of a car stopped in traffic and then demands payment from the driver: *squeegee guys at every corner | the squeegees wait at busy intersections.*
▶ **v.** (**squeegees, squeegeeing, squeegeed**) [with obj.] clean or scrape (something) with a squeegee: *squeegee the shower doors while the surfaces are still wet.*
– ORIGIN mid 19th cent.: from archaic *squeege* 'to press,' strengthened form of SQUEEZE.

squeeze /skwēz/ ▶ **v. 1** [with obj.] firmly press (something soft or yielding), typically with one's fingers: *Kate squeezed his hand affectionately |* [no obj.] *he squeezed with all his strength.* ■ extract (liquid or a soft substance) from something by compressing or twisting it firmly: ***squeeze out** as much juice as you can |* (as adj. with submodifier **squeezed**) *freshly squeezed orange juice.* ■ obtain (something) from someone with difficulty: *a governor who wants to **squeeze** as much money **out of** taxpayers as he can.* ■ informal pressure (someone) in order to obtain something from them: *she used the opportunity to squeeze him for information.* ■ (esp. in a financial or commercial context) have a damaging or restricting effect on: *the economy is being squeezed by foreign debt repayments.* ■ (**squeeze off**) informal shoot a round or shot from a gun: *squeeze off a few well-aimed shots.* ■ (**squeeze off**) informal take a photograph: *he squeezed off a half-dozen Polaroids.* ■ Bridge force (an opponent) to discard a guarding or potentially winning card.
2 [no obj.] manage to get into or through a narrow or restricted space: *Sarah squeezed in beside her | he found a hole in the hedge and **squeezed his way through**.* ■ [with obj.] manage to force into or through such a space: *she squeezed herself into her tightest pair of jeans.* ■ (**squeeze up**) move closer to someone or something so that one is pressed tightly against them or it: *he guided her toward a seat, motioning for everyone to squeeze up and make room.* ■ [with obj.] (**squeeze someone/something in**) manage to find time for someone or something: *the doctor can squeeze you in at noon.* ■ [with obj.] (**squeeze someone/something out**) force someone or something out of a domain or activity: *workers have been squeezed out of their jobs.*
▶ **n. 1** an act of pressing something with one's fingers: *a gentle squeeze of the trigger.* ■ a hug. ■ a state of forcing oneself or being forced into a small or restricted space: *it was **a tight squeeze** in the tiny hall.* ■ dated a crowded social gathering. ■ a small amount of liquid extracted from something by pressing it firmly with one's fingers: *a squeeze of lemon juice.* ■ a strong financial demand or pressure, typically a restriction on borrowing, spending, or investment in a financial crisis: *industry faced higher costs and **a squeeze on** profits.* ■ a molding or cast of an object, or an impression or copy of a design, obtained by pressing a pliable substance around or over it. ■ informal money illegally extorted or exacted from someone: *he was out to extract some squeeze from her.* ■ Bridge a tactic that forces an opponent to discard an important card. ■ (also **squeeze play** or **suicide squeeze**) Baseball an act of bunting a ball in order to enable a runner on third base to start for home as soon as the ball is pitched.
2 informal a person's girlfriend or boyfriend: *the poor guy just lost his **main squeeze**.*
– PHRASES **put the squeeze on** informal coerce or pressure (someone).
– DERIVATIVES **squeez·a·ble adj.**, **squeez·er n.**
– ORIGIN mid 16th cent.: from earlier *squise*, from obsolete *queise*, of unknown origin.

squeeze bot·tle ▶ **n.** a container made of flexible plastic that is squeezed to extract the contents.

squeeze-box /ˈskwēz,bäks/ (also **squeeze box**) ▶ **n.** informal an accordion or concertina.

squelch /skwelch/ ▶ **v.** [no obj.] make a soft sucking sound such as that made by walking heavily through mud: *bedraggled guests squelched across the lawn to seek shelter.* ■ [with obj.] informal forcefully silence or suppress: *property developers tried to squelch public protest.*
▶ **n. 1** a soft sucking sound made when pressure is applied to liquid or mud: *the squelch of their feet.*
2 (also **squelch circuit**) Electronics a circuit that suppresses the output of a radio receiver if the signal strength falls below a certain level.
– DERIVATIVES **squelch·er n.**, **squelch·y adj.**

– ORIGIN early 17th cent. (originally denoting a heavy crushing fall onto something soft): imitative.

squib /skwib/ ▶ **n. 1** a small firework that burns with a hissing sound before exploding. ■ a short piece of satirical writing. ■ a short news item or filler in a newspaper.
2 a small, slight, or weak person, esp. a child.
3 Football a short kick on a kickoff. ■ Baseball (also **squibber**) a blooper or infield grounder that becomes a base hit.
▶ **v.** (**squibs, squibbing, squibbed**) **1** [with obj.] Football kick (the ball) a comparatively short distance on a kickoff; execute (a kick) in this way. ■ Baseball hit (the ball) with little force, usually with the end of the bat, the typical result being a blooper or infield grounder.
2 [no obj.] archaic utter, write, or publish a satirical or sarcastic attack. ■ [with obj.] lampoon: *the mendicant parson, whom I am so fond of squibbing.*
– ORIGIN early 16th cent. (sense 1 of the noun): of unknown origin; perhaps imitative of a small explosion. The verb was first recorded in sense 2 of the noun (late 16th cent).

squick /skwik/ ▶ **v.** [with obj.] informal cause immediate and thorough revulsion: *was anyone else squicked by the potential adoptive parents?*
▶ **n.** a person or thing that causes immediate and thorough revulsion.

SQUID /skwid/ ▶ **n.** Physics a device used in particular in sensitive magnetometers, which consists of a superconducting ring containing one or more Josephson junctions. A change by one flux quantum in the ring's magnetic flux linkage produces a sharp change in its impedance.
– ORIGIN 1960s: acronym from *superconducting quantum interference device.*

squid /skwid/ ▶ **n.** (pl. **same** or **squids**) an elongated, fast-swimming cephalopod mollusk with ten arms (technically, eight arms and two long tentacles), typically able to change color. ● Order Teuthoidea and Vampyromorpha, class Cephalopoda, in particular the common genus *Loligo*. See also **GIANT SQUID**. ■ this mollusk used as food. ■ an artificial bait for fish imitating a squid in form.
▶ **v.** (**squidded, squidding**) [no obj.] fish using squid as bait.
– ORIGIN late 16th cent.: of unknown origin.

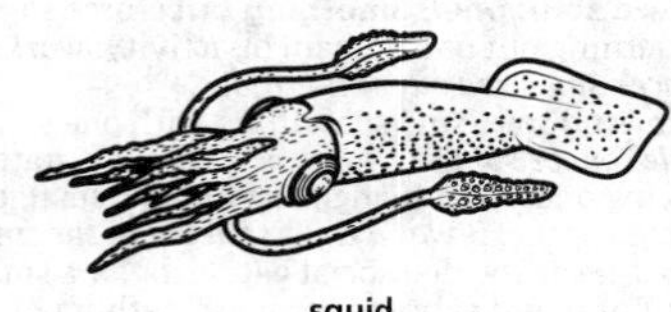
squid

squiffed /skwift/ ▶ **adj.** informal slightly drunk.
– ORIGIN late 19th cent.: variant of **SQUIFFY**.

squif·fy /ˈskwifē/ ▶ **adj.** (**squiffier, squiffiest**) informal, chiefly Brit. slightly drunk: *he's squiffy from the rum.*
– ORIGIN mid 19th cent.: of unknown origin.

squig·gle /ˈskwigəl/ ▶ **n.** a short line that curls and loops in an irregular way: *some prescriptions are a series of meaningless squiggles.*
▶ **v.** [no obj.] wriggle; squirm: *a worm that squiggled in his palm.* ■ [with obj.] squeeze (something) from a tube so as to make irregular, curly lines on a surface.
– DERIVATIVES **squig·gly** /ˈskwig(ə)lē/ **adj.**
– ORIGIN early 19th cent.: perhaps a blend of **SQUIRM** and **WIGGLE** or **WRIGGLE**.

squill /skwil/ ▶ **n. 1** (also **sea squill**) a coastal Mediterranean plant of the lily family, with broad leaves, white flowers, and a very large bulb. ● *Drimia* (or *Urginea*) *maritima*, family Liliaceae. ■ (also **squills**) an extract of the bulb of this plant, which is poisonous and has medicinal and other uses.
2 [usu. with modifier] a small plant of the lily family that resembles a hyacinth and has slender straplike leaves and small clusters of violet-blue or blue-striped flowers. ● Several species in the family Liliaceae, including the **spring squill** (*Scilla verna*), and the **striped squill** (*Puschkinia scilloides*).
– ORIGIN late Middle English: via Latin from Greek *skilla.*

squinch[1] /skwinCH/ ▶ **n.** a straight or arched structure across an interior angle of a square tower to carry a superstructure such as a dome.
– ORIGIN late 15th cent.: alteration of obsolete *scunch*, abbreviation of **SCUNCHEON**.

squinch[2] ▶ **v.** [with obj.] tense up the muscles of (one's eyes or face): *Gina squinched her face up.* ■ [no obj.] (of a person's eyes) narrow so as to be almost closed, typically in reaction to strong light: *he flicked on the light, which made my eyes squinch up.* ■ [no obj.] crouch down in order to make oneself seem smaller or to occupy less space: *I squinched down under the sheet.*
– ORIGIN early 19th cent.: perhaps a blend of the verbs **SQUEEZE** and **PINCH**.

squint /skwint/ ▶ **v. 1** [no obj.] look at someone or something with one or both eyes partly closed in an attempt to see more clearly or as a reaction to strong light: *the bright sun made them squint.* ■ [with obj.] partly close (one's eyes) for such reasons.
2 [no obj.] have eyes that look in different directions: *Melanie did not squint.* ■ (of a person's eye) have a deviation in the direction of its gaze: *her left eye squinted slightly.*
▶ **n. 1** [in sing.] a permanent deviation in the direction of the gaze of one eye: *I had a bad squint.*
2 [in sing.] informal a quick or casual look: *let me have a squint.*
3 an oblique opening through a wall in a church permitting a view of the altar from an aisle or side chapel.
– DERIVATIVES **squint·er n., squint·y adj.** [often in combination] *squinty-eyed.*
– ORIGIN mid 16th cent. (in the sense 'squinting,' as in **SQUINT-EYED**): shortening of **ASQUINT**.

squint-eyed ▶ **adj.** derogatory **1** (of a person) having a squint.
2 archaic spiteful.

squire /skwīr/ ▶ **n. 1** a man of high social standing who owns and lives on an estate in a rural area, esp. the chief landowner in such an area: *the squire of Radbourne Hall* | [as title] *Squire Hughes.* ■ Brit. informal used by a man as a friendly or humorous form of address to another man. ■ archaic a title given to a magistrate, lawyer, or judge in some rural districts.
2 historical a young nobleman acting as an attendant to a knight before becoming a knight himself.
▶ **v.** [with obj.] (of a man) accompany or escort (a woman): *she was squired around Rome by a reporter.* ■ dated (of a man) have a romantic relationship with (a woman).
– DERIVATIVES **squire·dom** /-dəm/ **n., squire·ship** /-ˌSHip/ **n.**
– ORIGIN Middle English (sense 2 of the noun): shortening of Old French *esquier* 'esquire.'

squire·arch /ˈskwīrärk/ ▶ **n.** a member of the squirearchy.
– DERIVATIVES **squire·ar·chi·cal** /ˌskwīˈrärkikəl/ **adj.**
– ORIGIN mid 19th cent.: back-formation from **SQUIREARCHY**, on the pattern of words such as *monarch.*

squire·ar·chy /ˈskwīrärkē/ ▶ **n.** (pl. **squirearchies**) landowners collectively, esp. when considered as a class having political or social influence.
– ORIGIN late 18th cent.: from **SQUIRE**, on the pattern of words such as *hierarchy.*

squirl /skwərl/ ▶ **n.** informal an ornamental flourish or curve, esp. in handwriting.
– ORIGIN mid 19th cent.: perhaps a blend of **SQUIGGLE** and **TWIRL** or **WHIRL**.

squirm /skwərm/ ▶ **v.** [no obj.] wriggle or twist the body from side to side, esp. as a result of nervousness or discomfort: *all my efforts to squirm out of his grasp were useless.* ■ show or feel embarrassment or shame.
▶ **n.** [in sing.] a wriggling movement.
– DERIVATIVES **squirm·er n., squirm·y adj.**
– ORIGIN late 17th cent.: symbolic of writhing movement; probably associated with **WORM**.

squir·rel /ˈskwər(ə)l/ ▶ **n.** an agile tree-dwelling rodent with a bushy tail, typically feeding on nuts and seeds. ● Family Sciuridae: several genera, in particular *Sciurus*, and numerous species. ■ a related rodent of this family. See **GROUND SQUIRREL, FLYING SQUIRREL**. ■ the fur of the squirrel.
▶ **v.** (**squirrels, squirreling, squirreled**) **1** [with obj.] (**squirrel something away**) hide money or something of value in a safe place: *the money was squirreled away in foreign bank accounts.*
2 [no obj.] move in an inquisitive and restless manner: *they were squirreling around in the woods in search of something.*
– ORIGIN Middle English: shortening of Old French *esquireul*, from a diminutive of Latin *sciurus*, from Greek *skiouros*, from *skia* 'shade' + *oura* 'tail.' Current verb senses date from the early 20th cent.

squir·rel cage ▶ **n.** a rotating cylindrical cage in which a small captive animal can exercise as on a treadmill. ■ a monotonous or repetitive activity or way of life: *running madly about in a squirrel cage of activity.* ■ a form of rotor used in small electric motors, resembling a cylindrical cage.

squir·rel·fish /ˈskwərlˌfiSH/ ▶ **n.** (pl. **same** or **squirrelfishes**) a chiefly nocturnal large-eyed marine fish that is typically brightly colored and lives around rocks or coral reefs in warm seas. ● Family Holocentridae: several genera and species.

squir·rel·ly /ˈskwər(ə)lē/ ▶ **adj. 1** relating to or resembling a squirrel: *the chipmunks were little squirrelly things.*
2 informal restless, nervous, or unpredictable. ■ eccentric or insane.

squir·rel mon·key ▶ **n.** a small South American monkey with a nonprehensile tail, typically moving through trees by leaping. ● Genus *Saimiri*, family Cebidae: five species, in particular *S. sciureus.*

squir·rel·tail /ˈskwərlˌtāl/ (also **squirreltail grass**) ▶ **n.** a kind of barley with bushy spikelets, sometimes cultivated as an ornamental grass. ● *Hordeum jubatum*, family Gramineae.

squirt /skwərt/ ▶ **v.** [with obj.] cause (a liquid) to be ejected from a small opening in something in a thin, fast stream or jet: *she squirted soda into a glass.* ■ cause (a container of liquid) to eject its contents in this way: *some youngsters squirted a water pistol in her face.* ■ wet (someone or something) with a jet or stream of liquid in this way: *she squirted me with the juice from her lemon wedge.* ■ [no obj.] (of a liquid) be ejected from something in this way. ■ [no obj.] (of an object) move suddenly and unpredictably: *he got his glove on the ball but it squirted away.* ■ transmit (information) in highly compressed or speeded-up form.
▶ **n. 1** a thin stream or small quantity of liquid ejected from something: *a quick squirt of perfume.* ■ a small device from which a liquid may be ejected in a thin, fast stream. ■ a compressed radio signal transmitted at high speed.
2 informal a person perceived to be insignificant, impudent, or presumptuous: *what did he see in this patronizing little squirt?*
– DERIVATIVES **squirt·er n.**
– ORIGIN Middle English (first recorded as a verb): imitative.

squirt boat ▶ **n.** a small, highly maneuverable kayak.

squirt gun ▶ **n.** a water pistol.

squish /skwiSH/ ▶ **v.** [no obj.] make a soft squelching sound when walked on or in: *the mud squished under my shoes.* ■ yield or cause to yield easily to pressure; squash: [no obj.] *strawberries so ripe that they squished if picked too firmly* | [with obj.] *Naomi was furiously squishing her ice cream in her bowl.*
▶ **n.** [in sing.] a soft squelching sound.
– DERIVATIVES **squish·y adj.** (**squishier, squishiest**).
– ORIGIN mid 17th cent.: imitative.

Sr ▶ **symbol** the chemical element strontium.

sr ▶ **abbr.** steradian(s).

Sr. ▶ **abbr.** ■ senior (in names): *E. T. Krebs, Sr.* ■ Señor. ■ Signor. ■ Sister (in a religious order): [as a title] *Sr. Agatha.*

Sra. ▶ **abbr.** ■ Senhora. ■ Señora.

SRAM /ˈesˌram/ ▶ **n.** Electronics a type of memory chip that is faster and requires less power than dynamic memory.
– ORIGIN acronym from *static random-access memory.*

Sra·nan /ˈsränən/ ▶ **n.** another term for **TAKI-TAKI**.
– ORIGIN from Taki-Taki *Sranan tongo*, literally 'Surinam tongue.'

Sri /srē/ (also **Shri**) ▶ **n.** Indian a title of respect used before the name of a man, a god, or a sacred book: *Sri Chaudhuri.*
– ORIGIN from Sanskrit *Śrī* 'beauty, fortune,' used as an honorific title.

Sri Lan·ka /ˌsrē ˈlänGkə, ˌSHrē, ˈlanGkə/ an island country off the southeastern coast of India; pop. 21,324,800 (est. 2009); capital, Colombo; languages, Sinhalese (official) and Tamil. Former name (until 1972) **CEYLON**.

> The island was ruled by a strong native dynasty from the 12th century but was successively dominated by the Portuguese, Dutch, and British from the 16th century; it was finally annexed by the British in 1815. A Commonwealth of Nations state from 1948, the country became an independent republic in 1972. Civil war between the government and Tamil separatists began in the 1980s and ended with a government victory in 2009.

– DERIVATIVES **Sri Lan·kan adj. & n.**

Sri·na·gar /srēˈnəgər, SHrē-/ a city in northwestern India, on the Jhelum River, in the foothills of the Himalayas; pop. 1,060,900 (est. 2009).

SRN ▶ **abbr.** State Registered Nurse.

sRNA ▶ **abbr.** soluble RNA.

SRO ▶ **abbr.** ■ (in the UK) self-regulatory organization, a body that regulates the activities of investment businesses. ■ single room occupancy. ■ standing room only.

Srta. ▶ **abbr.** ■ Senhorita. ■ Señorita.

SS[1] ▶ **abbr.** ■ Saints: *the Church of SS Peter and Paul.* ■ Baseball shortstop. ■ social security. ■ (in prescriptions) in the strict sense. [from Latin *sensu stricto*.] ■ steamship: *the SS Canberra.* ■ Sunday School.

SS[2] the Nazi special police force. Founded in 1925 by Hitler as a personal bodyguard, the SS provided security forces (including the Gestapo) and administered the concentration camps.
– ORIGIN abbreviation of German *Schutzstaffel* 'defense squadron.'

ss. ▶ **abbr.** ■ Law to wit; that is to say; namely (used on legal documents). [from Latin *scilicet*.] ■ sections. ■ Baseball shortstop.

s/s ▶ **abbr.** same size.

SSA ▶ **abbr.** ■ Social Security Act. ■ Social Security Administration.

SSB ▶ **abbr.** single sideband transmission, a type of amplitude modulation in which the carrier wave and one sideband are suppressed in order to occupy less bandwidth.

SSC ▶ **abbr.** ■ (in Scotland) Solicitor in the Supreme Court. ■ Physics superconducting super collider.

SSE ▶ **abbr.** south-south-east.

S.Sgt. (or **SSGT**) ▶ **abbr.** staff sergeant.

SSI ▶ **abbr.** ■ Electronics small-scale integration, the process of concentrating semiconductor devices in a single integrated circuit. ■ Supplemental Security Income.

SSL ▶ **abbr.** Secure Sockets Layer, a computing protocol that ensures the security of data sent via the Internet by using encryption.

SSN ▶ **abbr.** Social Security Number.

ssp. ▶ **abbr.** subspecies (usually singular).

sspp. ▶ **abbr.** subspecies (plural).

SSR ▶ **abbr.** historical Soviet Socialist Republic.

SSRC ▶ **abbr.** (in the UK) Social Science Research Council.

SSRI ▶ **abbr.** selective serotonin reuptake inhibitor, the designation for a class of antidepressants that work by increasing levels of serotonin in the brain.

SSS ▶ **abbr.** Selective Service System.

SSSI ▶ **abbr.** (in the UK) Site of Special Scientific Interest.

SST ▶ **abbr.** supersonic transport.

SSW ▶ **abbr.** south-southwest.

ST ▶ **abbr.** stokes.

st ▶ **abbr.** stone (in weight).

St. ▶ **abbr.** ■ Saint: *St. George.* ■ Street. ■ Physics stokes.

-st ▶ **suffix** variant spelling of **-EST**[2].

Sta. ▶ **abbr.** station (in particular, a railroad station).

stab /stab/ ▶ **v.** (**stabs, stabbing, stabbed**) [with obj.] (of a person) thrust a knife or other pointed weapon into (someone) so as to wound or kill: *he stabbed him in the stomach* | (as noun **stabbing**) *the fatal stabbings of four rival gang members.* ■ [no obj.] make a thrusting gesture or movement at something with a pointed object: *she stabbed at the earth with the fork* | [with obj.] *she stabbed the air with her forefinger.* ■ [no obj.] (**stab into/through**) (of a sharp or pointed object) violently pierce: *a sharp end of wicker stabbed into his sole.* ■ [no obj.] (**stab at**) (of a pain or painful thing) cause a sudden sharp sensation: (as adj. **stabbing**) *I felt a stabbing pain in my chest.*
▶ **n. 1** a thrust with a knife or other pointed weapon: [as modifier] *multiple stab wounds.* ■ a wound made in such a way: *she had a deep stab in the back.* ■ a thrusting movement with a finger or other pointed object: *impatient stabs of his finger.* ■ a sudden sharp feeling or pain: *she felt a stab of jealousy.*
2 (**stab at**) informal an attempt to do (something): *Meredith made a feeble stab at joining in.*
– PHRASES **a stab in the back** a treacherous act or statement. **stab someone in the back** betray someone. **a stab in the dark** see **DARK**.
– DERIVATIVES **stab·ber n.**
– ORIGIN late Middle English: of unknown origin.

Sta·bat Ma·ter /'stäbät 'mätər, 'stābat 'mātər/ ▶ **n.** a medieval Latin hymn on the suffering of the Virgin Mary at the Crucifixion.
– ORIGIN from the opening words *Stabat mater dolorosa* 'Stood the mother, full of grief.'

sta·bi·la·tor /'stābə,lātər/ ▶ **n.** a combined stabilizer and elevator at the tail of an aircraft.

sta·bile /'stā,bēl/ ▶ **n.** Art a freestanding abstract sculpture or structure, typically of wire or sheet metal, in the style of a mobile but rigid and stationary.
– ORIGIN 1940s: from Latin *stabilis* 'stable,' influenced by **MOBILE**.

sta·bil·i·ty /stə'bilitē/ ▶ **n.** the state of being stable: *there are fears for the political stability of the area.*
– ORIGIN Middle English: from Old French *stablete*, from Latin *stabilitas*, from *stabilis* 'stable.'

sta·bil·i·ty ball ▶ **n.** another term for **EXERCISE BALL**.

sta·bi·lize /'stābə,līz/ ▶ **v.** make or become unlikely to give way or overturn: [with obj.] *the craft was stabilized by throwing out the remaining ballast.* ■ make or become unlikely to change, fail, or decline: [with obj.] *an emergency program designed to stabilize the economy* | [no obj.] *his condition appears to have stabilized.*
– DERIVATIVES **sta·bi·li·za·tion** /,stābəli'zāshən/ **n.**

sta·bi·liz·er /'stābə,līzər/ ▶ **n.** a thing used to keep something steady or stable, in particular: ■ another term for **HORIZONTAL STABILIZER**. ■ a gyroscopically controlled system used to reduce the rolling of a ship. ■ a substance that prevents the breakdown of emulsions, esp. in foods and paints. ■ a financial mechanism that prevents unsettling fluctuation in an economic system.

sta·ble[1] /'stābəl/ ▶ **adj.** (**stabler, stablest**) not likely to change or fail; firmly established: *a stable relationship* | *prices have remained relatively stable.* ■ (of a patient or a medical condition) not deteriorating in health after an injury or operation: *he is now in a stable condition in the hospital.* ■ (of a person) sane and sensible; not easily upset or disturbed: *the officer concerned is mentally and emotionally stable.* ■ (of an object or structure) not likely to give way or overturn; firmly fixed: *specially designed dinghies that are very stable.* ■ not liable to undergo chemical decomposition, radioactive decay, or other physical change.
– DERIVATIVES **sta·bly** /-b(ə)lē/ **adv.**
– ORIGIN Middle English: from Anglo-Norman French, from Latin *stabilis*, from the base of *stare* 'to stand.'

sta·ble[2] ▶ **n.** a building set apart and adapted for keeping horses. ■ an establishment where racehorses are kept and trained. ■ the racehorses of a particular training establishment. ■ an organization or establishment providing the same background or training for its members: *the player comes from the same stable as Agassi.*
▶ **v.** [with obj.] put or keep (a horse) in a specially adapted building. ■ put or base (a train) in a depot.
– DERIVATIVES **sta·ble·ful** /'stābəl,fo͝ol/ **n.** (pl. **stablefuls**).
– ORIGIN Middle English: shortening of Old French *estable* 'stable, pigpen,' from Latin *stabulum*, from the base of *stare* 'to stand.'

sta·ble boy ▶ **n.** a boy or man employed in a stable.

sta·ble e·qui·lib·ri·um ▶ **n.** a state in which a body tends to return to its original position after being disturbed.

sta·ble fly ▶ **n.** a bloodsucking fly related to the housefly, biting large mammals including humans.
● *Stomoxis calcitrans*, family Muscidae.

sta·ble girl ▶ **n.** a girl or woman employed in a stable.

sta·ble·man /'stābəl,mən/ ▶ **n.** (pl. **stablemen**) a person employed in a stable.

sta·ble·mate /'stābəl,māt/ ▶ **n.** a horse, esp. a racehorse, from the same establishment as another. ■ a person or product from the same organization or background as another: *it is a marketing challenge for Fiat and its stablemate, Alfa Romeo.*

sta·bling /'stāb(ə)ling/ ▶ **n.** accommodations for horses.

stab·lish /'stablish/ ▶ **v.** archaic form of **ESTABLISH**.

stac·ca·to /stə'kätō/ chiefly Music ▶ **adv. & adj.** with each sound or note sharply detached or separated from the others: [as adj.] *a staccato rhythm.* Compare with **LEGATO, MARCATO**.
▶ **n.** (pl. **staccatos**) performance in this manner. ■ a noise or speech resembling a series of short, detached musical notes: *her heels made a rapid staccato on the polished boards.*
– ORIGIN Italian, literally 'detached.'

stack /stak/ ▶ **n. 1** a pile of objects, typically one that is neatly arranged: *a stack of boxes.* ■ (**a stack of/stacks of**) informal a large quantity of something: *there's stacks of work for me now.* ■ a rectangular or cylindrical pile of hay or straw or of grain in sheaf. ■ a vertical arrangement of stereo or guitar amplification equipment. ■ a number of aircraft flying in circles at different altitudes around the same point while waiting for permission to land at an airport. ■ a pyramidal group of rifles. ■ (**the stacks**) units of shelving in part of a library, used to store books compactly. ■ Computing a set of storage locations that store data in such a way that the most recently stored item is the first to be retrieved.
2 a chimney, esp. one on a factory, or a vertical exhaust pipe on a vehicle. ■ (also **sea stack**) a column of rock standing in the sea, remaining after erosion of cliffs.
▶ **v.** [with obj.] **1** arrange (a number of things) in a pile, typically a neat one: *the books had been stacked up in three piles* | *she stood up, beginning to stack the plates.* ■ fill or cover (a place or surface) with piles of things, typically neat ones: *he spent most of the time stacking shelves.* ■ cause (an aircraft) to fly in circles while waiting for permission to land at an airport: *I hope we aren't stacked for hours over Kennedy.*
2 shuffle or arrange (a deck of cards) dishonestly so as to gain an unfair advantage. ■ (**be stacked against/in favor of**) used to refer to a situation that is such that an unfavorable or a favorable outcome is overwhelmingly likely: *the odds were stacked against Fiji in the World Cup* | *they found the courts stacked in favor of timber interests.*
3 [no obj.] (in snowboarding) fall over.
– PHRASES **stack arms** place a number of rifles with their butts on the ground and the muzzles together.
– PHRASAL VERBS **stack up 1** (or **stack something up**) form or cause to form a large quantity; build up: *cars stack up behind every bus, while passengers stand in line to pay fares.* **2** informal measure up; compare: *our rural schools stack up well against their urban counterparts.* ■ [usu. with negative] make sense; correspond to reality: *to blame the debacle on the antics of a rogue trader is not credible—it doesn't stack up.*
– DERIVATIVES **stack·a·ble adj., stack·er n.**
– ORIGIN Middle English: from Old Norse *stakkr* 'haystack,' of Germanic origin.

stacked /stakt/ ▶ **adj. 1** (of a number of things) put or arranged in a stack or stacks: *the stacked chairs.* ■ (of a place or surface) filled or covered with goods: *the stacked shelves.* ■ (of a machine) having sections that are arranged vertically: *full-sized washer-dryers are replacing stacked units.* ■ (of a heel) made from thin layers of wood, plastic, or another material glued one on top of the other.
2 (of a deck of cards) shuffled or arranged dishonestly so as to gain an unfair advantage.
3 informal (of a woman) having large breasts.
4 Computing (of a task) placed in a queue for subsequent processing. ■ (of a stream of data) stored in such a way that the most recently stored item is the first to be retrieved.

stad·dle /'stadl/ ▶ **n.** a platform or framework supporting a stack or rick. ■ (also **staddle stone**) a stone, esp. one resembling a mushroom in shape, supporting a framework or rick.
– ORIGIN Old English *stathol* 'base, support,' of Germanic origin; related to the verb **STAND**.

sta·di·a rod /'stādēə/ ▶ **n.** another term for **LEVELING ROD**.

sta·di·um /'stādēəm/ ▶ **n.** (pl. **stadiums** or **stadia** /-dēə/) **1** a sports arena with tiers of seats for spectators. ■ (in ancient Rome or Greece) a track for a foot race or chariot race.
2 (pl. **stadia**) an ancient Roman or Greek measure of length, about 185 meters. [originally denoting the length of a stadium.]
– ORIGIN late Middle English (sense 2): via Latin from Greek *stadion*. Sense 1 dates from the mid 19th cent.

stadt·hold·er /'stat,hōldər/ (also **stadholder**) ▶ **n.** (from the 15th century to the late 18th century) the chief magistrate of the United Provinces of the Netherlands.
– DERIVATIVES **stadt·hold·er·ship** /-,ship/ **n.**
– ORIGIN mid 16th cent.: from Dutch *stadhouder* 'deputy,' from *stad* 'place' + *houder* 'holder,' translating medieval Latin *locum tenens*.

Staël /stäl/, Mme de, see **DE STAËL**.

staff[1] /staf/ ▶ **n. 1** [treated as sing. or pl.] all the people employed by a particular organization: *a staff of 600* | *hospital staff were not to blame.* ■ the teachers in a school or college: [as modifier] *a staff meeting.*
2 [treated as sing. or pl.] a group of officers assisting an officer in command of an army formation or administration headquarters. ■ (usu. **Staff**) short for **STAFF SERGEANT**.
3 a long stick used as a support when walking or climbing or as a weapon. ■ a rod or scepter held as a sign of office or authority. ■ short for **FLAGSTAFF**. ■ Surveying a rod for measuring distances or heights.
4 (pl. **staves** /stāvz/) (also **stave**) Music a set of five parallel lines and the spaces between them, on which notes are written to indicate their pitch.
▶ **v.** [with obj.] (usu. **be staffed**) provide (an organization, business, etc.) with staff: *legal advice centers are staffed by volunteer lawyers* | (as adj. **staffed**) *all units are fully staffed.*
– PHRASES **the staff of life** a staple food, esp. bread.

PRONUNCIATION KEY ə *ago, up*; ər *over, fur*; a *hat*; ā *ate*; ä *car*; e *let*; ē *see*; i *fit*; ī *by*; NG *sing*; ō *go*; ô *law, for*; oi *toy*; o͝o *good*; o͞o *goo*; ou *out*; TH *thin*; T͟H *then*; ZH *vision*

S

– ORIGIN Old English *stæf* (sense 3 of the noun), of Germanic origin; related to Dutch *staf* and German *Stab*.

staff² ▶ n. a mixture of plaster of Paris, cement, or a similar material, used for temporary building work.
– ORIGIN late 19th cent.: of unknown origin.

Staf·fa /'stafə/ a small uninhabited island in the Inner Hebrides, west of Mull.

staf·fage /'stafij/ ▶ n. accessory items in a painting, esp. figures or animals in a landscape picture.
– ORIGIN late 19th cent.: from German, from *staffieren* 'decorate,' perhaps from Old French *estoffer*, from *estoffe* 'stuff.'

staff·er /'stafər/ ▶ n. a member of the staff of an organization, esp. of a newspaper.

staff no·ta·tion ▶ n. Music notation by means of a stave, esp. as distinct from the tonic sol-fa.

staff of·fi·cer ▶ n. Military an officer serving on the staff of a military headquarters or government department.

Staf·ford·shire bull ter·ri·er /'stafərd,SHi(ə)r/ ▶ n. a dog of a small stocky breed of short-haired terrier, with a short, broad head and wide-set forelegs.

staff ser·geant ▶ n. a noncommissioned officer in the armed forces, in particular: ■ a noncommissioned officer in the US Army ranking above sergeant and below sergeant first class. ■ a noncommissioned officer in the US Air Force ranking above sergeant and below technical sergeant. ■ a noncommissioned officer in the US Marine Corps ranking above sergeant and below gunnery sergeant.

stag /stag/ ▶ n. **1** a male deer. ■ [usu. as modifier] a social gathering attended by men only: *a stag event.* ■ a person who attends a social gathering unaccompanied by a partner.
2 Brit. Stock Market a person who applies for shares in a new issue with a view to selling at once for a profit.
▶ adv. without a partner at a social gathering: *a lot of boys went stag.*
– ORIGIN Middle English (as a noun): related to Old Norse *steggr* 'male bird,' Icelandic *steggi* 'tomcat.'

stag bee·tle ▶ n. a large dark beetle, the male of which has large branched jaws that resemble a stag's antlers. ● Family Lucanidae: several species, including the European *Lucanus cervus.*

stage /stāj/ ▶ n. **1** a point, period, or step in a process or development: *there is no need at this stage to give explicit details | I was in the early stages of pregnancy.* ■ a section of a journey or race: *the final stage of the journey is made by taxi.* ■ each of two or more sections of a rocket or spacecraft that have their own engines and are jettisoned in turn when their propellant is exhausted. ■ [with modifier] Electronics a specified part of a circuit, typically one consisting of a single amplifying transistor or valve with the associated equipment.
2 a raised floor or platform, typically in a theater, on which actors, entertainers, or speakers perform: *there are only two characters on stage.* ■ (**the stage**) the acting or theatrical profession: *I've always wanted to go on the stage.* ■ [in sing.] a scene of action or forum of debate, esp. in a particular political context: *Argentina is playing a leading role on the international stage.*
3 a floor or level of a building or structure: *the upper stage was added in the 17th century.* ■ (on a microscope) a raised and usually movable plate on which a slide or object is placed for examination.
4 Geology (in chronostratigraphy) a range of strata corresponding to an age in time, forming a subdivision of a series. ■ (in paleoclimatology) a period of time marked by a characteristic climate: *the Boreal stage.*
5 archaic term for STAGECOACH.
▶ v. [with obj.] **1** present a performance of (a play or other show): *the show is being staged at the Goodspeed Opera House.* ■ (of a person or group) organize and participate in (a public event): *UDF supporters staged a demonstration in Sofia.* ■ cause (something dramatic or unexpected) to happen: *the president's attempt to stage a comeback | the dollar staged a partial recovery.*
2 Medicine diagnose or classify (a disease or patient) as having reached a particular stage in the expected progression of the disease.
– PHRASES **hold the stage** dominate a scene of action or forum of debate. **set the stage for** prepare the conditions for (the occurrence or beginning of something): *these churchmen helped to set the stage for popular reform.* **stage left** (or **right**) on the left (or right) side of a stage from the point of view of a performer facing the audience.
– DERIVATIVES **stage·a·bil·i·ty** /,stājə'bilitē/ n., **stage·a·ble** adj.
– ORIGIN Middle English (denoting a floor of a building, a platform, or a stopping place): shortening of Old French *estage* 'dwelling,' based on Latin *stare* 'to stand.' Current senses of the verb date from the early 17th cent.

stage·coach /'stāj,kōCH/ ▶ n. a large, closed horse-drawn vehicle formerly used to carry passengers and often mail along a regular route between two places.

stagecoach

stage·craft /'stāj,kraft/ ▶ n. skill or experience in writing or staging plays.

stage di·rec·tion ▶ n. an instruction in the text of a play, esp. one indicating the movement, position, or tone of an actor, or the sound effects and lighting.

stage-div·ing ▶ n. the practice (typically among audience members) of jumping from the stage at a rock concert or other event to be caught and carried aloft by the crowd below.
– DERIVATIVES **stage-dive** v. [no obj.], **stage-div·er** n.

stage door ▶ n. an actors' and workers' entrance from the street to the area of a theater behind the stage.

stage ef·fect ▶ n. an effect produced by the lighting, sound, or scenery in a play, movie, etc.: *there are some great stage effects.*

stage fright ▶ n. nervousness before or during an appearance before an audience.

stage·hand /'stāj,hand/ ▶ n. a person who moves scenery or props before or during the performance of a play.

stage-man·age ▶ v. [with obj.] be responsible for the lighting and other technical arrangements for (a stage play). ■ arrange and control (something) carefully in order to create a certain effect: *he stage-managed his image with astounding success.*
– DERIVATIVES **stage man·age·ment** n.

stage man·ag·er ▶ n. the person responsible for the lighting and other technical arrangements for a stage play.

stage name ▶ n. a name assumed for professional purposes by an actor or other performer.

stage play (also **stage production**) ▶ n. a play performed on stage rather than broadcast or made into a movie.

stage pres·ence ▶ n. the ability to command the attention of a theater audience by the impressiveness of one's manner or appearance.

stag·er /'stājər/ ▶ n. archaic an actor.

stage-struck ▶ adj. having a passionate desire to become an actor.

stage whis·per ▶ n. a loud whisper uttered by an actor on stage, intended to be heard by the audience but supposedly unheard by other characters in the play. ■ any loud whisper intended to be overheard.

stage·y ▶ adj. variant spelling of STAGY.

stag·fla·tion /,stag'flāSHən/ ▶ n. Economics persistent high inflation combined with high unemployment and stagnant demand in a country's economy.
– ORIGIN 1960s: blend of *stagnation* (see STAGNATE) and INFLATION.

stag·ger /'stagər/ ▶ v. **1** [no obj.] walk or move unsteadily, as if about to fall: *he staggered to his feet, swaying a little.* ■ [with adverbial of direction] continue in existence or operation uncertainly or precariously: *the council staggered from one crisis to the next.* ■ archaic waver in purpose; hesitate. ■ [with obj.] archaic (of a blow) cause (someone) to walk or move unsteadily, as if about to fall: *the collision staggered her and she fell.*
2 [with obj.] astonish or deeply shock: *I was staggered to find it was six o'clock* | (as adj. **staggering**) *the staggering bills for maintenance and repair.*
3 [with obj.] arrange (events, payments, hours, etc.) so that they do not occur at the same time; spread over a period of time: *meetings are staggered throughout the day.* ■ arrange (objects or parts of an object) in a zigzag order or so that they are not in line: *stagger the screws at each joint.*
▶ n. [in sing.] **1** an unsteady walk or movement: *she walked with a stagger.*
2 an arrangement of things in a zigzag order or so that they are not in line.
– DERIVATIVES **stag·ger·er** n., **stag·ger·ing·ly** adv. [as submodifier] *a staggeringly unjust society.*
– ORIGIN late Middle English (as a verb): alteration of dialect *stacker*, from Old Norse *stakra*, frequentative of *staka* 'push, stagger.' The noun dates from the late 16th cent.

stag·gers /'stagərz/ ▶ plural n. [usu. treated as sing.] any of several parasitic or acute deficiency diseases of farm animals characterized by staggering or loss of balance. ■ the inability to stand or walk steadily, esp. as a result of giddiness.

stag·horn cor·al /'stag,hôrn/ ▶ n. a large stony coral with antlerlike branches. ● Genus *Acropora*, order Scleractinia, in particular *A. cervicornis.*

stag·horn fern ▶ n. a fern with fronds that resemble antlers, occurring in tropical rain forests where it typically grows as an epiphyte. ● Genus *Platycerium*, family Polypodiaceae.

stag·horn su·mac /'stag,hôrn/ ▶ n. see SUMAC.

stag·hound /'stag,hound/ ▶ n. a large dog of a breed used for hunting deer by sight or scent.

stag·ing /'stājiNG/ ▶ n. **1** an instance or method of presenting a play or other dramatic performance: *one of the better stagings of this Shakespearean classic | the quality of staging and design.* ■ an instance of organizing a public event or protest: *the fourteenth staging of the championships.*
2 a stage or set of stages or temporary platforms arranged as a support for performers or between different levels of scaffolding.
3 Medicine diagnosis or classification of the particular stage reached by a progressive disease.
4 the arrangement of stages in a rocket or spacecraft. ■ the separation and jettisoning of a stage from the remainder of a rocket when its propellant is spent.

stag·ing ar·e·a (also **staging point** or **staging post**) ▶ n. a stopping place or assembly point en route to a destination: *a vast staging area for guerrilla attacks | the geese's major staging area on the St. Lawrence River.*

stag·nant /'stagnənt/ ▶ adj. (of a body of water or the atmosphere of a confined space) having no current or flow and often having an unpleasant smell as a consequence: *a stagnant ditch.* ■ showing no activity; dull and sluggish: *a stagnant economy.*
– DERIVATIVES **stag·nan·cy** /-nənsē/ n., **stag·nant·ly** adv.
– ORIGIN mid 17th cent.: from Latin *stagnant-* 'forming a pool of standing water,' from the verb *stagnare*, from *stagnum* 'pool.'

stag·nate /'stag,nāt/ ▶ v. [no obj.] (of water or air) cease to flow or move; become stagnant. ■ cease developing; become inactive or dull: *teaching can easily stagnate into a set of routines* | (as adj. **stagnating**) *stagnating consumer confidence.*
– DERIVATIVES **stag·na·tion** /stag'nāSHən/ n.
– ORIGIN mid 17th cent.: from Latin *stagnat-* 'settled as a still pool,' from the verb *stagnare*, from *stagnum* 'pool.'

stag par·ty ▶ n. a celebration held for a man shortly before his wedding, attended by his male friends only. ■ any party attended by men only.

stag·y /'stājē/ (also **stagey**) ▶ adj. (**stagier**, **stagiest**) excessively theatrical; exaggerated: *a stagy melodramatic voice.*
– DERIVATIVES **stag·i·ly** /-jilē/ adv., **stag·i·ness** n.

staid /stād/ ▶ adj. sedate, respectable, and unadventurous: *staid law firms.*
– DERIVATIVES **staid·ly** adv., **staid·ness** n.
– ORIGIN mid 16th cent.: archaic past participle of STAY¹.

stain /stān/ ▶ v. [with obj.] **1** mark (something) with colored patches or dirty marks that are not easily removed: *her clothing was stained with blood* | (as adj. **stained**) *a stained placemat* | [no obj.] *red ink can stain.* ■ [no obj.] be marked or be liable to be marked with such patches. ■ damage or bring disgrace to (the reputation or image of someone or something): *the awful events would unfairly stain the city's reputation.*
2 color (a material or object) by applying a penetrative dye or chemical: *wood can always be stained to a darker shade.*
▶ n. **1** a colored patch or dirty mark that is difficult to remove: *there were mud stains on my shoes.* ■ a thing that damages or brings disgrace to someone or something's reputation: *he regarded his time in jail as a stain on his character.*
2 a penetrative dye or chemical used in coloring a material or object. ■ Biology a special dye used to color organic tissue so as to make the structure visible for microscopic examination. ■ Heraldry any of the minor colors used in blazoning and liveries, esp. tenné and sanguine.
– DERIVATIVES **stain·a·ble** adj., **stain·er** n.

S

–ORIGIN late Middle English (as a verb): shortening of archaic *distain*, from Old French *desteindre* 'tinge with a color different from the natural one.' The noun was first recorded (mid 16th cent.) in the sense 'defilement, disgrace.'

stained glass ▶ **n.** colored glass used to form decorative or pictorial designs, notably for church windows, both by painting and esp. by setting contrasting pieces in a lead framework like a mosaic.

stain·less /ˈstānlis/ ▶ **adj.** unmarked by or resistant to stains or discoloration. ■ (of a person or their reputation) free from wrongdoing or disgrace: *her supposedly stainless past.*

stain·less steel ▶ **n.** a form of steel containing chromium, resistant to tarnishing and rust.

stair /ste(ə)r/ ▶ **n.** (usu. **stairs**) a set of steps leading from one floor of a building to another, typically inside the building: *he came up the stairs.* ■ single step in such a set: *the bottom stair.*
–ORIGIN Old English *stǣger*, of Germanic origin; related to Dutch *steiger* 'scaffolding,' from a base meaning 'climb.'

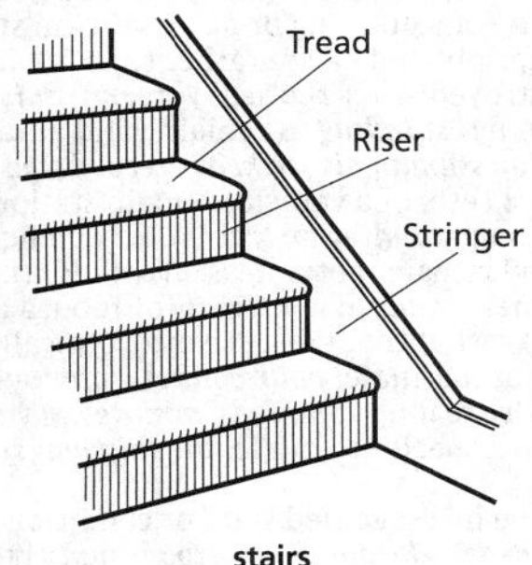

stairs

stair·case /ˈste(ə)rˌkās/ ▶ **n.** a set of stairs and its surrounding walls or structure.

stair·climb·er /ˈste(ə)rˌklīmər/ ▶ **n.** an exercise machine on which the user simulates the action of climbing a staircase.

stair·head /ˈste(ə)rˌhed/ ▶ **n.** chiefly Brit. a landing at the top of a set of stairs.

stair·lift /ˈste(ə)rˌlift/ ▶ **n.** a lift in the form of a chair that can be raised or lowered at the edge of a domestic staircase, used for carrying a person who is unable to go up or down the stairs.

stair·way /ˈste(ə)rˌwā/ ▶ **n.** a set of steps or stairs and its surrounding walls or structure.

stair·well /ˈste(ə)rˌwel/ ▶ **n.** a shaft in a building in which a staircase is built.

stake[1] /stāk/ ▶ **n. 1** a strong wooden or metal post with a point at one end, driven into the ground to support a tree, form part of a fence, act as a boundary mark, etc. ■ a long vertical rod used in basket-making. ■ a metalworker's small anvil, typically with a projection for fitting into a socket on a bench.
2 (**the stake**) historical a wooden post to which a person was tied before being burned alive as a punishment.
3 a territorial division of the Mormon Church under the jurisdiction of a president.
▶ **v.** [with obj.] **1** support (a tree or plant) with a stake or stakes.
2 (**stake something out**) mark an area with stakes so as to claim ownership of it: *the boundary between the two ranches was properly staked out* | figurative *the local dog staked out his territory.* ■ be assertive in defining and defending a position or policy: *Elena was staking out a role for herself as a formidable political force.*
–PHRASES **pull up stakes** move or go to live elsewhere. **stake a claim** assert one's right to something.
–PHRASAL VERBS **stake someone/something out** informal continuously watch a place or person in secret: *they'd staked out Culley's house for half a day.*
–ORIGIN Old English *staca*; related to Dutch *staak*, also to STICK[2].

stake[2] ▶ **n.** (usu. **stakes**) a sum of money or something else of value gambled on the outcome of a risky game or venture: *playing dice for high stakes* | figurative *the mayor raised the stakes in the battle for power* | *the stakes are high with a six-figure bonanza in television rights in the balance.* ■ a share or interest in a business, situation, or system: *GM acquired a 50 percent stake in Saab.* ■ (**stakes**) prize money, esp. in horse racing. ■ [in names] (**stakes**) a horse race in which all the owners of the racehorses running contribute to the prize money: *the horse is to run in the Lexington Stakes.* ■ [with modifier] (**stakes**) a situation involving competition in a specified area: *we will keep you one step ahead in the fashion stakes.*
▶ **v.** [with obj.] **1** gamble (money or something else of value) on the outcome of a game or race: *one gambler staked everything he'd got and lost* | figurative *it was risky to* **stake** *his reputation* **on** *one big success.*
2 informal give financial or other support to: *he staked him to an education at the École des Beaux-Arts.*
–PHRASES **at stake 1** to be won or lost; at risk: *people's lives could be at stake.* **2** at issue or in question: *the logical response is to give up, but there's more at stake than logic.*
–ORIGIN late Middle English: perhaps a specialized usage of STAKE[1], from the notion of an object being placed as a wager on a post or stake.

stake bod·y ▶ **n.** a body for a truck having a flat open platform with removable posts along the sides.

stake·hold·er /ˈstākˌhōldər/ ▶ **n. 1** (in gambling) an independent party with whom each of those who make a wager deposits the money or counters wagered.
2 a person with an interest or concern in something, esp. a business. ■ [as modifier] denoting a type of organization or system in which all the members or participants are seen as having an interest in its success: *a stakeholder economy.*

stake·out /ˈstākˌout/ ▶ **n.** informal a period of secret surveillance of a building or an area by police in order to observe someone's activities.

Sta·kha·nov·ite /stəˈkänəˌvīt/ ▶ **n.** a worker in the former Soviet Union who was exceptionally hardworking and productive. ■ an exceptionally hardworking or zealous person.
–DERIVATIVES **Sta·kha·nov·ism** /-ˌvizəm/ **n.**, **Sta·kha·nov·ist** /-vist/ **n. & adj.**
–ORIGIN 1930s: from the name of Aleksei Grigorevich *Stakhanov* (1906–77), Russian coal miner.

sta·lac·tite /stəˈlakˌtīt/ ▶ **n.** a tapering structure hanging like an icicle from the roof of a cave, formed of calcium salts deposited by dripping water. Compare with STALAGMITE.
–DERIVATIVES **sta·lac·tit·ic** /ˌstaləkˈtitik/ **adj.**
–ORIGIN late 17th cent.: from modern Latin *stalactites*, from Greek *stalaktos* 'dripping,' based on *stalassein* 'to drip.'

stalactites and stalagmites

Sta·lag /ˈstäˌläg/ ▶ **n.** (in World War II) a German prison camp, esp. for noncommissioned officers and privates.
–ORIGIN German, contraction of *Stammlager*, from *Stamm* 'base, main stock' + *Lager* 'camp.'

sta·lag·mite /stəˈlagˌmīt/ ▶ **n.** a mound or tapering column rising from the floor of a cave, formed of calcium salts deposited by dripping water and often uniting with a stalactite.
–DERIVATIVES **stal·ag·mit·ic** /ˌstaləgˈmitik/ **adj.**
–ORIGIN late 17th cent.: from modern Latin *stalagmites*, from Greek *stalagma* 'a drop,' based on *stalassein* (see STALACTITE).

stale[1] /stāl/ ▶ **adj.** (**staler, stalest**) (of food) no longer fresh and pleasant to eat; hard, musty, or dry: *stale bread.* ■ no longer new and interesting or exciting: *their marriage had gone stale.* ■ [predic.] (of a person) no longer able to perform well or creatively because of having done something for too long: *a top executive tends to get stale.* ■ (of a check or legal claim) invalid because out of date.
▶ **v.** make or become stale.
–DERIVATIVES **stale·ly** /ˈstā(l)lē/ **adv.**, **stale·ness n.**
–ORIGIN Middle English (describing beer in the sense 'clear from long standing, strong'): probably from Anglo-Norman French and Old French, from *estaler* 'to halt'; compare with the verb STALL.

stale[2] ▶ **v.** [no obj.] (of an animal, esp. a horse) urinate.
–ORIGIN late Middle English: perhaps from Old French *estaler* 'come to a stop, halt' (compare with STALE[1]).

stale·mate /ˈstālˌmāt/ ▶ **n.** Chess a position counting as a draw, in which a player is not in check but cannot move except into check. ■ a situation in which further action or progress by opposing or competing parties seems impossible: *the war had again reached stalemate.*
▶ **v.** [with obj.] bring to or cause to reach stalemate: (as adj. **stalemated**) *the currently stalemated peace talks.*
–ORIGIN mid 18th cent.: from obsolete *stale* (from Anglo-Norman French *estale* 'position,' from *estaler* 'be placed') + MATE[2].

Sta·lin /ˈstälin/, Joseph (1879–1953), Soviet statesman; general secretary of the Communist Party of the former Soviet Union 1922–53; born *Iosif Vissarionovich Dzhugashvili.* In 1928, he launched a succession of five-year plans for rapid industrialization and the enforced collectivization of agriculture. His large-scale purges of the intelligentsia in the 1930s were equally ruthless.

Joseph Stalin

Sta·lin·a·bad /ˌstälənəˈbäd/ former name (1929–61) for DUSHANBE.

Sta·lin·grad /ˈstälənˌgrad, -ˌgräd/ former name (1925–61) of VOLGOGRAD.

Sta·lin·ism /ˈstäləˌnizəm/ ▶ **n.** the ideology and policies adopted by Stalin, based on centralization, totalitarianism, and the pursuit of communism. ■ any rigid centralized authoritarian form of communism.
–DERIVATIVES **Sta·lin·ist n. & adj.**

Sta·lin Peak former name (1933-1962) of ISMAIL SAMANI PEAK.

stalk[1] /stôk/ ▶ **n.** the main stem of a herbaceous plant: *he chewed a stalk of grass.* ■ the slender attachment or support of a leaf, flower, or fruit: *the acorns grow on stalks.* ■ a similar support for a sessile animal, or for an organ in an animal. ■ a slender support or stem of something: *drinking glasses with long stalks.*
–DERIVATIVES **stalked adj.** [in combination] *rough-stalked meadow grass*, **stalk·less adj.**, **stalk·like** /-ˌlīk/ **adj.**, **stalk·y adj.**
–ORIGIN Middle English: probably a diminutive of dialect *stale* 'rung of a ladder, long handle.'

stalk[2] ▶ **v. 1** [with obj.] pursue or approach stealthily: *a cat stalking a bird.* ■ harass or persecute (someone) with unwanted and obsessive attention: *for five years she was stalked by a man who would taunt and threaten her.* ■ chiefly literary move silently or threateningly through (a place): *the tiger stalks the jungle* | figurative *fear stalked the camp.*
2 [no obj.] stride somewhere in a proud, stiff, or angry manner: *without another word she turned and stalked out.*
▶ **n. 1** a stealthy pursuit of someone or something.
2 a stiff, striding gait.
–ORIGIN late Old English *-stealcian* (in *bistealcian* 'walk cautiously or stealthily'), of Germanic origin; related to STEAL.

S

stalk·er /ˈstôkər/ ▶ **n.** a person who stealthily hunts or pursues an animal or another person. ■ a person who harasses or persecutes someone with unwanted and obsessive attention.

stalk·er·az·zi /ˌstôkəˈrätsē/ ▶ **plural n.** informal photojournalists who follow celebrities closely and persistently with the intention of obtaining sensational pictures.
–ORIGIN from *stalker* + *-azzi*, on the pattern of *paparazzi*.

stalk-eyed ▶ **adj.** (of a crustacean) having eyes mounted on stalks.

stalk·ing horse ▶ **n.** a screen traditionally made in the shape of a horse behind which a hunter can stay concealed when stalking prey. ■ a false pretext concealing someone's real intentions. ■ a political candidate who runs only in order to provoke the election and thus allow a stronger candidate to come forward.
–ORIGIN early 16th cent.: from the former practice of using a horse trained to allow a fowler to hide

behind it, or under its coverings, until within easy range of prey.

stall /stôl/ ▶ **n. 1** a stand, booth, or compartment for the sale of goods in a market or large covered area: *fruit and vegetable stalls.*
2 an individual compartment for an animal in a stable or barn, enclosed on three sides. ■ a stable. ■ a marked-out parking space for a vehicle. ■ a compartment for one person in a shower room, toilet, or similar facility.
3 a fixed seat in the choir or chancel of a church, more or less enclosed at the back and sides and often canopied, typically reserved for a particular member of the clergy.
4 (**stalls**) Brit. the seats on the ground floor in a theater.
5 an instance of an engine, vehicle, aircraft, or boat stalling: *speed must be maintained to avoid a stall and loss of control.*
▶ **v. 1** [no obj.] (of a motor vehicle or its engine) stop running, typically because of an overload on the engine: *her car stalled at the crossroads.* ■ (of an aircraft or its pilot) reach a condition where the speed is too low to allow effective operation of the controls. ■ Sailing have insufficient wind power in the sails to give controlled motion. ■ [with obj.] cause (an engine, vehicle, aircraft, or boat) to stall.
2 stop or cause to stop making progress: [no obj.] *his career had stalled, hers taken off* | [with obj.] *the government has stalled the much-needed project.* ■ speak or act in a deliberately vague way in order to gain more time to deal with a question or issue; prevaricate: *she was **stalling for time**.* ■ [with obj.] delay or divert (someone) by acting in such a way: *stall him until I've had time to take a look.*
3 [with obj.] put or keep (an animal) in a stall, esp. in order to fatten it.
– ORIGIN Old English *steall* 'stable or cattle shed,' of Germanic origin; related to Dutch *stal*, also to **STAND**. Early senses of the verb included 'reside, dwell' and 'bring to a halt.'

stal·lion /'stalyən/ ▶ **n.** an uncastrated adult male horse.
– ORIGIN Middle English: from an Anglo-Norman French variant of Old French *estalon*, from a derivative of a Germanic base shared by **STALL**.

Stal·lone /stə'lōn/, Sylvester Enzio (1946–), US actor, writer, and director; nickname **Sly**. He is best known for writing and starring in five *Rocky* movies (1976, 1979 1982, 1985, 1990) and three *Rambo* movies (1982, 1985, 1988). He also directed *Rocky II*, *Rocky III*, and *Rocky IV*.

stal·wart /'stôlwərt/ ▶ **adj.** loyal, reliable, and hardworking: *he remained a stalwart supporter of the cause.* ■ dated strongly built and sturdy: *he was of stalwart build.*
▶ **n.** a loyal, reliable, and hardworking supporter or participant in an organization or team: *the stalwarts of the Ladies' Auxiliary.*
– DERIVATIVES **stal·wart·ly** adv., **stal·wart·ness** n.
– ORIGIN late Middle English: Scots variant of obsolete *stalworth*, from Old English *stǣl* 'place' + *weorth* 'worth.'

Stam·boul /stam'bo͞ol, stäm-/ archaic name for **ISTANBUL**.

sta·men /'stāmin/ ▶ **n.** Botany the male fertilizing organ of a flower, typically consisting of a pollen-containing anther and a filament.
– ORIGIN mid 17th cent.: from Latin, literally 'warp in an upright loom, thread.'

S

Stam·ford /'stamfərd/ a commercial city in southwestern Connecticut, on Long Island Sound; pop. 119,303 (est. 2008).

stam·i·na /'stamənə/ ▶ **n.** the ability to sustain prolonged physical or mental effort: *their secret is stamina rather than speed.*
– ORIGIN late 17th cent. (in the sense 'rudiments, essential elements of something'): from Latin, plural of **STAMEN** in the sense 'threads spun by the Fates.'

stam·i·nate /'stamə,nāt/ ▶ **adj.** Botany (of a plant or flower) having stamens but no pistils. Compare with **PISTILLATE**.

stam·i·node /'stamə,nōd/ ▶ **n.** Botany a sterile or abortive stamen, frequently resembling a stamen without its anther.

stam·mer /'stamər/ ▶ **v.** [no obj.] speak with sudden involuntary pauses and a tendency to repeat the initial letters of words. ■ [with obj.] utter (words) in such a way: *I **stammered out** my history* | [with direct speech] *"I ... I can't," Isabel stammered.*
▶ **n.** [in sing.] a tendency to stammer: *as a young man, he had a dreadful stammer.*
– DERIVATIVES **stam·mer·er** n., **stam·mer·ing·ly** adv.
– ORIGIN late Old English *stamerian*; related to **STUMBLE**. The noun dates from the late 18th cent.

stamp /stamp/ ▶ **v.** [with obj.] **1** bring down (one's foot) heavily on the ground or on something on the ground: *he stamped his foot in frustration* | [no obj.] *he threw his cigarette down and stamped on it* | figurative *Robertson stamped on all these suggestions.* ■ crush, flatten, or remove with a heavy blow from one's feet: *she stamped the snow from her boots.* ■ [no obj.] walk with heavy, forceful steps: *John stamped off, muttering.*
2 impress a pattern or mark, esp. an official one, on (a surface, object, or document) using an engraved or inked block or die or other instrument: *the woman stamped my passport.* ■ impress (a pattern or mark) on something in such a way: *a key with a number **stamped on** the shaft* | figurative *it's one of those records that has 'classic' stamped all over it.* ■ make (something) by cutting it out with a die or mold: *the knives are **stamped out from** a flat strip of steel.* ■ reveal or mark out as having a particular character, quality, or ability: *his style **stamps him as** a player to watch.*
3 affix a postage stamp or stamps onto (a letter or package): *Annie stamped the envelope for her.*
4 crush or pulverize (ore).
▶ **n. 1** an instrument for stamping a pattern or mark, in particular an engraved or inked block or die. ■ a mark or pattern made by such an instrument, esp. one indicating official validation or certification: *passports with visa stamps* | figurative *the emperor gave them his **stamp of approval**.* ■ a characteristic or distinctive impression or quality: *the whole project has the stamp of authority.* ■ a particular class or type or person or thing: *empiricism of this stamp has been esp. influential in British philosophy.*
2 a small adhesive piece of paper stuck to something to show that an amount of money has been paid, in particular a postage stamp: *a first-class stamp.*
3 an act or sound of stamping with the foot: *the stamp of boots on the bare floor.*
4 a block for crushing ore in a stamp mill.
– PHRASES **stamp one's authority** (or **personality** or **style** etc.) **on** have a strong or permanent influence on: *he must be able to stamp his authority on the team.*
– PHRASAL VERBS **stamp something out 1** extinguish a fire by stamping on it: *he stamped out the flames before they could grow.* **2** suppress or put an end to something by taking decisive action: *urgent action is required to stamp out corruption.*
– DERIVATIVES **stamp·er** n.
– ORIGIN Middle English (in the sense 'crush to a powder'): of Germanic origin; related to German *stampfen* 'stamp with the foot'; reinforced by Old French *estamper* 'to stamp.' Compare with **STOMP**.

Stamp Act ▶ **n.** an act of the British Parliament in 1756 that exacted revenue from the American colonies by imposing a stamp duty on newspapers and legal and commercial documents. Colonial opposition led to the act's repeal in 1766 and helped encourage the revolutionary movement against the British Crown.

stam·pede /stam'pēd/ ▶ **n.** a sudden panicked rush of a number of horses, cattle, or other animals. ■ a sudden rapid movement or reaction of a mass of people in response to a particular circumstance or stimulus: *a stampede of bargain hunters.* ■ [often in titles] a rodeo: *the Calgary Stampede.*
▶ **v.** [no obj.] (of horses, cattle, or other animals) rush wildly in a sudden mass panic: *the nearby sheep stampeded as if they sensed impending danger.* ■ (of people) move rapidly in a mass: *the children stampeded through the kitchen, playing tag or hide-and-seek.* ■ [with obj.] cause (people or animals) to move in such a way: *the raiders stampeded 200 mules* | figurative *don't let them **stampede** us **into** anything.*
– DERIVATIVES **stam·ped·er** n.
– ORIGIN early 19th cent.: Mexican Spanish use of Spanish *estampida* 'crash, uproar,' of Germanic origin; related to the verb **STAMP**.

stamp·ing ground ▶ **n.** another term for **STOMPING GROUND**.

stamp mill ▶ **n.** a mill for crushing ore.

stance /stans/ ▶ **n. 1** the way in which someone stands, esp. when deliberately adopted (as in baseball, golf, and other sports); a person's posture: *she altered her stance, resting all her weight on one leg.* ■ the attitude of a person or organization toward something; a standpoint: *the party is changing its stance on the draft.*
2 Climbing a ledge or foothold on which a belay can be secured.
– ORIGIN Middle English (denoting a standing place): from French, from Italian *stanza*.

stanch[1] /stônCH, stänCH/ (also **staunch**) ▶ **v.** [with obj.] stop or restrict (a flow of blood) from a wound: *colleagues may have saved her life by stanching the flow* | figurative *the company did nothing to stanch the tide of rumors.* ■ stop the flow of blood from (a wound).
– ORIGIN Middle English: from Old French *estanchier*, from the base of **STAUNCH**[1].

stanch[2] ▶ **adj.** variant spelling of **STAUNCH**[1] (sense 2).

stan·chion /'stanCHən/ ▶ **n.** an upright bar, post, or frame forming a support or barrier.
– DERIVATIVES **stan·chioned** adj.
– ORIGIN Middle English: from Anglo-Norman French *stanchon*, from Old French *estanchon*, from *estance* 'a support,' probably based on Latin *stant-* 'standing,' from the verb *stare*.

stand /stand/ ▶ **v.** (past and past participle **stood** /sto͝od/) **1** [no obj.] have or maintain an upright position, supported by one's feet: *Lionel stood in the doorway* | *she stood still, heart hammering.* ■ rise to one's feet: *the two men **stood up** and shook hands.* ■ move to and remain in a specified position: *she stood aside to let them enter.* ■ [with obj.] place or set in an upright or specified position: *don't stand the plant in direct sunlight.*
2 [no obj.] (of an object, building, or settlement) be situated in a particular place or position: *the town stood on a hill* | *the hotel stands in three acres of gardens.* ■ (of a building or other vertical structure) remain upright and entire rather than fall into ruin or be destroyed: *after the heavy storms, only one house was left standing.* ■ remain valid or unaltered: *my decision stands* | *his strikeout record stood for 38 years.* ■ (esp. of a vehicle) remain stationary: *the train now standing on track 3.* ■ (of a liquid) collect and remain motionless: *avoid planting in soil where water stands in winter.* ■ (of food, a mixture, or liquid) rest without disturbance, typically so as to infuse or marinate: *pour boiling water over the fruit and leave it to stand for 5 minutes.* ■ (of a ship) remain on a specified course: *the ship was standing north.*
3 [no obj.] be in a specified state or condition: *since mother's death, the house had stood empty* | *sorry, darling—I stand corrected.* ■ adopt a particular attitude toward a matter or issue: *students should consider where they stand on this issue.* ■ be of a specified height: *Sampson was a small man, standing 5 ft. 4 in. tall.* ■ (**stand at**) be at (a particular level or value): *the budget stood at $14 million per annum.* ■ [no obj., with infinitive] be in a situation where one is likely to do something: *investors stood to lose heavily.* ■ act in a specified capacity: *he stood watch all night.* ■ (also **stand at stud**) (of a stallion) be available for breeding.
4 [with obj. and often modal] withstand (an experience or test) without being damaged: *small boats that could stand the punishment of heavy seas.* ■ [usu. with negative] informal be able to endure or tolerate: *I can't stand the way Mom talks to him.*
5 [no obj.] Brit. be a candidate in an election: *he **stood for** Parliament in 1968.*
6 [usu. with two objs.] provide (food or drink) for someone at one's own expense: *somebody in the bar would stand him a beer.*
▶ **n. 1** [usu. in sing.] an attitude toward a particular issue; a position taken in an argument: *the party's tough stand on welfare* | *his traditionalist stand.* ■ a determined effort to resist or fight for something: *this was not the moment to **make a stand for** independence* | *we have to **take a stand against** racism.* ■ an act of holding one's ground against or halting to resist an opposing force: *Custer's legendary last stand.*
2 a place where, or an object on which, someone or something stands, sits, or rests, in particular: ■ a large raised tiered structure for spectators, typically at a sports arena: *her parents watched from the stands.* ■ a rack, base, or piece of furniture for holding, supporting, or displaying something: *a microphone stand.* ■ a small stall or booth in a street, market, or public building from which goods are sold: *a hot-dog stand.* ■ a raised platform for a band, orchestra, or speaker. ■ (**the stand**) (also **witness stand**) a witness box: *Sergeant Harris took the stand.* ■ the place where someone typically stands or sits: *she took her stand in front of the desks.* ■ a place where vehicles, typically taxicabs, wait for passengers.
3 [usu. in sing.] a cessation from motion or progress: *the train drew to a stand by the signal box.* ■ each halt made on a touring theatrical production to give one or more performances.
4 a group of growing plants of a specified kind, esp. trees: *a stand of poplars.*
– PHRASES **as it stands** in its present condition: *there are no merits in the proposal as it stands.* ■ (also **as things stand**) in the present circumstances: *the country would struggle, as it stands, to host the next Winter Olympic Games.* **it stands to reason** see **REASON**. **stand a chance** see **CHANCE**. **stand one's ground** maintain one's position, typically in the face of opposition: *she stood her ground, refusing to let him intimidate her.* **stand someone in good stead** see **STEAD**. **stand on one's own (two) feet**

be or become self-reliant or independent. **stand out a mile** see MILE. **stand out like a sore thumb** see SORE. **stand pat** see PAT². **stand trial** be tried in a court of law. **stand up and be counted** state publicly one's support for someone or something. **will the real —— please stand up** informal used rhetorically to indicate that the specified person should clarify their position or reveal their true character: *he was so different from the unhappy man of a week ago—would the real Jack Lawrence please stand up?*

– PHRASAL VERBS **stand alone** be unequaled: *when it came to fun, Julia stood alone.* **stand aside** take no action to prevent, or not involve oneself in, something that is happening: *the army had stood aside as the monarchy fell.* ■ another way of saying STAND DOWN below. **stand back** withdraw from a situation emotionally in order to view it more objectively. ■ another way of saying STAND ASIDE above. **stand by 1** be present while something bad is happening but fail to take any action to stop it: *he was beaten to the ground as onlookers stood by.* **2** support or remain loyal to (someone), typically in a time of need: *she had stood by him during his years in prison.* ■ adhere to or abide by (something promised, stated, or decided): *the government must stand by its pledges.* **3** be ready to deal or assist with something: *two battalions were on their way, and a third was standing by.* **stand down 1** withdraw or resign from a position or office: *he stood down as leader of the party.* **2** (**stand down** or **stand someone down**) relax or cause to relax after a state of readiness: *if something doesn't happen soon, I guess they'll stand us down.* **3** (of a witness) leave the witness stand after giving evidence. **stand for 1** be an abbreviation of or symbol for: *NASA stands for National Aeronautics and Space Administration.* **2** [with negative] informal refuse to endure or tolerate: *I won't stand for any nonsense.* **3** support (a cause or principle): *we stand for animal welfare.* **stand in 1** deputize: *Brown stood in for the injured Simpson.* **2** Nautical sail closer to the shore. **stand off** move or keep away: *the women stood off at a slight distance.* ■ Nautical sail further away from the shore. **stand someone off** keep someone away: repel someone. **stand on 1** be scrupulous in the observance of: *call me Alex—let's not stand on formality.* **2** Nautical continue on the same course. **stand out 1** project from a surface: *the veins in his neck stood out.* ■ be easily noticeable: *he was one of those men who stood out in a crowd.* ■ be clearly better or more significant than someone or something: *four issues stand out as being of crucial importance.* **2** persist in opposition or support of something: *she **stood out against** public opinion | the company **stood out for** the product it wanted.* **stand over 1** stand close to (someone) so as to watch, supervise, or intimidate them. **2** (**stand over** or **stand something over**) be postponed or postpone to be dealt with at a later date: *a number of points were stood over to a further meeting.* **stand to** [often in imperative] Military stand ready for an attack, esp. one before dawn or after dark. **stand up** (of an argument, claim, evidence, etc.) remain valid after close scrutiny or analysis: *but will your story stand up in court?* **stand someone up** informal fail to keep an appointment with a boyfriend or girlfriend. **stand up for** speak or act in support of: *she learned to stand up for herself.* ■ act as best man for in a wedding. **stand up to 1** make a spirited defense against: *giving workers the confidence to stand up to their employers.* **2** be resistant to the harmful effects of (prolonged wear or use).

– DERIVATIVES **stand·er** n.

– ORIGIN Old English *standan* (verb), *stand* (noun), of Germanic origin, from an Indo-European root shared by Latin *stare* and Greek *histanai*, also by the noun STEAD.

stand-a·lone (also **standalone** /ˈstandə,lōn/) ▶ **adj.** (of computer hardware or software) able to operate independently of other hardware or software.

stand·ard /ˈstandərd/ ▶ **n. 1** a level of quality or attainment: *their restaurant offers a high standard of service | the governor's ambition to raise standards in schools.* ■ a required or agreed level of quality or attainment: *half of the beaches fail to comply with EPA standards | their tap water was not **up to standard**.*
2 an idea or thing used as a measure, norm, or model in comparative evaluations: *the wages are low by today's standards | the system had become an industry standard.* ■ (**standards**) principles of conduct informed by notions of honor and decency: *a decline in moral standards.* ■ a form of language that is widely accepted as the correct form. ■ the prescribed weight of fine metal in gold or silver coins: *the sterling standard for silver.* ■ a system by which the value of a currency is defined in terms of gold or silver or both.
3 an object that is supported in an upright position, in particular: ■ a military or ceremonial flag carried on a pole or hoisted on a rope. ■ a tree or shrub that grows on an erect stem of full height. ■ a shrub grafted on an erect stem and trained in tree form. ■ Botany the large frequently erect uppermost petal of a papilionaceous flower. Also called VEXILLUM. ■ Botany one of the inner petals of an iris flower, frequently erect. ■ an upright water or gas pipe.
4 a tune or song of established popularity.
▶ **adj. 1** used or accepted as normal or average: *the standard rate of income tax | it is standard practice in museums to register objects as they are acquired.* ■ (of a size, measure, design, etc.) such as is regularly used or produced; not special or exceptional: *all these doors come in a range of standard sizes.* ■ (of a work, repertoire, or writer) viewed as authoritative or of permanent value and so widely read or performed: *his essays on the interpretation of reality became a standard text.* ■ denoting or relating to the spoken or written form of a language widely accepted as usual and correct: *speakers of standard English.*
2 [attrib.] (of a tree or shrub) growing on an erect stem of full height. ■ (of a shrub) grafted on an erect stem and trained in tree form: *standard roses.*

– PHRASES **raise one's** (or **the**) **standard** take up arms; oppose: *he is the only one who has dared raise his standard against her.*

– DERIVATIVES **stand·ard·ly** adv.

– ORIGIN Middle English (denoting a flag raised on a pole as a rallying point, the authorized exemplar of a unit of measurement, or an upright timber): shortening of Old French *estendart*, from *estendre* 'extend'; sense 3 of the noun, influenced by the verb STAND.

Stand·ard & Poor's 500 /ˈstandərd ən po͝orz/ (abbr.: **S & P 500**) ▶ **n.** Finance a group of 500 companies whose average daily share prices are used to calculate an index of the day's security prices.

stand·ard-bear·er ▶ **n.** a soldier who is responsible for carrying the distinctive flag of a unit, regiment, or army. ■ a leading figure in a cause or movement: *the announcement made her a standard-bearer for gay rights.*

Stand·ard·bred /ˈstandərd,bred/ (also **standardbred**) ▶ **n.** a horse of a breed able to attain a specified speed, developed esp. for trotting.

stand·ard de·vi·a·tion ▶ **n.** Statistics a quantity calculated to indicate the extent of deviation for a group as a whole.

stand·ard er·ror ▶ **n.** Statistics a measure of the statistical accuracy of an estimate, equal to the standard deviation of the theoretical distribution of a large population of such estimates.

stand·ard gauge ▶ **n.** a railroad gauge of 56.5 inches (1.435 m), standard in the US, Britain, and many other parts of the world.

stand·ard·ize /ˈstandər,dīz/ ▶ **v.** [with obj.] cause (something) to conform to a standard: *the editors failed to standardize the spelling of geographic names.* ■ [no obj.] (**standardize on**) adopt (something) as one's standard: *we could standardize on U.S. equipment.* ■ determine the properties of by comparison with a standard.

– DERIVATIVES **stand·ard·iz·a·ble** adj., **stand·ard·i·za·tion** /,standərdiˈzāsʜən/ n., **stand·ard·iz·er** n.

stand·ard mod·el ▶ **n.** (**the standard model**) Physics a mathematical description of the elementary particles of matter and the electromagnetic, weak, and strong forces by which they interact.

stand·ard of liv·ing ▶ **n.** the degree of wealth and material comfort available to a person or community.

stand·ard time ▶ **n.** a uniform time for places in approximately the same longitude, established in a country or region by law or custom.

stand·by /ˈstan(d),bī/ ▶ **n.** (pl. **standbys**) readiness for duty or immediate deployment: *buses were placed **on standby** for the trip to Washington.* ■ the state of waiting to secure an unreserved place for a journey or performance, allocated on the basis of earliest availability: *passengers were obliged to **go on standby**.* ■ a person waiting to secure such a place. ■ a person or thing ready to be deployed immediately, esp. if needed as backup in an emergency: *a generator was kept as a standby in case of power failure | [as modifier] a standby rescue vessel.* ■ an operational mode of an electrical appliance in which the power is switched on but the appliance is not actually functioning.

stand-down ▶ **n.** chiefly Military a period of relaxation after a state of alert.

stand·ee /stanˈdē/ ▶ **n.** a person who stands, esp. in a passenger vehicle when all the seats are occupied or at a performance or sporting event.

stand-in ▶ **n.** a person who stands in for another, esp. in a performance; a substitute: *his stand-in does all the dancing sequences.*

stand·ing /ˈstandiɴɢ/ ▶ **n. 1** position, status, or reputation: *their standing in the community | a man of high social standing.* ■ (**standings**) the table of scores indicating the relative positions of competitors in a sports contest: *she heads the world championship standings.*
2 used to specify the length of time that something has lasted or that someone has fulfilled a particular role: *an interdepartmental squabble **of long standing**.*
▶ **adj.** [attrib.] **1** (of a jump or a start in a running race) performed from rest or an upright position, without a run-up or the use of starting blocks.
2 remaining in force or use; permanent: *he has a standing invitation to visit them | a standing army.*
3 (of water) stagnant or still.
4 (of grain) not yet reaped and so still erect.
5 Printing (of metal type) kept set up after use.

– PHRASES **all standing** Sailing (chiefly with reference to a boat's stopping) without time to lower the sails. **in good standing** in favor or on good terms with someone: *the companies wanted to stay **in good standing with** the government.* **leave someone/something standing** informal be much better or make much faster progress than someone or something else.

stand·ing com·mit·tee ▶ **n.** a permanent committee that meets regularly.

stand·ing count (also **standing eight count**) ▶ **n.** Boxing a count of eight taken on a boxer who has not been knocked down but who appears temporarily unfit to continue fighting.

stand·ing crop ▶ **n.** a growing crop, esp. of a grain. ■ Ecology the total biomass of an ecosystem or any of its components at a given time.

stand·ing joke ▶ **n.** something that regularly causes amusement or provokes ridicule.

stand·ing or·der ▶ **n. 1** an order or ruling governing the procedures of a society, council, or other deliberative body.
2 a military order or ruling that is retained irrespective of changing conditions.

stand·ing o·va·tion ▶ **n.** a period of prolonged applause during which those in the crowd or audience rise to their feet.

stand·ing part ▶ **n.** the end of a rope in a ship's rigging that is made fast, as distinct from the end to be hauled on. ■ (in knot-tying) the main part of the rope as opposed to the free end.

stand·ing rig·ging ▶ **n.** see RIGGING (sense 1).

Stand·ing Rock a Sioux Indian reservation that straddles the North Dakota–South Dakota border, west of the Missouri River.

stand·ing room ▶ **n.** space available for people to stand rather than sit in a vehicle, building, or stadium.

stand·ing stone ▶ **n.** another term for MENHIR.

stand·ing wave ▶ **n.** Physics a vibration of a system in which some particular points remain fixed while others between them vibrate with the maximum amplitude. Compare with TRAVELING WAVE.

Stan·dish /ˈstandisʜ/, Miles (*c.* 1584–1656), American colonist; born in England. He accompanied the Pilgrims to America in 1620 and became the military leader of Plymouth Colony. He was a cofounder of Duxbury, Massachusetts, in 1631. He is romanticized as the lovelorn suitor in Longfellow's fictional poem "The Courtship of Miles Standish" (1858).

stand·ish /ˈstandisʜ/ ▶ **n.** chiefly historical a stand for holding pens, ink, and other writing equipment.

– ORIGIN Middle English: commonly held to be from the verb STAND + DISH, but evidence of such a use of *dish* is lacking.

stand·off /ˈstand,ôf, -,äf/ ▶ **n.** a stalemate or deadlock between two equally matched opponents in a dispute or conflict: *the 16-day-old standoff was no closer to being resolved.*

stand·off·ish /,standˈôfisʜ, -ˈäfisʜ/ ▶ **adj.** informal distant and cold in manner; unfriendly.

– DERIVATIVES **stand·off·ish·ly** adv., **stand·off·ish·ness** n.

stand·out /ˈstand,out/ informal ▶ **n.** a person or thing of exceptional ability or high quality: *standouts include the homemade ravioli and the pizzas.*
▶ **adj.** [attrib.] exceptionally good: *he became a standout quarterback in the NFL.*

S

stand·pipe /ˈstan(d)ˌpīp/ ▶ **n.** a vertical pipe extending from a water supply, esp. one connecting a temporary tap to the main.

stand·point /ˈstan(d)ˌpoint/ ▶ **n.** an attitude to or outlook on issues, typically arising from one's circumstances or beliefs: *she writes on religion from the standpoint of a believer.* ■ the position from which someone is able to view a scene or an object.

stand·still /ˈstan(d)ˌstil/ ▶ **n.** [in sing.] a situation or condition in which there is no movement or activity at all: *the traffic came to a standstill.*

stand·still a·gree·ment ▶ **n.** Finance an agreement between two countries in which a debt owed by one to the other is held in abeyance for a specified period. ■ an agreement between a company and a bidder for the company in which the bidder agrees to buy no more shares for a specified period.

stand-to ▶ **n.** Military the state of readiness for action or attack. ■ the formal start to a day of military operations.

stand-up (also **standup** /ˈstandˌəp/) ▶ **adj.** [attrib.] **1** involving, done by, or engaged in by people standing up: *a stand-up party.* ■ such that people have to stand rather than sit: *a stand-up bar.* ■ (of a comedian) performing by standing in front of an audience and telling jokes. ■ (of comedy) performed in such a way: *his stand-up routine depends on improvised observations.*
2 informal courageous and loyal in a combative way: *he was a stand-up kind of guy.*
3 designed to stay upright or erect.
▶ **n.** a comedian who performs by standing in front of an audience and telling jokes. ■ comedy performed in such a way: *he began doing stand-up when he was fifteen.* ■ a brief monologue by a television news reporter.

Stan·ford /ˈstanfərd/, A(masa) Leland (1824–93), US railroad official and philanthropist. He was governor of California 1861–63; a member of the US Senate 1885–93; promoter, financier, and director of two railroads, the Central Pacific and the Southern Pacific; and founder of Stanford University in 1885.

Stan·ford-Bi·net test /ˌstanfərd bəˈnā/ ▶ **n.** an intelligence test based on the Binet-Simon scale, commonly administered to children.

stan·hope /ˈstanˌhōp, ˈstanəp/ ▶ **n.** historical a light open horse-drawn carriage for one person, with two or four wheels.
– ORIGIN early 19th cent.: named after Fitzroy *Stanhope* (1787–1864), an English clergyman for whom the first one was made.

Stan·is·laus, St. /ˈstanəˌslôs, -ˌsläs/ (1030–79), patron saint of Poland; Polish name *Stanisław*; known as **St. Stanislaus of Cracow**. As bishop of Cracow 1072–79, he excommunicated **King Boleslaus II**. According to tradition, Stanislaus was murdered by Boleslaus while attending Mass. Feast day, April 11 (formerly May 7).

Stan·i·slav·sky /ˌstanəˈsläfskē/, Konstantin (Sergeevich) (1863–1938), Russian theater director and actor; born *Konstantin Sergeevich Alekseev*. He trained actors to take a psychological approach and to use latent powers of self-expression when taking on roles; his theory and technique were later developed into method acting.

stank /staNGk/ past of **STINK**.

S

Stan·ley¹ /ˈstanlē/ (also **Port Stanley**) the chief port and town in the Falkland Islands, on the island of East Falkland; pop. 2,115 (2006).

Stan·ley², Sir Henry Morton (1841–1904), Welsh explorer; born *John Rowlands*. In 1871, he found David Livingstone (1813–73) at Lake Tanganyika in Africa. After Livingstone's death, Stanley continued his explorations in Africa, charting Lake Victoria (1874), tracing the course of the Congo (1874–77), and mapping Lake Albert (1889). In 1889, he was the first European to visit Lake Edward.

Stan·ley, Mount a mountain in the Ruwenzori range in central Africa, on the border between the Democratic Republic of the Congo (formerly Zaire) and Uganda. Margherita Peak, which rises to 16,765 feet (5,110 m), is the third-highest mountain in Africa. African name **NGALIEMA, MOUNT**.
– ORIGIN named after Sir Henry M. *Stanley*, the first European to reach it (1889).

Stan·ley crane ▶ **n.** another term for **BLUE CRANE**.

Stan·ley Cup a trophy awarded annually to the ice hockey team that wins the championship in the National Hockey League.
– ORIGIN named after Lord *Stanley* of Preston (1841–1908), the governor general of Canada who donated the trophy in 1893.

Stan·ley·ville /ˈstanlēˌvil/ former name (1882–1966) for **KISANGANI**.

stan·na·ry /ˈstanərē/ ▶ **n.** (pl. **stannaries**) (usu. **the stannaries**) Brit. chiefly historical a tin-mining district in Cornwall or Devon, England.
– ORIGIN late Middle English: from medieval Latin *stannaria* (plural), from late Latin *stannum* 'tin.'

stan·nic /ˈstanik/ ▶ **adj.** Chemistry of tin with a valence of four; of tin(IV). Compare with **STANNOUS**.
– ORIGIN late 18th cent.: from late Latin *stannum* 'tin' + **-IC**.

stan·nous /ˈstanəs/ ▶ **adj.** Chemistry of tin with a valence of two; of tin(II). Compare with **STANNIC**.
– ORIGIN mid 19th cent.: from late Latin *stannum* 'tin' + **-OUS**.

Stan·ton¹ /ˈstantən/, Edwin McMasters (1814–69), US lawyer and public official. As secretary of war 1862–67 and briefly during 1868, he served under President Lincoln and played a pivotal role in the impeachment proceedings against President Andrew Johnson. In 1869, he was appointed to the US Supreme Court but died before taking office.

Stan·ton², Elizabeth Cady (1815–1902), US social reformer. With Lucretia Mott, she organized the first US women's rights convention, in Seneca Falls, New York, in 1848. From 1852, she led the women's rights movement with Susan B. Anthony. She was president of the National Woman Suffrage Association 1869–90 and an editor of the radical feminist magazine *Revolution* 1868–70.

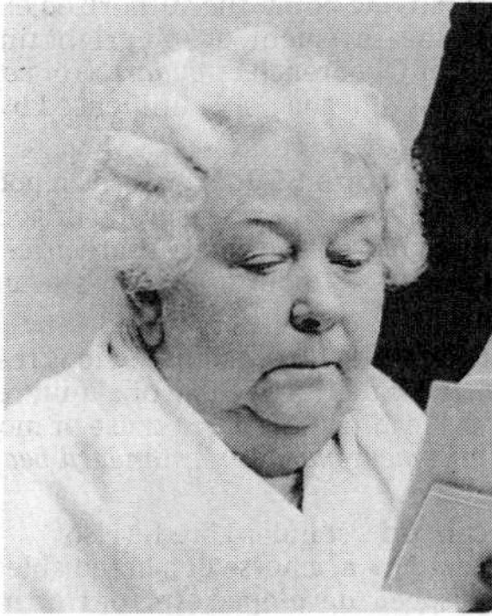

Elizabeth Cady Stanton

stan·za /ˈstanzə/ ▶ **n.** a group of lines forming the basic recurring metrical unit in a poem; a verse. ■ a group of four lines in some Greek and Latin meters.
– DERIVATIVES **stan·zaed** (also **stanza'd**) **adj.**, **stan·za·ic** /stanˈzā-ik/ **adj.**
– ORIGIN late 16th cent.: from Italian, literally 'standing place,' also 'stanza.'

sta·pe·di·al /stəˈpēdēəl/ ▶ **adj.** [attrib.] Anatomy & Zoology of or relating to the stapes.
– ORIGIN late 19th cent.: from modern Latin *stapedius* (denoting the muscle attached to the neck of the stapes) + **-AL**.

sta·pe·li·a /stəˈpēlyə/ ▶ **n.** a succulent African plant with large star-shaped fleshy flowers that have bold markings and a fetid carrionlike smell that attracts pollinating flies. Also called **CARRION FLOWER**. ● Genus *Stapelia*, family Asclepiadaceae.
– ORIGIN modern Latin, named after Jan Bode von *Stapel* (died 1636), Dutch botanist.

sta·pes /ˈstāpēz/ ▶ **n.** (pl. **same**) Anatomy a small stirrup-shaped bone in the middle ear, transmitting vibrations from the incus to the inner ear. Also called **STIRRUP**.
– ORIGIN mid 17th cent.: modern Latin, from medieval Latin *stapes* 'stirrup.'

staph /staf/ ▶ **n.** informal **1** Medicine short for **STAPHYLOCOCCUS**.
2 Entomology short for **STAPHYLINID**.

staph·y·lin·id /ˌstafəˈlinid/ ▶ **n.** Entomology a beetle of a family (Staphylinidae) that comprises the rove beetles.
– ORIGIN late 19th cent.: from modern Latin *Staphylinidae* (plural), from the genus name *Staphylinus*, from Greek *staphulinos*, denoting a kind of insect.

staph·y·lo·coc·cus /ˌstaf(ə)lōˈkäkəs/ ▶ **n.** (pl. **staphylococci** /-ˈkäkˌsī, -ˌsē/) a bacterium of a genus that includes many pathogenic kinds that cause pus formation, esp. in the skin and mucous membranes. ● Genus *Staphylococcus*; Gram-positive cocci in clusters.
– DERIVATIVES **staph·y·lo·coc·cal** /-ˈkäkəl/ **adj.**
– ORIGIN modern Latin, from Greek *staphulē* 'bunch of grapes' + *kokkos* 'berry.'

sta·ple¹ /ˈstāpəl/ ▶ **n.** a piece of bent metal or wire pushed through something or clipped over it as a fastening, in particular: ■ a piece of thin wire with a long center portion and two short end pieces that are driven by a stapler through sheets of paper to fasten them together. ■ a small U-shaped metal bar with pointed ends for driving into wood to hold attachments such as electric wires, battens, or sheets of cloth in place.
▶ **v.** [with obj.] attach or secure with a staple or staples: *Mark stapled a batch of papers together.*
– ORIGIN Old English *stapol*, of Germanic origin; related to Dutch *stapel* 'pillar' (a sense reflected in English in early use).

sta·ple² ▶ **n. 1** a main or important element of something, esp. of a diet: *bread, milk, and other staples | Greek legend was the staple of classical tragedy.* ■ a main item of trade or production: *rubber became the staple of the Malayan economy.*
2 the fiber of cotton or wool considered with regard to its length and degree of fineness: [in combination] *jackets made from long-staple Egyptian cotton.*
3 [often with modifier] historical a center of trade, esp. in a specified commodity: *proposals were made for a wool staple at Pisa.*
▶ **adj.** [attrib.] main or important, esp. in terms of consumption: *the staple foods of the poor* | figurative *violence is the staple diet of the video generation.* ■ most important in terms of trade or production: *rice was the staple crop grown in most villages.*
▶ **v.** [with obj.] sort or classify (wool, etc.) according to fiber.
– DERIVATIVES **stapled adj.** [in combination] *a long-stapled type of fiber.*
– ORIGIN Middle English (sense 3 of the noun): from Old French *estaple* 'market,' from Middle Low German and Middle Dutch *stapel* 'pillar, emporium'; related to **STAPLE¹**.

sta·ple gun ▶ **n.** a handheld mechanical tool for driving staples into a hard surface.

sta·pler /ˈstāp(ə)lər/ ▶ **n.** a device for fastening together sheets of paper with a staple or staples.

star /stär/ ▶ **n. 1** a fixed luminous point in the night sky that is a large, remote incandescent body like the sun.

> True stars were formerly known as the **fixed stars**, to distinguish them from the planets or **wandering stars**. They are gaseous spheres consisting primarily of hydrogen and helium, there being an equilibrium between the compressional force of gravity and the outward pressure of radiation resulting from internal thermonuclear fusion reactions. Some six thousand stars are visible to the naked eye, but there are actually more than a hundred billion in our own Galaxy, while billions of other galaxies are known.

2 a conventional or stylized representation of a star, typically one having five or more points: *the walls were painted with silver moons and stars.* ■ a symbol of this shape used to indicate a category of excellence: *the hotel has three stars.* ■ an asterisk. ■ a white patch on the forehead of a horse or other animal. ■ (also **star network**) [usu. as modifier] a data or communication network in which all nodes are independently connected to one central unit: *computers in a star layout.*
3 a famous or exceptionally talented performer in the world of entertainment or sports: *a pop star* | [as modifier] *singers of star quality.* ■ an outstandingly good or successful person or thing in a group: *a rising star in the party* | [as modifier] *Ellen was a star student.*
4 Astrology a planet, constellation, or configuration regarded as influencing someone's fortunes or personality: *his golf destiny was written in the stars.* ■ (**stars**) a horoscope published in a newspaper or magazine: *what do my stars say?*
▶ **v.** (**stars, starring, starred**) [with obj.] **1** (of a movie, play, or other show) have (someone) as a principal performer: *a film starring Liza Minnelli.* ■ [no obj.] (of a performer) have a principal role in a movie, play, or other show: *McQueen had starred in such epics as The Magnificent Seven* | (as adj. **starring**) *his first starring role.* ■ [no obj.] (of a person) perform brilliantly or prominently in a particular endeavor or event: *Vitt starred at third base for the Detroit Tigers.*
2 decorate or cover with star-shaped marks or objects: *thick grass starred with flowers.* ■ mark (something) for special notice or recommendation with an asterisk or other star-shaped symbol: *the activities listed below are starred according to their fitness ratings* | [as adj., in combination] (**-starred**) *Michelin-starred restaurants.*
– PHRASES **my stars!** informal, dated an expression of astonishment. **reach for the stars** have high or ambitious aims. **see stars** see flashes of light, esp. as a result of being hit on the head. **someone's star is rising** see **RISE**. **stars in one's eyes** used to describe someone who is idealistically hopeful or enthusiastic about their future: *a singer selected from hundreds of applicants with stars in their eyes.*

– DERIVATIVES **star·less** adj., **star·like** /-ˌlīk/ adj.
– ORIGIN Old English *steorra*, of Germanic origin; related to Dutch *ster*, German *Stern*, from an Indo-European root shared by Latin *stella* and Greek *astēr*.

star an·ise ▶ n. **1** a small star-shaped fruit with one seed in each arm. It has an aniseed flavor and is used unripe as a spice in Asian cooking.
2 the small Chinese evergreen tree from which this spice is obtained. Also called **CHINESE ANISE**. ● *Illicium verum*, family Illiciaceae.

star ap·ple ▶ n. an edible purple fruit with a star-shaped cross section. ● This is produced by the evergreen tropical American tree *Chrysophyllum cainito* (family Sapotaceae).

Sta·ra Za·go·ra /ˈstärə zəˈgôrə/ a city in east central Bulgaria; pop. 140,710 (2008).

star·board /ˈstärˌbôrd/ ▶ n. the side of a ship or aircraft that is on the right when one is facing forward. The opposite of **PORT**[3].
▶ v. [with obj.] turn (a ship or its helm) to starboard.
– ORIGIN Old English *stēorbord* 'rudder side' (see **STEER**[1], **BOARD**), because early Teutonic sailing vessels were steered with a paddle over the right side.

star·board watch ▶ n. see **WATCH** (sense 2 of the noun).

star·burst /ˈstärˌbərst/ ▶ n. a pattern of lines or rays radiating from a central object or source of light: [as modifier] *a starburst pattern*. ■ an explosion producing such an effect. ■ a camera lens attachment that produces a pattern of rays around the image of a source of light. ■ a period of intense activity in a galaxy involving the formation of stars.

starch /stärCH/ ▶ n. **1** an odorless tasteless white substance occurring widely in plant tissue and obtained chiefly from cereals and potatoes. It is a polysaccharide that functions as a carbohydrate store and is an important constituent of the human diet. ■ food containing this substance.
2 powder or spray made from this substance and used before ironing to stiffen fabric or clothing.
3 stiffness of manner or character: *the starch in her voice*.
▶ v. [with obj.] **1** stiffen (fabric or clothing) with starch: (as adj. **starched**) *his immaculately starched shirt*.
2 informal (of a boxer) defeat (an opponent) by a knockout: *Domenge starched Geddami in the first*.
– PHRASES **take the starch out of someone** deflate or humiliate someone.
– DERIVATIVES **starch·er** n.
– ORIGIN Old English (recorded only in the past participle *sterced* 'stiffened'), of Germanic origin; related to Dutch *sterken*, German *stärken* 'strengthen,' also to **STARK**.

Star Cham·ber an English court of civil and criminal jurisdiction that developed in the late 15th century, trying esp. those cases affecting the interests of the Crown. It was noted for its arbitrary and oppressive judgments and was abolished in 1641.

starch·y /ˈstärCHē/ ▶ adj. (**starchier**, **starchiest**)
1 (of food or diet) containing a relatively high amount of starch.
2 (of clothing) stiff with starch. ■ informal very stiff, formal, or prim in manner or character: *the manager is usually a bit starchy*.
– DERIVATIVES **starch·i·ly** /-CHəlē/ adv., **starch·i·ness** n.

star cloud ▶ n. a region where stars appear to be especially numerous and close together.

star-crossed ▶ adj. literary (of a person or a plan) thwarted by bad luck.

star·dom /ˈstärdəm/ ▶ n. the state or status of being a famous or exceptionally talented performer in the world of entertainment or sports.

star·dust /ˈstärˌdəst/ ▶ n. (esp. in the context of success in the world of entertainment or sports) a magical or charismatic quality or feeling: *a gang of Hollywood stars anointing us with sparkling stardust*.

stare /ste(ə)r/ ▶ v. [no obj.] look fixedly or vacantly at someone or something with one's eyes wide open: *he stared at her in amazement* | *Robin sat staring into space, her mind numb*. ■ (of a person's eyes) be wide open, with a fixed or vacant expression: *her gray eyes stared back at him*. ■ (of a thing) be unpleasantly prominent or striking: *the obituaries stared out at us*.
▶ n. a long fixed or vacant look: *she gave him a cold stare*.
– PHRASES **be staring something in the face** be on the verge of something inevitable or inescapable: *our team was staring defeat in the face*. **stare someone in the eye** (or **face**) look fixedly or boldly at someone. **stare someone in the face** be glaringly apparent or obvious: *the answer had been staring him in the face*.
– PHRASAL VERBS **stare someone down** look fixedly at someone until they feel forced to lower their eyes or turn away.
– DERIVATIVES **star·er** n.
– ORIGIN Old English *starian*, of Germanic origin, from a base meaning 'be rigid.'

sta·re de·ci·sis /ˈste(ə)rē diˈsīsis/ ▶ n. Law the legal principle of determining points in litigation according to precedent.
– ORIGIN Latin, literally 'stand by things decided.'

star·fish /ˈstärˌfiSH/ ▶ n. (pl. **same** or **starfishes**) a marine echinoderm with five or more radiating arms. The undersides of the arms bear tube feet for locomotion and, in predatory species, for opening the shells of mollusks. ● Class Asteroidea.

star·flow·er /ˈstärˌflou(-ə)r/ ▶ n. a plant with starlike flowers, in particular: ● a small North American woodland plant (*Trientalis borealis*, family Primulaceae). ● a star-of-Bethlehem.

star fruit (also **starfruit**) ▶ n. another term for **CARAMBOLA**.

star·gaz·er /ˈstärˌgāzər/ ▶ n. **1** informal an astronomer or astrologer. ■ a daydreamer.
2 a fish of warm seas that normally lies buried in the sand with only its eyes, which are on top of the head, protruding. ● a widely distributed fish that has electric organs (family Uranoscopidae: several genera). ● (**sand stargazer**) a western Atlantic fish (family Dactyloscopidae: several genera).
– DERIVATIVES **star·gaze** v.

Star·gell /ˈstärjəl/, Willie (1940–2001), US baseball player; full name *Wilver Dornell Stargell*. With the Pittsburgh Pirates 1962–82, he was noted for his hitting ability. Baseball Hall of Fame (1988).

stark /stärk/ ▶ adj. **1** severe or bare in appearance or outline: *the ridge formed a stark silhouette against the sky*. ■ unpleasantly or sharply clear; impossible to avoid: *his position on civil rights is **in stark contrast to** that of his liberal opponent* | *the stark reality of life for deprived minorities*.
2 [attrib.] complete; sheer: *he came running back in stark terror*. ■ rare completely naked.
3 archaic or literary stiff, rigid, or incapable of movement: *a human body lying stiff and stark by the stream*. ■ physically strong or powerful: *the dragoons were stark fellows*.
– PHRASES **stark naked** completely naked. **stark raving mad** informal completely crazy.
– DERIVATIVES **stark·ly** adv. [as submodifier] *the reality is starkly different*, **stark·ness** n.
– ORIGIN Old English *stearc* 'unyielding, severe,' of Germanic origin; related to Dutch *sterk* and German *stark* 'strong.'

Stark ef·fect /stärk/ ▶ n. Physics the splitting of a spectrum line into several components by the application of an electric field.
– ORIGIN early 20th cent.: named after Johannes *Stark* (1874–1957), German physicist.

stark·ers /ˈstärkərz/ ▶ adj. [predic.] informal, chiefly Brit.
1 completely naked: *they ran starkers across the stage!*
2 mad; crazy: *his lifestyle would **drive me starkers***.

star·let /ˈstärlit/ ▶ n. informal a young actress with aspirations to become a star: *a Hollywood starlet*.

star·light /ˈstärˌlīt/ ▶ n. the light that comes from the stars.

Star·ling /ˈstärliNG/, Ernest Henry (1866–1927), English physiologist and founder of the science of endocrinology. He demonstrated the existence of peristalsis and coined the term *hormone* for the substance secreted by the pancreas that stimulates the secretion of digestive juices.

star·ling[1] /ˈstärliNG/ ▶ n. a gregarious Old World songbird with a straight bill, typically with dark lustrous or iridescent plumage but sometimes brightly colored. ● Family Sturnidae (the **starling family**): many genera and numerous species, in particular the speckled **common** (or **European**) **starling** (*Sturnus vulgaris*), widely introduced elsewhere. The starling family also includes the mynahs, grackles, and (usually) the oxpeckers.
– ORIGIN Old English *stærlinc*, from *stær* 'starling' (of Germanic origin) + **-LING**.

star·ling[2] ▶ n. a wooden pile erected with others around or just upstream of a bridge or pier to protect it from the current or floating objects.
– ORIGIN late 17th cent.: perhaps a corruption of dialect *staddling* 'staddle.'

star·lit /ˈstärˌlit/ ▶ adj. lit or made brighter by stars: *a clear starlit night*.

star net·work ▶ n. another term for **STAR** (sense 2 of the noun).

star-nosed mole ▶ n. a mole with a number of fleshy radiating tentacles around its nostrils, native to northeastern North America. ● *Condylura cristata*, family Talpidae.

Star of Beth·le·hem ▶ n. a resplendent star that is said to have guided the Magi to the birthplace of the infant Jesus.

star-of-Beth·le·hem ▶ n. a plant of the lily family with star-shaped flowers that typically have green stripes on the outer surface, native to the temperate regions of the Old World. ● Genera *Ornithogalum* and *Gagea*, family Liliaceae: several species, including the white-flowered *O. umbellatum* and the yellow-flowered *G. luteum*.

Star of Da·vid ▶ n. a six-pointed figure consisting of two interlaced equilateral triangles, used as a Jewish and Israeli symbol. Also called **MAGEN DAVID**.

Star of David

Starr[1] /stär/, Bart (1934–), US football player; full name *Bryan Bartlett Starr*. A quarterback with the Greenbay Packers 1956–72, he led them to NFL championships 1965–68 and to Super Bowl wins in 1967 and 1968. Football Hall of Fame (1977).

Starr[2], Ringo (1940–), English rock and pop drummer; born *Richard Starkey*. He was the drummer for the Beatles, and occasionally a singer. After the band split up in 1970, he pursued a solo career as a musician, singer, and actor.

star route ▶ n. a postal delivery route served by a private contractor.
– ORIGIN from the use of a star or asterisk to mark the routes in postal records.

star ru·by ▶ n. a cabochon ruby reflecting an opalescent starlike image owing to its regular internal structure.

star·ry /ˈstärē/ ▶ adj. (**starrier**, **starriest**) full of or lit by stars: *a starry sky*. ■ resembling a star in brightness or shape: *tiny white starry flowers*.
– DERIVATIVES **star·ri·ness** n.

star·ry-eyed ▶ adj. naively enthusiastic or idealistic; failing to recognize the practical realities of a situation.

Stars and Bars ▶ plural n. [treated as sing.] historical the flag of the Confederate States of America. It had a horizontal white stripe between two red stripes, and in the upper left corner was a blue field with a circle of seven white stars, one for each of the original seven seceded states.

Stars and Stripes ▶ plural n. [treated as sing.] the national flag of the US. It has 13 horizontal stripes, alternating red and white, which represent the original Thirteen Colonies. In the upper left corner is a field of blue with 50 white stars, which represent the 50 states.

star sap·phire ▶ n. a cabochon sapphire that reflects a starlike image resulting from its regular internal structure.

star shell ▶ n. an explosive projectile designed to burst in the air and light up an enemy's position.

star·ship /ˈstärˌSHip/ ▶ n. (in science fiction) a large manned spaceship used for interstellar travel.

star-span·gled ▶ adj. literary covered, glittering, or decorated with stars: *the star-spangled horizon*. ■ glitteringly successful: *a star-spangled career*. ■ used humorously with reference to the US national flag and a perceived American identity: *star-spangled decency*.

Star-Span·gled Ban·ner the US national anthem, officially adopted in 1931. The words were written in 1814 by **Francis Scott Key** as a poem originally titled "Defence of Fort M'Henry" and were later put to a tune adapted from a popular English drinking song, "To Anacreon in Heaven."

star stream ▶ n. Astronomy a systematic drift of stars in the same general direction within a galaxy.

star-struck ▶ adj. fascinated or greatly impressed by famous people, esp. those connected with the entertainment industry: *I was a star-struck teenager*.

star-stud·ded ▶ adj. **1** (of the night sky) filled with stars.
2 informal featuring a number of famous people, esp. actors or sports players: *a star-studded cast*.

star sys·tem ▶ n. **1** a large number of stars with a perceptible structure; a galaxy.
2 the practice of promoting or otherwise favoring individuals who have become famous and popular, in particular in the motion-picture industry.

START /stärt/ ▶ abbr. Strategic Arms Reduction Talks.

start /stärt/ ▶ **v. 1** [no obj.] come into being; begin or be reckoned from a particular point in time or space: *the season starts in September* | *we ate before the show started* | *below Roaring Springs the real desert starts.* ■ [with infinitive or present participle] embark on a continuing action or a new venture: *I started to chat to him* | *we plan to start building in the fall.* ■ use a particular point, action, or circumstance as an opening for a course of action: *the teacher can* ***start*** *by capitalizing on children's curiosity* | *I shall* ***start with*** *the case you mention first.* ■ begin to move or travel: *we started out into the snow* | *he started for the door.* ■ [with obj.] begin to attend (an educational establishment) or engage in (an occupation, esp. a profession): *she will start school today* | *he started work at a travel agency.* ■ begin one's working life: *he started as a typesetter* | *she* ***started off*** *as a general practitioner.* ■ [with obj.] begin to live through (a period distinguished by a specified characteristic): *they started their married life.* ■ cost at least a specified amount: *fees* ***start at*** *around $300.*
2 [with obj.] cause (an event or process) to happen: *two men started the blaze that caused the explosion* | *those women started all the trouble.* ■ bring (a project or an institution) into being; cause to take effect or begin to work or operate: *I'm starting a campaign to get the law changed.* ■ cause (a machine) to begin to work: *we had trouble starting the car* | *he* ***starts up*** *his van.* ■ [no obj.] (of a machine or device) begin operating or being used: *the noise of a tractor* ***starting up*** | *there was a moment of silence before the organ started.* ■ cause or enable (someone or something) to begin doing or pursuing something: *his father* ***started*** *him* ***off*** *in business* | *what he said started me thinking.* ■ give a signal to (competitors) to start in a race.
3 [no obj.] give a small jump or make a sudden jerking movement from surprise or alarm: *"Oh my!" she said, starting.* ■ literary move or appear suddenly: *she had seen Meg start suddenly from a thicket.* ■ (of eyes) bulge so as to appear to burst out of their sockets: *his eyes* ***started out of*** *his head like a hare's.* ■ be displaced or displace by pressure or shrinkage: *the mortar in the joints had started.* ■ [with obj.] rouse (game) from its lair.
▶ **n.** [in sing.] **1** the point in time or space at which something has its origin; the beginning of something: *he takes over as chief executive at the start of next year* | *the event was a shambles from start to finish* | *his bicycle was found close to the start of a forest trail.* ■ the point or moment at which a race begins. ■ an act of beginning to do or deal with something: *I can* ***make a start on*** *cleaning up* | *an early start enabled us to avoid the traffic.* ■ used to indicate that a useful initial contribution has been made but that more remains to be done: *if he would tell her who had put him up to it, it would be a start.* ■ a person's position or circumstances at the beginning of their life, esp. a position of advantage: *she's anxious to give her baby the best* ***start in life.*** ■ an advantage consisting in having set out in a race or on journey earlier than one's rivals or opponents: *he would have a ninety-minute* ***start on*** *them.*
2 a sudden movement of surprise or alarm: *she awoke* ***with a start*** | *the woman* ***gave a*** *nervous* ***start.***
– PHRASES **don't start** (or **don't you start**) informal used to tell someone not to grumble or criticize: *don't start—I do my fair share.* **for a start** informal used to introduce or emphasize the first or most important of a number of considerations: *this side is at an advantage—for a start, there are more of them.* **get the start of** dated gain an advantage over. **start a family** conceive one's first child. **start something** informal cause trouble. **to start with** at the beginning of a series of events or period of time: *she wasn't very keen on the idea to start with.* ■ as the first thing to be taken into account: *to start with, I was feeling down.*
– PHRASAL VERBS **start again** chiefly Brit. another way of saying START OVER. **start in** informal begin doing something, esp. talking: *people groan when she starts in about her acting ambitions.* ■ (**start in on**) begin to do or deal with: *you vacuum the stairs and I'll start in on the laundry.* ■ (**start in on**) attack verbally; begin to criticize: *before you start in on me, let me explain.* **start off** (or **start someone/something off**) begin (or cause someone or something to begin) working, operating, or dealing with something: *treatment should start off with attention to diet* | *what started you off on this search?* ■ (**start off**) begin a meal: *she started off with soup.* **start on 1** begin to work on or deal with: *I'm starting on a new book.* **2** informal begin to talk to someone, esp. in a critical or hostile way: *she started on about my not having nice furniture.* **start out** (or **up**) embark on a venture or undertaking, esp. a commercial one: *the company will start out with a hundred employees.* **start over** make a new beginning: *could you face going back to school and starting over?*
– ORIGIN Old English *styrtan* 'to caper, leap,' of Germanic origin; related to Dutch *storten* 'push' and German *stürzen* 'fall headlong, fling.' From the sense 'sudden movement' arose the sense 'initiation of movement, setting out on a journey' and hence 'beginning (of a process, etc).'

start·er /ˈstärtər/ ▶ **n. 1** [with adj.] a person or thing that starts in a specified way: *he was a* ***late starter*** *in photography* | *I'm just a* ***slow starter.*** ■ a person who gives the signal for the start of a race. ■ [with adj.] a horse, competitor, or player taking part in a race or game at the start: *the trainer has confirmed Cool Ground as a definite starter.* ■ Baseball the pitcher who starts the game. ■ Baseball a pitcher who normally starts games, and seldom is used as a relief pitcher. ■ a topic, question, or other item with which to start a group discussion or course of study: *material to act as a* ***starter for*** *discussion.*
2 an automatic device for starting a machine, esp. the engine of a vehicle.
3 chiefly Brit. the first course of a meal; an appetizer.
4 (also **starter culture**) a bacterial culture used to initiate souring in making yogurt, cheese, or butter. ■ a preparation of chemicals to initiate the breakdown of vegetable matter in making compost.
– PHRASES **for starters** informal first of all; to start with.

start·er home ▶ **n.** a relatively small, economical house or condominium that meets the requirements of young people buying their first home.

start·er kit (also **starter set** or **starter pack**) ▶ **n.** a set of articles or equipment providing the essential items and instructions for taking up a particular activity or process for the first time.

start·er mar·riage ▶ **n.** informal a short-lived first marriage between young people that produces no offspring.

start·ing block ▶ **n.** (usu. **starting blocks**) a shaped rigid block for bracing the feet of a runner at the start of a race.

start·ing gate ▶ **n.** (usu. **the starting gate**) a restraining structure incorporating a barrier that is raised at the start of a race, typically in horse racing and skiing, to ensure a simultaneous start.

start·ing pis·tol ▶ **n.** a pistol used to give the signal for the start of a race.

star·tle /ˈstärtl/ ▶ **v.** [with obj.] cause (a person or animal) to feel sudden shock or alarm: *a sudden sound in the doorway startled her* | [with infinitive] *he was startled to see a column of smoke.*
– DERIVATIVES **star·tler n.**
– ORIGIN Old English *steartlian* 'kick, struggle,' from the base of START. The early sense gave rise to 'move quickly, caper' (typically said of cattle), whence '(cause to) react with fear' (late 16th cent).

star·tling /ˈstärtl-iNG/ ▶ **adj.** very surprising, astonishing, or remarkable: *he bore a startling likeness to their father* | *she had startling blue eyes.*
– DERIVATIVES **star·tling·ly adv.** [as submodifier] *a startlingly good memory.*

start-up (also **startup** /ˈstärt,əp/) ▶ **n.** the action or process of setting something in motion: *the start-up of marketing in Europe* | [as modifier] *start-up costs.* ■ a newly established business: *problems facing start-ups and small firms in rural areas.*

star turn ▶ **n.** the person or act that gives the most heralded or impressive performance in a program.

star·va·tion /stärˈvāSHən/ ▶ **n.** suffering or death caused by hunger: *thousands died of starvation.*

starve /stärv/ ▶ **v.** [no obj.] **1** (of a person or animal) suffer severely or die from hunger: *she left her animals to starve* | *seven million* ***starved to death*** | (as adj. **starving**) *the world's starving children.* ■ [with obj.] cause (a person or animal) to suffer severely or die from hunger: *for a while she had considered starving herself.* ■ (**be starving** or **starved**) informal feel very hungry: *I don't know about you, but I'm starving.* ■ (**starve someone out** or **into**) force someone out of a place or into a specified state by stopping supplies of food: *the Royalists were starved out after eleven days* | *German U-boats hoping to starve Britain into submission.* ■ [with obj.] (usu. **be starved of** or **for**) deprive of something necessary: *the arts are being starved of funds.*
2 archaic be freezing cold: *pull down that window for we are perfectly starving here.*
– ORIGIN Old English *steorfan* 'to die,' of Germanic origin, probably from a base meaning 'be rigid' (compare with STARE); related to Dutch *sterven* and German *sterben.*

starve·ling /ˈstärvliNG/ archaic ▶ **n.** an undernourished or emaciated person or animal.
▶ **adj.** (of a person or animal) lacking enough food; emaciated: *a starveling child.*

star·wort /ˈstärwərt, -,wôrt/ ▶ **n.** any of a number of plants with starlike flowers or leaves. ● *Stellaria* (family Caryophyllaceae), *Callitriche* (family Callitrichaceae), and other genera: several species, including the **lesser stitchwort** (*S. graminea*).

stash[1] /staSH/ informal ▶ **v.** [with obj.] store (something) safely and secretly in a specified place: *their wealth had been* ***stashed away*** *in Swiss banks.*
▶ **n. 1** a secret store of something: *the man grudgingly handed over a* ***stash of*** *notes.* ■ a quantity of an illegal drug, esp. one kept for personal use: *one prisoner tried to swallow his stash.*
2 dated a hiding place or hideout.
– ORIGIN late 18th cent.: of unknown origin.

stash[2] ▶ **n.** informal a mustache.
– ORIGIN 1940s: shortened form.

Sta·si /ˈstäzē/ the internal security force of the former German Democratic Republic, abolished in 1989.
– ORIGIN German, from *Sta(ats)si(cherheitsdienst)* 'state security service.'

sta·sis /ˈstāsis/ ▶ **n.** formal or technical **1** a period or state of inactivity or equilibrium. ■ Medicine a stoppage of flow of a body fluid.
2 civil strife.
– ORIGIN mid 18th cent.: modern Latin, from Greek, literally 'standing, stoppage,' from *sta-*, base of *histanai* 'to stand.'

-stasis ▶ **comb. form** (pl. **-stases**) Physiology slowing down; stopping: *hemostasis.*
– ORIGIN from Greek *stasis* 'standing, stoppage.'

stat[1] /stat/ informal ▶ **abbr.** ■ photostat. ■ statistic. ■ statistics: [as adj.] *a stat sheet.* ■ thermostat.

stat[2] ▶ **adv.** (in a medical direction or prescription) immediately.
– ORIGIN late 19th cent.: abbreviation of Latin *statim.*

stat. ▶ **abbr.** ■ (in prescriptions) immediately. [from Latin *statim.*] ■ statuary. ■ statue. ■ statute.

-stat ▶ **comb. form** denoting instruments, substances, etc., maintaining a controlled state: *thermostat* | *hemostat.*
– ORIGIN partly from (*helio*)*stat*, partly a back-formation from STATIC.

sta·tant /ˈstātnt/ ▶ **adj.** [usu. postpositive] Heraldry (of an animal) standing with all four paws on the ground.
– ORIGIN late 15th cent.: formed irregularly from Latin *stat-* 'fixed, stationary' (from the verb *stare* 'to stand') + -ANT.

state /stāt/ ▶ **n. 1** the particular condition that someone or something is in at a specific time: *the state of the company's finances* | *we're worried about her* ***state of mind.*** ■ a physical condition as regards internal or molecular form or structure: *water in a liquid state.* ■ [in sing.] (**a state**) informal an agitated or anxious condition: *don't* ***get into a state.*** ■ [in sing.] informal a dirty or untidy condition: *look at the state of you—what a mess!* ■ Physics short for QUANTUM STATE.
2 a nation or territory considered as an organized political community under one government: *Germany, Italy, and other European states.* ■ an organized political community or area forming part of a federal republic: *the German state of Bavaria.* ■ (**the States**) informal term for UNITED STATES.
3 the civil government of a country: *services provided by the state* | [in combination] *state-owned companies* | *King Fahd appointed a council to advise him on* ***affairs of state.*** ■ (**the States**) the legislative body in Jersey, Guernsey, and Alderney.
4 pomp and ceremony associated with monarchy or high levels of government: *he was buried* ***in state.***
5 [usu. with modifier] an impression taken from an etched or engraved plate at a particular stage. ■ a particular printed version of the first edition of a book, distinguished from others by prepublication changes.
▶ **adj.** [attrib.] **1** of, provided by, or concerned with the civil government of a country: *the future of state education* | *a state secret.*
2 used or done on ceremonial occasions; involving the ceremony associated with a head of state: *a state visit to Hungary by Queen Elizabeth.*
▶ **v. 1** [reporting verb] express something definitely or clearly in speech or writing: [with clause] *the report stated that more than 51 percent of voters failed to participate* | [with direct speech] *"Money hasn't changed me," she stated firmly* | [with obj.] *people will be invited to state their views.* ■ [with obj.] chiefly Law specify the facts of (a case) for consideration: *judges must give both sides an equal opportunity to state their case.*
2 [with obj.] Music present or introduce (a theme or melody) in a composition.
– PHRASES **state of affairs** (or **things**) a situation or set of circumstances: *the survey revealed a sorry state of affairs in schools.* **state of the art** the most recent stage in the development of a product, incorporating the newest ideas and the most up-to-date features. ■ (as adj. **state-of-the-art**) incorporating the newest ideas and the most up-to-date features: *a new state-of-the-art hospital.* **state of emergency** a situation of national danger or disaster in which a government suspends normal constitutional procedures in order to regain control: *the government has declared a state*

S

of emergency. **state of grace** a condition of being free from sin. **state of life** (in religious contexts) a person's occupation, calling, or status. **state of war** a situation when war has been declared or is in progress.
– DERIVATIVES **stat·a·ble adj.**
– ORIGIN Middle English (as a noun): partly a shortening of ESTATE, partly from Latin *status* 'manner of standing, condition' (see STATUS). The current verb senses date from the mid 17th cent.

state cap·i·tal·ism ▶ **n.** a political system in which the state has control of production and the use of capital.

State Col·lege a borough in central Pennsylvania, in the Nittany Valley, home to Pennsylvania State University; pop. 39,419 (est. 2008).

state·craft /ˈstātˌkraft/ ▶ **n.** the skillful management of state affairs; statesmanship: *issues of statecraft require great deliberation.*

stat·ed /ˈstātid/ ▶ **adj.** clearly expressed or identified; specified: *the stated aim of the program* | *do not exceed the stated dose.*

State De·part·ment the department in the US government dealing with foreign affairs.

state·hood /ˈstātˌho͝od/ ▶ **n.** the status of being a recognized independent nation: *the transition from late colonialism to political statehood.* ■ the status of being a state of the US: *a proposed referendum on statehood for Puerto Rico.*

state house (also **statehouse**) ▶ **n.** the building where a state legislature meets.

state·less /ˈstātlis/ ▶ **adj.** (of a person) not recognized as a citizen of any country.
– DERIVATIVES **state·less·ness** /ˈstātlisnis/ **n.**

state·let /ˈstātlit/ ▶ **n.** a small state, esp. one that is closely affiliated with or has emerged from the breakup of a larger state.

state·ly /ˈstātlē/ ▶ **adj.** (**statelier, stateliest**) having a dignified, unhurried, and grand manner; majestic in manner and appearance: *a stately procession* | *his tall and stately wife.*
– DERIVATIVES **state·li·ness n.**

state·ly home ▶ **n.** Brit. a large and fine house that is occupied or was formerly occupied by an aristocratic family.

state ma·chine ▶ **n.** Electronics a device that can be in one of a set number of stable conditions depending on its previous condition and on the present values of its inputs.

state·ment /ˈstātmənt/ ▶ **n.** a definite or clear expression of something in speech or writing: *do you agree with this statement?* | *this is correct as a statement of fact.* ■ an official account of facts, views, or plans, esp. one for release to the media: *the officials issued a joint statement calling for negotiations.* ■ a formal account of events given by a witness, defendant, or other party to the police or in a court of law: *she made a statement to the police.* ■ a document setting out items of debit and credit between a bank or other organization and a customer. ■ the expression of an idea or opinion through something other than words: *their humorous kitschiness makes a statement of serious wealth.* ■ Music the occurrence of a musical idea or motive within a composition: *a carefully structured musical and dramatic progression from the first statement of this theme.*

Stat·en Is·land /ˈstatn/ an island borough of New York City, in the southwestern part of the city; pop. 443,728 (2000).
– ORIGIN named after the *Staten* or States General of the Netherlands.

State of the Un·ion mes·sage (also **State of the Union address**) ▶ **n.** a yearly address delivered in January by the president of the US to Congress, giving the administration's view of the state of the nation and plans for legislation.

stat·er /ˈstātər/ ▶ **n.** historical an ancient Greek gold or silver coin.
– ORIGIN via late Latin from Greek *statēr*, from a base meaning 'weigh.'

state·room /ˈstātˌro͞om, -ˌro͝om/ ▶ **n.** a private compartment on a ship. ■ a captain's or superior officer's room on a ship. ■ a private compartment on a train. ■ a large room in a palace or public building, for use on formal occasions.

state's at·tor·ney ▶ **n.** a lawyer representing a state in court.

state school ▶ **n.** another term for STATE UNIVERSITY. ■ Brit. a school that is funded and controlled by the government and for which no fees are charged.

state se·cret ▶ **n.** a sensitive issue or piece of information that is kept secret by the government, usually to protect the public. ■ humorous a piece of information, usually of a trivial or personal nature, that is closely guarded and desired to be kept private: *she thought her affair with the boss was a state secret, but we all giggled about it behind her back.*

state's ev·i·dence ▶ **n.** Law evidence for the prosecution given by a participant in or accomplice to the crime being tried.
– PHRASES **turn state's evidence** give such evidence: *persuading one-time gang members to turn state's evidence.*

States-Gen·er·al ▶ **n.** **1** the bicameral legislative body in the Netherlands.
2 (also **Estates General**) historical the legislative body in France until 1789, representing the three estates of the realm (i.e., the clergy, the nobility, and the commons).

state·side /ˈstātˌsīd/ ▶ **adj. & adv.** informal of, in, or toward the US (used in reference to the US from elsewhere or from the geographically separate states of Alaska and Hawaii): [as adj.] *stateside police departments* | [as adv.] *they were headed stateside.*

states·man /ˈstātsmən/ ▶ **n.** (pl. **statesmen**) a skilled, experienced, and respected political leader or figure.
– DERIVATIVES **states·man·like** /-ˌlīk/ **adj.**, **states·man·ship** /-ˌship/ **n.**
– ORIGIN late 16th cent.: from *state's man*, translating French *homme d'état.*

state so·cial·ism ▶ **n.** a political system in which the state has control of industries and services.

states·per·son /ˈstātsˌpərsən/ ▶ **n.** (pl. **statespersons** or **statespeople**) a statesman or stateswoman (used as a neutral alternative).

states' rights ▶ **plural n.** the rights and powers held by individual US states rather than by the federal government.

States' Rights Dem·o·cra·tic Party ▶ **n.** a political party formed in 1948 advocating states' rights and opposing the presidential candidacy of Harry S Truman.

states·wom·an /ˈstātsˌwo͝omən/ ▶ **n.** (pl. **stateswomen**) a skilled, experienced, and respected female political leader.

state u·ni·ver·si·ty ▶ **n.** a university managed by the public authorities of a particular US state.

state vec·tor ▶ **n.** Physics a vector in a space whose dimensions correspond to all the independent wave functions of a system, the instantaneous value of the vector conveying all possible information about the state of the system at that instant.

state vis·it ▶ **n.** a ceremonial visit to a foreign country by a head of state.

state·wide /ˈstātˈwīd/ ▶ **adj. & adv.** extending throughout a particular US state: [as adj.] *a statewide health system* | [as adv.] *two stations will broadcast the final statewide.*

stat·ic /ˈstatik/ ▶ **adj.** **1** lacking in movement, action, or change, esp. in a way viewed as undesirable or uninteresting: *demand has grown in what was a fairly static market* | *the whole ballet appeared too static.* ■ Computing (of a process or variable) not able to be changed during a set period, for example, while a program is running.
2 Physics concerned with bodies at rest or forces in equilibrium. Often contrasted with DYNAMIC. ■ (of an electric charge) having gathered on or in an object that cannot conduct a current. ■ acting as weight but not moving. ■ of statics.
3 Computing (of a memory or store) not needing to be periodically refreshed by an applied voltage.
▶ **n.** crackling or hissing noises on a telephone, radio, or other telecommunications system. ■ short for STATIC ELECTRICITY. ■ informal angry or critical talk or behavior: *the reception was going sour, breaking up into static.*
– DERIVATIVES **stat·i·cal·ly** /-ik(ə)lē/ **adv.**, **stat·ick·y** /-ikē/ **adj.**
– ORIGIN late 16th cent. (denoting the science of weight and its effects): via modern Latin from Greek *statikē* (*tekhnē*) 'science of weighing'; the adjective from modern Latin *staticus*, from Greek *statikos* 'causing to stand,' from the verb *histanai.* Sense 1 of the adjective dates from the mid 19th cent.

-static ▶ **comb. form** in adjectives corresponding to nouns ending in *-stasis* (such as *hemostatic* corresponding to *hemostasis*).

stat·ic cling ▶ **n.** the adhering of a garment to the wearer's body or to another garment, caused by a buildup of static electricity.

stat·ice /ˈstatisē, ˈstatis/ ▶ **n.** another term for SEA LAVENDER, esp. when cultivated as a garden plant.
– ORIGIN mid 18th cent.: from modern Latin *statice* (former genus name), based on Greek, feminine of *statikos* 'causing to stand still' (with reference to medicinal use of the plant to stanch blood).

stat·ic e·lec·tric·i·ty ▶ **n.** a stationary electric charge, typically produced by friction, that causes sparks or crackling or the attraction of dust or hair.

stat·ic line ▶ **n.** a length of cord used instead of a ripcord for opening a parachute, attached at one end to the aircraft and temporarily snapped to the parachute at the other.

stat·ic pres·sure ▶ **n.** Physics the pressure of a fluid on a body when the body is at rest relative to the fluid.

stat·ics /ˈstatiks/ ▶ **plural n.** **1** [usu. treated as sing.] the branch of mechanics concerned with bodies at rest and forces in equilibrium. Compare with DYNAMICS (sense 1).
2 another term for STATIC.

stat·in /ˈstatn/ ▶ **n.** Medicine any of a group of drugs that act to reduce levels of fats, including triglycerides and cholesterol, in the blood.

sta·tion /ˈstāshən/ ▶ **n.** **1** a regular stopping place on a public transportation route, esp. one on a railroad line with a platform and often one or more buildings.
2 [usu. with modifier] a place or building where a specified activity or service is based: *a research station in the rain forest* | *coastal radar stations.* ■ a small military base, esp. of a specified kind: *a naval station.* ■ a police station. ■ a subsidiary post office. ■ Austral./NZ a large sheep or cattle farm.
3 [with adj.] a company involved in broadcasting of a specified kind: *a radio station.*
4 the place where someone or something stands or is placed on military or other duty: *the lookout resumed his station in the bow.* ■ dated one's social rank or position: *Karen was getting ideas above her station.*
5 Botany a particular site at which an interesting or rare plant grows.
6 short for STATIONS OF THE CROSS.
▶ **v.** [with obj.] put in or assign to a specified place for a particular purpose, esp. a military one: *troops were stationed in the town* | *a young girl had stationed herself by the door.*
– ORIGIN Middle English (as a noun): via Old French from Latin *statio(n-)*, from *stare* 'to stand.' Early use referred generally to 'position,' esp. 'position in life, status,' and specifically, in ecclesiastical use, to 'a holy place of pilgrimage (visited as one of a succession).' The verb dates from the late 16th cent.

sta·tion·ar·y /ˈstāshəˌnerē/ ▶ **adj.** not moving or not intended to be moved: *a car collided with a stationary vehicle.* ■ Astronomy (of a planet) having no apparent motion in longitude. ■ not changing in quantity or condition: *a stationary population.*
– ORIGIN late Middle English: from Latin *stationarius* (originally in the sense 'belonging to a military station'), from *station-* 'standing' (see STATION).

> **USAGE** The words **stationary** and **stationery** are often confused. **Stationary** is an adjective that means 'not moving or not intended to be moved,' as in *his car collided with a stationary vehicle*, whereas **stationery** is a noun that means 'writing and other office materials,' as in *I wrote to my father on the hotel stationery.*

sta·tion·ar·y bi·cy·cle (also **stationary bike**) ▶ **n.** an exercise bike.

sta·tion·ar·y en·gine ▶ **n.** an engine that remains in a fixed position, esp. one that drives generators or other machinery in a building.

sta·tion·ar·y state ▶ **n.** an unvarying condition in a physical process.

sta·tion·ar·y wave ▶ **n.** Physics another term for STANDING WAVE.

sta·tion bill ▶ **n.** a list showing the prescribed stations of a ship's crew in specified emergencies.

sta·tion break ▶ **n.** a pause between broadcast programs for an announcement of the identity of the station transmitting them, typically also containing commercials.

sta·tion·er /ˈstāsh(ə)nər/ ▶ **n.** a person or store selling paper, pens, and other writing and office materials.
– ORIGIN Middle English (in the sense 'bookseller'): from medieval Latin *stationarius* 'tradesman (at a fixed location, i.e., not itinerant).' Compare with STATIONARY.

sta·tion·er·y /ˈstāshəˌnerē/ ▶ **n.** writing paper, esp. with matching envelopes. ■ writing and other office materials.

> **USAGE** See usage at STATIONARY.

sta·tion house ▶ **n.** a police or fire station.

sta·tion·keep·ing /'stāsHən,kēpiNG/ ▶ **n.** the maintenance of a ship's proper position relative to others in a fleet.

sta·tion·mas·ter /'stāsHən,mastər/ ▶ **n.** an official in charge of a railroad station.

Sta·tions of the Cross ▶ **plural n.** a series of fourteen pictures or carvings representing successive incidents during Jesus' progress from his condemnation by Pilate to his crucifixion and burial, before which devotions are performed in some churches.

sta·tion wag·on ▶ **n.** a car with a longer body than usual, incorporating a large carrying area behind the seats and having an extra door at the rear for easy loading.

stat·ism /'stāt,izəm/ ▶ **n.** a political system in which the state has substantial centralized control over social and economic affairs: *the rise of authoritarian statism.*
– DERIVATIVES **stat·ist n. & adj.**

sta·tis·tic /stə'tistik/ ▶ **n.** a fact or piece of data from a study of a large quantity of numerical data: *the statistics show that the crime rate has increased.* ■ an event or person regarded as no more than such a piece of data (used to suggest an inappropriately impersonal approach): *he was just another statistic.*
▶ **adj.** another term for **STATISTICAL**.
– ORIGIN late 18th cent.: from German *statistisch* (adjective), *Statistik* (noun).

sta·tis·ti·cal /stə'tistikəl/ ▶ **adj.** of or relating to the use of statistics: *a statistical comparison.*
– DERIVATIVES **sta·tis·ti·cal·ly** /-ik(ə)lē/ **adv.** [sentence adverb] *these differences were not statistically significant.*

sta·tis·ti·cal in·fer·ence ▶ **n.** the theory, methods, and practice of forming judgments about the parameters of a population and the reliability of statistical relationships, typically on the basis of random sampling.

sta·tis·ti·cal me·chan·ics ▶ **plural n.** [treated as sing.] the description of physical phenomena in terms of a statistical treatment of the behavior of large numbers of atoms or molecules, esp. with regard to the distribution of energy among them.

sta·tis·ti·cal phys·ics ▶ **plural n.** [treated as sing.] a branch of physics concerned with large numbers of particles to which statistics can be applied.

sta·tis·ti·cal sig·nif·i·cance ▶ **n.** see **SIGNIFICANCE**.

sta·tis·ti·cal ta·bles ▶ **plural n.** the values of the cumulative distribution functions, probability functions, or probability density functions of certain common distributions presented as reference tables for different values of their parameters.

stat·is·ti·cian /,stati'stisHən/ ▶ **n.** an expert in the preparation and analysis of statistics.

sta·tis·tics /stə'tistiks/ ▶ **plural n.** [treated as sing.] the practice or science of collecting and analyzing numerical data in large quantities, esp. for the purpose of inferring proportions in a whole from those in a representative sample.

Sta·ti·us /'stāsH(ē)əs/, Publius Papinius (*c.* AD 45–96), Roman poet. He is best known for the *Silvae*, a miscellany of poems addressed to friends, and for the *Thebais*, an epic concerning the bloody quarrel between the sons of Oedipus.

sta·tive /'stātiv/ Linguistics ▶ **adj.** (of a verb) expressing a state or condition rather than an activity or event, such as *be* or *know*, as opposed to *run* or *grow*. Contrasted with **DYNAMIC**.
▶ **n.** a stative verb.
– ORIGIN mid 17th cent.: from Latin *stativus*, from *stat-* 'stopped, standing,' from the verb *stare*.

stato- ▶ **comb. form** relating to statics: *statocyst.*
– ORIGIN from Greek *statos* 'standing.'

stat·o·blast /'statə,blast/ ▶ **n.** Zoology (in bryozoans) a resistant reproductive body produced asexually.

stat·o·cyst /'statə,sist/ ▶ **n.** Zoology a small organ of balance and orientation in some aquatic invertebrates, consisting of a sensory vesicle or cell containing statoliths. Also called **OTOCYST**.

stat·o·lith /'statə,liTH/ ▶ **n.** Zoology a calcareous particle in the statocysts of invertebrates that stimulates sensory receptors in response to gravity, so enabling balance and orientation. ■ another term for **OTOLITH**.

sta·tor /'stātər/ ▶ **n.** the stationary portion of an electric generator or motor, esp. of an induction motor. ■ a row of small stationary airfoils attached to the casing of an axial-flow turbine, positioned between the rotors.
– ORIGIN late 19th cent.: from **STATIONARY**, on the pattern of *rotor*.

stat·o·scope /'statə,skōp/ ▶ **n.** a form of aneroid barometer for measuring minute variations of pressure, used esp. to indicate the altitude of an aircraft.
– ORIGIN early 20th cent.: from Greek *statos* 'standing' + **-SCOPE**.

stats /stats/ ▶ **plural n.** informal short for **STATISTICS**.

stat·u·ar·y /'staCHōō,erē/ ▶ **n.** sculpture consisting of statues; statues regarded collectively: *fragments of broken statuary | classical statuary.* ■ archaic the art or practice of making statues. ■ archaic a sculptor.
– ORIGIN mid 16th cent.: from Latin *statuarius*, from *statua* (see **STATUE**).

stat·ue /'staCHōō/ ▶ **n.** a carved or cast figure of a person or animal, esp. one that is life-size or larger.
– DERIVATIVES **stat·ued adj.**
– ORIGIN Middle English: from Old French, from Latin *statua*, from *stare* 'to stand.'

Stat·ue of Lib·er·ty a statue at the entrance to New York Harbor, a symbol of welcome to immigrants, representing a draped female figure carrying a book of laws in her left hand and holding aloft a torch in her right. Dedicated in 1886, it was designed by Frédéric-Auguste Bartholdi and was the gift of the French, commemorating the alliance of France and the US during the American Revolution.

Statue of Liberty

Stat·ue of Li·ber·ty play ▶ **n.** Football a trick play in which a ballcarrier takes the ball from the quarterback, who is poised as if to make a forward pass.

stat·u·esque /,staCHōō'esk/ ▶ **adj.** (esp. of a woman) attractively tall and dignified: *her statuesque beauty.*
– DERIVATIVES **stat·u·esque·ly adv.**, **stat·u·esque·ness n.**
– ORIGIN late 18th cent.: from **STATUE**, on the pattern of *picturesque*.

stat·u·ette /,staCHōō'et/ ▶ **n.** a small statue or figurine, esp. one that is smaller than life-size.
– ORIGIN mid 19th cent.: from French, diminutive of *statue*.

stat·ure /'staCHər/ ▶ **n.** a person's natural height: *a man of short stature | she was small in stature.* ■ importance or reputation gained by ability or achievement: *an architect of international stature.*
– DERIVATIVES **stat·ured adj.** [in combination] *a short-statured fourteen-year-old.*
– ORIGIN Middle English: via Old French from Latin *statura*, from *stare* 'to stand.' The sense 'importance' dates from the mid 19th cent.

sta·tus /'stātəs, 'statəs/ ▶ **n. 1** the relative social, professional, or other standing of someone or something: *an improvement in the status of women.* ■ high rank or social standing: *those who enjoy wealth and status.* ■ the official classification given to a person, country, or organization, determining their rights or responsibilities: *the duchy had been elevated to the status of a principality.*
2 the position of affairs at a particular time, esp. in political or commercial contexts: *an update on the status of the bill.*
– ORIGIN late 18th cent. (as a legal term meaning 'legal standing'): from Latin, literally 'standing,' from *stare* 'to stand.'

sta·tus asth·mat·i·cus /'stātəs az'matikəs, 'statəs/ ▶ **n.** Medicine a severe condition in which asthma attacks follow one another without pause.
– ORIGIN modern Latin.

sta·tus bar ▶ **n.** Computing a horizontal bar, typically at the bottom of the screen or window, showing information about a document being edited or a program running.

sta·tus ep·i·lep·ti·cus /'stātəs ,epə'leptikəs, 'statəs/ ▶ **n.** Medicine a dangerous condition in which epileptic seizures follow one another without recovery of consciousness between them.
– ORIGIN modern Latin.

sta·tus quo /'stātəs 'kwō, 'statəs/ ▶ **n.** (usu. **the status quo**) the existing state of affairs, esp. regarding social or political issues: *they have a vested interest in maintaining the status quo.*
– ORIGIN Latin, literally 'the state in which.'

sta·tus quo an·te /'stātəs kwō 'antē, statəs/ ▶ **n.** (usu. **the status quo rate**) the previously existing state of affairs.
– ORIGIN Latin, literally 'the state in which before.'

sta·tus sym·bol ▶ **n.** a possession that is taken to indicate a person's wealth or high social or professional status.

stat·ute /'staCHōōt/ ▶ **n.** a written law passed by a legislative body: *violation of the hate crimes statute | the tax is not specifically disallowed by statute.* ■ a rule of an organization or institution: *the appointment will be subject to the statutes of the university.* ■ archaic (in biblical use) a law or decree made by a sovereign, or by God.
– ORIGIN Middle English: from Old French *statut*, from late Latin *statutum*, neuter past participle of Latin *statuere* 'set up,' from *status* 'standing' (see **STATUS**).

stat·ute book ▶ **n.** a book in which laws are written.

stat·ute law ▶ **n.** the body of principles and rules of law laid down in statutes. Compare with **COMMON LAW, CASE LAW**.

stat·ute mile ▶ **n.** see **MILE**.

stat·ute of lim·i·ta·tions ▶ **n.** Law a statute prescribing a period of limitation for the bringing of certain kinds of legal action.

stat·utes at large ▶ **plural n.** a country's statutes in their original version, regardless of later modifications.

stat·u·to·ry /'staCHə,tôrē/ ▶ **adj.** required, permitted, or enacted by statute: *the courts did award statutory damages to each of the plaintiffs.* ■ (of a criminal offense) carrying a penalty prescribed by statute: *statutory theft.*
– DERIVATIVES **stat·u·to·ri·ly** /-,tôrəlē/ **adv.**

stat·u·to·ry in·stru·ment ▶ **n.** Law a government or executive order of subordinate legislation.

stat·u·to·ry rape ▶ **n.** Law sexual intercourse with a minor.

Stau·bach /'stô,bäk, 'stou-, -,bak/, Roger (Thomas) (1942–), US football player. A quarterback for the Dallas Cowboys 1969–79, he led them to Super Bowl wins in 1972 and 1978. He was a four-time passing leader in the NFL. Football Hall of Fame (1985).

staunch[1] /stônCH, stänCH/ ▶ **adj. 1** loyal and committed in attitude: *a staunch supporter of the antinuclear lobby | a staunch Catholic.*
2 (of a wall) of strong or firm construction. ■ (also **stanch**) archaic (of a ship) watertight.
– DERIVATIVES **staunch·ly adv.**, **staunch·ness n.**
– ORIGIN late Middle English (in the sense 'watertight'): from Old French *estanche*, feminine of *estanc*, from a Romance base meaning 'dried up, weary.' Sense 1 dates from the early 17th cent.

staunch[2] ▶ **v.** variant spelling of **STANCH**[1].

stau·ro·lite /'stôrə,līt/ ▶ **n.** a brown glassy mineral that occurs as hexagonal prisms often twinned in the shape of a cross. It consists of a silicate of aluminum and iron.
– ORIGIN early 19th cent.: from Greek *stauros* 'cross' + **-LITE**.

stave /stāv/ ▶ **n. 1** a vertical wooden post or plank in a building or other structure. ■ any of the lengths of wood attached side by side to make a barrel, bucket, or other container. ■ a strong wooden stick or iron pole used as a weapon.
2 Music another term for **STAFF**[1] (sense 4 of the noun).
3 a verse or stanza of a poem.
▶ **v.** [with obj.] **1** (past and past participle **staved** or **stove** /stōv/) (**stave something in**) break something by forcing it inward or piercing it roughly: *the door was staved in.*
2 (past and past participle **staved**) (**stave something off**) avert or delay something bad or dangerous: *a reassuring presence can stave off a panic attack.*
– ORIGIN Middle English: back-formation from *staves*. Current senses of the verb date from the early 17th cent.

barrel stave

stave church ▶ **n.** a church of a type built in Norway from the 11th to the 13th century, the walls of which were constructed of upright planks or staves.

staves·a·cre /'stāvz,ākər/ ▶ **n.** a southern European larkspur whose seeds were formerly used as an

insecticide. • *Delphinium staphisagria*, family Ranunculaceae.
– ORIGIN late Middle English: via Latin from Greek *staphis agria* 'wild raisin.'

Stav·ro·pol /'stävrəpəl, stav'rōpəl/ **1** an administrative territory in southern Russia, in the northern Caucasus. ■ its capital city; pop. 363,700 (est. 2008).
2 former name (until 1964) for TOGLIATTI.

stay[1] /stā/ ▶ **v. 1** [no obj.] remain in the same place: *you stay here and I'll be back soon | Jenny decided to stay at home with their young child | he stayed with the firm as a consultant.* ■ (**stay for/to**) delay leaving so as to join in (an activity): *why not stay for lunch?* ■ (**stay down**) (of food) remain in the stomach, rather than be thrown up as vomit.
2 [no obj.] remain in a specified state or position: *her ability to stay calm | tactics used to stay in power | I managed to stay out of trouble.*
3 [no obj.] (of a person) live somewhere temporarily as a visitor or guest: *the girls had gone to stay with friends | Minton invited him to stay the night.* ■ Scottish & S. African live permanently: *where do you stay?*
4 [with obj.] stop, delay, or prevent (something), in particular suspend or postpone (judicial proceedings) or refrain from pressing (charges). ■ assuage (hunger) for a short time: *I grabbed something to stay the pangs of hunger.* ■ literary curb; check: *he tries to stay the destructive course of barbarism.* ■ [no obj.] archaic wait a moment in order to allow someone time to think or speak: *stay, stand apart, I know not which is which.*
5 [with obj.] literary support or prop up.
▶ **n. 1** a period of staying somewhere, in particular of living somewhere temporarily as a visitor or guest: *an overnight stay at a luxury hotel.*
2 literary a curb or check: *there is likely to be a good public library as a stay against boredom.* ■ Law a suspension or postponement of judicial proceedings: *a stay of prosecution.*
3 a device used as a brace or support. ■ (**stays**) historical a corset made of two pieces laced together and stiffened by strips of whalebone.
4 archaic power of endurance.
– PHRASES **be here** (or **have come**) **to stay** informal be permanent or widely accepted: *the Internet is here to stay.* **stay the course** (or **distance**) keep going strongly to the end of a race or contest. ■ pursue a difficult task or activity to the end. **a stay of execution** a delay in carrying out a court order. **stay put** (of a person or object) remain somewhere without moving or being moved.
– PHRASAL VERBS **stay on** continue to study, work, or be somewhere after others have left: *75 percent of sixteen-year-olds stay on in full-time education.* **stay over** (of a guest or visitor) sleep somewhere, esp. at someone's home, for the night. **stay up** not go to bed: *they stayed up all night.* **stay with 1** remain in the mind or memory of (someone): *Gary's words stayed with her all evening.* **2** continue or persevere with (an activity or task): *the incentive needed to stay with a healthy diet.* **3** (of a competitor or player) keep up with (another) during a race or match.
– ORIGIN late Middle English (as a verb): from Anglo-Norman French *estai-*, stem of Old French *ester*, from Latin *stare* 'to stand'; in the sense 'support' (sense 5 of the verb and sense 3 of the noun), partly from Old French *estaye* (noun), *estayer* (verb), of Germanic origin.

stay[2] ▶ **n.** a large rope, wire, or rod used to support a ship's mast, leading from the masthead to another mast or spar or down to the deck. ■ a guy or rope supporting a flagpole or other upright pole. ■ a supporting wire or cable on an aircraft.
▶ **v.** [with obj.] secure or steady (a mast) by means of stays.
– PHRASES **be in stays** (of a sailing ship) be head to the wind while tacking.
– ORIGIN Old English *stæg*, of Germanic origin; related to Dutch *stag*, from a base meaning 'be firm.'

stay-at-home informal ▶ **adj.** [attrib.] preferring to be at home rather than to travel, socialize, or go out to work: *a stay-at-home family man.*
▶ **n.** a person who lives in such a way.

stay·ca·tion /,stā'kāsHn/ ▶ **n.** informal a vacation spent in one's home country rather than abroad, or one spent at home and involving day trips to local attractions.
– ORIGIN early 21st cent.: blend of STAY[1] and VACATION.

stay·er /'stāər/ ▶ **n. 1** a tenacious person or thing, esp. a horse able to hold out to the end of a race.
2 a person who lives somewhere temporarily as a visitor or guest.

stay·ing pow·er ▶ **n.** informal the ability to maintain an activity or commitment despite fatigue or difficulty; stamina: *do you have the staying power to study alone at home?*

stay-in strike ▶ **n.** Brit. a sit-down strike.

Stay·man /'stāmən/ (also **Stayman Winesap** /'wīn,sap/) ▶ **n.** an apple of a deep red variety with a mildly tart flavor, originating in the US.

stay·sail /'stāsəl, -,sāl/ ▶ **n.** a triangular fore-and-aft sail extended on a stay.

stay stitch·ing ▶ **n.** stitching placed along a bias or curved seam to prevent the fabric of a garment from stretching while the garment is being made.
– DERIVATIVES **stay stitch v.**

stbd. ▶ **abbr.** starboard.

STD ▶ **abbr.** ■ Doctor of Sacred Theology. [from Latin *Sanctae Theologiae Doctor*.] ■ sexually transmitted disease. ■ Brit. subscriber trunk dialing.

std. ▶ **abbr.** standard.

Ste. ▶ **abbr.** Saint (referring to a woman).
– ORIGIN from French *Sainte*.

stead /sted/ ▶ **n.** the place or role that someone or something should have or fill (used in referring to a substitute): *you wish to have him superseded and to be appointed in his stead.*
– PHRASES **stand someone in good stead** be advantageous or useful to someone over time or in the future: *his early training stood him in good stead.*
– ORIGIN Old English *stede* 'place,' of Germanic origin; related to Dutch *stad* 'town,' German *Statt* 'place,' *Stadt* 'town,' from an Indo-European root shared by the verb STAND.

stead·fast /'sted,fast/ ▶ **adj.** resolutely or dutifully firm and unwavering: *steadfast loyalty.*
– DERIVATIVES **stead·fast·ly adv.**, **stead·fast·ness n.**
– ORIGIN Old English *stedefæst* 'standing firm' (see STEAD, FAST[1]).

Stead·i·cam /'stedē,kam/ ▶ **n.** trademark a lightweight mounting for a movie camera that keeps it steady for filming when handheld or moving.

stead·ing /'stediNG/ ▶ **n.** Scottish & N. English a farm and its buildings; a farmstead.

stead·y /'stedē/ ▶ **adj.** (**steadier**, **steadiest**) **1** firmly fixed, supported, or balanced; not shaking or moving: *the lighter the camera, the harder it is to hold steady | he refilled her glass with a steady hand.* ■ not faltering or wavering; controlled: *a steady gaze | she tried to keep her voice steady.* ■ (of a person) sensible, reliable, and self-restrained: *a solid, steady young man.*
2 regular, even, and continuous in development, frequency, or intensity: *a steady decline in the national birth rate | sales remain steady.* ■ not changing; regular and established: *I thought I'd better get a steady job | a steady boyfriend.* ■ (of a ship) moving without deviation from its course.
▶ **v.** (**steadies**, **steadying**, **steadied**) make or become steady: [with obj.] *I took a deep breath to steady my nerves* | (as adj. **steadying**) *she's the one steadying influence in his life* | [no obj.] *by the beginning of May prices had steadied.*
▶ **exclam.** used as a warning to someone to keep calm or take care: *Steady now! We don't want you hurting yourself.*
▶ **n.** (pl. **steadies**) informal a person's regular boyfriend or girlfriend: *his steady chucked him two weeks ago.*
– PHRASES **go steady** informal have a regular romantic or sexual relationship with a particular person. **steady on!** Brit. used as a way of exhorting someone to calm down or be more reasonable in what they are saying or doing.
– DERIVATIVES **stead·i·er n.**, **stead·i·ly** /'stedl-ē/ **adv.**, **stead·i·ness n.**
– ORIGIN Middle English (in the sense 'unwavering, without deviation'): from STEAD + -Y[1]. The verb dates from the mid 16th cent.

stead·y-go·ing ▶ **adj.** (of a person) moderate and sensible in behavior; levelheaded.

stead·y state ▶ **n.** an unvarying condition in a physical process, esp. as in the theory that the universe is eternal and maintained by constant creation of matter.

> The steady state theory postulates that the universe maintains a constant average density, with more matter continuously created to fill the void left by galaxies that are receding from one another. The theory has now largely been abandoned in favor of the Big Bang theory and an evolving universe.

steak /stāk/ ▶ **n.** high-quality beef taken from the hindquarters of the animal, typically cut into thick slices that are cooked by broiling or frying: *he liked his steak rare.* ■ a thick slice of such beef or other high-quality meat or fish: *a salmon steak.* ■ poorer-quality beef that is cubed or ground and cooked more slowly by braising or stewing.
– ORIGIN Middle English: from Old Norse *steik*; related to *steikja* 'roast on a spit' and *stikna* 'be roasted.'

steak au poivre /ō 'pwävrə, 'pwäv/ ▶ **n.** steak coated liberally with crushed peppercorns before cooking.
– ORIGIN French, literally 'steak with pepper.'

steak Di·ane /dī'an/ ▶ **n.** a dish consisting of thin slices of steak fried with seasonings, esp. Worcestershire sauce.

steak·house /'stāk,hous/ ▶ **n.** a restaurant that specializes in serving steaks.

steak knife ▶ **n.** a knife with a serrated blade for use when eating steak.

steak tar·tare /tä(r)'tär/ ▶ **n.** a dish consisting of raw ground steak mixed with raw egg, onion, and seasonings.

steal /stēl/ ▶ **v.** (past **stole** /stōl/; past participle **stolen** /'stōlən/) **1** [with obj.] take (another person's property) without permission or legal right and without intending to return it: *thieves stole her bicycle* | [no obj.] *she was found guilty of stealing from her employers* | (as adj. **stolen**) *stolen goods.* ■ dishonestly pass off (another person's ideas) as one's own: *accusations that one group had stolen ideas from the other were soon flying.* ■ take the opportunity to give or share (a kiss) when it is not expected or when people are not watching: *he was allowed to steal a kiss in the darkness.* ■ (in various sports) gain (an advantage, a run, or possession of the ball) unexpectedly or by exploiting the temporary distraction of an opponent. ■ Baseball (of a base runner) advance safely to (the next base) by running to it as the pitcher begins the delivery: *Rickey stole third base.*
2 [no obj.] move somewhere quietly or surreptitiously: *he stole down to the kitchen* | figurative *a delicious languor was stealing over her.* ■ [with obj.] direct (a look) quickly and unobtrusively: *he stole a furtive glance at her.*
▶ **n.** [in sing.] **1** informal a bargain: *for $5 it was a steal.*
2 an act of stealing something: *New York's biggest art steal.* ■ an idea taken from another work. ■ Baseball an act of stealing a base.
– PHRASES **steal someone blind** see BLIND. **steal a march on** gain an advantage over (someone), typically by acting before they do: *stores that open on Sunday are stealing a march on their competitors.* **steal someone's heart** win someone's love. **steal the show** attract the most attention and praise. **steal someone's thunder** win praise for oneself by preempting someone else's attempt to impress. [from an exclamation by the English dramatist John Dennis (1657–1734), who invented a method of simulating the sound of thunder as a theatrical sound effect and used it in an unsuccessful play. Shortly after his play came to the end of its brief run he heard his new thunder effects used at a performance of Shakespeare's *Macbeth*, whereupon he is said to have exclaimed: "Damn them! They will not let my play run, but they steal my thunder!"]
– DERIVATIVES **steal·a·ble adj.**, **steal·er n.** [in combination] *a sheep-stealer*, **steal·ing n.**
– ORIGIN Old English *stelan* (verb), of Germanic origin; related to Dutch *stelen* and German *stehlen*.

stealth /stelTH/ ▶ **n.** cautious and surreptitious action or movement: *the silence and stealth of a hungry cat | why did you slip away by stealth like this?*
▶ **adj.** (chiefly of aircraft) designed in accordance with technology that makes detection by radar or sonar difficult: *a stealth bomber.*
– ORIGIN Middle English (in the sense 'theft'): probably representing an Old English word related to STEAL, + -TH[2].

S

stealth·y /'stelTHē/ ▶ **adj.** (**stealthier**, **stealthiest**) behaving, done, or made in a cautious and surreptitious manner, so as not to be seen or heard: *stealthy footsteps.*
– DERIVATIVES **stealth·i·ly** /-THəlē/ **adv.**, **stealth·i·ness n.**

steam /stēm/ ▶ **n.** the vapor into which water is converted when heated, forming a white mist of minute water droplets in the air. ■ the invisible gaseous form of water, formed by boiling, from which this vapor condenses. ■ the expansive force of this vapor used as a source of power for machines: *the equipment was originally powered by steam* | [as modifier] *a steam train.* ■ locomotives and railroad systems powered in this way: *the last years of steam.* ■ energy and momentum or impetus: *the anticorruption drive gathered steam.*
▶ **v. 1** [no obj.] give off or produce steam: *a mug of coffee was steaming at her elbow.* ■ (**steam up** or **steam something up**) become or cause to become covered or misted over with steam: *the glass keeps*

steaming up | [with obj.] *the warm air had begun to steam up the windows.* ■ (often **be/get steamed up**) informal be or become extremely agitated or angry: *you got all steamed up over nothing!* | *after steaming behind the closed door in his office, he came out and screamed at her.*
2 [with obj.] cook (food) by heating it in steam from boiling water: *steam the vegetables until just tender.* ■ [no obj.] (of food) cook in this way: *add the mussels and leave them to steam.* ■ clean or otherwise treat with steam: *he steamed his shirts in the bathroom to remove the wrinkles.* ■ [with obj. and complement or adverbial] apply steam to (something fixed with adhesive) so as to open or loosen it: *he'd steamed the letter open and then resealed it.* ■ operate (a steam locomotive).
3 [no obj., with adverbial of direction] (of a ship or train) travel somewhere under steam power: *the 11:54 steamed into the station.* ■ informal come, go, or move somewhere rapidly or in a forceful way: *Jerry steamed in ten minutes late* | figurative *the company has steamed ahead with its investment program.* ■ [no obj.] (**steam in**) Brit. informal start or join a fight. ■ [no obj.] (often as noun **steaming**) Brit. informal (of a gang of thieves) move rapidly through a public place, stealing things or robbing people on the way.
– PHRASES **pick up** (or **get up**) **steam 1** generate enough pressure to drive a steam engine. **2** (of a project in its early stages) gradually gain more impetus and driving force: *his campaign steadily picked up steam.* **have steam coming out of one's ears** informal be extremely angry or irritated. **in steam** (of a steam locomotive) ready for work, with steam in the boiler. **let** (or **blow**) **off steam** informal (of a person) get rid of pent-up energy or strong emotion. **run out of** (or **lose**) **steam** informal lose impetus or enthusiasm: *a rebellion that had run out of steam.* **under one's own steam** (with reference to travel) without assistance from others: *we're going to have to get there under our own steam.* **under steam** (of a machine) being operated by steam.
– ORIGIN Old English *stēam* 'vapor,' *stēman* 'emit a scent, be exhaled,' of Germanic origin; related to Dutch *stoom* 'steam.'

steam age ▶ n. the time when trains were drawn by steam locomotives.

steam bath ▶ n. a room that is filled with hot steam for the purpose of cleaning and refreshing the body and for relaxation. ■ a session in such a bath.

steam beer ▶ n. trademark an effervescent beer brewed chiefly in the western US.

steam·boat /ˈstēmˌbōt/ ▶ n. a boat that is propelled by a steam engine, esp. a paddle-wheel craft of a type used widely on rivers in the 19th century.

Steam·boat Springs a resort city in northwestern Colorado, a well-known skiing center; pop. 9,592 (est. 2008).

steam boil·er ▶ n. a container such as that in a steam engine in which water is boiled to generate steam.

steam dis·til·la·tion ▶ n. Chemistry distillation of a liquid in a current of steam, used esp. to purify liquids that are not very volatile and are immiscible with water.

steamed /stēmd/ ▶ adj. **1** having been cooked by steaming: *a cornucopia of steamed dumplings.*
2 [predic.] informal extremely angry: *you're simply steamed about some editor's bad treatment of you.* ■ Brit. informal extremely drunk: *we went out and got steamed.*

S

steam en·gine ▶ n. an engine that uses the expansion or rapid condensation of steam to generate power. ■ a steam locomotive.

steam·er /ˈstēmər/ ▶ n. **1** informal a ship, boat, or locomotive powered by steam.
2 a type of saucepan in which food can be steamed. ■ a device used to direct a jet of hot steam onto a garment in order to remove creases.
3 (in full **steamer clam**) another term for SOFT-SHELL CLAM.
4 informal a wetsuit.

steam·er duck ▶ n. a sturdily built grayish duck that churns the water with its wings when fleeing danger, typically flightless and native to southern South America. ● Genus *Tachyeres*, family Anatidae: several species, including the flightless *T. brachypterus* of the Falkland Islands.

steam·er rug ▶ n. a lap robe, esp. for use on board a passenger ship for keeping warm on deck.

steam·er trunk ▶ n. a sturdy trunk designed or intended for use on board a steamship.

steam gauge ▶ n. a pressure gauge attached to a steam boiler.

steam ham·mer ▶ n. a large steam-powered hammer used in forging.

steam heat ▶ n. heat produced by steam, esp. by a central heating system in a building or on a train or ship that uses steam.
▶ v. [with obj.] (**steam-heat**) heat (something) by passing hot steam through it, esp. at high pressure.

steam·ing /ˈstēmiNG/ ▶ adj. **1** giving off steam: *a basin of steaming water.*
2 informal very angry.
3 Brit. informal extremely drunk.
▶ adv. (as submodifier **steaming hot**) extremely hot.

steam i·ron ▶ n. an electric iron that emits steam from holes in its flat surface.

steam jack·et ▶ n. a steam-filled casing that is fitted around a cylinder in order to heat its contents.

steam or·gan ▶ n. a pipe organ that is driven by a steam engine and played by means of a keyboard or a system of punched cards.

steam·punk /ˈstēmˌpəNGk/ ▶ n. a genre of science fiction that typically features steam-powered machinery rather than advanced technology.

steam·roll /ˈstēmˌrōl/ ▶ v. another term for STEAMROLLER.

steam·roll·er /ˈstēmˌrōlər/ ▶ n. a heavy, slow-moving vehicle with a roller, used to flatten the surfaces of roads during construction. ■ an oppressive and relentless power or force: *victims of an ideological steamroller.*
▶ v. (also **steamroll**) [with obj.] (of a government or other authority) forcibly pass (a measure) by restricting debate or otherwise overriding opposition: *they would have to work together to steamroller the necessary bills past the smaller parties.* ■ force (someone) into doing or accepting something: *an attempt to **steamroller** the country **into** political reforms.*

steam·ship /ˈstēmˌSHip/ ▶ n. a ship that is propelled by a steam engine.

steam shov·el ▶ n. an excavator that is powered by steam.

steam ta·ble ▶ n. (in a cafeteria or restaurant) a table with slots to hold food containers that are kept hot by steam circulating beneath them.

steam·tight /ˈstēmˌtīt/ ▶ adj. not allowing steam to pass through: *steamtight joints.*

steam tur·bine ▶ n. a turbine in which a high-velocity jet of steam rotates a bladed disk or drum.

steam·y /ˈstēmē/ ▶ adj. (**steamier, steamiest**) producing, filled with, or clouded with steam: *a small steamy kitchen.* ■ (of a place or its atmosphere) hot and humid: *the hot, steamy jungle.* ■ informal depicting or involving erotic sexual activity: *steamy sex scenes* | *a steamy affair.*
– DERIVATIVES **steam·i·ly** /-məlē/ adv., **steam·i·ness** /-mēnis/ n.

ste·ar·ic ac·id /stēˈarik, ˈsti(ə)r-/ ▶ n. Chemistry a solid saturated fatty acid obtained from animal or vegetable fats. ● Chem. formula: $CH_3(CH_2)_{16}COOH$.
– DERIVATIVES **ste·a·rate** /ˈstē-əˌrāt, ˈsti(ə)rˌāt/ n.
– ORIGIN mid 19th cent.: *stearic* from French *stéarique*, from Greek *stear* 'tallow.'

ste·a·rin /ˈstēərin, ˈsti(ə)rin/ ▶ n. a white crystalline substance that is the main constituent of tallow and suet. It is a glyceryl ester of stearic acid. ■ a mixture of fatty acids used in candlemaking.
– ORIGIN early 19th cent.: from French *stéarine*, from Greek *stear* 'tallow.'

ste·a·tite /ˈstēəˌtīt/ ▶ n. the mineral talc occurring in consolidated form, esp. as soapstone.
– DERIVATIVES **ste·a·tit·ic** /ˌstēəˈtitik/ adj.
– ORIGIN mid 18th cent.: via Latin from Greek *steatītēs*, from *stear, steat-* 'tallow.'

steato- ▶ comb. form relating to fatty matter or tissue: *steatosis.*
– ORIGIN from Greek *stear, steat-* 'tallow, fat.'

ste·at·o·py·gi·a /ˌstēətəˈpijēə, stēˌatə-/ ▶ n. accumulation of large amounts of fat on the buttocks, esp. as a normal condition in the Khoikhoi and other peoples of arid parts of southern Africa.
– DERIVATIVES **ste·at·o·py·gous** /ˌstēətəˈpīgəs, ˌstēəˈtäpəgəs/ adj.
– ORIGIN early 19th cent.: modern Latin, from Greek *stear, steat-* 'tallow' + *pugē* 'rump.'

ste·at·or·rhe·a /ˌstēətəˈrēə, stēˌatə-/ (Brit. **steatorrhoea**) ▶ n. Medicine the excretion of abnormal quantities of fat with the feces owing to reduced absorption of fat by the intestine.

ste·a·to·sis /ˌstēəˈtōsis/ ▶ n. Medicine infiltration of liver cells with fat, associated with disturbance of the metabolism by, for example, alcoholism, malnutrition, pregnancy, or drug therapy.

steed /stēd/ ▶ n. archaic or literary a horse being ridden or available for riding.
– ORIGIN Old English *stēda* 'stallion'; related to STUD².

Steel /stēl/, Danielle (1947–), US writer. A prolific romance novelist, her works include *Changes* (1983), *Zoya* (1988), *The Ranch* (1997), *The Wedding* (2000), and *The House on Hope Street* (2000).

steel /stēl/ ▶ n. a hard, strong, gray or bluish-gray alloy of iron with carbon and usually other elements, used extensively as a structural and fabricating material. ■ used as a symbol or embodiment of strength and firmness: *nerves of steel* | [as modifier] *a steel will.* ■ a rod of roughened steel on which knives are sharpened.
▶ v. [with obj.] mentally prepare (oneself) to do or face something difficult: *I speak quickly, **steeling myself** for a mean reply.*
– ORIGIN Old English *stӯle, stēli*, of Germanic origin; related to Dutch *staal*, German *Stahl*, also to STAY².
The verb dates from the late 16th cent.

steel band ▶ n. a band that plays music on steel drums.

steel blue ▶ n. a dark bluish-gray color.

steel drum ▶ n. a percussion instrument originating in Trinidad, made out of an oil drum with one end beaten down and divided by grooves into sections to give different notes. Also called PAN¹ (esp. by players).

Steele /stēl/, Sir Richard (1672–1729), Irish essayist and playwright. He founded and wrote for the *Tatler* (1709–11) and the *Spectator* (1711–12), both periodicals, the latter in collaboration with Joseph Addison. Both had an important influence on the manners, morals, and literature of the time.

steel en·grav·ing ▶ n. the process or action of engraving a design into a steel plate. ■ a print made from an engraved steel plate.

steel gray ▶ n. a dark purplish-gray color: [as modifier] *the steel-gray November sky.*

steel·head /ˈstēlˌhed/ (also **steelhead trout**) ▶ n. a rainbow trout of a large migratory variety.

steel pan ▶ n. another term for STEEL DRUM.

steel wool ▶ n. fine strands of steel matted together into a mass, used as an abrasive.

steel·work /ˈstēlˌwərk/ ▶ n. articles of steel.

steel·works /ˈstēlˌwərks/ ▶ plural n. [usu. treated as sing.] a factory where steel is manufactured.
– DERIVATIVES **steel·work·er** /-ˌwərkər/ n.

steel·y /ˈstēlē/ ▶ adj. (**steelier, steeliest**)
1 resembling steel in color, brightness, or strength: *a steely blue.*
2 coldly determined; hard: *there was a steely edge to his questions.*
– DERIVATIVES **steel·i·ness** n.

steel·yard /ˈstēlˌyärd/ ▶ n. an apparatus for weighing that has a short arm taking the item to be weighed and a long graduated arm along which a weight is moved until it balances.

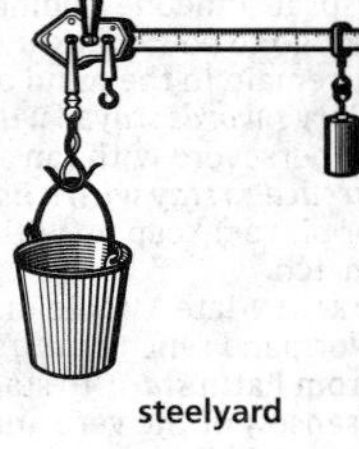
steelyard

steen·bok /ˈstēnˌbäk/ (also **steinbok** or **steenbuck**) ▶ n. a small African antelope with large ears, a small tail, and smooth upright horns. ● *Raphiceros campestris*, family Bovidae.
– ORIGIN late 18th cent.: from Dutch, from *steen* 'stone' + *bok* 'buck.'

steep¹ /stēp/ ▶ adj. **1** (of a slope, flight of stairs, angle, ascent, etc.) rising or falling sharply; nearly perpendicular: *she pushed the bike up the steep hill.* ■ (of a rise or fall in an amount) large or rapid: *the steep rise in unemployment.*
2 informal (of a price or demand) not reasonable; excessive: *a steep membership fee.* ■ dated (of a claim or account) exaggerated or incredible: *this is a rather steep statement.*
▶ n. chiefly Skiing or literary a steep mountain slope: *hair-raising steeps.*
– DERIVATIVES **steep·ish** adj., **steep·ly** adv., **steep·ness** n.
– ORIGIN Old English *stēap* 'extending to a great height'; related to STEEPLE and STOOP¹.

steep² ▶ v. [with obj.] **1** soak (food or tea) in water or other liquid so as to extract its flavor or to soften it: *the chilies are steeped in olive oil* | [no obj.] *the noodles should be left to steep for 3–4 minutes.* ■ soak or saturate (cloth) in water or other liquid.
2 (usu. **be steeped in**) surround or fill with a quality or influence: *a city steeped in history.*
– ORIGIN Middle English: of Germanic origin; related to STOUP.

steep·en /ˈstēpən/ ▶ v. become or cause to become steeper: [no obj.] *the snow improved as the slope steepened.*

stee·ple /ˈstēpəl/ ▶ **n.** a church tower and spire. ■ a spire on the top of a church tower or roof. ■ archaic a tall tower of a church or other building.
– DERIVATIVES **stee·pled** adj.
– ORIGIN Old English *stēpel*, of Germanic origin; related to STEEP[1].

stee·ple·chase /ˈstēpəl,CHās/ ▶ **n.** a horse race run on a racecourse having ditches and hedges as jumps. ■ a running race in which runners must clear hurdles and water jumps.
– DERIVATIVES **stee·ple·chas·er n.**, **stee·ple·chas·ing n.**
– ORIGIN late 18th cent.: from STEEPLE (because originally a steeple marked the finishing point across country) + CHASE[1].

stee·ple·jack /ˈstēpəl,jak/ ▶ **n.** a person who climbs tall structures such as chimneys and steeples in order to carry out repairs.

steer[1] /sti(ə)r/ ▶ **v.** [with obj.] (of a person) guide or control the movement of (a vehicle, vessel, or aircraft), for example by turning a wheel or operating a rudder: *he steered the boat slowly toward the busy quay* | [no obj.] *he let Lily steer.* ■ [no obj.] (of a vehicle, vessel, or aircraft) be guided in a specified direction in such a way: *the ship steered into port.* ■ follow (a course) in a specified direction: *the fishermen were steering a direct course for Kodiak.* ■ guide the movement or course of (someone or something): *he had steered her to a chair* | figurative *he made an attempt to steer the conversation back to Heather.*
▶ **n.** informal a piece of advice or information concerning the development of a situation: *the need for the school to be given a clear steer as to its future direction.*
– PHRASES **steer clear of** take care to avoid or keep away from: *his program steers clear of prickly local issues.* **steer a middle course** see MIDDLE.
– DERIVATIVES **steer·a·ble** /ˈsti(ə)rəbəl/ adj.
– ORIGIN Old English *stīeran*, of Germanic origin; related to Dutch *sturen* and German *steuern*.

steer[2] ▶ **n.** a male domestic bovine animal that has been castrated and is raised for beef.
– ORIGIN Old English *stēor*, of Germanic origin; related to Dutch *stier* and German *Stier*.

steer·age /ˈsti(ə)rij/ ▶ **n. 1** historical the part of a ship providing accommodations for passengers with the cheapest tickets: *poor emigrants in steerage.*
2 archaic or literary the action of steering a boat.

steer·age·way /ˈsti(ə)rij,wā/ ▶ **n.** (of a vessel) the minimum speed required for proper response to the helm.

steer-by-wire ▶ **n.** another term for DRIVE-BY-WIRE.

steer·er /ˈsti(ə)rər/ ▶ **n.** a person or mechanism that steers a vehicle or vessel. ■ informal a person who takes or entices someone to meet a racketeer or swindler.

steer·ing /ˈsti(ə)riNG/ ▶ **n.** the action of steering a vehicle, vessel, or aircraft. ■ the mechanism in a vehicle, vessel, or aircraft that makes it possible to steer it in different directions.

steer·ing col·umn ▶ **n.** a shaft that connects the steering wheel of a vehicle to the rest of the steering mechanism.

steer·ing com·mit·tee (Brit. also **steering group**) ▶ **n.** a committee that decides on the priorities or order of business of an organization and manages the general course of its operations.

steer·ing wheel ▶ **n.** a wheel that a driver rotates in order to steer a vehicle.

steers·man /ˈsti(ə)rzmən/ ▶ **n.** (pl. **steersmen**) a person who is steering a boat or ship.

steeve /stēv/ ▶ **n.** (in a sailing ship) the angle of the bowsprit in relation to a horizontal plane.
▶ **v.** [with obj.] (usu. **be steeved**) give (the bowsprit) a specified inclination.
– ORIGIN mid 17th cent.: of unknown origin.

Ste·fan–Boltz·mann law /ˈstefən ˈbōltsmən/ Physics a law stating that the total radiation emitted by a black body is proportional to the fourth power of its absolute temperature.
– ORIGIN late 19th cent.: named after Josef *Stefan* (1835–93), Austrian physicist, and L. BOLTZMANN.

Stef·fens /ˈstefənz/, Lincoln (1866–1936) US journalist; full name *Joseph Lincoln Steffens.* A leader of the muckraking movement, he was editor of *McClure's* magazine 1902–06 and, as an associate editor, contributed articles to *American* and *Everybody's* magazines 1906–11.

ste·ga·no·graph·y /,stegəˈnägrəfi/ ▶ **n.** the practice of concealing messages or information within other nonsecret text or data.
– ORIGIN late 16th cent.: modern Latin *steganographia*, from Greek *steganos* 'covered' + -GRAPHY.

Steg·ner /ˈstegnər/, Wallace (Earle) (1909–93) US writer, teacher, and environmentalist. He taught at Stanford University 1945–71 and was chairman of the National Parks Advisory Board 1965–66. His novels include *The Big Rock Candy Mountain* (1943), *The Spectator Bird* (1976), *Recapitulation* (1979), and *Crossing to Safety* (1987).

steg·o·saur /ˈstegə,sôr/ (also **stegosaurus** /,stegəˈsôrəs/) ▶ **n.** a small-headed quadrupedal herbivorous dinosaur of the Jurassic and early Cretaceous periods, with a double row of large bony plates or spines along the back. ● Infraorder Stegosauria, order Ornithischia: several genera, including *Stegosaurus.*
– ORIGIN modern Latin, from Greek *stegē* 'covering' + *sauros* 'lizard.'

Stei·chen /ˈstīkən/, Edward (1879–1973) US photographer; born in Luxembourg; born *Eduard Jean Steichen.* He is credited with transforming photography to an art form. He worked with Stieglitz in the early 1900s and then was chief photographer for *Vogue* and *Vanity Fair* 1923–38 and, from 1947, the director of photography for New York City's Museum of Modern Art.

Stein /stīn/, Gertrude (1874–1946), US writer. She developed an esoteric stream-of-consciousness style, notably in *The Autobiography of Alice B. Toklas* (1933). Her home in Paris became a focus for the avant-garde during the 1920s and 1930s.

stein /stīn/ ▶ **n.** a large earthenware beer mug.
– ORIGIN mid 19th cent.: from German *Stein*, literally 'stone.'

Stein·beck /ˈstīn,bek/, John (Ernst, Jr.) (1902–68), US novelist. *Of Mice and Men* (1937) and *The Grapes of Wrath* (1939) are among his works noted for their sympathetic and realistic portrayal of migrant farm workers and other common folk during the Great Depression. His later novels include *Cannery Row* (1945) and *East of Eden* (1952). Nobel Prize for Literature (1962).

stein·bok /ˈstīn,bäk/ ▶ **n.** variant spelling of STEENBOK.

Stein·em /ˈstīnəm/, Gloria (1934–), US social reformer and journalist. A women's rights activist, she cofounded the National Women's Political Caucus 1971 and cofounded *Ms.* magazine in 1972 and served as its editor until 1987. Her works include *Outrageous Acts and Everyday Rebellions* (1983) and *Revolution from Within* (1992).

Gloria Steinem

Stei·ner /ˈstīnər, ˈSHtī-/, Rudolf (1861–1925), Austrian philosopher; founder of anthroposophy. He founded the Anthroposophical Society in 1912, aiming to integrate the practical and psychological in education. The society has contributed to child-centered education, esp. with its Steiner schools.

Stein·way /ˈstīn,wā, ˈSHtīn-/, Henry (Engelhard) (1797–1871), German piano-maker; resident in the US from 1849; born *Heinrich Engelhard Steinweg.* He founded his piano-making firm in New York City in 1853.

ste·la /ˈstēlə/ ▶ **n.** (pl. **stelae** /-,lē/) Archaeology an upright stone slab or column typically bearing a commemorative inscription or relief design, often serving as a gravestone.
– ORIGIN late 18th cent.: via Latin from Greek (see STELE).

ste·le /stēl, ˈstēlē/ ▶ **n. 1** Botany the central core of the stem and root of a vascular plant, consisting of the vascular tissue (xylem and phloem) and associated supporting tissue. Also called VASCULAR CYLINDER.
2 Archaeology another term for STELA.
– DERIVATIVES **ste·lar** /ˈstēlər/ adj. (sense 1).
– ORIGIN early 19th cent.: from Greek *stēlē* 'standing block.'

Stel·la /ˈstelə/, Frank (Philip) (1936–), US painter, an important figure in minimalism known for his series of all-black paintings. He later experimented with shaped canvases and cut-out shapes in relief.

Stel·la Mar·is /ˈstelə ˈmaris/ ▶ **n.** chiefly literary a female protector or guiding spirit at sea (a title sometimes given to the Virgin Mary).
– ORIGIN Latin, literally 'star of the sea.'

stel·lar /ˈstelər/ ▶ **adj.** of or relating to a star or stars: *stellar structure and evolution.* ■ informal featuring or having the quality of a star performer or performers: *a stellar cast had been assembled.* ■ informal exceptionally good; outstanding: *his restaurant has received stellar ratings in the guides.*
– DERIVATIVES **stel·li·form** /ˈstelə,fôrm/ adj.
– ORIGIN mid 17th cent.: from late Latin *stellaris*, from Latin *stella* 'star.'

stel·lar·a·tor /ˈstelə,rātər/ ▶ **n.** Physics a toroidal apparatus for producing controlled fusion reactions in hot plasma, where all the controlling magnetic fields inside it are produced by external windings.
– ORIGIN 1950s: from STELLAR (with reference to the fusion processes in stars), on the pattern of *generator.*

stel·lar wind /wind/ ▶ **n.** Astronomy a continuous flow of charged particles from a star.

stel·late /ˈstelit, -,āt/ ▶ **adj.** technical arranged in a radiating pattern like that of a star.
– DERIVATIVES **stel·lat·ed** adj.
– ORIGIN mid 17th cent.: from Latin *stellatus*, from *stella* 'star.'

Stel·ler's jay /ˈstelərz ˈjā/ ▶ **n.** a blue jay with a dark crest, found in western North America. ● *Cyanocitta stelleri.*
– ORIGIN named after the German naturalist and geographer Georg Wilhelm *Steller* (1709–46).

Stel·ler's sea cow ▶ **n.** a very large relative of the dugong that was formerly found in the area of the Bering Sea and Kamchatka Peninsula, discovered and hunted to extinction in the 18th century. ● *Hydrodamalis gigas*, family Dugongidae.

stel·li·um /ˈstelēəm/ ▶ **n.** Astrology another term for SATELLITIUM.

stem[1] /stem/ ▶ **n. 1** the main body or stalk of a plant or shrub, typically rising above ground but occasionally subterranean. ■ the stalk supporting a fruit, flower, or leaf, and attaching it to a larger branch, twig, or stalk.
2 a long and thin supportive or main section of something: *the main stem of the wing feathers.* ■ the slender part of a wineglass between the base and the bowl. ■ the tube of a tobacco pipe. ■ a rod or cylinder in a mechanism, for example the sliding shaft of a bolt or the winding pin of a watch. ■ a vertical stroke in a letter or musical note.
3 Grammar the root or main part of a noun, adjective, or other word, to which inflections or formative elements are added. ■ archaic or literary the main line of descent of a family or nation: *the Hellenic tribes were derived from the Aryan stem.*
4 the main upright timber or metal piece at the bow of a ship, to which the ship's sides are joined.
5 informal a pipe used for smoking crack or opium.
▶ **v.** (**stems, stemming, stemmed**) **1** [no obj.] (**stem from**) originate in or be caused by: *many of the universities' problems stem from rapid expansion.*
2 [with obj.] remove the stems from (fruit or tobacco leaves).
3 [with obj.] (of a boat) make headway against (the tide or current).
– PHRASES **from stem to stern** from the front to the back, esp. of a ship: *surges of water rocked their boats from stem to stern.* ■ along the entire length of something; throughout: *the album is a joy from stem to stern.*
– DERIVATIVES **stem·less adj.**, **stem·like** /-,līk/ **adj.**
– ORIGIN Old English *stemn, stefn*, of Germanic origin; related to Dutch *stam* and German *Stamm.* Sense 4 of the noun is related to Dutch *steven*, German *Steven.*

stem[2] ▶ **v.** (**stems, stemming, stemmed**) **1** [with obj.] stop or restrict (the flow of something): *a nurse did her best to stem the bleeding.* ■ stop the spread or development of (something undesirable): *an attempt to stem the rising tide of unemployment.*
2 [no obj.] Skiing slide the tail of one ski or both skis outward in order to turn or slow down.
– ORIGIN Middle English (in the sense 'to stop, delay'): from Old Norse *stemma*, of Germanic origin. The skiing term (early 20th cent.) is from the German verb *stemmen.*

stem cell ▶ **n.** Biology an undifferentiated cell of a multicellular organism that is capable of giving rise to indefinitely more cells of the same type, and from which certain other kinds of cell arise by differentiation.

stem chris·tie /ˈkristē/ ▶ **n.** Skiing a turn made by stemming with the upper ski and then lifting the other one parallel to it for most of the turn.

stem·ma /ˈstemə/ ▶ **n.** (pl. **stemmata**) a recorded genealogy of a family; a family tree. ■ a diagram showing the relationship between a text and its various manuscript versions.
– ORIGIN mid 17th cent.: via Latin from Greek *stemma* 'wreath,' from *stephein* 'wreathe, crown.'

stem·ma·tics /stemˈatiks/ ▶ **plural n.** [treated as sing.] the branch of study concerned with analyzing the relationship of surviving variant versions of a text to each other, esp. so as to reconstruct a lost original.

stemmed /stemd/ ▶ **adj.** [attrib.] **1** [in combination] having a stem of a specified length or kind: *red-stemmed alder bushes.*
2 (of a glass, cup, or dish) having a slender supportive section between the base and bowl: *a stemmed goblet.*
3 (of fruit or leaves) having had the stems removed.

stem stitch ▶ **n.** an embroidery stitch forming a continuous line of long, overlapped stitches, typically used to represent narrow stems.

stem turn ▶ **n.** Skiing a turn made by stemming with the upper ski and lifting the lower one parallel to it toward the end of the turn.

stem·ware /ˈstemˌwe(ə)r/ ▶ **n.** goblets and stemmed glasses regarded collectively.

stem-wind·er /ˌwīndər/ (also **stemwinder**) ▶ **n.**
1 informal an entertaining and rousing speech: *the speech was a classic stem-winder in the best southern tradition.*
2 dated a watch wound by turning a knob on the end of a stem.
– ORIGIN Sense 1 from the notion of "winding up" or causing a lively reaction from those listening.

sten. ▶ **abbr.** ■ stenographer. ■ stenography.

stench /stenCH/ ▶ **n.** a strong and very unpleasant smell: *the stench of rotting fish.*
– ORIGIN Old English *stenc* 'smell,' of Germanic origin; related to Dutch *stank*, German *Gestank*, also to the verb STINK.

sten·cil /ˈstensəl/ ▶ **n.** a thin sheet of cardboard, plastic, or metal with a pattern or letters cut out of it, used to produce the cut design on the surface below by the application of ink or paint through the holes. ■ a design produced by such a sheet: *a floral stencil around the top of the room.*
▶ **v.** (**stencils, stenciling, stenciled**; Brit. **stencils, stencilling, stencilled**) [with obj.] decorate (a surface) with such a design: *the walls had been stenciled with designs* | (as noun **stenciling**) *the art of stenciling.* ■ produce (a design) with a stencil: *stencil a border around the door* | (as adj. **stenciled**) *the stenciled letters.*
– ORIGIN early 18th cent.: from earlier *stansel* 'ornament with various colors' (based on Latin *scintilla* 'spark').

STENCIL

stenciled lettering

Sten·dhal /stenˈdäl, steN-/ (1783–1842), French novelist; pseudonym of *Marie Henri Beyle.* His two best-known novels are *Le Rouge et le noir* (1830), relating the rise and fall of a young man from the provinces, and *La Chartreuse de Parme* (1839).

S

Sten·gel /ˈsteNGgəl/, Casey (c.1890–1975) US baseball player and manager; full name *Charles Dillon Stengel.* An outfielder 1910–31 and a manager 1931–48 for various minor and major league teams, he managed the New York Yankees 1949–60, guiding them to ten American League pennants and seven World Series. He also managed the New York Mets 1962–65. Baseball Hall of Fame (1966).

Casey Stengel

Sten gun /ˈsten/ ▶ **n.** a type of lightweight British submachine gun.
– ORIGIN 1940s: from the initials of the inventors' surnames, *S*hepherd and *T*urpin, suggested by BREN.

Sten·o /ˈstānō/, Nicolaus (1638–86), Danish anatomist and geologist; Danish name *Niels Steensen.* His ideas are now regarded as fundamental—that fossils are the petrified remains of living organisms, that many rocks arise from consolidation of sediments and occur in layers in the order in which they were laid down.

sten·o /ˈstenō/ ▶ **n.** (pl. **stenos**) informal a stenographer: *it was written by the steno herself.* ■ [as modifier] short for STENOGRAPHY: *the steno pool* | *I carry a steno pad and two pens.*

stenog. ▶ **abbr.** ■ stenographer. ■ stenographic. ■ stenography.

ste·nog·ra·phy /stəˈnägrəfē/ ▶ **n.** the action or process of writing in shorthand or taking dictation.
– DERIVATIVES **ste·nog·ra·pher** /-fər/ **n.**, **sten·o·graph·ic** /ˌstenəˈgrafik/ **adj.**
– ORIGIN early 17th cent.: from Greek *stenos* 'narrow' + -GRAPHY.

ste·no·ha·line /ˌstenəˈhālīn, -halīn/ ▶ **adj.** Ecology (of an aquatic organism) able to tolerate only a narrow range of salinity. Often contrasted with EURYHALINE.
– ORIGIN 1930s: from Greek *stenos* 'narrow' + *halinos* 'of salt.'

ste·no·sis /stəˈnōsis/ ▶ **n.** (pl. **stenoses** /-ˌsēz/) Medicine the abnormal narrowing of a passage in the body.
– DERIVATIVES **ste·nosed** /stəˈnōst, -nōzd/ **adj.**, **ste·nos·ing** /-ˈnōsiNG, -ˈnōz-/ **adj.**, **ste·not·ic** /stəˈnätik/ **adj.**
– ORIGIN late 19th cent.: modern Latin, from Greek *stenōsis* 'narrowing,' from *stenoun* 'make narrow,' from *stenos* 'narrow.'

sten·o·ther·mal /ˌstenəˈTHərməl/ ▶ **adj.** Ecology (of an organism) able to tolerate only a small range of temperature. Often contrasted with EURYTHERMAL.
– ORIGIN late 19th cent.: from Greek *stenos* 'narrow' + THERMAL.

sten·o·top·ic /ˌstenəˈtäpik/ ▶ **adj.** Ecology (of an organism) able to tolerate only a restricted range of habitats or ecological conditions. Often contrasted with EURYTOPIC.
– ORIGIN 1940s: from Greek *stenos* 'narrow' + *topos* 'place' + -IC.

sten·o·type /ˈstenəˌtīp/ ▶ **n.** a machine resembling a typewriter that is used for recording speech in syllables or phonemes.
– DERIVATIVES **sten·o·typ·ist** /-ˌtīpist/ **n.**, **sten·o·typ·y** /-ˌtīpē/ **n.**
– ORIGIN late 19th cent.: from STENOGRAPHY + TYPE.

stent /stent/ ▶ **n.** Medicine a tubular support placed temporarily inside a blood vessel, canal, or duct to aid healing or relieve an obstruction. ■ an impression or cast of a part or body cavity, used to maintain pressure so as to promote healing, esp. of a skin graft.
– ORIGIN late 19th cent.: from the name of Charles T. *Stent* (1807–85), English dentist. The sense 'tubular support' dates from the 1960s.

sten·tor /ˈstenˌtôr, ˈstentər/ ▶ **n. 1** literary a person with a powerful voice.
2 Zoology a sedentary trumpet-shaped single-celled animal that is widespread in fresh water. ● Genus *Stentor*, phylum Ciliophora, kingdom Protista.
– ORIGIN early 17th cent.: from Greek *Stentōr*, the name of a herald in the Trojan War.

sten·to·ri·an /stenˈtôrēən/ ▶ **adj.** (of a person's voice) loud and powerful: *he introduced me to the staff with a stentorian announcement.*

step /step/ ▶ **n. 1** an act or movement of putting one leg in front of the other in walking or running: *Ron took a step back* | *she turned and retraced her steps.* ■ the distance covered by such a movement: *Richard came a couple of steps nearer.* ■ [usu. in sing.] a person's particular way of walking: *she left the room with a springy step.* ■ one of the sequences of movement of the feet that make up a dance. ■ a short or easily walked distance: *the market is only a short step from the end of the lake.*
2 a flat surface, esp. one in a series, on which to place one's foot when moving from one level to another: *the bottom step of the staircase* | *a flight of marble steps.* ■ a doorstep: *there was a pint of milk on the step.* ■ a rung of a ladder. ■ (**steps**) (or **a pair of steps**) Brit. a stepladder. ■ Climbing a foothold cut in a slope of ice. ■ a block, typically fixed to the vessel's keel, on which the base of a mast is seated. ■ Physics an abrupt change in the value of a quantity, esp. voltage.
3 a measure or action, esp. one of a series taken in order to deal with or achieve a particular thing: *the government must take steps to discourage age discrimination* | *a major step forward in the fight for justice.* ■ a stage in a gradual process: *sales are up, which is a step in the right direction.* ■ a particular position or grade on an ascending or hierarchical scale: *the first step on the managerial ladder.*
4 Music an interval in a scale; a tone (whole step) or semitone (half step).
5 step aerobics: [as modifier] *a step class.*
▶ **v.** (**steps, stepping, stepped**) **1** [no obj.] lift and set down one's foot or one foot after the other in order to walk somewhere or move to a new position: *Claudia tried to step back* | *I accidentally stepped on his foot.* ■ [as imperative] used as a polite or deferential way of asking someone to walk a short distance for a particular purpose: *please step this way.* ■ (**step it**) dated perform a dance: *they stepped it down the room between the lines of dancers.* ■ take a particular course of action: *young men have temporarily stepped out of the labor market.*
2 [with obj.] Nautical set up (a mast) in its step.
– PHRASES **break step** stop walking or marching in step with others. **fall into step** change the way one is walking so that one is walking in step with another person. **in** (or **out of**) **step** putting (or not putting) one's feet forward alternately in the same rhythm as the people one is walking, marching, or dancing with. ■ conforming (or not conforming) to what others are doing or thinking: *the party is clearly out of step with voters.* ■ Physics (of two or more oscillations or other cyclic phenomena) having (or not having) the same frequency and always in the same phase. **keep step** remain walking, marching, or dancing in step. **one step ahead** managing to avoid competition or danger from someone or something: *I try to keep one step ahead of the rest of the staff.* **step by step** so as to progress gradually and carefully from one stage to the next: *I'll explain it to you step by step* | [as adj.] *a step-by-step guide.* **step into the breach** see BREACH. **step into someone's shoes** take control of a task or job from another person. **step on it** (or **step on the gas**) informal go faster, typically in a motor vehicle. **step** (or **tread**) **on someone's toes** offend someone by encroaching on their area of responsibility. **step out of line** behave inappropriately or disobediently. **step up to the plate** take action in response to an opportunity or crisis.
– PHRASAL VERBS **step aside** another way of saying STEP DOWN below. **step back** mentally withdraw from a situation in order to consider it objectively. **step down** withdraw or resign from an important position or office: *Mr. Krenz stepped down as party leader a week ago.* **step something down** decrease voltage by using a transformer. **step forward** offer one's help or services: *a company has stepped forward to sponsor the team.* **step in** become involved in a difficult or problematic situation, esp. in order to help or prevent something from happening. ■ act as a substitute for someone: *Lucy stepped in at very short notice to take Joan's place.* **step out 1** leave a room or building, typically for a short time. **2** informal go out to have a good time: *he was stepping out with a redheaded waitress.* **3** walk with long or vigorous steps: *she enjoyed the outing, stepping out manfully.* **step something up** increase the amount, speed, or intensity of something: *police decided to step up security plans for the game.* ■ increase voltage using a transformer.
– DERIVATIVES **step·like** /-ˌlīk/ **adj.**
– ORIGIN Old English *stæpe, stepe* (noun), *stæppan, steppan* (verb), of Germanic origin; related to Dutch *steppen* and German *stapfen*.

step- ▶ **comb. form** denoting a relationship resulting from a remarriage: *stepmother.*
– ORIGIN Old English *stēop-*, from a Germanic base meaning 'bereaved, orphaned.'

step aer·o·bics ▶ **plural n.** [often treated as sing.] a type of aerobics that involves stepping up onto and down from a portable block.

Ste·pa·na·kert /ˌstepənəˈkert, stiˌpänə-/ Russian name for XANKÄNDI.

step·broth·er /ˈstepˌbrəTHər/ ▶ **n.** a son of one's stepparent, by a marriage other than that with one's own father or mother.

step·child /ˈstepˌCHīld/ ▶ **n.** (pl. **stepchildren**) a child of one's husband or wife by a previous marriage.
– ORIGIN Old English *stēopcild* (see STEP-, CHILD).

step cut ▶ **n.** a cut for gemstones in the form of straight facets around the center.

step·dad /ˈstepˌdad/ ▶ **n.** informal term for STEPFATHER.

step·daugh·ter /ˈstepˌdôtər, ˈstepˌdätər/ ▶ **n.** a daughter of one's husband or wife by a previous marriage.

step·fam·i·ly /ˈstepˌfam(ə)lē/ ▶ **n.** (pl. **stepfamilies**) a family that is formed on the remarriage of a divorced or widowed person and that includes one or more children.

step·fa·ther /ˈstepˌfäT͟Hər/ ▶ **n.** a man who is married to one's mother after the divorce of one's parents or the death of one's father.

Step·ford /ˈstepˌfərd/ ▶ **n.** [as modifier] denoting someone who is regarded as robotically conformist or obedient: *it seems that colleges want to produce a generation of PC-driven Stepford students.*
– ORIGIN from *The Stepford Wives*, the title of a 1972 novel by Ira Levin (1929–2007), in which *Stepford* is the name of a fictional idyllic suburb where the men have replaced their wives with robots.

step func·tion ▶ **n.** Mathematics & Electronics a function that increases or decreases abruptly from one constant value to another.

steph·a·no·tis /ˌstefəˈnōtis/ ▶ **n.** a Madagascan climbing plant that is cultivated for its fragrant waxy white flowers. ● Genus *Stephanotis*, family Asclepiadaceae.
– ORIGIN modern Latin, from Greek, literally 'fit for a wreath,' from *stephanos* 'wreath.'

Ste·phen /ˈstēvən/ (*c.*1097–1154), grandson of William the Conqueror; king of England 1135–54. He seized the throne from Matilda a few months after the death of Henry I. Civil war followed until Matilda was defeated and forced to leave England in 1148.

Ste·phen, St.[1] (died *c.*35), Christian martyr. One of the original seven deacons in Jerusalem appointed by the Apostles, he was charged with blasphemy and stoned, thus becoming the first Christian martyr. Feast day (Western Church) December 26; (Eastern Church) December 27.

Ste·phen, St.[2] (*c.*977–1038), king and patron saint of Hungary; reigned 1000–38. The first king of Hungary, he took steps to Christianize the country. Feast day, September 2 or (in Hungary) August 20.

Ste·phen·son /ˈstēvənsən/, George (1781–1848), British engineer; a pioneer of steam locomotives and railroads. With his son **Robert** (1803–59) he built the *Rocket* (1829), the prototype for all future steam locomotives.

step-in ▶ **adj.** [attrib.] denoting a garment or pair of shoes that is put on by being stepped into and has no need for fasteners.
▶ **n.** (**step-ins**) **1** a pair of such shoes; slip-ons.
2 dated a pair of women's panties.

step·lad·der /ˈstepˌladər/ ▶ **n.** a short folding ladder with flat steps and a small platform.

step·mom /ˈstepˌmäm/ ▶ **n.** informal term for STEPMOTHER.

step·moth·er /ˈstepˌməT͟Hər/ ▶ **n.** a woman who is married to one's father after the divorce of one's parents or the death of one's mother.

step·par·ent /ˈste(p)ˌparənt, -ˌpe(ə)r-/ ▶ **n.** a stepfather or stepmother.

steppe /step/ ▶ **n.** (often **steppes**) a large area of flat unforested grassland in southeastern Europe or Siberia.
– ORIGIN late 17th cent.: from Russian *step'*.

stepped /stept/ ▶ **adj.** having or formed into a step or series of steps: *a building with stepped access.* ■ carried out or occurring in stages or with pauses rather than continuously: *a stepped scale of discounts.*

step·per /ˈstepər/ ▶ **n. 1** an electric motor or other device that moves or rotates in a series of small discrete steps.
2 a portable block used in step aerobics.
3 dated a horse with a brisk, attractive walking gait: *choosing a showy gray stepper for May's brougham.*

step·ping·stone /ˈstepiNGˌstōn/ ▶ **n.** a raised stone used singly or in a series as a place on which to step when crossing a stream or muddy area. ■ an undertaking or event that helps one to make progress toward a specified goal: *the school championships are a steppingstone to international competition.*

step re·sponse ▶ **n.** Electronics the output of a device in response to an abrupt change in voltage.

step·sis·ter /ˈstepˌsistər/ ▶ **n.** a daughter of one's stepparent by a marriage other than with one's own father or mother.

step·son /ˈstepˌsən/ ▶ **n.** a son of one's husband or wife by a previous marriage.
– ORIGIN Old English *stēopsunu* (see STEP-, SON).

step wedge ▶ **n.** Photography a series of contiguous, uniformly shaded rectangles growing progressively darker, from white (or light gray) at one end to black (or dark gray) at the other.

step·well /ˈstepˌwel/ ▶ **n.** the stairwell of a bus.

step·wise /ˈstepˌwīz/ ▶ **adv. & adj. 1** in a series of distinct stages; not continuously: [as adv.] *concentrations of the acid tend to decrease stepwise.*
2 Music (of melodic motion) moving by adjacent scale steps rather than leaps: *crackling solos and juicy, stepwise guitar counterpoints.*

-ster ▶ **suffix 1** denoting a person engaged in or associated with a particular activity or thing: *gangster | songster.*
2 denoting a person having a particular quality: *youngster.*
– ORIGIN Old English *-estre, -istre*, etc., of Germanic origin.

ste·ra·di·an /stəˈrādēən/ (abbr.: **sr**) ▶ **n.** the SI unit of solid angle, equal to the angle at the center of a sphere subtended by a part of the surface equal in area to the square of the radius.
– ORIGIN late 19th cent.: from Greek *stereos* 'solid' + RADIAN.

ster·ane /ˈsterˌān, ˈsti(ə)r-/ ▶ **n.** Chemistry any of a class of saturated polycyclic hydrocarbons that are found in crude oils and are derived from the sterols of ancient organisms.
– ORIGIN 1950s: from STEROID + -ANE².

ster·co·ra·ceous /ˌstərkəˈrāsHəs/ ▶ **adj.** technical consisting of or resembling dung or feces. ■ (of an insect) living in dung.
– ORIGIN mid 18th cent.: from Latin *stercus, stercor-* 'dung' + -ACEOUS.

stere /sti(ə)r/ ▶ **n.** a unit of volume equal to one cubic meter.
– ORIGIN late 18th cent.: from French *stère*, from Greek *stereos* 'solid.'

ster·e·o /ˈsterēˌō, ˈsti(ə)r-/ ▶ **n.** (pl. **stereos**) **1** sound that is directed through two or more speakers so that it seems to surround the listener and to come from more than one source; stereophonic sound. ■ a sound system, typically including a CD, tape, or record player, that has two or more speakers and produces stereo sound.
2 Photography another term for STEREOSCOPE.
3 Printing short for STEREOTYPE.
▶ **adj. 1** short for STEREOPHONIC: *stereo equipment | stereo sound.*
2 Photography short for STEREOSCOPIC (see STEREOSCOPE).

stereo- ▶ **comb. form** relating to solid forms having three dimensions: *stereography.* ■ relating to a three-dimensional effect, arrangement, etc.: *stereochemistry | stereophonic | stereoscope.*
– ORIGIN from Greek *stereos* 'solid.'

ster·e·o·bate /ˈsterēəˌbāt, ˈsti(ə)r-/ ▶ **n.** Architecture a solid mass of masonry serving as a foundation for a wall or row of columns.
– ORIGIN mid 19th cent.: from French *stéréobate*, via Latin from Greek *stereobatēs*, from *stereos* 'solid' + *batēs* 'base' (from *bainein* 'to walk').

ster·e·o·cam·e·ra /ˈsterē-ōˌkam(ə)rə, ˈsti(ə)r-/ ▶ **n.** Photography a camera for simultaneously taking two photographs of the same thing from adjacent viewpoints, so that they will form a stereoscopic pair.

ster·e·o·chem·is·try /ˌsterē-ōˈkeməstrē, ˌsti(ə)r-/ ▶ **n.** the branch of chemistry concerned with the three-dimensional arrangement of atoms and molecules and the effect of this on chemical reactions.
– DERIVATIVES **ster·e·o·chem·i·cal** /-ˈkemikəl/ **adj.**, **ster·e·o·chem·i·cal·ly adv.**

ster·e·og·no·sis /ˌsterē-ägˈnōsis, ˌsti(ə)r-/ ▶ **n.** Psychology the mental perception of depth or three-dimensionality by the senses, usually in reference to the ability to perceive the form of solid objects by touch.
– DERIVATIVES **ster·e·og·nos·tic** /-ˈnästik/ **adj.**
– ORIGIN early 20th cent.: from Greek *stereos* 'solid' + *gnōsis* 'knowledge.'

ster·e·o·gram /ˈsterēəˌgram, ˈsti(ə)r-/ ▶ **n. 1** a diagram or computer-generated image giving a three-dimensional representation of a solid object or surface.
2 another term for STEREOGRAPH (see STEREOGRAPHY).

ster·e·o·graph·ic pro·jec·tion /ˌsterēəˈgrafik, ˌsti(ə)r-/ ▶ **n.** Mathematics mathematical projection in which the angular relationships of lines and planes of the object represented are drawn in terms of their relationship to the great circle formed by the intersection of the equatorial plane with the surface of an imaginary sphere containing the object. This technique has applications in cartography and astronomy.

ster·e·og·ra·phy /ˌsterēˈägrəfē, ˌsti(ə)r-/ ▶ **n.** the depiction or representation of three-dimensional things by projection onto a two-dimensional surface, e.g., in cartography.
– DERIVATIVES **ster·e·o·graph** /ˈsterēəˌgraf, ˈsti(ə)r-/ **n.**, **ster·e·o·graph·ic** /ˌsterēəˈgrafik, ˌsti(ə)r-/ **adj.**

ster·e·o·i·so·mer /ˌsterē-ōˈīsəmər, ˌsti(ə)r-/ ▶ **n.** Chemistry each of two or more compounds differing only in the spatial arrangement of their atoms.
– DERIVATIVES **ster·e·o·i·so·mer·ic** /-ˌīsəˈmerik/ **adj.**, **ster·e·o·i·som·er·ism** /-īˈsäməˌrizəm/ **n.**

ster·e·o·li·thog·ra·phy /ˌsterē-ōliˈTHägrəfē, ˌsti(ə)r-/ ▶ **n.** a technique or process for creating three-dimensional objects, in which a computer-controlled moving laser beam is used to build up the required structure, layer by layer, from a liquid polymer that hardens on contact with laser light.
– DERIVATIVES **ster·e·o·lith·o·graph·ic** /-ˌliTHəˈgrafik/ **adj.**

ster·e·om·e·try /ˌsterēˈämitrē, ˌsti(ə)r-/ ▶ **n.** Geometry the measurement of solid bodies.

ster·e·o·mi·cro·scope /ˌsterē-ōˈmīkrəˌskōp, ˌsti(ə)r-/ ▶ **n.** a binocular microscope that gives a relatively low-power stereoscopic view of the subject.

ster·e·o·phon·ic /ˌsterēəˈfänik, ˌsti(ə)r-/ ▶ **adj.** (of sound recording and reproduction) using two or more channels of transmission and reproduction so that the reproduced sound seems to surround the listener and to come from more than one source.
– DERIVATIVES **ster·e·o·phon·i·cal·ly adv.**, **ster·e·oph·o·ny** /-ˈäfənē/ **n.**

ster·e·op·sis /ˌsterēˈäpsis/ ▶ **n.** the perception of depth produced by the reception in the brain of visual stimuli from both eyes in combination; binocular vision.
– DERIVATIVES **ster·e·op·tic** /-ˈäptik/ **adj.**
– ORIGIN early 20th cent.: from STEREO- 'three-dimensional' + Greek *opsis* 'sight.'

ster·e·op·ti·con /ˌsterēˈäptiˌkän, ˌsti(ə)r-/ ▶ **n.** a slide projector that combines two images to create a three-dimensional effect, or makes one image dissolve into another.
– ORIGIN mid 19th cent.: from STEREO- 'three-dimensional' + Greek *optikon*, neuter of *optikos* 'relating to vision.'

ster·e·o·scope /ˈsterēəˌskōp, ˈsti(ə)r-/ ▶ **n.** a device by which two photographs of the same object taken at slightly different angles are viewed together, creating an impression of depth and solidity.
– DERIVATIVES **ster·e·o·scop·ic** /ˌsterēəˈskäpik, ˌsti(ə)r-/ **adj.**, **ster·e·o·scop·i·cal·ly adv.**, **ster·e·os·co·py** /ˌsterēˈäskəpē, ˌsti(ə)r-/ **n.**

ster·e·o·se·lec·tive /ˌsterē-ōsəˈlektiv, ˌsti(ə)r-/ ▶ **adj.** Chemistry another term for STEREOSPECIFIC.
– DERIVATIVES **ster·e·o·se·lec·tiv·i·ty** /-səlekˈtivitē/ **n.**

ster·e·o sep·a·ra·tion ▶ **n.** see SEPARATION (sense 2).

ster·e·o·spe·cif·ic /ˌsterē-ōspəˈsifik, ˌsti(ə)r-/ ▶ **adj.** Chemistry (of a reaction) preferentially producing a particular stereoisomeric form of the product, irrespective of the configuration of the reactant.
– DERIVATIVES **ster·e·o·spe·cif·i·cal·ly adv.**, **ster·e·o·spec·i·fic·i·ty** /-ˌspesəˈfisitē/ **n.**

ster·e·o·spon·dyl /ˌsterēəˈspändl, ˌsti(ə)r-/ ▶ **n.** an extinct amphibian with a broad flat head, occurring in the Permian and Triassic periods. ● Suborder Stereospondyli, order Temnospondyli: several families.
– ORIGIN early 20th cent.: from modern Latin *Stereospondyli* (plural), from Greek *stereos* 'solid' + *spondulos* 'vertebra.'

ster·e·o·tac·tic /ˌsterēəˈtaktik, ˌsti(ə)r-/ (also **stereotaxic** /-ˈtaksik/) ▶ **adj.** relating to or denoting techniques for surgical treatment or scientific investigation that permit the accurate positioning of probes inside the brain or other parts of the body, based on three-dimensional diagrams.
– DERIVATIVES **ster·e·o·tac·ti·cal·ly adv.**

ster·e·o·tax·is /ˌsterēəˈtaksis, ˌsti(ə)r-/ (also **stereotaxy** /ˈsterēəˌtaksē, ˈstir-/) ▶ **n.** the use of stereotactic instruments or devices in surgery or research.
– ORIGIN late 19th cent.: from STEREO- 'three-dimensional' + Greek *taxis* 'orientation.'

ster·e·o·type /ˈsterēəˌtīp, ˈsti(ə)r-/ ▶ **n. 1** a widely held but fixed and oversimplified image or idea of a particular type of person or thing: *the stereotype of the woman as the carer | sexual and racial stereotypes.* ■ a person or thing that conforms to such an image: *don't treat anyone as a stereotype.*
2 a relief printing plate cast in a mold made from composed type or an original plate.
▶ **v.** [with obj.] view or represent as a stereotype: *the city is too easily stereotyped as an industrial wasteland.*
– DERIVATIVES **ster·e·o·typ·ic** /ˌsterēəˈtipik/ **adj.**, **ster·e·o·typ·i·cal adj.**, **ster·e·o·typ·i·cal·ly adv.**
– ORIGIN late 18th cent.: from French *stéréotype* (adjective).

ster·e·o·typed /ˈsterēəˌtīpt, ˈsti(ə)r-/ ▶ **adj.** viewed or represented as a stereotype: *the story is weakened by its stereotyped characters.*

ster·e·o·typ·y /ˈsterēəˌtīpē, ˈsti(ə)r-/ ▶ **n.** the persistent repetition of an act, esp. by an animal, for no obvious purpose.

ster·ic /ˈsterik, ˈsti(ə)r-/ ▶ **adj.** Chemistry of or relating to the spatial arrangement of atoms in a molecule, esp. as it affects chemical reactions.
– DERIVATIVES **ster·i·cal·ly** adv.
– ORIGIN late 19th cent.: formed irregularly from Greek *stereos* 'solid' + -IC.

ste·rig·ma /stəˈrigmə/ ▶ **n.** (pl. **sterigmata** /-mətə/) Botany (in some fungi) a spore-bearing projection from a cell.
– ORIGIN mid 19th cent.: modern Latin, from Greek *stērigma* 'a support,' from *stērizein* 'to support.'

ster·i·lant /ˈsterələnt/ ▶ **n.** an agent used to destroy microorganisms; a disinfectant. ■ a chemical agent used to destroy pests and diseases in the soil, esp. fungi and nematodes.

ster·ile /ˈsterəl/ ▶ **adj. 1** not able to produce children or young: *the disease had made him sterile.* ■ (of a plant) not able to produce fruit or seeds. ■ (of land or soil) too poor in quality to produce crops. ■ lacking in imagination, creativity, or excitement; uninspiring or unproductive: *he found the fraternity's teachings sterile.*
2 free from bacteria or other living microorganisms; totally clean: *a sterile needle and syringes.*
– DERIVATIVES **ster·ile·ly** /ˈsterə(l)lē/ adv.
– ORIGIN late Middle English: from Old French, or from Latin *sterilis*; related to Greek *steira* 'barren cow.' Sense 2 dates from the late 19th cent.

ste·ril·i·ty /stəˈrilitē/ ▶ **n.** the quality or condition of being sterile: *the disease can cause sterility in males | the sterility of debate in the party.*

ster·i·lize /ˈsterəˌlīz/ ▶ **v.** [with obj.] **1** make (something) free from bacteria or other living microorganisms: *babies' feeding equipment can be cleaned and sterilized* | (as adj. **sterilized**) *sterilized jars.*
2 (usu. **be sterilized**) deprive (a person or animal) of the ability to produce offspring, typically by removing or blocking the sex organs. ■ make (land or water) unable to produce crops or support life.
– DERIVATIVES **ster·i·liz·a·ble** adj., **ster·i·li·za·tion** /ˌsterəl(ə)ˈzāSHən/ n., **ster·i·liz·er** n.

ster·let /ˈstərlit/ ▶ **n.** a small sturgeon of the Danube basin and Caspian Sea area, farmed and commercially fished for its flesh and caviar. ● *Acipenser ruthenus*, family Acipenseridae.
– ORIGIN late 16th cent.: from Russian *sterlyad'.*

ster·ling /ˈstərliNG/ ▶ **n.** British money: *prices in sterling are shown* | [as modifier] *issues of sterling bonds.* ■ short for STERLING SILVER: [as modifier] *a sterling spoon.*
▶ **adj.** (of a person or their work, efforts, or qualities) excellent or valuable: *this organization does sterling work for youngsters.*
– ORIGIN Middle English: probably from *steorra* 'star' + -LING (because some early Norman pennies bore a small star). Until recently one popular theory was that the coin was originally made by *Easterling* moneyers (from the "eastern" Hansa towns), but the stressed first syllable would not have been dropped.

ster·ling ar·e·a a group of countries, most belonging to the Commonwealth of Nations, that formerly pegged their exchange rates to sterling or kept their reserves in sterling rather than gold or dollars. Also called **sterling bloc**.

S

Ster·ling Heights /ˈstərliNG/ a city in southeastern Michigan, north of Detroit; pop. 127,160 (est. 2008).

ster·ling sil·ver ▶ **n.** silver of 92½ percent purity.

Ster·li·ta·mak /ˌsterlitəˈmäk/ an industrial city in southern Russia, on the Belaya River, north of Orenburg; pop. 268,300 (est. 2008).

Stern /stərn/, Isaac (1920–2001), US violinist; born in Russia. He made his New York debut in 1937 at Carnegie Hall. In 1956, he was the first American to perform in Russia after World War II, and he was invited to China in 1979. He served as president of Carnegie Hall from 1960.

stern¹ /stərn/ ▶ **adj.** (of a person or their manner) serious and unrelenting, esp. in the assertion of authority and exercise of discipline: *a smile transformed his stern face | Mama looked stern.* ■ (of an act or statement) strict and severe; using extreme measures or terms: *stern measures to restrict growth of traffic.* ■ (of competition or opposition) putting someone or something under extreme pressure: *the past year has been a stern test of the ability of local industry.*
– PHRASES **be made of sterner stuff** have a stronger character and be more able to overcome problems than others: *whereas James was deeply wounded by the failure, George was made of sterner stuff.* [from Shakespeare's *Julius Caesar* (III. 2. 93).] **the sterner sex** archaic men regarded collectively and in contrast to women.
– DERIVATIVES **stern·ly** adv., **stern·ness** n.
– ORIGIN Old English *styrne*, probably from the West Germanic base of the verb STARE.

stern² ▶ **n.** the rearmost part of a ship or boat: *he stood at the stern of the yacht.* ■ humorous a person's bottom: *my stern can't take too much sun.*
– DERIVATIVES **sterned** /stərnd/ **adj.** [in combination] *a square-sterned vessel*, **stern·most** /-ˌmōst/ **adj.**, **stern·ward** /-wərd/ **adv.**
– ORIGIN Middle English: probably from Old Norse *stjórn* 'steering,' from *stýra* 'to steer.'

ster·nal /ˈstərnl/ ▶ **adj.** of or relating to the sternum: *the sternal area | sternal muscles.*

ster·nal rib ▶ **n.** another term for TRUE RIB.

stern·drive /ˈstərnˌdrīv/ ▶ **n.** an inboard engine connected to an outboard drive unit at the rear of a powerboat.

Stern Gang /ˈstərn/ a militant Zionist group that campaigned in Palestine during the 1940s for the creation of a Jewish state. Founded by **Avraham Stern** (1907–42) as an offshoot of Irgun, the group assassinated the British Minister for the Middle East, **Lord Moyne**, and **Count Folke Bernadotte** (1895–1948), the UN mediator for Palestine.

ster·nite /ˈstərˌnīt/ ▶ **n.** Entomology (in an insect) a sclerotized plate forming the sternum of a segment. Compare with TERGITE.

Sterno /ˈstərnō/ ▶ **n.** trademark flammable hydrocarbon jelly supplied in cans for use as fuel for cooking stoves or chafing dishes.
– ORIGIN early 20th cent.: from the name of *Sternau* and Co., New York, + -O.

ster·no·clei·do·mas·toid /ˌstərnōˌklīdəˈmastoid/ (also **sternocleidomastoid muscle**) ▶ **n.** Anatomy each of a pair of long muscles that connect the sternum, clavicle, and mastoid process of the temporal bone and serve to turn and nod the head.

ster·no·mas·toid /ˌstərnōˈmastoid/ ▶ **n.** another term for STERNOCLEIDOMASTOID.

stern·post /ˈstərnˌpōst/ ▶ **n.** the central upright structure at the stern of a vessel, typically bearing the rudder.

stern·sheets /ˈstərnˌSHēts/ ▶ **plural n.** the flooring planks in a boat's after section, or the seating in this section of an open boat.

ster·num /ˈstərnəm/ ▶ **n.** (pl. **sternums** or **sterna** /-nə/) the breastbone. ■ Zoology a thickened ventral plate on each segment of the body of an arthropod.
– ORIGIN mid 17th cent.: modern Latin, from Greek *sternon* 'chest.'

ster·nu·ta·tion /ˌstərnyəˈtāSHən/ ▶ **n.** formal the action of sneezing.
– ORIGIN late Middle English: from Latin *sternutatio(n-)*, from the verb *sternutare*, frequentative of *sternuere* 'to sneeze.'

ster·nu·ta·tor /ˈstərnyəˌtātər/ ▶ **n.** technical an agent that causes sneezing. ■ an agent used in chemical warfare that causes irritation to the nose and eyes, pain in the chest, and nausea.
– DERIVATIVES **ster·nu·ta·to·ry** /stərˈnyo͞otəˌtôrē/ **adj. & n.** (pl. **sternutatories**).

stern·way /ˈstərnˌwā/ ▶ **n.** backward movement of a ship: *we begin making sternway toward the shoal.*

stern·wheel·er /ˈstərnˌ(h)wēlər/ ▶ **n.** a steamer propelled by a paddle wheel positioned at the stern.

ste·roid /ˈsterˌoid, ˈsti(ə)r-/ ▶ **n.** Biochemistry any of a large class of organic compounds with a characteristic molecular structure containing four rings of carbon atoms (three six-membered and one five). They include many hormones, alkaloids, and vitamins. ■ short for ANABOLIC STEROID.
– PHRASES **on steroids** used to suggest a highly exaggerated, enhanced, or accelerated version of something: *high-protein gelatin squares, available in bright red or bright green, sort of like Jell-O on steroids.*
– DERIVATIVES **ste·roi·dal** /steˈroidl, sti-/ **adj.**
– ORIGIN 1930s: from STEROL + -OID.

ste·rol /ˈsterôl, -äl, ˈsti(ə)r-/ ▶ **n.** Biochemistry any of a group of naturally occurring unsaturated steroid alcohols, typically waxy solids.
– ORIGIN early 20th cent.: independent usage of the ending of words such as CHOLESTEROL and ERGOSTEROL.

ster·to·rous /ˈstərtərəs/ ▶ **adj.** (of breathing) noisy and labored.
– DERIVATIVES **ster·to·rous·ly** adv.
– ORIGIN early 19th cent.: from modern Latin *stertor* 'snoring sound' (from Latin *stertere* 'to snore') + -OUS.

stet /stet/ ▶ **v.** (**stets, stetting, stetted**) [no obj.] let it stand (used as an instruction on a printed proof to indicate that a correction or alteration should be ignored). ■ [with obj.] write such an instruction against (something corrected or deleted).
▶ **n.** such an instruction made on a printed proof.
– ORIGIN Latin, 'let it stand,' from *stare* 'to stand.'

steth·o·scope /ˈsteTHəˌskōp/ ▶ **n.** a medical instrument for listening to the action of someone's heart or breathing, typically having a small disk-shaped resonator that is placed against the chest and two tubes connected to earpieces.
– DERIVATIVES **steth·o·scop·ic** /ˌsteTHəˈskäpik/ **adj.**
– ORIGIN early 19th cent.: from French *stéthoscope*, from Greek *stēthos* 'breast' + *skopein* 'look at.'

stethoscope

Stet·son /ˈstetsən/ ▶ **n.** trademark a hat with a high crown and a wide brim, traditionally worn by cowboys and ranchers in the US.
– ORIGIN late 19th cent.: named after John B. *Stetson* (1830–1906), US hat manufacturer.

Stet·tin /SHteˈtēn/ German name for SZCZECIN.

Steu·ben /ˈSHtoibən, ˈst(y)o͞obən/, Friedrich (Wilhelm Ludolf Gerhard Augustin) von (1730–94), American army officer; born in Prussia. He came to America in December 1777 and joined Washington at Valley Forge, where he introduced European methods of training and discipline. Appointed inspector general of the Continental Army 1778, he was instrumental in shaping American forces into a legitimate military force.

ste·ve·dore /ˈstēvəˌdôr/ ▶ **n.** a person employed, or a contractor engaged, at a dock to load and unload cargo from ships.
– ORIGIN late 18th cent.: from Spanish *estivador*, from *estivar* 'stow a cargo,' from Latin *stipare.*

Ste·ven·graph /ˈstēvənˌgraf/ ▶ **n.** a type of small picture made from brightly colored woven silk, produced during the late 19th century.
– ORIGIN named after Thomas *Stevens* (1828–88), English weaver, whose firm made them.

Ste·vens¹ /ˈstēvənz/, John Paul (1920–), US Supreme Court associate justice 1975–2010. Appointed to the Court by President Ford, he is considered a moderate conservative.

Ste·vens², Wallace (1879–1955), US poet. He developed an original and colorful style, writing his poetry privately and mostly in isolation from the literary community. His *Collected Poems* (1954) won a Pulitzer Prize.

Ste·ven·son¹ /ˈstēvənsən/, Adlai Ewing (1900–65), US statesman and politician. A popular supporter of social reform and internationalism, he was governor of Illinois 1949–53 and was the unsuccessful Democratic candidate for the presidency 1952 and 1956. He later served as US ambassador to the United Nations 1960–65.

Ste·ven·son², Robert Louis (Balfour) (1850–94), Scottish novelist, poet, and travel writer. Stevenson, who wrote *Treasure Island* (1883), is also known for *A Child's Garden of Verses*, a collection of poetry first published as *Penny Whistles* in 1885. Other notable works: *The Strange Case of Dr. Jekyll and Mr. Hyde* and *Kidnapped* (both 1886).

ste·vi·a /ˈstēvēə, ˈstev-/ ▶ **n.** a composite herb native to South America (Genus *Stevia*, esp. *S. rebaudiana*, native to Paraguay) whose leaves are the source of a noncaloric sweetener.
– ORIGIN from modern Latin *Stevia*, from the name of the 16th-cent. Spanish botanist Pedro Jaime *Esteve.*

ste·vi·o·side /ˈstēvēəˌsīd, ˈstev-/ ▶ **n.** a sweet compound of the glycoside class obtained from the leaves of a Paraguayan shrub and used as a food sweetener. ● The shrub is *Stevia rebaudiana* (family Compositae).
– ORIGIN 1930s: from the genus name *Stevia* (from the name of P. J. *Esteve* (died 1566), Spanish botanist) + -OSE² + -IDE.

stew¹ /st(y)o͞o/ ▶ **n. 1** a dish of meat and vegetables cooked slowly in liquid in a closed dish or pan: *lamb stew | add to casseroles, stews, and sauces.*
2 [in sing.] informal a state of great anxiety or agitation: *I suppose he's all in a stew.*
3 archaic a heated public room used for hot steam baths. ■ a brothel.
▶ **v.** (with reference to meat, fruit, or other food) cook or be cooked slowly in liquid in a closed dish or pan: [with obj.] *a new way to stew rhubarb* | [no obj.] *let the tomato mixture stew for twenty minutes.*

■ [no obj.] informal remain in a heated or stifling atmosphere: *sweaty clothes left to stew in a plastic bag.* ■ [no obj.] informal worry about something, esp. on one's own: *James will be expecting us, so we will let him stew a bit.* ■ [no obj.] Brit. (of tea) become strong and bitter with prolonged brewing. ■ **(be stewed in)** literary be steeped in or imbued with: *politics there are stewed in sexual prejudice and privilege.*
– PHRASES **stew in one's own juice** informal suffer anxiety or the unpleasant consequences of one's own actions without the consoling intervention of others.
– ORIGIN Middle English (in the sense 'cauldron'): from Old French *estuve* (related to *estuver* 'heat in steam'), probably based on Greek *tuphos* 'smoke, steam.' Sense 1 of the noun (mid 18th cent.) is directly from the verb (dating from late Middle English).

stew² ▶ **n.** Brit. a pond or large tank for keeping fish for eating. ■ an artificial oyster bed.
– ORIGIN Middle English: from Old French *estui*, from *estoier* 'confine.'

stew³ ▶ **n.** informal an air steward or stewardess.
– ORIGIN 1970s: abbreviation.

stew·ard /'st(y)o͞oərd/ ▶ **n.** **1** a person who looks after the passengers on a ship, aircraft, or train and brings them meals. ■ a person responsible for supplies of food to a college, club, or other institution.
2 an official appointed to supervise arrangements or keep order at a large public event, for example a sporting event. ■ short for SHOP STEWARD.
3 a person employed to manage another's property, esp. a large house or estate. ■ a person whose responsibility it is to take care of something: *farmers pride themselves on being stewards of the countryside.*
▶ **v.** [with obj.] **1** (of an official) supervise arrangements or keep order at (a large public event): *the event was organized and stewarded properly.*
2 manage or look after (another's property).
– DERIVATIVES **stew·ard·ship n.**
– ORIGIN Old English *stīweard*, from *stig* (probably in the sense 'house, hall') + *weard* 'ward.' The verb dates from the early 17th cent.

stew·ard·ess /'st(y)o͞oərdis/ ▶ **n.** a woman who is employed to provide meals for and otherwise look after the passengers on a ship or aircraft.

Stew·art¹ ▶ **adj. & n.** variant spelling of STUART⁵.

Stew·art², James (Maitland) (1908–97), US actor, famous for roles that embody the all-American hero. His movies include *Mr. Smith Goes to Washington* (1939), *The Philadelphia Story* (1940), *It's a Wonderful Life* (1946), *The Man from Laramie* (1955), and *Vertigo* (1958).

James Stewart

Stew·art³, Martha (1941–), US businesswoman; born *Martha Kostyra*. She turned her home decorating and cooking ideas into an industry, including a radio talk show, a *Martha Stewart Living* television program and magazine, and a syndicated newspaper column. After serving prison time in 2004 for her part in fraudulent stock trading, her business ventures and personal marketability rebounded.

Stew·art⁴, Payne (1957–1999), US golfer; full name *William Payne Stewart*. His championship titles include the PGA (1989), and the US Open (1991, 1999). He owned a clothing line that featured his familiar plus fours (baggy knickers worn as traditional golfing attire). Stewart died in an airplane crash.

Stew·art⁵, Potter (1915–85) US Supreme Court associate justice 1958–81. Appointed to the Court by President Eisenhower, he was noted for his 1964 opinion on pornography, ". . . I know it when I see it." He upheld the First Amendment claim in the Pentagon Papers case in 1971.

stew·bum /'st(y)o͞o,bəm/ ▶ **n.** informal an alcoholic, esp. one who has become vagrant.

stewed /st(y)o͞od/ ▶ **adj.** (of food) cooked slowly in liquid in a closed dish or pan: *stewed apples.* ■ [predic.] informal drunk: *we got stewed at their party.* ■ Brit. (of tea) tasting strong and bitter because of prolonged brewing.

stew·ing /'st(y)o͞oiNG/ ▶ **adj.** [attrib.] (of meat or other food) suitable for stewing: *a stewing chicken.*

stew·pot /'st(y)o͞o,pät/ ▶ **n.** a large pot in which stews are cooked.

St. Ex. ▶ **abbr.** Stock Exchange.

stg ▶ **abbr.** sterling.

stge. ▶ **abbr.** storage.

Sth ▶ **abbr.** south.

sthen·ic /'sTHenik/ ▶ **adj.** Medicine, dated of or having a high or excessive level of strength and energy.
– ORIGIN late 18th cent.: from Greek *sthenos* 'strength,' on the pattern of *asthenic*.

stib·nite /'stibnīt/ ▶ **n.** a lead-gray mineral, typically occurring as striated prismatic crystals, that consists of antimony sulfide and is the chief ore of antimony.
– ORIGIN mid 19th cent.: from Latin *stibium* 'black antimony' + -INE⁴ + -ITE¹.

sti·cho·myth·i·a /,stikə'miTHēə/ ▶ **n.** dialogue in which two characters speak alternate lines of verse, used as a stylistic device in ancient Greek drama.
– ORIGIN mid 19th cent.: modern Latin, from Greek *stikhomuthia*, from *stikhos* 'row, line of verse' + *muthos* 'speech, talk.'

stick¹ /stik/ ▶ **n.** **1** a thin piece of wood that has fallen or been cut from a tree.
2 a thin piece of wood that has been trimmed for a particular purpose, in particular: ■ a long piece of wood used for support in walking or as a weapon with which to hit someone or something. ■ (in hockey, polo, and other games) a long implement, typically made of wood, with a head or blade of varying form that is used to hit or direct the ball or puck. ■ [usu. with modifier] a short piece of wood used to impale food: *Popsicle sticks.* ■ a piece of basic furniture: *every stick of furniture just vanished.* ■ **(sticks)** (in field hockey) the foul play of raising the stick above the shoulder. ■ Nautical, archaic a mast or spar. ■ **(the sticks)** Brit. informal goalposts.
3 something resembling or likened to a stick, in particular: ■ a long, thin piece of something: *a stick of dynamite | cinnamon sticks.* ■ a quarter-pound rectangular block of butter or margarine. ■ a conductor's baton. ■ a gear or control lever. ■ (in extended and metaphorical use) a very thin person or limb: *the girl was a stick | her arms were like sticks.* ■ a number of bombs or paratroopers dropped rapidly from an aircraft. ■ a small group of soldiers assigned to a particular duty: *a stick of heavily armed guards.* ■ informal a marijuana cigarette.
4 a threat of punishment or unwelcome measures (often contrasted with the offer of reward as a means of persuasion): *training that relies more on the carrot than on the stick.* ■ Brit. informal severe criticism or treatment: *I took a lot of stick from the press.*
5 **(the sticks)** informal, derogatory rural areas far from cities: *a small, dusty town out in the sticks.*
6 [with adj.] informal, dated a person of a specified kind: *Janet's not such a bad old stick sometimes.*
– PHRASES **up the stick** Brit. informal pregnant. **up sticks** Brit. informal go to live elsewhere. [from nautical slang *to up sticks* 'set up a boat's mast' (ready for departure).]
– DERIVATIVES **stick·like** /-,līk/ **adj.**
– ORIGIN Old English *sticca* 'peg, stick, spoon'; related to Dutch *stek* 'cutting from a plant' and German *Stecken* 'staff, stick.'

stick² ▶ **v.** (past and past participle **stuck** /stək/)
1 [with obj.] **(stick something in/into/through)** push a sharp or pointed object into or through (something): *he stuck his fork into the sausage | the candle was stuck in a straw-covered bottle.* ■ **(stick something on)** fix something on (a point or pointed object): *stick the balls of wool on knitting needles.* ■ [no obj.] **(stick in/into/through)** (of a pointed object) be or remain fixed with its point embedded in (something): *there was a slim rod sticking into the ground beside me.* ■ insert, thrust, or push: *a youth with a cigarette stuck behind one ear | she stuck out her tongue at him.* ■ [no obj.] protrude or extend in a certain direction: *his front teeth stick out | Sue's hair was sticking up at all angles.* ■ put somewhere, typically in a quick or careless way: *just stick that sandwich on my desk.* ■ informal used to express angry dismissal of a particular thing: *he told them they could stick the job—he didn't want it anyway.* ■ informal cause to incur an expense or loss: *she stuck me for all of last month's rent.* ■ stab or pierce with a sharp object: (as adj. **stuck**) *he screamed like a stuck pig.*
2 [no obj.] adhere or cling to a substance or surface: *the plastic seats stuck to my skin | if you heat the noodles in the microwave, they tend to stick together.* ■ [with obj.] fasten or cause to adhere to an object or surface: *she stuck the stamp on the envelope.* ■ be or become fixed or jammed in one place as a result of an obstruction: *he drove into a bog, where his wheels stuck fast.* ■ remain in a static condition; fail to progress: *he lost a lot of weight but had stuck at 210 pounds.* ■ informal be or become convincing, established, or regarded as valid: *the authorities couldn't make the charges stick | the name stuck and Anastasia she remained.* ■ (in blackjack and similar card games) decline to add to one's hand.
3 **(be stuck)** be fixed in a particular position or unable to move or be moved: *Sara tried to open the window but it was stuck | we got stuck in a traffic jam | the cat's stuck up a tree.* ■ be unable to progress with a task or find the answer or solution to something: *I'm doing the crossword and I'm stuck.* ■ [with adverbial of place] informal be or remain in a specified place or situation, typically one perceived as tedious or unpleasant: *I don't want to be stuck in an office all my life.* ■ **(be stuck for)** be at a loss for or in need of: *I'm not usually stuck for words.* ■ **(be stuck with)** informal be unable to get rid of or escape from: *like it or not, she and Grant were stuck with each other.* ■ **(be stuck on)** informal be infatuated with: *he's too good for Jenny, even though she's so stuck on him.*
4 [often with negative] Brit. informal accept or tolerate (an unpleasant or unwelcome person or situation): *I can't stick Geoffrey—he's a real old misery.* ■ **(stick it out)** informal put up with or persevere with something difficult or disagreeable.
– PHRASES **get stuck in** (or **into**) Brit. informal start doing (something) enthusiastically or with determination: *we got stuck into the decorating.* **stick at nothing** allow nothing to deter one from achieving one's aim, however wrong or dishonest: *he would stick at nothing to preserve his privileges.* **stick 'em up!** informal hands up! (spoken typically by a person threatening someone else with a gun). **stick in one's mind** (or **memory**) be remembered clearly and for a long time: *one particular incident sticks in my mind.* **stick in one's throat** (or **craw**) be difficult or impossible to accept; be a source of continuing annoyance. ■ (of words) be difficult or impossible to say: *she couldn't say "Thank you"—the words stuck in her throat.* **stick it to** informal treat (someone) harshly or severely. **stick one** (or **it**) **on** Brit. informal hit (someone). **stick one's neck out** informal risk incurring criticism or anger by acting or speaking boldly. **stick out a mile** see MILE. **stick out like a sore thumb** see SORE. **stick to one's guns** see GUN. **stick to one's ribs** (of food) be filling and nourishing: *a bowl of soup that will stick to your ribs.*
– PHRASAL VERBS **stick around** informal remain in or near a place: *I'd like to stick around and watch the game.* **stick at** informal persevere with (a task or endeavor) in a steady and determined way. **stick by 1** continue to support or be loyal to (someone), typically during difficult times: *I love him and whatever happens, I'll stick by him.* **2** another way of saying STICK TO below. **stick something on** informal place the blame for a mistake or wrongdoing on (someone). **stick out** be extremely noticeable: *many important things had happened to him, but one stuck out.* **stick out for** refuse to accept less than (what one has asked for); persist in demanding (something): *they offered him a Rover but Vic stuck out for a Jaguar.* **stick to 1** continue or confine oneself to doing or using (a particular thing): *I'll stick to bitter lemon, thanks.* ■ not move or digress from (a path or a subject). **2** adhere to (a commitment, belief, or rule): *the government stuck to its election pledges.* **stick together** informal remain united or mutually loyal: *we Europeans must stick together.* **stick someone/something up** informal rob someone at gunpoint. **stick up for** support or defend (a person or cause). **stick with** informal **1** persevere or continue with: *I'm happy to stick with the present team.* **2** another way of saying STICK BY above.
– ORIGIN Old English *stician*, of Germanic origin; related to German *sticken* 'embroider,' from an Indo-European root shared by Greek *stizein* 'to prick,' *stigma* 'a mark' and Latin *instigare* 'spur on.' Early senses included 'pierce' and 'remain fixed (by its embedded pointed end).'

stick·a·bil·i·ty /,stikə'bilitē/ ▶ **n.** informal a person's ability to persevere with something; staying power: *the secret of success is stickability.*

stick·ball /'stik,bôl/ ▶ **n.** an informal game resembling baseball, played with a stick and a (usually rubber) ball.

S

stick·built /ˈstikˌbilt/ ▶ **adj.** (of houses or other buildings) built piece-by-piece on the premises, rather than constructed from prefabricated units.

stick·er /ˈstikər/ ▶ **n.** an adhesive label or notice, generally printed or illustrated. ■ short for STICKER PRICE.

stick·er price ▶ **n.** the advertised retail price of an item, esp. the price listed on a sticker attached to the window of a new automobile.

stick·er shock ▶ **n.** informal shock or dismay experienced by the potential buyers of a particular product on discovering its high or increased price: *drugstore consumers are feeling the pain of sticker shock as never before.*

stick·han·dle /ˈstikˌhandl/ ▶ **v.** [no obj.] (as noun **stickhandling**) (in hockey and other games) control the puck or ball with one's stick.
– DERIVATIVES **stick·han·dler n.**

stick·ie /ˈstikē/ ▶ **n.** (pl. **stickies**) informal term for POST-IT.

stick·ing plas·ter ▶ **n.** chiefly Brit. an adhesive bandage, available in a roll or as individual patches.

stick·ing point ▶ **n.** an obstacle to progress toward an agreement or goal: *job security has emerged as a key sticking point in negotiations.*

stick in·sect ▶ **n.** another term for WALKING STICK (sense 2).

stick-in-the-mud ▶ **n.** informal a person who is dull and unadventurous and who resists change.

stick·le·back /ˈstikəlˌbak/ ▶ **n.** a small fish with sharp spines along its back, able to live in both salt and fresh water and found in both Eurasia and North America. ● Family Gasterosteidae: several genera and species, including the common and widespread **three-spined stickleback** (*Gasterosteus aculeatus*).
– ORIGIN late Middle English: from Old English *sticel* 'thorn, sting' + *bæc* 'back.'

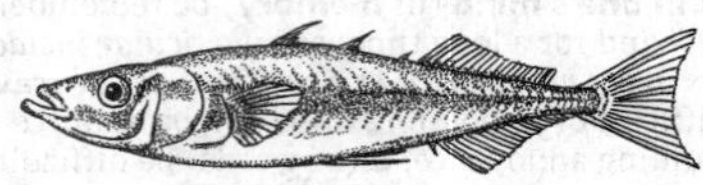

three-spined stickleback

stick·ler /ˈstik(ə)lər/ ▶ **n. 1** a person who insists on a certain quality or type of behavior: *a stickler for accuracy | a stickler when it comes to timekeeping.*
2 a difficult problem; a conundrum.
– ORIGIN mid 16th cent. (in the sense 'umpire'): from obsolete *stickle* 'be umpire,' alteration of obsolete *stightle* 'to control,' frequentative of Old English *stiht(i)an* 'set in order.'

stick-nest rat ▶ **n.** a fluffy-haired gregarious Australian rat that builds nests of interwoven sticks. ● Genus *Leporillus*, family Muridae: two species, in particular *L. conditor*.

stick·pin /ˈstikˌpin/ ▶ **n.** a straight pin with an ornamental head, worn to keep a tie in place or as a brooch.

stick·seed /ˈstikˌsēd/ ▶ **n.** a plant of the borage family that bears small barbed seeds. ● Genera *Hackelia* and *Lappula*, family Boraginaceae: several species, in particular *H. floribunda*, which resembles a forget-me-not.

stick shift ▶ **n.** a manual transmission.

stick-to-it·ive·ness /stik ˈto͞o itivnis/ ▶ **n.** informal perseverance; persistence.

stick·um /ˈstikəm/ ▶ **n.** informal a sticky or adhesive substance; gum or paste.
– ORIGIN early 20th cent.: from the verb STICK² + *-um* (representing the pronoun *them*).

stick·up /ˈstikˌəp/ ▶ **n.** informal an armed robbery in which a gun is used to threaten people.

stick·weed /ˈstikˌwēd/ ▶ **n.** any of a number of North American plants with hooked or barbed seeds, e.g., ragweed.

stick·y /ˈstikē/ ▶ **adj.** (**stickier, stickiest**) **1** tending or designed to stick to things on contact or covered with something that sticks: *her sticky bubblegum | sticky tape.* ■ (of a substance) glutinous; viscous: *the dough should be moist but not sticky.* ■ (of prices, interest rates, or wages) slow to change or react to change.
2 (of the weather) hot and damp; muggy: *it was an unusually hot and sticky summer.* ■ damp with sweat: *she felt hot and sticky and changed her clothes.*
3 informal involving problems; difficult or awkward: *the relationship is going through a sticky patch.*
4 (of a website) attracting a long visit or repeat visits from users: *make your site as sticky as possible to keep visitors there longer.*
▶ **n.** (on an Internet message board) a thread set to remain at the top of the list of threads regardless of when it was last updated.
– PHRASES **sticky fingers** informal a propensity to steal. **sticky wicket** see WICKET.
– DERIVATIVES **stick·i·ly** /ˈstikilē/ **adv.**, **stick·i·ness n.**

stick·y·beak /ˈstikēˌbēk/ Austral./NZ informal ▶ **n.** an inquisitive and prying person.
▶ **v.** [no obj.] pry into other people's affairs: *I don't mean to stickybeak, but when is he going to leave?*

stick·y end ▶ **n.** Biochemistry an end of a DNA double helix at which a few unpaired nucleotides of one strand extend beyond the other.

stick·y-fin·gered ▶ **adj.** informal given to stealing: *a sticky-fingered con artist.*

stic·tion /ˈstikSHən/ ▶ **n.** Physics the friction that tends to prevent stationary surfaces from being set in motion.

Stieg·litz /ˈstēglits/, Alfred (1864–1946), US photographer; husband of Georgia O'Keeffe. He pioneered the establishment of photography as a fine art in the US. He gained an international reputation in the 1890s when he experimented with such innovations as night-time photography.

sti·fa·do /stiˈfädō/ ▶ **n.** a Greek dish of meat stewed with onions and sometimes tomatoes.
– ORIGIN from modern Greek *stiphado.*

stiff /stif/ ▶ **adj. 1** not easily bent or changed in shape; rigid: *a stiff black collar | stiff cardboard.* ■ (of a semiliquid substance) viscous; thick: *add wheat until the mixture is quite stiff.* ■ not moving as freely as is usual or desirable; difficult to turn or operate: *a stiff drawer | the faucet in the shower is a little stiff.* ■ (of a person or part of the body) unable to move easily and without pain: *he was stiff from sitting on the desk | a stiff back.* ■ (of a person or their manner) not relaxed or friendly; constrained: *she greeted him with stiff politeness.*
2 severe or strong: *they face stiff fines and a possible jail sentence | a stiff increase in taxes.* ■ (of a wind) blowing strongly: *a stiff breeze stirring the lake.* ■ requiring strength or effort; difficult: *a long stiff climb up the bare hillside.* ■ (of an alcoholic drink) strong: *a stiff measure of brandy.*
3 [predic.] (**stiff with**) informal full of: *the place is stiff with alarm systems.*
4 (**—— stiff**) informal having a specified unpleasant feeling to an extreme extent: *she was scared stiff | I was bored stiff with my project.*
5 Bridge a card that is the only one of its suit in a hand: *two red aces and a stiff club.*
▶ **n.** informal **1** a dead body.
2 a boring, conventional person: *ordinary working stiffs in respectable offices.* ■ informal a fellow; an ordinary person: *the lucky stiff!*
▶ **v.** [with obj.] informal **1** cheat (someone) out of something, esp. money: *several workers were stiffed out of their pay.* ■ fail to leave (someone) a tip.
2 ignore deliberately; snub. ■ fail to appear for a promised engagement or appointment: *he stiffed us and didn't show up.*
3 kill: *I want to get those pigs who stiffed your doctor.* ■ [no obj.] be unsuccessful: *as soon as he began singing about the wife and kids, his albums stiffed.*
– PHRASES **stiff as a board** informal (of a person or part of the body) extremely stiff. **a stiff upper lip** a quality of uncomplaining stoicism: *senior managers had to keep a stiff upper lip and remain optimistic.*
– DERIVATIVES **stiff·ish adj.**, **stiff·ly adv.**, **stiff·ness n.**
– ORIGIN Old English *stīf*, of Germanic origin; related to Dutch *stijf.*

stiff-arm ▶ **v.** [with obj.] tackle or fend off (a person) by extending an arm rigidly.

stiff·en /ˈstifən/ ▶ **v.** make or become stiff or rigid: [with obj.] *he stiffened his knees in an effort to prevent them from trembling* | [no obj.] *my back stiffens up and I can't bend.* ■ [with obj.] support or strengthen (a garment or fabric), typically by adding tape or an adhesive layer. ■ make or become stronger or more steadfast: [with obj.] *outrage over the murders stiffened the government's resolve to confront the Mafia* | [no obj.] *the regime's resistance stiffened.*
– DERIVATIVES **stiff·en·er** /ˈstif(ə)nər/ **n.**

stiff·en·ing /ˈstif(ə)niNG/ ▶ **n.** material used to stiffen a garment, fabric, or other object.

stiff-necked ▶ **adj.** (of a person or their behavior) haughty and stubborn.

stiff·tail /ˈstifˌtāl/ (also **stiff-tailed duck**) ▶ **n.** a diving duck with a stiff tail of pointed feathers, often held up at an angle. ● Family Anatidae: four genera, in particular *Oxyura*, and several species, e.g., the ruddy duck.

stif·fy /ˈstifē/ (also **stiffie**) ▶ **n.** (pl. **stiffies**) chiefly Brit. vulgar slang an erection of a man's penis.

sti·fle¹ /ˈstīfəl/ ▶ **v.** [with obj.] **1** make (someone) unable to breathe properly; suffocate: *those in the streets were stifled by the fumes.*
2 restrain (a reaction) or stop oneself acting on (an emotion): *she stifled a giggle | she stifled a desire to turn and flee* | (as adj. **stifled**) *she gave a stifled cry of disappointment.* ■ prevent or constrain (an activity or idea): *high taxes were stifling private enterprise.*
– DERIVATIVES **sti·fler** /-f(ə)lər/ **n.**
– ORIGIN late Middle English: perhaps from a frequentative of Old French *estouffer* 'smother, stifle.'

sti·fle² (also **stifle joint**) ▶ **n.** a joint in the legs of horses, dogs, and other animals, equivalent to the knee in humans.
– ORIGIN Middle English: of unknown origin.

sti·fle bone ▶ **n.** the bone in front of a stifle.

sti·fling /ˈstīf(ə)liNG/ ▶ **adj. 1** (of heat, air, or a room) very hot and causing difficulties in breathing; suffocating: *stifling heat.*
2 making one feel constrained or oppressed: *the stifling formality of her family life.*
– DERIVATIVES **sti·fling·ly** /-f(ə)liNGlē/ **adv.** [as submodifier] *a stiflingly hot day.*

stig·ma /ˈstigmə/ ▶ **n.** (pl. **stigmas** or esp. in sense 2 **stigmata** /stigˈmätə, ˈstigmətə/) **1** a mark of disgrace associated with a particular circumstance, quality, or person: *the stigma of mental disorder | to be a nonreader carries a social stigma.*
2 (**stigmata**) (in Christian tradition) marks corresponding to those left on Jesus' body by the Crucifixion, said to have been impressed by divine favor on the bodies of St. Francis of Assisi and others.
3 Medicine a visible sign or characteristic of a disease. ■ a mark or spot on the skin.
4 Botany (in a flower) the part of a pistil that receives the pollen during pollination.
– ORIGIN late 16th cent. (denoting a mark made by pricking or branding): via Latin from Greek *stigma* 'a mark made by a pointed instrument, a dot'; related to STICK¹.

stig·mar·i·a /stigˈme(ə)rēə/ ▶ **n.** (pl. **stigmariae** /-ˈme(ə)rē-ē/) Paleontology a fossilized root of a giant lycopod, common in Carboniferous coal measures. ● Class Lycopsida, in particular the genera *Lepidodendron* and *Sigillaria*.
– DERIVATIVES **stig·mar·i·an adj.**
– ORIGIN mid 19th cent.: modern Latin, from Greek *stigma*, with reference to the scars where rootlets were attached, covering the fossils.

stig·mat·ic /stigˈmatik/ ▶ **adj. 1** of or relating to a stigma or stigmas, in particular constituting or conveying a mark of disgrace.
2 another term for ANASTIGMATIC.
▶ **n.** a person bearing stigmata.
– DERIVATIVES **stig·mat·i·cal·ly** /-ik(ə)lē/ **adv.**
– ORIGIN late 16th cent. (in the sense '(person) marked with a blemish or deformity'): from Latin *stigma, stigmat-* + -IC.

stig·ma·tist /ˈstigmətist/ ▶ **n.** another term for STIGMATIC.

stig·ma·tize /ˈstigməˌtīz/ ▶ **v.** [with obj.] **1** (usu. **be stigmatized**) describe or regard as worthy of disgrace or great disapproval: *the institution **was stigmatized** as a last resort for the destitute.*
2 mark with stigmata.
– DERIVATIVES **stig·ma·ti·za·tion** /ˌstigmətiˈzāSHən/ **n.**
– ORIGIN late 16th cent. (in the sense 'mark with a brand'): from French *stigmatiser* or medieval Latin *stigmatizare*, from Greek *stigmatizein*, from *stigma* (see STIGMA).

Stijl /stīl/ see DE STIJL.

stilb /stilb/ ▶ **n.** a unit of luminance equal to one candela per square centimeter.
– ORIGIN 1940s: from French, from Greek *stilbein* 'to glitter.'

stil·bene /ˈstilˌbēn/ ▶ **n.** Chemistry a synthetic aromatic hydrocarbon that forms phosphorescent crystals and is used in dye manufacture. ● Alternative name: *trans*-**1,2-diphenylethene**; chem. formula: $C_6H_5CH{\cdot}CHC_6H_5$.
– ORIGIN mid 19th cent.: from Greek *stilbein* 'to glitter' + -ENE.

stil·bes·trol /stilˈbesˌtrôl, -ˌträl/ (Brit. **stilboestrol**) ▶ **n.** Biochemistry a powerful synthetic estrogen used in hormone therapy, as a postcoital contraceptive, and as a growth-promoting agent for livestock.
– ORIGIN 1930s: from STILBENE + ESTRUS + -OL.

stile¹ /stīl/ ▶ **n.** an arrangement of steps that allows people but not animals to climb over a fence or wall.
– ORIGIN Old English *stigel*, from a Germanic root meaning 'to climb.'

stile² ▶ **n.** a vertical piece in the frame of a paneled door or sash window. Compare with RAIL¹ (sense 3 of the noun).
– ORIGIN late 17th cent.: probably from Dutch *stijl* 'pillar, doorpost.'

Stiles /stīlz/, Ezra (1727–95), US scholar, teacher, lawyer, and minister. A Congregational minister in Newport, Rhode Island 1755–86, he was a president of Yale College 1778–95 and founder of Rhode Island College (later Brown University) in 1764.

sti·let·to /stəˈletō/ ▶ **n.** (pl. **stilettos**) **1** a short dagger with a tapering blade. ■ a sharp-pointed tool for making eyelet holes.
2 (also **stiletto heel**) a thin, high, tapering heel on a woman's shoe: [as modifier] *the rapid click of stiletto heels on pavement.* ■ a shoe with such a heel.
– ORIGIN early 17th cent.: from Italian, diminutive of *stilo* 'dagger.'

still[1] /stil/ ▶ **adj.** not moving or making a sound: *the still body of the young man* | *the sheriff commanded him to* **stand still** *and drop the gun* | *she sat very still, her eyes closed.* ■ (of air or water) undisturbed by wind, sound, or current; calm and tranquil: *her voice carried on the still air* | *a still autumn day.* ■ (of a drink) not effervescent. Compare with SPARKLING (sense 2).
▶ **n. 1** deep silence and calm; stillness: *the still of the night.*
2 an ordinary static photograph as opposed to a motion picture, esp. a single shot from a movie.
▶ **adv. 1** up to and including the present or the time mentioned; even now (or then) as formerly: *he still lives with his mother* | *it was still raining.* ■ referring to something that will or may happen in the future: *we could still win.*
2 nevertheless; all the same: *I'm afraid he's crazy. Still, he's harmless.*
3 even (used with comparatives for emphasis): *write, or better still, type, captions for the pictures* | *Hank, already sweltering, began to sweat still more profusely.*
▶ **v.** make or become still; quieten: [with obj.] *she raised her hand, stilling Erica's protests* | [no obj.] *the din in the hall stilled.*
– PHRASES **still and all** informal nevertheless; even so. **still small voice** the voice of one's conscience (with reference to 1 Kings 19:12). **still waters run deep** proverb a quiet or placid manner may conceal a more passionate nature.
– DERIVATIVES **still·ness** n.
– ORIGIN Old English *stille* (adjective and adverb), *stillan* (verb), from a base meaning 'be fixed, stand.'

still[2] ▶ **n.** an apparatus for distilling alcoholic drinks such as whiskey.
– ORIGIN mid 16th cent.: from the rare verb *still* 'extract by distillation,' shortening of DISTILL.

stil·lage /ˈstilij/ ▶ **n.** a wooden rack or pallet for holding stored goods off the floor or separating goods in transit.
– ORIGIN late 16th cent. (originally denoting a stand for casks): apparently from Dutch *stellagie* 'scaffold,' from *stellen* 'to place.'

still·birth /ˈstilˌbərTH/ ▶ **n.** the birth of an infant that has died in the womb (strictly, after having survived through at least the first 28 weeks of pregnancy, earlier instances being regarded as abortion or miscarriage).

still·born /ˈstilˌbôrn/ ▶ **adj.** (of an infant) born dead. ■ (of a proposal or plan) having failed to develop or succeed; unrealized: *the proposed wealth tax was stillborn.*

still-hunt ▶ **v.** [no obj.] (often as noun **still-hunting**) hunt game stealthily; stalk.
▶ **n.** (**still hunt**) a stealthy hunt for game.

still life ▶ **n.** (pl. **still lifes** /ˌlīfs/) a painting or drawing of an arrangement of objects, typically including fruit and flowers and objects contrasting with these in texture, such as bowls and glassware. ■ this type or genre of painting or drawing.

still·room /ˈstilˌro͝om, -ˌro͞om/ ▶ **n.** Brit. historical a room in a large house used by the housekeeper for the storage of preserves, cakes, and liqueurs and the preparation of tea and coffee.
– ORIGIN early 18th cent.: a term used earlier for a room in a house where a still was kept for the distillation of perfumes and cordials.

Still·son /ˈstilsən/ (also **Stillson wrench**) ▶ **n.** a large wrench with jaws that tighten as pressure is increased.
– ORIGIN early 20th cent.: named after Daniel C. *Stillson* (1830–99), its US inventor.

Still·wa·ter /ˈstilˌwätər, -ˌwätər/ a city in north central Oklahoma, home to Oklahoma State University; pop. 47,653 (est. 2008).

stil·ly /ˈstil-lē/ literary ▶ **adv.** quietly and with little movement: *the birds rested stilly.*
▶ **adj.** still and quiet: *the stilly night.*

stilt /stilt/ ▶ **n. 1** either of a pair of upright poles with supports for the feet enabling the user to walk at a distance above the ground. ■ each of a set of posts or piles supporting a building above the ground. ■ a small, flat, three-pointed support for ceramic ware in a kiln.
2 a long-billed wading bird with predominantly black and white plumage and long slender reddish legs. ● Family Recurvirostridae: two genera, in particular *Himantopus*, and several species.
– PHRASES **on stilts 1** supported by stilts. **2** (of language) bombastic or stilted: *he is talking nonsense on stilts, and he knows it.*
– ORIGIN Middle English: of Germanic origin; related to Dutch *stelt* and German *Stelze*. Sense 2 dates from the late 18th cent.

stilt bug ▶ **n.** a plant bug with very long slender legs. ● Family Berytidae, suborder Heteroptera: many genera.

stilt·ed /ˈstiltid/ ▶ **adj. 1** (of a manner of talking or writing) stiff and self-conscious or unnatural: *we made stilted conversation.*
2 standing on stilts: *villages of stilted houses.* ■ Architecture (of an arch) with pieces of upright masonry between the imposts and the springers.
– DERIVATIVES **stilt·ed·ly** adv., **stilt·ed·ness** n.

Stil·ton /ˈstiltn/ ▶ **n.** trademark a kind of strong rich cheese, often with blue veins, originally made at various places in Leicestershire, England.
– ORIGIN so named because it was formerly sold to travelers at a coaching inn in Stilton, England.

Stil·well /ˈstilˌwel/, Joseph Warren (1883–1946), US army officer; known as **Uncle Joe** or **Vinegar Joe**. He commanded US troops in the China-Burma-India theater 1942–44, US army ground forces under Douglas MacArthur in 1945, and the US 10th Army in the Pacific 1945–46.

Stim·son /ˈstimsən/, Henry Lewis (1867–1950), US lawyer and statesman. He served five presidents—as secretary of war under President Taft 1911–13, as governor-general of the Philippines under President Coolidge 1927–29, as secretary of state under President Hoover 1929–33, as secretary of war under President Franklin D. Roosevelt 1940–45, and as chief adviser on atomic policy under Presidents Roosevelt and Truman.

stim·u·lant /ˈstimyələnt/ ▶ **n.** a substance that raises levels of physiological or nervous activity in the body. ■ something that increases activity, interest, or enthusiasm in a specified field: *population growth is a major stimulant to industrial development.*
▶ **adj.** raising levels of physiological or nervous activity in the body: *caffeine has stimulant effects on the heart.*
– ORIGIN early 18th cent.: from Latin *stimulant-* 'urging, goading,' from the verb *stimulare.*

stim·u·late /ˈstimyəˌlāt/ ▶ **v.** [with obj.] raise levels of physiological or nervous activity in (the body or any biological system): *the women are given fertility drugs to stimulate their ovaries.* ■ encourage interest or activity in (a person or animal): *the reader could not fail to be stimulated by the ideas presented.* ■ encourage development of or increased activity in (a state or process): *the courses stimulate a passion for learning* | *tax changes designed to stimulate economic growth.*
– DERIVATIVES **stim·u·la·ble** /-ləbəl/ adj., **stim·u·la·tion** /ˌstimyəˈlāSHən/ n., **stim·u·la·tive** /-ˌlātiv, -lətiv/ adj., **stim·u·la·tor** /-ˌlātər/ n., **stim·u·la·to·ry** /-ləˌtôrē/ adj.
– ORIGIN mid 16th cent. (in the sense 'sting, afflict'): from Latin *stimulat-* 'urged, goaded,' from the verb *stimulare.*

stim·u·lat·ing /ˈstimyəˌlātiNG/ ▶ **adj.** encouraging or arousing interest or enthusiasm: *a rich and stimulating working environment.*
– DERIVATIVES **stim·u·lat·ing·ly** adv.

stim·u·lus /ˈstimyələs/ ▶ **n.** (pl. **stimuli** /-ˌlī/) a thing or event that evokes a specific functional reaction in an organ or tissue: *areas of the brain which respond to auditory stimuli.* ■ a thing that rouses activity or energy in someone or something; a spur or incentive: *if the tax were abolished, it would act as a stimulus to exports.* ■ an interesting and exciting quality: *she loved the stimulus of the job.*
– ORIGIN late 17th cent.: from Latin, 'goad, spur, incentive.'

sting /stiNG/ ▶ **n. 1** a small sharp-pointed organ at the end of the abdomen of bees, wasps, ants, and scorpions, capable of inflicting a painful or dangerous wound by injecting poison. ■ any of a number of minute hairs or other organs of plants, jellyfishes, etc., that inject a poisonous or irritating fluid when touched. ■ a wound from such an animal or plant organ: *a wasp or bee sting.* ■ a sharp tingling or burning pain or sensation: *I felt the sting of the cold, bitter air.* ■ [in sing.] a hurtful quality or effect: *she smiled to take the sting out of her words.*
2 informal a carefully planned operation, typically one involving deception: *five blackmailers were jailed last week after they were snared in a police sting.*
▶ **v.** (past and past participle **stung** /stəNG/) **1** [with obj.] wound or pierce with a sting: *he was stung by a jellyfish* | [no obj.] *a nettle stings if you brush it lightly.*
2 feel or cause to feel a sharp tingling or burning pain or sensation: [no obj.] *her eyes stung* | [with obj.] *the brandy stung his throat* | (as adj. **stinging**) *a stinging pain.* ■ [with obj.] (typically of something said) hurt or upset (someone): *stung by her mockery, Frank hung his head.* ■ (**sting someone into**) provoke someone to do (something) by causing annoyance or offense: *he was stung into action by an article in the paper.*
3 [with obj.] informal swindle or exorbitantly overcharge (someone): *an elaborate fraud that stung a bank for thousands.*
– PHRASES **sting in the tail** an unexpected, typically unpleasant or problematic end to something: *the Budget comes with a sting in the tail—future tax increases.*
– DERIVATIVES **sting·ing·ly** adv., **sting·less** adj.
– ORIGIN Old English *sting* (noun), *stingan* (verb), of Germanic origin.

sting·a·ree /ˌstiNGəˈrē/ ▶ **n.** a cinnamon-brown stingray occurring on sand flats in shallow Australian waters. ● *Urolophus testaceus*, family Urolophidae. ■ informal any stingray.
– ORIGIN mid 19th cent.: alteration of STINGRAY.

stinge /stinj/ ▶ **n.** informal a mean or ungenerous person.
– ORIGIN early 20th cent.: back-formation from STINGY.

sting·er /ˈstiNGər/ ▶ **n. 1** an insect or animal that stings, such as a bee or jellyfish. ■ the part of an insect or animal that holds a sting. ■ informal a painful blow: *he suffered a stinger on his right shoulder.*
2 (**Stinger**) a heat-seeking ground-to-air missile that is launched from the shoulder.

sting·ing net·tle ▶ **n.** a Eurasian nettle covered in minute hairs that inject irritants when they are touched. These include histamine, which causes itching, and acetylcholine, which causes a burning sensation. ● Genus *Urtica*, family Urticaceae: several species, in particular *U. dioica*, well established in North America.

sting·ray /ˈstiNGˌrā/ ▶ **n.** a bottom-dwelling marine ray with a flattened diamond-shaped body and a long poisonous serrated spine at the base of the tail. ● Families Dasyatidae (the **long-tailed stingrays**) and Urolophidae (the **short-tailed stingrays**): several species, including the long-tailed **common stingray** (*Dasyatis centrourus*).

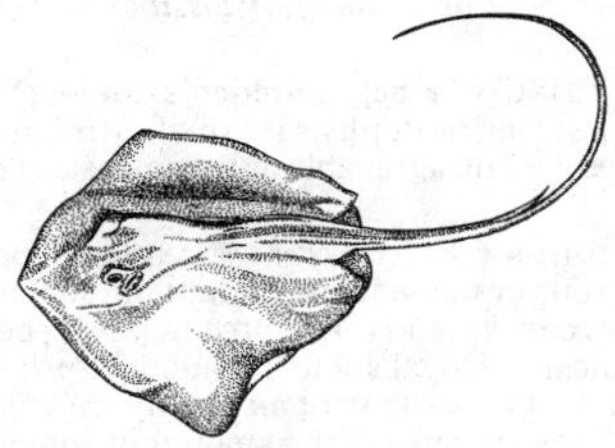

common stingray

stin·gy /ˈstinjē/ ▶ **adj.** (**stingier**, **stingiest**) unwilling to give or spend; ungenerous: *his employer is stingy and idle* | *he was stingy with his information.*
– DERIVATIVES **stin·gi·ly** /-lē/ adv., **stin·gi·ness** n.
– ORIGIN mid 17th cent.: perhaps a dialect variant of the noun STING + -Y[1].

stink /stiNGk/ ▶ **v.** (past **stank** /staNGk/ or **stunk** /stəNGk/; past participle **stunk**) [no obj.] **1** have a strong unpleasant smell: *the place stank like a sewer* | *his breath stank of drink.* ■ [with obj.] (**stink a place up**) fill a place with such a smell: *I hope they are not going to stink up the house with curry.*
2 informal be very unpleasant, contemptible, or scandalous: *the industry's reputation stinks.* ■ (**stink of**) be highly suggestive of (something regarded with disapproval): *the whole affair stinks of a setup.* ■ (**stink of**) have or appear to have a scandalously large amount of (something, esp. money): *the whole place was luxurious and stank of money.*
▶ **n.** [in sing.] **1** a strong unpleasant smell; a stench: *the stink of the place hit me as I went in.*
2 informal a commotion or fuss: *no matter how nice the restaurant is, wacko Meg has to make a big stink and embarrass the rest of us.*
– PHRASES **like stink** informal, chiefly Brit. extremely hard or intensely: *she's working like stink to get everything ready.*
– ORIGIN Old English *stincan*; related to Dutch and German *stinken*, also to STENCH.

stink·ard /ˈstiNGkərd/ ▶ **n. 1** archaic a smelly or despicable person.
2 a member of a lower social order in some American Indian communities.

PRONUNCIATION KEY ə *ago, up*; ər *over, fur*; a *hat*; ā *ate*; ä *car*; e *let*; ē *see*; i *fit*; ī *by*; NG *sing*; ō *go*; ô *law, for*; oi *toy*; o͝o *good*; o͞o *goo*; ou *out*; TH *thin*; TH *then*; ZH *vision*

S

stink bomb ▶ n. a small bomb that emits a strong and unpleasant smell when exploded.

stink bug ▶ n. a broad shield-shaped bug that is typically brightly colored or boldly marked. It emits a foul smell when handled or molested. ● Pentatomidae and other families, suborder Heteroptera.

stink·er /ˈstiNGkər/ ▶ n. informal a person or thing that smells very bad. ■ a very bad or unpleasant person or thing: *have those little stinkers been bullying you?* ■ a difficult task: *Tackled the crossword yet? It's a stinker.*

stink·horn /ˈstiNGk,hôrn/ ▶ n. a widely distributed fungus that has a tall whitish stem with a rounded greenish-brown gelatinous head that turns into a foul-smelling slime containing the spores. ● Family Phallaceae, class Gasteromycetes: many species, including the common European *Phallus impudicus.*

stink·ing /ˈstiNGkiNG/ ▶ adj. foul-smelling: *he was locked in a stinking cell.* ■ informal very bad or unpleasant: *a stinking cold.*
▶ adv. [as submodifier] informal extremely: *she is obviously stinking rich | I want to get stinking drunk and forget.*
– DERIVATIVES **stink·ing·ly** adv.

stink·ing ce·dar ▶ n. a tree of the yew family found only in Florida, with fetid leaves, branches, and timber. Also called **FLORIDA TORREYA**. ● *Torreya taxifolia*, family Taxaceae.

stink·ing smut ▶ n. another term for **BUNT**².

stink·o /ˈstiNGkō/ ▶ adj. informal **1** extremely drunk: *they took three-hour lunches and came back stinko.* **2** worthless or contemptible: *the plot and cast of characters are just plain stinko.*

stink·pot /ˈstiNGk,pät/ ▶ n. **1** informal an unpleasant person (used as a term of abuse). ■ a vehicle that emits foul-smelling exhaust fumes, esp. a motorboat as opposed to a sailboat.
2 another term for **MUSK TURTLE**.

stink·weed /ˈstiNGk,wēd/ ▶ n. any of a number of plants with a strong or fetid smell, e.g., jimson weed.

stink·wood /ˈstiNGk,wo͝od/ ▶ n. any of a number of trees that yield timber with an unpleasant odor, in particular: ● (**black stinkwood**) a South African tree (*Ocotea bullata*, family Lauraceae). ● a New Zealand tree (*Coprosoma foetidissima*, family Rubiaceae).

stink·y /ˈstiNGkē/ ▶ adj. (**stinkier, stinkiest**) informal having a strong or unpleasant smell: *stinky cigarette smoke.* ■ very disagreeable and unpleasant: *a stinky job.*

stint¹ /stint/ ▶ v. [with obj. often with negative] supply an ungenerous or inadequate amount of (something): *stowage room hasn't been stinted.* ■ [no obj.] be economical or frugal about spending or providing something: *he doesn't* **stint on** *wining and dining.* ■ restrict (someone) in the amount of something (esp. money) given or permitted: *to avoid having to stint yourself, budget in advance.*
▶ n. **1** a person's fixed or allotted period of work: *his varied career included a stint as a magician.*
2 limitation of supply or effort: *a collector with an eye for quality and the means to indulge it* **without stint***.*
– ORIGIN Old English *styntan* 'make blunt,' of Germanic origin; related to **STUNT**¹.

stint² ▶ n. a small short-legged sandpiper of northern Eurasia and Alaska, with a brownish back and white underparts. ● Genus *Calidris*, family Scolopacidae: four species.
– ORIGIN Middle English: of unknown origin.

stip. ▶ abbr. ■ stipend. ■ stipulation.

stipe /stīp/ ▶ n. Botany a stalk or stem, esp. the stem of a seaweed or fungus or the stalk of a fern frond.
– ORIGIN late 18th cent.: from French, from Latin *stipes* (see **STIPES**).

sti·pend /ˈstī,pend, -pənd/ ▶ n. a fixed regular sum paid as a salary or allowance.
– ORIGIN late Middle English: from Old French *stipendie* or Latin *stipendium*, from *stips* 'wages' + *pendere* 'to pay.'

sti·pen·di·ar·y /stīˈpendē,erē/ ▶ adj. receiving a stipend; working for payment rather than on a voluntary, unpaid basis: *stipendiary clergy.* ■ of, relating to, or of the nature of a stipend: *stipendiary obligations.*
▶ n. (pl. **stipendiaries**) a person receiving a stipend.
– ORIGIN late Middle English (as a noun): from Latin *stipendiarius*, from *stipendium* (see **STIPEND**).

sti·pes /ˈstī,pēz/ ▶ n. (pl. **stipites** /ˈstipə,tēz/) Zoology a part or organ resembling a stalk, esp. the second joint of the maxilla of an insect. ■ Botany more technical term for **STIPE**.
– ORIGIN mid 18th cent.: from Latin, literally 'log, tree trunk.'

stip·i·tate /ˈstipi,tāt/ ▶ adj. chiefly Botany (esp. of a fungus) having a stipe or a stipes.

stip·ple /ˈstipəl/ ▶ v. [with obj.] (in drawing, painting, and engraving) mark (a surface) with numerous small dots or specks: (as noun **stippling**) *the miniaturist's use of stippling.* ■ produce a decorative effect on (paint or other material) by roughening its surface when it is wet.
▶ n. the process or technique of stippling a surface, or the effect so created.
– DERIVATIVES **stip·pler** /ˈstip(ə)lər/ n.
– ORIGIN mid 17th cent.: from Dutch *stippelen*, frequentative of *stippen* 'to prick,' from *stip* 'a point.'

stip·u·late¹ /ˈstēpyə,lāt/ ▶ v. [with obj.] demand or specify (a requirement), typically as part of a bargain or agreement: *he stipulated certain conditions before their marriage* | (as adj. **stipulated**) *the stipulated time has elapsed.*
– DERIVATIVES **stip·u·la·tor** /-,lātər/ n.
– ORIGIN early 17th cent.: from Latin *stipulat-* 'demanded as a formal promise,' from the verb *stipulari.*

stip·u·late² ▶ adj. Botany (of a leaf or plant) having stipules.
– ORIGIN late 18th cent.: from Latin *stipula* (see **STIPULE**) + **-ATE**².

stip·u·la·tion /,stipyəˈlāsHən/ ▶ n. a condition or requirement that is specified or demanded as part of an agreement: *they donated their collection of prints with the stipulation that they never be publicly exhibited.*

stip·ule /ˈstipyo͞ol/ ▶ n. Botany a small leaflike appendage to a leaf, typically borne in pairs at the base of the leaf stalk.
– DERIVATIVES **stip·u·lar** /-yələr/ adj.
– ORIGIN late 18th cent.: from French *stipule* or Latin *stipula* 'straw.'

stir¹ /stər/ ▶ v. (**stirs, stirring, stirred**) **1** [with obj.] move a spoon or other implement around in (a liquid or other substance) in order to mix it thoroughly: *stir the batter until it is just combined.* ■ (**stir something in/into**) add an ingredient to (a liquid or other substance) in such a way: *stir in the flour and cook gently for two minutes.*
2 move or cause to move slightly: [no obj.] *nothing stirred except the wind* | [with obj.] *a gentle breeze stirred the leaves* | *cloudiness is caused by the fish* **stirring up** *mud.* ■ (of a person or animal) rise or wake from sleep: *no one else had stirred yet.* ■ (**stir from**) (of a person) leave or go out of (a place): *as he grew older, he seldom stirred from his apartment.* ■ begin or cause to begin to be active or to develop: [no obj.] *the 1960s, when the civil rights movement stirred* | [with obj.] *a voice* **stirred** *her* **from** *her reverie* | *he even* **stirred himself** *to play an encore.*
3 [with obj.] arouse strong feelings in (someone); move or excite: *they will be* **stirred to** *action by what is written* | *he* **stirred up** *the sweating crowd.* ■ arouse or prompt (a feeling or memory) or inspire (the imagination): *the story stirred many memories of my childhood* | *the rumors had* **stirred up** *his anger.*
▶ n. [in sing.] **1** a slight physical movement: *I stood, straining eyes and ears for the faintest stir.* ■ a commotion: *the event caused quite a stir.* ■ an initial sign of a specified feeling: *Caroline felt a stir of anger deep within her breast.*
2 an act of mixing food or drink with a spoon or other implement: *he gives his chocolate milk a stir.*
– PHRASES **stir someone's blood** make someone excited or enthusiastic. **stir one's stumps** [often in imperative] Brit. informal, dated (of a person) begin to move or act.
– PHRASAL VERBS **stir something up** cause or provoke trouble or bad feeling: *he accused me of trying to stir up trouble.*
– ORIGIN Old English *styrian*, of Germanic origin; related to German *stören* 'disturb.'

stir² ▶ n. informal prison: *I've spent twenty-eight years in stir.*
– ORIGIN mid 19th cent.: perhaps from Romany *sturbin* 'jail.'

stir·a·bout /ˈstərə,bout/ ▶ n. chiefly Irish porridge made by stirring oatmeal in boiling water or milk.

stir-cra·zy ▶ adj. informal psychologically disturbed, esp. as a result of being confined or imprisoned.

stir-fry ▶ v. [with obj.] fry (meat, fish, or vegetables) rapidly over a high heat while stirring briskly: (as adj. **stir-fried**) *stir-fried beef.*
▶ n. a dish cooked by such a method.

stirk /stərk/ ▶ n. Brit. a yearling bullock or heifer.
– ORIGIN Old English *stirc*, perhaps from *stēor* 'steer' + *-oc* (see **-OCK**).

Stir·ling en·gine /ˈstərliNG/ ▶ n. a machine used to provide power or refrigeration, operating on a closed cycle in which a working fluid is cyclically compressed and expanded at different temperatures.

stir·rer /ˈstərər/ ▶ n. an object or mechanical device used for stirring something. ■ Brit. informal a person who deliberately causes trouble between others by spreading rumors or gossip.

stir·ring /ˈstəriNG/ ▶ adj. **1** causing great excitement or strong emotion; rousing: *stirring songs.*
2 archaic moving briskly; active.
▶ n. an initial sign of activity, movement, or emotion: *the first stirrings of anger.*
– DERIVATIVES **stir·ring·ly** adv.

stir·rup /ˈstərəp, ˈstə-rəp, ˈstir-/ ▶ n. **1** each of a pair of devices attached to each side of a horse's saddle, in the form of a loop with a flat base to support the rider's foot.
2 (**stirrups**) a pair of metal supports in which a woman's heels may be placed during gynecological examinations and childbirth, to hold her legs in a position that will facilitate medical examination or intervention.
3 (also **stirrup bone**) another term for **STAPES**.
4 (**stirrups**) short for **STIRRUP PANTS**.
– ORIGIN Old English *stigrāp*, from the Germanic base of obsolete *sty* 'climb' + **ROPE**.

stirrup 1

stir·rup cup ▶ n. a cup of wine or other alcoholic drink offered to a person on horseback who is about to depart on a journey.

stir·rup i·ron ▶ n. the metal loop of a stirrup, in which the rider's foot rests.

stir·rup leath·er ▶ n. the strap attaching a stirrup iron to a saddle.

stir·rup pants ▶ plural n. a pair of women's or girls' stretch pants with a band of elastic at the bottom of each leg that passes under the arch of the foot.

stir·rup pump ▶ n. chiefly historical a portable hand-operated water pump with a footrest resembling a stirrup, used to extinguish small fires.

stish·ov·ite /ˈstisHə,vīt/ ▶ n. a mineral that is a dense polymorph of silica and is formed at very high pressures, esp. in meteorite craters.
– ORIGIN 1960s: from the name of Sergei M. *Stishov*, 20th-cent. Russian chemist, + **-ITE**¹.

stitch /sticH/ ▶ n. **1** a loop of thread or yarn resulting from a single pass or movement of the needle in sewing, knitting, or crocheting. ■ a loop of thread used to join the edges of a wound or surgical incision: *a neck wound requiring forty stitches.* ■ [usu. with adj.] a method of sewing, knitting, or crocheting producing a particular pattern or design: *basic embroidery stitches.* ■ [in sing., usu. with negative] informal the smallest item of clothing: *a man answered the door without a stitch on.*
2 a sudden sharp pain in the side of the body, caused by strenuous exercise: *she ran with a stitch in her side.*
▶ v. [with obj.] make, mend, or join (something) with stitches: *stitch a plain seam with right sides together* | *they stitched the cut on her face* | [as adj., in combination] (**stitched**) *hand-stitched English dresses.*
– PHRASES **in stitches** informal laughing uncontrollably: *his unique brand of droll self-mockery* **had** *his audiences* **in stitches***.* **a stitch in time saves nine** proverb if you sort out a problem immediately it may save a lot of extra work later.
– DERIVATIVES **stitch·er** n., **stitch·er·y** n.
– ORIGIN Old English *stice* 'a puncture, stabbing pain,' of Germanic origin; related to German *Stich* 'a sting, prick,' also to **STICK**². The sense 'loop' (in sewing, etc.) arose in Middle English.

stitch·bird /ˈsticH,bərd/ ▶ n. a rare New Zealand honeyeater with mainly dark brown or blackish plumage and a sharp call that resembles the word "stitch." ● *Notiomystis cincta*, family Meliphagidae.

stitch·ing /ˈsticHiNG/ ▶ n. a row of stitches sewn onto cloth: *the gloves were white with black stitching.* ■ the action or work of stitching or sewing: *one of the mares cut her leg and it required stitching.*

stitch-up ▶ n. Brit. informal an act of placing someone in a position in which they will be wrongly blamed for something, or of manipulating a situation to one's advantage.

stitch·wort /ˈsticHwərt, -,wôrt/ ▶ n. a straggling plant of the pink family with a slender stem and white starry flowers. It was formerly thought to cure a stitch in the side. ● Genus *Stellaria*, family Caryophyllaceae: several species, in particular **greater stitchwort** (*S. holostea*) and **lesser stitchwort** (*S. graminea*).

sti·ver /ˈstīvər/ ▶ n. a small coin formerly used in the Netherlands, equal to one twentieth of a guilder. ■ archaic any coin of low value. ■ [with negative] archaic a very small or insignificant amount: *they didn't care a stiver.*

–ORIGIN from Dutch *stuiver*, denoting a small coin; probably related to the noun STUB.

stk. ▶ abbr. stock.

STM ▶ abbr. scanning tunneling microscope.

sto·a /ˈstōə/ ▶ n. a classical portico or roofed colonnade. ■ (**the Stoa**) the great hall in Athens in which the ancient Greek philosopher Zeno gave the founding lectures of the Stoic school of philosophy.
–ORIGIN Greek.

stoat /stōt/ ▶ n. a small carnivorous mammal of the weasel family that has chestnut fur with white underparts and a black-tipped tail. It is native to both Eurasia and North America and in northern areas the coat turns white in winter. Also called SHORT-TAILED WEASEL. Compare with ERMINE, WEASEL. ● *Mustela erminea*, family Mustelidae.
–ORIGIN late Middle English: of unknown origin.

stob /stäb/ ▶ n. dialect a broken branch or a stump. ■ a stake used for fencing.
–ORIGIN Middle English: variant of STUB.

sto·chas·tic /stəˈkastik/ ▶ adj. randomly determined; having a random probability distribution or pattern that may be analyzed statistically but may not be predicted precisely.
–DERIVATIVES **sto·chas·ti·cal·ly** /-ik(ə)lē/ adv.
–ORIGIN mid 17th cent.: from Greek *stokhastikos*, from *stokhazesthai* 'aim at, guess,' from *stokhos* 'aim.'

stock /stäk/ ▶ n. **1** the goods or merchandise kept on the premises of a business or warehouse and available for sale or distribution: *the store has a very low turnover of stock | buy now, while stocks last! |* [as modifier] *stock shortages.* ■ a supply or quantity of something accumulated or available for future use: *I need to replenish my **stock of** wine | fish stocks are being dangerously depleted.* ■ farm animals such as cattle, pigs, and sheep, bred and kept for their meat or milk; livestock. ■ short for ROLLING STOCK. ■ (also **film stock**) photographic film that has not been exposed or processed. ■ (in some card games) the cards that have not yet been dealt, left on the table to be drawn.
2 the capital raised by a business or corporation through the issue and subscription of shares: *between 1982 and 1986, the value of the company's stock rose by 86%.* ■ (also **stocks**) a portion of this as held by an individual or group as an investment: *she owned $3000 worth of stock.* ■ (also **stocks**) the shares of a particular company, type of company, or industry: *blue-chip stocks.* ■ securities issued by the government in fixed units with a fixed rate of interest: *government gilt-edged stock.* ■ a person's reputation or popularity: *I felt I was right, but my stock was low with this establishment.*
3 liquid made by cooking bones, meat, fish, or vegetables slowly in water, used as a basis for the preparation of soup, gravy, or sauces: *a pint of chicken stock.* ■ [with modifier] the raw material from which a specified commodity can be manufactured: *the fat can be used as soap stock.*
4 [usu. with adj. or noun modifier] a person's ancestry or line of descent: *her mother was of French stock | both of them came from peasant stock.* ■ a breed, variety, or population of an animal or plant.
5 the trunk or woody stem of a living tree or shrub, esp. one into which a graft (scion) is inserted. ■ the perennial part of a herbaceous plant, esp. a rhizome.
6 a herbaceous European plant that is widely cultivated for its fragrant flowers, which are typically lilac, pink, or white. [mid 17th cent.: from *stock-gillyflower*.] ● Genus *Matthiola*, family Brassicaceae: several species.
7 (**the stocks**) [treated as sing. or pl.] historical an instrument of punishment consisting of an adjustable wooden structure with holes for securing a person's feet and hands, in which criminals were locked and exposed to public ridicule or assault.
8 the part of a rifle or other firearm to which the barrel and firing mechanism are attached, held against one's shoulder when firing the gun. ■ the crosspiece of an anchor. ■ the handle of something such as a whip or fishing rod. ■ short for HEADSTOCK (sense 1). ■ short for TAILSTOCK.
9 a band of white material tied like a cravat and worn as a part of formal horse-riding dress. ■ a piece of black material worn under a clerical collar.
10 (**stocks**) a frame used to support a ship or boat out of water, esp. when under construction.
▶ adj. [attrib.] **1** (of a product or type of product) usually kept in stock and thus regularly available for sale: *25 percent off stock items.*
2 (of a phrase or expression) so regularly used as to be automatic or hackneyed: *"Two weeks" was the stock reply.* ■ denoting a conventional character type or situation that recurs in a particular genre of literature, theater, or film: *the stock characters in every cowboy movie.* ■ denoting or relating to cinematic footage that can be regularly used in different productions, typically that of outdoor scenes used to add realism to a production shot in an indoor set.
▶ v. [with obj.] **1** have or keep a supply of (a particular product or type or product) available for sale: *most supermarkets now stock a range of organic produce.* ■ provide or fill with goods, items, or a supply of something: *I must **stock up** the fridge |* [as adj., with submodifier or in combination] (**stocked**) *a well-stocked store.* ■ [no obj.] (**stock up**) amass supplies of something, typically for a particular occasion or purpose: *I'm stocking up for Christmas | you'd better stock up with fuel.*
2 fit (a rifle or other firearm) with a stock.
–PHRASES **in** (or **out of**) **stock** (of goods) available (or unavailable) for immediate sale in a store. **on the stocks** in construction or preparation: *also on the stocks is a bill to bring about tax relief for these businesses.* **put stock in** [often with negative] have a specified amount of belief or faith in: *I don't put much stock in modern medicine.* **take stock** review or make an overall assessment of a particular situation, typically as a prelude to making a decision: *he needed a period of peace and quiet in order to **take stock of** his life.*
–DERIVATIVES **stock·less** adj.
–ORIGIN Old English *stoc(c)* 'trunk, block of wood, post,' of Germanic origin; related to Dutch *stok* and German *Stock* 'stick.' The notion 'store, fund' (sense 1 of the noun and sense 2 of the noun) arose in late Middle English and is of obscure origin, perhaps expressing 'growth from a central stem' or 'firm foundation.'

stock·ade /stäˈkād/ ▶ n. a barrier formed from upright wooden posts or stakes, esp. as a defense against attack or as a means of confining animals. ■ an enclosure bound by such a barrier: *we got ashore and into the stockade.* ■ a military prison.
▶ v. [with obj.] (usu. as adj. **stockaded**) enclose (an area) by erecting such a barrier.
–ORIGIN early 17th cent.: shortening of obsolete French *estocade*, alteration of *estacade*, from Spanish *estacada*, from the Germanic base of the noun STAKE[1].

stock·breed·er /ˈstäkˌbrēdər/ ▶ n. a farmer who breeds livestock.
–DERIVATIVES **stock·breed·ing** /-ˌbrēdiNG/ n.

stock brick ▶ n. a hard solid brick pressed in a mold.

Stock·bridge /ˈstäkˌbrij/ a resort town in western Massachusetts, in the Berkshire Hills; pop. 2,217 (est. 2008). Tanglewood estate, site of a noted summer music festival, is here.

stock·brok·er /ˈstäkˌbrōkər/ ▶ n. a broker who buys and sells securities on a stock exchange on behalf of clients.
–DERIVATIVES **stock·brok·er·age** /-ˌbrōk(ə)rij/ n., **stock·brok·ing** /-ˌbrōkiNG/ n.

stock·brok·er belt ▶ n. Brit. an affluent residential area outside a large city.

stock car ▶ n. **1** an ordinary car that has been modified for racing.
2 a railroad car for transporting livestock.

stock com·pa·ny ▶ n. a repertory company that is largely based in one theater.

stock dove /dəv/ ▶ n. a gray Eurasian and North African pigeon that resembles a small wood pigeon and nests in holes in trees. ● *Columba oenas*, family Columbidae.

stock·er /ˈstäkər/ ▶ n. **1** a farm animal, typically a young steer or heifer, destined for slaughter but kept until matured or fattened.
2 a person whose job is to fill the shelves of a store or supermarket with merchandise.
3 informal a stock car.

stock ex·change ▶ n. a market in which securities are bought and sold: *the company was **floated on the Stock Exchange**.* ■ (**the Stock Exchange**) the level of prices in such a market: *a plunge in the Stock Exchange during the election campaign.*

stock·feed /ˈstäkˌfēd/ ▶ n. food for livestock: *meat and bonemeal stockfeed has been banned for all livestock.*

stock·fish /ˈstäkˌfiSH/ ▶ n. (pl. **same** or **stockfishes**) **1** cod or a similar fish split and dried in the open air without salt.
2 a commercially valuable hake of coastal waters of southern Africa. ● *Merluccius capensis*, family Merlucciidae.
–ORIGIN Middle English (sense 1): from Middle Low German and Middle Dutch *stokvisch*, of unknown origin; sense 2 (early 19th cent.) from South African Dutch.

Stock·haus·en /ˈstäkˌhouzən/, Karlheinz (1928–2007), German composer, an important avant-garde composer and exponent of serialism.

stock·hold·er /ˈstäkˌhōldər/ ▶ n. a shareholder.
–DERIVATIVES **stock·hold·ing** /-ˌhōldiNG/ n.

Stock·holm /ˈstäkˌhō(l)m/ the capital of Sweden, a seaport on the eastern coast, on the mainland and on numerous adjacent islands; pop. 810,120 (2008).

Stock·holm syn·drome ▶ n. feelings of trust or affection felt in certain cases of kidnapping or hostage-taking by a victim toward a captor.
–ORIGIN 1970s: with reference to a bank robbery in Stockholm, Sweden.

Stock·holm tar ▶ n. a kind of tar prepared from resinous pinewood and used esp. in shipbuilding and as an ingredient of ointments.

stock horse ▶ n. a horse that is trained to herd livestock.

stock in·dex fu·tures ▶ plural n. contracts to buy a range of shares at an agreed price but delivered and paid for later.

stock·i·nette /ˌstäkəˈnet/ (also **stockinet**) ▶ n. **1** a soft, loosely knitted stretch fabric, formerly used for making underwear and now used for cleaning, wrapping, or bandaging.
2 (also **stockinette stitch**) a knitting stitch consisting of alternate rows of knit (plain) and purl stitch.
–ORIGIN late 18th cent.: probably an alteration of *stocking-net*.

stock·ing /ˈstäkiNG/ ▶ n. a women's garment, typically made of translucent nylon or silk, that fits closely over the foot and is held up by garters or an elasticized strip at the upper thigh. ■ short for CHRISTMAS STOCKING. ■ a long sock worn by men. ■ [usu. with modifier] a cylindrical bandage or other medical covering for the leg resembling a stocking, esp. an elasticized support used in the treatment of disorders of the veins. ■ a white marking of the lower part of a horse's leg, extending as far as, or just beyond, the knee or hock.
–PHRASES **in (one's) stocking feet** without shoes: *she stood five feet ten in her stocking feet.*
–DERIVATIVES **stock·inged** /ˈstäkiNGd/ adj. [in combination] *her black-stockinged legs*, **stock·ing·less** adj.
–ORIGIN late 16th cent.: from STOCK in the dialect sense 'stocking' + -ING[1].

stock·ing cap ▶ n. a knitted conical hat with a long tapered end, often bearing a tassel, that hangs down.

stock·ing mask ▶ n. a nylon stocking pulled over the face to disguise the features, used by criminals.

stock·ing stitch ▶ n. another term for STOCKINETTE (sense 2).

stock·ing stuff·er (Brit. **stocking filler**) ▶ n. a small present suitable for putting in a Christmas stocking.

stock-in-trade ▶ n. the typical subject or commodity a person, company, or profession uses or deals in: *information is our stock-in-trade.* ■ qualities, ideas, or behavior characteristic of a person or their work: *flippancy is his stock-in-trade.* ■ the goods kept on hand by a business for the purposes of its trade.

stock·ist /ˈstäkist/ ▶ n. Brit. a retailer that stocks goods of a particular type for sale: *one of the country's largest stockists of Italian designer labels.*

stock·job·ber /ˈstäkˌjäbər/ ▶ n. derogatory a stockbroker.
–DERIVATIVES **stock·job·bing** /-ˌjäbiNG/ n.

stock·man /ˈstäkmən, -ˌman/ ▶ n. (pl. **stockmen**) **1** a person who looks after livestock. ■ an owner of livestock.
2 a person who looks after a stockroom or warehouse.

stock mar·ket ▶ n. (usu. **the stock market**) a stock exchange.

stock op·tion ▶ n. a benefit in the form of an option given by a company to an employee to buy stock in the company at a discount or at a stated fixed price.

stock·out /ˈstäkˌout/ ▶ n. a situation in which an item is out of stock.

stock·pile /ˈstäkˌpīl/ ▶ n. a large accumulated stock of goods or materials, esp. one held in reserve for use at a time of shortage or other emergency.
▶ v. [with obj.] accumulate a large stock of (goods or materials): *he claimed that the weapons were being stockpiled.*
–DERIVATIVES **stock·pil·er** n.

Stock·port /ˈstäkˌpôrt/ an industrial town in northwestern England, near Manchester; pop. 133,400 (est. 2009).

stock·pot /ˈstäkˌpät/ ▶ n. a pot in which stock for soup is prepared by long, slow cooking.

stock·room /ˈstäkˌro͞om, -ˌro͝om/ ▶ n. a room in which quantities of goods are stored.

S

stock split ▸ **n.** an issue of new shares in a company to existing shareholders in proportion to their current holdings.

stock-still ▸ **adv.** without any movement; completely still: *he stood stock-still.*

stock swap ▸ **n. 1** acquisition of a company in which payment consists of stock in the buying company.
2 a means of exercising stock options in which shares already owned are traded for a greater number of shares at the exercise price.

stock·tak·ing /ˈstäk,tākiNG/ ▸ **n.** the action or process of recording the amount of stock held by a business: *the store is closed for stocktaking.* ■ the action of reviewing and assessing one's situation and options: *she had some mental stocktaking to do.*
– DERIVATIVES **stock·take n.**, **stock·tak·er** /-,tākər/ **n.**

Stock·ton /ˈstäktən/ an industrial city in north central California, a port on the San Joaquin River; pop. 287,037 (est. 2008).

Stock·ton-on-Tees /ˈstäktən än ˈtēz, ôn/ an industrial town in northeastern England, a port on the Tees River near its mouth on the North Sea; pop. 80,600 (est. 2009).

stock whip ▸ **n.** a whip used for driving cattle.

stock·y /ˈstäkē/ ▸ **adj.** (**stockier, stockiest**) (of a person) broad and sturdily built.
– DERIVATIVES **stock·i·ly** /ˈstäkəlē/ **adv.**, **stock·i·ness n.**

stock·yard /ˈstäk,yärd/ ▸ **n.** a large yard containing pens and sheds, typically adjacent to a slaughterhouse, in which livestock is kept and sorted.

stodge /stäj/ ▸ **n.** informal, chiefly Brit. **1** food that is heavy, filling, and high in carbohydrates: *she ate her way through a plateful of stodge.*
2 dull and uninspired material or work.
– ORIGIN late 17th cent. (as a verb in the sense 'stuff to stretching point'): symbolic, suggested by STUFF and PODGE.

stodg·y /ˈstäjē/ ▸ **adj.** (**stodgier, stodgiest**) **1** dull and uninspired: *some of the material is rather stodgy and top-heavy with facts.*
2 Brit. (of food) heavy, filling, and high in carbohydrates. ■ bulky or heavy in appearance: *this stodgy three-story building.*
– DERIVATIVES **stodg·i·ly** /ˈstäjəlē/ **adv.**, **stodg·i·ness n.**

stoep /sto͞op/ ▸ **n.** S. African a terraced porch in front of a house.
– ORIGIN Afrikaans, from Dutch; related to STEP.

stog /stäg/ ▸ **v.** (**be stogged**) dialect be stuck or bogged down: *people are stogged in their misery.*
– ORIGIN early 19th cent.: perhaps symbolic and suggested by STICK[2] and BOG.

sto·gie /ˈstōgē/ (also **stogy**) ▸ **n.** (pl. **stogies**) a long, thin, inexpensive cigar.
– ORIGIN mid 19th cent. (originally as *stoga*): from *Conestoga*, because the cigars are thought to have been smoked by the drivers of Conestoga wagons.

sto·ic /ˈstō-ik/ ▸ **n. 1** a person who can endure pain or hardship without showing their feelings or complaining.
2 (**Stoic**) a member of the ancient philosophical school of Stoicism.
▸ **adj. 1** another term for STOICAL.
2 (**Stoic**) of or belonging to the Stoics or their school of philosophy.
– ORIGIN late Middle English: via Latin from Greek *stōïkos*, from STOA (with reference to Zeno's teaching in the *Stoa Poikilē* or Painted Porch, at Athens).

sto·i·cal /ˈstō-ikəl/ ▸ **adj.** enduring pain and hardship without showing one's feelings or complaining: *he taught a stoical acceptance of suffering.*
– DERIVATIVES **sto·i·cal·ly** /-ik(ə)lē/ **adv.**

stoi·chi·o·met·ric /,stoikē-ōˈmetrik/ ▸ **adj.** Chemistry of or relating to stoichiometry. ■ relating to or denoting quantities of reactants in simple integral ratios, as prescribed by an equation or formula.
– DERIVATIVES **stoi·chi·o·met·ri·cal·ly** /-ik(ə)lē/ **adv.**

stoi·chi·om·e·try /,stoikēˈämitrē/ ▸ **n.** Chemistry the relationship between the relative quantities of substances taking part in a reaction or forming a compound, typically a ratio of whole integers.
– ORIGIN early 19th cent.: from Greek *stoikheion* 'element' + -METRY.

sto·i·cism /ˈstō-i,sizəm/ ▸ **n. 1** the endurance of pain or hardship without a display of feelings and without complaint.
2 (**Stoicism**) an ancient Greek school of philosophy founded at Athens by Zeno of Citium. The school taught that virtue, the highest good, is based on knowledge, and that the wise live in harmony with the divine Reason (also identified with Fate and Providence) that governs nature, and are indifferent to the vicissitudes of fortune and to pleasure and pain.

stoke /stōk/ ▸ **v.** [with obj.] add coal or other solid fuel to (a fire, furnace, or boiler). ■ encourage or incite (a strong emotion or tendency): *his composure had the effect of stoking her anger.* ■ (often as adj. **stoked**) informal excite or thrill: *when they told me I was on the team, I was stoked.* ■ [no obj.] informal consume a large quantity of food or drink to give one energy: *Carol was at the coffee machine, stoking up for the day.*
– ORIGIN mid 17th cent.: back-formation from STOKER.

stoke·hold /ˈstōk,hōld/ ▸ **n.** a compartment in a steamship from which the boiler fires are stoked.

stoke·hole /ˈstōk,hōl/ ▸ **n.** a space in front of a furnace in which a stoker works.

Stoke-on-Trent /ˈstōk än ˈtrent, ôn/ a city on the River Trent in central England; pop. 248,300 (est. 2009).

Stok·er /ˈstōkər/, Bram (1847–1912), Irish novelist and theater manager; full name *Abraham Stoker*. He is chiefly remembered as the author of the vampire story *Dracula* (1897).

stok·er /ˈstōkər/ ▸ **n.** a person who tends the furnace on a steamship or steam locomotive. ■ a mechanical device for supplying fuel to a firebox or furnace, esp. on a steam locomotive.
– ORIGIN mid 17th cent.: from Dutch, from *stoken* 'stoke (a furnace),' from Middle Dutch *stoken* 'push, poke'; related to STICK[1].

stokes /stōks/ (abbr.: **ST**) ▸ **n.** (pl. **same**) Physics the cgs unit of kinematic viscosity, corresponding to a dynamic viscosity of 1 poise and a density of 1 gram per cubic centimeter, equivalent to 10^{-4} square meters per second.
– ORIGIN mid 20th cent.: from the name of Sir G. *Stokes* (see STOKES' LAW).

Stokes' law /stōks/ Physics **1** a law stating that in fluorescence the wavelength of the emitted radiation is longer than that of the radiation causing it. This is not true in all cases.
2 an expression describing the resisting force on a particle moving through a viscous fluid and showing that a maximum velocity is reached in such cases, e.g., for an object falling under gravity through a fluid.
– ORIGIN late 19th cent.: named after Sir George *Stokes* (1819–1903), British physicist.

Stokes' the·o·rem Mathematics a theorem proposing that the surface integral of the curl of a function over any surface bounded by a closed path is equal to the line integral of a particular vector function around that path.
– ORIGIN late 19th cent.: named after Sir G. *Stokes* (see STOKES' LAW).

Sto·kow·ski /stəˈkôfskē, -ˈkou-/, Leopold (1882–1977), US conductor, born in Britain. He is best known for arranging and conducting the music for Walt Disney's movie *Fantasia* (1940), which sought to bring classical music to movie audiences by means of cartoons.

STOL /ˈestôl, stôl/ ▸ **abbr.** Aeronautics short takeoff and landing.

stole[1] /stōl/ ▸ **n.** a woman's long scarf or shawl, esp. fur or similar material, worn loosely over the shoulders. ■ of a strip of fabric used as an ecclesiastical vestment, worn over the shoulders and hanging down to the knee or below.
– ORIGIN Old English (in the senses 'long robe' and 'priest's vestment'), via Latin from Greek *stolē* 'clothing,' from *stellein* 'array.'

ecclesiastical stole

stole[2] past of STEAL.

sto·len /ˈstōlən/ past participle of STEAL.

sto·len gen·er·a·tion ▸ **n.** Austral. the Aboriginal people forcibly removed from their families as children between the 1900s and the 1960s, to be brought up by white foster families or in institutions.

stol·id /ˈstälid/ ▸ **adj.** (of a person) calm, dependable, and showing little emotion or animation.
– DERIVATIVES **sto·lid·i·ty** /stəˈliditē/ **n.**, **stol·id·ly adv.**, **stol·id·ness n.**
– ORIGIN late 16th cent.: from obsolete French *stolide* or Latin *stolidus* (perhaps related to *stultus* 'foolish').

stol·len /ˈstōlən, ˈSHtō-/ ▸ **n.** a rich German fruit and nut loaf.
– ORIGIN from German *Stollen*.

sto·lon /ˈstōlən/ ▸ **n. 1** Botany a creeping horizontal plant stem or runner that takes root at points along its length to form new plants. ■ an arching stem of a plant that roots at the tip to form a new plant, as in the bramble.
2 Zoology the branched stemlike structure of some colonial hydroid coelenterates, attaching the colony to the substrate.
– DERIVATIVES **sto·lon·ate** /-nit, -,nāt/ **adj.**, **sto·lo·nif·er·ous** /,stōləˈnif(ə)rəs/ **adj.**
– ORIGIN early 17th cent.: from Latin *stolo, stolon-* 'shoot, scion.'

sto·ma /ˈstōmə/ ▸ **n.** (pl. **stomas** or **stomata** /-mətə, ,stōˈmätə/) Botany any of the minute pores in the epidermis of the leaf or stem of a plant, forming a slit of variable width that allows movement of gases in and out of the intercellular spaces. Also called STOMATE. ■ Zoology a small mouthlike opening in some lower animals. ■ Medicine an artificial opening made into a hollow organ, esp. one on the surface of the body leading to the gut or trachea.
– DERIVATIVES **sto·mal adj.** (Medicine).
– ORIGIN late 17th cent.: modern Latin, from Greek *stoma* 'mouth.'

stom·ach /ˈstəmək/ ▸ **n. 1** the internal organ in which the first part of the digestion of food occurs, being (in humans and many mammals) a pear-shaped enlargement of the alimentary canal linking the esophagus to the small intestine. ■ each of four such organs in a ruminant (the rumen, reticulum, omasum, and abomasum). ■ any of a number of organs analogous to a stomach in lower animals. ■ the front part of the body between the chest and thighs; the belly: *Blake hit him in the stomach.* ■ [in sing.] the stomach viewed as the seat of hunger, nausea, anxiety, or other unsettling feelings: *Virginia had a sick feeling in her stomach.*
2 [in sing., usu. with negative] an appetite for food or drink: *she doesn't have the stomach to eat anything.* ■ a desire or inclination for something involving conflict, difficulty, or unpleasantness: *the teams proved to have **no stomach for a fight*** | [with infinitive] *frankly, I don't have the stomach to find out.*
▸ **v.** [with obj.] (usu. **cannot stomach**) consume (food or drink) without feeling or being sick: *if you cannot stomach orange juice, try apple juice.* ■ endure or accept (an obnoxious thing or person): *I can't stomach the self-righteous attitude of some managers.*
– PHRASES **an army marches on its stomach** a group of soldiers or workers can only fight or function effectively if they have been well fed. [translating French *c'est la soupe qui fait le soldat*, a maxim of Napoleon.] **on a full** (or **an empty**) **stomach** after having eaten (or having not eaten): *I think better on a full stomach.* **a strong stomach** an ability to see or do unpleasant things without feeling sick or squeamish.
– DERIVATIVES **stom·ach·ful** /-,fo͝ol/ **n.** (pl. **stomachfuls**).
– ORIGIN Middle English: from Old French *estomac, stomaque*, via Latin from Greek *stomakhos* 'gullet,' from *stoma* 'mouth.' The early sense of the verb was 'be offended at, resent' (early 16th cent).

stom·ach·ache /ˈstəmək,āk/ ▸ **n.** a pain in a person's belly: *most childhood stomachaches aren't serious.*

stom·ach·er /ˈstəməkər/ ▸ **n.** historical a V-shaped piece of decorative cloth, worn over the chest and stomach by men and women in the 16th century, later only by women.
– ORIGIN late Middle English: probably a shortening of Old French *estomachier*, from *estomac* (see STOMACH).

stom·ach flu ▸ **n.** a short-lived stomach disorder of unknown cause, popularly attributed to a virus.

sto·mach·ic /stəˈmakik/ dated ▸ **adj.** promoting the appetite or assisting digestion. ■ of or relating to the stomach.
▸ **n.** a medicine or tonic that promotes the appetite or assists digestion.

sto·mach mus·cles ▸ **plural n.** the muscles constituting the front wall of the abdomen.

sto·mach pump ▸ **n.** a syringe attached to a long tube, used for extracting the contents of a person's stomach (for example, if they have swallowed poison).

sto·ma·ta /ˈstōmətə, stōˈmätə/ plural form of STOMA.

stom·a·tal /ˈstōmətl, ˈstäm-/ ▸ **adj.** chiefly Botany of or relating to a stoma or stomata.

sto·mate /ˈstō,māt/ ▸ **n.** Botany another term for STOMA.
– ORIGIN mid 19th cent.: apparently an English singular of STOMATA.

sto·ma·ti·tis /,stōməˈtītis/ ▸ **n.** Medicine inflammation of the mucous membrane of the mouth.
– ORIGIN mid 19th cent.: modern Latin, from *stoma, stomat-* 'mouth' + -ITIS.

sto·ma·to·gas·tric /stō,matəˈgastrik, ,stōmətə-/ ▶ **adj.** chiefly Zoology relating to or connected with the mouth and stomach, particularly denoting a system of visceral nerves in invertebrates.
– ORIGIN mid 19th cent.: from Greek *stoma, stomat-* 'mouth' + **GASTRIC**.

stomp /stämp, stômp/ ▶ **v.** [no obj.] tread heavily and noisily, typically in order to show anger: *Martin stomped off to the spare room.* ■ (**stomp on**) tread heavily or stamp on: *I stomped on the accelerator.* ■ [with obj.] deliberately trample or tread heavily on: *Cobb proceeded to kick and stomp him viciously.* ■ [with obj.] stamp (one's feet). ■ dance with heavy stamping steps.
▶ **n.** informal (in jazz or popular music) a tune or song with a fast tempo and a heavy beat. ■ a lively dance performed to such music, involving heavy stamping.
– DERIVATIVES **stomp·er n.**, **stomp·y adj.**
– ORIGIN early 19th cent. (originally US dialect): variant of the verb **STAMP**.

stomp·ing /ˈstämpiNG, ˈstôm-/ ▶ **adj.** (of music) having a lively stamping rhythm.

stomp·ing ground (also **stamping ground**) ▶ **n.** a place where someone regularly spends time; a favorite haunt.

Stone[1] /stōn/, Edward Durell (1902–78), US architect. His notable designs include the Museum of Modern Art in New York City 1937–39; the US embassy in New Delhi, India 1954–58; and the John F. Kennedy Center for the Performing Arts in Washington, DC 1964–69.

Stone[2], Harlan Fiske (1872–1946), US chief justice 1941–46. He was the dean of the Columbia Law School 1910–24 and, briefly, US attorney general 1924 in President Coolidge's cabinet before he was appointed to the US Supreme Court as an associate justice 1925–41. He was named chief justice by President Franklin D. Roosevelt.

Stone[3], Lucy (1818–93), US feminist and abolitionist. The first woman in Massachusetts to earn a college degree (Oberlin College 1847), she traveled widely during the 1850s lecturing on women's rights. In 1869, she founded the American Woman Suffrage Association, which merged with the National Woman Suffrage Association in 1890 to form the National American Woman Suffrage Association.

Stone[4] /stōn/, Oliver (1946–), US movie director, screenwriter, and producer. He won Academy Awards for his adaptation of the novel *Midnight Express* (1978) and for his direction of *Platoon* (1986) and *Born on the Fourth of July* (1989), both of which indict US involvement in the Vietnam War. Other notable movies: *JFK* (1991) and *Natural Born Killers* (1994).

stone /stōn/ ▶ **n. 1** the hard, solid, nonmetallic mineral matter of which rock is made, esp. as a building material: *the houses are built of stone* | [as modifier] *high stone walls.* ■ a small piece of rock found on the ground. ■ (in metaphorical use) weight or lack of feeling, expression, or movement: *Isabel stood as if* ***turned to stone*** | *her face became* ***as hard as stone*** | *the elevator* ***dropped like a stone.*** ■ Astronomy a meteorite made of rock, as opposed to metal. ■ Medicine a calculus; a gallstone or kidney stone.
2 a piece of stone shaped for a purpose, esp. one of commemoration, ceremony, or demarcation: *a memorial stone* | *boundary stones.* ■ a gem or jewel. ■ short for **CURLING STONE**. ■ a round piece or counter, originally made of stone, used in various board games such as backgammon. ■ a large flat table or sheet, originally made of stone and later usually of metal, on which pages of type were made up.
3 a hard seed in a cherry, plum, peach, and some other fruits.
4 (pl. **same**) Brit. a unit of weight equal to 14 pounds (6.35 kg): *I weighed 10 stone.*
5 a natural shade of whitish-gray or brownish-gray: [as modifier] *stone stretch trousers.*
▶ **v.** [with obj.] **1** throw stones at: *policemen were stoned by the crowd.*
2 remove the stone from (a fruit): *halve, stone, and peel the avocados.*
3 build, face, or pave with stone.
– PHRASES **be written** (or **engraved** or **set**) **in stone** used to emphasize that something is fixed and unchangeable: *anything can change—nothing is written in stone.* **cast** (or **throw**) **the first stone** be the first to make an accusation (used to emphasize that a potential critic is not wholly blameless). [with biblical allusion to John 8:7.] **leave no stone unturned** try every possible course of action in order to achieve something. **stone me!** (or **stone the crows!**) Brit. informal an exclamation of surprise or shock. **a stone's throw** a short distance: *wild whales blowing a stone's throw from the boat.*
– DERIVATIVES **stone·less adj.**
– ORIGIN Old English *stān* (noun), of Germanic origin; related to Dutch *steen* and German *Stein*. The verb dates from Middle English (first recorded sense 1 of the noun).

Stone Age a prehistoric period when weapons and tools were made of stone or of organic materials such as bone, wood, or horn.

> The Stone Age covers a period of about 2.5 million years, from the first use of tools by the ancestors of man (*Australopithecus*) to the introduction of agriculture and the first towns. It is subdivided into the Paleolithic, Mesolithic, and Neolithic periods, and is succeeded in Europe by the Bronze Age (or, sometimes, the Copper Age) about 5,000–4,000 years ago.

stone boat ▶ **n.** a flat-bottomed sled used for transporting stones and other heavy objects.

stone broke ▶ **adj.** informal entirely without money.

stone·chat /ˈstōn,CHat/ ▶ **n.** a small Old World songbird of the thrush subfamily, having bold markings and a call that sounds like two stones being knocked together. ● Genus *Saxicola*, subfamily Turdinae, family Muscicapidae: three or four species, in particular the widespread *S. torquata*, the male of which has a black head and orange breast.

stone chi·na ▶ **n.** a kind of very hard earthenware resembling porcelain.

stone cold ▶ **adj.** completely cold.
▶ **adv.** (**stone-cold**) [as submodifier] completely: *stone-cold sober.*

stone crab ▶ **n.** a large, heavy, edible crab of the Gulf of Mexico and Caribbean area. ● *Menippe mercenaria*, family Xanthidae.

stone·crop /ˈstōn,kräp/ ▶ **n.** a small fleshy-leaved plant that typically has star-shaped yellow or white flowers and grows among rocks or on walls. ● Genus *Sedum*, family Crassulaceae: many species, including the **mossy stonecrop** (*S. acre*), whose tiny, thick leaves have a bitter, peppery taste.

stone cur·lew ▶ **n.** another term for **THICK-KNEE**.

stone·cut·ter /ˈstōn,kətər/ ▶ **n.** a person who cuts stone from a quarry or who shapes and carves it for use.

stoned /stōnd/ ▶ **adj.** informal under the influence of drugs, esp. marijuana: *he was up in the deck chair getting stoned.* ■ very drunk.

stone dead ▶ **adj.** [predic.] completely dead.

stone deaf ▶ **adj.** completely deaf: *the racket drove out any deer not stone deaf* | *the stone-deaf person relies entirely on sight.*

stone face ▶ **n.** informal a face that reveals no emotions.
– DERIVATIVES **stone-faced adj.**

stone·fish /ˈstōn,fiSH/ ▶ **n.** (pl. **same** or **stonefishes**) a chiefly marine fish of bizarre appearance that lives in the tropical Indo-Pacific. It rests motionless in the sand with its venomous dorsal spines projecting and is a frequent cause of injury to swimmers. ● Family Synanceiidae: several genera and species, including *Synanceia verrucosa* (also called **DEVILFISH**.).

stone·fly /ˈstōn,flī/ ▶ **n.** (pl. **stoneflies**) a slender insect with transparent membranous wings, the larvae of which live in clean running water. The adults are used as bait by fly fishermen. ● Order Plecoptera: many families.

stone fruit ▶ **n.** a fruit with flesh or pulp enclosing a stone, such as a peach, plum, or cherry.

stone·ground /ˈstōnˈground/ ▶ **adj.** (of flour) ground with millstones.

Stone·henge /ˈstōn,henj/ a megalithic monument on Salisbury Plain in Wiltshire, England. Completed in several constructional phases from *c.*2950 BC, it was probably used for ritual purposes.
– ORIGIN from Old English *stān* 'stone' + an element related to *hengan* 'to hang.'

stone lil·y ▶ **n.** (pl. **stone lilies**) dated a fossilized sea lily.

Stonehenge

stone mar·ten ▶ **n.** a Eurasian marten that has chocolate-brown fur with a white throat. Also called **BEECH MARTEN**. ● *Martes foina*, family Mustelidae.

stone·ma·son /ˈstōn,māsən/ ▶ **n.** a person who cuts, prepares, and builds with stone.
– DERIVATIVES **stone·ma·son·ry** /-,māsənrē/ **n.**

Stone Moun·tain a granite mass east of Atlanta, Georgia, site of the Confederate Memorial Carving, the world's largest bas-relief sculpture, which features the figures of Jefferson Davis, Robert E. Lee, and Thomas "Stonewall" Jackson, all on horseback.

stone pine ▶ **n.** an umbrella-shaped southern European pine tree with large needles, very large glossy brown cones, and edible seeds ("pine nuts"). Also called **UMBRELLA PINE**. ● *Pinus pinea*, family Pinaceae.

ston·er /ˈstōnər/ ▶ **n. 1** informal a person who regularly takes drugs, esp. marijuana: *I was a real stoner when I was a teenager.*
2 [in combination] Brit. a person or thing that weighs a specified number of stone: *a couple of 16-stoners.*

stone·roll·er ▶ **n.** a small freshwater fish of the minnow family that uses the hard ridge on its lower jaw to scrape food, esp. algae, from rocks. ● Genus *Campostoma*, family Cyprinidae: several species, including the **central stoneroller** (*C. anomalum*) of the eastern and central US, and the **Mexican stoneroller** (*C. ornatum*) of the southwestern US and northern Mexico.

stone·wall /ˈstōn,wôl/ ▶ **v.** [with obj.] delay or block (a request, process, or person) by refusing to answer questions or by giving evasive replies, esp. in politics: *the highest level of bureaucracy stonewalled us* | (as noun **stonewalling**) *the art of stonewalling and political intimidation.*
– DERIVATIVES **stone·wall·er n.**

Stone·wall Jack·son see **JACKSON**[9].

stoneware /ˈstōn,we(ə)r/ ▶ **n.** a type of pottery that is impermeable and partly vitrified but opaque.

stone·washed /ˈstōn,wôSHt, -,wäSHt/ (also **stonewash**) ▶ **adj.** (of a garment or fabric, esp. denim) washed with abrasives to produce a worn or faded appearance.

stone·work /ˈstōn,wərk/ ▶ **n.** the parts of a building that are made of stone. ■ the work of a mason: *a masterpiece of clever stonework.*
– DERIVATIVES **stone·work·er n.**

stone·wort /ˈstōnwərt, -,wôrt/ ▶ **n.** a freshwater plant with whorls of slender leaves, related to green algae. Many kinds become encrusted with chalky deposits, giving them a stony feel. ● *Chara* and other genera in the class Charophyceae, division Chlorophyta; sometimes placed in its own division (Charophyta).

stonk /stäNGk/ military slang ▶ **n.** a concentrated artillery bombardment.
▶ **v.** [with obj.] bombard with concentrated artillery fire.
– ORIGIN 1940s: said to be formed from elements of the artillery term *Standard Regimental Concentration.*

stonk·er /ˈstäNGkər, ˈstôNG-/ ▶ **n.** Brit. informal something that is very large or impressive of its kind: *it's a real stonker of a plan.*

stonk·ing /ˈstäNGkiNG, ˈstôNG-/ ▶ **adj.** Brit. informal used to emphasize something remarkable, exciting, or very large: *a stonking 207 mph maximum speed.*
– ORIGIN 1980s: from the verb **STONK**.

ston·y /ˈstōnē/ ▶ **adj.** (**stonier, stoniest**) covered with or full of small pieces of rock: *rough stony paths.* ■ made of or resembling stone: *stony steps.* ■ not having or showing feeling or sympathy: *Lorenzo's hard, stony eyes* | [in combination] *he walked away, stony-faced.* ■ Astronomy (of a meteorite) consisting mostly of rock, as opposed to metal.
– PHRASES **fall on stony ground** (of words or a suggestion) be ignored or badly received. [with biblical reference to the parable of the sower (Matt. 13:5).]
– DERIVATIVES **ston·i·ly** /-nəlē/ **adv.**, **ston·i·ness n.**
– ORIGIN Old English *stānig* (see **STONE**, **-Y**[1]).

ston·y cor·al ▶ **n.** see **CORAL** (sense 2).

ston·y-heart·ed ▶ **adj.** cruel or unfeeling.

ston·y-i·ron Astronomy ▶ **adj.** (of a meteorite) containing appreciable quantities of both rock and iron.
▶ **n.** a stony-iron meteorite.

stood /sto͝od/ past and past participle of **STAND**.

stooge /sto͞oj/ ▶ **n. 1** derogatory a person who serves merely to support or assist others, particularly in

S

doing unpleasant work: *you fell for that helpless-female act and let her make you a stooge.*
2 a performer whose act involves being the butt of a comedian's jokes.
▶ **v.** [no obj.] **1** move around aimlessly; drift or cruise: *she **stooged around** in the bathroom for a while.*
2 perform a role that involves being the butt of a comedian's jokes.
– ORIGIN early 20th cent.: of unknown origin.

stook /stŏŏk, stōōk/ Brit. ▶ **n.** a group of sheaves of grain stood on end in a field.
▶ **v.** [with obj.] arrange in stooks.
– ORIGIN Middle English (as a noun): from or related to Middle Low German *stūke.*

stool /stōōl/ ▶ **n. 1** a seat without a back or arms, typically resting on three or four legs or on a single pedestal. ■ short for FOOTSTOOL.
2 a piece of feces.
3 a root or stump of a tree or plant from which shoots spring.
4 a decoy bird in hunting.
▶ **v.** [no obj.] (of a plant) throw up shoots from the root. ■ [with obj.] cut back (a plant) to or near ground level in order to induce new growth.
– PHRASES **at stool** Medicine when defecating.
– ORIGIN Old English, of Germanic origin; related to Dutch *stoel,* German *Stuhl,* also to STAND. Current senses of the verb date from the late 18th cent.

stool·ie /ˈstōōlē/ ▶ **n.** informal short for STOOL PIGEON.

stool pi·geon ▶ **n.** a police informer. ■ a person acting as a decoy.
– ORIGIN late 19th cent.: so named from the original use of a pigeon fixed to a stool as a decoy.

stoop[1] /stōōp/ ▶ **v.** [no obj.] **1** bend one's head or body forward and downward: *he stooped down and reached toward the coin | Linda stooped to pick up the bottles |* [with obj.] *the man stoops his head.* ■ have the head and shoulders habitually bent forward: *he tends to stoop when he walks |* (as adj. **stooping**) *a thin, stooping figure.* ■ (of a bird of prey) swoop down on a quarry.
2 lower one's moral standards so far as to do something reprehensible: *Craig wouldn't stoop to thieving | she was unwilling to believe that anyone could **stoop so low** as to steal from a dead woman.* ■ [with infinitive] condescend to do something.
▶ **n. 1** [in sing.] a posture in which the head and shoulders are habitually bent forward: *a tall, thin man with a stoop.*
2 the downward swoop of a bird of prey.
– ORIGIN Old English *stūpian* (verb), of Germanic origin; related to the adjective STEEP[1]. Both senses of the noun date from the late 16th cent.

stoop[2] ▶ **n.** a porch with steps in front of a house or other building.
– ORIGIN mid 18th cent.: from Dutch *stoep* (see STOEP).

stoop ball ▶ **n.** a ball game resembling baseball in which the ball is thrown against a building or the steps of a stoop rather than to a batter.

stooped /stōōpt/ ▶ **adj.** (of a person) having the head and shoulders habitually bent forward: *a thin, stooped figure.* ■ (of the shoulders or another part of the body) habitually bent forward: *the man was slight, with stooped shoulders.*

stoop la·bor ▶ **n.** agricultural labor performed in a stooping or squatting position.

stop /stäp/ ▶ **v.** (**stops, stopping, stopped**) **1** [no obj.] (of an event, action, or process) come to an end; cease to happen: *his laughter stopped as quickly as it had begun | the rain had stopped and the clouds had cleared.* ■ [with present participle] cease to perform a specified action or have a specified experience: *she stopped giggling |* [with obj.] *he stopped work for tea.* ■ [with present participle] abandon a specified practice or habit: *I've stopped eating meat.* ■ stop moving or operating: *he stopped to look at the view | my watch has stopped.* ■ (of a bus or train) call at a designated place to pick up or let off passengers: *main-line trains stop at platform 7.* ■ Brit. informal stay somewhere for a short time: *you'll have to stop the night.*
2 [with obj.] cause (an action, process, or event) to come to an end: *this harassment has got to be stopped.* ■ prevent (an action or event) from happening: *a security guard was killed trying to stop a raid.* ■ prevent or dissuade (someone) from continuing in an activity or achieving an aim: *a campaign is under way to stop the bombers.* ■ prevent (someone or something) from performing a specified action or undergoing a specified experience: *you can't stop me from getting what I want.* ■ cause or order to cease moving or operating: *he stopped his car by the house | police were given powers to stop and search suspects.* ■ informal be hit by (a bullet). ■ instruct a bank to withhold payment on (a check). ■ refuse to supply as usual; withhold or deduct: *the union has threatened to stop the supply of minerals.* ■ Boxing defeat (an opponent) by a knockout: *he was stopped in the sixth by Tyson.*
3 [with obj.] block or close up (a hole or leak): *he tried to stop the hole with the heel of his boot | the drain has been stopped up.* ■ block the mouth of (a fox's earth) prior to a hunt. ■ plug the upper end of (an organ pipe), giving a note an octave lower. ■ obtain the required pitch from (the string of a violin or similar instrument) by pressing at the appropriate point with the finger. ■ make (a rope) fast with a stopper.
▶ **n. 1** a cessation of movement or operation: *all business **came to a stop** | there were constant stops and changes of pace.* ■ a break or halt during a journey: *allow an hour or so for driving and as long as you like for stops | the flight landed for a refueling stop.* ■ a place designated for a bus or train to halt and pick up or drop off passengers: *the bus was pulling up at her stop.* ■ an object or part of a mechanism that is used to prevent something from moving: *the shelves have special stops to prevent them from being pulled out too far.* ■ Brit. dated a punctuation mark, esp. a period. ■ used in telegrams to indicate a period: *MEET YOU AT THE AIRPORT STOP.* ■ Phonetics a consonant produced with complete closure of the vocal tract. ■ Bridge a high card that prevents the opponents from establishing a particular suit; a control. ■ Nautical a short length of cord used to secure something.
2 a set of organ pipes of a particular tone and range of pitch. ■ (also **stop knob**) a knob, lever, or similar device in an organ or harpsichord that brings into play a set of pipes or strings of a particular tone and range of pitch.
3 Photography the effective diameter of a lens. ■ a device for reducing this. ■ a unit of change of relative aperture or exposure (with a reduction of one stop equivalent to halving it).
– PHRASES **pull out all the stops** make a very great effort to achieve something: *the director pulled out all the stops to meet the impossible deadline.* ■ do something very elaborately or on a grand scale: *they gave a Christmas party and pulled out all the stops.* [with reference to the stops of an organ.] **put a stop to** cause (an activity) to end: *she would have to put a stop to all this nonsense.* **stop at nothing** be utterly ruthless or determined in one's attempt to achieve something: *he would stop at nothing to retain his position of power.* **stop dead** (or **short**) suddenly cease moving, speaking, or acting. **stop one's ears** put one's fingers in one's ears to avoid hearing something. **stop someone's mouth** induce someone to keep silent about something. **stop the show** (of a performer) provoke prolonged applause or laughter, causing an interruption.
– PHRASAL VERBS **stop by** (or **in**) call briefly and informally as a visitor. **stop something down** Photography reduce the aperture of a lens with a diaphragm. **stop off** (or **over**) pay a short visit en route to one's ultimate destination when traveling: *I stopped off to visit him and his wife | he decided to stop over in Paris.* **stop something out** cover an area that is not to be printed or etched when making a print or etching.
– DERIVATIVES **stop·pa·ble adj.**
– ORIGIN Old English (*for*)*stoppian* 'block up (an aperture)'; related to German *stopfen,* from late Latin *stuppare* 'to stuff.'

stop-and-go ▶ **n.** [usu. as modifier] alternate stopping and restarting of progress: *stop-and-go driving.*

stop·band /ˈstäp,band/ ▶ **n.** Electronics a band of frequencies that are attenuated by a filter.

stop·bank /ˈstäp,baNGk/ ▶ **n.** Austral./NZ an embankment built to prevent a river from flooding.

stop bath ▶ **n.** Photography a bath for stopping the action of a preceding bath by neutralizing any of its chemical still present.

stop bit ▶ **n.** Telecommunications (in asynchronous data transfers) one of a pattern of bits that indicate the end of a character or of the whole transmission.

stop·cock /ˈstäp,käk/ ▶ **n.** an externally operated valve regulating the flow of a liquid or gas through a pipe.

stope /stōp/ ▶ **n.** (usu. **stopes**) a steplike part of a mine where minerals are being extracted.
▶ **v.** [no obj.] (usu. as noun **stoping**) (in mining) excavate a series of steps or layers in (the ground or rock). ■ (as noun **stoping**) Geology the process by which country rock is broken up and removed by the upward movement of magma.
– ORIGIN mid 18th cent.: apparently related to the noun STEP.

stop·gap /ˈstäp,gap/ ▶ **n.** a temporary way of dealing with a problem or satisfying a need: *transplants are only a stopgap until more sophisticated alternatives can work.*

stop knob ▶ **n.** the knob controlling a stop on an organ or harpsichord.

stop·light /ˈstäp,līt/ ▶ **n. 1** another term for TRAFFIC LIGHT. ■ a red traffic light.
2 another term for BRAKE LIGHT.

stop list ▶ **n.** a list of words automatically omitted from a computer-generated concordance or index, typically the most frequent words, which would slow down processing unacceptably.

stop-loss ▶ **adj. 1** Finance denoting or relating to an order to sell a security or commodity at a specified price in order to limit a loss.
2 Military denoting or relating to a policy of forcibly retaining members of the armed forces on active duty beyond their original agreed period of enlistment.

stop-mo·tion ▶ **n.** [usu. as modifier] a cinematographic technique whereby the camera is repeatedly stopped and started, for example to give animated figures the impression of movement.

stop-off ▶ **n.** another term for STOPOVER.

stop-out ▶ **n.** Brit. informal a person who stays out late at night.

stop·o·ver /ˈstäp,ōvər/ ▶ **n.** a break in a journey: *the one-day stopover in Honolulu.* ■ a place where a journey is broken: *an inviting stopover between Quebec City and Montreal.*

stop·page /ˈstäpij/ ▶ **n.** an instance of movement, activity, or supply stopping or being stopped: *the result of the air raid was complete stoppage of production.* ■ a blockage in a narrow passage, such as the barrel of a gun. ■ a cessation of work by employees protesting the terms set by their employers. ■ Boxing a knockout.

stop·page time ▶ **n.** another term for INJURY TIME.

Stop·pard /ˈstäpərd, ˈstäp,ärd/, Sir Tom (1937–), British playwright, born in Czechoslovakia; born *Thomas Straussler.* His best-known plays are comedies, often dealing with metaphysical and ethical questions. His *Rosencrantz and Guildenstern Are Dead* (1966) is based on the characters from Shakespeare's *Hamlet.*

stop pay·ment ▶ **n.** an authorized withholding of payment on a check: *call the bank tomorrow and get a stop payment on that check.*
– ORIGIN the usage as a noun derives from the verb phrase *stop payment,* meaning "instruct a bank to withhold payment on a check."

stop·per /ˈstäpər/ ▶ **n. 1** a plug for sealing a hole, esp. in the neck of a bottle or other container.
2 a person or thing that halts or obstructs a specified thing: [in combination] *a crime-stopper.* ■ (in soccer and other sports) a player whose function is to block attacks on goal from the middle of the field. ■ Baseball a starting pitcher depended on to win a game or stop a losing streak, or a relief pitcher used to prevent the opposing team from scoring. ■ (in sailing or climbing) a rope or clamp for preventing a rope or cable from running out. ■ Bridge another term for CONTROL.
▶ **v.** (usu. as adj. **stoppered**) use a stopper to seal (a bottle or other container): *a small stoppered jar.*
– PHRASES **put a** (or **the**) **stopper on** informal prevent from happening or continuing.

stop·ping point ▶ **n.** a point or place at which it is convenient to stop during a journey or activity.

stop·ple /ˈstäpəl/ ▶ **n.** a stopper or plug.
▶ **v.** [with obj.] seal with a stopper.
– ORIGIN Middle English: partly a shortening of Old French *estouppail* 'bung,' reinforced by the verb STOP.

stop-start (also **stop-and-start**) ▶ **adj.** informal alternately stopping and starting; progressing with interruptions: *a $150 stop-start taxi ride.*

stop time ▶ **n.** (in jazz) a rhythmic device whereby a chord or accent is played only on the first beat of every bar or every other bar, typically accompanying a solo.

stop valve ▶ **n.** a valve used to stop the flow of liquid in a pipe.

stop vol·ley ▶ **n.** Tennis a volley played close to the net in which the player stops the ball without a forceful stroke, sending it just barely back over the net.

stop·watch /ˈstäp,wäCH/ ▶ **n.** a special watch with buttons that start, stop, and then zero the hands, used to time races.

stor·age /ˈstôrij/ ▶ **n.** the action or method of storing something for future use: *the chair can be folded flat for easy storage |* [as modifier] *the room lacked storage space.* ■ the retention of retrievable data on a computer or other electronic system; memory. ■ space available for storing something, esp. allocated space in a warehouse: *Cooper had put much of the furniture into storage.* ■ the cost of storing something in a warehouse.

stor·age bat·ter·y (also **storage cell**) ▶ **n.** a battery (or cell) used for storing electrical energy.

stor·age de·vice ▶ **n.** a piece of computer equipment on which information can be stored.

stor·age heat·er ▶ **n.** Brit. an electric heater that accumulates heat in water or bricks during the night (when electricity is cheaper) and releases it during the day.

stor·age ring ▶ **n.** Physics an approximately circular accelerator in which particles can be effectively stored by being made to circulate continuously at high energy.

sto·rax /ˈstôˌraks/ (also **styrax** /ˈstī-/) ▶ **n. 1** a rare fragrant gum resin obtained from an eastern Mediterranean tree, sometimes used in medicine, perfumery, and incense. ■ (**liquid storax**) a liquid balsam obtained from the Asian liquidambar tree. **2** a tropical or subtropical tree or shrub with showy white flowers in drooping clusters. ● Genus *Styrax*, family Styracaceae: several species, in particular *S. officinalis*, from which the resin storax is obtained.
– ORIGIN late Middle English: from Latin, from a variant of Greek *sturax*.

store /stôr/ ▶ **n. 1** a retail establishment selling items to the public: *a health-food store*. ■ [as modifier] store-bought: *there's a loaf of store bread*.
2 a quantity or supply of something kept for use as needed: *the squirrel has a store of food* | figurative *her vast store of knowledge*. ■ a place where things are kept for future use or sale: *a grain store*. ■ (**stores**) supplies of equipment and food kept for use by members of an army, navy, or other institution, or the place where they are kept. ■ Brit. a computer memory.
3 chiefly Brit. a sheep, steer, cow, or pig acquired or kept for fattening.
▶ **v.** [with obj.] keep or accumulate (something) for future use: *a small room used for storing furniture*. ■ retain or enter (information) for future electronic retrieval: *the data is stored on disk*. ■ (**be stored with**) have a supply of (something useful): *a mind well stored with esoteric knowledge*. ■ [no obj.] remain fresh while being stored: *they do not ship or store well*.
– PHRASES **in store 1** in a safe place while not being used or displayed: *items held in store*. **2** coming in the future; about to happen: *he did not yet know what lay in store for him*. **set** (or **lay** or **put**) **store by** (or **on**) consider (something) to be of a particular degree of importance or value: *many people set much store by privacy*.
– PHRASES **store something up** create problems for the future by failing to address a particular situation adequately at the time: *they're storing up trouble by denying opportunities to younger players*.
– DERIVATIVES **stor·a·ble** adj., **stor·er** n.
– ORIGIN Middle English: shortening of Old French *estore* (noun), *estorer* (verb), from Latin *instaurare* 'renew'; compare with RESTORE.

store-and-for·ward ▶ **adj.** [attrib.] Telecommunications relating to or denoting a data network in which messages are routed to one or more intermediate stations where they may be stored before being forwarded to their destinations.

store-bought ▶ **adj.** bought ready-made from a store; not homemade.

store brand ▶ **n.** a product manufactured specially for a retailer and bearing the retailer's name: [as modifier] *store-brand chocolate chip cookies*.

store·front /ˈstôrˌfrənt/ ▶ **n. 1** the facade of a store. **2** a room or set of rooms facing the street on the ground floor of a commercial building, typically used as a store: [as modifier] *a bright storefront eatery*.

store·house /ˈstôrˌhous/ ▶ **n.** a building used for storing goods. ■ a large supply of something: *an enormous storehouse of facts*.

store·keep·er /ˈstôrˌkēpər/ ▶ **n. 1** a person who owns or runs a store. **2** a person responsible for stored goods.

store·room /ˈstôrˌro͞om, -ˌro͝om/ ▶ **n.** a room in which items are stored.

sto·rey /ˈstôrē/ ▶ **n.** chiefly Brit. variant spelling of STORY².

sto·ri·at·ed /ˈstôrēˌātid/ ▶ **adj.** rare decorated with historical, legendary, or emblematic designs.
– DERIVATIVES **sto·ri·a·tion** /ˌstôrēˈāshən/ n.
– ORIGIN late 19th cent.: compare with HISTORIATED.

sto·ried¹ /ˈstôrēd/ ▶ **adj.** literary celebrated in or associated with stories or legends: *the island's storied past*.

sto·ried² /ˈstôrēd/ (Brit. also **storeyed**) ▶ **adj.** [in combination] (of a building) having a specified number of stories: *four-storied houses*.

stork /stôrk/ ▶ **n.** a tall long-legged wading bird with a long heavy bill and typically with white and black plumage. ● Family Ciconiidae: several genera and species, in particular the **white stork** (*Ciconia ciconia*), with black wing tips and a reddish bill and legs, often nesting on tall buildings in Europe. ■ the white stork as the pretended bringer of babies.
– ORIGIN Old English *storc*, of Germanic origin; probably related to STARK (because of its rigid stance).

storm /stôrm/ ▶ **n. 1** a violent disturbance of the atmosphere with strong winds and usually rain, thunder, lightning, or snow. ■ (also **storm system**) an intense low-pressure weather system; a cyclone. ■ a wind of force 10 on the Beaufort scale (48–55 knots or 55-63 mph). ■ a heavy discharge of missiles or blows: *two men were taken by a storm of bullets*.
2 [usu. in sing.] a tumultuous reaction; an uproar or controversy: *the book caused a storm in South America* | *she has been at the center of a storm concerning payments*. ■ a violent or noisy outburst of a specified feeling or reaction: *the disclosure raised a storm of protest*.
3 (**storms**) storm windows.
4 a direct assault by troops on a fortified place.
▶ **v. 1** [no obj.] move angrily or forcefully in a specified direction: *she burst into tears and stormed off* | *he stormed out of the house*. ■ [with direct speech] shout (something) angrily; rage: *"Don't patronize me!" she stormed*. ■ move forcefully and decisively to a specified position in a game or contest: *he barged past and stormed to the checkered flag*.
2 [with obj.] (of troops) suddenly attack and capture (a building or other place) by means of force: *Indian commandos stormed a hijacked plane early today* | (as noun **storming**) *the storming of the Bastille*.
3 [no obj.] (of the weather) be violent, with strong winds and usually rain, thunder, lightning, or snow: *when it stormed in the day, I shoveled the drive before Harry came home*.
– PHRASES **go down a storm** Brit. be enthusiastically received by an audience. **the calm** (or **lull**) **before the storm** a period of unusual tranquility or stability that seems likely to presage difficult times. **storm and stress** another term for STURM UND DRANG. **a storm in a teacup** British term for A TEMPEST IN A TEAPOT (see TEMPEST). **take something by storm** (of troops) capture a place by a sudden and violent attack. ■ have great and rapid success in a particular place or with a particular group of people: *his first collection took the fashion world by storm*. —— **up a storm** perform the specified action with great enthusiasm and energy: *the band could really play up a storm*.
– DERIVATIVES **storm·proof** /-ˌpro͞of/ adj.
– ORIGIN Old English, of Germanic origin; related to Dutch *storm* and German *Sturm*, probably also to the verb STIR¹. The verb dates from late Middle English in sense 3 of the verb.

storm beach ▶ **n.** an expanse of sand or gravel thrown up on the coast by storms.

storm·bound /ˈstôrmˌbound/ ▶ **adj.** prevented by storms from starting or continuing a journey.

storm cen·ter ▶ **n.** the point to which the wind blows spirally inward in a cyclonic storm. ■ the central point around which controversy or trouble happens.

storm cloud ▶ **n.** a heavy, dark rain cloud. ■ (**storm clouds**) used in reference to a threatening or ominous state of affairs: *the beginning of the decade saw storm clouds gathering over Europe*.

storm·cock /ˈstôrmˌkäk/ ▶ **n.** dialect the mistle thrush.

storm cuff ▶ **n.** a tight-fitting inner cuff, typically an elasticized one, that prevents rain or wind from getting inside a coat.

storm door ▶ **n.** an additional outer door for protection in bad weather or winter.

storm drain ▶ **n.** another term for STORM SEWER.

storm·er /ˈstôrmər/ ▶ **n.** [usu. in sing.] Brit. informal something particularly impressive or good of its kind: *a stormer of an album* | *the engine is a real stormer*.

storm flap ▶ **n.** a piece of material designed to protect an opening or fastener on a tent or coat from the effects of rain.

storm glass ▶ **n.** a sealed tube containing a solution whose clarity is thought to change when storms approach.

storm·ing /ˈstôrmiNG/ ▶ **adj.** [attrib.] Brit. informal (of a performance, esp. in sports or music) outstandingly vigorous or impressive: *his storming finish carried him into third place*.

Storm·in' Nor·man /ˈstôrmin/ see SCHWARZKOPF².

storm jib ▶ **n.** Sailing a small heavy jib for use in a high wind.

storm pet·rel ▶ **n.** a small seabird of the open ocean, typically having blackish plumage and a white rump, and formerly believed to be a harbinger of bad weather. ● Family Hydrobatidae: several genera and many species, e.g., *Hydrobates pelagicus* of the northeastern Atlantic and Mediterranean.

storm sail ▶ **n.** a sail used in stormy weather, of smaller size and stronger material than the corresponding one used in ordinary weather.

storm sew·er /ˈso͞oər/ ▶ **n.** a sewer built to carry away excess water in times of heavy rain.

storm sig·nal ▶ **n.** a lamp, flag, or other device used to give a visible warning of an approaching storm.

storm surge ▶ **n.** a rising of the sea as a result of atmospheric pressure changes and wind associated with a storm.

storm troops ▶ **plural n.** another term for SHOCK TROOPS. ■ (**Storm Troops**) historical the Nazi political militia.
– DERIVATIVES **storm troop·er** n.

storm wa·ter ▶ **n.** surface water in abnormal quantity resulting from heavy falls of rain or snow.

storm win·dow ▶ **n.** a window fixed outside a normal window for protection and insulation in bad weather or winter.

storm·y /ˈstôrmē/ ▶ **adj.** (**stormier, stormiest**) (of weather) characterized by strong winds and usually rain, thunder, lightning, or snow: *a dark and stormy night*. ■ (of the sea or sky) having large waves or dark clouds because of windy or rainy conditions: *gray and stormy skies*. ■ full of angry or violent outbursts of feeling: *a long and stormy debate* | *a stormy relationship*.
– DERIVATIVES **storm·i·ly** /-məlē/ adv., **storm·i·ness** n.

storm·y pet·rel ▶ **n.** another term for STORM PETREL.

Stor·ting /ˈstôrtiNG/ the Norwegian parliament.
– ORIGIN Norwegian, from *stor* 'great' + *ting* 'assembly.'

Stor·y /ˈstôrē/, Joseph (1779–1845), US Supreme Court associate justice 1811–45. Appointed to the Court by President Madison, he was the youngest associate justice ever to serve. He established the supremacy of Supreme Court rulings.

sto·ry¹ /ˈstôrē/ ▶ **n.** (pl. **stories**) **1** an account of imaginary or real people and events told for entertainment: *an adventure story* | *I'm going to tell you a story*. ■ a plot or story line: *the novel has a good story*. ■ a report of an item of news in a newspaper, magazine, or news broadcast: *stories in the local papers*. ■ a piece of gossip; a rumor: *there have been lots of stories going around, as you can imagine*. ■ informal a false statement or explanation; a lie: *Ellie never told stories—she had always believed in the truth*.
2 an account of past events in someone's life or in the evolution of something: *the story of modern farming* | *the film is based on a true story*. ■ a particular person's representation of the facts of a matter, esp. as given in self-defense: *during police interviews, Harper changed his story*. ■ [in sing.] a situation viewed in terms of the information known about it or its similarity to another: *having such information is useful, but it is not the whole story* | *many children with leukemia now survive—twenty years ago it was a very different story*.
– PHRASES **but that's another story** informal used after raising a matter to indicate that one does not want to expand on it for now. **end of story** informal used to emphasize that there is nothing to add on a matter just mentioned: *Men don't cry in public. End of story*. **it's a long story** informal used to indicate that, for now, one does not want to talk about something that is too involved or painful. **it's** (or **that's**) **the story of one's life** informal used to lament the fact that a particular misfortune has happened too often in one's experience: *"It's the story of my life," my mother would say when she returned home from a sale empty-handed*. **the same old story** used to indicate that a particular bad situation is tediously familiar: *are we not faced with the same old story of a badly managed project?* **the story goes** it is said or rumored: *the story goes that he's fallen out with his friends*. **to make** (or Brit. **cut**) **a long story short** used to end an account of events quickly: *to make a long story short, I married Stephen*.
– ORIGIN Middle English (denoting a historical account or representation): shortening of Anglo-Norman French *estorie*, from Latin *historia* (see HISTORY).

sto·ry² (Brit. also **storey**) ▶ **n.** (pl. **stories** or **storeys**) a part of a building comprising all the rooms that are on the same level: [in combination] *a three-story building*.
– ORIGIN late Middle English: shortening of Latin *historia* 'history, story,' a special use in Anglo-Latin, perhaps originally denoting a tier of painted

windows or sculptures on the front of a building (representing a historical subject).

sto·ry·board /ˈstôrēˌbôrd/ ▶ n. a sequence of drawings, typically with some directions and dialogue, representing the shots planned for a movie or television production.

sto·ry·book /ˈstôrēˌbo͝ok/ ▶ n. a book containing a story or collection of stories intended for children. ■ [as modifier] denoting something that is as idyllically perfect as things typically are in storybooks: *it was a storybook finish to an illustrious career*.

sto·ry ed·i·tor ▶ n. an editor who advises on the content and form of movie or television scripts.

sto·ry·line /ˈstôrēˌlīn/ ▶ n. the plot of a novel, play, movie, or other narrative form.

sto·ry·tell·er /ˈstôrēˌtelər/ ▶ n. a person who tells stories.
– DERIVATIVES **sto·ry·tell·ing** /-ˌteliNG/ n. & adj.

Sto·ry·ville /ˈstôrēˌvil/ a former red-light district in New Orleans, Louisiana, closed down in 1917 and associated with the early development of jazz music.

stot /stät/ ▶ v. (**stots, stotting, stotted**) [no obj.] another term for PRONK.
– ORIGIN early 16th cent.: of unknown origin.

sto·tin /stäˈtēn/ ▶ n. a former monetary unit of Slovenia, equal to one hundredth of a tolar.
– ORIGIN Slovene.

sto·tin·ka /stôˈtiNGkə/ ▶ n. (pl. **stotinki** /-kē/) a monetary unit of Bulgaria, equal to one hundredth of a lev.
– ORIGIN Bulgarian, literally 'one hundredth.'

stoup /sto͞op/ ▶ n. a basin for holy water, esp. on the wall near the door of a Roman Catholic church for worshipers to dip their fingers in before crossing themselves. ■ archaic or historical a flagon or beaker for drink.
– ORIGIN Middle English (in the sense 'pail, small cask'): from Old Norse *staup*, of Germanic origin; related to the verb STEEP[2].

stour /sto͝or/ (also **stoor**) ▶ n. Scottish & N. English dust forming a cloud or deposited in a mass.
– DERIVATIVES **stour·y** adj.
– ORIGIN late Middle English: of uncertain origin.

Stout /stout/, Rex (Todhunter) (1886–1975) US writer. He created the portly, food-loving, orchid aficionado Nero Wolfe, a detective who appeared in many of his novels; the first novel was *Fer de Lance* (1934) and the last, *A Family Affair* (1975).

stout /stout/ ▶ adj. **1** (of a person) somewhat fat or of heavy build: *stout middle-aged men*. ■ (of an object) strong and thick: *Billy had armed himself with a stout stick | stout walking boots*.
2 (of an act, quality, or person) brave and determined: *he put up a stout defense in court*.
▶ n. a kind of strong, dark beer brewed with roasted malt or barley.
– DERIVATIVES **stout·ish** adj. (sense 1 of the adjective), **stout·ly** adv., **stout·ness** n. (sense 1 of the adjective).
– ORIGIN Middle English: from Anglo-Norman French and Old French dialect, of West Germanic origin; perhaps related to STILT. The noun (late 17th cent.) originally denoted any strong beer and is probably elliptical for *stout ale*.

stout·heart·ed /ˈstoutˈhärtid/ ▶ adj. courageous or determined.
– DERIVATIVES **stout·heart·ed·ly** adv., **stout·heart·ed·ness** n.

S

stove[1] /stōv/ ▶ n. an apparatus for cooking or heating that operates by burning fuel or using electricity. ■ (also **stove house**) Brit. a hothouse for plants.
▶ v. [with obj.] **1** treat (an object) by heating it in a stove in order to apply a desired surface coating.
2 Brit. raise (plants) in a hothouse.
– ORIGIN Middle English (in the sense 'sweating room'): from Middle Dutch or Middle Low German *stove*; perhaps related to the noun STEW[1]. Current verb senses date from the early 17th cent.

stove[2] past and past participle of STAVE.

stoved /stōvd/ ▶ adj. [attrib.] Brit. (of vegetables or meat) stewed.

stove e·nam·el Brit. ▶ n. a heatproof enamel produced by heat treatment in a stove, or a paint imitating it.
▶ v. [with obj.] (usu. as adj. **stove-enamelled**) give (something) a finish of this kind.

stove·pipe /ˈstōvˌpīp/ ▶ n. **1** the pipe taking the smoke and gases from a stove up through a roof or to a chimney.
2 an information conduit that traverses vertical levels efficiently but does not disperse widely.
▶ v. [with obj.] transmit (information) directly through levels of a hierarchy: *neocons who stovepiped lies straight up to the White House*.

stove·pipe hat ▶ n. a silk hat resembling a top hat but much taller.

stove·top /ˈstōvˌtäp/ ▶ n. the upper surface of a cooking stove, including the burners.
▶ adj. of or relating to a stovetop: *healthy, no-oil stovetop grill pan*. ■ designed to be prepared on a stovetop, rather than in an oven: *beef noodle stovetop casserole*.

stow /stō/ ▶ v. [with obj.] pack or store (an object) carefully and neatly in a particular place: *the bathhouse offers baskets in which to stow your clothes | she* ***stowed*** *the map* ***away*** *in the glove compartment*.
– PHRASES **stow it!** informal used as a way of urging someone to be quiet or to stop doing something.
– PHRASAL VERBS **stow away** conceal oneself on a ship, aircraft, or other passenger vehicle in order to travel secretly or without paying the fare: *he stowed away on a ship bound for South Africa*.
– ORIGIN late Middle English: shortening of BESTOW.

stow·age /ˈstōij/ ▶ n. the action or manner of stowing something. ■ space for stowing something in: *there is plenty of stowage beneath the berth*.

stow·a·way /ˈstōəˌwā/ ▶ n. a person who stows away.

Stowe[1] /stō/ a town in north central Vermont, a noted skiing and resort center; pop. 4,919 (est. 2008).

Stowe[2], Harriet (Elizabeth) Beecher (1811–96), US novelist. She won fame with her novel *Uncle Tom's Cabin* (1852), which strengthened the contemporary abolitionist cause with its descriptions of the sufferings caused by slavery. She was the sister of Catharine Beecher and Henry Ward Beecher.

STP ▶ abbr. ■ Physiology short-term potentiation. ■ Chemistry standard temperature and pressure. ■ Professor of Sacred Theology. [from Latin *Sanctae Theologiae Professor*.]

STR ▶ abbr. synchronous transmitter receiver.

Str. ▶ abbr. ■ strait. ■ (**str.**) Rowing stroke.

stra·bis·mus /strəˈbizməs/ ▶ n. abnormal alignment of the eyes; the condition of having a squint.
– DERIVATIVES **stra·bis·mic** /-mik/ adj.
– ORIGIN late 17th cent.: modern Latin, from Greek *strabismos*, from *strabizein* 'to squint,' from *strabos* 'squinting.'

Stra·bo /ˈstrābō/ (*c.*63 BC–*c.* AD 23), historian and geographer. His only extant work, *Geographica*, in 17 volumes, provides a detailed physical and historical geography of the ancient world during the reign of Augustus.

strac·cia·tel·la /ˌsträCHəˈtelə/ ▶ n. an Italian soup containing eggs and cheese.
– ORIGIN Italian.

Stra·chey /ˈsträCHē/, Lytton (1880–1932), English biographer; full name *Giles Lytton Strachey*. A prominent member of the Bloomsbury Group, he achieved recognition with *Eminent Victorians* (1918).

Strad /strad/ ▶ n. informal a Stradivarius.
– ORIGIN late 19th cent.: abbreviation.

strad·dle /ˈstradl/ ▶ v. [with obj.] sit or stand with one leg on either side of: *he turned the chair around and straddled it*. ■ place (one's legs) wide apart: *he shifted his legs, straddling them to keep his balance*. ■ [no obj.] archaic stand, walk, or sit with one's legs wide apart. ■ extend across or be situated on both sides of: *a mountain range straddling the Franco-Swiss border*. ■ take up or maintain an equivocal position with regard to (a political issue): *a man who had straddled the issue of taxes*.
▶ n. **1** an act of sitting or standing with one's legs wide apart.
2 Stock Market a simultaneous purchase of options to buy and to sell a security or commodity at a fixed price, allowing the purchaser to make a profit whether the price of the security or commodity goes up or down.
– DERIVATIVES **strad·dler** n.
– ORIGIN mid 16th cent.: alteration of dialect *striddle*, back-formation from dialect *striddling* 'astride,' from STRIDE + the adverbial suffix *-ling*.

Stra·di·va·ri /ˌsträdəˈvärē, ˌstradəˈverē/, Antonio (*c.*1644–1737), Italian violin-maker. He devised the proportions of the modern violin, giving a more powerful and rounded sound than earlier instruments possessed. About 650 of his celebrated violins, violas, and violoncellos are still in existence.

Strad·i·var·i·us /ˌstradəˈve(ə)rēəs/ ▶ n. a violin or other stringed instrument made by Antonio Stradivari or his followers.
– ORIGIN mid 19th cent.: Latinized form of STRADIVARI.

strafe /strāf/ ▶ v. [with obj.] attack repeatedly with bombs or machine-gun fire from low-flying aircraft: *military aircraft strafed the village*.
▶ n. an attack from low-flying aircraft.
– ORIGIN early 20th cent.: humorous adaptation of the German World War I catchphrase *Gott strafe England* 'may God punish England.'

strag·gle /ˈstragəl/ ▶ v. [no obj.] move along slowly, typically in a small irregular group, so as to remain some distance behind the person or people in front: *half the men were already straggling back into the building* | (as adj. **straggling**) *only a few straggling kids remained*. ■ grow, spread, or be laid out in an irregular, untidy way: *her hair was straggling over her eyes*.
▶ n. an untidy or irregularly arranged mass or group of something: *a straggle of cottages*.
– DERIVATIVES **strag·gler** /ˈstrag(ə)lər/ n.
– ORIGIN late Middle English: perhaps from dialect *strake* 'go.'

strag·gly /ˈstrag(ə)lē/ ▶ adj. (**stragglier, straggliest**) growing or spreading in an irregular, untidy way: *his straggly dark hair*.

straight /strāt/ ▶ adj. **1** extending or moving uniformly in one direction only; without a curve or bend: *a long, straight road*. ■ Geometry (of a line) lying on the shortest path between any two of its points. ■ (of an aim, blow, or course) going direct to the intended target: *a straight punch to the face*. ■ (of hair) not curly or wavy. ■ (of a garment) not flared or fitted closely to the body: *a straight skirt*. ■ (of an arch) flat-topped.
2 properly positioned so as to be level, upright, or symmetrical: *he made sure his tie was straight*. ■ [predic.] in proper order or condition: *it'll take a long time to get the place straight*.
3 not evasive; honest: *a straight answer | thank you for being straight with me*. ■ simple; straightforward: *a straight choice between nuclear power and penury*. ■ (of a look) bold and steady: *he gave her a straight, no-nonsense look*. ■ (of thinking) clear, logical, and unemotional. ■ not addicted to drugs.
4 [attrib.] in continuous succession: *he scored his fourth straight win*. ■ supporting all the principles and candidates of one political party: *he generally voted a* ***straight ticket***.
5 (of an alcoholic drink) undiluted; neat: *straight brandy*.
6 (esp. of drama) serious as opposed to comic or musical; employing the conventional techniques of its art form: *a straight play*. ■ informal (of a person) conventional or respectable: *she looked pretty straight in her school clothes*. ■ informal heterosexual.
▶ adv. **1** in a straight line; directly: *he was gazing straight at her | keep* ***straight on***. ■ with no delay or diversion; directly or immediately: *after dinner we went straight back to our hotel | I fell into bed and went straight to sleep*. ■ archaic at once; immediately: *I'll fetch up the bath to you straight*.
2 in or into a level, even, or upright position: *he pulled his clothes straight | sit up straight!*
3 correctly; clearly: *I'm so tired I can hardly think straight*. ■ honestly and directly; in a straightforward manner: *I told her straight—the kid's right*.
4 without a break; continuously: *he remembered working sixteen hours straight*.
▶ n. **1** a part of something that is not curved or bent, esp. the concluding stretch of a racetrack: *he pulled away in the straight to win by half a second*. ■ archaic a form or position that is not curved or bent: *the rod flew back to the straight*.
2 Poker a continuous sequence of five cards.
3 informal a conventional person. ■ a heterosexual.
– PHRASES **get something straight** make a situation clear, esp. by reaching an understanding. **go straight** live an honest life after being a criminal. **a straight face** a blank or serious facial expression, esp. when trying not to laugh: *my father kept a straight face when he joked*. **the straight and narrow** the honest and morally acceptable way of living: *he's making a real effort to get back on the straight and narrow*. [a misinterpretation of Matt. 7:14, 'Strait is the gate, and narrow is the way which leadeth unto life, and few there be that find it'] **straight out** (or **off**) informal without hesitation or deliberation: *If you're not going to help me, just say so straight out*. **straight up** informal **1** unmixed; unadulterated: *a dry Martini served straight up*. **2** truthfully; honestly: *tell your friends straight up how you feel*.
– DERIVATIVES **straight·ish** adj., **straight·ly** adv., **straight·ness** n.
– ORIGIN Middle English (as an adjective and adverb): archaic past participle of STRETCH.

straight-a·head ▶ adj. (esp. of popular music) straightforward, simple, or unadorned.

straight an·gle ▶ n. Mathematics an angle of 180°.

straight-arm ▶ v. [with obj.] informal ward off (an opponent) or remove (an obstacle) with the arm straight: *I straight-armed the woman leaning in on her*.

straight ar·row ▶ **n.** informal an honest, morally upright person.

straight·a·way /ˈstrātəˌwā/ ▶ **adv.** immediately. ▶ **adj.** extending or moving in a straight line. ▶ **n.** a straight section of a road or racetrack.

straight chain ▶ **n.** Chemistry a chain of atoms in a molecule, usually carbon atoms, that is neither branched nor formed into a ring.

straight chair ▶ **n.** a straight-backed side chair.

straight·edge /ˈstrātˌej/ ▶ **n.** a bar with one accurately straight edge, used for testing whether something else is straight.
▶ **adj.** (esp. among fans of hardcore punk music) having an ascetic or abstinent lifestyle: *he's so straightedge that he won't even take Tylenol when he has a headache.*

straight·en /ˈstrātn/ ▶ **v.** make or become straight: [with obj.] *she helped him straighten his tie* | [no obj.] *where the river straightened he took his chance to check the barometer.* ■ [with obj.] make tidy or put in order again: *he sat down at his desk, straightening his things that Lee had moved* | *they are asking for help in* ***straightening out*** *their lives.* ■ [no obj.] stand or sit erect after bending: *he* ***straightened up****, using the bedside table for support.* ■ [no obj.] (**straighten up**) (of a vehicle, ship, or aircraft) stop turning and move in a straight line.
– DERIVATIVES **straight·en·er** n.

straight-faced ▶ **adj.** with a blank or serious facial expression.

straight flush ▶ **n.** (in poker or brag) a hand of cards all of one suit and in a continuous sequence (for example, the seven, eight, nine, ten, and jack of spades).

straight·for·ward /ˌstrātˈfôrwərd/ ▶ **adj.** uncomplicated and easy to do or understand: *in a straightforward case no fees will be charged.* ■ (of a person) honest and frank: *a straightforward young man.*
– DERIVATIVES **straight·for·ward·ly** adv., **straight·for·ward·ness** n.

straight·jack·et ▶ **n.** & **v.** variant spelling of STRAITJACKET.

straight-laced ▶ **adj.** variant spelling of STRAIT-LACED.

straight-line ▶ **adj.** containing, characterized by, or relating to straight lines or motion in a straight line: *a straight-line graph* | *the Porsche's straight-line stability.* ■ Finance of or relating to a method of depreciation allocating a given percentage of the cost of an asset each year for a fixed period.

straight man ▶ **n.** the person in a comedy duo who speaks lines that give a comedian the opportunity to make jokes.

straight pool ▶ **n.** a form of pool in which the players specify the ball they plan to pocket and which pocket the ball will drop into before taking a shot.

straight ra·zor ▶ **n.** a razor having a long blade set in a handle, usually folding like a penknife.

straight shoot·er ▶ **n.** informal an honest and forthright person.
– DERIVATIVES **straight-shoot·ing** adj.

straight-six ▶ **n.** an internal combustion engine with six cylinders in line. ■ a vehicle with an engine of this type.

straight stitch ▶ **n.** a single, short, separate embroidery stitch.

straight time ▶ **n.** normal working hours, paid at a regular rate.

straight-up ▶ **adj.** informal honest; trustworthy: *you sounded like a straight-up guy.* ■ truly so called; genuine: *a straight-up suspense tale.*

straight·way /ˈstrātˌwā/ ▶ **adv.** archaic form of STRAIGHTAWAY.

strain[1] /strān/ ▶ **v. 1** [with obj.] force (a part of one's body or oneself) to make a strenuous or unusually great effort: *I stopped and listened, straining my ears for any sound.* ■ injure (a limb, muscle, or organ) by overexerting it or twisting it awkwardly: *on cold days you are more likely to strain a muscle* | *glare from the screen can strain your eyes.* ■ [no obj.] make a strenuous and continuous effort: *his voice was so quiet that I had to strain to hear it.* ■ make severe or excessive demands on: *he strained her tolerance to the limit.* ■ [no obj.] pull or push forcibly at something: *the bear* ***strained at*** *the chain around its neck* | *his stomach was swollen,* ***straining against*** *the thin shirt.* ■ stretch (something) tightly: *the barbed wire fence was strained to posts six feet high.* ■ archaic embrace (someone) tightly: *she strained the infant to her bosom again.*
2 [with obj.] pour (a mainly liquid substance) through a porous or perforated device or material in order to separate out any solid matter: *strain the custard into a bowl.* ■ cause liquid to drain off (food that has been boiled, soaked, or canned) by using such a device. ■ drain off (liquid) in this way: *strain off the surplus fat.*
▶ **n. 1** a force tending to pull or stretch something to an extreme or damaging degree: *the usual type of chair puts an enormous strain on the spine* | *aluminum may bend under strain.* ■ Physics the magnitude of a deformation, equal to the change in the dimension of a deformed object divided by its original dimension. ■ an injury to a part of the body caused by overexertion or twisting a muscle awkwardly: *he has a slight groin strain.*
2 a severe or excessive demand on the strength, resources, or abilities of someone or something: *the accusations* ***put a strain on*** *relations between the two countries* | *she's obviously* ***under*** *considerable* ***strain.*** ■ a state of tension or exhaustion resulting from this: *the telltale signs of nervous strain.*
3 (usu. **strains**) the sound of a piece of music as it is played or performed: *through the open windows came the strains of a hurdy-gurdy playing in the street.*
– PHRASES **at (full) strain** archaic using the utmost effort. **strain every nerve** see NERVE. **strain at the leash** see LEASH.
– DERIVATIVES **strain·a·ble** adj.
– ORIGIN Middle English (as a verb): from Old French *estreindre*, from Latin *stringere* 'draw tight.' Current senses of the noun arose in the mid 16th cent.

strain[2] ▶ **n. 1** a breed, stock, or variety of an animal or plant developed by breeding. ■ a natural or cultured variety of a microorganism with a distinct form, biochemistry, or virulence.
2 a particular tendency as part of a person's character: *there was a powerful strain of insanity on her mother's side of the family.* ■ a variety of a particular abstract thing: *a strain of feminist thought.*
– ORIGIN Old English *strīon* 'acquisition, gain,' of Germanic origin; related to Latin *struere* 'to build up.'

strained /strānd/ ▶ **adj. 1** (of an atmosphere, situation, or relationship) not relaxed or comfortable; tense or uneasy: *there was a strained silence* | *relations between the two countries were strained.* ■ (of a person) showing signs of tiredness or nervous tension: *Jean's pale, strained face.* ■ (of an appearance or performance) produced by deliberate effort rather than natural impulse; artificial or forced: *I put on my strained smile for the next customer.* ■ (of a statement or representation) labored or far-fetched: *my example may seem a little strained and artificial.*
2 (of a limb or muscle) injured by overexertion or twisting.
3 (of a mainly liquid substance) having been strained to separate out any solid matter.

strain en·er·gy ▶ **n.** Mechanics energy stored in an elastic body under loading.

strain·er /ˈstrānər/ ▶ **n.** a device having holes punched in it or made of crossed wires for separating solid matter from a liquid: *a tea strainer.*

strain gauge ▶ **n.** a device for indicating the strain of a material or structure at the point of attachment.

strait /strāt/ ▶ **n. 1** (also **straits**) a narrow passage of water connecting two seas or two large areas of water: [in place names] *the Strait of Gibraltar.*
2 (**straits**) used in reference to a situation characterized by a specified degree of trouble or difficulty: *the economy is* ***in dire straits*** | *a crippling disease could leave anyone in serious financial straits.*
▶ **adj.** archaic (of a place) of limited spatial capacity; narrow or cramped: *the road was so strait that a handful of men might have defended it.* ■ close, strict, or rigorous: *my captivity was strait as ever.*
– DERIVATIVES **strait·ly** adv., **strait·ness** n.
– ORIGIN Middle English: shortening of Old French *estreit* 'tight, narrow,' from Latin *strictus* 'drawn tight' (see STRICT).

strait·en /ˈstrātn/ ▶ **v.** archaic make or become narrow: [with obj.] *the passage was straitened by tables.*

strait·ened /ˈstrātnd/ ▶ **adj. 1** characterized by poverty: *they lived in straitened circumstances.*
2 restricted in range or scope: *their straitened horizons.*

strait·jack·et /ˈstrātˌjakət/ (also **straightjacket**) ▶ **n.** a strong garment with long sleeves that can be tied together to confine the arms of a violent prisoner or mental patient. ■ used in reference to something that restricts freedom of action, development, or expression: *the government is operating in an economic straitjacket.*
▶ **v.** (**straitjackets, straitjacketing, straitjacketed**) [with obj.] restrain with a straitjacket. ■ impose severely restrictive measures on (a person or activity): *the treaty should not be used as a tool to straitjacket international trade.*

> **USAGE** See usage at STRAIT-LACED.

strait-laced (also **straight-laced**) ▶ **adj.** having or showing very strict moral attitudes.

> **USAGE** As an adjective, strait means 'narrow or cramped' and 'strict or rigorous': the idea behind **strait-laced** and **straitjacket** is of being tightly laced or confined. As **strait** is now old-fashioned and unfamiliar, however, people often interpret it as the more usual word **straight**. **Straight-laced** and **straightjacket** are now generally accepted in standard English, and the spelling **straight-laced** is more common than **strait-laced** in the Oxford English Corpus.

strake /strāk/ ▶ **n. 1** a continuous line of planking or plates from the stem to the stern of a ship or boat.
2 a protruding ridge fitted to an aircraft or other structure to improve aerodynamic stability.
– ORIGIN Middle English: from Anglo-Latin *stracus*, *straca*; probably from the Germanic base of the verb STRETCH.

stra·mo·ni·um /strəˈmōnēəm/ ▶ **n.** a preparation of the dried leaves or poisonous seeds of the jimson weed, with medical and other uses.
– ORIGIN mid 17th cent.: modern Latin (part of the plant's binomial), perhaps an alteration of Tartar *turman* 'horse medicine.'

strand[1] /strand/ ▶ **v.** [with obj.] drive or leave (a boat, sailor, or sea creature) aground on a shore: *the ships were stranded in shallow water* | (as adj. **stranded**) *a stranded whale.* ■ leave (someone) without the means to move from somewhere: *they were stranded in St. Louis by the blizzard.*
▶ **n.** literary the shore of a sea, lake, or large river: *a heron glided to rest on a pebbly strand.*
– ORIGIN Old English (as a noun), of unknown origin. The verb dates from the early 17th cent.

strand[2] ▶ **n.** a single thin length of something such as thread, fiber, or wire, esp. as twisted together with others: *a strand of cotton* | *strands of grass.* ■ a string of beads or pearls. ■ an element that forms part of a complex whole: *certain strands of postmodern thought.*
– ORIGIN late 15th cent.: of unknown origin.

strand·ed /ˈstrandid/ ▶ **adj.** [attrib.] (of thread, rope, or similar) arranged in single thin lengths twisted together: *stranded cotton* | [in combination] figurative *the many-stranded passions of the country.*

strand·wolf /ˈstrandˌwo͝olf/ ▶ **n.** S. African the brown hyena, which often frequents the shore, where it scavenges dead fish and birds. ● *Hyaena brunnea*, family Hyaenidae.
– ORIGIN late 18th cent.: from South African Dutch, from *strand* 'beach' + *wolf* 'wolf.'

strange /strānj/ ▶ **adj. 1** unusual or surprising in a way that is unsettling or hard to understand: *children have some strange ideas* | *he's a very strange man* | [with clause] ***it is strange how*** *things change.*
2 not previously visited, seen, or encountered; unfamiliar or alien: *she found herself in bed in a strange place* | *a harsh accent that was strange to his ears.* ■ [predic.] (**strange to/at/in**) archaic unaccustomed to or unfamiliar with: *I am strange to the work.*
3 Physics having a nonzero value for strangeness.
– PHRASES **feel strange** (of a person or part of the body) feel unwell; have unpleasant sensations: *her head still felt strange.* ■ be uncomfortable or ill at ease in a situation: *the family had expected to feel strange in Stephen's company.* **strange to say** (or literary **tell**) it is surprising or unusual that: *strange to say, I didn't really like carol singers.*
– DERIVATIVES **strange·ly** adv. [as submodifier] *the house was strangely quiet* | [sentence adverb] ***strangely enough****, people were able to perform this task without difficulty.*
– ORIGIN Middle English: shortening of Old French *estrange*, from Latin *extraneus* 'external, strange.'

strange at·trac·tor ▶ **n.** Mathematics an equation or fractal set representing a complex pattern of behavior in a chaotic system.

strange·ness /ˈstrānjnis/ ▶ **n. 1** the state or fact of being strange.
2 Physics one of six flavors of quark.

strange par·ti·cle ▶ **n.** Physics a subatomic particle classified as having a nonzero value for strangeness.

stran·ger /ˈstrānjər/ ▶ **n.** a person whom one does not know or with whom one is not familiar: *don't talk to strangers* | *she remained a stranger to him.* ■ a person who does not know, or is not known in, a particular place or community: *I'm a stranger in these parts* | *he must have been a stranger to the village.* ■ (**stranger to**) a person

S

entirely unaccustomed to (a feeling, experience, or situation): *he is no stranger to controversy*.
– PHRASES **hello, stranger!** humorous used to greet someone whom one has not seen for some time.
– ORIGIN late Middle English: shortening of Old French *estrangier*, from Latin *extraneus* (see STRANGE).

stran·gle /'straNGgəl/ ▶ v. [with obj.] squeeze or constrict the neck of (a person or animal), esp. so as to cause death: *the victim was strangled with a scarf*. ■ (as adj. **strangled**) sounding as though the speaker's throat is constricted: *a series of strangled gasps*. ■ suppress (an impulse, action, or sound): *she strangled a sob*. ■ hamper or hinder the development or activity of: *overrestrictive policies that strangle growth*.
– DERIVATIVES **stran·gler** /'straNGg(ə)lər/ n.
– ORIGIN Middle English: shortening of Old French *estrangler*, from Latin *strangulare*, from Greek *strangalan*, from *strangalē* 'halter,' related to *strangos* 'twisted.'

stran·gle·hold /'straNGgəl,hōld/ ▶ n. [in sing.] a grip around the neck of another person that can kill by asphyxiation if held for long enough. ■ complete or overwhelming control: *he broke the union that held a stranglehold on bus service*.

stran·gles /'straNGgəlz/ ▶ plural n. [usu. treated as sing.] a bacterial infection of the upper respiratory tract of horses, causing enlargement of the lymph nodes in the throat, which may impair breathing. ● This disease is caused by the bacterium *Streptococcus equi*.
– ORIGIN early 17th cent.: plural of obsolete *strangle* 'strangulation,' from STRANGLE.

stran·gu·late /'straNGgyə,lāt/ ▶ v. [with obj.] (often as adj. **strangulated**) **1** Medicine prevent circulation of the blood supply through (a part of the body, esp. a hernia) by constriction: *a strangulated hernia*.
2 informal strangle; throttle: *the poor woman died strangulated*. ■ (as adj. **strangulated**) sounding as though the speaker's throat is constricted: *a strangulated cry*.
– ORIGIN mid 17th cent. (in the sense 'suffocate'): from Latin *strangulat-* 'choked,' from the verb *strangulare* (see STRANGLE).

stran·gu·la·tion /,straNGgyə'lāsHən/ ▶ n. **1** the action or state of strangling or being strangled: *death due to strangulation*.
2 Medicine the condition in which circulation of blood to a part of the body (esp. a hernia) is cut off by constriction.

stran·gu·ry /'straNGgyərē/ ▶ n. a condition caused by blockage or irritation at the base of the bladder, resulting in severe pain and a strong desire to urinate.
– DERIVATIVES **stran·gu·ri·ous** /-'gyo͝orēəs/ adj.
– ORIGIN late Middle English: via Latin from Greek *strangouria*, from *stranx, strang-* 'drop squeezed out' + *ouron* 'urine.'

strap /strap/ ▶ n. a strip of leather, cloth, or other flexible material, often with a buckle, used to fasten, secure, or carry something or to hold onto something: *her bra strap* | *the strap of his shoulder bag*. ■ a strip of metal, often hinged, used to fasten or secure something. ■ **(the strap)** punishment by beating with a strip of leather. ■ variant form of STROP.
▶ v. **(straps, strapping, strapped) 1** [with obj.] fasten or secure in a specified place or position with a strap or seat belt: *I had to strap the bag to my bicycle* | *the children were strapped into their car seats*.
2 [with obj.] beat (someone) with a strip of leather: *I expected when my dad walked in that he'd strap him*.
– ORIGIN late 16th cent. (denoting a trap for birds, also a piece of timber fastening two objects together): dialect form of STROP.

strap·hang·er /'strap,haNGər/ ▶ n. informal a standing passenger in a bus or train. ■ a person who commutes to work by public transportation.
– DERIVATIVES **strap-hang** v.

strap hinge ▶ n. a hinge with long leaves or flaps for screwing onto the surface of a door or gate.

strap·less /'strapləs/ ▶ adj. (esp. of a dress or bra) without shoulder straps.

strap-on ▶ adj. able to be attached by a strap or straps.

strap·pa·do /strə'pādō, -'pä-/ ▶ n. (pl. **strappados**) (usu. **the strappado**) historical a form of punishment or torture in which the victim was secured to a rope and made to fall from a height almost to the ground before being stopped with an abrupt jerk. ■ the instrument used for inflicting this punishment or torture.
– ORIGIN mid 16th cent.: from French *(e)strapade*, from Italian *strappata*, from *strappare* 'to snatch.'

strapped /strapt/ ▶ adj. informal short of money: *I'm constantly strapped for cash*.

strap·ping¹ /'strapiNG/ ▶ adj. (esp. of a young person) big and strong: *they had three strapping sons*.

strap·ping² ▶ n. **1** adhesive plaster for binding injured parts of the body.
2 strips of leather or pliable metal used to hold, strengthen, or fasten something.

strap·py /'strapē/ ▶ adj. (of shoes or clothes) having eye-catching straps: *white strappy sandals*.

Stras·berg /'stras,bərg, 'sträs-/, Lee (1901–82), US actor, director, and drama teacher, born in Austria; born *Israel Strassberg*. As artistic director of the Actors' Studio in New York City (1948–82), he was the leading figure in the development of method acting in the US.

Stras·bourg /'sträs,bo͝org, 'sträz-, -,bərg/ a city in northeastern France, in Alsace, close to the border with Germany; pop. 276,867 (2006). It is the headquarters of the Council of Europe and of the European Parliament.

stra·ta /'strātə, 'strätə/ plural form of STRATUM.

strat·a·gem /'stratəjəm/ ▶ n. a plan or scheme, esp. one used to outwit an opponent or achieve an end: *a series of devious stratagems*. ■ archaic skill in devising such plans or schemes; cunning.
– ORIGIN late 15th cent. (originally denoting a military ploy): from French *stratagème*, via Latin from Greek *stratēgēma*, from *stratēgein* 'be a general,' from *stratēgos*, from *stratos* 'army' + *agein* 'to lead.'

stra·tal /'strātl/ ▶ adj. relating or belonging to strata or a stratum.

stra·te·gic /strə'tējik/ ▶ adj. relating to the identification of long-term or overall aims and interests and the means of achieving them: *the company should take strategic actions to cope with fundamental changes in the environment* | *strategic planning for the organization is the responsibility of top management*. ■ carefully designed or planned to serve a particular purpose or advantage: *alarms are positioned at strategic points around the prison*. ■ relating to the gaining of overall or long-term military advantage: *New Orleans was of strategic importance* | *a hazard to British strategic and commercial interests*. ■ (of human or material resources) essential in fighting a war: *the strategic forces on Russian territory*. ■ (of bombing or weapons) done or for use against industrial areas and communication centers of enemy territory as a long-term military objective: *strategic nuclear missiles*. Often contrasted with TACTICAL.
– DERIVATIVES **stra·te·gi·cal adj., stra·te·gi·cal·ly** /-ik(ə)lē/ **adv.** [as submodifier] *a strategically placed mirror*.
– ORIGIN early 19th cent.: from French *stratégique*, from Greek *stratēgikos*, from *stratēgos* (see STRATAGEM).

Stra·te·gic Arms Lim·i·ta·tion Talks (abbr. **SALT**) a series of negotiations between the US and the former Soviet Union aimed at the limitation or reduction of nuclear armaments, which produced the Strategic Arms Limitation Treaty. The talks were organized from 1968 onward and held in stages until superseded by the START negotiations in 1983.

Stra·te·gic Arms Re·duc·tion Talks (abbr.: **START**) a series of arms-reduction negotiations between the US and the former Soviet Union begun in 1983. The Intermediate Nuclear Forces (INF) treaty was signed in 1987 and the Strategic Arms Reduction Treaty in 1991.

strat·e·gist /'stratəjist/ ▶ n. a person skilled in planning action or policy, esp. in war or politics.

strat·e·gize /'stratə,jīz/ ▶ v. [no obj.] devise a strategy or strategies.

strat·e·gy /'stratəjē/ ▶ n. (pl. **strategies**) a plan of action or policy designed to achieve a major or overall aim: *time to develop a coherent economic strategy* | *shifts in marketing strategy*. ■ the art of planning and directing overall military operations and movements in a war or battle. Often contrasted with TACTICS (see TACTIC). ■ a plan for such military operations and movements: *nonprovocative defense strategies*.
– ORIGIN early 19th cent.: from French *stratégie*, from Greek *stratēgia* 'generalship,' from *stratēgos* (see STRATAGEM).

Strat·ford /'stratfərd/ **1** an industrial town in southwestern Connecticut, east of Bridgeport, former home to the American Shakespeare Festival; pop. 48,853 (est. 2008).
2 a city in southern Ontario in Canada, on the Avon River, noted for its summer Shakespeare Festival; pop. 30,461 (2006).

Strat·ford-up·on-A·von /'stratfərd ə,pän 'āvən, ə,pôn, 'ā,vän/ a town in central England, on the Avon River; pop. 23,100 (est. 2009). Noted as the birth and burial place of William Shakespeare, it is the site of the Royal Shakespeare Theatre.
– DERIVATIVES **Strat·for·di·an** /strat'fôrdēən/ n.

strath /straTH/ ▶ n. Scottish a broad mountain valley.
– ORIGIN mid 16th cent.: from Scottish Gaelic *srath*.

strath·spey /straTH'spā/ ▶ n. a slow Scottish dance. ■ a piece of music for such a dance, typically in four-four time.
– ORIGIN mid 18th cent.: from *Strathspey*, the name of the valley of the Spey River in Scotland.

strat·i·fied sam·ple /'stratə,fīd/ ▶ n. Statistics a sample that is drawn from a number of separate strata of the population, rather than at random from the whole population, in order that it should be representative.

strat·i·form /'stratə,fôrm/ ▶ adj. technical arranged in layers: *stratiform clouds*. ■ Geology (of a mineral deposit) formed parallel to the bedding planes of the surrounding rock.

strat·i·fy /'stratə,fī/ ▶ v. **(stratifies, stratifying, stratified)** [with obj.] (usu. as adj. **stratified**) form or arrange into strata: *socially stratified cities* | [no obj.] *the residues have begun to stratify*. ■ arrange or classify: *stratifying patients into well-defined risk groups*. ■ place (seeds) close together in layers in moist sand or peat to preserve them or to help them germinate. ■ [no obj.] (of seeds) be germinated by this method.
– DERIVATIVES **strat·i·fi·ca·tion** /,stratəfi'kāsHən/ n.

stra·tig·ra·phy /strə'tigrəfē/ ▶ n. the branch of geology concerned with the order and relative position of strata and their relationship to the geological time scale. ■ the analysis of the order and position of layers of archaeological remains. ■ the structure of a particular set of strata.
– DERIVATIVES **stra·tig·ra·pher** /-fər/ n., **strat·i·graph·ic** /,stratə'grafik/ adj., **strat·i·graph·i·cal** /,stratə'grafikəl/ adj.
– ORIGIN mid 19th cent.: from STRATUM + -GRAPHY.

stra·toc·ra·cy /strə'täkrəsē/ ▶ n. (pl. **stratocracies**) rare government by military forces. ■ a military government.

stra·to·cu·mu·lus /,stratō'kyo͞omyələs, ,strā-/ ▶ n. cloud forming a low layer of clumped or broken gray masses.

stra·to·pause /'stratə,pôz/ ▶ n. the interface between the stratosphere and the ionosphere.
– ORIGIN 1950s: from STRATOSPHERE, suggested by TROPOPAUSE.

strat·o·sphere /'stratə,sfi(ə)r/ ▶ n. the layer of the earth's atmosphere above the troposphere, extending to about 32 miles (50 km) above the earth's surface (the lower boundary of the mesosphere). ■ informal the very highest levels of a profession or other sphere, or of prices or other quantities: *her next big campaign launched her into the fashion stratosphere*.
– DERIVATIVES **strat·o·spher·ic** /,stratə'sfi(ə)rik, -'sferik/ adj.

strat·o·vol·ca·no /,stratōväl'kānō, ,strā-/ ▶ n. (pl. **stratovolcanoes**) a volcano built up of alternate layers of lava and ash.

stra·tum /'strātəm, 'stra-/ ▶ n. (pl. **strata** /'strātə, 'stra-/) **1** a layer or a series of layers of rock in the ground: *a stratum of flint*. ■ a thin layer within any structure: *thin strata of air*.
2 a level or class to which people are assigned according to their social status, education, or income: *members of other social strata*. ■ Statistics a group into which members of a population are divided in stratified sampling.
– ORIGIN late 16th cent. (in the sense 'layer or coat of a substance'): modern Latin, from Latin, literally 'something spread or laid down,' neuter past participle of *sternere* 'strew.'

> **USAGE** In Latin, the word **stratum** is singular and its plural form is **strata**. In English, this distinction is maintained. It is therefore incorrect to use **strata** as a singular: *a new* **stratum** *was uncovered* (not *a new* **strata** *was uncovered*). It is also wrong to create the form **stratums** or **stratas** as the plural: *a series of overlying* **strata** (not *overlying* **stratums** or *overlying* **stratas**).

stra·tum cor·ne·um /'strātəm ,kôrnēəm, 'stra-/ ▶ n. Anatomy the horny outer layer of the skin.
– ORIGIN Latin, literally 'horny layer.'

stra·tus /'strātəs, 'stra-/ ▶ n. cloud forming a continuous horizontal gray sheet, often with rain or snow.
– ORIGIN early 19th cent.: modern Latin, from Latin, literally 'strewn,' past participle of *sternere*.

Strauss¹ /strous, sHtrous/ the name of two Austrian composers. ■ **Johann** (1804–49), a leading composer of waltzes; known as **Strauss the Elder**. His best-known work is the *Radetzky March* (1838). ■ **Johann** (1825–99), son of Strauss the Elder; known as **Strauss the Younger** and as the **waltz**

S

king. He composed many famous waltzes, such as *The Blue Danube* (1867) and *Tales from the Vienna Woods* (1868). He is also noted for the operetta *Die Fledermaus* (1874).

Strauss², Levi (c.1829–1902), US manufacturer; born in Germany. He established Levi Strauss & Company in 1850 to sell pants made of tent canvas to gold miners. He eventually switched to denim cloth and made the work pants that became known as blue jeans or "Levi's."

Strauss³, Richard (1864–1949), German composer. With librettist Hugo von Hofmannsthal he produced operas such as *Der Rosenkavalier* (1911). He is often regarded as the last of the 19th-century romantic composers.

Stra·vin·sky /strə'vinskē/, Igor (Fyodorovich) (1882–1971), Russian composer, resident of the US from 1939. His ballets *The Firebird* (1910) and *The Rite of Spring* (1913) shocked Paris audiences with their irregular rhythms and frequent dissonances. He later developed a neoclassical style typified by the opera *The Rake's Progress* (1948–51) and experimented with serialism in *Threni* (1958).
– DERIVATIVES **Stra·vin·sky·an adj.**

straw /strô/ ▶ **n. 1** dried stalks of grain, used esp. as fodder or as material for thatching, packing, or weaving: [as modifier] *a straw hat.* ■ a pale yellow color like that of straw: [as modifier] *a dull straw color.*
2 a single dried stalk of grain: *the tramp sat chewing a straw.* ■ a stalk of grain or something similar used in drawing lots: *we had to **draw straws** for the food we had.*
3 a thin hollow tube of paper or plastic for sucking drink from a glass or bottle.
– PHRASES **grasp** (or **clutch** or **catch**) **at straws** (or **a straw**) be in such a desperate situation as to resort to even the most unlikely means of salvation. [from the proverb *a drowning man will clutch at a straw.*] **draw the short straw** be the unluckiest of a group of people, esp. in being chosen to perform an unpleasant task. **the last** (or **final**) **straw** a further difficulty or annoyance, typically minor in itself but coming on top of a whole series of difficulties, that makes a situation unbearable: *his affair was the last straw.* [from the proverb *the last straw breaks the (laden) camel's back.*] **a straw in the wind** a slight hint of future developments.
– DERIVATIVES **straw·y adj.**
– ORIGIN Old English *strēaw*, of Germanic origin; related to Dutch *stroo* and German *Stroh*, also to STREW.

straw·ber·ry /'strô,berē, -b(ə)rē/ ▶ **n.** (pl. **strawberries**) **1** a sweet soft red fruit with a seed-studded surface.
2 the low-growing plant that produces this fruit, having white flowers, lobed leaves, and runners, and found throughout north temperate regions. ● Genus *Fragaria*, family Rosaceae; the commercial strawberry is usually *F.* × *ananassa*.
3 a deep pinkish-red color.
– ORIGIN Old English *strēa(w)berige*, *strēowberige* (see STRAW, BERRY).

straw·ber·ry blond (also **strawberry blonde**) ▶ **adj.** denoting hair of a light reddish-blond color.
▶ **n.** ■ a person who has hair of such a color.

straw·ber·ry mark ▶ **n.** a soft red birthmark.

straw·ber·ry roan ▶ **adj.** denoting an animal's coat that is chestnut mixed with white or gray.
▶ **n.** a strawberry roan animal.

straw·ber·ry tree ▶ **n.** a small evergreen European tree of the heath family that bears clusters of whitish flowers late in the year, often at the same time as the strawberrylike fruit from the previous season's flowers. ● *Arbutus unedo*, family Ericaceae.

straw·board /'strô,bôrd/ ▶ **n.** board made of straw pulp, used in building (faced with paper) and in book covers.

straw boss ▶ **n.** informal a junior supervisor, esp. a worker who has some responsibility but little authority.

straw·flow·er /'strô,flou(-ə)r/ ▶ **n.** an everlasting flower of the daisy family. ● Several species in the family Compositae, in particular the Australian *Helichrysum bracteatum* and plants of the genus *Helipterum*.

straw man ▶ **n.** a person compared to a straw image; a sham. ■ a sham argument set up to be defeated.

straw poll (also **straw vote**) ▶ **n.** an unofficial ballot conducted as a test of opinion: *I took a straw poll among my immediate colleagues.*

straw pur·chase ▶ **n.** informal a criminal act in which a person who is prohibited from buying firearms uses another person to buy a gun on their behalf.

stray /strā/ ▶ **v.** [no obj.] move away aimlessly from a group or from the right course or place: *I strayed a few blocks in the wrong direction* | *dog owners are urged not to allow their dogs to stray* | *the military arrested anyone who **strayed into** the exclusion zone.* ■ (of the eyes or a hand) move idly or casually in a specified direction: *her eyes strayed to the telephone.* ■ (of a person who is married or in a long-term relationship) be unfaithful: *men who stray are seen as more exciting and desirable.* ■ literary wander or roam in a specified direction: *over these mounds the Kurdish shepherd strays.*
▶ **adj.** [attrib.] **1** not in the right place; separated from the group or target: *he pushed a few stray hairs from her face* | *she was killed by a stray bullet.* ■ (of a domestic animal) having no home or having wandered away from home: *stray dogs.*
2 Physics (of a physical quantity) arising as a consequence of the laws of physics, not by deliberate design, and usually having a detrimental effect on the operation or efficiency of equipment: *stray capacitance.*
▶ **n. 1** a stray person or thing, esp. a domestic animal.
2 (**strays**) electrical phenomena interfering with radio reception.
– DERIVATIVES **stray·er n.**
– ORIGIN Middle English: shortening of Anglo-Norman French and Old French *estrayer* (verb), Anglo-Norman French *strey* (noun), partly from ASTRAY.

streak /strēk/ ▶ **n. 1** a long, thin line or mark of a different substance or color from its surroundings: *a streak of oil.* ■ Microbiology a narrow line of bacteria smeared on the surface of a solid culture medium.
2 an element of a specified kind in someone's character: *there's a streak of insanity in the family* | *Lucy had a ruthless streak.* ■ [usu. with adj.] a continuous period of specified success or luck: *the theater is **on a winning streak*** | *the team closed the season with an 11-game **losing streak**.*
▶ **v. 1** [with obj.] cover (a surface) with streaks: *tears streaking her face, Cynthia looked up* | *his beard was **streaked with** gray.* ■ dye (hair) with long, thin lines of a different, typically lighter color than one's natural hair color: *hair that was **streaked blond**.* ■ Microbiology smear (a needle, swab, etc.) over the surface of a solid culture medium to initiate a culture.
2 [no obj.] move very fast in a specified direction: *the cat leaped free and streaked across the street.*
3 [no obj.] informal run naked in a public place so as to shock or amuse others.
– PHRASES **like a streak** informal very fast: *he is off like a streak.* **streak of lightning** a flash of lightning.
– DERIVATIVES **streak·er n.**
– ORIGIN Old English *strica*, of Germanic origin; related to Dutch *streek* and German *Strich*, also to STRIKE. The sense 'run naked' originated in the US in the 1970s.

streak·ing /'strēkiNG/ ▶ **n.** long, thin lines of a different color from their surroundings, esp. on dyed hair.

streak·y /'strēkē/ ▶ **adj.** (**streakier**, **streakiest**) having streaks of different colors or textures: *streaky blond hair.* ■ informal variable in quality; not predictable or reliable: *King has always been a famously streaky hitter.*
– DERIVATIVES **streak·i·ly** /-lē/ **adv.**, **streak·i·ness n.**

stream /strēm/ ▶ **n. 1** a small, narrow river.
2 a continuous flow of liquid, air, or gas: *Frank blew out **a stream of** smoke* | *the blood gushed out in scarlet streams.* ■ a mass of people or things moving continuously in the same direction: *there is **a steady stream of** visitors.* ■ a large number of things that happen or come one after the other: *a woman screamed **a stream of** abuse.*
3 Computing a continuous flow of data or instructions, typically one having a constant or predictable rate. ■ a continuous flow of video and audio material relayed over the Internet.
4 British term for TRACK¹ (sense 5 of the noun).
▶ **v. 1** [no obj.] (of liquid) run or flow in a continuous current in a specified direction: *she sat with tears **streaming down** her face* | figurative *sunlight **streamed through** the windows.* ■ (of a mass of people or things) move in a continuous flow in a specified direction: *he was watching the taxis **streaming past**.*
2 [no obj.] (usu. **be streaming**) (of a person or part of the body) produce a continuous flow of liquid; run with liquid: *my eyes were streaming* | *I woke up in the night, **streaming with** sweat* | [with obj.] *his mouth was streaming blood.*
3 [no obj.] (of hair, clothing, etc.) float or wave at full extent in the wind: *her black cloak **streamed behind** her.*
4 [with obj.] Computing transmit (audio or video data) continuously, so that the parts arriving first can be viewed or listened to while the remainder is downloading.
5 British term for TRACK¹ (sense 4 of the verb).
– PHRASES **against** (or **with**) **the stream** against (or with) the prevailing view or tendency: *a world in which the demand for quality does not run against the stream.* **on stream** in or into operation or existence; available: *more jobs are **coming on stream**.*
– ORIGIN Old English *strēam* (noun), of Germanic origin; related to Dutch *stroom*, German *Strom*, from an Indo-European root shared by Greek *rhein* 'to flow.'

stream·er /'strēmər/ ▶ **n.** a long, narrow strip of material used as a decoration or symbol: *plastic party streamers* | figurative *a streamer of smoke.* ■ [usu. as modifier] a banner headline in a newspaper: *his appearance was announced with a streamer headline.* ■ [usu. as modifier] Fishing a fly with feathers attached: *a streamer fly.* ■ Astronomy an elongated mass of luminous matter, e.g., in auroras or the sun's corona.

stream·flow /'strēm,flō/ ▶ **n.** the flow of water in a stream or river.

stream·ing /'strēmiNG/ ▶ **n.** a method of relaying data (esp. video and audio material) over a computer network as a steady continuous stream, allowing playback to proceed while subsequent data is being received.
▶ **adj.** [attrib.] Computing **1** relating to or making use of a form of tape transport, used mainly to provide backup storage, in which data may be transferred in bulk while the tape is in motion.
2 (of data) transmitted in a continuous stream while earlier parts are being used.

stream·let /'strēmlit/ ▶ **n.** a small stream.

stream·line /'strēm,līn/ ▶ **v.** [with obj.] (usu. as adj. **streamlined**) **1** design or provide with a form that presents very little resistance to a flow of air or water, increasing speed and ease of movement: *streamlined passenger trains.*
2 make (an organization or system) more efficient and effective by employing faster or simpler working methods: *the company streamlined its operations by removing whole layers of management.*
▶ **n.** a line along which the flow of a moving fluid is least turbulent.
▶ **adj. 1** (of fluid flow) free from turbulence.
2 dated having a streamlined shape: *a streamline airplane.*

stream of con·scious·ness ▶ **n.** Psychology a person's thoughts and conscious reactions to events, perceived as a continuous flow. The term was introduced by William James in his *Principles of Psychology* (1890). ■ a literary style in which a character's thoughts, feelings, and reactions are depicted in a continuous flow uninterrupted by objective description or conventional dialogue. James Joyce, Virginia Woolf, and Marcel Proust are among its notable early exponents.

Streep /strēp/, Meryl (1949–), US actress; born *Mary Louise Streep*. Notable movies: *Kramer vs. Kramer* (1980), *The French Lieutenant's Woman* (1981), *Sophie's Choice* (1982), *Out of Africa* (1986), *The Hours* (2002), and *The Manchurian Candidate* (2004).

street /strēt/ ▶ **n.** a public road in a city or town, typically with houses and buildings on one or both sides: *the narrow, winding streets of Greenwich Village* | [in place names] *45 Lake Street.* ■ (**the street**) used to refer to the financial markets and activities on Wall Street. ■ (**the street/streets**) the roads or public areas of a city or town: *every week, fans stop me in the street.* ■ [as modifier] of or relating to the outlook, values, or lifestyle of those young people who are perceived as composing a fashionable urban subculture: *New York City street culture.* ■ [as modifier] denoting someone who is homeless: *he ministered to street people in storefront missions.* ■ [as modifier] performing or being performed on the street: *street theater.*
– PHRASES **on the streets 1** homeless. **2** working as a prostitute. **streets ahead** Brit. informal greatly superior: *the restaurant is streets ahead of its local rivals.*
– DERIVATIVES **street·ed adj.** [in combination] *a many-streeted tangle of low, brick buildings*, **street·ward** /-wərd/ **adj. & adv.**
– ORIGIN Old English *strǣt*, from late Latin *strāta (via)* 'paved (way),' feminine past participle of *sternere* 'lay down.'

street Ar·ab ▶ **n.** archaic a raggedly dressed homeless child wandering the streets.

street·ball /'strēt,bôl/ ▶ **n.** an informal type of basketball played esp. in urban areas such as parking lots, playgrounds, etc.

street·car /'strēt,kär/ ▶ **n.** another term for TROLLEY CAR.

street clothes ▶ **plural n.** clothes suitable for everyday wear in public.

S

street cred·i·bil·i·ty (also informal **street cred**) ▶ **n.** acceptability among young black urban residents.

street cries ▶ **plural n.** the cries used by street vendors to advertise their wares.

street fur·ni·ture ▶ **n.** objects placed or fixed in the street for public use, such as mailboxes, road signs, and benches.

street hock·ey ▶ **n.** a form of hockey played on a paved surface using in-line skates.

street-le·gal ▶ **adj.** (of a vehicle) meeting all legal requirements for use on ordinary roads.

street·light /ˈstrēt,līt/ (also **streetlamp**) ▶ **n.** a light illuminating a road, typically mounted on a tall pole.

street name ▶ **n. 1** an informal term for something, esp. an illegal drug.
2 the name of a brokerage firm, bank, or dealer in which stock is held on behalf of a purchaser.

street-smart ▶ **adj.** informal having the skills and knowledge necessary for dealing with modern urban life, esp. the difficult or criminal aspects of it: *a street-smart hustler on a motorcycle.*
▶ **n.** (**street smarts**) these skills and knowledge: *take the advice of somebody who's got a little more street smarts than you.*

street val·ue ▶ **n.** the price for which something, esp. an amount of drugs, that is illegal or has been obtained illicitly can be sold: *detectives seized drugs with a street value of $300,000.*

street ven·dor ▶ **n.** a person who sells something in the street, either from a stall or van or with their goods laid out on the sidewalk.

street·walk·er /ˈstrēt,wôkər/ ▶ **n.** a prostitute who seeks customers in the street.
– DERIVATIVES **street·walk·ing** /-,wôkiNG/ **n. & adj.**

street·wise /ˈstrēt,wīz/ ▶ **adj.** another term for STREET-SMART. ■ reflective of modern urban life, esp. that of urban youth: *streetwise fashion.*

Stre·ga /ˈstrāgə/ ▶ **n.** trademark a kind of orange-flavored Italian liqueur.
– ORIGIN Italian, literally 'witch.'

Strei·sand /ˈstrī,zand, -zənd/, Barbra (Joan) (1942–), US singer, actress, and director. Notable movies: *Funny Girl* (1968), *The Way We Were* (1973), *A Star is Born* (1976), and *The Prince of Tides* (1991). She starred in, produced, and directed *Yentl* (1983).

strength /streNG(k)TH, strenTH/ ▶ **n. 1** the quality or state of being strong, in particular: ■ physical power and energy: *cycling can help you build up your strength.* ■ the emotional or mental qualities necessary in dealing with situations or events that are distressing or difficult: *many people find strength in religion | it takes strength of character to admit one needs help.* ■ the capacity of an object or substance to withstand great force or pressure: *they were taking no chances with the strength of the retaining wall.* ■ the influence or power possessed by a person, organization, or country: *the political and military strength of European governments.* ■ the degree of intensity of a feeling or belief: *street protests demonstrated the strength of feeling against the president.* ■ the cogency of an argument or case: *the strength of the argument for property taxation.* ■ the potency, intensity, or speed of a force or natural agency: *the wind had markedly increased in strength.* ■ the potency or degree of concentration of a drug, chemical, or drink: *it's double the strength of your average beer | the solution comes in two strengths.*
2 a good or beneficial quality or attribute of a person or thing: *the strengths and weaknesses of their sales and marketing operation | his strength was his obsessive single-mindedness.* ■ literary a person or thing perceived as a source of mental or emotional support: *he was my closest friend, my strength and shield.*
3 the number of people comprising a group, typically a team or army: *the peacetime strength of the army was 415,000.* ■ a number of people required to make such a group complete: *we are now more than 100 officers **below strength** | some units will be maintained **at full strength** while others will rely on reserves* | [in combination] *an under-strength side.*
– PHRASES **from strength** from a secure or advantageous position: *it makes sense to negotiate from strength.* **go from strength to strength** develop or progress with increasing success. **in strength** in large numbers: *security forces were out in strength.* **on the strength of** on the basis or with the justification of: *she got into Princeton on the strength of her essays.* **tower** (or **pillar**) **of strength** a person who can be relied upon to give a great deal of support and comfort to others.
– DERIVATIVES **strength·less adj.**
– ORIGIN Old English *strengthu*, from the Germanic base of STRONG.

strength·en /ˈstreNG(k)THən, ˈstren-/ ▶ **v.** make or become stronger: [with obj.] *he advises an application of fluoride to strengthen the teeth* | [no obj.] *the wind won't strengthen until after dark.*
– PHRASES **strengthen someone's hand** (or **hands**) enable or encourage a person to act more vigorously or effectively.
– DERIVATIVES **strength·en·er n.**

stren·u·ous /ˈstrenyo͞oəs/ ▶ **adj.** requiring or using great exertion: *all your muscles need more oxygen during strenuous exercise.*
– DERIVATIVES **stren·u·ous·ly adv.**, **stren·u·ous·ness n.**
– ORIGIN early 17th cent.: from Latin *strenuus* 'brisk' + -OUS.

strep /strep/ ▶ **n.** Medicine, informal short for STREPTOCOCCUS.

Strep·sip·ter·a /strepˈsiptərə/ Entomology an order of minute parasitic insects that comprises the stylopids.
– DERIVATIVES **strep·sip·ter·an n. & adj.**
– ORIGIN modern Latin (plural), from Greek *strepsi-* (combining form of *strephein* 'to turn') + *pteron* 'wing.'

strepto- ▶ **comb. form** twisted; in the form of a twisted chain: *streptomycete.* ■ associated with streptococci or streptomycetes: *streptokinase.*
– ORIGIN from Greek *streptos* 'twisted,' from *strephein* 'to turn.'

strep·to·coc·cus /,streptəˈkäkəs/ ▶ **n.** (pl. **streptococci** /-ˈkäksī, -sē/) a bacterium of a genus that includes the agents of souring of milk and dental decay, and hemolytic pathogens causing various infections such as scarlet fever and pneumonia. ● Genus *Streptococcus*; Gram-positive cocci in pairs and chains.
– DERIVATIVES **strep·to·coc·cal** /-ˈkäkəl/ **adj.**

strep·to·ki·nase /,streptəˈkīnās, -ˈkinās, -nāz/ ▶ **n.** Biochemistry an enzyme produced by some streptococci that is involved in breaking down red blood cells. It is used to treat inflammation and blood clots.

strep·to·my·cete /,streptəˈmīsēt/ ▶ **n.** a bacterium that occurs chiefly in soil as aerobic saprophytes resembling molds, several of which are important sources of antibiotics. ● *Streptomyces* and related genera, order Actinomycetales; Gram-positive filaments forming chains of spores.
– ORIGIN 1950s: anglicized singular of modern Latin *Streptomyces*, from STREPTO- 'twisted' + Greek *mukēs, mukēt-* 'fungus.'

strep·to·my·cin /,streptəˈmīsin/ ▶ **n.** Medicine an antibiotic that was the first drug to be successful against tuberculosis but is now chiefly used with other drugs because of its toxic side effects. ● This antibiotic is produced by the bacterium *Streptomyces griseus.*

stress /stres/ ▶ **n. 1** pressure or tension exerted on a material object: *the distribution of stress is uniform across the bar.* ■ the degree of this measured in units of force per unit area.
2 a state of mental or emotional strain or tension resulting from adverse or very demanding circumstances: *he's obviously **under a lot of stress*** | [in combination] *stress-related illnesses.* ■ something that causes such a state: *the stresses and strains of public life.*
3 particular emphasis or importance: *he has started to **lay** greater **stress on** the government's role in industry.* ■ emphasis given to a particular syllable or word in speech, typically through a combination of relatively greater loudness, higher pitch, and longer duration: *normally, the stress falls on the first syllable.*
▶ **v. 1** [reporting verb] give particular emphasis or importance to (a point, statement, or idea) made in speech or writing: [with obj.] *they stressed the need for reform* | [with clause] *she was anxious to stress that her daughter's safety was her only concern* | [with direct speech] *"I want it done very, very neatly," she stressed.* ■ [with obj.] give emphasis to (a syllable or word) when pronouncing it.
2 [with obj.] subject to pressure or tension: *this type of workout does stress the shoulder and knee joints.*
3 [with obj.] cause mental or emotional strain or tension in: *I avoid many of the things that used to stress me before* | (as adj. **stressed**) *she should see a doctor if she is feeling particularly **stressed out**.* ■ [no obj.] informal become tense or anxious; worry: *don't stress—there's plenty of time to get a grip on the situation.*
– DERIVATIVES **stress·less adj.**, **stres·sor** /-ər/ **n.** (sense 2 of the verb, sense 3 of the verb).
– ORIGIN Middle English (denoting hardship or force exerted on a person for the purpose of compulsion): shortening of DISTRESS, or partly from Old French *estresse* 'narrowness, oppression,' based on Latin *strictus* 'drawn tight' (see STRICT).

stress frac·ture ▶ **n.** a fracture of a bone caused by repeated (rather than sudden) mechanical stress.

stress·ful /ˈstresfəl/ ▶ **adj.** causing mental or emotional stress: *corporate finance work can be stressful.*
– DERIVATIVES **stress·ful·ly adv.**, **stress·ful·ness n.**

stress in·con·ti·nence ▶ **n.** a condition (found chiefly in women) in which there is involuntary emission of urine when pressure within the abdomen increases suddenly, as in coughing or jumping.

stress-timed ▶ **adj.** (of a language) characterized by a rhythm in which primary stresses occur at roughly equal intervals, irrespective of the number of unstressed syllables in between. English is a stress-timed language. Contrasted with SYLLABLE-TIMED.

stretch /strecH/ ▶ **v.** [no obj.] **1** (of something soft or elastic) be made or be capable of being made longer or wider without tearing or breaking: *my sweater stretched in the wash | rubber will stretch easily when pulled.* ■ [with obj.] cause to do this: *stretch the elastic | small squares of canvas were stretched over the bamboo frame.* ■ last or cause to last longer than expected: *her nap had stretched to two hours* | [with obj.] *stretch your weekend into a mini summer vacation.* ■ [with obj.] make great demands on the capacity or resources of: *the cost of the court case has **stretched their finances to the limit**.* ■ [with obj.] cause (someone) to make maximum use of their talents or abilities: *it's too easy—it doesn't stretch me.* ■ [with obj.] adapt or extend the scope of (something) in a way that exceeds a reasonable or acceptable limit: *to describe her as sweet would be stretching it a bit.*
2 straighten or extend one's body or a part of one's body to its full length, typically so as to tighten one's muscles or in order to reach something: *the cat yawned and stretched* | [with obj.] *stretching my cramped legs | we lay **stretched out** on the sand.*
3 extend or spread over an area or period of time: *the beach stretches for over four miles | the long hours of night stretched ahead of her.*
▶ **n. 1** an act of stretching one's limbs or body: *I got up and had a stretch.* ■ the fact or condition of a muscle being stretched: *she could feel the stretch and pull of the muscles in her legs.* ■ Baseball a phase of a pitcher's delivery, during which the arms are raised above and behind the head. ■ Baseball a shortened form of a pitcher's windup, typically used to prevent base runners from stealing or gaining a long lead. ■ [usu. as modifier] the capacity of a material or garment to stretch or be stretched; elasticity: *stretch jeans.* ■ a difficult or demanding task: *it was a stretch for me sometimes to come up with the rent.*
2 a continuous area or expanse of land or water: *a treacherous stretch of road.* ■ a continuous period of time: *long stretches of time.* ■ informal a period of time spent in prison: *a four-year stretch for tax fraud.* ■ a straight part of a racetrack, typically the homestretch: *he made a promising start, but faded down the stretch.* ■ Sailing the distance covered on one tack.
3 informal a stretch limo: *a chauffeur-driven stretch.*
– PHRASES **at a stretch** in one continuous period: *I often had to work for over twenty hours at a stretch.* **by no** (or **not by any**) **stretch of the imagination** used to emphasize that something is definitely not the case: *by no stretch of the imagination could Carl ever be called good-looking.* **stretch one's legs** go for a short walk, typically after sitting in one place for some time. **stretch one's wings** see WING.
– DERIVATIVES **stretch·a·bil·i·ty** /-əˈbilitē/ **n.**, **stretch·a·ble adj.**
– ORIGIN Old English *streccan*; related to Dutch *strekken* and German *strecken*. The noun dates from the late 16th cent.

stretch·er /ˈstrecHər/ ▶ **n. 1** a framework of two poles with a long piece of canvas slung between them, used for carrying sick, injured, or dead people. ■ a gurney.
2 a thing that stretches something, in particular: ■ a wooden frame over which a canvas is spread and tautened ready for painting. ■ archaic, informal an exaggeration or lie.
3 a rod or bar joining and supporting chair legs. ■ a crosspiece in the bottom of a boat on which a rower's feet are braced.
4 a brick or stone laid with its long side along the face of a wall. Compare with HEADER (sense 3).

stretch·er-bear·er ▶ **n.** a person who helps to carry the sick or injured on stretchers, esp. in time of war or at the scene of an accident.

stretch lim·o (also **stretch limousine**) ▶ **n.** a limousine that has an extended seating area.

stretch marks ▶ **plural n.** streaks or stripes on the skin, esp. on the abdomen, caused by distension of the skin from obesity or during pregnancy.

stretch re·cep·tor ▶ **n.** Physiology a sensory receptor that responds to the stretching of surrounding muscle tissue and so contributes to the coordination of muscle activity.

stretch·y /ˈstreCHē/ ▶ **adj.** (**stretchier, stretchiest**) (esp. of material or a garment) able to stretch or be stretched easily: *stretchy miniskirts.*
– DERIVATIVES **stretch·i·ness** **n.**

stret·to /ˈstretō/ Music ▶ **n.** (pl. **stretti** /ˈstretē/) a section at the end of a fugue in which successive introductions of the theme follow at shorter intervals than before, increasing the sense of excitement. ■ (also **stretta**) a passage, esp. at the end of an aria or movement, to be performed in quicker time.
▶ **adv.** (as a direction) in quicker time.
– ORIGIN Italian, literally 'narrow.'

streu·sel /ˈstro͞ozəl, ˈstroi-/ ▶ **n.** a crumbly topping or filling made from fat, flour, sugar, and often cinnamon. ■ a cake or pastry with such a topping.
– ORIGIN from German *Streusel*, from *streuen* 'sprinkle.'

strew /stro͞o/ ▶ **v.** (past participle **strewn** /stro͞on/ or **strewed**) [with obj.] (usu. **be strewn**) scatter or spread (things) untidily over a surface or area: *a small room with newspapers **strewn all over** the floor.* ■ (usu. **be strewn with**) cover (a surface or area) with untidily scattered things: *the table was strewn with books and papers* | [as adj., in combination] (**strewn**) *boulder-strewn slopes.* ■ be scattered or spread untidily over (a surface or area): *leaves strewed the path.*
– DERIVATIVES **strew·er** **n.**
– ORIGIN Old English *stre(o)wian*, of Germanic origin; related to Dutch *strooien*, German *streuen*, from an Indo-European root shared by Latin *sternere* 'lay flat.'

strewn field ▶ **n.** Geology a region of the earth's surface over which tektites of a similar age and presumed origin are found.

stri·a /ˈstrīə/ ▶ **n.** (pl. **striae** /ˈstrī-ē/) technical a linear mark, slight ridge, or groove on a surface, often one of a number of similar parallel features. ■ Anatomy any of a number of longitudinal collections of nerve fibers in the brain.
– ORIGIN late 17th cent. (as a scientific term): from Latin, literally 'furrow.'

stri·ate /ˈstrīˌāt/ technical ▶ **adj.** marked with striae: *the striate cortex.*
▶ **v.** [with obj.] (usu. as adj. **striated**) mark with striae: *striated bark.*
– DERIVATIVES **stri·a·tion** /strīˈāSHən/ **n.**

stri·at·ed mus·cle ▶ **n.** Physiology muscle tissue in which the contractile fibrils in the cells are aligned in parallel bundles, so that their different regions form stripes visible in a microscope. Muscles of this type are attached to the skeleton by tendons and are under voluntary control. Also called SKELETAL MUSCLE. Often contrasted with SMOOTH MUSCLE.

stri·a·tum /strīˈātəm/ ▶ **n.** (pl. **striata** /-ˈātə/) Anatomy short for CORPUS STRIATUM.
– DERIVATIVES **stri·a·tal** /-ˈātl/ **adj.**

strick·en /ˈstrikən/ past participle of STRIKE.
▶ **adj.** seriously affected by an undesirable condition or unpleasant feeling: *the pilot landed the stricken aircraft* | *Raymond was **stricken with** grief* | [in combination] *the farms were drought-stricken.* ■ (of a face or look) showing great distress: *she looked at Anne's stricken face, contorted with worry.*
– PHRASES **stricken in years** dated used euphemistically to describe someone old and feeble.

strick·le /ˈstrikəl/ ▶ **n.** **1** a rod used to level off a heaped measure.
2 a whetting tool.
– ORIGIN Old English *stricel* (sense 1); related to STRIKE. Sense 2 dates from the mid 17th cent.

strict /strikt/ ▶ **adj.** demanding that rules concerning behavior are obeyed and observed: *my father was very strict* | *a strict upbringing.* ■ (of a rule or discipline) demanding total obedience or observance; rigidly enforced: *civil servants are bound by strict rules on secrecy.* ■ (of a person) following rules or beliefs exactly: *a strict vegetarian.* ■ exact in correspondence or adherence to something; not allowing or admitting deviation or relaxation: *a strict interpretation of the law.*
– ORIGIN late Middle English (in the sense 'restricted in space or extent'): from Latin *strictus*, past participle of *stringere* 'tighten, draw tight.'

strict con·struc·tion ▶ **n.** Law a literal interpretation of a statute or document by a court.
– DERIVATIVES **strict con·struc·tion·ist** **n.**

strict li·a·bil·i·ty ▶ **n.** Law liability that does not depend on actual negligence or intent to harm.

strict·ly /ˈstrik(t)lē/ ▶ **adv.** **1** in a way that involves rigid enforcement or that demands obedience: *he's been brought up strictly.*
2 used to indicate that one is applying words or rules exactly or rigidly: [sentence adverb] ***strictly speaking**, ham is a cured, cooked leg of pork* | [as submodifier] *to be strictly accurate, there are two Wolvertons.* ■ with no exceptions; completely or absolutely: *these foods are strictly forbidden.* ■ no more than; purely: *that visit was strictly business* | *his attitude and manner were strictly professional.*

strict·ness /ˈstriktnis/ ▶ **n.** the quality or condition of being strict: *the strictness of his upbringing.*

stric·ture /ˈstrikCHər/ ▶ **n.** **1** a restriction on a person or activity: *religious strictures on everyday life.*
2 a sternly critical or censorious remark or instruction: *his strictures on their lack of civic virtue.*
3 Medicine abnormal narrowing of a canal or duct in the body: *a colonic stricture* | *jaundice caused by bile duct stricture.*
– DERIVATIVES **stric·tured** **adj.**
– ORIGIN late Middle English (sense 3): from Latin *strictura*, from *stringere* 'draw tight' (see STRICT). Another sense of the Latin verb, 'touch lightly,' gave rise to sense 2 via an earlier meaning 'incidental remark.'

stride /strīd/ ▶ **v.** (past **strode** /strōd/; past participle **stridden** /ˈstridn/) **1** [no obj.] walk with long, decisive steps in a specified direction: *he strode across the road* | figurative *striding confidently toward the future.* ■ [with obj.] walk about or along (a street or other place) in this way: *a woman striding the cobbled streets.*
2 [no obj.] (**stride across/over**) cross (an obstacle) with one long step: *by giving a little leap she could stride across like a grown-up.* ■ [with obj.] literary bestride: *new wealth enabled Britain to stride the world once more.*
▶ **n.** **1** a long, decisive step: *he crossed the room in a couple of strides.* ■ [in sing.] the length of a step or manner of taking steps in walking or running: *the horse shortened its stride* | *he followed her with an easy stride.*
2 (usu. **strides**) a step or stage in progress toward an aim: *great strides have been made toward equality.* ■ (**one's stride**) a good or regular rate of progress, esp. after a slow or hesitant start: *after months of ineffective campaigning, he seems to have **hit his stride**.*
3 [as modifier] denoting or relating to a rhythmic style of jazz piano playing in which the left hand alternately plays single bass notes on the downbeat and chords an octave higher on the upbeat: *a stride pianist.*
– PHRASES **break (one's) stride** slow or interrupt the pace at which one walks or moves. **match someone stride for stride** manage to keep up with a competitor. **take something in (one's) stride** deal with something difficult or unpleasant in a calm and accepting way: *we took each new disease in stride.*
– DERIVATIVES **strid·er** **n.**
– ORIGIN Old English *stride* (noun) 'single long step,' *strīdan* (verb) 'stand or walk with the legs wide apart,' probably from a Germanic base meaning 'strive, quarrel'; related to Dutch *strijden* 'fight' and German *streiten* 'quarrel.'

stri·dent /ˈstrīdnt/ ▶ **adj.** loud and harsh; grating: *his voice had become increasingly sharp, almost strident.* ■ presenting a point of view, esp. a controversial one, in an excessively and unpleasantly forceful way: *public pronouncements on the crisis became less strident.* ■ Phonetics another term for SIBILANT.
– DERIVATIVES **stri·den·cy** **n.**, **stri·dent·ly** **adv.**
– ORIGIN mid 17th cent.: from Latin *strident-* 'creaking,' from the verb *stridere.*

stri·dor /ˈstrīdər/ ▶ **n.** a harsh or grating sound: *the engines' stridor increased.* ■ Medicine a harsh vibrating noise when breathing, caused by obstruction of the windpipe or larynx.
– ORIGIN mid 17th cent.: from Latin, from *stridere* 'to creak.'

strid·u·late /ˈstrijəˌlāt/ ▶ **v.** [no obj.] (of an insect, esp. a male cricket or grasshopper) make a shrill sound by rubbing the legs, wings, or other parts of the body together.
– DERIVATIVES **strid·u·lant** /-lənt/ **adj.**, **strid·u·la·tion** /ˌstrijəˈlāSHən/ **n.**, **strid·u·la·to·ry** /-ləˌtôrē/ **adj.**
– ORIGIN mid 19th cent.: from French *striduler*, from Latin *stridulus* 'creaking,' from the verb *stridere.*

strife /strīf/ ▶ **n.** angry or bitter disagreement over fundamental issues; conflict: *strife within the community* | *ethnic and civil strife.*
– ORIGIN Middle English: shortening of Old French *estrif* (related to Old French *estriver* 'strive').

strig·il /ˈstrijəl/ ▶ **n.** an instrument with a curved blade used, esp. by ancient Greeks and Romans, to scrape sweat and dirt from the skin in a hot-air bath or after exercise; a scraper. ■ Entomology a comblike structure on the forelegs of some insects, used chiefly for grooming.
– ORIGIN from Latin *strigilis*, from *stringere* 'touch lightly.' The term in entomology dates from the late 19th cent.

stri·gose /ˈstrīˌgōs/ ▶ **adj.** Botany covered with short stiff adpressed hairs. ■ Entomology finely grooved or furrowed.
– ORIGIN late 18th cent.: from Latin *striga* 'swath, furrow' + -OSE¹.

strike /strīk/ ▶ **v.** (past and past participle **struck** /strək/) **1** [with obj.] hit forcibly and deliberately with one's hand or a weapon or other implement: *he raised his hand, as if to strike me* | *one man was struck on the head with a stick* | [no obj.] *Edgar **struck out** at her.* ■ inflict (a blow): [with two objs.] *he struck her two blows on the leg.* ■ accidentally hit (a part of one's body) against something: *she fell, striking her head against the side of the boat.* ■ come into forcible contact or collision with: *he was struck by a car on Whitepark Road.* ■ (of a beam or ray of light or heat) fall on (an object or surface): *the light struck her ring, reflecting off the diamond.* ■ (in sporting contexts) hit or kick (a ball) so as to score a run, point, or goal: *he struck the ball into the back of the net.* ■ [no obj.] (of a clock) indicate the time by sounding a chime or stroke: [with complement] *the church clock struck twelve.* ■ ignite (a match) by rubbing it briskly against an abrasive surface. ■ produce (fire or a spark) as a result of friction: *his iron stick struck sparks from the pavement.* ■ bring (an electric arc) into being. ■ produce (a musical note) by pressing or hitting a key.
2 [with obj.] (of a disaster, disease, or other unwelcome phenomenon) occur suddenly and have harmful or damaging effects on: *an earthquake struck the island* | [no obj.] *tragedy struck when he was killed in a car crash* | [as adj. in combination] (**struck**) *storm-struck areas.* ■ [no obj.] carry out an aggressive or violent action, typically without warning: *it was eight months before the murderer struck again.* ■ (usu. **be struck down**) kill or seriously incapacitate (someone): *he was struck down by a mystery virus.* ■ (**strike something into**) cause or create a particular strong emotion in (someone): *drugs—a subject guaranteed to strike fear into parents' hearts.* ■ [with obj. and complement] cause (someone) to be in a specified state: *he was struck dumb.*
3 [with obj.] (of a thought or idea) come into the mind of (someone) suddenly or unexpectedly: *a disturbing thought struck Melissa.* ■ cause (someone) to have a particular impression: [with clause] *it struck him that Marjorie was unusually silent* | *the idea **struck her as** odd.* ■ (**be struck by/with**) find particularly interesting, noticeable, or impressive: *Lucy was struck by the ethereal beauty of the scene.*
4 [no obj.] (of employees) refuse to work as a form of organized protest, typically in an attempt to obtain a particular concession or concessions from their employer: *workers may strike over threatened job losses.* ■ [with obj.] undertake such action against (an employer).
5 [with obj.] cancel, remove, or cross out with or as if with a pen: *strike his name **from** the list* | *striking words through with a pen.* ■ (**strike someone off**) officially remove someone from membership of a professional group: *he had been struck off as a disgrace to the profession.* ■ (**strike something down**) abolish a law or regulation: *the law was struck down by the Supreme Court.*
6 [with obj.] make (a coin or medal) by stamping metal. ■ (in cinematography) make (another print) of a film. ■ reach, achieve, or agree to (something involving agreement, balance, or compromise): *the team has **struck a deal** with a sports marketing agency* | *you have to **strike a happy medium**.* ■ (in financial contexts) reach (a figure) by balancing an account: *last year's loss was struck after allowing for depreciation of 67 million dollars.* ■ Canadian form (a committee): *the government struck a committee to settle the issue.*
7 [with obj.] discover (gold, minerals, or oil) by drilling or mining. ■ [no obj.] (**strike on/upon**) discover or think of, esp. unexpectedly or by chance: *pondering, she struck upon a brilliant idea.* ■ come to or reach: *several days out of the village, we struck the Gilgit Road.*
8 [no obj.] move or proceed vigorously or purposefully: *she **struck out** into the lake with a practiced crawl* | *he struck off down the track.* ■ (**strike out**) start out on a new or independent course or endeavor: *after two years he was able to strike out on his own.*
9 [with obj.] take down (a tent or the tents of an encampment): *it took ages to strike camp.* ■ dismantle (theatrical scenery): *the minute we finish this evening, they'll start striking the set.* ■ lower or take down (a flag or sail), esp. as a salute

S

PRONUNCIATION KEY ə *ago, up*; ər *over, fur*; a *hat*; ā *ate*; ä *car*; e *let*; ē *see*; i *fit*; ī *by*; NG *sing*; ō *go*; ô *law, for*; oi *toy*; o͝o *good*; o͞o *goo*; ou *out*; TH *thin*; T͟H *then*; ZH *vision*

or to signify surrender: *the ship struck her German colors.*
10 [with obj.] insert (a cutting of a plant) in soil to take root. ■ [no obj.] (of a plant or cutting) develop roots: *small conifers will strike from cuttings.* ■ [no obj.] (of a young oyster) attach itself to a bed.
11 [no obj.] Fishing secure a hook in the mouth of a fish by jerking or tightening the line after it has taken the bait or fly.
▶ **n. 1** a refusal to work organized by a body of employees as a form of protest, typically in an attempt to gain a concession or concessions from their employer: *dockers voted for an all-out strike* | *local government workers went on strike* | [as modifier] *strike action.* ■ [with modifier] a refusal to do something expected or required, typically by a body of people, with a similar aim: *a rent strike.*
2 a sudden attack, typically a military one: *the threat of nuclear strikes.* ■ (in bowling) an act of knocking down all the pins with one's first ball. ■ Fishing an act or instance of jerking or tightening the line to secure a fish that has already taken the bait or fly.
3 a discovery of gold, minerals, or oil by drilling or mining: *the Lena goldfields strike of 1912.*
4 Baseball a pitch that is counted against the batter, in particular one that the batter swings at and misses, or that passes through the strike zone without the batter swinging, or that the batter hits foul (unless two strikes have already been called). A batter accumulating three strikes is out. ■ a pitch that passes through the strike zone and is not hit. ■ something to one's discredit: *when they returned from Vietnam they had two strikes against them.*
5 the horizontal or compass direction of a stratum, fault, or other geological feature.
6 short for FLY STRIKE.
– PHRASES **strike a balance** see BALANCE. **strike a blow for** (or **at**/**against**) do something to help (or hinder) a cause, belief, or principle: *just by finishing the race, she hopes to strike a blow for womankind.* **strike a chord** see CHORD[2]. **strike at the root** (or **roots**) **of** see ROOT[1]. **strike hands** archaic (of two people) clasp hands to seal a deal or agreement. **strike home** see HOME. **strike it rich** informal acquire a great deal of money, typically in a sudden or unexpected way. **strike me pink** Brit. informal dated used to express astonishment or indignation. **strike a pose** (or **attitude**) hold one's body in a particular position to create an impression: *striking a dramatic pose, Antonia announced that she was leaving.* **strike while the iron is hot** make use of an opportunity immediately. [with reference to smithing.]
– PHRASAL VERBS **strike back 1** retaliate: *he struck back at critics who claim he is too negative.* **2** (of a gas burner) burn from an internal point before the gas has become mixed with air. **strike in** archaic intervene in a conversation or discussion. **strike someone out** (or **strike out**) Baseball put a batter out (or be put out) from play as a batter by means of three strikes. ■ (**strike out**) informal fail or be unsuccessful: *the company struck out the first time it tried to manufacture personal computers.* **strike up** (or **strike something up**) (of a band or orchestra) begin to play a piece of music: *they struck up the "Star-Spangled Banner."* ■ (**strike something up**) begin a friendship or conversation with someone, typically in a casual way.
– ORIGIN Old English *strīcan* 'go, flow' and 'rub lightly'; related to German *streichen* 'to stroke,' also to STROKE. The sense 'deliver a blow' dates from Middle English.

S

strike·break·er /ˈstrīkˌbrākər/ ▶ **n.** a person who works or is employed in place of others who are on strike, thereby making the strike ineffectual.
– DERIVATIVES **strike·break v.**, **strike·break·ing** /-ˌbrākiNG/ **n.**

strike force ▶ **n.** [treated as sing. or pl.] a military force equipped and organized for sudden attack.

strike·out /ˈstrīkˌout/ ▶ **n.** Baseball an out called when a batter accumulates three strikes.
▶ **adj.** Computing (of text) having a horizontal line through the middle; crossed out.

strike pay ▶ **n.** money paid to strikers by their labor union.

strike price ▶ **n.** Finance **1** the price fixed by the seller of a security after receiving bids in a tender offer, typically for a sale of bonds or a new stock market issue.
2 the price at which a put or call option can be exercised.

strik·er /ˈstrīkər/ ▶ **n. 1** an employee on strike.
2 the player who is to strike the ball in a game; a player considered in terms of ability to strike the ball: *a gifted striker of the ball.* ■ (chiefly in soccer) a forward or attacker.

strik·er plate ▶ **n.** a metal plate attached to a doorjamb or lidded container, against which the end of a spring-lock bolt strikes when the door or lid is closed.

strike-slip fault ▶ **n.** Geology a fault in which rock strata are displaced mainly in a horizontal direction, parallel to the line of the fault.

strike zone ▶ **n.** Baseball an area over home plate extending approximately from the armpits to the knees of a batter when in the batting position. The ball must be pitched through this area in order for a strike to be called.

strik·ing /ˈstrīkiNG/ ▶ **adj. 1** attracting attention by reason of being unusual, extreme, or prominent: *the murder bore a striking similarity to an earlier shooting* | [with clause] *it is striking that no research into the problem is occurring.* ■ dramatically good-looking or beautiful: *she is naturally striking* | *a striking landscape.*
2 [attrib.] (of an employee) on strike: *striking mine workers.*
▶ **n.** the action of striking: *substantial damage was caused by the striking of a submerged object.*
– PHRASES **within striking distance** see DISTANCE.
– DERIVATIVES **strik·ing·ly adv.** [as submodifier] *a strikingly beautiful girl.*

strik·ing price ▶ **n.** another term for STRIKE PRICE.

Strind·berg /ˈstrin(d)ˌbərg/, (Johan) August (1849–1912), Swedish playwright and novelist. His satire *The Red Room* (1879) is regarded as Sweden's first modern novel. His later plays are typically tense, psychic dramas, such as *A Dream Play* (1902).
– DERIVATIVES **Strind·berg·i·an adj.**

Strine /strīn/ (also **strine**) informal ▶ **n.** the English language as spoken by Australians; the Australian accent, esp. when considered striking or uneducated. ■ an Australian.
▶ **adj.** of or relating to Australians or Australian English: *he spoke with a broad Strine accent.*
– ORIGIN 1960s: representing the pronunciation of *Australian* in Strine.

string /striNG/ ▶ **n. 1** material consisting of threads of cotton, hemp, or other material twisted together to form a thin length. ■ a piece of such material used to tie around or attach to something. ■ a piece of catgut or similar material interwoven with others to form the head of a sports racket. ■ a length of catgut or wire on a musical instrument, producing a note by vibration. ■ (**strings**) the stringed instruments in an orchestra. ■ [as modifier] of, relating to, or consisting of stringed instruments: *a string quartet.*
2 a set of things tied or threaded together on a thin cord: *she wore a string of agates around her throat.* ■ a sequence of similar items or events: *a string of burglaries.* ■ Computing a linear sequence of characters, words, or other data. ■ a group of racehorses trained at one stable. ■ a team or player holding a specified position in an order of preference: *Gary was first string on the varsity football team.*
3 a tough piece of fiber in vegetables, meat, or other food, such as a tough elongated piece connecting the two halves of a bean pod.
4 short for STRINGBOARD.
5 a hypothetical one-dimensional subatomic particle having the dynamical properties of a flexible loop. ■ (also **cosmic string**) (in cosmology) a hypothetical threadlike concentration of energy within the structure of space-time.
▶ **v.** (past and past participle **strung** /strəNG/) **1** [with obj.] hang (something) so that it stretches in a long line: *lights were strung across the promenade.* ■ thread (a series of small objects) on a string: *he collected stones with holes in them and strung them on a strong cord.* ■ (**be strung**) be arranged in a long line: *the houses were strung along the road.* ■ (**string something together**) add items to one another to form a series or coherent whole: *he can't string two sentences together.*
2 [with obj.] fit a string or strings to (a musical instrument, a racket, or a bow): *the harp had been newly strung.*
3 [with obj.] remove the strings from (a bean).
4 Brit. Billiards another term for LAG[1] (sense 2 of the verb).
– PHRASES **no strings attached** informal used to show that an offer or opportunity carries no special conditions or restrictions. **on a string** under one's control or influence: *I've got the world on a string.*
– PHRASAL VERBS **string along** informal stay with or accompany a person or group casually or as long as it is convenient. **string someone along** informal mislead someone deliberately over a length of time, esp. about one's intentions: *she had no plans to marry him—she was just stringing him along.* **string something out** cause something to stretch out; prolong something. ■ (**string out**) stretch out into a long line: *the runners string out in a line across the road.* ■ (**be strung out**) be nervous or tense: *I often felt strung out by daily stresses.* ■ (**be strung out**) be under the influence of alcohol or drugs: *he died, strung out on booze and cocaine.* **string someone/something up** hang something up on strings. ■ kill someone by hanging.
– DERIVATIVES **string·less adj.**, **string·like** /-ˌlīk/ **adj.**
– ORIGIN Old English *streng* (noun), of Germanic origin; related to German *Strang*, also to STRONG. The verb (dating from late Middle English) is first recorded in the senses 'arrange in a row' and 'fit with a string.'

string bass /bās/ ▶ **n.** (esp. among jazz musicians) a double bass.

string bean ▶ **n. 1** any of various beans eaten in their fibrous pods, such as scarlet runners.
2 informal a tall thin person.

string bi·ki·ni ▶ **n.** a scant bikini with straps of thin cord.

string·board /ˈstriNGˌbôrd/ ▶ **n.** a board with which the ends of the steps in a staircase are covered.

string·course /ˈstriNGˌkôrs/ ▶ **n.** a raised horizontal band or course of bricks on a building. Also called CORDON.

stringed /striNGd/ ▶ **adj.** [attrib.] (of a musical instrument) having strings: [in combination] *a three-stringed fiddle.*

strin·gen·do /strēnˈjendō, strin-/ Music ▶ **adv. & adj.** (esp. as a direction) with increasing speed.
▶ **n.** (pl. **stringendos** or **stringendi** /-ˈjendē/) a passage marked to be performed in this way.
– ORIGIN Italian, literally 'squeezing, binding together.'

strin·gent /ˈstrinjənt/ ▶ **adj.** (of regulations, requirements, or conditions) strict, precise, and exacting: *California's air pollution guidelines are stringent.*
– DERIVATIVES **strin·gen·cy n.**, **strin·gent·ly adv.**
– ORIGIN mid 17th cent. (in the sense 'compelling, convincing'): from Latin *stringent-* 'drawing tight,' from the verb *stringere.*

string·er /ˈstriNGər/ ▶ **n. 1** a longitudinal structural piece in a framework, esp. that of a ship or aircraft.
2 informal a newspaper correspondent not on the regular staff of a newspaper, esp. one retained on a part-time basis to report on events in a particular place.
3 a side of a staircase, which supports the treads and risers.
4 [in combination] a sports player holding a specified position in an order of preference: *a third-stringer on the football team.*

string·halt /ˈstriNGˌhôlt/ ▶ **n.** a condition affecting one or both of a horse's hind legs, causing exaggerated bending of the hock.

string or·ches·tra ▶ **n.** an orchestra consisting only of bowed string instruments of the violin family.

string·piece /ˈstriNGˌpēs/ ▶ **n.** a long piece supporting and connecting the parts of a wooden framework.

string quar·tet ▶ **n.** a chamber music ensemble consisting of first and second violins, viola, and cello. ■ a piece of music for such an ensemble.

string the·o·ry ▶ **n.** a cosmological theory based on the existence of cosmic strings. See also STRING (sense 5 of the noun).

string tie ▶ **n.** a very narrow necktie.

string·y /ˈstriNGē/ ▶ **adj.** (**stringier**, **stringiest**) (esp. of hair) resembling string; long, thin, and lusterless. ■ (of a person) tall, wiry, and thin. ■ (of food) containing tough fibers and so hard to eat. ■ (of a liquid) viscous; forming strings.
– DERIVATIVES **string·i·ly** /-lē/ **adv.**, **string·i·ness n.**

strip[1] /strip/ ▶ **v.** (**strips, stripping, stripped**) [with obj.] **1** remove all coverings from: *they stripped the bed.* ■ remove the clothes from (someone): [with obj. and complement] *the man had been stripped naked.* ■ [no obj.] take off one's clothes: *they stripped and showered* | *she stripped down to her underwear.* ■ pull or tear off (a garment or covering): *she stripped off her shirt* | figurative *strip away the hype, and you'll find original thought.* ■ remove bark and branches from (a tree). ■ remove (paint or varnish) from (a surface): *the floorboards can be stripped, sanded, and polished* | *strip off the existing paint.* ■ remove the stems from (tobacco). ■ milk (a cow) to the last drop.
2 leave bare of accessories or fittings: *thieves stripped the room of luggage.* ■ remove the accessory fittings of or take apart (a machine, motor vehicle, etc.) to inspect or adjust it: *the tank was stripped down piece by piece.*
3 (**strip someone of**) deprive someone of (rank, power, or property): *the lieutenant was stripped of his rank.*
4 sell off (the assets of a company) for profit. ■ Finance divest (a bond) of its interest coupons so that it and they may be sold separately.
5 tear the thread or teeth from (a screw, gearwheel, etc.). ■ [no obj.] (of a screw, gearwheel, etc.) lose its thread or teeth.

6 [no obj.] (of a bullet) be fired from a rifled gun without spin owing to a loss of surface.
▶ n. an act of undressing, esp. in a striptease: *she got drunk and did a strip on top of the piano.* ■ [as modifier] used for or involving the performance of stripteases: *a campaigner against strip joints.*
– ORIGIN Middle English (as a verb): of Germanic origin; related to Dutch *stropen.*

strip² ▶ n. 1 a long, narrow piece of cloth, paper, plastic, or some other material: ***a strip of linen.*** ■ a long, narrow area of land. ■ a main road in or leading out of a town, lined with shops, restaurants, and other facilities. ■ steel or other metal in the form of narrow flat bars.
2 a comic strip.
– ORIGIN late Middle English: from or related to Middle Low German *strippe* 'strap, thong,' probably also to STRIPE.

strip club ▶ n. a club at which striptease performances are given in front of an audience.

strip crop·ping ▶ n. cultivation in which different crops are sown in alternate strips to prevent soil erosion.

stripe /strīp/ ▶ n. 1 a long narrow band or strip, typically of the same width throughout its length, differing in color or texture from the surface on either side of it: *a pair of blue shorts with pink stripes.* ■ archaic a blow with a scourge or lash.
2 a chevron sewn onto a uniform to denote military rank. ■ a type or category: *entrepreneurs of all stripes are joining in the offensive.*
▶ v. [with obj.] (usu. **be striped**) mark with stripes: *her body was striped with bands of sunlight.*
– ORIGIN late Middle English: perhaps a back-formation from STRIPED, of Dutch or Low German origin; compare with Middle Dutch and Middle Low German *stripe.*

striped /strīpt/ ▶ adj. marked with or having stripes: [in combination] *a green-striped coat.*

striped bass /bas/ ▶ n. a large bass of North American coastal waters, with dark horizontal stripes along the upper sides, migrating up streams to breed. ● *Morone* (or *Roccus*) *saxatilis*, family Percichthyidae.

striped hy·e·na ▶ n. a hyena with numerous black stripes on the body and legs, living in steppe and desert areas from northeastern Africa to India. ● *Hyaena hyaena*, family Hyaenidae.

striped ma·ple ▶ n. a compact North American maple with large leaves and vertically striped bark. Also called MOOSEWOOD (so named because moose often feed on the bark during severe winters). ● *Acer pennsylvanicum*, family Aceraceae.

striped pole·cat ▶ n. another term for ZORILLA.

strip·ey /'strīpē/ ▶ adj. variant spelling of STRIPY.

strip·ling /'stripliNG/ ▶ n. humorous a young man.
– ORIGIN Middle English: probably from STRIP² (from the notion of "narrowness," i.e., slimness) + -LING.

strip mall ▶ n. a shopping mall consisting of stores and restaurants typically in one-story buildings located on a busy main road.

strip-mine ▶ v. [with obj.] obtain (ore or coal) by open-pit mining: *lignite coal is strip-mined at depths of 45 to 100 feet* | (as noun **strip-mining**) *protected lands opened up to strip-mining for coal.* ■ subject (an area of land) to open-pit mining.
▶ n. (**strip mine**) a mine worked by this method.

stripped-down ▶ adj. reduced to essentials: *an interim, stripped-down funding bill.*

strip·per /'stripər/ ▶ n. 1 a device used for stripping something: *plier-style wire strippers.* ■ solvent for removing paint.
2 a striptease performer.

strip pok·er ▶ n. a form of poker in which a player with a losing hand takes off an item of clothing as a forfeit.

strip-search ▶ v. [with obj.] search (someone) for concealed items, typically drugs or weapons, in a way that involves the removal of all their clothes.
▶ n. (**strip search**) an act of searching someone in such a way.

strip·tease /'strip,tēz/ ▶ n. a form of entertainment in which a performer gradually undresses to music in a way intended to be sexually exciting.
– DERIVATIVES **strip·teas·er** n.

strip·y /'strīpē/ (also **stripey**) ▶ adj. striped: *a stripy T-shirt.*

strive /strīv/ ▶ v. (past **strove** /strōv/ or **strived**; past participle **striven** /strivən/ or **strived**) [no obj.] make great efforts to achieve or obtain something: *national movements were* ***striving for*** *independence* | [with infinitive] *we must strive to secure steady growth.* ■ struggle or fight vigorously: *scholars must* ***strive against*** *bias.*
– DERIVATIVES **striv·er** n.
– ORIGIN Middle English: shortening of Old French *estriver*; related to *estrif* 'strife.'

strobe /strōb/ informal ▶ n. 1 a stroboscope. ■ a stroboscopic lamp: [as modifier] *strobe lights dazzled her.*
2 an electronic flash for a camera.
▶ v. [no obj.] 1 flash intermittently: *the light of the fireworks strobed around the room.* ■ [with obj.] light as if with a stroboscope: *a neon sign strobed the room.*
2 exhibit or give rise to strobing: *he explained that the stripes I was wearing would strobe.*
– ORIGIN 1940s: abbreviation of *stroboscopic* (see STROBOSCOPE).

stro·bi·la /strə'bīlə/ ▶ n. (pl. **strobilae** /-lē/) Zoology
1 the segmented part of the body of a tapeworm that consists of a long chain of proglottids.
2 a stack of immature larval jellyfish formed on a sessile polyplike form by sequential budding.
– DERIVATIVES **strob·i·la·tion** /,strōbə'lāSHən/ n.
– ORIGIN mid 19th cent.: modern Latin, from Greek *strobilē* 'twisted plug of lint,' from *strephein* 'to twist.'

stro·bi·lus /'strōbələs/ ▶ n. (pl. **strobili** /-,lī/) Botany the cone of a pine, fir, or other conifer. ■ a conelike structure, such as the flower of the hop.
– ORIGIN mid 18th cent.: from late Latin, from Greek *strobilos*, from *strephein* 'to twist.'

strob·ing /'strōbiNG/ ▶ n. 1 irregular movement and loss of continuity sometimes seen in lines and stripes in a television picture.
2 jerkiness in what should be a smooth movement of an image on a screen.

stro·bo·scope /'strōbə,skōp/ ▶ n. Physics an instrument for studying periodic motion or determining speeds of rotation by shining a momentary bright light at intervals so that a moving object appears stationary. ■ a lamp made to flash intermittently, esp. for this purpose.
– DERIVATIVES **stro·bo·scop·ic** /,strōbə'skäpik/ adj., **stro·bo·scop·i·cal·ly** /,strōbə'skäpik(ə)lē/ adv.
– ORIGIN mid 19th cent.: from Greek *strobos* 'whirling' + -SCOPE.

strode /strōd/ past of STRIDE.

stro·ga·noff /'strôgə,nôf, 'strō-/ ▶ n. a dish in which the central ingredient, typically strips of beef, is cooked in a sauce containing sour cream.
– ORIGIN named after Count Pavel Stroganov (1772–1817), Russian diplomat.

stroke /strōk/ ▶ n. 1 an act of hitting or striking someone or something; a blow: *he received three strokes of the cane.* ■ a method of striking the ball in sports or games. ■ Golf an act of hitting the ball with a club, as a unit of scoring: *won by two strokes.* ■ the sound made by a striking clock.
2 an act of moving one's hand or an object across a surface, applying gentle pressure: *massage the cream into your skin using light upward strokes.* ■ a mark made by drawing a pen, pencil, or paintbrush in one direction across paper or canvas: *the paint had been applied in careful, regular strokes.* ■ a line forming part of a written or printed character. ■ a short printed or written diagonal line typically separating characters or figures.
3 a movement, esp. one of a series, in which something moves out of its position and back into it; a beat: *the ray swam with effortless strokes of its huge wings.* ■ the whole motion of a piston in either direction. ■ the rhythm to which a series of repeated movements is performed: *the rowers sing to keep their stroke.* ■ a movement of the arms and legs forming one of a series in swimming. ■ style of moving the arms and legs in swimming: *front crawl is a popular stroke.* ■ (in rowing) the mode or action of moving the oar. ■ (also **stroke oar**) the oar or oarsman nearest the stern of a boat, setting the timing for the other rowers.
4 a sudden disabling attack or loss of consciousness caused by an interruption in the flow of blood to the brain, esp. through thrombosis.
▶ v. [with obj.] 1 move one's hand with gentle pressure over (a surface, esp. hair, fur, or skin), typically repeatedly; caress: *he put his hand on her hair and stroked it.* ■ apply (something) to a surface using a gentle movement: *she strokes blue eyeshadow on her eyelids.* ■ informal reassure or flatter (someone), esp. in order to gain their cooperation: *production executives were expert at stroking stars and brokering talent.*
2 act as the stroke of (a boat or crew): *he stroked Penn's rowing eight to victory.*
3 hit or kick (a ball) smoothly and deliberately: *Miller calmly stroked three-pointers throughout the tournament.* ■ score (a run or point) in such a manner: *the senior stroked a two-run single.*
– PHRASES **at a** (or **one**) **stroke** by a single action having immediate effect: *attitudes cannot be changed at one stroke.* **not** (or **never**) **do a stroke of work** do no work at all. **on the stroke of ——** precisely at the specified time: *he arrived on the stroke of two.* **put someone off their stroke** disconcert someone so that they do not work or perform as well as they might; break the pattern or rhythm of someone's work. **stroke of business** a profitable transaction. **stroke of genius** an outstandingly brilliant and original idea. **stroke of luck** (or **good luck**) a fortunate occurrence that could not have been predicted or expected.
– ORIGIN Old English *strācian* 'caress lightly,' of Germanic origin; related to Dutch *streek* 'a stroke,' German *streichen* 'to stroke,' also to STRIKE. The earliest noun sense 'blow' is first recorded in Middle English.

stroke play ▶ n. a game of golf in which the score is reckoned by counting the number of strokes taken overall, as opposed to the number of holes won. Also called MEDAL PLAY.

stroll /strōl/ ▶ v. [no obj.] walk in a leisurely way: *I strolled around the city.*
▶ n. 1 a short leisurely walk.
2 a victory or objective that is easily achieved.
– ORIGIN early 17th cent. (in the sense 'roam as a vagrant'): probably from German *strollen, strolchen*, from *Strolch* 'vagabond,' of unknown ultimate origin.

stroll·er /'strōlər/ ▶ n. 1 a chair on wheels, typically folding, in which a baby or young child can be pushed along.
2 a person taking a leisurely walk: *shady gardens where strollers could relax.*

stroll·ing play·ers ▶ plural n. historical a troupe of itinerant actors.

stro·ma /'strōmə/ ▶ n. (pl. **stromata** /-mətə/)
1 Anatomy & Biology the supportive tissue of an epithelial organ, tumor, gonad, etc., consisting of connective tissues and blood vessels. ■ the spongy framework of protein fibers in a red blood cell or platelet. ■ Botany the matrix of a chloroplast, in which the grana are embedded.
2 Botany a cushionlike mass of fungal tissue, having spore-bearing structures either embedded in it or on its surface.
– DERIVATIVES **stro·mal** adj. (chiefly Anatomy), **stro·mat·ic** /strō'matik/ adj. (chiefly Botany).
– ORIGIN mid 19th cent.: modern Latin, via late Latin from Greek *strōma* 'coverlet.'

stro·mat·o·lite /strō'matə,līt/ ▶ n. a calcareous mound built up of layers of lime-secreting cyanobacteria and trapped sediment, found in Precambrian rocks as the earliest known fossils, and still being formed in lagoons in Australasia.
– ORIGIN 1930s: from modern Latin *stroma, stromat-* 'layer, covering' + -LITE.

stro·ma·top·o·roid /,strōmə'täpə,roid/ ▶ n. an extinct, sessile, corallike marine organism of uncertain relationship that built up calcareous masses composed of laminae and pillars, occurring from the Cambrian to the Cretaceous.
– ORIGIN late 19th cent.: from modern Latin *Stromatopora* (genus name), from *stroma, stromat-* 'layer, covering' + *-pora* (on the pattern of *madrepora*).

Strom·bo·li /'strämbəlē/ a volcanic island in the Mediterranean Sea, one of the Lipari Islands.

Strom·bo·li·an /sträm'bōlēən/ ▶ adj. Geology denoting volcanic activity of the kind typified by Stromboli, with continual mild eruptions in which lava fragments are ejected.

Strong /strôNG, sträNG/, William (1808–95), US Supreme Court associate justice 1870–80. Appointed to the Court by President Grant, he wrote the majority opinion in the Court's 1871 reversal of its decision that declared the Legal Tender Act of 1862 unconstitutional.

strong /strôNG/ ▶ adj. (**stronger** /'strôNGgər/, **strongest** /'strôNGgist/) 1 having the power to move heavy weights or perform other physically demanding tasks: *she cut through the water with her strong arms.* ■ [attrib.] able to perform a specified action well and powerfully: *he was not a strong swimmer.* ■ exerting great force: *a strong current.* ■ (of an argument or case) likely to succeed because of sound reasoning or convincing evidence: *there is a strong argument for decentralization.* ■ possessing skills and qualities that create a likelihood of success: *the competition was too strong.* ■ powerfully affecting the mind, senses, or emotions: *his imagery made a strong impression on the critics.* ■ used after a number to indicate the size of a group: *a hostile crowd several thousand strong.*
2 able to withstand great force or pressure: *cotton is strong, hard-wearing, and easy to handle.* ■ (of

S

a person's constitution) not easily affected by disease or hardship. ■ not easily disturbed, upset, or affected: *driving on these highways requires strong nerves.* ■ (of a person's character) showing determination, self-control, and good judgment: *only a strong will enabled him to survive.* ■ (of a market) having steadily high or rising prices. ■ firmly held or established: *a strong and trusting relationship.*
3 (of light) very intense. ■ (of something seen or heard) not soft or muted; clear or prominent: *she should wear strong colors.* ■ (of food or its flavor) distinctive and pungent: *strong cheese.* ■ (of a solution or drink) containing a large proportion of a particular substance; concentrated: *a cup of strong coffee.* ■ (of language or actions) forceful and extreme, esp. excessively or unacceptably so: *the government was urged to take strong measures against the perpetrators of violence.* ■ Chemistry (of an acid or base) fully ionized into cations and anions in solution; having (respectively) a very low or a very high pH.
4 Grammar denoting a class of verbs in Germanic languages that form the past tense and past participle by a change of vowel within the stem rather than by addition of a suffix (e.g., *swim, swam, swum*); contrasted with **WEAK**.
5 Physics of, relating to, or denoting the strongest of the known kinds of force between particles, which acts between nucleons and other hadrons when closer than about 10^{-13} cm (so binding protons in a nucleus despite the repulsion due to their charge), and which conserves strangeness, parity, and isospin.
– PHRASES **come on strong** informal **1** behave aggressively or assertively, esp. in making sexual advances to someone. **2** improve one's position considerably: *he came on strong toward the end of the round.* **going strong** informal continuing to be healthy, vigorous, or successful: *the program is still going strong after twelve episodes.* **strong on** good at: *he is strong on comedy.* ■ possessing large quantities of: *our pizza wasn't strong on pepperoni.* **one's strong point** something at which one excels: *arithmetic had never been my strong point.*
– DERIVATIVES **strong·ish** adj., **strong·ly** adv.
– ORIGIN Old English, of Germanic origin; related to Dutch and German *streng*, also to **STRING**.

strong-arm ▶ adj. [attrib.] using or characterized by force or violence: *they were furious at what they said were government strong-arm tactics.*
▶ v. [with obj.] use force or violence against: *the culprit shouted before being strong-armed out of the door.*

strong·box /ˈstrôNGˌbäks/ ▶ n. a small lockable box, typically made of metal, in which valuables may be kept.

strong breeze ▶ n. a wind of force 6 on the Beaufort scale (22–27 knots or 25–31 mph).

strong drink ▶ n. alcohol, esp. liquor.

strong gale ▶ n. a wind of force 9 on the Beaufort scale (41–47 knots or 47–54 mph).

strong·hold /ˈstrôNGˌhōld/ ▶ n. a place that has been fortified so as to protect it against attack. ■ a place where a particular cause or belief is strongly defended or upheld: *a Republican stronghold.*

strong in·ter·ac·tion ▶ n. interaction at short distances between certain subatomic particles mediated by the strong force. See **STRONG** (sense 5).

strong·man /ˈstrôNGˌman/ ▶ n. (pl. **strongmen**) a man of great physical strength, esp. one who performs feats of strength as a form of entertainment. ■ a leader who rules by the exercise of threats, force, or violence.

strong-mind·ed ▶ adj. not easily influenced by others; resolute and determined.
– DERIVATIVES **strong-mind·ed·ness** n.

strong·point /ˈstrôNGˌpoint/ ▶ n. a specially fortified defensive position.

strong·room /ˈstrôNGˌro͞om, -ˌro͝om/ ▶ n. a room, typically one in a bank, designed to protect valuable items against fire and theft.

strong safe·ty ▶ n. Football a defensive back positioned opposite the offensive team's stronger side, who often covers the tight end.

strong side ▶ n. Sports (on teams with an odd number of players) the half of an offensive or defensive alignment that has one player more.

strong suit ▶ n. (in bridge) a holding of a number of high cards of one suit in a hand. ■ a desirable quality that is particularly prominent in someone's character or an activity at which they excel: *compassion is not Jack's strong suit.*

strong-willed ▶ adj. determined to do as one wants even if other people advise against it.

stron·gyle /ˈstränˌjīl/ ▶ n. a nematode of a group that includes several common disease-causing parasites of mammals and birds. ● Genus *Strongylus* or family Strongylidae, class Phasmida. See also **RED WORM** (sense 2).
– ORIGIN mid 19th cent.: from modern Latin *Strongylus*, from Greek *strongulos* 'round.'

stron·gy·loi·di·a·sis /ˌstränjəloiˈdīəsis/ ▶ n. infestation with threadworms of a type found in tropical and subtropical regions, chiefly affecting the small intestine and causing ulceration and diarrhea. ● The worms belong to the genus *Strongyloides*, class Phasmida, in particular *S. stercoralis*.

stron·ti·a /ˈstränSH(ē)ə/ ▶ n. Chemistry strontium oxide, a white solid resembling quicklime. ● Chem. formula: SrO.
– ORIGIN early 19th cent.: from earlier *strontian*, denoting native strontium carbonate from *Strontian*, a parish in the Highland region of Scotland, where it was discovered.

stron·ti·an·ite /ˈstränSH(ē)əˌnīt/ ▶ n. a rare pale greenish-yellow or white mineral consisting of strontium carbonate.
– ORIGIN late 18th cent.: from *strontian* (see **STRONTIA**) + **-ITE**[1].

stron·ti·um /ˈstränCHēəm, -tēəm/ ▶ n. the chemical element of atomic number 38, a soft, silver-white metal of the alkaline earth series. Its salts are used in fireworks and flares because they give a brilliant red light. (Symbol: **Sr**)
– ORIGIN early 19th cent.: from **STRONTIA** + **-IUM**.

strop /sträp/ ▶ n. a device, typically a strip of leather, for sharpening straight razors. ■ (also **strap**) Nautical a rope sling for handling cargo.
▶ v. (**strops, stropping, stropped**) [with obj.] sharpen on or with a strop: *he stropped a knife razor-sharp on his belt.*
– ORIGIN late Middle English (in the sense 'thong,' also as a nautical term): probably a West Germanic adoption of Latin *stroppus* 'thong.'

stro·phan·thin /strōˈfanTHən/ ▶ n. Medicine a poisonous substance of the glycoside class, obtained from certain African trees and used as a heart stimulant. ● This substance is obtained from trees of the genera *Strophanthus* and *Acokanthera* (family Apocynaceae).
– ORIGIN late 19th cent.: from modern Latin *strophanthus* (from Greek *strophos* 'twisted cord' + *anthos* 'flower,' referring to the long segments of the corolla) + **-IN**[1].

stro·phe /ˈstrōfē/ ▶ n. the first section of an ancient Greek choral ode or of one division of it. Compare with **ANTISTROPHE** and **EPODE** (sense 2). ■ a structural division of a poem containing stanzas of varying line-length, esp. an ode or free verse poem.
– DERIVATIVES **stroph·ic** /-fik, ˈsträ-/ adj.
– ORIGIN early 17th cent.: from Greek *strophē*, literally 'turning,' from *strephein* 'to turn'; the term originally denoted a movement from right to left made by a Greek chorus, or lines of choral song recited during this.

stroud /stroud/ ▶ n. coarse woolen fabric, formerly used in the manufacture of blankets for sale to North American Indians.

strove /strōv/ past of **STRIVE**.

strow /strō/ ▶ v. (past participle **strown** /strōn/ or **strowed**) archaic variant of **STREW**.

struck /strək/ past and past participle of **STRIKE**.

struck joint ▶ n. a masonry joint in which the mortar between two courses of bricks is sloped inward so as to be flush with the surface of one but below that of the other.

struc·tur·al /ˈstrəkCHərəl/ ▶ adj. of, relating to, or forming part of the structure of a building or other item: *the blast left ten buildings with major structural damage.* ■ of or relating to the arrangement of and relations between the parts or elements of a complex whole: *there have been structural changes in the industry.*
– DERIVATIVES **struc·tur·al·ly** adv.

struc·tur·al en·gi·neer·ing ▶ n. the branch of civil engineering that deals with large modern buildings and similar structures.
– DERIVATIVES **struc·tur·al en·gi·neer** n.

struc·tur·al for·mu·la ▶ n. Chemistry a formula that shows the arrangement of atoms in the molecule of a compound. Compare with **EMPIRICAL FORMULA, MOLECULAR FORMULA**.

struc·tur·al·ism /ˈstrəkCHərəˌlizəm/ ▶ n. a method of interpretation and analysis of aspects of human cognition, behavior, culture, and experience that focuses on relationships of contrast between elements in a conceptual system that reflect patterns underlying a superficial diversity. ■ the doctrine that structure is more important than function.

> Originating in the structural linguistics of Ferdinand de Saussure and extended into anthropology by Claude Lévi-Strauss, structuralism was adapted to a wide range of social and cultural studies, esp. in the 1960s, by writers such as Roland Barthes, Louis Althusser, and Jacques Lacan.

– DERIVATIVES **struc·tur·al·ist** n. & adj.

struc·tur·al lin·guis·tics ▶ plural n. [treated as sing.] the branch of linguistics that deals with language as a system of interrelated structures, in particular the theories and methods of Leonard Bloomfield, emphasizing the accurate identification of syntactic and lexical form as opposed to meaning and historical development.

struc·tur·al steel ▶ n. strong mild steel in shapes suited to construction work.

struc·tur·al un·em·ploy·ment ▶ n. unemployment resulting from industrial reorganization, typically due to technological change, rather than fluctuations in supply or demand.

struc·tur·a·tion /ˌstrəkCHəˈrāSHən/ ▶ n. the state or process of organization in a structured form.

struc·ture /ˈstrəkCHər/ ▶ n. the arrangement of and relations between the parts or elements of something complex: *flint is extremely hard, like diamond, which has a similar structure.* ■ a building or other object constructed from several parts. ■ the quality of being organized: *we shall use three headings to give some structure to the discussion.*
▶ v. [with obj.] construct or arrange according to a plan; give a pattern or organization to: *the game is structured so that there are five ways to win.*
– DERIVATIVES **struc·ture·less** adj.
– ORIGIN late Middle English (denoting the process of building): from Old French, or from Latin *structura*, from *struere* 'to build.' The verb is rarely found before the 20th cent.

struc·tured set·tle·ment ▶ n. a legal settlement paid out as an annuity rather than in a lump sum, usually with certain tax advantages for the recipient and a savings for the payer.

stru·del /ˈstro͞odl/ ▶ n. a confection of thin pastry rolled up around a fruit filling and baked.
– ORIGIN from German *Strudel*, literally 'whirlpool.'

strug·gle /ˈstrəgəl/ ▶ v. [no obj.] make forceful or violent efforts to get free of restraint or constriction: *before she could struggle, he lifted her up* | [with infinitive] *he struggled to break free.* ■ strive to achieve or attain something in the face of difficulty or resistance: [with infinitive] *many families struggle to make ends meet* | *new authors are struggling in the present climate.* ■ (**struggle with**) have difficulty handling or coping with: *passengers struggle with bags and briefcases.* ■ engage in conflict: *politicians continued to struggle over familiar issues.* ■ make one's way with difficulty: *he struggled to the summit of the world's highest mountain.*
▶ n. a forceful or violent effort to get free of restraint or resist attack. ■ a conflict or contest: *a power struggle for the leadership* | *with a struggle, she pulled the stroller up the slope.* ■ a determined effort under difficulties: *the center is the result of the scientists' struggle to realize their dream.* ■ a very difficult task: *it was a struggle to make herself understood.*
– PHRASES **the struggle for existence** (or **life**) the competition between organisms, esp. as an element in natural selection, or between people seeking a livelihood.
– DERIVATIVES **strug·gler** /ˈstrəg(ə)lər/ n.
– ORIGIN late Middle English: frequentative, perhaps of imitative origin. The noun dates from the late 17th cent.

strum /strəm/ ▶ v. (**strums, strumming, strummed**) [with obj.] play (a guitar or similar instrument) by sweeping the thumb or a plectrum up or down across the strings. ■ play (a tune) in such a way: *he strummed a few chords.* ■ [no obj.] play casually or unskillfully on a stringed or keyboard instrument.
▶ n. [in sing.] the sound made by strumming: *the brittle strum of acoustic guitars.* ■ an instance or spell of strumming.
– DERIVATIVES **strum·mer** n.
– ORIGIN late 18th cent.: imitative; compare with **THRUM**[1].

stru·ma /ˈstro͞omə/ ▶ n. (pl. **strumae** /-mē/) Medicine a swelling of the thyroid gland; a goiter.
– ORIGIN mid 16th cent. (in the Latin sense): modern Latin, from Latin, 'scrofulous tumor.'

stru·mous /ˈstro͞oməs/ ▶ adj. archaic scrofulous.
– ORIGIN late 16th cent.: from Latin *strumosus*, from *struma* (see **STRUMA**).

strum·pet /ˈstrəmpət/ ▶ n. dated a female prostitute or a promiscuous woman.
– ORIGIN Middle English: of unknown origin.

strung /strəNG/ past and past participle of **STRING**.

strut /strət/ ▶ **n.** **1** a rod or bar forming part of a framework and designed to resist compression.
2 [in sing.] a stiff, erect, and apparently arrogant or conceited gait: *that old confident strut and swagger has returned.*
▶ **v.** (**struts, strutting, strutted**) **1** [no obj.] walk with a stiff, erect, and apparently arrogant or conceited gait: *peacocks strut through the grounds.*
2 [with obj.] brace (something) with a strut or struts: *the holes were close-boarded and strutted.*
– PHRASES **strut one's stuff** informal dance or behave in a confident and expressive way.
– DERIVATIVES **strut·ter n.**, **strut·ting·ly adv.**
– ORIGIN Old English *strūtian* 'protrude stiffly,' of Germanic origin. Current senses date from the late 16th cent.

Stru·ve /'SHtroōvə/, Otto (1897–1963), US astronomer, born in Russia. In 1938, he discovered the presence of ionized hydrogen in interstellar space.

strych·nine /'strik,nīn, -,nēn/ ▶ **n.** a bitter and highly poisonous compound obtained from nux vomica and related plants. An alkaloid, it has occasionally been used as a stimulant.
– ORIGIN early 19th cent.: from French, via Latin from Greek *strukhnos*, denoting a kind of nightshade.

Stryker /'strīkər/ (in full **Stryker Armored Vehicle**) ▶ **n.** an eight-wheeled armored vehicle used by the Army with defense capabilities similar to those of a tank, but with greater mobility and fewer logistical requirements.
– ORIGIN named for two different veterans of earlier wars who shared the surname *Stryker.*

Sts. ▶ **abbr.** Saints.

Stu·art[1] /'st(y)oōərt/, Charles Edward (1720–88), son of James Stuart; pretender to the British throne; known as **the Young Pretender** or **Bonnie Prince Charlie**.

Stu·art[2], Gilbert Charles (1755–1828), US artist. Considered the father of American portraiture, he is best known for his portraits of the first five presidents, painted between 1817 and 1821.

Stu·art[3], James (Francis Edward) (1688–1766), son of James II (James VII of Scotland); pretender to the British throne; known as **the Old Pretender**.

Stu·art[4], Jeb (1833–64), Confederate military officer; full name *James Ewell Brown Stuart.* He resigned from the US army in 1861 to join the Confederate army as a brigadier general. He was known for his brazen missions of reconnaissance during the Civil War, and his raid that surrounded McClellan's army in 1862 is praised as superb military strategy. He was mortally wounded at the Battle of Yellow Tavern in Virginia.

Stu·art[5], Mary, see **MARY, QUEEN OF SCOTS**.

Stu·art[6] (also **Stewart**) ▶ **adj.** of or relating to the royal family ruling Scotland 1371–1714 and Britain 1603–49 and 1660–1714.
▶ **n.** a member of this family.

stub /stəb/ ▶ **n.** **1** the truncated remnant of a pencil, cigarette, or similar-shaped object after use. ■ a truncated or unusually short thing: *he wagged his little stub of tail.* ■ [as modifier] denoting a projection or hole that goes only part of the way through a surface: *a stub tenon.*
2 the part of a check, receipt, ticket, or other document torn off and kept as a record.
▶ **v.** (**stubs, stubbing, stubbed**) [with obj.]
1 accidentally strike (one's toe) against something: *I stubbed my toe, swore, and tripped.*
2 extinguish (a lighted cigarette) by pressing the lighted end against something: *she* ***stubbed out*** *her cigarette in the overflowing ashtray.*
3 dig up (a plant) by the roots.
– ORIGIN Old English *stub(b)* 'stump of a tree,' of Germanic origin. The verb is first recorded (late Middle English) in sense 3 of the verb; sense 1 of the verb (mid 19th cent.) was originally a US usage.

stub ax·le ▶ **n.** an axle supporting only one wheel of a pair on opposite sides of a vehicle.

stub·ble /'stəbəl/ ▶ **n.** the cut stalks of grain plants left sticking out of the ground after the grain is harvested. ■ short, stiff hairs growing on a man's face when he has not shaved for a while.
– DERIVATIVES **stub·bled adj.**
– ORIGIN Middle English: from Anglo-Norman French *stuble*, from Latin *stupla, stupula*, variants of *stipula* 'straw.'

stub·bly /'stəb(ə)lē/ ▶ **adj.** (**stubblier, stubbliest**) covered with stubble: *a stubbly chin.*

stub·born /'stəbərn/ ▶ **adj.** having or showing dogged determination not to change one's attitude or position on something, esp. in spite of good arguments or reasons to do so: *he accused her of being a silly, stubborn old woman.* ■ difficult to move, remove, or cure: *the removal of stubborn screws.*
– DERIVATIVES **stub·born·ly adv.**, **stub·born·ness n.**
– ORIGIN Middle English (originally in the sense 'untamable, implacable'): of unknown origin.

stub·by /'stəbē/ ▶ **adj.** (**stubbier, stubbiest**) short and thick: *Bloom pointed with a stubby finger.*
– DERIVATIVES **stub·bi·ly** /-əlē/ **adv.**, **stub·bi·ness n.**

stuc·co /'stəkō/ ▶ **n.** fine plaster used for coating wall surfaces or molding into architectural decorations.
▶ **v.** (**stuccoes, stuccoing, stuccoed**) [with obj.] (usu. as adj. **stuccoed**) coat or decorate with such plaster: *a stuccoed house.*
– ORIGIN late 16th cent. (as a noun): from Italian, of Germanic origin.

stuck /stək/ past and past participle of **STICK**[2].

stuck-up ▶ **adj.** informal staying aloof from others because one thinks one is superior.

stud[1] /stəd/ ▶ **n.** **1** a large-headed piece of metal that pierces and projects from a surface, esp. for decoration. ■ a small, simple piece of jewelry for wearing in pierced ears or nostrils. ■ a fastener consisting of two buttons joined with a bar, used in formal wear to fasten a shirtfront or to fasten a collar to a shirt. ■ (usu. **studs**) a small projection fixed to the base of footwear, esp. athletic shoes, to allow the wearer to grip the ground. ■ (usu. **studs**) a small metal piece set into the tire of a motor vehicle to improve roadholding in slippery conditions.
2 an upright support in the wall of a building to which sheathing, drywall, etc., are attached. ■ the height of a room as indicated by the length of this.
3 a rivet or crosspiece in each link of a chain cable.
▶ **v.** (**studs, studding, studded**) [with obj.] (usu. **be studded**) decorate or augment (something) with many studs or similar small objects: *a dagger studded with precious diamonds.* ■ strew or cover (something) with a scattering of small objects or features: *the sky was clear and* ***studded with*** *stars.*
– ORIGIN Old English *studu, stuthu* 'post, upright prop'; related to German *stützen* 'to prop.' The sense 'ornamental metal knob' arose in late Middle English.

stud[2] ▶ **n.** **1** an establishment where horses or other domesticated animals are kept for breeding: [as modifier] *a stud farm | the horse was retired* ***to stud.*** ■ a collection of horses or other domesticated animals belonging to one person. ■ (also **stud horse**) a stallion. ■ informal a young man thought to be very active sexually or regarded as a good sexual partner.
2 (also **stud poker**) a form of poker in which the first card of a player's hand is dealt face down and the others face up, with betting after each round of the deal.
– ORIGIN Old English *stōd*, of Germanic origin; related to German *Stute* 'mare,' also to **STAND**.

stud. ▶ **abbr.** student.

stud book ▶ **n.** a book containing the pedigrees of horses.

stud·ded /'stədid/ ▶ **adj.** decorated or augmented with studs: *a studded leather belt.*

stud·ding /'stədiNG/ ▶ **n.** studs collectively. See **STUD**[1] (sense 2 of the noun).

stud·ding·sail /'stədiNG,sāl, 'stənsəl/ ▶ **n.** (on a square-rigged sailing ship) an additional sail set at the end of a yard in light winds.
– ORIGIN mid 16th cent.: *studding* perhaps from Middle Low German and Middle Dutch *stōtinge* 'a thrusting.'

stu·dent /'st(y)oōdnt/ ▶ **n.** a person who is studying at a school or college. ■ [as modifier] denoting someone who is studying in order to enter a particular profession: *a group of student nurses.* ■ a person who takes an interest in a particular subject: *a* ***student of*** *the free market.*
– DERIVATIVES **stu·dent·ship** /-,SHip/ **n.** (Brit.), **stu·dent·y adj.** (Brit. informal).
– ORIGIN late Middle English: from Latin *student-* 'applying oneself to,' from the verb *studere*, related to *studium* 'painstaking application.'

Stu·dent's t-test ▶ **n.** a test for statistical significance that uses tables of a statistical distribution called **Student's *t*-distribution**, which is that of a fraction (*t*) whose numerator is drawn from a normal distribution with a mean of zero, and whose denominator is the root mean square of *k* terms drawn from the same normal distribution (where *k* is the number of degrees of freedom).
– ORIGIN early 20th cent.: *Student*, the pseudonym of William Sealy Gosset (1876–1937), English brewery employee.

stud horse ▶ **n.** see **STUD**[2].

stud·ied /'stədēd/ ▶ **adj.** (of a quality or result) achieved or maintained by careful and deliberate effort: *he treated them with studied politeness.*
– DERIVATIVES **stud·ied·ly adv.**, **stud·ied·ness n.**

stu·di·o /'st(y)oōdē,ō/ ▶ **n.** (pl. **studios**) **1** a room where an artist, photographer, sculptor, etc., works. ■ a place where performers, esp. dancers, practice and exercise. ■ a room where musical or sound recordings can be made. ■ a room from which television or radio programs are broadcast, or in which they are recorded. ■ a place where movies are made or produced.
2 a film or television production company.
3 a studio apartment.
– ORIGIN early 19th cent.: from Italian, from Latin *studium* (see **STUDY**).

stu·di·o a·part·ment ▶ **n.** an apartment containing one main room.

stu·di·o couch ▶ **n.** a sofa bed.

stu·di·o por·trait ▶ **n.** a large photograph for which the sitter is posed, typically taken in the photographer's studio.

stu·di·o the·a·ter ▶ **n.** a small theater where experimental and innovative productions are staged.

stu·di·ous /'st(y)oōdēəs/ ▶ **adj.** spending a lot of time studying or reading: *he was quiet and studious.* ■ done deliberately or with a purpose in mind: *his studious absence from public view.* ■ showing great care or attention: *a studious inspection.*
– DERIVATIVES **stu·di·ous·ly adv.**, **stu·di·ous·ness n.**
– ORIGIN Middle English: from Latin *studiosus*, from *studium* 'painstaking application.'

stud·muf·fin /'stəd,məfin/ ▶ **n.** informal a man perceived as sexually attractive, typically one with well-developed muscles.

stud pok·er ▶ **n.** see **STUD**[2] (sense 2).

stud·y /'stədē/ ▶ **n.** (pl. **studies**) **1** the devotion of time and attention to acquiring knowledge on an academic subject, esp. by means of books: *the study of English | an application to continue full-time study.* ■ (**studies**) activity of this type as pursued by one person: *some students may not be able to resume their studies.* ■ an academic book or article on a particular topic: *a study of Jane Austen's novels.* ■ (**studies**) used in the title of an academic subject: *a major in East Asian studies.*
2 a detailed investigation and analysis of a subject or situation: *a study of a sample of 5,000 children | the study of global problems.* ■ a portrayal in literature or another art form of an aspect of behavior or character: *a study of a man devoured by awareness of his own mediocrity.* ■ archaic a thing that is or deserves to be investigated; the subject of an individual's study: *I have made it my study to examine the nature and character of the Indians.* ■ archaic the object or aim of someone's endeavors: *the acquisition of a fortune is the study of all.* ■ [with adj.] a person who learns a skill or acquires knowledge at a specified speed: *I'm a quick study.* [originally theatrical slang, referring to an actor who memorizes a role.]
3 a room used or designed for reading, writing, or academic work.
4 a piece of work, esp. a drawing, done for practice or as an experiment. ■ a musical composition designed to develop a player's technical skill.
5 (**a study in**) a thing or person that is an embodiment or good example of something: *he perched on the edge of the bed, a study in confusion and misery.* ■ informal an amusing or remarkable thing or person: *Ira's face was a study as he approached the car.*
▶ **v.** (**studies, studying, studied**) [with obj.] **1** devote time and attention to acquiring knowledge on (an academic subject), esp. by means of books: *she studied biology and botany.* ■ investigate and analyze (a subject or situation) in detail: *he has been studying mink for many years.* ■ [no obj.] apply oneself to study: *he spent his time listening to the radio rather than studying.* ■ [no obj.] acquire academic knowledge at an educational establishment: *he studied at the Kensington School of Art.* ■ [no obj.] (**study up**) learn intensively about something, esp. in preparation for a test of knowledge: *a graduate student studies up for her doctoral exams.* ■ (of an actor) try to learn (the words of one's role). ■ W. Indian give serious thought or consideration to: *the people here don't make so much noise, so you will find that the government doesn't have us to study.*
2 look at closely in order to observe or read: *she bent her head to study the plans.*
3 archaic make an effort to achieve (a result) or take into account (a person or their wishes): *with no husband to study, housekeeping is mere play.*

S

– PHRASES **in a brown study** absorbed in one's thoughts. [apparently originally from *brown* in the sense 'gloomy.']
– ORIGIN Middle English: shortening of Old French *estudie* (noun), *estudier* (verb), both based on Latin *studium* 'zeal, painstaking application.'

stud·y group ▸ n. a group of people who meet to study a particular subject and then report their findings or recommendations.

stud·y hall ▸ n. the period of time in a school curriculum set aside for the preparation of schoolwork. ■ a schoolroom used for such work.

stuff /stəf/ ▸ n. **1** matter, material, articles, or activities of a specified or indeterminate kind that are being referred to, indicated, or implied: *a pickup truck picked the stuff up* | *a girl who's good at the technical stuff.* ■ a person's belongings, equipment, or baggage: *he took his stuff and went.* ■ Brit. informal, dated worthless or foolish ideas, speech, or writing; rubbish: [as exclamation] *stuff and nonsense!* ■ informal drink or drugs. ■ (**one's stuff**) things in which one is knowledgeable and experienced; one's area of expertise: *he **knows his stuff** and can really write.*
2 the basic constituents or characteristics of something or someone: *Healey was made of sterner stuff* | *such a trip was the stuff of his dreams.*
3 Brit. dated woolen fabric, esp. as distinct from silk, cotton, and linen: [as modifier] *her dark stuff gown.*
4 (in sports) spin given to a ball to make it vary its course. ■ Baseball a pitcher's ability to produce such spin or control the speed of delivery of a pitch.
▸ v. [with obj.] **1** fill (a receptacle or space) tightly with something: *an old teapot **stuffed full of** cash* | figurative *his head has been **stuffed with** myths and taboos.* ■ informal force or cram (something) tightly into a receptacle or space: *he stuffed a thick wad of cash into his jacket pocket.* ■ informal hastily or clumsily push (something) into a space: *Sadie took the coin and stuffed it in her coat pocket.* ■ fill (the cavity of an item of food) with a savory or sweet mixture, esp. before cooking: *chicken stuffed with mushrooms and breadcrumbs.* ■ informal fill (oneself) with large amounts of food: *he **stuffed himself with** potato chips.* ■ fill out the skin of (a dead animal or bird) with material to restore the original shape and appearance: *he took the bird to a taxidermist to be stuffed* | (as adj. **stuffed**) *a stuffed parrot.* ■ informal fill (envelopes) with identical copies of printed matter: *they spent the whole time in a back room stuffing envelopes.* ■ place bogus votes in (a ballot box).
2 Brit. vulgar slang (of a man) have sexual intercourse with (someone).
3 Brit. informal defeat heavily in sport: *Town got stuffed every week.*
4 [usu. in imperative] Brit. informal used to express indifference toward or rejection of (something): *stuff the diet!*
– PHRASES **and stuff** informal said in vague reference to additional things of a similar nature to those specified: *all that running and swimming and stuff.* **be stuffed up** (of a person) have one's nose blocked up with mucus as a result of a cold. **get stuffed** [usu. in imperative] vulgar slang said in anger to tell someone to go away or as an expression of contempt. **stuff it** informal said to express indifference, resignation, or rejection: *Stuff it, I'm 61, what do I care?* **that's the stuff** informal said in approval of what has just been done or said.
– DERIVATIVES **stuff·er** n. [in combination] *a sausage-stuffer.*
– ORIGIN Middle English (denoting material for making clothes): shortening of Old French *estoffe* 'material, furniture,' *estoffer* 'equip, furnish,' from Greek *stuphein* 'draw together.'

> **WORD TRENDS** The e-commerce site Amazon has a section labeled 'Where's My Stuff?' to help customers find out about undelivered orders. The use of such a vague, casual term in an official context is an example of the informality of Internet language and, increasingly, of English in general. Although first found in Middle English, the noun **stuff** can also be seen as a very 21st century word, with the Oxford English Corpus showing that it's become steadily more common since 2000. It tends now to refer to objects or material (*we began writing new stuff straightaway; techniques for getting us to buy new stuff*) or to actions and events in general (*interesting stuff is happening*) rather than to physical matter (*a girl with red and green stuff in her hair*), and generally has positive connotations (it's usually found attached to words like *good, new, great, interesting,* and *cool*).

stuffed shirt ▸ n. informal a conservative, pompous person.

stuff·ing /ˈstəfiNG/ ▸ n. **1** a mixture used to stuff poultry or meat before cooking.
2 padding used to stuff cushions, furniture, or soft toys.
– PHRASES **knock** (or **take**) **the stuffing out of** informal severely impair the confidence or strength of (someone).

stuff·ing box ▸ n. a casing in which material such as greased wool is compressed around a shaft or axle to form a seal against gas or liquid, used for instance where the propeller shaft of a boat passes through the hull.

stuff sack ▸ n. a bag into which a sleeping bag, clothing, and other items can be stuffed or packed for ease of carrying or when not in use.

stuff·y /ˈstəfē/ ▸ adj. (**stuffier, stuffiest**) (of a place) lacking fresh air or ventilation: *a stuffy, overcrowded office.* ■ (of a person's nose) blocked up and making breathing difficult, typically as a result of illness. ■ (of a person) not receptive to new or unusual ideas and behavior; conventional and narrow-minded: *he was steady and rather stuffy.*
– DERIVATIVES **stuff·i·ly** /ˈstəfəlē/ adv., **stuff·i·ness** n.

Stu·ka /ˈsto͞okə, ˈSHto͞o-/ ▸ n. a type of German military aircraft (the Junkers Ju 87) designed for dive-bombing, much used in World War II.
– ORIGIN contraction of German *Sturzkampfflugzeug* 'dive-bomber.'

stul·ti·fy /ˈstəltəˌfī/ ▸ v. (**stultifies, stultifying, stultified**) [with obj.] **1** (usu. as adj. **stultifying**) cause to lose enthusiasm and initiative, esp. as a result of a tedious or restrictive routine: *the mentally stultifying effects of a disadvantaged home.*
2 cause (someone) to appear foolish or absurd: *Counsel is not expected to **stultify himself** in an attempt to advance his client's interests.*
– DERIVATIVES **stul·ti·fi·ca·tion** /ˌstəltəfiˈkāSHən/ n., **stul·ti·fi·er** n., **stul·ti·fy·ing·ly** adv.
– ORIGIN mid 18th cent.: from late Latin *stultificare*, from Latin *stultus* 'foolish.'

stum /stəm/ ▸ n. unfermented grape juice.
▸ v. (**stums, stumming, stummed**) [with obj.]
1 prevent or stop the fermentation of (wine) by fumigating a cask with burning sulfur.
2 renew the fermentation of (wine) by adding stum.
– ORIGIN mid 17th cent.: from Dutch *stom* (noun), *stommen* (verb), from *stom* 'dumb.'

stum·ble /ˈstəmbəl/ ▸ v. [no obj.] trip or momentarily lose one's balance; almost fall: *her foot caught a shoe and she stumbled.* ■ [with adverbial of direction] trip repeatedly as one walks: *his legs still weak, he stumbled after them.* ■ make a mistake or repeated mistakes in speaking: *she **stumbled over** the words.* ■ (**stumble across/on/upon**) find or encounter by chance: *they stumbled across a farmer selling 25 acres.*
▸ n. an act of stumbling. ■ a stumbling walk: *he parodied my groping stumble across the stage.*
– DERIVATIVES **stum·bler** /-b(ə)lər/ n., **stum·bling·ly** /-b(ə)liNGlē/ adv.
– ORIGIN Middle English (as a verb): from Old Norse, from the Germanic base of STAMMER.

stum·ble·bum /ˈstəmbəlbəm/ ▸ n. informal a clumsy or inept person.

stum·bling block ▸ n. a circumstance that causes difficulty or hesitation: *bashfulness is a great stumbling block to some men.*

stump /stəmp/ ▸ n. **1** the bottom part of a tree left projecting from the ground after most of the trunk has fallen or been cut down. ■ the small projecting remnant of something that has been cut or broken off or worn away: *the stump of an amputated arm.*
2 Cricket each of the three upright pieces of wood that form a wicket.
3 Art a cylinder with conical ends made of rolled paper or other soft material, used for softening or blending marks made with a crayon or pencil.
4 [as modifier] engaged in or involving political campaigning: *he is an inspiring stump speaker.* [referring to the use of a tree stump, from which an orator would speak.]
▸ v. [with obj.] **1** (usu. **be stumped**) (of a question or problem) be too hard for; baffle: *education chiefs were stumped by some of the exam questions.* ■ (**be stumped**) be at a loss; be unable to work out what to do or say: *detectives are **stumped for** a reason for the attack.*
2 [no obj.] walk stiffly and noisily: *he stumped away on short thick legs.*
3 travel around (a district) making political speeches: *there is no chance that he will be well enough to stump the country* | [no obj.] *the two men had come to the city to stump for the presidential candidate.*
4 use a stump on (a drawing, line, etc.).
– PHRASES **on the stump** informal engaged in political campaigning. **up a stump** informal in a situation too difficult for one to manage.
– PHRASAL VERBS **stump something up** Brit. informal pay a sum of money: *a buyer would have to stump up at least 8.5 million dollars for the site.*
– ORIGIN Middle English (denoting a part of a limb remaining after an amputation): from Middle Low German *stump(e)* or Middle Dutch *stomp*. The early sense of the verb was 'stumble.'

stump·age /ˈstəmpij/ ▸ n. a price on standing timber and the right to harvest it, reckoned as a unit value per stump. ■ such a price calculated in board feet, cubic meters, or some other measure.

stump·er /ˈstəmpər/ ▸ n. informal a puzzling question.

stump·nose /ˈstəmpˌnōz/ ▸ n. (pl. **same**) chiefly S. African a southern African sea bream, popular with anglers. ● *Rhabdosargus* and other genera, family Sparidae: several species, in particular the **white stumpnose** (*R. globiceps*), which is of commercial importance.

stump work ▸ n. a type of raised embroidery popular between the 15th and 17th centuries and characterized by elaborate designs padded with wool or hair.

stump·y /ˈstəmpē/ ▸ adj. (**stumpier, stumpiest**) short and thick; squat: *weak stumpy legs.*
– DERIVATIVES **stump·i·ly** /-pəlē/ adv., **stump·i·ness** n.

stun /stən/ ▸ v. (**stuns, stunning, stunned**) [with obj.] knock unconscious or into a dazed or semiconscious state: *the man was strangled after being stunned by a blow to the head.* ■ (usu. **be stunned**) astonish or shock (someone) so that they are temporarily unable to react: *the community was stunned by the tragedy.* ■ (of a sound) deafen temporarily: *a blast like that could stun anybody.*
– ORIGIN Middle English: shortening of Old French *estoner* 'astonish.'

stung /stəNG/ past and past participle of STING.

stun gre·nade ▸ n. a grenade that stuns people with its sound and flash, without causing serious injury.

stun gun ▸ n. a device used to immobilize an attacker without causing serious injury, typically by administering an electric shock.

stunk /stəNGk/ past and past participle of STINK.

stun·ner /ˈstənər/ ▸ n. informal a strikingly beautiful or impressive person or thing: *the girl was a stunner.* ■ an amazing turn of events.

stun·ning /ˈstəniNG/ ▸ adj. extremely impressive or attractive: *she looked stunning.*
– DERIVATIVES **stun·ning·ly** adv.

stun·sail /ˈstənsəl/ (also **stuns'l**) ▸ n. another term for STUDDINGSAIL.
– ORIGIN mid 18th cent.: contraction.

stunt[1] /stənt/ ▸ v. [with obj.] prevent from growing or developing properly: *some weeds produce chemicals that stunt the plant's growth* | figurative *the recovery of our industries is stunted by lack of funds* | (as adj. **stunted**) *an emotionally stunted young woman.*
– DERIVATIVES **stunt·ed·ness** n.
– ORIGIN late 16th cent. (in the sense 'bring to an abrupt halt'): from dialect *stunt* 'foolish, stubborn,' of Germanic origin; perhaps related to STUMP.

stunt[2] ▸ n. an action displaying spectacular skill and daring. ■ something unusual done to attract attention: *the story was spread as a publicity stunt to help sell books.*
▸ v. [no obj.] perform stunts, esp. aerobatics: *agile terns are stunting over the water.*
– ORIGIN late 19th cent. (originally US college slang): of unknown origin.

stunt cast·ing ▸ n. the casting of a very famous actor or other celebrity as a guest star in a film or TV show, in order to garner publicity.

stunt·man /ˈstəntˌman/ ▸ n. (pl. **stuntmen**) a man employed to take an actor's place in performing dangerous stunts.

stunt·wom·an /ˈstəntˌwo͝omən/ ▸ n. (pl. **stuntwomen**) a woman employed to take an actor's place in performing dangerous stunts.

stu·pa /ˈsto͞opə/ ▸ n. a dome-shaped structure erected as a Buddhist shrine.
– ORIGIN from Sanskrit *stūpa*.

stupe[1] /st(y)o͞op/ archaic ▸ n. a piece of soft cloth or absorbent cotton dipped in hot water and used to make a poultice.
▸ v. [with obj.] treat with such a poultice.
– ORIGIN late Middle English (as a noun): via Latin from Greek *stupē*.

stupe[2] ▸ n. informal a stupid person.
– ORIGIN mid 18th cent.: abbreviation of STUPID.

stu·pe·fa·cient /ˌst(y)o͞opəˈfāSHənt/ Medicine ▸ adj. (chiefly of a drug) causing semiconsciousness.
▸ n. a drug of this type.
– ORIGIN mid 17th cent.: from Latin *stupefacient-* 'stupefying,' from the verb *stupefacere*.

stu·pe·fac·tion /ˌst(y)o͞opəˈfakSHən/ ▸ n. the state of being stupefied: *salesmen stood in bored stupefaction.*

stu·pe·fy /ˈst(y)o͞opəˌfī/ ▸ v. (**stupefies, stupefying, stupefied**) [with obj.] make (someone) unable to think

or feel properly: *the offense of administering drugs to a woman with intent to stupefy her.* ■ astonish and shock: *the amount they spend on clothes would appall their parents and stupefy their grandparents.*
– DERIVATIVES **stu·pe·fi·er** n., **stu·pe·fy·ing·ly** adv. [as submodifier] *a stupefyingly tedious task.*
– ORIGIN late Middle English: from French *stupéfier*, from Latin *stupefacere*, from *stupere* 'be struck senseless.'

stu·pen·dous /st(y)o͞o'pendəs/ ▶ **adj.** informal extremely impressive: *a stupendous display of technique.*
– DERIVATIVES **stu·pen·dous·ly** adv., **stu·pen·dous·ness** n.
– ORIGIN mid 16th cent.: from Latin *stupendus* 'to be wondered at' (gerundive of *stupere*) + **-OUS**.

stu·pid /'st(y)o͞opid/ ▶ **adj.** (**stupider**, **stupidest**) lacking intelligence or common sense: *I was stupid enough to think she was perfect.* ■ dazed and unable to think clearly: *apprehension was numbing her brain and making her stupid.* ■ informal used to express exasperation or boredom: *she told him to stop messing with his stupid painting.*
▶ **n.** informal a stupid person (often used as a term of address): *you're not a coward, stupid!*
– DERIVATIVES **stu·pid·ly** adv.
– ORIGIN mid 16th cent.: from French *stupide* or Latin *stupidus*, from *stupere* 'be amazed or stunned.'

stu·pid·i·ty /st(y)o͞o'pidité/ ▶ **n.** behavior that shows a lack of good sense or judgment: *I can't believe my own stupidity | one of the stupidities of our age.* ■ the quality of being stupid or unintelligent: *a comedy of infantile stupidity.*

stu·pid·ness /'st(y)o͞opidnis/ ▶ **n.** W. Indian foolish or nonsensical talk or behavior: *girl, what stupidness are you talking?*

stu·por /'st(y)o͞opər/ ▶ **n.** [in sing.] a state of near-unconsciousness or insensibility: *a drunken stupor.*
– DERIVATIVES **stu·por·ous** /-rəs/ adj.
– ORIGIN late Middle English: from Latin, from *stupere* 'be amazed or stunned.'

Stur·bridge /'stər,brij/ a town in south central Massachusetts, noted for its historical recreation of Old Sturbridge Village; pop. 9,103 (est. 2008).

stur·dy /'stərdē/ ▶ **adj.** (**sturdier**, **sturdiest**) (of a person or their body) strongly and solidly built: *he had a sturdy, muscular physique.* ■ strong enough to withstand rough work or treatment: *the bike is sturdy enough to cope with bumpy tracks.* ■ showing confidence and determination: *the townspeople have a sturdy independence.*
▶ **n.** vertigo in sheep caused by a tapeworm larva encysted in the brain.
– DERIVATIVES **stur·di·ly** /-dl-ē/ adv., **stur·di·ness** n.
– ORIGIN Middle English (in the senses 'reckless, violent' and 'intractable, obstinate'): shortening of Old French *esturdi* 'stunned, dazed.' The derivation remains obscure; thought by some to be based on Latin *turdus* 'a thrush' (compare with the French phrase *soûl comme une grive* 'drunk as a thrush').

stur·geon /'stərjən/ ▶ **n.** a very large primitive fish with bony plates on the body. It occurs in temperate seas and rivers of the northern hemisphere, esp. central Eurasia, and is of commercial importance for its caviar and flesh. ● Family Acipenseridae: several genera and species.
– ORIGIN Middle English: from Anglo-Norman French, of Germanic origin; related to Dutch *steur* and German *Stör*.

Sturm·ab·tei·lung /,SHto͝orm'äp,tīlo͝oNG/ (abbr.: **SA**) see **BROWNSHIRT**.
– ORIGIN German, literally 'storm division.'

Stur·mer /'stərmər/ (also **Sturmer pippin**) ▶ **n.** an eating apple of a late-ripening variety with a mainly yellowish-green skin and firm yellowish flesh.
– ORIGIN mid 19th cent.: named after the village of *Sturmer* in eastern England, where it was first grown.

Sturm und Drang /'SHto͝orm o͝on(d) 'dräNG/ ▶ **n.** a literary and artistic movement in Germany in the late 18th century, influenced by Jean-Jacques Rousseau and characterized by the expression of emotional unrest and a rejection of neoclassical literary norms. ■ turbulent emotion or stress: *that casual morning meeting dragged into a brawling afternoon of Sturm und Drang.*
– ORIGIN German, literally 'storm and stress.'

Sturt's des·ert rose /,stərts ,dezərt 'rōz/ ▶ **n.** see **DESERT ROSE** (sense 3).

stut·ter /'stətər/ ▶ **v.** [no obj.] talk with continued involuntary repetition of sounds, esp. initial consonants: *the child was stuttering in fright.* ■ [with obj.] utter in such a way: *he shyly stuttered out an invitation to the movies* | [with direct speech] *"W-what's happened?" she stuttered.* ■ (of a machine or gun) produce a series of short, sharp sounds: *she flinched as a machine gun stuttered nearby.*
▶ **n.** a tendency to stutter while speaking. ■ a series of short, sharp sounds produced by a machine or gun.
– DERIVATIVES **stut·ter·er** n., **stut·ter·ing·ly** adv.
– ORIGIN late 16th cent. (as a verb): frequentative of dialect *stut*, of Germanic origin; related to German *stossen* 'strike against.'

stut·ter tone ▶ **n.** a dial tone interrupted by several short gaps, indicating the arrival of new voicemail messages to the user.

Stutt·gart /'SHto͝ot,gärt, 'sto͝ot-, 'stət-/ an industrial city in western Germany, the capital of Baden-Württemberg, on the Neckar River; pop. 593,900 (est. 2006).

Stuy·ves·ant /'stīvəsənt/, Peter (c.1610–72), Dutch administrator in North America. Appointed colonial governor of New Netherland (what are now the states of New York and New Jersey) in 1647, he served until the colony was captured by English forces in 1664. In 1655, he expanded the colony by taking over New Sweden in the Delaware River area.

sty[1] /stī/ ▶ **n.** a pigpen.
▶ **v.** (**sties**, **stying**, **stied**) [with obj.] archaic keep (a pig) in a sty: *the most beggarly place that ever pigs were stied in.*
– ORIGIN Old English *stī-* (in *stīfearh* 'sty pig'), probably identical with *stig* 'hall' (see **STEWARD**), of Germanic origin.

sty[2] (also **stye**) ▶ **n.** (pl. **sties** /stīz/ or **styes**) an inflamed swelling on the edge of an eyelid, caused by bacterial infection of the gland at the base of an eyelash.
– ORIGIN early 17th cent.: from dialect *styany*, from *styan* (from Old English *stīgend* 'riser') + **EYE**.

Styg·i·an /'stijēən/ ▶ **adj.** of or relating to the Styx River. ■ literary very dark: *the Stygian crypt.*

sty·lar /'stīlər/ ▶ **adj.** Botany of or relating to the style or styles of a flower.

style /stīl/ ▶ **n. 1** a manner of doing something: *different styles of management.* ■ a way of painting, writing, composing, building, etc., characteristic of a particular period, place, person, or movement. ■ a way of using language: *he never wrote in a journalistic style | students should pay attention to style and idiom.* ■ [usu. with negative] a way of behaving or approaching a situation that is characteristic of or favored by a particular person: *backing out isn't my style.* ■ an official or legal title: *the partnership traded* ***under the style of*** *Storr and Mortimer.*
2 a distinctive appearance, typically determined by the principles according to which something is designed: *the pillars are no exception to the general style.* ■ a particular design of clothing. ■ a way of arranging the hair.
3 elegance and sophistication: *a sophisticated nightspot with style and taste.*
4 a rodlike object or part, in particular: ■ archaic term for **STYLUS** (sense 2). ■ Botany (in a flower) a narrow, typically elongated extension of the ovary, bearing the stigma. ■ Zoology (in an invertebrate) a small slender pointed appendage; a stylet. ■ the gnomon of a sundial.
▶ **v.** [with obj.] **1** design or make in a particular form: *the yacht is well proportioned and conservatively styled.* ■ arrange (hair) in a particular way: *he styled her hair by twisting it up to give it body.*
2 [with obj. and complement] designate with a particular name, description, or title: *the official is styled principal and vice chancellor of the university.*
– PHRASES **in style** (or **in grand style**) in an impressive, grand, or luxurious way.
– DERIVATIVES **style·less** /'stīl(l)is/ adj., **style·less·ness** /'stīl(l)isnis/ n., **styl·er** n.
– ORIGIN Middle English (denoting a stylus, also a literary composition, an official title, or a characteristic manner of literary expression): from Old French *stile*, from Latin *stilus*. The verb dates (first sense 2 of the verb) from the early 16th cent.

-style ▶ **suffix** (forming adjectives and adverbs) in a manner characteristic of: *family-style | church-style.*
– ORIGIN from **STYLE**.

style sheet ▶ **n.** Computing a type of template file consisting of font and layout settings to give a standardized look to certain documents.

sty·let /stī'let, 'stīlit/ ▶ **n. 1** Medicine a slender probe. ■ a wire or piece of plastic run through a catheter or cannula in order to stiffen it or to clear it.
2 Zoology (in an invertebrate) a small style, esp. a piercing mouthpart of an insect.
– ORIGIN late 17th cent.: from French *stilet*, from Italian *stiletto* (see **STILETTO**).

sty·li /'stīlī/ plural form of **STYLUS**.

styl·ing /'stīliNG/ ▶ **n.** the way in which something is made, designed, or performed: *the car's subtle European styling | the musical stylings on his solo album.* ■ the action or process of arranging hair in a particular way: [as modifier] *styling gel.*

sty·lish /'stīliSH/ ▶ **adj.** having or displaying a good sense of style: *these are elegant and stylish performances.* ■ fashionably elegant: *a stylish and innovative range of jewelry.*
– DERIVATIVES **styl·ish·ly** adv., **styl·ish·ness** n.

styl·ist /'stīlist/ ▶ **n. 1** a designer of fashionable styles of clothing. ■ a hairdresser.
2 a person whose job is to arrange and coordinate food, clothes, etc. in a stylish and attractive way in photographs or films.
3 a person noted for elegant work or performance, in particular: ■ a writer noted for taking great pains over the style in which he or she writes. ■ (in sports or music) a person who performs with style.

sty·lis·tic /stī'listik/ ▶ **adj.** of or concerning style, esp. literary style: *the stylistic conventions of magazine stories.*
– DERIVATIVES **styl·is·ti·cal·ly** /-ik(ə)lē/ adv.
– ORIGIN mid 19th cent.: from **STYLIST**, suggested by German *stilistisch*.

sty·lis·tics /stī'listiks/ ▶ **plural n.** [treated as sing.] the study of the distinctive styles found in particular literary genres and in the works of individual writers.

sty·lite /'stī,līt/ ▶ **n.** historical an ascetic living on top of a pillar, esp. in ancient or medieval Syria, Turkey, and Greece in the 5th century AD.
– ORIGIN mid 17th cent.: from ecclesiastical Greek *stulitēs*, from *stulos* 'pillar.'

styl·ize /'stī,līz/ ▶ **v.** [with obj.] (usu. as adj. **stylized**) depict or treat in a mannered and nonrealistic style: *gracefully shaped vases decorated with stylized but recognizable white lilies.*
– DERIVATIVES **styl·i·za·tion** /,stīli'zāSHən/ n.
– ORIGIN late 19th cent.: from **STYLE**, suggested by German *stilisiren*.

sty·lo /'stīlō/ ▶ **n.** (pl. **stylos**) informal short for **STYLOGRAPH**.

sty·lo·bate /'stīlə,bāt/ ▶ **n.** a continuous base supporting a row of columns in classical Greek architecture.
– ORIGIN late 17th cent.: via Latin from Greek *stulobatēs*, from *stulos* 'pillar' + *batēs* 'base' (from *bainein* 'to walk').

sty·lo·graph /'stīlə,graf/ ▶ **n.** a kind of fountain pen having a fine perforated tube instead of a split nib.
– DERIVATIVES **sty·lo·graph·ic** /,stīlə'grafik/ adj.
– ORIGIN mid 19th cent.: from **STYLUS** + **-GRAPH**.

sty·loid /'stī,loid/ ▶ **adj.** technical resembling a stylus or pen.
▶ **n.** short for **STYLOID PROCESS**.

sty·loid proc·ess ▶ **n.** Anatomy a slender projection of bone, such as that from the lower surface of the temporal bone of the skull, or those at the lower ends of the ulna and radius.

sty·lo·lite /'stīlə,līt/ ▶ **n.** Geology an irregular surface or seam within a limestone or other sedimentary rock, characterized by irregular interlocking pegs and sockets around 1 cm in depth and a concentration of insoluble minerals. ■ a grooved peg forming part of such a seam.
– ORIGIN mid 19th cent.: from Greek *stulos* 'column' + **-LITE**.

sty·lom·e·try /stī'lämitrē/ ▶ **n.** the statistical analysis of variations in literary style between one writer or genre and another.
– DERIVATIVES **sty·lo·met·ric** /-lə'metrik/ adj.

sty·lo·phone /'stīlə,fōn/ ▶ **n.** a miniature electronic musical instrument producing a distinctive buzzing sound when a stylus is drawn along its metal keyboard.

S

sty·lo·pized /'stīlə,pēzd, -,pīzd/ ▶ **adj.** Entomology (of a bee or other insect) parasitized by a stylops.

sty·lops /'stī,läps/ ▶ **n.** (pl. **same**) a minute insect that spends part or all of its life as an internal parasite of other insects, esp. bees or wasps. The males are winged and the females typically retain a grublike form and remain parasitic. ● Order Strepsiptera, in particular genus *Stylops*, family Stylopidae.
– DERIVATIVES **sty·lo·pid** /-lə,pid/ n. & adj.
– ORIGIN late 19th cent.: modern Latin, from Greek *stulos* 'column' + *ōps* 'eye, face.'

sty·lus /'stīləs/ ▶ **n.** (pl. **styli** /-,lī/ or **styluses**) **1** a hard point, typically of diamond or sapphire, following a groove in a phonograph record and transmitting the recorded sound for reproduction. ■ a similar point producing such a groove when recording sound.
2 an ancient writing implement, consisting of a small rod with a pointed end for scratching letters on wax-covered tablets, and a blunt end for

obliterating them. ■ an implement of similar shape used esp. for engraving and tracing. ■ Computing a penlike device used to input handwritten text or drawings directly into a computer or for input on a touch-sensitive monitor.
– ORIGIN early 18th cent. (as a modern Latin term in botany: see **STYLE**): erroneous spelling of Latin *stilus*.

sty·mie /ˈstīmē/ ▶ v. (**stymies, stymieing, stymied**) [with obj.] informal prevent or hinder the progress of: *the changes must not be allowed to stymie new medical treatments*.
– ORIGIN mid 19th cent. (originally a golfing term, denoting a situation on the green where a ball obstructs the shot of another player): of unknown origin.

styp·tic /ˈstiptik/ Medicine ▶ adj. (of a substance) capable of causing bleeding to stop when it is applied to a wound.
▶ n. a substance of this kind.
– ORIGIN late Middle English: via Latin from Greek *stuptikos*, from *stuphein* 'to contract.'

styp·tic pen·cil ▶ n. a stick of a styptic substance, used to treat small cuts.

sty·rax /ˈstīˌraks/ ▶ n. variant of **STORAX**.

sty·rene /ˈstīˌrēn/ ▶ n. Chemistry an unsaturated liquid hydrocarbon obtained as a petroleum byproduct. It is easily polymerized and is used to make plastics and resins. ● Chem. formula: $C_6H_5CH{=}CH_2$.
– ORIGIN late 19th cent.: from **STYRAX** + **-ENE**.

sty·ro·foam /ˈstīrəˌfōm/ ▶ n. trademark a kind of expanded polystyrene.
– ORIGIN 1950s: from **POLYSTYRENE** + **FOAM**.

Sty·ron /ˈstīrən/, William (Clark, Jr.) (1925–2006), US writer. His works include *The Confessions of Nat Turner* (1967); *Sophie's Choice* (1979); *Darkness Visible* (1990), about his own battle with depression; and *A Tidewater Morning: Three Tales from Youth* (1993).

Styx /stiks/ Greek Mythology one of the rivers in the underworld, over which Charon ferried the souls of the dead.
– ORIGIN from Greek *Stux*, from *stugnos* 'hateful, gloomy.'

sua·sion /ˈswāZHən/ ▶ n. formal persuasion as opposed to force or compulsion.
– ORIGIN late Middle English: from Old French, or from Latin *suasio(n-)*, from *suadere* 'to urge.'

sua·sive /ˈswāsiv/ ▶ adj. serving to persuade. ■ Grammar denoting a class of English verbs, for example, *insist*, whose meaning includes the notion of persuading and that take a subordinate clause whose verb may either be in the subjunctive or take a modal.

suave /swäv/ ▶ adj. (**suaver, suavest**) (esp. of a man) charming, confident, and elegant: *all the waiters were suave and deferential*.
– DERIVATIVES **suave·ly** adv., **suave·ness** n.
– ORIGIN late Middle English (in the sense 'gracious, agreeable'): from Old French, or from Latin *suavis* 'agreeable.' The current sense dates from the mid 19th cent.

suav·i·ty /ˈswävitē/ ▶ n. (pl. **suavities**) the quality of being suave in manner: *he conveyed an air of polish and suavity*.

sub /səb/ informal ▶ n. **1** a submarine. ■ short for **SUBMARINE SANDWICH**.
2 a subscription.
3 a substitute.
▶ v. (**subs, subbing, subbed**) [no obj.] act as a substitute for someone: *he subbed for Scott as weatherman*.

sub. ▶ abbr. ■ subordinated. ■ subscription. ■ substitute. ■ suburb. ■ suburban. ■ subway.

sub- ▶ prefix **1** at, to, or from a lower level or position: *subalpine* | *sub-basement*. ■ lower in rank: *subdeacon*. ■ of a smaller size; of a subordinate nature: *subculture*. ■ of lesser quality; inferior: *subhuman* | *substandard*.
2 somewhat; nearly; more or less: *subantarctic*.
3 denoting a later or secondary action of the same kind: *sublet* | *subdivision* | *subsequent*.
4 denoting support: *subvention*.
5 Chemistry in names of compounds containing a relatively small proportion of a component: *suboxide*.
– ORIGIN from Latin *sub* 'under, close to.'

sub·ac·id /ˌsəbˈasid/ ▶ adj. (of a fruit) moderately sharp to the taste.
– ORIGIN mid 17th cent.: from Latin *subacidus* (see **SUB-**, **ACID**).

sub·a·cute /ˌsəbəˈkyo͞ot/ ▶ adj. **1** Medicine (of a condition) between acute and chronic.
2 moderately acute in shape or angle.

sub·a·dult /ˌsəbəˈdəlt/ ▶ n. Zoology an animal that is not fully adult.

sub·aer·i·al /ˌsəbˈe(ə)rēəl/ ▶ adj. Geology existing, occurring, or formed in the open air or on the earth's surface, not underwater or underground.
– DERIVATIVES **sub·aer·i·al·ly** adv.

sub·a·gen·cy /ˌsəbˈājənsē/ ▶ n. (pl. **subagencies**) a subordinate commercial, political, or other agency.
– DERIVATIVES **sub·a·gent** /-ˈājənt/ n.

sub·al·pine /ˌsəbˈalpīn/ ▶ adj. of or situated on the higher slopes of mountains just below the timberline.

sub·al·tern ▶ n. /səbˈôltərn/ an officer in the British army below the rank of captain, esp. a second lieutenant.
▶ adj. /səbˈôltərn/ **1** of lower status: *the private tutor was a recognized subaltern part of the bourgeois family*.
2 /ˈsəbəlˌtərn/ Logic, dated (of a proposition) implied by another proposition (e.g., as a particular affirmative is by a universal one), but not implying it in return.
– ORIGIN late 16th cent. (as an adjective): from late Latin *subalternus*, from Latin *sub-* 'below' + *alternus* 'every other.'

sub·ant·arc·tic /ˌsəbantˈärktik, -ˈärtik/ ▶ adj. of or relating to the region immediately north of the Antarctic Circle.

sub·a·quat·ic /ˌsəbəˈkwätik, -ˈkwa-/ ▶ adj. underwater: *a narrow, subaquatic microclimate*.

sub·a·que·ous /səbˈākwēəs, -ˈak-/ ▶ adj. existing, formed, or taking place underwater. ■ lacking in substance or strength: *the light that filtered through the leaves was pale, subaqueous*.

sub·a·rach·noid /ˌsəbəˈraknoid/ ▶ adj. Anatomy denoting or occurring in the fluid-filled space around the brain between the arachnoid membrane and the pia mater, through which major blood vessels pass.

sub·arc·tic /ˌsəbˈärktik, -ˈärtik/ ▶ adj. of or relating to the region immediately south of the Arctic Circle.

sub·as·sem·bly /ˌsəbəˈsemblē/ ▶ n. (pl. **subassemblies**) a unit assembled separately but designed to be incorporated with other units into a larger manufactured product.

Sub-At·lan·tic ▶ adj. Geology of, relating to, or denoting the fifth climatic stage of the postglacial period in northern Europe, following the Sub-Boreal stage (from about 2,800 years ago to the present day). The climate has been cooler and wetter than in the earlier postglacial periods. ■ (as noun **the Sub-Atlantic**) the Sub-Atlantic climatic stage.

sub·a·tom·ic /ˌsəbəˈtämik/ ▶ adj. smaller than or occurring within an atom.

sub·a·tom·ic par·ti·cle ▶ n. a particle smaller than an atom (e.g., a neutron) or a cluster of such particles (e.g., an alpha particle). Compare with **ELEMENTARY PARTICLE**.

sub·au·di·tion /ˌsəbôˈdiSHən/ ▶ n. a thing that is not stated, only implied or inferred.
– ORIGIN late 18th cent.: from late Latin *subauditio(n-)*, from *subaudire* 'understand.'

sub·base·ment ▶ n. a story below a basement.

Sub-Bo·re·al ▶ adj. Geology of, relating to, or denoting the fourth climatic stage of the postglacial period in northern Europe, between the Atlantic and Sub-Atlantic stages (about 5,000 to 2,800 years ago). The stage corresponds to the Neolithic period and Bronze Age, and the climate was cooler and drier than previously but still warmer than today. ■ (as noun **the Sub-Boreal**) the Sub-Boreal climatic stage.

sub·branch ▶ n. a secondary or subordinate branch of anything that has branches, such as a tree, a subject of study, or a bank.

sub·breed ▶ n. a minor variant of a breed; a secondary breed.

sub·car·ri·er /ˈsəbˌkarēər/ ▶ n. Telecommunications a carrier wave modulated by a signal wave and then used with other subcarriers to modulate the main carrier wave.

sub·cat·e·go·ry /ˈsəbˌkatəˌgôrē/ ▶ n. (pl. **subcategories**) a secondary or subordinate category.
– DERIVATIVES **sub·cat·e·go·ri·za·tion** /ˌsəbˌkatəgəriˈzāSHən/ n., **sub·cat·e·go·rize** /ˌsəbˈkatəgəˌrīz/ v.

sub·class /ˈsəbˌklas/ ▶ n. a secondary or subordinate class. ■ Biology a taxonomic category that ranks below class and above order.

sub·cla·vi·an /səbˈklāvēən/ ▶ adj. Anatomy relating to or denoting an artery or vein that serves the neck and arm on the left or right side of the body.
– ORIGIN mid 17th cent.: from modern Latin *subclavius*, from *sub* 'under' + *clavis* 'key' (see **CLAVICLE**), + **-IAN**.

sub·clin·i·cal /ˌsəbˈklinikəl/ ▶ adj. Medicine relating to or denoting a disease that is not severe enough to present definite or readily observable symptoms.

sub·com·mit·tee /ˈsəbkəˌmitē/ ▶ n. a committee composed of some members of a larger committee, board, or other body and reporting to it.

sub·com·pact /səbˈkämpakt/ ▶ n. a motor vehicle that is smaller than a compact.

sub·con·i·cal /səbˈkänikəl/ ▶ adj. approximately conical.

sub·con·scious /səbˈkänSHəs/ ▶ adj. of or concerning the part of the mind of which one is not fully aware but which influences one's actions and feelings: *my subconscious fear*.
▶ n. (**one's/the subconscious**) this part of the mind (not in technical use in psychoanalysis, where *unconscious* is preferred).
– DERIVATIVES **sub·con·scious·ly** adv., **sub·con·scious·ness** n.

sub·con·ti·nent /ˌsəbˈkäntnənt/ ▶ n. a large, distinguishable part of a continent, such as North America or southern Africa. See also **INDIAN SUBCONTINENT**.
– DERIVATIVES **sub·con·ti·nen·tal** /-ˌkäntəˈnen(t)l/ adj.

sub·con·tract ▶ v. /ˌsəbkənˈtrakt/ [with obj.] employ a business or person outside one's company to do (work) as part of a larger project: *we would subcontract the translation work out*. ■ [no obj.] (of a business or person) carry out work for a company as part of a larger project.
▶ n. /səbˈkäntrakt/ a contract for a company or person to do work for another company as part of a larger project.

sub·con·trac·tor /səbˈkänˌtraktər/ ▶ n. a business or person that carries out work for a company as part of a larger project.

sub·con·tra·ry /ˌsəbˈkäntrerē/ Logic, dated ▶ adj. denoting propositions that can both be true, but cannot both be false (e.g., *some X are Y* and *some X are not Y*).
▶ n. (pl. **subcontraries**) a proposition of this kind.
– ORIGIN late 16th cent.: from late Latin *subcontrarius*, translation of Greek *hupenantios*.

sub·cor·ti·cal /səbˈkôrtikəl/ ▶ adj. below the cortex. ■ Anatomy relating to or denoting the region of the brain below the cortex.

sub·cos·tal /səbˈkôstl, -ˈkästl/ ▶ adj. Anatomy beneath a rib; below the ribs.

sub·crit·i·cal /səbˈkritikəl/ ▶ adj. Physics below a critical threshold, in particular: ■ (in nuclear physics) containing or involving less than the critical mass. ■ (of a flow of fluid) slower than the speed at which waves travel in the fluid.

sub·cul·ture /ˈsəbˌkəlCHər/ ▶ n. a cultural group within a larger culture, often having beliefs or interests at variance with those of the larger culture.
– DERIVATIVES **sub·cul·tur·al** /ˌsəbˈkəlCHərəl/ adj.

sub·cu·ta·ne·ous /ˌsəbkyo͞oˈtānēəs/ ▶ adj. Anatomy & Medicine situated or applied under the skin: *subcutaneous fat*.
– DERIVATIVES **sub·cu·ta·ne·ous·ly** adv.

sub·dea·con /ˈsəbˌdēkən/ ▶ n. (in some Christian churches) a minister of an order ranking below deacon. Now largely obsolete in the Western church, the liturgical role has been taken by other ministers.
– DERIVATIVES **sub·di·ac·o·nate** /ˌsəbdīˈakənit, -ˌnāt/ n.

sub·di·rec·to·ry /ˌsəbdəˈrektərē/ ▶ n. (pl. **subdirectories**) Computing a directory below another directory in a hierarchy.

sub·di·vide /ˈsəbdəˌvīd/ ▶ v. [with obj.] divide (something that has already been divided or that is a separate unit): *the heading was subdivided into eight separate sections*.
– ORIGIN late Middle English: from Latin *subdividere* (see **SUB-**, **DIVIDE**).

sub·di·vi·sion /ˈsəbdəˌviZHən/ ▶ n. the action of subdividing or being subdivided. ■ a secondary or subordinate division. ■ an area of land divided into plots for sale. ■ an area of housing. ■ Biology any taxonomic subcategory, esp. (in botany) one that ranks below division and above class.

sub·dom·i·nant /səbˈdämənənt/ ▶ n. Music the fourth note of the diatonic scale of any key.

sub·duc·tion /səbˈdəkSHən/ ▶ n. Geology the sideways and downward movement of the edge of a plate of the earth's crust into the mantle beneath another plate.
– DERIVATIVES **sub·duct** /-ˈdəkt/ v.
– ORIGIN 1970s: via French from Latin *subductio(n-)*, from *subduct-* 'drawn from below,' from the verb *subducere*.

sub·due /səb'd(y)o͞o/ ▶ **v.** (**subdues, subduing, subdued**) [with obj.] overcome, quieten, or bring under control (a feeling or person): *she managed to subdue an instinct to applaud.* ■ bring (a country or people) under control by force: *Charles went on a campaign to subdue the Saxons.*
– DERIVATIVES **sub·du·a·ble** adj.
– ORIGIN late Middle English: from Anglo-Norman French *suduire*, from Latin *subducere*, literally 'draw from below.'

sub·dued /ˌsəb'd(y)o͞od/ ▶ **adj. 1** (of a person or their manner) quiet and rather reflective or depressed: *I felt strangely subdued as I drove home.* **2** (of color or lighting) soft and restrained: *a subdued plaid shirt.*

sub·du·ral /səb'd(y)o͝orəl/ ▶ **adj.** Anatomy situated or occurring between the dura mater and the arachnoid membrane of the brain and spinal cord.

sub·ed·it /səb'edit/ ▶ **v.** (**subedits, subediting, subedited**) [with obj.] chiefly Brit. check, correct, and adjust the extent of (the text of a newspaper or magazine before printing), typically also writing headlines and captions.
– DERIVATIVES **sub·ed·i·tor** /-'editər/ **n.**

su·ber·in /'so͞obərən/ ▶ **n.** Botany an inert impermeable waxy substance present in the cell walls of corky tissues.
– ORIGIN mid 19th cent.: from Latin *suber* 'cork' + -IN[1].

su·ber·ize /'so͞obəˌrīz/ ▶ **v.** [with obj.] (usu. as adj. **suberized**) Botany impregnate (the wall of a plant cell) with suberin: *suberized cell walls.*
– DERIVATIVES **su·ber·i·za·tion** /ˌso͞obəri'zāsʜən/ **n.**

sub·fam·i·ly /'səbˌfam(ə)lē/ ▶ **n.** (pl. **subfamilies**) a subdivision of a group. ■ Biology a taxonomic category that ranks below family and above tribe or genus, usually ending in *-inae* (in zoology) or *-oideae* (in botany).

sub·floor /'səbˌflôr/ ▶ **n.** the foundation for a floor in a building.

sub·form /'səbˌfôrm/ ▶ **n.** a subordinate or secondary form.

sub·frame /'səbˌfrām/ ▶ **n.** a supporting frame, esp. one into which a window or door is set, or one to which the engine or suspension of a car without a true chassis is attached.

sub·fusc /səb'fəsk/ ▶ **adj.** literary dull; gloomy: *the light was subfusc and aqueous.*
▶ **n.** Brit. the formal clothing worn for examinations and formal occasions at some universities.
– ORIGIN early 18th cent.: from Latin *subfuscus*, from *sub-* 'somewhat' + *fuscus* 'dark brown.'

sub·ge·nus /'səbˌjēnəs/ ▶ **n.** (pl. **subgenera** /-ˌjenərə/) Biology a taxonomic category that ranks below genus and above species.
– DERIVATIVES **sub·ge·ner·ic** /ˌsəbjə'nerik/ **adj.**

sub·gla·cial /ˌsəb'glāsʜəl/ ▶ **adj.** Geology situated or occurring underneath a glacier or ice sheet.

sub·group /'səbˌgro͞op/ ▶ **n.** a subdivision of a group. ■ Mathematics a group whose members are all members of another group, both being subject to the same operations.

sub·har·mon·ic /ˌsəbhär'mänik/ ▶ **n.** an oscillation with a frequency equal to an integral submultiple of another frequency.
▶ **adj.** denoting or involving a subharmonic.

sub·head·ing /'səbˌhediɴɢ/ (also **subhead**) ▶ **n.** a heading given to a subsection of a piece of writing.

sub·hu·man /səb'(h)yo͞omən/ ▶ **adj.** of a lower order of being than the human. ■ Zoology (of a primate) closely related to humans. ■ derogatory (of people or their behavior) not worthy of a human being; debased or depraved: *he regards all PR people as subhuman.*
▶ **n.** a subhuman creature or person.

Su·bic Bay /'so͞obik/ an inlet of the South China Sea in the Philippines, off central Luzon Island. A large US naval facility closed here in 1992.

subj. ▶ **abbr.** ■ subject. ■ subjective. ■ subjectively. ■ subjunctive.

sub·ja·cent /səb'jāsənt/ ▶ **adj.** technical situated below something else.
– DERIVATIVES **sub·ja·cen·cy** **n.**
– ORIGIN late 16th cent.: from Latin *subjacent-* 'lying underneath,' from *sub-* 'under' + *jacere* 'to lie.'

sub·ject ▶ **n.** /'səbjəkt/ **1** a person or thing that is being discussed, described, or dealt with: *I've said all there is to be said on the subject | he's the subject of a major new biography.* ■ a person or circumstance giving rise to a specified feeling, response, or action: *the incident was the **subject of** international condemnation.* ■ Grammar a noun phrase functioning as one of the main components of a clause, being the element about which the rest of the clause is predicated. ■ Logic the part of a proposition about which a statement is made. ■ Music a theme of a fugue or of a piece in sonata form; a leading phrase or motif. ■ a person who is the focus of scientific or medical attention or experiment.
2 a branch of knowledge studied or taught in a school, college, or university.
3 a citizen or member of a state other than its supreme ruler.
4 Philosophy a thinking or feeling entity; the conscious mind; the ego, esp. as opposed to anything external to the mind. ■ the central substance or core of a thing as opposed to its attributes.
▶ **adj.** /'səbjəkt/ [predic.] (**subject to**) **1** likely or prone to be affected by (a particular condition or occurrence, typically an unwelcome or unpleasant one): *he was subject to bouts of manic depression.*
2 dependent or conditional upon: *the proposed merger is subject to the approval of the shareholders.*
3 under the authority of: *legislation making Congress subject to the laws it passes.* ■ [attrib.] under the control or domination of (another ruler, country, or government): *the Greeks were the first subject people to break free from Ottoman rule.*
▶ **adv.** /'səbjəkt/ (**subject to**) conditionally upon: *subject to bankruptcy court approval, the company expects to begin liquidation of its inventory.*
▶ **v.** /səb'jekt/ [with obj.] **1** (**subject someone/something to**) cause or force to undergo (a particular experience of form of treatment): *he'd subjected her to a terrifying ordeal.*
2 bring (a person or country) under one's control or jurisdiction, typically by using force.
– DERIVATIVES **sub·ject·less** /'səbjək(t)ləs/ **adj.**
– ORIGIN Middle English (in the sense '(person) owing obedience'): from Old French *suget*, from Latin *subjectus* 'brought under,' past participle of *subicere*, from *sub-* 'under' + *jacere* 'throw.' Senses relating to philosophy, logic, and grammar are derived ultimately from Aristotle's use of *to hupokeimenon* meaning 'material from which things are made' and 'subject of attributes and predicates.'

sub·ject cat·a·log ▶ **n.** a catalog, esp. in a library, that is arranged according to the subjects treated.

sub·jec·tion /səb'jeksʜən/ ▶ **n.** the action of subjecting a country or person to one's control or the fact of being subjected: *the country's subjection to European colonialism.*

sub·jec·tive /səb'jektiv/ ▶ **adj. 1** based on or influenced by personal feelings, tastes, or opinions: *his views are highly subjective | there is always the danger of making a subjective judgment.* Contrasted with OBJECTIVE. ■ dependent on the mind or on an individual's perception for its existence.
2 Grammar of, relating to, or denoting a case of nouns and pronouns used for the subject of a sentence.
▶ **n.** (**the subjective**) Grammar the subjective case.
– DERIVATIVES **sub·jec·tive·ly** **adv.**, **sub·jec·tive·ness** **n.**, **sub·jec·tiv·i·ty** /ˌsəbjek'tivitē/ **n.**
– ORIGIN late Middle English (originally in the sense 'characteristic of a political subject, submissive'): from Latin *subjectivus*, from *subject-* 'brought under' (see SUBJECT).

sub·jec·tive case ▶ **n.** Grammar the nominative.

sub·jec·tiv·ism /səb'jektəˌvizəm/ ▶ **n.** Philosophy the doctrine that knowledge is merely subjective and that there is no external or objective truth.
– DERIVATIVES **sub·jec·tiv·ist** **n. & adj.**

sub·ject mat·ter ▶ **n.** the topic dealt with or the subject represented in a debate, exposition, or work of art.

sub·join /səb'join/ ▶ **v.** [with obj.] formal add (comments or supplementary information) at the end of a speech or text.
– ORIGIN late 16th cent.: from obsolete French *subjoindre*, from Latin *subjungere*, from *sub-* 'in addition' + *jungere* 'to join.'

sub ju·di·ce /ˌso͝ob 'yo͞odiˌkā, ˌsəb 'jo͞odiˌsē/ ▶ **adj.** Law under judicial consideration and therefore prohibited from public discussion elsewhere: *the cases were still sub judice.*
– ORIGIN Latin, literally 'under a judge.'

sub·ju·gate /'səbjəˌgāt/ ▶ **v.** [with obj.] bring under domination or control, esp. by conquest: *the invaders had soon subjugated most of the native population.* ■ (**subjugate someone/something to**) make someone or something subordinate to: *the new ruler firmly subjugated the Church to the state.*
– DERIVATIVES **sub·ju·ga·tion** /ˌsəbjə'gāsʜən/ **n.**, **sub·ju·ga·tor** /-ˌgātər/ **n.**
– ORIGIN late Middle English: from late Latin *subjugat-* 'brought under a yoke,' from the verb *subjugare*, based on *jugum* 'yoke.'

sub·junc·tive /səb'jəɴɢ(k)tiv/ Grammar ▶ **adj.** relating to or denoting a mood of verbs expressing what is imagined or wished or possible. Compare with INDICATIVE.
▶ **n.** a verb in the subjunctive mood. ■ (**the subjunctive**) the subjunctive mood.
– DERIVATIVES **sub·junc·tive·ly** **adv.**
– ORIGIN mid 16th cent.: from French *subjonctif, -ive* or late Latin *subjunctivus*, from *subjungere* (see SUBJOIN), rendering Greek *hupotaktikos* 'subjoined.'

> **USAGE** *... if I **were** you; the report recommends that he **face** the tribunal; it is important that they **be** aware of the provisions of the act.* These examples all contain a verb in the **subjunctive mood**. The subjunctive is used to express situations that are hypothetical or not yet realized and is typically used for what is imagined, hoped for, demanded, or expected. In English, the subjunctive mood is fairly uncommon (especially in comparison with other languages, such as Spanish), mainly because most of the functions of the subjunctive are covered by modal verbs such as **might**, **could**, and **should**. In fact, in English, the subjunctive is often indistinguishable from the ordinary **indicative mood** since its form in most contexts is identical. It is distinctive only in the third person singular, where the normal indicative **-s** ending is absent (*he **face*** rather than *he **faces*** in the example above), and in the verb 'to be' (*I **were*** rather than *I **was***, and *they **be*** rather than *they **are*** in the examples above). In modern English, the subjunctive mood still exists but is regarded in many contexts as optional. Use of the subjunctive tends to convey a more formal tone, but there are few people who would regard its absence as actually wrong. Today, it survives mostly in fixed expressions, as in ***be** that as it may; far **be** it from me; as it **were**; lest we **forget**; God **help** you; **perish** the thought;* and ***come** what may.*

sub·king·dom /'səbˌkiɴɢdəm/ ▶ **n.** Biology a taxonomic category that ranks below kingdom and above phylum or division.

sub·lan·guage /'səbˌlaɴɢgwij/ ▶ **n.** a specialized language or jargon associated with a specific group or context.

sub·late /sə'blāt/ ▶ **v.** [with obj.] Philosophy assimilate (a smaller entity) into a larger one: *fragmented aspects of the self the subject is unable to sublate.*
– DERIVATIVES **sub·la·tion** /-'blāsʜən/ **n.**
– ORIGIN mid 19th cent.: from Latin *sublat-* 'taken away,' from *sub-* 'from below' + *lat-* (from the stem of *tollere* 'take away').

sub·lat·er·al /'səbˌlatərəl/ ▶ **n.** a side shoot developing from a lateral shoot or branch of a plant.

sub·lease ▶ **n.** /'səbˌlēs/ a lease of a property by a tenant to a subtenant.
▶ **v.** /səb'lēs/ another term for SUBLET.

sub·les·see /ˌsəble'sē/ ▶ **n.** a person who holds a sublease.

sub·les·sor /ˌsəble'sôr/ ▶ **n.** a person who grants a sublease.

sub·let ▶ **v.** /səb'let/ (**sublets, subletting**; past and past participle **sublet**) [with obj.] lease (a property) to a subtenant: *I quit my job and sublet my apartment.*
▶ **n.** /'səbˌlet/ another term for SUBLEASE. ■ informal a property that has been subleased.

sub·le·thal /səb'lēтʜəl/ ▶ **adj.** having an effect less than lethal.

sub·li·cense /ˌsəb'līsəns/ ▶ **n.** a license granted to a third party by a licensee, extending some rights or privileges that the licensee enjoys.
▶ **v.** [with obj.] grant a sublicense to or for.

sub·lieu·ten·ant /ˌsəbˌlo͞o'tenənt/ ▶ **n.** an officer in the British Royal Navy ranking above midshipman and below lieutenant.

S

sub·li·mate ▶ **v.** /'sabləˌmāt/ **1** [with obj.] (esp. in psychoanalytic theory) divert or modify (an instinctual impulse) into a culturally higher or socially more acceptable activity: *people who will **sublimate** sexuality **into** activities which help to build up and preserve civilization | he sublimates his hurt and anger into humor.*
2 [no obj.] Chemistry another term for SUBLIME.
▶ **n.** /-ˌmit, -ˌmāt/ Chemistry a solid deposit of a substance that has sublimed.
– DERIVATIVES **sub·li·ma·tion** /ˌsəblə'māsʜən/ **n.**
– ORIGIN late Middle English (in the sense 'raise to a higher status'): from Latin *sublimat-* 'raised up,' from the verb *sublimare*.

sub·lime /sə'blīm/ ▶ **adj.** (**sublimer, sublimest**) of such excellence, grandeur, or beauty as to inspire great admiration or awe: *Mozart's sublime piano concertos* | (as noun **the sublime**) *experiences that ranged **from the sublime to the ridiculous**.* ■ used to denote the extreme or unparalleled nature of a person's attitude or behavior: *he had the sublime confidence of youth.*

PRONUNCIATION KEY ə *ago, up*; ər *over, fur*; a *hat*; ā *ate*; ä *car*; e *let*; ē *see*; i *fit*; ī *by*; NG *sing*; ō *go*; ô *law, for*; oi *toy*; o͝o *good*; o͞o *goo*; ou *out*; TH *thin*; T͟H *then*; ZH *vision*

▶ **v. 1** [no obj.] Chemistry (of a solid substance) change directly into vapor when heated, typically forming a solid deposit again on cooling. ■ [with obj.] cause (a substance) to do this: *these crystals could be sublimed under a vacuum.*
2 [with obj.] archaic elevate to a high degree of moral or spiritual purity or excellence.
– DERIVATIVES **sub·lime·ly** adv., **sub·lim·i·ty** /-ˈblimitē/ n.
– ORIGIN late 16th cent. (in the sense 'dignified, aloof'): from Latin *sublimis*, from *sub-* 'up to' + a second element perhaps related to *limen* 'threshold,' *limus* 'oblique.'

Sub·lime Porte /səˈblīm ˈpôrt/ ▶ **n.** see PORTE.

sub·lim·i·nal /səˈblimənl/ ▶ **adj.** Psychology (of a stimulus or mental process) below the threshold of sensation or consciousness; perceived by or affecting someone's mind without their being aware of it.
– DERIVATIVES **sub·lim·i·nal·ly** adv.
– ORIGIN late 19th cent.: from SUB- 'below' + Latin *limen, limin-* 'threshold' + -AL.

sub·lim·i·nal ad·ver·tis·ing ▶ **n.** the use by advertisers of images and sounds to influence consumers' responses without their being conscious of it.

sub·lin·gual /ˌsəbˈliNGgwəl/ ▶ **adj.** Anatomy & Medicine situated or applied under the tongue. ■ denoting a pair of small salivary glands beneath the tongue.
– DERIVATIVES **sub·lin·gual·ly** adv.

sub·lit·to·ral /ˌsəbˈlitərəl/ chiefly Ecology ▶ **adj.** (of a marine animal, plant, or deposit) living, growing, or accumulating near to or just below the shore. ■ relating to or denoting a biogeographic zone extending (in the sea) from the average line of low tide to the edge of the continental shelf or (in a large lake) beyond the littoral zone but still well lit.
▶ **n.** (**the sublittoral**) the sublittoral zone.

Sub-Lt. ▶ **abbr.** Sublieutenant.

sub·lu·nar /səbˈlo͞onər/ ▶ **adj.** Astronomy within the moon's orbit and subject to its influence.

sub·lu·nar·y /səbˈlo͞onərē/ ▶ **adj.** literary belonging to this world as contrasted with a better or more spiritual one: *the concept was irrational to sublunary minds.*
– ORIGIN late 16th cent. (in the sense 'terrestrial'): from modern Latin *sublunaris*.

sub·lux·a·tion /ˌsəbləkˈsāSHən/ ▶ **n.** Medicine a partial dislocation. ■ a slight misalignment of the vertebrae, regarded in chiropractic theory as the cause of many health problems.
– ORIGIN late 17th cent.: from modern Latin *subluxatio(n-)* (see SUB-, LUXATE).

sub·ma·chine gun /ˌsəbməˈSHēn/ ▶ **n.** a handheld, lightweight machine gun.

sub·man·dib·u·lar /ˌsəbmanˈdibyələr/ ▶ **adj.** Anatomy situated beneath the jaw or mandible. ■ relating to or affecting a submandibular gland.

sub·man·dib·u·lar gland ▶ **n.** Anatomy either of a pair of salivary glands situated below the lower jaw. Also called SUBMAXILLARY GLAND.

sub·mar·gin·al /səbˈmärjənl/ ▶ **adj.** (of land) not allowing profitable farming or cultivation.

sub·ma·rine /ˌsəbməˈrēn, ˈsəbməˌrēn/ ▶ **n.** a warship with a streamlined hull designed to operate completely submerged in the sea for long periods, equipped with an internal store of air and a periscope and typically armed with torpedoes and/or missiles. ■ a submersible craft of any kind. ■ a submarine sandwich.
▶ **adj.** existing, occurring, done, or used under the surface of the sea: *submarine volcanic activity.*
– DERIVATIVES **sub·ma·rin·er** /səbˈmarənər, -məˈrēnər/ n.

sub·ma·rine sand·wich ▶ **n.** a sandwich made of a long roll typically filled with meat, cheese, and vegetables such as lettuce, tomato, and onions.

sub·max·il·lar·y gland /səbˈmaksəˌlerē/ ▶ **n.** another term for SUBMANDIBULAR GLAND.

sub·me·di·ant /ˌsəbˈmēdēənt/ ▶ **n.** Music the sixth note of the diatonic scale of any key.

sub·men·u /ˈsəbˌmenyo͞o/ ▶ **n.** Computing a menu accessed from a more general menu.

sub·merge /səbˈmərj/ ▶ **v.** [with obj.] (usu. **be submerged**) cause to be under water: *houses had been flooded and cars submerged.* ■ [no obj.] descend below the surface of an area of water: *the U-boat had had time to submerge.* ■ completely cover or obscure: *the tensions submerged earlier in the campaign now came to the fore.*
– DERIVATIVES **sub·mer·gence** /-jəns/ n., **sub·mer·gi·ble** /-jəbəl/ adj.
– ORIGIN early 17th cent.: from Latin *submergere*, from *sub-* 'under' + *mergere* 'to dip.'

sub·merse /səbˈmərs/ ▶ **v.** [with obj.] submerge: *pellets were then submersed in agar.*
▶ **adj.** (**submersed**) Botany denoting or characteristic of a plant growing entirely underwater. Contrasted with EMERSED.
– DERIVATIVES **sub·mer·sion** /-ˈmərZHən, -SHən/ n.
– ORIGIN late Middle English: from Latin *submers-* 'plunged below,' from the verb *submergere* (see SUBMERGE).

sub·mers·i·ble /səbˈmərsəbəl/ ▶ **adj.** designed to be completely submerged or to operate while submerged.
▶ **n.** a small boat or other craft of this kind, esp. one designed for research and exploration.

sub·mi·cro·scop·ic /ˌsəbmīkrəˈskäpik/ ▶ **adj.** too small to be seen by an ordinary light microscope.

sub·min·i·a·ture /səbˈmin(ē)əCHər, -ˌCHo͝or/ ▶ **adj.** of greatly reduced size. ■ (of a camera) very small and using 16-mm film.

sub·mis·sion /səbˈmiSHən/ ▶ **n. 1** the action or fact of accepting or yielding to a superior force or to the will or authority of another person: *they were forced into submission.* ■ Wrestling an act of surrendering to a hold by one's opponent. ■ archaic humility; meekness: *servile flattery and submission.*
2 the action of presenting a proposal, application, or other document for consideration or judgment: *reports should be prepared for submission at partners' meetings.* ■ a proposal, application, or other document presented in this way. ■ Law a proposition or argument presented by a lawyer to a judge or jury.
– ORIGIN late Middle English: from Old French, or from Latin *submissio(n-)*, from the verb *submittere* (see SUBMIT).

sub·mis·sive /səbˈmisiv/ ▶ **adj.** ready to conform to the authority or will of others; meekly obedient or passive.
– DERIVATIVES **sub·mis·sive·ly** adv.
– ORIGIN late 16th cent.: from SUBMISSION, on the pattern of pairs such as *remission, remissive.*

sub·mis·sive·ness /səbˈmisivnis/ ▶ **n.** the quality of being submissive: *he didn't confuse respect with submissiveness.*

sub·mit /səbˈmit/ ▶ **v.** (**submits, submitting, submitted**) **1** [no obj.] accept or yield to a superior force or to the authority or will of another person: *the original settlers were forced to submit to Bulgarian rule.* ■ (**submit oneself**) consent to undergo a certain treatment: *he submitted himself to a body search.* ■ [with obj.] subject to a particular process, treatment, or condition: *samples submitted to low pressure.* ■ agree to refer a matter to a third party for decision or adjudication: *the U.S. refused to submit to arbitration.*
2 [with obj.] present (a proposal, application, or other document) to a person or body for consideration or judgment: *the panel's report was submitted to a parliamentary committee.* ■ [with clause] (esp. in judicial contexts) suggest; argue: *he submitted that such measures were justified.*
– DERIVATIVES **sub·mit·ter** n.
– ORIGIN late Middle English: from Latin *submittere*, from *sub-* 'under' + *mittere* 'send, put.' Sense 2 'present for judgment' dates from the mid 16th cent.

sub·mod·i·fi·er /səbˈmädəˌfīər/ ▶ **n.** Grammar an adverb used in front of an adjective or another adverb to modify its meaning, for example *very* in *very cold* or *unusually* in *an unusually large house.*
– DERIVATIVES **sub·mod·i·fi·ca·tion** /səbˌmädəfiˈkāSHən/ n., **sub·mod·i·fy** /-ˌfī/ v.

sub·mon·tane /səbˈmäntān/ ▶ **adj.** passing under or through mountains. ■ situated in the foothills or lower slopes of a mountain range.

sub·mu·co·sa /ˌsəbmyo͞oˈkōsə/ ▶ **n.** (pl. **submucosae** /-sē/) Physiology the layer of areolar connective tissue lying beneath a mucous membrane.
– DERIVATIVES **sub·mu·co·sal** adj.
– ORIGIN late 19th cent.: from modern Latin *submucosa (membrana)*, feminine of *submucosus* 'submucous.'

sub·mul·ti·ple /səbˈməltəpəl/ ▶ **n.** a number that can be divided exactly into a specified number.
▶ **adj.** of or pertaining to such a number.

sub·mu·ni·tion /ˌsəbmyo͞oˈniSHən/ ▶ **n.** a small weapon or device that is part of a larger warhead and separates from it prior to impact.

sub·net·work /səbˈnetwərk/ (also **subnet** /səbˈnet/) ▶ **n.** Computing a part of a larger network such as the Internet.

sub·nor·mal /səbˈnôrməl/ ▶ **adj.** not meeting standards or reaching a level regarded as usual, esp. with respect to intelligence or development.
– DERIVATIVES **sub·nor·mal·i·ty** /ˌsəbnôrˈmalitē/ n.

sub·nu·cle·ar /səbˈn(y)o͞okliər/ ▶ **adj.** Physics occurring in or smaller than an atomic nucleus.

sub·op·ti·mal /səbˈäptəməl/ ▶ **adj.** technical of less than the highest standard or quality.

sub·or·bit·al /səbˈôrbitl/ ▶ **adj. 1** situated below or behind the orbit of the eye.
2 of, relating to, or denoting a trajectory that does not complete a full orbit of the earth or other celestial body.

sub·or·der /ˈsəbˌôrdər/ ▶ **n.** Biology a taxonomic category that ranks below order and above family.

sub·or·di·nar·y /ˌsəbˈôrdnˌerē/ ▶ **n.** (pl. **subordinaries**) Heraldry a simple device or bearing that is less common than the ordinaries (e.g., roundel, orle, lozenge).

sub·or·di·nate ▶ **adj.** /səˈbôrdnit/ lower in rank or position: *his subordinate officers.* ■ of less or secondary importance: *in adventure stories, character must be subordinate to action.*
▶ **n.** /səˈbôrdnit/ a person under the authority or control of another within an organization.
▶ **v.** /-ˌāt/ [with obj.] treat or regard as of lesser importance than something else: *practical considerations were subordinated to political expediency.* ■ make subservient to or dependent on something else.
– DERIVATIVES **sub·or·di·nate·ly** adv., **sub·or·di·na·tive** /-ətiv/ adj.
– ORIGIN late Middle English: from medieval Latin *subordinatus* 'placed in an inferior rank,' from Latin *sub-* 'below' + *ordinare* 'ordain.'

sub·or·di·nate clause ▶ **n.** a clause, typically introduced by a conjunction, that forms part of and is dependent on a main clause (e.g., "when it rang" in "she answered the phone when it rang").

sub·or·di·nat·ed debt /səbˈôrdnˌātid/ ▶ **n.** Finance a debt owed to an unsecured creditor that can only be paid, in the event of a liquidation, after the claims of secured creditors have been met.

sub·or·di·nat·ing con·junc·tion /səˈbôrdnˌātiNG/ ▶ **n.** a conjunction that introduces a subordinate clause, e.g., *although, because.* Contrasted with COORDINATING CONJUNCTION.

sub·or·di·na·tion /səˌbôrdnˈāSHən/ ▶ **n.** the action or state of subordinating or of being subordinate: *the subordination of medicine to political expediency.*

sub·orn /səˈbôrn/ ▶ **v.** [with obj.] bribe or otherwise induce (someone) to commit an unlawful act such as perjury: *he was accused of conspiring to suborn witnesses.*
– DERIVATIVES **sub·or·na·tion** /ˌsəbôrˈnāSHən/ n., **sub·orn·er** n.
– ORIGIN mid 16th cent.: from Latin *subornare* 'incite secretly,' from *sub-* 'secretly' + *ornare* 'equip.'

sub·os·cine /səbˈäsin, -īn/ Ornithology ▶ **adj.** of, relating to, or denoting passerine birds of a division that includes those other than songbirds, found chiefly in America. Compare with OSCINE.
● Suborder Deutero-Oscines, order Passeriformes.
▶ **n.** a bird of this division.

sub·ox·ide /səbˈäkˌsīd/ ▶ **n.** Chemistry an oxide containing the lowest or an unusually small proportion of oxygen.

sub·par /səbˈpär/ ▶ **adj.** below an average level.

sub·par·al·lel /səbˈparəˌlel/ ▶ **adj.** chiefly Geology almost parallel.

sub·phy·lum /ˈsəbˌfīləm/ ▶ **n.** (pl. **subphyla** /-ˌfīlə/) Zoology a taxonomic category that ranks below phylum and above class.

sub·plot /ˈsəbˌplät/ ▶ **n.** a subordinate plot in a play, novel, or similar work.

sub·poe·na /səˈpēnə/ Law ▶ **n.** (in full **subpoena ad testificandum**) a writ ordering a person to attend a court: *a subpoena may be issued to compel their attendance | they were all under subpoena to appear.*
▶ **v.** (**subpoenas, subpoenaing, subpoenaed** /-nəd/) [with obj.] summon (someone) with a subpoena: *the Queen is above the law and cannot be subpoenaed.* ■ require (a document or other evidence) to be submitted to a court of law: *the decision to subpoena government records.*
– ORIGIN late Middle English (as a noun): from Latin *sub poena* 'under penalty' (the first words of the writ). Use as a verb dates from the mid 17th cent.

sub·poe·na du·ces te·cum /səˈpēnə ˈdo͞osēz ˈtēkəm/ ▶ **n.** Law a writ ordering a person to attend a court and bring relevant documents.
– ORIGIN Latin, literally 'under penalty you shall bring with you.'

sub·prime /səbˈprīm/ ▶ **adj.** referring to credit or loan arrangements for borrowers with a poor credit history, typically having unfavorable conditions such as high interest rates: *a coalition of subprime lenders.*

sub·pro·gram /ˈsəbˌprōgram, -grəm/ ▶ **n.** Computing another term for SUBROUTINE.

sub·re·gion /ˈsəbˌrējən/ ▶ **n.** a division of a region.
– DERIVATIVES **sub·re·gion·al** /ˌsəbˈrēj(ə)nəl/ adj.

sub·ro·ga·tion /ˌsəbrəˈgāSHən/ ▶ **n.** Law the substitution of one person or group by another in

respect of a debt or insurance claim, accompanied by the transfer of any associated rights and duties.
– DERIVATIVES **sub·ro·gate** /ˈsəbrəˌgāt/ **v.**
– ORIGIN late Middle English (in the general sense 'substitution'): from late Latin *subrogatio(n-)*, from *subrogare* 'choose as substitute,' from *sub-* 'in place of another' + *rogare* 'ask.'

sub ro·sa /ˌsəb ˈrōzə/ ▶ **adj. & adv.** formal happening or done in secret: [as adv.] *the committee operates sub rosa* | [as adj.] *sub rosa inspections.*
– ORIGIN Latin, literally 'under the rose,' as an emblem of secrecy.

sub·rou·tine /ˈsəbrōōˌtēn/ ▶ **n.** Computing a set of instructions designed to perform a frequently used operation within a program.

subs. ▶ **abbr.** subscription.

sub-Sa·har·an ▶ **adj.** [attrib.] from or forming part of the African regions south of the Sahara desert.

sub·sam·ple ▶ **n.** /ˈsəbˌsampəl/ a sample drawn from a larger sample.
▶ **v.** /səbˈsampəl/ [with obj.] take such a sample from.

sub·scribe /səbˈskrīb/ ▶ **v. 1** [no obj.] arrange to receive something regularly, typically a publication, by paying in advance: ***subscribe to** the magazine for twelve months and receive a free T-shirt.* ■ arrange for access to an electronic mailing list or online service: *some 40,000 users have **subscribed to** the service at $ 2.99 per month.* ■ chiefly Brit. contribute or undertake to contribute a certain sum of money to a particular fund, project, or charitable cause, typically on a regular basis: *he is one of the millions who **subscribe to** the NSPCC* | [with obj.] *he **subscribed** £400 to the campaign.* ■ [with obj.] apply to participate in: *the course has been fully subscribed.* ■ apply for or undertake to pay for an offering of shares of stock: *investors would **subscribe** electronically **to** the initial stock offerings* | [with obj.] *yesterday's offering was fully subscribed.* ■ [with obj.] (of a bookseller) agree before publication to take (a certain number of copies of a book): *most of the first print run of 15,000 copies has been subscribed.*
2 (**subscribe to**) express or feel agreement with (an idea or proposal): *we prefer to subscribe to an alternative explanation.*
3 [with obj.] formal sign (a will, contract, or other document): *he subscribed the will as a witness.* ■ sign (one's name) on such a document. ■ (**subscribe oneself**) [with complement] archaic sign oneself as: *he ventured still to subscribe himself her most obedient servant.*
– ORIGIN late Middle English (in the sense 'sign at the bottom of a document'): from Latin *subscribere*, from *sub-* 'under' + *scribere* 'write.'

sub·scrib·er /səbˈskrībər/ ▶ **n.** a person who receives a publication regularly by paying in advance: *I have been a subscriber to your magazine for many years.* ■ a person who pays to receive or access a service: *the company has 2.6 million subscribers to its digital service* | *cable TV subscribers.* ■ chiefly Brit. a person who regularly contributes money to a fund, project, or cause.

sub·script /ˈsəbˌskript/ ▶ **adj.** (of a letter, figure, or symbol) written or printed below the line.
▶ **n.** a subscript letter, figure, or symbol. ■ Computing a symbol (notionally written as a subscript but in practice usually not) used in a program, alone or with others, to specify one of the elements of an array.
– ORIGIN early 18th cent.: from Latin *subscript-* 'written below,' from the verb *subscribere* (see SUBSCRIBE).

sub·scrip·tion /səbˈskripSHən/ ▶ **n. 1** the action of making or agreeing to make an advance payment in order to receive or participate in something: *the newsletter is available only on subscription* | *take out a one-year subscription.* ■ an arrangement by which access is granted to an online service. ■ chiefly Brit. an advance payment made to receive or participate in something: *membership is available at an annual subscription of £300.* ■ a system in which the production of a book is wholly or partly financed by advance orders.
2 formal a signature or short piece of writing at the end of a document: *he signed the letter and added a subscription.* ■ archaic a signed declaration or agreement.
– ORIGIN late Middle English (sense 2): from Latin *subscriptio(n-)*, from *subscribere* 'write below' (see SUBSCRIBE).

sub·scrip·tion con·cert ▶ **n.** one of a series of concerts for which tickets are sold mainly in advance.

sub·sea /səbˈsē/ ▶ **adj.** (esp. of processes or equipment used in the oil industry) situated or occurring beneath the surface of the sea.

sub·sec·tion /ˈsəbˌsekSHən/ ▶ **n.** a division of a section.

sub·sel·li·um /ˌsəbˈselēəm/ ▶ **n.** (pl. **subsellia** /-ˈselēə/) another term for MISERICORD (sense 1).
– ORIGIN Latin, from *sub-* 'secondary' + *sella* 'seat.'

sub·sense /ˈsəbˌsens/ ▶ **n.** a subsidiary sense of a word defined in a dictionary.

sub·se·quence[1] /ˈsəbsəkwəns/ ▶ **n.** formal the state of following something, esp. as a result or effect: *an affair which appeared in due subsequence in the newspapers.*

sub·se·quence[2] /ˈsəbˌsēkwəns/ ▶ **n.** a sequence contained in or forming part of another sequence. ■ Mathematics a sequence derived from another by the omission of a number of terms.

sub·se·quent /ˈsəbsəkwənt/ ▶ **adj.** coming after something in time; following: *the theory was developed **subsequent to** the earthquake of 1906.* ■ Geology (of a stream or valley) having a direction or character determined by the resistance to erosion of the underlying rock, and typically following the strike of the strata.
– ORIGIN late Middle English: from Old French, or from Latin *subsequent-* 'following after' (from the verb *subsequi*).

sub·se·quent·ly /ˈsəbsəkwəntlē/ ▶ **adv.** after a particular thing has happened; afterward: *Mel's offhand remark subsequently became their rallying cry.*

sub·serve /səbˈsərv/ ▶ **v.** [with obj.] help to further or promote: *officers are appointed to subserve their own profit and convenience.*
– ORIGIN mid 17th cent.: from Latin *subservire* (see SUB-, SERVE).

sub·ser·vi·ent /səbˈsərvēənt/ ▶ **adj.** prepared to obey others unquestioningly: *she was **subservient** to her parents.* ■ less important; subordinate: *he expected her career to become **subservient to** his.* ■ serving as a means to an end: *the whole narration is **subservient to** the moral plan of exemplifying twelve virtues in twelve knights.*
– DERIVATIVES **sub·ser·vi·ence** **n.**, **sub·ser·vi·en·cy** **n.**, **sub·ser·vi·ent·ly** **adv.**
– ORIGIN mid 17th cent.: from Latin *subservient-* 'subjecting to, complying with,' from the verb *subservire* (see SUBSERVE).

sub·set /ˈsəbˌset/ ▶ **n.** a part of a larger group of related things. ■ Mathematics a set of which all the elements are contained in another set.

sub·shrub /ˈsəbˌSHrəb/ ▶ **n.** Botany a dwarf shrub, esp. one that is woody only at the base.
– DERIVATIVES **sub·shrub·by** **adj.**

sub·side /səbˈsīd/ ▶ **v.** [no obj.] **1** become less intense, violent, or severe: *I'll wait a few minutes until the storm subsides.* ■ lapse into silence or inactivity: *Fred opened his mouth to protest again, then subsided.*
2 (of water) go down to a lower or the normal level: *the floods subside almost as quickly as they arise.* ■ (of the ground) cave in; sink: *the island is subsiding.* ■ (of a swelling) reduce until gone: *it took seven days for the swelling to subside completely.*
– ORIGIN late 17th cent.: from Latin *subsidere*, from *sub-* 'below' + *sidere* 'settle' (related to *sedere* 'sit').

sub·sid·ence /səbˈsīdns, ˈsəbsidns/ ▶ **n.** the gradual caving in or sinking of an area of land.
– ORIGIN mid 17th cent.: from Latin *subsidentia* 'sediment,' from the verb *subsidere* (see SUBSIDE).

sub·sid·i·ar·y /səbˈsidēˌerē/ ▶ **adj.** less important than but related or supplementary to: *many environmentalists argue that the cause of animal rights is subsidiary to that of protecting the environment.* ■ (of a company) controlled by a holding or parent company.
▶ **n.** (pl. **subsidiaries**) a company controlled by a holding company. ■ rare a thing that is of lesser importance than but related to something else.
– DERIVATIVES **sub·sid·i·ar·i·ly** /-ˌsidēˈe(ə)rəlē/ **adv.** (rare).
– ORIGIN mid 16th cent. (in the sense 'serving to help or supplement'): from Latin *subsidiarius*, from *subsidium* 'support, assistance' (see SUBSIDY).

sub·si·dize /ˈsəbsəˌdīz/ ▶ **v.** [with obj.] support (an organization or activity) financially: *it was beyond the power of a state to subsidize a business.* ■ pay part of the cost of producing (something) to reduce prices for the buyer: *the government subsidizes basic goods including sugar, petroleum, and wheat.*
– DERIVATIVES **sub·si·di·za·tion** /ˌsəbsədiˈzāSHən/ **n.**, **sub·si·diz·er** **n.**

sub·si·dy /ˈsəbsidē/ ▶ **n.** (pl. **subsidies**) **1** a sum of money granted by the government or a public body to assist an industry or business so that the price of a commodity or service may remain low or competitive: *a farm subsidy* | *they disdain government subsidy.* ■ a sum of money granted to support an arts organization or other undertaking held to be in the public interest. ■ a grant or contribution of money.
2 historical a parliamentary grant to the sovereign for state needs. ■ a tax levied on a particular occasion.
– ORIGIN late Middle English: from Anglo-Norman French *subsidie*, from Latin *subsidium* 'assistance.'

sub·sist /səbˈsist/ ▶ **v.** [no obj.] **1** maintain or support oneself, esp. at a minimal level: *thousands of refugees **subsist on** international handouts.* ■ [with obj.] archaic provide sustenance for: *the problem of subsisting the poor in a period of high bread prices.*
2 chiefly Law remain in being, force, or effect. ■ (**subsist in**) be attributable to: *the effect of genetic maldevelopment may subsist in chromosomal mutation.*
– DERIVATIVES **sub·sist·ent** /-ənt/ **adj.**
– ORIGIN mid 16th cent. (in the sense 'continue to exist'): from Latin *subsistere* 'stand firm,' from *sub-* 'from below' + *sistere* 'set, stand.'

sub·sist·ence /səbˈsistəns/ ▶ **n. 1** the action or fact of maintaining or supporting oneself at a minimum level: *the minimum income needed for subsistence.* ■ the means of doing this: *the garden provided not only subsistence but a little cash crop* | *the agricultural working class were deprived of a subsistence.* ■ [as modifier] denoting or relating to production at a level sufficient only for one's own use or consumption, without any surplus for trade: *subsistence agriculture.*
2 chiefly Law the state of remaining in force or effect: *rights of occupation normally only continue during the subsistence of the marriage.*

sub·sist·ence lev·el (also **subsistence wage**) ▶ **n.** a standard of living (or wage) that provides only the bare necessities of life.

sub·soil /ˈsəbˌsoil/ ▶ **n.** the soil lying immediately under the surface soil.
▶ **v.** [with obj.] (usu. as noun **subsoiling**) plow (land) so as to cut into the subsoil.

sub·soil·er /ˈsəbˌsoilər/ ▶ **n.** a kind of plow with no moldboard, used to loosen the soil at some depth below the surface without turning it over.

sub·song /ˈsəbˌSÔNG, -ˌsäNG/ ▶ **n.** Ornithology birdsong that is softer and less well defined than the usual territorial song, sometimes heard only at close quarters as a quiet warbling.

sub·son·ic /ˌsəbˈsänik/ ▶ **adj.** relating to or flying at a speed or speeds less than that of sound.
– DERIVATIVES **sub·son·i·cal·ly** /-ik(ə)lē/ **adv.**

subsp. ▶ **abbr.** subspecies.

sub·space /ˈsəbˌspās/ ▶ **n. 1** Mathematics a space that is wholly contained in another space, or whose points or elements are all in another space.
2 (in science fiction) a hypothetical space-time continuum used for communication at a speed faster than that of light.

sub spe·cie ae·ter·ni·ta·tis /ˈsəb ˈspēSHē ēˌtərniˈtätis, ˈspēsē/ ▶ **adv.** viewed in relation to the eternal; in a universal perspective: *sub specie aeternitatis the authors have got it about right.*
– ORIGIN Latin, literally 'under the aspect of eternity.'

sub·spe·cies /ˈsəbˌspēSHēz, -sēz/ (abbr.: **subsp.** or **ssp.**) ▶ **n.** (pl. **same**) Biology a taxonomic category that ranks below species, usually a fairly permanent geographically isolated race. Subspecies are designated by a Latin trinomial, e.g., (in zoology) *Ursus arctos horribilis* or (in botany) *Beta vulgaris* subsp. *crassa*. Compare with FORM (sense 3 of the noun) and VARIETY (sense 2).
– DERIVATIVES **sub·spe·cif·ic** /ˌsəbspəˈsifik/ **adj.**

subst. ▶ **abbr.** ■ substantive. ■ substantively. ■ substitute.

sub·stage /ˈsəbˌstāj/ ▶ **n.** [usu. as modifier] an apparatus fixed beneath the ordinary stage of a compound microscope to support mirrors and other accessories.

sub·stance /ˈsəbstəns/ ▶ **n. 1** a particular kind of matter with uniform properties: *a steel tube coated with a waxy substance.* ■ an intoxicating, stimulating, or narcotic chemical or drug, esp. an illegal one.
2 the real physical matter of which a person or thing consists and which has a tangible, solid presence: *proteins compose much of the actual substance of the body.* ■ the quality of having a solid basis in reality or fact: *the claim has no substance.* ■ the quality of being dependable or stable: *some were inclined to knock her for her lack of substance.*
3 the quality of being important, valid, or significant: *he had yet to accomplish anything of substance.* ■ the most important or essential part of something; the real or essential meaning: *the substance of the treaty.* ■ the subject matter of a text, speech, or work of art, esp. as contrasted with the form or style in which it is presented. ■ wealth and possessions: *a woman of substance.* ■ Philosophy

S

the essential nature underlying phenomena, which is subject to changes and accidents.
– PHRASES **in substance** essentially: *basic rights are equivalent in substance to human rights.*
– ORIGIN Middle English (denoting the essential nature of something): from Old French, from Latin *substantia* 'being, essence,' from *substant-* 'standing firm,' from the verb *substare.*

sub·stance a·buse ▶ **n.** overindulgence in or dependence on an addictive substance, esp. alcohol or drugs.

sub·stance P ▶ **n.** Biochemistry a compound thought to be involved in the synaptic transmission of pain and other nerve impulses. It is a polypeptide with eleven amino-acid residues.

sub·stand·ard /səb'standərd/ ▶ **adj. 1** below the usual or required standard: *substandard housing.* **2** another term for NONSTANDARD.

sub·stan·tial /səb'stanCHəl/ ▶ **adj. 1** of considerable importance, size, or worth: *a substantial amount of cash.* ■ strongly built or made: *a row of substantial Victorian villas.* ■ (of a meal) large and filling. ■ important in material or social terms; wealthy: *a substantial Devon family.* **2** concerning the essentials of something: *there was substantial agreement on changing policies.* **3** real and tangible rather than imaginary: *spirits are shadowy, human beings substantial.*
– DERIVATIVES **sub·stan·ti·al·i·ty** /-ˌstanCHē'alitē/ **n.**
– ORIGIN Middle English: from Old French *substantiel* or Christian Latin *substantialis,* from *substantia* 'being, essence' (see SUBSTANCE).

sub·stan·tial·ism /səb'stanCHəˌlizəm/ ▶ **n.** Philosophy the doctrine that behind phenomena there are substantial realities.
– DERIVATIVES **sub·stan·tial·ist n. & adj.**

sub·stan·tial·ize /səb'stanCHəˌlīz/ ▶ **v.** [with obj.] give (something) substance or actual existence: *the universe is a series of abstract truths, substantialized by their reference to God.*

sub·stan·tial·ly /səb'stanCHəlē/ ▶ **adv. 1** to a great or significant extent: *profits grew substantially* | [as submodifier] *substantially higher earnings.* **2** for the most part; essentially: *things will remain substantially the same over the next ten years.*

sub·stan·ti·ate /səb'stanCHēˌāt/ ▶ **v.** [with obj.] provide evidence to support or prove the truth of: *they had found nothing to substantiate the allegations.*
– DERIVATIVES **sub·stan·ti·a·tion** /-ˌstanCHē'āSHən/ **n.**
– ORIGIN mid 17th cent.: from medieval Latin *substantiat-* 'given substance,' from the verb *substantiare.*

sub·stan·tive /'səbstəntiv/ ▶ **adj. 1** having a firm basis in reality and therefore important, meaningful, or considerable: *there is no substantive evidence for the efficacy of these drugs.* **2** having a separate and independent existence. ■ (of a dye) not needing a mordant. **3** (of law) defining rights and duties as opposed to giving the rules by which such things are established.
▶ **n.** Grammar a noun.
– DERIVATIVES **sub·stan·ti·val** /ˌsəbstən'tīvəl/ **adj., sub·stan·tive·ly adv.**
– ORIGIN late Middle English (in the sense 'having an independent existence'): from Old French *substantif, -ive* or late Latin *substantivus,* from *substantia* 'essence' (see SUBSTANCE).

sub·sta·tion /'səbˌstāSHən/ ▶ **n. 1** a set of equipment reducing the high voltage of electrical power transmission to that suitable for supply to consumers. **2** a subordinate station for the police or fire department. ■ a small post office, for example one situated within a larger store.

sub·stel·lar /'səbˌstelər/ ▶ **adj.** Astronomy relating to or denoting a body much smaller than a typical star whose mass is not great enough to support main sequence hydrogen burning.

sub·stit·u·ent /səb'stiCHōōənt/ ▶ **n.** Chemistry an atom or group of atoms taking the place of another atom or group or occupying a specified position in a molecule.
– ORIGIN late 19th cent.: from Latin *substituent-* 'standing in place of,' from the verb *substituere* (see SUBSTITUTE).

sub·sti·tute /'səbstiˌt(y)ōōt/ ▶ **n.** a person or thing acting or serving in place of another: *soy milk is used as a substitute for dairy milk.* ■ a sports player nominated as eligible to replace another after a game has begun. ■ Psychology a person or thing that becomes the object of love or other emotion deprived of its natural outlet: *a father substitute.*
▶ **v.** [with obj.] use or add in place of: *dried rosemary can be* ***substituted for*** *the fresh herb.* ■ [no obj.] act or serve as a substitute: *I found someone to* ***substitute for*** *me.* ■ replace (someone or something) with another: *customs officers* ***substituted*** *the drugs* ***with*** *another substance* | *this was substituted by a new clause.* ■ replace (a sports player) with a substitute during a contest: *he was substituted for Nichols in the fifth inning.* ■ Chemistry replace (an atom or group in a molecule, esp. a hydrogen atom) with another. ■ (as adj. **substituted**) Chemistry (of a compound) in which one or more hydrogen atoms have been replaced by other atoms or groups: *a substituted alkaloid.*
– DERIVATIVES **sub·sti·tut·a·bil·i·ty** /ˌsəbstəˌt(y)ōōtə'bilitē/ **n., sub·sti·tut·a·ble adj., sub·sti·tu·tive** /-ˌt(y)ōōtiv/ **adj.**
– ORIGIN late Middle English (denoting a deputy or delegate): from Latin *substitutus* 'put in place of,' past participle of *substituere,* based on *statuere* 'set up.'

> **USAGE** Traditionally, the verb **substitute** is followed by **for** and means 'put (someone or something) in place of another,' as in *she* ***substituted*** *the fake vase* ***for*** *the real one.* From the late 17th century, **substitute** has also been used to mean 'replace (someone or something) with someone or something else,' as in *she* ***substituted*** *the real vase* ***with*** *the fake one.* This can be confusing, since the two sentences shown above mean the same thing, yet the object of the verb and the object of the preposition have swapped positions. Despite the potential confusion, the second, newer use is well established, especially in some scientific contexts and in sports (*the top scorer was substituted with almost half an hour still to play*), and is now generally regarded as part of standard English.

sub·sti·tu·tion /ˌsəbsti't(y)ōōSHən/ ▶ **n.** the action of replacing someone or something with another person or thing: *the* ***substitution of*** *pediatricians* ***for*** *grandmothers in guiding baby care* | *a tactical substitution.*
– DERIVATIVES **sub·sti·tu·tion·al** /-SHənl/ **adj., sub·sti·tu·tion·ar·y** /-ˌnerē/ **adj.**

sub·storm /'səbˌstôrm/ ▶ **n.** a localized disturbance of the earth's magnetic field in high latitudes, typically manifested as an aurora.

sub·strain /'səbˌstrān/ ▶ **n.** a strain of a virus derived from another strain.

sub·strate /'səbˌstrāt/ ▶ **n.** a substance or layer that underlies something, or on which some process occurs, in particular: ■ the surface or material on or from which an organism lives, grows, or obtains its nourishment. ■ the substance on which an enzyme acts. ■ a material that provides the surface on which something is deposited or inscribed, for example the silicon wafer used to manufacture integrated circuits.
– ORIGIN early 19th cent.: anglicized form of SUBSTRATUM.

sub·stra·tum /'səbˌstrātəm, -ˌstra-/ ▶ **n.** (pl. **substrata** /-tə/) an underlying layer or substance, in particular, a layer of rock or soil beneath the surface of the ground. ■ a foundation or basis of something: *there is a broad* ***substratum of*** *truth in it.*
– ORIGIN mid 17th cent.: modern Latin, neuter past participle (used as a noun) of Latin *substernere,* from *sub-* 'below' + *sternere* 'strew.' Compare with STRATUM.

sub·struc·ture /'səbˌstrəkCHər/ ▶ **n.** an underlying or supporting structure.
– DERIVATIVES **sub·struc·tur·al** /ˌsəb'strəkCHərəl/ **adj.**

sub·sume /səb'sōōm/ ▶ **v.** [with obj.] include or absorb (something) in something else: *most of these phenomena can be* ***subsumed under*** *two broad categories.*
– DERIVATIVES **sub·sum·a·ble adj., sub·sump·tion** /-'səm(p)SHən/ **n.**
– ORIGIN mid 16th cent. (in the sense 'subjoin, add'): from medieval Latin *subsumere,* from *sub-* 'from below' + *sumere* 'take.' The current sense dates from the early 19th cent.

sub·sur·face /'səbsərfəs/ ▶ **n.** the stratum or strata below the earth's surface.

sub·sys·tem /'səbˌsistəm/ ▶ **n.** a self-contained system within a larger system.

sub·ten·ant /səb'tenənt/ ▶ **n.** a person who leases property from a tenant.
– DERIVATIVES **sub·ten·an·cy** /-'tenənsē/ **n.**

sub·tend /səb'tend/ ▶ **v.** [with obj.] **1** (of a line, arc, or figure) form (an angle) at a particular point when straight lines from its extremities are joined at that point. ■ (of an angle or chord) have bounding lines or points that meet or coincide with those of (a line or arc). **2** Botany (of a bract) extend under (a flower) so as to support or enfold it.
– ORIGIN late 16th cent. (sense 1): from Latin *subtendere,* from *sub-* 'under' + *tendere* 'stretch.' Sense 2 dates from the late 19th cent.

sub·tense /səb'tens/ ▶ **n.** Geometry a subtending line, esp. the chord of an arc. ■ the angle subtended by a line at a point.
– ORIGIN early 17th cent.: from modern Latin *subtensa (linea),* feminine past participle of *subtendere* (see SUBTEND).

sub·ter·fuge /'səbtərˌfyōōj/ ▶ **n.** deceit used in order to achieve one's goal.
– ORIGIN late 16th cent.: from French, or from late Latin *subterfugium,* from Latin *subterfugere* 'escape secretly,' from *subter-* 'beneath' + *fugere* 'flee.'

sub·ter·mi·nal /'səbˌtərmənl/ ▶ **adj.** technical near the end of a chain or other structure.

sub·ter·ra·ne·an /ˌsəbtə'rānēən/ ▶ **adj.** existing, occurring, or done under the earth's surface. ■ secret; concealed: *the subterranean world of the behind-the-scenes television powerbrokers.*
– DERIVATIVES **sub·ter·ra·ne·ous·ly** /-'rānēəslē/ **adv.**
– ORIGIN early 17th cent.: from Latin *subterraneus* (from *sub-* 'below' + *terra* 'earth') + -AN.

sub·text /'səbˌtekst/ ▶ **n.** an underlying and often distinct theme in a piece of writing or conversation.
– DERIVATIVES **sub·text·u·al adj.**

sub·til·ize /'sətlˌīz/ ▶ **v.** [with obj.] archaic make more subtle; refine.
– DERIVATIVES **sub·til·i·za·tion** /ˌsətl-i'zāSHən/ **n.**

sub·ti·tle /'səbˌtītl/ ▶ **n. 1** (**subtitles**) captions displayed at the bottom of a movie or television screen that translate or transcribe the dialogue or narrative. **2** a subordinate title of a published work or article giving additional information about its content.
▶ **v.** [with obj.] (usu. **be subtitled**) **1** provide (a movie or program) with subtitles: *much of the film is subtitled.* **2** provide (a published work or article) with a subtitle: *the novel was aptly subtitled.*

sub·tle /'sətl/ ▶ **adj.** (**subtler, subtlest**) (esp. of a change or distinction) so delicate or precise as to be difficult to analyze or describe: *his language expresses rich and subtle meanings.* ■ (of a mixture or effect) delicately complex and understated: *subtle lighting.* ■ making use of clever and indirect methods to achieve something: *he tried a more subtle approach.* ■ capable of making fine distinctions: *a subtle mind.* ■ arranged in an ingenious and elaborate way. ■ archaic crafty; cunning.
– DERIVATIVES **sub·tle·ness n., sub·tly adv.**
– ORIGIN Middle English (also in the sense 'not easily understood'): from Old French *sotil,* from Latin *subtilis* 'fine, delicate.'

sub·tle·ty /'sətltē/ ▶ **n.** (pl. **subtleties**) the quality or state of being subtle: *the textural subtlety of Degas.* ■ a subtle distinction, feature, or argument: *the subtleties of English grammar.*
– ORIGIN Middle English: from Old French *soutilte,* from Latin *subtilitas,* from *subtilis* 'fine, delicate' (see SUBTLE).

sub·ton·ic /səb'tänik/ ▶ **n.** Music the note below the tonic, the seventh note of the diatonic scale of any key.

sub·to·tal /'səbˌtōtl/ ▶ **n.** the total of one set of a larger group of figures to be added.
▶ **v.** (**subtotals, subtotaling, subtotaled**; Brit. **subtotals, subtotalling, subtotalled**) [with obj.] add (numbers) so as to obtain a subtotal.
▶ **adj.** Medicine (of an injury or a surgical operation) partial; not total.

sub·tract /səb'trakt/ ▶ **v.** [with obj.] take away (a number or amount) from another to calculate the difference: *subtract 43 from 60.* ■ take away (something) from something else so as to decrease the size, number, or amount: *programs were added and subtracted as called for.*
– DERIVATIVES **sub·tract·er n., sub·trac·tive** /-tiv/ **adj.**
– ORIGIN mid 16th cent.: from Latin *subtract-* 'drawn away,' from *sub-* 'from below' + *trahere* 'to draw.'

sub·trac·tion /səb'trakSHən/ ▶ **n.** the process or skill of taking one number or amount away from another: ***subtraction of*** *this figure* ***from*** *the total.* ■ Mathematics the process of taking a matrix, vector, or other quantity away from another under specific rules to obtain the difference.

sub·tra·hend /'səbtrəˌhend/ ▶ **n.** Mathematics a quantity or number to be subtracted from another.
– ORIGIN late 17th cent.: from Latin *subtrahendus* 'to be taken away,' gerundive of *subtrahere* (see SUBTRACT).

sub·trop·ics /səb'träpiks/ ▶ **plural n.** (**the subtropics**) the regions adjacent to or bordering on the tropics.
– DERIVATIVES **sub·trop·i·cal** /-'träpikəl/ **adj.**

sub·type /ˈsəbˌtīp/ ▶ **n.** a secondary or subordinate type. ■ a subdivision of a type of microorganism: *HIV-1infections reflect a diverse range of non-B subtypes.*

Su·bud /so͞oˈbo͞od/ a movement, founded in 1947 and led by the Javanese mystic Pak Muhammad Subuh, based on a system of exercises by which the individual seeks to approach a state of perfection through divine power.
– ORIGIN contraction of Javanese *susila budhi dharma*, from Sanskrit *suśīla* 'good disposition' + *buddhi* 'understanding' + *dharma* 'religious duty.'

su·bu·late /ˈsəbyəlit, -ˌlāt/ ▶ **adj.** Botany & Zoology (of a part) slender and tapering to a point; awl-shaped.
– ORIGIN mid 18th cent.: from Latin *subula* 'awl' + **-ATE**[2].

sub·um·brel·la /ˌsəbəmˈbrelə/ ▶ **n.** Zoology the concave inner surface of the umbrella of a jellyfish or other medusa.
– DERIVATIVES **sub·um·brel·lar** adj.

sub·un·gu·late /səbˈəNGgyəlit, -ˌlāt/ ▶ **n.** Zoology a mammal of a diverse group that probably evolved from primitive ungulates, comprising the elephants, hyraxes, sirenians, and perhaps the aardvark.

sub·u·nit /ˈsəbˌyo͞onit/ ▶ **n.** a distinct component of something: *chemical subunits of human DNA.*

sub·urb /ˈsəbərb/ ▶ **n.** an outlying district of a city, esp. a residential one.
– ORIGIN Middle English: from Old French *suburbe* or Latin *suburbium*, from *sub-* 'near to' + *urbs, urb-* 'city.'

sub·ur·ban /səˈbərbən/ ▶ **adj.** of or characteristic of a suburb: *suburban life.* ■ contemptibly dull and ordinary: *Elizabeth despised Ann's house-proudness as deeply suburban.*
– DERIVATIVES **sub·ur·ban·ite** n., **sub·ur·ban·i·za·tion** /səˌbərbənəˈzāSHən/ n., **sub·ur·ban·ize** v.

sub·ur·bi·a /səˈbərbēə/ ▶ **n.** the suburbs or their inhabitants viewed collectively.

sub·vent /səbˈvent/ ▶ **v.** [with obj.] formal support or assist by the payment of a subvention.
– ORIGIN early 20th cent.: from Latin *subvent-* 'assisted,' from the verb *subvenire* (see **SUBVENTION**).

sub·ven·tion /səbˈvenCHən/ ▶ **n.** a grant of money, esp. from a government.
– ORIGIN late Middle English (in the sense 'provision of help'): from Old French, from late Latin *subventio(n-)*, from Latin *subvenire* 'assist,' from *sub-* 'from below' + *venire* 'come.'

sub·ver·sive /səbˈvərsiv/ ▶ **adj.** seeking or intended to subvert an established system or institution: *subversive literature.*
▶ **n.** a person with such aims.
– DERIVATIVES **sub·ver·sive·ly** adv., **sub·ver·sive·ness** n.
– ORIGIN mid 17th cent.: from medieval Latin *subversivus*, from the verb *subvertere* (see **SUBVERT**).

sub·vert /səbˈvərt/ ▶ **v.** [with obj.] undermine the power and authority of (an established system or institution): *an attempt to subvert democratic government.*
– DERIVATIVES **sub·ver·sion** /-ˈvərZHən, -SHən/ n., **sub·vert·er** n.
– ORIGIN late Middle English: from Old French *subvertir* or Latin *subvertere*, from *sub-* 'from below' + *vertere* 'to turn.'

sub·vo·cal /səbˈvōkəl/ ▶ **adj.** Psychology & Philosophy relating to or denoting an unarticulated level of speech comparable to thought: *almost all of what is called "thinking" is subvocal talk.*

sub·vo·cal·ize /səbˈvōkəˌlīz/ ▶ **v.** [with obj.] utter (words or sounds) with the lips silently or with barely audible sound, esp. when talking to oneself, memorizing something, or reading.
– DERIVATIVES **sub·vo·cal·i·za·tion** /-ˌvōkəliˈzāSHən/ n.

sub·way /ˈsəbˌwā/ ▶ **n. 1** an underground electric railroad.
2 Brit. a tunnel under a road for use by pedestrians.

sub·web /ˈsəbˌweb/ ▶ **n.** an isolated part of a website, esp. one that is password-protected or that is not obviously accessible from the main page.

sub·woof·er /ˈsəbˌwo͝ofər/ ▶ **n.** a loudspeaker component designed to reproduce very low bass frequencies.

sub·ze·ro /ˌsəbˈzi(ə)rō/ ▶ **adj.** below zero on the Fahrenheit scale (−18 Celsius); very cold. ■ below zero on the Celsius scale; below freezing.

suc- ▶ **prefix** variant spelling of **SUB-** assimilated before *c* (as in *succeed, succussion*).

suc·cah /so͞oˈkä, ˈso͞okə/ (also **sukkah**) ▶ **n.** a temporary shelter covered in natural materials, built near a synagogue or house and used esp. for meals during the Jewish festival of Succoth.
– ORIGIN late 19th cent.: from Hebrew *sukkāh* 'hut.'

suc·ce·da·ne·um /ˌsəksiˈdānēəm/ ▶ **n.** (pl. **succedanea** /-nēə/) dated or literary a substitute, esp. for a medicine or drug.
– DERIVATIVES **suc·ce·da·ne·ous** /-nēəs/ adj.
– ORIGIN early 17th cent.: modern Latin, neuter of Latin *succedaneus* 'following after,' from *succedere* 'come close after' (see **SUCCEED**).

suc·ceed /səkˈsēd/ ▶ **v. 1** [no obj.] achieve the desired aim or result: *a mission which could not possibly succeed* | *he succeeded in winning a pardon.*
2 [with obj.] take over a throne, inheritance, office, or other position from: *he would succeed Hawke as prime minister.* ■ [no obj.] become the new rightful holder of an inheritance, office, title, or property: *he succeeded to his father's kingdom.* ■ come after and take the place of: *her embarrassment was succeeded by fear.*
– PHRASES **nothing succeeds like success** proverb success leads to opportunities for further and greater successes.
– DERIVATIVES **suc·ceed·er** n. (archaic).
– ORIGIN late Middle English: from Old French *succeder* or Latin *succedere* 'come close after,' from *sub-* 'close to' + *cedere* 'go.'

suc·ceed·ing /səkˈsēdiNG/ ▶ **adj.** [attrib.] coming after something in time; subsequent: *over the succeeding decades, recording equipment got cheaper.*

suc·cen·tor /səkˈsen(t)ər/ ▶ **n.** a precentor's deputy in some cathedrals.
– ORIGIN early 17th cent.: from late Latin, from Latin *succinere* 'sing to, chime in,' from *sub-* 'subordinately' + *canere* 'sing.'

suc·cès de scan·dale /so͞okˌsä də ˌskänˈdäl/ ▶ **n.** a success due to notoriety or a thing's scandalous nature.
– ORIGIN French, literally 'success of scandal.'

suc·cès d'es·time /so͞okˌsä desˈtēm/ ▶ **n.** (pl. **same**) a success through critical appreciation, as opposed to popularity or commercial gain.
– ORIGIN French, literally 'success of opinion.'

suc·cess /səkˈses/ ▶ **n.** the accomplishment of an aim or purpose: *the president had some success in restoring confidence.* ■ the attainment of popularity or profit: *the success of his play.* ■ a person or thing that achieves desired aims or attains prosperity: *I must make a success of my business.* ■ archaic the outcome of an undertaking, specified as achieving or failing to achieve its aims: *the good or ill success of their maritime enterprises.*
– ORIGIN mid 16th cent.: from Latin *successus*, from the verb *succedere* 'come close after' (see **SUCCEED**).

suc·cess·ful /səkˈsesfəl/ ▶ **adj.** accomplishing an aim or purpose: *a successful attack on the town.* ■ having achieved popularity, profit, or distinction: *a successful actor.*
– DERIVATIVES **suc·cess·ful·ly** adv., **suc·cess·ful·ness** n.

suc·ces·sion /səkˈseSHən/ ▶ **n. 1** a number of people or things sharing a specified characteristic and following one after the other: *she had been secretary to a succession of board directors.* ■ Geology a group of strata representing a single chronological sequence.
2 the action or process of inheriting a title, office, property, etc.: *the new king was already elderly at the time of his succession.* ■ the right or sequence of inheriting a position, title, etc.: *the succession to the Crown was disputed.* ■ Ecology the process by which a plant or animal community successively gives way to another until a stable climax is reached. Compare with **SERE**[2].
– PHRASES **in quick** (or **rapid**) **succession** following one another at short intervals. **in succession** following one after the other without interruption: *she won the race for the second year in succession.* **in succession to** inheriting or elected to the place of: *he is not first in succession to the presidency.* **settle the succession** determine who shall succeed someone.
– DERIVATIVES **suc·ces·sion·al** /-SHənl/ adj.
– ORIGIN Middle English (denoting legal transmission of an estate or the throne to another, also in the sense 'successors, heirs'): from Old French, or from Latin *successio(n-)*, from the verb *succedere* (see **SUCCEED**). The term in ecology dates from the mid 19th cent.

Suc·ces·sion, Act of (in English history) each of three Acts of Parliament passed during the reign of Henry VIII regarding the succession of his children.

> The first (1534) declared Henry's marriage to Catherine of Aragon to be invalid, fixing the succession on any child born to Henry's new wife Anne Boleyn. The second (1536) canceled this, asserting the rights of Jane Seymour and her issue, while the third (1544) determined the order of succession of Henry's three children, the future Edward VI, Mary I, and Elizabeth I.

suc·ces·sive /səkˈsesiv/ ▶ **adj.** [attrib.] following one another or following others: *they were looking for their fifth successive win.*
– DERIVATIVES **suc·ces·sive·ly** adv., **suc·ces·sive·ness** n.
– ORIGIN late Middle English: from medieval Latin *successivus*, from *success-* 'followed closely,' from the verb *succedere* (see **SUCCEED**).

suc·ces·sor /səkˈsesər/ ▶ **n.** a person or thing that succeeds another: *Schoenberg saw himself as a natural successor to the German romantic school.*

suc·cess sto·ry ▶ **n.** informal a successful person or thing.

suc·cinct /sə(k)ˈsiNG(k)t/ ▶ **adj.** (esp. of something written or spoken) briefly and clearly expressed: *use short, succinct sentences.*
– DERIVATIVES **suc·cinct·ly** adv., **suc·cinct·ness** n.
– ORIGIN late Middle English (in the sense 'encircled'): from Latin *succinctus* 'tucked up,' past participle of *succingere*, from *sub-* 'from below' + *cingere* 'gird.'

suc·cin·ic ac·id /səkˌsinik/ ▶ **n.** Biochemistry a crystalline organic acid which occurs in living tissue as an intermediate in glucose metabolism. ● Chem. formula: $HOOC(CH_2)_2COOH$.
– DERIVATIVES **suc·ci·nate** /ˈsəksəˌnāt/ n.
– ORIGIN late 18th cent.: *succinic* from French *succinique*, from Latin *succinum* 'amber' (from which it was first derived).

suc·ci·nyl·cho·line /ˌsəksənlˈkōlēn/ ▶ **n.** Medicine a synthetic compound used as a short-acting muscle relaxant and local anesthetic. It is an ester of choline with succinic acid.

suc·cor /ˈsəkər/ (Brit. **succour**) ▶ **n.** assistance and support in times of hardship and distress. ■ (**succors**) archaic reinforcements of troops.
▶ **v.** [with obj.] give assistance or aid to: *prisoners of war were liberated and succored.*
– DERIVATIVES **suc·cor·less** adj.
– ORIGIN Middle English: via Old French from medieval Latin *succursus*, from Latin *succurrere* 'run to the help of,' from *sub-* 'from below' + *currere* 'run.'

suc·co·ry /ˈsəkərē/ ▶ **n.** another term for **CHICORY** (sense 1).
– ORIGIN mid 16th cent.: alteration of obsolete French *cicorée*.

suc·co·tash /ˈsəkəˌtaSH/ ▶ **n.** a dish of corn and lima beans cooked together.
– ORIGIN mid 18th cent.: from Narragansett *msíckquatash* (plural).

Suc·coth /so͞oˈkōt, ˈso͞okəs/ (also **Sukkot, Sukkoth**) ▶ **n.** a major Jewish festival held in the autumn (beginning on the 15th day of Tishri) to commemorate the sheltering of the Israelites in the wilderness. Also called **FEAST OF TABERNACLES**. See also **SUCCAH**.
– ORIGIN from Hebrew *sukkōt*, plural of *sukkāh* 'thicket, hut.'

suc·cour ▶ **n. & v.** British spelling of **SUCCOR**.

suc·cu·bous /ˈsəkyəbəs/ ▶ **adj.** Botany (of a liverwort) having leaves obliquely inserted on the stem so that their upper edges are overlapped by the lower edges of the leaves above. Often contrasted with **INCUBOUS**.
– ORIGIN mid 19th cent.: from late Latin *succubare* 'lie under' + **-OUS**.

suc·cu·bus /ˈsəkyəbəs/ ▶ **n.** (pl. **succubi** /-ˌbī/) a female demon believed to have sexual intercourse with sleeping men.
– ORIGIN late Middle English: from medieval Latin *succubus* 'prostitute,' from *succubare*, from *sub-* 'under' + *cubare* 'to lie.'

suc·cu·lent /ˈsəkyələnt/ ▶ **adj.** (of food) tender, juicy, and tasty. ■ Botany (of a plant, esp. a xerophyte) having thick fleshy leaves or stems adapted to storing water.
▶ **n.** Botany a succulent plant.
– DERIVATIVES **suc·cu·lence** n., **suc·cu·lent·ly** adv.
– ORIGIN early 17th cent.: from Latin *succulentus*, from *succus* 'juice.'

suc·cumb /səˈkəm/ ▶ **v.** [no obj.] fail to resist (pressure, temptation, or some other negative force): *he has become the latest to succumb to the strain.* ■ die from the effect of a disease or injury.
– ORIGIN late 15th cent. (in the sense 'bring low, overwhelm'): from Old French *succomber* or Latin *succumbere*, from *sub-* 'under' + a verb related to *cubare* 'to lie.'

suc·cur·sal /səˈkərsəl/ ▶ **adj.** (of a religious establishment such as a monastery) subsidiary to a principal establishment.

S

– ORIGIN mid 19th cent.: from French *succursale*, from medieval Latin *succursus*, from the verb *succurrere* (see SUCCOR).

suc·cuss /sə'kəs/ ▶ **v.** [with obj.] (in preparing homeopathic remedies) shake (a solution) vigorously.
– DERIVATIVES **suc·cus·sion** /-'kəSHən/ **n.**
– ORIGIN mid 19th cent.: from Latin *succuss-* 'shaken,' from the verb *succutere*, from *sub-* 'away' + *quatere* 'to shake.'

such /səCH/ ▶ **determiner, predeterminer, & pron. 1** of the type previously mentioned: [as determiner] *I have been involved in many such courses* | [as predeterminer] *I longed to find a kindred spirit, and in him I thought I had found such a person* | [as pronoun] *we were second-class citizens and they treated us as such.*
2 (**such —— as/that**) of the type about to be mentioned: [as determiner] *there is no such thing as a free lunch* | [as predeterminer] *the farm is organized in such a way that it can be run by two adults* | [as pronoun] *the wound was such that I had to have stitches.*
3 to so high a degree; so great (often used to emphasize a quality): [as determiner] *this material is of* ***such*** *importance* ***that*** *it has a powerful bearing on the case* | [as predeterminer] *autumn's such a beautiful season* | [as pronoun] ***such*** *is the elegance of his typeface* ***that*** *it is still a favorite of designers.*
– PHRASES **and such** and similar things: *he had activities like the scouts and Sunday school and such.* **as such** [often with negative] in the exact sense of the word: *it is possible to stay overnight here although there is no guest house as such.* **such and such** (or **such-and-such**) used to refer vaguely to a person or thing that does not need to be specified: *they'll want to know what actor played such-and-such a character.* **such as 1** for example: *wildflowers such as daisies and red clover.* **2** of a kind that; like: *an event such as we've shared.* **such as it is** (or **they are**) what little there is; for what it's worth: *the law, such as it is, will be respected.* **such a one** such a person or thing: *what was the reward for such a one as Fox?* **such that** to the extent that: *the linking of sentences such that they constitute a narrative.*
– ORIGIN Old English *swilc, swylc*; related to Dutch *zulk*, German *solch*, from the Germanic bases of SO[1] and ALIKE.

such·like /'səCH,līk/ ▶ **pron.** things of the type mentioned: *carpets, old chairs, tables, and suchlike.*
▶ **determiner** of the type mentioned: *food, drink, clothing, and suchlike provisions.*

suck /sək/ ▶ **v. 1** [with obj.] draw into the mouth by contracting the muscles of the lip and mouth to make a partial vacuum: *they suck mint juleps through straws.* ■ hold (something) in the mouth and draw at it by contracting the lip and cheek muscles: *she sucked a mint* | [no obj.] *the child* ***sucked on*** *her thumb.* ■ draw milk, juice, or other fluid from (something) into the mouth or by suction: *she sucked each segment of the orange carefully.* ■ draw in a specified direction by creating a vacuum: *he was sucked under the surface of the river.* ■ [no obj.] (of a pump) make a gurgling sound as a result of drawing air.
2 involve (someone) in something without their choosing: *I didn't want to be* ***sucked into*** *the role of dutiful daughter.*
3 [no obj.] informal be very bad, disagreeable, or disgusting: *I love your country, but the weather sucks.*
▶ **n.** an act of sucking something. ■ the sound made by water retreating and drawing at something: *the soft suck of the sea against the sand.*
– PHRASES **give suck** archaic give milk from the breast or teat; suckle. **suck someone dry** exhaust someone's physical, material, or emotional resources. **suck it up** informal accept a hardship.
– PHRASAL VERBS **suck someone in** cheat or deceive someone: *we were sucked in by his charm and good looks.* **suck someone off** vulgar slang perform fellatio on someone. **suck up** informal behave obsequiously, esp. for one's own advantage: *he has risen to where he is mainly by* ***sucking up to*** *the president.*
– ORIGIN Old English *sūcan* (verb), from an Indo-European imitative root; related to SOAK.

S

suck·er /'səkər/ ▶ **n. 1** a person or thing that sucks, in particular: ■ a flat or concave organ enabling an animal to cling to a surface by suction. ■ the piston of a suction pump. ■ a pipe through which liquid is drawn by suction.
2 informal a gullible or easily deceived person. ■ (**a sucker for**) a person particularly susceptible to or fond of a specified thing: *I always was a sucker for a good fairy tale.*
3 informal a thing or person not specified by name: *he's one strong sucker.*
4 Botany a shoot springing from the base of a tree or other plant, esp. one arising from the root below ground level at some distance from the main stem or trunk. ■ a side shoot from an axillary bud, as in tomato plants.
5 a freshwater fish with thick lips that are used to suck up food from the bottom, native to North America and Asia. ● Family Catostomidae: many genera and species.
6 informal a lollipop.
▶ **v. 1** [no obj.] Botany (of a plant) produce suckers: *it spread rapidly after being left undisturbed to sucker.*
2 [with obj.] informal fool or trick (someone): *they got suckered into accepting responsibility.*

suck·er·fish /'səkər,fiSH/ ▶ **n.** (pl. **same** or **suckerfishes**) another term for REMORA.

suck·er punch ▶ **n.** an unexpected punch or blow.
▶ **v.** (**sucker-punch**) [with obj.] hit (someone) with such a punch or blow: *Joe sucker-punched him and knocked him out.*

suck·le /'səkəl/ ▶ **v.** [with obj.] feed (a baby or young animal) from the breast or teat: *a mother pig suckling a huge litter.* ■ [no obj.] (of a baby or young animal) feed by sucking the breast or teat: *the infant's biological need to suckle.*
– ORIGIN late Middle English: probably a back-formation from SUCKLING.

suck·ler /'səkələr/ ▶ **n.** an unweaned animal, esp. a calf. ■ a cow used to breed and suckle calves for beef.

suck·ling /'səkliNG/ ▶ **n.** an unweaned child or animal: [as modifier] *roast suckling pig.*
– ORIGIN Middle English: from the verb SUCK + -LING.

suck-up ▶ **n.** informal a person who behaves obsequiously, esp. to earn approval or favoritism.

suck·y /'səkē/ ▶ **adj.** (**suckier, suckiest**) informal disagreeable; unpleasant: *her sucky job.*

su·cral·fate /'so͞okrəl,fāt/ ▶ **n.** Medicine a drug used in the treatment of gastric and duodenal ulcers. It is a complex of aluminum hydroxide and a sulfate derivative of sucrose.
– ORIGIN 1960s: blend of SUCROSE, ALUMINUM, and SULFATE.

su·crase /'so͞o,krās, -,krāz/ ▶ **n.** another term for INVERTASE.

Su·cre[1] /'so͞okrā/ the judicial capital and seat of the judiciary of Bolivia; pop. 274,576 (2009). Located in the Andes, at an altitude of 8,860 feet (2,700 m), it was named Chuquisaca by the Spanish in 1539. It was renamed in 1825 in honor of Antonio José de Sucre.

Su·cre[2] /'so͞o,krā/, Antonio José de (1795–1830), Venezuelan revolutionary and statesman; president of Bolivia 1826–28. He served as Simón Bolívar's chief of staff, liberating Ecuador, Peru, and Bolivia from the Spanish. He was the first president of Bolivia.

su·cre /'so͞o,krā/ ▶ **n.** the basic monetary unit of Ecuador until 2000, equal to 100 centavos.
– ORIGIN named after A. J. de *Sucre* (see SUCRE[2]).

su·crose /'so͞o,krōs/ ▶ **n.** Chemistry a compound that is the chief component of cane or beet sugar. ● A disaccharide containing glucose and fructose units; chem. formula: $C_{12}H_{22}O_{11}$.
– ORIGIN mid 19th cent.: from French *sucre* 'sugar' + -OSE[2].

suc·tion /'səkSHən/ ▶ **n.** the production of a partial vacuum by the removal of air in order to force fluid into a vacant space or procure adhesion.
▶ **v.** [with obj.] remove (something) using suction: *physicians used a tube to suction out the gallstones.*
– ORIGIN early 17th cent.: from late Latin *suctio(n-)*, from Latin *sugere* 'suck.'

suc·tion pump ▶ **n.** a pump for drawing liquid through a pipe into a chamber emptied by a piston.

suc·to·ri·al /,sək'tôrēəl/ ▶ **adj.** chiefly Zoology adapted for sucking (descriptive, for example, of the mouthparts of some insects). ■ (of an animal) having a sucker for feeding or adhering to something.
– DERIVATIVES **suc·to·ri·al·ly adv.**
– ORIGIN mid 19th cent.: from modern Latin *suctorius* (from Latin *sugere* 'suck') + -AL.

Su·dan /so͞o'dan/ (also **the Sudan**) **1** a country in northeastern Africa, south of Egypt, with a coastline on the Red Sea; pop. 41,087,800 (est. 2009); capital, Khartoum; languages, Arabic (official), Dinka, Hausa, and others.

> Under Arab rule from the 13th century, the country was conquered by Egypt in 1820–22. Sudan was separated from its northern neighbor by the Mahdist revolt of 1881–98 and administered after the reconquest of 1898 as an Anglo-Egyptian condominium. It became an independent republic in 1956, but has suffered severely as a result of protracted civil war between the Islamic government in the north and separatist forces in the south and west, in particular the Darfur region.

2 a vast region in North Africa that extends across the width of the continent from the southern edge of the Sahara to the tropical equatorial zone in the south.
– DERIVATIVES **Su·da·nese** /,so͞odn'ēz, -'ēs/ **adj. & n.**
– ORIGIN from Arabic *sūdān*, literally 'country of the blacks.'

su·dan grass /so͞o'dan/ ▶ **n.** a Sudanese sorghum cultivated for fodder in dry regions of the US. ● *Sorghum sudanense*, family Gramineae.

Sud·bur·y /'səd,berē, -b(ə)rē/ a city in central Ontario; pop. 157,857 (2006). It lies at the center of Canada's largest mining region.

sudd /səd/ ▶ **n.** (**the sudd**) an area of floating vegetation in a stretch of the White Nile, thick enough to impede navigation.
– ORIGIN Arabic, literally 'obstruction.'

sud·den /'sədn/ ▶ **adj.** occurring or done quickly and unexpectedly or without warning: *a sudden bright flash.*
▶ **adv.** literary or informal suddenly: *sudden there swooped an eagle downward.*
– PHRASES **all of a sudden** suddenly: *I feel really tired all of a sudden.*
– DERIVATIVES **sud·den·ness n.**
– ORIGIN Middle English: from Anglo-Norman French *sudein*, from an alteration of Latin *subitaneus*, from *subitus* 'sudden.'

sud·den death ▶ **n.** informal a means of deciding the winner in a tied contest, in which play continues and the winner is the first side or player to score: [as modifier] *a sudden-death playoff.*

sud·den in·fant death syn·drome (abbr.: **SIDS**) ▶ **n.** the death of a seemingly healthy baby in its sleep, due to an apparent spontaneous cessation of breathing.

sud·den·ly /'sədn-lē/ ▶ **adv.** quickly and unexpectedly: *the ambassador died suddenly* | [sentence adverb] *suddenly I heard a loud scream.*

sud·den oak death ▶ **n.** a disease of various oaks and other forest trees, sometimes resulting in sudden death as a result of bark cankers that encircle the trunk. ● The infecting organism is the water mold *Phytophthora Ramorum.*

Su·de·ten·land /so͞o'dātn,land, -,länt/ an area in the northwestern part of the Czech Republic, on the border with Germany. Allocated to Czechoslovakia after World War I, it became an object of Nazi expansionist policies and was ceded to Germany as a result of the Munich Agreement of September 1938. In 1945, the area was returned to Czechoslovakia. Czech name **Sudety**.

su·do·ku /so͞o'dōko͞o/ ▶ **n.** a puzzle in which players insert the numbers one to nine into a grid consisting of nine squares subdivided into a further nine smaller squares in such a way that every number appears once in each horizontal line, vertical line, and square.
– ORIGIN 21st cent.: from Japanese *Sūdoku*, from *sū-* (in *sūji* 'number') + *-doku* (in *dokushin* 'single status'), elements of the puzzle's former name.

su·dor·if·er·ous /,so͞odə'rif(ə)rəs/ ▶ **adj.** (of a gland) secreting sweat.
– ORIGIN late 16th cent. (in the sense 'sudorific'): from late Latin *sudorifer* (from Latin *sudor* 'sweat') + -OUS.

su·dor·if·ic /,so͞odə'rifik/ Medicine ▶ **adj.** relating to or causing sweating.
▶ **n.** a drug that induces sweating.
– ORIGIN early 17th cent.: from modern Latin *sudorificus*, from Latin *sudor* 'sweat.'

suds /sədz/ ▶ **plural n.** short for SOAPSUDS. ■ informal beer.
▶ **v.** [with obj.] lather, cover, or wash in soapy water: *Martha sudsed my back.* ■ [no obj.] form suds: *soft baby soap that sudsed.*
– DERIVATIVES **suds·y adj.**
– ORIGIN mid 19th cent.: of uncertain sense development but perhaps originally denoting the flood water of the English Fens; compare with Middle Low German *sudde*, Middle Dutch *sudse* 'marsh, bog'; probably related to SEETHE.

suds·er /'sədzər/ ▶ **n.** informal a soap opera.

sue /so͞o/ ▶ **v.** (**sues, suing, sued**) **1** [with obj.] institute legal proceedings against (a person or institution), typically for redress: *she is to sue the baby's father* | [no obj.] *I* ***sued for*** *breach of contract.*
2 [no obj.] formal appeal formally to a person for something: *the rebels were forced to* ***sue for peace.***
– DERIVATIVES **su·er** /'so͞oər/ **n.**
– ORIGIN Middle English: from Anglo-Norman French *suer*, based on Latin *sequi* 'follow.' Early senses were very similar to those of the verb *follow.*

suede /swād/ ▶ **n.** leather with the flesh side rubbed to make a velvety nap.
– ORIGIN mid 17th cent.: from French (*gants de*) *Suède* '(gloves of) Sweden.'

suede·head /'swād,hed/ ▶ **n.** chiefly Brit. a person, esp. a youth, whose appearance is similar to that of a skinhead but generally characterized by slightly longer hair and neater, more stylish clothes.

su·et /ˈso͞oit/ ▶ **n.** the hard white fat on the kidneys and loins of cattle, sheep, and other animals, used to make foods including puddings, pastry, and mincemeat.
– DERIVATIVES **su·et·y adj.**
– ORIGIN Middle English: from Anglo-Norman French, from the synonymous word *su*, from Latin *sebum* 'tallow.'

Sue·to·ni·us /so͞oəˈtōnēəs, swēˈtō-/ (*c.*69–*c.*150), Roman biographer and historian; full name *Gaius Suetonius Tranquillus*. His surviving works include *Lives of the Caesars*.

Su·ez, Isthmus of /so͞oˈez, ˈso͞oˌez/ an isthmus between the Mediterranean and the Red seas that connects Egypt and Africa to the Sinai Peninsula and Asia. The port of Suez lies in the south, and the isthmus is traversed by the Suez Canal.

Su·ez Ca·nal a shipping canal that connects the Mediterranean Sea at Port Said with the Red Sea. It was constructed between 1859 and 1869 under the direction of Ferdinand de Lesseps. From 1888 it was a neutral zone under British protection; its nationalization by Egypt in 1956 prompted the Suez crisis.

suf. ▶ **abbr.** suffix.

suf- ▶ **prefix** variant spelling of **SUB-** assimilated before *f* (as in *suffocate, suffuse*).

Suff. ▶ **abbr.** ■ Suffolk. ■ suffragan.

suff. ▶ **abbr.** ■ sufficient. ■ suffix.

suf·fer /ˈsəfər/ ▶ **v.** [with obj.] **1** experience or be subjected to (something bad or unpleasant): *he'd suffered intense pain* | [no obj.] *he'd suffered a great deal since his arrest.* ■ [no obj.] (**suffer from**) be affected by or subject to (an illness or ailment): *his daughter suffered from agoraphobia.* ■ [no obj.] become or appear worse in quality: *his relationship with Anne did suffer.* ■ [no obj.] archaic undergo martyrdom or execution.
2 dated tolerate: *France will no longer suffer the existing government.* ■ allow (someone) to do something: [with obj. and infinitive] *my conscience would not suffer me to accept any more.*
– PHRASES **not suffer fools gladly** be impatient or intolerant toward people one regards as foolish or unintelligent. [with biblical allusion to 2 Cor. 11–19.]
– DERIVATIVES **suf·fer·a·ble** /ˈsəf(ə)rəbəl/ **adj.**, **suf·fer·er** /ˈsəf(ə)rər/ **n.** (sense 1).
– ORIGIN Middle English: from Anglo-Norman French *suffrir*, from Latin *sufferre*, from *sub-* 'from below' + *ferre* 'to bear.'

suf·fer·ance /ˈsəf(ə)rəns/ ▶ **n. 1** absence of objection rather than genuine approval; toleration: *Charles was only here* ***on sufferance.*** ■ Law the condition of the holder of an estate who continues to hold it after the title has ceased, without the express permission of the owner: *an estate at sufferance.* ■ archaic patient endurance.
2 archaic the suffering or undergoing of something bad or unpleasant.
– ORIGIN Middle English (sense 2): from Anglo-Norman French *suffraunce*, from late Latin *sufferentia*, from *sufferre* (see **SUFFER**).

suf·fer·ing /ˈsəf(ə)riNG/ ▶ **n.** the state of undergoing pain, distress, or hardship: *weapons that cause unnecessary suffering* | *his disregard for the sufferings of his fellow countrymen.*

suf·fice /səˈfīs/ ▶ **v.** [no obj.] be enough or adequate: *a quick look should suffice* | [with infinitive] *two examples should suffice to prove the contention.* ■ [with obj.] meet the needs of: *simple mediocrity cannot suffice them.*
– PHRASES **suffice (it) to say** used to indicate that one is saying enough to make one's meaning clear while withholding something for reasons of discretion or brevity: *suffice it to say that they were not considered suitable for this project.*
– ORIGIN Middle English: from Old French *suffis-*, stem of *suffire*, from Latin *sufficere* 'put under, meet the need of,' from *sub-* 'under' + *facere* 'make.'

suf·fi·cien·cy /səˈfiSHənsē/ ▶ **n.** (pl. **sufficiencies**) the condition or quality of being adequate or sufficient. ■ [in sing.] an adequate amount of something, esp. of something essential: ***a sufficiency of*** *good food.* ■ archaic self-sufficiency or independence of character, esp. of an arrogant or imperious sort.
– ORIGIN late 15th cent. (denoting sufficient means or wealth): from late Latin *sufficientia*, from the verb *sufficere* (see **SUFFICE**).

suf·fi·cient /səˈfiSHənt/ ▶ **adj. & determiner** enough; adequate: [as adj.] *a small income that was sufficient for her needs* | [as determiner] *they had sufficient resources to survive.*
– DERIVATIVES **suf·fi·cient·ly adv.**
– ORIGIN Middle English (in the sense 'legally satisfactory'): from Old French, or from Latin *sufficient-* 'meeting the need of' (see **SUFFICE**).

suf·fix ▶ **n.** /ˈsəfiks/ a morpheme added at the end of a word to form a derivative, e.g., *-ation, -fy, -ing, -itis*.
▶ **v.** /ˈsəfiks, səˈfiks/ [with obj.] append, esp. as a suffix.
– DERIVATIVES **suf·fix·a·tion** /ˌsəfikˈsāSHən/ **n.**
– ORIGIN late 18th cent. (as a noun): from modern Latin *suffixum*, neuter past participle (used as a noun) of Latin *suffigere*, from *sub-* 'subordinately' + *figere* 'fasten.'

suf·fo·cate /ˈsəfəˌkāt/ ▶ **v.** die or cause to die from lack of air or inability to breathe: [no obj.] *ten detainees suffocated in an airless police cell* | [with obj.] *she was suffocated by the fumes.* ■ have or cause to have difficulty in breathing: [no obj.] *he was suffocating, his head jammed up against the back of the sofa* | [with obj.] *you're suffocating me—I can scarcely breathe* | (as adj. **suffocating**) *the suffocating heat.* ■ feel or cause to feel trapped and oppressed: (as adj. **suffocated**) *I felt suffocated by my marriage.*
– DERIVATIVES **suf·fo·cat·ing·ly adv.**, **suf·fo·ca·tion** /ˌsəfəˈkāSHən/ **n.**
– ORIGIN late 15th cent.: from Latin *suffocat-* 'stifled,' from the verb *suffocare*, from *sub-* 'below' + *fauces* 'throat.'

Suf·folk¹ /ˈsəfək/ **1** a county in eastern England, on the coast of East Anglia; county town, Ipswich.
2 a commercial and agricultural city in southern Virginia, in the Hampton Roads area; pop. 82,302 (est. 2008).

Suf·folk² (also **Suffolk sheep**) ▶ **n.** a sheep of a large black-faced breed with a short fleece.

Suf·folk Coun·ty a suburban, agricultural, and resort county in southeastern New York, on the eastern end of Long Island; pop. 1,512,224 (est. 2008).

suf·fra·gan /ˈsəfrəgən/ (also **suffragan bishop** or **bishop suffragan**) ▶ **n.** a bishop appointed to help a diocesan bishop. ■ a bishop in relation to his archbishop or metropolitan.
– ORIGIN late Middle English: from Anglo-Norman French and Old French, representing medieval Latin *suffraganeus* 'assistant (bishop),' from Latin *suffragium* (see **SUFFRAGE**).

suf·frage /ˈsəfrij/ ▶ **n. 1** the right to vote in political elections. ■ archaic a vote given in assent to a proposal or in favor of the election of a particular person.
2 (usu. **suffrages**) a series of intercessory prayers or petitions.
– ORIGIN late Middle English (in the sense 'intercessory prayers,' also 'assistance'): from Latin *suffragium*, reinforced by French *suffrage*. The modern sense of 'right to vote' was originally US (dating from the late 18th cent).

suf·fra·gette /ˌsəfrəˈjet/ ▶ **n.** historical a woman seeking the right to vote through organized protest.

suf·fra·gist /ˈsəfrəjist/ ▶ **n.** chiefly historical a person advocating the extension of suffrage, esp. to women.
– DERIVATIVES **suf·fra·gism** /-jizəm/ **n.**

suf·fuse /səˈfyo͞oz/ ▶ **v.** [with obj.] gradually spread through or over: *her cheeks were suffused with color* | *the first half of the poem is suffused with idealism.*
– DERIVATIVES **suf·fu·sion** /-ˈfyo͞oZHən/ **n.**, **suf·fu·sive** /-ˈfyo͞osiv/ **adj.**
– ORIGIN late 16th cent.: from Latin *suffus-* 'poured into,' from *sub-* 'below, from below' + *fundere* 'pour.'

Su·fi /ˈso͞ofē/ ▶ **n.** (pl. **Sufis**) a Muslim ascetic and mystic.
– DERIVATIVES **Su·fic** /-fik/ **adj.**
– ORIGIN mid 17th cent.: from Arabic *ṣūfī*, perhaps from *ṣūf* 'wool' (referring to the woolen garment worn).

Su·fism /ˈso͞oˌfizəm/ ▶ **n.** the mystical system of the Sufis.

> Sufism is the esoteric dimension of the Islamic faith, the spiritual path to mystical union with God. It is influenced by other faiths, such as Buddhism, and reached its peak in the 13th century. There are many Sufi orders, the best known being the dervishes.

sug /səg/ ▶ **v.** (**sugs, sugging, sugged**) [no obj.] informal, chiefly Brit. sell or attempt to sell a product under the guise of conducting market research: *a market researcher claims the firm is sugging.*
– ORIGIN 1980s: acronym from *sell under the guise*.

sug- ▶ **prefix** variant spelling of **SUB-**. assimilated before *g* (as in *suggest*).

sug·ar /ˈSHo͝ogər/ ▶ **n. 1** a sweet crystalline substance obtained from various plants, esp. sugar cane and sugar beet, consisting essentially of sucrose, and used as a sweetener in food and drink. ■ a lump or teaspoonful of this, used to sweeten tea or coffee: *I'll have mine black with two sugars.* ■ informal used as a term of endearment or an affectionate form of address: *what's wrong, sugar?* ■ [as exclamation] informal used as a euphemism for "shit." ■ informal a psychoactive drug in the form of white powder, esp. heroin or cocaine.
2 Biochemistry any of the class of soluble, crystalline, typically sweet-tasting carbohydrates found in living tissues and exemplified by glucose and sucrose.
▶ **v.** [with obj.] **1** sweeten, sprinkle, or coat with sugar: *she absentmindedly sugared her tea* | (as adj. **sugared**) *sugared almonds.*
2 make more agreeable or palatable: *the novel was preachy but sugared heavily with jokes.*
– PHRASES **sugar the pill** see **PILL¹**.
– DERIVATIVES **sug·ar·less adj.**
– ORIGIN Middle English: from Old French *sukere*, from Italian *zucchero*, probably via medieval Latin from Arabic *sukkar*.

sug·ar ap·ple ▶ **n.** another term for **SWEETSOP**.

sug·ar beet ▶ **n.** beet of a variety from which sugar is extracted. It provides an important alternative sugar source to cane, and the pulp that remains after processing is used as feed for livestock.

sug·ar·bird /ˈSHo͝ogərˌbərd/ (also **sugar bird**) ▶ **n. 1** a southern African songbird with a long fine bill and very long tail, feeding on nectar and insects. ● Genus *Promerops*, family Promeropidae (or Meliphagidae): two species.
2 another term for **BANANAQUIT**.

sug·ar bush (also **sugarbush** /ˈSHo͝ogərˌbo͝oSH/) ▶ **n.** a plantation of sugar maples.

sug·ar can·dy ▶ **n.** another term for **CANDY**, esp. hard candy.

sug·ar cane (also **sugarcane** /ˈSHo͝ogərˌkān/) ▶ **n.** a perennial tropical grass with tall stout jointed stems from which sugar is extracted. The fibrous residue can be used as fuel, in fiberboard, and for a number of other purposes. ● Genus *Saccharum*, family Gramineae: several species, in particular *S. officinarum* and its hybrids.

sug·ar·coat /ˈSHo͝ogərˌkōt/ ▶ **v.** [with obj.] coat (an item of food) with sugar: (as adj. **sugarcoated**) *sugarcoated almonds.* ■ make superficially attractive or acceptable: *you won't see him sugarcoat the truth.* ■ make excessively sentimental: *the filmmakers' proficiency is overpowered by their tendency to sugarcoat the material.*

sug·ar cube ▶ **n.** a small cube of compacted sugar used esp. for sweetening hot drinks.

sug·ar dad·dy ▶ **n.** informal a rich older man who lavishes gifts on a young woman in return for her company or sexual favors.

sug·ar glid·er ▶ **n.** a flying phalanger that feeds on wattle gum and eucalyptus sap, native to Australia, New Guinea, and Tasmania. ● *Petaurus breviceps*, family Petauridae.

sug·ar·ing /ˈSHo͝ogəriNG/ ▶ **n. 1** (also **sugaring off**) the boiling down of maple sap until it thickens into syrup or crystallizes into sugar.
2 a method of removing unwanted hair by applying a mixture of lemon juice, sugar, and water to the skin and then peeling it off together with the hair.

sug·ar·loaf /ˈSHo͝ogərˌlōf/ ▶ **n.** a conical molded mass of sugar (now used chiefly in similes and metaphors to describe the shape of other objects): [as modifier] *a sugarloaf hat.*

Sug·ar Loaf Moun·tain a rocky peak in Brazil, northeast of Rio de Janeiro's Copacabana Beach. It rises to a height of 1,296 feet (390 m).

sug·ar ma·ple ▶ **n.** a North American maple, from the sap of which maple sugar and maple syrup are made. Also called **ROCK MAPLE**. ● *Acer saccharum*, family Aceraceae.

sug·ar of lead /led/ ▶ **n.** Chemistry, dated lead acetate, a soluble white crystalline salt. ● Chem. formula: $Pb(CH_3CO_2)_2$.
– ORIGIN mid 17th cent.: so named for its sweet taste.

sug·ar pine ▶ **n.** a tall pine tree, the heartwood of which exudes a sweet substance, hence its name. Found primarily in California and Oregon, sugar pines have very long cones, some reaching 26 inches in length. ● *Pinus lambertiana*.

sug·ar·plum /ˈSHo͝ogərˌpləm/ ▶ **n.** a small round candy of flavored boiled sugar.

sug·ar snap (also **sugar snap pea**) ▶ **n.** a snow pea, esp. of a variety with distinctively thick and rounded pods.

sug·ar·y /ˈSHo͝ogərē/ ▶ **adj.** containing much sugar: *energy-restoring, sugary drinks.* ■ resembling or

coated in sugar: *a sugary texture.* ■ excessively sentimental: *sugary romance.*
– DERIVATIVES **sug·ar·i·ness** n.

sug·gest /sə(g)ˈjest/ ▶ v. [reporting verb] put forward for consideration: [with clause] *I suggest that we wait a day or two* | [with direct speech] *"Maybe you ought to get an expert," she suggested* | [with obj.] *Ruth suggested a vacation.* ■ [with obj.] cause one to think that (something) exists or is the case: *finds of lead coffins suggested a cemetery north of the river* | [with clause] *the temperature wasn't as tropical as the bright sunlight may have suggested.* ■ state or express indirectly: [with clause] *are you suggesting that I should ignore her?* | [with obj.] *the seduction scenes suggest his guilt and her loneliness.* ■ [with obj.] evoke: *the theatrical interpretation of weather and water almost suggests El Greco.* ■ (**suggest itself**) (of an idea) come into one's mind.
– DERIVATIVES **sug·gest·er** n.
– ORIGIN early 16th cent.: from Latin *suggest-* 'suggested, prompted,' from the verb *suggerere,* from *sub-* 'from below' + *gerere* 'bring.'

sug·gest·i·ble /sə(g)ˈjestəbəl/ ▶ adj. open to suggestion; easily swayed: *a suggestible client would comply.*
– DERIVATIVES **sug·gest·i·bil·i·ty** /-ˌjestəˈbilitē/ n.

sug·ges·tion /sə(g)ˈjesCHən/ ▶ n. an idea or plan put forward for consideration. ■ the action of doing this: ***at my suggestion**, the museum held an exhibition of his work.* ■ something that implies or indicates a certain fact or situation: *there is no suggestion that he was involved in any wrongdoing.* ■ a slight trace or indication of something: *there was a suggestion of a smile on his lips.* ■ the action or process of calling up an idea or thought in someone's mind by associating it with other things: *the power of suggestion.* ■ Psychology the influencing of a person to accept an idea, belief, or impulse uncritically, esp. as a technique in hypnosis or other therapies. ■ Psychology a belief or impulse of this type.
– ORIGIN Middle English (in the sense 'an incitement to evil'): via Old French from Latin *suggestio(n-),* from the verb *suggerere* (see SUGGEST).

sug·ges·tive /sə(g)ˈjestiv/ ▶ adj. tending to suggest an idea: *there were various suggestive pieces of evidence.* ■ indicative or evocative: *flavors **suggestive of** coffee and blackberry.* ■ making someone think of sex and sexual relationships: *a suggestive remark.*
– DERIVATIVES **sug·ges·tive·ly** adv., **sug·ges·tive·ness** n.

suh /sə(r)/ ▶ n. nonstandard spelling of SIR, used in representing chiefly southern US, black, or British dialect: *my dear suh, we are shocked by your candor* | *I'm not gonna do it, no suh.*

Su·har·to /so͞oˈhärtō/, Raden (1921–2008), Indonesian president 1968–98. As president, he restored political, social, and economic stability to Indonesia, but after the economy began to falter in 1997 and opposition to his authoritarian rule spread in 1998, he resigned from office.

Sui /swā/ a dynasty that ruled in China AD 581–618 and reunified the country.

su·i·cid·al /ˌso͞oiˈsīdl/ ▶ adj. deeply unhappy or depressed and likely to commit suicide: *far from being suicidal, he was clearly enjoying life.* ■ relating to or likely to lead to suicide: *I began to take her suicidal tendencies seriously.* ■ likely to have a disastrously damaging effect on oneself or one's interests: *a suicidal career move.*
– DERIVATIVES **su·i·cid·al·i·ty** n., **su·i·cid·al·ly** adv.

su·i·cide /ˈso͞oiˌsīd/ ▶ n. the action of killing oneself intentionally: *he **committed suicide** at the age of forty* | *drug-related suicides.* ■ a person who does this. ■ a course of action that is disastrously damaging to oneself or one's own interests: *it would be political suicide to restrict criteria for unemployment benefits.* ■ [as modifier] relating to or denoting a violent act or attack carried out by a person who does not expect to survive it: *a suicide bombing.*
▶ v. [no obj.] intentionally kill oneself: *he leaves the service and then suicides.*
– ORIGIN mid 17th cent.: from modern Latin *suicida* 'act of suicide,' *suicidium* 'person who commits suicide,' from Latin *sui* 'of oneself' + *caedere* 'kill.'

su·i·cide gene ▶ n. an introduced gene that causes a tumor cell to produce an enzyme that will attract a drug lethal to the tumor.

su·i·cide pact ▶ n. an agreement between two or more people to commit suicide together.

su·i ge·ne·ris /ˌso͞oˌī ˈjenərəs, ˌso͞oē/ ▶ adj. unique: *the sui generis nature of animals.*
– ORIGIN Latin, literally 'of its own kind.'

su·i ju·ris /ˌso͞oˌī ˈjo͝oris, ˌso͞oē/ ▶ adj. Law of age; independent: *the beneficiaries are all sui juris.*
– ORIGIN Latin, literally 'of one's own right.'

su·int /ˈso͞oənt, swint/ ▶ n. a natural greasy substance in sheep's wool, from which lanolin is obtained.
– ORIGIN late 18th cent.: from French, from *suer* 'sweat.'

Suisse /swēs/ French name for **SWITZERLAND**.

suit /so͞ot/ ▶ n. **1** a set of outer clothes made of the same fabric and designed to be worn together, typically consisting of a jacket and trousers or a jacket and skirt. ■ a set of clothes to be worn on a particular occasion or for a particular activity: *a jogging suit.* ■ a complete set of pieces of armor for covering the whole body. ■ a complete set of sails required for a ship or for a set of spars. ■ (usu. **suits**) informal an executive in a business or organization, typically one regarded as exercising influence in an impersonal way: *maybe now the suits in Washington will listen.*
2 any of the sets distinguished by their pictorial symbols into which a deck of playing cards is divided, in conventional decks comprising spades, hearts, diamonds, and clubs.
3 short for LAWSUIT. ■ the process of trying to win a woman's affection, typically with a view to marriage: *he could not compete with John's charms in Marian's eyes and his suit came to nothing.* ■ literary a petition or entreaty made to a person in authority.
▶ v. **1** [with obj.] be convenient for or acceptable to: *he lied whenever it suited him* | [no obj.] *the apartment has two bedrooms—if it suits, you can have one of them.* ■ (**suit oneself**) [often in imperative] act entirely according to one's own wishes (often used to express the speaker's annoyance): *"I'm not going to help you." "Suit yourself."* ■ go well with or enhance the features, figure, or character of (someone): *the dress didn't suit her.* ■ (**suit something to**) archaic adapt or make appropriate for (something): *they took care to suit their answers to the questions put to them.*
2 [no obj.] put on clothes, typically for a particular activity: *I **suited up** and entered the water.*
– PHRASES **follow suit** see FOLLOW.
– ORIGIN Middle English: from Anglo-Norman French *siwte,* from a feminine past participle of a Romance verb based on Latin *sequi* 'follow.' Early senses included 'attendance at a court' and 'legal process'; sense 1 of the noun and sense 2 of the noun derive from an earlier meaning 'set of things to be used together.' The verb sense 'make appropriate' dates from the late 16th cent.

suit·a·ble /ˈso͞otəbəl/ ▶ adj. right or appropriate for a particular person, purpose, or situation: *these toys are not **suitable for** children under five.*
– DERIVATIVES **suit·a·bil·i·ty** /ˌso͞otəˈbilitē/ n., **suit·a·ble·ness** n., **suit·a·bly** /-blē/ adv.
– ORIGIN late 16th cent.: from the verb SUIT, on the pattern of *agreeable.*

suit·case /ˈso͞otˌkās/ ▶ n. a case with a handle and a hinged lid, used for carrying clothes and other personal possessions.
– DERIVATIVES **suit·case·ful** /-ˌfo͝ol/ n. (pl. **suitcasefuls**).

suite /swēt/ ▶ n. **1** a set of things belonging together, in particular: ■ a set of rooms designated for one person's or family's use or for a particular purpose. ■ a set of furniture of the same design. ■ Music a set of instrumental compositions, originally in dance style, to be played in succession. ■ Music a set of selected pieces from an opera or musical, arranged to be played as one instrumental work. ■ Computing a set of programs with a uniform design and the ability to share data. ■ Geology a group of minerals, rocks, or fossils occurring together and characteristic of a location or period.
2 a group of people in attendance on a monarch or other person of high rank.
– ORIGIN late 17th cent.: from French, from Anglo-Norman French *siwte* (see SUIT).

suit·ed /ˈso͞otid/ ▶ adj. **1** [predic.] right or appropriate for a particular person, purpose, or situation: *the task is ideally **suited to** a computer.*
2 [in combination] wearing a suit of clothes of a specified type, fabric, or color: *a dark-suited man* | *sober-suited lawyers.*

suit·ing /ˈso͞otiNG/ ▶ n. fabric of a suitable quality for making suits, trousers, jackets, and skirts. ■ suits collectively.

suit·or /ˈso͞otər/ ▶ n. a man who pursues a relationship with a particular woman, with a view to marriage. ■ a prospective buyer of a business or corporation.
– ORIGIN late Middle English (in the sense 'member of a retinue'): from Anglo-Norman French *seutor,* from Latin *secutor,* from *sequi* 'follow.'

suk /so͞ok/ (also **sukh**) ▶ n. variant spelling of SOUK.

Su·kar·no /so͞oˈkärnō/, Achmad (1901–70), Indonesian statesman; president 1945–67. He led the struggle for independence, which was formally granted in 1949, but lost power in the 1960s after having been implicated in the abortive communist coup of 1965.

su·ki·ya·ki /so͞okēˈyäkē/ ▶ n. a Japanese dish of sliced meat, esp. beef, fried rapidly with vegetables and sauce.
– ORIGIN Japanese.

suk·kah ▶ n. variant spelling of SUCCAH.

Sukkot (also **Sukkoth**) ▶ n. variant form of SUCCOTH.

Suk·kur /ˈso͝okər/ a city in southeastern Pakistan, on the Indus River; pop. 476,800 (est. 2009). Nearby is the Sukkur Barrage, a dam constructed across the Indus that directs water through irrigation channels to a large area of the Indus valley.

Su·la·we·si /ˌso͞oləˈwāsē/ a mountainous island in the Greater Sunda group in Indonesia, east of Borneo; chief town, Ujung Pandang. Former name **CELEBES**.

Su·lay·ma·ni·yah /ˌso͞olīmäˈnē(y)ə/ (also **Sulaimaniya**) (Full name **As Sulaymaniyah**) a town in northeastern Iraq, in the mountainous region of southern Kurdistan; pop. 759,500 (est. 2009). It is the capital of a Kurdish governorate of the same name.

sul·cate /ˈsəlˌkāt/ ▶ adj. Botany & Zoology marked with parallel grooves.
– ORIGIN mid 18th cent.: from Latin *sulcatus* 'furrowed,' past participle of *sulcare.*

sul·cus /ˈsəlkəs/ ▶ n. (pl. **sulci** /ˈsəlˌsī, -ˌsē/) Anatomy a groove or furrow, esp. one on the surface of the brain.
– ORIGIN mid 17th cent.: from Latin, 'furrow, wrinkle.'

Su·lei·man I /ˌso͞oläˈmän/ (also **Soliman** or **Solyman**) (c.1494–1566), sultan of the Ottoman Empire 1520–66; also known as **Suleiman the Magnificent** or **Suleiman the Lawgiver**. The Ottoman Empire reached its fullest extent under his rule.

sul·fa /ˈsəlfə/ (chiefly Brit. also **sulpha**) ▶ n. [usu. as modifier] the sulfonamide family of drugs: *a succession of life-saving sulfa drugs.*
– ORIGIN 1940s: abbreviation (see SULFA-).

sulfa- (chiefly Brit. also **sulph-**) ▶ comb. form in names of drugs derived from sulfanilamide.
– ORIGIN abbreviation of SULFANILAMIDE.

sul·fa·di·a·zine /ˌsəlfəˈdīəˌzēn/ (chiefly Brit. also **sulphadiazine**) ▶ n. Medicine a sulfonamide antibiotic used to treat meningococcal meningitis.

sul·fa·dim·i·dine /ˌsəlfəˈdīmiˌdēn/ (chiefly Brit. also **sulphadimidine**) ▶ n. Medicine a sulfonamide antibiotic used chiefly to treat human urinary infections and to control respiratory disease in pigs.
– ORIGIN mid 20th cent.: from SULFA- + DI-[1] + PYRIMIDINE.

sul·fa·meth·ox·a·zole /ˌsəlfəmeˈTHäksəˌzōl/ (chiefly Brit. also **sulphamethoxazole**) ▶ n. Medicine a sulfonamide antibiotic used to treat respiratory and urinary tract infections, and as a component of the preparation co-trimoxazole.

sul·fa·mic ac·id /səlˈfamik/ (chiefly Brit. also **sulphamic acid**) ▶ n. Chemistry a strongly acid crystalline compound used in cleaning agents and to make weed killers. ● Chem. formula: $HOSO_2NH_2$.
– DERIVATIVES **sul·fa·mate** /ˈsəlfəˌmāt/ n.
– ORIGIN mid 19th cent.: *sulfamic* from SULFUR + AMIDE + -IC.

sul·fa·nil·a·mide /ˌsəlfəˈniləˌmīd/ (chiefly Brit. also **sulphanilamide**) ▶ n. Medicine a synthetic compound with antibacterial properties that is the basis of the sulfonamide drugs. ● Alternative name: ***p*-aminobenzenesulfonamide**; chem. formula: $(H_2N)C_6H_4(SO_2NH_2)$.
– ORIGIN 1930s: from *sulfanilic* (from SULFUR + ANILINE + -IC) + AMIDE.

sul·fa·pyr·i·dine /ˌsəlfəˈpirəˌdēn/ (chiefly Brit. also **sulphapyridine**) ▶ n. Medicine a sulfonamide antibiotic used to treat some forms of dermatitis.

sul·fa·sal·a·zine /ˌsəlfəˈsaləˌzēn/ (chiefly Brit. also **sulphasalazine**) ▶ n. Medicine a sulfonamide antibiotic used to treat ulcerative colitis and Crohn's disease.
– ORIGIN mid 20th cent.: from SULFA- + *sal(icylic acid)* + AZINE.

sul·fate /ˈsəlˌfāt/ (chiefly Brit. also **sulphate**) ▶ n. Chemistry a salt or ester of sulfuric acid, containing the anion SO_4^{2-} or the divalent group $-OSO_2O-$.
– ORIGIN late 18th cent.: French, from Latin *sulfur* (see SULFUR).

sul·fide /ˈsəlˌfīd/ (chiefly Brit. also **sulphide**) ▶ n. Chemistry a binary compound of sulfur with another element or group.

sul·fite /ˈsəlˌfīt/ (chiefly Brit. also **sulphite**) ▶ n. Chemistry a salt of sulfurous acid, containing the anion SO_3^{2-}.
– ORIGIN late 18th cent.: French, alteration of *sulfate* (see SULFATE).

sul·fon·a·mide /səlˈfänəˌmīd/ (chiefly Brit. also **sulphonamide**) ▶ **n.** Medicine any of a class of synthetic drugs, derived from sulfanilamide, that are able to prevent the multiplication of some pathogenic bacteria.
– ORIGIN late 19th cent.: from SULFONE + AMIDE.

sul·fo·nate /ˈsəlfəˌnāt/ (chiefly Brit. also **sulphonate**) Chemistry ▶ **n.** a salt or ester of a sulfonic acid.
▶ **v.** [with obj.] convert (a compound) into a sulfonate, typically by reaction with sulfuric acid.
– DERIVATIVES **sul·fo·na·tion** /ˌsəlfəˈnāSHən/ **n.**

sul·fone /ˈsəlˌfōn/ (chiefly Brit. also **sulphone**) ▶ **n.** Chemistry an organic compound containing a sulfonyl group linking two organic groups.
– ORIGIN late 19th cent.: from German *Sulfon*, from *Sulfur* (see SULFUR).

sul·fon·ic ac·id /səlˈfänik/ (chiefly Brit. also **sulphonic**) ▶ **n.** Chemistry an organic acid containing the group $-SO_2OH$.

sul·fo·nyl /ˈsəlfənil/ (chiefly Brit. also **sulphonyl**) ▶ **n.** [as modifier] Chemistry of or denoting a divalent radical, $-SO_2-$, derived from a sulfonic acid group.

sul·fur /ˈsəlfər/ (also chiefly Brit. **sulphur**) ▶ **n.** **1** the chemical element of atomic number 16, a yellow combustible nonmetal. (Symbol: **S**) ■ the material of which hellfire and lightning were believed to consist. ■ a pale greenish-yellow color: [as modifier] *the bird's sulfur-yellow throat.*

> Sulfur occurs uncombined in volcanic and sedimentary deposits, as well as being a constituent of many minerals and petroleum. It is normally a bright yellow crystalline solid, but several other allotropic forms can be made. Sulfur is an ingredient of gunpowder, and is used in making matches and as an antiseptic and fungicide.

2 an American butterfly with predominantly yellow wings that may bear darker patches. ● *Colias*, *Phoebis*, and other genera, family Pieridae.
▶ **v.** [with obj.] disinfect or fumigate with sulfur.
– DERIVATIVES **sul·fur·y** **adj.**
– ORIGIN Middle English: from Anglo-Norman French *sulfre*, from Latin *sulfur*, *sulphur*.

> **USAGE** In general use, the standard US spelling is **sulfur** and the standard British spelling is **sulphur**. In chemistry, however, **sulfur** is now the standard form in the field in both US and British contexts.

sul·fu·rate /ˈsəlf(y)əˌrāt/ (chiefly Brit. also **sulphurate**) ▶ **v.** [with obj.] impregnate, fumigate, or treat with sulfur, esp. in bleaching.
– DERIVATIVES **sul·fu·ra·tion** /ˌsəlf(y)əˈrāSHən/ **n.**, **sul·fu·ra·tor** /-ˌrātər/ **n.**

sul·fur di·ox·ide ▶ **n.** Chemistry a colorless pungent toxic gas formed by burning sulfur in air. ● Chem. formula: SO_2.

sul·fu·re·ous /səlˈfyo͝orēəs/ (chiefly Brit. also **sulphureous**) ▶ **adj.** of, like, or containing sulfur.
– ORIGIN early 16th cent.: from Latin *sulfureus* (from SULFUR) + -OUS.

sul·fu·ret·ed hy·dro·gen ▶ **n.** Chemistry archaic term for HYDROGEN SULFIDE.

sul·fu·ric /səlˈfyo͝orik/ (chiefly Brit. also **sulphuric**) ▶ **adj.** containing sulfur or sulfuric acid: *the sulfuric byproducts of wood fires.*
– ORIGIN late 18th cent.: from French *sulfurique*, from Latin (as SULFUR).

sul·fu·ric ac·id ▶ **n.** a strong acid made by oxidizing solutions of sulfur dioxide and used in large quantities as an industrial and laboratory reagent. The concentrated form is an oily, dense, corrosive liquid. ● Chem. formula: H_2SO_4.

sul·fu·rize /ˈsəlf(y)əˌrīz/ (chiefly Brit. also **sulphurize**) ▶ **v.** another term for SULFURATE.
– DERIVATIVES **sul·fu·ri·za·tion** /ˌsəlf(y)ərəˈzāSHən/ **n.**

sul·fur·ous /ˈsəlfərəs/ (chiefly Brit. also **sulphurous**) ▶ **adj.** (chiefly of vapor or smoke) containing or derived from sulfur: *wafts of sulfurous fumes.* ■ sulfureous. ■ like sulfur in color; pale yellow. ■ marked by bad temper, anger, or profanity: *a sulfurous glance.*
– ORIGIN late Middle English: from Latin *sulfurosus*, from *sulfur* (see SULFUR).

sul·fur·ous ac·id ▶ **n.** Chemistry an unstable weak acid formed when sulfur dioxide dissolves in water. It is used as a reducing and bleaching agent. ● Chem. formula: H_2SO_3.

sul·fur spring ▶ **n.** a spring of which the water contains sulfur or its compounds.

sulk /səlk/ ▶ **v.** [no obj.] be silent, morose, and bad-tempered out of annoyance or disappointment: *he was sulking over the breakup of his band.*
▶ **n.** a period of gloomy and bad-tempered silence stemming from annoyance and resentment: *she was in a fit of the sulks.*
– DERIVATIVES **sulk·er** **n.**
– ORIGIN late 18th cent.: perhaps a back-formation from SULKY.

sulk·y /ˈsəlkē/ ▶ **adj.** (**sulkier**, **sulkiest**) morose, bad-tempered, and resentful; refusing to be cooperative or cheerful: *disappointment was making her sulky.* ■ expressing or suggesting gloom and bad temper: *she had a sultry, sulky mouth.*
▶ **n.** (pl. **sulkies**) a light two-wheeled horse-drawn vehicle for one person, used chiefly in harness racing.
– DERIVATIVES **sulk·i·ly** /-kəlē/ **adv.**, **sulk·i·ness** **n.**
– ORIGIN mid 18th cent.: perhaps from obsolete *sulke* 'hard to dispose of,' of unknown origin.

sulky

sull /səl/ ▶ **v.** [no obj.] informal or dialect (of an animal) refuse to go on. ■ (of a person) become sullen; sulk: *don't sull up on me, let's get it aired.*
– ORIGIN mid 19th cent.: back-formation from SULLEN.

Sul·la /ˈso͝olə/ (138–78 BC), Roman general and politician; full name *Lucius Cornelius Sulla Felix*. After a victorious campaign against Mithridates VI, Sulla invaded Italy in 83. He was elected dictator in 82 and implemented constitutional reforms in favor of the Senate.

sul·lage /ˈsəlij/ ▶ **n.** waste from household sinks, showers, and baths, but not toilets. ■ archaic refuse, esp. sewage.
– ORIGIN mid 16th cent.: perhaps from Anglo-Norman French *suillage*, from *suiller* 'to soil.'

sul·len /ˈsələn/ ▶ **adj.** bad-tempered and sulky; gloomy: *a sullen pout.* ■ (of the sky) full of dark clouds: *a sullen sunless sky.*
▶ **n.** (**the sullens**) archaic a sulky or depressed mood.
– DERIVATIVES **sul·len·ly** **adv.**, **sul·len·ness** **n.**
– ORIGIN Middle English (in the senses 'solitary, averse to company,' and 'unusual'): from Anglo-Norman French *sulein*, from *sol* 'sole.'

Sul·li·van[1] /ˈsələvən/, Sir Arthur (Seymour) (1842–1900), English composer. He is best known for the 14 light operas that he wrote in collaboration with librettist W. S. Gilbert.

Sul·li·van[2], Ed (1901–74), US television host and journalist; full name *Edward Vincent Sullivan*. As host of television's *Ed Sullivan Show* 1948–71, he gave national exposure to many performers who were on their way to stardom, including Elvis Presley and the Beatles.

Sul·li·van[3], John L. (1858–1918), US boxer; full name *John Lawrence Sullivan*. Fighting with his bare knuckles, he was proclaimed the world heavyweight champion in 1882. In 1892, when boxing rules changed and padded gloves were used, he fought James J. Corbett for the heavyweight championship and lost, being knocked out in the 21st round.

Sul·li·van[4], Louis Henry (1856–1924), US architect. He developed modern functionalism in architecture by designing skyscrapers. Among his works were the Auditorium (1886–90), the Stock Exchange (1893–94), and the Carson, Pirie, Scott (1899–1904) buildings in Chicago, as well as the Wainwright building in St. Louis (1890–91).

Sul·ly /ˈsəlē/, Thomas (1783–1872), US artist; born in England. Chiefly a portrait painter, his works include portraits of Queen Victoria, the Marquis de Lafayette, Thomas Jefferson, and James Monroe. His other paintings include "The Passage of the Delaware" (1819) and "Mother and Child" (1827).

sul·ly /ˈsəlē/ ▶ **v.** (**sullies**, **sullying**, **sullied**) [with obj.] literary or ironic damage the purity or integrity of; defile: *they were outraged that anyone should sully their good name.*
– ORIGIN late 16th cent.: perhaps from French *souiller* 'to soil.'

sulpha- ▶ **comb. form** chiefly British spelling of SULFA-.

sul·phur, etc. ▶ **n.** chiefly British spelling of SULFUR.

> **USAGE** See usage at SULFUR.

Sul·pi·cian /səlˈpiSHən/ ▶ **n.** a member of a congregation of secular Roman Catholic priests founded in 1642 by a priest of St. Sulpice, Paris, mainly to train candidates for holy orders.
▶ **adj.** relating to or denoting this congregation.

sul·tan /ˈsəltn/ ▶ **n.** a Muslim sovereign. ■ (**the Sultan**) historical the sultan of Turkey.
– DERIVATIVES **sul·tan·ate** /-ˌāt/ **n.**
– ORIGIN mid 16th cent.: from French, or from medieval Latin *sultanus*, from Arabic *sulṭān* 'power, ruler.'

sul·tan·a /səlˈtanə/ ▶ **n.** **1** a small, light brown, seedless raisin used in foods such as puddings and cakes.
2 a wife or concubine of a sultan. ■ any other woman in a sultan's family.
– ORIGIN late 16th cent. (sense 2): from Italian, feminine of *sultano* (see SULTAN). Sense 1 dates from the mid 19th cent.

sul·try /ˈsəltrē/ ▶ **adj.** (**sultrier**, **sultriest**) **1** (of the air or weather) hot and humid.
2 (of a person, esp. a woman) attractive in a way that suggests a passionate nature.
– DERIVATIVES **sul·tri·ly** /-trəlē/ **adv.**, **sul·tri·ness** **n.**
– ORIGIN late 16th cent.: from obsolete *sulter* 'swelter.'

su·lu /ˈso͞olo͞o/ ▶ **n.** (pl. **sulus**) a length of cotton or other light fabric wrapped about the body as a sarong, worn from the waist by men and full-length by women from the Melanesian Islands.
– ORIGIN Fijian.

Su·lu Sea /ˈso͞olo͞o/ a sea in the Malay Archipelago, surrounded by the northeastern coast of Borneo and the western islands of the Philippines.

Sulz·ber·ger /ˈsəltsˌbərgər/, Arthur Ochs (1926–) US publisher. He worked for *The New York Times* from 1951, serving as its president from 1963 until 1979. He was responsible for modernizing and broadening the newspaper's editorial range and for reorganizing the staff and day-to-day operations.

sum /səm/ ▶ **n.** **1** a particular amount of money: *they could not afford such a sum.*
2 (**the sum of**) the total amount resulting from the addition of two or more numbers, amounts, or items: *the sum of two prime numbers.* ■ the total amount of something that exists: *the sum of his own knowledge.*
3 an arithmetical problem, esp. at an elementary level.
▶ **v.** (**sums**, **summing**, **summed**) [with obj.] technical find the sum of (two or more amounts): *if we sum these equations we obtain x.* ■ [no obj.] (**sum to**) (of two or more amounts) add up to a specified total: *these additional probabilities must sum to 1.*
– PHRASES **in sum** to sum up; in summary: *this interpretation does little, in sum, to add to our understanding.*
– PHRASAL VERBS **sum up** give a brief summary of something: *Gerard will open the debate and I will sum up.* ■ Law (of a judge) review the evidence at the end of a case, and direct the jury regarding points of law. **sum someone/something up** express a concise idea of the nature or character of a person or thing: *selfish—that summed her up.*
– ORIGIN Middle English: via Old French from Latin *summa* 'main part, sum total,' feminine of *summus* 'highest.'

su·mac /ˈso͞omak, ˈSHo͞o-/ (also **sumach**) ▶ **n.** a shrub or small tree of the cashew family, with compound leaves, fruits in conical clusters, and bright autumn colors. ● Genera *Rhus* and *Cotinus*, family Anacardiaceae: several species, including the North American **staghorn sumac** (*R. typhina*), with densely clustered reddish hairy fruits, and **poison sumac** (*R. vernix*), with loosely clustered greenish-white fruits. Touching any part of the poison sumac can cause severe dermatitis.
– ORIGIN Middle English (denoting the dried and ground leaves of *R. coriaria* used in tanning and dyeing): from Old French *sumac* or medieval Latin *sumac(h)*, from Arabic *summāḳ*.

Su·ma·tra /səˈmätrə/ a large island in Indonesia, southwest of the Malay Peninsula, from which it is separated by the Strait of Malacca; chief city, Medan.
– DERIVATIVES **Su·ma·tran** **adj.** & **n.**

Su·ma·tran rhi·noc·er·os /səˈmätrən/ ▶ **n.** a rare hairy two-horned rhinoceros found in montane rain forests from Malaysia to Borneo. ● *Dicerorhinus sumatrensis*, family Rhinocerotidae.

Sum·ba /ˈso͞ombə/ an island of the Lesser Sunda group in Indonesia, south of the islands of Flores and Sumbawa; chief town, Waingapu. Also called SANDALWOOD ISLAND.

Sum·ba·wa /so͞omˈbäwə/ an island in the Lesser Sunda group in Indonesia, situated between the islands of Lombok and Flores.

S

Su·mer /'so͞omər/ an ancient region in southwestern Asia, in present-day Iraq, comprising the southern part of Mesopotamia. From the 4th millennium BC it was the site of city states that became part of ancient Babylonia.

Su·me·ri·an /sə'merēən, -'miər-/ ▶ **adj.** of or relating to Sumer, its ancient language, or the early, non-Semitic element it contributed to Babylonian civilization.
▶ **n. 1** a member of the indigenous non-Semitic people of ancient Babylonia.
2 the Sumerian language.

> The Sumerians had the oldest known written language, whose relationship to any other language is unclear. Theirs is the first historically attested civilization, and they invented cuneiform writing, the sexagesimal system of mathematics, and the sociopolitical institution of the city state. Their art, literature, and theology had a profound influence long after their demise c.2000 BC.

– ORIGIN late 19th cent.: from French *sumérien*, from SUMER.

Sum·ga·it /ˌso͞omgä'ēt/ Russian name for SUMQAYIT.

su·mi /'so͞omē/ ▶ **n.** a type of black Japanese ink prepared in solid sticks and used for painting and writing.
– ORIGIN early 20th cent.: Japanese, literally 'ink, blacking.'

su·mi-e /'so͞omē e/ ▶ **n.** Japanese ink painting using sumi.
– ORIGIN early 20th cent.: from SUMI + Japanese *e* 'painting.'

sum·ma /'səmə, 'so͞omə/ ▶ **n.** (pl. **summae** /'səmē, 'so͞omī/) chiefly archaic a summary of a subject.
– ORIGIN early 18th cent.: from Latin, literally 'sum total' (a sense reflected in Middle English).

sum·ma cum lau·de /'so͞omə ˌko͝om 'loudə, 'loudē/ ▶ **adv. & adj.** with the highest distinction: [as adv.] *he graduated summa cum laude* | [as adj.] *three scientific degrees, all summa cum laude.*
– ORIGIN Latin, literally 'with highest praise.'

sum·mand /'səmand, sə'mand/ ▶ **n.** Mathematics a quantity to be added to another.
– ORIGIN mid 19th cent.: from Latin *summandus* 'to be added,' gerundive of *summare*.

sum·mar·i·ly /sə'me(ə)rəlē, 'səmərəlē/ ▶ **adv.** in a summary manner; without the customary formalities: *she was summarily dismissed.*

sum·ma·rize /'səməˌrīz/ ▶ **v.** [with obj.] give a brief statement of the main points of (something): *these results can be summarized in the following table* | [no obj.] *to summarize, there are three main categories.*
– DERIVATIVES **sum·ma·ri·za·tion** /ˌsəməri'zāSHən/ **n.**, **sum·ma·riz·er n.**

sum·ma·ry /'səmərē/ ▶ **n.** (pl. **summaries**) a brief statement or account of the main points of something: *a summary of Chapter Three.*
▶ **adj. 1** dispensing with needless details or formalities; brief: *summary financial statements.*
2 Law (of a judicial process) conducted without the customary legal formalities: *summary arrest.* ■ (of a conviction) made by a judge or magistrate without a jury.
– PHRASES **in summary** in short: *in summary, there is no clear case for one tax system compared to another.*
– DERIVATIVES **sum·mar·i·ness** /sə'merēnis/ **n.**
– ORIGIN late Middle English (as an adjective): from Latin *summarius*, from *summa* 'sum total' (see SUM).

S

sum·ma·tion /sə'māSHən/ ▶ **n. 1** the process of adding things together: *the summation of numbers of small pieces of evidence.* ■ a sum total of things added together.
2 the process of summing something up: *these will need summation in a single document.* ■ a summary. ■ Law an attorney's closing speech at the conclusion of the giving of evidence.
– DERIVATIVES **sum·ma·tion·al** /-SHənl/ **adj.**, **sum·ma·tive** /'səmətiv/ **adj.**

sum·mer[1] /'səmər/ ▶ **n.** the warmest season of the year, in the northern hemisphere from June to August and in the southern hemisphere from December to February: *the plant flowers in late summer* | *a long hot summer* | [as modifier] *summer vacation* | figurative *the golden summer of her life.* ■ Astronomy the period from the summer solstice to the autumnal equinox. ■ (**summers**) literary years, esp. of a person's age: *a girl of sixteen or seventeen summers.*
▶ **v.** [no obj.] spend the summer in a particular place: *well over 100 birds summered there in 1976.* ■ [with obj.] pasture (cattle) for the summer.
– DERIVATIVES **sum·mer·y adj.**
– ORIGIN Old English *sumor*, of Germanic origin; related to Dutch *zomer*, German *Sommer*, also to Sanskrit *samā* 'year.'

sum·mer[2] (also **summertree** /'səmərˌtrē/) ▶ **n.** a horizontal bearing beam, esp. one supporting joists or rafters. ■ a capstone that supports an arch or lintel. ■ a lintel.
– ORIGIN Middle English: from Old French *somier* 'packhorse,' from late Latin *sagmarius*, from Greek *sagma* 'packsaddle.'

sum·mer camp ▶ **n.** a camp providing recreational and athletic facilities for children during the summer vacation period.

sum·mer cy·press ▶ **n.** another term for KOCHIA.

sum·mer·house /'səmərˌhous/ (also **summer house**) ▶ **n.** a small, typically rustic building in a garden or park, used for sitting in during the summer months. ■ (usu. **summer house**) a cottage or house use as a second residence, esp. during the summer.

Sum·mer Pal·ace a palace (now in ruins) of the former Chinese emperors near Beijing.

sum·mer·sault ▶ **n. & v.** archaic spelling of SOMERSAULT.

sum·mer sau·sage ▶ **n.** a type of hard dried and smoked sausage that is similar to salami in preparation and can be kept without refrigeration.

sum·mer school ▶ **n.** courses held during school summer vacations, taken for remedial purposes, as part of an academic program, or for professional or personal purposes.

sum·mer sol·stice ▶ **n.** the solstice that marks the onset of summer, at the time of the longest day, about June 21 in the northern hemisphere and December 22 in the southern hemisphere. ■ Astronomy the solstice in June.

sum·mer squash ▶ **n.** a squash that is eaten before the seeds and rind have hardened. Unlike winter squash, summer squash does not keep well. ● Cultivars of *Cucurbita pepo* var. *melopepo*, family Cucurbitaceae.

sum·mer stock ▶ **n.** theatrical productions by a repertory company organized for the summer season, esp. at vacation resorts or in a suburban area.

sum·mer tan·a·ger ▶ **n.** a tanager (bird), the adult male of which is rosy red, and which is a common summer visitor in the central and southern US. ● *Piranga rubra.*

sum·mer·time /'səmərˌtīm/ ▶ **n.** the season or period of summer: *in summertime trains run every ten minutes.*

sum·mer·tree /'səmərˌtrē/ ▶ **n.** see SUMMER[2].

Sum·mer·ville /'səmərˌvil/ a city in southeastern South Carolina, northwest of North Charleston; pop. 45,193 (est. 2008).

sum·mer-weight ▶ **adj.** (of clothes) made of light fabric and therefore cool to wear.

sum·ming-up ▶ **n.** a restatement of the main points of an argument, case, etc.

sum·mit /'səmit/ ▶ **n. 1** the highest point of a hill or mountain. ■ the highest attainable level of achievement: *the dramas are considered to form one of the summits of world literature.*
2 a meeting between heads of government: [as modifier] *a summit conference.*
– ORIGIN late Middle English (in the general sense 'top part'): from Old French *somete*, from *som* 'top,' from Latin *summum*, neuter of *summus* 'highest.'

sum·mit·eer /ˌsəmi'ti(ə)r/ ▶ **n.** a participant in a meeting between heads of government.

sum·mon /'səmən/ ▶ **v.** [with obj.] authoritatively or urgently call on (someone) to be present, esp. as a defendant or witness in a law court: *the pope summoned Anselm to Rome.* ■ urgently demand (help): *she summoned medical assistance.* ■ call people to attend (a meeting): *he summoned a meeting of head delegates.* ■ bring to the surface (a particular quality or reaction) from within oneself: *she managed to summon up a smile.* ■ (**summon something up**) call an image to mind: *names that summon up images of far-off places.*
– DERIVATIVES **sum·mon·a·ble adj.**, **sum·mon·er n.**
– ORIGIN Middle English: from Old French *somondre*, from Latin *summonere* 'give a hint,' later 'call, summon,' from *sub-* 'secretly' + *monere* 'warn.'

sum·mons /'səmənz/ ▶ **n.** (pl. **summonses**) an order to appear before a judge or magistrate, or the writ containing it: *a summons for nonpayment of a parking ticket.* ■ an authoritative or urgent call to someone to be present or to do something: [with infinitive] *they might receive a summons to fly to France next day.*
▶ **v.** [with obj.] chiefly Law serve (someone) with a summons: [with obj. and infinitive] *he has been summonsed to appear in court next month.*
– ORIGIN Middle English: from Old French *sumunse*, from an alteration of Latin *summonita*, feminine past participle of *summonere* (see SUMMON).

sum·mum bo·num /'so͞oməm 'bōnəm/ ▶ **n.** the highest good, esp. as the ultimate goal according to which values and priorities are established in an ethical system.
– ORIGIN Latin.

su·mo /'so͞omō/ ▶ **n.** (pl. **sumos**) a Japanese form of heavyweight wrestling, in which a wrestler wins a bout by forcing his opponent outside a marked circle or by making him touch the ground with any part of his body except the soles of his feet. ■ a sumo wrestler.
– ORIGIN from Japanese *sūmo*.

sump /səmp/ ▶ **n.** a pit or hollow in which liquid collects, in particular: ■ the base of an internal combustion engine, which serves as a reservoir of oil for the lubrication system. ■ a depression in the floor of a mine or basement in which water collects. ■ a cesspool.
– ORIGIN Middle English (in the sense 'marsh'): from Middle Dutch or Low German *sump*, or (in the mining sense) from German *Sumpf*; related to SWAMP.

sump·ter /'səmptər/ ▶ **n.** archaic a pack animal.
– ORIGIN Middle English: from Old French *sommetier*, via late Latin from Greek *sagma*, *sagmat-* 'packsaddle'; compare with SUMMER[2].

sump·tu·ary /'səm(p)CHo͞oˌerē/ ▶ **adj.** [attrib.] chiefly historical relating to or denoting laws that limit private expenditure on food and personal items.
– ORIGIN early 17th cent.: from Latin *sumptuarius*, from *sumptus* 'cost, expenditure,' from *sumere* 'take.'

sump·tu·ous /'səm(p)CHo͞oəs/ ▶ **adj.** splendid and expensive-looking: *the banquet was a sumptuous, luxurious meal.*
– DERIVATIVES **sump·tu·os·i·ty** /ˌsəm(p)CHo͞o'äsitē/ **n.**, **sump·tu·ous·ly adv.**, **sump·tu·ous·ness n.**
– ORIGIN late Middle English (in the sense 'made or produced at great cost'): from Old French *somptueux*, from Latin *sumptuosus*, from *sumptus* 'expenditure' (see SUMPTUARY).

Sum·qay·it /ˌso͞omgä'(y)ēt/ an industrial city in eastern Azerbaijan, on the Caspian Sea; pop. 299,700 (est. 2008). Russian name SUMGAIT.

sum to·tal ▶ **n.** another term for SUM (sense 2 of the noun).

Su·my /'so͞omē/ an industrial city in northeastern Ukraine, near the border with Russia; pop. 273,900 (est. 2009).

sun /sən/ ▶ **n. 1** (also **Sun**) the star around which the earth orbits. ■ any similar star in the universe, with or without planets.

> The sun is the central body of the solar system. It provides the light and energy that sustains life on earth, and its position relative to the earth's axis determines the terrestrial seasons. The sun is a star of a type known as a G2 dwarf, a sphere of hydrogen and helium 870,000 miles (1.4 million km) in diameter that obtains its energy from nuclear fusion reactions in its interior, where the temperature is about 15 million°C. The surface is a little under 6,000°C.

2 (usu. **the sun**) the light or warmth received from the earth's sun: *we sat outside in the sun.* ■ literary a person or thing regarded as a source of glory or inspiration or understanding: *the rhetoric faded before the sun of reality.* ■ literary used with reference to someone's success or prosperity: *the sun of the Plantagenets went down in clouds.*
3 literary a day or a year: *after going so many suns without food, I was sleeping.*
▶ **v.** (**suns, sunning, sunned**) (**sun oneself**) sit or lie in the sun: *Buzz could see Clare sunning herself on the terrace below.* ■ [with obj.] expose (something) to the sun, esp. to warm or dry it: *the birds are sunning their wings.*
– PHRASES **against the sun** Nautical against the direction of the sun's apparent movement in the northern hemisphere; from right to left or counterclockwise. **catch the sun** see CATCH. **make hay while the sun shines** see HAY[1]. **on which the sun never sets** (of an empire) worldwide. [applied in the 17th cent. to the Spanish dominions, later to the British Empire.] **place in the sun** see PLACE. **shoot the sun** Nautical ascertain the altitude of the sun with a sextant in order to determine one's latitude. **under the sun** on earth; in existence (used in expressions emphasizing the large number of something): *they exchanged views on every subject under the sun.* **with the sun** Nautical in the direction of the sun's apparent movement in the northern hemisphere; from left to right or clockwise.
– DERIVATIVES **sun·like** /-ˌlīk/ **adj.**, **sun·ward** /-wərd/ **adj. & adv.**, **sun·wards** /-wərdz/ **adv.**

–ORIGIN Old English *sunne*, of Germanic origin; related to Dutch *zon* and German *Sonne*, from an Indo-European root shared by Greek *hēlios* and Latin *sol*.

Sun. ▶ **abbr.** Sunday.

sun-and-plan·et gear ▶ **n.** a system of gearwheels consisting of a central wheel (a **sun gear** or **sun wheel**) around which one or more outer wheels (**planet gears** or **planet wheels**) travel.

sun-baked ▶ **adj.** (esp. of the ground) exposed to the heat of the sun and therefore dry and hard.

sun·bath /ˈsənˌbaTH/ ▶ **n.** a period of sunbathing: *an upstairs deck on which you could take a sunbath.*

sun·bathe /ˈsənˌbāT͟H/ ▶ **v.** [no obj.] sit or lie in the sun, esp. to tan the skin: (as noun **sunbathing**) *it was too hot for sunbathing.*
–DERIVATIVES **sun·bath·er** **n.**

sun·beam /ˈsənˌbēm/ ▶ **n.** a ray of sunlight.

sun bear (also **Malayan sun bear**) ▶ **n.** a small mainly nocturnal bear that has a brownish-black coat with a light-colored mark on the chest, native to Southeast Asia. ● *Helarctos malayanus*, family Ursidae.

sun·belt /ˈsənˌbelt/ (also **sun belt**) ▶ **n.** a strip of territory receiving a high amount of sunshine, esp.: ■ (**Sunbelt** or **Sun Belt**) the southern US from California to Florida, noted for resort areas and for the movement of businesses and population into these states from the colder northern states.

sun·bird /ˈsənbərd/ ▶ **n.** a small, brightly colored Old World songbird with a long down-curved bill, feeding on nectar and resembling a hummingbird (but not able to hover). ● Family Nectariniidae: four genera, in particular *Nectarinia*, and numerous species.

sun·bit·tern /ˈsənˌbitərn/ (also **sun bittern**) ▶ **n.** a tropical American wading bird with a long bill, neck, and legs, having mainly grayish plumage but showing chestnut and orange on the wings when they are spread in display. ● *Eurypyga helias*, the only member of the family Eurypygidae.
–ORIGIN late 19th cent.: so named because of the pattern on the spread wings, which resembles a sunset.

sun·block /ˈsənˌbläk/ ▶ **n.** a cream or lotion for protecting the skin from the sun and preventing sunburn.

sun·bon·net /ˈsənˌbänit/ ▶ **n.** a close-fitting brimmed cotton hat that protects the head and neck from the sun, worn esp. by infants and formerly by women.

sun·burn /ˈsənˌbərn/ ▶ **n.** reddening, inflammation, and, in severe cases, blistering and peeling of the skin caused by overexposure to the ultraviolet rays of the sun.
▶ **v.** (**sunburns**, **sunburning**, past and past participle **sunburned** or **sunburnt**) (**be sunburned**) (of a person or bodily part) suffer from sunburn: *most of us managed to get sunburnt.* ■ (usu. as adj. **sunburned** or **sunburnt**) ruddy from exposure to the sun: *a handsome sunburned face.* ■ [no obj.] suffer from sunburn: *a complexion that sunburned easily.*

sun·burst /ˈsənˌbərst/ ▶ **n.** a sudden brief appearance of the full sun from behind clouds. ■ a decoration or ornament resembling the sun and its rays: [as modifier] *a pair of sunburst diamond earrings.* ■ a pattern of irregular concentric bands of color with the brightest at the center.

sun·dae /ˈsənˌdā/ ▶ **n.** a dish of ice cream with added ingredients such as fruit, nuts, syrup, and whipped cream.
–ORIGIN late 19th cent. (originally US): perhaps an alteration of **SUNDAY**, either because the dish was made with ice cream left over from Sunday and sold cheaply on Monday, or because it was sold only on Sundays, a practice devised (according to some accounts) to circumvent Sunday legislation.

Sun·da Is·lands /ˈsəndə, ˈso͞on-/ a chain of islands in the southwestern part of the Malay Archipelago. They are divided into two groups: the **Greater Sunda Islands**, which include Sumatra, Java, Borneo, and Sulawesi, and the **Lesser Sunda Islands**, which lie to the east of Java and include Bali, Sumbawa, Flores, Sumba, and Timor.

sun dance ▶ **n.** a dance performed by North American Plains Indians in honor of the sun and to prove bravery by overcoming pain.

Sun·da·nese /ˌsəndəˈnēz, -ˈnēs/ ▶ **n.** (pl. **same**) **1** a member of a mainly Muslim people of western Java. **2** the Indonesian language of this people.
▶ **adj.** of or relating to the Sundanese or their language.
–ORIGIN from Sundanese *Sunda*, the western part of Java, + **-ESE**.

Sun·day /ˈsəndā, -dē/ ▶ **n.** the day of the week before Monday and following Saturday, observed by Christians as a day of rest and religious worship and (together with Saturday) forming part of the weekend: *they left town on Sunday* | *many people work on Sundays* | [as modifier] *Sunday evening.*
▶ **adv.** on Sunday: *the concert will be held Sunday.* ■ (**Sundays**) on Sundays; each Sunday: *the program is repeated Sundays at 9 p.m.*
–ORIGIN Old English *Sunnandæg* 'day of the sun,' translation of Latin *dies solis*; compare with Dutch *zondag* and German *Sonntag.*

Sun·day best ▶ **n.** (**one's Sunday best**) a person's best clothes, worn to church or on special occasions.

Sun·day driv·er ▶ **n.** a person perceived as driving in an inexperienced or unskillful way, esp. one who drives slowly.

Sun·day-go-to-meet·ing ▶ **adj.** (of a hat, clothes, etc.) suitable for going to church in.

Sun·day punch ▶ **n.** informal a powerful or devastating punch or other attacking action.

Sun·day school ▶ **n.** a class held on Sundays to teach children about their religion.

sun deck ▶ **n.** **1** the deck, or part of a deck, of a yacht or cruise ship that is open to the sky. **2** a terrace or balcony positioned to catch the sun.

sun·der /ˈsəndər/ ▶ **v.** [with obj.] literary split apart: *the crunch of bone when it is sundered.*
–PHRASES **in sunder** apart or into pieces: *hew their bones in sunder!*
–ORIGIN late Old English *sundrian*; related to German *sondern.*

Sun·der·land /ˈsəndərlənd/ an industrial city in northeastern England, a port at the mouth of the Wear River; pop. 171,300 (est. 2009).

sun·dew /ˈsənˌd(y)o͞o/ ▶ **n.** a small carnivorous plant of boggy places, with rosettes of leaves that bear sticky glandular hairs. These trap insects, which are then digested. ● Genus *Drosera*, family Droseraceae: many species, including the common European *D. rotundifolia.*

sun·di·al /ˈsənˌdīl/ ▶ **n.** **1** an instrument showing the time by the shadow of a pointer cast by the sun onto a plate marked with the hours of the day. **2** (also **sundial shell**) a mollusk with a flattened spiral shell that is typically patterned in shades of brown, living in tropical and subtropical seas. ● Family Architectonicidae, class Gastropoda.

sundial 1

sun disk ▶ **n.** (esp. in ancient Egypt) a winged disk representing a sun god.

sun dog (also **sundog** /ˈsənˌdôg/) ▶ **n.** another term for **PARHELION**.

sun·down /ˈsənˌdoun/ ▶ **n.** [in sing.] the time in the evening when the sun disappears or daylight fades.

sun·down·er /ˈsənˌdounər/ ▶ **n.** **1** Brit. informal an alcoholic drink taken at sunset. **2** Austral. a tramp arriving at a sheep station in the evening under the pretense of seeking work, so as to obtain food and shelter.

sun-drenched ▶ **adj.** (of a place) receiving a great deal of sunlight: *the sun-drenched beaches of Southern California.*

sun·dress /ˈsənˌdres/ ▶ **n.** a light, loose, sleeveless dress, typically having a wide neckline and thin shoulder straps.

sun·drops /ˈsənˌdräps/ ▶ **n.** a day-flowering North American plant with yellow flowers, related to the evening primrose. ● Genera *Oenothera* and *Calylophus*, family Onagraceae.

sun·dry /ˈsəndrē/ ▶ **adj.** [attrib.] of various kinds; several: *lemon rind and sundry herbs.*
▶ as **plural n.** (**sundries**) various items not important enough to be mentioned individually: *a drugstore selling magazines, newspapers, and sundries.*
–PHRASES **all and sundry** see **ALL**.
–ORIGIN Old English *syndrig* 'distinct, separate'; related to **SUNDER**.

sun-dry ▶ **v.** [with obj.] (usu. as adj. **sun-dried**) dry (something, esp. food) in the sun, as opposed to using artificial heat: *sun-dried tomatoes.*

sun·fast /ˈsənˌfast/ ▶ **adj.** (of a dye or fabric) not prone to fade in sunlight.

sun·fish /ˈsənˌfiSH/ ▶ **n.** (pl. **same** or **sunfishes**) **1** a large deep-bodied marine fish of warm seas, with tall dorsal and anal fins near the rear of the body and a very short tail. Also called **MOLA**. ● Family Molidae: three genera and several species, in particular the very large **ocean sunfish** (*Mola mola*), also commonly called **mola mola**. **2** a nest-building freshwater fish that is native to North America and popular in aquariums, e.g., the pumpkinseed. ● Several genera and species in the family Centrarchidae (the **sunfish family**). This family also includes sport fish such as the black basses, rock bass, bluegill, and crappies.

ocean sunfish

sun·flow·er /ˈsənˌflou(-ə)r/ ▶ **n.** a tall North American plant of the daisy family, with very large golden-rayed flowers. Sunflowers are cultivated for their edible seeds, which are an important source of oil for cooking and margarine. ● *Helianthus annus*, family Compositae.

sunflower

sun·flow·er seed ▶ **n.** the hard-shelled edible seed of a plant of the daisy family, yielding an oil used in cooking and margarine.

Sun·flow·er State a nickname for the state of **KANSAS**.

Sung /so͝oNG/ (also **Song**) a dynasty that ruled in China AD 960–1279. The period was marked by the first use of paper money and by advances in printing, firearms, shipbuilding, clockmaking, and medicine.

sung /səNG/ past participle of **SING**.

sun·glass·es /ˈsənˌglasiz/ ▶ **plural n.** glasses tinted to protect the eyes from sunlight or glare.

sun hat (also **sunhat** /ˈsənˌhat/) ▶ **n.** a broad-brimmed hat that protects the head and neck from the sun.

sunk /səNGk/ past and past participle of **SINK**[1].

USAGE See usage at **SINK**[1].

sunk·en /ˈsəNGkən/ ▶ **adj.** **1** [attrib.] having sunk or been submerged in water: *the wreck of a sunken ship.* **2** [attrib.] at a lower level than the surrounding area: *a sunken garden.* ■ (of a person's eyes or cheeks) deeply recessed, esp. as a result of illness, hunger, or stress: *her face was white, with sunken cheeks.*
–ORIGIN late Middle English: past participle of **SINK**[1].

sunk fence ▶ **n.** a ditch with one side formed by a wall or with a fence running along the bottom.

Sun King the nickname of Louis XIV of France (see **LOUIS**[1]).

sun-kissed ▶ **adj.** made warm or brown by the sun: *the sun-kissed resort of Acapulco* | *her sun-kissed shoulders.*

sun·lamp /ˈsənˌlamp/ ▶ **n.** **1** a lamp emitting ultraviolet rays used as a substitute for sunlight, typically to produce an artificial suntan or in therapy. **2** a large lamp with a parabolic reflector used in filmmaking.

sun·less /ˈsənlis/ ▶ **adj.** without any sun: *a sunless winter day.* ■ (of a place) receiving no sunlight: *the windowless, sunless headquarters.*
–DERIVATIVES **sun·less·ness** **n.**

sun·light /ˈsənˌlīt/ ▶ **n.** light from the sun: *a shaft of sunlight.*

sun·lit /ˈsənˌlit/ ▶ **adj.** illuminated by direct light from the sun: *clear sunlit waters.*

sunn /sən/ (also **sunn hemp**) ▶ **n.** a hemplike fiber from southern Asia.
–ORIGIN late 18th cent.: from Urdu and Hindi *san*, from Sanskrit *śaṇá* 'hempen.'

Sun·na /ˈsənə/ ▶ **n.** the traditional portion of Muslim law based on Muhammad's words or acts, accepted (together with the Koran) as authoritative

by Muslims and followed particularly by Sunni Muslims.
– ORIGIN Arabic, literally 'form, way, course, rule.'

Sun·ni /ˈso͞onē/ ▶ **n.** (pl. **same** or **Sunnis**) one of the two main branches of Islam, commonly described as orthodox, and differing from Shia in its understanding of the Sunna and in its acceptance of the first three caliphs. Compare with **SHIA**. ■ a Muslim who adheres to this branch of Islam.
– DERIVATIVES **Sun·nite** /ˈso͞onīt/ **adj. &n.**
– ORIGIN from the Arabic for 'an adherent of Sunna.'

Sun·ni Tri·an·gle ▶ **n.** an area of Iraq bounded roughly by Baghdad in the southeast, Ramadi in the southwest, and Tikrit in the north. It is predominantly Sunni and has been a focus of opposition to occupation forces.

sun·ny /ˈsənē/ ▶ **adj.** (**sunnier**, **sunniest**) bright with sunlight: *a sunny day.* ■ (of a place) receiving much sunlight: *find a sunny patch for the dahlia tubers.* ■ (of a person or their temperament) cheery and bright: *he had a sunny disposition.*
– DERIVATIVES **sun·ni·ly** /ˈsənəlē/ **adv.**, **sun·ni·ness n.**

sun·ny side ▶ **n.** the side of something that receives the sun for longest: *a well-known hotel on the sunny side of the island.* ■ the more cheerful or pleasant aspect of a state of affairs: *he was fond of the sunny side of life.*
– PHRASES **sunny side up** (of an egg) fried on one side only.

Sun·ny·vale /ˈsənēˌvāl/ a city in north central California, one of the technological centers of Silicon Valley; pop. 132,109 (est. 2008).

sun porch (also **sunporch** /ˈsənˌpôrCH/) ▶ **n.** another term for **SUNROOM**.

Sun·rise /ˈsənˌrīz/ a city in southeastern Florida, west of Fort Lauderdale; pop. 89,026 (est. 2008).

sun·rise /ˈsənˌrīz/ ▶ **n.** [in sing.] the time in the morning when the sun appears or full daylight arrives: *an hour before sunrise.* ■ the colors and light visible in the sky on an occasion of the sun's first appearance in the morning, considered as a view or spectacle: *a spectacular sunrise over the summit of the mountain.*

sun·rise in·dus·try ▶ **n.** a new and growing industry, esp. in electronics or telecommunications.

sun·roof /ˈsənˌro͞of, -ˌro͝of/ ▶ **n.** a panel in the roof of a car that can be opened for extra ventilation.

sun·room /ˈsənˌro͞om, -ˌro͝om/ ▶ **n.** a room with large windows and sometimes a glass roof, designed to allow in a lot of sunlight.

sun·scald /ˈsənˌskôld/ (also **sun scald**) ▶ **n.** damage to plant tissue, esp. bark or fruit, caused by exposure to excessive sunlight.

sun·screen /ˈsənˌskrēn/ ▶ **n.** a cream or lotion rubbed onto the skin to protect it from the sun. ■ an active ingredient of creams and lotions of this kind and other preparations for the skin.

sun·set /ˈsənˌset/ ▶ **n.** [in sing.] the time in the evening when the sun disappears or daylight fades: *sunset was still a couple of hours away.* ■ the colors and light visible in the sky on an occasion of the sun's disappearance in the evening, considered as a view or spectacle: *a blue and gold sunset.* ■ a period of decline, esp. the last years of a person's life: *the sunset of his life.*

Sun·set Boul·e·vard a road that links the center of Los Angeles with the Pacific Ocean 30 miles (48 km) to the west. The eastern section between Fairfax Avenue and Beverly Hills is known as Sunset Strip.

sun·set in·dus·try ▶ **n.** an old and declining industry.

sun·set law ▶ **n.** Law a law that automatically terminates a regulatory agency, board, or function of government on a certain date, unless renewed: *in accordance with the state sunset law, the act sets the expiration date for the committee three years after the date of its creation.*

sun·set pro·vi·sion ▶ **n.** a stipulation that an agency or program be disbanded or terminated at the end of a fixed period unless it is formally renewed.

sun·shade /ˈsənˌSHād/ ▶ **n.** a parasol, awning, or other device giving protection from the sun.

sun·shine /ˈsənˌSHīn/ ▶ **n.** direct sunlight unbroken by cloud, esp. over a comparatively large area: *we walked in the warm sunshine.* ■ cheerfulness; happiness: *their colorful music can bring a ray of sunshine.*
– DERIVATIVES **sun·shin·y adj.**

sun·shine law ▶ **n.** a law requiring certain proceedings of government agencies to be open or available to the public.

Sun·shine State a nickname for the state of **FLORIDA**.

sun·space /ˈsənˌspās/ ▶ **n.** a room or area in a building having a glass roof and walls and intended to maximize the power of the sun's rays.

sun spi·der ▶ **n.** a fast-moving predatory arachnid with a pair of massive vertical pincers (chelicerae). Sun spiders live chiefly in warm deserts, many are active by day, and some grow to a large size. ● Order Solifugae (or Solpugida).

sun·spot /ˈsənˌspät/ ▶ **n.** Astronomy a spot or patch appearing from time to time on the sun's surface, appearing dark by contrast with its surroundings.

> Sunspots are regions of lower surface temperature and are believed to form where loops in the sun's magnetic field intersect the surface; an individual spot may persist for several weeks. The number of sunspots on the solar surface fluctuates according to a regular cycle, with times of maximum sunspot activity recurring every eleven years.

sun·star /ˈsənˌstär/ ▶ **n.** a widely distributed starfish with a large number of arms. ● Genus *Solaster*, class Asteroidea.

sun·stone /ˈsənˌstōn/ ▶ **n.** a chatoyant gem consisting of feldspar, with a red or gold color.

sun·stroke /ˈsənˌstrōk/ ▶ **n.** heatstroke brought about by excessive exposure to the sun.

sun·suit /ˈsənˌso͞ot/ ▶ **n.** a child's one- or two-piece suit of clothes, typically consisting of shorts and sleeveless top, worn in hot sunny weather.

sun·tan /ˈsənˌtan/ ▶ **n.** a browning of skin caused by exposure to the sun: *he had acquired quite a suntan.*
▶ **v.** [with obj.] (usu. as adj. **suntanned**) expose to the sun in order to achieve such a brown color: *a suntanned face.*

sun·up /ˈsənˌəp/ ▶ **n.** [in sing.] the time in the morning when the sun appears or full daylight arrives: *they worked from sunup to sundown.*

Sun Valley a city in south central Idaho, a well-known winter sports resort; pop. 1,466 (est. 2008).

sun vi·sor ▶ **n.** a small screen above a vehicle's windshield, attached by a hinge so that it can be lowered to protect the occupants' eyes from bright sunlight.

sun·ya·ta /ˈSHo͞onyəˌtä, ˈso͞on-/ ▶ **n.** variant of **SHUNYATA**.

Sun Yat-sen /ˈso͞on ˈyät ˈsen/ (also **Sun Yixian** /ˈyēSHēˈän/) (1866–1925), Chinese statesman; provisional president of the Republic of China 1911–12 and president of the Southern Chinese Republic 1923–25. He organized the Kuomintang force and established a secessionist government at Guangzhou.

Sun Yat-sen

Suo·mi /ˈso͞o-ōmē/ Finnish name for **FINLAND**.

sup¹ /səp/ ▶ **v.** (**sups**, **supping**, **supped**) [with obj.] dated or dialect take (drink or liquid food) by sips or spoonfuls: *she supped up her soup delightedly* | [no obj.] *he was supping straight from the bottle.*
▶ **n.** a sip of liquid: *he took another sup of wine.*
– ORIGIN Old English *sūpan* (verb), *sūpa* (noun), of Germanic origin; related to Dutch *zuipen*, German *saufen* 'to drink.'

sup² ▶ **v.** (**sups**, **supping**, **supped**) [no obj.] dated eat supper: *you'll sup on seafood delicacies.*
– ORIGIN Middle English: from Old French *super*, of Germanic origin; related to **SUP¹**.

sup. ▶ **abbr.** ■ superior. ■ superlative. ■ supine. ■ supplement. ■ supplementary. ■ supply. ■ supra.

sup- ▶ **prefix** variant spelling of **SUB-** assimilated before *p* (as in *suppurate*).

Sup. Ct. ▶ **abbr.** ■ Superior Court. ■ Supreme Court.

su·per /ˈso͞opər/ ▶ **adj. 1** informal very good or pleasant; excellent: *Julie was a super girl* | [as exclamation] *You're both coming in? Super!*
2 (of a manufactured product) superfine: *a super quality binder.*
▶ **adv.** [as submodifier] informal especially; particularly: *he's been super understanding.*
▶ **n.** informal **1** a superintendent.
2 archaic an extra, unwanted, or unimportant person; a supernumerary. ■ theatrical slang, dated an extra.
3 superphosphate.
4 superfine fabric or manufacture.
– ORIGIN mid 19th cent.: abbreviation.

super. ▶ **abbr.** ■ superintendent. ■ superior.

super- ▶ **comb. form** above; over; beyond: *superlunary* | *superstructure.* ■ to a great or extreme degree: *superabundant* | *supercool.* ■ extra large of its kind: *supercontinent.* ■ having greater influence, capacity, etc., than another of its kind: *superbike* | *superpower.* ■ of a higher kind (esp. in names of classificatory divisions): *superfamily.*
– ORIGIN from Latin *super-*, from *super* 'above, beyond.'

su·per·a·ble /ˈso͞opərəbəl/ ▶ **adj.** able to be overcome.
– ORIGIN early 17th cent.: from Latin *superabilis*, from *superare* 'overcome.'

su·per·a·bound /ˌso͞opərəˈbound/ ▶ **v.** [no obj.] archaic be very or too abundant: *the capitalists do not need to combine when labor superabounds.*
– ORIGIN late Middle English (in the sense 'be more abundant'): from late Latin *superabundare* (see **SUPER-**, **ABOUND**).

su·per·a·bun·dant /ˌso͞opərəˈbəndənt/ ▶ **adj.** excessive in quantity; more than sufficient; overabundant.
– DERIVATIVES **su·per·a·bun·dance n.**, **su·per·a·bun·dant·ly adv.**
– ORIGIN late Middle English (in the sense 'very plentiful'): from late Latin *superabundant-* 'abounding to excess,' from the verb ***superabundare***.

su·per·ac·id /ˈso͞opərˌasid/ ▶ **n.** Chemistry a solution of a strong acid in a very acidic (usually nonaqueous) solvent, functioning as a powerful protonating agent.
– DERIVATIVES **su·per·a·cid·i·ty** /ˌso͞opərəˈsiditē/ **n.**

su·per·add /ˌso͞opərˈad/ ▶ **v.** [with obj.] rare add (something) to what has already been added: (as adj. **superadded**) *the presence of superadded infection by bacteria.*
– DERIVATIVES **su·per·ad·di·tion** /-əˈdiSHən/ **n.**
– ORIGIN late Middle English: from Latin *superaddere* (see **SUPER-**, **ADD**).

su·per·ad·i·a·bat·ic /ˌso͞opərˌādīəˈbatik, -ˌadēə-/ ▶ **adj.** chiefly Meteorology relating to or denoting a temperature gradient which is steeper than that occurring in adiabatic conditions.

su·per·al·loy /ˈso͞opərˌaloi/ ▶ **n.** an alloy capable of withstanding high temperatures, high stresses, and often highly oxidizing atmospheres.

su·per·an·nu·ate /ˌso͞opərˈanyo͞oˌāt/ ▶ **v.** [with obj.] (usu. **be superannuated**) retire (someone) with a pension: *his pilot's license was withdrawn and he was superannuated.*
– DERIVATIVES **su·per·an·nu·a·ble** /-ˈanyo͞oəbəl/ **adj.**
– ORIGIN mid 17th cent.: back-formation from *superannuated*, from medieval Latin ***superannuatus***, from Latin *super-* 'over' + *annus* 'year.'

su·per·an·nu·at·ed /ˌso͞opərˈanyo͞oˌātid/ ▶ **adj.** (of a position or employee) belonging to a superannuation plan: *she is not superannuated and has no paid vacation.* ■ obsolete through age or new technological or intellectual developments: *superannuated computing equipment.*

su·per·an·nu·a·tion /ˌso͞opərˌanyo͞oˈāSHən/ ▶ **n.** [usu. as modifier] regular payment made into a fund by an employee toward a future pension: *a superannuation fund.* ■ a pension of this type paid to a retired person. ■ the process of superannuating an employee.

su·perb /so͞oˈpərb, sə-/ ▶ **adj. 1** excellent: *a superb performance.*
2 impressively splendid: *a superb Egyptian statue of Osiris.*
– DERIVATIVES **su·perb·ly adv.**, **su·perb·ness n.**
– ORIGIN mid 16th cent. (sense 2): from Latin *superbus* 'proud, magnificent.'

Su·per Bowl ▶ **n.** the National Football League championship game, played annually between the champions of the National and the American Football Conferences.

su·per·bug /ˈso͞opərˌbəg/ ▶ **n. 1** a bacterium that is useful in biotechnology, typically one that has been genetically engineered to enhance its usefulness for a particular purpose.
2 a strain of bacteria that has become resistant to antibiotic drugs. ■ an insect that is difficult to control or eradicate, esp. because it has become immune to insecticides.

su·per·cal·en·der /ˈso͞opərˌkaləndər/ ▶ **v.** [with obj.] give a highly glazed finish to (paper) by calendering it more than normally calendered paper: (as adj. **supercalendered**) *a supercalendered art paper.*

su·per·car·go /ˈso͞opərˌkärgō/ ▶ **n.** (pl. **supercargoes** or **supercargos**) a representative of the ship's owner on board a merchant ship, responsible for overseeing the cargo and its sale.
– ORIGIN late 17th cent.: alteration of earlier *supracargo*, from Spanish *sobrecargo*, from *sobre* 'over' + *cargo* 'cargo.'

su·per·cede ▶ **v.** variant spelling of SUPERSEDE.

> **USAGE** The standard spelling is **supersede**, not **supercede**. The word is derived from the Latin verb *supersedere* but has been influenced by the presence of other words in English spelled with **-cede**, such as **intercede** and **accede**. The spelling **supercede** is recorded as early as the 16th century, but is still regarded as incorrect.

su·per·cell /ˈso͞opərˌsel/ ▶ **n.** Meteorology a system producing severe thunderstorms and featuring rotating winds sustained by a prolonged updraft that may result in hail or tornadoes.

su·per·charge /ˈso͞opərˌchärj/ ▶ **v.** [with obj.] fit or design (an internal combustion engine) with a supercharger: (as adj. **supercharged**) *a supercharged 3.8-liter V6*. ■ (usu. as adj. **supercharged**) supply with extra energy or power: *a supercharged computer*. ■ (as adj. **supercharged**) having powerful emotional overtones or associations: *his trademark supercharged hot-air statements*.

su·per·charg·er /ˈso͞opərˌchärjər/ ▶ **n.** a device that increases the pressure of the fuel-air mixture in an internal combustion engine, used in order to achieve greater efficiency.

su·per·cil·i·ar·y /ˌso͞opərˈsilēˌerē/ ▶ **adj.** [attrib.] Anatomy of or relating to the eyebrow or the region over the eye.
– ORIGIN mid 18th cent.: from Latin *supercilium* 'eyebrow' (from *super-* 'above' + *cilium* 'eyelid') + -ARY[1].

su·per·cil·i·ous /ˌso͞opərˈsilēəs/ ▶ **adj.** behaving or looking as though one thinks one is superior to others: *a supercilious lady's maid*.
– DERIVATIVES **su·per·cil·i·ous·ly** adv., **su·per·cil·i·ous·ness** n.
– ORIGIN early 16th cent.: from Latin *superciliosus* 'haughty,' from *supercilium* 'eyebrow.'

su·per·class /ˈso͞opərˌklas/ ▶ **n.** Biology a taxonomic category that ranks above class and below phylum.

su·per·clus·ter /ˈso͞opərˌkləstər/ ▶ **n.** Astronomy a cluster of galaxies which themselves occur as clusters.

su·per·coil /ˈso͞opərˌkoil/ Biochemistry ▶ **n.** another term for SUPERHELIX.
▶ **v.** [with obj.] form (a substance) into a superhelix: (as adj. **supercoiled**) *a supercoiled circular DNA molecule*.

su·per·col·lid·er /ˈso͞opərkəˌlīdər/ ▶ **n.** Physics a collider in which superconducting magnets are used to accelerate particles to energies of millions of megavolts.

su·per·com·put·er /ˈso͞opərkəmˌpyo͞otər/ ▶ **n.** a particularly powerful mainframe computer.
– DERIVATIVES **su·per·com·put·ing** /-ˌpyo͞otiNG/ n.

su·per·con·duc·tiv·i·ty /ˌso͞opərˌkänˌdəkˈtivitē/ ▶ **n.** Physics the property of zero electrical resistance in some substances at very low absolute temperatures.
– DERIVATIVES **su·per·con·duct** /-kənˈdəkt/ v., **su·per·con·duct·ing** /-kənˈdəktiNG/ adj., **su·per·con·duc·tive** /-kənˈdəktiv/ adj.

su·per·con·duc·tor /ˈso͞opərkənˌdəktər/ ▶ **n.** Physics a substance capable of becoming superconducting at sufficiently low temperatures. ■ a substance in the superconducting state.

su·per·con·scious /ˌso͞opərˈkänsHəs/ ▶ **adj.** transcending human or normal consciousness: *the superconscious, universal mind of God*.
– DERIVATIVES **su·per·con·scious·ly** adv., **su·per·con·scious·ness** n.

su·per·con·ti·nent /ˈso͞opərˌkäntn-ənt/ ▶ **n.** each of several large landmasses (notably Pangaea, Gondwana, and Laurasia) thought to have divided to form the present continents in the geological past.

su·per·cool /ˌso͞opərˈko͞ol/ ▶ **v.** [with obj.] Chemistry cool (a liquid) below its freezing point without solidification or crystallization. ■ [no obj.] Biology (of a living organism) survive body temperatures below the freezing point of water.
▶ **adj.** informal extremely attractive, impressive, or calm: *the supercool tracks in this collection*.

su·per·crit·i·cal /ˌso͞opərˈkritikəl/ ▶ **adj.** Physics above a critical threshold, in particular: ■ (in nuclear physics) containing or involving more than the critical mass. ■ (of a flow of fluid) faster than the speed at which waves travel in the fluid. ■ denoting an airfoil or aircraft wing designed to tolerate shock-wave formation at transonic speeds. ■ of, relating to, or denoting a fluid at a temperature and pressure greater than its critical temperature and pressure.

su·per·del·e·gate /ˈso͞opərˌdeləgət/ ▶ **n.** (in the Democratic Party) an unelected delegate who is free to support any candidate for the presidential nomination at the party's national convention.

su·per-du·per /ˌso͞opər ˈdo͞opər/ ▶ **adj.** humorous very good; marvelous: *this new line of toys is super-duper*.

su·per·e·go /ˌso͞opərˈēgō/ ▶ **n.** (pl. **superegos**) Psychoanalysis the part of a person's mind that acts as a self-critical conscience, reflecting social standards learned from parents and teachers. Compare with EGO and ID.

su·per·el·e·va·tion /ˌso͞opərˌeləˈvāsHən/ ▶ **n.** the amount by which the outer edge of a curve on a road or railroad is banked above the inner edge.

su·per·em·i·nent /ˌso͞opərˈemənənt/ ▶ **adj.** chiefly dated term for PREEMINENT.
– DERIVATIVES **su·per·em·i·nence** n., **su·per·em·i·nent·ly** adv.
– ORIGIN mid 16th cent.: from Latin *supereminent-* 'rising above,' from the verb *supereminere* 'rise above' (see SUPER-, EMINENT).

su·per·er·o·ga·tion /ˌso͞opərˌerəˈgāsHən/ ▶ **n.** the performance of more work than duty requires.
– PHRASES **works of supererogation** (in the Roman Catholic Church) actions believed to form a reserve fund of merit that can be drawn on by prayer in favor of sinners.
– DERIVATIVES **su·per·e·rog·a·to·ry** /-əˈrägəˌtôrē/ adj.
– ORIGIN early 16th cent.: from late Latin *supererogatio(n-)*, from *supererogare* 'pay in addition,' from *super-* 'over' + *erogare* 'pay out.'

su·per·ette /ˌso͞opərˈet/ ▶ **n.** a small supermarket.
– ORIGIN 1930s: from SUPERMARKET + -ETTE.

su·per·fam·i·ly /ˈso͞opərˌfam(ə)lē/ ▶ **n.** (pl. **superfamilies**) Biology a taxonomic category that ranks above family and below order. ■ Linguistics another term for PHYLUM.

su·per·fe·cun·da·tion /ˌso͞opərˌfekənˈdāsHən/ ▶ **n.** Medicine & Zoology another term for SUPERFETATION.

su·per·fe·ta·tion /ˌso͞opərˌfēˈtāsHən/ ▶ **n.** Medicine & Zoology the occurrence of a second conception during pregnancy, giving rise to embryos of different ages in the uterus. ■ the accretion of one thing on another: *the superfetation of ideas*.
– ORIGIN early 17th cent.: from French *superfétation* or modern Latin *superfetatio(n-)*, from Latin *superfetare*, from *super-* 'above' + *fetus* 'fetus.'

su·per·fi·cial /ˌso͞opərˈfisHəl/ ▶ **adj.** existing or occurring at or on the surface: *the building suffered only superficial damage*. ■ situated or occurring on the skin or immediately beneath it: *the superficial muscle groups*. ■ appearing to be true or real only until examined more closely: *the resemblance between the breeds is superficial*. ■ not thorough, deep, or complete; cursory: *he had only the most superficial knowledge of foreign countries*. ■ not having or showing any depth of character or understanding: *perhaps I was a superficial person*.
– DERIVATIVES **su·per·fi·ci·al·i·ty** /-ˌfisHēˈalitē/ n. (pl. **superficialities**), **su·per·fi·cial·ness** n.
– ORIGIN late Middle English: from late Latin *superficialis*, from Latin *superficies* (see SUPERFICIES).

su·per·fi·cial·ly /ˌso͞opərˈfisHəlē/ ▶ **adv.** **1** as to the outward appearance only; on the surface: [as submodifier] *the theory is superficially attractive* | [sentence adverb] *superficially, they have little in common*.
2 not thoroughly or deeply: *I understood the issue only superficially*.
3 at or on the surface or skin: *he was superficially wounded in the neck*.

su·per·fi·ci·es /ˌso͞opərˈfisHēz, -ˈfisHē-ēz/ ▶ **n.** (pl. **same**) archaic a surface: *the superficies of a sphere*. ■ an outward part or appearance: *the superficies of life*.
– ORIGIN mid 16th cent.: from Latin, from *super-* 'above' + *facies* 'face.'

su·per·fine /ˌso͞opərˈfīn/ ▶ **adj.** **1** of especially high quality: *superfine upholstery*.
2 (of fibers or an instrument) very thin: *superfine tweezers*. ■ consisting of especially small particles: *superfine sugar*.
– ORIGIN late 16th cent. (in the sense 'excessively elegant'): from SUPER- 'to a high degree' + FINE[1].

su·per·fine sug·ar ▶ **n.** finely granulated white sugar that dissolves quickly and is used in cold drinks and baking.

su·per·flu·id·i·ty /ˌso͞opərˌflo͞oˈiditē/ ▶ **n.** Physics the property of flowing without friction or viscosity, as in liquid helium below about 2.18 kelvins.
– DERIVATIVES **su·per·flu·id** /ˈso͞opərˌflo͞o-id/ n. & adj.

su·per·flu·i·ty /ˌso͞opərˈflo͞o-itē/ ▶ **n.** (pl. **superfluities**) [in sing.] an unnecessarily or excessively large amount or number of something: *a superfluity of unoccupied time*. ■ an unnecessary thing: *they thought the garrison a superfluity*. ■ the state of being superfluous: *servants who had nothing to do but to display their own superfluity*.
– ORIGIN late Middle English: from Old French *superfluite*, from late Latin *superfluitas*, from Latin *superfluus* 'running over' (see SUPERFLUOUS).

su·per·flu·ous /so͞oˈpərfləwəs/ ▶ **adj.** unnecessary, esp. through being more than enough: *the purchaser should avoid asking for superfluous information*.
– DERIVATIVES **su·per·flu·ous·ly** adv., **su·per·flu·ous·ness** n.
– ORIGIN late Middle English: from Latin *superfluus*, from *super-* 'over' + *fluere* 'to flow.'

su·per·food /ˈso͞opərˌfo͞od/ ▶ **n.** a nutrient-rich food considered to be especially beneficial for health and well-being: *he touts broccoli sprouts and salmon as two of the most perfect superfoods*.

su·per·fund /ˈso͞opərˌfənd/ ▶ **n.** a fund established to finance a long-term, expensive project. ■ (**Superfund**) a US federal government program designed to fund the cleanup of toxic wastes: *billions have been spent on Superfund since 1980*.

su·per·gal·ax·y /ˈso͞opərˌgaləksē/ ▶ **n.** (pl. **supergalaxies**) another term for SUPERCLUSTER.

su·per·gene[1] /ˈso͞opərˌjēn/ ▶ **adj.** [attrib.] Geology relating to or denoting the deposition or enrichment of mineral deposits by solutions moving downward through the rocks.

su·per·gene[2] ▶ **n.** Genetics a group of closely linked genes, typically having related functions.

su·per·gi·ant /ˈso͞opərˌjīənt/ ▶ **n.** Astronomy a very large star that is even brighter than a giant, often despite being relatively cool.

su·per·glue /ˈso͞opərˌglo͞o/ ▶ **n.** a very strong quick-setting adhesive, based on cyanoacrylates or similar polymers.
▶ **v.** (**superglues**, **supergluing** or **superglueing**, **superglued**) [with obj.] stick with superglue: *he superglued his hands together*.

su·per·grav·i·ty /ˌso͞opərˈgravitē/ ▶ **n.** Physics gravity as described or predicted by a supersymmetric quantum field theory.

su·per·group /ˈso͞opərˌgro͞op/ ▶ **n.** an exceptionally successful rock group, in particular one formed by musicians already famous from playing in other groups.

su·per·heat /ˌso͞opərˈhēt/ Physics ▶ **v.** [with obj.] heat (a liquid) under pressure above its boiling point without vaporization. ■ heat (a vapor) above its temperature of saturation. ■ heat to a very high temperature.
▶ **n.** the excess of temperature of a vapor above its temperature of saturation.
– DERIVATIVES **su·per·heat·er** n.

su·per·heav·y /ˌso͞opərˈhevē/ ▶ **adj.** Physics relating to or denoting an element with an atomic mass or atomic number greater than those of the naturally occurring elements, esp. one belonging to a group above atomic number 110 having proton/neutron ratios that in theory confer relatively long half-lives.

su·per·he·lix /ˈso͞opərˌhēliks/ ▶ **n.** (pl. **superhelices** /-ˌheləˌsēz, -ˌhēlə,sēz/ or **superhelixes**) Biochemistry a helical structure formed from a number of protein or nucleic acid chains that are individually helical.
– DERIVATIVES **su·per·hel·i·cal** /ˌso͞opərˈhelikəl, -ˈhēli-/ adj.

su·per·he·ro /ˈso͞opərˌhirō/ ▶ **n.** (pl. **superheroes**) a benevolent fictional character with superhuman powers, such as Superman.

S

su·per·het /ˈso͞opərˌhet/ ▶ **n.** informal short for SUPERHETERODYNE.

su·per·het·er·o·dyne /ˌso͞opərˈhetərəˌdīn/ ▶ **adj.** denoting or using a system of radio and television reception in which the receiver produces a tunable signal that is combined with the incoming signal to produce a predetermined intermediate frequency, on which most of the amplification is formed.
▶ **n.** a superheterodyne receiver.
– ORIGIN 1920s: from SUPERSONIC + HETERODYNE.

su·per·high·way /ˈso͞opərˌhīwā, ˌso͞opərˈhīˌwā/ ▶ **n.** **1** an expressway.
2 (also **information superhighway**) an extensive electronic network such as the Internet, used for the rapid transfer of information such as sound, video, and graphics.

su·per·hu·man /ˌso͞opərˈ(h)yo͞omən/ ▶ **adj.** having or showing exceptional ability or powers: *the pilot made one last superhuman effort not to come down right on our heads*.
– DERIVATIVES **su·per·hu·man·ly** adv.

– ORIGIN mid 17th cent.: from late Latin *superhumanus* (see **SUPER-**, **HUMAN**).

su·per·im·pose /ˌso͞opərimˈpōz/ ▶ **v.** [with obj.] place or lay (one thing) over another, typically so that both are still evident: *the number will appear on the screen, superimposed on a flashing button* | (as adj. **superimposed**) *different stone tools were found in superimposed layers.*
– DERIVATIVES **su·per·im·pos·a·ble** adj., **su·per·im·po·si·tion** /-ˌimpəˈzisHən/ **n.**

su·per·in·cum·bent /ˌso͞opərinˈkəmbənt, -iNGˈkəm-/ ▶ **adj.** literary lying on something else: *the crushing effect of the superincumbent masonry.*

su·per·in·duce /ˌso͞opərinˈd(y)o͞os/ ▶ **v.** [with obj.] introduce or induce in addition: *both genes are known to be superinduced in fibroblasts by inhibition of protein synthesis.*
– ORIGIN mid 16th cent.: from Latin *superinducere* 'cover over, bring from outside' (see **SUPER-**, **INDUCE**).

su·per·in·fec·tion /ˌso͞opərinˈfeksHən/ ▶ **n.** Medicine infection occurring after or on top of an earlier infection, esp. following treatment with broad-spectrum antibiotics.

su·per·in·tend /ˌso͞opərinˈtend/ ▶ **v.** [with obj.] be responsible for the management or arrangement of (an activity or organization); oversee: *he superintended a land reclamation program.*
– DERIVATIVES **su·per·in·tend·ence** /-dəns/ **n.**, **su·per·in·tend·en·cy** /-dənsē/ **n.**
– ORIGIN early 17th cent.: from ecclesiastical Latin *superintendere*, translating Greek *episkopein*.

su·per·in·tend·ent /ˌso͞opərinˈtendənt/ ▶ **n.** a person who manages or superintends an organization or activity: *the construction superintendent* | [as modifier] *the superintendent registrar.* ■ a high-ranking official, esp. the head of a large urban police department. ■ the caretaker of a building.
– ORIGIN mid 16th cent.: from ecclesiastical Latin *superintendent-* 'overseeing,' from the verb *superintendere* (see **SUPERINTEND**).

su·pe·ri·or /səˈpi(ə)rēər/ ▶ **adj. 1** higher in rank, status, or quality: *a superior officer* | *it is superior to every other car on the road.* ■ of high standard or quality: *superior malt whiskeys.* ■ greater in size or power: *deploying superior force.* ■ [predic.] (**superior to**) above yielding to or being influenced by: *I felt superior to any accusation of anti-Semitism.* ■ having or showing an overly high opinion of oneself; supercilious: *that girl was frightfully superior.*
2 chiefly Anatomy further above or out; higher in position. ■ (of a letter, figure, or symbol) written or printed above the line. ■ Astronomy (of a planet) having an orbit further from the sun than the earth's. ■ Botany (of the ovary of a flower) situated above the sepals and petals.
▶ **n. 1** a person or thing superior to another in rank, status, or quality, esp. a colleague in a higher position: *obeying their superiors' orders.* ■ the head of a monastery or other religious institution.
2 Printing a superior letter, figure, or symbol.
– DERIVATIVES **su·pe·ri·or·ly** adv.
– ORIGIN late Middle English: from Old French *superiour*, from Latin *superior*, comparative of *superus* 'that is above,' from *super* 'above.'

Su·pe·ri·or, Lake the largest of the five Great Lakes of North America, on the border between Canada and the US. With an area of 31,800 square miles (82,350 sq km), it is the largest freshwater lake in the world.

su·pe·ri·or con·junc·tion ▶ **n.** Astronomy a conjunction of Mercury or Venus with the sun, when the planet and the earth are on opposite sides of the sun.

su·pe·ri·or court ▶ **n.** Law **1** (in many states of the US) a court of appeals or a court of general jurisdiction.
2 a court with general jurisdiction over other courts; a higher court.

su·pe·ri·or·i·ty /səˌpi(ə)rēˈôritē, -ˈäritē/ ▶ **n.** the state of being superior: *an attempt to establish superiority over others* | *the allies have achieved air superiority.* ■ a supercilious manner or attitude: *he attacked the media's smug superiority.*

su·pe·ri·or·i·ty com·plex ▶ **n.** an attitude of superiority that conceals actual feelings of inferiority and failure.

su·pe·ri·or plan·et ▶ **n.** Astronomy any of the planets (Mars, Jupiter, Saturn, Uranus, and Neptune) whose orbits are further from the sun than the Earth's. Compare with **INFERIOR PLANET**.

su·pe·ri·us /səˈpi(ə)rēəs/ ▶ **n.** the highest voice part in early choral music; the cantus.
– ORIGIN late 18th cent.: from Latin, neuter (used as a noun) of *superior* (see **SUPERIOR**).

su·per·ja·cent /ˌso͞opərˈjāsənt/ ▶ **adj.** technical lying over or above something else; overlying.
– ORIGIN late 16th cent.: from Latin *superjacent-*, from *super-* 'over' + *jacere* 'to lie.'

su·per·la·tive /səˈpərlətiv/ ▶ **adj. 1** of the highest quality or degree: *a superlative piece of skill.*
2 Grammar (of an adjective or adverb) expressing the highest or a very high degree of a quality (e.g., *bravest, most fiercely*). Contrasted with **POSITIVE** and **COMPARATIVE**.
▶ **n. 1** Grammar a superlative adjective or adverb. ■ (**the superlative**) the highest degree of comparison.
2 (usu. **superlatives**) an exaggerated or hyperbolical expression of praise: *the critics ran out of superlatives to describe him.*
3 something or someone embodying excellence.
– DERIVATIVES **su·per·la·tive·ly** adv. [as submodifier] *he was superlatively fit*, **su·per·la·tive·ness** n.
– ORIGIN late Middle English: from Old French *superlatif, -ive*, from late Latin *superlativus*, from Latin *superlatus* 'carried beyond,' past participle of *superferre*.

su·per·lat·tice /ˈso͞opərˌlatis/ ▶ **n.** Metallurgy & Physics an ordered arrangement of certain atoms that occurs in a solid solution and which is superimposed on the solvent crystal lattice.

su·per·lu·mi·nal /ˌso͞opərˈlo͞omənl/ ▶ **adj.** Physics denoting or having a speed greater than that of light.
– ORIGIN 1950s: from **SUPER-** 'above' + Latin *lumen, lumin-* 'a light' + **-AL**.

su·per·lu·na·ry /ˌso͞opərˈlo͞onərē/ ▶ **adj.** belonging to a higher world; celestial.
– ORIGIN early 17th cent.: from medieval Latin *superlunaris* (see **SUPER-**, **LUNAR**).

su·per·ma·jor·i·ty /ˈso͞opərməˌjôritē, -ˌjär-/ ▶ **n.** (pl. **supermajorities**) a number that is much more than half of a total, esp. in a vote.

su·per·man /ˈso͞opəˌman/ ▶ **n.** (pl. **supermen**) **1** chiefly Philosophy the ideal superior man of the future. See **ÜBERMENSCH**.
2 (**a superman**) informal a man with exceptional physical or mental ability.
– ORIGIN early 20th cent.: from **SUPER-** 'exceptional' + **MAN**, coined by G. B. Shaw in imitation of German *Übermensch* (used by Nietzsche).

su·per·mar·ket /ˈso͞opərˌmärkit/ ▶ **n.** a large self-service store selling foods and household goods.

su·per·mas·sive /ˈso͞opərˌmasiv/ ▶ **adj.** Astronomy having a mass many times (typically between 10^6 and 10^9 times) that of the sun: *a supermassive star.*

su·per·max /ˈso͞opərˌmaks/ ▶ **adj.** denoting or relating to an extremely high-security prison or part of a prison, intended for particularly dangerous prisoners.
▶ **n.** a supermax prison.
– ORIGIN 1970s: shortened from *super-maximum*, i.e., 'greater than the expected or conventional maximum.'

su·per·min·i /ˈso͞opərˌminē/ (also **superminicomputer**) ▶ **n.** (pl. **superminis**) a microcomputer with the speed, power, and capabilities of a mainframe.

su·per·mod·el /ˈso͞opərˌmädl/ ▶ **n.** a successful fashion model who has reached the status of a celebrity.

su·per·nal /səˈpərnl/ ▶ **adj.** chiefly literary of or relating to the sky or the heavens; celestial. ■ of exceptional quality or extent: *he is the supernal poet of our age* | *supernal erudition.*
– DERIVATIVES **su·per·nal·ly** adv.
– ORIGIN late Middle English: from Old French, or from medieval Latin *supernalis*, from Latin *supernus*, from *super* 'above.'

su·per·na·tant /ˌso͞opərˈnātnt/ technical ▶ **adj.** denoting the liquid lying above a solid residue after crystallization, precipitation, centrifugation, or other process.
▶ **n.** a volume of supernatant liquid.

su·per·nat·u·ral /ˌso͞opərˈnacH(ə)rəl/ ▶ **adj.** (of a manifestation or event) attributed to some force beyond scientific understanding or the laws of nature: *a supernatural being.* ■ unnaturally or extraordinarily great: *a woman of supernatural beauty.*
▶ **n.** (**the supernatural**) manifestations or events considered to be of supernatural origin, such as ghosts.
– DERIVATIVES **su·per·nat·u·ral·ism** n., **su·per·nat·u·ral·ist** n., **su·per·nat·u·ral·ly** adv. [as submodifier] *the monster was supernaturally strong.*

su·per·nor·mal /ˌso͞opərˈnôrməl/ ▶ **adj.** exceeding or beyond the normal; exceptional: *a supernormal human.*
– DERIVATIVES **su·per·nor·mal·i·ty** /-ˌnôrˈmalitē/ **n.**

su·per·no·va /ˈso͞opərˌnōvə/ ▶ **n.** (pl. **supernovae** /-ˌnōvē/ or **supernovas**) Astronomy a star that suddenly increases greatly in brightness because of a catastrophic explosion that ejects most of its mass.

su·per·nu·mer·ar·y /ˌso͞opərˈn(y)o͞oməˌrerē/ ▶ **adj.** present in excess of the normal or requisite number, in particular: ■ (of a person) not belonging to a regular staff but engaged for extra work. ■ not wanted or needed; redundant: *books were obviously supernumerary, and he began jettisoning them.* ■ Botany & Zoology denoting a structure or organ occurring in addition to the normal ones: *a pair of supernumerary teats.* ■ (of an actor) appearing on stage but not speaking.
▶ **n.** (pl. **supernumeraries**) a supernumerary person or thing.
– ORIGIN early 17th cent.: from late Latin *supernumerarius* '(soldier) added to a legion after it is complete,' from Latin *super numerum* 'beyond the number.'

su·per·or·der /ˈso͞opərˌôrdər/ ▶ **n.** Biology a taxonomic category that ranks above order and below class.

su·per·or·di·nate /ˌso͞opərˈôrdn-ət/ ▶ **n.** a thing that represents a superior order or category within a system of classification: *a pair of compatibles must have a common superordinate.* ■ a person who has authority over or control of another within an organization. ■ Linguistics a word whose meaning includes the meaning of one or more other words: *"bird" is the superordinate of "canary."*
▶ **adj.** superior in status: *senior staff's superordinate position.*
– ORIGIN early 17th cent.: from **SUPER-** 'above,' on the pattern of *subordinate*.

su·per·ox·ide /ˌso͞opərˈäkˌsīd/ ▶ **n.** Chemistry an oxide containing the anion O_2^-.

su·per·phos·phate /ˈso͞opərˌfäsˌfāt/ ▶ **n.** a fertilizer made by treating phosphate rock with sulfuric or phosphoric acid.

su·per·plas·tic /ˈso͞opərˌplastik/ Metallurgy ▶ **adj.** (of a metal or alloy) capable of extreme plastic extension under load.
▶ **n.** a metal or alloy having this property.
– DERIVATIVES **su·per·plas·tic·i·ty** /ˌso͞opərplasˈtisitē/ **n.**

su·per·pose /ˌso͞opərˈpōz/ ▶ **v.** [with obj.] place (something) on or above something else, esp. so that they coincide: (as adj. **superposed**) *a border of superposed triangles.*
– DERIVATIVES **su·per·pos·a·ble** adj., **su·per·po·si·tion** /-pəˈzisHən/ **n.**
– ORIGIN early 19th cent.: from French *superposer*, from *super-* 'above' + *poser* 'to place.'

su·per·pow·er /ˈso͞opərˌpouər/ ▶ **n.** a very powerful and influential nation (used esp. with reference to the US and the former Soviet Union when these were perceived as the two most powerful nations in the world).

su·per·sat·u·rate /ˌso͞opərˈsacHəˌrāt/ ▶ **v.** [with obj.] Chemistry increase the concentration of (a solution) beyond saturation point.
– DERIVATIVES **su·per·sat·u·ra·tion** /-ˌsacHəˈrāsHən/ **n.**

su·per·sca·lar /ˌso͞opərˈskālər/ ▶ **adj.** denoting a computer architecture where several instructions are loaded at once and, as far as possible, are executed simultaneously, shortening the time taken to run the whole program.

su·per·scribe /ˌso͞opərˈskrīb/ ▶ **v.** [with obj.] write or print (an inscription) at the top of or on the outside of a document: *they had superscribed "Top Secret" across the cover page.* ■ write or print an inscription at the top of or on the outside of (a document): *he invariably will want to superscribe the memo with one of his banal mottoes.* ■ write or print (a letter, word, symbol, or line of writing or printing) above an existing letter, word, or line.
– DERIVATIVES **su·per·scrip·tion** /-ˈskripsHən/ **n.**
– ORIGIN late 15th cent.: from Latin *superscribere*, from *super-* 'over' + *scribere* 'write.'

su·per·script /ˈso͞opərˌskript/ ▶ **adj.** (of a letter, figure, or symbol) written or printed above the line.
▶ **n.** a superscript letter, figure, or symbol.
– ORIGIN late 19th cent. (as an adjective): from Latin *superscriptus* 'written above,' past participle of *superscribere*.

su·per·sede /ˌso͞opərˈsēd/ ▶ **v.** [with obj.] take the place of (a person or thing previously in authority or use); supplant: *the older models have now been superseded.*
– DERIVATIVES **su·per·ses·sion** /-ˈsesHən/ **n.**
– ORIGIN late 15th cent. (in the sense 'postpone, defer'): from Old French *superseder*, from Latin *supersedere* 'be superior to,' from *super-* 'above' + *sedere* 'sit.' The current sense dates from the mid 17th cent.

USAGE See usage at **SUPERCEDE**.

S

su·per·set /ˈso͞opərˌset/ ▶ **n.** Mathematics a set that includes another set or sets.

su·per·size /ˈso͞opərˌsīz/ ▶ **v.** [with obj.] produce or serve (something) in a larger size: *click here to supersize the picture.*
▶ **adj.** larger than average or standard sizes; extremely large: *a pair of supersize sunglasses.*

su·per·son·ic /ˌso͞opərˈsänik/ ▶ **adj.** involving or denoting a speed greater than that of sound.
– DERIVATIVES **su·per·son·i·cal·ly** /-ik(ə)lē/ **adv.**

su·per·son·ics /ˌso͞opərˈsäniks/ ▶ **plural n.** [treated as sing.] another term for ULTRASONICS.

su·per·space /ˈso͞opərˌspās/ ▶ **n.** Physics a concept of space-time in which points are defined by more than four coordinates. ■ a space of infinitely many dimensions postulated to contain actual space-time and all possible spaces.

su·per·star /ˈso͞opərˌstär/ ▶ **n.** a high-profile and extremely successful performer or athlete.
– DERIVATIVES **su·per·star·dom** /-dəm/ **n.**

su·per·state /ˈso͞opərˌstāt/ ▶ **n.** a large and powerful state or union formed from a federation of nations: *we are not advocates of a European superstate.*

su·per·sta·tion /ˈso͞opərˌstāsHən/ ▶ **n.** a television station that broadcasts widely via cable or satellite.

su·per·sti·tion /ˌso͞opərˈstisHən/ ▶ **n.** excessively credulous belief in and reverence for supernatural beings: *he dismissed the ghost stories as mere superstition.* ■ a widely held but unjustified belief in supernatural causation leading to certain consequences of an action or event, or a practice based on such a belief: *she touched her locket for luck, a superstition she had had since childhood.*
– ORIGIN Middle English: from Old French, or from Latin *superstitio(n-)*, from *super-* 'over' + *stare* 'to stand' (perhaps from the notion of "standing over" something in awe).

su·per·sti·tious /ˌso͞opərˈstisHəs/ ▶ **adj.** having or showing a belief in superstitions: *many superstitious beliefs and practices are connected with sneezing.*
– DERIVATIVES **su·per·sti·tious·ly** /-ˈstisHəslē/ **adv.**, **su·per·sti·tious·ness** /-ˈstisHəsnəs/ **n.**

su·per·store /ˈso͞opərˌstôr/ ▶ **n.** a retail store, as a grocery store or bookstore, with more than the average amount of space and variety of stock.

su·per·stra·tum /ˈso͞opərˌstrātəm, -ˌstratəm/ ▶ **n.** (pl. **superstrata** /-tə/) an overlying stratum.

su·per·string /ˈso͞opərˌstriNG/ ▶ **n.** Physics a subatomic particle in a version of string theory that incorporates supersymmetry.

su·per·struc·ture /ˈso͞opərˌstrəkCHər/ ▶ **n.** a structure built on top of something else. ■ the parts of a ship, other than masts and rigging, built above its hull and main deck. ■ the part of a building above its foundations. ■ a concept or idea based on others. ■ (in Marxist theory) the institutions and culture considered to result from or reflect the economic system underlying a society.
– DERIVATIVES **su·per·struc·tur·al** /ˌso͞opərˈstrəkCHərəl/ **adj.**

su·per·sym·me·try /ˈso͞opərˌsimitrē/ ▶ **n.** Physics a very general type of mathematical symmetry that relates fermions and bosons.
– DERIVATIVES **su·per·sym·met·ric** /-siˈmetrik/ **adj.**

su·per·tank·er /ˈso͞opərˌtaNGkər/ ▶ **n.** a very large oil tanker, specifically one whose dead-weight capacity exceeds 75,000 tons.

su·per·tax /ˈso͞opərˌtaks/ ▶ **n.** an additional tax on something already taxed.

su·per·ti·tle /ˈso͞opərˌtītl/ ▶ **n.** (usu. **supertitles**) a caption projected on a screen above the stage in an opera, translating the text being sung.
▶ **v.** [with obj.] provide (an opera) with supertitles.

su·per·ton·ic /ˈso͞opərˌtänik/ ▶ **n.** Music the second note of the diatonic scale of any key; the note above the tonic.

Su·per Tues·day ▶ **n.** informal a day on which several US states hold primary elections.

su·per·us·er /ˈso͞opərˌyo͞ozər/ ▶ **n.** a user of a computer system with special privileges needed to administer and maintain the system; a system administrator.

su·per·vene /ˌso͞opərˈvēn/ ▶ **v.** [no obj.] occur later than a specified or implied event or action, typically in such a way as to change the situation: (as adj. **supervening**) *any plan that is made is liable to be disrupted by supervening events.* ■ Philosophy (of a fact or property) be entailed by or consequent on the existence or establishment of another: *the view that mental events supervene upon physical ones.*
– DERIVATIVES **su·per·ven·ient** /-ˈvēnyənt/ **adj.**, **su·per·ven·tion** /-ˈvenCHən/ **n.**
– ORIGIN mid 17th cent.: from Latin *supervenire*, from *super-* 'in addition' + *venire* 'come.'

su·per·vise /ˈso͞opərˌvīz/ ▶ **v.** [with obj.] observe and direct the execution of (a task, project, or activity): *the sergeant left to supervise the loading of the trucks.* ■ observe and direct the work of (someone): *nurses were supervised by a consulting psychiatrist.* ■ keep watch over (someone) in the interest of their or others' security: *prisoners were supervised by two officers.*
– ORIGIN late 15th cent. (in the sense 'survey, peruse'): from medieval Latin *supervis-* 'surveyed, supervised,' from *supervidere*, from *super-* 'over' + *videre* 'to see.'

su·per·vi·sion /ˌso͞opərˈvizHən/ ▶ **n.** the action of supervising someone or something: *students were under the supervision of the faculty member at all times.*

su·per·vi·sor /ˈso͞opərˌvīzər/ ▶ **n.** a person who supervises a person or an activity.
– DERIVATIVES **su·per·vi·so·ry** /ˌso͞opərˈvīzərē/ **adj.**

su·per·vol·tage /ˈso͞opərˌvōltij/ ▶ **n.** [usu. as modifier] Medicine a voltage in excess of 200 kV used in X-ray radiotherapy: *supervoltage therapy.*

su·per·wom·an /ˈso͞opərˌwo͝omən/ ▶ **n.** (pl. **superwomen**) informal a woman with exceptional strength or ability, esp. one who successfully manages a home, brings up children, and has a full-time job.

su·pi·nate /ˈso͞opəˌnāt/ ▶ **v.** [with obj.] Anatomy turn or hold (a hand, foot, or limb) so that the palm or sole is facing upward or outward: (as adj. **supinated**) *a supinated foot.* Compare with PRONATE. ■ [no obj.] walk or run with most of the weight on the outside of the feet.
– DERIVATIVES **su·pi·na·tion** /ˌso͞opəˈnāsHən/ **n.**
– ORIGIN mid 19th cent.: back-formation from *supination*, from Latin *supinatio(n-)*, from *supinare* 'lay backward,' from *supinus* (see SUPINE).

su·pi·na·tor /ˈso͞opəˌnātər/ ▶ **n.** Anatomy **1** a muscle whose contraction produces or assists in the supination of a limb or part of a limb.
2 a person who supinates when walking or running.

su·pine /ˈso͞oˌpīn/ ▶ **adj.** **1** (of a person) lying face upward. ■ technical having the front or ventral part upward. ■ (of the hand) with the palm upward.
2 failing to act or protest as a result of moral weakness or indolence: *supine in the face of racial injustice.*
▶ **n.** a Latin verbal noun used only in the accusative and ablative cases, esp. to denote purpose (e.g., *dictu* in *mirabile dictu* "wonderful to relate").
– DERIVATIVES **su·pine·ly** **adv.**, **su·pine·ness** **n.**
– ORIGIN late Middle English: the adjective from Latin *supinus* 'bent backward' (related to *super* 'above'); the noun from late Latin *supinum*, neuter of *supinus*.

supp. ▶ **abbr.** ■ supplement. ■ supplementary.

sup·per /ˈsəpər/ ▶ **n.** an evening meal, typically a light or informal one: *we had a delicious cold supper* | *I was sent to bed without any supper.*
– PHRASES **sing for one's supper** earn a favor or benefit by providing a service in return: *the cruise lecturers are academics singing for their supper.*
– DERIVATIVES **sup·per·less** **adj.**
– ORIGIN Middle English: from Old French *super* 'to sup' (used as a noun) (see SUP[2]).

sup·per club ▶ **n.** a restaurant or nightclub serving suppers and usually providing entertainment.

suppl. ▶ **abbr.** ■ supplement. ■ supplementary.

sup·plant /səˈplant/ ▶ **v.** [with obj.] supersede and replace: *another discovery could supplant the original finding.*
– DERIVATIVES **sup·plant·er** **n.**
– ORIGIN Middle English: from Old French *supplanter* or Latin *supplantare* 'trip up,' from *sub-* 'from below' + *planta* 'sole.'

sup·ple /ˈsəpəl/ ▶ **adj.** (**suppler**, **supplest**) bending and moving easily and gracefully; flexible: *her supple fingers* | figurative *my mind is becoming more supple.* ■ not stiff or hard; easily manipulated: *this body oil leaves your skin feeling deliciously supple.*
▶ **v.** [with obj.] make more flexible.
– DERIVATIVES **sup·ple·ly** /ˈsəp(ə)lē/ (also **supply**) **adv.**, **sup·ple·ness** **n.**
– ORIGIN Middle English: from Old French *souple*, from Latin *supplex*, *supplic-* 'submissive,' from *sub-* 'under' + *placere* 'propitiate.'

sup·ple·jack /ˈsəpəlˌjak/ ▶ **n.** either of two New World twining plants. ● a tall North American climber (*Berchemia scandens*, family Rhamnaceae). ● a plant of the Caribbean and tropical America (*Paullinia plumieri*, family Sapindaceae).

sup·ple·ment ▶ **n.** /ˈsəpləmənt/ **1** something that completes or enhances something else when added to it: *the handout is a supplement to the official manual.* ■ a substance taken to remedy the deficiencies in a person's diet: *multivitamin supplements.* ■ a separate section, esp. a color magazine, added to a newspaper or periodical.
2 Geometry the amount by which an angle is less than 180°.
▶ **v.** /ˈsəpləˌment, -mənt/ [with obj.] add an extra element or amount to: *she took the job to supplement her husband's income.*
– DERIVATIVES **sup·ple·men·tal** /ˌsəpləˈmentl/ **adj.**, **sup·ple·men·tal·ly** /ˌsəpləˈmentl-ē/ **adv.**, **sup·ple·men·ta·tion** /ˌsəpləˌmenˈtāsHən/ **n.**
– ORIGIN late Middle English: from Latin *supplementum*, from *supplere* 'fill up, complete' (see SUPPLY[1]).

sup·ple·men·ta·ry /ˌsəpləˈmentərē/ ▶ **adj.** completing or enhancing something: *the center's work was to be seen as supplementary to orthodox treatment and not a substitute for it.*
▶ **n.** a supplementary person or thing.
– DERIVATIVES **sup·ple·men·tar·i·ly** /-ˌmenˈte(ə)rəlē/ **adv.**

sup·ple·men·ta·ry an·gle ▶ **n.** Mathematics either of two angles whose sum is 180°.

sup·ple·tion /səˈplēsHən/ ▶ **n.** Linguistics the occurrence of an unrelated form to fill a gap in a conjugation (e.g., *went* as the past tense of *go*).
– DERIVATIVES **sup·ple·tive** /səˈplētiv, ˈsəplətiv/ **adj.**
– ORIGIN Middle English: from Old French, from medieval Latin *suppletio(n-)*, from *supplere* 'fill up, make full' (see SUPPLY[1]).

Sup·plex /ˈsəpleks/ ▶ **n.** trademark a synthetic stretchable fabric which is permeable to air and water vapor, used in sports and outdoor clothing.

sup·pli·ant /ˈsəplēənt/ ▶ **n.** a person making a humble plea to someone in power or authority.
▶ **adj.** making or expressing a plea, esp. to someone in power or authority: *their faces were suppliant.*
– DERIVATIVES **sup·pli·ant·ly** **adv.**
– ORIGIN late Middle English (as a noun): from French, 'beseeching,' present participle of *supplier*, from Latin *supplicare* (see SUPPLICATE).

sup·pli·cate /ˈsəpliˌkāt/ ▶ **v.** [no obj.] ask or beg for something earnestly or humbly: [with infinitive] *the plutocracy supplicated to be made peers.*
– DERIVATIVES **sup·pli·cant** /-kənt/ **adj. & n.**, **sup·pli·ca·to·ry** /-kəˌtôrē/ **adj.**
– ORIGIN late Middle English: from Latin *supplicat-* 'implored,' from the verb *supplicare*, from *sub-* 'from below' + *placere* 'propitiate.'

sup·pli·ca·tion /ˌsəpliˈkāsHən/ ▶ **n.** the action of asking or begging for something earnestly or humbly: *he fell to his knees in supplication.*

sup·ply[1] /səˈplī/ ▶ **v.** (**supplies**, **supplying**, **supplied**) [with obj.] make (something needed or wanted) available to someone; provide: *the farm supplies apples to cider makers.* ■ provide (someone) with something needed or wanted: *they struggled to supply the besieged island with aircraft.* ■ be adequate to satisfy (a requirement or demand): *the two reservoirs supply about 1% of the city's needs.* ■ archaic take over (a place or role left by someone else): *when she died, no one could supply her place.*
▶ **n.** (pl. **supplies**) a stock of a resource from which a person or place can be provided with the necessary amount of that resource: *there were fears that the drought would limit the exhibition's water supply.* ■ the action of providing what is needed or wanted: *the deal involved the supply of forty fighter aircraft.* ■ Economics the amount of a good or service offered for sale. ■ (**supplies**) the provisions and equipment necessary for an army or for people engaged in a particular project or expedition. ■ (**supplies**) Brit. a grant of money by Parliament for the costs of government. ■ [usu. as modifier] a person acting as a temporary substitute for another. ■ [as modifier] providing necessary goods and equipment: *a supply ship.*
– PHRASES **in short supply** not easily obtainable; scarce: *he meant to go, but time and gas were in short supply.* **supply and demand** the amount of a commodity, product, or service available and the desire of buyers for it, considered as factors regulating its price: *by the law of supply and demand the cost of health care will plummet.*
– DERIVATIVES **sup·pli·er** **n.**
– ORIGIN late Middle English: from Old French *soupleer*, from Latin *supplere* 'fill up,' from *sub-* 'from below' + *plere* 'fill.' The early sense of the noun was 'assistance, relief' (chiefly a Scots use).

sup·ply[2] /ˈsəp(ə)lē/ ▶ **adv.** variant spelling of SUPPLELY (see SUPPLE).

sup·ply chain ▶ **n.** the sequence of processes involved in the production and distribution of a commodity.

PRONUNCIATION KEY ə *ago, up*; ər *over, fur*; a *hat*; ā *ate*; ä *car*; e *let*; ē *see*; i *fit*; ī *by*; NG *sing*; ō *go*; ô *law, for*; oi *toy*; o͝o *good*; o͞o *goo*; ou *out*; TH *thin*; T͟H *then*; ZH *vision*

S

sup·ply-side ▶ **adj.** [attrib.] Economics denoting or relating to a policy designed to increase output and employment by changing the conditions under which goods and services are supplied, esp. by measures that reduce government involvement in the economy and allow the free market to operate.
– DERIVATIVES **sup·ply-sid·er n.**

sup·port /sə'pôrt/ ▶ **v.** [with obj.] **1** bear all or part of the weight of; hold up: *the dome was supported by a hundred white columns.* ■ produce enough food and water for; be capable of sustaining: *the land had lost its capacity to support life.* ■ be capable of fulfilling (a role) adequately: *tutors gain practical experience that helps them support their tutoring role.* ■ endure; tolerate: *at work during the day I could support the grief.*
2 give assistance to, esp. financially; enable to function or act: *the government gives $2.5 billion a year to support the activities of the voluntary sector.* ■ provide with a home and the necessities of life: *my main concern was to support my family.* ■ give approval, comfort, or encouragement to: *I like to visit her to support her | the proposal was supported by many delegates.* ■ suggest the truth of; corroborate: *the studies support our findings.* ■ be actively interested in and concerned for the success of (a particular sports team). ■ (as adj. **supporting**) (of an actor or a role) important in a play or film but subordinate to the leading parts. ■ (of a pop or rock group or performer) function as a secondary act to (another) at a concert.
3 Computing (of a computer or operating system) allow the use or operation of (a program, language, or device): *the new versions do not support the graphical user interface standard.*
▶ **n. 1** a thing that bears the weight of something or keeps it upright: *the best support for a camera is a tripod.* ■ the action or state of bearing the weight of something or someone or of being so supported: *she clutched the sideboard for support.*
2 material assistance: *he urged that military support be sent to protect humanitarian convoys* | [as modifier] *support staff.* ■ comfort and emotional help offered to someone in distress: *she's been through a bad time and needs our support.* ■ approval and encouragement: *the policies of reform enjoy widespread support.* ■ a secondary act at a pop or rock concert. ■ technical help given to the user of a computer or other product.
– PHRASES **in support of** giving assistance to: *air operations in support of the land forces.* ■ showing approval of: *the paper printed many letters in support of the government.* ■ attempting to promote or obtain: *a strike in support of an 8.5% pay raise.*
– DERIVATIVES **sup·port·a·bil·i·ty** /sə,pôrtə'bilitē/ **n.**, **sup·port·a·ble adj.**
– ORIGIN Middle English (originally in the sense 'tolerate, put up with'): from Old French *supporter*, from Latin *supportare*, from *sub-* 'from below' + *portare* 'carry.'

sup·port·er /sə'pôrtər/ ▶ **n. 1** a person who approves of and encourages someone or something (typically a public figure, a movement or party, or a policy): *Reagan supporters | supporters of the boycott.* ■ a person who is actively interested in and wishes success for a particular sports team.
2 Heraldry a representation of an animal or other figure, typically one of a pair, holding up or standing beside an escutcheon.
3 (in full **athletic supporter**) another term for JOCKSTRAP.

S

sup·port group ▶ **n. 1** a group of people who are available to support one another emotionally, socially, and sometimes financially: *a support group for gay teens.*
2 a system implemented with the aim of providing support for an enterprise, product line, or project: *Unix system support group.*

sup·port·ive /sə'pôrtiv/ ▶ **adj.** providing encouragement or emotional help: *the staff are extremely supportive of each other.*
– DERIVATIVES **sup·port·ive·ly adv.**, **sup·port·ive·ness n.**

sup·port·ive ther·a·py ▶ **n.** treatment designed to improve, reinforce, or sustain a patient's physiological well-being or psychological self-esteem and self-reliance.

sup·pose /sə'pōz/ ▶ **v. 1** [with clause] assume that something is the case on the basis of evidence or probability but without proof or certain knowledge: *I suppose I got there about half past eleven.* ■ used to make a reluctant or hesitant admission: *I'm quite a good actress, I suppose.* ■ used to introduce a hypothesis and trace or ask about what follows from it: *suppose he had been murdered—what then?* ■ [in imperative] used to introduce a suggestion: *suppose we leave this to the police.* ■ (of a theory or argument) assume or require that something is the case as a precondition: *the procedure supposes that a will has already been proved* | [with obj.] *the theory supposes a predisposition to interpret utterances.* ■ [with obj.] believe to exist or to possess a specified characteristic: *he supposed the girl to be about twelve.*
2 (**be supposed to do something**) be required to do something because of the position one is in or an agreement one has made: *I'm supposed to be meeting someone at the airport.* ■ [with negative] be forbidden to do something: *I shouldn't have been in the kitchen—I'm not supposed to go in there.*
– PHRASES **I suppose so** used to express hesitant or reluctant agreement.
– DERIVATIVES **sup·pos·a·ble adj.**
– ORIGIN Middle English: from Old French *supposer*, from Latin *supponere* (from *sub-* 'from below' + *ponere* 'to place'), but influenced by Latin *suppositus* 'set under' and Old French *poser* 'to place.'

sup·posed /sə'pōzd, sə'pōzid/ ▶ **adj.** [attrib.] generally assumed or believed to be the case, but not necessarily so: *people admire their supposed industriousness.*

sup·pos·ed·ly /sə'pōzidlē/ ▶ **adv.** [sentence adverb] according to what is generally assumed or believed (often used to indicate that the speaker doubts the truth of the statement): *the ads are aimed at women, supposedly because they do the shopping.*

sup·po·si·tion /,səpə'zisHən/ ▶ **n.** an uncertain belief: *they were working on the supposition that his death was murder | their outrage was based on supposition and hearsay.*
– DERIVATIVES **sup·po·si·tion·al** /-SHənl/ **adj.**
– ORIGIN late Middle English (as a term in scholastic logic): from Old French, or from late Latin *suppositio(n-)* (translating Greek *hupothesis* 'hypothesis'), from the verb *supponere* (see SUPPOSE).

sup·po·si·tious /,səpə'zisHəs/ ▶ **adj.** based on assumption rather than fact: *most of the evidence is purely suppositious.*
– DERIVATIVES **sup·po·si·tious·ly adv.**, **sup·po·si·tious·ness n.**
– ORIGIN early 17th cent. (in the sense 'supposititious'): partly a contraction of SUPPOSITITIOUS, reinforced by SUPPOSITION.

sup·pos·i·ti·tious /sə,päzə'tisHəs/ ▶ **adj.** substituted for the real thing; not genuine: *the supposititious heir to the throne.*
– DERIVATIVES **sup·pos·i·ti·tious·ly adv.**, **sup·pos·i·ti·tious·ness n.**
– ORIGIN early 17th cent.: from Latin *supposititius* (from *supponere* 'to substitute') + -OUS.

sup·pos·i·to·ry /sə'päzə,tôrē/ ▶ **n.** (pl. **suppositories**) a solid medical preparation in a roughly conical or cylindrical shape, designed to be inserted into the rectum or vagina to dissolve.
– ORIGIN late Middle English: from medieval Latin *suppositorium*, neuter (used as a noun) of late Latin *suppositorius* 'placed underneath.'

sup·press /sə'pres/ ▶ **v.** [with obj.] forcibly put an end to: *the uprising was savagely suppressed.* ■ prevent the development, action, or expression of (a feeling, impulse, idea, etc.); restrain: *she could not suppress a rising panic.* ■ prevent the dissemination of (information): *the report had been suppressed.* ■ prevent or inhibit (a process or reaction): *use of the drug suppressed the immune response.* ■ partly or wholly eliminate (electrical interference). ■ Psychoanalysis consciously inhibit (an unpleasant idea or memory) to avoid considering it.
– DERIVATIVES **sup·press·i·ble adj.**, **sup·pres·sive** /-siv/ **adj.**, **sup·pres·sor** /-sər/ **n.**
– ORIGIN late Middle English: from Latin *suppress-* 'pressed down,' from the verb *supprimere*, from *sub-* 'down' + *premere* 'to press.'

sup·pres·sant /sə'presənt/ ▶ **n.** a drug or other substance that acts to suppress or restrain something: *an appetite suppressant.*

sup·pres·sion /sə'presHən/ ▶ **n.** the action of suppressing something such as an activity or publication: *the forcible suppression of campus protests.* ■ Medicine stoppage or reduction of a discharge or secretion. ■ Biology the absence or nondevelopment of a part or organ that is normally present. ■ Genetics the canceling of the effect of one mutation by a second mutation. ■ Psychology the restraint or repression of an idea, activity, or reaction by something more powerful. ■ Psychoanalysis the conscious inhibition of unacceptable memories, impulses, or desires. ■ prevention of electrical interference.

sup·pres·sor cell /sə'presər/ (also **suppressor T cell**) ▶ **n.** Physiology a lymphocyte that can suppress antibody production by other lymphoid cells.

sup·pu·rate /'səpyə,rāt/ ▶ **v.** [no obj.] undergo the formation of pus; fester.
– DERIVATIVES **sup·pu·ra·tion** /,səpyə'rāsHən/ **n.**, **sup·pu·ra·tive** /-,rātiv/ **adj.**
– ORIGIN late Middle English (in the sense 'cause to form pus'): based on Latin *sub-* 'below' + *pus, pur-* 'pus.'

supr. ▶ **abbr.** ■ superior. ■ supreme.

su·pra /'so͞oprə/ ▶ **adv.** formal used in academic or legal texts to refer to someone or something mentioned above or earlier: *the recent work by McAuslan and others (supra).*
– ORIGIN Latin.

supra- ▶ **prefix 1** beyond; transcending: *supranational.*
2 above: *suprarenal.*
– ORIGIN from Latin *supra* 'above, beyond, before in time.'

su·pra·chi·as·mat·ic nu·cle·us /'so͞oprə,kīəz'matik/ ▶ **n.** Anatomy each of a pair of small nuclei in the hypothalamus of the brain, above the optic chiasma, thought to be concerned with the regulation of physiological circadian rhythms.

su·pra·mo·lec·u·lar /,so͞oprəmə'lekyələr/ ▶ **adj.** Biochemistry relating to or denoting structures composed of several or many molecules.

su·pra·na·tion·al /,so͞oprə'nasHənl/ ▶ **adj.** having power or influence that transcends national boundaries or governments: *supranational law.*
– DERIVATIVES **su·pra·na·tion·al·ism** /-,izəm/ **n.**, **su·pra·na·tion·al·i·ty** /-,nasHə'nalitē/ **n.**

su·pra·op·tic /,so͞oprə'äptik/ ▶ **adj.** Anatomy situated above the optic chiasma.

su·pra·or·bit·al /,so͞oprə'ôrbitl/ ▶ **adj.** Anatomy situated above the orbit of the eye.

su·pra·re·nal /,so͞oprə'rēnl/ ▶ **adj.** Anatomy another term for ADRENAL.

su·pra·seg·men·tal /,so͞oprə,seg'mentl/ Linguistics ▶ **adj.** denoting a feature of an utterance other than the consonantal and vocalic components, e.g., (in English) stress and intonation.
▶ **n.** such a feature.

su·prem·a·cist /sə'preməsist, so͞o-/ ▶ **n.** an advocate of the supremacy of a particular group, esp. one determined by race or sex: *a white supremacist.*
▶ **adj.** relating to or advocating such supremacy.
– DERIVATIVES **su·prem·a·cism** /-,sizəm/ **n.**

su·prem·a·cy /sə'preməsē, so͞o-/ ▶ **n.** the state or condition of being superior to all others in authority, power, or status: *the supremacy of the king.*

su·prem·a·tism /sə'premə,tizəm, so͞o-/ ▶ **n.** the Russian abstract art movement developed by Kazimir Malevich *c.*1915, characterized by simple geometric shapes and associated with ideas of spiritual purity.
– DERIVATIVES **su·prem·a·tist n.**

su·preme /sə'prēm, so͞o-/ ▶ **adj.** (of authority or an office, or someone holding it) superior to all others: *a unified force with a supreme commander.* ■ strongest, most important, or most powerful: *on the racetrack he reigned supreme.* ■ very great or intense; extreme: *he was nerving himself for a supreme effort.* ■ (of a penalty or sacrifice) involving death: *our comrades who made the supreme sacrifice.* ■ [postpositive] used to indicate that someone or something is very good at or well known for a specified activity: *here was the gift supreme.*
▶ **n.** (also **suprême**) a rich cream sauce. ■ a dish served in such a sauce: *chicken supreme.* [from French *suprême.*]
– PHRASES **the Supreme Being** a name for God.
– DERIVATIVES **su·preme·ly adv.**
– ORIGIN late 15th cent. (in the sense 'highest'): from Latin *supremus*, superlative of *superus* 'that is above,' from *super* 'above.'

Su·preme Court ▶ **n.** the highest judicial court in a country or state. ■ (in full **US Supreme Court**) the highest federal court in the US, consisting of nine justices and taking judicial precedence over all other courts in the nation.

su·preme pon·tiff ▶ **n.** see PONTIFF.

Su·preme So·vi·et ▶ **n.** the governing council of the former Soviet Union or one of its constituent republics. That of the Soviet Union was its highest legislative authority and was composed of two equal chambers: the Soviet of Union and the Soviet of Nationalities.

Supt. ▶ **abbr.** Superintendent.

supvr. ▶ **abbr.** supervisor.

suq ▶ **n.** variant spelling of SOUK.

sur. ▶ **abbr.** ■ surface. ■ surplus.

sur-[1] ▶ **prefix** equivalent to SUPER- (as in *surcharge, surmount*).
– ORIGIN from French.

sur-[2] ▶ **prefix** variant spelling of SUB- assimilated before *r* (as in *surrogate*).

su·ra /ˈsŏŏrə/ (also **surah**) ▶ **n.** a chapter or section of the Koran.
– ORIGIN from Arabic *sūra*.

Su·ra·ba·ya /ˌsŏŏrəˈbīə/ a seaport in Indonesia, on the northern coast of Java; pop. 2,336,800 (est. 2009). It is Indonesia's principal naval base and its second largest city.

su·rah /ˈsŏŏrə/ ▶ **n.** a soft twilled silk fabric used in dressmaking.
– ORIGIN late 19th cent.: representing the French pronunciation of SURAT, where it was originally made.

su·ral /ˈsŏŏrəl/ ▶ **adj.** Anatomy of or relating to the calf of the leg.
– ORIGIN early 17th cent.: from modern Latin *suralis*, from Latin *sura* 'calf.'

Su·rat /ˈsŏŏrˌat, sŏŏˈrat/ a city in the state of Gujarat in western India, a port on the Tapti River near its mouth on the Gulf of Cambay; pop. 3,234,000 (est. 2009).

sur·cease /sərˈsēs/ ▶ **n.** cessation: *he teased us without surcease.* ■ relief or consolation: *drugs are taken to provide surcease from intolerable psychic pain.*
▶ **v.** [no obj.] archaic cease.
– ORIGIN late Middle English (as a verb): from Old French *sursis*, past participle of Old French *surseoir* 'refrain, delay,' from Latin *supersedere* (see SUPERSEDE). The change in the ending was due to association with CEASE; the noun dates from the late 16th cent.

sur·charge /ˈsərˌCHärj/ ▶ **n. 1** an additional charge or payment: *we guarantee that no surcharges will be added to the cost of your trip.* ■ a charge made by assessors as a penalty for false returns of taxable property. ■ the showing of an omission in an account for which credit should have been given.
2 a mark printed on a postage stamp changing its value.
▶ **v.** [with obj.] **1** exact an additional charge or payment from: *retailers will be able to surcharge credit-card users.*
2 mark (a postage stamp) with a surcharge.
– ORIGIN late Middle English (as a verb): from Old French *surcharger* (see SUR-¹, CHARGE). The early sense of the noun (late 15th cent.) was 'excessive load.'

sur·cin·gle /ˈsərˌsiNGgəl/ ▶ **n.** a wide strap that runs over the back and under the belly of a horse, used to keep a blanket or other equipment in place.
– ORIGIN Middle English: from Old French *surcengle*, based on *cengle* 'girth,' from Latin *cingula*, from *cingere* 'gird.'

sur·coat /ˈsərˌkōt/ ▶ **n.** historical a loose robe worn over armor. ■ a similar sleeveless garment worn as part of the insignia of an order of knighthood. ■ an outer coat of rich material.
– ORIGIN Middle English: from Old French *surcot*, from *sur* 'over' + *cot* 'coat.'

sur·cu·lose /ˈsərkyəˌlōs, -ˌlōz/ ▶ **adj.** Botany producing suckers.
– ORIGIN mid 19th cent.: from Latin *surculosus*, from *surculus* 'twig.'

surd /sərd/ ▶ **adj. 1** Mathematics (of a number) irrational.
2 Phonetics (of a speech sound) uttered with the breath and not the voice (e.g., *f, k, p, s, t*).
▶ **n. 1** Mathematics a surd number, esp. the irrational root of an integer.
2 Phonetics a surd consonant.
– ORIGIN mid 16th cent.: from Latin *surdus* 'deaf, mute'; as a mathematical term, translating Greek (Euclid) *alogos* 'irrational, speechless,' apparently via Arabic *jidr aṣamm*, literally 'deaf root.' The phonetics senses date from the mid 18th cent.

sure /SHŏŏr/ ▶ **adj.** [predic. often with clause] confident in what one thinks or knows; having no doubt that one is right: *I'm sure I've seen that dress before | she had to check her diary to be* **sure of** *the day of the week.* ■ (**sure of**) having a certain prospect or confident anticipation of: *Ripken can be sure of a place in the Hall of Fame.* ■ [with infinitive] certain to do something: *it's sure to rain before morning.* ■ true beyond any doubt: *what is sure is that learning is a complex business.* ■ [attrib.] able to be relied on or trusted: *her neck was red—a sure sign of agitation.* ■ confident; assured: *the drawings impress by their sure sense of rhythm.*
▶ **adv.** informal certainly (used for emphasis): *Texas sure was a great place to grow up.* ■ [as an exclamation] used to show assent: *"Are you serious?" "Sure."*
– PHRASES **be sure** [usu. in imperative] do not fail (used to emphasize an invitation or instruction): [with infinitive] *be sure to drop by* | [with clause] *be sure that you know what is required.* **for sure** informal without doubt: *I can't say for sure what George really wanted.* **make sure** [usu. with clause] establish that something is definitely so; confirm: *go and make sure she's all right.* ■ ensure that something is done or happens: *he made sure that his sons were well educated.* **sure enough** informal used to introduce a statement that confirms something previously predicted: *when X-rays were taken, sure enough, there was the needle.* **sure of oneself** very confident of one's own abilities or views: *he's very sure of himself.* **sure thing** informal a certainty. ■ [as exclamation] certainly; of course: *"Can I watch?" "Sure thing."* **to be sure** used to concede the truth of something that conflicts with another point that one wishes to make: *the ski runs are very limited, to be sure, but excellent for beginners.* ■ used for emphasis: *what an extraordinary woman she was, to be sure.*
– DERIVATIVES **sure·ness** n.
– ORIGIN Middle English: from Old French *sur*, from Latin *securus* 'free from care.'

sure-fire ▶ **adj.** [attrib.] informal certain to succeed: *bad behavior is a sure-fire way of getting attention.*

sure-foot·ed (also **surefooted**) ▶ **adj.** unlikely to stumble or slip: *tough, sure-footed ponies.* ■ confident and competent: *the challenges of the 1990s demand a responsible and sure-footed government.*
– DERIVATIVES **sure-foot·ed·ly** adv., **sure-foot·ed·ness** n.

sure·ly /ˈSHŏŏrlē/ ▶ **adv. 1** [sentence adverb] used to emphasize the speaker's firm belief that what they are saying is true and often their surprise that there is any doubt of this: *if there is no will, then surely the house goes automatically to you.* ■ without doubt; certainly: *if he did not heed the warning, he would surely die.* ■ [as exclamation] informal of course; yes: *"You'll wait for me?" "Surely."*
2 with assurance or confidence: *no one knows how to move the economy quickly and surely in that direction.*

Sûre·té /sYrˈtā/ (also **Sûreté nationale** /näsyôNˈnäl/) the French police department of criminal investigation.
– ORIGIN French, literally '(National) Security.'

sur·e·ty /ˈSHŏŏritē/ ▶ **n.** (pl. **sureties**) a person who takes responsibility for another's performance of an undertaking, for example their appearing in court or the payment of a debt. ■ money given to support an undertaking that someone will perform a duty, pay their debts, etc.; a guarantee: *the judge granted bail with a surety of $500.* ■ the state of being sure or certain of something: *I was enmeshed in the surety of my impending fatherhood.*
– PHRASES **of** (or **for**) **a surety** archaic for certain: *who can tell that for a surety?*
– DERIVATIVES **sur·e·ty·ship** /-ˌSHip/ n.
– ORIGIN Middle English (in the sense 'something given to support an undertaking that someone will fulfill an obligation'): from Old French *surte*, from Latin *securitas* (see SECURITY).

surf /sərf/ ▶ **n.** the mass or line of foam formed by waves breaking on a seashore or reef: *the roar of the surf.* ■ [in sing.] a spell of surfing: *he went for an early surf.*
▶ **v.** [no obj.] ride on the crest of a wave, typically toward the shore while riding on a surfboard: *learning to surf.* ■ [with obj.] ride (a wave) toward the shore in such a way: *he has built a career out of surfing big waves.* ■ informal ride on the roof or outside of a fast-moving vehicle, typically a train, for excitement: *he fell to his death while surfing on a 70 mph train.* ■ short for CHANNEL-SURF. ■ [with obj.] move from site to site on (the Internet).
– DERIVATIVES **surf·er** n., **surf·y** adj.
– ORIGIN late 17th cent.: apparently from obsolete *suff*, of unknown origin, perhaps influenced by the spelling of *surge*.

sur·face /ˈsərfis/ ▶ **n. 1** the outside part or uppermost layer of something (often used when describing its texture, form, or extent): *the earth's surface | poor road surfaces.* ■ the level top of something: *roll out the dough on a floured surface.* ■ (also **surface area**) the area of such an outer part or uppermost layer: *the surface area of a cube.* ■ [in sing.] the upper limit of a body of liquid: *fish floating on the surface of the water.* ■ [in sing.] what is apparent on a casual view or consideration of someone or something, esp. as distinct from feelings or qualities that are not immediately obvious: *Tom was a womanizer, but on the surface he remained respectable* | [as modifier] *we need to go beyond surface appearances.*
2 Geometry a continuous set of points that has length and breadth but no thickness.
▶ **adj.** [attrib.] of, relating to, or occurring on the upper or outer part of something: *surface workers at the copper mines.* ■ denoting ships that travel on the surface of the water as distinct from submarines: *the surface fleet.* ■ carried by or denoting transportation by sea or overland as contrasted with by air: *surface mail.*
▶ **v. 1** [no obj.] rise or come up to the surface of the water or the ground: *he surfaced from his dive.* ■ come to people's attention; become apparent: *the quarrel first surfaced two years ago.* ■ informal (of a person) appear after having been asleep: *it was almost noon before Anthony surfaced.*
2 [with obj.] (usu. **be surfaced**) provide (something, esp. a road) with a particular upper or outer layer: *a small path surfaced with terra-cotta tiles.*
– DERIVATIVES **sur·faced** adj. [often in combination] *a smooth-surfaced cylinder*, **sur·fac·er** n.
– ORIGIN early 17th cent.: from French (see SUR-¹, FACE), suggested by Latin *superficies*.

sur·face-ac·tive ▶ **adj.** (of a substance, such as a detergent) tending to reduce the surface tension of a liquid in which it is dissolved.

sur·face bound·a·ry lay·er ▶ **n.** Meteorology the lowest layer of the earth's atmosphere extending to about one kilometer. Winds within it are affected by friction with the earth's surface.

sur·face chem·is·try ▶ **n.** the branch of chemistry concerned with the processes occurring at interfaces between phases, esp. that between liquid and gas.

sur·face-mount ▶ **adj.** (of an electronic component) having leads that are designed to be soldered on the side of a circuit board that the body of the component is mounted on.

sur·face noise ▶ **n.** extraneous noise in playing a phonograph record, caused by imperfections in the grooves or in the pickup system.

sur·face struc·ture ▶ **n.** (in generative grammar) the structure of a well-formed phrase or sentence in a language, as opposed to its underlying abstract representation. Contrasted with DEEP STRUCTURE.

sur·face ten·sion ▶ **n.** the tension of the surface film of a liquid caused by the attraction of the particles in the surface layer by the bulk of the liquid, which tends to minimize surface area.

sur·face-to-air ▶ **adj.** [attrib.] (of a missile) designed to be fired from the ground or a vessel at an aircraft.

sur·face-to-sur·face ▶ **adj.** [attrib.] (of a missile) designed to be fired from one point on the ground or a vessel at another such point or vessel.

sur·face wa·ter ▶ **n. 1** water that collects on the surface of the ground.
2 (also **surface waters**) the top layer of a body of water: *the surface water of a pond or lake.*

sur·fac·tant /sərˈfaktənt/ ▶ **n.** a substance that tends to reduce the surface tension of a liquid in which it is dissolved.
– ORIGIN 1950s: from *surf(ace)-act(ive)* + -ANT.

surf·bird /ˈsərfbərd/ ▶ **n.** a small migratory wader of the sandpiper family, with mainly dark gray plumage and a short bill and legs, breeding in Alaska. ● *Aphriza virgata*, family Scolopacidae.

surf·board /ˈsərfˌbôrd/ ▶ **n.** a long, narrow streamlined board used in surfing.

surf·cast·ing /ˈsərfˌkastiNG/ ▶ **n.** fishing by casting a line into the sea from the shore or near the shore.
– DERIVATIVES **surf·cast·er** /-ˌkastər/ n.

sur·feit /ˈsərfət/ ▶ **n.** [usu. in sing.] an excessive amount of something: *a surfeit of food and drink.* ■ archaic an illness caused or regarded as being caused by excessive eating or drinking: *he died of a surfeit.*
▶ **v.** (**surfeits, surfeiting, surfeited**) [with obj.] (usu. **be surfeited with**) cause (someone) to desire no more of something as a result of having consumed or done it to excess: *I am surfeited with shopping.* ■ [no obj.] archaic consume too much of something: *he never surfeited on rich wine.*
– ORIGIN Middle English: from Old French *surfeit*, based on Latin *super-* 'above, in excess' + *facere* 'do.'

sur·fi·cial /sərˈfiSHəl/ ▶ **adj.** Geology of or relating to the earth's surface: *surficial deposits.*
– DERIVATIVES **sur·fi·cial·ly** adv.
– ORIGIN late 19th cent.: from SURFACE, on the pattern of *superficial*.

surf·ing /ˈsərfiNG/ ▶ **n.** the sport or pastime of being carried to the shore on the crest of large waves while standing or lying on a surfboard.

surf mu·sic ▶ **n.** a style of popular music originating in the US in the early 1960s, characterized by high harmony vocals and typically having lyrics relating to surfing.

surf 'n' turf /ˈsərf ən ˈtərf/ (also **surf and turf**) ▶ **n.** a dish containing both seafood and meat, typically shellfish and steak.

surf·perch /ˈsərfˌpərCH/ ▶ **n.** (pl. **same** or **surfperches**) a deep-bodied livebearing fish of the North Pacific, living chiefly in coastal waters. Also called SEA PERCH. ● Family Embiotocidae: several genera and species.

S

surg. ▸ abbr. ▪ surgeon. ▪ surgery. ▪ surgical.

surge /sərj/ ▸ n. a sudden powerful forward or upward movement, esp. by a crowd or by a natural force such as the waves or tide: *flooding caused by tidal surges.* ▪ a sudden large increase, typically a brief one that happens during an otherwise stable or quiescent period: *the firm predicted a 20% surge in sales.* ▪ a major deployment of military forces to reinforce those already in a particular area. ▪ a powerful rush of an emotion or feeling: *Sophie felt a surge of anger.* ▪ a sudden marked increase in voltage or current in an electric circuit.
▸ v. [no obj.] (of a crowd or a natural force) move suddenly and powerfully forward or upward: *the journalists surged forward.* ▪ increase suddenly and powerfully, typically during an otherwise stable or quiescent period: *shares surged to a record high.* ▪ (of an emotion or feeling) affect someone powerfully and suddenly: *indignation surged up within her.* ▪ (of an electric voltage or current) increase suddenly. ▪ Nautical (of a rope, chain, or windlass) slip back with a jerk.
– ORIGIN late 15th cent. (in the sense 'fountain, stream'): the noun (in early use) from Old French *sourgeon*; the verb partly from the Old French stem *sourge-*, based on Latin *surgere* 'to rise.' Early senses of the verb included 'rise and fall on the waves' and 'swell with great force.'

surge cham·ber ▸ n. another term for SURGE TANK.

sur·geon /'sərjən/ ▸ n. a medical practitioner qualified to practice surgery.
– ORIGIN Middle English: from Anglo-Norman French *surgien*, contraction of Old French *serurgien*, based on Latin *chirurgia*, from Greek *kheirourgia* 'handiwork, surgery,' from *kheir* 'hand' + *ergon* 'work.'

sur·geon·fish /'sərjən,fisʜ/ ▸ n. (pl. **same** or **surgeonfishes**) a deep-bodied and typically brightly colored tropical marine fish with a scalpellike spine on each side of the tail. ● Family Acanthuridae: several genera and many species. See also TANG³.

sur·geon gen·er·al ▸ n. (pl. **surgeons general**) the head of a public health service or of an armed forces medical service.

sur·geon's knot ▸ n. a square knot with one or more extra turns in the first half knot.
– ORIGIN from the use of such a knot to tie a ligature in surgery.

sur·ger·y /'sərjərē/ ▸ n. (pl. **surgeries**) **1** the treatment of injuries or disorders of the body by incision or manipulation, esp. with instruments: *cardiac surgery | he had surgery on his ankle.*
2 Brit. a place where a doctor, dentist, or other medical practitioner treats or advises patients. ▪ [in sing.] an occasion on which such treatment or consultation occurs: *Doctor Bailey had finished his evening surgery.*
– ORIGIN Middle English: from Old French *surgerie*, contraction of *serurgerie*, from *serurgien* (see SURGEON).

surge tank ▸ n. a tank connected to a pipe carrying a liquid and intended to neutralize sudden changes of pressure in the flow by filling when the pressure increases and emptying when it drops.

sur·gi·cal /'sərjikəl/ ▸ adj. **1** of, relating to, or used in surgery: *a surgical dressing | a surgical ward.* ▪ (of a special garment or appliance) worn to correct or relieve an injury, illness, or deformity: *surgical stockings.*
2 denoting something done with great precision, esp. a swift and highly accurate military attack from the air: *surgical bombing.*
– DERIVATIVES **sur·gi·cal·ly** /-ik(ə)lē/ adv.
– ORIGIN late 18th cent. (earlier as *chirurgical*): from French *cirurgical*, from Old French *sirurgie* (see SURGERY).

S

Su·ri·ba·chi, Mount /,so͝orə'bäcʜē/ a small dormant volcano on Iwo Jima, in the western Pacific Ocean, site of a February 1945 flag-raising by US Marines that was the subject of a well-known World War II photograph and a monument adjacent to Arlington National Cemetery in Virginia.

su·ri·cate /'so͝ori,kāt/ ▸ n. a gregarious burrowing meerkat with dark bands on the back and a black-tipped tail, native to southern Africa. ● *Suricata suricatta*, family Herpestidae.
– ORIGIN late 18th cent.: via French from a local African word.

suricate

su·ri·mi /sə'rēmē/ ▸ n. fish (often pollock) that is minced to make a gelatinous paste that is then flavored, reformed into flakes, sticks, or other shapes, and colored. It is used as a crab substitute.
– ORIGIN from Japanese,'formed fish.'

Su·ri·na·me /,so͝orə'nämə, 'so͝orə,näm, -,nam/ (also **Surinam** /'so͝orə,näm, -,nam/) a country on the northeastern coast of South America; pop. 481,300 (est. 2009); capital, Paramaribo; languages, Dutch (official), Creoles, and Hindi. Former name (until 1948) DUTCH GUIANA.

> Colonized by the Dutch and the English from the 17th century, Suriname became fully independent in 1975. The population is descended largely from African slaves and Asian laborers brought in to work on sugar plantations; there is also a small American Indian population.

– DERIVATIVES **Su·ri·nam·er** /,so͝orə'nämər/ n., **Su·ri·na·mese** /,so͝orənə'mēz, -'mēs/ adj. & n.

Su·ri·nam toad /'so͝orə,nam/ ▸ n. an aquatic South American toad with a flat body and long webbed feet, the female of which carries the eggs and tadpoles in pockets on her back. ● *Pipa pipa*, family Pipidae.

sur·ly /'sərlē/ ▸ adj. (**surlier**, **surliest**) bad-tempered and unfriendly: *he left with a surly expression.*
– DERIVATIVES **sur·li·ly** /-ləlē/ adv., **sur·li·ness** n.
– ORIGIN mid 16th cent. (in the sense 'lordly, haughty, arrogant'): alteration of obsolete *sirly* (see SIR, -LY¹).

sur·mise ▸ v. /sər'mīz/ [no obj., usu. with clause] suppose that something is true without having evidence to confirm it: *he surmised that something must be wrong* | [with direct speech] *"I don't think they're locals," she surmised.*
▸ n. /sər'mīz, 'sər,mīz/ a supposition that something may be true, even though there is no evidence to confirm it: *Charles was glad to have his surmise confirmed | all these observations remain surmise.*
– ORIGIN late Middle English (in the senses 'formal allegation' and 'allege formally'): from Anglo-Norman French and Old French *surmise*, feminine past participle of *surmettre* 'accuse,' from late Latin *supermittere* 'put in afterward,' from *super-* 'over' + *mittere* 'send.'

sur·mount /sər'mount/ ▸ v. [with obj.] **1** overcome (a difficulty or obstacle): *all manner of cultural differences were surmounted.*
2 (usu. **be surmounted**) stand or be placed on top of: *the tomb was surmounted by a sculptured angel.*
– DERIVATIVES **sur·mount·a·ble** adj.
– ORIGIN late Middle English (also in the sense 'surpass, be superior to'): from Old French *surmonter* (see SUR-¹, MOUNT¹).

sur·mul·let /sər'məlit/ ▸ n. a red mullet that is widely distributed in the tropical Indo-Pacific. ● *Pseudupeneus fraterculus*, family Mullidae.
– ORIGIN late 17th cent.: from French *surmulet*, from Old French *sor* 'red' + *mulet* 'mullet.'

sur·name /'sər,nām/ ▸ n. a hereditary name common to all members of a family, as distinct from a given name. ▪ archaic a name, title, or epithet added to a person's name, esp. one indicating their birthplace or a particular quality or achievement: *by his successes there, he acquired the surname of "the African."*
▸ v. [with obj.] give a surname to: *Eddie Penham, so aptly surnamed, had produced a hand-painted sign for us.*
– ORIGIN Middle English: partial translation of Anglo-Norman French *surnoun*, suggested by medieval Latin *supernomen.*

sur·pass /sər'pas/ ▸ v. [with obj.] exceed; be greater than: *prewar levels of production were surpassed in 1929.* ▪ be better than: *he continued to surpass me at all games.* ▪ (**surpass oneself**) do or be better than ever before: *the organist was surpassing himself.*
– DERIVATIVES **sur·pass·a·ble** adj.
– ORIGIN mid 16th cent.: from French *surpasser*, from *sur-* 'above' + *passer* 'to pass.'

sur·pass·ing /sər'pasiɴɢ/ ▸ adj. dated or literary incomparable or outstanding: *a picture of surpassing beauty.*
– DERIVATIVES **sur·pass·ing·ly** adv.

sur·plice /'sərplis/ ▸ n. a loose white linen vestment varying from hip-length to calf-length, worn over a cassock by clergy, acolytes, and choristers at Christian church services.
– DERIVATIVES **sur·pliced** adj.
– ORIGIN Middle English: from Old French *sourpelis*, from medieval Latin *superpellicium*, from *super-* 'above' + *pellicia* 'fur garment.'

surplice

sur·plus /'sərpləs/ ▸ n. an amount of something left over when requirements have been met; an excess of production or supply over demand: *exports of food surpluses.* ▪ an excess of income or assets over expenditure or liabilities in a given period, typically a fiscal year: *a trade surplus of $1.4 billion.* ▪ the excess value of a company's assets over the face value of its stock.
▸ adj. more than what is needed or used; excess: *make the most of your surplus cash.* ▪ denoting a store selling excess or out-of-date military equipment or clothing: *she had picked up her boots in an army surplus store.*
– ORIGIN late Middle English: from Old French *sourplus*, from medieval Latin *superplus*, from *super-* 'in addition' + *plus* 'more.'

sur·plus val·ue ▸ n. Economics (in Marxist theory) the excess of value produced by the labor of workers over the wages they are paid.

Sur, Point /'sər/ see BIG SUR.

sur·prise /sə(r)'prīz/ ▸ n. **1** an unexpected or astonishing event, fact, or thing: *the announcement was a complete surprise.* ▪ a feeling of mild astonishment or shock caused by something unexpected: *much to her surprise, she'd missed him.* ▪ [as modifier] denoting something made, done, or happening unexpectedly: *a surprise attack.*
2 [as modifier] Bell-ringing denoting a class of complex methods of change-ringing: *surprise major.*
▸ v. [with obj.] (of something unexpected) cause (someone) to feel mild astonishment or shock: *I was surprised at his statement* | [with obj. and infinitive] *Joe was surprised that he enjoyed the journey* | [with infinitive] *she was surprised to learn that he was forty.* ▪ capture, attack, or discover suddenly and unexpectedly; catch unawares: *he surprised a gang stealing scrap metal.*
– PHRASES **surprise, surprise** informal said when giving someone a surprise. ▪ said ironically when one believes that something was entirely predictable: *we entrust you with Jason's care and, surprise surprise, you make a mess of it.* **take someone/something by surprise** attack or capture someone or something unexpectedly. ▪ (**take someone by surprise**) happen when someone is not prepared or is expecting something different: *the question took David by surprise.*
– ORIGIN late Middle English (in the sense 'unexpected seizure of a place, or attack on troops'): from Old French, feminine past participle of *surprendre*, from medieval Latin *superprehendere* 'seize.'

sur·prised /sə(r)'prīzd/ ▸ adj. feeling or showing surprise: *there was a surprised silence.*
– DERIVATIVES **sur·pris·ed·ly** /-z(i)dlē/ adv.

sur·pris·ing /sə(r)'prīziɴɢ/ ▸ adj. causing surprise; unexpected: *a surprising sequence of events.*
– DERIVATIVES **sur·pris·ing·ly** adv. [as submodifier] *the profit margin in advertising is surprisingly low* | [sentence adverb] *not surprisingly, his enthusiasm knew no bounds*, **sur·pris·ing·ness** n.

surr. ▸ abbr. surrender.

sur·ra /'so͝orə, 'sərə/ ▸ n. a parasitic disease of camels and other mammals caused by trypanosomes, transmitted by biting flies and occurring chiefly in North Africa and Asia.
– ORIGIN late 19th cent.: from Marathi *sūra* 'air breathed through the nostrils.'

sur·re·al /sə'rēəl/ ▸ adj. having the qualities of surrealism; bizarre: *a surreal mix of fact and fantasy.*
– DERIVATIVES **sur·re·al·i·ty** /,sərē'alitē/ n., **sur·re·al·ly** adv.
– ORIGIN 1930s: back-formation from SURREALISM.

sur·re·al·ism /sə'rēə,lizəm/ ▸ n. a 20th-century avant-garde movement in art and literature that sought to release the creative potential of the unconscious mind, for example by the irrational juxtaposition of images.

> Launched in 1924 by a manifesto of André Breton and having a strong political content, the movement grew out of symbolism and Dada and was strongly influenced by Sigmund Freud. In the visual arts its most notable exponents were André Masson, Jean Arp, Joan Miró, René Magritte, Salvador Dalí, Max Ernst, Man Ray, and Luis Buñuel.

– DERIVATIVES **sur·re·al·ist** n. & adj., **sur·re·al·is·tic** /sə,rēə'listik/ adj., **sur·re·al·is·ti·cal·ly** /sə,rēə'listik(ə)lē/ adv.
– ORIGIN early 20th cent.: from French *surréalisme* (see SUR-¹, REALISM).

sur·re·but·tal /'sərə,bətl/ ▸ n. another term for SURREBUTTER.

sur·re·but·ter /,sərə'bətər/ ▸ n. Law, archaic a plaintiff's reply to the defendant's rebutter.
– ORIGIN late 16th cent.: from SUR-¹ 'in addition' + REBUTTER, on the pattern of *surrejoinder*.

sur·re·join·der /ˌsərəˈjoindər/ ▶ **n.** Law, archaic a plaintiff's reply to the defendant's rejoinder.
– ORIGIN mid 16th cent.: from **SUR-**[1] 'in addition' + **REJOINDER**.

sur·ren·der /səˈrendər/ ▶ **v.** [no obj.] cease resistance to an enemy or opponent and submit to their authority: *over 140 rebels surrendered to the authorities.* ■ [with obj.] give up or hand over (a person, right, or possession), typically on compulsion or demand: *in 1815 Denmark **surrendered** Norway **to** Sweden | they refused to surrender their weapons.* ■ [with obj.] (in a sports contest) lose (a point, game, or advantage): *she surrendered only twenty games in her five qualifying matches.* ■ (**surrender to**) abandon oneself entirely to (a powerful emotion or influence); give in to: *he was surprised that Miriam should surrender to this sort of jealousy | he **surrendered himself** to the mood of the hills.* ■ [with obj.] (of an insured person) cancel (a life insurance policy) and receive back a proportion of the premiums paid.
▶ **n.** the action of surrendering. ■ the action of surrendering a life insurance policy.
– ORIGIN late Middle English (chiefly in legal use): from Anglo-Norman French (see **SUR-**[1], **RENDER**).

sur·ren·der val·ue ▶ **n.** the amount payable to a person who surrenders a life insurance policy.

sur·rep·ti·tious /ˌsərəpˈtiSHəs/ ▶ **adj.** kept secret, esp. because it would not be approved of: *they carried on a surreptitious affair.*
– DERIVATIVES **sur·rep·ti·tious·ly** **adv.**, **sur·rep·ti·tious·ness** **n.**
– ORIGIN late Middle English (in the sense 'obtained by suppression of the truth'): from Latin *surreptitius* (from the verb *surripere*, from *sub-* 'secretly' + *rapere* 'seize') + **-OUS**.

Sur·rey /ˈsərē/ a county in southeastern England; county town, Kingston upon Thames.

sur·rey /ˈsərē/ ▶ **n.** (pl. **surreys**) historical a light four-wheeled carriage with two seats facing forward.
– ORIGIN late 19th cent.: originally denoting a *Surrey cart*, first made in **SURREY**, from which the carriage was later adapted.

surrey

sur·ro·ga·cy /ˈsərəgəsē/ ▶ **n.** the action or state of being a surrogate. ■ the process of giving birth as a surrogate mother or of arranging such a birth.

sur·ro·gate /ˈsərəgit, -ˌgāt/ ▶ **n.** a substitute, esp. a person deputizing for another in a specific role or office: *she was regarded as the **surrogate for** the governor during his final illness.* ■ (in the Christian Church) a bishop's deputy who grants marriage licenses. ■ a judge in charge of probate, inheritance, and guardianship.
– ORIGIN early 17th cent.: from Latin *surrogatus*, past participle of *surrogare* 'elect as a substitute,' from *super-* 'over' + *rogare* 'ask.'

sur·ro·gate moth·er ▶ **n.** **1** a person, animal, or thing that takes on all or part of the role of mother to another person or animal.
2 a woman who bears a child on behalf of another woman, either from her own egg fertilized by the other woman's partner, or from the implantation in her uterus of a fertilized egg from the other woman.

sur·round /səˈround/ ▶ **v.** [with obj.] (usu. **be surrounded**) be all around (someone or something): *the hotel is surrounded by its own gardens |* figurative *he loves to **surround himself with** family and friends.* ■ (of troops, police, etc.) encircle (someone or something) so as to cut off communication or escape: *troops surrounded the parliament building.* ■ be associated with: *the killings were surrounded by controversy.*
▶ **n.** a thing that forms a border or edging around an object: *an oak fireplace surround.* ■ (usu. **surrounds**) the area encircling something; surroundings: *the beautiful surrounds of Moosehead Lake.*
– ORIGIN late Middle English (in the sense 'overflow'): from Old French *souronder*, from late Latin *superundare*, from *super-* 'over' + *undare* 'to flow' (from *unda* 'a wave'); later associated with **ROUND**. Current senses of the noun date from the late 19th cent.

sur·round·ing /səˈroundiNG/ ▶ **adj.** [attrib.] all around a particular place or thing: *the surrounding countryside | Nashville and the surrounding area.*

sur·round·ings /səˈroundiNGz/ ▶ **plural n.** the things and conditions around a person or thing: *I took up the time admiring my surroundings.*

sur·round sound ▶ **n.** a system of stereophonic sound involving three or more speakers surrounding the listener so as to create a more realistic effect.

sur·tax /ˈsərˌtaks/ ▶ **n.** an additional tax on something already taxed, such as a higher rate of tax on incomes above a certain level.
– ORIGIN late 19th cent.: from French *surtaxe* (see **SUR-**[1], **TAX**).

sur·ti·tle /ˈsərtītl/ **n.** & **v.** another term for **SUPERTITLE**.

sur·tout /sərˈtoo͞(t)/ ▶ **n.** historical a man's overcoat of a style similar to a frock coat.
– ORIGIN late 17th cent.: from French, from *sur* 'over' + *tout* 'everything.'

Surt·sey /ˈsərtsē/ a small island south of Iceland, formed by a volcanic eruption in 1963.

sur·veil·lance /sərˈvāləns/ ▶ **n.** close observation, esp. of a suspected spy or criminal: *he found himself **put under surveillance** by military intelligence.*
– ORIGIN early 19th cent.: from French, from *sur-* 'over' + *veiller* 'watch' (from Latin *vigilare* 'keep watch').

sur·vey ▶ **v.** /sərˈvā/ [with obj.] **1** (of a person or their eyes) look carefully and thoroughly at (someone or something), esp. so as to appraise them: *her green eyes surveyed him coolly | I surveyed the options.* ■ investigate the opinions or experience of (a group of people) by asking them questions: *95% of patients surveyed were satisfied with the health service.* ■ investigate (behavior or opinions) by questioning a group of people: *the investigator surveyed the attitudes and beliefs held by residents.*
2 examine and record the area and features of (an area of land) so as to construct a map, plan, or description: *he surveyed the coasts of New Zealand.*
▶ **n.** /ˈsərˌvā/ **1** a general view, examination, or description of someone or something: *the author provides a survey of the relevant literature.* ■ an investigation of the opinions or experience of a group of people, based on a series of questions.
2 an act of surveying an area of land: *the flight involved a detailed aerial survey of military bases.* ■ a map, plan, or detailed description obtained in such a way. ■ a department carrying out the surveying of land: *the U.S. Geological Survey.*
– ORIGIN late Middle English (in the sense 'examine and ascertain the condition of'): from Anglo-Norman French *surveier*, from medieval Latin *supervidere*, from *super-* 'over' + *videre* 'to see.' The early sense of the noun (late 15th cent.) was 'supervision.'

Sur·vey·or /sərˈvāər/ a series of unmanned US spacecraft sent to the moon between 1966 and 1968, five of which successfully made soft landings.

sur·vey·or /sərˈvāər/ ▶ **n.** a person who surveys, esp. one whose profession is the surveying of land. ■ a person who investigates or examines something, esp. boats for seaworthiness: *a marine surveyor.*
– DERIVATIVES **sur·vey·or·ship** /-ˌSHip/ **n.**
– ORIGIN late Middle English (denoting a supervisor): from Anglo-Norman French *surveiour*, from the verb *surveier* (see **SURVEY**).

sur·viv·a·ble /sərˈvīvəbəl/ ▶ **adj.** (of an accident or ordeal) able to be survived; not fatal.
– DERIVATIVES **sur·viv·a·bil·i·ty** **n.**

sur·viv·al /sərˈvīvəl/ ▶ **n.** the state or fact of continuing to live or exist, typically in spite of an accident, ordeal, or difficult circumstances: *the animal's chances of survival were low |* figurative *he was fighting for his political survival.* ■ an object or practice that has continued to exist from an earlier time: *his shorts were a survival from his army days.*
– PHRASES **survival of the fittest** Biology the continued existence of organisms that are best adapted to their environment, with the extinction of others, as a concept in the Darwinian theory of evolution. Compare with **NATURAL SELECTION**.

sur·viv·al curve ▶ **n.** a graph showing the proportion of a population living after a given age, or at a given time after contracting a serious disease or receiving a radiation dose.

sur·viv·al·ism /sərˈvīvəˌlizəm/ ▶ **n.** **1** the policy of trying to ensure one's own survival or that of one's social or national group.
2 the practicing of outdoor survival skills as a sport or hobby.
– DERIVATIVES **sur·viv·al·ist** **n.** & **adj.**

sur·viv·al kit ▶ **n.** a pack of emergency equipment, including food, medical supplies, and tools, esp. as carried by members of the armed forces. ■ a collection of items to help someone in a particular situation: *a substitute teacher survival kit.*

sur·viv·al val·ue ▶ **n.** the property of an ability, faculty, or characteristic that makes individuals possessing it more likely to survive, thrive, and reproduce: *everyone knows that a bad smell is of survival value to the skunk.*

sur·vive /sərˈvīv/ ▶ **v.** [no obj.] continue to live or exist, esp. in spite of danger or hardship: *against all odds the child survived.* ■ [with obj.] continue to live or exist in spite of (an accident or ordeal): *he has survived several assassination attempts.* ■ [with obj.] remain alive after the death of (a particular person): *he was survived by his wife and six children |* (as adj. **surviving**) *there were no surviving relatives.* ■ [no obj.] manage to keep going in difficult circumstances: *she had to work day and night and **survive on** two hours sleep.*
– ORIGIN late Middle English: from Old French *sourvivre*, from Latin *supervivere*, from *super-* 'in addition' + *vivere* 'live.'

sur·vi·vor /sərˈvīvər/ ▶ **n.** a person who survives, esp. a person remaining alive after an event in which others have died: *the sole survivor of the massacre.* ■ the remainder of a group of people or things: *a survivor from last year's team.* ■ a person who copes well with difficulties in their life: *she is a born survivor.* ■ Law a joint tenant who has the right to the whole estate on the other's death.

sur·vi·vor·ship /sərˈvīvərˌSHip/ ▶ **n.** the state or condition of being a survivor; survival. ■ Law a right depending on survival, esp. the right of a survivor of people with a joint interest to take the whole on the death of the others.

Sus. ▶ **abbr.** (in biblical references) Susanna (Apocrypha).

sus- ▶ **prefix** variant spelling of **SUB-** before *c, p, t* (as in *susceptible, suspend, sustain.*).

Su·sa /ˈsoo͞zə, -sə/ **1** an ancient city in southwestern Asia, one of the chief cities of the kingdom of Elam and later capital of the Persian Achaemenid dynasty.
2 another name for **SOUSSE**.

sus·cep·ti·bil·i·ty /səˌseptəˈbilitē/ ▶ **n.** (pl. **susceptibilities**) **1** the state or fact of being likely or liable to be influenced or harmed by a particular thing: *lack of exercise increases **susceptibility to** disease.* ■ (**susceptibilities**) a person's feelings, typically considered as being easily hurt: *I was so careful not to offend their susceptibilities.*
2 Physics the ratio of magnetization to a magnetizing force.

sus·cep·ti·ble /səˈseptəbəl/ ▶ **adj.** **1** likely or liable to be influenced or harmed by a particular thing: *patients with liver disease may be **susceptible to** infection.* ■ (of a person) easily influenced by feelings or emotions; sensitive: *they only do it to tease him—he's too susceptible.*
2 [predic.] (**susceptible of**) capable or admitting of: *the problem is not susceptible of a simple solution.*
– DERIVATIVES **sus·cep·ti·bly** /-blē/ **adv.**
– ORIGIN early 17th cent.: from late Latin *susceptibilis*, from Latin *suscipere* 'take up, sustain,' from *sub-* 'from below' + *capere* 'take.'

sus·cep·tive /səˈseptiv/ ▶ **adj.** archaic receptive or sensitive to something; susceptible.
– ORIGIN late Middle English: from late Latin *susceptivus*, from *suscept-* 'taken up,' from the verb *suscipere* (see **SUSCEPTIBLE**).

su·shi /ˈsoo͞SHē/ ▶ **n.** a Japanese dish consisting of small balls or rolls of vinegar-flavored cold cooked rice served with a garnish of raw fish, vegetables, or egg.
– ORIGIN Japanese.

sus·lik /ˈsəsˌlik/ ▶ **n.** variant spelling of **SOUSLIK**.

sus·pect ▶ **v.** /səˈspekt/ [with obj.] **1** have an idea or impression of the existence, presence, or truth of (something) without certain proof: *if you suspect a gas leak, do not turn on an electric light |* [with clause] *she suspected that he might be bluffing |* (as adj. **suspected**) *a suspected heart condition.* ■ believe or feel that (someone) is guilty of an illegal, dishonest, or unpleasant act, without certain proof: *parents **suspected of** child abuse.*
2 doubt the genuineness or truth of: *a broker whose honesty he had no reason to suspect.*
▶ **n.** /ˈsəsˌpekt/ a person thought to be guilty of a crime or offense: *the police have arrested a suspect.*
▶ **adj.** /ˈsəsˌpekt/ not to be relied on or trusted; possibly dangerous or false: *a suspect package was found on the platform.*
– ORIGIN Middle English (originally as an adjective): from Latin *suspectus* 'mistrusted,' past participle of *suspicere*, from *sub-* 'from below' + *specere* 'to look.'

sus·pend /səˈspend/ ▶ **v.** [with obj.] **1** temporarily prevent from continuing or being in force or effect: *work on the dam was suspended.* ■ officially

S

prohibit (someone) from holding their usual post or carrying out their usual role for a particular length of time: *two officers were **suspended from** duty pending the outcome of the investigation.* ■ defer or delay (an action, event, or judgment): *the judge suspended judgment until January 15.* ■ Law (of a judge or court) cause (an imposed sentence) not to be enforced as long as no further offense is committed within a specified period: *the sentence was suspended for six months* | (as adj. **suspended**) *a suspended jail sentence.*
2 hang (something) from somewhere: *the light was **suspended from** the ceiling.*
3 (**be suspended**) (of solid particles) be dispersed throughout the bulk of a fluid: *the paste contains collagen suspended in a salt solution.*
– PHRASES **suspend disbelief** temporarily allow oneself to believe something that isn't true, esp. in order to enjoy a work of fiction. **suspend payment** (of a company) cease to meet its financial obligations as a result of insolvency or insufficient funds.
– ORIGIN Middle English: from Old French *suspendre* or Latin *suspendere*, from *sub-* 'from below' + *pendere* 'hang.'

sus·pend·ed an·i·ma·tion ▶ **n.** the temporary cessation of most vital functions without death, as in a dormant seed or a hibernating animal.

sus·pend·ers /sə'spendərz/ ▶ **plural n.** a pair of straps that pass over the shoulders and fasten to the waistband of a pair of trousers or a skirt at the front and back to hold it up.

sus·pense /sə'spens/ ▶ **n. 1** a state or feeling of excited or anxious uncertainty about what may happen: *come on, Fran, don't keep me **in suspense**!* ■ a quality in a work of fiction that arouses excited expectation or uncertainty about what may happen: *a tale of mystery and suspense* | [as modifier] *a suspense novel.*
2 chiefly Law the temporary cessation or suspension of something.
– DERIVATIVES **sus·pense·ful** /-fəl/ **adj.**
– ORIGIN late Middle English: from Old French *suspens* 'abeyance,' based on Latin *suspensus* 'suspended, hovering, doubtful,' past participle of *suspendere* (see SUSPEND).

sus·pense ac·count ▶ **n.** an account in the books of an organization in which items are entered temporarily before allocation to the correct or final account.

sus·pen·sion /sə'spenSHən/ ▶ **n. 1** the action of suspending someone or something or the condition of being suspended, in particular: ■ the temporary prevention of something from continuing or being in force or effect: *the suspension of military action.* ■ the official prohibition of someone from holding their usual post or carrying out their usual role for a particular length of time: *the investigation led to the suspension of several officers* | *a four-game suspension.* ■ Music a discord made by prolonging a note of a chord into the following chord.
2 the system of springs and shock absorbers by which a vehicle is cushioned from road conditions: *the car's rear suspension.*
3 a mixture in which particles are dispersed throughout the bulk of a fluid: *a suspension of corn starch in peanut oil.* ■ the state of being dispersed in such a way: *the agitator in the vat keeps the slurry **in suspension**.*
– ORIGIN late Middle English: from French, or from Latin *suspensio(n-)*, from the verb *suspendere* (see SUSPEND).

sus·pen·sion bridge ▶ **n.** a bridge in which the weight of the deck is supported by vertical cables suspended from larger cables that run between towers and are anchored in abutments at each end.

sus·pen·sive /sə'spensiv/ ▶ **adj. 1** of or relating to the deferral or suspension of an event, action, or legal obligation.
2 causing suspense.
– DERIVATIVES **sus·pen·sive·ly adv.**, **sus·pen·sive·ness n.**

sus·pen·so·ry /sə'spensərē/ ▶ **adj. 1** holding and supporting an organ or part: *a suspensory ligament.*
2 of or relating to the deferral or suspension of an event, action, or legal obligation: *a suspensory requirement.*
– ORIGIN late Middle English: from medieval Latin *suspensorius* 'used for hanging something up,' from Latin *suspendere* (see SUSPEND).

sus·pi·cion /sə'spiSHən/ ▶ **n. 1** a feeling or thought that something is possible, likely, or true: *she had a sneaking **suspicion that** he was laughing at her.* ■ a feeling or belief that someone is guilty of an illegal, dishonest, or unpleasant action: *police would not say what aroused their suspicions* | *he was arrested **on suspicion of** murder.* ■ cautious distrust: *her activities were regarded with suspicion by the headmistress.*
2 a very slight trace of something: *a **suspicion of** a smile.*
– PHRASES **above suspicion** too obviously good or honest to be thought capable of wrongdoing. **under suspicion** thought to be guilty of wrongdoing.
– ORIGIN Middle English: from Anglo-Norman French *suspeciun*, from medieval Latin *suspectio(n-)*, from *suspicere* 'mistrust.' The change in the second syllable was due to association with Old French *suspicion* (from Latin *suspicio(n-)* 'suspicion').

sus·pi·cious /sə'spiSHəs/ ▶ **adj.** having or showing a cautious distrust of someone or something: *he was **suspicious of** her motives* | *she gave him a suspicious look.* ■ causing one to have the idea or impression that something or someone is of questionable, dishonest, or dangerous character or condition: *they are not treating the fire as suspicious.* ■ having the belief or impression that someone is involved in an illegal or dishonest activity: *police were called when staff became suspicious.*
– DERIVATIVES **sus·pi·cious·ly adv.** [as submodifier] *it's suspiciously cheap*, **sus·pi·cious·ness n.**
– ORIGIN Middle English: from Old French *suspicious*, from Latin *suspiciosus*, from *suspicio(n-)* (see SUSPICION).

sus·pire /sə'spīr/ ▶ **v.** [no obj.] literary breathe.
– DERIVATIVES **sus·pi·ra·tion** /,səspə'rāSHən/ **n.**
– ORIGIN late Middle English (in the sense 'yearn after'): from Latin *suspirare*, from *sub-* 'from below' + *spirare* 'breathe.'

Sus·que·han·na /,səskwə'hanə/ a river in the northeastern US. It has two headstreams, one that rises in New York and one in Pennsylvania, both of which meet in central Pennsylvania. The river then flows 150 miles (240 km) south to Chesapeake Bay.

suss /səs/ informal, chiefly Brit. ▶ **v.** (**susss, sussing, sussed**) [with obj.] realize; grasp: *he's sussed it* | [with clause] *she **sussed out** right away that there was something fishy going on.*
– ORIGIN 1930s: abbreviation of SUSPECT, SUSPICION.

Sus·sex /'səsəks/ ▶ **n.** a speckled or red bird of a domestic English breed of chicken.

sus·tain /sə'stān/ ▶ **v.** [with obj.] **1** strengthen or support physically or mentally: *this thought had sustained him throughout the years* | (as adj. **sustaining**) *a sustaining breakfast of bacon and eggs.* ■ cause to continue or be prolonged for an extended period or without interruption: *he cannot sustain a normal conversation.* ■ (of a performer) represent (a part or character) convincingly: *he sustained the role with burly resilience.* ■ bear (the weight of an object) without breaking or falling: *he sagged against her so that she could barely sustain his weight* | figurative *his health will no longer enable him to sustain the heavy burdens of office.*
2 undergo or suffer (something unpleasant, esp. an injury): *he died after sustaining severe head injuries.*
3 uphold, affirm, or confirm the justice or validity of: *the allegations of discrimination were sustained.*
▶ **n.** Music an effect or facility on a keyboard or electronic instrument whereby a note can be sustained after the key is released.
– DERIVATIVES **sus·tain·er n.**, **sus·tain·ment n.**
– ORIGIN Middle English: from Old French *soustenir*, from Latin *sustinere*, from *sub-* 'from below' + *tenere* 'hold.'

sus·tain·a·ble /sə'stānəbəl/ ▶ **adj. 1** able to be maintained at a certain rate or level: *sustainable fusion reactions.* ■ conserving an ecological balance by avoiding depletion of natural resources: *our fundamental commitment to sustainable development.*
2 able to be upheld or defended: *sustainable definitions of good educational practice.*
– DERIVATIVES **sus·tain·a·bil·i·ty** /sə,stānə'bilitē/ **n.**, **sus·tain·a·bly** /-blē/ **adv.**

sus·tained /sə'stānd/ ▶ **adj.** continuing for an extended period or without interruption: *several years of sustained economic growth.*
– DERIVATIVES **sus·tain·ed·ly** /-nidlē/ **adv.**

sus·tained-re·lease ▶ **adj.** [attrib.] Medicine denoting a drug preparation in a capsule containing numerous tiny pellets with different coatings that release their contents steadily over a long period.

sus·tained yield ▶ **n.** a level of exploitation or crop production that is maintained by restricting the quantity harvested to avoid long-term depletion.

sus·te·nance /'səstənəns/ ▶ **n.** food and drink regarded as a source of strength; nourishment: *poor rural economies turned to potatoes for sustenance.* ■ the maintaining of someone or something in life or existence: *he kept two or three cows for the sustenance of his family* | *the sustenance of democracy.*
– ORIGIN Middle English: from Old French *soustenance*, from the verb *soustenir* (see SUSTAIN).

sus·ten·ta·tion /,səst(ə)n'tāSHən/ ▶ **n.** formal the support or maintenance of someone or something, esp. through the provision of money: *provision is made for the sustentation of preachers.*
– ORIGIN late Middle English: from Old French, or from Latin *sustentatio(n-)*, from *sustentare* 'uphold, sustain,' frequentative of *sustinere* (see SUSTAIN).

Su·su /'so͞o,so͞o/ ▶ **n.** (pl. **same**) **1** a member of a people of northwestern Sierra Leone and the southern coast of Guinea.
2 the Mande language of this people.
▶ **adj.** of or relating to this people or their language.
– ORIGIN the name in Susu.

su·sur·rus /so͞o'sərəs/ (also **susurration** /,so͞osə'rāSHən/) ▶ **n.** literary whispering, murmuring, or rustling: *the susurrus of the stream.*
– DERIVATIVES **su·sur·rant** /so͞o'sərənt/ **adj.**, **su·sur·rate** /'so͞osə,rāt, so͞o'sər,āt/ **v.**, **su·sur·rous** /so͞o'sərəs/ **adj.**
– ORIGIN late Middle English: from late Latin *susurratio(n-)*, from Latin *susurrare* 'to murmur, hum.'

Suth·er·land[1], George (1862–1942), US Supreme Court associate justice 1922–38. Appointed to the Court by President Harding, he was a conservative and strongly opposed many of President Franklin D. Roosevelt's New Deal programs.

Suth·er·land[2], Graham (Vivian) (1903–80), English painter. During World War II he was an official war artist. His postwar work included the tapestry *Christ in Majesty* (1962) in Coventry cathedral.

Suth·er·land[3], Dame Joan (1926–), Australian opera singer. She is noted for her dramatic coloratura roles, particularly the title role in Donizetti's *Lucia di Lammermoor.*

Sut·lej /'sətlij/ a river in northern India and Pakistan that rises in the Himalayas in southwestern Tibet and flows for 900 miles (1,450 km) west through India into Punjab province in Pakistan, where it joins the Chenab River to form the Panjnad River, which eventually joins the Indus River. It is one of the five rivers that gave Punjab its name.

sut·ler /'sətlər/ ▶ **n.** historical a person who followed an army and sold provisions to the soldiers.
– ORIGIN late 16th cent.: from obsolete Dutch *soeteler*, from *soetelen* 'perform menial duties.'

su·tra /'so͞otrə/ ▶ **n.** a rule or aphorism in Sanskrit literature, or a set of these on a technical subject. See also KAMA SUTRA. ■ a Buddhist or Jain scripture.
– ORIGIN from Sanskrit *sūtra* 'thread, rule,' from *siv* 'sew.'

sut·tee ▶ **n.** variant spelling of SATI.

su·ture /'so͞oCHər/ ▶ **n. 1** a stitch or row of stitches holding together the edges of a wound or surgical incision. ■ a thread or wire used for this. ■ the action of stitching together the edges of a wound or incision.
2 a seamlike immovable junction between two bones, such as those of the skull. ■ Zoology a similar junction, such as between the sclerites of an insect's body. ■ Geology a line of junction formed by two crustal plates that have collided.
▶ **v.** [with obj.] stitch up (a wound or incision) with a suture: *the small incision was sutured.*
– DERIVATIVES **su·tur·al** /-CHərəl/ **adj.**
– ORIGIN late Middle English: from French, or from Latin *sutura*, from *suere* 'sew.'

SUV ▶ **n.** (pl. **SUVs**) a sport utility vehicle.

Su·va /'so͞ovə/ the capital of Fiji, on the southeastern coast of the island of Viti Levu; pop. 224,000 (est. 2007).

Su·wan·nee /'swänē, sə'wänē/ (also **Swanee** /'swä-/) a river in southeastern US. Rising in southeastern Georgia, it flows for about 250 miles (400 km) southwest through northern Florida to the Gulf of Mexico.

su·ze·rain /'so͞ozərən, -,rān/ ▶ **n.** a sovereign or state having some control over another state that is internally autonomous. ■ historical a feudal overlord.
– DERIVATIVES **su·ze·rain·ty** /-rəntē, -,rāntē/ **n.**
– ORIGIN early 19th cent.: from French, apparently from *sus* 'above' (from Latin *su(r)sum* 'upward'), suggested by *souverain* 'sovereign.'

Su·zhou /'so͞o'jō/ (also **Suchou** or **Soochow** /-'CHou, -'jō/) a city in eastern China, in the province of Jiangsu, west of Shanghai on the Grand Canal; pop. 1,416,200 (est. 2006).

Su·zu·ki /sə'zo͞okē/ ▶ **adj.** relating to or denoting a method of teaching the violin, typically to very young children in large groups, developed by Shin'ichi Suzuki (1898–1998), Japanese educator and violin teacher.

Sv ▶ **abbr.** sievert(s).

s.v. ▶ **abbr.** used in textual references before a word or heading to indicate that a specified item can be found under it: *the dictionary defines "sweet dreams" (s.v. "sweet").*

S

– ORIGIN from Latin *sub voce* or *sub verbo*, literally 'under the word or voice.'

Sval·bard /ˈsväl,bär(d)/ a group of islands in the Arctic Ocean about 400 miles (640 km) north of Norway; pop. 2,100 (est. 2009). They came under Norwegian sovereignty in 1925. The chief settlement (on Spitsbergen) is Longyearbyen.

svc (also **svce**) ▶ **abbr.** service.

Sved·berg /ˈsfed,bərg, ˈsved-/ (also **Svedberg unit**) (abbr.: **S**) ▶ **n.** Biochemistry a unit of time equal to 10^{-13} seconds, used in expressing sedimentation coefficients.
– ORIGIN 1940s: named after Theodor S. *Svedberg* (1884–1971), Swedish chemist.

svelte /svelt, sfelt/ ▶ **adj.** (of a person) slender and elegant.
– ORIGIN early 19th cent.: from French, from Italian *svelto.*

Sven·ga·li /svenˈgälē, sfen-/ a musician in George du Maurier's novel *Trilby* (1894) who trains Trilby's voice and controls her stage singing hypnotically. ■ (as noun **a Svengali**) a person who exercises a controlling or mesmeric influence on another, esp. for a sinister purpose.

Sverd·lovsk /sverdˈlôfsk, svərd-/ former name (1924–91) of **Yekaterinburg**.

Sve·ri·ge /ˈsvaryə/ Swedish name for **Sweden**.

Sve·tam·ba·ra /sHveˈtämbərə/ ▶ **n.** a member of one of the two principal sects of Jainism, which was formed as a result of doctrinal schism *c.* AD 80 and survives today in parts of India. Ascetic adherents of the sect traditionally wear white clothing. See also **Digambara**.
– ORIGIN from Sanskrit *śvetāmbara*, literally 'white-clad.'

SVGA ▶ **abbr.** super video graphics array, a high-resolution standard for computer monitors and display screens.

svgs. ▶ **abbr.** savings.

Sviz·ze·ra /ˈzvētsə,rä/ Italian name for **Switzerland**.

SW ▶ **abbr.** ■ southwest. ■ southwestern.

Sw. (also **Swed**) ▶ **abbr.** ■ Sweden. ■ Swedish.

sw. ▶ **abbr.** switch.

swab /swäb/ ▶ **n. 1** an absorbent pad or piece of material used in surgery and medicine for cleaning wounds, applying medication, or taking specimens. ■ a specimen of a secretion taken with a swab for examination: *he had taken throat swabs.* ■ a piece of absorbent material used for cleaning the bore of a firearm, a woodwind instrument, etc.
2 a mop or other absorbent device for cleaning or mopping up a floor or other surface.
3 another term for **swabbie**.
▶ **v.** (**swabs, swabbing, swabbed**) [with obj.] clean (a wound or surface) with a swab: ***swabbing down** the decks* | *swab a patch of skin with alcohol.* ■ [with adverbial] absorb or clear (moisture) with a swab: *the blood was swabbed away.*
– ORIGIN mid 17th cent. (in the sense 'mop for cleaning the decks'): back-formation from *swabber* 'sailor detailed to swab decks,' from early modern Dutch *zwabber*, from a Germanic base meaning 'splash' or 'sway.'

swab·bie /ˈswäbē/ (also **swabby**) ▶ **n.** (pl. **swabbies**) Nautical slang a member of the navy, typically one who is of low rank.

Swa·bi·a /ˈswābēə/ a former duchy of medieval Germany, now divided between southwestern Germany, Switzerland, and France. German name **Schwaben**.
– DERIVATIVES **Swa·bi·an adj. & n.**

swacked /swakt/ ▶ **adj.** informal drunk.
– ORIGIN 1930s: past participle of Scots *swack* 'fling, strike heavily.'

swad·dle /ˈswädl/ ▶ **v.** [with obj.] wrap (someone, esp. a baby) in garments or cloth: *she swaddled the baby tightly* | figurative *they have grown up swaddled in consumer technology.*
– ORIGIN Middle English: frequentative of **swathe**.

swad·dling clothes /ˈswädliNG/ ▶ **plural n.** narrow bands of cloth formerly wrapped around a newborn child to restrain its movements and quiet it.

swag /swag/ ▶ **n. 1** an ornamental festoon of flowers, fruit, and greenery: *ribbon-tied swags of flowers.* ■ a carved or painted representation of such a festoon: *fine plaster swags.* ■ a curtain or piece of fabric fastened so as to hang in a drooping curve.
2 informal money or goods taken by a thief or burglar: *garden machinery is the most popular swag.* ■ informal a large number, amount, or variety: *a swag of events including fleece competitions, poultry and water fowl competitions, and a tractor pull.*
3 Austral./NZ a traveler's or miner's bundle of personal belongings.
▶ **v.** (**swags, swagging, swagged**) [with obj.] **1** arrange in or decorate with a swag or swags of fabric: *swag the fabric gracefully over the curtain tie-backs* | (as adj. **swagged**) *the swagged contours of nomads' tents.*
2 Austral./NZ travel with one's personal belongings in a bundle: ***swagging it** in Queensland* | ***swagging my way** up to the Northern Territory.*
3 [no obj.] chiefly literary hang heavily: *the crinkly old hide swags here and there.* ■ sway from side to side: *the stout chief sat swagging from one side of the carriage to the other.*
– ORIGIN Middle English (in the sense 'bulging bag'): probably of Scandinavian origin. The original sense of the verb (early 16th cent.) was 'cause to sway or sag.'

swage /swāj/ ▶ **n. 1** a shaped tool or die for giving a desired form to metal by hammering or pressure.
2 a groove, ridge, or other molding on an object.
▶ **v.** [with obj.] shape (metal) using a swage, esp. in order to reduce its cross section. ■ [with adverbial] join (metal pieces) together by this process.
– ORIGIN late Middle English (sense 2 of the noun): from Old French *souage* 'decorative groove,' of unknown origin.

swage block ▶ **n.** a grooved or perforated block for shaping metal.

swag·ger /ˈswagər/ ▶ **v.** [no obj.] walk or behave in a very confident and typically arrogant or aggressive way: *he swaggered along the corridor* | (as adj. **swaggering**) *a swaggering gait.*
▶ **n.** [in sing.] a very confident and typically arrogant or aggressive gait or manner: *they strolled around the camp with an exaggerated swagger.*
▶ **adj.** [attrib.] denoting a coat or jacket cut with a loose flare from the shoulders.
– DERIVATIVES **swag·ger·er** /ˈswag(ə)rər/ **n.**, **swag·ger·ing·ly** /ˈswag(ə)riNGlē/ **adv.**
– ORIGIN early 16th cent.: apparently a frequentative of the verb **swag**.

swag·ger stick ▶ **n.** a short cane carried by a military officer.

swag·man /ˈswagmən/ ▶ **n.** (pl. **swagmen**) Austral./NZ a person carrying a swag.

Swa·hi·li /swäˈhēlē/ ▶ **n.** (pl. **same**) **1** a Bantu language widely used as a lingua franca in East Africa and having official status in several countries. Also called **Kiswahili**.
2 a member of a people of Zanzibar and nearby coastal regions, descendants of the original speakers of Swahili.
▶ **adj.** of or relating to this language or to the people who are its native speakers.
– ORIGIN from Arabic *sawāḥil*, plural of *sāḥil* 'coast.'

swain /swān/ ▶ **n.** archaic a country youth. ■ literary a young lover or suitor.
– ORIGIN late Old English (denoting a young man attendant on a knight), from Old Norse *sveinn* 'lad.'

Swain·son's hawk /ˈswānsənz/ ▶ **n.** a dark-colored, narrow-winged buteo of western North America. ● *Buteo swainsoni*, family Accipitridae.
– ORIGIN mid 19th cent.: named after William *Swainson* (1789–1855), English naturalist.

SWAK ▶ **abbr.** sealed with a kiss (written on the flap of an envelope).

swale /swāl/ ▶ **n.** a low or hollow place, esp. a marshy depression between ridges.
– ORIGIN early 16th cent.: British, of unknown origin.

swal·low[1] /ˈswälō/ ▶ **v.** [with obj.] cause or allow (something, esp. food or drink) to pass down the throat: *she swallowed a mouthful slowly.* ■ [no obj.] perform the muscular movement of the esophagus required to do this, esp. through fear or nervousness: *she swallowed hard, sniffing back her tears.* ■ put up with or meekly accept (something insulting or unwelcome): *he seemed ready to swallow any insult.* ■ believe unquestioningly (a lie or unlikely assertion): *she had swallowed his story hook, line, and sinker.* ■ resist expressing (a feeling) or uttering (words): *he swallowed his pride.* ■ take in and cause to disappear; engulf: *the dark mist swallowed her up.* ■ completely use up (money or resources): *debts **swallowed up** most of the money he had gotten for the house.*
▶ **n.** an act of swallowing something, esp. food or drink: *he downed his drink in one swallow.* ■ an amount of something swallowed in one action: *he said he'd like just a swallow of pie.*
– DERIVATIVES **swal·low·a·ble adj.**, **swal·low·er n.**
– ORIGIN Old English *swelgan*, of Germanic origin; related to Dutch *zwelgen* and German *schwelgen*.

swal·low[2] ▶ **n.** a migratory swift-flying songbird with a forked tail and long pointed wings, feeding on insects in flight. ● Family Hirundinidae: several genera, in particular *Hirundo*, and numerous species, including the widespread **barn swallow** (*H. rustica*).
– PHRASES **one swallow does not make a summer** proverb a single fortunate event does not mean that what follows will also be good.
– ORIGIN Old English *swealwe*, of Germanic origin; related to Dutch *zwaluw* and German *Schwalbe*.

barn swallow

swal·low dive ▶ **n.** British term for **swan dive**.

swal·low·tail /ˈswälō,tāl/ ▶ **n. 1** (also **swallowtail butterfly**) a large brightly colored butterfly with taillike projections (suggestive of a swallow's tail) on the hind wings. ● Family Papilionidae: many genera and species, including the **pipevine swallowtail** (*Battus philenor*) of southern North America and the **eastern tiger swallowtail** (*Papilio glaucus*) of eastern North America.
2 [usu. as modifier] a deeply forked tail; a thing resembling such a tail in shape: *swallowtail suits.*
– DERIVATIVES **swal·low-tailed adj.**

eastern tiger swallowtail

swal·low·wort /ˈswälōwərt, -,wôrt/ ▶ **n. 1** a plant of the milkweed family, the follicles of which suggest a swallow with outstretched wings, often becoming a weed. ● Several species in the family Asclepiadaceae, in particular the **black swallowwort** (*Cynanchum* (or *Vincetoxicum*) *nigrum*).
2 chiefly Brit. the greater celandine, formerly believed to be used by swallows to restore their sight.

swam /swam/ past of **swim**.

swa·mi /ˈswämē/ ▶ **n.** (pl. **swamis**) a Hindu male religious teacher: [as title] *Swami Satchidananda.*
– ORIGIN from Hindi *swāmī* 'master, prince,' from Sanskrit *svāmin.*

Swam·mer·dam /ˈsvämər,däm/, Jan (1637–80), Dutch naturalist and microscopist. He classified insects into four groups and was the first to observe red blood cells.

swamp /swämp/ ▶ **n.** an area of low-lying, uncultivated ground where water collects; a bog or marsh. ■ used to emphasize the degree to which a piece of ground is waterlogged: *the ceaseless deluge had turned the lawn into a swamp.*
▶ **v.** [with obj.] overwhelm or flood with water: *a huge wave swamped the canoes.* ■ overwhelm with an excessive amount of something; inundate: *feelings of guilt suddenly swamped her* | *the country was **swamped with** goods from abroad.* ■ [no obj.] (of a boat) become overwhelmed with water and sink.
– ORIGIN early 17th cent.: probably ultimately from a Germanic base meaning 'sponge' or 'fungus.'

swamp bug·gy ▶ **n.** an amphibious vehicle with wheels or a continuous track and an elevated body, used for navigating marshes or swamps.

swamp cab·bage ▶ **n.** skunk cabbage, esp. the species of western North America (*Lysichitum americanum*), the leaves of which are sometimes used in cooking.

swamp cool·er ▶ **n.** informal term for **evaporative cooler**.

swamp cy·press ▶ **n.** chiefly British term for **bald cypress**.

swamp·er /ˈswämpər/ ▶ **n.** informal, dated **1** a laborer, esp. one employed as a general assistant to a riverboat captain. ■ a worker who trims felled trees and clears a road for lumberers in a forest.
2 a native or inhabitant of a swampy region.

swamp fe·ver ▶ **n. 1** a contagious viral disease of horses that causes anemia and emaciation and is usually fatal.
2 dated malaria.

swamp gas ▶ **n.** another term for **marsh gas**.

swamp·land /ˈswämp,land/ ▶ **n.** (also **swamplands**) land consisting of swamps.

S

swamp·y /ˈswämpē/ ▶ **adj.** (**swampier**, **swampiest**) characteristic of or resembling a swamp: *a swampy area.*

Swan /swän/, Sir Joseph Wilson (1828–1914), English physicist and chemist. He devised an electric light bulb in 1860, and in 1883 he formed a partnership with Thomas Edison to manufacture it.

swan /swän/ ▶ **n.** a large waterbird with a long flexible neck, short legs, webbed feet, a broad bill, and typically all-white plumage. ● Genus *Cygnus* (and *Coscoroba*): several species.
▶ **v.** (**swans**, **swanning**, **swanned**) [no obj.] informal move about or go somewhere in a casual, relaxed way, typically perceived as irresponsible or ostentatious by others: *swanning around in a $2,000 sharkskin suit doesn't make you a Renaissance prince.*
– DERIVATIVES **swan·like** /-ˌlīk/ **adj.**
– ORIGIN Old English, of Germanic origin; related to Dutch *zwaan* and German *Schwan.*

swan dive ▶ **n.** a dive performed with one's arms outspread until close to the water.
▶ **v.** [no obj.] (**swan-dive**) perform a swan drive.

swank /swaNGk/ informal ▶ **v.** [no obj.] display one's wealth, knowledge, or achievements in a way that is intended to impress others: ***swanking about,** playing the dashing young master spy.*
▶ **n.** behavior, talk, or display intended to impress others: *a little money will buy you a good deal of swank.*
▶ **adj.** another term for **SWANKY**: *coming out of some swank nightclub.*
– ORIGIN early 19th cent.: of unknown origin.

swank·y /ˈswaNGkē/ ▶ **adj.** (**swankier**, **swankiest**) informal stylishly luxurious and expensive: *directors with swanky company cars.* ■ using one's wealth, knowledge, or achievements to try to impress others.
– DERIVATIVES **swank·i·ly** /-kəlē/ **adv.**, **swank·i·ness n.**

swan neck ▶ **n.** a curved structure shaped like a swan's neck: [as modifier] *a small swan-neck dispenser.* ■ another term for **GOOSENECK**.
– DERIVATIVES **swan-necked adj.**

swan·ner·y /ˈswänərē/ ▶ **n.** (pl. **swanneries**) a place set aside for swans to breed.

Swan Riv·er a river in western Australia. Rising as the Avon River southeast of Perth, it flows north and west through Perth to the Indian Ocean at Fremantle. It was the site of the first free European settlement in the state of Western Australia.

swans·down /ˈswänzˌdoun/ (also **swan's down**) ▶ **n. 1** the fine down of a swan, used for trimmings and powder puffs.
2 a thick cotton fabric with a soft nap on one side, used esp. for baby clothes. ■ a soft, thick fabric made from wool mixed with a little silk or cotton.

Swan·sea /ˈswänzē/ a city in southern Wales, on the Bristol Channel; pop. 173,500 (est. 2009). Welsh name **ABERTAWE**.

Swan·son /ˈswänsən/, Gloria (1899–1983), US actress; born *Gloria May Josephine Svensson.* She was a major star of silent movies, such as *Sadie Thompson* (1928), but is chiefly known for her performance as the fading movie star in *Sunset Boulevard* (1950).

swan song ▶ **n.** a person's final public performance or professional activity before retirement: *he has decided to make this tour his swan song.*
– ORIGIN early 19th cent.: suggested by German *Schwanengesang*, a song like that fabled to be sung by a dying swan.

swan-up·ping ▶ **n.** Brit. the annual practice of catching the swans on the River Thames and marking them to indicate their ownership.

swap /swäp/ (also **swop**) ▶ **v.** (**swaps**, **swapping**, **swapped**) [with obj.] take part in an exchange of: *we swapped phone numbers* | *I'd swap places with you any day* | [no obj.] *I was wondering if you'd like to swap with me.* ■ give (one thing) and receive something else in exchange: ***swap** one of your sandwiches **for** a cheese and pickle?* ■ substitute (one thing) for another: *I **swapped** my busy life on Wall Street **for** a peaceful mountain retreat.*
▶ **n.** an act of exchanging one thing for another: *let's **do a swap**.* ■ a thing that has been or may be given in exchange for something else: *I've got one already, but I'll keep this as a swap.* ■ Finance an exchange of liabilities between two borrowers, either so that each acquires access to funds in a currency they need or so that a fixed interest rate is exchanged for a floating rate.
– DERIVATIVES **swap·pa·ble adj.**, **swap·per n.**
– ORIGIN Middle English (originally in the sense 'throw forcibly'): probably imitative of a resounding blow. Current senses have arisen from an early use meaning 'clasp hands as a token of agreement.'

swap·file /ˈswäpˌfīl/ ▶ **n.** Computing a file on a hard disk used to provide space for programs that have been transferred from the processor's memory.

swap meet ▶ **n.** a gathering at which enthusiasts or collectors trade or exchange items of common interest: *a computer swap meet.* ■ a flea market.

SWAPO /ˈswäpō/ (also **Swapo**) ▶ **abbr.** South West Africa People's Organization.

swap shop ▶ **n.** informal an agency that provides a communication channel for people with articles to exchange or trade: *radio swap shops remain popular ways to exchange goods in farm communities.* ■ an event to which people are invited to bring articles for exchange or trade.

swap·tion /ˈswäpSHən/ ▶ **n.** Finance an option giving the right but not the obligation to engage in a swap.
– ORIGIN 1980s: blend of **SWAP** and **OPTION**.

sward /swôrd/ ▶ **n.** an expanse of short grass. ■ Farming the upper layer of soil, esp. when covered with grass.
– DERIVATIVES **sward·ed adj.**
– ORIGIN Old English *sweard* 'skin.' The sense 'upper layer of soil' developed in late Middle English (at first in phrases such as *sward of the earth*).

sware /swe(ə)r/ archaic past of **SWEAR**.

swarm /swôrm/ ▶ **n.** a large or dense group of insects, esp. flying ones. ■ a large number of honeybees that leave a hive en masse with a newly fertilized queen in order to establish a new colony. ■ (**a swarm/swarms of**) a large number of people or things: *a swarm of journalists.* ■ a series of similar-sized earthquakes occurring together, typically near a volcano. ■ Astronomy a large number of minor celestial objects occurring together in space, esp. a dense shower of meteors.
▶ **v. 1** [no obj.] (of insects) move in or form a swarm: (as adj. **swarming**) *swarming locusts.* ■ (of honeybees, ants, or termites) issue from the nest in large numbers with a newly fertilized queen in order to found new colonies: *the bees had swarmed and left the hive.*
2 [no obj.] move somewhere in large numbers: *protesters were swarming into the building.* ■ (**swarm with**) (of a place) be crowded or overrun with (moving people or things): *the place was swarming with police.*
– PHRASAL VERBS **swarm up** climb (something) rapidly by gripping it with one's hands and feet, alternately hauling and pushing oneself upward: *I swarmed up the mast.* [mid 16th cent.: of unknown origin.]
– ORIGIN Old English *swearm* (noun), of Germanic origin; related to German *Schwarm*, probably also to the base of Sanskrit *svarati* 'it sounds.'

swarm·er /ˈswôrmər/ (also **swarmer cell**) ▶ **n.** Biology another term for **ZOOSPORE**.

swart /swôrt/ ▶ **adj.** archaic or literary swarthy.
– ORIGIN Old English *sweart*, of Germanic origin; related to Dutch *zwart* and German *schwarz.*

swarth·y /ˈswôrT͟Hē/ ▶ **adj.** (**swarthier**, **swarthiest**) dark-skinned: *she looked frail standing next to her strong and swarthy brother.*
– DERIVATIVES **swarth·i·ly** /-T͟Hәlē/ **adv.**, **swarth·i·ness n.**
– ORIGIN late 16th cent.: alteration of obsolete *swarty* (see **SWART**).

swash[1] /swôSH, swäSH/ ▶ **v.** [no obj.] **1** (of water or an object in water) move with a splashing sound: *the water swashed and rippled around the car wheels.*
2 archaic (of a person) flamboyantly swagger about or wield a sword: *he swashed about self-confidently.*
▶ **n.** the rush of seawater up the beach after the breaking of a wave. ■ archaic the motion or sound of water dashing or washing against something.
– ORIGIN mid 16th cent. (in the sense 'make a noise like swords clashing or beating on shields'): imitative.

swash[2] ▶ **adj.** Printing denoting an ornamental written or printed character, typically a capital letter.
– ORIGIN late 17th cent.: of unknown origin.

swash·buck·le /ˈswôSHˌbəkəl, ˈswäSH-/ ▶ **v.** [no obj.] (usu. as adj. **swashbuckling**) engage in daring and romantic adventures with ostentatious bravado or flamboyance: *a crew of swashbuckling buccaneers.*
– ORIGIN late 19th cent.: back-formation from **SWASHBUCKLER**.

swash·buck·ler /ˈswôSHˌbəklər, ˈswäSH-/ ▶ **n.** a swashbuckling person.
– ORIGIN mid 16th cent.: from **SWASH**[1] + **BUCKLER**.

swash plate ▶ **n.** an inclined disk revolving on an axle and giving reciprocating motion to a part in contact with it.

swas·ti·ka /ˈswästikə/ ▶ **n.** an ancient symbol in the form of an equal-armed cross with each arm continued at a right angle, used (in clockwise form) as the emblem of the German Nazi Party.
– ORIGIN late 19th cent.: from Sanskrit *svastika*, from *svasti* 'well-being,' from *su* 'good' + *asti* 'being.'

swastika

swat /swät/ ▶ **v.** (**swats**, **swatting**, **swatted**) [with obj.] hit or crush (something, esp. an insect) with a sharp blow from a flat object: *I swatted a mosquito that had landed on my wrist* | [no obj.] ***swatting at** a fly.* ■ hit (someone) with a sharp blow: *she swatted him over the head with a rolled-up magazine.*
▶ **n.** such a sharp blow: *the dog gave the hedgehog a sideways swat.*
– ORIGIN early 17th cent. (in the sense 'sit down'): northern English dialect and US variant of **SQUAT**.

swatch /swäCH/ ▶ **n.** a sample, esp. of fabric. ■ a collection of such samples, esp. in the form of a book. ■ a patch or area of a material or surface: *the sunset had filled the sky with swatches of deep orange.*
– ORIGIN early 16th cent. (originally Scots and northern English, denoting the counterfoil of a tally, and later a tally fixed to a piece of cloth before dyeing): of unknown origin.

swath /swäTH, swôTH/ (also **swathe** /swäT͟H, swôT͟H, swāT͟H/) ▶ **n.** (pl. **swaths** /swäTHS, swôTHS/ or **swathes** /swāT͟Hz/) **1** a row or line of grass, grain, or other crop as it lies when mown or reaped. ■ a strip left clear by the passage of a mowing machine or scythe: *the combine had cut a deep swath around the border of the fields.*
2 a broad strip or area of something: *vast **swaths of** countryside* | figurative ***a significant swath of** popular opinion.*
– PHRASES **cut a swath through** pass through (something) causing great damage, destruction, or change: *a tornado cut a two-mile long swath through residential neighborhoods.* **cut a wide swath** attract a great deal of attention by trying to impress others.
– ORIGIN Old English *swæth*, *swathu* 'track, trace'; related to Dutch *zwad(e)* and German *Schwade.* In Middle English the term denoted a measure of the width of grassland, probably reckoned by a sweep of the mower's scythe.

swathe /swäT͟H, swāT͟H/ ▶ **v.** [with obj.] (usu. **be swathed in**) wrap in several layers of fabric: *his hands were swathed in bandages.*
▶ **n.** a piece or strip of material in which something is wrapped.
– ORIGIN late Old English *swath-* (noun), *swathian* (verb); compare with **SWADDLE**.

swath·er /ˈswäT͟Hər, ˈswäTH-/ ▶ **n.** a device on a mowing machine for raising uncut fallen grain and marking the line between cut and uncut grain.

Swa·tow /ˈswäˈtou/ former name of **SHANTOU**.

SWAT team /swät/ ▶ **n.** a group of elite police marksmen who specialize in high-risk tasks such as hostage rescue. ■ any group of specialists brought in to solve a difficult or urgent problem: *an economic SWAT team that aims to bolster the region's hunting and outdoor recreation industry.*
– ORIGIN 1980s: acronym from *Special Weapons and Tactics.*

sway /swā/ ▶ **v.** move or cause to move slowly or rhythmically backward and forward or from side to side: [no obj.] *he swayed slightly on his feet* | (as adj. **swaying**) *swaying palm trees* | [with obj.] *wind rattled and swayed the trees.* ■ [with obj.] control or influence (a person or course of action): *he's easily swayed by other people.* ■ literary rule; govern: *now let the Lord forever reign and sway us as he will.*
▶ **n. 1** a rhythmical movement from side to side: *the easy sway of her hips.*
2 rule; control: *the part of the continent **under** Russia's **sway**.*
– PHRASES **hold sway** have great power or influence over a particular person, place, or domain.
– PHRASAL VERBS **sway something up** Nautical hoist a mast into position.
– ORIGIN Middle English: corresponding in sense to Low German *swājen* 'be blown to and fro' and Dutch *zwaaien* 'swing, walk in a tottering way.'

sway·back /ˈswāˌbak/ ▶ **n.** an abnormally hollowed back, esp. in a horse; lordosis.
– DERIVATIVES **sway-backed adj.**

Swayne /swān/, Noah Haynes (1804–84), US Supreme Court associate justice 1862–81. Appointed to the Court by President Lincoln, he opposed slavery and advocated expanded federal powers.

Swa·zi /ˈswäzē/ ▶ **n.** (pl. **same** or **Swazis**) **1** a member of a people inhabiting Swaziland and parts of eastern Transvaal. ■ a native or inhabitant of Swaziland.
2 the Nguni language of this people, an official language in Swaziland and South Africa.
▶ **adj.** of or relating to Swaziland, the Swazis, or their language.

–ORIGIN from the name of *Mswati*, a 19th-century king of the Swazis.

Swa·zi·land /'swäzē,land/ a small landlocked kingdom in southern Africa, bounded by South Africa and Mozambique; pop. 1,337,200 (est. 2009); capital, Mbabane; languages, Swazi and English (both official).

> Swaziland was a South African protectorate from 1894 and came under British rule in 1902 after the Second Boer War. In 1968 it became a fully independent Commonwealth of Nations state.

SWB ▶ **abbr.** short wheelbase.

swbd. ▶ **abbr.** switchboard.

SWbS ▶ **abbr.** southwest by south.

SWbW ▶ **abbr.** southwest by west.

Swe. ▶ **abbr.** ■ Sweden. ■ Swedish.

swear /swe(ə)r/ ▶ **v.** (**swears, swearing**; past **swore** /swôr/; past participle **sworn** /swôrn/) **1** [reporting verb] make a solemn statement or promise undertaking to do something or affirming that something is the case: [with clause] *Maria made me swear I would never tell anyone* | *I* **swear by** *all I hold dear that I had nothing to do with it* | [with infinitive] *he swore to obey the rules* | [with direct speech] *"Never again," she swore, "will I be short of money"* | [with obj.] *they were reluctant to swear allegiance.* ■ [with obj.] take (an oath): *he forced them to swear an oath of loyalty to him.* ■ [with obj.] take a solemn oath as to the truth of (a statement): *I asked him if he would swear a statement to this effect.* ■ [with obj.] make (someone) promise to observe a certain course of action: *I've been* **sworn to** *secrecy.*
2 [no obj.] use offensive language, esp. as an expression of anger: *Peter swore under his breath.*
–PHRASES **swear up and down** informal affirm something emphatically: *he swore up and down they'd never get him up on that stage.*
–PHRASAL VERBS **swear by** informal have or express great confidence in the use, value, or effectiveness of: *Iris swears by her yoga.* **swear someone in** admit someone to a particular office or position by directing them to take a formal oath: *he was sworn in as president on July 10.* **swear off** informal promise to abstain from: *I'd sworn off alcohol.* **swear something out** Law obtain the issue of (a warrant for arrest) by making a charge on oath. **swear to** express one's assurance that something is the case: *I couldn't swear to it, but I'm pretty sure it's his writing.*
–DERIVATIVES **swear·er n., swear·y adj.** (informal).
–ORIGIN Old English *swerian*, of Germanic origin; related to Dutch *zweren*, German *schwören*, also to ANSWER.

swear·ing /'swe(ə)riNG/ ▶ **n.** the use of offensive language: *there's a lot of swearing in the show.*

swear word ▶ **n.** an offensive word, used esp. as an expression of anger.

sweat /swet/ ▶ **n. 1** moisture exuded through the pores of the skin, typically in profuse quantities as a reaction to heat, physical exertion, fever, or fear. ■ an instance of exuding moisture in this way over a period of time: *even thinking about him made me* **break out in a sweat** | *we'd all* **worked up a sweat** *in spite of the cold.* ■ informal a state of flustered anxiety or distress: *I don't believe he'd* **get into such a sweat** *about a girl.* ■ informal hard work; effort: *computer graphics take a lot of the sweat out of animation.*
2 (**sweats**) informal term for SWEATSUIT or SWEATPANTS. ■ [as modifier] denoting loose casual garments made of thick, fleecy cotton: *sweat tops and bottoms.*
▶ **v.** (**sweats, sweating**; past **sweated** or **sweat**)
1 [no obj.] exude sweat: *he was sweating profusely.* ■ [with obj.] (**sweat something out/off**) get rid of (something) from the body by exuding sweat: *a well-hydrated body sweats out waste products more efficiently.* ■ [with obj.] cause (a person or animal) to exude sweat by exercise or exertion: *cold as it was, the climb had sweated him.* ■ (of food or an object) ooze or exude beads of moisture onto its surface: *cheese stored at room temperature will quickly begin to sweat.* ■ (of a person) exert a great deal of strenuous effort: *I've* **sweated over** *this for six months.* ■ (of a person) be or remain in a state of extreme anxiety, typically for a prolonged period: *I let her sweat for a while, then I asked her out again.* ■ [with obj.] informal worry about (something): *he's not going to have a lot of time to sweat the details.*
2 [with obj.] heat (chopped vegetables) slowly in a pan with a small amount of fat, so that they cook in their own juices: *sweat the celery and onions with olive oil and seasoning.* ■ [no obj.] (of chopped vegetables) be cooked in this way: *let the chopped onion sweat gently for five minutes.*
3 [with obj.] subject (metal) to surface melting, esp. to fasten or join by solder without a soldering iron: *the tire is sweated onto the wooden parts.*
–PHRASES **break a sweat** informal exert oneself physically. **by the sweat of one's brow** by one's own hard work, typically manual labor. **don't sweat it** used to urge someone not to worry. **no sweat** informal used to convey that one perceives no difficulty or problem with something: *"We haven't any decaf, I'm afraid." "No sweat."* **sweat blood** informal make an extraordinarily strenuous effort to do something: *she's sweated blood to support her family.* ■ be extremely anxious: *we've been sweating blood over the question of what is right.* **sweat buckets** informal sweat profusely. **sweat bullets** informal be extremely anxious or nervous. **sweat it out** informal endure an unpleasant experience, typically one involving physical exertion in great heat: *about 1,500 runners are expected to sweat it out in this year's run.* ■ wait in a state of extreme anxiety for something to happen or be resolved: *he sweated it out until the lab report was back.* **sweat the small stuff** worry about trivial things.
–ORIGIN Old English *swāt* (noun), *swǣtan* (verb), of Germanic origin; related to Dutch *zweet* and German *Schweiss*, from an Indo-European root shared by Latin *sudor*.

sweat·band /'swet,band/ ▶ **n.** a band of absorbent material worn around the head or wrist to soak up sweat, esp. by participants in sports. ■ a band of absorbent material lining a hat.

sweat·box /'swet,bäks/ ▶ **n. 1** a confined space in which one or more individuals are punished or tortured with conditions of extreme heat and dehydration.
2 a heated compartment in which perspiration is induced, to encourage weight loss, pore cleansing, etc.

sweat eq·ui·ty ▶ **n.** informal an interest or increased value in a property earned from labor toward upkeep or restoration.

sweat·er /'swetər/ ▶ **n. 1** a knitted garment typically with long sleeves, worn over the upper body.
2 dated an employer who works employees hard in poor conditions for low pay.

sweat·er set ▶ **n.** another term for TWINSET.

sweat gland ▶ **n.** a small gland that secretes sweat, situated in the dermis of the skin. Such glands are found over most of the body, and have a simple coiled tubular structure.

sweat·ing sick·ness ▶ **n.** any of various fevers with intense sweating, epidemic in England in the 15th–16th centuries.

sweat lodge ▶ **n.** a hut, typically dome-shaped and made with natural materials, used by North American Indians for ritual steam baths as a means of purification.

sweat·pants /'swet,pants/ ▶ **plural n.** loose, warm trousers with an elasticized or drawstring waist, worn when exercising or as leisurewear.

sweat·shirt /'swet,SHərt/ ▶ **n.** a loose, heavy shirt, typically made of cotton, worn when exercising or as leisurewear.

sweat·shop /'swet,SHäp/ ▶ **n.** a factory or workshop, esp. in the clothing industry, where manual workers are employed at very low wages for long hours and under poor conditions.

sweat sock ▶ **n.** a thick, absorbent, calf-length sock, often worn with athletic shoes.

sweat·suit /'swet,so͞ot/ ▶ **n.** a suit consisting of a sweatshirt and sweatpants, worn when exercising or as leisurewear.

sweat·y /'swetē/ ▶ **adj.** (**sweatier, sweatiest**) exuding, soaked in, or inducing sweat: *my feet got so hot and sweaty.*
–DERIVATIVES **sweat·i·ly** /'swetəlē/ **adv.**, **sweat·i·ness n.**

Swede /swēd/ ▶ **n.** a native or inhabitant of Sweden, or a person of Swedish descent.
–ORIGIN from Middle Low German and Middle Dutch *Swēde*, probably from Old Norse *Svíthjóth*, from *Svíar* 'Swedes' + *thjóth* 'people.'

swede /swēd/ ▶ **n.** British term for RUTABAGA.
–ORIGIN early 19th cent.: from SWEDE, being first introduced into Scotland from Sweden in 1781–82.

Swe·den /'swēdn/ a country that occupies the eastern part of the Scandinavian peninsula; pop. 9,059,700 (est. 2009); capital, Stockholm; language, Swedish (official). Swedish name SVERIGE.

> Originally united in the 12th century, Sweden formed part of the Union of Kalmar with Denmark and Norway from 1397 until its re-emergence as an independent kingdom in 1523. Between 1814 and 1905, it was united with Norway. A constitutional monarchy, Sweden has pursued a policy of nonalignment, and it remained neutral in the two world wars. Sweden joined the European Union in 1995.

Swe·den·borg /'swēdn,bôrg/, Emanuel (1688–1772), Swedish scientist, philosopher, and mystic. The spiritual beliefs that he expounded after a series of mystical experiences blended Christianity with pantheism and theosophy.
–DERIVATIVES **Swe·den·bor·gi·an** /,swēdən'bôrgēən/ **adj. & n.**

Swede saw ▶ **n.** chiefly Canadian a type of saw with a bowlike tubular frame and many cutting teeth.
–ORIGIN *Swede* in the sense 'Swedish.'

Swed·ish /'swēdiSH/ ▶ **adj.** of or relating to Sweden, its people, or their language.
▶ **n.** the North Germanic language of Sweden, also spoken in parts of Finland.

Swed·ish mas·sage ▶ **n.** a popular general-purpose system of massage, devised in Sweden.

sweep /swēp/ ▶ **v.** (**sweeps, sweeping**; past and past participle **swept** /swept/) **1** [with obj.] clean (an area) by brushing away dirt or litter: *I've swept the floor* | *Greg swept out the kitchen.* ■ move or remove (dirt or litter) in such a way: *she swept the tea leaves into a dustpan.* ■ move or push (someone or something) with great force: *I was swept along by the crowd.* ■ brush (hair) back from one's face or upward: *long hair swept up into a high chignon.* ■ search (an area) for something: *the detective swept the room for hair and fingerprints.* ■ examine (a place or thing) for electronic listening devices: *the line is swept every fifteen minutes.* ■ cover (an entire area) with a gun: *they were trying to get the Lewis gun up behind some trees from where they would sweep the trench.*
2 [no obj.] move swiftly and smoothly: *a large black car swept past the open windows* | figurative *a wave of sympathy swept over him.* ■ [with obj.] cause to move swiftly and smoothly: *he swept his hand around the room.* ■ (of a person) move in a confident and stately manner: *she swept magnificently from the hall.* ■ (of a geographical or natural feature) extend continuously in a particular direction, esp. in a curve: *green forests swept down the hillsides.* ■ affect (an area or place) swiftly and widely: *the rebellion had swept through all four of the country's provinces* | [with obj.] *violence swept the country.* ■ [with obj.] win all the games in (a series); take each of the winning or main places in (a contest or event): *we knew we had to sweep these three home games.*
▶ **n. 1** an act of sweeping something with a brush: *I was giving the floor a quick sweep.* ■ short for CHIMNEY SWEEP.
2 a long, swift, curving movement: *a grandiose sweep of his hand.* ■ Electronics the movement of a beam across the screen of a cathode ray tube.
3 a comprehensive search or survey of a place or area: *the police finished their sweep through the woods.* ■ (often **sweeps**) a survey of the ratings of broadcast stations, carried out at regular intervals to determine advertising rates.
4 a long, typically curved stretch of road, river, country, etc.: *we could see a wide sweep of country perhaps a hundred miles across.* ■ a curved part of a driveway in front of a building: *one fork of the driveway continued on to the gravel sweep.* ■ the range or scope of something: *the whole sweep of the history of the USSR.*
5 informal a sweepstake.
6 an instance of winning every event, award, or place in a contest: *a World Series sweep.*
7 a long heavy oar used to row a barge or other vessel: [as modifier] *a big, heavy sweep oar.*
8 a sail of a windmill.
9 a long pole mounted as a lever for raising buckets from a well.
–PHRASES **a clean sweep** see CLEAN. **sweep the board** (or **boards**) win every event or prize in a contest. **sweep someone off their feet** see FOOT. **sweep something under the rug** (or **carpet**) conceal or ignore a problem or difficulty in the hope that it will be forgotten.
–PHRASAL VERBS **sweep something away** (or **aside**) remove, dispel, or abolish something in a swift and sudden way: *Nahum's smile swept away the air of apprehensive gloom.*
–ORIGIN Old English *swāpan* (verb), of Germanic origin; related to German *schweifen* 'sweep in a curve.'

sweep·back /'swēp,bak/ ▶ **n.** the angle at which an aircraft's wing is set back from a right angle to the body.

sweep·er /'swēpər/ ▶ **n. 1** a person or device that cleans a floor or road by sweeping.
2 a small nocturnal shoaling fish of reefs and coastal waters, occurring chiefly in the tropical Indo-Pacific. ● Family Pempheridae: several genera and species,

S

PRONUNCIATION KEY ə *ago, up*; ər *over, fur*; a *hat*; ā *ate*; ä *car*; e *let*; ē *see*; i *fit*; ī *by*; NG *sing*; ō *go*; ô *law, for*; oi *toy*; o͝o *good*; o͞o *goo*; ou *out*; TH *thin*; T̲H̲ *then*; ZH *vision*

including the western Atlantic **glassy sweeper** (*Pempheris schomburgki*), with transparent young.

sweep·ing /ˈswēpiNG/ ▶ **adj.** wide in range or effect: *we cannot recommend any sweeping alterations.* ■ extending or performed in a long, continuous curve: *sweeping, desolate moorlands | a smooth sweeping motion.* ■ (of a statement) taking no account of particular cases or exceptions; too general: *a sweeping assertion.*
▶ **n.** (**sweepings**) dirt or refuse collected by sweeping: *the sweepings from the house.*
– DERIVATIVES **sweep·ing·ly adv.**, **sweep·ing·ness n.**

sweep sec·ond hand ▶ **n.** a second hand on a clock or watch, moving on the same dial as the other hands.

sweep·stake /ˈswēpˌstāk/ ▶ **n.** (also **sweepstakes**) a form of gambling, esp. on horse races, in which all the stakes are divided among the winners: [as modifier] *a sweepstake ticket.* ■ a race on which money is bet in this way. ■ a prize or prizes won in a sweepstake.

Sweet /swēt/, Sarah C., see **JEWETT**.

sweet /swēt/ ▶ **adj. 1** having the pleasant taste characteristic of sugar or honey; not salty, sour, or bitter: *a cup of hot sweet tea* | figurative *a sweet taste of success.* ■ (of air, water, or food) fresh, pure, and untainted: *lungfuls of the clean, sweet air.* ■ [often in combination] smelling pleasant like flowers or perfume; fragrant: *sweet-smelling flowers.*
2 pleasing in general; delightful: *it was the sweet life he had always craved.* ■ highly satisfying or gratifying: *some sweet, short-lived revenge.* ■ [often as exclamation] informal used in expressions of assent or approval: *Yeah, I'd like to come to the party. Sweet.* ■ working, moving, or done smoothly or easily: *the sweet handling of this motorcycle.* ■ (of sound) melodious or harmonious: *the sweet notes of the flute.* ■ denoting music, esp. jazz, played at a steady tempo without improvisation.
3 (of a person or action) pleasant and kind or thoughtful: *a very sweet nurse came along.* ■ (esp. of a person or animal) charming and endearing: *a sweet little cat.* ■ [predic.] (**sweet on**) informal, dated infatuated or in love with: *she seemed quite sweet on him.* ■ dear; beloved: *my sweet love.* ■ archaic used as a respectful form of address: *go to thy rest, sweet sir.*
4 used for emphasis in various phrases and exclamations: *What had happened? Sweet nothing.* ■ (**one's own sweet ——**) used to emphasize the unpredictable individuality of someone's actions: *I'd rather carry on in my own sweet way.*
▶ **n. 1** chiefly Brit. a small shaped piece of confectionery made with sugar: *a bag of sweets.*
2 (**sweets**) sweet foods, collectively: *Americans eat too many sweets.* ■ Brit. a sweet dish forming a course of a meal; a dessert: *she served up a lovely sweet made with whipped chestnuts and almond paste.*
3 used as an affectionate form of address to a person one is very fond of: *hello, my sweet.*
4 (**the sweet**) archaic or literary the sweet part or element of something: *you have had the bitter, now comes the sweet.* ■ (**sweets**) the pleasures or delights found in something: *the sweets of office.*
– PHRASES **sweet dreams** used to express good wishes to a person going to bed. **sweet sixteen** used to refer to the age of sixteen as characterized by prettiness and innocence in a girl.
– DERIVATIVES **sweet·ish adj.**, **sweet·ly adv.**
– ORIGIN Old English *swēte*, of Germanic origin; related to Dutch *zoet*, German *süss*, from an Indo-European root shared by Latin *suavis* and Greek *hēdus*.

sweet a·ca·cia ▶ **n.** another term for **HUISACHE**.

sweet alys·sum ▶ **n.** see **ALYSSUM**.

sweet-and-sour ▶ **adj.** [attrib.] (esp. of Chinese-style food) cooked in a sauce containing sugar and either vinegar or lemon.

sweet balm ▶ **n.** see **BALM** (sense 3).

sweet bas·il ▶ **n.** see **BASIL**.

sweet bay ▶ **n.** see **BAY²**.

sweet birch ▶ **n.** a North American birch, esp. of Appalachian forests, with brown or black bark and smooth twigs that smell of wintergreen when broken or crushed. The leaves and sap of sweet birch yield oil of wintergreen (see **WINTERGREEN**). Also called **BLACK BIRCH**. ● *Betula lenta*, family Betulaceae.

sweet·bread /ˈswētˌbred/ ▶ **n.** the thymus gland (or, rarely, the pancreas) of an animal, esp. as used for food.

sweet·bri·er /ˈswētˌbrīər/ (also **sweetbriar**) ▶ **n.** a Eurasian wild rose with fragrant leaves and flowers. ● *Rosa eleganteria*, family Rosaceae.

sweet but·ter ▶ **n.** a type of unsalted butter made from fresh pasteurized cream.

sweet cher·ry ▶ **n.** another term for **MAZZARD**.

sweet chest·nut ▶ **n.** see **CHESTNUT**.

sweet cic·e·ly ▶ **n.** another term for **CICELY**.

sweet clov·er /swēt ˈklōvər/ ▶ **n.** another term for **MELILOT**.

sweet corn ▶ **n.** corn of a variety with kernels that have a high sugar content. It is grown for human consumption and is harvested while slightly immature. ■ the kernels of this plant eaten as a vegetable.

sweet·en /ˈswētn/ ▶ **v.** make or become sweet or sweeter, esp. in taste: [with obj.] *a cup of coffee sweetened with saccharin* | [no obj.] *her smile sweetened.* ■ [with obj.] make more agreeable or acceptable: *there is no way to sweeten the statement.* ■ [with obj.] informal induce (someone) to be well disposed or helpful to oneself: *I am in the process of sweetening him up.*
– PHRASES **sweeten the pill** see **PILL¹**. **sweeten the pot** add to the total sum of bets made in poker. ■ add an inducement, typically in the form of money or a concession: *he is trying to sweeten the pot, offering workers a 50-cent raise.*

sweet·en·er /ˈswētn-ər, ˈswētnər/ ▶ **n.** a substance used to sweeten food or drink, esp. one other than sugar. ■ informal an inducement, typically in the form of money or a concession: *these sweeteners made rental cars a bargain.*

sweet fen·nel ▶ **n.** see **FENNEL**.

sweet flag (also **sweetflag**) ▶ **n.** an Old World waterside plant of the arum family, with leaves that resemble those of the iris. It is used medicinally and as a flavoring. Also called **CALAMUS**. ● *Acorus calamus*, family Araceae.

sweet gale ▶ **n.** a deciduous shrub of boggy places, with short upright catkins and aromatic gray-green leaves. It has insecticidal properties. Also called **BOG MYRTLE**. ● *Myrica gale*, family Myricaceae.
– ORIGIN mid 17th cent.: *gale* from Old English *gagel*, *gagelle*, of Germanic origin; related to Dutch *gagel*, German *Gagel*.

sweet gal·in·gale ▶ **n.** another term for **GALINGALE** (sense 1).

sweet·grass /ˈswētˌgras/ ▶ **n.** any of a number of grasses that possess a sweet flavor, making them attractive to livestock, or a sweet smell, resulting in their former use as herbs for strewing or burning. ● *Glyceria*, *Hierochloe*, and other genera, family Gramineae.

sweet gum ▶ **n.** the North American liquidambar, which yields a balsam and decorative heartwood that is marketed as satin walnut. ● *Liquidambar styraciflua*, family Hamamelidaceae.

sweet·heart /ˈswētˌhärt/ ▶ **n.** used as a term of endearment or affectionate form of address: *don't worry, sweetheart, I've got it all worked out.* ■ a person that one is in love with: *the pair were childhood sweethearts.* ■ a particularly lovable or pleasing person or thing: *he is an absolute sweetheart.* ■ [as modifier] informal denoting an arrangement reached privately by two sides, esp. an employer and a labor union, in their own interests: *a sweetheart agreement.*

sweet·heart neck·line ▶ **n.** a neckline on a dress or blouse that is low at the front and shaped like the top of a stylized heart.

sweet·heart rose ▶ **n.** a rose with small pink, white, or yellow flowers that are particularly attractive as buds.

sweet·ie /ˈswētē/ informal ▶ **n. 1** (also **sweetie pie**) used as a term of endearment (esp. as a form of address).
2 a green-skinned grapefruit of a variety noted for its sweet taste.

sweet·ing /ˈswētiNG/ ▶ **n. 1** an apple of a sweet-flavored variety.
2 archaic darling.

sweet·lips /ˈswētˌlips/ (also **sweetlip**) ▶ **n.** (pl. **same**) a patterned grunt (fish) that changes its color and markings with age, occurring in the Indo-Pacific. ● *Plectorhynchus* and other genera, family Pomadasyidae: several species, including the **oriental sweetlips** (*P. orientalis*).

sweet mar·jo·ram ▶ **n.** see **MARJORAM**.

sweet·meat /ˈswētˌmēt/ ▶ **n.** archaic an item of confectionery or sweet food.

sweet milk ▶ **n.** fresh whole milk, as opposed to buttermilk.

sweet·ness /ˈswētnis/ ▶ **n.** the quality of being sweet. ■ used as an affectionate form of address, though often ironically: *I've just got to go, sweetness.*
– PHRASES **sweetness and light** social or political harmony: *the relationship was by no means all sweetness and light.* ■ a reasonable and peaceable person: *when he's around she's all sweetness and light.* [taken from Swift and used with aesthetic or moral reference, first by Arnold in *Culture and Anarchy* (1869).]

sweet pea ▶ **n.** a climbing plant of the pea family, widely cultivated for its colorful fragrant flowers. ● Genus *Lathyrus*, family Leguminosae: several species, in particular *L. odoratus*, which originated in southern Italy and Sicily.

sweet pep·per ▶ **n.** a large green, yellow, orange, or red variety of capsicum that has a mild or sweet flavor and is often eaten raw. Also called **BELL PEPPER**. ● *Capsicum annuum* var. *annuum*, 'grossum' group (or var. *grossum*).

sweet po·ta·to ▶ **n. 1** an edible tropical tuber with pinkish orange, slightly sweet flesh.
2 the Central American climbing plant that yields this tuber, widely cultivated in warm countries. ● *Ipomoea batatas*, family Convolvulaceae.
3 informal another term for **OCARINA**.

sweet rock·et ▶ **n.** a herbaceous plant of the cabbage family, cultivated for its long spikes of mauve or white flowers that are fragrant in the evening. ● *Hesperis matronalis*, family Brassicaceae.

sweet·sop /ˈswētˌsäp/ ▶ **n. 1** a round or heart-shaped custard apple that has a green scaly rind and a sweet pulp. Also called **SUGAR APPLE**.
2 the tropical American evergreen shrub that yields this fruit. ● *Annona squamosa*, family Annonaceae.

sweet spot ▶ **n.** informal the point or area on a bat, club, or racket at which it makes most effective contact with the ball.

sweet sul·tan ▶ **n.** a Near Eastern plant of the daisy family, with sweet-scented flowers, slender stems, and narrow gray-green leaves, cultivated for garden plantings. ● *Centaurea moschata*, family Compositae.

sweet talk informal ▶ **v.** (**sweet-talk**) [with obj.] insincerely praise (someone) in order to persuade them to do something: *detectives sweet-talked them into confessing.*
▶ **n.** insincere praise used to persuade someone to do something.

sweet tooth ▶ **n.** [usu. in sing.] (pl. **sweet tooths**) a great liking for sweet-tasting foods.
– DERIVATIVES **sweet-toothed adj.**

sweet ver·nal grass ▶ **n.** see **VERNAL GRASS**.

sweet vi·o·let ▶ **n.** a sweet-scented Old World violet with heart-shaped leaves, used in perfumery and as a flavoring. ● *Viola odorata*, family Violaceae.

sweet wil·liam (also **sweet William**) ▶ **n.** a fragrant garden pink with flattened clusters of vivid red, pink, or white flowers. ● *Dianthus barbatus*, family Caryophyllaceae.

sweet wood·ruff ▶ **n.** see **WOODRUFF**.

swell /swel/ ▶ **v.** (**swells, swelling**; past participle **swollen** /ˈswōlən/ or **swelled**) [no obj.] (esp. of a part of the body) become larger or rounder in size, typically as a result of an accumulation of fluid: *her bruised knee was already* ***swelling up*** | figurative *the sky was black and swollen with rain* | (as adj. **swollen**) *swollen glands.* ■ become or make greater in intensity, number, amount, or volume: [no obj.] *the murmur swelled to a roar* | (as adj. **swelling**) *the swelling ranks of Irish singer-songwriters* | [with obj.] *the city's population was swollen by refugees.* ■ be intensely affected or filled with a particular emotion: *she felt herself* ***swell with pride.***
▶ **n. 1** [in sing.] a full or gently rounded shape or form: *the soft swell of her breast.* ■ a gradual increase in sound, amount, or intensity: *there was a swell of support in favor of him.* ■ a welling up of a feeling: *a swell of pride swept over George.*
2 [usu. in sing.] a slow, regular movement of the sea in rolling waves that do not break: *there was a heavy swell.*
3 a mechanism for producing a crescendo or diminuendo in an organ or harmonium.
4 informal, dated a person of wealth or high social position, typically one perceived as fashionable or stylish: *a crowd of city swells.*
▶ **adj.** informal, dated excellent; very good: *you're looking swell.* ■ archaic smart; fashionable: *a swell boulevard.*
▶ **adv.** informal, dated excellently; very well: *everything was just going swell.*
– PHRASES **someone's head swells** someone becomes conceited: *I am not saying this to make your head swell* | *if I say this, you'll get* ***swollen-headed.***
– ORIGIN Old English *swellan* (verb), of Germanic origin; related to German *schwellen*. Current senses of the noun date from the early 16th cent.; the informal adjectival use derives from sense 4 of the noun (late 18th cent).

swell box ▶ **n.** a part of a large organ in which some of the pipes are enclosed, with a movable shutter for controlling the sound level.

swell·ing /ˈsweliNG/ ▶ **n.** an abnormal enlargement of a part of the body, typically as a result of an accumulation of fluid. ■ a natural rounded protuberance: *the lobes are prominent swellings on the base of the brain.*

swell or·gan ▶ **n.** a section of a large organ consisting of pipes enclosed in a swell box, usually played with an upper keyboard.

swel·ter /ˈsweltər/ ▶ **v.** [no obj.] (of a person or the atmosphere at a particular time or place) be uncomfortably hot: *Barney sweltered in his doorman's uniform.*
▶ **n.** [in sing.] an uncomfortably hot atmosphere: *the swelter of an August day.*
– ORIGIN Middle English: from the base of dialect *swelt* 'perish,' of Germanic origin.

swel·ter·ing /ˈswelt(ə)riNG/ ▶ **adj.** uncomfortably hot: *the sweltering afternoon heat.*
– DERIVATIVES **swel·ter·ing·ly adv.**

swept /swept/ past and past participle of **SWEEP**.

swept-back ▶ **adj.** [attrib.] (of an aircraft wing) positioned to point somewhat backward.

swept-up ▶ **adj.** another term for **UPSWEPT**.

swept-wing ▶ **adj.** [attrib.] (of an aircraft) having swept-back wings.

swerve /swərv/ ▶ **v.** change or cause to change direction abruptly: [no obj.] *a car swerved around a corner* | [with obj.] *he swerved the truck, narrowly missing a teenager on a skateboard.*
▶ **n.** an abrupt change of direction: *do not make sudden swerves, particularly around parked vehicles.*
– DERIVATIVES **swerv·er n.**
– ORIGIN Old English *sweorfan* 'depart, leave, turn aside,' of Germanic origin; related to Middle Dutch *swerven* 'to stray.'

Sweyn I /sven, svān/ (also **Sven** /sven/) (died 1014), king of Denmark c.985–1014; known as **Sweyn Forkbeard**. From 1003, he launched a series of attacks on England, finally causing Ethelred the Unready to flee to Normandy at the end of 1013. Sweyn then became king of England but died five weeks later.

SWF ▶ **abbr.** ■ single white female (used in personal ads). ■ sovereign wealth fund.

swid·den /ˈswidn/ ▶ **n.** an area of land cleared for cultivation by slashing and burning vegetation. ■ the method of clearing land in this way: *the practice of swidden.*
– ORIGIN late 18th cent. (as a verb, originally dialect): variant of dialect *swithen* 'to burn.'

Swift /swift/, Jonathan (1667–1745), Irish satirist, poet, and Anglican cleric; known as **Dean Swift**. He is best known for *Gulliver's Travels* (1726), a satire on human society in the form of a fantastic tale of travels in imaginary lands.

swift /swift/ ▶ **adj.** happening quickly or promptly: *a remarkably swift recovery.* ■ moving or capable of moving at high speed: *the water was very swift* | *the swiftest horse in his stable.*
▶ **adv.** literary except in combination swiftly: *streams that ran swift and clear* | *a swift-acting poison.*
▶ **n. 1** a swift-flying insectivorous bird with long slender wings and a superficial resemblance to a swallow, spending most of its life on the wing. ● Family Apodidae: several genera and numerous species, including the common **Eurasian swift** (*Apus apus*).
2 (also **swift moth**) a moth, typically yellow-brown in color, with fast darting flight. The eggs are scattered in flight and the larvae live underground feeding on roots, where they can be a serious pest. ● Family Hepialidae: *Hepialus* and other genera.
3 a light, adjustable reel for holding a skein of silk or wool.
– DERIVATIVES **swift·ly adv.**, **swift·ness n.**
– ORIGIN Old English (as an adjective), from the Germanic base of Old English *swīfan* 'move in a course, sweep.' The bird name dates from the mid 17th cent.

swift fox ▶ **n.** a small fox with a yellowish-buff coat and a black-tipped tail, living on the plains of North America. ● *Vulpes velox*, family Canidae.

swift·let /ˈswif(t)lit/ ▶ **n.** a small swift found in southern Asia and Australasia. ● Genera *Aerodramus* and *Collocalia*, family Apodidae: many species.

swig /swig/ informal ▶ **v.** (**swigs, swigging, swigged** /swigd/) [with obj.] drink in large gulps: *Dave swigged the wine in five gulps* | [no obj.] *old men swigged from bottles of plum brandy.*
▶ **n.** a large draft of drink: *he took a swig of tea.*
– DERIVATIVES **swig·ger n.**
– ORIGIN mid 16th cent. (as a noun in the obsolete sense 'liquor'): of unknown origin.

swill /swil/ ▶ **v. 1** [with obj.] Brit. wash or rinse out (an area or container) by pouring large amounts of water or other liquid over or into it: *I swilled out the mug.* ■ cause (liquid) to swirl around in a container or cavity: *she gently swilled her brandy around her glass.* ■ [no obj.] (of a liquid) move or splash about over a surface: *the icy water swilled around us.*
2 [with obj.] drink (something) greedily or in large quantities: *they whiled away their evening swilling pints of beer* | (as adj. **swilling**) *his beer-swilling pals.* ■ accompany (food) with large quantities of drink: *a feast swilled down with pints of cider.*
▶ **n. 1** kitchen refuse and scraps of waste food mixed with water for feeding to pigs. ■ alcohol of inferior quality: *the beer was just warm swill.*
2 a large mouthful of a drink: *a swill of ale.*
– DERIVATIVES **swill·er n.** [usu. in combination] *beer-swillers.*
– ORIGIN Old English *swillan, swilian* (verb), of unknown origin. The noun dates from the mid 16th cent.

swim /swim/ ▶ **v.** (**swims, swimming**; past **swam** /swam/; past participle **swum** /swəm/) **1** [no obj.] propel the body through water by using the limbs, or (in the case of a fish or other aquatic animal) by using fins, tail, or other bodily movement: *they swam ashore* | *Adrian taught her to swim breaststroke.* ■ [with obj.] cross (a particular stretch of water) in this way: *she swam the Channel.* ■ float on or at the surface of a liquid: *bubbles swam on the surface.* ■ [with obj.] cause to float or move across water: *the Russians were able to swim their infantry carriers across.*
2 [no obj.] be immersed in or covered with liquid: *mashed potatoes swimming in gravy.*
3 [no obj.] appear to reel or whirl before one's eyes: *Emily rubbed her eyes as the figures swam before her eyes.* ■ experience a dizzily confusing sensation in one's head: *the drink made his head swim.*
▶ **n. 1** an act or period of swimming: *we went for a swim in the river.*
2 a pool in a river that is a particularly good spot for fishing: *he landed two 5-lb chub from the same swim.*
– PHRASES **in the swim** involved in or aware of current affairs or events. **swim with** (or **against**) **the tide** act in accordance with (or against) the prevailing opinion or tendency.
– DERIVATIVES **swim·ma·ble adj.**, **swim·mer n.**
– ORIGIN Old English *swimman* (verb), of Germanic origin; related to Dutch *zwemmen* and German *schwimmen.*

> **USAGE** In standard English, the past tense of **swim** is **swam** (*she swam to the shore*) and the past participle is **swum** (*she had never swum there before*). In the 17th and 18th centuries, **swam** and **swum** were used interchangeably for the past participle, but this is not acceptable in standard modern English.

swim blad·der ▶ **n.** Zoology a gas-filled sac present in the body of many bony fishes, used to maintain and control buoyancy.

swim·mer·et /ˌswiməˈret/ ▶ **n.** another term for **PLEOPOD**.

swim·ming /ˈswimiNG/ ▶ **n.** the sport or activity of propelling oneself through water using the limbs.

swim·ming bath /ˈswimiNG ˌbaTH/ ▶ **n.** (also **swimming baths**) Brit. a swimming pool, esp. a public indoor one.

swim·ming crab ▶ **n.** a coastal crab that has paddlelike rear legs for swimming. ● Family Portunidae: many species, including the **velvet swimming crab** (*Macropipus puber*).

swim·ming hole ▶ **n.** a deep place for swimming in a stream or river.

swim·ming·ly /ˈswimiNGlē/ ▶ **adv.** smoothly and satisfactorily: *things are going swimmingly.*

swim·ming pool ▶ **n.** an artificial pool for swimming in.

swim·suit /ˈswimˌso͞ot/ ▶ **n.** a garment worn for swimming.
– DERIVATIVES **swim·suit·ed adj.**

swim trunks (also **swimming trunks**) ▶ **plural n.** shorts worn by men for swimming.

swim·wear /ˈswimˌwe(ə)r/ ▶ **n.** clothing worn for swimming.

Swin·burne /ˈswinˌbərn/, Algernon Charles (1837–1909), English poet and critic. Associated as a poet with the Pre-Raphaelites, he also contributed to the revival of interest in Elizabethan and Jacobean drama and produced influential studies of William Blake and the Brontës.

swin·dle /ˈswindl/ ▶ **v.** [with obj.] use deception to deprive (someone) of money or possessions: *a businessman swindled investors out of millions of dollars.* ■ obtain (money) fraudulently: *he was said to have swindled $62.5 million from the pension fund.*
▶ **n.** a fraudulent scheme or action: *he is mixed up in a $10 million insurance swindle.*
– DERIVATIVES **swin·dler n.**
– ORIGIN late 18th cent.: back-formation from *swindler*, from German *Schwindler* 'extravagant maker of schemes, swindler,' from *schwindeln* 'be giddy,' also 'tell lies.'

Swin·don /ˈswindən/ a town in central England; pop. 158,400 (est. 2009).

swine /swīn/ ▶ **n.** (pl. **same**) **1** a pig.
2 (pl. **same** or **swines**) informal a person regarded by the speaker with contempt and disgust: *what an arrogant, unfeeling swine!*
– DERIVATIVES **swin·ish adj.**, **swin·ish·ly adv.**, **swin·ish·ness n.**
– ORIGIN Old English *swīn*, of Germanic origin; related to Dutch *zwijn* and German *Schwein*, also to **SOW**[2].

swine fe·ver ▶ **n.** an intestinal viral disease of pigs.

swine flu ▶ **n.** a form of influenza that affects pigs, or a form of human influenza that is caused by a related virus.

swine·herd /ˈswīnˌhərd/ ▶ **n.** chiefly historical a person who tends pigs.
– ORIGIN Old English, from **SWINE** + obsolete *herd* 'herdsman.'

swine ve·sic·u·lar dis·ease /vəˈsikyələr/ ▶ **n.** an infectious viral disease of pigs causing mild fever and blisters around the mouth and feet.

swing /swiNG/ ▶ **v.** (**swings, swinging**; past and past participle **swung** /swəNG/) **1** move or cause to move back and forth or from side to side while suspended or on an axis: [no obj.] *her long black skirt swung about her legs* | [with obj.] *a priest began swinging a censer* | (as adj. **swinging**) *local girls with their castanets and their swinging hips.* ■ [with obj.] turn (a ship or aircraft) to all compass points in succession, in order to test compass error. ■ [no obj.] informal be executed by hanging: *now he was going to swing for it.*
2 [no obj.] move by grasping a support from below and leaping: *we swung across like two trapeze artists* | (**swing oneself**) *the Irishman swung himself into the saddle.* ■ move quickly around to the opposite direction: *Ronni had swung around to face him.* ■ move with a rhythmic swaying gait: *the riflemen swung along smartly.*
3 [with adverbial of direction] move or cause to move in a smooth, curving line: [with obj.] *he swung her bag up onto the rack* | [no obj.] *the cab swung into the parking lot.* ■ [with obj.] bring down (something held) with a curving movement, typically in order to hit an object: *I swung the club and missed the ball.* ■ [no obj.] (**swing at**) attempt to hit or punch, typically with a wide curving movement of the arm: *he swung at me with the tire iron.* ■ [with obj.] throw (a punch) with such a movement: *she swung a punch at him.*
4 shift or cause to shift from one opinion, mood, or state of affairs to another: [no obj.] *opinion swung in the chancellor's favor* | [with obj.] *the failure to seek a peace could swing sentiment the other way.* ■ [with obj.] have a decisive influence on (something, esp. a vote or election): *an attempt to swing the vote in their favor.* ■ [with obj.] informal succeed in bringing about: *with us backing you we might be able to swing something.*
5 [no obj.] play music with an easy flowing but vigorous rhythm: *the band swung on.* ■ (of music) be played with such a rhythm.
6 [no obj.] informal (of an event, place, or way of life) be lively, exciting, or fashionable.
7 [no obj.] informal be promiscuous, typically by engaging in group sex or swapping sexual partners.
▶ **n. 1** a seat suspended by ropes or chains, on which someone may sit and swing back and forth. ■ a spell of swinging on such an apparatus.
2 an act of swinging: *with the swing of her arm, the knife flashed through the air.* ■ the manner in which a golf club or a bat is swung: *improve your golf swing.* ■ the motion of swinging: *this short cut gave her hair new movement and swing.*
3 a discernible change in opinion: *the South's swing to the right.*
4 a style of jazz or dance music with an easy flowing but vigorous rhythm. ■ the rhythmic feeling or drive of such music.
5 a swift tour involving a number of stops, esp. one undertaken as part of a political campaign.
– PHRASES **get** (**back**) **into the swing of things** informal get used to (or return to) being easy and relaxed about an activity or routine one is engaged in. **in full swing** at the height of activity: *by nine-thirty the dance was in full swing.* **swing into action** quickly begin acting or operating.
– DERIVATIVES **swing·er n.**
– ORIGIN Old English *swingan* 'to beat, whip,' also 'rush,' *geswing* 'a stroke with a weapon,' of Germanic origin; related to German *schwingen* 'brandish.'

swing bridge ▶ **n.** a bridge over water that can be rotated horizontally to allow ships through.

S

swing·by /ˈswiNG,bī/ ▶ n. a change in the flight path of a spacecraft using the gravitational pull of a celestial body. Compare with SLINGSHOT.

swing coat ▶ n. a coat cut so as to swing when the wearer moves.

swinge /swinj/ ▶ v. (**swinges, swingeing, swinged**) [with obj.] literary strike hard; beat.
– ORIGIN Old English *swengan* 'shake, shatter, move violently,' of Germanic origin.

swinge·ing /ˈswinjiNG/ ▶ adj. chiefly Brit. severe or otherwise extreme: *swingeing cuts in public expenditure.*
– DERIVATIVES **swinge·ing·ly** adv.

swing·ing /ˈswiNGiNG/ ▶ adj. informal (of a person, place, or way of life) lively, exciting, and fashionable: *a swinging resort | the Swinging Sixties.* ■ sexually liberated or promiscuous.
– DERIVATIVES **swing·ing·ly** adv.

swing·ing door ▶ n. a door that can be opened in either direction and is closed by a spring device when released.

swin·gle /ˈswiNGgəl/ ▶ n. **1** a wooden tool for beating flax and removing the woody parts from it.
2 the swinging part of a flail.
▶ v. [with obj.] beat (flax) with such a tool.
– ORIGIN Middle English: from Middle Dutch *swinghel*, from the base of the verb SWING.

swin·gle·tree /ˈswiNGgəl,trē/ ▶ n. chiefly British term for SINGLETREE.

swing·man /ˈswiNGmən, -,man/ ▶ n. (pl. **swingmen**) Basketball a player who can play both guard and forward.

swing set ▶ n. a frame for children to play on, typically including one or more swings and a slide.

swing shift ▶ n. a work shift from mid-afternoon to around midnight.

swing state ▶ n. a marginal US state where voters are liable to swing from one political party to another, important in determining the overall result of an election.

swing vote ▶ n. a vote that has a decisive influence on the result of an election.
– DERIVATIVES **swing vot·er** n.

swing-wing ▶ n. [usu. as modifier] an aircraft wing that can move from a right-angled to a swept-back position: *swing-wing fighter bombers.* ■ an aircraft with wings of this design.

swing·y /ˈswiNGē/ ▶ adj. (**swingier, swingiest**) **1** (of music) characterized by swing (see SWING (sense 4 of the noun)).
2 (of a skirt, coat, or other garment) cut so as to swing as the wearer moves.

swipe /swīp/ informal ▶ v. [with obj.] **1** hit or try to hit with a swinging blow: *she swiped me right across the nose* | [no obj.] *she lifted her hand to swipe at a cat.*
2 steal: *someone swiped one of his sausages.*
3 pass (a card with a magnetic strip) through an electronic device that reads it.
▶ n. a sweeping blow: *he missed the ball with his first swipe.* ■ an attack or criticism: *he took a swipe at his critics.*
– DERIVATIVES **swip·er** n.
– ORIGIN mid 18th cent.: perhaps a variant of SWEEP.

swipe card ▶ n. a plastic card such as a credit card or ID card bearing magnetically encoded information that is read when the edge of the card is slid through an electronic device.

S

swip·ple /ˈswipəl/ ▶ n. dialect the swinging part of a flail.
– ORIGIN late Middle English: probably based on the verb SWEEP.

swirl /swərl/ ▶ v. [no obj.] move in a twisting or spiraling pattern: *the smoke was swirling around him* | (as adj. **swirling**) figurative *a flood of swirling emotions.* ■ [with obj.] cause to move in such a pattern: *swirl a little cream into the soup.*
▶ n. a quantity of something moving in such a pattern: *swirls of dust swept across the floor.* ■ a twisting or spiraling movement or pattern: *she emerged with a swirl of skirts | swirls of color.*
– DERIVATIVES **swirl·y** adj.
– ORIGIN late Middle English (originally Scots in the sense 'whirlpool'): perhaps of Low German or Dutch origin; compare with Dutch *zwirrelen* 'to whirl.'

swish /swisH/ ▶ v. **1** [no obj.] move with a hissing or rushing sound: *a car swished by.* ■ [with obj.] cause to move with such a sound: *a girl came in, swishing her long skirts.* ■ aim a swinging blow at something: *he swished at a bramble with a piece of stick.*
2 [with obj.] Basketball sink (a shot) without the ball touching the backboard or rim.
▶ n. **1** a hissing or rustling sound: *he could hear the swish of a distant car.* ■ a rapid swinging movement: *the cow gave a swish of its tail.*
2 Basketball, informal a shot that goes through the basket without touching the backboard or rim.
3 informal, offensive an effeminate male homosexual.
▶ adj. **1** informal, offensive (of a man) effeminate.
2 Brit. informal impressively attractive and fashionable: *dinner at a swish hotel.*
– ORIGIN mid 18th cent.: imitative.

swish·y /ˈswisHē/ ▶ adj. **1** making a swishing sound or movement.
2 informal, offensive (of a man) effeminate.

Swiss /swis/ ▶ adj. of or relating to Switzerland or its people. ■ (as plural noun **the Swiss**) the people of Switzerland.
▶ n. (pl. **same**) a native or inhabitant of Switzerland, or a person of Swiss descent.
– ORIGIN early 16th cent.: from French *Suisse*, from Middle High German *Swīz* 'Switzerland.'

Swiss ar·my knife ▶ n. a penknife incorporating several blades and other tools such as scissors and screwdrivers.

Swiss chard ▶ n. see CHARD.

Swiss cheese ▶ n. cheese of a style originating in Switzerland, typically containing large holes. ■ used figuratively to refer to something that is full of holes, gaps, or defects: *the team has Swiss cheese for a defense.*

Swiss cheese plant ▶ n. a large monstera with perforated leaves (supposedly resembling the holes in a Swiss cheese), popularly grown as a house plant while young. ● *Monstera deliciosa*, family Araceae.

Swiss Con·fed·er·a·tion the confederation of cantons that form Switzerland.

Swiss guard ▶ n. [often treated as pl.] Swiss mercenaries employed as a special guard, formerly by sovereigns of France, now only at the Vatican.

Swiss roll ▶ n. Brit. a jelly roll.

switch /swicH/ ▶ n. **1** a device for making and breaking the connection in an electric circuit: *the guard hit a switch and the gate swung open.* ■ Computing a program variable that activates or deactivates a certain function of a program.
2 an act of adopting one policy or way of life, or choosing one type of item, in place of another; a change, esp. a radical one: *his friends were surprised at his switch from newspaper owner to farmer.*
3 a slender flexible shoot cut from a tree.
4 a junction of two railroad tracks, with a pair of linked tapering rails that can be moved laterally to allow a train to pass from one line to the other.
5 a tress of false or detached hair tied at one end, used in hairdressing to supplement natural hair.
▶ v. [with obj.] **1** change the position, direction, or focus of: *the company switched the boats to other routes.* ■ adopt (something different) in place of something else; change: [with obj.] *she's managed to switch careers* | [no obj.] *she worked as a librarian and then switched to journalism.* ■ substitute (two items) for each other; exchange: *after ten minutes, listener and speaker switch roles.*
2 archaic beat or flick with or as if with a switch.
– PHRASAL VERBS **switch something off** turn off an electrical device. ■ (**switch off**) informal cease to pay attention: *as he waffles on, I switch off.* **switch something on** turn on an electrical device.
– DERIVATIVES **switch·a·ble** adj.
– ORIGIN late 16th cent. (denoting a thin tapering riding whip): probably from Low German.

switch·back /ˈswicH,bak/ ▶ n. **1** a 180° bend in a road or path, esp. one leading up the side of a mountain.
2 Brit. a road, path, or railroad with alternate sharp ascents and descents. ■ a roller coaster.
▶ v. [no obj.] (of a road or vehicle) make a series of switchback turns: *a road that switchbacked up blue and distant hills.*

switch·blade /ˈswicH,blād/ ▶ n. a knife with a blade that springs out from the handle when a button is pressed.

switch·board /ˈswicH,bôrd/ ▶ n. an installation for the manual control of telephone connections in an office, hotel, or other large building. ■ another term for HELPLINE. ■ an apparatus for varying connections between electric circuits in other applications.

switch·er /ˈswicHər/ ▶ n. **1** a shunting engine.
2 a piece of electronic equipment used to select or combine different video and audio signals.

switch·er·oo /,swicHəˈro͞o/ ▶ n. informal a change, reversal, or exchange, esp. a surprising or deceptive one.
– ORIGIN late 20th cent.: from the noun SWITCH + *-eroo*, a humorous suffix probably imitative of *buckaroo*.

switch·gear /ˈswicH,gi(ə)r/ ▶ n. **1** switching equipment used in the transmission of electricity.
2 the switches or electrical controls in a motor vehicle.

switch·grass /ˈswicH,gras/ ▶ n. a tall North American panic grass that forms large clumps. ● *Panicum virgatum*, family Gramineae.

switch-hit·ter ▶ n. Baseball a batter who can hit from either side of home plate. ■ informal a bisexual.
– DERIVATIVES **switch-hit** v., **switch-hit·ting** adj.

switch·man /ˈswicH,mən/ ▶ n. (pl. **switchmen**) a railroad worker responsible for operating signals and switches. Also called SIGNALMAN.

switch·o·ver (also **switchover**) ▶ n. an instance of adopting a new policy, position, way of life, etc.: *a product switchover in its mainframe computer line.*

switch·yard /ˈswicH,yärd/ ▶ n. **1** the part of a railroad yard taken up by junctions, in which trains are made up.
2 an enclosed area of a power system containing the switchgear.

Swith·in, St. /ˈswi*TH*ən/ (also **Swithun**) (died 862), English ecclesiastic; bishop of Winchester 852–862. The tradition that if it rains on St. Swithin's Day it will do so for the next 40 days may have its origin in the heavy rain said to have occurred when his relics were to be transferred to a shrine in Winchester Cathedral. Feast day, July 15.

Switz·er·land /ˈswitsərlənd/ a mountainous, landlocked country in central Europe; pop. 7,604,500 (est. 2009); capital, Berne; languages, French, German, Italian, and Romansh (all official). French name SUISSE, German name SCHWEIZ, Italian name SVIZZERA; also called by its Latin name HELVETIA.

> Switzerland emerged as an independent country in the 14th and 15th centuries, when the states or cantons formed a confederation to defeat first their Habsburg overlords and then their Burgundian neighbors. After a period of French domination (1798–1815) the Swiss Confederation's neutrality was guaranteed by the other European powers. Neutral in both world wars, Switzerland emerged as an international financial center and as the headquarters of several international organizations such as the Red Cross.

swive /swīv/ ▶ v. [with obj.] archaic or humorous have sexual intercourse with.
– ORIGIN Middle English: apparently from the Old English verb *swīfan* 'move (along a course), sweep.'

swiv·el /ˈswivəl/ ▶ n. a coupling between two parts enabling one to revolve without turning the other.
▶ v. (**swivels, swiveling, swiveled**; Brit. **swivels, swivelling, swivelled**) [often with adverbial] turn around a point or axis or on a swivel: [no obj.] *he swiveled in the chair* | [with obj.] *she swiveled her eyes around.*
– ORIGIN Middle English, from the base of Old English *swīfan* 'to move (along a course), sweep.'

swiv·el chair ▶ n. a chair with a seat able to be turned on its base to face in any direction.

swiv·et /ˈswivit/ ▶ n. [in sing.] a fluster or panic: *the incomprehensible did not throw him into a swivet.*
– ORIGIN late 19th cent.: of unknown origin.

swiz·zle /ˈswizəl/ ▶ n. a mixed alcoholic drink, esp. a frothy one of rum or gin and bitters.
▶ v. [with obj.] stir (a drink) with a swizzle stick.
– ORIGIN early 19th cent.: of unknown origin.

swiz·zle stick ▶ n. a stick used for stirring still drinks or taking the fizz out of sparkling ones.

SWM ▶ abbr. single white male (used in personal ads).

swol·len /ˈswōlən/ past participle of SWELL.

swoon /swo͞on/ ▶ v. [no obj.] faint from extreme emotion: *I don't want a nurse who swoons at the sight of blood.* ■ be emotionally affected by someone or something that one admires; become ecstatic: *teenagers* **swoon over** *Japanese pop singers.*
▶ n. an occurrence of fainting: *her strength ebbed away and she fell into a swoon.*
– ORIGIN Middle English: the verb from obsolete *swown* 'fainting,' the noun from *aswoon* 'in a faint,' both from Old English *geswōgen* 'overcome.'

swoop /swo͞op/ ▶ v. **1** [no obj.] (esp. of a bird) move rapidly downward through the air: *the barn owl can swoop down on a mouse in total darkness | the aircraft swooped in to land.* ■ carry out a sudden attack, esp. in order to make a capture or arrest: *investigators* **swooped on** *the Graf family home.*
2 [with obj.] informal seize with a sweeping motion: *she* **swooped up** *the hen in her arms.*
▶ n. a swooping or snatching movement or action: *four members were arrested following a swoop by detectives on their homes.*
– PHRASES **at** (or **in**) **one fell swoop** see FELL[4].
– ORIGIN mid 16th cent. (in the sense 'sweep along in a stately manner'): perhaps a dialect variant of Old English *swāpan* (see SWEEP). The early sense of the noun was 'a blow, stroke.'

swoosh /swo͝osH, swo͞osH/ ▶ n. the sound produced by a sudden rush of air or liquid: *the swoosh of surf.*
▶ v. [no obj.] move with such a sound: *swooshing down beautiful ski slopes.*
– ORIGIN mid 19th cent.: imitative.

swop /swäp/ ▶ **v. & n.** chiefly Brit. variant spelling of **SWAP**.

sword /sôrd/ ▶ **n.** a weapon with a long metal blade and a hilt with a hand guard, used for thrusting or striking and now typically worn as part of ceremonial dress. ■ (**the sword**) literary military power, violence, or destruction: *not many perished by the sword*. ■ (**swords**) one of the suits in a tarot pack.
– PHRASES **beat** (or **turn**) **swords into ploughshares** devote resources to peaceful rather than warlike ends. [with biblical allusion to Is. 2:4 and Mic. 4:3.] **he who lives by the sword dies by the sword** proverb those who commit violent acts must expect to suffer violence themselves. **put to the sword** kill, esp. in war. **the sword of justice** judicial authority.
– DERIVATIVES **sword·like** /-ˌlīk/ **adj.**
– ORIGIN Old English *sw(e)ord*, of Germanic origin; related to Dutch *zwaard* and German *Schwert*.

sword and sor·cer·y ▶ **n.** a genre of fiction characterized by heroic adventures and elements of fantasy.

sword-bear·er ▶ **n.** an official who carries a sword for a sovereign or other dignitary on formal occasions.

sword·bill /ˈsôrdˌbil/ (also **sword-billed hummingbird**) ▶ **n.** a mainly green hummingbird with a very long bill, found in northern South America. ● *Ensifera ensifera*, family Trochilidae.

sword dance ▶ **n.** a dance in which the performers brandish swords or step around swords laid on the ground, originally as a tribal preparation for war or as a victory celebration.

sword fern ▶ **n.** a fern with long slender fronds. ● Genera *Polystichum* and *Nephrolepis*, family Dryopteridaceae: several species, including the North American *P. munitum* and the tropical *N. exaltata*.

sword·fish /ˈsôrdˌfisн/ ▶ **n.** (pl. **same** or **swordfishes**) a large edible marine fish with a streamlined body and a long flattened swordlike snout, related to the billfishes and popular as a game fish. ● *Xiphias gladius*, the only member of the family Xiphiidae.

swordfish

sword knot ▶ **n.** a ribbon or tassel attached to a sword hilt, originally for securing it to the wrist.

sword lil·y ▶ **n.** a gladiolus.

sword of Dam·o·cles ▶ **n.** see **DAMOCLES**.

sword of state ▶ **n.** the sword carried in front of a sovereign on state occasions.

sword·play /ˈsôrdˌplā/ ▶ **n.** the activity or skill of fencing with swords or foils. ■ repartee; skillful debate: *this intellectual swordplay went on for several minutes*.

swords·man /ˈsôrdzmən/ ▶ **n.** (pl. **swordsmen**) a man who fights with a sword (typically with his level of skill specified): *an expert swordsman*.
– DERIVATIVES **swords·man·ship** /-ˌsнip/ **n.**

sword swal·low·er ▶ **n.** a person who passes (or pretends to pass) a sword blade down the throat and gullet as entertainment.

sword·tail /ˈsôrdˌtāl/ ▶ **n.** a livebearing freshwater fish of Central America, popular in aquariums. The lower edge of the tail is elongated and brightly marked in the male. ● *Xiphophorus helleri*, family Poeciliidae.

swore /swôr/ past of **SWEAR**.

sworn /swôrn/ past participle of **SWEAR**.
▶ **adj.** [attrib.] **1** (of testimony or evidence) given under oath: *he made a sworn statement*.
2 determined to remain in the role or condition specified: *they were sworn enemies*.

swot /swät/ Brit. informal ▶ **v.** (**swots, swotting, swotted**) [no obj.] study assiduously: *kids swotting for exams*.
▶ **n.** a person who studies hard, esp. one regarded as spending too much time studying.
– PHRASAL VERBS **swot up on** study (a subject) intensively, esp. in preparation for something: *teachers spend their evenings swotting up on jargon* | (**swot something up**) *I've always been interested in old furniture and I've swotted it up a bit*.
– DERIVATIVES **swot·ty adj.**
– ORIGIN mid 19th cent.: dialect variant of **SWEAT**.

SWOT a·nal·y·sis /ˈswät/ ▶ **n.** a study undertaken by an organization to identify its internal strengths and weaknesses, as well as its external opportunities and threats.
– ORIGIN acronym from *strengths, weaknesses, opportunities, threats*.

swum /swəm/ past participle of **SWIM**.

swung /swəNG/ past and past participle of **SWING**.

swung dash ▶ **n.** a dash (~) in the form of a reverse *s* on its side.

SY ▶ **abbr.** steam yacht: *the SY Morning*.

-sy ▶ **suffix** forming diminutive nouns and adjectives such as *folksy, mopsy*, also nicknames or hypocoristics such as *Patsy*.
– ORIGIN variant of **-Y²**.

syb·a·rite /ˈsibəˌrīt/ ▶ **n.** a person who is self-indulgent in their fondness for sensuous luxury.
– DERIVATIVES **syb·a·rit·ism** /-rītˌizəm/ **n.**
– ORIGIN mid 16th cent. (originally denoting an inhabitant of Sybaris, an ancient Greek city in southern Italy, noted for luxury): via Latin from Greek *Subaritēs*.

syb·a·rit·ic /ˌsibəˈritik/ ▶ **adj.** fond of sensuous luxury or pleasure; self-indulgent: *their opulent and sybaritic lifestyle*.

syc·a·mine /ˈsikəˌmīn, -min/ ▶ **n.** (in biblical use) the black mulberry tree (see Luke 17:6; in modern versions translated as "mulberry tree").
– ORIGIN early 16th cent.: via Latin from Greek *sukaminos* 'mulberry tree,' from Hebrew *šiqmāh* 'sycamore,' assimilated to Greek *sukon* 'fig.'

syc·a·more /ˈsikəˌmôr/ ▶ **n. 1** an American plane tree. ● Genus *Platanus*, family Platanaceae: several species, in particular *P. occidentalis* (also called **BUTTONWOOD** or **BUTTONBALL TREE**), which is the largest deciduous tree in the US. ■ the timber of this tree.
2 (in full **sycamore maple**) a large Eurasian maple with winged fruits, native to central and southern Europe. ● *Acer pseudoplatanus*, family Aceraceae.
– ORIGIN Middle English: from Old French *sic(h)amor*, via Latin from Greek *sukomoros*, from *sukon* 'fig' + *moron* 'mulberry.'

syce /sīs/ ▶ **n.** (esp. in India) a groom (taking care of horses).
– ORIGIN from Persian and Urdu *sā'is*, from Arabic.

sy·con /ˈsīˌkän/ ▶ **n.** Zoology a sponge of intermediate structure, showing some folding of the body wall with choanocytes lining only radial canals. Compare with **ASCON** and **LEUCON**.
– DERIVATIVES **sy·co·noid** /-kəˌnoid/ **adj.**
– ORIGIN late 19th cent.: adopted as a genus name from Greek *sukon* 'fig.'

sy·co·ni·um /sīˈkōnēəm/ ▶ **n.** (pl. **syconia** /-nēə/) Botany a fleshy hollow receptacle that develops into a multiple fruit, as in the fig.
– ORIGIN mid 19th cent.: modern Latin, from Greek *sukon* 'fig.'

syc·o·phant /ˈsikəfənt, -ˌfant/ ▶ **n.** a person who acts obsequiously toward someone important in order to gain advantage.
– DERIVATIVES **syc·o·phan·cy** /-fənsē, -ˌfansē/ **n.**
– ORIGIN mid 16th cent. (denoting an informer): from French *sycophante*, or via Latin from Greek *sukophantēs* 'informer,' from *sukon* 'fig' + *phainein* 'to show'; the association with informing against the illegal exportation of figs from ancient Athens (recorded by Plutarch) is not substantiated.

syc·o·phan·tic /ˌsikəˈfantik/ ▶ **adj.** behaving or done in an obsequious way in order to gain advantage: *a sycophantic interview*.
– DERIVATIVES **syc·o·phan·ti·cal·ly** /ˌsikəˈfantik(ə)lē/ **adv.**

sy·co·sis /sīˈkōsis/ ▶ **n.** inflammation of the hair follicles in the bearded part of the face, caused by bacterial infection.
– ORIGIN late 16th cent. (originally denoting any fig-shaped skin ulcer): modern Latin, from Greek *sukōsis*, from *sukon* 'fig.'

Sy·den·ham /ˈsidn-əm, ˈsidnəm/, Thomas (*c.*1624–89), English physician; known as **the English Hippocrates**. He emphasized the healing power of nature, made a study of epidemics, and explained the nature of the type of chorea that is named after him.

Sy·den·ham's cho·rea /ˈsidnəmz kôˈrēə/ ▶ **n.** a form of chorea chiefly affecting children, associated with rheumatic fever. Formerly called **ST. VITUS'S DANCE**.

Syd·ney /ˈsidnē/ the capital of New South Wales in southeastern Australia, the country's largest city and chief port; pop. 4,399,722 (2008). It has a fine natural harbor, crossed by the Sydney Harbour Bridge (1932), and a striking opera house (1973).

sy·e·nite /ˈsīəˌnīt/ ▶ **n.** Geology a coarse-grained gray igneous rock composed mainly of alkali feldspar and ferromagnesian minerals such as hornblende.
– DERIVATIVES **sy·e·nit·ic** /ˌsīəˈnitik/ **adj.**
– ORIGIN late 18th cent.: from French *syénite*, from Latin *Syenites (lapis)* '(stone) of *Syene*' (from Greek *Suēnē* 'Aswan,' a town in Egypt).

Syk·tyv·kar /ˌsiktifˈkär/ a city in northwestern Russia, capital of the autonomous republic of Komi; pop. 231,000 (est. 2008).

syl. ▶ **abbr.** syllable.

syl- ▶ **prefix** variant spelling of **SYN-** assimilated before *l* (as in *syllogism*).

syll. ▶ **abbr.** ■ syllable. ■ syllabus.

syl·la·bar·y /ˈsiləˌberē/ ▶ **n.** (pl. **syllabaries**) a set of written characters representing syllables and (in some languages or stages of writing) serving the purpose of an alphabet.
– ORIGIN mid 19th cent.: from modern Latin *syllabarium*, from Latin *syllaba* (see **SYLLABLE**).

syl·la·bi /ˈsiləˌbī/ plural form of **SYLLABUS**.

syl·lab·ic /səˈlabik/ ▶ **adj.** of, relating to, or based on syllables: *a system of syllabic symbols*. ■ Prosody based on the number of syllables in a line: *the recreation of classical syllabic meters*. ■ (of a consonant, esp. a nasal or other continuant) constituting a whole syllable, such as the *m* in *Mbabane* or the *l* in *bottle*. ■ articulated in syllables: *syllabic singing*.
▶ **n.** a written character that represents a syllable: *Inuit syllabics*.
– DERIVATIVES **syl·lab·i·cal·ly** /-ik(ə)lē/ **adv.**, **syl·la·bic·i·ty** /ˌsiləˈbisitē/ **n.**
– ORIGIN early 18th cent.: from French *syllabique* or late Latin *syllabicus*, from Greek *sullabikos*, from *sullabē* 'syllable.'

syl·lab·i·fi·ca·tion /səˌlabəfiˈkāsнən/ (also **syllabication** /səˈlabiˈkāsнən/) ▶ **n.** the division of words into syllables, either in speech or in writing.
– DERIVATIVES **syl·lab·i·fy** /səˈlabəˌfī/ **v.** (**syllabifies, syllabifying, syllabified**).

syl·la·bize /ˈsiləˌbīz/ ▶ **v.** [with obj.] divide into or articulate by syllables.
– ORIGIN late 16th cent.: via medieval Latin from Greek *sullabizein*, from *sullabē* 'syllable.'

syl·la·ble /ˈsiləbəl/ ▶ **n.** a unit of pronunciation having one vowel sound, with or without surrounding consonants, forming the whole or a part of a word; e.g., there are two syllables in *water* and three in *inferno*. ■ a character or characters representing a syllable. ■ [usu. with negative] the least amount of speech or writing; the least mention of something: *I'd never have breathed a syllable if he'd kept quiet*.
▶ **v.** [with obj.] pronounce (a word or phrase) clearly, syllable by syllable.
– DERIVATIVES **syl·la·bled adj.** [usu. in combination] *poems of few-syllabled lines*.
– ORIGIN late Middle English: from an Anglo-Norman French alteration of Old French *sillabe*, via Latin from Greek *sullabē*, from *sun-* 'together' + *lambanein* 'take.'

syl·la·ble-timed ▶ **adj.** (of a language) characterized by a rhythm in which syllables occur at roughly equivalent time intervals, irrespective of the stress placed on them. French is a syllable-timed language. Contrasted with **STRESS-TIMED**.

syl·la·bub /ˈsiləˌbəb/ ▶ **n.** a whipped cream dessert, typically flavored with white wine or sherry.
– ORIGIN of unknown origin.

syl·la·bus /ˈsiləbəs/ ▶ **n.** (pl. **syllabuses** or **syllabi** /-ˌbī/) **1** an outline of the subjects in a course of study or teaching: *there isn't time to cover the syllabus* | *the history syllabus*.
2 (in the Roman Catholic Church) a summary of points decided by papal decree regarding heretical doctrines or practices.
– ORIGIN mid 17th cent. (in the sense 'concise table of headings of a discourse'): modern Latin, originally a misreading of Latin *sittybas*, accusative plural of *sittyba*, from Greek *sittuba* 'title slip, label.'

syl·lep·sis /səˈlepsis/ ▶ **n.** (pl. **syllepses** /-sēz/) a figure of speech in which a word is applied to two others in different senses (e.g., *caught the train and a bad cold*) or to two others of which it grammatically suits only one (e.g., *neither they nor it is working*). Compare with **ZEUGMA**.
– DERIVATIVES **syl·lep·tic** /-tik/ **adj.**
– ORIGIN late Middle English: via late Latin from Greek *sullēpsis* 'taking together.'

syl·lo·gism /ˈsiləˌjizəm/ ▶ **n.** an instance of a form of reasoning in which a conclusion is drawn (whether validly or not) from two given or assumed propositions (premises), each of which shares a term with the conclusion, and shares a common or middle term not present in the conclusion (e.g., *all dogs are animals; all animals have four legs; therefore*

S

all dogs have four legs). ■ deductive reasoning as distinct from induction: *logic is rules or syllogism.*
– DERIVATIVES **syl·lo·gis·tic** /ˌsiləˈjistik/ **adj.**, **syl·lo·gis·ti·cal·ly** /ˌsiləˈjistik(ə)lē/ **adv.**
– ORIGIN late Middle English: via Old French or Latin from Greek *sullogismos*, from *sullogizesthai*, from *sun-* 'with' + *logizesthai* 'to reason' (from *logos* 'reasoning').

syl·lo·gize /ˈsiləˌjīz/ ▶ **v.** [no obj.] use syllogisms. ■ [with obj.] put (facts or an argument) in the form of syllogism.
– ORIGIN late Middle English: via Old French or late Latin from Greek *sullogizesthai* (see SYLLOGISM).

sylph /silf/ ▶ **n. 1** an imaginary spirit of the air. ■ a slender woman or girl.
2 a mainly dark green and blue hummingbird, the male of which has a long forked tail. ● Genus *Aglaiocercus* (and *Neolesbia*), family Trochilidae: three species.
– ORIGIN mid 17th cent.: from modern Latin *sylphes*, *sylphi* and the German plural *Sylphen*, perhaps based on Latin *sylvestris* 'of the woods' + *nympha* 'nymph.'

sylph·like /ˈsilfˌlīk/ ▶ **adj.** (of a woman or girl) slender and graceful.

syl·van /ˈsilvən/ (also **silvan**) ▶ **adj.** chiefly literary consisting of or associated with woods; wooded: *trees and contours all add to a sylvan setting.* ■ pleasantly rural or pastoral: *vistas of sylvan charm.*
– ORIGIN mid 16th cent. (as a noun denoting an inhabitant of the woods): from French *sylvain* or Latin *Silvanus* 'woodland deity,' from *silva* 'a wood.'

Syl·va·ner /silˈvänər, -ˈvanər/ ▶ **n.** a variety of wine grape first developed in German-speaking districts, the dominant form being a white grape. ■ a white wine made from this grape.
– ORIGIN German.

syl·vat·ic /silˈvatik/ ▶ **adj.** Veterinary Medicine relating to or denoting certain diseases when contracted by wild animals, and the pathogens causing them: *an epidemic of sylvatic plague among prairie dogs.*
– ORIGIN 1930s: from Latin *silvaticus*, from *silva* 'wood.'

Syl·vi·an fis·sure /ˈsilvēən/ (also **fissure of Sylvius** /ˈsilvēəs/) ▶ **n.** Anatomy a large diagonal fissure on the lateral surface of the brain that separates off the temporal lobe.
– ORIGIN mid 19th cent.: named after François de la Boë *Sylvius* (1614–72), Flemish anatomist.

syl·vine ▶ **n.** another term for SYLVITE.

syl·vin·ite /ˈsilvəˌnīt/ ▶ **n.** a mixture of the minerals sylvite and halite, mined as a source of potash.
– ORIGIN late 19th cent.: from SYLVINE + -ITE[1].

syl·vite /ˈsilˌvīt/ ▶ **n.** a colorless or white mineral consisting of potassium chloride, occurring typically as cubic crystals. Also called SYLVINE.
– ORIGIN mid 19th cent.: from modern Latin (*sal digestivus*) *Sylvii*, the old name of this salt, + -ITE[1].

sym. ▶ **abbr.** ■ symbol. ■ Chemistry symmetrical. ■ symphony. ■ symptom.

sym- ▶ **prefix** variant spelling of SYN- assimilated before *b*, *m*, *p* (as in *symbiosis*, *symmetry*, *symphysis*).

sym·bi·ont /ˈsimbēˌänt, -bī-/ ▶ **n.** Biology either of two organisms that live in symbiosis with one another.
– ORIGIN late 19th cent.: formed irregularly from Greek *sumbiōn* 'living together,' present participle of *sumbioun* (see SYMBIOSIS).

S

sym·bi·o·sis /ˌsimbēˈōsis, -bī-/ ▶ **n.** (pl. **symbioses** /-ˌsēz/) Biology interaction between two different organisms living in close physical association, typically to the advantage of both. Compare with ANTIBIOSIS. ■ a mutually beneficial relationship between different people or groups: *a perfect mother and daughter symbiosis.*
– DERIVATIVES **sym·bi·ot·ic** /-ˈätik/ **adj.**, **sym·bi·ot·i·cal·ly** /-ˈätik(ə)lē/ **adv.**
– ORIGIN late 19th cent.: modern Latin, from Greek *sumbiōsis* 'a living together,' from *sumbioun* 'live together,' from *sumbios* 'companion.'

sym·bol /ˈsimbəl/ ▶ **n.** a thing that represents or stands for something else, esp. a material object representing something abstract: *the limousine was another symbol of his wealth and authority.* ■ a mark or character used as a conventional representation of an object, function, or process, e.g., the letter or letters standing for a chemical element or a character in musical notation. ■ a shape or sign used to represent something such as an organization, e.g., a red cross or a Star of David.
▶ **v.** (**symbols, symboling, symboled**; Brit. **symbols, symbolling, symbolled**) [with obj.] archaic symbolize.
– ORIGIN late Middle English (denoting the Apostles' Creed): from Latin *symbolum* 'symbol, Creed (as the mark of a Christian),' from Greek *sumbolon* 'mark, token,' from *sun-* 'with' + *ballein* 'to throw.'

sym·bol·ic /simˈbälik/ ▶ **adj. 1** serving as a symbol: *a repeating design symbolic of eternity.* ■ significant purely in terms of what is being represented or implied: *the release of the dissident was an important symbolic gesture.*
2 involving the use of symbols or symbolism: *the symbolic meaning of motifs and designs.*
– DERIVATIVES **sym·bol·i·cal adj.**, **sym·bol·i·cal·ly** /-ik(ə)lē/ **adv.**
– ORIGIN mid 17th cent.: from French *symbolique* or late Latin *symbolicus*, from Greek *sumbolikos*. The adjective *symbolical* dates from the early 17th cent.

sym·bol·ic in·ter·ac·tion·ism ▶ **n.** Sociology the view of social behavior that emphasizes linguistic or gestural communication and its subjective understanding, esp. the role of language in the formation of the child as a social being.

sym·bol·ic log·ic ▶ **n.** the use of symbols to denote propositions, terms, and relations in order to assist reasoning.

sym·bol·ism /ˈsimbəˌlizəm/ ▶ **n.** the use of symbols to represent ideas or qualities: *he has always believed in the importance of symbolism in garden art.* ■ symbolic meaning attributed to natural objects or facts: *the old-fashioned symbolism of flowers.* ■ (also **Symbolism**) an artistic and poetic movement or style using symbolic images and indirect suggestion to express mystical ideas, emotions, and states of mind. It originated in late 19th century France and Belgium, with important figures including Mallarmé, Maeterlinck, Verlaine, Rimbaud, and Redon.
– DERIVATIVES **sym·bol·ist n. & adj.**

sym·bol·ize /ˈsimbəˌlīz/ ▶ **v.** [with obj.] be a symbol of: *the ceremonial dagger symbolizes justice.* ■ represent by means of symbols: *a tendency to symbolize the father as the sun.*
– DERIVATIVES **sym·bol·i·za·tion** /ˌsimbəliˈzāsHən/ **n.**

sym·bol·o·gy /simˈbäləjē/ ▶ **n.** the study or use of symbols. ■ symbols collectively: *the use of religious symbology.*

sym·met·ri·cal /səˈmetrikəl/ ▶ **adj.** made up of exactly similar parts facing each other or around an axis; showing symmetry.
– DERIVATIVES **sym·met·ric adj.**, **sym·met·ri·cal·ly** /-ik(ə)lē/ **adv.**

sym·me·try /ˈsimitrē/ ▶ **n.** (pl. **symmetries**) the quality of being made up of exactly similar parts facing each other or around an axis: *this series has a line of symmetry through its center | a crystal structure with hexagonal symmetry.* ■ correct or pleasing proportion of the parts of a thing: *an overall symmetry making the poem pleasant to the ear.* ■ similarity or exact correspondence between different things: *a lack of **symmetry between** men and women | history sometimes exhibits weird symmetries between events.* ■ Physics & Mathematics a law or operation in which a physical property or process has an equivalence in two or more directions.
– DERIVATIVES **sym·me·trize** /-ˌtrīz/ **v.**
– ORIGIN mid 16th cent. (denoting proportion): from French *symétrie* or Latin *symmetria*, from Greek, from *sun-* 'with' + *metron* 'measure.'

sym·me·try break·ing ▶ **n.** Physics the absence or reduction of manifest symmetry in a situation despite its presence in the laws of nature underlying it.

sym·path·ec·to·my /ˌsimpəˈTHektəmē/ ▶ **n.** the surgical cutting of a sympathetic nerve or removal of a ganglion to relieve a condition affected by its stimulation.

sym·pa·thet·ic /ˌsimpəˈTHetik/ ▶ **adj. 1** feeling, showing, or expressing sympathy: *he was **sympathetic toward** staff with family problems | he spoke in a sympathetic tone.* ■ [predic.] showing approval of or favor toward an idea or action: *he was **sympathetic to** evolutionary ideas.*
2 pleasant or agreeable, in particular: ■ (of a person) attracting the liking of others: *Audrey develops as a sympathetic character.* ■ (of a structure) designed in a sensitive or fitting way: *buildings that were **sympathetic to** their surroundings.*
3 relating to or denoting the part of the autonomic nervous system consisting of nerves arising from ganglia near the middle part of the spinal cord, supplying the internal organs, blood vessels, and glands, and balancing the action of the parasympathetic nerves.
4 relating to, producing, or denoting an effect that arises in response to a similar action elsewhere.
– DERIVATIVES **sym·pa·thet·i·cal·ly** /-ik(ə)lē/ **adv.**
– ORIGIN mid 17th cent. (in the sense 'relating to an affinity or paranormal influence,' as in SYMPATHETIC MAGIC): from SYMPATHY, on the pattern of *pathetic*.

sym·pa·thet·ic mag·ic ▶ **n.** primitive or magical ritual using objects or actions resembling or symbolically associated with the event or person over which influence is sought.

sym·pa·thet·ic string ▶ **n.** each of a group of additional wire strings fitted to certain stringed instruments to give extra resonance.

sym·pa·thize /ˈsimpəˌTHīz/ ▶ **v.** [no obj.] **1** feel or express sympathy: *it is easy to understand and **sympathize with** his predicament.*
2 agree with a sentiment or opinion: *they **sympathize with** critiques of traditional theory.*
– ORIGIN late 16th cent. (in the sense 'suffer with another person'): from French *sympathiser*, from *sympathie* 'sympathy, friendly understanding' (see SYMPATHY).

sym·pa·thiz·er /ˈsimpəˌTHīzər/ ▶ **n.** a person who agrees with or supports a sentiment or opinion: *a Nazi sympathizer.*

sym·pa·tho·lyt·ic /ˌsimpəTHōˈlitik/ Medicine ▶ **adj.** (of a drug) antagonistic to or inhibiting the transmission of nerve impulses in the sympathetic nervous system.
▶ **n.** a drug having this effect, often used in the treatment of high blood pressure.

sym·pa·tho·mi·met·ic /ˌsimpəTHōməˈmetik/ Medicine ▶ **adj.** (of a drug) producing physiological effects characteristic of the sympathetic nervous system by promoting the stimulation of sympathetic nerves.
▶ **n.** a drug having this effect, often used in nasal decongestants.

sym·pa·thy /ˈsimpəTHē/ ▶ **n.** (pl. **sympathies**)
1 feelings of pity and sorrow for someone else's misfortune: *they had great **sympathy for** the flood victims.* ■ (**one's sympathies**) formal expression of such feelings; condolences: *all Tony's friends joined in sending their sympathies to his widow Jean.*
2 understanding between people; common feeling: *the special sympathy between the two boys was obvious to all.* ■ (**sympathies**) support in the form of shared feelings or opinions: *his **sympathies lay with** his constituents.* ■ agreement with or approval of an opinion or aim; a favorable attitude: *I have some **sympathy for** this view.* ■ (**in sympathy**) relating harmoniously to something else; in keeping: *repairs had to be **in sympathy with** the original structure.* ■ the state or fact of responding in a way similar or corresponding to an action elsewhere: *the magnetic field oscillates **in sympathy**.*
– ORIGIN late 16th cent. (sense 2): via Latin from Greek *sumpatheia*, from *sumpathēs*, from *sun-* 'with' + *pathos* 'feeling.'

sym·pat·ric /simˈpatrik/ ▶ **adj.** Biology (of animals or plants, esp. of related species or populations) occurring within the same geographical area; overlapping in distribution. Compare with ALLOPATRIC. ■ (of speciation) taking place without geographical separation.
– DERIVATIVES **sym·pa·try** /ˈsimˌpatrē, -pətrē/ **n.**
– ORIGIN early 20th cent.: from SYM- 'with, together' + Greek *patra* 'fatherland' + -IC.

sym·pet·al·ous /simˈpetl-əs/ ▶ **adj.** Botany (of a flower or corolla) having the petals united along their margins to form a tubular shape.
– DERIVATIVES **sym·pet·a·ly n.**

sym·phon·ic /simˈfänik/ ▶ **adj.** (of music) relating to or having the form or character of a symphony: *Franck's Symphonic Variations.* ■ relating to or written for a symphony orchestra: *symphonic and chamber music.*
– DERIVATIVES **sym·phon·i·cal·ly** /-ik(ə)lē/ **adv.**

sym·phon·ic po·em ▶ **n.** another term for TONE POEM.

sym·pho·nist /ˈsimfənist/ ▶ **n.** a composer of symphonies.

sym·pho·ny /ˈsimfənē/ ▶ **n.** (pl. **symphonies**) an elaborate musical composition for full orchestra, typically in four movements, at least one of which is traditionally in sonata form. ■ chiefly historical an orchestral interlude in a large-scale vocal work. ■ something regarded, typically favorably, as a composition of different elements: ***autumn is a symphony of texture and pattern.*** ■ (esp. in names of orchestras) short for SYMPHONY ORCHESTRA: *the Boston Symphony.*
– ORIGIN Middle English (denoting any of various instruments such as the dulcimer or the virginal): from Old French *symphonie*, via Latin from Greek *sumphōnia*, from *sumphōnos* 'harmonious,' from *sun-* 'together' + *phōnē* 'sound.'

sym·pho·ny or·ches·tra ▶ **n.** a large classical orchestra, including string, wind, brass, and percussion instruments.

Sym·phy·la /ˈsimfələ/ Zoology a small class of myriapod invertebrates that resemble the centipedes. They are small eyeless animals with one pair of legs per segment, typically living in soil and leaf mold.
– DERIVATIVES **sym·phy·lan n. & adj.**

– ORIGIN modern Latin (plural), from **SYM-** 'together' + Greek *phulē, phulon* 'tribe.'

sym·phy·sis /'simfəsis/ ▶ **n.** (pl. **symphyses** /-ˌsēz/) **1** the process of growing together. **2** a place where two bones are closely joined, either forming an immovable joint (as between the pubic bones in the center of the pelvis) or completely fused (as at the midline of the lower jaw).
– DERIVATIVES **sym·phys·e·al** /sim'fizēəl/ **adj.**, **sym·phys·i·al** /sim'fizēəl/ **adj.**
– ORIGIN late 16th cent. (sense 2): modern Latin, from Greek *sumphusis*, from *sun-* 'together' + *phusis* 'growth.'

sym·plasm /'simˌplazəm/ ▶ **n.** Botany a symplast, esp. the cytoplasm of which it is composed.
– DERIVATIVES **sym·plas·mic** /sim'plazmik/ **adj.**

sym·plast /'simˌplast/ ▶ **n.** Botany a continuous network of interconnected plant cell protoplasts.
– DERIVATIVES **sym·plas·tic** /sim'plastik/ **adj.**
– ORIGIN 1930s: from German *Symplast*.

sym·po·di·um /sim'pōdēəm/ ▶ **n.** (pl. **sympodia** /-dēə/) Botany the apparent main axis or stem of a plant, made up of successive secondary axes due to the death of each season's terminal bud, as in the vine.
– DERIVATIVES **sym·po·di·al** /-dēəl/ **adj.**
– ORIGIN mid 19th cent.: modern Latin, from Greek *syn-* 'together' + *pous, pod-* 'foot.'

sym·po·si·ast /sim'pōzēəst/ ▶ **n.** a participant in a symposium.

sym·po·si·um /sim'pōzēəm/ ▶ **n.** (pl. **symposia** /-zēə/ or **symposiums**) a conference or meeting to discuss a particular subject. ■ a collection of essays or papers on a particular subject by a number of contributors. ■ a drinking party or convivial discussion, esp. as held in ancient Greece after a banquet (and notable as the title of a work by Plato).
– ORIGIN late 16th cent. (denoting a drinking party): via Latin from Greek *sumposion*, from *sumpotēs* 'fellow drinker,' from *sun-* 'together' + *potēs* 'drinker.'

symp·tom /'sim(p)təm/ ▶ **n.** Medicine a physical or mental feature that is regarded as indicating a condition of disease, particularly such a feature that is apparent to the patient: *dental problems may be a symptom of other illness*. Compare with **SIGN** (sense 1 of the noun). ■ a sign of the existence of something, esp. of an undesirable situation: *the government was plagued by leaks—a symptom of divisions and poor morale*.
– DERIVATIVES **symp·tom·less** **adj.**
– ORIGIN late Middle English *synthoma*, from medieval Latin, based on Greek *sumptōma* 'chance, symptom,' from *sumpiptein* 'happen'; later influenced by French *symptome*.

symp·to·mat·ic /ˌsim(p)tə'matik/ ▶ **adj.** serving as a symptom or sign, esp. of something undesirable: *the closings are symptomatic of a decaying city*. ■ exhibiting or involving symptoms: *patients with symptomatic celiac disease | symptomatic patients*.
– DERIVATIVES **symp·to·mat·i·cal·ly** /-ik(ə)lē/ **adv.**

symp·tom·a·tol·o·gy /ˌsim(p)təmə'täləjē/ (also **symptomology**) ▶ **n.** the set of symptoms characteristic of a medical condition or exhibited by a patient.

symp·tom·ize /'simptəˌmīz/ ▶ **v.** [with obj.] be a symptom or sign of: ***hypothermia is symptomized by** confusion, slurred speech, and stiff muscles*.

syn. ▶ **abbr.** ■ synonym. ■ synonymous. ■ synonymy.

syn- ▶ **prefix** united; acting or considered together: *synchrony | syncarpous*.
– ORIGIN from Greek *sun* 'with.'

syn·aes·the·sia ▶ **n.** British spelling of **SYNESTHESIA**.

syn·a·gogue /'sinəˌgäg/ ▶ **n.** the building where a Jewish assembly or congregation meets for religious worship and instruction. ■ such a Jewish assembly or congregation.
– DERIVATIVES **syn·a·gog·al** /ˌsinə'gägəl, -'gôgəl/ **adj.**, **syn·a·gog·i·cal** /ˌsinə'gäjikəl/ **adj.**
– ORIGIN Middle English: via Old French and late Latin from Greek *sunagōgē* 'meeting,' from *sun-* 'together' + *agein* 'bring.'

syn·ap·o·mor·phy /si'napəˌmôrfē/ ▶ **n.** (pl. **synapomorphies**) Biology the possession by two organisms of a characteristic (not necessarily the same in each) that is derived from one characteristic in an organism from which they both evolved. ■ a characteristic derived in this way.
– ORIGIN 1960s: from **SYN-** 'together' + **APO-** 'away from' + Greek *morphē* 'form.'

syn·apse /'sinˌaps/ ▶ **n.** a junction between two nerve cells, consisting of a minute gap across which impulses pass by diffusion of a neurotransmitter.
– ORIGIN late 19th cent.: from Greek *sunapsis*, from *sun-* 'together' + *hapsis* 'joining,' from *haptein* 'to join.'

syn·ap·sid /sə'napsid/ ▶ **n.** a fossil reptile of a Permian and Triassic group, the members of which show increasingly mammalian characteristics and include the ancestors of mammals. Also called **MAMMALLIKE REPTILE**. ● Subclass Synapsida; includes the pelycosaurs and the therapsids.
– ORIGIN early 20th cent.: from modern Latin *Synapsida*, from Greek *sun-* 'together' + *apsis, apsid-* 'arch.'

syn·ap·sis /sə'napsis/ ▶ **n.** Biology the fusion of chromosome pairs at the start of meiosis.
– ORIGIN late 19th cent.: modern Latin, from Greek *sunapsis* 'connection, junction.'

syn·ap·tic /sə'naptik/ ▶ **adj.** Anatomy of or relating to a synapse or synapses between nerve cells: *the synaptic membrane*.
– DERIVATIVES **syn·ap·ti·cal·ly** /-ik(ə)lē/ **adv.**

syn·ap·to·ne·mal com·plex /səˌnaptə'nēməl/ ▶ **n.** Biology a ladderlike series of parallel threads visible in electron microscopy adjacent to and coaxial with pairing chromosomes in meiosis.
– ORIGIN 1950s: from *synapto-* (combining form of **SYNAPSIS**) + Greek *nēma* 'thread' + **-AL**.

syn·ar·chy /'sinərkē/ ▶ **n.** joint rule or government by two or more individuals or parties.
– DERIVATIVES **synarchic** /sə'närkik/ **adj.**, **synarchist** /-kist/ **n.**
– ORIGIN mid 18th cent.: from Greek *sunarkhia*, from *sunarkhein* 'rule jointly.'

syn·ar·thro·sis /ˌsinär'THrōsis/ ▶ **n.** (pl. **synarthroses** /-ˌsēz/) Anatomy an immovably fixed joint between bones connected by fibrous tissue (for example, the sutures of the skull).
– ORIGIN late 16th cent.: from modern Latin, from Greek *sunarthrōsis*, from *sun-* 'together' + *arthrōsis* 'jointing' (from *arthron* 'joint').

syn·as·try /sə'nastrē, 'sinəstrē/ ▶ **n.** Astrology comparison between the horoscopes of two or more people in order to determine their likely compatibility and relationship.
– ORIGIN mid 17th cent.: via late Latin from Greek *sunastria*, from *sun-* 'together' + *astēr, astr-* 'star.'

sync /siNGk/ (also **synch**) informal ▶ **n.** synchronization: *images flash onto your screen in sync with the music*.
▶ **v.** [with obj.] synchronize: *the flash needs to be synced to your camera*.
– PHRASES **in** (or **out of**) **sync** working well (or badly) together; in (or out of) agreement: *her eyes and her brain seemed to be seriously out of sync*.
– ORIGIN 1920s: abbreviation.

syn·car·pous /sin'kärpəs/ ▶ **adj.** Botany (of a flower, fruit, or ovary) having the carpels united. Often contrasted with **APOCARPOUS**.
– ORIGIN mid 19th cent.: from **SYN-** 'together' + Greek *karpos* 'fruit' + **-OUS**.

syn·chon·dro·sis /ˌsiNGkən'drōsis/ ▶ **n.** (pl. **synchondroses** /-ˌsēz/) Anatomy an almost immovable joint between bones bound by a layer of cartilage, as in the vertebrae.
– ORIGIN late 16th cent.: from modern Latin, from Greek *sunkhondrōsis*, from *sun-* 'together' + *khondros* 'cartilage.'

syn·chro /'siNGkrō/ ▶ **n. 1** short for **SYNCHROMESH**. **2** synchronized or synchronization: *tape editing with synchro start*. **3** short for **SYNCHRONIZED SWIMMING**.

synchro- ▶ **comb. form** synchronous: *synchrotron*.

syn·chro·cy·clo·tron /ˌsiNGkrō'sīkləˌträn/ ▶ **n.** Physics a cyclotron able to achieve higher energies by decreasing the frequency of the accelerating electric field as the particles increase in energy and mass.

syn·chro·mesh /'siNGkrōˌmesH/ ▶ **n.** a system of gear changing, esp. in motor vehicles, in which the driving and driven gearwheels are made to revolve at the same speed during engagement by means of a set of friction clutches, thereby easing the change.
– ORIGIN 1920s: contraction of *synchronized mesh*.

syn·chron·ic /siNG'kränik/ ▶ **adj.** concerned with something, esp. a language, as it exists at one point in time: *synchronic linguistics*. Often contrasted with **DIACHRONIC**.
– DERIVATIVES **syn·chron·i·cal·ly** /-ik(ə)lē/ **adv.**
– ORIGIN 1920s: from late Latin *synchronus* (see **SYNCHRONOUS**) + **-IC**.

syn·chro·nic·i·ty /ˌsiNGkrə'nisitē/ ▶ **n. 1** the simultaneous occurrence of events that appear significantly related but have no discernible causal connection: *such synchronicity is quite staggering*. **2** another term for **SYNCHRONY** (sense 1).
– ORIGIN 1950s: coined (in sense 1) by C. G. Jung.

syn·chro·nism /'siNGkrəˌnizəm/ ▶ **n.** another term for **SYNCHRONY**.
– DERIVATIVES **syn·chro·nis·tic** /ˌsiNGkrə'nistik/ **adj.**, **syn·chro·nis·ti·cal·ly** /ˌsiNGkrə'nistik(ə)lē/ **adv.**
– ORIGIN late 16th cent.: from Greek *sunkhronismos*, from *sunkhronos* (see **SYNCHRONOUS**).

syn·chro·nize /'siNGkrəˌnīz/ ▶ **v.** [with obj.] cause to occur or operate at the same time or rate: *soldiers used watches to synchronize movements | synchronize your hand gestures with your main points*. ■ [no obj.] occur at the same time or rate: *sometimes converging swells will synchronize to produce a peak*. ■ adjust (a clock or watch) to show the same time as another: *It is now 5:48. Synchronize watches*. ■ [no obj.] tally; agree: ***their version failed to synchronize with the** police view*. ■ coordinate; combine: *both media **synchronize** national interests **with** multinational scope*.
– DERIVATIVES **syn·chro·ni·za·tion** /ˌsiNGkrənə'zāSHən/ **n.**, **syn·chro·niz·er** **n.**

syn·chro·nized swim·ming ▶ **n.** a sport in which members of a team of swimmers perform coordinated or identical movements in time to music.
– DERIVATIVES **syn·chro·nized swim·mer** **n.**

syn·chro·nous /'siNGkrənəs/ ▶ **adj. 1** existing or occurring at the same time: *glaciations were approximately synchronous in both hemispheres*. **2** (of a satellite or its orbit) making or denoting an orbit around the earth or another celestial body in which one revolution is completed in the period taken for the body to rotate about its axis.
– DERIVATIVES **syn·chro·nous·ly** **adv.**
– ORIGIN mid 17th cent.: from late Latin *synchronus* (from Greek *sunkhronos*, from *sun-* 'together' + *khronos* 'time') + **-OUS**.

syn·chro·nous mo·tor ▶ **n.** an electric motor having a speed exactly proportional to the current frequency.

syn·chro·ny /'siNGkrənē/ ▶ **n. 1** simultaneous action, development, or occurrence. ■ the state of operating or developing according to the same time scale as something else: *some individuals do not remain **in synchrony with** the twenty-four-hour day*. **2** synchronic treatment or study: *the structuralist distinction between synchrony and diachrony*.
– ORIGIN mid 19th cent.: from Greek *sunkhronos* (see **SYNCHRONOUS**).

syn·chro·tron /'siNGkrəˌträn/ ▶ **n.** Physics a cyclotron in which the magnetic field strength increases with the energy of the particles to keep their orbital radius constant.

syn·chro·tron ra·di·a·tion ▶ **n.** Physics polarized radiation emitted by a charged particle spinning in a magnetic field.

syn·cline /'sinˌklīn/ ▶ **n.** Geology a trough or fold of stratified rock in which the strata slope upward from the axis. Compare with **ANTICLINE**.
– DERIVATIVES **syn·cli·nal** /sin'klīnl/ **adj.**
– ORIGIN late 19th cent.: from **SYN-** 'together' + Greek *klinein* 'to lean,' on the pattern of *incline*.

syn·co·pate /'siNGkəˌpāt/ ▶ **v.** [with obj.] **1** (usu. as adj. **syncopated**) displace the beats or accents in (music or a rhythm) so that strong beats become weak and vice versa: *syncopated dance music*. **2** shorten (a word) by dropping sounds or letters in the middle, as in *symbology* for *symbolology*, or *Gloster* for *Gloucester*.
– DERIVATIVES **syn·co·pa·tion** /ˌsiNGkə'pāSHən/ **n.**, **syn·co·pa·tor** /-ˌpātər/ **n.**
– ORIGIN early 17th cent.: from late Latin *syncopat-* 'affected with syncope,' from the verb *syncopare* 'to swoon' (see **SYNCOPE**).

syn·co·pe /'siNGkəpē/ ▶ **n. 1** Medicine temporary loss of consciousness caused by a fall in blood pressure. **2** Grammar the omission of sounds or letters from within a word, e.g., when *probably* is pronounced /'präblē/.
– DERIVATIVES **syn·co·pal** /-pəl/ **adj.**
– ORIGIN late Middle English: via late Latin from Greek *sunkopē*, from *sun-* 'together' + *koptein* 'strike, cut off.'

syn·cre·tism /'siNGkrəˌtizəm/ ▶ **n. 1** the amalgamation or attempted amalgamation of different religions, cultures, or schools of thought. **2** Linguistics the merging of different inflectional varieties of a word during the development of a language.
– DERIVATIVES **syn·cret·ic** /siNG'kretik/ **adj.**, **syn·cre·tist** **n. & adj.**, **syn·cre·tis·tic** /ˌsiNGkrə'tistik/ **adj.**
– ORIGIN early 17th cent.: from modern Latin *syncretismus*, from Greek *sunkrētismos*, from *sunkrētizein* 'unite against a third party,' from *sun-* 'together' + *krēs* 'Cretan' (originally with reference to ancient Cretan communities).

syn·cre·tize /'siNGkriˌtīz/ ▶ **v.** [with obj.] attempt to amalgamate or reconcile (differing things, esp.

S

religious beliefs, cultural elements, or schools of thought).
– DERIVATIVES **syn·cre·ti·za·tion** /ˌsiNGkritəˈzāSHən/ **n.**

syn·cy·tium /sinˈsiSHəm/ ▶ **n.** (pl. **syncytia** /-ˈsiSHə/) Biology a single cell or cytoplasmic mass containing several nuclei, formed by fusion of cells or by division of nuclei. ■ Embryology material of this kind forming the outermost layer of the trophoblast.
– DERIVATIVES **syn·cy·tial** /-SHəl/ **adj.**
– ORIGIN late 19th cent.: from SYN- 'together' + -CYTE 'cell' + -IUM.

synd. ▶ **abbr.** ■ syndicate. ■ syndicated.

syn·dac·tyl·y /sinˈdaktəlē/ ▶ **n.** Medicine & Zoology the condition of having some or all of the fingers or toes wholly or partly united, either naturally (as in web-footed animals) or as a malformation.
– ORIGIN mid 19th cent.: from SYN- 'united' + Greek *daktulos* 'finger' + -Y³.

syn·des·mo·sis /ˌsinˌdezˈmōsis/ ▶ **n.** (pl. **syndesmoses** /-ˌsēz/) Anatomy an immovable joint in which bones are joined by connective tissue (e.g., between the fibula and tibia at the ankle).
– ORIGIN late 16th cent.: modern Latin, from Greek *sundesmos* 'binding, fastening.'

syn·det·ic /sinˈdetik/ ▶ **adj.** Grammar of or using conjunctions.
– ORIGIN early 17th cent.: from Greek *sundetikos*, from *sundein* 'bind together.'

syn·dic /ˈsindik/ ▶ **n. 1** a government official in various countries.
2 (in the UK) a business agent of certain universities and corporations.
– DERIVATIVES **syn·di·cal adj.**
– ORIGIN early 17th cent.: from French, via late Latin from Greek *sundikos*, from *sun-* 'together' + *dikē* 'justice.'

syn·di·cal·ism /ˈsindəkəˌlizəm/ ▶ **n.** historical a movement for transferring the ownership and control of the means of production and distribution to workers' unions. Influenced by Proudhon and by the French social philosopher **Georges Sorel** (1847–1922), syndicalism developed in French labor unions during the late 19th century and was at its most vigorous between 1900 and 1914, particularly in France, Italy, Spain, and the US.
– DERIVATIVES **syn·di·cal·ist n. & adj.**
– ORIGIN early 20th cent.: from French *syndicalisme*, from *syndical*, from *syndic* 'a delegate' (see SYNDIC).

syn·di·cate ▶ **n.** /ˈsindikit/ a group of individuals or organizations combined to promote some common interest: *large-scale buyouts involving a syndicate of financial institutions | a crime syndicate.* ■ an association or agency supplying material simultaneously to a number of newspapers or periodicals. ■ a committee of syndics.
▶ **v.** /ˈsindiˌkāt/ [with obj.] control or manage by a syndicate: *the loans are syndicated to a group of banks.* ■ publish or broadcast (material) simultaneously in a number of newspapers, television stations, etc.: *his reports were syndicated to 200 other papers.* ■ sell (a horse) to a syndicate: *the stallion was syndicated for a record $5.4 million.*
– DERIVATIVES **syn·di·ca·tion** /ˌsindiˈkāSHən/ **n.**, **syn·di·ca·tor** /-ˌkātər/ **n.**
– ORIGIN early 17th cent. (denoting a committee of syndics): from French *syndicat*, from medieval Latin *syndicatus*, from late Latin *syndicus* 'delegate of a corporation' (see SYNDIC). Current verb senses date from the late 19th cent.

S

syn·di·o·tac·tic /ˌsindīōˈtaktik, sinˌdī-/ ▶ **adj.** Chemistry (of a polymer or polymeric structure) in which the repeating units have alternating stereochemical configurations.
– ORIGIN 1950s: from Greek *sunduo* 'two together' + *taktos* 'arranged' + -IC.

syn·drome /ˈsinˌdrōm/ ▶ **n.** a group of symptoms that consistently occur together or a condition characterized by a set of associated symptoms: *a rare syndrome in which the production of white blood cells is damaged.* ■ a characteristic combination of opinions, emotions, or behavior: *the "Not In My Backyard" syndrome.*
– DERIVATIVES **syn·drom·ic** /sinˈdrämik/ **adj.**
– ORIGIN mid 16th cent.: modern Latin, from Greek *sundromē*, from *sun-* 'together' + *dramein* 'to run.'

syndrome X ▶ **n.** a group of risk factors (including glucose intolerance, high triglycerides, obesity, and hypertension) that indicate predisposition to diabetes.

syne /sīn/ ▶ **adv.** Scottish ago. See also AULD LANG SYNE, LANG SYNE.
– ORIGIN Middle English: contraction of dialect *sithen* 'ever since.'

syn·ec·do·che /siˈnekdəkē/ ▶ **n.** a figure of speech in which a part is made to represent the whole or vice versa, as in *Cleveland won by six runs* (meaning "Cleveland's baseball team").
– DERIVATIVES **syn·ec·doch·ic** /ˌsinekˈdäkik/ **adj.**, **syn·ec·doch·i·cal** /ˌsinekˈdäkikəl/ **adj.**, **syn·ec·doch·i·cal·ly** /-ˈdäkik(ə)lē/ **adv.**
– ORIGIN late Middle English: via Latin from Greek *sunekdokhē*, from *sun-* 'together' + *ekdekhesthai* 'take up.'

syn·e·col·o·gy /ˌsiniˈkäləjē/ ▶ **n.** the ecological study of whole plant or animal communities. Contrasted with AUTECOLOGY.
– DERIVATIVES **syn·ec·o·log·i·cal** /sinˌekəˈläjikəl, -ˌēkə-/ **adj.**, **syn·e·col·o·gist** /-jist/ **n.**
– ORIGIN early 20th cent.: from SYN- 'together' + ECOLOGY.

syn·ec·tics /səˈnektiks/ ▶ **plural n.** [treated as sing.] trademark a problem-solving technique that seeks to promote creative thinking, typically among small groups of people of diverse experience and expertise.
– ORIGIN 1960s: from late Latin *synecticus* (based on Greek *sunekhein* 'hold together'), on the pattern of *dialectics*.

syn·er·e·sis /səˈnerəsis/ ▶ **n.** (pl. **synereses** /-ˌsēz/) **1** the contraction of two vowels into a diphthong or single vowel.
2 Chemistry the contraction of a gel accompanied by the separating out of liquid.
– ORIGIN late 16th cent.: via late Latin from Greek *sunairesis*, based on *sun-* 'together' + *hairein* 'take.'

syn·er·gist /ˈsinərjist/ ▶ **n.** a substance, organ, or other agent that participates in an effect of synergy.
– DERIVATIVES **syn·er·gis·tic** /ˌsinərˈjistik/ **adj.**, **syn·er·gis·ti·cal·ly** /ˈˌsinərˈjistik(ə)lē/ **adv.**

syn·er·gy /ˈsinərjē/ (also **synergism** /-ˌjizəm/) ▶ **n.** the interaction or cooperation of two or more organizations, substances, or other agents to produce a combined effect greater than the sum of their separate effects: *the synergy between artist and record company.*
– DERIVATIVES **syn·er·get·ic** /ˌsinərˈjetik/ **adj.**, **syn·er·gic** /səˈnərjik/ **adj.**
– ORIGIN mid 19th cent.: from Greek *sunergos* 'working together,' from *sun-* 'together' + *ergon* 'work.'

syn·es·the·sia /ˌsinəsˈTHēZHə/ (Brit. **synaesthesia**) ▶ **n.** Physiology & Psychology the production of a sense impression relating to one sense or part of the body by stimulation of another sense or part of the body.
– DERIVATIVES **syn·es·thete** /ˈsinisˌTHēt/ **n.**, **syn·es·thet·ic** /-ˈTHetik/ **adj.**
– ORIGIN late 19th cent.: modern Latin, from SYN- 'with,' on the pattern of *anesthesia*.

syn·fu·el /ˈsinˌfyo͞oəl/ ▶ **n.** fuel made from coal, corn, etc., as a substitute for a petroleum product.

syn·ga·my /ˈsiNGgəmē/ ▶ **n.** Biology the fusion of two cells, or of their nuclei, in reproduction.
– ORIGIN early 20th cent.: from SYN- 'with' + Greek *gamos* 'marriage.'

syn·gas /ˈsinˌgas/ ▶ **n.** short for SYNTHESIS GAS.

Synge /siNG/, J. M. (1871–1909), Irish playwright; full name *Edmund John Millington Synge*. His *The Playboy of the Western World* (1907) caused riots at the Abbey Theatre, Dublin, because of its explicit language and its implication that Irish peasants would condone a brutal murder.

syn·ge·ne·ic /ˌsinjəˈnēik/ ▶ **adj.** Medicine & Biology (of organisms or cells) genetically similar or identical and hence immunologically compatible, esp. so closely related that transplantation does not provoke an immune response.
– ORIGIN 1960s: from SYN- 'together' + Greek *genea* 'race, stock' + -IC.

syn·ge·net·ic /ˌsinjəˈnetik/ ▶ **adj.** Geology relating to or denoting a mineral deposit or formation produced at the same time as the enclosing or surrounding rock.

syng·na·thid /ˈsiNGnəˌTHid, ˈsiNGgnə-/ ▶ **n.** any of a family of fish with an elongated snout and no ventral and first dorsal fins. It includes the sea moths, seahorses, and trumpet fish.

syn·od /ˈsinəd/ ▶ **n. 1** an assembly of the clergy and sometimes also the laity in a diocese or other division of a particular church.
2 a Presbyterian ecclesiastical court above the presbyteries and subject to the General Assembly.
– ORIGIN late Middle English: via late Latin from Greek *sunodos* 'meeting,' from *sun-* 'together' + *hodos* 'way.'

syn·od·ic /səˈnädik/ ▶ **adj.** Astronomy relating to or involving the conjunction of stars, planets, or other celestial objects.
– ORIGIN mid 17th cent.: via late Latin from Greek *sunodikos*, from *sunodos* (see SYNOD).

syn·od·i·cal /səˈnädikəl/ ▶ **adj. 1** Christian Church of, relating to, or constituted as a synod: *synodical government.*
2 Astronomy another term for SYNODIC.
– DERIVATIVES **syn·od·al** /ˈsinədl/ **adj.** (sense 1).

syn·od·ic month ▶ **n.** Astronomy another term for LUNAR MONTH.

syn·od·ic pe·ri·od ▶ **n.** Astronomy the time between successive conjunctions of a planet with the sun.

syn·o·nym /ˈsinəˌnim/ ▶ **n.** a word or phrase that means exactly or nearly the same as another word or phrase in the same language, for example *shut* is a synonym of *close.* ■ a person or thing so closely associated with a particular quality or idea that the mention of their name calls it to mind: *the Victorian age is a synonym for sexual puritanism.* ■ Biology a taxonomic name that has the same application as another, esp. one that has been superseded and is no longer valid.
– DERIVATIVES **syn·o·nym·ic** /ˌsinəˈnimik/ **adj.**, **syn·o·nym·i·ty** /ˌsinəˈnimitē/ **n.**
– ORIGIN late Middle English: via Latin from Greek *sunōnumon*, neuter (used as a noun) of the adjective *sunōnumos*, from *sun-* 'with' + *onuma* 'name.'

syn·on·y·mous /səˈnänəməs/ ▶ **adj.** (of a word or phrase) having the same or nearly the same meaning as another word or phrase in the same language: ***aggression is often taken as synonymous with violence.*** ■ closely associated with or suggestive of something: *his deeds had made his name synonymous with victory.*
– DERIVATIVES **syn·on·y·mous·ly adv.**, **syn·on·y·mous·ness n.**

syn·on·y·my /səˈnänəmē/ ▶ **n.** the state of being synonymous.
– ORIGIN mid 16th cent.: via late Latin from Greek *sunōnumia*, from *sunōnumos* (see SYNONYM).

syn·op·sis /səˈnäpsis/ ▶ **n.** (pl. **synopses** /-ˌsēz/) a brief summary or general survey of something: *a synopsis of the accident.* ■ an outline of the plot of a book, play, movie, or episode of a television show.
– DERIVATIVES **syn·op·size** /-ˌsīz/ **v.**
– ORIGIN early 17th cent.: via late Latin from Greek, from *sun-* 'together' + *opsis* 'seeing.'

syn·op·tic /səˈnäptik/ ▶ **adj. 1** of or forming a general summary or synopsis: *a synoptic outline of the contents.* ■ taking or involving a comprehensive mental view: *a synoptic model of higher education.*
2 of or relating to the Synoptic Gospels.
▶ **n.** (**Synoptics**) the Synoptic Gospels.
– DERIVATIVES **syn·op·ti·cal adj.**, **syn·op·ti·cal·ly** /-ik(ə)lē/ **adv.**
– ORIGIN early 17th cent.: from Greek *sunoptikos*, from *sunopsis* (see SYNOPSIS).

Syn·op·tic Gos·pels ▶ **plural n.** the Gospels of Matthew, Mark, and Luke, which describe events from a similar point of view, as contrasted with that of John.

syn·op·tist /səˈnäptist/ ▶ **n.** the writer of a Synoptic Gospel.

syn·os·to·sis /ˌsinäˈstōsis/ ▶ **n.** (pl. **synostoses** /-sēz/) Physiology & Medicine the union or fusion of adjacent bones by the growth of bony substance, either as a normal process during growth or as the result of ankylosis.
– ORIGIN mid 19th cent.: from SYN- 'together' + Greek *osteon* 'bone' + -OSIS.

syn·o·vi·al /səˈnōvēəl/ ▶ **adj.** relating to or denoting a type of joint that is surrounded by a thick flexible membrane forming a sac into which is secreted a viscous fluid that lubricates the joint.
– ORIGIN mid 18th cent.: from modern Latin *synovia*, probably formed arbitrarily by Paracelsus.

syn·o·vi·tis /ˌsinəˈvītis/ ▶ **n.** Medicine inflammation of a synovial membrane.

syn·sac·rum /sinˈsakrəm, -ˈsā-/ ▶ **n.** (pl. **synsacra** /-ˈsakrə, -ˈsākrə/ or **synsacrums**) Zoology an elongated composite sacrum containing a number of fused vertebrae, present in birds and some extinct reptiles.

syn·tac·tic /sinˈtaktik/ ▶ **adj.** of or according to syntax: *syntactic analysis.*
– DERIVATIVES **syn·tac·ti·cal adj.**, **syn·tac·ti·cal·ly** /-ik(ə)lē/ **adv.**
– ORIGIN early 19th cent.: from Greek *suntaktikos*, from *suntassein* 'arrange together' (see SYNTAX).

syn·tagm /ˈsinˌtam/ (also **syntagma** /sinˈtagmə/) ▶ **n.** (pl. **syntagms** or **syntagmas** or **syntagmata** /sinˈtagmətə/) a linguistic unit consisting of a set of linguistic forms (phonemes, words, or phrases) that are in a sequential relationship to one another. Often contrasted with PARADIGM. ■ the relationship between any two such forms.
– ORIGIN mid 17th cent.: via late Latin from Greek *suntagma*, from *suntassein* 'arrange together.'

syn·tag·mat·ic /ˌsintagˈmatik/ ▶ **adj.** of or denoting the relationship between two or more linguistic units used sequentially to make well-formed structures. Contrasted with PARADIGMATIC.

–DERIVATIVES **syn·tag·mat·i·cal·ly** /-ik(ə)lē/ **adv.**, **syn·tag·mat·ics plural n.** [treated as sing.].

syn·tax /'sinˌtaks/ ▶ **n.** the arrangement of words and phrases to create well-formed sentences in a language: *the syntax of English*. ■ a set of rules for or an analysis of this: *generative syntax*. ■ the branch of linguistics that deals with this.
–ORIGIN late 16th cent.: from French *syntaxe*, or via late Latin from Greek *suntaxis*, from *sun-* 'together' + *tassein* 'arrange.'

syn·tax er·ror ▶ **n.** Computing a character or string incorrectly placed in a command or instruction that causes a failure in execution.

syn·ten·ic /sin'tenik/ ▶ **adj.** Genetics (of genes) occurring on the same chromosome: *syntenic sequences*.
–DERIVATIVES **syn·te·ny** /'sintənē/ **n.**
–ORIGIN 1970s: from **SYN-** 'together' + Greek *tainia* 'band, ribbon' + **-IC**.

synth /sinTH/ ▶ **n.** informal short for **SYNTHESIZER**.

synth·ase /'sinˌTHās, -ˌTHāz/ ▶ **n.** [often with modifier] Biochemistry an enzyme that catalyzes the linking together of two molecules, esp. without the direct involvement of ATP: *nitric oxide synthases*. Compare with **LIGASE**.

syn·the·sis /'sinTHəsis/ ▶ **n.** (pl. **syntheses** /-ˌsēz/) combination or composition, in particular: ■ the combination of ideas to form a theory or system: *the synthesis of intellect and emotion in his work | the ideology represented a synthesis of certain ideas*. Often contrasted with **ANALYSIS**. ■ the production of chemical compounds by reaction from simpler materials: *the synthesis of methanol from carbon monoxide and hydrogen*. ■ (in Hegelian philosophy) the final stage in the process of dialectical reasoning, in which a new idea resolves the conflict between thesis and antithesis. ■ Grammar the process of making compound and derivative words. ■ Linguistics the use of inflected forms rather than word order to express grammatical structure.
–DERIVATIVES **syn·the·sist n.**
–ORIGIN early 17th cent.: via Latin from Greek *sunthesis*, from *suntithenai* 'place together.'

syn·the·sis gas ▶ **n.** a mixture of carbon monoxide and hydrogen produced industrially, esp. from coal, and used as a feedstock in making synthetic chemicals.

syn·the·size /'sinTHiˌsīz/ (also **synthetize** /-ˌtīz/) ▶ **v.** [with obj.] make (something) by synthesis, esp. chemically: *man synthesizes new chemical poisons and sprays the countryside wholesale*. ■ combine (a number of things) into a coherent whole: *pupils should synthesize the data they have gathered | Darwinian theory has been synthesized with modern genetics*. ■ produce (sound) electronically: *trigger chips that synthesize speech* | (as adj. **synthesized**) *synthesized chords*.

syn·the·siz·er /'sinTHəˌsīzər/ ▶ **n.** an electronic musical instrument, typically operated by a keyboard, producing a wide variety of sounds by generating and combining signals of different frequencies.

syn·thes·pi·an /sin'THespēən/ ▶ **n.** a computer-generated three-dimensional human character, designed to simulate a lifelike performance on film: *her first little-girl crush was on a synthespian, none other than Buzz Lightyear*.
–ORIGIN blend of *synthetic* and *thespian*.

syn·thet·ic /sin'THetik/ ▶ **adj. 1** (of a substance) made by chemical synthesis, esp. to imitate a natural product: *synthetic rubber*. ■ (of an emotion or action) not genuine; insincere: *their tears are a bit synthetic*.
2 Logic (of a proposition) having truth or falsity determinable by recourse to experience. Compare with **ANALYTIC**.
3 Linguistics (of a language) characterized by the use of inflections rather than word order to express grammatical structure. Contrasted with **AGGLUTINATIVE** and **ANALYTIC**.
▶ **n.** (often **synthetics**) a synthetic material or chemical, esp. a textile fiber.
–DERIVATIVES **syn·thet·i·cal adj.**, **syn·thet·i·cal·ly** /-ik(ə)lē/ **adv.**
–ORIGIN late 17th cent.: from French *synthétique* or modern Latin *syntheticus*, from Greek *sunthetikos*, based on *suntithenai* 'place together.'

syn·thet·ic res·in ▶ **n.** see **RESIN**.

syn·thon /'sinˌTHän/ ▶ **n.** Chemistry a constituent part of a molecule to be synthesized that is regarded as the basis of a synthetic procedure.
–ORIGIN 1960s: from **SYNTHESIS** + **-ON**.

syn·ton·ic /sin'tänik/ ▶ **adj.** Psychology (of a person) responsive to and in harmony with their environment so that affect is appropriate to the given situation: *culturally syntonic*. ■ [in combination] (of a psychiatric condition or psychological process) consistent with other aspects of an individual's personality and belief system: *this phobia was ego-syntonic*. ■ historical relating to or denoting the lively and responsive type of temperament that was considered liable to manic-depressive psychosis. See also **CYCLOTHYMIA**.
–DERIVATIVES **syn·tone** /'sinˌtōn/ **n.**
–ORIGIN late 19th cent.: from German *Syntonie* 'state of being syntonic' + **-IC**.

syn·type /'sinˌtīp/ ▶ **n.** Botany & Zoology each of a set of type specimens of equal status, upon which the description and name of a new species is based. Compare with **HOLOTYPE**.

syph·i·lis /'sifəlis/ ▶ **n.** a chronic bacterial disease that is contracted chiefly by infection during sexual intercourse, but also congenitally by infection of a developing fetus. ● This is caused by the spirochete *Treponema pallidum*. The infection progresses in four successive stages: **primary syphilis**, characterized by a chancre in the part infected; **secondary syphilis**, affecting chiefly the skin, lymph nodes, and mucous membranes; **tertiary syphilis**, involving the spread of tumorlike lesions (gummas) throughout the body, frequently damaging the cardiovascular and central nervous systems; **quaternary syphilis** neurosyphilis.
–DERIVATIVES **syph·i·lit·ic** /ˌsifə'litik/ **adj. & n.**
–ORIGIN early 18th cent.: modern Latin, from *Syphilis, sive Morbus Gallicus*, the title of a Latin poem (1530), from the name of the character *Syphilus*, the supposed first sufferer of the disease.

sy·phon ▶ **n. & v.** variant spelling of **SIPHON**.

Syr·a·cuse /'siraˌkyo͞os, -ˌkyo͞oz/ **1** a port on the eastern coast of Sicily; pop. 125,000. Italian name **SIRACUSA**.
2 a city in New York, southeast of Lake Ontario; pop. 138,068 (est. 2008). The site of salt springs, it was an important center of salt production during the 19th century.

Sy·rah /sə'rä, 'sirə/ ▶ **n.** another term for **SHIRAZ**[2].

syr·ette /si'ret/ ▶ **n.** Medicine, trademark a disposable injection unit comprising a collapsible tube with an attached hypodermic needle and a single dose of a drug, commonly morphine.
–ORIGIN 1940s: from **SYRINGE** + **-ETTE**.

Syr·i·a /'si(ə)rēə/ a country in the Middle East, on the eastern Mediterranean Sea; pop. 21,763,000 (est. 2009); capital, Damascus; language, Arabic (official).

> Syria was the site of various early civilizations, most notably that of the Phoenicians. Falling successively within the empires of Persia, Macedon, and Rome, it became a center of Islamic power and civilization from the 7th century and a province of the Ottoman Empire in 1516. After the Turkish defeat in World War I, Syria was mandated to France and became independent with the ejection of Vichy troops by the Allies in 1941. From 1958 to 1961, Syria was united with Egypt as the United Arab Republic. It lost the Golan Heights to Israel in the 1967 war.

–DERIVATIVES **Syr·i·an adj. & n.**

Syr·i·ac /'si(ə)rēˌak/ ▶ **n.** the language of ancient Syria, a western dialect of Aramaic in which many important early Christian texts are preserved, and that is still used by Syrian Christians as a liturgical language.
▶ **adj.** of or relating to this language.

sy·rin·ga /sə'riNGgə/ ▶ **n. 1** a plant of the genus *Syringa* (family Oleaceae), esp. (in gardening) the lilac.
2 informal another term for **MOCK ORANGE**.
–ORIGIN modern Latin, from Greek *surinx, suring-* 'tube' (with reference to the use of its stems as pipe stems).

sy·ringe /sə'rinj, 'sirinj/ ▶ **n.** a tube with a nozzle and piston or bulb for sucking in and ejecting liquid in a thin stream, used for cleaning wounds or body cavities, or fitted with a hollow needle for injecting or withdrawing fluids. ■ any similar device used in gardening or cooking.
▶ **v.** (**syringes, syringing, syringed**) [with obj.] spray liquid into (the ear or a wound) with a syringe: *I had my ears syringed*. ■ spray liquid over (plants) with a syringe: *syringe the leaves frequently during warm weather*.
–ORIGIN late Middle English: from medieval Latin *syringa*, from *syrinx* (see **SYRINX**).

medical syringe

sy·rin·go·my·e·li·a /səˌriNGgōˌmī'ēlēə, -'ēlyə/ ▶ **n.** Medicine a chronic progressive disease in which longitudinal cavities form in the cervical region of the spinal cord. This characteristically results in wasting of the muscles in the hands and a loss of sensation.
–ORIGIN late 19th cent.: modern Latin, from Greek *surinx, suring-* 'tube, channel' + *muelos* 'marrow.'

syr·inx /'siriNGks/ ▶ **n.** (pl. **syrinxes**) **1** a set of panpipes.
2 Ornithology the lower larynx or voice organ in birds, situated at or near the junction of the trachea and bronchi and well developed in songbirds.
–ORIGIN early 17th cent.: via Latin from Greek *surinx* 'pipe, channel.'

Syro- ▶ **comb. form** Syrian; Syrian and ...: *Syro-Palestinian*. ■ relating to Syria.

syr·phid /'sərfid/ ▶ **n.** Entomology a fly of the hoverfly family (Syrphidae).
–ORIGIN late 19th cent.: from modern Latin *Syrphidae* (plural), from the genus name *Syrphus*, from Greek *surphos* 'gnat.'

syr·ta·ki /sər'takē, -'tākē/ (also **sirtaki**) ▶ **n.** (pl. **syrtakis** or **syrtakia** /-kyä/) a Greek folk dance in which dancers form a line or chain.
–ORIGIN modern Greek, from Greek *surtos* 'drawn, led' + the diminutive suffix *-aki*.

syr·up /'sirəp, 'sər-/ (also **sirup**) ▶ **n.** a thick sweet liquid made by dissolving sugar in boiling water, often used for preserving fruit. ■ a thick sweet liquid containing medicine or used as a drink: *cough syrup*. ■ a thick sticky liquid derived from a sugar-rich plant, esp. sugar cane, corn, and maple. ■ excessive sweetness or sentimentality of style or manner: *Mr. Gurney's poems are almost all of them syrup*.
–ORIGIN late Middle English: from Old French *sirop* or medieval Latin *siropus*, from Arabic *šarāb* 'beverage'; compare with **SHERBET** and **SHRUB**[2].

syr·up of figs ▶ **n.** a laxative syrup made from dried figs, typically with senna and carminatives.

syr·up·y /'sirəpē, 'sər-/ (also **sirupy**) ▶ **adj.** having the consistency or sweetness of syrup: *syrupy desserts*. ■ excessively sentimental: *a particularly syrupy moment from a corny film*.

sys·op /'siˌsäp/ ▶ **n.** Computing a system operator.
–ORIGIN 1980s: abbreviation.

syst. ▶ **abbr.** system.

sys·tem /'sistəm/ ▶ **n. 1** a set of connected things or parts forming a complex whole, in particular: ■ a set of things working together as parts of a mechanism or an interconnecting network: *the state railroad system | fluid is pushed through a system of pipes or channels*. ■ Physiology a set of organs in the body with a common structure or function: *the digestive system*. ■ the human or animal body as a whole: *you need to get the cholesterol out of your system*. ■ Computing a group of related hardware units or programs or both, esp. when dedicated to a single application. ■ Geology (in chronostratigraphy) a major range of strata that corresponds to a period in time, subdivided into series. ■ Astronomy a group of celestial objects connected by their mutual attractive forces, esp. moving in orbits about a center: *the system of bright stars known as the Gould Belt*. ■ short for **CRYSTAL SYSTEM**.
2 a set of principles or procedures according to which something is done; an organized scheme or method: *a multiparty system of government | the public school system*. ■ orderliness; method: *there was no system at all in the company*. ■ a method of choosing one's procedure in gambling. ■ a set of rules used in measurement or classification: *the metric system*. ■ (**the system**) the prevailing political or social order, esp. when regarded as oppressive and intransigent: *don't try bucking the system*.
3 Music a set of staves in a musical score joined by a brace.
–PHRASES **get something out of one's system** informal get rid of a preoccupation or anxiety: *she let her get the crying out of her system*.
–DERIVATIVES **sys·tem·less adj.**
–ORIGIN early 17th cent.: from French *système* or late Latin *systema*, from Greek *sustēma*, from *sun-* 'with' + *histanai* 'set up.'

sys·tem·at·ic /ˌsistə'matik/ ▶ **adj.** done or acting according to a fixed plan or system; methodical: *a systematic search of the whole city*.
–DERIVATIVES **sys·tem·at·i·cal·ly** /-ik(ə)lē/ **adv.**, **sys·tem·a·tist** /'sistəməˌtist/ **n.**
–ORIGIN early 18th cent.: from French *systématique*, via late Latin from late Greek *sustēmatikos*, from *sustēma* (see **SYSTEM**).

sys·tem·at·ic de·sen·si·ti·za·tion ▶ **n.** Psychiatry a treatment for phobias in which the patient is exposed to progressively more anxiety-provoking stimuli and taught relaxation techniques.

sys·tem·at·ic er·ror ▶ **n.** Statistics an error having a nonzero mean, so that its effect is not reduced when observations are averaged.

sys·tem·at·ic name ▶ **n.** a standardized name, esp. for a chemical element or compound, a biological taxon, or a star or other astronomical object. Compare with **TRIVIAL NAME**.

sys·tem·at·ics /ˌsistəˈmatiks/ ▶ **plural n.** [treated as sing.] the branch of biology that deals with classification and nomenclature; taxonomy.

sys·tem·at·ic the·ol·o·gy ▶ **n.** a form of theology in which the aim is to arrange religious truths in a self-consistent whole.
– DERIVATIVES **sys·tem·at·ic the·o·lo·gian n.**

sys·tem·a·tize /ˈsistəməˌtīz/ ▶ **v.** [with obj.] arrange according to an organized system; make systematic: *Galen set about systematizing medical thought* | (as adj. **systematized**) *systematized reading schemes.*
– DERIVATIVES **sys·tem·a·ti·za·tion** /ˌsistəmətiˈzāsHən/ **n.**, **sys·tem·a·tiz·er n.**

sys·tem·ic /səˈstemik/ ▶ **adj. 1** of or relating to a system, esp. as opposed to a particular part: *the disease is localized rather than systemic.* ■ (of an insecticide, fungicide, or similar substance) entering the plant via the roots or shoots and passing through the tissues. **2** Physiology denoting the part of the circulatory system concerned with the transportation of oxygen to and carbon dioxide from the body in general, esp. as distinct from the pulmonary part concerned with the transportation of oxygen from and carbon dioxide to the lungs.
– DERIVATIVES **sys·tem·i·cal·ly** /-ik(ə)lē/ **adv.**
– ORIGIN early 19th cent.: formed irregularly from **SYSTEM** + **-IC**.

sys·tem in·te·gra·tor (also **systems integrator**) ▶ **n.** see **INTEGRATOR**.

sys·tem·ize /ˈsistəˌmīz/ ▶ **v.** another term for **SYSTEMATIZE**.
– DERIVATIVES **sys·tem·i·za·tion** /ˌsistəmiˈzāsHən/ **n.**, **sys·tem·iz·er n.**

sys·tem op·er·a·tor (also **systems operator**) ▶ **n.** a person who manages the operation of a computer system, such as a message board.

sys·tems an·a·lyst ▶ **n.** a person who analyzes a complex process or operation in order to improve its efficiency, esp. by applying a computer system.
– DERIVATIVES **sys·tems a·nal·y·sis n.**

sys·to·le /ˈsistəlē/ ▶ **n.** Physiology the phase of the heartbeat when the heart muscle contracts and pumps blood from the chambers into the arteries. Often contrasted with **DIASTOLE**.
– DERIVATIVES **sys·tol·ic** /siˈstälik/ **adj.**
– ORIGIN late 16th cent.: via late Latin from Greek *sustolē*, from *sustellein* 'to contract.'

syz·y·gy /ˈsizijē/ ▶ **n.** (pl. **syzygies**) Astronomy a conjunction or opposition, esp. of the moon with the sun: *the planets were aligned in syzygy.* ■ a pair of connected or corresponding things: ***animus** and **anima** represent a supreme pair of opposites, the syzygy.*
– ORIGIN early 17th cent.: via late Latin from Greek *suzugia*, from *suzugos* 'yoked, paired,' from *sun-* 'with, together' + the stem of *zeugnunai* 'to yoke.'

Szcze·cin /ˈSHCHeCHēn/ a city in northwestern Poland, a port on the Oder River, near the border with Germany; pop. 408,583 (2007). German name **STETTIN**.

Sze·chuan /ˈseCHˈwän/ (also **Szechwan**) variant of **SICHUAN**.

Sze·ged /ˈsegˌed/ a city in southern Hungary, a port on the Tisza River, near the border with Serbia; pop. 169,030 (2009).

Szent-Györ·gyi /sānt ˈjôrj(ē)/, Albert von (1893–1986), US biochemist, born in Hungary. He discovered ascorbic acid, which was later identified with vitamin C.

Szi·lard /ˈzilˌärd, ˈsil-, -ərd/, Leo (1898–1964), US physicist and molecular biologist, born in Hungary. He fled from Nazi Germany to the US, where he became a central figure in the Manhattan Project, which developed the atom bomb.

S

Tt

T[1] /tē/ (also **t**) ▶ **n.** (pl. **Ts** or **T's**) **1** the twentieth letter of the alphabet. ■ denoting the next after S in a set of items, categories, etc.
2 (**T**) (also **tee**) a shape like that of a capital T: [in combination] *make a T-shaped wound in the rootstock and insert the cut bud.* See also **T-SQUARE**, etc.
– PHRASES **cross the T** historical (of a naval force) cross in front of an enemy force approximately at right angles, securing a tactical advantage for gunnery. **to a T** informal exactly; to perfection: *I baked it to a T, and of course it was delicious.*

T[2] ▶ **abbr.** ■ [in combination] (in units of measurement) tera- (10^{12}): *12 Tbytes of data storage.* ■ tesla. ■ tablespoon(s). ■ Brit. (in names of sports clubs) Town: *Mansfield T.* ▶ **symbol** ■ temperature. ■ Chemistry the hydrogen isotope tritium.

t ▶ **abbr.** ■ long or metric ton(s). ■ teaspoon(s). ▶ **symbol** (*t*) Statistics a number characterizing the distribution of a sample taken from a population with a normal distribution (see **STUDENT'S T-TEST**).

't /t/ ▶ **contraction** the word "it," attached to the end of a verb, esp. in the transcription of regional spoken use: *I'll never do 't again.*

-t[1] ▶ **suffix** equivalent to **-ED**[2] (as in *crept, sent, slept*).

-t[2] ▶ **suffix** equivalent to **-EST**[2] (as in *shalt*).

T-1 ▶ **n.** (also **T-3**) Computing a high-speed data transmission line.

Ta ▶ **symbol** the chemical element tantalum.

ta /tä/ ▶ **exclam.** Brit. informal thank you.
– ORIGIN late 18th cent.: a child's word.

TAB /tab/ ▶ **abbr.** typhoid–paratyphoid A and B vaccine.

tab[1] /tab/ ▶ **n. 1** a small flap or strip of material attached to or projecting from something, used to hold or manipulate it, or for identification and information. ■ a strip or ring of metal attached to the top of a canned drink and pulled to open the can.
2 Computing a second or further document or page that can be opened on a spreadsheet or Internet browser.
3 informal a restaurant or bar bill.
4 Aeronautics a part of a control surface, typically hinged, that modifies the action or response of the surface.
▶ **v.** (**tabs, tabbing, tabbed**) [with obj.] mark or identify with a projecting piece of material: *he opened the book at a page tabbed by a cloth bookmark.* ■ identify as being of a specified type or suitable for a specified position: *he was tabbed by the president as the next Republican National Committee chairman.*
– PHRASES **keep tabs** (or **a tab**) **on** informal monitor the activities or development of; keep under observation. **pick up the tab** informal pay for something: *my company will pick up the tab for all moving expenses.*
– DERIVATIVES **tabbed** adj.
– ORIGIN late Middle English: perhaps related to **TAG**[1].

tab[2] ▶ **n.** a facility in a word-processing program, or a device on a keyboard, for advancing to a sequence of set positions in tabular work: *set tabs at 1.4 inches and 3.4 inches* | [as modifier] *the tab key.*
▶ **v.** (**tabs, tabbing, tabbed**) **1** [no obj.] use the tab key on a computer or typewriter keyboard: *the user can tab to the phrase and press Enter.*
2 [with obj.] short for **TABULATE**.
– ORIGIN early 20th cent.: short for **TABULATOR**.

tab[3] ▶ **n.** informal a tablet containing a dose of a drug.
– ORIGIN 1960s: abbreviation.

tab[4] ▶ **n.** informal a tabloid newspaper: *she tries to cover up his peccadillos before they make the tabs' front pages.*

tab. ▶ **abbr.** ■ tables. ■ (in prescriptions) tablet. [from Latin *tabella*.]

ta·bac /tä'bäk/ ▶ **n.** (pl. pronunc. **same**) (in French-speaking regions) a tobacconist's shop.
– ORIGIN French, literally *tobacco.*

tab·ard /'tabərd/ ▶ **n.** a sleeveless jerkin consisting only of front and back pieces with a hole for the head. ■ historical a coarse garment of this kind as the outer dress of medieval peasants and clerics, or worn as a surcoat over armor. ■ a herald's official coat emblazoned with the arms of the sovereign.
– ORIGIN Middle English: from Old French *tabart*, of unknown origin.

tab·a·ret /'tabərit/ ▶ **n.** an upholstery fabric of alternate satin and watered silk stripes.
– ORIGIN late 18th cent.: probably from **TABBY**.

Ta·bas·co[1] /tə'baskō, -'bäs-/ a state in southeastern Mexico, on the Gulf of Mexico; capital, Villahermosa.

Ta·bas·co[2] /tə'baskō/ (also **Tabasco sauce**) ▶ **n.** trademark a pungent sauce made from the fruit of a capsicum pepper. ● The plant is *Capsicum frutescens* (or *C. anuum*), family Solanaceae.
– ORIGIN late 19th cent.: named after the state of *Tabasco* (see **TABASCO**[1]).

tab·bou·leh /tə'bo͞olē/ (also **tabouli**) ▶ **n.** an Arab salad of cracked wheat mixed with finely chopped ingredients such as tomatoes, onions, and parsley.
– ORIGIN from Arabic *tabbūla.*

tab·by /'tabē/ ▶ **n.** (pl. **tabbies**) **1** (also **tabby cat**) a cat whose fur is mottled or streaked with dark stripes. [late 17th cent. (as *tabby cat*): said to be so named from its striped coloring.] ■ informal any domestic cat.
2 a fabric with a watered pattern, typically silk.
3 a plain weave.
4 a type of concrete made of lime, shells, gravel, and stones that dries very hard. [early 19th cent. (originally *tabby work*): perhaps a different word, or from a resemblance in color to that of a tabby cat.]
▶ **adj.** (of a cat) gray or brownish in color and streaked with dark stripes.
– ORIGIN late 16th cent. (denoting a kind of silk taffeta, originally striped, later with a watered finish: sense 2 of the noun): from French *tabis*, based on Arabic *al-'Attābiyya*, the name of the quarter of Baghdad where tabby was manufactured.

tab·er·nac·le /'tabər,nakəl/ ▶ **n. 1** (in biblical use) a fixed or movable habitation, typically of light construction. ■ a tent used as a sanctuary for the Ark of the Covenant by the Israelites during the Exodus and until the building of the Temple.
2 a meeting place for worship used by some Protestants or Mormons.
3 an ornamented receptacle or cabinet in which a pyx or ciborium containing the reserved sacrament may be placed in Catholic churches, usually on or above an altar. ■ archaic a canopied niche or recess in the wall of a church.
4 a partly open socket or double post on a sailboat's deck into which a mast is fixed, with a pivot near the top so that the mast can be lowered.
– DERIVATIVES **tab·er·nac·led** adj.
– ORIGIN Middle English: via French from Latin *tabernaculum* 'tent,' diminutive of *taberna* 'hut, tavern.'

ta·bes /'tābēz/ ▶ **n.** Medicine emaciation. See also **TABES DORSALIS**.
– DERIVATIVES **ta·bet·ic** /tə'betik/ adj.
– ORIGIN late 16th cent.: from Latin, literally 'wasting away.'

ta·bes·cent /tə'besənt/ ▶ **adj.** wasting away.
– ORIGIN late 19th cent.: from Latin *tabescent-* 'beginning to waste away,' from the verb *tabescere*, from *tabere* 'waste away.'

ta·bes dor·sal·is /'tābēz dôr'salis, -'sālis/ ▶ **n.** Medicine loss of coordination of movement, esp. as a result of syphilitic infection of the spinal cord. Also called **LOCOMOTOR ATAXIA**.
– ORIGIN modern Latin, literally 'wasting of the back.'

ta·bi /'täbē/ ▶ **n.** (pl. **same**) a thick-soled Japanese ankle sock with a separate section for the big toe.
– ORIGIN Japanese.

ta·bla /'täblə/ ▶ **n.** a pair of small hand drums attached together, used in Indian music; one is slightly larger than the other and is played using pressure from the heel of the hand to vary the pitch.
– ORIGIN from Persian and Urdu *tablah*, Hindi *tablā*, from Arabic *tabl* 'drum.'

tab·la·ture /'tabləCHər, -,CHo͝or/ ▶ **n.** chiefly historical a form of musical notation indicating fingering rather than the pitch of notes, written on lines corresponding to, for example, the strings of a lute or the holes on a flute.
– ORIGIN late 16th cent.: from French, probably from Italian *tavolatura*, from *tavolare* 'set to music.'

ta·ble /'tābəl/ ▶ **n. 1** a piece of furniture with a flat top and one or more legs, providing a level surface on which objects may be placed, and that can be used for such purposes as eating, writing, working, or playing games. ■ [in sing.] food provided in a restaurant or household: *he was reputed to have the finest French table of the time.* ■ a group seated at a table for a meal: *the whole table was in gales of laughter.* ■ (**the table**) a meeting place or forum for formal discussions held to settle an issue or dispute: *the negotiating table.* ■ [in sing.] Bridge the dummy hand (which is exposed on the table): *they made the hand easily with the aid of a club ruff **on the table**.*
2 a set of facts or figures systematically displayed, esp. in columns: *the population has grown, as shown in table 1* | *a table of contents.* ■ Computing a collection of data stored in memory as a series of records, each defined by a unique key stored with it.
3 a flat surface, in particular: ■ Architecture a flat, typically rectangular, vertical surface. ■ a horizontal molding, esp. a cornice. ■ a slab of wood or stone bearing an inscription. ■ a flat surface of a gem. ■ a cut gem with two flat faces. ■ each half or quarter of a folding board for backgammon.
▶ **v.** [with obj.] **1** postpone consideration of: *I'd like the issue to be tabled for the next few months.*
2 Brit. present formally for discussion or consideration at a meeting: *an MP tabled an amendment to the bill.*
– PHRASES **at table** seated at a table eating a meal. **lay something on the table 1** make something known so that it can be freely and sensibly discussed. **2** postpone something indefinitely. **on the table** offered for discussion: *our offer remains on the table.* **turn the tables** reverse one's position relative to someone else, esp. by turning a position of disadvantage into one of advantage: *police invited householders to a seminar on how to **turn the tables on burglars**.* **under the table 1** informal very drunk: *by 3:30 everybody was under the table.* **2** (esp. of making a payment) secretly or covertly: *he accepted a slew of payoffs under the table.* ■ another term for **UNDER THE COUNTER** (see **COUNTER**[1]).
– DERIVATIVES **ta·ble·ful** /-,fo͝ol/ **n.** (pl. **tablefuls**).

PRONUNCIATION KEY ə *ago, up*; ər *over, fur*; a *hat*; ā *ate*; ä *car*; e *let*; ē *see*; i *fit*; ī *by*; NG *sing*; ō *go*; ô *law, for*; oi *toy*; o͝o *good*; o͞o *goo*; ou *out*; TH *thin*; TH *then*; ZH *vision*

– ORIGIN Old English *tabule* 'flat slab, inscribed tablet,' from Latin *tabula* 'plank, tablet, list,' reinforced in Middle English by Old French *table*.

tab·leau /ˌtaˈblō/ ▶ **n.** (pl. **tableaux** /ˌtaˈblōz/) a group of models or motionless figures representing a scene from a story or from history; a tableau vivant.
– ORIGIN late 17th cent. (in the sense 'picture,' figuratively 'picturesque description'): from French, literally 'picture,' diminutive of *table* (see **TABLE**).

tab·leau vi·vant /täˈblō vēˈväN, -ˈvänt/ ▶ **n.** (pl. **tableaux vivants** pronunc. **same**) chiefly historical a silent and motionless group of people arranged to represent a scene or incident.
– ORIGIN French, literally 'living picture.'

ta·ble·cloth /ˈtābəlˌklôTH, -ˌkläTH/ ▶ **n.** a cloth spread over a table, esp. during meals.

ta·ble d'hôte /ˌtäbəl ˈdōt, ˌtäblə, ˌtabəl/ ▶ **n.** a restaurant meal offered at a fixed price and with few if any choices.
– ORIGIN early 17th cent.: French, literally 'host's table.' The term originally denoted a table in a hotel or restaurant where all guests ate together, hence a meal served there at a stated time and for a fixed price.

ta·ble lamp ▶ **n.** a small lamp designed to stand on a table.

ta·ble·land /ˈtābəl,(l)and/ ▶ **n.** a broad, high, level region; a plateau.

ta·ble lin·en ▶ **n.** fabric items used at mealtimes, such as tablecloths and napkins, collectively.

ta·ble man·ners ▶ **plural n.** a pattern of behavior that is conventionally required of someone while eating.

Ta·ble Moun·tain a flat-topped mountain near the southwestern tip of South Africa that overlooks Cape Town and Table Bay. It is 3,563 feet (1,087 m) high.

ta·ble nap·kin ▶ **n.** see **NAPKIN** (sense 1).

ta·ble salt ▶ **n.** salt suitable for sprinkling on food at meals.

ta·ble saw ▶ **n.** a circular saw mounted under a table or bench so that the blade projects up through a slot.

table saw

ta·ble·spoon /ˈtābəlˌspo͞on/ ▶ **n.** a large spoon for serving food. ■ (abbr.: **tbsp.** or **T**) a measurement in cooking, equivalent to 1/2 fluid ounce, three teaspoons, or 15 ml.
– DERIVATIVES **ta·ble·spoon·ful** /-ˌfo͝ol/ **n.** (pl. **tablespoonfuls**).

tab·let /ˈtablit/ ▶ **n. 1** a flat slab of stone, clay, or wood, used esp. for an inscription. ■ Architecture another term for **TABLE** (sense 3 of the noun).
2 a small disk or cylinder of a compressed solid substance, typically a measured amount of a medicine or drug; a pill. ■ Brit. a small flat piece of soap.
3 a writing pad. ■ (also **tablet PC**) (trademark in the UK) a computer that accepts input directly onto an LCD screen rather via than a keyboard or mouse.
– ORIGIN Middle English: from Old French *tablete*, from a diminutive of Latin *tabula* (see **TABLE**).

ta·ble talk ▶ **n.** informal conversation carried on at meals.

ta·ble ten·nis ▶ **n.** an indoor game based on tennis, played with small paddles and a ball bounced on a table divided by a net.

ta·ble·top /ˈtābəlˌtäp/ ▶ **n.** the horizontal top part of a table. ■ [as modifier] small or portable enough to be placed or used on a table: *a tabletop hockey game.*

ta·ble·ware /ˈtābəlˌwer/ ▶ **n.** dishes, utensils, and glassware used for serving and eating meals at a table.

ta·ble wine ▶ **n.** wine of moderate quality considered suitable for drinking with a meal.

ta·blier /tāblēˈā/ ▶ **n.** historical a part of a woman's dress resembling an apron.
– ORIGIN mid 19th cent.: from French, based on Latin *tabula* (see **TABLE**).

tab·loid /ˈtabˌloid/ ▶ **n.** a newspaper having pages half the size of those of a standard newspaper, typically popular in style and dominated by headlines, photographs, and sensational stories. ■ [as modifier] sensational in a lurid or vulgar way: *they argued about who made what allegation on what tabloid TV show.*
– ORIGIN late 19th cent.: from **TABLET** + **-OID**. Originally the proprietary name of a medicine sold in tablets, the term came to denote any small medicinal tablet; the current sense reflects the notion of "concentrated, easily assimilable."

tab·loid·i·za·tion /ˌtabloidəˈzāsHən/ ▶ **n.** a change in emphasis from the factual to the sensational, esp. in television news: *the tabloidization of the nightly news during sweeps week.*

ta·boo /təˈbo͞o, ta-/ ▶ **n.** (pl. **taboos**) a social or religious custom prohibiting or forbidding discussion of a particular practice or forbidding association with a particular person, place, or thing. ■ a practice that is prohibited or restricted in this way: *speaking about sex is a taboo in his country.*
▶ **adj.** prohibited or restricted by social custom: *sex was a taboo subject.* ■ designated as sacred and prohibited: *the burial ground was seen as a taboo place.*
▶ **v.** (**taboos, tabooing, tabooed** /-ˈbo͞od/) [with obj.] place under such prohibition: *traditional societies taboo female handling of food during this period.*
– ORIGIN late 18th cent.: from Tongan *tabu* 'set apart, forbidden'; introduced into English by Captain Cook.

ta·bor /ˈtābər/ ▶ **n.** historical a small drum, esp. one used simultaneously by the player of a simple pipe.
– ORIGIN Middle English: from Old French *tabour* 'drum'; perhaps related to Persian *tabīra* 'drum.' Compare with **TAMBOUR**.

tab·o·ret /tabəˈret, ˈtabərit/ (**tabouret**) ▶ **n.** a low stool or small table.
– ORIGIN mid 17th cent.: from French, 'stool,' diminutive of *tabour* 'drum' (see **TABOR**).

ta·bou·li ▶ **n.** variant spelling of **TABBOULEH**.

Ta·briz /təˈbrēz/ a city in northwestern Iran; pop. 1,398,060 (2006). It lies at about 4,485 feet (1,367 m) above sea level at the center of a volcanic region and has been subject to frequent destructive earthquakes.

Ta·briz rug ▶ **n.** a rug made in Tabriz, the older styles of which typically have a rich decorative medallion pattern.

ta·bu ▶ **n.** (pl. **tabus**) & **adj.** variant form of **TABOO** in archaic or anthropological use.

tab·u·lar /ˈtabyələr/ ▶ **adj. 1** (of data) consisting of or presented in columns or tables: *a tabular presentation of running costs.*
2 broad and flat like the top of a table: *a huge tabular iceberg.* ■ (of a crystal) relatively broad and thin, with two well-developed parallel faces.
– DERIVATIVES **tab·u·lar·ly adv.**
– ORIGIN mid 17th cent. (sense 2): from Latin *tabularis*, from *tabula* (see **TABLE**).

ta·bu·la ra·sa /ˈtäbyo͞olə ˈräsə, ˈräzə/ ▶ **n.** (pl. **tabulae rasae** /ˈtäbyo͞olē ˈräsē, ˈräzē/) an absence of preconceived ideas or predetermined goals; a clean slate: *the team did not have complete freedom and a tabula rasa from which to work.* ■ the human mind, esp. at birth, viewed as having no innate ideas.
– ORIGIN Latin, literally 'scraped tablet,' denoting a tablet with the writing erased.

tab·u·late /ˈtabyəˌlāt/ ▶ **v.** [with obj.] arrange (data) in tabular form: (as adj. **tabulated**) *tabulated results.*
– DERIVATIVES **tab·u·la·tion** /ˌtabyəˈlāsHən/ **n.**
– ORIGIN early 17th cent. (originally Scots in the sense 'enter on a roll'): in modern use from **TABLE** + **-ATE**[3].

tab·u·la·tor /ˈtabyəlātər/ ▶ **n. 1** a person or thing that arranges data in tabular form.
2 another term for **TAB**[2].

ta·bun /ˈtäbo͝on/ ▶ **n.** an organophosphorus nerve gas, developed in Germany during World War II.
– ORIGIN German, of unknown origin.

TAC ▶ **abbr.** Tactical Air Command.

tac·a·ma·hac /ˈtakəməˌhak/ ▶ **n.** another term for **BALSAM POPLAR**.
– ORIGIN late 16th cent. (originally denoting the aromatic resin of *Bursera simaruba*: see **ELEMI**): from obsolete Spanish *tacamahaca*, from Aztec *tecomahiyac.*

tac·an /ˈtakən/ ▶ **n.** an electronic ultrahigh-frequency navigational aid system for aircraft that measures bearing and distance from a ground beacon.
– ORIGIN 1950s: from *tac(tical) a(ir) n(avigation).*

ta·cet /ˈtāsit, ˈtas-, ˈtäket/ ▶ **v.** [no obj.] Music (as a direction) indicating that a voice or instrument is silent.
– ORIGIN Latin, literally 'is silent,' from *tacere* 'be silent.'

tach /tak/ ▶ **n.** informal short for **TACHOMETER**.

tach·ism /ˈtaˌsHizəm/ (also **tachisme**) ▶ **n.** a style of painting adopted by some French artists from the 1940s, involving the use of dabs or splotches of color, similar in aims to abstract expressionism.
– ORIGIN 1950s: from French *tachisme*, from *tache* 'a stain.'

ta·chis·to·scope /təˈkistəˌskōp/ ▶ **n.** an instrument used for exposing objects to the eye for a very brief measured period of time.
– DERIVATIVES **ta·chis·to·scop·ic** /-ˌkistəˈskäpik/ **adj.**, **ta·chis·to·scop·i·cal·ly** /-ˈskäpik(ə)lē/ **adv.**
– ORIGIN late 19th cent.: from Greek *takhistos* 'swiftest' + **-SCOPE**.

tacho- ▶ **comb. form** relating to speed: *tachograph.*
– ORIGIN from Greek *takhos* 'speed.'

tach·o·graph /ˈtakəˌgraf/ ▶ **n.** a tachometer providing a record of engine speed over a period, esp. in a commercial road vehicle.

ta·chom·e·ter /taˈkämitər, tə-/ ▶ **n.** an instrument that measures the working speed of an engine (esp. in a road vehicle), typically in revolutions per minute.

tachy- ▶ **comb. form** rapid: *tachycardia.*
– ORIGIN from Greek *takhus* 'swift.'

tach·y·car·di·a /ˌtakiˈkärdēə/ ▶ **n.** an abnormally rapid heart rate.
– ORIGIN late 19th cent.: from **TACHY-** 'swift' + Greek *kardia* 'heart.'

ta·chyg·ra·phy /taˈkigrəfē, tə-/ ▶ **n.** stenography or shorthand, esp. that of ancient or medieval scribes.
– DERIVATIVES **tach·y·graph·ic** /ˌtakiˈgrafik/ **adj.**

tach·y·kin·in /ˌtakəˈkīnin/ ▶ **n.** Biochemistry any of a class of substances formed in bodily tissue in response to injury and having a rapid stimulant effect on smooth muscle.

ta·chym·e·ter /taˈkimitər, tə-/ ▶ **n. 1** a theodolite for the rapid measurement of distances in surveying.
2 a facility on a watch for measuring speed.
– DERIVATIVES **tach·y·met·ric** /ˌtakəˈmetrik/ **adj.**

tach·y·on /ˈtakēˌän/ ▶ **n.** Physics a hypothetical particle that travels faster than light.
– ORIGIN 1960s: from **TACHY-** 'swift' + **-ON**.

tach·y·phy·lax·is /ˌtakəfiˈlaksis/ ▶ **n.** Medicine rapidly diminishing response to successive doses of a drug, rendering it less effective. The effect is common with drugs acting on the nervous system.

tach·yp·ne·a /ˌtakə(p)ˈnēə/ (Brit. **tachypnoea**) ▶ **n.** Medicine abnormally rapid breathing.
– ORIGIN late 19th cent.: from **TACHY-** 'swift' + Greek *pnoē* 'breathing.'

tac·it /ˈtasit/ ▶ **adj.** understood or implied without being stated: *your silence may be taken to mean tacit agreement.*
– DERIVATIVES **tac·it·ly adv.**
– ORIGIN early 17th cent. (in the sense 'wordless, noiseless'): from Latin *tacitus*, past participle of *tacere* 'be silent.'

tac·i·turn /ˈtasiˌtərn/ ▶ **adj.** (of a person) reserved or uncommunicative in speech; saying little.
– DERIVATIVES **tac·i·turn·i·ty** /ˌtasiˈtərnitē/ **n.**, **tac·i·turn·ly adv.**
– ORIGIN late 18th cent.: from Latin *taciturnus*, from *tacitus* (see **TACIT**).

Tac·i·tus /ˈtasətəs/ (*c.* 56–120), Roman historian; full name *Publius* (or *Gaius*) *Cornelius Tacitus*. His *Annals* (covering the years 14–68) and *Histories* (69–96) are major works on the history of the Roman Empire.

tack[1] /tak/ ▶ **n. 1** a small, sharp, broad-headed nail. ■ a thumbtack.
2 a long stitch used to fasten fabrics together temporarily, prior to permanent sewing.
3 a method of dealing with a situation or problem; a course of action or policy: *as she could not stop him from going she tried another tack and insisted on going with him.*
4 Sailing an act of changing course by turning a vessel's head into and through the wind, so as to bring the wind on the opposite side. ■ a boat's course relative to the direction of the wind: *the brig bowled past on the opposite tack.* ■ a distance sailed between such changes of course.
5 Sailing a rope for securing the weather clew of a course. ■ the weather clew of a course, or the lower forward corner of a fore-and-aft sail.
6 the quality of being sticky: *cooking the sugar to caramel gives tack to the texture.*
▶ **v. 1** [with obj.] fasten or fix in place with tacks: *he used the tool to tack down sheets of fiberboard.* ■ fasten (pieces of cloth) together temporarily with long stitches. ■ (**tack something on**) add or append something to something already existing: *long-term savings plans with some life insurance tacked on.*
2 [no obj.] Sailing change course by turning a boat's head into and through the wind. Compare with **WEAR**[2]. [from the practice of shifting ropes (sense 5

of the noun) to change direction.] ■ [with obj.] alter the course of (a boat) in such a way. ■ [with adverbial of direction] make a series of such changes of course while sailing: *she spent the entire night tacking back and forth.*
– PHRASES **on the port** (or **starboard**) **tack** Sailing with the wind coming from the port (or starboard) side of the boat.
– DERIVATIVES **tack·er** n.
– ORIGIN Middle English (in the general sense 'something that fastens one thing to another'): probably related to Old French *tache* 'clasp, large nail.'

tack² ▶ n. equipment used in horseback riding, including the saddle and bridle.
– ORIGIN late 18th cent. (originally dialect in the general sense 'apparatus, equipment'): shortening of TACKLE. The noun sense dates from the 1920s.

tack coat ▶ n. (in roadmaking) a thin coating of tar or asphalt applied before a road is based to form an adhesive bond.

tack·le /'takəl/ ▶ n. **1** the equipment required for a task or sport: *fishing tackle.*
2 a mechanism consisting of ropes, pulley blocks, hooks, or other things for lifting heavy objects. ■ the running rigging and gear used to work a boat's sails.
3 Football & Rugby an act of seizing and stopping a player in possession of the ball by knocking them to the ground. ■ (in soccer and other games) an act of taking the ball, or attempting to take the ball, from an opponent.
4 Football a player who lines up inside the end along the line of scrimmage.
▶ v. [with obj.] make determined efforts to deal with (a problem or difficult task): *police have launched an initiative to tackle rising crime.* ■ Football & Rugby stop the forward progress of (the ball carrier) by seizing them and knocking them to the ground. ■ chiefly Soccer try to take the ball from (an opponent) by intercepting them.
– DERIVATIVES **tack·ler** /'tak(ə)lər/ n.
– ORIGIN Middle English (denoting equipment for a specific task): probably from Middle Low German *takel,* from *taken* 'lay hold of.' Early senses of the verb (late Middle English) described the provision and handling of a ship's equipment.

tack·le block ▶ n. a pulley over which a rope runs.

tack·le fall ▶ n. a rope for applying force to the blocks of a tackle. See TACKLE (sense 2 of the noun).

tack room ▶ n. a room in a stable building where saddles, bridles, and other equipment are kept.

tack·y¹ /'takē/ ▶ adj. **(tackier, tackiest)** (of glue, paint, or other substances) retaining a slightly sticky feel; not fully dry: *the paint was still tacky.*
– DERIVATIVES **tack·i·ness** n.

tack·y² ▶ adj. **(tackier, tackiest)** informal showing poor taste and quality: *even in her faintly tacky costumes, she won our hearts.*
– DERIVATIVES **tack·i·ly** /'takəlē/ adv., **tack·i·ness** n.
– ORIGIN early 19th cent.: of unknown origin. Early use was as a noun denoting a horse of little value, later applied to a poor white in some southern states, hence 'shabby, cheap, in bad taste' (mid 19th cent).

ta·co /'täkō/ ▶ n. (pl. **tacos**) a Mexican dish consisting of a fried tortilla, typically folded, filled with various mixtures, such as seasoned meat, beans, lettuce, and tomatoes.
– ORIGIN Mexican Spanish, from Spanish, literally 'plug, wad.'

ta·co chip ▶ n. a fried fragment of a taco, flavored with spices and eaten as a snack.

Ta·co·ma /tə'kōmə/ an industrial port city in west central Washington, on Puget Sound, south of Seattle; pop. 197,181 (est. 2008).

Ta·con·ic Moun·tains /tə'känik/ a range of the Appalachian system, along the eastern border of New York with three states: Connecticut, Massachusetts, and Vermont.

tac·o·nite /'takə,nīt/ ▶ n. a low-grade iron ore consisting largely of chert, occurring in the US chiefly around Lake Superior.
– ORIGIN early 20th cent.: from the name of the *Taconic* Mountains (in southeastern New York State, western Massachusetts, and southwestern Vermont) + -ITE¹.

tac·rine /'tak,rēn/ ▶ n. Medicine a synthetic drug used in Alzheimer's disease to inhibit the breakdown of acetylcholine by cholinesterase and thereby enhance neurological function. ● An acridine derivative; chem. formula: $C_{13}H_{15}N_2Cl$.
– ORIGIN 1960s: from *t(etra-)* + *acr(id)ine.*

tact /takt/ ▶ n. adroitness and sensitivity in dealing with others or with difficult issues: *the inspector broke the news to me with tact and consideration.*
– ORIGIN mid 17th cent. (denoting the sense of touch): via French from Latin *tactus* 'touch, sense of touch,' from *tangere* 'to touch.'

Tac·tel /'tak,tel/ ▶ n. trademark a polyamide fabric or fiber with a soft, silky feel.

tact·ful /'tak(t)fəl/ ▶ adj. having or showing tact: *they need a tactful word of advice | they were too tactful to say anything.*
– DERIVATIVES **tact·ful·ly** adv., **tact·ful·ness** n.

tac·tic /'taktik/ ▶ n. an action or strategy carefully planned to achieve a specific end. ■ **(tactics)** [also treated as sing.] the art of disposing armed forces in order of battle and of organizing operations, esp. during contact with an enemy. Often contrasted with STRATEGY.
– DERIVATIVES **tac·ti·cian** /tak'tisHən/ n.
– ORIGIN mid 18th cent.: from modern Latin *tactica,* from Greek *taktikē* (*tekhnē*) '(art) of tactics,' feminine of *taktikos,* from *taktos* 'ordered, arranged,' from the base of *tassein* 'arrange.'

tac·ti·cal /'taktikəl/ ▶ adj. of, relating to, or constituting actions carefully planned to gain a specific military end: *as a tactical officer in the field he had no equal.* ■ (of bombing or weapons) done or for use in immediate support of military or naval operations. Often contrasted with STRATEGIC. ■ (of a person or their actions) showing adroit planning; aiming at an end beyond the immediate action: *in a tactical retreat, she moved into a hotel with her daughters.*
– DERIVATIVES **tac·ti·cal·ly** /-ik(ə)lē/ adv.
– ORIGIN late 16th cent. (in the sense 'relating to military or naval tactics'): from Greek *taktikos* (see TACTIC) + -AL.

tac·tile /'taktl, 'tak,tīl/ ▶ adj. of or connected with the sense of touch: *vocal and visual signals become less important as tactile signals intensify.* ■ perceptible by touch or apparently so; tangible: *she had a distinct, almost tactile memory.* ■ designed to be perceived by touch: *tactile exhibitions help blind people enjoy the magic of sculpture.* ■ (of a person) given to touching others, esp. as an unselfconscious expression of sympathy or affection.
– DERIVATIVES **tac·til·i·ty** /tak'tilitē/ n.
– ORIGIN early 17th cent. (in the sense 'perceptible by touch, tangible'): from Latin *tactilis,* from *tangere* 'to touch.'

tact·less /'taktləs/ ▶ adj. having or showing a lack of adroitness and sensitivity in dealing with others or with difficult issues: *a tactless remark.*
– DERIVATIVES **tact·less·ly** adv., **tact·less·ness** n.

tac·tu·al /'takCHōōəl/ ▶ adj. another term for TACTILE.

tac·tus /'täktōōs/ ▶ n. Music a principal accent or rhythmic unit, esp. in 15th- and 16th-century music.
– ORIGIN Latin.

tad /tad/ informal ▶ adv. **(a tad)** to a small extent; somewhat: *Mark looked a tad embarrassed.*
▶ n. [in sing.] a small amount of something: *biscuits sweetened with a tad of honey.*
– ORIGIN late 19th cent. (denoting a small child): origin uncertain, perhaps from TADPOLE. The current usage dates from the 1940s.

ta-da /tä 'dä/ (also **ta-dah**) ▶ exclam. an imitation of a fanfare, used typically to call attention to an impressive entrance or a dramatic announcement.
– ORIGIN late 20th cent.: imitative.

Ta·djik ▶ n. & adj. variant spelling of TAJIK.

tad·pole /'tad,pōl/ ▶ n. the tailed aquatic larva of an amphibian (frog, toad, newt, or salamander), breathing through gills and lacking legs until its later stages of development.
– ORIGIN late 15th cent.: from Old English *tāda* 'toad' + POLL (probably because the tadpole seems to consist of a large head and a tail in its early development stage).

Ta·dzhik ▶ n. & adj. variant spelling of TAJIK.

tae-bo /'tī 'bō/ ▶ n. trademark an exercise system combining elements of aerobics and kick-boxing.
– ORIGIN 1990s: from Korean *t'ae* 'foot' + *bo,* short for *boxing.*

tae·di·um vi·tae /'tēdēəm 'vē,tī, 'vītē/ ▶ n. a state of extreme ennui; weariness of life.
– ORIGIN Latin.

Tae·gu /'ta,gōō/ a city in southeastern South Korea; pop. 2,512,600 (est. 2008). Nearby is the Haeinsa temple, which was established in AD 802 and contains 80,000 Buddhist printing blocks dating from the 13th century.

Tae·jon /'ta'jən, -'jôn/ a city in central South Korea; pop. 1,495,000 (est. 2008).

tae kwon do /'tī 'kwän 'dō/ ▶ n. a modern Korean martial art similar to karate.
– ORIGIN Korean, literally 'art of hand and foot fighting,' from *t'ae* 'kick' + *kwon* 'fist' + *do* 'art, method.'

tael /tāl/ ▶ n. a weight used in China and East Asia, originally of varying amount but later fixed at about 38 grams (1¹/₃ oz.). ■ a former Chinese monetary unit based on the value of this weight of standard silver.
– ORIGIN from Malay *tahil* 'weight.'

tae·ni·a /'tēnēə/ (also **tenia**) ▶ n. (pl. **taeniae** /-nē,ē, -nē,ī/ or **taenias**) **1** Anatomy a flat ribbonlike structure in the body. ■ **(taeniae coli** /'kōlī/) the smooth longitudinal muscles of the colon.
2 Architecture a fillet between a Doric architrave and frieze.
3 (in ancient Greece) a band or ribbon worn around a person's head.
4 a large tapeworm that parasitizes mammals. ● Genus *Taenia,* class Cestoda: several species, in particular *T. saginata* and *T. soleum.*
– DERIVATIVES **tae·ni·oid** /-nē,oid/ adj.
– ORIGIN mid 16th cent. (sense 2): via Latin from Greek *tainia* 'band, ribbon.'

taen·ite /'tē,nīt/ ▶ n. a nickel-iron alloy occurring as lamellae and strips in meteorites.
– ORIGIN mid 19th cent.: from TAENIA + -ITE¹.

taf·fe·ta /'tafitə/ ▶ n. a fine lustrous silk or similar synthetic fabric with a crisp texture.
– ORIGIN late Middle English (originally denoting a plain-weave silk): from Old French *taffetas* or medieval Latin *taffata,* based on Persian *tāftan* 'to shine.'

taff·rail /'taf,rāl, -rəl/ ▶ n. a rail and ornamentation around a ship's stern.
– ORIGIN early 19th cent.: alteration (by association with RAIL¹) of obsolete *tafferel* 'panel,' used to denote the flat part of a ship's stern above the transom, from Dutch *tafereel.*

taf·fy /'tafē/ ▶ n. (pl. **taffies**) **1** a candy similar to toffee, made from sugar or molasses, boiled with butter and pulled until glossy.
2 informal insincere flattery.
– ORIGIN early 19th cent.: earlier form of TOFFEE.

taf·fy pull ▶ n. dated a social occasion on which young people meet to make taffy.

taf·i·a /'tafēə/ ▶ n. W. Indian a drink similar to rum, distilled from molasses or waste from the production of brown sugar.
– ORIGIN via French from West Indian Creole, alteration of RATAFIA.

Taft /taft/, William Howard (1857–1930), 27th president of the US 1909–13. A Republican, he succeeded Theodore Roosevelt to the presidency. His administration is remembered for its use of dollar diplomacy, enforcement of antitrust laws, and enactment of tariff laws. He later served as chief justice of the US 1921–30.

William Howard Taft

tag¹ /tag/ ▶ n. **1** a label attached to someone or something for the purpose of identification or to give other information. ■ an electronic device that can be attached to someone or something for monitoring purposes, e.g., to deter shoplifters. ■ a nickname or description popularly given to someone or something. ■ a license plate of a motor vehicle. ■ informal a nickname or other identifying mark written as the signature of a graffiti artist: *scrawled felt-tip tags on city walls.* ■ Computing a character or set of characters appended to or enclosing a piece of text or data in order to identify or categorize it.
2 a small piece or part that is attached to a main body. ■ a ragged lock of wool on a sheep. ■ the tip of an animal's tail when it is distinctively colored. ■ a loose or spare end of something; a leftover. ■ a metal or plastic point at the end of a shoelace that stiffens it, making it easier to insert through an eyelet.

PRONUNCIATION KEY ə *ago, up;* ər *over, fur;* a *hat;* ā *ate;* ä *car;* e *let;* ē *see;* i *fit;* ī *by;* NG *sing;* ō *go;* ô *law, for;* oi *toy;* ŏŏ *good;* ōō *goo;* ou *out;* TH *thin;* TH *then;* ZH *vision*

t

3 a frequently repeated quotation or stock phrase. ■ Theater a closing speech addressed to the audience. ■ a refrain or musical phrase in a song or piece of music. ■ Grammar a short phrase or clause added to an already complete sentence, as in *I like it, I do*. See also **TAG QUESTION**.
▶ v. (**tags, tagging, tagged**) [with obj.] **1** attach a label to: *the bears were tagged and released.* ■ attach an electronic tag to: (as noun **tagging**) *laser tattooing is used in the tagging of cattle.* ■ [with obj. or complement] give a specified name or description to: *he left because he didn't want to be tagged as a soap star.* ■ informal (of a graffiti artist) write one's nickname or mark on (a surface): *storefronts are shuttered with metal roll-down barricades tagged with graffiti.* ■ Computing add a character or set of characters to (a piece of text or data) in order to identify or categorize it. ■ Biology & Chemistry label (something) with a radioactive isotope, fluorescent dye, or other marker: *pieces of DNA tagged with radioactive particles.*
2 add to something, esp. as an afterthought or with no real connection: *she meant to* **tag** *her question* **on** *at the end of her remarks.* ■ [no obj.] follow or accompany someone, esp. without invitation: *that'll teach you not to* **tag along** *where you're not wanted.*
3 shear away ragged locks of wool from (sheep).
– ORIGIN late Middle English (denoting a narrow hanging section of a decoratively slashed garment): of unknown origin. The verb dates from the early 17th cent.

tag[2] ▶ n. a children's game in which one chases the rest, and anyone who is touched then becomes the pursuer. ■ Baseball the action of tagging out a runner or tagging a base: *he narrowly avoided a sweeping tag by the first baseman.* ■ [as modifier] denoting a form of wrestling involving tag teams. See **TAG TEAM**.
▶ v. (**tags, tagging, tagged**) [with obj.] touch (someone being chased) in a game of tag. ■ (**tag out**) Baseball put out (a runner) by touching them with the ball or with the glove holding the ball: *catching their fastest runner in a rundown and tagging him out.* ■ Baseball (of a base runner, or a fielder with the ball) touch (a base) with the foot: *the short center fielder could field the ball and tag second base for a force out.* ■ [no obj.] (usu. **tag up**) Baseball (of a base runner) touch the base one has occupied after a fly ball is caught, before running to the next base: *when the ball was hit, he went back to the bag to tag up.*

Ta·ga·log /tə'gäləg, -lôg/ ▶ n. **1** a member of a people originally of central Luzon in the Philippine Islands.
2 the Austronesian language of this people. Its vocabulary has been much influenced by Spanish and English, and it is the basis of a standardized national language of the Philippines (Filipino).
▶ adj. of or relating to this people or their language.
– ORIGIN the name in Tagalog, from *tagá* 'native' + *ilog* 'river.'

Tag·a·met /'tagə,met/ ▶ n. trademark for **CIMETIDINE**.
– ORIGIN 1970s: an arbitrary formation.

Ta·gan·rog /,tagən'rôk, 'tagən,räg, -,rôg/ an industrial port in southwestern Russia on the Gulf of Taganrog, which is an inlet of the Sea of Azov; pop. 260,700 (est. 2008). It was founded in 1698 by Peter the Great as a fortress and naval base.

tag·board /'tag,bôrd/ ▶ n. a kind of sturdy cardboard used esp. for making luggage labels and posters. Also called **OAKTAG**.

tag cloud ▶ n. a visual depiction of the word content of a website, or of user-generated tags attached to online content, typically using color and font size to represent the prominence or frequency of the words or tags depicted.

t

tag day ▶ n. dated a day on which money is collected for a charity in the street and donors are given tags to show that they have contributed.

tag end ▶ n. the last remaining part of something: *the tag end of the season.*

tag·ger /'tagər/ ▶ n. **1** a person who writes graffiti using their nickname or identifying mark.
2 Computing a piece of software that adds identifying or classifying tags to pieces of text or data.

ta·gine /tə'ZHēn, tə'jēn/ ▶ n. a North African stew of spiced meat and vegetables prepared by slow cooking in a shallow earthenware cooking dish with a tall, conical lid.
– ORIGIN from Moroccan Arabic: *ṭažin* from Arabic *ṭājin* 'frying pan.'.

ta·gli·a·tel·le /,tälyə'telē/ ▶ n. pasta in long ribbons.
– ORIGIN Italian, from *tagliare* 'to cut.'

tag line ▶ n. informal a catchphrase or slogan, esp. as used in advertising, or the punchline of a joke.

Ta·gore /tə'gôr/, Rabindranath (1861–1941), Indian writer and philosopher. His poetry pioneered the use of colloquial Bengali. Nobel Prize for Literature (1913).

tag ques·tion ▶ n. Grammar a question converted from a statement by an appended interrogative formula, e.g., *it's nice out, isn't it?*

tag sale ▶ n. a rummage sale or garage sale.

tag team ▶ n. a pair of wrestlers who fight as a team, taking the ring alternately. One team member cannot enter the ring until touched or tagged by the one leaving. ■ informal a pair of people working together.

ta·gua nut /'tägwə/ ▶ n. another term for **IVORY NUT**.
– ORIGIN mid 19th cent.: *tagua*, via Spanish from Quechua *tawa*.

Ta·gus /'tāgəs/ a river in southwestern Europe, the longest river on the Iberian peninsula. It rises in the mountains of eastern Spain and flows over 625 miles (1,000 km) west into Portugal, where it turns southwest and empties into the Atlantic Ocean near Lisbon. Spanish name **TAJO**, Portuguese name **TEJO**.

tag wres·tling ▶ n. a form of wrestling involving tag teams.

ta·hi·ni /tə'hēnē/ (also **tahina** /-nə/) ▶ n. a Middle Eastern paste or sauce made from ground sesame seeds.
– ORIGIN from modern Greek *takhini*, based on Arabic *ṭaḥana* 'to crush.'

Ta·hi·ti /tə'hētē, tä-/ an island in the central South Pacific Ocean, one of the Society Islands that forms part of French Polynesia; pop. 178,173 (2007); capital, Papeete. One of the largest islands in the South Pacific, it was declared a French colony in 1880.

Ta·hi·tian /tə'hēSHən/ ▶ n. **1** a native or inhabitant of Tahiti, or a person of Tahitian descent.
2 the Polynesian language of Tahiti.
▶ adj. of or relating to Tahiti, its people, or their language.

Ta·hoe, Lake /'tähō/ a mountain lake on the border of north central California with Nevada.

tahr /tär/ ▶ n. a goatlike mammal inhabiting cliffs and mountain slopes in Oman, southern India, and the Himalayas. ● Genus *Hemitragus*, family Bovidae: three species.
– ORIGIN mid 19th cent.: a local word in Nepal.

Tai /tī/ ▶ adj. of, relating to, or denoting a family of tonal Southeast Asian languages, including Thai and Lao, of uncertain affinity to other language groups, but sometimes linked with the Sino-Tibetan family.

tai /tī/ ▶ n. (pl. **same**) a deep red-brown Pacific sea bream, eaten as a delicacy in Japan. ● *Pagrus major*, family Sparidae.
– ORIGIN early 17th cent.: from Japanese.

Tai·'an /'tī'än/ a city in northeastern China, in Shandong province; pop. 698,200 (est. 2006).

t'ai chi ch'uan /'tī ,CHē 'CHwän, ,jē/ (also **t'ai chi** /'tī 'CHē/) ▶ n. **1** a Chinese martial art and system of calisthenics, consisting of sequences of very slow controlled movements.
2 (in Chinese philosophy) the ultimate source and limit of reality, from which spring yin and yang and all of creation.
– ORIGIN Chinese, literally 'great ultimate boxing,' from *tài* 'extreme' + *ji* 'limit' + *quán* 'fist, boxing.'

Tai·chung /'tī'CHOOSNG/ a city in west central Taiwan; pop. 1,055,900 (est. 2007).

Ta·'if /'tä-if/ a city in western Saudi Arabia, southeast of Mecca, in the Asir Mountains; pop. 521,300 (est. 2004). It is the unofficial seat of government of Saudi Arabia during the summer.

tai·ga /'tīgə/ ▶ n. (often **the taiga**) the sometimes swampy coniferous forest of high northern latitudes, esp. that between the tundra and steppes of Siberia and North America.
– ORIGIN late 19th cent.: from Russian *taĭga*, from Mongolian.

tai·ko /'tīkō/ ▶ n. (pl. **same** or **taikos**) a Japanese barrel-shaped drum.
– ORIGIN late 19th cent.: Japanese.

tai·ko·naut /'tīkə,nôt/ ▶ n. a Chinese astronaut.
– ORIGIN 1990s: blend of Chinese *taikong*, 'outer space' + *astronaut*.

tail[1] /tāl/ ▶ n. **1** the hindmost part of an animal, esp. when prolonged beyond the rest of the body, such as the flexible extension of the backbone in a vertebrate, the feathers at the hind end of a bird, or a terminal appendage in an insect. ■ a thing resembling an animal's tail in its shape or position, typically something extending downward or outward at the end of something: *the trailed tail of a capital Q* | *the cars were head to tail.* ■ the rear part of an airplane, with the horizontal stabilizer and rudder. ■ the lower or hanging part of a garment, esp. the back of a shirt or coat. ■ (**tails**) informal a tailcoat; a man's formal evening suit with such a coat: *the men looked debonair in white tie and tails.* ■ the luminous trail of particles following a comet. ■ the lower end of a pool or stream. ■ the exposed end of a slate or tile in a roof.
2 the end of a long train or line of people or vehicles: *an armored truck at the tail of the convoy.* ■ [in sing.] the final, more distant, or weaker part of something: *the forecast says we're in for the tail of a hurricane.* ■ informal a person secretly following another to observe their movements.
3 informal a person's buttocks: *fireworks followed when the coach kicked Ryan in his tail.* ■ vulgar slang a woman's genitals. ■ informal women collectively regarded as a means of sexual gratification: *my wife thinks going out with you guys will keep me from chasing tail.*
4 (**tails**) the reverse side of a coin (used when tossing a coin).
▶ v. [with obj.] **1** informal follow and observe (someone) closely, esp. in secret: *a flock of paparazzi had tailed them all over Paris.* ■ [no obj.] follow: *they went to their favorite cafe—Bill and Sally tailed along.*
2 [no obj.] (of an object in flight) drift or curve in a particular direction: *the next pitch tailed in on me at the last second.*
3 rare provide with a tail: *her calligraphy was topped by banners of black ink and tailed like the haunches of fabulous beasts.*
4 archaic join (one thing) to another: *each new row of houses tailed on its drains to those of its neighbors.*
– PHRASES **chase one's (own) tail** informal rush around ineffectually. **on someone's tail** following someone closely: *a police car stayed on his tail for half a mile.* **a piece of tail** see **PIECE**. **the tail wags the dog** the less important or subsidiary factor, person, or thing dominates a situation; the usual roles are reversed: *the financing system is becoming the tail that wags the dog.* **with one's tail between one's legs** informal in a state of dejection or humiliation.
– PHRASAL VERBS **tail something in** (or **into**) insert the end of a beam, stone, or brick into (a wall).
tail off (or **away**) gradually diminish in amount, strength, or intensity: *the economic boom was beginning to tail off.*
– DERIVATIVES **tailed** adj. [in combination] *a white-tailed deer*, **tail·less** adj., **tail·less·ness** n.
– ORIGIN Old English *tæg(e)l*, from a Germanic base meaning 'hair, hairy tail'; related to Middle Low German *tagel* 'twisted whip, rope's end.' The early sense of the verb (early 16th cent.) was 'fasten to the back of something.'

tail[2] ▶ n. Law, chiefly historical limitation of ownership, esp. of an estate or title limited to a person and their heirs: *the land was held* **in tail general**. See also **FEE TAIL**.
– ORIGIN Middle English (denoting a tallage): from Old French *taille* 'notch, tax,' from *taillier* 'to cut,' based on Latin *talea* 'twig, cutting.'

tail·back /'tāl,bak/ ▶ n. Football (in some offensive formations) the back who is positioned farthest from the line of scrimmage.

tail·board /'tāl,bôrd/ ▶ n. chiefly British term for **TAILGATE**.

tail·bone /'tāl,bōn/ ▶ n. less technical term for **COCCYX**.

tail·coat /'tāl,kōt/ ▶ n. a man's formal morning or evening coat, with a long skirt divided at the back into tails and cut away in front.

tail cov·ert ▶ n. (in a bird's tail) each of the smaller feathers covering the bases of the main feathers.

tail·drag·ger /'tāl,dragər/ ▶ n. an airplane that lands and taxis on a tail wheel or tail skid, its nose off the ground.

tail end ▶ n. [in sing.] the last or hindmost part of something: *the tail end of the 19th century* | *the tail end of a herd of cattle.*

tail fin ▶ n. Zoology a fin at the posterior extremity of a fish's body, typically continuous with the tail. Also called **CAUDAL FIN**. ■ Aeronautics a projecting vertical surface on the tail of an aircraft, providing stability and typically housing the rudder. ■ an upswept projection on each rear corner of an automobile, popular in the 1950s.

tail gas ▶ n. gas produced in a refinery and not required for further processing.

tail·gate /'tāl,gāt/ ▶ n. a hinged flap at the back of a truck that can be lowered or removed when loading or unloading the vehicle. ■ the door at the back of a station wagon. ■ [as modifier] relating to or denoting an informal meal served from the back of a parked vehicle, typically in the parking lot of a sports stadium: *a tailgate lunch* | *they turned the parking lot into a huge tailgate party.* ■ [as modifier] denoting a style of jazz trombone playing characterized by improvisation in the manner of the early New Orleans musicians.
▶ v. informal **1** [with obj.] drive too closely behind another vehicle: *he started tailgating the car in front* | [no obj.] *drivers who will tailgate at 90 mph.* ■ gain unauthorized entry to a secured area by closely

following someone with authority to enter: *a Toyota pickup tailgated the delivery vehicle into the prison.* **2** [no obj.] eat an informal meal served from the back of a parked vehicle.
– DERIVATIVES **tail·gat·er** n.

tail·ing /'tāliNG/ ▶ n. **1** (**tailings**) the residue of something, esp. ore.
2 the part of a beam or projecting brick or stone embedded in a wall.

taille /tāl, 'täyə/ ▶ n. (pl. **same**) **1** (in France before 1789) a tax levied on the common people by the king or an overlord. [compare with TAIL².]
2 the juice produced from a second pressing of the grapes during winemaking, generally considered inferior because it contains less sugar and more tannin and has lower acidity than the first pressing. ■ low-quality wine made from this residue.
– ORIGIN French.

Tail·le·ferre /,tīə'fer/, Germaine (1892–1983), French composer and pianist. A member of Les Six, she composed concertos for unusual combinations of instruments.

tail·leur /tä'yər/ ▶ n. (pl. **same**) dated or formal a woman's tailor-made suit.
– ORIGIN French.

tail·light /'tāl,(l)īt/ (also **taillamp**) ▶ n. a red light at the rear of a motor vehicle, train, or bicycle.

tai·lor /'tālər/ ▶ n. **1** a person whose occupation is making fitted clothes such as suits, pants, and jackets to fit individual customers.
2 (also **tailorfish**) another term for BLUEFISH.
▶ v. [with obj.] (usu. **be tailored**) (of a tailor) make (clothes) to fit individual customers: *he was wearing a sports coat that had obviously been tailored in New York.* ■ make or adapt for a particular purpose or person: *arrangements can be tailored to meet individual requirements.*
– ORIGIN Middle English: from Anglo-Norman French *taillour*, literally 'cutter,' based on late Latin *taliare* 'to cut.' The verb dates from the mid 17th cent.

tai·lor·bird /'tālər,bərd/ ▶ n. a small southern Asian warbler that makes a row of holes in one or two large leaves and stitches them together with cottony fibers or silk to form a container for the nest. ● Genus *Orthotomus*, family Sylviidae: several species.

tai·lored /'tālərd/ ▶ adj. (of clothes) smart, fitted, and well cut: *a tailored charcoal-gray suit.*

tai·lor·ing /'tāləriNG/ ▶ n. the activity or trade of a tailor. ■ the style or cut of a garment or garments.

tai·lor-made ▶ adj. (of clothes) made by a tailor for a particular customer: *tailor-made suits.* ■ made, adapted, or suited for a particular purpose or person: *he was tailor-made for the job.*
▶ n. a garment that has been specially made for a particular customer: *a lady in a red tailor-made.*

tai·lor's chalk ▶ n. hard chalk or soapstone used in tailoring and dressmaking for marking fabric.

tail·piece /'tāl,pēs/ ▶ n. a final or end part of something, in particular: ■ a part added to the end of a story or piece of writing. ■ a small decorative design at the foot of a page or the end of a chapter or book. ■ the piece at the base of a violin or other stringed instrument to which the strings are attached.

tail·pipe /'tāl,pīp/ ▶ n. the rear section of the exhaust system of a motor vehicle.

tail·plane /'tāl,plān/ ▶ n. Brit. another term for HORIZONTAL STABILIZER.

tail·race /'tāl,rās/ ▶ n. a water channel below a dam or water mill.

tail ro·tor ▶ n. Aeronautics an auxiliary rotor at the tail of a helicopter designed to counterbalance the torque of the main rotor.

tail skid ▶ n. a support for the tail of an aircraft when on the ground.

tail slide ▶ n. a backward movement of an aircraft from a vertical stalled position.

tail·spin /'tāl,spin/ ▶ n. an aircraft's diving descent combined with rotation. ■ a state or situation characterized by chaos, panic, or loss of control: *the rise in interest rates sent the stock market into a tailspin.*
▶ v. (**tailspins, tailspinning**; past and past participle **tailspun**) [no obj.] become out of control: *an economy tailspinning into chaos.*

tail·stock /'tāl,stäk/ ▶ n. the adjustable part of a lathe holding the fixed spindle.

tail·wa·ter /'tāl,wôtər, -,wätər/ ▶ n. the water in a tailrace.

tail·wheel /'tāl,(h)wēl/ ▶ n. a wheel supporting the tail of an aircraft, designed to ease handling while on the ground.

tail·wind /'tāl,wind/ ▶ n. a wind blowing in the direction of travel of a vehicle or aircraft; a wind blowing from behind.

tai·men /'tīmen/ ▶ n. (pl. **same**) a food fish that is closely related to the huchen, widespread in Siberia and eastern Asia. ● *Hucho taimen*, family Salmonidae.
– ORIGIN 1970s: from Russian.

Tai·myr Pen·in·su·la /tī'mi(ə)r/ (also **Taymyr**) a vast, almost uninhabited peninsula on the northern coast of central Russia that extends into the Arctic Ocean and separates the Kara Sea from the Laptev Sea. Its northern tip is the northernmost point in Asia.

Tai·nan /'tī'nän/ a city on the southwestern coast of Taiwan; pop. 764,700 (est. 2007). Its original name was Taiwan, the name later given to the whole island.

Tai·no /'tīnō/ ▶ n. (pl. **same** or **Tainos**) **1** a member of an extinct Arawak people formerly inhabiting the Greater Antilles and the Bahamas.
2 the extinct Arawakan language of this people.
▶ adj. relating to or denoting this people or their language.
– ORIGIN from Taino *taino* 'noble, lord.'

taint /tānt/ ▶ n. a trace of a bad or undesirable quality or substance: *the taint of corruption that adhered to the regime.* ■ a thing whose influence or effect is perceived as contaminating or undesirable: *the taint that threatens to stain most of the company's other partners.* ■ an unpleasant smell: *the lingering taint of creosote.*
▶ v. [with obj.] contaminate or pollute (something): *the air was tainted by fumes from the cars.* ■ affect with a bad or undesirable quality: *his administration was tainted by scandal.* ■ [no obj.] archaic (of food or water) become contaminated or polluted.
– DERIVATIVES **taint·less** adj. (literary).
– ORIGIN Middle English (as a verb in the sense 'convict, prove guilty'): partly from Old French *teint* 'tinged,' based on Latin *tingere* 'to dye, tinge'; partly a shortening of ATTAINT.

tai·pan¹ /'tī,pan/ ▶ n. a foreigner who is head of a business in China or Hong Kong.
– ORIGIN mid 19th cent.: from Chinese (Cantonese dialect) *daaihbāan*.

tai·pan² ▶ n. a large, brown, highly venomous Australian snake. ● Genus *Oxyuranus*, family Elapidae: two species, in particular *O. scutellatus*.
– ORIGIN 1930s: from Wik Munkan (an extinct Aboriginal language of northern Queensland) *dhayban*.

Tai·pei /,tī'pā, -'bā/ the capital of Taiwan, in the northern part of the country; pop. 2,629,300 (est. 2007).

Tai·wan /,tī'wän/ an island country off the southeastern coast of China; pop. 22,974,300 (est. 2009); capital, Taipei; language, Mandarin Chinese (official). Official name CHINA, REPUBLIC OF. Former name FORMOSA.

> In 1949, toward the end of the war with the communist regime of mainland China, Chiang Kai-shek withdrew here with 500,000 nationalist Kuomintang troops. Taiwan became the headquarters of the Kuomintang, which held power continuously until defeated in presidential elections in 2000. Since the 1950s Taiwan has undergone steady economic growth, esp. in its export industries.

– DERIVATIVES **Tai·wan·ese** /,tīwə'nēz, -wä-, -'nēs/ adj. & n.

Tai·yuan /'tīyoo'än/ a city in northern China, capital of Shanxi province; pop. 2,162,000 (est. 2006).

Tai Yue Shan /'tī yoo'ä 'SHän/ Chinese name for LANTAU.

Ta·'iz /tä'ēz/ a city in southwestern Yemen; pop. 467,000 (est. 2004). It was the administrative capital of Yemen 1948–62.

taj /täZH, täj/ ▶ n. a tall conical cap worn by a dervish. ■ historical a crown worn by an Indian prince of high rank.
– ORIGIN mid 19th cent.: from Persian *tāj* 'crown.'

Ta·jik /tä'jik/ (also **Tadjik** or **Tadzhik**) ▶ n. **1** a member of a mainly Muslim people inhabiting Tajikistan and parts of neighboring countries. ■ a native or inhabitant of the republic of Tajikistan.
2 (also **Tajiki** /-'jikē/) the Iranian language of the Tajiks.
▶ adj. of or relating to Tajikistan, the Tajiks, or their language.
– ORIGIN from Persian *tājik* 'a Persian, someone who is neither an Arab nor a Turk.'

Ta·jik·i·stan /tə'jēkə,stan, tä-, -'jikə, -,stän/ (also **Tadzhikistan**) a mountainous republic in central Asia, north of Afghanistan; pop. 7,349,100 (est. 2009); capital, Dushanbe; languages, Tajik (official) and Russian.

> The region was conquered by the Mongols in the 13th century and absorbed into the Russian empire during the 1880s and 1890s. From 1929, Tajikistan formed a constituent republic of the former Soviet Union; it became an independent republic within the Commonwealth of Independent States in 1991.

Taj Ma·hal /'täZH mə'häl, 'täj/ a mausoleum at Agra, India, built by the Mogul emperor **Shah Jahan** (1592–1666) in memory of his favorite wife, completed *c.*1649. Set in formal gardens, the domed building in white marble is reflected in a pool flanked by cypresses.
– ORIGIN perhaps a corruption of Persian *Mumtaz Mahal*, from *mumtāz* 'chosen one' (the title of the wife of Shah Jahan) and *mahal* 'abode.'

Taj Mahal

Ta·jo /'tähō/ Spanish name for TAGUS.

ta·ka /'täkə/ ▶ n. (pl. **same**) the basic monetary unit of Bangladesh, equal to 100 poisha.
– ORIGIN from Bengali *ṭākā*.

ta·ka·he /tə'kī/ ▶ n. a large, rare, flightless rail with bluish-black and olive-green plumage and a large red bill, found in mountain grassland in New Zealand. ● *Porphyrio mantelli*, family Rallidae.
– ORIGIN mid 19th cent.: from Maori.

take /tāk/ ▶ v. (past **took** /to͝ok/; past participle **taken** /'tākən/) [with obj.] **1** lay hold of (something) with one's hands; reach for and hold: *he leaned forward to take her hand.* ■ remove (someone or something) from a particular place: *he took an envelope from his inside pocket | the police took him away.* ■ consume as food, drink, medicine, or drugs: *take an aspirin and lie down.* ■ capture or gain possession of by force or military means: *twenty of their ships were sunk or taken | the French took Ghent.* ■ (in bridge, hearts, and similar card games) win (a trick). ■ Chess capture (an opposing piece or pawn). ■ dispossess someone of (something); steal or illicitly remove: *someone must have sneaked in here and taken it.* ■ cheat (someone) of something: *can I get taken by buying mutual funds?* ■ subtract: *take two from ten | add the numbers together and take away five.* ■ occupy (a place or position): *we found that all the seats were taken.* ■ buy or rent (a house). ■ agree to buy (an item): *I'll take the one on the end.* ■ gain or acquire (possession or ownership of something): *he took possession of a unique Picasso ceramic piece.* ■ (**be taken**) humorous (of a person) already be married or in an emotional relationship. ■ [in imperative] use or have ready to use: *take half the marzipan and roll out.* ■ [usu. in imperative] use as an instance or example in support of an argument: *let's take Napoleon, for instance.* ■ regularly buy or subscribe to (a particular newspaper or periodical). ■ ascertain by measurement or observation: *the nurse takes my blood pressure.* ■ write down: *he was taking notes.* ■ make (a photograph) with a camera. ■ (esp. of illness) suddenly strike or afflict (someone): *he was taken with a seizure of some kind.* ■ have sexual intercourse with.
2 carry or bring with one; convey: *he took along a portfolio of his drawings | the drive takes you through some wonderful scenery* | [with two objs.] *I took him a letter.* ■ accompany or guide (someone) to a specified place: *I'll take you to your room.* ■ bring into a specified state: *the invasion took Europe to the brink of war.* ■ use as a route or a means of transportation: *take 95 north to Baltimore | we took the night train to Scotland.*
3 accept or receive (someone or something): *she was advised to take any job offered | they don't take children.* ■ understand or accept as valid: *I take your point.* ■ acquire or assume (a position, state, or form): *teaching methods will take various forms | he took office in September.* ■ achieve or attain (a victory or result): *John Martin took the men's title.*

t

■ act on (an opportunity): *he took his chance to get out while the house was quiet.* ■ experience or be affected by: *the lad took a savage beating.* ■ tolerate, stand: *I can't take the humidity.* ■ react to or regard (news or an event) in a specified way: *she took the news well | everything you say, he takes it the wrong way.* ■ deal with (a physical obstacle or course) in a specified way: *he takes the corners with no concern for his own safety.* ■ Baseball (of a batter) allow (a pitch) to go by without attempting to hit the ball. ■ regard or view in a specified way: *he somehow took it as a personal insult* | [with obj. and infinitive] *I fell over what I took to be a heavy branch.* ■ (**be taken by/with**) be attracted or charmed by: *Billie was very taken with him.* ■ submit to, tolerate, or endure: *they refused to take it any more | some people found her hard to take.* ■ (**take it**) [with clause] assume: *I take it that someone is coming to meet you.*
4 make, undertake, or perform (an action or task): *Lucy took a deep breath | he took the oath of office.* ■ be taught or examined in (a subject): *some degrees require a student to take a secondary subject.* ■ Brit. obtain (an academic degree) after fulfilling the required conditions: *she took a degree in English.*
5 require or use up (a specified amount of time): *the jury took an hour and a half to find McPherson guilty* | [with two objs.] *it takes me about a quarter of an hour to walk to work.* ■ (of a task or situation) need or call for (a particular person or thing): *it will take an electronics expert to dismantle it.* ■ hold; accommodate: *an exclusive island hideaway that takes just twenty guests.* ■ wear or require (a particular size of garment or type of complementary article): *he takes size 5 boots.*
6 [no obj.] (of a plant or seed) take root or begin to grow; germinate: *the fuchsia cuttings had taken and were looking good.* ■ (of an added substance) become successfully established.
7 Grammar have or require as part of the appropriate construction: *verbs that take both the infinitive and the finite clause as their object.*
▶ **n. 1** a scene or sequence of sound or vision photographed or recorded continuously at one time: *he completed a particularly difficult scene in two takes.* ■ a particular version of or approach to something: *his own whimsical* ***take on*** *life.*
2 an amount of something gained or acquired from one source or in one session: *the take from commodity taxation.* ■ the money received at a theater, arena, etc., for seats.
3 Printing an amount of copy set up at one time or by one compositor.
– PHRASES **be on the take** informal take bribes. **be taken ill** become ill suddenly. **have what it takes** informal have the necessary qualities for success. **take a chair** sit down. **take advantage of** (**take advice**, etc.) see ADVANTAGE, ADVICE, etc. **take something as read** Brit. accept something without considering or discussing it; assume something. **take the cake** informal (of a person or incident) be the most remarkable or foolish of their kind. **take five** (or **ten**) take a five (or ten) minute break before resuming work or another activity. **take a lot of** (or **some**) —— be difficult to do or effect in the specified way: *he might take some convincing.* **take someone in hand** undertake to control or reform someone. **take something in hand** start doing or dealing with a task. **take the heat** informal accept blame or withstand disapproval: *"Don't worry about it," Mulder said, "we'll take the heat. You can tell him we pulled rank."* **take something ill** archaic resent something done or said: *I did not mean for you to take my comments ill.* **take it from me** I can assure you: *take it from me, kid—I've been there.* **take it on one** (or **oneself**) **to do something** decide to do something without asking for permission or advice. **take it or leave it** [usu. in imperative] said to express that the offer one has made is not negotiable and that one is indifferent to another's reaction to it: *that's the deal—take it or leave it.* **take it out of** exhaust the strength of (someone): *parties and tours can take it out of you, especially if you are over 65.* **take sick** (or **ill**) informal become ill, esp. suddenly. **take the stand** testify at a trial. **take someone out of themselves** make a person forget their worries. **take that!** exclaimed when hitting someone or taking decisive action against them. **take one's time** not hurry.
– PHRASAL VERBS **take after** resemble (a parent or ancestor): *the rest of us take after our mother.* **take something apart** dismantle something. ■ (**take someone/something apart**) informal attack, criticize, or defeat someone or something in a vigorous or forceful way. **take something away** Brit. another way of saying TAKE SOMETHING OUT. **take away from** detract from: *that shouldn't take away from the achievement of the French.* **take someone back** strongly remind someone of a past time: *if "Disco Inferno" doesn't take you back, the bell-bottom pants will.* **take something back 1** retract a statement: *I take back nothing of what I said.* **2** return unsatisfactory goods to a store. ■ (of a store) accept such goods. **3** Printing transfer text to the previous line. **take something down 1** write down spoken words: *I took down the address.* **2** dismantle and remove a structure: *the old Norman church was taken down in 1819.* **take from** another way of saying TAKE AWAY FROM. **take someone in 1** accommodate someone as a lodger or because they are homeless or in difficulties. **2** cheat, fool, or deceive someone: *she tried to pass this off as an amusing story, but nobody was taken in.* **take something in 1** undertake work at home: *she took in laundry on weekends.* **2** make a garment tighter by altering its seams. ■ Sailing furl a sail. **3** receive a specified amount of money as payment or earnings: *our club took in nearly $800,000 in its first year.* **4** include or encompass something: *the sweep of his arm took in most of Main Street.* ■ fully understand or absorb something heard or seen: *she took in the scene at a glance.* **5** visit or attend a place or event in a casual way or on the way to another: *he'd maybe take in a movie, or just relax.* **take off 1** (of an aircraft or bird) become airborne. ■ (of an enterprise) become successful or popular: *the newly launched electronic newspaper has really taken off.* **2** depart hastily: *the officer took off after his men.* **take something off 1** remove clothing from one's or another's body: *she took off her cardigan.* **2** deduct part of an amount. **3** choose to have a period away from work: *I took the next day off.* **take someone on 1** hire an employee. **2** be willing or ready to meet an adversary or opponent, esp. a stronger one: *a group of villagers has taken on the planners.* **take something on 1** undertake a task or responsibility, esp. a difficult one: *whoever takes on the trout farm will have their work cut out.* **2** acquire a particular meaning or quality: *the subject has taken on a new significance in the past year.* **take someone out 1** escort someone to a social event or place of entertainment: *I finally get to take her out on Saturday night.* **2** Bridge respond to a bid or double by one's partner by bidding a different suit. **take someone/something out** informal kill, destroy, or disable someone or something. **take something out 1** obtain an official document or service: *you can take out a loan for a specific purchase.* ■ get a license or summons issued. **2** buy food at a cafe or restaurant for eating elsewhere: *he ordered a lamb madras to take out.* **take something out on** relieve frustration or anger by attacking or mistreating (a person or thing not responsible for such feelings). **take something over 1** (also **take over**) assume control of something: *British troops had taken over the German trenches.* ■ (of a company) buy out another. ■ become responsible for a task in succession to another: *he will take over as chief executive in April.* **2** Printing transfer text to the next line. **take to 1** begin or fall into the habit of: *he took to hiding some secret supplies in his desk.* **2** form a liking for: *Mrs. Brady never took to Moran.* ■ develop an ability for (something), esp. quickly or easily: *I took to pole-vaulting right away.* **3** go to (a place) to escape danger or an enemy: *they took to the hills.* **take something up 1** become interested or engaged in a pursuit: *she took up tennis at the age of 11.* ■ begin to hold or fulfill a position or post: *he left to take up an appointment as a missionary.* ■ accept an offer or challenge. **2** occupy time, space, or attention: *I don't want to take up any more of your time.* **3** pursue a matter later or further: *he'll have to take it up with the bishop.* ■ (also **take up**) resume speaking after an interruption: *I took up where I had left off.* **4** shorten a garment by turning up the hem. **take someone up on 1** accept (an offer or challenge) from someone: *I'd like to take you up on that offer.* **2** challenge or question a speaker on (a particular point): *the interviewer did not take him up on his quotation.* **take up with** begin to associate with (someone), esp. in a way disapproved of by the speaker: *he's taken up with a divorced woman, I understand.*
– DERIVATIVES **tak·a·ble** /ˈtākəbəl/ (also **takeable**) **adj.**
– ORIGIN late Old English *tacan* 'get (esp. by force), capture,' from Old Norse *taka* 'grasp, lay hold of,' of unknown ultimate origin.

take·a·way /ˈtākəˌwā/ ▶ **n. 1** Sports (in football and hockey) an act of regaining the ball or puck from the opposing team.
2 Brit. a takeout restaurant: *a fast-food takeaway.* ■ a meal or dish of such food.
3 Golf another term for BACKSWING.

take·down /ˈtākˌdoun/ ▶ **n. 1** a wrestling maneuver in which an opponent is swiftly brought to the mat from a standing position.
2 informal a police raid or arrest.
3 [as modifier] denoting a firearm with the capacity to have the barrel and magazine detached from the stock.

take-home pay ▶ **n.** the pay received by an employee after the deduction of taxes and other obligations.

take·off /ˈtākˌôf, -ˌäf/ ▶ **n. 1** the action of becoming airborne: *the plane accelerated down the runway for takeoff.*
2 an act of mimicking someone or something: *a pleasant* ***takeoff on*** *some Everly Brothers routine.*

take·out /ˈtākˌout/ ▶ **n. 1** food that is cooked and sold by a restaurant or store to be eaten elsewhere: *let's just order takeout* | [as modifier] *takeout pizza.*
2 Bridge a bid in a different suit made in response to a bid or double by one's partner.

take·out dou·ble ▶ **n.** Bridge a double that, by convention, requires one's partner to bid, used to convey information rather than to score penalty points. Often contrasted with BUSINESS DOUBLE.

take·o·ver /ˈtākˌōvər/ ▶ **n.** an act of assuming control of something, esp. the buying out of one company by another.

tak·er /ˈtākər/ ▶ **n. 1** [in combination] a person who takes a specified thing: *a drug-taker | a risk-taker.*
2 a person who takes a bet or accepts an offer or challenge: *there were plenty of takers when I offered a small wager.*

take-up ▶ **n. 1** a device for taking up slack or excess: [as modifier] *a take-up reel.*
2 the action of taking something up: *automatic bobbin thread take-up.*
3 chiefly Brit. the acceptance of something offered: *practices that discourage take-up of legal advice.*

ta·kin /ˈtäˌkēn/ ▶ **n.** a large heavily built goat-antelope found in steep, dense woodlands of the eastern Himalayas. ● *Budorcas taxicolor*, family Bovidae.
– ORIGIN mid 19th cent.: a local word.

tak·ing /ˈtākiNG/ ▶ **n. 1** the action or process of taking something: *the taking of life.*
2 (**takings**) the amount of money earned by a business from the sale of goods or services: *box-office takings were scant.*
▶ **adj.** dated (of a person) captivating in manner; charming: *he was not a very taking person, she felt.*
– PHRASES **for the taking** ready or available for someone to take advantage of: *the big money is out there for the taking.*
– DERIVATIVES **tak·ing·ly adv.**

Ta·ki-Ta·ki /ˌtākē ˈtākē/ ▶ **n.** an English-based Creole language of Suriname. Also called SRANAN.
– ORIGIN an alteration and reduplication of TALK.

Ta·kli·ma·kan Des·ert /ˌtākləməˈkän/ (also **Takla Makan**) a desert in the Xinjiang autonomous region of northwestern China that lies between the Kunlun Shan and Tien Shan mountains and forms the greater part of the Tarim Basin.

Ta·ko·ra·di /ˌtäkəˈrädē/ a seaport in western Ghana, on the Gulf of Guinea; pop. 308,300 (est. 2009).

ta·la[1] /ˈtälə/ ▶ **n.** a traditional rhythmic pattern in classical Indian music.
– ORIGIN from Sanskrit *tāla* 'handclapping, musical time.'

ta·la[2] ▶ **n.** (pl. **same** or **talas** /ˈtäləz/) the basic monetary unit of Western Samoa, equal to 100 sene.
– ORIGIN from Samoan *tālā*.

tal·a·poin /ˈtaləˌpoin/ ▶ **n.** a small West African monkey that lives in large groups near watercourses and in swamp forest. ● *Miopithecus talapoin*, family Cercopithecidae.
– ORIGIN late 16th cent.: from Portuguese *talapão*, from Mon *tala pôi*, literally 'lord of merit,' used as a respectful title for a Buddhist monk.

ta·laq /təˈläk/ ▶ **n.** (in Islamic law) divorce effected by the husband's threefold repetition of the word "talaq," this constituting a formal repudiation of his wife.
– ORIGIN from Arabic *ṭalāq*, from *ṭalaqa* 'repudiate.'

ta·lar·i·a /təˈle(ə)rēə/ ▶ **plural n.** (in Roman mythology) winged sandals as worn by certain gods and goddesses, esp. Mercury.
– ORIGIN Latin, neuter plural of *talaris*, from *talus* 'ankle.'

tal·bot /ˈtalbət, ˈtôl-/ ▶ **n.** a dog of an extinct light-colored breed of hound with large ears and heavy jaws.
– ORIGIN late Middle English: probably from the family name *Talbot*; the term was also used to denote the representation of such a dog in the coat of arms of the Talbot family, earls of Shrewsbury (a town in western England).

talc /talk/ ▶ **n.** talcum powder. ■ a white, gray, or pale green soft mineral with a greasy feel, occurring as translucent masses or laminae and consisting of magnesium hydroxyl silicate.
▶ **v.** (**talcs, talcing, talced**) [with obj.] powder or treat (something) with talc.
– DERIVATIVES **talc·ose** /ˈtalkōs/ **adj.** (Geology), **talc·y** /ˈtalkē/ **adj.**

t

– ORIGIN late 16th cent. (denoting the mineral): from medieval Latin *talcum* (see **TALCUM**).

tal·cum /ˈtalkəm/ (also **talcum powder**) ▶ **n.** a cosmetic or toilet preparation consisting of the mineral talc in powdered form, typically perfumed. ▶ **v.** (**talcums, talcuming, talcumed**) [with obj.] powder (something) with this substance.
– ORIGIN mid 16th cent.: from medieval Latin, from Arabic *ṭalk*, from Persian.

tale /tāl/ ▶ **n.** **1** a fictitious or true narrative or story, esp. one that is imaginatively recounted. ■ a lie. **2** archaic a number or total: *an exact tale of the dead bodies.*
– PHRASES **tell tales** see **TELL¹**.
– ORIGIN Old English *talu* 'telling, something told,' of Germanic origin; related to Dutch *taal* 'speech' and German *Zahl* 'number,' also to **TELL¹**. Sense 2 is probably from Old Norse.

tale·bear·er /ˈtālˌbe(ə)rər/ ▶ **n.** dated a person who maliciously gossips or reveals secrets.
– DERIVATIVES **tale·bear·ing** /-ˌbe(ə)riNG/ **n. & adj.**

ta·leg·gio /təˈlejē-ō/ ▶ **n.** a type of soft Italian cheese made from cows' milk.
– ORIGIN named after the *Taleggio* valley in Lombardy.

tal·ent /ˈtalənt/ ▶ **n.** **1** natural aptitude or skill: *he possesses more talent than any other player* | *she displayed a talent for garden design.* ■ people possessing such aptitude or skill: *I signed all the talent in Rome* | *Simon is a talent to watch.* ■ informal people regarded as sexually attractive or as prospective sexual partners: *most Saturday nights I have this urge to go on the hunt for new talent.* **2** a former weight and unit of currency, used esp. by the ancient Romans and Greeks.
– DERIVATIVES **tal·ent·less adj.**
– ORIGIN Old English *talente, talentan* (as a unit of weight), from Latin *talenta*, plural of *talentum* 'weight, sum of money,' from Greek *talanton*. Sense 1 is a figurative use with biblical allusion to the parable of the talents (Matt. 25:14–30).

tal·ent·ed /ˈtaləntid/ ▶ **adj.** having a natural aptitude or skill for something: *a talented young musician.*

tal·ent scout ▶ **n.** a person whose job is to search for talented performers who can be employed or promoted, esp. in sports and entertainment.

tales /tālz, ˈtālēz/ ▶ **n.** Law a writ for summoning substitute jurors when the original jury has become deficient in number.
– ORIGIN from Latin *tales* (*de circumstantibus*) 'such (of the bystanders),' the first words of the writ.

tales·man /ˈtālzmən/ ▶ **n.** (pl. **talesmen**) Law a person summoned by a tales.

tale-tell·er ▶ **n.** a person who tells stories. ■ a person who spreads gossip or reveals secrets.
– DERIVATIVES **tale-tell·ing n.**

ta·li /ˈtāˌlī/ plural form of **TALUS¹**.

Tal·i·ban /ˈtaliˌban/ a fundamentalist Muslim movement whose militia took control of much of Afghanistan from early 1995, and in 1996 took Kabul and set up a radical Islamic state. The movement was forcibly removed from power by the US and its allies after the September 11, 2001, attacks.
– DERIVATIVES **Tal·i·ban·i·za·tion n.**, **Tal·i·ban·ize v.**
– ORIGIN from Pashto or Dari, from Persian, literally 'students, seekers of knowledge.'

ta·lik /ˈtälik, ˈtal-/ ▶ **n.** Geology an area of unfrozen ground surrounded by permafrost.
– ORIGIN 1940s: from Russian, from *tayat'* 'melt.'

tal·i·pes /ˈtaləˌpēz/ ▶ **n.** Medicine technical term for **CLUB FOOT**.
– ORIGIN mid 19th cent.: modern Latin, from Latin *talus* 'ankle' + *pes* 'foot.'

tal·i·pot /ˈtaləˌpät/ ▶ **n.** a tall Indian palm with very large fan-shaped leaves that are used as sunshades and for thatching, and to make the material upon which books were traditionally written. When the talipot matures, at about 40–60 years, it sends up a 25-foot (8-m) stalk bearing millions of flowers, and subsequently the tree dies. ● *Corypha umbraculifera*, family Palmae.
– ORIGIN late 17th cent.: from Malayalam *tālipat*, from Sanskrit *tālīpatra*, from *tālī* 'palm' + *patra* 'leaf.'

tal·is·man /ˈtalismən, -iz-/ ▶ **n.** (pl. **talismans**) an object, typically an inscribed ring or stone, that is thought to have magic powers and to bring good luck.
– DERIVATIVES **tal·is·man·ic** /ˌtalizˈmanik/ **adj.**
– ORIGIN mid 17th cent.: based on Arabic *tilsam*, apparently from an alteration of late Greek *telesma* 'completion, religious rite,' from *telein* 'complete, perform a rite,' from *telos* 'result, end.'

talk /tôk/ ▶ **v.** [no obj.] speak in order to give information or express ideas or feelings; converse or communicate by spoken words: *the two men talked* | *we'd sit and* **talk about** *jazz* | *it was no use* **talking to** *Anthony* | [with obj.] *you're talking rubbish.* ■ have the power of speech: *he can talk as well as you or I can.* ■ discuss personal or intimate feelings: *we need to talk, Maggie.* ■ have formal dealings or discussions; negotiate: *they won't* **talk to** *the regime that killed their families.* ■ [with obj.] (**be talking**) informal used to emphasize the seriousness, importance, or extent of the thing one is mentioning or in the process of discussing: *we're talking big money.* ■ [with obj.] use (a particular language) in speech: *we were talking German.* ■ [with obj.] persuade or cause (someone) to do something by talking: *don't try to talk me into acting as a go-between.* ■ reveal secret or confidential information; betray secrets. ■ gossip: *you'll have the whole school talking.* ▶ **n.** conversation; discussion: *there was a slight but noticeable lull in the talk.* ■ a period of conversation or discussion, esp. a relatively serious one: *my mother had a talk with Louis.* ■ an informal address or lecture. ■ rumor, gossip, or speculation: *there is talk of an armistice.* ■ empty promises or boasting: *he's all talk.* ■ (**the talk of**) a current subject of widespread gossip or speculation in (a particular place): *within days I was* **the talk of the town.** ■ (**talks**) formal discussions or negotiations over a period: *peace talks.*
– PHRASES **don't talk to me about ——** informal said in protest when someone introduces a subject of which the speaker has had bitter personal experience. **know what one is talking about** be expert or authoritative on a specified subject. **look who's talking** another way of saying **YOU SHOULDN'T TALK**. **now you're talking** see **NOW**. **you shouldn't** (or **should**) (or chiefly Brit. **can't** or **can**) **talk** informal used to convey that a criticism made applies equally well to the person who has made it: *"He'd chase anything in a skirt!" "You shouldn't talk!"* **talk a blue streak** see **BLUE**. **talk about ——!** informal used to emphasize that something is an extreme or striking example of a particular situation, state, or experience: *Talk about hangovers! But aching head or not we were getting ready.* **talk big** informal talk boastfully or overconfidently. **talk dirty** see **DIRTY**. **talk the hind leg off a donkey** Brit. informal talk incessantly. **talk nineteen to the dozen** see **DOZEN**. **talk of the devil** see **DEVIL**. **talk sense into** persuade (someone) to behave more sensibly. **talk shop** see **SHOP**. **talk through one's hat** (or **ass** or **backside** or Brit. **arse**) informal talk foolishly, wildly, or ignorantly. **talk the talk** informal speak fluently or convincingly about something or in a way intended to please or impress others: *we may not look like true rock jocks yet, but we talk the talk.* **talk turkey** see **TURKEY**.
– PHRASAL VERBS **talk someone around** (or Brit. **round**) bring someone to a particular point of view by talking. **talk at** address (someone) in a hectoring or self-important way without listening to their replies: *he never talked at you.* **talk back** reply defiantly or insolently. **talk down to** speak patronizingly or condescendingly to. **talk something out** Brit. (in Parliament) block the course of a bill by prolonging discussion to the time of adjournment. **talk someone out of** persuade someone not to do (something unwise). **talk something over** (or **through**) discuss something thoroughly. **talk someone through** enable someone to perform (a task) by giving them continuous instruction. **talk to** *someone will have to talk to Lily.* **talk someone/something up** (or **down**) discuss someone or something in a way that makes them seem more (or less) interesting or attractive.
– DERIVATIVES **talk·er n.**
– ORIGIN Middle English: frequentative verb from the Germanic base of **TALE** or **TELL¹**.

talk·a·thon /ˈtôkəˌTHän/ ▶ **n.** informal a prolonged discussion or debate.
– ORIGIN 1930s (denoting a debate artificially prolonged to prevent the progress of a bill): blend of **TALK** and **MARATHON**.

talk·a·tive /ˈtôkətiv/ ▶ **adj.** fond of or given to talking: *the talkative driver hadn't stopped chatting.*
– DERIVATIVES **talk·a·tive·ly adv.**, **talk·a·tive·ness n.**

talk·back /ˈtôkˌbak/ ▶ **n.** a system of two-way communication by loudspeaker.

talk·fest /ˈtôkˌfest/ ▶ **n.** informal a session of lengthy discussion, conversation, or debate.

talk·ie /ˈtôkē/ ▶ **n.** informal a movie with a soundtrack, as distinct from a silent film.
– ORIGIN early 20th cent. (in the phrase *the talkies*): from **TALK**, on the pattern of *movie*.

talk·ing /ˈtôkiNG/ ▶ **adj.** [attrib.] engaging in speech. ■ (of an animal or object) able to make sounds similar to those of speech: *the world's greatest talking bird.* ■ silently expressive: *he did have talking eyes.* ▶ **n.** the action of talking; speech or discussion: *I'll do the talking—you just back me up.*
– PHRASES **talking of ——** while we are on the subject of —— (said when one is reminded of something by the present topic of conversation): *talking of cards, you'd better take a couple of my business cards.*

talk·ing blues ▶ **plural n.** a style of blues music in which the lyrics are more or less spoken rather than sung.

talk·ing book ▶ **n.** a recorded reading of a book, originally designed for use by blind people.

talk·ing cure ▶ **n.** a form of psychotherapy that relies on verbal interaction, esp. psychoanalysis.

talk·ing drum ▶ **n.** one of a set of West African drums, each having a different pitch, that are beaten to transmit a tonal language.

talk·ing head ▶ **n.** informal a commentator or reporter on television who addresses the camera and is viewed in close-up.

talk·ing pic·ture (also **talking film**) ▶ **n.** a movie with a soundtrack, as distinct from a silent film.

talk·ing point ▶ **n.** a topic that invites discussion or argument.

talk·ing-to ▶ **n.** [in sing.] informal a sharp reprimand in which someone is told that they have done wrong.

talk ra·di·o ▶ **n.** a type of radio broadcast in which the presenter talks about topical issues and encourages listeners to call in to air their opinions.

talk show ▶ **n.** a television or radio show in which various topics are discussed informally and listeners, viewers, or the studio audience are invited to participate in the discussion.

talk time ▶ **n.** the time during which a mobile telephone is in use to handle calls, esp. as a measure of the duration of the telephone's battery.

tall /tôl/ ▶ **adj.** **1** of great or more than average height, esp. (with reference to an object) relative to width: *a tall, broad-shouldered man* | *a tall glass of iced tea.* ■ (after a measurement and in questions) measuring a specified distance from top to bottom: *he was over six feet tall* | *how tall are you?* ■ [as adv.] used in reference to proud and confident movement or behavior: *stop wishing that you were somehow different—start to walk tall!* **2** [attrib.] informal (of an account) fanciful and difficult to believe; unlikely: *sometimes it's hard to tell a legend from a tall tale.*
– PHRASES **a tall order** an unreasonable or difficult demand.
– DERIVATIVES **tall·ish adj.**, **tall·ness n.**
– ORIGIN late Middle English: probably from Old English *getæl* 'swift, prompt' Early senses also included 'fine, handsome' and 'bold, strong, good at fighting.'

tal·lage /ˈtalij/ ▶ **n.** historical a form of arbitrary taxation levied by kings on the towns and lands of the Crown, abolished in the 14th century. ■ a tax levied on feudal dependents by their superiors.
– ORIGIN Middle English: from Old French *taillage*, from *tailler* 'to cut' (see **TAIL²**).

Tal·la·has·see /ˌtaləˈhasē/ the capital of Florida, in the northwestern part of the state; pop. 171,922 (est. 2008).

Tal·la·poo·sa Riv·er /ˌtaləˈpo͞osə/ a river that flows for 268 miles (430 km) from northwestern Georgia to Alabama, where it joins the Coosa River to form the Alabama River.

tall·boy /ˈtôlˌboi/ ▶ **n.** chiefly Brit. a tall chest of drawers, typically one mounted on legs and in two sections, one standing on the other. Compare with **HIGHBOY**.

Tal·ley·rand /ˈtaliˌrand, ˌtälēˈräN/, Charles Maurice de (1754–1838), French statesman; full surname *Talleyrand-Périgord*. He became head of the new government after the fall of Napoleon in 1814 and was later instrumental in the overthrow of Charles X and the accession of Louis Philippe in 1830.

tall hat ▶ **n.** another term for **TOP HAT**.

Tal·linn /ˈtälən, ˈtalən/ the capital of Estonia, a port on the Gulf of Finland; pop. 397,000 (est. 2007).

tal·lith /ˈtälis, täˈlēt/ (also **tallis**) ▶ **n.** a fringed shawl traditionally worn by Jewish men at prayer.
– ORIGIN from Rabbinical Hebrew *ṭallīt*, from biblical Hebrew *ṭillēl* 'to cover.'

tal·low /ˈtalō/ ▶ **n.** a hard fatty substance made from rendered animal fat, used in making candles and soap. ▶ **v.** [with obj.] archaic smear (something, esp. the bottom of a boat) with such a substance.
– DERIVATIVES **tal·low·y adj.**

PRONUNCIATION KEY ə *ago, up*; ər *over, fur*; a *hat*; ā *ate*; ä *car*; e *let*; ē *see*; i *fit*; ī *by*; NG *sing*; ō *go*; ô *law, for*; oi *toy*; o͝o *good*; o͞o *goo*; ou *out*; TH *thin*; T͟H *then*; ZH *vision*

– ORIGIN Middle English: perhaps from Middle Low German; related to Dutch *talk* and German *Talg*.

tal·low·wood /ˈtalō,wo͝od/ ▶ **n.** see HOG PLUM.

tall pop·py syn·drome ▶ **n.** informal, chiefly Austral. a perceived tendency to discredit or disparage those who have achieved notable wealth or prominence in public life.

tall ship ▶ **n.** a sailing ship with high masts.

tall tim·ber ▶ **n.** dense and uninhabited forest. ■ (usu. **tall timbers**) informal a remote or unknown place.

tal·ly /ˈtalē/ ▶ **n.** (pl. **tallies**) **1** a current score or amount: *that takes his tally to 10 goals in 10 games*. ■ a record of a score or amount: *I **kept a running tally** of David's debt on a note above my desk*. ■ a particular number taken as a group or unit to facilitate counting. ■ a mark registering such a number. ■ (also **tally stick**) historical a piece of wood scored across with notches for the items of an account and then split into halves, each party keeping one. ■ an account kept in such a way. ■ archaic a counterpart or duplicate of something.
2 a label attached to a plant or tree, or stuck in the ground beside it, that gives information about it, such as its name and class.
▶ **v.** (**tallies, tallying, tallied**) **1** [no obj.] agree or correspond: *their signatures should tally with their names on the register*.
2 [with obj.] calculate the total number of: *the votes were being tallied with abacuses*.
– DERIVATIVES **tal·li·er n.**
– ORIGIN late Middle English (denoting a notched tally stick): from Anglo-Norman French *tallie*, from Latin *talea* 'twig, cutting.' Compare with TAIL[2].

tal·ly·ho /ˈtalēˈhō/ ▶ **exclam.** a huntsman's cry to the hounds on sighting a fox.
▶ **n.** (pl. **tallyhos**) **1** an utterance of this.
2 historical a fast horse-drawn coach.
▶ **v.** (**tallyhoes, tallyhoing, tallyhoed**) [no obj.] utter a cry of "tallyho."
– ORIGIN late 18th cent.: apparently an alteration of French *taïaut*, of unknown origin.

tal·ly·man /ˈtalēmən, -ˌman/ ▶ **n.** (pl. **tallymen**) **1** a person who keeps a score or record of something.
2 Brit. a person who sells merchandise on credit, esp. from door to door.

Tal·mud /ˈtälˌmo͝od, ˈtalməd/ ▶ **n.** (**the Talmud**) the body of Jewish civil and ceremonial law and legend comprising the Mishnah and the Gemara. There are two versions of the Talmud: the Babylonian Talmud (which dates from the 5th century AD but includes earlier material) and the earlier Palestinian or Jerusalem Talmud.
– DERIVATIVES **Tal·mud·ic** /talˈm(y)o͞odik, -ˈmo͝odik/ **adj.**, **Tal·mud·i·cal** /talˈm(y)o͞odikəl, -ˈmo͝od-/ **adj.**, **Tal·mud·ist** /ˈtälmo͝odist, ˈtalməd-/ **n.**
– ORIGIN from late Hebrew *talmūḏ* 'instruction,' from Hebrew *lāmaḏ* 'learn.'

Tal·mud To·rah /ˈtälmo͝od ˈtôrə, ˈtalməd, ˈtôrə, tälˈmo͝od tôˈrä/ ▶ **n.** Judaism the field of study that deals with the Jewish law. ■ a communal school where children are instructed in Judaism.

tal·on /ˈtalən/ ▶ **n. 1** a claw, esp. one belonging to a bird of prey.
2 the part of a bolt against which the key presses to slide it in a lock.
3 (in various card games) the cards that have not yet been dealt.
– DERIVATIVES **tal·oned adj.**
– ORIGIN late Middle English (denoting any heellike part or object): from Old French, literally 'heel,' from Latin *talus* 'ankle bone, heel.'

t

ta·lus[1] /ˈtāləs/ ▶ **n.** (pl. **tali** /ˈtālī/) Anatomy the large bone in the ankle that articulates with the tibia of the leg and the calcaneum and navicular bone of the foot. Also called ASTRAGALUS.
– ORIGIN late 16th cent.: from Latin, literally 'ankle, heel.'

ta·lus[2] ▶ **n.** (pl. **taluses**) a sloping mass of rock fragments at the foot of a cliff. ■ the sloping side of an earthwork, or of a wall that tapers to the top.
– ORIGIN mid 17th cent.: from French, of unknown origin.

TAM ▶ **abbr.** television audience measurement.

tam /tam/ ▶ **n.** a tam-o'-shanter.
– ORIGIN late 19th cent.: abbreviation.

ta·ma·got·chi /ˌtäməˈgōCHē, ˌtam-, -ˈgäCHē/ ▶ **n.** an electronic toy displaying a digital image of a creature, which has to be looked after and responded to by the "owner" as if it were a pet.
– ORIGIN Japanese.

ta·ma·le /təˈmälē/ ▶ **n.** a Mexican dish of seasoned meat wrapped in cornmeal dough and steamed or baked in corn husks.
– ORIGIN from Mexican Spanish *tamal*, plural *tamales*, from Nahuatl *tamalli*.

ta·man·du·a /təˈmando͞oə/ ▶ **n.** a small nocturnal arboreal anteater with a naked prehensile tail, native to tropical America. ● Genus *Tamandua*, family Myrmecophagidae: two species.
– ORIGIN early 17th cent.: via Portuguese from Tupi *tamanduá*, from *taly* 'ant' + *monduar* 'hunter.'

Tam·a·rac /ˈtaməˌrak/ a city in southeastern Florida, northwest of Fort Lauderdale; pop. 59,340 (est. 2008).

tam·a·rack /ˈtaməˌrak/ ▶ **n.** a slender North American larch. ● *Larix laricina*, family Pinaceae.
– ORIGIN early 19th cent.: from Canadian French *tamarac*, probably of Algonquian origin.

ta·ma·rau /ˌtaməˈrou/ ▶ **n.** a small brownish-black buffalo similar to the anoa, found only on Mindoro in the Philippines. ● *Bubalus mindorensis*, family Bovidae.
– ORIGIN late 19th cent.: from Tagalog.

ta·ma·ri /təˈmärē/ (also **tamari sauce**) ▶ **n.** a variety of rich, naturally fermented soy sauce.
– ORIGIN Japanese.

ta·ma·ril·lo /ˌtaməˈrilō, -ˈrē(y)ō/ ▶ **n.** (pl. **tamarillos**) a tropical South American plant of the nightshade family that bears edible egg-shaped red fruits. Also called TREE TOMATO. ● *Cyphomandra betacea*, family Solanaceae. ■ the fruit of this plant.
– ORIGIN 1960s (originally NZ): an invented name, perhaps suggested by Spanish *tomatillo*, diminutive of *tomate* 'tomato.'

tam·a·rin /ˈtamərin, -ˌran/ ▶ **n.** a small forest-dwelling South American monkey of the marmoset family, typically brightly colored and with tufts and crests of hair around the face and neck. ● Genera *Saguinus* and *Leontopithecus*, family Callitrichidae (or Callithricidae): several species.
– ORIGIN late 18th cent.: from French, from Galibi.

tam·a·rind /ˈtaməˌrind/ ▶ **n. 1** sticky brown acidic pulp from the pod of a tree of the pea family, widely used as a flavoring in Asian cooking. ■ the pod from which this pulp is extracted.
2 the tropical African tree that yields these pods, cultivated throughout the tropics and also grown as an ornamental and shade tree. ● *Tamarindus indica*, family Leguminosae.
– ORIGIN late Middle English: from medieval Latin *tamarindus*, from Arabic *tamr hindī* 'Indian date.'

tam·a·risk /ˈtaməˌrisk/ ▶ **n.** an Old World shrub or small tree with tiny scalelike leaves borne on slender branches, giving it a feathery appearance. ● Genus *Tamarix*, family Tamaricaceae: many species.
– ORIGIN late Middle English: from late Latin *tamariscus*, variant of Latin *tamarix*, of unknown origin.

ta·mas /ˈtəməs/ ▶ **n.** (in Vedanta) the element or mode of prakriti associated with lethargy, darkness, and ignorance.

ta·ma·sha /təˈmäsHə/ ▶ **n.** Indian a grand show, performance, or celebration, esp. one involving dance. ■ [in sing.] a fuss or confusion: *what a tamasha!*
– ORIGIN via Persian and Urdu from Arabic *tamāšā* 'walk around together.'

Tam·a·shek /ˈtaməˌsHek/ ▶ **n.** the dialect of Berber spoken by the Tuareg, sometimes regarded as a separate language.
– ORIGIN the name in Berber.

ta·mas·ic /təˈmasik/ ▶ **adj.** (in Ayurveda) denoting a class of foods that are dry, old, foul, or unpalatable, and are thought to promote pessimism, ignorance, laziness, criminal tendencies, and doubt. Compare RAJASIC, SATTVIC.

Ta·mau·li·pas /ˌtämouˈlēpäs/ a state in northeastern Mexico, on the Gulf of Mexico; capital, Ciudad Victoria.

tam·ba·la /tämˈbälə/ ▶ **n.** (pl. **same** or **tambalas**) a monetary unit of Malawi, equal to one hundredth of a kwacha.
– ORIGIN from Nyanja, literally 'cockerel.'

tam·bour /ˈtamˌbo͝or/ ▶ **n. 1** historical a small drum.
2 something resembling a drum in shape or construction, in particular: ■ a circular frame for holding fabric taut while it is being embroidered. ■ Architecture a wall of circular plan, such as one supporting a dome or surrounded by a colonnade. ■ Architecture each of a sequence of cylindrical stones forming the shaft of a column. ■ a projecting part of the wall of a tennis court. ■ [usu. as modifier] a sliding flexible shutter or door on a piece of furniture, made of strips of wood attached to a backing of canvas: *a tambour door*.
▶ **v.** [with obj.] (often as adj. **tamboured**) decorate or embroider on a tambour: *a tamboured waistcoat*.
– ORIGIN late 15th cent.: from French *tambour* 'drum'; perhaps related to Persian *tabīra* 'drum.' Compare with TABOR.

tam·bou·ra /tamˈbo͝orə/ (also **tambura**) ▶ **n. 1** a large four-stringed lute used in Indian music as a drone accompaniment.
2 a long-necked lute or mandolin of Balkan countries.
– ORIGIN late 16th cent. (denoting a type of long-necked lute): from Arabic *ṭanbūr* or Persian *tunbūra*, both from Persian *dunbara*, literally 'lamb's tail.'

tam·bou·rin /ˈtambo͝orin, taNbo͞oˈraN/ ▶ **n.** a long narrow drum used in Provence. ■ a dance accompanied by such a drum.
– ORIGIN French, diminutive of *tambour* (see TAMBOUR).

tam·bou·rine /ˌtambəˈrēn/ ▶ **n.** a percussion instrument resembling a shallow drum with small metal disks in slots around the edge, played by being shaken or hit with the hand.
– DERIVATIVES **tam·bou·rin·ist** /-nist/ **n.**
– ORIGIN late 16th cent.: from French *tambourin* (see TAMBOURIN).

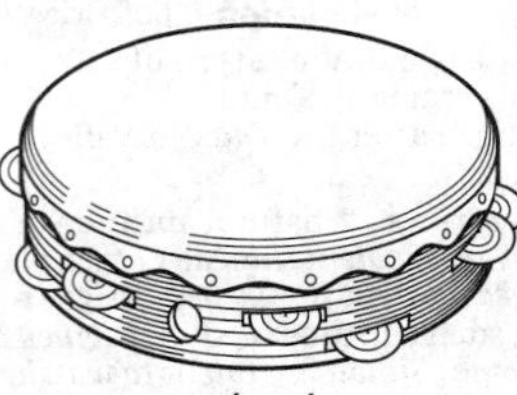

tambourine

Tam·bov /tämˈbôf, -ˈbôv/ an industrial city in southwestern Russia; pop. 279,800 (est. 2008).

tam·bu·ra ▶ **n.** variant spelling of TAMBOURA.

tam·bu·rit·za /tamˈbo͝oritsə, ˌtambəˈritsə/ ▶ **n.** a kind of long-necked mandolin played in Croatia and neighboring countries.
– ORIGIN Croatian, diminutive of *tambura* TAMBOURA.

tame /tām/ ▶ **adj. 1** (of an animal) not dangerous or frightened of people; domesticated: *the fish are so tame you have to push them away from your face mask*. ■ not exciting, adventurous, or controversial: *network TV on Saturday night is a pretty tame affair*. ■ informal (of a person) willing to cooperate.
2 (of a plant) produced by cultivation. ■ (of land) cultivated.
▶ **v.** [with obj.] domesticate (an animal): *wild rabbits can be kept in captivity and eventually tamed*. ■ make less powerful and easier to control: *the battle to tame inflation*. ■ cultivate (land or wilderness).
– DERIVATIVES **tam·a·ble** (also **tameable**) **adj.**, **tame·ly adv.**, **tame·ness n.**, **tam·er n.**
– ORIGIN Old English *tam* (adjective), *temmian* (verb), of Germanic origin; related to Dutch *tam* and German *zahm*, from an Indo-European root shared by Latin *domare* and Greek *daman* 'tame, subdue.'

Tam·er·lane /ˈtamərˌlān-/ (also **Tamburlaine** /ˈtambər-/) (1336–1405), Mongol ruler of Samarkand 1369–1405; Tartar name *Timur Lenk* ("lame Timur"). Leading a force of Mongols and Turks, he conquered Persia, northern India, and Syria and established his capital at Samarkand. He was the ancestor of the Mogul dynasty in India.

Tam·il /ˈtaməl/ ▶ **n. 1** a member of a people inhabiting parts of southern India and Sri Lanka.
2 the Dravidian language of the Tamils.
▶ **adj.** of or relating to this people or their language.
– DERIVATIVES **Tam·il·i·an** /təˈmilēən/ **adj. & n.**
– ORIGIN the name in Tamil.

Tam·il Na·du /ˈtaməl ˈnädo͞o/ a state in southeastern India, on the Coromandel Coast, with a largely Tamil-speaking Hindu population; capital, Chennai (Madras). Former name (until 1968) MADRAS.

Tam·il Ti·gers a Sri Lankan guerrilla organization founded in 1972 that seeks the establishment of an independent state (Eelam) in the northeast of the country for the Tamil community. Also called LIBERATION TIGERS OF TAMIL EELAM.

Tam·la Mo·town /ˈtamlə ˈmōˌtoun/ ▶ **n.** trade name for MOTOWN (sense 1).

Tam·ma·ny /ˈtamənē/ (also **Tammany Hall**) a powerful organization within the Democratic Party that was widely associated with corruption. Founded as a fraternal and benevolent society in 1789, it came to dominate political life in New York City in the 19th and early 20th centuries, before being reduced in power by Franklin D. Roosevelt in the early 1930s. ■ (as noun **a Tammany**) a corrupt political organization or group.
– DERIVATIVES **Tam·ma·ny·ite** /-nēˌīt/ **n.**
– ORIGIN named after an American Indian chief of the late 17th cent., said to have welcomed William Penn, and regarded as "patron saint" of Pennsylvania and other northern colonies.

tam·mar wal·la·by /ˈtamər/ ▶ **n.** a small grayish-brown wallaby found in southwestern Australia. ● *Macropus eugenii*, family Macropodidae.

– ORIGIN mid 19th cent.: from Gaurna (an Aboriginal language) *tamma*.

Tam·mer·fors /ˌtämərˈfô(r)SH/ Swedish name for **TAMPERE**.

Tam·muz[1] /ˈtämo͝oz, ˈtaməz/ Near Eastern Mythology a Mesopotamian god, lover of Ishtar and similar in some respects to the Greek Adonis. He became the personification of the seasonal death and rebirth of crops.
– ORIGIN from Ezek. 8:14, from Akkadian *Dumuzi*.

Tam·muz[2] variant spelling of **THAMMUZ**.

tam-o'-shan·ter /ˈtam əˌSHantər/ ▶ **n.** a round woolen or cloth cap of Scottish origin, with a pom-pom in the center.
– ORIGIN mid 19th cent.: named after the hero of Burns's poem *Tam o' Shanter* (1790).

tam-o'-shanter

ta·mox·i·fen /təˈmäksəfən/ ▶ **n.** Medicine a synthetic drug used to treat breast cancer and infertility in women. It acts as an estrogen antagonist.
– ORIGIN 1970s: an arbitrary formation based on **TRANS-**, **AMINE**, **OXY-**[2], **PHENOL**, elements of the drug's chemical name.

tamp /tamp/ ▶ **v.** [with obj.] pack (a blast hole) full of clay or sand to concentrate the force of the explosion: *when the hole was tamped to the top, gunpowder was inserted.* ■ ram or pack (a substance) down or into something firmly: *he **tamped down** the tobacco with his thumb.*
– ORIGIN early 19th cent.: probably a back-formation from *tampin* (interpreted as 'tamping'), variant of **TAMPION**.

Tam·pa /ˈtampə/ a port and resort on the western coast of Florida; pop. 340,882 (est. 2008).

Tam·pa Bay an inlet of the Gulf of Mexico, in southwestern Florida. Tampa and St. Petersburg are among the cities that lie along its shores.

tam·per /ˈtampər/ ▶ **v. 1** [no obj.] (**tamper with**) interfere with (something) in order to cause damage or make unauthorized alterations: *someone tampered with the brakes on my car.*
2 [no obj.] (**tamper with**) exert a secret or corrupt influence upon (someone).
▶ **n.** a person or thing that tamps something down, esp. a machine or tool for tamping down earth or ballast.
– DERIVATIVES **tam·per·er n.**
– ORIGIN mid 16th cent. (in the sense 'busy oneself to a particular end, machinate'): alteration of the verb **TEMPER**.

Tam·pe·re /ˈtämpəˌrā, ˈtam-, ˈtampərə/ a city in southwestern Finland; pop. 209,690 (2009). Swedish name **TAMMERFORS**.

tam·per-ev·i·dent ▶ **adj.** (of packaging) designed to reveal any interference with the contents.

tam·per-proof ▶ **adj.** made so that it cannot be interfered with or changed.

Tam·pi·co /tamˈpēkō, täm-/ a principal seaport in Mexico, on the Gulf of Mexico; pop. 303,635 (2005).

tam·pi·on /ˈtampēən/ (also **tompion** /ˈtämpēən/) ▶ **n.** a wooden stopper for the muzzle of a gun. ■ a plug for the top of an organ pipe.
– ORIGIN late Middle English: from French *tampon* 'tampon.'

tam·pon /ˈtamˌpän/ ▶ **n.** a plug of soft material inserted into the vagina to absorb menstrual blood. ■ Medicine a plug of material used to stop a wound or block an opening in the body and absorb blood or secretions.
▶ **v.** (**tampons, tamponing, tamponed**) [with obj.] plug with a tampon.
– ORIGIN mid 19th cent.: from French, nasalized variant of *tapon* 'plug, stopper,' ultimately of Germanic origin and related to **TAP**[1].

tam·pon·ade /ˌtampəˈnād/ ▶ **n.** Medicine **1** (in full **cardiac tamponade**) compression of the heart by an accumulation of fluid in the pericardial sac.
2 the surgical use of a plug of absorbent material.

tam-tam /ˈtəm ˌtəm, ˈtam ˌtam/ ▶ **n.** a large metal gong with indefinite pitch.
– ORIGIN mid 19th cent.: perhaps from Hindi *tam-tam* (see **TOM-TOM**).

Tan /tan/, Amy, (1952–) US writer. Her works include *The Joy Luck Club* (1989), *The Kitchen God's Wife* (1991), *The Bonesetter's Daughter* (2000), and *Saving Fish from Drowning* (2005). She also wrote children's stories, such as *The Moon Lady* (1992) and *Sagwa, the Chinese Siamese Cat* (1994).

tan[1] /tan/ ▶ **n. 1** a yellowish-brown color: *the overall color scheme of tan and cream.* ■ a golden-brown shade of skin developed by pale-skinned people after exposure to the sun.
2 (also **tanbark** /ˈtanˌbärk/) bark of oak or other trees, bruised and used as a source of tannin for converting hides into leather. ■ (also **spent tan**) such bark from which the tannin has been extracted, used for covering the ground for walking, riding, children's play, etc., and in gardening.
▶ **v.** (**tans, tanning, tanned**) **1** [no obj.] (of a pale-skinned person or their skin) become brown or browner after exposure to the sun: *you'll tan very quickly in the pure air.* ■ [with obj.] (usu. as adj. **tanned**) (of the sun) cause (a pale-skinned person or their skin) to become brown or browner: *he looked tanned and fit.*
2 [with obj.] convert (animal skin) into leather by soaking in a liquid containing tannic acid, or by the use of other chemicals.
3 [with obj.] informal, dated beat (someone) repeatedly, esp. as a punishment: *"If Mickey touches a fishing net, I'll **tan his hide**!"*
▶ **adj.** of a yellowish-brown color: *a tan baseball cap with orange piping.* ■ (of a pale-skinned person) having golden-brown skin after exposure to the sun: *she looks tall, tan, and healthy.*
– DERIVATIVES **tan·ning n.**, **tan·nish adj.**
– ORIGIN late Old English *tannian* 'convert into leather,' probably from medieval Latin *tannare*, perhaps of Celtic origin; reinforced in Middle English by Old French *tanner*. Early use of the noun (late Middle English) was sense 2 of the noun.

tan[2] ▶ **abbr.** tangent.

Ta·na, Lake /ˈtänə/ a lake in northern Ethiopia, the source of the Blue Nile.

tan·a·ger /ˈtanəjər/ ▶ **n.** a small American songbird of the bunting family, the male of which typically has brightly colored plumage. ● Family Emberizidae (subfamily Thraupinae): many genera, in particular *Tangara*, and numerous species.
– ORIGIN early 17th cent. (originally as *tangara*): from Tupi *tangará*, later refashioned on the pattern of the modern Latin genus name *Tanagra*.

Ta·na·na·rive /ˌtanənəˈrēv, təˌnanə-/ former name (until 1975) of **ANTANANARIVO**.

Tan·a·na Riv·er /ˈtanəˌnô/ a river that flows for 600 miles (1,000 km) from Yukon Territory across Alaska, to meet the Yukon River west of Fairbanks.

tan·bark /ˈtanˌbärk/ ▶ **n.** see **TAN**[1] (sense 2 of the noun).

T & A ▶ **abbr.** vulgar slang tits and ass.

tan·dem /ˈtandəm/ ▶ **n.** (also **tandem bicycle**) a bicycle with seats and pedals for two riders, one behind the other. ■ a carriage driven by two animals harnessed one in front of the other. ■ a group of two people or machines working together.
▶ **adv.** with two or more horses harnessed one behind another: *I rode tandem to Paris.* ■ alongside each other; together.
▶ **adj.** having two things arranged one in front of the other: *a tandem trailer.*
– PHRASES **in tandem** alongside each other; together: *a tight fiscal policy working in tandem with a tight foreign exchange policy.* ■ one behind another.
– ORIGIN late 18th cent.: humorously from Latin, literally 'at length.'

tan·door /tanˈdo͝or, tän-/ ▶ **n.** a clay oven of a type used originally in northern India and Pakistan.
– ORIGIN from Urdu *tandūr*, from Persian *tanūr*, based on Arabic *tannūr* 'oven.'

tan·door·i /tanˈdo͝orē, tän-/ ▶ **adj.** denoting or relating to a style of Indian cooking based on the use of a tandoor: *tandoori chicken.*
▶ **n.** food or cooking of this type. ■ a restaurant serving such food.
– ORIGIN from Urdu and Persian *tandūrī*, from *tandūr* (see **TANDOOR**).

Tan·ey /ˈtônē/, Roger Brooke, (1777–1864) US chief justice 1836–64. He was active in Maryland politics and was the US attorney general 1831–33 before being appointed chief justice. He upheld the principle of federal supremacy over states' rights. In the *Dred Scott* v. *Sandford* case 1857, he expressed the opinion that blacks could not be citizens and that Congress had no control over slavery in the territories.

TANF ▶ **abbr.** Temporary Assistance for Needy Families, a federal assistance program since 1997.

Tang /taNG/ a dynasty ruling China 618–*c.*906, a period noted for territorial conquest and great wealth and regarded as the golden age of Chinese poetry and art.

tang[1] /taNG/ ▶ **n. 1** [in sing.] a strong taste, flavor, or smell: *the clean salty tang of the sea.* ■ a characteristic quality: *the tang of finality hovers throughout Tolstoy's story.*
2 the projection on the blade of a tool such as a knife, by which the blade is held firmly in the handle.
– ORIGIN Middle English (denoting a snake's tongue, formerly believed to be a stinging organ; also denoting the sting of an insect): from Old Norse *tangi* 'point, tang of a knife.'

tang[2] ▶ **v.** [no obj.] make a loud ringing or clanging sound: *the bronze bell tangs.*
▶ **n.** a tanging sound.
– ORIGIN mid 16th cent.: imitative.

tang[3] ▶ **n.** a surgeonfish that occurs around reefs and rocky areas, where it browses on algae. ● Genus *Acanthurus*, family Acanthuridae: several species, in particular the **blue tang** (*A. coeruleus*) of the western Atlantic.
– ORIGIN mid 18th cent.: from **TANG**[1].

Tan·ga /ˈtaNGgə, ˈtäNG-/ one of the principal ports in Tanzania, situated in the northeastern part of the country, on the Indian Ocean; pop. 240,000 (est. 2009).

tan·ga /ˈtaNGgə/ (also **tanga briefs**) ▶ **n.** Brit. a pair of briefs consisting of small panels connected by strings at the sides.
– ORIGIN early 20th cent. (denoting a loincloth worn by indigenous peoples in tropical America): from Portuguese, ultimately of Bantu origin. The current sense dates from the 1970s.

Tan·gan·yi·ka, Lake /ˌtan-gənˈyēkə, ˌtaNG-/ a lake in East Africa in the Great Rift Valley. The deepest lake in Africa and the longest freshwater lake in the world, it forms most of the border of the Democratic Republic of the Congo (formerly Zaire) with Tanzania and Burundi.

tan·ge·lo /ˈtanjəˌlō/ ▶ **n.** (pl. **tangelos**) a hybrid of the tangerine and grapefruit.
– ORIGIN early 20th cent.: blend of **TANGERINE** and **POMELO**.

tan·gent /ˈtanjənt/ ▶ **n. 1** a straight line or plane that touches a curve or curved surface at a point, but if extended does not cross it at that point.
2 a completely different line of thought or action: *he quickly **went off on a tangent** about wrestling.*
3 Mathematics the trigonometric function that is equal to the ratio of the sides (other than the hypotenuse) opposite and adjacent to an angle in a right triangle.
▶ **adj.** (of a line or plane) touching, but not intersecting, a curve or curved surface.
– DERIVATIVES **tan·gen·cy** /-jənsē/ **n.**
– ORIGIN late 16th cent. (sense 3 of the noun and as an adjective): from Latin *tangent-* 'touching,' from the verb *tangere*.

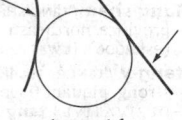

tangent 1

tan·gen·tial /tanˈjenCHəl/ ▶ **adj.** of, relating to, or along a tangent: *a tangential line.* ■ diverging from a previous course or line; erratic: *tangential thoughts.* ■ hardly touching a matter; peripheral: *the reforms were tangential to efforts to maintain a basic standard of life.*
– DERIVATIVES **tan·gen·tial·ly adv.**

tan·ge·rine /ˌtanjəˈrēn/ ▶ **n. 1** a small citrus fruit with a loose skin, esp. one of a variety with deep orange-red skin. ■ a deep orange-red color.
2 the citrus tree that bears this fruit. ● *Citrus reticulata*, family Rutaceae.
– ORIGIN mid 19th cent.: from *Tanger* (former name of **TANGIER**) + **-INE**[1]. The fruit, exported from Tangier, was originally called the *tangerine orange*.

tan·gi·ble /ˈtanjəbəl/ ▶ **adj.** perceptible by touch: *the atmosphere of neglect and abandonment was **almost tangible**.* ■ clear and definite; real: *the emphasis is now on tangible results.*
▶ **n.** (usu. **tangibles**) a thing that is perceptible by touch.
– DERIVATIVES **tan·gi·bil·i·ty** /ˌtanjəˈbilitē/ **n.**, **tan·gi·ble·ness n.**, **tan·gi·bly** /-blē/ **adv.**
– ORIGIN late 16th cent.: from French, or from late Latin *tangibilis*, from *tangere* 'to touch.'

Tan·gier /tanˈji(ə)r/ (also **Tangiers**) a seaport on the northern coast of Morocco, on the Strait of Gibraltar where it stands guard at the western entrance to the Mediterranean Sea; pop. 762,583 (2004).

tan·gle[1] /ˈtaNGgəl/ ▶ **v.** [with obj.] (usu. **be tangled**) twist together into a confused mass: *the broom somehow got **tangled up** in my long skirt.* ■ [no obj.] (**tangle with**) informal become involved in a conflict or fight with: *I know there'll be trouble if I try to tangle with him.*
▶ **n.** a confused mass of something twisted together: *a tangle of golden hair.* ■ a confused or complicated state; a muddle. ■ informal a fight, argument, or disagreement.
– DERIVATIVES **tan·gly** /-g(ə)lē/ **adj.**

t

– ORIGIN Middle English (in the sense 'entangle, catch in a tangle'): probably of Scandinavian origin and related to Swedish dialect *taggla* 'disarrange.'

tan·gle² ▶ **n.** any of a number of brown seaweeds, esp. oarweed.
– ORIGIN mid 16th cent.: probably from Norwegian *tongul.*

tan·gled /'taNGgəld/ ▶ **adj.** twisted together untidily; matted: *his hair was a tangled mess.* ■ complicated and confused; chaotic: *a tangled tale.*
– PHRASES **a tangled web** a complex, difficult, and confusing situation or thing. [from 'O what a tangled web we weave, When first we practise to deceive' (Scott's *Marmion*).]

tan·gle·foot /'taNGgəl,fo͝ot/ ▶ **n. 1** trademark material applied to a tree trunk as a grease band, esp. to prevent infestation by insects.
2 informal intoxicating liquor, esp. cheap whiskey.

tan·go /'taNGgō/ ▶ **n.** (pl. **tangos**) **1** a ballroom dance originating in Buenos Aires, characterized by marked rhythms and postures and abrupt pauses. ■ a piece of music written for or in the style of this dance, typically in a slow dotted duple rhythm.
2 a code word representing the letter T, used in voice communication by radio.
▶ **v.** (**tangoes, tangoing, tangoed**) [no obj.] dance the tango.
– PHRASES **it takes two to tango** informal both parties involved in a situation or argument are responsible for it.
– ORIGIN late 19th cent.: from Latin American Spanish, perhaps of African origin.

tan·gram /'taNG,grəm/ ▶ **n.** a Chinese geometric puzzle consisting of a square cut into seven pieces that can be arranged to make various other shapes.
– ORIGIN mid 19th cent.: of unknown origin.

Tang·shan /'täNG'SHän/ an industrial city in Hebei province, northeastern China; pop. 1,658,200 (est.2006). It was rebuilt after an earthquake in 1976.

tang·y /'taNGē/ ▶ **adj.** (**tangier, tangiest**) having a strong, piquant flavor or smell: *a tangy salad.*
– DERIVATIVES **tang·i·ness n.**

tanh ▶ **abbr.** Mathematics hyperbolic tangent.

tan·ist /'tanist, 'THô-/ ▶ **n.** the heir apparent to a Celtic chief, typically the most vigorous adult of his kin, elected during the chief's lifetime.
– DERIVATIVES **tan·ist·ry** /-istrē/ **n.**
– ORIGIN mid 16th cent.: from Irish and Scottish Gaelic *tánaiste*, literally 'second in excellence.'

Tan·jung·ka·rang /,tänjo͝oNG'käräNG/ see **BANDAR LAMPUNG.**

tank /taNGk/ ▶ **n. 1** a large receptacle or storage chamber, esp. for liquid or gas. ■ the container holding the fuel supply in a motor vehicle. ■ a receptacle with transparent sides in which to keep fish; an aquarium.
2 a heavy armored fighting vehicle carrying guns and moving on a continuous articulated metal track. [from the use of *tank* as a secret code word during manufacture in 1915.]
3 informal a cell in a police station or jail.
▶ **v.** [no obj.] **1** fill the tank of a vehicle with fuel: *the cars stopped to tank up.* ■ (**be/get tanked up**) informal drink heavily; become drunk: *they get tanked up before the game.*
2 informal fail completely, esp. at great financial cost. ■ [with obj.] informal (in sports) deliberately lose or fail to finish (a game): *the lackluster performance prompted speculation that he tanked the second set.*
– DERIVATIVES **tank·ful** /-fo͝ol/ **n.** (pl. **tankfuls**), **tank·less adj.**
– ORIGIN early 17th cent.: perhaps from Gujarati *tānku-* or Marathi *tānkē* 'underground cistern,' from Sanskrit *tadāga* 'pond,' probably influenced by Portuguese *tangue* 'pond,' from Latin *stagnum.*

t

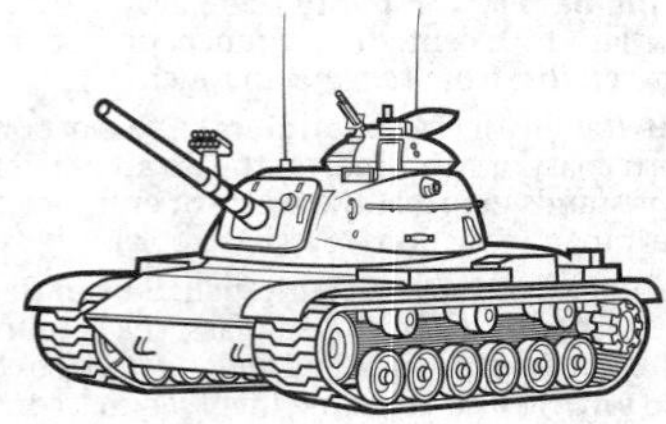

tank 2

tan·ka¹ /'täNGkə/ ▶ **n.** (pl. **same** or **tankas**) a Japanese poem consisting of five lines, the first and third of which have five syllables and the other seven, making 31 syllables in all and giving a complete picture of an event or mood.
– ORIGIN Japanese, from *tan* 'short' + *ka* 'song.'

tan·ka² ▶ **n.** (pl. **tankas**) a Tibetan religious painting on a scroll, hung as a banner in temples and carried in processions.
– ORIGIN from Tibetan *t'án-ka* 'image, painting.'

tank·age /'taNGkij/ ▶ **n. 1** the storage capacity of a tank. ■ the storage of something in a tank or a charge made for such storage.
2 a fertilizer or animal feed obtained from the residue from tanks in which animal carcasses have been rendered.

tan·kard /'taNGkərd/ ▶ **n.** a tall beer mug, typically made of silver or pewter, with a handle and sometimes a hinged lid. ■ the contents of or an amount held by such a mug: *I've downed a tankard of ale.*
– ORIGIN Middle English (denoting a large tub for carrying liquid): perhaps related to Dutch *tanckaert.*

tank·er /'taNGkər/ ▶ **n. 1** a ship, road vehicle, or aircraft for carrying liquids, esp. petroleum, in bulk.
2 Military member of a tank crew.

tank farm ▶ **n.** an area of oil or gas storage tanks.

tank·i·ni /taNG'kēnē/ ▶ **n.** a two-piece bathing suit consisting of a tank top and a bikini bottom.

tank kill·er ▶ **n.** an aircraft, vehicle, or missile effective against tanks.

tank top ▶ **n.** a close-fitting sleeveless top.

tank town ▶ **n.** a small unimportant town (used originally of a town at which trains stopped to take on water).

tan·ner¹ /'tanər/ ▶ **n. 1** a person who tans animal hides, esp. to earn a living.
2 a lotion or cream designed to promote the development of a suntan or produce a similar skin color artificially.

tan·ner² ▶ **n.** Brit. informal a sixpence.
– ORIGIN early 19th cent.: of unknown origin.

tan·ner·y /'tanərē/ ▶ **n.** (pl. **tanneries**) a place where animal hides are tanned; the workshop of a tanner.

Tann·häu·ser /'tän,hoizər/ (*c.*1200–*c.*1270), German poet. In reality a minnesinger whose works included lyrics and love poetry, he became a legendary figure as a knight who visited Venus's grotto. He spent seven years in debauchery, then repented and sought absolution from the pope.

tan·nic /'tanik/ ▶ **adj.** of or relating to tannin: *a dry wine with a slightly tannic aftertaste.*
– ORIGIN mid 19th cent.: from French *tannique*, from *tanin* (see **TANNIN**).

tan·nic ac·id ▶ **n.** another term for **TANNIN.**
– DERIVATIVES **tan·nate** /'tanāt/ **n.**

tan·nin /'tanin/ ▶ **n.** a yellowish or brownish bitter-tasting organic substance present in some galls, barks, and other plant tissues, consisting of derivatives of gallic acid, used in leather production and ink manufacture.
– ORIGIN early 19th cent.: from French *tanin*, from *tan* 'tanbark' (ultimately related to **TAN¹**) + **-IN¹**.

tan·ning bed ▶ **n.** an apparatus used for tanning, consisting of a bank of sunlamp tubes, typically horizontal for lying on, with another above.

Tan·nu-Tu·va /,täno͞o 'to͞ovə/ former name for **TUVA.**

Ta·no·an /'tänōən/ ▶ **n.** a small language family comprising a number of Pueblo Indian languages, including Tewa and Tiwa, and related to Kiowa.
▶ **adj.** of or relating to this language family.
– ORIGIN from Spanish *Tano* + **-AN.**

tan·su /'tänso͞o, 'tan-/ ▶ **n.** (pl. **same**) a Japanese chest of drawers or cabinet.
– ORIGIN Japanese.

tan·sy /'tanzē/ ▶ **n.** a plant of the daisy family with yellow flat-topped buttonlike flower heads and aromatic leaves, formerly used in cooking and medicine. ● Genus *Tanacetum*, family Compositae: several species, in particular **common tansy** (*T. vulgare*).
– ORIGIN Middle English: from Old French *tanesie*, probably from medieval Latin *athanasia* 'immortality,' from Greek.

tan·ta·lite /'tantl,īt/ ▶ **n.** a rare, dense, black mineral consisting of a mixed oxide of tantalum, of which it is the principal source, and iron.
– ORIGIN early 19th cent.: from **TANTALUM** + **-ITE¹**.

tan·ta·lize /'tantl,īz/ ▶ **v.** [with obj.] torment or tease (someone) with the sight or promise of something that is unobtainable: *such ambitious questions have long tantalized the world's best thinkers.* ■ excite the senses or desires of (someone): *she still tantalized him* | (as adj. **tantalizing**) *the tantalizing fragrance of fried bacon.*
– DERIVATIVES **tan·ta·li·za·tion** /,tantli'zāSHən/ **n.**, **tan·ta·liz·er n.**, **tan·ta·liz·ing·ly adv.**
– ORIGIN late 16th cent.: from **TANTALUS** + **-IZE.**

tan·ta·lum /'tantl-əm/ ▶ **n.** the chemical element of atomic number 73, a hard silver-gray metal of the transition series. (Symbol: **Ta**)
– DERIVATIVES **tan·tal·ic** /tan'talik/ **adj.**
– ORIGIN early 19th cent.: from **TANTALUS**, with reference to its frustrating insolubility in acids.

Tan·ta·lus /'tantl-əs/ Greek Mythology a Lydian king, son of Zeus and father of Pelops. As punishment for his crimes (which included killing Pelops), he was forced to remain in chin-deep water with fruit-laden branches over his head, neither of which he could reach to drink or eat. His name is the origin of the word *tantalize.*

tan·ta·lus /'tantl-əs/ ▶ **n.** chiefly Brit. a stand in which decanters of liquor can be locked up though still visible.

tan·ta·mount /'tantə,mount/ ▶ **adj.** [predic.] (**tantamount to**) equivalent in seriousness to; virtually the same as: *the resignations were tantamount to an admission of guilt.*
– ORIGIN mid 17th cent.: from the earlier verb *tantamount* 'amount to as much,' from Italian *tanto montare.*

tante /tänt, 'täntə/ ▶ **n.** (esp. among those of French or German origin) a mature or elderly woman who is related or well known to the speaker (often used as a respectful form of address).
– ORIGIN French and Dutch *tante*, German *Tante* 'aunt.'

tan·tiv·y /tan'tivē/ archaic ▶ **n.** (pl. **tantivies**) a rapid gallop or ride.
▶ **exclam.** used as a hunting cry.
▶ **adj.** moving or riding swiftly.
– ORIGIN mid 17th cent.: probably imitative of the sound of galloping.

tant mieux /'täN 'myə/ ▶ **exclam.** so much the better.
– ORIGIN French.

tan·to¹ /'täntō/ ▶ **n.** (pl. **tantos**) a Japanese short sword or dagger.
– ORIGIN Japanese.

tan·to² ▶ **adv.** [usu. with negative] Music (esp. as a direction after a tempo marking) too much: *allegro non tanto.*
– ORIGIN Italian.

tant pis /'täN 'pē/ ▶ **exclam.** so much the worse; the situation is regrettable but now beyond retrieval.
– ORIGIN French.

Tan·tra /'təntrə, 'tan-/ ▶ **n.** a Hindu or Buddhist mystical or ritual text, dating from the 6th to the 13th centuries. ■ adherence to the doctrines or principles of the tantras, involving mantras, meditation, yoga, and ritual.
– DERIVATIVES **tan·tric** /-trik/ **adj.**, **tan·trism** /-,trizəm/ **n.**, **tan·trist** /-trist/ **n.**
– ORIGIN Sanskrit, literally 'loom, groundwork, doctrine,' from *tan* 'stretch.'

tan·trum /'tantrəm/ ▶ **n.** an uncontrolled outburst of anger and frustration, typically in a young child: *he has temper tantrums if he can't get his own way.*
– ORIGIN early 18th cent.: of unknown origin.

Tan·za·ni·a /,tanzə'nēə/ a country in East Africa, on the Indian Ocean; pop. 41,048,500 (est. 2009); capital, Dodoma; languages, Swahili and English (both official).

> Tanzania consists of a mainland area (the former Tanganyika) and the island of Zanzibar. A German colony (German East Africa) from the late 19th century, Tanganyika became a British mandate after World War I and a trust territory, administered by Britain, after World War II, before becoming independent within the Commonwealth of Nations in 1961. It was named Tanzania after its union with Zanzibar in 1964.

– DERIVATIVES **Tan·za·ni·an adj. & n.**

tan·za·nite /'tanzə,nīt/ ▶ **n.** a blue or violet gem variety of zoisite, containing vanadium.
– ORIGIN 1960s: from **TANZANIA** + **-ITE¹**.

Tao /dou, tou/ ▶ **n.** (in Chinese philosophy) the absolute principle underlying the universe, combining within itself the principles of yin and yang and signifying the way, or code of behavior, that is in harmony with the natural order. The interpretation of Tao in the Tao-te-Ching developed into the philosophical religion of Taoism.
– ORIGIN Chinese, literally '(right) way.'

Taoi·seach /'tēSHək, -SHəKH, 'THē-/ ▶ **n.** the prime minister of the Republic of Ireland.
– ORIGIN Irish, literally 'chief, leader.'

Tao·ism /'dou,izəm, 'tou-/ ▶ **n.** a Chinese philosophy based on the writings of Lao-tzu (*fl.* 6th century BC), advocating humility and religious piety.

> The central concept and goal is the Tao, and its most important text is the Tao-te-Ching. Taoism has both a philosophical and a religious aspect. Philosophical Taoism emphasizes inner contemplation and mystical union with nature; wisdom, learning, and purposive action should be abandoned in favor of simplicity and **wu-wei** (nonaction, or letting things take their natural course). The religious aspect of Taoism developed later, c.3rd century AD, incorporating certain

Buddhist features and developing a monastic system.

– DERIVATIVES **Tao·ist** n. & adj., **Tao·is·tic** /tou'istik/ adj.

Ta·or·mi·na /ˌtour'mēnə/ a resort town on the eastern coast of Sicily; pop. 11,096 (est. 2008). It was founded by Greek colonists in the 4th century BC.

Taos[1] /tous, 'tä-ōs/ a town in northern New Mexico, in the Sangre de Cristo Mountains; pop. 5,551 (est. 2008).

Taos[2] ▶ n. (pl. **same**) a North American people native to New Mexico. ■ a member of this people. ■ the language of this people.

Tao-te-Ching /'dou də 'jiNG/ ▶ n. the central Taoist text, ascribed to Lao-tzu, the traditional founder of Taoism. Apparently written as a guide for rulers, it defined the Tao, or way, and established the philosophical basis of Taoism.
– ORIGIN Chinese, literally 'the Book of the Way and its Power.'

tap[1] /tap/ ▶ n. **1** a device by which a flow of liquid or gas from a pipe or container can be controlled. ■ a device connected to a telephone used for listening secretly to someone's conversations. ■ an act of listening secretly to someone's telephone conversation. ■ (also **tapping**) an electrical connection made to some point between the end terminals of a transformer coil or other component.
2 an instrument for cutting a threaded hole in a material.
3 Brit. a taproom.
▶ v. (**taps, tapping, tapped**) [with obj.] **1** draw liquid through the tap or spout of (a cask, barrel, or other container): *bragging of tests they had aced and kegs they had tapped.* ■ draw (liquid) from a cask, barrel, or other container: *the butlers were tapping new ale.* ■ connect a device to (a telephone) so that conversation can be listened to secretly: *the telephones were tapped by the state security police.* ■ informal obtain money or information from (someone): *he considered whom he could **tap for information**.* ■ exploit or draw a supply from (a resource): *clients from industry seeking to tap Philadelphia's resources of expertise* | [no obj.] *these magazines have **tapped into** a target market of consumers.* ■ draw sap from (a tree) by cutting into it.
2 cut a thread in (something) to accept a screw.
– PHRASES **on tap** ready to be poured from a tap. ■ informal freely available whenever needed. ■ informal on schedule to occur.
– DERIVATIVES **tap·pa·ble** adj.
– ORIGIN Old English *tæppa* 'peg for the vent hole of a cask,' *tæppian* 'provide (a cask) with a stopper,' of Germanic origin; related to Dutch *tap* and German *Zapfen* (nouns).

tap[2] ▶ v. (**taps, tapping, tapped**) [with obj.] **1** strike (someone or something) with a quick light blow or blows: *one of my staff tapped me on the shoulder.* ■ strike (something) against something else with a quick light blow or blows: *Gloria was tapping her feet in time to the music.* ■ (**tap something out**) produce (a rhythm) with a series of quick light blows on a surface: *drums that tapped out a rumba beat.* ■ write or enter (something) using a keyboard or keypad: *he tapped out a few words on the keyboard.*
2 (usu. **be tapped**) informal designate or select (someone) for a task or honor, esp. membership in an organization or committee: *he had been tapped earlier to serve in Costa Rica.*
▶ n. **1** a quick light blow or the sound of such a blow.
2 tap dancing. ■ a piece of metal attached to the toe and heel of a tap dancer's shoe to make a tapping sound.
3 (**taps**) [treated as sing. or pl.] a bugle call for lights to be put out in army quarters. [so named because the signal was originally sounded on a drum.] ■ a similar call sounded at a military funeral.
– DERIVATIVES **tap·per** n.
– ORIGIN Middle English: from Old French *taper*, or of imitative origin; compare with CLAP[1] and RAP[1].

ta·pa /'täpə/ ▶ n. the bark of the paper mulberry tree. ■ (also **tapa cloth**) cloth made from such bark, used in the Pacific islands.
– ORIGIN early 19th cent.: of Polynesian origin.

ta·pas /'täpəs/ ▶ plural n. small Spanish savory dishes, typically served with drinks at a bar.
– ORIGIN Spanish *tapa*, literally 'cover, lid' (because the dishes were given free with the drink, served on a dish balanced on, therefore "covering," the glass).

tap dance ▶ n. a dance performed wearing shoes fitted with metal taps, characterized by rhythmical tapping of the toes and heels.
▶ v. [no obj.] (**tap-dance**) perform such a dance.
– DERIVATIVES **tap danc·er** n., **tap danc·ing** n.

tape /tāp/ ▶ n. a narrow strip of material, typically used to hold or fasten something: *a roll of tape* | *a dirty apron fastened with thin tapes.* ■ [often with modifier] long narrow flexible material with magnetic properties, used for recording sound, pictures, or computer data. ■ a cassette or reel containing such material. ■ a recording on such a cassette or reel. ■ (also **adhesive tape**) a strip of paper or plastic coated with adhesive, used to stick things together. ■ a strip of material stretched across the finish line of a race, to be broken by the winner. ■ a strip of white material at the top of a tennis net. ■ a strip of material used to mark off an area. ■ a tape measure.
▶ v. [with obj.] **1** record (sound or pictures) on audio or videotape: *it is not known who taped the conversation.*
2 fasten or attach (something) with adhesive tape.
3 (**tape something off**) seal or mark off an area or thing with tape.
– PHRASES **on tape** recorded on magnetic tape.
– ORIGIN Old English *tæppa, tæppe*; perhaps related to Middle Low German *teppen* 'pluck, tear.'

tape deck ▶ n. a piece of equipment for playing audiotapes, esp. as part of a stereo system.

tape grass ▶ n. a submerged aquatic plant of the frog's-bit family, with narrow grasslike leaves. Also called EELGRASS and RIBBON GRASS. ● Genus *Vallisneria*, family Hydrocharitaceae: several species.

tape ma·chine ▶ n. a tape recorder.

tape meas·ure ▶ n. a length of tape or thin flexible metal, marked at intervals for measuring.

ta·pe·nade /ˌtäpə'näd/ ▶ n. a Provençal paste or dip, made from black olives, capers, and anchovies.
– ORIGIN French, from Provençal.

ta·per /'tāpər/ ▶ n. a slender candle. ■ a wick coated with wax, used for conveying a flame. ■ a gradual narrowing: *the current industry standard taper of 5 degrees.*
▶ v. diminish or reduce or cause to diminish or reduce in thickness toward one end: [no obj.] *the tail tapers to a rounded tip* | [with obj.] *David asked my dressmaker to taper his trousers.* ■ [no obj.] gradually lessen: *the impact of the dollar's depreciation started to **taper off**.*
– ORIGIN Old English (denoting any wax candle), dissimilated form (by alteration of *p-* to *t-*) of Latin *papyrus* (see PAPYRUS), the pith of which was used for candle wicks.

tape re·cord·er ▶ n. an apparatus for recording sounds on magnetic tape and later reproducing them.
– DERIVATIVES **tape-re·cord** v., **tape re·cord·ing** n.

ta·per pin ▶ n. a short round metal rod having a small degree of taper that enables it to act as a stop or wedge when driven into a hole.

tap·es·try /'tapistrē/ ▶ n. (pl. **tapestries**) a piece of thick textile fabric with pictures or designs formed by weaving colored weft threads or by embroidering on canvas, used as a wall hanging or furniture covering. ■ used in reference to an intricate or complex combination of things or sequence of events: *a tapestry of cultures, races, and customs.*
– DERIVATIVES **tap·es·tried** adj.
– ORIGIN late Middle English: from Old French *tapisserie*, from *tapissier* 'tapestry worker' or *tapisser* 'to carpet,' from *tapis* 'carpet, tapis.'

tap·es·try moth ▶ n. another term for CARPET MOTH.

ta·pe·tum /tə'pētəm/ ▶ n. Zoology a reflective layer of the choroid in the eyes of many animals, causing them to shine in the dark.
– ORIGIN early 18th cent.: from late Latin, from Latin *tapete* 'carpet.'

tape·worm /'tāpˌwərm/ ▶ n. a parasitic flatworm, the adult of which lives in the intestine of humans and other vertebrates. It has a long ribbonlike body with many segments that can become independent, and a small head bearing hooks and suckers. ● Class Cestoda, phylum Platyhelminthes.

ta·phon·o·my /tə'fänəmē/ ▶ n. the branch of paleontology that deals with the processes of fossilization.
– DERIVATIVES **taph·o·nom·ic** /ˌtafə'nämik/ adj., **ta·phon·o·mist** /-mist/ n.
– ORIGIN 1940s: from Greek *taphos* 'grave' + -NOMY.

tap-in ▶ n. chiefly Golf, Soccer, & Basketball a relatively easy, close-range putt, shot, or tap of the ball into the goal or hole.

tap·i·o·ca /ˌtapē'ōkə/ ▶ n. a starchy substance in the form of hard white grains, obtained from cassava and used in cooking puddings and other dishes.
– ORIGIN early 18th cent.: from Tupi-Guarani *tipioca*, from *tipi* 'dregs' + *og, ok* 'squeeze out.'

tap·i·o·ca milk tea ▶ n. another term for BUBBLE TEA.

ta·pir /'tāpər/ ▶ n. a nocturnal hoofed mammal with a stout body, sturdy limbs, and a short flexible proboscis, native to the forests of tropical America and Malaysia. ● Family Tapiridae and genus *Tapirus*: four species, including the black and white **Malayan tapir** (*T. indicus*) and the reddish-brown or black **mountain tapir** (*T. pinchaque*), which is the smallest tapir.
– ORIGIN late 18th cent.: via Spanish and Portuguese from Tupi *tapyra*.

mountain tapir

tap·is /'tapē, 'tapis, tä'pē/ ▶ n. (pl. **same**) archaic a tapestry or richly decorated cloth, used as a hanging or a covering for something.
– ORIGIN French, from Old French *tapiz*, via late Latin from Greek *tapētion*, diminutive of *tapēs* 'tapestry.'

ta·pote·ment /tə'pōtmənt/ ▶ n. rapid and repeated striking of the body as a technique in massage.
– ORIGIN late 19th cent.: French, from *tapoter* 'to tap.'

tap pants ▶ plural n. a pair of brief lingerie shorts, usually worn with a camisole top.
– ORIGIN so named because such shorts were formerly worn for tap dancing.

Tap·pan Zee /'tapən ˌzē/ a broadening of the Hudson River in southeastern New York, near the village of Tarrytown.

tap·pet /'tapit/ ▶ n. a lever or projecting part on a machine that intermittently makes contact with a cam or other part so as to give or receive motion.
– ORIGIN mid 18th cent.: apparently an irregular diminutive of TAP[2].

tap·ping /'tapiNG/ ▶ n. the action of a person or things that taps. ■ a sound made by this.

tap·room /'tapˌro͞om, -ˌro͝om/ ▶ n. a room in which alcoholic drinks, esp. beer, are available on tap; a bar in a hotel or inn.

tap·root /'tapˌro͞ot, -ˌro͝ot/ ▶ n. a straight tapering root growing vertically downward and forming the center from which subsidiary rootlets spring.

tap shoe ▶ n. a shoe with a specially hardened sole or attached metal plates at toe and heel to make a tapping sound in tap dancing.

tap·ster /'tapstər/ ▶ n. archaic a person who draws and serves alcoholic drinks at a bar.
– ORIGIN Old English *tæppestre*, denoting a woman serving ale (see TAP[1], -STER).

tap wa·ter ▶ n. water from a piped supply.

ta·que·ri·a /ˌtäkə'rēə, ˌtak-/ ▶ n. a Mexican restaurant specializing in tacos.
– ORIGIN Mexican Spanish.

tar[1] /tär/ ▶ n. a dark, thick, flammable liquid distilled from wood or coal, consisting of a mixture of hydrocarbons, resins, alcohols, and other compounds. It is used in roadmaking and for coating and preserving timber. ■ a similar substance formed by burning tobacco or other material: [in combination] *low-tar cigarettes.*
▶ v. (**tars, tarring, tarred**) [with obj.] (usu. as adj. **tarred**) cover (something) with tar: *a newly tarred road.*
– PHRASES **beat** (or **whale**) **the tar out of** informal beat or thrash severely. **tar and feather** smear with tar and then cover with feathers as a punishment. **tar people with the same brush** consider specified people to have the same faults.
– ORIGIN Old English *teru, teoru*, of Germanic origin; related to Dutch *teer*, German *Teer*, and perhaps ultimately to TREE.

tar[2] ▶ n. informal, dated a sailor.
– ORIGIN mid 17th cent.: perhaps an abbreviation of TARPAULIN, also used as a nickname for a sailor at this time.

Ta·rab·u·lus al-Gharb /tə'räbələs al'gärb/ Arabic name for TRIPOLI (sense 1).

Ta·rab·u·lus ash-Sham /tə'räbələs ash'sham/ Arabic name for TRIPOLI (sense 2).

tar·a·did·dle /'tarəˌdidl/ (also **tarradiddle**) ▶ n. informal, chiefly Brit. a petty lie. ■ pretentious nonsense.
– ORIGIN late 18th cent.: perhaps related to DIDDLE.

Ta·ra·hu·ma·ra /ˌtärəho͞o'märə/ ▶ n. (pl. **same**)
1 a member of an American Indian people of northwestern Mexico.
2 the Uto-Aztecan language of this people.

▶ adj. of or relating to this people or their language.
– ORIGIN Spanish from Tarahumara *rarámuri*.

ta·ra·ma·sa·la·ta /ˌtärəməsəˈlätə/ (also **tarama** /ˌtärəˈmä/) ▶ n. a pinkish paste or dip made from the roe of certain fish, mixed with olive oil and seasoning.
– ORIGIN from modern Greek *taramas* 'roe' (from Turkish *tarama*, denoting a preparation of soft roe or red caviar) + *salata* 'salad.'

tar·an·tel·la /ˌtarənˈtelə/ (also **tarantelle** /-ˈtel/) ▶ n. a rapid whirling dance originating in southern Italy. ■ a piece of music written in fast 6/8 time in the style of this dance.
– ORIGIN late 18th cent.: Italian, from the name of the seaport TARANTO; so named because it was thought to be a cure for tarantism, the victim dancing the tarantella until exhausted. See also TARANTULA.

Ta·ran·ti·no /ˌtarənˈtēnō/, Quentin (Jerome) (1963–), US movie director, screenwriter, and actor. His screenplays for *Reservoir Dogs* (1992) and *Pulp Fiction* (1994) aroused controversy for their amorality and violence but also won admiration for their wit and style.

tar·ant·ism /ˈtarənˌtizəm/ ▶ n. a psychological illness characterized by an extreme impulse to dance, prevalent in southern Italy from the 15th to the 17th century, and widely believed at the time to have been caused by the bite of a tarantula.
– ORIGIN mid 17th cent.: from Italian *tarantismo*, from the name of the seaport TARANTO, after which the tarantula is also named. Compare with TARANTELLA.

Ta·ran·to /ˈtärənˌtō, təˈrantō/ a seaport and naval base in southeastern Italy; pop. 194,021 (2008).

ta·ran·tu·la /təˈranCHələ/ ▶ n. **1** a large hairy spider found chiefly in tropical and subtropical America, some kinds of which are able to catch small lizards, frogs, and birds. ● Family Theraphosidae, suborder Mygalomorphae: numerous species.
2 a large black wolf spider of southern Europe whose bite was formerly believed to cause tarantism. ● *Lycosa tarentula*, family Lycosidae.
– ORIGIN mid 16th cent.: from medieval Latin, from Old Italian *tarantola* 'tarantula,' from the name of the seaport TARANTO. Compare with TARANTELLA and TARANTISM.

tarantula 1

ta·ran·tu·la hawk ▶ n. a large spider-hunting wasp of the southwestern US. ● Genus *Pepsis*, family Pompilidae.

Ta·ras·can /təˈraskən/ ▶ n. (pl. **same** or **Tarascans**) **1** a member of an American Indian people of a mountainous area in Michoacán, Mexico.
2 the language of this people.
▶ adj. of or relating to this people or their language.
– ORIGIN from Spanish *Tarasco* (a Meso-American Indian language of Mexico) + -AN.

Ta·ra·wa /təˈräwə, ˈtarəˌwä/ an atoll in the South Pacific Ocean, one of the Gilbert Islands in Kiribati; pop. 45,989 (2005). Bairiki, Kiribati's capital, is located here.

ta·rax·a·cum /təˈraksəkəm/ ▶ n. any plant of the genus *Taraxacum* (daisy family), including the dandelion. ■ a preparation of the dried roots of this, used medicinally.
– ORIGIN early 18th cent.: from medieval Latin *altaraxacon*, via Arabic from Persian *talḵ* 'bitter' + *čakūk* 'purslane.'

t

tar ba·by ▶ n. informal a difficult problem that is only aggravated by attempts to solve it.
– ORIGIN with allusion to the doll smeared with tar as a trap for Brer Rabbit, in J. C. Harris's *Uncle Remus*.

Tar·bell /ˈtärbəl/, Ida Minerva, (1857–1944), US writer. She was a leader of the muckraking movement and a writer for *McClure's* magazine 1896–1904 and for *American* magazine 1906–15. Her books include the exposé *The History of the Standard Oil Company* (1904) and *The Business of Being a Woman* (1912).

tar·boosh /tärˈbo͞osH/ ▶ n. a man's cap similar to a fez, typically of red felt with a tassel at the top.
– ORIGIN early 18th cent.: from Egyptian Arabic *ṭarbūš*, based on Persian *sarpūš*, from *sar* 'head' + *pūš* 'cover.'

tar·brush /ˈtärˌbrəsH/ ▶ n. (**the tarbrush**) offensive black or Indian ancestry.

Tar·di·gra·da /tärˈdigrədə/ Zoology a small phylum that comprises the water bears.
– ORIGIN modern Latin (plural), from Latin *tardigradus*, from *tardus* 'slow' + *gradi* 'to walk.'

tar·di·grade /ˈtärdəˌgrād/ ▶ n. Zoology a minute animal of the phylum Tardigrada; a water bear.

tar·di·ness /ˈtärdēnis/ ▶ n. the quality or fact of being late; lateness: *forgive my tardiness, I had some very important business to attend to.*

Tar·dis /ˈtärdis/ ▶ n. **1** a time machine.
2 a building or container that is larger inside than it appears to be from outside.
– ORIGIN the name (said to be an acronym from *time and relative dimensions in space*) of a time machine that had the exterior of a police telephone box in the British TV science-fiction series *Doctor Who*, first broadcast in 1963.

tar·dive dys·ki·ne·sia /ˌtärdiv ˌdiskəˈnēzH(ē)ə/ ▶ n. Medicine a neurological disorder characterized by involuntary movements of the face and jaw.
– ORIGIN 1960s: *tardive* from French *tardif, tardive* (see TARDY).

tar·dy /ˈtärdē/ ▶ adj. (**tardier**, **tardiest**) delaying or delayed beyond the right or expected time; late: *please forgive this tardy reply.* ■ slow in action or response; sluggish.
– DERIVATIVES **tar·di·ly** /ˈtärdl-ē/ adv.
– ORIGIN mid 16th cent.: from French *tardif, -ive*, from Latin *tardus* 'slow.'

tare[1] /te(ə)r/ ▶ n. **1** a vetch, esp. the common vetch.
2 (**tares**) (in biblical use) an injurious weed resembling wheat when young (Matt. 13:24–30).
– ORIGIN Middle English: of unknown origin.

tare[2] ▶ n. an allowance made for the weight of the packaging in order to determine the net weight of goods. ■ the weight of a motor vehicle, railroad car, or aircraft without its fuel or load.
– ORIGIN late Middle English: from French, literally 'deficiency, tare,' from medieval Latin *tara*, based on Arabic *ṭaraḥa* 'reject, deduct.'

tar·ga /ˈtärgə/ ▶ n. [usu. as modifier] a type of convertible sports car with hood or panel that can be removed, esp. leaving a central roll bar for passenger safety: *a targa roof.*
– ORIGIN Italian, literally 'shield,' given as a name to a model of Porsche with a detachable hood (1965), probably suggested by the *Targa Florio* ('Florio Shield'), a motor time trial held annually in Sicily.

targe /tärj/ ▶ n. archaic term for TARGET (sense 2 of the noun).
– ORIGIN Old English *targa, targe*, of Germanic origin; reinforced in Middle English by Old French *targe*.

tar·get /ˈtärgit/ ▶ n. **1** a person, object, or place selected as the aim of an attack. ■ a mark or point at which someone fires or aims, esp. a round or rectangular board marked with concentric circles used in archery or shooting. ■ an objective or result toward which efforts are directed: *the car met its sales target in record time.* ■ Phonetics an idealization of the articulation of a speech sound, with reference to which actual utterances can be described. ■ a person or thing against whom criticism or abuse is or may be directed.
2 historical a small, round shield or buckler.
▶ v. (**targets, targeting, targeted**) [with obj.] (usu. **be targeted**) select as an object of attention or attack: *two men were targeted by the attackers.* ■ aim or direct (something): *a significant nuclear capability targeted on the US.*
– PHRASES **on** (or **off**) **target** hitting (or missing) the thing aimed at. ■ proceeding or improving at a rate good enough (or not good enough) to achieve an objective: *the new police station is on target for a June opening.*
– DERIVATIVES **tar·get·a·ble** adj.
– ORIGIN late Middle English (sense 2 of the noun): diminutive of TARGE. The noun came to denote various round objects. The verb dates from the early 17th cent.

tar·get cell ▶ n. **1** Physiology a cell that bears receptors for a hormone, drug, or other signaling molecule, or is the focus of contact by a virus, phagocyte, nerve fiber, etc.
2 Medicine an abnormal form of red blood cell that appears as a dark ring surrounding a dark central spot, typical of certain kinds of anemia.

tar·get lan·guage ▶ n. the language into which a text, document, or speech is translated. ■ a foreign language that a person intends to learn.

tar·get of op·por·tu·ni·ty ▶ n. an object to which effort or study is diverted as soon as it becomes known. ■ a military target that is attacked while in pursuit of another.

tar·get or·gan ▶ n. Physiology & Medicine a specific organ on which a hormone, drug, or other substance acts.

Tar·gum /ˈtärˌgo͝om, -ˌgo͞om/ ▶ n. an ancient Aramaic paraphrase or interpretation of the Hebrew Bible, of a type made from about the 1st century AD when Hebrew was declining as a spoken language.
– ORIGIN from Aramaic *targūm* 'interpretation.'

Tar Heel State a nickname for the state of NORTH CAROLINA.

tar·iff /ˈtarif/ ▶ n. a tax or duty to be paid on a particular class of imports or exports. ■ a list of these taxes. ■ a table of the fixed charges made by a business, esp. in a hotel or restaurant.
▶ v. [with obj.] fix the price of (something) according to a tariff: *these services are tariffed by volume.*
– ORIGIN late 16th cent. (also denoting an arithmetical table): via French from Italian *tariffa*, based on Arabic *'arrafa* 'notify.'

Ta·rim /ˈtäˈrēm/ a river in northwestern China, in Xinjiang autonomous region. It rises as the Yarkand in the Kunlun Shan mountains and flows for over 1,250 miles (2,000 km) east through the dry Tarim Basin, petering out in the Lop Nor depression. For much of its course, the river follows no clearly defined bed and is subject to much evaporation.

ta·ri·qa /təˈrēkə/ (also **tariqat** /-kət/) ▶ n. the Sufi doctrine or path of spiritual learning. ■ a Sufi missionary.
– ORIGIN from Arabic *ṭarīka* 'manner, way, creed.'

Tar·king·ton /ˈtärkiNGtən/, Booth, (1869–1946), US writer; full name *Newton Booth Tarkington*. His novels include *The Magnificent Ambersons* (1918) and *Alice Adams* (1921). He is also known for his young adult novels such as *Penrod* (1914) and *Seventeen* (1916).

Tar·kov·sky /tärˈkôfskē/, Andrei (Arsenevich) (1932–86), Russian movie director. Featuring a poetic and impressionistic style, his movies include *Ivan's Childhood* (1962), *Solaris* (1972), and *The Sacrifice* (1986), which won the special grand prize at Cannes.

tar·la·tan /ˈtärlətn/ ▶ n. a thin, starched, open-weave muslin fabric, used for stiffening evening gowns.
– ORIGIN early 18th cent.: from French *tarlatane*, probably of Indian origin.

Tar·mac /ˈtärˌmak/ ▶ n. (usu. **tarmac**) trademark material used for surfacing roads or other outdoor areas, consisting of crushed rock mixed with tar. ■ (**the tarmac**) a runway or other area surfaced with such material.
– ORIGIN early 20th cent.: abbreviation of TARMACADAM.

tar·mac·ad·am /ˈtärməˌkadəm/ ▶ n. chiefly Brit. another term for TARMAC.
– DERIVATIVES **tar·mac·ad·amed** adj.
– ORIGIN late 19th cent.: from TAR[1] + MACADAM.

Tarn /tärn/ a river in southern France that rises in the Cévennes and flows 235 miles (380 km) southwest through deep gorges before meeting the Garonne River northwest of Toulouse.

tarn /tärn/ ▶ n. a small mountain lake.
– ORIGIN Middle English (originally northern English dialect): from Old Norse *tjǫrn*.

tar·na·tion /tärˈnāsHən/ ▶ n. & exclam. used as a euphemism for "damnation."
– ORIGIN late 18th cent.: alteration.

tar·nish /ˈtärnisH/ ▶ v. lose or cause to lose luster, esp. as a result of exposure to air or moisture: [no obj.] *silver tarnishes too easily* | [with obj.] *lemon juice would tarnish the gilded metal.* ■ make or become less valuable or respected: [with obj.] *his regime had not been tarnished by human rights abuses.*
▶ n. dullness of color; loss of brightness. ■ a film or stain formed on an exposed surface of a mineral or metal. ■ damage or harm done to something.
– DERIVATIVES **tar·nish·a·ble** adj.
– ORIGIN late Middle English (as a verb): from French *terniss-*, lengthened stem of *ternir*, from *terne* 'dark, dull.'

tar·nished plant bug ▶ n. either of two brownish mirid bugs that are pests of numerous fruits, vegetables, and other crops. ● *Lygus lineolaris* (in North America) and *Lygus rugulipennis* (in Europe).

ta·ro /ˈtarō, ˈte(ə)rō/ ▶ n. a tropical Asian plant of the arum family that has edible starchy corms and edible fleshy leaves, esp. a variety with a large central corm grown as a staple in the Pacific. Also called DASHEEN. Compare with EDDO. ● *Colocasia esculenta* var. *esculenta*, family Araceae. ■ the corm of this plant.
– ORIGIN mid 18th cent.: of Polynesian origin.

ta·rot /ˈtarō, ˈte(ə)rō, təˈrō/ ▶ n. (**the Tarot**) playing cards, traditionally a pack of 78 with five suits, used for fortune-telling and (esp. in Europe) in certain games. The suits are typically swords, cups, coins (or pentacles), batons (or wands), and a permanent suit of trump. ■ a card game played with such cards. ■ a card from such a set.
– ORIGIN late 16th cent.: from French, from Italian *tarocchi*, of unknown origin.

tarp /tärp/ ▶ n. informal a tarpaulin sheet or cover.
– ORIGIN early 20th cent.: abbreviation.

tar·pan /ˈtärˌpan/ ▶ n. a grayish wild horse that was formerly common in eastern Europe and western

Asia, exterminated in 1919. ● *Equus caballus gomelini*, family Equidae.
– ORIGIN Kyrgyz.

tar·pa·per /ˈtärˌpāpər/ ▶ **n.** a heavy paper impregnated with tar and used as a waterproofing material in building.

tar·pau·lin /tärˈpôlən, ˈtärpə-/ ▶ **n. 1** heavy-duty waterproof cloth, originally of tarred canvas. ■ a sheet or covering of this.
2 historical a sailor's tarred or oilskin hat. ■ archaic a sailor.
– ORIGIN early 17th cent.: probably from **TAR**[1] + **PALL**[1] + **-ING**[1].

Tar·pe·ia /tärˈpēə/ one of the Vestal Virgins, the daughter of a commander of the Capitol in ancient Rome. According to legend she betrayed the citadel to the Sabines in return for whatever they wore on their arms, hoping to receive their golden bracelets; however, the Sabines killed her by throwing their shields onto her.

tar pit ▶ **n. 1** a hollow in which natural tar accumulates by seepage.
2 a complicated or difficult situation or problem: *the tar pit of municipal poverty*.

tar·pon /ˈtärpən/ ▶ **n.** a large tropical marine fish of herringlike appearance. ● Two species in the family Megalopidae: *Tarpon atlanticus*, a prized Atlantic game fish, and *Megalops cyprinoides* of the Indo-Pacific.
– ORIGIN late 17th cent.: probably from Dutch *tarpoen*, perhaps from a Central American language.

Tar·quin·i·us /tärˈkwinēəs/ the name of two semilegendary Etruscan kings of ancient Rome; anglicized name *Tarquin*. ■ **Tarquinius Priscus**, reigned *c.*616–*c.*578 BC; full name *Lucius Tarquinius Priscus*. According to tradition he was murdered by the sons of the previous king. ■ **Tarquinius Superbus**, reigned *c.*534–*c.*510 BC; full name *Lucius Tarquinius Superbus*; known as **Tarquin the Proud**. According to tradition he was the son or grandson of Tarquinius Priscus. Noted for his cruelty, he was expelled from the city, and the republic was founded.

tar·ra·did·dle /ˈtarəˌdidl/ ▶ **n.** variant spelling of **TARADIDDLE**.

tar·ra·gon /ˈtarəˌgän, -gən/ ▶ **n.** a perennial plant of the daisy family, with narrow aromatic leaves that are used as a culinary herb. ● *Artemisia dracunculus*, family Compositae.
– ORIGIN mid 16th cent.: representing medieval Latin *tragonia* and *tarchon*, perhaps from an Arabic alteration of Greek *drakōn* 'dragon' (by association with *drakontion* 'green dragon').

tar·ra·gon vin·e·gar ▶ **n.** a culinary seasoning made by steeping the young shoots and leaves of tarragon in wine vinegar.

Tar·ra·sa /təˈräsə/ (also **Terrassa** /təˈräsə/) an industrial city in Catalonia, in northeastern Spain; pop. 206,245 (2008).

tar·ry[1] /ˈtärē/ ▶ **adj.** (**tarrier, tarriest**) of, like, or covered with tar: *a length of tarry rope*.
– DERIVATIVES **tar·ri·ness n.**

tar·ry[2] /ˈtarē/ ▶ **v.** (**tarries, tarrying, tarried**) [no obj.] dated stay longer than intended; delay leaving a place: *she could tarry a bit and not get home until four*.
– DERIVATIVES **tar·ri·er n.** (rare).
– ORIGIN Middle English: of unknown origin.

tar·sal /ˈtärsəl/ Anatomy & Zoology ▶ **adj.** of or relating to the tarsus: *the tarsal claws of beetles*.
▶ **n.** a bone of the tarsus.
– ORIGIN early 19th cent.: from **TARSUS** + **-AL**.

tar sand ▶ **n.** (often **tar sands**) Geology a deposit of sand impregnated with bitumen.

tar·si /ˈtärsī, -sē/ plural form of **TARSUS**.

tar·si·er /ˈtärsēər/ ▶ **n.** a small insectivorous, tree-dwelling, nocturnal primate with large eyes, a long tufted tail, and long hind limbs, native to the islands of Southeast Asia. ● Family Tarsiidae and genus *Tarsius*, suborder Prosimii: four species.
– ORIGIN late 18th cent.: from French, from *tarse* 'tarsus,' with reference to the animal's long tarsal bones.

tar·so·met·a·tar·sus /ˈtärsōˌmetəˈtärsəs/ ▶ **n.** (pl. **tarsometatarsi** /-ˈtärsī, -ˌsē/) Zoology a long bone in the lower leg of birds and some reptiles, formed by fusion of tarsal and metatarsal structures.
– DERIVATIVES **tar·so·met·a·tar·sal** /-ˈtärsəl/ **adj.**

Tar·sus /ˈtärsəs/ an ancient city in southern Turkey, now a market town. It is the birthplace of St. Paul.

tar·sus /ˈtärsəs/ ▶ **n.** (pl. **tarsi** /ˈtärsī, -sē/) **1** Anatomy a group of small bones between the main part of the hind limb and the metatarsus in terrestrial vertebrates. The seven bones of the human tarsus form the ankle and upper part of the foot. They are the talus, calcaneus, navicular, and cuboid and the three cuneiform bones. ■ Zoology the shank or tarsometatarsus of the leg of a bird or reptile. ■ Zoology the foot or fifth joint of the leg of an insect or other arthropod, typically consisting of several small segments and ending in a claw.
2 Anatomy a thin sheet of fibrous connective tissue that supports the edge of each eyelid.
– ORIGIN late Middle English: modern Latin, from Greek *tarsos* 'flat of the foot, the eyelid.'

tart[1] /tärt/ ▶ **n.** an open pastry case containing a filling.
– DERIVATIVES **tart·let** /-lit/ **n.**
– ORIGIN late Middle English (denoting a savory pie): from Old French *tarte* or medieval Latin *tarta*, of unknown origin.

tart[2] ▶ **n.** informal, derogatory a prostitute or a promiscuous woman.
▶ **v.** [with obj.] (**tart oneself up**) informal, chiefly Brit. dress or make oneself up in order to look attractive or eye-catching. ■ (**tart something up**) decorate or improve the appearance of something: *the page layouts have been tarted up with cartoons*.
– ORIGIN mid 19th cent.: probably an abbreviation of **SWEETHEART**.

tart[3] ▶ **adj.** sharp or acid in taste: *a tart apple*. ■ (of a remark or tone of voice) cutting, bitter, or sarcastic: *I bit back a tart reply*.
– DERIVATIVES **tart·ly adv.**, **tart·ness n.**
– ORIGIN Old English *teart* 'harsh, severe,' of unknown origin.

tar·tan[1] /ˈtärtn/ ▶ **n.** a woolen cloth woven in one of several patterns of plaid, esp. of a design associated with a particular Scottish clan.
▶ **adj.** used allusively in reference to Scotland or the Scots.
– ORIGIN late 15th cent. (originally Scots): perhaps from Old French *tertaine*, denoting a kind of cloth; compare with *tartarin*, a rich fabric formerly imported from the east through Tartary.

tartan[1]

tar·tan[2] ▶ **n.** historical a lateen-rigged, single-masted ship used in the Mediterranean.
– ORIGIN early 17th cent.: from French *tartane*, from Italian *tartana*, perhaps from Arabic *ṭarīda*.

Tar·tar /ˈtärtər/ ▶ **n.** historical a member of the combined forces of central Asian peoples, including Mongols and Turks, who under the leadership of Genghis Khan conquered much of Asia and eastern Europe in the early 13th century, and under Tamerlane (14th century) established an empire with its capital at Samarkand. See also **TATAR**.
■ (**tartar**) a harsh, fierce, or intractable person: *"Merciful God! but you're a tartar, miss!" said the sheriff, ruefully*.
– DERIVATIVES **Tar·tar·i·an** /tärˈte(ə)rēən/ **adj.**
– ORIGIN from Old French *Tartare* or medieval Latin *Tartarus*, alteration (influenced by **TARTARUS**) of **TATAR**.

tar·tar /ˈtärtər/ ▶ **n.** a hard calcified deposit that forms on the teeth and contributes to their decay. ■ a deposit of impure potassium hydrogen tartrate formed during the fermentation of wine. See also **CREAM OF TARTAR**.
– DERIVATIVES **tar·tar·ic** /tärˈtarik/ **adj.**
– ORIGIN late Middle English: via medieval Latin from medieval Greek *tartaron*, of unknown origin.

tar·tare /tärˈtär, ˈtärtər/ ▶ **adj.** [postpositive] (of fish) served raw, typically seasoned and shaped into small cakes. See also **STEAK TARTARE**.
– ORIGIN French, literally 'Tartar.'

tar·tar e·met·ic ▶ **n.** a toxic compound used in treating protozoal disease in animals, as a mordant in dyeing, and formerly as an emetic. ● Alternative name: **potassium antimony tartrate**; chem. formula: $K(SbO)C_4H_4O_6$.

tar·tar·ic ac·id ▶ **n.** Chemistry a crystalline organic acid that is present esp. in unripe grapes and is used in baking powders and as a food additive. ● A dibasic acid; chem. formula: $COOH(CHOH)_2COOH$.
– ORIGIN late 18th cent.: *tartaric* from obsolete French *tartarique*, from medieval Latin *tartarum* (see **TARTAR**).

tar·tar sauce (also **tartare sauce**) ▶ **n.** a cold sauce, typically eaten with fish, consisting of mayonnaise mixed with chopped pickles, capers, etc.

Tar·ta·rus /ˈtärtərəs/ Greek Mythology **1** a primeval god, offspring of Chaos.
2 a part of the underworld where the wicked suffered punishment for their misdeeds, esp. those such as Ixion and Tantalus who had committed some outrage against the gods.
– DERIVATIVES **Tar·tar·e·an** /tärˈte(ə)rēən/ **adj.**

Tar·ta·ry /ˈtärtərē/ a historical region of Asia and eastern Europe, esp. the high plateau of central Asia and its northwestern slopes, which formed part of the Tartar empire in the Middle Ages.

tarte Ta·tin /ˈtärt taˈtaN/ ▶ **n.** a type of upside-down apple tart consisting of pastry baked over slices of fruit arranged in caramelized sugar, served fruit side up after cooking.
– ORIGIN French, from *tarte* 'tart' + *Tatin*, the surname of the sisters said to have created the dish.

tar·trate /ˈtärtrāt/ ▶ **n.** Chemistry a salt or ester of tartaric acid.
– ORIGIN late 18th cent.: from French, from *tartre* 'tartar' + **-ATE**[1].

tar·tra·zine /ˈtärtrəˌzēn, -zin/ ▶ **n.** Chemistry a brilliant yellow synthetic dye derived from tartaric acid and used to color food, drugs, and cosmetics.
– ORIGIN late 19th cent.: from French *tartre* 'tartar' + **AZO-** + **-INE**[4].

Tar·tuffe /tärˈto͝of/ ▶ **n.** literary or humorous a religious hypocrite, or a hypocritical pretender to excellence of any kind. [from the name of the principal character (a religious hypocrite) in Molière's *Tartuffe* (1664).]
– DERIVATIVES **Tar·tuf·fer·ie** /-ˈto͝ofərē/ (also **Tartuffery**) **n.**

tar·tu·fo /tärˈto͞ofō/ ▶ **n.** (pl. **tartufos**) **1** an edible fungus, esp. the white truffle.
2 an Italian dessert, containing chocolate, of a creamy mousselike consistency.
– ORIGIN Italian, literally 'truffle.'

tart·y /ˈtärtē/ ▶ **adj.** (**tartier, tartiest**) informal (of a woman) dressed in a sexually provocative manner that is considered to be in bad taste. ■ (of clothes) contributing to a sexually provocative appearance.
– DERIVATIVES **tart·i·ly** /ˈtärtəlē/ **adv.**, **tart·i·ness n.**

tar·weed /ˈtärˌwēd/ ▶ **n.** any of a number of American plants of the daisy family with sticky leaves and heavy scent. ● *Madia*, *Grindelia*, *Hemizonia*, and related genera, family Compositae.

Tar·zan /ˈtärzan, -zən/ a fictitious character created by Edgar Rice Burroughs. Tarzan (Lord Greystoke by birth) is orphaned in West Africa in his infancy and reared by apes in the jungle. ■ (as noun **a Tarzan**) a man of great agility and powerful physique.

TAS ▶ **abbr.** ■ telephone answering system. ■ true airspeed.

Tas. ▶ **abbr.** chiefly Austral. Tasmania.

Ta·sa·day /ˈtasəˌdā, təˈsädī/ ▶ **n.** (pl. **same** or **Tasadays**) a member of a small group of people living on the Philippine island of Mindanao, formerly said to represent a long-isolated Stone Age people discovered only in the 1960s.
▶ **adj.** of or relating to this people.
– ORIGIN apparently from Tasaday *tau* 'person' + *sa* (expressing location) + *dáya* 'inland.'

tas·ca /ˈtäskə, ˈtas-/ ▶ **n.** (in Spain and Portugal) a tavern or bar, esp. one serving food.
– ORIGIN Spanish and Portuguese.

Ta·ser /ˈtāzər/ ▶ **n.** trademark a weapon firing barbs attached by wires to batteries, causing temporary paralysis.
▶ **v.** (**taser** or **tase**) [with obj.] fire a Taser at (someone) in order to incapacitate them temporarily.
– ORIGIN 1970s: from the initial letters of *Tom Swift's electric rifle* (a fictitious weapon), on the pattern of *laser*.

Ta·shi La·ma /ˈtäsнē ˈlämə/ ▶ **n.** another name for **PANCHEN LAMA**.

Tash·kent /ˌtasнˈkent, ˌtäsн-/ the capital of Uzbekistan, in the northeast part of the country, in the western foothills of the Tien Shan mountains: pop. 2,192,700 (est. 2007). One of the oldest cities in central Asia, it was an important center on the trade route between Europe and the Orient. It became part of the Mongol empire in the 13th century, was captured by the Russians in 1865, and replaced Samarkand as capital of Uzbekistan in 1930.

task /task/ ▶ **n.** a piece of work to be done or undertaken.
▶ **v.** [with obj.] (usu. **be tasked**) assign such a piece of work to: *NATO troops are tasked with separating the warring parties*. ■ make great demands on (someone's resources or abilities): *it tasked his diplomatic skill to effect his departure in safety*.
– PHRASES **take someone to task** reprimand or criticize someone severely for a fault or mistake.
– ORIGIN Middle English: from an Old Northern French variant of Old French *tasche*, from medieval Latin *tasca*, alteration of *taxa*, from Latin *taxare* 'censure, charge' (see **TAX**). An early sense of the verb was 'impose a tax on.'

t

task force ▶ **n.** an armed force organized for a special operation. ■ a unit specially organized for a task: *aides say his plans include a task force on hate crimes.*

task·mas·ter /ˈtask,mastər/ ▶ **n.** a person who imposes a harsh or onerous workload on someone.

Tas·man /ˈtazmən/, Abel (Janszoon) (1603–c.1659), Dutch navigator. Sent in 1642 by Anthony van Diemen (1593–1645), the governor general of the Dutch East Indies, to explore Australian waters, he reached Tasmania (which he named Van Diemen's Land) and New Zealand. He arrived at Tonga and Fiji in 1643.

Tas·ma·ni·a /tazˈmānēə, -ˈmānyə/ a state in Australia that consists of the mountainous island of Tasmania itself and several smaller islands; separated from the southeast coast of mainland Australia by the Bass Strait; pop. 497,529 (2008); capital, Hobart. It was known as Van Diemen's Land until 1855.
– DERIVATIVES **Tas·ma·ni·an adj. & n.**

Tas·ma·ni·an dev·il /tazˈmānēən, -ˈmānyən/ ▶ **n.** a heavily built marsupial with a large head, powerful jaws, and mainly black fur, found only in Tasmania. It is slow-moving and aggressive, feeding mainly on carrion. ● *Sarcophilus harrisii*, family Dasyuridae.

Tas·ma·ni·an wolf (also **Tasmanian tiger**) ▶ **n.** another term for **THYLACINE**.

Tas·man Sea /ˈtazmən/ an arm of the South Pacific Ocean that lies between Australia and New Zealand.

Tass /täs, tas/ the official news agency of the former Soviet Union, renamed ITAR-Tass in 1992.
– ORIGIN Russian acronym, from *Telegrafnoe agentstvo Sovetskogo Soyuza* 'Telegraphic Agency of the Soviet Union.'

tas·sel /ˈtasəl/ ▶ **n.** a tuft of loosely hanging threads, cords, or other material knotted at one end and attached for decoration to home furnishings, clothing, or other items. ■ the tufted head of some plants, esp. a flower head with prominent stamens at the top of a cornstalk.
▶ **v.** (**tassels, tasseling, tasseled**; Brit. **tassels, tasselling, tasselled**) **1** [with obj.] (usu. as adj. **tasseled**) provide with a tassel or tassels: *a tasseled tablecloth.*
2 [no obj.] (of corn or other plants) form tassels.
– ORIGIN Middle English (also denoting a clasp for a cloak): from Old French *tassel* 'clasp,' of unknown origin.

tas·so /ˈtäsō/ ▶ **n.** spicy cured pork cut into strips.
– ORIGIN perhaps from Spanish *tasajo* 'slice of dried meat.'

taste /tāst/ ▶ **n. 1** the sensation of flavor perceived in the mouth and throat on contact with a substance: *the wine had a fruity taste.* ■ the faculty of perceiving this quality: *birds do not have a highly developed sense of taste.* ■ a small portion of food or drink taken as a sample: *try a taste of Gorgonzola.* ■ a brief experience of something, conveying its basic character: *it was his first taste of serious action.*
2 a person's liking for particular flavors: *this pudding is too sweet for my taste.* ■ a person's tendency to like and dislike certain things: *he found the aggressive competitiveness of the profession was not to his taste.* ■ (**taste for**) a liking for or interest in (something): *have you lost your taste for fancy restaurants?* ■ the ability to discern what is of good quality or of a high aesthetic standard: *she has awful taste in literature.* ■ conformity or failure to conform with generally held views concerning what is offensive or acceptable: *that's a joke in very bad taste.*
▶ **v.** [with obj.] perceive or experience the flavor of: *she had never tasted ice cream before.* ■ [no obj.] have a specified flavor: [with complement] *the spinach tastes delicious.* ■ sample or test the flavor of (food or drink) by taking it into the mouth: *the waiter poured some wine for him to taste.* ■ eat or drink a small portion of. ■ have experience of: *the team has not yet tasted victory at home.*
– PHRASES **a bad** (or **bitter**) **taste in someone's mouth** informal a feeling of distress or disgust following an experience: *this incident has left a bad taste in all our mouths.* **taste blood** see **BLOOD**. **to taste** in the amount needed to give a flavor pleasing to someone eating a dish: *add salt and pepper to taste.*
– ORIGIN Middle English (also in the sense 'touch'): from Old French *tast* (noun), *taster* (verb) 'touch, try, taste,' perhaps based on a blend of Latin *tangere* 'to touch' and *gustare* 'to taste.'

taste bud ▶ **n.** (usu. **taste buds**) any of the clusters of bulbous nerve endings on the tongue and in the lining of the mouth that provide the sense of taste.

taste·ful /ˈtāstfəl/ ▶ **adj.** showing good aesthetic judgment or appropriate behavior: *Sarah's modest, tasteful apartment.*
– DERIVATIVES **taste·ful·ly adv.**, **taste·ful·ness n.**

taste·less /ˈtāstlis/ ▶ **adj. 1** lacking flavor.
2 considered to be lacking in aesthetic judgment or to offend against what is regarded as appropriate behavior: *a tasteless joke.*
– DERIVATIVES **taste·less·ly adv.**, **taste·less·ness n.**

taste·mak·er /ˈtāst,mākər/ ▶ **n.** a person who decides or influences what is or will become fashionable.

tast·er /ˈtāstər/ ▶ **n. 1** a person employed to test food or drink for quality by tasting it: *experienced tasters can tell which plantation coffee beans are from.* ■ a small cup used by a person tasting wine in such a way. ■ an instrument for extracting a small sample from within a cheese.
2 Brit. a small quantity or brief experience of something, intended as a sample; a taste: *the song is a taster for the band's new LP.*
– ORIGIN late Middle English: in early use from Anglo-Norman French *tastour*, from Old French *taster* 'to taste'; later from **TASTE** + **-ER**[1].

tas·te·vin /,tastəˈvan/ ▶ **n.** (pl. **same**) a small, shallow silver cup for tasting wines, of a type used in France.
– ORIGIN French, literally 'wine taster.'

tast·ing /ˈtāstiNG/ ▶ **n.** a gathering at which people sample, compare, and evaluate different wines, or other drinks or food: *we did a tasting of over forty of the cheaper champagnes.* See also **WINE TASTING**.

tast·ing men·u ▶ **n.** a type of meal offered in certain restaurants, consisting of sample portions of many different dishes served in several courses for a set price.

tast·y /ˈtāstē/ ▶ **adj.** (**tastier, tastiest**) (of food) having a pleasant, distinct flavor: *a tasty snack.* ■ informal, chiefly Brit. attractive; very appealing: *some tasty acoustic piano licks.*
– DERIVATIVES **tast·i·ly** /-stilē/ **adv.**, **tast·i·ness n.**

tat[1] /tat/ ▶ **v.** (**tats, tatting, tatted**) [with obj.] make (a decorative mat or edging) by tying knots in thread and using a small shuttle to form lace.
– ORIGIN late 19th cent.: back-formation from **TATTING**.

tat[2] ▶ **n.** (in phrase **tit for tat**) see **TIT**[3].

tat[3] ▶ **n.** Brit. informal tasteless or shoddy clothes, jewelry, or ornaments.
– ORIGIN mid 19th cent. (in the senses 'rag' and 'person in rags'): probably a back-formation from **TATTY**.

tat[4] ▶ **n.** informal a tattoo.

ta-ta /täˈtä/ ▶ **exclam.** informal, chiefly Brit. goodbye.
– ORIGIN early 19th cent.: of unknown origin; compare with earlier *da-da*.

ta·ta·ki /təˈtäki/ ▶ **n.** (in Japanese cooking) a dish consisting of meat or fish steak, served either raw or lightly seared.
– ORIGIN Japanese, literally 'pounded, minced.'

ta·ta·mi /təˈtämē/ (also **tatami mat**) ▶ **n.** (pl. **same** or **tatamis**) a rush-covered straw mat forming a traditional Japanese floor covering.
– ORIGIN Japanese.

Ta·tar /ˈtätər/ ▶ **n. 1** a member of a Turkic people living in Tatarstan and various other parts of Russia and Ukraine. They are the descendants of the Tartars who ruled central Asia in the 14th century.
2 the Turkic language of this people.
▶ **adj.** of or relating to this people or their language.
– ORIGIN the Turkic name of a Tartar tribe.

Ta·tar·stan /ˈtätər,stan, -,stän/ an autonomous republic in western Russia, in the valley of the Volga River; pop. 3,755,800 (est. 2009); capital, Kazan.

Tate /tāt/, Nahum (1652–1715), Irish playwright and poet, resident in London from the 1670s. He was appointed poet laureate in 1692.

ta·ter /ˈtātər/ ▶ **n.** informal a potato.
– ORIGIN mid 18th cent.: alteration.

Ta·tha·ga·ta /təˈtägətə/ ▶ **n.** an honorific title of a buddha.
– ORIGIN from Pali *Tathāgata*, from *tathā* 'in that manner' + *gata* 'gone.'

ta·tha·ta /ˈtətə,tä/ ▶ **n.** Buddhism the ultimate inexpressible nature of all things. Compare with **SUNYATA**.
– ORIGIN Pali, literally 'true state of things.'

Ta·ti /täˈtē/, Jacques (1908–82), French movie director and actor; born *Jacques Tatischeff*. He introduced the comically inept character Monsieur Hulot in *Monsieur Hulot's Holiday* (1953), seen again in movies that included *Mon oncle* (1958).

Ta·tra Moun·tains /ˈtätrə/ (also **the Tatras**) a range of mountains in eastern Europe on the Polish–Slovak border, the highest range in the Carpathian Mountains, that rise to 8,710 feet (2,655 m) at Mount Gerlachovsky.

tat·soi /tatˈsoi/ ▶ **n.** a kind of Chinese cabbage with glossy dark green leaves. ● *Brassica rapa* var. *rosularis*.
– ORIGIN Chinese *daat-choi*, from *daat-* 'sink, fall flat' + *choi* 'vegetable.'

tat·tered /ˈtatərd/ ▶ **adj.** old and torn; in poor condition: *an old woman in tattered clothes* | figurative *the tattered remnants of his dreams.*
– ORIGIN Middle English (in the sense 'dressed in decoratively slashed or jagged clothing'): apparently originally from the noun *tatter* 'scrap of cloth' + **-ED**[2]; later treated as a past participle.

tat·ters /ˈtatərz/ ▶ **plural n.** irregularly torn pieces of cloth, paper, or other material.
– PHRASES **in tatters** informal torn in many places; in shreds: *wallpaper hung in tatters.* ■ destroyed; ruined: *the ceasefire was in tatters within hours.*
– ORIGIN late Middle English (also in the singular meaning 'scrap of cloth'): from Old Norse *tǫtrar* 'rags.'

tat·ter·sall /ˈtatər,sôl/ (also **tattersall check**) ▶ **n.** a woolen fabric with a pattern of colored checks and intersecting lines, resembling a tartan.
– ORIGIN late 19th cent.: named after *Tattersalls*, an English firm of horse auctioneers (named after the horseman Richard *Tattersall* (1724–95)), by association with the traditional design of horse blankets.

tat·ting /ˈtatiNG/ ▶ **n.** a kind of knotted lace made by hand with a small shuttle, used chiefly for trimming. ■ the process of making such lace.
– ORIGIN mid 19th cent.: of unknown origin.

tat·tle /ˈtatl/ ▶ **v.** [no obj.] report another's wrongdoing: *he never tattled or told tales* | *I would tattle on her whenever I had hard evidence.* ■ gossip idly.
▶ **n.** gossip; idle talk.
– ORIGIN late 15th cent. (in the sense 'falter, stammer,' also 'make meaningless sounds,' referring to a small child): from Middle Flemish *tatelen, tateren*, of imitative origin.

tat·tler /ˈtatl-ər, ˈtatlər/ ▶ **n. 1** a person who tattles.
2 a migratory sandpiper with mainly gray plumage, breeding in northwestern Canada or eastern Siberia. ● Genus *Heteroscelus*, family Scolopacidae: two species, in particular the **wandering tattler** (*H. incanus*) of Canada, noted for its loud cry.

tat·tle·tale /ˈtatl,tāl/ ▶ **n.** a person, esp. a child, who reveals secrets or informs on others; a telltale.

tat·too[1] /taˈto͞o/ ▶ **n.** (pl. **tattoos**) an evening drum or bugle signal recalling soldiers to their quarters. ■ an entertainment consisting of music, marching, and the performance of displays and exercises by military personnel. ■ a rhythmic tapping or drumming.
– ORIGIN mid 17th cent. (originally as *tap-too*): from Dutch *taptoe!*, literally 'close the tap (of the cask)!'

tat·too[2] ▶ **v.** (**tattoos, tattoing, tattooed** /-ˈto͞od/) [with obj.] mark (a person or a part of the body) with an indelible design by inserting pigment into punctures in the skin: *his cheek was tattooed with a winged fist.* ■ make (a design) in such a way: *he has a heart tattooed on his left hand.*
▶ **n.** (pl. **tattoos**) a design made in such a way.
– DERIVATIVES **tat·too·er n.**, **tat·too·ist** /taˈto͞oist/ **n.**
– ORIGIN mid 18th cent.: from Tahitian, Tongan, and Samoan *ta-tau* or Marquesan *ta-tu*.

tat·ty /ˈtatē/ ▶ **adj.** (**tattier, tattiest**) informal worn and shabby; in poor condition: *the room was furnished in slightly tatty upholstered furniture.* ■ of poor quality: *his gap-toothed smile and tatty haircut.*
– DERIVATIVES **tat·ti·ly** /ˈtatəlē/ **adv.**, **tat·ti·ness n.**
– ORIGIN early 16th cent. (originally Scots, in the sense 'tangled, matted, shaggy'): apparently ultimately related to Old English *tættec* 'rag,' of Germanic origin; compare with **TATTERED**.

Ta·tum /ˈtätəm/, Art (1910–56), US jazz pianist; full name *Arthur Tatum, Jr.* Almost completely blind, he was known for his solo and trio work in the 1930s.

tau /tou, tô/ ▶ **n.** the nineteenth letter of the Greek alphabet (Τ, τ), transliterated as 't.' ■ (**Tau**) [followed by Latin genitive] Astronomy the nineteenth star in a constellation: *Tau Ceti.* ■ (in full **tau particle** or **tau lepton**) Physics an unstable subatomic particle of the lepton class, with a charge of −1 and a mass roughly 3,500 times that of the electron.

tau cross ▶ **n.** a T-shaped cross.

taught /tôt/ past and past participle of **TEACH**.

tau neu·tri·no ▶ **n.** Physics a neutrino of the type associated with the tau particle.

taunt /tônt/ ▶ **n.** a remark made in order to anger, wound, or provoke someone.
▶ **v.** [with obj.] provoke or challenge (someone) with insulting remarks: *students began taunting her about her weight.* ■ reproach (someone) with something in a contemptuous way: *she had taunted him with going to another man.*
– DERIVATIVES **taunt·er n.**, **taunt·ing·ly adv.**
– ORIGIN early 16th cent.: from French *tant pour tant* 'like for like, tit for tat,' from *tant* 'so much,' from

t

Latin *tantum*, neuter of *tantus*. An early use of the verb was 'exchange banter.'

Taun·ton /'tôntn/ an industrial city in southeastern Massachusetts; pop. 55,702 (est. 2008).

tau par·ti·cle ▶ **n.** see TAU.

taupe /tōp/ ▶ **n.** gray with a tinge of brown: [as modifier] *a taupe overcoat.*
– ORIGIN early 20th cent.: from French, literally 'mole, moleskin,' from Latin *talpa.*

Tau·po, Lake /'toupō/ the largest lake of New Zealand, in the center of North Island. The town of Taupo is situated on its northern shore. Maori name **Taupomoana**.

tau·rine[1] /'tô,rēn/ ▶ **n.** Biochemistry a sulfur-containing amino acid important in the metabolism of fats. ● Chem. formula: $NH_2CH_2CH_2SO_3H$.
– ORIGIN mid 19th cent.: from Greek *tauros* 'bull' (because it was originally obtained from ox bile) + -INE[4].

tau·rine[2] /'tô,rīn/ ▶ **adj.** of or like a bull. ■ of or relating to bullfighting: *taurine skill.*
– ORIGIN early 17th cent.: from Latin *taurinus*, from *taurus* 'bull.'

tau·ro·cho·lic ac·id /,tôrə'kōlik, -'kälik/ ▶ **n.** Biochemistry an acid formed by the combination of taurine with cholic acid, occurring in bile.
– DERIVATIVES **tau·ro·cho·late** /-'kōlāt/ **n.**
– ORIGIN mid 19th cent.: from Greek *tauros* 'bull' + *kholē* 'bile' + -IC.

tau·rom·a·chy /tô'räməkē/ ▶ **n.** (pl. **tauromachies**) rare bullfighting. ■ a bullfight.
– DERIVATIVES **tau·ro·ma·chi·an** /,tôrə'mākēən/ **adj.**, **tau·ro·mach·ic** /,tôrə'makik/ **adj.**
– ORIGIN mid 19th cent.: from Greek *tauromakhia*, from *tauros* 'bull' + *makhē* 'battle.'

Tau·rus /'tôrəs/ **1** Astronomy a constellation (the Bull), said to represent a bull with brazen feet that was tamed by Jason. Its many bright stars include Aldebaran (the bull's eye), and it contains the Crab Nebula and the star clusters of the Hyades and the Pleiades. ■ (as genitive **Tauri** /'tôrē, 'tôrī/) used with a preceding letter or numeral to designate a star in this constellation: *the star Beta Tauri.*
2 Astrology the second sign of the zodiac, which the sun enters on about April 21. ■ (**a Taurus**) a person born when the sun is in this sign.
– DERIVATIVES **Tau·re·an** /'tôrēən, tô'rēən/ **n. & adj.** (sense 2).
– ORIGIN Latin.

Tau·rus Moun·tains a range of mountains in southern Turkey, parallel to the Mediterranean coast. Rising to 12,250 feet (3,734 m) at Mount Aladaë, the range forms the southern edge of the Anatolian plateau.

taut /tôt/ ▶ **adj.** **1** stretched or pulled tight; not slack: *the fabric stays taut without adhesive.* ■ (esp. of muscles or nerves) tense; not relaxed.
2 (of writing, music, etc.) concise and controlled: *a taut text of only a hundred and twenty pages.*
3 (of a ship) having a disciplined and efficient crew.
– DERIVATIVES **taut·en** /'tôtn/ **v.**, **taut·ly adv.**, **taut·ness n.**
– ORIGIN Middle English *tought* 'distended,' perhaps originally a variant of TOUGH.

tauto- ▶ **comb. form** same: *tautology.*
– ORIGIN from Greek *tauto*, contraction of *to auto* 'the same.'

tau·tog /tô'tôg, tô'täg/ ▶ **n.** a grayish-olive edible wrasse (fish) that occurs off the Atlantic coast of North America. ● *Tautoga onitis*, family Labridae.
– ORIGIN mid 17th cent.: from Narragansett *tautauog*, plural of *taut.*

tau·tol·o·gy /tô'täləjē/ ▶ **n.** (pl. **tautologies**) the saying of the same thing twice in different words, generally considered to be a fault of style (e.g., *they arrived one after the other in succession*). ■ a phrase or expression in which the same thing is said twice in different words. ■ Logic a statement that is true by necessity or by virtue of its logical form.
– DERIVATIVES **tau·to·log·i·cal** /,tôtl'äjikəl/ **adj.**, **tau·to·log·i·cal·ly** /,tôtl'äjik(ə)lē/ **adv.**, **tau·tol·o·gist** /-jist/ **n.**, **tau·tol·o·gize** /-,jīz/ **v.**, **tau·tol·o·gous** /-gəs/ **adj.**
– ORIGIN mid 16th cent.: via late Latin from Greek, from *tautologos* 'repeating what has been said,' from *tauto-* 'same' + *-logos* (see -LOGY).

tau·to·mer /'tôtəmər/ ▶ **n.** Chemistry each of two or more isomers of a compound that exist together in equilibrium, and are readily interchanged by migration of an atom or group within the molecule.
– DERIVATIVES **tau·to·mer·ic** /,tôtə'merik/ **adj.**, **tau·tom·er·ism** /tô'tämə,rizəm/ **n.**
– ORIGIN early 20th cent.: blend of TAUTO- 'same' and ISOMER.

tau·to·nym /'tôtə,nim/ ▶ **n.** Botany & Zoology a scientific name in which the same word is used for both genus and species, for example *Vulpes vulpes* (the red fox). ■ Linguistics a word that designates different objects or concepts in different dialects (e.g., *corn* is *wheat* in England and *oats* in Scotland).
– DERIVATIVES **tau·ton·y·my** /tô'tänəmē/ **n.**

Ta·vel /tä'vel/ ▶ **n.** a fine rosé wine produced at Tavel in the south of France.

tav·ern /'tavərn/ ▶ **n.** an establishment for the sale of beer and other drinks to be consumed on the premises, sometimes also serving food.
– ORIGIN Middle English: from Old French *taverne*, from Latin *taberna* 'hut, tavern.' Compare with TABERNACLE.

ta·ver·na /tə'vərnə/ ▶ **n.** a small Greek restaurant or cafe.
– ORIGIN modern Greek, from Latin *taberna* (see TAVERN).

taw[1] /tô/ ▶ **v.** [with obj.] make (hide) into leather without the use of tannin, esp. by soaking it in a solution of alum and salt.
– DERIVATIVES **taw·er n.**
– ORIGIN Old English *tawian* 'prepare raw material for use or further processing,' of Germanic origin; related to TOOL.

taw[2] ▶ **n.** a large marble. ■ a game of marbles. ■ a line from which players throw marbles.
– ORIGIN early 18th cent.: of unknown origin.

taw·dry /'tôdrē/ ▶ **adj.** (**tawdrier**, **tawdriest**) showy but cheap and of poor quality: *tawdry jewelry.* ■ sordid or unpleasant: *the tawdry business of politics.*
▶ **n.** archaic cheap and gaudy finery.
– DERIVATIVES **taw·dri·ly** /-drəlē/ **adv.**, **taw·dri·ness n.**
– ORIGIN early 17th cent.: short for *tawdry lace*, a fine silk lace or ribbon worn as a necklace in the 16th–17th centuries, contraction of *St. Audrey's lace*: *Audrey* was a later form of *Etheldrida* (died 679), patron saint of Ely, England, where tawdry laces, along with cheap imitations and other cheap finery, were traditionally sold at a fair.

taw·ny /'tônē/ ▶ **adj.** (**tawnier**, **tawniest**) of an orange-brown or yellowish-brown color: *tawny eyes.*
▶ **n.** an orange-brown or yellowish-brown color: *pine needles turning from tawny to amber.*
– DERIVATIVES **taw·ni·ness n.**
– ORIGIN Middle English: from Old French *tane*, from *tan* 'tanbark'; related to TAN[1].

taw·ny owl ▶ **n.** a common Eurasian owl with either reddish-brown or gray plumage and a quavering hoot. ● *Strix aluco*, family Strigidae.

taw·ny port ▶ **n.** a port wine made from a blend of several vintages matured in wood.

tawse /tôz/ (also **taws**) ▶ **n.** Scottish a thong with a slit end, formerly used in schools for punishing children.
– ORIGIN early 16th cent. (denoting a whip for driving a spinning top): apparently the plural of obsolete *taw* 'tawed leather,' from TAW[1].

tax /taks/ ▶ **n.** **1** a compulsory contribution to state revenue, levied by the government on workers' income and business profits or added to the cost of some goods, services, and transactions.
2 [in sing.] a strain or heavy demand: *a heavy tax on the reader's attention.*
▶ **v.** [with obj.] **1** impose a tax on (someone or something): *hardware and software is taxed at 7.5 percent.*
2 make heavy demands on (someone's powers or resources): *she knew that the ordeal to come would tax all her strength.*
3 confront (someone) with a fault or wrongdoing: *why are you taxing me with these preposterous allegations?*
4 Law examine and assess (the costs of a case).
– DERIVATIVES **tax·a·ble adj.**, **tax·er n.**
– ORIGIN Middle English (also in the sense 'estimate or determine the amount of a penalty or damages,' surviving sense 4 of the verb): from Old French *taxer*, from Latin *taxare* 'to censure, charge, compute,' perhaps from Greek *tassein* 'fix.'

tax·a /'taksə/ plural form of TAXON.

tax al·low·ance ▶ **n.** a sum to be deducted from gross income in the calculation of taxable income.

tax-and-spend ▶ **n.** a policy, usually associated with the political left, of increasing taxes in order to fund an increase in government spending: [as modifier] *they remain committed to their tax-and-spend philosophy.*
– DERIVATIVES **tax-and-spend·er n.**

tax·a·tion /tak'sāSHən/ ▶ **n.** the levying of tax. ■ money paid as tax.
– ORIGIN Middle English (in the sense 'the assessment of a penalty or damages'; compare with TAX): via Old French from Latin *taxatio(n-)*, from *taxare* 'to censure, charge.'

tax a·void·ance ▶ **n.** the arrangement of one's financial affairs to minimize tax liability within the law. Compare with TAX EVASION.

tax brack·et ▶ **n.** Economics a range of incomes taxed at a given rate.

tax break ▶ **n.** informal a tax concession or advantage allowed by a government.

tax cred·it ▶ **n.** an amount of money that can be offset against a tax liability.

tax-de·duct·i·ble ▶ **adj.** able to be deducted from taxable income when calculating income tax due.

tax e·va·sion ▶ **n.** the illegal nonpayment or underpayment of tax. Compare with TAX AVOIDANCE.

tax ex·ile ▶ **n.** a person with a high income or considerable wealth who chooses to live in a country or area with low tax rates.

tax-free ▶ **adj. & adv.** (of goods, income, etc.) exempt from tax: [as adj.] *a tax-free lump sum* | [as adv.] *your return is paid to you tax-free.*

tax ha·ven ▶ **n.** a country or independent area where taxes are levied at a low rate.

tax·i /'taksē/ ▶ **n.** (pl. **taxis**) short for TAXICAB. ■ a boat or other means of transportation used to convey passengers in return for payment of a fare.
▶ **v.** (**taxis, taxiing, taxied**) [no obj.] **1** (of an aircraft) move slowly along the ground before takeoff or after landing: *the plane taxis up to a waiting limousine.* ■ [with obj.] (of a pilot) cause (an aircraft) to move in such a way: *he taxied it to the very end of the airstrip.*
2 take a taxi as a means of transport: *I would taxi home and sleep till eight.*
– ORIGIN early 20th cent.: abbreviation of *taxicab* or *taximeter cab* (see TAXIMETER).

tax·i·cab /'taksē,kab/ ▶ **n.** a car licensed to transport passengers in return for payment of a fare, usually fitted with a taximeter.
– ORIGIN early 20th cent.: shortened form of *taximeter cab.*

tax·i danc·er ▶ **n.** a dancing partner available for a fee.

tax·i·der·mist /'taksə,dərmist/ ▶ **n.** a person who practices taxidermy.

tax·i·der·my /'taksə,dərmē/ ▶ **n.** the art of preparing, stuffing, and mounting the skins of animals with lifelike effect.
– DERIVATIVES **tax·i·der·mal** /,taksə'dərməl/ **adj.**, **tax·i·der·mic** /,taksə'dərmik/ **adj.**, **tax·i·der·mi·cal·ly** /,taksə'dərmik(ə)lē/ **adv.**
– ORIGIN early 19th cent.: from Greek *taxis* 'arrangement' + *derma* 'skin.'

tax·i·me·ter /'taksē,mētər/ ▶ **n.** a device used in taxicabs that automatically records the distance traveled and the fare payable.
– ORIGIN late 19th cent.: from French *taximètre*, from *taxe* 'tariff,' from the verb *taxer* 'to tax' + *-mètre* '(instrument) measuring.'

tax·ing /'taksiNG/ ▶ **adj.** physically or mentally demanding: *they find the work too taxing.*

tax·is /'taksis/ ▶ **n.** (pl. **taxes** /'tak,sēz/) **1** Surgery the restoration of displaced bones or organs by manual pressure alone.
2 Biology a motion or orientation of a cell, organism, or part in response to an external stimulus. Compare with KINESIS.
3 Linguistics the systematic arrangement of linguistic units (phonemes, morphemes, words, phrases, or clauses) in linear sequence.
– ORIGIN mid 18th cent. (sense 1): from Greek, literally 'arrangement,' from *tassein* 'arrange.' Sense 2 dates from the late 19th cent.

tax·i squad ▶ **n.** Football a group of players who take part in practices and may be called on as reserves for the team.

tax·i stand (Brit. **taxi rank**) ▶ **n.** a place where taxicabs park while waiting to be engaged.

tax·i·way /'taksē,wā/ ▶ **n.** a route along which an aircraft can taxi when moving to or from a runway.

tax loss ▶ **n.** Economics a loss that can be offset against taxable profit earned elsewhere or in a different period.

tax·man /'taks,man/ ▶ **n.** (pl. **taxmen**) informal, chiefly Brit. a collector of taxes. ■ (**the taxman**) the government department that collects tax: *he denies conspiracy to cheat the taxman.*

Tax·ol /'taksôl, -säl/ (also **taxol**) ▶ **n.** Medicine, trademark a compound, originally obtained from the bark of the Pacific yew tree, that has been found to inhibit the growth of certain cancers.
– ORIGIN 1970s: from Latin *taxus* 'yew' + -OL.

tax·on /'taksän/ ▶ **n.** (pl. **taxa** /'taksə/) Biology a taxonomic group of any rank, such as a species, family, or class.

– ORIGIN 1920s: back-formation from TAXONOMY.

tax·on·o·my /tak'sänəmē/ ▶ n. chiefly Biology the branch of science concerned with classification, esp. of organisms; systematics. ■ the classification of something, esp. organisms: *the taxonomy of these fossils.* ■ a scheme of classification: *a taxonomy of smells.*
– DERIVATIVES **tax·o·nom·ic** /ˌtaksə'nämik/ adj., **tax·o·nom·i·cal** /ˌtaksə'nämikəl/ adj., **tax·o·nom·i·cal·ly** /ˌtaksə'nämik(ə)lē/ adv., **tax·on·o·mist** /-mist/ n.
– ORIGIN early 19th cent.: coined in French from Greek *taxis* 'arrangement' + *-nomia* 'distribution.'

tax·pay·er /'taksˌpāər/ ▶ n. a person who pays taxes.
– DERIVATIVES **tax·pay·ing** adj.

tax re·turn ▶ n. a form on which a taxpayer makes an annual statement of income and personal circumstances, used by the tax authorities to assess liability for tax.

tax shel·ter ▶ n. a financial arrangement made to avoid or minimize taxes.

Tay /tā/ the longest river in Scotland, which flows 120 miles (192 km) east through Loch Tay and enters the North Sea through the Firth of Tay.

Tay, Firth of the estuary of the Tay River, on the North Sea coast of Scotland.

Tay·lor[1] /'tālər/ a city in southeastern Michigan, southwest of Detroit; pop. 60,619 (est. 2008).

Tay·lor[2], Elizabeth (1932–), US actress, born in England. Notable movies include *National Velvet* (1944), *Cat on a Hot Tin Roof* (1958), *Butterfield 8* (1960), *Cleopatra* (1963), and *Who's Afraid of Virginia Woolf?* (1966).

Elizabeth Taylor

Tay·lor[3], Lawrence, (1959–) US football player. A linebacker for the New York Giants 1981–93, he was voted the NFL's most valuable player in 1986. He played in ten Pro Bowl games. Football Hall of Fame (1999).

Tay·lor[4], Zachary (1784–1850), 12th president of the US. 1849–50. Long in the military 1808–49, he became a national hero after his victories in the war with Mexico 1846–48. He negotiated the Clayton-Bulwer Treaty of 1850 with Great Britain that stated that any canal built in Central America would be under the joint control of Great Britain and the US. As the last Whig president, he came into conflict with Congress over his desire to admit California to the Union as a free state (without slavery) and died before the problem was resolved.

Zachary Taylor

Tay·lor·ism /'tāləˌrizəm/ ▶ n. the principles or practice of scientific management.
– DERIVATIVES **Tay·lor·ist** n. & adj.
– ORIGIN mid 19th cent.: from the name of Frederick W. *Taylor* (1856–1915), the American engineer who expounded the system, + -ISM.

Tay·lor se·ries ▶ n. Mathematics an infinite sum giving the value of a function $f(z)$ in the neighborhood of a point a in terms of the derivatives of the function evaluated at a.
– ORIGIN early 19th cent.: named after Brook *Taylor* (1685–1731), English mathematician.

Tay·lors·ville /'tālərzˌvil/ a city in northwestern Utah, a southwestern suburb of Salt Lake City; pop. 58,785 (est. 2008). It was incorporated as a city in 1995.

tay·ra /'tīrə/ ▶ n. a large, agile, tree-dwelling animal of the weasel family, with a short dark coat, native to Central and South America. ● *Eira barbara*, family Mustelidae.
– ORIGIN mid 19th cent.: from Tupi *taira*.

Tay–Sachs dis·ease /'tā ˌsaks/ ▶ n. an inherited metabolic disorder in which certain lipids accumulate in the brain, causing spasticity and death in childhood.
– ORIGIN early 20th cent.: from the names of Warren *Tay* (1843–1927), English ophthalmologist, and Bernard *Sachs* (1858–1944), American neurologist, who described it in 1881 and 1887, respectively.

taz·za /'tätsə/ ▶ n. a saucer-shaped cup mounted on a foot.
– ORIGIN early 19th cent.: from Italian, from Arabic *ṭasa* 'bowl.'

TB ▶ abbr. ■ terabyte(s). ■ (also **t.b.**) tubercle bacillus. ■ (also **t.b.**) tuberculosis.

Tb ▶ abbr. ■ terabyte(s). ■ Bible Tobit. ▶ symbol the chemical element terbium.

t.b. ▶ abbr. trial balance.

TBA ▶ abbr. to be announced (or arranged).

T-back ▶ n. a high-cut undergarment or swimsuit having only a thin strip of material passing between the buttocks. ■ a style of back on a bra or bikini top in which the shoulder straps meet a supporting lateral strap below the shoulder blades.

t-ball ▶ n. TEE-BALL.

T-bar ▶ n. **1** a beam or bar shaped like the letter T. ■ (also **T-bar lift**) a type of ski lift in the form of a series of inverted T-shaped bars for towing two skiers at a time uphill.
2 the horizontal line of the letter *T*.

TBC ▶ abbr. to be confirmed.

Tbi·li·si /ˌtəbə'lēsē/ the capital of Georgia; pop. 1,100,000 (est. 2007). From 1845 until 1936, its name was Tiflis.

T-bill ▶ n. informal short for TREASURY BILL.

T-bond ▶ n. informal short for TREASURY BOND.

T-bone ▶ n. (also **T-bone steak**) a large choice piece of loin steak containing a T-shaped bone.
▶ v. [with obj.] crash head-on into the side of (another vehicle): *his car rolled over and was T-boned by an oncoming vehicle.*

tbsp. (also **tbs.**) ▶ abbr. (pl. **same** or **tbsps.**) ■ tablespoon(s). ■ tablespoonful(s).

Tc ▶ symbol the chemical element technetium.

TCA ▶ abbr. TRICHLORANISOLE.

TCD ▶ abbr. Trinity College, Dublin.

TCDD ▶ abbr. tetrachlorodibenzoparadioxin (see DIOXIN).

T cell ▶ n. Physiology a lymphocyte of a type produced or processed by the thymus gland and actively participating in the immune response. Also called T LYMPHOCYTE. Compare with B CELL.
– ORIGIN 1970s: from *T* for *thymus*.

tch /CH/ ▶ exclam. used to express irritation, annoyance, or impatience.

Tchai·kov·sky /CHī'kôfskē/, Pyotr (Ilich) (1840–93), Russian composer. His music is characterized by melodiousness and depth of expression and is often melancholy. Notable works include the ballets *Swan Lake* (1877) and *The Nutcracker* (1892) and the overture *1812* (1880).

tchotch·ke /'CHäCHkə/ (also **tsatske**) ▶ n. informal **1** a small object that is decorative rather than strictly functional; a trinket.
2 a pretty girl or woman.
– ORIGIN 1960s: Yiddish.

tchr. ▶ abbr. teacher.

TCP/IP ▶ abbr. Computing, trademark transmission control protocol/Internet protocol, used to govern the connection of computer systems to the Internet.

TD ▶ abbr. ■ technical drawing. ■ Football touchdown. ■ Treasury Department.

TDD ▶ abbr. telecommunications device for the deaf.

TDN (also **t.d.n.**) ▶ abbr. totally digestible nutrients.

TDY ▶ abbr. temporary duty.

Te ▶ symbol the chemical element tellurium.

tea /tē/ ▶ n. **1** a hot drink made by infusing the dried, crushed leaves of the tea plant in boiling water. ■ the dried leaves used to make such a drink. ■ [usu. with adj. or noun modifier] a hot drink made from the infused leaves, fruits, or flowers of other plants: *herbal tea | fruit teas.*
2 (also **tea plant**) the evergreen shrub or small tree that produces these leaves, native to South and eastern Asia and grown as a major cash crop. ● *Camellia sinensis*, family Theaceae.
3 chiefly Brit. a light afternoon meal consisting typically of tea to drink, sandwiches, and cakes. ■ Brit. a cooked evening meal. See also HIGH TEA.
– ORIGIN mid 17th cent.: probably via Malay from Chinese (Min dialect) *te*; related to Mandarin *chá*. Compare with CHAR[3].

tea bag ▶ n. a small porous bag containing tea leaves or powdered tea, onto which boiling water is poured in order to make a drink of tea.

tea ball ▶ n. a hollow ball of perforated metal to hold tea leaves, over which boiling water is poured in order to make a drink of tea.

tea cad·dy ▶ n. a small container in which tea is kept for daily use.

tea·cake /'tēˌkāk/ ▶ n. Brit. a light yeast-raised sweet bun with dried fruit, typically served toasted and buttered.

tea cer·e·mo·ny ▶ n. an elaborate Japanese ritual of serving and drinking tea, as an expression of Zen Buddhist philosophy.

teach /tēCH/ ▶ v. (past and past participle **taught** /tôt/) [with obj. and infinitive or clause] show or explain to (someone) how to do something: *she taught him to read | he taught me how to ride a bike.* ■ [with obj.] give information about or instruction in (a subject or skill): *he came one day each week to teach painting* | [with two objs.] *she teaches me French.* ■ [no obj.] give such instruction professionally: *she teaches at the local high school.* ■ [with obj.] encourage someone to accept (something) as a fact or principle: *the philosophy teaches self-control.* ■ cause (someone) to learn or understand something by example or experience: *she'd been taught that it paid to be passive | my upbringing taught me never to be disrespectful to elders.* ■ informal make (someone) less inclined to do something: *"I'll teach you to mess with young girls!"*
▶ n. informal a teacher.
– PHRASES **teach someone a lesson** see LESSON. **teach school** be a schoolteacher.
– ORIGIN Old English *tǣcan* 'show, present, point out,' of Germanic origin; related to TOKEN, from an Indo-European root shared by Greek *deiknunai* 'show,' and Latin *dicere* 'say.'

teach·a·ble /'tēCHəbəl/ ▶ adj. **1** (of a person) able to learn by being taught.
2 (of a subject) able to be taught.
– DERIVATIVES **teach·a·bil·i·ty** /ˌtēCHə'bilitē/ n., **teach·a·ble·ness** n.

teach·er /'tēCHər/ ▶ n. a person who teaches, esp. in a school.
– DERIVATIVES **teach·er·ly** adj.

teach·er·age /'tēCHərij/ ▶ n. a house or accommodations provided for a teacher by a school.

teach·ers col·lege (also **Teachers College**) ▶ n. a four-year college with a special curriculum for training primary and secondary school teachers.

tea chest ▶ n. a light metal-lined wooden box in which tea is transported.

teach-in ▶ n. informal an informal lecture and discussion or series of lectures on a subject of public interest.

teach·ing /'tēCHiNG/ ▶ n. **1** the occupation, profession, or work of a teacher.
2 (**teachings**) ideas or principles taught by an authority: *the teachings of the Koran.*

teach·ing fel·low ▶ n. a postgraduate student who carries out teaching or laboratory duties in return for accommodations, tuition, or expenses.

teach·ing hos·pi·tal ▶ n. a hospital that is affiliated with a medical school, in which medical students receive practical training.

teach·ing ma·chine ▶ n. a machine or computer that gives instruction to a student according to a program, reacting to their responses.

tea co·zy ▶ n. a thick or padded cover placed over a teapot to keep the tea hot.

tea·cup /'tēˌkəp/ ▶ n. a cup from which tea is drunk. ■ an amount held by this, about 150 ml.
– DERIVATIVES **tea·cup·ful** /-ˌfo͝ol/ n. (pl. **teacupfuls**).

tea dance ▶ n. an afternoon tea with dancing, originating in 19th-century society.

Tea·gar·den /'tēˌgärdn/, Jack (1905–64) US jazz trombonist and singer; full name *Weldon John Teagarden*. He had his own big band 1939–46 and then played with Louis Armstrong's All-Stars 1947–51.

tea gar·den ▶ n. **1** a garden in which tea and other refreshments are served to the public.
2 a tea plantation.

tea gown ▶ **n.** dated a long, loose-fitting dress, typically made of fine fabric and lace-trimmed, worn at afternoon tea and popular in the late 19th and early 20th centuries.

tea·head /ˈtēˌhed/ ▶ **n.** informal, dated a habitual user of marijuana.

tea·house /ˈtēhous/ ▶ **n.** a place serving tea and other refreshments.

teak /tēk/ ▶ **n. 1** hard durable timber used in shipbuilding and for making furniture.
2 the large deciduous tree native to India and Southeast Asia that yields this timber. ● *Tectona grandis*, family Verbenaceae.
– ORIGIN late 17th cent.: from Portuguese *teca*, from Tamil and Malayalam *tēkku*.

tea·ket·tle /ˈtēˌketl/ ▶ **n.** a metal or plastic vessel with a lid, spout, and handle, used for boiling water.

teal /tēl/ ▶ **n.** (pl. **same** or **teals**) a small freshwater duck, typically with a greenish band on the wing that is most prominent in flight. ● Genus *Anas*, family Anatidae: several species, in particular the common Eurasian and Canadian (**green-winged**) **teal** (*A. crecca*). ■ (also **teal blue**) a dark greenish-blue color.
– ORIGIN Middle English: of unknown origin; related to Dutch *teling*.

tea leaf ▶ **n.** a dried leaf of tea. ■ (**tea leaves**) dried leaves of tea after they have been used to make tea or as dregs.

tea light ▶ **n.** a small, squat candle in a metal case, used for decoration or within a stand to keep food or drink warm.

team /tēm/ ▶ **n.** [treated as sing. or pl.] a group of players forming one side in a competitive game or sport. ■ two or more people working together: ***a team of** researchers* | [as modifier] *a team effort.* ■ two or more animals, esp. horses, harnessed together to pull a vehicle.
▶ **v. 1** [no obj.] (**team up**) come together as a team to achieve a common goal: *he **teamed up with** the band to produce the album.*
2 [with obj.] (usu. **team something with**) match or coordinate a garment with (another): *a pinstripe suit teamed with a crisp white shirt.*
3 [with obj.] harness (animals, esp. horses) together to pull a vehicle: *the horses are teamed in pairs.*
– ORIGIN Old English *tēam* 'team of draft animals,' of Germanic origin; related to German *Zaum* 'bridle,' also to TEEM[1] and TOW[1], from an Indo-European root shared by Latin *ducere* 'to lead.'

team·mate /ˈtē(m)ˌmāt/ ▶ **n.** a fellow member of a team.

team play·er ▶ **n.** a person who plays or works well as a member of a team or group.

team spir·it ▶ **n.** feelings of camaraderie among the members of a group, enabling them to cooperate and work well together.

team·ster /ˈtēmstər/ ▶ **n. 1** a truck driver. ■ a member of the Teamsters Union, including truck drivers, chauffeurs, and warehouse workers.
2 a driver of a team of animals.

team teach·ing ▶ **n.** coordinated teaching by a team of teachers working together.

team·work /ˈtēmˌwərk/ ▶ **n.** the combined action of a group of people, esp. when effective and efficient.

tea oil ▶ **n.** an oil resembling olive oil obtained from the seeds of the sasanqua and related plants, used chiefly in China and Japan.

tea par·ty ▶ **n.** a social gathering in the afternoon at which tea, cakes, and other light refreshments are served.

tea·pot /ˈtēˌpät/ ▶ **n.** a pot with a handle, spout, and lid, in which tea is brewed and from which it is poured.

Tea·pot Dome an oil field in southeastern Wyoming that, as a naval reserve, was the focus of a 1920s corruption scandal.

tea·poy /ˈtēˌpoi/ ▶ **n.** a small three-legged table or stand, esp. one that holds a tea caddy.
– ORIGIN early 19th cent.: from Hindi *tī-* 'three' + Urdu and Persian *pāī* 'foot,' the sense and spelling influenced by TEA.

tear[1] /te(ə)r/ ▶ **v.** (past **tore** /tôr/; past participle **torn** /tôrn/) **1** [with obj.] pull or rip (something) apart or to pieces with force: *I **tore up** the letter.* ■ remove by pulling or ripping forcefully: *he tore up the floorboards* | *he **tore off** his belt* | *Joe tore the sack **from** her hand.* ■ make a hole or split in (something) by pulling it or piercing it with a sharp implement: *she was always tearing her clothes.* ■ make (a hole or split) in something by force: *the blast tore a hole in the wall.* ■ [no obj.] come apart; rip: *the material wouldn't tear.* ■ damage (a muscle or ligament) by overstretching it: *he tore a ligament playing squash.*
2 [no obj.] informal move very quickly, typically in a reckless or excited manner: *she tore along the footpath on her bike.*
3 (**be torn**) be in a state of uncertainty between two conflicting options or parties: ***he was torn between** his duty and his better instincts.*
▶ **n. 1** a hole or split in something caused by it having been pulled apart forcefully.
2 informal a spell of great success or excellence in performance: *he went **on a tear**, winning three out of every four hands.* ■ informal a brief spell of erratic behavior; a binge or spree: *every so often she goes **on a tear**, walking around town and zapping people with orange spray paint.*
– PHRASES **tear one's hair out** informal act with or show extreme desperation. **that's torn it** Brit. informal used to express dismay when something unfortunate has happened to disrupt someone's plans: *a friend of her father's arrived. "That's torn it," she said.*
– PHRASAL VERBS **tear someone/something apart 1** destroy something, esp. good relations between people: *a bloody civil war had torn the country apart.* **2** upset someone greatly: *stop crying—it's tearing me apart.* **3** criticize someone or something harshly. **tear oneself away** [often with negative] leave despite a strong desire to stay: *she couldn't tear herself away from the view.* **tear someone/something down 1** demolish something, esp. a building. **2** informal criticize or punish someone severely. **tear into 1** attack verbally: *she tore into him: "Don't you realize what you've done to me?"* **2** make an energetic or enthusiastic start on: *a jazz trio is tearing into the tune with gusto.*
– DERIVATIVES **tear·a·ble adj.**, **tear·er n.**
– ORIGIN Old English *teran*, of Germanic origin; related to Dutch *teren* and German *zehren*, from an Indo-European root shared by Greek *derein* 'flay.' The noun dates from the early 17th cent.

tear[2] /ti(ə)r/ ▶ **n.** a drop of clear salty liquid secreted from glands in a person's eye when they cry or when the eye is irritated. ■ (**tears**) the state or action of crying: *he was so hurt by her attitude he was nearly **in tears*** | *puppets that **moved** Jack **to tears**.*
▶ **v.** [no obj.] (of the eye) produce tears: *the freezing wind made her eyes tear.*
– DERIVATIVES **tear·like** /-ˌlīk/ **adj.**
– ORIGIN Old English *tēar*, of Germanic origin; related to German *Zähre*, from an Indo-European root shared by Old Latin *dacruma* (classical Latin *lacrima*) and Greek *dakru*.

tear·a·way /ˈte(ə)rəˌwā/ ▶ **n.** Brit. a person who behaves in a wild or reckless manner.

tear·down /ˈte(ə)rdoun/ ▶ **n.** informal an act of completely dismantling something: *an engine teardown.* ■ an act of demolishing a building, usually to build a new one on the same plot: *every teardown has an impact on the look and feel of a community.* ■ a building bought solely for this purpose: *a $2 million teardown.*

tear·drop /ˈti(ə)rˌdräp/ ▶ **n.** a single tear. ■ [as modifier] shaped like a single tear: *a wardrobe with brass teardrop handles.*

tear duct /ti(ə)r/ ▶ **n.** a passage through which tears pass from the lachrymal glands to the eye or from the eye to the nose.

tear·ful /ˈti(ə)rfəl/ ▶ **adj.** crying or inclined to cry: *a tearful infant* | *Stephen felt tearful.* ■ causing tears; sad or emotional: *a tearful farewell.*
– DERIVATIVES **tear·ful·ly adv.**, **tear·ful·ness n.**

tear gas /ti(ə)r/ ▶ **n.** gas that causes severe irritation to the eyes, chiefly used in riot control to force crowds to disperse.
▶ **v.** (**tear-gas**) [with obj.] (usu. **be tear-gassed**) attack with tear gas.

tear·ing /ˈte(ə)riNG/ ▶ **adj.** [attrib.] violent; extreme: *he did seem to be in a tearing hurry* | *the tearing wind.*

tear·jerk·er /ˈti(ə)rˌjərkər/ ▶ **n.** informal a sentimental story, movie, or song, calculated to evoke sadness or sympathy.
– DERIVATIVES **tear·jerk·ing** /-ˌjərkiNG/ **n. & adj.**

tear·less /ˈti(ə)rlis/ ▶ **adj.** not crying: *Mary watched in tearless silence as the coffin was lowered.*
– DERIVATIVES **tear·less·ly adv.**, **tear·less·ness n.**

tear-off /te(ə)r/ ▶ **adj.** denoting something that is removed by being torn off, typically along a perforated line: *please complete the tear-off slip.*

tea·room /ˈtēˌro͞om, -ˌro͝om/ (also **tea room**) ▶ **n. 1** a small restaurant or cafe where tea and other light refreshments are served.
2 informal a public restroom used as a meeting place for homosexual encounters.

tea rose ▶ **n.** a garden rose with flowers that have a delicate scent said to resemble that of tea. ● Numerous cultivars of the Chinese hybrid *Rosa* × *odorata*.

tear sheet /te(ə)r/ ▶ **n.** a page that can be or has been removed from a newspaper, magazine, or book for use separately.

tear-stained /ti(ə)r/ ▶ **adj.** wet with tears: *I looked at the man's tear-stained face.*

Teas·dale /ˈtēzˌdāl/, Sara, (1884–1933) US poet; born *Sarah Trevor*. Her poetry is collected in *Helen of Troy and Other Poetry* (1911), *River to the Sea* (1915), *Love Songs* (1917), *Flame and Shadow* (1920), and *Strange Victory* (1933).

tease /tēz/ ▶ **v.** [with obj.] **1** make fun of or attempt to provoke (a person or animal) in a playful way: *Brenda teased her father about the powerboat that he bought but seldom used* | [no obj.] *she was just teasing* | [with direct speech] *"Think you're clever, don't you?" she teased.* ■ tempt (someone) sexually with no intention of satisfying the desire aroused.
2 gently pull or comb (something tangled, esp. wool or hair) into separate strands: *she was teasing out the curls into her usual hairstyle.* ■ (**tease something out**) find something out from a mass of irrelevant information: *a historian who tries to tease out the truth.* ■ comb (hair) in the reverse direction of its natural growth in order to make it appear fuller. ■ archaic comb (the surface of woven cloth) to raise a nap.
▶ **n.** informal a person who makes fun of someone playfully or unkindly. ■ a person who tempts someone sexually with no intention of satisfying the desire aroused. ■ [in sing.] an act of making fun of or tempting someone: *she couldn't resist a gentle tease.*
– DERIVATIVES **teas·ing·ly adv.**
– ORIGIN Old English *tǣsan* (sense 2 of the verb); related to Dutch *teezen* and German dialect *zeisen*, also to TEASEL. Sense 1 is a development of the earlier and more serious 'irritate by annoying actions' (early 17th cent.), a figurative use of the word's original sense.

tea·sel /ˈtēzəl/ (also **teazle** or **teazel**) ▶ **n.** a tall prickly Eurasian plant with spiny purple flower heads. ● Genus *Dipsacus*, family Dipsacaceae: several species, including **fuller's teasel**. ■ a large, dried, spiny head from such a plant, or a device serving as a substitute for one of these, used in the textile industry to raise a nap on woven cloth.
▶ **v.** [with obj.] (often as noun **teaseling**) chiefly archaic raise a nap on (cloth) with or as if with teasels.
– ORIGIN Old English *tǣsl*, *tǣsel*; related to TEASE.

teas·er /ˈtēzər/ ▶ **n. 1** informal a difficult or tricky question or task.
2 a person who makes fun of or provokes others in a playful or unkind way. ■ a person who tempts someone sexually with no intention of satisfying the desire aroused. ■ a short introductory advertisement for a product, esp. one that does not mention the name of the thing being advertised. ■ Fishing a lure or bait trailed behind a boat to attract fish. ■ an inferior stallion or ram used to excite mares or ewes before they are served by the stud animal.

tea set (also **tea service**) ▶ **n.** a set of dishes, typically of china or silver, used for serving tea.

tea shop ▶ **n.** another term for TEAROOM (sense 1).

tea·spoon /ˈtēˌspo͞on/ ▶ **n.** a small spoon used typically for adding sugar to and stirring hot drinks or for eating some soft foods. ■ (abbr.: **tsp.** or **t**) a measurement used in cooking, equivalent to 1/6 fluid ounce, 1/3 tablespoon, or 4.9 ml.
– DERIVATIVES **tea·spoon·ful** /-ˌfo͝ol/ **n.** (pl. **teaspoonfuls**).

tea strain·er ▶ **n.** a small device incorporating a fine mesh for straining tea.

teat /tēt/ ▶ **n.** a nipple of the mammary gland of a female mammal, from which the milk is sucked by the young. ■ Brit. a thing resembling this, esp. a perforated plastic bulb by which an infant or young animal can suck milk from a bottle.
– ORIGIN Middle English (superseding earlier TIT[2]): from Old French *tete*, probably of Germanic origin.

tea·time /ˈtēˌtīm/ ▶ **n.** chiefly Brit. the time in the afternoon when tea is traditionally served.

tea tow·el ▶ **n.** chiefly British term for DISH TOWEL.

tea tray ▶ **n.** a tray from which tea is served.

tea tree ▶ **n.** an Australasian flowering shrub or small tree with leaves that are sometimes used for tea. Some species yield an oil used for its antiseptic properties. ● Genus *Leptospermum*, family Myrtaceae: several species, in particular *Melaleuca alternifolia*, whose leaves yield an essential oil.

tea·zle (also **teazel**) ▶ **n.** variant spelling of TEASEL.

Te·bet /'tāvās, -vāt, te'vet/ (also **Tevet**) ▶ **n.** (in the Jewish calendar) the fourth month of the civil and tenth of the religious year, usually coinciding with parts of December and January.
– ORIGIN from Hebrew *ṭēbēt*.

tec. ▶ **abbr.** ■ technical. ■ technician.

tech /tek/ (Brit. also **tec**) ▶ **n.** informal technology. See also **HIGH-TECH, LOW-TECH.** ■ a technician. ■ Basketball a technical.
▶ **adj.** technical: *I was in tech school then.*
– ORIGIN early 20th cent.: abbreviation.

tech. ▶ **abbr.** ■ technic. ■ technical. ■ technology.

Teche /tesH/ (**the Teche**) another name for **BAYOU TECHE.**

tech·ie /'tekē/ (also **tekkie** or **techy**) ▶ **n.** (pl. **techies**) informal a person who is expert in or enthusiastic about technology, esp. computing.
– ORIGIN 1960s: from **TECH** + **-IE.** First recorded as a US slang term for a technical college student, the word was later used as British service slang, denoting a technician. Sense 1 dates from the 1980s.

tech·ne·ti·um /tek'nēsH(ē)əm/ ▶ **n.** the chemical element of atomic number 43, a radioactive metal. Technetium was the first element to be created artificially, in 1937, by bombarding molybdenum with deuterons. (Symbol: **Tc**)
– ORIGIN 1940s: modern Latin, from Greek *tekhnētos* 'artificial,' from *tekhnasthai* 'make by art,' from *tekhnē* 'art.'

tech·nic /'teknik/ ▶ **n. 1** technique.
2 (**technics**) [treated as sing. or pl.] technical terms, details, and methods; technology.
– DERIVATIVES **tech·ni·cist** /-nisist/ **n.**
– ORIGIN early 17th cent. (as an adjective in the sense 'to do with art or an art'): from Latin *technicus*, from Greek *tekhnikos*, from *tekhnē* 'art.' The noun dates from the 19th cent.

tech·ni·cal /'teknikəl/ ▶ **adj. 1** of or relating to a particular subject, art, or craft, or its techniques: *technical terms | a test of an artist's technical skill.* ■ (esp. of a book or article) requiring special knowledge to be understood: *a technical report.*
2 of, involving, or concerned with applied and industrial sciences: *an important technical achievement.*
3 resulting from mechanical failure: *a technical fault.*
4 according to a strict application or interpretation of the law or rules: *the arrest was a technical violation of the treaty.*
▶ **n.** Basketball short for **TECHNICAL FOUL.**

tech·ni·cal ar·e·a ▶ **n.** Soccer a designated area around a team's dugout, from where a coach or manager may give instructions to players on the field.

tech·ni·cal col·lege ▶ **n.** a college providing courses in a range of practical subjects, such as information technology, applied sciences, engineering, agriculture, and secretarial skills.

tech·ni·cal draw·ing ▶ **n.** the practice or skill of delineating objects in a precise way using certain techniques of draftsmanship, as employed in architecture or engineering. ■ a drawing produced in such a way.

tech·ni·cal foul ▶ **n.** Basketball a violation of certain rules of the game, not usually involving physical contact, but often involving unsportsmanlike actions.

tech·ni·cal·i·ty /,tekni'kalitē/ ▶ **n.** (pl. **technicalities**) a point of law or a small detail of a set of rules: *their convictions were overturned on a technicality.* ■ (**technicalities**) the specific details or terms belonging to a particular field: *he has great expertise in the technicalities of the game.* ■ the state of being technical; the use of technical terms or methods: *the extreme technicality of the proposed constitution.*

tech·ni·cal knock·out (abbr.: **TKO**) ▶ **n.** Boxing the ending of a fight by the referee on the grounds of one contestant's inability to continue, the opponent being declared the winner.

tech·ni·cal·ly /'teknik(ə)lē/ ▶ **adv. 1** [usu. sentence adverb] according to the facts or exact meaning of something; strictly: *technically, a nut is a single-seeded fruit.*
2 with reference to the technique displayed: *a technically brilliant boxing contest.*
3 involving or regarding the technology available: *technically advanced tools.*

tech·ni·cal ser·geant ▶ **n.** a noncommissioned officer in the US Air Force ranking above staff sergeant and below master sergeant.

tech·ni·cal sup·port ▶ **n.** Computing a service provided by a hardware or software company that provides registered users with help and advice about their products.

tech·ni·cian /tek'nisHən/ ▶ **n.** a person employed to look after technical equipment or do practical work in a laboratory. ■ an expert in the practical application of a science. ■ a person skilled in the technique of an art or craft.

Tech·ni·col·or /'tekni,kələr/ ▶ **n.** trademark a process of color cinematography using synchronized monochrome films, each of a different color, to produce a movie in color. ■ (**technicolor**) informal vivid color: [as modifier] *a technicolor bruise.*
– DERIVATIVES **tech·ni·col·ored adj.**
– ORIGIN early 20th cent.: blend of **TECHNICAL** and **COLOR.**

tech·ni·col·or yawn ▶ **n.** informal, humorous an act of vomiting.

tech·nique /tek'nēk/ ▶ **n.** a way of carrying out a particular task, esp. the execution or performance of an artistic work or a scientific procedure. ■ skill or ability in a particular field: *he has excellent technique* | [in sing.] *an established athlete with a very good technique.* ■ a skillful or efficient way of doing or achieving something: *tape recording is a good technique for evaluating our own communications.*
– ORIGIN early 19th cent.: from French, from Latin *technicus* (see **TECHNIC**).

tech·no /'teknō/ ▶ **n.** a style of fast, heavy electronic dance music, typically with few or no vocals.
– ORIGIN 1980s: abbreviation of **TECHNOLOGICAL.**

techno- ▶ **comb. form** relating to technology or its use: *technophobe.*
– ORIGIN from Greek *tekhnē* 'art, craft.'

tech·no·bab·ble /'teknō,babəl/ ▶ **n.** informal incomprehensible technical jargon.

tech·noc·ra·cy /tek'näkrəsē/ ▶ **n.** (pl. **technocracies**) the government or control of society or industry by an elite of technical experts. ■ an instance or application of this. ■ an elite of technical experts.
– ORIGIN early 20th cent.: from Greek *tekhnē* 'art, craft' + **-CRACY.**

tech·no·crat /'teknə,krat/ ▶ **n.** an exponent or advocate of technocracy. ■ a member of a technically skilled elite.
– DERIVATIVES **tech·no·crat·ic** /,teknə'kratik/ **adj.**, **tech·no·crat·i·cal·ly** /,teknə'kratik(ə)lē/ **adv.**

tech·no·fear /'teknō,fi(ə)r/ ▶ **n.** informal, chiefly Brit. fear of using technological equipment, esp. computers.

technol. ▶ **abbr.** technology.

tech·no·log·i·cal /,teknə'läjikəl/ ▶ **adj.** of, relating to, or using technology: *the quickening pace of technological change.*
– DERIVATIVES **tech·no·log·i·cal·ly** /-ik(ə)lē/ **adv.**

tech·nol·o·gy /tek'näləjē/ ▶ **n.** (pl. **technologies**) the application of scientific knowledge for practical purposes, esp. in industry: *advances in computer technology | recycling technologies.* ■ machinery and equipment developed from such scientific knowledge. ■ the branch of knowledge dealing with engineering or applied sciences.
– DERIVATIVES **tech·nol·o·gist** /-jist/ **n.**, **tech·nol·o·gize** /-jīz/ **v.**
– ORIGIN early 17th cent.: from Greek *tekhnologia* 'systematic treatment,' from *tekhnē* 'art, craft' + *-logia* (see **-LOGY**).

tech·nol·o·gy park ▶ **n.** a science park.

tech·nol·o·gy trans·fer ▶ **n.** the transfer of new technology from the originator to a secondary user, esp. from developed to less developed countries in an attempt to boost their economies.

tech·no·phile /'teknə,fil/ ▶ **n.** a person who is enthusiastic about new technology.
– DERIVATIVES **tech·no·phil·i·a** /,teknə'filēə/ **n.**, **tech·no·phil·ic** /,teknə'filik/ **adj.**

tech·no·phobe /'teknə,fōb/ ▶ **n.** a person who fears, dislikes, or avoids new technology.
– DERIVATIVES **tech·no·pho·bi·a** /,teknə'fōbēə/ **n.**, **tech·no·pho·bic** /,teknə'fōbik/ **adj.**

tech·no·speak /'teknə,spēk/ ▶ **n.** another term for **TECHNOBABBLE.**

tech·no·stress /'teknō,stres/ ▶ **n.** informal stress or psychosomatic illness caused by working with computer technology on a daily basis.

tech·no·struc·ture /'teknō,strəkCHər/ ▶ **n.** [treated as sing. or pl.] a group of technologists or technical experts having considerable control over the workings of industry or government.
– ORIGIN 1960s: coined by J. K. Galbraith.

tech·y /'teCHē/ ▶ **n.** variant spelling of **TECHIE.**

tec·ton·ic /tek'tänik/ ▶ **adj. 1** Geology of or relating to the structure of the earth's crust and the large-scale processes that take place within it. ■ (of a change or development) very significant or considerable: *the last decade has witnessed a tectonic shift in world affairs.*
2 of or relating to building or construction.
– DERIVATIVES **tec·ton·i·cal·ly** /-ik(ə)lē/ **adv.**
– ORIGIN mid 17th cent. (sense 2): via late Latin from Greek *tektonikos*, from *tektōn* 'carpenter, builder.'

tec·ton·ics /tek'täniks/ ▶ **plural n.** [treated as sing. or pl.] Geology large-scale processes affecting the structure of the earth's crust.

tec·to·no·phys·ics /tek,tänō'fiziks, ,tektənō-/ ▶ **plural n.** [treated as sing.] the branch of geophysics that deals with the forces that cause movement and deformation in the earth's crust.
– DERIVATIVES **tec·to·no·phys·i·cist** /-'fizəsist/ **n.**
– ORIGIN 1950s: from **TECTONICS** + **PHYSICS.**

tec·to·ri·al /tek'tôrēəl/ ▶ **adj.** Anatomy forming a covering. ■ denoting the membrane covering the organ of Corti in the inner ear.
– ORIGIN late 19th cent.: from Latin *tectorium* 'covering, a cover' (from *tegere* 'to cover') + **-AL.**

tec·trix /'tek,triks/ ▶ **n.** (pl. **tectrices** /-,trisēz/) Ornithology a covert of a bird.
– ORIGIN late 19th cent.: modern Latin, from Latin *tect-* 'covered,' from the verb *tegere.*

tec·tum /'tektəm/ ▶ **n.** Anatomy the uppermost part of the midbrain, lying to the rear of the cerebral aqueduct. ■ (in full **optic tectum**) a rounded swelling (colliculus) forming part of this and containing cells involved in the visual system.
– ORIGIN early 20th cent.: from Latin, literally 'roof.'

Te·cum·seh /ti'kəmsə/ (1768–1813) Shawnee Indian chief; also *Tecumtha.* His plan to organize a military confederacy of tribes to resist US encroachment was thwarted by the defeat of his brother, **Tenskwatawa** (c.1768–1834) (also called *the Prophet*), at Tippecanoe 1811. An ally of the British in the War of 1812, Tecumseh fought and died at the Battle of the Thames.

Tecumseh

ted /ted/ ▶ **v.** (**teds, tedding, tedded**) [with obj.] (often as noun **tedding**) turn over and spread out (grass, hay, or straw) to dry or for bedding.
– DERIVATIVES **ted·der n.**
– ORIGIN Middle English: from Old Norse *tethja* 'spread manure' (past tense *tadda*), related to *tad* 'dung.'

ted·dy /'tedē/ ▶ **n.** (pl. **teddies**) **1** (also **teddy bear**) a soft toy bear.
2 a woman's all-in-one undergarment.
– ORIGIN early 20th cent.: from *Teddy*, nickname for the given name *Theodore*: sense 1 alluding to *Theodore* **ROOSEVELT**[3], an enthusiastic bear hunter.

Ted·dy boy ▶ **n.** Brit. (in the 1950s) a young man of a subculture characterized by a style of dress based on Edwardian fashion and a liking for rock and roll music.
– ORIGIN from *Teddy*, nickname for the given name *Edward* (with reference to Edward VII's reign).

Te De·um /tā 'dāəm, tē 'dēəm/ ▶ **n.** a hymn beginning *Te Deum laudamus*, "We praise Thee, O God," sung at matins or on special occasions such as a thanksgiving. ■ a musical setting of this. ■ an expression of thanksgiving or exultation.
– ORIGIN Latin.

te·di·ous /'tēdēəs/ ▶ **adj.** too long, slow, or dull: tiresome or monotonous: *a tedious journey.*
– DERIVATIVES **te·di·ous·ly adv.**, **te·di·ous·ness n.**
– ORIGIN late Middle English: from Old French *tedieus* or late Latin *taediosus*, from Latin *taedium* (see **TEDIUM**).

te·di·um /'tēdēəm/ ▶ **n.** the state of being tedious: *cousins and uncles filled the tedium of winter nights with many a tall tale.*
– ORIGIN mid 17th cent.: from Latin *taedium*, from *taedere* 'be weary of.'

tee[1] /tē/ ▶ **n.** see **T**[1] (sense 2).

tee[2] ▶ **n. 1** a cleared space on a golf course, from which the ball is struck at the beginning of play for each hole. ■ a small peg with a concave head that can be placed in the ground to support a golf ball before it is struck from such an area. ■ Football a small stand on which the ball is placed for a

t

kickoff. ■ a waist-high or higher stand used in tee-ball to hold a baseball before it is hit with a bat. [late 17th cent. (originally Scots, as *teaz*): of unknown origin.]
2 a mark aimed at in lawn bowling, quoits, curling, and other similar games. [late 18th cent. (originally Scots): perhaps the same word as TEE[1].]
▶ **v.** (**tees, teeing, teed**) [no obj.] (usu. **tee up**) Golf place the ball on a tee ready to make the first stroke of the round or hole: *he had not missed a par as he teed up for the last hole* | [with obj.] *she fished in her pocket for a ball and teed it.* ■ [with obj.] place (something) in position, esp. to be struck: *a shining white radar dome was teed up on top of the mountain.*
– PHRASAL VERBS **tee off** Golf play the ball from a tee; begin a round or hole of golf: *we spend ten minutes practicing putting before we tee off.* ■ informal make a start on something. **tee off on someone/something** informal sharply attack someone or something: *he will tee off on conservative politicians* | *Chang teed off on his opponent's serve.* **tee someone off** (usu. **be teed off**) informal make someone angry or annoyed: *Tommy was really teed off at Ernie.*

tee[3] ▶ **n.** informal a T-shirt.

tee-ball (also **t-ball**) ▶ **n.** a game for young children, played by the rules of baseball, in which the ball is not pitched but hit from a stationary tee.

tee-hee /ˌtē ˈhē/ ▶ **n.** a giggle or titter.
▶ **v.** (**tee-hees, tee-heeing, tee-heed**) [no obj.] titter or giggle in such a way.
– ORIGIN Middle English (as a verb): imitative.

teem[1] /tēm/ ▶ **v.** [no obj.] (**teem with**) be full of or swarming with: *every garden is teeming with wildlife* | (as adj. **teeming**) *she walked briskly through the teeming streets.*
– ORIGIN Old English *tēman, tīeman*, of Germanic origin; related to TEAM. The original senses included 'give birth to,' also 'be or become pregnant,' giving rise to 'be full of' in the late 16th cent.

teem[2] ▶ **v.** [no obj.] (of water, esp. rain) pour down; fall heavily: *with the rain teeming down at the manor, Italy seemed a long way off.*
– ORIGIN Middle English: from Old Norse *tœma* 'to empty,' from *tómr* 'empty.' The original sense was 'to empty,' specifically 'to drain liquid from, pour liquid out'; the current sense (originally dialect) dates from the early 19th cent.

teen /tēn/ informal ▶ **adj.** [attrib.] of or relating to teenagers: *a teen idol.*
▶ **n.** a teenager.
– ORIGIN early 19th cent. (as a noun): abbreviation. The adjective dates from the 1940s.

-teen ▶ **suffix** forming the names of numerals from 13 to 19: *fourteen* | *eighteen.*
– ORIGIN Old English, inflected form of TEN.

teen·age /ˈtēnˌāj/ ▶ **adj.** [attrib.] denoting a person between 13 and 19 years old: *a teenage girl.*
■ relating to or characteristic of people of this age: *teenage magazines.*
– DERIVATIVES **teen·aged** adj.

teen·ag·er /ˈtēnˌājər/ ▶ **n.** a person aged from 13 to 19 years.

WORD TRENDS See YOUTH.

teens /tēnz/ ▶ **plural n.** the years of a person's age from 13 to 19: *they were both in their late teens.*
– ORIGIN late 17th cent.: plural of *teen*, independent usage of -TEEN.

teen·sy /ˈtēnsē/ ▶ **adj.** (**teensier, teensiest**) informal tiny: *the dress just needs to be altered a teensy bit.*
– ORIGIN late 19th cent. (originally dialect): probably an extension of TEENY.

teen·sy-ween·sy /ˌtēnsē ˈwēnsē/ ▶ **adj.** informal tiny: *do we detect a teensy-weensy bit of animosity?*

tee·ny /ˈtēnē/ ▶ **adj.** (**teenier, teeniest**) informal tiny: *a teeny bit of criticism.*
– ORIGIN early 19th cent.: variant of TINY.

tee·ny·bop·per /ˈtēnēˌbäpər/ ▶ **n.** informal a young teenager, esp. a girl, who keenly follows the latest fashions in clothes and pop music.
– DERIVATIVES **tee·ny·bop** adj.

tee·ny-wee·ny /ˌtēnē ˈwēnē/ ▶ **adj.** informal tiny: *doesn't he have a teeny-weeny twinge of conscience?*

tee·pee ▶ **n.** variant spelling of TEPEE.

Tees /tēz/ a river in northeastern England that flows southeast for 80 miles (128 km) to the North Sea at Middlesbrough.

tee shirt ▶ **n.** variant spelling of T-SHIRT.

tee·ter /ˈtētər/ ▶ **v.** [no obj.] move or balance unsteadily; sway back and forth: *she teetered after him in her high-heeled sandals.* ■ (often **teeter between**) be unable to decide between different courses; waver: *she teetered between tears and anger.*
– PHRASES **teeter on the brink** (or **edge**) be very close to a difficult or dangerous situation: *the country teetered on the brink of civil war.*
– ORIGIN mid 19th cent.: variant of dialect *titter*, from Old Norse *titra* 'shake, shiver.'

tee·ter-tot·ter /ˈtētər ˌtätər/ ▶ **n.** a seesaw.
▶ **v.** [no obj.] teeter; waver.
– ORIGIN late 19th cent.: reduplication of TEETER or TOTTER.

teeth /tēTH/ plural form of TOOTH.

teethe /tē<u>TH</u>/ ▶ **v.** [no obj.] grow or cut teeth, esp. milk teeth.
– ORIGIN late Middle English: from TEETH.

teeth·ing /ˈtē<u>TH</u>iNG/ ▶ **n.** the process of growing one's teeth, esp. milk teeth.

teeth·ing ring ▶ **n.** a small ring for an infant to bite on while teething.

tee·to·tal /ˈtēˌtōtl/ ▶ **adj.** choosing or characterized by abstinence from alcohol: *a teetotal lifestyle.*
– DERIVATIVES **tee·to·tal·ism** /-ˌizəm/ **n.**
– ORIGIN mid 19th cent.: emphatic extension of TOTAL, apparently first used by Richard Turner, a worker from Preston, England, in a speech (1833) urging total abstinence from all alcohol, rather than mere abstinence from spirits, advocated by some early temperance reformers.

tee·to·tal·er /ˈtēˌtōtl-ər/ (Brit. **teetotaller**) ▶ **n.** a person who never drinks alcohol.

tee·to·tum /tēˈtōtəm/ ▶ **n.** a small spinning top spun with the fingers, esp. one with four sides lettered to determine whether the spinner has won or lost.
– ORIGIN early 18th cent. (as *T totum*): from *T* (representing *totum*, inscribed on the side of the toy) + Latin *totum* 'the whole' (stake). The letters on the sides (representing Latin words) were *T* (= *totum*), *A* (= *auferre* 'take away'), *D* (= *deponere* 'put down'), and *N* (= *nihil* 'nothing').

tee·vee /tēˈvē/ ▶ **n.** nonstandard spelling of **TV**.

teff /tef/ ▶ **n.** an African cereal that is cultivated almost exclusively in Ethiopia, used mainly to make flour. ● *Eragrostis tef*, family Gramineae.
– ORIGIN late 18th cent.: from Amharic *têf*.

te·fil·lin /təˈfilin, -fēˈlēn/ ▶ **plural n.** collective term for Jewish phylacteries.
– ORIGIN from Aramaic *tĕpillīn* 'prayers.'

TEFL /ˈtefəl/ ▶ **abbr.** teaching of English as a foreign language.

Tef·lon /ˈtefˌlän/ ▶ **n.** trademark a tough synthetic resin made by polymerizing tetrafluoroethylene, used to coat nonstick cooking utensils and to make seals and bearings. Also called POLYTETRAFLUOROETHYLENE. ■ [as modifier] used to refer to someone able to withstand criticism or attack with no apparent effect: *the head of the crime family is known as the Teflon Don because of his acquittals in three previous trials.*
– ORIGIN 1940s: from TETRA- 'four' + FLUORO- + *-on* on the pattern of words such as *nylon* and *rayon*.

teg /teg/ ▶ **n.** a sheep in its second year.
– ORIGIN early 16th cent. (as a contemptuous term for a woman; later applied specifically to a ewe in her second year): perhaps related to Swedish *tacka* 'ewe.'

teg·men /ˈtegmən/ ▶ **n.** (pl. **tegmina** /-mənə/) Biology a covering structure or roof of an organ, in particular: ■ Entomology a sclerotized forewing serving to cover the hind wing in grasshoppers and related insects. ■ Botany the delicate inner protective layer of a seed. ■ (also **tegmen tympani**) Anatomy a plate of thin bone forming the roof of the middle ear, a part of the temporal bone.
– ORIGIN early 19th cent.: from Latin, 'covering,' from *tegere* 'to cover.'

teg·men·tum /tegˈmentəm/ ▶ **n.** (pl. **tegmenta** /-ˈmentə/) Anatomy a region of gray matter on either side of the cerebral aqueduct in the midbrain.
– DERIVATIVES **teg·men·tal** /tegˈmentl/ **adj.**
– ORIGIN mid 19th cent.: from Latin, variant of *tegumentum* 'tegument.'

te·gu /tiˈgo͞o/ ▶ **n.** (pl. **same** or **tegus**) a large stocky lizard that has dark skin with pale bands of small spots, native to the tropical forests of South America. ● Genus *Tupinambis*, family Teiidae: several species, in particular the **common tegu** (*T. teguixin*).
– ORIGIN 1950s: abbreviation of *teguexin*, from Aztec *tecoixin* 'lizard.'

Te·gu·ci·gal·pa /təˌgo͞osəˈgalpə, -sēˈgäl-/ the capital of Honduras; pop. 967,200 (est. 2008).

teg·u·la /ˈtegyələ/ ▶ **n.** (pl. **tegulae** /-ˌlē/) **1** Entomology a small scalelike sclerite covering the base of the forewing in many insects.
2 Archaeology a flat roof tile, used esp. in Roman roofs.
– ORIGIN early 19th cent.: from Latin, literally 'tile,' from *tegere* 'to cover.'

teg·u·ment /ˈtegyəmənt/ ▶ **n.** chiefly Zoology the integument of an organism, esp. a parasitic flatworm.
– DERIVATIVES **teg·u·men·tal** /ˌtegyəˈmentl/ **adj.**, **teg·u·men·ta·ry** /ˌtegyəˈmen(t)ərē/ **adj.**
– ORIGIN late Middle English (in the general sense 'a covering or coating'): from Latin *tegumentum*, from *tegere* 'to cover.'

Te·hach·a·pi Moun·tains /təˈhaCHəˌpē/ a range that lies across California, north of the Transverse Ranges, sometimes considered the divider between north and south California.

Teh·ran /ˌte(ə)ˈran, -ˈrän/ (also **Teheran**) the capital of Iran, in the foothills of the Elburz Mountains; pop. 7,088,287 (2006). It replaced Isfahan as the capital of Persia in 1788.

tei·cho·ic ac·id /tīˈkō-ik, tā-/ ▶ **n.** Biochemistry a compound present in the walls of Gram-positive bacteria. It is a polymer of ribitol or glycerol phosphate.
– ORIGIN 1950s: *teichoic* from Greek *teikhos* 'wall' + -IC.

Teil·hard de Char·din /tāˈyär də SHärˈdaN/, Pierre (1881–1955), French Jesuit philosopher and paleontologist. His theory, which blends science and Christianity, is that man is evolving mentally and socially toward a perfect spiritual state. The Roman Catholic Church declared that his views were unorthodox.

te·in /ˈtā-in/ ▶ **n.** (pl. **same** or **teins**) a monetary unit of Kazakhstan, equal to one hundredth of a tenge.

Te·ja·no /təˈhänō/ ▶ **n.** (pl. **Tejanos**) a Mexican-American inhabitant of southern Texas: [as modifier] *the Tejano upper classes.* ■ a style of folk or popular music originating among such people, with elements from Mexican-Spanish vocal traditions and Czech and German dance tunes and rhythms, traditionally played by small groups featuring accordion and guitar.
– ORIGIN American Spanish, alteration of *Texano* 'Texan.'

Te·jo /ˈtāZHo͞o/ Portuguese name for TAGUS.

tek·kie ▶ **n.** variant spelling of TECHIE.

tek·tite /ˈtekˌtīt/ ▶ **n.** Geology a small black glassy object, many of which are found over certain areas of the earth's surface, believed to have been formed as molten debris in meteorite impacts and scattered widely through the air.
– ORIGIN early 20th cent.: coined in German from Greek *tēktos* 'molten' (from *tēkein* 'melt') + -ITE[1].

tel. (also **Tel.**) ▶ **abbr.** telephone.

tel·a·mon /ˈteləˌmän/ ▶ **n.** (pl. **telamones** /ˌteləˈmōnēz/) Architecture a male figure used as a pillar to support an entablature or other structure.
– ORIGIN early 17th cent.: via Latin from Greek *telamōnes*, plural of *Telamōn*, the name of a mythical hero.

tel·an·gi·ec·ta·sia /telˌanjē-ekˈtāZHə/ (also **telangiectasis** /-ˈektəsis/) ▶ **n.** Medicine a condition characterized by dilation of the capillaries, which causes them to appear as small red or purple clusters, often spidery in appearance, on the skin or the surface of an organ.
– DERIVATIVES **tel·an·gi·ec·tat·ic** /-ˈtatik/ **adj.**
– ORIGIN mid 19th cent.: modern Latin, from Greek *telos* 'end' + *angeion* 'vessel' + *ektasis* 'dilatation.'

Tel A·viv /ˌtel əˈvēv/ (also **Tel Aviv–Jaffa**) a city on the Mediterranean coast of Israel; pop. (with Jaffa) 392,500 (est. 2008). It was founded as a suburb of Jaffa by Russian Jewish immigrants in 1909 and named Tel Aviv a year later.

tel·co /ˈtelkō/ ▶ **n.** (pl. **telcos**) a telecommunications company.
– ORIGIN late 20th cent.: abbreviation.

tele- ▶ **comb. form 1** to or at a distance: *telekinesis.* ■ used in names of instruments for operating over long distances: *telemeter.* [from Greek *tēle-* 'far off.']
2 relating to television: *telecine.* [abbreviation.]
3 done by means of the telephone: *telemarketing.* [abbreviation.]

tel·e·cast /ˈteləˌkast/ ▶ **n.** a television broadcast.
▶ **v.** (past and past participle **telecast**) [with obj.] transmit by television: *the program will be telecast simultaneously to nearly 150 cities.*
– DERIVATIVES **tel·e·cast·er** **n.**

tel·e·cin·e /ˈteləˌsinē/ ▶ **n.** the broadcasting of a movie on television. ■ equipment used in such broadcasting.

tel·e·com /ˈteləˌkäm/ (Brit. also **telecoms**) ▶ **plural n.** [treated as sing.] telecommunications.
– ORIGIN 1960s: abbreviation.

PRONUNCIATION KEY ə *ago, up*; ər *over, fur*; a *hat*; ā *ate*; ä *car*; e *let*; ē *see*; i *fit*; ī *by*; NG *sing*; ō *go*; ô *law, for*; oi *toy*; o͝o *good*; o͞o *goo*; ou *out*; TH *thin*; <u>TH</u> *then*; ZH *vision*

tel·e·com·mu·ni·ca·tion /ˌteləkəˌmyo͞oniˈkāSHən/ ▶ **n.** communication over a distance by cable, telegraph, telephone, or broadcasting. ■ (**telecommunications**) [treated as sing.] the branch of technology concerned with such communication. ■ formal a message sent by such means.
– ORIGIN 1930s: from French *télécommunication*, from *télé-* 'at a distance' + *communication* 'communication.'

tel·e·com·mute /ˌteləkəˈmyo͞ot/ ▶ **v.** [no obj.] (usu. as noun **telecommuting**) work from home, making use of the Internet, e-mail, and the telephone.
– DERIVATIVES **tel·e·com·mut·er n.**

tel·e·con /ˈteləˌkän/ ▶ **n.** informal a teleconference.

tel·e·con·fer·ence /ˈteləˌkänf(ə)rəns/ ▶ **n.** a conference with participants in different locations linked by telecommunications devices.
– DERIVATIVES **tel·e·con·fer·enc·ing** /ˌteləˈkänf(ə)rənsiNG/ **n.**

tel·e·con·nec·tion /ˌteləkəˈnekSHən/ ▶ **n.** a causal connection or correlation between meteorological or other environmental phenomena that occur a long distance apart.

tel·e·con·vert·er /ˌteləkənˈvərtər/ ▶ **n.** Photography a camera lens designed to be fitted in front of a standard lens to increase its effective focal length.

Tel·e·cop·i·er /ˈteləˌkäpēər/ ▶ **n.** trademark a device that transmits and reproduces facsimile copies over a telephone line.

tel·e·du /ˈteləˌdo͞o/ ▶ **n.** a badgerlike animal that has brownish-black fur with a white stripe along the top of the head and back, and anal glands that contain a foul-smelling liquid that can be squirted at an attacker. It is native to Sumatra, Java, and Borneo. ● *Mydaus javanensis*, family Mustelidae.
– ORIGIN early 19th cent.: from Javanese.

tel·e·fac·sim·i·le /ˌteləˌfakˈsiməlē/ ▶ **n.** another term for FAX.

tel·e·fax /ˈteləˌfaks/ trademark ▶ **n.** the transmission of documents by fax: *for more information contact us by telefax.* ■ a document sent in such a way. ■ a fax machine.
▶ **v.** [with obj.] (usu. as adj. **telefaxed**) send (a message) by fax: *telefaxed bills of lading.*
– ORIGIN 1940s: abbreviation of TELEFACSIMILE.

tel·e·film /ˈteləˌfilm/ ▶ **n.** a movie made for or broadcast on television.

teleg. ▶ **abbr.** ■ telegram. ■ telegraph. ■ telegraphy.

tel·e·gen·ic /ˌteləˈjenik/ ▶ **adj.** having an appearance or manner that is appealing on television: *his telegenic charm appears to be his major asset.*
– DERIVATIVES **tel·e·gen·i·cal·ly** /-ik(ə)lē/ **adv.**
– ORIGIN 1930s (originally US): from TELE- 'television' + -GENIC 'well suited to,' on the pattern of *photogenic*.

tel·e·gram /ˈteləˌgram/ ▶ **n.** a message sent by telegraph and then delivered in written or printed form.
– ORIGIN mid 19th cent.: from TELE- 'at a distance' + -GRAM[1], on the pattern of *telegraph*.

tel·e·graph /ˈteləˌgraf/ ▶ **n.** a system for transmitting messages from a distance along a wire, esp. one creating signals by making and breaking an electrical connection: *news came from the outside world by telegraph.* ■ a device for transmitting messages in such a way.
▶ **v.** [with obj.] send (someone) a message by telegraph: *I must go and telegraph Mom.* ■ send (a message) by telegraph: *she would rush off to telegraph news to her magazine.* ■ convey (an intentional or unconscious message), esp. with facial expression or body language: *a tiny movement of her arm telegraphed her intention to strike.*
– DERIVATIVES **te·leg·ra·pher** /təˈlegrəfər/ **n.**
– ORIGIN early 18th cent.: from French *télégraphe*, from *télé-* 'at a distance' + *-graphe* (see -GRAPH).

tel·e·graph·ese /ˌteləgraˈfēz/ ▶ **n.** informal the terse, abbreviated style of language used in telegrams.

Tel·e·graph Hill a hill neighborhood in San Francisco in California, named for the signal stations that surmounted it in the 19th century.

tel·e·graph·ic /ˌteləˈgrafik/ ▶ **adj. 1** of or by telegraphs or telegrams: *the telegraphic transfer of the funds.*
2 (esp. of speech) omitting inessential words; concise.
– DERIVATIVES **tel·e·graph·i·cal·ly** /-ik(ə)lē/ **adv.**

te·leg·ra·phist /təˈlegrəfist/ ▶ **n.** a person skilled or employed in telegraphy. ■ a person whose job is to operate telegraph equipment.

tel·e·graph key ▶ **n.** a button that is pressed to produce a signal when transmitting Morse code.

tel·e·graph plant ▶ **n.** a tropical Asian plant of the pea family whose leaves have a spontaneous jerking motion. ● *Codariocalyx motorius* (formerly *Desmodium gyrans*), family Leguminosae.

te·leg·ra·phy /təˈlegrəfē/ ▶ **n.** the science or practice of using or constructing communications systems for the transmission or reproduction of information.

Tel·e·gu ▶ **n.** variant spelling of TELUGU.

tel·e·im·mer·sion /ˌteləiˈmərZHən, -SHən/ ▶ **n.** two-way remote communication in which each party gets an audio and three-dimensional visual representation of the other, via high-speed data exchange: *tele-immersion allows users to climb into a computer screen.*

tel·e·ki·ne·sis /ˌteləkiˈnēsis/ ▶ **n.** the supposed ability to move objects at a distance by mental power or other nonphysical means.
– DERIVATIVES **tel·e·ki·net·ic** /-ˈnetik/ **adj.**
– ORIGIN late 19th cent.: from TELE- 'at a distance' + Greek *kinēsis* 'motion' (from *kinein* 'to move').

Te·lem·a·chus /təˈleməkəs/ Greek Mythology the son of Odysseus and Penelope.

Te·le·mann /ˈtāləˌmän, ˈtel-/, Georg Philipp (1681–1767), German composer and organist. His works include church music, oratorios, and a great deal of instrumental music.

tel·e·mark /ˈteləˌmärk/ Skiing ▶ **n.** a turn in downhill skiing or a landing style in ski jumping with one ski advanced and the knees bent.
▶ **v.** [no obj.] perform such a turn while skiing: *they went telemarking silently through the trees.*
– ORIGIN early 20th cent.: named after *Telemark*, the district in Norway, where it originated.

tel·e·mar·ket·ing /ˌteləˈmärkitiNG/ ▶ **n.** the marketing of goods or services by means of telephone calls, typically unsolicited, to potential customers.
– DERIVATIVES **tel·e·mar·ket·er** /-ˌmärkitər/ **n.**

tel·e·mat·ics /ˌteləˈmatiks/ ▶ **plural n.** [treated as sing.] the branch of information technology that deals with the long-distance transmission of computerized information.
– DERIVATIVES **tel·e·mat·ic adj.**
– ORIGIN 1970s: blend of TELECOMMUNICATION and INFORMATICS.

tel·e·med·i·cine /ˈteləˌmedisin/ ▶ **n.** the remote diagnosis and treatment of patients by means of telecommunications technology.

te·lem·e·ter ▶ **n.** /təˈlemitər, ˈteləˌmētər/ an apparatus for recording the readings of an instrument and transmitting them by radio.
▶ **v.** /ˈteləˌmētər/ [with obj.] transmit (readings) to a distant receiving set or station.
– DERIVATIVES **tel·e·met·ric** /ˌteləˈmetrik/ **adj.**, **te·lem·e·try** /təˈlemitrē/ **n.**

tel·en·ceph·a·lon /ˌtelənˈsefəlän, -lən/ ▶ **n.** Anatomy the most highly developed and anterior part of the forebrain, consisting chiefly of the cerebral hemispheres. Compare with DIENCEPHALON.
– ORIGIN late 19th cent.: from TELE- 'far' + ENCEPHALON.

tel·e·no·vel·a /ˌtelənōˈvelə/ ▶ **n.** (in Latin America) a television soap opera. Also called NOVELA.
– ORIGIN Spanish.

tel·e·o·log·i·cal ar·gu·ment /ˌtelēəˈläjikəl, ˌtēlē-/ ▶ **n.** Philosophy the argument for the existence of God from the evidence of order, and hence design, in nature. Compare with ARGUMENT FROM DESIGN, COSMOLOGICAL ARGUMENT, and ONTOLOGICAL ARGUMENT.

tel·e·ol·o·gy /ˌtelēˈäləjē, ˌtēlē-/ ▶ **n.** (pl. **teleologies**) Philosophy the explanation of phenomena by the purpose they serve rather than by postulated causes. ■ Theology the doctrine of design and purpose in the material world.
– DERIVATIVES **tel·e·o·log·ic** /-əˈläjik/ **adj.**, **tel·e·o·log·i·cal** /-əˈläjikəl/ **adj.**, **tel·e·o·log·i·cal·ly** /-əˈläjik(ə)lē/ **adv.**, **tel·e·ol·o·gism** /-ˌjizəm/ **n.**, **tel·e·ol·o·gist** /-jist/ **n.**
– ORIGIN mid 18th cent. (denoting the branch of philosophy that deals with ends or final causes): from modern Latin *teleologia*, from Greek *telos* 'end' + *-logia* (see -LOGY).

tel·e·op·er·a·tion /ˌteləˌäpəˈrāSHən/ ▶ **n.** the electronic remote control of machines.
– DERIVATIVES **tel·e·op·er·ate** /-ˈäpəˌrāt/ **v.**

tel·e·op·er·a·tor /ˌteləˈäpəˌrātər/ ▶ **n.** a machine operated by remote control so as to imitate the movements of its operator.

tel·e·ost /ˈtelēˌäst, ˈtēlē-/ ▶ **n.** Zoology a fish of a large group that comprises all ray-finned fishes apart from the primitive bichirs, sturgeons, paddlefishes, freshwater garfishes, and bowfins. ● Division (or infraclass) Teleostei, subclass Actinopterygii: many orders.
– ORIGIN mid 19th cent.: from Greek *teleos* 'complete' + *osteon* 'bone.'

tel·e·path /ˈteləpaTH/ ▶ **n.** a person with the ability to communicate using telepathy.
– ORIGIN late 19th cent. (as a verb, meaning 'to use telepathy'): back-formation from TELEPATHY.

tel·e·path·ic /ˌteləˈpaTHik/ ▶ **adj.** supposedly capable of transmitting thoughts to other people and of knowing their thoughts; psychic: *a team of telepathic superheroes who can read each other's thoughts.* ■ relating to or characteristic of telepathy: *suppose that telepathic communication between human minds occurs.*
– DERIVATIVES **tel·e·path·i·cal·ly** /ˌteləˈpaTHik(ə)lē/ **adv.**

te·lep·a·thy /təˈlepəTHē/ ▶ **n.** the supposed communication of thoughts or ideas by means other than the known senses.
– DERIVATIVES **te·lep·a·thist** /-THist/ **n.**

tel·e·phone /ˈteləˌfōn/ ▶ **n. 1** a system that converts acoustic vibrations to electrical signals in order to transmit sound, typically voices, over a distance using wire or radio. ■ an instrument used as part of such a system, typically a single unit including a handset with a transmitting microphone and a set of numbered buttons by which a connection can be made to another such instrument.
2 a game in which a message is distorted by being passed around in a whisper. Also called CHINESE WHISPERS.
▶ **v.** [with obj.] contact (someone) using the telephone: *he telephoned his wife at 9.30.* ■ [no obj.] make a telephone call: *she **telephoned for help**.* ■ send (a message) by telephone: *Barbara had telephoned the news.*
– DERIVATIVES **tel·e·phon·er n.**, **tel·e·phon·ic** /ˌteləˈfänik/ **adj.**, **tel·e·phon·i·cal·ly** /ˌteləˈfänik(ə)lē/ **adv.**

tel·e·phone bank·ing ▶ **n.** a method of banking in which the customer conducts transactions by telephone, typically by means of a computerized system using touch-tone dialing or voice-recognition technology.

tel·e·phone book ▶ **n.** a telephone directory.

tel·e·phone booth (Brit. also **telephone box**) ▶ **n.** a public booth or enclosure housing a pay phone.

tel·e·phone card ▶ **n.** another term for CALLING CARD (sense 2).

tel·e·phone di·rec·to·ry ▶ **n.** a book listing the names, addresses, and telephone numbers of the people in a particular area.

tel·e·phone ex·change ▶ **n.** a set of equipment that connects telephone lines during a call.

tel·e·phone num·ber ▶ **n.** a number assigned to a particular telephone and used in making connections to it.

tel·e·phone op·er·a·tor ▶ **n.** a person who works at the switchboard of a telephone exchange.

tel·e·phone pole /ˈteləˌfōn pōl/ ▶ **n.** a tall pole used to carry telephone wires and other utility lines above the ground.

tel·e·phone tag ▶ **n.** informal a situation in which two people trying to communicate by telephone continually miss each other.

te·leph·o·nist /ˈteləˌfōnist, təˈlefə-/ ▶ **n.** Brit. an operator of a switchboard.

te·leph·o·ny /təˈlefənē, ˈteləˌfōnē/ ▶ **n.** the working or use of telephones.

tel·e·pho·to /ˈteləˌfōtō/ (also **telephoto lens**) ▶ **n.** (pl. **telephotos**) a lens with a longer focal length than standard, giving a narrow field of view and a magnified image.

tel·e·pic /ˈteləˌpik/ ▶ **n.** informal a movie made for television.
– ORIGIN blend of *television* and *epic*.

tel·e·play /ˈteləˌplā/ ▶ **n.** a play written or adapted for television.

tel·e·port /ˈteləˌpôrt/ ▶ **v.** (esp. in science fiction) transport or be transported across space and distance instantly.
▶ **n. 1** a center providing interconnections between different forms of telecommunications, esp. one that links satellites to ground-based communications. [1980s: originally the name of such a center in New York.]
2 an act of teleporting.
– DERIVATIVES **tel·e·por·ta·tion** /ˌteləˌpôrˈtāSHən/ **n.**
– ORIGIN 1950s: back-formation from *teleportation* (1930s), from TELE- 'at a distance' + a shortened form of TRANSPORTATION.

tel·e·pres·ence /ˈteləˌprezəns/ ▶ **n.** the use of virtual reality technology, esp. for remote control of machinery or for apparent participation in distant events. ■ a sensation of being elsewhere, created in such a way.

tel·e·print·er /ˈteləˌprin(t)ər/ ▶ **n.** a device for transmitting telegraph messages as they are keyed, and for printing messages received.

Tel·e·Promp·Ter /ˈteləˌpräm(p)tər/ ▶ **n.** trademark a device used in television and moviemaking to project a speaker's script out of sight of the audience.

t

tel·e·sales /ˈteləˌsālz/ ▶ **plural n.** the selling of goods or services over the telephone: *sales personnel work on fully automated telesales systems.*

tel·e·scope /ˈteləˌskōp/ ▶ **n.** an optical instrument designed to make distant objects appear nearer, containing an arrangement of lenses, or of curved mirrors and lenses, by which rays of light are collected and focused and the resulting image magnified. ■ short for RADIO TELESCOPE.
▶ **v.** (with reference to an object made of concentric tubular parts) slide or cause to slide into itself, so that it becomes smaller: [no obj.] *five steel sections that telescope into one another.* ■ [with obj.] crush (a vehicle) by the force of an impact. ■ [with obj.] condense or conflate so as to occupy less space or time: *a way of telescoping many events into a relatively brief period.*
– ORIGIN mid 17th cent.: from Italian *telescopio* or modern Latin *telescopium*, from *tele-* 'at a distance' + *-scopium* (see -SCOPE).

telescope

tel·e·scop·ic /ˌteləˈskäpik/ ▶ **adj. 1** of, relating to, or made with a telescope. ■ capable of viewing and magnifying distant objects. ■ Astronomy visible only through a telescope.
2 having or consisting of concentric tubular sections designed to slide into one another: *a telescopic umbrella.*
– DERIVATIVES **tel·e·scop·i·cal·ly** /-ik(ə)lē/ **adv.**

tel·e·scop·ic sight ▶ **n.** a small telescope used for sighting, typically mounted on a rifle.

tel·e·shop·ping /ˈteləˌSHäpiNG/ ▶ **n.** the ordering of goods by customers using a telephone or direct computer link.

tel·e·sur·ger·y /ˈteləˌsərjərē/ ▶ **n.** surgery performed by a doctor considerably distant from the patient, using medical robotics and multimedia image communication.
– DERIVATIVES **tel·e·sur·geon** /ˈteləˌsərjən/ **n.**

tel·e·text /ˈteləˌtekst/ ▶ **n.** a news and information service in the form of text and graphics, transmitted using the spare capacity of existing television channels to televisions with appropriate receivers.

tel·e·the·sia /ˌteləsˈTHĒZH(ē)ə/ (Brit. **telaesthesia**) ▶ **n.** the supposed perception of distant occurrences or objects otherwise than by the recognized senses.
– DERIVATIVES **tel·es·thet·ic** /-ˈTHetik/ **adj.**
– ORIGIN late 19th cent.: from TELE- + Greek *aisthēsis* 'perception.'

tel·e·thon /ˈteləˌTHän/ ▶ **n.** a very long television program, typically one broadcast to raise money for a charity.
– ORIGIN 1940s (originally US): from TELE- 'at a distance' + *-thon* on the pattern of *marathon.*

Tel·e·type /ˈteləˌtīp/ (often **teletype**) ▶ **n.** trademark a kind of teleprinter. ■ a message received and printed by a teleprinter.
▶ **v.** [with obj.] send (a message) by means of a teleprinter.

tel·e·type·writ·er /ˌteləˈtīpˌrītər/ ▶ **n.** a teleprinter.

tel·e·van·ge·list /ˌteləˈvanjəlist/ ▶ **n.** an evangelical preacher who appears regularly on television to preach and appeal for funds.
– DERIVATIVES **tel·e·van·gel·i·cal** /ˌteləˌvanˈjelikəl/ **adj.**, **tel·e·van·ge·lism** /-ˌlizəm/ **n.**

tel·e·view·er /ˈteləˌvyo͞oər/ ▶ **n.** a person who watches television.
– DERIVATIVES **tel·e·view·ing** /-ˌvyo͞o-iNG/ **n. & adj.**

tel·e·vise /ˈteləˌvīz/ ▶ **v.** [with obj.] (usu. as adj. **televised**) transmit by television: *a live televised debate between the party leaders.*
– DERIVATIVES **tel·e·vis·a·ble adj.**
– ORIGIN 1920s: back-formation from TELEVISION.

tel·e·vi·sion /ˈteləˌviZHən/ ▶ **n. 1** a system for transmitting visual images and sound that are reproduced on screens, chiefly used to broadcast programs for entertainment, information, and education. ■ the activity, profession, or medium of broadcasting on television: *neither of my children showed the merest inclination to follow me into television* | [as modifier] *television news.* ■ television programs: *Dan was sitting on the sofa watching television.*
2 (also **television set**) a device that receives television signals and reproduces them on a screen.
– PHRASES **on (the) television** being broadcast by television; appearing in a television program: *Norman was on television yesterday.*
– ORIGIN early 20th cent.: from TELE- 'at a distance' + VISION.

tel·e·vi·sion sta·tion ▶ **n.** an organization transmitting television programs.

tel·e·vis·u·al /ˌteləˈviZHo͞oəl/ ▶ **adj.** relating to or suitable for television: *the world of televisual images.*
– DERIVATIVES **tel·e·vis·u·al·ly adv.**

tel·e·work /ˈteləˌwərk/ ▶ **v.** another term for TELECOMMUTE.
▶ **n.** the practice of working from home, making use of the Internet, e-mail, and the telephone.
– DERIVATIVES **tel·e·work·er n.**, **tel·e·work·ing n.**

tel·ex /ˈteleks/ ▶ **n.** an international system of telegraphy with printed messages transmitted and received by teleprinters using the public telecommunications network. ■ a device used for this. ■ a message sent by this system.
▶ **v.** [with obj.] communicate with (someone) by telex. ■ send (a message) by telex.
– ORIGIN 1930s: blend of TELEPRINTER and EXCHANGE.

Tel·ford[1] /ˈtelfərd/ a town in west central England; pop. 161,700 (est. 2007).

Tel·ford[2], Thomas (1757–1834), Scottish civil engineer. He built hundreds of miles of roads, more than a thousand bridges, and some canals, including the Caledonian Canal across Scotland that opened in 1822.

tel·ic /ˈtelik, ˈtē-/ ▶ **adj.** (of an action or attitude) directed or tending to a definite end. ■ Linguistics (of a verb, conjunction, or clause) expressing goal, result, or purpose.
– DERIVATIVES **te·lic·i·ty** /təˈlisitē/ **n.**
– ORIGIN mid 19th cent.: from Greek *telikos* 'final,' from *telos* 'end.'

Tell /tel/, William, a legendary hero of the liberation of Switzerland from Austrian oppression. He was required to hit with an arrow an apple placed on the head of his son, which he did successfully. The events are placed in the 14th century, but there is no evidence for a historical person of this name, and similar legends are of widespread occurrence.

tell[1] /tel/ ▶ **v.** (past and past participle **told** /tōld/)
1 [reporting verb] communicate information, facts, or news to someone in spoken or written words: [with obj. and clause] *I told her you were coming* | [with obj. and direct speech] *"We have nothing in common," she told him* | [with obj.] *he's telling the truth* | [with two objs.] *we must be told the facts.* ■ [with obj. and infinitive] order, instruct, or advise (someone) to do something: *tell him to go away.* ■ [with obj.] narrate or relate (a tale or story). ■ [with obj.] reveal (information) to someone in a nonverbal way: *the figures tell a different story* | [with two objs.] *the smile on her face told him everything.* ■ [no obj.] divulge confidential or private information: *promise you won't tell.* ■ [no obj.] (**tell on**) informal inform someone of the misdemeanors of: *friends don't tell on each other.*
2 [with clause] decide or determine correctly or with certainty: *you can tell they're in love.* ■ [with obj.] distinguish (one person or thing) from another; perceive (the difference) between one person or thing and another: *I can't tell the difference between margarine and butter.*
3 [no obj.] (of an experience or period of time) have a noticeable, typically harmful, effect on someone: *the strain of supporting the family was beginning to tell on him.* ■ (of a particular factor) play a part in the success or otherwise of someone or something: *lack of fitness told against him on his first run of the season.*
4 [with obj.] archaic count (the members of a series or group): *the shepherd had told all his sheep.*
▶ **n.** (esp. in poker) an unconscious action that is thought to betray an attempted deception.
– PHRASES **as far as one can tell** judging from the available information. **I tell you** (or **I can tell you**) used to emphasize a statement: *that took me by surprise, I can tell you!* **I** (or **I'll**) **tell you what** used to introduce a suggestion: *I tell you what, why don't we meet for lunch tomorrow?* **I told you** (**so**) used as a way of pointing out that one's warnings, although ignored, have been proved to be well founded. **tell one's beads** see BEAD. **tell someone's fortune** see FORTUNE. **tell it like it is** informal describe the facts of a situation no matter how unpleasant they may be. **tell its own tale** (or **story**) be significant or revealing, without any further explanation or comment being necessary: *the worried expression on Helen's face told its own tale.* **tell me about it** informal used as an ironic acknowledgment of one's familiarity with a difficult or unpleasant situation or experience described by someone else. **tell me another** informal used as an expression of disbelief or incredulity. **tell something a mile off** see MILE. **tell tales** make known or gossip about another person's secrets, wrongdoings, or faults. **tell it to the marines** see MARINE. **tell time** be able to ascertain the time from reading the face of a clock or watch. **tell someone where to get off** (or **where they get off**) informal angrily dismiss or rebuke someone. **tell someone where to put** (or **what to do with**) **something** informal angrily or emphatically reject something: *I told him what he could do with his diamond.* **that would be telling** informal used to convey that one is not prepared to divulge secret or confidential information. **there is no telling** used to convey the impossibility of knowing what has happened or will happen: *there's no telling how she will react.* **to tell** (**you**) **the truth** used as a preface to a confession or admission of something. **you're telling me!** informal used to emphasize that one is already well aware of something or in complete agreement with a statement.
– PHRASAL VERBS **tell someone off** informal reprimand or scold someone: *my parents told me off for coming home late.*
– DERIVATIVES **tell·a·ble adj.**
– ORIGIN Old English *tellan* 'relate, count, estimate,' of Germanic origin; related to German *zählen* 'reckon, count,' *erzählen* 'recount, relate,' also to TALE.

tell[2] ▶ **n.** Archaeology (in the Middle East) an artificial mound formed by the accumulated remains of ancient settlements.
– ORIGIN mid 19th cent.: from Arabic *tall* 'hillock.'

tell-all ▶ **adj.** revealing private or salacious details: *a tell-all article in the tabloids.*
▶ **n.** a biography or memoir that reveals intimate details about its subject.

Tell·er /ˈtelər/, Edward, (1908–2003), US physicist, born in Hungary. He worked on the first atomic reactor and the first atom bombs, and work under his guidance led to the detonation of the first hydrogen bomb in 1952.

tell·er /ˈtelər/ ▶ **n. 1** a person employed to deal with customers' transactions in a bank. ■ an automated teller machine.
2 a person who tells something: *a foul-mouthed teller of lies.*
3 a person appointed to count votes, esp. in a legislature.
– DERIVATIVES **tell·er·ship** /-ˌSHip/ **n.** (chiefly historical) (sense 1).

tell·ing /ˈteliNG/ ▶ **adj.** having a striking or revealing effect; significant: *a telling argument against this theory.*
– DERIVATIVES **tell·ing·ly adv.**

tell·tale /ˈtelˌtāl/ ▶ **adj.** [attrib.] revealing, indicating, or betraying something: *the telltale bulge of a concealed weapon.*
▶ **n. 1** a person, esp. a child, who reports others' wrongdoings or reveals their secrets.
2 a device or object that automatically gives a visual indication of the state or presence of something. ■ (on a sailboat) a piece of string or fabric that shows the direction and force of the wind.

tel·lu·ri·an /təˈlo͝orēən/ ▶ **adj.** formal or literary of or inhabiting the earth.
▶ **n.** formal or literary an inhabitant of the earth.
– ORIGIN mid 19th cent.: from Latin *tellus, tellur-* 'earth' + -IAN.

tel·lu·ric /təˈlo͝orik/ ▶ **adj.** of the earth as a planet. ■ of the soil.
– ORIGIN mid 19th cent.: from Latin *tellus, tellur-* 'earth' + -IC.

tel·lu·ric ac·id ▶ **n.** Chemistry a crystalline acid made by oxidizing tellurium dioxide. ● Chem. formula: $Te(OH)_6$.
– DERIVATIVES **tel·lu·rate** /ˈtelyəˌrāt/ **n.**

Tel·lu·ride /ˈtelyəˌrīd/ a resort town in southwestern Colorado, a former mining center, now a popular ski resort; pop. 2,361 (est. 2008).

tel·lu·ride ▶ **n.** Chemistry a compound of tellurium with another more electropositive element or a radical.

tel·lu·rite /ˈtelyəˌrīt/ ▶ **n.** Chemistry a salt of the anion TeO_3^{2-}.

tel·lu·ri·um /təˈlo͝orēəm/ ▶ **n.** the chemical element of atomic number 52, a brittle, shiny silvery-white semimetal resembling selenium and occurring

mainly in small amounts in metallic sulfide ores. It is a semiconductor and is used in some electrical devices and in specialized alloys. (Symbol: **Te**)
– ORIGIN early 19th cent.: modern Latin, from Latin *tellus, tellur-* 'earth,' probably named in contrast to **URANIUM**.

tel·ly /'telē/ ▶ **n.** (pl. **tellies**) Brit. informal term for **TELEVISION**.

tel·net /'tel,net/ Computing ▶ **n.** a network protocol that allows a user on one computer to log onto another computer that is part of the same network. ■ a program that establishes a connection from one computer to another by means of such a protocol. ■ a link established in such a way.
▶ **v.** (**telnets, telnetting, telnetted**) [no obj.] informal log onto a remote computer using a telnet program.
– DERIVATIVES **tel·net·ta·ble** adj.
– ORIGIN 1970s: blend of **TELECOMMUNICATION** and **NETWORK**.

tel·o·lec·i·thal /,telō'lesəTHəl, ,tēlō-/ ▶ **adj.** Zoology (of an egg or egg cell) having a large yolk situated at or near one end.
– ORIGIN late 19th cent.: from Greek *telos* 'end' + *lekithos* 'egg yolk' + **-AL**.

te·lom·er·ase /tə'lämə,rās, tə'lō, -,rāz/ ▶ **n.** an enzyme that adds nucleotides to telomeres, esp. in cancer cells.

tel·o·mere /'telə,mi(ə)r, 'telə-/ ▶ **n.** Genetics a compound structure at the end of a chromosome.
– DERIVATIVES **tel·o·mer·ic** /,tēlə'merik, ,telə-/ adj.
– ORIGIN 1940s: from Greek *telos* 'end' + *meros* 'part.'

tel·o·phase /'tēlə,fāz, 'telə-/ ▶ **n.** Biology the final phase of cell division, between anaphase and interphase, in which the chromatids or chromosomes move to opposite ends of the cell and two nuclei are formed.
– ORIGIN late 19th cent.: from Greek *telos* 'end' + **PHASE**.

te·los /'teläs, 'tē-/ ▶ **n.** (pl. **teloi** /'teloi, 'tēloi/) chiefly Philosophy or literary an ultimate object or aim.
– ORIGIN Greek, literally 'end.'

tel·son /'telsən/ ▶ **n.** Zoology the last segment in the abdomen, or a terminal appendage to it, in crustaceans, chelicerates, and embryonic insects.
– ORIGIN mid 19th cent.: from Greek, literally 'limit.'

Tel·star /'tel,stär/ the first of the active communications satellites (i.e., both receiving and retransmitting signals, not merely reflecting signals from the earth). It was launched by the US in 1962 and used in the transmission of television broadcasting and telephone communication.

Tel·u·gu /'telə,gōō/ (also **Telegu**) ▶ **n.** (pl. **same** or **Telugus**) **1** a member of a people of southeastern India.
2 the Dravidian language of this people, spoken mainly in the state of Andhra Pradesh.
▶ **adj.** of or relating to this people or their language.
– ORIGIN from the name in Telugu, *telungu*.

tem·blor /'temblər, -,blôr/ ▶ **n.** an earthquake.
– ORIGIN late 19th cent.: from American Spanish.

tem·er·ar·i·ous /,temə're(ə)rēəs/ ▶ **adj.** literary reckless; rash.
– ORIGIN mid 16th cent.: from Latin *temerarius* (from *temere* 'rashly') + **-OUS**.

te·mer·i·ty /tə'meritē/ ▶ **n.** excessive confidence or boldness; audacity: *no one had the temerity to question his conclusions.*
– ORIGIN late Middle English: from Latin *temeritas*, from *temere* 'rashly.'

t

Tem·es·vár /'temesH,vär/ Hungarian name for **TIMIŞOARA**.

Tem·ne /'temnē/ ▶ **n.** (pl. **same** or **Temnes**) **1** a member of a people of Sierra Leone.
2 the Niger–Congo language of this people, the main language of Sierra Leone.
▶ **adj.** of or relating to this people or their language.
– ORIGIN the name in Temne.

tem·no·spon·dyl /,temnō'spändl/ ▶ **n.** an extinct amphibian of a large group that was dominant from the Carboniferous to the Triassic. ● Order (or grade) Temnospondyli: many families.
– ORIGIN early 20th cent.: from modern Latin *Temnospondyli* (plural), from Greek *temnein* 'to cut' + *spondulos* 'vertebra.'

temp[1] /temp/ informal ▶ **n.** a temporary employee, typically an office worker who finds employment through an agency.
▶ **v.** [no obj.] work as a temporary employee.
– ORIGIN 1930s: abbreviation.

temp[2] ▶ **abbr.** temperature.

temp. ▶ **abbr.** in or from the time of: *a Roman aqueduct temp. Augustus.*
– ORIGIN from Latin *tempore*, ablative of *tempus* 'time.'

Tem·pe /tem'pē, 'tempē/ a city in south central Arizona, east of Phoenix, home to Arizona State University; pop. 175,523 (est. 2008).

tem·peh /'tempā/ ▶ **n.** an Indonesian dish made by deep-frying fermented soybeans.
– ORIGIN from Indonesian *tempe*.

tem·per /'tempər/ ▶ **n. 1** [in sing.] a person's state of mind seen in terms of their being angry or calm: *he rushed out in a very bad temper.* ■ a tendency to become angry easily: *I know my temper gets the better of me at times.* ■ an angry state of mind: *Drew had walked out in a temper | I only said it in a fit of temper.*
2 the degree of hardness and elasticity in steel or other metal: *the blade rapidly heats up and the metal loses its temper.*
▶ **v.** [with obj.] **1** improve the hardness and elasticity of (steel or other metal) by reheating and then cooling it. ■ improve the consistency or resiliency of (a substance) by heating it or adding particular substances to it.
2 (often **be tempered with**) serve as a neutralizing or counterbalancing force to (something): *their idealism is tempered with realism.*
3 tune (a piano or other instrument) so as to adjust the note intervals correctly.
– PHRASES **keep** (or **lose**) **one's temper** refrain (or fail to refrain) from becoming angry. **out of temper** in an irritable mood.
– DERIVATIVES **tem·per·er** n.
– ORIGIN Old English *temprian* 'bring something into the required condition by mixing it with something else,' from Latin *temperare* 'mingle, restrain oneself.' Sense development was probably influenced by Old French *temprer* 'to temper, moderate.' The noun originally denoted a proportionate mixture of elements or qualities, also the combination of the four bodily humors, believed in medieval times to be the basis of temperament, hence sense 1 of the noun (late Middle English). Compare with **TEMPERAMENT**.

tem·per·a /'tempərə/ ▶ **n.** a method of painting with pigments dispersed in an emulsion miscible with water, typically egg yolk. The method was used in Europe for fine painting, mainly on wood panels, from the 12th or early 13th century until the 15th, when it began to give way to oils. ■ emulsion used in this method of painting.
– ORIGIN mid 19th cent.: from Italian, in the phrase *pingere a tempera* 'paint in distemper.'

tem·per·a·ment /'temp(ə)rəmənt/ ▶ **n. 1** a person's or animal's nature, esp. as it permanently affects their behavior: *she had an artistic temperament.* ■ the tendency to behave angrily or emotionally: *he had begun to show signs of temperament.*
2 the adjustment of intervals in tuning a piano or other musical instrument so as to fit the scale for use in different keys; in **equal temperament**, the octave consists of twelve equal semitones.
– ORIGIN late Middle English: from Latin *temperamentum* 'correct mixture,' from *temperare* 'mingle.' In early use the word was synonymous with the noun **TEMPER**.

tem·per·a·men·tal /,temp(ə)rə'mentl/ ▶ **adj. 1** (of a person) liable to unreasonable changes of mood.
2 of or relating to a person's temperament: *they were firm friends in spite of temperamental differences.*
– DERIVATIVES **tem·per·a·men·tal·ly** adv.

tem·per·ance /'temp(ə)rəns/ ▶ **n.** abstinence from alcoholic drink: [as modifier] *the temperance movement.* ■ moderation or self-restraint, esp. in eating and drinking.
– ORIGIN Middle English: from Anglo-Norman French *temperaunce*, from Latin *temperantia* 'moderation,' from *temperare* 'restrain.'

tem·per·ate /'temp(ə)rət/ ▶ **adj. 1** of, relating to, or denoting a region or climate characterized by mild temperatures.
2 showing moderation or self-restraint: *Charles was temperate in his consumption of both food and drink.*
– DERIVATIVES **tem·per·ate·ly** adv., **tem·per·ate·ness** n.
– ORIGIN late Middle English (in the sense 'not affected by passion or emotion'): from Latin *temperatus* 'mingled, restrained,' from the verb *temperare*.

tem·per·ate zone (also **Temperate Zone**) ▶ **n.** each of the two belts of latitude between the torrid zone and the northern and southern frigid zones.

tem·per·a·ture /'temp(ə)rəCHər, -,CHŏŏr/ ▶ **n.** the degree or intensity of heat present in a substance or object, esp. as expressed according to a comparative scale and shown by a thermometer or perceived by touch. ■ Medicine the degree of internal heat of a person's body: *I'll take her temperature.* ■ informal a body temperature above the normal; fever: *he was running a temperature.* ■ the degree of excitement or tension in a discussion or confrontation: *the temperature of the debate was lower than before.*
– ORIGIN late Middle English: from French *température* or Latin *temperatura*, from *temperare* 'restrain.' The word originally denoted the state of being tempered or mixed, later becoming synonymous with **TEMPERAMENT**. The modern sense dates from the late 17th cent.

tem·per·a·ture in·ver·sion ▶ **n.** see **INVERSION** (sense 2).

-tempered ▶ **comb. form** having a specified temper or disposition: *ill-tempered.*

-temperedly ▶ **comb. form** in adverbs corresponding to adjectives ending in *-tempered* (such as *bad-temperedly* corresponding to *bad-tempered*).

-temperedness ▶ **comb. form** in nouns corresponding to adjectives ending in *-tempered* (such as *bad-temperedness* corresponding to *bad-tempered*).

tem·pest /'tempist/ ▶ **n.** a violent windy storm.
– PHRASES **a tempest in a teapot** great anger or excitement about a trivial matter.
– ORIGIN Middle English: from Old French *tempeste*, from Latin *tempestas* 'season, weather, storm,' from *tempus* 'time, season.'

tem·pes·tu·ous /tem'pesCHōōəs/ ▶ **adj.**
1 characterized by strong and turbulent or conflicting emotion: *he had a reckless and tempestuous streak.*
2 very stormy: *a tempestuous wind.*
– DERIVATIVES **tem·pes·tu·ous·ly** adv., **tem·pes·tu·ous·ness** n.
– ORIGIN late Middle English: from late Latin *tempestuosus*, from Latin *tempestas* (see **TEMPEST**).

tem·pi /'tempē/ plural form of **TEMPO**.

Tem·plar /'templər/ ▶ **n.** historical a member of the Knights Templar.
– ORIGIN Middle English: from Old French *templier*, from medieval Latin *templarius*, from Latin *templum* (see **TEMPLE**[1]).

tem·plate /'templət/ ▶ **n. 1** a shaped piece of metal, wood, card, plastic, or other material used as a pattern for processes such as painting, cutting out, shaping, or drilling. ■ something that serves as a model for others to copy: *the plant was to serve as the template for change throughout the company.* ■ Computing a preset format for a document or file, used so that the format does not have to be recreated each time it is used: *a memo template.* ■ Biochemistry a nucleic acid molecule that acts as a pattern for the sequence of assembly of a protein, nucleic acid, or other large molecule.
2 a timber or plate used to distribute the weight in a wall or under a support.
– ORIGIN late 17th cent. (as *templet*): probably from **TEMPLE**[3] + **-ET**[1]. The change in the ending in the 19th cent. was due to association with **PLATE**.

Tem·ple[1] /'tempəl/ an industrial and commercial city in central Texas; pop. 59,654 (est. 2008).

Tem·ple[2], Shirley (1928–), US child star; married name *Shirley Temple Black*. In the 1930s, she appeared in movies such as *The Little Colonel* (1935) and *Rebecca of Sunnybrook Farm* (1938). She later became active in Republican politics and represented the US at the United Nations and as an ambassador.

Shirley Temple

tem·ple[1] /'tempəl/ ▶ **n.** a building devoted to the worship, or regarded as the dwelling place, of a god or gods or other objects of religious reverence. ■ (**the Temple**) either of two successive religious buildings of the Jews in Jerusalem. The first (957–586 BC) was built by Solomon and destroyed by Nebuchadnezzar; it contained the Ark of the Covenant. The second (515 BC–AD 70) was enlarged by Herod the Great from 20 BC and destroyed by the Romans during a Jewish revolt; all that remains is the Western Wall. ■ (**the Temple**) a group of buildings in Fleet Street in London that stand on land formerly occupied by the headquarters of

the Knights Templar. Located there are the Inner and Outer Temple, two of the Inns of Court. ■ a synagogue. ■ a place of Christian public worship, esp. a Protestant church in France.
– ORIGIN Old English *templ, tempel*, reinforced in Middle English by Old French *temple*, both from Latin *templum* 'open or consecrated space.'

tem·ple² ▶ n. the flat part of either side of the head between the forehead and the ear.
– ORIGIN Middle English: from Old French, from an alteration of Latin *tempora*, plural of *tempus* 'temple of the head.'

tem·ple³ ▶ n. a device in a loom for keeping the cloth stretched.
– ORIGIN late Middle English: from Old French, perhaps ultimately the same word as TEMPLE².

tem·ple block ▶ n. a percussion instrument consisting of a hollow block of wood that is struck with a stick.

tem·po /ˈtempō/ ▶ n. (pl. **tempos** or **tempi** /-pē/)
1 Music the speed at which a passage of music is or should be played.
2 the rate or speed of motion or activity; pace: *the tempo of life dictated by a heavy workload.*
– ORIGIN mid 17th cent. (as a fencing term denoting the timing of an attack): from Italian, from Latin *tempus* 'time.'

tem·po·ral¹ /ˈtemp(ə)rəl/ ▶ adj. **1** relating to worldly as opposed to spiritual affairs; secular.
2 of or relating to time. ■ Grammar relating to or denoting time or tense.
– DERIVATIVES **tem·po·ral·ly** adv.
– ORIGIN Middle English: from Old French *temporel* or Latin *temporalis*, from *tempus, tempor-* 'time.'

tem·po·ral² ▶ adj. Anatomy of or situated in the temples of the head.
– ORIGIN late Middle English: from late Latin *temporalis*, from *tempora* 'the temples' (see TEMPLE²).

tem·po·ral bone ▶ n. Anatomy either of a pair of bones that form part of the side of the skull on each side and enclose the middle and inner ear.

tem·po·ral·is /ˌtempəˈraləs, -ˈrālis/ ▶ n. Anatomy a fan-shaped muscle that runs from the side of the skull to the back of the lower jaw and is involved in closing the mouth and chewing.
– ORIGIN late 17th cent.: from late Latin.

tem·po·ral·i·ty /ˌtempəˈralitē/ ▶ n. (pl. **temporalities**) **1** the state of existing within or having some relationship with time.
2 (usu. **temporalities**) a secular possession, esp. the properties and revenues of a religious body or a member of the clergy.
– ORIGIN late Middle English (denoting temporal matters or secular authority): from late Latin *temporalitas*, from *temporalis* (see TEMPORAL¹).

tem·po·ral lobe ▶ n. each of the paired lobes of the brain lying beneath the temples, including areas concerned with the understanding of speech.

tem·po·ral pow·er ▶ n. the power of a bishop or cleric, esp. the pope, in secular matters.

tem·po·rar·y /ˈtempəˌrerē/ ▶ adj. lasting for only a limited period of time; not permanent: *a temporary job.*
▶ n. (pl. **temporaries**) a person employed on a temporary basis, typically an office worker who finds employment through an agency. See also TEMP¹.
– DERIVATIVES **tem·po·rar·i·ly** /ˌtempəˈre(ə)rəlē, ˈtempəˌrer-/ adv., **tem·po·rar·i·ness** n.
– ORIGIN mid 16th cent.: from Latin *temporarius*, from *tempus, tempor-* 'time.'

tem·po·rize /ˈtempəˌrīz/ ▶ v. **1** [no obj.] avoid making a decision or committing oneself in order to gain time: *the opportunity was missed because the mayor still temporized.*
2 temporarily adopt a particular course in order to conform to the circumstances: *their unwillingness to temporize had driven their country straight into conflict with France.*
– DERIVATIVES **tem·po·ri·za·tion** /ˌtempəriˈzāsHən/ n., **tem·po·riz·er** n.
– ORIGIN late 16th cent.: from French *temporiser* 'bide one's time,' from medieval Latin *temporizare* 'to delay,' from Latin *tempus, tempor-* 'time.'

tem·po·ro·man·dib·u·lar joint /ˌtemporōˌmanˈdibyələr/ ▶ n. Anatomy the hinge joint between the temporal bone and the lower jaw.

tem·po ru·ba·to /ˈtempō ro͞oˈbätō/ ▶ n. fuller term for RUBATO.

Tem·pra·ni·llo /ˌtempräˈnē(y)ō/ ▶ n. a variety of wine grape grown in Spain, used to make Rioja wine. ■ a red wine made from this grape.
– ORIGIN named after a village in northern Spain.

tempt /tem(p)t/ ▶ v. [with obj.] entice or attempt to entice (someone) to do or acquire something that they find attractive but know to be wrong or not beneficial: *don't allow impatience to tempt you into overexposure and sunburn* | *there'll always be someone tempted by the rich pickings of poaching* | [with obj. and infinitive] *jobs that involve entertaining may tempt you to drink more than you intend.*
■ (**be tempted to do something**) have an urge or inclination to do something: *I was tempted to look at my watch, but didn't dare.* ■ attract; allure: *he was tempted out of retirement to save the team.* ■ archaic risk provoking (a deity or abstract force), usually with undesirable consequences.
– PHRASES **tempt fate** (or **providence**) do something that is risky or dangerous.
– DERIVATIVES **tempt·a·bil·i·ty** /ˌtem(p)təˈbilitē/ n. (rare), **tempt·a·ble** adj. (rare).
– ORIGIN Middle English: from Old French *tempter* 'to test,' from Latin *temptare* 'handle, test, try.'

temp·ta·tion /tem(p)ˈtāsHən/ ▶ n. a desire to do something, esp. something wrong or unwise: *he resisted the temptation to call Celia at the office* | *we almost gave in to temptation.* ■ a thing or course of action that attracts or tempts someone: *the temptations of life in New York.* ■ (**the Temptation**) the tempting of Jesus by the Devil (see Matt. 4).
– ORIGIN Middle English: from Old French *temptacion*, from Latin *temptatio(n-)*, from *temptare* 'handle, test, try.'

tempt·er /ˈtem(p)tər/ ▶ n. a person or thing that tempts. ■ (**the Tempter**) the Devil.
– ORIGIN late Middle English: from Old French *tempteur*, from ecclesiastical Latin *temptator*, from Latin *temptare* 'to handle, test, try.'

tempt·ing /ˈtem(p)tiNG/ ▶ adj. appealing to or attracting someone, even if wrong or inadvisable: *a tempting financial offer* | [with infinitive] *it is often tempting to bring about change rapidly.*
– DERIVATIVES **tempt·ing·ly** adv.

tempt·ress /ˈtem(p)tris/ ▶ n. a woman who tempts someone to do something, typically a sexually attractive woman who sets out to allure or seduce someone.

tem·pu·ra /temˈpo͝orə/ ▶ n. a Japanese dish of fish, shellfish, or vegetables, fried in batter.
– ORIGIN Japanese, probably from Portuguese *tempêro* 'seasoning.'

ten /ten/ ▶ cardinal number equivalent to the product of five and two; one more than nine; 10: *the last ten years* | *the house comfortably sleeps ten* | *a ten-foot shrub.* (Roman numeral: **x, X**) ■ a group or unit of ten people or things: *count in tens.* ■ ten years old: *the boy was no more than ten.* ■ ten o'clock: *at about ten at night, I got a call.* ■ a size of garment or other merchandise denoted by ten. ■ a ten-dollar bill: *he took the money in tens.* ■ a playing card with ten pips. ■ (**a ten**) used to indicate that someone has done something well; the highest mark on a scale of one to ten: *I would have to give them a ten for all the work they did.*
– PHRASES **be ten a penny** see PENNY. **ten to one** very probably: *ten to one you'll never find out who did this.*
– ORIGIN Old English *tēn, tīen*, of Germanic origin; related to Dutch *tien* and German *zehn*, from an Indo-European root shared by Sanskrit *daśa*, Greek *deka*, and Latin *decem*.

ten. ▶ abbr. Music tenuto.

ten·a·ble /ˈtenəbəl/ ▶ adj. **1** able to be maintained or defended against attack or objection: *such a simplistic approach is no longer tenable.*
2 (of an office, position, scholarship, etc.) able to be held or used: *the post is tenable for three years.*
– DERIVATIVES **ten·a·bil·i·ty** /ˌtenəˈbilitē/ n.
– ORIGIN late 16th cent.: from French, from *tenir* 'to hold,' from Latin *tenere*.

ten·ace /ˈtenˌās, ˈtenis/ ▶ n. (in bridge, whist, and similar card games) a pair of cards in one hand that rank immediately above and below a card held by an opponent, e.g., the ace and queen in a suit of which an opponent holds the king.
– ORIGIN mid 17th cent.: from French, from Spanish *tenaza*, literally 'pincers.'

te·na·cious /təˈnāsHəs/ ▶ adj. tending to keep a firm hold of something; clinging or adhering closely: *a tenacious grip.* ■ not readily relinquishing a position, principle, or course of action; determined: *you're tenacious and you get at the truth* | *the most tenacious politician.* ■ persisting in existence; not easily dispelled: *a tenacious local legend.*
– DERIVATIVES **te·na·cious·ly** adv., **te·na·cious·ness** n.
– ORIGIN early 17th cent.: from Latin *tenax, tenac-* (from *tenere* 'to hold') + -IOUS.

te·nac·i·ty /təˈnasitē/ ▶ n. the quality or fact of being able to grip something firmly; grip: *the sheer tenacity of the limpet.* ■ the quality or fact of being very determined; determination: *you have to admire the tenacity of these two guys.* ■ the quality or fact of continuing to exist; persistence: *the tenacity of certain myths within the historical record.*

te·nac·u·lum /təˈnakyələm/ ▶ n. (pl. **tenacula** /-yələ/) a surgical clamp with sharp hooks at the end, used to hold or pick up small pieces of tissue such as the ends of arteries.
– ORIGIN late 17th cent.: from Latin, literally 'holder, holding instrument,' from *tenere* 'to hold.'

ten·an·cy /ˈtenənsē/ ▶ n. (pl. **tenancies**) possession of land or property as a tenant: *Holding took over the tenancy of the farm.*

ten·an·cy in com·mon ▶ n. Law a shared tenancy in which each holder has a distinct, separately transferable interest.

ten·ant /ˈtenənt/ ▶ n. a person who occupies land or property rented from a landlord. ■ Law a person holding real property by private ownership.
▶ v. [with obj.] (usu. **be tenanted**) occupy (property) as a tenant.
– DERIVATIVES **ten·ant·a·ble** adj. (formal), **ten·ant·less** adj.
– ORIGIN Middle English: from Old French, literally 'holding,' present participle of *tenir*, from Latin *tenere*.

ten·ant at will ▶ n. (pl. **tenants at will**) Law a tenant that can be evicted without notice.

ten·ant farm·er ▶ n. a person who farms rented land.

ten·ant·ry /ˈtenəntrē/ ▶ n. **1** [treated as sing. or pl.] the tenants of an estate.
2 tenancy.

Ten·cel /ˈtensel/ ▶ n. trademark a cellulosic fiber obtained from wood pulp using recyclable solvents; a fabric made from this.
– ORIGIN 1960s (proprietary name of various yarns and fabrics): an invented word.

tench /tencH/ ▶ n. (pl. **same**) a European freshwater fish of the minnow family, popular with anglers and widely introduced elsewhere, including several US states. ● *Tinca tinca*, family Cyprinidae.
– ORIGIN Middle English: from Old French *tenche*, from late Latin *tinca*.

Ten Com·mand·ments (in the Bible) the divine rules of conduct given by God to Moses on Mount Sinai, according to Exod. 20:1–17.

> The commandments are generally enumerated as: have no other gods; do not make or worship idols; do not take the name of the Lord in vain; keep the sabbath holy; honor one's father and mother; do not kill; do not commit adultery; do not steal; do not give false evidence; do not covet another's property or wife.

tend¹ /tend/ ▶ v. [no obj.] regularly or frequently behave in a particular way or have a certain characteristic: [no obj., with infinitive] *written language tends to be formal* | *her hair tended to come loose.* ■ (**tend to/toward**) be liable to possess or display (a particular characteristic): *Walter tended toward corpulence.* ■ go or move in a particular direction: *the road tends west around small mountains.* ■ (**tend to**) Mathematics approach (a quantity or limit): *the Fourier coefficients tend to zero.*
– ORIGIN Middle English (in the sense 'move or be inclined to move in a certain direction'): from Old French *tendre* 'stretch, tend,' from Latin *tendere*.

tend² ▶ v. [with obj.] care for or look after; give one's attention to: *Viola tended plants on the roof* | [no obj.] *for two or three months he tended to business.* ■ direct or manage; work in: *I've been tending bar at the airport lounge.* ■ archaic wait on as an attendant or servant.
– DERIVATIVES **tend·ance** /ˈtendəns/ n. (archaic).
– ORIGIN Middle English: shortening of ATTEND.

ten·den·cy /ˈtendənsē/ ▶ n. (pl. **tendencies**) an inclination toward a particular characteristic or type of behavior: *for students, there is a* **tendency to** *socialize in the evenings* | *criminal tendencies.* ■ a group within a larger political party or movement: *the dominant tendency in the party remained right-wing.*
– ORIGIN early 17th cent.: from medieval Latin *tendentia*, from *tendere* 'to stretch' (see TEND¹).

ten·den·tious /tenˈdensHəs/ ▶ adj. expressing or intending to promote a particular cause or point of view, esp. a controversial one: *a tendentious reading of history.*
– DERIVATIVES **ten·den·tious·ly** adv., **ten·den·tious·ness** n.
– ORIGIN early 20th cent.: suggested by German *tendenziös*.

ten·der¹ /ˈtendər/ ▶ adj. (**tenderer, tenderest**)
1 showing gentleness and concern or sympathy: *he was being so kind and tender.* ■ [predic.] (**tender of**)

t

archaic solicitous of; concerned for: *be tender of a lady's reputation.*
2 (of food) easy to cut or chew; not tough: *tender green beans.* ■ (of a plant) easily injured by severe weather and therefore needing protection. ■ (of a part of the body) sensitive to pain: *the pale, tender skin of her forearm.* ■ young, immature, and vulnerable: *at the tender age of five.* ■ requiring tact or careful handling: *the issue of conscription was a particularly tender one.* ■ Nautical (of a ship) leaning or readily inclined to roll in response to the wind.
– PHRASES **tender mercies** used ironically to imply that someone cannot be trusted to look after or treat someone else kindly or well: *they have abandoned their children to the tender mercies of the social services.*
– DERIVATIVES **ten·der·ly adv.**, **ten·der·ness n.**
– ORIGIN Middle English: from Old French *tendre*, from Latin *tener* 'tender, delicate.'

ten·der² ▶ **v.** [with obj.] offer or present (something) formally: *he tendered his resignation as leader.* ■ offer (money) as payment: *she tendered her fare.* ■ [no obj.] make a formal written offer to carry out work, supply goods, or buy land, shares, or another asset for a stated fixed price: *firms of interior decorators have been **tendering** for the work.* ■ [with obj.] make such an offer giving (a stated fixed price): *what price should we tender for a contract?*
▶ **n.** an offer to carry out work, supply goods, or buy land, shares, or another asset at a stated fixed price.
– PHRASES **put something out to tender** seek offers to carry out work or supply goods at a stated fixed price.
– DERIVATIVES **ten·der·er n.**
– ORIGIN mid 16th cent. (as a legal term meaning 'formally offer a plea or evidence, or money to discharge a debt,' also as a noun denoting such an offer): from Old French *tendre*, from Latin *tendere* 'to stretch, hold forth' (see **TEND¹**).

ten·der³ ▶ **n. 1** [usu. in combination or with modifier] a person who looks after someone else or a machine or place: *Alexei signaled to one of the engine tenders.*
2 a boat used to ferry people and supplies to and from a ship.
3 a railcar coupled to a steam locomotive to carry fuel and water.
– ORIGIN late Middle English (in the sense 'attendant, nurse'): from **TEND²** or shortening of *attender* (see **ATTEND**).

ten·der-eyed ▶ **adj. 1** having gentle eyes. **2** having sore or weak eyes.

ten·der·foot /ˈtendərˌfo͝ot/ ▶ **n.** (pl. **tenderfoots** or **tenderfeet**) **1** a newcomer or novice, esp. a person unaccustomed to the hardships of pioneer life.
2 a Boy Scout of the lowest rank.

ten·der·heart·ed /ˈtendərˈhärtid/ ▶ **adj.** having a kind, gentle, or sentimental nature.
– DERIVATIVES **ten·der·heart·ed·ness n.**

ten·der·ize /ˈtendəˌrīz/ ▶ **v.** make (meat) more tender by beating or slow cooking.

ten·der·iz·er /ˈtendəˌrīzər/ ▶ **n.** a thing used to make meat tender, in particular: ■ a substance such as papain that is rubbed onto meat or used as a marinade to soften the fibers. ■ a small hammer with teeth on the head, used to beat meat.

ten·der·loin /ˈtendərˌloin/ ▶ **n. 1** the tenderest part of a loin of beef, pork, etc., taken from under the short ribs in the hindquarters. ■ the undercut of a sirloin.
2 informal a district of a city where vice and corruption are prominent. [late 19th cent.: originally a term applied to a district of New York, seen as a 'choice' assignment by police because of the bribes offered to them to turn a blind eye.]

ten·di·ni·tis /ˌtendəˈnītis/ (also **tendonitis**) ▶ **n.** inflammation of a tendon, most commonly from overuse but also from infection or rheumatic disease.

ten·don /ˈtendən/ ▶ **n.** a flexible but inelastic cord of strong fibrous collagen tissue attaching a muscle to a bone. ■ the hamstring of a quadruped.
– DERIVATIVES **ten·di·nous** /-dənəs/ **adj.**
– ORIGIN late Middle English: from French or medieval Latin *tendo(n-)*, translating Greek *tenōn* 'sinew,' from *teinein* 'to stretch.'

ten·don or·gan ▶ **n.** Anatomy a sensory receptor within a tendon that responds to tension and relays impulses to the central nervous system.

ten·dril /ˈtendrəl/ ▶ **n.** a slender threadlike appendage of a climbing plant, often growing in a spiral form, that stretches out and twines around any suitable support. ■ something resembling a plant tendril, esp. a slender curl or ringlet of hair.
– ORIGIN mid 16th cent.: probably a diminutive of Old French *tendron* 'young shoot,' from Latin *tener* 'tender.'

ten·du /tänˈdo͞o, tänˈdʏ/ ▶ **adj.** [postpositive] Ballet (of a position) stretched out or held tautly: *battement tendu.*
– ORIGIN French.

ten·du leaf ▶ **n.** the leaves of an Asian ebony tree, gathered in India as a cheap tobacco substitute. ● *Diospyros melanoxylon*, family Ebenaceae.
– ORIGIN Hindi *tendu.*

Ten·e·brae /ˈtenəˌbrā, -ˌbrē/ ▶ **plural n.** (in the Roman Catholic Church) matins and lauds for the last three days of Holy Week, at which candles are successively extinguished. Several composers have set parts of the office to music.
– ORIGIN Latin, literally 'darkness.'

ten·e·brous /ˈtenəbrəs/ ▶ **adj.** literary dark; shadowy or obscure.
– ORIGIN late Middle English: via Old French from Latin *tenebrosus*, from *tenebrae* 'darkness.'

ten·e·ment /ˈtenəmənt/ ▶ **n. 1** a room or a set of rooms forming a separate residence within a house or block of apartments. ■ (also **tenement house**) a house divided into and rented in such separate residences, esp. one that is run-down and overcrowded.
2 a piece of land held by an owner. ■ Law any kind of permanent property, e.g., lands or rents, held from a superior.
– ORIGIN Middle English (in the sense 'tenure, property held by tenure'): via Old French from medieval Latin *tenementum*, from *tenere* 'to hold.'

Ten·er·ife /ˌtenəˈrēf, -ˈrif, -ˈrēfā/ a volcanic island in the Atlantic Ocean, the largest of the Canary Islands; pop. 866,033 (2008); capital, Santa Cruz.

te·nes·mus /təˈnezməs/ ▶ **n.** Medicine a continual or recurrent inclination to evacuate the bowels, caused by disorder of the rectum or other illness.
– ORIGIN early 16th cent.: via medieval Latin from Greek *teinesmos* 'straining,' from *teinein* 'stretch, strain.'

ten·et /ˈtenit/ ▶ **n.** a principle or belief, esp. one of the main principles of a religion or philosophy: *the tenets of classical liberalism.*
– ORIGIN late 16th cent. (superseding earlier *tenent*): from Latin, literally 'he holds,' from the verb *tenere.*

ten·fold /ˈtenˌfōld/ ▶ **adj.** ten times as great or as numerous: *a tenfold increase in the use of insecticides.* ■ having ten parts or elements.
▶ **adv.** by ten times; to ten times the number or amount: *production increased tenfold.*

ten-gal·lon hat ▶ **n.** a large, broad-brimmed hat, traditionally worn by cowboys.

ten·ge /ˈteNGgä/ ▶ **n.** (pl. **same** or **tenges**) **1** the basic monetary unit of Kazakhstan, equal to 100 teins.
2 a monetary unit of Turkmenistan, equal to one hundredth of a manat.

te·ni·a ▶ **n.** variant spelling of **TAENIA**.

Ten·iers /ˈtenyərz, təˈni(ə)rs/, David (1610–90), Flemish painter; known as **David Teniers the Younger**.

Ten Lost Tribes of Is·ra·el see **LOST TRIBES**.

Tenn. ▶ **abbr.** Tennessee.

ten·nant·ite /ˈtenənˌtīt/ ▶ **n.** a gray-black mineral consisting of a sulfide of copper, iron, and arsenic. It is an important ore of copper.
– ORIGIN mid 19th cent.: from the name of Smithson *Tennant* (1761–1815), English chemist, + **-ITE¹**.

ten·né /ˈtenē/ (also **tenny**) Heraldry ▶ **n.** orange-brown, as a stain used in blazoning.
▶ **adj.** [usu. postpositive] of this color.
– ORIGIN mid 16th cent.: obsolete French, variant of Old French *tane* (see **TAWNY**).

ten·ner /ˈtenər/ ▶ **n.** Brit. informal a ten-pound note.

Ten·nes·see /ˌtenəˈsē/ **1** a river in the southeastern US, flowing in a great loop, generally west and then north, for about 875 miles (1,400 km) to join the Ohio River in western Kentucky.
2 a state in the central southeastern US; pop. 6,214,888 (est. 2008); capital, Nashville; statehood, June 1, 1796 (16). It was the site of many Civil War battles, including those at Shiloh and Chattanooga.
– DERIVATIVES **Ten·nes·see·an** /-ˈsēən/ **n. & adj.**

Ten·nes·see Val·ley Au·thor·i·ty (abbr.: **TVA**) an independent federal government agency in the US, created in 1933 as part of the New Deal proposals. Responsible for the development of the whole Tennessee river basin, it provides one of the world's greatest irrigation and hydroelectric power systems.

Ten·nes·see Walk·ing Horse ▶ **n.** a powerful riding horse of a breed with a characteristic fast walking pace.

ten·nies /ˈtenēz/ ▶ **plural n.** informal tennis shoes.

ten·nis /ˈtenis/ ▶ **n.** a game in which two or four players strike a ball with rackets over a net stretched across a court. The usual form (originally called **lawn tennis**) is played with a felt-covered hollow rubber ball on a grass, clay, or artificial surface. See also **COURT TENNIS**.
– ORIGIN late Middle English *tenetz, tenes* 'court tennis,' apparently from Old French *tenez* 'take, receive' (called by the server to an opponent), imperative of *tenir.*

ten·nis brace·let ▶ **n.** a bracelet containing many small gems, usually diamonds, linked together in a narrow chain.

ten·nis court ▶ **n.** a rectangular area marked with lines on which tennis is played.

ten·nis el·bow ▶ **n.** inflammation of the tendons of the elbow (epicondylitis) caused by overuse of the muscles of the forearm.

ten·nis shoe ▶ **n.** a light canvas or leather soft-soled shoe suitable for tennis or casual wear.

Ten·no /ˈtenō/ ▶ **n.** (pl. **Tennos**) the Emperor of Japan.
– ORIGIN Japanese.

ten·ny /ˈtenē/ ▶ **n. & adj.** var. of **TENNÉ**.

Ten·ny·son /ˈtenəsən/, Alfred, 1st Baron Tennyson of Aldworth and Freshwater (1809–92), English poet; poet laureate from 1850. His reputation was established by *In Memoriam* (1850), a long poem concerned with immortality, change, and evolution. Other notable works: "The Charge of the Light Brigade" (1854) and *Idylls of the King* (1859).

Ten·ny·so·ni·an /ˌteniˈsōnēən/ ▶ **adj.** relating to or in the style of Tennyson.
▶ **n.** an admirer or student of Tennyson or his work.

Te·noch·ti·tlán /təˌnôCHtētˈlän/ the ancient capital of the Aztec empire, founded *c.*1320. In 1521, the Spanish conquistador Cortés destroyed it and established Mexico City on its site.

ten·on /ˈtenən/ ▶ **n.** a projecting piece of wood made for insertion into a mortise in another piece.
▶ **v.** [with obj.] (usu. **be tenoned**) join by means of a tenon. ■ cut as a tenon.
– DERIVATIVES **ten·on·er n.**
– ORIGIN late Middle English: from French, from *tenir* 'to hold,' from Latin *tenere.*

ten·or¹ /ˈtenər/ ▶ **n.** a singing voice between baritone and alto or countertenor, the highest of the ordinary adult male range. ■ a singer with such a voice. ■ a part written for such a voice. ■ [usu. as modifier] an instrument, esp. a saxophone, trombone, tuba, or viol, of the lowest pitch but one in its family: *a tenor sax.* ■ (in full **tenor bell**) the largest and deepest bell of a ring or set.
– ORIGIN late Middle English: via Old French from medieval Latin, based on *tenere* 'to hold'; so named because the tenor part was allotted (and therefore "held") the melody.

ten·or² ▶ **n. 1** [in sing.] (usu. **the tenor of**) the general meaning, sense, or content of something: *the general tenor of the debate.*
2 [in sing.] (usu. **the tenor of**) a settled or prevailing character or direction, esp. the course of a person's life or habits: *the even tenor of life in the kitchen was disrupted the following day.*
3 Law the actual wording of a document.
4 Finance the time that must elapse before a bill of exchange or promissory note becomes due for payment.
– ORIGIN Middle English: from Old French *tenour*, from Latin *tenor* 'course, substance, import of a law,' from *tenere* 'to hold.'

ten·or clef ▶ **n.** Music a clef placing middle C on the second-highest line of the stave, used chiefly for cello and bassoon music.

te·no·ri·no /ˌtenəˈrēnō/ ▶ **n.** (pl. **tenorini** /-ˈrēnē/) a high tenor.
– ORIGIN Italian, diminutive of *tenore* 'tenor.'

ten·or·ist /ˈtenərist/ ▶ **n.** a person who plays a tenor instrument, esp. the tenor saxophone.

ten·o·syn·o·vi·tis /ˌtenōˌsinəˈvītis/ ▶ **n.** Medicine inflammation and swelling of a tendon, typically in the wrist, often caused by repetitive movements such as typing.
– ORIGIN late 19th cent.: from Greek *tenōn* 'tendon' + **SYNOVITIS**.

te·not·o·my /təˈnätəmē/ ▶ **n.** the surgical cutting of a tendon, esp. as a remedy for club foot.
– ORIGIN mid 19th cent.: coined in French from Greek *tenōn* 'tendon' + *-tomia* (see **-TOMY**).

ten·pin /ˈtenˌpin/ ▶ **n.** a wooden pin used in tenpin bowling. ■ (**tenpins**) [treated as sing.] tenpin bowling.

ten·pin bowl·ing ▶ **n.** a game in which ten wooden pins are set up at the end of a track (typically one of several in a large, automated alley) and bowled down with hard rubber or plastic balls.

ten·pound·er /ˈtenˈpoundər/ ▶ **n.** a large, silvery-blue, herringlike fish of tropical seas that is popular as a game fish. Also called **LADYFISH**. ● *Elops saurus* (or *machnata*), family Elopidae.

ten·rec /ˈtenˌrek/ ▶ **n.** a small, insectivorous mammal native to Madagascar, different kinds of which

resemble hedgehogs, shrews, or small otters. ● Several genera in the family Tenrecidae: many species, including the **common** (or **tailless**) **tenrec** (*Tenrec ecaudatus*), also found in the Comoro islands.
– ORIGIN late 18th cent.: from French *tanrec*, from Malagasy *tàndraka*.

TENS /tenz/ ▶ **abbr.** transcutaneous electrical nerve stimulation, a technique intended to provide pain relief by applying electrodes to the skin to block impulses in underlying nerves.

tense[1] /tens/ ▶ **adj.** (esp. of a muscle or someone's body) stretched tight or rigid: *she tried to relax her tense muscles.* ■ (of a person) unable to relax because of nervousness, anxiety, or stimulation: *he was tense with excitement.* ■ (of a situation, event, etc.) causing or showing anxiety and nervousness: *relations between the two neighboring states had been tense in recent years.* ■ Phonetics (of a speech sound, esp. a vowel) pronounced with the vocal muscles stretched tight. The opposite of LAX.
▶ **v.** [no obj.] become tense, typically through anxiety or nervousness: *her body tensed up.* ■ [with obj.] make (a muscle or one's body) tight or rigid: *carefully stretch and then tense your muscles.*
– DERIVATIVES **tense·ly adv.**, **tense·ness n.**, **ten·si·ty** /'tensitē/ **n.** (dated).
– ORIGIN late 17th cent.: from Latin *tensus* 'stretched,' from the verb *tendere*.

tense[2] ▶ **n.** Grammar a set of forms taken by a verb to indicate the time (and sometimes also the continuance or completeness) of the action in relation to the time of the utterance: *the past tense.*
– DERIVATIVES **tense·less adj.**
– ORIGIN Middle English (in the general sense 'time'): from Old French *tens*, from Latin *tempus* 'time.'

ten·seg·ri·ty /ten'segritē/ ▶ **n.** Architecture the characteristic property of a stable three-dimensional structure consisting of members under tension that are contiguous and members under compression that are not.
– ORIGIN 1950s: from *tensional integrity*.

ten·sile /'tensəl, -ˌsīl/ ▶ **adj. 1** of or relating to tension.
2 capable of being drawn out or stretched.
– DERIVATIVES **ten·sil·i·ty** /ten'silitē/ **n.**
– ORIGIN early 17th cent. (sense 2): from medieval Latin *tensilis*, from Latin *tendere* 'to stretch.'

ten·sile strength ▶ **n.** the resistance of a material to breaking under tension. Compare with COMPRESSIVE STRENGTH.

ten·sion /'tenSHən/ ▶ **n. 1** the state of being stretched tight: *the parachute keeps the cable under tension as it drops.* ■ the state of having the muscles stretched tight, esp. as causing strain or discomfort: *the elimination of neck tension can relieve headaches.* ■ a strained state or condition resulting from forces acting in opposition to each other. ■ the degree of tightness of stitches in knitting and machine sewing. ■ electromotive force.
2 mental or emotional strain: *a mind that is affected by stress or tension cannot think as clearly.* ■ a strained political or social state or relationship: *the coup followed months of tension between the military and the government | racial tensions.* ■ a relationship between ideas or qualities with conflicting demands or implications: *the basic tension between freedom and control.*
▶ **v.** [with obj.] apply a force to (something) that tends to stretch it.
– DERIVATIVES **ten·sion·al** /-SHənl/ **adj.**, **ten·sion·al·ly** /-SHənl-ē/ **adv.**, **ten·sion·er n.**, **ten·sion·less adj.**
– ORIGIN mid 16th cent. (as a medical term denoting a condition or feeling of being physically stretched or strained): from French, or from Latin *tensio(n-)*, from *tendere* 'stretch.'

ten·sive /'tensiv/ ▶ **adj.** causing or expressing tension.

Tens·kwa·ta·wa /ten(t)'skwätəˌwä/ see TECUMSEH.

ten·sor /'tensər, 'tenˌsôr/ ▶ **n. 1** Mathematics a mathematical object analogous to but more general than a vector, represented by an array of components that are functions of the coordinates of a space.
2 Anatomy a muscle that tightens or stretches a part of the body.
– DERIVATIVES **ten·so·ri·al** /ten'sôrēəl/ **adj.**
– ORIGIN early 18th cent.: modern Latin, from Latin *tendere* 'to stretch.'

tent /tent/ ▶ **n.** a portable shelter made of cloth, supported by one or more poles and stretched tight by cords or loops attached to pegs driven into the ground. ■ Medicine short for OXYGEN TENT.
▶ **v. 1** [with obj.] cover with or as if with a tent: *the garden had been completely tented over for supper.* ■ arrange in a shape that looks like a tent: *Tim tented his fingers.* ■ (as adj. **tented**) composed of or provided with tents: *they were living in large tented camps.*
2 [no obj.] (esp. of traveling circus people) live in a tent.
– ORIGIN Middle English: from Old French *tente*, based on Latin *tent-* 'stretched,' from the verb *tendere*. The verb dates from the mid 16th cent.

ten·ta·cle /'tentəkəl/ ▶ **n.** a slender flexible limb or appendage in an animal, esp. around the mouth of an invertebrate, used for grasping, moving about, or bearing sense organs. ■ (in a plant) a tendril or a sensitive glandular hair. ■ something resembling a tentacle in shape or flexibility: *trailing tentacles of vapor.* ■ (usu. **tentacles**) an insidious spread of influence and control: *the Party's tentacles reached into every nook and cranny of people's lives.*
– DERIVATIVES **ten·ta·cled adj.** [also in combination], **ten·tac·u·lar** /ten'takyələr/ **adj.**, **ten·tac·u·late** /ten'takyələt/ **adj.**
– ORIGIN mid 18th cent.: anglicized from modern Latin *tentaculum*, from Latin *tentare*, *temptare* 'to feel, try.'

ten·ta·tive /'tentətiv/ ▶ **adj.** not certain or fixed; provisional: *a tentative conclusion.* ■ done without confidence; hesitant: *he eventually tried a few tentative steps round his hospital room.*
– DERIVATIVES **ten·ta·tive·ly adv.**, **ten·ta·tive·ness n.**
– ORIGIN late 16th cent.: from medieval Latin *tentativus*, from *tentare*, variant of *temptare* 'handle, try.'

tent cat·er·pil·lar ▶ **n.** a chiefly American moth caterpillar that lives in groups inside communal silken webs in a tree, which it often defoliates. ● Several species in the family Lasiocampidae, esp. *Malacosoma americana*.

tent cit·y ▶ **n.** a large collection of tents, typically one forming temporary or makeshift accommodations for refugees or homeless people.

tent dress ▶ **n.** a full, loose-fitting dress that is narrow at the shoulders and very wide at the hem, having no waistline or darts.

ten·ter /'tentər/ ▶ **n.** a framework on which fabric can be held taut for drying or other treatment during manufacture.
– ORIGIN Middle English: from medieval Latin *tentorium*, from *tent-* 'stretched,' from the verb *tendere*.

ten·ter·hook /'tentərˌho͝ok/ ▶ **n.** historical a hook used to fasten cloth on a drying frame or tenter.
– PHRASES **on tenterhooks** in a state of suspense or agitation because of uncertainty about a future event.

tenth /tenTH/ ▶ **n.** constituting number ten in a sequence; 10th: *the tenth century | the tenth of September | the tenth-floor locker room.* ■ (**a tenth/one tenth**) each of ten equal parts into which something is or may be divided: *a tenth of a second.* ■ the tenth grade of a school. ■ Music an interval or chord spanning an octave and a third in the diatonic scale, or a note separated from another by this interval.
– DERIVATIVES **tenth·ly adv.**

tenth-rate ▶ **adj.** informal of extremely poor quality.

ten·to·ri·um /ten'tôrēəm/ ▶ **n.** (pl. **tentoria** /-'tôrēə/) **1** Anatomy a fold of the dura mater forming a partition between the cerebrum and cerebellum.
2 Entomology an internal skeletal framework in the head of an insect.
– ORIGIN early 19th cent.: from Latin, literally 'tent.'

tent peg ▶ **n.** see PEG (sense 1 of the noun).

tent pole ▶ **n. 1** a pole supporting a tent.
2 [usu. as modifier] informal a movie that is expected to be very successful and therefore able to fund a range of related products or movies: *tent-pole movies can run to three hundred million or more in total costs.*

tent stitch ▶ **n.** a series of parallel diagonal stitches.

te·nu·i·ty /te'n(y)o͞oitē, tə-/ ▶ **n.** lack of solidity or substance; thinness.
– ORIGIN late Middle English: from Latin *tenuitas*, from *tenuis* 'thin.'

ten·u·ous /'tenyo͞oəs/ ▶ **adj.** very weak or slight: *the tenuous link between interest rates and investment.* ■ very slender or fine; insubstantial: *a tenuous cloud.*
– DERIVATIVES **ten·u·ous·ly adv.**, **ten·u·ous·ness n.**
– ORIGIN late 16th cent.: formed irregularly from Latin *tenuis* 'thin' + -OUS.

ten·ure /'tenyər, -yo͝or/ ▶ **n. 1** the conditions under which land or buildings are held or occupied.
2 the holding of an office: *his tenure of the premiership would be threatened.* ■ a period for which an office is held.
3 guaranteed permanent employment, esp. as a teacher or professor, after a probationary period.
▶ **v.** [with obj.] give (someone) a permanent post, esp. as a teacher or professor: *I had recently been tenured and then promoted to full professor.* ■ (as adj. **tenured**) having or denoting such a post: *a tenured faculty member.*
– ORIGIN late Middle English: from Old French, from *tenir* 'to hold,' from Latin *tenere*.

ten·ure track ▶ **n.** [usu. as modifier] an employment structure whereby the holder of a post, typically an academic one, is guaranteed consideration for eventual tenure: *a tenure-track position.*

te·nu·to /te'no͞otō/ Music ▶ **adv. & adj.** (of a note) held for its full time value or slightly more.
▶ **n.** (pl. **tenutos** or **tenuti** /-'no͞otē/) a note or chord performed in this way.
– ORIGIN Italian, literally 'held,' past participle of *tenere*.

Ten·zing Nor·gay /'tenziNG 'nôrˌgā/ (1914–86), Sherpa mountaineer. In 1953, as members of the British expedition, he and Sir Edmund Hillary were the first to reach the summit of Mount Everest.

te·o·cal·li /ˌtē-ō'kälē, ˌtā-/ ▶ **n.** (pl. **teocallis**) a temple of the Aztecs or other Mexican peoples, typically standing on a truncated pyramid.
– ORIGIN American Spanish, from Nahuatl *teo:kalli*, from *teo:tl* 'god' + *kalli* 'house.'

te·o·sin·te /ˌtē-ō'sintē, ˌtā-/ ▶ **n.** a Mexican grass that is grown as fodder and is considered to be one of the parent plants of modern corn. ● *Zea mays* subsp. *mexicana*, family Gramineae.
– ORIGIN late 19th cent.: from French *téosinté*, from Nahuatl *teocintli*, apparently from *teo:tl* 'god' + *cintli* 'dried ear of maize.'

Te·o·ti·hua·c·án /ˌtēəˌtēwä'kän/ the largest city in pre-Columbian America, 25 miles (40 km) northeast of Mexico City. Built *c.*300 BC, it reached its zenith *c.* AD 300–600, when it was the center of an influential culture that spread throughout Meso-America. It was sacked by the invading Toltecs *c.*900.

te·pa·che /tə'päCHē/ ▶ **n.** a Mexican drink, typically made with pineapple, water, and brown sugar and partially fermented.
– ORIGIN Mexican Spanish.

te·pal /'tēpəl, 'tepəl/ ▶ **n.** Botany a segment of the outer whorl in a flower that has no differentiation between petals and sepals.
– ORIGIN mid 19th cent.: from French *tépale*, blend of *pétale* 'petal' and *sépal* 'sepal.'

tep·a·ry bean /'tepərē/ ▶ **n.** a bean plant native to the southwestern US, cultivated in Mexico and Arizona for its drought-resistant qualities. ● *Phaseolus acutifolius*, family Leguminosae.
– ORIGIN early 20th cent.: from Spanish *tepari*, from Pima.

te·pee /'tēˌpē/ (also **teepee** or **tipi**) ▶ **n.** a portable conical tent made of skins, cloth, or canvas on a frame of poles, used by American Indians of the Plains and Great Lakes regions.
– ORIGIN mid 18th cent.: from Sioux *tīpi* 'dwelling.'

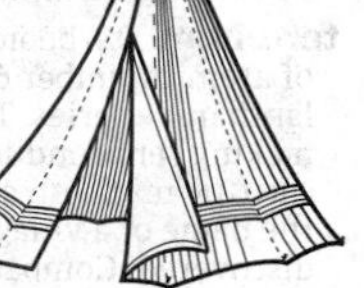
tepee

teph·ra /'tefrə/ ▶ **n.** Geology rock fragments and particles ejected by a volcanic eruption.
– ORIGIN 1940s: from Greek, literally 'ash, ashes.'

Te·pic /te'pēk/ a city in western Mexico, capital of the state of Nayarit; pop. 288,253 (2009).

tep·id /'tepid/ ▶ **adj. 1** (esp. of a liquid) only slightly warm; lukewarm.
2 showing little enthusiasm: *the applause was tepid.*
– DERIVATIVES **te·pid·i·ty** /tə'piditē/ **n.**, **tep·id·ly adv.**, **tep·id·ness n.**
– ORIGIN late Middle English: from Latin *tepidus*, from *tepere* 'be warm.'

TEPP ▶ **abbr.** Chemistry tetraethyl pyrophosphate.

tep·pan-ya·ki /ˌtepän'yäkē/ ▶ **n.** a Japanese dish of meat, fish, or both, fried with vegetables on a hot steel plate forming the center of the dining table.
– ORIGIN Japanese, from *teppan* 'steel plate' + *yaki* 'to fry.'

te·qui·la /tə'kēlə/ ▶ **n.** a Mexican liquor made from an agave.
– ORIGIN Mexican Spanish, named after the town of *Tequila* in Mexico, where the drink was first produced.

te·qui·la sun·rise ▶ **n.** a cocktail containing tequila, orange juice, and grenadine.

ter. ▶ **abbr.** ■ (in prescriptions) rub. [from Latin *tere*.] ■ terrace. ■ territorial. ■ territory.

t

ter- ▶ comb. form three; having three: *tercentenary*.
– ORIGIN from Latin *ter* 'thrice.'

USAGE The combining-form prefix **ter-** is commonly replaced by **tri-**, as in **tricentenary**.

tera- ▶ comb. form used in units of measurement.
1 denoting a factor of 10^{12}: *terawatt*.
2 Computing denoting a factor of 2^{40}.
– ORIGIN from Greek *teras* 'monster.'

ter·a·byte /ˈterə,bīt/ (abbr.: **Tb** or **TB**) ▶ n. Computing a unit of information equal to one million million (10^{12}) or strictly, 2^{40} bytes.

ter·a·flop /ˈterə,fläp/ ▶ n. Computing a unit of computing speed equal to one million million (10^{12}) floating-point operations per second.

te·rai /təˈrī/ (also **terai hat**) ▶ n. a wide-brimmed felt hat, typically with a double crown, worn chiefly by travelers in subtropical regions.
– ORIGIN late 19th cent.: from *Terai*, the name of a belt of marshy jungle between the Himalayan foothills and plains, from Hindi *tarāī* 'marshy lowlands.'

ter·a·phim /ˈterə,fim/ ▶ plural n. [also treated as sing.] small images or cult objects used as domestic deities or oracles by ancient Semitic peoples.
– ORIGIN late Middle English: via late Latin from Greek *theraphin*, from Hebrew *tĕrāpīm*.

terato- ▶ comb. form relating to monsters or abnormal forms: *teratology*.
– ORIGIN from Greek *teras, terat-* 'monster.'

ter·at·o·car·ci·no·ma /,terətō,kärsəˈnōmə/ ▶ n. (pl. **teratocarcinomata** /-mətə/ or **teratocarcinomas**) Medicine a form of malignant teratoma occurring esp. in the testis.

te·rat·o·gen /teˈratəjən, -,jen, ˈterətəjən/ ▶ n. an agent or factor that causes malformation of an embryo.
– DERIVATIVES **te·rat·o·gen·ic** /tə,ratəˈjenik, ,terətə-/ adj., **te·rat·o·ge·nic·i·ty** /tə,ratəjəˈnisitē, ,terə,tō-/ n.

te·rat·o·gen·e·sis /,terətōˈjenəsis, tə,ratō-/ ▶ n. the process by which congenital malformations are produced in an embryo or fetus.

ter·a·tol·o·gy /,terəˈtäləjē/ ▶ n. **1** Medicine & Biology the scientific study of congenital abnormalities and abnormal formations.
2 mythology relating to fantastic creatures and monsters.
– DERIVATIVES **ter·a·to·log·i·cal** /,terətəˈläjikəl/ adj., **ter·a·tol·o·gist** /-jist/ n.

ter·a·to·ma /,terəˈtōmə/ ▶ n. (pl. **teratomas** or **teratomata** /-mətə/) Medicine a tumor composed of tissues not normally present at the site (the site being typically in the gonads).

ter·a·watt /ˈterə,wät/ ▶ n. a unit of power equal to 10^{12} watts or a million megawatts.

ter·bi·um /ˈtərbēəm/ ▶ n. the chemical element of atomic number 65, a silvery-white metal of the lanthanide series. The main use of terbium is in making semiconductors. (Symbol: **Tb**)
– ORIGIN mid 19th cent.: modern Latin, from *Ytterby*, the name of a village in Sweden where it was discovered. Compare with ERBIUM and YTTERBIUM.

ter·bu·ta·line /tərˈbyo͞otl,ēn/ ▶ n. Medicine a synthetic compound with bronchodilator properties, used esp. in the treatment of asthma. ● Chem. formula: $C_{12}H_{19}NO_3$.
– ORIGIN 1960s: from TER- + BUTYL (elements of the systematic name), on the pattern of words such as *isoprenaline*.

terce /tərs/ ▶ n. a service forming part of the Divine Office of the Western Christian Church, traditionally said (or chanted) at the third hour of the day (i.e., 9 a.m.).
– ORIGIN late Middle English: from Old French, from Latin *tertia*, feminine of *tertius* 'third.' Compare with TIERCE.

ter·cel /ˈtərsəl/ ▶ n. variant spelling of TIERCEL.
– ORIGIN Middle English: from Old French, based on Latin *tertius* 'third,' perhaps from the belief that the third egg of a clutch produced a male.

ter·cen·ten·ar·y /,tərsenˈtenərē, terˈsentn,erē/ ▶ adj. & n. (pl. **tercentenaries**) another term for TRICENTENNIAL.

ter·cen·ten·ni·al /,tərsenˈtenēəl/ ▶ adj. & n. another term for TRICENTENNIAL.

ter·cet /ˈtərsit/ ▶ n. Prosody a set or group of three lines of verse rhyming together or connected by rhyme with an adjacent tercet.
– ORIGIN late 16th cent.: from French, from Italian *terzetto*, diminutive of *terzo* 'third,' from Latin *tertius*.

ter·e·binth /ˈterə,binTH/ ▶ n. a small southern European tree of the cashew family that was formerly a source of turpentine. ● *Pistacia terebinthus*, family Anacardiaceae.
– ORIGIN late Middle English: from Old French *therebinte*, or via Latin from Greek *terebinthos*.

te·re·do /təˈrēdō/ ▶ n. Zoology (pl. **teredos**) a wormlike bivalve mollusk with reduced shells that it uses to drill into wood. It can cause substantial damage to wooden structures and vessels.
Also called SHIPWORM. ● Genus *Teredo*, family Teredinidae: several species, in particular *T. navalis*.
– ORIGIN late Middle English: via Latin from Greek *terēdōn*; related to *teirein* 'rub hard, wear away.'

Ter·ence /ˈterəns/ (*c.*190–159 BC), Roman comic playwright; Latin name *Publius Terentius Afer*. His six surviving comedies are based on the Greek New Comedy; they are marked by more realism and a greater consistency of plot than are the works of Plautus.

ter·eph·thal·ic ac·id /ˈterəf,THalik/ ▶ n. Chemistry a crystalline organic acid used in making polyester resins and other polymers. ● The *para*-isomer of phthalic acid; chem. formula: $C_6H_4(COOH)_2$.
– DERIVATIVES **ter·eph·thal·ate** /,terəfˈTHal,āt/ n.
– ORIGIN mid 19th cent.: blend of *terebic* 'of or from turpentine' (from TEREBINTH) and PHTHALIC ACID.

te·res /ˈti(ə)rēz, ˈterēz/ ▶ n. Anatomy either of two muscles passing below the shoulder joint from the scapula to the upper part of the humerus, one (**teres major**) drawing the arm toward the body and rotating it inward, the other (**teres minor**) rotating it outward.
– ORIGIN early 18th cent.: modern Latin, from Latin, literally 'rounded.'

Te·re·sa, Moth·er /təˈrēsə, təˈrāsə/ (also **Theresa**) (1910–97), Roman Catholic nun and missionary, born of Albanian parentage in what is now Macedonia; born *Agnes Gonxha Bojaxhiu*. She became an Indian citizen in 1948. She founded the Order of Missionaries of Charity, noted for its work among the poor in Kolkata (Calcutta). Nobel Peace Prize (1979).

Mother Teresa

Te·re·sa of Á·vi·la, St. /ˈävilə/ (1515–82), Spanish Carmelite nun and mystic. She instituted the "discalced" reform movement with St. John of the Cross. Her writings include *The Way of Perfection* (1583) and *The Interior Castle* (1588). Feast day, October 15.

Te·re·sa of Li·sieux, St. /lēsˈyœ/ (also **Thérèse** /teˈrez/) (1873–97), French Carmelite nun; born *Marie-Françoise Thérèse Martin*. In her autobiography *L'Histoire d'une âme* (1898) she taught that sanctity can be attained through continual renunciation in small matters. Feast day, October 3.

Te·resh·ko·va /,tərəSHˈkôvə, ,ter-/, Valentina (Vladimirovna) (1937–), Russian cosmonaut. In June 1963, she was the first woman to go into space.

Te·re·si·na /,terəˈzēnə, -ˈsē-/ a river port in northeastern Brazil, on the Parnaíba River, capital of the state of Piauí; pop. 779,939 (2007).

te·rete /təˈrēt, ˈter,ēt/ ▶ adj. chiefly Botany cylindrical or slightly tapering, and without substantial furrows or ridges.
– ORIGIN early 17th cent.: from Latin *teres, teret-* 'rounded off.'

ter·gal /ˈtərgəl/ ▶ adj. Zoology of or relating to a tergum of an arthropod.
– ORIGIN mid 19th cent.: from Latin *tergum* 'back' + -AL.

ter·gite /ˈtər,jīt/ ▶ n. Entomology (in an insect) a sclerotized plate forming the tergum of a segment. Compare with STERNITE.
– ORIGIN late 19th cent.: from TERGUM + -ITE[1].

ter·gi·ver·sate /tərˈjivər,sāt, ˈtərjivər-/ ▶ v. [no obj.] **1** make conflicting or evasive statements; equivocate: *the more she tergiversated, the greater grew the ardency of the reporters for an interview*.
2 change one's loyalties; be apostate.
– DERIVATIVES **ter·gi·ver·sa·tion** /,tərjivərˈsāSHən/ n., **ter·gi·ver·sa·tor** /-,sātər/ n.
– ORIGIN mid 17th cent.: from Latin *tergiversat-* 'with one's back turned,' from the verb *tergiversari*, from *tergum* 'back' + *vertere* 'to turn.'

ter·gum /ˈtərgəm/ ▶ n. (pl. **terga** /-gə/) Zoology a thickened dorsal plate on each segment of the body of an arthropod.
– ORIGIN early 19th cent.: from Latin, literally 'back.'

Ter·hune /tərˈhyo͞on/, Albert Payson, (1872–1942) US writer. His fiction for young readers about dogs, esp. collies, includes *Lad: A Dog* (1919), *Treve* (1924), *My Friend the Dog* (1926), and *Loot* (1940).

-teria ▶ suffix denoting self-service establishments: *washeteria*.
– ORIGIN on the pattern of (*cafe*)*teria*.

ter·i·ya·ki /,terēˈyäkē/ ▶ n. a Japanese dish consisting of fish or meat marinated in soy sauce and grilled. ■ (also **teriyaki sauce**) a mixture of soy sauce, sake, ginger, and other flavorings, used in Japanese cooking as a marinade or glaze for such dishes.
– ORIGIN Japanese.

Ter·kel /ˈtərkəl/, Studs, (1912–2008), US writer, radio and television journalist, and historian; full name *Louis Terkel*. He had his own television show 1950–53 and radio show 1953–98. Thought of as the voice of the common man, he wrote *Division Street: America* (1967), *The Good War* (1984), *Coming of Age* (1995), and *My American Century* (1997).

term /tərm/ ▶ n. **1** a word or phrase used to describe a thing or to express a concept, esp. in a particular kind of language or branch of study: *the musical term "leitmotiv" | a term of abuse*. ■ (**terms**) language used on a particular occasion; a way of expressing oneself: *a protest in the strongest possible terms*. ■ Logic a word or words that may be the subject or predicate of a proposition.
2 a fixed or limited period for which something, e.g., office, imprisonment, or investment, lasts or is intended to last: *the president is elected for a single four-year term*. ■ archaic the duration of a person's life. ■ (also **full term**) the completion of a normal length of pregnancy: *the pregnancy went to full term | low birthweight at term*. ■ (also **term for years** or Brit. **term of years**) Law a tenancy of a fixed period. ■ archaic a boundary or limit, esp. of time.
3 each of the periods in the year, alternating with holidays or vacations, during which instruction is given in a school, college, or university, or during which a court holds sessions: *the summer term | term starts tomorrow*.
4 (**terms**) conditions under which an action may be undertaken or agreement reached; stipulated or agreed-upon requirements: *the union and the company agreed upon the contract's terms | he could only be dealt with on his own terms*. ■ conditions with regard to payment for something; stated charges: *loans on favorable terms*. ■ agreed conditions under which a war or other dispute is brought to an end: *a deal in Bosnia that could force the Serbs to come to terms*.
5 Mathematics each of the quantities in a ratio, series, or mathematical expression.
6 Architecture another term for TERMINUS.
▶ v. [with obj. and usu. with complement] give a descriptive name to; call by a specified name: *he has been termed the father of modern theology*.
– PHRASES **come to terms with** come to accept (a new and painful or difficult event or situation); reconcile oneself to: *she had come to terms with the tragedies in her life*. **in terms of** (or **in —— terms**) with regard to the particular aspect or subject specified: *replacing the printers is difficult to justify in terms of cost | sales are down by nearly 7 percent in real terms*. **the long/short/medium term** used to refer to a time that is a specified way into the future. **on —— terms** in a specified relation or on a specified footing: *we are all on friendly terms*.
– ORIGIN Middle English (denoting a limit in space or time, or (in the plural) limiting conditions): from Old French *terme*, from Latin *terminus* 'end, boundary, limit.'

term. ▶ abbr. ■ terminal. ■ termination.

ter·ma·gant /ˈtərməgənt/ ▶ n. **1** a harsh-tempered or overbearing woman.
2 (**Termagant**) historical an imaginary deity of violent and turbulent character, often appearing in morality plays.
– ORIGIN Middle English (sense 2): via Old French from Italian *Trivigante*, taken to be from Latin *tri-* 'three' + *vagant-* 'wandering,' and to refer to the moon "wandering" between heaven, earth, and hell under the three names *Selene*, *Artemis*, and *Persephone*.

term for years ▶ n. see TERM (sense 2 of the noun).

ter·mi·na·ble /ˈtərmənəbəl/ ▶ **adj. 1** able to be terminated.
2 coming to an end after a certain time.

ter·mi·nal /ˈtərmənl/ ▶ **adj. 1** [attrib.] of, forming, or situated at the end or extremity of something: *a terminal date | the terminal tip of the probe.* ■ of or forming a transportation terminal: *terminal platforms.* ■ Zoology situated at, forming, or denoting the end of a part or series of parts furthest from the center of the body. ■ Botany (of a flower, inflorescence, etc.) borne at the end of a stem or branch. Often contrasted with **AXILLARY**.
2 (of a disease) predicted to lead to death, esp. slowly; incurable: *terminal cancer.* ■ [attrib.] suffering from or relating to such a disease: *a hospice for terminal cases.* ■ [attrib.] (of a condition) forming the last stage of such a disease. ■ informal extreme and usually beyond cure or alteration (used to emphasize the extent of something regarded as bad or unfortunate): *you're making a terminal ass of yourself.*
▶ **n. 1** an end or extremity of something, in particular: ■ the end of a railroad or other transport route, or a station at such a point. ■ a departure and arrival building for air passengers at an airport. ■ an installation where oil or gas is stored at the end of a pipeline or at a port.
2 a point of connection for closing an electric circuit.
3 a device at which a user enters data or commands for a computer system and that displays the received output.
4 (also **terminal figure**) another term for **TERMINUS** (sense 3).
– DERIVATIVES **ter·mi·nal·ly adv.** [as submodifier] *a terminally ill woman.*
– ORIGIN early 19th cent.: from Latin *terminalis*, from *terminus* 'end, boundary.'

ter·mi·nal mo·raine ▶ **n.** Geology a moraine deposited at the point of furthest advance of a glacier or ice sheet.

ter·mi·nal ve·loc·i·ty ▶ **n.** Physics the constant speed that a freely falling object eventually reaches when the resistance of the medium through which it is falling prevents further acceleration.

ter·mi·nate /ˈtərməˌnāt/ ▶ **v.** [with obj.] bring to an end: *he was advised to terminate the contract.* ■ [no obj.] (**terminate in**) (of a thing) have its end at (a specified place) or of (a specified form): *the chain terminated in an iron ball covered with spikes.* ■ [no obj.] (of a train, bus, or boat service) end its journey: *the train will terminate at Stratford.* ■ end (a pregnancy) before term by artificial means. ■ end the employment of (someone); dismiss: *Adamson's putting pressure on me to terminate you.* ■ assassinate (someone, esp. an intelligence agent): *he was terminated by persons unknown.* ■ archaic form the physical end or extremity of (an area).
– PHRASES **terminate someone with extreme prejudice** murder or assassinate someone (used as a euphemism).
– ORIGIN late 16th cent. (in the sense 'direct an action toward a specified end'): from Latin *terminat-* 'limited, ended,' from the verb *terminare*, from *terminus* 'end, boundary.'

ter·mi·na·tion /ˌtərməˈnāsʜən/ ▶ **n. 1** the action of bringing something or coming to an end: *the termination of a contract.* ■ an act of dismissing someone from employment. ■ an induced abortion. ■ an assassination, esp. of an intelligence agent.
2 an ending or final point of something, in particular: ■ the final letter or letters or syllable of a word, esp. when constituting an element in inflection or derivation. ■ [with adj.] archaic an ending or result of a specified kind: *a good result and a happy termination.*
– DERIVATIVES **ter·mi·na·tion·al** /-sʜənl/ **adj.**
– ORIGIN late Middle English (in the sense 'determination, decision'): from Old French, or from Latin *terminatio(n-)*, from *terminare* 'to limit, end.'

ter·mi·na·tor /ˈtərməˌnātər/ ▶ **n.** a person or thing that terminates something. ■ Astronomy the dividing line between the light and dark part of a planetary body. ■ Biochemistry a sequence of polynucleotides that causes transcription to end and the newly synthesized nucleic acid to be released from the template molecule.

ter·mi·ner /ˈtərmənər/ ▶ **n.** see **OYER AND TERMINER**.

ter·mi·ni /ˈtərmənī/ plural form of **TERMINUS**.

ter·mi·nol·o·gy /ˌtərməˈnäləjē/ ▶ **n.** (pl. **terminologies**) the body of terms used with a particular technical application in a subject of study, theory, profession, etc.: *the terminology of semiotics | specialized terminologies for higher education.*
– DERIVATIVES **ter·mi·no·log·i·cal** /-nəˈläjikəl/ **adj.**, **ter·mi·no·log·i·cal·ly** /-nəˈläjik(ə)lē/ **adv.**, **ter·mi·nol·o·gist** /-jist/ **n.**
– ORIGIN early 19th cent.: from German *Terminologie*, from medieval Latin *terminus* 'term.'

ter·mi·nus /ˈtərmənəs/ ▶ **n.** (pl. **termini** /-nī/ or **terminuses**) **1** a final point in space or time; an end or extremity: *the exhibition's terminus is 1962.* ■ Biochemistry the end of a polypeptide or polynucleotide chain or similar long molecule.
2 chiefly Brit. the end of a railroad or other transportation route, or a station at such a point; a terminal. ■ an oil or gas terminal.
3 Architecture a figure of a human bust or an animal ending in a square pillar from which it appears to spring, originally used as a boundary marker in ancient Rome.
– ORIGIN mid 16th cent. (in the sense 'final point in space or time'): from Latin, 'end, limit, boundary.'

ter·mi·nus ad quem /ˈtərmənəs äd ˈkwem/ ▶ **n.** the point at which something ends or finishes. ■ an aim or goal.
– ORIGIN Latin, literally 'end to which.'

ter·mi·nus an·te quem /ˈtərmənəs ˈantē ˈkwem/ ▶ **n.** the latest possible date for something.
– ORIGIN Latin, literally 'end before which.'

ter·mi·nus a quo /ˈtərmənəs ä ˈkwō/ ▶ **n.** the earliest possible date for something. ■ a starting point or initial impulse.
– ORIGIN Latin, literally 'end from which.'

ter·mi·nus post quem /ˈtərmənəs ˈpōst ˈkwem/ ▶ **n.** the earliest possible date for something.
– ORIGIN Latin, literally 'end after which.'

ter·mi·tar·i·um /ˌtərmiˈte(ə)rēəm/ ▶ **n.** (pl. **termitaria** /-ˈte(ə)rēə/) a colony of termites, typically within a mound of cemented earth.
– ORIGIN mid 19th cent.: modern Latin, from Latin *termes, termit-* 'termite.'

ter·mi·ta·ry /ˈtərmiˌterē/ ▶ **n.** (pl. **termitaries**) another term for **TERMITARIUM**.

ter·mite /ˈtərˌmīt/ ▶ **n.** a small, pale soft-bodied insect that lives in large colonies with several different castes, typically within a mound of cemented earth. Many kinds feed on wood and can be highly destructive to trees and timber. Also called **WHITE ANT**. ● Order Isoptera: several families.
– ORIGIN late 18th cent.: from Latin *termes, termit-* 'woodworm,' alteration of Latin *tarmes*, perhaps by association with *terere* 'to rub.'

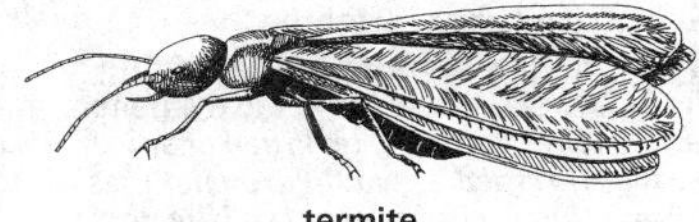
termite

term life in·sur·ance ▶ **n.** life insurance that pays a benefit in the event of the death of the insured during a specified term. Compare with **WHOLE LIFE INSURANCE**.

term of years ▶ **n.** see **TERM** (sense 2 of the noun).

term pa·per ▶ **n.** a student's lengthy essay on a subject drawn from the work done during a school or college term.

terms of trade ▶ **plural n.** Economics the ratio of an index of a country's export prices to an index of its import prices.

tern[1] /tərn/ ▶ **n.** a seabird related to the gulls, typically smaller and more slender, with long pointed wings and a forked tail. ● Family Sternidae (or Laridae): several genera, in particular *Sterna*, and many species.
– ORIGIN late 17th cent.: of Scandinavian origin; related to Danish *terne* and Swedish *tärna*, both from Old Norse *therna*.

tern[2] ▶ **n.** rare a set of three, esp. three lottery numbers that when drawn together win a large prize.
– ORIGIN late Middle English: apparently from French *terne*, from Latin *terni* 'three at once, three each,' from *ter* 'thrice.'

ter·na·ry /ˈtərnərē/ ▶ **adj.** composed of three parts. ■ Mathematics using three as a base.
– ORIGIN late Middle English: from Latin *ternarius*, from *terni* 'three at once.'

ter·na·ry form ▶ **n.** Music the form of a movement in which the first subject is repeated after an interposed second subject in a related key.

terne /tərn/ ▶ **n.** (also **terne metal**) a lead alloy containing about 20 percent tin and often some antimony. ■ (also **terneplate**) thin sheet iron or steel coated with this.
– ORIGIN mid 19th cent. (denoting terneplate): probably from French *terne* 'dull, tarnished.'

ter·pene /ˈtərˌpēn/ ▶ **n.** Chemistry any of a large group of volatile unsaturated hydrocarbons found in the essential oils of plants, esp. conifers and citrus trees. They are based on a cyclic molecule having the formula $C_{10}H_{16}$.
– ORIGIN late 19th cent.: from German *Terpentin* 'turpentine' + **-ENE**.

ter·pe·noid /ˈtərpəˌnoid/ Chemistry ▶ **n.** any of a large class of organic compounds including terpenes, diterpenes, and sesquiterpenes. They have unsaturated molecules composed of linked isoprene units, generally having the formula $(C_5H_8)n$.
▶ **adj.** denoting such a compound.

ter·pol·y·mer /tərˈpäləmər/ ▶ **n.** Chemistry a polymer synthesized from three different monomers.

Terp·sich·o·re /ˌtərpˈsikərē/ Greek & Roman Mythology the Muse of lyric poetry and dance.
– ORIGIN Greek, literally 'delighting in dancing.'

terp·si·cho·re·an /ˌtərpsikəˈrēən, -ˈkôrēən/ ▶ **adj.** formal or humorous of or relating to dancing.
▶ **n.** formal or humorous a dancer.
– ORIGIN early 19th cent.: from *Terpsichore* (used in the 18th cent. to denote a female dancer or the art of dance) + **-AN**.

terr. ▶ **abbr.** ■ terrace. ■ territorial. ■ territory.

ter·ra /ˈterə/ ▶ **n. 1** [usu. with adj.] land or territory.
2 (**Terra**) (in science fiction) the planet earth.
– ORIGIN Latin, literally 'earth.'

ter·ra al·ba /ˈterə ˈalbə/ ▶ **n.** pulverized gypsum, esp. as an ingredient of medicines.
– ORIGIN Latin, literally 'white earth.'

ter·race /ˈteris/ ▶ **n. 1** a level paved area or platform next to a building; a patio or veranda. ■ each of a series of flat areas made on a slope, used for cultivation. ■ Geology a natural horizontal shelflike formation, such as a raised beach.
2 chiefly Brit. a block of row houses. ■ a row house.
▶ **v.** [with obj.] make or form (sloping land) into a number of level flat areas resembling a series of steps.
– ORIGIN early 16th cent. (denoting an open gallery, later a platform or balcony in a theater): from Old French, literally 'rubble, platform,' based on Latin *terra* 'earth.'

ter·raced /ˈterist/ ▶ **adj. 1** (of land) having been formed into a number of level areas resembling a series of steps.
2 chiefly Brit. (of a house) in the style of a row house.

ter·ra cot·ta /ˈterə ˈkätə/ (also **terracotta**) ▶ **n.** unglazed, typically brownish-red earthenware, used chiefly as an ornamental building material and in modeling. ■ a statuette or other object made of such earthenware. ■ a strong brownish-red or brownish-orange color.
– ORIGIN early 18th cent.: from Italian *terra cotta* 'baked earth,' from Latin *terra cocta*.

ter·ra fir·ma /ˈterə ˈfərmə/ ▶ **n.** dry land; the ground as distinct from the sea or air.
– ORIGIN early 17th cent. (denoting the territories on the Italian mainland that were subject to the state of Venice): from Latin, literally 'firm land.'

ter·ra·form /ˈterəˌfôrm/ ▶ **v.** [with obj.] (esp. in science fiction) transform (a planet) so as to resemble the earth, esp. so that it can support human life.
– DERIVATIVES **ter·ra·form·er n.**
– ORIGIN 1940s: from Latin *terra* 'earth' + the verb **FORM**.

ter·rain /təˈrān/ ▶ **n. 1** a stretch of land, esp. with regard to its physical features: *they were delayed by rough terrain.*
2 Geology variant form of **TERRANE**.
– ORIGIN early 18th cent. (denoting part of the training ground in a riding school): from French, from a popular Latin variant of Latin *terrenum*, neuter of *terrenus* (see **TERRENE**).

ter·ra in·cog·ni·ta /ˈterə ˌinkägˈnētə, inˈkägnitə/ ▶ **n.** unknown or unexplored territory.
– ORIGIN Latin, 'unknown land.'

ter·rain park ▶ **n.** a specially designed outdoor area for skiing and snowboarding, containing a variety of ramps, jumps, etc.

Ter·ra·my·cin /ˌterəˈmīsin/ ▶ **n.** trademark for **OXYTETRACYCLINE**.
– ORIGIN 1950s: from Latin *terra* 'earth' + **-MYCIN**.

Ter·ran /ˈterən/ ▶ **n.** (in science fiction) an inhabitant of the planet Earth.
▶ **adj.** (in science fiction) of or relating to the planet Earth or its inhabitants.

ter·rane /təˈrān, ˈterˌān/ (also **terrain**) ▶ **n.** Geology a fault-bounded area or region with a distinctive stratigraphy, structure, and geological history.
– ORIGIN early 19th cent: from popular Latin *terranum*. Compare with **TERRAIN**.

ter·ra·pin /ˈterəˌpin/ ▶ **n. 1** (also **diamondback terrapin**) a small edible turtle with lozenge-shaped markings on its shell, found in coastal marshes of the eastern US. ● *Malaclemys terrapin*, family Emydidae.

t

2 a freshwater turtle, esp. one of the smaller kinds of the Old World. Also called **TURTLE**. ● Emydidae and other families, order Chelonia: several genera and species.
– ORIGIN early 17th cent. (denoting the diamondback terrapin): of Algonquian origin.

diamondback terrapin

ter·ra·que·ous /terˈākwēəs, -ˈak-/ ▶ **adj.** consisting of, or formed of, land and water.
– ORIGIN mid 17th cent.: from Latin *terra* 'land' + **AQUEOUS**.

ter·rar·i·um /təˈre(ə)rēəm/ ▶ **n.** (pl. **terrariums** or **terraria** /-ˈre(ə)rēə/) a vivarium for smaller land animals, esp. reptiles, amphibians, or terrestrial invertebrates, typically in the form of a glass-fronted case. ■ a sealed transparent globe or similar container in which plants are grown.
– ORIGIN late 19th cent.: modern Latin, from Latin *terra* 'earth,' on the pattern of *aquarium*.

ter·rasse /teˈräs/ ▶ **n.** (pl. **same**) (in France) a flat, paved area outside a cafe where people sit to take refreshments.
– ORIGIN French, literally 'terrace.'

ter·raz·zo /təˈräzō, tiˈrätsō/ ▶ **n.** flooring material consisting of chips of marble or granite set in concrete and polished to give a smooth surface.
– ORIGIN early 20th cent.: Italian, literally 'terrace,' based on Latin *terra* 'earth.'

Ter·re Haute /ˌtər(ə) ˈhōt/ a city in western Indiana, on the Wabash River, near the border with Illinois; pop. 60,007 (est. 2008).

ter·rene /təˈrēn, ˈterˌēn/ ▶ **adj.** archaic of or like earth; earthy. ■ occurring on or inhabiting dry land. ■ of the world; secular rather than spiritual.
– ORIGIN Middle English: from Anglo-Norman French, from Latin *terrenus*, from *terra* 'earth.'

terre·plein /ˈterəˌplān/ ▶ **n.** chiefly historical a level space where a battery of guns is mounted.
– ORIGIN late 16th cent. (denoting a sloping bank behind a rampart): from French *terre-plein*, from Italian *terrapieno*, from *terrapienare* 'fill with earth.'

ter·res·tri·al /təˈrestrēəl, -ˈresCHəl/ ▶ **adj.** of, on, or relating to the earth: *increased ultraviolet radiation may disrupt terrestrial ecosystems*. ■ denoting television broadcasting using equipment situated on the ground rather than by satellite: *terrestrial and cable technology*. ■ of or on dry land: *a submarine eruption will be much more explosive than its terrestrial counterpart*. ■ (of an animal) living on or in the ground; not aquatic, arboreal, or aerial. ■ (of a plant) growing on land or in the soil; not aquatic or epiphytic. ■ Astronomy (of a planet) similar in size or composition to the earth, esp. being one of the four inner planets of our solar system. ■ archaic of or relating to the earth as opposed to heaven.
▶ **n.** an inhabitant of the earth.
– DERIVATIVES **ter·res·tri·al·ly adv.**
– ORIGIN late Middle English (in the sense 'temporal, worldly, mundane'): from Latin *terrestris* (from *terra* 'earth') + **-AL**.

ter·res·tri·al globe ▶ **n.** a spherical representation of the earth with a map on the surface.

ter·res·tri·al mag·net·ism ▶ **n.** the magnetic properties of the earth as a whole.

ter·res·tri·al tel·e·scope ▶ **n.** a telescope that is used for observing terrestrial objects and gives an uninverted image.

ter·ret /ˈterit/ ▶ **n.** each of the loops or rings on a harness pad for the driving reins to pass through.
– ORIGIN late 15th cent. (denoting either of two rings by which a leash is attached to a hawk's jesses): from Old French *touret*, diminutive of *tour* 'a turn.'

terre verte /ˈter ˈvert/ ▶ **n.** a grayish-green pigment made from glauconite and used esp. for watercolors and tempera. Also called **GREEN EARTH**.
– ORIGIN mid 17th cent.: French, literally 'green earth.'

ter·ri·bi·li·tà /ˌterəˌbilēˈtä/ ▶ **n.** awesomeness or emotional intensity of conception and execution in an artist or work of art, originally as a quality attributed to Michelangelo by his contemporaries.
– ORIGIN Italian.

ter·ri·ble /ˈterəbəl/ ▶ **adj.** extremely or distressingly bad or serious: *a terrible crime | terrible pain | the terrible conditions in which the ordinary people lived*. ■ extremely unpleasant or disagreeable: *the weather was terrible*. ■ [attrib.] informal used to emphasize the extent of something unpleasant or bad: *what a terrible mess*. ■ [as complement] extremely unwell or troubled: *I was sick all night and felt terrible for two solid days | Maria felt terrible because she had forgotten the woman's name*. ■ causing or likely to cause terror; sinister: *the stranger gave a terrible smile*.
– PHRASES **terrible twos** informal a period in a child's early social development (typically around the age of two years) that is associated with defiant or unruly behavior.
– DERIVATIVES **ter·ri·ble·ness n.**
– ORIGIN late Middle English (in the sense 'causing terror'): via French from Latin *terribilis*, from *terrere* 'frighten.'

ter·ri·bly /ˈterəblē/ ▶ **adv. 1** [usu. as submodifier] very; extremely: *I'm terribly sorry | it was all terribly frustrating*.
2 very badly or unpleasantly: *they beat me terribly*. ■ very greatly (used to emphasize something bad, distressing, or unpleasant): *your father misses you terribly*.

ter·ric·o·lous /teˈrikələs/ ▶ **adj.** Zoology (of an animal such as an earthworm) living on the ground or in the soil. ■ Botany (of a plant, esp. a lichen) growing on soil or on the ground.
– ORIGIN mid 19th cent.: from Latin *terricola* 'earth dweller' (from *terra* 'earth' + *colere* 'inhabit') + **-OUS**.

ter·ri·er /ˈterēər/ ▶ **n.** a small dog of a breed originally used for turning out foxes and other burrowing animals from their lairs. ■ used in similes to emphasize tenacity or eagerness: *she would fight like a terrier for every penny*.
– ORIGIN late Middle English: from Old French (*chien*) *terrier* 'earth (dog),' from medieval Latin *terrarius*, from Latin *terra* 'earth.'

ter·rif·ic /təˈrifik/ ▶ **adj. 1** of great size, amount, or intensity: *there was a terrific bang*. ■ informal extremely good; excellent: *it's been such a terrific day | you look terrific*.
2 archaic causing terror.
– DERIVATIVES **ter·rif·i·cal·ly** /-ik(ə)lē/ **adv.** [as submodifier] *she's been terrifically busy lately*.
– ORIGIN mid 17th cent. (sense 2): from Latin *terrificus*, from *terrere* 'frighten.'

ter·ri·fy /ˈterəˌfī/ ▶ **v.** (**terrifies, terrifying, terrified**) [with obj.] cause to feel extreme fear: *the thought terrifies me | he is terrified of spiders* | [with obj.] *she was terrified he would drop her* | (as adj. **terrifying**) *the terrifying events of the past few weeks*.
– DERIVATIVES **ter·ri·fi·er n., ter·ri·fy·ing·ly** /ˈterəˌfī-iNGlē/ **adv.** [as submodifier] *the bombs are terrifyingly accurate*.
– ORIGIN late 16th cent.: from Latin *terrificare*, from *terrificus* 'frightening' (see **TERRIFIC**).

ter·rig·e·nous /teˈrijənəs/ ▶ **adj.** Geology (of a marine deposit) made of material eroded from the land.
– ORIGIN late 17th cent. (in the sense 'produced from the earth, earth-born'): from Latin *terrigenus* (from *terra* 'earth' + *-genus* 'born') + **-OUS**.

ter·rine /təˈrēn/ ▶ **n.** a meat, fish, or vegetable mixture that has been cooked or otherwise prepared in advance and allowed to cool or set in its container, typically served in slices. ■ a container used for such a dish, typically of an oblong shape and made of earthenware.
– ORIGIN early 18th cent. (denoting a tureen): from French, literally 'large earthenware pot,' from *terrin* 'earthen.' Compare with **TUREEN**.

ter·ri·to·ri·al /ˌteriˈtôrēəl/ ▶ **adj. 1** of or relating to the ownership of an area of land or sea: *territorial disputes*. ■ Zoology (of an animal or species) defending a territory: *these sharks are aggressively territorial*. ■ of or relating to an animal's territory or its defense: *territorial growls*.
2 of or relating to a particular territory, district, or locality: *a bizarre territorial rite*. ■ (usu. **Territorial**) of or relating to a Territory, in the US (historically) or Canada.
▶ **n.** (**Territorial**) (in the UK) a member of the Territorial Army, a volunteer force locally organized to provide a reserve of trained and disciplined manpower for use in an emergency.
– DERIVATIVES **ter·ri·to·ri·al·i·ty** /-ˌtôrēˈalitē/ **n., ter·ri·to·ri·al·ly adv.**
– ORIGIN early 17th cent.: from late Latin *territorialis*, from Latin *territorium* (see **TERRITORY**).

ter·ri·to·ri·al im·per·a·tive ▶ **n.** [usu. in sing.] Zoology & Psychology the need to claim and defend a territory.

ter·ri·to·ri·al wa·ters ▶ **plural n.** the waters under the jurisdiction of a state, esp. the part of the sea within a stated distance of the shore (traditionally three miles from low-water mark).

ter·ri·to·ry /ˈterəˌtôrē/ ▶ **n.** (pl. **territories**) **1** an area of land under the jurisdiction of a ruler or state: *the government was prepared to give up the nuclear weapons on its territory | sorties into enemy territory*. ■ Zoology an area defended by an animal or group of animals against others of the same sex or species. Compare with **HOME RANGE**. ■ an area defended by a team or player in a game or sport. ■ an area in which one has certain rights or for which one has responsibility with regard to a particular type of activity: *a sales rep for a large territory*. ■ [with modifier] land with a specified characteristic: *woodland territory*.
2 (**Territory**) (esp. in the US, Canada, or Australia) an organized division of a country that is not yet admitted to the full rights of a state.
3 an area of knowledge, activity, or experience: *the contentious territory of clinical standards | the way she felt now—she was in unknown territory*.
– PHRASES **go** (or **come**) **with the territory** be an unavoidable result of a particular situation.
– ORIGIN late Middle English: from Latin *territorium*, from *terra* 'land.' The word originally denoted the district surrounding and under the jurisdiction of a town or city, specifically a Roman or provincial city.

ter·roir /terˈwär/ ▶ **n.** the complete natural environment in which a particular wine is produced, including factors such as the soil, topography, and climate. ■ (also **goût de terroir** /gōō də/) the characteristic taste and flavor imparted to a wine by the environment in which it is produced.
– ORIGIN French, *land*, from medieval Latin *terratorium*.

ter·ror /ˈterər/ ▶ **n. 1** extreme fear: *people fled in terror* | [in sing.] *a terror of darkness*. ■ the use of such fear to intimidate people, esp. for political reasons; terrorism: *weapons of terror*. ■ [in sing.] a person or thing that causes extreme fear: *his unyielding scowl became the terror of the Chicago mob*. ■ (**the Terror**) the period of the French Revolution between mid 1793 and July 1794 when the ruling Jacobin faction, dominated by Robespierre, ruthlessly executed anyone considered a threat to their regime. Also called **REIGN OF TERROR**.
2 (also **holy terror**) informal a person, esp. a child, who causes trouble or annoyance: *placid and obedient in their parents' presence, but holy terrors when left alone*.
– PHRASES **have** (or **hold**) **no terrors for someone** not frighten or worry someone.
– ORIGIN late Middle English: from Old French *terrour*, from Latin *terror*, from *terrere* 'frighten.'

> **WORD TRENDS** When George W. Bush declared a 'War on Terror' in September 2001 he was employing a new, and highly charged, synonym for terrorism. Before 2001, **terror** was a fairly uncommon word in the Oxford English Corpus, but it has since shown a steady rise in use, with the majority of examples being used synonymously with **terrorism**. It is now commonly seen as a modifier, with *attack*, *bombing*, *suspect*, and *plot* all common collocates. However, the use of **terror** has dropped off since a peak in 2007. In March 2009, the US Defense Department officially changed the name of its operations from 'Global War on Terror' to 'Overseas Contingency Operation.'

ter·ror·ism /ˈterəˌrizəm/ ▶ **n.** the use of violence and intimidation in the pursuit of political aims.

ter·ror·ist /ˈterərist/ ▶ **n.** a person who uses terrorism in the pursuit of political aims.
– DERIVATIVES **ter·ror·is·tic** /ˌterəˈristik/ **adj., ter·ror·is·ti·cal·ly adv.**
– ORIGIN late 18th cent.: from French *terroriste*, from Latin *terror* (see **TERROR**). The word was originally applied to supporters of the Jacobins in the French Revolution, who advocated repression and violence in pursuit of the principles of democracy and equality.

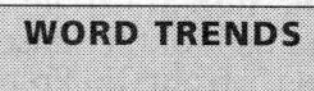

> **WORD TRENDS** See **FIGHTER**.

ter·ror·ize /ˈterəˌrīz/ ▶ **v.** [with obj.] create and maintain a state of extreme fear and distress in (someone); fill with terror: *he used his private army to terrorize the population | the union said staff would not be terrorized into ending their strike*.
– DERIVATIVES **ter·ror·i·za·tion** /ˌterərəˈzāSHən/ **n., ter·ror·iz·er n.**

ter·ror-strick·en (also **terror-struck**) ▶ **adj.** feeling or expressing extreme fear.

ter·ry /ˈterē/ (also **terry cloth**) ▶ **n.** (pl. **terries**) a fabric with raised uncut loops of thread covering both surfaces, used esp. for towels.
– ORIGIN late 18th cent.: of unknown origin.

terse /tərs/ ▶ **adj.** (**terser, tersest**) sparing in the use of words; abrupt: *a terse statement*.
– DERIVATIVES **terse·ly adv., terse·ness n.**
– ORIGIN early 17th cent.: from Latin *tersus* 'wiped, polished,' from the verb *tergere*. The original sense was 'polished, trim, spruce,' (relating to language)

'polished, polite,' hence 'concise and to the point' (late 18th cent).

ter·tian /'tərsHən/ ▶ **adj.** [attrib.] Medicine denoting a form of malaria causing a fever that recurs every second day: *tertian fever.* ● The common benign tertian malaria (or tertian ague) is caused by infection with *Plasmodium vivax* or *P. ovale*, and malignant tertian malaria is caused by *P. falciparum*. Compare with QUARTAN.
– ORIGIN late Middle English (*fever*) *terciane*, from Latin (*febris*) *tertiana*, from *tertius* 'third' (the fever recurring every third day by inclusive reckoning).

ter·ti·ar·y /'tərsHē,erē, -sHərē/ ▶ **adj.** **1** third in order or level: *most of the enterprises were of tertiary importance | the tertiary stage of the disease.* ■ chiefly Brit. relating to or denoting education at a level beyond that provided by schools, esp. that provided by a college or university. ■ relating to or denoting the medical treatment provided at a specialist institution.
2 (**Tertiary**) Geology of, relating to, or denoting the first period of the Cenozoic era, between the Cretaceous and Quaternary periods, and comprising the Paleogene and Neogene subperiods.
3 Chemistry (of an organic compound) having its functional group located on a carbon atom that is itself bonded to three other carbon atoms. ■ Chemistry (chiefly of amines) derived from ammonia by replacement of three hydrogen atoms by organic groups.
▶ **n.** **1** (**the Tertiary**) Geology the Tertiary period or the system of rocks deposited during it.

The Tertiary lasted from about 65 million to 1.6 million years ago. The mammals diversified following the demise of the dinosaurs and became dominant, as did the flowering plants.

2 a lay associate of certain Christian monastic organizations: *a Franciscan tertiary.*
– ORIGIN mid 16th cent. (sense 2 of the noun): from Latin *tertiarius* 'of the third part or rank,' from *tertius* 'third.'

ter·ti·ar·y struc·ture ▶ **n.** Biochemistry the overall three-dimensional structure resulting from folding and covalent cross-linking of a protein or polynucleotide molecule.

ter·ti·um quid /'tərsHēəm 'kwid, 'tərtēəm/ ▶ **n.** a third thing that is indefinite and undefined but is related to two definite or known things.
– ORIGIN early 18th cent.: from late Latin, translation of Greek *triton ti* 'some third thing.'

Ter·tul·li·an /tər'təlēən, -'təlyən/ (*c.*160–*c.*240), early Christian theologian; Latin name *Quintus Septimius Florens Tertullianus*. His writings include Christian apologetics and attacks on pagan idolatry and Gnosticism.

ter·va·lent /tər'vālənt/ ▶ **adj.** Chemistry another term for TRIVALENT.

ter·za ri·ma /,tertsə 'rēmə/ ▶ **n.** Prosody an arrangement of triplets, esp. in iambs, that rhyme *aba bcb cdc*, etc., as in Dante's *Divine Comedy*.
– ORIGIN Italian, literally 'third rhyme.'

TESL /'tesəl/ ▶ **abbr.** teaching of English as a second language.

Tes·la /'teslə/, Nikola (1856–1943), US electrical engineer and inventor, born in what is now Croatia. He developed the first alternating-current induction motor, as well as several forms of oscillators, the Tesla coil, and a wireless guidance system for ships.

tes·la /'teslə/ (abbr.: **T**) ▶ **n.** Physics the SI unit of magnetic flux density.
– ORIGIN 1960s: named after N. TESLA.

Tes·la coil ▶ **n.** a form of induction coil for producing high-frequency alternating currents.

TESOL /'te,säl, -,sôl, 'tesəl/ ▶ **abbr.** teaching of English to speakers of other languages.

tes·sel·late /'tesə,lāt/ (also **tesselate**) ▶ **v.** [with obj.] decorate (a floor) with mosaics. ■ Mathematics cover (a plane surface) by repeated use of a single shape, without gaps or overlapping.
– DERIVATIVES **tes·sel·la·tion** /,tesə'lāsHən/ (also **tesselation**) **n.**
– ORIGIN late 18th cent.: from late Latin *tessellat-*, from the verb *tessellare*, from *tessella*, diminutive of *tessera* (see TESSERA).

tes·ser·a /'tesərə/ ▶ **n.** (pl. **tesserae** /'tesərē/) a small block of stone, tile, glass, or other material used in the construction of a mosaic. ■ (in ancient Greece and Rome) a small tablet of wood or bone used as a token.
– DERIVATIVES **tes·ser·al** /-rəl/ **adj.**
– ORIGIN mid 17th cent.: via Latin from Greek, neuter of *tesseres*, variant of *tessares* 'four.'

Tes·sin /te'saN, te'sēn/ French and German name for TICINO.

tes·si·tu·ra /,tesi'to͝orə/ ▶ **n.** Music the range within which most notes of a vocal part fall.
– ORIGIN Italian, literally 'texture,' from Latin *textura* (see TEXTURE).

test[1] /test/ ▶ **n.** **1** a procedure intended to establish the quality, performance, or reliability of something, esp. before it is taken into widespread use: *no sparking was visible during the tests.* ■ a short written or spoken examination of a person's proficiency or knowledge: *a spelling test.* ■ an event or situation that reveals the strength or quality of someone or something by putting them under strain: *this is the first serious test of the peace agreement.* ■ an examination of part of the body or a body fluid for medical purposes, esp. by means of a chemical or mechanical procedure rather than simple inspection: *a test for HIV | eye tests.* ■ Chemistry a procedure employed to identify a substance or to reveal the presence or absence of a constituent within a substance. ■ the result of a medical examination or analytical procedure: *a positive test for protein.* ■ a means of establishing whether an action, item, or situation is an instance of a specified quality, esp. one held to be undesirable: *a statutory test of obscenity.*
2 Metallurgy a movable hearth in a reverberating furnace, used for separating gold or silver from lead.
▶ **v.** [with obj.] take measures to check the quality, performance, or reliability of (something), esp. before putting it into widespread use or practice: *this range has not been tested on animals* | (as noun **testing**) *the testing and developing of prototypes* | figurative *a useful way to **test out** ideas before implementation.* ■ reveal the strengths or capabilities of (someone or something) by putting them under strain: *such behavior would severely test any marriage.* ■ give (someone) a short written or oral examination of their proficiency or knowledge: *all children are tested at eleven.* ■ judge or measure (someone's proficiency or knowledge) by means of such an examination. ■ carry out a medical test on (a person, a part of the body, or a body fluid). ■ [no obj.] produce a specified result in a medical test, esp. a drug test or AIDS test: *he **tested positive** for steroids after the race.* ■ Chemistry examine (a substance) by means of a reagent. ■ touch or taste (something) to check that it is acceptable before proceeding further: *she tested the water with the tip of her elbow.*
– PHRASES **put someone/something to the test** find out how useful, strong, or effective someone or something is. **stand the test of time** last or remain popular for a long time. **test the water** judge people's feelings or opinions before taking further action.
– DERIVATIVES **test·a·bil·i·ty** /,testə'bilitē/ **n.**, **test·a·ble adj.**, **test·ee** /-'tē/ **n.**
– ORIGIN late Middle English (denoting a cupel used to treat gold or silver alloys or ore): via Old French from Latin *testu*, *testum* 'earthen pot,' variant of *testa* 'jug, shell.' Compare with TEST[2]. The verb dates from the early 17th cent.

test[2] ▶ **n.** Zoology the shell or integument of some invertebrates and protozoans, esp. the chalky shell of a foraminiferan or the tough outer layer of a tunicate.
– ORIGIN mid 19th cent.: from Latin *testa* 'tile, jug, shell.' Compare with TEST[1].

Test. ▶ **abbr.** Testament.

test. ▶ **abbr.** ■ testator. ■ testimony.

tes·ta /'testə/ ▶ **n.** (pl. **testae** /-tē/) Botany the protective outer covering of a seed; the seed coat.
– ORIGIN late 18th cent.: from Latin, literally 'tile, shell.'

tes·ta·ceous /te'stāsHəs/ ▶ **adj.** chiefly Entomology of a dull brick-red color.
– ORIGIN mid 17th cent.: from Latin *testaceus* (from *testa* 'tile') + -OUS.

tes·ta·ment /'testəmənt/ ▶ **n.** **1** a person's will, esp. the part relating to personal property.
2 something that serves as a sign or evidence of a specified fact, event, or quality: *growing attendance figures are a testament to the event's popularity.*
3 (in biblical use) a covenant or dispensation. ■ (**Testament**) a division of the Bible. See also OLD TESTAMENT, NEW TESTAMENT. ■ (**Testament**) a copy of the New Testament.
– ORIGIN Middle English: from Latin *testamentum* 'a will' (from *testari* 'testify'), in Christian Latin also translating Greek *diathēkē* 'covenant.'

tes·ta·men·ta·ry /,testə'men(t)ərē/ ▶ **adj.** of, relating to, or bequeathed or appointed through a will.
– ORIGIN late Middle English: from Latin *testamentarius*, from *testamentum* 'a will,' from *testari* 'testify.'

tes·tate /'tes,tāt/ ▶ **adj.** [predic.] having made a valid will before one dies.
▶ **n.** a person who has died leaving such a will.
– ORIGIN late Middle English (as a noun): from Latin *testatus* 'testified, witnessed,' past participle of *testari*, from *testis* 'a witness.'

tes·ta·tion /te'stāsHən/ ▶ **n.** Law the disposal of property by will.

tes·ta·tor /'testātər/ ▶ **n.** Law a person who has made a will or given a legacy.
– ORIGIN Middle English: from Anglo-Norman French *testatour*, from Latin *testator*, from the verb *testari* 'testify.'

tes·ta·trix /te'stātriks/ ▶ **n.** (pl. **testatrices** /-trisēz/ or **testatrixes**) Law, dated a woman who has made a will or given a legacy.
– ORIGIN late 16th cent.: from late Latin, feminine of *testator* (see TESTATOR).

Test-Ban Trea·ty an international agreement not to test nuclear weapons in the atmosphere, in space, or underwater, signed in 1963 by the US, the UK, and the former Soviet Union, and later by more than 100 governments.

test bed ▶ **n.** a piece of equipment used for testing new machinery, esp. aircraft engines.

test case ▶ **n.** Law a case that sets a precedent for other cases involving the same question of law.

test drive ▶ **n.** an act of driving a motor vehicle that one is considering buying in order to determine its quality. ■ a test of a product before purchase or release.
▶ **v.** (**test-drive**) [with obj.] drive (a vehicle) to determine its qualities with a view to buying it. ■ test (a product) before purchase or release: *a laboratory where they can test-drive new tools and techniques.*

test·er[1] /'testər/ ▶ **n.** a person who tests something, esp. a new product. ■ a person who tests another's proficiency. ■ a device that tests the functioning of something: *a cake tester.* ■ a sample of a product provided so that customers can try it before buying it.

test·er[2] ▶ **n.** a canopy over a four-poster bed.
– ORIGIN late Middle English: from medieval Latin *testerium*, *testrum*, from a Romance word meaning 'head,' based on Latin *testa* 'tile.'

tes·tes /'testēz/ plural form of TESTIS.

test flight ▶ **n.** a flight during which the performance of an aircraft or its equipment is tested.
– DERIVATIVES **test-fly v.**

tes·ti·cle /'testikəl/ ▶ **n.** either of the two oval organs that produce sperm in men and other male mammals, enclosed in the scrotum behind the penis. Also called TESTIS.
– DERIVATIVES **tes·tic·u·lar** /te'stikyələr/ **adj.**
– ORIGIN late Middle English: from Latin *testiculus*, diminutive of *testis* 'a witness' (i.e., to virility).

tes·tic·u·lar fem·i·ni·za·tion ▶ **n.** a condition produced in genetically male people by the failure of tissue to respond to male sex hormones, resulting in normal female anatomy but with testes in place of ovaries.

tes·tic·u·late /te'stikyəlit/ ▶ **adj.** Botany (esp. of the twin tubers of some orchids) shaped like a pair of testicles.
– ORIGIN mid 18th cent.: from late Latin *testiculatus*, from *testiculus* (see TESTICLE).

tes·ti·fy /'testə,fī/ ▶ **v.** (**testifies**, **testifying**, **testified**) [no obj.] give evidence as a witness in a law court: *he testified against his own commander* | [with clause] *he testified that he had supplied Barry with crack.* ■ serve as evidence or proof of something's existing or being the case: *the bleak lines testify to inner torment.*
– DERIVATIVES **tes·ti·fi·er n.**
– ORIGIN late Middle English: from Latin *testificari*, from *testis* 'a witness.'

tes·ti·mo·ni·al /,testə'mōnēəl/ ▶ **n.** a formal statement testifying to someone's character and qualifications. ■ a public tribute to someone and to their achievements. ■ [often as modifier] (in sports) a game or event held in honor of a player, who typically receives part of the income generated: *the Yankees held a testimonial day for Gehrig.*
– ORIGIN late Middle English: from Old French *testimonial* 'testifying, serving as evidence,' from late Latin *testimonialis*, from Latin *testimonium* (see TESTIMONY).

tes·ti·mo·ny /'testə,mōnē/ ▶ **n.** (pl. **testimonies**) a formal written or spoken statement, esp. one given in a court of law. ■ evidence or proof provided by the existence or appearance of something: *his blackened finger was **testimony to** the fact that he had*

t

played in pain. ■ a public recounting of a religious conversion or experience. ■ archaic a solemn protest or declaration.
– ORIGIN Middle English: from Latin *testimonium*, from *testis* 'a witness.'

test·ing ground ▶ n. an area or field of activity used for the testing of a product or an idea, esp. a military site used for the testing of weapons.

tes·tis /'testis/ ▶ n. (pl. **testes** /-ˌtēz/) Anatomy & Zoology an organ that produces spermatozoa (male reproductive cells). Compare with TESTICLE.
– ORIGIN early 18th cent.: from Latin, literally 'a witness' (i.e., to virility). Compare with TESTICLE.

Test match ▶ n. an international cricket or rugby match.

test meal ▶ n. Medicine a portion of food of specified quantity and composition, eaten to stimulate digestive secretions which can then be analyzed.

tes·tos·ter·one /te'stästəˌrōn/ ▶ n. a steroid hormone that stimulates development of male secondary sexual characteristics, produced mainly in the testes, but also in the ovaries and adrenal cortex.
– ORIGIN 1930s: from TESTIS + *sterone* (blend of STEROL and KETONE).

test pa·per ▶ n. Chemistry a paper impregnated with an indicator that changes color under known conditions, used esp. to test for acidity.

test pat·tern ▶ n. a geometric design broadcast by a television station so that viewers can adjust the quality of their reception.

test pi·lot ▶ n. a pilot who flies an aircraft to test its performance.

test strip ▶ n. a strip of material used in testing, esp. (in photography) a strip of sensitized material, sections of which are exposed for varying lengths of time to assess its response.

test tube ▶ n. a thin glass tube closed at one end, used to hold small amounts of material for laboratory testing or experiments. ■ [as modifier] denoting things produced or processes performed in a laboratory: *new forms of test-tube life.*

test-tube ba·by ▶ n. informal a baby conceived by in vitro fertilization.

Tes·tu·di·nes /te'st(y)o͞odnˌēz/ Zoology an order of reptiles that comprises the turtles, terrapins, and tortoises. They are distinguished by having a shell of bony plates covered with horny scales, and many kinds are aquatic. Also called (esp. formerly) CHELONIA.
– ORIGIN modern Latin (plural), based on Latin *testa* 'shell.'

tes·tu·do /te'st(y)o͞odō/ ▶ n. (pl. **testudos** or **testudines** /-dnˌēz/) (in ancient Rome) a screen on wheels and with an arched roof, used to protect besieging troops. ■ a protective screen formed by a body of troops holding their shields above their heads in such a way that the shields overlap.
– ORIGIN late Middle English: from Latin, literally 'tortoise,' from *testa* 'tile, shell.'

tes·ty /'testē/ ▶ adj. easily irritated; impatient and somewhat bad-tempered.
– DERIVATIVES **tes·ti·ly** /'testəlē/ adv., **tes·ti·ness** n.
– ORIGIN late Middle English (in the sense 'headstrong, impetuous'): from Anglo-Norman French *testif*, from Old French *teste* 'head,' from Latin *testa* 'shell.'

te·tan·ic /te'tanik/ ▶ adj. relating to or characteristic of tetanus, esp. in connection with tonic muscle spasm.
– DERIVATIVES **te·tan·i·cal·ly** /-ik(ə)lē/ adv.
– ORIGIN early 18th cent.: via Latin from Greek *tetanikos*, from *tetanos* (see TETANUS).

tet·a·nus /'tetn-əs/ ▶ n. **1** a bacterial disease marked by rigidity and spasms of the voluntary muscles. See also TRISMUS. ● This disease is caused by the bacterium *Clostridium tetani*; Gram-positive anaerobic rods.
2 Physiology the prolonged contraction of a muscle caused by rapidly repeated stimuli.
– DERIVATIVES **tet·a·nize** /-ˌīz/ v., **tet·a·noid** /-ˌoid/ adj.
– ORIGIN late Middle English: from Latin, from Greek *tetanos* 'muscular spasm,' from *teinein* 'to stretch.'

tet·a·ny /'tetn-ē/ ▶ n. a condition marked by intermittent muscular spasms, caused by malfunction of the parathyroid glands and a consequent deficiency of calcium.
– ORIGIN late 19th cent.: from French *tétanie*, from Latin *tetanus* (see TETANUS).

tetch·y /'tecHē/ (also **techy**) ▶ adj. bad-tempered and irritable.
– DERIVATIVES **tetch·i·ly** /'tecHəlē/ adv., **tetch·i·ness** n.
– ORIGIN late 16th cent.: probably from a variant of Scots *tache* 'blotch, fault,' from Old French *teche*.

tête-à-tête /ˌtāt ə 'tāt, ˌtet ə 'tet/ ▶ n. (pl. **tête-à-têtes** pronounced **same**) **1** a private conversation between two people.
2 an S-shaped sofa on which two people can sit face to face.
▶ adj. & adv. involving or happening between two people in private: [as adj.] *a tête-à-tête meal* | [as adv.] *his business was conducted tête-à-tête.*
– ORIGIN late 17th cent.: French, literally 'head-to-head.'

tête-bêche /tet 'besH/ ▶ adj. (of a postage stamp) printed upside down or sideways relative to another.
– ORIGIN French, from *tête* 'head' and *bêche*, contraction of obsolete *béchevet* 'placed with the head of one against the foot of the other.'

teth·er /'teTHər/ ▶ n. a rope or chain with which an animal is tied to restrict its movement.
▶ v. [with obj.] tie (an animal) with a rope or chain so as to restrict its movement: *the horse had been tethered to a post.*
– PHRASES **the end of one's tether** see END.
– ORIGIN late Middle English: from Old Norse *tjóthr*, from a Germanic base meaning 'fasten.'

teth·er·ball /'teTHərˌbôl/ ▶ n. a game in which two people use their hands or paddles to hit a ball suspended on a cord from an upright post, the winner being the first person to wind the cord completely around the post.

Te·thys /'teTHis/ **1** Greek Mythology a goddess of the sea, daughter of Uranus (Heaven) and Gaia (Earth).
2 Astronomy a satellite of Saturn, the ninth closest to the planet, discovered by Cassini in 1684. It is probably composed mainly of ice and has a diameter of 659 miles (1,060 km).
3 Geology an ocean formerly separating the supercontinents of Gondwana and Laurasia, the forerunner of the present-day Mediterranean.

Tet Of·fen·sive /tet/ (in the Vietnam War) an offensive launched in January–February 1968 by the Vietcong and the North Vietnamese army. Timed to coincide with the first day of the Tet (Vietnamese New Year), it was a surprise attack on South Vietnamese cities, notably Saigon. Although repulsed after initial successes, the attack shook US confidence and hastened the withdrawal of its forces.

Te·ton /'tēˌtän/ (also **Teton Sioux**) ▶ n. another term for LAKOTA.
– ORIGIN via North American French or directly from the name in Lakota *thíthu-wã*, possibly meaning 'dwellers on the prairie.'

Té·touan /tā'twän/ a city in northern Morocco; pop. 613,506 (2004).

tet·ra /'tetrə/ ▶ n. a small tropical freshwater fish that is typically brightly colored. Native to Africa and America, many tetras are popular in aquariums. ● Numerous genera and species in the family Characidae, including the **neon tetra**.
– ORIGIN mid 20th cent.: abbreviation of modern Latin *Tetragonopterus* (former genus name), literally 'tetragonal-finned.'

tetra- (also **tetr-** before a vowel) ▶ comb. form **1** four; having four: *tetramerous* | *tetragram* | *tetrode.*
2 Chemistry (in names of compounds) containing four atoms or groups of a specified kind: *tetracycline.*
– ORIGIN from Greek, from *tettares* 'four.'

tet·ra·chord /'tetrəˌkôrd/ ▶ n. Music a scale of four notes, the interval between the first and last being a perfect fourth. ■ historical a musical instrument with four strings.

tet·ra·cy·clic /ˌtetrə'sīklik/ ▶ adj. Chemistry (of an organic compound) having four fused rings of atoms in its molecule.
– ORIGIN early 20th cent.: from TETRA- 'four' + Greek *kuklos* 'circle' + -IC.

tet·ra·cy·cline /ˌtetrə'sīˌklēn, -klin/ ▶ n. Medicine any of a large group of antibiotics with a molecular structure containing four rings. ● These antibiotics are often obtained from bacteria of the genus *Streptomyces*.
– ORIGIN 1950s: from TETRA- + CYCLIC + -INE[4].

tet·rad /'teˌtrad/ ▶ n. technical a group or set of four.
– ORIGIN mid 17th cent.: from Greek *tetras*, *tetrad-* 'four, a group of four.'

tet·ra·dac·tyl /ˌtetrə'daktl/ ▶ adj. Zoology (of a vertebrate limb) having four toes or fingers.

tet·ra·eth·yl lead /ˌtetrə'eTHəl 'led/ ▶ n. Chemistry a toxic colorless oily liquid made synthetically and used as an antiknock agent in leaded gasoline. ● Chem. formula: $Pb(C_2H_5)_4$.

tet·ra·fluo·ro·eth·yl·ene /ˌtetrəˌflo͝orō'eTHəˌlēn/ ▶ n. Chemistry a dense colorless gas that is polymerized to make plastics such as polytetrafluoroethylene. ● Chem. formula: $F_2C{=}CF_2$.

te·trag·o·nal /te'tragənl/ ▶ adj. of or denoting a crystal system or three-dimensional geometric arrangement having three axes at right angles, two of them equal.
– DERIVATIVES **te·trag·o·nal·ly** adv.
– ORIGIN late 16th cent.: via late Latin from Greek *tetragōnon* (neuter of *tetragōnos* 'four-angled') + -AL.

tet·ra·gram /'tetrəˌgram/ ▶ n. a word consisting of four letters or characters.

Tet·ra·gram·ma·ton /ˌtetrə'gramәˌtän/ ▶ n. the Hebrew name of God transliterated in four letters as *YHWH* or *JHVH* and articulated as *Yahweh* or *Jehovah*.
– ORIGIN Greek, neuter of *tetragrammatos* 'having four letters,' from *tetra-* 'four' + *gramma*, *grammat-* 'letter.'

tet·ra·he·drite /ˌtetrə'hēdrīt/ ▶ n. a gray mineral consisting of a sulfide of antimony, iron, and copper, typically occurring as tetrahedral crystals.

tet·ra·he·dron /ˌtetrə'hēdrən/ ▶ n. (pl. **tetrahedra** /-drə/ or **tetrahedrons**) a solid having four plane triangular faces; a triangular pyramid.

tetrahedron

– DERIVATIVES **tet·ra·he·dral** /-drəl/ adj.
– ORIGIN late 16th cent.: from late Greek *tetraedron*, neuter (used as a noun) of *tetraedros* 'four-sided.'

tet·ra·hy·dro·can·nab·i·nol /ˌtetrəˌhīdrəkə'nabəˌnôl, -ˌnäl/ ▶ n. Chemistry a crystalline compound that is the main active ingredient of cannabis. ● Chem. formula: $C_{21}H_{30}O_2$.

tet·ra·hy·dro·fu·ran /ˌtetrəˌhīdrō'fyo͝orˌan/ ▶ n. Chemistry a colorless liquid used chiefly as a solvent for plastics and as an intermediate in organic syntheses. ● A heterocyclic compound; chem. formula: C_4H_8O.

te·tral·o·gy /te'träləjē/ ▶ n. (pl. **tetralogies**) **1** a group of four related literary or operatic works. ■ a series of four ancient Greek dramas, three tragedies and one satyr play, originally presented together. [from Greek *tetralogia*.]
2 Medicine a set of four related symptoms or abnormalities frequently occurring together.

te·tral·o·gy of Fal·lot /fa'lō/ ▶ n. Medicine a congenital heart condition involving four abnormalities occurring together, including a defective septum between the ventricles and narrowing of the pulmonary artery, and accompanied by cyanosis.
– ORIGIN 1920s: named after Etienne L. A. *Fallot* (1850–1911), French physician.

tet·ra·mer /'tetrəmər/ ▶ n. Chemistry a polymer comprising four monomer units.
– DERIVATIVES **tet·ra·mer·ic** /ˌtetrə'merik/ adj.

te·tram·er·ous /te'tramərəs/ ▶ adj. Botany & Zoology having parts arranged in groups of four. ■ consisting of four joints or parts.

te·tram·e·ter /te'tramitər/ ▶ n. Prosody a verse of four measures.
– ORIGIN early 17th cent.: from late Latin *tetrametrus*, from Greek *tetrametros*, from *tetra-* 'four' + *metron* 'measure.'

tet·ra·ple·gi·a /ˌtetrə'plēj(ē)ə/ ▶ n. another term for QUADRIPLEGIA.
– DERIVATIVES **tet·ra·ple·gic** /-'plējik/ adj. & n.
– ORIGIN early 20th cent.: from TETRA- 'four' + PARAPLEGIA.

tet·ra·ploid /'tetrəˌploid/ Biology ▶ adj. (of a cell or nucleus) containing four homologous sets of chromosomes. ■ (of an organism or species) composed of such cells.
▶ n. an organism, variety, or species of this type.
– DERIVATIVES **tet·ra·ploi·dy** n.

tet·ra·pod /'tetrəˌpäd/ ▶ n. Zoology a four-footed animal, esp. a member of a group that includes all vertebrates higher than fishes. ● Superclass Tetrapoda: the amphibians, reptiles, birds, and mammals. ■ an object or structure with four feet, legs, or supports.
– ORIGIN early 19th cent.: from modern Latin *tetrapodus*, from Greek *tetrapous*, *tetrapod-* 'four-footed,' from *tetra-* 'four' + *pous* 'foot.'

te·trap·ter·ous /te'traptərəs/ ▶ adj. Entomology (of an insect) having two pairs of wings.
– ORIGIN early 19th cent.: from modern Latin *tetrapterus* (from Greek *tetrapteros*, from *tetra-* 'four' + *pteron* 'wing') + -OUS.

te·trarch /'teˌträrk/ ▶ n. (in the Roman Empire) the governor of one of four divisions of a country or province. ■ one of four joint rulers. ■ archaic a subordinate ruler.

– DERIVATIVES **te·trar·chy** n. (pl. **tetrarchies**).
– ORIGIN Old English, from late Latin *tetrarcha*, from Latin *tetrarches*, from Greek *tetrarkhēs*, from *tetra-* 'four' + *arkhein* 'to rule.'

tet·ra·spore /'tetrə,spôr/ ▶ n. Botany a spore occurring in groups of four, in particular (in a red alga) each of four spores produced together, two of which produce male plants and two female.

tet·ra·stich /'tetrə,stik/ ▶ n. Prosody a group of four lines of verse.
– ORIGIN late 16th cent.: via Latin from Greek *tetrastikhon* 'having four rows,' from *tetra-* 'four' + *stikhon* 'row, line of verse.'

tet·ra·tom·ic /,tetrə'tämik/ ▶ adj. Chemistry consisting of four atoms.

tet·ra·va·lent /,tetrə'vālənt/ ▶ adj. Chemistry having a valence of four.

tet·ra·zole /'tetrə,zōl/ ▶ n. Chemistry an acidic crystalline compound whose molecule is a five-membered ring of one carbon and four nitrogen atoms. ● Chem. formula: CH_2N_4.
– ORIGIN late 19th cent.: from TETRA- 'four' + AZO- + -OLE.

tet·ra·zo·li·um /,tetrə'zōlēəm/ ▶ n. [as modifier] Chemistry a cation derived from tetrazole or one of its derivatives, esp. the triphenyl derivative. ■ (also **nitroblue tetrazolium**) a yellow dye used as a test for viability in biological material.

Tet·raz·zi·ni /,tetrə'zēnē/ ▶ adj. [postpositive] served over pasta with mushrooms and almonds in a cream sauce, sprinkled with cheese, and baked in the oven: *turkey Tetrazzini*.
– ORIGIN early 20th cent.: named after *Luisa Tetrazzini* (1871–1940), Italian operatic soprano.

tet·rode /'te,trōd/ ▶ n. a thermionic tube having four electrodes.
– ORIGIN early 20th cent.: from TETRA- 'four' + Greek *hodos* 'way.'

te·tro·do·tox·in /te,trōdə'täksin/ ▶ n. a poisonous compound present in the ovaries of certain pufferfishes. It is a powerful neurotoxin.
– ORIGIN early 20th cent.: from modern Latin *Tetrodon* (former genus name, from Greek *tetra-* 'fourfold' + *odous, odont-* 'tooth') + TOXIN.

tet·rose /'tetrōs, -trōz/ ▶ n. Chemistry any of a group of monosaccharide sugars whose molecules contain four carbon atoms.

te·trox·ide /te'träk,sīd/ ▶ n. Chemistry an oxide containing four atoms of oxygen in its molecule or empirical formula.

tet·ter /'tetər/ ▶ n. chiefly archaic a skin disease in humans or animals causing itchy or pustular patches, such as eczema or ringworm.
– ORIGIN Old English *teter*, of Germanic origin; from an Indo-European root shared by Sanskrit *dadru* 'skin disease.'

Teut. ▶ abbr. ■ Teuton. ■ Teutonic.

Teu·ton /'t(y)o͞otn/ ▶ n. a member of a people who lived in Jutland in the 4th century BC and fought the Romans in France in the 2nd century BC. ■ often derogatory a German.
– ORIGIN from Latin *Teutones, Teutoni* (plural), from an Indo-European root meaning 'people' or 'country.'

Teu·ton·ic /t(y)o͞o'tänik/ ▶ adj. **1** of or relating to the Teutons. ■ often derogatory displaying the characteristics popularly attributed to Germans: *making preparations with Teutonic thoroughness*.
2 archaic denoting the Germanic branch of the Indo-European language family.
▶ n. archaic the language of the Teutons.
– DERIVATIVES **Teu·ton·i·cism** /-'tänə,sizəm/ n.

Teu·ton·ic Knights a military and religious order of German knights, priests, and lay brothers, originally enrolled c.1191 as the Teutonic Knights of St. Mary of Jerusalem.

> They became a great sovereign power through conquests made in campaigns against Germany's non-Christian neighbors, such as Prussia and Livonia, from 1225. Abolished by Napoleon in 1809, the order was re-established in Vienna as an honorary ecclesiastical institution in 1834 and maintains a titular existence.

Te·ve·re /'tāvə,rā/ Italian name for TIBER.

Te·vet ▶ n. variant spelling of TEBET.

Te·wa /'tāwə, 'tē-/ ▶ n. (pl. **same** or **Tewas**) **1** a member of a Pueblo Indian people of the Rio Grande area in the southwestern US.
2 the Tanoan language of this people. Do not confuse with TIWA.
▶ adj. of or relating to this people or their language.
– ORIGIN from Spanish *Tegua* or directly from the Tewa self-designation *téwa*.

Tex. ▶ abbr. Texas.

Tex·ar·kana /,teksär'kanə/ twin cities on the Texas-Arkansas border. The Texas city, in the northeastern part of the state, is home to an army ordnance center; pop. 36,611 (est. 2008). The Arkansas city is in the southwestern part of the state; pop. 30,087 (est. 2008).

Tex·as /'teksəs/ a state in the southern US, on the border with Mexico, with a coastline on the Gulf of Mexico; pop. 24,326,974 (est. 2008); capital, Austin; statehood, Dec. 29, 1845 (28). The area was part of Mexico until 1836, when it declared independence, became a republic, and began to work for admittance to the US as a state.
– DERIVATIVES **Tex·an** /'teksən/ adj. & n.

Tex·as Cit·y a port city in southeastern Texas, on Galveston Bay, southeast of Houston; pop. 44,491 (est. 2008).

Tex·as fe·ver ▶ n. the disease babesiosis in cattle.

Tex·as hold 'em /'hōldəm/ ▶ n. a poker game in which players compose their hands from cards dealt to them combined with community cards dealt face up and shared among them.

Tex·as lea·guer ▶ n. Baseball a pop fly that falls to the ground between the infield and the outfield and results in a base hit.

Tex·as Rang·er ▶ n. a member of the Texas State police force (formerly, of certain locally mustered regiments in the federal service during the Mexican War).

Tex-Mex /'teks 'meks/ ▶ adj. (esp. of cooking and music) having a blend of Mexican and southern American features originally characteristic of the border regions of Texas and Mexico.
▶ n. **1** music or cooking of such a type.
2 a variety of Mexican Spanish spoken in Texas.
– ORIGIN 1940s: blend of *Texan* and *Mexican*.

text /tekst/ ▶ n. **1** a book or other written or printed work, regarded in terms of its content rather than its physical form: *a text that explores pain and grief*. ■ a piece of written or printed material regarded as conveying the authentic or primary form of a particular work: *in some passages it is difficult to establish the original text* | *the text of the lecture was available to guests*. ■ written or printed words, typically forming a connected piece of work: *stylistic features of journalistic text*. ■ Computing data in the form of words or alphabetic characters.
2 [in sing.] the main body of a book or other piece of writing, as distinct from other material such as notes, appendices, and illustrations: *the pictures are clear and relate well to the text*. ■ a script or libretto.
3 a written work chosen or assigned as a subject of study: *the book is intended as a secondary text for religion courses*. ■ a textbook. ■ a passage from the Bible or other religious work, esp. when used as the subject of a sermon. ■ a subject or theme for a discussion or exposition: *he took as his text the fact that Australia is paradise*.
4 a text message.
5 (also **text-hand**) fine, large handwriting, used esp. for manuscripts.
▶ v. [with obj.] send a text message to: *I thought it was fantastic that he took the trouble to text me* | (as noun **texting**) *stricter regulations against texting while driving*.
– DERIVATIVES **text·er** n., **text·less** adj.
– ORIGIN late Middle English: from Old Northern French *texte*, from Latin *textus* 'tissue, literary style' (in medieval Latin, 'Gospel'), from *text-* 'woven,' from the verb *texere*.

text·book /'teks(t),bo͝ok/ ▶ n. a book used as a standard work for the study of a particular subject.
▶ adj. [attrib.] conforming to or corresponding to a standard or type that is prescribed or widely held by theorists: *he had the presence of mind to carry out a textbook emergency descent*.
– DERIVATIVES **text·book·ish** adj.

text ed·i·tor ▶ n. Computing a system or program that allows a user to edit text.

tex·tile /'tek,stīl/ ▶ n. **1** (usu. **textiles**) a type of cloth or woven fabric: *a fascinating range of pottery, jewelry, and textiles*. ■ (**textiles**) the branch of industry involved in the manufacture of cloth.
2 informal used by nudists to describe someone wearing clothes, esp. on a beach.
▶ adj. **1** [attrib.] of or relating to fabric or weaving: *the textile industry*.
2 informal used by nudists to describe something relating to or restricted to people wearing clothes.
– ORIGIN early 17th cent.: from Latin *textilis*, from *text-* 'woven,' from the verb *texere*.

text mes·sage ▶ n. an electronic communication sent and received by cellular phone.
– DERIVATIVES **text mes·sag·ing** n.

text·phone /'tekst,fōn/ ▶ n. a telephone for use by hearing-impaired people, having a small screen on which a message can be received and a keyboard on which an outgoing message may be typed to another textphone.

text proc·ess·ing ▶ n. Computing the manipulation of text, esp. the transformation of text from one format to another.

tex·tu·al /'teksCHo͞oəl/ ▶ adj. of or relating to a text or texts: *textual analysis*.
– DERIVATIVES **tex·tu·al·ly** adv.
– ORIGIN late Middle English: from medieval Latin *textualis*, from Latin *textus* (see TEXT).

tex·tu·al crit·i·cism ▶ n. the process of attempting to ascertain the original wording of a text.

tex·tu·al·ist /'teksCHo͞oəlist/ ▶ n. a person who adheres strictly to a text, esp. that of religious scriptures.
– DERIVATIVES **tex·tu·al·ism** /-,lizəm/ n.

tex·tu·al·i·ty /,teksCHo͞o'alitē/ ▶ n. **1** the quality or use of language characteristic of written works as opposed to spoken usage.
2 strict adherence to a text; textualism.

tex·ture /'teksCHər/ ▶ n. the feel, appearance, or consistency of a surface or a substance: *skin texture and tone* | *the cheese is firm in texture* | *the different colors and textures of bark*. ■ the character or appearance of a textile fabric as determined by the arrangement and thickness of its threads: *a dark shirt of rough texture*. ■ Art the tactile quality of the surface of a work of art. ■ the quality created by the combination of the different elements in a work of music or literature: *a closely knit symphonic texture*.
▶ v. [with obj.] (usu. as adj. **textured**) give (a surface, esp. of a fabric or wall covering) a rough or raised texture: *wallcoverings which create a textured finish*.
– DERIVATIVES **tex·tur·al** /-rəl/ adj., **tex·tur·al·ly** /-rəlē/ adv., **tex·ture·less** adj.
– ORIGIN late Middle English (denoting a woven fabric or something resembling this): from Latin *textura* 'weaving,' from *text-* 'woven,' from the verb *texere*.

tex·tured veg·e·ta·ble pro·tein ▶ n. a type of protein obtained from soybeans and made to resemble minced meat.

tex·ture map·ping ▶ n. Computing the application of patterns or images to three-dimensional graphics to enhance the realism of their surfaces.

tex·tur·ing /'teksCHəriNG/ ▶ n. the representation or use of texture, esp. in music, fine art, and interior design.

tex·tur·ize /'teksCHə,rīz/ ▶ v. [with obj.] impart a particular texture to (a product, esp. a fabric or foodstuff) in order to make it more attractive.

text wrap ▶ n. (in word processing) a facility allowing text to surround embedded features such as pictures.

TF ▶ abbr. Territorial Force.

T-for·ma·tion ▶ n. Football a T-shaped offensive formation, with the halfbacks and fullback positioned in a line parallel to the line of scrimmage.

tfr. ▶ abbr. transfer.

TFT ▶ abbr. Electronics thin-film transistor, denoting a technology used to make flat color display screens, usually for high-end portable computers.

TG ▶ abbr. transformational grammar or transformational-generative grammar.

t.g. ▶ abbr. Biology type genus.

TGIF ▶ abbr. informal thank God it's Friday.

T-group ▶ n. Psychology a group of people undergoing therapy or training in which they observe and seek to improve their own interpersonal relationships or communication skills.
– ORIGIN 1950s: *T* for *training*.

tgt. ▶ abbr. target.

TGV ▶ n. a French high-speed electric passenger train.
– ORIGIN abbreviation of French *train à grande vitesse*.

Th ▶ symbol the chemical element thorium.

Th. ▶ abbr. Thursday.

-th[1] (also **-eth**) ▶ suffix forming ordinal and fractional numbers from *four* onwards: *fifth* | *sixty-sixth*.
– ORIGIN Old English *-(o)tha, -(o)the*.

-th[2] ▶ suffix forming nouns: **1** (from verbs) denoting an action or process: *birth* | *growth*.
2 (from adjectives) denoting a state: *filth* | *health* | *width*.
– ORIGIN Old English *-thu, -tho, -th*.

-th[3] ▶ suffix variant spelling of -ETH[2] (as in *doth*).

Thack·er·ay /'THak(ə)rē, 'THakə,rā/, William Makepeace (1811–63), British novelist, born in India. He established his reputation with *Vanity Fair* (1847–48), a satire of the upper middle class of early-19th-century society. Other novels included *The History of Henry Esmond* (1852).

Thad·dae·us /ˈTHadēəs/ an apostle named in St. Matthew's gospel, traditionally identified with St. Jude.

Thai /tī/ ▶ **adj.** of or relating to Thailand, its people, or their language.
▶ **n.** (pl. **same** or **Thais**) **1** a native or inhabitant of Thailand. ■ a member of the largest ethnic group in Thailand. ■ a person of Thai descent.
2 the Tai language that is the official language of Thailand.
– ORIGIN Thai, literally 'free.'

Thai box·ing ▶ **n.** a traditional Thai martial art in which the fists, elbows, knees, and bare feet may all be used to deliver blows.
– DERIVATIVES **Thai box·er n.**

Thai·land /ˈtīˌland/ a kingdom in Southeast Asia, on the Gulf of Thailand; pop. 65,998,400 (est. 2009); capital, Bangkok; language, Thai (official). Former name (until 1939) **Siam**.

> A powerful Thai kingdom emerged in the 14th century. In the 19th century, it lost territory in the east to France and in the south to Britain. Thailand was occupied by the Japanese during World War II; it supported the US in the Vietnam War, later experiencing a large influx of refugees from Cambodia, Laos, and Vietnam. Absolute monarchy was abolished in 1932, the king remaining head of state.

Thai·land, Gulf of an inlet of the South China Sea between the Malay Peninsula on the west and Thailand and Cambodia on the east. It was formerly known as the Gulf of Siam.

Thai stick ▶ **n.** strong cannabis in leaf form, twisted into a small, tightly packed cylinder ready for smoking.

thal·a·mus /ˈTHaləməs/ ▶ **n.** (pl. **thalami** /-ˌmī/) Anatomy either of two masses of gray matter lying between the cerebral hemispheres on either side of the third ventricle, relaying sensory information and acting as a center for pain perception.
– DERIVATIVES **tha·lam·ic** /THəˈlamik/ **adj.**
– ORIGIN late 17th cent. (denoting the part of the brain at which a nerve originates): via Latin from Greek *thalamos*.

thal·as·se·mi·a /ˌTHaləˈsēmēə/ (Brit. **thalassaemia**) ▶ **n.** Medicine any of a group of hereditary hemolytic diseases caused by faulty hemoglobin synthesis, widespread in Mediterranean, African, and Asian countries.
– ORIGIN 1930s: from Greek *thalassa* 'sea' (because the diseases were first known around the Mediterranean) + **-emia**.

tha·las·sic /THəˈlasik/ ▶ **adj.** literary or technical of or relating to the sea.
– ORIGIN mid 19th cent.: from French *thalassique*, from Greek *thalassa* 'sea.'

tha·las·so·ther·a·py /THəˌlasōˈTHerəpē, ˌTHaləsō-/ ▶ **n.** the use of seawater in cosmetic and health treatment.
– ORIGIN late 19th cent.: from Greek *thalassa* 'sea' + **therapy**.

thale cress /THāl/ ▶ **n.** a small white-flowered plant of north temperate regions, widely used in genetics experiments due to its small number of chromosomes and short life cycle. ● *Arabidopsis thaliana*, family Brassicaceae.
– ORIGIN late 18th cent.: named after Johann *Thal* (1542–83), German physician.

tha·ler /ˈtälər/ ▶ **n.** historical a German silver coin.
– ORIGIN German, earlier form of *Taler* (see **dollar**).

Tha·les /ˈTHāˌlēz/ (*c.*624–*c.*545 BC), Greek philosopher, mathematician, and astronomer, living at Miletus. Judged by Aristotle to be the founder of physical science, he is also credited with founding geometry. He proposed that water was the primary substance from which all things were derived.

Tha·li·a /ˈTHālēə/ **1** Greek & Roman Mythology the Muse of comedy.
2 Greek Mythology one of the Graces.
– ORIGIN Greek, literally 'rich, plentiful.'

tha·lid·o·mide /THəˈlidəˌmīd/ ▶ **n.** a drug formerly used as a sedative, but withdrawn in the early 1960s after it was found to cause congenital malformation or absence of limbs in children whose mothers took the drug during early pregnancy.
– ORIGIN 1950s: from *(ph)thal(ic acid)* + *(im)ido* + *(i)mide*.

thal·li /ˈTHalī/ plural form of **thallus**.

thal·li·um /ˈTHalēəm/ ▶ **n.** the chemical element of atomic number 81, a soft silvery-white metal that occurs naturally in small amounts in pyrite and other ores. Its compounds are very poisonous. (Symbol: **Tl**)
– ORIGIN mid 19th cent.: modern Latin, from Greek *thallos* 'green shoot,' because of the green line in its spectrum.

thal·lo·phyte /ˈTHaləˌfīt/ ▶ **n.** Botany a plant that consists of a thallus.
– DERIVATIVES **thal·lo·phyt·ic adj.**
– ORIGIN mid 19th cent.: from modern Latin *Thallophyta* (former taxon), from Greek *thallos* (see **thallus**) + **-phyte**.

thal·lus /ˈTHaləs/ ▶ **n.** (pl. **thalli** /ˈTHalī/) Botany a plant body that is not differentiated into stem and leaves and lacks true roots and a vascular system. Thalli are typical of algae, fungi, lichens, and some liverworts.
– DERIVATIVES **thal·loid** /ˈTHaloid/ **adj.**
– ORIGIN early 19th cent.: from Greek *thallos* 'green shoot,' from *thallein* 'to bloom.'

thal·weg /ˈtälˌveg/ ▶ **n.** Geology a line connecting the lowest points of successive cross-sections along the course of a valley or river.
– ORIGIN mid 19th cent.: from German, from obsolete *Thal* 'valley, dale' + *Weg* 'way.'

Thames /temz/ **1** a river that flows for 160 miles (260 km) across southern Ontario in Canada. It was the scene of an 1813 battle in which Tecumseh died.
2 a river in southern England that flows 210 miles (338 km) east from the Cotswolds in Gloucestershire through London to the North Sea.
3 /ˈTHāmz, ˈtāmz, ˈtemz/ an estuarial river in southeastern Connecticut that flows from Norwich past New London and Groton to Long Island Sound.

Tham·muz /ˈtämo͝oz, täˈmo͞oz/ (also **Tammuz**) ▶ **n.** (in the Jewish calendar) the tenth month of the civil and fourth of the religious year, usually coinciding with parts of June and July.
– ORIGIN from Hebrew *tammūz*.

than /T͟Han, T͟Hən/ ▶ **conj. & prep. 1** introducing the second element in a comparison: [as prep.] *he was much smaller than his son* | [as conjunction] *Jack doesn't know any more than I do.*
2 used in expressions introducing an exception or contrast: [as prep.] *he claims not to own anything other than his home* | [as conjunction] *they observe rather than act.*
3 [conjunction] used in expressions indicating one thing happening immediately after another: *scarcely was the work completed than it was abandoned.*
– ORIGIN Old English *than(ne), thon(ne), thænne*, originally the same word as **then**.

> **USAGE** Traditional grammar holds that personal pronouns following **than** should be in the subjective rather than the objective case: *he is smaller **than she*** (rather than *he is smaller **than her***). This is based on an analysis of **than** by which **than** is a conjunction and the personal pronoun ('she') is standing in for a full clause: *he is smaller **than she is***. However, it is arguable that **than** in this context is not a conjunction but a preposition, similar grammatically to words like **with, between,** or **for**. In this case, the personal pronoun is objective: *he is smaller **than her*** is standard in just the same way as, for example, *I work **with her*** is standard (not *I work with she*). Whatever the grammatical analysis, the evidence confirms that sentences like *he is smaller **than she*** are uncommon in modern English except in the most formal contexts. Uses such as *he is smaller **than her***, on the other hand, are almost universally accepted. For more explanation, see usage at **personal pronoun** and **between**.

than·age /ˈTHānij/ ▶ **n.** historical the tenure, land, and rank granted to a thane.
– ORIGIN late Middle English: from Anglo-Norman French (see **thane, -age**).

than·a·tol·o·gy /ˌTHanəˈtäləjē/ ▶ **n.** the scientific study of death and the practices associated with it, including the study of the needs of the terminally ill and their families.
– DERIVATIVES **than·a·to·log·i·cal** /-ətəˈläjikəl/ **adj., than·a·tol·o·gist** /-jist/ **n.**
– ORIGIN mid 19th cent.: from Greek *thanatos* 'death' + **-logy**.

Than·a·tos /ˈTHanəˌtōs, -ˌtäs/ (in Freudian theory) the death instinct. Often contrasted with **Eros**.
– ORIGIN from Greek *thanatos* 'death.'

thane /THān/ ▶ **n.** historical (in Anglo-Saxon England) a man who held land granted by the king or by a military nobleman, ranking between an ordinary freeman and a hereditary noble. ■ (in Scotland) a man, often the chief of a clan, who held land from a Scottish king and ranked with an earl's son.
– DERIVATIVES **thane·dom** /-dəm/ **n.**
– ORIGIN Old English *theg(e)n* 'servant, soldier,' of Germanic origin; related to German *Degen* 'warrior,' from an Indo-European root shared by Greek *teknon* 'child,' *tokeus* 'parent.'

thang /THaNG/ ▶ **n.** informal nonstandard spelling of **thing** representing southern US pronunciation, and typically used to denote a feeling or tendency: *I'm doing the wild thang now.*

thank /THaNGk/ ▶ **v.** [with obj.] express gratitude to (someone), esp. by saying "Thank you": *Mac **thanked** her for the meal and left.* ■ used ironically to assign blame or responsibility for something: *you have only yourself to thank for the plight you are in.*
– PHRASES **I will thank you to do something** used to make a request or command and implying a reproach or annoyance: *I'll thank you not to interrupt me again.* **thank goodness** (or **God** or **heavens**) an expression of relief: *thank goodness no one was badly injured.* **thank one's lucky stars** feel grateful for one's good fortune.
– ORIGIN Old English *thancian*, of Germanic origin; related to Dutch and German *danken*; compare with **thanks**.

thank·ful /ˈTHaNGkfəl/ ▶ **adj.** pleased and relieved: [with clause] *they were thankful that the war was finally over* | [with infinitive] *I was very thankful to be alive.* ■ expressing gratitude and relief: *an earnest and thankful prayer.*
– DERIVATIVES **thank·ful·ness n.**
– ORIGIN Old English *thancful* (see **thank, -ful**).

thank·ful·ly /ˈTHaNGkfəlē/ ▶ **adv.** in a thankful manner: *she thankfully accepted the armchair she was offered.* ■ [sentence adverb] used to express pleasure or relief at the situation or outcome that one is reporting; fortunately: *thankfully, everything went smoothly.*
– ORIGIN Old English *thancfullīce* (see **thankful, -ly**[2]).

> **USAGE** **Thankfully** has been used for centuries to mean 'in a thankful manner,' as in *she accepted the offer **thankfully***. Since the 1960s, it has also been used as a sentence adverb to mean 'fortunately,' as in ***thankfully**, we didn't have to wait.* Although this use has not attracted the same amount of attention as **hopefully**, it has been criticized for the same reasons. It is, however, far more common now than is the traditional use. For further explanation, see usage at **hopefully** and **sentence adverb**.

thank·less /ˈTHaNGklis/ ▶ **adj.** (of a job or task) difficult or unpleasant and not likely to bring one pleasure or the appreciation of others. ■ (of a person) not expressing or feeling gratitude.
– DERIVATIVES **thank·less·ly adv., thank·less·ness n.**

thank-of·fer·ing ▶ **n.** an offering made as an act of thanksgiving.

thanks /THaNGks/ ▶ **plural n.** an expression of gratitude: *festivals were held to give **thanks** for the harvest* | *a letter of thanks.* ■ another way of saying **thank you**: *thanks for being so helpful* | *many thanks.*
– PHRASES **no thanks to** used to imply that someone has failed to contribute to, or has hindered, a successful outcome: *we've won, but no thanks to you.* **thanks a million** informal thank you very much. **thanks to** as a result of; due to: *it's thanks to you that he's in this mess.*
– ORIGIN Old English *thancas*, plural of *thanc* '(kindly) thought, gratitude,' of Germanic origin; related to Dutch *dank* and German *Dank*, also to **think**.

thanks·giv·ing /ˌTHaNGksˈgiviNG/ ▶ **n. 1** the expression of gratitude, esp. to God: *he offered prayers **in thanksgiving for** his safe arrival* | *he described the service as a thanksgiving.*
2 (**Thanksgiving** or **Thanksgiving Day**) (in North America) an annual national holiday marked by religious observances and a traditional meal including turkey. The holiday commemorates a harvest festival celebrated by the Pilgrims in 1621, and is held in the US on the fourth Thursday in November. A similar holiday is held in Canada, usually on the second Monday in October.

thank you ▶ **exclam.** a polite expression used when acknowledging a gift, service, or compliment, or accepting or refusing an offer: ***thank you** for your letter* | *no thank you, I don't believe I will.*
▶ **n.** an instance or means of expressing thanks: *Lucy planned a party as a thank you to the nurses* | [as modifier] *thank-you letters.*

Thant /THänt, THant/, U, (1909–74), Burmese statesman. He served as the representative of Burma (Myanmar) to the United Nations 1957–61 before becoming UN secretary-general 1961–71. As secretary general, he worked to settle the 1962 Cuban missile crisis diplomatically, to end the

Congolese civil war in 1962, and to keep peace in Cyprus in 1964.

U Thant

Thar Des·ert /tär/ a desert region to the east of the Indus River that lies in the states of Rajasthan and Gujarat in northwestern India and in the Punjab and Sind regions of southeastern Pakistan. Also called **Great Indian Desert**.

Tharp /THärp/, Twyla, (1941–) US dancer and choreographer. She performed with the Paul Taylor Dance Company 1963–65 and then formed her own modern dance troupe 1965–88. She choreographed dances such as "Push Comes to Shove" (1976) and did pieces for movies such as *Hair* (1979), *Ragtime* (1981), and *Amadeus* (1984). She served as an artistic associate for the American Ballet Theater 1988–90.

that /T͟Hat, T͟Hət/ ▶ **pron.** (pl. **those** /T͟Hōz/) **1** used to identify a specific person or thing observed by the speaker: *that's his wife over there*. ■ referring to the more distant of two things near to the speaker (the other, if specified, being identified by "this"): *this is stronger than that*.
2 referring to a specific thing previously mentioned, known, or understood: *that's a good idea | what are we going to do about that?*
3 [often with clause] used in singling out someone or something and ascribing a distinctive feature to them: *it is part of human nature to be attracted to* **that which** *is aesthetically pleasing | his appearance was* **that of** *an undergrown man | they care about the rights of those less privileged than themselves*.
4 (pl. **that**) [relative pronoun] used to introduce a defining or restrictive clause, esp. one essential to identification. ■ instead of "which," "who," or "whom": *the book that I've just written*. ■ instead of "when" after an expression of time: *the year that Anna was born*.
▶ **determiner** (pl. **those**) **1** used to identify a specific person or thing observed or heard by the speaker: *look at that man there | how much are those brushes?* ■ referring to the more distant of two things near to the speaker (the other, if specified, being identified by "this").
2 referring to a specific thing previously mentioned, known, or understood: *he lived in Mysore at that time | seven people died in that incident*.
3 [usu. with clause] used in singling out someone or something and ascribing a distinctive feature to them: *I have always envied those people who make their own bread*.
4 referring to a specific person or thing assumed as understood or familiar to the person being addressed: *where is that son of yours? | I let him spend all that money on me | Dad got that hunted look*.
▶ **adv.** [as submodifier] to such a degree; so: *I would not go that far*. ■ used with a gesture to indicate size: *it was that big, perhaps even bigger*. ■ [with negative] informal very: *he wasn't that far away*.
▶ **conj. 1** introducing a subordinate clause expressing a statement or hypothesis: *she said that she was satisfied | it is possible that we have misunderstood*. ■ expressing a reason or cause: *he seemed pleased that I wanted to continue*. ■ expressing a result: *she was* **so** *tired* **that** *she couldn't think*. ■ [usu. with modal] expressing a purpose, hope, or intention: *we pray that the coming year may be a year of peace | I eat that I may live*.
2 [usu. with modal] literary expressing a wish or regret: *oh that he could be restored to health*.
– PHRASES **and all that** informal and that sort of thing; and so on: *other people depend on them for food and clothing and all that*. **at that** see AT[1]. **like that 1** of that nature or in that manner: *we need more people like that | don't talk like that*. **2** informal with no preparation or introduction; instantly or effortlessly: *he can't just leave like that*. **not all that ——** not very ——: *it was not all that long ago*. **that is** (or **that is to say**) a formula introducing or following an explanation or further clarification of a preceding word or words: *androcentric—that is to say, male-dominated—concepts | He was a long-haired kid with freckles. Last time I saw him, that is*. **that said** even so (introducing a concessive statement): *It's just a gimmick. That said, I'd love to do it*. **that's it** see IT. **that's that** there is nothing more to do or say about the matter. **—— that was** as the specified person or thing was formerly known: *General Dunstaple had married Miss Hughes that was*. **that will do** no more is needed or desirable.
– ORIGIN Old English *þæt*, nominative and accusative singular neuter of *se* 'the,' of Germanic origin; related to Dutch *dat* and German *das*.

> **USAGE 1** The word **that** can be omitted in standard English where it introduces a *subordinate* clause, as in *she said* (*that*) *she was satisfied*. *That* can also be dropped in a *relative* clause where it is the *object* of the clause, as in *the book* (*that*) *I've just written*. *That*, however, is obligatory when it is the *subject* of the relative clause, as in *the company* **that** *employs Jack*. **2** It is sometimes argued that, in relative clauses, **that** should be used for *nonhuman* references and **who** should be used for *human* references: *a house* **that** *overlooks the park*, but *the woman* **who** *lives next door*. In practice, while it is true to say that *who* is restricted to human references, the function of *that* is flexible. It has been used for both human and nonhuman references since at least the 11th century. In standard English, it is interchangeable with *who* in this context. **3** Is there any difference between the use of **that** and **which** in sentences such as *any book* **that** *gets children reading is worth having*, and *any book* **which** *gets children reading is worth having*? The general rule is that, in *restrictive* relative clauses, where the relative clause serves to define or restrict the reference to the particular one described, *that* is the preferred relative pronoun. However, in *nonrestrictive* relative clauses, where the relative clause serves only to give additional information, *which* must be used: *this book,* **which** *is set in the last century, is very popular with teenagers*, but not *this book,* **that** *is set in the last century, is very popular with teenagers*. For more details, see usage at RESTRICTIVE.

that·a·way /ˈT͟Hatəˌwā/ ▶ **adv.** informal **1** in that direction.
2 in that way; like that.

thatch /THaCH/ ▶ **n.** a roof covering of straw, reeds, palm leaves, or a similar material. ■ straw or a similar material used for such a covering. ■ informal the hair on a person's head, esp. if thick or unruly. ■ a matted layer of dead stalks, moss, and other material in a lawn.
▶ **v.** [with obj.] cover (a roof or a building) with straw or a similar material: (as adj. **thatched**) *thatched cottages*.
– DERIVATIVES **thatch·er** n.
– ORIGIN Old English *theccan* 'cover,' of Germanic origin; related to Dutch *dekken* and German *decken*.

Thatch·er /ˈTHaCHər/, Margaret (Hilda), Baroness Thatcher of Kesteven (1925–), British Conservative stateswoman; prime minister 1979–90. The country's first woman prime minister and the longest-serving British prime minister of the 20th century, her period in office was marked by an emphasis on monetarist policies, privatization of nationalized industries, and trade union legislation.
– DERIVATIVES **Thatch·er·ism** /-ˌrizəm/ **n.**, **Thatch·er·ite** /-ˌrīt/ **n. & adj.**

thau·ma·tin /ˈTHômətən, -mətn/ ▶ **n.** a sweet-tasting protein isolated from a West African fruit (*Thaumatococcus danielli*, family Marantaceae), used as a sweetener in food.
– ORIGIN 1970s: from modern Latin *thaumat-* (from Greek *thauma, thaumat-* 'marvel') + -IN[1].

thau·ma·turge /ˈTHôməˌtərj/ ▶ **n.** a worker of wonders and performer of miracles; a magician.
– DERIVATIVES **thau·ma·tur·gic** /ˌTHôməˈtərjik/ **adj.**, **thau·ma·tur·gi·cal adj.**, **thau·ma·tur·gist n.**, **thau·ma·tur·gy n.**
– ORIGIN early 18th cent. (as *thaumaturg*): via medieval Latin from Greek *thaumatourgos*, from *thauma* 'marvel' + *-ergos* '-working.'

thaw /THô/ ▶ **v.** [no obj.] (of ice, snow, or another frozen substance, such as food) become liquid or soft as a result of warming: *the river thawed and barges of food began to reach the capital* | (as noun **thawing**) *catastrophic summer floods caused by thawing*. ■ (**it thaws, it is thawing**, etc.) the weather becomes warmer and melts snow and ice. ■ [with obj.] make (something) warm enough to become liquid or soft: *European exporters simply thawed their beef before unloading*. ■ (of a part of the body) become warm enough to stop feeling numb: *Ryan began to feel his ears and toes* **thaw out**. ■ make or become friendlier or more cordial: [no obj.] *she* **thawed out** *sufficiently to allow a smile to appear*.
▶ **n.** a period of warmer weather that thaws ice and snow: *the thaw came yesterday afternoon*. ■ an increase in friendliness or cordiality: *a thaw in relations between the two countries*.
– ORIGIN Old English *thawian* (verb); related to Dutch *dooien*. The noun (first recorded in Middle English) developed its figurative use in the mid 19th cent.

Th.B. ▶ **abbr.** Bachelor of Theology.
– ORIGIN New Latin *Theologicae Baccalaureus*.

THC ▶ **abbr.** tetrahydrocannabinol.

Th.D. ▶ **abbr.** Doctor of Theology.
– ORIGIN New Latin *Theologicae Doctor*.

the /T͟Hē, T͟Hə/ [called the definite article] ▶ **determiner**
1 denoting one or more people or things already mentioned or assumed to be common knowledge: *what's the matter? | call the doctor | the phone rang*. Compare with A. ■ used to refer to a person, place, or thing that is unique: *the Queen | the Mona Lisa | the Nile*. ■ informal denoting a disease or affliction: *I've got the flu*. ■ (with a unit of time) the present; the current: *dish of the day | man of the moment*. ■ informal used instead of a possessive to refer to someone with whom the speaker or person addressed is associated: *I'm meeting the boss | how's the family?* ■ used with a surname to refer to a family or married couple: *the Johnsons were not wealthy*. ■ used before the surname of the chief of a Scottish or Irish clan: *the O'Donoghue*.
2 used to point forward to a following qualifying or defining clause or phrase: *the fuss that he made of her | the top of a bus | I have done the best I could*. ■ (chiefly with rulers and family members with the same name) used after a name to qualify it: *George the Sixth | Edward the Confessor | Jack the Ripper*.
3 used to make a generalized reference to something rather than identifying a particular instance: *he taught himself to play the violin | worry about the future*. ■ used with a singular noun to indicate that it represents a whole species or class: *they placed the African elephant on their endangered list*. ■ used with an adjective to refer to those people who are of the type described: *the unemployed*. ■ used with an adjective to refer to something of the class or quality described: *they are trying to accomplish the impossible*. ■ used with the name of a unit to state a rate: *they can do 120 miles to the gallon*.
4 enough of (a particular thing): *he hoped to publish monthly, if only he could find the money*.
5 (pronounced stressing "the") used to indicate that someone or something is the best known or most important of that name or type: *he was* **the** *hot young piano prospect in jazz*.
6 used adverbially with comparatives to indicate how one amount or degree of something varies in relation to another: **the more** *she thought about it,* **the more** *devastating it became*. ■ (usu. **all the ——**) used to emphasize the amount or degree to which something is affected: *commodities made all the more desirable by their rarity*.
– ORIGIN Old English (Northumbrian and North Mercian dialects) *thē*; related to Dutch *de, dat*, and German *der, die, das*.

the·an·throp·ic /ˌTHēənˈTHräpik/ ▶ **adj.** embodying deity in a human form; both divine and human.
– ORIGIN mid 17th cent.: from ecclesiastical Greek *theanthrōpos* 'god-man' (from *theos* 'god' + *anthrōpos* 'human being') + -IC.

the·ar·chy /ˈTHēˌärkē/ ▶ **n.** (pl. **thearchies**) archaic rule by a god or gods.
– ORIGIN mid 17th cent.: from ecclesiastical Greek *thearkhia* 'godhead,' from *theos* 'god' + *arkhein* 'to rule.'

theat. ▶ **abbr.** ■ theater. ■ theatrical.

the·a·ter /ˈTHēətər/ (also **theatre**) ▶ **n.** a building or outdoor area in which plays and other dramatic performances are given. ■ (often **the theater**) the activity or profession of acting in, producing, directing, or writing plays: *what made you want to go into the theater?* ■ a play or other activity or presentation considered in terms of its dramatic quality: *this is intense, moving, and inspiring theater*. ■ a movie theater. ■ a room or hall for lectures, etc., with seats in tiers. ■ the area in which something happens: *a new* **theater of war** *has been opened up*. ■ [as modifier] denoting weapons for use in a particular region between tactical and strategic: *he was working on theater defense missiles*.
– ORIGIN late Middle English (originally as 'theatre'), from Old French, or from Latin *theatrum*, from Greek *theatron*, from *theasthai* 'behold.'

the·a·ter-in-the-round ▶ **n.** a form of theatrical presentation in which the audience is seated in a

t

PRONUNCIATION KEY ə ago, up; ər over, fur; a hat; ā ate; ä car; e let; ē see; i fit; ī by; NG sing; ō go; ô law, for; oi toy; o͝o good; o͞o goo; ou out; TH thin; T͟H then; ZH vision

circle around the stage or on at least three of its sides.

The·a·ter of the Ab·surd ▶ **n.** (**the Theater of the Absurd**) drama using the abandonment of conventional dramatic form to portray the futility of human struggle in a senseless world. Major exponents include Samuel Beckett, Eugène Ionesco, and Harold Pinter.

the·at·ric /THē'atrik/ ▶ **adj.** another term for THEATRICAL.

the·at·ri·cal /THē'atrikəl/ ▶ **adj.** of, for, or relating to acting, actors, or the theater: *theatrical productions.* ■ exaggerated and excessively dramatic: *Henry looked over his shoulder with theatrical caution.*
– DERIVATIVES **the·at·ri·cal·ism** /-ˌlizəm/ **n.**, **the·at·ri·cal·i·ty** /-ˌatri'kalitē/ **n.**, **the·at·ri·cal·i·za·tion** /-ˌatrikəli'zāSHən/ **n.**, **the·at·ri·cal·ize** /-ˌlīz/ **v.**, **the·at·ri·cal·ly** /-ik(ə)lē/ **adv.**
– ORIGIN mid 16th cent.: via late Latin from Greek *theatrikos* (from *theatron* 'theater') + -AL.

the·at·ri·cals /THē'atrikəlz/ ▶ **plural n.** dramatic performances: *I was persuaded to act in some amateur theatricals.*

the·at·rics /THē'atriks/ ▶ **plural n.** dramatic performances. ■ excessively emotional and dramatic behavior: *stop your theatrics.*

the·be /'tebe/ ▶ **n.** (pl. **same**) a monetary unit of Botswana, equal to one hundredth of a pula.
– ORIGIN Setswana, literally 'shield.'

Thebes /THēbz/ **1** the Greek name for an ancient city in Upper Egypt, the ruins of which are located on the Nile River about 420 miles (675 km) south of Cairo. The capital of ancient Egypt under the 18th dynasty (*c.*1550–1290 BC), it is the site of the major temples of Luxor and Karnak.
2 a city in Greece, in Boeotia, northwest of Athens. A major military power in Greece following the defeat of the Spartans at the battle of Leuctra in 371 BC, it was destroyed by Alexander the Great in 336 BC. Greek name **THÍVAI**.
– DERIVATIVES **The·ban** /'THēbən/ **adj. & n.**

the·ca /'THēkə/ ▶ **n.** (pl. **thecae** /'THēsē/) a receptacle, sheath, or cell enclosing an organ, part, or structure, in particular: ■ Anatomy the loose sheath enclosing the spinal cord. ■ Zoology a cuplike or tubular structure containing a coral polyp. ■ Botany either of the lobes of an anther, each containing two pollen sacs. ■ (also **theca folliculi** /fə'likyəˌlī/) Anatomy the outer layer of cells of a Graafian follicle.
– DERIVATIVES **the·cal adj.**, **the·cate** /-ˌkāt/ **adj.**
– ORIGIN early 17th cent.: via Latin from Greek *thēkē* 'case.'

the·co·dont /'THēkəˌdänt/ ▶ **n.** a fossil quadrupedal or partly bipedal reptile of the Triassic period, having teeth fixed in sockets in the jaw. Thecodonts are ancestral to the dinosaurs and other archosaurs. ● Order Thecodontia, subdivision Archosauria.
– ORIGIN mid 19th cent.: from modern Latin *Thecodontia*, from Greek *thēkē* 'case' + *odous, odont-* 'tooth.'

thee /T͟Hē/ ▶ **pron.** [second person singular] archaic or dialect form of YOU, as the singular object of a verb or preposition: *we beseech thee O lord.* Compare with THOU[1].
– ORIGIN Old English *thē*, accusative and dative case of *thū* 'thou.'

> **USAGE** The word **thee** is still used in some traditional dialects (e.g., in northern England) and among certain religious groups (e.g., Quakers), but in standard English it is restricted to archaic or religious contexts. For more details on **thee** and thou, see usage at THOU[1].

theft /THeft/ ▶ **n.** the action or crime of stealing: *he was convicted of theft | the latest theft happened at a garage.*
– ORIGIN Old English *thiefth, thēofth*, of Germanic origin; related to THIEF.

thegn /THān/ ▶ **n.** historical an English thane.
– ORIGIN mid 19th cent.: modern representation of Old English *theg(e)n*, adopted to distinguish the Old English use of THANE from the Scots use made familiar by Shakespeare.

the·ine /'THē-ēn, -in/ ▶ **n.** caffeine, esp. when it occurs in tea.
– ORIGIN mid 19th cent.: from modern Latin *Thea* (former genus name of the tea plant, from Dutch *thee*) + -INE[4].

their /T͟He(ə)r/ ▶ **possessive determiner 1** belonging to or associated with the people or things previously mentioned or easily identified: *her taunts had lost their power to touch him.* ■ belonging to or associated with a person of unspecified sex: *she heard someone blow their nose loudly.*
2 (**Their**) used in titles: *a double portrait of Their Majesties.*
– ORIGIN Middle English: from Old Norse *their(r)* a 'of them,' genitive plural of the demonstrative *sá*; related to THEM and THEY.

> **USAGE 1** On the use of **their** in the singular to mean 'his or her,' see usage at THEY. **2** On the differences between **their, they're,** and **there**, see usage at THEY.

theirs /T͟He(ə)rz/ ▶ **possessive pron.** used to refer to a thing or things belonging to or associated with two or more people or things previously mentioned: *they think everything is theirs | a favorite game of theirs.*
– ORIGIN Middle English: from THEIR + -'S[1].

their·selves /T͟He(ə)r'selvz/ ▶ **pron.** [third person plural] dialect form of THEMSELVES.

the·ism /'THēˌizəm/ ▶ **n.** belief in the existence of a god or gods, esp. belief in one god as creator of the universe, intervening in it and sustaining a personal relation to his creatures. Compare with DEISM.
– DERIVATIVES **the·ist n.**, **the·is·tic** /THē'istik/ **adj.**
– ORIGIN late 17th cent.: from Greek *theos* 'god' + -ISM.

The·lon River /'THēˌlän/ a river that rises in the Northwest Territories in Canada and flows for 550 miles (900 km) across Nunavut to Hudson Bay.

them /T͟Hem, T͟Həm/ ▶ **pron.** [third person plural] **1** used as the object of a verb or preposition to refer to two or more people or things previously mentioned or easily identified: *I bathed the kids and read them stories | rows of doors, most of them locked.* Compare with THEY. ■ used after the verb "to be" and after "than" or "as": *you think that's them? | we're better than them.* ■ [singular] referring to a person of unspecified sex: *how well do you have to know someone before you call them a friend?*
2 archaic themselves: *they bethought them of a new expedient.*
▶ **determiner** informal or dialect those: *look at them eyes.*
– ORIGIN Middle English: from Old Norse *theim* 'to those, to them,' dative plural of *sá*; related to THEIR and THEY.

> **USAGE** On the use of **them** in the singular to mean 'him or her,' see usage at THEY.

the·mat·ic /THi'matik/ ▶ **adj. 1** having or relating to subjects or a particular subject: *the orientation of this anthology is essentially thematic.* ■ Linguistics belonging to, relating to, or denoting the theme of a sentence. ■ Music of, relating to, or containing melodic subjects: *the concerto relies on the frequent repetition of thematic fragments.* ■ Philately British term for TOPICAL.
2 Linguistics of or relating to the theme of an inflected word. ■ (of a vowel) connecting the theme of a word to its inflections. ■ (of a word) having a vowel connecting its theme to its inflections.
▶ **n. 1** (**thematics**) [treated as sing. or pl.] a body of topics for study or discussion.
2 Philately British term for TOPICAL.
– DERIVATIVES **the·mat·i·cal·ly** /-ik(ə)lē/ **adv.**
– ORIGIN late 17th cent.: from Greek *thematikos*, from *thema* (see THEME).

The·mat·ic Ap·per·cep·tion Test ▶ **n.** Psychology a projective test designed to reveal a person's social drives or needs by their interpretation of a series of pictures of emotionally ambiguous situations.

the·ma·tize /'THēməˌtīz/ ▶ **v.** [with obj.] present or select (a subject) as a theme. ■ Linguistics place (a word or phrase) at the start of a sentence in order to focus attention on it.
– DERIVATIVES **the·mat·i·za·tion** /ˌTHēməti'zāSHən/ **n.**

theme /THēm/ ▶ **n. 1** the subject of a talk, a piece of writing, a person's thoughts, or an exhibition; a topic: *the theme of the sermon was reverence | a show on the theme of waste and recycling.* ■ Linguistics the first major constituent of a clause, indicating the subject-matter, typically being the subject but optionally other constituents, as in "*poor* he is not." Contrasted with RHEME. ■ an idea that recurs in or pervades a work of art or literature. ■ Music a prominent or frequently recurring melody or group of notes in a composition. ■ [as modifier] (of music) frequently recurring in or accompanying the beginning and end of a film, play, or musical: *a theme song.* ■ [usu. as modifier] a setting given to a leisure venue or activity, intended to evoke a particular country, historical period, culture, etc.: *a family fun park with a western theme | a New Deal theme restaurant.* ■ an essay written by a student on an assigned subject.
2 Linguistics the stem of a noun or verb; the part to which inflections are added, esp. one composed of the root and an added vowel.
3 historical any of the twenty-nine provinces in the Byzantine empire.
▶ **v.** [with obj.] give a particular setting or ambience to (a venue or activity): (as adj. **themed**) *Independence Day was celebrated with special themed menus* | [in combination] *a golf-themed business park.*
– ORIGIN Middle English: via Old French from Latin *thema*, from Greek, literally 'proposition'; related to *tithenai* 'to set or place.'

theme park ▶ **n.** an amusement park with a unifying setting or idea.

The·mis /'THēmis/ Greek Mythology a goddess, daughter of Uranus (Heaven) and Gaia (Earth). In Homer she was the personification of order and justice, who convened the assembly of the gods.

The·mis·to·cles /THə'mistəˌklēz/ (*c.*528–462 BC), Athenian statesman. He helped build up the Athenian fleet and defeated the Persian fleet at Salamis in 480.

them·self /T͟Həm'self, T͟Hem-/ ▶ **pron.** [third person singular] used instead of "himself" or "herself" to refer to a person of unspecified sex: *the casual observer might easily think themself back in 1945.*

> **USAGE** The standard reflexive form corresponding to **they** and **them** is **themselves**, as in *they can do it **themselves**.* The singular form **themself**, first recorded in the 14th century, has re-emerged in recent years corresponding to the singular gender-neutral use of **they**, as in *this is the first step in helping someone to help **themself**.* The form is not widely accepted in standard English, however. For more details, see usage at THEY.

them·selves /T͟Həm'selvz, T͟Hem-/ ▶ **pron.** [third person plural] **1** [reflexive] used as the object of a verb or preposition to refer to a group of people or things previously mentioned as the subject of the clause: *countries unable to look after themselves.*
2 [emphatic] used to emphasize a particular group of people or things mentioned: *excellent at organizing others, they may well be disorganized themselves.*
3 [singular] used instead of "himself" or "herself" to refer to a person of unspecified sex: *anyone who fancies themselves as a racing driver.*
– PHRASES **(not) be themselves** see BE ONESELF, NOT BE ONESELF at BE. **by themselves** see THEMSELVES at BY.

> **USAGE** On the use of **themselves** in the singular to mean 'himself or herself,' see usage at THEY.

then /T͟Hen/ ▶ **adv. 1** at that time; at the time in question: *I was living in Cairo then* | [after prep.] *Phoebe by then was exhausted* | [as adj.] *a hotel where the then prime minister, Margaret Thatcher, was staying.*
2 after that; next; afterward: *she won the first and then the second game.* ■ also; in addition: *I'm paid a generous salary, and then there's the money I've made at the races.*
3 in that case; therefore: *if you do what I tell you, then there's nothing to worry about | well, that's okay then.* ■ used at the end of a sentence to emphasize an inference being drawn: *so you're still here, then.* ■ used to finish off a conversation: *see you in an hour, then.*
– PHRASES **but then (again)** after all; on the other hand (introducing a contrasting comment): *it couldn't help, but then again, it probably couldn't hurt.* **then and there** immediately: *she made up her mind then and there.*
– ORIGIN Old English *thænne, thanne, thonne*, of Germanic origin; related to Dutch *dan* and German *dann*, also to THAT and THE.

the·nar /'THēnär/ Anatomy ▶ **adj.** of or relating to the rounded fleshy part of the hand at the base of the thumb (the ball of the thumb).
▶ **n.** this part of the hand.
– ORIGIN mid 17th cent.: from Greek, literally 'palm of the hand, sole of the foot.'

the·nard·ite /THə'närdīt, tə-/ ▶ **n.** a white to brownish translucent crystalline mineral occurring in evaporated salt lakes, consisting of anhydrous sodium sulfate.
– ORIGIN mid 19th cent.: from the name of Baron Louis-Jacques *Thénard* (1777–1857), French chemist, + -ITE[1].

thence /T͟Hens/ (also **from thence**) ▶ **adv.** formal from a place or source previously mentioned: *they intended to cycle on into France and thence home via Belgium.* ■ as a consequence: *studying maps to assess past latitudes and thence an indication of climate.*
– ORIGIN Middle English *thennes*, from earlier *thenne* (from Old English *thanon*) + -S[3] (later respelled *-ce* to denote the unvoiced sound).

thence·forth /T͟Hens'fôrTH/ (also **from thenceforth**) ▶ **adv.** archaic or literary from that time, place, or point onward: *thenceforth he made his life in England.*

thence·for·ward /T͟Hens'fôrwərd/ ▶ **adv.** another term for THENCEFORTH.

theo- ▶ **comb. form** relating to God or deities: *theocentric | theocracy.*

–ORIGIN from Greek *theos* 'god.'

the·o·bro·mine /ˌTHēəˈbrōˌmēn, -min/ ▶ **n.** Chemistry a bitter, volatile compound obtained from cacao seeds. It is an alkaloid resembling caffeine in its physiological effects. ● Chem. formula: $C_7H_8N_4O_2$.
–ORIGIN mid 19th cent.: from modern Latin *Theobroma* (genus name, from Greek *theos* 'god' and *brōma* 'food') + **-INE⁴**.

the·o·cen·tric /ˌTHēōˈsentrik/ ▶ **adj.** having God as a central focus: *a theocentric civilization*.

the·oc·ra·cy /THēˈäkrəsē/ ▶ **n.** (pl. **theocracies**) a system of government in which priests rule in the name of God or a god. ■ (**the Theocracy**) the commonwealth of Israel from the time of Moses until the election of Saul as King.
–DERIVATIVES **the·o·crat** /ˈTHēəˌkrat/ **n.**, **the·o·crat·ic** /THēəˈkratik/ **adj.**, **the·o·crat·i·cal·ly** /THēəˈkratik(ə)lē/ **adv.**
–ORIGIN early 17th cent.: from Greek *theokratia* (see **THEO-**, **-CRACY**).

The·oc·ri·tus /THēˈäkrətəs/ (*c.*310–*c.*250 BC), Greek poet, born in Sicily. He is chiefly known for his *Idylls*, which were hexameter poems presenting the lives of imaginary shepherds and which became the model for Virgil's *Eclogues*.

the·od·i·cy /THēˈädəsē/ ▶ **n.** (pl. **theodicies**) the vindication of divine goodness and providence in view of the existence of evil.
–DERIVATIVES **the·od·i·ce·an** /-ˌädəˈsēən/ **adj.**
–ORIGIN late 18th cent.: from French *Théodicée*, the title of a work by Leibniz, from Greek *theos* 'god' + *dikē* 'justice.'

the·od·o·lite /THēˈädəˌlīt/ ▶ **n.** a surveying instrument with a rotating telescope for measuring horizontal and vertical angles.
–DERIVATIVES **the·od·o·lit·ic** /-ˌädəˈlitik/ **adj.**
–ORIGIN late 16th cent. (originally denoting an instrument for measuring horizontal angles): from modern Latin *theodelitus*, of unknown origin.

The·o·do·ra /ˌTHēəˈdôrə/ (*c.*500–548), Byzantine empress; wife of Justinian. As Justinian's closest adviser, she exercised considerable influence on political affairs and the theological questions of the time.

The·o·do·ra·kis /ˌTHēədəˈräkis/, Mikis (1925–), Greek composer and politician. He was imprisoned by the military government for his left-wing political activities (1967–70). His compositions include the ballet *Antigone* (1958) and the score for the movie *Zorba the Greek* (1965).

The·o·dore Roo·se·velt Na·tion·al Park /ˈTHēəˌdôr ˈrōzəˌvelt/ a preserve in western North Dakota that incorporates Roosevelt's ranch home as well as extensive badlands areas.

The·od·o·ric /THēˈädərik/ (*c.*454–526), king of the Ostrogoths 471–526; known as **Theodoric the Great**. At its greatest extent, his empire included Italy, Sicily, Dalmatia, and parts of Germany.

The·o·do·si·us I /ˌTHēəˈdōsH(ē)əs/ (*c.*346–395), Roman emperor 379–395; full name *Flavius Theodosius*; known as **Theodosius the Great**. He took control of the Eastern Empire and ended the war with the Visigoths. A pious Christian, in 391 he banned all forms of pagan worship.

the·og·o·ny /THēˈägənē/ ▶ **n.** (pl. **theogonies**) the genealogy of a group or system of gods.
–ORIGIN early 17th cent.: from Greek *theogonia*, from *theos* 'god' + *-gonia* '-begetting.'

theol. ▶ **abbr.** ■ theologian. ■ theological. ■ theology.

the·o·lo·gian /THēəˈlōjən/ ▶ **n.** a person who engages or is an expert in theology.
–ORIGIN late 15th cent.: from French *théologien*, from *théologie* or Latin *theologia* (see **THEOLOGY**).

the·o·log·i·cal /THēəˈläjikəl/ ▶ **adj.** of or relating to the study of theology.
–DERIVATIVES **the·o·log·i·cal·ly** /-ik(ə)lē/ **adv.** [sentence adverb].
–ORIGIN late Middle English (in the sense 'relating to the word of God or the Bible'): from medieval Latin *theologicalis*, from late Latin *theologicus*, from Greek *theologikos*, from *theologia* (see **THEOLOGY**).

the·o·log·i·cal vir·tue ▶ **n.** each of the three virtues of faith, hope, and charity as defined by St. Paul. Often contrasted with **CARDINAL VIRTUE**.

the·ol·o·gize /THēˈäləjīz/ ▶ **v. 1** [no obj.] engage in theological reasoning or speculation.
2 [with obj.] treat (a person or subject) in theological terms: *he even theologizes writing problems*.

the·ol·o·gy /THēˈäləjē/ ▶ **n.** (pl. **theologies**) the study of the nature of God and religious belief. ■ religious beliefs and theory when systematically developed: *Augustine assimilated Roman ideals into Christian theology | a willingness to tolerate new theologies*.
–DERIVATIVES **the·ol·o·gist** /-jist/ **n.**
–ORIGIN late Middle English (originally applying only to Christianity): from French *théologie*, from Latin *theologia*, from Greek, from *theos* 'god' + *-logia* (see **-LOGY**).

the·om·a·chy /THēˈäməkē/ ▶ **n.** (pl. **theomachies**) a war or struggle against God or among or against the gods.
–ORIGIN late 16th cent. (denoting fighting against God): from Greek *theomakhia*, from *theos* 'god' + *-makhia* 'fighting.'

the·oph·a·ny /THēˈäfənē/ ▶ **n.** (pl. **theophanies**) a visible manifestation to humankind of God or a god.
–ORIGIN Old English, via ecclesiastical Latin from Greek *theophaneia*, from *theos* 'god' + *phainein* 'to show.'

the·o·phor·ic /THēəˈfôrik/ (also **theophorous** /THēˈäfərəs/) ▶ **adj.** bearing the name of a god.

The·o·phras·tus /ˌTHēəˈfrastəs/ (*c.*370–*c.*287 BC), Greek philosopher and scientist, the student and successor of Aristotle. The most influential of his works was *Characters*, a collection of sketches of psychological types.

the·o·phyl·line /THēˈäfəlin, ˌTHēəˈfilēn/ ▶ **n.** Chemistry a bitter crystalline compound present in small quantities in tea leaves, isomeric with theobromine.
–ORIGIN late 19th cent.: from modern Latin *Thea* (former genus name of the tea plant, from Dutch *thee*) + Greek *phullon* 'leaf' + **-INE⁴**.

the·or·bo /THēˈôrbō/ ▶ **n.** (pl. **theorbos**) a large lute with the neck extended to carry several long bass strings, used for accompaniment in 17th- and early-18th-century music.
–ORIGIN early 17th cent.: from Italian *tiorba*, of unknown origin.

the·o·rem /ˈTHēərəm, ˈTHi(ə)r-/ ▶ **n.** Physics & Mathematics a general proposition not self-evident but proved by a chain of reasoning; a truth established by means of accepted truths. ■ a rule in algebra or other branches of mathematics expressed by symbols or formulae.
–DERIVATIVES **the·o·re·mat·ic** /ˌTHēərəˈmatik, ˌTHi(ə)rə-/ **adj.**
–ORIGIN mid 16th cent.: from French *théorème*, or via late Latin from Greek *theōrēma* 'speculation, proposition,' from *theōrein* 'look at,' from *theōros* 'spectator.'

the·o·ret·ic /THēəˈretik/ ▶ **adj.** another term for **THEORETICAL**.
–ORIGIN early 17th cent. (in the sense 'conjectural'): via late Latin from Greek *theōrētikos*, from *theōrētos* 'that may be seen,' from *theōrein* (see **THEOREM**).

the·o·ret·i·cal /THēəˈretikəl/ ▶ **adj.** concerned with or involving the theory of a subject or area of study rather than its practical application: *a theoretical physicist | the training is task-related rather than theoretical*. ■ based on or calculated through theory rather than experience or practice: *the theoretical value of their work*.
–DERIVATIVES **the·o·ret·i·cal·ly** /-ik(ə)lē/ **adv.** [sentence adverb] *theoretically we might expect this to be true*.

the·o·re·ti·cian /ˌTHēərəˈtisHən, ˌTHi(ə)rə-/ ▶ **n.** a person who forms, develops, or studies the theoretical framework of a subject.

the·o·rist /ˈTHēərist, ˈTHi(ə)r-/ ▶ **n.** a person concerned with the theoretical aspects of a subject; a theoretician.

the·o·rize /ˈTHēəˌrīz, ˈTHi(ə)ˌrīz/ ▶ **v.** [no obj.] form a theory or set of theories about something: (as noun **theorizing**) *they are more interested in obtaining results than in political theorizing*. ■ [with obj.] create a theoretical premise or framework for (something): *women should be doing feminism rather than theorizing it*.
–DERIVATIVES **the·o·ri·za·tion** /ˌTHēərəˈzāsHən, ˌTHi(ə)r-/ **n.**, **the·o·riz·er n.**

the·o·ry /ˈTHēərē, ˈTHi(ə)rē/ ▶ **n.** (pl. **theories**) a supposition or a system of ideas intended to explain something, esp. one based on general principles independent of the thing to be explained: *Darwin's theory of evolution*. ■ a set of principles on which the practice of an activity is based: *a theory of education | music theory*. ■ an idea used to account for a situation or justify a course of action: *my theory would be that the place has been seriously mismanaged*. ■ Mathematics a collection of propositions to illustrate the principles of a subject.
–PHRASES **in theory** used in describing what is supposed to happen or be possible, usually with the implication that it does not in fact happen: *in theory, things can only get better; in practice, they may well become a lot worse*.
–ORIGIN late 16th cent. (denoting a mental scheme of something to be done): via late Latin from Greek *theōria* 'contemplation, speculation,' from *theōros* 'spectator.'

the·o·ry-lad·en ▶ **adj.** denoting a term, concept, or statement that has meaning only as part of some theory, so that its use implies the acceptance of that theory.

the·o·ry of games ▶ **n.** another term for **GAME THEORY**.

the·os·o·phy /THēˈäsəfē/ ▶ **n.** any of a number of philosophies maintaining that a knowledge of God may be achieved through spiritual ecstasy, direct intuition, or special individual relations, esp. the movement founded in 1875 as the Theosophical Society by Helena Blavatsky and **Henry Steel Olcott** (1832–1907).
–DERIVATIVES **the·os·o·pher** /-fər/ **n.**, **the·o·soph·ic** /ˌTHēəˈsäfik/ **adj.**, **the·o·soph·i·cal** /ˌTHēəˈsäfikəl/ **adj.**, **the·o·soph·i·cal·ly** /ˌTHēəˈsäfik(ə)lē/ **adv.**, **the·os·o·phist** /-fist/ **n.**
–ORIGIN mid 17th cent.: from medieval Latin *theosophia*, from late Greek, from *theosophos* 'wise concerning God,' from *theos* 'god' + *sophos* 'wise.'

The·o·to·kos /ˌTHēəˈtäkəs/ ▶ **n.** (**the Theotokos**) Mother of God (used in the Eastern Orthodox Church as a title of the Virgin Mary).
–ORIGIN from ecclesiastical Greek, from *theos* 'god' + *-tokos* 'bringing forth.'

The·ra /ˈTHi(ə)rə/ a Greek island in the southern Cyclades. It suffered a violent volcanic eruption in about 1500 BC; remains of an ancient Minoan civilization have been discovered beneath the volcanic debris. Also called **SANTORINI**. Greek name **THÍRA**.

therap. ▶ **abbr.** therapeutic; therapeutics.

ther·a·peu·tic /ˌTHerəˈpyo͞otik/ ▶ **adj.** of or relating to the healing of disease: *diagnostic and therapeutic facilities*. ■ administered or applied for reasons of health: *a therapeutic shampoo*. ■ having a good effect on the body or mind; contributing to a sense of well-being: *a therapeutic silence*.
▶ **n. 1** (**therapeutics**) the branch of medicine concerned with the treatment of disease and the action of remedial agents.
2 a treatment, therapy, or drug: *current therapeutics for asthma*.
–DERIVATIVES **ther·a·peu·ti·cal adj.**, **ther·a·peu·ti·cal·ly** /-ik(ə)lē/ **adv.**, **ther·a·peu·tist** /-tist/ **n.** (archaic).
–ORIGIN mid 17th cent.: via modern Latin from Greek *therapeutikos*, from *therapeuein* 'minister to, treat medically.'

ther·a·pist /ˈTHerəpist/ ▶ **n.** a person skilled in a particular kind of therapy: *a certified massage therapist*. ■ a psychoanalyst, psychologist, etc., who treats psychological problems; a psychotherapist: *cost is one factor keeping them from the therapist's couch*.

ther·a·pize /ˈTHerəˌpīz/ ▶ **v.** [with obj.] subject to psychological therapy: *you don't need to therapize or fix each other*.

the·rap·sid /THəˈrapsid/ ▶ **n.** an extinct reptile of a Permian and Triassic order, the members of which are related to the ancestors of mammals. ● Order Therapsida, subclass Synapsida: many families and numerous genera, including the cynodonts.
–ORIGIN early 20th cent.: from modern Latin *Therapsida*, from Greek *thēr* 'beast' + *hapsis, hapsid-* 'arch' (referring to the structure of the skull).

ther·a·py /ˈTHerəpē/ ▶ **n.** (pl. **therapies**) treatment intended to relieve or heal a disorder: *a course of antibiotic therapy | cancer therapies*. ■ the treatment of mental or psychological disorders by psychological means: *he is currently in therapy* | [as modifier] *therapy sessions*.
–ORIGIN mid 19th cent.: from modern Latin *therapia*, from Greek *therapeia* 'healing,' from *therapeuein* 'minister to, treat medically.'

Ther·a·va·da /ˌTHerəˈvädə/ (also **Theravada Buddhism**) ▶ **n.** the more conservative of the two major traditions of Buddhism (the other being Mahayana), and a school of Hinayana Buddhism. It is practiced mainly in Sri Lanka, Burma (Myanmar), Thailand, Cambodia, and Laos.
–ORIGIN from Pali *theravāda*, literally 'doctrine of the elders,' from *thera* 'elder, old' + *vāda* 'speech, doctrine.'

there /T͟He(ə)r/ ▶ **adv. 1** in, at, or to that place or position: *we went on to Paris and stayed there eleven days* | [after prep.] *I'm not going in there—it's freezing* | figurative *the opportunity is right there in front of you*. ■ used when pointing or gesturing to indicate the place in mind: *there on the right | if anyone wants out, there's the door!* ■ at that point (in speech, performance, writing, etc.): *"I'm quite—" There she stopped*. ■ in that respect; on that issue: *I don't agree*

PRONUNCIATION KEY ə ago, up; ər over, fur; a hat; ā ate; ä car; e let; ē see; i fit; ī by; NG sing; ō go; ô law, for; oi toy; o͝o good; o͞o goo; ou out; TH thin; T͟H then; ZH vision

with you there. ■ [with infinitive] used to indicate one's role in a particular situation: *at the end of the day, we are there to make money.*
2 used in attracting someone's attention or calling attention to someone or something: *hello there!* | *there goes the phone.*
3 (usu. **there is/are**) used to indicate the fact or existence of something: *there's a restaurant around the corner* | *there comes a point where you give up.*
▶ **exclam. 1** used to focus attention on something and express satisfaction or annoyance at it: *there, I told you she wouldn't mind!*
2 used to comfort someone: ***there, there,** you must take all of this philosophically.*
– PHRASES **been there, done that** informal used to express past experience of or familiarity with something, esp. something now regarded as boring or unwelcome. **be there for someone** be available to provide support or comfort for someone, esp. at a time of adversity. **have been there before** informal know all about a situation from experience. **here and there** see HERE. **not all there** (of a person) not fully alert and functioning: *he's not all there—give him a couple of days to readjust.* **so there** informal used to express one's defiance or awareness that someone will not like what one has decided or is saying: *you can't share, so there!* **there and then** immediately. **there goes ——** used to express the destruction or failure of something: *there goes my career.* **there it is** that is the situation: *pretty ridiculous, I know, but there it is.* **there or thereabouts** in or very near a particular place or position. ■ approximately: *forty years, there or thereabouts, had elapsed.* **there you are** (or **go**) informal **1** this is what you wanted: *there you are—that'll be $3.80 please.* **2** expressing confirmation, triumph, or resignation: *there you are! I told you the problem was a political one* | *sometimes it is embarrassing, but there you go.* **there you go again** used to criticize someone for behaving in a way that is typical of them. **there you have it** used to emphasize or draw attention to a particular fact: *so there you have it—the ultimate grand unified theory.* ■ used to draw attention to the simplicity of a process or action: *simply turn the handle three times and there you have it.*
– ORIGIN Old English *thǣr, thēr*, of Germanic origin; related to Dutch *daar* and German *da*, also to THAT and THE.

> **USAGE** On the differences between **their**, **they're**, and **there**, see usage at THEY.

there·a·bouts /ˈT͟He(ə)rəˌbouts/ (also **thereabout**) ▶ **adv.** near that place: *the land is dry in places thereabouts.* ■ used to indicate that a date of figure is approximate: *the notes were written in 1860 or thereabouts.*

there·af·ter /T͟He(ə)rˈaftər/ ▶ **adv.** formal after that time: *thereafter their fortunes suffered a steep decline.*

there·at /T͟He(ə)rˈat/ ▶ **adv.** archaic or formal **1** at that place.
2 on account of or after that.

there·by /T͟He(ə)rˈbī/ ▶ **adv.** by that means; as a result of that: *students perform in hospitals, thereby gaining a deeper awareness of the therapeutic power of music.*
– PHRASES **thereby hangs a tale** used to indicate that there is more to say about something.

there·for /ˌT͟He(ə)rˈfôr/ ▶ **adv.** archaic for that object or purpose.

there·fore /ˈT͟He(ə)rˌfôr/ ▶ **adv.** for that reason; consequently: *he was injured and therefore unable to play.*

t

there·from /T͟He(ə)rˈfrəm/ ▶ **adv.** archaic or formal from that or that place.

there·in /T͟He(ə)rˈin/ ▶ **adv.** archaic or formal in that place, document, or respect: *it shall be sufficient evidence of the facts therein contained.*

there·in·af·ter /ˌT͟He(ə)rinˈaftər/ ▶ **adv.** archaic or formal in a later part of that document.

there·in·be·fore /ˌT͟He(ə)rinbiˈfôr/ ▶ **adv.** archaic or formal in an earlier part of that document.

there·in·to /T͟He(ə)rˈinˌto͞o/ ▶ **adv.** archaic or formal into that place.

ther·e·min /ˈTHerəˌmin/ ▶ **n.** an electronic musical instrument in which the tone is generated by two high-frequency oscillators and the pitch controlled by the movement of the performer's hand toward and away from the circuit.
– ORIGIN early 20th cent.: named after Lev *Theremin* (1896–1993), its Russian inventor.

there·of /T͟He(ə)rˈəv/ ▶ **adv.** formal of the thing just mentioned; of that: *the member state or a part thereof.*

there·on /T͟He(ə)rˈän, -ˈôn/ ▶ **adv.** formal on or following from the thing just mentioned: *the order of the court and the taxation consequent thereon.*

there·out /T͟He(ə)rˈout/ ▶ **adv.** archaic out of that; from that source.

there's /T͟He(ə)rz/ ▶ **contraction** there is: *there's nothing there.* ■ informal, chiefly Brit. used to make a request or express approval of an action in a patronizing manner: *make a cup of tea, there's a good girl.*

The·re·sa, Moth·er see TERESA, MOTHER.

there·through /T͟He(ə)rˈTHro͞o/ ▶ **adv.** archaic through or by reason of that; thereby.

there·to /T͟He(ə)rˈto͞o/ ▶ **adv.** archaic or formal to that or that place: *the third party assents thereto.*

there·to·fore /ˌT͟He(ə)rtəˈfôr/ ▶ **adv.** archaic or formal before that time.

there·un·der /T͟He(ə)rˈəndər/ ▶ **adv.** archaic or formal in accordance with the thing mentioned: *the act and the regulations made thereunder.*

there·un·to /ˌT͟He(ə)rˌənˈto͞o/ ▶ **adv.** archaic or formal to that: *his agent thereunto lawfully authorized in writing or by will.*

there·up·on /ˈT͟He(ə)rəˌpän/ ▶ **adv.** formal immediately or shortly after that: *he thereupon returned to Moscow.*

there·with /T͟He(ə)rˈwiT͟H, -ˈwiTH/ ▶ **adv.** archaic or formal **1** with or in the thing mentioned: *documents lodged therewith.*
2 soon or immediately after that; forthwith: *therewith he rose.*

there·with·al /ˈT͟He(ə)rwiˌTHôl, -wiT͟H-/ ▶ **adv.** archaic together with that; besides: *he was to make a voyage and his fortune therewithal.*

The·ria /ˈTHi(ə)rēə/ Zoology a major group of mammals that comprises the marsupials and placentals. Compare with PROTOTHERIA. ● Subclass Theria, class Mammalia.
– ORIGIN modern Latin (plural), from Greek *thēria* 'wild animals.'

the·ri·ac /ˈTHi(ə)rēˌak/ ▶ **n.** archaic an ointment or other medicinal compound used as an antidote to snake venom or other poison.
– ORIGIN late Middle English: from Latin *theriaca* (see TREACLE).

the·ri·an /ˈTHi(ə)rēən/ Zoology ▶ **n.** a mammal of the major group Theria, which comprises the marsupials and placentals.
▶ **adj.** relating to or denoting therians.

the·ri·an·throp·ic /ˌTHi(ə)rēˌanˈTHräpik/ ▶ **adj.** (esp. of a deity) combining the form of an animal with that of a man.
– ORIGIN late 19th cent.: from Greek *thērion* 'wild animal' + *anthrōpos* 'human being' + -IC.

the·ri·o·mor·phic /ˌTHi(ə)rēəˈmôrfik/ ▶ **adj.** (esp. of a deity) having an animal form.
– ORIGIN late 19th cent.: from Greek *thērion* 'wild beast' + -MORPH + -IC.

therm /THərm/ ▶ **n.** a unit of heat equivalent to 100,000 Btu or 1.055×10^8 joules.
– ORIGIN 1920s: from Greek *thermē* 'heat.'

therm. ▶ **abbr.** thermometer.

ther·mal /ˈTHərməl/ ▶ **adj.** of or relating to heat. ■ another term for GEOTHERMAL. ■ (of a garment) made of a fabric that provides exceptional insulation to keep the body warm: *thermal underwear.*
▶ **n. 1** an upward current of warm air, used by gliders, balloons, and birds to gain height.
2 (usu. **thermals**) a thermal garment, esp. underwear.
– DERIVATIVES **ther·mal·ly** adv.
– ORIGIN mid 18th cent. (in the sense 'relating to hot springs'): from French, from Greek *thermē* 'heat.'

ther·mal de·po·lym·er·i·za·tion ▶ **n.** a process of breaking down complex hydrocarbons in an oxygen-deprived, heated and pressurized environment to yield simpler compounds that can be used to produce fuels.

ther·mal ef·fi·cien·cy ▶ **n.** the efficiency of a heat engine measured by the ratio of the work done by it to the heat supplied to it.

ther·mal im·ag·ing ▶ **n.** the technique of using the heat given off by an object to produce an image of it or locate it.

ther·mal in·ver·sion ▶ **n.** see INVERSION (sense 2).

ther·mal·ize /ˈTHərməˌlīz/ ▶ **v.** attain or cause to attain thermal equilibrium with the environment.
– DERIVATIVES **ther·mal·i·za·tion** /ˌTHərməliˈzāSHən/ **n.**

ther·mal neu·tron ▶ **n.** a neutron in thermal equilibrium with its surroundings. Compare with SLOW NEUTRON.

ther·mal noise ▶ **n.** Electronics electrical fluctuations arising from the random thermal motion of electrons.

ther·mal pa·per ▶ **n.** heat-sensitive paper used in thermal printers.

ther·mal print·er ▶ **n.** a printer in which small heated pins form characters on heat-sensitive paper.

ther·mal re·ac·tor ▶ **n.** a nuclear reactor using thermal neutrons.

ther·mal spring ▶ **n.** a spring of naturally hot water.

ther·mal u·nit ▶ **n.** a unit for measuring heat.

ther·mic /ˈTHərmik/ ▶ **adj.** of or relating to heat.
– ORIGIN mid 19th cent.: from Greek *thermē* 'heat' + -IC.

Ther·mi·dor /ˈTHərmiˌdôr/ **n.** the eleventh month of the French Republican calendar (1793–1805), originally running from July 19 to August 17. ■ a reaction of moderates following a revolution, such as that which occurred in Paris on 9 Thermidor (July 27) 1794 and resulted in the fall of Robespierre.
– DERIVATIVES **Ther·mi·do·ri·an** /ˌTHərməˈdôrēən/ **adj.**
– ORIGIN French, from Greek *thermē* 'heat' + *dōron* 'gift.'

therm·i·on /ˈTHərmˌīən/ ▶ **n.** an ion or electron emitted by a substance at high temperature.
– ORIGIN early 20th cent.: from THERMO- 'of heat' + ION.

therm·i·on·ic /ˌTHərmīˈänik/ ▶ **adj.** of or relating to electrons emitted from a substance at very high temperature.

therm·i·on·ic e·mis·sion ▶ **n.** the emission of electrons from a heated source.

therm·i·on·ics /ˌTHərmīˈäniks/ ▶ **plural n.** [treated as sing.] the branch of science and technology concerned with thermionic emission.

therm·i·on·ic tube (Brit. **thermionic valve**) ▶ **n.** Electronics an electron tube giving a unidirectional flow of electrons emitted from a hot cathode, used esp. in the rectification of a current and in radio reception.

therm·is·tor /ˈTHərˌmistər/ ▶ **n.** an electrical resistor whose resistance is greatly reduced by heating, used for measurement and control.
– ORIGIN 1940s: contraction of *thermal resistor*.

ther·mite /ˈTHərˌmīt/ (also trademark **Thermit** /-mit/) ▶ **n.** a mixture of finely powdered aluminum and iron oxide that produces a very high temperature on combustion, used in welding and for incendiary bombs.
– ORIGIN early 20th cent.: coined in German from THERMO- 'of heat' + -ITE[1].

thermo- ▶ **comb. form** relating to heat: *thermodynamics* | *thermoelectric.*
– ORIGIN from Greek *thermos* 'hot,' *thermē* 'heat.'

ther·mo·chem·is·try /ˌTHərmōˈkemistrē/ ▶ **n.** the branch of chemistry concerned with the quantities of heat evolved or absorbed during chemical reactions.
– DERIVATIVES **ther·mo·chem·i·cal** /-ˈkemikəl/ **adj.**

ther·mo·cline /ˈTHərmōˌklīn/ ▶ **n.** a steep temperature gradient in a body of water such as a lake, marked by a layer above and below which the water is at different temperatures.

ther·mo·cou·ple /ˈTHərmōˌkəpəl/ ▶ **n.** a thermoelectric device for measuring temperature, consisting of two wires of different metals connected at two points, a voltage being developed between the two junctions in proportion to the temperature difference.

ther·mo·dy·nam·ics /ˌTHərmōdīˈnamiks/ ▶ **plural n.** [treated as sing.] the branch of physical science that deals with the relations between heat and other forms of energy (such as mechanical, electrical, or chemical energy), and, by extension, of the relationships between all forms of energy.

> The **first law of thermodynamics** states the equivalence of heat and work and reaffirms the principle of conservation of energy. The **second law** states that heat does not of itself pass from a cooler to a hotter body. Another, equivalent, formulation of the second law is that the entropy of a closed system can only increase. The **third law** (also called Nernst's heat theorem) states that it is impossible to reduce the temperature of a system to absolute zero in a finite number of operations.

– DERIVATIVES **ther·mo·dy·nam·ic** adj., **ther·mo·dy·nam·i·cal** /-ikəl/ **adj.**, **ther·mo·dy·nam·i·cal·ly** /-ik(ə)lē/ **adv.**, **ther·mo·dy·nam·i·cist** /-ˌdīˈnamisist/ **n.**

ther·mo·e·las·tic /ˌTHərmō-iˈlastik/ ▶ **adj.** of or relating to elasticity in connection with heat.

ther·mo·e·lec·tric /ˌTHərmō-iˈlektrik/ ▶ **adj.** producing electricity by a difference of temperatures.

– DERIVATIVES **ther·mo·e·lec·tri·cal·ly** adv., **ther·mo·e·lec·tric·i·ty** /-iˌlek'trisitē, -ˌēlek-/ n.

ther·mo·form·ing /'THərməˌfôrmiNG/ ▶ n. the process of heating a thermoplastic material and shaping it in a mold.

ther·mo·gen·e·sis /ˌTHərmō'jenəsis/ ▶ n. the production of heat, esp. in a human or animal body.
– DERIVATIVES **ther·mo·gen·ic** /-mə'jenik/ adj.

ther·mo·gram /'THərməˌgram/ ▶ n. a record made by a thermograph.

ther·mo·graph /'THərməˌgraf/ ▶ n. an instrument that produces a trace or image representing a record of the varying temperature or infrared radiation over an area or during a period of time.

ther·mog·ra·phy /THər'mägrəfē/ ▶ n. **1** the use of thermograms to study heat distribution in structures or regions, for example in detecting tumors.
2 a printing technique in which a wet ink image is fused by heat or infrared radiation with a resinous powder to produce a raised impression.
– DERIVATIVES **ther·mo·graph·ic** /ˌTHərmə'grafik/ adj.

ther·mo·karst /'THərməˌkärst/ ▶ n. Geology a form of periglacial topography resembling karst, with hollows produced by the selective melting of permafrost.

ther·mo·la·bile /ˌTHərmō'lāˌbīl, -bəl/ ▶ adj. chiefly Biochemistry (of a substance) readily destroyed or deactivated by heat.

ther·mo·lu·mi·nes·cence /ˌTHərmōˌlo͞omə'nesəns/ ▶ n. the property of some materials that have accumulated energy over a long period of becoming luminescent when pretreated and subjected to high temperatures, used as a means of dating ancient ceramics and other artifacts.
– DERIVATIVES **ther·mo·lu·mi·nes·cent** adj.

ther·mol·y·sis /THər'mäləsis/ ▶ n. Chemistry the breakdown of molecules by the action of heat.
– DERIVATIVES **ther·mo·lyt·ic** /ˌTHərmə'litik/ adj.

ther·mom·e·ter /THər'mämitər/ ▶ n. an instrument for measuring and indicating temperature, typically one consisting of a narrow, hermetically sealed glass tube marked with graduations and having at one end a bulb containing mercury or alcohol that expands and contracts in the tube with heating and cooling.
– DERIVATIVES **ther·mo·met·ric** /ˌTHərmə'metrik/ adj., **ther·mo·met·ri·cal** /ˌTHərmə'metrikəl/ adj., **ther·mom·e·try** /-trē/ n.
– ORIGIN mid 17th cent.: from French *thermomètre* or modern Latin *thermometrum*, from THERMO- 'of heat' + *-metrum* 'measure.'

ther·mo·nu·cle·ar /ˌTHərmō'n(y)o͞oklēər, -kli(ə)r/ ▶ adj. relating to or using nuclear reactions that occur only at very high temperatures. ■ of, relating to, or involving weapons in which explosive force is produced by thermonuclear reactions.

ther·mo·phile /'THərməˌfīl/ ▶ n. Microbiology a bacterium or other microorganism that grows best at higher than normal temperatures.
– DERIVATIVES **ther·mo·phil·ic** /ˌTHərmə'filik/ adj.

ther·mo·pho·to·vol·ta·ic /ˌTHərmōˌfōtōväl'tā-ik, -vōl-, -vôl-/ ▶ adj. (abbr. **TPV**) denoting or relating to the capacity to convert infrared radiation (i.e. radiant heat) into electricity.

ther·mo·pile /'THərməˌpīl/ ▶ n. a set of thermocouples arranged for measuring small quantities of radiant heat.

ther·mo·plas·tic /ˌTHərmə'plastik/ Chemistry ▶ adj. denoting substances (esp. synthetic resins) that become plastic on heating and harden on cooling and are able to repeat these processes. Often contrasted with THERMOSETTING.
▶ n. (usu. **thermoplastics**) a substance of this kind.

Ther·mop·y·lae /THər'mäpəˌlē, -ˌlī/ a narrow pass between the mountains and the sea in Greece, about 120 miles (200 km) northwest of Athens, now much widened by the recession of the sea. In 480 BC it was the scene of the defense against the Persian army of Xerxes I by 6,000 Greeks; among them were 300 Spartans, all of whom, including their king Leonidas, were killed.

ther·mo·reg·u·late /ˌTHərmō'regyəˌlāt/ ▶ v. [no obj.] regulate temperature, esp. one's own body temperature.
– DERIVATIVES **ther·mo·reg·u·la·tion** /-ˌregyə'lāSHən/ n., **ther·mo·reg·u·la·to·ry** /-ləˌtôrē/ adj.

ther·mos /'THərməs/ (also **thermos bottle**) ▶ n. a container that keeps a drink or other fluid hot or cold by means of a double wall enclosing a vacuum.
– ORIGIN early 20th cent.: from Greek, literally 'hot.'

ther·mo·set·ting /'THərmōˌsetiNG/ ▶ adj. Chemistry denoting substances (esp. synthetic resins) that set permanently when heated. Often contrasted with THERMOPLASTIC.
– DERIVATIVES **ther·mo·set** adj. & n.

ther·mo·sphere /'THərmōˌsfir/ ▶ n. the region of the atmosphere above the mesosphere and below the height at which the atmosphere ceases to have the properties of a continuous medium. The thermosphere is characterized throughout by an increase in temperature with height.

ther·mo·sta·ble /'THərmōˌstābəl/ ▶ adj. chiefly Biochemistry (of a substance) not readily destroyed or deactivated by heat.

ther·mo·stat /'THərməˌstat/ ▶ n. a device that automatically regulates temperature, or that activates a device when the temperature reaches a certain point.
– DERIVATIVES **ther·mo·stat·ic** /ˌTHərmə'statik/ adj., **ther·mo·stat·i·cal·ly** /ˌTHərmə'statik(ə)lē/ adv.

ther·mot·ro·pism /THər'mätrəˌpizəm/ ▶ n. Biology the turning or bending of a plant or other organism in response to a directional source of heat.
– DERIVATIVES **ther·mo·trop·ic** /ˌTHərmə'trōpik, -'träpik/ adj.

the·ro·pod /'THi(ə)rəˌpäd/ ▶ n. a carnivorous dinosaur of a group whose members are typically bipedal and range from small and delicately built to very large. ● Suborder Theropoda, order Saurischia; includes the carnosaurs, ornithomimosaurs, coelurosaurs, and dromaeosaurids.
– ORIGIN 1930s: from Greek *thēr* 'beast' + *pous, pod-* 'foot.'

The·roux /THə'ro͞o/, Paul, (1941–) US writer. His fiction includes *The Mosquito Coast* (1982), *My Other Life* (1996), and *Kowloon Tong* (1997). His nonfiction travel books include *The Great Railway Bazaar* (1975), *The Pillars of Hercules* (1995), and *Ghost Train to the Eastern Star* (2008).

the·sau·rus /THə'sôrəs/ ▶ n. (pl. **thesauri** /-'sôrī/ or **thesauruses**) a book that lists words in groups of synonyms and related concepts. ■ archaic a dictionary or encyclopedia.
– ORIGIN late 16th cent.: via Latin from Greek *thēsauros* 'storehouse, treasure.' The original sense 'dictionary or encyclopedia' was narrowed to the current meaning by the publication of Roget's *Thesaurus of English Words and Phrases* (1852).

these /T͟Hēz/ plural form of THIS.

The·se·us /'THēsēəs, -syo͞os/ Greek Mythology the legendary hero of Athens, son of Poseidon (or, in another account, of Aegeus, king of Athens) and husband of Phaedra. He slew the Cretan Minotaur with the help of Ariadne.

the·sis /'THēsis/ ▶ n. (pl. **theses** /-sēz/) **1** a statement or theory that is put forward as a premise to be maintained or proved: *his central thesis is that psychological life is not part of the material world.* ■ (in Hegelian philosophy) a proposition forming the first stage in the process of dialectical reasoning. Compare with ANTITHESIS, SYNTHESIS.
2 a long essay or dissertation involving personal research, written by a candidate for a college degree: *a doctoral thesis.*
3 Prosody an unstressed syllable or part of a metrical foot in Greek or Latin verse. Often contrasted with ARSIS.
– ORIGIN late Middle English (sense 3): via late Latin from Greek, literally 'placing, a proposition,' from the root of *tithenai* 'to place.'

thesp ▶ abbr. informal thespian.

thes·pi·an /'THespēən/ formal humorous ▶ adj. of or relating to drama and the theater: *thespian talents.*
▶ n. an actor or actress.
– ORIGIN late 17th cent.: from the name THESPIS + -IAN.

Thes·pis /'THespəs/ (6th century BC), Greek dramatic poet. He is regarded as the founder of Greek tragedy.

Thess. ▶ abbr. Bible Thessalonians.

Thes·sa·lo·ni·ans /ˌTHesə'lōnēənz/ either of two books of the New Testament, epistles of St. Paul to the new church at Thessalonica.

Thes·sa·lo·ní·ki /ˌTHesəlō'nēkē/ a seaport in northeastern Greece, the second largest city in Greece and capital of the Greek region of Macedonia; pop. 348,900 (est. 2009). Latin name **Thessalonica**. Also called SALONICA.

Thes·sa·ly /'THesəlē/ a region of northeastern Greece. Greek name **Thessalía**.
– DERIVATIVES **Thes·sa·li·an** /THe'sālēən, -'sālyən/ adj. & n.

the·ta /'THātə, 'THē-/ ▶ n. the eighth letter of the Greek alphabet (Θ, θ), transliterated as 'th.' ■ (**Theta**) [followed by Latin genitive] Astronomy the eighth star in a constellation: *Theta Draconis.* ■ [as modifier] Chemistry denoting a temperature at which a polymer solution behaves ideally as regards its osmotic pressure. ■ [as modifier] denoting electrical activity observed in the brain under certain conditions, consisting of oscillations having a frequency of 4 to 7 hertz: *theta rhythm.* ▶ symbol ■ (θ) temperature (esp. in degrees Celsius). ■ (θ) a plane angle. ■ (θ) a polar coordinate. Often coupled with PHI.

The·tis /'THētis/ Greek Mythology a sea nymph, mother of Achilles.

the·ur·gy /'THēərjē/ ▶ n. the operation or effect of a supernatural or divine agency in human affairs. ■ a system of white magic practiced by the early Neoplatonists.
– DERIVATIVES **the·ur·gic** /THē'ərjik/ adj., **the·ur·gi·cal** adj., **the·ur·gist** n.
– ORIGIN mid 16th cent.: via late Latin from Greek *theourgia* 'sorcery,' from *theos* 'god' + *-ergos* 'working.'

thew /TH(y)o͞o/ ▶ n. literary muscular strength. ■ (**thews**) muscles and tendons perceived as generating such strength.
– DERIVATIVES **thew·y** adj.
– ORIGIN Old English *thēaw* 'usage, custom,' (plural) '(personal) manner of behaving,' of unknown origin. The sense 'good bodily proportions, muscular development' arose in Middle English.

they /T͟Hā/ ▶ pron. [third person plural] **1** used to refer to two or more people or things previously mentioned or easily identified: *the two men could get life sentences if they are convicted.* ■ people in general: *the rest, as they say, is history.* ■ informal a group of people in authority regarded collectively: *they cut my water off.*
2 [singular] used to refer to a person of unspecified sex: *ask someone if they could help.*
– ORIGIN Middle English: from Old Norse *their*, nominative plural masculine of *sá*; related to THEM and THEIR, also to THAT and THE.

> **USAGE** 1 The word **they** (with its counterparts **them, their, and themselves**) as a singular pronoun to refer to a person of unspecified sex has been used since at least the 16th century. In the late 20th century, as the traditional use of **he** to refer to a person of either sex came under scrutiny on the grounds of sexism, this use of **they** has become more common. It is now generally accepted in contexts where it follows an indefinite pronoun such as **anyone, no one, someone,** or **a person**: *anyone can join if they are a resident; each to their own.* In other contexts, coming after singular nouns, the use of **they** is now common, although less widely accepted, especially in formal contexts. Sentences such as *ask a friend if they could help* are still criticized for being ungrammatical. Nevertheless, in view of the growing acceptance of **they** and its obvious practical advantages, **they** is used in this dictionary in many cases where **he** would have been used formerly. See also usage at HE and SHE.
> 2 Don't confuse **their, they're,** and **there. Their** is a possessive pronoun: *I like their new car.* **They're** is a contraction of 'they are': *they're parking the car.* **There** is an adverb meaning 'at that place': *park the car over there.*

they'd /T͟Hād/ ▶ contraction they had. ■ they would.

they'll /T͟Hāl/ ▶ contraction they shall; they will.

they're /T͟He(ə)r/ ▶ contraction they are.

> **USAGE** On the differences between **their, they're,** and **there**, see usage at THEY.

they've /T͟Hāv/ ▶ contraction they have.

THG ▶ abbr. tetrahydrogestrinone, an artificial anabolic steroid taken for enhancement of athletic performance.

THI ▶ abbr. temperature-humidity index.

thi·a·ben·da·zole /ˌTHīə'bendəˌzōl/ ▶ n. Medicine a synthetic compound with anthelmintic properties, derived from thiazole and used chiefly to treat infestation with intestinal nematodes.
– ORIGIN 1960s: from elements from THIAZOLE + BENZENE + IMIDAZOLE.

thi·a·mine /'THīəmin, -mēn/ (also **thiamin** /-min/) ▶ n. Biochemistry a vitamin of the B complex, found in unrefined grains, beans, and liver, a deficiency of which causes beriberi. It is a sulfur-containing derivative of thiazole and pyrimidine. Also called VITAMIN B1 (see VITAMIN B).

thi·a·zide /'THīəˌzīd/ ▶ n. Medicine any of a class of sulfur-containing drugs that increase the excretion of sodium and chloride and are used as diuretics and as a method of lowering the blood pressure.
– ORIGIN 1950s: from elements of THIO- + AZINE + OXIDE.

t

thi·a·zine /ˈTHīəˌzēn/ ▶ **n.** any of a class of molecules containing a ring of one nitrogen, one sulfur, and four carbon atoms, used in dyes and more recently in sedatives.
– ORIGIN late 19th cent.: from *thio-* + *azine*.

thi·a·zole /ˈTHīəˌzōl/ ▶ **n.** Chemistry a foul-smelling synthetic liquid whose molecule is a ring of one nitrogen, one sulfur, and three carbon atoms. ● Chem. formula: C_3H_3NS.

thick /THik/ ▶ **adj. 1** with opposite sides or surfaces that are a great or relatively great distance apart: *thick slices of bread* | *the walls are 5 feet thick* | *thick metal cables*. ■ (of a garment or other knitted or woven item) made of heavy material for warmth or comfort: *a thick sweater*. ■ (of script or type) consisting of broad lines: *a headline in thick black type*.
2 made up of a large number of things or people close together: *his hair was long and thick* | *the road winds through thick forest*. ■ [predic.] (**thick with**) densely filled or covered with: *the room was thick with smoke* | figurative *the air was thick with tension*. ■ (of the air or atmosphere, or a substance in the air) opaque, dense, or heavy: *the shore was obscured by thick fog* | *a thick cloud of smoke*.
3 (of a liquid or a semiliquid substance) relatively firm in consistency; not flowing freely: *thick mud*.
4 informal of low intelligence; stupid: *he's a bit thick* | *I've got to shout to get it into your thick head*.
5 (of a voice) not clear or distinct; hoarse or husky. ■ (of an accent) very marked and difficult to understand.
6 [predic.] informal having a very close, friendly relationship: *he's very thick with the new boss*.
▶ **n.** (**the thick**) the busiest or most crowded part of something; the middle of something: *the thick of battle*.
▶ **adv.** in or with deep, dense, or heavy mass: *bread spread thick with butter*.
– PHRASES **be thick on the ground** see GROUND[1]. **a bit thick** Brit. informal unfair or unreasonable. **have a thick skin** see SKIN. **thick and fast** rapidly and in great numbers. **(as) thick as a brick** very stupid. **(as) thick as thieves** informal (of two or more people) very close or friendly; sharing secrets. **through thick and thin** under all circumstances, no matter how difficult: *they stuck together through thick and thin*.
– DERIVATIVES **thick·ish** adj., **thick·ly** adv. [as submodifier] *thickly carpeted corridors*.
– ORIGIN Old English *thicce*, of Germanic origin; related to Dutch *dik* and German *dick*.

thick·en /ˈTHikən/ ▶ **v.** make or become thick or thicker: [with obj.] *thicken the sauce with flour* | [no obj.] *the fog had thickened*.
– PHRASES **the plot thickens** used when a situation is becoming more and more complicated and puzzling.

thick·en·er /ˈTHikənər/ ▶ **n.** a substance added to a liquid to make it firmer, esp. in cooking. ■ Chemistry an apparatus for the sedimentation of solids from suspension in a liquid.

thick·en·ing /ˈTHikəniNG/ ▶ **n. 1** the process or result of becoming broader, deeper, or denser. ■ a broader, deeper, or denser area of animal or plant tissue.
2 another term for THICKENER.
▶ **adj.** becoming broader, deeper, or denser: *a hazardous journey through thickening fog*.

thick·et /ˈTHikit/ ▶ **n.** a dense group of bushes or trees.
– ORIGIN Old English *thiccet* (see THICK, -ET[1]).

thick·head /ˈTHikˌhed/ ▶ **n.** informal a stupid person.
– DERIVATIVES **thick·head·ed** adj., **thick·head·ed·ness** n.

t

thick-knee ▶ **n.** a large-eyed ploverlike bird with mottled brownish plumage, inhabiting open stony or sandy country. Also called STONE CURLEW. ● Family Burhinidae: two genera and several species, in particular *Burhinus oedicnemus* of Eurasia and Africa.

thick·ness /ˈTHiknis/ ▶ **n. 1** the distance between opposite sides of something: *the gateway is several feet in thickness* | *paving slabs can be obtained in varying thicknesses*. ■ a layer of a specified material: *the framework has to support two thicknesses of plasterboard*. ■ [in sing.] a broad or deep part of a specified thing: *the beams were set into the thickness of the wall*.
2 the state or quality of being thick: *he gave his eyes time to adjust to the thickness of the fog* | *the thickness of his hair*.
– ORIGIN Old English *thicness* (see THICK, -NESS).

thick·set /ˈTHikˌset/ ▶ **adj.** (of a person or animal) heavily or solidly built; stocky.

thick-skinned ▶ **adj.** insensitive to criticism or insults: *you have to be thick-skinned and none too squeamish*.

thick-wit·ted (also **thick-skulled**) ▶ **adj.** dull and stupid.

thief /THēf/ ▶ **n.** (pl. **thieves** /THēvz/) a person who steals another person's property, esp. by stealth and without using force or violence.
– ORIGIN Old English *thiof*, *thēof*, of Germanic origin; related to Dutch *dief* and German *Dieb*, also to THEFT.

thieve /THēv/ ▶ **v.** [no obj.] be a thief; steal something: *they began thieving again* | (as adj. **thieving**) *get lost, you thieving swine*.
– ORIGIN Old English *thēofian*, from *thēof* 'thief.' Transitive uses began in the late 17th cent.

thiev·er·y /ˈTHēv(ə)rē/ ▶ **n.** the action of stealing another person's property.

thieves /THēvz/ plural form of THIEF.

thiev·ish /ˈTHēviSH/ ▶ **adj.** of, relating to, or given to stealing.
– DERIVATIVES **thiev·ish·ly** adv., **thiev·ish·ness** n.

thigh /THī/ ▶ **n.** the part of the human leg between the hip and the knee. ■ the corresponding part in other animals.
– DERIVATIVES **thighed** adj. [in combination].
– ORIGIN Old English *thēh*, *thēoh*, *thīoh*, of Germanic origin; related to Dutch *dij*.

thigh bone ▶ **n.** the femur.

thigh-high ▶ **adj.** reaching as high as a person's thigh: [as adj.] *black thigh-high boots* | [as adv.] *skirts are sexily split thigh-high*.

thigh-slap·per ▶ **n.** informal a joke or anecdote considered to be exceptionally funny.
– DERIVATIVES **thigh-slap·ping** adj.

thig·mo·tax·is /ˌTHigməˈtaksis/ ▶ **n.** Biology the motion or orientation of an organism in response to a touch stimulus.
– DERIVATIVES **thig·mo·tac·tic** /-ˈtaktik/ adj.
– ORIGIN early 20th cent.: from Greek *thigma* 'touch' + TAXIS.

thig·mot·ro·pism /THigˈmätrəˌpizəm/ ▶ **n.** Biology the turning or bending of a plant or other organism in response to a touch stimulus.
– DERIVATIVES **thig·mo·trop·ic** /ˌTHigməˈtrōpik, -ˈträpik/ adj.
– ORIGIN early 20th cent.: from Greek *thigma* 'touch' + TROPISM.

thill /THil/ ▶ **n.** historical a shaft, esp. one of a pair, used to attach a cart or carriage to the animal drawing it.
– ORIGIN Middle English: of unknown origin.

thim·ble /ˈTHimbəl/ ▶ **n.** a metal or plastic cap with a closed end, worn to protect the finger and push the needle in sewing. ■ a short metal tube or ferrule. ■ Nautical a metal ring, concave on the outside, around which a loop of rope is spliced.
– ORIGIN Old English *thȳmel* 'finger protector' (see THUMB, -LE[1].).

thim·ble·ber·ry /ˈTHimbəlˌberē/ ▶ **n.** (pl. **thimbleberries**) a North American blackberry or raspberry with thimble-shaped fruit. ● Genus *Rubus*, family Rosaceae: several species, including *R. parviflorus*, which has white flowers and juicy, somewhat tasteless fruit.

thim·ble·ful /ˈTHimbəlˌfo͝ol/ ▶ **n.** (pl. **thimblefuls**) a small quantity of liquid, esp. alcohol: *a thimbleful of brandy*.

thim·ble·rig /ˈTHimbəlˌrig/ ▶ **n.** another term for SHELL GAME.
– DERIVATIVES **thim·ble·rig·ger** n.
– ORIGIN early 19th cent.: from THIMBLE + RIG[2] in the sense 'trick, dodge.'

thi·mer·o·sal /THīˈmerəsəl/ ▶ **n.** a local antiseptic for abrasions and minor cuts. ● Chem. formula: $C_9H_9HgNaO_2S$.

Thim·phu /timˈpo͞o, THim-/ (also **Thimbu** /-ˈbo͞o/) the capital of Bhutan, in the Himalayas at an altitude of 8,000 feet (2,450 m); pop. 98,676 (2005).

thin /THin/ ▶ **adj.** (**thinner**, **thinnest**) **1** having opposite surfaces or sides close together; of little thickness or depth: *thin slices of bread*. ■ (of a person) having little, or too little, flesh or fat on their body: *she was painfully thin*. ■ (of a garment or other knitted or woven item) made of light material for coolness or elegance. ■ (of a garment) having had a considerable amount of fabric worn away. ■ (of script or type) consisting of narrow lines: *tall, thin lettering*.
2 having few parts or members relative to the area covered or filled; sparse: *a depressingly thin crowd* | *his hair was going thin*. ■ not dense: *the thin cold air of the mountains*. ■ containing much liquid and not much solid substance: *thin soup*. ■ Climbing denoting a route on which the holds are small or scarce.
3 (of a sound) faint and high-pitched: *a thin, reedy little voice*. ■ (of a smile) weak and forced. ■ too weak to justify a result or effect; inadequate: *the evidence is rather thin*.
▶ **adv.** [often in combination] with little thickness or depth: *thin-sliced ham* | *cut it as thin as possible*.
▶ **v.** (**thins**, **thinning**, **thinned**) **1** make or become less dense, crowded, or numerous: [with obj.] *the remorseless fire of archers thinned their ranks* | [no obj.] *the trees began to thin out* | (as adj. **thinning**) *thinning hair*. ■ [with obj.] remove some plants from (a row or area) to allow the others more room to grow: *thin out overwintered rows of peas*. ■ make or become weaker or more watery: [with obj.] *if the soup is too thick, add a little water to thin it down* | [no obj.] *the blood thins*.
2 make or become smaller in width or thickness: [with obj.] *their effect in thinning the ozone layer is probably slowing the global warming trend* | [no obj.] *the trees have thinned and diminished in size*.
3 [with obj.] Golf hit (a ball) above its center.
– PHRASES **on thin ice** see ICE. **thin air** used to refer to the state of being invisible or nonexistent: *she just vanished into thin air* | *they seemed to pluck numbers out of thin air*. **the thin blue line** informal used to refer to the police, typically in the context of situations of civil unrest. **thin end of the wedge** see WEDGE. **thin on top** informal balding.
– DERIVATIVES **thin·ly** adv., **thin·ness** n., **thin·nish** adj.
– ORIGIN Old English *thynne*, of Germanic origin; related to Dutch *dun* and German *dünn*, from an Indo-European root shared by Latin *tenuis*.

-thin ▶ **comb. form** denoting a specified degree of thinness: *gossamer-thin* | *wafer-thin*.

thine /T͟Hīn/ ▶ **possessive pron.** archaic form of YOURS; the thing or things belonging to or associated with thee: *his spirit will take courage from thine*.
▶ **possessive determiner** form of THY used before a vowel: *inquire into thine own heart*.
– ORIGIN Old English *thīn*, of Germanic origin; related to German *dein*, also to THOU[1].

> **USAGE** The use of **thine** is still found in certain religious groups and in some traditional British dialects, but elsewhere it is restricted to archaic contexts. See also usage at THOU[1].

thin-film ▶ **adj.** (of a process or device) using or involving a very thin solid or liquid film. ■ Electronics denoting a miniature circuit or device consisting of a thin layer of metal or semiconductor on a ceramic or glass substrate.

thing /THiNG/ ▶ **n. 1** an object that one need not, cannot, or does not wish to give a specific name to: *look at that metal rail thing over there* | *there are lots of things I'd like to buy* | *she was wearing this pink thing*. ■ (**things**) personal belongings or clothing: *she began to unpack her things*. ■ [with modifier] (**things**) objects, equipment, or utensils used for a particular purpose: *they cleared away the last few lunch things*. ■ [with negative] (**a thing**) anything (used for emphasis): *she couldn't find a thing to wear*. ■ used to express one's disapproval or contempt for something: *you won't find me smoking those filthy things*. ■ [with postpositive adj.] (**things**) all that can be described in the specified way: *his love for all things Italian*. ■ used euphemistically to refer to a man's penis.
2 an inanimate material object as distinct from a living sentient being: *I'm not a thing, not a work of art to be cherished*. ■ [with adj.] a living creature or plant: *the sea is the primal source of all living things on earth*. ■ [with adj.] used to express and give a reason for one's pity, affection, approval, or contempt for a person or animal: *have a nice weekend in the country, you lucky thing!* | *the lamb was a puny little thing*.
3 an action, activity, event, thought, or utterance: *she said the first thing that came into her head* | *the only thing I could do well was cook*. ■ (**things**) circumstances, conditions, or matters that are unspecified: *things haven't gone entirely according to plan* | *how are things with you?* ■ an abstract entity or concept: *mourning and depression are not the same thing*. ■ a quality or attribute: *they had one thing in common—they were men of action*. ■ a specimen or type of something: *the game is the latest thing in family fun*. ■ (**one's thing**) informal one's special interest or concern: *reading isn't my thing*. ■ [with modifier] (**a thing**) informal a situation or activity of a specified type or quality: *your being here is just a friendship thing, OK?*
4 (**the thing**) informal what is needed or required: *you need a tonic–and here's just the thing*. ■ what is socially acceptable or fashionable: *it wouldn't be quite the thing to go to a royal garden party in boots*. ■ used to introduce or draw attention to an important fact or consideration: *the thing is, I am going to sell this house*.
– PHRASES **be all things to all men** (or **people**) please everyone, typically by regularly altering one's behavior or opinions in order to conform to those of others. ■ be able to be interpreted or used differently by different people to their own satisfaction. **be onto a good thing** informal have found a job, situation, or lifestyle that is pleasant,

profitable, or easy. **be hearing** (or **seeing**) **things** imagine that one can hear (or see) something that is not in fact there. **a close** (or **near**) **thing** a narrow avoidance of something unpleasant. **do one's own thing** informal follow one's own interests or inclinations regardless of others. **do the —— thing** informal engage in the kind of behavior typically associated with someone or something: *a film in which he does the bad-guy thing.* **do things to** informal have a powerful emotional effect on: *it just does things to me when we kiss.* **for one thing** used to introduce one of two or more possible reasons for something, the remainder of which may or may not be stated: *Why hadn't he arranged to see her at the house? For one thing, it would have been warmer.* **have a thing about** informal have an obsessive interest in or dislike of: *she had a thing about men who wore glasses.* **—— is one thing, —— is another** used to indicate that the second item mentioned is much more serious or important than the first, and cannot be compared to it: *physical attraction was one thing, love was quite another.* **make a** (**big**) **thing of** (or **about**) informal make (something) seem more important than it actually is. **of all things** out of all conceivable possibilities (used to express surprise): *What had he been thinking about? A kitten, of all things.* (**just**) **one of those things** informal used to indicate that one wishes to pass over an unfortunate event or experience by regarding it as unavoidable or to be accepted. **one thing leads to another** used to suggest that the exact sequence of events is too obvious to need recounting, the listener or reader being able to guess easily what happened. **a thing of the past** a thing that no longer happens or exists. **a thing or two** informal used to refer to useful information that can be imparted or learned: *Teddy taught me a thing or two about wine.* **things that go bump in the night** informal, humorous unexplained and frightening noises at night, regarded as being caused by ghosts.
– ORIGIN Old English, of Germanic origin; related to German *Ding*. Early senses included 'meeting' and 'matter, concern' as well as 'inanimate object.'

thing·a·ma·jig /'THiNGəmə,jig/ (also **thingumajig**; **thingamabob** or **thingumabob** /-,bäb/) ▶ **n.** informal used to refer to or address a person or thing whose name one has forgotten, does not know, or does not wish to mention: *one of those thingamajigs for keeping all the fireplace tools together.*
– ORIGIN early 19th cent.: arbitrary extension of earlier *thingum* (from THING + a meaningless suffix). *Thingumabob* dates from the mid 18th cent.

thing·um·my /'THiNGəmē/ (also **thingamy**) ▶ **n.** (pl. **thingummies**) British term for THINGAMAJIG.

thing·y /'THiNGē/ ▶ **n.** (pl. **thingies**) another term for THINGAMAJIG.

think /THiNGk/ ▶ **v.** (past and past participle **thought** /THôt/) **1** [with clause] have a particular opinion, belief, or idea about someone or something: *she thought that nothing would be the same again* | [no obj.] *what would John think of her?* | (**be thought**) *it's thought he may have collapsed from shock* | [with infinitive] *up to 300 people were thought to have died.* ■ used in questions to express anger or surprise: *What do you think you're doing?* ■ (**I think**) used in speech to reduce the force of a statement or opinion, or to politely suggest or refuse something: *I thought we could go out for a meal.*
2 [no obj.] direct one's mind toward someone or something; use one's mind actively to form connected ideas: *he was thinking about Colin* | *Jack thought for a moment* | [with obj.] *any writer who so rarely produces a book is not thinking deep thoughts.* ■ (**think of/about**) take into account or consideration when deciding on a possible action: *you can live how you like, but there's the children to think about.* ■ (**think of/about**) consider the possibility or advantages of (a course of action): *he was thinking of becoming a zoologist.* ■ have a particular mental attitude or approach: *he thought like a general* | [with complement] *one should always think positive.* ■ (**think of**) have a particular opinion of: *I think of him as a friend* | *she did not think highly of modern art.* ■ call something to mind; remember: *lemon thyme is a natural pair with any chicken dish you can think of* | [with infinitive] *I hadn't thought to warn Rachel about him.* ■ imagine (an actual or possible situation): *think of being paid a salary to hunt big game!* ■ [usu. with clause] expect: *I never thought we'd raise so much money* | [with infinitive] *she said something he'd never thought to have heard said again.* ■ (**think oneself into**) concentrate on imagining what it would be like to be in (a position or role): *she tried to think herself into the part of Peter's fiancée.*
▶ **n.** [in sing.] informal an act of thinking: *I went for a walk to have a think.*
– PHRASES **have** (**got**) **another think coming** informal used to express the speaker's disagreement with or unwillingness to do something suggested by someone else: *if they think I'm going to do physical exercises, they've got another think coming.* **think again** reconsider something, typically so as to alter one's intentions or ideas. **think out loud** express one's thoughts as soon as they occur. **think better of** decide not to do (something) after reconsideration. **think big** see BIG. **think fit** see FIT[1]. **think for oneself** have an independent mind or attitude. **think nothing** (or **little**) **of** consider (an activity others regard as odd, wrong, or difficult) as straightforward or normal. **think nothing of it** see NOTHING. **think on one's feet** see FOOT. **think twice** consider a course of action carefully before embarking on it. **think the world of** see WORLD.
– PHRASAL VERBS **think back** recall a past event or time: *I keep thinking back to school.* **think on** think of or about. **think something out** consider something in all its aspects before taking action: *the plan had not been properly thought out.* **think something over** consider something carefully. **think something through** consider all the possible effects or implications of something: *they had failed to think the policy through.* **think something up** informal use one's ingenuity to invent or devise something.
– DERIVATIVES **think·a·ble** /'THiNGkəbəl/ **adj.**
– ORIGIN Old English *thencan*, of Germanic origin; related to Dutch and German *denken*.

think·er /'THiNGkər/ ▶ **n.** a person who thinks deeply and seriously. ■ a person with highly developed intellectual powers, esp. one whose profession involves intellectual activity: *a leading scientific thinker.*

think·ing /'THiNGkiNG/ ▶ **adj.** [attrib.] using thought or rational judgment; intelligent: *he seemed to be a thinking man.*
▶ **n.** the process of using one's mind to consider or reason about something: *they have done some thinking about welfare reform.* ■ a person's ideas or opinions: *his thinking is reflected in his later autobiography.* ■ (**thinkings**) archaic thoughts; meditations.
– PHRASES **good** (or **nice**) **thinking** used as an expression of approval for an ingenious plan, explanation, or observation. **put on one's thinking cap** informal meditate on a problem.

think piece ▶ **n.** an article in a newspaper, magazine, or journal presenting personal opinions, analysis, or discussion, rather than bare facts.

think tank ▶ **n.** a body of experts providing advice and ideas on specific political or economic problems.
– DERIVATIVES **think tank·er n.**

thin-lay·er chro·ma·tog·ra·phy ▶ **n.** Chemistry chromatography in which compounds are separated on a thin layer of adsorbent material, typically a coating of silica gel on a glass plate or plastic sheet.

thin·ner /'THinər/ ▶ **n.** a volatile solvent used to make paint or other mixtures less viscous.

thin sec·tion ▶ **n.** a thin, flat piece of material prepared for examination with a microscope, in particular a piece of rock about 0.03 millimeters thick, or, for electron microscopy, a piece of tissue about 30 nanometers thick.
▶ **v.** (**thin-section**) [with obj.] prepare (something) for examination in this way.

thin-skinned ▶ **adj.** sensitive to criticism or insults: *these bloggers sure are a thin-skinned crowd.*

Thin·su·late /'THinsəlit/ ▶ **n.** trademark a thin, highly insulating fabric made from polypropylene fibers, used to make outdoor clothing and sleeping bags.
– ORIGIN a blend of THIN + INSULATE.

thio- ▶ **comb. form** Chemistry denoting replacement of oxygen by sulfur in a compound: *thiosulphate.*
– ORIGIN from Greek *theion* 'sulfur.'

thi·o·cy·a·nate /,THī-ō'sīə,nāt/ ▶ **n.** Chemistry a salt containing the anion SCN^-.

thi·ol /'THī,ôl, -,äl/ ▶ **n.** Chemistry an organic compound containing the group –SH, i.e., a sulfur-containing analog of an alcohol.

thi·o·nyl /'THīə,nil/ ▶ **n.** [as modifier] Chemistry of or denoting the divalent radical =SO.
– ORIGIN 1857: so named by Hugo Schiff (1834–1915), German chemist.

thi·o·pen·tal /,THī-ō'pen,tal, -tôl/ ▶ **n.** Medicine a sulfur-containing barbiturate drug used as a general anesthetic and hypnotic, and (reputedly) as a truth serum.
– ORIGIN 1940s: from THIO- + a contraction of PENTOBARBITAL.

thi·o·pen·tone /,THī-ō'pen,tōn/ ▶ **n.** British term for PENTOTHAL.

thi·o·rid·a·zine /,THīə'ridə,zēn, -zin/ ▶ **n.** Medicine a synthetic compound derived from phenothiazine, used as a tranquilizer, chiefly in the treatment of mental illness.
– ORIGIN 1950s: from THIO- + (*pipe*)*rid*(*ine*) + AZINE.

thi·o·sul·fate /,THī-ō'səl,fāt/ ▶ **n.** Chemistry a salt containing the anion $S_2O_3^{2-}$, i.e., a sulfate with one oxygen atom replaced by sulfur.

thi·o·u·re·a /,THī-ōyə'rēə/ ▶ **n.** Chemistry a synthetic crystalline compound used in photography and the manufacture of synthetic resins. ● The sulfur analog of urea; chem. formula: $SC(NH_2)_2$.

Thí·ra /'THi(ə)rə/ modern Greek name for THERA.

thi·ram /'THī,ram/ ▶ **n.** Chemistry a synthetic sulfur-containing compound used as a fungicide and seed protectant. ● Chem. formula: $C_6H_{12}N_2S_4$.
– ORIGIN 1950s: from THIO-, (*u*)*r*(*ea*), and *am*(*ine*), elements of the systematic name.

third /THərd/ ▶ **ordinal number** constituting number three in a sequence; 3rd: *the third century* | *the third of October* | *Edward the Third.* ■ (**a third/one third**) each of three equal parts into which something is or may be divided: *a third of a mile.* ■ the third finisher or position in a race or competition: *Hill finished third.* ■ the third in a sequence of a vehicle's gears: *he took the corner in third.* ■ Baseball third base. ■ the third grade of a school. ■ thirdly (used to introduce a third point or reason): *second, they are lightly regulated; and third, they do business with nonresident clients.* ■ Music an interval spanning three consecutive notes in a diatonic scale, e.g., C to E (**major third**, equal to two tones) or A to C (**minor third**, equal to a tone and a semitone). ■ Music the note that is higher by this interval than the tonic of a diatonic scale or root of a chord. ■ Brit. a place in the third-highest grade in an examination, esp. that for a degree.
– PHRASES **third time is a charm** (or Brit. **third time lucky**) used to express the hope that, after twice failing to accomplish something, one may succeed in the third attempt.
– ORIGIN Old English *thridda*, of Germanic origin; related to Dutch *derde* and German *dritte*, also to THREE. The spelling *thrid* was dominant until the 16th cent. (but *thirdda* is recorded in Northumbrian dialect as early as the 10th cent).

third class ▶ **n.** [in sing.] a group of people or things considered together as third best. ■ Brit. a university degree or examination result in the third-highest classification. ■ a cheap class of mail for advertising and other printed material that weighs less than 16 ounces and is unsealed. ■ chiefly historical the cheapest and least comfortable accommodations in a train or ship.
▶ **adj. & adv.** of the third-best quality or of lower status: [as adj.] *many indigenous groups are still viewed as third-class citizens.* ■ [as adj.] Brit. of or relating to the third-highest division in a university examination: *he left university with a third-class degree.* ■ of or relating to a cheap class of mail including advertising and other printed material weighing less than 16 ounces: [as adj.] *third-class mail.* ■ chiefly historical of or relating to the cheapest and least comfortable accommodations in a train or ship: [as adj.] *a suffocating third-class compartment* | [as adv.] *I traveled third class across Europe.*

third coun·try ▶ **n.** a Third World country.

third cous·in ▶ **n.** see COUSIN.

third-de·gree ▶ **adj.** [attrib.] **1** denoting burns of the most severe kind, affecting tissue below the skin.
2 Law denoting the least serious category of a crime, esp. murder.
▶ **n.** (**the third degree**) long and harsh questioning, esp. by police, to obtain information or a confession.

third es·tate ▶ **n.** [treated as sing. or pl.] the commons. [the first two estates were formerly represented by the clergy, and the barons and knights; later the Lords spiritual and the Lords temporal.] ■ (**the Third Estate**) the French bourgeoisie and working class before the French Revolution. [translating French *le tiers état*.]

third eye ▶ **n.** **1** Hinduism the locus of occult power and wisdom in the forehead of a deity, esp. the god Shiva. ■ the "eye of insight" located in the forehead, which can be activated through the practice of yoga.
2 informal term for PINEAL EYE.

third eye·lid ▶ **n.** informal term for NICTITATING MEMBRANE.

third force ▶ **n.** [in sing.] a political group or party acting as a check on conflict between two extreme or opposing groups.

third-hand (also **thirdhand**) ▶ **adj.** **1** (of goods) having had two previous owners: *a thirdhand dinner suit.*
2 (of information) acquired from or via several intermediate sources and consequently not

t

authoritative or reliable: *the accounts are thirdhand, told years after the event.*
▶ **adv.** from or via several intermediate sources: *I heard about the case thirdhand.*

Third In·ter·na·tion·al see INTERNATIONAL (sense 2 of the noun).

third·ly /ˈTHərdlē/ ▶ **adv.** in the third place (used to introduce a third point or reason).

third mar·ket ▶ **n.** Finance used to refer to over-the-counter trading in listed stocks outside the stock exchange.

third par·ty ▶ **n.** a person or group besides the two primarily involved in a situation, esp. a dispute. ■ a political party organized as an alternative to the major parties in a two-party system.
▶ **adj.** [attrib.] of or relating to a person or group besides the two primarily involved in a situation: *third-party suppliers.*

third per·son ▶ **n. 1** a third party.
2 see PERSON (sense 2).

third po·si·tion ▶ **n. 1** Ballet a posture in which the turned-out feet are placed one in front of the other, so that the heel of the front foot fits into the hollow of the instep of the back foot. ■ a position of the arms in which one is held curved in front of the body and the other curved to the side, both at waist level.
2 Music a position of the left hand on the fingerboard of a stringed instrument nearer to the bridge than the second position, enabling a higher set of notes to be played.

third rail ▶ **n.** an additional rail supplying electric current, used in some electric railroad systems. ■ informal a subject or issue considered by politicians to be too controversial to discuss.

third-rate ▶ **adj.** of inferior or very poor quality.
– DERIVATIVES **third-rat·er n.**

third read·ing ▶ **n.** a third presentation of a bill to a legislative assembly, in the US to consider it for the last time, and in the UK to debate committee reports.

Third Reich the Nazi regime, 1933–45.

Third Re·pub·lic the republican regime in France between the fall of Napoleon III in 1870 and the German occupation of 1940.

third ven·tri·cle ▶ **n.** Anatomy the central cavity of the brain, lying between the thalamus and hypothalamus of the two cerebral hemispheres.

third way (also **Third Way**) ▶ **n.** an option regarded as an alternative to two extremes, esp. a political agenda that is centrist and consensus-based rather than left- or right-wing: *the Third Way espoused by Europe's new leaders doesn't challenge the supremacy of the marketplace.*

Third World ▶ **n.** (usu. **the Third World**) the developing countries of Asia, Africa, and Latin America.
– ORIGIN translation of French *tiers monde* first used in the 1950s to distinguish the developing countries from the capitalist and communist blocs.

thirst /THərst/ ▶ **n.** a feeling of needing or wanting to drink something: *they quenched their thirst with spring water.* ■ lack of the liquid needed to sustain life: *tens of thousands died of thirst and starvation.* ■ (usu. **thirst for**) literary a strong desire for something: *his thirst for knowledge was mainly academic.*
▶ **v.** [no obj.] archaic (of a person or animal) feel a need to drink something. ■ (usu. **thirst for/after**) literary have a strong desire for something: *an opponent thirsting for revenge.*
– ORIGIN Old English *thurst* (noun), *thyrstan* (verb), of Germanic origin; related to Dutch *dorst, dorsten* and German *Durst, dürsten.*

thirst·y /ˈTHərstē/ ▶ **adj.** (**thirstier, thirstiest**) feeling a need to drink something: *the hikers were hot and thirsty.* ■ (of land, plants, or skin) in need of water: dry or parched. ■ (of an engine, plant, or crop) consuming a lot of fuel or water. ■ having or showing a strong desire for something: *Jake was as thirsty for scandal as anyone else.* ■ [attrib.] informal (of activity, weather, or a time) causing the feeling of a need to drink something: *modeling is thirsty work.*
– DERIVATIVES **thirst·i·ly** /-stəlē/ **adv.**, **thirst·i·ness n.**

thir·teen /ˌTHərˈtēn, ˈTHərˌtēn/ ▶ **cardinal number** equivalent to the sum of six and seven; one more than twelve, or seven less than twenty; 13: *thirteen miles away | a rise of 13 percent | thirteen of the bishops voted against the motion.* (Roman numeral: **xiii, XIII**) ■ a size of garment or other merchandise denoted by thirteen. ■ thirteen years old: *two boys aged eleven and thirteen.*
– DERIVATIVES **thir·teenth** /ˌTHərˈtēnTH, ˈTHərˌtēnTH/ **ordinal number.**
– ORIGIN Old English *thrēotīene* (see THREE, -TEEN). The spelling with initial *thi-* is recorded in late Middle English.

Thir·teen Col·o·nies the British colonies that ratified the Declaration of Independence in 1776 and thereby became founding states of the US. The colonies were Virginia, Massachusetts, Maryland, Connecticut, Rhode Island, North Carolina, South Carolina, New York, New Jersey, Delaware, New Hampshire, Pennsylvania, and Georgia.

thir·ty /ˈTHərtē/ ▶ **cardinal number** (pl. **thirties**) the number equivalent to the product of three and ten; ten less than forty; 30: *thirty or forty years ago | thirty were hurt | thirty of her school friends.* (Roman numeral: **xxx, XXX**) ■ (**thirties**) the numbers from thirty to thirty-nine, esp. the years of a century or of a person's life: *a woman in her thirties | she was a famous actress in the thirties.* ■ thirty years old: *I've got a long way to go before I'm thirty.* ■ thirty miles an hour: *doing about thirty.*
– DERIVATIVES **thir·ti·eth** /-iTH/ **ordinal number**, **thir·ty·fold** /-ˌfōld/ **adj. & adv.**
– ORIGIN Old English *thrītig* (see THREE, -TY[2]). The spelling with initial *thi-* is recorded in the 15th cent., and has been the prevalent form since the 16th cent.

thir·ty-eight ▶ **n.** a revolver of .38 caliber.

Thir·ty-nine Ar·ti·cles ▶ **plural n.** a series of points of doctrine historically accepted as representing the teaching of the Church of England.

thir·ty-sec·ond note ▶ **n.** Music a note having the time value of half a sixteenth note, represented by a large dot with a three-hooked stem. Also called DEMISEMIQUAVER.

thir·ty-two-mo /ˌTHərtē ˈto͞o mō/ ▶ **n.** (pl. **thirty-two-mos**) a size of book page that results from folding each printed sheet into thirty-two leaves (sixty-four pages). ■ a book of this size.

Thir·ty Years War a European war of 1618–48 that broke out between the Catholic Holy Roman Emperor and some of his German Protestant states and developed into a struggle for continental hegemony with France, Sweden, Spain, and the Holy Roman Empire as the major protagonists. It was ended by the Treaty of Westphalia.

Thi·ru·van·an·tha·pur·am /ˌtiro͞oˌvənəntəˈpo͝orəm/ ˌtiruːˌvʌnʌntʌˈpuːrʌm/ a port on the southwestern coast of India, capital of the state of Kerala; pop. 822,400 (est. 2009). Also called TRIVANDRUM.

this /T͟His/ ▶ **pron.** (pl. **these** /T͟Hēz/) **1** used to identify a specific person or thing close at hand or being indicated or experienced: *is this your bag? | he soon knew that this was not the place for him.* ■ used to introduce someone or something: *this is the captain speaking | listen to this.* ■ referring to the nearer of two things close to the speaker (the other, if specified, being identified by "that"): *this is different from that.*
2 referring to a specific thing or situation just mentioned: *the company was transformed, and Ward had played a vital role in bringing this about.*
▶ **determiner** (pl. **these**) **1** used to identify a specific person or thing close at hand or being indicated or experienced: *don't listen to this guy | these croissants are delicious.* ■ referring to the nearer of two things close to the speaker (the other, if specified, being identified by "that"): *this one or that one?*
2 referring to a specific thing or situation just mentioned: *there was a court case resulting from this incident.*
3 used with periods of time related to the present: *I thought you were busy all this week | how are you this morning?* ■ referring to a period of time that has just passed: *I haven't left my bed these three days.*
4 informal used (chiefly in narrative) to refer to a person or thing previously unspecified: *I turned around, and there was this big mummy standing next to us! | I've got this problem and I need help.*
▶ **adv.** [as submodifier] to the degree or extent indicated: *they can't handle a job this big | he's not used to this much attention.*
– PHRASES **this and that** (or **this, that, and the other**) informal various unspecified things: *they stayed up chatting about this and that.* **this here** informal used to draw attention emphatically to someone or something: *I've slept in this here bed for forty years.*
– ORIGIN Old English, neuter of *thes*; related to THAT and THE.

This·be /ˈTHizbē/ Roman Mythology a Babylonian girl, lover of Pyramus.

this·tle /ˈTHisəl/ ▶ **n.**
1 a widely distributed herbaceous plant of the daisy family, which typically has a prickly stem and leaves and rounded heads of purple flowers. ● *Carlina, Cirsium, Carduus,* and other genera, family Compositae: numerous species, including **bull thistle** (*Cirsium vulgare*) and **nodding** (or **musk**) **thistle** (*Carduus nutans*).
2 a plant of this type as the Scottish national emblem. ● This is usually identified as the **Scotch** (or **cotton**) **thistle** (*Onopordum acanthium*).
– DERIVATIVES **this·tly** /ˈTHis(ə)lē/ **adj.**
– ORIGIN Old English *thistel*, of Germanic origin; related to Dutch *distel* and German *Distel.*

bull thistle

this·tle·down /ˈTHisəlˌdoun/ ▶ **n.** light fluffy down that is attached to thistle seeds, enabling them to be blown about in the wind.

this-world·ly ▶ **adj.** relating to or concerned with the physical or material world, as opposed to a spiritual one: *his distrust of this-worldly pleasures.*

thith·er /ˈTHiT͟Hər/ ▶ **adv.** archaic or literary to or toward that place: *no trickery had been necessary to attract him thither.*
– ORIGIN Old English *thider*, alteration (by association with HITHER) of *thæder*, of Germanic origin; related to THAT and THE.

Thí·vai /ˈTHēvē/ modern Greek name for THEBES (sense 2).

thix·ot·ro·py /THikˈsätrəpē/ ▶ **n.** Chemistry the property of becoming less viscous when subjected to an applied stress, shown for example by some gels that become temporarily fluid when shaken or stirred.
– DERIVATIVES **thix·o·trop·ic** /ˌTHiksəˈträpik, -ˈtrōpik/ **adj.**
– ORIGIN 1920s: from Greek *thixis* 'touching' + *tropē* 'turning.'

THM ▶ **abbr.** TRIHALOMETHANE.

Th.M. ▶ **abbr.** Master of Theology.

tho /T͟Hō/ (also **tho'**) ▶ **conj. & adv.** informal spelling of THOUGH.

thole /THōl/ ▶ **v.** [with obj.] Scottish or archaic endure (something) without complaint or resistance; tolerate.
– ORIGIN Old English *tholian*, of Germanic origin.

thole pin ▶ **n.** a pin, typically one of a pair, fitted to the gunwale of a rowboat to act as the fulcrum for an oar.
– ORIGIN Old English, of Germanic origin; related to Dutch *dol.*

Thom·as[1] /ˈtäməs/, Clarence, (1948–) US Supreme Court associate justice 1991– . He chaired the Equal Employment Opportunity Commission (EEOC) 1982–90 and was a judge on the US Court of Appeals before being nominated to replace Thurgood Marshall on the Court. His appointment was approved only after a lengthy and controversial Senate hearing in which he had to respond to charges of sexual harassment brought by former colleague Anita Hill (1956–).

Thom·as[2], Danny, (1914–91) US television producer and actor; born *Amos Jacobs.* He starred in the television series *Make Room for Daddy* 1953–64 and *The Danny Thomas Hour* 1967–68. He also was known for his sponsorship of St. Jude's Children's Research Hospital in Memphis, Tennessee.

Thom·as[3], Dylan (Marlais) (1914–53), Welsh poet. In 1953, on radio, he narrated *Under Milk Wood,* a portrait of a small Welsh town, interspersing poetic alliterative prose with songs and ballads. Other notable works: *Portrait of the Artist as a Young Dog* (prose, 1940).

Thom·as[4], Norman (Mattoon), (1884–1968) US social reformer, minister, and politician. A minister 1911–31, he helped found the American Civil Liberties Union 1920 and was a Socialist Party presidential candidate six times between 1928 and 1948.

Thom·as, St. an apostle; known as **Doubting Thomas.** He earned his nickname by saying that he would not believe that Jesus had risen again until he had seen and touched his wounds (John 20:24–29). Feast day, December 21.

Thom·as à Kem·pis /ˈtäməs ə ˈkempəs/ (*c.*1380–1471), German theologian; born *Thomas Hemerken.* He is the probable author of *On the Imitation of Christ* (*c.*1415–24), a manual of spiritual devotion.

Thom·as A·qui·nas, St. /ˈtäməs əˈkwīnəs/, see AQUINAS, ST. THOMAS.

Thom·as More, St. see MORE.

Tho·mism /ˈtōˌmizəm/ ▶ **n.** the theology of Thomas Aquinas or of his followers.
– DERIVATIVES **Tho·mist n. & adj.**, **Tho·mis·tic** /təˈmistik/ **adj.**

Thomp·son[1], Francis (1859–1907), English poet. His work, such as "The Hound of Heaven" (1893), contains powerful imagery to convey intense religious experience.

Thomp·son² /ˈtämpsən/, Sir John Sparrow David (1845–94), Canadian Conservative statesman; prime minister 1892–94.

Thomp·son³, Smith (1768–1843), US Supreme Court associate justice 1823–43. Appointed to the Court by President Monroe, he was an advocate of states' rights.

Thom·son's ga·zelle ▶ **n.** a light brown gazelle with a conspicuous dark band along the flanks, living in large herds on the open plains of East Africa. ● *Gazella thomsonii*, family Bovidae.
– ORIGIN late 19th cent.: named after Joseph *Thomson* (1858–94), Scottish explorer.

thong /THÔNG, THÄNG/ ▶ **n. 1** a narrow strip of leather or other material, used esp. as a fastening or as the lash of a whip.
2 an item of clothing fastened by or including such a narrow strip, in particular: ■ a skimpy bathing suit or pair of underpants like a G-string. ■ another term for FLIP-FLOP (sense 1 of the noun).
▶ **v.** [with obj.] archaic flog or lash (someone) with a whip.
– DERIVATIVES **thonged adj.**, **thong·y adj.**
– ORIGIN Old English *thwang*, *thwong*, of Germanic origin; related to German *Zwang* 'compulsion.' Compare with WHANG.

Thor /THôr/ Scandinavian Mythology the god of thunder, the weather, agriculture, and the home, the son of Odin and Freya (Frigga). Thursday is named after him.

thor·a·ces /ˈTHôrəˌsēz/ plural form of THORAX.

tho·rac·ic /THəˈrasik/ ▶ **adj.** Anatomy & Zoology of or relating to the thorax.

tho·rac·ic duct ▶ **n.** Anatomy the main vessel of the lymphatic system, passing upward in front of the spine and draining into the left innominate vein near the base of the neck.

tho·rac·ic ver·te·bra ▶ **n.** Anatomy each of the twelve bones of the backbone to which the ribs are attached.

tho·ra·co·lum·bar /ˌTHôrəkəˈləmbər/ ▶ **adj.** Anatomy of or relating to the thoracic and lumbar regions of the spine. ■ denoting the sympathetic nervous system.

tho·ra·cot·o·my /ˌTHôrəˈkätəmē/ ▶ **n.** surgical incision into the chest wall.
– ORIGIN late 19th cent.: from Greek *thōrax*, *thōrāc-* 'chest' + -TOMY.

tho·rax /ˈTHôrˌaks/ ▶ **n.** (pl. **thoraxes** or **thoraces** /ˈTHôrəˌsēz/) Anatomy & Zoology the part of the body of a mammal between the neck and the abdomen, including the cavity enclosed by the ribs, breastbone, and dorsal vertebrae, and containing the chief organs of circulation and respiration; the chest. ■ Zoology the corresponding part of a bird, reptile, amphibian, or fish. ■ Entomology the middle section of the body of an insect, between the head and the abdomen, bearing the legs and wings.
– ORIGIN late Middle English: via Latin from Greek *thōrax*.

Tho·ra·zine /ˈTHôrəˌzēn/ ▶ **n.** trademark for CHLORPROMAZINE.
– ORIGIN 1950s: formed from elements of the systematic name.

Tho·reau /THəˈrō, THôˈrō, ˈTHôrō/, Henry David (1817–62), US essayist and poet. A key proponent of transcendentalism, he is best known for *Walden, or Life in the Woods* (1854), an account of a two-year experiment in self-sufficiency. His essay on civil disobedience (1849) influenced Mahatma Gandhi's policy of passive resistance.

tho·ri·a /ˈTHôrēə/ ▶ **n.** Chemistry thorium dioxide, a white refractory solid used in making gas mantles and other materials for high-temperature applications. ● Chem. formula: ThO_2.
– ORIGIN mid 19th cent.: from THORIUM, on the pattern of words such as *alumina* and *magnesia*.

tho·ri·um /ˈTHôrēəm/ ▶ **n.** the chemical element of atomic number 90, a white radioactive metal of the actinide series. (Symbol: **Th**)
– ORIGIN mid 19th cent.: named after the god THOR.

Thorn /tôrn/ German name for TORUN.

thorn /THôrn/ ▶ **n. 1** a stiff, sharp-pointed, straight or curved woody projection on the stem or other part of a plant. ■ a source of discomfort, annoyance, or difficulty; an irritation or an obstacle: *the issue has become a thorn in renewing the peace talks*. See also A THORN IN SOMEONE'S SIDE below.
2 (also **thorn bush** or **thorn tree**) a thorny bush, shrub, or tree, esp. a hawthorn.
3 an Old English and Icelandic runic letter, Þ or þ, representing the dental fricatives /TH/ and /TH/. In English it was eventually superseded by the digraph *th*. Compare with ETH. [so named from the word of which it was the first letter.]
– PHRASES **there is no rose without a thorn** proverb every apparently desirable situation has its share of trouble or difficulty. **a thorn in someone's side** (or **flesh**) a source of continual annoyance or trouble: *the pastor has long been a thorn in the side of the regime*.
– DERIVATIVES **thorn·less adj.** (sense 1), **thorn·proof** /-ˌpro͞of/ **adj.** (sense 1).
– ORIGIN Old English, of Germanic origin; related to Dutch *doorn* and German *Dorn*.

thorn ap·ple ▶ **n.** chiefly Brit. another term for JIMSON WEED.

thorn·back /ˈTHôrnˌbak/ (also **thornback ray**) ▶ **n.** a ray of shallow inshore waters that has spines on the back and tail, in particular: ● a prickly skinned European ray that is often eaten as "skate" (*Raja clavata*, family Rajidae). ● a ray that lives in the warm waters of the Pacific (*Platyrhinoidis triseriata*, family Platyrhinidae).

Thorn·ton /ˈTHôrntn/ a city in north central Colorado, just northeast of Denver; pop. 113,429 (est. 2008).

thorn·y /ˈTHôrnē/ ▶ **adj.** (**thornier**, **thorniest**) having many thorns or thorn bushes. ■ causing distress, difficulty, or trouble: *a thorny problem for our team to solve*.
– DERIVATIVES **thorn·i·ly** /-nəlē/ **adv.**, **thorn·i·ness n.**

thorn·y-head·ed worm ▶ **n.** a parasitic worm with a thornlike proboscis for attachment to the gut of vertebrates. ● Phylum Acanthocephala.

thorn·y oys·ter ▶ **n.** a bivalve mollusk of warm seas, whose pinkish-brown shell is heavily ribbed and bears blunt or flattened spines. ● Family Spondylidae: *Spondylus* and other genera.

thor·ough /ˈTHərō/ ▶ **adj.** complete with regard to every detail; not superficial or partial: *planners need a thorough understanding of the subject*. ■ performed or written with great care and completeness: *officers have made a thorough examination of the wreckage*. ■ taking pains to do something carefully and completely: *the Canadian authorities are very thorough*. ■ [attrib.] absolute (used to emphasize the degree of something, typically something unwelcome or unpleasant): *the child is being a thorough nuisance*.
– DERIVATIVES **thor·ough·ness n.**
– ORIGIN Old English *thuruh*, alteration of *thurh* 'through.' Original use was as an adverb and preposition, in senses of *through*. The adjective dates from the late 15th cent., when it also had the sense 'that goes or extends through something,' surviving in *thoroughfare*.

thor·ough bass /bās/ ▶ **n.** Music basso continuo (see CONTINUO).

thor·ough·bred /ˈTHərəˌbred/ ▶ **adj.** (of a horse) of pure breed, esp. of a breed originating from English mares and Arab stallions and widely used as racehorses. ■ informal of outstanding quality: *this thoroughbred car affords the luxury of three spoilers*.
▶ **n.** a horse of a thoroughbred breed. ■ informal an outstanding or first-class person or thing: *this is a real thoroughbred of a record*.

thor·ough·fare /ˈTHərəˌfe(ə)r/ ▶ **n.** a road or path forming a route between two places. ■ a main road in a town.

thor·ough·go·ing /ˈTHərəˌgōiNG/ ▶ **adj.** involving or attending to every detail or aspect of something: *a thoroughgoing reform of the whole economy*. ■ [attrib.] exemplifying a specified characteristic fully; absolute: *a thoroughgoing chocoholic*.

thor·ough·ly /ˈTHərōlē/ ▶ **adv. 1** in a thorough manner: *he searched the house thoroughly*.
2 very much; greatly: *I thoroughly enjoyed the day* | [as submodifier] *she was soon thoroughly bored*.

thor·ough-paced ▶ **adj.** archaic highly skilled or trained. ■ absolute (used to emphasize the degree to which someone or something exemplifies a characteristic).

thor·ough·pin /ˈTHərəˌpin/ ▶ **n.** a swelling of the tendon sheath above the hock of a horse, which may be pressed from inside to outside and vice versa.

thorp /THôrp/ (also **thorpe**) ▶ **n.** (in place names) a village or hamlet: *Scunthorpe*.
– ORIGIN Old English *thorp*, *throp*, of Germanic origin; related to Dutch *dorp* and German *Dorf*.

Thorpe /THôrp/, Jim, (1888–1953) US athlete; full name *James Francis Thorpe*. After starring as an All-American football player at the Carlisle Indian Industrial School 1911–12, he won Olympic gold medals in the pentathlon and decathlon 1912 and played baseball 1913–19 and football 1917–29 professionally. Although he was required to return his Olympic medals because he had played semi-professional baseball in 1909, they were returned to his family in 1984.

Thor·vald·sen /ˈto͝orˌvälsən/ (also **Thorwaldsen**), Bertel (*c.*1770–1844), Danish neoclassical sculptor. Major works include a statue of Jason (1803) in Rome and the tomb of Pius VII (1824–31).

Thos. ▶ **abbr.** Thomas.

those /THōz/ plural form of THAT.

Thoth /THôTH, tōt/ Egyptian Mythology a moon god, the god of wisdom, justice, and writing, patron of the sciences, and messenger of Ra.

thou¹ /THou/ ▶ **pron.** [second person singular] archaic or dialect form of YOU, as the singular subject of a verb: *thou art fair, o my beloved*. Compare with THEE.
– ORIGIN Old English *thu*, of Germanic origin; related to German *du*, from an Indo-European root shared by Latin *tu*.

> **USAGE** In modern English, the personal pronoun **you** (together with the possessives **your** and **yours**) covers a number of uses: it is both singular and plural, both objective and subjective, and both formal and familiar. This has not always been the case. In Old English and Middle English, some of these different functions of **you** were supplied by different words. Thus, **thou** was at one time the singular subjective case (*thou art a beast*), while **thee** was the singular objective case (*he cares not for thee*). In addition, the form **thy** (modern equivalent **your**) was the singular possessive determiner, and **thine** (modern equivalent **yours**) the singular possessive pronoun, both corresponding to **thee**. The forms **you** and **ye**, on the other hand, were at one time reserved for plural uses. By the 19th century, these forms were universal in standard English for both singular and plural, polite and familiar. In present day use, **thou, thee, thy,** and **thine** survive in certain religious groups and in some traditional British dialects, but otherwise are found only in archaic contexts.

thou² /THou/ ▶ **n.** (pl. **same** or **thous**) informal a thousand. ■ one thousandth of an inch.
– ORIGIN mid 19th cent.: abbreviation.

though /THō/ ▶ **conj.** despite the fact that; although: *though they were speaking in undertones, Philip could hear them*. ■ [with modal] even if (introducing a possibility): *you will be informed of its progress, slow though that may be*. ■ however; but (introducing something opposed to or qualifying what has just been said): *her first name was Rose, though no one called her that*.
▶ **adv.** however (indicating that a factor qualifies or imposes restrictions on what was said previously): *I was hunting for work. Jobs were scarce though*.
– PHRASES **as though** see AS¹. **even though** see EVEN¹.
– ORIGIN Old English *thēah*, of Germanic origin; related to Dutch and German *doch*; superseded in Middle English by forms from Old Norse *thó*, *thau*.

> **USAGE** On the differences in use between **though** and **although**, see usage at ALTHOUGH.

thought¹ /THôt/ ▶ **n. 1** an idea or opinion produced by thinking or occurring suddenly in the mind: *Maggie had a sudden thought* | *I asked him if he had any thoughts on how it had happened* | *Mrs. Oliver's first thought was to get help*. ■ (**one's thoughts**) one's mind or attention: *he's very much **in our thoughts** and prayers*. ■ an act of considering or remembering someone or something: *she hadn't **given a thought to** Max for some time*. ■ (usu. **thought of**) an intention, hope, or idea of doing or receiving something: *he had given up all thoughts of making Manhattan his home*.
2 the action or process of thinking: *Sophie sat **deep in thought***. ■ the formation of opinions, esp. as a philosophy or system of ideas, or the opinions so formed: *the freedom of thought and action* | *the traditions of Western thought*. ■ careful consideration or attention: *I haven't **given it** much **thought***. ■ concern for another's well-being or convenience: *he is carrying on the life of a single man, with **no thought for** me*.
– PHRASES **don't give it another thought** informal used to tell someone not to worry when they have apologized for something. **it's the thought that counts** informal used to indicate that it is the kindness behind an act that matters, however imperfect or insignificant the act may be. **a second thought** [with negative] more than the slightest consideration: *not one of them **gave a second thought** to the risks involved*. **take thought** dated reflect or consider. **that's a thought!** informal used to express approval of a comment or suggestion.
– ORIGIN Old English *thōht*, of Germanic origin; related to Dutch *gedachte*, also to THINK.

thought² past and past participle of THINK.

thought con·trol ▶ **n.** the attempt to restrict ideas and impose opinions through censorship and the control of school curricula.

t

thought·crime /ˈTHôtˌkrīm/ ▶ **n.** an instance of unorthodox or controversial thinking, considered as a criminal offense or as socially unacceptable: *academia is pandering to politicized pressure groups with courses on feminism and homosexuality, and persecuting colleagues who are guilty of thoughtcrimes.*

thought dis·or·der ▶ **n.** Psychiatry a disorder of cognitive organization, characteristic of psychotic mental illness, in which thoughts and conversation appear illogical and lacking in sequence and may be delusional or bizarre in content.

thought ex·per·i·ment ▶ **n.** an experiment carried out only in the imagination.

thought form ▶ **n.** (often **thought forms**) (esp. in Christian theology) a combination of presuppositions, imagery, and vocabulary current at a particular time or place and forming the context for thinking on a subject.

thought·ful /ˈTHôtfəl/ ▶ **adj.** absorbed in or involving thought: *brows drawn together in thoughtful consideration.* ■ showing consideration for the needs of other people: *he was attentive and thoughtful* | *how very **thoughtful of** you!* ■ showing careful consideration or attention: *her work is thoughtful and provocative.*
– DERIVATIVES **thought·ful·ly** **adv.**, **thought·ful·ness** **n.**

thought lead·er ▶ **n.** one whose views on a subject are taken to be authoritative and influential.

thought·less /ˈTHôtləs/ ▶ **adj.** (of a person or their behavior) not showing consideration for the needs of other people: *it was **thoughtless of** her to have rushed out and not said where she would be going.* ■ without consideration of the possible consequences: *to think a few minutes of thoughtless pleasure could end in this.*
– DERIVATIVES **thought·less·ly** **adv.**, **thought·less·ness** **n.**

thought pat·tern ▶ **n.** a habit of thinking in a particular way, using particular assumptions. ■ a quality characterizing someone's thought processes as expressed in language: *thought patterns such as overgeneralization and illogicality.* ■ another term for **THOUGHT FORM**.

thought po·lice ▶ **n.** [treated as pl.] a group of people who aim or are seen as aiming to suppress ideas that deviate from the way of thinking that they believe to be correct.

thought-pro·vok·ing ▶ **adj.** stimulating careful consideration or attention: *thought-provoking questions.*

thought re·form ▶ **n.** the systematic alteration of a person's mode of thinking, esp. (in communist China) a process of individual political indoctrination.

thought trans·fer·ence ▶ **n.** another term for **TELEPATHY**.

thought wave ▶ **n.** a supposed pattern of energy by which it is claimed that thoughts are transferred from one person to another.

thou·sand /ˈTHouzənd/ ▶ **cardinal number** (pl. **thousands** /ˈTHouzndz/ or (with numeral or quantifying word) **same**) (**a/one thousand**) the number equivalent to the product of a hundred and ten; 1,000: *a thousand meters* | *two thousand acres* | *thousands have been killed.* (Roman numeral: **m**, **M**) ■ (**thousands**) the numbers from one thousand to 9,999: *the cost of repairs could be in the thousands.* ■ (usu. **thousands**) informal an unspecified large number: *you'll meet thousands of girls before you find the one you like* | *I have imagined it a thousand times.*
– DERIVATIVES **thou·sand·fold** /-ˌfōld/ **adj. & adv.**, **thou·sandth** /-zən(t)TH/ **ordinal number.**
– ORIGIN Old English *thūsend*, of Germanic origin; related to Dutch *duizend* and German *Tausend*.

Thou·sand and One Nights another name for **ARABIAN NIGHTS**.

Thou·sand Is·land dress·ing ▶ **n.** a dressing for salad or seafood consisting of mayonnaise with ketchup and chopped pickles.

Thou·sand Is·lands **1** a group of about 1,500 islands in a widening of the St. Lawrence River, just below Kingston, Ontario, Canada. Some of the islands belong to Canada and some to the US. **2** a group of about 100 small islands off the northern coast of Java that form part of Indonesia. Indonesian name **PULAU SERIBU**.

Thou·sand Oaks an industrial city in southwestern California, northwest of Los Angeles; pop. 123,091 (est. 2008).

thp (also **t.hp.**) ▶ **abbr.** thrust horsepower.

Thrace /THrās/ an ancient country that was west of the Black Sea and north of the Aegean Sea. It is now divided between Turkey, Bulgaria, and Greece.
– DERIVATIVES **Thra·cian** /ˈTHrāSHən/ **adj. & n.**

thrall /THrôl/ ▶ **n.** literary the state of being in someone's power or having great power over someone: *she was **in thrall to** her abusive husband.* ■ historical a slave, servant, or captive.
– DERIVATIVES **thrall·dom** /-dəm/ (also **thraldom**) **n.**
– ORIGIN Old English *thrǣl* 'slave,' from Old Norse *thræll*.

thrash /THrasH/ ▶ **v.** [with obj.] beat (a person or animal) repeatedly and violently with a stick or whip: *she thrashed him across the head and shoulders* | (as noun **thrashing**) *what he needs is a good thrashing.* ■ hit (something) hard and repeatedly: *the wind screeched and the mast thrashed the deck.* ■ [no obj.] move in a violent and convulsive way: *he lay on the ground **thrashing around** in pain* | [with obj.] *she thrashed her arms, attempting to swim.* ■ [no obj.] (**thrash around**) struggle in a wild or desperate way to do something: *two months of thrashing around on my own have produced nothing.* ■ informal defeat (someone) heavily in a contest or match: *I thrashed Pete at cards* | [with obj. and complement] *the Braves were thrashed 8–1 by the Mets.* ■ [no obj.] move with brute determination or violent movements: *I wrench the steering wheel back and thrash on up the hill.* ■ rare term for **THRESH** (sense 1).
▶ **n. 1** [usu. in sing.] a violent or noisy movement, typically involving hitting something repeatedly: *the thrash of the waves.*
2 (also **thrash metal**) a style of fast, loud, harsh-sounding rock music, combining elements of punk and heavy metal. ■ a short, fast, loud piece or passage of rock music.
– PHRASAL VERBS **thrash something out** discuss something thoroughly and honestly.■
– ORIGIN Old English, variant of **THRESH** (an early sense). Current senses of the noun date from the mid 19th cent.

thrash·er[1] /ˈTHrasHər/ ▶ **n. 1** a person or thing that thrashes.
2 archaic spelling of **THRESHER** (sense 1).

thrash·er[2] ▶ **n.** a thrushlike American songbird of the mockingbird family, with mainly brown or gray plumage, a long tail, and a down-curved bill. ● Family Mimidae: five genera, in particular *Toxostoma*, and several species.
– ORIGIN early 19th cent.: perhaps from English dialect *thrusher, thresher* 'thrush.'

thrawn /THrôn/ ▶ **adj.** Scottish perverse; ill-tempered: *your mother's looking a bit thrawn this morning.* ■ twisted; crooked: *a slightly thrawn neck.*
– ORIGIN late Middle English: Scots form of *thrown* (see **THROW**), in the obsolete sense 'twisted, wrung.'

thread /THred/ ▶ **n. 1** a long, thin strand of cotton, nylon, or other fibers used in sewing or weaving. ■ cotton, nylon, or other fibers spun into long, thin strands and used for sewing. ■ (**threads**) informal clothes.
2 a thing resembling a thread in length or thinness, in particular: ■ chiefly literary a long, thin line or piece of something: *the river was a thread of silver below them.* ■ a theme or characteristic, typically forming one of several, running throughout a situation or piece of writing: *a **common thread** running through the scandals was the failure to conduct audits.*
3 a group of linked messages posted on an Internet forum that share a common subject or theme. ■ a programming structure or process formed by linking a number of separate elements or subroutines, esp. each of the tasks executed concurrently in multithreading.
4 (also **screw thread**) a helical ridge on the outside of a screw, bolt, etc., or on the inside of a cylindrical hole, to allow two parts to be screwed together.
▶ **v.** [with obj.] **1** pass a thread through the eye of (a needle) or through the needle and guides of (a sewing machine). ■ pass (a long, thin object or piece of material) through something and into the required position for use: *he threaded the rope through a pulley.* ■ [no obj.] move carefully or skillfully in and out of obstacles: *she **threaded her way** through the tables.* ■ interweave or intersperse as if with threads: *his hair had become ill-kempt and **threaded with** gray.* ■ put (beads, chunks of food, or other small objects) together or singly on a thread, chain, or skewer that runs through the center of each one: *Connie sat threading beads.*
2 (usu. as adj. **threaded**) cut a screw thread in or on (a hole, screw, or other object).
– PHRASES **hang by a thread** be in a highly precarious state. **lose the** (or **one's**) **thread** be unable to follow what someone is saying or remember what one is going to say next.
– DERIVATIVES **thread·like** /-ˌlīk/ **adj.**
– ORIGIN Old English *thrǣd* (noun), of Germanic origin; related to Dutch *draad* and German *Draht*, also to the verb **THROW**. The verb dates from late Middle English.

thread·bare /ˈTHredˌber/ ▶ **adj.** (of cloth, clothing, or soft furnishings) becoming thin and tattered with age: *shabby rooms with threadbare carpets.* ■ (of a person, building, or room) poor or shabby in appearance. ■ (of an argument, excuse, idea, etc.) used so often that it is no longer effective: *the song was a tissue of threadbare clichés.*

thread·er /ˈTHredər/ ▶ **n. 1** a device for passing a thread through the needle and guides of a sewing machine. ■ a factory worker who attaches spools of yarn to a loom.
2 a device for cutting a spiral ridge on the outside of a screw or the inside of a hole.

thread·fin /ˈTHredˌfin/ ▶ **n.** a tropical marine fish that has long streamers or rays arising from its pectoral fins, locally important as a food fish. ● Family Polynemidae: several genera and species.

thread·ing /ˈTHrediNG/ ▶ **n. 1** a process in which unwanted facial hair is removed by using twisted cotton thread to pull the hair from the follicle.
2 Computing the system by which consecutive messages relating to a single subject on a message board or newsgroup are stored for retrieval.

thread·worm /ˈTHredˌwərm/ ▶ **n.** a very slender parasitic nematode worm, esp. a pinworm.

thread·y /ˈTHredē/ ▶ **adj.** (**threadier**, **threadiest**)
1 of, relating to, or resembling a thread.
2 (of a sound, esp. the voice) scarcely audible: *he managed a thready whisper.* ■ Medicine (of a person's pulse) scarcely perceptible.

threat /THret/ ▶ **n. 1** a statement of an intention to inflict pain, injury, damage, or other hostile action on someone in retribution for something done or not done: *members of her family have received **death threats**.* ■ Law a menace of bodily harm, such as may restrain a person's freedom of action.
2 a person or thing likely to cause damage or danger: *hurricane damage poses a major **threat to** many coastal communities.* ■ [in sing.] the possibility of trouble, danger, or ruin: *the company faces the threat of bankruptcy* | *thousands of railroad jobs came **under threat**.*
– ORIGIN Old English *thrēat* 'oppression,' of Germanic origin; related to Dutch *verdrieten* 'grieve,' German *verdriessen* 'irritate.'

threat·en /ˈTHretn/ ▶ **v.** [reporting verb] state one's intention to take hostile action against someone in retribution for something done or not done: [with obj.] *the unions threatened a general strike* | [with infinitive] *she made a scene and Tom threatened to leave* | [with direct speech] *"I might sue for damages," he threatened.* ■ [with obj.] express one's intention to harm or kill (someone): *the men **threatened** the customers **with** a handgun.* ■ [with obj.] cause (someone or something) to be vulnerable or at risk; endanger: *a broken finger threatened his career* | *one of four hospitals **threatened with** closure.* ■ [with infinitive] (of a situation or weather conditions) seem likely to produce an unpleasant or unwelcome result: *the dispute threatened to spread to other cities* | [with obj.] *the air was raw and threatened rain.* ■ [no obj.] (of something undesirable) seem likely to occur: *unless war threatened, national politics remained the focus of attention.*
– DERIVATIVES **threat·en·er** /ˈTHretn-ər, -nər/ **n.**
– ORIGIN Old English *thrēatnian* 'urge or induce, esp. by using threats,' from *thrēat* (see **THREAT**).

threat·en·ing /ˈTHretn-iNG/ ▶ **adj.** having a hostile or deliberately frightening quality or manner: *her mother had received a threatening letter.* ■ Law (of behavior) showing an intention to cause bodily harm. ■ (of a person or situation) causing someone to feel vulnerable or at risk: *she was a type he found threatening.* ■ (of weather conditions) indicating that bad weather is likely: *black threatening clouds.*
– DERIVATIVES **threat·en·ing·ly** **adv.**

three /THrē/ ▶ **cardinal number** equivalent to the sum of one and two; one more than two; 3: *her three children* | *a crew of three* | *a three-bedroom house* | *all three of them are buried there.* (Roman numeral: **iii**, **III**) ■ a group or unit of three people or things: *students clustered in twos or threes.* ■ three years old: *she is only three.* ■ three o'clock: *I'll come at three.* ■ a size of garment or other merchandise denoted by three. ■ a playing card or domino with three pips.
– ORIGIN Old English *thrīe* (masculine), *thrīo, thrēo* (feminine), of Germanic origin; related to Dutch *drie* and German *drei*, from an Indo-European root shared by Latin *tres* and Greek *treis*.

three-card mon·te ▶ **n.** a game traditionally associated with con men, in which the dealer shows the player three cards then moves them around face-down, the player being obliged to pick the specified card from among the three.

three cheers ▶ **plural n.** see **CHEER**.

three-col·or proc·ess ▶ **n.** Photography a means of reproducing natural colors by combining photographic images in the three primary colors.

three-cor·nered ▶ **adj.** triangular. ■ (esp. of a contest) between three people or groups.

three-cush·ion bil·liards ▶ **plural n.** [usu. treated as sing.] a type of billiards in which the cue ball must strike one object ball and three or more cushions before the second object ball.

three-deck·er ▶ **n.** a thing with three levels or layers: [as modifier] *three-decker sandwiches.* ■ historical a sailing warship with three gun decks.

three-di·men·sion·al ▶ **adj.** having or appearing to have length, breadth, and depth: *a three-dimensional object.* ■ (of a literary or dramatic work) sufficiently full in characterization and representation of events to be believable.
– DERIVATIVES **three-di·men·sion·al·i·ty** /di͵mensHəˈnalətē/ **n.**, **three-di·men·sion·al·ly adv.**

three·fold /ˈTHrē͵fōld/ ▶ **adj.** three times as great or as numerous: *a threefold increase in the number of stolen cars.* ■ having three parts or elements: *the differences are threefold.*
▶ **adv.** by three times; to three times the number or amount: *the aftershocks intensify threefold each time.*

Three Grac·es see **GRACE**.

three-leg·ged race /ˈlegəd/ ▶ **n.** a race run by pairs of people, one member of each pair having their left leg tied to the right leg of the other.

Three Mile Is·land an island in the Susquehanna River near Harrisburg, Pennsylvania, site of a nuclear power station. In 1979, an accident caused damage to the reactor core, provoking strong reactions against the nuclear industry in the US.

three-mile lim·it ▶ **n.** Law the outer boundary of the area extending 3 miles (4.8 km) out to sea from the coast of a state or country, considered to be within its jurisdiction.

three-peat ▶ **v.** [no obj.] win a particular sports championship three times, esp. consecutively: *the Bulls rate as the favorite to three-peat.*
▶ **n.** [in sing.] a third win of a particular sports championship, esp. the third of three consecutive wins: *all eyes were on the 49ers' bid for a three-peat.*
– ORIGIN 1980s: from **THREE** + a shortened form of **REPEAT**.

three·pence /ˈTHrepəns, ˈTHrəp-, ˈTHrē͵pens/ ▶ **n.** Brit. the sum of three pence, esp. before decimalization (1971).

three·pen·ny /ˈTHrip(ə)nē, ˈTHrəp-, ˈTHrē͵penē/ ▶ **adj.** [attrib.] Brit. costing or worth three pence, esp. before decimalization (1971). ■ trifling or paltry; of little worth: *a threepenny production.*

three-phase ▶ **adj.** (of an electric generator, motor, or other device) designed to supply or use simultaneously three separate alternating currents of the same voltage, but with phases differing by a third of a period.

three-piece ▶ **adj.** [attrib.] consisting of three separate and complementary items, in particular: ■ (of a set of furniture) consisting of a sofa and two armchairs. ■ (of a set of clothes) consisting of slacks or a skirt with a vest and jacket.
▶ **n.** a set of three separate and complementary items. ■ a group consisting of three musicians.

three-ply ▶ **adj.** (of material) having three layers or strands.
▶ **n. 1** knitting wool made of three strands.
2 plywood made by gluing together three layers with the grain in different directions.

three-point land·ing ▶ **n.** a landing of an aircraft on the two main wheels and the tailwheel or skid simultaneously.

three-point turn ▶ **n.** a method of turning a vehicle around in a narrow space by moving forward, backward, and forward again in a sequence of arcs.

three-quar·ter ▶ **adj.** [attrib.] consisting of three quarters of something (used esp. with reference to size or length): *a three-quarter length cashmere coat.* ■ (of a view or depiction of a person's face) at an angle between full face and profile.

three-ring cir·cus ▶ **n.** a public spectacle, esp. one with little substance: *his attempt at a dignified resignation turned into a three-ring circus.*

three·score /ˈTHrēˈskôr/ ▶ **cardinal number** literary sixty.

Three Sis·ters glacier-covered volcanic peaks in west central Oregon, in the Cascade Range, in a noted wilderness area.

three·some /ˈTHrēsəm/ ▶ **n.** a group of three people engaged in the same activity. ■ a game or activity for three people.

three-star ▶ **adj.** (esp. of a hotel or restaurant) given three stars in a grading system, typically one in which this denotes a high or average class or quality (four- or five-star denoting the highest standard). ■ (in the US armed services) having or denoting the rank of lieutenant general, distinguished by three stars on the uniform.

Three Stoog·es, US comedy team, comprising various partners from the early 1930s to 1970. The most popular trio (1934–46) were **Moe Howard** (born *Moses Horwitz*) (1897–1975), **Curly Howard** (Moe's brother; born *Jerome Lester Horwitz*) (1903–52), and **Larry Fine** (born *Louis Feinberg*) (1902–75). The Stooges' nearly 200 movie shorts include *Men in Black* (1934), *Hold That Lion!* (1947), and *Quiz Whizz* (1958).

three strikes ▶ **n.** [usu. as modifier] legislation providing that an offender's third felony is punishable by life imprisonment or another severe sentence.
– ORIGIN 1990s: from the phrase *three strikes and you're out* (with allusion to baseball).

three-way ▶ **adj.** involving three directions, processes, or participants: *a three-way race for the presidency* | *a three-way switch.*

three-wheel·er ▶ **n.** a vehicle with three wheels, esp. a child's tricycle.

Three Wise Men another name for **MAGI**.

threm·ma·tol·o·gy /͵THreməˈtäləjē/ ▶ **n.** the science of breeding animals and plants.
– ORIGIN late 19th cent.: from Greek *thremma*, *thremmat-* 'nursling' + **-LOGY**.

thren·o·dy /ˈTHrenədē/ ▶ **n.** (pl. **threnodies**) a lament.
– DERIVATIVES **thre·no·di·al** /THrəˈnōdēəl/ **adj.**, **thre·nod·ic** /THrəˈnädik/ **adj.**, **thren·o·dist** /-dist/ **n.**
– ORIGIN mid 17th cent.: from Greek *thrēnōidia*, from *thrēnos* 'wailing' + *ōidē* 'song.'

thre·o·nine /ˈTHrēə͵nēn, -nin/ ▶ **n.** Biochemistry a hydrophilic amino acid that is a constituent of most proteins. It is an essential nutrient in the diet of vertebrates. ● Chem. formula: $CH_3CH(OH)CH(NH_2)COOH$.
– ORIGIN 1930s: from *threose* (the name of a tetrose sugar) + **-INE**[4].

thresh /THresH/ ▶ **v.** [with obj.] **1** separate grain from (a plant), typically with a flail or by the action of a revolving mechanism: *machinery that can reap and thresh corn in the same process* | (as noun **threshing**) *farm workers started the afternoon's threshing.*
2 variant spelling of **THRASH**.
– ORIGIN Old English *therscan*, later *threscan*, of Germanic origin; related to Dutch *dorsen* and German *dreschen*. Compare with **THRASH**.

thresh·er /ˈTHresHər/ ▶ **n. 1** a person or machine that separates grain from the plants by beating.
2 (also **thresher shark**) a surface-living shark with a long upper lobe to the tail. Threshers often hunt in pairs, lashing the water with their tails to herd fish into a tightly packed shoal. ● *Alopias vulpinus*, family Alopidae.

thresh·ing floor ▶ **n.** a hard, level surface on which grain is threshed with a flail.

thresh·ing ma·chine ▶ **n.** a power-driven machine for separating grain from plants.

thresh·old /ˈTHresH͵(h)ōld/ ▶ **n. 1** a strip of wood, metal, or stone forming the bottom of a doorway and crossed in entering a house or room. ■ [in sing.] a point of entry or beginning: *she was **on the threshold** of a dazzling career.* ■ the beginning of an airport runway on which an aircraft is attempting to land.
2 the magnitude or intensity that must be exceeded for a certain reaction, phenomenon, result, or condition to occur or be manifested: *nothing happens until the signal passes the threshold* | [as modifier] *a threshold level.* ■ the maximum level of radiation or a concentration of a substance considered to be acceptable or safe: *their water would meet the safety threshold of 50 milligrams of nitrates per liter.* ■ Physiology & Psychology a limit below which a stimulus causes no reaction: *everyone has a different pain threshold.* ■ a level, rate, or amount at which something comes into effect: *the tax threshold has risen to $10,492 of adjusted gross income.*
– ORIGIN Old English *therscold*, *threscold*; related to German dialect *Drischaufel*; the first element is related to **THRESH** (in a Germanic sense 'tread'), but the origin of the second element is unknown.

threw /THrōō/ past of **THROW**.

thrice /THrīs/ ▶ **adv.** chiefly formal literary three times: *a dose of 25 mg thrice daily.* ■ [as submodifier] extremely; very: *I was thrice blessed.*
– ORIGIN Middle English *thries*, from earlier *thrie* (from Old English *thriga*, related to **THREE**) + **-S**[3] (later respelled *-ce* to denote the unvoiced sound); compare with **ONCE**.

thrift /THrift/ ▶ **n. 1** the quality of using money and other resources carefully and not wastefully: *the values of thrift and self-reliance.* ■ another term for **SAVINGS AND LOAN**.
2 a European plant that forms low-growing tufts of slender leaves with rounded pink flower heads, growing chiefly on sea cliffs and mountains. Also called **SEA PINK**. ● *Armeria maritima*, family Plumbaginaceae.
– ORIGIN Middle English (in the sense 'prosperity, acquired wealth, success'): from Old Norse, from *thrífa* 'grasp, get hold of.' Compare with **THRIVE**.

thrift·less /ˈTHriftlis/ ▶ **adj.** (of a person or their behavior) spending money in an extravagant and wasteful way.
– DERIVATIVES **thrift·less·ly adv.**, **thrift·less·ness n.**

thrift shop (also **thrift store**) ▶ **n.** a store selling secondhand clothes and other household goods, typically to raise funds for a charitable institution.

thrift·y /ˈTHriftē/ ▶ **adj.** (**thriftier**, **thriftiest**) **1** (of a person or their behavior) using money and other resources carefully and not wastefully.
2 chiefly archaic dialect (of livestock or plants) strong and healthy. ■ archaic prosperous.
– DERIVATIVES **thrift·i·ly** /-lē/ **adv.**, **thrift·i·ness n.**

thrill /THril/ ▶ **n.** a sudden feeling of excitement and pleasure: *the thrill of jumping out of an airplane.* ■ an experience that produces such a feeling. ■ a wave or nervous tremor of emotion or sensation: *a thrill of excitement ran through her.* ■ archaic a throb or pulsation. ■ Medicine a vibratory movement or resonance heard through a stethoscope.
▶ **v. 1** [with obj.] cause (someone) to have a sudden feeling of excitement and pleasure: *his kiss thrilled and excited her* | *I'm **thrilled to death*** | *they were **thrilled to pieces*** | (as adj. **thrilling**) *a thrilling adventure.* ■ [no obj.] experience such feeling: ***thrill to** the magic of the world's greatest guitarist.*
2 [no obj.] (of an emotion or sensation) pass with a nervous tremor: *the shock of alarm **thrilled through** her.* ■ literary quiver or throb.
– PHRASES **thrills and chills** the excitement of dangerous sports or entertainments, as experienced by spectators.
– DERIVATIVES **thrill·ing·ly adv.**
– ORIGIN Middle English (as a verb in the sense 'pierce or penetrate'): alteration of dialect *thirl* 'pierce, bore.'

thrill·er /ˈTHrilər/ ▶ **n.** a novel, play, or movie with an exciting plot, typically involving crime or espionage. ■ a very exciting contest or experience: *a 17–14 overtime thriller against Tampa Bay.*

thrips /THrips/ (also **thrip**) ▶ **n.** (pl. **same**) a minute black winged insect that sucks plant sap and can be a serious pest of ornamental and food plants when present in large numbers. ● Order Thysanoptera: many species.
– ORIGIN late 18th cent.: via Latin from Greek, literally 'woodworm.'

thrive /THrīv/ ▶ **v.** (**thrives**, **thriving**; past **throve** /THrōv/ or **thrived**; past participle **thriven** /ˈTHrivən/ or **thrived**) [no obj.] (of a child, animal, or plant) grow or develop well or vigorously: *the new baby thrived.* ■ prosper; flourish: *education groups **thrive on** organization* | (as adj. **thriving**) *a thriving economy.*
– ORIGIN Middle English (originally in the sense 'grow, increase'): from Old Norse *thrífask*, reflexive of *thrífa* 'grasp, get hold of.' Compare with **THRIFT**.

thro' /THrōō/ (or **thro**) ▶ **prep., adv., & adj.** literary spelling of **THROUGH**.

throat /THrōt/ ▶ **n.** the passage that leads from the back of the mouth of a person or animal. ■ the front part of a person's or animal's neck, behind which the esophagus, trachea, and blood vessels serving the head are situated: *a gold pendant gleamed at her throat.* ■ literary a voice of a person or a songbird: *from a hundred throats came the cry "Vive l'Empereur!"* ■ a thing compared to a throat, esp. a narrow passage, entrance, or exit. ■ Sailing the forward upper corner of a quadrilateral fore-and-aft sail.
– PHRASES **be at each other's throats** (of people or organizations) quarrel or fight persistently. **cut one's own throat** bring about one's own downfall by one's actions. **force** (or **shove** or **ram**) **something down someone's throat** force ideas or material on a person's attention by repeatedly putting them forward. **grab** (or **take**) **someone by the throat** put one's hands around someone's throat, typically in an attempt to throttle them. ■ (**grab something by the throat**) seize control of something: *in the second half, the Huskies took the game by the throat.* ■ attract someone's undivided attention: *the movie grabs you by the throat and refuses to let go.* **jump down someone's throat** see **JUMP**. **stick in one's throat** see **STICK**[2].
– DERIVATIVES **throat·ed adj.** [in combination] *a full-throated baritone* | *a ruby-throated hummingbird.*

PRONUNCIATION KEY ə *ago, up*; ər *over, fur*; a *hat*; ā *ate*; ä *car*; e *let*; ē *see*; i *fit*; ī *by*; NG *sing*; ō *go*; ô *law, for*; oi *toy*; ŏŏ *good*; ōō *goo*; ou *out*; TH *thin*; T̲H̲ *then*; ZH *vision*

t

– ORIGIN Old English *throte*, *throtu*, of Germanic origin; related to German *Drossel*. Compare with **THROTTLE**.

throat·latch /'THrōt,laCH/ (also **throatlash** /-,lasH/) ▶ **n.** a strap passing under a horse's throat to help keep the bridle in position.

throat·y /'THrōtē/ ▶ **adj.** (**throatier, throatiest**) (of a sound such as a person's voice or the noise of an engine) deep and rasping: *rich, throaty laughter*.
– DERIVATIVES **throat·i·ly** /-təlē/ **adv.**, **throat·i·ness n.**

throb /THräb/ ▶ **v.** (**throbs, throbbing, throbbed**) [no obj.] beat or sound with a strong, regular rhythm; pulsate steadily: *the war drums throbbed* | figurative *the crowded streets **throbbed with** life*. ■ feel pain in a series of regular beats: *her foot **throbbed with** pain* | (as adj. **throbbing**) *a throbbing headache*.
▶ **n.** [usu. in sing.] a strong, regular beat or sound; a steady pulsation: *the throb of the ship's engines*. ■ a feeling of pain in a series of regular beats.
– ORIGIN late Middle English: probably imitative.

throes /THrōz/ ▶ **plural n.** intense or violent pain and struggle, esp. accompanying birth, death, or great change: *he convulsed in his **death throes***.
– PHRASES **in the throes of** in the middle of doing or dealing with something very difficult or painful: *a friend was in the throes of a divorce*.
– ORIGIN Middle English *throwe* (singular); perhaps related to Old English *thrēa*, *thrawu* 'calamity,' influenced by *thrōwian* 'suffer.'

Throgs Neck /'THrôgz ,nek, 'THrägz/ a peninsula in the southeast Bronx in New York City that gives its name to a major bridge, which crosses Long Island South to Queens on Long Island.

throm·bi /'THräm,bī/ plural form of **THROMBUS**.

throm·bin /'THrämbin/ ▶ **n.** Biochemistry an enzyme in blood plasma that causes the clotting of blood by converting fibrinogen to fibrin.
– ORIGIN late 19th cent.: from Greek *thrombos* 'blood clot' + **-IN**[1].

thrombo- ▶ **comb. form** relating to the clotting of blood: *thromboembolism*.
– ORIGIN from Greek *thrombos* 'blood clot.'

throm·bo·cyte /'THrämbə,sīt/ ▶ **n.** another term for **PLATELET**.

throm·bo·cy·to·pe·ni·a /,THrämbō,sītə'pēnēə/ ▶ **n.** Medicine deficiency of platelets in the blood. This causes bleeding into the tissues, bruising, and slow blood clotting after injury.
– ORIGIN 1920s: from **THROMBOCYTE** + Greek *penia* 'poverty.'

throm·bo·em·bo·lism /,THrämbō'embə,lizəm/ ▶ **n.** Medicine obstruction of a blood vessel by a blood clot that has become dislodged from another site in the circulation.
– DERIVATIVES **throm·bo·em·bol·ic** /-,em'bälik/ **adj.**

throm·bo·phle·bi·tis /,THrämbōflə'bītis/ ▶ **n.** Medicine inflammation of the wall of a vein with associated thrombosis, often occurring in the legs during pregnancy.

throm·bo·plas·tin /,THrämbō'plastən/ ▶ **n.** Biochemistry an enzyme released from damaged cells, esp. platelets, that converts prothrombin to thrombin during the early stages of blood coagulation.

throm·bo·sis /THräm'bōsis/ ▶ **n.** (pl. **thromboses** /-,sēz/) local coagulation or clotting of the blood in a part of the circulatory system: *increased risk of thrombosis* | *he died of a coronary thrombosis*.
– DERIVATIVES **throm·bot·ic** /-'bätik/ **adj.**
– ORIGIN early 18th cent.: modern Latin, from Greek *thrombōsis* 'curdling,' from *thrombos* 'blood clot.'

throm·box·ane /THräm'bäksān/ ▶ **n.** Biochemistry a hormone of the prostacyclin type released from blood platelets. It induces platelet aggregation and arterial constriction.

throm·bus /'THrämbəs/ ▶ **n.** (pl. **thrombi** /-,bī/) a blood clot formed in situ within the vascular system of the body and impeding blood flow.
– ORIGIN mid 19th cent.: modern Latin, from Greek *thrombos* 'lump, blood clot.'

throne /THrōn/ ▶ **n.** a ceremonial chair for a sovereign, bishop, or similar figure. ■ (**the throne**) used to signify sovereign power: *the heir to the throne*. ■ humorous a toilet. ■ (**thrones**) (in traditional Christian angelology) the third-highest order of the ninefold celestial hierarchy.
▶ **v.** [with obj.] (usu. **be throned**) literary place (someone) on a throne: *the king was throned on a rock*.
– ORIGIN Middle English: from Old French *trone*, via Latin from Greek *thronos* 'elevated seat.'

throng /THrôNG, THräNG/ ▶ **n.** a large, densely packed crowd of people or animals: *he pushed his way through the throng* | ***a throng of** birds*.
▶ **v.** [with obj.] (of a crowd) fill or be present in (a place or area): *a crowd thronged the station* | *the streets are **thronged with** people*. ■ [no obj.] flock or be present in great numbers: *tourists thronged to the picturesque village*.
– ORIGIN Old English *(ge)thrang* 'crowd, tumult,' of Germanic origin. The early sense of the verb (Middle English) was 'press violently, force one's way.'

thros·tle /'THrôsəl/ ▶ **n. 1** Brit. old-fashioned term for **SONG THRUSH**.
2 (also **throstle frame**) historical a machine for continuously spinning wool or cotton.
– ORIGIN Old English, of Germanic origin, from an Indo-European root shared by Latin *turdus* 'thrush.' Sense 2 dates from the early 19th cent. and was apparently named from the humming sound of the machine.

throt·tle /'THrätl/ ▶ **n. 1** a device controlling the flow of fuel or power to an engine: *the engines were **at full throttle***.
2 archaic a throat, gullet, or windpipe.
▶ **v.** [with obj.] **1** attack or kill (someone) by choking or strangling them: *she was sorely tempted to throttle him* | figurative *the revolution has throttled the free exchange of information and opinion*.
2 control (an engine or vehicle) with a throttle. ■ [no obj.] (**throttle back** or **down**) reduce the power of an engine or vehicle by use of the throttle.
– DERIVATIVES **throt·tler** /'THrätl-ər, 'THrätlər/ **n.**
– ORIGIN late Middle English (as a verb): perhaps a frequentative, from **THROAT**; the noun (sense 2, dating from the mid 16th cent.) is perhaps a diminutive of **THROAT**, but the history of the word is not clear.

throt·tle·hold /'THrätl,hōld/ ▶ **n.** another term for **STRANGLEHOLD**.

through /THrōō/ ▶ **prep. & adv. 1** moving in one side and out of the other side of (an opening, channel, or location): [as prep.] *stepping boldly through the doorway* | [as adv.] *as soon as we opened the gate, they came streaming through*. ■ so as to make a hole or opening in (a physical object): [as prep.] *the truck smashed through a brick wall* | [as adv.] *a cucumber, slit, but not all the way through*. ■ moving around or from one side to the other within (a crowd or group): [as prep.] *making my way through the guests*. ■ so as to be perceived from the other side of (an intervening obstacle): [as prep.] *the sun was streaming in through the window* | [as adv.] *the glass in the front door where the moonlight streamed through*. ■ [prep.] expressing the position or location of something beyond or at the far end of (an opening or an obstacle): *the approach to the church is through a gate*. ■ expressing the extent of turning from one orientation to another: [as prep.] *each joint can move through an angle within fixed limits*.
2 continuing in time toward completion of (a process or period): [as prep.] *he showed up halfway through the second act* | [as adv.] *to struggle through until payday*. ■ so as to complete (a particular stage or trial) successfully: [as prep.] *she had come through her sternest test* | [as adv.] *I will struggle through alone rather than ask for help*. ■ from beginning to end of (an experience or activity, typically a tedious or stressful one): [as prep.] *we sat through some very boring speeches* | *she's been through a bad time* | [as adv.] *Karl will see you through, Ingrid*.
3 so as to inspect all or part of (a collection, inventory, or publication): [as prep.] *flipping through the pages of a notebook* | [as adv.] *she read the letter through carefully*.
4 [prep.] up to and including (a particular point in an ordered sequence): *they will be in town from March 24 through May 7*.
5 [prep.] by means of (a process or intermediate stage): *dioxins get into mothers' milk through contaminated food*. ■ by means of (an intermediary or agent): *seeking justice through the proper channels*.
6 [adv.] so as to be connected by telephone: *he put a call through to the senator*.
▶ **adj. 1** [attrib.] (of a means of public transportation or a ticket) continuing or valid to the final destination: *a through train from Boston*.
2 [attrib.] denoting traffic that passes from one side of a place to another in the course of a longer journey: *neighborhoods from which through traffic would be excluded*. ■ denoting a road that is open at both ends, allowing traffic free passage from one end to the other: *the shopping center is on a busy through road*.
3 [attrib.] (of a room) running the whole length of a building.
4 [predic.] informal having no prospect of any future relationship, dealings, or success: *she told him she was through with him* | *you and I are through*.
– PHRASES **through and through** in every aspect; thoroughly or completely: *Harriet was a political animal through and through*.
– ORIGIN Old English *thurh* (preposition and adverb), of Germanic origin; related to Dutch *door* and German *durch*. The spelling change to *thr-* appears *c*.1300, becoming standard from Caxton onward.

through-com·posed ▶ **adj.** Music (of a composition, esp. a song) not based on repeated sections or verses, esp. having different music for each verse. Also called **DURCHKOMPONIERT**.

through line ▶ **n.** a connecting theme or plot in a movie, play, book, etc.

through·out /THrōō'out/ ▶ **prep. & adv.** all the way through, in particular: ■ in every part of (a place or object): [as prep.] *it had repercussions throughout Europe* | [as adv.] *the house is in good order throughout*. ■ from beginning to end of (an event or period of time): [as prep.] *the Church of which she was a faithful member throughout her life* | [as adv.] *both sets of parents retained a smiling dignity throughout*.

through·put /'THrōō,po͝ot/ ▶ **n.** the amount of material or items passing through a system or process.

through·way ▶ **n.** another spelling of **THRUWAY**.

throve /THrōv/ past of **THRIVE**.

throw /THrō/ ▶ **v.** (**throws, throwing**; past **threw** /THrōō/; past participle **thrown** /THrōn/) **1** [with obj.] propel (something) with force through the air by a movement of the arm and hand: *I threw a brick through the window*. ■ [with obj. or complement] push or force (someone or something) violently and suddenly into a particular physical position or state: *the pilot and one passenger were thrown clear and survived* | *the door was thrown open, and a uniformed guard entered the room*. ■ put in place or erect quickly: *the stewards had thrown a cordon across the fairway*. ■ move (a part of the body) quickly or suddenly in a particular direction: *she threw her head back and laughed*. ■ project or cast (light or shadow) in a particular direction: *a chandelier threw its bright light over the walls*. ■ deliver (a punch). ■ direct (a particular kind of look or facial expression): *she threw a withering glance at him*. ■ project (one's voice) so that it appears to come from someone or something else, as in ventriloquism. ■ (**throw something off/on**) put on or take off a garment hastily: *I threw on my housecoat and went to the door*. ■ move (a switch or lever) so as to operate a device. ■ roll (dice). ■ obtain (a specified number) by rolling dice. ■ informal lose (a race or contest) intentionally, esp. in return for a bribe.
2 [with obj.] cause to enter suddenly a particular state or condition: *he threw all her emotions into turmoil* | *the bond market was thrown into confusion*. ■ put (someone) in a particular place or state, esp. in a rough, abrupt, or summary fashion: *these guys should be thrown in jail*. ■ disconcert; confuse: *she frowned, thrown by this apparent change of tack*.
3 [with obj.] send (one's opponent) to the ground in wrestling, judo, or similar activity. ■ (of a horse) unseat (its rider). ■ (of a horse) lose (a shoe). ■ (of an animal) give birth to (young, of a specified kind): *sometimes a completely black calf is thrown*.
4 [with obj.] form (ceramic ware) on a potter's wheel: *further on, a potter was throwing pots*. ■ turn (wood or other material) on a lathe. ■ twist (silk or other fabrics) into thread or yarn.
5 [with obj.] have (a fit or tantrum).
6 [with obj.] give or hold (a party).
▶ **n. 1** an act of throwing something: *Jeter's throw to first base was too late*. ■ an act of throwing one's opponent in wrestling, judo, or similar sport: *a shoulder throw*.
2 a light cover for furniture. ■ short for **THROW RUG**.
3 short for **ROLL OF THE DICE** (see **DICE**).
4 Geology the extent of vertical displacement between the two sides of a fault.
5 [usu. in sing.] the action or motion of a slide valve or of a crank, eccentric wheel, or cam. ■ the extent of such motion. ■ the distance moved by the pointer of an instrument.
6 (**a throw**) informal used to indicate how much a single item, turn, or attempt costs: *he was offering to draw on-the-spot portraits at $25 a throw*.
– PHRASES **be thrown back on** be forced to rely on (something) because there is no alternative: *we are once again thrown back on the resources of our imagination*. **throw away the key** used to suggest that someone who has been put in prison should or will never be released: *the judge should lock up these robbers and throw away the key*. **throw the baby out with the bathwater** see **BABY**. **throw something back in someone's face** see **FACE**. **throw the book at** see **BOOK**. **throw cold water on** see **COLD**. **throw down the gauntlet** see **GAUNTLET**[1]. **throw someone for a loop** see **LOOP**. **throw dust in someone's eyes** seek to mislead or deceive someone by misrepresentation or distraction. **throw good money after bad** incur further loss in a hopeless attempt to recoup a previous loss. **throw one's hand in** withdraw from a card game, poker, because one has a poor hand. ■ withdraw from a contest or activity; give up. **throw in one's lot with**

see LOT. **throw in the towel** (or **sponge**) (of boxers or their seconds) throw a towel (or sponge) into the ring as a token of defeat. ■ abandon a struggle; admit defeat. **throw light on** see LIGHT[1]. **throw money at something** see MONEY. **throw of the dice** see DICE. **throw oneself on** (or **upon**) **someone's mercy** abjectly ask someone for help, forgiveness, or leniency. **throw up one's hands** raise both hands in the air as an indication of one's exasperation. **throw one's weight around** see WEIGHT. **throw one's weight behind** see WEIGHT.
– PHRASAL VERBS **throw money around** spend money freely and ostentatiously. **throw oneself at** appear too eager to become the sexual partner of. **throw something away 1** discard something as useless or unwanted. ■ waste or fail to make use of an opportunity or advantage: *I've thrown away my chances in life.* ■ discard a playing card in a game. **2** (of an actor) deliver a line with deliberate underemphasis for increased dramatic effect. **throw something in 1** include something, typically at no extra cost, with something that is being sold or offered: *they cut the price by $100 and threw in an AC adaptor.* **2** make a remark casually as an interjection in a conversation: *he threw in a sensible remark about funding.* **throw oneself into** start to do (something) with enthusiasm and vigor: *Eve threw herself into her work.* **throw something off 1** rid oneself of something: *he was struggling to throw off a viral-hepatitis problem.* **2** write or utter in an offhand manner: *Thomas threw off the question lightly.* **throw oneself on** (or **upon**) attack (someone) vigorously: *they threw themselves on the enemy.* **throw something open** make something accessible: *the market was thrown open to any supplier to compete for contracts.* ■ invite general discussion of or participation in a subject or a debate or other event: *the debate will be thrown open to the audience.* **throw someone out 1** expel someone unceremoniously from a place, organization, or activity. **2** Baseball put out a runner by a throw to the base being approached, followed by a tag. **throw something out 1** discard something as unwanted. **2** (of a court, legislature, or other body) dismiss or reject something brought before it: *the charges were thrown out by the judge.* **3** put forward a suggestion tentatively: *a suggestion that Dunne threw out caught many a reader's fancy.* **4** cause numbers or calculations to become inaccurate: *an undisclosed stock option throws out all your figures.* **5** emit or radiate something: *a big range fire that threw out heat like a furnace.* **6** (of a plant) rapidly develop a side shoot, bud, etc. **throw someone over** abandon or reject someone as a lover. **throw people together** bring people into contact, esp. by chance. **throw something together** make or produce something hastily, without careful planning or arrangement: *the meal was quickly thrown together at news of Rose's arrival.* **throw up** vomit. **throw something up 1** abandon or give up something, esp. one's job: *why has he thrown up a promising career in politics?* **2** informal vomit something one has eaten or drunk. **3** produce something and bring it to notice: *he saw the prayers of the Church as a living and fruitful tradition that threw up new ideas.* **4** erect a building or structure hastily.
– DERIVATIVES **throw·a·ble** adj., **throw·er** n.
– ORIGIN Old English *thrāwan* 'to twist, turn'; related to Dutch *draaien* and German *drehen*, from an Indo-European root shared by Latin *terere* 'to rub,' Greek *teirein* 'wear out.' Sense 1 of the verb, expressing propulsion and sudden action, dates from Middle English.

throw·a·way /ˈTHrōəˌwā/ ▶ adj. **1** denoting or relating to products that are intended to be discarded after being used once or a few times: *a throwaway camera | we live in a throwaway society.* **2** (of a remark) expressed in a casual or understated way: *some people overreacted to a few throwaway lines.*
▶ n. a thing intended or destined to be discarded after brief use or appeal.

throw·back /ˈTHrōˌbak/ ▶ n. a reversion to an earlier ancestral characteristic: *the eyes could be an ancestral throwback.* ■ a person or thing having the characteristics of a former time: *a lot of his work is a throwback to the fifties.*

throw·down /ˈTHrōˌdoun/ ▶ n. informal a performance by or competition between rappers, breakdancers, etc.: *a funky hip-hop throwdown.*

throw-in ▶ n. Soccer the act of throwing the ball from the sideline to restart play after the ball has gone out of bounds.

throw pil·low ▶ n. a small decorative pillow placed on a chair or couch.

throw rug ▶ n. a small decorative rug designed to be placed with a casual effect and moved as required.

throw·ster /ˈTHrōstər/ ▶ n. a person who twists silk fibers into thread.

thru /THroo͞/ ▶ prep., adv., & adj. informal spelling of THROUGH.

thrum[1] /THrəm/ ▶ v. (**thrums, thrumming, thrummed**) [no obj.] make a continuous rhythmic humming sound: *the boat's huge engines thrummed in his ears.* ■ [with obj.] strum (the strings of a musical instrument) in a rhythmic way.
▶ n. [usu. in sing.] a continuous rhythmic humming sound: *the steady thrum of rain on the windows.*
– ORIGIN late 16th cent. (as a verb): imitative.

thrum[2] ▶ n. (in weaving) an unwoven end of a warp thread, or a fringe of such ends, left in the loom when the finished cloth is cut away. ■ any short loose thread.
▶ v. (**thrums, thrumming, thrummed**) [with obj.] cover or adorn (cloth or clothing) with ends of thread.
– DERIVATIVES **thrum·mer** n., **thrum·my** adj.
– ORIGIN Old English *thrum* (only in *tungethrum* 'ligament of the tongue'): of Germanic origin; related to Dutch *dreum* 'thrum' and German *Trumm* 'endpiece.' The current sense dates from Middle English.

thrush[1] /THrəSH/ ▶ n. a small or medium-sized songbird, typically having a brown back, spotted breast, and loud song. ● Subfamily Turdinae (the **thrush subfamily**), family Muscicapidae: many genera, in particular *Turdus*, and numerous species. The thrush subfamily includes the chats, robins, bluebirds, blackbirds, nightingales, redstarts, and wheatears.
– ORIGIN Old English *thrysce*, of Germanic origin; related to THROSTLE.

thrush[2] ▶ n. **1** infection of the mouth and throat by a yeastlike fungus, causing whitish patches. Also called CANDIDIASIS. ● The fungus belongs to the genus *Candida*, subdivision Deuteromycotina, in particular *C. albicans.* ■ infection of the female genitals with the same fungus.
2 a chronic condition affecting the frog of a horse's foot, causing the accumulation of a dark, foul-smelling substance. Also called CANKER.
– ORIGIN mid 17th cent.: origin uncertain; sense 1 possibly related to Swedish *torsk* and Danish *troske*; sense 2 perhaps from dialect *frush* in the same sense, perhaps from Old French *fourchette* 'frog of a horse's hoof.'

thrust /THrəst/ ▶ v. (**thrusts, thrusting**; past and past participle **thrust**) [with obj.] push (something or someone) suddenly or violently in the specified direction: *she thrust her hands into her pockets |* figurative *Howard was thrust into the limelight |* [no obj.] *he thrust at his opponent with his sword.* ■ [no obj.] (of a person) move or advance forcibly: *she thrust through the bramble canes | he tried to* ***thrust his way*** *past her.* ■ [no obj.] (of a thing) extend so as to project conspicuously: *beside the boathouse a jetty thrust out into the water.* ■ (**thrust something on/upon**) force (someone) to accept or deal with something: *he felt that fame had been thrust upon him.*
▶ n. **1** a sudden or violent lunge with a pointed weapon or a bodily part: *he drove the blade upward with one powerful thrust.* ■ a forceful attack or effort: *executives led a new thrust in business development.* ■ [in sing.] the principal purpose or theme of a course of action or line of reasoning: *anti-Americanism became* ***the main thrust*** *of their policy.*
2 the propulsive force of a jet or rocket engine. ■ the lateral pressure exerted by an arch or other support in a building.
3 (also **thrust fault**) Geology a reverse fault of low angle, with older strata displaced horizontally over younger.
– PHRASES **cut and thrust** see CUT.
– ORIGIN Middle English (as a verb): from Old Norse *thrýsta*; perhaps related to Latin *trudere* 'to thrust.' The noun is first recorded (early 16th cent.) in the sense 'act of pressing.'

thrust·er /ˈTHrəstər/ ▶ n. a person or thing that thrusts, in particular: ■ a small rocket engine on a spacecraft, used to make alterations in its flight path or altitude. ■ a secondary jet or propeller on a ship or offshore rig, used for accurate maneuvering and maintenance of position.

thrust·ing /ˈTHrəstiNG/ ▶ n. the motion of pushing or lunging suddenly or violently. ■ Geology the pushing upward of the earth's crust.

thrust stage ▶ n. a stage that extends into the auditorium so that the audience is seated around three sides.

thru·way /ˈTHroo͞ˌwā/ (also **throughway**) ▶ n. a major road or highway.

Thu·cyd·i·des /THoo͞ˈsidēˌdēz/ (*c.*455–*c.*400 BC), Greek historian. Remembered for his *History of the Peloponnesian War*, he fought in the conflict on the Athenian side.

thud /THəd/ ▶ n. a dull, heavy sound, such as that made by an object falling to the ground: *Jean heard the thud of the closing door.*
▶ v. (**thuds, thudding, thudded**) [no obj.] move, fall, or strike something with a dull, heavy sound: *the bullets thudded into the dusty ground.*
– PHRASES **with a thud** used to describe a sudden and disillusioning reminder of reality in contrast to someone's dreams or aspirations: *dropouts have now come back down to earth with a thud.*
– ORIGIN late Middle English (originally Scots): probably from Old English *thyddan* 'to thrust, push'; related to *thoden* 'violent wind.' The noun is recorded first denoting a sudden blast or gust of wind, later the sound of a thunderclap, whence a dull, heavy sound. The verb dates from the early 16th cent.

thud·ding /ˈTHədiNG/ ▶ n. the action of moving, falling, or striking something with a dull, heavy sound: *he heard the hollow thudding of hooves.*
▶ adj. [attrib.] used to emphasize the clumsiness or awkwardness of something, esp. a remark: *great thudding conversation-stoppers.*
– DERIVATIVES **thud·ding·ly** adv.

thug /THəg/ ▶ n. **1** a violent person, esp. a criminal. [mid 19th cent.: extension of sense 2.]
2 (**Thug**) historical a member of a religious organization of robbers and assassins in India. Devotees of the goddess Kali, the Thugs waylaid and strangled their victims, usually travelers, in a ritually prescribed manner. They were suppressed by the British in the 1830s.
– DERIVATIVES **thug·ger·y** /-gərē/ n., **thug·gish** adj., **thug·gish·ly** adv., **thug·gish·ness** n., **thug·gism** /-ˌgizəm/ n.
– ORIGIN early 19th cent. (sense 2): from Hindi *ṭhag* 'swindler, thief,' based on Sanskrit *sthagati* 'he covers or conceals.'

thug·gee /ˈTHəgē/ ▶ n. historical the robbery and murder practiced by the Thugs in accordance with their ritual.
– ORIGIN from Hindi *ṭhagī*, from *ṭhag* (see THUG).

thu·ja /ˈTHoo͞jə/ (also **thuya** /ˈTHoo͞yə/) ▶ n. a North American and eastern Asian evergreen coniferous tree of a genus that includes the arbor vitaes. ● Genus *Thuja*, family Cupressaceae.
– ORIGIN modern Latin (genus name), from Greek *thuia*, denoting an African tree formerly included in the genus.

Thu·le 1 /ˈTHoo͞lē, THoo͞l/ a country described by the ancient Greek explorer Pytheas (*c.*310 BC) as being six days' sail north of Britain, most plausibly identified with Norway. It was regarded by the ancients as the northernmost part of the world.
2 /ˈtoo͞lē/ an Eskimo culture existing from Alaska to Greenland *c.* AD 500–1400.
3 /ˈtoo͞lē/ a settlement on the northwestern coast of Greenland, founded in 1910 by Danish explorer Knud Rasmussen (1879–1933).

thu·li·um /ˈTH(y)oo͞lēəm/ ▶ n. the chemical element of atomic number 69, a soft silvery-white metal of the lanthanide series. (Symbol: **Tm**)
– ORIGIN late 19th cent.: modern Latin, from Latin *Thule* THULE (sense 1), from Greek *Thoulē*, of unknown origin.

Thumb /THəm/, General Tom, (1838–83) US circus entertainer; born *Charles S. Stratton.* A 40-inch-tall dwarf, he worked as a sideshow attraction in the shows of P. T. Barnum.

thumb /THəm/ ▶ n. the short, thick first digit of the human hand, set lower and apart from the other four and opposable to them. ■ the corresponding digit of primates or other mammals. ■ the part of a glove intended to cover the thumb.
▶ v. [with obj.] press, move, or touch (something) with one's thumb: *as soon as she thumbed the button, the door slid open.* ■ turn over (pages) with or as if with one's thumb: *I've thumbed my address book and found quite a range of smaller hotels |* [no obj.] *he was* ***thumbing through*** *that magazine for the umpteenth time.* ■ (usu. **be thumbed**) wear or soil (a book's pages) by repeated handling: *his dictionaries were thumbed and ink-stained.* ■ request or obtain (a free ride in a passing vehicle) by signaling with one's thumb: *three cars passed me and I tried to* ***thumb a ride*** *|* [no obj.] *he* ***was thumbing his way*** *across France.*
– PHRASES **be all thumbs** informal be clumsy or awkward in one's actions: *I'm all thumbs when it comes to making bows.* **thumb one's nose at** informal show disdain or contempt for. **thumbs up** (or **down**) informal an indication of satisfaction or approval (or of rejection or failure): *plans to build a house on the site have been given the thumbs down by the Department of the Environment.* [with reference

PRONUNCIATION KEY ə ago, up; ər over, fur; a hat; ā ate; ä car; e let; ē see; i fit; ī by; NG sing; ō go; ô law, for; oi toy; o͝o good; o͞o goo; ou out; TH thin; T͟H then; ZH vision

to the signal of approval or disapproval, used by spectators at a Roman amphitheater; the sense has been reversed, as the Romans used 'thumbs down' to signify that a beaten gladiator had performed well and should be spared, and 'thumbs up' to call for his death.] **under someone's thumb** completely under someone's influence or control.
– DERIVATIVES **thumbed adj., thumb·less adj.**
– ORIGIN Old English *thūma*; related to Dutch *duim* and German *Daumen*, from an Indo-European root shared by Latin *tumere* 'to swell.' The verb dates from the late 16th cent., first in the sense 'play (a musical instrument) with the thumbs.'

thumb drive ▶ **n.** Computing another term for **USB FLASH DRIVE.**

thumb in·dex ▶ **n.** a set of lettered or marked grooves cut down the side of a book, esp. a diary or dictionary, for easy reference.
– DERIVATIVES **thumb-in·dexed adj.**

thumb·nail /'THəm,nāl/ ▶ **n. 1** the nail of the thumb.
2 [usu. as modifier] a very small or concise description, representation, or summary: *a thumbnail sketch.* ■ Computing a small picture of an image or page layout.

thumb pi·an·o ▶ **n.** any of various musical instruments, mainly of African origin, made from strips of metal fastened to a resonator and played by plucking with the fingers and thumbs. Also called **KALIMBA, MBIRA,** or **SANSA.**

thumb·print /'THəm,print/ ▶ **n.** an impression or mark made on a surface by the inner part of the top joint of the thumb, esp. as used for identifying individuals from the unique pattern of whorls and lines. ■ a distinctive identifying characteristic: *it has an individuality and thumbprint of its own.*

thumb·screw /'THəm,skrōō/ ▶ **n. 1** a screw with a protruding winged or flattened head for turning with the thumb and forefinger.
2 (usu. **thumbscrews**) an instrument of torture for crushing the thumbs.

thumb·suck·er /'THəm,səkər/ ▶ **n.** informal, often derogatory a serious piece of journalism that concentrates on the background and interpretation of events rather than on the news or action; a think piece. ■ a journalist who writes in this style: *in a few days we'll be inundated with thumbsuckers assessing the first hundred days of the Clinton administration.*

thumb·tack /'THəm,tak/ ▶ **n.** a short flat-headed pin, used for fastening paper to a wall or other surface.

thumb·wheel /'THəm,(h)wēl/ ▶ **n.** a control device for electrical or mechanical equipment in the form of a wheel operated with the thumb.

Thum·mim ▶ **n.** see **URIM AND THUMMIM.**

thump /THəmp/ ▶ **v.** [with obj.] hit (someone or something) heavily, esp. with the fist or a blunt implement: *Holman thumped the desk with his hand* | [no obj.] *she thumped on the door.* ■ move (something) forcefully, noisily, or decisively: *she picked up the kettle then thumped it down again.* ■ [no obj.] move or do something with a heavy deadened sound: *Philip thumped down on the sofa.* ■ [no obj.] (of a person's heart or pulse) beat or pulsate strongly, typically because of fear or excitement. ■ (**thump something out**) play a tune enthusiastically but heavy-handedly. ■ informal defeat heavily: *Tampa Bay thumped Toronto 8–0.*
▶ **n.** a heavy dull blow with a person's fist or a blunt implement: *I felt a thump on my back.* ■ a loud deadened sound: *his wife put down her iron with a thump.* ■ a strong heartbeat, esp. one caused by fear or excitement.
– DERIVATIVES **thump·er n.**
– ORIGIN mid 16th cent.: imitative.

thump·ing /'THəmpiNG/ ▶ **adj.** [attrib.] **1** pounding; throbbing: *the thumping beat of her heart.*
2 informal of an impressive size, extent, or amount: *a thumping 64 percent majority* | [as submodifier] *a thumping great lie.*

thun·der /'THəndər/ ▶ **n.** a loud rumbling or crashing noise heard after a lightning flash due to the expansion of rapidly heated air. ■ a resounding loud deep noise: *you can hear the thunder of the falls in the distance.* ■ used in similes and comparisons to refer to an angry facial expression or tone of voice: *"I am Brother Joachim," he announced in a voice like thunder.* ■ [as exclamation] dated used to express anger, annoyance, or incredulity: *none of this did the remotest good, but, by thunder, it kept the union activists feeling good.*
▶ **v.** [no obj.] (**it thunders, it is thundering,** etc.) thunder sounds: *it began to thunder.* ■ make a loud, deep resounding noise: *the motorcycle thundered into life* | *the train thundered through the night.* ■ [with obj.] strike powerfully: *McGwire thundered that one out of the stadium.* ■ speak loudly and forcefully or angrily, esp. to denounce or criticize: *he thundered against the evils of the age* | [with direct speech] *"Sit down!" thundered Morse with immense authority.*
– PHRASES **steal someone's thunder** see **STEAL.**
– DERIVATIVES **thun·der·er n., thun·der·y** /-d(ə)rē/ **adj.**
– ORIGIN Old English *thunor* (noun), *thunrian* (verb), of Germanic origin; related to Dutch *donder* and German *Donner*, from an Indo-European root shared by Latin *tonare* 'to thunder.'

Thun·der Bay a city on a large bay of Lake Superior in western Ontario; pop. 109,140 (2006). It is one of Canada's major ports.

thun·der·bird /'THəndər,bərd/ ▶ **n.** a mythical bird thought by some North American Indians to bring thunder.

thun·der·bolt /'THəndər,bōlt/ ▶ **n.** literary a flash of lightning with a simultaneous crash of thunder. ■ a supposed bolt or shaft believed to be the destructive agent in a lightning flash, esp. as an attribute of a god such as Jupiter or Thor. ■ used in similes and comparisons to refer to a very sudden or unexpected event or item of news, esp. of an unpleasant nature: *the full force of what she had been told hit her like a thunderbolt.* ■ informal a very fast and powerful shot, throw, or stroke.

thun·der·clap /'THəndər,klap/ ▶ **n.** a crash of thunder: *the door opened like a thunderclap.* ■ used in similes to refer to something startling or unexpected: *the invasion of the Falklands came as a thunderclap.*

thun·der·cloud /'THəndər,kloud/ ▶ **n.** a cumulus cloud with a towering or spreading top, charged with electricity and producing thunder and lightning.

thun·der·head /'THəndər,hed/ ▶ **n.** a rounded, projecting head of a cumulus cloud, which portends a thunderstorm.

thun·der·ing /'THənd(ə)riNG/ ▶ **adj.** [attrib.] making a resounding, loud, deep noise: *thundering waterfalls.* ■ informal extremely great, severe, or impressive: *a thundering bore* | [as submodifier] *a thundering good read.*
– DERIVATIVES **thun·der·ing·ly adv.** [as submodifier] *it was so thunderingly dull.*

thun·der·ous /'THənd(ə)rəs/ ▶ **adj.** of, relating to, or giving warning of thunder: *a thunderous gray cloud.* ■ very loud: *thunderous applause.* ■ very powerful or intense: *thunderous romantic situations and adventures* | *the hockey game against Sweden included several thunderous collisions.*
– DERIVATIVES **thun·der·ous·ly adv., thun·der·ous·ness n.**

thun·der·show·er /'THəndər,SHou(ə)r/ ▶ **n.** a shower of rain accompanied by thunder and lightning.

thun·der·storm /'THəndər,stôrm/ ▶ **n.** a storm with thunder and lightning and typically also heavy rain or hail.

thun·der·struck /'THəndər,strək/ ▶ **adj.** extremely surprised or shocked: *they were thunderstruck by this revelation.*

thun·der thighs ▶ **n.** informal large thighs, esp. those with a great deal of cellulite.

thunk[1] /THəNGk/ ▶ **n. & v.** informal term for **THUD.**

thunk[2] informal or humorous past and past participle of **THINK:** *who would've thunk it?*

Thur. ▶ **abbr.** Thursday.

Thur·ber /'THərbər/, James (Grover) (1894–1961), US humorist and cartoonist. He published many of his essays, stories, and sketches in *The New Yorker* magazine. His collections of essays, stories, and sketches include *My Life and Hard Times* (1933) and *My World—And Welcome to It* (1942), which contains the story "The Secret Life of Walter Mitty."

thu·ri·ble /'THŏŏrəbəl/ ▶ **n.** a censer.
– ORIGIN late Middle English: from Old French, or from Latin *thuribulum*, from *thus, thur-* 'incense' (see **THURIFER**).

thu·ri·fer /'THŏŏrəfər/ ▶ **n.** an acolyte carrying a censer.
– ORIGIN mid 19th cent.: from late Latin, from Latin *thus, thur-* 'incense' (from Greek *thuos* 'sacrifice') + *-fer* '-bearing.'

Thu·rin·gi·a /THŏŏ'rinj(ē)ə/ a densely forested state of central Germany; capital, Erfurt. German name **Thüringen.**

Thur·mond /'THərmənd/, Strom, (1902–2003) US politician; full name *James Strom Thurmond.* He was governor of South Carolina 1947–51 and a member of the US Senate from South Carolina 1954–2003. An ardent segregationist, he ran for president on the States' Rights Party (Dixiecrat) ticket in 1948. Originally a Democrat, he switched to the Republican Party in 1964.

Thurs. ▶ **abbr.** Thursday.

Thurs·day /'THərzdā, -dē/ ▶ **n.** the day of the week before Friday and following Wednesday: *the committee met* **on Thursday** | *the music program for Thursdays in April* | [as modifier] *Thursday morning.*
▶ **adv.** on Thursday: *he called her up Thursday.* ■ (**Thursdays**) on Thursdays; each Thursday: *the column is published Thursdays.*
– ORIGIN Old English *Thu(n)resdæg* 'day of thunder,' translation of late Latin *Jovis dies* 'day of Jupiter' (god associated with thunder): compare with Dutch *donderdag* and German *Donnerstag.*

thus /T͟Həs/ ▶ **adv.** literary or formal **1** as a result or consequence of this; therefore: *Burke knocked out Byrne, thus becoming champion.*
2 in the manner now being indicated or exemplified; in this way: *she phoned Susan, and while she was thus engaged, Charles summoned the doctor.*
3 [as submodifier] to this point; so: *the website has been cracked three times* **thus far.**
– ORIGIN Old English, of unknown origin.

thus·ly /'T͟Həslē/ ▶ **adv.** informal another term for **THUS** (sense 2): *the review was conducted thusly.*

thu·ya /'THōōyə/ ▶ **n.** variant spelling of **THUJA.**

thwack /THwak/ ▶ **v.** [with obj.] strike forcefully with a sharp blow: *she thwacked the back of their knees with a cane.*
▶ **n.** a sharp blow: *he hit it with a hefty thwack.*
– ORIGIN late Middle English: imitative.

thwart /THwôrt/ ▶ **v.** [with obj.] prevent (someone) from accomplishing something: *he never did anything to thwart his father* | *he was thwarted in his desire to punish Uncle Fred.* ■ oppose (a plan, attempt, or ambition) successfully: *the government had been able to thwart all attempts by opposition leaders to form new parties.*
▶ **n.** a structural crosspiece sometimes forming a seat for a rower in a boat.
▶ **prep. & adv.** archaic or literary from one side to another side of; across: [as prep.] *a pink-tinged cloud spread thwart the shore.*
– ORIGIN Middle English *thwerte*, from the adjective *thwert* 'perverse, obstinate, adverse,' from Old Norse *thvert*, neuter of *thverr* 'transverse,' from an Indo-European root shared by Latin *torquere* 'to twist.'

thy /T͟HĪ/ (also **thine** before a vowel) ▶ **possessive determiner** archaic or dialect form of **YOUR:** *honor thy father and thy mother.*
– ORIGIN Middle English *thi* (originally before words beginning with any consonant except *h*), reduced from *thin*, from Old English *thīn* (see **THINE**).

USAGE The use of **thy** is still found in certain religious groups and in some traditional British dialects, but elsewhere it is restricted to archaic contexts. See also usage at **THOU**[1].

Thy·es·tes /THĪ'estēz/ Greek Mythology the brother of Atreus and father of Aegisthus.
– DERIVATIVES **Thy·es·te·an** /-tēən/ **adj.**

thy·la·cine /'THīlə,sīn, -sin/ ▶ **n.** a doglike carnivorous marsupial with stripes across the rump, found only in Tasmania. There have been no confirmed sightings since one was captured in 1933, and it may now be extinct. Also called **TASMANIAN WOLF.** ● *Thylacinus cynocephalus*, family Thylacinidae.
– ORIGIN mid 19th cent.: from modern Latin *Thylacinus* (genus name), from Greek *thulakos* 'pouch.'

thy·la·koid /'THīlə,koid/ ▶ **n.** Botany each of a number of flattened sacs inside a chloroplast, bounded by pigmented membranes on which the light reactions of photosynthesis take place, and arranged in stacks or grana.
– ORIGIN 1960s: from German *Thylakoid*, from Greek *thulakoeidēs* 'pouchlike,' from *thulakos* 'pouch.'

thyme /tīm/ ▶ **n.** a low-growing aromatic plant of the mint family. The small leaves are used as a culinary herb, and the plant yields a medicinal oil. ● Genus *Thymus*, family Labiatae: many species, in particular **common** (or **garden**) **thyme** (*T. vulgaris*).
– DERIVATIVES **thym·y** /'tīmē/ **adj.**
– ORIGIN Middle English: from Old French *thym*, via Latin from Greek *thumon*, from *thuein* 'burn, sacrifice.'

thy·mec·to·my /THī'mektəmē/ ▶ **n.** (pl. **thymectomies**) surgical removal of the thymus gland.

thy·mi /'THīmī/ plural form of **THYMUS.**

thy·mic /'THīmik/ ▶ **adj.** Physiology of or relating to the thymus gland or its functions.

thy·mi·dine /'THīmə,dēn/ ▶ **n.** Biochemistry a crystalline nucleoside present in DNA, consisting of thymine linked to deoxyribose.
– ORIGIN early 20th cent.: from **THYMINE** + **-IDE** + **-INE**[4].

thy·mine /ˈTHīˌmēn, -min/ ▶ **n.** Biochemistry a compound that is one of the four constituent bases of nucleic acids. A pyrimidine derivative, it is paired with adenine in double-stranded DNA. ● Alternative name; **5-methyluracil**; chem. formula: $C_5H_6N_2O_2$.
– ORIGIN late 19th cent.: from THYMUS + -INE[4].

thy·mo·cyte /ˈTHīməˌsīt/ ▶ **n.** Physiology a lymphocyte within the thymus gland.
– ORIGIN 1920s: from THYMUS + -CYTE.

thy·mol /ˈTHīˌmôl, -ˌmōl/ ▶ **n.** Chemistry a white crystalline compound present in oil of thyme and used as a flavoring and preservative. ● Alternative name: **2-isopropyl-5-methylphenol**; chem. formula: $C_{10}H_{13}OH$.
– ORIGIN mid 19th cent.: from Greek *thumon* 'thyme' + -OL.

thy·mo·ma /THīˈmōmə/ ▶ **n.** (pl. **thymomas** or **thymomata** /-mətə/) Medicine a rare, usually benign tumor arising from thymus tissue and sometimes associated with myasthenia gravis.
– ORIGIN early 20th cent.: from THYMUS + -OMA.

thy·mus /ˈTHīməs/ (also **thymus gland**) ▶ **n.** (pl. **thymuses** or **thymi** /-mī/) a lymphoid organ situated in the neck of vertebrates that produces T cells for the immune system. The human thymus becomes much smaller at the approach of puberty.
– ORIGIN late 16th cent. (denoting a growth or tumor resembling a bud): from Greek *thumos* 'excrescence like a thyme bud, thymus gland.'

thy·ris·tor /THīˈristər/ ▶ **n.** Electronics a four-layered semiconductor rectifier in which the flow of current between two electrodes is triggered by a signal at a third electrode.
– ORIGIN 1950s: blend of *thyratron*, denoting a kind of thermionic tube (from Greek *thura* 'gate') and TRANSISTOR.

thyro- ▶ **comb. form** representing THYROID.

thy·ro·cal·ci·to·nin /ˌTHīrōˌkalsiˈtōnin/ ▶ **n.** another term for CALCITONIN, believed until the late 1960s to denote a different hormone.

thy·ro·glob·u·lin /ˌTHīrōˈglābyəlin/ ▶ **n.** Biochemistry a protein present in the thyroid gland, from which thyroid hormones are synthesized.

thy·roid /ˈTHīˌroid/ ▶ **n. 1** (also **thyroid gland**) a large ductless gland in the neck that secretes hormones regulating growth and development through the rate of metabolism. ■ an extract prepared from the thyroid gland of animals and used in treating deficiency of thyroid hormones.
2 (also **thyroid cartilage**) a large cartilage of the larynx, a projection of which forms the Adam's apple in humans.
– ORIGIN early 18th cent. (as an adjective): from Greek (*khondros*) *thureoeidēs* 'shield-shaped (cartilage),' from *thureos* 'oblong shield.'

thy·roid·ec·to·my /ˌTHīroiˈdektəmē/ ▶ **n.** (pl. **thyroidectomies**) removal of the thyroid gland by surgery.

thy·roid·i·tis /ˌTHīroiˈdītis/ ▶ **n.** inflammation of the thyroid.

thy·roid-stim·u·lat·ing hor·mone ▶ **n.** another term for THYROTROPIN.

thy·ro·tox·i·co·sis /ˌTHīrōˌtäksiˈkōsis/ ▶ **n.** another term for HYPERTHYROIDISM.

thy·ro·tro·pin /ˌTHīrōˈtrōpin, THīˈrätrə-/ (also **thyrotrophin** /-fin/) ▶ **n.** Biochemistry a hormone secreted by the pituitary gland that regulates the production of thyroid hormones.

thy·ro·tro·pin-re·leas·ing hor·mone (also **thyrotropin-releasing factor**) ▶ **n.** Biochemistry a hormone secreted by the hypothalamus that stimulates release of thyrotropin.

thy·rox·ine /THīˈräksēn, -sin/ (also **thyroxin** /-sin/) ▶ **n.** Biochemistry the main hormone produced by the thyroid gland, acting to increase metabolic rate and so regulating growth and development. ● An iodine-containing amino acid; chem. formula: $C_{15}H_{11}NO_4I_4$.
– ORIGIN early 20th cent.: from THYROID + OX- 'oxygen' + *in* from INDOLE (because of an early misunderstanding of its chemical structure), altered by substitution of -INE[4].

thyr·sus /ˈTHərsəs/ ▶ **n.** (pl. **thyrsusi** /-sī/) (in ancient Greece and Rome) a staff or spear tipped with an ornament like a pine cone, carried by Dionysus and his followers.
– ORIGIN Latin, from Greek *thursos* 'plant stalk, Bacchic staff.'

Thy·sa·nop·ter·a /ˌTHīsəˈnäptərə, ˌTHis-/ Entomology an order of insects that comprises the thrips. ■ (as plural noun **thysanoptera**) insects of this order; thrips.
– DERIVATIVES **thy·sa·nop·ter·an** n. & adj.
– ORIGIN modern Latin (plural), from Greek *thusanos* 'tassel' + *pteron* 'wing.'

Thy·sa·nu·ra /ˌTHīsəˈn(y)o͝orə/ Entomology an order of insects that comprises the true, or three-pronged, bristletails. ■ (as plural noun **thysanura**) insects of this order; bristletails.
– DERIVATIVES **thy·sa·nu·ran** n. & adj.
– ORIGIN modern Latin (plural), from Greek *thusanos* 'tassel' + *oura* 'tail.'

thy·self /T͟Hīˈself/ ▶ **pron.** [second person singular] archaic or dialect form of YOURSELF, corresponding to the subject THOU[1]: *thou shalt love thy neighbor as thyself.*

Thz ▶ **abbr.** terahertz.

Ti ▶ **symbol** the chemical element titanium.

ti /tē/ ▶ **n.** (in solmization) the seventh note of a major scale. ■ the note B in the fixed-do system.
– ORIGIN mid 19th cent.: alteration of SI, adopted to avoid having two notes (*sol* and *si*) beginning with the same letter (see SOLMIZATION).

TIA ▶ **abbr.** Medicine transient ischemic attack.

Ti·a·mat /ˈtyämät/ Babylonian Mythology a monstrous she-dragon who was the mother of the first Babylonian gods. She was slain by Marduk.

tian /tyan/ ▶ **n.** (pl. **same**) a dish of finely chopped vegetables cooked in olive oil and then baked au gratin. ■ a large oval earthenware cooking pot traditionally used in Provence.
– ORIGIN Provençal, based on Greek *tēganon* 'frying pan.'

Tian·an·men Square /tēˈenə(n)ˌmen, tyˈänän-/ a square in the center of Beijing adjacent to the Forbidden City, the largest public open space in the world.
– ORIGIN Chinese, literally 'square of heavenly peace.'

Tiananmen Square

Tian·jin /ˈtyenˈjin/ (also **Tientsin** /ˈtyenˈjin, ˈtyentˈsin/) a port in northeastern China, in Hebei province; pop. 5,332,100 (est. 2006).

ti·ar·a /tēˈärə, -ˈarə, -ˈe(ə)rə/ ▶ **n. 1** a jeweled ornamental band worn on the front of a woman's hair.
2 a high diadem encircled with three crowns and worn by a pope. ■ historical a turban worn by ancient Persian kings.
– ORIGIN mid 16th cent. (denoting the Persian royal headdress): via Latin from Greek, partly via Italian. Sense 1 dates from the early 18th cent.

ti·a·rel·la /ˌtēəˈrelə, ˌtī-/ ▶ **n.** a small chiefly North American plant of the saxifrage family. ● Genus *Tiarella*, family Saxifragaceae, esp. the **foamflower** (*T. cordifolia*).
– ORIGIN modern Latin, from Latin *tiara* 'turban, tiara' + the diminutive suffix *-ella*.

Tib·bett /ˈtibit/, Lawrence, (1896–1960) US opera singer. A baritone, he sang with the Metropolitan Opera 1923–50. He also appeared in movies, such as *The Rogue Song* (1930), and sang on the radio.

Ti·ber /ˈtībər/ a river in central Italy that rises in the Tuscan Apennines and flows southwest for 252 miles (405 km), entering the Tyrrhenian Sea at Ostia. The city of Rome is on its banks. Italian name TEVERE.

Ti·be·ri·as, Lake /tīˈbi(ə)rēəs/ another name for Sea of Galilee (see GALILEE, SEA OF).

Ti·be·ri·us /tīˈbi(ə)rēəs/ (42 BC–AD 37), Roman emperor AD 14–37; full name *Tiberius Julius Caesar Augustus*.

Ti·bes·ti Moun·tains /təˈbestē/ a mountain range in north central Africa, in the Sahara in northern Chad and southern Libya. It rises to 11,201 feet (3,415 m) at Emi Koussi, the highest point in the Sahara.

Ti·bet /təˈbet/ a mountainous region in Asia on the northern side of the Himalayas, since 1965 forming an autonomous region in the west of China; pop. 2,840,000 (est. 2007); official languages, Tibetan and Chinese; capital, Lhasa. Chinese name XIZANG.

> Most of Tibet forms a high plateau with an average elevation of over 12,500 feet (4,000 m). Ruled by Buddhist lamas since the 7th century, it was conquered by the Mongols in the 13th century and the Manchus in the 18th. China extended its authority over Tibet in 1951 but gained full control only after crushing a revolt in 1959, during which the country's spiritual leader, the Dalai Lama, escaped to India; he remains in exile and sporadic unrest has continued.

Ti·bet·an /təˈbetn/ ▶ **n. 1** a native of Tibet or a person of Tibetan descent.
2 the Tibeto-Burman language of Tibet, also spoken in neighboring areas of China, India, and Nepal.
▶ **adj.** of or relating to Tibet, its people, or its language.

Ti·bet·an an·te·lope ▶ **n.** another term for CHIRU.

Ti·bet·an Bud·dhism ▶ **n.** the religion of Tibet, a form of Mahayana Buddhism. It was formed in the 8th century AD from a combination of Buddhism and the indigenous Tibetan religion. The head of the religion is the Dalai Lama.

Ti·bet·an mas·tiff ▶ **n.** an animal of a breed of large black-and-tan dog with a thick coat and drop ears.

Ti·bet·an span·iel ▶ **n.** an animal of a breed of small white, brown, or black dog with a silky coat of medium length.

Ti·bet·an ter·ri·er ▶ **n.** an animal of a breed of gray, black, cream, or particolored terrier with a thick shaggy coat.

Ti·bet·o-Bur·man /təˌbetō ˈbərmən/ ▶ **adj.** of, relating to, or denoting a division of the Sino-Tibetan language family that includes Tibetan, Burmese, and a number of other languages spoken in mountainous regions of central southern Asia.

tib·i·a /ˈtibēə/ ▶ **n.** (pl. **tibiae** /ˈtibēˌē/ or **tibias**) Anatomy the inner and typically larger of the two bones between the knee and the ankle (or the equivalent joints in other terrestrial vertebrates), parallel with the fibula. ■ Zoology the tibiotarsus of a bird. ■ Entomology the fourth segment of the leg of an insect, between the femur and the tarsus.
– DERIVATIVES **tib·i·al** adj.
– ORIGIN late Middle English: from Latin, 'shin bone.'

tib·i·a·lis /ˌtibēˈalis, -ˈālis/ ▶ **n.** Anatomy any of several muscles and tendons in the calf of the leg concerned with movements of the foot.
– ORIGIN late 19th cent.: from Latin, 'relating to the shin bone.'

tib·i·o·tar·sus /ˌtibēōˈtärsəs/ ▶ **n.** (pl. **tibiotarsi** /-sī/) Zoology the bone in a bird's leg corresponding to the tibia, fused at the lower end with some bones of the tarsus.
– ORIGIN late 19th cent.: blend of TIBIA and TARSUS.

tic /tik/ ▶ **n.** a habitual spasmodic contraction of the muscles, most often in the face. ■ a characteristic or recurrent behavioral trait; idiosyncrasy: *I began with the kind of generalization that was one of my primary tics as a writer.*
– ORIGIN early 19th cent.: from French, from Italian *ticchio*.

tic dou·lou·reux /ˈtik ˌdo͞oləˈro͞o/ ▶ **n.** another term for TRIGEMINAL NEURALGIA.
– ORIGIN early 19th cent.: French, literally 'painful tic.'

Ti·ci·no /tiˈCHēnō/ a predominantly Italian-speaking canton in southern Switzerland, on the Italian border; capital, Bellinzona. It joined the Swiss Confederation in 1803. French name TESSIN, German name TESSIN.

tick[1] /tik/ ▶ **n. 1** a regular short, sharp sound, esp. that made every second by a clock or watch. ■ Brit. informal a moment (used esp. to reassure someone that one will return or be ready very soon): *I'll be with you in a tick.*
2 chiefly Brit. a check mark.
3 Stock Market the smallest recognized amount by which a price of a security or future may fluctuate.
▶ **v. 1** [no obj.] (of a clock or other mechanical device) make regular short sharp sounds, typically for every second of time passing: *I could hear the clock ticking.* ■ (**tick away/by/past**) (of time) pass (used esp. when someone is pressed for time or keenly awaiting an event): *the minutes were ticking away till the actor's appearance.* ■ [with obj.] (**tick something away**) (of a clock or watch) mark the passing of time with regular short sharp sounds: *the little clock ticked the precious minutes away.* ■ proceed or progress: *her book was ticking along nicely.*
2 [with obj.] chiefly Brit. mark (an item) with a check mark, typically to show that it has been chosen, checked, approved, or dealt with: *just tick the appropriate box below.*
– PHRASES **what makes someone tick** informal what motivates someone: *people are curious to know what makes these men tick.*
– PHRASAL VERBS **tick someone off 1** informal make someone annoyed or angry. **2** Brit. informal reprimand or rebuke someone: *he was ticked off by Angela* | (as noun **ticking off**) *he got a ticking off from the boss.* **tick something off** chiefly Brit. **1** mark an item

PRONUNCIATION KEY ə *ago, up*; ər *over, fur*; a *hat*; ā *ate*; ä *car*; e *let*; ē *see*; i *fit*; ī *by*; NG *sing*; ō *go*; ô *law, for*; oi *toy*; o͝o *good*; o͞o *goo*; ou *out*; TH *thin*; T͟H *then*; ZH *vision*

in a list with a tick to show that it has been dealt with: *I ticked several items off my "to do" list.* **2** list items one by one in one's mind or during a speech: *he ticked the points off on his fingers.* **tick over** (of an engine) idle. ■ work or function at a basic or minimum level: *they are keeping things ticking over until their father returns.*
– ORIGIN Middle English (as a verb in the sense 'pat, touch'): probably of Germanic origin and related to Dutch *tik* (noun), *tikken* (verb) 'pat, touch.' The noun was recorded in late Middle English as 'a light tap'; current senses date from the late 17th cent.

tick² ▶ n. a parasitic arachnid that attaches itself to the skin of a terrestrial vertebrate from which it sucks blood, leaving the host when sated. Some species transmit diseases, including tularemia and Lyme disease. ● Suborder Ixodida, order Acarina (or Acari). ■ informal a parasitic louse fly.
– ORIGIN Old English *ticia*, of Germanic origin; related to Dutch *teek* and German *Zecke*.

tick³ ▶ n. a fabric case stuffed with feathers or other material to form a mattress or pillow. ■ short for TICKING.
– ORIGIN late Middle English: probably Middle Low German and Middle Dutch *tēke*, or Middle Dutch *tīke*, via West Germanic from Latin *theca* 'case,' from Greek *thēkē*.

tick⁴ ▶ n. (in phrase **on tick**) chiefly Brit. or dated on credit.
– ORIGIN mid 17th cent.: apparently short for TICKET in the phrase *on the ticket*, referring to an IOU or promise to pay.

tick-borne ▶ adj. transmitted or carried by ticks: *babesiosis is a tick-borne, malaria-like disease.*

tick·er /ˈtikər/ ▶ n. **1** informal a watch. ■ a person's heart.
2 a telegraphic or electronic machine that prints out data on a strip of paper, esp. stock market information or news reports. ■ another term for NEWS TICKER.

tick·er tape ▶ n. a paper strip on which messages are recorded in a telegraphic tape machine. ■ [as modifier] denoting a parade or other event in which this or similar material is thrown from windows.

tick·et /ˈtikit/ ▶ n. **1** a piece of paper or small card that gives the holder a certain right, esp. to enter a place, travel by public transport, or participate in an event: *admission is by ticket only.* ■ (**ticket to/out of**) a method of getting into or out of (a specified state or situation): *drugs are seen as the only ticket out of poverty | companies that appeared to have a **one-way ticket to** profitability.*
2 a certificate or warrant, in particular: ■ an official notice of a traffic offense. ■ a certificate of qualification as a ship's master, pilot, or other crew member.
3 a label attached to a retail product, giving its price, size, and other details.
4 [in sing.] a list of candidates put forward by a party in an election: *his presence on the Republican ticket.* ■ a set of principles or policies supported by a party in an election: *he stood for office on a strong right-wing, no-nonsense ticket.*
5 (**the ticket**) informal, dated the desirable or correct thing: *a wet spring would be **just the ticket** for the garden.*
▶ v. (**tickets, ticketing, ticketed**) [with obj.] **1** issue (someone) with an official notice of a traffic or other offense: *park illegally and you are likely to be ticketed.*
2 (**be ticketed**) (of a passenger) be issued with a travel ticket: *passengers can now get electronically ticketed.* ■ be destined or heading for a specified state or position: *they were sure that Downing was ticketed for greatness.*
3 (**be ticketed**) (of a retail product) be marked with a label giving its price, size, and other details.
– PHRASES **punch one's ticket** informal deliberately undertake particular assignments that are likely to lead to promotion at work. ■ (in sports) ensure one's progress to a further contest or tournament: *in scoring 13 points, they punched their ticket to the Super Bowl in Jacksonville.* **write one's (own) ticket** informal dictate one's own terms.
– ORIGIN early 16th cent. (in the general senses 'short written note' and 'a license or permit'): shortening of obsolete French *étiquet*, from Old French *estiquet(te)*, from *estiquier* 'to fix,' from Middle Dutch *steken*. Compare with ETIQUETTE.

tick·et·less /ˈtikitlis/ ▶ adj. & adv. **1** not requiring a paper ticket: [as adj.] *all seats are assigned, all travel is ticketless, and all fares are one-way.*
2 not in possession of a valid ticket: [as adv.] *activists on Monday traveled ticketless in suburban trains to protest the hike in fares.*

tick·et of·fice ▶ n. an office or kiosk where tickets are sold, esp. for entertainment events or travel accommodations.

tick·et·y-boo /ˌtikitēˈbo͞o/ ▶ adj. [predic.] Brit. informal, dated in good order; fine: *everything is tickety-boo.*
– ORIGIN 1930s: perhaps from Hindi *ṭhīk hai* 'all right.'

tick fe·ver ▶ n. any fever transmitted by the bite of a tick.

tick·ing /ˈtiking/ ▶ n. a strong, durable material, typically striped, used to cover mattresses and pillows.
– ORIGIN mid 17th cent.: from TICK³ + -ING¹.

tick·le /ˈtikəl/ ▶ v. [with obj.] **1** lightly touch or prod (a person or a part of the body) in a way that causes itching and often laughter: *she tickled me under the chin.* ■ [no obj.] (of a part of the body) give a sensation of mild discomfort similar to that caused by being touched in this way: *his throat had stopped tickling.* ■ touch with light finger movements: [with obj. and complement] *tickling the safe open took nearly ninety minutes.*
2 appeal to (someone's taste, sense of humor, curiosity, etc.): *here are a couple of anecdotes that might tickle your fancy.* ■ (usu. **be tickled**) cause (someone) amusement or pleasure: *he is tickled by the idea.*
▶ n. [in sing.] an act of tickling someone: *Dad gave my chin a little tickle.* ■ a sensation like that of being lightly touched or prodded: *I had a tickle between my shoulder blades.*
– PHRASES **be tickled pink** (or **to death**) informal be extremely amused or pleased. **tickle the ivories** informal play the piano.
– ORIGIN Middle English (in the sense 'be delighted or thrilled'): perhaps a frequentative of TICK¹, or an alteration of Scots and dialect *kittle* 'to tickle' (compare with KITTLE).

tick·ler /ˈtik(ə)lər/ ▶ n. a thing that tickles. ■ a memorandum.

tick·lish /ˈtik(ə)lish/ ▶ adj. **1** sensitive to being tickled: *Lhasa apsos are ticklish on their feet.* ■ (of a cough) characterized by persistent irritation in the throat.
2 (of a situation or problem) difficult to deal with; requiring careful handling: *her skill in evading ticklish questions.* ■ (of a person) easily upset.
– DERIVATIVES **tick·lish·ly** adv., **tick·lish·ness** n.

tick·ly /ˈtik(ə)lē/ ▶ adj. another term for TICKLISH.

tick mark ▶ n. another term for CHECK MARK.

tick·seed /ˈtikˌsēd/ ▶ n. another term for COREOPSIS.
– ORIGIN mid 16th cent.: so named because of the resemblance of the seed to a parasitic tick.

tick-tack-toe ▶ n. variant spelling of TIC-TAC-TOE.

tick-tock /ˈtik ˌtäk/ ▶ n. [in sing.] the sound of a large clock ticking.
▶ v. [no obj.] make a ticking sound: *the clock on the wall was tick-tocking.*
– ORIGIN mid 19th cent.: imitative; compare with TICK¹.

tick tre·foil ▶ n. a tall, spindly leguminous North American plant, the pods of which break up into one-seeded joints that adhere to clothing, animals' fur, etc. ● Genus *Desmodium*, family Leguminosae: several species.

tick·y-tack·y /ˈtikē ˌtakē/ informal ▶ n. inferior or cheap material, esp. as used in suburban building.
▶ adj. (esp. of a building or housing development) made of inferior material; cheap or in poor taste: *ticky-tacky little houses.*
– ORIGIN 1960s: probably a reduplication of TACKY².

Ti·con·der·o·ga /ˌtīkändəˈrōgə/ an industrial village in northeastern New York, in lowlands between lakes George and Champlain; its nearby fort was fought over repeatedly in the 1750s–80s; pop. 4,963 (est. 2008).

tic-tac-toe /ˈtik ˌtak ˈtō/ (also **tick-tack-toe**) ▶ n. a game in which two players seek in alternate turns to complete a row, a column, or a diagonal with either three O's or three X's drawn in the spaces of a grid of nine squares.
– ORIGIN imitative; from *tick-tack*, used earlier to denote games in which the pieces made clicking sounds.

t.i.d. ▶ abbr. (in prescriptions) three times a day.
– ORIGIN from Latin *ter in die.*

tid·al /ˈtīdl/ ▶ adj. of, relating to, or affected by tides: *the river here is not tidal | strong tidal currents.*
– DERIVATIVES **tid·al·ly** adv.

tid·al ba·sin ▶ n. a basin for boats that is accessible or navigable only at high tide.

tid·al bore ▶ n. a large wave caused by the funneling of a flood tide as it enters a long, narrow, shallow inlet.

tid·al farm ▶ n. an installation of turbines used to generate electricity from tidal forces.

tid·al wave ▶ n. an exceptionally large ocean wave, esp. one caused by an underwater earthquake or volcanic eruption (used as a nontechnical term for TSUNAMI). ■ a widespread or overwhelming manifestation of an emotion or phenomenon: *a tidal wave of crime.*

tid·bit /ˈtidˌbit/ (also chiefly Brit. **titbit** /ˈtit-/) ▶ n. a small piece of tasty food. ■ a small and particularly interesting item of gossip or information.
– ORIGIN mid 17th cent. (as *tyd bit, tid-bit*): from dialect *tid* 'tender' (of unknown origin) + BIT¹.

tid·dle·dy·wink /ˈtidl-dēˌwingk/ ▶ n. variant spelling of TIDDLYWINK.

tid·dly /ˈtidlē/ ▶ adj. (**tiddlier, tiddliest**) informal, chiefly Brit. slightly drunk.
– ORIGIN mid 19th cent. (as a noun denoting an alcoholic drink, particularly of spirits): perhaps from slang *tiddlywink*, denoting an unlicensed bar. The current sense dates from the early 20th cent.

tid·dly·wink /ˈtidlēˌwingk/ (also **tiddledywink** /ˈtidl-dē-/) ▶ n. **1** (**tiddlywinks**) a game in which small plastic counters are flicked into a central receptacle by being pressed on the edge with a larger counter.
2 a counter used in such a game.
– ORIGIN mid 19th cent.: of unknown origin; perhaps related to TIDDLY. The word originally denoted an unlicensed bar, also a game of dominoes. Current senses date from the late 19th cent.

tide /tīd/ ▶ n. the alternate rising and falling of the sea, usually twice in each lunar day at a particular place, due to the attraction of the moon and sun: *the changing patterns of the tides | they were driven on by wind and tide.* ■ the water as affected by this: *the rising tide covered the wharf.* ■ a powerful surge of feeling or trend of events: *he drifted into sleep on a tide of euphoria | we must reverse the growing tide of racism sweeping the country.*
▶ v. [no obj.] archaic drift with or as if with the tide. ■ (of a ship) float or drift in or out of a harbor by taking advantage of favoring tides.
– PHRASES **turn the tide** reverse the trend of events: *the air power that helped to turn the tide of battle.*
– PHRASAL VERBS **tide someone over** help someone through a difficult period, esp. with financial assistance: *she needed a small loan to tide her over.*
– DERIVATIVES **tide·less** adj.
– ORIGIN Old English *tīd* 'time, period, era,' of Germanic origin; related to Dutch *tijd* and German *Zeit*, also to TIME. The sense relating to the sea dates from late Middle English.

-tide ▶ comb. form literary denoting a specified time or season: *springtide.* ■ denoting a festival of the Christian Church: *Shrovetide.*

tide·land /ˈtīdˌland/ ▶ n. (also **tidelands**) land that is submerged at high tide.

tide·line /ˈtīdˌlīn/ (also **tide line**) ▶ n. a line left or reached by the sea on a shore at the highest point of a tide.

tide·mark /ˈtīdˌmärk/ ▶ n. a mark left or reached by the sea on a shore at the highest or lowest point of a tide.

tide rip ▶ n. an area of rough water typically caused by opposing currents or by a rapid current passing over an uneven bottom.

tide ta·ble ▶ n. a table indicating the times of high and low tides at a particular place.

tide·wait·er /ˈtīdˌwātər/ ▶ n. historical a customs officer who boarded ships on their arrival to enforce the customs regulations.

Tide·wa·ter /ˈtīdˌwôtər, -ˌwätər/ (**the Tidewater**) coastal regions of eastern Virginia where tidal water flows up the Potomac, Rappahannock, York, James, and smaller rivers. Early-17th-century British settlement was focused here.

tide·wa·ter ▶ n. water brought or affected by tides. ■ an area that is affected by tides: [as modifier] *a large area of tidewater country.*

tide·way /ˈtīdˌwā/ ▶ n. a channel in which a tide runs, esp. the tidal part of a river.

ti·dings /ˈtīdingz/ ▶ plural n. literary news; information: *the bearer of glad tidings.*
– ORIGIN late Old English *tīdung* 'announcement, piece of news,' probably from Old Norse *títhindi* 'news of events,' from *títhr* 'occurring.'

ti·dy /ˈtīdē/ ▶ adj. (**tidier, tidiest**) **1** arranged neatly and in order: *his scrupulously tidy apartment |* figurative *the lives they lead don't fit into tidy patterns.* ■ (of a person) inclined to keep things or one's appearance neat and in order: *she was a tidy little girl.* ■ not messy; neat and controlled: *he wrote down her replies in a small, tidy hand.*
2 [attrib.] informal (of an amount, esp. of money) considerable: *the book will bring in a tidy sum.*
▶ n. (pl. **tidies**) **1** [usu. with modifier] a receptacle for holding small objects or waste scraps: *a desk tidy.*
2 another term for ANTIMACASSAR.
▶ v. (**tidies, tidying, tidied**) [with obj.] bring order to; arrange neatly: *the boys have finally tidied their*

t

bedroom | figurative *the bill is intended to tidy up the law on this matter* | [no obj.] *I'll just go and tidy up.*
– DERIVATIVES **ti·di·ly** /-dilē/ **adv.**, **ti·di·ness n.**
– ORIGIN Middle English: from the noun TIDE + -Y[1]. The original meaning was 'timely, opportune'; it later had various senses expressing approval, usually of a person, including 'attractive,' 'healthy,' and 'skillful'; the sense 'orderly, neat' dates from the early 18th cent.

tie /tī/ ▶ **v.** (**ties, tying** /'tī-iNG/, **tied**) **1** [with obj.] attach or fasten (someone or something) with string or similar cord: *they tied Max to a chair* | *her long hair was tied back in a bow.* ■ fasten (something) to or around someone or something by means of its strings or by forming the ends into a knot or bow: *Lewis tied on his apron.* ■ form (a string, ribbon, or lace) into a knot or bow: *Rick bent to tie his shoelaces.* ■ form (a knot or bow) in this way: *tie a knot in one end of the cotton.* ■ [no obj.] be fastened with a knot or bow: *a sarong that ties at the waist.* ■ restrict or limit (someone) to a particular situation, occupation, or place: *she didn't want to be like her mother, tied to a feckless man.*
2 [with obj.] connect; link: *self-respect is closely* **tied up with** *the esteem in which one is held by one's peers.* ■ hold together by a crosspiece or tie: *ceiling joists are used to tie the rafter feet.* ■ Music unite (written notes) by a tie. ■ Music perform (two notes) as one unbroken note.
3 [no obj.] achieve the same score or ranking as another competitor or team: *he* **tied for** *second in the league* | [with obj.] *Toronto tied the score in the fourth inning.*
▶ **n.** (pl. **ties**) **1** a piece of string, cord, or the like used for fastening or tying something: *he tightened the tie of his robe.* ■ a shoe tied with a lace.
2 a rod or beam holding parts of a structure together. ■ a wooden or concrete beam laid transversely under a railroad track to support it. ■ Music a curved line above or below two notes of the same pitch indicating that they are to be played for the combined duration of their time values.
3 (usu. **ties**) a thing that unites or links people: *it is important that we keep family ties strong.* ■ a thing that restricts someone's freedom of action: *some cities and merchants were freed from feudal ties.*
4 a strip of material worn around the collar and tied in a knot at the front with the ends hanging down, typically forming part of a man's business or formal outfit; a necktie.
5 a result in a game or other competitive situation in which two or more competitors or teams have the same score or ranking; a draw: *there was a tie for first place.*
– PHRASES **fit to be tied** see FIT[1]. **tie someone (up) in knots** see KNOT[1]. **tie the knot** see KNOT[1]. **tie one on** informal get drunk.
– PHRASAL VERBS **tie someone down** restrict someone to a particular situation or place: *she didn't want to be tied down by a full-time job.* **tie something in** (or **tie in**) cause something to fit or harmonize with something else (or fit or harmonize with something): *her husband is able to* **tie in** *his shifts* **with** *hers at the hospital* | *she may have developed ideas that don't necessarily* **tie in with** *mine.* **tie into** informal attack or get to work on vigorously: *tie into breakfast now and let's get a move on.* **tie someone up** bind someone's legs and arms together or bind someone to something so that they cannot move or escape: *robbers tied her up and ransacked her home.* ■ (usu. **be tied up**) informal occupy someone to the exclusion of any other activity: *she would be tied up at the meeting all day.* **tie something up 1** bind or fasten something securely with rope, cord, or string. ■ moor a vessel. ■ (often **be tied up**) invest or reserve capital so that it is not immediately available for use: *money tied up in accounts must be left to grow.* **2** bring something to a satisfactory conclusion; settle: *he said he had a business deal to tie up.*
– DERIVATIVES **tie·less adj.**
– ORIGIN Old English *tīgan* (verb), *tēah* (noun), of Germanic origin.

tie-back (also **tieback**) ▶ **n.** a decorative strip of fabric or cord, typically used for holding an open curtain off to the side of the window.

tie beam ▶ **n.** a horizontal beam connecting two rafters in a roof or roof truss.

tie·break·er /'tī,brākər/ ▶ **n.** a means of deciding a winner from competitors who have tied, in particular (in tennis) a special game to decide the winner of a set when the score is six games all.

tie clasp (also **tie clip**) ▶ **n.** an ornamental clip for holding a tie in place.

tie-down ▶ **n.** rope, cord, straps, or chains used to attach or secure an item. ■ a stationary ring, post, or the like to which items are secured with tie-downs.

tie-dye ▶ **n.** [often as modifier] a method of producing textile patterns by tying parts of the fabric to shield it from the dye: *tie-dye T-shirts.*
▶ **v.** [with obj.] dye (a garment or piece of cloth) by such a process.

tie-in ▶ **n.** a connection or association: *there's a tie-in to another case I'm working on.* ■ a book, movie, or other product produced to take advantage of a related work in another medium. ■ [as modifier] denoting sales made conditional on the purchase of an additional item or items from the same supplier.

tie line ▶ **n.** a transmission line connecting parts of a system, esp. a telephone line connecting two private branch exchanges.

Tien Shan /'tyen 'SHän/ (also **Tian Shan**) a range of mountains that lies north of the Tarim Basin in the Xinjiang autonomous region and eastern Kyrgyzstan. Extending for about 1,500 miles (2,500 km), it rises to 24,406 feet (7,439 m) at Pik Pobedy.

tie·pin /'tī,pin/ ▶ **n.** an ornamental pin for holding a tie in place.

tier /ti(ə)r/ ▶ **n.** a row or level of a structure, typically one of a series of rows placed one above the other and successively receding or diminishing in size: *a tier of seats* | [in combination] *the room was full of three-tier metal bunks.* ■ one of a number of successively overlapping ruffles or flounces on a garment. ■ a level or grade within the hierarchy of an organization or system: *companies have taken out a tier of management to save money.*
– DERIVATIVES **tiered** /ti(ə)rd/ **adj.**
– ORIGIN late 15th cent.: from French *tire* 'sequence, order,' from *tirer* 'elongate, draw.'

tierce /ti(ə)rs/ ▶ **n. 1** another term for TERCE.
2 Music an organ stop sounding two octaves and a major third above the pitch of the diapason.
3 (in piquet) a sequence of three cards of the same suit.
4 Fencing the third of eight standard parrying positions.
5 a former measure of wine equal to one third of a pipe, usually equivalent to 35 gallons (about 156 liters). ■ archaic a cask containing a certain quantity of provisions, the amount varying with the goods.
– ORIGIN late Middle English: variant of TERCE.

tier·cel /'ti(ə)rsəl/ (also **tercel**) ▶ **n.** Falconry the male of a hawk, esp. a peregrine or a goshawk. Compare with FALCON.

tie rod ▶ **n.** a rod acting as a tie in a building or other structure, or in the steering gear of a motor vehicle.

Tier·ra del Fue·go /tē'erə del 'fwāgō/ an island off the southern tip of South America, separated from the mainland by the Strait of Magellan. Discovered by Ferdinand Magellan in 1520, it is now divided between Argentina and Chile.
– ORIGIN Spanish, literally 'land of fire.'

tie tack (also **tie tac**) ▶ **n.** a short pin with an ornamental head, used to attach the ends of a necktie to a shirt front.

tie-up ▶ **n. 1** a link or connection, esp. one between commercial companies: *marketing tie-ups.* ■ a telecommunications link or network.
2 a building where cattle are tied up for the night. ■ a place for mooring a boat.
3 a traffic holdup.

TIFF /tif/ ▶ **n.** Computing a format for image files: [as modifier] *a TIFF image.*
– ORIGIN 1990s: acronym from *tagged image file format.*

tiff /tif/ ▶ **n.** informal a petty quarrel, esp. one between friends or lovers: *Joanna had a tiff with her boyfriend.*
– ORIGIN early 18th cent. (denoting a slight outburst of temper): probably of dialect origin.

Tif·fa·ny /'tifənē/, Louis Comfort (1848–1933), US glassmaker and interior decorator. A leading exponent of art nouveau in the US, he established an interior decorating firm in New York City that produced stained glass, vases, lamps, and mosaic.

tif·fa·ny /'tifənē/ ▶ **n.** thin gauze muslin.
– ORIGIN early 17th cent.: from Old French *tifanie*, via ecclesiastical Latin from Greek *theophaneia* 'epiphany.' The word is usually taken to be short for *Epiphany silk* or *muslin*, i.e., that worn on Twelfth Night, but may be a humorous allusion to *epiphany* in the sense 'manifestation,' tiffany being semitransparent.

tif·fin /'tifin/ ▶ **n.** Indian or dated a light meal, esp. lunch.
– ORIGIN early 19th cent.: apparently from dialect *tiffing* 'sipping,' of unknown origin.

Tif·lis /'tiflis, tə'flēs/ official Russian name (1845–1936) for TBILISI.

Ti·gard /'tīgərd/ a city in northwestern Oregon, a southwestern suburb of Portland; pop. 48,713 (est. 2008).

ti·ger /'tīgər/ ▶ **n.** a very large solitary cat with a yellow-brown coat striped with black, native to the forests of Asia but becoming increasingly rare. ● *Panthera tigris*, family Felidae. ■ used to refer to someone fierce, determined, or ambitious: *despite his wound, he still fought like a tiger* | *one of the sport's young tigers.* ■ (also **tiger economy**) a dynamic economy of one of the smaller eastern Asian countries, esp. that of Singapore, Taiwan, or South Korea.
– PHRASES **have a tiger by the tail** have embarked on a course of action that proves unexpectedly difficult but that cannot easily or safely be abandoned.
– ORIGIN Middle English: from Old French *tigre*, from Latin *tigris*, from Greek.

tiger

ti·ger bee·tle ▶ **n.** a fast-running predatory beetle that has spotted or striped wing cases and flies in sunshine. The larvae live in tunnels from which they snatch passing insect prey. ● Family Cicindelidae: *Cicindela* and other genera.

ti·ger cat ▶ **n.** a small forest cat that has a light brown coat with dark stripes and blotches, native to Central and South America. ● *Felis tigrina*, family Felidae. ■ any moderate-sized striped cat, such as the ocelot, serval, or margay. ■ a domestic cat with markings like a tiger's.

ti·ger e·con·o·my ▶ **n.** see TIGER.

ti·ger·ish /'tīgəriSH/ ▶ **adj.** resembling or likened to a tiger, esp. in being fierce and determined: *she was in a tigerish mood.*
– DERIVATIVES **ti·ger·ish·ly adv.**

ti·ger lil·y ▶ **n.** a tall lily that has orange flowers spotted with black or purple. ● *Lilium lancifolium* (or *tigrinum*), family Liliaceae.

ti·ger ma·ple ▶ **n.** the wood from an American maple that contains contrasting light and dark lines.

ti·ger moth ▶ **n.** a stout moth that has boldly spotted and streaked wings. ● *Arctia* and other genera, family Arctiidae: many species.

ti·ger sal·a·man·der ▶ **n.** a large North American salamander that is blackish with yellow patches or stripes. ● *Ambystoma tigrinum*, family Ambystomatidae.

ti·ger's eye (also **tiger eye**) ▶ **n.** a yellowish-brown semiprecious variety of quartz with a silky or chatoyant luster, formed by replacement of crocidolite with chalcedony.

ti·ger shark ▶ **n.** an aggressive shark of warm seas, with dark vertical stripes on the body. ● *Galeocerdo cuvieri*, family Carcharhinidae.

ti·ger shrimp ▶ **n.** a large edible shrimp marked with dark bands, found in the Indian and Pacific oceans. ● Genus *Penaeus*, class Malacostraca: several species, in particular the widely farmed *P. monodon.*

ti·ger team ▶ **n.** a team of specialists in a particular field brought together to work on specific tasks.

tight /tīt/ ▶ **adj. 1** fixed, fastened, or closed firmly; hard to move, undo, or open: *she twisted her handkerchief into a tight knot.* ■ (of clothes or shoes) close-fitting, esp. uncomfortably so: *the dress was too tight for her.* ■ (of a grip) very firm so as not to let go: *she released her tight hold on the dog* | figurative *presidential advisers* **keep a tight grip on** *domestic policy.* ■ (of a ship, building, or object) well sealed against something such as water or air: [in combination] *a light-tight container.* ■ (of a formation or a group of people or things) closely or densely packed together: *he levered the bishop out from a tight knot of clerical wives.* ■ (of a community or other group of people) having close relations; secretive: *the tenants were far too tight to let anyone know.*
2 (of a rope, fabric, or surface) stretched so as to leave no slack; not loose: *the drawcord pulls tight.* ■ (of a part of the body or a bodily sensation) feeling painful and constricted, as a result of anxiety or illness: *there was a tight feeling in his gut.* ■ (of appearance or manner) tense, irritated, or angry: *she gave him a tight smile.* ■ (of a rule, policy, or form of control) strictly imposed: *security was tight at yesterday's ceremony.* ■ (of a game or contest) with evenly matched competitors; very close: *he won in a tight finish.* ■ (of a written work or form)

PRONUNCIATION KEY ə *ago, up*; ər *over, fur*; a *hat*; ā *ate*; ä *car*; e *let*; ē *see*; i *fit*; ī *by*; NG *sing*; ō *go*; ô *law, for*; oi *toy*; o͝o *good*; o͞o *goo*; ou *out*; TH *thin*; TH *then*; ZH *vision*

concise, condensed, or well structured: *a tight argument.* ■ (of an organization or group of people) disciplined or professional; well coordinated: *the vocalists are strong, and the band is tight.*
3 (of an area or space) having or allowing little room for maneuver: *a tight parking spot* | *it was a tight squeeze in the tiny vestibule.* ■ (of a bend, turn, or angle) changing direction sharply; having a short radius. ■ (of money or time) limited or restricted: *David was out of work and money was tight* | *an ability to work to tight deadlines.* ■ informal (of a person) not willing to spend or give much money; stingy.
4 [predic.] informal drunk: *later, at the club, he got tight on brandy.*
▶ **adv.** very firmly, closely, or tensely: *he went downstairs, holding tight to the banisters.*
– PHRASES **run a tight ship** be very strict in managing an organization or operation. **a tight corner** (or **spot** or **place**) a difficult situation: *her talent for talking her way out of tight corners.*
– DERIVATIVES **tight·ly** adv., **tight·ness** n.
– ORIGIN Middle English (in the sense 'healthy, vigorous,' later 'firm, solid'): probably an alteration of *thight* 'firm, solid,' later 'close-packed, dense,' of Germanic origin; related to German *dicht* 'dense, close.'

tight-ass ▶ **n.** informal an inhibited, repressed, or excessively conventional person.
– DERIVATIVES **tight-assed** adj.

tight·en /ˈtītn/ ▶ **v.** make or become tight or tighter: [with obj.] *tighten the bolts* | [no obj.] *the revenue laws were tightening up.*
– PHRASES **tighten one's belt** see BELT. **tighten the screw** see SCREW.

tight end ▶ **n.** Football an offensive end who lines up close to the tackle.

tight·fist·ed /ˈtītˈfistid/ ▶ **adj.** informal not willing to spend or give much money; miserly.

tight-fit·ting ▶ **adj.** (of a garment) fitting close to and showing the contours of the body. ■ (of a lid or cover) forming a tight seal when placed on a container.

tight junc·tion ▶ **n.** Biology a specialized connection of two adjacent animal cell membranes such that the space usually lying between them is absent.

tight-knit (also **tightly knit**) ▶ **adj.** (of a group of people) united or bound together by strong relationships and common interests: *tight-knit mining communities.*

tight-lipped ▶ **adj.** with the lips firmly closed, esp. as a sign of suppressed emotion or determined reticence: *she stayed tight-lipped and shook her head* | figurative *a group of tight-lipped air force officers.*

tight mon·ey ▶ **n.** Finance money or financing that is available only at high rates of interest.

tight·rope /ˈtītˌrōp/ ▶ **n.** a rope or wire stretched tightly high above the ground, on which acrobats perform feats of balancing: [as modifier] *a tightrope walker* | figurative *he continues to walk a tightrope between success and failure.*
▶ **v.** [no obj.] walk or perform on such a rope.

tights /tīts/ ▶ **plural n.** a woman's thin, close-fitting garment, typically made of nylon, cotton, or wool, covering the lower half of the body. ■ a similar garment worn by a dancer or acrobat.

tight·wad /ˈtītˌwäd/ ▶ **n.** informal a mean or miserly person.

tigh·ty-whi·ties /ˌtītē ˈ(h)wītēz/ ▶ **n.** informal men's white cotton briefs.

t

Tig·lath-pi·le·ser /ˌtiglaTH pīˈlēzər/ the name of three kings of Assyria, notably. ■ **Tiglath-pileser I**, reigned *c.*1115–*c.*1077 BC. He extended Assyrian territory by taking Cappadocia, reaching Syria, and defeating the king of Babylonia. ■ **Tiglath-pileser III**, reigned *c.*745–727 BC. He brought the Assyrian empire to the height of its power by subduing large parts of Syria and Palestine, and he conquered Babylonia.

ti·gnon /ˈtēyôN, tēˈyôN/ ▶ **n.** a piece of cloth worn as a turban headdress by Creole women from Louisiana.
– ORIGIN Louisana French, from French *tigne*, dialect variant of *teigne* 'moth.'

ti·gon /ˈtīgən/ (also **tiglon** /-glən/) ▶ **n.** the hybrid offspring of a male tiger and a lioness.
– ORIGIN 1920s: portmanteau word from TIGER and LION.

Ti·gray /təˈgrā/ (also **Tigre**) a province of Ethiopia, in the north of the country, bordering Eritrea. Tigray engaged in a bitter guerrilla war against the government of Ethiopia 1975–91, during which time the region suffered badly from drought and famine.
– DERIVATIVES **Ti·gray·an** /-ˈgrāən/ (also **Tigrean**) adj. & n.

Ti·gre /ˈtēgrā/ ▶ **n.** a Semitic language spoken in Eritrea and adjoining parts of Sudan. It is not the language of Tigray, which is Tigrinya.
– ORIGIN the name in Tigre.

ti·gress /ˈtīgris/ ▶ **n.** a female tiger. ■ a fierce or passionate woman.

Ti·grin·ya /tiˈgrēnyə/ ▶ **n.** a Semitic language spoken in Tigray. Compare with TIGRE.
– ORIGIN the name in Tigrinya.

Ti·gris /ˈtīgris/ a river in southwestern Asia. It rises in the mountains of eastern Turkey and flows southeast for 1,150 miles (1,850 km) through Iraq, passing through Baghdad, to join the Euphrates River to form the Shatt al-Arab, which flows into the Persian Gulf.

Ti·hwa /ˈdēˈhwä/ former name (until 1954) for URUMQI.

Ti·jua·na /ˌtēəˈwänə, tēˈhwänə/ a town in northwestern Mexico, just south of the US border; pop. 1,286,187 (2005).

Ti·kal /tēˈkäl/ an ancient Mayan city in northern Guatemala. It flourished AD 300–800.

tike ▶ **n.** variant spelling of TYKE.

ti·ki /ˈtēkē/ ▶ **n.** (pl. **tikis**) NZ a large wooden or small greenstone image of a human figure.
– ORIGIN Maori, literally 'image.'

tik·ka /ˈtikə, ˈtē-/ ▶ **n.** [usu. with modifier] an Indian dish of small pieces of meat or vegetables marinated in a spice mixture.
– ORIGIN from Punjabi *ṭikkā.*

til·ak /ˈtilək/ ▶ **n.** a mark worn by a Hindu on the forehead to indicate caste, status, or sect, or as an ornament.
– ORIGIN from Sanskrit *tilaka.*

ti·la·pi·a /təˈläpēə/ ▶ **n.** an African freshwater cichlid fish that has been widely introduced to many areas for food. ● *Tilapia* and related genera, family Cichlidae: several species.
– ORIGIN modern Latin, of unknown origin.

Til·burg /ˈtilˌbərg/ an industrial city in the southern Netherlands, in the province of North Brabant; pop. 202,091 (2008).

Til·bur·y /ˈtilbərē, -ˌberē/ the principal container port of London and southeastern England, on the northern bank of the Thames River.

til·bur·y /ˈtilˌberē, -bərē/ ▶ **n.** (pl. **tilburies**) historical a light, open two-wheeled carriage.
– ORIGIN early 19th cent.: named after its inventor.

til·de /ˈtildə/ ▶ **n.** an accent (~) placed over Spanish *n* when pronounced *ny* (as in *señor*) or Portuguese *a* or *o* when nasalized (as in *São Paulo*), or over a vowel in phonetic transcription, indicating nasalization. ■ the same symbol as a part of a URL. ■ a similar symbol used in mathematics to indicate similarity, and in logic to indicate negation.
– ORIGIN mid 19th cent.: from Spanish, based on Latin *titulus* (see TITLE).

Til·den /ˈtildən/, Bill (1893–1953), US tennis player; full name *William Tatem Tilden II.* During 1920–30, he won the men's singles title at seven US Open and three Wimbledon tournaments. He led the US to seven straight Davis Cup victories 1920–26.

tile /tīl/ ▶ **n.** a thin rectangular slab of baked clay, concrete, or other material, used in overlapping rows for covering roofs. ■ a thin square slab of glazed ceramic, cork, linoleum, or other material for covering floors, walls, or other surfaces. ■ a thin, flat piece used in Scrabble, mah-jongg, and certain other games. ■ Mathematics a plane shape used in tiling.
▶ **v.** [with obj.] (usu. **be tiled**) cover (something) with tiles: *the lobby was tiled in blue.* ■ Computing arrange (two or more windows) on a computer screen so that they do not overlap.
– PHRASES **on the tiles** informal, chiefly Brit. having a lively night out: *it won't be the first time he's spent a night on the tiles.*
– ORIGIN Old English *tigele*, from Latin *tegula*, from an Indo-European root meaning 'cover.'

tile·fish /ˈtīlˌfiSH/ ▶ **n.** (pl. **same** or **tilefishes**) a long, slender bottom-dwelling fish of warm seas. ● Several species in the family Malacanthidae (or Branchiostegidae), in particular the large and edible *Lopholatilus chamaeleonticeps* of the Atlantic coast of North America.

til·er /ˈtīlər/ ▶ **n. 1** a person who lays tiles: *a roof tiler.*
2 the doorkeeper of a Masonic lodge, who prevents outsiders from entering.

til·ing /ˈtīliNG/ ▶ **n.** a surface covered by tiles: *an area of plain tiling.* ■ Mathematics a way of arranging identical plane shapes so that they completely cover an area without overlapping.

till[1] /til/ ▶ **prep. & conj.** less formal way of saying UNTIL.
– ORIGIN Old English *til*, of Germanic origin; related to Old Norse *til* 'to,' also ultimately to TILL[3].

> **USAGE** In most contexts, till and until have the same meaning and are interchangeable. The main difference is that till is generally considered to be more informal than until. Until occurs much more frequently than till in writing. In addition, until tends to be the natural choice at the beginning of a sentence: *until very recently, there was still a chance of rescuing the situation.* Interestingly, while it is commonly assumed that till is an abbreviated form of until (the spellings 'till and 'til reflect this), till is in fact the earlier form. Until appears to have been formed by the addition of Old Norse *und* ('as far as') several hundred years after the date of the first records for till.

till[2] ▶ **n.** a cash register or drawer for money in a store, bank, or restaurant.
– PHRASES **have** (or **with**) **one's fingers** (or **hand**) **in the till** used in reference to theft from one's place of work: *he was caught with his hand in the till and sacked.*
– ORIGIN late Middle English (in the general sense 'drawer or compartment for valuables'): of unknown origin.

till[3] ▶ **v.** [with obj.] prepare and cultivate (land) for crops: *no land was being tilled or crops sown.*
– DERIVATIVES **till·a·ble** adj.
– ORIGIN Old English *tilian* 'strive for, obtain by effort,' of Germanic origin; related to Dutch *telen* 'produce, cultivate' and German *zielen* 'aim, strive,' also ultimately to TILL[1]. The current sense dates from Middle English.

till[4] ▶ **n.** Geology a sediment consisting of particles of various sizes and deposited by melting glaciers or ice sheets.
– ORIGIN late 17th cent. (originally Scots, denoting shale): of unknown origin.

till·age /ˈtilij/ ▶ **n.** the preparation of land for growing crops. ■ land under cultivation: *forty acres of tillage.*

till·er[1] /ˈtilər/ ▶ **n.** a horizontal bar fitted to the head of a boat's rudder post and used as a lever for steering.
– ORIGIN late Middle English: from Anglo-Norman French *telier* 'weaver's beam, stock of a crossbow,' from medieval Latin *telarium*, from Latin *tela* 'web.'

till·er[2] ▶ **n.** an implement or machine for breaking up soil; a plow or cultivator.

till·er[3] ▶ **n.** a lateral shoot from the base of the stem, esp. in a grass or cereal.
▶ **v.** [no obj.] (usu. as noun **tillering**) develop tillers.
– ORIGIN mid 17th cent. (denoting a sapling arising from the stool of a felled tree): apparently based on Old English *telga* 'bough,' of Germanic origin.

Til·lich /ˈtilik/, Paul (Johannes) (1886–1965), US theologian and philosopher, born in Germany. He proposed a form of Christian existentialism, outlining a reconciliation of religion and secular society, as expounded in *Systematic Theology* (1951–63).

till·ite /ˈtilīt/ ▶ **n.** Geology sedimentary rock composed of lithified glacial till.

Til·sit /ˈtilsit, -zit/ ▶ **n.** a semihard mildly flavored cheese.
– ORIGIN named after the town in East Prussia (now Sovetsk, Russia) where it was first produced.

tilt /tilt/ ▶ **v. 1** move or cause to move into a sloping position: [no obj.] *the floor tilted slightly* | [with obj.] *he tilted his head to one side.* ■ change or cause to change in favor of one person or thing as opposed to another: [no obj.] *the balance of industrial power tilted towards the workers.* ■ [with obj.] move (a camera) in a vertical plane.
2 [no obj.] (**tilt at**) historical (in jousting) thrust at with a lance or other weapon: *he tilts at his prey* | figurative *the lonely hero tilting at the system.* ■ (**tilt with**) archaic engage in a contest with: *I resolved never to tilt with a French lady in compliment.*
▶ **n. 1** a sloping position or movement: *the tilt of her head* | *the coffee cup was on a tilt.* ■ an upward or downward pivoting movement of a camera: *pans and tilts.* ■ an inclination or bias: *the paper's tilt toward the Republicans.* ■ short for TILT HAMMER.
2 historical a combat for exercise or sport between two men on horseback with lances; a joust. ■ (**tilt at**) an attempt at winning (something) or defeating (someone), esp. in sports: *a tilt at the championship.*
– PHRASES (**at**) **full tilt** with maximum energy or force; at top speed. **tilt at windmills** attack imaginary enemies or evils. [with allusion to the story of Don Quixote tilting at windmills, believing they were giants.]
– DERIVATIVES **tilt·er** n.
– ORIGIN late Middle English (in the sense 'fall or cause to fall, topple'): perhaps related to Old English *tealt* 'unsteady,' or perhaps of Scandinavian origin

and related to Norwegian *tylten* 'unsteady' and Swedish *tulta* 'totter.'

tilth /tilTH/ ▶ **n.** cultivation of land; tillage. ■ [in sing.] the condition of tilled soil, esp. in respect to suitability for sowing seeds: *he could determine whether the soil was of the right tilth.* ■ prepared surface soil.
– ORIGIN Old English *tilth, tilthe*, from *tilian* (see TILL[3]).

tilt ham·mer ▶ **n.** a heavy pivoted hammer used in forging, raised mechanically and allowed to drop on the metal being worked.

tilt yard ▶ **n.** historical a place where jousts took place.

Tim. ▶ **abbr.** Bible Timothy.

tim·bal /'timbəl/ (also **tymbal**) ▶ **n. 1** archaic a kettledrum.
2 a membrane that forms part of the sound-producing organ in various insects, as the cicada.
– ORIGIN late 17th cent.: from French *timbale*, alteration (influenced by *cymbale* 'cymbal') of obsolete *tamballe*, from Spanish *atabal*, from Arabic *at-tabl* 'the drum.'

tim·bale /'timbəl, tim'bäl/ ▶ **n. 1** a dish of finely minced meat or fish cooked with other ingredients in a pastry shell or in a mold.
2 (**timbales**) paired cylindrical drums played with sticks in Latin American dance music.
– ORIGIN French, 'drum' (in sense 1 with reference to the shape of the prepared dish; in sense 2 short for *timbales cubains* or *timbales creoles* 'Cuban' or 'creole drums').

tim·ber /'timbər/ ▶ **n.** wood prepared for use in building and carpentry: *the exploitation of forests for timber* | [as modifier] *a small timber building.* ■ trees grown for such wood: *contracts to cut timber.* ■ (usu. **timbers**) a wooden beam or board used in building a house, ship, or other structure. ■ [as exclamation] used to warn that a tree is about to fall after being cut: *we cried "Timber!" as our tree fell.* ■ [usu. with adj.] personal qualities or character, esp. as seen as suitable for a particular role: *she is frequently hailed as presidential timber.*
– ORIGIN Old English in the sense 'a building,' also 'building material,' of Germanic origin; related to German *Zimmer* 'room,' from an Indo-European root meaning 'build.'

tim·bered /'timbərd/ ▶ **adj. 1** (of a building) made wholly or partly of timber: *black-and-white timbered buildings.* ■ (of the walls or other surface of a room) covered with wooden panels: *the timbered banqueting hall.*
2 having many trees; wooded.

tim·ber hitch ▶ **n.** a knot used to attach a rope to a log or spar.
– DERIVATIVES **tim·ber-hitch** **v.**

tim·ber·ing /'timb(ə)riNG/ ▶ **n.** wood as a building material, or finished work built from wood.

tim·ber·land /'timbər,land/ ▶ **n.** (also **timberlands**) land covered with forest suitable or managed for timber.

tim·ber·line /'timbər,līn/ ▶ **n.** (on a mountain) the line or altitude above which no trees grow. Also called TREE LINE. ■ (in high northern (or southern) latitudes) the line north (or south) of which no trees grow.

tim·ber wolf ▶ **n.** a wolf of a large variety found mainly in northern North America, with gray brindled fur. Also called GRAY WOLF.

tim·ber yard ▶ **n.** Brit. a lumberyard.

tim·bre /'tambər, 'tänbrə/ ▶ **n.** the character or quality of a musical sound or voice as distinct from its pitch and intensity: *trumpet mutes with different timbres* | *a voice high in pitch but rich in timbre.*
– ORIGIN mid 19th cent.: from French, from medieval Greek *timbanon*, from Greek *tumpanon* 'drum.'

tim·brel /'timbrəl/ ▶ **n.** archaic a tambourine or similar instrument.
– ORIGIN early 16th cent.: perhaps a diminutive of obsolete *timbre*, in the same sense, from Old French (see TIMBRE).

Tim·buk·tu /,timbək'tōō/ (also **Timbuctoo**) a town in northern Mali; pop. 35,600 (est. 2009). Formerly a major trading center for gold and salt on the trans-Saharan trade routes, it reached the height of its prosperity in the 16th century but fell into decline after its capture by the Moroccans in 1591. French name **Tombouctou**. ■ used in reference to a remote or extremely distant place: *from here to Timbuktu.*

time /tīm/ ▶ **n. 1** the indefinite continued progress of existence and events in the past, present, and future regarded as a whole: *travel through space and time* | *one of the greatest wits of all time.* ■ the progress of this as affecting people and things: *things were getting better as time passed.* ■ time or an amount of time as reckoned by a conventional standard: *it's eight o'clock Eastern Standard Time.* ■ (**Time** or **Father Time**) the personification of time, typically as an old man with a scythe and hourglass.
2 a point of time as measured in hours and minutes past midnight or noon: *the time is 9:30.* ■ a moment or definite portion of time allotted, used, or suitable for a purpose: *the scheduled departure time* | *should we set a time for the meeting?* ■ (often **time for/to do something**) the favorable or appropriate time to do something; the right moment: *it was time to go* | *it's time for bed.* ■ (**a time**) an indefinite period: *traveling always distorts one's feelings for a time.* ■ (also **times**) a more or less definite portion of time in history or characterized by particular events or circumstances: *Victorian times* | *at the time of Galileo* | *the park is beautiful at this time of year.* ■ (also **times**) the conditions of life during a particular period: *times have changed.* ■ (**the Times**) used in names of newspapers: *The New York Times.* ■ (**one's time**) one's lifetime: *I've known a lot of women in my time.* ■ (**one's time**) the successful, fortunate, or influential part of a person's life or career: *in my time that was unheard of.* ■ (**one's time**) the appropriate or expected time for something, in particular childbirth or death: *he seemed old before his time.* ■ an apprenticeship: *all of our foremen **served their time** on the loading dock.* ■ dated a period of menstruation or pregnancy. ■ the normal rate of pay for time spent working: *if called out on weekends, they are paid **time and a half**.* ■ the length of time taken to run a race or complete an event or journey: *his time for the mile was 3:49.31.* ■ (in sports) a moment at which play is stopped temporarily within a game, or the act of calling for this: *the umpire **called time**.* ■ Soccer the end of the game: *he scored five minutes from time.*
3 time as allotted, available, or used: *we need more time* | *it would be a waste of time.* ■ informal a prison sentence: *he was **doing time** for fraud.*
4 an instance of something happening or being done; an occasion: *this is the first time I have gotten into debt* | *the nurse came in four times a day.* ■ an event, occasion, or period experienced in a particular way: *we had a good time* | *she was **having a rough time of it**.*
5 (**times**) (following a number) expressing multiplication: *five goes into fifteen three times* | *it burns calories four times faster than walking.*
6 the rhythmic pattern of a piece of music, as expressed by a time signature: *tunes **in** waltz **time**.* ■ the tempo at which a piece of music is played or marked to be played.
▶ **v. 1** [with obj. or infinitive] plan, schedule, or arrange when (something) should happen or be done: *the first track race is timed for 11:15* | *the bomb had been timed to go off an hour later.* ■ perform (an action) at a particular moment: *Williams timed his pass perfectly from about thirty yards.*
2 [with obj.] measure the time taken by (a process or activity, or a person doing it): *we were timed and given certificates according to our speed* | [with clause] *I timed how long it took to empty that tanker.*
3 [with obj.] (**time something out**) Computing (of a computer or a program) cancel an operation automatically because a predefined interval of time has passed without a certain event happening. ■ (**time out**) (of an operation) be canceled in this way.
– PHRASES **about time** used to convey that something now happening or about to happen should have happened earlier: *it's about time I came clean and admitted it.* **against time** with utmost speed, so as to finish by a specified time: *he was working against time.* **ahead of time** earlier than expected or required. **ahead of one's time** having ideas too enlightened or advanced to be accepted by one's contemporaries. **all the time** at all times. ■ very frequently or regularly: *we were in and out of each other's houses all the time.* **at one time** in or during a known but unspecified past period: *she was a nurse at one time.* **at the same time 1** simultaneously; at once. **2** nevertheless (used to introduce a fact that should be taken into account): *I can't really explain it, but at the same time I'm not convinced.* **at a time** separately in the specified groups or numbers: *he took the stairs two at a time.* **at times** sometimes; on occasions. **before time** before the due or expected time. **behind time** late. **behind the times** not aware of or using the latest ideas or techniques; out of date. **for the time being** for the present; until some other arrangement is made. **give someone the time of day** [usu. with negative] be pleasantly polite or friendly to someone: *I wouldn't give him the time of day if I could help it.* **half the time** as often as not. **have no time for** be unable or unwilling to spend time on: *he had no time for anything except essays and projects.* ■ dislike or disapprove of: *he's got no time for airheads.* **have the time 1** be able to spend the time needed to do something: *she didn't have the time to look very closely.* **2** know from having a watch what time it is. **in (less than) no time** very quickly or very soon: *the video has sold 30,000 copies in no time.* **in one's own time** (also **in one's own good time**) at a time and a rate decided by oneself. **in time 1** not late; punctual: *I came back **in time for** Molly's party.* **2** eventually: *there is the danger that he might, in time, not be able to withstand temptation.* **3** in accordance with the appropriate musical rhythm or tempo. **keep good** (or **bad**) **time 1** (of a clock or watch) record time accurately (or inaccurately). **2** (of a person) be habitually punctual (or not punctual). **keep time** play or rhythmically accompany music in time. **lose no time** do a specified thing immediately or as soon as possible: *the administration **lost no time** in trying to regain the initiative.* **no time** a very short interval or period: *the renovations were done **in no time**.* **on one's own time** outside working hours; without being paid. **on time** punctual; punctually: *the train was on time* | *we paid our bills on time.* **out of time 1** at the wrong time or period: *I felt that I was born out of time.* ■ not following or maintaining the correct rhythm (of music): *every time we get to this part in the song, you are out of time.* **2** with no time remaining to continue or complete something, esp. a task for which a specific amount of time had been allowed: *I knew the answers to all the essay questions, but I **ran out of time**.* **pass the time of day** exchange greetings or casual remarks. **time after time** (also **time and again** or **time and time again**) on very many occasions; repeatedly. **time and tide wait for no man** proverb if you don't make use of a favorable opportunity, you may never get the same chance again. **time immemorial** used to refer to a point of time in the past that was so long ago that people have no knowledge or memory of it: *markets had been held there **from time immemorial**.* **time is money** proverb time is a valuable resource, therefore it is better to do things as quickly as possible. **the time of one's life** a period or occasion of exceptional enjoyment. **time out of mind** another way of saying TIME IMMEMORIAL. **time was** there was a time when: *time was, each street had its own specialized trade.* (**only**) **time will tell** the truth or correctness of something will (only) be established at some time in the future.
– ORIGIN Old English *tīma*, of Germanic origin; related to TIDE, which it superseded in temporal senses. The earliest of the current verb senses (dating from late Middle English) is 'do (something) at a particular moment.'

time-and-mo·tion stud·y ▶ **n.** a procedure in which the efficiency of an industrial or other operation is evaluated.

time base ▶ **n.** Electronics a signal for uniformly and repeatedly deflecting the electron beam of a cathode ray tube. ■ a line on the display produced in this way and serving as a time axis.

time bomb ▶ **n.** a bomb designed to explode at a preset time. ■ a process or procedure causing a problem that will eventually become dangerous if not addressed: *an environmental time bomb.*

time cap·sule ▶ **n.** a container storing a selection of objects chosen as being typical of the present time, buried for discovery in the future.

time·card /'tīm'kärd/ ▶ **n.** a card used to record an employee's starting and quitting times, usually stamped by a time clock.

time clock ▶ **n.** a clock with a device for recording employees' times of arrival and departure.

time code ▶ **n.** Electronics a coded signal on videotape or film giving information about such things as frame number, time of recording, or exposure.

time con·stant ▶ **n.** Physics a time that represents the speed with which a particular system can respond to change, typically equal to the time taken for a specified parameter to vary by a factor of $1-1/e$ (approximately 0.6321).

time-con·sum·ing ▶ **adj.** taking a lot of or too much time: *an extremely time-consuming process.*

time de·pos·it ▶ **n.** a deposit in a bank account that cannot be withdrawn before a set date or for which notice of withdrawal is required.

time dif·fer·ence ▶ **n. 1** the difference in standard time between places in different time zones.
2 the difference in the time at which two things happen or in how long they occur.

time di·vi·sion mul·ti·plex·ing ▶ **n.** Telecommunications a technique for transmitting two or more signals over the same telephone line, radio channel, or other medium. Each signal is sent as a series of pulses or packets, which are interleaved with those of the other signal or signals and transmitted as a continuous stream. Compare with FREQUENCY DIVISION MULTIPLEXING.

PRONUNCIATION KEY ə *ago, up*; ər *over, fur*; a *hat*; ā *ate*; ä *car*; e *let*; ē *see*; i *fit*; ī *by*; NG *sing*; ō *go*; ô *law, for*; oi *toy*; ŏŏ *good*; ōō *goo*; ou *out*; TH *thin*; TH *then*; ZH *vision*

t

time do·main ▶ **n.** Physics time considered as an independent variable in the analysis or measurement of time-dependent phenomena.

time do·main re·flec·tom·e·ter ▶ **n.** see REFLECTOMETER.

time ex·po·sure ▶ **n.** the exposure of photographic film for longer than the maximum normal shutter setting.

time frame ▶ **n.** a period of time, esp. a specified period in which something occurs or is planned to take place: *the work had to be done in a time frame of fourteen working days.*

time-hon·ored ▶ **adj.** [attrib.] (of a custom or tradition) respected or valued because it has existed for a long time.

time·keep·er /ˈtīmˌkēpər/ ▶ **n. 1** a person who measures or records the amount of time taken, esp. in a sports competition.
2 [usu. with adj.] a person regarded as being punctual or not punctual: *we were good timekeepers.*
■ a watch or clock regarded as recording time accurately or inaccurately: *these watches are accurate timekeepers.* ■ archaic a clock.
– DERIVATIVES **time·keep·ing** /-ˌkēpiNG/ **n.**

time lag ▶ **n.** see LAG¹ (sense 1 of the noun).

time-lapse ▶ **adj.** denoting the photographic technique of taking a sequence of frames at set intervals to record changes that take place slowly over time. When the frames are shown at normal speed, or in quick succession, the action seems much faster.

time·less /ˈtīmlis/ ▶ **adj.** not affected by the passage of time or changes in fashion: *antiques add to the timeless atmosphere of the dining room.*
– DERIVATIVES **time·less·ly adv.**, **time·less·ness n.**

time lim·it ▶ **n.** a limit of time within which something must be done.

time·line /ˈtīmˌlīn/ (also **time line**) ▶ **n.** a graphic representation of the passage of time as a line.

time lock ▶ **n.** a lock fitted with a device that prevents it from being unlocked until a set time. ■ a device built into a computer program to stop it from operating after a certain time.
▶ **v.** (**time-lock**) [with obj.] secure (a door or other locking mechanism) with a time lock. ■ link (something) inextricably to a certain period of time: *an overdone theme tends to time-lock a setting and stifle imagination.*

time·ly /ˈtīmlē/ ▶ **adj.** done or occurring at a favorable or useful time; opportune: *a timely warning.*
– DERIVATIVES **time·li·ness n.**

time ma·chine ▶ **n.** (in science fiction) a machine capable of transporting a person backward or forward in time.

time off ▶ **n.** time for rest or recreation away from one's usual work or studies: *we're too busy to take time off.*

time·ous /ˈtīməs/ ▶ **adj.** chiefly Scottish in good time; sufficiently early: *ensure timeous completion and posting of applications.*
– DERIVATIVES **time·ous·ly adv.**

time out ▶ **n. 1** time for rest or recreation away from one's usual work or studies: *she is taking time out from her hectic tour.* ■ (usu. **timeout** or **time-out**) a brief break in play in a game or sport: *he inadvertently called for a timeout with two seconds remaining.* ■ (also **timeout** or **time-out**) an imposed temporary suspension of activities, esp. the separation of a misbehaving child from one or more playmates as a disciplinary measure: *it's the third time this week he's been in time-out.*
2 (usu. **timeout**) Computing a cancellation or cessation that automatically occurs when a predefined interval of time has passed without a certain event occurring.

time·piece /ˈtīmˌpēs/ ▶ **n.** an instrument, such as a clock or watch, for measuring time.

tim·er /ˈtīmər/ ▶ **n. 1** an automatic mechanism for activating a device at a preset time: *a video timer.* ■ a person or device that measures or records the amount of time taken by a process or activity.
2 [in combination] used to indicate how many times someone has done something: *for most first-timers the success rate is 45 percent.*

time-re·lease ▶ **adj.** denoting something, esp. a medicine, that releases an active substance gradually.

times /tīmz/ ▶ **prep.** multiplied by: *eleven times four is forty-four.*
– ORIGIN see TIME (sense 5 of the noun).

time·sav·ing /ˈtīmˌsāviNG/ ▶ **adj.** (of a device, method, etc.) reducing the time spent or required through greater efficiency or a shorter route.
– DERIVATIVES **time·sav·er** /-ˌsāvər/ **n.**

time·scale /ˈtīmˌskāl/ ▶ **n.** the time allowed for or taken by a process or sequence of events: *climatic changes on a timescale of thousands of years.*

time se·ries ▶ **n.** Statistics a series of values of a quantity obtained at successive times, often with equal intervals between them.

time-serv·er ▶ **n. 1** a person who changes their views to suit the prevailing circumstances or fashion.
2 a person who makes very little effort at work because they are waiting to leave or retire.
3 (**time server**) Computing a server that distributes synchronized time information to all members of a network.
– DERIVATIVES **time-serv·ing adj.**

time·share /ˈtīmˌSHe(ə)r/ ▶ **n.** the arrangement whereby several joint owners have the right to use a property as a vacation home under a time-sharing scheme: *a growing interest in timeshare.* ■ a property owned in such a way.

time-shar·ing ▶ **n. 1** the operation of a computer system by several users for different operations at the same time.
2 the use of a property as a vacation home at specified times by several joint owners.

time sheet (also **timesheet** /ˈtīmˌSHēt/) ▶ **n.** a piece of paper for recording the number of hours worked.

time-shift ▶ **v. 1** [no obj.] move from one period in time to another.
2 [with obj.] record (a television program) for later viewing.
▶ **n.** (**time shift**) a movement from one period in time to another, esp. in a play or movie.

time sig·na·ture ▶ **n.** Music an indication of rhythm following a clef, generally expressed as a fraction with the denominator defining the beat as a division of a whole note and the numerator giving the number of beats in each bar.

time slice ▶ **n.** Computing a short interval of time during which a computer or its central processor deals uninterruptedly with one user or program, before switching to another.

Times Square /tīmz/ a focal point of Manhattan in New York City, around the intersection of Broadway and 42nd Street.

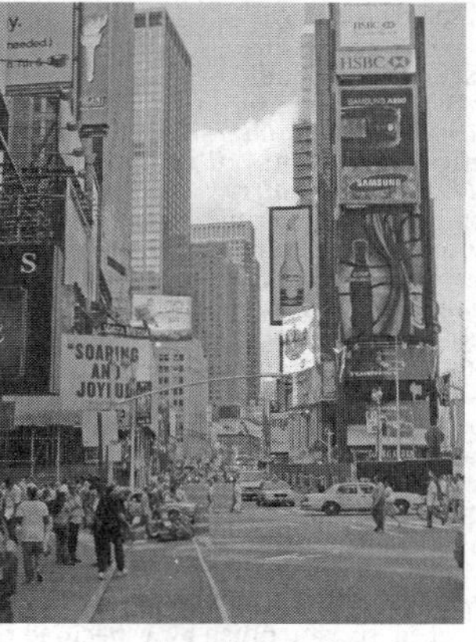

Times Square

times ta·ble ▶ **n.** informal term for MULTIPLICATION TABLE.

time·ta·ble /ˈtīmˌtābəl/ ▶ **n.** a chart showing the departure and arrival times of trains, buses, or planes. ■ a plan of times at which events are scheduled to take place, esp. toward a particular end: *the timetable for a military coup.*
▶ **v.** [with obj.] schedule (something) to take place at a particular time: *German lessons were timetabled on Wednesday and Friday.*

time trav·el ▶ **n.** (in science fiction) the action of traveling through time into the past or the future.
– DERIVATIVES **time-trav·el v.**, **time trav·el·er n.**

time tri·al ▶ **n.** (in various sports) a test of a competitor's individual speed over a set distance, esp. a cycling race in which competitors are separately timed.

time warp ▶ **n.** (esp. in science fiction) an imaginary distortion of space in relation to time whereby people or objects of one period can be moved to another.

time·worn /ˈtīmˌwôrn/ ▶ **adj.** damaged or impaired, or made less striking or attractive, as a result of age or much use: *the timeworn faces of the veterans | a timeworn aphorism.*

time zone ▶ **n.** see ZONE (sense 1 of the noun).

tim·id /ˈtimid/ ▶ **adj.** (**timider**, **timidest**) showing a lack of courage or confidence; easily frightened: *I was too timid to ask for what I wanted.*
– DERIVATIVES **ti·mid·i·ty** /təˈmiditē/ **n.**, **tim·id·ly adv.**, **tim·id·ness n.**
– ORIGIN mid 16th cent.: from Latin *timidus*, from *timere* 'to fear.'

tim·ing /ˈtīmiNG/ ▶ **n.** the choice, judgment, or control of when something should be done: *one of the secrets of golf is good timing.* ■ a particular point or period of time when something happens. ■ (in an internal combustion engine) the times when the valves open and close, and the time of the ignition spark, in relation to the movement of the piston in the cylinder.

tim·ing chain ▶ **n.** a metal chain or reinforced rubber belt that drives the camshaft of an internal combustion engine. Also called **timing belt**.

Ti·mi·şoa·ra /ˌtēmēSHˈwärə/ an industrial city in western Romania; pop. 303,796 (2006). Formerly part of Hungary, the city has substantial Hungarian- and German-speaking populations. Hungarian name TEMESVÁR.

ti·moc·ra·cy /təˈmäkrəsē/ ▶ **n.** (pl. **timocracies**) chiefly Philosophy **1** a form of government in which possession of property is required in order to hold office.
2 a form of government in which rulers are motivated by ambition or love of honor.
– DERIVATIVES **ti·mo·crat·ic** /ˌtīməˈkratik/ **adj.**
– ORIGIN late 15th cent.: from Old French *timocracie*, via medieval Latin from Greek *timokratia*, from *timē* 'honor, worth' + *-kratia* 'power.' Sense 1 reflects Aristotle's usage, sense 2 Plato's.

tim·o·lol /ˈtīməˌlôl, -ˌläl/ ▶ **n.** Medicine a synthetic compound that acts as a beta blocker and is used to treat hypertension, migraines, and glaucoma.
● Chem. formula: $C_{13}H_{24}N_4O_3S$.
– ORIGIN 1970s: from *tim-* (of unknown origin) + *(propran)olol*.

Ti·mor /ˈtēˌmôr/ the largest of the Lesser Sunda Islands, in the southern Malay Archipelago. The island was formerly divided into Dutch West Timor and Portuguese East Timor. In 1950, West Timor was absorbed into the newly formed Republic of Indonesia. In 1975, East Timor declared itself independent but was invaded and occupied by Indonesia; it finally became an independent state in 2002 (see EAST TIMOR).
– DERIVATIVES **Ti·mo·rese** /ˌtēməˈrēz, -ˈrēs/ **adj. & n.**

Ti·mor Les·te /tēˈmôr ˈlesHtā/ official name of EAST TIMOR.

tim·or·ous /ˈtimərəs/ ▶ **adj.** showing or suffering from nervousness, fear, or a lack of confidence: *a timorous voice.*
– DERIVATIVES **tim·or·ous·ly adv.**, **tim·or·ous·ness n.**
– ORIGIN late Middle English (in the sense 'feeling fear'): from Old French *temoreus*, from medieval Latin *timorosus*, from Latin *timor* 'fear,' from *timere* 'to fear.'

Ti·mor Sea an arm of the Indian Ocean between Timor and northwestern Australia.

Tim·o·thy /ˈtiməTHē/ either of two books of the New Testament, epistles of St. Paul addressed to St. Timothy.

tim·o·thy /ˈtiməTHē/ (also **timothy grass**) ▶ **n.** a Eurasian grass that is widely grown for grazing and hay. It is naturalized in North America, where many cultivars have been developed. ● *Phleum pratense*, family Gramineae.
– ORIGIN mid 18th cent.: named after *Timothy* Hanson, the American farmer who introduced it to the Carolinas from New York (*c.*1720).

Tim·o·thy, St. (1st century AD), convert and disciple of St. Paul. Traditionally, he was the first bishop of Ephesus and was martyred in the reign of Roman emperor Nerva. Feast day, January 22 or 26.

tim·pa·ni /ˈtimpənē/ (also **tympani**) ▶ **plural n.** kettledrums, esp. when played by one musician in an orchestra.
– DERIVATIVES **tim·pa·nist** /-nist/ **n.**
– ORIGIN late 19th cent.: from Italian, plural of *timpano* 'kettledrum,' from Latin *tympanum* 'drum' (see TYMPANUM).

tin /tin/ ▶ **n. 1** a silvery-white metal, the chemical element of atomic number 50. (Symbol: **Sn**) ■ short for TINPLATE. ■ Brit. informal, dated money.

> Tin is quite a rare element, occurring chiefly in the mineral cassiterite. Pure crystalline tin exists in two allotropic modifications, the metallic form (**white tin**), and a semimetallic form (**gray tin**). It is used in various alloys, notably bronze, and for electroplating iron or steel sheets to make tinplate.

2 a metal container, in particular: ■ chiefly Brit. another term for TIN CAN: *she had opened a tin of beans.* ■ a lidded airtight container made of tinplate

t

or aluminum: *Albert got out the cookie tin.* ■ chiefly Brit. an open metal container for baking food: *grease a loaf tin.*
▶ v. (**tins, tinning, tinned** /tind/) [with obj.] cover with a thin layer of tin: *the copper pans are tinned inside.*
– PHRASES **have a tin ear** be tone-deaf.
– ORIGIN Old English, of Germanic origin; related to Dutch *tin* and German *Zinn.*

tin·a·mou /ˈtinəˌmo͞o/ ▶ n. a ground-dwelling tropical American bird that looks somewhat like a grouse. ● Family Tinamidae: several genera and many species.
– ORIGIN late 18th cent.: via French from Galibi *tinamu.*

Tin·ber·gen[1] /ˈtinˌbergə(n)/, Jan (1903–94), Dutch economist. A pioneer in econometrics, he was the brother of zoologist Nikolaas Tinbergen. Nobel Prize for Economics (1969), shared with Ragnar Frisch.

Tin·ber·gen[2], Nikolaas (1907–88), Dutch zoologist. He found that much animal behavior is innate and stereotyped, and he introduced the concept of displacement activity. He was the brother of economist Jan Tinbergen. Nobel Prize for Physiology or Medicine (1973), shared with Konrad Lorenz and Karl von Frisch.

tin can ▶ n. a tinplate or aluminum container for preserving food, esp. an empty one. ■ Nautical slang a destroyer or a submarine.

tinct. ▶ abbr. tincture.

tinc·to·ri·al /tiNG(k)ˈtôrēəl/ ▶ adj. technical of or relating to dyeing, coloring, or staining properties.
– ORIGIN mid 17th cent.: from Latin *tinctorius* (from *tinctor* 'dyer,' from *tingere* 'to dye or color') + -AL.

tinc·ture /ˈtiNGkCHər/ ▶ n. **1** a medicine made by dissolving a drug in alcohol: *the remedies can be administered in the form of tinctures | a bottle containing tincture of iodine.*
2 a slight trace of something: *she could not keep a tincture of bitterness out of her voice.*
3 Heraldry any of the conventional colors (including the metals and stains, and often the furs) used in coats of arms.
▶ v. (**be tinctured**) be tinged, flavored, or imbued with a slight amount of: *Arthur's affability was tinctured with faint sarcasm.*
– ORIGIN late Middle English (denoting a dye or pigment): from Latin *tinctura* 'dyeing,' from *tingere* 'to dye or color.' Sense 2 of the noun (early 17th cent.) comes from the obsolete sense 'imparted quality,' likened to a tint imparted by a dye.

tin·der /ˈtindər/ ▶ n. dry, flammable material, such as wood or paper, used for lighting a fire.
– DERIVATIVES **tin·der·y** adj.
– ORIGIN Old English *tynder, tyndre,* of Germanic origin; related to Dutch *tonder* and German *Zunder.*

tin·der·box /ˈtindərˌbäks/ ▶ n. **1** a thing that is readily ignited: *dry winds and no rain have turned parts of the state into a tinderbox |* figurative *food riots were a potential tinderbox in the city.*
2 historical a box containing tinder, flint, a steel, and other items for kindling fires.

tin·der-dry ▶ adj. (of vegetation) extremely dry and flammable.

tine /tīn/ ▶ n. a prong or sharp point, such as that on a fork or antler.
– DERIVATIVES **tined** adj. [in combination] *a three-tined fork.*
– ORIGIN Old English *tind,* of Germanic origin; related to German *Zinne* 'pinnacle.'

tin·e·a /ˈtinēə/ ▶ n. technical term for RINGWORM.
– ORIGIN late Middle English: from Latin, 'worm.'

tin·foil /ˈtinˌfoil/ (also **tin foil**) ▶ n. foil made of aluminum or a similar silvery-gray metal, used esp. for covering or wrapping food.

ting /tiNG/ ▶ n. a sharp, clear ringing sound, such as when a glass is struck by a metal object.
▶ v. [no obj.] emit such a sound.
– ORIGIN late Middle English (as a verb): imitative. The noun dates from the early 17th cent.

tinge /tinj/ ▶ v. (**tinges, tinging** or **tingeing, tinged**) [with obj.] color slightly: *a mass of white blossom tinged with pink |* [with obj. and complement] *toward the sun the sky was tinged crimson.* ■ have a slight influence on; imbue slightly with a feeling or quality: *this visit will be tinged with sadness.*
▶ n. a tendency toward or trace of some color: *there was a faint pink tinge to the sky.* ■ a slight trace of a feeling or quality.
– ORIGIN late 15th cent.: from Latin *tingere* 'to dip or color.' The noun dates from the mid 18th cent.

tin·gle /ˈtiNGgəl/ ▶ v. experience or cause to experience a slight prickling or stinging sensation: [no obj.] *she was tingling with excitement |* [with obj.] *a standing ovation that tingled your spine.*
▶ n. a slight prickling or stinging sensation: *she felt a tingle in the back of her neck | a tingle of anticipation.*
– ORIGIN late Middle English: perhaps a variant of TINKLE. The original notion was perhaps 'ring in response to a loud noise,' but the term was very early applied to the result of hearing something shocking.

tin·gly /ˈtiNG(g)(ə)lē/ ▶ adj. (**tinglier, tingliest**) causing or experiencing a slight prickling or stinging sensation: *a tingly sense of excitement.*

tin god ▶ n. a person, esp. a minor official, who is pompous and self-important. ■ an object of unjustified veneration or respect.

tin·horn /ˈtinˌhôrn/ ▶ n. informal a contemptible person, esp. one pretending to have money, influence, or ability: *he portrayed Wyatt Earp as a narcissistic tinhorn |* [as modifier] *tinhorn politicians.*

tin·ker /ˈtiNGkər/ ▶ n. **1** (esp. in former times) a person who travels from place to place mending metal utensils as a way of making a living. ■ a person who makes minor mechanical repairs, esp. on a variety of appliances and apparatuses, usually for a living. ■ Brit., chiefly derogatory a Gypsy or other person living in an itinerant community.
2 an act of attempting to repair something.
▶ v. [no obj.] attempt to repair or improve something in a casual or desultory way, often to no useful effect: *he spent hours tinkering with the car.* ■ [with obj.] archaic attempt to mend (something) in such a way.
– PHRASES **not give a tinker's damn** informal not care at all.
– DERIVATIVES **tin·ker·er** n.
– ORIGIN Middle English (first recorded in Anglo-Latin as a surname): of unknown origin.

Tin·ker·toy /ˈtiNGkərˌtoi/ ▶ n. trademark a children's building toy consisting of pieces held together by pegs in holes.

tin·kle /ˈtiNGkəl/ ▶ v. **1** make or cause to make a light, clear ringing sound: [no obj.] *cool water tinkled in the stone fountains |* [with obj.] *the maid tinkled a bell.*
2 [no obj.] informal urinate.
▶ n. **1** a light, clear ringing sound: *the distant tinkle of a cowbell.* ■ Brit. informal a telephone call: *I'll give them a tinkle.*
2 informal an act of urinating.
– DERIVATIVES **tin·kly** /-k(ə)lē/ adj.
– ORIGIN late Middle English (also in the sense 'tingle'): frequentative of obsolete *tink* 'to chink or clink,' of imitative origin.

Tin Liz·zie /ˈlizē/ (also **tin lizzie**) ▶ n. informal, dated a cheap, old, or run-down automobile (originally used as a nickname for early Ford cars, esp. the Model T).
– ORIGIN early 20th cent.: *Lizzie,* a nickname for the given name *Elizabeth.*

tinned /tind/ ▶ adj. **1** [attrib.] covered or coated in tin or a tin alloy.
2 chiefly Brit. (of food) preserved in a tin can: *tinned fruit.*

tin·ner /ˈtinər/ ▶ n. a tin miner or tinsmith.

tin·ni·tus /ˈtinitəs, tiˈnī-/ ▶ n. Medicine ringing or buzzing in the ears.
– ORIGIN mid 19th cent.: from Latin, from *tinnire* 'to ring, tinkle,' of imitative origin.

tin·ny /ˈtinē/ ▶ adj. (**tinnier, tinniest**) having a displeasingly thin, metallic sound: *tinny music played in the background.* ■ (of an object) made of thin or poor-quality metal: *a tinny little car.* ■ having an unpleasantly metallic taste: *canned artichokes taste somewhat tinny.*
– DERIVATIVES **tin·ni·ly** /ˈtinilē/ adv., **tin·ni·ness** n.

Tin Pan Al·ley the name given to a district in New York City (not associated with any particular street, but with the area around 28th Street, between 5th Avenue and Broadway) where many songwriters, arrangers, and music publishers were formerly based. ■ [as noun, usu. as adj.] the world of composers and publishers of popular music, particularly with reference to the works of such composers as Irving Berlin, Jerome Kern, George Gershwin, Cole Porter, and Richard Rodgers.

tin·plate /ˈtinˌplāt/ (also **tin plate**) ▶ n. sheet steel or iron coated with tin.
▶ v. [with obj.] (often as adj. **tinplated** or **tin-plated**) coat (an object) with tin.

tin·pot /ˈtinˌpät/ ▶ adj. [attrib.] informal (esp. of a country or its leader) having or showing poor leadership or organization: *a tinpot dictator.*

tin·sel /ˈtinsəl/ ▶ n. a form of decoration consisting of thin strips of shiny metal foil. ■ showy or superficial attractiveness or glamour: *his taste for the tinsel of the art world.*
– DERIVATIVES **tin·sel·ly** adj.
– ORIGIN late Middle English (denoting fabric either interwoven with metallic thread or spangled): from Old French *estincele* 'spark,' or *estinceler* 'to sparkle,' based on Latin *scintilla* 'a spark.'

tin·seled /ˈtinsəld/ (also chiefly Brit. **tinselled**) ▶ adj. decorated or adorned with tinsel. ■ showily or superficially attractive or glamorous: *his tinseled sentiments.*

Tin·sel·town /ˈtinsəlˌtoun/ ▶ n. informal Hollywood, or the superficially glamorous world it represents.

tin·smith /ˈtinˌsmiTH/ ▶ n. a person who makes or repairs articles of tin or tinplate.

tin snips (also **tinsnips**) ▶ plural n. a pair of clippers for cutting sheet metal.

tin sol·dier ▶ n. a toy soldier made of metal.

tin·stone /ˈtinˌstōn/ ▶ n. another term for CASSITERITE.

tint /tint/ ▶ n. **1** a shade or variety of color: *the sky was taking on an apricot tint.* ■ Printing an area of faint even color printed as a halftone, used for highlighting overprinted text. ■ a set of parallel engraved lines to give uniform shading. ■ a trace of something: *a tint of glamour.*
2 an artificial dye for coloring the hair. ■ an application of such a substance: *peering into the mirror to see if any white hair showed after her last tint.*
▶ v. [with obj.] (usu. **be tinted**) color (something) slightly; tinge: *her skin was tinted with delicate color |* (as adj. **tinted**) *a black car with tinted windows.* ■ dye (someone's hair) with a tint.
– DERIVATIVES **tint·er** n.
– ORIGIN early 18th cent.: alteration (perhaps influenced by Italian *tinta*) of obsolete *tinct* 'to color, tint,' from Latin *tinctus* 'dyeing,' from *tingere* 'to dye or color.'

tin·tin·nab·u·la·tion /ˌtintəˌnabyəˈlāSHən/ ▶ n. a ringing or tinkling sound.
– ORIGIN mid 19th cent.: from Latin *tintinnabulum* 'tinkling bell' (from *tintinnare,* reduplication of *tinnire* 'to ring, tinkle') + -ATION.

Tin·to·ret·to /ˌtintəˈretō/ (1518–94), Italian painter; born *Jacopo Robusti.* His work is typified by a mannerist style, including unusual viewpoints and chiaroscuro effects.

tin·type /ˈtinˌtīp/ ▶ n. historical a photograph taken as a positive on a thin tin plate.

tin·ware /ˈtinˌwe(ə)r/ ▶ n. kitchen utensils or other articles made of tin or tinplate.

tin whis·tle ▶ n. a small flutelike instrument made from a thin metal tube, with six finger holes of varying size on top and no thumb holes.

ti·ny /ˈtīnē/ ▶ adj. (**tinier, tiniest**) very small: *a tiny hummingbird.*
– DERIVATIVES **ti·ni·ly** /-nəlē/ adv., **ti·ni·ness** n.
– ORIGIN late 16th cent.: extension of obsolete *tine* 'small, diminutive,' of unknown origin.

-tion ▶ suffix forming nouns of action, condition, etc., such as *completion, relation.*
– ORIGIN from Latin participial stems ending in *-t* + -ION.

tip[1] /tip/ ▶ n. the pointed or rounded end or extremity of something slender or tapering: *George pressed the tips of his fingers together | the northern tip of Maine.* ■ a small piece or part fitted to the end of an object: *the rubber tip of the walking stick.*
▶ v. (**tips, tipping, tipped**) [with obj.] **1** (usu. as adj. **tipped**) attach to or cover the end or extremity of: *mountains tipped with snow |* [in combination] *steel-tipped spears.* ■ color (something) at its end or edge: *velvety red petals tipped with white.*
2 (**tip a page in**) (in bookbinding) paste a single page, typically an illustration, to the neighboring page of a book by a thin line of paste down its inner margin.
– PHRASES **on the tip of one's tongue** used to indicate that someone is almost but not quite able to bring a particular word or name to mind: *his name's on the tip of my tongue!* ■ used to indicate that someone is about to utter a comment or question but thinks better of it: *it was on the tip of his tongue to ask what was the matter.* **the tip of the iceberg** see ICEBERG.
– ORIGIN late Middle English: from Old Norse *typpi* (noun), *typpa* (verb), *typptr* 'tipped'; related to TOP[1].

tip[2] ▶ v. (**tips, tipping, tipped**) **1** overbalance or cause to overbalance so as to fall or turn over: [no obj.] *the hay caught fire when the candle tipped over |* [with obj.] *a youth sprinted past, tipping over her glass.* ■ be or cause to be in a sloping position with one end or side higher than the other: [with obj.] *I tipped my seat back, preparing myself for sleep |* [no obj.] *the car had tipped to one side.*
2 [with obj.] strike or touch lightly: *I tipped his hoof with the handle of a knife.* ■ [with obj.] cause (an object) to move somewhere by striking or touching it in this way: *the ball was tipped over the rim by Erving.*

3 [no obj.] (**tip off**) Basketball put the ball in play by throwing it up between two opponents.
▶ **n. 1** Brit. a place where trash is deposited; a dump.
2 Baseball a pitched ball that is slightly deflected by the bat.
– PHRASES **tip one's hand** informal reveal one's intentions inadvertently. **tip one's hat** (or **cap**) raise or touch one's hat or cap as a way of greeting or acknowledging someone. **tip the scales** (or **balance**) (of a circumstance or event) be the deciding factor; make the critical difference: *her proven current form tips the scales in her favor.* **tip the scales at** have a weight of (a specified amount): *this phone tips the scales at only 5 ounces.*
– ORIGIN late Middle English: perhaps of Scandinavian origin, influenced later by TIP[1] in the sense 'touch with a tip or point' Current senses of the noun date from the mid 19th cent.

tip³ ▶ **n. 1** a sum of money given to someone as a reward for their services.
2 a small but useful piece of practical advice. ■ a very reliable prediction or piece of inside information: *are those tips you're getting legal?*
▶ **v.** (**tips, tipping, tipped**) [with obj.] **1** give (someone) a sum of money as a way of rewarding them for their services: [with two objs.] *I tipped her five dollars* | [no obj.] *that sort of person never tips.*
2 (usu. **be tipped**) Brit. predict as likely to win or achieve something: *she was widely **tipped to** get the job.*
– PHRASES **tip someone off** informal give someone information about something, typically in a discreet or confidential way: *they were arrested after police were tipped off by local residents.*
– ORIGIN early 17th cent. (in the sense 'give, hand, pass'): probably from TIP[1].

tip·cat /ˈtipˌkat/ ▶ **n.** chiefly historical a game in which a piece of wood tapered at both ends is struck at one end with a stick so as to spring up and is then knocked away by the same player. ■ a tapered piece of wood of this kind.

ti·pi ▶ **n.** variant spelling of TEPEE.

tip-in ▶ **n.** Basketball a score made by tipping a rebound into the basket.

tip-off (also **tipoff**) ▶ **n. 1** informal a piece of information, typically one given in a discreet or confidential way.
2 (usu. **tipoff**) a jump ball that begins each period in a basketball game (used esp. in reference to the first tipoff of the game): *the news of his injury came just two hours before tipoff.*

Tip·pe·ca·noe Riv·er /ˌtipikəˈno͞o/ a river that flows for 170 miles (275 km) through Indiana to join the Wabash River. Battle Ground, along the river, is the site of the 1811 Battle of Tippecanoe.

tip·per /ˈtipər/ ▶ **n.** [usu. with adj.] a person who leaves a specified sort of tip as a reward for services they have received: *he's a big tipper.*

Tip·per·ar·y /ˌtipəˈre(ə)rē/ a county in the Republic of Ireland, in the central part of the country, in the province of Munster; county town, Clonmel.

tip·pet /ˈtipit/ ▶ **n.** a woman's long fur scarf or shawl worn around the neck and shoulders. ■ a similar ceremonial garment worn esp. by the clergy. ■ historical a long, narrow strip of cloth forming part of or attached to a hood or sleeve.
– ORIGIN Middle English: probably from an Anglo-Norman derivative of the noun TIP[1].

Tip·pett /ˈtipit/, Sir Michael (Kemp) (1905–98), English composer. He established his reputation with *A Child of Our Time* (1941), an oratorio that draws on jazz, madrigals, and spirituals as well as on classical sources.

tip·ping point ▶ **n.** the point at which a series of small changes or incidents becomes significant enough to cause a larger, more important change.

tip·ple¹ /ˈtipəl/ ▶ **v.** [no obj.] drink alcohol, esp. habitually: *those who liked to tipple and gamble.*
▶ **n.** informal an alcoholic drink.
– ORIGIN late 15th cent. (in the sense 'sell (alcoholic drink) at retail'): back-formation from TIPPLER[1].

tip·ple² ▶ **n.** a revolving frame or cage in which a truck or freight car is inverted to discharge its load. ■ a place where such loads, esp. from a coal mine, are dumped.
– ORIGIN early 19th cent.: from dialect *tipple* 'tumble over.'

tip·pler¹ /ˈtip(ə)lər/ ▶ **n.** a habitual drinker of alcohol.
– ORIGIN late Middle English (denoting a retailer of alcoholic liquor): of unknown origin.

tip·pler² ▶ **n.** a person who operates or works at a tipple, esp. at a mine.

tip·py /ˈtipē/ ▶ **adj.** inclined to tilt or overturn; unsteady: *they crossed the water in tippy canoes.*

tip·py-toe ▶ **v.** [no obj.] informal walk on the tips of one's toes; tiptoe: *he tippy-toed around the house.*
– PHRASES **on tippy-toe** (or **tippy-toes**) on the tips of one's toes; on tiptoe: *Kurt was mincing around on tippy-toes.*
– ORIGIN late 19th cent.: alteration of TIPTOE.

tip·staff /ˈtipˌstaf/ ▶ **n.** a sheriff's officer; a bailiff.
– ORIGIN mid 16th cent. (first denoting a metal-tipped staff): contraction of *tipped staff* (carried by a bailiff).

tip·ster /ˈtipstər/ ▶ **n.** a person who gives tips, esp. about the likely winner of a race or contest, and esp. for a fee.

tip·sy /ˈtipsē/ ▶ **adj.** (**tipsier, tipsiest**) slightly drunk.
– DERIVATIVES **tip·si·ly** /-səlē/ **adv.**, **tip·si·ness n.**
– ORIGIN late 16th cent.: from the verb TIP[2] + -SY.

tip·toe /ˈtipˌtō/ ▶ **v.** (**tiptoes, tiptoeing, tiptoed**) [no obj.] walk quietly and carefully with one's heels raised and one's weight on the balls of the feet: *Liz tiptoed out of the room.* ■ (**tiptoe around**) carefully avoid discussing or dealing with (a difficult or sensitive subject): *he admits he has never been one to tiptoe around controversial issues.*
– PHRASES **on tiptoe** (or **tiptoes**) (also **on one's tiptoes**) with one's heels raised and one's weight on the balls of the feet, esp. in order to move quietly or make oneself taller: *Jane stood on tiptoe to kiss him* | *the children danced on their tiptoes.*

tip-top (also **tiptop**) ▶ **adj.** of the very best class or quality; excellent: *an athlete in tip-top condition.*
▶ **n. 1** the highest part or point of excellence.
2 a line guide on a fishing rod.

tip-up ▶ **n.** a device used in ice fishing in which a wire attached to the rod is tripped, raising a signal flag, when a fish takes the bait.

ti·rade /ˈtiˌrād, ˌtīˈrād/ ▶ **n.** a long, angry speech of criticism or accusation: *a tirade of abuse.*
– ORIGIN early 19th cent.: from French, literally 'long speech,' from Italian *tirata* 'volley,' from *tirare* 'to pull.'

tir·a·mi·su /ˌtirəmēˈso͞o, -ˈmēso͞o/ (also **tiramisù**) ▶ **n.** an Italian dessert consisting of layers of sponge cake soaked in coffee and brandy or liqueur with powdered chocolate and mascarpone cheese.
– ORIGIN Italian, from the phrase *tirami sù* 'pick me up.'

Ti·ra·na /tiˈränə/ (also **Tiranë**) the capital of Albania, in the central part of the country, on the Ishm River; pop. 407,000 (est. 2009).

tire¹ /tīr/ ▶ **v.** feel or cause to feel in need of rest or sleep: [no obj.] *soon the ascent grew steeper and he began to tire* | [with obj.] *the journey had tired her* | *the training tired us out.* ■ (**tire of**) lose interest in; become bored with: *she will stay with him until he tires of her.* ■ [with obj.] exhaust the patience or interest of; bore: *it tired her that Eddie felt important because he was involved behind the scenes.*
– DERIVATIVES **tir·ing adj.**
– ORIGIN Old English *tēorian* 'fail, come to an end,' also 'become physically exhausted,' of unknown origin.

tire² (Brit. **tyre**) ▶ **n.** a rubber covering, typically inflated or surrounding an inflated inner tube, placed around a wheel to form a flexible contact with the road. ■ a strengthening band of metal fitted around the rim of a wheel.
– ORIGIN late 15th cent. (denoting the curved pieces of iron plate with which carriage wheels were formerly shod): perhaps a shortening of ATTIRE (because the tire was the "clothing" of the wheel).

tired /tīrd/ ▶ **adj.** in need of sleep or rest; weary: *Fisher rubbed his tired eyes* | *she was **tired out** now that the strain was over.* ■ [predic.] (**tired of**) bored with: *I have to look after these animals when you get tired of them.* ■ (of a thing) no longer fresh or in good condition: *a few boxes of tired vegetables.* ■ (esp. of a statement or idea) boring or uninteresting because overfamiliar: *tired clichés like the "information revolution."*
– DERIVATIVES **tired·ly adv.**, **tired·ness n.**

Ti·ree /tīˈrē/ an island in the Inner Hebrides, west of Mull and Coll.

tire gauge (Brit. **tyre gauge**) ▶ **n.** a portable gauge for measuring the air pressure in a tire.

tire i·ron (Brit. **tyre iron**) ▶ **n.** a steel lever for removing tires from wheel rims.

tire·less /ˈtīrlis/ ▶ **adj.** having or showing great effort or energy: *a tireless campaigner.*
– DERIVATIVES **tire·less·ly adv.**, **tire·less·ness n.**

Ti·re·si·as /tiˈrēsēəs/ (also **Teiresias**) Greek Mythology a blind Theban prophet, so wise that even his ghost had its wits and was not a mere phantom. Legends account variously for his wisdom and blindness; some stories hold also that he spent seven years as a woman.

tire·some /ˈtīrsəm/ ▶ **adj.** causing one to feel bored or annoyed: *weeding is a tiresome but essential job.*
– DERIVATIVES **tire·some·ly adv.** [as submodifier] *a tiresomely predictable attitude*, **tire·some·ness n.**

Tîr·gu Mur·eş /ˈtərgo͞o ˈmo͞oresH, ˈti(ə)r-/ a city in central Romania, on the Mureş River; pop. 146,448 (2006).

Ti·rich Mir /ˈtiricH ˈmir/ the highest peak in the Hindu Kush, in northwestern Pakistan. It rises to 25,230 feet (7,690 m).

ti·ro ▶ **n.** variant spelling of TYRO.

Tir·ol /təˈrōl, tiˈrōl, ˈtīˌrōl/ German name for TYROL.

Tir·u·chi·ra·pal·li /ˌtirəcHəˈräpəlē/ a city in Tamil Nadu, southern India; pop. 813,400 (est. 2009). Also called TRICHINOPOLY.

'tis /tiz/ chiefly literary ▶ **contraction** it is.

Ti·sa /ˈtēsä/ Serbian name for TISZA.

ti·sane /tiˈzan, -ˈzän/ ▶ **n.** an herbal tea, consumed esp. for its medicinal properties.
– ORIGIN 1930s: from French.

Tish·ri /ˈtisHrē, -rā/ (also **Tisri** /ˈtiz-/) ▶ **n.** (in the Jewish calendar) the first month of the civil and seventh of the religious year, usually coinciding with parts of September and October.
– ORIGIN from Hebrew *tišrī*.

Ti·siph·o·ne /tiˈsifənē/ Greek Mythology one of the Furies.
– ORIGIN Greek, literally 'the avenger of blood.'

tis·sue /ˈtisHo͞o/ ▶ **n. 1** any of the distinct types of material of which animals or plants are made, consisting of specialized cells and their products: *inflammation is a reaction of living tissue to infection or injury* | (**tissues**) *the organs and tissues of the body.*
2 tissue paper. ■ a disposable piece of absorbent paper, used esp. as a handkerchief or for cleaning the skin. ■ rich or fine material of a delicate or gauzy texture: [as modifier] *the blue and silver tissue sari.*
3 [in sing.] an intricate structure or network made from a number of connected items: *such scandalous stories are **a tissue of** lies.*
– DERIVATIVES **tis·su·ey adj.** (sense 2).
– ORIGIN late Middle English: from Old French *tissu* 'woven,' past participle of *tistre*, from Latin *texere* 'to weave.' The word originally denoted a rich material, often interwoven with gold or silver threads, later (mid 16th cent.) any woven fabric, hence the notion of 'intricacy.'

tis·sue cul·ture ▶ **n.** Biology & Medicine the growth in an artificial medium of cells derived from living tissue. ■ a cell culture of this kind.

tis·sue flu·id ▶ **n.** Physiology extracellular fluid that bathes the cells of most tissues, arriving via blood capillaries and being removed via the lymphatic vessels.

tis·sue pa·per ▶ **n.** thin, soft paper, typically used for wrapping or protecting fragile or delicate articles.

Ti·sza /ˈtisˌä/ a river in southeastern Europe, the longest tributary of the Danube River. It rises in the Carpathian Mountains of western Ukraine and flows west for 600 miles (960 km) into Hungary and then south to join the Danube River in Serbia northwest of Belgrade. Serbian name TISA.

tit¹ /tit/ ▶ **n.** a titmouse. ■ used in names of similar or related birds, e.g., **New Zealand tit**.
– ORIGIN mid 16th cent.: probably of Scandinavian origin and related to Icelandic *titlingur* 'sparrow'; compare with TITMOUSE. Earlier senses were 'small horse' and 'girl'; the current sense dates from the early 18th cent.

tit² ▶ **n.** vulgar slang a woman's breast or nipple.
– PHRASES **suck the hind tit** informal receive less of something than others who are competing for it. **tits and ass** (also chiefly Brit. **tits and bums**) vulgar slang used in reference to the use of crudely sexual images of women.
– ORIGIN Old English *tit* 'teat, nipple,' of Germanic origin; related to Dutch *tit* and German *Zitze*. The vulgar slang use was originally US and dates from the early 20th cent.

tit³ ▶ **n.** (in phrase **tit for tat**) the infliction of an injury or insult in return for one that one has suffered: [as modifier] *the conflict staggered on with tit-for-tat assassinations.*
– ORIGIN mid 16th cent.: variant of obsolete *tip for tap*.

Tit. ▶ **abbr.** Bible Titus.

Ti·tan /ˈtītn/ **1** Greek Mythology any of the older gods who preceded the Olympians and were the children of Uranus (Heaven) and Gaia (Earth). Led by Cronus, they overthrew Uranus; Cronus' son, Zeus, then rebelled against his father and eventually defeated the Titans. ■ (as noun, usu. **a titan**) a person or thing of very great strength, intellect, or importance: *a titan of American industry.*
2 Astronomy the largest satellite of Saturn, the fifteenth closest to the planet, discovered by C. Huygens in 1655, and having a diameter of

3,200 miles (5,150 km). It is unique in having a hazy atmosphere of nitrogen, and methane and other hydrocarbons.

ti·tan·ate /ˈtītn,āt/ ▶ **n.** Chemistry a salt in which the anion contains both titanium and oxygen, in particular one of the anion TiO_3^{2-}.
– ORIGIN mid 19th cent.: from **TITANIUM** + **-ATE**[1].

Ti·tan·ess /ˈtītn-is/ ▶ **n.** a female Titan. ■ (**titaness**) a female person of very great strength, intellect, or importance.

Ti·ta·ni·a /tīˈtānēə/ Astronomy the largest satellite of Uranus, the fourteenth closest to the planet, discovered by W. Herschel in 1787. It has an icy surface and a diameter 1,000 miles (1,610 km).
– ORIGIN the name of the queen of the fairies in Shakespeare's *A Midsummer Night's Dream*.

Ti·tan·ic /tīˈtanik/ a British passenger liner, the largest ship in the world when it was built and supposedly unsinkable, that struck an iceberg in the North Atlantic on its maiden voyage in April 1912 and sank with the loss of 1,490 lives.

ti·tan·ic[1] /tīˈtanik/ ▶ **adj.** of exceptional strength, size, or power: *a series of titanic explosions*.
– DERIVATIVES **ti·tan·i·cal·ly** /-ik(ə)lē/ **adv.**
– ORIGIN mid 17th cent. (in the sense 'relating to the sun'): from Greek *titanikos*, from *Titan* (see **TITAN**).

ti·tan·ic[2] ▶ **adj.** Chemistry of titanium with a valence of four; of titanium(IV). Compare with **TITANOUS**.
– ORIGIN early 19th cent.: from **TITANIUM** + **-IC**.

ti·tan·if·er·ous /,tītnˈifərəs/ ▶ **adj.** (of rocks and minerals) containing or yielding titanium.

ti·tan·ite /ˈtītn,īt/ ▶ **n.** another term for **SPHENE**.
– ORIGIN late 18th cent.: from **TITANIUM** + **-ITE**[1].

ti·ta·ni·um /tīˈtānēəm/ ▶ **n.** the chemical element of atomic number 22, a hard silver-gray metal of the transition series, used in strong, light, corrosion-resistant alloys. (Symbol: **Ti**)

> One of the transition metals, titanium is a common element in the earth's crust; the main sources are the minerals ilmenite and rutile. Very large quantities of the dioxide are manufactured for use as a white pigment in paper, paint, etc.

– ORIGIN late 18th cent.: from **TITAN**, on the pattern of *uranium*.

ti·ta·ni·um di·ox·ide (also **titanium oxide**) ▶ **n.** a white unreactive solid that occurs naturally as the mineral rutile and is used extensively as a white pigment. ● Chem. formula: TiO_2.

ti·ta·ni·um white ▶ **n.** a white pigment consisting chiefly or wholly of titanium dioxide.

ti·tan·ous /tīˈtanəs/ ▶ **adj.** Chemistry of titanium with a lower valence, usually three. Compare with **TITANIC**[2].
– ORIGIN mid 19th cent.: from **TITANIUM**, on the pattern of words such as *ferrous*.

tit·bit /ˈtit,bit/ ▶ **n.** chiefly British spelling of **TIDBIT**.

ti·ter /ˈtītər/ (Brit. **titre**) ▶ **n.** Chemistry the concentration of a solution as determined by titration. ■ the minimum volume of a solution needed to reach the endpoint in a titration. ■ Medicine the concentration of an antibody, as determined by finding the highest dilution at which it is still able to cause agglutination of the antigen.
– ORIGIN mid 19th cent.: from French *titre*, from *titrer* (see **TITRATE**).

tithe /tīT͟H/ ▶ **n.** one tenth of annual produce or earnings, formerly taken as a tax for the support of the church and clergy. ■ (in certain religious denominations) a tenth of an individual's income pledged to the church. ■ [in sing.] archaic a tenth of a specified thing: *he hadn't said a tithe of the prayers he knew*.
▶ **v.** [with obj.] pay or give as a tithe: *he tithes 10 percent of his income to the church*. ■ historical subject to a tax of one tenth of income or produce.
– DERIVATIVES **tith·a·ble adj.**
– ORIGIN Old English *tēotha* (adjective in the ordinal sense 'tenth,' used in a specialized sense as a noun), *tēothian* (verb).

tith·ing /ˈtīT͟HiNG/ ▶ **n. 1** the practice of taking or paying a tithe.
2 historical (in England) a group of ten householders who lived close together and were collectively responsible for each other's behavior.
– ORIGIN Old English *tēothung* (see **TITHE**, **-ING**[1]).

Ti·tho·nus /tīˈTHōnəs/ Greek Mythology a Trojan prince with whom the goddess Aurora fell in love. She asked Zeus to make him immortal but omitted to ask for eternal youth, and he became very old and decrepit although he talked perpetually. Tithonus begged her to remove him from this world, and she changed him into a grasshopper, which chirps ceaselessly.

ti·ti[1] /tēˈtē/ (also **titi monkey**) ▶ **n.** (pl. **titis**) a small forest-dwelling monkey of South America. ● Genus *Callicebus*, family Cebidae: several species.
– ORIGIN mid 18th cent.: from Aymara.

ti·ti[2] /ˈtī,tī, ˈtē,tē/ ▶ **n.** (pl. **titis**) a shrub or small tree with leathery leaves. ● Family Cyrillaceae: three genera, esp. *Cyrilla* and *Cliftonia* of the coastal southeastern US, each of which contains a single species: *Cyrilla racemiflora* (**leatherwood**) and *Cliftonia monophylla* (**buckwheat tree** or **titi tree**).
– ORIGIN early 19th cent.: perhaps of American Indian origin.

Ti·tian[1] /ˈtisHən/ (*c.*1488–1576), Italian painter; Italian name *Tiziano Vecellio*. The most important painter of the Venetian school, he experimented with vivid colors and often broke conventions of composition. He painted many sensual mythological works, including *Bacchus and Ariadne* (*c.*1518–23).

Ti·tian[2] (also **titian**) ▶ **adj.** (of hair) bright golden auburn: *a mass of Titian curls*.
– ORIGIN early 19th cent.: from **TITIAN**[1], by association with the bright auburn hair portrayed in many of his works.

Ti·ti·ca·ca, Lake /,titēˈkäkə/ a lake in the Andes, on the border between Peru and Bolivia. At an altitude of 12,497 feet (3,809 m), it is the highest large lake in the world.

tit·il·late /ˈtitl,āt/ ▶ **v.** [with obj.] stimulate or excite (someone), esp. in a sexual way: *these journalists are paid to titillate the public*. ■ archaic lightly touch; tickle.
– DERIVATIVES **tit·il·la·tion** /,titlˈāsHən/ **n.**
– ORIGIN early 17th cent.: from Latin *titillat-* 'tickled,' from the verb *titillare*.

tit·il·lat·ing /ˈtitl,ātiNG/ ▶ **adj.** arousing mild sexual excitement or interest; salacious: *she let slip titillating details about her clients*.
– DERIVATIVES **tit·il·lat·ing·ly adv.**

tit·i·vate /ˈtitə,vāt/ ▶ **v.** [with obj.] informal make small enhancing alterations to (something): *she slapped on her warpaint and titivated her hair*. ■ (**titivate oneself**) make oneself look attractive.
– DERIVATIVES **tit·i·va·tion** /,titəˈvāsHən/ **n.**
– ORIGIN early 19th cent. (in early use, also as *tidivate*): perhaps from **TIDY**, on the pattern of *cultivate*.

> **USAGE** The verbs titillate and titivate sound alike but do not have the same meaning. **Titillate**, a much more common word, means 'stimulate or excite,' as in *the press are paid to* ***titillate*** *the public*. **Titivate**, on the other hand, means 'adorn or smarten up,' as in *she* ***titivated*** *her hair*.

tit·lark /ˈtit,lärk/ ▶ **n.** dialect a pipit.

ti·tle /ˈtītl/ ▶ **n. 1** the name of a book, composition, or other artistic work: *the author and title of the book*. ■ (usu. as **titles**) a caption or credit in a movie or broadcast. ■ a book, magazine, or newspaper considered as a publication: *the company publishes 400 titles a year*.
2 a name that describes someone's position or job: *Leese assumed the title of director general*. ■ a word such as *Senator* or *Dame* that is used before someone's name, or a form that is used instead of someone's name, to indicate high social or official rank: *he will inherit the title of Duke of Marlborough*. ■ a word such as *Mrs.* or *Dr.* that is used before someone's name to indicate their profession or marital status. ■ a descriptive or distinctive name that is earned or chosen: *Nata's deserved the title of Best Restaurant of the Year*.
3 the position of being the champion of a major sports competition: *Davis won the world title for the first time in 1981*.
4 Law a right or claim to the ownership of property or to a rank or throne: *a local family had title to the property* | *the buyer acquires a good title to the merchandise*.
5 (in church use) a fixed sphere of work and source of income as a condition for ordination. ■ a parish church in Rome under a cardinal.
▶ **v.** [with obj. and complement] (usu. **be titled**) give a name to (a book, composition, or other work): *a song titled "You Rascal, You."*
– ORIGIN Old English *titul*, reinforced by Old French *title*, both from Latin *titulus* 'inscription, title.' The word originally denoted a placard or inscription placed on an object, giving information about it, hence a descriptive heading in a book or other composition.

ti·tle bar ▶ **n.** Computing a horizontal bar at the top of a window, bearing the name of the program and typically the name of the currently active document.

ti·tled /ˈtītld/ ▶ **adj.** (of a person) having a title indicating high social or official rank.

ti·tle deed ▶ **n.** a legal deed or document constituting evidence of a right, esp. to ownership of property.

ti·tle·hold·er /ˈtītl,hōldər/ (also **title holder**) ▶ **n.** a person who holds a title, esp. a sports champion.

ti·tle page ▶ **n.** a page at the beginning of a book giving its title, the names of the author and publisher, and other publication information.

ti·tle role ▶ **n.** the part in a play, movie, television show, etc., from which the work's title is taken.

tit·mouse /ˈtit,mous/ ▶ **n.** (pl. **titmice**) a small songbird that searches acrobatically for insects among foliage and branches. ● Family Paridae: three genera, esp. *Parus*, and numerous species, including the chickadees and the **tufted titmouse** (*P. bicolor*).
– ORIGIN Middle English: from **TIT**[1] + obsolete *mose* 'titmouse.' The change in the ending in the 16th cent. was due to association with **MOUSE**, probably because of the bird's size and quick movements.

Ti·to /ˈtētō/ (1892–1980), Yugoslav marshal and statesman; prime minister 1945–53 and president 1953–80; born *Josip Broz*. He organized a communist resistance movement against the German invasion of Yugoslavia in 1941. He became head of the new government at the end of World War II and established Yugoslavia as a nonaligned communist state with a federal constitution.

Ti·to·grad /ˈtētō,grad, -,gräd/ former name (1946–93) for **PODGORICA**.

ti·trate /ˈtī,trāt/ ▶ **v.** [with obj.] Chemistry ascertain the amount of a constituent in (a solution) by measuring the volume of a known concentration of reagent required to complete a reaction with it, typically using an indicator. ■ Medicine continuously measure and adjust the balance of (a physiological function or drug dosage).
– DERIVATIVES **ti·tra·ta·ble adj.**, **ti·tra·tion** /,tīˈtrāsHən/ **n.**
– ORIGIN late 19th cent.: from French *titrer* (from *titre* in the sense 'fineness of alloyed gold or silver') + **-ATE**[3].

ti·tre ▶ **n.** British spelling of **TITER**.

tit·ter /ˈtitər/ ▶ **v.** [no obj.] give a short, half-suppressed laugh; giggle: *her stutter caused the children to titter*.
▶ **n.** a short, half-suppressed laugh.
– DERIVATIVES **tit·ter·er n.**, **tit·ter·ing·ly adv.**
– ORIGIN early 17th cent.: imitative.

tit·ti·vate ▶ **v.** archaic spelling of **TITIVATE**.

tit·tle /ˈtitl/ ▶ **n.** [in sing.] a tiny amount or part of something: *the rules have* ***not*** *been altered* ***one jot or tittle*** *since*. ■ archaic a small written or printed stroke or dot, indicating omitted letters in a word.
– ORIGIN late Middle English: from Latin *titulus* (see **TITLE**), in medieval Latin 'small stroke, accent'; the phrase *jot or tittle* is from Matt. 5:18.

tit·tle-tat·tle ▶ **n.** idle talk; gossip.
▶ **v.** [no obj.] engage in such talk.
– ORIGIN early 16th cent.: reduplication of **TATTLE**.

tit·tup /ˈtitəp/ ▶ **v.** (**tittups, tittuping, tittuped** or **tittups, tittupping, tittupped**) [no obj.] chiefly Brit. move with jerky or exaggerated movements: *Nicky came tittupping along in a rakish mood*.
– ORIGIN late 17th cent. (as a noun): perhaps imitative of hoofbeats.

tit·ty /ˈtitē/ (also **tittie**) ▶ **n.** vulgar slang (pl. **titties**) another term for **TIT**[2].

tit·u·ba·tion /,ticHəˈbāsHən/ ▶ **n.** Medicine nodding movement of the head or body, esp. as caused by a nervous disorder.
– ORIGIN mid 17th cent.: from Latin *titubatio(n-)*, from *titubare* 'to totter.'

tit·u·lar /ˈticHələr/ ▶ **adj. 1** holding or constituting a purely formal position or title without any real authority: *the queen is titular head of the Church of England* | *a titular post*. ■ [attrib.] (of a cleric) nominally appointed to serve a diocese, abbey, or other foundation no longer in existence, and typically in fact having authority in another capacity.
2 denoting a person or thing from whom or which the name of an artistic work or similar is taken: *the work's titular song*. ■ [attrib.] denoting any of the parish churches in Rome to which cardinals are formally appointed: *the priests of the titular churches*.
– ORIGIN late 16th cent. (in the sense 'existing only in name'): from French *titulaire* or modern Latin *titularis*, from *titulus* (see **TITLE**).

tit·u·lar·ly /ˈticHələrlē/ ▶ **adv.** in name or in name only: *he was titularly a chief petty officer*.

PRONUNCIATION KEY ə *ago, up*; ər *over, fur*; a *hat*; ā *ate*; ä *car*; e *let*; ē *see*; i *fit*; ī *by*; NG *sing*; ō *go*; ô *law, for*; oi *toy*; o͝o *good*; o͞o *goo*; ou *out*; TH *thin*; T͟H *then*; ZH *vision*

Ti·tus[1] /ˈtītəs/ (AD 39–81), Roman emperor 79–81; son of Vespasian; full name *Titus Vespasianus Augustus*; born *Titus Flavius Vespasianus*. In 70, he ended a revolt in Judaea with the conquest of Jerusalem.

Ti·tus[2] a book of the New Testament, an epistle of St. Paul addressed to St. Titus.

Ti·tus, St. (1st century AD), Greek churchman. A convert and St. Paul's helper, he was traditionally the first bishop of Crete. Feast day (Eastern Church) August 23; (Western Church) February 6.

Ti·tus·ville /ˈtītəsˌvil/ **1** a commercial and resort city in east central Florida, near Cape Canaveral; pop. 44,756 (est. 2008).
2 a historic city in northwestern Pennsylvania, on Oil Creek, site of the first operative oil well (1859); pop. 5,774 (est. 2008).

Tiv /tiv/ ▶ **n.** (pl. **same** or **Tivs**) **1** a member of a people of southeastern Nigeria.
2 the Benue-Congo language of this people.
▶ **adj.** of or relating to this people or their language.
– ORIGIN the name in Tiv.

Ti·wa /ˈtēwə/ ▶ **n.** (pl. **same** or **Tiwas**) **1** a member of a Pueblo Indian people living mainly in the region of Taos, New Mexico.
2 the Tanoan language of this people. Do not confuse with **Tewa**.
▶ **adj.** of or relating to this people or their language.
– ORIGIN from Spanish *Tigua*, from a Tanoan name like the Southern Tiwa self-designation *tiwáde*.

ti·yin /tēˈ(y)in/ ▶ **n.** (pl. **same** or **tiyins**) a monetary unit of Kyrgyzstan, equal to one hundredth of a som.

tiz·zy /ˈtizē/ ▶ **n.** (pl. **tizzies**) [in sing.] informal a state of nervous excitement or agitation: *he got **into a tizzy** and was talking absolute nonsense.*
– ORIGIN 1930s (originally US): of unknown origin.

tk. ▶ **abbr.** ■ tank. ■ truck.

TKO ▶ **abbr.** Boxing technical knockout.

tkt. ▶ **abbr.** ticket.

Tl ▶ **symbol** the chemical element thallium.

t.l. ▶ **abbr.** (in the insurance industry) total loss.

TLA ▶ **abbr.** three-letter acronym.

Tlax·ca·la /tläˈskälə/ a state in eastern central Mexico.

TLC ▶ **abbr.** informal tender loving care.

Tlem·cen /tlemˈsen/ a city in northwestern Algeria; pop. 122,300 (est. 2009).

Tlin·git /ˈtliNG(g)it/ ▶ **n.** (pl. **same** or **Tlingits**) **1** a member of an American Indian people of the coasts and islands of southeastern Alaska and adjacent British Columbia.
2 the Na-Dene language of this people.
▶ **adj.** of or relating to this people or their language.
– ORIGIN the name in Tlingit.

t.l.o. ▶ **abbr.** (in the insurance industry) total loss only.

tlr. ▶ **abbr.** tailor.

T lym·pho·cyte ▶ **n.** another term for **T cell**.

TM ▶ **abbr.** trademark Transcendental Meditation.

Tm ▶ **symbol** the chemical element thulium.

t.m. ▶ **abbr.** true mean.

tme·sis /təˈmēsis/ ▶ **n.** (pl. **tmeses** /-sēz/) the separation of parts of a compound word by an intervening word or words, heard mainly in informal speech (e.g., *a whole nother story*; *shove it back any-old-where in the pile*).
– ORIGIN mid 16th cent.: from Greek *tmēsis* 'cutting,' from *temnein* 'to cut.'

TMJ ▶ **abbr.** temporormandibular joint.

TN ▶ **abbr.** Tennessee (in official postal use).

tn ▶ **abbr.** ■ ton(s). ■ town. ■ train.

tng. ▶ **abbr.** training.

tnpk. ▶ **abbr.** turnpike.

TNT ▶ **n.** a high explosive formed from toluene by substitution of nitro groups for three hydrogen atoms. It is relatively insensitive to shock and can be conveniently melted. ● Alternative name: **trinitrotoluene**; chem. formula: $C_7H_5(NO_2)_3$.

to /to͞o/ ▶ **prep. 1** expressing motion in the direction of (a particular location): *walking down to the mall* | *my first visit to Africa.* ■ expressing location, typically in relation to a specified point of reference: *forty miles to the south of the site* | *place the cursor to the left of the first word.* ■ expressing a point reached at the end of a range or after a period of time: *a drop in profits from $105 million to around $75 million* | *from 1938 to 1945.* ■ (in telling the time) before (the hour specified): *it's five to ten.* ■ approaching or reaching (a particular condition): *Christopher's expression changed from amazement to joy* | *she was close to tears.* ■ expressing the result of a process or action: *smashed to smithereens.*
2 identifying the person or thing affected: *you were terribly unkind to her.* ■ identifying the recipient or intended recipient of something: *he wrote a heart-rending letter to the parents* | *I am deeply grateful to my parents.*
3 identifying a particular relationship between one person and another: *he is married to Jan's cousin* | *economic adviser to the president.* ■ in various phrases indicating how something is related to something else (often followed by a noun without a determiner): *made to order* | *a prelude to disaster.* ■ indicating a rate of return on something, e.g., the distance traveled in exchange for fuel used, or an exchange rate that can be obtained in one currency for another: *it only does ten miles to the gallon.* ■ (**to the**) Mathematics indicating the power (exponent) to which a number is raised: *ten to the minus thirty-three.*
4 indicating that two things are attached: *he had left his bike chained to a fence* | figurative *they are inextricably linked to this island.*
5 concerning or likely to concern (something, esp. something abstract): *a threat to world peace* | *a reference to Psalm 22:18.*
6 governing a phrase expressing someone's reaction to something: *to her astonishment, he smiled.*
7 used to introduce the second element in a comparison: *it's nothing to what it once was.*
▶ **infinitive marker 1** used with the base form of a verb to indicate that the verb is in the infinitive, in particular: ■ expressing purpose or intention: *I set out to buy food* | *we tried to help* | *I am **going to** tell you a story.* ■ expressing an outcome, result, or consequence: *he was left to die* | *he managed to escape.* ■ expressing a cause: *I'm sorry to hear that.* ■ indicating a desired or advisable action: *I'd love to go to France this summer* | *we asked her to explain* | *the leaflet explains how to start a recycling program.* ■ indicating a proposition that is known, believed, or reported about a specified person or thing: *a house that people believed to be haunted.* ■ (**about to**) forming a future tense with reference to the immediate future: *he was about to sing.* ■ after a noun, indicating its function or purpose: *a chair to sit on* | *something to eat.* ■ after a phrase containing an ordinal number: *the first person to arrive.*
2 used without a verb following when the missing verb is clearly understood: *he asked her to come but she said she didn't want to.*
▶ **adv.** so as to be closed or nearly closed: *he pulled the door to behind him.*
– ORIGIN Old English *tō* (adverb and preposition); related to Dutch *toe* and German *zu*.

t.o. ▶ **abbr.** ■ turnover. ■ turn over.

toad /tōd/ ▶ **n. 1** a tailless amphibian with a short stout body and short legs, typically having dry warty skin that can exude poison. ● Several families in the order Anura, in particular Bufonidae, which includes the **common toad** (*Bufo bufo*).
2 a contemptible or detestable person (used as a general term of abuse): *you're an arrogant little toad.*
– DERIVATIVES **toad·ish adj.**
– ORIGIN Old English *tādde*, *tāda*, abbreviation of *tādige*, of unknown origin.

toad·fish /ˈtōdˌfisH/ ▶ **n.** (pl. **same** or **toadfishes**) any of a number of fishes with a wide flattened head. ● a chiefly bottom-dwelling large-mouthed fish of warm seas that can produce loud grunts (family Batrachoididae: several genera).

toad·flax /ˈtōdˌflaks/ ▶ **n.** a Eurasian plant of the figwort family, typically having yellow or purplish snapdragonlike flowers and slender leaves. ● *Linaria* and related genera, family Scrophulariaceae: several species, in particular **butter-and-eggs** (*L. vulgaris*), with yellow and orange flowers and found widely as a naturalized North American weed.

toad-in-the-hole ▶ **n.** Brit. a dish consisting of sausages baked in batter.

toad·stone /ˈtōdˌstōn/ ▶ **n.** a gem, fossil tooth, or other stone formerly supposed to have been formed in the body of a toad, and credited with therapeutic or protective properties.

toad·stool /ˈtōdˌsto͞ol/ ▶ **n.** the spore-bearing fruiting body of a fungus, typically in the form of a rounded cap on a stalk, esp. one that is believed to be inedible or poisonous. See also **mushroom**.
– ORIGIN late Middle English: a fanciful name.

toad·y /ˈtōdē/ ▶ **n.** (pl. **toadies**) a person who behaves obsequiously to someone important.
▶ **v.** (**toadies**, **toadying**, **toadied**) [no obj.] act in an obsequious way: *she imagined him **toadying to** his rich clients.*
– DERIVATIVES **toad·y·ish adj.**, **toad·y·ism** /-ˌizəm/ **n.**
– ORIGIN early 19th cent.: said to be a contraction of *toad-eater*, a charlatan's assistant who ate toads; toads were regarded as poisonous, and the assistant's survival was thought to be due to the efficacy of the charlatan's remedy.

to and fro ▶ **adv.** in a constant movement backward and forward or from side to side: *she cradled him, rocking him to and fro.*
▶ **v.** [no obj.] (**be toing and froing**) move constantly backward and forward: *the ducks were toing and froing.* ■ repeatedly discuss or think about something without making any progress.
▶ **n.** [in sing.] constant movement backward and forward: *Wilkie watched the to and fro of their dancing.* ■ constant change in action, attitude, or focus.

toast[1] /tōst/ ▶ **n. 1** sliced bread browned on both sides by exposure to radiant heat.
2 a call to a gathering of people to raise their glasses and drink together in honor of a person or thing, or an instance of drinking in this way: *he raised his glass in a toast to his son.* ■ [in sing.] a person or thing that is very popular or held in high regard by a particular group of people: *he found himself **the toast of** the baseball world.*
▶ **v.** [with obj.] **1** cook or brown (food, esp. bread or cheese) by exposure to a grill, fire, or other source of radiant heat: *he sat by the fire and toasted a piece of bread* | (as adj. **toasted**) *toasted marshmallows.* ■ [no obj.] (of food) cook or become brown in this way: *broil until the nuts have toasted.* ■ warm (oneself or part of one's body) in front of a fire or other source or heat.
2 drink to the health or in honor of (someone or something) by raising one's glass together with others: *happy families toasting each other's health* | figurative *he is toasted by the trade as the outstanding dealer in children's books.*
– PHRASES **be toast** informal be or be likely to become finished, defunct, or dead: *one mistake and you're toast.*
– ORIGIN late Middle English (as a verb in the sense 'burn as the sun does, parch'): from Old French *toster* 'roast,' from Latin *torrere* 'parch.' The practice of drinking a toast (sense 2 of the noun) goes back to the late 17th cent., and originated in naming a lady whose health the company was requested to drink, the idea being that the lady's name flavored the drink like the pieces of spiced toast that were formerly placed in drinks such as wine.

toast[2] ▶ **v.** [no obj.] (usu. as noun **toasting**) (of a DJ) accompany a reggae backing track or music with improvised rhythmic speech.
– ORIGIN 1970s: perhaps the same word as **toast**[1].

toast·er /ˈtōstər/ ▶ **n. 1** an electrical device for making toast.
2 a DJ who accompanies reggae with improvised rhythmic speech.

toast·mas·ter /ˈtōs(t)ˌmastər/ ▶ **n.** an official responsible for proposing toasts, introducing speakers, and making other formal announcements at a large social event.

toast·mis·tress /ˈtōs(t)ˌmistris/ ▶ **n.** a female toastmaster.

toast·y /ˈtōstē/ ▶ **adj.** of or resembling toast. ■ comfortably warm: *a roaring fire may make a home seem toasty.*

Tob. ▶ **abbr.** (in biblical references) Tobit (Apocrypha).

to·bac·co /təˈbakō/ ▶ **n.** (pl. **tobaccos**) **1** a preparation of the nicotine-rich leaves of an American plant, which are cured by a process of drying and fermentation for smoking or chewing.
2 (also **tobacco plant**) the plant of the nightshade family that yields these leaves, native to tropical America. It is widely cultivated in warm regions, esp. in the US and China. ● *Nicotiana tabacum*, family Solanaceae. See also **nicotiana**.
– ORIGIN mid 16th cent.: from Spanish *tabaco*.

to·bac·co mo·sa·ic vi·rus ▶ **n.** a virus that causes mosaic disease in tobacco, much used in biochemical research.

to·bac·co·nist /təˈbakənist/ ▶ **n.** a dealer in cigarettes, tobacco, cigars, and other items used by smokers.

to·bac·co plant ▶ **n.** the plant that yields tobacco. See **tobacco** (sense 2). ■ an ornamental plant related to this. See **nicotiana**.

To·ba·go /təˈbāgō/ see **Trinidad and Tobago**.

To·bit /ˈtōbət/ a pious Israelite living in exile in Assyria, described in the Apocrypha. ■ a book of the Apocrypha telling the story of Tobit.

to·bog·gan /təˈbägən/ ▶ **n.** a long narrow sled used for the sport of coasting downhill over snow or ice. It typically is made of a lightweight board that is curved upward and backward at the front.
▶ **v.** [no obj.] (usu. as noun **tobogganing**) ride on a toboggan: *he thought he would enjoy the tobogganing.*

– DERIVATIVES **to·bog·gan·er** n., **to·bog·gan·ist** /-nist/ n.
– ORIGIN early 19th cent.: from Canadian French *tabaganne*, from Micmac *topāĝan* 'sled.'

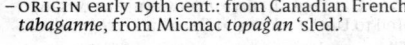

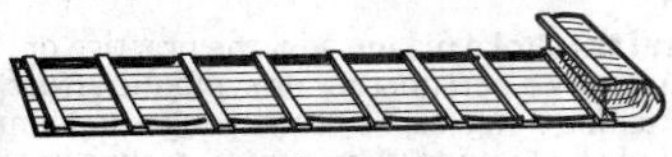
toboggan

to·bra·my·cin /ˌtōbrəˈmīsin/ ▶ n. Medicine a bacterial antibiotic used chiefly to treat pseudomonas infections. ● The drug is obtained from the bacterium *Streptomyces tenebrarius*.
– ORIGIN 1970s: from *to-* (of unknown origin) + Latin (*tene*)*bra*(*rius*) 'belonging to darkness' (part of the name of the bacterium) + **-MYCIN**.

To·bruk /təˈbro͝ok, ˈtōˌbro͝ok/ a port on the Mediterranean coast of northeastern Libya; pop. 134,600 (est. 2009). It was the scene of fierce fighting during the North African campaign in World War II. Arabic name **TUBRUQ**.

To·by jug /ˈtōbē/ (also **toby jug**) ▶ n. a beer jug or mug in the form of a stout old man wearing a three-cornered hat.
– ORIGIN mid 19th cent.: nickname for the given name *Tobias*, and said to come from an 18th-cent. poem about *Toby Philpot* (with a pun on *fill pot*), a soldier who liked to drink.

To·can·tins /ˌtōkənˈtēns/ a river in South America that rises in central Brazil and flows 1,640 miles (2,640 km) north, joining the Pará River to enter the Atlantic Ocean through a large estuary at Belém.

toc·ca·ta /təˈkätə/ ▶ n. a musical composition for a keyboard instrument designed to exhibit the performer's touch and technique.
– ORIGIN early 18th cent.: from Italian, feminine past participle of *toccare* 'to touch.'

To·char·i·an /tōˈke(ə)rēən, -ˈkär-/ ▶ n. **1** a member of a central Asian people who inhabited the Tarim Basin in the 1st millennium AD.
2 either of two extinct languages (**Tocharian A** and **Tocharian B**) spoken by this people, the most easterly of known ancient Indo-European languages, surviving in a few documents and inscriptions and showing affinities to Celtic and Italic languages.
▶ **adj.** of or relating to this people or their language.
– ORIGIN from French *tocharien*, via Latin from Greek *Tokharoi*, the name of a Scythian tribe (almost certainly unrelated to the Tocharians).

to·co /ˈtōkō/ (also **toco toucan**) ▶ n. (pl. **tocos**) the largest and most familiar South American toucan, with mainly black plumage, a white throat and breast, and a massive black-tipped orange bill. ● *Ramphastos toco*, family Ramphastidae.
– ORIGIN late 18th cent.: via Portuguese from Tupi; compare with **TOUCAN**.

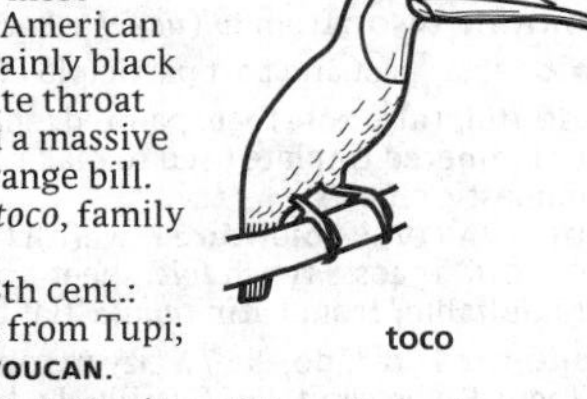
toco

to·coph·er·ol /təˈkäfəˌrôl, -ˌräl/ ▶ n. Biochemistry any of several closely related compounds, found in wheat germ oil, egg yolk, and leafy vegetables, that collectively constitute vitamin E. They are fat-soluble alcohols with antioxidant properties, important in the stabilization of cell membranes.
– ORIGIN 1930s: from Greek *tokos* 'offspring' + *pherein* 'to bear' + **-OL**.

Tocque·ville /ˈtōkˌvil, ˈtäk-/, Alexis de, (1805–59) French politician and historian; full name *Alexis Charles Henri Maurice Clérel de Tocqueville*. He is best known for his classic work of political analysis, *Democracy in America* (1835–40), which he wrote after a visit to the US to study the American penal system.

toc·sin /ˈtäksən/ ▶ n. an alarm bell or signal.
– ORIGIN late 16th cent.: from Old French *toquassen*, from Provençal *tocasenh*, from *tocar* 'to touch' + *senh* 'signal bell.'

tod /täd/ ▶ n. a bushy mass of foliage, esp. ivy.

to·day /təˈdā/ ▶ adv. on or in the course of this present day: *she's thirty today* | *he will appear in court today*. ■ at the present period of time; nowadays: *millions of people today cannot afford adequate housing*.
▶ n. this present day: *today is a day of rest* | *today's game against the Blue Jays*. ■ the present period of time: *the powerful computers of today* | *today's society*.
– ORIGIN Old English *tō dæg* 'on (this) day' Compare with **TOMORROW** and **TONIGHT**.

Todd /täd/, Thomas (1765–1826) US Supreme Court associate justice 1807–26. Appointed to the Court by President Jefferson, he was noted for his expertise in land law.

tod·dle /ˈtädl/ ▶ v. [no obj.] (of a young child) move with short unsteady steps while learning to walk: *William toddled curiously toward the TV crew*. ■ informal walk or go somewhere in a casual or leisurely way: *they would go for a drink and then toddle off home*.
▶ n. [in sing.] a young child's unsteady walk.
– ORIGIN late 16th cent.: of unknown origin.

tod·dler /ˈtädlər/ ▶ n. a young child who is just beginning to walk.
– DERIVATIVES **tod·dler·hood** /-ˌho͝od/ n.

tod·dy /ˈtädē/ ▶ n. (pl. **toddies**) **1** a drink made of alcoholic liquor with hot water, sugar, and sometimes spices.
2 the sap of some kinds of palm, fermented to produce arrack.
– ORIGIN early 17th cent. (sense 2): from Marathi *tāḍī*, Hindi *tāṛī*, from Sanskrit *tāḍī* 'palmyra.'

to-do /təˈdo͞o/ ▶ n. [in sing.] informal a commotion or fuss: *he ignored the to-do in the hall*.
– ORIGIN late 16th cent.: from *to do* as in *much to do*, originally meaning 'much needing to be done' but later interpreted as the adjective *much* and a noun; compare with **ADO**.

to·dy /ˈtōdē/ ▶ n. (pl. **todies**) a small insectivorous Caribbean bird related to the motmots, with a large head, long bill, bright green upper parts, and a red throat. ● Family Todidae and genus *Todus*: five species.
– ORIGIN late 18th cent.: from French *todier*, from Latin *todus*, the name of a small bird.

toe /tō/ ▶ n. **1** any of the five digits at the end of the human foot: *he cut his big toe on a sharp stone*. ■ any of the digits of the foot of a quadruped or bird. ■ the part of an item of footwear that covers a person's toes.
2 the lower end, tip, or point of something, in particular: ■ the tip of the head of a golf club, furthest from the shaft. ■ the foot or base of a cliff, slope, or embankment. ■ a flattish portion at the foot of an otherwise steep curve on a graph. ■ a section of a rhizome or similar fleshy root from which a new plant may be propagated.
▶ v. (**toes, toeing, toed**) **1** [with obj.] push, touch, or kick (something) with one's toe: *he toed off his shoes and flexed his feet*. ■ Golf strike (the ball) with the toe of the club.
2 [no obj.] (**toe in/out**) walk with the toes pointed in (or out): *he toes out when he walks*. ■ (of a pair of wheels) converge (or diverge) slightly at the front: *on a turn, the inner wheel toes out more*.
– PHRASES **make someone's toes curl** informal bring about an extreme reaction in someone, either of pleasure or of disgust. **on one's toes** ready for any eventuality; alert: *he carries out random spot checks to keep everyone on their toes*. **toe the line** accept the authority, principles, or policies of a particular group, esp. under pressure. [from the literal sense 'stand with the tips of the toes exactly touching a line.'] **toe to toe** (of two people) standing directly in front of one another, esp. in order to fight or argue.
– DERIVATIVES **toed** adj. [in combination] *three-toed feet*, **toe·less** adj.
– ORIGIN Old English *tā*, of Germanic origin; related to Dutch *tee* and German *Zeh, Zehe*. Current senses of the verb date from the mid 19th cent.

toe·a /ˈtoi-ə/ ▶ n. (pl. **same**) a monetary unit of Papua New Guinea, equal to one hundredth of a kina.
– ORIGIN Motu, a Melanesian language, literally 'cone-shaped shell.'

toe cap (also **toecap**) ▶ n. a piece of steel or leather constituting or fitted over the front part of a boot or shoe as protection or reinforcement.

toe clip ▶ n. a clip on a bicycle pedal to prevent the foot from slipping.

toe·hold /ˈtōˌhōld/ ▶ n. a small place where a person's foot can be lodged to support them, esp. while climbing. ■ a relatively insignificant position from which further progress may be made: *the importance of networking at conventions to gain a toehold in the industry*.

toe-in ▶ n. a slight forward convergence of a pair of wheels so that they are closer together in front than behind.

toe loop ▶ n. Figure Skating a jump, initiated with the help of the supporting foot, in which the skater makes a full turn in the air, taking off from and landing on the outside edge of the same foot.

toe·nail /ˈtōˌnāl/ ▶ n. **1** the nail at the tip of each toe.
2 a nail driven obliquely through a piece of wood to secure it.
▶ v. [with obj.] fasten (a piece of wood) in this way.

toe-out ▶ n. a slight forward divergence of a pair of wheels so that they are closer together behind than in front.

toe-tap·ping ▶ adj. informal (of music) making one want to tap one's feet; lively.

toff /täf/ Brit. informal, derogatory ▶ n. a rich or upper-class person.
– ORIGIN mid 19th cent.: perhaps an alteration of **TUFT**, used to denote a gold tassel worn on the cap by titled undergraduates at Oxford and Cambridge.

tof·fee /ˈtôfē, ˈtäfē/ ▶ n. (pl. **toffees**) a kind of firm or hard candy that softens when sucked or chewed, made by boiling together sugar and butter, often with other ingredients or flavorings added. ■ a small shaped piece of such candy.
– ORIGIN early 19th cent.: alteration of **TAFFY**.

tof·fee-nosed ▶ adj. informal, chiefly Brit. pretentiously superior; snobbish.
– DERIVATIVES **tof·fee nose** n.

Toff·ler /ˈtôflər/, Alvin, (1928–) US futurist and writer. He first gained popularity with the publication of *Future Shock* (1970), coauthored with his wife, **Heidi Toffler**. Their other coauthored works include *The Third Wave* (1980), *Powershift* (1991), and *Revolutionary Wealth* (2006).

to·fu /ˈtōfo͞o/ ▶ n. curd made from mashed soybeans, used chiefly in Asian and vegetarian cooking.
– ORIGIN from Japanese *tōfu*, from Chinese *dòufu*, from *dòu* 'beans' + *fŭ* 'rot, turn sour.'

tog /täg/ informal ▶ n. (**togs**) clothes: *running togs*.
▶ v. (**togs, togging, togged**) (**be/get togged up/out**) be or get dressed for a particular occasion or activity: *we got togged up in our glad rags*.
– ORIGIN early 18th cent. (as a slang term for a coat or outer garment): apparently an abbreviation of obsolete criminals' slang *togeman(s)* 'a light cloak,' from French *toge* or Latin *toga* (see **TOGA**).

to·ga /ˈtōgə/ ▶ n. a loose flowing outer garment worn by the citizens of ancient Rome, made of a single piece of cloth and covering the whole body apart from the right arm. ■ a robe of office; a mantle of responsibility, etc.
– ORIGIN Latin; related to *tegere* 'to cover.'

toga

to·geth·er /təˈgeT͟Hər/ ▶ adv. **1** with or in proximity to another person or people: *together they climbed the dark stairs* | *they stood together in the kitchen*. ■ so as to touch or combine: *she held her hands together as if she were praying* | *pieces of wood nailed together*. ■ in combination; collectively: *taken together, these measures would significantly improve people's chances of surviving a tornado*. ■ into companionship or close association: *the experience has brought us together*. ■ (of two people) married or in a sexual relationship with each other: *they split up after ten years together*. ■ so as to be united or in agreement: *he won the confidence of the government and the rebels, but could not bring the two sides together*.
2 at the same time: *they both spoke together*.
3 without interruption; continuously: *she sits for hours together in the lotus position*.
▶ **adj.** informal self-confident, level-headed, or well organized: *she seems a very together young woman*.
– PHRASES **together with** as well as; along with: *their meal arrived, together with a carafe of red wine*.
– ORIGIN Old English *tōgædere*, based on the preposition **TO** + a West Germanic word related to **GATHER**. The adjective dates from the 1960s.

to·geth·er·ness /təˈgeT͟Hərnəs/ ▶ n. the state of being close to another person or other people: *the sense of family togetherness was strong and excluded neighbors*.

tog·ger·y /ˈtägərē/ ▶ n. informal, humorous clothes.

tog·gle /ˈtägəl/ ▶ n. **1** a short rod of wood or plastic sewn to one side of a coat or other garment, pushed through a hole or loop on the other side and twisted so as to act as a fastener. ■ a pin or other crosspiece put through the eye of a rope or a link of a chain to keep it in place. ■ (also **toggle bolt**) a kind of wall fastener for use on hollow walls, having a part that springs open or turns through 90° after it is inserted so as to prevent withdrawal. ■ a movable pivoted crosspiece acting as a barb on a harpoon.

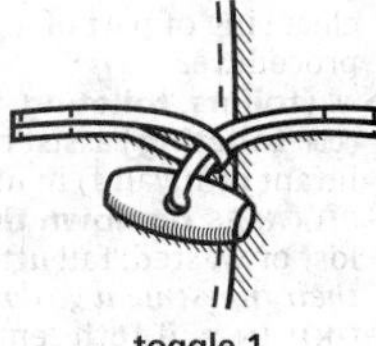
toggle 1

PRONUNCIATION KEY ə *ago, up*; ər *over, fur*; a *hat*; ā *ate*; ä *car*; e *let*; ē *see*; i *fit*; ī *by*; NG *sing*; ō *go*; ô *law, for*; oi *toy*; o͝o *good*; o͞o *goo*; ou *out*; TH *thin*; T͟H *then*; ZH *vision*

2 (also **toggle switch** or **toggle key**) Computing a key or command that is operated the same way but with opposite effect on successive occasions.
▶ **v. 1** [no obj.] Computing switch from one effect, feature, or state to another by using a toggle.
2 [with obj.] provide or fasten with a toggle or toggles.
– ORIGIN mid 18th cent. (originally in nautical use): of unknown origin.

tog·gle switch ▶ **n. 1** an electric switch operated by means of a projecting lever that is moved up and down.
2 Computing another term for **TOGGLE**.

To·gliat·ti /tôl'yätē, täl-/ an industrial city and river port in southwestern Russia, on the Volga River; pop. 705,500 (est. 2008). Former name (until 1964) **STAVROPOL**. Russian name **TOLYATTI**.
– ORIGIN renamed in 1964 after Palmiro *Togliatti* (1893–1964), leader of the Italian Communist Party.

To·go /'tōgō/ a country in West Africa with a short coastline on the Gulf of Guinea; pop. 6,031,800 (est. 2009); capital, Lomé; languages, French (official) and West African languages. Official name **Togolese Republic**.

The region formerly known as Togoland lay between the military powers of Ashanti and Dahomey and became a center of the slave trade. It was annexed by Germany in 1884 and divided between France and Britain after World War I. The western, British section joined Ghana when the latter became independent in 1957. The remainder, administered by France under a UN mandate after World War II, became an independent republic called Togo in 1960.

– DERIVATIVES **To·go·lese** /,tōgō'lēz, ,tōgə-, -'lēs/ **adj. & n.**

to·hu·bo·hu /'tōhōō'bōhōō/ ▶ **n.** informal a state of chaos; utter confusion: *a fearful tohubohu*.
– ORIGIN from Hebrew *tōhū wa-bōhū* 'emptiness and desolation,' translated in Gen. 1:2 (Bible of 1611) as 'without form and void.'

toil /toil/ ▶ **v.** [no obj.] work extremely hard or incessantly: *we toiled away* | [with infinitive] *Richard toiled to build his editorial team.* ■ [with adverbial of direction] move slowly and with difficulty: *she began to toil up the cliff path.*
▶ **n.** exhausting physical labor: *a life of toil.*
– DERIVATIVES **toil·er n.**
– ORIGIN Middle English (in the senses 'contend verbally' and 'strife'): from Anglo-Norman French *toiler* 'strive, dispute,' *toil* 'confusion,' from Latin *tudiculare* 'stir around,' from *tudicula* 'machine for crushing olives,' related to *tundere* 'crush.'

toile /twäl/ ▶ **n. 1** an early version of a finished garment made up in cheap material so that the design can be tested and perfected.
2 a translucent linen or cotton fabric, used for making clothes. ■ short for **TOILE DE JOUY**.
– ORIGIN late Middle English (denoting cloth or canvas for painting on): from French *toile* 'cloth, web,' from Latin *tela* 'web.'

toile de Jouy /,twäl də 'zhwē/ ▶ **n.** a type of printed calico with a characteristic floral, figure, or landscape design on a light background, typically used for upholstery or curtains.
– ORIGIN originally made at *Jouy*-en-Josas, near Paris.

toi·let /'toilit/ ▶ **n. 1** a large bowl for urinating or defecating into, typically plumbed into a sewage system and with a flushing mechanism: *Liz heard the toilet flush* | figurative *my tenure was down the toilet.* ■ a room, building, or cubicle containing one or more of these.
2 [in sing.] the process of washing oneself, dressing, and attending to one's appearance: *her toilet completed, she finally went back downstairs.* ■ [as modifier] denoting articles used in this process: *a bathroom cabinet stocked with toilet articles.* ■ the cleansing of part of a person's body as a medical procedure.
▶ **v.** (**toilets, toileting, toileted**) [with obj.] (usu. as noun **toileting**) assist or supervise (someone, esp. an infant or invalid) in using a toilet.
– PHRASES **go down the toilet** informal be completely lost or wasted; fail utterly: *they didn't want to see their investment go down the toilet.*
– ORIGIN mid 16th cent.: from French *toilette* 'cloth, wrapper,' diminutive of *toile* (see **TOILE**). The word originally denoted a cloth used as a wrapper for clothes; then (in the 17th cent.) a cloth cover for a dressing table, the articles used in dressing, and the process of dressing, later also of washing oneself (sense 2 of the noun). In the 19th cent. the word came to denote a dressing room, and, in the US, one with washing facilities; hence, a lavatory (early 20th cent).

toi·let pa·per ▶ **n.** paper in sheets or on a roll for wiping oneself clean after urination or defecation.

toi·let·ries /'toilitrēz/ ▶ **plural n.** articles used in washing and taking care of one's body, such as soap, shampoo, and toothpaste.

toi·lette /twä'let/ ▶ **n.** [in sing.] dated the process of washing oneself, dressing, and attending to one's appearance: *Emily got up to begin her morning toilette.*
– ORIGIN late 17th cent.: French (see **TOILET**).

toi·let tis·sue ▶ **n.** another term for **TOILET PAPER**.

toi·let-train ▶ **v.** [with obj.] teach (a young child) to use the toilet: *she was toilet-trained by the age of one* | (as noun **toilet-training**) *books on toilet-training.*

toi·let wa·ter ▶ **n.** a dilute form of perfume. Also called **EAU DE TOILETTE**.

toils /toilz/ ▶ **plural n.** literary used in reference to a situation regarded as a trap: *Henry had become caught in the toils of his own deviousness.*
– ORIGIN early 16th cent. (denoting a net into which a hunted quarry is driven): plural of *toil*, from Old French *toile* 'net, trap' (see **TOILE**).

toil·some /'toilsəm/ ▶ **adj.** archaic or literary involving hard or tedious work.
– DERIVATIVES **toil·some·ly adv., toil·some·ness n.**

toil·worn /'toil,wôrn/ ▶ **adj.** literary exhausted by hard physical labor.

To·jo /'tō'jō/, Hideki (1884–1948), Japanese military leader and statesman; prime minister 1941–44. He initiated the Japanese attack on Pearl Harbor and by 1944 had assumed virtual control of all political and military decision-making. After Japan's surrender, he was tried and hanged as a war criminal.

to·ka·mak /'tōkə,mak, 'täk-/ ▶ **n.** Physics a toroidal apparatus for producing controlled fusion reactions in hot plasma.
– ORIGIN 1960s: Russian, from *to(roidal'naya) kam(era s) ak(sial'nym magnitnym polem)* 'toroidal chamber with axial magnetic field.'

To·kay /tō'kā/ ▶ **n.** a sweet aromatic wine, originally made near Tokaj in Hungary.

to·kay /tō'kā/ (also **tokay gecko**) ▶ **n.** a large gray Southeast Asian gecko with orange and blue spots, having a loud call that resembles its name. ● *Gekko gecko*, family Gekkonidae.
– ORIGIN mid 18th cent.: from Malay dialect *toke?*, from Javanese *tekèk*, imitative of its call.

toke /tōk/ informal ▶ **n.** the drawing of a puff from a cigarette or pipe, typically one containing marijuana.
▶ **v.** [no obj.] smoke marijuana or tobacco: *he muses while toking on a cigarette* | [with obj.] *we toked some grass.*
– DERIVATIVES **tok·er n.**
– ORIGIN 1950s: of unknown origin.

to·ken /'tōkən/ ▶ **n. 1** a thing serving as a visible or tangible representation of a fact, quality, feeling, etc.: *mistletoe was cut from an oak tree as a token of good fortune* | *I wanted to offer you a small token of my appreciation.* ■ archaic a characteristic or distinctive sign or mark, esp. a badge or favor worn to indicate allegiance to a particular person or party. ■ archaic a word or object conferring authority on or serving to authenticate the speaker or holder. ■ chiefly Brit. a staff or other object given to a locomotive engineer on a single-track railroad as authority to proceed over a given section of line. ■ Computing a sequence of bits used in a certain network architecture in which the ability to transmit information is conferred on a particular node by the arrival there of this sequence, which is passed continuously between nodes in a fixed order. ■ a person chosen by way of tokenism as a nominal representative of a minority or underrepresented group.
2 a voucher that can be exchanged for goods or services, typically one given as a gift or offered as part of a promotional offer: *redeem this token for a free dessert.* ■ a metal or plastic disk used to operate a machine or in exchange for particular goods or services.
3 an individual occurrence of a symbol or string, in particular: ■ Linguistics an individual occurrence of a linguistic unit in speech or writing, as contrasted with the type or class of linguistic unit of which it is an instance. Contrasted with **TYPE**. ■ Computing the smallest meaningful unit of information in a sequence of data for a compiler.
▶ **adj.** done for the sake of appearances or as a symbolic gesture: *cases like these often bring just token fines from the courts.* ■ [attrib.] (of a person) chosen by way of tokenism as a representative of a particular minority or underrepresented group: *she took offense at being called the token woman on the force.*
– PHRASES **by the same token** in the same way or for the same reason: *there was little evidence to substantiate the gossip and, by the same token, there was little to disprove it.* **in token of** as a sign or symbol of: *we bought each other drinks in token of the holiday season.*
– ORIGIN Old English *tāc(e)n*, of Germanic origin; related to Dutch *teken* and German *Zeichen*, also to **TEACH**.

to·ken·ism /'tōkə,nizəm/ ▶ **n.** the practice of making only a perfunctory or symbolic effort to do a particular thing, esp. by recruiting a small number of people from underrepresented groups in order to give the appearance of sexual or racial equality within a workforce.
– DERIVATIVES **to·ken·is·tic** /,tōkə'nistik/ **adj.**

to·ken ring ▶ **n.** Computing a local area network in which a node can transmit only when in possession of a sequence of bits (called the token) that is passed to each node in turn.

Tok·las /'tōkləs/, Alice B. (1877–1967), US writer; full name *Alice Babette Toklas*. She was a companion and secretary to Gertrude Stein. A collection of her letters, *Staying on Alone* (1973) was published posthumously.

to·ko·no·ma /,tōkə'nōmə/ ▶ **n.** (in a Japanese house) a recess or alcove, typically a few inches above floor level, for displaying flowers, pictures, and ornaments.
– ORIGIN Japanese.

Tok Pis·in /,täk 'pisin/ ▶ **n.** an English-based Creole used as a commercial and administrative language by over 2 million people in Papua New Guinea. Also called **NEO-MELANESIAN**.
– ORIGIN the name in Tok Pisin, literally 'pidgin talk.'

To·ku·ga·wa /,tōkōō'gäwə/ the last shogunate in Japan (1603–1867), founded by **Tokugawa Ieyasu** (1543–1616).The shogunate was followed by the restoration of imperial power under Meiji Tenno.

To·ky·o /'tōkē,ō/ the capital of Japan, located on the northwestern shores of Tokyo Bay, on the southeastern part of the island of Honshu; pop. 12,758,000 (est. 2007). Formerly called Edo, it was the center of the military government under the shoguns 1603–1867. Renamed Tokyo in 1868, it replaced Kyoto as the imperial capital.

to·lar /'tälär/ ▶ **n.** the former basic monetary unit of Slovenia, equal to 100 stotins.
– ORIGIN Slovene; compare with **THALER**.

Tol·bu·khin /tôl'bōōkin, -khin/ former name (1949–91) of **DOBRICH**.

tol·bu·ta·mide /täl'byōōtə,mīd/ ▶ **n.** Medicine a synthetic compound used to lower blood sugar levels in the treatment of diabetes. ● Alternative name: **1-butyl-3-tosylurea**; chem. formula: $C_{12}H_{18}N_2O_3S$.
– ORIGIN 1950s: from *tol(uene)* + *but(yl)* + **AMIDE**.

told /tōld/ past and past participle of **TELL**[1].

tole /tōl/ (also **tôle**) ▶ **n.** painted, enameled, or lacquered tinplate used to make decorative domestic objects.
– DERIVATIVES **tole·ware** /-,we(ə)r/ **n.**
– ORIGIN 1940s: French *tôle* 'sheet iron,' from dialect *taule* 'table,' from Latin *tabula* 'flat board.'

To·le·do 1 /tə'lādō, -'lē-/ a city in central Spain on the Tagus River, capital of Castilla–La Mancha region; pop. 80,810 (2008). Toledan steel and sword blades have been well known since the first century BC.
2 /tə'lēdō/ an industrial city and port on Lake Erie, in northwestern Ohio; pop. 293,201 (est. 2008).
– DERIVATIVES **To·le·dan** /tə'lēdn/ **adj. & n.**

tol·er·a·ble /'tälərəbəl/ ▶ **adj.** able to be endured: *a stimulant to make life more tolerable.* ■ fairly good; mediocre: *he was fond of music and had a tolerable voice.*
– DERIVATIVES **tol·er·a·bil·i·ty** /,täl(ə)rə'bilitē/ **n.**, **tol·er·a·bly** /-blē/ **adv.** [as submodifier] *the welfare state works tolerably well.*
– ORIGIN late Middle English: via Old French from Latin *tolerabilis*, from *tolerare* (see **TOLERATE**).

tol·er·ance /'täl(ə)rəns/ ▶ **n. 1** the ability or willingness to tolerate something, in particular the existence of opinions or behavior that one does not necessarily agree with: *the tolerance of corruption* | *an advocate of religious tolerance.* ■ the capacity to endure continued subjection to something, esp. a drug, transplant, antigen, or environmental conditions, without adverse reaction: *the desert camel shows the greatest tolerance to dehydration* | *species were grouped according to pollution tolerance* | *various species of diatoms display different tolerances to acid.* ■ diminution in the body's response to a drug after continued use.
2 an allowable amount of variation of a specified quantity, esp. in the dimensions of a machine or part: *250 parts in his cars were made to tolerances of one thousandth of an inch.*
– ORIGIN late Middle English (denoting the action of bearing hardship, or the ability to bear pain and hardship): via Old French from Latin *tolerantia*, from *tolerare* (see **TOLERATE**).

tol·er·ance dose ▶ **n.** a dose of something toxic, in particular of nuclear radiation, believed to be the maximum that can be taken without harm.

tol·er·ant /ˈtälərənt/ ▶ **adj. 1** showing willingness to allow the existence of opinions or behavior that one does not necessarily agree with: *we must be* ***tolerant of*** *others* | *a more tolerant attitude toward other religions.*
2 (of a plant, animal, or machine) able to endure (specified conditions or treatment): *rye is reasonably* ***tolerant of*** *drought* | [in combination] *fault-tolerant computer systems.*
– DERIVATIVES **tol·er·ant·ly adv.** (sense 1).
– ORIGIN late 18th cent.: from French *tolérant*, present participle of *tolérer*, from Latin *tolerare* (see TOLERATE). Compare with earlier INTOLERANT.

tol·er·ate /ˈtäləˌrāt/ ▶ **v.** [with obj.] allow the existence, occurrence, or practice of (something that one does not necessarily like or agree with) without interference: *a regime unwilling to tolerate dissent.* ■ accept or endure (someone or something unpleasant or disliked) with forbearance: *how was it that she could tolerate such noise?* ■ be capable of continued subjection to (a drug, toxin, or environmental condition) without adverse reaction: *lichens grow in conditions that no other plants tolerate.*
– DERIVATIVES **tol·er·a·tor** /-ˌrātər/ **n.**
– ORIGIN early 16th cent. (in the sense 'endure (pain)'): from Latin *tolerat-* 'endured,' from the verb *tolerare.*

tol·er·a·tion /ˌtäləˈrāsʜən/ ▶ **n.** the practice of tolerating something, in particular differences of opinion or behavior: *the king demanded greater religious toleration.*
– ORIGIN late 15th cent. (denoting the granting of permission by authority): from French *tolération*, from Latin *toleratio(n-)*, from *tolerare* (see TOLERATE).

Tol·kien /ˈtōlˌkēn, ˈtäl-/, J. R. R. (1892–1973), British novelist and literary scholar, born in South Africa; full name *John Ronald Reuel Tolkien.* He is known for *The Hobbit* (1937) and *The Lord of the Rings* (1954–55), fantasy adventures set in Middle Earth.

toll[1] /tōl/ ▶ **n. 1** a charge payable for permission to use a particular bridge or road: *turnpike tolls* | [as modifier] *a toll bridge.* ■ a charge for a long-distance telephone call.
2 [in sing.] the number of deaths, casualties, or injuries arising from particular circumstances, such as a natural disaster, conflict, or accident: *the toll of dead and injured mounted.* ■ the cost or damage resulting from something: *the environmental toll of the policy has been high.*
▶ **v.** [with obj.] (usu. as noun **tolling**) charge a toll for the use of (a bridge or road): *the report advocates expressway tolling.*
– PHRASES **take its toll** (or **take a heavy toll**) have an adverse effect, esp. so as to cause damage, suffering, or death: *years of pumping iron have taken their toll on his body.*
– ORIGIN Old English (denoting a charge, tax, or duty), from medieval Latin *toloneum*, alteration of late Latin *teloneum*, from Greek *telōnion* 'tollhouse,' from *telos* 'tax.' Sense 2 of the noun (late 19th cent.) arose from the notion of paying a toll or tribute in human lives (to an adversary or to death).

toll[2] ▶ **v.** (with reference to a bell) sound or cause to sound with a slow, uniform succession of strokes, as a signal or announcement: [no obj.] *the bells of the cathedral began to* ***toll for*** *evening service* | [with obj] *the priest began tolling the bell.* ■ (of a bell) announce or mark (the time, a service, or a person's death): *the bell of St. Mary's began to toll the curfew.*
▶ **n.** [in sing.] a single ring of a bell.
– ORIGIN late Middle English: probably a special use of dialect *toll* 'drag, pull.'

toll·booth /ˈtōlˌbo͞otʜ/ ▶ **n.** a booth where drivers must pay to use a bridge or road.

toll bridge ▶ **n.** a bridge where drivers or pedestrians must pay to cross.

toll·gate /ˈtōlˌgāt/ ▶ **n.** a barrier across a road where drivers or pedestrians must pay to go further.

toll·house /ˈtōlˌhous/ ▶ **n.** a small house by a tollgate or toll bridge where money is collected from road users.

toll·house cook·ie ▶ **n.** a cookie made with flour, brown sugar, chocolate chips, and usually chopped nuts.
– ORIGIN named after the *Toll House* in Whitman, Massachusetts, source of the original recipe.

toll pla·za ▶ **n.** a row of tollbooths on a toll road.

toll road ▶ **n.** a road that drivers must pay to use.

toll·way /ˈtōlˌwā/ ▶ **n.** a highway for the use of which a charge is made.

Tol·stoy /ˈtôlˌstoi, ˈtōl-/, Count Leo (1828–1910), Russian writer; Russian name *Lev Nikolaevich Tolstoi.* He is noted for the novels *War and Peace* (1863–69), an epic tale of the Napoleonic invasion, and *Anna Karenina* (1873–77).

Leo Tolstoy

Tol·tec /ˈtōlˌtek, ˈtäl-/ ▶ **n. 1** a member of an American Indian people that flourished in Mexico before the Aztecs.
2 the language of this people.
▶ **adj.** of or relating to this people.
– DERIVATIVES **Tol·tec·an** /tōlˈtekən, täl-/ **adj.**
– ORIGIN via Spanish from Nahuatl *toltecatl*, literally 'a person from *Tula*' (see TULA).

to·lu /təˈlo͞o/ (also **tolu balsam**) ▶ **n.** a fragrant brown balsam obtained from a South American tree, used in perfumery and medicine. ● This balsam is obtained mainly from *Myroxylon balsamum*, family Leguminosae.
– ORIGIN late 17th cent.: named after *Santiago de Tolú* in Colombia, from where it was exported.

To·lu·ca /təˈlo͝okə/ a city in central Mexico, capital of the state of Mexico; pop. 467,712 (2005). It lies at the foot of Nevado de Toluca, an extinct volcano, at an altitude of 8,793 feet (2,680 m). Full name **Toluca de Lerdo.**

tol·u·ene /ˈtälyo͞oˌēn/ ▶ **n.** Chemistry a colorless liquid hydrocarbon present in coal tar and petroleum and used as a solvent and in organic synthesis. ● Alternative name: **methylbenzene**; chem. formula: $C_6H_5CH_3$.
– ORIGIN late 19th cent.: from TOLU + -ENE.

to·lu·i·dine blue /təˈlo͞oəˌdēn/ ▶ **n.** a synthetic blue dye used chiefly as a stain in biology. ● A thiazine dye; chem. formula: $C_{15}H_{16}ClN_3S$.
– ORIGIN late 19th cent.: *toluidine* from TOLUENE + -IDE + -INE[4].

To·lyat·ti /tôlˈyätē, täl-/ Russian name for TOGLIATTI.

tom /täm/ ▶ **n. 1** the male of various animals, esp. a turkey or domestic cat.
2 (**Tom**) informal short for UNCLE TOM.
▶ **v.** (**Tom**) (**toms, Tomming, Tommed**) [no obj.] informal, derogatory (of a black person) behave in an excessively obedient or servile way.
– ORIGIN late Middle English (denoting an ordinary man, surviving in *tomfool, tomboy*, and the phrase *Tom, Dick, and Harry*): abbreviation of the given name *Thomas*. Sense 1 of the noun dates from the mid 18th cent.

tom·a·hawk /ˈtäməˌhôk/ ▶ **n.** a light ax used as a tool or weapon by American Indians.
▶ **v.** [with obj.] strike or cut with or as if with a tomahawk.
– ORIGIN early 17th cent.: from a Virginia Algonquian language.

tomahawk

tom·al·ley /ˈtämˌalē/ ▶ **n.** the digestive gland of a lobster, which turns green when cooked. It is sometimes considered a delicacy.
– ORIGIN mid 17th cent.: from French *taumalin*, from Carib *taumali*.

Tom and Jer·ry /täm and ˈjerē/ ▶ **n.** (pl. **Tom and Jerries**) a kind of hot spiced rum cocktail, made with eggs.

to·ma·til·lo /ˌtōməˈtē(y)ō/ ▶ **n.** (pl. **tomatillos**) **1** a small edible fruit that is purplish or yellow when ripe, but is most often used when green for salsas and preserves.
2 the Mexican plant, related to the cape gooseberry, that bears this fruit. ● *Physalis philadelphica*, family Solanaceae.
– ORIGIN early 20th cent.: from Spanish, diminutive of *tomate* 'tomato.'

to·ma·to /təˈmātō, -ˈmätō/ ▶ **n.** (pl. **tomatoes**) **1** a glossy red, or occasionally yellow, pulpy edible fruit that is typically eaten as a vegetable or in salad. ■ the bright red color of a ripe tomato.
2 the South American plant of the nightshade family that produces this fruit. It is widely grown as a cash crop, and many varieties have been developed. ● *Lycopersicon esculentum*, family Solanaceae.
– DERIVATIVES **to·ma·to·ey** /-ˈmātō-ē, -ˈmätō-ē/ **adj.**
– ORIGIN early 17th cent.: from French, Spanish, or Portuguese *tomate*, from Nahuatl *tomatl*.

to·ma·to fruit·worm ▶ **n.** another term for CORN EARWORM.

tomb /to͞om/ ▶ **n.** a large vault, typically an underground one, for burying the dead. ■ an enclosure for a corpse cut in the earth or in rock. ■ a monument to the memory of a dead person, erected over their burial place. ■ used in similes and metaphors to refer to a place or situation that is extremely cold, quiet, or dark, or that forms a confining enclosure: *the house was as quiet as a tomb.* ■ (**the tomb**) literary death: *none escape the tomb.*
– ORIGIN Middle English: from Old French *tombe*, from late Latin *tumba*, from Greek *tumbos*.

Tom·baugh /ˈtämˌbô/, Clyde William (1906–97), US astronomer. He discovered Pluto on March 13, 1930, and subsequently discovered numerous asteroids.

Tom·big·bee Riv·er /tämˈbigbē/ a river that flows for 400 miles (640 km) from northeastern Mississippi through western Alabama, to the Alabama River. In the 1980s, the ***Tennessee-Tombigbee Waterway*** connected it with the Tennessee River.

tom·bo·lo /ˈtämbəˌlō/ ▶ **n.** (pl. **tombolos**) a bar of sand or shingle joining an island to the mainland.
– ORIGIN late 19th cent.: from Italian, literally 'sand dune.'

Tom·bouc·tou /ˌtôɴbo͝okˈto͞o, ˌtämbək-/ French name for TIMBUKTU.

tom·boy /ˈtämˌboi/ ▶ **n.** a girl who enjoys rough, noisy activities traditionally associated with boys.
– DERIVATIVES **tom·boy·ish adj., tom·boy·ish·ness n.**

Tomb·stone /ˈto͞omˌstōn/ a historic frontier city in southeastern Arizona, the site of the 1881 gunfight at the O.K. Corral; pop. 1,566 (2008).

tomb·stone /ˈto͞omˌstōn/ ▶ **n. 1** a large, flat inscribed stone standing or laid over a grave.
2 (also **tombstone advertisement** or **tombstone ad**) an advertisement listing the underwriters or firms associated with a new issue of securities.

tom·cat /ˈtämˌkat/ ▶ **n.** a male domestic cat. ■ informal a sexually aggressive man; a womanizer.
▶ **v.** (**tomcats, tomcatting, tomcatted**) [no obj.] informal pursue women promiscuously for sexual gratification: *tomcatting all night and sleeping until afternoon.*

tom·cod /ˈtämˌkäd/ ▶ **n.** (pl. **same** or **tomcods**) a small edible greenish-brown North American fish of the cod family, popular with anglers. ● Genus *Microgradus*, family Gadidae: *M. proximus* of the Pacific coasts, and *M. tomcod* of the Atlantic coasts and fresh water.

Tom Col·lins /täm ˈkälənz/ ▶ **n.** a cocktail made from gin mixed with soda water, sugar, and lemon or lime juice.
– ORIGIN sometimes said to have been named after a 19th-cent. London bartender.

Tom, Dick, and Har·ry /ˈtäm ˈdik and ˈharē/ (also **Tom, Dick, or Harry**) ▶ **n.** used to refer to ordinary people in general: *he didn't want every Tom, Dick, and Harry knowing their business.*

tome /tōm/ ▶ **n.** chiefly humorous a book, esp. a large, heavy, scholarly one: *a weighty tome.*
– ORIGIN early 16th cent. (denoting one volume of a larger work): from French, via Latin from Greek *tomos* 'section, roll of papyrus, volume'; related to *temnein* 'to cut.'

-tome ▶ **comb. form 1** denoting an instrument for cutting: *microtome.*
2 denoting a section or segment: *myotome.*
– ORIGIN Sense 1 from Greek *-tomon* (neuter) 'that cuts'; sense 2 from Greek *tomē* 'a cutting,' both from *temnein* 'to cut.'

to·men·tum /tōˈmentəm/ ▶ **n.** (pl. **tomenta** /-tə/) Botany a layer of matted woolly down on the surface of a plant.
– DERIVATIVES **to·men·tose** /tōˈmentōs, ˈtōmənˌtōs/ **adj., to·men·tous** /-təs/ **adj.**

PRONUNCIATION KEY ə *ago, up*; ər *over, fur*; a *hat*; ā *ate*; ä *car*; e *let*; ē *see*; i *fit*; ī *by*; ɴɢ *sing*; ō *go*; ô *law, for*; oi *toy*; o͝o *good*; o͞o *goo*; ou *out*; ᴛʜ *thin*; ᴛʜ *then*; ᴢʜ *vision*

– ORIGIN late 17th cent.: from Latin, literally 'cushion stuffing.'

tom·fool /'tämˈfo͞ol/ ▶ n. dated a foolish person: [as modifier] *she was destined to take part in some tomfool caper.*

tom·fool·er·y /tämˈfo͞ol(ə)rē/ ▶ n. foolish or silly behavior: *he was no longer amused by Ozzie's youthful tomfoolery.*

To·mis /'tōməs/ ancient name for CONSTANȚA.

Tom·my /'tämē/ (also **tommy**) ▶ n. (pl. **Tommies**) informal a British private soldier. [nickname for the given name *Thomas*; from a use of the name *Thomas Atkins* in specimens of completed official forms in the British army during the 19th cent.]

tom·my gun /'tämē/ ▶ n. informal a type of submachine gun.
– ORIGIN 1920s: contraction of *Thompson gun*, named by its designer after John T. *Thompson* (1860–1940), the US army officer who conceived the idea for it.

Tom·my John sur·ger·y ▶ n. a surgical procedure in which a healthy tendon extracted from an arm (or sometimes a leg) is used to replace an arm's torn ligament. The healthy tendon is threaded through holes drilled into the bone above and below the elbow.
– ORIGIN 1970s: named after *Tommy John* (1943–), a US major-league pitcher who, after a debilitating injury, was able to resume his career after undergoing this surgery. The procedure was devised specifically for John by US orthopedic surgeon Dr. Frank Jobe in 1974.

tom·my·rot /'tämē,rät/ ▶ n. informal, dated nonsense; rubbish: *did you ever hear such awful tommyrot?*

to·mo·gram /'tōmə,gram/ ▶ n. a record obtained by tomography.

to·mog·ra·phy /tə'mägrəfē/ ▶ n. a technique for displaying a representation of a cross section through a human body or other solid object using X-rays or ultrasound.
– DERIVATIVES **to·mo·graph·ic** /,tōmə'grafik/ adj.
– ORIGIN 1930s: from Greek *tomos* 'slice, section' + -GRAPHY.

to·mor·row /tə'môrō, -'märō/ ▶ adv. on the day after today: *the show opens tomorrow.* ■ in the future, esp. the near future: *East Germany will not disappear tomorrow.*
▶ n. the day after today: *tomorrow is going to be a special day.* ■ the future, esp. the near future: *today's engineers are tomorrow's buyers.*
– PHRASES **as if there was** (or **as though there were**) **no tomorrow** with no regard for the future consequences: *I ate as if there was no tomorrow.* **tomorrow morning** (or **afternoon**, etc.) in the morning (or afternoon, etc.) of tomorrow. **tomorrow is another day** used after a bad experience to express one's belief that the future will be better.
– ORIGIN Middle English (as two words): from the preposition TO + MORROW. Compare with TODAY and TONIGHT.

Tom·pi·on /'tämpēən/, Thomas (*c.*1639–1713), English clock- and watchmaker. He made one of the first balance-spring watches and made two large pendulum clocks for the Royal Greenwich Observatory.

tom·pi·on /'tämpēən/ ▶ n. variant spelling of TAMPION.

Tomsk /tämsk, tômsk/ an industrial city in southern Siberia in Russia, a port on the Tom River; pop. 496,500 (est. 2008).

Tom Thumb ▶ n. [usu. as modifier] a dwarf variety of a cultivated flower or vegetable: *Tom Thumb lettuce.*
– ORIGIN late 19th cent.: from the name of the hero of a children's story, a plowman's son who was only as tall as his father's thumb.

tom·tit /tämˈtit/ ▶ n. a popular name for any of a number of small active songbirds, esp. a tit or a chickadee.

tom-tom ▶ n. a medium-sized cylindrical drum used in jazz bands, etc. ■ an early drum, of Native American or Asian origin, typically played with the hands.
– ORIGIN late 17th cent.: from Hindi *ṭam ṭam*, Telugu *ṭamaṭama*, of imitative origin.

-tomy ▶ comb. form cutting, esp. as part of a surgical process: *episiotomy.*
– ORIGIN from Greek *-tomia* 'cutting,' from *temnein* 'to cut.'

ton¹ /tən/ (abbr.: **t** also **tn**) ▶ n. **1** (also **short ton**) a unit of weight equal to 2,000 pounds avoirdupois (907.19 kg). ■ (also **long ton**) a unit of weight equal to 2,240 pounds avoirdupois (1016.05 kg). ■ short for METRIC TON. ■ (also **displacement ton**) a unit of measurement of a ship's weight representing the weight of water it displaces, equal to 2,240 pounds or 35 cubic feet (0.99 cu m). ■ (also **freight ton**) a unit of weight or volume of sea cargo, equal to a metric ton (1,000 kg) or 40 cubic feet. ■ (also **gross ton**) a unit of gross internal capacity, equal to 100 cubic feet (2.83 cu m). ■ (also **net** or **register ton**) an equivalent unit of net internal capacity. ■ a unit of refrigerating power able to freeze 2,000 pounds of water at 0°C in 24 hours. ■ a measure of capacity for various materials, esp. 40 cubic feet of timber.
2 (usu. **a ton of/tons of**) informal a large number or amount: *all of a sudden I had tons of friends | that bag of yours weighs a ton.*
– PHRASES **like a ton of bricks** see BRICK.
– ORIGIN Middle English: variant of TUN, both spellings being used for the container and the weight. The senses were differentiated in the late 17th cent.

ton² /tôN/ ▶ n. fashionable style or distinction. ■ (**the ton**) [treated as sing. or pl.] fashionable society.
– ORIGIN French, from Latin *tonus* (see TONE).

ton·al /'tōnl/ ▶ adj. of or relating to the tone of music, color, or writing: *his ear for tonal color | the poem's tonal lapses.* ■ of or relating to music written using conventional keys and harmony. ■ Phonetics (of a language) expressing semantic differences by varying the intonation given to words or syllables of a similar sound.
– DERIVATIVES **ton·al·ly** adv.
– ORIGIN late 18th cent. (designating church music in plainsong mode): from medieval Latin *tonalis*, from Latin *tonus* (see TONE).

to·nal·i·ty /tō'nalitē/ ▶ n. (pl. **tonalities**) **1** the character of a piece of music as determined by the key in which it is played or the relations between the notes of a scale or key. ■ the harmonic effect of being in a particular key: *the first bar would seem set to create a tonality of C major.* ■ the use of conventional keys and harmony as the basis of musical composition.
2 the color scheme or range of tones used in a picture.

ton·do /'tändō/ ▶ n. (pl. **tondi** /-dē/) a circular painting or relief.
– ORIGIN late 19th cent.: from Italian, literally 'round object,' from *rotondo* 'round,' from Latin *rotundus.*

tone /tōn/ ▶ n. **1** a musical or vocal sound with reference to its pitch, quality, and strength: *the piano tone appears monochrome or lacking in warmth.* ■ a modulation of the voice expressing a particular feeling or mood: *a firm tone of voice.* ■ a musical note, warble, or other sound used as a particular signal on a telephone or answering machine.
2 the general character or attitude of a place, piece of writing, situation, etc.: *trust her to lower the tone of the conversation | there was a general tone of ill-concealed glee in the reporting.* ■ informal an atmosphere of respectability or class: *they don't feel he gives the place tone.*
3 Phonetics (in some languages, such as Chinese) a particular pitch pattern on a syllable used to make semantic distinctions. ■ Phonetics (in some languages, such as English) intonation on a word or phrase used to add functional meaning.
4 (also **whole tone**) a basic interval in classical Western music, equal to two semitones and separating, for example, the first and second notes of an ordinary scale (such as C and D, or E and F sharp); a major second or whole step.
5 the particular quality of brightness, deepness, or hue of a tint or shade of a color: *an attractive color that is even in tone and texture | stained glass in vivid tones of red and blue.* ■ the general effect of color or of light and shade in a picture. ■ a slight degree of difference in the intensity of a color.
6 (also **muscle tone**) the normal level of firmness or slight contraction in a resting muscle. ■ Physiology the normal level of activity in a nerve fiber.
▶ v. [with obj.] **1** give greater strength or firmness to (the body or a part of it): *exercise tones up the muscles.* ■ [no obj.] (**tone up**) (of a muscle or bodily part) became stronger or firmer.
2 [no obj.] (**tone with**) harmonize with (something) in terms of color: *the rich orange color of the wood tones beautifully with the yellow roses.*
3 Photography give (a monochrome picture) an altered color in finishing by means of a chemical solution.
– PHRASAL VERBS **tone something down** make something less harsh in sound or color. ■ make something less extreme or intense: *she saw the need to tone down her protests.*
– DERIVATIVES **toned** adj. [in combination] *the fresh-toned singing,* **tone·less** adj., **tone·less·ly** adv.
– ORIGIN Middle English: from Old French *ton*, Latin *tonus*, from Greek *tonos* 'tension, tone,' from *teinein* 'to stretch.'

tone arm (also **tonearm** /'tōn,ärm/) ▶ n. the movable arm supporting the pickup of a record player.

tone clus·ter ▶ n. another term for NOTE CLUSTER.

tone col·or ▶ n. Music another term for TIMBRE.

tone-deaf ▶ adj. (of a person) unable to perceive differences of musical pitch accurately.
– DERIVATIVES **tone-deaf·ness** n.

tone dialing ▶ n. a method of telephone dialing in which each digit is transmitted as a different tone. Compare with PULSE DIALING.

tone lan·guage ▶ n. Linguistics a language in which variations in pitch distinguish different words.

ton·eme /'tōnēm/ ▶ n. Phonetics a phoneme distinguished from another only by its tone.
– DERIVATIVES **to·ne·mic** /tō'nēmik/ adj.
– ORIGIN 1920s: from TONE, on the pattern of *phoneme.*

tone-on-tone ▶ adj. (of a fabric or design) dyed with or using different shades of the same color.

tone po·em ▶ n. a piece of orchestral music, typically in one movement, on a descriptive or rhapsodic theme.

ton·er /'tōnər/ ▶ n. **1** an astringent liquid applied to the skin to reduce oiliness and improve its condition. ■ [with modifier] a device or exercise for making a specified part of the body firmer and stronger: *a tummy toner.*
2 a black or colored powder used in xerographic copying processes. ■ [usu. with adj. or noun modifier] a chemical bath for changing the color or shade of a photographic print, esp. as specified: *sepia or blue toners.*

tone row ▶ n. a particular sequence of the twelve notes of the chromatic scale used as a basis for twelve-tone (serial) music.

tong¹ /tôNG, täNG/ ▶ n. a Chinese association or secret society in the US, frequently associated with underworld criminal activity.
– ORIGIN late 19th cent.: from Chinese (Cantonese dialect) *t'ong*, literally 'meeting place.'

tong² ▶ v. [with obj.] collect, lift, or handle (items such as logs or oysters) using tongs.

Ton·ga /'täNGgə/ a country in the South Pacific Ocean that consists of an island group southeast of Fiji; pop. 120,900 (est. 2009); capital, Nuku'alofa; languages, Tongan and English (both official). Also called the FRIENDLY ISLANDS.

> The kingdom of Tonga consists of about 170 volcanic and coral islands, of which 36 are inhabited. Visited by the Dutch in the early 17th century, Tonga became a British protectorate in 1900 and an independent Commonwealth of Nations state in 1970. It has been a constitutional monarchy since 1875.

ton·ga /'täNGgə/ ▶ n. a light horse-drawn two-wheeled vehicle used in India.
– ORIGIN from Hindi *tāgā.*

Ton·gan /'täNGgən/ ▶ adj. of or relating to Tonga or its people or language.
▶ n. **1** a native or inhabitant of Tonga.
2 the Polynesian language spoken in Tonga.

Ton·gass Na·tion·al For·est /'täNGgəs/ a preserve in southeastern Alaska, the largest US national forest, in the panhandle and on islands in the Alexander Archipelago, the focus of 1990s disputes over logging.

tongs /tôNGz, täNGz/ ▶ plural n. (also **a pair of tongs**) an instrument with two movable arms that are joined at one end, used for picking up and holding things: *ice tongs.*
– ORIGIN Old English *tang(e)* (singular), of Germanic origin; related to Dutch *tang* and German *Zange.*

Tong·shan /'to͝oNG'SHän/ former name (1912–45) of XUZHOU.

tongue /təNG/ ▶ n. **1** the fleshy muscular organ in the mouth of a mammal, used for tasting, licking, swallowing, and (in humans) articulating speech. ■ the equivalent organ in other vertebrates, sometimes used (in snakes) as a scent organ or (in chameleons) for catching food. ■ an analogous organ in insects, formed from some of the mouthparts and used in feeding. ■ the tongue of a hoofed mammal, in particular an ox or lamb, as food. ■ used in reference to a person's style or manner of speaking: *he was a redoubtable debater with a caustic tongue.* ■ a particular language: *the prioress chatted to the peddler in a strange tongue.* ■ (**tongues**) see THE GIFT OF TONGUES below.
2 a thing resembling or likened to a tongue, in particular: ■ a long, low promontory of land. ■ a strip of leather or fabric under the laces in a shoe, attached only at the front end. ■ the pin of a buckle. ■ a projecting strip on a wooden board fitting into a groove on another. ■ the vibrating reed of a musical instrument or organ pipe. ■ a jet of flame: *a tongue of flame flashes four feet from the gun.*
▶ v. (**tongues, tonguing** /'təNGiNG/, **tongued**) [with obj.] **1** Music sound (a note) distinctly on a wind instrument by interrupting the air flow with the tongue.

2 lick or caress with the tongue: *the other horse tongued every part of the colt's mane.*
– PHRASES **find** (or **lose**) **one's tongue** be able (or unable) to express oneself after a shock. **get one's tongue around** pronounce (words): *she found it very difficult to get her tongue around the unfamiliar words.* **the gift of tongues** the power of speaking in unknown languages, regarded as one of the gifts of the Holy Spirit (Acts 2). **give tongue** (of hounds) bark, esp. on finding a scent. ■ express one's feelings or opinions freely, sometimes objectionably so. **keep a civil tongue in one's head** speak politely. **speak in tongues** speak in an unknown language during religious worship. (**with**) **tongue in cheek** without really meaning what one is saying or writing. **someone's tongue is hanging out** someone is very eager for something: *the tabloids have their tongues hanging out for this stuff.*
– DERIVATIVES **tongue·less** adj.
– ORIGIN Old English *tunge*, of Germanic origin; related to Dutch *tong*, German *Zunge* and Latin *lingua*.

tongue and groove ▶ n. wooden planking in which adjacent boards are joined by means of interlocking ridges and grooves down their sides.
– DERIVATIVES **tongued-and-grooved** adj.

tongued /təNGd/ ▶ adj. **1** [in combination] having a specified kind of tongue: *the blue-tongued lizard.* ■ (in carpentry) constructed using a tongue.
2 (of a note) played by tonguing.

tongue de·pres·sor ▶ n. an instrument, typically a small flat piece of wood, used by health practitioners to press down the tongue in order to allow inspection of the mouth or throat.

tongue-in-cheek ▶ adj. & adv. with ironic or flippant intent: [as adj.] *her delightful tongue-in-cheek humor* | [as adv.] *"I swear there's a female conspiracy against men!" he complained, tongue-in-cheek.*

tongue-lash·ing ▶ n. [in sing.] a loud or severe scolding: *the incensed boss gave him a tongue-lashing.*
– DERIVATIVES **tongue-lash** v.

tongue-tie ▶ n. a malformation that restricts the movement of the tongue and causes a speech impediment.

tongue-tied ▶ adj. **1** too shy or embarrassed to speak.
2 having a malformation restricting the movement of the tongue.

tongue-twist·er ▶ n. a sequence of words or sounds, typically of an alliterative kind, that are difficult to pronounce quickly and correctly, as, for example, *tie twine to three tree twigs.*
– DERIVATIVES **tongue-twist·ing** adj.

tongue worm ▶ n. a flattened wormlike parasite that infests vertebrates, esp. reptiles, having a sucking mouth with hooks for attachment to the lining of the respiratory tract. ● Subphylum Pentastomida, phylum Arthropoda; sometimes regarded as a class of crustacean.

ton·ic /ˈtänik/ ▶ n. **1** a medicinal substance taken to give a feeling of vigor or well-being. ■ something with an invigorating effect: *being needed is a tonic for someone at my age.*
2 short for TONIC WATER.
3 Music the first note in a scale that, in conventional harmony, provides the keynote of a piece of music.
▶ adj. **1** giving a feeling of vigor or well-being; invigorating.
2 Music relating to or denoting the first degree of a scale.
3 Phonetics denoting or relating to the syllable within a tone group that has greatest prominence, because it carries the main change of pitch.
4 relating to or restoring normal tone to muscles or other organs. ■ Physiology relating to, denoting, or producing continuous muscular contraction.
– DERIVATIVES **ton·i·cal·ly** /-ik(ə)lē/ adv.
– ORIGIN mid 17th cent.: from French *tonique*, from Greek *tonikos* 'of or for stretching,' from *tonos* (see TONE).

ton·ic–clon·ic /ˌtänik ˈklänik, ˈklōnik/ ▶ adj. Medicine of or characterized by successive phases of tonic and clonic spasm (as in *grand mal* epilepsy).

to·nic·i·ty /tōˈnisitē/ ▶ n. **1** muscle tone.
2 Linguistics the pattern of tones or stress in speech.
3 Biology the state of a solution in respect of osmotic pressure: *the tonicity of the fluid.*

ton·ic sol-fa /ˌsōl ˈfä/ ▶ n. a system of naming the notes of the scale (usually **do, re, mi, fa, sol, la, ti**) developed in England and used esp. to teach singing, with do as the keynote of all major keys and la as the keynote of all minor keys. See SOLMIZATION.

ton·ic wa·ter ▶ n. a bitter carbonated soft drink made with quinine, used esp. as a mixer with gin or other liquors (originally used as a stimulant of appetite and digestion).

ton·i·fy /ˈtōnəˌfī, ˈtän-/ ▶ v. (**tonifies, tonifying, tonified**) [with obj.] impart tone to (the body or a part of it). ■ (of acupuncture or herbal medicine) increase the available energy of (an organ, part, or system of the body).
– DERIVATIVES **ton·i·fi·ca·tion** /ˌtōnəfiˈkāSHən/ n.

to·night /təˈnīt/ ▶ adv. on the present or approaching evening or night: *are you doing anything tonight?*
▶ n. the evening or night of the present day: *tonight is a night to remember.*
– ORIGIN Old English *tō niht*, from the preposition TO + NIGHT. Compare with TODAY and TOMORROW.

ton·ka bean /ˈtäNGkə/ ▶ n. the black seed of a South American tree, which has a vanillalike fragrance. The dried beans are cured in rum or other alcohol and then used in perfumery and for scenting and flavoring tobacco, ice cream, and other products. ● The tree is *Dipteryx odorata*, family Leguminosae.
– ORIGIN late 18th cent.: *tonka*, a local word in Guyana.

Ton·kin /ˈtäNGkən, ˈtänˈkin/ a mountainous region in northern Vietnam, centered on the Red River delta.

Ton·kin, Gulf of an arm of the South China Sea, bounded by the coasts of southern China and northern Vietnam. Its chief port is Haiphong. An incident in 1964 led to increased US military involvement in the area.

Ton·lé Sap /tōnˈlā ˈsap/ a lake in central Cambodia, linked to the Mekong River by the Tonlé Sap River. The ruins of the ancient city Angkor stand on its northwestern shore.

ton-mile /ˈtən ˌmīl/ ▶ n. one ton of freight carried one mile, as a unit of traffic.

ton·nage /ˈtənij/ ▶ n. weight in tons, esp. of cargo or freight: *road convoys carry more tonnage.* ■ the size or carrying capacity of a ship measured in tons. ■ shipping considered in terms of total carrying capacity: *the port's total tonnage.*
– ORIGIN early 17th cent. (denoting a charge per ton on cargo): from TON¹ + -AGE.

tonne /tən/ ▶ n. another term for METRIC TON.
– ORIGIN late 19th cent.: from French; compare with TON¹.

ton·neau /təˈnō, ˈtänō/ ▶ n. (pl. **tonneaus** or **tonneaux** /təˈnōz, ˈtänōz/) the part of an automobile, typically an open car, occupied by the back seats. ■ short for TONNEAU COVER.

ton·neau cov·er ▶ n. a protective cover for the seats in an open car or cabin cruiser when they are not in use.

to·nom·e·ter /tōˈnämitər/ ▶ n. **1** a tuning fork or other instrument for measuring the pitch of musical tones.
2 an instrument for measuring the pressure in a part of the body, such as the eyeball (to test for glaucoma) or a blood vessel.
– ORIGIN early 18th cent.: from Greek *tonos* (see TONE) + -METER.

ton·o·plast /ˈtänəˌplast, ˈtō-/ ▶ n. Botany a membrane that bounds the chief vacuole of a plant cell.
– ORIGIN late 19th cent.: from Greek *tonos* 'tension, tone' + *plastos* 'formed.'

ton·sil /ˈtänsəl/ ▶ n. either of two small masses of lymphoid tissue in the throat, one on each side of the root of the tongue.
– DERIVATIVES **ton·sil·lar** /-sələr/ adj.
– ORIGIN late 16th cent.: from French *tonsilles* or Latin *tonsillae* (plural).

ton·sil·lec·to·my /ˌtänsəˈlektəmē/ ▶ n. (pl. **tonsillectomies**) a surgical operation to remove the tonsils.

ton·sil·li·tis /ˌtänsəˈlītis/ ▶ n. inflammation of the tonsils.

ton·so·ri·al /tänˈsôrēəl/ ▶ adj. formal or humorous of or relating to hairdressing.
– ORIGIN early 19th cent.: from Latin *tonsorius* (from *tonsor* 'barber,' from *tondere* 'shear, clip') + -AL.

ton·sure /ˈtänSHər/ ▶ n. a part of a monk's or priest's head left bare on top by shaving off the hair. ■ [in sing.] an act of shaving the top of a monk's or priest's head as a preparation for entering a religious order.
▶ v. [with obj.] (often as adj. **tonsured**) shave the hair on the crown of.
– ORIGIN late Middle English: from Old French, or from Latin *tonsura*, from *tondere* 'shear, clip.'

ton·tine /ˈtänˌtēn, tänˈtēn/ ▶ n. an annuity shared by subscribers to a loan or common fund, the shares increasing as subscribers die until the last survivor enjoys the whole income. ■ a scheme for life insurance in which the beneficiaries are those who survive and maintain a policy to the end of a given period.
– ORIGIN mid 18th cent.: from French, named after Lorenzo *Tonti* (1630–95), a Neapolitan banker who started such a program to raise government loans in France (*c.*1653).

Ton·ton Ma·coute /ˈtôNˌtôNməˈko͞ot/ ▶ n. (pl. **Tontons Macoutes** pronunc. **same**) a member of a notoriously brutal militia formed by President François Duvalier of Haiti, active from 1961 to 1986.
– ORIGIN Haitian French, apparently with reference to an ogre of folk tales.

to·nus /ˈtōnəs/ ▶ n. the constant low-level activity of a body tissue, esp. muscle tone.
– ORIGIN late 19th cent.: from Latin, from Greek *tonos* 'tension.'

Ton·y /ˈtōnē/ ▶ n. (pl. **Tonys**) any of a number of awards given annually in the US for outstanding achievement in the theater in various categories.
– ORIGIN from the nickname of Antoinette Perry (1888–1946), US actress and director.

ton·y /ˈtōnē/ ▶ adj. (**tonier, toniest**) informal fashionable among wealthy or stylish people: *a tony restaurant.*
– ORIGIN late 19th cent.: from the noun TONE + -Y¹.

too /to͞o/ ▶ adv. **1** [as submodifier] to a higher degree than is desirable, permissible, or possible; excessively: *he was driving too fast* | *he wore suits that seemed a size **too small for** him.* ■ informal very: *you're too kind.*
2 in addition; also: *is he coming too?* ■ moreover (used when adding a further point): *she is a grown woman, and a strong one too.*
– PHRASES **all too ——** used to emphasize that something is the case to an extreme or unwelcome extent: *failures are all too common.* **none too ——** far from; not very: *her sight's none too good.* **only too** see ONLY. **too bad** see BAD. **too far** see FAR. **too much** see MUCH.
– ORIGIN Old English, stressed form of TO, spelled *too* from the 16th cent.

too·dle-oo /ˌto͞odl ˈo͞o/ ▶ exclam. informal, dated goodbye: *we'll see you later, toodle-oo!*
– ORIGIN early 20th cent.: perhaps an alteration of French *à tout à l'heure* 'see you soon.'

took /to͝ok/ past of TAKE.

tool /to͞ol/ ▶ n. **1** a device or implement, esp. one held in the hand, used to carry out a particular function: *gardening tools.* ■ a thing used in an occupation or pursuit: *computers are an essential tool* | *the ability to write clearly is **a tool of the trade**.* ■ a person used or exploited by another: *the beautiful Estella is Miss Havisham's tool.* ■ Computing a piece of software that carries out a particular function, typically creating or modifying another program.
2 a distinct design in the tooling of a book. ■ a small stamp or roller used to make such a design.
3 vulgar slang a man's penis. ■ informal a dull, slow-witted, or socially inept person.
▶ v. **1** [with obj.] (usu. **be tooled**) impress a design on (leather, esp. a leather book cover): *volumes bound in green leather and tooled in gold.* ■ dress (stone) with a chisel.
2 equip or be equipped with tools for industrial production: [with obj.] *the factory must be tooled to produce the models* | [no obj.] *they were **tooling up** for production.*
3 [no obj.] informal drive or ride in a casual or leisurely manner: *tooling around town in a pink Rolls-Royce.*
– DERIVATIVES **tool·er** n.
– ORIGIN Old English *tōl*, from a Germanic base meaning 'prepare'; compare with TAW¹. The verb dates from the early 19th cent.

tool·bar /ˈto͞olˌbär/ ▶ n. Computing (in a program with a graphical user interface) a strip of icons used to perform certain functions.

tool·box /ˈto͞olˌbäks/ ▶ n. a box or container for keeping tools in. ■ Computing a set of software tools. ■ Computing the set of programs or functions accessible from a single menu.

tool·ing /ˈto͞oliNG/ ▶ n. **1** assorted tools, esp. ones required for a mechanized process. ■ the process of making or working something with tools.
2 the ornamentation of a leather book cover with designs impressed by heated tools.

tool kit ▶ n. a set of tools, esp. one kept in a bag or box and used for a particular purpose. ■ Computing a set of software tools.

tool·mak·er /ˈto͞olˌmākər/ ▶ n. a maker of tools, esp. a person who makes and maintains tools for use in a manufacturing process.
– DERIVATIVES **tool·mak·ing** /-ˌmākiNG/ n.

tool push·er (also **toolpusher**) ▶ n. a person who directs the drilling on an oil rig.

tool·set /ˈto͞olset/ ▶ n. Computing a set of software tools.

tool·shed /ˈto͞olˌsHed/ (also **tool shed**) ▶ n. a one-story structure, typically in a backyard, used for storing tools.

tool·tip /ˈto͞oltip/ ▶ n. Computing a message that appears when a cursor is positioned over an icon, image, hyperlink, or other element in a graphical user interface.

toon /to͞on/ ▶ n. informal a cartoon film. ■ a character in such a film.
– ORIGIN 1930s: shortening of CARTOON.

too·nie /ˈto͞onē/ (also **twoonie**) ▶ n. Canadian informal the Canadian two-dollar coin.
– ORIGIN after LOONIE.

toot /to͞ot/ ▶ n. **1** a short, sharp sound made by a horn, trumpet, or similar instrument.
2 informal a snort of a drug, esp. cocaine. ■ cocaine.
3 informal a spell of drinking and lively enjoyment; a spree: *a sales manager **on a toot**.*
▶ v. [with obj.] **1** sound (a horn or similar instrument) with a short, sharp sound: *behind us an impatient driver tooted a horn.* ■ [no obj.] make such a sound: *a car tooted at us.*
2 informal snort (cocaine).
– DERIVATIVES **toot·er** n.
– ORIGIN early 16th cent.: probably from Middle Low German *tūten*, but possibly an independent imitative formation.

tooth /to͞oTH/ ▶ n. (pl. **teeth** /tēTH/) **1** each of a set of hard, bony enamel-coated structures in the jaws of most vertebrates, used for biting and chewing. ■ a similar hard, pointed structure in invertebrate animals, typically functioning in the mechanical breakdown of food. ■ (**teeth**) genuine force or effectiveness of a body or in a law or agreement: *the Charter would be fine if it had teeth and could be enforced.*
2 a projecting part on a tool or other instrument, esp. one of a series that function or engage together, such as a cog on a gearwheel or a point on a saw or comb. ■ a projecting part on an animal or plant, esp. one of a jagged or dentate row on the margin of a leaf or shell.
3 an appetite or liking for a particular thing: *what a tooth for fruit a monkey has!*
4 roughness given to a surface to allow color or glue to adhere.
– PHRASES **armed to the teeth** formidably armed. **fight tooth and nail** fight fiercely. **get** (or **sink**) **one's teeth into** work energetically and productively on (a task): *the course gives students something to get their teeth into.* **in the teeth of** directly against (the wind). ■ in spite of or contrary to (opposition or difficulty): *we defended it in the teeth of persecution.* **set someone's teeth on edge** see EDGE.
– DERIVATIVES **toothed** adj., **tooth·like** /-ˌlīk/ adj.
– ORIGIN Old English *tōth* (plural *tēth*), of Germanic origin; related to Dutch *tand* and German *Zahn*, from an Indo-European root shared by Latin *dent-*, Greek *odont-*.

tooth·ache /ˈto͞oTHˌāk/ ▶ n. a pain in a tooth or teeth: *he has a toothache.*

tooth·ache tree ▶ n. another term for NORTHERN PRICKLY-ASH (see PRICKLY-ASH).

tooth·brush /ˈto͞oTHˌbrəsH/ ▶ n. a small brush with a long handle, used for cleaning the teeth.

tooth·brush mus·tache ▶ n. a short bristly mustache trimmed to a rectangular shape.

toothed whale ▶ n. a predatory whale having teeth rather than baleen plates. Toothed whales include sperm whales, killer whales, beaked whales, narwhals, dolphins, and porpoises. ● Suborder Odontoceti, order Cetacea: six families and numerous species.

tooth fair·y ▶ n. a fairy said to leave a gift, esp. a coin, under a child's pillow in exchange for a baby tooth that has fallen out and been put under the pillow.

tooth·less /ˈto͞oTHlis/ ▶ adj. having no teeth, typically through old age: *a toothless old man.* ■ lacking genuine force or effectiveness: *laws that are well intentioned but toothless.*
– DERIVATIVES **tooth·less·ly** adv., **tooth·less·ness** n.

tooth·paste /ˈto͞oTHˌpāst/ ▶ n. a paste used on a toothbrush for cleaning the teeth.

tooth·pick /ˈto͞oTHˌpik/ ▶ n. a short pointed piece of wood or plastic used for removing bits of food lodged between the teeth.

tooth pow·der ▶ n. powder used for cleaning the teeth.

tooth shell ▶ n. a burrowing mollusk with a slender tusk-shaped shell, which is open at both ends and typically white, and a three-lobed foot. Also called TUSK SHELL. ● Class Scaphopoda, in particular the genus *Dentalium*.

tooth·some /ˈto͞oTHsəm/ ▶ adj. (of food) temptingly tasty: *a toothsome morsel.* ■ informal (of a person) good-looking; attractive.
– DERIVATIVES **tooth·some·ly** adv., **tooth·some·ness** n.

tooth·y /ˈto͞oTHē/ ▶ adj. (**toothier**, **toothiest**) having or showing large, numerous, or prominent teeth: *a toothy smile.*
– DERIVATIVES **tooth·i·ly** /-THəlē/ adv.

toot·in' /ˈto͞otn/ ▶ adj. informal used for emphasis: *he said he was damned tootin' he was right.*

too·tle /ˈto͞otl/ ▶ v. **1** [no obj.] casually make a series of sounds on a horn, trumpet, or similar instrument: *he tootled on the horn.* ■ [with obj.] play (an instrument) or make (a sound or tune) in such a way: *the video games tootled their tunes.*
2 [no obj.] informal go or travel in a leisurely way: *they were **tootling along** the coast.*
▶ n. [usu. in sing.] **1** an act or sound of casual playing on an instrument such as a horn or trumpet.
2 informal a leisurely journey.
– ORIGIN early 19th cent.: frequentative of TOOT.

too-too ▶ adv. & adj. informal, dated used affectedly to convey that one finds something excessively annoying or fatiguing: [as adv.] *it had become too-too tiring* | [as adj.] *it is all just too-too.*
– ORIGIN late 19th cent.: reduplication of TOO.

toot·sie /ˈto͞otsē/ (also **tootsy**) ▶ n. (pl. **tootsies**) informal **1** a person's foot.
2 a young woman, esp. one perceived as being sexually available.
– ORIGIN mid 19th cent.: humorous diminutive of FOOT.

toot sweet ▶ adv. informal immediately: *hop down here toot sweet and let's have a look at it.*
– ORIGIN early 20th cent.: anglicized form of French *tout de suite*.

top[1] /täp/ ▶ n. **1** [usu. in sing.] the highest or uppermost point, part, or surface of something: *Eileen stood at the top of the stairs* | *fill the cup almost to the top.* ■ (usu. **tops**) the leaves, stems, and shoots of a plant, esp. those of a vegetable grown for its root. ■ chiefly Brit. the end of something that is furthest from the speaker or a point of reference: *the bus shelter at the top of the road.*
2 a thing or part placed on, fitted to, or covering the upper part of something, in particular: ■ a garment covering the upper part of the body and worn with a skirt, pants, or shorts. ■ a lid, cover, or cap for something: *the pen dries out if you leave the top off.* ■ a platform at the head of a ship's mast, esp. (in a sailing ship) a platform around the head of each of the lower masts, serving to extend the topmast shrouds.
3 (**the top**) the highest or most important rank, level, or position: *her talent will take her right to the top* | *the people **at the top** must be competent.* ■ (**tops**) informal a person or thing regarded as particularly good or pleasant: *Davison is tops in its market.* ■ the utmost degree or the highest level: *she shouted at the top of her voice.* ■ Brit. the highest gear of a motor vehicle. ■ the high-frequency component of reproduced sound.
4 Baseball the first half of an inning: *the top of the eighth.*
5 short for TOPSPIN.
6 (usu. **tops**) a bundle of long wool fibers prepared for spinning.
7 Physics one of six flavors of quark.
8 informal a male who takes the active role in homosexual intercourse, esp. anal intercourse.
▶ adj. [attrib.] highest in position, rank, or degree: *the top button of his shirt* | *a top executive.*
▶ v. (**tops**, **topping**, **topped**) [with obj.] **1** exceed (an amount, level, or number); be more than: *losses are expected to top $100 million this year.* ■ be at the highest place or rank in (a list, poll, chart, or league): *her debut album topped the charts for five weeks.* ■ be taller than: *he topped her by several inches.* ■ surpass (a person or previous achievement or action); outdo: *he was baffled as to how he could top his past work.* ■ appear as the chief performer or attraction at: *Hopper topped a great night of boxing.* ■ reach the top of (a hill or other stretch of rising ground): *they topped a rise and began a slow descent.*
2 (usu. **be topped**) provide with a top or topping: *baked potatoes topped with melted cheese.* ■ complete (an outfit) with an upper garment, hat, or item of jewelry: *a white dress topped by a dark cardigan.* ■ remove the top of (a vegetable or fruit) in preparation for cooking.
3 Golf mishit (the ball or a stroke) by hitting above the center of the ball.
▶ adv. (**tops**) informal at the most: *he makes $28,000 a year, tops.*
– PHRASES **at the top of one's game** informal at the height of one's powers: *this film is the work of a director at the top of his game.* **at the top of one's lungs** as loudly as possible. **from top to bottom** completely; thoroughly: *we searched the place from top to bottom.* **from top to toe** completely; all over: *she seemed to glow from top to toe.* **from the top** informal from the beginning: *they rehearsed Act One from the top.* **off the top of one's head** see HEAD. **on top 1** on the highest point or uppermost surface: *a hill with a flat rock on top.* ■ on the upper part of the head: *my hair's thinning on top.* **2** in a leading or the dominant position: *his party came out on top in last month's elections.* **on top of 1** on the highest point or uppermost surface of: *a town perched on top of a hill.* ■ so as to cover; over: *trays stacked one on top of another.* ■ in close proximity to: *we all lived on top of each other.* **2** in command or control of: *he couldn't get on top of his work.* **3** in addition to: *on top of everything else, he's a brilliant linguist.* **on top of the world** informal happy and elated. **over the top** /ˌōvər T͟Hə ˈtäp/ **1** informal to an excessive or exaggerated degree, in particular so as to go beyond reasonable or acceptable limits: *his reactions had been a bit over the top.* **2** chiefly historical over the parapet of a trench and into battle. **top dollar** informal a very high price: *I pay top dollar for my materials.* **top forty** (or **ten**, etc.) the first forty (or ten, etc.) records in the pop music charts. **to top it all** as a culminating, typically unpleasant, event or action in a series: *her father had a fatal heart attack, and to top it all her mother disowned her.* **up top** see UP.
– PHRASAL VERBS **top something off 1** (often **be topped off**) finish something in a memorable or notable way: *the festivities were topped off with the awarding of prizes.* **2** informal fill up a nearly full tank with fuel. **top out** reach an upper limit: *collectors whose budgets tend to top out at about $50,000.* **top something out** put the highest structural feature on a building, typically as a ceremony to mark the building's completion. **top something up** chiefly Brit. add to a number or amount to bring it up to a certain level: *a 0.5 percent bonus is offered to top up savings rates.* ■ fill up a glass or other partly full container.
– DERIVATIVES **topped** adj. [in combination] *a glass-topped table.*
– ORIGIN late Old English *topp* (noun), of Germanic origin; related to Dutch *top* 'summit, crest.'

top[2] ▶ n. (also **spinning top**) a conical, spherical, or pear-shaped toy that with a quick or vigorous twist may be set to spin.
– ORIGIN late Old English, of unknown origin.

Top 40 ▶ plural n. the forty most popular songs of a given time period.
▶ adj. made up of, or broadcasting the Top 40: *a Top 40 countdown.*

to·paz /ˈtōpaz/ ▶ n. **1** a precious stone, typically colorless, yellow, or pale blue, consisting of a fluorine-containing aluminum silicate. ■ a dark yellow color.
2 a large tropical American hummingbird with a yellowish throat and a long tail. ● Genus *Topaza*, family Trochilidae: two species.
– ORIGIN Middle English (denoting a yellow sapphire): from Old French *topace*, via Latin from Greek *topazos*.

to·paz·o·lite /tōˈpazəˌlīt/ ▶ n. a yellowish-green variety of andradite (garnet).
– ORIGIN early 19th cent.: from TOPAZ + -LITE.

top boot ▶ n. chiefly historical a high boot with a broad band of a different material or color at the top.

top brass ▶ n. see BRASS.

top·coat /ˈtäpˌkōt/ ▶ n. **1** an overcoat.
2 an outer coat of paint.

top dead cen·ter ▶ n. the furthest point of a piston's travel, at which it changes from an upward to a downward stroke.

top dog ▶ n. informal a person who is successful or dominant in their field: *he was a top dog in the City.*

top-down ▶ adj. **1** denoting a system of government or management in which actions and policies are initiated at the highest level; hierarchical.
2 proceeding from the general to the particular: *a top-down approach to research.* ■ Computing working from the top or root of a treelike system toward the branches.

top draw·er ▶ n. (**the top drawer**) informal high social position or class: *George and Madge were not out of the top drawer.*
▶ adj. (**top-drawer**) informal of the highest quality or social class: *a top-drawer performance.*

top dress·ing ▶ n. an application of manure or fertilizer to the surface layer of soil or a lawn.
– DERIVATIVES **top-dress** v.

tope[1] /tōp/ ▶ v. [no obj.] archaic or literary drink alcohol to excess, esp. on a regular basis.
– DERIVATIVES **top·er** n.
– ORIGIN mid 17th cent.: perhaps an alteration of obsolete *top* 'overbalance'; perhaps from Dutch *toppen* 'slant or tilt a ship's yard.'

t

tope² ▶ **n.** another term for STUPA.
– ORIGIN from Punjabi *thūp, thop* 'barrow, mound,' apparently related to Sanskrit *stūpa*.

tope³ ▶ **n.** a small grayish slender-bodied shark, occurring chiefly in inshore waters. ● Genus *Galeorhinus*, family Carcharhinidae: the eastern Atlantic *G. galeus*, and the commercially important *G. australis* of Australia.
– ORIGIN late 17th cent.: perhaps of Cornish origin.

to·pee ▶ **n.** variant spelling of TOPI¹.

To·pe·ka /tə'pēkə/ the capital of Kansas, in the east central part of the state; pop. 123,446 (est. 2008).

top-end ▶ **adj.** (of a product) at the top of a range; high quality or sophisticated: *top-end automobiles.*

top fer·men·ta·tion ▶ **n.** the process by which ale-type beers are fermented, proceeding for a relatively short period at high temperature with the yeast rising to the top.

top flight ▶ **n.** (**the top flight**) the highest rank or level.
▶ **adj.** [attrib.] of the highest rank or level: *a top-flight investment bank.*

top·gal·lant /täp'galənt, tə'gal-/ ▶ **n.** (also **topgallant mast**) the section of a square-rigged sailing ship's mast immediately above the topmast. ■ (also **topgallant sail**) a sail set on such a mast.

top ham·per ▶ **n.** Sailing sails, rigging, or other things above decks creating top-heaviness or catching too much wind.

top hat ▶ **n.** a man's formal hat with a high cylindrical crown.

top hat

top-heav·y ▶ **adj.** disproportionately heavy at the top so as to be in danger of toppling. ■ (of an organization) having a disproportionately large number of people in senior administrative positions. ■ informal (of a woman) having a disproportionately large bust.
– DERIVATIVES **top-heav·i·ly** **adv.**, **top-heav·i·ness** **n.**

To·phet /'tōfet/ ▶ **n.** a term for hell.
– ORIGIN late Middle English: from Hebrew *tōpet*, the name of a place in the Valley of Hinnom near Jerusalem used for idolatrous worship, including the sacrifice of children (see Jer. 19:6), and later for burning refuse.

top-hole ▶ **adj.** Brit. informal, dated excellent; first-rate.

to·phus /'tōfəs/ ▶ **n.** (pl. **tophi** /-fī/) Medicine a deposit of crystalline uric acid and other substances at the surface of joints or in skin or cartilage, typically as a feature of gout.
– ORIGIN early 17th cent.: from Latin, denoting loose porous stones of various kinds.

to·pi¹ /'tōpē/ (also **topee**) ▶ **n.** (pl. **topis** also **topees**) chiefly Indian a hat, esp. a sola topi.
– ORIGIN from Hindi *ṭopī* 'hat.'

to·pi² ▶ **n.** (pl. **same** or **topis**) a large African antelope related to the hartebeests, with a pattern of bold black patches on a reddish coat, and thick ridged horns. ● *Damaliscus lunatus*, family Bovidae, in particular the race *D. l. topi* of East Africa. Compare with SASSABY.
– ORIGIN late 19th cent.: from Mende.

to·pi·ar·y /'tōpē,erē/ ▶ **n.** (pl. **topiaries**) the art or practice of clipping shrubs or trees into ornamental shapes. ■ shrubs or trees clipped into ornamental shapes in such a way: *a cottage surrounded by topiary and flowers.*
– DERIVATIVES **to·pi·ar·i·an** /,tōpē'e(ə)rēən/ **adj.**, **to·pi·a·rist** /-ərist/ **n.**
– ORIGIN late 16th cent.: from French *topiaire*, from Latin *topiarius* 'ornamental gardener,' from *topia opera* 'fancy gardening,' from a diminutive of Greek *topos* 'place.'

topiary

top·ic /'täpik/ ▶ **n.** a matter dealt with in a text, discourse, or conversation; a subject: *her favorite topic of conversation is her partner.* ■ Linguistics that part of a sentence about which something is said, typically the first major constituent.
– ORIGIN late 15th cent. (originally denoting a set or book of general rules or ideas): from Latin *topica*, from Greek *ta topika*, literally 'matters concerning commonplaces' (the title of a treatise by Aristotle), from *topos* 'a place.'

top·i·cal /'täpikəl/ ▶ **adj.** **1** (of a subject) of immediate relevance, interest, or importance owing to its relation to current events: *a wide variety of subjects of topical interest.* ■ relating to a particular subject; classified according to subject: *annotated links to resources in eleven topical categories.* ■ Philately relating to the collecting of postage stamps with designs connected with the same subject.
2 chiefly Medicine relating or applied directly to a part of the body.
▶ **n.** Philately a postage stamp forming part of a set or collection with designs connected with the same subject.
– DERIVATIVES **top·i·cal·i·ty** /,täpə'kalitē/ **n.**, **top·i·cal·ly** /-ik(ə)lē/ **adv.**
– ORIGIN late 16th cent.: from Greek *topikos* + -AL. Early use was as a term in logic and rhetoric describing a rule or argument as 'applicable in most but not all cases.'

top·i·cal·ize /'täpikə,līz/ ▶ **v.** [with obj.] Linguistics cause (a subject, word, or phrase) to be the topic of a sentence or discourse, typically by placing it first.
– DERIVATIVES **top·i·cal·i·za·tion** /,täpəkəli'zāsнən/ **n.**

top·ic sen·tence ▶ **n.** a sentence that expresses the main idea of the paragraph in which it occurs.

top·knot /'täp,nät/ ▶ **n.** a knot of hair arranged on the top of the head. ■ a decorative knot or bow of ribbon worn on the top of the head, popular in the 18th century. ■ (in an animal or bird) a tuft or crest of hair or feathers.

top·less /'täpləs/ ▶ **adj.** (of a woman or a woman's item of clothing) having or leaving the breasts uncovered: *a topless dancer | a topless swimsuit.* ■ (of a place such as a bar or beach) where there are women wearing such clothes: *a topless beach.*
– DERIVATIVES **top·less·ness** **n.**

top-lev·el ▶ **adj.** of the highest level of importance or prestige: *top-level talks.*

top light (also **toplight**) ▶ **n.** **1** a skylight: (as adj. **top-lighted**) *a top-lighted gallery.*
2 Brit. a small pane above a main window, typically opening outward and upward.

top-line ▶ **adj.** [attrib.] of the highest quality or ranking: *a top-line act.*

top·loft·y /'täp,lôftē/ ▶ **adj.** informal haughty and arrogant.

top·mast /'täp,mast, -məst/ ▶ **n.** the second section of a square-rigged sailing ship's mast, immediately above the lower mast.

top·min·now /'täp,minō/ ▶ **n.** a small surface-swimming fish related to the killifishes, found in fresh, brackish, and salt water throughout North America. ● Genus *Fundulus*, family Fundulidae: many species, including the **banded topminnow** (*F. cingulatus*) and the **eastern starhead topminnow** (*F. escambiae*).

top·most /'täp,mōst/ ▶ **adj.** highest in physical position; highest: *we watched a squirrel negotiate the topmost branches of a nearby tree.* ■ highest in status or importance; foremost: *the rider's safety must be the topmost priority.*

top-notch ▶ **adj.** informal of the highest quality; excellent: *a top-notch hotel.*
– DERIVATIVES **top-notch·er** **n.**

top note ▶ **n.** **1** a dominant scent in a perfume: *fragrant musk with a fresh citrus top note.*
2 the highest or a very high note in a piece of music or a singer's vocal range.

top·o /'täpō/ ▶ **n.** (pl. **topos**) informal a topographic map: *a topo drawn for the Hell Cave area.* ■ Climbing a diagram of a mountain with details of routes to the top marked on it.
▶ **adj.** short for TOPOGRAPHICAL: *the topo map showed a watering hole.*
– ORIGIN 1970s: abbreviation of *topographic* (see TOPOGRAPHICAL).

topog. ▶ **abbr.** ■ topographical. ■ topography.

top·o·graph·i·cal /,täpə'grafikəl/ ▶ **adj.** of or relating to the arrangement or accurate representation of the physical features of an area: *the topographical features of the river valley.* ■ (of a work of art or an artist) dealing with or depicting places (esp. towns), buildings, and natural prospects in a realistic and detailed manner. ■ Anatomy & Biology relating to or representing the physical distribution of parts or features on the surface of or within an organ or organism.
– DERIVATIVES **top·o·graph·ic** **adj.**, **top·o·graph·i·cal·ly** /-ik(ə)lē/ **adv.**

to·pog·ra·phy /tə'pägrəfē/ ▶ **n.** the arrangement of the natural and artificial physical features of an area: *the topography of the island.* ■ a detailed description or representation on a map of such features. ■ Anatomy & Biology the distribution of parts or features on the surface of or within an organ or organism.
– DERIVATIVES **to·pog·ra·pher** /-fər/ **n.**
– ORIGIN late Middle English: via late Latin from Greek *topographia*, from *topos* 'place' + *-graphia* (see -GRAPHY).

to·poi /'tōpoi/ plural form of TOPOS.

top·o·i·so·mer /,täpō'īsəmər/ ▶ **n.** Biochemistry a topologically distinct isomer, esp. of DNA.

top·o·i·som·er·ase /,täpō,ī'sämə,rās, -,rāz/ ▶ **n.** Biochemistry an enzyme that alters the supercoiled form of a DNA molecule.
– ORIGIN 1970s: from Greek *topos* 'place' + ISOMER + -ASE.

top·o·log·i·cal space /,täpə'läjikəl/ ▶ **n.** Mathematics a space that has an associated family of subsets that constitute a topology. The relationships between members of the space are mathematically analogous to those between points in ordinary two- and three-dimensional space.

to·pol·o·gy /tə'päləjē/ ▶ **n.** **1** Mathematics the study of geometric properties and spatial relations unaffected by the continuous change of shape or size of figures. ■ a family of open subsets of an abstract space such that the union and the intersection of any two of them are members of the family, and that includes the space itself and the empty set.
2 the way in which constituent parts are interrelated or arranged: *the topology of a computer network.*
– DERIVATIVES **top·o·log·i·cal** /,täpə'läjikəl/ **adj.**, **top·o·log·i·cal·ly** /,täpə'läjik(ə)lē/ **adv.**, **to·pol·o·gist** /-jist/ **n.**
– ORIGIN late 19th cent.: via German from Greek *topos* 'place' + -LOGY.

top·o·nym /'täpə,nim/ ▶ **n.** a place name, esp. one derived from a topographical feature.
– ORIGIN 1930s: from Greek *topos* 'place' + *onuma* 'name.'

to·pon·y·my /tə'pänəmē/ ▶ **n.** the study of place names.
– DERIVATIVES **top·o·nym·ic** /,täpə'nimik/ **adj.**
– ORIGIN late 19th cent.: from Greek *topos* 'place' + *onuma* 'name.'

to·pos /'tōpōs/ ▶ **n.** (pl. **topoi** /-poi/) a traditional theme or formula in literature.
– ORIGIN 1940s: from Greek, literally 'place.'

top·per /'täpər/ ▶ **n.** **1** something that culminates a situation; a clincher: *the topper was a late-evening interview with an old man who ran the place.*
2 a hard protective lightweight cover or shell mounted on the back or bed of a pickup truck. ■ a type of camper mounted on a truck bed.
3 informal a top hat.
4 Brit. informal, dated an exceptionally good person or thing.
5 a woman's loose, short coat.

top·ping /'täpiNG/ ▶ **n.** a layer of food poured or spread over a base of a different type of food to add flavor: *a cake with a marzipan topping.*
▶ **adj.** Brit. informal, dated excellent: *that really is a topping dress.*

top·ping lift ▶ **n.** a rope or cable on a sailing vessel that supports the weight of a boom or yard and can be used to lift it.

top·ple /'täpəl/ ▶ **v.** [no obj.] overbalance or become unsteady and fall slowly: *she toppled over when I touched her.* ■ [with obj.] cause to fall in such a way: *the push almost toppled him to the ground |* figurative *disagreement had threatened to topple the government.*
– ORIGIN mid 16th cent. (in the sense 'roll around'): frequentative of TOP¹.

top quark (abbr.: **t**) ▶ **n.** a hypothetical quark with a mass of 360,000 times that of an electron and a charge of $+^2/_3$.

top rope Climbing ▶ **n.** a rope lowered from above to the lead climber in a group, typically to give assistance at a difficult part of a climb.
▶ **v.** (**top-rope**) [with obj.] climb (a route or part of one) using a top rope.

top round ▶ **n.** a cut of meat taken from an inner section of a round of beef.

top·sail /'täpsəl, -,sāl/ ▶ **n.** a sail set on a ship's topmast. ■ a fore-and-aft sail set above the gaff.

top se·cret ▶ **adj.** of the highest secrecy; highly confidential: *the experiments were top secret | a top-secret mission.*

top-shelf ▶ **adj.** **1** of a high quality; excellent: *top-shelf vocal talent.*
2 Brit. (of a magazine or other publication) pornographic.

top·side /'täp,sīd/ ▶ **n.** (often **topsides**) the upper part of a ship's side, above the waterline.
▶ **adv.** on or toward the upper decks of a ship: *we stayed topside.*

PRONUNCIATION KEY ə *ago, up*; ər *over, fur*; a *hat*; ā *ate*; ä *car*; e *let*; ē *see*; i *fit*; ī *by*; NG *sing*; ō *go*; ô *law, for*; oi *toy*; o͝o *good*; o͞o *goo*; ou *out*; TH *thin*; T͟H *then*; ZH *vision*

t

Top-Sid·er ▶ **n.** trademark a casual shoe, typically made of leather or canvas with a rubber sole, designed to be worn on boats.

top·soil /ˈtäpˌsoil/ ▶ **n.** the top layer of soil.

top·spin /ˈtäpˌspin/ ▶ **n.** a fast forward spinning motion imparted to a ball when throwing or hitting it, often resulting in a curved path or a strong forward motion on rebounding.
– DERIVATIVES **top·spin·ner n.**

top·stitch /ˈtäpˌstiCH/ ▶ **v.** [no obj.] make a row of continuous stitches on the top or right side of a garment or other article as a decorative feature.

top·sy-tur·vy /ˌtäpsē ˈtərvē/ ▶ **adj.** upside down: *the fairground ride turned riders topsy-turvy.* ■ in a state of confusion: *the topsy-turvy months of the invasion.*
▶ **n.** [in sing.] a state of utter confusion.
– DERIVATIVES **top·sy·tur·vi·ly** /ˈtərvəlē/ **adv.**, **top·sy·tur·vi·ness n.**
– ORIGIN early 16th cent.: a jingle apparently based on TOP[1] and obsolete *terve* 'overturn.'

top-tier ▶ **adj.** of the highest level or quality: *a top-tier medical school.*

top·wa·ter /ˈtäpˌwôtər, -ˌwätər/ ▶ **adj.** Fishing (of a bait) floating on or near the top of the water.

toque /tōk/ ▶ **n.** a woman's small hat, typically having a narrow, closely turned-up brim. ■ historical a small cap or bonnet of such a type worn by a man or woman. ■ a tall white hat with a full pouched crown, worn by chefs.
– ORIGIN early 16th cent.: from French, of unknown origin.

to·qui·lla /tōˈkē(y)ə/ ▶ **n.** a palmlike tree, *Carludovica palmata*, native to South America. ■ the fiber obtained from this plant, used esp. to make hats.
– ORIGIN late 19th cent.: from an American Spanish use of Spanish *toquilla* 'small gauze headdress,' diminutive of *toca* 'toque.'

tor /tôr/ ▶ **n.** a hill or rocky peak.
– ORIGIN Old English *torr*, perhaps of Celtic origin and related to Welsh *tor* 'belly' and Scottish Gaelic *tòrr* 'bulging hill.'

To·rah /ˈtôrə, ˈtō-, tôˈrä/ ▶ **n.** (usu. **the Torah**) (in Judaism) the law of God as revealed to Moses and recorded in the first five books of the Hebrew scriptures (the Pentateuch). ■ a scroll containing this.
– ORIGIN from Hebrew *tōrāh* 'instruction, doctrine, law,' from *yārāh* 'show, direct, instruct.'

torc /tôrk/ (also **torque**) ▶ **n.** historical a neck ornament consisting of a band of twisted metal, worn esp. by the ancient Gauls and Britons.
– ORIGIN mid 19th cent.: from French *torque*, from Latin *torques* (see TORCH).

torch /tôrCH/ ▶ **n. 1** chiefly historical a portable means of illumination such as a piece of wood or cloth soaked in tallow or an oil lamp on a pole, sometimes carried ceremonially. ■ (usu. **the torch**) used to refer to a valuable quality, principle, or cause that needs to be protected and maintained: *mountain warlords carried the torch of Greek independence.* ■ a blowtorch. ■ informal an arsonist.
2 British term for FLASHLIGHT (sense 1).
▶ **v.** [with obj.] informal set fire to: *the shops had been looted and torched.*
– PHRASES **carry a torch for** suffer from unrequited love for. **put to the torch** (or **put a torch to**) destroy by burning.
– ORIGIN Middle English: from Old French *torche*, from Latin *torqua*, variant of *torques* 'necklace, wreath,' from *torquere* 'to twist.' The current verb sense was originally US slang and dates from the 1930s.

torch·bear·er /ˈtôrCHˌbe(ə)rər/ ▶ **n.** a person who carries a ceremonial torch. ■ a person who leads or inspires others in working toward a valued goal.

tor·chière /tôrˈSHer, tôrˈSHē-er/ (also **torchère**) ▶ **n.** a tall ornamental flat-topped stand, traditionally used as a stand for a candlestick.
– ORIGIN early 20th cent.: French, from *torche* (see TORCH).

torch·light /ˈtôrCHˌlīt/ ▶ **n.** the light of a torch or torches.
– DERIVATIVES **torch·lit** /-lit/ **adj.**

tor·chon lace /ˈtôrSHän/ ▶ **n.** coarse bobbin lace with geometric designs.
– ORIGIN mid 19th cent.: from French, literally 'duster, dishcloth,' from *torcher* 'to wipe.'

torch song ▶ **n.** a sad or sentimental song, typically about unrequited love.
– DERIVATIVES **torch sing·er n.**
– ORIGIN 1920s: *torch* from the phrase 'carry a torch for' (see TORCH).

tore[1] /tôr/ past of TEAR[1].

tore[2] ▶ **n.** archaic term for TORUS.

– ORIGIN mid 17th cent.: from French.

tor·e·a·dor /ˈtôrēəˌdôr/ ▶ **n.** a bullfighter.
– ORIGIN Spanish, from *torear* 'fight bulls,' from *toro* 'bull.'

tor·e·a·dor pants ▶ **plural n.** women's tight-fitting calf-length trousers.

to·re·ro /təˈre(ə)rō/ ▶ **n.** (pl. **toreros**) a bullfighter.
– ORIGIN Spanish, from *toro* 'bull' (see TOREADOR).

to·reu·tics /təˈro͞otiks/ ▶ **plural n.** [treated as sing.] the art of making designs in relief or intaglio, esp. by chasing, carving, and embossing in metal.
– DERIVATIVES **to·reu·tic adj.**
– ORIGIN mid 19th cent.: from Greek *toreutikos*, from *toreuein* 'to work in relief.'

to·ri /ˈtôrī/ plural form of TORUS.

tor·ic /ˈtôrik/ ▶ **adj.** Geometry having the form of a torus or part of a torus. ■ (of a contact lens) having two different curves instead of one, used to correct both astigmatism and near- or farsightedness.

to·ri·i /ˈtôrēˌē/ ▶ **n.** (pl. **same**) the gateway of a Shinto shrine, with two uprights and two crosspieces.
– ORIGIN Japanese, from *tori* 'bird' + *i* 'sit, perch.'

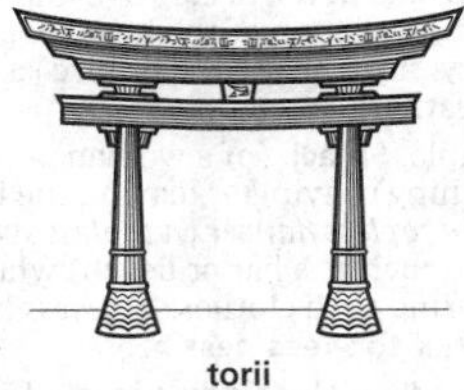

torii

To·ri·no /təˈrēnō/ Italian name for TURIN.

tor·ment ▶ **n.** /ˈtôrment/ severe physical or mental suffering: *their deaths have left both families in torment.* ■ a cause of such suffering: *the journey must have been a torment for them.*
▶ **v.** /tôrˈment/ [with obj.] cause to experience severe mental or physical suffering: *he was tormented by jealousy.* ■ annoy or provoke in a deliberately unkind way: *every day I have kids tormenting me because they know I live alone.*
– DERIVATIVES **tor·ment·ed·ly** /tôrˈmentədlē/ **adv.**, **tor·ment·ing·ly** /tôrˈmentiNGlē/ **adv.**, **tor·men·tor** /tôrˈmentər/ **n.**
– ORIGIN Middle English (as both noun and verb referring to the infliction or suffering of torture): from Old French *torment* (noun), *tormenter* (verb), from Latin *tormentum* 'instrument of torture,' from *torquere* 'to twist.'

tor·men·til /ˈtôrmənˌtil/ ▶ **n.** a low-growing Eurasian plant with bright yellow flowers. The root is used in herbal medicine to treat diarrhea. ● *Potentilla erecta*, family Rosaceae.
– ORIGIN late Middle English: from French *tormentille*, from medieval Latin *tormentilla*, of unknown origin.

torn /tôrn/ past participle of TEAR[1].

tor·na·do /tôrˈnādō/ ▶ **n.** (pl. **tornadoes** or **tornados**) a mobile, destructive vortex of violently rotating winds having the appearance of a funnel-shaped cloud and advancing beneath a large storm system. ■ a person or thing characterized by violent or devastating action or emotion: *a tornado of sexual confusion.*
– DERIVATIVES **tor·nad·ic** /-ˈnādik, -ˈnadik/ **adj.**
– ORIGIN mid 16th cent. (denoting a violent thunderstorm of the tropical Atlantic Ocean): perhaps an alteration of Spanish *tronada* 'thunderstorm' (from *tronar* 'to thunder') by association with Spanish *tornar* 'to turn.'

Tor·na·do Al·ley ▶ **n.** an area of the Great Plains centered on eastern Kansas and Oklahoma and including parts of the surrounding states, where tornadoes are frequent.

Tor·ni·o /ˈtôrnēˌō/ a river that rises in northeastern Sweden and flows south for 356 miles (566 km) to form the border between Sweden and Finland before it empties into the Gulf of Bothnia. Swedish name **Torne Älv**.

to·ro /ˈtôrō/ ▶ **n.** a pale, fatty cut of tuna used for sushi and sashimi.
– ORIGIN Japanese, 'tuna belly.'

to·roid /ˈtôroid/ ▶ **n.** Geometry a figure with a shape resembling a torus. ■ Electronics a coil shaped like a torus or doughnut.

to·roi·dal /tôˈroidl/ ▶ **adj.** Geometry of or resembling a torus.
– DERIVATIVES **to·roi·dal·ly adv.**

To·ron·to /təˈräntō/ a city in Canada, capital of Ontario, on the northern shore of Lake Ontario; pop. 2,503,281 (2006).
– ORIGIN originally named York but renamed *Toronto* in 1834, from an Iroquoian word of uncertain meaning.

tor·pe·do /tôrˈpēdō/ ▶ **n.** (pl. **torpedoes**) **1** a cigar-shaped self-propelled underwater missile designed to be fired from a ship or submarine or dropped into the water from an aircraft and to explode on reaching a target. ■ a signal placed on a railroad track, exploding as the train passes over it. ■ a firework exploding on impact with a hard surface. ■ informal a submarine sandwich. ■ informal a gangster hired to commit a murder or other violent act. ■ an explosive device lowered into oil wells to clear obstructions.
2 (also **torpedo ray**) an electric ray.
▶ **v.** (**torpedoes, torpedoing, torpedoed**) [with obj.] attack or sink (a ship) with a torpedo or torpedoes. ■ destroy or ruin (a plan or project): *fighting between the militias torpedoed peace talks.*
– DERIVATIVES **tor·pe·do·like** /-ˌlīk/ **adj.**
– ORIGIN early 16th cent. (sense 2 of the noun): from Latin, literally 'stiffness, numbness,' by extension 'electric ray' (which gives a shock causing numbness), from *torpere* 'be numb or sluggish.' Sense 1 of the noun dates from the late 18th cent. and first described a timed explosive device for detonation under water.

tor·pe·do boat ▶ **n.** a small, fast, light warship armed with torpedoes.

tor·pe·do net ▶ **n.** historical a net made of steel wire, hung in the water around an anchored ship to intercept torpedoes.

tor·pe·do tube ▶ **n.** a tube in a submarine or other ship from which torpedoes are fired by the use of compressed air or an explosive charge.

tor·pe·fy /ˈtôrpəˌfī/ ▶ **v.** (**torpefies, torpefying, torpefied**) [with obj.] formal make (someone or something) numb, paralyzed, or lifeless.
– ORIGIN early 19th cent.: from Latin *torpefacere*, from *torpere* 'be numb or sluggish.'

tor·pid /ˈtôrpid/ ▶ **adj.** mentally or physically inactive; lethargic: *we sat around in a torpid state.* ■ (of an animal) dormant, esp. during hibernation.
– DERIVATIVES **tor·pid·i·ty** /tôrˈpiditē/ **n.**, **tor·pid·ly adv.**
– ORIGIN late Middle English: from Latin *torpidus*, from *torpere* 'be numb or sluggish.'

tor·por /ˈtôrpər/ ▶ **n.** a state of physical or mental inactivity; lethargy: *they veered between apathetic torpor and hysterical fanaticism.*
– ORIGIN late Middle English: from Latin, from *torpere* 'be numb or sluggish.'

torque /tôrk/ ▶ **n. 1** Mechanics a twisting force that tends to cause rotation.
2 variant spelling of TORC.
▶ **v.** [with obj.] apply torque or a twisting force to (an object): *he gently torqued the hip joint.*
– DERIVATIVES **tor·quey adj.**
– ORIGIN late 19th cent.: from Latin *torquere* 'to twist.'

torque con·vert·er ▶ **n.** a device that transmits or multiplies torque generated by an engine.

Tor·que·ma·da /ˌtôrkəˈmädə, ˌtôrkāˈmäTHä/, Tomás de (*c.*1420–98), Spanish cleric and Grand Inquisitor. A Dominican monk and confessor to Ferdinand and Isabella, he was the prime mover behind the Inquisition in 1478 and the expulsion of the Jews from Spain beginning in 1492.

torque wrench ▶ **n.** a tool for setting and adjusting the tightness of nuts and bolts to a desired value.

torr /tôr/ ▶ **n.** (pl. **same**) a unit of pressure used in measuring partial vacuums, equal to 133.32 pascals.
– ORIGIN 1940s: named after E. TORRICELLI.

Tor·rance /ˈtôrəns, ˈtär-/ a commercial and industrial city in southwestern California, south of Los Angeles; pop. 140,820 (est. 2008).

Tor·rens sys·tem /ˈtôrənz, ˈtär-/ ▶ **n.** Law a system of land title registration, adopted originally in Australia and later in some states of the US.
– ORIGIN mid 19th cent.: named after Sir Robert *Torrens* (1814–84), first premier of South Australia.

tor·rent /ˈtôrənt, ˈtär-/ ▶ **n.** a strong and fast-moving stream of water or other liquid: *rain poured down in torrents | after the winter rains, the stream becomes a raging torrent.* ■ (**a torrent of** or **torrents of**) a sudden, violent, and copious outpouring of (something, typically words or feelings): *she was subjected to a torrent of abuse | banks plowed torrents of money into the booming stock and property markets.*
– ORIGIN late 16th cent.: from French, from Italian *torrente*, from Latin *torrent-* 'boiling, roaring,' from *torrere* 'parch, scorch.'

tor·ren·tial /tôˈrenCHəl, tə-/ ▶ **adj.** (of rain) falling rapidly and in copious quantities: *a torrential downpour.* ■ (of water) flowing rapidly and with force.
– DERIVATIVES **tor·ren·tial·ly adv.**

Tor·res Strait /ˈtôrˌez, -ēs/ a channel that separates the northern tip of Queensland, Australia, from the

island of New Guinea and links the Arafura Sea and the Coral Sea.
– ORIGIN named after Spanish explorer Luis V. de *Torres*, the first European to sail along the southern coast of New Guinea 1606.

Tor·ri·cel·li /ˌtôrəˈCHelē/, Evangelista (1608–47), Italian mathematician and physicist. He invented the mercury barometer, with which he demonstrated that the atmosphere exerts a pressure sufficient to support a column of mercury in an inverted closed tube.

tor·rid /ˈtôrəd, ˈtär-/ ▶ **adj. 1** very hot and dry: *the torrid heat of the afternoon.* ■ full of passionate or highly charged emotions arising from sexual love: *a torrid love affair.*
2 full of difficulty or tribulation: *Wall Street is in for a torrid time in the next few weeks.*
– DERIVATIVES **tor·rid·i·ty** /təˈriditē/ **n.**, **tor·rid·ly adv.**
– ORIGIN late 16th cent.: from French *torride* or Latin *torridus*, from *torrere* 'parch, scorch.'

tor·rid zone (also **Torrid Zone**) ▶ **n.** the hot central belt of the earth bounded by the tropics of Cancer and Capricorn.

Tor·ring·ton /ˈtôriNGtən, ˈtär-/ a historic industrial and commercial city in northwestern Connecticut, on the Naugatuck River; pop. 35,312 (est. 2008).

tor·sade /tôrˈsäd, -ˈsād/ ▶ **n.** a decorative twisted braid, ribbon, or other strand used as trimming. ■ an artificial plait of hair.
– ORIGIN late 19th cent.: from French, from Latin *tors-* 'twisted,' from *torquere* 'to twist.'

tor·sade de poin·tes /tôrˈsäd də ˈpwänt/ ▶ **n.** Medicine a form of tachycardia in which the electrical pulse in the heart undergoes a cyclical variation in strength, giving a characteristic electrocardiogram resembling a twisted fringe of spikes.
– ORIGIN 1960s: French, literally 'twist of spikes.'

torse /tôrs/ ▶ **n.** Heraldry a wreath.
– ORIGIN late 16th cent.: from obsolete French, from Latin *torta*, feminine past participle of *torquere* 'twist.'

tor·sion /ˈtôrSHən/ ▶ **n.** the action of twisting or the state of being twisted, esp. of one end of an object relative to the other. ■ Mathematics the extent to which a curve departs from being planar. ■ Zoology (in a gastropod mollusk) the spontaneous twisting of the visceral hump through 180° during larval development.
– DERIVATIVES **tor·sion·al** /-SHənl/ **adj.**, **tor·sion·al·ly** /-SHənl-ē/ **adv.**, **tor·sion·less adj.**
– ORIGIN late Middle English (as a medical term denoting colic or in the sense 'twisting' (esp. of a loop of the intestine)): via Old French from late Latin *torsio(n-)*, variant of *tortio(n-)* 'twisting, torture,' from Latin *torquere* 'to twist.'

tor·sion bal·ance ▶ **n.** an instrument for measuring very weak forces by their effect on a system of fine twisted wire.

tor·sion bar ▶ **n.** a bar forming part of a vehicle suspension, twisting in response to the motion of the wheels and absorbing their vertical movement.

tor·sion pen·du·lum ▶ **n.** a pendulum that rotates rather than swings.

torsk /tôrsk/ ▶ **n.** a North Atlantic fish of the cod family, occurring in deep water and of some commercial importance. Also called **CUSK**. ● *Brosme brosme*, family Gadidae.
– ORIGIN early 18th cent.: from Norwegian *torsk*, from Old Norse *thorskr*; probably related to *thurr* 'dry.'

tor·so /ˈtôrsō/ ▶ **n.** (pl. **torsos** or **torsi** /-sē/) the trunk of the human body. ■ the trunk of a statue without, or considered independently of, the head and limbs. ■ an unfinished or mutilated thing, esp. a work of art or literature: *the Requiem torso was preceded by the cantata.*
– ORIGIN late 18th cent.: from Italian, literally 'stalk, stump,' from Latin *thyrsus* (see **THYRSUS**).

tort /tôrt/ ▶ **n.** Law a wrongful act or an infringement of a right (other than under contract) leading to civil legal liability.
– ORIGIN Middle English (in the general sense 'wrong, injury'): from Old French, from medieval Latin *tortum* 'wrong, injustice,' neuter past participle of Latin *torquere* 'to twist.'

torte /tôrt, ˈtôrtə/ ▶ **n.** (pl. **tortes** or German **torten** /ˈtôrtn/) a sweet cake or tart.
– ORIGIN from German *Torte*, via Italian from late Latin *torta* 'round loaf, cake.' Compare with **TORTILLA**.

tor·tel·li /tôrˈtelē/ ▶ **n.** small pasta parcels stuffed with a cheese or vegetable mixture.
– ORIGIN Italian, plural of *tortello* 'small cake, fritter.'

tor·tel·li·ni /ˌtôrtlˈēnē/ ▶ **n.** small squares of pasta that are stuffed with meat or cheese and then rolled and formed into small rings.
– ORIGIN Italian, plural of *tortellino*, diminutive of *tortello* 'small cake, fritter.'

tort·fea·sor /ˈtôrtˌfēzər, -zôr/ ▶ **n.** Law a person who commits a tort.
– ORIGIN mid 17th cent.: from Old French *tort-fesor*, from *tort* 'wrong' and *fesor* 'doer.'

tor·ti·col·lis /ˌtôrtiˈkälis/ ▶ **n.** Medicine a condition in which the head becomes persistently turned to one side, often associated with painful muscle spasms. Also called **WRYNECK**.
– ORIGIN early 19th cent.: modern Latin, from Latin *tortus* 'crooked, twisted' + *collum* 'neck.'

tor·til·la /tôrˈtē(y)ə/ ▶ **n.** (in Mexican cooking) a thin, flat pancake of cornmeal or flour, eaten hot or cold, typically with a savory filling. ■ (in Spanish cooking) a thick omelet containing potato and other vegetables, typically served cut into wedges.
– ORIGIN Spanish, diminutive of *torta* 'cake.' Compare with **TORTE**.

tor·tious /ˈtôrSHəs/ ▶ **adj.** Law constituting a tort; wrongful.
– DERIVATIVES **tor·tious·ly adv.**
– ORIGIN late Middle English: from Anglo-Norman French *torcious*, from the stem of *torcion* 'extortion, violence,' from late Latin *tortio(n-)* (see **TORSION**). The original sense was 'injurious.'

tor·toise /ˈtôrtəs/ ▶ **n. 1** a turtle, typically a herbivorous one that lives on land. ■ informal anything exceptionally slow-moving: *you are a tortoise on the uptake today.*
2 another term for **TESTUDO**.
– DERIVATIVES **tor·toise-like** /-ˌlīk/ **adj. & adv.**
– ORIGIN late Middle English *tortu*, *tortuce*: from Old French *tortue* and Spanish *tortuga*, both from medieval Latin *tortuca*, of uncertain origin. The current spelling dates from the mid 16th cent.

tor·toise bee·tle ▶ **n.** a small flattened leaf beetle with an enlarged thorax, having wing cases that cover the entire insect and provide camouflage and protection. The larva carries a construction of feces and molted skins for camouflage. ● *Cassida* and other genera, family Chrysomelidae.

tor·toise·shell /ˈtôrtə(s),SHel/ ▶ **n. 1** the semitransparent mottled yellow and brown shell of certain turtles, typically used to make jewelry or ornaments. ■ a synthetic substance made in imitation of this.
2 short for **TORTOISESHELL CAT**.
3 short for **TORTOISESHELL BUTTERFLY**.

tor·toise·shell but·ter·fly ▶ **n.** a butterfly with mottled orange, yellow, and black markings, and wavy wing margins. ● Genera *Aglais* and *Nymphalis*, subfamily Nymphalinae, family Nymphalidae: several species.

tor·toise·shell cat ▶ **n.** a domestic cat with markings resembling tortoiseshell.

Tor·to·la /tôrˈtōlə/ the principal island of the British Virgin Islands in the Caribbean Sea. Its chief town, Road Town, is the capital of the British Virgin Islands.
– ORIGIN Spanish, literally 'turtledove.'

tor·to·ni /tôrˈtōnē/ ▶ **n.** an Italian ice cream made with eggs and cream, typically served in a small cup and topped with chopped almonds or crumbled macaroons.
– ORIGIN early 20th cent.: the name of a 19th-cent. Italian cafe owner in Paris.

tor·trix /ˈtôrtriks/ (also **tortrix moth**) ▶ **n.** (pl. **tortrices** /-trisēz/) a small moth with typically green caterpillars that live inside rolled leaves and can be a serious pest of fruit and other trees. ● Family Tortricidae: many species.
– DERIVATIVES **tor·tri·cid** /-trisid/ **n. & adj.**
– ORIGIN late 18th cent.: modern Latin, feminine of Latin *tortor* 'twister,' from *torquere* 'to twist.'

tor·tu·ous /ˈtôrCHōōəs/ ▶ **adj.** full of twists and turns: *the route is remote and tortuous.* ■ excessively lengthy and complex: *a tortuous argument.*
– DERIVATIVES **tor·tu·os·i·ty** /ˌtôrCHōōˈäsitē/ **n.** (pl. **tortuosities**), **tor·tu·ous·ly adv.**, **tor·tu·ous·ness n.**
– ORIGIN late Middle English: via Old French from Latin *tortuosus*, from *tortus* 'twisting, a twist,' from Latin *torquere* 'to twist.'

> **USAGE** On the difference between **tortuous** and **torturous**, see usage at **TORTUROUS**.

tor·ture /ˈtôrCHər/ ▶ **n.** the action or practice of inflicting severe pain on someone as a punishment or to force them to do or say something, or for the pleasure of the person inflicting the pain. ■ great physical or mental suffering or anxiety: *the torture I've gone through because of loving you so.* ■ a cause of such suffering or anxiety: *dances were absolute torture because I was so small.*
▶ **v.** [with obj.] inflict severe pain on: *most of the victims had been brutally tortured.* ■ cause great mental suffering or anxiety to: *he was tortured by grief.*
– DERIVATIVES **tor·tur·er n.**
– ORIGIN late Middle English (in the sense 'distortion, twisting,' or a physical disorder characterized by this): via French from late Latin *tortura* 'twisting, torment,' from Latin *torquere* 'to twist.'

tor·tur·ous /ˈtôrCHərəs/ ▶ **adj.** characterized by, involving, or causing excruciating pain or suffering: *a torturous eight weeks in their prison camp.*
– DERIVATIVES **tor·tur·ous·ly adv.**
– ORIGIN late 15th cent.: from Anglo-Norman French, from *torture* 'torture.'

> **USAGE** **Tortuous** and **torturous** have different core meanings. **Tortuous** means 'full of twists and turns' or 'devious, circuitous': *both paths were tortuous and strewn with boulders.* **Torturous** is derived from *torture* and means 'involving torture or excruciating pain'. **Torturous** should be reserved for agonized suffering; it is not a fancy word for 'painful' or 'discomforting,' as in *I found the concert torturous because of the music's volume.*

tor·u·la /ˈtôr(y)ələ/ ▶ **n.** (pl. **torulae** /-lē, -lī/)
1 (also **torula yeast**) a yeast cultured for use in medicine and as a food additive, esp. as a source of vitamins and protein. ● *Candida utilis*, subdivision Deuteromycotina.
2 a yeastlike fungus composed of chains of rounded cells, several kinds growing on dead vegetation and some causing infections. ● Genus *Torula* (or formerly this genus), subdivision Deuteromycotina: several species, in particular *T. herbarum*, which grows on dead grasses.
– ORIGIN modern Latin (genus name), diminutive of Latin *torus* 'swelling, bolster.'

To·ruń /ˈtôr,ōōn/ an industrial city in northern Poland, on the Vistula River; pop. 206,765 (2007). German name **THORN**.

to·rus /ˈtôrəs/ ▶ **n.** (pl. **tori** /ˈtôrī/ or **toruses**)
1 Geometry a surface or solid formed by rotating a closed curve, esp. a circle, around a line that lies in the same plane but does not intersect it (e.g., like a ring-shaped doughnut). ■ a thing of this shape, esp. a large ring-shaped chamber used in physical research.
2 Architecture a large convex molding, typically semicircular in cross section, esp. as the lowest part of the base of a column.
3 Anatomy a ridge of bone or muscle: *the maxillary torus.*
4 Botany the receptacle of a flower.
– ORIGIN mid 16th cent. (sense 2): from Latin, literally 'swelling, bolster, round molding.' The other senses date from the 19th cent.

To·ry /ˈtôrē/ ▶ **n.** (pl. **Tories**) **1** an American colonist who supported the British side during the American Revolution.
2 (in the UK) a member or supporter of the Conservative Party. ■ a member of the English political party opposing the exclusion of James II from the succession. It remained the name for members of the English, later British, parliamentary party supporting the established religious and political order until the emergence of the Conservative Party in the 1830s. Compare with **WHIG** (sense 1).
▶ **adj.** of or relating to the British Conservative Party or its supporters: *Tory voters.*
– DERIVATIVES **To·ry·ism** /-ˌizəm/ **n.**
– ORIGIN mid 17th cent.: probably from Irish *toraidhe* 'outlaw, highwayman,' from *tóir* 'pursue.' The word was used of Irish peasants dispossessed by English settlers and living as robbers, and extended to other marauders esp. in the Scottish Highlands. It was then adopted *c.*1679 as an abusive nickname for supporters of the Catholic James II.

to·sa /ˈtōsə/ ▶ **n.** a dog of a breed of mastiff originally kept for dogfighting.
– ORIGIN 1940s: from *Tosa*, the name of a former province in Japan.

Tos·ca·na /tôˈskänä/ Italian name for **TUSCANY**.

Tos·ca·ni·ni /ˌtäskəˈnēnē/, Arturo (1867–1957), Italian conductor. He was musical director at La Scala in Milan 1898–1903 and 1906–08 before becoming a conductor at the Metropolitan Opera in New York City 1908–21 and the New York Philharmonic Orchestra 1928–38. He founded the NBC Symphony Orchestra in 1937.

tosh /täSH/ ▶ **n.** Brit. informal rubbish; nonsense: *it's sentimental tosh.*
– ORIGIN late 19th cent.: of unknown origin.

toss /tôs, täs/ ▶ **v. 1** [with obj.] throw (something) somewhere lightly, easily, or casually: *Suzy tossed her bag onto the sofa* | [with two objs.] *she tossed me a*

t

box of matches. ■ (of a horse) throw (a rider) off its back. ■ throw (a coin) into the air in order to make a decision between two alternatives, based on which side of the coin faces up when it lands: *we could just toss a coin.* ■ settle a matter with (someone) by doing this: *I'll* ***toss you for*** *it.* ■ move or cause to move from side to side or back and forth: [no obj.] *the tops of the olive trees swayed and tossed* | [with obj.] *the yachts were tossed around in the harbor like toys* | [as adj. in combination] (**-tossed**) *a storm-tossed sea.* ■ jerk (one's head or hair) sharply backward: *Paula pursed her lips and tossed her head.* ■ shake or turn (food) in a liquid, so as to coat it lightly: *toss the pasta in the sauce.*
2 [with obj.] informal search (a place): *I could demand her keys and toss her office.*
▶ **n.** an action or instance of tossing something: *a defiant toss of her head* | *the toss of a coin.* ■ (**the toss**) the action of tossing a coin as a method of deciding which team has the right to make a particular decision at the beginning of a game: *we'd win the toss and keep the ball.*
– PHRASES **toss one's cookies** informal vomit. **tossing the caber** see **CABER**.
– PHRASAL VERBS **toss something off 1** drink something rapidly or all at once: *Roger tossed off a full glass of Sauternes.* **2** produce something rapidly or without thought or effort: *some of the best letters are tossed off in a burst of inspiration.*
– DERIVATIVES **toss·er n.**
– ORIGIN early 16th cent.: of unknown origin.

toss·pot /'tôs,pät, 'täs-/ ▶ **n.** informal a habitual drinker (also used as a general term of abuse).

toss-up ▶ **n.** informal the tossing of a coin to make a decision between two alternatives. ■ a situation in which all outcomes or options are equally possible or equally attractive: *employment-wise, at this stage it's a toss-up between two jobs.*

tos·ta·da /tō'städə/ (also **tostado** /-dō/) ▶ **n.** (pl. **tostadas** also **tostados**) a Mexican deep-fried tortilla topped with a seasoned mixture of beans, ground meat, and vegetables.
– ORIGIN Spanish, literally 'toasted,' past participle of *tostar*.

tos·to·ne /täs'tōnā/ ▶ **n.** a Mexican dish of fried plantains, typically served with a dip.
– ORIGIN Spanish.

tos·yl /'täsəl/ ▶ **n.** [as modifier] Chemistry of or denoting the toluene-4-sulphonyl radical $-SO_2C_6H_4CH_3$, used in organic synthesis.
– ORIGIN 1930s: from German, from *to(luol)* and *s(ulphon)yl*.

tos·yl·ate /'täsə,lāt/ ▶ **n.** Chemistry an ester containing a tosyl group.

tot[1] /tät/ ▶ **n. 1** a very young child.
2 chiefly Brit. a small amount of a strong alcoholic drink such as whiskey or brandy: *a* ***tot of*** *brandy.*
– ORIGIN early 18th cent. (originally dialect): of unknown origin.

tot[2] ▶ **v.** (**tots, totting, totted**) [with obj.] chiefly Brit. (**tot something up**) add up numbers or amounts. ■ accumulate something over a period of time: *he has already totted up 89 victories.*
– ORIGIN mid 18th cent.: from archaic *tot* 'set of figures to be added up,' abbreviation of **TOTAL** or of Latin *totum* 'the whole.'

to·tal /'tōtl/ ▶ **adj. 1** [attrib.] comprising the whole number or amount: *a total cost of $4,000.*
2 complete; absolute: *a total stranger* | *they drove home in total silence.*
▶ **n.** the whole number or amount of something: *he scored a total of thirty-three points* | ***in total****, 200 people were interviewed.*
▶ **v.** (**totals, totaling, totaled**; Brit. **totals, totalling, totalled**) **1** [with obj.] amount in number to: *they were left with debts totaling $6,260.* ■ add up the full number or amount of: *the scores were totaled.*
2 [with obj.] informal damage (something, typically a vehicle) beyond repair; wreck.
– ORIGIN late Middle English: via Old French from medieval Latin *totalis*, from *totum* 'the whole,' neuter of Latin *totus* 'whole, entire.' The verb, at first in the sense 'add up,' dates from the late 16th cent.

to·tal de·prav·i·ty ▶ **n.** Christian Theology the Calvinist doctrine that human nature is thoroughly corrupt and sinful as a result of the Fall.

to·tal e·clipse ▶ **n.** an eclipse in which the whole of the disk of the sun or moon is obscured.

to·tal har·mon·ic dis·tor·tion ▶ **n.** the distortion produced by an amplifier, as measured in terms of the harmonics of the sinusoidal components of the signal that it introduces.

to·tal heat ▶ **n.** another term for **ENTHALPY**.

to·tal·i·tar·i·an /tō,tali'te(ə)rēən/ ▶ **adj.** of or relating to a system of government that is centralized and dictatorial and requires complete subservience to the state: *a totalitarian regime.*
▶ **n.** a person advocating such a system of government.
– DERIVATIVES **to·tal·i·tar·i·an·ism** /-,nizəm/ **n.**

to·tal·i·ty /tō'talitē/ ▶ **n.** the whole of something: *the totality of their current policies.* ■ Astronomy the moment or duration of total obscuration of the sun or moon during an eclipse.
– PHRASES **in its totality** as a whole: *a deeper exploration of life in its totality.*

to·tal·i·za·tor /'tōtl-i,zātər/ ▶ **n.** a device showing the number and amount of bets staked on a race, to facilitate the division of the total among those backing the winner.

to·tal·ize /'tōtl,īz/ ▶ **v.** [with obj.] (usu. as adj. **totalizing**) comprehend in an all-encompassing way: *grand ideas and totalizing worldviews.*
– DERIVATIVES **to·tal·i·za·tion** /-'zāSHən/ **n.**

to·tal·iz·er /'tōtl,īzər/ ▶ **n.** another term for **TOTALIZATOR**.

to·tal·ly /'tōtl-ē/ ▶ **adv.** completely; absolutely: *the building was totally destroyed by the fire* | [as submodifier] *they came from totally different backgrounds.*

To·tal Qual·i·ty Man·age·ment ▶ **n.** a system of management based on the principle that every staff member must be committed to maintaining high standards of work in every aspect of a company's operations.

to·tal re·call ▶ **n.** the ability to remember with clarity every detail of the events of one's life or of a particular event, object, or experience.

to·tal war ▶ **n.** a war that is unrestricted in terms of the weapons used, the territory or combatants involved, or the objectives pursued, esp. one in which the laws of war are disregarded.

Tote /tōt/ ▶ **n.** (**the Tote**) Brit. a system of betting based on the use of the totalizator, in which dividends are calculated according to the amount staked rather than odds offered.
– ORIGIN late 19th cent.: abbreviation.

tote /tōt/ ▶ **v.** [with obj.] informal carry, wield, or convey (something heavy or substantial): *here are books well worth toting home* | [as adj., in combination] (**-toting**) *a gun-toting loner.*
▶ **n.** short for **TOTE BAG**.
– DERIVATIVES **tot·er n.** [in combination] *a gun-toter.*
– ORIGIN late 17th cent.: probably of dialect origin.

tote bag ▶ **n.** a large bag used for carrying a number of items.

to·tem /'tōtəm/ ▶ **n.** a natural object or animal believed by a particular society to have spiritual significance and adopted by it as an emblem.
– DERIVATIVES **to·tem·ic** /tō'temik/ **adj.**, **to·tem·ism** /-,mizəm/ **n.**, **to·tem·ist** /-mist/ **n.**, **to·tem·is·tic** /,tōdə'mistik/ **adj.**
– ORIGIN mid 18th cent.: from Ojibwa *nindoodem* 'my totem.'

to·tem pole ▶ **n. 1** a pole on which totems are hung or on which the images of totems are carved.
2 a hierarchy: *the social totem pole.*

totem pole

t'oth·er /'təTHər/ (also **tother**) ▶ **adj. & pron.** dialect or humorous the other: [as adj.] *I was talking about it t'other day* | [as pronoun] *we were talking of this, that, and t'other.*
– ORIGIN Middle English *the tother*, wrong division of *thet other* 'the other' (*thet*, from Old English *thaet*, the obsolete neuter form of *the*).

to·tip·o·tent /tō'tipətənt/ ▶ **adj.** Biology (of an immature or stem cell) capable of giving rise to any cell type or (of a blastomere) a complete embryo.
– ORIGIN early 20th cent.: from Latin *totus* 'whole' + **POTENT**[1].

To·to·nac /,tōtə'näk/ ▶ **n.** (pl. **same** or **Totonacs**) **1** a member of an American Indian people of east central Mexico.
2 the language of this people.
▶ **adj.** of or relating to this people or their language.
– ORIGIN from Spanish *Totonaca*, from Nahuatl *Totonacatl*.

tot·ter /'tätər/ ▶ **v.** [no obj.] move in a feeble or unsteady way: *a hunched figure tottering down the path.* ■ (usu. as adj. **tottering**) (of a building) shake or rock as if about to collapse: *tottering, gutted houses.* ■ be insecure or about to fail: *the pharmaceutical industry has tottered from crisis to crisis.*
▶ **n.** [in sing.] a feeble or unsteady gait.
– DERIVATIVES **tot·ter·er n.**, **tot·ter·y adj.**
– ORIGIN Middle English: from Middle Dutch *touteren* 'to swing' (the original sense in English).

tou·can /'tōō,kan, -,kän/ ▶ **n.** a tropical American fruit-eating bird with a massive bill and typically brightly colored plumage. ● Genera *Ramphastos* and *Andigena*, family Ramphastidae: several species.
– ORIGIN mid 16th cent.: via French and Portuguese from Tupi *tucan*, imitative of its call.

tou·can·et /,tōōkə'net/ ▶ **n.** a small tropical American toucan with mainly green plumage. ● Family Ramphastidae: three genera, in particular *Aulacorhynchus* and *Selenidera*, and several species.
– ORIGIN early 19th cent.: diminutive of **TOUCAN**.

touch /təCH/ ▶ **v.** [with obj.] **1** come so close to (an object) as to be or come into contact with it: *the dog had one paw outstretched, not quite touching the ground.* ■ bring one's hand or another part of one's body into contact with: *he touched a strand of her hair* | *she lowered her head to touch his fingers with her lips.* ■ come or bring into mutual contact: [no obj.] *for a moment their fingers touched* | [with obj.] *we touched wheels and nearly came off the road.* ■ Geometry be tangent to (a curve or surface) at a certain point. ■ informal reach (a specified level or amount): *sales touched twenty grand last year.* ■ [usu. with negative] informal be comparable to in quality or excellence: *there's no one who can touch him at lightweight judo.*
2 handle in order to manipulate, alter, or otherwise affect, esp. in an adverse way: *I didn't play her records or touch any of her stuff.* ■ cause harm to (someone): *I've got friends who'll pull strings—nobody will dare touch me.* ■ consume or use (food, drink, money, etc.): *the beer by his right hand was hardly touched* | *in three years I haven't touched a cent of the money.* ■ [with negative] used to indicate that something is avoided or rejected: *he was good only for the jobs that nobody else would touch.* ■ (**touch someone for**) informal ask someone for (money or some other commodity) as a loan or gift: *he touched me for his fare.*
3 have an effect on; make a difference to: *a tenth of state companies have been touched by privatization.* ■ (of a quality or expression) be or become visible or apparent in: *a wry smile touched his lips* | *the voice was touched by hysteria.* ■ (**touch something in**) chiefly Art lightly mark in features or other details with a brush or pencil. ■ produce feelings of affection, gratitude, or sympathy in: *she was touched by her friend's loyalty.* ■ (as adj. **touched**) informal slightly insane.
▶ **n. 1** an act of touching someone or something: *her touch on his shoulder was hesitant* | *expressions of love through words and touch* | *you can manipulate images on the screen* ***at the touch of*** *a key.* ■ the faculty of perception through physical contact, esp. with the fingers: *reading by touch.* ■ a musician's manner of playing keys or strings. ■ the manner in which a musical instrument's keys or strings respond to being played: *Viennese instruments with their too delicate touch.* ■ a light stroke with a pen, pencil, etc. ■ [in sing.] informal, dated an act of asking for and getting money or some other commodity from someone as a loan or gift: *I only tolerated him because he was good for a touch now and then.* ■ [in sing.] archaic a thing or an action that tries out the worth or character of something; a test: *you must* ***put*** *your fate* ***to the touch****.*
2 a small amount; a trace: *add a* ***touch of*** *vinegar* | *he retired to bed with* ***a touch of*** *the flu.* ■ a detail or feature, typically one that gives something a distinctive character: *the film's most inventive touch.* ■ [in sing.] a distinctive manner or method of dealing with something: *later he showed a surer political touch.* ■ [in sing.] an ability to deal with something successfully: *getting caught looks so incompetent, as though we're losing our touch.*
3 Bell-ringing a series of changes shorter than a peal.
4 short for **TOUCH FOOTBALL**.
– PHRASES **a touch** to a slight degree; a little: *the water was a touch too chilly for us.* **in touch 1** in or into communication: *she said that you* ***kept in touch****, that you wrote* | *ask someone to* ***put you in touch with*** *other suppliers.* **2** possessing up-to-date knowledge: *we need to keep in touch with the latest developments.* ■ having an intuitive or empathetic awareness: *you need to be in touch with your feelings.* **lose touch 1** cease to correspond or be in communication: *I lost touch with him when he joined the air force.* **2** cease to be aware or informed: *we cannot* ***lose touch with*** *political reality.* **out of touch** lacking knowledge or information concerning current events and developments: *he seems surprisingly out of touch with recent economic thinking.* ■ lacking in awareness or sympathy: *we have been betrayed by a government out of touch with our values.* **to the touch** used to describe the qualities of something perceived by touching it or the sensations felt by someone who is touched: *the silk was slightly rough to the touch* | *the ankle was swollen and painful to the touch.* **touch base** (**with**) see **BASE**[1]. **touch bottom** reach the bottom of a body of water with one's feet or a pole. ■ be at the lowest or worst point:

the housing market has touched bottom. **touch a chord** see CHORD². **touch wood** see WOOD. **would not touch something with a ten-foot pole** informal used to express a refusal to have anything to do with someone or something: *relax, I wouldn't touch you with a ten-foot pole!*
– PHRASAL VERBS **touch at** (of a ship or someone in it) call briefly at (a port). **touch down** (of an aircraft or spacecraft) make contact with the ground in landing. **touch something off** cause something to ignite or explode by touching it with a match. ■ cause something to happen, esp. suddenly: *there was concern that the move could touch off a trade war.* **touch on** (or **upon**) **1** deal briefly with (a subject) in written or spoken discussion: *he touches upon several themes from the last chapter.* **2** come near to being: *a self-confident manner touching on the arrogant.* **touch something up** make small improvements to something: *these paints are handy for touching up small areas on walls or ceilings.*
– DERIVATIVES **touch·a·ble** adj., **touch·er** n.
– ORIGIN Middle English: the verb from Old French *tochier*, probably from a Romance word of imitative origin; the noun originally from Old French *touche*, later (in certain senses) directly from the verb.

touch and go ▶ adj. (also **touch-and-go**) (of an outcome, esp. one that is desired) possible but very uncertain: *it was touch and go there for a while whether they would make it.*
▶ n. (**touch-and-go**) (pl. **touch-and-goes**) a maneuver in which an aircraft touches the ground as in landing, and immediately takes off again.

touch·back /ˈtəCH,bak/ ▶ n. Football a ball one downs deliberately behind one's own goal line or that is kicked through one's end zone. It is taken to the 20-yard line to resume play.

touch·down /ˈtəCH,doun/ ▶ n. **1** the moment at which an aircraft's wheels or part of a spacecraft make contact with the ground during landing: *two hours until touchdown.*
2 Football a six-point score made by carrying or passing the ball into the end zone of the opposing side, or by recovering it there following a fumble or blocked kick. ■ Rugby an act of touching the ground with the ball behind the opponents' goal line, scoring a try.

tou·ché /to͞oˈSHā/ ▶ exclam. (in fencing) used as an acknowledgment of a hit by one's opponent. ■ used as an acknowledgment during a discussion of a good or clever point made at one's expense by another person.
– ORIGIN French, literally 'touched,' past participle of *toucher*.

touch foot·ball ▶ n. a form of football in which a ball carrier is downed by touching instead of tackling.

touch·hole /ˈtəCH,hōl/ ▶ n. a small hole in early firearms through which the charge is ignited.

touch·ing /ˈtəCHiNG/ ▶ adj. arousing strong feelings of sympathy, appreciation, or gratitude: *your loyalty is very touching | a touching reconciliation scene.* [early 16th cent.: from TOUCH + -ING².]
▶ prep. concerning; about: *evidence touching the facts of Roger's case.* [late Middle English: from French *touchant*, present participle of *toucher* 'to touch.']
– DERIVATIVES **touch·ing·ly** adv., **touch·ing·ness** n.

touch·line /ˈtəCH,līn/ ▶ n. Rugby & Soccer the boundary line on each side of the field.

touch-me-not ▶ n. a plant of the balsam family whose ripe seed capsules open explosively when touched, scattering seeds over some distance.
● Genus *Impatiens*, family Balsaminaceae: several species, in particular the orange-flowered **spotted touch-me-not** (*I. capensis*).

touch·pad /ˈtəCH,pad/ ▶ n. a computer input device in the form of a small panel containing different touch-sensitive areas.

touch·point /ˈtəCH,point/ ▶ n. **1** Commerce any point of contact between a buyer and a seller.
2 Computing on some laptop computers, a device like a miniature joystick with a rubber tip, manipulated with a finger to move the screen pointer.
3 a time, condition, or circumstance that is vulnerable or unstable enough to precipitate a highly unfavorable, possibly devastating outcome: *a touchpoint for world conflagration.* ■ Psychology the time in a child's development that precedes an appreciable leap in physical, emotional, or cognitive growth. [1990s: from the usage coined in the book *Touchpoints* (1992) by US pediatrician T. Berry Brazelton (1918–) and US child psychiatrist Joshua D. Sparrow.]

touch screen (also **touchscreen**) ▶ n. a display device that allows a user to interact with a computer by touching areas on the screen.

touch·stone /ˈtəCH,stōn/ ▶ n. a piece of fine-grained dark schist or jasper formerly used for testing alloys of gold by observing the color of the mark that they made on it. ■ a standard or criterion by which something is judged or recognized: *they tend to regard grammar as the touchstone of all language performance.*

touch-tone (also **Touch-Tone**) ▶ adj. (of a telephone) having push buttons and generating tones to dial rather than pulses. ■ (of a service) accessed or controlled by the tones generated by these telephones.
▶ n. trademark a telephone of this type. ■ one of the set of tones generated by these telephones.

touch-type ▶ v. [no obj.] (often as noun **touch-typing**) type using all one's fingers and without looking at the keys.
– DERIVATIVES **touch-typ·ist** n.

touch-up ▶ n. a quick restoration or improvement made to the appearance or state of something: *the hotels had undergone more than the customary touch-ups and refurbishing.*

touch·wood /ˈtəCH,wo͝od/ ▶ n. archaic readily flammable wood used as tinder, esp. when made soft by fungi.

touch·y /ˈtəCHē/ ▶ adj. (**touchier**, **touchiest**) (of a person) oversensitive and irritable. ■ (of an issue or situation) requiring careful handling; delicate: *the monarchy has become a touchy topic.*
– DERIVATIVES **touch·i·ly** /ˈtəCHəlē/ adv., **touch·i·ness** n.
– ORIGIN early 17th cent.: perhaps an alteration of TETCHY, influenced by TOUCH.

touch·y-feel·y /ˈfēlē/ ▶ adj. informal, often derogatory openly expressing affection or other emotions, esp. through physical contact: *touchy-feely guys calling home to talk baby talk to their kids.* ■ characteristic of or relating to such behavior: *such touchy-feely topics as employees' personal values.*

tough /təf/ ▶ adj. **1** (of a substance or object) strong enough to withstand adverse conditions or rough or careless handling: *tough backpacks for climbers.* ■ (of a person or animal) able to endure hardship or pain; physically robust: *even at this ripe old age, he's still as tough as old boots.* ■ able to protect one's own interests or maintain one's own opinions without being intimidated by opposition; confident and determined: *she's both sensitive and tough.* ■ demonstrating a strict and uncompromising attitude or approach: *police have been getting tough with drivers | tough new laws on tobacco advertising.* ■ (of a person) strong and prone to violence: *tough young teenagers.* ■ (of an area) notorious for violence and crime. ■ (of food, esp. meat) difficult to cut or chew.
2 involving considerable difficulty or hardship; requiring great determination or effort: *the training has been quite tough | he had a tough time getting into a good college.* ■ used to express sympathy with someone in an unpleasant or difficult situation: *Poor kid. It's tough on her.* ■ [often as exclamation] used to express a lack of sympathy with someone: *I feel the way I feel, and if you don't like it, tough.*
▶ n. a tough person, esp. a gangster or criminal: *young toughs sporting their state-of-the-art firearms.*
– PHRASES **tough it out** informal endure a period of hardship or difficulty. **tough shit** (or **titty**) vulgar slang used to express a lack of sympathy with someone.
– DERIVATIVES **tough·ish** adj., **tough·ly** adv., **tough·ness** n.
– ORIGIN Old English *tōh*, of Germanic origin; related to Dutch *taai* and German *zäh*.

tough·en /ˈtəfən/ ▶ v. make or become tougher: [with obj.] *he tried to toughen his son up by sending him to public school* | [no obj.] *if removed from the oven too soon meringues shrink and toughen.* ■ [with obj.] make (rules or a policy) stricter and more harsh: *new congressional efforts to toughen the laws.*
– DERIVATIVES **tough·en·er** n.

tough·ie /ˈtəfē/ ▶ n. informal **1** a person who is tough, determined, and not easily daunted.
2 a difficult problem or question: *Whom do you admire most? That's a toughie.*

tough love ▶ n. promotion of a person's welfare, esp. that of an addict, child, or criminal, by enforcing certain constraints on them, or requiring them to take responsibility for their actions. ■ a political policy designed to encourage self-help by restricting state benefits.

tough-mind·ed ▶ adj. strong, determined, and able to face up to reality.
– DERIVATIVES **tough-mind·ed·ness** n.

Tou·lon /to͞oˈlôN/ a port and naval base on the Mediterranean coast of southern France; pop. 170,041 (2006).

Tou·louse /to͞oˈlo͞oz/ a city in southwestern France on the Garonne River, principal city of the Midi-Pyrénées region; pop. 444,392 (2006).

Tou·louse-Lau·trec /to͞o,lo͞oz lōˈtrek/, Henri (Marie Raymond) de (1864–1901), French painter and lithographer. His color lithographs depict actors, music-hall singers, prostitutes, and waitresses from the 1890s in Montmartre: the *Moulin Rouge* series (1894) is particularly well known.

tou·pee /to͞oˈpā/ ▶ n. a small wig or artificial hairpiece worn to cover a bald spot.
– ORIGIN early 18th cent. (denoting a curl or lock of artificial hair): alteration of French *toupet* 'hair tuft,' diminutive of Old French *toup* 'tuft,' ultimately of Germanic origin and related to TOP¹.

tour /to͝or/ ▶ n. **1** a journey for pleasure in which several different places are visited: *three couples from Kansas on an airline tour of Alaska.* ■ a short trip to or through a place in order to view or inspect something: *a tour of the White House.*
2 a journey made by performers or an athletic team, in which they perform or play in several different places: *she joined the Royal Shakespeare Company on tour.* ■ (**the tour**) (in golf, tennis, and other sports) the annual round of events in which top professionals compete.
3 (also **tour of duty**) a period of duty on military or diplomatic service: *he was haunted by his tour of duty in Vietnam.*
▶ v. [with obj.] make a tour of (an area): *he decided to tour France* | [no obj.] *they had toured in a little minivan.* ■ take (a performer, production, etc.) on tour.
– ORIGIN Middle English (sense 3 of the noun): from Old French, 'turn,' via Latin from Greek *tornos* 'lathe.' Sense 1 dates from the mid 17th cent.

tou·ra·co /ˈto͝orə,kō/ (also **turaco**) ▶ n. (pl. **touracos**) a fruit-eating African bird with brightly colored plumage, a prominent crest, and a long tail.
● Family Musophagidae (the **touraco family**): three genera, esp. *Musophaga* and *Tauraco*, and several species. The touraco family also includes the plantain-eaters.
– ORIGIN mid 18th cent.: French, from a West African word.

Tou·rane /to͞oˈrän/ former name of DA NANG.

tour de force /ˈto͝or də ˈfôrs/ ▶ n. (pl. **tours de force** pronunc. **same** or /ˈto͝orz/) an impressive performance or achievement that has been accomplished or managed with great skill: *his novel is a tour de force.*
– ORIGIN French, literally 'feat of strength.'

Tour de France /ˈto͝or də ˈfrans/ a French race for professional cyclists held annually since 1903, covering approximately 3,000 miles (4,800 km) of roads in about three weeks, renowned for its mountain stages.

tour d'ho·ri·zon /ˈto͝or dôrēˈzôN/ ▶ n. (pl. **tours d'horizon** pronunc. **same**) a broad general survey or summary of an argument or event.
– ORIGIN French, literally 'tour of the horizon.'

tour en l'air /ˈto͝or än ˈle(ə)r/ ▶ n. (pl. **tours en l'air** /ˈto͝orz/) Ballet a movement in which a dancer jumps straight upward and completes at least one full revolution in the air before landing.
– ORIGIN French, literally 'turn in the air.'

tour·er /ˈto͝orər/ ▶ n. a car, camper, or bicycle designed for touring. ■ a person touring with such a vehicle.

Tou·rette's syn·drome /to͞oˈrets/ ▶ n. Medicine a neurological disorder characterized by involuntary tics and vocalizations and often the compulsive utterance of obscenities.
– ORIGIN late 19th cent.: named after Gilles de la *Tourette* (1857–1904), French neurologist.

tour·ing car ▶ n. a car designed with room for passengers and luggage. ■ a car of this type used in auto racing, as distinct from a specially designed race car.

tour·ism /ˈto͝or,izəm/ ▶ n. the commercial organization and operation of vacations and visits to places of interest.

tour·ist /ˈto͝orist/ ▶ n. **1** a person who is traveling or visiting a place for pleasure: *the pyramids have drawn tourists to Egypt.*
2 short for TOURIST CLASS.
▶ v. [no obj.] rare travel as a tourist: *American families touristing abroad.*
– DERIVATIVES **tour·is·tic** /to͞oˈristik/ adj., **tour·is·ti·cal·ly** /to͞oˈristik(ə)lē/ adv.

tour·ist class ▶ n. the cheapest accommodations or seating for passengers in a ship, aircraft, or hotel.
▶ adj. & adv. of, relating to, or by such accommodations or seating: [as adj.] *a tourist-class hotel* | [as adv.] *they had come tourist class from Cairo.*

tour·ist·y /ˈto͝oristē/ ▶ adj. informal relating to, appealing to, or visited by tourists (often used to suggest tawdriness or lack of authenticity): *a touristy shopping street.*

tour·ma·line /'to͝orməlan, -ˌlēn/ ▶ **n.** a brittle gray or black mineral that occurs as prismatic crystals in granitic and other rocks. It consists of a boron aluminosilicate and has pyroelectric and polarizing properties, and is used in electrical and optical instruments and as a gemstone.
– ORIGIN mid 18th cent.: from French, based on Sinhalese *tōramalli* 'carnelian.'

tour·na·ment /'tərnəmənt, 'to͝or-/ ▶ **n. 1** (in a sport or game) a series of contests between a number of competitors, who compete for an overall prize.
2 (in the Middle Ages) a sporting event in which two knights (or two groups of knights) jousted on horseback with blunted weapons, each trying to knock the other off, the winner receiving a prize.
– ORIGIN Middle English (sense 2): from Anglo-Norman French variants of Old French *torneiement*, from *torneier* 'take part in a tourney' (see TOURNEY).

tour·ne·dos /'to͝ornəˌdō/ ▶ **n.** (pl. **same**) a small round thick cut from a fillet of beef.
– ORIGIN French, from *tourner* 'to turn' + *dos* 'back.'

tour·ney /'tərnē, 'to͝or-/ ▶ **n.** (pl. **tourneys**) a tournament.
▶ **v.** (**tourneys, tourneying, tourneyed**) [no obj.] take part in a tournament.
– ORIGIN Middle English: from Old French *tornei* (noun), *torneier* (verb), based on Latin *tornus* 'a turn.'

tour·ni·quet /'tərnikit, 'to͝or-/ ▶ **n.** a device for stopping the flow of blood through a vein or artery, typically by compressing a limb with a cord or tight bandage.
– ORIGIN late 17th cent.: from French, probably from Old French *tournicle* 'coat of mail,' influenced by *tourner* 'to turn.'

tourniquet

tour op·er·a·tor ▶ **n.** a travel agent specializing in package vacations.

Tours /to͝or/ an industrial city in western central France, on the Loire River; pop. 140,252 (2006).

tour·tière /to͝or'tyer/ ▶ **n.** (pl. **same**) a kind of meat pie traditionally eaten at Christmas in Canada.
– ORIGIN French.

tou·sle /'touzəl/ ▶ **v.** [with obj.] (usu. as adj. **tousled**) make (something, esp. a person's hair) untidy: *Nathan's tousled head appeared in the hatchway.*
– ORIGIN late Middle English (in the sense 'handle roughly or rudely'): frequentative of dialect *touse* 'handle roughly,' of Germanic origin and related to German *zausen*. Compare with TUSSLE.

Tous·saint L'Ou·ver·ture /to͞o'saN ˌlo͞over'tʏr/, Pierre Dominique (*c.*1743–1803), Haitian revolutionary leader. One of the leaders of a rebellion that emancipated the island's slaves in 1791, he was appointed governor general in 1797 by the revolutionary government of France. In 1802, Napoleon, wishing to restore slavery, took over the island, and Toussaint died in prison in France.

tout[1] /tout/ ▶ **v. 1** [with obj.] attempt to sell (something), typically by pestering people in an aggressive or bold manner: *Jim was touting his wares.* ■ attempt to persuade people of the merits of (someone or something): *the headquarters facility was touted as the best in the country.* ■ Brit. scalp (a ticket).
2 [no obj.] offer racing tips for a share of any resulting winnings. ■ [with obj.] chiefly Brit. spy out the movements and condition of (a racehorse in training) in order to gain information to be used when betting.
▶ **n. 1** a person soliciting custom or business, typically in an aggressive or bold manner. ■ Brit. a person who buys tickets for an event to resell them at a profit; a scalper.
2 a person who offers racing tips for a share of any resulting winnings.
3 N. Irish & Scottish informal an informer.
– DERIVATIVES **tout·er n.**
– ORIGIN Middle English *tute* 'look out,' of Germanic origin; related to Dutch *tuit* 'spout, nozzle.' Later senses were 'watch, spy on' (late 17th cent.) and 'solicit business' (mid 18th cent). The noun was first recorded (early 18th cent.) in the slang use 'thieves' lookout.'

tout[2] /to͞o/ ▶ **determiner** (often **le tout**) used before the name of a city to refer to its high society or people of importance: *le tout Washington adored him.*
– ORIGIN French, suggested by *le tout Paris* 'all (of) Paris,' used to refer to Parisian high society.

tout court /ˌto͞o 'ko͝or/ ▶ **adv.** with no addition or qualification; simply: *he saw it as an illusion, tout court.*
– ORIGIN French, literally 'very short.'

tout de suite /ˌto͞ot 'swēt/ ▶ **adv.** immediately; at once: *she left tout de suite.*
– ORIGIN French, literally 'quite in sequence.'

tout le monde /ˌto͞o lə 'mônd/ ▶ **n.** [treated as sing. or pl.] everyone: *he shouted "Bon appetit, tout le monde!"*
– ORIGIN French.

to·va·rish /tə'värisн/ (also **tovarich**) ▶ **n.** (in the former Soviet Union) a comrade (often used as a form of address).
– ORIGIN from Russian *tovarishch*, from Turkic.

TOW /tō/ ▶ **abbr.** tube-launched, optically guided, wire-guided (missile).

tow[1] /tō/ ▶ **v.** [with obj.] (of a motor vehicle or boat) pull (another vehicle or boat) along with a rope, chain, or tow bar. ■ (of a person) pull (someone or something) along behind one: *she saw Frank towing Nicky along by the hand.*
▶ **n.** [in sing.] an act of towing a vehicle or boat. ■ a rope or line used to tow a vehicle or boat.
– PHRASES **in tow 1** being towed by another vehicle or boat: *his boat was taken in tow by a trawler.* **2** accompanying or following someone: *trying to shop with three children in tow is no joke.*
– DERIVATIVES **tow·a·ble adj.**
– ORIGIN Old English *togian* 'draw, drag,' of Germanic origin; related to TUG. The noun dates from the early 17th cent.

tow[2] ▶ **n.** the coarse and broken part of flax or hemp prepared for spinning. ■ a bundle of untwisted natural or man-made fibers.
– DERIVATIVES **tow·y adj.**
– ORIGIN Old English (recorded in *towcræft* 'spinning'), of Germanic origin.

tow·age /'tō-ij/ ▶ **n. 1** [usu. as modifier] the action or process of towing.
2 a charge for towing a boat or vehicle.

to·ward /tôrd, t(ə)'wôrd/ ▶ **prep.** (also **towards** /tôrdz, t(ə)'wôrdz/) **1** in the direction of: *I walked toward the front door.* ■ getting closer to achieving (a goal): *an irresistible move toward freedom.* ■ close or closer to (a particular time): *toward the end of April.*
2 as regards; in relation to: *he was warm and tender toward her | our attitude toward death.*
3 contributing to the cost of (something): *the council provided a grant toward the cost of new buses.*
▶ **adj.** [predic.] archaic going on; in progress: *is something new toward?*
– ORIGIN Old English *tōweard* (see TO, -WARD).

tow bar ▶ **n.** a bar fitted to the back of a vehicle, used in towing a trailer.

tow-col·ored ▶ **adj.** (of hair) very light blond.

tow·el /'toul/ ▶ **n.** a piece of thick absorbent cloth or paper used for drying oneself or wiping things dry.
▶ **v.** (**towels, toweling, toweled**; Brit. **towels, towelling, towelled**) [with obj.] wipe or dry (a person or thing) with a towel: [with obj. and complement] *she toweled her hair dry* | [no obj.] *quickly we'd towel off and dress for dinner.*
– PHRASES **throw in the towel** see THROW.
– ORIGIN Middle English: from Old French *toaille*, of Germanic origin. The verb, originally meaning 'beat or thrash,' dates from the early 18th cent. The sense 'wipe with a towel' arose in the mid 19th cent.

tow·el·ette /tou(ə)'let/ ▶ **n.** a small paper or cloth towel, usually premoistened in a sealed package, used for cleansing.

tow·el·head /'tou(ə)l ˌhed/ ▶ **n.** informal, offensive a person who wears a turban or a kaffiyeh.

tow·el·ing /'touliNG/ (Brit. **towelling**) ▶ **n.** thick absorbent cloth, typically cotton with uncut loops, used for towels and robes.

tow·er /'tou(ə)r/ ▶ **n. 1** a tall narrow building, either freestanding or forming part of a building such as a church or castle. ■ [with modifier] a tall structure that houses machinery, operators, etc. ■ [with modifier] a tall structure used as a receptacle or for storage: *a CD tower.* ■ a tall pile or mass of something: *a titanic tower of garbage.* ■ (**the Tower**) see TOWER OF LONDON.
2 a place of defense; a protection.
▶ **v.** [no obj.] **1** rise to or reach a great height: *he seemed to tower over everyone else.*
2 (of a bird) soar to a great height, esp. (of a falcon) so as to be able to swoop down on the quarry.
– PHRASES **tower of strength** see STRENGTH.
– DERIVATIVES **tow·ered adj.** (chiefly literary), **tow·er·y adj.** (literary).
– ORIGIN Old English *torr*, reinforced in Middle English by Old French *tour*, from Latin *turris*, from Greek.

tow·er·ing /'tou(-ə)riNG/ ▶ **adj.** [attrib.] extremely tall, esp. in comparison with the surroundings: *Hari looked up at the towering buildings.* ■ of exceptional importance or influence: *a majestic, towering album.* ■ of great intensity: *his towering anger.*

Tow·er of Ba·bel /'babəl, 'bā-/ (in the Bible) a tower built in an attempt to reach heaven, which God frustrated by confusing the languages of its builders so that they could not understand one another (Genesis 11:1–9).
– ORIGIN *Babel* from Hebrew *Bābel* 'Babylon,' from Akkadian *bāb ili* 'gate of god.'

Tow·er of Lon·don (also **the Tower**) a fortress by the Thames River just east of the City of London. The oldest part, the White Tower, was begun in 1078. It was later used as a state prison, and is now open to the public as a repository of ancient armor and weapons, and of the Crown jewels.

Tower of London

tow·head /'tōˌhed/ ▶ **n.** a head of tow-colored or very blond hair. ■ a person with such hair.
– DERIVATIVES **tow·head·ed adj.**

tow·hee /'tōˌhē, 'tou-/ ▶ **n.** a North American songbird of the bunting family, typically with brownish plumage but sometimes black and rufous. ● Genus *Pipilo* (and *Chlorurus*), family Emberizidae (subfamily Emberizinae): several species.
– ORIGIN mid 18th cent.: imitative of the call of *Pipilo erythrophthalmus*.

tow·line /'tōˌlīn/ ▶ **n.** a rope, cable, or other line used in towing.

town /toun/ ▶ **n.** an urban area that has a name, defined boundaries, and local government, and that is generally larger than a village and smaller than a city. ■ the particular town under consideration, esp. one's own town: *Carson was in town.* ■ the central part of a neighborhood, with its business or shopping area: *Rachel left to drive back into town.* ■ Brit. dated the chief city or town of a region: *he has moved to town.* ■ a densely populated area, esp. as contrasted with the country or suburbs: *the cultural differences between town and country.* ■ the permanent residents of a college town as distinct from the members of the college: *a rift between the city's town and gown that resulted in a petition to the college.* Often contrasted with GOWN. ■ another term for TOWNSHIP (sense 3).
– PHRASES **go to town** informal do something thoroughly, enthusiastically, or extravagantly: *I thought I'd go to town on the redecoration.* **on the town** informal enjoying the entertainments, esp. the nightlife, of a city or town: *a lot of guys out for a night on the town.*
– DERIVATIVES **town·ish adj.**, **town·let** /-lit/ **n.**, **town·ward** /-wərd/ **adj. & adv.**, **town·wards** /-wərdz/ **adv.**
– ORIGIN Old English *tūn* 'enclosed piece of land, homestead, village,' of Germanic origin; related to Dutch *tuin* 'garden' and German *Zaun* 'fence.'

town car ▶ **n.** a limousine.

town clerk ▶ **n.** a public official in charge of the records of a town.

town coun·cil ▶ **n.** an elected governing body in a town.
– DERIVATIVES **town coun·ci·lor n.**

town cri·er ▶ **n.** historical a person employed to make public announcements in the streets or marketplace of a town.

Townes /tounz/, Charles Hard (1915–), US physicist. His development of microwave oscillators and amplifiers led to his invention of the maser in 1954. He later showed that an optical maser (a laser) was possible. He shared the 1964 Nobel Prize for Physics with Nicolay Basov (1922–2001) and Aleksandr Prokhorov (1916–2002).

town hall ▶ **n.** a building used for the administration of local government.

town·house /'tounˌhous/ (also **town house**) ▶ **n.**
1 a tall, narrow, traditional row house, generally having three or more floors. ■ a modern two- or three-story house built as one of a group of similar houses.
2 a house in a town or city belonging to someone who has another property in the country.

town·ie /'tounē/ ▶ **n.** a person who lives in a town (used esp. with reference to their supposed lack of familiarity with rural affairs). ■ a resident in a college town, rather than a student: *any differences there might have been between townies and students.*

town ma·jor ▶ **n.** historical the chief executive officer in a garrison town or fortress.

town meet·ing ▶ **n.** a meeting of the voters of a town for the transaction of public business.

Town 'n' Coun·try a residential community in western Florida, northwest of Tampa; pop. 72,523 (2000).

town plan·ning ▶ **n.** another term for CITY PLANNING.
– DERIVATIVES **town plan·ner n.**

town·scape /'toun,skāp/ ▶ **n.** the visual appearance of a town or urban area; an urban landscape: *the building's contribution to the townscape | an industrial townscape.* ■ a picture of a town.

towns·folk /'tounz,fōk/ ▶ **plural n.** another term for TOWNSPEOPLE.

town·ship /'toun,SHip/ ▶ **n.** **1** a division of a county with some corporate powers. ■ a district six miles square.
2 (in South Africa) a suburb or city of predominantly black occupation, formerly officially designated for black occupation by apartheid legislation.
3 Brit. historical a manor or parish as a territorial division. ■ a small town or village forming part of a large parish.
– ORIGIN Old English *tūnscipe* 'the inhabitants of a village' (see TOWN, -SHIP).

town·site /'toun,sīt/ ▶ **n.** a tract of land set apart by legal authority to be occupied by a town and usually surveyed and laid out with streets.

towns·man /'tounzmən/ ▶ **n.** (pl. **townsmen**) a man living in a particular town or city.

towns·peo·ple /'tounz,pēpəl/ (also **townsfolk** /-,fōk/) ▶ **plural n.** the people living in a particular town or city.

Towns·ville /'tounz,vil/ an industrial port and resort on the coast of Queensland, in northeastern Australia; pop. 175,542 (2008).

towns·wom·an /'tounz,wo͝omən/ ▶ **n.** (pl. **townswomen**) a woman living in a particular town or city.

tow·path /'tō,paTH/ ▶ **n.** a path beside a river or canal, originally used as a pathway for horses towing barges.

tow·plane /'tō,plān/ ▶ **n.** an aircraft that tows gliders.

tow rope ▶ **n.** another term for TOWLINE.

Tow·son /'tousən/ a suburban community in northern Maryland, north of Baltimore; pop. 51,793 (2000).

tow truck /'tō ,trək/ ▶ **n.** a truck used to tow or pick up damaged or disabled vehicles.

tox·a·phene /'täksə,fēn/ ▶ **n.** a synthetic amber waxy solid with an odor of chlorine and camphor, used as an insecticide. It is a chlorinated terpene.
– ORIGIN 1940s: from TOXIN + (*cam*)*phene*, a related terpene.

tox·e·mi·a /täk'sēmēə/ (Brit. **toxaemia**) ▶ **n.** blood poisoning by toxins from a local bacterial infection. ■ (also **toxemia of pregnancy**) another term for PREECLAMPSIA.
– DERIVATIVES **tox·e·mic** /-'sēmik/ **adj.**
– ORIGIN mid 19th cent.: from TOXI- + -EMIA.

toxi- ▶ **comb. form** representing TOXIC or TOXIN.

tox·ic /'täksik/ ▶ **adj. 1** poisonous: *the dumping of toxic waste | alcohol is toxic to the ovaries.* ■ relating to or caused by poison: *toxic hazards | toxic liver injury.* ■ very bad, unpleasant, or harmful: *a toxic relationship.*
2 Finance denoting or relating to debt that has a high risk of default. ■ denoting securities that are based on toxic debt and for which there is not a healthy or functioning market: *the financial system has become clogged with toxic assets.*
▶ **n.** (**toxics**) poisonous substances.
– DERIVATIVES **tox·i·cal·ly** /-sik(ə)lē/ **adv.**, **tox·ic·i·ty** /täk'sisitē/ **n.**
– ORIGIN mid 17th cent.: from medieval Latin *toxicus* 'poisoned,' from Latin *toxicum* 'poison,' from Greek *toxikon* (*pharmakon*) '(poison for) arrows,' from *toxon* 'bow.'

WORD TRENDS The financial sense of **toxic** describes debts that are unlikely to be repaid and assets suddenly found to be worthless: *banks will be pressured to come clean on the amount of toxic debt they hold | no one wants to buy any of these toxic assets.* **Toxic** has been used metaphorically to describe something very bad or harmful since the late 20th century (*the scandal could be politically toxic*), and the specific financial sense is first recorded around 1990. Before that, though, risky stocks and bonds were referred to as *toxic waste*—they are dangerous to (financial) health and very difficult to dispose of.

tox·i·cant /'täksikənt/ ▶ **n.** a toxic substance introduced into the environment, e.g., a pesticide.
– ORIGIN late 19th cent.: variant of INTOXICANT, differentiated in sense.

toxico- ▶ **comb. form** equivalent to TOXI-.
– ORIGIN from Greek *toxicon* 'poison.'

tox·i·col·o·gy /,täksi'käləjē/ ▶ **n.** the branch of science concerned with the nature, effects, and detection of poisons.
– DERIVATIVES **tox·i·co·log·ic** /-kə'läjik/ **adj.**, **tox·i·co·log·i·cal** /-kə'läjikəl/ **adj.**, **tox·i·co·log·i·cal·ly adv.**, **tox·i·col·o·gist** /-'käləjist/ **n.**

tox·ic shock syn·drome (abbr.: **TSS**) ▶ **n.** acute septicemia in women, typically caused by bacterial infection from a retained tampon or IUD.

tox·i·drome /'täksi,drōm/ ▶ **n.** a group of signs and symptoms constituting the basis for a diagnosis of poisoning.

tox·i·gen·ic /,täksi'jenik/ ▶ **adj.** (esp. of a bacterium) producing a toxin or toxic effect.
– DERIVATIVES **tox·i·ge·nic·i·ty** /-jə'nisitē/ **n.**

tox·in /'täksin/ ▶ **n.** an antigenic poison or venom of plant or animal origin, esp. one produced by or derived from microorganisms and causing disease when present at low concentration in the body.
– ORIGIN late 19th cent.: from TOXIC + -IN[1].

toxo- ▶ **comb. form** equivalent to TOXI-.

tox·o·car·a /,täksə'karə/ ▶ **n.** a parasitic nematode worm, esp. a common worm of dogs or cats that is transmissible to humans. ● Genus *Toxocara*, class Phasmida, in particular *T. canis* (in dogs) and *T. cati* (in cats).
– ORIGIN modern Latin, from TOXO- (see TOXI-) + Greek *kara* 'head.'

tox·o·car·i·a·sis /,täksəkə'rīəsis/ ▶ **n.** infection of a human with the larvae of toxocara worms, causing illness and a risk of blindness from cyst formation in the eye.

tox·oid /'täk,soid/ ▶ **n.** Medicine a chemically modified toxin from a pathogenic microorganism, which is no longer toxic but is still antigenic and can be used as a vaccine.

tox·oph·i·lite /täk'säfə,līt/ rare ▶ **n.** a student or lover of archery.
▶ **adj.** of or relating to archers and archery.
– DERIVATIVES **tox·oph·i·ly** /-'säfəlē/ **n.**
– ORIGIN late 18th cent.: from *Toxophilus* (a name invented by Ascham, used as the title of his treatise on archery (1545), from Greek *toxon* 'bow' + *-philos* 'loving') + -ITE[1].

tox·o·plas·ma /,täksə'plazmə/ ▶ **n.** a parasitic spore-forming protozoan that can sometimes cause disease in humans. ● Genus *Toxoplasma*, phylum Sporozoa, in particular *T. gondii.*

tox·o·plas·mo·sis /,täksōplaz'mōsis/ ▶ **n.** a disease caused by toxoplasmas, transmitted chiefly through undercooked meat, or in soil or cat feces. Symptoms generally pass unremarked in adults, but infection can be dangerous to unborn children.

toy /toi/ ▶ **n. 1** an object for a child to play with, typically a model or miniature replica of something: [as modifier] *a toy car.* ■ an object, esp. a gadget or machine, regarded as providing amusement for an adult: *in 1914 the car was still a rich man's toy.* ■ a person treated by another as a source of pleasure or amusement rather than with due seriousness: *a man needed a friend, an ally, not an idol or a toy.*
2 [as modifier] denoting a diminutive breed or variety of dog: *a toy poodle.*
– PHRASAL VERBS **toy with 1** consider (an idea, movement, or proposal) casually or indecisively. ■ treat (someone) without due seriousness, esp. in a superficially amorous way. **2** move or handle (an object) absentmindedly or nervously. ■ eat or drink in an unenthusiastic or restrained way.
– DERIVATIVES **toy·like** /-,līk/ **adj.**
– ORIGIN late Middle English: of unknown origin. The word originally denoted a funny story or remark, later an antic or trick, or a frivolous entertainment. The verb dates from the early 16th cent.

toy boy ▶ **n.** Brit. informal a male lover who is much younger than his partner.

Toyn·bee[1] /'toinbē/, Arnold (1852–83), English economist and social reformer. He is best known for his pioneering work *The Industrial Revolution* (1884).

Toyn·bee[2], Arnold (Joseph) (1889–1975), English historian. He is best known for his 12-volume *Study of History* (1934–61), in which he traced the pattern of growth, maturity, and decay of different civilizations. He was the nephew of the economist Arnold Toynbee.

to·yon /'toi-än/ ▶ **n.** an evergreen Californian shrub of the rose family, the fruiting branches of which are used for Christmas decorations. ● *Heteromeles arbutifolia*, family Rosaceae.
– ORIGIN mid 19th cent.: from Mexican Spanish *tollón.*

tp. ▶ **abbr.** ■ township. ■ troop.

t.p. ▶ **abbr.** ■ title page. ■ toilet paper. ■ (in surveying) turning point.
▶ **v.** (also **TP**) cover things such as trees and buildings with toilet paper, as a prank or in celebration of a school sports victory, graduation, etc.

TPA ▶ **abbr.** tissue plasminogen activator.

tpk. ▶ **abbr.** turnpike.

TPV ▶ **abbr.** thermophotovoltaic.

TQM ▶ **abbr.** Total Quality Management.

tr. ▶ **abbr.** ■ tare. ■ tincture. ■ trace. ■ train. ■ transaction. ■ transitive. ■ translated. ■ translation. ■ translator. ■ transpose. ■ transposition. ■ treasurer. ■ Music trill. ■ troop. ■ trust. ■ trustee.

tra·be·a·tion /,trābē'āsHən/ ▶ **n.** the use of beams in architectural construction, rather than arches or vaulting.
– DERIVATIVES **tra·be·at·ed** /'trābē,ātid/ **adj.**
– ORIGIN mid 16th cent. (denoting a horizontal beam): formed irregularly from Latin *trabs, trab-* 'beam, timber' + -ATION.

tra·bec·u·la /trə'bekyələ/ ▶ **n.** (usu. in pl. **trabeculae** /-lē/) **1** Anatomy each of a series or group of partitions formed by bands or columns of connective tissue, esp. a plate of the calcareous tissue forming cancellous bone.
2 Botany any of a number of rodlike structures in plants, e.g., a strand of sterile tissue dividing the cavity in a sporangium.
– DERIVATIVES **tra·bec·u·lar adj.**, **tra·bec·u·late** /-lit/ **adj.**
– ORIGIN mid 19th cent.: from Latin, diminutive of *trabs* 'beam, timber.'

Trâ·blous Arabic name for TRIPOLI (sense 2).

Trab·zon /trab'zän/ a port on the Black Sea in northern Turkey; pop. 228,800 (est. 2007). Also called TREBIZOND.

trace[1] /trās/ ▶ **v.** [with obj.] **1** find or discover by investigation: *police are trying to trace a white van seen in the area.* ■ find or describe the origin or development of: *Bob's book traces his flying career with the Marines.* ■ follow or mark the course or position of (something) with one's eye, mind, or finger: *through the binoculars, I traced the path I had taken the night before.* ■ take (a particular path or route): *a tear traced a lonely path down her cheek.*
2 copy (a drawing, map, or design) by drawing over its lines on a superimposed piece of transparent paper. ■ draw (a pattern or line), esp. with one's finger or toe. ■ give an outline of: *the article traces out some of the connections between education, qualifications, and the labor market.*
▶ **n. 1** a mark, object, or other indication of the existence or passing of something: *remove all traces of the old adhesive | the aircraft disappeared without trace.* ■ a beaten path or small road; a track. ■ a physical change in the brain presumed to be caused by a process of learning or memory. ■ a procedure to investigate the source of something, such as the place from which a telephone call was made, or the origin of an error in a computer program.
2 a very small quantity, esp. one too small to be accurately measured: *his body contained traces of amphetamines* | [as modifier] *trace quantities of PCBs.* ■ a slight indication or barely discernible hint of something: *just a trace of a smile.*
3 a line or pattern displayed by an instrument using a moving pen or a luminous spot on a screen to show the existence or nature of something that is being investigated. ■ a line that represents the projection of a curve or surface on a plane or the intersection of a curve or surface with a plane.
4 Mathematics the sum of the elements in the principle diagonal of a square matrix.
– DERIVATIVES **trace·a·bil·i·ty** /,trāsə'bilitē/ **n.**, **trace·a·ble adj.**, **trace·less adj.**
– ORIGIN Middle English (first recorded as a noun in the sense 'path that someone or something takes'): from Old French *trace* (noun), *tracier* (verb), based on Latin *tractus* (see TRACT[1]).

PRONUNCIATION KEY ə *ago, up*; ər *over, fur*; a *hat*; ā *ate*; ä *car*; e *let*; ē *see*; i *fit*; ī *by*; NG *sing*; ō *go*; ô *law, for*; oi *toy*; o͝o *good*; o͞o *goo*; ou *out*; TH *thin*; T͟H *then*; ZH *vision*

t

trace[2] ▶ **n.** each of the two side straps, chains, or ropes by which a horse is attached to a vehicle that it is pulling.
– ORIGIN Middle English (denoting a pair of traces): from Old French *trais*, plural of *trait* (see TRAIT).

trace el·e·ment ▶ **n.** a chemical element present only in minute amounts in a particular sample or environment. ■ a chemical element required only in minute amounts by living organisms for normal growth.

trace fos·sil ▶ **n.** Geology a fossil of a footprint, trail, burrow, or other trace of an animal rather than of the animal itself.

trace min·er·al ▶ **n.** a trace element required for nutrition: *selenium and other trace minerals are vital to good health.*

trac·er /ˈtrāsər/ ▶ **n.** a person or thing that traces something or by which something may be traced, in particular: ■ a bullet or shell whose course is made visible in flight by a trail of flames or smoke, used to assist in aiming. ■ a substance introduced into a biological organism or other system so that its subsequent distribution can be readily followed from its color, fluorescence, radioactivity, or other distinctive property. ■ a device that transmits a signal and so can be located when attached to a moving vehicle or other object.

trac·er·y /ˈtrāsərē/ ▶ **n.** (pl. **traceries**) Architecture ornamental stone openwork, typically in the upper part of a Gothic window. ■ a delicate branching pattern: *a tracery of red veins.*
– DERIVATIVES **trac·er·ied adj.**

tra·che·a /ˈtrākēə/ ▶ **n.** (pl. **tracheae** /-kēˌē/ or **tracheas**) Anatomy a large membranous tube reinforced by rings of cartilage, extending from the larynx to the bronchial tubes and conveying air to and from the lungs; the windpipe. ■ Entomology each of a number of fine chitinous tubes in the body of an insect, conveying air directly to the tissues. ■ Botany any duct or vessel in a plant, providing support and conveying water and salts.
– DERIVATIVES **tra·che·al adj.**, **tra·che·ate** /-it, -ˌāt/ **adj.**
– ORIGIN late Middle English: from medieval Latin, from late Latin *trachia*, from Greek *trakheia (artēria)* 'rough (artery),' from *trakhus* 'rough.'

tra·che·id /ˈtrākēid/ ▶ **n.** Botany a type of water-conducting cell in the xylem that lacks perforations in the cell wall.
– ORIGIN late 19th cent.: from German *Tracheïde*, from medieval Latin *trachea* (see TRACHEA).

tra·che·i·tis /ˌtrākēˈītis/ ▶ **n.** Medicine inflammation of the trachea, usually secondary to a nose or throat infection.

tracheo- ▶ **comb. form** relating to the trachea: *tracheotomy.*

tra·che·ot·o·my /ˌtrākēˈätəmē/ (also **tracheostomy** /-ˈästəmē/) ▶ **n.** (pl. **tracheotomies**) Medicine an incision in the windpipe made to relieve an obstruction to breathing.

tra·cho·ma /trəˈkōmə/ ▶ **n.** a contagious bacterial infection of the eye in which there is inflamed granulation on the inner surface of the lids. ● The disease is caused by the chlamydial organism *Chlamydia trachomatis.*
– DERIVATIVES **tra·chom·a·tous** /-mətəs/ **adj.**
– ORIGIN late 17th cent.: from Greek *trakhōma* 'roughness,' from *trakhus* 'rough.'

tra·chyte /ˈtrakˌīt, ˈtrā-/ ▶ **n.** Geology a gray fine-grained volcanic rock consisting largely of alkali feldspar.
– ORIGIN early 19th cent. (denoting a volcanic rock with a rough or gritty surface): from Greek *trakhus* 'rough' or *trakhutēs* 'roughness.'

tra·chyt·ic /trəˈkitik/ ▶ **adj.** Geology relating to or denoting a rock texture (characteristic of trachyte) in which crystals show parallel alignment due to flow in the magma.

trac·ing /ˈtrāsiNG/ ▶ **n.** a copy of a drawing, map, or design made by tracing it. ■ a faint or delicate mark or pattern: *tracings of apple blossoms against the deep greens of pines.* ■ another term for TRACE[1] (sense 3 of the noun). ■ Figure Skating the marking out of a figure on the ice when skating.

trac·ing pa·per ▶ **n.** transparent paper used for tracing maps, drawings, or designs.

track[1] /trak/ ▶ **n. 1** a rough path or minor road, typically one beaten by use rather than constructed: *follow the track to the farm | a forest track.* ■ a prepared course or circuit for athletes, horses, motor vehicles, bicycles, or dogs to race on: *a Formula One Grand Prix track.* ■ the sport of running on such a track. ■ (usu. **tracks**) a mark or line of marks left by a person, animal, or vehicle in passing: *he followed the tracks made by the police cars in the snow.* ■ the course or route followed by someone or something (used esp. in talking about their pursuit by others): *I didn't want the Russians **on my track**.* ■ a course of action; a way of proceeding: *defense budgeting and procurement do not move along different tracks from defense policy as a whole.*
2 a continuous line of rails on a railroad. ■ a metal or plastic strip or rail from which a curtain or spotlight may be hung or fitted. ■ a continuous articulated metal band around the wheels of a heavy vehicle such as a tank or bulldozer, intended to facilitate movement over rough or soft ground. ■ Electronics a continuous line of copper or other conductive material on a printed circuit board, used to connect parts of a circuit. ■ Sailing a strip on the mast, boom, or deck of a yacht along which a slide attached to a sail can be moved, used to adjust the position of the sail.
3 a recording of one song or piece of music: *the CD contains early Elvis Presley tracks.* ■ a lengthwise strip of magnetic tape containing one sequence of signals. ■ the soundtrack of a film or video.
4 the transverse distance between a vehicle's wheels.
5 a group in which schoolchildren of the same age and ability are taught.
▶ **v.** [with obj.] **1** follow the course or trail of (someone or something), typically in order to find them or note their location at various points: *secondary radars that track the aircraft in flight | he tracked Anna to her room.* ■ follow and note the course or progress of: *they are tracking the girth and evolution of stars.* ■ [no obj.] follow a particular course: *the storm was tracking across the ground at 30 mph.* ■ (of a stylus) follow (a groove in a record). ■ [no obj.] (of a film or television camera) move in relation to the subject being filmed: *the camera eventually tracked away.* [with reference to early filming when a camera was mobile by means of a track.] ■ (**track something up**) leave a trail of dirty footprints on a surface. ■ (**track something in**) leave a trail of dirt, debris, or snow from one's feet: *the road salt I'd tracked in from the street.*
2 [no obj.] (of wheels) run so that the back ones are exactly in the track of the front ones.
3 [no obj.] Electronics (of a tunable circuit or component) vary in frequency in the same way as another circuit or component, so that the frequency difference between them remains constant.
4 assign (a student) to a course of study according to ability.
– PHRASES **in one's tracks** informal where one or something is at that moment; suddenly: *Turner immediately **stopped dead in his tracks**.* **keep** (or **lose**) **track of** keep (or fail to keep) fully aware of or informed about: *she had lost all track of time and had fallen asleep.* **make tracks (for)** informal leave hurriedly (for a place). **off the beaten track** see BEATEN. **on the right** (or **wrong**) **track** acting or thinking in a way that is likely to result in success (or failure): *we are on the right track for continued growth.* **on track** acting or thinking in a way that is likely to achieve what is required: *formulas for keeping the economy on track.* **the wrong** (or **right**) **side of the tracks** informal a poor, less prestigious (or wealthy, prestigious) part of town.
– PHRASAL VERBS **track someone/something down** find someone or something after a thorough or difficult search. **track up** (of a horse at the trot) create sufficient impulsion in its hindquarters to cause the hind feet to step onto or slightly ahead of the former position of the forefeet.
– ORIGIN late 15th cent. (in the sense 'trail, marks left behind'): the noun from Old French *trac*, perhaps from Low German or Dutch *trek* 'drawing, pull'; the verb (current senses dating from the mid 16th cent.) from French *traquer* or directly from the noun.

track[2] ▶ **v.** [with obj.] tow (a boat) along a waterway from the bank.
– ORIGIN early 18th cent.: apparently from Dutch *trekken* 'to draw, pull, or travel.' The change in the vowel was due to association with TRACK[1].

track·age /ˈtrakij/ ▶ **n.** the tracks or lines of a railroad system collectively.

track and field ▶ **n.** athletic events that take place on a running track and a nearby field; track events and field events.

track·ball /ˈtrakˌbôl/ ▶ **n.** a small ball set in a holder that can be rotated by hand to move a cursor on a computer screen.

track·bed /ˈtrakˌbed/ ▶ **n.** a roadbed for a railroad.

track·er /ˈtrakər/ ▶ **n. 1** a person who tracks someone or something by following their trail. ■ a device that follows and records the movements of someone or something: *electronic trackers are now showing ornithologists where the birds go.*
2 Music a connecting rod in the mechanism of some organs.

track·er fund ▶ **n.** Finance a mutual fund whose holdings mirror the composition of a stock market index or group of indexes.

track e·vents ▶ **plural n.** track-and-field contests that take place on a running track, as opposed to those involving throwing or other activities. Compare with FIELD EVENTS.

track·ing /ˈtrakiNG/ ▶ **n. 1** Electronics the maintenance of a constant difference in frequency between two or more connected circuits or components. ■ the alignment of the wheels of a vehicle. ■ the formation of a conducting path for an electric current over the surface of an insulating material.
2 the practice of putting schoolchildren in groups of the same age and ability to be taught together: *Japan allows virtually no tracking or ability grouping before high school.*

track·ing sta·tion ▶ **n.** a place from which the movements of missiles, aircraft, or satellites are tracked by radar or radio.

track·lay·er /ˈtrakˌlāər/ ▶ **n. 1** a tractor or other vehicle equipped with continuous tracks.
2 another term for TRACKMAN (sense 1).

track·less /ˈtrakləs/ ▶ **adj. 1** (of land) having no paths or tracks on it: *leading travelers into trackless wastelands.* ■ literary not leaving a track or trace.
2 (of a vehicle or component) not running on a track or tracks.

track light·ing ▶ **n.** a lighting system in which the lights are fitted on tracks, allowing variable positioning.
– DERIVATIVES **track lights plural n.**

track·man /ˈtrakmən, -ˌman/ ▶ **n.** (pl. **trackmen**) **1** a person employed in laying and maintaining railroad track.
2 an athlete in track events.

track rec·ord ▶ **n.** the best recorded performance in a particular track-and-field event at a particular track. ■ the past achievements or performance of a person, organization, or product: *he has an excellent track record as an author.*

track shoe ▶ **n.** a running shoe.

track·side /ˈtrakˌsīd/ ▶ **n.** the area alongside a railroad track or sports track.

track suit ▶ **n.** a loose, warm set of clothes consisting of a sweatshirt or light jacket and pants with an elastic or drawstring waist, worn when exercising or as casual wear.

track·way /ˈtrakˌwā/ ▶ **n.** a path formed by the repeated treading of people or animals. ■ an ancient roadway.

tract[1] /trakt/ ▶ **n. 1** an area of indefinite extent, typically a large one: *large tracts of natural forest.* ■ literary an indefinitely large extent of something: *the vast tracts of time required to account for the deposition of the strata.*
2 a major passage in the body, large bundle of nerve fibers, or other continuous elongated anatomical structure or region: *the digestive tract.*
– ORIGIN late Middle English (in the sense 'duration or course (of time)'): from Latin *tractus* 'drawing, dragging,' from *trahere* 'draw, pull.'

tract[2] ▶ **n.** a short treatise in pamphlet form, typically on a religious subject.
– ORIGIN late Middle English (denoting a written work treating a particular topic), apparently an abbreviation of Latin *tractatus* (see TRACTATE). The current sense dates from the early 19th cent.

trac·ta·ble /ˈtraktəbəl/ ▶ **adj.** (of a person or animal) easy to control or influence: *the tractable dogs that have had some obedience training.* ■ (of a situation or problem) easy to deal with: *trying to make the mathematics tractable.*
– DERIVATIVES **trac·ta·bil·i·ty** /ˌtraktəˈbilitē/ **n.**, **trac·ta·bly** /-blē/ **adv.**
– ORIGIN early 16th cent.: from Latin *tractabilis*, from *tractare* 'to handle' (see TRACTATE).

Trac·tar·i·an·ism /trakˈte(ə)rēəˌnizəm/ ▶ **n.** another name for OXFORD MOVEMENT.
– DERIVATIVES **Trac·tar·i·an adj. & n.**
– ORIGIN mid 19th cent.: from *Tracts for the Times*, the title of a series of pamphlets on theological topics started by J. H. Newman and published in Oxford 1833–41, which set out the doctrines on which the movement was based.

trac·tate /ˈtrakˌtāt/ ▶ **n.** formal a treatise.
– ORIGIN late 15th cent.: from Latin *tractatus*, from *tractare* 'to handle,' frequentative of *trahere* 'draw.'

trac·tion /ˈtrakSHən/ ▶ **n. 1** the action of drawing or pulling a thing over a surface, esp. a road or track: *a primitive vehicle used in animal traction.* ■ motive power provided for such movement, esp. on a railroad: *the changeover to diesel and electric traction.* ■ locomotives collectively.
2 the grip of a tire on a road or a wheel on a rail: *his car hit a patch of ice and lost traction.*

3 the extent to which a product, idea, etc., gains popularity or acceptance: *analysts predicted that the technology would rapidly* ***gain traction*** *in the corporate market.*
4 Medicine the application of a sustained pull on a limb or muscle, esp. in order to maintain the position of a fractured bone or to correct a deformity: *his leg is* ***in traction.***
– ORIGIN late Middle English (denoting contraction, such as that of a muscle): from French, or from medieval Latin *traction-*, from Latin *trahere* 'draw, pull.' Current senses date from the early 19th cent.

WORD TRENDS Fast cars and successful businesses seem to go together, so it's appropriate that the world of commerce has borrowed expressions from the road. **Traction** still has its literal senses of 'the action of pulling something' and 'the grip of a tire on the road,' with *traction control* the most common compound in the Oxford English Corpus. The new figurative sense, which refers to the popularity and success of a product or service, is steadily rising in use, however, with the most common accompanying verbs being *gain, get,* and *lose*: *they are losing traction in foreign markets | his product has gained national traction.* The sense can now also express progress in any sphere or the extent to which an idea has been accepted by the general public: *polls in key states showed he wasn't gaining traction | deranged conspiracy theories are circulating through the media and have now gained serious traction.*

trac·tion en·gine ▶ **n.** a steam or diesel-powered road vehicle used (esp. formerly) for pulling very heavy loads.

trac·tive /'traktiv/ ▶ **adj.** [attrib.] relating to or denoting the power exerted in pulling, esp. by a vehicle or other machine.

trac·tor /'traktər/ ▶ **n.** a powerful motor vehicle with large rear wheels, used chiefly on farms for hauling equipment and trailers. ■ a short truck consisting of the driver's cab, designed to pull a large trailer.
– ORIGIN late 18th cent. (in the general sense 'someone or something that pulls'): from Latin, from *tract-* 'pulled,' from the verb *trahere*.

trac·tor beam ▶ **n.** (in science fiction) a hypothetical beam of energy that can be used to move objects such as space ships or hold them stationary.

trac·tor-trail·er ▶ **n.** a transport vehicle consisting of a semi-tractor and attached trailer.

trac·tot·o·my /trak'tätəmē/ ▶ **n.** the surgical severing of nerve tracts esp. in the medulla of the brain, typically to relieve intractable pain or mental illness, or in research.

trac·trix /'traktriks/ ▶ **n.** (pl. **tractrices** /ˌtrak'trīsēz, 'traktrəˌsēz/) Geometry a curve whose tangents all intercept the *x*-axis at the same distance from the point of contact, being the involute of a catenary. ■ one of a class of curves similarly traced by one end of a rigid rod, whose other end moves along a fixed line or curve.
– ORIGIN early 18th cent.: modern Latin, feminine of late Latin *tractor* 'that which pulls' (see **TRACTOR**).

Tra·cy[1] /'trāsē/ a commercial and industrial city in north central California, in the San Joaquin Valley; pop. 79,196 (est. 2008).

Tra·cy[2], Spencer (1900–67), US actor. He is particularly known for his screen partnership with Katharine Hepburn, with whom he costarred in movies such as *Adam's Rib* (1949) and *Guess Who's Coming to Dinner?* (1967). Other notable movies include *Captains Courageous* (1937) and *Boys' Town* (1938).

trad /trad/ informal ▶ **adj.** (esp. of music) traditional: *trad jazz.*
▶ **n.** traditional jazz or folk music.
– ORIGIN 1950s: abbreviation.

trade /trād/ ▶ **n. 1** the action of buying and selling goods and services: *a move to ban all* ***trade in*** *ivory | a significant increase in foreign trade | the meat trade.* ■ dated, chiefly derogatory the practice of making one's living in business, as opposed to in a profession or from unearned income: *the aristocratic classes were contemptuous of those* ***in trade.*** ■ (in sports) a transfer; an exchange: *players can demand a trade after five years of service.*
2 a skilled job, typically one requiring manual skills and special training: *the fundamentals of the construction trade | a carpenter by trade.* ■ (**the trade**) [treated as sing. or pl.] the people engaged in a particular area of business: *in the trade this sort of computer is called "a client-based system."* ■ (**the trade**) [treated as sing. or pl.] Brit. people licensed to sell alcoholic drink. ■ informal a person in gay male sexual encounters who is not penetrated sexually and usually considers himself to be heterosexual.
3 (usu. **trades**) a trade wind: *the north-east trades.*
▶ **v. 1** [no obj.] buy and sell goods and services: *middlemen* ***trading in*** *luxury goods.* ■ [with obj.] buy or sell (a particular item or product): *she has traded millions of dollars' worth of metals.* ■ (esp. of shares or currency) be bought and sold at a specified price: *the dollar was trading where it was in January.*
2 [with obj.] exchange (something) for something else, typically as a commercial transaction: *they trade mud-shark livers for fish oil | the hostages were* ***traded for*** *arms.* ■ give and receive (something, typically insults or blows): *they traded a few punches.* ■ transfer (a player) to another club or team.
– PHRASES **trade places** change places.
– PHRASAL VERBS **trade down** (or **up**) sell something in order to buy something similar but less (or more) expensive. **trade something in** exchange a used article in part payment for another: *she* ***traded in*** *her Ford* ***for*** *a BMW.* **trade something off** exchange something of value, esp. as part of a compromise: *the government* ***traded off*** *economic advantages* ***for*** *political gains.* **trade on** take advantage of (something), esp. in an unfair way: *the government is trading on fears of inflation.*
– DERIVATIVES **trad·a·ble** (or **tradeable**) **adj.**
– ORIGIN late Middle English (as a noun): from Middle Low German, literally 'track'; related to **TREAD**. Early senses included 'course, way of life,' which gave rise in the 16th cent. to 'habitual practice of an occupation,' 'skilled handicraft.' The current verb senses date from the late 16th cent.

trade book ▶ **n.** a book published by a commercial publisher and intended for general readership.

trade def·i·cit ▶ **n.** the amount by which the cost of a country's imports exceeds the value of its exports.

trade dis·count ▶ **n.** a discount on the retail price of something allowed or agreed between traders or to a retailer by a wholesaler.

trad·ed op·tion ▶ **n.** Finance an option on a stock exchange or futures exchange which can itself be bought and sold.

trade e·di·tion ▶ **n.** an edition of a book intended for general sale rather than for book clubs or specialist suppliers.

trade gap ▶ **n.** another term for **TRADE DEFICIT**.

trade-in ▶ **n.** [usu. as modifier] a used article accepted by a retailer in partial payment for another: *the trade-in value of the old car.*

trade jour·nal (also **trade magazine**) ▶ **n.** a periodical containing news and items of interest concerning a particular trade.

trade-last ▶ **n.** dated a compliment from a third person that is relayed to the person complimented in exchange for a similarly relayed compliment.

trade·mark /'trādˌmärk/ ▶ **n.** a symbol, word, or words legally registered or established by use as representing a company or product. ■ a distinctive characteristic or object: *it had all the trademarks of a Mafia hit.*
▶ **v.** [with obj.] (usu. as adj. **trademarked**) provide with a trademark: *they are counterfeiting trademarked goods.* ■ identify (a habit, quality, or way of life) as typical of someone: *his trademarked grandiose style.*

trade name ▶ **n. 1** a name that has the status of a trademark.
2 a name by which something is known in a particular trade or profession.

trade-off ▶ **n.** a balance achieved between two desirable but incompatible features; a compromise: *a trade-off between objectivity and relevance.*

trade pa·per ▶ **n.** another term for **TRADE JOURNAL**.

trad·er /'trādər/ ▶ **n.** a person who buys and sells goods, currency, or stocks. ■ a merchant ship.

Trade·scant /trə'deskənt, 'tradəˌskant/, John (1570–1638), English botanist and horticulturalist. He was the earliest known collector of plants and other natural history specimens.

trad·es·can·tia /ˌtradə'skanCH(ē)ə, -tēə/ ▶ **n.** an American plant with triangular three-petaled flowers, esp. a tender kind widely grown as a houseplant for its trailing, typically variegated, foliage. Compare with **SPIDERWORT**. ● Genus *Tradescantia*, family Commelinaceae.
– ORIGIN modern Latin, named in honor of J. **TRADESCANT**.

trade se·cret ▶ **n.** a secret device or technique used by a company in manufacturing its products.

trades·man /'trādzmən/ ▶ **n.** (pl. **tradesmen**) a person engaged in trading or a trade, typically on a relatively small scale.

trades·peo·ple /'trādzˌpēpəl/ ▶ **plural n.** people engaged in trade.

trade sur·plus ▶ **n.** the amount by which the value of a country's exports exceeds the cost of its imports.

trade un·ion (Brit. also **trades union**) ▶ **n.** another term for **LABOR UNION**.

trade-up ▶ **n.** a sale of an article in order to buy something similar but more expensive and of higher quality.

trade war ▶ **n.** a situation in which countries try to damage each other's trade, typically by the imposition of tariffs or quota restrictions.

trade wind /wind/ ▶ **n.** a wind blowing steadily toward the equator from the northeast in the northern hemisphere or the southeast in the southern hemisphere, esp. at sea. Two belts of trade winds encircle the earth, blowing from the tropical high-pressure belts to the low-pressure zone at the equator.
– ORIGIN mid 17th cent.: from the phrase *blow trade* 'blow steadily in the same direction.' Because of the importance of these winds to navigation, 18th-cent. etymologists were led erroneously to connect the word *trade* with "commerce."

trad·ing /'trādiNG/ ▶ **n.** the action of engaging in trade.

trad·ing card ▶ **n.** one of a set of cards, such as those depicting professional athletes, that are collected and traded, esp. by children.

trad·ing floor ▶ **n.** an area within an exchange or a bank or securities house where dealers trade in stocks or other securities.

trad·ing post ▶ **n.** a store or small settlement established for trading, typically in a remote place.

trad·ing stamp ▶ **n.** a stamp given by some stores to a customer according to the amount spent, and exchangeable in the appropriate number for various articles.

tra·di·tion /trə'disHən/ ▶ **n. 1** the transmission of customs or beliefs from generation to generation, or the fact of being passed on in this way: *every shade of color is fixed* ***by tradition*** *and governed by religious laws.* ■ a long-established custom or belief that has been passed on in this way: *Japan's unique cultural traditions.* ■ [in sing.] an artistic or literary method or style established by an artist, writer, or movement, and subsequently followed by others: *visionary works* ***in the tradition of*** *William Blake.*
2 Theology a doctrine believed to have divine authority though not in the scriptures, in particular: ■ (in Christianity) doctrine not explicit in the Bible but held to derive from the oral teaching of Jesus and the Apostles. ■ (in Judaism) an ordinance of the oral law not in the Torah but held to have been given by God to Moses. ■ (in Islam) a saying or act ascribed to the Prophet but not recorded in the Koran. See **HADITH**.
– DERIVATIVES **tra·di·tion·ar·y** /-ˌnerē/ **adj.**, **tra·di·tion·ist** /-nist/ **n.**, **tra·di·tion·less adj.**
– ORIGIN late Middle English: from Old French *tradicion*, or from Latin *traditio(n-)*, from *tradere* 'deliver, betray,' from *trans-* 'across' + *dare* 'give.'

tra·di·tion·al /trə'disHənl/ ▶ **adj.** existing in or as part of a tradition; long-established: *the traditional festivities of the church year.* ■ produced, done, or used in accordance with tradition: *a traditional fish soup.* ■ habitually done, used, or found: *the traditional drinks in the clubhouse.* ■ (of a person or group) adhering to tradition, or to a particular tradition: *traditional Elgarians.* ■ (of jazz) in the style of the early 20th century.
– DERIVATIVES **tra·di·tion·al·ly adv.**

tra·di·tion·al·ism /trə'disHənlˌizəm/ ▶ **n.** the upholding or maintenance of tradition, esp. so as to resist change. ■ chiefly historical the theory that all moral and religious truth comes from divine revelation passed on by tradition, human reason being incapable of attaining it.
– DERIVATIVES **tra·di·tion·al·ist n. & adj.**, **tra·di·tion·al·is·tic** /trəˌdisHənl'istik/ **adj.**

tra·duce /trə'd(y)o͞os/ ▶ **v.** [with obj.] speak badly of or tell lies about (someone) so as to damage their reputation.
– DERIVATIVES **tra·duce·ment n.**, **tra·duc·er n.**
– ORIGIN mid 16th cent. (in the sense 'transport, transmit'): from Latin *traducere* 'lead in front of others, expose to ridicule,' from *trans-* 'over, across' + *ducere* 'to lead.'

Tra·fal·gar, Bat·tle of /trə'falgər/ a decisive naval battle fought on October 21, 1805, off the cape of Trafalgar on the south coast of Spain during the Napoleonic Wars. The British fleet under Horatio Nelson (who was killed in the action) defeated the combined fleets of France and Spain, which were attempting to clear the way for Napoleon's projected invasion of Britain.

traf·fic /ˈtrafik/ ▶ n. **1** vehicles moving on a road or public highway: *a stream of heavy traffic.* ■ a large number of such vehicles: *we were caught in traffic on the expressway.* ■ the movement of other forms of transportation or of pedestrians: *managing the air traffic was a mammoth task.* ■ the transportation of goods or passengers: *the increased use of railroads for goods traffic.* ■ the messages or signals transmitted through a communications system: *data traffic between remote workstations.*
2 the action of dealing or trading in something illegal: *the traffic in stolen cattle.*
3 archaic dealings or communication between people.
▶ v. (**traffics, trafficking, trafficked**) [no obj.] deal or trade in something illegal: *the government will vigorously pursue individuals who traffic in drugs.*
– DERIVATIVES **traf·fick·er** n., **traf·fic·less** adj.
– ORIGIN early 16th cent. (denoting commercial transportation of merchandise or passengers): from French *traffique,* Spanish *tráfico,* or Italian *traffico,* of unknown origin. Sense 1 dates from the early 19th cent.

traf·fic calm·ing ▶ n. the deliberate slowing of traffic in residential areas by building speed bumps or other obstructions.
– ORIGIN 1980s: translation of German *Verkehrsberuhigung.*

traf·fic cir·cle ▶ n. a road junction at which traffic moves in one direction around a central island.

traf·fic is·land ▶ n. a small raised area in the middle of a road that provides a safe place for pedestrians to stand and marks a division between two opposing streams of traffic.

traf·fic jam ▶ n. road traffic at or near a standstill because of road construction, an accident, or heavy congestion.

traf·fic light (also **traffic signal**) ▶ n. a set of automatically operated colored lights, typically red, amber, and green, for controlling traffic at road junctions and crosswalks.

traf·fic pat·tern ▶ n. a pattern in the air above an airport of permitted lanes for aircraft to follow after takeoff or prior to landing. ■ the characteristic distribution of traffic on a route: *the filming had screwed up the traffic patterns in town.*

traf·fic sign ▶ n. a sign conveying information, an instruction, or a warning to drivers.

trag·a·canth /ˈtragəˌkanTH, ˈtraj-/ (also **gum tragacanth**) ▶ n. a white or reddish plant gum used in the food, textile, and pharmaceutical industries. ● This gum is obtained from plants of the genus *Astragalus,* family Leguminosae, in particular the Eurasian *A. gummifer.*
– ORIGIN late 16th cent.: from French *tragacante,* via Latin from Greek *tragakantha* 'goat's thorn,' from *tragos* 'goat' (because it is browsed by goats) + *akantha* 'thorn' (referring to the shrub's spines).

tra·ge·di·an /trəˈjēdēən/ ▶ n. an actor who specializes in tragic roles. ■ a writer of tragedies.
– ORIGIN late Middle English (denoting a writer of tragedies): from Old French *tragediane,* from *tragedie* (see TRAGEDY).

tra·ge·di·enne /trəˌjēdēˈen/ ▶ n. an actress who specializes in tragic roles.
– ORIGIN mid 19th cent.: from French *tragédienne,* feminine of *tragédien.*

trag·e·dy /ˈtrajidē/ ▶ n. (pl. **tragedies**) **1** an event causing great suffering, destruction, and distress, such as a serious accident, crime, or natural catastrophe: *a tragedy that killed 95 people* | *his life had been plagued by tragedy.*
2 a play dealing with tragic events and having an unhappy ending, esp. one concerning the downfall of the main character. ■ the dramatic genre represented by such plays: *Greek tragedy.* Compare with COMEDY.
– ORIGIN late Middle English: from Old French *tragedie,* via Latin from Greek *tragōidia,* apparently from *tragos* 'goat' (the reason remains unexplained) + *ōidē* 'song, ode.' Compare with TRAGIC.

tra·ghet·to /träˈgetō/ ▶ n. (pl. **traghetti** /-ˈgetē/) (in Venice) a landing place or jetty for gondolas. ■ a gondola ferry.
– ORIGIN Italian.

trag·ic /ˈtrajik/ ▶ adj. causing or characterized by extreme distress or sorrow: *the shooting was a tragic accident.* ■ suffering extreme distress or sorrow: *the tragic parents reached the end of their tether.* ■ of or relating to tragedy in a literary work.
– DERIVATIVES **trag·i·cal** adj., **trag·i·cal·ly** /-ik(ə)lē/ adv.
– ORIGIN mid 16th cent.: from French *tragique,* via Latin from Greek *tragikos,* from *tragos* 'goat,' but associated with *tragōidia* (see TRAGEDY).

trag·ic flaw ▶ n. less technical term for HAMARTIA.

trag·ic i·ro·ny ▶ n. see IRONY[1].

trag·i·com·e·dy /ˌtrajəˈkämidē/ ▶ n. (pl. **tragicomedies**) a play or novel containing elements of both comedy and tragedy. ■ such works as a genre.
– DERIVATIVES **trag·i·com·ic** /-ˈkämik/ adj., **trag·i·com·i·cal·ly** /-ˈkämik(ə)lē/ adv.
– ORIGIN late 16th cent.: from French *tragicomédie* or Italian *tragicomedia,* based on Latin *tragicocomoedia,* from *tragicus* (see TRAGIC) + *comoedia* (see COMEDY).

trag·o·pan /ˈtragəˌpan/ ▶ n. an Asian pheasant of highland forests, the male of which has brightly colored plumage used in courtship. ● Genus *Tragopan,* family Phasianidae: five species.
– ORIGIN modern Latin, from Greek, the name of a horned bird, from *tragos* 'goat' + the name *Pan* (see PAN).

tra·gus /ˈtrāgəs/ ▶ n. (pl. **tragi** /-jī, -gī/) Anatomy & Zoology a prominence on the inner side of the external ear, in front of and partly closing the passage to the organs of hearing.
– ORIGIN late 17th cent.: from late Latin, via Latin from Greek *tragos* 'goat' (with reference to the characteristic tuft of hair that is often present, likened to a goat's beard).

Tra·herne /trəˈhərn/, Thomas (1637–74), English religious writer and metaphysical poet. His major prose work *Centuries* (1699) was rediscovered in 1896 and republished as *Centuries of Meditation* (1908). It consists of brief meditations showing his joy in creation and in divine love and is noted for its description of his childhood.

tra·hi·son des clercs /trä-ēˈzôN dā ˈkler/ ▶ n. literary a betrayal of intellectual, artistic, or moral standards by writers, academics, or artists.
– ORIGIN French, literally 'treason of the scholars,' the title of a book by Julien Benda (1927).

trail /trāl/ ▶ n. **1** a mark or a series of signs or objects left behind by the passage of someone or something: *a trail of blood on the grass.* ■ a track or scent used in following someone or hunting an animal: *police followed his trail to Atlantic City.* ■ a part, typically long and thin, stretching behind or hanging down from someone or something: *smoke trails* | *trails of ivy.* ■ a line of people or things following behind each other: *a trail of ants.*
2 a beaten path through rough country such as a forest or moor. ■ a route planned or followed for a particular purpose: *a Democratic candidate on the campaign trail.* ■ (also **ski trail**) a downhill ski run or cross-country ski route.
3 short for TRAILER (sense 2 of the noun).
4 the rear end of a gun carriage, resting or sliding on the ground when the gun is unlimbered.
▶ v. **1** [with adverbial] draw or be drawn along the ground or other surface behind someone or something: [with obj.] *Alex trailed a hand through the clear water* | [no obj.] *her robe trailed along the ground.* ■ [no obj.] (typically of a plant) grow or hang over the edge of something or along the ground: *the roses grew wild, their stems trailing over the banks.* ■ [with obj.] follow (a person or animal), typically by using marks, signs, or scent left behind. ■ [no obj.] be losing to an opponent in a game or contest: [with complement] *the Packers were trailing 10–6 at halftime.*
2 [no obj.] walk or move slowly or wearily: *she trailed behind, whimpering at intervals.* ■ (of the voice or a speaker) fade gradually before stopping: *her voice trailed away.*
3 [with obj.] advertise (something, esp. a film or program) in advance by broadcasting extracts or details.
4 [with obj.] apply (slip) through a nozzle or spout to decorate ceramic ware.
– ORIGIN Middle English (as a verb): from Old French *traillier* 'to tow,' or Middle Low German *treilen* 'haul (a boat),' based on Latin *tragula* 'dragnet,' from *trahere* 'to pull.' Compare with TRAWL. The noun originally denoted the train of a robe, later generalized to denote something trailing.

trail bike ▶ n. a light motorcycle for use in rough terrain.

trail·blaz·er /ˈtrālˌblāzər/ ▶ n. a person who makes a new track through wild country. ■ a pioneer; an innovator: *he was a trailblazer for many ideas that are now standard fare.*
– DERIVATIVES **trail·blaz·ing** /-ˌblāziNG/ n. & adj.

trail boss ▶ n. a foreman in charge of a cattle drive.

trail·er /ˈtrālər/ ▶ n. **1** an unpowered vehicle towed by another, in particular: ■ the rear section of a tractor-trailer. ■ an open cart. ■ a platform for transporting a boat. ■ an unpowered vehicle equipped for living in, typically used during vacations.
2 an excerpt or series of excerpts from a movie or program used to advertise it in advance; a preview.
3 a thing that trails, esp. a trailing plant.
▶ v. [with obj.] **1** advertise (a movie or program) in advance by broadcasting excerpts or details.
2 transport (something) by trailer.

trail·er park (also **trailer court**) ▶ n. an area with special amenities where trailers are parked and used for recreation or as permanent homes. ■ [as modifier] lacking refinement, taste, or quality; coarse: *her trailer-park bleached perm.*

trail·er trash ▶ n. informal, derogatory poor lower-class white people typified as living in trailers.

trail·er truck ▶ n. a tractor-trailer.

trail·head /ˈtrālˌhed/ ▶ n. the place where a trail begins: *we camped amid the pines at the trailhead.*

trail·ing ar·bu·tus ▶ n. see ARBUTUS.

trail·ing edge ▶ n. the rear edge of a moving body, esp. an aircraft wing or propeller blade. ■ Electronics the part of a pulse in which the amplitude diminishes.

trail mix ▶ n. a mixture of dried fruit and nuts eaten as a snack food, originally by hikers and campers.

train /trān/ ▶ v. **1** [with obj.] teach (a person or animal) a particular skill or type of behavior through practice and instruction over a period of time: *the plan trains people for promotion* | [with obj. and infinitive] *the dogs are trained to sniff out illegal stowaways.* ■ [no obj.] be taught in such a way: *he trained as a classicist.* ■ (usu. as adj. **trained**) cause (a mental or physical faculty) to be sharp, discerning, or developed as a result of instruction or practice: *an alert mind and trained eye give astute evaluations.* ■ cause (a plant) to grow in a particular direction or into a required shape: *they trained roses over their houses.* ■ [no obj.] undertake a course of exercise and diet in order to reach or maintain a high level of physical fitness, typically in preparation for participating in a specific sport or event: *she trains three times a week.* ■ cause to undertake such a course of exercise: *the horse was trained in Paris.* ■ [no obj.] (**train down**) reduce one's weight through diet and exercise in order to be fit for a particular event: *he trained down to middleweight.*
2 [with obj.] (**train something on**) point or aim something, typically a gun or camera, at: *the detective trained his gun on the side door.*
3 [no obj.] dated go by train: *Charles trained to Chicago with Emily.*
4 [with obj.] archaic entice (someone) by offering pleasure or a reward.
▶ n. **1** a series of railroad cars moved as a unit by a locomotive or by integral motors: *a freight train* | *the journey took two hours* ***by train.***
2 a succession of vehicles or pack animals traveling in the same direction: *a camel train.* ■ a retinue of attendants accompanying an important person. ■ a series of connected events: *you may be setting in motion a train of events that will cause harm.* ■ a series of gears or other connected parts in machinery: ***a train of gears.***
3 a long piece of material attached to the back of a formal dress or robe that trails along the ground.
4 a trail of gunpowder for firing an explosive charge.
– PHRASES **in train** (of arrangements) well organized or in progress: *an investigation is in train.* **in someone/something's train** (or **in the train of**) following behind someone or something. ■ as a sequel or consequence: *unemployment brings great difficulties in its train.* **train of thought** the way in which someone reaches a conclusion; a line of reasoning: *I failed to follow his train of thought.*
– DERIVATIVES **train·a·bil·i·ty** /ˌtrānəˈbilitē/ n., **train·a·ble** adj.
– ORIGIN Middle English (as a noun in the sense 'delay'): from Old French *train* (masculine), *traine* (feminine), from *trahiner* (verb), from Latin *trahere* 'pull, draw.' Early noun senses were 'trailing part of a robe' and 'retinue'; the latter gave rise to 'line of traveling people or vehicles,' later 'a connected series of things.' The early verb sense 'cause (a plant) to grow in a desired shape' was the basis of the sense 'educate, instruct, teach.'

train·band /ˈtrānˌband/ ▶ n. historical a division of civilian soldiers in London and other areas of England, in particular in the Stuart period.

train·ee /trāˈnē/ ▶ n. a person undergoing training for a particular job or profession.
– DERIVATIVES **train·ee·ship** /-ˌSHip/ n.

train·er /ˈtrānər/ ▶ n. **1** a person who trains people or animals. ■ informal an aircraft or simulator used to train pilots.
2 a person whose job is to provide medical assistance to athletes.
3 Brit. a soft sports shoe suitable for casual wear.

train·ing /ˈtrāniNG/ ▶ n. the action of teaching a person or animal a particular skill or type of behavior: *in-service training for staff.* ■ the action of undertaking a course of exercise and diet in preparation for a sporting event: *you'll have to go into strict training.*

– PHRASES **in** (or **out of**) **training** undergoing (or no longer undergoing) physical training for a sporting event. ■ physically fit (or unfit) as a result of the amount of training one has undertaken.

train·ing ship ▶ n. a ship on which people are taught sailing and related skills.

train·ing shoe ▶ n. a soft shoe designed to be used for athletic training.

train·ing ta·ble ▶ n. a table in a dining hall where athletes in training are served specially prepared meals.

train·ing wheels ▶ plural n. a pair of small supporting wheels fitted on either side of the rear wheel of a child's bicycle.

train·load /ˈtrān,lōd/ ▶ n. a number of people or a quantity of a commodity transported by train.

train·man /ˈtrānmən, -,man/ ▶ n. (pl. **trainmen**) a railroad employee who works on trains.

train oil ▶ n. chiefly historical oil obtained from the blubber of a whale (and formerly of other sea creatures), esp. the right whale.
– ORIGIN mid 16th cent.: from obsolete *train* 'train-oil,' from Middle Low German *trān*, Middle Dutch *traen*, literally 'tear' (because it was extracted in droplets).

train set ▶ n. **1** a set of trains, tracks, and other things making up a child's model railroad.
2 a set of railroad cars, often with a locomotive, coupled together for a particular service.

train shed ▶ n. a large structure providing a shelter over the tracks and platforms of a railroad station.

train·sick /ˈtrān,sik/ ▶ adj. affected with nausea by the motion of a train.

train wreck ▶ n. informal a chaotic or disastrous situation that holds a peculiar fascination for observers: *his train wreck of a private life guaranteed front-page treatment.*

traipse /trāps/ ▶ v. [no obj.] walk or move wearily or reluctantly: *students had to traipse all over Washington to attend lectures.* ■ walk about casually or needlessly: *there's people traipsing in and out all the time.*
▶ n. **1** [in sing.] a tedious or tiring journey on foot.
2 archaic a slovenly woman.
– ORIGIN late 16th cent. (as a verb): of unknown origin. The noun (sense 2) is first recorded in the late 17th cent.

trait /trāt/ ▶ n. a distinguishing quality or characteristic, typically one belonging to a person: *he was a letter-of-the-law man, a common trait among coaches.* ■ a genetically determined characteristic.
– ORIGIN mid 16th cent.: from French, from Latin *tractus* 'drawing, pulling' (see TRACT[1]). An early sense was 'stroke of the pen or pencil in a picture,' giving rise to the sense 'a particular feature of mind or character' (mid 18th cent).

trai·tor /ˈtrātər/ ▶ n. a person who betrays a friend, country, principle, etc.: *they see me as a traitor, a sellout to the enemy.*
– PHRASES **turn traitor** betray a group or person: *to think of a man like you turning traitor to his class.*
– ORIGIN Middle English: from Old French *traitour*, from Latin *traditor*, from *tradere* 'hand over.'

trai·tor·ous /ˈtrātərəs/ ▶ adj. relating to or characteristic of a traitor; treacherous: *when his traitorous actions were discovered, he was imprisoned.*
– DERIVATIVES **trai·tor·ous·ly** adv.

Tra·jan /ˈtrājən/ (*c.*53–117), Roman emperor 98–117; Latin name *Marcus Ulpius Traianus*. His reign is noted for the Dacian wars (101–106), which ended in the annexation of Dacia as a province.

tra·jec·to·ry /trəˈjektərē/ ▶ n. (pl. **trajectories**)
1 the path followed by a projectile flying or an object moving under the action of given forces: *the missile's trajectory was preset* | figurative *the rapid upward trajectory of Rich's career.*
2 Geometry a curve or surface cutting a family of curves or surfaces at a constant angle.
– ORIGIN late 17th cent.: from modern Latin *trajectoria* (feminine), from Latin *traject-* 'thrown across,' from the verb *traicere*, from *trans-* 'across' + *jacere* 'to throw.'

Tra·keh·ner /trəˈkānər/ ▶ n. **1** a saddle horse of a light breed first developed at the Trakehnen stud farm near Kaliningrad in Russia.
2 a type of fence used in horse trials, consisting of a ditch spanned by center rails.
– ORIGIN early 20th cent.: from German.

tra la /trä ˈlä/ (also **tra-la-la**) ▶ exclam. chiefly ironic expressing joy or gaiety: *off to his life, kids, and wife, tra la*
– ORIGIN early 19th cent.: imitative of a fanfare or of the refrain of a song.

Tra·lee /trəˈlē/ a port on the southwestern coast of the Republic of Ireland, the county town of Kerry; pop. 20,288 (2006).

tram /tram/ (also **tramcar**) ▶ n. **1** Brit. a trolley car.
2 a cable car.
3 historical a low four-wheeled cart or barrow used in coal mines.
– ORIGIN early 16th cent. (sense 3): from Middle Low German and Middle Dutch *trame* 'beam, barrow shaft.' In the early 19th cent. the word denoted the parallel wheel tracks used in a mine, on which the public streetcar system was modeled; hence sense 1 (late 19th cent.).

Tra·mi·ner /trəˈmēnər/ ▶ n. a variety of white wine grape grown chiefly in Germany and Alsace. ■ a white wine with a perfumed bouquet made from this grape.
– ORIGIN named after the Italian village *Termeno*.

tram·lines /ˈtram,līnz/ ▶ n. a pair of parallel lines, in particular the long lines at the sides of a tennis court (enclosing the extra width used in doubles play) or at the sides or back of a badminton court.
– ORIGIN late 19th cent.: from the resemblance to the rails for a tram (trolley car).

tram·mel /ˈtraməl/ ▶ n. **1** (usu. **trammels**) literary a restriction or impediment to someone's freedom of action: *we will forge our own future, free from the trammels of materialism.*
2 (also **trammel net**) a set-net consisting of three layers of netting, designed so that a fish entering through one of the large-meshed outer sections will push part of the finer-meshed central section through the large meshes on the further side, forming a pocket in which the fish is trapped.
3 an instrument consisting of a board with two grooves intersecting at right angles, in which the two ends of a beam compass can slide to draw an ellipse. [early 18th cent.: so named because the motion of the beam is 'restricted' by the grooves.] ■ a beam compass.
4 a hook in a fireplace for a kettle.
▶ v. (**trammels, trammeling, trammeled**; Brit. **trammels, trammelling, trammelled**) [with obj.] deprive of freedom of action: *those less trammeled by convention than himself.*
– ORIGIN late Middle English (sense 2 of the noun): from Old French *tramail*, from a medieval Latin variant of *trimaculum*, perhaps from Latin *tri-* 'three' + *macula* 'mesh.'

tra·mon·ta·na /,trämənˈtänə/ ▶ n. a cold north wind blowing in Italy or the adjoining regions of the Adriatic and Mediterranean.
– ORIGIN Italian, 'north wind, North Star' (see TRAMONTANE).

tra·mon·tane /trəˈmän,tān, ˈtramən-/ ▶ adj. rare traveling to, situated on, or living on the other side of mountains. ■ archaic (esp. from the Italian point of view) foreign; barbarous.
▶ n. **1** another term for TRAMONTANA.
2 archaic a person who lives on the other side of mountains (used in particular by Italians to refer to people beyond the Alps).
– ORIGIN Middle English (as a noun denoting the Pole Star): from Italian *tramontana* 'North Star, north wind,' *tramontani* 'people living beyond the Alps,' from Latin *transmontanus* 'beyond the mountains,' from *trans-* 'across' + *mons, mont-* 'mountain.'

tramp /tramp/ ▶ v. [no obj.] walk heavily or noisily: *he tramped around the room.* ■ walk through or over a place wearily or reluctantly and for long distances: *we have tramped miles over mountain and moorland.* ■ [with obj.] tread or stamp on: *one of the few wines still tramped by foot.*
▶ n. **1** a person who travels from place to place on foot in search of work or as a vagrant or beggar.
2 [in sing.] the sound of heavy steps, typically of several people: *the tramp of marching feet.*
3 [in sing.] a long walk, typically a tiring one: *they start off on a tramp from Roxbury to New York.*
4 [usu. as modifier] a cargo vessel that carries goods among many different ports rather than sailing a fixed route: *a tramp steamer.*
5 informal a promiscuous woman.
6 a metal plate protecting the sole of a boot. ■ the top of the blade of a spade.
– DERIVATIVES **tramp·er** n., **tramp·ish** adj.
– ORIGIN late Middle English (as a verb): probably of Low German origin. The noun dates from the mid 17th cent.

tram·ple /ˈtrampəl/ ▶ v. [with obj.] tread on and crush: *the fence had been trampled down* | [no obj.] *her dog trampled on his tulips.* ■ [no obj.] (**trample on/over**) treat with contempt: *a drug-testing device that doesn't trample on employees' civil liberties.*
▶ n. literary an act or the sound of trampling.
– DERIVATIVES **tram·pler** /-p(ə)lər/ n.
– ORIGIN late Middle English (in the sense 'tread heavily'): frequentative of TRAMP.

tram·po·line /ˈtrampə,lēn/ ▶ n. a strong fabric sheet connected by springs to a frame, used as a springboard and landing area in doing acrobatic or gymnastic exercises.
▶ v. [no obj.] (usu. as noun **trampolining**) do acrobatic or gymnastic exercises on a trampoline as a recreation or sport: *his hobby is trampolining.* ■ leap or rebound from something with a springy base: *she trampolined across the bed.*
– DERIVATIVES **tram·po·lin·er** n., **tram·po·lin·ist** /-nist/ n.
– ORIGIN late 18th cent.: from Italian *trampolino*, from *trampoli* 'stilts.'

tramp stamp ▶ n. informal a tattoo on a woman's lower back.

tram road ▶ n. historical a road with wooden, stone, or metal tracks for wheels, used by wagons in mining districts.

tram·way /ˈtram,wā/ ▶ n. **1** Brit. a set of rails that forms the route for a streetcar. ■ a streetcar system.
2 another term for CABLE CAR.
3 historical another term for TRAM ROAD.

trance /trans/ ▶ n. a half-conscious state characterized by an absence of response to external stimuli, typically as induced by hypnosis or entered by a medium: *she put him into a light trance.* ■ a state of abstraction: *the kind of trance he went into whenever illness was discussed.* ■ (also **trance music**) a type of electronic dance music characterized by hypnotic rhythms and sounds.
▶ v. [with obj.] literary put into a trance: *she's been tranced and may need waking.*
– DERIVATIVES **tranced·ly** /ˈtranstlē, ˈtransid-/ adv., **trance·like** /-,līk/ adj.
– ORIGIN Middle English (originally as a verb in the sense 'be in a trance'): from Old French *transir* 'depart, fall into trance,' from Latin *transire* 'go across.'

tranche /tränsh/ ▶ n. a portion of something, esp. money: *they released the first **tranche of** the loan.*
– ORIGIN late 15th cent.: from Old French, literally 'slice.'

trank /traNGk/ (also **tranq**) ▶ n. informal term for TRANQUILIZER.
– DERIVATIVES **tranked** adj.

tran·ny /ˈtranē/ (also **trannie**) ▶ n. informal **1** a transvestite.
2 the transmission in a motor vehicle.
3 a photographic transparency.
4 chiefly Brit. a transistor radio.
– ORIGIN 1960s: abbreviation.

tran·quil /ˈtraNGkwəl/ ▶ adj. free from disturbance; calm: *her tranquil gaze* | *the sea was tranquil.*
– DERIVATIVES **tran·quil·ly** adv.
– ORIGIN late Middle English: from French *tranquille* or Latin *tranquillus*.

tran·quil·i·ty /,traNGˈkwilitē/ (also **tranquillity**) ▶ n. the quality or state of being tranquil; calm: *passing cars are the only noise that disturbs the tranquility of rural life.*

tran·quil·ize /ˈtraNGkwə,līz/ (Brit. **tranquillize**) ▶ v. [with obj.] (usu. as adj. **tranquilizing**) (of a drug) have a calming or sedative effect on: *the majority regarded tranquilizing drugs as the chief therapeutic weapon.* ■ administer such a drug to (a person or animal): *the stray elk was tranquilized and relocated.* ■ literary make tranquil: *joys that tranquilize the mind.*

tran·quil·iz·er /ˈtraNGkwə,līzər/ (Brit. **tranquillizer**) ▶ n. a medicinal drug taken to reduce tension or anxiety.

trans /tranz, trans/ ▶ adj. Chemistry denoting or relating to a molecular structure in which two particular atoms or groups lie on opposite sides of a given plane in the molecule, in particular denoting an isomer in which substituents at opposite ends of a carbon–carbon double bond are also on opposite sides of the bond: *the trans isomer of stilbene.* Compare with CIS.
– ORIGIN independent usage of TRANS-.

trans. ▶ abbr. ■ transaction; transactions. ■ transfer. ■ transferred. ■ transformer. ■ transit. ■ transitive. ■ translated. ■ translation. ■ translator. ■ transparent. ■ transportation. ■ transpose. ■ transverse.

trans- ▶ prefix **1** across; beyond: *transcontinental* | *transgress.* ■ on or to the other side of: *transatlantic* | *transalpine.* Often contrasted with CIS-.
2 through: *transonic.* ■ into another state or place: *transform* | *translate.* ■ surpassing; transcending: *transfinite.*

t

3 Chemistry (usu. *trans-*) denoting molecules with trans arrangements of substituents: *trans-1,2-dichloroethylene.* ■ Genetics denoting alleles on different chromosomes.
– ORIGIN from Latin *trans* 'across.'

trans·act /tranˈsakt, -ˈzakt/ ▶ v. [with obj.] conduct or carry out (business).
– DERIVATIVES **trans·ac·tor** /-tər/ n.
– ORIGIN late 16th cent.: from Latin *transact-* 'driven through,' from the verb *transigere*, from *trans-* 'through' + *agere* 'do, lead.'

trans·ac·tion /tranˈsakSHən, -ˈzak-/ ▶ n. an instance of buying or selling something; a business deal: *in an ordinary commercial transaction a delivery date is essential.* ■ the action of conducting business. ■ an exchange or interaction between people: *intellectual transactions in the classroom.* ■ (**transactions**) published reports of proceedings at the meetings of a learned society. ■ an input message to a computer system that must be dealt with as a single unit of work.
– DERIVATIVES **trans·ac·tion·al** /-SHənl/ adj., **trans·ac·tion·al·ly** /-SHənl-ē/ adv.
– ORIGIN late Middle English (as a term in Roman law): from late Latin *transactio(n-)*, from *transigere* 'drive through' (see TRANSACT).

trans·ac·tion·al a·nal·y·sis ▶ n. a system of popular psychology based on the idea that one's behavior and social relationships reflect an interchange between parental (critical and nurturing), adult (rational), and childlike (intuitive and dependent) aspects of personality established early in life.

trans·ac·ti·va·tion /tran,saktəˈvāSHən, -zakt-/ ▶ n. Biochemistry activation of a gene at one locus by the presence of a particular gene at another locus, typically following infection by a virus.

Trans-A·las·ka Pipe·line /ˌtranzəˈlaskə/ an oil pipeline that extends for 800 miles (1,300 km) from Prudhoe Bay on the North Slope of Alaska to Valdez on Prince William Sound.

trans·al·pine /transˈalpīn, tranz-/ ▶ adj. of, related to, or situated in the area beyond the Alps, in particular as viewed from Italy. See also GAUL[1]. ■ crossing the Alps: *transalpine road freight.*
– ORIGIN late 16th cent.: from Latin *transalpinus*, from *trans-* 'across' + *alpinus* (see ALPINE).

trans·am·i·nase /transˈamə,nās, tranz-, -,nāz/ ▶ n. Biochemistry an enzyme that catalyzes a particular transamination reaction.

trans·am·i·na·tion /trans,aməˈnāSHən, tranz-/ ▶ n. Biochemistry the transfer of an amino group from one molecule to another, esp. from an amino acid to a keto acid.
– DERIVATIVES **trans·am·i·nate** /-,nāt/ v.

trans·at·lan·tic /ˌtransətˈlantik, ˌtranz-/ ▶ adj. crossing the Atlantic: *a transatlantic flight.* ■ concerning countries on both sides of the Atlantic: *the transatlantic relationship.* ■ of, relating to, or situated on the other side of the Atlantic; British or European (from an American point of view).
– DERIVATIVES **trans·at·lan·ti·cal·ly** /-ik(ə)lē/ adv.

trans·ax·le /transˈaksəl, tranz-/ ▶ n. an integral driving axle and differential gear in a motor vehicle.

trans·bor·der /tranzˈbôrdər/ ▶ adj. crossing or extending across a border between two countries: *transborder trade* | *transborder regions.*

Trans-Can·a·da High·way /ˌtransˈkanədə, ˌtranz-/ a route, 4,860 miles (7,820 km) long, between Victoria in British Columbia and Saint John's in Newfoundland.

Trans·cau·ca·sia /ˌtrans,kôˈkāZHə, ˌtranz-/ a region that lies to the south of the Caucasus Mountains, between the Black Sea and the Caspian Sea, and that comprises the present-day republics of Georgia, Armenia, and Azerbaijan. It was created as the Transcaucasian Soviet Federated Socialist Republic, a republic of the former Soviet Union, in 1922, but was broken up into its constituent republics in 1936.
– DERIVATIVES **Trans·cau·ca·sian** adj.

trans·ceiv·er /tranˈsēvər/ ▶ n. a device that can both transmit and receive communications, in particular a combined radio transmitter and receiver.
– ORIGIN 1930s: blend of TRANSMITTER and RECEIVER.

tran·scend /tranˈsend/ ▶ v. [with obj.] be or go beyond the range or limits of (something abstract, typically a conceptual field or division): *this was an issue transcending party politics.* ■ surpass (a person or an achievement).
– ORIGIN Middle English: from Old French *transcendre* or Latin *transcendere*, from *trans-* 'across' + *scandere* 'climb.'

tran·scend·ence /tranˈsendəns/ (also **transcendency** /sī/) ▶ n. existence or experience beyond the normal or physical level: *the possibility of spiritual transcendence in the modern world.*

tran·scend·ent /tranˈsendənt/ ▶ adj. beyond or above the range of normal or merely physical human experience: *the search for a transcendent level of knowledge.* ■ surpassing the ordinary; exceptional: *the conductor was described as a "transcendent genius."* ■ (of God) existing apart from and not subject to the limitations of the material universe. Often contrasted with IMMANENT. ■ (in scholastic philosophy) higher than or not included in any of Aristotle's ten categories. ■ (in Kantian philosophy) not realizable in experience.
– DERIVATIVES **tran·scend·ent·ly** adv.
– ORIGIN late Middle English: from Latin *transcendent-* 'climbing over,' from the verb *transcendere* (see TRANSCEND).

tran·scen·den·tal /ˌtransenˈdentl/ ▶ adj. **1** of or relating to a spiritual or nonphysical realm: *the transcendental importance of each person's soul.* ■ (in Kantian philosophy) presupposed in and necessary to experience; a priori. ■ relating to or denoting Transcendentalism.
2 Mathematics (of a number, e.g., e or π) real but not a root of an algebraic equation with rational roots. ■ (of a function) not capable of being produced by the algebraical operations of addition, multiplication, and involution, or the inverse operations.
– DERIVATIVES **tran·scen·den·tal·ize** /-,īz/ v., **tran·scen·den·tal·ly** adv.
– ORIGIN early 17th cent.: from medieval Latin *transcendentalis* (see TRANSCENDENT).

tran·scen·den·tal·ism /ˌtran,senˈdentl,izəm/ ▶ n. **1** (**Transcendentalism**) an idealistic philosophical and social movement that developed in New England around 1836 in reaction to rationalism. Influenced by romanticism, Platonism, and Kantian philosophy, it taught that divinity pervades all nature and humanity, and its members held progressive views on feminism and communal living. Ralph Waldo Emerson and Henry David Thoreau were central figures.
2 a system developed by Immanuel Kant, based on the idea that, in order to understand the nature of reality, one must first examine and analyze the reasoning process that governs the nature of experience.
– DERIVATIVES **tran·scen·den·tal·ist** (also **Transcendentalist**) n. & adj.

Tran·scen·den·tal Med·i·ta·tion (abbr.: **TM**) ▶ n. trademark a technique for detaching oneself from anxiety and promoting harmony and self-realization by meditation, repetition of a mantra, and other yogic practices, promulgated by an international organization founded by the Indian guru Maharishi Mahesh Yogi (*c.*1911–2008).

trans·code /transˈkōd, tranz-/ ▶ v. [with obj.] convert (language or information) from one form of coded representation to another.

trans·con·duct·ance /ˌtranskənˈdəktəns, ˌtranz-/ ▶ n. Electronics the ratio of the change in current at the output terminal to the change in the voltage at the input terminal of an active device.

trans·con·ti·nen·tal /ˌtranskäntəˈnentl, ˌtranz-/ ▶ adj. (esp. of a railroad line) crossing a continent. ■ extending across or relating to two or more continents: *a transcontinental radio audience.*
▶ n. Canadian a transcontinental railroad or train.
– DERIVATIVES **trans·con·ti·nen·tal·ly** adv.

trans·cor·ti·cal /transˈkôrtikəl, tranz-/ ▶ adj. Physiology of or relating to nerve pathways that cross the cerebral cortex of the brain.

tran·scribe /tranˈskrīb/ ▶ v. [with obj.] put (thoughts, speech, or data) into written or printed form: *each interview was taped and transcribed.* ■ transliterate (foreign characters) or write or type out (shorthand, notes, or other abbreviated forms) into ordinary characters or full sentences. ■ arrange (a piece of music) for a different instrument, voice, or group of these: *his largest early work was transcribed for organ.* ■ Biochemistry synthesize (a nucleic acid, typically RNA) using an existing nucleic acid, typically DNA, as a template, thus copying the genetic information in the latter.
– DERIVATIVES **tran·scrib·er** n.
– ORIGIN mid 16th cent. (in the sense 'make a copy in writing'): from Latin *transcribere*, from *trans-* 'across' + *scribere* 'write.'

tran·script /ˈtran,skript/ ▶ n. a written or printed version of material originally presented in another medium. ■ Biochemistry a length of RNA or DNA that has been transcribed respectively from a DNA or RNA template. ■ an official record of a student's work, showing courses taken and grades achieved.
– DERIVATIVES **tran·scrip·tive** /ˌtranˈskriptiv/ adj.
– ORIGIN Middle English: from Old French *transcrit*, from Latin *transcriptum*, neuter past participle of *transcribere* (see TRANSCRIBE). The spelling change in the 15th cent. was due to association with the Latin.

tran·scrip·tase /tranˈskrip,tās, -,tāz/ ▶ n. Biochemistry an enzyme that catalyzes the formation of RNA from a DNA template during transcription. Also called **RNA polymer**.

tran·scrip·tion /tranˈskripSHən/ ▶ n. a written or printed representation of something. ■ the action or process of transcribing something: *the funding covers transcription of nearly illegible photocopies.* ■ an arrangement of a piece of music for a different instrument, voice, or number of these: *a transcription for voice and lute.* ■ a form in which a speech sound or a foreign character is represented. ■ Biochemistry the process by which genetic information represented by a sequence of DNA nucleotides is copied into newly synthesized molecules of RNA, with the DNA serving as a template.
– DERIVATIVES **tran·scrip·tion·al** /-SHənl/ adj., **tran·scrip·tion·al·ly** /-SHənl-ē/ adv., **tran·scrip·tion·ist** /-nist/ n.
– ORIGIN late 16th cent.: from French, or from Latin *transcriptio(n-)*, from the verb *transcribere* (see TRANSCRIBE).

trans·cul·tur·al /transˈkəlCHərəl, tranz-/ ▶ adj. relating to or involving more than one culture; cross-cultural: *the possibility of transcultural understanding.*

trans·cu·ta·ne·ous /ˌtranskyo͞oˈtānēəs, ˌtranz-/ ▶ adj. existing, applied, or measured across the depth of the skin.

trans·der·mal /transˈdərməl, tranz-/ ▶ adj. relating to or denoting the application of a medicine or drug through the skin, typically by using an adhesive patch, so that it is absorbed slowly into the body.

trans·dif·fer·en·ti·a·tion /tranz,difə,renSHēˈāSHən, trans-/ ▶ n. Biology the rare natural transformation of cells other than stem cells into a different cell type.
– DERIVATIVES **trans·dif·fer·en·ti·ate** /-SHē,āt/ v. [no obj.].

trans·duc·er /transˈd(y)o͞osər, tranz-/ ▶ n. a device that converts variations in a physical quantity, such as pressure or brightness, into an electrical signal, or vice versa.
– DERIVATIVES **trans·duce** v., **trans·duc·tion** /-ˈdəkSHən/ n.
– ORIGIN 1920s: from Latin *transducere* 'lead across' (from *trans-* 'across' + *ducere* 'lead') + -ER[1].

tran·sect /tranˈsekt/ technical ▶ v. [with obj.] cut across or make a transverse section in.
▶ n. a straight line or narrow section through an object or natural feature or across the earth's surface, along which observations are made or measurements taken.
– DERIVATIVES **tran·sec·tion** /-ˈsekSHən/ n.
– ORIGIN mid 17th cent. (as a verb): from TRANS- 'through' + Latin *sect-* 'divided by cutting' (from the verb *secare*).

tran·sept /ˈtran,sept/ ▶ n. (in a cross-shaped church) either of the two parts forming the arms of the cross shape, projecting at right angles from the nave: *the north transept.*
– DERIVATIVES **tran·sep·tal** /tranˈseptl/ adj.
– ORIGIN mid 16th cent.: from modern Latin *transeptum* (see TRANS-, SEPTUM).

transf. ▶ abbr. ■ transfer. ■ transferred. ■ transformer.

trans-fat /ˈtransˈfat/ ▶ n. another term for TRANS-FATTY ACID.

trans-fat·ty ac·id /ˌtransˈfatē/ ▶ n. an unsaturated fatty acid with a trans arrangement of the carbon atoms adjacent to its double bonds. Such acids occur esp. in margarines and cooking oils as a result of the hydrogenation process.

trans·fect /transˈfekt/ ▶ v. [with obj.] Microbiology infect (a cell) with free nucleic acid. ■ introduce (genetic material) in this way.
– DERIVATIVES **trans·fec·tant** /-ənt/ n., **trans·fec·tion** /transˈfekSHən/ n.
– ORIGIN 1960s: from TRANS- 'across' + INFECT, or a blend of TRANSFER and INFECT.

trans·fer ▶ v. /transˈfər, ˈtransfər/ (**transfers, transferring, transferred**) **1** move from one place to another: [with obj.] *he would have to transfer money to his own account* | [no obj.] *I went to sleep on the couch before transferring to my bedroom later in the night.* ■ move to another group, occupation, or service: [no obj.] *she transferred to the Physics Department* | [with obj.] *employees have been transferred to the installation team.* ■ [no obj.] enroll in a different school or college: *Ron transferred to the University of Idaho.* ■ (in professional sports) move or cause to move to another team: [no obj.] *he transferred to the Dodgers* | [with obj.] *when a player is transferred to the minors by a major league club.* ■ redirect (a telephone call) to another line or extension. ■ [with obj.] copy (a drawing or design) from one surface to another. ■ [with obj.] copy (data,

music, etc.) from one medium or device to another: *you can easily transfer your personal data to another PC using the export feature.*
2 [no obj.] change to another place, route, or means of transportation during a journey: *John advised him to transfer from Rome airport to the railroad station.*
3 [with obj.] make over the possession of (property, a right, or a responsibility) to someone else.
4 [with obj.] (usu. as adj. **transferred**) change (the sense of a word or phrase) by extension or metaphor: *a transferred use of the Old English noun.*
▶ **n.** /ˈtransfər/ **1** an act of moving something or someone to another place: *a transfer of wealth to the poorer nations | she was going to ask her boss for a transfer to the city | a patient had died after transfer from the County Hospital to St. Peter's.* ■ Brit. an act of selling or moving an athlete to another team: *his transfer from Rangers cost £800,000.* ■ a student who has enrolled in a different school or college. ■ a conveyance of property, esp. stocks, from one person to another. ■ the action of copying data from one medium or device to another.
2 a small colored picture or design on paper that can be transferred to another surface by being pressed or heated: *T-shirts with iron-on transfers.*
3 an act of changing to another place, route, or means of transportation during a journey: *it took three hours and several bus transfers to get there.* ■ a ticket allowing a passenger to change from one public transportation vehicle to another as part of a single journey.
– DERIVATIVES **trans·fer·ee** /ˌtransfəˈrē/ **n.**, **trans·fer·or** /transˈfərər, ˈtransfərər/ **n.** (chiefly Law), **trans·fer·rer n.**
– ORIGIN late Middle English (as a verb): from French *transférer* or Latin *transferre*, from *trans-* 'across' + *ferre* 'to bear.' The earliest use of the noun (late 17th cent.) was as a legal term in the sense 'conveyance of property.'

trans·fer·a·ble /transˈfərəbəl, ˈtransfərə-/ ▶ **adj.** (typically of financial assets, liabilities, or legal rights) able to be transferred or made over to the possession of another person.
– DERIVATIVES **trans·fer·a·bil·i·ty** /ˌtransfərəˈbilitē/ **n.**

trans·fer·ase /ˈtransfəˌrās, -ˌrāz/ ▶ **n.** Biochemistry an enzyme that catalyzes the transfer of a particular group from one molecule to another.

trans·fer·ence /transˈfərəns, ˈtransfərəns/ ▶ **n.** the action of transferring something or the process of being transferred: *education involves the transference of knowledge.* ■ Psychoanalysis the redirection to a substitute, usually a therapist, of emotions that were originally felt in childhood (in a phase of analysis called **transference neurosis**).

trans·fer fac·tor ▶ **n.** Biology a substance released by antigen-sensitized lymphocytes and capable of transferring the response of delayed hypersensitivity to a nonsensitized cell or individual into which it is introduced.

trans·fer func·tion ▶ **n.** Electronics a mathematical function relating the output or response of a system such as a filter circuit to the input or stimulus.

trans·fer or·bit ▶ **n.** a trajectory by which a spacecraft can pass from one orbit to another at a higher altitude, esp. a geostationary orbit.

trans·fer pay·ment ▶ **n.** Economics a payment made or income received in which no goods or services are being paid for, such as a benefit payment or subsidy.

trans·fer·ral /transˈfərəl/ ▶ **n.** an act of transferring someone or something.

trans·fer·rin /transˈferin/ ▶ **n.** Biochemistry a protein of the beta globulin group that binds and transports iron in blood serum.
– ORIGIN 1940s: from TRANS- 'across' + Latin *ferrum* 'iron' + -IN¹.

trans·fer RNA ▶ **n.** Biochemistry RNA consisting of folded molecules that transport amino acids from the cytoplasm of a cell to a ribosome.

trans·fig·u·ra·tion /transˌfigyəˈrāSHən/ ▶ **n.** a complete change of form or appearance into a more beautiful or spiritual state: *in this light the junk undergoes a transfiguration; it shines.* ■ (**the Transfiguration**) Christ's appearance in radiant glory to three of his disciples (Matthew 17:2, Mark 9:2–3, Luke 9:28–36). ■ the church festival commemorating this, held on August 6.
– ORIGIN late Middle English (with biblical reference): from Old French, or from Latin *transfiguratio(n-)*, from the verb *transfigurare* (see TRANSFIGURE).

trans·fig·ure /transˈfigyər/ ▶ **v.** [with obj.] (usu. **be transfigured**) transform into something more beautiful or elevated: *the world is made luminous and is transfigured.*
– ORIGIN Middle English: from Old French *transfigurer* or Latin *transfigurare*, from *trans-* 'across' + *figura* 'figure.'

trans·fi·nite /transˈfīˌnīt/ ▶ **adj. 1** Mathematics relating to or denoting a number corresponding to an infinite set in the way that a natural number denotes or counts members of a finite set.
2 beyond or surpassing the finite.

trans·fix /transˈfiks/ ▶ **v.** [with obj.] **1** (usu. **be transfixed**) cause (someone) to become motionless with horror, wonder, or astonishment: *he was transfixed by the pain in her face | she stared at him, transfixed.*
2 pierce with a sharp implement or weapon: *a field mouse is transfixed by the curved talons of an owl.*
– DERIVATIVES **trans·fix·ion** /-ˈfikSHən/ **n.**
– ORIGIN late 16th cent. (sense 2): from Latin *transfix-* 'pierced through,' from the verb *transfigere*, from *trans-* 'across' + *figere* 'fix, fasten.'

trans·form /transˈfôrm/ ▶ **v.** [with obj.] make a thorough or dramatic change in the form, appearance, or character of: *lasers have transformed cardiac surgery | he wanted to **transform** himself **into** a successful businessman.* ■ [no obj.] undergo such a change: *an automobile that **transformed into** a boat.* ■ change the voltage of (an electric current). ■ Mathematics change (a mathematical entity) by transformation.
▶ **n.** /ˈtransfôrm/ Mathematics & Linguistics the product of a transformation. ■ a rule for making a transformation.
– DERIVATIVES **trans·form·a·ble adj.**, **trans·form·a·tive** /-mətiv/ **adj.**
– ORIGIN Middle English (as a verb): from Old French *transformer* or Latin *transformare* (see TRANS-, FORM).

trans·for·ma·tion /ˌtransfərˈmāSHən/ ▶ **n.** a thorough or dramatic change in form or appearance: *its landscape has undergone a radical transformation.* ■ a metamorphosis during the life cycle of an animal. ■ Physics the induced or spontaneous change of one element into another by a nuclear process. ■ Mathematics & Logic a process by which one figure, expression, or function is converted into another that is equivalent in some important respect but is differently expressed or represented. ■ Linguistics a process by which an element in the underlying deep structure of a sentence is converted to an element in the surface structure. ■ Biology the genetic alteration of a cell by introduction of extraneous DNA, esp. by a plasmid. ■ Biology the heritable modification of a cell from its normal state to a malignant state.
– ORIGIN late Middle English: from Old French, or from late Latin *transformatio(n-)*, from the verb *transformare* (see TRANSFORM).

trans·for·ma·tion·al /ˌtransfərˈmāSHənl/ ▶ **adj.** relating to or involving transformation or transformations. ■ of or relating to transformational grammar.
– DERIVATIVES **trans·for·ma·tion·al·ly adv.**

trans·for·ma·tion·al gram·mar ▶ **n.** Linguistics a type of grammar that describes a language in terms of transformations applied to an underlying deep structure in order to generate the surface structure of sentences that can actually occur. See also GENERATIVE GRAMMAR.

trans·form·er /transˈfôrmər/ ▶ **n. 1** an apparatus for reducing or increasing the voltage of an alternating current.
2 a person or thing that transforms something.

trans·form fault ▶ **n.** Geology a strike-slip fault occurring at the boundary between two plates of the earth's crust.

trans·fuse /transˈfyo͞oz/ ▶ **v.** [with obj.] **1** Medicine transfer (blood or its components) from one person or animal to another. ■ inject (liquid) into a blood vessel to replace lost fluid.
2 cause (something or someone) to be permeated or infused by something: *we became transfused by a radiance of joy.*
– ORIGIN late Middle English (in the sense 'cause to pass from one person to another'): from Latin *transfus-* 'poured from one container to another,' from the verb *transfundere*, from *trans-* 'across' + *fundere* 'pour.'

trans·fu·sion /transˈfyo͞oZHən/ ▶ **n.** an act of transfusing donated blood, blood products, or other fluid into the circulatory system of a person or animal.

trans·gen·der /tranzˈjendər, trans-/ (also **transgendered**) ▶ **adj.** identified with a gender other than the biological one: *a transgender activist and author.*

trans·gen·ic /transˈjenik, tranz-/ ▶ **adj.** Biology of, relating to, or denoting an organism that contains genetic material into which DNA from an unrelated organism has been artificially introduced.
– ORIGIN 1980s: from TRANS- 'across' + GENE + -IC.

trans·gen·ics /transˈjeniks, tranz-/ ▶ **plural n.** [usu. treated as sing.] the branch of biology concerned with transgenic organisms.

trans·glob·al /transˈglōbəl/ ▶ **adj.** (of an expedition, enterprise, search, or network) moving or extending across or around the world.

trans·gress /transˈgres, tranz-/ ▶ **v.** [with obj.] infringe or go beyond the bounds of (a moral principle or other established standard of behavior): *she had transgressed an unwritten social law |* [no obj.] *they must control the impulses that lead them to transgress.* ■ Geology (of the sea) spread over (an area of land).
– DERIVATIVES **trans·gres·sor** /-ˈgresər/ **n.**
– ORIGIN late 15th cent.: from Old French *transgresser* or Latin *transgress-* 'stepped across,' from the verb *transgredi*, from *trans-* 'across' + *gradi* 'go.'

trans·gres·sion /transˈgreSHən, tranz-/ ▶ **n.** an act that goes against a law, rule, or code of conduct; an offense: *I'll be keeping an eye out for further transgressions | her transgression of etiquette.*

trans·gres·sive /transˈgresiv, tranz-/ ▶ **adj.** involving a violation of accepted or imposed boundaries, esp. those of social acceptability: *her experiences of transgressive love with both sexes.* ■ of or relating to fiction, cinematography, or art in which orthodox cultural, moral, and artistic boundaries are challenged by the representation of unconventional behavior and the use of experimental forms. ■ Geology (of a stratum) overlapping others unconformably, esp. as a result of marine transgression.

tran·ship ▶ **v.** variant spelling of TRANSSHIP.

trans·his·tor·i·cal /ˌtrans-hiˈstôrikəl, ˌtranz-, -ˈstär-/ ▶ **adj.** transcending historical boundaries; eternal: *femininity may not be a transhistorical absolute.*

trans·hu·mance /transˈ(h)yo͞oməns, tranz-/ ▶ **n.** the action or practice of moving livestock from one grazing ground to another in a seasonal cycle, typically to lowlands in winter and highlands in summer.
– DERIVATIVES **trans·hu·mant** /-mənt/ **adj.**
– ORIGIN early 20th cent.: from French, from the verb *transhumer*, based on Latin *trans-* 'across' + *humus* 'ground.'

trans·hu·man·ism /tranzˈhyo͞oməˌnizəm/ ▶ **n.** the belief or theory that the human race can evolve beyond its current physical and mental limitations, esp. by means of science and technology.
– DERIVATIVES **trans·hu·man·ist adj. & n.**

tran·sience /ˈtransHəns, -ZHəns, -zēəns/ (also **transiency** /-sē/) ▶ **n.** the state or fact of lasting only for a short time; transitory nature: *the transience of life and happiness.*

tran·sient /ˈtransHənt, -ZHənt, -zēənt/ ▶ **adj.** lasting only for a short time; impermanent: *a transient cold spell.* ■ staying or working in a place for only a short time: *the transient nature of the labor force in catering.*
▶ **n. 1** a person who is staying or working in a place for only a short time.
2 a momentary variation in current, voltage, or frequency.
– DERIVATIVES **tran·sient·ly adv.**
– ORIGIN late 16th cent.: from Latin *transient-* 'going across,' from the verb *transire*, from *trans-* 'across' + *ire* 'go.'

tran·si·ent is·che·mic at·tack (abbr.: **TIA**) ▶ **n.** technical term for MINISTROKE.

trans·il·lu·mi·nate /ˌtransəˈlo͞oməˌnāt, ˌtranz-/ ▶ **v.** [with obj.] pass strong light through (an organ or part of the body) in order to detect disease or abnormality.
– DERIVATIVES **trans·il·lu·mi·na·tion** /-əˌlo͞oməˈnāSHən/ **n.**

tran·sis·tor /tranˈzistər/ ▶ **n.** a semiconductor device with three connections, capable of amplification in addition to rectification. ■ (also **transistor radio**) a portable radio using circuits containing transistors rather than vacuum tubes.
– ORIGIN 1940s: from TRANSCONDUCTANCE, on the pattern of words such as *varistor.*

tran·sis·tor·ize /tranˈzistəˌrīz/ ▶ **v.** [with obj.] (usu. as adj. **transistorized**) design or make with transistors rather than vacuum tubes: *a transistorized tape recorder.*
– DERIVATIVES **tran·sis·tor·i·za·tion** /-ˌzistəriˈzāSHən/ **n.**

tran·sit /ˈtranzit/ ▶ **n. 1** the carrying of people, goods, or materials from one place to another: *a painting was damaged in transit.* ■ an act of passing

t

through or across a place: *the first west-to-east transit of the Northwest Passage* | [as modifier] *a transit airline passenger.* ■ the conveyance of passengers on public transportation. ■ Astronomy the passage of an inferior planet across the face of the sun, or of a moon or its shadow across the face of a planet. ■ Astronomy the apparent passage of a celestial body across the meridian of a place. ■ Astrology the passage of a celestial body through a specified sign, house, or area of a chart.
2 informal (in full **transit theodolite**) a tool used by surveyors to measure horizontal angles.
▶ **v.** (**transits, transiting, transited**) [with obj.] pass across or through (an area): *the new large ships will be too big to transit the Panama Canal.* ■ Astronomy (of a planet or other celestial body) pass across (a meridian or the face of another body). ■ Astrology (of a celestial body) pass across (a specified sign, house, or area of a chart).
– ORIGIN late Middle English (denoting passage from one place to another): from Latin *transitus*, from *transire* 'go across.'

tran·sit camp ▶ **n.** a camp for the temporary accommodation of groups of people, e.g., refugees or soldiers, who are traveling through a country or region.

tran·sit cir·cle (also **transit instrument**) ▶ **n.** another term for MERIDIAN CIRCLE.

tran·si·tion /tran'zisʜən, -'sisʜən/ ▶ **n.** the process or a period of changing from one state or condition to another: *students **in transition** from one program to another* | *a transition to multiparty democracy.* ■ a passage in a piece of writing that smoothly connects two topics or sections to each other. ■ Music a momentary modulation from one key to another. ■ Physics a change of an atom, nucleus, electron, etc., from one quantum state to another, with emission or absorption of radiation.
▶ **v.** undergo or cause to undergo a process or period of transition: [with obj.] *the network ought to be built by the federal government and then transitioned into private industry* | [no obj.] *we have transitioned from a high-intensity combat operation to a support role in the community.*
– DERIVATIVES **tran·si·tion·a·ry** /-ˌnerē/ **adj.**
– ORIGIN mid 16th cent.: from French, or from Latin *transitio(n-)*, from *transire* 'go across.'

tran·si·tion·al /tran'zisʜənl/ ▶ **adj.** relating to or characteristic of a process or period of transition: *a transitional government was appointed.* ■ (**Transitional**) Architecture of or denoting the last stage of Romanesque style, in which Gothic elements begin to appear.
– DERIVATIVES **tran·si·tion·al·ly** /-sʜənlē/ **adv.**

tran·si·tion met·al (also **transition element**) ▶ **n.** Chemistry any of the set of metallic elements occupying a central block (Groups IVB–VIII, IB, and IIB, or 4–12) in the periodic table, e.g., iron, manganese, chromium, and copper. Chemically they show variable valence and a strong tendency to form coordination compounds, and many of their compounds are colored.

tran·si·tion point ▶ **n.** Chemistry the set of conditions of temperature and pressure at which different phases of the same substance can be in equilibrium.

tran·si·tion prob·a·bil·i·ty ▶ **n.** Physics the probability of the occurrence of a transition between two quantum states of an atom, nucleus, electron, etc.

tran·si·tion tem·per·a·ture ▶ **n.** Physics the temperature at which a substance acquires or loses some distinctive property, in particular superconductivity.

tran·si·tive /'transitiv, 'tranz-/ ▶ **adj.** **1** Grammar (of a verb or a sense or use of a verb) able to take a direct object (expressed or implied), e.g., *saw* in *he saw the donkey*. The opposite of INTRANSITIVE.
2 Logic & Mathematics (of a relation) such that, if it applies between successive members of a sequence, it must also apply between any two members taken in order. For instance, if A is larger than B, and B is larger than C, then A is larger than C.
▶ **n.** a transitive verb.
– DERIVATIVES **tran·si·tive·ly adv.**, **tran·si·tive·ness n.**, **tran·si·tiv·i·ty** /ˌtransə'tivitē, -zə-/ **n.**
– ORIGIN mid 16th cent. (in the sense 'transitory'): from late Latin *transitivus*, from *transit-* 'gone across' (see TRANSIT).

tran·sit lounge ▶ **n.** a lounge at an airport for passengers waiting between flights.

tran·si·to·ry /'transiˌtôrē, 'tranzi-/ ▶ **adj.** not permanent: *transitory periods of medieval greatness.*
– DERIVATIVES **tran·si·to·ri·ly** /-rəlē/ **adv.**, **tran·si·to·ri·ness n.**
– ORIGIN late Middle English: from Old French *transitoire*, from Christian Latin *transitorius*, from *transit-* 'gone across' (see TRANSIT).

tran·sit vi·sa ▶ **n.** a visa allowing its holder to pass through a country but not to stay there.

Trans·jor·dan /trans'jôrdn, tranz-/ former name (until 1949) of the region east of the Jordan River that now forms the main part of Jordan.
– DERIVATIVES **Trans·jor·da·ni·an** /ˌtransˌjôr'dānēən, ˌtranz-/ **adj.**

Trans·kei /tran'skī, -'skā/ a former homeland established in South Africa for the Xhosa people, now part of the province of Eastern Cape.

trans·ke·to·lase /tranz'kētlˌās, -ˌāz/ ▶ **n.** Biochemistry an enzyme that catalyzes the transfer of an alcohol group between sugar molecules.

trans·late /trans'lāt, tranz-/ ▶ **v.** [with obj.] **1** express the sense of (words or text) in another language: *the German original has been translated into English.* ■ [no obj.] be expressed or be capable of being expressed in another language: *shiatsu literally translates as "finger pressure."* ■ (**translate something into/translate into**) convert or be converted into (another form or medium): [with obj.] *few of Shakespeare's other works have been translated into ballets.*
2 move from one place or condition to another: *she had been translated from familiar surroundings to a foreign court.* ■ formal move (a bishop) to another see or pastoral charge. ■ formal remove (a saint's relics) to another place. ■ literary convey (someone, typically still alive) to heaven. ■ Biology convert (a sequence of nucleotides in messenger RNA) to an amino-acid sequence in a protein or polypeptide during synthesis.
3 Physics cause (a body) to move so that all its parts travel in the same direction, without rotation or change of shape. ■ Mathematics transform (a geometric figure) in an analogous way.
– DERIVATIVES **trans·lat·a·bil·i·ty** /ˌtransˌlātə'bilətē, ˌtranz-/ **n.**, **trans·lat·a·ble adj.**
– ORIGIN Middle English: from Latin *translatus* 'carried across,' past participle of *transferre* (see TRANSFER).

trans·la·tion /trans'lāsʜən, tranz-/ ▶ **n.** **1** the process of translating words or text from one language into another: *Constantine's translation of Arabic texts into Latin.* ■ a written or spoken rendering of the meaning of a word, speech, book, or other text, in another language: *a German translation of Oscar Wilde's play* | *a term for which there is no adequate English translation.* ■ the conversion of something from one form or medium into another: *the translation of research findings into clinical practice.* ■ Biology the process by which a sequence of nucleotide triplets in a messenger RNA molecule gives rise to a specific sequence of amino acids during synthesis of a polypeptide or protein.
2 formal or technical the process of moving something from one place to another: *the translation of the relics of St. Thomas of Canterbury.* ■ Mathematics movement of a body from one point of space to another such that every point of the body moves in the same direction and over the same distance, without any rotation, reflection, or change in size.
– DERIVATIVES **trans·la·tion·al** /-sʜənl/ **adj.**, **trans·la·tion·al·ly** /-sʜənl-ē/ **adv.**
– ORIGIN Middle English: from Old French, or from Latin *translatio(n-)*, from *translat-* 'carried across' (see TRANSLATE).

trans·la·tor /'transˌlātər, 'tranz-/ ▶ **n.** a person who translates from one language into another, esp. as a profession. ■ a program that translates from one programming language into another.

trans·lit·er·ate /trans'litəˌrāt, tranz-/ ▶ **v.** [with obj.] (usu. **be transliterated**) write or print (a letter or word) using the closest corresponding letters of a different alphabet or language: *names from one language are often transliterated into another.*
– DERIVATIVES **trans·lit·er·a·tion** /transˌlitə'rāsʜən, tranz-/ **n.**, **trans·lit·er·a·tor** /-ˌrātər/ **n.**
– ORIGIN mid 19th cent.: from TRANS- 'across' + Latin *littera* 'letter' + -ATE[3].

trans·lo·cate /trans'lōˌkāt, tranz-/ ▶ **v.** [with obj.] chiefly technical move from one place to another: *translocating rhinos to other reserves* | [no obj.] *the cell bodies translocate into the other side of the brain.* ■ Physiology & Biochemistry transport (a dissolved substance) within an organism, esp. in the phloem of a plant, or actively across a cell membrane. ■ Genetics move (a portion of a chromosome) to a new position on the same or another chromosome.
– DERIVATIVES **trans·lo·ca·tion** /ˌtransˌlō'kāsʜən, tranz-/ **n.**

trans·lu·cent /trans'lo͞osnt, tranz-/ ▶ **adj.** (of a substance) allowing light, but not detailed images, to pass through; semitransparent: *fry until the onions become translucent.*
– DERIVATIVES **trans·lu·cence n.**, **trans·lu·cen·cy n.**, **trans·lu·cent·ly adv.**
– ORIGIN late 16th cent. (in the Latin sense): from Latin *translucent-* 'shining through,' from the verb *translucere*, from *trans-* 'through' + *lucere* 'to shine.'

trans·lu·nar /trans'lo͞onər, tranz-/ ▶ **adj.** of, relating to, or denoting the trajectory of a spacecraft traveling between the earth and the moon.

trans·man /'tranzˌman, 'trans-/ ▶ **n.** (pl. **transmen**) a transsexual male.

trans·ma·rine /ˌtransmə'rēn, ˌtranz-/ ▶ **adj.** dated situated or originating on the other side of the sea: *an alien, or a transmarine stranger.* ■ of or involving crossing the sea: *some birds make long transmarine migrations.*
– ORIGIN late 16th cent.: from Latin *transmarinus*, from *trans-* 'across' + *marinus* 'marine, of the sea.'

trans·mem·brane /trans'memˌbrān, tranz-/ ▶ **adj.** Biology existing or occurring across a cell membrane: *transmembrane conductance.*

trans·mi·grant /trans'mīgrənt, tranz-/ ▶ **n.** rare a person passing through a country or region in the course of emigrating to another region.
– ORIGIN early 17th cent.: from Latin *transmigrant-* 'migrating across,' from the verb *transmigrare* (see TRANSMIGRATE).

trans·mi·grate /trans'mīˌgrāt, tranz-/ ▶ **v.** [no obj.] **1** (of the soul) pass into a different body after death.
2 rare migrate.
– DERIVATIVES **trans·mi·gra·tion** /ˌtransˌmī'grāsʜən, ˌtranz-/ **n.**, **trans·mi·gra·tor** /-ˌgrātər/ **n.**, **trans·mi·gra·to·ry** /-grəˌtôrē/ **adj.**
– ORIGIN late Middle English (as an adjective in the sense 'transferred'): from Latin *transmigrat-* 'removed from one place to another,' from the verb *transmigrare* (see TRANS-, MIGRATE).

trans·mis·sion /trans'misʜən, tranz-/ ▶ **n.** **1** the action or process of transmitting something or the state of being transmitted: *the transmission of the HIV virus.* ■ a program or signal that is broadcast or sent out: *television transmissions.*
2 the mechanism by which power is transmitted from an engine to the wheels of a motor vehicle.
– ORIGIN early 17th cent.: from Latin *transmissio* (see TRANS-, MISSION).

trans·mis·sion e·lec·tron mi·cro·scope ▶ **n.** a form of electron microscope in which an image is derived from electrons that have passed through the specimen, in particular one in which the whole image is formed at once rather than by scanning.

trans·mis·sion line ▶ **n.** a conductor or conductors designed to carry electricity or an electrical signal over large distances with minimum losses and distortion.

trans·mis·siv·i·ty /ˌtransmi'sivitē, ˌtranz-/ ▶ **n.** (pl. **transmissivities**) the degree to which a medium allows something, in particular electromagnetic radiation, to pass through it.

trans·mit /tranz'mit, trans-/ ▶ **v.** (**transmits, transmitting, transmitted**) [with obj.] cause (something) to pass on from one place or person to another: *knowledge is transmitted from teacher to student.* ■ broadcast or send out (an electrical signal or a radio or television program): *the program was transmitted on October 7.* ■ pass on (a disease or trait) to another: (as adj. **transmitted**) *sexually transmitted diseases.* ■ allow (heat, light, sound, electricity, or other energy) to pass through a medium: *the three bones transmit sound waves to the inner ear.* ■ communicate or be a medium for (an idea or emotion): *the theatrical gift of being able to transmit emotion.*
– DERIVATIVES **trans·mis·si·bil·i·ty** /-ˌmisə'bilitē/ **n.** (chiefly Medicine), **trans·mis·si·ble** /-'misəbəl/ **adj.** (chiefly Medicine), **trans·mis·sive** /-'misiv/ **adj.**, **trans·mit·ta·ble adj.**, **trans·mit·tal** /-'mitl/ **n.**
– ORIGIN late Middle English: from Latin *transmittere*, from *trans-* 'across' + *mittere* 'send.'

trans·mit·tance /trans'mitns, tranz-/ ▶ **n.** Physics the ratio of the light energy falling on a body to that transmitted through it.

trans·mit·ter /trans'mitər, tranz-/ ▶ **n.** a set of equipment used to generate and transmit electromagnetic waves carrying messages or signals, esp. those of radio or television. ■ a person or thing that transmits something: *reggae has established itself as the principal transmitter of the Jamaican language.* ■ short for NEUROTRANSMITTER.

trans·mog·ri·fy /trans'mägrəˌfī, tranz-/ ▶ **v.** (**transmogrifies, transmogrifying, transmogrified**) [with obj.] chiefly humorous transform, esp. in a surprising or magical manner: *the cucumbers that were ultimately transmogrified into pickles.*
– DERIVATIVES **trans·mog·ri·fi·ca·tion** /-ˌmägrəfi'kāsʜən/ **n.**
– ORIGIN mid 17th cent.: of unknown origin.

trans·mon·tane /trans'män,tān, tranz-/ ▶ **adj.** another term for **TRAMONTANE**.

trans·mu·ral /trans'myo͝orəl, tranz-/ ▶ **adj.** Medicine existing or occurring across the entire wall of an organ or blood vessel.

trans·mu·ta·tion /,transmyo͞o'tāsHən, ,tranz-/ ▶ **n.** the action of changing or the state of being changed into another form: *the transmutation of the political economy of the postwar years was complete.* ■ Physics the changing of one element into another by radioactive decay, nuclear bombardment, or similar processes. ■ Biology, chiefly historical the conversion or transformation of one species into another. ■ the supposed alchemical process of changing base metals into gold.
– DERIVATIVES **trans·mu·ta·tion·al** /-sHənl/ **adj.**, **trans·mu·ta·tion·ist** /-nist/ **n.**

trans·mute /trans'myo͞ot, tranz-/ ▶ **v.** change in form, nature, or substance: [with obj.] *the raw material of his experience was **transmuted into** stories* | [no obj.] *the discovery that elements can transmute by radioactivity.* ■ [with obj.] subject (base metals) to alchemical transmutation: *the quest to **transmute** lead into gold.*
– DERIVATIVES **trans·mut·a·bil·i·ty** /-,myo͞otə'bilitē/ **n.**, **trans·mut·a·ble adj.**, **trans·mut·a·tive** /-'myo͞otətiv/ **adj.**, **trans·mut·er n.**
– ORIGIN late Middle English: from Latin *transmutare*, from *trans-* 'across' + *mutare* 'to change.'

trans·na·tion·al /trans'nasHənl, tranz-/ ▶ **adj.** extending or operating across national boundaries: *transnational advertising agencies.*
▶ **n.** a large company operating internationally; a multinational.
– DERIVATIVES **trans·na·tion·al·ism** /-,izəm/ **n.**, **trans·na·tion·al·ly adv.**

trans·o·ce·an·ic /,transōsHē'anik, ,tranz-/ ▶ **adj.** crossing an ocean: *the transoceanic cable system.* ■ coming from or situated beyond an ocean: *there is a higher rate for letters intended for transoceanic countries.*

tran·som /'transəm/ ▶ **n.** the flat surface forming the stern of a vessel. ■ a horizontal beam reinforcing the stern of a vessel. ■ a strengthening crossbar, in particular one set above a window or door. Compare with **MULLION**. ■ short for **TRANSOM WINDOW**.
– PHRASES **over the transom** informal offered or sent without prior agreement; unsolicited: *the editors receive about ten manuscripts a week over the transom.*
– DERIVATIVES **tran·somed adj.**
– ORIGIN late Middle English (earlier as *traversayn*): from Old French *traversin*, from the verb *traverser* 'to cross' (see **TRAVERSE**).

tran·som win·dow ▶ **n.** a window set above the transom of a door or larger window; a fanlight.

tran·son·ic /tran'sänik/ (also **transsonic**) ▶ **adj.** denoting or relating to speeds close to that of sound.
– ORIGIN 1940s: from **TRANS-** 'through, across' + **SONIC**, on the pattern of words such as *supersonic*.

trans-Pa·cif·ic /,transpə'sifik, ,tranz-/ ▶ **adj.** crossing the Pacific: *new trans-Pacific routes to India, Korea, and Japan.* ■ of or relating to an area beyond the Pacific.

trans·par·ence /tran'sparəns/ ▶ **n.** rare term for **TRANSPARENCY** (sense 1).

trans·par·en·cy /tran'sparənsē/ ▶ **n.** (pl. **transparencies**) **1** the condition of being transparent: *the transparency of ice.*
2 an image, text, or positive transparent photograph printed on transparent plastic or glass, able to be viewed using a projector.
– ORIGIN late 16th cent. (as a general term denoting a transparent object): from medieval Latin *transparentia*, from *transparent-* 'shining through' (see **TRANSPARENT**).

trans·par·ent /tran'spe(ə)rənt, -'spar-/ ▶ **adj.** (of a material or article) allowing light to pass through so that objects behind can be distinctly seen: *transparent blue water.* ■ easy to perceive or detect: *the residents will see through any transparent attempt to buy their votes* | *the meaning of the poem is by no means transparent.* ■ having thoughts, feelings, or motives that are easily perceived: *you'd be no good at poker—you're too transparent.* ■ (of an organization or its activities) open to public scrutiny: *if you had transparent government procurement, corruption would go away.* ■ Physics transmitting heat or other electromagnetic rays without distortion. ■ Computing (of a process or interface) functioning without the user being aware of its presence.
– DERIVATIVES **trans·par·ent·ly adv.** [as submodifier] *a transparently feeble argument.*
– ORIGIN late Middle English: from Old French, from medieval Latin *transparent-* 'shining through,' from Latin *transparere*, from *trans-* 'through' + *parere* 'appear.'

trans·per·son·al /trans'pərsənl, tranz-/ ▶ **adj.** of, denoting, or dealing with states or areas of consciousness beyond the limits of personal identity: *transpersonal states of consciousness.*

tran·spic·u·ous /tran'spikyo͞oəs/ ▶ **adj.** rare transparent. ■ easily understood; lucid.
– ORIGIN mid 17th cent.: from modern Latin *transpicuus* (from Latin *transpicere* 'look through') + **-OUS**.

trans·pierce /trans'pi(ə)rs/ ▶ **v.** [with obj.] literary pierce through (someone or something).

tran·spi·ra·tion stream /,transpə'rāsHən/ ▶ **n.** Botany the flow of water through a plant, from the roots to the leaves, via the xylem vessels.

tran·spire /tran'spī(ə)r/ ▶ **v.** [no obj.] **1** occur; happen: *I'm going to find out exactly what transpired.* ■ prove to be the case: *as it transpired, he was right.* ■ [with clause] (usu. **it transpires**) (of a secret or something unknown) come to be known; be revealed: *Yaddo, it transpired, had been under FBI surveillance for some time.*
2 Botany (of a plant or leaf) give off water vapor through the stomata.
– DERIVATIVES **tran·spi·ra·tion** /-spə'rāsHən/ **n.** (sense 2).
– ORIGIN late Middle English (in the sense 'emit as vapor through the surface'): from French *transpirer* or medieval Latin *transpirare*, from Latin *trans-* 'through' + *spirare* 'breathe.' The sense 'be revealed' (mid 18th cent.) is a figurative use comparable with 'leak out.'

> **USAGE** The common use of **transpire** to mean 'occur, happen' (*I'm going to find out exactly what transpired*) is a loose extension of an earlier meaning, 'come to be known' (*it transpired that Mark had been baptized a Catholic*). This loose sense of 'happen,' which is now more common in American usage than the sense of 'come to be known,' was first recorded in US English toward the end of the 18th century and has been listed in US dictionaries from the 19th century. It is often criticized as jargon, an unnecessarily long word used where *occur* or *happen* would do just as well.

trans·plant ▶ **v.** /trans'plant/ [with obj.] move or transfer (something) to another place or situation, typically with some effort or upheaval: *his endeavor to transplant people from Russia to the Argentine* | (as adj. **transplanted**) *a transplanted Easterner.* ■ replant (a plant) in another place. ■ remove (living tissue or an organ) and implant it in another part of the body or in another body.
▶ **n.** /'trans,plant/ an operation in which an organ or tissue is transplanted: *a heart transplant* | *kidneys available for transplant.* ■ an organ or tissue that is transplanted. ■ a plant that has been or is to be transplanted. ■ a person or thing that has been moved to a new place or situation.
– DERIVATIVES **trans·plant·a·ble** /trans'plantəbəl/ **adj.**, **trans·plan·ta·tion** /-,plan'tāsHən/ **n.**, **trans·plant·er n.**
– ORIGIN late Middle English (as a verb describing the repositioning of a plant): from late Latin *transplantare*, from Latin *trans-* 'across' + *plantare* 'to plant.' The noun, first in the sense 'something or someone moved to a new place,' dates from the mid 18th cent.

tran·spon·der /tran'spändər/ ▶ **n.** a device for receiving a radio signal and automatically transmitting a different signal.
– ORIGIN 1940s: blend of **TRANSMIT** and **RESPOND**, + **-ER**[1].

trans·pon·tine /trans'pän,tin/ ▶ **adj.** dated **1** on or from the other side of an ocean, in particular the Atlantic. [late 19th cent.: from **TRANS-** 'across' + Latin *pontus* 'sea' + **-INE**[1].]
2 on or from the other side of a bridge. [mid 19th cent.: from **TRANS-** 'across' + Latin *pons, pont-* 'bridge' + **-INE**[1].]

trans·port ▶ **v.** /trans'pôrt/ [with obj.] **1** take or carry (people or goods) from one place to another by means of a vehicle, aircraft, or ship: *the bulk of freight traffic was transported by truck.* ■ cause (someone) to feel that they are in another place or time: *for a moment she was transported to a warm summer garden on the night of a ball.* ■ historical send (a convict) to a penal colony.
2 overwhelm (someone) with a strong emotion, esp. joy: *she was **transported with** pleasure.*
▶ **n.** /'trans,pôrt/ **1** a system or means of conveying people or goods from place to place by means of a vehicle, aircraft, or ship: *many possess their own forms of transport* | *air transport.* ■ the action of transporting something or the state of being transported: *the transport of crude oil.* ■ a large vehicle, ship, or aircraft used to carry troops or stores. ■ historical a convict who was transported to a penal colony.
2 (usu. **transports**) an overwhelmingly strong emotion: *art can send people into **transports of** delight.*
– ORIGIN late Middle English: from Old French *transporter* or Latin *transportare*, from *trans-* 'across' + *portare* 'carry.'

trans·port·a·ble /trans'pôrtəbəl/ ▶ **adj. 1** able to be carried or moved: *the first transportable phones.*
2 historical (of an offender or an offense) punishable by transportation.
– DERIVATIVES **trans·port·a·bil·i·ty** /,trans,pôrtə'bilitē/ **n.**

trans·por·ta·tion /,transpər'tāsHən/ ▶ **n. 1** the action of transporting someone or something or the process of being transported: *the era of global mass transportation.* ■ a system or means of transporting people or goods: *transportation on the site includes a monorail.*
2 historical the action or practice of transporting convicts to a penal colony.

trans·port·er /trans'pôrtər/ ▶ **n.** a person or thing that transports something, in particular: ■ a large vehicle used to carry heavy objects, e.g., cars. ■ (in science fiction) a device that conveys people or things instantaneously from one place to another.

trans·pose /trans'pōz/ ▶ **v.** [with obj.] **1** cause (two or more things) to change places with each other: *the captions describing the two state flowers were accidentally transposed.*
2 transfer to a different place or context: *the problems of civilization are transposed into a rustic setting.* ■ write or play (music) in a different key from the original: *the basses are **transposed down** an octave.* ■ Mathematics transfer (a term), with its sign changed, to the other side of an equation.
▶ **n.** Mathematics a matrix obtained from a given matrix by interchanging each row and the corresponding column.
– DERIVATIVES **trans·pos·a·ble adj.**, **trans·pos·al** /-'spōzəl/ **n.**, **trans·pos·er n.**
– ORIGIN late Middle English (also in the sense 'transform, convert'): from Old French *transposer*, from *trans-* 'across' + *poser* 'to place.'

trans·pos·ing in·stru·ment ▶ **n.** an orchestral instrument whose notated pitch is different from its sounded pitch, e.g., the clarinet and many brass instruments.

trans·po·si·tion /,transpə'zisHən/ ▶ **n.** the action of transposing something: *transposition of word order* | *a transposition of an old story into a contemporary context.* ■ a thing that has been produced by transposing something: *in China, the dragon is a transposition of the serpent.*
– DERIVATIVES **trans·po·si·tion·al** /-sHənl/ **adj.**
– ORIGIN mid 16th cent.: from late Latin *transpositio(n-)* (see **TRANS-**, **POSITION**).

trans·po·son /trans'pō,zän/ ▶ **n.** Genetics a chromosomal segment that can undergo transposition, esp. a segment of bacterial DNA that can be translocated as a whole between chromosomal, phage, and plasmid DNA in the absence of a complementary sequence in the host DNA. Also called **JUMPING GENE**.
– ORIGIN 1970s: from **TRANSPOSITION** + **-ON**.

trans·put·er /trans'pyo͞otər/ ▶ **n.** a microprocessor with integral memory designed for parallel processing.
– ORIGIN 1970s: blend of **TRANSISTOR** and **COMPUTER**.

trans·ra·cial /tranz'rāsHəl, trans-/ ▶ **adj.** across or crossing racial boundaries.

trans·sex·u·al /tran(s)'seksHo͞oəl/ ▶ **n.** a person who emotionally and psychologically feels that they belong to the opposite sex. ■ a person who has undergone treatment in order to acquire the physical characteristics of the opposite sex.
▶ **adj.** of or relating to transsexuals.
– DERIVATIVES **trans·sex·u·al·ism** /-,lizəm/ **n.**, **trans·sex·u·al·i·ty** /-,seksHo͞o'alitē/ **n.**

trans·ship /tran(s)'sHip/ (also **tranship**) ▶ **v.** (**transships**, **transshipping**, **transshipped**) [with obj.] transfer (cargo) from one ship or other form of transport to another.
– DERIVATIVES **trans·ship·ment n.**

trans·son·ic ▶ **adj.** variant spelling of **TRANSONIC**.

trans·syn·ap·tic /,tran(s)sə'naptik, ,tranz-/ ▶ **adj.** Physiology occurring or existing across a nerve synapse.

tran·sub·stan·ti·ate /,transəb'stancHē,āt/ ▶ **v.** [with obj.] (usu. **be transubstantiated**) Christian Theology convert (the substance of the Eucharistic elements) into the body and blood of Christ. ■ formal

change the form or substance of (something) into something different.
– ORIGIN late Middle English: from medieval Latin *transubstantiat-* 'changed in substance,' from the verb *transubstantiare*, from Latin *trans-* 'across' + *substantia* 'substance.'

tran·sub·stan·ti·a·tion /ˌtransəbˌstanCHēˈāSHən/ ▶ **n.** Christian Theology (esp. in the Roman Catholic Church) the conversion of the substance of the Eucharistic elements into the body and blood of Christ at consecration, only the appearances of bread and wine still remaining.

tran·sude /tranˈso͞od/ ▶ **v.** archaic (with reference to a fluid) discharge or be discharged gradually through pores in a membrane, esp. within the body.
– DERIVATIVES **tran·su·date** /ˈtrans(y)o͞oˌdāt/ **n.**, **tran·su·da·tion** /ˌtrans(y)o͞oˈdāSHən/ **n.**
– ORIGIN mid 17th cent.: from French *transsuder* (in Old French *tressuer*), from Latin *trans-* 'across' + *sudare* 'to sweat.'

trans·u·ran·ic /ˌtransyəˈranik, tranz-/ ▶ **adj.** Chemistry (of an element) having a higher atomic number than uranium (92).

trans·u·re·thral /ˌtransyo͞oˈrēTHrəl, ˌtranz-/ ▶ **adj.** (of a medical procedure) performed via the urethra.

Trans·vaal /transˈväl, tranz-, -ˈfäl/ (also **the Transvaal**) a former province in northeastern South Africa, north of the Vaal River. Resistance to Britain's annexation of Transvaal in 1877 led to the Boer Wars, after which the Transvaal became a Crown Colony. It became a founding province of the Union of South Africa in 1910 and in 1994 was divided into the provinces of Northern Transvaal, Eastern Transvaal, Pretoria-Witwatersrand-Vereeniging, and the eastern part of North-West Province.

Trans·vaal dai·sy ▶ **n.** a South African gerbera, grown for its large brightly colored daisylike flowers. • *Gerbera jamesonii*, family Compositae.

trans·val·ue /transˈvalyo͞o, tranz-/ ▶ **v.** (**transvalues, transvaluing, transvalued**) [with obj.] represent (something, typically an idea, custom, or quality) in a different way, altering people's judgment of or reaction to it: *survival strategies are aesthetically* ***transvalued into*** *weapons of attack.*
– DERIVATIVES **trans·val·u·a·tion** /ˌtransvalyo͞oˈāSHən, ˌtranz-/ **n.**

trans·ver·sal /transˈvərsəl, tranz-/ Geometry ▶ **adj.** (of a line) intersecting a system of lines.
▶ **n.** a transversal line.
– DERIVATIVES **trans·ver·sal·i·ty** /ˌtransvərˈsalitē, ˌtranz-/ **n.**, **trans·ver·sal·ly adv.**
– ORIGIN late Middle English (as a synonym of TRANSVERSE): from medieval Latin *transversalis*, from Latin *transversus* 'lying across.'

trans·verse /transˈvərs, tranz-/ ▶ **adj.** situated or extending across something: *a transverse beam supports the dashboard.*
– DERIVATIVES **trans·verse·ly adv.**
– ORIGIN late Middle English: from Latin *transversus* 'turned across,' past participle of *transvertere*, from *trans-* 'across' + *vertere* 'to turn.'

trans·verse co·lon ▶ **n.** Anatomy the middle part of the large intestine, passing across the abdomen from right to left below the stomach.

trans·verse flute ▶ **n.** a flute that is held horizontally when played, e.g., the modern flute as opposed to the recorder.

trans·verse mag·net ▶ **n.** a magnet with poles at the sides and not the ends.

trans·verse proc·ess ▶ **n.** Anatomy a lateral process of a vertebra.

Trans·verse Ranges a term for various mountain ranges that cross southern California and are often considered the divider between north and south. See also TEHACHAPI MOUNTAINS.

trans·verse wave ▶ **n.** Physics a wave vibrating at right angles to the direction of its propagation.

trans·ves·tite /transˈvesˌtīt, tranz-/ ▶ **n.** a person, typically a man, who derives pleasure from dressing in clothes appropriate to the opposite sex.
– DERIVATIVES **trans·ves·tism** /-ˌtizəm/ **n.**, **trans·ves·tist** /-tist/ **n.** (dated), **trans·ves·ti·tism** /-tiˌtizəm/ **n.**
– ORIGIN 1920s: from German *Transvestit*, from Latin *trans-* 'across' + *vestire* 'clothe.'

Tran·syl·va·nia /ˌtransəlˈvānyə, -ˈvānēə/ **1** a large tableland region of northwestern Romania, separated from the rest of the country by the Carpathian Mountains and the Transylvanian Alps. Part of Hungary until it became a principality of the Ottoman Empire in the 16th century, it was returned to Hungary at the end of the 17th century and was incorporated into Romania in 1918.
2 (in US history) an unrecognized fourteenth colony that was proposed in the 1770s in what is now central Kentucky and neighboring Tennessee.
– DERIVATIVES **Tran·syl·va·ni·an adj.**
– ORIGIN based on Latin *trans* 'across, beyond' + *silva* 'forest.'

trap^{1} /trap/ ▶ **n. 1** a device or enclosure designed to catch and retain animals, typically by allowing entry but not exit or by catching hold of a part of the body. ■ a curve in the waste pipe from a bathtub, sink, or toilet that is always full of liquid and prevents gases from coming up the pipe into the building. ■ [with modifier] a container or device used to collect a specified thing: *one fuel filter and water trap are sufficient on the fuel system.* ■ a bunker or other hollow on a golf course. ■ the compartment from which a greyhound is released at the start of a race.

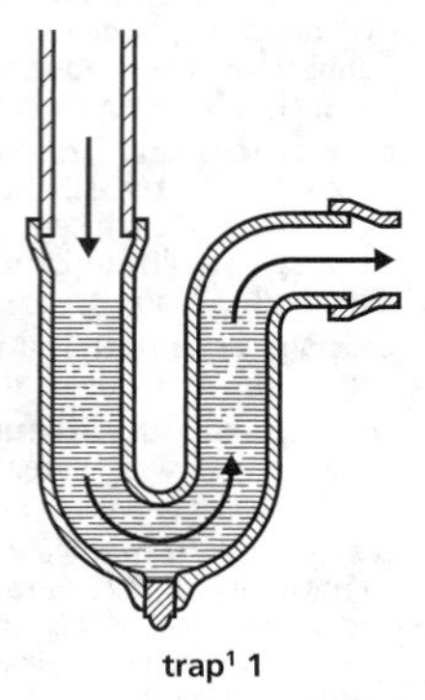
trap^{1} 1

2 a situation in which people lie in wait to make a surprise attack: *police deliberately herded 400 demonstrators into a trap and then attacked and arrested them.* ■ an unpleasant situation from which it is hard to escape: *they* ***fell into the trap*** *of relying too little on equity financing.* ■ a trick by which someone is misled into acting contrary to their interests or intentions: *by keeping quiet I was* ***walking into a trap.***
3 a device for hurling an object such as a clay pigeon into the air to be shot at. ■ (in the game of trapball) the shoe-shaped device that is hit with a bat to send the ball into the air.
4 chiefly historical a light, two-wheeled carriage pulled by a horse or pony.
5 short for TRAPDOOR.
6 informal a person's mouth (used in expressions to do with speaking): *keep your trap shut!*
7 (usu. **traps**) informal percussion instruments, typically in a jazz band.
8 Baseball & Football an act of trapping the ball.
▶ **v.** (**traps, trapping, trapped**) [with obj.] catch (an animal) in a trap. ■ prevent (someone) from escaping from a place: *twenty workers were trapped by flames.* ■ have (something, typically a part of the body) held tightly by something so that it cannot move or be freed: *he had trapped his finger in a spring-loaded hinge.* ■ induce (someone), by means of trickery or deception, to do something they would not otherwise want to do: *I hoped to* ***trap him into an admission.*** ■ Baseball & Football catch (the ball) after it has briefly touched the ground. ■ Soccer bring (the ball) under control with the feet or other part of the body on receiving it.
– DERIVATIVES **trap·like** /-ˌlīk/ **adj.**
– ORIGIN Old English *træppe* (in *coltetræppe* 'Christ's thorn'); related to Middle Dutch *trappe* and medieval Latin *trappa*, of uncertain origin. The verb dates from late Middle English.

trap^{2} ▶ **v.** (**traps, trapping, trapped**) [with obj.] (usu. as adj. **trapped**) archaic put trappings on (a horse, etc.): *gaily trapped mules.*
– ORIGIN late Middle English: from the obsolete noun *trap* 'trappings,' from Old French *drap* 'drape.'

trap^{3} (also **traprock**) ▶ **n.** basalt or a similar dark, fine-grained igneous rock.
– ORIGIN late 18th cent.: from Swedish *trapp*, from *trappa* 'stair' (because of the often stairlike appearance of its outcroppings).

trap·ball /ˈtrapˌbôl/ ▶ **n.** historical a game in which the player uses a bat to hit a trap (see TRAP^{1} (sense 2 of the noun)) to send a ball into the air and then hits the ball itself. ■ the ball used in this game.

trap crop ▶ **n.** a crop planted to attract insect pests from another crop, esp. one in which the pests fail to survive or reproduce.

trap·door /ˈtrapˌdôr/ (also **trap door**) ▶ **n.** a hinged or removable panel in a floor, ceiling, or roof. ■ a feature or defect of a computer system that allows surreptitious unauthorized access to data.

trapes ▶ **v. & n.** archaic spelling of TRAIPSE.

tra·peze /trəˈpēz, tra-/ ▶ **n. 1** (also **flying trapeze**) a horizontal bar hanging by two ropes (usually high in the air) and free to swing, used by acrobats in a circus.
2 Sailing a harness attached by a cable to a dinghy's mast, enabling a sailor to balance the boat by leaning backward out over the windward side.
– ORIGIN mid 19th cent.: from French *trapèze*, from late Latin *trapezium* (see TRAPEZIUM).

Tra·pe·zi·um /trəˈpēzēəm/ (**the Trapezium**) Astronomy the multiple star Theta Orionis, which lies within the Great Nebula of Orion and illuminates it. Four stars are visible in a small telescope and two more with a larger telescope.

tra·pe·zi·um /trəˈpēzēəm/ ▶ **n.** (pl. **trapezia** /-zēə/ or **trapeziums**) **1** Geometry a type of quadrilateral. ■ a quadrilateral with no sides parallel. Compare with TRAPEZOID. ■ Brit. a quadrilateral with one pair of sides parallel.

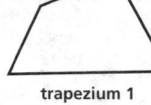

trapezium 1

2 (also **os trapezium**) Anatomy a bone in the wrist below the base of the thumb.
– ORIGIN late 16th cent.: via late Latin from Greek *trapezion*, from *trapeza* 'table.' The term has been used in anatomy since the mid 19th cent.

tra·pe·zi·us /trəˈpēzēəs/ (also **trapezius muscle**) ▶ **n.** (pl. **trapezii** /-zēˌī/ or **trapeziuses**) Anatomy either of a pair of large triangular muscles extending over the back of the neck and shoulders and moving the head and shoulder blade.
– ORIGIN early 18th cent.: from modern Latin, from Greek *trapezion* 'trapezium' (because of the shape formed by the muscles).

tra·pe·zo·he·dron /trəˌpēzōˈhēdrən, ˌtrapizō-/ ▶ **n.** (pl. **trapezohedra** /-drə/ or **trapezohedrons**) a solid figure whose faces are trapeziums or trapezoids.
– DERIVATIVES **tra·pe·zo·he·dral** /-drəl/ **adj.**
– ORIGIN early 19th cent.: from TRAPEZIUM + -HEDRON, on the pattern of words such as *polyhedron*.

trap·e·zoid /ˈtrapiˌzoid/ ▶ **n. 1** Geometry a type of quadrilateral. ■ N. Amer. a quadrilateral with only one pair of parallel sides. ■ Brit. a quadrilateral with no sides parallel. Compare with TRAPEZIUM.

trapezoid 1

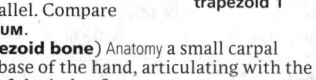

2 (also **trapezoid bone**) Anatomy a small carpal bone in the base of the hand, articulating with the metacarpal of the index finger.
– DERIVATIVES **trap·e·zoi·dal** /ˌtrapiˈzoidl/ **adj.**
– ORIGIN early 18th cent.: from modern Latin *trapezoides*, from late Greek *trapezoeidēs*, from *trapeza* 'table' (see TRAPEZIUM).

trap·line /ˈtrapˌlīn/ ▶ **n.** a series of traps for game.

trap·per /ˈtrapər/ ▶ **n.** a person who traps wild animals, esp. for their fur.

trap·pings /ˈtrapiNGz/ ▶ **plural n.** the outward signs, features, or objects associated with a particular situation, role, or thing: *I had the trappings of success.* ■ a horse's ornamental harness.
– ORIGIN late Middle English: derivative of TRAP^{2}.

Trap·pist /ˈtrapist/ ▶ **adj.** of, relating to, or denoting a branch of the Cistercian order of monks founded in 1664 and noted for an austere rule that includes remaining silent for much of the time.
▶ **n.** a member of this order.
– ORIGIN early 19th cent.: from French *trappiste*, from *La Trappe* in Normandy.

trap·rock /ˈtrapˌräk/ ▶ **n.** see TRAP^{3}.

traps /traps/ ▶ **plural n.** informal personal belongings; baggage: *I was ready to pack my traps and leave.*
– ORIGIN early 19th cent.: perhaps a contraction of TRAPPINGS.

trap·shoot·ing /ˈtrapˌSHo͞otiNG/ ▶ **n.** the sport of shooting at clay pigeons released from a spring trap.
– DERIVATIVES **trap·shoot·er** /-ˌSHo͞otər/ **n.**

trash /traSH/ ▶ **n.** discarded matter; refuse. ■ cultural items, ideas, or objects of poor quality: *if they read at all, they read trash.* ■ a person or people regarded as being of very low social standing: *she would have been considered trash.*
▶ **v.** [with obj.] **1** informal damage or wreck: *my apartment's been totally trashed.* ■ discard: *they trashed the tapes and sent her back into the studio.* ■ Computing kill (a file or process) or wipe (a disk): *she almost trashed the e-mail window.* ■ criticize severely: *trade associations trashed the legislation as deficient.* ■ (as adj. **trashed**) intoxicated with alcohol or drugs: *there was pot, there was booze, but nobody really got trashed.*
2 strip (sugar cane) of its outer leaves to ripen it faster.
– ORIGIN late Middle English: of unknown origin. The verb is first recorded (mid 18th cent.) in sense 2 of the verb; the other senses have arisen in the 20th cent.

trash can ▶ **n.** another term for GARBAGE CAN.

trash talk (also **trash talking**) informal ▶ **n.** insulting or boastful speech intended to demoralize, intimidate, or humiliate someone, esp. an opponent in an athletic contest: *he heard more trash talk from the Giants before the game than during the game | stop the trash talking and stop the violence.*
▶ **v.** [no obj.] (**trash-talk**) use insulting or boastful speech for such a purpose: *their players do not swear*

or tussle or trash-talk | (as adj. **trash-talking**) *the worst trash-talking team they had ever encountered.*
– DERIVATIVES **trash talk·er** (also **trash-talker**) **n.**

trash·y /'trasHē/ ▶ **adj.** (**trashier, trashiest**) (esp. of items of popular culture) of poor quality: *trashy novels and formulaic movies.*
– DERIVATIVES **trash·i·ly** /'trasHəlē/ **adv.**, **trash·i·ness n.**

trass /tras/ ▶ **n.** a light-colored variety of volcanic ash resembling pozzolana, used in making water-resistant cement.
– ORIGIN late 18th cent.: from Dutch *tras*, German *Trass*, based on Latin *terra* 'earth.'

trat·to·ri·a /,trätə'rēə/ ▶ **n.** an Italian restaurant serving simple food.
– ORIGIN Italian.

trau·ma /'troumə, 'trô-/ ▶ **n.** (pl. **traumas** or **traumata** /-mətə/) a deeply distressing or disturbing experience: *they were reluctant to talk about the traumas of the revolution.* ■ emotional shock following a stressful event or a physical injury, which may be associated with physical shock and sometimes leads to long-term neurosis. ■ Medicine physical injury.
– ORIGIN late 17th cent.: from Greek, literally 'wound.'

trau·mat·ic /trə'matik, trou-, trô-/ ▶ **adj.** emotionally disturbing or distressing: *she was going through a traumatic divorce.* ■ relating to or causing psychological trauma. ■ Medicine relating to or denoting physical injury.
– DERIVATIVES **trau·mat·i·cal·ly** /-ik(ə)lē/ **adv.**
– ORIGIN mid 19th cent.: via late Latin from Greek *traumatikos*, from *trauma* (see TRAUMA).

trau·ma·tism /'troumə,tizəm/ ▶ **n.** chiefly technical a traumatic effect or condition.

trau·ma·tize /'troumə,tīz, 'trô-/ ▶ **v.** [with obj.] subject to lasting shock as a result of an emotionally disturbing experience or physical injury: *the children were traumatized by separation from their families.* ■ Medicine cause physical injury to: *the dressings can be removed without traumatizing newly formed tissue.*
– DERIVATIVES **trau·ma·ti·za·tion** /,troumətiˈzāsHən, ,trô-/ **n.**

trav. ▶ **abbr.** ■ traveler. ■ travels.

tra·vail /trə'vāl, 'trav,āl/ literary ▶ **n.** (also **travails**) painful or laborious effort: *advice for those who wish to save great sorrow and travail.* ■ labor pains: *a woman in travail.*
▶ **v.** [no obj.] engage in painful or laborious effort. ■ (of a woman) be in labor.
– ORIGIN Middle English: via Old French from medieval Latin *trepalium* 'instrument of torture,' from Latin *tres* 'three' + *palus* 'stake.'

trav·el /'travəl/ ▶ **v.** (**travels, traveling, traveled**; also chiefly Brit. **travels, travelling, travelled**) **1** [no obj.] make a journey, typically of some length or abroad: *the vessel had been traveling from Libya to Ireland | we traveled thousands of miles.* ■ [with obj.] journey along (a road) or through (a region): *he traveled the world with the army.* ■ (usu. as adj. **traveling**) go or be moved from place to place: *a traveling exhibition.* ■ informal resist motion sickness, damage, or some other impairment on a journey: *he usually travels well.* ■ be enjoyed or successful away from the place of origin: *accordion music travels well.* ■ dated go from place to place as a sales representative: *he traveled for a shoe company through Mississippi.* ■ (of an object or radiation) move, typically in a constant or predictable way: *light travels faster than sound.* ■ informal (esp. of a vehicle) move quickly.
2 [no obj.] Basketball take more than the allowed number of steps (typically two) while holding the ball without dribbling it.
▶ **n.** the action of traveling, typically abroad: *I have a job that involves a lot of travel.* ■ (**travels**) journeys, esp. long or exotic ones: *perhaps you'll write a book about your travels.* ■ [as modifier] (of a device) designed so as to be sufficiently compact for use on a journey: *a travel iron.* ■ the range, rate, or mode of motion of a part of a machine.
– ORIGIN Middle English: variant of TRAVAIL and originally in the same sense.

trav·el a·gen·cy (also **travel bureau**) ▶ **n.** an agency that makes the necessary arrangements for travelers, esp. the booking of airline tickets and hotel rooms.
– DERIVATIVES **trav·el a·gent n.**

trav·el·a·tor /'travəlātər/ (also **travolator**) ▶ **n.** a moving walkway, typically at an airport.
– ORIGIN 1950s: from TRAVEL, suggested by ESCALATOR.

trav·el card ▶ **n.** a prepaid card allowing unlimited travel on buses or trains for a specified period of time: *a one-day travel card.*

trav·eled /'travəld/ ▶ **adj.** [with submodifier or in combination] **1** having traveled to many places: *he was widely traveled.*
2 used by people traveling: *a less well-traveled route.*

trav·el·er /'trav(ə)lər/ (Brit. **traveller**) ▶ **n.** a person who is traveling or who often travels.

trav·el·er's check ▶ **n.** a check for a fixed amount that can be cashed or used in payment after endorsement with the holder's signature.

trav·el·er's joy ▶ **n.** a tall scrambling clematis with small fragrant flowers and tufts of gray hairs around the seeds. Native to Eurasia and North Africa, it grows chiefly on calcareous soils. Also called OLD MAN'S BEARD. ● *Clematis vitalba*, family Ranunculaceae.

trav·el·er's tale ▶ **n.** a story about the unusual characteristics or customs of a foreign country, regarded as probably exaggerated or untrue.

trav·el·ing crane ▶ **n.** a crane able to move on rails, esp. along an overhead support.

trav·el·ing peo·ple ▶ **plural n.** people whose lifestyle is nomadic, for example gypsies (a term typically used by such people of themselves).

trav·el·ing sales·man ▶ **n.** a representative of a company who visits stores and other businesses to show samples and gain orders.

trav·el·ing sales·man prob·lem ▶ **n.** a mathematical problem in which one tries to find the shortest route that passes through each of a set of points once and only once.

trav·el·ing wave ▶ **n.** Physics a wave in which the medium moves in the direction of propagation.

trav·e·logue /'travə,lôg, -,läg/ ▶ **n.** a movie, book, or illustrated lecture about the places visited and experiences encountered by a traveler.
– ORIGIN early 20th cent.: from TRAVEL, on the pattern of *monologue*.

trav·ers /'travərs, trə'vərs/ (also **traverse**) ▶ **n.** a movement performed in dressage, in which the horse moves parallel to the side of the arena, with its shoulders carried closer to the wall than its hindquarters and its body curved toward the center.
– ORIGIN French, from *pied de travers* 'foot askew.'

trav·erse /trə'vərs/ ▶ **v.** [with obj.] **1** travel across or through: *he traversed the forest.* ■ extend across or through: *a moving catwalk that traversed a vast cavernous space.* ■ [no obj.] cross a hill or mountain by means of a series of sideways movements from one practicable line of ascent or descent to another: *I often use this route, eventually traversing around the cliff.* ■ ski diagonally across (a slope), with only a slight descent. ■ consider or discuss the whole extent of (a subject): *he would traverse a number of subjects and disciplines.*
2 move (something) back and forth or sideways: *a probe is traversed along the tunnel.* ■ turn (a large gun or other device on a pivot) to face a different direction.
3 Law deny (an allegation) in pleading. ■ archaic oppose or thwart (a plan).
▶ **n. 1** an act of traversing something. ■ a hill or mountain where traversing is necessary: *a narrow traverse made lethal by snow and ice.* ■ a movement following a diagonal course made by a skier descending a slope. ■ a zigzag course followed by a ship because winds or currents prevent it from sailing directly toward its destination.
2 a part of a structure that extends or is fixed across something. ■ a gallery extending from side to side of a church or other building.
3 a mechanism enabling a large gun to be turned to face a different direction. ■ the sideways movement of a part in a machine.
4 a single line of survey, usually plotted from compass bearings and chained or paced distances between angular points. ■ a tract surveyed in this way.
5 Military a pair of right-angled bends incorporated in a trench to avoid enfilading fire.
6 variant spelling of TRAVERS.
▶ **adj.** (of a curtain rod) allowing the curtain to be opened and closed by sliding it along the rod.
– DERIVATIVES **tra·vers·a·ble adj.**, **tra·vers·al** /-səl/ **n.**, **tra·vers·er n.**
– ORIGIN Middle English (sense 3 of the verb): from Old French *traverser*, from late Latin *traversare*; the noun is from Old French *travers* (masculine), *traverse* (feminine), partly based on *traverser*.

trav·er·tine /'travər,tēn, -tin/ ▶ **n.** white or light-colored calcareous rock deposited from mineral springs, used in building.
– ORIGIN late 18th cent.: from Italian *travertino*, *tivertino*, from Latin *tiburtinus* 'of Tibur' (now Tivoli, a district near Rome).

trav·es·ty /'travistē/ ▶ **n.** (pl. **travesties**) a false, absurd, or distorted representation of something: *the absurdly lenient sentence is* ***a travesty of*** *justice.*
▶ **v.** (**travesties, travestying, travestied**) [with obj.] represent in such a way: *Michael has betrayed the family by travestying them in his plays.*
– ORIGIN mid 17th cent. (as an adjective in the sense 'dressed to appear ridiculous'): from French *travesti* 'disguised,' past participle of *travestir*, from Italian *travestire*, from *trans-* 'across' + *vestire* 'clothe.'

tra·vois /trə'voi, 'trav,oi/ ▶ **n.** (pl. **same**) a type of sled formerly used by North American Indians to carry goods, consisting of two joined poles dragged by a horse or dog.
– ORIGIN mid 19th cent.: alteration of synonymous *travail*, from French.

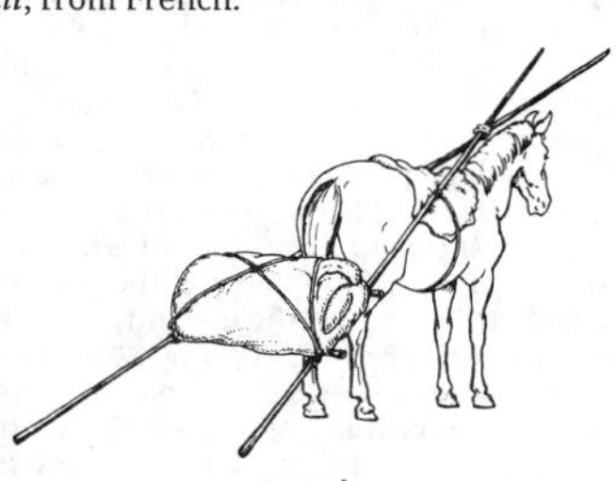
travois

trav·ol·a·tor ▶ **n.** variant spelling of TRAVELATOR.

trawl /trôl/ ▶ **v.** [no obj.] fish with a trawl net or seine: *the boats* ***trawled for*** *flounder* | (as noun **trawling**) *restrictions on excessive trawling were urgently needed.* ■ [with obj.] catch with a trawl net. ■ sift through as part of a search: *they* ***trawled through*** *twenty-five-year-old confidential files* | [with obj.] *he trawled his memory and remembered locking the door.* ■ [with obj.] drag or trail (something) through water or other liquid: *she trawled a toe to test the temperature.*
▶ **n. 1** an act of fishing with a trawl net: *they had caught two trout on the lazy trawl.* ■ an act of sifting through something as part of a search: *we did a trawl of supermarkets and health-food stores | a constant* ***trawl for*** *information.*
2 (also **trawl net**) a large wide-mouthed fishing net dragged by a vessel along the bottom or in the midwater of the sea or a lake.
3 (also **trawl line**) another term for LONGLINE.
– ORIGIN mid 16th cent. (as a verb): probably from Middle Dutch *traghelen* 'to drag' (related to *traghel* 'dragnet'), perhaps from Latin *tragula* 'dragnet.'

trawl·er /'trôlər/ ▶ **n.** a fishing boat used for trawling.

tray /trā/ ▶ **n.** a flat, shallow container with a raised rim, typically used for carrying food and drink, or for holding small items.
– DERIVATIVES **tray·ful** /-,fo͝ol/ **n.** (pl. **trayfuls**).
– ORIGIN late Old English *trīg*, from the Germanic base of TREE; the primary sense may have been 'wooden container.'

trayf /trāf/ (also **treyf** or **treyfa** /'trāfə/) ▶ **adj.** (of food) not satisfying the requirements of Jewish law: *I asked her if she ever ate food that was trayf.*
– ORIGIN mid 19th cent.: from Hebrew *ṭĕrēpāh* 'the flesh of an animal torn or mauled,' from *ṭārap* 'rend.'

treach·er·ous /'trecHərəs/ ▶ **adj.** guilty of or involving betrayal or deception: *a treacherous Gestapo agent | memory is particularly treacherous.* ■ (of ground, water, conditions, etc.) hazardous because of presenting hidden or unpredictable dangers: *a vacationer was swept away by treacherous currents.*
– DERIVATIVES **treach·er·ous·ly adv.**, **treach·er·ous·ness n.**
– ORIGIN Middle English (in the sense 'involving betrayal'): from Old French *trecherous*, from *trecheor* 'a cheat,' from *trechier* 'to cheat.'

treach·er·y /'trecHərē/ ▶ **n.** (pl. **treacheries**) betrayal of trust; deceptive action or nature: *his resignation was perceived as an act of treachery | the treachery of language.*
– ORIGIN Middle English: from Old French *trecherie*, from *trechier* 'to cheat.'

trea·cle /'trēkəl/ ▶ **n. 1** British term for MOLASSES.
2 cloying sentimentality or flattery: *enough of this treacle—let's get back to business.*
– DERIVATIVES **trea·cly** /'trēk(ə)lē/ **adj.**
– ORIGIN Middle English (originally denoting an antidote against venom): from Old French *triacle*, via Latin from Greek *thēriakē* 'antidote against venom,' feminine of *thēriakos* (adjective), from *thērion* 'wild beast.' The sense 'molasses' dates from the late 17th cent.; 'sentimentality' arose in the late 18th cent.

PRONUNCIATION KEY ə *ago, up*; ər *over, fur*; a *hat*; ā *ate*; ä *car*; e *let*; ē *see*; i *fit*; ī *by*; NG *sing*; ō *go*; ô *law, for*; oi *toy*; o͝o *good*; o͞o *goo*; ou *out*; TH *thin*; T͟H *then*; ZH *vision*

t

tread /tred/ ▶ **v.** (past **trod** /träd, träd/; past participle **trodden** /ˈträdn/ or **trod**) [no obj.] walk in a specified way: *he trod lightly, trying to make as little contact with the mud as possible* | figurative *the administration had to **tread carefully** so as not to offend the judiciary.* ■ (**tread on**) set one's foot down on top of. ■ [with obj.] walk on or along: *shoppers will soon be treading the floors of the new shopping mall.* ■ [with obj.] press down into the ground or another surface with the feet: *food and cigarette butts had been **trodden into** the carpet.* ■ [with obj.] crush or flatten something with the feet: *the snow had been **trodden down** by the horses* | (as adj. **trodden**) *she stood on the floor of trodden earth.*
▶ **n. 1** [in sing.] a manner or the sound of someone walking: *I heard the heavy tread of Dad's boots.*
2 the top surface of a step or stair.
3 the thick molded part of a vehicle tire that grips the road. ■ the part of a wheel that touches the ground or rail. ■ the upper surface of a railroad track, in contact with the wheels. ■ the part of the sole of a shoe that rests on the ground.
– PHRASES **tread the boards** (or **stage**) see BOARD. **tread on someone's toes** see STEP ON SOMEONE'S TOES at STEP. **tread water** (past **treaded**) maintain an upright position in deep water by moving the feet with a walking movement and the hands with a downward circular motion. ■ fail to advance or make progress: *men who are treading water in their careers.*
– DERIVATIVES **tread·er** n.
– ORIGIN Old English *tredan* (as a verb); related to Dutch *treden* and German *treten.*

trea·dle /ˈtredl/ ▶ **n.** a lever worked by the foot that imparts motion to a machine. ■ any of a row of metal spikes set on an angle on a spring within a plate laid across the entrance or exit of a parking facility, used to prevent drivers from using the facility without paying.
▶ **v.** [with obj.] operate (a machine) using a treadle.
– ORIGIN Old English *tredel* 'stair, step' (see TREAD).

tread·mill /ˈtredˌmil/ ▶ **n.** a device formerly used for driving machinery, consisting of a large wheel with steps fitted into its inner surface. It was turned by the weight of people or animals treading the steps. ■ an exercise machine, typically with a continuous belt, that allows one to walk or run in place. ■ a job or situation that is tiring, boring, or unpleasant and from which it is hard to escape: *the soulless treadmill of urban existence.*

treas. ▶ **abbr.** ■ treasurer. ■ (also **Treas.**) Treasury.

trea·son /ˈtrēzən/ ▶ **n.** (also **high treason**) the crime of betraying one's country, esp. by attempting to kill the sovereign or overthrow the government: *they were convicted of treason.* ■ the action of betraying someone or something: *doubt is the ultimate treason against faith.* ■ (**petty treason**) historical the crime of murdering someone to whom the murderer owed allegiance, such as a master or husband.
– DERIVATIVES **trea·son·ous** /ˈtrēzənəs/ **adj.**
– ORIGIN Middle English: from Anglo-Norman French *treisoun*, from Latin *traditio(n-)* 'handing over,' from the verb *tradere.*

> **USAGE** Formerly, there were two types of crime to which the term **treason** was applied: **petty treason** (the crime of murdering one's master) and **high treason** (the crime of betraying one's country). As a classification of offense, the crime of **petty treason** was abolished in 1828. In modern use, the term **high treason** is now often simply called **treason.**

t

trea·son·a·ble /ˈtrēzənəbəl/ ▶ **adj.** (of an offense or offender) punishable as treason or as committing treason: *there was no evidence of treasonable activity.*
– DERIVATIVES **trea·son·a·bly** /-blē/ **adv.**

treas·ure /ˈtreZHər/ ▶ **n.** a quantity of precious metals, gems, or other valuable objects. ■ a very valuable object: *she set out to look at the art treasures.* ■ informal a person whom the speaker loves or who is valued for the assistance they can give: *the housekeeper is a real treasure—I don't know what he would do without her.*
▶ **v.** [with obj.] keep carefully (a valuable or valued item). ■ value highly: *the island is treasured by walkers and conservationists* | (as adj. **treasured**) *his library was his most treasured possession.*
– ORIGIN Middle English: from Old French *tresor*, based on Greek *thēsauros* (see THESAURUS).

treas·ure hunt ▶ **n.** a search for treasure. ■ a game in which players search for hidden objects by following a trail of clues.

treas·ur·er /ˈtreZHərər/ ▶ **n.** a person appointed to administer or manage the financial assets and liabilities of a society, company, local authority, or other body.
– DERIVATIVES **treas·ur·er·ship** /-ˌSHip/ **n.**
– ORIGIN Middle English: from Old French *tresorier*, from *tresor* (see TREASURE), influenced by late Latin *thesaurarius.*

Treas·ure State a nickname for the state of MONTANA[1].

treas·ure trove ▶ **n.** valuables of unknown ownership that are found hidden, in some cases declared the property of the finder. ■ a hidden store of valuable or delightful things: *your book is a treasure trove of unspeakable delights.*
– ORIGIN late Middle English: from Anglo-Norman French *tresor trové*, literally 'found treasure.'

treas·ur·y /ˈtreZHərē/ ▶ **n.** (pl. **treasuries**) **1** the funds or revenue of a government, corporation, or institution: *the country's pledge not to spend more than it has in its treasury.* ■ (**Treasury**) (in some countries) the government department responsible for budgeting for and controlling public expenditure, management of the national debt, and the overall management of the economy.
2 a place or building where treasure is stored. ■ a store or collection of valuable or delightful things: *the old town is a treasury of ancient monuments.*
– ORIGIN Middle English: from Old French *tresorie* (see TREASURE).

Treas·ur·y bill ▶ **n.** a short-dated government security, yielding no interest but issued at a discount on its redemption price.

Treas·ur·y bond ▶ **n.** a government bond issued by the US Treasury.

Treas·ur·y note ▶ **n.** a note issued by the US Treasury for use as currency.

treat /trēt/ ▶ **v.** [with obj.] **1** behave toward or deal with in a certain way: *she had been brutally treated* | *he **treated** her **with** grave courtesy.* ■ (**treat something as**) regard something as being of a specified nature with implications for one's actions concerning it: *the names are being treated as classified information.* ■ give medical care or attention to; try to heal or cure: *the two were **treated for** cuts and bruises.* ■ apply a process or a substance to (something) to protect or preserve it or to give it particular properties: *linen creases badly unless it is **treated with** the appropriate finish.* ■ present or discuss (a subject): *the lectures show a striking variation in the level at which subjects are treated.*
2 (**treat someone to**) provide someone with (food, drink, or entertainment) at one's own expense: *the old man had treated him to a drink or two.* ■ give someone (something) as a favor: *he treated her to one of his smiles.* ■ (**treat oneself**) do or have something that gives one great pleasure: *treat yourself—you can diet tomorrow.*
3 [no obj.] negotiate terms with someone, esp. an opponent: *propagandists claimed that he was **treating with** the enemy.*
▶ **n.** an event or item that is out of the ordinary and gives great pleasure: *he wanted to take her to the movies as a treat.* ■ used with a possessive adjective to indicate that the person specified is paying for food, entertainment, etc., for someone else: *"My treat," he insisted, reaching for the bill.*
– PHRASES **—— a treat** Brit. informal used to indicate that someone or something does something specified very well or satisfactorily: *their tactics worked a treat.* ■ used to indicate that someone is looking attractive: *I don't know whether she can act, but she **looks a treat**.*
– DERIVATIVES **treat·a·ble adj.**, **treat·er n.**
– ORIGIN Middle English (in the senses 'negotiate' and 'discuss (a subject)'): from Old French *traitier*, from Latin *tractare* 'handle,' frequentative of *trahere* 'draw, pull.' The current noun sense dates from the mid 17th cent.

trea·tise /ˈtrētis/ ▶ **n.** a written work dealing formally and systematically with a subject: *a comprehensive **treatise on** electricity and magnetism.*
– ORIGIN late Middle English: from Anglo-Norman French *tretis*, from Old French *traitier* (see TREAT).

treat·ment /ˈtrētmənt/ ▶ **n.** the manner in which someone behaves toward or deals with someone or something: *the directive required equal treatment for men and women.* ■ medical care given to a patient for an illness or injury: *I'm receiving **treatment for** an injured shoulder.* ■ a session of medical care or the administration of a dose of medicine: *the patient was given repeated treatments as required.* ■ the use of a chemical, physical, or biological agent to preserve or give particular properties to something: *the treatment of hazardous waste is particularly expensive.* ■ the presentation or discussion of a subject: *analysis of the treatment of women in her painting.* ■ (**the full treatment**) informal used to indicate that something is done enthusiastically, vigorously, or to an extreme degree: *I gave them the full treatment, and they were just falling over themselves.*

trea·ty /ˈtrētē/ ▶ **n.** (pl. **treaties**) a formally concluded and ratified agreement between countries.
– ORIGIN late Middle English: from Old French *traite*, from Latin *tractatus* 'treatise' (see TRACTATE).

trea·ty port ▶ **n.** historical a port bound by treaty to be open to foreign trade, esp. in 19th- and early-20th-century China and Japan.

Treb·bia·no /trebˈyänō/ ▶ **n.** a variety of wine grape widely cultivated in Italy and elsewhere. ■ a wine made from this grape.
– ORIGIN Italian, from the name of the *Trebbia* River, in northern central Italy.

Treb·i·zond /ˈtrebiˌzänd/ another name for TRABZON.

tre·ble[1] /ˈtrebəl/ ▶ **adj.** [attrib.] consisting of three parts; threefold: *the fish were caught with large treble hooks dragged through the water.* ■ multiplied or occurring three times: *she turned back to make a double and treble check.*
▶ **predeterminer** three times as much or as many: *the tip was at least treble what she would normally have given.*
▶ **n.** a threefold quantity or thing, in particular: ■ (in show jumping) a fence consisting of three elements. ■ a crochet stitch made with three loops of wool on the hook at a time. ■ a drink of liquor of three times the standard measure.
▶ **pron.** a number or amount that is three times as large as a contrasting or usual number or amount: *by virtue of having paid treble, he had a double room to himself.*
▶ **v.** make or become three times as large or numerous: [with obj.] *rents were doubled and probably trebled* | [no obj.] *his salary has trebled in a couple of years.*
– ORIGIN Middle English: via Old French from Latin *triplus* (see TRIPLE).

tre·ble[2] ▶ **n.** a high-pitched voice, esp. a boy's singing voice. ■ a boy or girl with such a singing voice. ■ a part written for a high voice or an instrument of a high pitch. ■ [as modifier] denoting a relatively high-pitched member of a family of similar instruments: *a treble viol.* ■ (also **treble bell**) the smallest and highest-pitched bell of a set. ■ the high-frequency output of an audio system or radio, corresponding to the treble in music.
– ORIGIN late Middle English: from TREBLE[1], because it was the highest part in a three-part contrapuntal composition.

tre·ble clef ▶ **n.** a clef placing G above middle C on the second-lowest line of the staff.

Tre·blin·ka /trəˈbliNGkə, tre-/ a Nazi concentration camp in Poland during World War II, where a great many of the Jews of the Warsaw ghetto were murdered.

tre·bly /ˈtreblē/ ▶ **adj.** (of sound, esp. recorded music) having much or excessive treble.
▶ **adv.** [as submodifier] three times as much: *to Katherine, the house was trebly impressive.*

treb·u·chet /ˌtrebyəˈSHet/ ▶ **n.** a machine used in medieval siege warfare for hurling large stones or other missiles.
– ORIGIN Middle English: from Old French, from *trebucher* 'overthrow.'

tre·cen·to /trāˈCHentō/ ▶ **n.** (**the trecento**) the 14th century as a period of Italian art, architecture, or literature.
– ORIGIN Italian, literally '300,' shortened from *milletrecento* '1300,' used with reference to the years 1300–99.

tree /trē/ ▶ **n. 1** a woody perennial plant, typically having a single stem or trunk growing to a considerable height and bearing lateral branches at some distance from the ground. Compare with SHRUB[1]. ■ (in general use) any bush, shrub, or herbaceous plant with a tall erect stem, e.g., a banana plant.
2 a wooden structure or part of a structure. ■ archaic or literary the cross on which Jesus Christ was crucified. ■ archaic a gallows or gibbet.
3 a thing that has a branching structure resembling that of a tree. ■ (also **tree diagram**) a diagram with a structure of branching connecting lines, representing different processes and relationships.
▶ **v.** (**trees, treeing, treed**) [with obj.] **1** force (a hunted animal) to take refuge in a tree. ■ informal force (someone) into a difficult situation.
2 (as adj. **treed**) (of an area) planted with trees: *sparsely treed grasslands.*
– PHRASES **out of one's tree** informal completely stupid; insane. **up a tree** informal in a difficult situation without escape; cornered.
– DERIVATIVES **tree·less adj.**, **tree·less·ness n.**, **tree·like** /-ˌlīk/ **adj.**
– ORIGIN Old English *trēow, trēo*: from a Germanic variant of an Indo-European root shared by Greek *doru* 'wood, spear,' *drus* 'oak.'

white ash
(Fraxinus americana)

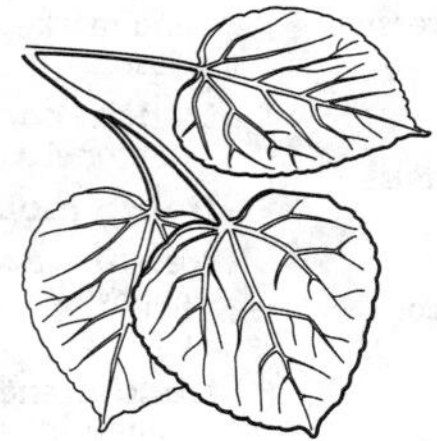
quaking aspen
(Populus tremuloides)

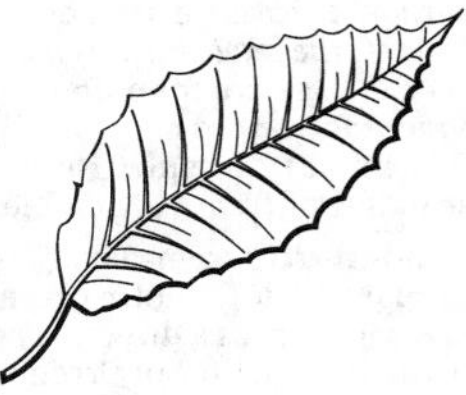
American beech
(Fagus grandifolia)

paper birch
(Betula papyrifera)

Eastern cottonwood
(Populus deltoides)

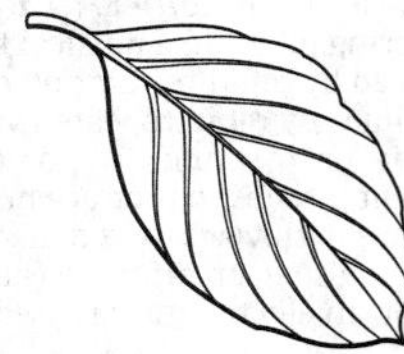
flowering dogwood
(Cornus florida)

American holly
(Ilex opaca)

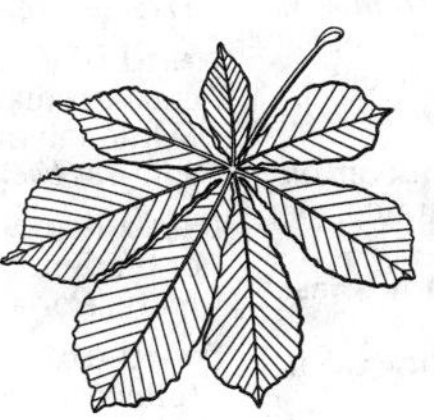
horse chestnut
(Aesculus hippocastanum)

black locust
(Robinia pseudoacacia)

silver maple
(Acer saccharinum)

sugar maple
(Acer saccharum)

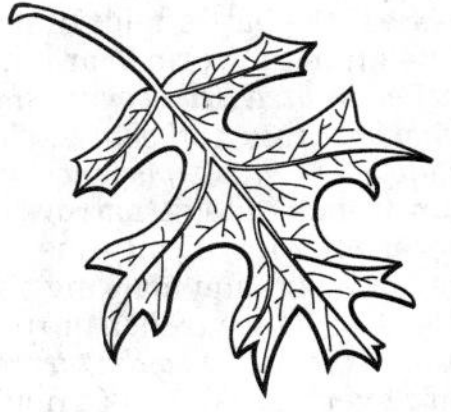
pin oak
(Quercus palustris)

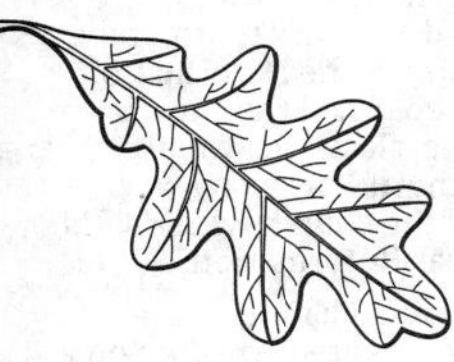
white oak
(Quercus alba)

tulip tree (yellow poplar)
(Liriodendron tulipifera)

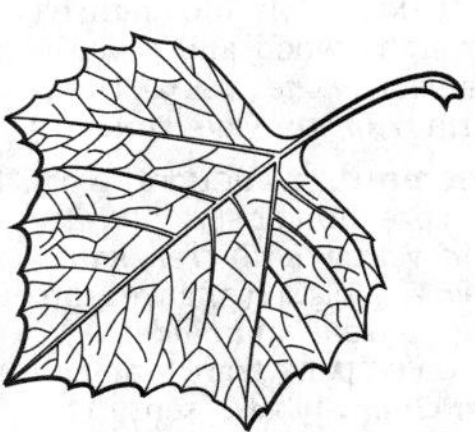
sycamore
(Platanus occidentalis)

leaves of familiar trees of North America

tree calf ▶ **n.** calfskin stained with a treelike design and used in bookbinding.

tree·creep·er /ˈtrēˌkrēpər/ ▶ **n.** a small songbird with drab plumage and a down-curved bill that creeps around on the trunks of trees to search for insects. Compare with **CREEPER** (sense 2). ● a Eurasian and North American bird (*Certhia*, family Certhiidae, in particular the common *C. familiaris*). ● an Australasian bird (family Climacteridae and genus *Climacteris*).

tree di·a·gram ▶ **n.** see **TREE** (sense 3 of the noun).

tree duck ▶ **n.** another term for **WHISTLING DUCK**.

tree fern ▶ **n.** a large palmlike fern with a trunklike stem bearing a crown of large fronds, sometimes reaching a height of 24 m and occurring chiefly in the tropics, particularly the southern hemisphere. ● Cyatheaceae and related families, class Filicopsida: seven genera, in particular *Cyathea* and *Dicksonia*.

tree frog ▶ **n.** an arboreal frog that has long toes with adhesive disks and is typically small and brightly colored. ● Families Hylidae (of Eurasia, America, and Australia) and Rhacophoridae (of Africa and Asia): numerous species, including the common **green tree frog** (*Hyla arborea*) of southern Europe.

tree·hop·per /ˈtrēˌhäpər/ ▶ **n.** a tree-dwelling jumping bug that lives chiefly in the tropics. A tall backward-curving projection of the thorax gives the bug a thornlike appearance for camouflage. ● Family Membracidae, suborder Homoptera: species, including the bright green **buffalo treehopper** (*Stictocephalus bisonia*) of North America.

tree house (also **treehouse**) ▶ **n.** a structure built in the branches of a tree for children to play in.

tree-hug·ger ▶ **n.** informal, chiefly derogatory an environmental campaigner (used in reference to the practice of embracing a tree in an attempt to prevent it from being felled).
– DERIVATIVES **tree-hug·ging n.**

tree kan·ga·roo ▶ **n.** an agile tree-climbing kangaroo with a long furred tail, and fore- and hind limbs that are of almost equal length, found in the rain forests of Australia and New Guinea. ● Genus *Dendrolagus*, family Macropodidae: six species.

tree line ▶ **n.** another term for **TIMBERLINE**.

treen /trēn/ ▶ **n.** (also **treenware** /-ˌwe(ə)r/) [treated as pl.] small domestic wooden objects, esp. antiques. ▶ **adj.** chiefly archaic wooden.
– ORIGIN Old English *trēowen* 'wooden' (see **TREE**, **-EN**[2]).

tree·nail /ˈtrēˌnāl, ˈtrenl/ ▶ **n.** a trunnel.

tree of heav·en ▶ **n.** a fast-growing Chinese ailanthus that is widely cultivated as an ornamental. ● *Ailanthus altissima*, family Simaroubaceae.

tree of know·ledge (also **tree of the knowledge of good and evil**) ▶ **n.** (in the Bible) the tree in the Garden of Eden bearing the forbidden fruit that Adam and Eve disobediently ate (Gen. 2:9, 3).

tree of life ▶ **n. 1** (**Tree of Life**) (in the Bible) a tree in the Garden of Eden whose fruit imparts eternal life (Gen. 3:22–24). ■ an imaginary branching, treelike structure representing the evolutionary divergence of all living creatures. ■ (in cabalism) a diagram in the form of a tree bearing spheres that represent the sephiroth.
2 the thuja or arbor vitae.

tree pip·it ▶ **n.** a widespread Old World pipit that inhabits open country with scattered trees. ● *Anthus trivialis*, family Motacillidae.

Tree Plant·ers' State a nickname for the state of **NEBRASKA**.

tree ring ▶ **n.** each of a number of concentric rings in the cross section of a tree trunk, representing a single year's growth.

tree shrew ▶ **n.** a small squirrellike insectivorous mammal with a pointed snout, native to Southeast Asia, esp. Borneo. ● Family Tupaiidae and order Scandentia: several genera, in particular *Tupaia*; tree shrews were formerly placed with either the insectivores or the primates.

tree snake ▶ **n.** a harmless arboreal snake, typically very slender and able to mimic a twig. ● Several genera in the family Colubridae, e.g., *Dendrelaphis* and *Ahaetulla* (of Asia), and *Leptophis* and *Oxybelis* (of America).

tree spar·row ▶ **n. 1** a Eurasian sparrow with a chocolate-brown cap in both sexes, inhabiting agricultural land. ● *Passer montanus*, family Passeridae (or Ploceidae).
2 a migratory sparrowlike songbird of the bunting family, breeding on the edge of the North American tundra. ● *Spizella arborea*, family Emberizidae (subfamily Emberizidae).

tree squir·rel ▶ **n.** an arboreal squirrel that is typically active in daylight and does not hibernate. ● *Sciurus* and other genera, family Sciuridae: numerous species.

tree struc·ture ▶ **n.** Computing a structure that has successive branchings or subdivisions.

tree sur·geon ▶ **n.** a person who prunes and treats old or damaged trees in order to preserve them.
– DERIVATIVES **tree sur·ger·y n.**

tree swal·low ▶ **n.** a North American swallow that nests in trees. ● *Tachycineta bicolor*.

tree toad ▶ **n.** another term for **TREE FROG**.

tree to·ma·to ▶ **n.** another term for **TAMARILLO**.

tree·top /ˈtrēˌtäp/ ▶ **n.** (usu. **treetops**) the uppermost part of a tree.

tre·foil /ˈtrēˌfoil, ˈtrefˌoil/ ▶ **n.** a small European plant of the pea family with yellow flowers and three-lobed cloverlike leaves. ● Genera *Trifolium* and *Lotus*, family Leguminosae: several species, in particular the **bird's-foot trefoil**. ■ a similar or related plant with three-lobed leaves. ■ an ornamental design of three rounded lobes like a clover leaf, used typically in architectural tracery. ■ a thing having three parts; a set of three: *a trefoil of parachutes lowers the shuttle's used rockets to Earth.* ■ [as modifier] denoting something shaped in the form of a trefoil leaf: *trefoil windows*.

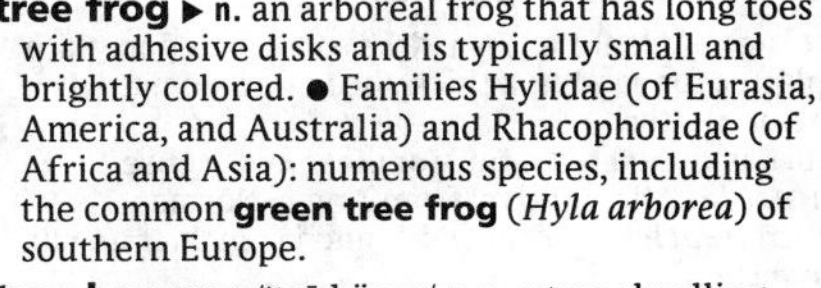
trefoil design

PRONUNCIATION KEY ə *ago, up*; ər *over, fur*; a *hat*; ā *ate*; ä *car*; e *let*; ē *see*; i *fit*; ī *by*; NG *sing*; ō *go*; ô *law, for*; oi *toy*; o͝o *good*; o͞o *goo*; ou *out*; TH *thin*; T͟H *then*; ZH *vision*

t

– DERIVATIVES **tre·foiled** adj.
– ORIGIN Middle English: from Anglo-Norman French *trifoil*, from Latin *trifolium*, from *tri-* 'three' + *folium* 'leaf.'

tre·ha·lose /trəˈhäˌlōs/ ▶ **n.** Chemistry a sugar of the disaccharide class produced by some fungi, yeasts, and similar organisms.
– ORIGIN mid 19th cent.: from *trehala* (from Turkish, denoting a sweet substance derived from insect cocoons) + -OSE[2].

trek /trek/ ▶ **n.** a long arduous journey, esp. one made on foot: *a trek to the South Pole.* ■ a tourist hike.
▶ **v.** (**treks, trekking, trekked**) [no obj.] go on a long arduous journey, typically on foot: *we trekked through the jungle.* ■ chiefly S. African historical migrate or journey with one's belongings by ox-wagon. ■ S. African (of an ox) draw a vehicle or pull a load. ■ S. African travel constantly from place to place; lead a nomadic life: *my plan is to trek about seeing the world.*
– DERIVATIVES **trek·ker** n.
– ORIGIN mid 19th cent.: from South African Dutch *trek* (noun), *trekken* (verb) 'pull, travel.'

Trek·kie /ˈtrekē/ ▶ **n.** (pl. **Trekkies**) informal a fan of the US science-fiction television program *Star Trek*.

trel·lis /ˈtrelis/ ▶ **n.** a framework of light wooden or metal bars, chiefly used as a support for fruit trees or climbing plants.
▶ **v.** (**trelliss, trellising, trellised**) [with obj.] (usu. as adj. **trellised**) provide with or enclose in a trellis: *a trellised archway.* ■ support (a climbing plant) with a trellis.
– ORIGIN late Middle English (denoting any latticed screen): from Old French *trelis*, from Latin *trilix* 'three-ply,' from *tri-* 'three' + *licium* 'warp thread.' Current senses date from the early 16th cent.

trellis

trem /trem/ (also **trem arm**) ▶ **n.** informal a tremolo arm.

Trem·a·to·da /ˌtreməˈtōdə, ˌtrē-/ Zoology a class of flatworms that comprises those flukes that are internal parasites. The monogenean flukes are sometimes also placed in this class. See FLUKE[2] (sense 1) and DIGENEAN.
– ORIGIN modern Latin (plural), from Greek *trēmatōdēs* 'perforated,' from *trēma* 'hole.'

trem·a·tode /ˈtreməˌtōd, ˈtrē-/ ▶ **n.** any parasitic flatworm of the class Trematoda, esp. a fluke, having hookers or suckers.

trem·ble /ˈtrembəl/ ▶ **v.** [no obj.] shake involuntarily, typically as a result of anxiety, excitement, or frailty: *Isobel was trembling with excitement.* ■ be in a state of extreme apprehension: [with infinitive] *I **tremble to think** that we could ever return to conditions like these.* ■ (usu. as adj. **trembling**) (of a person's voice) sound unsteady or hesitant. ■ shake or quiver slightly: *the earth trembled beneath their feet.*
▶ **n. 1** a trembling feeling, movement, or sound: *there was a slight tremble in his voice.*
2 (**the trembles**) informal a physical or emotional condition marked by trembling. ■ another term for MILK SICKNESS.
– DERIVATIVES **trem·bling·ly** /-b(ə)liNGlē/ **adv.**
– ORIGIN Middle English (as a verb): from Old French *trembler*, from medieval Latin *tremulare*, from Latin *tremulus* (see TREMULOUS).

trem·bler /ˈtremb(ə)lər/ ▶ **n. 1** informal an earthquake.
2 a songbird related to the thrashers, found in the Lesser Antilles and named from its habit of violent shaking. ● Genera *Cinclocerthia* and *Ramphocinclus*, family Mimidae: three species.

trem·blor /ˈtremblər, -ˌblôr/ ▶ **n.** an earth tremor.
– ORIGIN early 20th cent.: alteration of Spanish *temblor* 'shudder,' influenced by TREMBLER.

trem·bly /ˈtremb(ə)lē/ ▶ **adj.** (**tremblier, trembliest**) informal shaking or quivering involuntarily: *her eyes were tearful, her hands trembly | she gave a queer trembly laugh.*

tre·men·dous /trəˈmendəs/ ▶ **adj.** very great in amount, scale, or intensity: *Penny put in a tremendous amount of time | there was a tremendous explosion.* ■ informal extremely good or impressive; excellent: *the crew did a tremendous job.*
– DERIVATIVES **tre·men·dous·ly** adv., **tre·men·dous·ness** n.
– ORIGIN mid 17th cent.: from Latin *tremendus* (gerundive of *tremere* 'tremble') + -OUS.

trem·o·lan·do /ˌtreməˈländō/ Music ▶ **n.** (pl. **tremolandi** /-dē/) another term for TREMOLO.
▶ **adv. & adj.** (esp. as a direction) with tremolo.
– ORIGIN Italian, literally 'trembling.'

trem·o·lite /ˈtreməˌlīt/ ▶ **n.** a white to gray amphibole mineral that is characteristic of metamorphosed dolomitic limestones.
– ORIGIN late 18th cent.: from *Tremola* Valley, Switzerland, + -ITE[1].

trem·o·lo /ˈtreməˌlō/ ▶ **n.** (pl. **tremolos**) Music a wavering effect in a musical tone, typically produced by rapid reiteration of a note, or sometimes by rapid repeated variation in the pitch of a note or by sounding two notes of slightly different pitches to produce prominent overtones. Compare with VIBRATO. ■ a mechanism in an organ producing such an effect. ■ (also **tremolo arm**) a lever on an electric guitar, used to produce such an effect.
– ORIGIN mid 18th cent.: from Italian.

trem·or /ˈtremər/ ▶ **n.** an involuntary quivering movement: *a disorder that causes tremors and muscle rigidity.* ■ (also **earth tremor**) a slight earthquake. ■ a sudden feeling of fear or excitement: *a tremor of unease.* ■ a tremble or quaver in a person's voice.
– ORIGIN early 17th cent.: from Latin *tremor*, from *tremere* 'to tremble.'

trem·u·lous /ˈtremyələs/ ▶ **adj.** shaking or quivering slightly: *Barbara's voice was tremulous.* ■ timid; nervous: *he gave a tremulous smile.*
– DERIVATIVES **trem·u·lous·ly** adv., **trem·u·lous·ness** n.
– ORIGIN early 17th cent.: from Latin *tremulus* (from *tremere* 'tremble') + -OUS.

tre·nail ▶ **n.** British term for TREENAIL.

trench /trenCH/ ▶ **n.** a long, narrow ditch. ■ such a ditch dug by troops to provide a place of shelter from enemy fire. ■ (**trenches**) a connected system of such ditches forming an army's line. ■ (**the trenches**) the battlefields of northern France and Belgium in World War I: *the slaughter in the trenches created a new cynicism* | figurative *entry-level teachers are taught the latest classroom techniques by colleagues with experience **in the trenches**.* ■ (also **ocean trench**) a long, narrow, deep depression in the ocean floor, typically one running parallel to a plate boundary and marking a subduction zone.
▶ **v. 1** [with obj.] dig a trench or trenches in (the ground): *she trenched the terrace to a depth of 6 feet.* ■ turn over the earth of (a field or garden) by digging a succession of adjoining ditches.
2 [no obj.] (**trench on/upon**) archaic border closely on; encroach upon: *this would surely trench very far on the dignity and liberty of citizens.*
– ORIGIN late Middle English (in the senses 'track cut through a wood' and 'sever by cutting'): from Old French *trenche* (noun), *trenchier* (verb), based on Latin *truncare* (see TRUNCATE).

trench·ant /ˈtrenCHənt/ ▶ **adj. 1** vigorous or incisive in expression or style: *she heard angry voices, not loud, yet certainly trenchant.*
2 archaic or literary (of a weapon or tool) having a sharp edge: *a trenchant blade.*
– DERIVATIVES **trench·an·cy** /-CHənsē/ **n.** (sense 1), **trench·ant·ly** **adv.** (sense 1).
– ORIGIN Middle English (sense 2): from Old French, literally 'cutting,' present participle of *trenchier* (see TRENCH).

trench coat ▶ **n.** a loose, belted, double-breasted raincoat in a military style. ■ a lined or padded waterproof coat worn by soldiers.

trench·er[1] /ˈtrenCHər/ ▶ **n. 1** historical a wooden plate or platter for food. ■ a thick slice of bread used as a plate or platter.
2 old-fashioned term for MORTARBOARD (sense 1).
– ORIGIN Middle English: from Anglo-Norman French *trenchour*, from Old French *trenchier* 'to cut' (see TRENCH).

trench·er[2] ▶ **n.** a machine or attachment used in digging trenches.

trench·er·man /ˈtrenCHərmən/ ▶ **n.** (pl. **trenchermen**) [usu. with adj.] humorous a person who eats in a specified manner, typically heartily: *he is a hearty trencherman, as befits a man of his girth.*

trench fe·ver ▶ **n.** a highly contagious rickettsial disease transmitted by lice, that infected soldiers in the trenches in World War I.

trench foot ▶ **n.** a painful condition of the feet caused by long immersion in cold water or mud and marked by blackening and death of surface tissue.

trench mor·tar ▶ **n.** a light simple mortar designed to propel a bomb into enemy trenches.

trench mouth ▶ **n.** ulcerative gingivitis.

trench war·fare ▶ **n.** a type of combat in which opposing troops fight from trenches facing each other.

trend /trend/ ▶ **n.** a general direction in which something is developing or changing: *an upward trend in sales and profit margins.* ■ a fashion: *the latest trends in modern dance.*
▶ **v.** [no obj.] (esp. of geographical features) bend or turn away in a specified direction: *the Richelieu River trending northward from Lake Champlain.* ■ change or develop in a general direction: *unemployment has been trending upward.*
– ORIGIN Old English *trendan* 'revolve, rotate,' of Germanic origin; compare with TRUNDLE. The verb sense 'turn in a specified direction' dates from the late 16th cent. and gave rise to the figurative use 'assume a general tendency' in the mid 19th cent., a development paralleled in the noun.

Tren·de·len·burg po·si·tion /trenˈdelənˌbərg/ ▶ **n.** a position, used for pelvic surgery and to treat shock, in which a patient lies face upward on a tilted table or bed with the pelvis higher than the head.
– ORIGIN late 19th cent.: named after Friedrich *Trendelenburg* (1844–1924), German surgeon.

trend·i·fy /ˈtrendəˌfī/ ▶ **v.** [with obj.] informal, chiefly derogatory make (something or someone) very fashionable or up to date in style or influence: *the cafe has been trendified to look like a wine bar.*

trend line ▶ **n.** a line indicating the general course or tendency of something, e.g., a geographical feature or a set of points on a graph.

trend·oid /ˈtrendoid/ informal ▶ **n.** a person who follows fashion blindly or excessively.
▶ **adj.** following fashion blindly or extravagantly.

trend·set·ter /ˈtren(d)ˌsetər/ ▶ **n.** a person who leads the way in fashion or ideas.
– DERIVATIVES **trend·set·ting** /-ˌsetiNG/ **adj.**

trend·y /ˈtrendē/ informal ▶ **adj.** (**trendier, trendiest**) very fashionable or up to date in style or influence: *I enjoyed being able to go out and buy trendy clothes.*
▶ **n.** (pl. **trendies**) a person who is very fashionable or up to date.
– DERIVATIVES **trend·i·ly** /-dəlē/ **adv.**, **trend·i·ness** **n.**

Treng·ga·nu /trenGˈgänoo/ (also **Terengganu** /ˌtereNG-/) a state of Malaysia, on the eastern coast of the Malay Peninsula; capital, Kuala Trengganu.

Trent /trent/ the chief river in central England. It rises in Staffordshire and flows northeast for 170 miles (275 km) to join the Ouse River 15 miles (25 km) west of Hull to form the Humber estuary.

Trent, Coun·cil of an ecumenical council of the Roman Catholic Church, held in three sessions between 1545 and 1563 in Trento, Italy. Prompted by the opposition of the Reformation, the council clarified and redefined the church's doctrine, abolished many ecclesiastical abuses, and strengthened the authority of the papacy. These measures provided the church with a solid foundation for the Counter-Reformation.

trente et qua·rante /ˈtränt ā kaˈränt/ ▶ **n.** a gambling game in which cards are turned up on a table marked with red and black diamonds.
– ORIGIN French, literally 'thirty and forty,' these being winning and losing numbers respectively in the game.

Tren·to /ˈtrentō/ a city in northern Italy, on the Adige River; pop. 114,236 (2008).

Tren·ton /ˈtrentn/ the capital of New Jersey, in the west central part of the state; pop. 82,883 (est. 2008).

tre·pan /trəˈpan/ ▶ **n.** chiefly historical a trephine (hole saw) used by surgeons for perforating the skull.
▶ **v.** (**trepans, trepanning, trepanned**) [with obj.] perforate (a person's skull) with a trepan.
– DERIVATIVES **trep·a·na·tion** /ˌtrepəˈnāSHən/ **n.**
– ORIGIN late Middle English: the noun via medieval Latin from Greek *trupanon*, from *trupan* 'to bore,' from *trupē* 'hole'; the verb from Old French *trepaner*.

tre·pang /trəˈpaNG/ ▶ **n.** another term for BÊCHE-DE-MER (sense 1).
– ORIGIN late 18th cent.: from Malay *teripang*.

tre·phine /triˈfīn/ ▶ **n.** a hole saw used in surgery to remove a circle of tissue or bone.
▶ **v.** [with obj.] operate on with a trephine.

– DERIVATIVES **treph·i·na·tion** /ˌtrefəˈnāsʜən/ **n.**
– ORIGIN early 17th cent.: from Latin *tres fines* 'three ends,' apparently influenced by TREPAN.

trep·i·da·tion /ˌtrepiˈdāsʜən/ ▶ **n. 1** a feeling of fear or agitation about something that may happen: *the men set off in fear and trepidation.*
2 archaic trembling motion.
– DERIVATIVES **trep·i·da·tious** /-sʜəs/ **adj.**
– ORIGIN late 15th cent.: from Latin *trepidatio(n-)*, from *trepidare* 'be agitated, tremble,' from *trepidus* 'alarmed.'

trep·o·ne·me /ˈtrepəˌnēm/ (also **treponema** /ˌtrepəˈnēmə/) ▶ **n.** a spirochete bacterium that is parasitic or pathogenic in humans and warm-blooded animals, including the causal agents of syphilis and yaws. ● Genus *Treponema*, order Spirochaetales; Gram-negative.
– DERIVATIVES **trep·o·ne·mal** /-ˈnēməl/ **adj.**
– ORIGIN early 20th cent.: from modern Latin *Treponema*, from Greek *trepein* 'to turn' + *nēma* 'thread.'

très /trā/ ▶ **adv.** (usually with reference to a fashionable quality) very: *très macho, très chic.*
– ORIGIN French.

tres·pass /ˈtrespəs, -ˌpas/ ▶ **v.** [no obj.] **1** enter the owner's land or property without permission: *there is no excuse for **trespassing on** railroad property.*
■ (**tresspass on**) make unfair claims on or take advantage of (something): *she really must not trespass on his hospitality.*
2 (**trespass against**) archaic or literary commit an offense against (a person or a set of rules): *a man who had trespassed against Judaic law.*
▶ **n. 1** Law entry to a person's land or property without their permission: *the defendants were guilty of trespass | a mass trespass on the hills.*
2 archaic or literary a sin; an offense: *the worst trespass against the goddess Venus is to see her naked and asleep.*
– ORIGIN Middle English (sense 2 of the verb): from Old French *trespasser* 'pass over, trespass,' *trespas* 'passing across,' from medieval Latin *transpassare* (see TRANS-, PASS¹).

tres·pass·er /ˈtrespəsər, -ˌpasər/ ▶ **n.** a person entering someone's land or property without permission: ***a trespasser on** his land.*

tress /tres/ ▶ **n.** (usu. **tresses**) a long lock of a woman's hair: *she was tugging a comb through her long tresses.*
▶ **v.** [with obj.] archaic arrange (a person's hair) into long locks.
– DERIVATIVES **tressed adj.** [often in combination] *a blonde-tressed sex symbol*, **tress·y adj.**
– ORIGIN Middle English: from Old French *tresse*, perhaps based on Greek *trikha* 'threefold.'

tres·sure /ˈtresʜər/ ▶ **n.** Heraldry a thin border inset from the edge of a shield, narrower than an orle and usually borne double. ■ an ornamental enclosure containing a figure or distinctive device, formerly found on various gold and silver coins.
– ORIGIN Middle English (denoting a ribbon or band for the hair): from Old French *tressour* (see TRESS).

tres·tle /ˈtresəl/ ▶ **n.** a framework consisting of a horizontal beam supported by two pairs of sloping legs, used in pairs to support a flat surface such as a tabletop. ■ (also **trestlework**) an open cross-braced framework used to support an elevated structure such as a bridge. ■ short for TRESTLE TABLE.
■ (also **trestletree**) each of a pair of horizontal pieces on a sailing ship's lower mast supporting the topmast.
– ORIGIN Middle English: from Old French *trestel*, based on Latin *transtrum* 'beam.'

tres·tle ta·ble ▶ **n.** a table consisting of a board or boards laid on trestles.

tret /tret/ ▶ **n.** historical an allowance of extra weight made to purchasers of certain goods to compensate for waste during transportation.
– ORIGIN late 15th cent: from an Old French variant of *trait* 'act of dragging' (see TRAIT).

tre·tin·o·in /trəˈtinō-in/ ▶ **n.** a drug related to retinol (Vitamin A), used as a topical ointment in the treatment of acne and other disorders of the skin.

tre·val·ly /trəˈvalē/ ▶ **n.** (pl. **trevallies**) a marine sporting fish of the Indo-Pacific that is sometimes caught in large quantities for food. ● *Caranx* and other genera, family Carangidae: several species.
– ORIGIN late 19th cent.: probably an alteration of *cavally* 'horse mackerel,' from Spanish *caballo* 'horse.'

Trèves /trev/ French name for **TRIER**.

Tre·vi Foun·tain /ˈtrevē/ the largest and most famous of the fountains of Rome, situated at the intersection of three roads, built in 1735 by architect Nicola Salvi (1697–1751), and decorated by artists of the Bernini school.
– ORIGIN from Italian *tri vie* 'three roads.'

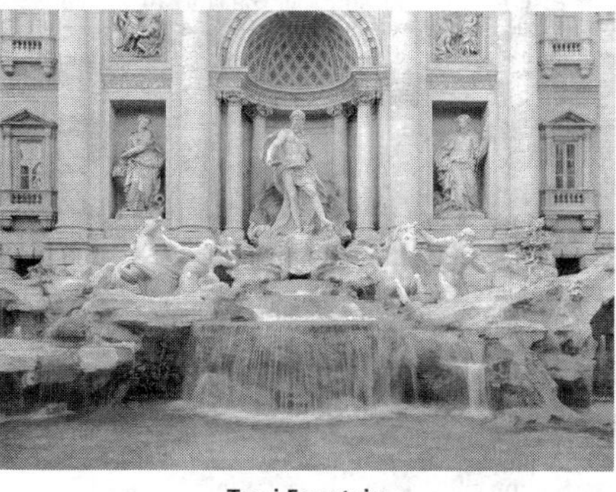

Trevi Fountain

Tre·vi·no /trəˈvēnō/, Lee (Buck) (1939–), US golfer; known as **Supermex**. In 1971, he became the first man to win the Canadian, US, and British open championships in the same year. His other championship titles include the 1974 and 1984 PGA, the 1968 US Open, and the 1972 British Open.

Trev·i·thick /trəˈvɪᴛʜik/, Richard (1771–1833), English engineer. He built the world's first railroad locomotive in 1804.

trews /tro͞oz/ ▶ **plural n.** chiefly Brit. trousers. ■ close-fitting tartan trousers worn by certain Scottish regiments.
– ORIGIN mid 16th cent.: from Irish *triús*, Scottish Gaelic *triubhas* (singular); compare with TROUSERS.

trey /trā/ ▶ **n.** (pl. **treys**) a thing having three of something, in particular: ■ (in basketball) a shot scoring three points. ■ a playing card or die with three spots.
– ORIGIN late Middle English: from Old French *trei* 'three,' from Latin *tres.*

trey·fa /ˈtrāfə/ (also **treyf** /ˈtrāf/) ▶ **adj.** another term for TRAYF.

TRH ▶ **abbr.** ■ Their Royal Highnesses. ■ Biochemistry thyrotropin-releasing hormone.

tri- ▶ **comb. form** three; having three: *triathlon.*
■ Chemistry (in names of compounds) containing three atoms or groups of a specified kind: *trichloroethane.*
– ORIGIN from Latin and Greek, from Latin *tres*, Greek *treis* 'three.'

USAGE See usage at TER-.

tri·a·ble /ˈtrīəbəl/ ▶ **adj.** Law (of an offense) liable to a judicial trial. ■ (of a case or issue) able to be investigated and decided judicially.
– ORIGIN late Middle English: from Anglo-Norman French, from Old French *trier* 'sift' (see TRY).

tri·ac /ˈtrīak/ ▶ **n.** Electronics a three-electrode semiconductor device that will conduct in either direction when triggered by a positive or negative signal at the gate electrode.
– ORIGIN 1960s: from TRIODE + **AC** (short for *alternating current*).

tri·ac·e·tate /trīˈasiˌtāt/ (also **cellulose triacetate**) ▶ **n.** a form of cellulose acetate containing three acetate groups per glucose monomer, used as a basis for man-made fibers.

tri·ad /ˈtrīˌad/ ▶ **n. 1** a group or set of three connected people or things: *the triad of medication, diet, and exercise are necessary in diabetes care.* ■ a chord of three musical notes, consisting of a given note with the third and fifth above it. ■ a Welsh form of literary composition with an arrangement of subjects or statements in groups of three.
2 (also **Triad**) a secret society originating in China, typically involved in organized crime. ■ a member of such a society.
– DERIVATIVES **tri·ad·ic** /trīˈadik/ **adj.** (sense 1).
– ORIGIN mid 16th cent.: from French *triade*, or via late Latin from Greek *trias, triad-*, from *treis* 'three.'

tri·age /trēˈäzʜ, ˈtrēˌäzʜ/ ▶ **n.** (in medical use) the assignment of degrees of urgency to wounds or illnesses to decide the order of treatment of a large number of patients or casualties. ■ the process of determining the most important people or things from amongst a large number that require attention.
▶ **v.** [with obj.] assign degrees of urgency to (wounded or ill patients).
– ORIGIN early 18th cent.: from French, from *trier* 'separate out.' The medical sense dates from the 1930s, from the military system of assessing the wounded on the battlefield.

tri·al /ˈtrī(ə)l/ ▶ **n. 1** a formal examination of evidence before a judge, and typically before a jury, in order to decide guilt in a case of criminal or civil proceedings: *the newspaper accounts of the trial | the editor was summoned to **stand trial** for libel.*
2 a test of the performance, qualities, or suitability of someone or something: *clinical trials must establish whether the new hip replacements are working.* ■ an athletic contest to test the ability of players eligible for selection to a team. ■ (**trials**) an event in which horses, dogs, or other animals compete or perform: *horse trials.*
3 a person, thing, or situation that tests a person's endurance or forbearance: ***the trials and tribulations** of married life.*
▶ **v.** (**trials, trialing, trialed**; Brit. **trials, trialling, trialled**) **1** [with obj.] test (something, esp. a new product) to assess its suitability or performance: *all seeds are carefully trialed in a variety of growing conditions.*
2 [no obj.] (of a horse, dog, or other animal) compete in trials: *the pup trialed on Saturday.*
– PHRASES **on trial** being tried in a court of law. **trial and error** the process of experimenting with various methods of doing something until one finds the most successful.
– ORIGIN late Middle English (as a noun): from Anglo-Norman French, or from medieval Latin *triallum*. The verb dates from the 1980s.

tri·al bal·ance ▶ **n.** a statement of all debits and credits in a double-entry account book, with any disagreement indicating an error.

tri·al bal·loon ▶ **n.** a tentative measure taken or statement made to see how a new policy will be received.
– ORIGIN 1930s: a translation of French *ballon d'essai.*

tri·al court ▶ **n.** a court of law where cases are tried in the first place, as opposed to an appeals court.

tri·al·ist /ˈtrīəlist/ ▶ **n.** a person who participates in a trial, in particular: ■ a person who takes part in a sports trial or motorcycle trial. ■ a person who takes part in a clinical or market test of a new product.

tri·al law·yer ▶ **n.** a lawyer who practices in a trial court.

tri·a·logue /ˈtrīəˌlôg, -ˌläg/ ▶ **n.** a dialogue between three people.
– ORIGIN mid 16th cent.: formed irregularly from TRI- 'three' + DIALOGUE (*di-* being misinterpreted as 'two').

tri·al run ▶ **n.** a test of the operation of a new system or product.

tri·an·gle /ˈtrīˌaɴɢgəl/ ▶ **n.** a plane figure with three straight sides and three angles: *an equilateral triangle.* ■ a thing shaped like such a figure: *a small triangle of grass.* ■ a situation involving three people or things, esp. an emotional relationship involving a couple and a third person with whom one of them is involved. ■ a musical instrument consisting of a steel rod bent into a triangle and sounded by being struck with a small steel rod.
■ a frame used to position the balls in pool and snooker. ■ a drawing instrument in the form of a right triangle. ■ (**triangles**) historical a frame of three halberds joined at the top to which a soldier was bound for flogging.
– ORIGIN late Middle English: from Old French *triangle* or Latin *triangulum*, neuter of *triangulus* 'three-cornered' (see TRI-, ANGLE¹).

tri·an·gle of forc·es ▶ **n.** Physics a triangle whose sides represent in magnitude and direction three forces in equilibrium.

tri·an·gu·lar /trīˈaɴɢgyələr/ ▶ **adj.** shaped like a triangle; having three sides and three corners: *dainty triangular sandwiches.* ■ involving three people or parties: *a triangular relationship.* ■ (of a pyramid) having a three-sided base.
– DERIVATIVES **tri·an·gu·lar·i·ty** /trīˌaɴɢgyəˈlaritē/ **n.**, **tri·an·gu·lar·ly adv.**
– ORIGIN mid 16th cent.: from late Latin *triangularis*, from Latin *triangulum* (see TRIANGLE).

tri·an·gu·lar num·ber ▶ **n.** any of the series of numbers (1, 3, 6, 10, 15, etc.) obtained by continued summation of the natural numbers 1, 2, 3, 4, 5, etc.

tri·an·gu·lar trade ▶ **n.** a multilateral system of trading in which a country pays for its imports from one country by its exports to another.
■ used to refer to the trade in the eighteenth and nineteenth centuries that involved shipping goods from Britain to West Africa to be exchanged for slaves, these slaves being shipped to the West Indies and exchanged for sugar, rum, and other commodities, which were in turn shipped back to Britain.

tri·an·gu·late /trīˈaNGgyəˌlāt/ ▶ **v. 1** [with obj.] divide (an area) into triangles for surveying purposes. ■ measure and map (an area) by the use of triangles with a known base length and base angles. ■ determine (a height, distance, or location) in this way.
2 [with obj.] form into a triangle or triangles: *the brackets triangulate the frame.*
3 [no obj.] (in politics) position oneself in such a way as to appeal to or appease both left-wing and right-wing standpoints: *will the president decide to triangulate?*
– ORIGIN mid 19th cent.: from Latin *triangulum* 'triangle' (see TRIANGLE) + -ATE[3].

tri·an·gu·la·tion /ˌtrīˌaNGgyəˈlāSHən/ ▶ **n. 1** (in surveying) the tracing and measurement of a series or network of triangles in order to determine the distances and relative positions of points spread over a territory or region, esp. by measuring the length of one side of each triangle and deducing its angles and the length of the other two sides by observation from this baseline.
2 formation of or division into triangles.
3 (in politics) the action or process of positioning oneself in such a way as to appeal to or appease both left-wing and right-wing standpoints.

tri·an·gu·la·tion point ▶ **n.** a reference point on high ground used in surveying, typically marked by a small pillar.

Tri·an·gu·lum /trīˈaNGgyələm/ Astronomy a small northern constellation (the Triangle), between Andromeda and Aries. ■ (as genitive **Trianguli** /trīˈaNGgyəlē, -ˌlī/) used with a preceding letter or numeral to designate a star in this constellation: *the star Beta Trianguli.*
– ORIGIN Latin.

Tri·an·gu·lum Aus·tra·le /ôˈstrālē/ Astronomy a small southern constellation (the Southern Triangle), lying in the Milky Way near the south celestial pole. ■ (as genitive **Trianguli Australis** /trīˈaNGgyəlē ôˈstrālis, trīˈaNGgyəˌlī/) used with a preceding letter or numeral to designate a star in this constellation: *the star Alpha Trianguli Australis.*
– ORIGIN Latin.

Tri·a·non /ˈtrēəˌnän/ either of two small palaces in the great park at Versailles in France. The larger was built by Louis XIV in 1687; the smaller, built by Louis XV 1762–68, was used first by his mistress **Madame du Barry** (1743–93) and afterward by Marie Antoinette.

Tri·as·sic /trīˈasik/ ▶ **adj.** Geology of, relating to, or denoting the earliest period of the Mesozoic era, between the Permian and Jurassic periods. See also PERMO-TRIASSIC. ■ (as noun **the Triassic** or **the Trias**) the Triassic period or the system of rocks deposited during it.

> The Triassic lasted from about 245 million to 208 million years ago. Many new organisms appeared following the mass extinctions of the end of the Paleozoic era, including the earliest dinosaurs and ammonites and the first primitive mammals.

– ORIGIN mid 19th cent.: from late Latin *trias* (see TRIAD), because the strata are divisible into three groups, + -IC.

tri·ath·lon /trīˈaTHlən, -ˌlän/ ▶ **n.** an athletic contest consisting of three different events, typically swimming, cycling, and long-distance running.
– DERIVATIVES **tri·ath·lete** /-ˌlēt/ **n.**
– ORIGIN 1970s: from TRI- 'three,' on the pattern of *decathlon.*

tri·a·tom·ic /ˌtrīəˈtämik/ ▶ **adj.** Chemistry consisting of three atoms.

tri·ax·i·al /trīˈaksēəl/ ▶ **adj.** having or relating to three axes, esp. in mechanical or astronomical contexts.

tri·a·zine /ˈtrīəˌzēn/ ▶ **n.** Chemistry any of a group of compounds whose molecules contain an unsaturated ring of three carbon and three nitrogen atoms.

tri·a·zole /ˈtrīəˌzōl, trīˈazôl/ ▶ **n.** any compound whose molecule contains a ring of three nitrogen and two carbon atoms, in particular each of five isomeric compounds containing such a ring with two double bonds. ● Chem. formula: $C_2H_3N_3$.

trib. ▶ **abbr.** tributary.

trib·ade /ˈtribəd/ ▶ **n.** a lesbian, esp. one who lies on top of her partner and simulates the movements of the male in heterosexual intercourse.
– DERIVATIVES **trib·a·dism** /-ˌdizəm/ **n.**
– ORIGIN early 17th cent.: from French *tribade,* or via Latin from Greek *tribas,* from *tribein* 'to rub.'

trib·al /ˈtrībəl/ ▶ **adj.** of or characteristic of a tribe or tribes: *tribal people in Malaysia.* ■ chiefly derogatory characterized by a tendency to form groups or by strong group loyalty: *British industrial operatives remained locked in primitive tribal attitudes.*
▶ **n.** (**tribals**) members of tribal communities, esp. in South Asia.
– DERIVATIVES **trib·al·ly adv.**

trib·al·ism /ˈtrībəˌlizəm/ ▶ **n.** the state or fact of being organized in a tribe or tribes. ■ chiefly derogatory the behavior and attitudes that stem from strong loyalty to one's own tribe or social group: *a society motivated by cultural tribalism.*

trib·al·ist /ˈtrībəlist/ ▶ **n.** chiefly derogatory an advocate or practitioner of strong loyalty to one's own tribe or social group.
– DERIVATIVES **tri·bal·is·tic** /ˌtrībəˈlistik/ **adj.**

tri·band ▶ **adj.** (of a cellular phone) having three frequencies, enabling it to be used in different regions (typically Europe and the US).

tri·ba·sic /trīˈbāsik/ ▶ **adj.** Chemistry (of an acid) having three replaceable hydrogen atoms.

tribe /trīb/ ▶ **n. 1** a social division in a traditional society consisting of families or communities linked by social, economic, religious, or blood ties, with a common culture and dialect, typically having a recognized leader: *indigenous Indian tribes | the Celtic tribes of Europe.* ■ (in ancient Rome) each of several political divisions, originally three, later thirty, ultimately thirty-five. ■ informal family: *the entire tribe is coming for Thanksgiving.* ■ derogatory a distinctive close-knit group: *she made a stand against the social codes of her English middle-class tribe | an outburst against the whole tribe of theoreticians.* ■ informal a large number of people or animals: *tribes of children playing under the watchful eyes of nurses.*
2 Biology a taxonomic category that ranks above genus and below family or subfamily, usually ending in *-ini* (in zoology) or *-eae* (in botany).
– ORIGIN Middle English: from Old French *tribu* or Latin *tribus* (singular and plural); perhaps related to *tri-* 'three' and referring to the three divisions of the early people of Rome.

> **USAGE** In historical contexts, the word **tribe** is broadly accepted (*the area was inhabited by Slavic tribes*), but in contemporary contexts, it is problematic when used to refer to a community living within a traditional society. It is strongly associated with past attitudes of white colonialists toward so-called primitive or uncivilized peoples living in remote undeveloped places. For this reason it is generally preferable to use alternative terms such as **community** or **people.**

Tri·Be·Ca /trīˈbekə/ a residential and commercial section of southern Manhattan in New York City, noted for its factory lofts converted into apartments. Its name is derived from *Tri*angle *Be*low *Ca*nal Street.

tribes·man /ˈtrībzmən/ ▶ **n.** (pl. **tribesmen**) a man belonging to a tribe in a traditional society or group.

Tribes of Is·ra·el the twelve divisions of ancient Israel, each traditionally descended from one of the twelve sons of Jacob. Ten of the tribes (Asher, Dan, Gad, Issachar, Levi, Manasseh, Naphtali, Reuben, Simeon, and Zebulun, known as the LOST TRIBES) were deported to captivity in Assyria *c.*720 BC, leaving only the tribes of Judah and Benjamin. Also called TWELVE TRIBES OF ISRAEL.

tribes·peo·ple /ˈtrībzˌpēpəl/ ▶ **plural n.** people belonging to a tribe in a traditional society or group.

tribes·wom·an /ˈtrībzˌwo͝omən/ ▶ **n.** (pl. **tribeswomen**) a woman belonging to a tribe in a traditional society or group.

tribo- ▶ **comb. form** relating to friction: *triboelectricity.*
– ORIGIN from Greek *tribos* 'rubbing.'

tri·bo·e·lec·tric·i·ty /ˌtrībō-iləkˈtrisitē, -ˌēlek-/ ▶ **n.** electric charge generated by friction.

tri·bol·o·gy /trīˈbäləjē/ ▶ **n.** the study of friction, wear, lubrication, and the design of bearings; the science of interacting surfaces in relative motion.
– DERIVATIVES **tri·bo·log·i·cal** /-bəˈläjikəl/ **adj.**, **tri·bol·o·gist** /-jist/ **n.**

tri·bo·lu·mi·nes·cence /ˌtrībōˌlo͞oməˈnesəns/ ▶ **n.** the emission of light from a substance caused by rubbing, scratching, or similar frictional contact.
– DERIVATIVES **tri·bo·lu·mi·nes·cent adj.**

tri·bom·e·ter /trīˈbämitər/ ▶ **n.** an instrument for measuring friction in sliding.

Tri·bor·ough Bridge /ˈtrībərō/ a bridge complex opened in 1936 that links the Bronx, Queens, and Manhattan boroughs in New York City.

tri·brach /ˈtrīˌbrak/ ▶ **n.** Prosody a metrical foot of three short or unstressed syllables.
– DERIVATIVES **tri·brach·ic** /trīˈbrakik/ **adj.**
– ORIGIN late 16th cent.: via Latin from Greek *tribrakhus,* from *tri-* 'three' + *brakhus* 'short.'

trib·u·la·tion /ˌtribyəˈlāSHən/ ▶ **n.** (usu. **tribulations**) a cause of great trouble or suffering: *the tribulations of being a megastar.* ■ a state of great trouble or suffering: *his time of tribulation was just beginning.*
– ORIGIN Middle English: via Old French from ecclesiastical Latin *tribulatio(n-),* from Latin *tribulare* 'press, oppress,' from *tribulum* 'threshing board (constructed of sharp points),' based on *terere* 'rub.'

tri·bu·nal /trīˈbyo͞onl, trə-/ ▶ **n.** a court of justice: *an international war crimes tribunal.* ■ a seat or bench for a judge or judges.
– ORIGIN late Middle English (denoting a seat for judges): from Old French, or from Latin *tribunal* 'raised platform provided for magistrates' seats,' from *tribunus* (see TRIBUNE[1]).

trib·une[1] /ˈtribyo͞on, trīˈbyo͞on/ ▶ **n.** (also **tribune of the people**) an official in ancient Rome chosen by the plebeians to protect their interests. ■ (also **military tribune**) a Roman legionary officer. ■ a popular leader; a champion of the people.
– DERIVATIVES **trib·u·nate** /ˈtribyənit, trīˈbyo͞onit, -ˌnāt/ **n.**, **trib·une·ship** /-ˌSHip/ **n.**
– ORIGIN late Middle English: from Latin *tribunus,* literally 'head of a tribe,' from *tribus* 'tribe.'

trib·une[2] ▶ **n. 1** an apse in a basilica.
2 a dais or rostrum, esp. in a church. ■ a raised area or gallery with seats, esp. in a church.
– ORIGIN mid 17th cent. (denoting the principal room in an Italian mansion): via French from Italian, from medieval Latin *tribuna,* alteration of Latin *tribunal* (see TRIBUNAL).

trib·u·tar·y /ˈtribyəˌterē/ ▶ **n.** (pl. **tributaries**) **1** a river or stream flowing into a larger river or lake: *the Illinois River, a tributary of the Mississippi.*
2 historical a person or state that pays tribute to another state or ruler: *tributaries of the Ottoman empire.*
– ORIGIN late Middle English (sense 2): from Latin *tributarius,* from *tributum* (see TRIBUTE). Sense 1 dates from the early 19th cent.

trib·ute /ˈtribyo͞ot/ ▶ **n. 1** an act, statement, or gift that is intended to show gratitude, respect, or admiration: *the video is a tribute to the musicals of the '40s | a symposium organized to* ***pay tribute*** *to Darwin.* ■ [in sing.] something resulting from something else and indicating its worth: *his victory in the championship was* ***a tribute to*** *his persistence.* ■ [as modifier] denoting or relating to a group or musician that performs the music of a more famous one and typically imitates them in appearance and style of performance: *an Abba tribute band.*
2 historical payment made periodically by one state or ruler to another, esp. as a sign of dependence: *the king had at his disposal plunder and tribute amassed through warfare.*
3 historical a proportion of ore or its equivalent, paid to a miner for his work, or to the owner or lessor of a mine.
– ORIGIN late Middle English (sense 2): from Latin *tributum,* neuter past participle (used as a noun) of *tribuere* 'assign' (originally 'divide between tribes'), from *tribus* 'tribe.'

tri·cam·er·al /trīˈkamərəl/ ▶ **adj.** of or relating to the parliamentary system operating in South Africa between 1983 and 1994, in which the legislature consisted of three ethnically based houses.

tri·car·box·yl·ic ac·id cy·cle /ˌtrīkärbäkˈsilik/ ▶ **n.** another term for KREBS CYCLE.

trice /trīs/ ▶ **n.** (in phrase **in a trice**) in a moment; very quickly.
– ORIGIN late Middle English *trice* 'a tug,' figuratively 'an instant,' from Middle Dutch *trīsen* 'pull sharply,' related to *trīse* 'pulley.'

tri·cen·ten·ar·y /trīˈsentnˌerē, ˌtrīsenˈtenərē/ ▶ **n.** (pl. **tricentenaries**) another term for TRICENTENNIAL.

tri·cen·ten·ni·al /ˌtrīsenˈtenēəl/ ▶ **n.** the three-hundredth anniversary of a significant event.
▶ **adj.** of or relating to a three-hundredth anniversary: *the tricentennial year.*

tri·ceps /ˈtrīˌseps/ ▶ **n.** (pl. **same** or **tricepses**) Anatomy any of several muscles having three points of attachment at one end, particularly (also **triceps brachii** /ˈbrākēˌī, -kēˌē, ˈbrak-/) the large muscle at the back of the upper arm.
– DERIVATIVES **tri·cep adj.** *tricep tendonitis.*
– ORIGIN late 16th cent.: from Latin, literally 'three-headed,' from *tri-* 'three' + *-ceps* (from *caput* 'head').

tri·cer·a·tops /trīˈserəˌtäps/ ▶ **n.** a large quadrupedal herbivorous dinosaur living at the end of the Cretaceous period, having a massive head with two large horns, a smaller horn on the beaked snout, and a bony frill above the neck. ● Genus *Triceratops,* infraorder Ceratopsia, order Ornithischia.
– ORIGIN modern Latin, from Greek *trikeratos* 'three-horned' + *ōps* 'face.'

tri·chi·a·sis /triˈkīəsis/ ▶ **n.** Medicine ingrowth or introversion of the eyelashes.

t

– ORIGIN mid 17th cent.: via late Latin from Greek *trikhiasis*, from *trikhian* 'be hairy.'

tri·chi·na /trī'kīnə/ ▶ n. (pl. **trichinae** /-nē/) a parasitic nematode worm of humans and other mammals, the adults of which live in the small intestine. The larvae form hard cysts in the muscles, where they remain until eaten by the next host. ● Genus *Trichinella*, class Aphasmida (or Adenophorea).
– ORIGIN mid 19th cent.: from modern Latin (former genus name), from Greek *trikhinos* 'of hair.'

Trich·i·nop·o·ly /,trikə'näpəlē, ,tricH-/ another name for **TIRUCHIRAPALLI**.

trich·i·no·sis /,trikə'nōsis/ ▶ n. a disease caused by trichinae, typically from infected meat, esp. pork, characterized by digestive disturbance, fever, and muscular rigidity. ● This disease is typically caused by *Trichinella spiralis*.

tri·chlor·an·i·sole /,trīklôr'anə,ōl/ ▶ n. a chemical released by a fungus whose smell is detectable in minute concentrations. It is responsible for the musty smell that taints wines bottled with infected corks(. abbr. **TCA**).

tri·chlo·ro·a·ce·tic ac·id /trī,klôrōə'sētik/ (also **trichloracetic acid** /-,klôrə'setik/) ▶ n. Chemistry a toxic deliquescent crystalline solid used as a solvent, analgesic, and anesthetic. ● Chem. formula: CCl_3COOH.
– DERIVATIVES **tri·chlo·ro·ac·e·tate** /-'asi,tāt/ n.

tri·chlo·ro·eth·ane /trī,klôrō'eTHān/ ▶ n. Chemistry a colorless, nonflammable volatile liquid, used as a solvent and cleaner. ● Alternative name: **1,1,1-trichloroethane**; chem. formula: CCl_3CH_3.

tri·chlo·ro·eth·yl·ene /trī,klôrō'eTHə,lēn/ ▶ n. Chemistry a colorless volatile liquid used as a solvent and formerly as an anesthetic. ● Chem. formula: $CCl_2{\cdot}CHCl$.

tri·chlo·ro·phe·nol /trī,klôrō'fēnôl, -nōl/ ▶ n. Chemistry a synthetic crystalline compound used as an insecticide and preservative and in the synthesis of pesticides. ● Chem. formula: $C_6H_2Cl_3(OH)$; six isomers.

tricho- ▶ comb. form of or relating to hair: *trichology*.
– ORIGIN from Greek *thrix*, *trikhos* 'hair.'

trich·o·cyst /'trikə,sist/ ▶ n. Biology any of numerous minute, rodlike structures, each containing a protrusible filament, found near the surface of ciliates and dinoflagellates.

tri·chol·o·gy /tri'käləjē/ ▶ n. the branch of medical and cosmetic study and practice concerned with the hair and scalp.
– DERIVATIVES **trich·o·log·i·cal** /,trikə'läjikəl/ adj., **tri·chol·o·gist** /-jist/ n.

trich·ome /'trī,kōm, 'trikōm/ ▶ n. Botany a small hair or other outgrowth from the epidermis of a plant, typically unicellular and glandular.
– ORIGIN late 19th cent.: from Greek *trikhōma*, from *trikhoun* 'cover with hair.'

trich·o·mon·ad /,trikə'mänad, -'mō-/ ▶ n. Zoology & Medicine a parasitic protozoan with four to six flagella and an undulating membrane, infesting the urogenital or digestive system. ● Order Trichomonadida, phylum Parabasilia, kingdom Protista.
– DERIVATIVES **trich·o·mon·al** /-'mänl, -'mōnl/ adj.
– ORIGIN mid 19th cent.: from modern Latin *Trichomonadida* (plural), from Greek *thrix*, *trikh-* 'hair' + *monas*, *monad-* 'unit.'

trich·o·mo·ni·a·sis /,trikəmə'nīəsis/ ▶ n. Medicine an infection caused by parasitic trichomonads, chiefly affecting the urinary tract, vagina, or digestive system. ● Genus *Trichomonas*, in particular *T. vaginalis* (in the reproductive tract) and *T. hominis* (in the large intestine).

Tri·chop·ter·a /trī'käptərə/ Entomology an order of insects that comprises the caddisflies. ■ (as plural noun **trichoptera**) insects of this order.
– ORIGIN modern Latin (plural), from **TRICHO-** 'hair' + Greek *pteron* 'wing.'

tri·chop·ter·an /trī'käptərən/ Entomology ▶ n. an insect of the order Trichoptera; a caddisfly.
▶ adj. relating to or denoting trichopterans.

tri·chot·o·my /trī'kätəmē/ ▶ n. (pl. **trichotomies**) a division into three categories: *the pragmatics–semantics–syntax trichotomy*.
– DERIVATIVES **tri·chot·o·mous** /-məs/ adj.
– ORIGIN 17th cent.: from Greek *trikha* 'threefold,' from *treis* 'three,' on the pattern of *dichotomy*.

tri·chro·ic /trī'krōik/ ▶ adj. Crystallography (of a crystal) appearing with different colors when viewed along the three crystallographic directions.
– DERIVATIVES **tri·chro·ism** /'trīkrə,wizəm/ n.
– ORIGIN late 19th cent.: from Greek *trikhroos* (from *tri-* 'three' + *khrōs* 'color') + **-IC**.

tri·chro·mat·ic /,trīkrō'matik/ ▶ adj. having or using three colors. ■ having normal color vision, which is sensitive to all three primary colors.
– DERIVATIVES **tri·chro·ma·tism** /-'krōmə,tizəm/ n.

tri·chrome /'trī,krōm/ ▶ adj. Biology denoting a stain or method of histological staining in which different tissues are stained, each in one of three different colors.
– ORIGIN early 20th cent.: from **TRI-** 'three' + Greek *khrōma* 'color.'

trick /trik/ ▶ n. **1** a cunning or skillful act or scheme intended to deceive or outwit someone: *he's a double-dealer capable of any mean trick*. ■ a mischievous practical joke: *she thought Elaine was **playing some trick on her***. ■ a skillful act performed for entertainment or amusement: *he did conjuring tricks for his daughters*. ■ an illusion: *I thought I saw a flicker of emotion, but it was probably **a trick of the light***. ■ a clever or particular way of doing something: *the trick is to put one ski forward and kneel*.
2 a peculiar or characteristic habit or mannerism: *she had a trick of clipping off certain words and phrases*.
3 (in bridge, whist, and similar card games) a sequence of cards forming a single round of play. One card is laid down by each player, the highest card being the winner.
4 informal a prostitute's client.
5 a sailor's turn at the helm, usually lasting for two or four hours.
▶ v. [with obj.] **1** deceive or outwit (someone) by being cunning or skillful: *buyers can be tricked by savvy sellers*. ■ (**trick someone into**) use deception to make someone do (something): *he tricked her into parting with the money*. ■ (**trick someone out of**) use deception to deprive someone of (something): *the king was tricked out of his land*.
2 Heraldry sketch (a coat of arms) in outline, with the colors indicated by letters or signs.
▶ adj. [attrib.] **1** intended or used to deceive or mystify, or to create an illusion: *a trick question*.
2 liable to fail; defective: *a trick knee*.
– PHRASES **do the trick** informal achieve the required result. **every trick in the book** informal every available method of achieving what one wants. **how's tricks?** informal used as a friendly greeting: *"How's tricks in your neck of the woods?"* **not miss a trick** see **MISS**[1]. **the oldest trick in the book** a ruse so hackneyed that it should no longer deceive anyone. **tricks of the trade** special ingenious techniques used in a profession or craft, esp. those that are little known by outsiders. **turn a trick** informal (of a prostitute) have a session with a client. **up to one's (old) tricks** informal misbehaving in a characteristic way.
– PHRASAL VERBS **trick someone/something out** (or **up**) (usu. **be tricked out**) dress or decorate someone or something in an elaborate or showy way: *a Marine **tricked out** in World War II kit and weaponry*. [late 15th cent.: perhaps associated with obsolete French *s'estriquer*.]
– DERIVATIVES **trick·er** n., **trick·ish** adj. (dated).
– ORIGIN late Middle English (as a noun): from an Old French dialect variant of *triche*, from *trichier* 'deceive,' of unknown origin. Current senses of the verb date from the mid 16th cent.

trick cy·clist ▶ n. Brit. informal used as a humorous euphemism for a psychiatrist.

trick·er·y /'trikərē/ ▶ n. (pl. **trickeries**) the practice of deception: *the dealer resorted to trickery*.

trick·le /'trikəl/ ▶ v. [no obj.] (of a liquid) flow in a small stream: *a solitary tear trickled down her cheek* | (as adj. **trickling**) *a trickling brook*. ■ [with obj.] cause (a liquid) to flow in a small stream: *he trickled the vodka onto the rocks*. ■ come or go slowly or gradually: *the details began to trickle out*.
▶ n. a small flow of liquid: *a trickle of blood*. ■ a small group or number of people or things moving slowly: *the traffic had dwindled to a trickle*.
– PHRASAL VERBS **trickle down** (of wealth) gradually benefit the poorest as a result of the increasing wealth of the richest.
– ORIGIN Middle English (as a verb): imitative.

trick·le charg·er ▶ n. a battery charger that produces a very small current.

trick·le-down ▶ adj. (of an economic system) in which the poorest gradually benefit as a result of the increasing wealth of the richest.

trick·le ir·ri·ga·tion ▶ n. the supply of a controlled flow of water to a number of points in a cultivated area.

trick or treat ▶ n. a children's custom of calling at houses at Halloween with the threat of pranks if they are not given a small gift (often used as a greeting by children doing this).
▶ v. [no obj.] (**trick-or-treat**) take part in the custom of trick or treat: *kids are going to go trick-or-treating tomorrow night*.
– DERIVATIVES **trick-or-treat·er** n.

trick·ster /'trikstər/ ▶ n. a person who cheats or deceives people.

trick·sy /'triksē/ ▶ adj. (**tricksier**, **tricksiest**) clever in an ingenious or deceptive way: *a typically tricksy beginning to his latest venture*. ■ (of a person) playful or mischievous.
– DERIVATIVES **trick·si·ly** /-səlē/ adv., **trick·si·ness** n.

trick·y /'trikē/ ▶ adj. (**trickier**, **trickiest**) (of a task, problem, or situation) requiring care and skill because difficult or awkward: *applying eyeliner can be a tricky business* | *some things are very tricky to explain*. ■ (of a person or act) deceitful, crafty, or skillful.
– DERIVATIVES **trick·i·ly** /'trikəlē/ adv., **trick·i·ness** n.

tri·clad /'trī,klad/ ▶ n. Zoology a free-living flatworm of an order characterized by having a gut with three branches, including the planarians. ● Order Tricladida, class Turbellaria.
– ORIGIN late 19th cent.: from modern Latin *Tricladida*, from **TRI-** 'three' + Greek *klados* 'branch.'

tri·clin·ic /trī'klinik/ ▶ adj. of or denoting a crystal system or three-dimensional geometric arrangement having three unequal oblique axes.
– ORIGIN mid 19th cent.: from Greek **TRI-** 'three' + *-clinic*, on the pattern of *monoclinic*.

tri·clin·i·um /trī'klinēəm/ ▶ n. (pl. **triclinia** /-'klinēə/) a dining table with couches along three sides used in ancient Rome. ■ a room containing such a table.
– ORIGIN Latin, from Greek *triklinion*, from *tri-* 'three' + *klinē* 'couch.'

tri·col·or /'trī,kələr/ (Brit. **tricolour**) ▶ n. a flag with three bands or blocks of different colors, esp. the French national flag with equal upright bands of blue, white, and red.
▶ adj. (also **tricolored**) having three colors.
– ORIGIN late 18th cent.: from French *tricolore*, from late Latin *tricolor* (see **TRI-**, **COLOR**).

tri·corne /'trī,kôrn/ (also **tricorn**) ▶ adj. [attrib.] (of a hat) having a brim turned up on three sides.
▶ n. a hat of this kind.
– ORIGIN mid 19th cent.: from French *tricorne* or Latin *tricornis*, from *tri-* 'three' + *cornu* 'horn.'

tri·cot /'trēkō/ ▶ n. a fine knitted fabric made of a natural or man-made fiber.
– ORIGIN late 18th cent.: from French, literally 'knitting,' from *tricoter* 'to knit,' of unknown origin.

tri·co·teuse /,trēkō'tœz/ ▶ n. (pl. **same**) a woman who sits and knits (used esp. in reference to a number of women who did this, during the French Revolution, while attending public executions).
– ORIGIN French, from *tricoter* 'to knit.'

tric-trac /'trik ,trak/ ▶ n. historical a form of backgammon.
– ORIGIN late 17th cent.: from French, from the clicking sound made by the game pieces.

tri·cus·pid /trī'kəspid/ ▶ adj. having three cusps or points, in particular: ■ denoting a tooth with three cusps or points. ■ denoting or relating to a valve formed of three triangular segments, particularly that between the right atrium and ventricle of the heart.
– ORIGIN late 17th cent.: from **TRI-** 'three' + Latin *cuspis*, *cuspid-* 'cusp.'

tri·cy·cle /'trīsikəl, -,sikəl/ ▶ n. a vehicle similar to a bicycle, but having three wheels, two at the back and one at the front.
▶ v. [no obj.] (often as noun **tricycling**) ride on a tricycle.
– DERIVATIVES **tri·cy·clist** /-ist/ n.

tri·cy·clic /trī'sīklik, -'sik-/ ▶ adj. Chemistry (of an organic compound) having three fused rings of atoms in its molecule.
▶ n. (usu. **tricyclics**) Medicine any of a class of antidepressant drugs having molecules with three fused rings.
– ORIGIN late 19th cent.: from **TRI-** 'three' + Greek *kuklos* 'circle' + **-IC**.

tri·dac·tyl /trī'daktl/ ▶ adj. Zoology (of a vertebrate limb) having three toes or fingers.
– ORIGIN early 19th cent.: from **TRI-** 'three' + Greek *daktulos* 'finger.'

tri·dent /'trīdnt/ ▶ n. a three-pronged spear, esp. as an attribute of Poseidon (Neptune) or Britannia.

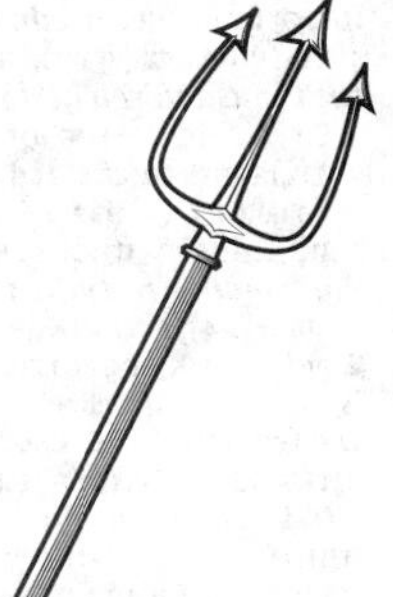

trident

PRONUNCIATION KEY ə *ago, up*; ər *over, fur*; a *hat*; ā *ate*; ä *car*; e *let*; ē *see*; i *fit*; ī *by*; NG *sing*; ō *go*; ô *law, for*; oi *toy*; o͝o *good*; o͞o *goo*; ou *out*; TH *thin*; T͟H *then*; ZH *vision*

t

■ (**Trident**) a US design of submarine-launched long-range ballistic missile.
– ORIGIN late Middle English: from Latin *trident-*, from *tri-* 'three' + *dens, dent-* 'tooth.'

Tri·den·tine /trī'den,tēn, -,tin/ ▶ **adj.** of or relating to the Council of Trent, esp. as the basis of Roman Catholic doctrine.
– ORIGIN from medieval Latin *Tridentinus*, from *Tridentum* 'Trent.'

Tri·den·tine mass ▶ **n.** the Latin Eucharistic liturgy used by the Roman Catholic Church from 1570 to 1964.

trid·y·mite /'tridə,mīt/ ▶ **n.** a high-temperature form of quartz found as thin hexagonal crystals in some igneous rocks and stony meteorites.
– ORIGIN mid 19th cent.: from German *Tridymit*, from Greek *tridumos* 'threefold,' from *tri-* 'three' + *-dumos* (as in *didumos* 'twin'), because of its occurrence in groups of three crystals.

tried /trīd/ past and past participle of **TRY**.
▶ **adj.** [attrib.] used in various phrases to describe something that has proved effective or reliable before: *novel applications of tried-and-tested methods* | *a tried-and-true recipe.*

tri·ene /'trī,ēn/ ▶ **n.** Chemistry an unsaturated hydrocarbon containing three double bonds between carbon atoms.

tri·en·ni·al /trī'enēəl/ ▶ **adj.** recurring every three years: *the triennial meeting of the Association.* ■ lasting for or relating to a period of three years.
▶ **n.** a visitation of an Anglican diocese by its bishop every three years.
– DERIVATIVES **tri·en·ni·al·ly** adv.
– ORIGIN mid 16th cent.: from late Latin *triennis* (from Latin *tri-* 'three' + *annus* 'year') + **-AL**.

tri·en·ni·um /trī'enēəm/ ▶ **n.** (pl. **triennia** /-'enēə/ or **trienniums**) a specified period of three years.
– ORIGIN mid 19th cent.: from Latin, from *tri-* 'three' + *annus* 'year.'

Tri·er /tri(ə)r/ a city on the Mosel River in Rhineland-Palatinate, in western Germany; pop. 103,500 (est. 2006). French name **TRÈVES** Established by a Germanic tribe, the Treveri, *c.*400 BC, Trier is one of the oldest cities in Europe.

tri·er /'trīər/ ▶ **n. 1** a person who always makes an effort, however unsuccessful they may be: *Kelly was described by her teachers as a real trier.*
2 a person or body responsible for investigating and deciding a case judicially: *the jury is the trier of fact.*

Tri·este /trē'est, -'estā/ a city in northeastern Italy, the largest port on the Adriatic Sea; pop. 205,341 (2008). Formerly held by Austria (1382–1918), Trieste was annexed by Italy after World War I. The Free Territory of Trieste was created after World War II but it was returned to Italy in 1954.

tri·fa·cial nerve /trī'fāsHəl/ ▶ **n.** another term for **TRIGEMINAL NERVE**.

tri·fect·a /trī'fektə/ ▶ **n.** a bet in which the person betting forecasts the first three finishers in a race in the correct order. ■ [in sing.] a run of three wins or grand events: *today is a trifecta of birthdays.*
– ORIGIN 1970s: from **TRI-** 'three' + **PERFECTA**.

trif·fid /'trifid/ (also **Triffid**) ▶ **n.** (in science fiction) one of a race of predatory plants that are capable of growing to a gigantic size and are possessed of locomotor ability and a poisonous sting.
– ORIGIN coined by John Wyndham in *Day of the Triffids* (1951).

tri·fid /'trīfid/ ▶ **adj.** chiefly Biology partly or wholly split into three divisions or lobes.
– ORIGIN mid 18th cent.: from Latin *trifidus*, from *tri-* 'three' + *fid-* 'split, divided' (from the verb *findere*).

t

tri·fle /'trīfəl/ ▶ **n. 1** a thing of little value or importance: *we needn't trouble the headmaster over such trifles.* ■ [in sing.] a small amount of something: *the thousand yen he'd paid seemed the merest trifle.*
2 Brit. a cold dessert of sponge cake and fruit covered with layers of custard, jelly, and cream.
▶ **v.** [no obj.] **1** (**trifle with**) treat (someone or something) without seriousness or respect: *he is not a man to be trifled with* | *men who trifle with women's affections.*
2 archaic talk or act frivolously: *we will not trifle—life is too short.* ■ [with obj.] (**trifle something away**) waste something, esp. time, frivolously.
– PHRASES **a trifle** a little; somewhat: *his methods are a trifle eccentric.*
– DERIVATIVES **tri·fler** /-f(ə)lər/ **n.**
– ORIGIN Middle English (also denoting an idle story told to deceive or amuse): from Old French *trufle*, by-form of *trufe* 'deceit,' of unknown origin. The verb derives from Old French *truffler* 'mock, deceive.'

tri·fling /'trīf(ə)liNG/ ▶ **adj.** unimportant or trivial: *a trifling sum.*
– DERIVATIVES **tri·fling·ly** adv.

tri·flu·o·per·a·zine /trī,flo͞o-ō'perə,zēn/ ▶ **n.** Medicine an antipsychotic and sedative drug related to phenothiazine.
– ORIGIN mid 20th cent.: from **TRI-** + *fluo(rine)* + *(pi) perazine.*

tri·fo·cal /'trī,fōkəl/ ▶ **adj.** (of a pair of glasses) having lenses with three parts with different focal lengths.
▶ **n.** (**trifocals**) a pair of glasses with such lenses.

tri·fold /'trī,fōld/ ▶ **adj.** triple; threefold: *an ingenious trifold partnership between government, employers, and students.*

tri·fo·li·ate /trī'fōlē-it, -,āt/ ▶ **adj.** (of a compound leaf) having three leaflets: *dark green trifoliate leaves.* ■ (of a plant) having such leaves. ■ (of an object or design) having the form of such a leaf: *a bronze trifoliate key handle.*
▶ **n.** a plant with such leaves: *poison ivy is a thornless trifoliate.*

tri·fo·ri·um /trī'fôrēəm/ ▶ **n.** (pl. **triforia** /-'fôrēə/) a gallery or arcade above the arches of the nave, choir, and transepts of a church.
– ORIGIN early 18th cent.: from Anglo-Latin, of unknown origin.

tri·form /'trī,fôrm/ ▶ **adj.** technical composed of three parts: *strawberries nestling among their triform leaves.*

tri·fur·cate ▶ **v.** /'trīfər,kāt/ [no obj.] divide into three branches or forks.
▶ **adj.** (also **trifurcated**) divided into three branches or forks.
– DERIVATIVES **tri·fur·ca·tion** /,trīfər'kāsHən/ **n.**
– ORIGIN mid 19th cent.: from Latin *trifurcus* 'three-forked' (from *tri-* 'three' + *furca* 'fork') + **-ATE**².

trig¹ /trig/ ▶ **n.** informal trigonometry.
– ORIGIN late 19th cent.: abbreviation.

trig² ▶ **adj.** neat and smart in appearance: *two trig little boys, each in a gray flannel suit.*
▶ **v.** (**trigs, trigging, trigged**) [with obj.] make neat and smart in appearance: *he has rigged her and trigged her with paint and spar.*
– ORIGIN Middle English (in the sense 'faithful, trusty'): from Old Norse *tryggr*; related to **TRUE**. The current verb sense dates from the late 17th cent.

trig. ▶ **abbr.** ■ trigonometric. ■ trigonometrical. ■ trigonometry.

trig·a·mous /'trigəməs/ ▶ **adj.** having three wives or husbands at the same time.
– DERIVATIVES **trig·a·mist** /-mist/ **n.**, **trig·a·my** /-mē/ **n.**
– ORIGIN mid 19th cent.: from Greek *trigamos* (from *tri-* 'three' + *gamos* 'marriage') + **-OUS**. The nouns *trigamist* and *trigamy* date from the mid 17th cent.

tri·gem·i·nal nerve /trī'jemənl/ ▶ **n.** Anatomy each of the fifth and largest pair of cranial nerves, supplying the front part of the head and dividing into the ophthalmic, maxillary, and mandibular nerves.

tri·gem·i·nal neu·ral·gia ▶ **n.** Medicine neuralgia involving one or more of the branches of the trigeminal nerves, and often causing severe pain.

tri·gem·i·nus /trī'jemənəs/ ▶ **n.** (pl. **trigemini** /-,nī/) Anatomy the trigeminal nerve.
– ORIGIN late 19th cent.: from Latin, literally 'three born at the same birth,' extended to mean 'threefold.'

trig·ger /'trigər/ ▶ **n.** a small device that releases a spring or catch and so sets off a mechanism, esp. in order to fire a gun: *he pulled the trigger of the shotgun.* ■ an event or thing that causes something to happen: *the trigger for the strike was the closure of a mine.*
▶ **v.** [with obj.] cause (an event or situation) to happen or exist: *an allergy can be triggered by stress or overwork.* ■ cause (a device) to function.
– PHRASES **quick on the trigger** quick to respond.
– DERIVATIVES **trig·gered** adj.
– ORIGIN early 17th cent.: from dialect *tricker*, from Dutch *trekker*, from *trekken* 'to pull.'

trig·ger fin·ger ▶ **n. 1** the forefinger of the hand, as that with which the trigger of a gun is typically pulled.
2 Medicine a defect in a tendon causing a finger to jerk or snap straight when the hand is extended.

trig·ger·fish /'trigər,fisH/ ▶ **n.** (pl. **same** or **triggerfishes**) a marine fish occurring chiefly in tropical inshore waters. It has a large, stout dorsal spine that can be erected and locked into place, allowing the fish to wedge itself into crevices.
● Family Balistidae: numerous genera and species.

trig·ger hair ▶ **n.** a hairlike structure that triggers a rapid movement when touched, in particular: ■ Zoology (in a coelenterate) a filament at the mouth of a nematocyst, triggering the emission of the stinging hair. ■ Botany a bristle on the leaf of a Venus flytrap, triggering the closure of the leaf around an insect.

trig·ger-hap·py ▶ **adj.** ready to react violently, esp. by shooting, on the slightest provocation: *territory controlled by trigger-happy bandits.*

trig·ger point ▶ **n.** a particular circumstance or situation that causes an event to occur: *the army's refusal to withdraw from the territory was the trigger point for military action.* ■ Physiology & Medicine a sensitive area of the body, stimulation or irritation of which causes a specific effect in another part, esp. a tender area in a muscle that causes generalized musculoskeletal pain when overstimulated.

Tri·glav /'trē,gläf, -,gläv/ a mountain in the Julian Alps, in northwestern Slovenia, near the Italian border. Rising to 9,392 feet (2,863 m), it is the highest peak in the mountains east of the Adriatic Sea.

tri·glyc·er·ide /trī'glisə,rīd/ ▶ **n.** Chemistry & Medicine an ester formed from glycerol and three fatty acid groups. Triglycerides are the main constituents of natural fats and oils, and high concentrations in the blood indicate an elevated risk of stroke.

tri·glyph /'trī,glif/ ▶ **n.** Architecture a tablet in a Doric frieze with three vertical grooves. Triglyphs alternate with metopes.
– DERIVATIVES **tri·glyph·ic** /trī'glifik/ **adj.**
– ORIGIN mid 16th cent.: via Latin from Greek *trigluphos*, from *tri-* 'three' + *gluphē* 'carving.'

tri·gon /'trī,gän/ ▶ **n.** archaic term for **TRIANGLE**. ■ an ancient triangular lyre or harp. ■ a triangular cutting region formed by three cusps on an upper molar tooth.
– ORIGIN early 17th cent. (in the sense 'triangle'): via Latin from Greek *trigōnon*, neuter of *trigōnos* 'three-cornered.'

trigon. ▶ **abbr.** ■ trigonometric. ■ trigonometrical. ■ trigonometry.

trig·o·nal /'trigənl/ ▶ **adj.** triangular: *square or trigonal double-sided inserts.* ■ chiefly Biology triangular in cross section: *large trigonal shells.* ■ of or denoting a crystal system or three-dimensional geometric arrangement having three equal axes separated by equal angles that are not right angles.
– DERIVATIVES **trig·o·nal·ly** adv.
– ORIGIN late 16th cent.: from medieval Latin *trigonalis*, from Latin *trigonum* (see **TRIGON**).

tri·gone /'trī,gōn/ ▶ **n.** Anatomy a triangular region or tissue, particularly the area at the base of the urinary bladder, between the openings of the ureters and urethra.
– ORIGIN mid 19th cent.: from French, from Latin *trigonum* 'triangle.'

trig·o·no·met·ric func·tion ▶ **n.** Mathematics a function of an angle, or of an abstract quantity, used in trigonometry, including the sine, cosine, tangent, cotangent, secant, and cosecant, and their hyperbolic counterparts. Also called **CIRCULAR FUNCTION**.

trig·o·nom·e·try /,trigə'nämitrē/ ▶ **n.** the branch of mathematics dealing with the relations of the sides and angles of triangles and with the relevant functions of any angles.
– DERIVATIVES **trig·o·no·met·ric** /-nə'metrik/ **adj.**, **trig·o·no·met·ri·cal** /-nə'metrikəl/ **adj.**
– ORIGIN early 17th cent.: from modern Latin *trigonometria* (see **TRIGON**, **-METRY**).

tri·gram /'trī,gram/ ▶ **n. 1** another term for **TRIGRAPH**.
2 each of the eight figures formed of three parallel lines, each either whole or broken, combined to form the sixty-four hexagrams of the *I Ching.*

tri·graph /'trī,graf/ ▶ **n.** a group of three letters representing one sound, for example German *sch-*.

tri·hal·o·meth·ane (abbr.: **THM**) ▶ **n.** another term for **HALOFORM**.

tri·he·dral /trī'hēdrəl/ ▶ **adj.** (of a solid figure or body) having three sides or faces (in addition to the base or ends); triangular in cross section.
▶ **n.** a trihedral figure.
– ORIGIN late 18th cent.: from Greek *tri-* 'three' + *hedra* 'base' + **-AL**.

tri·he·dron /trī'hēdrən/ ▶ **n.** (pl. **trihedrons** or **trihedra** /-drə/) a solid figure having three sides or faces (in addition to the base or ends).
– ORIGIN early 19th cent.: from **TRI-** 'three' + **-HEDRON**, on the pattern of words such as *polyhedron*.

tri·hy·dric /trī'hīdrik/ ▶ **adj.** Chemistry (of an alcohol) containing three hydroxyl groups.
– ORIGIN mid 19th cent.: from **TRI-** 'three' + **HYDROGEN** + **-IC**.

tri·i·o·do·meth·ane /,trī-īōdō'meTHān, -,ädō-/ ▶ **n.** another term for **IODOFORM**.

tri·i·o·do·thy·ro·nine /,trī-ī,ōdō'THīrə,nēn, -ī,ädō-/ ▶ **n.** Biochemistry a thyroid hormone similar to thyroxine but having greater potency.

tri·jet /'trī,jet/ ▶ **n.** an aircraft powered by three jet engines.

trike /trīk/ informal ▶ **n.** a tricycle.
– ORIGIN late 19th cent.: abbreviation.

tri·lat·er·al /trīˈlatərəl/ ▶ **adj.** shared by or involving three parties: *trilateral negotiations.* ■ Geometry of, on, or with three sides.
▶ **n.** a triangle.

tril·by /ˈtrilbē/ ▶ **n.** (pl. **trilbies**) chiefly Brit. a soft felt hat with a narrow brim and indented crown.
– DERIVATIVES **tril·bied adj.**
– ORIGIN late 19th cent.: from the name of the heroine in G. du Maurier's novel *Trilby* (1894), in the stage version of which such a hat was worn.

tri·lin·e·ar /trīˈlinēər/ ▶ **adj.** Mathematics of or having three lines.

tri·lin·gual /trīˈliNGgwəl/ ▶ **adj.** (of a person) speaking three languages fluently. ■ (of a text or an activity) written or conducted in three languages: *trilingual magazines in Chinese, Indonesian, and English.*
– DERIVATIVES **tri·lin·gual·ism** /-ˌlizəm/ **n.**
– ORIGIN mid 19th cent.: from **TRI-** 'three' + Latin *lingua* 'tongue' + **-AL**.

trill /tril/ ▶ **n.** a quavering or vibratory sound, esp. a rapid alternation of sung or played notes: *they heard the muffled trill of the telephone | the caged bird launched into a piercing trill.* ■ the pronunciation of a consonant, esp. *r*, with rapid vibration of the tongue against the hard or soft palate or the uvula.
▶ **v.** [no obj.] produce a quavering or warbling sound: *a skylark was trilling overhead* | [with direct speech] *"Coming sir," they both trilled* | [with obj.] *trilling a love ballad, she led him to her chair.* ■ [with obj.] pronounce (a consonant) by rapid vibration of the tongue against the hard or soft palate or the uvula.
– ORIGIN mid 17th cent.: from Italian *trillo* (noun), *trillare* (verb).

trill·er /ˈtrilər/ ▶ **n.** an Australasian and Southeast Asian songbird of the cuckoo-shrike family, with mainly black and white plumage. ● Family Campephagidae: two genera, in particular *Lalage*, and several species.

Tril·lin /ˈtrilən/, Calvin (1935–), US writer. He became a staff writer for *The New Yorker* magazine in 1963 and had a syndicated newspaper column 1986–95 and a weekly column in *Time* magazine 1995–2001. He was a columnist 1978–85 for *The Nation*, to which he has contributed a weekly satirical verse since 1990. Among his many books are *Remembering Denny* (1993), a story of a college friend, and *Messages from My Father* (1996).

tril·lion /ˈtrilyən/ ▶ **cardinal number** (pl. **trillions** or (with numeral) **same**) a million million (1,000,000,000,000 or 10^{12}). ■ (**trillions**) informal a very large number or amount: *the yammering of trillions of voices.* ■ dated, chiefly Brit. a million million million (1,000,000,000,000,000,000 or 10^{18}).
– DERIVATIVES **tril·lionth** /-yənTH/ **ordinal number.**
– ORIGIN late 17th cent.: from French, from *million*, by substitution of the prefix *tri-* 'three' for the initial letters.

tril·li·um /ˈtrilēəm/ ▶ **n.** a plant with a solitary three-petaled flower above a whorl of three leaves, native to North American and Asia. ● Genus *Trillium*, family Liliaceae (or Trilliaceae): several species, in particular **red** (or **purple**) **trillium** (*T. erectum*).
– ORIGIN modern Latin, apparently an alteration of Swedish *trilling* 'triplet.'

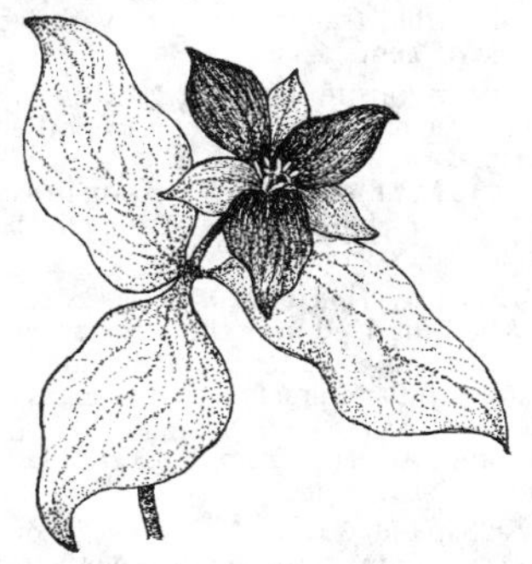

red trillium

tri·lo·bite /ˈtrīləˌbīt/ ▶ **n.** an extinct marine arthropod that occurred abundantly during the Paleozoic era, with a carapace over the forepart, and a segmented hind part divided longitudinally into three lobes. ● Subphylum Trilobita, phylum Arthropoda: numerous classes and orders.
– ORIGIN mid 19th cent.: from modern Latin *Trilobites*, from Greek *tri-* 'three' + *lobos* 'lobe' + **-ITE**[1].

tril·o·gy /ˈtriləjē/ ▶ **n.** (pl. **trilogies**) a group of three related novels, plays, films, operas, or albums. ■ (in ancient Greece) a series of three tragedies performed one after the other. ■ a group or series of three related things: *a trilogy of cases reflected this development.*
– ORIGIN from Greek *trilogia*, from *tri-* 'three times' + *logos* 'story.'

trim /trim/ ▶ **v.** (**trims**, **trimming**, **trimmed**) [with obj.] **1** make (something) neat or of the required size or form by cutting away irregular or unwanted parts: *trim the grass using a sharp mower.* ■ cut off (irregular or unwanted parts): *he was **trimming the fat off** some pork chops.* ■ reduce the size, amount, or number of (something, typically expenditure or costs): *Congress had to decide which current defense programs should be trimmed.* ■ [no obj.] (**trim down**) (of a person) lose weight; become slimmer: *he works on trimming down and eating right.* ■ firm up or lose weight from (a part of one's body).
2 (usu. **be trimmed**) decorate (something), typically with contrasting items or pieces of material: *a pair of black leather gloves **trimmed with** fake fur.*
3 adjust (sails) to take best advantage of the wind. ■ adjust the forward and after drafts of (a vessel) by changing the distribution of weight on board, esp. cargo and ballast. ■ keep or adjust the degree to which (an aircraft) can be maintained at a constant altitude without any control forces being present. ■ [no obj.] adapt one's views to the prevailing political trends for personal advancement.
4 informal, dated get the better of (someone), typically by cheating them out of money.
5 informal, dated rebuke (someone) angrily.
▶ **n. 1** additional decoration, typically along the edges of something and in contrasting color or material: *suede sandals with gold trim | we painted the buildings off-white with a blue trim.* ■ decorative additions to a vehicle, typically the upholstery or interior lining of a car.
2 [in sing.] an act of cutting off part of something in order to neaten it: *his hair needs a trim.* ■ a short piece of film cut out during the final editing stage.
3 the state of being in good order or condition: *no one had been there for months—everything was out of trim.*
4 the degree to which an aircraft can be maintained at a constant altitude without any control forces being present: *the pilot's only problem was the need to constantly readjust the trim.*
5 the difference between a vessel's forward and after drafts, esp. as it affects its navigability.
▶ **adj.** (**trimmer**, **trimmest**) neat and smart in appearance; in good order: *she kept her husband's clothes neat and trim | a trim little villa.* ■ (of a person or their body) slim and fit: *she has a trim, athletic figure.*
– PHRASES **in trim** slim and fit. ■ Nautical in good order. **trim one's sails** (**to the wind**) make changes to suit one's new circumstances.
– DERIVATIVES **trim·ly adv.**, **trim·ness n.**
– ORIGIN Old English *trymman, trymian* 'make firm, arrange,' of which the adjective appears to be a derivative. The word's history is obscure; current verb senses date from the early 16th cent. when usage became frequent and served many purposes: this is possibly explained by spoken or dialect use in the Middle English period not recorded in extant literature.

tri·ma·ran /ˈtrīməˌran/ ▶ **n.** a yacht with three hulls in parallel.
– ORIGIN 1940s: from **TRI-** + **CATAMARAN**.

Trim·ble /ˈtrimbəl/, Robert (1776–1828), US Supreme Court associate justice 1826–28. Appointed to the Court by President John Quincy Adams, he was an advocate of federal supremacy.

tri·mer /ˈtrīmər/ ▶ **n.** Chemistry a polymer comprising three monomer units.
– DERIVATIVES **tri·mer·ic** /trīˈmerik/ **adj.**

trim·er·ous /ˈtrimərəs/ ▶ **adj.** Botany & Zoology having parts arranged in groups of three. ■ consisting of three joints or parts.

tri·mes·ter /trīˈmestər, ˈtrīˌmes-/ ▶ **n.** a period of three months, esp. as a division of the duration of pregnancy. ■ each of the three terms in an academic year.
– DERIVATIVES **tri·mes·tral** /trīˈmestrəl/ **adj.**, **tri·mes·tri·al** /trīˈmestrēəl/ **adj.**
– ORIGIN early 19th cent.: from French *trimestre*, from Latin *trimestris*, from *tri-* 'three' + *mensis* 'month.'

trim·e·ter /ˈtrimitər/ ▶ **n.** Prosody a line of verse consisting of three metrical feet.
– DERIVATIVES **tri·met·ric** /trīˈmetrik/ **adj.**, **tri·met·ri·cal** /trīˈmetrikəl/ **adj.**
– ORIGIN mid 16th cent.: via Latin from Greek *trimetros*, from *tri-* 'three' + *metron* 'measure.'

tri·meth·o·prim /trīˈmeTHəˌprim/ ▶ **n.** Medicine a synthetic antibiotic used to treat malaria and respiratory and urinary infections (usually in conjunction with a sulfonamide).
– ORIGIN 1960s: from *trimeth(yl)* + *o(xy-)* + *p(y)rim(idine)*.

tri·mix /ˈtrīˌmiks/ ▶ **n.** a breathing mixture for deep-sea divers, composed of nitrogen, helium, and oxygen.

trim·mer /ˈtrimər/ ▶ **n. 1** an implement used for trimming off the unwanted or untidy parts of something: *a hedge trimmer.*
2 a person who adapts their views to the prevailing political trends for personal advancement.
3 a person who decorates something: *window trimmers.*
4 (also **trimmer joist**) Architecture a crosspiece fixed between full-length joists (and often across the end of truncated joists) to form part of the frame of an opening in a floor or roof.
5 a person responsible for trimming the sails of a yacht. ■ a person employed to arrange cargo or fuel in a ship's hold.
6 a small capacitor or other component used to tune a circuit such as a radio set.

trim·ming /ˈtrimiNG/ ▶ **n. 1** (**trimmings**) small pieces trimmed off something: *hedge trimmings.*
2 decoration, esp. for clothing: *a party dress with lace trimming.* ■ (**the trimmings**) informal the traditional accompaniments to something, esp. a meal or special occasion: *roast turkey **with all the trimmings**.*

Tri·mon·ti·um /trīˈmäntēəm/ Roman name for **PLOVDIV**.

trim·pot /ˈtrimˌpät/ ▶ **n.** a small potentiometer used to make small adjustments to the value of resistance or voltage in an electronic circuit.

trim tab (also **trimming tab**) ▶ **n.** Aeronautics an adjustable tab or airfoil attached to a control surface, used to trim an aircraft in flight.

Tri·mur·ti /triˈmo͝ortē/ Hinduism the trinity of Brahma the creator, Vishnu the preserver, and Shiva the destroyer.
– ORIGIN from Sanskrit *tri* 'three' + *mūrti* 'form.'

trine /trīn/ Astrology ▶ **n.** an aspect of 120° (one third of a circle): ***Venus in trine to** Mars* | [as modifier] *a trine aspect.* See also **GRAND TRINE**.
▶ **v.** [with obj.] (of a planet) be in a trine aspect with (another planet or position): *Jupiter trines Pluto all month.*
– ORIGIN late Middle English (in the sense 'made up of three parts'): from Old French *trin(e)*, from Latin *trinus* 'threefold,' from *tres* 'three.'

Trin·i /ˈtrinē/ ▶ **n.** W. Indian a Trinidadian.
– ORIGIN abbreviation.

Trin·i·dad and To·ba·go /ˈtrinəˌdad and təˈbāgō/ a country in the Caribbean Sea comprising two islands off the northeastern coast of Venezuela; pop. 1,230,000 (est. 2009); capital, Port-of-Spain (on Trinidad); languages, English (official) and Creole.

> The larger of the two islands is Trinidad, with Tobago to the northeast. Trinidad, inhabited by Arawaks, was visited by Columbus in 1498 and settled by the Spanish; Tobago, occupied by Caribs, was colonized by the French and later the British in the 18th century. Trinidad became British during the Napoleonic Wars and was formally amalgamated with Tobago as a Crown Colony in 1888. Trinidad and Tobago became an independent member state of the Commonwealth of Nations in 1962 and finally a republic in 1976.

– DERIVATIVES **Trin·i·da·di·an** /ˌtrinəˈdadēən, -ˈdādē-/ **adj. & n.**, **To·ba·gan** /təˈbāgən/ **adj. & n.**, **To·ba·go·ni·an** /ˌtōbəˈgōnēən/ **adj. & n.**

Trin·i·tar·i·an /ˌtrinəˈte(ə)rēən/ ▶ **adj.** of or relating to belief in the doctrine of the Trinity.
▶ **n.** a person who believes in the doctrine of the Trinity.
– DERIVATIVES **Trin·i·tar·i·an·ism** /-ˌnizəm/ **n.**

tri·ni·tro·tol·u·ene /trīˌnītrōˈtälyəˌwēn/ ▶ **n.** see **TNT**.

trin·i·ty /ˈtrinitē/ ▶ **n.** (pl. **trinities**) (also **the Trinity** or **the Holy Trinity**) the Christian Godhead as one God in three persons: Father, Son, and Holy Spirit. ■ a group of three people or things: *the wine was the first of a trinity of three excellent vintages.* ■ the state of being three: *God is said to be trinity in unity.*
– ORIGIN Middle English: from Old French *trinite*, from Latin *trinitas* 'triad,' from *trinus* 'threefold' (see **TRINE**).

Trin·i·ty Moun·tains a forested range of the Klamath Mountains in northwestern California.

Trin·i·ty Riv·er a river that flows for 550 miles (900 km) from the Trinity Mountains across Texas to the Gulf of Mexico.

t

Trin·i·ty Sun·day ▶ n. the next Sunday after Pentecost, observed in the Western Christian Church as a feast in honor of the Holy Trinity.

trin·ket /ˈtriNGkit/ ▶ n. a small ornament or item of jewelry that is of little value.
– DERIVATIVES **trin·ket·ry** /-trē/ n.
– ORIGIN mid 16th cent.: of unknown origin.

tri·no·mi·al /trīˈnōmēəl/ ▶ adj. **1** (of an algebraic expression) consisting of three terms.
2 Biology (of a systematic name for a taxon) consisting of three terms of which the first is the name of the genus, the second that of the species, and the third that of the subspecies or variety.
▶ n. **1** an algebraic expression of three terms.
2 Biology a trinomial taxonomic name.
– ORIGIN late 17th cent.: from TRI- 'three,' on the pattern of *binomial*.

tri·o /ˈtrē-ō/ ▶ n. (pl. **trios**) a set or group of three people or things: *the hotel was run by a trio of brothers*. ■ a group of three musicians: *a jazz trio*. ■ a composition written for three musicians: *Chopin's G minor Trio*. ■ the central, typically contrastive, section of a minuet, scherzo, or march. ■ (in piquet) a set of three aces, kings, queens, jacks, or tens held in one hand.
– ORIGIN early 18th cent.: from Italian, from Latin *tres* 'three,' on the pattern of *duo*.

tri·ode /ˈtrīˌōd/ ▶ n. a vacuum tube having three electrodes. ■ a semiconductor rectifier having three connections.
– ORIGIN early 20th cent.: from TRI- 'three' + ELECTRODE.

tri·o·let /ˈtrēəlit, ˈtrī-, ˌtrēəˈlā/ ▶ n. a poem of eight lines, typically of eight syllables each, rhyming *abaaabab* and so structured that the first line recurs as the fourth and seventh and the second as the eighth.
– ORIGIN mid 17th cent.: from French.

tri·ose /ˈtrīˌōs/ ▶ n. Chemistry any of a group of monosaccharide sugars whose molecules contain three carbon atoms.

tri·o so·na·ta ▶ n. a baroque composition written in three parts, two upper parts and one bass, and usually performed with a keyboard continuo.

tri·ox·ide /trīˈäkˌsīd/ ▶ n. Chemistry an oxide containing three atoms of oxygen in its molecule or empirical formula.

trip /trip/ ▶ v. (**trips, tripping, tripped**) **1** [no obj.] catch one's foot on something and stumble or fall: *he **tripped over** his cat* | *she **tripped up** during the penultimate lap*. ■ [with obj.] cause (someone) to do this: *she shot out her foot to trip him up*. ■ (**trip up**) make a mistake: *taxpayers often trip up by not declaring taxable income*. ■ [with obj.] (**trip someone up**) detect or expose someone in an error, blunder, or inconsistency: *the man was determined to trip him up on his economics*.
2 [no obj.] walk, run, or dance with quick light steps: *they tripped up the terrace steps*. ■ (of words) flow lightly and easily: *a name that **trips off the tongue*** | *the guest list tripped from her lips*.
3 [with obj.] activate (a mechanism), esp. by contact with a switch, catch, or other electrical device: *an intruder trips the alarm*. ■ [no obj.] (of part of an electric circuit) disconnect automatically as a safety measure: *the plugs will trip as soon as any change in current is detected*.
4 [with obj.] Nautical release and raise (an anchor) from the seabed by means of a buoyed line attached to the anchor's crown. ■ turn (a yard or other object) from a horizontal to a vertical position for lowering.
5 [no obj.] informal experience hallucinations induced by taking a psychedelic drug, esp. LSD: *they prance around **tripping out** on their hallucinogens*.
6 [no obj.] go on a short journey: *when tripping through the Yukon, take some time to explore our museums*.
▶ n. **1** an act of going to a place and returning; a journey or excursion, esp. for pleasure: *Sally's gone on a school trip* | *a trip to the North Pole* | *a quick trip to the store*.
2 a stumble or fall due to catching one's foot on something. ■ archaic a mistake: *an occasional trip in the performance*.
3 informal a hallucinatory experience caused by taking a psychedelic drug, esp. LSD: *acid trips*. ■ an exciting or stimulating experience: *it was a trip seeing him again*. ■ a self-indulgent attitude or activity: *politics was a sixties trip*.
4 a device that activates or disconnects a mechanism, circuit, etc.
5 archaic a light, lively movement of a person's feet: *yonder comes Dalinda; I know her by her trip*.
– PHRASES **trip the light fantastic** humorous dance, in particular engage in ballroom dancing. [from "Trip it as you go / On the light fantastic toe" (Milton's *L'Allegro*).]
– ORIGIN Middle English: from Old French *triper*, from Middle Dutch *trippen* 'to skip, hop.'

tri·par·tite /trīˈpärˌtīt/ ▶ adj. consisting of three parts: *a tripartite classification*. ■ shared by or involving three parties: *a tripartite coalition government*.
– DERIVATIVES **tri·par·tite·ly** adv., **tri·par·ti·tion** /ˌtrīpärˈtisHən/ n.
– ORIGIN late Middle English: from Latin *tripartitus*, from *tri-* 'three' + *partitus* 'divided' (past participle of *partiri*).

trip com·pu·ter ▶ n. an electronic odometer, typically with extra capabilities such as the ability to calculate fuel consumption.

tripe /trīp/ ▶ n. **1** the first or second stomach of a cow or other ruminant used as food.
2 informal nonsense; rubbish: *you do talk tripe sometimes*.
– ORIGIN Middle English: from Old French, of unknown origin.

trip ham·mer ▶ n. a large, heavy pivoted hammer used in forging, raised by a cam or lever and allowed to drop on the metal being worked.

trip-hop ▶ n. a style of dance music, usually slow in tempo, that combines elements of hip-hop and dub reggae with softer, more ambient sounds.

triph·thong /ˈtrifˌTHôNG, ˈtrip-/ ▶ n. a union of three vowels (letters or sounds) pronounced in one syllable (as in some pronunciations of *our*). Contrasted with DIPHTHONG, MONOPHTHONG. ■ a vowel trigraph (as in *beau*).
– DERIVATIVES **triph·thong·al** /trifˈTHôNG(g)əl, trip-, -ˈTHäNG(g)əl/ adj.
– ORIGIN mid 16th cent.: from French *triphtongue*, from *tri-* 'three,' on the pattern of *diphthong*.

Tri·pit·a·ka /triˈpitikə/ ▶ n. (**the Tripitaka**) the discourses of the Buddha, collected in the first century and arranged into the three divisions of sermons, monastic law, and metaphysics. Only the compilation of the Theravada school, written in Pali, survives in its entirety.
– ORIGIN from Sanskrit *tripiṭaka*, literally 'the three baskets or collections.'

tripl. ▶ abbr. triplicate.

tri·plane /ˈtrīˌplān/ ▶ n. an early type of airplane with three pairs of wings, one above the other.

tri·ple /ˈtripəl/ ▶ adj. [attrib.] consisting of or involving three parts, things, or people: *a triple murder* | *triple somersaults*. ■ having three times the usual size, quality, or strength: *a triple dark rum*.
▶ predeterminer three times as much or as many: *the copper energy cells had triple the efficiency of silicon cells*.
▶ n. **1** a thing that is three times as large as usual or is made up of three standard units or items.
2 (**triples**) a sporting contest in which each side has three players.
3 (**Triples**) Bell-ringing a system of change ringing using seven bells, with three pairs changing places each time.
4 Baseball a hit that enables the batter to reach third base.
5 another term for TRIFECTA.
▶ v. [no obj.] **1** become three times as much or as many: *grain prices were expected to triple*. ■ [with obj.] multiply (something) by three: *the party more than tripled its share of the vote*.
2 Baseball hit a triple: *he tripled into right field*.
– DERIVATIVES **trip·ly** /ˈtriplē/ adv.
– ORIGIN Middle English (as an adjective and adverb): from Old French, or from Latin *triplus*, from Greek *triplous*.

tri·ple A (also **AAA**) ▶ n. **1** [usu. as modifier] Finance the highest grading available from credit rating agencies.
2 the highest competitive level in minor league baseball.

Tri·ple Al·li·ance ▶ n. a union or association between three powers or states, in particular that made in 1668 between England, the Netherlands, and Sweden against France, and that in 1882 between Germany, Austria-Hungary, and Italy against France and Russia.

tri·ple bond ▶ n. Chemistry a chemical bond in which three pairs of electrons are shared between two atoms.

tri·ple crown ▶ n. **1** (**Triple Crown**) an award or honor for winning a group of three important events in a sport, in particular victory by one horse in the Kentucky Derby, the Preakness, and the Belmont Stakes.
2 the papal tiara.

Tri·ple En·tente /änˈtänt/ an early-20th-century alliance between Great Britain, France, and Russia. Originally a series of loose agreements, the Triple Entente began to assume the nature of a more formal alliance as the prospect of war with the Central Powers became more likely, and formed the basis of the Allied powers in World War I.

tri·ple jump ▶ n. **1** (**the triple jump**) a track-and-field event in which competitors attempt to jump as far as possible by performing a hop, a step, and a jump from a running start.
2 Skating a jump in which the skater makes three full turns while in the air.
▶ v. (**triple-jump**) [no obj.] (of an athlete) perform a triple jump.
– DERIVATIVES **tri·ple jump·er** n.

tri·ple play ▶ n. Baseball a defensive play in which three runners are put out.

tri·ple point ▶ n. Chemistry the temperature and pressure at which the solid, liquid, and vapor phases of a pure substance can coexist in equilibrium.

tri·ple rhyme ▶ n. a feminine rhyme involving one stressed and two unstressed syllables in each rhyming line.

tri·plet /ˈtriplit/ ▶ n. **1** (usu. **triplets**) one of three children or animals born at the same birth.
2 a set or succession of three similar things. ■ Music a group of three equal notes to be performed in the time of two or four. ■ a set of three rhyming lines of verse.
3 Physics & Chemistry an atomic or molecular state characterized by two unpaired electrons with parallel spins. ■ a group of three associated lines close together in a spectrum or electrophoretic gel.
– ORIGIN mid 17th cent.: from TRIPLE, on the pattern of *doublet*.

tri·plet code ▶ n. Biology the standard version of the genetic code, in which a sequence of three nucleotides in a DNA or RNA molecule codes for a specific amino acid in protein synthesis.

tri·ple time ▶ n. musical time with three beats to the bar.

tri·ple tongu·ing ▶ n. Music a technique in which alternate movements of the tongue are made (typically as in sounding *ttk*) to facilitate rapid playing of a wind instrument.

tri·plex /ˈtripleks, ˈtrī-/ ▶ n. **1** a building divided into three self-contained residences. ■ an apartment or other residence on three floors. ■ a movie theater with three separate screening rooms.
2 Biochemistry a triple-stranded polynucleotide molecule.
▶ adj. having three parts, in particular (of a residence) on three floors: *his vast triplex apartment*.
▶ v. (**be triplexed**) (of electrical equipment or systems) be provided or fitted in triplicate so as to ensure reliability.
– ORIGIN early 17th cent. (as an adjective in the sense 'threefold'): from Latin, 'threefold,' from *tri-* 'three' + *plicare* 'to fold.' Current specific senses date from the 1920s.

trip·li·cate ▶ adj. /ˈtriplikit/ [attrib.] existing in three copies or examples: *triplicate measurements*.
▶ n. /ˈtriplikit/ archaic a thing that is part of a set of three copies or corresponding parts: *the triplicate of a letter to the Governor*.
▶ v. /-ˌkāt/ [with obj.] make three copies of (something); multiply by three.
– PHRASES **in triplicate** three times in exactly the same way: *the procedure was repeated in triplicate*. ■ existing as a set of three exact copies: *this form is in triplicate and must be handed to all employees*.
– DERIVATIVES **trip·li·ca·tion** /ˌtripləˈkāSHən/ n.
– ORIGIN late Middle English: from Latin *triplicat-* 'made three,' from the verb *triplicare*, from *triplex*, *triplic-* 'threefold' (see TRIPLEX). The verb dates from the early 17th cent.

tri·plic·i·ty /triˈplisitē/ ▶ n. (pl. **triplicities**) rare a group of three people or things. ■ archaic the state of being triple.
– ORIGIN late Middle English (as a term in astrology): from late Latin *triplicitas*, from Latin *triplex*, *triplic-* 'threefold' (see TRIPLEX).

trip·lo·blas·tic /ˌtriplōˈblastik/ ▶ adj. Zoology having a body derived from three embryonic cell layers (ectoderm, mesoderm, and endoderm), as in all multicellular animals except sponges and coelenterates.
– ORIGIN late 19th cent.: from Greek *triploos* 'threefold' + -BLAST + -IC.

trip·loid /ˈtriploid/ Genetics ▶ adj. (of a cell or nucleus) containing three homologous sets of chromosomes. ■ (of an organism or species) composed of triploid cells.
▶ n. a triploid organism, variety, or species.
– DERIVATIVES **trip·loi·dy** /ˈtriˌploidē/ n.

trip·me·ter /ˈtripˌmētər/ ▶ n. a vehicle instrument that can be set to record the distance of individual journeys.

tri·pod /ˈtrīpäd/ ▶ n. **1** a three-legged stand for supporting a camera or other apparatus.
2 archaic a stool, table, or cauldron resting on three legs. ■ historical the bronze altar at Delphi on which a priestess sat to utter oracles.
– DERIVATIVES **trip·o·dal** /ˈtripədl/ adj.

– ORIGIN early 17th cent.: via Latin from Greek *tripous, tripod-*, from *tri-* 'three' + *pous, pod-* 'foot.'

Trip·o·li /'tripəlē/ **1** the capital and chief port of Libya, on the Mediterranean coast in the northwestern part of the country; pop. 1,065,400 (est. 2006). Founded by Phoenicians in the 7th century BC, its ancient name was Oea. Arabic name **TARABULUS AL-GHARB**, 'western Tripoli.' **2** a port in northwestern Lebanon; pop. 190,800 (est. 2009). It was founded *c.*700 BC and was the capital of the Phoenician triple federation formed by the city states Sidon, Tyre, and Arvad. Today it is a major port and commercial center. Arabic name **TARABULUS ASH-SHAM**, 'eastern Tripoli,' **TRÂBLOUS**.

trip·o·li /'tripəlē/ ▶ **n.** another term for **ROTTENSTONE**.
– ORIGIN early 17th cent.: from French, from **TRIPOLI**.

Trip·o·li·ta·ni·a /ˌtripələ'tānēə, triˌpälə-, -'tānyə/ a coastal region that surrounds Tripoli in North Africa, in what is now northeastern Libya.
– DERIVATIVES **Trip·o·li·ta·ni·an** adj. & n.
– ORIGIN based on Latin *tripolis* 'three cities,' referring to the Phoenician cities, Oea (now Tripoli), Leptis Magna, and Sabratha, established here in the 7th cent. BC.

tri·pos /'trīˌpäs/ ▶ **n.** [in sing.] the final honors examination for a BA degree at Cambridge University.
– ORIGIN late 16th cent.: alteration of Latin *tripus* 'tripod,' with reference to the stool on which a designated graduate (known as the "Tripos") sat.

trip·pant /'tripənt/ ▶ **adj.** [usu. postpositive] Heraldry (of a stag or deer) represented as walking. Compare with **PASSANT**.
– ORIGIN mid 17th cent.: from Old French, literally 'walking or springing lightly,' present participle of *tripper*.

trip·per /'tripər/ ▶ **n.** informal a person who goes on a pleasure trip or excursion.

trip·py /'tripē/ ▶ **adj.** (**trippier**, **trippiest**) informal resembling or inducing the hallucinatory effect produced by taking a psychedelic drug: *trippy house music*.

trip·tych /'triptik/ ▶ **n.** a picture or relief carving on three panels, typically hinged together side by side and used as an altarpiece. ■ a set of three associated artistic, literary, or musical works intended to be appreciated together.
– ORIGIN mid 18th cent. (denoting a set of three writing tablets hinged or tied together): from **TRI-** 'three,' on the pattern of *diptych*.

trip·tyque /trip'tēk, 'triptik/ ▶ **n.** dated a customs permit serving as a passport for a motor vehicle.
– ORIGIN early 20th cent.: from French, literally 'triptych' (because originally the document had three sections).

Trip·u·ra /'tripŏŏrə/ a small state in northeastern India, on the eastern border of Bangladesh; capital, Agartala.

trip·wire /'tripˌwīr/ ▶ **n.** a wire stretched close to the ground, working a trap, explosion, or alarm when disturbed and serving to detect or prevent people or animals entering an area. ■ a comparatively weak military force employed as a first line of defense, engagement with which will trigger the intervention of strong forces.

tri·que·tra /trī'kwētrə, -'kwetrə/ ▶ **n.** (pl. **triquetrae** /-trē/) a symmetrical triangular ornament of three interlaced arcs used on metalwork and stone crosses.
– ORIGIN late 16th cent. (originally denoting a triangle): from Latin, feminine of *triquetrus* 'three-cornered.'

tri·que·tral /trī'kwētrəl, -'kwetrəl/ (also **triquetral bone**) ▶ **n.** Anatomy a carpal bone on the outside of the wrist, articulating with the lunate, hamate, and pisiform bones.
– ORIGIN mid 17th cent.: from Latin *triquetrus* 'three-cornered' + **-AL**.

tri·reme /'trīˌrēm/ ▶ **n.** an ancient Greek or Roman war galley with three banks of oars. The rowers are believed to have sat in threes on angled benches, rather than in three superimposed banks.
– ORIGIN from Latin *triremis*, from *tri-* 'three' + *remus* 'oar.'

tris[1] /tris/ (also **tris buffer**) ▶ **n.** a flammable compound that forms a corrosive solution in water and is used as a buffer and emulsifying agent. ● Alternative name: **trishydroxymethylaminomethane**; chem. formula: $(HOCH_2)_3CNH_2$.
– ORIGIN 1950s: from *tris-*, the prefix of the systematic name.

tris[2] ▶ **n.** an organophosphorus compound, used as a flame retardant. ● Alternative name: **tris-2,3-dibromopropylphosphate**; chem. formula: $(Br_2C_3H_5)_3PO_4$.
– ORIGIN 1970s: from *tris-*, the prefix of the systematic name.

tri·sac·cha·ride /trī'sakəˌrīd/ ▶ **n.** Chemistry any of the class of sugars whose molecules contain three monosaccharide molecules.

Tris·agion /trē'sagēən, -'säyôn/ ▶ **n.** a hymn, esp. in the Orthodox Church, with a triple invocation of God as holy.
– ORIGIN late Middle English: from Greek, neuter of *trisagios*, from *tris* 'three times' + *hagios* 'holy.'

tri·sect /trī'sekt/ ▶ **v.** [with obj.] divide (something) into three parts, typically three equal parts.
– DERIVATIVES **tri·sec·tion** /-'seksʜən/ **n.**, **tri·sec·tor** /-tər/ **n.**
– ORIGIN late 17th cent.: from **TRI-** 'three' + Latin *sect-* 'divided, cut' (from the verb *secare*).

tri·shaw /'trīˌsʜô/ ▶ **n.** a light three-wheeled vehicle with pedals, used in East Asia.
– ORIGIN 1940s: from **TRI-** 'three' + **RICKSHA**.

tris·kai·dek·a·pho·bi·a /ˌtriskīˌdekə'fōbēə, ˌtriskə-/ ▶ **n.** extreme superstition regarding the number thirteen.
– ORIGIN early 20th cent.: from Greek *treiskaideka* 'thirteen' + **-PHOBIA**.

tris·kel·i·on /trī'skelēən, tri-/ ▶ **n.** a Celtic symbol consisting of three legs or lines radiating from a center.
– ORIGIN mid 19th cent.: from **TRI-** 'three' + Greek *skelos* 'leg.'

tris·mus /'trizməs/ ▶ **n.** Medicine spasm of the jaw muscles, causing the mouth to remain tightly closed, typically as a symptom of tetanus. Also called **LOCKJAW**.
– ORIGIN late 17th cent.: from modern Latin, from Greek *trismos* 'a scream, grinding.'

tri·so·my /'trīˌsōmē, 'trīsō-/ ▶ **n.** Medicine a condition in which an extra copy of a chromosome is present in the cell nuclei, causing developmental abnormalities.
– ORIGIN 1930s: from **TRI-** 'three' + **-SOME**[3].

tri·so·my-21 ▶ **n.** Medicine the most common form of Down syndrome, caused by an extra copy of chromosome number 21.

Tris·tan /'trisˌtän, -tən/ variant spelling of **TRISTRAM**.

tris·tesse /trē'stes/ ▶ **n.** literary a state of melancholy sadness.
– ORIGIN French.

Tris·tram /'tristrəm/ (also **Tristan** /'trisˌtän, -tən/) (in medieval legend) a knight who was the lover of Iseult.

tri·syl·la·ble /trī'siləbəl/ ▶ **n.** a word or metrical foot of three syllables.
– DERIVATIVES **tri·syl·lab·ic** /ˌtrīsə'labik/ **adj.**

tri·tag·o·nist /trī'tagənist/ ▶ **n.** the person who is third in importance, after the protagonist and deuteragonist, in an ancient Greek drama.
– ORIGIN late 19th cent.: from Greek *tritagōnistēs*, from *tritos* 'third' + *agōnistēs* 'actor.'

trit·an·ope /'trītnˌōp/ ▶ **n.** a person suffering from tritanopia.

trit·an·o·pi·a /ˌtrītn'ōpēə/ ▶ **n.** a rare form of color-blindness resulting from insensitivity to blue light, causing confusion of greens and blues. Compare with **PROTANOPIA**.
– ORIGIN early 20th cent.: from **TRITO-** 'third' (referring to blue as the third color in the spectrum) + **AN-**[1] 'without' + **-OPIA**.

trite /trīt/ ▶ **adj.** (of a remark, opinion, or idea) overused and consequently of little import; lacking originality or freshness: *this point may now seem obvious and trite*.
– DERIVATIVES **trite·ly** adv., **trite·ness** n.
– ORIGIN mid 16th cent.: from Latin *tritus*, past participle of *terere* 'to rub.'

tri·ter·pene /trī'tərpēn/ ▶ **n.** Chemistry any of a group of terpenes found in plant gums and resins, having unsaturated molecules based on a unit with the formula $C_{30}H_{48}$.
– DERIVATIVES **tri·ter·pe·noid** /-pəˌnoid/ **adj. & n.**

tri·the·ism /trī'ᴛʜēˌizəm/ ▶ **n.** (in Christian theology) the doctrine of or belief in the three persons of the Trinity as three distinct gods.
– DERIVATIVES **tri·the·ist** n.

tri·ti·at·ed /'tritēˌātid, 'trisʜ-/ ▶ **adj.** Chemistry (of a compound) in which the ordinary isotope of hydrogen has been replaced with tritium.
– DERIVATIVES **tri·ti·a·tion** /ˌtrisʜē'āsʜən/ **n.**

trit·i·ca·le /ˌtriti'kālē/ ▶ **n.** a hybrid grain produced by crossing wheat and rye, grown as a fodder crop.
– ORIGIN 1950s: modern Latin, from a blend of the genus names *Triticum* 'wheat' and *Secale* 'rye.'

trit·i·um /'tritēəm, 'trisʜ-/ ▶ **n.** Chemistry a radioactive isotope of hydrogen with a mass approximately three times that of the common protium isotope. (Symbol: **T**)

> Discovered in 1934, tritium has two neutrons as well as a proton in the nucleus. It occurs in minute traces in nature and can be made artificially from lithium or deuterium in nuclear reactors; it is used as a fuel in thermonuclear bombs.

– ORIGIN 1930s: from modern Latin, from Greek *tritos* 'third.'

trito- ▶ **comb. form** third: *tritocerebrum*.
– ORIGIN from Greek *tritos* 'third.'

tri·to·cer·e·brum /ˌtrītōsə'rēbrəm, -'serə-/ ▶ **n.** (pl. **tritocerebra** /-brə/) Entomology the third and hindmost segment of an insect's brain.

Tri·ton /'trītn/ **1** Greek Mythology a minor sea god usually represented as a man with a fish's tail and carrying a trident and shell trumpet. **2** Astronomy the largest satellite of Neptune, the seventh closest to the planet, discovered in 1846. It has a retrograde orbit, a thin nitrogen atmosphere, and a diameter of 1,678 miles (2,700 km).

tri·ton[1] /'trītn/ ▶ **n.** a large mollusk that has a tall spiral shell with a large aperture, living in tropical and subtropical seas. ● Genus *Charonia*, family Cymatiidae, class Gastropoda, in particular *C. tritonis*, which is used as a trumpet shell.
– ORIGIN late 18th cent.: from **TRITON**.

tri·ton[2] ▶ **n.** a nucleus of a tritium atom, consisting of a proton and two neutrons.
– ORIGIN 1940s: from **TRITIUM** + **-ON**.

tri·tone /'trīˌtōn/ ▶ **n.** Music an interval of three whole tones (an augmented fourth), as between C and F sharp.

trit·u·rate /'tricʜəˌrāt/ ▶ **v.** [with obj.] technical grind to a fine powder. ■ chew or grind (food) thoroughly.
– DERIVATIVES **trit·u·ra·tion** /ˌtricʜə'rāsʜən/ **n.**, **trit·u·ra·tor** /-ˌrātər/ **n.**
– ORIGIN mid 18th cent.: from Latin *triturat-* '(of corn) threshed,' from *tritura* 'rubbing' (from the verb *terere*).

tri·umph /'trīəmf/ ▶ **n.** **1** a great victory or achievement: *a garden built to celebrate Napoleon's many triumphs*. ■ the state of being victorious or successful: *the king returned home **in triumph***. ■ joy or satisfaction resulting from a success or victory: *"Here it is!" Helen's voice rose **in triumph***. ■ a highly successful example of something: *the marriage had been **a triumph of** togetherness*. **2** the processional entry of a victorious general into ancient Rome.
▶ **v.** [no obj.] **1** achieve a victory; be successful: *spectacle has once again **triumphed over** content*. ■ rejoice or exult at a victory or success: *"There!" triumphed Alima*. **2** (of a Roman general) ride into ancient Rome after a victory.
– ORIGIN late Middle English: from Old French *triumphe* (noun), from Latin *triump(h)us*, probably from Greek *thriambos* 'hymn to Bacchus.' Current senses of the verb date from the early 16th cent.

tri·um·phal /trī'əmfəl/ ▶ **adj.** made, carried out, or used in celebration of a great victory or achievement: *a vast triumphal arch* | *a triumphal procession*.
– ORIGIN late Middle English: from Old French *triumphal* or Latin *triumphalis*, from *triump(h)us* (see **TRIUMPH**).

> **USAGE** On the differences in use of **triumphal** and **triumphant**, see usage at **TRIUMPHANT**.

tri·um·phal·ism /trī'əmfəˌlizəm/ ▶ **n.** excessive exultation over one's success or achievements (used esp. in a political context): *an air of triumphalism reigns in his administration*.
– DERIVATIVES **tri·um·phal·ist** adj. & n.

tri·um·phant /trī'əmfənt/ ▶ **adj.** having won a battle or contest; victorious: *the triumphant winner rose from his seat* | [postpositive] *a comic fairy tale about innocence triumphant*. ■ feeling or expressing jubilation after having won a victory or mastered a difficulty: *he couldn't suppress a triumphant smile*.
– DERIVATIVES **tri·um·phant·ly** adv.
– ORIGIN late Middle English (in the sense 'victorious'): from Old French, or from Latin *triumphant-* 'celebrating a triumph,' from the verb *triumphare* (see **TRIUMPH**).

> **USAGE** Of the two words **triumphant** and **triumphal**, the more common is **triumphant**, which means 'victorious' or 'exultant': *she led an arduous campaign to its triumphant conclusion; he returned triumphant with a patent for his device*. **Triumphal** means 'used in or celebrating a triumph': *a triumphal parade*.

t

tri·um·vir /trīˈəmvər/ ▶ **n.** (pl. **triumvirs** or **triumviri** /-vəˌrī/) (in ancient Rome) each of three public officers jointly responsible for overseeing any of the administrative departments.
– DERIVATIVES **tri·um·vi·ral** /-rəl/ **adj.**
– ORIGIN Latin, originally as *triumviri* (plural), back-formation from *trium virorum* 'of three men,' genitive of *tres viri*.

tri·um·vi·rate /trīˈəmvərit, -ˌrāt/ ▶ **n. 1** (in ancient Rome) a group of three men holding power, in particular (**the First Triumvirate**) the unofficial coalition of Julius Caesar, Pompey, and Crassus in 60 BC and (**the Second Triumvirate**) a coalition formed by Antony, Lepidus, and Octavian in 43 BC. ■ a group of three powerful or notable people or things existing in relation to each other: *a triumvirate of three former executive vice presidents*.
2 the office of triumvir in ancient Rome.
– ORIGIN late 16th cent.: from Latin *triumviratus*, from *triumvir* (see TRIUMVIR).

tri·une /ˈtrīˌ(y)o͞on/ ▶ **adj.** consisting of three in one (used esp. with reference to the Trinity): *the triune Godhead*.
– DERIVATIVES **tri·u·ni·ty** /trīˈyo͞onitē/ **n.** (pl. **triunities**).
– ORIGIN early 17th cent.: from TRI- 'three' + Latin *unus* 'one.'

tri·va·lent /trīˈvālənt/ ▶ **adj.** Chemistry having a valence of three.

Tri·van·drum /trəˈvandrəm/ another name for THIRUVANANTHAPURAM.

triv·et /ˈtrivit/ ▶ **n.** an iron tripod placed over a fire for a cooking pot or kettle to stand on. ■ an iron bracket designed to hook onto bars of a grate for a similar purpose. ■ a small plate placed under a hot serving dish to protect a table.
– ORIGIN late Middle English: apparently from Latin *tripes, triped-* 'three-legged,' from *tri-* 'three' + *pes, ped-* 'foot.'

triv·i·a /ˈtrivēə/ ▶ **plural n.** details, considerations, or pieces of information of little importance or value: *we fill our days with meaningless trivia*.
– ORIGIN early 20th cent.: from modern Latin, plural of *trivium* 'place where three roads meet,' influenced in sense by TRIVIAL.

triv·i·al /ˈtrivēəl/ ▶ **adj.** of little value or importance: *huge fines were imposed for trivial offenses | trivial details*. ■ (of a person) concerned only with trifling or unimportant things. ■ Mathematics denoting a subgroup that either contains only the identity element or is identical with the given group.
– DERIVATIVES **triv·i·al·ly adv.**
– ORIGIN late Middle English (in the sense 'belonging to the trivium'): from medieval Latin *trivialis*, from Latin *trivium* (see TRIVIUM).

triv·i·al·i·ty /ˌtrivēˈalitē/ ▶ **n.** (pl. **trivialities**) lack of seriousness or importance; insignificance: *the mediocrity and triviality of current popular culture*. ■ an insignificant detail; a trifle: *an over-concentration on trivialities*.

triv·i·al·ize /ˈtrivēəˌlīz/ ▶ **v.** [with obj.] make (something) seem less important, significant, or complex than it really is: *the problem was either trivialized or ignored by teachers*.
– DERIVATIVES **triv·i·al·i·za·tion** /ˌtrivēəliˈzāsHən/ **n.**

triv·i·al name ▶ **n.** chiefly Chemistry a name that is in general use although not part of systematic nomenclature: *its common trivial name is citric acid*. Compare with SYSTEMATIC NAME. ■ chiefly Zoology another term for SPECIFIC EPITHET.

triv·i·um /ˈtrivēəm/ ▶ **n.** historical an introductory curriculum at a medieval university involving the study of grammar, rhetoric, and logic. Compare with QUADRIVIUM.
– ORIGIN early 19th cent.: from Latin, literally 'place where three roads meet,' from *tri-* 'three' + *via* 'road.'

t

-trix ▶ **suffix** (pl. **-trices** or **-trixes**) (chiefly in legal terms) forming feminine agent nouns corresponding to masculine nouns ending in *-tor* (such as *executrix* corresponding to *executor*).
– ORIGIN from Latin.

tRNA ▶ **abbr.** Biology transfer RNA.

Tro·ad /ˈtrōˌad/ an ancient region of northwestern Asia Minor. Troy was its chief city.

Tro·bri·and Is·lands /ˈtrōbrēˌand, -ˌänd/ a small group of islands in the southwestern Pacific Ocean, in Papua New Guinea, located off the southeastern tip of the island of New Guinea.

tro·car /ˈtrōˌkär/ ▶ **n.** a surgical instrument with a three-sided cutting point enclosed in a tube, used for withdrawing fluid from a body cavity.
– ORIGIN early 18th cent.: from French *trocart, trois-quarts*, from *trois* 'three' + *carre* 'side, face of an instrument.'

tro·cha·ic /trōˈkā-ik/ Prosody ▶ **adj.** consisting of or featuring trochees.
▶ **n.** (usu. **trochaics**) a type of verse that consists of or features trochees.
– ORIGIN late 16th cent.: via Latin from Greek *trokhaikos*, from *trokhaios* (see TROCHEE).

tro·chal disk /ˈtrōkəl disk/ ▶ **n.** Zoology (in a rotifer) a ring of cilia that is used in feeding and (in most kinds) swimming.
– ORIGIN mid 19th cent.: *trochal* from Greek *trokhos* 'wheel' + -AL.

tro·chan·ter /trōˈkantər/ ▶ **n. 1** Anatomy any of two bony protuberances by which muscles are attached to the upper part of the thigh bone.
2 Entomology the small second segment of the leg of an insect, between the coxa and the femur.
– ORIGIN early 17th cent.: from French, from Greek *trokhantēr*, from *trekhein* 'to run.'

tro·chee /ˈtrōkē/ ▶ **n.** Prosody a foot consisting of one long or stressed syllable followed by one short or unstressed syllable.
– ORIGIN late 16th cent.: via Latin from Greek *trokhaios* (*pous*) 'running (foot),' from *trekhein* 'to run.'

troch·le·a /ˈträklēə/ ▶ **n.** (pl. **trochleae** /-lēˌē/) Anatomy a structure resembling or acting like a pulley, such as the groove at the lower end of the humerus forming part of the elbow joint.
– ORIGIN late 17th cent.: Latin, 'pulley'; compare with Greek *trokhilia* 'sheave of a pulley.'

troch·le·ar /ˈträklēər/ ▶ **adj.** Anatomy of or relating to a part of the body resembling a pulley.

troch·le·ar nerve ▶ **n.** Anatomy each of the fourth pair of cranial nerves, supplying the superior oblique muscle of the eyeball.

tro·choid /ˈtrōˌkoid/ ▶ **adj. 1** Anatomy denoting a joint in which one element rotates on its own axis (e.g., the atlas vertebra).
2 Geometry denoting a curve traced by a point on a radius of a circle rotating along a straight line or another circle (a cycloid, epicycloid, or hypocycloid).
3 Zoology having or denoting a form of mollusk shell that is conical with a flat base, like a top shell.
▶ **n. 1** a trochoid curve.
2 a trochoid joint.
– DERIVATIVES **tro·choi·dal** /trōˈkoidl/ **adj.**
– ORIGIN early 18th cent.: from Greek *trokhoeidēs* 'wheellike,' from *trokhos* 'wheel.'

troch·o·phore /ˈträkəˌfôr/ ▶ **n.** Zoology the planktonic larva of certain invertebrates, including some mollusks and polychaete worms, having a roughly spherical body, a band of cilia, and a spinning motion.
– ORIGIN late 19th cent.: from Greek *trokhos* 'wheel' + -PHORE.

Troc·ken·bee·ren·aus·le·se /ˈträkənˌberənˌous-ˌlāzə/ ▶ **n.** a sweet German white wine made from selected individual grapes picked later than the general harvest and affected by noble rot.
– ORIGIN German, from *trocken* 'dry' + BEERENAUSLESE.

troc·to·lite /ˈträktəˌlīt/ ▶ **n.** Geology gabbro made up mainly of olivine and calcic plagioclase, often having a spotted appearance likened to a trout's back.
– ORIGIN late 19th cent.: from German *Troklotit*, from Greek *trōktēs*, a marine fish (taken to be 'trout').

trod /träd/ past and past participle of TREAD.

trod·den /ˈträdn/ past participle of TREAD.

trog·lo·dyte /ˈträgləˌdīt/ ▶ **n.** (esp. in prehistoric times) a person who lived in a cave. ■ a hermit. ■ a person who is regarded as being deliberately ignorant or old-fashioned.
– DERIVATIVES **trog·lo·dyt·ic** /ˌträgləˈditik/ **adj.**, **trog·lo·dyt·ism** /-dīˌtizəm/ **n.**
– ORIGIN late 15th cent.: via Latin from Greek *trōglodutēs*, alteration of the name of an Ethiopian people, influenced by *trōglē* 'hole.'

tro·gon /ˈtrōˌgän/ ▶ **n.** a bird of tropical American forests, with a long tail and brilliantly colored plumage. ● Family Trogonidae: several genera, in particular *Trogon*, and many species; the quetzals also belong to this family.
– ORIGIN late 18th cent.: from modern Latin, from Greek *trōgōn*, from *trōgein* 'gnaw.'

troi·ka /ˈtroikə/ ▶ **n. 1** a Russian vehicle pulled by a team of three horses abreast. ■ a team of three horses for such a vehicle.
2 a group of three people working together, esp. in an administrative or managerial capacity.
– ORIGIN Russian, from *troe* 'set of three.'

troil·ism /ˈtroiˌlizəm/ ▶ **n.** sexual activity involving three participants.
– ORIGIN 1950s: perhaps based on French *trois* 'three.'

Troi·lus /ˈtroiləs/ Greek Mythology a Trojan prince, the son of Priam and Hecuba, killed by Achilles. In medieval legends of the Trojan War he is portrayed as the forsaken lover of Cressida.

Tro·jan /ˈtrōjən/ ▶ **adj.** of or relating to ancient Troy in Asia Minor: *Trojan legends*.
▶ **n.** a native or inhabitant of ancient Troy.
– PHRASES **work like a Trojan** (or **Trojans**) work extremely hard.
– ORIGIN Middle English: from Latin *Troianus*, from *Troia* 'Troy.'

Tro·jan as·ter·oid ▶ **n.** an asteroid belonging to one of two groups that orbit the sun at the same distance as Jupiter, at the Lagrangian points roughly 60 degrees ahead of it and behind it.
– ORIGIN early 20th cent.: so named because the first asteroids discovered were named after heroes of the Trojan War.

Tro·jan Horse ▶ **n.** Greek Mythology a hollow wooden statue of a horse in which the Greeks concealed themselves in order to enter Troy. ■ (also **Trojan horse**) a person or thing intended secretly to undermine or bring about the downfall of an enemy or opponent: *the rebels may use this peace accord as a Trojan horse to try and take over*. ■ (also **Trojan horse**) Computing a program designed to breach the security of a computer system while ostensibly performing some innocuous function.

Tro·jan War the legendary ten-year siege of Troy by a coalition of Greeks, described in Homer's *Iliad*.

> The Greeks were attempting to recover Helen, wife of Menelaus, who had been abducted by the Trojan prince Paris. The war ended with the capture of the city by a trick: the Greeks ostensibly ended the siege but left behind a group of men concealed in a hollow wooden horse so large that the city walls had to be breached for it to be drawn inside.

troll[1] /trōl/ ▶ **n.** a mythical, cave-dwelling being depicted in folklore as either a giant or a dwarf, typically having a very ugly appearance.
– ORIGIN from Old Norse and Swedish *troll*, Danish *trold*; adopted into English from Scandinavian in the mid 19th cent.

troll[2] ▶ **v. 1** [no obj.] fish by trailing a baited line along behind a boat: *we trolled for mackerel*. ■ search for something: *a group of companies trolling for partnership opportunities* | [with obj.] *I spent tonight trolling the Internet for expensive lighting gear*.
2 [with obj.] sing (something) in a happy and carefree way: *troll the ancient Yuletide carol*.
3 [with obj.] Computing, informal send or submit (a provocative e-mail or Internet posting) with the intention of inciting an angry response.
4 [no obj., with adverbial of direction] chiefly Brit. walk; stroll: *we all trolled into town*.
▶ **n. 1** a line or bait used in trolling for fish.
2 Computing, informal a provocative e-mail or posting on the Internet intended to incite an angry response. ■ informal a person who sends such an e-mail or submits such a posting.
– DERIVATIVES **troll·er n.**
– ORIGIN late Middle English (in the sense 'stroll, roll'): origin uncertain; compare with Old French *troller* 'wander here and there (in search of game)' and Middle High German *trollen* 'stroll.'

trol·ley /ˈträlē/ ▶ **n.** (pl. **trolleys**) **1** short for TROLLEY CAR or TROLLEY BUS.
2 (also **trolley wheel**) a wheel attached to a pole, used for collecting current from an overhead electric wire to drive a streetcar or trolley bus.
3 chiefly Brit. a large metal basket or frame on wheels, used for transporting heavy or large items, such as supermarket purchases or luggage at an airport or railroad station. ■ Brit. a small table on wheels or casters, typically used to convey food and drink.
– PHRASES **off one's trolley** informal mad; insane.
– ORIGIN early 19th cent.: of dialect origin, perhaps from TROLL[2].

trol·ley bus ▶ **n.** a bus powered by electricity obtained from an overhead cable by means of a trolley wheel.

trol·ley car ▶ **n.** a passenger vehicle powered by electricity obtained from an overhead cable by means of a trolley wheel. Also called STREETCAR.

trol·ley dol·ly ▶ **n.** Brit. informal a flight attendant.

trol·lop /ˈträləp/ ▶ **n.** dated or humorous a woman perceived as sexually disreputable or promiscuous.
– ORIGIN early 17th cent.: perhaps related to TRULL.

Trol·lope /ˈträləp/, Anthony (1815–82), English novelist. He is noted for the six "Barsetshire" novels, including *The Warden* (1855) and *Barchester Towers* (1857), and for the six political "Palliser" novels.

trom·bone /trämˈbōn, trəm-/ ▶ **n.** a large brass wind instrument with straight tubing in three sections, ending in a bell over the player's left shoulder, different fundamental notes being made using a forward-pointing extendable slide. ■ an organ stop with the quality of such an instrument.

– DERIVATIVES **trom·bon·ist** /-nist/ **n.**
– ORIGIN early 18th cent.: from French or Italian, from Italian *tromba* 'trumpet.'

trombone

trom·mel /'träməl/ ▶ **n.** Mining a rotating cylindrical sieve or screen used for washing and sorting pieces of ore or coal.
– ORIGIN late 19th cent.: from German, literally 'drum.'

trompe l'oeil /,trômp 'loi/ ▶ **n.** (pl. **trompe l'oeils** pronunc. **same**) visual illusion in art, esp. as used to trick the eye into perceiving a painted detail as a three-dimensional object. ■ a painting or design intended to create such an illusion.
– ORIGIN French, literally 'deceives the eye.'

-tron ▶ **suffix** Physics **1** denoting a subatomic particle: *positron.*
2 denoting a particle accelerator: *cyclotron.*
3 denoting a vacuum tube: *ignitron.*
– ORIGIN from (*elec*)*tron.*

tro·na /'trōnə/ ▶ **n.** a gray mineral that occurs as an evaporite in salt deposits and consists of a hydrated carbonate and bicarbonate of sodium.
– ORIGIN late 18th cent.: from Swedish, from Arabic *naṭrūn* (see **NATRON**).

Trond·heim /'trän,hām, 'trôn-/ a fishing port in western central Norway; pop. 152,845 (2007). It was the capital of Norway during the Viking period.

troop /tro͞op/ ▶ **n. 1** a group of soldiers, esp. a cavalry unit commanded by a captain, or an airborne unit. ■ (**troops**) soldiers or armed forces: *UN peacekeeping troops* | (as modifier **troop**) *troop withdrawals.* ■ a unit of 18 to 24 Girl Scouts or Boy Scouts organized under a troop leader.
2 a group of people or animals of a particular kind: ***a troop of** musicians.*
▶ **v.** [no obj.] (of a group of people) come or go together or in large numbers: *the girls **trooped in** for dinner.* ■ (of a lone person) walk at a slow or steady pace: *Caroline trooped wearily home from work.*
– ORIGIN mid 16th cent.: from French *troupe,* back-formation from *troupeau,* diminutive of medieval Latin *troppus* 'flock,' probably of Germanic origin.

troop car·ri·er ▶ **n.** a large aircraft or armored vehicle or ship designed for transporting troops.

troop·er /'tro͞opər/ ▶ **n. 1** a state police officer. ■ a mounted police officer.
2 a private soldier in a cavalry, armored, or airborne unit. ■ a cavalry horse. ■ chiefly Brit. a ship used for transporting troops.
– PHRASES **swear like a trooper** swear a great deal.

troop·ship /'tro͞op,SHip/ ▶ **n.** a ship designed or used for transporting troops.

trop. ▶ **abbr.** ■ tropic. ■ tropical.

trope /trōp/ ▶ **n.** a figurative or metaphorical use of a word or expression: *he used the two-Americas trope to explain how a nation free and democratic at home could act wantonly abroad.* ■ a significant or recurrent theme; a motif: *she uses the Eucharist as a pictorial trope.*
▶ **v.** [no obj.] create a trope.
– ORIGIN mid 16th cent.: via Latin from Greek *tropos* 'turn, way, trope,' from *trepein* 'to turn.'

troph·al·lax·is /,träfə'laksis, ,trō-/ ▶ **n.** Entomology the mutual exchange of regurgitated liquids between adult social insects or between them and their larvae.
– ORIGIN early 20th cent.: from **TROPHO-** 'nourishment' + Greek *allaxis* 'exchange.'

troph·ec·to·derm /träf'ektə,dərm, trō-/ ▶ **n.** another term for **TROPHOBLAST**.

troph·ic /'trōfik, 'träf-/ ▶ **adj.** Ecology of or relating to feeding and nutrition. ■ Physiology (of a hormone or its effect) stimulating the activity of another endocrine gland.
– ORIGIN late 19th cent.: from Greek *trophikos,* from *trophē* 'nourishment,' from *trephein* 'nourish.'

-trophic ▶ **comb. form 1** relating to nutrition: *oligotrophic.*
2 relating to maintenance or regulation of a bodily organ or function, esp. by a hormone: *gonadotrophic.*
– ORIGIN from Greek *trophikos,* from *trophē* 'nourishment.'

troph·ic lev·el ▶ **n.** Ecology each of several hierarchical levels in an ecosystem, comprising organisms that share the same function in the food chain and the same nutritional relationship to the primary sources of energy.

-trophism ▶ **comb. form** in nouns corresponding to adjectives ending in *-trophic* (such as *phototropism* corresponding to *phototrophic*).

tropho- ▶ **comb. form** relating to nourishment: *trophoblast.*
– ORIGIN from Greek *trophē* 'nourishment.'

troph·o·blast /'träfə,blast, 'trō-/ ▶ **n.** Embryology a layer of tissue on the outside of a mammalian blastula, supplying the embryo with nourishment and later forming the major part of the placenta.
– DERIVATIVES **troph·o·blas·tic** /,träfə'blastik/ **adj.**

troph·o·zo·ite /,träfə'zō,īt, ,trō-/ ▶ **n.** Zoology & Medicine a growing stage in the life cycle of some sporozoan parasites, when they are absorbing nutrients from the host.

tro·phy /'trōfē/ ▶ **n.** (pl. **trophies**) **1** a cup or other decorative object awarded as a prize for a victory or success. ■ a souvenir of an achievement, esp. a part of an animal taken when hunting.
2 (in ancient Greece or Rome) the weapons and other spoils of a defeated army set up as a memorial of victory. ■ a representation of such a memorial; an ornamental group of symbolic objects arranged for display.
– ORIGIN late 15th cent. (sense 2, denoting a display of weapons): from French *trophée,* via Latin from Greek *tropaion,* from *tropē* 'a rout,' from *trepein* 'to turn.'

-trophy ▶ **comb. form** in nouns corresponding to adjectives ending in *-trophic* (such as *phototrophy* corresponding to *phototrophic*).

tro·phy wife ▶ **n.** informal, derogatory a young, attractive wife regarded as a status symbol for an older man.

trop·ic¹ /'träpik/ ▶ **n.** the parallel of latitude 23°26' north (**tropic of Cancer**) or south (**tropic of Capricorn**) of the equator. ■ Astronomy each of two corresponding circles on the celestial sphere where the sun appears to turn after reaching its greatest declination, marking the northern and southern limits of the ecliptic. ■ (**the tropics**) the region between the tropics of Cancer and Capricorn.
▶ **adj.** another term for **TROPICAL** (sense 1).
– ORIGIN late Middle English (denoting the point on the ecliptic reached by the sun at the solstice): via Latin from Greek *tropikos,* from *tropē* 'turning,' from *trepein* 'to turn.'

trop·ic² ▶ **adj. 1** Biology relating to, consisting of, or exhibiting tropism.
2 Physiology variant spelling of **TROPHIC**.

-tropic ▶ **comb. form 1** turning toward: *heliotropic.*
2 affecting: *psychotropic.*
3 (esp. in names of hormones) equivalent to **-TROPHIC**.
– ORIGIN from Greek *tropē* 'turn, turning.'

trop·i·cal /'träpəkəl/ ▶ **adj. 1** of, typical of, or peculiar to the tropics: *tropical countries* | *a tropical rain forest.* ■ resembling the tropics, esp. in being very hot and humid: *some plants thrived in last year's tropical summer heat.*
2 archaic of or involving a trope; figurative.
– DERIVATIVES **trop·i·cal·ly** /-ik(ə)lē/ **adv.**

trop·i·cal sprue ▶ **n.** see **SPRUE²**.

trop·i·cal storm (also **tropical cyclone**) ▶ **n.** a localized, very intense low-pressure wind system, forming over tropical oceans and with winds of hurricane force.

trop·i·cal year ▶ **n.** see **YEAR** (sense 1).

trop·ic·bird /'träpik,bərd/ ▶ **n.** a tropical seabird with mainly white plumage and very long central tail feathers. ● Family Phaethontidae and genus *Phaethon*: three species.

trop·ic of Can·cer ▶ **n.** see **TROPIC¹**.

trop·ic of Cap·ri·corn ▶ **n.** see **TROPIC¹**.

tro·pism /'trō,pizəm/ ▶ **n.** Biology the turning of all or part of an organism in a particular direction in response to an external stimulus.
– ORIGIN late 19th cent.: from Greek *tropos* 'turning' (from *trepein* 'to turn') + **-ISM**.

tro·pol·o·gy /trə'päləjē/ ▶ **n.** the figurative use of language. ■ Christian Theology the figurative interpretation of the scriptures as a source of moral guidance.
– DERIVATIVES **trop·o·log·i·cal** /,träpə'läjikəl/ **adj.**
– ORIGIN late Middle English: via late Latin from Greek *tropologia,* from *tropos* (see **TROPE**).

trop·o·lone /'träpə,lōn, 'trō-/ ▶ **n.** Chemistry an organic compound present in various plants, with a molecule based on a seven-membered carbon ring. ● Chem. formula: $C_7H_6O_2$.
– ORIGIN 1940s: from *tropilidine* (a liquid hydrocarbon) + **-OL** + **-ONE**.

trop·o·my·o·sin /,träpō'mīəsən, ,trō-/ ▶ **n.** Biochemistry a protein involved in muscle contraction. It is related to myosin and occurs together with troponin in the thin filaments of muscle tissue.
– ORIGIN 1940s: from Greek *tropos* 'turning' + **MYOSIN**.

tro·po·nin /'träpənən, 'trō-/ ▶ **n.** Biochemistry a globular protein complex involved in muscle contraction. It occurs with tropomyosin in the thin filaments of muscle tissue.
– ORIGIN 1960s: from **TROPOMYOSIN** + *-n-* + **-IN¹**.

trop·o·pause /'träpə,pôz, 'trō-/ ▶ **n.** the interface between the troposphere and the stratosphere.
– ORIGIN early 20th cent.: from Greek *tropos* 'turning' + **PAUSE**.

trop·o·sphere /'träpə,sfi(ə)r, 'trō-/ ▶ **n.** the lowest region of the atmosphere, extending from the earth's surface to a height of about 3.7–6.2 miles (6–10 km), which is the lower boundary of the stratosphere.
– DERIVATIVES **trop·o·spher·ic** /,träpə'sfi(ə)rik, -'sferik, ,trō-/ **adj.**
– ORIGIN early 20th cent.: from Greek *tropos* 'turning' + **SPHERE**.

trop·po¹ /'träpō/ ▶ **adv.** [usu. with negative] Music (in directions) too much; excessively.
– PHRASES **ma non troppo** /mä ,nôn 'trôpō/ (as a direction) but not too much (used to suggest moderate application of another direction): *allegro ma non troppo.*
– ORIGIN Italian.

trop·po² ▶ **adj.** Austral./NZ informal mentally disturbed, supposedly as a result of spending too much time in a tropical climate: *have you gone troppo?*
– ORIGIN 1940s: from **TROPIC¹** + **-O**.

trot /trät/ ▶ **v.** (**trots, trotting, trotted**) (with reference to a horse or other quadruped) proceed or cause to proceed at a pace faster than a walk, lifting each diagonal pair of legs alternately: [no obj] *the horses trotted slowly through the night* | [with obj.] *he trotted his horse forward.* ■ [no obj.] (of a person) run at a moderate pace, typically with short steps. ■ [no obj.] informal go or walk briskly: *he trotted over to the bonfire.*
▶ **n. 1** a trotting pace: *our horses slowed to a trot.*
2 (**the trots**) informal diarrhea: *a bad case of the trots.*
3 informal a literal translation of a foreign language text for use by students, esp. in a surreptitious way: *adult readers who can turn to translations without being penalized for depending on trots.*
– PHRASES **on the trot** informal **1** continually busy: *I've been on the trot all day.* **2** Brit. in succession: *they lost seven matches on the trot.*
– PHRASAL VERBS **trot something out** informal produce the same information, story, or explanation that has been produced many times before: *everyone trots out the old excuse.*
– ORIGIN Middle English: from Old French *trot* (noun), *troter* (verb), from medieval Latin *trottare,* of Germanic origin.

troth /trôTH, trōTH/ ▶ **n. 1** archaic or formal faith or loyalty when pledged in a solemn agreement or undertaking: *a token of troth.*
2 archaic truth.
– PHRASES **pledge** (or **plight**) **one's troth** make a solemn pledge of commitment or loyalty, esp. in marriage.
– ORIGIN Middle English: variant of **TRUTH**.

Trot·sky /'trätskē/, Leon (1879–1940), Russian revolutionary; born *Lev Davidovich Bronshtein.* He helped to organize the October Revolution with Lenin and built up the Red Army. Expelled from the party by Stalin in 1927, he was exiled in 1929. He settled in Mexico in 1937, where he was later murdered by a Stalinist assassin.

Trot·sky·ism /'trätskē,izəm/ ▶ **n.** the political or economic principles of Leon Trotsky, esp. the theory that socialism should be established throughout the world by continuing revolution. Trotskyism has generally included elements of anarchism and syndicalism, but the term has come to be used indiscriminately to describe a great many forms of radical socialism.
– DERIVATIVES **Trot·sky·ist n. & adj., Trot·sky·ite** /-,īt/ **n. & adj.** (derogatory).

trot·ter /'trätər/ ▶ **n. 1** a horse bred or trained for the sport of harness racing.
2 a pig's foot used as food. ■ humorous a human foot.

trot·ting /'trätiNG/ ▶ **n.** another term for **HARNESS RACING**.

trou·ba·dour /'tro͞obə,dôr, -,do͝or/ ▶ **n.** a French medieval lyric poet composing and singing in Provençal in the 11th to 13th centuries, esp. on the theme of courtly love. ■ a poet who writes verse to music.
– ORIGIN French, from Provençal *trobador,* from *trobar* 'find, invent, compose in verse.'

trou·ble /'trəbəl/ ▶ **n. 1** difficulty or problems: *I had trouble finding somewhere to park* | *friends should support each other when they are **in trouble*** | *the government's policies **ran into trouble*** | *our troubles are just beginning.* ■ the malfunction of

t

something such as a machine or a part of the body: *their helicopter developed engine trouble.* ■ effort or exertion made to do something, esp. when inconvenient: *I wouldn't want to put you to any trouble | he's* ***gone to a lot of trouble*** *to help you.* ■ a cause of worry or inconvenience: *the kid had been* ***no trouble*** *up to now.* ■ a particular aspect or quality of something regarded as unsatisfactory or as a source of difficulty: *that's* ***the trouble with*** *capitalism.* ■ a situation in which one is liable to incur punishment or blame: *he's been* ***in trouble with*** *the police.* ■ informal, dated used to refer to the condition of a pregnant unmarried woman: *she's not the first girl who's* ***gotten herself into trouble.***
2 public unrest or disorder: *the cops are preparing for trouble by bringing in tear gas.*
▶ **v.** [with obj.] cause distress or anxiety to: *he was not troubled by doubts.* ■ [no obj.] (**trouble about/over/with**) be distressed or anxious about: *there is nothing you need trouble about.* ■ cause (someone) pain: *my legs started to trouble me.* ■ cause (someone) inconvenience (typically used as a polite way of asking someone to do or provide something): *sorry to trouble you | could I* ***trouble*** *you* ***for*** *a receipt?* ■ [no obj.] make the effort required to do something: *oh, don't trouble to answer.*
– PHRASES **ask for trouble** informal act in a way that is likely to incur problems or difficulties: *hitching a lift is asking for trouble.* **look for trouble** informal behave in a way that is likely to provoke an argument or fight: *youths take a cocktail of drink and drugs before going out to look for trouble.* **trouble and strife** Brit. rhyming slang wife. **a trouble shared is a trouble halved** proverb talking to someone else about one's problems helps to alleviate them.
– DERIVATIVES **trou·bler** /-b(ə)lər/ **n.**
– ORIGIN Middle English: from Old French *truble* (noun), *trubler* (verb), based on Latin *turbidus* (see TURBID).

trou·bled /ˈtrəbəld/ ▶ **adj.** beset by problems or conflict: *his troubled private life.* ■ showing distress or anxiety: *his troubled face.*
– PHRASES **troubled waters** a difficult situation or time.

trou·ble·mak·er /ˈtrəbəlˌmākər/ ▶ **n.** a person who habitually causes difficulty or problems, esp. by inciting others to defy those in authority.
– DERIVATIVES **trou·ble·mak·ing** /-ˌmākiNG/ **n. & adj.**

trou·ble·shoot /ˈtrəbəlˌSHo͞ot/ ▶ **v.** [no obj.] (usu. as noun **troubleshooting**) solve serious problems for a company or other organization. ■ trace and correct faults in a mechanical or electronic system.
– DERIVATIVES **trou·ble·shoot·er n.**

trou·ble·some /ˈtrəbəlsəm/ ▶ **adj.** causing difficulty or annoyance: *a troublesome knee injury.*
– DERIVATIVES **trou·ble·some·ly adv.**, **trou·ble·some·ness n.**

trou·ble spot ▶ **n.** a place where difficulties regularly occur, esp. a country or area where there is a continuous cycle of violence.

trou·bling /ˈtrəb(ə)liNG/ ▶ **adj.** causing distress or anxiety: *this is a troubling development for the president | the lack of attention to security is equally troubling.*
– DERIVATIVES **trou·bling·ly adv.**

trou·blous /ˈtrʌbləs/ ▶ **adj.** archaic or literary full of difficulty or agitation: *those were troublous times.*
– ORIGIN late Middle English: from Old French *troubleus*, from *truble* (see TROUBLE).

trough /trôf/ ▶ **n.** a long, narrow open container for animals to eat or drink out of: *a water trough.* ■ a container of a similar shape used for a purpose such as growing plants or mixing chemicals. ■ a channel used to convey a liquid. ■ a long hollow in the earth's surface: *a vast glacial trough.* ■ an elongated region of low atmospheric pressure. ■ a hollow between two wave crests in the sea. ■ Mathematics a region around the minimum on a curve of variation of a quantity. ■ a point of low activity, achievement, or satisfaction: *learning a language is a series of peaks and troughs.*
– ORIGIN Old English *trog*, of Germanic origin; related to Dutch *trog* and German *Trog*, also to TREE.

trough shell ▶ **n.** a burrowing marine bivalve mollusk with a thin, smooth shell. ● Family Mactridae: *Spisula* and other genera.

trounce /trouns/ ▶ **v.** [with obj.] defeat heavily in a contest: *the Knicks trounced the Rockets on Sunday.* ■ rebuke or punish severely: *some shows were trounced by critics.*
– DERIVATIVES **trounc·er n.**
– ORIGIN mid 16th cent. (also in the sense 'afflict'): of unknown origin.

troupe /tro͞op/ ▶ **n.** a group of dancers, actors, or other entertainers who tour to different venues.
– ORIGIN early 19th cent.: from French, literally 'troop.'

troup·er /ˈtro͞opər/ ▶ **n.** an actor or other entertainer, typically one with long experience. ■ a reliable and uncomplaining person: *a real trouper, Ma concealed her troubles.*

troup·i·al /ˈtro͞opēəl/ ▶ **n.** a gregarious songbird of the American oriole family, typically having orange and black plumage and yellow eyes. ● Genus *Icterus*, family Icteridae: several species, in particular the tropical American *Icterus icterus*.
– ORIGIN early 19th cent.: from French *troupiale*, alteration of American Spanish *turpial*, of unknown origin.

trou·ser /ˈtrouzər/ ▶ **n.** [as modifier] relating to trousers: *his trouser pocket | a trouser press.* ■ a trouser leg: *his trouser was torn.*

trou·sers /ˈtrouzərz/ (also **a pair of trousers**) ▶ **plural n.** an outer garment covering the body from the waist to the ankles, with a separate part for each leg.
– DERIVATIVES **trou·sered** /-zərd/ **adj.**
– ORIGIN early 17th cent.: from archaic *trouse* (singular), from Irish *triús* and Scottish Gaelic *triubhas* (see TREWS), on the pattern of *drawers*.

trous·seau /ˈtro͞oˌsō, ˌtro͞oˈsō/ ▶ **n.** (pl. **trousseaux** pronunc. **same**, or **trousseaus**) the clothes, household linen, and other belongings collected by a bride for her marriage.
– ORIGIN mid 19th cent.: from French, diminutive of *trousse* 'bundle' (a sense also found in Middle English).

trout /trout/ ▶ **n.** (pl. **same** or **trouts**) a chiefly freshwater fish of the salmon family, found in both Eurasia and North America and highly valued as food and game. ● Genera *Salmo* (several species of true trouts, including the European **brown trout** and the **rainbow trout**), and *Salvelinus* (several North American species), family Salmonidae. See also LAKE TROUT, SEA TROUT.
– PHRASES **old trout** informal an annoying or bad-tempered old person, esp. a woman.
– ORIGIN late Old English *truht*, from late Latin *tructa*, based on Greek *trōgein* 'gnaw.'

trout·ing /ˈtroutiNG/ ▶ **n.** the activity of catching or trying to catch trout, either for food or as a sport.

trout lil·y ▶ **n.** a North American dogtooth violet with yellow flowers, so called from its mottled leaves. Also called ADDER'S TONGUE. ● *Erythronium americanum*, family Liliaceae.

trou·vaille /tro͞oˈvī/ ▶ **n.** a lucky find: *one of numerous trouvailles to be gleaned from his book.*
– ORIGIN French, from *trouver* 'find.'

trou·vère /tro͞oˈver/ ▶ **n.** a medieval epic poet in northern France in the 11th–14th centuries.
– ORIGIN from Old French *trovere*, from *trover* 'to find'; compare with TROUBADOUR.

trove /trōv/ ▶ **n.** a store of valuable or delightful things: *the museum's trove of antique treasure.*
– ORIGIN late 19th cent.: from TREASURE TROVE.

tro·ver /ˈtrōvər/ ▶ **n.** Law common-law action to recover the value of personal property that has been wrongfully disposed of by another person.
– ORIGIN late 16th cent.: from an Anglo-Norman French noun use of Old French *trover* 'to find.'

trow /trō/ ▶ **v.** [with obj.] archaic think or believe: *why, this is strange, I trow!*
– ORIGIN Old English *trūwian*, *trēowian* 'to trust'; related to TRUCE.

trow·el /ˈtrouəl/ ▶ **n. 1** a small handheld tool with a flat, pointed blade, used to apply and spread mortar or plaster.
2 a small handheld tool with a curved scoop for lifting plants or earth.
▶ **v.** (**trowels, troweling, troweled**; Brit. **trowels, trowelling, trowelled**) [with obj.] apply or spread with or as if with a trowel.
– ORIGIN Middle English (as a noun): from Old French *truele*, from medieval Latin *truella*, alteration of Latin *trulla* 'scoop,' diminutive of *trua* 'skimmer.'

Troy /troi/ **1** (in Homeric legend) the city of King Priam, besieged for ten years by the Greeks during the Trojan War. It was regarded as having been a purely legendary city until Heinrich Schliemann identified the mound of Hissarlik on the northeast Aegean coast of Turkey as the site of Troy. The city was apparently sacked and destroyed by fire in the mid 13th century BC, a period coinciding with the Mycenaean civilization of Greece. Also called ILIUM.
2 a residential and commercial city in southeastern Michigan; pop. 80,264 (est. 2008).
3 an industrial city in eastern New York, on the Hudson River, northeast of Albany; pop. 47,459 (est. 2008).

troy /troi/ (in full **troy weight**) ▶ **n.** a system of weights used mainly for precious metals and gems, with a pound of 12 ounces or 5,760 grains. Compare with AVOIRDUPOIS.
– ORIGIN late Middle English: from a weight used at the fair of *Troyes*.

Troyes /trwä/, Chrétien de, see CHRÉTIEN DE TROYES.

trp. ▶ **abbr.** troop.

tru·an·cy /ˈtro͞oənsē/ ▶ **n.** the action of staying away from school without good reason; absenteeism: *he had a history of truancy and expulsion from school.*

tru·ant /ˈtro͞oənt/ ▶ **n.** a student who stays away from school without leave or explanation.
▶ **adj.** (of a student) being a truant: *truant children.* ■ wandering; straying: *her truant husband.*
▶ **v.** [no obj.] another way of saying PLAY TRUANT below.
– PHRASES **play truant** stay away from school or work without permission or explanation; play hooky.
– ORIGIN Middle English (denoting a person begging through choice rather than necessity): from Old French, probably ultimately of Celtic origin; compare with Welsh *truan*, Scottish Gaelic *truaghan* 'wretched.'

truce /tro͞os/ ▶ **n.** an agreement between enemies or opponents to stop fighting or arguing for a certain time: *the guerrillas called a three-day truce.*
– ORIGIN Middle English *trewes*, *trues* (plural), from Old English *trēowa*, plural of *trēow* 'belief, trust,' of Germanic origin; related to Dutch *trouw* and German *Treue*, also to TRUE.

Tru·cial States /ˈtro͞oSHəl/ former name (until 1971) of the UNITED ARAB EMIRATES.

truck[1] /trək/ ▶ **n. 1** a wheeled vehicle, in particular: ■ a large, heavy motor vehicle, used for transporting goods, materials, or troops. ■ Brit. a railroad vehicle for carrying freight, esp. a small open one. ■ a low flat-topped cart used for moving heavy items.
2 a undercarriage with four to six wheels pivoted beneath the end of a railroad car. ■ each of two axle units on a skateboard, to which the wheels are attached.
3 a wooden disk at the top of a ship's mast or flagstaff, with sheaves for signal halyards.
▶ **v.** [with obj.] convey by truck: *the food was trucked to St. Petersburg* | (as noun **trucking**) *industries such as trucking.* ■ [no obj.] drive a truck. ■ [no obj.] informal go or proceed, esp. in a casual or leisurely way: *he walked confidently behind them and trucked on through!*
– DERIVATIVES **truck·age** /-kij/ **n.**
– ORIGIN Middle English (denoting a solid wooden wheel): perhaps short for TRUCKLE[1] in the sense 'wheel, pulley' The sense 'wheeled vehicle' dates from the late 18th cent.

truck[2] ▶ **n. 1** archaic barter. ■ chiefly historical the payment of workers in kind or with vouchers rather than money.
2 chiefly archaic small wares. ■ informal odds and ends.
3 market-garden produce, esp. vegetables: [as modifier] *a truck garden.*
▶ **v.** [with obj.] archaic barter or exchange.
– PHRASES **have** (or **want**) **no truck with** avoid or wish to avoid dealings or being associated with: *we have no truck with that style of gutter journalism.*
– ORIGIN Middle English (as a verb): probably from Old French, of unknown origin; compare with medieval Latin *trocare*.

truck·er /ˈtrəkər/ ▶ **n.** a long-distance truck driver.

truck farm ▶ **n.** a farm that produces vegetables for the market.

truck·le[1] /ˈtrəkəl/ ▶ **n.** a small barrel-shaped cheese, esp. cheddar.
– ORIGIN late Middle English (denoting a wheel or pulley): from Anglo-Norman French *trocle*, from Latin *trochlea* 'sheave of a pulley.' The current sense dates from the early 19th cent. and was originally dialect.

truck·le[2] ▶ **v.** [no obj.] submit or behave obsequiously: *she despised her husband, who* ***truckled to*** *her.*
– DERIVATIVES **truck·ler** /ˈtrək(ə)lər/ **n.**
– ORIGIN mid 17th cent.: figuratively, from TRUCKLE BED; an earlier use of the verb was in the sense *sleep in a truckle bed.*

truck·le bed ▶ **n.** chiefly Brit. a trundle bed.
– ORIGIN late Middle English: from TRUCKLE[1] in the sense 'wheel' + BED.

truck·load /ˈtrəkˌlōd/ ▶ **n.** a quantity of goods that can be transported in a truck: *a truckload of chemicals caught fire.* ■ (**a truckload/truckloads of**) informal a large quantity or number of something: *the government had plowed* ***truckloads of*** *money into this land.*
– PHRASES **by the truckload** informal in large quantities or numbers: *he had charm by the truckload.*

truck stop ▶ **n.** a large roadside service station and restaurant for truck drivers on interstate highways.

truc·u·lent /ˈtrəkyələnt/ ▶ **adj.** eager or quick to argue or fight; aggressively defiant: *his days of truculent defiance were over.*
– DERIVATIVES **truc·u·lence n.**, **truc·u·lent·ly adv.**
– ORIGIN mid 16th cent.: from Latin *truculentus*, from *trux*, *truc-* 'fierce.'

Tru·deau[1] /tro͞o'dō/, Garry (1948–), US editorial cartoonist; full name *Garretson Beekman Trudeau.* He created *Doonesbury*, a satirical comic strip that began in 1970.

Tru·deau[2], Pierre Elliott (1919–2000), Canadian Liberal statesman; prime minister 1968–79 and 1980–84. Noted for his commitment to federalism, he made both English and French official languages of the Canadian government in 1969, held a provincial referendum in Quebec in 1980 that rejected independence, and saw the transfer of residual constitutional powers from Britain to Canada in 1982.

trudge /trəj/ ▶ **v.** [no obj.] walk slowly and with heavy steps, typically because of exhaustion or harsh conditions: *I trudged up the stairs | she trudged through blinding snow.*
▶ **n.** a difficult or laborious walk: *he began the long trudge back.*
– DERIVATIVES **trudg·er n.**
– ORIGIN mid 16th cent. (as a verb): of unknown origin.

trudg·en /'trəjən/ ▶ **n.** [in sing.] a swimming stroke like the crawl with a scissors movement of the legs.
– ORIGIN late 19th cent.: named after John *Trudgen* (1852–1902), English swimmer.

true /tro͞o/ ▶ **adj.** (**truer, truest**) **1** in accordance with fact or reality: *a true story | of course it's true | that is not true of the people I am talking about.* ■ [attrib.] rightly or strictly so called; genuine: *people are still willing to pay for true craftsmanship | we believe in true love.* ■ [attrib.] real or actual: *he has guessed my true intentions.* ■ said when conceding a point in argument or discussion: *true, it faced north, but you got used to that.*
2 accurate or exact: *it was a true depiction.* ■ (of a note) exactly in tune. ■ (of a compass bearing) measured relative to true north: *steer 085 degrees true.* ■ correctly positioned, balanced, or aligned; upright or level.
3 loyal or faithful: *he was a true friend.* ■ [predic.] (**true to**) accurately conforming to (a standard or expectation); faithful to: *this entirely new production remains true to the essence of Lorca's play.*
4 chiefly archaic honest: *we appeal to all good men and true to rally to us.*
▶ **adv. 1** chiefly literary truly: *Hobson spoke truer than he knew.*
2 accurately or without variation.
▶ **v.** (**trues, truing** or **trueing, trued**) [with obj.] bring (an object, wheel, or other construction) into the exact shape, alignment, or position required.
– PHRASES **come true** actually happen or become the case: *dreams can come true.* **out of true** not in the correct or exact shape or alignment: *take care not to pull the frame out of true.* **many a true word is spoken in jest** proverb a humorous remark not intended to be taken seriously may turn out to be accurate after all. **true to form** (or **type**) being or behaving as expected: *true to form, they took it well.* **true to life** accurately representing real events or objects: *artworks of the period were often composed in strident colors not true to life.*
– DERIVATIVES **true·ness n.**
– ORIGIN Old English *trēowe, trȳwe* 'steadfast, loyal'; related to Dutch *getrouw*, German *treu*, also to TRUCE.

true bill ▶ **n.** Law a bill of indictment found by a grand jury to be supported by sufficient evidence to justify the hearing of a case.

true-blue ▶ **adj.** extremely loyal or orthodox: *I'm a dyed-in-the-wool, true-blue patriot.*

true-born ▶ **adj.** [attrib.] of a specified kind by birth; genuine: *a true-born criminal.*

true bug ▶ **n.** see BUG (sense 2 of the noun).

true-false test ▶ **n.** a test consisting of statements that must be marked as either true or false.

true·heart·ed /'tro͞o'härtəd/ ▶ **adj.** literary loyal or faithful: *a truehearted paladin.*

true leaf ▶ **n.** Botany a foliage leaf of a plant, as opposed to a seed leaf or cotyledon.

true-life ▶ **adj.** true to life; realistic: *a story adapted from the true-life confessions of a Bayonne Mafioso.*

true-love knot (also **true-lover's knot**) ▶ **n.** a kind of knot with interlacing bows on each side, symbolizing the bonds of love.

true north ▶ **n.** north according to the earth's axis, not magnetic north.

true rib ▶ **n.** a rib that is attached directly to the breastbone. Compare with FLOATING RIB.

Truf·faut /tro͞o'fō/, François (1932–84), French movie director. His first movie, *The 400 Blows* (1959), established him as a leading director of the *nouvelle vague.* Other movies include *Jules et Jim* (1961) and *The Last Metro* (1980).

truf·fle /'trəfəl/ ▶ **n. 1** a strong-smelling underground fungus that resembles an irregular, rough-skinned potato, growing chiefly in broadleaved woodland on calcareous soils. It is considered a culinary delicacy and found, esp. in France, with the aid of trained dogs or pigs. ● Family Tuberaceae, subdivision Ascomycotina: *Tuber* and other genera.
2 a soft candy made of a chocolate mixture, typically flavored with rum and covered with cocoa.
– ORIGIN late 16th cent.: probably via Dutch from obsolete French *truffle*, perhaps based on Latin *tubera*, plural of *tuber* 'hump, swelling.' Sense 2 dates from the 1920s.

truf·fled /'trəfəld/ ▶ **adj.** (of food) cooked, garnished, or stuffed with truffles: *a truffled turkey.*

truf·fling /'trəf(ə)liNG/ ▶ **n.** the activity of hunting or rooting for truffles.

trug /trəg/ (also **trug basket**) ▶ **n.** Brit. a shallow oblong basket made of strips of wood, traditionally used for carrying garden flowers and produce.
– ORIGIN late Middle English (denoting a basin): perhaps a dialect variant of TROUGH.

tru·ism /'tro͞o,izəm/ ▶ **n.** a statement that is obviously true and says nothing new or interesting: *the truism that you get what you pay for.* ■ Logic a proposition that states nothing beyond what is implied by any of its terms.
– DERIVATIVES **tru·is·tic** /tro͞o'istik/ **adj.**

truite au bleu /,trwēt ō 'blœ/ ▶ **n.** a dish consisting of trout cooked with vinegar, which turns the fish blue.
– ORIGIN French, literally 'trout in the blue.'

Tru·ji·llo[1] /tro͞o'hē(y)ō/ a city on the coast of northwestern Peru; pop. 682,800 (est. 2007).

Tru·ji·llo[2], Rafael (1891–1961), Dominican statesman; president of the Dominican Republic 1930–38 and 1942–52; born *Rafael Leónidas Trujillo Molina*; known as **Generalissimo**. Although he was formally president for only two periods, he wielded dictatorial powers from 1930 until his death.

Truk Is·lands /trək, tro͝ok/ former name for CHUUK ISLANDS.

trull /trəl/ ▶ **n.** archaic a prostitute.
– ORIGIN early 16th cent.: from German *Trulle.*

tru·ly /'tro͞olē/ ▶ **adv. 1** in a truthful way: *he speaks truly.* ■ used to emphasize emotional sincerity or seriousness: *time to reflect on what we truly want | it is truly a privilege to be here* | [as submodifier] *I'm truly sorry, but I can't join you today* | [sentence adverb] *truly, I don't understand you sometimes.*
2 to the fullest degree; genuinely or properly: *management does not truly understand or care about the residents* | [as submodifier] *a truly free press.* ■ [as submodifier] absolutely or completely (used to emphasize a description): *a truly dreadful song.*
3 in fact or without doubt; really: *this is truly a miracle.*
4 archaic loyally or faithfully: *why cannot all masters be served truly?*
– PHRASES **yours truly** used as a formula for ending a letter. ■ humorous used to refer to oneself: *the demos will be organized by yours truly.*
– ORIGIN Old English *trēowlīce* 'faithfully' (see TRUE, -LY[2]).

Tru·man /'tro͞omən/, Harry S. (1884–1972), 33rd president of the US 1945–53. A Democrat, he served in the US Senate 1934–45. As vice president 1945, he succeeded to the presidency upon the death of Franklin D. Roosevelt during World War II. He authorized the use of the atom bomb against Hiroshima and Nagasaki in 1945, initiated the Truman Doctrine in 1947, introduced the Marshall Plan in 1948, and helped to establish NATO the following year. The US became involved in the Korean War in 1950. Truman's victory over Thomas E. Dewey in the 1948 presidential election was one of the closest in US history.

Harry S. Truman

Tru·man Doc·trine the principle that the US should give support to countries or peoples threatened by Soviet forces or communist insurrection. First expressed in 1947 by US President Truman in a speech to Congress seeking aid for Greece and Turkey, the doctrine was seen by the communists as an open declaration of the Cold War.

Trum·bull, John (1756–1843), US artist. He is noted for his large scenes, particularly of the American Revolution, and created paintings for the rotunda of the Capitol building in Washington, DC. He also painted "The Declaration of Independence" (1796) and several portraits of George Washington.

tru·meau /tro͞o'mō/ ▶ **n.** (pl. **trumeaux** /-'mōz, -'mō/) a section of wall or a pillar between two openings, esp. a pillar dividing a large doorway in a church.
– ORIGIN late 19th cent.: from French, literally 'calf of the leg.'

Trump /trəmp/, Donald John (1946–) US real estate developer. He was noted for building Trump Tower in New York City and the Taj Mahal gambling complex in Atlantic City in New Jersey.

trump[1] /trəmp/ ▶ **n.** (in bridge, whist, and similar card games) a playing card of the suit chosen to rank above the others, which can win a trick where a card of a different suit has been led. ■ (**trumps**) the suit having this rank in a particular hand: *the ace of trumps.* ■ (in a tarot pack) any of a special suit of 22 cards depicting symbolic and typical figures and scenes. ■ (also **trump card**) a valuable resource that may be used, esp. as a surprise, in order to gain an advantage: *in this month General Haig decided to play his trump card: the tank.* ■ informal, dated a helpful or admirable person.
▶ **v.** [with obj.] (in bridge, whist, and similar card games) play a trump on (a card of another suit), having no cards of the suit led. ■ beat (someone or something) by saying or doing something better: *taste trumps most if not all other factors when consumers choose food products.*
– PHRASAL VERBS **trump something up** invent a false accusation or excuse: *they've trumped up charges against her.*
– ORIGIN early 16th cent.: alteration of TRIUMPH, once used in card games in the same sense.

trump[2] ▶ **n.** archaic a trumpet or a trumpet blast.
– ORIGIN Middle English: from Old French *trompe*, of Germanic origin; probably imitative.

trump·er·y /'trəmpərē/ archaic ▶ **n.** (pl. **trumperies**) attractive articles of little value or use. ■ practices or beliefs that are superficially or visually appealing but have little real value or worth.
▶ **adj.** showy but worthless: *trumpery jewelry.* ■ delusive or shallow: *that trumpery hope which lets us dupe ourselves.*
– ORIGIN late Middle English (denoting trickery): from Old French *tromperie*, from *tromper* 'deceive.'

trum·pet /'trəmpit/ ▶ **n. 1** a brass musical instrument with a flared bell and a bright, penetrating tone. The modern instrument has the tubing looped to form a straight-sided coil, with three valves. ■ an organ reed stop with a quality resembling that of a trumpet. ■ something shaped like a trumpet, esp. the tubular corona of a daffodil flower. ■ a sound resembling that of a trumpet, esp. the loud cry of an elephant.
2 (**trumpets**) a North American pitcher plant. ● Genus *Sarracenia*, family Sarraceniaceae: several species, in particular **yellow trumpets** (*S. alata*).
▶ **v.** (**trumpets, trumpeting, trumpeted**) **1** [no obj.] play a trumpet: (as adj. **trumpeting**) *figures of two trumpeting angels.* ■ make a loud, penetrating sound resembling that of a trumpet: *wild elephants trumpeting in the bush.*
2 [with obj.] proclaim widely or loudly: *the press trumpeted another defeat for the government.*
– PHRASES **blow one's (own) trumpet** talk openly and boastfully about one's achievements: *he refused to blow his own trumpet and blushingly declined to speak.*
– ORIGIN Middle English: from Old French *trompette*, diminutive of *trompe* (see TRUMP[2]). The verb dates from the mid 16th cent.

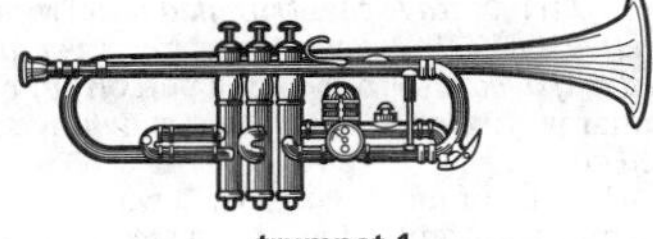

trumpet 1

trum·pet creep·er ▶ **n.** another term for TRUMPET VINE.

trum·pet·er /'trəmpitər/ ▶ **n. 1** a person who plays a trumpet.

2 a large gregarious ground-dwelling bird of tropical South American forests, with mainly black plumage and loud trumpeting and booming calls. ● Family Psophiidae and genus *Psophia*: three species.
3 a pigeon of a domestic breed that makes a trumpetlike sound.
4 an edible marine fish with a spiny dorsal fin, found chiefly in cool Australasian waters and said to make a grunting or trumpeting sound when taken out of the water. ● Family Latridae: several genera and species, including the **Tasmanian trumpeter** (*Latris lineata*), prized as food.

trum·pet·er swan ▶ **n.** a large migratory swan with a black and yellow bill and a honking call, breeding in northern North America. ● *Cygnus buccinator*, family Anatidae.

trum·pet·fish /ˈtrəmpit,fiSH/ ▶ **n.** (pl. **same** or **trumpetfishes**) an elongated marine fish with a long narrow snout, resembling a pipefish. It lives around reefs and rocks in tropical waters and typically hangs in a semivertical position. ● Family Aulostomidae and genus *Aulostomus*: several species.

trum·pet ma·jor ▶ **n.** the chief trumpeter of a cavalry regiment, typically a principal musician in a regimental band.

trum·pet shell ▶ **n.** the shell of a large marine mollusk that can be blown to produce a loud note. ● Several species in the class Gastropoda, in particular the triton (*Charonia tritonis*, family Cymatiidae).

trum·pet tree ▶ **n.** any of a number of tropical American trees, in particular: ● a tree grown in the Caribbean for its numerous trumpet-shaped flowers, which bloom when the tree is leafless (genus *Tabebuia*, family Bignoniaceae). ● a cecropia whose hollow branches are used to make wind instruments (*Cecropia peltata*, family Cecropiaceae).

trum·pet vine (also **trumpet creeper**) ▶ **n.** a climbing shrub with orange or red trumpet-shaped flowers, cultivated as an ornamental. ● Genus *Campsis*, family Bignoniaceae: the North American *C. radicans* and the Chinese *C. grandiflora*.

North American trumpet vine

trun·cal /ˈtrəNGkəl/ ▶ **adj.** Medicine of or affecting the trunk of the body, or of a nerve.

trun·cate /ˈtrəNG,kāt/ ▶ **v.** [with obj.] (often as adj. **truncated**) shorten (something) by cutting off the top or the end: *a truncated cone shape* | *discussion was truncated by the arrival of tea.* ■ Crystallography replace (an edge or an angle) by a plane, typically so as to make equal angles with the adjacent faces.
▶ **adj.** Botany & Zoology (of a leaf, feather, or other part) ending abruptly as if cut off across the base or tip.
– DERIVATIVES **trun·ca·tion** /,trəNGˈkāSHən/ **n.**
– ORIGIN late 15th cent. (as a verb): from Latin *truncat-* 'maimed,' from the verb *truncare*.

trun·cheon /ˈtrənCHən/ ▶ **n.** chiefly Brit. a short, thick stick carried as a weapon by a police officer. ■ a staff or baton acting as a symbol of authority.
– ORIGIN Middle English (denoting a piece broken off (esp. from a spear), also a cudgel): from Old French *tronchon* 'stump,' based on Latin *truncus* 'trunk.'

t

trun·dle /ˈtrəndl/ ▶ **v.** (with reference to a wheeled vehicle or its occupants) move or cause to move slowly and heavily, typically in a noisy or uneven way: [no obj.] *ten vintage cars trundled past* | [with obj.] *we trundled a wheelbarrow down to the river and collected driftwood.* ■ [no obj.] (of a person) move in a similar way: *she could hear him coughing as he trundled out.*
▶ **n.** [in sing.] an act of moving in such a way.
– ORIGIN mid 16th cent. (denoting a small wheel or roller): a parallel formation to obsolete or dialect *trendle*, *trindle* '(cause to) revolve'; related to TREND.

trun·dle bed ▶ **n.** a low bed on wheels that can be stored under a larger bed.

trunk /trəNGk/ ▶ **n.** **1** the main woody stem of a tree as distinct from its branches and roots. ■ the main part of an artery, nerve, or other anatomical structure from which smaller branches arise. ■ short for TRUNK LINE. ■ an enclosed shaft or conduit for cables or ventilation.
2 a person's or animal's body apart from the limbs and head.
3 the elongated, prehensile nose of an elephant.
4 a large box with a hinged lid for storing or transporting clothes and other articles. ■ the space at the back of a car for carrying luggage and other goods.
– DERIVATIVES **trunk·ful** /-,fo͝ol/ **n.** (pl. **trunkfuls**), **trunk·less adj.**
– ORIGIN late Middle English: from Old French *tronc*, from Latin *truncus*.

trunk call ▶ **n.** dated, chiefly Brit. a long-distance telephone call made within the same country.

trunk·fish /ˈtrəNGk,fiSH/ ▶ **n.** (pl. **same** or **trunkfishes**) another term for BOXFISH.

trunk·ing /ˈtrəNGkiNG/ ▶ **n.** **1** a system of shafts or conduits for cables or ventilation.
2 the use or arrangement of trunk lines.

trunk line ▶ **n.** a main line of a railroad, telephone system, or other network.

trunk road ▶ **n.** chiefly Brit. an important main road used for long-distance travel.

trunks /trəNGks/ ▶ **plural n.** men's shorts, worn esp. for swimming or boxing.
– ORIGIN late 19th cent. (originally US): from an earlier theatrical use denoting short breeches of thin material worn over tights.

trun·nel /ˈtrənəl/ ▶ **n.** a hard wooden pin used for fastening timbers together.

trun·nion /ˈtrənyən/ ▶ **n.** a pin or pivot forming one of a pair on which something is supported. ■ a supporting cylindrical projection on each side of a cannon or mortar.
– ORIGIN early 17th cent.: from French *trognon* 'core, tree trunk,' of unknown origin.

Tru·ro /ˈtro͝orō/ a resort town in eastern Massachusetts, near the tip of Cape Cod, a well-known arts colony; pop. 2,125 (est. 2008).

truss /trəs/ ▶ **n.** **1** a framework, typically consisting of rafters, posts, and struts, supporting a roof, bridge, or other structure: *roof trusses.* ■ a surgical appliance worn to support a hernia, typically a padded belt. ■ a large projection of stone or timber, typically one supporting a cornice.
2 Brit. chiefly historical a bundle of old hay (56 lb), new hay (60 lb), or straw (36 lb).
3 a compact cluster of flowers or fruit growing on one stalk.
4 Sailing a heavy metal ring securing a lower yard to its mast.
▶ **v.** [with obj.] **1** tie up the wings and legs of (a chicken or other bird) before cooking. ■ tie up (someone) with their arms at their sides: *I found him **trussed up** in his closet.* ■ (usu. **be trussed up in**) dress (someone) in elaborate or uncomfortable clothing: *he was trussed up in a heavily padded suit, complete with face mask and protective gloves.*
2 (usu. as adj. **trussed**) support (a roof, bridge, or other structure) with a truss or trusses.
– DERIVATIVES **truss·er n.**
– ORIGIN Middle English (in the sense 'bundle'): from Old French *trusse* (noun), *trusser* 'pack up, bind in,' based on late Latin *tors-* 'twisted,' from the verb *torquere*. Sense 1 of the noun dates from the mid 17th cent.

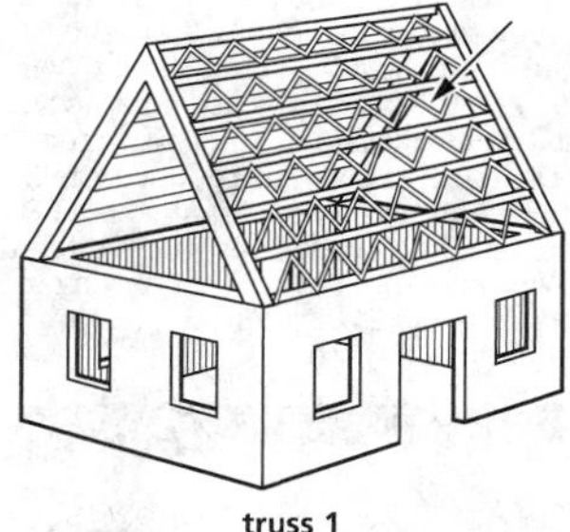
truss 1

trust /trəst/ ▶ **n.** **1** firm belief in the reliability, truth, ability, or strength of someone or something: *relations have to be built on trust* | *they have been able to win the trust of the others.* ■ acceptance of the truth of a statement without evidence or investigation: *I used only primary sources, taking nothing **on trust**.* ■ the state of being responsible for someone or something: *a man in a position of trust.* ■ literary a person or duty for which one has responsibility: *rulership is a trust from God.* ■ literary a hope or expectation: *all the great trusts of womanhood.*
2 Law confidence placed in a person by making that person the nominal owner of property to be held or used for the benefit of one or more others. ■ an arrangement whereby property is held in such a way: *a trust was set up* | *the property is to be **held in trust** for his son.*
3 a body of trustees. ■ an organization or company managed by trustees: *a charitable trust* | [in names] *the National Trust for Historic Preservation.* ■ dated a large company that has or attempts to gain monopolistic control of a market.
4 W. Indian or archaic commercial credit: *my master lived on trust at an alehouse.*
▶ **v.** [with obj.] **1** believe in the reliability, truth, ability, or strength of: *I should never have trusted her* | [with obj. and infinitive] *he can be trusted to carry out an impartial investigation* | (as adj. **trusted**) *a trusted adviser.* ■ (**trust someone with**) allow someone to have, use, or look after (someone or something of importance or value) with confidence: *I'd trust you with my life.* ■ (**trust someone/something to**) commit (someone or something) to the safekeeping of: *they don't like to **trust** their money **to** anyone outside the family.* ■ [with clause] have confidence; hope (used as a polite formula in conversation): *I trust that you have enjoyed this book.* ■ [no obj.] have faith or confidence: *she **trusted in** the powers of justice.* ■ [no obj.] (**trust to**) place reliance on (luck, fate, or something else over which one has little control): *trusting to the cover of night, I ventured out.*
2 chiefly archaic allow credit to (a customer).
– PHRASES **not trust someone as far as one can throw them** informal not trust or hardly trust a particular person at all. **trust someone to ——** it is characteristic or predictable for someone to act in the specified way: *trust Sam to have all the inside information.*
– DERIVATIVES **trust·a·ble adj.**, **trust·er n.**
– ORIGIN Middle English: from Old Norse *traust*, from *traustr* 'strong'; the verb from Old Norse *treysta*, assimilated to the noun.

trust·a·far·i·an /,trəstəˈfe(ə)rēən/ ▶ **n.** informal a rich young person who adopts a bohemian lifestyle and lives in a nonaffluent area.
– ORIGIN 1990s: blend of *trust fund* and *Rastafarian*.

trust·bust·er /ˈtrəstbəstər/ ▶ **n.** informal a person or agency employed to enforce antitrust legislation.

trust com·pa·ny ▶ **n.** a company formed to act as a trustee or to deal with trusts.

trust deed ▶ **n.** Law a deed of conveyance creating and setting out the conditions of a trust.

trust·ee /trəˈstē/ ▶ **n.** Law an individual person or member of a board given control or powers of administration of property in trust with a legal obligation to administer it solely for the purposes specified. ■ a state made responsible for the government of a trust territory by the United Nations.
– DERIVATIVES **trust·ee·ship** /-,SHip/ **n.**

trust·ee in bank·rupt·cy ▶ **n.** Law a person taking administrative responsibility for the financial affairs of a bankrupt and the distribution of assets to creditors.

trust·ful /ˈtrəstfəl/ ▶ **adj.** having or marked by a total belief in the reliability, truth, ability, or strength of someone.
– DERIVATIVES **trust·ful·ly adv.**, **trust·ful·ness n.**

trust fund ▶ **n.** a fund consisting of assets belonging to a trust, held by the trustees for the beneficiaries.

trust·ing /ˈtrəstiNG/ ▶ **adj.** showing or tending to have a belief in a person's honesty or sincerity; not suspicious: *it is foolish to be too **trusting of** other people* | *a shy and trusting child.*
– DERIVATIVES **trust·ing·ly adv.**, **trust·ing·ness n.**

trust ter·ri·to·ry ▶ **n.** a territory under the trusteeship of the United Nations or of a country designated by it.

trust·wor·thy /ˈtrəst,wərT͟Hē/ ▶ **adj.** able to be relied on as honest or truthful: *leave a spare key with a trustworthy neighbor.*
– DERIVATIVES **trust·wor·thi·ly** /-T͟Həlē/ **adv.**, **trust·wor·thi·ness n.**

trust·y /ˈtrəstē/ ▶ **adj.** (**trustier**, **trustiest**) [attrib.] archaic or humorous having served for a long time and regarded as reliable or faithful: *his trusty Corona typewriter* | *their trusty steeds.*
▶ **n.** (pl. **trusties**) a prisoner who is given special privileges or responsibilities in return for good behavior.
– DERIVATIVES **trust·i·ly** /-təlē/ **adv.**, **trust·i·ness n.**

Truth /tro͞oTH/, Sojourner (*c.*1797–1883), US evangelist and reformer; previously *Isabella Van Wagener*. Born into slavery, she was sold to **Isaac Van Wagener**, who released her in 1827. She became a zealous evangelist and preached in favor of black rights and women's suffrage. In 1864, she was received at the White House by President Lincoln.

truth /tro͞oTH/ ▶ **n.** (pl. **truths** /tro͞oT͟Hz, tro͞oTHs/) the quality or state of being true: *he had to accept the truth of her accusation.* ■ (also **the truth**) that which is true or in accordance with fact or reality: *tell me the truth* | *she found out the truth about*

him. ■ a fact or belief that is accepted as true: *the emergence of scientific truths.*
– PHRASES **in truth** really; in fact: *in truth, she was more than a little unhappy.* **of a truth** archaic certainly: *of a truth, such things used to happen.* **to tell the truth** (or **truth to tell** or **if truth be told**) to be frank (used esp. when making an admission or when expressing an unwelcome or controversial opinion): *I think, if truth be told, we were all a little afraid of him.* **the truth, the whole truth, and nothing but the truth** used to emphasize the absolute veracity of a statement. [part of a statement sworn by witnesses in court.]
– ORIGIN Old English *trīewth, trēowth* 'faithfulness, constancy' (see TRUE, -TH[2]).

truth con·di·tion ▶ **n.** Logic the condition under which a given proposition is true. ■ a statement of this condition, sometimes taken to be the meaning of the proposition.

truth·ful /ˈtro͞oTHfəl/ ▶ **adj.** (of a person or statement) telling or expressing the truth; honest: *I think you're confusing being rude with being truthful* | *I want a truthful answer.* ■ (of artistic or literary representation) characterized by accuracy or realism; true to life: *astonishingly truthful acting.*
– DERIVATIVES **truth·ful·ly** adv.

truth·ful·ness /ˈtro͞oTHfəlnis/ ▶ **n.** the fact of being true; truth: *we have had to judge the truthfulness of the evidence.* ■ the fact of being realistic or true to life; realism: *the truthfulness of her playing of an aging American spinster.*

truth func·tion ▶ **n.** Logic a function whose truth value is dependent on the truth value of its arguments.

truth·i·ness /ˈtro͞oTHēnis/ ▶ **n.** informal the quality of seeming or being felt to be true, even if not necessarily true.
– ORIGIN early 19th cent. (in the sense 'truthfulness'): coined in the modern sense by US humorist Stephen Colbert (1964–).

truth se·rum (also **truth drug**) ▶ **n.** a drug supposedly able to induce a state in which a person answers questions truthfully.

truth ta·ble ▶ **n.** Logic a diagram in rows and columns showing how the truth or falsity of a proposition varies with that of its components. ■ Electronics a similar diagram of the outputs from all possible combinations of input.

truth val·ue ▶ **n.** Logic the attribute assigned to a proposition in respect of its truth or falsehood, which in classical logic has only two possible values (true or false).

try /trī/ ▶ **v.** (**tries, trying, tried**) **1** [no obj.] make an attempt or effort to do something: [with infinitive] *he tried to regain his breath* | *I started to **try and** untangle the mystery* | *I decided to try writing fiction* | *none of them tried very hard* | [with obj.] *three times he tried the maneuver and three times he failed.* ■ (**try for**) attempt to achieve or attain: *they decided to try for another baby.* ■ [with obj.] use, test, or do (something new or different) in order to see if it is suitable, effective, or pleasant: *everyone wanted to know if I'd tried jellied eel* | *these methods are **tried and tested**.* ■ (**try out for**) compete or audition in order to join (a team) or be given (a position): *she tried out for the team.* ■ [with obj.] go to (a place) or attempt to contact (someone), typically in order to obtain something: *I've tried the apartment, but the number is busy.* ■ [with obj.] push or pull (a door or window) to determine whether it is locked: *I tried the doors, but they were locked.* ■ [with obj.] make severe demands on (a person or a quality, typically patience): *Mary tried everyone's patience to the limit.* **2** [with obj.] (usu. **be tried**) subject (someone) to trial: *he was arrested and tried for the murder.* ■ investigate and decide (a case or issue) in a formal trial: *such cases must be tried by a jury.* **3** [with obj.] chiefly Brit. smooth (roughly planed wood) with a plane to give an accurately flat surface. **4** [with obj.] extract (oil or fat) by heating: *some of the fat may be tried out and used.*
▶ **n.** (pl. **tries**) **1** an effort to accomplish something; an attempt: *Mitterrand was elected president on his third try.* ■ an act of doing, using, or testing something new or different to see if it is suitable, effective, or pleasant: *they should give the idea a try.* **2** Rugby an act of touching the ball down behind the opposing goal line, scoring points and entitling the scoring side to a goal kick.
– PHRASES **I** (or **he**, etc.) **will try anything once** used to indicate willingness to do or experience something new. **try something on for size** assess whether something is suitable: *he was trying on the role for size.* **try one's hand at** attempt to do (something) for the first time, typically in order to find out if one is good at it: *a chance to try your hand at the ancient art of drystone walling.* **try it on** Brit. informal attempt to deceive or seduce someone: *he was trying it on with my wife.* ■ deliberately test someone's patience to see how much one can get away with. **try one's luck** see LUCK. **try me** used to suggest that one may be willing to do something unexpected or unlikely: *"You won't use a gun up here." "Try me."*
– PHRASAL VERBS **try something on** put on an item of clothing to see if it fits or suits one. **try someone/something out** test someone or something new or different to assess their suitability or effectiveness: *I try out new recipes on my daughter.*
– ORIGIN Middle English: from Old French *trier* 'sift,' of unknown origin. Sense 1 of the noun dates from the early 17th cent.

> **USAGE** In practice, there is little discernible difference in meaning between **try to** plus infinitive (*we should **try to** help them*) and **try and** plus infinitive (*we should **try and** help them*), but there is a difference in formality, with **try to** being regarded as more formal than **try and.** Beyond the issue of formality, the construction **try and** is grammatically odd, in that it cannot be inflected for tense—that is, sentences like *she **tried and** fix it* or *they are **trying and** renew their visa* are not acceptable, while their equivalents *she **tried to** fix it* or *they are **trying to** renew their visa* obviously are. For this reason, **try and** is best regarded as a fixed idiom used only in its infinitive and imperative form. See also usage at AND.

try·ing /ˈtrī-iNG/ ▶ **adj.** difficult or annoying; hard to endure: *it had been a very trying day.*
– DERIVATIVES **try·ing·ly** adv.

try·out /ˈtrīˌout/ ▶ **n.** a test of the potential of someone or something, esp. in the context of entertainment or sports: *she would be too distraught to compete in cheerleader tryouts.*

try·pan blue /ˈtripən, trəˈpan/ ▶ **n.** a diazo dye used as a biological stain due to its absorption by macrophages of the reticuloendothelial system.
– ORIGIN early 20th cent.: *trypan* from TRYPANOSOME.

try·pan·o·some /trəˈpanəˌsōm, ˈtripənə-/ ▶ **n.** Medicine & Zoology a single-celled parasitic protozoan with a trailing flagellum, infesting the blood. ● Genus *Trypanosoma*, phylum Kinetoplastida, kingdom Protista.
– ORIGIN early 20th cent.: from Greek *trupanon* 'borer' + -SOME[3].

try·pan·o·so·mi·a·sis /trəˌpanəsōˈmīəsis, ˈtripənə-/ ▶ **n.** Medicine any tropical disease caused by trypanosomes and typically transmitted by biting insects, esp. sleeping sickness and Chagas' disease.

tryp·sin /ˈtripsin/ ▶ **n.** Biochemistry a digestive enzyme that breaks down proteins in the small intestine. It is secreted by the pancreas in an inactive form, trypsinogen.
– DERIVATIVES **tryp·tic** /-tik/ adj.
– ORIGIN late 19th cent.: from Greek *tripsis* 'friction,' from *tribein* 'to rub' (because it was first obtained by rubbing down the pancreas with glycerine), + -IN[1].

tryp·sin·o·gen /tripˈsinəjən, -ˌjen/ ▶ **n.** Biochemistry an inactive substance secreted by the pancreas, from which the digestive enzyme trypsin is formed in the duodenum.

tryp·ta·mine /ˈtriptəˌmēn/ ▶ **n.** Biochemistry a compound, of which serotonin is a derivative, produced from tryptophan by decarboxylation. ● A heterocyclic amine; chem. formula: $C_8H_6NCH_2CH_2NH$.

tryp·to·phan /ˈtriptəˌfan/ ▶ **n.** Biochemistry an amino acid that is a constituent of most proteins. It is an essential nutrient in the diet of vertebrates. ● An indole derivative; chem. formula: $C_8H_6NCH_2CH(NH_2)COOH$.
– ORIGIN late 19th cent.: from *tryptic* 'relating to trypsin' + Greek *phainein* 'appear.'

try·sail /ˈtrīsəl, -ˌsāl/ ▶ **n.** a small, strong fore-and-aft sail set on the mast of a sailing vessel in heavy weather.

try square ▶ **n.** an implement used to check and mark right angles in construction work.

tryst /trist/ literary ▶ **n.** a private, romantic rendezvous between lovers: *a moonlight tryst.*
▶ **v.** [no obj.] keep a rendezvous of this kind: (as noun **trysting**) *a trysting place.*
– DERIVATIVES **trys·ter** n.
– ORIGIN late Middle English (originally Scots): variant of obsolete *trist* 'an appointed place in hunting,' from French *triste* or medieval Latin *trista.*

TS ▶ **abbr.** tensile strength.

Tsao-chuang /ˈjou jo͞oˈäNG/ variant of ZAOZHUANG.

tsar /zär, (t)sär/ (also **czar** or **tzar**) ▶ **n. 1** an emperor of Russia before 1917: *Tsar Nicholas II.* ■ a South Slav ruler in former times, esp. one reigning over Serbia in the 14th century. **2** (often **czar**) [usu. with adj. or noun modifier] a person appointed by government to advise on and coordinate policy in a particular area: *America's new drug czar.*
– DERIVATIVES **tsar·dom** /-dəm/ n., **tsar·ism** /-ˌizəm/ n., **tsar·ist** /-ist/ n. & adj.
– ORIGIN from Russian *tsar'*, representing Latin *Caesar.*

> **WORD TRENDS** There seem to be so many **tsars** or **czars** involved in politics these days, you could be forgiven for thinking that the government had been overrun by Russian autocrats. In the US, the word has been used since the 1930s to describe an official appointed to coordinate policy in a particular area, and it is now familiar in British English as well. A modifiying word usually specifies the **czar's** area of responsibility: *drug* is the most common, followed by terms such as *health, border, security,* and *counterterrorism.* Many people are uncomfortable with the power and influence of these modern **czars**, a feeling that can't be helped by the choice of a name traditionally associated with authoritarian rule. See also OLIGARCH.

tsar·e·vich /ˈzärəˌviCH, ˈ(t)sär-/ (also **czarevich** or **tzarevitch**) ▶ **n.** historical the eldest son of an emperor of Russia.
– ORIGIN early 18th cent.: Russian, literally 'son of a tsar.'

tsa·rev·na /zäˈrevnə, (t)sä-/ ▶ **n. 1** a daughter of a tsar.
2 the wife of a tsarevich.

tsa·ri·na /zäˈrēnə, (t)sä-/ (also **czarina** or **tzarina**) ▶ **n.** historical an empress of Russia before 1917.

Tsa·ri·tsyn /(t)säˈrētsin/ former name (until 1925) of VOLGOGRAD.

tsats·ke /ˈtsätskə/ ▶ **n.** variant spelling of TCHOTCHKE.

TSE ▶ **abbr.** transmissible spongiform encephalopathy; any spongiform encephalopathy, including BSE and vCJD, that is transmissible between animals, or between animals and humans.

tses·se·bi /ˈ(t)sesəbē/ (also **tsessebe**) ▶ **n.** variant spelling of SASSABY.
– ORIGIN mid 19th cent.: from Setswana.

tset·se /ˈ(t)sētsē, ˈ(t)set-/ (also **tsetse fly**) ▶ **n.** an African bloodsucking fly that bites humans and other mammals, transmitting sleeping sickness and nagana. ● Genus *Glossina*, family Tabanidae: several species.
– ORIGIN mid 19th cent.: from Setswana.

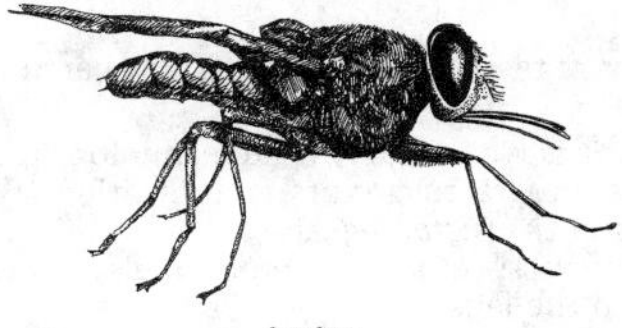

tsetse

TSgt ▶ **abbr.** technical sergeant.

TSH ▶ **abbr.** thyroid-stimulating hormone.

T-shirt (also **tee shirt**) ▶ **n.** a short-sleeved casual top, generally made of cotton, having the shape of a T when spread out flat.

tsim·mes /ˈtsimis/ (also **tzimmes** or **tzimmis**) ▶ **n.** (pl. **same**) a Jewish stew of sweetened vegetables or vegetables and fruit, sometimes with meat. ■ a fuss or muddle.
– ORIGIN Yiddish.

Tsim·shi·an /ˈCHimsHēən, ˈtsim-/ ▶ **n.** (pl. **same**) **1** a member of an American Indian people of coastal British Columbia.
2 the language of this people.
▶ **adj.** of or relating to this people or their language.
– ORIGIN from the Tsimshian self-designation *c'msyan*, literally 'inside the Skeena River.'

Tsi·nan /ˈjēˈnän/ variant of JINAN.

Tsing·hai /ˈtsiNGˈhī, ˈCHiNG/ variant of QINGHAI.

tsk tsk /tisk tisk/ ▶ **exclam.** expressing disapproval or annoyance: *you of all people, Goldie—tsk, tsk.*
▶ **v.** (**tsk-tsk**) [no obj.] make such an exclamation.
– ORIGIN 1940s: imitative.

tsp. ▶ **abbr.** (pl. **same** or **tsps.**) ■ teaspoon(s). ■ teaspoonful(s).

T-square (also **T square**) ▶ **n.** a T-shaped instrument for drawing or testing right angles.

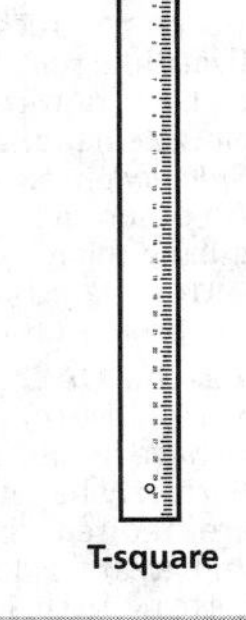

T-square

PRONUNCIATION KEY ə *ago, up*; ər *over, fur*; a *hat*; ā *ate*; ä *car*; e *let*; ē *see*; i *fit*; ī *by*; NG *sing*; ō *go*; ô *law, for*; oi *toy*; o͝o *good*; o͞o *goo*; ou *out*; TH *thin*; T͟H *then*; ZH *vision*

t

TSR ▶ **abbr.** Computing terminate and stay resident, denoting a type of program that remains in the memory of a computer after it has finished running and that can be quickly reactivated.

TSS ▶ **abbr.** toxic shock syndrome.

T-storm /ˈtē ˌstôrm/ ▶ **n.** informal short for THUNDERSTORM.

tsu·ba /ˈtso͞obə/ ▶ **n.** (pl. **same** or **tsubas**) a Japanese sword guard, typically elaborately decorated and made of steel.
– ORIGIN Japanese.

tsu·bo /ˈtso͞obō/ ▶ **n.** (pl. **same** or **tsubos**) **1** a Japanese unit of area equal to approximately 3.95 square yards (3.30 sq m).
2 (in complementary medicine) a point on the face or body to which pressure or other stimulation is applied during treatment.
– ORIGIN Japanese.

tsu·ke·mo·no /ˈ(t)so͞okēˈmōnō/ ▶ **n.** (pl. **tsukemonos**) a Japanese side dish of pickled vegetables, usually served with rice.
– ORIGIN Japanese, from *tsukeru* 'pickle' + *mono* 'thing.'

tsu·na·mi /(t)so͞oˈnämē/ ▶ **n.** (pl. **same** or **tsunamis**) a long high sea wave caused by an earthquake, submarine landslide, or other disturbance.
– ORIGIN late 19th cent.: from Japanese, from *tsu* 'harbor' + *nami* 'wave.'

tsu·ris /ˈtso͝oris, ˈtsər/ ▶ **n.** informal trouble or woe; aggravation.
– ORIGIN early 20th cent.: from Hebrew.

Tsu·shi·ma /(t)so͞oˈsʜēmə/ a Japanese island in Korea Strait, between South Korea and Japan. In 1905 it was the scene of a defeat for the Russian navy during the Russo-Japanese War.

tsu·tsu·ga·mu·shi dis·ease /ˌ(t)so͞otsəgəˈmo͞osʜē/ ▶ **n.** another term for SCRUB TYPHUS.
– ORIGIN early 20th cent.: *tsutsugamushi*, from the Japanese name of the mite that transmits the disease.

Tswa·na /ˈ(t)swänə/ ▶ **n.** (pl. **same**, **Tswanas**, or **Batswana** /bätˈswänə/) **1** a member of a people living in Botswana, South Africa, and neighboring areas.
2 the Bantu language of this people. Also called SETSWANA.
▶ **adj.** of or relating to the Tswana or their language.
– ORIGIN stem of Setswana *moTswana*, plural *baTswana*.

TT ▶ **abbr.** ■ teetotal. ■ teetotaler. ■ tuberculin-tested.

TTL ▶ **n.** Electronics a widely used technology for making integrated circuits. [abbreviation of *transistor transistor logic*.]
▶ **adj.** Photography (of a camera focusing system) through-the-lens.

T-top /ˈtē ˌtäp/ ▶ **n.** a car roof with removable panels.

TTS ▶ **abbr.** text-to-speech, a form of speech synthesis used to create a spoken version of the text in an electronic document.

TTY ▶ **abbr.** teletypewriter.

TTYL ▶ **abbr.** informal talk to you later: *Anyway, gotta run now! TTYL.*

Tu. ▶ **abbr.** Tuesday.

Tu·a·mo·tu Ar·chi·pel·a·go /ˌto͞oəˈmōto͞o/ a group of about 80 coral islands that form part of French Polynesia, in the South Pacific Ocean; pop. 18,317 (2007). It is the largest group of coral atolls in the world.

Tua·reg /ˈtwäˌreg/ ▶ **n.** (pl. **same** or **Tuaregs**) a member of a Berber people of the western and central Sahara, living mainly in Algeria, Mali, Niger, and western Libya, traditionally as nomadic pastoralists.
▶ **adj.** of or relating to this people.
– ORIGIN from Arabic *tawāriq*.

tu·a·ta·ra /ˌto͞oəˈtärə/ ▶ **n.** a nocturnal burrowing lizardlike reptile with a crest of soft spines along its back, now confined to some small islands off New Zealand. ● Order Rhynchocephalia and genus *Sphenodon*: two species, in particular *S. punctatum*. All other members of the order became extinct during the Mesozoic era.
– ORIGIN late 19th cent.: from Maori, from *tua* 'on the back' + *tara* 'spine.'

Tu·a·tha Dé Da·nann /ˈto͞oəhə dā ˈdänən/ ▶ **plural n.** Irish Mythology the members of an ancient race said to have inhabited Ireland before the historical Irish. Formerly believed to have been a real people, they are credited with the possession of magical powers and great wisdom.
– ORIGIN Irish, literally 'people of the goddess Danann.'

tub /təb/ ▶ **n.** **1** a wide, open, deep, typically round container with a flat bottom used for holding liquids, growing plants, etc.: *hydrangeas in a patio tub.* ■ a similar small plastic or cardboard container in which food is bought or stored: *a margarine tub.* ■ the contents of such a container or the amount it can contain: *she ate a tub of yogurt.* ■ a washtub. ■ informal a bathtub. ■ Mining a container for conveying ore, coal, etc.
2 informal an old, awkward, or run-down vessel.
▶ **v.** (**tubs**, **tubbed**, **tubbing**) [with obj.] **1** (usu. as adj. **tubbed**) plant in a tub: *tubbed fruit trees.*
2 dated wash or bathe (someone or something) in or as in a tub or bath. ■ [no obj.] Brit. informal take a bath.
– DERIVATIVES **tub·ba·ble adj.** (informal), **tub·ful** /-ˌfo͝ol/ **n.** (pl. **tubfuls**).
– ORIGIN Middle English: probably of Low German or Dutch origin; compare with Middle Low German and Middle Dutch *tubbe*.

tu·ba /ˈt(y)o͞obə/ ▶ **n.** a large brass wind instrument of bass pitch, with three to six valves and a broad bell typically facing upward. ■ a powerful reed stop on an organ with the quality of a tuba.
– ORIGIN mid 19th cent.: via Italian from Latin, 'trumpet.'

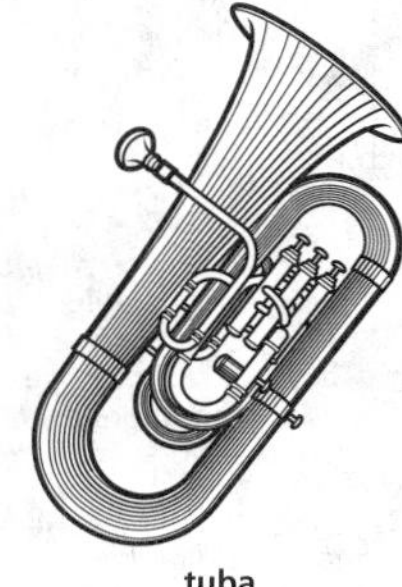
tuba

tub·al /ˈt(y)o͞obəl/ ▶ **adj.** of, relating to, or occurring in a tube, esp. the fallopian tubes.

tub·al li·ga·tion ▶ **n.** a surgical procedure for female sterilization that involves severing and tying the fallopian tubes.

tub·al preg·nan·cy ▶ **n.** Medicine an ectopic pregnancy in which the fetus develops in a fallopian tube.

tub·by /ˈtəbē/ ▶ **adj.** (**tubbier**, **tubbiest**) **1** informal (of a person) short and rather fat. [referring to the shape of a tub.]
2 (of a sound) lacking resonance; dull. [referring to the sound of a tub when struck.]
– DERIVATIVES **tub·bi·ness n.**

tub chair ▶ **n.** a chair with solid arms continuous with a semicircular back.

tube /t(y)o͞ob/ ▶ **n.** **1** a long, hollow cylinder of metal, plastic, glass, etc., for holding or transporting something, chiefly liquids or gases. ■ the inner tube of a bicycle tire. ■ material in such a cylindrical form; tubing: *the firm manufactures steel tube for a wide variety of applications.*
2 a thing in the form of or resembling such a cylinder, in particular: ■ a flexible metal or plastic container sealed at one end and having a screw cap at the other, for holding a semiliquid substance ready for use: *a tube of toothpaste.* ■ a rigid cylindrical container: *a tube of lipstick.* ■ [usu. with modifier] Anatomy, Zoology, & Botany a hollow cylindrical organ or structure in an animal body or in a plant: *Eustachian tube | sieve tube.* ■ (**tubes**) informal a woman's fallopian tubes. ■ a woman's close-fitting garment, typically without darts or other tailoring and made from a single piece of knitted or elasticized fabric: [as modifier] *stretchy tube skirts.* ■ (in surfing) the hollow curve under the crest of a breaking wave.
3 (**the Tube**) Brit. trademark the subway system in London. ■ a train running on this system: *I caught the tube home.*
4 a sealed container, typically of glass and either evacuated or filled with gas, containing two electrodes between which an electric current can be made to flow. ■ a cathode ray tube, esp. in a television set. ■ (**the tube**) informal television: *another wasted evening, sitting in front of the tube.* ■ a vacuum tube.
▶ **v.** [with obj.] **1** (usu. as adj. **tubed**) provide with a tube or tubes: [in combination] *a giant eight-tubed hookah.*
2 informal fit (a person or animal) with a tube to assist breathing, esp. after a laryngotomy.
– PHRASES **go down the tubes** (or **tube**) informal be completely lost or wasted; fail utterly: *we watched his political career go down the tubes.*
– DERIVATIVES **tube·less adj.**, **tube·like** /-ˌlīk/ **adj.**
– ORIGIN mid 17th cent.: from French *tube* or Latin *tubus*.

tu·bec·to·my /t(y)o͞oˈbektəmē/ ▶ **n.** (pl. **tubectomies**) another term for SALPINGECTOMY.

tube foot ▶ **n.** (usu. **tube feet**) Zoology (in an echinoderm) each of a large number of small, flexible, hollow appendages protruding through the ambulacra, used either for locomotion or for collecting food and operated by hydraulic pressure within the water-vascular system.

tube·less tire /ˈto͞oblis/ ▶ **n.** a rubber tire designed for use without an inner tube.

tube-nosed bat ▶ **n.** an Old World bat with tubular nostrils. ● a fruit bat found chiefly in New Guinea and Sulawesi (genus *Nyctimene*, family Pteropodidae). ● an insectivorous Asian bat (genus *Murina*, family Vespertilionidae).

tube pan ▶ **n.** a round cake pan with a hollow, cone-shaped center, used for baking ring-shaped cakes.

tu·ber /ˈt(y)o͞obər/ ▶ **n.** **1** a much thickened underground part of a stem or rhizome, e.g., in the potato, serving as a food reserve and bearing buds from which new plants arise. ■ a tuberous root, e.g., of the dahlia.
2 Anatomy a rounded swelling or protuberant part.
– ORIGIN mid 17th cent.: from Latin, literally 'hump, swelling.'

tu·ber ci·ne·re·um /siˈne(ə)rēəm/ ▶ **n.** Anatomy the part of the hypothalamus to which the pituitary gland is attached.
– ORIGIN Latin *cinereum*, neuter of *cinereus* 'ash-colored.'

tu·ber·cle /ˈt(y)o͞obərkəl/ ▶ **n.** **1** Anatomy, Zoology, & Botany a small rounded projection or protuberance, esp. on a bone or on the surface of an animal or plant.
2 Medicine a small nodular lesion in the lungs or other tissues, characteristic of tuberculosis.
– DERIVATIVES **tu·ber·cu·late** /t(y)o͞oˈbərkyəˌlāt, -lit/ **adj.** (sense 1).
– ORIGIN late 16th cent.: from Latin *tuberculum*, diminutive of *tuber* (see TUBER).

tu·ber·cle ba·cil·lus ▶ **n.** a bacterium that causes tuberculosis.

tu·ber·cu·lar /təˈbərkyələr/ ▶ **adj.** Medicine of, relating to, or affected with tuberculosis: *a tubercular kidney.* ■ Biology & Medicine having or covered with tubercles.
▶ **n.** a person with tuberculosis.

tu·ber·cu·la·tion /t(y)o͞oˌbərkyəˈlāsʜən/ ▶ **n.** chiefly Biology the formation or presence of tubercles, esp. of a specified type.
– ORIGIN mid 19th cent.: from Latin *tuberculum* (see TUBERCLE) + -ATION.

tu·ber·cu·lin /t(y)o͞oˈbərkyəlin/ ▶ **n.** a sterile protein extract from cultures of tubercle bacillus, used in a test by hypodermic injection for infection with or immunity to tuberculosis, and also formerly in the treatment of the disease.
– ORIGIN late 19th cent.: from Latin *tuberculum* (see TUBERCLE) + -IN[1].

tu·ber·cu·lin-test·ed ▶ **adj.** (of cows or their milk) giving, or from cows giving, a negative response to a tuberculin test.

tu·ber·cu·loid /t(y)o͞oˈbərkyəˌloid/ ▶ **adj.** Medicine resembling tuberculosis or its symptoms, in particular: ■ relating to or denoting the milder of the two principal forms of leprosy, marked by few, well-defined lesions similar to those of tuberculosis, often with loss of feeling in the affected areas. Compare with LEPROMATOUS.

tu·ber·cu·lo·sis /təˌbərkyəˈlōsis, t(y)o͞o-/ (abbr.: **TB**) ▶ **n.** an infectious bacterial disease characterized by the growth of nodules (tubercles) in the tissues, esp. the lungs. ● The disease is caused by the bacterium *Mycobacterium tuberculosis* or (esp. in animals) a related species; Gram-positive acid-fast rods.

> The most common form, **pulmonary tuberculosis** (formerly known as 'consumption'), is caused by inhalation of the bacteria. It was widespread in 19th-century Europe, and still causes 3 million deaths each year in developing countries. The disease can affect other parts of the body, notably the bones and joints and the central nervous system. Its spread was largely countered by vaccination and by the pasteurization of milk to prevent transmission from cattle. Today, the rise in HIV infection has helped cause a resurgence of tuberculosis, especially of drug-resistant strains.

– ORIGIN mid 19th cent.: modern Latin, from Latin *tuberculum* (see TUBERCLE) + -OSIS.

tu·ber·cu·lous /təˈbərkyələs, t(y)o͞o-/ ▶ **adj.** another term for TUBERCULAR.

tu·ber·ose /ˈt(y)o͞obəˌrōs, -ˌrōz/ ▶ **n.** **1** a Mexican plant of the agave family, with heavily scented white waxy flowers and a bulblike base. Unknown in the wild, it was formerly cultivated as a flavoring for chocolate; the flower oil is used in perfumery. ● *Polianthes tuberosa*, family Agavaceae.
2 variant spelling of TUBEROUS.
– ORIGIN mid 17th cent.: sense 1 from Latin *tuberosa*, feminine of *tuberosus* 'with protuberances'; sense 2 from Latin *tuberosus*.

tu·ber·ous /ˈt(y)o͞obərəs/ (also **tuberose** /-bəˌrōs/) ▶ **adj.** **1** Botany of the nature of a tuber. See TUBEROUS ROOT. ■ (of a plant) having tubers or a tuberous root.
2 Medicine characterized by or affected by rounded swellings: *tuberous sclerosis.*
– DERIVATIVES **tu·ber·os·i·ty** /ˌt(y)o͞obəˈräsitē/ **n.**

– ORIGIN mid 17th cent.: from French *tubéreux* or Latin *tuberosus*, from *tuber* (see TUBER).

tu·ber·ous root ▶ n. a thick and fleshy root like a tuber but without buds, as in the dahlia.

tube·snout /'t(y)o͞ob,snout/ ▶ n. a small inshore fish with a very elongated snout, head, and body, living along the Pacific coast of North America. ● *Aulorynchus flavidus*, the only member of the family Aulorhynchidae.

tube sock ▶ n. a sock without a shaped heel.

tube top ▶ n. a tight-fitting strapless top made of stretchy material and worn by women or girls.

tube well ▶ n. Brit. another term for SAND POINT WELL.

tube worm ▶ n. a marine bristle worm, esp. a fan worm, that lives in a tube made from sand particles or in a calcareous tube that it secretes. ● Families Serpulidae and Sabellidae, phylum Polychaeta. ■ a pogonophoran or vestimentiferan worm.

tu·bic·o·lous /t(y)o͞o'bikələs/ ▶ adj. Zoology (of a marine worm) living in a tube.

tu·bi·fex /'t(y)o͞obə,feks/ ▶ n. a small red annelid worm that lives in fresh water, partly buried in the mud. Also called BLOODWORM. ● Genus *Tubifex*, family Tubificidae, class Oligochaeta.

– ORIGIN modern Latin, from Latin *tubus* 'tube' + *-fex* from *facere* 'make.'

tub·ing /'t(y)o͞obiNG/ ▶ n. **1** a length or lengths of metal, plastic, glass, etc., in tubular form: *use the plastic tubing to siphon the beer into the bottles.*
2 the leisure activity of riding on water or snow on a large inflated inner tube.

Tub·man /'təbmən/, Harriet Ross (*c.*1820–1913), US abolitionist; born *Araminta Ross*; known as the *Moses of Her People*. She was born a slave in Maryland, but escaped via the Underground Railroad in 1849. Following what she called direct messages from God, she returned to Maryland numerous times to lead about 300 slaves to safety in the North. During the Civil War, she spied and served as a scout for the Union.

Harriet Tubman

tu·bo·cu·ra·rine /,t(y)o͞obōk(y)o͞o'rä,rēn/ ▶ n. Medicine a compound of the alkaloid class obtained from curare and used to produce relaxation of voluntary muscles before surgery and in tetanus, encephalitis, and poliomyelitis.

– ORIGIN late 19th cent.: from Latin *tubus* 'tube' + CURARE + -INE[4].

Tu·bruq /tō'bro͝ok, to͞o-/ Arabic name for TOBRUK.

tub-thump·ing informal, derogatory ▶ adj. [attrib.] expressing opinions in a loud and violent or dramatic manner: *a tub-thumping speech.*
▶ n. the expression of opinions in such a way.

– DERIVATIVES **tub-thump·er** n.

Tu·bu·a·i Is·lands /to͞ob'wä-ē/ a group of volcanic islands in the South Pacific Ocean that form part of French Polynesia; pop. 6,669 (2007). The chief town, Mataura, is on the island of Tubuai. Also called the AUSTRAL ISLANDS.

tu·bu·lar /'t(y)o͞obyələr/ ▶ adj. **1** long, round, and hollow like a tube: *tubular flowers of deep crimson.* ■ made from a tube or tubes: *tubular steel chairs.* ■ Surfing (of a wave) hollow and well curved. ■ informal, dated excellent: *U2's brand of really tubular new-wave sounds.*
2 Medicine of or involving tubules or other tube-shaped structures.
▶ n. **1** short for TUBULAR TIRE.
2 (**tubulars**) oil-drilling equipment made from tubes.

– ORIGIN late 17th cent.: from Latin *tubulus* 'small tube' + -AR[1].

tu·bu·lar bells ▶ plural n. an orchestral instrument consisting of a row of vertically suspended metal tubes struck with a mallet.

tu·bu·lar tire ▶ n. a completely enclosed tire cemented onto the wheel rim, used on racing bicycles.

tu·bule /'t(y)o͞o,byo͞ol/ ▶ n. a minute tube, esp. as an anatomical structure: *kidney tubules.*

– ORIGIN late 17th cent.: from Latin *tubulus*, diminutive of *tubus* 'tube.'

Tu·bu·li·den·ta·ta /,t(y)o͞obyəliden'tätə/ Zoology an order of mammals that comprises only the aardvark.

– ORIGIN modern Latin (plural), from TUBULE + Greek *odous, odont-* 'tooth.'

tu·bu·lin /'t(y)o͞obyəlin/ ▶ n. Biochemistry a protein that is the main constituent of the microtubules of living cells.

– ORIGIN 1960s: from TUBULE + -IN[1].

Tu·ca·na /t(y)o͞o'kānə, -'kanə/ Astronomy a southern constellation (the Toucan), south of Grus and Phoenix. It contains the Small Magellanic Cloud. ■ (as genitive **Tucanae** /t(y)o͞o'kānē, -'kanē/) used with a preceding letter or numeral to designate a star in this constellation: *the star Delta Tucanae.*

– ORIGIN modern Latin.

Tuch·man /'təkmən/, Barbara (1912–89), US historian and writer. Her many works include *The Guns of August* (1962), *Stilwell and the American Experience in China, 1911–45* (1971), *A Distant Mirror* (1978), and *The First Salute* (1988).

tuck /tək/ ▶ v. **1** [with obj.] push, fold, or turn (the edges or ends of something, esp. a garment or bedclothes) so as to hide them or hold them in place: *he tucked his shirt into his trousers.* ■ (**tuck someone in**) make someone, esp. a child, comfortable in bed by pulling the edges of the bedclothes firmly under the mattress: *he carried her back to bed and tucked her in.* ■ draw (something, esp. part of one's body) together into a small space: *she tucked her legs under her.* ■ put (something) away in a specified place or way so as to be hidden, safe, comfortable, or tidy: *the colonel was coming toward her, his gun tucked under his arm.*
2 [with obj.] make a flattened, stitched fold in (a garment or material), typically so as to shorten or tighten it, or for decoration.
▶ n. **1** a flattened, stitched fold in a garment or material, typically one of several parallel folds put in a garment for shortening, tightening, or decoration: *a dress with tucks along the bodice.* ■ [usu. with modifier] informal a surgical operation to reduce surplus flesh or fat: *a tummy tuck.*
2 Brit. informal food, typically cakes and candy, eaten by children at school as a snack: [as modifier] *a tuck shop.*
3 (also **tuck position**) (in diving, gymnastics, downhill skiing, etc.) a position with the knees bent and held close to the chest, often with the hands clasped around the shins.

– PHRASAL VERBS **tuck something away 1** store something in a secure place: *employees can tuck away a percentage of their pretax salary.* ■ (**be tucked away**) be located in an inconspicuous or concealed place: *the police station was tucked away in a square behind the main street.* **2** informal eat a lot of food. **tuck in** (or **into**) informal eat food heartily: *I tucked into the bacon and scrambled eggs.*

– ORIGIN Old English *tūcian* 'to punish, ill-treat'; related to TUG. Influenced in Middle English by Middle Dutch *tucken* 'pull sharply.'

tuck·a·hoe /'təkə,hō/ ▶ n. a root or other underground plant part formerly eaten by North American Indians, in particular: ● the starchy rhizome of an arum that grows chiefly in marshland (*Peltandra virginica*, family Araceae). ● the underground sclerotium of a bracket fungus (*Poria cocos*, class Hymenomycetes).

– ORIGIN early 17th cent.: from Virginia Algonquian *tockawhoughe*.

Tuck·er /'təkər/, Richard (1913–75) US opera singer; born *Rubin Ticker*. A tenor, he sang with the Metropolitan Opera for 30 seasons, beginning with his debut in 1945.

tuck·er /'təkər/ ▶ n. historical a piece of lace or linen worn in or around the top of a bodice or as an insert at the front of a low-cut dress. See also ONE'S BEST BIB AND TUCKER at BIB[1].
▶ v. [with obj.] (usu. **be tuckered out**) informal exhaust; wear out.

tuck·et /'təkit/ ▶ n. archaic a flourish on a trumpet.

– ORIGIN late 16th cent.: from obsolete *tuck* 'beat (a drum),' from Old Northern French *toquer*, from the base of TOUCH.

tuck-in ▶ n. Brit. informal, dated a large meal.

tuck·ing /'təkiNG/ ▶ n. a series of stitched tucks in a garment.

tuck-point ▶ v. [with obj.] point (brickwork) with colored mortar so as to have a narrow groove that is filled with fine white lime putty allowed to project slightly.

tuck po·si·tion ▶ n. see TUCK (sense 3 of the noun).

tu·co-tu·co /,to͞okō 'to͞okō/ ▶ n. (pl. **tuco-tucos**) a burrowing ratlike rodent native to South America. ● Family Ctenomyidae and genus *Ctenomys*: numerous species.

– ORIGIN mid 19th cent.: imitative of the call of some species.

Tuc·son /'to͞o,sän, to͞o'sän/ a city in southeastern Arizona; pop. 541,811 (est. 2008). Its desert climate makes it a tourist resort.

tu·cu·xi /to͞o'ko͞ohē/ ▶ n. (pl. **same**) a small stout-bodied dolphin with a gray back and pinkish underparts, living along the coasts and rivers from Panama to Brazil and in the Amazon. ● *Sotalia fluviatilis*, family Delphinidae.

'tude /t(y)o͞od/ ▶ n. informal short for ATTITUDE: *the song bristles with lotsa 'tude.*

-tude ▶ suffix forming abstract nouns such as *beatitude, solitude.*

– ORIGIN from French *-tude*, from Latin *-tudo*.

Tu·deh /'to͞odā/ (also **Tudeh Party**) the Communist Party of Iran.

– ORIGIN Persian, literally 'mass.'

Tu·dor[1] /'t(y)o͞odər/ ▶ adj. of or relating to the English royal dynasty that held the throne from the accession of Henry VII in 1485 until the death of Elizabeth I in 1603. ■ of, denoting, or relating to the prevalent architectural style of the Tudor period, characterized esp. by half-timbering.
▶ n. a member of the Tudor dynasty.

Tu·dor[2], Henry, Henry VII of England (see HENRY[1]).

Tu·dor[3], Mary, Mary I of England (see MARY[2]).

Tu·dor rose ▶ n. a conventionalized, typically five-lobed figure of a rose used in architectural and other decoration in the Tudor period, in particular a combination of the red and white roses of Lancaster or York adopted as a badge by Henry VII.

Tues. (also **Tue.**) ▶ abbr. Tuesday.

Tues·day /'t(y)o͞ozdā, -dē/ ▶ n. the day of the week before Wednesday and following Monday: *come to dinner on Tuesday* | *the following Tuesday* | [as modifier] *Tuesday afternoons.*
▶ adv. on Tuesday: *they're all leaving Tuesday.* ■ (**Tuesdays**) on Tuesdays; each Tuesday: *she works late Tuesdays.*

– ORIGIN Old English *Tīwesdæg*, named after the Scandinavian god *Tyr* (associated with Mars); translation of Latin *dies Marti* 'day of Mars.'

tu·fa /'t(y)o͞ofə/ ▶ n. a porous rock composed of calcium carbonate and formed by precipitation from water, e.g., around mineral springs. ■ another term for TUFF.

– DERIVATIVES **tu·fa·ceous** /t(y)o͞o'fāSHəs/ adj.

– ORIGIN late 18th cent.: from Italian, variant of *tufo* (see TUFF).

tuff /təf/ ▶ n. a light, porous rock formed by consolidation of volcanic ash.

– DERIVATIVES **tuff·a·ceous** /tə'fāSHəs/ adj.

– ORIGIN mid 16th cent.: via French from Italian *tufo*, from late Latin *tofus*, Latin *tophus* (see TOPHUS).

tuf·fet /'təfit/ ▶ n. **1** a tuft or clump of something: *grass tuffets.*
2 a footstool or low seat.

– ORIGIN mid 16th cent.: alteration of TUFT.

tuft /təft/ ▶ n. a bunch or collection of something, typically threads, grass, or hair, held or growing together at the base: *scrubby tufts of grass.* ■ Anatomy & Zoology a bunch of small blood vessels, respiratory tentacles, or other small anatomical structures.
▶ v. [with obj.] **1** (usu. **be tufted**) provide (something) with a tuft or tufts.
2 Needlework make depressions at regular intervals in (a mattress or cushion) by passing a thread through it.

– DERIVATIVES **tuft·y** adj.

– ORIGIN late Middle English: probably from Old French *tofe*, of unknown origin. The final *-t* is typical of phonetic confusion between *-f* and *-ft* at the end of words; compare with GRAFT[1].

tuft·ed /'təftid/ ▶ adj. having or growing in a tuft or tufts: *tufted grass.*

tuft·ed duck ▶ n. a Eurasian freshwater diving duck with a drooping crest, the male having mainly black and white plumage. ● *Aythya fuligula*, family Anatidae.

Tu Fu /'do͞o 'fo͞o/ (also **Du Fu**) (AD 712–770), Chinese poet. He is noted for his bitter satiric poems that attacked social injustice and corruption at court.

tug /təg/ ▶ v. (**tugs, tugging, tugged**) [with obj.] pull (something) hard or suddenly: *she tugged off her boots* | [no obj.] *he tugged at Tom's coat sleeve.*
▶ n. **1** a hard or sudden pull: *another tug and it came loose* | figurative *an overwhelming tug of attraction.*

PRONUNCIATION KEY ə ago, up; ər over, fur; a hat; ā ate; ä car; e let; ē see; i fit; ī by; NG sing; ō go; ô law, for; oi toy; o͝o good; o͞o goo; ou out; TH thin; T͟H then; ZH vision

t

2 short for TUGBOAT. ■ an aircraft towing a glider. 3 a loop from a horse's saddle that supports a shaft or trace.
– DERIVATIVES **tug·ger** n.
– ORIGIN Middle English: from the base of TOW[1]. The noun is first recorded (late Middle English) in sense 3 of the noun.

tug·boat ▶ n. a powerful boat used for towing larger vessels, esp. in harbor.

tugboat

tug of war ▶ n. a contest in which two teams pull at opposite ends of a rope until one drags the other over a central line. ■ a situation in which two evenly matched people or factions are striving to keep or obtain the same thing: *a tug of war between builders and environmentalists*.

tu·grik /'to͞ogrik/ ▶ n. (pl. **same** or **tugriks**) the basic monetary unit of Mongolia, equal to 100 mongos.
– ORIGIN Mongolian.

tu·i /'to͞oē/ ▶ n. a large New Zealand honeyeater with glossy blackish plumage and two white tufts at the throat. ● *Prosthemadura novaeseelandiae*, family Meliphagidae.
– ORIGIN mid 19th cent.: from Maori.

tuile /twē/ ▶ n. (pl. **same**) a thin curved cookie, typically made with almonds.
– ORIGIN French, literally 'tile.'

Tui·ler·ies /'twēlərē(z)/ (also **Tuileries Gardens**) formal gardens next to the Louvre in Paris. The gardens are all that remain of the Tuileries Palace, a royal residence begun in 1564 and burned down in 1871 during the Commune of Paris.
– ORIGIN French, literally 'Tile works,' so named because the palace was built on the site of an ancient tile works.

Tu·i·nal /'to͞oə,nôl, -,nal/ ▶ n. Medicine, trademark a sedative and hypnotic drug consisting of a combination of the barbiturates amobarbital and secobarbital.

tu·i·tion /t(y)o͞o'isHən/ ▶ n. a sum of money charged for teaching or instruction by a school, college, or university: *I'm not paying next year's tuition*. ■ teaching or instruction, esp. of individual pupils or small groups: *private tuition in French*.
– DERIVATIVES **tu·i·tion·al** /-sHənl/ adj.
– ORIGIN late Middle English (in the sense 'custody, care'): via Old French from Latin *tuitio(n-)*, from *tueri* 'to watch, guard.' Current senses date from the late 16th cent.

tuk-tuk /'to͝ok ,to͝ok/ ▶ n. (in Thailand) a three-wheeled motorized vehicle used as a taxi.
– ORIGIN imitative.

Tu·la /'to͞olə/ 1 an industrial city in western Russia, south of Moscow; pop. 500,000 (est. 2008). 2 the ancient capital city of the Toltecs, usually identified with a site near the town of Tula in Hidalgo State, in central Mexico.

Tu·lar·e /to͞o'le(ə)rē, -le(ə)r/ a commercial city in south central California, in the San Joaquin Valley; pop. 56,654 (est. 2008).

tu·la·re·mi·a /,t(y)o͞olə'rēmēə/ (Brit. **tularaemia**) ▶ n. a severe infectious bacterial disease of animals transmissible to humans, characterized by ulcers at the site of infection, fever, and loss of weight. Compare with RABBIT FEVER. ● This disease is caused by the bacterium *Francisella tularensis*; Gram-negative rods or cocci.
– DERIVATIVES **tu·la·re·mic** /'rēmik/ adj.
– ORIGIN 1920s: modern Latin, from *Tulare*, the county in California where it was first observed.

tu·le /'to͞olē/ ▶ n. a large bulrush that is abundant in marshy areas of California. ● Genus *Scirpus*, family Cyperaceae: two species, *S. acutus* and *S. validus*.
– ORIGIN mid 19th cent.: via Spanish from Nahuatl *tullin*.

Tu·le Lake /'to͞olē/ a lake in northern California, on the Modoc Plateau, a noted wildfowl refuge and site of fighting during the 1870s Modoc War.

tu·lip /'t(y)o͞oləp/ ▶ n. a bulbous spring-flowering plant of the lily family, with boldly colored cup-shaped flowers. ● Genus *Tulipa*, family Liliaceae: numerous complex hybrids.
– ORIGIN late 16th cent.: from French *tulipe*, via Turkish from Persian *dulband* 'turban,' from the shape of the expanded flower.

tu·lip shell ▶ n. a predatory marine mollusk with a sculptured spiral shell resembling that of a whelk. ● Family Fasciolariidae, class Gastropoda, in particular *Fasciolaria tulipa*, which is common in the Caribbean.

tu·lip tree (also **tuliptree**) ▶ n. a deciduous North American tree with large distinctively lobed leaves and large green and orange tuliplike flowers. Also called YELLOW POPLAR. ● *Liriodendron tulipifera*, family Magnoliaceae.

tu·lip·wood /'t(y)o͞oləp,wo͝od/ ▶ n. 1 an Australian tree of rain forest and scrub, with heavy black and yellow timber that is used mainly for cabinetmaking. ● *Harpullia pendula*, family Sapindaceae. 2 the pale timber of the tulip tree.

Tull /təl/, Jethro (1674–1741), English agriculturalist. In 1701, he invented the seed drill, a machine that could sow seeds in accurately spaced rows at a controlled rate, reducing the need for farm laborers.

tulle /to͞ol/ ▶ n. a soft, fine silk, cotton, or nylon material like net, used for making veils and dresses.
– ORIGIN early 19th cent.: from *Tulle*, a town in southwestern France, where it was first made.

tul·li·bee /'tələ,bē/ ▶ n. (pl. **same** or **tullibees**) a lake cisco (fish) of a deep-bodied race living in the Great Lakes of Canada. ● *Coregonus artedii tullibee*, family Salmonidae.
– ORIGIN late 18th cent.: from Canadian French *toulibi*, *outolouby*, from Ojibwa *otōlipī*.

Tul·sa /'təlsə/ a port city on the Arkansas River in northeastern Oklahoma; pop. 385,635 (est. 2008).

tul·si /'to͞olsē/ ▶ n. another term for HOLY BASIL.
– ORIGIN from Hindi *tulsī*.

tum /təm/ ▶ n. informal a person's stomach or abdomen.
– ORIGIN mid 19th cent.: abbreviation of TUMMY.

tum·ba·ga /to͞om'bägə/ ▶ n. an alloy of gold and copper commonly used in pre-Columbian South and Central America.
– ORIGIN 1930s: from Spanish, from Malay *tembaga* 'copper, brass.'

tum·ble /'təmbəl/ ▶ v. 1 [no obj.] (typically of a person) fall suddenly, clumsily, or headlong: *she pitched forward, tumbling down the remaining stairs*. ■ move or rush in a headlong or uncontrolled way: *police and dogs tumbled from the vehicle*. ■ (of something abstract) fall rapidly in amount or value: *property prices tumbled*. ■ [with obj.] rumple; disarrange: (as adj. **tumbled**) *his tumbled bedclothes*. ■ [with obj.] informal have sexual intercourse with (someone). 2 [no obj.] Brit. (**tumble to**) informal understand the meaning or hidden implication of (a situation): *she tumbled to our scam*. 3 [no obj.] perform acrobatic or gymnastic exercises, typically handsprings and somersaults in the air. ■ (of tumbler pigeons) repeatedly turn over backward in flight. 4 [with obj.] clean (castings, gemstones, etc.) in a tumbling barrel.
▶ n. 1 a sudden or headlong fall: *I took a tumble in the nettles*. ■ a rapid fall in amount or value: *a tumble in share prices*. ■ an untidy or confused arrangement or state: *her hair was a tumble of untamed curls*. ■ informal an act of sexual intercourse. ■ a handspring, somersault in the air, or other acrobatic feat. 2 informal a friendly sign of recognition, acknowledgment, or interest: *not a soul gave him a tumble*.
– ORIGIN Middle English (as a verb, also in the sense 'dance with contortions'): from Middle Low German *tummelen*; compare with Old English *tumbian* 'to dance' The sense was probably influenced by Old French *tomber* 'to fall.' The noun, first in the sense 'tangled mass,' dates from the mid 17th cent.

tum·ble·bug /'təmbəl,bəg/ ▶ n. a dung beetle that rolls balls of dung along the ground.

tum·ble·down /'təmbəl,doun/ ▶ adj. (of a building or structure) falling or fallen into ruin; dilapidated.

tum·ble dry ▶ v. (**dries**, **tumble drying**, **dried**) dry washed clothes by spinning them in hot air inside a dryer.

tum·ble·home /'təmbəl,hōm/ ▶ n. the inward slope of the upper part of the sides of a boat or ship.

tum·bler /'təmblər/ ▶ n. 1 a drinking glass with straight sides and no handle or stem. [formerly having a rounded bottom so as not to stand upright.] 2 an acrobat or gymnast, esp. one who performs somersaults. ■ a pigeon of a breed that repeatedly turns over backward in flight. 3 a pivoted piece in a lock that holds the bolt until lifted by a key. ■ a notched pivoted plate in a gunlock. 4 another term for TUMBLING BARREL.
– DERIVATIVES **tum·bler·ful** /-,fo͝ol/ n. (pl. **tumblerfuls**).

tum·ble·weed /'təmbəl,wēd/ ▶ n. a plant of dry regions that breaks off near the ground in late summer and is tumbled about by the wind, thereby dispersing its seeds. ● Genera *Salsola* (family Chenopodiaceae) and *Amaranthus* (family Amaranthaceae).

tum·bling bar·rel /'təmb(ə)liNG/ (also **tumbling box**) ▶ n. a revolving device containing an abrasive substance, in which castings, gemstones, or other hard objects can be cleaned and polished by friction.

tum·bril /'təmbrəl/ (also **tumbrel**) ▶ n. historical an open cart that tilted backward to empty out its load, in particular one used to convey condemned prisoners to the guillotine during the French Revolution. ■ a two-wheeled covered cart that carried tools or ammunition for an army.
– ORIGIN Middle English (originally denoting a type of cucking stool): from Old French *tomberel*, from *tomber* 'to fall.'

tu·me·fy /'t(y)o͞omə,fī/ ▶ v. (**tumefies**, **tumefying**, **tumefied**) [no obj.] become swollen.
– DERIVATIVES **tu·me·fac·tion** /,t(y)o͞omə'faksHən/ n.
– ORIGIN late 16th cent. (in the sense 'cause to swell'): from French *tuméfier*, from Latin *tumefacere*, from *tumere* 'to swell.'

tu·mes·cent /t(y)o͞o'mesənt/ ▶ adj. 1 swollen or becoming swollen, esp. as a response to sexual arousal. 2 (esp. of language or literary style) pompous or pretentious; tumid: *his prose is tumescent, full of orotund language*.
– DERIVATIVES **tu·mes·cence** n., **tu·mes·cent·ly** adv.
– ORIGIN mid 19th cent.: from Latin *tumescent-* 'beginning to swell,' from the verb *tumescere*, from *tumere* 'to swell.'

tu·mid /'t(y)o͞omid/ ▶ adj. 1 (esp. of a part of the body) swollen: *a tumid belly*. 2 (esp. of language or literary style) pompous or bombastic: *tumid oratory*.
– DERIVATIVES **tu·mid·i·ty** /t(y)o͞o'midətē/ n., **tu·mid·ly** adv.
– ORIGIN mid 16th cent.: from Latin *tumidus*, from *tumere* 'to swell.'

tumm·ler /'to͞omlər/ ▶ n. a person who makes things happen, in particular a professional entertainer or comedian whose function is to encourage an audience, guests at a resort, etc., to participate in the entertainments or activities.
– ORIGIN 1960s: Yiddish, from German *tummeln* 'to stir.'

tum·my /'təmē/ ▶ n. (pl. **tummies**) informal a person's stomach or abdomen.
– ORIGIN mid 19th cent.: child's pronunciation of STOMACH.

tum·my tuck ▶ n. informal an abdominoplasty.

tu·mor /'t(y)o͞omər/ (Brit. **tumour**) ▶ n. a swelling of a part of the body, generally without inflammation, caused by an abnormal growth of tissue, whether benign or malignant. ■ archaic a swelling of any kind.
– DERIVATIVES **tu·mor·ous** /-mərəs/ adj.
– ORIGIN late Middle English: from Latin *tumor*, from *tumere* 'to swell.'

tu·mor·i·gen·e·sis /,t(y)o͞omərə'jenəsis/ ▶ n. the production or formation of a tumor or tumors.

tu·mor·i·gen·ic /,t(y)o͞omərə'jenik/ ▶ adj. capable of forming or tending to form tumors.
– DERIVATIVES **tu·mor·i·ge·nic·i·ty** /-jə'nisitē/ n.

tump /təmp/ ▶ n. [often in place names] Brit. chiefly dialect 1 a small rounded hill or mound; a tumulus. 2 a clump of trees, shrubs, or grass.
– ORIGIN late 16th cent.: of unknown origin.

tump·line /'təmp,līn/ ▶ n. a sling for carrying a load on the back, with a strap that passes around the forehead. ■ a strap of this kind.
– ORIGIN late 18th cent.: based on Algonquian *(mat)tump* + the noun LINE[1].

tu·mult /'t(y)o͞o,məlt/ ▶ n. [usu. in sing.] a loud, confused noise, esp. one caused by a large mass of people: *a tumult of shouting and screaming broke out*. ■ confusion or disorder: *the whole neighborhood was in a state of fear and tumult* | figurative *his personal tumult ended when he began writing songs*.
– ORIGIN late Middle English: from Old French *tumulte* or Latin *tumultus*.

tu·mul·tu·ous /t(y)o͞o'məlcHo͞oəs, tə-/ ▶ adj. making a loud, confused noise; uproarious: *tumultuous applause*. ■ excited, confused, or disorderly: *a tumultuous crowd* | figurative *a tumultuous personal life*.
– DERIVATIVES **tu·mul·tu·ous·ly** adv., **tu·mul·tu·ous·ness** n.
– ORIGIN mid 16th cent.: from Old French *tumultuous* or Latin *tumultuosus*, from *tumultus* (see TUMULT).

tu·mu·lus /'t(y)o͞omyələs/ ▶ n. (pl. **tumuli** /-,lī/) an ancient burial mound; a barrow.
– ORIGIN late Middle English: from Latin; related to *tumere* 'swell.'

t

tun /tən/ ▶ **n. 1** a large beer or wine cask. ■ a brewer's fermenting vat.
2 an imperial measure of capacity, equal to 4 hogsheads.
3 (also **tun shell**) a large marine mollusk that has a rounded barrellike shell with broad spirals. ● Family Tonnidae, class Gastropoda.
▶ **v.** (**tuns, tunning, tunned**) [with obj.] archaic store (wine or other alcoholic drinks) in a tun.
– ORIGIN Old English *tunne*, from medieval Latin *tunna*, probably of Gaulish origin.

tu·na[1] /ˈt(y)o͞onə/ ▶ **n.** (pl. **same** or **tunas**) a large and active predatory schooling fish of the mackerel family. Found in warm seas, it is extensively fished commercially and is popular as a game fish. ● *Thunnus* and other genera, family Scombridae: several species, including the albacore, bigeye, bluefin, skipjack, and yellowfin. ■ (also **tuna fish**) the flesh of this fish as food, usually canned.
– ORIGIN late 19th cent.: from American Spanish, from Spanish *atún*.

tu·na[2] ▶ **n. 1** the edible fruit of a prickly pear cactus.
2 a cactus that produces such fruit, widely cultivated in Mexico. ● Genus *Opuntia*, family Cactaceae: many species, in particular *O. tuna* of Central America and the Caribbean.
– ORIGIN mid 16th cent.: via Spanish from Taino.

tun·dra /ˈtəndrə/ ▶ **n.** a vast, flat, treeless Arctic region of Europe, Asia, and North America in which the subsoil is permanently frozen.
– ORIGIN late 16th cent.: from Lappish.

tun·dra swan ▶ **n.** an Arctic-breeding migratory swan with a yellow and black bill often known by the names of its constituent races, e.g., whistling swan. ● *Cygnus columbianus*, family Anatidae.

tune /t(y)o͞on/ ▶ **n.** a melody, esp. one that characterizes a certain piece of music: *she left the theater humming a cheerful tune.*
▶ **v.** [with obj.] **1** adjust (a musical instrument) to the correct or uniform pitch: *he tuned the harp for me.*
2 adjust (a receiver circuit such as a radio or television) to the frequency of the required signal: *the radio was **tuned to** the CBC* | [no obj.] *they **tuned in** to watch the game.*
3 (often **tune up**) adjust (an engine) or balance (mechanical parts) so that a vehicle runs smoothly and efficiently: *the suspension was tuned for a softer ride* | figurative *state officials have been tuning up an emergency plan.*
4 adjust or adapt (something) to a particular purpose or situation: *the animals are finely **tuned to** life in the desert.*
– PHRASES **call the tune** see CALL. **change one's tune** see CHANGE. **in** (or **out of**) **tune** with correct (or incorrect) pitch or intonation. ■ (of an engine or other machine) properly (or poorly) adjusted. ■ in (or not in) agreement or harmony: *he was **out of tune with** conventional belief.* **to the tune of** informal amounting to or involving (a specified considerable sum): *he was in debt to the tune of forty thousand dollars.*
– PHRASAL VERBS **be tuned in** informal be aware of, sensitive to, or able to understand something: *it's important to **be tuned in to** your child's needs.* **tune into** become sensitive to: *you must tune into the needs of loved ones.* **tune out** informal stop listening or paying attention. **tune someone/something out** not listen or pay attention to someone or something. **tune something out** exclude a sound or transmission of a particular frequency. **tune up** (of a musician) adjust one's instrument to the correct or uniform pitch: *we could hear the band tuning up.*
– DERIVATIVES **tun·a·ble** (also **tuneable**) **adj.**, **tun·ing n.**
– ORIGIN late Middle English: unexplained alteration of TONE. The verb is first recorded (late 15th cent.) in the sense 'celebrate in music, sing.'

tune·ful /ˈt(y)o͞onfəl/ ▶ **adj.** having a pleasing tune; melodious.
– DERIVATIVES **tune·ful·ly adv.**, **tune·ful·ness n.**

tune·less /ˈt(y)o͞onləs/ ▶ **adj.** not pleasing to listen to; not melodious.
– DERIVATIVES **tune·less·ly adv.**, **tune·less·ness n.**

tun·er /ˈt(y)o͞onər/ ▶ **n.** a person who tunes musical instruments, esp. pianos. ■ an electronic device for tuning a guitar or other instrument. ■ an electronic device for varying the frequency to which a radio or television is tuned. ■ a separate unit for detecting and preamplifying a program signal and supplying it to an audio amplifier.

tune·smith /ˈt(y)o͞onˌsmiTH/ ▶ **n.** informal a composer of popular music.

tune-up (also **tuneup**) ▶ **n.** an act of tuning something up: *take your car in for a tune-up if it's an older model.* ■ a sporting event that serves as a practice for a subsequent event: *a tune-up for the college's fall league.*

tung oil ▶ **n.** an oil used as a drying agent in inks, paints, and varnishes. ● This oil is obtained from the seeds of trees of the genus *Aleurites*, family Euphorbiaceae.
– ORIGIN late 19th cent.: *tung*, from Chinese.

tung·state /ˈtəNGˌstāt/ ▶ **n.** Chemistry a salt in which the anion contains both tungsten and oxygen, esp. one of the anion WO_4^{2-}.
– ORIGIN early 19th cent.: from TUNGSTEN + -ATE[1].

tung·sten /ˈtəNGstən/ ▶ **n.** the chemical element of atomic number 74, a hard steel-gray metal of the transition series. It has a very high melting point (3410°C) and is used to make electric light filaments. (Symbol: **W**)
– ORIGIN late 18th cent.: from Swedish, from *tung* 'heavy' + *sten* 'stone.'

tung·sten car·bide ▶ **n.** a very hard gray compound made by reaction of tungsten and carbon at high temperatures, used in making engineering dies, cutting and drilling tools, etc. ● Chem. formula: WC; some forms also contain W_2C.

tung·stite /ˈtəNGˌstīt/ ▶ **n.** a yellow mineral consisting of hydrated tungsten oxide, typically occurring as a powdery coating on tungsten ores.
– ORIGIN mid 19th cent.: from TUNGSTEN + -ITE[1].

Tun·gus /ˈto͝oNGˈgo͞oz, tən-/ ▶ **n.** (pl. **same**) a member of the northern Evenki people of Siberia. ■ older term for EVENKI (the language).
– ORIGIN Russian, from a Turkic language.

Tun·gus·ic /to͝oNGˈgo͞ozik/ ▶ **adj.** of, relating to, or denoting a small family of Altaic languages of Siberia and northern China.
▶ **n.** this family of languages collectively.

Tun·gu·ska /to͝oNGˈgo͞oskə, təNG-/ two rivers in Siberia in Russia, the **Lower Tunguska** and the **Stony Tunguska**, that flow west through the forested, sparsely populated Tunguska Basin into the Yenisei River.

tu·nic /ˈt(y)o͞onik/ ▶ **n. 1** a loose garment, typically sleeveless and reaching to the wearer's knees, as worn in ancient Greece and Rome. ■ a loose, thigh-length garment, worn typically by women over a skirt or trousers.
2 a close-fitting short coat as part of a uniform, esp. a police or military uniform.
3 Biology & Anatomy an integument or membrane enclosing or lining an organ or part. ■ Botany any of the concentric layers of a plant bulb, e.g., an onion. ■ Zoology the rubbery outer coat of a sea squirt.
– ORIGIN Old English, from Old French *tunique* or Latin *tunica*.

tu·ni·ca /ˈt(y)o͞onikə/ ▶ **n.** (pl. **tunicae** /-nəkē, -sē/) **1** Anatomy a membranous sheath enveloping or lining an organ.
2 Botany the outer layer or layers of cells in an apical meristem, which contribute to surface growth.
– ORIGIN late 17th cent.: from Latin, literally 'tunic.'

tu·ni·cate /ˈt(y)o͞oniˌkāt/ ▶ **n.** Zoology a marine invertebrate of a group that includes the sea squirts and salps. They have a rubbery or hard outer coat and two siphons to draw water into and out of the body. ● Subphylum Urochordata: three classes.
▶ **adj.** (usu. **tunicated**) Botany (of a plant bulb, e.g., an onion) having concentric layers.
– ORIGIN mid 18th cent.: from Latin *tunicatus*, past participle of *tunicare* 'clothe with a tunic,' from *tunica* (see TUNICA).

tu·ni·cle /ˈt(y)o͞onikəl/ ▶ **n.** a short liturgical vestment that is traditionally worn over the alb by a subdeacon at celebrations of the Mass.
– ORIGIN late Middle English: from Old French *tunicle* or Latin *tunicula*, diminutive of *tunica* (see TUNICA).

tun·ing fork ▶ **n.** a two-pronged steel device used by musicians, which vibrates when struck to give a note of specific pitch.

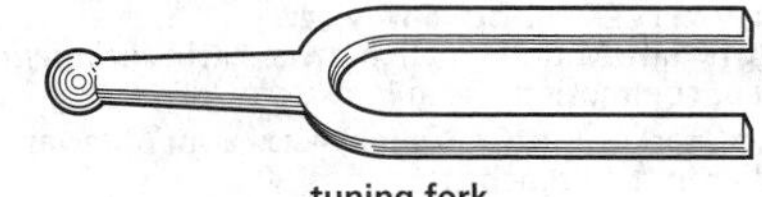

tuning fork

tun·ing pin /ˈt(y)o͞oniNG/ ▶ **n.** a pin to which the strings of a piano or harpsichord are attached.

Tu·nis /ˈt(y)o͞onəs/ the capital of Tunisia, a port on the Mediterranean coast of North Africa; pop. 745,000 (est. 2007).

Tu·ni·sia /t(y)o͞oˈnēZHə/ a country in North Africa, on the Mediterranean Sea and extending south into the Sahara Desert; pop. 10,486,300 (est. 2009); capital, Tunis; language, Arabic (official).

> Phoenician coastal settlements developed into the commercial empire of Carthage (near modern Tunis). The area was conquered by the Arabs in the 7th century and became part of the Ottoman Empire in the 16th century; a French protectorate was established in 1886. The rise of nationalism led to independence and the establishment of a republic in 1956–57.

– DERIVATIVES **Tu·ni·sian adj. & n.**

tun·nel /ˈtənl/ ▶ **n.** an artificial underground passage, esp. one built through a hill or under a building, road, or river. ■ an underground passage dug by a burrowing animal. ■ [in sing.] a passage in a sports stadium by which players enter or leave the field.
▶ **v.** (**tunnels, tunneling, tunneled**; Brit. **tunnels, tunnelling, tunnelled**) **1** [no obj.] dig or force a passage underground or through something: *he **tunneled under the fence*** | (**tunnel one's way**) *the insect tunnels its way out of the plant.*
2 [no obj.] Physics (of a particle) pass through a potential barrier.
– PHRASES **light at the end of the tunnel** see LIGHT[1].
– DERIVATIVES **tun·nel·er n.**
– ORIGIN late Middle English (in the senses 'tunnel net' and 'flue of a chimney'): from Old French *tonel*, diminutive of *tonne* 'cask.' Sense 1 of the verb of the noun dates from the mid 18th cent.

tun·nel di·ode ▶ **n.** Electronics a two-terminal semiconductor diode using tunneling electrons to perform high-speed switching operations.

tun·nel kiln ▶ **n.** an industrial kiln in which ceramic items being fired are carried on trucks along a continuously heated passage.

tun·nel of love ▶ **n.** a fairground amusement for couples involving a train or boat ride through a darkened tunnel.

tun·nel vi·sion ▶ **n.** defective sight in which objects cannot be properly seen if not close to the center of the field of view. ■ informal the tendency to focus exclusively on a single or limited goal or point of view.

Tun·ney /ˈtənē/, Gene (1898–1978), US boxer; born *James Joseph Tunney*. He became world heavyweight champion in 1926 by defeating Jack Dempsey. After defending his title several times, he retired as the undefeated world heavyweight champion in 1928.

tun·ny /ˈtənē/ (also **tunny fish**) ▶ **n.** chiefly Brit. (pl. **same** or **tunnies**) a tuna, esp. the bluefin. ■ tuna as food.
– ORIGIN mid 16th cent.: from French *thon*, via Latin from Greek *thunnos*.

tun shell ▶ **n.** see TUN (sense 3 of the noun).

Tu·ol·um·ne River /to͞oˈäləmē/ a river that flows from Yosemite National Park in California to the San Joaquin River. It is impounded in the Hetch Hetchy and Don Pedro reservoirs.

tup /təp/ ▶ **n.** chiefly Brit. a ram.
▶ **v.** (**tups, tupping, tupped**) [with obj.] (often as noun **tupping**) chiefly Brit. (of a ram) copulate with (a ewe). ■ vulgar slang (of a man) have sexual intercourse with (a woman).
– ORIGIN Middle English: of unknown origin.

Tu·pa·ma·ro /ˌto͞opəˈmäˌrō/ ▶ **n.** (pl. **Tupamaros**) a member of a Marxist urban guerrilla organization in Uruguay that was active mainly in the late 1960s and early 1970s.
– ORIGIN 1960s: from *Tupac Amarú*, the name of an 18th-cent. Inca leader.

Tu·pe·lo /ˈt(y)o͞opəˌlō/ a city in northeastern Mississippi; pop. 36,233 (est. 2008). The site of some Civil War battles, it is also the birthplace of Elvis Presley.

tu·pe·lo /ˈt(y)o͞opəˌlō/ ▶ **n.** (pl. **tupelos**) a North American or Asian tree of damp and swampy habitats that yields useful timber. ● Genus *Nyssa*, family Nyssaceae: several species, including the **water tupelo** (*N. aquatica*), which grows in the coastal-plain swamps of the southeastern US.
– ORIGIN mid 18th cent.: from Creek, from *ito* 'tree' + *opilwa* 'swamp.'

Tu·pi /ˈto͞opē, to͞oˈpē/ ▶ **n.** (pl. **same** or **Tupis**) **1** a member of a group of American Indian peoples living in scattered areas throughout the Amazon basin.
2 any of the languages of these peoples, a branch of the Tupi-Guarani language family.
▶ **adj.** of or relating to these peoples or their languages.
– DERIVATIVES **Tu·pi·an** /-pēən/ **adj.**
– ORIGIN a local name.

Tu·pi-Gua·ra·ni /ˌto͞opē ˌgwäräˈnē/ ▶ **n.** a South American Indian language family whose principal members are Guarani and the Tupian languages.
▶ **adj.** of, relating to, or denoting these languages.

tup·pence ▶ **n.** Brit. variant spelling of TWOPENCE.

tup·pen·ny /ˈtəp(ə)nē/ ▶ **adj.** Brit. variant spelling of TWOPENNY.

Tup·per /ˈtəpər/, Sir Charles (1821–1915), Canadian Conservative statesman. His 69-day term as prime minister in 1896 was the shortest in Canada's history.

Tup·per·ware /ˈtəpərˌwer/ ▶ **n.** trademark a range of plastic containers used chiefly for storing food.
– ORIGIN 1950s: from *Tupper*, the name of the American manufacturer, + WARE[1].

tuque /t(y)o͞ok/ ▶ **n.** Canadian a close-fitting knitted stocking cap.
– ORIGIN Canadian French form of TOQUE.

tur /to͝or/ ▶ **n.** a wild goat native to the Caucasian mountains. ● Genus *Capra*, family Bovidae: two species.
– ORIGIN late 19th cent.: from Russian.

tu·ra·co ▶ **n.** variant spelling of TOURACO.

Tu·ra·ni·an /t(y)o͝oˈrānēən/ ▶ **adj.** dated of, relating to, or denoting the languages of central Asia, particularly those of the Uralic and Altaic families, or the peoples that speak them.
– ORIGIN late 18th cent.: from Persian *Tūrān*, the region beyond the Oxus, + -IAN.

tur·ban /ˈtərbən/ ▶ **n.** **1** a man's headdress, consisting of a long length of cotton or silk wound around a cap or the head, worn esp. by Muslims and Sikhs.
2 (also **turban shell**) a marine mollusk with a sculptured spiral shell and a distinctive operculum which is smooth on the inside and sculptured and typically patterned on the outside. ● Family Turbinidae, class Gastropoda: *Turbo* and other genera.
– DERIVATIVES **tur·baned** adj.
– ORIGIN mid 16th cent.: via French from Turkish *tülbent*, from Persian *dulband*. Compare with TULIP.

turban 1

tur·ban squash ▶ **n.** a winter squash with a green and orange rind, shaped somewhat like a turban.

Tur·bel·lar·ia /ˌtərbəˈle(ə)rēə/ Zoology a class of typically free-living flatworms that have a ciliated surface and a simple branched gut with a single opening.
– DERIVATIVES **tur·bel·lar·i·an** /ˌtərbəˈle(ə)rēən/ adj. & n.
– ORIGIN modern Latin (plural), from Latin *turbella* 'bustle, stir,' diminutive of *turba* 'crowd.'

tur·bid /ˈtərbid/ ▶ **adj.** (of a liquid) cloudy, opaque, or thick with suspended matter: *the turbid estuary.* ■ confused or obscure in meaning or effect: *a turbid piece of cinéma vérité.*
– DERIVATIVES **tur·bid·i·ty** /tərˈbiditē/ n., **tur·bid·ly** adv., **tur·bid·ness** n.
– ORIGIN late Middle English (in the figurative sense): from Latin *turbidus*, from *turba* 'a crowd, a disturbance.'

> **USAGE** Is it **turbid** or **turgid**? **Turbid** is used of a liquid or color to mean 'muddy, not clear': *turbid water.* **Turgid** means 'swollen, inflated, enlarged': *turgid veins.* Both **turbid** and **turgid** can also be used to describe language or literary style: as such, **turbid** means 'confused, muddled' (*the turbid utterances of Carlyle*), and **turgid** means 'pompous, bombastic' (*a turgid and pretentious essay*).

t

tur·bi·dim·e·ter /ˌtərbiˈdimitər/ ▶ **n.** an instrument for measuring the turbidity of a liquid suspension, usually as a means of determining the surface area of the suspended particles.
– DERIVATIVES **tur·bi·di·met·ric** /-dəˈmetrik/ adj., **tur·bi·dim·e·try** /-trē/ n.

tur·bi·dite /ˈtərbiˌdīt/ ▶ **n.** Geology a sediment or rock deposited by a turbidity current.
– DERIVATIVES **tur·bi·dit·ic** /ˌtərbiˈditik/ adj.
– ORIGIN 1950s: from *turbid* (see TURBID) + -ITE[1].

tur·bid·i·ty cur·rent /tərˈbiditē/ ▶ **n.** an underwater current flowing swiftly downslope owing to the weight of sediment it carries.

tur·bi·nal /ˈtərbənl/ ▶ **n.** (usu. **turbinals**) Anatomy & Zoology each of three thin curved shelves of bone in the sides of the nasal cavity in humans and other warm-blooded vertebrates, covered in mucous membrane.
– ORIGIN late 16th cent. (as an adjective in the sense 'top-shaped'): from Latin *turbo, turbin-* 'spinning top' + -AL.

tur·bi·nate /ˈtərbənit, -ˌnāt/ ▶ **adj.** chiefly Zoology (esp. of a shell) shaped like a spinning top or inverted cone. ■ Anatomy relating to or denoting the turbinals.
▶ **n.** (also **turbinate bone**) Anatomy another term for TURBINAL.
– ORIGIN mid 17th cent.: from Latin *turbinatus*, from *turbo, turbin-* (see TURBINE).

tur·bine /ˈtərˌbīn, -bin/ ▶ **n.** a machine for producing continuous power in which a wheel or rotor, typically fitted with vanes, is made to revolve by a fast-moving flow of water, steam, gas, air, or other fluid.
– ORIGIN mid 19th cent.: from French, from Latin *turbo, turbin-* 'spinning top, whirl.'

tur·bit /ˈtərbit/ ▶ **n.** a stoutly built pigeon of a domestic breed with a neck frill and short beak.
– ORIGIN late 17th cent.: apparently from Latin *turbo* 'spinning top,' from its shape.

tur·bo /ˈtərbō/ ▶ **n.** (pl. **turbos**) short for TURBOCHARGER. ■ a motor vehicle equipped with a turbocharger.

turbo- ▶ **comb. form** having or driven by a turbine: *turboshaft.*
– ORIGIN from TURBINE.

tur·bo·boost /ˈtərbōˌbo͞ost/ ▶ **n.** the increase in speed or power produced by turbocharging a car's engine or, specifically, when the turbocharger becomes activated.

tur·bo·charge /ˈtərbōˌCHärj/ ▶ **v.** [with obj.] (often as adj. **turbocharged**) equip (an engine or vehicle) with a turbocharger. ■ add speed or energy to (something): *his turbocharged style of choreography.*

tur·bo·charg·er /ˈtərbōˌCHärjər/ ▶ **n.** a supercharger driven by a turbine powered by the engine's exhaust gases.

tur·bo die·sel ▶ **n.** a turbocharged diesel engine. ■ a vehicle equipped with such an engine.

tur·bo·fan /ˈtərbōˌfan/ ▶ **n.** a jet engine in which a turbine-driven fan provides additional thrust. ■ an aircraft powered by such an engine.

tur·bo·gen·er·a·tor /ˌtərbōˈjenəˌrātər/ ▶ **n.** a large electricity generator driven by a steam turbine.

tur·bo·jet /ˈtərbōˌjet/ ▶ **n.** a jet engine in which the jet gases also operate a turbine-driven compressor for compressing the air drawn into the engine. ■ an aircraft powered by such an engine.

tur·bo·prop /ˈtərbōˌpräp/ ▶ **n.** a jet engine in which a turbine is used to drive a propeller. ■ an aircraft powered by such an engine.

tur·bo·shaft /ˈtərbōˌSHaft/ ▶ **n.** a gas turbine engine in which the turbine drives a shaft other than a propeller shaft.

tur·bo·su·per·charg·er /ˌtərbōˈso͞opərˌCHärjər/ ▶ **n.** another term for TURBOCHARGER.

tur·bot /ˈtərbət/ ▶ **n.** (pl. **same** or **turbots**) a European flatfish of inshore waters that has large bony tubercles on the body and is prized as food. ● *Scophthalmus maximus*, family Scophthalmidae (or Bothidae). ■ used in names of similar flatfishes, e.g., **black turbot**.
– ORIGIN Middle English: from Old French, of Scandinavian origin.

tur·bu·lence /ˈtərbyələns/ ▶ **n.** violent or unsteady movement of air or water, or of some other fluid: *the plane shuddered as it entered some turbulence.* ■ conflict; confusion: *a time of political turbulence.*
– ORIGIN late Middle English: from Old French, or from late Latin *turbulentia*, from *turbulentus* 'full of commotion' (see TURBULENT).

tur·bu·lent /ˈtərbyələnt/ ▶ **adj.** characterized by conflict, disorder, or confusion; not controlled or calm: *the country's turbulent 20-year history | her turbulent emotions.* ■ (of air or water) moving unsteadily or violently: *the turbulent sea.* ■ technical of, relating to, or denoting flow of a fluid in which the velocity at any point fluctuates irregularly and there is continual mixing rather than a steady or laminar flow pattern.
– DERIVATIVES **tur·bu·lent·ly** adv.
– ORIGIN late Middle English: from Latin *turbulentus* 'full of commotion,' from *turba* 'crowd.'

Tur·co /ˈtərkō/ ▶ **n.** (pl. **Turcos**) historical an Algerian soldier in the French army.
– ORIGIN mid 19th cent.: from Spanish, Portuguese, and Italian, literally 'Turk.'

Turco- (also **Turko-**) ▶ **comb. form** Turkish; Turkish and ...: *Turco-Tartar.* ■ relating to Turkey.

Tur·co·man ▶ **n.** variant spelling of TURKOMAN.

turd /tərd/ ▶ **n.** vulgar slang a lump of excrement. ■ a person regarded as obnoxious or contemptible.
– ORIGIN Old English *tord*, of Germanic origin.

tur·duck·en /tərˈdəkən/ ▶ **n.** a roast dish consisting of a boned chicken inside a boned duck, which is then placed inside a partially boned turkey.
– ORIGIN 1980s: blend of TURKEY and DUCK[1] and CHICKEN.

tu·reen /t(y)o͝oˈrēn/ ▶ **n.** a deep covered dish from which soup is served.
– ORIGIN mid 18th cent.: alteration of earlier *terrine*, from French *terrine* (see TERRINE), feminine of Old French *terrin* 'earthen,' based on Latin *terra* 'earth.'

turf /tərf/ ▶ **n.** (pl. **turfs** or **turves** /tərvz/) **1** grass and the surface layer of earth held together by its roots: *they walked across the springy turf.* ■ Brit. a piece of such grass and earth cut from the ground. ■ peat used for fuel.
2 (**the turf**) horse racing or racecourses generally: *he spent his money gambling on the turf.*
3 informal an area regarded as someone's personal territory; one's home ground: *the team will play Canada on their home turf this summer.* ■ a person's sphere of influence or activity: *we're in similar businesses but we cover different turf.*
▶ **v. 1** [with obj.] informal, chiefly Brit. force (someone) to leave somewhere: *they were turfed off the bus.*
2 [with obj.] (often as adj. **turfed**) cover (a patch of ground) with turf: *a turfed lawn.*
– ORIGIN Old English, of Germanic origin; related to Dutch *turf* and German *Torf*, from an Indo-European root shared by Sanskrit *darbha* 'tuft of grass.'

turf·man /ˈtərfmən/ ▶ **n.** (pl. **turfmen**) a devotee of horse racing, esp. one who owns or trains horses.

turf war (also **turf battle**) ▶ **n.** informal an acrimonious dispute between rival groups over territory or a particular sphere of influence.
– ORIGIN 1970s: from the notion of a *war* over *turf* in the informal sense 'area regarded as personal territory' (originally the area controlled by, for example, a street gang or criminal).

turf·y /ˈtərfē/ ▶ **adj.** (**turfier**, **turfiest**) covered with or consisting of turf; grassy: *a turfy plain.* ■ of or like peat; peaty: *I inhaled the turfy air.*

Tur·ge·nev /to͝orˈgānyəf/, Ivan (Sergeevich) (1818–83), Russian novelist, playwright, and short-story writer. His novels, such as *Fathers and Sons* (1862), examine individual lives to illuminate the social, political, and philosophical issues of the day.

tur·ges·cent /tərˈjesənt/ ▶ **adj.** chiefly technical becoming or seeming swollen or distended.
– DERIVATIVES **tur·ges·cence** n.
– ORIGIN early 18th cent.: from Latin *turgescent-* 'beginning to swell,' from the verb *turgescere*, from *turgere* 'to swell.'

tur·gid /ˈtərjid/ ▶ **adj.** swollen and distended or congested: *a turgid and fast-moving river.* ■ (of language or style) tediously pompous or bombastic: *some turgid verses on the death of Prince Albert.*
– DERIVATIVES **tur·gid·i·ty** /tərˈjiditē/ n., **tur·gid·ly** adv.
– ORIGIN early 17th cent.: from Latin *turgidus*, from *turgere* 'to swell.'

> **USAGE** On the differences in use between **turgid** and **turbid**, see usage at TURBID.

tur·gor /ˈtərgər/ ▶ **n.** chiefly Botany the state of turgidity and resulting rigidity of cells (or tissues), typically due to the absorption of fluid.
– ORIGIN late 19th cent.: from late Latin, from *turgere* 'to swell.'

Tu·rin /ˈt(y)o͝orən, t(y)o͝oˈrin/ a city in northwestern Italy on the Po River, capital of Piedmont region; pop. 908,825 (2008). It was the capital of the kingdom of Sardinia from 1720 and became the first capital of a unified Italy (1861–64). Italian name TORINO.

Tu·rin, Shroud of a relic, preserved at Turin since 1578, venerated as the winding sheet in which Christ's body was wrapped for burial. It bears the apparent imprint of the front and back of a human body as well as markings that correspond to the traditional stigmata. Scientific tests carried out in 1988 dated the shroud to the 13th–14th centuries.

Tu·ring /ˈt(y)o͝oriNG/, Alan Mathison (1912–54), English mathematician. He developed the concept of a theoretical computing machine and carried out important code-breaking work during World War II. He also investigated artificial intelligence.

Tu·ring ma·chine ▶ **n.** a mathematical model of a hypothetical computing machine that can use a predefined set of rules to determine a result from a set of input variables.

Tu·ring test ▶ **n.** a test for intelligence in a computer, requiring that a human being should be unable to distinguish the machine from another human being by using the replies to questions put to both.

tu·ri·on /ˈt(y)o͝orēˌän/ ▶ **n.** Botany (in some aquatic plants) a wintering bud that becomes detached and remains dormant at the bottom of the water.
– ORIGIN early 18th cent.: from French, from Latin *turio(n-)* 'a shoot.'

tu·ris·ta /to͞oˈrēstə/ ▶ **n.** informal diarrhea as suffered by travelers when visiting certain foreign countries.
– ORIGIN Spanish, literally 'tourist.'

Turk /tərk/ ▶ **n. 1** a native or inhabitant of Turkey, or a person of Turkish descent.
2 historical a member of any of the ancient central Asian peoples who spoke Turkic languages, including the Seljuks and Ottomans.
3 archaic a member of the ruling Muslim population of the Ottoman Empire.
– ORIGIN late Middle English: via Old French from Turkish *türk*.

Tur·ka·na /tər'känə/ ▶ **n.** (pl. **same**) **1** a member of an East African people living between Lake Turkana and the Nile.
2 the Nilotic language of the Turkana, spoken by about 250,000 people.
▶ **adj.** of or relating to the Turkana or their language.
– ORIGIN a local name.

Tur·ka·na, Lake /tər'kanə, -'känə/ a salt lake in northwestern Kenya, with no outlet. It was visited in 1888 by Hungarian explorer **Count Teleki** (1845–1916), who named it Lake Rudolf after the crown prince of Austria. It was given its present name in 1979.

Tur·ke·stan /'tərkə,stan, -,stän/ (also **Turkistan**) a region in central Asia between the Caspian Sea and the Gobi Desert, inhabited mainly by Turkic peoples. It is divided by the Pamir and Tien Shan mountains into eastern Turkestan, now the Xinjiang autonomous region of China, and western Turkestan, which consists of present-day Turkmenistan, Kazakhstan, Uzbekistan, Tajikistan, and Kyrgyzstan.

Tur·key /'tərkē/ a country located on the Anatolian peninsula in western Asia, with a small enclave in southeastern Europe west of Istanbul; pop. 76,805,500 (est. 2009); capital, Ankara; language, Turkish (official).

Turkey was the center of the Ottoman Empire, established in the late Middle Ages and largely maintained until its collapse at the end of World War I, in which Turkey supported the Central Powers. The nationalist leader Kemal Atatürk established the modern republic of Turkey in the 1920s. Turkey was neutral in World War II but is a member of NATO.

tur·key /'tərkē/ ▶ **n.** (pl. **turkeys**) **1** a large mainly domesticated game bird native to North America, having a bald head and (in the male) red wattles. It is prized as food, esp. on festive occasions such as Thanksgiving and Christmas. ● *Meleagris gallopavo*, family Meleagridae (or Phasianidae). ■ the flesh of the turkey as food.

turkey 1

2 informal something that is extremely or completely unsuccessful, esp. a play or movie. ■ a stupid or inept person.
– PHRASES **talk turkey** informal discuss something frankly and straightforwardly.
– ORIGIN mid 16th cent.: short for TURKEY COCK or *turkey hen*, originally applied to the guinea fowl (which was imported through Turkey), and then erroneously to the American bird.

tur·key buz·zard ▶ **n.** another term for TURKEY VULTURE.

tur·key call ▶ **n.** an instrument used by hunters to decoy the wild turkey by imitating its characteristic gobbling sound.

tur·key cock ▶ **n.** a male turkey. ■ a pompous or self-important person.

tur·key oak ▶ **n.** a small oak of the coastal plains of the southeastern US, with leathery three-lobed leaves shaped like the outline of a turkey track. ● *Quercus laevis*, family Fagaceae.

Tur·key red ▶ **n.** a scarlet textile dye obtained from madder or alizarin. ■ the color of this dye. ■ cotton cloth dyed with this, popular in the 19th century.

tur·key shoot ▶ **n.** informal a situation, typically in a war, in which one side has an overwhelming advantage.

tur·key trot ▶ **n.** a kind of ballroom dance to ragtime music that was popular in the early 20th century.

tur·key vul·ture ▶ **n.** a common American vulture with black plumage and a bare red head. ● *Cathartes aura*, family Cathartidae.

Tur·kic /'tərkik/ ▶ **adj.** of, relating to, or denoting a large group of closely related Altaic languages of western and central Asia, including Turkish, Azerbaijani, Kazakh, Kyrgyz, Uighur, Uzbek, and Tatar.
▶ **n.** the Turkic languages collectively.
– ORIGIN mid 19th cent.: from TURK + -IC.

Turk·ish /'tərkisH/ ▶ **adj.** of or relating to Turkey or to the Turks or their language. ■ historical relating to or associated with the Ottoman Empire.
▶ **n.** the Turkic language that is the official language of Turkey.

Turk·ish bath ▶ **n.** a cleansing or relaxing treatment that involves a period of time spent sitting in a room filled with very hot air or steam, generally followed by washing and massage. ■ a building or room where such a treatment is available.

Turk·ish car·pet (also **Turkish rug**) ▶ **n.** a rug woven in Turkey in a traditional fashion, typically with a bold colored design and thick wool pile, or made elsewhere in this style.

Turk·ish cof·fee ▶ **n.** very strong black coffee served with the fine grounds in it.

Turk·ish de·light ▶ **n.** a gelatinous sweet confection traditionally made of syrup and cornflour, dusted with icing sugar.

Turk·ish slip·per ▶ **n.** a soft heelless slipper with a turned-up toe.

Turk·ish tow·el ▶ **n.** a towel made of cotton terry toweling.

Turk·ish Van (in full **Turkish Van cat**) ▶ **n.** a cat of a long-haired breed, with a white body, auburn markings on the head and tail, and light orange eyes.
– ORIGIN 1960s: named after the town of *Van*, Turkey.

Tur·ki·stan variant spelling of TURKESTAN.

Turk·men /'tərkmen, -mən/ ▶ **n.** (pl. **same** or **Turkmens**) **1** a member of a group of Turkic peoples inhabiting the region east of the Caspian Sea and south of the Aral Sea, now comprising Turkmenistan and parts of Iran and Afghanistan.
2 the Turkic language of these peoples.
▶ **adj.** of or relating to the Turkmens, their language, or the region that they inhabit.
– ORIGIN from Persian *turkmān*, from Turkish *türkmen*; also influenced by Russian *turkmen*.

Turk·me·ni·stan /tərk'menə,stan, -,stän/ a republic in central Asia that lies between the Caspian Sea and Afghanistan; pop. 4,884,900 (est. 2009); capital, Ashgabat; languages, Turkoman (official) and Russian. Also called **Turkmenia**.

Turkmenistan is dominated by the Karakum Desert, which occupies about 90 percent of the country. Previously part of Turkestan, from 1924 it formed a separate constituent republic of the former Soviet Union; Turkmenistan became an independent republic within the Commonwealth of Independent States in 1991.

Turko- ▶ **comb. form** variant spelling of TURCO-.

Tur·ko·man /'tərkəmən/ (also **Turcoman**) ▶ **n.** (pl. **Turkomans**) another term for TURKMEN.
– ORIGIN early 17th cent.: from medieval Latin *Turcomannus*, French *turcoman*, from Persian *turkmān* (see TURKMEN).

Turks and Cai·cos Is·lands /'tərks and 'kākəs, 'kākōs/ a British overseas territory in the Caribbean Sea that is composed of two island groups between Haiti and the Bahamas; pop. 22,900 (est. 2009); capital, Cockburn Town (on the island of Grand Turk).

Turk's-cap lil·y ▶ **n.** a lily with orange flowers that resemble turbans due to the almost completely reflexed petals. ● *Lilium superbum*, family Liliaceae.

Turk's-cap lily

Turk's head ▶ **n.** an ornamental knot resembling a turban in shape, made in the end of a rope to form a stopper.

Turk's-head cac·tus ▶ **n.** a barrel-shaped Jamaican cactus that bears red flowers from a terminal part that resembles a fez. Also called **Turk's-cap cactus**. ● *Melocactus communis*, family Cactaceae.

Tur·ku /'to͝orko͞o/ an industrial port in southwestern Finland; pop. 175,279 (2009). It was the capital of Finland until 1812. Swedish name ÅBO.

Tur·lock /'tər,läk/ a commercial city in north central California, in the San Joaquin Valley; pop. 68,404 (est. 2008).

tur·lough /'tər,lôKH/ ▶ **n.** (in Ireland) a low-lying area on limestone that becomes flooded in wet weather through the welling up of groundwater.
– ORIGIN late 17th cent.: from Irish *turloch*, from *tur* 'dry' + *loch* 'lake.'

tur·mer·ic /'tərmərik/ ▶ **n. 1** a bright yellow aromatic powder obtained from the rhizome of a plant of the ginger family, used for flavoring and coloring in Asian cooking and formerly as a fabric dye.
2 the Asian plant from which this rhizome is obtained. ● *Curcuma longa*, family Zingiberaceae.
– ORIGIN late Middle English (earlier as *tarmaret*): perhaps from French *terre mérite* and modern Latin *terra merita*, literally 'deserving earth,' perhaps an alteration of an Asian word.

tur·moil /'tər,moil/ ▶ **n.** a state of great disturbance, confusion, or uncertainty: *the country was in turmoil* | *he endured years of inner turmoil*.
– ORIGIN early 16th cent.: of unknown origin.

turn /tərn/ ▶ **v. 1** move or cause to move in a circular direction wholly or partly around an axis or point: [no obj.] *the big wheel was turning* | [with obj.] *I turned the key in the door and crept in*. ■ [with obj.] move (something) so that it is in a different position in relation to its surroundings or its previous position: *we waited in suspense for him to turn the cards over*. ■ [with obj.] move (a page) over so that it is flat against the previous or next page: *she turned a page noisily* | [no obj.] *turn to page five for the answer*. ■ change or cause to change direction: [no obj.] *we turned around and headed back to the house*. ■ [with obj.] aim, point, or direct (something): *she turned her head toward me* | *the government has now turned its attention to primary schools*. ■ [no obj.] change the position of one's body so that one is facing in a different direction: *Charlie turned and looked at his friend*. ■ [no obj.] (of the tide) change from flood to ebb or vice versa. ■ [with obj.] pass around (the flank or defensive lines of an army) so as to attack it from the side or rear. ■ [with obj.] perform (a somersault or cartwheel). ■ [with obj.] twist or sprain (an ankle). ■ [with obj.] fold or unfold (fabric or a piece of a garment) in the specified way: *he turned up the collar of his coat*. ■ [with obj.] remake (a garment or a sheet), putting the worn outer side on the inside. ■ [with obj.] (usu. as adj. **turned**) Printing set or print (a type or letter) upside down. ■ [with obj.] archaic bend back (the edge of a blade) so as to make it blunt.
2 [no obj.] change in nature, state, form, or color; become: *Emmeline turned pale*. ■ [with obj. or adverbial] cause to change in such a way; cause to become: *potatoes are covered with sacking to keep the light from turning them green*. ■ (of leaves) change color in the autumn. ■ [with obj.] pass the age or time of: *I've just turned forty*. ■ (with reference to milk) make or become sour: [with obj.] *the thunder had turned the milk*. ■ (with reference to the stomach) make or become nauseated: [with obj.] *the smell was bad enough to turn the strongest stomach*. ■ [with obj. or adverbial] send or put into a specified place or condition: *the dogs were turned loose on the crowd*.
3 [no obj.] (**turn to**) start doing or becoming involved with: *in 1939 he turned to films in earnest*. ■ go on to consider next: *we can now turn to another aspect of the problem*. ■ go to for help, advice, or information: *who can she turn to?* ■ have recourse to (something, esp. something dangerous or unhealthy): *he turned to drink and drugs for solace*.
4 [with obj.] shape (something) on a lathe: *the faceplate is turned rather than cast*. ■ give a graceful or elegant form to: (as adj. with submodifier **turned**) *a production full of so many finely turned words*. ■ make (a profit).
▶ **n. 1** an act of moving something in a circular direction around an axis or point: *a safety lock requiring four turns of the key*. ■ a change of direction when moving: *they made a left turn and picked up speed*. ■ a development or change in circumstances or a course of events: *life has **taken a turn for the better***. ■ a time when one specified period of time ends and another begins: *the turn of the century*. ■ a bend or curve in a road, path, river, etc.: *the twists and turns in the passageways*. ■ a place where a road meets or branches off another. ■ (**the turn**) the beginning of the second nine holes of a round of golf: *he made the turn in one under par*. ■ a change of the tide from ebb to flow or vice versa. ■ one round in a coil of rope or other material.
2 an opportunity or obligation to do something that comes successively to each of a number of people: *it was his turn to speak*. ■ a short performance, esp. one of a number given by different performers in succession: *a comic turn*. ■ a performer giving such a performance.
3 a short walk or ride: *why don't you take a turn around the garden?*
4 informal a shock: *you gave us quite a turn!* ■ a brief feeling or experience of illness: *tell me how you feel when you have these funny turns*.
5 the difference between the buying and selling price of stocks or other financial products. ■ a profit made from such a difference.

PRONUNCIATION KEY ə *ago, up*; ər *over, fur*; a *hat*; ā *ate*; ä *car*; e *let*; ē *see*; i *fit*; ī *by*; NG *sing*; ō *go*; ô *law, for*; oi *toy*; o͝o *good*; o͞o *goo*; ou *out*; TH *thin*; T͟H *then*; ZH *vision*

6 Music a melodic ornament consisting of the principal note with those above and below it.
– PHRASES **at every turn** on every occasion; continually: *her name seemed to come up at every turn.* **by turns** one after the other; alternately: *he was by turns amused and mildly annoyed by her.* **do someone a good** (or **bad**) **turn** do something that is helpful (or unhelpful) for someone. **in turn** in succession; one after the other: *four men prayed in turn.* ■ (also **in one's/its turn**) used to convey that an action, process, or situation is the result or product of a previous one: *he would shout until she, in her turn, lost her temper.* **not know which way** (or **where**) **to turn** not know what to do; be completely at a loss. **not turn a hair** see HAIR. **one good turn deserves another** proverb if someone does you a favor, you should take the chance to repay it. **on the turn** at a turning point; in a state of change: *my luck is on the turn.* **out of turn** at a time when it is not one's turn. **speak** (or **talk**) **out of turn** speak in a tactless or foolish way. **take turns** (of two or more people) do something alternately or in succession. **to a turn** to exactly the right degree (used esp. in relation to cooking): *hamburgers done to a turn.* **turn and turn about** chiefly Brit. one after another; in succession: *the two men were working in rotation, turn and turn about.* **turn one's back on** see BACK. **turn the corner** pass the critical point and start to improve. **turn a deaf ear** see DEAF. **turn one's hand to something** see HAND. **turn one's head** see HEAD. **turn heads** see HEAD. **turn an honest penny** see HONEST. **turn in one's grave** see GRAVE[1]. **turn of mind** a particular way of thinking: *people with a practical turn of mind.* **turn of speed** the ability to go fast when necessary. **turn on one's heel** see HEEL[1]. **turn the other cheek** see CHEEK. **turn over a new leaf** start to act or behave in a better or more responsible way. **turn something over in one's mind** think about or consider something thoroughly. **turn around and do** (or **say**) **something** informal used to convey that someone's actions or words are perceived as unexpected, unwelcome, or confrontational: *then she just turned around and said she wasn't coming after all.* **turn the tables** see TABLE. **turn tail** informal turn around and run away. **turn the tide** see TIDE. **turn something to (good) account** see ACCOUNT. **turn a trick** see TRICK. **turn turtle** see TURTLE. **turn up one's nose at** see NOSE.
– PHRASAL VERBS **turn against** (or **turn someone against**) become (or cause someone to become) hostile toward: *public opinion turned against him.* **turn around** move so as to face in the opposite direction: *Alice turned around and walked down the corridor.* **turn something around 1** prepare a ship or aircraft for its return journey. **2** reverse the previously poor performance of something, esp. a company, and make it successful. **turn someone away** refuse to allow someone to enter or pass through a place. **turn back** (or **turn someone/something back**) go (or cause to go) back in the direction in which one has come: *they turned back before reaching the church.* **turn someone down** reject an offer or application made by someone: *the Air Force turned him down on medical grounds.* **turn something down 1** reject something offered or proposed: *his novel was turned down by publisher after publisher.* **2** adjust a control on a device to reduce the volume, heat, etc. **turn in** informal go to bed in the evening. **turn someone in** hand someone over to the authorities. **turn something in** give something to someone in authority: *I've turned in my resignation.* ■ produce or achieve a particular score or a performance of a specified quality. **turn into** become (a particular kind of thing or person); be transformed into: *the slight drizzle turned into a downpour | that dream turned into a nightmare | in the next instant he turned into a tiny mouse.* **turn someone/something into** cause to become (a particular kind of thing or person); transform into: *the town was turned into a thriving seaside destination | every single good children's book has been turned into a feature-length cartoon.* **turn off** leave one road in order to join another. **turn someone off** informal induce a feeling of boredom or disgust in someone. **turn something off** stop the operation or flow of something by means of a valve, switch, or button: *remember to turn off the gas.* ■ operate a valve or switch in order to do this. **turn on 1** suddenly attack (someone) physically or verbally: *he turned on her with cold savagery.* **2** have as the main topic or point of interest: *for most businessmen, the central questions will turn on taxation.* **turn someone on** informal excite or stimulate the interest of someone, esp. sexually. **turn something on** start the flow or operation of something by means of a valve, switch, or button: *she turned on the TV.* ■ operate a valve or switch in order to do this. **turn someone on to** informal cause someone to become interested or involved in (something, esp. drugs): *he turned her on to heroin.* **turn out 1** prove to be the case: *the job turned out to be beyond his rather limited abilities.* **2** go somewhere in order to do something, esp. to attend a meeting, to play a game, or to vote: *over 75 percent of the electorate turned out to vote.* **turn someone out 1** eject or expel someone from a place. **2** Military call a guard from the guardroom. **3** (**be turned out**) be dressed in the manner specified: *she was smartly turned out and as well groomed as always.* **turn something out 1** extinguish a light. **2** produce something: *the plant takes 53 hours to turn out each car.* **3** empty something, esp. one's pockets. **4** tip prepared food from a mold or other container. **turn over** (of an engine) start or continue to run properly. **turn someone over to** deliver someone to the care or custody of (another person or body, esp. one in authority): *they turned him over to the police.* **turn something over 1** cause an engine to run. **2** transfer control or management of something to someone else: *a plan to **turn** the bar **over to** a new manager.* **3** change the function or use of something: *the works was **turned over to** the production of aircraft parts.* **4** informal rob a place. **5** (of a business) have a turnover of a specified amount: *last year the company turned over $12 million.* **turn up 1** be found, esp. by chance, after being lost: *all the missing documents had turned up.* **2** put in an appearance; arrive: *half the guests failed to turn up.* **turn something up 1** increase the volume or strength of sound, heat, etc., by turning a knob or switch on a device. **2** reveal or discover something: *New Yorkers confidently expect the inquiry to turn up nothing.* **3** shorten a garment by raising the hem.
– ORIGIN Old English *tyrnan, turnian* (verb), from Latin *tornare*, from *tornus* 'lathe,' from Greek *tornos* 'lathe, circular movement'; probably reinforced in Middle English by Old French *turner*. The noun (Middle English) is partly from Anglo-Norman French *tourn*, partly from the verb.

turn·a·bout /ˈtərnəˌbout/ ▶ **n.** a sudden and complete change or reversal of policy or opinion, or of a situation: *the move was a significant turnabout for the company.*

turn·a·round /ˈtərnəˌround/ ▶ **n. 1** an abrupt or unexpected change, esp. one that results in a more favorable situation: *it was **a** remarkable **turnaround** in his fortunes.*
2 the process of completing or the time needed to complete a task, esp. one involving receiving something, processing it, and sending it out again: *a seven-day turnaround.* ■ the process of or time taken for unloading and reloading a ship, aircraft, or vehicle.
3 a space for vehicles to turn around in, esp. one at the end of a driveway or dead-end street.

turn·back /ˈtərn ˌbak/ ▶ **n.** a part of a garment that is folded back: [as modifier] *the jacket has turn-back cuffs.*

turn·buck·le /ˈtərnˌbəkəl/ ▶ **n.** a coupling with female screw threads used to connect two rods, lengths of boat rigging, etc., lengthwise and to regulate their length or tension.

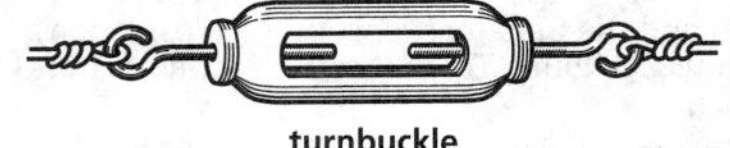

turnbuckle

turn·coat /ˈtərnˌkōt/ ▶ **n.** a person who deserts one party or cause in order to join an opposing one.

turn·cock /ˈtərnˌkäk/ ▶ **n.** historical a waterworks official responsible for turning on water at the mains.

turn·down /ˈtərnˌdoun/ ▶ **n. 1** a rejection or refusal.
2 a decline in something; a downturn.
▶ **adj.** (of a collar) turned down.

Tur·ner[1] /ˈtərnər/, Frederick Jackson (1861–1932), US historian, educator, and writer. He revolutionized the study of the American frontier with his paper entitled "The Significance of the Frontier in American History" (1893). He also wrote *The Frontier in American History* (1920) and *The Significance of Sections in American History* (1932).

Tur·ner[2], J. M. W. (1775–1851), English painter; full name *Joseph Mallord William Turner*. He painted landscapes and stormy seascapes and became increasingly concerned with depicting the power of light with primary colors, often arranged in a swirling vortex. Notable works: *Rain, Steam, Speed* (1844) and *The Fighting Téméraire* (1838).

Tur·ner[3], John Napier Wyndham (1929–), Canadian Liberal statesman; prime minister for just 79 days in 1984.

Tur·ner[4], Nat (1800–1831), US slave leader. He was convicted of murder and insurrection and hanged for organizing a slave uprising in Southampton, Virginia, in August 1831, in which at least 50 whites were killed.

Tur·ner[5], Ted (1938–), US broadcasting executive; full name *Robert Edward Turner III*. His Turner Broadcasting System included the television networks TBS, CNN, TCM, and the Cartoon Network. He bought the Atlanta Braves baseball team in 1976 and the Atlanta Hawks basketball team in 1977 and started the Atlanta Thrashers hockey team in 1999. An accomplished yachtsman, he won the America's Cup in 1977.

turn·er /ˈtərnər/ ▶ **n. 1** a person who is skilled in turning wood on a lathe.
2 an implement that can be used to turn or flip something over: *a pancake turner.*
– ORIGIN Middle English: from Old French *torneor*, from late Latin *tornator*, from the verb *tornare* (see TURN).

Turn·er's syn·drome ▶ **n.** Medicine a genetic defect in which affected women have only one X chromosome, causing developmental abnormalities and infertility.
– ORIGIN named after Henry Hubert *Turner* (1892–1970), the US physician who described it.

turn·er·y /ˈtərnərē/ ▶ **n.** the action or skill of making objects on a lathe. ■ objects made on a lathe.

turn·ing /ˈtərniNG/ ▶ **n. 1** a place where a road branches off another: *take the first turning on the right.*
2 the action or skill of using a lathe. ■ (**turnings**) shavings of wood or metal resulting from turning something on a lathe.

turn·ing point ▶ **n.** a time at which a decisive change in a situation occurs, esp. one with beneficial results: *this could be the turning point in Nancy's career.*

tur·nip /ˈtərnəp/ ▶ **n. 1** a round root with white or cream flesh that is eaten as a vegetable and also has edible leaves. ■ a similar or related root, esp. a rutabaga.
2 the European plant of the cabbage family that produces this root. ● *Brassica rapa*, family Brassicaceae: 'rapifera' group.
3 informal a large, thick, old-fashioned pocket watch.
– DERIVATIVES **tur·nip·y** adj.
– ORIGIN mid 16th cent.: first element of unknown origin + NEEP.

turn·key /ˈtərnˌkē/ ▶ **n.** (pl. **turnkeys**) archaic a jailer.
▶ **adj.** of or involving the provision of a complete product or service that is ready for immediate use: *turnkey systems for telecommunications customers.*

turn·off /ˈtərnˌôf/ ▶ **n. 1** a junction at which a road branches off from a main road: *Adam missed the turnoff to the village.*
2 [usu. in sing.] informal a person or thing that causes someone to feel bored, disgusted, or sexually repelled: *he smelled of carbolic soap, a dreadful turnoff.*
3 an instance of turning or switching something off.

turn-on ▶ **n.** [usu. in sing.] informal a person or thing that causes someone to feel excited or sexually aroused: *tight jeans are a real turn-on.*

turn·out /ˈtərnˌout/ ▶ **n. 1** [usu. in sing.] the number of people attending or taking part in an event, esp. the number of people voting in an election.
2 a turn in a road. ■ a point at which a railroad track diverges. ■ a widened place in a road for cars to pass each other or park temporarily.
3 a carriage or other horse-drawn vehicle with its horse or horses.
4 [in sing.] the way in which a person or thing is equipped or dressed: *his turnout was exceedingly elegant.*
5 Ballet the ability to rotate the legs outward at the hips.

turn·o·ver /ˈtərnˌōvər/ ▶ **n. 1** the amount of money taken by a business in a particular period: *a turnover approaching $4 million.*
2 the rate at which employees leave a workforce and are replaced. ■ the rate at which goods are sold and replaced in a store.
3 a small pie made by folding a piece of pastry over on itself to enclose a sweet filling: *an apple turnover.*
4 (in a game) a loss of possession of the ball to the opposing team.

turn·pike /ˈtərnˌpīk/ ▶ **n. 1** an expressway, esp. one on which a toll is charged. ■ historical a toll gate. ■ (also **turnpike road**) historical a road on which a toll was collected at such a gate.
2 historical a spiked barrier fixed in or across a road or passage as a defense against sudden attack.

turn sig·nal ▶ **n.** a flashing light on a vehicle to show that it is about to change lanes or turn.

turn·sole /ˈtərnˌsōl/ ▶ **n.** a Mediterranean plant of the spurge family, whose flowers are said to turn with the sun. ● *Chrozophora tinctoria* (family Euphorbiaceae), from which a blue or purple dye was formerly obtained.
– ORIGIN late Middle English: from Old French *tournesole*, based on Latin *tornare* (see **TURN**) + *sol* 'sun.'

turn·spit /ˈtərnˌspit/ ▶ **n.** historical a servant (or a small dog running on a treadmill) whose job was to turn a spit on which meat was roasting.

turns ra·tio ▶ **n.** the ratio of the number of turns on the primary coil of an electrical transformer to the number on the secondary, or vice versa.

turn·stile /ˈtərnˌstīl/ ▶ **n.** a mechanical gate consisting of revolving horizontal arms fixed to a vertical post, allowing only one person at a time to pass through.

turn·stone /ˈtərnˌstōn/ ▶ **n.** a small, short-billed wading bird of the sandpiper family that turns over stones to feed on small animals beneath them. ● Genus *Arenaria*, family Scolopacidae: two species, in particular the **ruddy turnstone** (*A. interpres*), breeding in northern Eurasia and northern Canada.

turn·ta·ble /ˈtərnˌtābəl/ ▶ **n.** a circular revolving plate supporting a phonograph record as it is played. ■ a circular revolving platform for turning a railroad locomotive or other vehicle.

turn-up ▶ **n.** Brit. (usu. **turn-ups**) a pant cuff.

Tur·ow /ˈto͝orō/, Scott (1949–), US lawyer and writer. His legal thrillers, all of which take place in the fictional Kindle County, include *Presumed Innocent* (1987), *The Burden of Proof* (1990), and *Limitations* (2006).

tur·pen·tine /ˈtərpənˌtīn/ ▶ **n. 1** (also **oil of turpentine**) a volatile pungent oil distilled from gum turpentine or pine wood, used in mixing paints and varnishes and in liniment. ● Chem. formula $C_{10}H_{16}$. ■ (also **crude turpentine** or **gum turpentine**) an oleoresin secreted by certain trees, esp. pines, and distilled to make rosin and oil of turpentine.
2 (also **turpentine tree**) any of a number of trees that yield turpentine or a similar resin, in particular: ● a coniferous tree of the pine family (*Larix*, *Pinus*, and other genera, family Pinaceae). ● the terebinth.
▶ **v.** [with obj.] apply turpentine to.
– ORIGIN Middle English: from Old French *ter(e)bentine*, from Latin *ter(e)binthina (resina)* '(resin) of the turpentine tree,' from *terebinthus* (see **TEREBINTH**).

Tur·pin /ˈtərpən/, Dick (1706–39), English robber. He was a cattle and deer thief in Essex before entering into partnership with **Tom King**, a notorious highway robber. He was hanged for horse-stealing.

tur·pi·tude /ˈtərpiˌt(y)o͞od/ ▶ **n.** formal depravity; wickedness: *acts of **moral turpitude**.*
– ORIGIN late 15th cent.: from French, or from Latin *turpitudo*, from *turpis* 'disgraceful, base.'

turps /tərps/ ▶ **n.** informal turpentine.
– ORIGIN early 19th cent.: abbreviation.

tur·quoise /ˈtərˌk(w)oiz/ ▶ **n. 1** a semiprecious stone, typically opaque and of a greenish-blue or sky-blue color, consisting of a hydrated hydroxyl phosphate of copper and aluminum.
2 a greenish-blue color like that of this stone: [as modifier] *the turquoise waters of the bay.*
– ORIGIN late Middle English: from Old French *turqueise* 'Turkish (stone).'

tur·ret /ˈtərit/ ▶ **n. 1** a small tower on top of a larger tower or at the corner of a building or wall, typically of a castle. ■ a low, flat armored gun emplacement, typically one that revolves, in a ship, aircraft, fort, or tank. ■ a rotating holder for tools, esp. on a lathe.
2 (also **turret shell**) a mollusk with a long, slender, pointed spiral shell, typically brightly colored and living in tropical seas. ● Family Turitellidae, class Gastropoda: *Turitella* and other genera.
– DERIVATIVES **tur·ret·ed** adj.
– ORIGIN Middle English: from Old French *tourete*, diminutive of *tour* 'tower.'

turret 1

tur·ron /to͝orˈōn, -ˈän/ ▶ **n.** a kind of Spanish confectionery resembling nougat, made from almonds and honey.
– ORIGIN from Spanish *turrón*.

tur·tle /ˈtərtl/ ▶ **n. 1** a slow-moving reptile, enclosed in a scaly or leathery domed shell into which it can retract its head and thick legs. ● Family Testudinidae: numerous genera and species, including the **European tortoise** (*Testudo graeca*).
2 (also **sea turtle**) a large marine reptile with a bony or leathery shell and flippers, coming ashore annually on sandy beaches to lay eggs. ● Families Cheloniidae (seven species) and Dermochelyidae (the leatherback). ■ the flesh of a sea turtle, esp. the green turtle, used chiefly for soup.
3 a freshwater reptile related to the turtles, typically having a flattened shell. Called **TERRAPIN** in South Africa and India and **TORTOISE** in Australia. ● Order Chelonia: several families, in particular Emydidae and Kinosternidae. ■ any reptile of this order, including the terrapins and tortoises.
4 Computing a directional cursor in a computer graphics system that can be instructed to move around a screen.
5 short for **TURTLENECK**.
– PHRASES **turn turtle** (chiefly of a boat) capsize.
– ORIGIN mid 16th cent.: apparently an alteration of French *tortue* (see **TORTOISE**).

tur·tle bug ▶ **n.** a bug or beetle with a turtlelike carapace, esp. an olive-brown shield bug that frequents grassy places.

tur·tle·dove /ˈtərdl dōv/ ▶ **n.** a small Old World dove with a soft purring call, noted for the apparent affection shown for its mate. ● Genus *Streptopelia*, family Columbidae: several species, in particular the migratory European and North African *S. turtur*, with a reddish-brown back and pinkish breast.
– ORIGIN Middle English: *turtle* from Old English *turtla*, *turtle* 'turtle dove' (from Latin *turtur*, of imitative origin).

tur·tle grass ▶ **n.** a submerged marine flowering plant found in the Caribbean, with long grasslike leaves. ● *Thalassia testudinum*, family Hydrocharitaceae.

tur·tle·head /ˈtərtlˌhed/ ▶ **n.** a North American plant of the figwort family that produces spikes of pink or white flowers that are said to resemble the head of a turtle. ● Genus *Chelone*, family Scrophulariaceae.

tur·tle·neck /ˈtərtlˌnek/ ▶ **n.** a high, close-fitting, turned-over collar on a garment, typically a shirt or sweater: [as modifier] *a turtleneck sweater.* ■ a shirt or sweater with a neck of this type.

turtleneck

tur·tle·shell /ˈtərtlˌsHel/ ▶ **n.** another term for **TORTOISESHELL**.

turves /tərvz/ plural form of **TURF**.

Tus·ca·loo·sa /ˌtəskəˈlo͞osə/ an industrial city in west central Alabama, on the Black Warrior River, home to the University of Alabama; pop. 90,221 (est. 2008).

Tus·can /ˈtəskən/ ▶ **adj. 1** of or relating to Tuscany, its inhabitants, or the form of Italian spoken there, which is the standard variety taught to foreign learners.
2 relating to or denoting a classical order of architecture resembling the Doric but lacking all ornamentation.
▶ **n. 1** a native or inhabitant of Tuscany.
2 the form of Italian spoken in Tuscany.
3 the Tuscan order of architecture.
– ORIGIN late Middle English (as a noun denoting an Etruscan): via French from Latin *Tuscanus*, from *Tuscus* 'an Etruscan.'

Tus·ca·ny /ˈtəskənē/ a region in west central Italy, on the Ligurian Sea; capital, Florence. Italian name **TOSCANA**.

Tus·ca·ro·ra /ˌtəskəˈrôrə/ ▶ **n.** (pl. **same** or **Tuscaroras**) **1** an American Indian people forming part of the Six Nations, originally inhabiting the Carolinas and later New York.
2 the Iroquoian language of this people.
▶ **adj.** of or relating to the Tuscarora or their language.
– ORIGIN from an Iroquoian name, perhaps from Catawba (a Siouan language spoken in South Carolina) *taskarudē*.

Tus·ca·ro·ra Moun·tains /ˌtəskəˈrôrə/ a range in northeastern Nevada that has been the scene of gold and silver booms.

tusch·e /ˈto͝osH(ə)/ ▶ **n.** a greasy black composition, in liquid form or to be mixed with liquids, used as ink for making lithographic drawings.
– ORIGIN early 20th cent.: from German *tuschen*, from French *toucher* 'to touch.'

tush[1] /təsH/ ▶ **exclam.** archaic or humorous expressing disapproval, impatience, or dismissal: *tush, these are trifles and mere old wives' tales.*
– ORIGIN natural utterance: first recorded in late Middle English.

tush[2] /təsH/ ▶ **n.** a long pointed tooth, in particular a canine tooth of a male horse. ■ a stunted tusk of some Indian elephants.
– ORIGIN Old English *tusc* (see **TUSK**).

tush[3] /to͝osH/ ▶ **n.** informal a person's buttocks.
– ORIGIN 1960s (as *tushie*): from Yiddish *tokhes*, from Hebrew *taḥat* 'beneath.'

tush·y /ˈto͝osHē/ ▶ **n.** (pl. **tushies**) another term for **TUSH**[3].

tusk /təsk/ ▶ **n.** a long, pointed tooth, esp. one specially developed so as to protrude from the closed mouth, as in the elephant, walrus, or wild boar. ■ a long, tapering object or projection resembling such a tooth.
– DERIVATIVES **tusked** adj., **tusk·y** adj. (literary).
– ORIGIN Old English *tux*, variant of *tusc* (see **TUSH**[2]).

Tus·ke·gee /təˈskēgē/ a city in east central Alabama, home to Tuskegee University; pop. 11,357 (est. 2008).

tusk·er /ˈtəskər/ ▶ **n.** an elephant or wild boar with well-developed tusks.

tusk shell ▶ **n.** another term for **TOOTH SHELL**.

tus·sah /ˈtəsə, -sô/ ▶ **n.** variant form of **TUSSORE**.

Tus·saud /ˈto͞osō, təˈsôd, təˈsōd/, Madame (1761–1850), French founder of Madame Tussaud's waxworks; resident of Britain from 1802; née *Marie Grosholtz*. She was imprisoned during the French Revolution and compelled to make death masks in wax of prominent victims of the guillotine. In 1835, she founded a permanent waxworks exhibition in Baker Street, London.

tus·sie-mus·sie /ˌtəsē ˈməsē/ ▶ **n.** (pl. **tussie-mussies**) a small bunch of flowers or aromatic herbs.
– ORIGIN late Middle English: of unknown origin.

tus·sive /ˈtəsiv/ ▶ **adj.** Medicine relating to coughing.
– ORIGIN mid 19th cent.: from Latin *tussis* 'a cough' + **-IVE**.

tus·sle /ˈtəsəl/ ▶ **n.** a vigorous struggle or scuffle, typically in order to obtain or achieve something: *there was a tussle for the ball.*
▶ **v.** [no obj.] engage in such a struggle or scuffle: *the demonstrators tussled with police.*
– ORIGIN late Middle English (as a verb, originally Scots and northern English): perhaps a diminutive of dialect *touse* 'handle roughly' (see **TOUSLE**).

tus·sock /ˈtəsək/ ▶ **n. 1** a small area of grass that is thicker or longer than the grass growing around it.
2 (also **tussock moth**) a woodland moth whose adults and brightly colored caterpillars both bear tufts of irritant hairs. The caterpillars can be a pest of trees, damaging fruit and stripping leaves. ● Family Lymantriidae: many genera.
– DERIVATIVES **tus·sock·y** adj.
– ORIGIN mid 16th cent.: perhaps an alteration of dialect *tusk* 'tuft,' of unknown origin.

tus·sock grass ▶ **n.** a grass that grows in tussocks. ● Genera *Poa*, *Nassella*, or *Deschampsia*, family Gramineae: several species, in particular *D. cespitosa*, a coarse fodder grass of the northern hemisphere.

tus·sore /ˈtəsôr/ (also **tussah** /ˈtəsə, -sô/) ▶ **n.** (also **tussore silk**) coarse silk from the larvae of the tussore moth and related species.
– ORIGIN late 16th cent.: from Hindi *tasar*, from Sanskrit *tasara* 'shuttle.'

tus·sore moth ▶ **n.** a silkworm moth that is sometimes kept in India and China, with caterpillars (**tussore silkworms**) that yield a strong but coarse brown silk. ● *Antheraea mylitta*, family Saturniidae.

Tus·tin /ˈtəstin/ a city in southwestern California, southeast of Los Angeles; pop. 71,814 (est. 2008).

tut /tət/ ▶ **exclam., n., & v.** short for **TUT-TUT**.

Tut·ankh·a·men /ˌto͞oˌtaNGˈkämən, ˌto͞oˌtäNG-/ (also **Tutankhamun**) (died *c.*1352 BC), Egyptian pharaoh of the 18th dynasty; reigned *c.*1361–*c.*1352 BC. His

PRONUNCIATION KEY ə *ago, up*; ər *over, fur*; a *hat*; ā *ate*; ä *car*; e *let*; ē *see*; i *fit*; ī *by*; NG *sing*; ō *go*; ô *law, for*; oi *toy*; o͝o *good*; o͞o *goo*; ou *out*; TH *thin*; T͟H *then*; ZH *vision*

tomb, which contained a wealth of rich and varied contents, was discovered virtually intact by English archaeologist **Howard Carter** in 1922.

Tutankhamen

tu·tee /t(y)o͞oˈtē/ ▶ **n.** a student or pupil of a tutor.

tu·te·lage /ˈt(y)o͞otl-ij/ ▶ **n.** protection of or authority over someone or something; guardianship: *the organizations remained under firm government tutelage.* ■ instruction; tuition: *he felt privileged to be **under the tutelage of** an experienced actor.*
– ORIGIN early 17th cent.: from Latin *tutela* 'keeping' (from *tut-* 'watched,' from the verb *tueri*) + **-AGE**.

tu·te·lar·y /ˈt(y)o͞otl,erē/ (also **tutelar** /-tl-ər/) ▶ **adj.** serving as a protector, guardian, or patron: *the tutelary spirits of these regions.* ■ of or relating to protection or a guardian: *the state maintained a tutelary relation with the security police.*
– ORIGIN early 17th cent.: from Latin *tutelarius*, from *tutela* 'keeping' (see **TUTELAGE**).

Tuth·mo·sis III /to͝otˈmōsəs/ (died *c.*1450 BC), son of Tuthmosis II; Egyptian pharaoh of the 18th dynasty *c.*1504–*c.*1450. His reign was marked by extensive building projects, including Cleopatra's Needles (*c.*1475).

tu·tor /ˈt(y)o͞otər/ ▶ **n.** a private teacher, typically one who teaches a single student or a very small group. ■ chiefly Brit. a university or college teacher responsible for the teaching and supervision of assigned students. ■ an assistant lecturer in a college or university.
▶ **v.** [with obj.] act as a tutor to (a single student or a very small group): *his children were privately tutored.* ■ [no obj.] work as a tutor.
– DERIVATIVES **tu·tor·age** /-rij/ **n.**, **tu·tor·ship** /-,SHip/ **n.**
– ORIGIN late Middle English: from Old French *tutour* or Latin *tutor*, from *tueri* 'to watch, guard.'

tu·to·ri·al /t(y)o͞oˈtôrēəl/ ▶ **adj.** of or relating to a tutor or a tutor's instruction: *tutorial sessions.*
▶ **n.** a period of instruction given by a university or college tutor to an individual or very small group. ■ an account or explanation of a subject, printed or on a computer screen, intended for private study.
– ORIGIN early 18th cent.: from Latin *tutorius* (see **TUTOR**) + **-AL**.

Tut·si /ˈto͞otsē/ ▶ **n.** (pl. **same** or **Tutsis**) a member of a people forming a minority of the population of Rwanda and Burundi, who formerly dominated the Hutu majority. Historical antagonism between the peoples led in 1994 to large-scale ethnic violence, esp. in Rwanda.
▶ **adj.** of or relating to this people.
– ORIGIN a local name. See also **WATUSI**.

tut·ti /ˈto͞otē/ Music ▶ **adv. & adj.** (esp. as a direction after a solo section) with all voices or instruments together.
▶ **n.** (pl. **tuttis**) a passage to be performed in this way.
– ORIGIN Italian, plural of *tutto* 'all,' from Latin *totus*.

tut·ti-frut·ti /,to͞otē ˈfro͞otē/ ▶ **n.** (pl. **tutti-fruttis**) a type of ice cream containing or flavored with mixed fruits and sometimes nuts.
– ORIGIN Italian, literally 'all fruits.'

tut-tut /,tət ˈtət/ (also **tut**) ▶ **exclam.** expressing disapproval or annoyance: *tut-tut, Robin, you disappoint me.*
▶ **n.** such an exclamation: *tut-tuts of disapproval.*
▶ **v.** (**tut-tuts, tut-tutting, tut-tutted**) [no obj.] make such an exclamation: *Aunt Mary tut-tutted at all the goings-on.*
– ORIGIN natural utterance (representing a reduplicated clicking sound made by the tongue against the teeth): first recorded in English in the early 16th cent.

Tu·tu /ˈto͞o,to͞o/, Desmond (Mpilo) (1931–), South African Anglican clergyman. As general secretary of the South African Council of Churches from 1979 until 1984, he became a leading voice in the struggle against apartheid. He was archbishop of Cape Town 1986–96. Nobel Peace Prize (1984).

tu·tu /ˈto͞o,to͞o/ ▶ **n.** a female ballet dancer's costume consisting of a bodice and an attached skirt incorporating numerous layers of fabric, this being either short and stiff and projecting horizontally from the waist (the **classical tutu**) or long, soft, and bell-shaped (the **romantic tutu**).
– ORIGIN early 20th cent.: from French, child's alteration of *cucu*, informal diminutive of *cul* 'buttocks.'

classical tutu

Tu·va /ˈto͞ovə/ an autonomous republic in south central Russia, on the border with Mongolia; pop. 310,600 (est. 2009); capital, Kyzyl. Former name **TANNU-TUVA**.

Tu·va·lu /to͞oˈvälo͞o/ a country in the southwestern Pacific Ocean that consists of a group of nine main islands, formerly called the Ellice Islands; pop. 12,400 (est. 2009); capital, Funafuti; languages, English and Tuvaluan (both official).

The islands formed part of the British colony of the Gilbert and Ellice Islands but separated from the Gilberts after a referendum in 1975. Tuvalu became independent within the Commonwealth of Nations in 1978.

– DERIVATIVES **Tu·va·lu·an** /-lo͞oən/ **adj. & n.**

tu-whit tu-whoo /to͞o ,(h)wit tə ˈ(h)wo͞o/ ▶ **n.** a stylized representation of the cry of the tawny owl.
– ORIGIN late 16th cent.: imitative.

tux /təks/ ▶ **n.** informal a tuxedo.

tux·e·do /təkˈsēdō/ ▶ **n.** (pl. **tuxedos** or **tuxedoes**) a man's dinner jacket. ■ a suit of formal evening clothes including such a jacket.
– DERIVATIVES **tux·e·doed** **adj.**
– ORIGIN late 19th cent.: from *Tuxedo* Park, the site of a country club in New York, where it was first worn.

Tux·e·do Park /təkˈsēdō/ a village in southeastern New York; pop. 719 (est. 2008). Developed in the 1880s as a retreat for the rich, it gave its name to the evening jacket.

Tux·tla Gu·tiér·rez /ˈto͞ostlə go͞oˈtyeres/ a city in southeastern Mexico, capital of the state of Chiapas; pop. 490,455 (2005).

tu·yère /to͞oˈyer, twē-/ ▶ **n.** a nozzle through which air is forced into a smelter, furnace, or forge.
– ORIGIN late 18th cent.: French, from *tuyau* 'pipe.'

Tuz·la /ˈto͞ozlə/ a town in northeastern Bosnia; pop. 83,800 (est. 2008). The town, a Muslim enclave, suffered damage and heavy casualties when besieged by Bosnian Serb forces between 1992 and 1994.

TV ▶ **abbr.** ■ television (the system or a set): *anything good on TV tonight?* ■ transvestite.

TVA ▶ **abbr.** Tennessee Valley Authority.

TV din·ner ▶ **n.** a prepared prepackaged meal that only requires heating before it is ready to eat.

Tver /tver/ an industrial port in western Russia, on the Volga River, northwest of Moscow; pop. 402,700 (est. 2009). It was known as Kalinin 1931–91 in honor of President Kalinin.

TVP ▶ **abbr.** trademark textured vegetable protein.

Twa /twä/ ▶ **n.** (pl. **same, Twas,** or **Batwa** /baˈtwä/) a member of a pygmy people inhabiting parts of Burundi, Rwanda, and the Democratic Republic of the Congo (formerly Zaire).
▶ **adj.** of or relating to the Twa.
– ORIGIN a local word meaning 'foreigner, outsider.'

twad·dle /ˈtwädl/ informal ▶ **n.** trivial or foolish speech or writing; nonsense: *he dismissed the novel as self-indulgent twaddle.*
▶ **v.** [no obj.] archaic talk or write in a trivial or foolish way: *what is that old fellow twaddling about?*
– DERIVATIVES **twad·dler** /ˈtwädlər, ˈtwädl-ər/ **n.**
– ORIGIN late 18th cent.: alteration of earlier *twattle*, of unknown origin.

Twain /twān/, Mark (1835–1910), US novelist and humorist; pseudonym of *Samuel Langhorne Clemens*. After gaining a reputation as a humorist with his early work, he wrote his best-known novels, *The Adventures of Tom Sawyer* (1876) and *The Adventures of Huckleberry Finn* (1885); both give a vivid evocation of Mississippi River life.

Mark Twain

twain /twān/ ▶ **cardinal number** archaic term for **TWO**: *he split it in twain.*
– PHRASES **never the twain shall meet** used to suggest that two things are too different to coexist: *Ulster people are British and Irish people are Irish, and never the twain shall meet.* [from Rudyard Kipling's "Oh, East is East, and West is West, and never the twain shall meet." (*Barrack-room Ballads* (1892)).]
– ORIGIN Old English *twegen*, masculine of *twā* (see **TWO**).

twaite shad /ˈtwāt ,SHad/ ▶ **n.** a European shad (fish) with a deep blue back, silvery sides, and some spotting. ● *Alosa fallax*, family Clupeidae.
– ORIGIN early 17th cent. (as *twaite*): of unknown origin.

twang /twaNG/ ▶ **n.** a strong ringing sound such as that made by the plucked string of a musical instrument or a released bowstring. ■ a nasal or other distinctive manner of pronunciation or intonation characteristic of the speech of an individual, area, or country: *an American twang.*
▶ **v.** make or cause to make such a sound: [no obj.] *a spring twanged beneath him* | [with obj.] *some old men were twanging banjos.* ■ [with obj.] utter (something) with a nasal twang: *the announcer was twanging out all the details.*
– DERIVATIVES **twang·y** **adj.**
– ORIGIN mid 16th cent.: imitative.

'twas /twəz/ ▶ **contraction** archaic or literary it was.

twat /twät/ ▶ **n.** vulgar slang a woman's genitals. ■ a person regarded as stupid or obnoxious.
– ORIGIN mid 17th cent.: of unknown origin.

tway·blade /ˈtwā,blād/ ▶ **n.** an orchid with a slender spike of greenish or mauve flowers and a single pair of broad leaves near the base or midway up the stem. ● Genera *Listera* and *Liparis*, family Orchidaceae: several species, including the North American **heartleaf twayblade** (*Listera cordata*) and the Eurasian **common twayblade** (*Listera ovata*).
– ORIGIN late 16th cent.: from *tway* (variant of **TWAIN**) + **BLADE**, translating Latin *bifolium*.

tweak /twēk/ ▶ **v.** [with obj.] **1** twist or pull (something) sharply: *he tweaked the boy's ear.* **2** informal improve (a mechanism or system) by making fine adjustments to it: *engineers tweak the car's operating systems during the race.*
▶ **n.** **1** a sharp twist or pull. **2** informal a fine adjustment to a mechanism or system.
– ORIGIN early 17th cent.: probably an alteration of dialect *twick* 'pull sharply'; related to **TWITCH**.

twee /twē/ ▶ **adj.** Brit. chiefly derogatory excessively or affectedly quaint, pretty, or sentimental: *although the film's a bit twee, it's watchable.*
– ORIGIN early 20th cent.: representing a child's pronunciation of **SWEET**.

Tweed[1] /twēd/ a river that rises in southeastern Scotland and flows east for 97 miles (155 km) before it crosses into northeastern England and enters the North Sea. Part of its lower course forms the border between Scotland and England.

Tweed[2], William M. (1823–78) US politician; known as **Boss Tweed**. As a New York City official and a state senator 1867–71, he became the leader of Tammany Hall, the executive committee of New York City's Democratic Party and a ring of political corruption, which swindled the state treasury out of as much as $200 million. Convicted in 1873, he fled to Cuba and then Spain, but was extradited in 1876 and returned to a New York jail, where he died.

tweed /twēd/ ▶ **n.** a rough-surfaced woolen cloth, typically of mixed flecked colors, originally

produced in Scotland: [as modifier] *a tweed sports jacket.* ■ (**tweeds**) clothes made of this material: *boisterous Englishwomen in tweeds.*
– ORIGIN mid 19th cent.: originally a misreading of *tweel*, Scots form of TWILL, influenced by association with the *Tweed* River.

Twee·dle·dum and Twee·dle·dee /ˌtwēdlˈdəm and ˌtwēdlˈdē/ ▶ **n.** a pair of people or things that are virtually indistinguishable.
– ORIGIN originally names applied to the composers Bononcini (1670–1747) and Handel, in a 1725 satire by John Byrom (1692–1763); they were later used for two identical characters in Lewis Carroll's *Through the Looking Glass.*

tweed·y /ˈtwēdē/ ▶ **adj.** (**tweedier, tweediest**) (of a garment) made of tweed cloth: *a tweedy suit.* ■ informal (of a person) habitually wearing tweed clothes: *a stout, tweedy woman.* ■ informal of a refined, traditional, upscale character: *the tweedy world of books.*
– DERIVATIVES **tweed·i·ly** /-dilē/ **adv.**, **tweed·i·ness n.**

Tween /twēn/ ▶ **n.** trademark any of a class of compounds used esp. as emulsifiers and surfactants. They are derivatives of fatty acid esters of sorbitan.
– ORIGIN 1940s: of unknown origin.

tween /twēn/ (also **tweenie** /ˈtwēnē/) ▶ **n.** short for TWEENAGER.

'tween /twēn/ ▶ **contraction** archaic or literary between.

tween·ag·er /ˈtwēnˌājər/ ▶ **n.** informal a preteen or a young teenager: *the hot Nickelodeon show for tweenagers.*

'tween decks ▶ **plural n.** Nautical the space between the decks of a ship, esp. that below the upper deck.

tween·er /ˈtwēnər/ ▶ **n.** informal a person or thing considered to be between two other recognized categories or types: *Price considered him a tweener, too small for a lineman and too big for a linebacker.* ■ short for TWEENAGER.

tween·y /ˈtwēnē/ ▶ **n.** (pl. **tweenies**) archaic, informal a maid who assisted two other members of a domestic staff.
– ORIGIN late 19th cent.: from *between-maid*, a servant assisting two others.

tweet /twēt/ ▶ **n. 1** the chirp of a small or young bird.
2 a posting made on the social networking site Twitter: *he started posting 'tweets' via his cell phone to let his parents know he was safe.*
▶ **v.** [no obj.] **1** make a chirping noise: *the birds were tweeting in the branches.*
2 make a posting on the social networking site Twitter: *it's easy to tweet all the time.*
– ORIGIN mid 19th cent.: imitative.

> **WORD TRENDS** Once invoking nothing beyond the sound of birds gently chirping, **tweet** is a striking example of the influence the Internet has on language trends. Since the social networking service Twitter was set up in 2006, 'tweeting' (posting short messages, known as **tweets**, over the Web) has become so popular that the frequency of the noun **tweet** in the Oxford English Corpus has risen tenfold. The millions of people using Twitter may take themselves and their tweets very seriously, but the site's name suggests otherwise: the Corpus shows that the majority of uses of **twitter** in the sense 'talk rapidly and at length' imply foolishness or triviality: *I was never asked to sit with the cheerleaders who twittered and giggled their way through every lunch period | twittering on about the good old days.*

tweet·er /ˈtwētər/ ▶ **n.** a loudspeaker designed to reproduce high frequencies.

tweeze /twēz/ ▶ **v.** [with obj.] pluck, grasp, or pull with or as if with tweezers: *the brows were tweezed to an almost invisible line.*
– ORIGIN 1930s: back-formation from *tweezer* (see TWEEZERS).

tweez·ers /ˈtwēzərz/ ▶ **plural n.** (also **a pair of tweezers**) a small instrument like a pair of pincers for plucking out hairs and picking up small objects.
– ORIGIN mid 17th cent.: extended form of obsolete *tweeze* 'case of surgical instruments,' shortening of *etweese*, plural of ETUI.

twelfth /twelfTH/ ▶ **ordinal number** constituting number twelve in a sequence; 12th: *the twelfth of November | his twelfth birthday | the twelfth in a series of essays.* ■ (**a twelfth/one twelfth**) each of twelve equal parts into which something is or may be divided. ■ the twelfth grade of a school. ■ Music an interval or chord spanning an octave and a fifth in the diatonic scale, or a note separated from another by this interval. ■ (**the Twelfth**) July 12, celebrated by upholders of Protestant supremacy in Ireland as the anniversary of William III's victory over James II at the Battle of the Boyne.
– DERIVATIVES **twelfth·ly adv.**, **twelve·fold** /ˈtwel(v)ˌfōld/ **adj. & adv.**

Twelfth Day ▶ **n.** archaic term for TWELFTH NIGHT.

Twelfth Night ▶ **n.** January 6, the feast of the Epiphany. ■ strictly, the evening of January 5, the eve of the Epiphany and formerly the twelfth and last day of Christmas festivities.

twelve /twelv/ ▶ **cardinal number** equivalent to the product of three and four; two more than ten; 12: *he walked twelve miles | there are just twelve of us in all | a twelve-string guitar.* (Roman numeral: **xii, XII**) ■ a group or unit of twelve people or things. ■ twelve years old: *a small blond girl of about twelve.* ■ twelve o'clock: *it's half past twelve.* ■ a size of garment or other merchandise denoted by twelve. ■ (**the Twelve**) the twelve Apostles.
– ORIGIN Old English *twelf(e)*, from the base of TWO + a second element (probably expressing the sense 'left over'); of Germanic origin and related to Dutch *twaalf* and German *zwölf*. Compare with ELEVEN.

twelve-bar ▶ **adj.** denoting or relating to a musical structure based on a sequence lasting twelve bars and typically consisting of three chords, the basic unit of much blues and rock and roll music.
▶ **n.** a song or piece of music having such a structure.

twelve-bore ▶ **n.** British term for TWELVE-GAUGE.

twelve-gauge ▶ **n.** a shotgun with a gauge corresponding to the diameter of a round bullet of which twelve constitute a pound in weight.

twelve·mo /ˈtwelvˌmō/ ▶ **n.** another term for DUODECIMO.

twelve·month /ˈtwelvˌmənTH/ ▶ **n.** archaic a year.

twelve step ▶ **adj.** denoting or relating to a process of recovery from addiction by following a twelve-stage program, esp. one modeled on that of Alcoholics Anonymous.
▶ **v.** (often as noun **twelve-stepping**) (of an addict) undergo such a program.

Twelve Ta·bles a set of laws drawn up in ancient Rome in 451 and 450 BC, embodying the most important rules of Roman law.

twelve-tone (also **twelve-note**) ▶ **adj.** denoting a system of musical composition using the twelve chromatic notes of the octave on an equal basis without dependence on a key system. Developed by Arnold Schoenberg, the technique is central to serialism and involves the transposition and inversion of a fixed sequence of pitches.

Twelve Tribes of Is·ra·el see TRIBES OF ISRAEL.

Twen·ti·eth Cen·tu·ry Fox /ˈtwentē-iTH/ a US film production company formed in 1935 by the merger of the Fox Company with Twentieth Century. Under production head **Darryl F. Zanuck** (1902–79) the company pioneered widescreen film techniques.

twen·ty /ˈtwentē/ ▶ **cardinal number** (pl. **twenties**) the number equivalent to the product of two and ten; ten less than thirty; 20: *twenty or thirty years ago | twenty of us stood and waited | a twenty-foot aerial.* (Roman numeral: **xx, XX**) ■ (**twenties**) the numbers from twenty to twenty-nine, esp. the years of a century or of a person's life: *he's in his late twenties.* ■ twenty years old: *he's about twenty.* ■ twenty miles an hour. ■ a size of garment or other merchandise denoted by twenty. ■ a twenty-dollar bill.
– DERIVATIVES **twen·ti·eth** /-tēiTH/ **ordinal number**, **twen·ty·fold** /-ˌfōld/ **adj. & adv.**
– ORIGIN Old English *twentig*, from the base of TWO + -TY².

twen·ty-eight ▶ **n.** Austral. a ringneck parrot of a race having a call that resembles the word "twenty-eight." ● *Barnardius zonarius semitorquatus*, family Psittacidae; a subspecies of the Port Lincoln parrot.

twen·ty-four-hour clock (also **24-hour clock**) ▶ **n.** a method of measuring the time based on the full twenty-four hours of the day, rather than dividing it into two units of twelve hours.

twen·ty-four hours ▶ **n.** W. Indian a long-legged arboreal lizard of tropical America, related to the anoles. ● *Polychrus marmoratus*, family Iguanidae.
– ORIGIN so named from the superstition that a person touched by one will die within twenty-four hours.

twen·ty-one ▶ **n.** the card game blackjack.

twen·ty-twen·ty (also **20/20**) ▶ **adj.** denoting vision of normal sharpness.
– ORIGIN the Snellen fraction for normal visual acuity (see SNELLEN TEST).

'twere /twər/ archaic literary ▶ **contraction** it were.

twerp /twərp/ (also **twirp**) ▶ **n.** informal a silly or annoying person.
– ORIGIN late 19th cent.: of unknown origin.

Twi /twē/ ▶ **n.** (pl. **same** or **Twis**) **1** a member of an Akan-speaking people of Ghana.
2 another term for AKAN (the language).
▶ **adj.** of or relating to this people or their language.
– ORIGIN the name in Akan.

twi·bill /ˈtwīˌbil/ ▶ **n.** archaic a double-bladed battle-ax.
– ORIGIN Old English *twibile* 'ax with two cutting edges,' from *twi-* 'double' + BILL³.

twice /twīs/ ▶ **adv.** two times; on two occasions: *she had been married twice | the tablets should be taken twice a day.* ■ double in degree or quantity: *I'm twice your age | an engine **twice as big as** the original.*
– PHRASES **once bitten, twice shy** see BITE. **think twice** see THINK.
– ORIGIN late Old English *twiges*, from the base of TWO + -S³ (later respelled *-ce* to denote the unvoiced sound); compare with ONCE.

twice-baked ▶ **adj.** (of bread or cookie dough) baked in a loaf and then sliced and returned to the oven to bake again until crisp.

twice-born ▶ **adj.** having undergone a renewal of faith or life, in particular: ■ (of a Hindu) belonging to one of the three highest castes, esp. as an initiated Brahman. ■ (of a Christian) born-again.

twid·dle /ˈtwidl/ ▶ **v.** [with obj.] twist, move, or fiddle with (something), typically in a purposeless or nervous way: *she twiddled the dials on the radio |* [no obj.] *he began twiddling with the curtain cord.* ■ [no obj.] archaic turn or move in a twirling way.
▶ **n.** an act of twisting or fiddling with something: *one twiddle of a button.*
– PHRASES **twiddle one's thumbs** rotate one's thumbs around each other with the fingers linked together. ■ be bored or idle because one has nothing to do.
– DERIVATIVES **twid·dler** /ˈtwidlər, ˈtwidl-ər/ **n.**, **twid·dly** /ˈtwidlē, ˈtwidl-ē/ **adj.**
– ORIGIN mid 16th cent. (in the sense 'trifle'): apparently imitative, combining the notion *twirl* or *twist* with that of trifling action expressed by *fiddle*.

twig¹ /twig/ ▶ **n.** a slender woody shoot growing from a branch or stem of a tree or shrub. ■ Anatomy a small branch of a blood vessel or nerve.
– DERIVATIVES **twigged adj.**, **twig·gy adj.**
– ORIGIN Old English *twigge*, of Germanic origin; related to Dutch *twijg* and German *Zweig*, also to TWAIN and TWO.

twig² ▶ **v.** (**twigs, twigging, twigged**) [no obj.] Brit. informal understand or realize something: *it was amazing that Graham hadn't twigged before.* ■ [with obj.] archaic perceive; observe: *nine days now since my eyes have twigged any terra firma.*
– ORIGIN mid 18th cent.: of unknown origin.

twig fur·ni·ture ▶ **n.** a rustic style of furniture in which the natural state of the wood is retained as an aesthetic feature.

twi·light /ˈtwīˌlīt/ ▶ **n. 1** the soft glowing light from the sky when the sun is below the horizon, caused by the refraction and scattering of the sun's rays from the atmosphere. ■ the period of the evening during which this takes place, between daylight and darkness: *a pleasant walk in the woods at twilight.*
2 [in sing.] a period or state of obscurity, ambiguity, or gradual decline: *he was **in the twilight of** his career |* [as modifier] *a **twilight world** of secrecy.*
– ORIGIN late Middle English: from Old English *twi-* 'two' (used in an obscure sense in this compound) + LIGHT¹.

twi·light of the gods Scandinavian & Germanic Mythology the destruction of the gods and the world in a final conflict with the powers of evil. Also called GÖTTERDÄMMERUNG, RAGNARÖK.
– ORIGIN translating Icelandic *ragna rökr* (see RAGNARÖK).

twi·light sleep ▶ **n.** Medicine a state of partial narcosis or stupor without total loss of consciousness, in particular a state induced by an injection of morphine and scopolamine, formerly popular for use during childbirth.

twi·light zone ▶ **n. 1** a conceptual area that is undefined or intermediate: *the twilight zone between the middle and working classes.* ■ a sphere of experience that appears sinister or dangerous because of its uncertainty, unpredictability, or ambiguity: *they languish in a twilight zone of unemployment and despair.*
2 the lowest level of the ocean to which light can penetrate.

twi·lit /ˈtwīˌlit/ ▶ **adj.** dimly illuminated by or as if by twilight: *the deserted twilit street.* ■ relating to or denoting the period of twilight: *twilit hours.*

– ORIGIN mid 19th cent.: past participle of the literary verb *twilight*.

twill /twil/ ▶ **n.** a fabric so woven as to have a surface of diagonal parallel ridges.
▶ **v.** [with obj.] (usu. as adj. **twilled**) weave (fabric) in this way: *twilled cotton*.
– ORIGIN Middle English: from a Scots and northern English variant of obsolete *twilly*, from Old English *twi-* 'two,' suggested by Latin *bilix* 'two-threaded.'

'twill /twil/ archaic literary ▶ **contraction** it will.

twin /twin/ ▶ **n. 1** one of two children or animals born at the same birth. ■ a person or thing that is exactly like another: *there was a bruise on his cheek, a twin to the one on mine.* ■ (**the Twins**) the zodiacal sign or constellation Gemini.
2 something containing or consisting of two matching or corresponding parts, in particular: ■ a twin-bedded room. ■ a twin-engined aircraft. ■ a twinned crystal.
▶ **adj.** [attrib.] forming, or being one of, a pair born at one birth: *she gave birth to twin boys | her twin sister.* ■ forming a matching, complementary, or closely connected pair: *the twin problems of economic failure and social disintegration.* ■ Botany growing in pairs: *twin seed leaves.* ■ (of a bedroom) containing two single beds. ■ (of a crystal) twinned.
▶ **v.** (**twins, twinning, twinned**) [with obj.] (usu. **be twinned**) link; combine: *the company twinned its core business of brewing with that of distilling.*
– ORIGIN late Old English *twinn* 'double,' from *twi-* 'two'; related to Old Norse *tvinnr*. Current verb senses date from late Middle English.

twin bed ▶ **n.** a bed designed or suitable for one person; a single bed, esp. one of a pair of matching single beds.
– DERIVATIVES **twin-bed·ded adj.**

twin-cam ▶ **adj.** denoting an engine having two camshafts.

twin cit·y ▶ **n.** either of two neighboring cities lying close together. ■ (**the Twin Cities**) Minneapolis and St. Paul in Minnesota.

twine /twīn/ ▶ **n.** strong thread or string consisting of two or more strands of hemp, cotton, or nylon twisted together.
▶ **v.** [with obj.] cause to wind or spiral round something: *she twined her arms around his neck.* ■ [no obj.] (of a plant) grow so as to spiral around a support: *runner beans twined around canes.* ■ interlace: *a spray of jasmine was twined in her hair.*
– DERIVATIVES **twin·er n.**
– ORIGIN Old English *twīn* 'thread, linen,' from the Germanic base of *twi-* 'two'; related to Dutch *twijn*.

twin-en·gined (also **twin-engine**) ▶ **adj.** (chiefly of an aircraft) having two engines.

Twin Falls a commercial and industrial city in south central Idaho, on the Snake River; pop. 42,197 (est. 2008).

twin·flow·er /ˈtwin,flou(-ə)r/ ▶ **n.** a slender evergreen trailing plant of the honeysuckle family, with pairs of very small trumpet-shaped pink flowers in the leaf axils, native to coniferous woodlands in northern latitudes. ● *Linnaea borealis*, family Caprifoliaceae.

twinge /twinj/ ▶ **n.** a sudden, sharp localized pain: *he felt a twinge in his knee.* ■ a brief experience of an emotion, typically an unpleasant one: *Kate felt a twinge of guilt.*
▶ **v.** (**twinges, twingeing** or **twinging** /-jiNG/, **twinged**) [no obj.] (of a part of the body) suffer a sudden, sharp localized pain: *the ankle still twinged, but the pain was slight.*
– ORIGIN Old English *twengan* 'pinch, wring,' of Germanic origin. The noun dates from the mid 16th cent.

twin-jet ▶ **adj.** (of an aircraft) having two jet engines.
▶ **n.** (**twin jet**) a twin-jet aircraft.

Twin·kie /ˈtwiNGkē/ ▶ **n.** (pl. **Twinkies**) **1** trademark a small finger-shaped sponge cake with a white synthetic cream filling.
2 (also **twinkie**) informal, offensive a gay or effeminate man. ■ a young gay male who is meticulous about his dress, hair, weight, and other aspects of his personal appearance.
– ORIGIN late 20th cent.: probably related to TWINKLE.

twin·kle /ˈtwiNGkəl/ ▶ **v.** [no obj.] (of a star or light, or a shiny object) shine with a gleam that varies repeatedly between bright and faint: *the lights twinkled in the distance* | (as adj. **twinkling**) *twinkling harbor lights.* ■ (of a person's eyes) sparkle, esp. with amusement. ■ smile so that one's eyes sparkle: *"Aha!" he said, twinkling at her* | (as adj. **twinkling**) *a twinkling smile.* ■ (of a person's feet) move lightly and rapidly: *his sandaled feet twinkled over the ground.*
▶ **n.** a sparkle or gleam in a person's eyes. ■ a light that appears continually to grow brighter and fainter: *the distant twinkle of the lights.*
– PHRASES **in a twinkling** (or **the twinkling of an eye**) in an instant; very quickly.
– DERIVATIVES **twin·kler** /-k(ə)lər/ **n.**, **twin·kly** /-k(ə)lē/ **adj.**
– ORIGIN Old English *twinclian* (verb), of Germanic origin.

twin·kle·toes /ˈtwiNGkəl,tōz/ ▶ **n.** informal a person who is nimble and quick on their feet.

twin-lens ▶ **adj.** (of a camera) having two identical sets of lenses, either for taking stereoscopic pictures, or with one forming an image for viewing and the other an image to be photographed (**twin-lens reflex**).

twinned /twind/ ▶ **adj.** (of a crystal) that is a composite consisting of two (or sometimes more) parts that are reversed in orientation with respect to each other (typically by reflection in a particular plane).

twin·ning /ˈtwiniNG/ ▶ **n.** the bearing of twins: *the study showed an increased level of twinning in cattle.* ■ the occurrence or formation of twinned crystals.

twin par·a·dox ▶ **n.** Physics the apparent paradox arising from relativity theory that if one of a pair of twins makes a long journey at near the speed of light and then returns, he or she will have aged less than the twin who remains behind.

twin-screw ▶ **adj.** (of a ship) having two propellers on separate shafts that rotate in opposite directions.

twin·set /ˈtwin,set/ ▶ **n.** a woman's matching cardigan and pullover sweater.

twin·spot /ˈtwin,spät/ ▶ **n.** an African waxbill with white-spotted black underparts, the male typically having a reddish face and breast. ● *Hypargos* and related genera, family Estrildidae: several species.

twirl /twərl/ ▶ **v.** [no obj.] spin quickly and lightly around, esp. repeatedly: *she twirled in delight to show off her new dress.* ■ [with obj.] cause to rotate: *she twirled her fork in the pasta.* ■ [with obj.] Baseball pitch (the ball).
▶ **n.** an act of spinning: *Kate did a twirl in front of the mirror.* ■ a spiraling or swirling shape, esp. a flourish made with a pen.
– DERIVATIVES **twirl·er n.**, **twirl·y adj.**
– ORIGIN late 16th cent.: probably an alteration (by association with WHIRL) of *tirl*, a variant of archaic *trill* 'twiddle, spin.'

twirp ▶ **n.** variant spelling of TWERP.

twist /twist/ ▶ **v.** [with obj.] **1** form into a bent, curling, or distorted shape: *a strip of metal is twisted to form a hollow tube | her pretty features twisted into a fearsome expression.* ■ form (something) into a particular shape by taking hold of one or both ends and turning them: *she twisted her handkerchief into a knot.* ■ turn or bend into a specified position or in a specified direction: *he grabbed the man and twisted his arm behind his back.* ■ (**twist something off**) remove something by pulling and rotating it: *beets can be stored once the leaves have been twisted off.* ■ [no obj.] move one's body so that the shoulders and hips are facing in different directions: *she twisted in her seat to look at the buildings.* ■ [no obj.] move in a wriggling or writhing fashion: *he twisted himself free.* ■ injure (a joint) by wrenching it: *he twisted his ankle trying to avoid his opponent's lunge.* ■ distort or misrepresent the meaning of (words): *he twisted my words to make it seem that I'd claimed she was a drug addict.*
2 cause to rotate around something that remains stationary; turn: *she twisted her ring around and around on her finger.* ■ wind around or through something: *she twisted a lock of hair around her finger.* ■ move or cause to move around each other; interlace: *she twisted her hands together nervously | the machine twists together strands to make a double yarn.* ■ make (something) by interlacing or winding strands together. ■ [no obj.] take or have a winding course: *the road twisted through a dozen tiny villages.*
3 [no obj.] dance the twist.
4 Brit. informal cheat; defraud.
▶ **n. 1** an act of turning something so that it moves in relation to something that remains stationary: *the taps needed a single twist to turn them on.* ■ an act of turning one's body or part of one's body: *with a sudden twist, she got away from him.* ■ (**the twist**) a dance with a twisting movement of the body, popular in the 1960s. ■ the extent of twisting of a rod or other object. ■ force producing twisting; torque. ■ forward motion combined with rotation about an axis. ■ the rifling in the bore of a gun: *barrels with a 1:24 inch twist.*
2 a thing with a spiral shape: *a licorice twist.* ■ a curled piece of lemon peel used to flavor a drink.
3 a distorted shape: *he had a cruel twist to his mouth.* ■ an unusual feature of a person's personality, typically an unhealthy one.
4 a point at which something turns or bends: *the car negotiated the twists and turns of the mountain road.* ■ an unexpected development of events: *it was soon time for the next twist of fate in his extraordinary career.* ■ a new treatment or outlook; a variation: *she takes conventional subjects and gives them a twist.*
5 a fine strong thread consisting of twisted strands of cotton or silk.
6 Brit. a drink consisting of two ingredients mixed together.
7 a carpet with a tightly curled pile.
– PHRASES **twist someone's arm** informal persuade someone to do something that they are or might be reluctant to do. **twist in the wind** be left in a state of suspense or uncertainty. **twist someone around one's little finger** see LITTLE FINGER. **twists and turns** intricate or convoluted dealings or circumstances: *the twists and turns of her political career.*
– ORIGIN Old English (as a noun), of Germanic origin; probably from the base of TWIN and TWINE. Current verb senses date from late Middle English.

twist drill ▶ **n.** a drill with a twisted body like that of an auger.

twist·ed /ˈtwistid/ ▶ **adj. 1** forced out of its natural or proper shape; crumpled: *the crash left a trail of twisted metal across the highway.* ■ (of a joint) injured by wrenching; sprained: *suffering a twisted ankle, he was carried from the field.*
2 (of a personality or a way of thinking) unpleasantly or unhealthily abnormal; warped: *a man with a twisted mind.*

twist·ed pair ▶ **n.** Electronics a cable consisting of two wires twisted around each other, used esp. for telephone or computer applications.

twist·ed-stalk ▶ **n.** a plant of the lily family with bell-shaped flowers carried on bent or twisted stalks, native to the temperate regions of Russia and North America. ● Genus *Streptopus*, family Liliaceae: several species, including the **rosy twisted-stalk** (*S. roseus*), which grows in the coastal mountain regions from British Columbia to Oregon.

twist·er /ˈtwistər/ ▶ **n.** a tornado.

twist-grip ▶ **n.** a control operated manually by twisting, esp. one serving as a handgrip for operating the throttle on a motorcycle or for changing gear on a bicycle.

twist-lock ▶ **n.** a locking device for securing freight containers to the trailers on which they are transported.

twist·or /ˈtwistər/ ▶ **n.** Physics a complex variable used in some descriptions of space-time.

twist tie ▶ **n.** a small piece of paper- or plastic-covered wire, to be twisted around the neck of a plastic bag as a closure.

twist·y /ˈtwistē/ ▶ **adj.** (**twistier, twistiest**) not arranged or moving in a straight line; winding: *a twisty country road.*

twit[1] /twit/ ▶ **n.** informal a silly or foolish person.
– DERIVATIVES **twit·tish adj.**
– ORIGIN 1930s (earlier dialect, in the sense 'talebearer'): perhaps from TWIT[2].

twit[2] ▶ **v.** (**twits, twitting, twitted**) [with obj.] dated tease or taunt (someone), esp. in a good-humored way.
▶ **n.** [in sing.] a state of nervous excitement: *we're in a twit about your visit.*
– ORIGIN Old English *ætwītan* 'reproach with,' from *æt* 'at' + *wītan* 'to blame.'

twitch /twiCH/ ▶ **v. 1** give or cause to give a short, sudden jerking or convulsive movement: [no obj.] *he saw her lips twitch and her eyelids flutter* | [with obj.] *the dog twitched his ears.* ■ [with obj.] cause to move in a specified direction by giving a sharp pull: *he twitched a cigarette out of a packet.*
2 [with obj.] apply a sudden pull or jerk to (a horse).
▶ **n. 1** a short, sudden jerking or convulsive movement: *his mouth gave a slight twitch.* ■ a sudden pull or jerk: *he gave a twitch at his mustache.* ■ a sudden sharp sensation; a pang: *he felt a twitch of annoyance.*
2 a stick with a small noose attached to one end. The noose may be twisted around the upper lip or the ear of a horse to subdue it, esp. during veterinary procedures.
– ORIGIN Middle English: of Germanic origin; related to Old English *twiccian* 'to pluck, pull sharply.'

twitch·er /ˈtwiCHər/ ▶ **n.** a person or thing that twitches. ■ Brit. informal a birdwatcher whose main aim is to collect sightings of rare birds.

twitch grass ▶ **n.** another term for COUCH GRASS.
– ORIGIN late 16th cent.: *twitch*, alteration of QUITCH.

twitch·y /ˈtwiCHē/ ▶ **adj.** (**twitchier, twitchiest**) informal nervous; anxious: *she felt twitchy about the man hovering in the background.* ■ given to twitching: *a mouse with a twitchy nose.*

twite /twīt/ ▶ **n.** a Eurasian moorland finch related to the linnet, having streaky brown plumage and a pink rump. ● *Acanthis flavirostris*, family Fringillidae.
– ORIGIN mid 16th cent.: imitative of its call.

twit·ter /ˈtwitər/ ▶ **v.** [no obj.] **1** (of a bird) give a call consisting of repeated light tremulous sounds. ■ talk in a light, high-pitched voice: *old ladies in the congregation twittered.* ■ talk rapidly and at length in an idle or trivial way: *he **twittered on about** buying a new workshop.*
2 make a posting on the social networking site Twitter: *many active bloggers are twittering more and more these days.*
▶ **n.** a series of short, high-pitched calls or sounds: *his words were cut off by a faint electronic twitter.* ■ idle or ignorant talk: *drawing-room twitter.*
– PHRASES **in** (or **of**) **a twitter** informal in a state of agitation or excitement.
– DERIVATIVES **twit·ter·er n.**, **twit·ter·y adj.**
– ORIGIN late Middle English (as a verb): imitative.

WORD TRENDS See **TWEET**.

'twixt /twikst/ ▶ **contraction** betwixt.

two /to͞o/ ▶ **cardinal number** equivalent to the sum of one and one; one less than three; 2: *two years ago | a romantic weekend for two in Paris | two of Amy's friends.* (Roman numeral: **ii, II**) ■ a group or unit of two people or things: *they would straggle home in ones and twos.* ■ two years old: *he is only two.* ■ two o'clock: *the bar closed at two.* ■ a size of garment or other merchandise denoted by two. ■ a playing card or domino with two pips.
– PHRASES **a —— or two** (or **two or three ——**) used to denote a small but unspecified number: *a minute or two had passed.* **be two a penny** see **PENNY**. **in two** in or into two halves or pieces: *he tore the piece of paper in two.* **in two shakes** (**of a lamb's tail**) see **SHAKE**. **it takes two to tango** see **TANGO**. **put two and two together** draw an obvious conclusion from what is known or evident. **that makes two of us** one is in the same position or holds the same opinion as the previous speaker: *"I haven't a clue!" "That makes two of us."* **two by two** side by side in pairs. **two can play that game** used to assert that another person's bad behavior can be copied to that person's disadvantage. **two's company, three's a crowd** used to indicate that two people, esp. lovers, should be left alone together. **two heads are better than one** proverb it's helpful to have the advice or opinion of a second person.
– ORIGIN Old English *twā* (feminine and neuter), of Germanic origin; related to Dutch *twee* and German *zwei*, from an Indo-European root shared by Latin and Greek *duo*. Compare with **TWAIN**.

two-bit ▶ **adj.** [attrib.] informal insignificant, cheap, or worthless: *some two-bit town.*

two-by-four ▶ **n.** a piece of lumber with a rectangular cross section nominally two inches by four inches. ■ [usu. as modifier] a small or insignificant thing, typically a building: *they lived in a two-by-four shack of one bedroom.*

two-cy·cle ▶ **adj.** another term for **TWO-STROKE**.

two-di·men·sion·al ▶ **adj.** having or appearing to have length and breadth but no depth. ■ lacking depth or substance; superficial: *a nether world of two-dimensional heroes and villains.*
– DERIVATIVES **two-di·men·sion·al·i·ty n.**, **two-di·men·sion·al·ly adv.**

two-edged ▶ **adj.** double-edged.

two-faced ▶ **adj.** insincere and deceitful.

two·fer /ˈto͞ofər/ ▶ **n.** informal an item or offer that comprises two items but is sold for the price of one.
– ORIGIN 20th cent.: representing a pronunciation of *two for* in 'two for the price of one.'

two fin·gers ▶ **plural n.** [often treated as sing.] Brit. another term for **V-SIGN** (sense 2).

two-fist·ed ▶ **adj.** strong, virile, and straightforward.

two·fold /ˈto͞oˌfōld/ ▶ **adj.** twice as great or as numerous: *a twofold increase in the risk.* ■ having two parts or elements: *the twofold demands of the business and motherhood.*
▶ **adv.** so as to double; to twice the number or amount: *use increased more than twofold from 1979 to 1989.*

two-four ▶ **n.** Canadian informal a case of twenty-four bottles of beer.

two-hand·ed ▶ **adj. & adv.** having, using, or requiring the use of two hands.
– DERIVATIVES **two-hand·ed·ly adv.**

two-hand·er ▶ **n. 1** a play for two actors.
2 Tennis a shot taken with both hands on the racket.

two·ness /ˈto͞onəs/ ▶ **n.** the fact or state of being two; duality.

two·pence /ˈtəpəns/ ▶ **n.** Brit. the sum of two pence, esp. before decimalization (1971). ■ [with negative] informal a trivial sum; anything at all: *he didn't care **twopence for** her.*

two·pen·ny /ˈtəp(ə)nē, ˈto͞oˌpenē/ ▶ **adj.** [attrib.] Brit. costing or worth two pence, esp. before decimalization (1971).

two-phase ▶ **adj.** (of an electric generator, motor, or other device) designed to supply or use simultaneously two separate alternating currents of the same voltage, but with phases differing by half a period.

two-piece ▶ **adj.** denoting something consisting of two matching items: *a two-piece suit.*
▶ **n.** a thing consisting of two matching parts, esp. a suit or swimsuit.

two-ply ▶ **adj.** (of a material or yarn) consisting of two layers or strands.
▶ **n. 1** a yarn consisting of two strands.
2 plywood made by gluing together two layers with the grain in different directions.

two-seat·er ▶ **n.** a vehicle or piece of furniture with seating for two people.

two shot ▶ **n.** a movie or television shot of two people together.

two-sid·ed ▶ **adj.** having two sides: *a colorful two-sided leaflet.* ■ having two aspects: *the two-sided nature of the debate.*

two·some /ˈto͞osəm/ ▶ **n.** a pair of people considered together. ■ a game or dance for or involving two people.

two-star ▶ **adj.** given two stars in a grading system, typically one in which this denotes a low middle standard (four- or five-star denoting the highest standard): *a two-star award in the Michelin guide.* ■ (in the US armed forces) having or denoting the rank of major general, distinguished by two stars on the uniform.

two-step ▶ **n.** a round dance with a sliding step in march or polka time.

two-stroke ▶ **adj.** denoting an internal combustion engine whose power cycle is completed in one up-and-down movement of the piston. ■ denoting a vehicle having such an engine.
▶ **n.** a two-stroke engine or vehicle. Compare with **FOUR-STROKE**.

two-tailed ▶ **adj.** Statistics (of a test) testing for deviation from the null hypothesis in both directions.

two-tailed pa·sha ▶ **n.** see **PASHA**.

two-time ▶ **v.** [with obj.] informal deceive or be unfaithful to (a lover or spouse): *he was two-timing a fiancée back in England.*
▶ **adj.** [attrib.] denoting someone who has done or experienced something twice: *a two-time winner of the event.*
– DERIVATIVES **two-tim·er n.**, **two-tim·ing adj.**

two-tone (also **two-toned**) ▶ **adj.** having two different shades or colors: *a two-tone jacket.* ■ emitting or consisting of two different sounds, typically alternately and at intervals: *a two-tone pulse signal.*

'twould /two͝od/ archaic ▶ **contraction** it would.

two-way ▶ **adj.** allowing or involving movement or communication in opposite directions: *a two-way radio | make the interview a two-way process.* ■ involving two participants: *a two-way presidential race.* ■ (of a switch) permitting a current to be switched on or off from either of two points.
– PHRASES **two-way street** a situation or relationship involving mutual or reciprocal action or obligation: *trust is a two-way street.*

two-way mir·ror ▶ **n.** a panel of glass that can be seen through from one side but is a mirror on the other.

two-wheel drive ▶ **n.** a transmission system in a motor vehicle, providing power to either the front or the rear wheels only.

two-wheel·er ▶ **n.** a bicycle or motorcycle.

twp. ▶ **abbr.** township.

TWX ▶ **abbr.** teletypewriter exchange.

TX ▶ **abbr.** Texas (in official postal use).

-ty[1] ▶ **suffix** forming nouns denoting quality or condition such as *beauty, royalty.*
– ORIGIN via Old French from Latin *-tas, -tat-.*

-ty[2] ▶ **suffix** denoting specified groups of ten: *forty | ninety.*
– ORIGIN Old English *-tig.*

ty·chism /ˈtīˌkizəm/ ▶ **n.** Philosophy the doctrine that account must be taken of the element of chance in reasoning or explanation of the universe.
– ORIGIN late 19th cent.: from Greek *tukhē* 'chance' + **-ISM**.

ty·coon /tīˈko͞on/ ▶ **n. 1** a wealthy, powerful person in business or industry: *a newspaper tycoon.*
2 a title applied by foreigners to the shogun of Japan in power between 1857 and 1868.
– ORIGIN mid 19th cent.: from Japanese *taikun* 'great lord.'

ty·ing /ˈtī-iNG/ present participle of **TIE**.

ty·ing-up ▶ **n.** another term for **AZOTURIA** in horses.

tyke /tīk/ (also **tike**) ▶ **n. 1** [usu. with adj.] informal a small child: *is the little tyke up to his tricks again?* ■ [usu. as modifier] Canadian an initiation level of sports competition for young children: *tyke hockey.*
2 dated, chiefly Brit. an unpleasant or coarse man.
3 a dog, esp. a mongrel.
– ORIGIN late Middle English (sense 2 and sense 3): from Old Norse *tík* 'bitch.'

Ty·le·nol /ˈtīləˌnôl, -ˌnäl/ ▶ **n.** trademark for **ACETAMINOPHEN**.

Ty·ler[1] /ˈtīlər/ an industrial city in eastern Texas, noted for its roses; pop. 97,705 (est. 2008).

Tyl·er[2], Anne (1941–), US writer. Her novels include *The Accidental Tourist* (1986), *Breathing Lessons* (1988), *Ladder of Years* (1995), and *A Patchwork Planet* (1998).

Ty·ler[3], John (1790–1862), 10th president of the US 1841–45. A Virginia Whig, he served as US congressman 1817–21, governor of Virginia 1825–27, US senator 1827–36, and US vice president 1841. He succeeded to the presidency upon the death of President William H. Harrison. Noted for securing the annexation of Texas (1845), throughout his political career he advocated states' rights. His alliance with Southern Democrats on this issue accentuated the divide between North and South prior to the Civil War.

John Tyler

Ty·ler[4], Wat (died 1381), English leader of the Peasants' Revolt of 1381. He captured Canterbury and went on to take London and secure Richard II's concession to the rebels' demands, which included the lifting of the newly imposed poll tax. He was killed by royal supporters.

ty·lo·pod /ˈtīləˌpäd/ ▶ **n.** Zoology an even-toed ungulate mammal of a group that comprises the camels, llamas, and their extinct relatives. They are distinguished by bearing their weight on the sole-pads of the feet rather than on the hoofs, and they do not chew the cud. ● Suborder Tylopoda, order Artiodactyla: family Camelidae.
– ORIGIN late 19th cent.: from modern Latin *Tylopoda*, from Greek *tulos* 'knob' or *tulē* 'callus, cushion' + *pous, pod-* 'foot.'

ty·lo·sin /ˈtīləˌsin/ ▶ **n.** an antibiotic that is routinely fed to livestock as a growth promoter and that may contribute to antibiotic resistance in humans.

tym·bal ▶ **n.** variant spelling of **TIMBAL**.

tym·pan /ˈtimpən/ ▶ **n. 1** (in letterpress printing) a layer of packing, typically of paper, placed between the platen and the paper to be printed to equalize the pressure over the whole forme.
2 Architecture another term for **TYMPANUM**.
– ORIGIN late 16th cent. (sense 1): from French *tympan* or Latin *tympanum* (see **TYMPANUM**). Sense 2 dates from the early 18th cent.

tym·pa·na /ˈtimpənə/ plural form of **TYMPANUM**.

tym·pa·ni ▶ **plural n.** variant spelling of **TIMPANI**.

tym·pan·ic /timˈpanik/ ▶ **adj. 1** Anatomy of, relating to, or having a tympanum.
2 resembling or acting like a drumhead.

tym·pan·ic bone ▶ **n.** Zoology a small bone supporting the tympanic membrane in some vertebrates.

t

tym·pan·ic mem·brane ▶ **n.** a membrane forming part of the organ of hearing, which vibrates in response to sound waves. In humans and other higher vertebrates it forms the eardrum, between the outer and middle ear.

tym·pa·ni·tes /ˌtimpəˈnītēz/ ▶ **n.** Medicine swelling of the abdomen with air or gas.
– DERIVATIVES **tym·pa·nit·ic** /-ˈnitik/ **adj.**
– ORIGIN late Middle English: via late Latin from Greek *tumpanitēs*, from *tumpanon* (see **TYMPANUM**).

tym·pa·num /ˈtimpənəm/ ▶ **n.** (pl. **tympanums** or **tympana** /-nə/) **1** Anatomy & Zoology the tympanic membrane or eardrum. ■ Entomology a membrane covering the hearing organ on the leg or body of some insects, sometimes adapted (as in cicadas) for producing sound. ■ archaic a drum.
2 Architecture a vertical recessed triangular space forming the center of a pediment, typically decorated. ■ a similar space over a door between the lintel and the arch.
– ORIGIN early 17th cent.: via Latin from Greek *tumpanon* 'drum,' based on *tuptein* 'to strike.'

tym·pa·ny /ˈtimpənē/ ▶ **n.** another term for **TYMPANITES** (used esp. in veterinary medicine).
– ORIGIN early 16th cent.: from Greek *tumpanias*, from *tumpanon* (see **TYMPANUM**).

Tyn·dall /ˈtindəl/, John (1820–93), Irish physicist. He is best known for his work on heat but he also worked on the transmission of sound and the scattering of light by suspended particles.

Tyne /tīn/ a river in northeastern England, formed by the confluence of two headstreams, the North Tyne, which rises in the Cheviot Hills, and the South Tyne, which rises in the northern Pennines. It flows east and enters the North Sea at Tynemouth.

typ. ▶ **abbr.** ■ typographer. ■ typographic. ■ typographical. ■ typography.

type /tīp/ ▶ **n.** **1** a category of people or things having common characteristics: *this type of heather grows better in a drier habitat* | *blood types.* ■ a person, thing, or event considered as a representative of such a category: *it's not the type of car I'd want my daughter to drive* | *I'm an adventurous type.* ■ [with modifier] informal a person of a specified character or nature: *professor types in tweed.* ■ **(one's type)** informal the sort of person one likes or finds attractive: *she's not really my type.* ■ Linguistics an abstract category or class of linguistic item or unit, as distinct from actual occurrences in speech or writing. Contrasted with **TOKEN**.
2 a person or thing symbolizing or exemplifying the ideal or defining characteristics of something: *she characterized his witty sayings as the type of modern wisdom.* ■ an object, conception, or work of art serving as a model for subsequent artists. ■ Botany & Zoology an organism or taxon chosen as having the essential characteristics of its group. ■ short for **TYPE SPECIMEN**.
3 printed characters or letters: *bold or italic type.* ■ a piece of metal with a raised letter or character on its upper surface, for use in letterpress printing. ■ such pieces collectively.
4 a design on either side of a medal or coin.
5 Theology a foreshadowing in the Old Testament of a person or event of the Christian tradition.
▶ **v.** [with obj.] **1** write (something) on a typewriter or computer by pressing the keys: *he* ***typed out*** *the second draft* | [no obj.] *I am learning how to type.*
2 Medicine determine the type to which (a person or their blood or tissue) belongs: *the kidney was typed.*
3 short for **TYPECAST**.
– PHRASES **in type** Printing composed and ready for printing.
– DERIVATIVES **typ·al** /-pəl/ **adj.** (rare).
– ORIGIN late 15th cent. (in the sense 'symbol, emblem'): from French, or from Latin *typus*, from Greek *tupos* 'impression, figure, type,' from *tuptein* 'to strike.' The use in printing dates from the early 18th cent.; the general sense 'category with common characteristics' arose in the mid 19th cent.

a **a** *a*

roman **boldface** *italic*
type 3

-type ▶ **suffix** (forming adjectives) resembling or having the characteristics of a specified thing: *the dish-type radio telescope* | *a champagne-type fizzy wine.*

Type A ▶ **n.** a personality type characterized by ambition, high energy, and competitiveness, and thought to be susceptible to stress and heart disease.

Type B ▶ **n.** a personality type characterized as easygoing and thought to have low susceptibility to stress.

type·cast /ˈtīpˌkast/ ▶ **v.** (past and past participle **typecast**) [with obj.] (usu. **be typecast**) assign (an actor or actress) repeatedly to the same type of role, as a result of the appropriateness of their appearance or previous success in such roles: *he tends to be typecast as the caring, intelligent male.* ■ represent or regard (a person or their role) as a stereotype: *people are not as likely to be typecast by their accents as they once were.*

type·face /ˈtīpˌfās/ ▶ **n.** Printing a particular design of type.

type found·er ▶ **n.** Printing a designer and maker of metal type.
– DERIVATIVES **type found·ry** **n.**

type lo·cal·i·ty ▶ **n.** **1** Botany & Zoology the place in which a type specimen was found.
2 Geology a place where deposits regarded as defining the characteristics of a particular geological formation or period occur.

type met·al ▶ **n.** Printing an alloy of lead, tin, and antimony, used for casting type.

type·script /ˈtīpˌskript/ ▶ **n.** a typed copy of a text.

type·set /ˈtīpˌset/ ▶ **v.** (**typesets**, **typesetting**; past and past participle **typeset**) [with obj.] arrange the type or process the data for (text that is to be printed).
– DERIVATIVES **type·set·ting** **n.**

type·set·ter /ˈtīpˌsetər/ ▶ **n.** Printing a person who typesets text. ■ a typesetting machine.

type spe·cies ▶ **n.** Botany & Zoology the particular species on which the description of a genus is based and with which the genus name remains associated during any taxonomic revision.

type spec·i·men ▶ **n.** Botany & Zoology the specimen, or each of a set of specimens, on which the description and name of a new species is based. See also **HOLOTYPE**, **SYNTYPE**.

type·writ·er /ˈtīpˌrītər/ ▶ **n.** an electric, electronic, or manual machine with keys for producing printlike characters one at a time on paper inserted around a roller.
– DERIVATIVES **type·writ·ing** /-ˌrīting/ **n.**, **type·writ·ten** /-ˌritn/ **adj.**

typh·li·tis /tifˈlītis/ ▶ **n.** Medicine inflammation of the cecum.
– DERIVATIVES **typh·lit·ic** /-ˈlitik/ **adj.**
– ORIGIN mid 19th cent.: modern Latin, from Greek *tuphlon* 'cecum or blind gut' (from *tuphlos* 'blind') + **-ITIS**.

ty·phoid /ˈtīˌfoid/ (also **typhoid fever**) ▶ **n.** an infectious bacterial fever with an eruption of red spots on the chest and abdomen and severe intestinal irritation. ● Typhoid is caused by the bacterium *Salmonella typhi*; Gram-negative rods.
– DERIVATIVES **ty·phoi·dal** /tīˈfoidl/ **adj.**
– ORIGIN early 19th cent.: from **TYPHUS** + **-OID**.

Ty·phoid Mar·y ▶ **n.** (pl. **Typhoid Marys**) informal a transmitter of undesirable opinions, sentiments, or attitudes.
– ORIGIN the nickname of *Mary* Mallon (see **MALLON**), an Irish-born cook who transmitted typhoid fever in the US.

ty·phoon /tīˈfo͞on/ ▶ **n.** a tropical storm in the region of the Indian or western Pacific oceans.
– DERIVATIVES **ty·phon·ic** /-ˈfänik/ **adj.**
– ORIGIN late 16th cent.: partly via Portuguese from Arabic *ṭūfān* (perhaps from Greek *tuphōn* 'whirlwind'); reinforced by Chinese dialect *tai fung* 'big wind.'

ty·phus /ˈtīfəs/ ▶ **n.** an infectious disease caused by rickettsiae, characterized by a purple rash, headaches, fever, and usually delirium, and historically a cause of high mortality during wars and famines. There are several forms, transmitted by vectors such as lice, ticks, mites, and rat fleas. Also called **SPOTTED FEVER**.
– DERIVATIVES **ty·phous** /-fəs/ **adj.**
– ORIGIN mid 17th cent.: modern Latin, from Greek *tuphos* 'smoke, stupor,' from *tuphein* 'to smoke.'

typ·i·cal /ˈtipikəl/ ▶ **adj.** having the distinctive qualities of a particular type of person or thing: *a typical day* | *a typical example of 1930s art deco* | *typical symptoms.* ■ characteristic of a particular person or thing: *he brushed the incident aside with typical good humor.* ■ informal showing the characteristics expected of or popularly associated with a particular person, situation, or thing: *"Typical woman!" John said disapprovingly.* ■ representative as a symbol; symbolic: *the pit is typical of hell.*
– DERIVATIVES **typ·i·cal·i·ty** /ˌtipiˈkalitē/ **n.**, **typ·i·cal·ly** /-ik(ə)lē/ **adv.** [sentence adverb] *typically, she showed no alarm* | [as submodifier] *a typically British stiff upper lip.*
– ORIGIN early 17th cent.: from medieval Latin *typicalis*, via Latin from Greek *tupikos*, from *tupos* (see **TYPE**).

typ·i·fy /ˈtipəˌfī/ ▶ **v.** (**typifies**, **typifying**, **typified**) [with obj.] be characteristic or a representative example of: *tough, low-lying vegetation typifies this arctic area.* ■ represent; symbolize: *the sun typified the Greeks, and the moon the Persians.*
– DERIVATIVES **typ·i·fi·ca·tion** /ˌtipəfiˈkāshən/ **n.**, **typ·i·fi·er** **n.**
– ORIGIN mid 17th cent.: from Latin *typus* (see **TYPE**) + **-FY**.

typ·ing /ˈtīping/ ▶ **n.** the action or skill of writing something by means of a typewriter or computer: *they learned shorthand and typing* | [as modifier] *typing errors.* ■ writing produced in such a way: *five pages of typing.*

typ·ist /ˈtīpist/ ▶ **n.** a person who is skilled in using a typewriter or computer keyboard, esp. one who is employed for this purpose.

ty·po /ˈtīpō/ ▶ **n.** (pl. **typos**) informal a typographical error.
– ORIGIN early 19th cent.: abbreviation.

typo. ▶ **abbr.** ■ typographer. ■ typographic. ■ typographical. ■ typography.

ty·pog·ra·phy /tīˈpägrəfē/ ▶ **n.** the style and appearance of printed matter. ■ the art or procedure of arranging type or processing data and printing from it.
– DERIVATIVES **ty·pog·ra·pher** /-fər/ **n.**, **ty·po·graph·ic** /ˌtīpəˈgrafik/ **adj.**, **ty·po·graph·i·cal** /ˌtīpəˈgrafikəl/ **adj.**, **ty·po·graph·i·cal·ly** /ˌtīpəˈgrafik(ə)lē/ **adv.**
– ORIGIN early 17th cent.: from French *typographie* or modern Latin *typographia* (see **TYPE**, **-GRAPHY**).

ty·pol·o·gy /tīˈpäləjē/ ▶ **n.** (pl. **typologies**) **1** a classification according to general type, esp. in archaeology, psychology, or the social sciences: *a typology of Saxon cremation vessels.* ■ study or analysis using such classification.
2 the study and interpretation of types and symbols, originally esp. in the Bible.
– DERIVATIVES **ty·po·log·i·cal** /ˌtīpəˈläjikəl/ **adj.**, **ty·pol·o·gist** /-jist/ **n.**
– ORIGIN mid 19th cent. (sense 2): from Greek *tupos* 'type' + **-LOGY**.

Tyr /ti(ə)r/ Scandinavian Mythology the god of battle, identified with Mars, after whom Tuesday is named.

ty·ra·mine /ˈtīrəˌmēn/ ▶ **n.** Biochemistry a compound that occurs naturally in cheese and other foods and can cause dangerously high blood pressure in people taking a monoamine oxidase inhibitor. ● An amine related to tyrosine; chem. formula: $C_6H_4(OH)CH_2CH_2NH_2$.
– ORIGIN early 20th cent.: from *tyr(osine)* + **AMINE**.

ty·ran·ni·cal /təˈranikəl/ ▶ **adj.** exercising power in a cruel or arbitrary way: *her father was portrayed as tyrannical and unloving.* ■ characteristic of tyranny; oppressive and controlling: *a momentary quieting of her tyrannical appetite.*
– DERIVATIVES **ty·ran·ni·cal·ly** /-ik(ə)lē/ **adv.**
– ORIGIN mid 16th cent.: from Old French *tyrannique*, via Latin from Greek *turannikos*, from *turannos* (see **TYRANT**).

ty·ran·ni·cide /təˈraniˌsīd/ ▶ **n.** the killing of a tyrant. ■ the killer of a tyrant.
– DERIVATIVES **ty·ran·ni·cid·al** /təˌraniˈsīdl/ **adj.**
– ORIGIN mid 17th cent.: from French, from Latin *tyrannicida* 'killer of a tyrant,' *tyrannicidium* 'killing of a tyrant' (see **TYRANT**, **-CIDE**).

tyr·an·nize /ˈtirəˌnīz/ ▶ **v.** [with obj.] rule or treat (someone) despotically or cruelly: *she tyrannized her family* | [no obj.] *he* ***tyrannizes over*** *the servants.*
– ORIGIN late 15th cent.: from French *tyranniser*, from *tyran* 'tyrant.'

ty·ran·no·saur /təˈranəˌsôr/ (also **tyrannosaurus** /təˌranəˈsôrəs/) ▶ **n.** a very large bipedal carnivorous dinosaur of the late Cretaceous period, with powerful jaws and small clawlike front legs. ● Family Tyrannosauridae, infraorder Carnosauria, suborder Theropoda: several species, in particular *Tyrannosaurus rex.*
– ORIGIN modern Latin, from Greek *turannos* 'tyrant' + *sauros* 'lizard,' on the pattern of *dinosaur*.

ty·ran·nu·let /təˈranyəlit/ ▶ **n.** a small tropical American bird of the tyrant flycatcher family, typically with drab grayish or greenish plumage. ● Family Tyrannidae: several genera and many species.
– ORIGIN diminutive based on modern Latin *Tyrannus* (genus name), from Greek *turannos* 'tyrant.'

tyr·an·ny /ˈtirənē/ ▶ **n.** (pl. **tyrannies**) cruel and oppressive government or rule: *people who survive war and escape tyranny* | *the removal of the regime may be the end of a tyranny.* ■ a nation under such cruel and oppressive government. ■ cruel,

unreasonable, or arbitrary use of power or control: *she resented his rages and his tyranny* | figurative *the tyranny of the nine-to-five day* | *his father's tyrannies.* ■ (esp. in ancient Greece) rule by one who has absolute power without legal right.
– DERIVATIVES **tyr·an·nous** /-nəs/ **adj.**, **tyr·an·nous·ly** /-nəslē/ **adv.**
– ORIGIN late Middle English: from Old French *tyrannie*, from late Latin *tyrannia*, from Latin *turannus* (see TYRANT).

ty·rant /'tīrənt/ ▶ **n. 1** a cruel and oppressive ruler: *the tyrant was deposed by popular demonstrations.* ■ a person exercising power or control in a cruel, unreasonable, or arbitrary way: *her father was a tyrant and a bully.* ■ (esp. in ancient Greece) a ruler who seized power without legal right.
2 a tyrant flycatcher.
– ORIGIN Middle English: from Old French, via Latin from Greek *turannos*.

ty·rant fly·catch·er ▶ **n.** a New World perching bird that resembles the Old World flycatchers in behavior, typically with brightly colored plumage. ● Family Tyrannidae: many genera and numerous species.
– ORIGIN mid 18th cent.: so named because of its aggressive behavior toward other birds approaching its nest.

Tyre /tī(ə)r/ a port on the Mediterranean Sea in southern Lebanon; pop. 41,800 (est. 2009). Founded in the 2nd millennium BC as a colony of Sidon, it was for centuries a Phoenician port and trading center.
– DERIVATIVES **Tyr·i·an** /'tirēən/ **adj. & n.**

tyre ▶ **n.** British spelling of TIRE[2].

Tyr·i·an pur·ple /'tirēən/ ▶ **n.** see PURPLE.

ty·ro /'tīrō/ (also **tiro**) ▶ **n.** (pl. **tyros**) a beginner or novice.
– ORIGIN late Middle English: from Latin *tiro*, medieval Latin *tyro* 'recruit.'

Ty·rode's so·lu·tion /'tīrōdz/ (also **Tyrode's**) ▶ **n.** Biology & Medicine a type of physiological saline solution.
– ORIGIN 1920s: named after Maurice V. *Tyrode* (1878–1930), American pharmacologist.

Ty·rol /tə'rōl, tī'rōl, 'tī,rōl/ an Alpine state in western Austria; capital, Innsbruck. The southern part was ceded to Italy after World War I. German name **TIROL**.
– DERIVATIVES **Ty·ro·le·an** /tə'rōlēən, tī-/ **adj. & n.**, **Tyr·o·lese** /,tirə'lēz, ,tīrə-, -'lēs/ **adj. & n.**

Ty·rone /tī'rōn/ one of the six counties of Northern Ireland, formerly an administrative area; pop. 180,700 (est. 2007); chief town, Omagh.

ty·ro·si·nase /tī'räsə,nās, -,nāz/ ▶ **n.** Biochemistry a copper-containing enzyme that catalyzes the formation of quinones from phenols and polyphenols (e.g., melanin from tyrosine).
– ORIGIN late 19th cent.: from TYROSINE + -ASE.

ty·ro·sine /'tīrə,sēn/ ▶ **n.** Biochemistry a hydrophilic amino acid that is a constituent of most proteins and is important in the synthesis of some hormones. ● Chem. formula: $C_6H_4(OH)CH_2CH(NH_2)COOH$.
– ORIGIN mid 19th cent.: formed irregularly from Greek *turos* 'cheese' + -INE[4].

Tyr·rhe·ni·an /tə'rēnēən/ ▶ **adj.** of, relating to, or denoting the Tyrrhenian Sea or the surrounding region. ■ archaic Etruscan.
▶ **n.** archaic an Etruscan.

Tyr·rhe·ni·an Sea a part of the Mediterranean Sea between mainland Italy and the islands of Sicily and Sardinia.

Ty·son /'tīsən/, Mike (1966–), US heavyweight boxing champion during the 1980s and 1990s; full name *Michael Gerald Tyson.*

Tyu·men /tyōō'men/ a city in west Siberian Russia, in the eastern foothills of the Ural Mountains; pop. 560,000 (est. 2008). Founded in 1586, it is thought to be one of the oldest cities in Siberia.

tyu·ya·mu·nite /,tyōōyə'mōōnīt/ ▶ **n.** a yellowish earthy mineral that is an ore of uranium. It consists of a hydrated vanadate of calcium and uranium.
– ORIGIN early 20th cent.: from *Tyuya Muyun*, the name of a Kyrgyz village, + -ITE[1].

tzar ▶ **n.** variant spelling of CZAR.

Tza·ra /'tsärə/, Tristan (1896–1963), French poet, born in Romania; born *Samuel Rosenstock*. One of the founders of the Dada movement in 1916, he wrote its manifestos. His poetry, with its continuous flow of unconnected images, helped form the basis for surrealism.

tza·ri·na ▶ **n.** variant spelling of CZARINA.

tza·tzi·ki /tsä'tsēkē/ (also **tzatziki sauce**) ▶ **n.** a sauce of Greek origin, made from yogurt, garlic, and cucumbers.
– ORIGIN mid 20th cent.: modern Greek, from Turkish *cacık*.

tze·da·kah /tsi'dôkə, tsədä'kä/ ▶ **n.** (among the Jews) charitable giving, typically seen as a moral obligation.
– ORIGIN from Hebrew *ṣĕḏāqāh* 'righteousness.'

Tzel·tal /(t)sel'täl/ ▶ **n.** (pl. **same** or **Tzeltals**) **1** a member of an American Indian people inhabiting parts of southern Mexico.
2 the Mayan language of this people.
▶ **adj.** of or relating to this people or their language.
– ORIGIN Spanish name of one of the three regions of the Mexican state of Chiapas, of uncertain origin.

tzi·gane /(t)si'gän/ ▶ **n.** (pl. **same** or **tziganes**) a Hungarian Gypsy.
– ORIGIN mid 18th cent.: from French, from Hungarian *c(z)igány*.

tzim·mes (also **tzimmis**) ▶ **n.** variant spelling of TSIMMES.

T-zone ▶ **n.** the central part of a person's face, including the forehead, nose, and chin, esp. as having oilier skin than the rest of the face.
– ORIGIN *T* designating the shape of the area defined.

Tzo·tzil /'(t)sōt'sēl/ ▶ **n.** (pl. **same** or **Tzotzils**) **1** a member of an American Indian people of southern Mexico.
2 the Mayan language of this people.
▶ **adj.** of or relating to this people or their language.
– ORIGIN the name in Tzotzil.

Tzu-po variant of ZIBO.

Uu

U¹ /yo͞o/ (also **u**) ▸ **n.** (pl. **Us** or **U's**) **1** the twenty-first letter of the alphabet. ■ denoting the next after T in a set of items, categories, etc.
2 (**U**) a shape like that of a capital U, esp. a cross section: [in combination] *U-shaped glaciated valleys.*

U² ▸ **symbol** the chemical element uranium.

U³ ▸ **adj.** informal, chiefly Brit. (of language or social behavior) characteristic of or appropriate to the upper social classes: *U manners.*
– ORIGIN abbreviation of **upper class**; coined in 1954 by Alan S. C. Ross, professor of linguistics, the term was popularized by its use in Nancy Mitford's *Noblesse Oblige* (1956).

U⁴ /o͞o/ ▸ **n.** a Burmese title of respect before a man's name, equivalent to Mr: *U Thien San.*

u ▸ **abbr.** Physics denoting quantum states or wave functions that change sign on inversion through the origin. The opposite of **g**. [from German *ungerade* 'odd.'] ▸ **symbol** [in combination] (in units of measurement) micro- (10^{-6}): *direct readout of concentration in ug or mg/l.*
– ORIGIN substituted for **mu**.

UAE ▸ **abbr.** United Arab Emirates.

U·ban·ghi Sha·ri /(y)o͞o'banGgē 'sHärē, -'bäNG-/ former name (until 1958) of **Central African Republic**.

U·ban·gi Riv·er /(y)o͞o'baNGgē/ a river that flows for 660 miles (1,060 km) from the border of the Central African Republic and the Democratic Republic of the Congo (formerly Zaire), along the border of the latter with Congo, to join the Congo River, of which it is the chief northern tributary.

uber- /'o͞obər/ (also **über-** /'Ybər/) ▸ **comb. form** denoting an outstanding or supreme example of a particular kind of person or thing: *an uberbabe | the uberregulator.*
– ORIGIN German *über* 'over,' after **Übermensch**.

Ü·ber·mensch /'o͞obər,mencH, 'Ybər-/ ▸ **n.** (pl. **Übermenschen** /-,mencHən/) the ideal superior man of the future who could rise above conventional Christian morality to create and impose his own values, originally described by Nietzsche in *Thus Spake Zarathustra* (1883–85). Also called **superman, overman**.
– ORIGIN German, literally 'superhuman person.'

-ubility ▸ **suffix** forming nouns from or corresponding to adjectives ending in *-uble* (such as *solubility* from *soluble*).

u·bi·qui·none /yo͞o'bikwə,nōn/ ▸ **n.** Biochemistry any of a class of compounds that occur in all living cells and that act as electron-transfer agents in cell respiration. They are substituted quinones.
– ORIGIN 1950s: blend of **ubiquitous** and **quinone**.

u·bi·qui·tin /yo͞o'bikwitin/ ▸ **n.** Biochemistry a compound found in living cells that plays a role in the degradation of defective and superfluous proteins. It is a single-chain polypeptide.
– ORIGIN 1970s: from **ubiquitous** + **-in¹**.

u·biq·ui·tous /yo͞o'bikwətəs/ ▸ **adj.** present, appearing, or found everywhere: *his ubiquitous influence was felt by all the family | cowboy hats are ubiquitous among the male singers.*
– DERIVATIVES **u·biq·ui·tous·ly adv.**, **u·biq·ui·tous·ness n.**, **u·biq·ui·ty** /-wətē/ **n.**
– ORIGIN mid 19th cent.: from modern Latin *ubiquitas* (from Latin *ubique* 'everywhere,' from *ubi* 'where') + **-ous**.

-uble ▸ **suffix** (forming adjectives) able to: *voluble.* ■ able to be: *soluble.* Compare with **-able**.
– ORIGIN from French, from Latin *-ubilis*.

-ubly ▸ **suffix** forming adverbs corresponding to adjectives ending in *-uble* (such as *volubly* corresponding to *voluble*).

U-boat ▸ **n.** a German submarine used in World War I or World War II.
– ORIGIN from German *U-Boot*, abbreviation of *Unterseeboot* 'undersea boat.'

u·bun·tu /o͞o'bo͝ontōo/ ▸ **n.** a quality that includes the essential human virtues; compassion and humanity.
– ORIGIN Xhosa and Zulu.

u.c. ▸ **abbr.** uppercase.

Uca·ya·li River /,o͞okə'yälē/ a river that flows for 1,000 miles (1,600 km) through central and northern Peru to join the Marañón River to form the Amazon River.

UCC ▸ **abbr.** Uniform Commercial Code.

ud·der /'ədər/ ▸ **n.** the mammary gland of female cattle, sheep, goats, horses, and related ungulates, a baglike organ with two or more teats hanging near the hind legs.
– DERIVATIVES **ud·dered adj.** [in combination].
– ORIGIN Old English *ūder*; related to Dutch *uier* and German *Euter*.

Ud·mur·ti·a /o͝od'mo͝orsHə/ an autonomous republic in central Russia; pop. 1,527,800 (est. 2009); capital, Izhevsk. Also called **Udmurt Republic**.

u·don /'o͞o,dän/ ▸ **n.** (in Japanese cooking) wheat pasta made in thick strips.
– ORIGIN Japanese.

UEFA /yo͞o'(w)efə/ ▸ **abbr.** Union of European Football Associations, the governing body of soccer in Europe.

U·fa /o͞o'fä/ the capital of Bashkiria, in the Ural Mountains, in southwestern Russia; pop. 1,021,500 (est. 2008).

UFO ▸ **n.** (pl. **UFOs**) a mysterious object seen in the sky for which, it is claimed, no orthodox scientific explanation can be found.
– ORIGIN 1950s: acronym from *unidentified flying object.*

u·fol·o·gy /yo͞o'fäləjē/ ▸ **n.** the study of UFOs.
– DERIVATIVES **u·fo·log·i·cal** /,yo͞ofə'läjikəl/ **adj.**, **u·fol·o·gist** /-jist/ **n.**

U·gan·da /yo͞o'gandə/ a landlocked country in East Africa; pop. 32,369,600 (est. 2009); capital, Kampala; languages, English (official), Swahili, and other languages.

> Ethnically and culturally diverse, Uganda became a British protectorate in 1894 and an independent Commonwealth of Nations state in 1962. The country was ruled 1971–79 by dictator Idi Amin, who came to power after an army coup. His overthrow, with Tanzanian military support, was followed by several years of conflict, partly resolved in 1986 by the formation of a government under President Yoweri Museveni.

– DERIVATIVES **U·gan·dan adj. & n.**

U·ga·rit /'(y)o͞ogərit, (y)o͞o'gärit/ an ancient port and Bronze Age trading city in northern Syria. Its people spoke a Semitic language written in a distinctive cuneiform alphabet.
– DERIVATIVES **U·ga·rit·ic** /(y)o͞ogə'ritik/ **adj. & n.**

Ugg boot /'əg ,bo͞ot/ (also **Ugh boot**) ▸ **n.** trademark a type of soft sheepskin boot originating in Australia.
– ORIGIN 1960s: probably named after *Ugh*, a series of cartoon characters.

ugh /əg, əKH, o͝oKH/ ▸ **exclam.** informal used to express disgust or horror: *Ugh! What's this disgusting object?*
– ORIGIN mid 18th cent.: imitative.

Ug·li fruit /'əglē/ ▸ **n.** (pl. **same**) trademark a mottled green and yellow citrus fruit that is a hybrid of grapefruit and tangerine. ● This fruit is obtained from the tree *Citrus* × tangelo, family Rutaceae.
– ORIGIN 1930s: *ugli*, alteration of **ugly**.

ug·ly /'əglē/ ▸ **adj.** (**uglier, ugliest**) unpleasant or repulsive, esp. in appearance: *she thought she was ugly and fat | the ugly sound of a fire alarm* | (as noun **the ugly**) *he instinctively shrinks from the ugly.* ■ (of a situation or mood) involving or likely to involve violence or other unpleasantness: *the mood in the room turned ugly.* ■ unpleasantly suggestive; causing disquiet: *ugly rumors persisted that there had been a cover-up.* ■ morally repugnant: *racism and its most ugly manifestations, racial attacks and harassment.*
– DERIVATIVES **ug·li·fi·ca·tion** /,əgləfi'kāsHən/ **n.**, **ug·li·fy** /'əglə,fī/ **v.** (**uglifies, uglifying, uglified**), **ug·li·ly** /-ləlē/ **adv.**, **ug·li·ness n.**
– ORIGIN Middle English: from Old Norse *uggligr* 'to be dreaded,' from *ugga* 'to dread.'

ug·ly A·mer·i·can ▸ **n.** informal an American who behaves offensively when abroad.

ug·ly duck·ling ▸ **n.** a person, esp. a child, who turns out to be beautiful or talented against all expectations.
– ORIGIN from the title of one of Hans Christian Andersen's fairy tales, in which the "ugly duckling" becomes a swan.

U·gri·an /'(y)o͞ogrēən/ ▸ **adj.** another term for **Ugric**.

U·gric /'(y)o͞ogrik/ ▸ **adj.** of, relating to, or denoting a branch of the Finno-Ugric language family comprising Hungarian and the Ob-Ugric languages.
– ORIGIN from Russian *Ugry* (the name of a people dwelling east of the Urals) + **-ic**.

uh¹ /ə, əN/ ▸ **exclam. 1** used to express hesitation: *"I was just, uh, passing by."*
2 another way of saying **huh**.
– ORIGIN 1960s: imitative.

uh² /ə/ ▸ **adj.** nonstandard spelling of the indefinite article **a**, used to represent black English: *crabs in uh basket.*
▸ **prep.** nonstandard spelling of **of**, used to represent black English: *a house full uh young 'uns.*

UHF ▸ **abbr.** ultrahigh frequency.

uh-huh /ə 'hə, əN 'həN/ ▸ **exclam.** used to express assent or as a noncommittal response to a question or remark: *"Do you understand?" "Uh-huh."*
– ORIGIN 1920s: imitative.

uh·lan /o͞o'län, '(y)o͞olən/ ▸ **n.** historical a cavalryman armed with a lance as a member of various European armies.
– ORIGIN mid 18th cent.: via French and German from Polish (*h*)*ulan*, from Turkish *oğlan* 'youth, servant.'

uh-oh /'ə ,ō/ ▸ **exclam.** used to express alarm, dismay, or realization of a difficulty: *"Uh-oh! Take cover!"*

uh-uh /'əN ,əN, 'əN 'əN/ ▸ **exclam.** used to express a negative response to a question or remark.
– ORIGIN 1920s: imitative.

Ui·ghur /'wē,go͝or/ (also **Uigur, Uygur**) ▸ **n. 1** a member of a people of northwestern China, particularly the Xinjiang region, and adjoining areas.
2 the Turkic language of this people.
▸ **adj.** of or relating to this people or their language.
– ORIGIN the name in Uighur.

uil·lean pipes /'ilən, 'ilyən/ ▸ **plural n.** Irish bagpipes played resting on the knee using bellows worked by the elbow, and having three extra pipes on which chords can be played.

– ORIGIN early 20th cent.: from Irish *píob uilleann*, literally 'pipe of the elbow.'

U·in·ta Moun·tains /yo͞oʹintə/ a range of the Rocky Mountains in northeastern Utah that rises to 13,528 feet (4,123 m) at Kings Peak.

U·ist /ˈyo͞o-ist/ two islands in the Outer Hebrides, **North Uist** and **South Uist**, that lie to the south of the island of Lewis and Harris.

Uit·land·er /ˈīt,landər, ˈāt-, ˈout-/ ▶ **n.** S. African historical a British immigrant living in the Transvaal who was denied citizenship by the Boers for cultural and economic reasons.
– ORIGIN Afrikaans, from Dutch *uit* 'out' + *land* 'land.'

U·ji·ya·ma·da /ˈo͞ojēyäˈmädə/ former name (until 1956) of **Ise**.

Uj·jain /ˈo͞o,jīn/ a city in west central India, in Madhya Pradesh; pop. 483,300 (est. 2009). It is one of the seven holy cities of Hinduism.

U·jung Pan·dang /ˈo͞o,jo͞ong ˈpän,däng/ the chief seaport in the southwest of the island of Sulawesi in Indonesia; pop. 1,168,300 (est. 2005). Former name (until 1973) **Makassar**.

UK ▶ **abbr.** United Kingdom.

u·kase /yo͞oˈkās, -ˈkāz/ ▶ **n.** an edict of the Russian government: *Tsar Alexander I issued his famous ukase unilaterally decreeing the North Pacific Coast Russian territory.* ■ an arbitrary command: *defying the publisher in the very building from which he had issued his ukase.*
– ORIGIN from Russian *ukaz* 'ordinance, edict,' from *ukazat'* 'to show, decree.'

uke /yo͞ok/ ▶ **n.** informal short for **ukulele**.

u·ke·le·le ▶ **n.** variant spelling of **ukulele**.

u·ki·yo-e /,o͞okē(y)ō ˈā, ˈyo͞o-/ ▶ **n.** a school of Japanese art depicting subjects from everyday life, dominant in the 17th–19th centuries.
– ORIGIN Japanese, from *ukiyo* 'fleeting world' + *e* 'picture.'

U·kraine /yo͞oˈkrān, ˈyo͞o,krān/ a country in eastern Europe, north of the Black Sea; pop. 45,700,400 (est. 2009); capital, Kiev; languages, Ukrainian and Russian.

> Large portion of Ukraine's current territory formed part of the medieval state of Kievan Rus'. After the breakup of Kievan Rus', instigated by the Mongol invasion, the country was divided for several centuries between the kingdom of Poland, the grand duchy of Lithuania, and the Ottoman Empire, and by the 18th century it had been largely integrated into the Russian Empire and the Austro-Hungarian Empire. Briefly independent following the 1917 revolution, Ukraine became one of the original constituent republics (and the third largest) of the USSR. In 1991, on the dissolution of the Soviet Union, Ukraine became an independent republic.

– ORIGIN from obsolete Russian *ukraina* 'frontier regions,' from *u* 'at' + *kraĭ* 'edge.'

U·krain·i·an /yo͞oˈkrānēən/ ▶ **n. 1** a native or inhabitant of Ukraine, or a person of Ukrainian descent.
2 the East Slavic language of Ukraine.
▶ **adj.** of or relating to Ukraine, its people, or their language.

u·ku·le·le /,yo͞okəˈlālē/ (also **ukelele**) ▶ **n.** a small four-stringed guitar of Hawaiian origin.
– ORIGIN late 19th cent.: from Hawaiian, literally 'jumping flea.'

U·laan·baa·tar /ˈo͞oˈlän'bä,tär/ (also **Ulan Bator** /ˈo͞oˈlän ,bäˈtôr/) a city in northeastern Mongolia, the capital of the country; pop. 922,100 (est. 2009). Former name (until 1924) **Urga**.

u·la·ma ▶ **n.** variant spelling of **ulema**.

U·lan-U·de /o͞o,län o͞oˈdā/ an industrial city in southern Siberia, in southern Russia, capital of the republic of Buryatia; pop. 340,800 (est. 2008). Former name (until 1934) **Verkhneudinsk**.

-ular ▶ **suffix** forming adjectives, sometimes corresponding to nouns ending in *-ule* (such as *pustular* corresponding to *pustule*), but often without diminutive force (as in *angular*, *granular*).
– ORIGIN from Latin *-ularis*.

-ularity ▶ **suffix** forming nouns corresponding to adjectives ending in *-ular* (such as *modularity* corresponding to *modular*).
– ORIGIN see **-ular**, **-ity**.

ul·cer /ˈəlsər/ ▶ **n.** an open sore on an external or internal surface of the body, caused by a break in the skin or mucous membrane that fails to heal. ■ a moral blemish or corrupting influence: *he's a con man with an incurable ulcer called gambling.*
– DERIVATIVES **ul·cered adj.**
– ORIGIN late Middle English: from Latin *ulcus, ulcer-*.

ul·cer·ate /ˈəlsə,rāt/ ▶ **v.** [no obj.] develop into or become affected by an ulcer.
– DERIVATIVES **ul·cer·a·tion** /,əlsəˈrāshən/ **n.**, **ul·cer·a·tive** /-rətiv, -,rātiv/ **adj.**
– ORIGIN late Middle English: from Latin *ulcerat-* 'made ulcerous,' from the verb *ulcerare*.

ul·cer·ous /ˈəls(ə)rəs/ ▶ **adj.** having or constituting an ulcer: *the parasites created ulcerous sores.*

-ule ▶ **suffix** forming diminutive nouns such as *capsule* and *pustule*.
– ORIGIN from Latin *-ulus, -ula, -ulum*.

u·le·ma /ˈo͞olə,mä/ (also **ulama**) ▶ **n.** [treated as sing. or pl.] a body of Muslim scholars recognized as having specialist knowledge of Islamic sacred law and theology. ■ a member of such a body.
– ORIGIN from Arabic *'ulamā'*, plural of *'ālim* 'learned,' from *'alima* 'know.'

-ulence ▶ **suffix** forming nouns corresponding to adjectives ending in *-ulent* (such as *virulence* corresponding to *virulent*).
– ORIGIN see **-ulent**.

-ulent ▶ **suffix** (forming adjectives) abounding in; full of: *fraudulent | purulent | virulent*. Compare with **-lent**.
– ORIGIN from Latin *-ulentus*.

u·lex·ite /ˈyo͞olək,sīt/ ▶ **n.** a mineral occurring on alkali flats as rounded masses of small white crystals. It is a hydrated borate of sodium and calcium.
– ORIGIN mid 19th cent.: from George L. *Ulex* (died 1883), German chemist, + **-ite**[1].

Ul·has·na·gar /,o͞olhəsˈnəgər, -ˈnägər/ a city in western India, in the state of Maharashtra; pop. 563,800 (est. 2009).

U·li·thi /o͞oˈlēthē/ an atoll in the western Caroline Islands, in the Federated States of Micronesia, site of a US victory over the Japanese in 1944.

ul·lage /ˈəlij/ ▶ **n.** the amount by which a container falls short of being full. ■ loss of liquid by evaporation or leakage.
– ORIGIN late Middle English: from Anglo-Norman French *ulliage*, from Old French *euillier* 'fill up,' based on Latin *oculus* 'eye' (with reference to a container's bunghole).

ul·lage rock·et ▶ **n.** an auxiliary rocket engine used in weightless conditions to provide sufficient acceleration to maintain the flow of liquid propellant from the fuel tank.

Ulm /o͞olm/ an industrial city on the Danube River in Baden-Württemberg, in southern Germany; pop. 120,900 (est. 2006).

ul·na /ˈəlnə/ ▶ **n.** (pl. **ulnae** /-,nē, -,nī/ or **ulnas**) the thinner and longer of the two bones in the human forearm, on the side opposite to the thumb. Compare with **radius** (sense 2). ■ the corresponding bone in a quadruped's foreleg or a bird's wing.
– DERIVATIVES **ul·nar adj.**
– ORIGIN late Middle English (denoting the humerus): from Latin; related to **ell**[1].

U-lock ▶ **n.** a mechanism used to secure a bicycle when parked, consisting of a U-shaped bar and crosspiece of hardened steel.

-ulous ▶ **suffix** forming adjectives such as *incredulous*, *garrulous*.
– ORIGIN from Latin *-ulosus*, *-ulus*.

Ul·san /ˈo͞olˈsän/ an industrial port on the southern coast of South Korea; pop. 1,126,900 (est. 2008).

Ul·ster /ˈəlstər/ a former province of Ireland, in the north of the island. The nine counties of Ulster are now divided between Northern Ireland (Antrim, Down, Armagh, Londonderry, Tyrone, and Fermanagh) and the Republic of Ireland (Cavan, Donegal, and Monaghan). ■ (in general use) Northern Ireland.
– DERIVATIVES **Ul·ster·man** /-mən/ **n.** (pl. **Ulstermen**), **Ul·ster·wom·an** /-,wo͝omən/ **n.** (pl. **Ulsterwomen**).

ul·ster /ˈəlstər/ ▶ **n.** a man's long, loose overcoat of rough cloth, typically with a belt at the back.
– ORIGIN late 19th cent.: from **Ulster**, where it was originally sold.

Ul·ster Coun·ty /ˈəlstər/ a county in southeastern New York, west of the Hudson River, the site of Catskill resorts; pop. 181,670 (est. 2008).

ult. ▶ **abbr.** ■ ultimate. ■ ultimo.

ul·te·ri·or /,əlˈti(ə)rēər/ ▶ **adj.** existing beyond what is obvious or admitted; intentionally hidden: *could there be an ulterior motive behind his request?* ■ beyond what is immediate or present; coming in the future: *ulterior pay promised to the mariners.*
– ORIGIN mid 17th cent.: from Latin, literally 'further, more distant.'

ul·ti·ma·ta /,əltəˈmātə, -ˈmätə/ plural form of **ultimatum**.

ul·ti·mate /ˈəltəmit/ ▶ **adj.** being or happening at the end of a process; final: *their ultimate aim was to force his resignation.* ■ being the best or most extreme example of its kind: *the ultimate accolade.* ■ basic or fundamental: *the ultimate constituents of anything that exists are atoms.* ■ Physics denoting the maximum possible strength or resistance beyond which an object breaks.
▶ **n. 1** (**the ultimate**) the best achievable or imaginable of its kind: *the ultimate in decorative luxury.*
2 a final or fundamental fact or principle.
– DERIVATIVES **ul·ti·ma·cy** /-məsē/ **n.** (pl. **ultimacies**).
– ORIGIN mid 17th cent.: from late Latin *ultimatus*, past participle of *ultimare* 'come to an end.'

ul·ti·mate·ly /ˈəltəmitlē/ ▶ **adv.** finally; in the end: *the largest firms may ultimately become unstoppable.* ■ at the most basic level: *ultimately he has only himself to blame.*

ul·ti·ma Thu·le /ˈəltəmə ˈtho͞olē, ˈtho͞ol/ ▶ **n.** a distant unknown region; the extreme limit of travel and discovery.
– ORIGIN Latin, literally 'furthest Thule' (see **Thule**).

ul·ti·ma·tum /,əltəˈmātəm, -ˈmät-/ ▶ **n.** (pl. **ultimatums** or **ultimata** /-ˈmātə, -ˈmätə/) a final demand or statement of terms, the rejection of which will result in retaliation or a breakdown in relations: *their employers issued an ultimatum demanding an immediate return to work | a "Marry me or else" ultimatum.*
– ORIGIN mid 18th cent.: from Latin, neuter past participle of *ultimare* 'come to an end.'

ul·ti·mo /ˈəltə,mō/ (abbr.: **ult.** or **ulto**) ▶ **adj.** [postpositive] dated of last month: *the 3rd ultimo.* Compare with **instant**, **proximo**.
– ORIGIN from Latin *ultimo mense* 'in the last month.'

ul·ti·mo·bran·chi·al /,əltəmōˈbrangkēəl/ ▶ **adj.** Zoology relating to or denoting a gland in the neck that in many lower vertebrates regulates the calcium level in the body.

ul·ti·mo·gen·i·ture /,əltəmōˈjenichər, -,cho͝or/ ▶ **n.** Law a principle of inheritance in which the right of succession belongs to the youngest son. Compare with **primogeniture**.

ul·ti·sol /ˈəltə,säl, -,sôl/ ▶ **n.** Soil Science a highly weathered leached red or reddish-yellow acid soil with a clay-rich B horizon (subsoil), occurring in warm, humid climates.
– ORIGIN 1960s: from **ultimate** + Latin *solum* 'soil.'

ul·tra /ˈəltrə/ informal ▶ **n.** an extremist.
▶ **adv.** [as submodifier] very; extremely: *the play was not just boring, it was ultra boring.*
– ORIGIN early 19th cent.: an independent usage of **ultra-**, originally as an abbreviation of French *ultra-royaliste*.

ultra- ▶ **prefix 1** beyond; on the other side of: *ultramontane*. Often contrasted with **cis-**.
2 extreme; to an extreme degree: *ultramicroscopic | ultraradical.*
– ORIGIN from Latin *ultra* 'beyond.'

ul·tra·ba·sic /,əltrəˈbāsik/ ▶ **adj.** Geology relating to or denoting igneous rocks having a silica content less than 45 percent by weight, most of which are also ultramafic. Compare with **ultramafic**.

ul·tra·cen·tri·fuge /,əltrəˈsentrə,fyo͞oj/ ▶ **n.** a very fast centrifuge used to precipitate large biological molecules from solution or separate them by their different rates of sedimentation.
▶ **v.** [with obj.] subject to the action of an ultracentrifuge.
– DERIVATIVES **ul·tra·cen·tri·fug·al adj.**, **ul·tra·cen·tri·fu·ga·tion** /-,sentrəfyo͞oˈgāshən, -sen,trif(y)ə-/ **n.**

ul·tra·con·serv·a·tive /,əltrəkənˈsərvətiv/ ▶ **adj.** extremely conservative in politics or in the observance of religion: *an effort by an ultraconservative faction to limit believers' freedom to follow their consciences.*
▶ **n.** a person who is extremely conservative in politics or religion: *the literature of the well-organized ultraconservatives is more plentiful.*
– DERIVATIVES **ul·tra·con·serv·a·tism** /-və,tizəm/ **n.**

ul·tra·di·an /əlˈtrādēən/ ▶ **adj.** Physiology (of a rhythm or cycle) having a period of recurrence shorter than a day but longer than an hour. Compare with **infradian**.
– ORIGIN 1960s: from **ultra-** 'beyond' (being of greater frequency than circadian) + **-ian**.

ul·tra·fil·tra·tion /,əltrəfilˈtrāshən/ ▶ **n.** filtration using a medium fine enough to retain colloidal particles, viruses, or large molecules.
– DERIVATIVES **ul·tra·fil·ter** /ˈəltrə,filtər/ **n. & v.**

ul·tra·high fre·quen·cy /ˈəltrə,hī, ,əltrəˈhī/ (abbr.: **UHF**) ▶ **n.** a radio frequency in the range 300 to 3,000 MHz.

PRONUNCIATION KEY ə *ago, up*; ər *over, fur*; a *hat*; ā *ate*; ä *car*; e *let*; ē *see*; i *fit*; ī *by*; NG *sing*; ō *go*; ô *law, for*; oi *toy*; o͝o *good*; o͞o *goo*; ou *out*; TH *thin*; T͟H *then*; ZH *vision*

U

ul·tra·ism /ˈəltrəˌizəm/ ▶ **n.** the holding of extreme opinions.
– DERIVATIVES **ul·tra·ist n.**

ul·tra·light ▶ **adj.** /ˌəltrəˈlīt, ˈəltrəˌlīt/ extremely lightweight.
▶ **n.** /ˈəltrəˌlīt/ a small, light, single-seater aircraft.

ul·tra·maf·ic /ˌəltrəˈmafik/ ▶ **adj.** Geology relating to or denoting igneous rocks composed chiefly of mafic minerals. Compare with ULTRABASIC.

ul·tra·ma·rine /ˌəltrəməˈrēn/ ▶ **n.** a brilliant deep blue pigment originally obtained from lapis lazuli. ■ an imitation of such a pigment, made from powdered fired clay, sodium carbonate, sulfur, and resin. ■ a brilliant deep blue color.
– ORIGIN late 16th cent.: from medieval Latin *ultramarinus* 'beyond the sea' with reference to the foreign origin of lapis lazuli.

ul·tra·mi·cro·scope /ˌəltrəˈmīkrəˌskōp/ ▶ **n.** an optical microscope used to detect particles smaller than the wavelength of light by illuminating them at an angle and observing the light scattered by the Tyndall effect against a dark background.

ul·tra·mi·cro·scop·ic /ˌəltrəˌmīkrəˈskäpik/ ▶ **adj.** too small to be seen by an ordinary optical microscope. ■ of or relating to an ultramicroscope.

ul·tra·mod·ern /ˌəltrəˈmädərn/ ▶ **adj.** incorporating ideas, styles, or techniques only recently developed or available: *a wave of ultramodern architecture.*

ul·tra·mon·tane /ˌəltrəˌmänˈtān, -ˈmänˌtān/ ▶ **adj.** **1** advocating supreme papal authority in matters of faith and discipline. Compare with **GALLICAN**. **2** situated on the other side of the Alps from the point of view of the speaker.
▶ **n.** a person advocating supreme papal authority.
– DERIVATIVES **ul·tra·mon·ta·nism** /-ˈmäntəˌnizəm/ **n.**
– ORIGIN late 16th cent. (denoting a representative of the Roman Catholic Church north of the Alps): from medieval Latin *ultramontanus*, from Latin *ultra* 'beyond' + *mons, mont-* 'mountain.'

ul·tra·mun·dane /ˌəltrəˈmənˌdān, -ˌmənˈdān/ ▶ **adj.** literary existing outside the known world, the solar system, or the universe.
– ORIGIN mid 17th cent.: from late Latin *ultramundanus*, from *ultra* 'beyond' + *mundanus* (from *mundus* 'world').

ul·tra·nat·ion·al·ism /ˌəltrəˈnasHənəˌlizəm/ ▶ **n.** extreme nationalism that promotes the interest of one state or people above all others: *the Yugoslav president is fanning the flames of ultranationalism.*
– DERIVATIVES **ul·tra·nat·ion·al·ist n. & adj., ul·tra·nat·ion·al·ist·ic** /-ˌnasHənəˈlistik/ **adj.**

ul·tra·por·ta·ble /ˌəltrəˈpôrtəbl/ ▶ **n.** a type of laptop computer that is very slim and lightweight.

ul·tra·sau·rus /ˈəltrəˌsôrəs, ˌəltrəˈsôrəs/ ▶ **n.** a late Jurassic dinosaur related to the brachiosaurus, known from only a few bones but probably the tallest animal ever, and possibly the heaviest at up to 130 tons. ● Genus *Ultrasaurus*, infraorder Sauropoda, order Saurischia.
– ORIGIN modern Latin, from Latin *ultra* 'beyond' + Greek *sauros* 'lizard.'

ul·tra·short /ˌəltrəˈsHôrt/ ▶ **adj.** (of radio waves) having a wavelength significantly shorter than that of the usual shortwaves, in particular shorter than 10 meters (i.e., of a VHF frequency above 30 MHz).

ul·tra·son·ic /ˌəltrəˈsänik/ ▶ **adj.** of or involving sound waves with a frequency above the upper limit of human hearing.
– DERIVATIVES **ul·tra·son·i·cal·ly** /-ik(ə)lē/ **adv.**

ul·tra·son·ics /ˌəltrəˈsäniks/ ▶ **plural n.** [treated as sing.] the science and application of ultrasonic waves. ■ [treated as sing. or pl.] ultrasonic waves; ultrasound.

ul·tra·so·nog·ra·phy /ˌəltrəsəˈnägrəfē/ ▶ **n.** Medicine a technique using echoes of ultrasound pulses to delineate objects or areas of different density in the body.
– DERIVATIVES **ul·tra·son·o·graph·ic** /ˌəltrəˌsänəˈgrafik, -ˌsōnə-/ **adj.**

ul·tra·sound /ˈəltrəˌsound/ ▶ **n.** sound or other vibrations having an ultrasonic frequency, particularly as used in medical imaging. ■ an ultrasound scan, esp. one of a pregnant woman to examine the fetus.

ul·tra·struc·ture /ˈəltrəˌstrəkCHər/ ▶ **n.** Biology a fine structure, esp. within a cell, that can be seen only with the high magnification obtainable with an electron microscope.
– DERIVATIVES **ul·tra·struc·tur·al** /-CHərəl/ **adj.**

ul·tra·vi·o·let /ˌəltrəˈvī(ə)lət/ Physics ▶ **adj.** (of electromagnetic radiation) having a wavelength shorter than that of the violet end of the visible spectrum but longer than that of X-rays. ■ (of equipment or techniques) using or concerned with this radiation: *an ultraviolet telescope.*
▶ **n.** the ultraviolet part of the spectrum; ultraviolet radiation.

> Ultraviolet radiation spans wavelengths from about 10 nm to 400 nm and is an important component of sunlight although the ozone layer prevents much of it from reaching the earth's surface. While ultraviolet is necessary for the production of vitamin D_2 in the skin, excessive exposure can be harmful, causing skin cancer and genetic mutation.

ul·tra·vi·o·let lamp ▶ **n.** a lamp with a bulb that produces ultraviolet light.

ul·tra vi·res /ˌəltrə ˈvīrēz/ ▶ **adj. & adv.** Law beyond one's legal power or authority: [as adj.] *jurisdictional errors render the decision ultra vires.*
– ORIGIN Latin, literally 'beyond the powers.'

u·lu /ˈo͞oˌlo͞o/ ▶ **n.** (pl. **ulus**) a short-handled knife with a broad crescent-shaped blade, used by Eskimo women.
– ORIGIN Inuit.

ul·u·late /ˈəlyəˌlāt, ˈyo͞ol-/ ▶ **v.** [no obj.] howl or wail as an expression of strong emotion, typically grief: *women were ululating as the body was laid out.*
– DERIVATIVES **ul·u·lant** /-lənt/ **adj., ul·u·la·tion** /ˌəlyəˈlāsHən, ˌyo͞ol-/ **n.**
– ORIGIN early 17th cent.: from Latin *ululat-* 'howled, shrieked,' from the verb *ululare*, of imitative origin.

Ul·u·ru /ˌo͞oləˈro͞o/ Aboriginal name for **AYERS ROCK**.

Ul·ya·nov /o͞olˈyänəf/, Vladimir Ilich, see **LENIN**.

Ul·ya·novsk /o͞olˈyänəfsk, -ˌnôfsk/ former name (1924–92) of **SIMBIRSK**.

U·lys·ses /yo͞oˈlisēz/ Roman Mythology Roman name for **ODYSSEUS**.

um /əm/ ▶ **exclam.** expressing hesitation or a pause in speech: *anyway, um, where was I?*
– ORIGIN natural utterance: first recorded in English in the early 17th cent.

-um ▶ **suffix** variant spelling of -IUM (sense 1).

u·ma·mi /o͞oˈmämē/ ▶ **n.** a category of taste in food (besides sweet, sour, salt, and bitter), corresponding to the flavor of glutamates, esp. monosodium glutamate.
– ORIGIN Japanese, literally 'deliciousness.'

U·may·yad /o͞oˈmī(y)əd, -ˌ(y)ad/ (also **Omayyad** /ōˈmī-/) ▶ **n.** a member of a Muslim dynasty that ruled the Islamic world from AD 660 (or 661) to 750 and Moorish Spain from 756 to 1031. The dynasty claimed descent from Umayya, a distant relative of Muhammad.
▶ **adj.** of or relating to this dynasty.

Um·ban·da /o͞omˈbändə/ ▶ **n.** a Brazilian folk religion combining elements of macumba, Roman Catholicism, and South American Indian practices.
– ORIGIN Portuguese.

um·bel /ˈəmbəl/ ▶ **n.** Botany a flower cluster in which stalks of nearly equal length spring from a common center and form a flat or curved surface, characteristic of the parsley family.
– DERIVATIVES **um·bel·late** /ˈəmbəlit, -ˌlāt, ˌəmˈbelit/ **adj.**
– ORIGIN late 16th cent.: from obsolete French *umbelle* or Latin *umbella* 'sunshade,' diminutive of *umbra* (see UMBRA).

um·bel·lif·er /ˌəmˈbeləfər/ ▶ **n.** Botany a plant of the parsley family. ● Family Umbelliferae: numerous genera and species.
– DERIVATIVES **um·bel·lif·er·ous** /-bəˈlif(ə)rəs/ **adj.**
– ORIGIN early 18th cent.: from obsolete French *umbellifère*, from Latin *umbella* 'parasol' + *-fer* 'bearing.'

um·ber /ˈəmbər/ ▶ **n. 1** a natural pigment resembling but darker than ocher, normally dark yellowish-brown in color (**raw umber**) or dark brown when roasted (**burnt umber**). ■ the color of this pigment. **2** a brownish-gray moth with coloring that resembles tree bark. ● Several species in the family Geometridae.
– ORIGIN mid 16th cent.: from French *(terre d')ombre* or Italian *(terra di) ombra*, literally '(earth of) shadow,' from Latin *umbra* 'shadow' or *Umbra* (feminine) 'Umbrian.'

um·bil·i·cal /ˌəmˈbilikəl/ ▶ **adj.** relating to or affecting the navel or umbilical cord: *the umbilical artery.* ■ extremely close; inseparable: *their umbilical attachment to the state.* ■ (of a pipe, cable, etc.) connecting someone or something to a source of essential supplies: *our standard dive gear, with 300-foot umbilical hoses.*
▶ **n.** short for UMBILICAL CORD.
– DERIVATIVES **um·bil·i·cal·ly** /-ik(ə)lē/ **adv.**
– ORIGIN mid 16th cent.: from French *ombilical*, or based on Latin *umbilicus* (see UMBILICUS).

um·bil·i·cal cord ▶ **n.** a flexible cordlike structure containing blood vessels and attaching a human or other mammalian fetus to the placenta during gestation. ■ a flexible cable, pipe, or other line carrying essential services or supplies.

um·bil·i·cate /ˌəmˈbilikit, -ˌkāt/ ▶ **adj.** Botany & Zoology (esp. of the cap of a fungus) having a central depression. ■ (of a shell) having an umbilicus.

um·bil·i·co·plas·ty /ˌəmˈbilikōˌplastē/ ▶ **n.** (pl. **umbilicoplasties**) plastic surgery performed on the navel, usu. for cosmetic purposes.

um·bil·i·cus /ˌəmˈbilikəs/ ▶ **n.** (pl. **umbilici** /-ˌkī, -ˌsī, -ˌkē/ or **umbilicuses**) Anatomy the navel. ■ Zoology a depression or hole at the center of the shell whorls of some gastropod mollusks and many ammonites. ■ Zoology a hole at each end of the hollow shaft of a feather.
– ORIGIN late 17th cent.: from Latin: related to Greek *omphalos*, also to NAVEL.

um·bles /ˈəmbəlz/ ▶ **plural n.** variant spelling of NUMBLES.

um·bo /ˈəmbō/ ▶ **n.** (pl. **umbones** /ˌəmˈbōnēz/ or **umbos**) **1** historical the central boss of a shield. **2** Biology a rounded knob or protuberance. ■ Zoology the highest point of each valve of a bivalve shell. ■ Botany a central swelling on the cap of a mushroom or toadstool.
– DERIVATIVES **um·bo·nal** /ˈəmbənəl, əmˈbōnəl/ **adj.** (chiefly Zoology), **um·bo·nate** /ˈəmbənit, -ˌnāt/ **adj.** (chiefly Botany).
– ORIGIN early 18th cent.: from Latin, 'shield boss.'

um·bra /ˈəmbrə/ ▶ **n.** (pl. **umbras** or **umbrae** /-ˌbrē, -ˌbrī/) the fully shaded inner region of a shadow cast by an opaque object, esp. the area on the earth or moon experiencing the total phase of an eclipse. Compare with PENUMBRA. ■ Astronomy the dark central part of a sunspot. ■ chiefly literary shadow or darkness.
– DERIVATIVES **um·bral adj.**
– ORIGIN late 16th cent. (denoting a phantom or ghost): from Latin, literally 'shade.'

um·brage /ˈəmbrij/ ▶ **n. 1** offense or annoyance: *she took umbrage at his remarks.* **2** archaic shade or shadow, esp. as cast by trees.
– DERIVATIVES **um·bra·geous** /ˌəmˈbrājəs/ **adj.**
– ORIGIN late Middle English (sense 2): from Old French, from Latin *umbra* 'shadow.' An early sense was 'shadowy outline,' giving rise to 'ground for suspicion,' whence the current notion of 'offense.'

um·brel·la /ˌəmˈbrelə/ ▶ **n. 1** a device consisting of a circular canopy of cloth on a folding metal frame supported by a central rod, used as protection against rain or sometimes sun. **2** a protecting force or influence: *the American nuclear umbrella over the West.* ■ a screen of fighter aircraft or antiaircraft artillery. **3** [usu. as modifier] a thing that includes or contains many different elements or parts: *an umbrella organization.* **4** Zoology the gelatinous disk of a jellyfish, which it contracts and expands to move through the water.
– DERIVATIVES **um·brel·laed adj., um·brel·la·like** /-ˌlīk/ **adj.**
– ORIGIN early 17th cent.: from Italian *ombrella*, diminutive of *ombra* 'shade,' from Latin *umbra* (see UMBRA).

um·brel·la bird (also **umbrellabird**) ▶ **n.** a large tropical American cotinga with black plumage, a radiating crest, and typically long wattles. ● Genus *Cephalopterus*, family Cotingidae: three species.

um·brel·la pine ▶ **n. 1** another term for STONE PINE. **2** a tall Japanese evergreen conifer related to the redwoods, with leaves growing in umbrellalike whorls. ● *Sciadopitys verticillata*, family Taxodiaceae.

um·brel·la plant ▶ **n.** a tropical Old World sedge that has stiff green stems, each terminating in a whorl of arching green leaflike bracts. It is commonly grown as a houseplant. ● *Cyperus alternifolius* (or *involucratus*), family Cyperaceae.

um·brel·la tree ▶ **n.** either of two small trees or shrubs with leaves or leaflets arranged in umbrellalike whorls. ● (also **umbrella magnolia**) a North American magnolia (*Magnolia tripetala*, family Magnoliaceae). ● an Australian plant that is widely grown elsewhere as a houseplant (*Schefflera actinophylla*, family Araliaceae).

Um·bri·a /ˈəmbrēə/ a region in central Italy, in the valley of the Tiber River; capital, Perugia.

Um·bri·an /ˈəmbrēən/ ▶ **adj.** of or relating to Umbria, its people, or their languages.
▶ **n. 1** a native or inhabitant of Umbria, esp. in pre-Roman times. **2** an extinct Italic language of central Italy, related to Oscan and surviving in inscriptions mainly of the 2nd and 1st centuries BC.

Um·bri·el /ˈəmbrēəl/ Astronomy a satellite of Uranus, the thirteenth closest to the planet, discovered in 1851, having a diameter of 739 miles (1,190 km).
– ORIGIN named after a sprite in *The Rape of the Lock* by Alexander Pope.

Um·bun·du /əmˈbo͝onˌdo͞o/ see **MBUNDU**.

u·mi·ak /ˈo͞omēˌak/ ▸ **n.** an Eskimo open boat made with skin stretched over a wooden frame.
– ORIGIN from Inuit *umiaq*.

um·laut /ˈo͞omˌlout/ Linguistics ▸ **n.** a mark (¨) used over a vowel, as in German or Hungarian, to indicate a different vowel quality, usually fronting or rounding. ■ (esp. in Germanic languages) the process by which a back vowel becomes front in the context of another front vowel, resulting, e.g., in the differences between modern German *Mann* and *Männer* or (after loss of the inflection) English *man* and *men*.
▸ **v.** [with obj.] modify (a form or a sound) by using an umlaut.
– ORIGIN mid 19th cent.: from German *Umlaut*, from *um* 'about' + *Laut* 'sound.'

um·ma /ˈo͞omə/ (also **ummah**) ▸ **n.** the whole community of Muslims bound together by ties of religion.
– ORIGIN Arabic, literally 'people, community.'

Umm al-Qai·wain /ˈo͞om älkīˈwīn, al/ one of the seven member states of the United Arab Emirates; pop. 69,900 (est. 2009).

ump /əmp/ ▸ **n. & v.** informal short for **UMPIRE**.
– ORIGIN early 20th cent.: abbreviation.

umph ▸ **n.** variant spelling of **OOMPH**.

um·pire /ˈəmˌpī(ə)r/ ▸ **n.** (in some sports) an official who watches a game or match closely to enforce the rules and arbitrate on matters arising from the play. ■ a person chosen to arbitrate between contending parties.
▸ **v.** [no obj.] act as an umpire. ■ [with obj.] act as umpire in (a game or match).
– DERIVATIVES **um·pir·age** /-ˌpīrij/ **n.**, **um·pire·ship** /-ˌsHip/ **n.**
– ORIGIN late Middle English (originally as *noumpere*) (denoting an arbitrator): from Old French *nonper* 'not equal.' The *n* was lost by wrong division of *a noumpere*; compare with **ADDER**.

ump·teen /ˈəm(p)ˌtēn/ informal ▸ **cardinal number** indefinitely many; a lot of: *you need umpteen pieces of identification to cash a check.*
– DERIVATIVES **ump·teenth** /-ˌtēnTH/ **ordinal number.**
– ORIGIN early 20th cent.: humorous formation based on **-TEEN**.

um·rah /ˈo͞omˌrä/ ▸ **n.** the nonmandatory lesser pilgrimage made by Muslims to Mecca, which may be performed at any time of the year.
– ORIGIN Arabic *'umra*.

Um·ta·li /o͞omˈtälē/ former name (until 1982) of **MUTARE**.

UMTS ▸ **abbr.** Universal Mobile Telephone System.

u·mu /ˈo͞omo͞o/ ▸ **n.** a Maori oven consisting of a hollow in the earth in which food is cooked on heated stones.
– ORIGIN Maori.

Um·welt /ˈo͞omˌvelt/ ▸ **n.** (pl. **Umwelten** /-ˌvelt(ə)n/) (in ethology) the world as it is experienced by a particular organism.
– ORIGIN German, literally 'environment.'

UN ▸ **abbr.** United Nations.

'un /ən/ informal or dialect ▸ **pron.** one: *a good 'un | a wild 'un.*
– ORIGIN patterned after a contraction.

un-¹ ▸ **prefix 1** (added to adjectives, participles, and their derivatives) denoting the absence of a quality or state; not: *unabashed | unacademic | unrepeatable.* ■ the reverse of (usually with an implication of approval or disapproval, or with another special connotation): *unselfish | unprepossessing | unworldly.*
2 (added to nouns) a lack of: *unrest | untruth.*
– ORIGIN Old English, of Germanic origin; from an Indo-European root shared by Latin *in-* and Greek *a-*.

> **USAGE** The prefixes **un-** and **non-** both mean 'lacking' or 'not,' but there is a distinction in terms of perspective. The prefix **un-** tends to be stronger and less neutral than **non-**. Consider, for example, the differences between **unacademic** and **nonacademic**, as in *his language was refreshingly unacademic; a nonacademic life suits him.*

un-² ▸ **prefix** [added to verbs:] **1** denoting the reversal or cancellation of an action or state: *untie | unsettle.*
2 denoting deprivation, separation, or reduction to a lesser state: *unmask | unman.* ■ denoting release: *unburden | unhand.*
– ORIGIN Old English *un-, on-*, of Germanic origin; related to Dutch *ont-* and German *ent-*.

un·a·bashed /ˌənəˈbasHt/ ▸ **adj.** not embarrassed, disconcerted, or ashamed: *he was unabashed by the furor his words provoked.*
– DERIVATIVES **un·a·bash·ed·ly** /-ˈbasHədlē/ **adv.**

un·a·bat·ed /ˌənəˈbātid/ ▸ **adj.** without any reduction in intensity or strength: *the storm was raging unabated.*
– DERIVATIVES **un·a·bat·ed·ly adv.**

un·a·ble /ˌənˈābəl/ ▸ **adj.** [with infinitive] lacking the skill, means, or opportunity to do something: *she was unable to conceal her surprise.*

un·a·bridged /ˌənəˈbrijd/ ▸ **adj.** (of a text) not cut or shortened; complete: *an unabridged edition.*

un·ab·sorbed /ˌənəbˈzôrbd, /-ˈsôrbd/ ▸ **adj.** not taken in or soaked up; not absorbed: *unabsorbed nutrients.*

un·ac·a·dem·ic /ˌənakəˈdemik/ ▸ **adj.** not adopting or characteristic of a scholarly approach or language: *his language was refreshingly unacademic.* ■ (of a person) not suited or drawn to academic study.

un·ac·cent·ed /ˌənˈakˌsentid/ ▸ **adj.** having no accent, stress, or emphasis: *his English is fluent and unaccented.*

un·ac·cept·a·ble /ˌənəkˈseptəbəl/ ▸ **adj.** not satisfactory or allowable: *unacceptable behavior.*
– DERIVATIVES **un·ac·cept·a·bil·i·ty** /-ˌseptəˈbilətē/ **n.**, **un·ac·cept·a·bly** /-blē/ **adv.**

un·ac·com·mo·dat·ing /ˌənəˈkäməˌdātiNG/ ▸ **adj.** not in harmony with the wishes or demands of others; unhelpful.

un·ac·com·pa·nied /ˌənəˈkəmp(ə)nēd/ ▸ **adj.** having no companion or escort: *no unaccompanied children allowed.* ■ (of a piece of music) sung or played without instrumental accompaniment: *an unaccompanied violin elegy.* ■ (of a state, condition, or event) taking place without something specified taking place at the same time: *the political change was unaccompanied by social change.*

un·ac·com·plished /ˌənəˈkämplisHt/ ▸ **adj.**
1 showing little skill.
2 not carried out.

un·ac·count·a·ble /ˌənəˈkountəbəl/ ▸ **adj. 1** unable to be explained: *a strange and unaccountable fact.* ■ (of a person or their behavior) unpredictable and strange.
2 (of a person, organization, or institution) not required or expected to justify actions or decisions; not responsible for results or consequences.
– DERIVATIVES **un·ac·count·a·bil·i·ty** /-ˌkountəˈbilətē/ **n.**, **un·ac·count·a·bly** /-blē/ **adv.**

un·ac·count·ed /ˌənəˈkountid/ ▸ **adj.** (**unaccounted for**) not included in (an account or calculation) through being lost or disregarded: *a substantial amount of money is unaccounted for.*

un·ac·cred·it·ed /ˌənəˈkreditid/ ▸ **adj.** not recognized as having attained an acceptable standard: *a mail-order degree from an unaccredited correspondence school.*

un·ac·cus·tomed /ˌənəˈkəstəmd/ ▸ **adj.** not familiar or usual; out of the ordinary: *they finished their supper with unaccustomed speed.* ■ [predic.] (**unaccustomed to**) not familiar with or used to: *the visitors were unaccustomed to country roads.*
– DERIVATIVES **un·ac·cus·tomed·ly adv.**

un·a·chiev·a·ble /ˌənəˈCHēvəbəl/ ▸ **adj.** (of an aim or objective) too difficult to be achieved: *an unachievable political goal.*

un·ac·knowl·edged /ˌənakˈnälijd/ ▸ **adj. 1** existing or having taken place but not accepted, recognized, or admitted to: *her unacknowledged feelings.*
2 (of a person or their work) deserving but not receiving praise or recognition.

u·na cor·da /ˈo͞onə ˈkôrdə/ Music ▸ **adv. & adj.** (esp. as a direction) using the soft pedal on a piano.
▸ **n.** a device in a piano that shifts the mechanism slightly to one side when the soft pedal is depressed, so that the hammers do not strike all of the strings when sounding each note and the tone is therefore quieter.
– ORIGIN Italian, literally 'one string.'

un·ac·quaint·ed ▸ **adj.** (of two or more people) not having met before; not knowing each other. ■ (**unacquainted with**) having no experience of or familiarity with: *I regret that I am unacquainted with the place.*

un·a·dapt·ed /ˌənəˈdaptəd/ ▸ **adj.** not adapted: *animals unadapted for surviving shocks.*

un·ad·dressed /ˌənəˈdrest/ ▸ **adj. 1** not considered or dealt with: *wider questions remain unaddressed.*
2 (of a letter or other item sent in the mail) having no address written or printed on it.

un·ad·just·ed /ˌənəˈjəstid/ ▸ **adj.** (esp. of figures or statistics) not adjusted or refined: *the unadjusted jobless total increased last month.*

un·a·dorned /ˌənəˈdôrnd/ ▸ **adj.** not adorned; plain.

un·a·dul·ter·at·ed /ˌənəˈdəltəˌrātid/ ▸ **adj.** not mixed or diluted with any different or extra elements; complete and absolute: *pure, unadulterated jealousy.* ■ (of food or drink) having no inferior added substances; pure: *unadulterated whole-milk yogurt.*

un·ad·ven·tur·ous /ˌənadˈvencHərəs/ ▸ **adj.** not offering, involving, or eager for new or stimulating things: *he was the unadventurous type | an unadventurous menu.*
– DERIVATIVES **un·ad·ven·tur·ous·ly adv.**

un·ad·ver·tised /ˌənˈadvərˌtīzd/ ▸ **adj.** existing or taking place without being made public.

un·ad·vis·a·ble /ˌənədˈvīzəbəl/ ▸ **adj.** likely to have unfortunate consequences; unwise.

un·ad·vis·ed·ly /ˌənədˈvīzidlē/ ▸ **adv.** in an unwise or rash manner: *they enter into nothing lightly or unadvisedly.*

un·aes·thet·ic /ˌənesˈTHetik/ ▸ **adj.** not visually pleasing; unattractive. ■ not motivated by aesthetic principles.

un·af·fect·ed /ˌənəˈfektid/ ▸ **adj. 1** feeling or showing no effects or changes: *the walks are suitable only for people who are unaffected by vertigo.*
2 (of a person) without artificiality or insincerity: *his manner was natural and unaffected.*
– DERIVATIVES **un·af·fect·ed·ly adv.**, **un·af·fect·ed·ness n.**

un·af·fil·i·at·ed /ˌənəˈfilēˌātid/ ▸ **adj.** not officially attached to or connected with an organization or group.

un·af·ford·a·ble /ˌənəˈfôrdəbəl/ ▸ **adj.** too expensive to be afforded by the average person: *medical care has become unaffordable.*

un·a·fraid /ˌənəˈfrād/ ▸ **adj.** [predic.] feeling no fear or anxiety: *she was calm and unafraid.*

un·aid·ed /ˌənˈādid/ ▸ **adj.** needing or having no assistance; without help: *she can no longer walk unaided.*

un·aired /ˌənˈe(ə)rd/ ▸ **adj. 1** not exposed to the open air for ventilation.
2 not previously broadcast: *the original unaired pilot episode.*

Un·a·las·ka /ˌənəˈlaskə/ an island in the eastern Aleutian Islands of Alaska, on which the naval base of Dutch Harbor and the city of Unalaska (pop. 3,532; est. 2008) are the chief settlements.

un·al·ien·a·ble /ˌənˈālyənəbəl, -ˈālēə-/ ▸ **adj.** another term for **INALIENABLE**.

un·a·ligned /ənəˈlīnd/ ▸ **adj. 1** not placed or arranged in a straight line, in parallel, or in correct relative positions.
2 not allied with or giving support to a particular organization or cause.

un·a·like /ˌənəˈlīk/ ▸ **adj.** [predic.] (of two or more things) differing from each other; not similar: *they are unalike in personality.*

un·al·le·vi·at·ed /ˌənəˈlēvēˌātid/ ▸ **adj.** not alleviated; relentless: *a time of unalleviated misery.*

un·al·lo·cat·ed /ənˈaləkātəd/ ▸ **adj.** (of resources or duties) not yet allocated: *$2.8m of the state's stimulus funds remained unallocated.*

un·al·loyed /ˌənəˈloid/ ▸ **adj.** (of metal) not alloyed; pure: *unalloyed copper.* ■ (chiefly of emotions) complete and unreserved: *unalloyed delight.*

un·al·ter·a·ble /ˌənˈôlt(ə)rəbəl/ ▸ **adj.** not able to be changed.
– DERIVATIVES **un·al·ter·a·ble·ness n.**, **un·al·ter·a·bly** /-blē/ **adv.**

un·al·tered /ˌənˈôltərd/ ▸ **adj.** remaining the same; unchanged: *many buildings survive unaltered.*

un·am·big·u·ous /ˌənamˈbigyo͞oəs/ ▸ **adj.** not open to more than one interpretation: *instructions should be unambiguous.*
– DERIVATIVES **un·am·bi·gu·i·ty** /-ˌambəˈgyo͞oətē/ **n.**, **un·am·big·u·ous·ly adv.**

un·am·bi·tious /ˌənamˈbisHəs/ ▸ **adj.** not motivated or driven by a strong desire or determination to succeed. ■ (of a plan or piece of work) not involving anything new, exciting, or demanding.
– DERIVATIVES **un·am·bi·tious·ly adv.**, **un·am·bi·tious·ness n.**

un-A·mer·i·can /ˌənəˈmerikən/ ▸ **adj.** not in accordance with American characteristics: *such un-American concepts as subsidized medicine.* ■ chiefly historical contrary to the interests of the US and therefore treasonable.
– DERIVATIVES **un-A·mer·i·can·ism** /-ˌnizəm/ **n.**

U·na·mi /o͞oˈnämē/ ▸ **n.** see **DELAWARE²** (sense 2 of the noun).
– ORIGIN the name in Unami.

PRONUNCIATION KEY ə *ago, up*; ər *over, fur*; a *hat*; ā *ate*; ä *car*; e *let*; ē *see*; i *fit*; ī *by*; NG *sing*; ō *go*; ô *law, for*; oi *toy*; o͝o *good*; o͞o *goo*; ou *out*; TH *thin*; T͟H *then*; ZH *vision*

U

un·a·mused /ˌənəˈmyo͞ozd/ ▶ **adj.** not responding in a positive way to something intended to be amusing; feeling somewhat annoyed or disapproving: *she was unamused by some of the things written about her.*

un·an·a·lyz·a·ble /ˌənˈanlˌīzəbəl/ (Brit. **unanalysable**) ▶ **adj.** not able to be explained or interpreted through methodical examination: *unanalyzable recorded data.*

un·an·a·lyzed /ˌənˈanlˌīzd/ (Brit. **unanalysed**) ▶ **adj.** not revealed, explained, or interpreted through methodical examination.

un·an·chored /ənˈaNGkərd/ ▶ **adj.** not anchored or securely fixed.

un·a·neled /ˌənəˈnēld/ ▶ **adj.** archaic having died without receiving extreme unction; not anointed.

U·na·ni /yo͞oˈnänē/ ▶ **n.** [usu. as modifier] a system of medicine practiced in parts of India, thought to be derived via medieval Muslim physicians from Byzantine Greece. It is sometimes contrasted with the Ayurvedic system.
– ORIGIN from Arabic *Yūnānī* 'Greek.'

u·na·nim·i·ty /ˌyo͞onəˈnimətē/ ▶ **n.** agreement by all people involved; consensus: *there is almost complete unanimity on this issue.*

u·nan·i·mous /yo͞oˈnanəməs/ ▶ **adj.** (of two or more people) fully in agreement: *the doctors were unanimous in their diagnoses.* ■ (of an opinion, decision, or vote) held or carried by everyone involved.
– ORIGIN early 17th cent.: from Latin *unanimus* (from *unus* 'one' + *animus* 'mind') + **-ous**.

u·nan·i·mous·ly /yo͞oˈnanəməslē/ ▶ **adv.** without opposition; with the agreement of all people involved: *a bipartisan law passed unanimously by Congress.*

un·an·nounced /ˌənəˈnounst/ ▶ **adj.** not made known; not publicized: *the company has justified its recent unannounced addition of chlorine to its water.* ■ without previous notice or arrangement and therefore unexpected: *he arrived unannounced.*

un·an·swer·a·ble /ˌənˈans(ə)rəbəl/ ▶ **adj.** unable to be answered: *unanswerable questions concerning our own mortality.* ■ unable to be disclaimed or proved wrong: *the case for abolishing the fee is unanswerable.*
– DERIVATIVES **un·an·swer·a·bly** /-blē/ **adv.**

un·an·swered /ˌənˈansərd/ ▶ **adj.** not answered or responded to: *unanswered letters.*

un·an·tic·i·pat·ed /ˌənanˈtisəˌpātid/ ▶ **adj.** not expected or predicted.

un·a·pol·o·get·ic /ˌənəˌpäləˈjetik/ ▶ **adj.** not acknowledging or expressing regret: *he remained unapologetic about his decision.*
– DERIVATIVES **un·a·pol·o·get·i·cal·ly** /-ik(ə)lē/ **adv.**

un·ap·par·ent /ˌənəˈparənt/ ▶ **adj.** not visible or in evidence.

un·ap·peal·a·ble /ˌənəˈpēləbəl/ ▶ **adj.** Law (of a case or ruling) not able to be referred to a higher court for review.

un·ap·peal·ing /ˌənəˈpēliNG/ ▶ **adj.** not inviting or attractive: *the company faces some unappealing choices.*
– DERIVATIVES **un·ap·peal·ing·ly** **adv.**

un·ap·peas·a·ble /ˌənəˈpēzəbəl/ ▶ **adj.** not able to be pacified, placated, or satisfied.

un·ap·pe·tiz·ing /ˌənˈapəˌtīziNG/ ▶ **adj.** not inviting or attractive; unwholesome.
– DERIVATIVES **un·ap·pe·tiz·ing·ly** **adv.**

un·ap·pre·ci·at·ed /ˌənəˈprēSHēˌātid/ ▶ **adj.** not fully understood, recognized, or valued: *she had been brought up in a family where she felt unappreciated and undervalued.*

un·ap·pre·ci·a·tive /ˌənəˈprēSH(ē)ətiv/ ▶ **adj.** not fully understanding, recognizing, or valuing something: *one daughter of an unappreciative mother says, "Nothing I ever did for her was enough."*

un·ap·proach·a·ble /ˌənəˈprōCHəbəl/ ▶ **adj.** (of a person or institution) not welcoming or friendly. ■ archaic (of a place) remote and inaccessible.
– DERIVATIVES **un·ap·proach·a·bil·i·ty** /-ˌprōCHəˈbilətē/ **n.**, **un·ap·proach·a·bly** /-blē/ **adv.**

un·ap·pro·pri·at·ed /ˌənəˈprōprēˌātid/ ▶ **adj.** not allocated, assigned, or taken into possession: *vacant and unappropriated land.*

un·ap·proved /ˌənəˈpro͞ovd/ ▶ **adj.** not officially accepted or sanctioned: *they deposit waste on unapproved sites.*

un·ar·gu·a·ble /ˌənˈärgyo͞oəbəl/ ▶ **adj.** not open to disagreement; indisputable: *unarguable proof of conspiracy.*
– DERIVATIVES **un·ar·gu·a·bly** /-blē/ **adv.**

un·armed /ˌənˈärmd/ ▶ **adj.** not equipped with or carrying weapons: *he was shooting unarmed civilians.*

un·ar·tic·u·lat·ed /ˌənärˈtikyəˌlātid/ ▶ **adj.** not mentioned or coherently expressed: *repressed hurt and previously unarticulated anger are explored.*

u·na·ry /ˈyo͞onərē/ ▶ **adj.** (esp. of a mathematical operation) consisting of or involving a single component or element.

un·a·shamed /ˌənəˈSHāmd/ ▶ **adj.** expressed or acting openly and without guilt or embarrassment: *an unashamed emotionalism.*
– DERIVATIVES **un·a·sham·ed·ly** /-ˈSHāmidlē/ **adv.**, **un·a·sham·ed·ness** /-ˈSHām(i)dnis/ **n.**

un·asked /ˌənˈas(k)t/ ▶ **adj.** (of a question) not asked. ■ (often **unasked for**) not sought or requested: *unasked-for advice | the memories he had poured unasked into her head.*

un·as·pi·rat·ed /ˌənˈaspəˌrātid/ ▶ **adj.** Phonetics (of a sound) not aspirated.

un·as·sail·a·ble /ˌənəˈsāləbəl/ ▶ **adj.** unable to be attacked, questioned, or defeated: *an unassailable lead.*
– DERIVATIVES **un·as·sail·a·bil·i·ty** /-ˌsāləˈbilətē/ **n.**, **un·as·sail·a·bly** /-blē/ **adv.**

un·as·ser·tive /ˌənəˈsərtiv/ ▶ **adj.** (of a person) not having or showing a confident and forceful personality.
– DERIVATIVES **un·as·ser·tive·ly** **adv.**, **un·as·ser·tive·ness** **n.**

un·as·signed /ˌənəˈsīnd/ ▶ **adj.** not allocated or set aside for a specific purpose: *as cell phones proliferate, the number of unassigned numbers is being exhausted.*
– DERIVATIVES **un·as·sign·a·ble** **adj.**

un·as·sim·i·lat·ed /ˌənəˈsiməˌlātid/ ▶ **adj.** (esp. of a people, an idea, or a culture) not absorbed or integrated into a wider society or culture.
– DERIVATIVES **un·as·sim·i·la·ble** /-ləbəl/ **adj.**

un·as·sist·ed /ˌənəˈsistid/ ▶ **adj.** not helped by anyone or anything: *medically unassisted births | I could never find the place unassisted.* ■ (of a play in a team sport) done by one player, without an assist from another player: *he made two unassisted tackles.*

un·as·so·ci·at·ed /ˌənəˈsōsēˌātid/ ▶ **adj.** not connected or associated: *the issue is being raised by thousands of unassociated individuals.*

un·as·suaged /ˌənəˈswājd/ ▶ **adj.** not soothed or relieved: *her unassuaged grief.*
– DERIVATIVES **un·as·suage·a·ble** /-əˈswājəbəl/ **adj.**

un·as·sum·ing /ˌənəˈso͞omiNG/ ▶ **adj.** not pretentious or arrogant; modest: *he was an unassuming and kindly man.*
– DERIVATIVES **un·as·sum·ing·ly** **adv.**, **un·as·sum·ing·ness** **n.**

un·at·tached /ˌənəˈtaCHt/ ▶ **adj.** not working for or belonging to a particular body or organization. ■ not married or having an established partner; single.

un·at·tain·a·ble /ˌənəˈtānəbəl/ ▶ **adj.** not able to be reached or achieved: *an unattainable goal.*
– DERIVATIVES **un·at·tain·a·ble·ness** **n.**, **un·at·tain·a·bly** /-blē/ **adv.**

un·at·tempt·ed /ˌənəˈtem(p)tid/ ▶ **adj.** not previously attempted or embarked upon; untried.

un·at·tend·ed /ˌənəˈtendid/ ▶ **adj.** not noticed or dealt with: *her behavior went unnoticed and unattended to.* ■ not supervised or looked after: *it is not acceptable for parents to leave children unattended at that age.*

un·at·test·ed /ˌənəˈtestid/ ▶ **adj.** not existing in any documented form: *if a will contains unattested changes, the changes will be disregarded | although large masonry instruments were not unattested in the world, they were constructed infrequently.* ■ Linguistics denoting a form or usage or pronunciation of a word for which there is no evidence: *logically possible but unattested word-formation.*

un·at·trac·tive /ˌənəˈtraktiv/ ▶ **adj.** not pleasing or appealing to look at. ■ having no inviting or beneficial features: *if the revised bid is unattractive, it may not be accepted.*
– DERIVATIVES **un·at·trac·tive·ly** **adv.**, **un·at·trac·tive·ness** **n.**

un·at·trib·ut·ed /ˌənəˈtribyətid/ ▶ **adj.** (of a quotation, story, or work of art) not ascribed to any source; of unknown or unpublished provenance.
– DERIVATIVES **un·at·trib·ut·a·ble** /-yətəbəl/ **adj.**, **un·at·trib·ut·a·bly** /-yətəblē/ **adv.**

un·au·dit·ed /ˌənˈôditid/ ▶ **adj.** (of financial accounts) not having been officially examined.

un·au·then·tic /ˌənôˈTHentik/ ▶ **adj.** not made or done in a way that reflects tradition or faithfully resembles an original.
– DERIVATIVES **un·au·then·ti·cal·ly** /-ik(ə)lē/ **adv.**

un·au·then·ti·cat·ed /ˌənôˈTHentiˌkātid/ ▶ **adj.** not proven or validated: *an unauthenticated report.*

un·au·thor·ized /ˌənˈôTHəˌrīzd/ ▶ **adj.** not having official permission or approval: *unauthorized access to the computer system.*

un·a·vail·a·ble /ˌənəˈvāləbəl/ ▶ **adj.** **1** not able to be used or obtained; not at someone's disposal: *material that is* ***unavailable to*** *the researcher.*
2 (of a person) not free to do something; otherwise occupied: *the men were* ***unavailable for*** *work.*
– DERIVATIVES **un·a·vail·a·bil·i·ty** **n.**

un·a·vail·ing /ˌənəˈvāliNG/ ▶ **adj.** achieving little or nothing; ineffective: *their efforts were unavailing.*
– DERIVATIVES **un·a·vail·ing·ly** **adv.**

un·a·void·a·ble /ˌənəˈvoidəbəl/ ▶ **adj.** not able to be avoided, prevented, or ignored; inevitable: *the natural and unavoidable consequences of growing old.*
– DERIVATIVES **un·a·void·a·bil·i·ty** /-ˌvoidəˈbilətē/ **n.**, **un·a·void·a·bly** /-blē/ **adv.**

un·a·wak·ened /ˌənəˈwākənd/ ▶ **adj.** not aware of or roused to particular sensations or feelings.

un·a·ware /ˌənəˈwe(ə)r/ ▶ **adj.** [predic.] having no knowledge of a situation or fact: *they were* ***unaware of*** *his absence.*
▶ **adv.** variant of **UNAWARES**.
– DERIVATIVES **un·a·ware·ness** **n.**

un·a·wares /ˌənəˈwe(ə)rz/ (also **unaware**) ▶ **adv.** without being aware of a situation: *it will be flagged so that people don't stumble on it unawares.*
– PHRASES **catch** (or **take**) **someone unawares** take someone by surprise: *this morning she caught me unawares before I'd had a single cup of coffee.*
– ORIGIN mid 16th cent.: from **UNAWARE** + **-S**[3].

un·backed /ˌənˈbakt/ ▶ **adj.** **1** having no financial, material, or moral support.
2 (of a horse) having no backers in a race.
3 having no backing layer: *unbacked hessian.*

un·bal·ance /ˌənˈbaləns/ ▶ **v.** [with obj.] make (someone or something) unsteady so that they tip or fall. ■ upset or disturb the equilibrium of (a state of affairs or someone's state of mind): *this sharing can often unbalance even the closest of relationships.*
▶ **n.** a lack of symmetry, balance, or stability.

un·bal·anced /ˌənˈbalənst/ ▶ **adj.** not keeping or showing an even balance; not evenly distributed. ■ (of a person) emotionally or mentally disturbed. ■ (of an account) not giving accurate, fair, or equal coverage to all aspects; partial: *this may give an unbalanced impression of the competition.*

un·ban /ˌənˈban/ ▶ **v.** (**unbans, unbanning, unbanned**) [with obj.] remove a ban on (a person, group, or activity).

un·banked /ˌənˈbaNGkt/ ▶ **adj.** not served by a bank or similar financial institution.

un·bar /ˌənˈbär/ ▶ **v.** (**unbars, unbarring, unbarred**) [with obj.] remove the bars from (a gate or door); unlock.

un·bear·a·ble /ˌənˈbe(ə)rəbəl/ ▶ **adj.** not able to be endured or tolerated: *the heat was getting unbearable.*
– DERIVATIVES **un·bear·a·ble·ness** **n.**, **un·bear·a·bly** /-blē/ **adv.** [as submodifier] *it was unbearably hot.*

un·beat·a·ble /ˌənˈbētəbəl/ ▶ **adj.** not able to be defeated or exceeded in a contest or commercial market: *the shop sells bikes at unbeatable prices.* ■ extremely good; outstanding: *views from the patio are unbeatable.*
– DERIVATIVES **un·beat·a·bly** /-blē/ **adv.**

un·beat·en /ˌənˈbētn/ ▶ **adj.** not defeated or surpassed: *they were the only team to remain unbeaten.*

un·beau·ti·ful /ˌənˈbyo͞otəfəl/ ▶ **adj.** without beauty.
– DERIVATIVES **un·beau·ti·ful·ly** **adv.**

un·be·com·ing /ˌənbiˈkəmiNG/ ▶ **adj.** (esp. of clothing or a color) not flattering: *a stout lady in an unbecoming striped sundress.* ■ (of a person's attitude or behavior) not fitting or appropriate; unseemly: *it was* ***unbecoming for*** *a university to do anything so crass as advertising its wares.*
– DERIVATIVES **un·be·com·ing·ly** **adv.**, **un·be·com·ing·ness** **n.**

un·be·fit·ting /ˌənbiˈfitiNG/ ▶ **adj.** not appropriate; unsuitable: *unbefitting conduct.*
– DERIVATIVES **un·be·fit·ting·ly** **adv.**, **un·be·fit·ting·ness** **n.**

un·be·got·ten /ˌənbəˈgätn/ ▶ **adj.** archaic not brought into existence by the process of reproduction.

un·be·known /ˌənbiˈnōn/ (also **unbeknownst** /-ˈnōnst/) ▶ **adj.** [predic.] (**unbeknown to**) without the knowledge of (someone): *unbeknown to me, she made some inquiries.*
– ORIGIN mid 17th cent.: from **UN-**[1] 'not' + archaic *beknown* 'known.'

un·be·lief /ˌənbəˈlēf/ ▶ **n.** lack of religious belief; an absence of faith. ■ another term for **DISBELIEF**.

un·be·liev·a·ble /ˌənbəˈlēvəbəl/ ▶ **adj.** not able to be believed; unlikely to be true: *unbelievable or not, it*

u

happened. ■ so great or extreme as to be difficult to believe; extraordinary: *your audacity is unbelievable.*
– DERIVATIVES **un·be·liev·a·bil·i·ty** /-ˌlēvəˈbilətē/ **n.**, **un·be·liev·a·bly** /-ˈlēvəblē/ **adv.** [as submodifier] *he worked unbelievably long hours.*

un·be·liev·er /ˌənbəˈlēvər/ ▶ **n.** someone who has no religious beliefs, or who does not follow a particular religion.

un·be·liev·ing /-ˌənbəˈlēviNG/ ▶ **adj.** not believing someone or something; incredulous: *Drew could only stand there, wide-eyed and unbelieving.* ■ having no religious beliefs, or not following a particular religion: *they were to preach to the unbelieving people.*
– DERIVATIVES **un·be·liev·ing·ly** /-ˈlēviNGlē/ **adv.**

un·belt /ˌənˈbelt/ ▶ **v.** [with obj.] remove or undo the belt of (a garment): *he unbelted his kimono.*

un·belt·ed /ˌənˈbeltid/ ▶ **adj.** (of a garment) without a belt. ■ (of a person) not wearing a belt, in particular a vehicle seat belt.

un·bend /ˌənˈbend/ ▶ **v.** (past and past participle **unbent**) **1** make or become straight from a bent or twisted form or position: [with obj.] *I had trouble unbending my cramped knees* | [no obj.] *he unbent from the cockpit as she passed.* ■ [no obj.] become less reserved, formal, or strict: *you could be fun too, you know, if you'd only unbend a little.*
2 [with obj.] Sailing unfasten (sails) from yards or stays. ■ untie or cast loose (a rope or cable).

un·bend·ing /ˌənˈbendiNG/ ▶ **adj.** strict and austere in one's behavior or attitudes: *they were unbending in their demands* | *his unbending iron will.*
– DERIVATIVES **un·bend·ing·ly** **adv.**, **un·bend·ing·ness** **n.**

un·bi·ased /ˌənˈbīəst/ ▶ **adj.** showing no prejudice for or against something; impartial.

un·bib·li·cal /ˌənˈbiblikəl/ ▶ **adj.** not found in, authorized by, or based on the Bible.

un·bid·da·ble /ˌənˈbidəbəl/ ▶ **adj.** **1** not easily controlled; unruly or disobedient.
2 (of a card, suit, or hand) that cannot be bid or bid on: *some hands would be unbiddable if we applied that rule to them.*

un·bid·den /ˌənˈbidn/ ▶ **adj.** without having been commanded or invited: *unbidden guests.* ■ (esp. of a thought or feeling) arising without conscious effort: *unbidden tears came to his eyes.*

un·bind /ˌənˈbīnd/ ▶ **v.** (past and past participle **unbound**) [with obj.] release from bonds or restraints.

un·birth·day /ˌənˈbərTH,dā/ ▶ **n.** humorous any day except one's birthday: [as modifier] *an unbirthday present.*
– ORIGIN 1871: coined by Lewis Carroll in *Through the Looking Glass.*

un·bleached /ənˈblēCHd/ ▶ **adj.** (esp. of paper or cloth) not made whiter or lighter by a chemical process: *unbleached cotton.*

un·blem·ished /ˌənˈblemisHt/ ▶ **adj.** not damaged or marked in any way; perfect.

un·blessed /ˌənˈblest/ (also **unblest**) ▶ **adj.** not blessed: *unblessed food* | *a desolate and unblest extent of buffalo-grass.*

un·blind /ˌənˈblīnd/ ▶ **v.** [with obj.] conduct (a test or experiment) in such a way that it is not blind.

un·blink·ing /ˌənˈbliNGkiNG/ ▶ **adj.** (of a person or their gaze or eyes) not blinking. ■ (of an assessment or account) direct, thorough, and honest: *they have helped him paint an unblinking portrait of the man and the writer.*
– DERIVATIVES **un·blink·ing·ly** **adv.**

un·block /ˌənˈbläk/ ▶ **v.** [with obj.] **1** remove an obstruction from (something, esp. a pipe or drain): *balloon catheters are used to unblock occluded arteries.*
2 restore access to or the use of (e-mail or a website or cellular phone): *crooks are using software to unblock the phones so they can be resold.*
– DERIVATIVES **un·block·er** **n.**

un·blush·ing /ˌənˈbləsHiNG/ ▶ **adj.** not feeling or showing embarrassment or shame.
– DERIVATIVES **un·blush·ing·ly** **adv.**

un·bolt /ˌənˈbōlt/ ▶ **v.** [with obj.] open (a door or window) by drawing back a bolt.

un·bolt·ed /ˌənˈbōltid/ ▶ **adj.** **1** (of a door or window) not bolted.
2 (of flour, etc.) not sifted.

un·born /ˌənˈbôrn/ ▶ **adj.** (of a baby) not yet born: *the sound of an unborn baby's heartbeat* | figurative *without training, your full talent remains unborn* | [as plural noun] *the side with the most power will determine how America treats its unborn.*

un·bos·om /ˌənˈbo͝ozəm/ ▶ **v.** [with obj.] archaic disclose (one's thoughts or secrets): *she* **unbosomed herself** *to a trusty female friend.*

un·both·ered /ˌənˈbäT͟Hərd/ ▶ **adj.** showing or feeling a lack of concern about or interest in something: *she was unbothered by the mess in the sink.*

un·bound[1] /ˌənˈbound/ ▶ **adj.** not bound or tied up: *her hair was unbound* | figurative *they were unbound by convention.* ■ (of printed sheets) not bound together. ■ (of a book) not provided with a proper or permanent cover. ■ Chemistry & Physics not held by a chemical bond, gravity, or other physical force: *unbound electrons.*

un·bound[2] past and past participle of **UNBIND**.

un·bound·ed /ˌənˈboundid/ ▶ **adj.** having or appearing to have no limits: *the possibilities are unbounded.*
– DERIVATIVES **un·bound·ed·ly** **adv.**, **un·bound·ed·ness** **n.**

un·bowed /ˌənˈboud/ ▶ **adj.** not having submitted to pressure or demands: *they are unbowed by centuries of colonial rule.*

un·brace /ˌənˈbrās/ ▶ **v.** [with obj.] remove a support from.

un·braid /ˌənˈbrād/ ▶ **v.** [with obj.] untie (something braided): *she may never unbraid her hair in the soft candlelight of a shared bedroom.*

un·brand·ed /ˌənˈbrandid/ ▶ **adj.** **1** (of a product) not bearing a brand name: *unbranded computer systems.*
2 (of livestock) not branded with the owner's mark.

un·breach·a·ble /ˌənˈbrēCHəbəl/ ▶ **adj.** not able to be breached or overcome: *a virtually unbreachable position.*

un·break·a·ble /ˌənˈbrākəbəl/ ▶ **adj.** not liable to break to be break easily: *plastic bottles that are essentially unbreakable* | *an unbreakable code.*

un·bridge·a·ble /ˌənˈbrijəbəl/ ▶ **adj.** (of a gap or difference) not able to be bridged or made less significant: *a seemingly unbridgeable cultural abyss.*

un·bri·dle /ənˈbrīdl/ ▶ **v.** [with obj.] remove the bridle from (a horse or mule): *learn how to bridle and unbridle a horse.* ■ release from restraint: [as adj.] *the forces of the world capitalist market were unbridled and spread quickly.*

un·bri·dled /ˌənˈbrīdld/ ▶ **adj.** uncontrolled; unconstrained: *a moment of unbridled ambition* | *unbridled lust.*

un·bro·ken /ˌənˈbrōkən/ ▶ **adj.** not broken, fractured, or damaged: *an unbroken glass.* ■ not interrupted or disturbed; continuous: *a night of sleep unbroken by nightmares.* ■ (of a record) not surpassed: *a 13-year unbroken record of increasing profits.* ■ (of a horse) not tamed or accustomed to being ridden. ■ (of land) not cultivated.
– DERIVATIVES **un·bro·ken·ly** **adv.**, **un·bro·ken·ness** **n.**

un·buck·le /ˌənˈbəkəl/ ▶ **v.** [with obj.] unfasten the buckle of (something, esp. a belt).

un·build /ˌənˈbild/ ▶ **v.** (past and past participle **unbuilt**) [with obj.] demolish or destroy (something, esp. a building or system). ■ (as adj. **unbuilt**) (of buildings or land) not yet built or built on: *a slope of unbuilt land.*

un·bun·dle /ˌənˈbəndl/ ▶ **v.** [with obj.] **1** market or charge for (items or services) separately rather than as part of a package.
2 split (a company or conglomerate) into its constituent businesses, esp. before selling them off.
– DERIVATIVES **un·bun·dler** **n.** (sense 2).

un·bur·den /ˌənˈbərdn/ ▶ **v.** [with obj.] relieve (someone) of something that is causing anxiety or distress: *the need to* **unburden yourself** *to someone who will listen.*

un·bur·dened /ənˈbərdnd/ ▶ **adj.** not burdened or encumbered: *they are unburdened by expectations of success.*

un·bur·ied /ənˈberēd/ ▶ **adj.** (esp. of a dead body) not buried.

un·burned /ˌənˈbərnd/ (also **unburnt**) ▶ **adj.** not damaged or destroyed by fire. ■ (of energy sources) not used or consumed: *unburned calories.* ■ (esp. of bricks) not exposed to heat in a kiln.

un·bur·y /ˌənˈberē/ ▶ **v.** (**unburies**, **unburying**, **unburied**) [with obj.] remove (something) from under the ground.

un·but·ton /ˌənˈbətn/ ▶ **v.** [with obj.] unfasten the buttons of (a garment). ■ [no obj.] informal relax and become less inhibited: *unbutton a little, Molly.*

un·caged /ˌənˈkājd/ ▶ **adj.** released from or not confined in a cage.

un·called /ˌənˈkôld/ ▶ **adj.** not summoned or invited. ■ (**uncalled for**) (esp. of a person's behavior) undesirable and unnecessary: *uncalled-for remarks.*

un·can·ny /ˌənˈkanē/ ▶ **adj.** (**uncannier**, **uncanniest**) strange or mysterious, esp. in an unsettling way: *an uncanny feeling that she was being watched.*
– DERIVATIVES **un·can·ni·ly** /-ˈkanəl-ē/ **adv.**, **un·can·ni·ness** **n.**
– ORIGIN late 16th cent. (originally Scots in the sense 'relating to the occult, malicious'): from **UN-**[1] 'not' + **CANNY**.

un·cap /ˌənˈkap/ ▶ **v.** (**uncaps**, **uncapping**, **uncapped**) [with obj.] remove the lid or cover from. ■ remove a limit or restriction on (a price, rate, or amount).

un·cared /ˌənˈke(ə)rd/ ▶ **adj.** (**uncared for**) not looked after properly: *it was sad to see the old place uncared for and neglected* | *he grinned, showing surprisingly uncared-for teeth.*

un·car·ing /ˌənˈke(ə)riNG/ ▶ **adj.** not displaying sympathy or concern for others: *an uncaring father.* ■ not feeling interest in or attaching importance to something: *she fled out into the weather,* **uncaring** *of the rain.*
– DERIVATIVES **un·car·ing·ly** **adv.**

Un·cas /ˈəNGkəs/ (c.1588–1683) chief of the Mohegan Indians in what is now eastern Connecticut. He fought on the side of the British in the Pequot War 1637 and King Philip's War 1675–76.

un·case /ˌənˈkās/ ▶ **v.** [with obj.] remove from a cover or case.

un·cashed /ənˈkasHd/ ▶ **adj.** (of a check, lottery ticket, etc.) not converted to cash.

un·cat·a·loged /ənˈkatl,ôgd, -ˌägd/ (also **uncatalogued**) ▶ **adj.** (of a book, document, etc.) not yet cataloged.

un·catch·a·ble /ˌənˈkaCHəbəl/ ▶ **adj.** not able to be caught, caught up to, or captured.

un·ceas·ing /ˌənˈsēsiNG/ ▶ **adj.** not coming to an end; continuous: *the unceasing efforts of the staff.*
– DERIVATIVES **un·ceas·ing·ly** **adv.**

un·cel·e·brat·ed /ˌənˈseləˌbrātid/ ▶ **adj.** not publicly acclaimed: *an uncelebrated but indispensable role.*

un·cen·sored /ənˈsensərd/ ▶ **adj.** not censored.

un·cer·e·mo·ni·ous /ˌənserəˈmōnēəs/ ▶ **adj.** having or showing a lack of courtesy; rough or abrupt.
– DERIVATIVES **un·cer·e·mo·ni·ous·ly** **adv.**, **un·cer·e·mo·ni·ous·ness** **n.**

un·cer·tain /ˌənˈsərtn/ ▶ **adj.** not able to be relied on; not known or definite: *an uncertain future.* ■ (of a person) not completely confident or sure of something: *I was uncertain how to proceed.*
– PHRASES **in no uncertain terms** clearly and forcefully: *she refused me, in no uncertain terms.*
– DERIVATIVES **un·cer·tain·ly** **adv.**

un·cer·tain·ty /ˌənˈsərtntē/ ▶ **n.** (pl. **uncertainties**) the state of being uncertain: *times of uncertainty and danger.* ■ (usu. **uncertainties**) something that is uncertain or that causes one to feel uncertain: *financial uncertainties.*

un·cer·tain·ty prin·ci·ple ▶ **n.** Physics the principle that the momentum and position of a particle cannot both be precisely determined at the same time.

un·cer·ti·fied /ˌənˈsərtəˌfīd/ ▶ **adj.** not officially recognized as having a certain status or meeting certain standards: *uncertified accountants.* ■ not attested or confirmed in a formal statement.

un·chain /ˌənˈCHān/ ▶ **v.** [with obj.] remove the chains fastening or securing (someone or something).

un·chal·lenge·a·ble /ˌənˈCHalənjəbəl/ ▶ **adj.** not able to be disputed, opposed, or defeated: *the unchallengeable truth of these basic facts.*
– DERIVATIVES **un·chal·lenge·a·bly** /-blē/ **adv.**

un·chal·lenged /ˌənˈCHalənjd/ ▶ **adj.** not disputed or questioned: *the report's findings did not go unchallenged.* ■ (esp. of a person in power) not opposed or defeated: *a position of unchallenged supremacy.* ■ not called on to prove one's identity or allegiance: *they walked unchallenged into a hospital and stole a baby.*

un·chal·leng·ing /ˌənˈCHalənjiNG/ ▶ **adj.** (of a task or situation) not testing one's abilities: *my job was unchallenging.* ■ not threatening someone's position: *his voice was gentle and unchallenging.*

un·chanc·y /ˌənˈCHansē/ ▶ **adj.** (**unchancier**, **unchanciest**) chiefly Scottish unlucky, inauspicious, or dangerous.

un·change·a·ble /ˌənˈCHānjəbəl/ ▶ **adj.** not liable to variation or able to be altered: *personality characteristics are virtually unchangeable.*
– DERIVATIVES **un·change·a·bil·i·ty** **n.**, **un·change·a·ble·ness** **n.**, **un·change·a·bly** **adv.**

un·changed /ˌənˈCHānjd/ ▶ **adj.** not changed; unaltered: *the landscape has remained unchanged for a thousand years.*

un·chang·ing /ˌənˈCHānjiNG/ ▶ **adj.** not changing; remaining the same: *the party stood for unchanging principles.*
– DERIVATIVES **un·chang·ing·ly** **adv.**

PRONUNCIATION KEY ə *ago, up*; ər *over, fur*; a *hat*; ā *ate*; ä *car*; e *let*; ē *see*; i *fit*; ī *by*; NG *sing*; ō *go*; ô *law, for*; oi *toy*; o͝o *good*; o͞o *goo*; ou *out*; TH *thin*; T͟H *then*; ZH *vision*

un·chap·er·oned /ˌənˈsHapəˌrōnd/ ▶ **adj.** unaccompanied or unsupervised.

un·char·ac·ter·is·tic /ˌənˌkariktəˈristik/ ▶ **adj.** not typical of a particular person or thing: *an uncharacteristic display of temper.*
– DERIVATIVES **un·char·ac·ter·is·ti·cal·ly adv.**

un·charged /ˌənˈCHärjd/ ▶ **adj.** not charged, in particular: ■ not accused of an offense under the law: *she was released uncharged.* ■ not carrying an electric charge. ■ not charged to a particular account: *an uncharged fixed cost.*

un·char·is·mat·ic /ˌənˌkarizˈmatik/ ▶ **adj.** lacking the charm and attractiveness that can inspire enthusiasm in others.

un·char·i·ta·ble /ˌənˈCHaritəbəl/ ▶ **adj.** (of a person's behavior or attitude toward others) unkind; unsympathetic: *this uncharitable remark possibly arose out of jealousy.*
– DERIVATIVES **un·char·i·ta·ble·ness n., un·char·i·ta·bly** /-blē/ **adv.**

un·chart·ed /ˌənˈCHärtid/ ▶ **adj.** (of an area of land or sea) not mapped or surveyed: *an uncharted region of space* | figurative *the present study is a foray into uncharted territory.*

> **USAGE** **Uncharted** means 'not yet mapped or surveyed.' Especially in the phrase **uncharted territory**, it is confused with **unchartered**, a far less common word that means 'not having a charter or written constitution.' **Unchartered territory** constitutes around 10 percent of the total citations for the phrase in the Oxford English Corpus.

un·char·tered /ˌənˈCHärtərd/ ▶ **adj.** not having a charter or written constitution.

un·chaste /ˌənˈCHāst/ ▶ **adj.** relating to or engaging in sexual activity, esp. of an illicit or extramarital nature: *unchaste subjects in art.*
– DERIVATIVES **un·chaste·ly adv., un·chas·ti·ty** /-ˈCHastətē/ **n.**

un·chas·tened /ˌənˈCHāsənd/ ▶ **adj.** (of a person) not restrained or subdued: *he was unchastened and ready for fresh mischief.*

un·checked /ˌənˈCHekt/ ▶ **adj.** (esp. of something undesirable) not controlled or restrained: *unchecked population growth.* ■ not examined, esp. in order to determine the accuracy, quality, or condition of something.

un·cho·sen /ˌənˈCHōzən/ ▶ **adj.** not chosen.

un·chris·tian /ˌənˈkrisCHən/ ▶ **adj.** not professing Christianity or its teachings. ■ (of a person or their behavior) unkind, unfair, or morally wrong.
– DERIVATIVES **un·chris·tian·ly adv.**

un·church /ˌənˈCHərCH/ ▶ **v.** [with obj.] officially exclude (someone) from participation in the Christian sacraments; excommunicate. ■ deprive (a building) of its status as a church.

un·churched /ˌənˈCHərCHt/ ▶ **adj.** not belonging to or connected with a church.

un·ci·al /ˈənsHəl, -sēəl/ ▶ **adj. 1** of or written in a majuscule script with rounded unjoined letters that is found in European manuscripts of the 4th–8th centuries and from which modern capital letters are derived.
2 rare of or relating to an inch or an ounce.
▶ **n.** an uncial letter or script. ■ a manuscript in uncial script.
– ORIGIN mid 17th cent.: from Latin *uncialis*, from *uncia* 'inch.' Sense 1 of the adjective is in the late Latin sense of *unciales litterae* 'uncial letters,' the original application of which is unclear.

uncial

uncial

un·ci·form /ˈənsəˌfôrm/ ▶ **adj.** another term for **UNCINATE.** ■ dated denoting the hamate bone of the wrist.

un·ci·na·ri·a·sis /ˌənsənəˈrīəsis/ ▶ **n.** another term for **ANCYLOSTOMIASIS.**
– ORIGIN early 20th cent.: from modern Latin *Uncinaria* (the name of a genus of hookworms) + **-IASIS.**

un·ci·nate /ˈənsənit, -ˌnāt/ ▶ **adj.** chiefly Anatomy having a hooked shape.
– ORIGIN mid 18th cent.: from Latin *uncinatus*, from *uncinus* 'hook.'

un·cir·cu·lat·ed /ˌənˈsərkyəˌlātid/ ▶ **adj.** (esp. of paper money or coin) not having been in circulation.

un·cir·cum·cised /ˌənˈsərkəmˌsīzd/ ▶ **adj.** (of a boy or man) not circumcised. ■ archaic irreligious or heathen.
– DERIVATIVES **un·cir·cum·ci·sion** /-ˌsərkəmˈsizHən/ **n.**

un·civ·il /ˌənˈsivəl/ ▶ **adj.** discourteous; impolite.
– DERIVATIVES **un·civ·il·ly adv.**

un·civ·i·lized /ˌənˈsivəˌlīzd/ ▶ **adj.** (of a place or people) not considered to be socially, culturally, or morally advanced. ■ impolite; bad-mannered.

un·clad /ˌənˈklad/ ▶ **adj. 1** unclothed; naked.
2 not provided with cladding: *unclad girders.*

un·claimed /ˌənˈklāmd/ ▶ **adj.** not demanded or requested as being something one has a right to: *unclaimed benefits.*

un·clamp /ˌənˈklamp/ ▶ **v.** [with obj.] release or loosen the clamp of; remove the clamp from: *he unclamped its jaws and climbed out of its cage.*

un·clasp /ˌənˈklasp/ ▶ **v.** [with obj.] unfasten (a clasp or similar device): *they unclasped their seat belts.* ■ release the grip of: *I unclasped her fingers from my hair.*

un·clas·si·fi·a·ble /ˌənˈklasəˌfīəbəl/ ▶ **adj.** not able to be assigned to a particular class or category.

un·clas·si·fied /ˌənˈklasəˌfīd/ ▶ **adj.** not arranged in or assigned to classes or categories: *many texts remain unclassified or uncatalogued.* ■ (of information or documents) not designated as secret.

un·cle /ˈəNGkəl/ ▶ **n.** the brother of one's father or mother or the husband of one's aunt. ■ informal an unrelated older male friend, esp. of a child. ■ archaic informal a pawnbroker.
– PHRASES **cry** (or **say**) **uncle** informal surrender or admit defeat.
– ORIGIN Middle English: from Old French *oncle*, from late Latin *aunculus*, alteration of Latin *avunculus* 'maternal uncle' (see **AVUNCULAR**).

-uncle ▶ **suffix** forming chiefly diminutive nouns: *carbuncle* | *peduncle.*
– ORIGIN from Old French *-oncle, -uncle*, or from Latin *-unculus*, a special form of *-ulus.*

un·clean /ˌənˈklēn/ ▶ **adj.** dirty: *the company was fined for operating in unclean premises.* ■ morally wrong: *unclean thoughts.* ■ (of food) regarded in a particular religion as impure and unfit to be eaten: *pork is an unclean meat for Muslims.* ■ (in biblical use) ritually impure; (of a spirit) evil.
– DERIVATIVES **un·clean·ness n.**
– ORIGIN Old English *unclǣne* (see **UN-**[1], **CLEAN**).

un·clean·li·ness /ˌənˈklenlēnis/ ▶ **n.** the state of being dirty: *head lice and general uncleanliness in schools.*

un·clean·ly /ˌənˈklenlē/ ▶ **adj.** archaic term for **UNCLEAN.**

un·clear /ˌənˈkli(ə)r/ ▶ **adj.** not easy to see, hear, or understand: *the motive for this killing is unclear.* ■ not obvious or definite; ambiguous: *their future remains unclear.* ■ having or feeling doubt or confusion: *users are still unclear about what middleware does.*
– DERIVATIVES **un·clear·ly adv., un·clear·ness n.**

un·cleared /ˌənˈkli(ə)rd/ ▶ **adj.** not having been cleared or cleared up, in particular: ■ (of a check) not having passed through a clearinghouse and been paid into the payee's account. ■ (of land) not cleared of vegetation before cultivation.

un·clench /ˌənˈklenCH/ ▶ **v.** [with obj.] release (a clenched part of the body): *slowly she unclenched her fist.* ■ [no obj.] relax from a clenched state.

Un·cle Sam /sam/ a personification of the federal government or citizens of the US, typically portrayed as a tall, thin, bearded man wearing a suit of red, white, and blue.
– ORIGIN early 19th cent.: said (from the time of the first recorded instances) to have arisen as a facetious expansion of the letters US.

Uncle Sam

Un·cle Tom /täm/ ▶ **n.** derogatory a black man considered to be excessively obedient or servile.
– DERIVATIVES **Un·cle Tom·ism** /ˈtämˌizəm/ **n.**
– ORIGIN 1920s: from the name of the hero of H. B. Stowe's *Uncle Tom's Cabin* (1852).

un·climbed /ˌənˈklīmd/ ▶ **adj.** (of a mountain or rock face) not previously climbed: *the unclimbed south ridge.*
– DERIVATIVES **un·climb·a·ble** /-ˈklīməbəl/ **adj.**

un·cloak /ˌənˈklōk/ ▶ **v.** [with obj.] literary uncover; reveal.

un·clog /ˌənˈklôg, -ˈkläg/ ▶ **v.** (**unclogs, unclogging, unclogged**) [with obj.] remove accumulated matter from: *exfoliation unclogs pores and prevents blackheads.*

un·close /ˌənˈklōz/ ▶ **v.** rare open.

un·clothe /ˌənˈklōT͟H/ ▶ **v.** [with obj.] remove the clothes from (oneself or someone).

un·clothed /ˌənˈklōT͟Hd/ ▶ **adj.** not wearing clothes; naked: *her unclothed body.*

un·cloud·ed /ˌənˈkloudid/ ▶ **adj.** (of the sky) not dark or overcast: *you wake up to sunshine and unclouded skies.* ■ not troubled or spoiled by anything: *six months of unclouded happiness.*

un·clut·tered /ˌənˈklətərd/ ▶ **adj.** not having or impeded by too many objects, details, or elements: *the rooms were plain and uncluttered.*

un·co /ˈəNGkō, -kə/ Scottish ▶ **adj.** unusual or remarkable.
▶ **adv.** [as submodifier] remarkably; very: *it's got an unco fine taste.*
▶ **n.** (pl. **uncos**) a stranger. ■ (**uncos**) news.
– ORIGIN late Middle English (in the sense 'unknown, strange'): alteration of **UNCOUTH.**

un·coat·ed /ˌənˈkōtid/ ▶ **adj.** not covered with a coating of a particular substance.

un·coil /ˌənˈkoil/ ▶ **v.** straighten or cause to straighten from a coiled or curled position: [no obj.] *the rope uncoiled like a snake* | [with obj.] *she uncoiled her feather boa.*

un·col·lect·ed /ˌənkəˈlektid/ ▶ **adj.** not collected or claimed: *the reward remained uncollected.*

un·col·o·nized /ənˈkäləˌnīzd/ ▶ **adj.** (of a place) not yet colonized.

un·col·ored /ˌənˈkələrd/ (Brit. **uncoloured**) ▶ **adj.** having no color; neutral in color. ■ not influenced, esp. in a negative way: *explanations that are uncolored by the observer's feelings.*

un·combed /ənˈkōmd/ ▶ **adj.** (of a person's hair) not combed.

un·com·fort·a·ble /ˌənˈkəmfərtəbəl, -ˈkəmftərbəl/ ▶ **adj.** causing or feeling slight pain or physical discomfort: *athlete's foot is a painful and uncomfortable condition.* ■ causing or feeling unease or awkwardness: *he began to feel uncomfortable at the man's hard stare* | *an uncomfortable silence.*
– DERIVATIVES **un·com·fort·a·ble·ness n., un·com·fort·a·bly** /-blē/ **adv.** [as submodifier] *the house was dark and uncomfortably cold.*

un·com·fy /ˌənˈkəmfē/ ▶ **adj.** informal not comfortable.

un·com·ment /ˌənˈkämˌent/ ▶ **v.** [with obj.] Computing change (a piece of text within a program) from being a comment to being part of the program that is run by the computer by removing tagging that identifies the text as a comment.

un·com·mer·cial /ˌənkəˈmərsHəl/ ▶ **adj.** not making, intended to make, or allowing a profit.

un·com·mer·cial·ized /ˌənkəˈmərsHəˌlīzd/ ▶ **adj.** not having profit as a primary aim.

un·com·mit·ted /ˌənkəˈmitid/ ▶ **adj.** not committed to a cause, activity, etc.: *uncommitted voters.* ■ (of resources) not pledged or set aside for future use: *there is very little uncommitted money to fund new policies.*

un·com·mon /ˌənˈkämən/ ▶ **adj.** out of the ordinary; unusual: *prostate cancer is not uncommon in men over 60* | *an uncommon name.* ■ [attrib.] remarkably great (used for emphasis): *an uncommon amount of noise.*
▶ **adv.** [as submodifier] archaic remarkably: *he was uncommon afraid.*

un·com·mon·ly ▶ **adv.** [usu. as submodifier] exceptionally; very: *he is an uncommonly good talker.*

un·com·mu·ni·ca·tive /ˌənkəˈmyo͞onəkətiv, -ˌkātiv/ ▶ **adj.** (of a person) unwilling to talk or impart information. ■ (of something such as writing or art) not conveying much or any meaning or sense.
– DERIVATIVES **un·com·mu·ni·ca·tive·ly adv., un·com·mu·ni·ca·tive·ness n.**

un·com·pen·sat·ed /ˌənˈkämpənˌsātid/ ▶ **adj.** not compensated or reimbursed: *the plaintiff remained uncompensated for his original injuries* | *workers who performed uncompensated "off-the-clock" work* *for Ernst in violation of the law.* ■ (of an action) not compensated for: *uncompensated exploitation of the Third World.*

un·com·pet·i·tive /ˌənkəmˈpetətiv/ ▶ **adj.** (with reference to business or commerce) not competitive: *that would destroy jobs and make industry uncompetitive.* ■ characterized by a desire to avoid fair competition: *uncompetitive practices.*
– DERIVATIVES **un·com·pet·i·tive·ly adv.**, **un·com·pet·i·tive·ness n.**

un·com·plain·ing /ˌənkəmˈplāniNG/ ▶ **adj.** not complaining; resigned: *she was uncomplaining, accepting of her lot.*
– DERIVATIVES **un·com·plain·ing·ly adv.**

un·com·plet·ed /ˌənkəmˈplētid/ ▶ **adj.** not completed.

un·com·plexed /ənˈkämpleksd/ ▶ **adj.** Chemistry (of an atom or molecule) not combined in a complex.

un·com·pli·cat·ed /ˌənˈkämpləˌkātid/ ▶ **adj.** simple or straightforward: *he was an extraordinarily uncomplicated man.*

un·com·pli·men·ta·ry /ˌənˌkämpləˈmentərē/ ▶ **adj.** not complimentary; negative or insulting: *uncomplimentary remarks.*

un·com·pre·hend·ing /ˌənˌkämpriˈhendiNG/ ▶ **adj.** showing or having an inability to comprehend something: *an uncomprehending silence.*
– DERIVATIVES **un·com·pre·hend·ing·ly adv.**

un·com·pressed /ˌənkəmˈprest/ ▶ **adj.** (of data) not compressed.

un·com·pro·mis·ing /ˌənˈkämprəˌmīziNG/ ▶ **adj.** showing an unwillingness to make concessions to others, esp. by changing one's ways or opinions. ■ harsh or relentless: *the uncompromising ugliness of her home.*
– DERIVATIVES **un·com·pro·mis·ing·ly adv.**, **un·com·pro·mis·ing·ness n.**

un·con·cealed /ˌənkənˈsēld/ ▶ **adj.** (esp. of an emotion) not concealed; obvious: *Sophie looked around her with unconcealed curiosity.*

un·con·cern /ˌənkənˈsərn/ ▶ **n.** a lack of worry or interest, esp. when surprising or callous.

un·con·cerned /ˌənkənˈsərnd/ ▶ **adj.** showing a lack of worry or interest, esp. when this is surprising or callous: *Scott seemed unconcerned by his companion's problem.*
– DERIVATIVES **un·con·cern·ed·ly** /-ˈsərnədlē/ **adv.**

un·con·di·tion·al /ˌənkənˈdisHənl, -ˈdisHnəl/ ▶ **adj.** not subject to any conditions: *unconditional surrender.*
– DERIVATIVES **un·con·di·tion·al·i·ty** /-ˌdisHəˈnalətē/ **n.**, **un·con·di·tion·al·ly adv.**

un·con·di·tioned /ˌənkənˈdisHənd/ ▶ **adj. 1** not subject to conditions or to an antecedent condition; unconditional: *pure and unconditioned love.* **2** relating to or denoting instinctive reflexes or other behavior not formed or influenced by conditioning or learning: *an unconditioned response.* **3** not subjected to a conditioning process: *waste in its raw, unconditioned form.*

un·con·fessed /ˌənkənˈfest/ ▶ **adj.** not acknowledged: *the hope that remains unconfessed.* ■ (of a sin) not confessed to a priest.

un·con·fi·dent /ˌənˈkänfədənt/ ▶ **adj.** not confident; hesitant.
– DERIVATIVES **un·con·fi·dent·ly adv.**

un·con·fined /ˌənkənˈfīnd/ ▶ **adj.** not confined to a limited space: *sows should be unconfined at farrowing.* ■ (of joy or excitement) very great: *joy was unconfined.*

un·con·firmed /ˌənkənˈfərmd/ ▶ **adj.** not confirmed as to truth or validity: *an unconfirmed report of shots being fired.*

un·con·form·a·ble /ˌənkənˈfôrməbəl/ ▶ **adj.** Geology (of rock strata in contact) marking a discontinuity in the geological record, and typically not having the same direction of stratification.
– DERIVATIVES **un·con·form·a·bly** /-blē/ **adv.**

un·con·form·i·ty /ˌənkənˈfôrmətē/ ▶ **n.** Geology a surface of contact between two groups of unconformable strata. ■ the condition of being unconformable.

un·con·gen·ial /ˌənkənˈjēnyəl/ ▶ **adj.** (of a person) not friendly or pleasant to be with: *uncongenial dining companions.* ■ unsuitable and therefore unlikely to promote success or well-being: *the religious climate proved uncongenial* **to** *such ideas.*

un·con·nect·ed /ˌənkəˈnektid/ ▶ **adj.** not joined together or to something else: *the ground wire was left unconnected.* ■ not associated or linked in a sequence: *two unconnected events* | *the question was unconnected* **to** *anything they had been discussing.*
– DERIVATIVES **un·con·nect·ed·ly adv.**, **un·con·nect·ed·ness n.**

un·con·quer·a·ble /ˌənˈkäNGk(ə)rəbəl/ ▶ **adj.** (esp. of a place, people, or emotion) not conquerable: *an unconquerable pride.*
– DERIVATIVES **un·con·quer·a·bly** /-blē/ **adv.**

un·con·quered /ˌənˈkäNGkərd/ ▶ **adj.** not conquered.

un·con·scion·a·ble /ˌənˈkänsH(ə)nəbəl/ ▶ **adj.** not right or reasonable: *the unconscionable conduct of his son.* ■ unreasonably excessive: *shareholders have had to wait an unconscionable time for the facts to be established.*
– DERIVATIVES **un·con·scion·a·bly** /-blē/ **adv.**
– ORIGIN mid 16th cent.: from UN-¹ 'not' + obsolete *conscionable*, from CONSCIENCE (interpreted as a plural) + -ABLE.

un·con·scious /ˌənˈkänsHəs/ ▶ **adj.** not conscious: *the boy was beaten unconscious.* ■ done or existing without one realizing: *he would wipe back his hair in an unconscious gesture of annoyance.* ■ [predic.] (**unconscious of**) unaware of: *"What is it?" he said again, unconscious of the repetition.*
▶ **n.** (**the unconscious**) the part of the mind that is inaccessible to the conscious mind but that affects behavior and emotions.
– DERIVATIVES **un·con·scious·ly adv.**

un·con·scious·ness /ˌənˈkänCHəsnəs/ ▶ **n.** the state of being unconscious: *someone gave me a crack across the head and I slipped into unconsciousness.* ■ the state of being uninformed or unaware: *part of her beauty was her unconsciousness of it.*

un·con·sid·ered /ˌənkənˈsidərd/ ▶ **adj.** disregarded and unappreciated: *a penchant for picking up unconsidered trifles.* ■ (of a statement or action) not thought about in advance, and therefore rash or harsh: *I realize that my unconsidered remarks were dangerously indiscreet.*

un·con·sol·a·ble /ˌənkənˈsōləbəl/ ▶ **adj.** inconsolable.
– DERIVATIVES **un·con·sol·a·bly** /-blē/ **adv.**

un·con·sti·tu·tion·al /ˌənˌkänstəˈt(y)o͞osHənl/ ▶ **adj.** not in accordance with a political constitution, esp. the US Constitution, or with procedural rules.
– DERIVATIVES **un·con·sti·tu·tion·al·i·ty** /-ˌt(y)o͞osHəˈnalətē/ **n.**, **un·con·sti·tu·tion·al·ly adv.**

un·con·strained /ˌənkənˈstrānd/ ▶ **adj.** not restricted or limited: *unconstrained growth.*
– DERIVATIVES **un·con·strain·ed·ly adv.**

un·con·straint /ˌənkənˈstrānt/ ▶ **n.** freedom from constraint.

un·con·struct·ed /ˌənkənˈstrəktid/ ▶ **adj.** (of a garment) unstructured.

un·con·sumed /ˌənkənˈso͞omd/ ▶ **adj.** (esp. of food or fuel) not consumed.

un·con·sum·mat·ed /ˌənˈkänsəˌmātid/ ▶ **adj.** (of a marriage or other relationship) not having been consummated.

un·con·tain·a·ble /ˌənkənˈtānəbəl/ ▶ **adj.** (esp. of an emotion) very strong: *his uncontainable enthusiasm.*

un·con·tam·i·nat·ed /ˌənkənˈtaməˌnātid/ ▶ **adj.** not contaminated: *uncontaminated air and food.*

un·con·test·ed /ˌənkənˈtestid/ ▶ **adj.** not contested: *these claims have not gone uncontested.*
– DERIVATIVES **un·con·test·ed·ly adv.**

un·con·trived /ˌənkənˈtrīvd/ ▶ **adj.** not appearing artificial: *the whole effect was uncontrived.*

un·con·trol·la·ble /ˌənkənˈtrōləbəl/ ▶ **adj.** not controllable: *her brother had an uncontrollable temper.*
– DERIVATIVES **un·con·trol·la·bil·i·ty n.**, **un·con·trol·la·bly adv.**, **un·con·trolled adj.**

un·con·tro·ver·sial /ˌənˌkäntrəˈvərsHəl/ ▶ **adj.** not controversial.
– DERIVATIVES **un·con·tro·ver·sial·ly adv.**

un·con·tro·vert·ed /ˌənˌkäntrəˈvərtid/ ▶ **adj.** of which the truth or validity is not disputed or denied.

un·con·ven·tion·al /ˌənkənˈvensHənl/ ▶ **adj.** not based on or conforming to what is generally done or believed: *his unconventional approach to life.*
– DERIVATIVES **un·con·ven·tion·al·i·ty** /-ˌvensHəˈnalətē/ **n.**, **un·con·ven·tion·al·ly adv.**

un·con·vert·ed /ˌənkənˈvərtid/ ▶ **adj.** not converted, in particular: ■ (of a building) not adapted to a different use. ■ not having adopted a different religion, belief, or practice: *unconverted pagans.*

un·con·vinced /ˌənkənˈvinst/ ▶ **adj.** not certain that something is true or can be relied on or trusted: *Parisians remain unconvinced* **that** *the project will be approved.*

un·con·vinc·ing /ˌənkənˈvinsiNG/ ▶ **adj.** failing to make someone believe that something is true or valid: *she felt the lie was unconvincing.* ■ failing to impress: *a slightly bizarre and unconvincing fusion of musical forces.*
– DERIVATIVES **un·con·vinc·ing·ly adv.**

un·cooked /ənˈko͝okt/ ▶ **adj.** not cooked; raw.

un·cool /ˌənˈko͞ol/ ▶ **adj.** informal not fashionable or impressive: *an uncool haircut.*

un·co·op·er·a·tive /ˌənkōˈäp(ə)rətiv/ ▶ **adj.** unwilling to help others or do what they ask.
– DERIVATIVES **un·co·op·er·a·tive·ly adv.**

un·co·or·di·nat·ed /ˌənkōˈôrdnˌātid/ ▶ **adj. 1** badly organized: *expensive mistakes resulting from uncoordinated manufacturing strategies.* **2** (of a person or their movements) clumsy.

un·cork /ˌənˈkôrk/ ▶ **v.** [with obj.] pull the cork out of (a bottle or other container). ■ informal (in a game or sport) deliver (a kick, throw, or punch): *he uncorked the best throw of his career.*

un·cor·rect·ed /ˌənkəˈrektid/ ▶ **adj.** not corrected.

un·cor·re·lat·ed /ənˈkôrəˌlātid, -ˈkär-/ ▶ **adj.** not correlated; lacking a mutual relationship or connection.

un·cor·rob·o·rat·ed /ˌənkəˈräbəˌrātid/ ▶ **adj.** not confirmed or supported by other evidence or information: *the unreliability of uncorroborated confessions.*

un·cor·rupt·ed /ˌənkəˈrəptid/ ▶ **adj.** not corrupted: *Lucinda is uncorrupted by nefarious influences.*

un·count·a·ble /ˌənˈkountəbəl/ ▶ **adj.** too many to be counted (usually in hyperbolic use): *she'd spent uncountable nights in this very bed.*
– DERIVATIVES **un·count·a·bil·i·ty** /-ˌkountəˈbilətē/ **n.**, **un·count·a·bly** /-blē/ **adv.**

un·count·ed /ˌənˈkountid/ ▶ **adj.** not counted. ■ very numerous: *uncounted millions of dollars.*

un·cou·ple /ˌənˈkəpəl/ ▶ **v.** [with obj.] disconnect (something, esp. a railroad vehicle that has been coupled to another). ■ [no obj.] become disconnected: *the groups of cells commonly uncouple from surrounding tissue* | figurative *I have seen marriages uncouple under the strain.* ■ release (hunting dogs) from being fastened together in couples.

un·court·ly /ˌənˈkôrtlē/ ▶ **adj.** not courteous or refined.

un·couth /ˌənˈko͞oTH/ ▶ **adj.** (of a person or their appearance or behavior) lacking good manners, refinement, or grace: *he is unwashed, uncouth, and drunk most of the time.* ■ (esp. of art or language) lacking sophistication or delicacy: *uncouth sketches of peasants.* ■ archaic (of a place) uncomfortable, esp. because of remoteness or poor conditions.
– DERIVATIVES **un·couth·ly adv.**, **un·couth·ness n.**
– ORIGIN Old English *uncūth* 'unknown,' from UN-¹ 'not' + *cūth* (past participle of *cunnan* 'know, be able').

un·cov·e·nant·ed /ˌənˈkəv(ə)nəntid/ ▶ **adj.** not bound by or in accordance with a covenant or agreement. ■ not promised by or based on a covenant, esp. a covenant with God.

un·cov·er /ˌənˈkəvər/ ▶ **v.** [with obj.] remove a cover or covering from: *he uncovered the face of the dead man.* ■ discover (something previously secret or unknown): *further evidence has been uncovered.* ■ [no obj.] archaic remove one's hat, esp. as a mark of respect.

un·cov·ered /ˌənˈkəvərd/ ▶ **adj.** not covered: *no uncovered heads are seen on the street.*

un·crate /ˈənˌkrāt/ ▶ **n.** [with obj.] an item of merchandise removed from its shipping container.

un·cre·ate /ˌənkrēˈāt/ ▶ **v.** [with obj.] literary destroy.

un·cre·at·ed /ˌənkrēˈātid/ ▶ **adj.** (esp. of a divine being) existing without having been created. ■ not yet created.

un·cre·a·tive /ˌənkrēˈātiv/ ▶ **adj.** not having or involving imagination or original ideas.

un·cred·it·ed /ˌənˈkreditid/ ▶ **adj.** (of a person or their work) not publicly acknowledged as being part of something, esp. a publication or broadcast.

un·crit·i·cal /ˌənˈkritikəl/ ▶ **adj.** not expressing criticism or using one's critical faculties: *the technique had received uncritical acclaim in the media.* ■ not in accordance with the principles of critical analysis: *uncritical reasoning.*
– DERIVATIVES **un·crit·i·cal·ly** /-ik(ə)lē/ **adv.**

un·cross /ˌənˈkrôs, -ˈkräs/ ▶ **v.** [with obj.] move (something) back from a crossed position: *the reporter uncrossed his legs.*

un·crowd·ed /ˌənˈkroudid/ ▶ **adj.** not filled with a large number of people: *miles of uncrowded beaches.*

un·crown /ˌənˈkroun/ ▶ **v.** [with obj.] deprive (a monarch) of their ruling position.

un·crowned /ˌənˈkround/ ▶ **adj.** not formally crowned as a monarch.

PRONUNCIATION KEY ə **a**go, **u**p; ər **over**, **fur**; a **hat**; ā **ate**; ä **car**; e **let**; ē **see**; i **fit**; ī **by**; NG **sing**; ō **go**; ô **law**, **for**; oi **toy**; o͝o **good**; o͞o **goo**; ou **out**; TH **thin**; T̲H̲ **then**; ZH **vision**

UNCSTD ▶ **abbr.** United Nations Conference on Science and Technology for Development.

UNCTAD /ˈəNGkˌtad/ ▶ **abbr.** United Nations Conference on Trade and Development.

unc·tion /ˈəNG(k)SHən/ ▶ **n.** **1** formal the action of anointing someone with oil or ointment as a religious rite or as a symbol of investiture as a monarch. ■ short for EXTREME UNCTION.
2 archaic treatment with a medicinal oil or ointment. ■ an ointment: *mercury in the form of unctions.*
3 a manner of expression arising or apparently arising from deep emotion, esp. as intended to flatter: *he spoke the last two words with exaggerated unction.*
– ORIGIN late Middle English: from Latin *unctio(n-)*, from *unguere* 'anoint.' Sense 3 arises from the link between religious fervor and "anointing" with the Holy Spirit.

unc·tu·ous /ˈəNG(k)CHo͞oəs/ ▶ **adj.** **1** (of a person) excessively or ingratiatingly flattering; oily: *he seemed anxious to please but not in an unctuous way.*
2 (chiefly of minerals) having a greasy or soapy feel.
– DERIVATIVES **unc·tu·ous·ly** adv., **unc·tu·ous·ness** n.
– ORIGIN late Middle English (in the sense 'greasy'): from medieval Latin *unctuosus*, from Latin *unctus* 'anointing,' from *unguere* 'anoint.'

un·cul·ti·vat·ed /ˌənˈkəltəˌvātid/ ▶ **adj.** (of land) not used for growing crops. ■ (of a person) not highly educated or socially adept.

un·cul·tured /ˌənˈkəlCHərd/ ▶ **adj.** not characterized by good taste, manners, or education: *to my uncultured palate most of the wines were good.* ■ (of organisms) not cultivated; not maintained by means of a culture: *uncultured soil microbes.*

un·cured /ˌənˈkyo͝ord/ ▶ **adj.** **1** (of a person) not restored to health.
2 (of meat, fish, tobacco, or animal skins) not preserved by salting, drying, or smoking.

un·curl /ˌənˈkərl/ ▶ **v.** straighten or cause to straighten from a curled position: [no obj.] *in spring the new leaves uncurl* | [with obj.] *the doctor uncurled his fingers.*

un·cut /ˌənˈkət/ ▶ **adj.** not cut: *her hair was left uncut.* ■ (of a text, movie, or performance) complete; unabridged. ■ (of a stone, esp. a diamond) not shaped by cutting. ■ (of alcohol or a drug) not diluted or adulterated: *large amounts of uncut heroin.* ■ chiefly historical (of a book) with the edges of its pages not slit open or trimmed off. ■ (of fabric) having its pile loops intact.

un·dam·aged /ˌənˈdamijd/ ▶ **adj.** not harmed or damaged: *buildings undamaged during the war.*

un·dat·ed /ˌənˈdātid/ ▶ **adj.** not provided or marked with a date: *most of his letters are undated.*

un·daunt·ed /ˌənˈdôntid, -ˈdänt-/ ▶ **adj.** not intimidated or discouraged by difficulty, danger, or disappointment: *they were undaunted by the huge amount of work needed.*
– DERIVATIVES **un·daunt·ed·ly** adv., **un·daunt·ed·ness** n.

un·dead /ˌənˈded/ ▶ **adj.** (of a fictional being, esp. a vampire) technically dead but still animate.

un·dec·a·gon /ˌənˈdekəˌgän/ ▶ **n.** another term for HENDECAGON.
– ORIGIN early 18th cent.: formed irregularly from Latin *undecim* 'eleven,' on the pattern of *decagon.*

un·de·ceive /ˌəndiˈsēv/ ▶ **v.** [with obj.] tell (someone) that an idea or belief is mistaken: *they took her for a nun, and Mary said nothing to undeceive them.*

un·de·cid·a·ble /ˌəndiˈsīdəbəl/ ▶ **adj.** not able to be firmly established or refuted. ■ Logic (of a proposition or theorem) not able to be proved or disproved.
– DERIVATIVES **un·de·cid·a·bil·i·ty** /-ˌsīdəˈbilətē/ n.

un·de·cid·ed /ˌəndiˈsīdid/ ▶ **adj.** (of a person) not having made a decision: *the jury remained undecided.* ■ not settled or resolved: *the match was still undecided.*
▶ **n.** a person who has not decided how they are going to vote in an election.
– DERIVATIVES **un·de·cid·ed·ly** adv.

un·de·ci·pher·a·ble /ˌəndiˈsīf(ə)rəbəl/ ▶ **adj.** (of speech or writing) not able to be read or understood.
– DERIVATIVES **un·de·ci·phered** adj.

un·de·clared /ˌəndiˈkle(ə)rd/ ▶ **adj.** not publicly announced, admitted, or acknowledged: *his undeclared candidacy, which surged in the polls last spring.* ■ (esp. of taxable income or dutiable goods) not declared.

un·dec·o·rat·ed /ˌənˈdekəˌrātid/ ▶ **adj.** **1** not adorned or decorated: *the walls were completely undecorated.*
2 (of a member of the armed forces) not honored with an award.

un·de·feat·ed /ˌəndiˈfētid/ ▶ **adj.** not defeated, esp. in a battle or other contest: *the undefeated champion.*

un·de·fend·ed /ˌəndiˈfendid/ ▶ **adj.** not defended: *undefended frontiers* | *legal aid for undefended divorces.*

un·de·filed /ˌəndiˈfīld/ ▶ **adj.** not defiled; pure.

un·de·fined /ˌəndiˈfīnd/ ▶ **adj.** not clear or defined: *undefined areas of jurisdiction* | *he felt an undefined longing.*
– DERIVATIVES **un·de·fin·a·ble** /-ˈfīnəbəl/ adj., **un·de·fin·a·bly** /-ˈfīnəblē/ adv.

un·de·lete /ˌəndiˈlēt/ ▶ **v.** [with obj.] Computing cancel the deletion of (text or a file).

un·de·liv·ered /əndiˈlivərd/ ▶ **adj.** not delivered: *undelivered letters.*
– DERIVATIVES **un·de·liv·er·a·ble** adj.

un·de·mand·ing /ˌəndəˈmandiNG, ˌəndēˈmandiNG/ ▶ **adj.** (esp. of a task or person) not demanding: *undemanding clerical jobs.*

un·dem·o·crat·ic /ˌənˌdeməˈkratik/ ▶ **adj.** not relating or according to democratic principles: *an undemocratic regime.*
– DERIVATIVES **un·dem·o·crat·i·cal·ly** adv.

un·de·mon·stra·tive /ˌəndiˈmänstrətiv/ ▶ **adj.** (of a person) not tending to express feelings, esp. of affection, openly: *John is silent and undemonstrative, like Dad.*
– DERIVATIVES **un·de·mon·stra·tive·ly** adv., **un·de·mon·stra·tive·ness** n.

un·de·ni·a·ble /ˌəndiˈnīəbəl/ ▶ **adj.** unable to be denied or disputed: *it is an undeniable fact that some dogs are easier to train than others* | *ornate fireplaces give the place undeniable class.*
– DERIVATIVES **un·de·ni·a·bly** /-blē/ adv. [sentence adverb] *the topic is undeniably an important one.*

un·de·pend·a·ble ▶ **adj.** not trustworthy and reliable: *evidence is scarce and often undependable.*

un·der /ˈəndər/ ▶ **prep.** **1** extending or directly below: *vast stores of oil under Alaska* | *the streams that ran under the melting glaciers.* ■ below (something covering or protecting): *under several feet of water* | *a hot plate under an insulated lid.*
2 at a lower level than: *the room under his study.* ■ behind (a physical surface): *it was written on the new canvas under a gluey coating.* ■ behind or hidden behind (an appearance or disguise): *he had a deep sense of fun under his quiet exterior.* ■ lower in grade or rank than: *under him in the hierarchy.*
3 controlled, managed, or governed by: *the country is now under martial law* | *I was under his spell.* ■ during (a specified time period, reign, or administration): *it occurred under the pontificate of Paul II.* ■ as a reaction to or undergoing the pressure of (something): *the sofa creaked under his weight* | *certain institutions may be under threat.* ■ as provided for by the rules of; in accordance with: *flowers supplied under contract by a local florist.* ■ used to express grouping or classification: *file it under "lost"* | *published under his own name.* ■ Computing within the environment of (a particular operating system): *the program runs under DOS.*
4 lower than (a specified amount, rate, norm, or age): *they averaged just under 2.8 percent.*
5 undergoing (a process): *under construction.* ■ in an existent state of: *children living under difficult circumstances.* ■ planted with: *fields under wheat.*
▶ **adv.** **1** extending or directly below something: *weaving the body through the crossbars, over and under, over and under.*
2 under water: *he was floating for some time but suddenly went under.*
▶ **adj.** **1** denoting the lowest part or surface of something; on the underside: *the under part of the shell is concave.*
2 unconscious, typically as a result of general anesthesia: *the operation was quick—she was only under for 15 minutes.*
– DERIVATIVES **un·der·most** /-ˌmōst/ adj.
– ORIGIN Old English, of Germanic origin; related to Dutch *onder* and German *unter.*

under- ▶ **prefix** **1** below; beneath: *underclothes* | *undercover.* ■ lower in status; subordinate: *undersecretary.*
2 insufficiently; incompletely: *undernourished.*

un·der·a·chieve /ˌəndərəˈCHēv/ ▶ **v.** [no obj.] do less well than is expected, esp. in schoolwork.
– DERIVATIVES **un·der·a·chieve·ment** n., **un·der·a·chiev·er** n.

un·der·act /ˌəndərˈakt/ ▶ **v.** [no obj.] act a part in a play or film in an overly restrained or unemotional way.

un·der·act·ive /ˌəndərˈaktiv/ ▶ **adj.** insufficiently active: *a health problem such as an underactive thyroid.*

un·der·age /ˌəndərˈāj/ ▶ **adj.** (of a person) too young to engage legally in a particular activity, esp. drinking alcohol or having sex. ■ [attrib.] (of an activity) engaged in by people who are underage: *underage drinking.*

un·der·ap·pre·ci·ate /ˌəndərəˈprēSHiˌāt/ ▶ **v.** [with obj.] (usu. as adj. **underappreciated**) fail to value (someone or something) highly enough: *one of the jazz world's most underappreciated artists.*
– DERIVATIVES **un·der·ap·pre·ci·a·tion** n.

un·der·arm /ˈəndərˌärm/ ▶ **adj. & adv.** another term for UNDERHAND (sense 2).
▶ **n.** a person's armpit: [as modifier] *use an underarm deodorant.*

un·der·banked /ˌəndərˈbaNGkt/ ▶ **adj.** **1** (of an area) with insufficient banks to meet market demand. ■ (of consumers) lacking full use of banking facilities.
2 (of an investment issue) not adequately underwritten by financing institutions.

un·der·bel·ly /ˈəndərˌbelē/ ▶ **n.** (pl. **underbellies**) the soft underside or abdomen of an animal. ■ an area vulnerable to attack: *these multinationals have a soft underbelly.* ■ a hidden unpleasant or criminal part of society.

un·der·bid ▶ **v.** /ˌəndərˈbid/ (**underbids**, **underbidding**; past and past participle **underbid**) [with obj.] (in an auction or when seeking a contract) make a lower bid than (someone): *they were underbid by competitors who charged less.* ■ Bridge make a lower bid on (one's hand) than its strength warrants.
▶ **n.** /ˈəndərˌbid/ a bid that is lower than another or than is justified.
– DERIVATIVES **un·der·bid·der** /ˌəndərˈbidər/ n.

un·der·bite /ˈəndərˌbīt/ ▶ **n.** (in nontechnical use) the projection of the lower teeth beyond the upper.

un·der·bod·y /ˈəndərˌbädē/ ▶ **n.** (pl. **underbodies**) the underside of a road vehicle, ship, or animal's body.

un·der·boss /ˈəndərˌbôs, -ˌbäs/ ▶ **n.** a boss's deputy, esp. in a criminal organization.

un·der·bred /ˌəndərˈbred/ ▶ **adj.** dated ill-mannered; rude.

un·der·brush /ˈəndərˌbrəSH/ ▶ **n.** shrubs and small trees forming the undergrowth in a forest.

un·der·cap·i·tal·ize /ˌəndərˈkapətlˌīz/ ▶ **v.** [with obj.] provide (a company) with insufficient capital to achieve desired results.
– DERIVATIVES **un·der·cap·i·tal·i·za·tion** /-ˌkapətl-əˈzāSHən/ n.

un·der·card /ˈəndərˌkärd/ ▶ **n.** the list of less important bouts on the same bill as a main boxing match.

un·der·car·riage /ˈəndərˌkarij/ ▶ **n.** a wheeled structure beneath an aircraft, typically retracted when not in use, that receives the impact on landing and supports the aircraft on the ground. ■ the supporting frame under the body of a vehicle.

un·der·cast /ˌəndərˈkast/ ▶ **v.** (past and past participle **undercast**) [with obj.] (usu. **be undercast**) allocate the parts in (a play or movie) to insufficiently skilled actors.

un·der·charge ▶ **v.** /ˌəndərˈCHärj/ [with obj.] **1** charge (someone) a price or amount that is too low.
2 give less than the proper charge to (an electric battery).
▶ **n.** /ˈəndərˌCHärj/ a charge that is insufficient.

un·der·class /ˈəndərˌklas/ ▶ **n.** the lowest social stratum in a country or community, consisting of the poor and unemployed.

un·der·class·man /ˌəndərˈklasmən/ ▶ **n.** (pl. **underclassmen**) a student in high school or college who is not a senior: *one of the talented underclassmen leaving campus life early for the NFL.*

un·der·cling /ˈəndərˌkliNG/ Climbing ▶ **n.** a handhold that faces down the rock face.
▶ **v.** [no obj.] climb using such handholds.

un·der·clothes /ˈəndərˌklō(TH)z/ ▶ **plural n.** clothes worn under others, typically next to the skin.

un·der·cloth·ing /ˈəndərˌklōTHiNG/ ▶ **n.** underclothes.

un·der·coat /ˈəndərˌkōt/ ▶ **n.** **1** a layer of paint applied after the primer and before the topcoat.
2 an animal's underfur or down.
▶ **v.** [with obj.] apply a coat of undercoat to (something).

un·der·con·sump·tion /ˌəndərkənˈsəm(p)SHən/ ▶ **n.** Economics purchase of goods and services at a level lower than that of their supply.

un·der·cook /ˌəndərˈko͝ok, ˈəndərˌko͝ok/ ▶ **v.** [with obj.] (usu. as adj. **undercooked**) cook (something) insufficiently: *undercooked meats.*

un·der·cool /ˌəndərˈko͞ol/ ▶ **v.** another term for SUPERCOOL.

un·der·count ▶ **v.** /ˌəndərˈkount/ [with obj.] enumerate (something, esp. a sector of a population in a census) at a lower figure than the actual figure.

▶ **n.** /ˈəndərˌkount/ a count or figure that is inaccurately low. ■ the amount by which such a count or figure falls short of the actual figure.

un·der·cov·er /ˌəndərˈkəvər/ ▶ **adj.** (of a person or their activities) involved in or involving secret work within a community or organization, esp. for the purposes of police investigation or espionage: *an undercover police operation.*
▶ **adv.** as an undercover agent: *a special unit of the police that operates undercover.*

un·der·croft /ˈəndərˌkrôft, -ˌkräft/ ▶ **n.** the crypt of a church.
– ORIGIN late Middle English: from UNDER- + the rare term *croft* 'crypt,' from Middle Dutch *crofte* 'cave,' from Latin *crypta.*

un·der·cur·rent /ˈəndərˌkərənt/ ▶ **n.** **1** a current of water below the surface, moving in a different direction from any surface current.
2 an underlying feeling or influence, esp. one that is contrary to the prevailing atmosphere and is not expressed openly: *an undercurrent of anger and discontent.*

un·der·cut ▶ **v.** /ˌəndərˈkət/ (**undercuts, undercutting**; past and past participle **undercut**) [with obj.] **1** offer goods or services at a lower price than (a competitor): *these industries have been undercut by more efficient foreign producers.*
2 cut or wear away the part below or under (something, esp. a cliff). ■ cut away material to leave (a carved design) in relief.
3 weaken; undermine: *the chairman denied his authority was being undercut.*
4 (in sports such as tennis or golf) strike (a ball) with a chopping motion so as to give it backspin.
▶ **n.** /ˈəndərˌkət/ **1** a space formed by the removal or absence of material from the lower part of something, such as a cliff, a coal seam, or part of a carving in relief. ■ a notch cut in a tree trunk to guide its fall when felled.
2 Brit. the underside of a sirloin of beef.

un·der·damp /ˌəndərˈdamp/ ▶ **v.** [with obj.] Physics damp (a system) incompletely, so as to allow a few oscillations after a single disturbance.

un·der·de·ter·mine /ˌəndərdiˈtərmən/ ▶ **v.** [with obj.] (usu. **be underdetermined**) account for (a theory or phenomenon) with less than the amount of evidence needed for proof or certainty.
– DERIVATIVES **un·der·de·ter·mi·na·tion** /-ˌtərməˈnāSHən/ **n.**

un·der·de·vel·oped /ˌəndərdiˈveləpt/ ▶ **adj.** not fully developed: *underdeveloped kidneys* | *the community services are underfunded and underdeveloped.* ■ (of a country or region) not advanced economically. ■ (of photographic film) not developed sufficiently to give a normal image.
– DERIVATIVES **un·der·de·vel·op·ment** /-əpmənt/ **n.**

un·der·dog /ˈəndərˌdôg, -ˌdäg/ ▶ **n.** a competitor thought to have little chance of winning a fight or contest. ■ a person who has little status in society.
– ORIGIN late 19th cent.: with reference to the beaten dog in a dogfight.

un·der·done /ˌəndərˈdən/ ▶ **adj.** (of food) insufficiently cooked.

un·der·draw·ing /ˈəndərˌdrôiNG/ ▶ **n.** sketched lines made by a painter as a preliminary guide, and subsequently covered with layers of paint.

un·der·dress /ˌəndərˈdres/ ▶ **v.** [no obj.] (also **be underdressed**) dress too plainly or too informally: *without a pinstripe you'd be underdressed.*

un·der·ed·u·cat·ed /ˌəndərˈejəˌkātid/ ▶ **adj.** inadequately educated.

un·der·em·pha·size /ˌəndərˈemfəˌsīz/ ▶ **v.** [with obj.] (usu. **be underemphasized**) place insufficient emphasis on: *history is underemphasized in the curriculum.*
– DERIVATIVES **un·der·em·pha·sis** /-sis/ **n.**

un·der·em·ployed /ˌəndərimˈploid/ ▶ **adj.** (of a person) not having enough paid work or not doing work that makes full use of their skills and abilities.
– DERIVATIVES **un·der·em·ploy·ment** /-ˈploimənt/ **n.**

un·der·es·ti·mate ▶ **v.** /ˌəndərˈestəˌmāt/ [with obj.] estimate (something) to be smaller or less important than it actually is: *the administration has grossly underestimated the extent of the problem.* ■ regard (someone) as less capable than they really are: *he had underestimated the new president.*
▶ **n.** /-mit/ [usu. in sing.] an estimate that is too low.
– DERIVATIVES **un·der·es·ti·ma·tion** /-ˌestəˈmāSHən/ **n.**

un·der·ex·pose /ˌəndərikˈspōz/ ▶ **v.** [with obj.] Photography expose (film or an image) for too short a time.
– DERIVATIVES **un·der·ex·po·sure** /-ˈspōZHər/ **n.**

un·der·fed /ˌəndərˈfed/ ▶ **adj.** insufficiently fed or nourished.

un·der·fi·nanced /ˌəndərfəˈnanst, ˌəndərˈfīnanst/ ▶ **adj.** not having or receiving sufficient funding: *the chronically underfinanced state budget.*

un·der·floor /ˌəndərˈflôr/ ▶ **adj.** situated or operating beneath the floor.

un·der·flow /ˈəndərˌflō/ ▶ **n. 1** an undercurrent. ■ a horizontal flow of water through the ground, esp. one underneath a riverbed.
2 Computing the generation of a number that is too small to be represented in the device meant to store it.

un·der·foot /ˌəndərˈfo͝ot/ ▶ **adv.** under one's feet; on the ground: *it was very muddy underfoot* | figurative *genuine rights were being trodden underfoot.* ■ constantly present and in one's way: *the last thing my mother wanted was a child underfoot.*

un·der·fund /ˌəndərˈfənd/ ▶ **v.** [with obj.] (usu. **be underfunded**) provide with insufficient funding.
– DERIVATIVES **un·der·fund·ing n.**

un·der·fur /ˈəndərˌfər/ ▶ **n.** an inner layer of short, fine fur or down underlying an animal's outer fur, providing warmth and waterproofing.

un·der·gar·ment /ˈəndərˌgärmənt/ ▶ **n.** an article of underclothing.

un·der·gird /ˌəndərˈgərd/ ▶ **v.** [with obj.] secure or fasten from the underside, esp. by a rope or chain passed underneath. ■ formal provide support or a firm basis for.

un·der·glaze /ˈəndərˌglāz/ ▶ **n.** a color or design applied to pottery before it is glazed.

un·der·go /ˌəndərˈgō/ ▶ **v.** (**undergoes, undergoing**; past **underwent**; past participle **undergone**) [with obj.] experience or be subjected to (something, typically something unpleasant, painful, or arduous): *the baby underwent a life-saving brain operation.*
– ORIGIN Old English *undergān* 'undermine' (see UNDER-, GO[1]).

un·der·grad /ˈəndərˌgrad/ ▶ **n.** informal an undergraduate.

un·der·grad·u·ate /ˌəndərˈgrajəwit/ ▶ **n.** a student at a college or university who has not yet earned a bachelor's or equivalent degree.

un·der·ground ▶ **adv.** /ˌəndərˈground/ beneath the surface of the ground: *miners working underground.* ■ in or into secrecy or hiding, esp. as a result of carrying out subversive political activities: *many were forced to* **go underground** *by the government.*
▶ **adj.** /ˈəndərˌground/ situated beneath the surface of the ground: *underground parking garages.* ■ of or relating to the secret activities of people working to subvert an established order: *Czech underground literature.* ■ of or denoting a group or movement seeking to explore alternative forms of lifestyle or artistic expression; radical and experimental: *the New York underground art scene.*
▶ **n.** /ˈəndərˌground/ **1** a group or movement organized secretly to work against an existing regime: *I got involved with the French underground.* ■ a group or movement seeking to explore alternative forms of lifestyle or artistic expression: *the late-sixties underground.*
2 (**the Underground**) Brit. a subway, esp. the one in London: *travel chaos on the Underground.*

un·der·ground e·con·o·my ▶ **n.** the part of a country's economic activity that is unrecorded and untaxed by its government.

Un·der·ground Rail·road a secret network for helping slaves escape from the South to the North and to Canada in the years before the Civil War.

un·der·growth /ˈəndərˌgrōTH/ ▶ **n.** a dense growth of shrubs and other plants, esp. under trees in woodland.

un·der·hand /ˈəndərˌhand/ ▶ **adj. 1** (of a throw or stroke in sports) made with the arm or hand below shoulder level: *he has a surprisingly good motion, more sidearm than underhand* | [as adv.] *I served underhand.* ■ with the palm of the hand upward or outward: *an underhand grip.*
2 another term for UNDERHANDED: *Laura would never agree to anything that smacked of underhand snooping.*
– ORIGIN Old English in the sense 'in or into subjection, under control' (see UNDER-, HAND).

un·der·hand·ed /ˌəndərˈhandəd/ ▶ **adj.** acting or done in a secret or dishonest way: *an underhanded method of snatching clients from rivals.*
– DERIVATIVES **un·der·hand·ed·ly adv.**

un·der·hung /ˌəndərˈhəNG/ ▶ **adj.** another term for UNDERSHOT (sense 2 of the adjective).

un·der·in·sured /ˌəndərinˈSHo͝ord/ ▶ **adj.** (of a person) having inadequate insurance coverage.
– DERIVATIVES **un·der·in·sur·ance** /ˈəndərinˌSHo͝orəns/ **n.**

un·der·in·vest /ˌəndərinˈvest/ ▶ **v.** [no obj.] fail to invest sufficient money or resources in a project or enterprise: *we persistently underinvest in historic buildings.*
– DERIVATIVES **un·der·in·vest·ment n.**

un·der·lay[1] ▶ **v.** /ˌəndərˈlā/ (past and past participle **underlaid**) [with obj.] place something under (something else), esp. to support or raise it: *the green fields are underlaid with limestone* | figurative *a whine underlaid by an occasional choking sob.*
▶ **n.** /ˈəndərˌlā/ something placed under or behind something else, esp. material laid under a carpet for protection or support. ■ Music the manner in which the words are fitted to the notes in a piece of vocal music.
– ORIGIN Old English *underlecgan* (see UNDER-, LAY[1]).

un·der·lay[2] past tense of UNDERLIE.

un·der·lay·ment /ˌəndərˈlāmənt/ ▶ **n.** a layer between a subfloor and a finished floor that facilitates leveling and adhesion.

un·der·let /ˌəndərˈlet/ ▶ **v.** [with obj.] (**underlets, underletting**; past and past participle **underlet**) another term for SUBLET. ■ lease (land or property) at less than the true value.

un·der·lie /ˌəndərˈlī/ ▶ **v.** (**underlies, underlying**; past **underlay**; past participle **underlain**) [with obj.] (esp. of a layer of rock or soil) lie or be situated under (something). ■ be the cause or basis of (something): *the fundamental issue that underlies the conflict* | (as adj. **underlying**) *the underlying causes of poverty and drug addiction.*
– ORIGIN Old English *underlicgan* 'be subject or subordinate to' (see UNDER-, LIE[1]).

un·der·life /ˈəndərˌlīf/ ▶ **n.** a way of living that the general public does not normally encounter.

un·der·line /ˌəndərˈlīn/ ▶ **v.** [with obj.] draw a line under (a word or phrase) to give emphasis or indicate special type. ■ emphasize (something): *the improvement in retail sales was underlined by these figures.*
▶ **n. 1** a line drawn under a word or phrase, esp. for emphasis.
2 the line of the lower part of an animal's body.

un·der·lin·en /ˈəndərˌlinin/ ▶ **n.** archaic underclothes, esp. those made of linen.

un·der·ling /ˈəndərliNG/ ▶ **n.** (usu. **underlings**) chiefly derogatory a person lower in status or rank.

un·der·lip /ˈəndərˌlip/ ▶ **n.** the lower lip of a person or animal.

un·der·ly·ing /ˌəndərˈlī-iNG/ present participle of UNDERLIE.

un·der·man /ˌəndərˈman/ ▶ **v.** (**undermans, undermanning, undermanned**) [with obj.] (usu. **be undermanned**) fail to provide with enough workers or crew: *the public prosecutor's offices are hopelessly undermanned.*

un·der·men·tioned /ˌəndərˈmenCHənd/ ▶ **adj.** Brit. mentioned at a later place in a book or document.

un·der·mine /ˌəndərˈmīn, ˈəndərˌmīn/ ▶ **v.** [with obj.] **1** erode the base or foundation of (a rock formation). ■ dig or excavate beneath (a building or fortification) so as to make it collapse.
2 damage or weaken (someone or something), esp. gradually or insidiously: *this could undermine years of hard work.*
– DERIVATIVES **un·der·min·er n.**
– ORIGIN Middle English: from UNDER- + the verb MINE[2], probably suggested by Middle Dutch *ondermineren.*

un·der·neath /ˌəndərˈnēTH/ ▶ **prep. & adv. 1** situated directly below (something else): [as prep.] *our bedroom is right underneath theirs* | [as adv.] *his eyes were red-rimmed with black bags underneath* | [as adj.] *on longer hair, the underneath layers can be permed to give extra body.*
2 so as to be concealed by (something else): [as prep.] *money changed hands underneath the table* | figurative *underneath his aloof air, Nicky was a warm and open young man* | [as adv.] *paint was peeling off in flakes to reveal grayish plaster underneath.* ■ partly or wholly concealed by (a garment): [as prep.] *she could easily see the broadness of his shoulders underneath a tailored white shirt* | [as adv.] *I wear button-downs, and my T-shirts show underneath.*
▶ **n.** [in sing.] the part or side of something facing toward the ground; the underside.
– ORIGIN Old English *underneothan*; compare with BENEATH.

un·der·nour·ished /ˌəndərˈnərisht, -ˈnə-risht/ ▶ **adj.** having insufficient food or other substances for good health and condition: *undernourished children.*
– DERIVATIVES **un·der·nour·ish·ment n.**

PRONUNCIATION KEY ə *ago, up*; ər *over, fur*; a *hat*; ā *ate*; ä *car*; e *let*; ē *see*; i *fit*; ī *by*; NG *sing*; ō *go*; ô *law, for*; oi *toy*; o͝o *good*; o͞o *goo*; ou *out*; TH *thin*; T͟H *then*; ZH *vision*

un·der·paid /ˌəndərˈpād/ past and past participle of UNDERPAY.

un·der·paint·ing /ˈəndərˌpāntiNG/ ▶ **n.** paint subsequently overlaid with another layer or with a finishing coat.

un·der·pants /ˈəndərˌpan(t)s/ ▶ **plural n.** an undergarment covering the lower part of the torso and having two holes for the legs.

un·der·part /ˈəndərˌpärt/ ▶ **n.** a lower part or portion of something. ■ (**underparts**) the underside of an animal's body, esp. when of a specified color or pattern.

un·der·pass /ˈəndərˌpas/ ▶ **n.** a road or pedestrian tunnel passing under another road or a railroad.

un·der·pay /ˌəndərˈpā/ ▶ **v.** (past and past participle **underpaid**) [with obj.] pay too little to (someone). ■ pay less than is due for (something): (as adj. **underpaid**) *late or underpaid tax.*
– DERIVATIVES **un·der·pay·ment** /ˌəndərˈpāmənt, ˈəndərˌpā-/ **n.**

un·der·per·form /ˌəndərpərˈfôrm/ ▶ **v.** [no obj.] perform less well than expected. ■ [with obj.] increase in value less than: *the shares have underperformed the market.*
– DERIVATIVES **un·der·per·for·mance** /-ˈfôrməns/ **n.**

un·der·pin /ˌəndərˈpin/ ▶ **v.** (**underpins, underpinning, underpinned**) [with obj.] support (a building or other structure) from below by laying a solid foundation below ground level or by substituting stronger for weaker materials. ■ support, justify, or form the basis for: *the theme of honor underpinning the two books.*

un·der·pin·ning /ˈəndərˌpiniNG/ ▶ **n.** a solid foundation laid below ground level to support or strengthen a building. ■ a set of ideas, motives, or devices that justify or form the basis for something: *the theoretical underpinning for free-market economics.*

un·der·plant /ˌəndərˈplant/ ▶ **v.** [with obj.] plant or cultivate the ground around (a tall plant) with smaller plants: *the roses* ***are underplanted with*** *pink and white bulbs.*

un·der·play /ˌəndərˈplā, ˈəndərˌplā/ ▶ **v.** [with obj.] perform (something) in a restrained way: *the violins underplayed the romantic element in the music.* ■ represent (something) as being less important than it actually is: *I do not wish to underplay the tragedies that have occurred.*

un·der·plot /ˈəndərˌplät/ ▶ **n.** a subordinate plot in a play, novel, or similar work.

un·der·pop·u·lat·ed /ˌəndərˈpäpyəˌlātid/ ▶ **adj.** having an insufficient or very small population.
– DERIVATIVES **un·der·pop·u·la·tion** /-ˌpäpyəˈlāSHən/ **n.**

un·der·pow·ered /ˌəndərˈpou(-ə)rd/ ▶ **adj.** lacking sufficient mechanical, electrical, or other power.

un·der·pre·pared /ˌəndərpriˈpe(ə)rd/ ▶ **adj.** not having prepared sufficiently to carry out a task.

un·der·price /ˌəndərˈprīs/ ▶ **v.** [with obj.] sell or offer (something) at too low a price: *we try not to underprice our books, while making sure they are still a good buy.* ■ sell or offer something at a lower price than (the competition): *Wal-Mart has underpriced its traditional competitors.*

un·der·priv·i·leged /ˌəndərˈpriv(ə)lijd/ ▶ **adj.** (of a person) not enjoying the same standard of living or rights as the majority of people in a society.

un·der·pro·duce /ˌəndərprəˈd(y)o͞os/ ▶ **v.** [with obj.]
1 produce less of (a commodity) than is wanted or needed.
2 (often as adj. **underproduced**) record or produce (a song or movie) in such a basic way that it appears rough or unfinished: *many of the album's best tracks are relatively underproduced.*
– DERIVATIVES **un·der·pro·duc·tion** /-prəˈdəkSHən/ **n.**

U

un·der·proof /ˌəndərˈpro͞of/ ▶ **adj.** containing less alcohol than proof spirit does.

un·der·prop /ˌəndərˈpräp/ ▶ **v.** (**underprops, underpropping, underpropped**) [with obj.] archaic support, esp. with a prop.

un·der·rate /ˌəndə(r)ˈrāt/ ▶ **v.** [with obj.] (often as adj. **underrated**) underestimate the extent, value, or importance of (someone or something): *a very underrated film.*

un·der·re·hearsed /ˌəndə(r)riˈhərst/ ▶ **adj.** (of a performance or performer) having had insufficient rehearsals.

un·der·re·port /ˌəndə(r)riˈpôrt/ ▶ **v.** [with obj.] fail to report (something) fully: *athletes are inclined to underreport their use of drugs* | (as adj. **underreported**) *underreported domestic violence.*

un·der·rep·re·sent /ˌəndə(r)ˌrepriˈzent/ ▶ **v.** [with obj.] provide with insufficient or inadequate representation: *women are underrepresented at high levels.*
– DERIVATIVES **un·der·rep·re·sen·ta·tion** /-zenˈtāSHən, -zən-/ **n.**

un·der·re·sourced /ˌəndə(r)rēˈsôrst, -riˈsôrst/ ▶ **adj.** chiefly Brit. provided with insufficient resources: *an overstretched and under-resourced service.*
– DERIVATIVES **un·der·re·sourc·ing** /-ˈrēˌsôrsiNG, -riˈsôrs-/ **n.**

un·der·sat·u·rat·ed /ˌəndərˈsaCHəˌrātid/ ▶ **adj.** technical falling short of being saturated with a particular constituent.
– DERIVATIVES **un·der·sat·u·ra·tion** /-ˌsaCHəˈrāSHən/ **n.**

un·der·score ▶ **n.** /ˈəndərˌskôr/ a line drawn under a word or phrase for emphasis. ■ (on a computer or typewriter keyboard) a short horizontal line (_) on the baseline.
▶ **v.** /ˈəndərˌskôr, ˌəndərˈskôr/ [with obj.] underline (something). ■ emphasize: *the company underscored the progress made with fuel cells.*

un·der·sea /ˌəndərˈsē/ ▶ **adj.** below the sea or the surface of the sea: *undersea cables.*

un·der·sec·re·tar·y /ˌəndərˈsekriˌterē/ ▶ **n.** (pl. **undersecretaries**) a subordinate official, in particular (in the US) the principal assistant to a member of the cabinet, or (in the UK) a junior minister or senior civil servant.

un·der·sell /ˌəndərˈsel/ ▶ **v.** (past and past participle **undersold**) [with obj.] sell something at a lower price than (a competitor): *we can equal or undersell mail order.* ■ promote or rate (something) insufficiently; undervalue: *don't undersell yourself.*

un·der·set ▶ **v.** /ˌəndərˈset/ (**undersets, undersetting**; past and past participle **underset**) [with obj.] rare place (something) under something else, esp. for support.
▶ **n.** /ˈəndərˌset/ another term for UNDERCURRENT.

un·der·sexed /ˌəndərˈsekst/ ▶ **adj.** having unusually weak sexual desires.

un·der·sher·iff /ˈəndərˌsherif/ ▶ **n.** a deputy sheriff.

un·der·shirt /ˈəndərˌSHərt/ ▶ **n.** an undergarment worn under a shirt.

un·der·shoot ▶ **v.** /ˌəndərˈSHo͞ot/ (past and past participle **undershot**) [with obj.] fall short of (a point or target): *the figure undershot the government's original estimate.* ■ (of an aircraft) land short of (the runway).
▶ **n.** /ˈəndərˌSHo͞ot/ an act of undershooting.

un·der·shorts /ˈəndərˌSHôrts/ ▶ **plural n.** underpants, esp. those worn by men or boys.

un·der·shot /ˈəndərˌSHät/ past and past participle of UNDERSHOOT.
▶ **adj. 1** (of a waterwheel) turned by water flowing under it.
2 denoting or having a lower jaw that projects beyond the upper jaw.

un·der·side /ˈəndərˌsīd/ ▶ **n.** the bottom or lower side or surface of something: *the butterfly's wings have a mottled brown pattern on the underside.* ■ the less favorable aspect of something: *the sordid underside of the glamorous 1980s.*

un·der·signed /ˈəndərˌsīnd/ ▶ **adj.** (usu. as plural noun **the undersigned**) formal whose signature is appended: *we, the undersigned, wish to protest the current activities of the company.*

un·der·sized /ˌəndərˈsīzd/ (also **undersize**) ▶ **adj.** of less than the usual size.

un·der·skirt /ˈəndərˌskərt/ ▶ **n.** a skirt worn under another; a petticoat.

un·der·slung /ˌəndərˈsləNG/ ▶ **adj.** suspended from the underside of something: *helicopters hover to lift underslung loads.* ■ (of a vehicle chassis) hanging lower than the axles.

un·der·soil /ˈəndərˌsoil/ ▶ **n.** subsoil.

un·der·sold /ˌəndərˈsōld/ past and past participle of UNDERSELL.

un·der·spend /ˌəndərˈspend/ ▶ **v.** (past and past participle **underspent**) [no obj.] spend too little. ■ [with obj.] spend less than (a specified or allocated amount): *schools have underspent their training budgets.*

un·der·staff /ˌəndərˈstaf/ ▶ **v.** [with obj.] provide (an organization) with too few staff members to operate effectively: (as adj. **understaffed**) *the department is understaffed and overworked.*
– DERIVATIVES **un·der·staff·ing** **n.**

un·der·stand /ˌəndərˈstand/ ▶ **v.** (past and past participle **understood**) **1** [with obj.] perceive the intended meaning of (words, a language, or speaker): *he didn't understand a word I said* | *he could usually* ***make himself understood*** | [with clause] *she understood what he was saying.* ■ perceive the significance, explanation, or cause of (something): *she didn't really understand the situation* | [with clause] *he couldn't understand why we burst out laughing* | [no obj.] *you don't understand—she has left me.* ■ be sympathetically or knowledgeably aware of the character or nature of: *Picasso understood color* | [with clause] *I understand how you feel.* ■ interpret or view (something) in a particular way: *as the term is usually understood, legislation refers to regulations and directives.*
2 [with clause] infer something from information received (often used as a polite formula in conversation): *I understand you're at art school* | [with obj.] *as I understood it, she was flying back to New Zealand tomorrow.* ■ [with obj.] regard (a missing word, phrase, or idea) as present; supply mentally: *"present company excepted" is always understood when sweeping generalizations are being made.* ■ [with obj.] assume to be the case; take for granted: *he liked to play the field—that was understood.*
– DERIVATIVES **un·der·stand·er** **n.**
– ORIGIN Old English *understandan* (see UNDER-, STAND).

un·der·stand·a·ble /ˌəndərˈstandəbəl/ ▶ **adj.** able to be understood: *though his accent was strange, the words were perfectly understandable.* ■ to be expected; natural, reasonable, or forgivable: *such fears are understandable.*
– DERIVATIVES **un·der·stand·a·bil·i·ty** /-ˌstandəˈbilətē/ **n.**, **un·der·stand·a·bly** /-blē/ **adv.** [sentence adverb] *understandably, Richard did not believe me.*

un·der·stand·ing /ˌəndərˈstandiNG/ ▶ **n.** the ability to understand something; comprehension: *foreign visitors with little understanding of English.* ■ the power of abstract thought; intellect: *a child of sufficient intelligence and understanding.* ■ an individual's perception or judgment of a situation: *my understanding was that he would try to find a new supplier.* ■ sympathetic awareness or tolerance: *a problem that needs to be handled with understanding.* ■ an informal or unspoken agreement or arrangement: *he and I have an understanding* | *he had only been allowed to come* ***on the understanding that*** *he would be on his best behavior.*
▶ **adj. 1** sympathetically aware of other people's feelings; tolerant and forgiving: *people expect their doctor to be understanding.*
2 archaic having insight or good judgment.
– DERIVATIVES **un·der·stand·ing·ly** **adv.**

un·der·state /ˌəndərˈstāt/ ▶ **v.** [with obj.] describe or represent (something) as being smaller, worse, or less important than it actually is: *the press has understated the extent of the problem.*
– DERIVATIVES **un·der·stat·er** /ˈəndərˌstātər/ **n.**

un·der·stat·ed /ˌəndərˈstātid/ ▶ **adj.** presented or expressed in a subtle and effective way: *understated elegance.*
– DERIVATIVES **un·der·stat·ed·ly** **adv.**

un·der·state·ment /ˈəndərˌstātmənt/ ▶ **n.** the presentation of something as being smaller, worse, or less important than it actually is: *a master of English understatement* | *to say I am delighted is an understatement.*

un·der·steer ▶ **v.** /ˌəndərˈsti(ə)r/ [no obj.] (of a motor vehicle) have a tendency to turn less sharply than is intended: *the car understeers on very fast bends.*
▶ **n.** /ˈəndərˌstir/ the tendency of a vehicle to turn in such a way.

un·der·stood /ˌəndərˈsto͝od/ past and past participle of UNDERSTAND.

un·der·stored /ˈəndərˈstôrd/ ▶ **adj.** supplied with fewer retail stores than the market demands: *specific market niches in which Chicago is understored compared to Los Angeles and New York.*

un·der·sto·ry /ˈəndərˌstôrē/ (Brit. **understorey**) ▶ **n.** (pl. **understories**) Ecology a layer of vegetation beneath the main canopy of a forest.

un·der·strap·per /ˈəndərˌstrapər/ ▶ **n.** informal, dated an assistant or junior official.

un·der·stud·y /ˈəndərˌstədē/ ▶ **n.** (pl. **understudies**) (in the theater) a person who learns another's role in order to be able to act as a replacement at short notice.
▶ **v.** (**understudies, understudying, understudied**) [with obj.] learn (a role) or the role played by (an actor): *he had to understudy Prospero.*

un·der·sub·scribed /ˌəndərsəbˈskrībd/ ▶ **adj.** (of a course or event) having more places available than applications.

un·der·sur·face /ˈəndərsərfəs/ ▶ **n.** the lower surface of something; the surface underneath, or on the bottom of, something.

un·der·take /ˌəndərˈtāk/ ▶ **v.** (past **undertook**; past participle **undertaken**) [with obj.] commit oneself to and begin (an enterprise or responsibility); take on: *a firm of builders undertook the construction* *work*. ■ [usu. with infinitive] promise to do a particular thing: *the firm undertook to keep price increases to a minimum*. ■ [with clause] guarantee or affirm something; give as a formal pledge: *a truck driver implicitly* ***undertakes that*** *he is reasonably skilled as a driver*.

un·der·tak·er /ˈəndərˌtākər/ ▶ **n.** a person whose business is preparing dead bodies for burial or cremation and making arrangements for funerals.

un·der·tak·ing /ˈəndərˌtākiNG, ˌəndərˈtā-/ ▶ **n.** **1** a formal pledge or promise to do something: *I give* ***an undertaking that*** *we shall proceed with the legislation*. ■ a task that is taken on; an enterprise: *a mammoth undertaking that involved digging into the side of a cliff face*. ■ the action of undertaking to do something: *the knowing undertaking of an obligation*.
2 /ˈəndərˌtākiNG/ the management of funerals as a profession.

un·der·things /ˈəndərˌTHiNGz/ ▶ **plural n.** underclothes, esp. those worn by a woman or girl.

un·der·thrust /ˌəndərˈTHrəst/ Geology ▶ **v.** (past and past participle **underthrust**) [with obj.] force (a crustal plate or other body of rock) beneath another plate or block. ■ be forced underneath (another plate or block).
▶ **n.** an instance of such forced movement.

un·der·tint /ˈəndərˌtint/ ▶ **n.** a subdued or delicate tint.

un·der·tip /ˈəndərˈtip/ ▶ **v.** (**undertips, undertipping, undertipped**) give (someone) an excessively small tip.

un·der·tone /ˈəndərˌtōn/ ▶ **n.** a subdued or muted tone of sound or color: *they were talking in undertones* | *a pallid undertone to her tanned skin*. ■ an underlying quality or feeling: *the sexual undertones of most advertising*.

un·der·took /ˌəndərˈto͝ok/ past participle of **UNDERTAKE**.

un·der·tow /ˈəndərˌtō/ ▶ **n.** another term for **RIP CURRENT**, used in the incorrect belief that rip currents drag swimmers below the surface: *I was swept away by the undertow*. ■ an implicit quality, emotion, or influence underlying the superficial aspects of something and leaving a particular impression: *there's a dark undertow of loss that links the novel with earlier works*.

un·der·trained /ˌəndərˈtrānd/ ▶ **adj.** with insufficient training for a job, sport, etc.

un·der·trick /ˈəndərˌtrik/ ▶ **n.** Bridge a trick by which the declarer falls short of their contract.

un·der·use ▶ **v.** /ˌəndərˈyo͞oz/ [with obj.] (usu. as adj. **underused**) use (something) below the optimum level: *the owner noted a lot of underused space in that garage*.
▶ **n.** /ˌəndərˈyo͞os/ insufficient use: *underuse of existing services*.

un·der·u·ti·lize /ˌəndərˈyo͞otlˌīz/ ▶ **v.** [with obj.] underuse (something).
– DERIVATIVES **un·der·u·ti·li·za·tion** /-ˌyo͞otl-əˈzāSHən/ **n.**

un·der·val·ue /ˌəndərˈvalyo͞o/ ▶ **v.** (**undervalues, undervaluing, undervalued**) [with obj.] (often as adj. **undervalued**) rate (something) insufficiently highly; fail to appreciate: *the skills of the housewife remain undervalued in society*. ■ underestimate the financial value of (something): *the company's assets were undervalued in its balance sheet*.
– DERIVATIVES **un·der·val·u·a·tion** /-ˌvalyo͞oˈāSHən/ **n.**

un·der·vest /ˈəndərˌvest/ ▶ **n.** chiefly Brit. an undershirt.

un·der·vote /ˈəndərˌvōt/ ▶ **n.** a ballot not counted because of unclear marking by the voter.

un·der·wa·ter /ˌəndərˈwôtər, -ˈwätər/ ▶ **adj. & adv.** situated, occurring, or done beneath the surface of the water: [as adj.] *there are underwater volcanoes in the region* | [as adv.] *they learn to navigate underwater at night*.

un·der·way /ˌəndərˈwā/ (also **under way**) ▶ **adv.** **1** having started and in progress; being done or carried out: *the remodeling should be underway by July*.
2 (of a boat) moving through the water: *the ship was so huge and silent, I hadn't realized we had gotten underway*.
– ORIGIN mid 18th cent. (as a nautical term): from Dutch *onderweg*.

un·der·wear /ˈəndərˌwer/ ▶ **n.** clothing worn under other clothes, typically next to the skin.

un·der·weight /ˈəndərˌwāt, ˌəndərˈwāt/ ▶ **adj.** below a weight considered normal or desirable: *he was thirty pounds underweight*. ■ Finance (also **underweighted**) having less investment in a particular area than is considered desirable or appropriate: *the company is still underweight in Japan* | *underweighted in technology*.
▶ **v.** [with obj.] apply too little weight to (something): *we feared the hot-air balloon had been underweighted* | figurative *clinicians tend to overweight parent and underweight child information when deriving diagnoses*.
▶ **n.** insufficient weight.

un·der·went /ˌəndərˈwent/ past of **UNDERGO**.

un·der·whelm /ˌəndərˈ(h)welm/ ▶ **v.** [with obj.] (usu. **be underwhelmed**) humorous fail to impress or make a positive impact on (someone); disappoint: *American voters seem underwhelmed by the choices for president*.
– ORIGIN 1950s: suggested by **OVERWHELM**.

un·der·wing /ˈəndərˌwiNG/ ▶ **n.** **1** the hind wing of an insect, esp. when it is normally hidden by a forewing.
2 the underside of a bird's wing.
3 (also **underwing moth**) [usu. with modifier] a moth with drab forewings and brightly colored hind wings, typically yellow or red with a black terminal band. ● Several genera in the family Noctuidae.

un·der·wire /ˈəndərˌwīr/ ▶ **n.** a semicircular wire support stitched under each cup of a bra.
– DERIVATIVES **un·der·wired adj.**

un·der·wood /ˈəndərˌwo͝od/ ▶ **n.** small trees and shrubs growing beneath taller timber trees.

un·der·work /ˌəndərˈwərk/ ▶ **v.** [with obj.] (usu. **be underworked**) impose too little work on (someone): *its members are viewed by the public as overpaid and underworked*.

un·der·world /ˈəndərˌwərld/ ▶ **n.** **1** the world of criminals or of organized crime.
2 the mythical abode of the dead, imagined as being under the earth.

un·der·write /ˈəndə(r)ˌrīt, ˌəndə(r)ˈrīt/ ▶ **v.** (past **underwrote**; past participle **underwritten**) [with obj.] **1** sign and accept liability under (an insurance policy), thus guaranteeing payment in case loss or damage occurs. ■ accept (a liability or risk) in this way.
2 (of a bank or other financial institution) engage to buy all the unsold shares in (an issue of new securities). ■ undertake to finance or otherwise support or guarantee (something): *they were willing to underwrite the construction of a ship*.
3 archaic write (something) below something else, esp. other written matter.
– DERIVATIVES **un·der·writ·er** /ˈəndə(r)ˌrītər/ **n.**

un·de·scend·ed /ˌəndiˈsendid/ ▶ **adj.** Medicine (of a testicle) remaining in the abdomen instead of having descended normally into the scrotum.

un·de·served /ˌəndiˈzərvd/ ▶ **adj.** not warranted, merited, or earned: *an undeserved term of imprisonment*.
– DERIVATIVES **un·de·serv·ed·ly** /-ˈzərvədlē/ **adv.**

un·de·serv·ing /ˌəndiˈzərviNG/ ▶ **adj.** not deserving or worthy of something positive, esp. help or praise.
– DERIVATIVES **un·de·serv·ing·ly adv.**

un·de·signed ▶ **adj.** unintended. ■ arising from causes other than design: *undesigned buildings*.
– DERIVATIVES **un·de·sign·ed·ly adv.**

un·de·sir·a·ble /ˌəndiˈzīrəbəl/ ▶ **adj.** not wanted or desirable because harmful, objectionable, or unpleasant: *the drug's undesirable side effects*.
▶ **n.** a person considered to be objectionable in some way.
– DERIVATIVES **un·de·sir·a·bil·i·ty n., un·de·sir·a·ble·ness n., un·de·sir·a·bly** /-blē/ **adv.**

un·de·sired /ˌəndiˈzīrd/ ▶ **adj.** (esp. of an act or consequence) not wanted or desired.

un·de·tect·a·ble /ˌəndiˈtektəbəl/ ▶ **adj.** not able to be detected.
– DERIVATIVES **un·de·tect·a·bil·i·ty n., un·de·tect·a·bly adv.**

un·de·tect·ed /ˌəndiˈtektid/ ▶ **adj.** not detected or discovered: *the thieves escaped undetected*.

un·de·ter·mined /ˌəndiˈtərmənd/ ▶ **adj.** not authoritatively decided or settled: *the acquisition will result in an as yet undetermined number of layoffs*. ■ not known: *the bus was traveling with an undetermined number of passengers when it crashed*.

un·de·terred ▶ **adj.** persevering with something despite setbacks: *he was undeterred by these disasters*.

un·det·o·nat·ed /ənˈdetnˌātid/ ▶ **adj.** (of a bomb or other explosive weapon) not having been detonated.

un·de·vel·oped /ˌəndiˈveləpt/ ▶ **adj.** not having been developed: *undeveloped coal reserves*. ■ not having developed: *undeveloped buds and shoots*.

un·de·vi·at·ing /ˌənˈdēvēˌātiNG/ ▶ **adj.** showing no deviation; constant and steady: *the undeviating loyalty of his wife*.
– DERIVATIVES **un·de·vi·at·ing·ly adv.**

un·di·ag·nosed ▶ **adj.** not diagnosed or having been subject to diagnosis.

un·did /ˌənˈdid/ past of **UNDO**.

un·dies /ˈəndēz/ ▶ **plural n.** informal articles of underwear, esp. those of a woman or girl.
– ORIGIN early 20th cent.: abbreviation.

un·dif·fer·enced /ˌənˈdif(ə)rənst/ ▶ **adj.** Heraldry (of arms) not made distinct by a mark of difference.

un·dif·fer·en·ti·at·ed /ˌənˌdifəˈrenCHēˌātid/ ▶ **adj.** not different or differentiated: *ideologically undifferentiated candidates*.

un·di·gest·ed /ˌəndiˈjestid/ ▶ **adj.** (of food) not digested. ■ (of information, facts, or ideas) not having been properly assessed, considered, or understood: *undigested and conflicting intelligence*.

un·dig·ni·fied /ˌənˈdigniˌfīd/ ▶ **adj.** appearing foolish and unseemly; lacking in dignity: *an undignified exit*.

un·di·lut·ed /ˌəndiˈlo͞otid/ ▶ **adj.** (of a liquid) not diluted. ■ not moderated or weakened in any way: *a sudden surge of pure, undiluted happiness*.

un·di·min·ished /ˌəndiˈminisHt/ ▶ **adj.** not diminished, reduced, or lessened: *his enthusiasm for the game remains undiminished*.

un·dine /ˌənˈdēn, ˈənˌdēn/ ▶ **n.** a female spirit or nymph inhabiting water.
– ORIGIN early 19th cent.: from modern Latin *undina* (a word invented by Paracelsus), from Latin *unda* 'a wave.'

un·dip·lo·mat·ic /ˌənˌdipləˈmatik/ ▶ **adj.** being or appearing insensitive and tactless.
– DERIVATIVES **un·dip·lo·mat·i·cal·ly** /-ik(ə)lē/ **adv.**

un·di·rect·ed /ˌəndəˈrektəd, -ˌdī-/ ▶ **adj.** lacking direction; without a particular aim, purpose, or target: *she was full of ineffectual undirected anger*.

un·dis·cern·ing /ˌəndiˈsərniNG/ ▶ **adj.** lacking judgment, insight, or taste: *an undiscerning audience*.

un·dis·ci·plined /ˌənˈdisəplind/ ▶ **adj.** lacking in discipline; uncontrolled in behavior or manner.

un·dis·closed /ˌəndisˈklōzd/ ▶ **adj.** not revealed or made known publicly: *an out-of-court settlement for an undisclosed amount*.

un·dis·cov·ered /ˌəndisˈkəvərd/ ▶ **adj.** not discovered: *the novel had lain undiscovered for years among his papers*.

un·dis·crim·i·nat·ing /ˌəndisˈkriməˌnātiNG/ ▶ **adj.** not having or showing good judgment or taste.

un·dis·cussed /ˌəndisˈkəst/ ▶ **adj.** not discussed.

un·dis·guised /ˌəndisˈgīzd/ ▶ **adj.** (of a feeling) not disguised or concealed; open: *she looked at him with undisguised contempt*.
– DERIVATIVES **un·dis·guis·ed·ly** /-ˈgīzidlē/ **adv.**

un·dis·mayed /ˌəndisˈmād/ ▶ **adj.** not dismayed or discouraged by a setback.

un·dis·put·ed /ˌəndiˈspyo͞otid/ ▶ **adj.** not disputed or called into question; accepted.

un·dis·so·ci·at·ed /ˌəndiˈsōsHēˌātid, -ˈsōsē/ ▶ **adj.** Chemistry (of a molecule) not dissociated into oppositely charged ions.

un·dis·tin·guish·a·ble /ˌəndiˈstiNGgwisHəbəl/ ▶ **adj.** indistinguishable.

un·dis·tin·guished /ˌəndiˈstiNGgwisHt/ ▶ **adj.** lacking distinction; unexceptional: *an undistinguished career*.

un·dis·tort·ed /ˌəndisˈtôrtid/ ▶ **adj.** not distorted: *it may be difficult to provide undistorted information*.

un·dis·tract·ed /ˌəndiˈstraktəd/ ▶ **adj.** able to concentrate fully on something; not distracted: *she was undistracted by the flashing cameras*.

un·dis·trib·ut·ed /ˌəndisˈtribyo͞otid/ ▶ **adj.** not distributed.

un·dis·trib·ut·ed mid·dle ▶ **n.** Logic a fallacy arising from the failure of the middle term of a syllogism to refer to all the members of a class in at least one premise.

un·dis·turbed /ˌəndisˈtərbd/ ▶ **adj.** not disturbed: *a quiet weekend of undisturbed tranquillity* | *the tombs had lain undisturbed for 2,500 years*.

un·di·vid·ed /ˌəndəˈvīdid/ ▶ **adj.** not divided, separated, or broken into parts. ■ concentrated on or devoted completely to one object: *I can now give you my undivided attention*.

un·do /ˌənˈdo͞o/ ▶ **v.** (**undoes** /-ˈdəz/, **undoing**; past **undid**; past participle **undone**) [with obj.] **1** unfasten, untie, or loosen (something): *the knot was difficult to undo*.

2 cancel or reverse the effects or results of (a previous action or measure): *there wasn't any way Evelyn could undo the damage.* ■ cancel (the last one or more commands executed by a computer). **3** formal cause the downfall or ruin of: *Iago's hatred of women undoes him.*
▶ **n.** Computing a feature of a computer program that allows a user to cancel or reverse the last one or more commands executed.
– ORIGIN Old English *undōn* (see UN-², DO¹).

un·dock /ˌən'däk/ ▶ **v.** [with obj.] **1** separate (a spacecraft) from another in space: *Conrad undocked Gemini and used his thruster to back slowly away* | [no obj.] *Atlantis is scheduled to undock from Mir today.* **2** take (a ship) out of or away from a dock.

un·doc·u·ment·ed /ˌən'däkyəˌmentid/ ▶ **adj. 1** not recorded in or proved by documents. **2** not having the appropriate legal document or license: *undocumented immigrants.*

un·do·ing /ˌən'do͞o-iNG/ ▶ **n.** [in sing.] a person's ruin or downfall: *he knew of his ex-partner's role in his undoing.* ■ the cause of such ruin or downfall: *that complacency was to be their undoing.*

un·do·mes·ti·cat·ed /ˌəndə'mestiˌkātid/ ▶ **adj.** not domesticated: *I never cook for him and I am totally undomesticated.*

un·done /ˌən'dən/ past participle of UNDO.
▶ **adj. 1** not tied or fastened: *the top few buttons of his shirt were undone.* **2** not done or finished: *he had left his homework undone.* **3** formal or humorous (of a person) ruined by a disastrous or devastating setback or reverse: *I am undone!*

un·doubt·a·ble /ˌən'doutəbəl/ ▶ **adj.** rare not able to be doubted; indubitable.
– DERIVATIVES **un·doubt·a·bly** /-blē/ **adv.**

un·doubt·ed /ˌən'doutid/ ▶ **adj.** not questioned or doubted by anyone: *her undoubted ability.*

un·doubt·ed·ly /ˌən'doutidlē/ ▶ **adv.** without doubt; certainly: *they are undoubtedly guilty.*

UNDP ▶ **abbr.** United Nations Development Program.

un·drained /ˌən'drānd/ ▶ **adj.** not emptied of water; not drained: *undrained marshes.*

un·dra·mat·ic /ˌəndrə'matik/ ▶ **adj.** lacking the qualities expected in drama: *an undramatic libretto.* ■ unexciting: *research tends to be undramatic and unglamorous.*

un·draped /ˌən'drāpt/ ▶ **adj.** not covered with cloth or drapery. ■ (esp. of a model or subject in art) nude.

un·dreamed /ˌən'drēmd/ (Brit. also **undreamt** /-'dremt/) ▶ **adj.** (**undreamed of**) not thought to be possible (used to express pleasant surprise at the amount, extent, or level of something): *a level of comfort undreamed of in earlier times* | *she is now enjoying undreamed-of success.*

un·dress /ˌən'dres/ ▶ **v.** [no obj.] take off one's clothes: *she undressed and climbed into bed* | *I went into the bathroom to get undressed.* ■ [with obj.] take the clothes off (someone else).
▶ **n. 1** the state of being naked or only partially clothed: *women in various states of undress.* **2** Military ordinary clothing or uniform, as opposed to that worn on ceremonial occasions. Compare with FULL DRESS.

un·dressed /ˌən'drest/ ▶ **adj. 1** wearing no clothes: *he was undressed and ready for bed.* **2** not treated, processed, or prepared for use: *undressed deerskin* | *a rough, undressed stone slab.* **3** (of food) not having a dressing: *an undressed salad.*

un·drink·a·ble /ˌən'driNGkəbəl/ ▶ **adj.** not fit to be drunk because of impurity or poor quality.

UNDRO ▶ **abbr.** United Nations Disaster Relief Office.

un·due /ˌən'd(y)o͞o/ ▶ **adj.** unwarranted or inappropriate because excessive or disproportionate: *this figure did not give rise to undue concern.*
– DERIVATIVES **un·du·ly** /-'d(y)o͞olē/ **adv.**

un·due in·flu·ence ▶ **n.** Law influence by which a person is induced to act otherwise than by their own free will or without adequate attention to the consequences.

un·du·lant /'ənjələnt, 'əndyə-/ ▶ **adj.** having a rising and falling motion or appearance like that of waves; undulating.
– DERIVATIVES **un·du·lance** **n.**
– ORIGIN mid 19th cent.: from Latin *undulant-* 'moving like a wave,' from the verb *undulare.*

un·du·lant fe·ver ▶ **n.** brucellosis in humans.
– ORIGIN late 19th cent.: so named because of the intermittent fever associated with the disease.

un·du·late ▶ **v.** /'ənjəˌlāt, 'əndyə-/ [no obj.] move with a smooth wavelike motion: *her body undulated to the thumping rhythm of the music.* ■ (usu. adj. **undulating**) have a wavy form or outline: *delightful views over undulating countryside.*
▶ **adj.** /-lit, -ˌlāt/ Botany & Zoology (esp. of a leaf) having a wavy surface or edge.
– DERIVATIVES **un·du·late·ly** /-litlē/ **adv.**, **un·du·la·tion** /ˌənjə'lāSHən, ˌəndyə-/ **n.**, **un·du·la·to·ry** /'ənjələˌtôrē, 'əndyə-/ **adj.**
– ORIGIN mid 17th cent.: from late Latin *undulatus,* from Latin *unda* 'a wave.'

un·dy /'əndē/ ▶ **adj.** [usu. postpositive] Heraldry another term for WAVY.

un·dyed /ən'dīd/ ▶ **adj.** (esp. of fabric) not dyed; of its natural color.

un·dy·ing /ˌən'dī-iNG/ ▶ **adj.** (esp. of an emotion) lasting forever: *promises of undying love.*
– DERIVATIVES **un·dy·ing·ly** **adv.**

un·earned /ˌən'ərnd/ ▶ **adj.** not earned or deserved: *unearned privileges.* ■ Baseball (of a run) scored as the result of or following an error made by the fielding side, and not recorded in the pitcher's earned run average.

un·earned in·come ▶ **n.** income from investments rather than from work.

un·earned in·cre·ment ▶ **n.** an increase in the value of land or property without labor or expenditure on the part of the owner.

un·earth /ˌən'ərTH/ ▶ **v.** [with obj.] find (something) in the ground by digging. ■ discover (something hidden, lost, or kept secret) by investigation or searching: *they have done all they can to unearth the truth.*

un·earth·ly /ˌən'ərTHlē/ ▶ **adj. 1** unnatural or mysterious, esp. in a disturbing way: *unearthly quiet.* **2** informal unreasonably early or inconvenient: *a job that involves getting up at an unearthly hour.*
– DERIVATIVES **un·earth·li·ness** **n.**

un·ease /ˌən'ēz/ ▶ **n.** anxiety or discontent: *public unease about defense policy.*

un·eas·y /ˌən'ēzē/ ▶ **adj.** (**uneasier, uneasiest**) causing or feeling anxiety; troubled or uncomfortable: *she felt guilty now and a little uneasy* | *an uneasy silence.*
– DERIVATIVES **un·eas·i·ly** /-zəlē/ **adv.**, **un·eas·i·ness** **n.**

un·eat·en /ən'ētn/ ▶ **adj.** not eaten: *salad lying uneaten on the plate.*

un·ec·o·nom·ic /ˌənˌekə'nämik, -ˌēkə-/ ▶ **adj.** unprofitable: *costs for seven huge, uneconomic reactors.* ■ constituting an inefficient use of money or other resources: *it may be uneconomic to repair some goods.*

un·ec·o·nom·i·cal /ˌənˌekə'nämikəl, -ˌēkə-/ ▶ **adj.** wasteful of money or other resources; not economical: *the old buses eventually become uneconomical to run.*
– DERIVATIVES **un·ec·o·nom·i·cal·ly** /-ik(ə)lē/ **adv.**

un·ed·i·fy·ing /ˌən'edəˌfī-iNG/ ▶ **adj.** (esp. of an event taking place in public) distasteful; unpleasant: *the unedifying sight of the two leaders screeching conflicting proposals.*
– DERIVATIVES **un·ed·i·fy·ing·ly** **adv.**

un·ed·it·ed /ˌən'editid/ ▶ **adj.** (of material for publication or broadcasting) not edited.

un·ed·u·cat·ed /ˌən'ejəˌkātid/ ▶ **adj.** lacking an education; poorly educated.
– DERIVATIVES **un·ed·u·ca·ble** /-kəbəl/ **adj.**

un·e·lect·a·ble /ˌəni'lektəbəl/ ▶ **adj.** (of a candidate or party) unable to be elected.

un·e·lect·ed /ˌəni'lektid/ ▶ **adj.** (of an official) not elected: *unelected bureaucrats.*

un·em·bar·rassed /ˌənem'barəst/ ▶ **adj.** not feeling or showing embarrassment.

un·em·bel·lished /ˌənem'belisHt/ ▶ **adj.** not embellished or decorated: *the unembellished truth.*

un·e·mo·tion·al /ˌəni'mōSHənl/ ▶ **adj.** not having or showing strong feelings: *a flat, unemotional voice.*
– DERIVATIVES **un·e·mo·tion·al·ly** /-SHənl-ē/ **adv.**

un·em·ploy·a·ble /ˌənim'ploi-əbəl/ ▶ **adj.** (of a person) not able or likely to get paid employment, esp. because of a lack of skills or qualifications.
▶ **n.** an unemployable person.
– DERIVATIVES **un·em·ploy·a·bil·i·ty** /-ˌploi-ə'bilətē/ **n.**

un·em·ployed /ˌənim'ploid/ ▶ **adj.** (of a person) without a paid job but available to work: *I was unemployed for three years* | (as plural noun **the unemployed**) *a training program for the long-term unemployed.* ■ (of a thing) not in use.

un·em·ploy·ment /ˌənim'ploimənt/ ▶ **n.** the state of being unemployed. ■ the number or proportion of unemployed people: *a time of high unemployment* ■ short for UNEMPLOYMENT BENEFIT.

un·em·ploy·ment ben·e·fit (also **unemployment compensation**) ▶ **n.** a payment made by a government or a labor union to an unemployed person.

un·em·ploy·ment com·pen·sa·tion ▶ **n.** money that substitutes for wages or salary, paid to recently unemployed workers under a program administered by a government or labor union.

un·en·closed /ˌənen'klōzd/ ▶ **adj.** not enclosed by walls or fences: *the main staircase is unenclosed at the lobby level.*

un·en·crypt·ed /ˌənin'kriptəd/ ▶ **adj.** Computing (of information or data) not converted into a code that would prevent unauthorized access: *unencrypted passwords.*

un·en·cum·bered /ˌənen'kəmbərd/ ▶ **adj.** not having any burden or impediment: *he needed to travel light and unencumbered.* ■ free of debt or other financial liability.

un·end·ing /ˌən'endiNG/ ▶ **adj.** having or seeming to have no end: *the charity rescues children from unending poverty.* ■ countless or continual: *unending demands.*
– DERIVATIVES **un·end·ing·ly** **adv.**, **un·end·ing·ness** **n.**

un·en·dur·a·ble /ˌənin'd(y)o͝orəbəl/ ▶ **adj.** not able to be tolerated or endured: *cries of unendurable suffering.*
– DERIVATIVES **un·en·dur·a·bly** /-blē/ **adv.**

un·en·force·a·ble /ˌənen'fôrsəbəl/ ▶ **adj.** (esp. of an obligation or law) impossible to enforce.

un·en·gaged /ˌənen'gājd/ ▶ **adj.** not occupied or engaged.

un·Eng·lish /ˌən'iNG(g)liSH/ ▶ **adj.** not considered characteristic of English people or the English language.

un·en·light·ened /ˌənen'lītnd/ ▶ **adj.** not having or showing an enlightened outlook: *unenlightened thinking.*
– DERIVATIVES **un·en·light·en·ing** **adj.**, **un·en·light·en·ment** **n.**

un·en·riched /ˌənen'riCHt/ ▶ **adj. 1** (of foodstuffs or soil) without additional nutrients added: *unenriched white flour.* **2** (of uranium) in the natural state, containing less than one percent U-235 (an unstable, fissionable isotope of uranium ore).

un·en·tan·gle /ˌənin'taNGgəl/ ▶ **v.** another term for DISENTANGLE.

un·en·thu·si·as·tic /ˌənenˌTHo͞ozē'astik/ ▶ **adj.** not having or showing enthusiasm: *an unenthusiastic response.*
– DERIVATIVES **un·en·thu·si·as·ti·cal·ly** **adv.**

un·en·vi·a·ble /ˌən'envēəbəl/ ▶ **adj.** difficult, undesirable, or unpleasant: *he had the unenviable task of trying to reconcile their disparate interests* | *an unenviable reputation for drunkenness.*
– DERIVATIVES **un·en·vi·a·bly** /-blē/ **adv.**

UNEP ▶ **abbr.** United Nations Environment Programme.

un·e·qual /ˌən'ēkwəl/ ▶ **adj. 1** not equal in quantity, size, or value: *two rooms of unequal size* | *unequal odds.* ■ not fair, evenly balanced, or having equal advantage: *the ownership of capital is unequal in this country.* **2** [predic.] not having the ability or resources to meet a challenge: *she felt **unequal to** the task before her.*
▶ **n.** a person or thing considered to be different from another in status or level.
– DERIVATIVES **un·e·qual·ly** **adv.**

un·e·qualed /ˌən'ēkwəld/ (Brit. **unequalled**) ▶ **adj.** superior to all others in performance or extent: *a range of facilities unequaled in Chicago* | *trout of unequaled quality.*

un·e·quipped /ˌəni'kwipt/ ▶ **adj.** not equipped with the necessary items or skills: *kids unequipped to deal with the situation.*

un·e·quiv·o·cal /ˌəni'kwivəkəl/ ▶ **adj.** leaving no doubt; unambiguous: *an unequivocal answer* | *he was unequivocal in condemning the violence.*
– DERIVATIVES **un·e·quiv·o·cal·ly** /-ik(ə)lē/ **adv.**, **un·e·quiv·o·cal·ness** **n.**

un·err·ing /ˌən'əriNG, -'er-/ ▶ **adj.** always right or accurate: *an unerring sense of direction.*
– DERIVATIVES **un·err·ing·ly** **adv.**, **un·err·ing·ness** **n.**

un·es·cap·a·ble /ˌənə'skāpəbəl/ ▶ **adj.** another term for INESCAPABLE.

UNESCO /yo͞o'neskō/ (also **Unesco**) an agency of the United Nations established in 1945 to promote the exchange of information, ideas, and culture. In 1984 the US withdrew from the organization, but in 2003 after satisfied with certain reforms, it rejoined.

– ORIGIN acronym from *United Nations Educational, Scientific, and Cultural Organization.*

un·es·cort·ed /ˌənəˈskôrtid, -ˈesˌkôrtid/ ▶ **adj.** not escorted, esp. for protection, security, or as a mark of rank: *their task was to prey on unescorted enemy merchant ships and sink them.* ■ unaccompanied by a social partner: *in some bars unescorted women were not served.*

un·es·sen·tial /ˌənəˈsenCHəl/ ▶ **adj. & n.** another term for **INESSENTIAL**.

un·eth·i·cal /ˌənˈeTHikəl/ ▶ **adj.** not morally correct: *it is unethical to torment any creature for entertainment.*
– DERIVATIVES **un·eth·i·cal·ly** /-ik(ə)lē/ **adv.**

un·e·ven /ˌənˈēvən/ ▶ **adj.** not level or smooth: *the floors are cracked and uneven.* ■ not regular, consistent, or equal: *the uneven distribution of resources.* ■ (of a contest) not equally balanced: *Fran struggled briefly but soon gave up the uneven contest.*
– DERIVATIVES **un·e·ven·ly adv.**, **un·e·ven·ness n.**
– ORIGIN Old English *unefen* 'not corresponding exactly' (see **UN-**[1], **EVEN**[1]).

un·e·ven bars (also **uneven parallel bars**) ▶ **plural n.** a pair of parallel bars set at different heights, used in women's gymnastics.

un·e·vent·ful /ˌəniˈventfəl/ ▶ **adj.** not marked by interesting or exciting events.
– DERIVATIVES **un·e·vent·ful·ly adv.**, **un·e·vent·ful·ness n.**

un·ex·am·ined /ˌənigˈzamənd/ ▶ **adj.** not investigated or examined: *widely held but largely unexamined preconceptions.*

un·ex·am·pled /ˌənigˈzampəld/ ▶ **adj.** formal having no precedent or parallel: *a regime that brought such unexampled disaster on its people.*

un·ex·cep·tion·a·ble /ˌənikˈsepSH(ə)nəbəl/ ▶ **adj.** not open to objection: *the unexceptionable belief that society should be governed by law.*
– DERIVATIVES **un·ex·cep·tion·a·ble·ness n.**, **un·ex·cep·tion·a·bly** /-blē/ **adv.**

USAGE There is a clear distinction in meaning between **exceptionable** ('open to objection') and **exceptional** ('out of the ordinary, very good'). However, this distinction has become blurred in the negative forms **unexceptionable** and **unexceptional**. Strictly speaking, **unexceptionable** means 'not open to objection' (*this request is* ***unexceptionable*** *in itself*), while **unexceptional** means 'not out of the ordinary, usual' (*the hotel was adequate but* ***unexceptional***). But, although the distinction may be clear in these two examples, the meaning of **unexceptionable** is often indeterminate between 'not open to objection' and 'ordinary,' as in *the food was bland and* ***unexceptionable*** *or the candidates were pretty* ***unexceptionable***. See also usage at **EXCEPTIONABLE**.

un·ex·cep·tion·al /ˌənikˈsepSHənl/ ▶ **adj.** not out of the ordinary; usual: *an unexceptional movie.*
– DERIVATIVES **un·ex·cep·tion·al·ly adv.**

USAGE See usage at **UNEXCEPTIONABLE**.

un·ex·cit·a·ble /ˌənikˈsītəbəl/ ▶ **adj.** (of a person) not easily excited.
– DERIVATIVES **un·ex·cit·a·bil·i·ty** /-ˌsītəˈbilətē/ **n.**

un·ex·cit·ing /ˌənikˈsītiNG/ ▶ **adj.** not exciting; dull.

un·ex·er·cised /ˌənˈeksərˌsīzd/ ▶ **adj. 1** not made use of or put into practice: *unexercised stock options.* **2** (of a person) not taking exercise; unfit.

un·ex·pect·ed /ˌənikˈspektid/ ▶ **adj.** not expected or regarded as likely to happen: *his death was totally unexpected* | (as noun **the unexpected**) *he seemed to have a knack for saying the unexpected.*
– DERIVATIVES **un·ex·pect·ed·ly adv.** [as submodifier] *an unexpectedly high price*, **un·ex·pect·ed·ness n.**

un·ex·pired /ˌənikˈspīrd/ ▶ **adj.** (of an agreement or period of time) not yet having come to an end: *the unexpired portion of the lease.*

un·ex·plain·a·ble /ˌənikˈsplānəbəl/ ▶ **adj.** unable to be explained or accounted for: *unexplainable rages.*
– DERIVATIVES **un·ex·plain·a·bly** /-blē/ **adv.**

un·ex·plained /ˌənikˈsplānd/ ▶ **adj.** not described or made clear; unknown: *the reason for her summons was as yet unexplained.* ■ not accounted for or attributable to an identified cause: *SIDS is still an unexplained phenomenon.*

un·ex·plod·ed /ˌənikˈsplōdid/ ▶ **adj.** (of a bomb or other explosive device) not having exploded.

un·ex·ploit·ed /ˌənikˈsploitid/ ▶ **adj.** (of resources) not used to maximum benefit: *unexploited reserves of natural gas.*

un·ex·plored /ˌənikˈsplôrd/ ▶ **adj.** (of a country or area) not investigated or mapped. ■ not evaluated or discussed in detail: *the research focuses on an unexplored theme in European history.*

un·ex·posed /ˌənikˈspōzd/ ▶ **adj.** covered or protected; not vulnerable. ■ [predic.] not introduced to or acquainted with something: *a person* ***unexposed to*** *spiritualist traditions.* ■ [predic.] not made public; concealed: *no secrets were left unexposed.* ■ (of photographic film) not subjected to light.

un·ex·pressed /ˌənikˈsprest/ ▶ **adj.** (of a thought or feeling) not communicated or made known: *he thought it best to leave his doubts unexpressed.* ■ Genetics (of a gene) not appearing in a phenotype.

un·ex·pres·sive /ˌənikˈspresiv/ ▶ **adj.** showing no expression; emotionless: *his big brown eyes were dull and unexpressive.*
– DERIVATIVES **un·ex·pres·sive·ly adv.**

un·ex·pur·gat·ed /ˌənˈekspərˌgātid/ ▶ **adj.** (of a text) complete and containing all the original material; uncensored.

un·face·a·ble /ˌənˈfāsəbəl/ ▶ **adj.** (of a situation or circumstance) not able to be confronted or dealt with.

un·fad·ing /ˌənˈfādiNG/ ▶ **adj.** not losing brightness, vitality, or strength.
– DERIVATIVES **un·fad·ing·ly adv.**

un·fail·ing /ˌənˈfāliNG/ ▶ **adj.** without error or fault: *his unfailing memory for names.* ■ reliable or constant: *his mother had always been an unfailing source of reassurance.*
– DERIVATIVES **un·fail·ing·ly adv.**, **un·fail·ing·ness n.**

un·fair /ˌənˈfe(ə)r/ ▶ **adj.** not based on or behaving according to the principles of equality and justice: *at times like these the legal system appears inhumane and unfair.* ■ unkind, inconsiderate, or unreasonable: *you're unfair to criticize like that when she's never done you any harm.* ■ not following the rules of a game or sport.
– DERIVATIVES **un·fair·ly adv.**, **un·fair·ness n.**
– ORIGIN Old English *unfæger* 'not beautiful' (see **UN-**[1], **FAIR**[1]).

un·faith·ful /ˌənˈfāTHfəl/ ▶ **adj.** not faithful, in particular: ■ engaging in sexual relations with a person other than one's regular partner in contravention of a previous promise or understanding: *you haven't* ***been unfaithful to*** *him, have you?* | *her unfaithful husband.* ■ disloyal, treacherous, or insincere: *she felt that to sell the house would be* ***unfaithful*** *to her parents' memory.*
– DERIVATIVES **un·faith·ful·ly adv.**, **un·faith·ful·ness n.**

un·fal·ter·ing /ˌənˈfôltəriNG/ ▶ **adj.** not faltering; steady; resolute: *her unfaltering energy and determination.*
– DERIVATIVES **un·fal·ter·ing·ly adv.**

un·fa·mil·iar /ˌənfəˈmilyər/ ▶ **adj.** not known or recognized: *his voice was* ***unfamiliar to*** *her.* ■ unusual or uncharacteristic: *the yellow taxicab was an unfamiliar sight on these roads.* ■ [predic.] (**unfamiliar with**) not having knowledge or experience of: *the organization was set up to advise people who might be unfamiliar with legal procedures.*
– DERIVATIVES **un·fa·mil·i·ar·i·ty** /-ˌmilēˈe(ə)ritē, -fəmilˈyer-/ **n.**

un·fash·ion·a·ble /ˌənˈfasH(ə)nəbəl/ ▶ **adj.** not fashionable or popular at a particular time: *they lived in an unfashionable part of Houston.*
– DERIVATIVES **un·fash·ion·a·ble·ness n.**, **un·fash·ion·a·bly adv.**

un·fash·ioned /ˌənˈfasHənd/ ▶ **adj.** chiefly literary not made into a specific shape; formless.

un·fas·ten /ˌənˈfasən/ ▶ **v.** [with obj.] open the fastening of; undo (something): *Allie stands before the mirror unfastening her earrings* | (as adj. **unfastened**) *he had left the door unfastened.* ■ [no obj.] become loose or undone.

un·fa·thered /ˌənˈfäTHərd/ ▶ **adj.** dated having no known or acknowledged father; illegitimate. ■ chiefly literary of unknown or obscure origin: *unfathered rumors.*

un·fath·om·a·ble /ˌənˈfaTHəməbəl/ ▶ **adj.** **1** incapable of being fully explored or understood: *her gray eyes were dark with some unfathomable emotion.* **2** (of water or a natural feature) impossible to measure the extent of.
– DERIVATIVES **un·fath·om·a·bly adv.**

un·fath·omed /ˌənˈfaTHəmd/ ▶ **adj. 1** not fully explored or understood. **2** (of water) of unascertained depth.

un·fa·vor·a·ble /ˌənˈfāv(ə)rəbəl/ (Brit. **unfavourable**) ▶ **adj. 1** expressing or showing a lack of approval or support: *single mothers are often the target of unfavorable press attention.* **2** adverse; inauspicious: *it would be unwise to sell the company while the economic circumstances are so unfavorable.*
– DERIVATIVES **un·fa·vor·a·ble·ness n.**, **un·fa·vor·a·bly** /-blē/ **adv.**

un·fazed /ˌənˈfāzd/ ▶ **adj.** not disconcerted or perturbed: *the protestors were unfazed by the prospect of arrest.*

un·fea·si·ble ▶ **adj.** inconvenient or impractical: *childcare is expensive, making the return to work unfeasible for many women.*
– DERIVATIVES **un·fea·si·bil·i·ty n.**, **un·fea·si·bly adv.**

un·fed ▶ **adj.** not having been fed.

un·feel·ing /ˌənˈfēliNG/ ▶ **adj.** unsympathetic, harsh, or callous. ■ lacking physical sensation or sensitivity.
– DERIVATIVES **un·feel·ing·ly adv.**, **un·feel·ing·ness n.**
– ORIGIN late Old English *unfēlende* 'insensible' (see **UN-**[1], **FEELING**).

un·feigned /ˌənˈfānd/ ▶ **adj.** genuine; sincere: *a broad smile of unfeigned delight.*
– DERIVATIVES **un·feign·ed·ly** /-ˈfānidlē/ **adv.**

un·felt /ˌənˈfelt/ ▶ **adj.** not felt or experienced: *he had no desire to trade unfelt greetings with his mother-in-law.*

un·fem·i·nine /ˌənˈfemənin/ ▶ **adj.** not having or showing qualities traditionally associated with women.
– DERIVATIVES **un·fem·i·nin·i·ty n.**

un·fenced /ˌənˈfenst/ ▶ **adj.** not provided with fences.

un·fer·ment·ed /ˌənfərˈmentid/ ▶ **adj.** not fermented.

un·fer·ti·lized /ˌənˈfərtlˌīzd/ ▶ **adj.** not fertilized: *an unfertilized egg* | *unfertilized land.*

un·fet·ter /ˌənˈfetər/ ▶ **v.** [with obj.] (usu. as adj. **unfettered**) release from restraint or inhibition: *his imagination is unfettered by the laws of logic.*

un·fil·i·al /ˌənˈfilēəl, -ˈfilyəl/ ▶ **adj.** not having or showing the qualities associated with a son or daughter.
– DERIVATIVES **un·fil·i·al·ly adv.**

un·filled /ˌənˈfild/ ▶ **adj.** not filled: *12% of IT jobs in the city are unfilled.*

un·film·a·ble /ənˈfilməbl/ ▶ **adj.** (esp. of a novel) not suitable to be adapted for a movie.

un·fil·tered /ˌənˈfiltərd/ ▶ **adj. 1** not having been filtered: *unfiltered tap water.* **2** (of a cigarette) not provided with a filter.

un·fin·ished /ˌənˈfinisHt/ ▶ **adj.** not finished or concluded; incomplete: *her last novel is unfinished.* ■ (of an object) not having been given an attractive surface appearance as the final stage of manufacture.

un·fit /ˌənˈfit/ ▶ **adj. 1** [predic.] (of a thing) not of the necessary quality or standard to meet a particular purpose: *the land is* ***unfit for*** *food crops.* ■ (of a person) not having the requisite qualities or skills to undertake something competently: *she is unfit to have care and control of her children.* ■ Biology (of a species) not able to produce viable offspring or survive in a particular environment. **2** (of a person) not in good physical condition, typically as a result of failure to exercise regularly.
▶ **v.** (**unfits, unfitting, unfitted**) [with obj.] archaic make (something or someone) unsuitable; disqualify.
– DERIVATIVES **un·fit·ly adv.**, **un·fit·ness n.**

un·fit·ted /ˌənˈfitid/ ▶ **adj. 1** [predic.] (of a person) not fitted or suited for a particular task or vocation: *he seemed to know he was* ***unfitted for*** *such a role.* **2** (of furniture) not fitted.

un·fit·ting /ˌənˈfitiNG/ ▶ **adj.** not fitting or suitable; unbecoming.
– DERIVATIVES **un·fit·ting·ly adv.**

un·fix·a·ble /ənˈfiksəbl/ ▶ **adj.** not able to be repaired or put right: *I do not think the problem is unfixable.*

un·fixed /ˌənˈfikst/ ▶ **adj.** not fixed, in particular: ■ not fixed in a definite place or position; unfastened; loose: *the green cloth cover had become unfixed in a dozen places.* ■ uncertain or variable: *a being of unfixed gender.* ■ informal (of a venture or situation) doubtful or unsuccessful; coming to nothing: *you don't have to do anything unless the deal comes unfixed.*
– DERIVATIVES **un·fix v.**

un·flag·ging /ˌənˈflagiNG/ ▶ **adj.** tireless; persistent: *his apparently unflagging enthusiasm impressed her.*
– DERIVATIVES **un·flag·ging·ly adv.**

PRONUNCIATION KEY ə *ago, up*; ər *over, fur*; a *hat*; ā *ate*; ä *car*; e *let*; ē *see*; i *fit*; ī *by*; NG *sing*; ō *go*; ô *law, for*; oi *toy*; o͝o *good*; o͞o *goo*; ou *out*; TH *thin*; T͟H *then*; ZH *vision*

U

un·flap·pa·ble /ˌənˈflapəbəl/ ▶ **adj.** informal having or showing calmness in a crisis.
– DERIVATIVES **un·flap·pa·bil·i·ty** /-ˌflapəˈbilətē/ **n.**, **un·flap·pa·bly** /-blē/ **adv.**

un·flash·y /ənˈflaSHē/ ▶ **adj.** not seeking attention through ostentation; restrained or tasteful: *a solid, unflashy performance.*

un·flat·ter·ing /ˌənˈflatəriNG/ ▶ **adj.** not flattering: *the reviews of the book were very unflattering | an unflattering portrait.*
– DERIVATIVES **un·flat·ter·ing·ly adv.**

un·fla·vored /ˌənˈflāvərd/ (Brit. **unflavoured**) ▶ **adj.** (of food or drink) not containing additional flavorings.

un·fledged /ˌənˈflejd/ ▶ **adj.** (of a bird) not yet fledged. ■ (of a person) inexperienced; youthful.

un·fleshed /ˌənˈfleSHt/ ▶ **adj.** chiefly literary not covered with flesh.

un·flinch·ing /ˌənˈflinCHiNG/ ▶ **adj.** not showing fear or hesitation in the face of danger or difficulty: *he has shown unflinching determination throughout the campaign.*
– DERIVATIVES **un·flinch·ing·ly adv.**

un·flus·tered /ənˈfləstərd/ ▶ **adj.** not agitated; calm and self-controlled: *she seemed surprisingly unflustered by the delay.*

un·fo·cused /ˌənˈfōkəst/ (also **unfocussed**) ▶ **adj.** (of a person or their eyes) not seeing clearly; appearing glazed or expressionless. ■ (of an optical device) not adjusted to focus: *perpetually unfocused binoculars.* ■ (of a lens) not making incident light rays meet at a single point. ■ (of an object of vision) not in focus; indistinct. ■ (of feelings or plans) without a specific aim or direction: *my aspirations to write history were real but unfocused.*

un·fold /ˌənˈfōld/ ▶ **v.** open or spread out from a folded position: [with obj.] *he unfolded the map and laid it out on the table* | [no obj.] *the white flowers were just starting to unfold.* ■ [with obj.] reveal or disclose (thoughts or information): *Miss Eva* ***unfolded*** *her secret exploits* ***to*** *Mattie.* ■ [no obj.] (of information or a sequence of events) be revealed or disclosed: *there was a fascinating scene unfolding before me.*
– DERIVATIVES **un·fold·ment n.**
– ORIGIN Old English *unfealdan* (see **UN-**[2], **FOLD**[1]).

un·forced /ˌənˈfôrst/ ▶ **adj.** not produced by effort; natural: *an unforced cheerfulness.* ■ not compelled or constrained: *his retirement was an unforced departure.*
– DERIVATIVES **un·forc·ed·ly** /-ˈfôrsədlē/ **adv.**

unforced er·ror ▶ **n.** Sports a mistake made on an easy shot by a competitor in a nonpressure situation.

un·fore·see·a·ble /ˌənfôrˈsēəbəl/ ▶ **adj.** not able to be anticipated or predicted: *unforeseeable political consequences could arise.*

un·fore·seen /ˌənfôrˈsēn/ ▶ **adj.** not anticipated or predicted: *insurance to protect yourself against unforeseen circumstances.*

un·fore·told /ˌənfôrˈtōld, -fər-/ ▶ **adj.** literary not foretold; unpredicted.

un·for·get·ta·ble /ˌənfərˈgetəbəl/ ▶ **adj.** impossible to forget; very memorable: *that unforgettable first kiss.*
– DERIVATIVES **un·for·get·ta·bly** /-blē/ **adv.**

un·for·giv·a·ble /ˌənfərˈgivəbəl/ ▶ **adj.** so bad as to be unable to be forgiven or excused: *losing your temper with him was unforgivable.*
– DERIVATIVES **un·for·giv·a·bly** /-blē/ **adv.**

un·for·giv·en /ˌənfərˈgivən/ ▶ **adj.** not forgiven: *I could see some unforgiven issues between them.*

un·for·giv·ing /ˌənfərˈgiviNG/ ▶ **adj.** not willing to forgive or excuse people's faults or wrongdoings: *he was always a proud and unforgiving man.* ■ (of conditions) harsh; hostile: *the moor can be a wild and unforgiving place in bad weather.*
– DERIVATIVES **un·for·giv·ing·ly adv.**, **un·for·giv·ing·ness n.**

un·for·mat·ted /ənˈfôrmatid/ ▶ **adj.** Computing (of a document, storage medium, etc.) not formatted.

un·formed /ˌənˈfôrmd/ ▶ **adj.** without a definite form or shape: *she packed the unformed butter into the mold.* ■ not having developed or been developed fully: *he had an ambitious, albeit unformed, idea for a novel | unformed youths.*

un·forth·com·ing /ˌənfôrTHˈkəmiNG/ ▶ **adj.** [predic.] **1** (of a person) not willing to divulge information: *the sergeant seemed unforthcoming, so he inquired at the gate.*
2 (of something required) not ready or made available when wanted or needed: *with money unforthcoming from the company, the project has had to be delayed.*

un·for·ti·fied /ənˈfôrtəˌfīd/ ▶ **adj. 1** not fortified against attack: *there seems to have been an unfortified village on the site.*
2 (of food) without added nutritional supplements: *check with your doctor if you are giving your baby an unfortified formula.*

un·for·tu·nate /ˌənˈfôrCHənət/ ▶ **adj.** having or marked by bad fortune; unlucky: *the unfortunate Cunningham was fired.* ■ (of a circumstance) unfavorable or inauspicious: *the delay at the airport was an unfortunate start to our vacation.* ■ regrettable or inappropriate: *his unfortunate remark silenced the gathering.*
▶ **n.** (often **unfortunates**) a person who suffers bad fortune. ■ archaic a person who is considered immoral or lacking in religious faith or instruction, esp. a prostitute.

un·for·tu·nate·ly /ˌənˈfôrCHənətlē/ ▶ **adv.** [sentence adverb] it is unfortunate that: *unfortunately, we do not have the time to interview every applicant.*

un·found·ed /ˌənˈfoundid/ ▶ **adj.** having no foundation or basis in fact: *her persistent fear that she had cancer was unfounded.*
– DERIVATIVES **un·found·ed·ly adv.**, **un·found·ed·ness n.**

UNFPA ▶ **abbr.** United Nations Fund for Population Activities.

un·framed /ˌənfrāmd/ ▶ **adj.** (esp. of a picture) not having a frame.

un·free /ˌənˈfrē/ ▶ **adj.** deprived or devoid of liberty.
– DERIVATIVES **un·free·dom** /-dəm/ **n.**

un·freeze /ˌənˈfrēz/ ▶ **v.** (past **unfroze**; past participle **unfrozen**) [with obj.] cause (something) to thaw. ■ [no obj.] become thawed. ■ remove restrictions on the use or transfer of (an asset).

un·fre·quent·ed /ˌənˈfrēkwəntid, -frēˈkwen-/ ▶ **adj.** (of a place) visited only rarely: *an unfrequented dirt path off the road to the beach.*

un·friend /ˌənˈfrend/ ▶ **v.** [with obj.] informal remove (someone) from a list of friends or contacts on a social networking site: *she broke up with her boyfriend, but she hasn't unfriended him.*

WORD TRENDS See **FRIEND**.

un·friend·ed /ˌənˈfrendid/ ▶ **adj.** literary without friends: *murder left innocent people bereft and unfriended.*

un·friend·ly /ˌənˈfren(d)lē/ ▶ **adj.** (**unfriendlier**, **unfriendliest**) not friendly: *she shot him an unfriendly glance | Mildred felt unfriendly toward her | environmentally unfriendly activities.*
– DERIVATIVES **un·friend·li·ness n.**

un·frock /ˌənˈfräk/ ▶ **v.** another term for **DEFROCK**.

un·fro·zen /ˌənˈfrōzən/ past participle of **UNFREEZE**.
▶ **adj.** not or no longer frozen: *larvae remain unfrozen under the ice.*

un·fruit·ful /ˌənˈfro͞otfəl/ ▶ **adj. 1** not producing good or helpful results; unproductive: *the meeting was unfruitful.*
2 not producing fruit or crops; unfertile.
– DERIVATIVES **un·fruit·ful·ly adv.**, **un·fruit·ful·ness n.**

un·ful·filled /ˌənfo͝o(l)ˈfild/ ▶ **adj.** not carried out or brought to completion: *it was his unfulfilled ambition to write.* ■ not having fully utilized or exploited one's abilities or character.
– DERIVATIVES **un·ful·fill·a·ble** /-ˈfiləbəl/ **adj.**, **un·ful·fill·ing** /-ˈfiliNG/ **adj.**

un·fund·ed /ˌənˈfəndid/ ▶ **adj.** not funded, in particular: ■ not receiving public funds: *a new education bill remained unfunded.* ■ planned but not provided for financially: *unfunded owner buyouts.* ■ (of a debt) repayable on demand rather than having been converted into a more or less permanent debt at fixed interest.

un·fun·ny /ˌənˈfənē/ ▶ **adj.** (**unfunnier**, **unfunniest**) (typically of something intended to be funny) not amusing: *a hideously unfunny spoof film.*
– DERIVATIVES **un·fun·ni·ly** /-ˈfənəlē/ **adv.**, **un·fun·ni·ness n.**

un·furl /ˌənˈfərl/ ▶ **v.** make or become spread out from a rolled or folded state, esp. in order to be open to the wind: [with obj.] *a man was unfurling a sail* | [no obj.] *the flags unfurl.*

un·fur·nished /ˌənˈfərnisHt/ ▶ **adj. 1** (of a house or apartment) without furniture, esp. available to be rented without furniture: *an unfurnished apartment.*
2 archaic not supplied: *he is* ***unfurnished with*** *the ideas of justice.*

un·fused /ˌənˈfyo͞ozd/ ▶ **adj. 1** not fused or joined: *Darwin had predicted that a proto-bird would one day turn up with unfused wing fingers.*
2 not fitted or supplied with a fuse: *unfused electrical terminals.*

un·fus·sy ▶ **adj.** not fussy: *a simple unfussy design.*
– DERIVATIVES **un·fus·si·ly adv.**

un·gain·ly /ˌənˈgānlē/ ▶ **adj.** (of a person or movement) awkward; clumsy: *an ungainly walk.*
– DERIVATIVES **un·gain·li·ness n.**
– ORIGIN mid 17th cent.: from **UN-**[1] 'not' + obsolete *gainly* 'graceful,' based on Old Norse *gegn* 'straight.'

un·gen·er·ous /ˌənˈjenərəs/ ▶ **adj.** not generous; selfish.
– DERIVATIVES **un·gen·er·ous·ly adv.**, **un·gen·er·ous·ness n.**

un·gen·tle·man·ly /ˌənˈjentlmənlē/ ▶ **adj.** not appropriate to or behaving like a gentleman: *an ungentlemanly lack of sportsmanship.*
– DERIVATIVES **un·gen·tle·man·li·ness n.**

un·get·at·a·ble /ˌənˌgetˈatəbəl/ ▶ **adj.** informal inaccessible.

un·gift·ed /ˌənˈgiftid/ ▶ **adj.** not having any exceptional talents.

un·gird /ənˈgərd/ ▶ **v.** [with obj.] archaic release or take off by undoing a belt or girth.

un·giv·ing /ˌənˈgiviNG/ ▶ **adj.** (of a person) cold or stubborn in relationships with other people. ■ (of a material) not bending or pliable; stiff.

un·glam·or·ous /ˌənˈglamərəs/ ▶ **adj.** lacking glamour and excitement: *an unglamorous family car.*

un·glazed /ˌənˈglāzd/ ▶ **adj.** not glazed: *unglazed porcelain.*

un·gloved /ənˈgləvd/ ▶ **adj.** not wearing a glove or gloves.

un·glued /ˌənˈglo͞od/ ▶ **adj.** not or no longer stuck: *grease particles* ***come unglued*** *from the plate* | figurative *it was only a matter of time before the whole operation came unglued.* ■ informal (of a person or state of mind) confused and emotionally strained: *it had been a long day, and tempers were* ***becoming unglued.***

un·god·ly /ˌənˈgädlē/ ▶ **adj.** irreligious or immoral: *ungodly lives of self-obsession, lust, and pleasure.* ■ informal unreasonably early or inconvenient: *I've been troubled by telephone calls at ungodly hours.*
– DERIVATIVES **un·god·li·ness n.**

un·gov·ern·a·ble /ˌənˈgəvərnəbəl/ ▶ **adj.** impossible to control or govern.
– DERIVATIVES **un·gov·ern·a·bil·i·ty** /-ˌgəvərnəˈbilətē/ **n.**, **un·gov·ern·a·bly** /-blē/ **adv.**

un·grace·ful /ˌənˈgrāsfəl/ ▶ **adj.** lacking grace; clumsy.
– DERIVATIVES **un·grace·ful·ly adv.**, **un·grace·ful·ness n.**

un·gra·cious /ˌənˈgrāSHəs/ ▶ **adj. 1** not polite or friendly: *after Anna's kindness I wouldn't want to seem ungracious.*
2 not graceful or elegant.
– DERIVATIVES **un·gra·cious·ly adv.**, **un·gra·cious·ness n.**

un·grad·ed /ˌənˈgrādid/ ▶ **adj. 1** not divided into grades or separate levels: *students are in ungraded classrooms.*
2 not required or subject to evaluation: *the ungraded part of the assignment.*

un·gram·mat·i·cal /ˌəngrəˈmatikəl/ ▶ **adj.** not conforming to grammatical rules; not well formed: *ungrammatical sentences.*
– DERIVATIVES **un·gram·mat·i·cal·i·ty** /-ˌmatiˈkalətē/ **n.** (pl. **ungrammaticalities**), **un·gram·mat·i·cal·ly** /-ik(ə)lē/ **adv.**, **un·gram·mat·i·cal·ness n.**

un·grasp·a·ble /ˌənˈgraspəbəl/ ▶ **adj.** impossible to comprehend or understand.

un·grate·ful /ˌənˈgrātfəl/ ▶ **adj.** not feeling or showing gratitude: *she's so ungrateful for everything we do.* ■ not pleasant or acceptable: *he turned to the ungrateful task of forming a police cordon.*
– DERIVATIVES **un·grate·ful·ly adv.**, **un·grate·ful·ness n.**

un·green /ˌənˈgrēn/ ▶ **adj.** (of a product or practice) harmful to the environment; not ecologically acceptable: *an ungreen commercial development.* ■ (of a person or organization) not supporting protection of the environment.
– DERIVATIVES **un·green·ly adv.**

un·ground /ˌənˈground/ ▶ **v.** [with obj.] remove from a grounded state: *It's easy to jump in and ground airplanes. It's not so easy to unground them.*

un·ground·ed /ˌənˈgroundid/ ▶ **adj. 1** having no basis or justification; unfounded: *ungrounded fears.*
2 not electrically grounded.
3 [predic.] (**ungrounded in**) not properly instructed or proficient in (a subject or activity).

un·group /ˌənˈgro͞op/ ▶ **v.** [with obj.] Computing separate (items) from a group formed within a word-processing or graphics package.

un·grudg·ing /ˌənˈgrəjiNG/ ▶ **adj.** not grudging: *he showed her ungrudging courtesy and kindness.*
– DERIVATIVES **un·grudg·ing·ly adv.**

un·gual /ˈəNGg(yə)wəl/ ▶ **adj.** Zoology & Medicine of, relating to, or affecting a nail, hoof, or claw.
– ORIGIN mid 19th cent.: from Latin *unguis* 'nail' + **-AL**.

un·guard·ed /ˌənˈgärdid/ ▶ **adj.** without protection or a guard: *the museum was unguarded at night.* ■ not well considered; careless: *an unguarded remark.*
– DERIVATIVES **un·guard·ed·ly adv.**, **un·guard·ed·ness n.**

un·guent /ˈəNGgwənt/ ▶ **n.** a soft greasy or viscous substance used as an ointment or for lubrication.
– ORIGIN late Middle English: from Latin *unguentum*, from *unguere* 'anoint.'

un·guic·u·late /ˌəNGˈgwikyəˌlāt, -lət/ ▶ **adj.** Zoology having one or more nails or claws. ■ Botany (of a petal) having a narrow stalklike base.
– ORIGIN early 19th cent.: from modern Latin *unguiculatus*, from Latin *unguiculus* 'fingernail, toenail,' diminutive of *unguis* 'nail.'

un·guid·ed /ˌənˈgīdid/ ▶ **adj.** not guided in a particular path or direction; left to take its own course. ■ (of a missile) not directed by remote control or internal equipment. Compare with **BALLISTIC MISSILE** and **GUIDED**.

un·guis /ˈəNGgwis/ ▶ **n.** (pl. **ungues** /ˈəNGgwēz/) Zoology a nail, claw, or fang.
– ORIGIN early 18th cent.: from Latin.

un·gu·late /ˈəNGgyələt, -ˌlāt/ ▶ **n.** Zoology a hoofed mammal. See also **EVEN-TOED UNGULATE**, **ODD-TOED UNGULATE**. ● Former order Ungulata, now divided into two unrelated orders (see **ARTIODACTYLA** and **PERISSODACTYLA**).
– ORIGIN early 19th cent.: from late Latin *ungulatus*, from Latin *ungula* 'hoof.'

un·guled /ˈəNGˌgyo͞old/ ▶ **adj.** Heraldry (of an animal) having hoofs of a specified different tincture.

un·hal·lowed /ˌənˈhalōd/ ▶ **adj.** not formally consecrated: *unhallowed ground.* ■ unholy; wicked: *unhallowed retribution.*

un·ham·pered /ˌənˈhampərd/ ▶ **adj.** not impeded or encumbered: *a press unhampered by government censorship.*

un·hand /ˌənˈhand/ ▶ **v.** [with obj., usu. in imperative] archaic or humorous release (someone) from one's grasp: *"Unhand me, sir!" she cried.*

un·hand·some /ˌənˈhan(d)səm/ ▶ **adj.** [often with negative] not handsome: *Bobby was not unhandsome in his uniform.*

un·hand·y /ˌənˈhandē/ ▶ **adj. 1** not easy to handle or manage; awkward.
2 not skillful in using the hands.
– DERIVATIVES **un·hand·i·ly** /-dəlē/ **adv.**, **un·hand·i·ness n.**

un·hang /ˌənˈhaNG/ ▶ **v.** (past and past participle **unhung**) [with obj.] rare take down from a hanging position.

un·hap·pen /ˌənˈhapən/ ▶ **v.** [no obj.] (of an occurrence) become as though never having happened; be reversed: *things had happened that could never unhappen.* ■ [with obj.] cause (something) not to have happened: *you can't unhappen it just by saying we won't speak of it again.*

un·hap·pi·ly /ˌənˈhapəlē/ ▶ **adv.** in an unhappy manner. ■ [sentence adverb] unfortunately: *unhappily, such days do not come too often.*

un·hap·pi·ness ▶ **n.** the feeling of not being happy; sadness: *I've seen too much unhappiness caused by broken marriages.* ■ the feeling of not being satisfied or pleased with a situation: *residents expressed their unhappiness at the council's decision.*

un·hap·py /ˌənˈhapē/ ▶ **adj.** (**unhappier**, **unhappiest**) not happy: *an unhappy marriage* | *Aunt Millie looked unhappy.* ■ [predic.] (**unhappy at/about/with**) not satisfied or pleased with (a situation): *many were unhappy about the scale of the cuts.* ■ unfortunate: *an unhappy coincidence.*

un·harmed /ˌənˈhärmd/ ▶ **adj.** [often as complement] not harmed; uninjured: *all the hostages were released unharmed.*

un·har·ness /ˌənˈhärnəs/ ▶ **v.** [with obj.] remove a harness from (a horse or other animal).

un·hasp /ˌənˈhasp/ ▶ **v.** [with obj.] archaic unfasten.

un·hatched /ˌənˈhacht/ ▶ **adj.** (of an egg or young bird) not yet hatched.

UNHCR an agency of the United Nations set up in 1951 to aid, protect, and monitor refugees.
– ORIGIN abbreviation of *United Nations High Commissioner for Refugees.*

un·healed /ˌənˈhēld/ ▶ **adj.** not yet healed.

un·health·ful /ˌənˈhelTHfəl/ ▶ **adj.** harmful to health: *radon can build up to unhealthful levels.*
– DERIVATIVES **un·health·ful·ness n.**

un·health·y /ˌənˈhelTHē/ ▶ **adj.** (**unhealthier**, **unhealthiest**) harmful to health: *an unhealthy diet.* ■ not having or showing good health: *his face looked pale and unhealthy.* ■ (of a person's attitude or behavior) not sensible or well balanced; abnormal and harmful: *an unhealthy obsession with fast cars.*
– DERIVATIVES **un·health·i·ly** /-THəlē/ **adv.**, **un·health·i·ness n.**

un·heard /ˌənˈhərd/ ▶ **adj.** not heard or listened to: *my protests went unheard.* ■ (**unheard of**) not previously known of or done: *sales tax was unheard of in Kansas up until 1937* | *wines from unheard-of villages.*

un·heat·ed ▶ **adj.** not heated.

un·hedged /ˌənˈhejd/ ▶ **adj. 1** not bounded by a hedge: *an unhedged field.*
2 (of an investment or investor) not protected against loss by balancing or compensating contracts or transactions: *the bank collapsed due to unhedged trading.*

un·heed·ed /ˌənˈhēdid/ ▶ **adj.** heard or noticed but disregarded: *my protest went unheeded.*

un·heed·ful /ˌənˈhēdfəl/ ▶ **adj.** [predic.] not noticing or paying attention: *I charged down the stairs, unheedful of the missing bannister.*

un·heed·ing /ˌənˈhēdiNG/ ▶ **adj.** not paying attention: *Mary, unheeding, watched the television.*
– DERIVATIVES **un·heed·ing·ly adv.**

un·heim·lich /ˌo͞onˈhīmliKH, ˌən-/ ▶ **adj.** uncanny; weird.
– ORIGIN German.

un·help·ful /ˌənˈhelpfəl/ ▶ **adj.** not helpful: *several complained that the staff were unhelpful.*
– DERIVATIVES **un·help·ful·ly adv.**, **un·help·ful·ness n.**

un·her·ald·ed /ˌənˈherəldid/ ▶ **adj.** not previously announced, expected, or recognized.

un·he·ro·ic /ˌənhəˈrōik/ ▶ **adj.** not heroic: *an unheroic death.*
– DERIVATIVES **un·he·ro·i·cal·ly adv.**

un·hes·i·tat·ing /ˌənˈheziˌtātiNG/ ▶ **adj.** without doubt or hesitation; immediate: *unequivocal and unhesitating condemnation.*
– DERIVATIVES **un·hes·i·tat·ing·ly adv.**

un·hin·dered /ˌənˈhindərd/ ▶ **adj.** not hindered or obstructed.

un·hinge /ˌənˈhinj/ ▶ **v.** (**unhinges**, **unhinging**, **unhinged**) [with obj.] **1** make (someone) mentally unbalanced: *the loneliness had nearly unhinged him.* ■ deprive of stability or fixity; throw into disorder.
2 take (a door) off its hinges.

un·hinged /ˌənˈhinjd/ ▶ **adj.** mentally unbalanced; deranged: *the violent acts of unhinged minds.*

un·hip /ˌənˈhip/ ▶ **adj.** (**unhipper**, **unhippest**) informal unaware of or unaffected by current fashions or trends: *while it was remote and decidedly unhip, the town was otherwise right up-to-date.*

un·his·tor·ic /ˌənhiˈstôrik, -ˈstär-/ ▶ **adj.** not historic or historical.

un·his·tor·i·cal /ˌənhiˈstôrikəl, -ˈstär-/ ▶ **adj.** not in accordance with history or with historical analysis.
– DERIVATIVES **un·his·tor·i·cal·ly** /-ik(ə)lē/ **adv.**

un·hitch /ˌənˈhiCH/ ▶ **v.** [with obj.] unhook or unfasten (something tethered to or caught on something else).

un·hol·ster /ˌənˈhōlstər/ ▶ **v.** [with obj.] remove (a gun) from a holster.

un·ho·ly /ˌənˈhōlē/ ▶ **adj.** (**unholier**, **unholiest**) sinful; wicked. ■ denoting an alliance with potentially harmful implications between two or more parties that are not natural allies: *an unholy alliance between economic and political power.* ■ informal awful; dreadful (used for emphasis): *she was making an unholy racket.*
– DERIVATIVES **un·ho·li·ness n.**
– ORIGIN Old English *unhālig* (see **UN-**[1], **HOLY**).

un·hood /ˌənˈho͝od/ ▶ **v.** [with obj.] remove the hood from (something, esp. a falcon or horse).

un·hook /ˌənˈho͝ok/ ▶ **v.** [with obj.] unfasten or detach (something that is held or caught by a hook).

un·hoped /ˌənˈhōpt/ ▶ **adj.** (**unhoped for**) exceeding hope or expectation: *an unhoped-for piece of good luck.*

un·horse /ˌənˈhôrs/ ▶ **v.** [with obj.] cause to fall from a horse: *having unhorsed each other, the two men finished the fight on foot* | figurative *her mission is to unhorse fashionable literary theories.*

un·housed /ˌənˈhouzd/ ▶ **adj.** having no accommodation or shelter: *the poor remain unhoused.*

un·hou·seled /ˌənˈhouzəld/ ▶ **adj.** archaic (of a person) not having received the Eucharist.
– ORIGIN mid 16th cent.: from **UN-**[1] 'not' + the past participle of obsolete *housel* 'offer the Eucharist to,' from *housel* 'Eucharist.'

un·hu·man /ˌən(h)yo͞omən/ ▶ **adj.** not resembling or having the qualities of a human being.

un·hung[1] /ˌənˈhəNG/ ▶ **adj. 1** (esp. of a picture) not hanging or hung.
2 [predic.] (of a wicked person) still living when expected to be executed by hanging.

un·hung[2] past and past participle of **UNHANG**.

un·hur·ried /ˌənˈhərēd, -ˈhə-rēd/ ▶ **adj.** moving, acting, or taking place without haste or urgency.
– DERIVATIVES **un·hur·ried·ly adv.**

un·hurt /ˌənˈhərt/ ▶ **adj.** not hurt or harmed.

un·husk /ənˈhəsk/ ▶ **v.** [with obj.] remove a husk or shell from (a seed or fruit): (as adj. **unhusked**) *unhusked rice.*

un·hy·gi·en·ic /ˌənhīˈjēnik, ˌənhīˈjenik/ ▶ **adj.** not clean or sanitary: *damp, unhygienic accommodations.*
– DERIVATIVES **un·hy·gi·en·i·cal·ly** /ˌənhīˈjenək(ə)lē, ˌənhīˈjēnək(ə)lē/ **adv.**

uni- ▶ **comb. form** one; having or consisting of one: *unicellular* | *unicycle.*
– ORIGIN from Latin *unus* 'one.'

U·ni·ate /ˈyo͞onēˌat, -it, -ˌāt/ (also **Uniat**) ▶ **adj.** denoting or relating to any community of Christians in eastern Europe or the Near East that acknowledges papal supremacy but retains its own liturgy: *the Uniate churches.*
▶ **n.** a member of such a community.
– ORIGIN mid 19th cent.: from Russian *uniat*, from *uniya*, from Latin *unio* (see **UNION**).

u·ni·ax·i·al /ˌyo͞onēˈaksēəl/ ▶ **adj.** having or relating to a single axis. ■ (of crystals) having one optic axis, as in the hexagonal, trigonal, and tetragonal systems.

u·ni·bod·y /ˈyo͞onəˌbädē/ ▶ **n.** (pl. **unibodies**) a single molded unit forming both the bodywork and chassis of a vehicle.

u·ni·brow /ˈyo͞onəˌbrou/ ▶ **n.** a pair of eyebrows that meet above the nose, giving the appearance of a single eyebrow. Also called **MONOBROW**.
– DERIVATIVES **u·ni·browed adj.**

u·ni·cam·er·al /ˌyo͞onəˈkam(ə)rəl/ ▶ **adj.** (of a legislative body) having a single legislative chamber.
– ORIGIN mid 19th cent.: from **UNI-** 'one' + Latin *camera* 'chamber' + **-AL**.

u·ni·cast /ˈyo͞oniˌkast/ ▶ **n.** transmission of a data package or an audiovisual signal to a single recipient: [as modifier] *the unicast method wastes a lot of bandwidth by sending duplicate information.*
– ORIGIN 1990s: on the pattern of *broadcast.*

UNICEF /ˈyo͞onəˌsef/ an agency of the United Nations established in 1946 to help governments (esp. in developing countries) improve the health and education of children and their mothers.
– ORIGIN acronym from *United Nations Children's* (originally *International Children's Emergency*) *Fund.*

u·ni·cel·lu·lar /ˌyo͞onəˈselyələr/ ▶ **adj.** Biology (of protozoans, certain algae and spores, etc.) consisting of a single cell. ■ (of an evolutionary or developmental stage) characterized by the formation or presence of a single cell or cells.

u·ni·cit·y /yo͞oˈnisətē/ ▶ **n.** rare the fact of being or consisting of one, or of being united as a whole. ■ the fact or quality of being unique.

U·ni·code /ˈyo͞oniˌkōd/ ▶ **n.** Computing an international encoding standard for use with different languages and scripts, by which each letter, digit, or symbol is assigned a unique numeric value that applies across different platforms and programs.

u·ni·col·or /ˈyo͞onəˌkələr/ (also **unicolored**) (Brit. **-colour** or **-coloured**) ▶ **adj.** of one color.

u·ni·com /ˈyo͞onəˌkäm/ ▶ **n.** a radio communications system of a type used at small airports.

u·ni·corn /ˈyo͞onəˌkôrn/ ▶ **n. 1** a mythical animal typically represented as a horse with a single straight horn projecting from its forehead. ■ a heraldic representation of such an animal, with a twisted horn, a deer's feet, a goat's beard, and a lion's tail.

U

PRONUNCIATION KEY ə *ago, up*; ər *over, fur*; a *hat*; ā *ate*; ä *car*; e *let*; ē *see*; i *fit*; ī *by*; NG *sing*; ō *go*; ô *law, for*; oi *toy*; o͝o *good*; o͞o *goo*; ou *out*; TH *thin*; T͟H *then*; ZH *vision*

2 historical a carriage drawn by three horses, two abreast and one leader. ■ a team of three horses arranged in such a way.
– ORIGIN Middle English: via Old French from Latin *unicornis*, from *uni-* 'single' + *cornu* 'horn,' translating Greek *monokerōs*.

unicorn 1

u·ni·corn root ▶ **n.** any of a number of plants in the lily family, esp. those with roots having medicinal uses, in particular devil's bit and colicroot.

u·ni·cum /'yo͞onəkəm/ ▶ **n.** (pl. **unica** /-kə/) a unique example or specimen.
– ORIGIN late 19th cent.: from Latin, neuter of *unicus* 'unique.'

u·ni·cur·sal /,yo͞onə'kərsəl/ ▶ **adj.** Mathematics relating to or denoting a curve or surface that is closed and can be drawn or swept out in a single movement.
– ORIGIN mid 19th cent.: from **UNI-** 'one' + Latin *cursus* 'course' + **-AL**.

u·ni·cus·pid /,yo͞onə'kəspid/ ▶ **adj.** having one cusp or point.
▶ **n.** a tooth with a single cusp, esp. a canine tooth.

u·ni·cy·cle /'yo͞onə,sīkəl/ ▶ **n.** a cycle with a single wheel, typically used by acrobats.
– DERIVATIVES **u·ni·cy·clist** /-,sīklist/ **n.**

un·i·den·ti·fi·a·ble /,ənī'denti,fīəbəl/ ▶ **adj.** unable to be identified: *an unidentifiable accent*.

un·i·den·ti·fied /,ənī'denti,fīd/ ▶ **adj.** not recognized or identified: *a picture of an unidentified motorcyclist*.

un·i·den·ti·fied fly·ing ob·ject ▶ **n.** see **UFO**.

u·ni·di·men·sion·al /,yo͞onədə'mensHənl, -SHnəl/ ▶ **adj.** having one dimension: *a unidimensional model*.

u·ni·di·rec·tion·al /,yo͞onidi'reksHənl/ ▶ **adj.** moving or operating in a single direction.
– DERIVATIVES **u·ni·di·rec·tion·al·i·ty** /-,reksHə'nalitē/ **n.**, **u·ni·di·rec·tion·al·ly adv.**

UNIDO ▶ **abbr.** United Nations Industrial Development Organization.

u·ni·fi·ca·tion /,yo͞onəfi'kāsHən/ ▶ **n.** the process of being united or made into a whole.
– DERIVATIVES **u·ni·fi·ca·to·ry** /-'kātərē/ **adj.**

U·ni·fi·ca·tion Church an evangelistic religious and political organization founded in 1954 in Korea by Sun Myung Moon. Also called **HOLY SPIRIT ASSOCIATION FOR THE UNIFICATION OF WORLD CHRISTIANITY**.

u·ni·fied field the·o·ry ▶ **n.** Physics a theory that describes two or more of the four interactions (electromagnetic, gravitational, weak, and strong) previously described by separate theories.

u·ni·form /'yo͞onə,fôrm/ ▶ **adj. 1** not changing in form or character; remaining the same in all cases and at all times: *blocks of stone of uniform size* | *the decline in fertility was not uniform across social classes*. ■ of a similar form or character to another or others: *a uniform package of amenities at a choice of hotels*.
2 denoting a garment forming part of a person's uniform: *black uniform jackets*.
▶ **n. 1** the distinctive clothing worn by members of the same organization or body or by children attending certain schools: *airline pilots in dark blue uniforms* | *an officer in uniform*. ■ informal a police officer wearing a uniform: *uniforms were already on the scene*.
2 a code word representing the letter U, used in radio communication.
▶ **v.** [with obj.] make uniform.
– DERIVATIVES **u·ni·form·ly** /'yo͞onə,fôrmlē, ,yo͞onə'fôrm-/ **adv.**
– ORIGIN mid 16th cent. (as an adjective): from French *uniforme* or Latin *uniformis* (see **UNI-**, **FORM**). Sense 1 of the noun dates from the mid 18th cent.

U·ni·form Com·mer·ci·al Code (abbr.: **UCC**) ▶ **n.** the body of laws governing commercial transactions in the US.

u·ni·formed /'yo͞onə,fôrmd/ ▶ **adj.** (of a person) wearing a uniform: *uniformed police officers*.

u·ni·form·i·tar·i·an·ism /,yo͞onə,fôrmə'te(ə)rēə,nizəm/ ▶ **n.** Geology the theory that changes in the earth's crust during geological history have resulted from the action of continuous and uniform processes. Often contrasted with *noun* **CATASTROPHISM**.
– DERIVATIVES **u·ni·form·i·tar·i·an adj. & n.**

u·ni·form·i·ty /,yo͞onə'fôrmətē/ ▶ **n.** (pl. **uniformities**) the quality or state of being uniform: *an attempt to impose administrative and cultural uniformity*.
– ORIGIN late Middle English: from Old French *uniformite* or late Latin *uniformitas*, from Latin *uniformis* (see **UNIFORM**).

u·ni·form re·source lo·ca·tor (abbr.: **URL**) ▶ **n.** a location or address identifying where documents can be found on the Internet.

u·ni·fy /'yo͞onə,fī/ ▶ **v.** (**unifies, unifying, unified**) make or become united, uniform, or whole: [with obj.] *the government hoped to centralize and unify the nation* | [no obj.] *opposition groups struggling to unify around the goal of replacing the regime* | (as adj. **unified**) *a unified system of national education*.
– DERIVATIVES **u·ni·fi·er n.**
– ORIGIN early 16th cent.: from French *unifier* or late Latin *unificare* 'make into a whole.'

u·ni·lat·er·al /,yo͞onə'latərəl, -'latrəl/ ▶ **adj. 1** (of an action or decision) performed by or affecting only one person, group, or country involved in a particular situation, without the agreement of another or the others: *unilateral nuclear disarmament*.
2 relating to, occurring on, or affecting only one side of an organ or structure, or of the body.
– DERIVATIVES **u·ni·lat·er·al·ly adv.**

u·ni·lat·er·al·ism /,yo͞onə'latərə,lizəm, -'latrə-/ ▶ **n.** the process of acting, reaching a decision, or espousing a principle unilaterally. ■ the pursuit of or belief in unilateral nuclear disarmament: *the party's commitment to unilateralism*.
– DERIVATIVES **u·ni·lat·er·al·ist n. & adj.**

u·ni·lin·e·ar /,yo͞onə'linēər/ ▶ **adj.** developing or arranged serially and predictably, without deviation: *there is a unilinear path of language learning with a finite end*. ■ (of websites) allowing or designed for controlled navigation, following a single path.
– DERIVATIVES **u·ni·lin·e·ar·ly adv.**

u·ni·lin·gual /,yo͞onə'liNGg(yə)wəl/ ▶ **adj.** conducted in, concerned with, or speaking only one language.
– DERIVATIVES **u·ni·lin·gual·ly adv.**

u·ni·loc·u·lar /,yo͞onə'läkyələr/ ▶ **adj.** Botany & Zoology having, consisting of, or characterized by only one loculus or cavity; single-chambered.

un·im·ag·i·na·ble /,ənə'maj(ə)nəbəl/ ▶ **adj.** difficult or impossible to imagine or comprehend: *lives of almost unimaginable deprivation*.
– DERIVATIVES **un·im·ag·i·na·bly** /-blē/ **adv.**

un·im·ag·i·na·tive /,əni'maj(ə)nətiv/ ▶ **adj.** not readily using or demonstrating the use of the imagination; stolid and somewhat dull.
– DERIVATIVES **un·im·ag·i·na·tive·ly adv.**, **in·im·ag·i·na·tive·ness n.**

un·i·mag·ined /,əni'majind/ ▶ **adj.** not having been imagined or thought of as possible: *a previously unimagined degree of economic and social freedom*.

u·ni·mod·al /,yo͞onə'mōdl/ ▶ **adj.** having or involving one mode. ■ (of a statistical distribution) having one maximum.

u·ni·mo·lec·u·lar /,yo͞onəmə'lekyələr/ ▶ **adj.** Chemistry consisting of or involving a single molecule.

un·im·paired /,ənim'pe(ə)rd/ ▶ **adj.** not weakened or damaged: *unimpaired mobility*.

un·im·peach·a·ble /,ənim'pēcHəbəl/ ▶ **adj.** not able to be doubted, questioned, or criticized; entirely trustworthy: *an unimpeachable witness*.
– DERIVATIVES **un·im·peach·a·bly** /-blē/ **adv.**

un·im·ped·ed /,ənim'pēdid/ ▶ **adj.** not obstructed or hindered: *an unimpeded view across the headland*.
– DERIVATIVES **un·im·ped·ed·ly adv.**

un·im·por·tance /,ənim'pôrtns/ ▶ **n.** the state or fact of lacking in importance or significance: *her tone conveyed the unimportance of anything that might have happened*.

un·im·por·tant /,ənim'pôrtnt/ ▶ **adj.** lacking in importance or significance: *trivial and unimportant details*.

un·im·pos·ing /,ənim'pōziNG/ ▶ **adj.** not imposing or impressive in appearance.
– DERIVATIVES **un·im·pos·ing·ly adv.**

un·im·pressed /,ənim'prest/ ▶ **adj.** feeling no admiration, interest, or respect.

un·im·pres·sive /,ənim'presiv/ ▶ **adj.** evoking no admiration or respect; not striking.
– DERIVATIVES **un·im·pres·sive·ly adv.**, **un·im·pres·sive·ness n.**

un·im·proved /,ənim'pro͞ovd/ ▶ **adj.** not made better. ■ (of land) not cleared or cultivated.

un·in·cor·po·rat·ed /,ənin'kôrpə,rātid, ,əniNG-/ ▶ **adj. 1** (of a company or other organization) not formed into a legal corporation: *an unincorporated business*.
2 not included as part of a whole. ■ (of territory) not designated as belonging to a particular country, town, or area.

un·in·fect·ed ▶ **adj.** not harboring a pathogen. ■ Computing not affected with a virus.

un·in·flect·ed /,ənin'flektid/ ▶ **adj. 1** Grammar (of a word or a language) not undergoing changes to express grammatical functions or attributes: *English is largely uninflected*.
2 not varying in intonation or pitch: *her voice was flat and uninflected*.

un·in·flu·enced /ən'inflo͞oənsd/ ▶ **adj.** not influenced or affected: *styles of dress relatively uninfluenced by popular fashion*.

un·in·form·a·tive /,ənin'fôrmətiv/ ▶ **adj.** not providing particularly useful or interesting information.

un·in·formed /,ənin'fôrmd/ ▶ **adj.** not having or showing awareness or understanding of the facts: *uninformed criticism of conservation projects*.

un·in·hab·it·a·ble /,ənin'habətəbəl/ ▶ **adj.** (of a place) unsuitable for living in.

un·in·hab·it·ed /,ənin'habitid/ ▶ **adj.** (of a place) without inhabitants: *small uninhabited islands*.

un·in·hib·it·ed /,ənin'hibitid/ ▶ **adj.** expressing one's feelings or thoughts unselfconsciously and without restraint: *fits of uninhibited laughter*.
– DERIVATIVES **un·in·hib·it·ed·ly adv.**, **un·in·hib·it·ed·ness n.**

un·in·i·ti·at·ed /,ənə'nisHē,ātid/ ▶ **adj.** without special knowledge or experience: *a bachelor neither prudish nor uninitiated* | (as plural noun **the uninitiated**) *the discussion wasn't easy to follow for the uninitiated*.

un·in·jured /,ən'injərd/ ▶ **adj.** (of a person or part of the body) not harmed or damaged.

un·in·spired /,ənin'spīrd/ ▶ **adj. 1** lacking in imagination or originality: *he writes repetitive and uninspired poetry*.
2 (of a person) not filled with excitement: *they were uninspired by the Nationalist Party*.

un·in·spir·ing /,ənin'spīriNG/ ▶ **adj.** not producing excitement or interest: *an uninspiring game that Chicago scarcely deserved to win*.
– DERIVATIVES **un·in·spir·ing·ly adv.**

un·in·stall /,ənin'stôl/ (Brit. also **uninstal**) ▶ **v.** (**uninstalls** or Brit. **uninstals, uninstalling, uninstalled**) [with obj.] remove (an application or file) from a computer.
– DERIVATIVES **un·in·stal·la·tion** /,ən-instə'lāsHən/ **n.**, **un·in·stall·er n.**

un·in·struct·ed /,ənin'strəktid/ ▶ **adj.** (of a person) not taught or having learned a subject or skill. ■ (of behavior) not acquired by teaching; natural or spontaneous: *her own instinctive, uninstructed response*.

un·in·su·lat·ed /,ən'ins(y)ə,lātid/ ▶ **adj.** not insulated: *the roofs were uninsulated in both housing types*.

un·in·sur·a·ble /,ənin'sHo͞orəbəl/ ▶ **adj.** not eligible for insurance coverage: *some risky activities are uninsurable at any price*.

un·in·sured ▶ **adj.** not covered by insurance: *an uninsured driver*.

un·in·tel·li·gent /,ənin'teləjənt/ ▶ **adj.** having or showing a low level of intelligence: *a good-natured but unintelligent boy*.
– DERIVATIVES **un·in·tel·li·gence n.**, **un·in·tel·li·gent·ly adv.**

un·in·tel·li·gi·ble /,ənin'teləjəbəl/ ▶ **adj.** impossible to understand: *dolphin sounds are* ***unintelligible to*** *humans*.
– DERIVATIVES **un·in·tel·li·gi·bil·i·ty** /-,teləjə'bilətē/ **n.**, **un·in·tel·li·gi·bly** /-blē/ **adv.**

un·in·tend·ed /,ənin'tendid/ ▶ **adj.** not planned or meant: *the unintended consequences of people's actions*.

un·in·ten·tion·al /,ənin'tencHənl/ ▶ **adj.** not done on purpose: *the translation added a layer of unintentional comedy*.
– DERIVATIVES **un·in·ten·tion·al·ly adv.**

un·in·ter·est·ed /,ən'intristid, -'intə,restid/ ▶ **adj.** not interested in or concerned about something or someone: *I was totally* ***uninterested in*** *boys* | *an uninterested voice*.

– DERIVATIVES **un·in·ter·est·ed·ly** adv., **un·in·ter·est·ed·ness** n.

USAGE On the difference between **uninterested** and **disinterested**, see usage at **DISINTERESTED**.

un·in·ter·est·ing /ˌənˈint(ə)ristiNG, ˌənˈintəˌrestiNG/ ▶ adj. not arousing curiosity or interest: *the scenery is dull and uninteresting.*
– DERIVATIVES **un·in·ter·est·ing·ly** adv., **un·in·ter·est·ing·ness** n.

un·in·ter·pret·a·ble /ˌəninˈtərprətəbəl/ ▶ adj. impossible to explain or understand in terms of meaning or significance.

un·in·ter·rupt·ed /ˌənˌintəˈrəptid/ ▶ adj. without a break in continuity: *an uninterrupted flow of traffic.* ■ (of a view) unobstructed.
– DERIVATIVES **un·in·ter·rupt·ed·ly** adv.

un·in·ter·rupt·i·ble /ˌənˌintəˈrəptəbəl/ ▶ adj. not able to be broken in continuity: *an uninterruptible power supply.*

u·ni·nu·cle·ate /ˌyo͞onəˈn(y)o͞oklēit/ ▶ adj. Biology having a single nucleus.

un·in·ven·tive /ˌəninˈventiv/ ▶ adj. not showing creativity or original thought: *the oils were sensitively painted but uninventive in design.*
– DERIVATIVES **un·in·ven·tive·ly** adv., **un·in·ven·tive·ness** n.

un·in·ves·ti·gat·ed /ˌəninˈvestiˌgātid/ ▶ adj. not systematically investigated: *uninvestigated deaths in custody.*

un·in·vit·ed /ˌəninˈvītid/ ▶ adj. (of a person) attending somewhere or doing something without having been asked: *their privacy was disrupted by a series of uninvited guests.* ■ (of a thought or act) involuntary, unwelcome, or unwarranted: *strange uninvited thoughts crossed her mind.*
– DERIVATIVES **un·in·vit·ed·ly** adv.

un·in·vit·ing /ˌəninˈvītiNG/ ▶ adj. (esp. of a place or prospect) not attractive: *the house was dark and uninviting.*
– DERIVATIVES **un·in·vit·ing·ly** adv.

un·in·voked /ˌəninˈvōkt/ ▶ adj. (of a god, spirit, or power) not invoked or called on in prayer.

un·in·volved /ˌəninˈvälvd/ ▶ adj. not connected or concerned with someone or something, esp. on an emotional level.

un·in·volv·ing /ˌəninˈvälviNG/ ▶ adj. failing to engage someone's interest or attention; dull: *a pointless and uninvolving storyline.*

Un·ion /ˈyo͞onyən/ an industrial and residential township in northeastern New Jersey; pop. 53,673 (est. 2008).
2 an industrial city in northeastern New Jersey, across the Hudson River from New York City; pop. 62,183 (est. 2008).

un·ion /ˈyo͞onyən/ ▶ n. **1** the action or fact of joining or being joined, esp. in a political context: *he was opposed to closer political or economic union with Europe | a currency union between the two countries.* ■ a state of harmony or agreement: *they live in perfect union.* ■ a marriage: *their union had not been blessed with children.*
2 an organized association of workers formed to protect and further their rights and interests; a labor union: *the National Farmers' Union.* ■ a club, society, or association formed by people with a common interest or purpose: *members of the Students' Union.* ■ Brit. historical a number of parishes consolidated for the purposes of administering the Poor Laws. ■ Brit. an association of independent churches for purposes of cooperation.
3 (also **Union**) a political unit consisting of a number of states or provinces with the same central government, in particular: ■ the US, esp. from its founding by the original thirteen states in 1787–90 to the secession of the Confederate states in 1860–61. ■ (also **the Federal Union**) the northern states of the US that opposed the seceding Confederate states in the Civil War.
4 a building at a college or university used by students for recreation and other nonacademic activities.
5 Mathematics the set that comprises all the elements (and no others) contained in any of two or more given sets. ■ the operation of forming such a set.
6 a pipe coupling.
7 a part of a flag with an emblem symbolizing national union, typically occupying the upper corner next to the staff.
8 a fabric made of two or more different yarns, typically cotton and linen or silk.
– ORIGIN late Middle English: from Old French, or from ecclesiastical Latin *unio(n-)* 'unity,' from Latin *unus* 'one.'

un·ion-bash·ing ▶ n. informal active or vocal opposition to labor unions and their rights.

un·ion cat·a·log ▶ n. a list of the combined holdings of several libraries.

Un·ion Cit·y 1 a city in north central California, south of Oakland; pop. 72,123 (est. 2008).

un·ion·ist /ˈyo͞onyənist/ ▶ n. **1** a member of a labor union. ■ an advocate or supporter of labor unions.
2 (**Unionist**) a person who opposed secession during the Civil War. ■ a person in Northern Ireland, esp. a member of a political party, supporting or advocating union with Great Britain.
– DERIVATIVES **un·ion·ism** /-ˌnizəm/ n., **un·ion·is·tic** /ˌyo͞onyəˈnistik/ adj.

un·ion·ize /ˈyo͞onyəˌnīz/ ▶ v. become or cause to become members of a labor union.
– DERIVATIVES **un·ion·i·za·tion** /ˌyo͞onyəniˈzāSHən, -ˌnīˈzā-/ n.

un·ion·ized /ˈyo͞onyəˌnīzd/ ▶ adj. (of workers or their workplace) belonging to, or having workers belonging to, a labor union: *unionized factories.*

un·i·o·nized /ˌənˈīəˌnīzd/ ▶ adj. not ionized.

Un·ion Jack ▶ n. **1** the national flag of the United Kingdom, consisting of red and white crosses on a blue background. [originally a small British union flag flown as the jack of a ship; compare with **UNION**.]
2 (**union jack**) (in the US) a small flag consisting of the union from the national flag, flown at the bows of vessels in harbor.

Un·ion of My·an·mar official name for **BURMA**.

Un·ion of So·vi·et So·cial·ist Re·pub·lics (abbr.: **USSR**) full name of the **SOVIET UNION**.

un·ion shop ▶ n. a place of work where employers may hire nonunion workers who must join a labor union within an agreed time. Compare with **CLOSED SHOP**, **OPEN SHOP**.

Un·ion Square a park in southern Manhattan in New York City, noted as a former theater and, later, labor union hub.

un·ion suit ▶ n. dated a single undergarment combining shirt and pants.

Un·ion Ter·ri·to·ry any of several territories of India that are administered by the central government.

u·nip·ar·ous /yo͞oˈnip(ə)rəs/ ▶ adj. chiefly Zoology producing a single young at a birth.
– ORIGIN mid 17th cent.: from modern Latin *uniparus* (from Latin *uni-* 'one' + *-parus* 'bearing') + **-OUS**.

u·ni·per·son·al /ˌyo͞onəˈpərsənəl/ ▶ adj. rare comprising, or existing as, one person only.

u·ni·pla·nar /ˌyo͞onəˈplānər/ ▶ adj. lying in one plane.

u·ni·po·lar /ˌyo͞onəˈpōlər/ ▶ adj. having or relating to a single pole or kind of polarity: *a unipolar magnetic charge.* ■ (of psychiatric illness) characterized by either depressive or (more rarely) manic episodes but not both. Compare with **BIPOLAR DISORDER**. ■ (of a nerve cell) having only one axon or process. ■ Electronics (of a transistor or other device) using charge carriers of a single polarity.
– DERIVATIVES **u·ni·po·lar·i·ty** /-pəˈlaritē, -pō-/ n.

u·nip·o·tent /yo͞oˈnipətənt/ ▶ adj. **1** Mathematics (of a subgroup) having only one idempotent element.
2 Biology (of an immature or stem cell) capable of giving rise to only one cell type.

u·nique /yo͞oˈnēk/ ▶ adj. being the only one of its kind; unlike anything else: *the situation was unique in modern politics | original and unique designs.* ■ particularly remarkable, special, or unusual: *a unique opportunity to see the spectacular Bolshoi Ballet.* ■ [predic.] (**unique to**) belonging or connected to (one particular person, group, or place): *a style of architecture that is unique to Portugal.*
▶ n. archaic a unique person or thing.
– DERIVATIVES **u·nique·ly** adv., **u·nique·ness** n.
– ORIGIN early 17th cent.: from French, from Latin *unicus*, from *unus* 'one.'

USAGE There is a set of adjectives—including **unique, complete, equal,** and **perfect**—whose core meaning embraces a mathematically absolute concept and which therefore, according to a traditional argument, cannot be modified by adverbs such as **really, quite,** or **very**. For example, since the core meaning of **unique** (from Latin 'one') is 'being only one of its kind,' it is logically impossible, the argument goes, to submodify it: it either is 'unique' or it is not, and there are no stages in between. In practice, the situation in the language is more complex than this. Words like **unique** have a core sense, but they often also have a secondary, less precise (nonabsolute) sense of 'very remarkable or unusual,' as in *a really unique opportunity*. It is advisable, however, to use **unique** in this sense sparingly and not to modify it with *very, quite, really*, etc.

u·ni·sex /ˈyo͞onəˌseks/ ▶ adj. (esp. of clothing or hairstyles) designed to be suitable for both sexes.
▶ n. a style in which men and women look and dress in a similar way.

u·ni·sex·u·al /ˌyo͞onəˈsekSHo͞oəl/ ▶ adj. (of an organism) either male or female; not hermaphrodite. ■ Botany (of a flower) having either stamens or pistils but not both.
– DERIVATIVES **u·ni·sex·u·al·i·ty** /-ˌsekSHo͞oˈalitē/ n., **u·ni·sex·u·al·ly** adv.

un-Is·lam·ic /ˌəniˈslämik/ ▶ adj. contrary to the tenets of Islam.

u·ni·son /ˈyo͞onəsən, -zən/ ▶ n. **1** simultaneous performance of action or utterance of speech: *"Yes, sir," said the girls in unison.*
2 Music coincidence in pitch of sounds or notes: *the flutes play in unison with the violas.* ■ a combination of notes, voices, or instruments at the same pitch or (esp. when singing) in octaves: *good unisons are formed by flutes, oboes, and clarinets.*
▶ adj. [attrib.] performed in unison.
– DERIVATIVES **u·nis·o·nous** /yo͞oˈnisənəs/ adj.
– ORIGIN late Middle English (sense 2 of the noun): from Old French, or from late Latin *unisonus*, from Latin *uni-* 'one' + *sonus* 'sound.'

un·is·sued /ˌənˈisHo͞od/ ▶ adj. (esp. of shares of stock) not yet issued: *his rights to acquire any unissued shares were eliminated.*

u·nit /ˈyo͞onit/ ▶ n. **1** an individual thing or person regarded as single and complete but which can also form an individual component of a larger or more complex whole: *the family unit | large areas of land made up of smaller units | the sentence as a unit of grammar.* ■ a device that has a specified function, esp. one forming part of a complex mechanism: *the gearbox and transmission unit.* ■ a piece of furniture or equipment for fitting with others like it or made of complementary parts: *a sink unit.* ■ a self-contained section of accommodations in a larger building or group of buildings: *one- and two-bedroom units.* ■ a part of an institution such as a hospital having a special function: *the intensive care unit.* ■ a subdivision of a larger military grouping: *he returned to Germany with his unit.* ■ an amount of educational instruction, typically determined by the number of hours spent in class: *students take three compulsory core units.* ■ an item manufactured: [as modifier] *unit cost.* ■ a police car: *he eased into his unit and flicked the siren on.*
2 a quantity chosen as a standard in terms of which other quantities may be expressed: *a unit of measurement | fifty units of electricity.*
3 the number one. ■ (**units**) the digit before the decimal point in decimal notation, representing an integer less than ten.
– ORIGIN late 16th cent. (as a mathematical term): from Latin *unus*, probably suggested by **DIGIT**.

UNITA /ˌyo͞oˈnētə/ an Angolan nationalist movement founded in 1966 by **Jonas Savimbi** (1934–2002) to fight Portuguese rule. After independence was achieved in 1975, UNITA continued to fight against the ruling Marxist MPLA, with help from South Africa.
– ORIGIN acronym from Portuguese *União Nacional para a Independencia Total de Angola.*

u·ni·tard /ˈyo͞onəˌtärd/ ▶ n. a tight-fitting one-piece garment of stretchable fabric that covers the body from the neck to the knees or feet.
– ORIGIN 1960s: from **UNI-** 'single' + **LEOTARD**.

U·ni·tar·i·an /ˌyo͞oniˈte(ə)rēən/ ▶ n. Theology a person, esp. a Christian, who asserts the unity of God and rejects the doctrine of the Trinity. ■ a member of a church or religious body maintaining such beliefs and typically rejecting formal dogma in favor of a rationalist approach to belief.
▶ adj. of or relating to the Unitarians.
– DERIVATIVES **U·ni·tar·i·an·ism** /-ˌnizəm/ n.
– ORIGIN late 17th cent.: from modern Latin *unitarius* (from Latin *unitas* 'unity') + **-AN**.

U·ni·tar·i·an U·ni·ver·sal·ism /ˌyo͞onəˈvərsəˌlizəm/ ▶ n. the religious denomination formed in 1961 by the merger of the Unitarians and the Universalists.
– DERIVATIVES **U·ni·tar·i·an U·ni·ver·sal·ist** adj.

u·ni·tar·y /ˈyo͞oniˌterē/ ▶ adj. **1** forming a single or uniform entity: *a sort of unitary wholeness.* ■ of or relating to a system of government or organization in which the powers of the separate constituent parts are vested in a central body: *a unitary rather than a federal state.*
2 of or relating to a unit or units.
– DERIVATIVES **u·ni·tar·i·ly** /ˈyo͞onəˌterəlē, ˌyo͞onəˈte(ə)r-/ adv., **u·ni·tar·i·ty** /ˌyo͞onəˈte(ə)ritē/ n.

U·ni·tas /yo͞oˈnītəs/, Johnny (1933–2002), US football player; full name *John Constantine Unitas.*

U

PRONUNCIATION KEY ə *ago, up*; ər *over, fur*; a *hat*; ā *ate*; ä *car*; e *let*; ē *see*; i *fit*; ī *by*; NG *sing*; ō *go*; ô *law, for*; oi *toy*; o͝o *good*; o͞o *goo*; ou *out*; TH *thin*; T͟H *then*; ZH *vision*

A quarterback with the Baltimore Colts 1956–72, he led them to three NFL titles in 1958, 1959, and 1968 and a Super Bowl win in 1971. He also played for the San Diego Chargers 1972–73. Football Hall of Fame (1979).

u·nit cell ▶ **n.** Crystallography the smallest group of atoms of a substance that has the overall symmetry of a crystal of that substance, and from which the entire lattice can be built up by repetition in three dimensions.

u·nite /yo͞oˈnīt/ ▶ **v.** come or bring together for a common purpose or action: [no obj.] *he called on the party to unite* | [with obj.] *they are united by their love of cars.* ■ come or bring together to form a unit or whole, esp. in a political context: [no obj.] *the two Germanys officially united* | [with obj.] *he aimed to unite Italy and Sicily under his imperial crown* | *his work unites theory and practice.* ■ [with obj.] archaic join in marriage.
– DERIVATIVES **u·ni·tive** /ˈyo͞onətiv, yo͞oˈnī-/ **adj.**
– ORIGIN late Middle English: from Latin *unit-* 'joined together,' from the verb *unire*, from *unus* 'one.'

u·nit·ed /yo͞oˈnītid/ ▶ **adj.** joined together politically, for a common purpose, or by common feelings: *women acting together in a united way.* ■ chiefly Brit. used in names of soccer and other sports teams formed by amalgamation: *Oxford United.*
– DERIVATIVES **u·nit·ed·ly adv.**

U·nit·ed Ar·ab E·mir·ates (abbr.: **UAE**) an independent state on the southern coast of the Persian Gulf, west of the Gulf of Oman; pop. 4,798,500 (est. 2009); capital, Abu Dhabi; official language, Arabic.

> The United Arab Emirates was formed in 1971 by the federation of the independent sheikhdoms formerly called the Trucial States: Abu Dhabi, Ajman, Dubai, Fujairah, Ras al-Khaimah (joined early 1972), Sharjah, and Umm al-Qaiwain.

U·nit·ed Ar·ab Re·pub·lic (abbr.: **UAR**) a former political union established by Egypt and Syria in 1958. It was seen as the first step toward the creation of a pan-Arab union in the Middle East, but only Yemen entered into loose association with it 1958–66 and Syria withdrew in 1961. Egypt retained the name United Arab Republic until 1971.

U·nit·ed Art·ists a movie production company founded in 1919 by Charlie Chaplin, Douglas Fairbanks, Mary Pickford, and D. W. Griffith.

U·nit·ed Breth·ren ▶ **plural n.** a Protestant denomination founded in the US in 1800.

U·nit·ed King·dom (abbr.: **UK**) a country in western Europe that consists of England, Wales, Scotland, and Northern Ireland; pop. 61,113,200 (est. 2009); capital, London. Full name **United Kingdom of Great Britain and Northern Ireland**.

> England (which had incorporated Wales in the 16th century) and Scotland have had the same monarch since 1603, when James VI of Scotland succeeded to the English crown as James I; the kingdoms were formally united by the Act of Union in 1707. An Act of Parliament joined Great Britain and Ireland in 1801, but the Irish Free State (later the Republic of Ireland) broke away in 1921. The UK became a member of the EC (now the EU) in 1973.

U·nit·ed Na·tions (abbr.: **UN**) an international organization of countries set up in 1945, in succession to the League of Nations, to promote international peace, security, and cooperation.

> The members of the United Nations, originally the countries that fought against the Axis Powers in the Second World War, now number 192 and include most sovereign states of the world. Administration is by a secretariat headed by a secretary general. The chief deliberative body is the General Assembly, in which each member state has one vote; recommendations are passed but are not binding on members and generally have had little effect on world politics. The Security Council bears the primary responsibility for the maintenance of peace and security and may call on members to take action, chiefly peacekeeping action, to enforce its decisions. The UN's headquarters are in New York City.

U·nit·ed Prov·inc·es historical **1** the seven provinces united in 1579 that formed the basis of the republic of the Netherlands.
2 an Indian administrative division formed by the union of Agra and Oudh that has been called Uttar Pradesh since 1950.

U·nit·ed States (abbr.: **US** or **U.S.**) a country that occupies most of the southern half of North America as well as Alaska and the Hawaiian Islands; pop. 304,059,724 (est. 2008); capital, Washington, DC. Full name **United States of America**.

> The US is a federal republic comprising 50 states and the Federal District of Columbia. It originated in the American Revolution, the successful rebellion of the colonies on the eastern coast against British rule in 1775–83. The original 13 states that formed the Union drew up a federal constitution in 1787, and George Washington was elected the first president in 1789. In the 19th century the territory of the US was extended across the continent through the westward spread of pioneers and settlers and acquisitions such as that of Texas and California from Mexico in the 1840s. After a long period of isolation in foreign affairs, the US participated on the Allied side in both world wars and emerged from the Cold War as the world's leading military and economic power.

u·nit·ize /ˈyo͞onəˌtīz/ ▶ **v.** [with obj.] (usu. as adj. **unitized**) form into a single unit by combining parts into a whole: *a six-cylinder engine and a unitized body with thousands of welds.* ■ package (cargo) into unit loads: *a unitized load.*

u·nit mem·brane ▶ **n.** Biology a lipoprotein membrane that encloses many cells and cell organelles and is composed of two electron-dense layers enclosing a less dense layer.

u·nit pric·ing ▶ **n.** identification of and labeling of items for sale with the retail price per unit, permitting easier price comparisons among similar products in different sized containers.

u·nit train ▶ **n.** a train transporting a single commodity.

u·nit trust ▶ **n.** British term for **MUTUAL FUND**.

u·nit vec·tor ▶ **n.** Mathematics a vector that has a magnitude of one.

u·ni·ty /ˈyo͞onətē/ ▶ **n.** (pl. **unities**) **1** the state of being united or joined as a whole: *European unity* | *their leaders called for unity between opposing factions.* ■ the state of forming a complete and pleasing whole, esp. in an artistic context: *the repeated phrase gives the piece unity and cohesion.* ■ a thing forming a complex whole: *they speak of the three parts as a unity.* ■ in Aristotle's *Poetics*, each of the three dramatic principles requiring limitation of the supposed time of a drama to that occupied in acting it or to a single day (**unity of time**), use of one scene throughout (**unity of place**), and concentration on the development of a single plot (**unity of action**).
2 Mathematics chiefly Brit. the number one.
– ORIGIN Middle English: from Old French *unite*, from Latin *unitas*, from *unus* 'one.'

Univ. ▶ **abbr.** University.

univ. ▶ **abbr.** universal.

u·ni·va·lent ▶ **adj.** /ˌyo͞onəˈvālənt/ **1** Biology (of a chromosome) remaining unpaired during meiosis.
2 Chemistry another term for **MONOVALENT**.
▶ **n.** /yo͞oˈnivələnt/ Biology a univalent chromosome.

u·ni·valve /ˈyo͞onəˌvalv/ Zoology ▶ **adj.** having one valve or shell.
▶ **n.** another term for **GASTROPOD**.

u·ni·var·i·ate /ˈyo͞oniˈve(ə)riət/ ▶ **adj.** Statistics involving one variate or variable quantity.

U·ni·ver·sal /ˌyo͞onəˈvərsəl/ a movie production company formed by Carl Laemmle in 1912, one of the first studios to move from New York to the Los Angeles area. The company merged with MCA (Music Corporation of America) in 1962. The company produced movies starring Abbott and Costello, the series of Sherlock Holmes movies featuring Basil Rathbone and Nigel Bruce, and blockbusters such as *ET The Extra-Terrestrial* (1982).

u·ni·ver·sal /ˌyo͞onəˈvərsəl/ ▶ **adj.** of, affecting, or done by all people or things in the world or in a particular group; applicable to all cases: *universal adult suffrage* | *the incidents caused universal concern.* ■ Logic denoting a proposition in which something is asserted of all of a class. Contrasted with **PARTICULAR**. ■ Linguistics denoting or relating to a grammatical rule, set of rules, or other linguistic feature that is found in all languages. ■ (of a tool or machine) adjustable to or appropriate for all requirements; not restricted to a single purpose or position.
▶ **n.** a person or thing having universal effect, currency, or application, in particular: ■ Logic a universal proposition. ■ Philosophy a term or concept of general application. ■ Philosophy a nature or essence signified by a general term. ■ Linguistics a universal grammatical rule or linguistic feature.
– DERIVATIVES **u·ni·ver·sal·i·ty** /-vərˈsalətē/ **n.**
– ORIGIN late Middle English: from Old French, or from Latin *universalis*, from *universus* (see **UNIVERSE**).

Uni·ver·sal Cit·y /ˈyo͞onəˌvərsəl/ a district in northwestern Los Angeles in California, in the San Fernando Valley, home to Universal Studios and other entertainment facilities.

u·ni·ver·sal do·nor ▶ **n.** a person of blood group O, who can in theory donate blood to recipients of any ABO blood group.

u·ni·ver·sal·ist /ˌyo͞onəˈvərsəlist/ ▶ **n.** **1** Christian Theology a person who believes that all humankind will eventually be saved. ■ (usu. **Universalist**) a member of an organized body of Christians who hold such beliefs.
2 a person advocating loyalty to and concern for others without regard to national or other allegiances.
▶ **adj.** **1** Christian Theology of or relating to universalists.
2 universal in scope or character.
– DERIVATIVES **u·ni·ver·sal·ism** /-ˌlizəm/ **n.**, **u·ni·ver·sal·is·tic** /-ˌvərsəˈlistik/ **adj.**

u·ni·ver·sal·ize /ˌyo͞onəˈvərsəˌlīz/ ▶ **v.** [with obj.] give a universal character or application to (something, esp. something abstract): *theories that universalize experience.* ■ bring into universal use; make available for all: *attempts to universalize basic education.*
– DERIVATIVES **u·ni·ver·sal·iz·a·bil·i·ty** /-ˌvərsəˌlīzəˈbilətē/ **n.**, **u·ni·ver·sal·i·za·tion** /-ˌvərsəliˈzāsʜən/ **n.**

u·ni·ver·sal joint (also **universal coupling**) ▶ **n.** a coupling or joint that can transmit rotary power by a shaft over a range of angles.

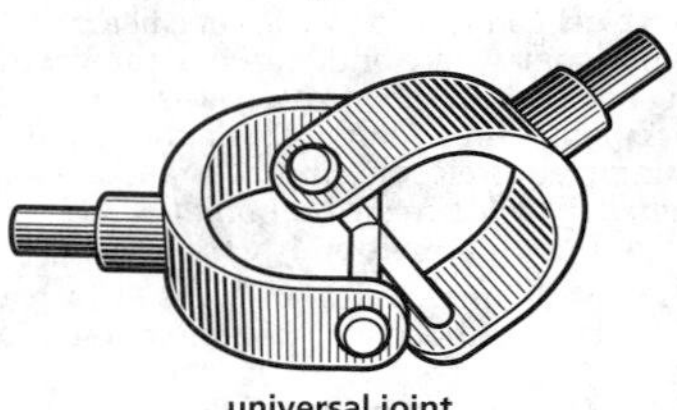
universal joint

u·ni·ver·sal·ly /ˌyo͞onəˈvərsəlē/ ▶ **adv.** by everyone; in every case: *progress is not always universally welcomed.*

U·ni·ver·sal Prod·uct Code ▶ **n.** more formal term for **BARCODE**.

u·ni·ver·sal quan·ti·fi·er ▶ **n.** Logic a formal expression used in asserting that a stated general proposition is true of all the members of the delineated universe or class.

u·ni·ver·sal re·cip·i·ent ▶ **n.** a person of blood group AB, who can in theory receive donated blood of any ABO blood group.

u·ni·ver·sal set ▶ **n.** Mathematics & Logic the set containing all objects or elements and of which all other sets are subsets.

U·ni·ver·sal Time (also **Universal Time Coordinated**) another term for **GREENWICH MEAN TIME**.

u·ni·verse /ˈyo͞onəˌvərs/ ▶ **n.** (**the universe**) all existing matter and space considered as a whole; the cosmos. The universe is believed to be at least 10 billion light years in diameter and contains a vast number of galaxies; it has been expanding since its creation in the Big Bang about 13 billion years ago. ■ a particular sphere of activity, interest, or experience: *the front parlor was the hub of her universe.* ■ (Logic also **universe of discourse**) another term for **UNIVERSAL SET**.
– ORIGIN late Middle English: from Old French *univers* or Latin *universum*, neuter of *universus* 'combined into one, whole,' from *uni-* 'one' + *versus* 'turned' (past participle of *vertere*).

u·ni·ver·si·ty /ˌyo͞onəˈvərsətē/ ▶ **n.** (pl. **universities**) an educational institution designed for instruction, examination, or both, of students in many branches of advanced learning, conferring degrees in various faculties, and often embodying colleges and similar institutions: [in names] *Oxford University* | *the University of California* | [as modifier] *the university buildings* | *a university professor.*
– PHRASES **at university** chiefly Brit. studying at a university. **the university of life** the experience of life regarded as a means of instruction.
– ORIGIN Middle English: from Old French *universite*, from Latin *universitas* 'the whole,' in late Latin 'society, guild,' from *universus* (see **UNIVERSE**).

U·ni·ver·si·ty Cit·y /ˌyo͞onəˈvərsitē/ a city in eastern Missouri, west of St. Louis, home to Washington University; pop. 36,289 (est. 2008).

U·ni·ver·si·ty Park a city in northeastern Texas, enclosed by northern Dallas, home to Southern Methodist University; pop. 24,853 (est. 2008).

u·niv·o·cal /ˌyo͞onəˈvōkəl, yo͞oˈnivə-/ ▶ **adj.** Philosophy & Linguistics (of a word or term) having only one

possible meaning; unambiguous: *a univocal set of instructions.*
– DERIVATIVES **u·niv·o·cal·i·ty** /ˌyo͞onəˌvōˈkalətē/ **n.**, **u·niv·o·cal·ly adv.**

U·nix /ˈyo͞oniks/ (also **UNIX**) ▶ **n.** Computing, trademark a widely used multiuser operating system.
– ORIGIN 1970s: from **UNI-** 'one' + a respelling of **-ICS**, on the pattern of an earlier less compact system called *Multics.*

un·joint /ˌənˈjoint/ ▶ **v.** [with obj.] rare separate or dislocate the joints of.

un·just /ˌənˈjəst/ ▶ **adj.** not based on or behaving according to what is morally right and fair: *resistance to unjust laws.*
– DERIVATIVES **un·just·ly adv.**, **un·just·ness n.**

un·jus·ti·fi·a·ble /ˌənˈjəstəˌfīəbəl, -ˌjəstəˈfī-/ ▶ **adj.** not able to be shown to be right or reasonable: *an unjustifiable restriction on their freedom.*
– DERIVATIVES **un·jus·ti·fi·a·bly** /-blē/ **adv.** [sentence adverb] *they seemed, unjustifiably, to be taking things out on the students.*

un·jus·ti·fied /ˌənˈjəstəˌfīd/ ▶ **adj. 1** not shown to be right or reasonable: *unjustified price increases.*
2 Printing (of printed text) not justified.

un·kempt /ˌənˈkem(p)t/ ▶ **adj.** (esp. of a person) having an untidy or disheveled appearance: *they were unwashed and unkempt.*
– DERIVATIVES **un·kempt·ly adv.**, **un·kempt·ness n.**
– ORIGIN late Middle English: from **UN-**[1] 'not' + *kempt* 'combed' (past participle of archaic *kemb*, related to **COMB**).

un·kept /ˌənˈkept/ ▶ **adj. 1** (of a commitment or undertaking) not honored or fulfilled: *unkept appointments and broken promises.*
2 not tidy or cared for.

un·kind /ˌənˈkīnd/ ▶ **adj.** inconsiderate and harsh to others: *you were terribly **unkind to** her | he was the butt of some unkind jokes | it was **unkind of** her to criticize.*
– DERIVATIVES **un·kind·ly adv.**

un·kind·ness /ˌənˈkīn(d)nis/ ▶ **n.** inconsiderate and harsh behavior: *she had had enough of her father's unkindness.*

un·king /ˌənˈkiNG/ ▶ **v.** [with obj.] archaic remove (a monarch) from power.

un·kink /ˌənˈkiNGk/ ▶ **v.** straighten or become straight.

un·knit /ˌənˈnit/ ▶ **v.** (**unknits**, **unknitting**, **unknitted**) [with obj.] separate (things that are joined, knotted, or interlocked).

un·knot /ˌənˈnät/ ▶ **v.** (**unknots**, **unknotting**, **unknotted**) **1** [with obj.] release or untie the knot or knots in: *he swiftly unknotted his tie.*
2 [no obj.] (of a muscle) relax after being tense and hard: *his shoulders unknotted.*

un·know·a·ble /ˌənˈnōəbəl/ ▶ **adj.** not able to be known: *the total cost is unknowable.*
– DERIVATIVES **un·know·a·bil·i·ty** /-ˌnōəˈbilətē/ **n.**

un·know·ing /ˌənˈnō-iNG/ ▶ **adj.** not knowing or aware: *the lions moved stealthily toward their unknowing victims.*
▶ **n.** lack of awareness or knowledge.
– DERIVATIVES **un·know·ing·ly adv.**, **un·know·ing·ness n.**

un·known /ˌənˈnōn/ ▶ **adj.** not known or familiar: *exploration into unknown territory | his whereabouts are **unknown to** his family.* ■ (of a performer or artist) not well known or famous.
▶ **n.** an unknown person or thing: *she is a relative unknown.* ■ Mathematics an unknown quantity or variable: *find the unknown in the following equations.* ■ (**the unknown**) that which is unknown: *our fear of the unknown.*
– PHRASES **unknown to** without the knowledge of: *unknown to Miller, the police had taped their telephone conversation.*
– DERIVATIVES **un·known·ness n.**

un·known quan·ti·ty ▶ **n.** a person or thing whose nature, value, or significance cannot be determined or is not yet known: *the producers replaced her with an unknown quantity.*

Un·known Sol·dier ▶ **n.** an unidentified representative member of a country's armed forces killed in war, given burial with special honors in a national memorial.

un·la·beled /ˌənˈlābəld/ (Brit. **unlabelled**) ▶ **adj.** without a label; not labeled: *bottles of unlabeled white wine.*

un·lace /ˌənˈlās/ ▶ **v.** [with obj.] undo the laces of (a shoe or garment).

un·lade /ˌənˈlād/ ▶ **v.** [with obj.] archaic unload (a ship or cargo).

un·lad·en /ˌənˈlādn/ ▶ **adj.** not carrying a load: *unladen, the boat heeled to starboard.*

un·la·dy·like /ˌənˈlādēˌlīk/ ▶ **adj.** not appropriate for or typical of a well-bred woman or girl: *Sharon gave an unladylike snort.*

un·laid /ˌənˈlād/ past and past participle of **UNLAY**.
▶ **adj.** not laid: *the table was still unlaid.*

un·la·ment·ed /ˌənləˈmentid/ ▶ **adj.** (of a person who has died or something that has gone or finished) not mourned or regretted.

un·lash /ˌənˈlasH/ ▶ **v.** [with obj.] unfasten (something securely tied with a cord or rope): *he unlashed the dinghy.*

un·latch /ˌənˈlacH/ ▶ **v.** [with obj.] unfasten the latch of (a door or gate).

un·law·ful /ˌənˈlôfəl/ ▶ **adj.** not conforming to, permitted by, or recognized by law or rules: *the use of unlawful violence | they claimed the ban was unlawful.*
– DERIVATIVES **un·law·ful·ly** /-f(ə)lē/ **adv.**, **un·law·ful·ness n.**

un·lay /ˌənˈlā/ ▶ **v.** (past and past participle **unlaid**) [with obj.] Nautical untwist (a rope) into separate strands.
– ORIGIN early 18th cent.: from **UN-**[2] (expressing reversal) + **LAY**[1].

un·lead·ed /ˌənˈledid/ ▶ **adj. 1** (esp. of gasoline) without added tetraethyl lead.
2 not covered, weighted, or framed with lead.
3 Printing (of type) with no space or leads added between lines.
▶ **n.** gasoline without added lead.

un·learn /ˌənˈlərn/ ▶ **v.** (past and past participle **unlearned** or chiefly Brit. **unlearnt**) [with obj.] discard (something learned, esp. a bad habit or false or outdated information) from one's memory: *teachers are being asked to unlearn rigid rules for labeling and placing children.*

un·learn·ed[1] /ˌənˈlərnid/ ▶ **adj.** (of a person) not well educated.
– DERIVATIVES **un·learn·ed·ly adv.**

un·learned[2] /ˌənˈlərnd/ ▶ **adj.** not having been learned: *she found herself on the stage, lines unlearned.* ■ not needing to be learned because innate: *the unlearned responses of our inner world.*

un·leash /ˌənˈlēsH/ ▶ **v.** [with obj.] release from a leash or restraint: *we unleashed the dog and carried it down to our car |* figurative *the failure of the talks could unleash more fighting.* ■ cause (a strong or violent force) to be released or become unrestrained: *the failure of the talks could unleash more fighting | his comment unleashed a storm of protest in India.*

un·leav·ened /ˌənˈlevənd/ ▶ **adj.** (of bread) made without yeast or other leavening agent.

un·less /ənˈles, ən-/ ▶ **conj.** except if (used to introduce a case in which a statement being made is not true or valid): *unless you have a photographic memory, repetition is vital | manuscripts cannot be returned unless accompanied by a self-addressed envelope.*
– ORIGIN late Middle English: from **ON** or **IN** (assimilated through lack of stress to **UN-**[1]) + **LESS**.

un·let·tered /ˌənˈletərd/ ▶ **adj.** (of a person) poorly educated or illiterate.

un·li·censed /ˌənˈlīsənst/ (Brit. also **unlicenced**) ▶ **adj.** not having an official license: *unlicensed weapons.* ■ chiefly Brit. (of a bar or restaurant) not having a license for the sale of liquor: *unlicensed clubs do not seek publicity.*

un·light·ed /ˌənˈlītid/ ▶ **adj.** unlit.

un·lik·a·ble /ˌənˈlīkəbəl/ (also **unlikeable**) ▶ **adj.** (esp. of a person) not likable: *a thoroughly unlikable bully.*

un·like /ˌənˈlīk/ ▶ **prep.** different from; not similar to: *they were unlike anything ever seen before | a large house not unlike Mr. Shaw's.* ■ in contrast to; differently from: *unlike Helen, he was not superstitious.* ■ uncharacteristic of (someone): *he sounded irritable, which was unlike him.*
▶ **adj.** [predic.] dissimilar or different from each other: *they seemed utterly unlike, despite being twins.* ■ (**unlike to/from**) archaic not like; different from: *he was very unlike to any other man.*
– DERIVATIVES **un·like·ness n.**
– ORIGIN Middle English: perhaps originally an alteration of Old Norse *úlíkr*; compare with Old English *ungelīc* 'not of the same kind, not comparable.'

USAGE The use of unlike as a conjunction, as in *she was behaving **unlike** she'd ever behaved before*, is not considered standard English. It can be avoided by using as with a negative instead: *she was behaving **as** she'd **never** behaved before.*

un·like·ly /ˌənˈlīklē/ ▶ **adj.** (**unlikelier**, **unlikeliest**) not likely to happen, be done, or be true; improbable: *an unlikely explanation | **it is unlikely that** they will ever be used |* [with infinitive] *the change is unlikely to affect many people.*
– DERIVATIVES **un·like·li·hood** /-ˌho͝od/ **n.**, **un·like·li·ness n.**

un·lim·ber /ˌənˈlimbər/ ▶ **v.** [with obj.] detach (a gun) from its limber so that it can be used. ■ unpack or unfasten (something) ready for use: *we had to unlimber some of the gear.*

un·lim·it·ed /ˌənˈlimitid/ ▶ **adj.** not limited or restricted in terms of number, quantity, or extent: *the range of possible adaptations was unlimited.* ■ Brit. (of a company) not limited. ■ Mathematics (of a problem) having an infinite number of solutions.
– DERIVATIVES **un·lim·it·ed·ly adv.**, **un·lim·it·ed·ness n.**

un·lined[1] /ˌənˈlīnd/ ▶ **adj.** not marked or covered with lines: *her face was still unlined | unlined paper.*

un·lined[2] ▶ **adj.** (of a container or garment) without a lining: *unlined curtains.*

un·link /ˌənˈliNGk/ ▶ **v.** [with obj.] make no longer connected: *all three loops are linked, but cutting any one unlinks the other two.* ■ (as adj. **unlinked**) unconnected: *three previously unlinked murders.*

un·liq·ui·dat·ed /ˌənˈlikwəˌdātid/ ▶ **adj.** (of a debt) not cleared or paid off.

un·list·ed /ˌənˈlistid/ ▶ **adj.** not included on a list. ■ (of a person or telephone number) not listed in a telephone directory or available through directory assistance, at the wish of the subscriber: *the nuisance calls stopped after he obtained an unlisted number.* ■ denoting or relating to a company whose shares are not listed on a stock exchange.

un·lis·ten·a·ble /ˌənˈlisənəbəl/ ▶ **adj.** (esp. of music) impossible or unbearable to listen to: *today, his recordings seem unlistenable.*

un·lit /ˌənˈlit/ ▶ **adj. 1** not provided with lighting: *an unlit staircase.*
2 not having been set alight: *his unlit pipe.*

un·liv·a·ble /ˌənˈlivəbəl/ ▶ **adj.** not able to be lived in; uninhabitable: *the pollution that has made life virtually unlivable for our people there.*

un·lived-in /ˌənˈliv ˌdin/ ▶ **adj.** not appearing to be used or inhabited; not homey or comfortable.

un·load /ˌənˈlōd/ ▶ **v.** [with obj.] **1** remove goods from (a vehicle, ship, container, etc.): *she hadn't finished unloading the car.* ■ remove (goods) from a vehicle, ship, container, etc.: *the men unloaded the wheat into the bays.* ■ [no obj.] (of a vehicle, ship, container, etc.) have goods removed: *the street was jammed with trucks unloading.* ■ informal get rid of (something unwanted): *he had **unloaded** his depreciating stock **on** his unsuspecting wife.* ■ informal give expression to (oppressive thoughts or feelings): *the meeting had been a chance for her to unload some of her feelings about her son.*
2 remove (ammunition) from a gun or (film) from a camera.
– DERIVATIVES **un·load·er n.**

un·lock /ənˈläk/ ▶ **v.** [with obj.] undo the lock of (something) by using a key: *he unlocked the door to his room.* ■ make (something previously inaccessible or unexploited) available for use: *the campaign has helped us unlock rich reserves of talent among our employees.*

un·locked /ənˈläkt/ ▶ **adj.** not locked: *unlocked doors.*

un·looked-for /ˌənˈlo͝okt ˌfôr/ ▶ **adj.** unexpected; unforeseen: *in his family he found unlooked-for happiness.*

un·loose /ˌənˈlo͞os/ (also **unloosen**) ▶ **v.** [with obj.] undo; let free: *he rushed across to unloose the dog.*

un·lov·a·ble /ənˈləvəbəl/ (also **unloveable**) ▶ **adj.** not lovable: *a very unlovable child.*
– DERIVATIVES **un·lov·a·bil·i·ty** /-ˌləvəˈbilətē/ **n.**

un·loved /ˌənˈləvd/ ▶ **adj.** not loved.

un·love·ly /ˌənˈləvlē/ ▶ **adj.** not attractive; ugly.
– DERIVATIVES **un·love·li·ness n.**

un·lov·ing /ˌənˈləviNG/ ▶ **adj.** not loving: *an unloving father.*
– DERIVATIVES **un·lov·ing·ly adv.**

un·luck·y /ˌənˈləkē/ ▶ **adj.** (**unluckier**, **unluckiest**) having, bringing, or resulting from bad luck: *an unlucky defeat |* [with infinitive] *the visitors were unlucky to have a goal disallowed.*
– DERIVATIVES **un·luck·i·ly** /-ˈləkəlē/ **adv.**, **un·luck·i·ness n.**

un·made /ˌənˈmād/ ▶ **adj. 1** (of a bed) not having the bedclothes neatly arranged for sleeping in.
2 Brit. (of a road) without a hard, smooth surface.

un·maid·en·ly /ˌənˈmādn-lē/ ▶ **adj.** not befitting or characteristic of a young, sexually inexperienced woman.

U

PRONUNCIATION KEY ə *ago, up*; ər *over, fur*; a *hat*; ā *ate*; ä *car*; e *let*; ē *see*; i *fit*; ī *by*; NG *sing*; ō *go*; ô *law, for*; oi *toy*; o͝o *good*; o͞o *goo*; ou *out*; TH *thin*; T͟H *then*; ZH *vision*

– DERIVATIVES **un·maid·en·li·ness** n.

un·make /ˌənˈmāk/ ▶ v. (past and past participle **unmade**) [with obj.] reverse or undo the making of; annul: *Watergate made the independent prosecutor law necessary; Whitewater may unmake it.* ■ ruin; destroy: *human beings make cities and unmake them.*

un·man /ˌənˈman/ ▶ v. (**unmans, unmanning, unmanned**) [with obj.] literary deprive of qualities traditionally associated with men, such as self-control or courage: *sitting in the dock awaiting a sentence will unman the stoutest heart.*

un·man·age·a·ble /ˌənˈmanijəbəl/ ▶ adj. difficult or impossible to manage, manipulate, or control: *his behavior was becoming unmanageable at home.*
– DERIVATIVES **un·man·age·a·ble·ness** n., **un·man·age·a·bly** /-blē/ adv.

un·man·aged /ˌənˈmanijd/ ▶ adj. **1** not controlled or regulated: *a critique of unmanaged capitalism.*
2 (of land) left wild; in a natural state.

un·man·ly /ˌənˈmanlē/ ▶ adj. not manly; weak or cowardly: *unmanly behavior.*
– DERIVATIVES **un·man·li·ness** n.

un·manned /ˌənˈmand/ ▶ adj. not having or needing a crew or staff: *an unmanned space flight.*

un·man·nered /ˌənˈmanərd/ ▶ adj. not affected or artificial in style.

un·man·ner·ly /ˌənˈmanərlē/ ▶ adj. not having or showing good manners: *uncouth, unmannerly fellows.*
– DERIVATIVES **un·man·ner·li·ness** n.

un·mapped /ˌənˈmapt/ ▶ adj. (of an area or feature) not represented on a geographical map. ■ unexplored: *unmapped corners of Africa.* ■ Biology (of a gene or chromosome) not yet mapped.

un·marked /ˌənˈmärkt/ ▶ adj. **1** not marked: *an unmarked police car | his skin was unmarked.* ■ Linguistics (of a word or other linguistic unit) having a more general meaning or use than a corresponding marked term: *"duck" is unmarked, whereas "drake" is marked.*
2 not noticed: *it's a pleasure to reward them for work which might otherwise go unmarked.*

un·mar·ket·a·ble /ˌənˈmärkitəbəl/ ▶ adj. without qualities that attract sales; not marketable.

un·mar·ried /ˌənˈmarēd/ ▶ adj. not married; single.

un·mask /ˌənˈmask/ ▶ v. [with obj.] expose the true character of or hidden truth about: *the trial unmasked him as a complete charlatan.* ■ (often as adj. **unmasked**) remove the mask from: *an unmasked gunman.*
– DERIVATIVES **un·mask·er** n.

un·match·a·ble /ˌənˈmacHəbəl/ ▶ adj. incapable of being matched, equaled, or rivaled.
– DERIVATIVES **un·match·a·bly** /-blē/ adv.

un·matched /ˌənˈmacHt/ ▶ adj. not matched or equaled: *he has a talent unmatched by any other politician.*

un·mean·ing /ˌənˈmēniNG/ ▶ adj. having no meaning or significance; meaningless: *a sweet, unmeaning smile.*
– DERIVATIVES **un·mean·ing·ly** adv.

un·meas·ur·a·ble /ˌənˈmeZH(ə)rəbəl/ ▶ adj. not able to be measured objectively: *the unmeasurable qualities of a scientist.*
– DERIVATIVES **un·meas·ur·a·bly** /-blē/ adv.

un·meas·ured /ˌənˈmeZHərd/ ▶ adj. **1** not having been measured: *unmeasured risk factors.*
2 chiefly literary immense; limitless: *he is regarded by his congregation with unmeasured adoration.*

un·me·di·at·ed /ˌənˈmēdēˌātid/ ▶ adj. without anyone or anything intervening or acting as an intermediate; direct.

un·melt·ed /ˌənˈmeltid/ ▶ adj. not melted: *unmelted snow.*

u

un·mem·o·ra·ble /ˌənˈmem(ə)rəbəl/ ▶ adj. not memorable.
– DERIVATIVES **un·mem·o·ra·bly** adv.

un·men·tion·a·ble /ˌənˈmenCHənəbəl/ ▶ adj. too embarrassing, offensive, or shocking to be spoken about: *the unmentionable subject of incontinence.*
▶ n. (usu. **unmentionables**) chiefly humorous a person or thing that is too shocking or embarrassing to be mentioned by name: *wearing nothing but fig leaves over their unmentionables.* ■ (**unmentionables**) underwear.
– DERIVATIVES **un·men·tion·a·bil·i·ty** /-ˌmenCHənəˈbilətē/ n., **un·men·tion·a·ble·ness** n., **un·men·tion·a·bly** /-blē/ adv.

un·men·tioned /ˌənˈmenCHənd/ ▶ adj. not mentioned: *a monument unmentioned in all the architectural guides.*

un·mer·ci·ful /ənˈmərsəfəl/ ▶ adj. cruel or harsh; showing no mercy.
– DERIVATIVES **un·mer·ci·ful·ly** /-f(ə)lē/ adv., **un·mer·ci·ful·ness** n.

un·mer·it·ed /ˌənˈmeritid/ ▶ adj. not deserved or merited: *an unmerited insult.*

un·met /ˌənˈmet/ ▶ adj. (of a requirement) not achieved or fulfilled: *an unmet need.*

un·me·tered /ˌənˈmētərd/ ▶ adj. **1** not charged for according to amount or time used.
2 not supplied or fitted with a meter: *an unmetered taxi.*
3 not canceled or franked using a postage meter: *agents warned the public to be on the alert for unmetered packages.*

un·met·ri·cal /ˌənˈmetrikəl/ ▶ adj. not composed in or using meter: *an unmetrical poet.*

un·mil·i·tar·y /ˌənˈmiliˌterē/ ▶ adj. not typical of, suitable for, or connected with the military.

un·mind·ful /ˌənˈmīn(d)fəl/ ▶ adj. [predic.] not conscious or aware: *Danielle seemed* ***unmindful of*** *her parents' plight.*
– DERIVATIVES **un·mind·ful·ly** adv., **un·mind·ful·ness** n.

un·miss·a·ble /ˌənˈmisəbəl/ ▶ adj. **1** so good that it should not be missed: *the special effects make this an unmissable treat.*
2 so clear or obvious that it cannot be missed.

un·mis·tak·a·ble /ˌənməˈstākəbəl/ (also **unmistakeable**) ▶ adj. not able to be mistaken for anything else; very distinctive: *the unmistakable sound of his laughter.*
– DERIVATIVES **un·mis·tak·a·bil·i·ty** /-ˌstākəˈbilətē/ n., **un·mis·tak·a·bly** /-blē/ adv.

un·mis·tak·en /ˌənməˈstākən/ ▶ adj. not mistaken; right, correct.

un·mit·i·gat·ed /ˌənˈmitəˌgātid/ ▶ adj. [attrib.] absolute; unqualified: *the tour had been* ***an unmitigated disaster.***
– DERIVATIVES **un·mit·i·gat·ed·ly** adv.

un·mixed /ˌənˈmikst/ ▶ adj. not mixed: *bold unmixed colors.*

un·mixed bless·ing ▶ n. [usu. with negative] a situation or thing having advantages and no disadvantages: *motherhood is not an unmixed blessing.*

un·mod·ern·ized /ˌənˈmädərˌnīzd/ ▶ adj. not modernized; retaining the original form or features: *unmodernized spelling.*

un·mod·u·lat·ed /ˌənˈmäjəˌlātid/ ▶ adj. not modulated: *an unmodulated video signal.*

un·mo·lest·ed /ˌənməˈlestid/ ▶ adj. not pestered or molested; left in peace: *they allowed him to pass unmolested.*

un·mon·i·tored /ənˈmänitərd/ ▶ adj. not monitored or kept under observation: *unmonitored patients | unmonitored Internet access.*

un·moor /ˌənˈmo͝or/ ▶ v. [with obj.] release the moorings of (a vessel).

un·mor·al /ˌənˈmôrəl, -ˈmär-/ ▶ adj. not influenced by or concerned with morality. Compare with IMMORAL.
– DERIVATIVES **un·mo·ral·i·ty** /-məˈralətē, -mô-/ n.

un·moth·er·ly /ˌənˈməTHərlē/ ▶ adj. not having or showing the affectionate feelings associated with a mother.

un·mo·ti·vat·ed /ˌənˈmōtəˌvātid/ ▶ adj. **1** not having interest in or enthusiasm for something, esp. work or study.
2 without a reason or motive: *an unmotivated attack.*

un·mount·ed /ˌənˈmountid/ ▶ adj. not mounted.

un·mourned /ˌənˈmôrnd/ ▶ adj. not mourned: *he would die alone and unmourned.*

un·moved /ˌənˈmo͞ovd/ ▶ adj. [predic.] not affected by emotion or excitement: *he was unmoved by her outburst.* ■ not changed in one's purpose or intention: *her opponents were unmoved and plan to return to court.* ■ not changed in position: *shares in some companies were initially unmoved.*
– DERIVATIVES **un·mov·a·ble** /-vəbəl/ (also **unmoveable**) adj.

un·mov·ing /ˌənˈmo͞oviNG/ ▶ adj. **1** not moving; still: *Claudia sat unmoving behind her desk.*
2 not stirring any emotion.

un·muf·fle /ənˈməfəl/ ▶ v. [with obj.] free (something) from something that muffles or conceals.

un·muf·flered /ˌənˈməflərd/ ▶ adj. **1** (of an engine or vehicle) not fitted with a muffler: *the crescendo of unmufflered 400-horsepower engines.*
2 not restrained, muffled, or suppressed in any way: *unmufflered fun.*

un·mur·mur·ing /ˌənˈmərməriNG/ ▶ adj. literary not complaining.
– DERIVATIVES **un·mur·mur·ing·ly** adv.

un·mu·si·cal /ˌənˈmyo͞ozikəl/ ▶ adj. not pleasing to the ear. ■ unskilled in or indifferent to music.
– DERIVATIVES **un·mu·si·cal·i·ty** /-ˌmyo͞oziˈkalətē/ n., **un·mu·si·cal·ly** /-zik(ə)lē/ adv., **un·mu·si·cal·ness** n.

un·muz·zle /ənˈməzəl/ ▶ v. [with obj.] remove a muzzle from (an animal). ■ allow (a person or the press) to express their views freely and without censorship.

un·muz·zled /ənˈməzəld/ ▶ adj. (of an animal) not wearing a muzzle.

un·name·a·ble /ˌənˈnāməbəl/ (also **unnamable**) ▶ adj. not able to be named, esp. because too bad or horrific: *his mind was blank with an unnameable fear.*

un·named /ˌənˈnāmd/ ▶ adj. not having a name: *a new but yet unnamed African violet.* ■ not identified by name: *an old couple in an unnamed American city.*

un·nat·u·ral /ˌənˈnacH(ə)rəl/ ▶ adj. contrary to the ordinary course of nature; abnormal: *death by unnatural causes.* ■ not existing in nature; artificial: *the artificial turf looks an unnatural green.* ■ affected or stilted: *the formal tone of the programs caused them to sound stilted and unnatural.* ■ lacking feelings of kindness and sympathy that are considered to be natural: *they condemned her as an unnatural woman.*
– DERIVATIVES **un·nat·u·ral·ly** adv., **un·nat·u·ral·ness** n.

un·nav·i·ga·ble /ˌənˈnavəgəbəl/ ▶ adj. (of a waterway or sea) not able to be sailed on by ships or boats.
– DERIVATIVES **un·nav·i·ga·bil·i·ty** /-ˌnavəgəˈbilətē/ n.

un·nec·es·sar·y /ˌənˈnesəˌserē/ ▶ adj. not needed: *a fourth Chicago airport is unnecessary.* ■ more than is needed; excessive: *the police used unnecessary force.* ■ (of a remark) not appropriate and likely to be offensive or impertinent.
▶ plural n. (**unnecessaries**) unnecessary things.
– DERIVATIVES **un·nec·es·sar·i·ly** /-ˌnesəˈse(ə)rəlē/ adv., **un·nec·es·sar·i·ness** n.

un·need·ed /ˌənˈnēdid/ ▶ adj. not needed: *the disposal of unneeded assets.*

un·nerve /ˌənˈnərv/ ▶ v. [with obj.] make (someone) lose courage or confidence: *the bleakness of his gaze unnerved her* | (as adj. **unnerving**) *an unnerving experience.*
– DERIVATIVES **un·nerv·ing·ly** adv.

un·no·tice·a·ble /ˌənˈnōtisəbəl/ ▶ adj. not easily observed or noticed: *the reverberation will be so slight as to be unnoticeable.*
– DERIVATIVES **un·no·tice·a·bly** /-blē/ adv.

un·no·ticed /ˌənˈnōtist/ ▶ adj. [usu. as complement] not noticed: *a deliberate kick that went unnoticed by the referee.*

un·num·bered /ˌənˈnəmbərd/ ▶ adj. **1** not marked with or assigned a number.
2 not counted, typically because very great.

UNO /ˈyo͞onō/ ▶ abbr. United Nations Organization.

un·ob·jec·tion·a·ble /ˌənəbˈjeksHənəbəl/ ▶ adj. not objectionable; acceptable: *he thought he would become a storyteller, an unobjectionable hobby.*
– DERIVATIVES **un·ob·jec·tion·a·bly** /-blē/ adv.

un·o·blig·ing /ˌənəˈblījiNG/ ▶ adj. not helpful or cooperative.

un·ob·scured /ˌənəbˈskyo͝ord/ ▶ adj. not obscured.

un·ob·serv·a·ble /ˌənəbˈzərvəbəl/ ▶ adj. not able to be observed.

un·ob·serv·ant /ˌənəbˈzərvənt/ ▶ adj. not observant.
– DERIVATIVES **un·ob·serv·ant·ly** adv.

un·ob·served /ˌənəbˈzərvd/ ▶ adj. not observed: *their courtship has not gone unobserved by Mildred.*

un·ob·struct·ed /ˌənəbˈstrəktid/ ▶ adj. not obstructed: *an unobstructed view of the water.*

un·ob·tain·a·ble /ˌənəbˈtānəbəl/ ▶ adj. not able to be obtained.

un·ob·tain·i·um /ˌənəbˈtānēəm/ (also **unobtanium**) ▶ n. a fictional material with supernatural properties: *what type of cabling are we talking about, steel, composite, unobtainium?* ■ a material that it extremely rare and difficult to obtain.

un·ob·tru·sive /ˌənəbˈtro͞osiv/ ▶ adj. not conspicuous or attracting attention: *corrections should be neat and unobtrusive.*
– DERIVATIVES **un·ob·tru·sive·ly** adv., **un·ob·tru·sive·ness** n.

un·oc·cu·pied /ˌənˈäkyəˌpīd/ ▶ adj. **1** (of ground) not occupied by inhabitants. ■ (of premises) having fixtures and furniture but no inhabitants or occupants. Compare with VACANT.
2 not engaged in work or a pursuit; idle.
3 not occupied by enemy troops.

un·of·fi·cial /ˌənəˈfisHəl/ ▶ adj. not officially authorized or confirmed: *unofficial reports that dozens of people were injured.*
– DERIVATIVES **un·of·fi·cial·ly** adv.

un·o·pened /ənˈōpənd/ ▶ adj. not opened: *unopened mail.*

un·op·posed /ˌənəˈpōzd/ ▶ adj. not opposed; unchallenged: *she was elected unopposed as leader.*

un·or·dained /ˌənôrˈdānd/ ▶ **adj.** not having been ordained as a priest or minister.

un·or·dered /ˌənˈôrdərd/ ▶ **adj.** not put in order; unarranged or disorderly. ■ not ordered or asked for.

un·or·gan·ized /ˌənˈôrgəˌnīzd/ ▶ **adj.** not organized: *a sea of unorganized data.* ■ not represented by or formed into a labor union: *unorganized white-collar workers.*

un·o·rig·i·nal /ˌənəˈrijənl/ ▶ **adj.** lacking originality; derivative: *an uninteresting and unoriginal essay.*
– DERIVATIVES **un·o·rig·i·nal·i·ty** /-ˌrijəˈnalətē/ **n.**, **un·o·rig·i·nal·ly adv.**

un·or·na·ment·ed /ˌənˈôrnəməntid/ ▶ **adj.** not having any decoration.

un·or·tho·dox /ˌənˈôrTHəˌdäks/ ▶ **adj.** contrary to what is usual, traditional, or accepted; not orthodox: *he frequently upset other scholars with his unorthodox views.*
– DERIVATIVES **un·or·tho·dox·ly adv.**, **un·or·tho·dox·y** /-ˌdäksē/ **n.**

un·os·ten·ta·tious /ˌənˌästənˈtāsHəs/ ▶ **adj.** not ostentatious: *he was generous in a quiet, unostentatious way.*
– DERIVATIVES **un·os·ten·ta·tious·ly adv.**, **un·os·ten·ta·tious·ness n.**

un·owned /ˌənˈōnd/ ▶ **adj. 1** not having an owner. **2** not admitted to; unacknowledged: *the unowned anger of all the smiling females of unenlightened times.*

un·ox·i·dized /ənˈäksiˌdīzd/ ▶ **adj.** not oxidized.

un·pack /ˌənˈpak/ ▶ **v.** [with obj.] open and remove the contents of (a suitcase, bag, or package): *she unpacked her suitcase* | [no obj.] *he unpacked and put everything away.* ■ remove (something) from a suitcase, bag, or package: *we unpacked the sandwiches.* ■ analyze (something) into its component elements: *let us unpack this question.* ■ Computing convert (data) from a compressed form to a usable form.
– DERIVATIVES **un·pack·er n.**

un·pack·aged /ˌənˈpakijd/ ▶ **adj.** chiefly Brit. (of a vacation) not organized as an inclusive package.

un·paged /ˌənˈpājd/ ▶ **adj.** (of a book) not having the pages numbered: *a rare unpaged leaf.*

un·pag·i·nat·ed /ˌənˈpajəˌnātid/ ▶ **adj.** unpaged.

un·paid /ˌənˈpād/ ▶ **adj. 1** (of a debt) not yet discharged by payment: *unpaid bills.* **2** (of work or a period of leave) undertaken without payment: *unpaid labor in the home.* ■ (of a person) not receiving payment for work done.

un·paint·ed /ˌənˈpāntid/ ▶ **adj.** not painted.

un·paired /ˌənˈpe(ə)rd/ ▶ **adj. 1** not arranged in pairs. **2** not forming one of a pair.

un·pal·at·a·ble /ˌənˈpalətəbəl/ ▶ **adj.** not pleasant to taste. ■ difficult to tolerate or accept: *the unpalatable fact that many of the world's people are starving.*
– DERIVATIVES **un·pal·at·a·bil·i·ty** /-ˌpalətəˈbilitē/ **n.**, **un·pal·at·a·bly** /-blē/ **adv.**

un·par·al·leled /ˌənˈparəˌleld/ ▶ **adj.** having no parallel or equal; exceptional: *the sudden rise in unemployment is unparalleled in the postwar period.*

un·par·don·a·ble /ˌənˈpärdn-əbəl, -ˈpärdnə-/ ▶ **adj.** (of a fault or offense) too severe to be pardoned; unforgivable: *an unpardonable sin.*
– DERIVATIVES **un·par·don·a·ble·ness n.**, **un·par·don·a·bly** /-blē/ **adv.**

un·par·lia·men·ta·ry /ˌənˌpärləˈmentərē/ ▶ **adj.** (esp. of language) contrary to the rules or procedures of a parliament: *an unparliamentary expression.*

un·pas·teur·ized ▶ **adj.** not pasteurized: *unpasteurized milk.*

un·pa·tri·ot·ic /ˌənˌpātrēˈätik/ ▶ **adj.** not patriotic.
– DERIVATIVES **un·pa·tri·ot·i·cal·ly adv.**

un·paved /ˌənˌpāvd/ ▶ **adj.** not paved: *unpaved streets.*

un·peeled /ˌənˈpēld/ ▶ **adj.** not peeled: *an unpeeled orange.*

un·peg /ˌənˈpeg/ ▶ **v.** (**unpegs**, **unpegging**, **unpegged**) [with obj.] unfasten by the removal of pegs. ■ cease to maintain a fixed relationship between (a currency) and another currency.

un·peo·ple /ˌənˈpēpəl/ ▶ **v.** [with obj.] (usu. as adj. **unpeopled**) empty of people; depopulate.

un·per·ceived /ˌənpərˈsēvd/ ▶ **adj.** [usu. as complement] not perceived; unobserved: *the full significance of this went unperceived.*

un·per·formed /ˌənpərˈfôrmd/ ▶ **adj.** not having been performed: *an unperformed play.*

un·per·son /ˈənˈpərsən, -ˌpər-/ ▶ **n.** (pl. **unpersons**) a person whose name or existence is denied or ignored, esp. because of a political misdemeanor.
– ORIGIN 1949: coined by George Orwell in the novel *Nineteen Eighty-Four.*

un·per·suad·ed /ˌənpərˈswādid/ ▶ **adj.** not persuaded; unconvinced.

un·per·sua·sive /ˌənpərˈswāsiv/ ▶ **adj.** not persuasive.
– DERIVATIVES **un·per·sua·sive·ly adv.**

un·per·turbed /ˌənpərˈtərbd/ ▶ **adj.** not perturbed or concerned: *Kenneth seems unperturbed by the news.*
– DERIVATIVES **un·per·turbed·ly** /-ˈtərbədlē/ **adv.**

un·phil·o·soph·i·cal /ˌənˌfiləˈsäfikəl/ ▶ **adj.** not following philosophical principles or method.
– DERIVATIVES **un·phil·o·soph·ic adj.** (archaic), **un·phil·o·soph·i·cal·ly** /-ik(ə)lē/ **adv.**

un·phys·i·cal /ˌənˈfizikəl/ ▶ **adj.** not in accordance with the laws or principles of physics; not corresponding to a physically possible situation.

un·phys·i·o·log·i·cal /ˌənˌfizēəˈläjikəl/ ▶ **adj.** not in accordance with normal physiological conditions.
– DERIVATIVES **un·phys·i·o·log·ic adj.**, **un·phys·i·o·log·i·cal·ly** /-ik(ə)lē/ **adv.**

un·pick /ˌənˈpik/ ▶ **v.** [with obj.] undo the sewing of (stitches or a garment): *I unpicked the seams of his trousers.* ■ carefully analyze the different elements of, esp. in order to find faults.

un·picked /ˌənˈpikt/ ▶ **adj. 1** (of a flower, fruit, or vegetable) not picked: *unpicked tomatoes.* **2** not selected.

un·pin /ˌənˈpin/ ▶ **v.** (**unpins**, **unpinning**, **unpinned**) [with obj.] unfasten or detach by removing a pin or pins. ■ Chess release (a pinned piece or pawn), e.g., by moving away the piece it is shielding.

un·pit·y·ing /ˌənˈpitē-iNG/ ▶ **adj.** not feeling or showing pity.
– DERIVATIVES **un·pit·y·ing·ly adv.**

un·place·a·ble /ˌənˈplāsəbəl/ ▶ **adj.** not able to be placed or classified: *an unplaceable accent.*

un·placed /ˌənˈplāst/ ▶ **adj.** not having or assigned to a specific place. ■ chiefly Horse Racing not one of the first three to finish in a race or competition. ■ not appropriate or correct in the circumstances: *a feeling of unplaced alarm.*

un·planned /ˌənˈpland/ ▶ **adj.** not planned: *an unplanned pregnancy.*

un·plant·ed /ˌənˈplantid/ ▶ **adj.** (of land) uncultivated.

un·play·a·ble /ˌənˈplāəbəl/ ▶ **adj.** not able to be played or played on: *hit a high-bouncing, unplayable chop over second* | *an unplayable golf course.* ■ (of music) too difficult or bad to perform.
– DERIVATIVES **un·play·a·bly** /-blē/ **adv.**

un·pleas·ant /ˌənˈplezənt/ ▶ **adj.** causing discomfort, unhappiness, or revulsion; disagreeable: *an unpleasant smell* | *the symptoms are extremely unpleasant.* ■ (of a person or their manner) unfriendly and inconsiderate; rude: *when drunk, he could become very unpleasant.*
– DERIVATIVES **un·pleas·ant·ly adv.**

un·pleas·ant·ness /ˌənˈplezəntnəs/ ▶ **n.** the state or quality of being unpleasant. ■ bad feeling or quarreling between people.

un·pleas·ant·ry /ˌənˈplezəntrē/ ▶ **n.** (pl. **unpleasantries**) **1** (**unpleasantries**) disagreeable matters or comments: *the day-to-day unpleasantries of dealing with an alien administration.* **2** dated quarreling or other disagreeable behavior: *a little unpleasantry with the authorities.*

un·pleas·ing /ˌənˈplēziNG/ ▶ **adj.** not giving satisfaction, esp. of an aesthetic kind: *the sound was not unpleasing.*
– DERIVATIVES **un·pleas·ing·ly adv.**

un·plea·sure /ˌənˈplezHər/ ▶ **n.** Psychoanalysis the sense of inner pain, discomfort, or anxiety that results from the blocking of an instinctual impulse by the ego.

un·plowed /ˌənˈploud/ (Brit. **unploughed**) ▶ **adj. 1** (of an area of land) not having been plowed. **2** (of a road) not cleared of snow by a snowplow.

un·plug /ˌənˈpləg/ ▶ **v.** (**unplugs**, **unplugging**, **unplugged**) [with obj.] **1** disconnect (an electrical device) by removing its plug from a socket: *she unplugged the fridge.* ■ sever the connection between a peripheral device and a computer: *the only thing you can do is to unplug the RJ45* | *Why do I have to unplug the mouse to get the printer to work?* **2** remove an obstacle or blockage from: *a procedure to unplug blocked arteries.* **3** [no obj.] informal relax by disengaging from normal activities: *they've gone up to the cabin to unplug.*

un·plugged /ənˈpləgd/ ▶ **adj.** trademark (of pop or rock music) performed or recorded with acoustic rather than electrically amplified instruments.

un·plumbed /ənˈpləmd/ ▶ **adj. 1** unsounded; unfathomed: *loomed to the surface like a stingray from unplumbed depths.* ■ not fully explored or understood: *one-dimensional performances that leave the play's psychological depths unplumbed.* **2** (of a building or room) not having water and drainage pipes installed and connected: *an indoor, unplumbed outhouse.*
– DERIVATIVES **un·plumb·a·ble** /-ˈpləməbəl/ **adj.**

un·po·et·ic /ˌənpōˈetik/ ▶ **adj.** not having a style of expression characteristic of poetry.
– DERIVATIVES **un·po·et·i·cal adj.**

un·point·ed /ˌənˈpointid/ ▶ **adj. 1** not having a sharpened or tapered tip. **2** (of a Semitic alphabet) written without dots or small strokes to indicate vowels or distinguish consonants. **3** (of brickwork, a brick structure, or tiling) having joints that are not filled in or repaired.

un·pol·ished /ˌənˈpälisHt/ ▶ **adj.** not having a polished surface: *his shoes were unpolished.* ■ unrefined in style or behavior: *his work is unpolished and sometimes incoherent.*

un·pol·i·tic /ˌənˈpäliˌtik/ ▶ **adj.** rare term for IMPOLITIC.

un·po·lit·i·cal /ˌənpəˈlitikəl/ ▶ **adj.** not concerned with politics; apolitical: *large numbers of otherwise unpolitical people responded to the war.*

un·polled /ˌənˈpōld/ ▶ **adj. 1** (of a voter) not having voted, or registered to vote, at an election. ■ (of a vote) not cast at or registered for an election. **2** (of a person) not included in an opinion poll.

un·pol·lut·ed ▶ **adj.** not contaminated with noxious or poisonous substances.

un·pop·u·lar /ˌənˈpäpyələr/ ▶ **adj.** not liked or popular: *unpopular measures* | *Luke was* ***unpopular with*** *most of the teachers.*
– DERIVATIVES **un·pop·u·lar·i·ty** /-ˌpäpyəˈlaritē/ **n.**

un·pop·u·lat·ed /ˌənˈpäpyəˌlātid/ ▶ **adj.** (of a place) having no inhabitants: *three missiles landed in unpopulated areas.* ■ (of a printed circuit board) having no components fitted.

un·posed /ˌənˈpōzd/ ▶ **adj.** (of a photograph) not having an artificially posed subject.

un·pos·sessed /ˌənpəˈzest/ ▶ **adj.** not owned. ■ [predic.] (**unpossessed of**) not having (an ability, quality, or characteristic): *the money men are unpossessed of the social graces.*

un·pow·ered /ˌənˈpou(-ə)rd/ ▶ **adj.** having no mechanical source of power for propulsion.

un·prac·ti·cal /ˌənˈpraktikəl/ ▶ **adj.** another term for IMPRACTICAL (sense 1).
– DERIVATIVES **un·prac·ti·cal·i·ty** /-ˌpraktiˈkalətē/ **n.**

un·prac·ticed /ˌənˈpraktist/ (Brit. **unpractised**) ▶ **adj.** (of a person or faculty) not trained or experienced: *to the unpracticed eye, the result might appear a hodgepodge.* ■ (of an action or performance) not often done before.

un·prec·e·dent·ed /ˌənˈpresəˌdəntid/ ▶ **adj.** never done or known before: *the government took the unprecedented step of releasing confidential correspondence.*
– DERIVATIVES **un·prec·e·dent·ed·ly adv.**

un·pre·dict·a·ble /ˌənpriˈdiktəbəl/ ▶ **adj.** not able to be predicted: *the unpredictable weather of the Scottish islands.* ■ (of a person) behaving in a way that is not easily predicted: *he is emotional and unpredictable.*
– DERIVATIVES **un·pre·dict·a·bil·i·ty** /-ˌdiktəˈbilətē/ **n.**, **un·pre·dict·a·bly** /-blē/ **adv.**

un·pre·dict·ed /ˌənpriˈdiktid/ ▶ **adj.** (of an event or result) unforeseen: *the unpredicted change of weather.*

un·prej·u·diced /ˌənˈprejədist/ ▶ **adj.** not having or showing a dislike or distrust based on fixed or preconceived ideas.

un·pre·med·i·tat·ed /ˌənpriˈmedəˌtātid, -prē-/ ▶ **adj.** (of an act, remark, or state) not thought out or planned beforehand: *it was a totally unpremeditated attack.*
– DERIVATIVES **un·pre·med·i·tat·ed·ly adv.**

un·pre·pared /ˌənpriˈpe(ə)rd/ ▶ **adj.** [predic.] not ready or able to deal with something: *she was totally* ***unprepared for*** *what happened next* | *the transformation caught them* ***unprepared.*** ■ [with infinitive] not willing to do something: *they were unprepared to accept what was proposed.* ■ (of

U

a thing) not made ready for use: *paintings on unprepared canvas.*
– DERIVATIVES **un·pre·par·ed·ness** /-ˈpe(ə)r(i)dnis/ **n.**

un·pre·pos·ses·sing /ˌənˌprēpəˈzesiNG/ ▶ **adj.** not particularly attractive or appealing to the eye: *despite his unprepossessing appearance he had an animal magnetism.*

un·pre·sent·a·ble /ˌənpriˈzentəbəl/ ▶ **adj.** not clean, well-dressed, or decent enough to be seen in public.

un·pressed /ˌənˈprest/ ▶ **adj.** (of food or drink) not shaped, squeezed, or obtained by pressure. ■ (of clothing) unironed.

un·pres·sur·ized /ˌənˈpresHəˌrīzd/ ▶ **adj.** (of a gas or its container) not having raised pressure that is produced or maintained artificially. ■ (of an aircraft cabin) not having normal atmospheric pressure maintained at a high altitude.

un·pre·sum·ing /ənpriˈzo͞omiNG/ ▶ **adj.** modest; unassuming: *a quiet, unpresuming man.*

un·pre·tend·ing /ˌənpriˈtendiNG/ ▶ **adj.** archaic not pretentious or false; genuine: *unpretending sympathy.*

un·pre·ten·tious /ˌənpriˈtenCHəs/ ▶ **adj.** not attempting to impress others with an appearance of greater importance, talent, or culture than is actually possessed. ■ (of a place) pleasantly simple and functional; modest.
– DERIVATIVES **un·pre·ten·tious·ly adv.**, **un·pre·ten·tious·ness n.**

un·pre·vent·a·ble /ˌənprəˈventəbl/ ▶ **adj.** not able to be prevented or avoided: *until now this devastating disease has been unpreventable.*

un·priced /ˌənˈprīst/ ▶ **adj.** having no marked or stated price.

un·primed /ˌənˈprīmd/ ▶ **adj.** not made ready for use or action, in particular: ■ (of wood, canvas, or metal) not covered with primer or undercoat. ■ Biology & Medicine (of a cell) not having an induced susceptibility or proclivity.

un·prin·ci·pled /ˌənˈprinsəpəld/ ▶ **adj.** (of a person or their behavior) not acting in accordance with moral principles: *the public's dislike of unprincipled press behavior.*

un·print·a·ble /ˌənˈprintəbəl/ ▶ **adj.** (of words, comments, or thoughts) too offensive or shocking to be published: *Peter's first reply was unprintable.*
– DERIVATIVES **un·print·a·bly** /-blē/ **adv.**

un·print·ed /ˌənˈprintid/ ▶ **adj.** (of a book or piece of writing) not published: *unprinted law reports.*

un·priv·i·leged /ˌənˈpriv(ə)lijd/ ▶ **adj.** not having special rights, advantages, or immunities.

un·prob·lem·at·ic /ˌənˌpräbləˈmatik/ ▶ **adj.** not constituting or presenting a problem or difficulty: *none of these approaches is unproblematic.*
– DERIVATIVES **un·prob·lem·at·i·cal adj.**, **un·prob·lem·at·i·cal·ly** /-ik(ə)lē/ **adv.**

un·proc·essed /ˌənˈpräˌsest, -səst-, -ˈprō-/ ▶ **adj.** unaltered from an original or natural state; not processed: *fresh, unprocessed food.*

un·pro·duc·tive /ˌənprəˈdəktiv/ ▶ **adj.** not producing or able to produce large amounts of goods, crops, or other commodities: *unproductive land must be reforested.* ■ (of an activity or period) not achieving much; not very useful: *unproductive meetings.*
– DERIVATIVES **un·pro·duc·tive·ly adv.**, **un·pro·duc·tive·ness n.**

un·pro·fes·sion·al /ˌənprəˈfesHənl/ ▶ **adj.** below or contrary to the standards expected in a particular profession: *a report on unprofessional conduct.*
– DERIVATIVES **un·pro·fes·sion·al·ism** /-ˌizəm/ **n.**, **un·pro·fes·sion·al·ly adv.**

un·prof·it·a·ble /ˌənˈpräfitəbəl/ ▶ **adj.** (of a business or activity) not yielding profit or financial gain: *the mines became increasingly unprofitable.* ■ (of an activity) not beneficial or useful: *there has been much unprofitable speculation.*
– DERIVATIVES **un·prof·it·a·bil·i·ty** /-ˌpräfitəˈbilitē/ **n.**, **un·prof·it·a·bly** /-blē/ **adv.**

un·pro·gres·sive /ˌənprəˈgresiv/ ▶ **adj.** not favoring or implementing social reform or new, typically liberal, ideas.

un·prom·is·ing /ˌənˈpräməsiNG/ ▶ **adj.** not giving hope of future success or good results: *the boy's natural intellect had survived in unpromising circumstances.*
– DERIVATIVES **un·prom·is·ing·ly adv.**

un·prompt·ed /ˌənˈpräm(p)tid/ ▶ **adv.** without being encouraged or assisted to say or do something: *unprompted, helpful conductors advised me to change at Thornaby | those are the notions they volunteered unprompted.*
▶ **adj.** said, done, or acting without being encouraged or assisted: *unprompted remarks.*

un·pro·nounce·a·ble /ˌənprəˈnounsəbəl/ ▶ **adj.** (of a word or name) too difficult to say.
– DERIVATIVES **un·pro·nounce·a·bly** /-blē/ **adv.**

un·pro·pi·tious /ˌənprəˈpisHəs/ ▶ **adj.** (of a circumstance) not giving or indicating a good chance of success; unfavorable: *his reports were submitted at a financially unpropitious time.*
– DERIVATIVES **un·pro·pi·tious·ly adv.**

un·pros·per·ous /ˌənˈpräspərəs/ ▶ **adj.** rare not enjoying or bringing financial success.

un·pro·tect·ed /ˌənprəˈtektid/ ▶ **adj.** not protected or kept safe from harm or injury: *a high, unprotected plateau | health care workers remained **unprotected against** hepatitis B infection.* ■ (of a dangerous machine or mechanism) not fitted with safety guards. ■ (of sex) engaged in without a condom. ■ Computing (of data or a memory location) able to be accessed or used without restriction.

un·pro·test·ing /ˌənprəˈtestiNG, -prō-, -ˈprōˌtest-/ ▶ **adj.** not objecting to what someone has said or done.
– DERIVATIVES **un·pro·test·ing·ly adv.**

un·prov·a·ble /ˌənˈpro͞ovəbəl/ ▶ **adj.** unable to be demonstrated by evidence or argument as true or existing: *the hypothesis is not merely unprovable, but false.*
– DERIVATIVES **un·prov·a·bil·i·ty** /-ˌpro͞ovəˈbilətē/ **n.**

un·prov·en /ˌənˈpro͞ovən/ (also **unproved** /-ˈpro͞ovd/) ▶ **adj.** not demonstrated by evidence or argument as true or existing: *long-standing but unproven allegations | the risks are unproven.* ■ (of a new or alternative product, system, or treatment) not tried and tested.

un·pro·vid·ed /ˌənprəˈvīdid/ ▶ **adj.** [predic.] not provided. ■ (**unprovided with**) not equipped with (something useful or necessary). ■ (**unprovided for**) (of a dependent) not supplied with sufficient money to cover the cost of living: *he left a widow and children totally unprovided for.*

un·pro·voked /ˌənprəˈvōkt/ ▶ **adj.** (of an attack, or a display of aggression or emotion) not caused by anything done or said: *acts of unprovoked aggression.* ■ (of a person) not provoked to do something.

un·pruned /ˌənˈpro͞ond/ ▶ **adj.** not subjected to any reducing, trimming, or refining process: *structured, unpruned data.*

un·pub·li·cized /ˌənˈpəbləˌsīzd/ ▶ **adj.** not made widely known.

un·pub·lished /ˌənˈpəblisHt/ ▶ **adj.** (of a piece of writing or music) not issued in print for public sale or consumption. ■ (of an author) having no writings issued in print.
– DERIVATIVES **un·pub·lish·a·ble** /-lisHəbəl/ **adj.**

un·punc·tu·al /ˌənˈpəNGkCHo͞oəl/ ▶ **adj.** not happening or doing something at the agreed or proper time.
– DERIVATIVES **un·punc·tu·al·i·ty** /-ˌpəNG(k)CHo͞oˈalitē/ **n.**

un·punc·tu·at·ed /ˌənˈpəNGkCHo͞oˌātid/ ▶ **adj.** (of a continuing event) not interrupted or marked by something occurring at intervals: *we wished for sleep unpunctuated by the cry of gulls.* ■ (of text) not containing punctuation marks.

un·pun·ished /ˌənˈpənisHt/ ▶ **adj.** [as complement] (of an offense or offender) not receiving a penalty or sanction as retribution for transgression: *I can't allow such a mistake to **go unpunished**.*

un·pu·ri·fied ▶ **adj.** not made pure: *unpurified water.*

un·put·down·a·ble /ˌənˌpo͝otˈdounəbəl/ ▶ **adj.** informal (of a book) so engrossing that one cannot stop reading it.

un·qual·i·fied /ˌənˈkwäləˌfīd/ ▶ **adj. 1** (of a person) not officially recognized as a practitioner of a particular profession or activity through having satisfied the relevant conditions or requirements. ■ [usu. with infinitive] not competent or sufficiently knowledgeable to do something: *I am singularly unqualified to write about football.*
2 without reservation or limitation; total: *the experiment was not an unqualified success.*
– DERIVATIVES **un·qual·i·fied·ly** /-ˌfī(i)dlē/ **adv.**

un·quan·ti·fi·a·ble /ˌənˈkwäntəˌfīəbəl, -ˌkwäntəˈfī-/ ▶ **adj.** impossible to express or measure in terms of quantity.

un·quan·ti·fied /ˌənˈkwäntəˌfīd/ ▶ **adj.** not expressed or measured in terms of quantity: *we now have abundant, if unquantified, evidence.*

un·quench·a·ble /ˌənˈkwenCHəbəl/ ▶ **adj.** not able to be quenched: *his enthusiasm was unquenchable.*
– DERIVATIVES **un·quench·a·bly adv.**

un·quenched /ˌənˈkwenCHt/ ▶ **adj.** not quenched.

un·ques·tion·a·ble /ˌənˈkwesCHənəbəl/ ▶ **adj.** not able to be disputed or doubted: *his musicianship is unquestionable.*
– DERIVATIVES **un·ques·tion·a·bil·i·ty** /-ˈkwesCHənəˈbilətē/ **n.**, **un·ques·tion·a·bly** /-blē, -ˈkwesH-/ **adv.** [sentence adverb] *unquestionably, the loss of his father was a grievous blow.*

un·ques·tioned /ˌənˈkwesCHənd/ ▶ **adj.** not disputed or doubted; certain: *his loyalty to John is unquestioned.* ■ not examined or inquired into: *an unquestioned assumption.* ■ not subjected to questioning.

un·ques·tion·ing /ˌənˈkwesCHəniNG/ ▶ **adj.** accepting something without dissent or doubt: *an unquestioning acceptance of the traditional curriculum.*
– DERIVATIVES **un·ques·tion·ing·ly adv.**

un·qui·et /ˌənˈkwīət/ ▶ **adj.** not inclined to be quiet or inactive; restless: *she prowled at night like an unquiet spirit.* ■ uneasy; anxious: *her unquiet desperation.*
– DERIVATIVES **un·qui·et·ly adv.**, **un·qui·et·ness n.**

un·quote /ˌənˈkwōt, ˈənˌkwōt/ ▶ **v.** see QUOTE — UNQUOTE at QUOTE.

un·quot·ed /ˌənˈkwōtid/ ▶ **adj.** not quoted or listed on a stock exchange: *an unquoted company.*

un·rat·ed /ˌənˈrātid/ ▶ **adj.** not having received a rating or assessment. ■ (of a film) not allocated an official classification, typically because regarded as unsuitable for general release. ■ informal not highly regarded.

un·rav·el /ˌənˈravəl/ ▶ **v.** (**unravels, unraveling, unraveled**; Brit. **unravels, unravelling, unravelled**) [with obj.] **1** undo (twisted, knitted, or woven threads). ■ [no obj.] (of twisted, knitted, or woven threads) become undone: *part of the crew neck had unraveled.* ■ unwind (something wrapped around another object): *he unraveled the cellophane from a small cigar.*
2 investigate and solve or explain (something complicated or puzzling): *they were attempting to unravel the cause of death.* ■ [no obj.] begin to fail or collapse: *his painstaking diplomacy of the last eight months could quickly unravel.*

un·reach·a·ble /ˌənˈrēCHəbəl/ ▶ **adj.** unable to be reached or contacted.
– DERIVATIVES **un·reach·a·bly adv.**

un·reached /ˌənˈrēCHt/ ▶ **adj.** not yet reached, esp. by people seeking to convert others to Christianity.

un·re·act·ive /ˌənrēˈaktiv/ ▶ **adj.** having little tendency to react chemically.

un·read /ˌənˈred/ ▶ **adj.** (of a book or document) not read. ■ archaic (of a person) not well-read.

un·read·a·ble /ˌənˈrēdəbəl/ ▶ **adj. 1** not clear enough to read; illegible. ■ too dull or difficult to be worth reading: *a heavy, unreadable novel.*
2 (of data or a storage medium or device) not capable of being processed or interpreted by a computer or other electronic device.
– DERIVATIVES **un·read·a·bil·i·ty** /-ˌrēdəˈbilətē/ **n.**, **un·read·a·bly** /-blē/ **adv.**

un·read·y /ˌənˈredē/ ▶ **adj.** [predic.] not prepared for a situation or activity: *she was young and unready for motherhood.* ■ archaic slow to act; hesitant.
– DERIVATIVES **un·read·i·ness n.**

un·re·al /ˌənˈrē(ə)l/ ▶ **adj.** so strange as to appear imaginary; not seeming real: *in the half-light the tiny cottages seemed unreal.* ■ unrealistic: *unreal expectations.* ■ informal incredible; amazing.
– DERIVATIVES **un·re·al·i·ty** /-rēˈalətē/ **n.**, **un·re·al·ly adv.**

un·re·al·is·tic /ˌənˌrēəˈlistik/ ▶ **adj.** not realistic: *it was unrealistic to expect changes to be made overnight.*
– DERIVATIVES **un·re·al·is·ti·cal·ly adv.**

un·re·al·iz·a·ble /ˌənˈrēəˌlīzəbəl, -ˌrēəˈlī-/ ▶ **adj.** not able to be achieved or made to happen: *the summit might generate unrealizable public expectations.*

un·re·al·ized /ˌənˈrēəˌlīzd/ ▶ **adj.** not achieved or created: *an unrealized plan for a full-length novel.* ■ not converted into money: *unrealized property assets.*

un·rea·son /ˌənˈrēzən/ ▶ **n.** inability to act or think reasonably.
– ORIGIN Middle English (in the senses 'unreasonable intention' and 'impropriety'): from UN-[1] 'lack of' + REASON.

un·rea·son·a·ble /ˌənˈrēz(ə)nəbəl/ ▶ **adj.** not guided by or based on good sense: *your attitude is completely unreasonable.* ■ beyond the limits of acceptability or fairness: *an unreasonable request.*
– DERIVATIVES **un·rea·son·a·ble·ness n.**, **un·rea·son·a·bly** /-blē/ **adv.**

un·rea·soned /ˌənˈrēzənd/ ▶ **adj.** not based on good sense or logic: *an unreasoned reaction to the idea.*

un·rea·son·ing /ˌənˈrēz(ə)niNG/ ▶ **adj.** not guided by or based on good sense; illogical: *unreasoning panic.*
– DERIVATIVES **un·rea·son·ing·ly adv.**

un·re·cep·tive /ˌənriˈseptiv/ ▶ **adj.** not receptive, esp. to new suggestions or ideas.

un·re·cip·ro·cat·ed /ˌənriˈsiprəˌkātid/ ▶ **adj.** not reciprocated: *his feelings for her were unreciprocated.*

un·reck·oned /ˌənˈrekənd/ ▶ **adj.** not calculated or taken into account.

un·re·claimed /ˌənriˈklāmd/ ▶ **adj.** (esp. of land) not reclaimed.

un·rec·og·niz·a·ble /ˌənˌrekigˈnīzəbəl/ ▶ **adj.** not able to be recognized or identified.
– DERIVATIVES **un·rec·og·niz·a·bly** adv.

un·rec·og·nized /ˌənˈrekəgˌnīzd/ ▶ **adj.** not identified from previous encounters or knowledge. ■ not acknowledged as valuable or valid.

un·rec·on·ciled /ˌənˈrekənˌsīld/ ▶ **adj.** not reconciled: *unreconciled conflict.*

un·re·con·struct·ed /ˌənˌrēkənˈstrəktid/ ▶ **adj.** not reconciled or converted to the current political theory or movement: *an unreconstructed elitist.*

un·re·cord·ed /ˌənriˈkôrdid/ ▶ **adj.** not recorded.

un·re·cov·er·a·ble /ˌənriˈkəvərəbəl/ ▶ **adj.** not able to be recovered or corrected.

un·re·deem·a·ble /ˌənriˈdēməbəl/ ▶ **adj.** not able to be redeemed: *an unredeemable defect.*

un·re·deemed /ˌənriˈdēmd/ ▶ **adj.** not redeemed.

un·reel /ˌənˈrēl/ ▶ **v.** [with obj.] unwind (something wrapped around another object): *she unreeled the plug from her headset.* ■ [no obj.] (of a film) wind from one reel to another during projection: *the film sequence unreeled meaninglessly in front of her.*

un·reeve /ˌənˈrēv/ ▶ **v.** (**unreeves, unreeving;** past **unrove** /-ˈrōv/) [with obj.] Nautical withdraw (a rope) from a pulley block or other object.

un·re·fined /ˌənriˈfīnd/ ▶ **adj.** not processed to remove impurities or unwanted elements: *unrefined sugar.* ■ (of a person or their behavior) not elegant or cultured.

un·re·flect·ing /ˌənriˈflektiNG/ ▶ **adj. 1** not engaging in reflection or thought: *an unreflecting hedonist.*
2 not reflecting light.
– DERIVATIVES **un·re·flect·ing·ly** adv., **un·re·flect·ing·ness** n., **un·re·flec·tive** /-tiv/ adj.

un·re·formed /ˌənriˈfôrmd/ ▶ **adj.** not changed or improved.

un·re·gard·ed /ˌənriˈgärdid/ ▶ **adj.** not respected or considered; ignored: *her sarcasm went unregarded.*

un·re·gen·er·ate /ˌənriˈjenərət/ ▶ **adj.** not reforming or showing repentance; obstinately wrong or bad.
– DERIVATIVES **un·re·gen·er·a·cy** /-rəsē/ n., **un·re·gen·er·ate·ly** adv.

un·reg·is·tered /ˌənˈrejəstərd/ ▶ **adj.** not officially recognized and recorded: *unregistered births.*

un·reg·u·lat·ed /ˌənˈregyəˌlātid/ ▶ **adj.** not controlled or supervised by regulations or laws.

un·re·hearsed /ˌənriˈhərst/ ▶ **adj.** not practiced before a performance: *spontaneous and unrehearsed music.*

un·re·lat·ed /ˌənriˈlātid/ ▶ **adj.** not related or linked: *unrelated facts | households containing two or more unrelated people.*
– DERIVATIVES **un·re·lat·ed·ness** n.

un·re·laxed /ˌənriˈlakst/ ▶ **adj.** tense.

un·re·leased /ˌənriˈlēst/ ▶ **adj.** (esp. of a film or recording) not released.

un·re·lent·ing /ˌənriˈlentiNG/ ▶ **adj.** not yielding in strength, severity, or determination: *the heat was unrelenting.* ■ (of a person or their behavior) not giving way to kindness or compassion: *unrelenting opponents.*
– DERIVATIVES **un·re·lent·ing·ly** adv., **un·re·lent·ing·ness** n.

un·re·li·a·ble /ˌənriˈlīəbəl/ ▶ **adj.** not able to be relied upon: *he's lazy and unreliable | unreliable information.*
– DERIVATIVES **un·re·li·a·bil·i·ty** n., **un·re·li·a·bly** adv.

un·re·lieved /ˌənriˈlēvd/ ▶ **adj.** lacking variation or change; monotonous: *flowing gowns of unrelieved black.* ■ not provided with relief; not aided or assisted.
– DERIVATIVES **un·re·liev·ed·ly** /-ˈlēvidlē/ adv.

un·re·li·gious /ˌənriˈlijəs/ ▶ **adj.** indifferent or hostile to religion. ■ not connected with religion.

un·re·mark·a·ble /ˌənriˈmärkəbəl/ ▶ **adj.** not particularly interesting or surprising: *his early childhood was unremarkable | an unremarkable house.*
– DERIVATIVES **un·re·mark·a·bly** /-blē/ adv.

un·re·marked /ˌənriˈmärkt/ ▶ **adj.** not mentioned or remarked upon; unnoticed: *she let his bitterness go unremarked.*

un·re·mem·bered /ˌənriˈmembərd/ ▶ **adj.** not remembered; forgotten.

un·re·mit·ting /ˌənriˈmitiNG/ ▶ **adj.** never relaxing or slackening; incessant: *unremitting drizzle.*
– DERIVATIVES **un·re·mit·ting·ly** adv., **un·re·mit·ting·ness** n.

un·re·mu·ner·a·tive /ˌənriˈmyo͞onərətiv, -ˌrātiv/ ▶ **adj.** bringing little or no profit or income: *unremunerative research work.*
– DERIVATIVES **un·re·mu·ner·a·tive·ly** adv.

un·re·peat·a·ble /ˌənriˈpētəbəl/ ▶ **adj.** not able to be done or made again. ■ too offensive or shocking to be said again.
– DERIVATIVES **un·re·peat·a·bil·i·ty** /-ˌpētəˈbilətē/ n.

un·re·pent·ant /ˌənriˈpentənt/ ▶ **adj.** showing no regret for one's wrongdoings: *he was unrepentant and said that his comments were completely accurate.*
– DERIVATIVES **un·re·pent·ant·ly** adv.

un·re·port·ed /ˌənriˈpôrtid/ ▶ **adj.** not reported: *many human rights abuses went unreported.*

un·rep·re·sent·a·tive /ˌənˌrepriˈzentətiv/ ▶ **adj.** not typical of a class, group, or body of opinion: *an unrepresentative survey.*
– DERIVATIVES **un·rep·re·sen·ta·tive·ness** n.

un·rep·re·sent·ed /ˌənˌrepriˈzentid/ ▶ **adj.** not represented.

un·re·quest·ed /ˌənriˈkwestid/ ▶ **adj.** not asked for.

un·re·quit·ed /ˌənriˈkwītid/ ▶ **adj.** (of a feeling, esp. love) not returned or rewarded.
– DERIVATIVES **un·re·quit·ed·ly** adv., **un·re·quit·ed·ness** n.

un·re·serve /ˌənriˈzərv/ ▶ **n.** archaic lack of reserve; frankness.

un·re·served /ˌənriˈzərvd/ ▶ **adj. 1** without reservations; complete: *he has had their unreserved support.* ■ frank and open: *a tall, unreserved young man.*
2 not set apart for a particular purpose or booked in advance: *unreserved grandstand seats.*
– DERIVATIVES **un·re·serv·ed·ly** /-ˈzərvidlē/ adv., **un·re·serv·ed·ness** /-ˈzərvədnəs/ n.

un·re·sist·ing /ˌənriˈzistiNG/ ▶ **adj.** not showing, producing, or putting up any resistance.
– DERIVATIVES **un·re·sist·ing·ly** adv.

un·re·solv·a·ble /ˌənriˈzälvəbəl, -ˈzôlvəbəl/ ▶ **adj.** not able to be resolved.

un·re·solved /ˌənriˈzälvd, -ˈzôlvd/ ▶ **adj.** (of a problem, question, or dispute) not resolved: *a number of issues remain unresolved.* ■ archaic (of a person) uncertain of what to think or do.
– DERIVATIVES **un·re·solv·ed·ly** /-ˈzälvidlē, -ˈzôl-/ adv., **un·re·solv·ed·ness** /-ˈzälvidnəs, -ˈzôl-/ n.

un·re·spon·sive /ˌənriˈspänsiv/ ▶ **adj.** not responsive: *these symptoms may be* ***unresponsive to*** *conventional treatment.*
– DERIVATIVES **un·re·spon·sive·ly** adv., **un·re·spon·sive·ness** n.

un·rest /ˌənˈrest/ ▶ **n.** a state of dissatisfaction, disturbance, and agitation in a group of people, typically involving public demonstrations or disorder: *the very worst years of industrial unrest.* ■ a feeling of disturbance and dissatisfaction in a person: *the frenzy and unrest of her own life.*

un·rest·ed /ˌənˈrestid/ ▶ **adj.** (of a person) not refreshed by rest: *she woke feeling unrested.*

un·rest·ing /ˌənˈrestiNG/ ▶ **adj.** ceaselessly active.
– DERIVATIVES **un·rest·ing·ly** adv.

un·re·stored /ˌənriˈstôrd/ ▶ **adj.** not repaired or renovated: *an unrestored farmhouse.*

un·re·strained /ˌənriˈstrānd/ ▶ **adj.** not restrained or restricted: *a display of unrestrained delight.*
– DERIVATIVES **un·re·strain·ed·ly** /-ˈstrānidlē/ adv., **un·re·strain·ed·ness** /-ˈstrānidnis/ n.

un·re·straint /ˌənriˈstrānt/ ▶ **n.** lack of restraint, or freedom from it; wildness: *they enjoyed the unrestraint of drunkenness.*

un·re·strict·ed /ˌənriˈstriktid/ ▶ **adj.** not limited or restricted: *unrestricted access to both military bases.*
– DERIVATIVES **un·re·strict·ed·ly** adv.

un·re·turned /ˌənriˈtərnd/ ▶ **adj.** not reciprocated or responded to: *phone calls go unreturned.*

un·re·vealed /ˌənriˈvēld/ ▶ **adj.** not revealed; secret: *some feelings can run so deep that they are better left unrevealed.*
– DERIVATIVES **un·re·veal·ing** adj.

un·re·versed /ˌənrəˈvərst/ ▶ **adj.** (esp. of a decision, etc.) not reversed.

un·re·vised /ˌənriˈvīzd/ ▶ **adj.** not revised; in an original form: *the manuscript was unrevised when he died.*

un·re·ward·ed /ˌənriˈwôrdid/ ▶ **adj.** not rewarded: *he gave untiring and unrewarded service.*

un·re·ward·ing /ˌənrəˈwôrdiNG/ ▶ **adj.** not rewarding or satisfying: *it was dull, unrewarding work.*

un·rhymed /ˌənˈrīmd/ ▶ **adj.** without rhymes; not rhymed.

un·rid·den /ˌənˈridn/ ▶ **adj.** not ridden or never having been ridden or broken in.

un·rid·dle /ˌənˈridl/ ▶ **v.** [with obj.] rare solve; explain.

un·ride·a·ble /ˌənˈrīdəbəl/ (also **unridable**) ▶ **adj.** not able to be ridden.

un·rig /ˌənˈrig/ ▶ **v.** (**unrigs, unrigging, unrigged**) [with obj.] remove the rigging from (a ship).

un·right·eous /ˌənˈrīCHəs/ ▶ **adj.** formal not righteous; wicked.
– DERIVATIVES **un·right·eous·ly** adv., **un·right·eous·ness** n.
– ORIGIN Old English *unrihtwīs* (see UN-[1], RIGHTEOUS).

un·rip /ˌənˈrip/ ▶ **v.** (**unrips, unripping, unripped**) [with obj.] rare open by ripping: *he carefully unripped one of the seams.*

un·ripe /ˌənˈrīp/ ▶ **adj.** not ripe: *unripe fruit.*

un·ri·valed /ˌənˈrīvəld/ (Brit. **unrivalled**) ▶ **adj.** better than everyone or everything of the same type: *the paper's coverage of foreign news is unrivaled.*

un·riv·et /ˌənˈrivit/ ▶ **v.** (**unrivets, unriveting, unriveted**) [with obj.] rare undo, unfasten, or detach by the removal of rivets.

un·road·wor·thy /ˌnˈrōdˌwərT͟Hē/ ▶ **adj.** (of a vehicle) not roadworthy.

un·robe /ˌənˈrōb/ ▶ **v.** less common term for DISROBE.

un·roll /ˌənˈrōl/ ▶ **v.** open or cause to open out from a rolled-up state: [no obj.] *the blanket unrolled as he tugged it* | [with obj.] *two carpets had been unrolled.*

un·ro·man·tic /ˌənrōˈmantik/ ▶ **adj.** not romantic.
– DERIVATIVES **un·ro·man·ti·cal·ly** adv.

un·roof /ˌənˈro͞of, -ˈro͝of/ ▶ **v.** [with obj.] rare remove the roof of.

un·roofed /ˌənˈro͞oft, -ˈro͝oft/ ▶ **adj.** not provided with a roof.

un·root /ˌənˈro͞ot, -ˈro͝ot/ ▶ **v.** [with obj.] uproot (something).

un·rope /ˌənˈrōp/ ▶ **v.** [no obj.] Climbing detach oneself from a rope.

un·round·ed /ˌənˈroundid/ ▶ **adj.** not rounded. ■ Phonetics (of a vowel) pronounced with the lips not rounded.

un·rove /ˌənˈrōv/ past of UNREEVE.

un·ruf·fled /ˌənˈrəfəld/ ▶ **adj.** not disordered or disarranged: *the unruffled waters of the lake.* ■ (of a person) not agitated or disturbed; calm.

un·ruled /ˌənˈro͞old/ ▶ **adj. 1** literary not ruled, governed, or under control: *men with passions unruled.*
2 (of paper) not having ruled lines.

un·ru·ly /ˌənˈro͞olē/ ▶ **adj.** (**unrulier, unruliest**) disorderly and disruptive and not amenable to discipline or control: *complaints about unruly behavior* | figurative *Kate tried to control her unruly emotions.*
– DERIVATIVES **un·ru·li·ness** n.
– ORIGIN late Middle English: from UN-[1] 'not' + archaic *ruly* 'amenable to discipline or order' (from RULE).

UNRWA /ˈənrə/ ▶ **abbr.** United Nations Relief and Works Agency.

un·sad·dle /ˌənˈsadl/ ▶ **v.** [with obj.] remove the saddle from (a horse or other ridden animal). ■ dislodge from a saddle.

un·safe ▶ **adj.** not safe; dangerous: *drinking water in some areas may be unsafe.*
– DERIVATIVES **un·safe·ly** adv., **un·safe·ness** n.

un·safe sex ▶ **n.** sexual activity in which precautions are not taken to reduce the risk of spreading sexually transmitted diseases, esp. AIDS.

un·said[1] /ˌənˈsed/ past and past participle of UNSAY.

un·said[2] ▶ **adj.** not said or uttered: *the rest of the remark he left unsaid.*

un·sal·a·ble /ˌənˈsāləbəl/ (also **unsaleable**) ▶ **adj.** not able to be sold: *the house proved unsalable.*
– DERIVATIVES **un·sal·a·bil·i·ty** /-ˌsāləˈbilətē/ n.

un·sal·a·ried /ˌənˈsalərēd/ ▶ **adj.** not being paid or involving the payment of a salary: *an unsalaried post.*

un·salt·ed /ˌənˈsôltid/ ▶ **adj.** not salted: *unsalted butter.*

PRONUNCIATION KEY ə *ago, up;* ər *over, fur;* a *hat;* ā *ate;* ä *car;* e *let;* ē *see;* i *fit;* ī *by;* NG *sing;* ō *go;* ô *law, for;* oi *toy;* o͝o *good;* o͞o *goo;* ou *out;* TH *thin;* T͟H *then;* ZH *vision*

U

un·sanc·tioned /ˌənˈsaNG(k)SHənd/ ▶ **adj.** not sanctioned: *unsanctioned rallies against high unemployment.*

un·san·i·tar·y ▶ **adj.** not sanitary: *the unsanitary conditions in the orphanage.*

un·sat·is·fac·to·ry /ˌənˌsatəsˈfakt(ə)rē/ ▶ **adj.** unacceptable because poor or not good enough: *an unsatisfactory situation.*
– DERIVATIVES **un·sat·is·fac·to·ri·ly** /-ˈfakt(ə)rəlē/ **adv.**, **un·sat·is·fac·to·ri·ness** **n.**

un·sat·is·fied /ˌənˈsatisˌfīd/ ▶ **adj.** not satisfied: *the compromise left all sides unsatisfied.*

un·sat·is·fy·ing /ənˈsatisˌfī-iNG/ ▶ **adj.** not satisfying: *an unsatisfying relationship.*
– DERIVATIVES **un·sat·is·fy·ing·ly** **adv.**

un·sat·u·rat·ed /ˌənˈsaCHəˌrātid/ ▶ **adj.** Chemistry (of organic molecules) having carbon–carbon double or triple bonds and therefore not containing the greatest possible number of hydrogen atoms for the number of carbons.
– DERIVATIVES **un·sat·u·ra·tion** /-ˌsaCHəˈrāSHən/ **n.**

un·saved /ˌənˈsāvd/ ▶ **adj.** not saved, in particular (in Christian use) not having had one's soul saved from damnation.

un·sa·vor·y /ˌənˈsāv(ə)rē/ (Brit. **unsavoury**) ▶ **adj.** disagreeable to taste, smell, or look at. ■ disagreeable and unpleasant because morally disreputable: *an unsavory reputation.*
– DERIVATIVES **un·sa·vor·i·ly** /-rəlē/ **adv.**, **un·sa·vor·i·ness** **n.**

un·say /ˌənˈsā/ ▶ **v.** (**unsays**, **unsaying**; past and past participle **unsaid**) [with obj.] withdraw or retract (a statement).

un·say·a·ble /ˌənˈsāəbəl/ ▶ **adj.** not able to be said, esp. because considered too controversial or offensive to mention.

un·scal·a·ble /ˌənˈskāləbəl/ ▶ **adj.** not able to be scaled or climbed: *a prison with unscalable walls.*

un·scaled /ˌənˈskāld/ ▶ **adj.** (of a mountain) not yet climbed: *they had climbed a hitherto unscaled peak.*

un·scarred /ˌənˈskärd/ ▶ **adj.** not scarred or damaged: *he did not escape unscarred.*

un·scathed /ˌənˈskāT͟Hd/ ▶ **adj.** [predic.] without suffering any injury, damage, or harm: *I came through all those perils unscathed.*

un·scent·ed ▶ **adj.** not scented: *unscented soap.*

un·sched·uled /ˌənˈskeˌjo͞old/ ▶ **adj.** not scheduled: *his plane made an unscheduled stop.*

un·schol·ar·ly /ˌənˈskälərlē/ ▶ **adj.** not showing the learning, reasoning, and attention to detail characteristic of a scholar.
– DERIVATIVES **un·schol·ar·li·ness** **n.** (rare).

un·schooled /ˌənˈsko͞old/ ▶ **adj.** not educated at or made to attend school: *unschooled children.* ■ lacking knowledge or training in a particular field: *she was* **unschooled in** *the niceties of royal behavior.* ■ not affected or artificial; natural and spontaneous.

un·sci·en·tif·ic /ˌənˌsīənˈtifik/ ▶ **adj.** **1** not in accordance with scientific principles or methodology: *our whole approach is hopelessly unscientific.*
2 lacking knowledge of or interest in science.
– DERIVATIVES **un·sci·en·tif·i·cal·ly** /-ik(ə)lē/ **adv.**

un·scram·ble /ˌənˈskrambəl/ ▶ **v.** [with obj.] restore (something that has been scrambled) to an intelligible, readable, or viewable state.
– DERIVATIVES **un·scram·bler** /-b(ə)lər/ **n.**

un·screened /ˌənˈskrēnd/ ▶ **adj.** **1** not subjected to testing or investigation by screening: *a transfusion with unscreened blood.* ■ not filtered or sorted using a screen.
2 (of a movie or television program) not shown or broadcast: *copies of the unscreened episodes.*
3 not provided with or hidden by a screen.

un·screw /ˌənˈskro͞o/ ▶ **v.** (with reference to a lid or other object held in place by a spiral thread) unfasten or be unfastened by twisting: [with obj.] *Will unscrewed the cap from a metal flask* | [no obj.] *the spout usually unscrews or lifts off easily.* ■ [with obj.] detach, open, or slacken (something) by removing or loosening the screws holding it in place.

un·script·ed /ˌənˈskriptid/ ▶ **adj.** said or delivered without a prepared script; impromptu.

un·scrip·tur·al /ˌənˈskripCHərəl/ ▶ **adj.** not in accordance with the Bible: *sacraments deemed unscriptural by Luther.*

un·scru·pu·lous /ˌənˈskro͞opyələs/ ▶ **adj.** having or showing no moral principles; not honest or fair.
– DERIVATIVES **un·scru·pu·lous·ly** **adv.**, **un·scru·pu·lous·ness** **n.**

un·seal /ˌənˈsēl/ ▶ **v.** [with obj.] remove or break the seal of: *she slowly unsealed the envelope.*

un·search·a·ble /ˌənˈsərCHəbəl/ ▶ **adj.** literary unable to be clearly understood; inscrutable: *their motives in coming were complex and unsearchable.*
– DERIVATIVES **un·search·a·ble·ness** **n.**, **un·search·a·bly** /-blē/ **adv.**

un·sea·son·a·ble /ˌənˈsēzənəbəl/ ▶ **adj.** (of weather) unusual for the time of year: *an unseasonable warm spell.* ■ untimely; inopportune: *we visited the place at an unseasonable time.*
– DERIVATIVES **un·sea·son·a·ble·ness** **n.**, **un·sea·son·a·bly** /-blē/ **adv.**

un·sea·son·al /ˌənˈsēzənəl/ ▶ **adj.** (esp. of weather) unusual or inappropriate for the time of year: *unseasonal heavy rains have brought a great influx of snakes.*

un·sea·soned /ˌənˈsēzənd/ ▶ **adj.** **1** (of food) not flavored with salt, pepper, or other spices or seasonings.
2 (of timber) not treated or matured. ■ (of a person) inexperienced.

un·seat /ˌənˈsēt/ ▶ **v.** [with obj.] cause (someone) to fall from a horse or bicycle. ■ remove from a position of power or authority.

un·sea·wor·thy /ˌənˈsēˌwərT͟Hē/ ▶ **adj.** (of a boat or ship) not in a good enough condition to sail on the sea.
– DERIVATIVES **un·sea·wor·thi·ness** **n.**

un·se·cured /ˌənsiˈkyo͝ord/ ▶ **adj.** **1** (of a loan) made without an asset given as security. ■ (of a creditor) having made such a loan.
2 not made secure or safe.

un·see·a·ble /ˌənˈsēəbəl/ ▶ **adj.** not able to be seen; invisible.

un·seed·ed /ˌənˈsēdid/ ▶ **adj.** (chiefly of a competitor in a sports tournament) not seeded.

un·see·ing /ˌənˈsēiNG/ ▶ **adj.** with one's eyes open but without noticing or seeing anything.
– DERIVATIVES **un·see·ing·ly** **adv.**

un·seem·ly /ˌənˈsēmlē/ ▶ **adj.** (of behavior or actions) not proper or appropriate: *an unseemly squabble.*
– DERIVATIVES **un·seem·li·ness** **n.**

un·seen /ˌənˈsēn/ ▶ **adj.** not seen or noticed: *it seemed she might escape unseen.* ■ not foreseen or predicted: *unseen problems.* ■ chiefly Brit. (of a passage for translation in a test or examination) not previously read or prepared.

un·se·lect /ˌənsəˈlekt/ ▶ **v.** [with obj.] cancel the selection of.

un·se·lect·ed /ˌənsəˈlektid/ ▶ **adj.** not selected or chosen: *a large, unselected sample of pregnant mothers.*

un·self·con·scious /ˌənˌselfˈkänSHəs/ ▶ **adj.** not suffering from or exhibiting self-consciousness; not shy or embarrassed.
– DERIVATIVES **un·self·con·scious·ly** **adv.**, **un·self·con·scious·ness** **n.**

un·sel·fish /ˌənˈselfiSH/ ▶ **adj.** willing to put the needs or wishes of others before one's own: *unselfish devotion.*
– DERIVATIVES **un·self·ish·ly** **adv.**, **un·self·ish·ness** **n.**

un·sell·a·ble /ənˈseləbl/ ▶ **adj.** not able to be sold, or very difficult to sell: *many of the houses are unsellable.*

un·sen·sa·tion·al /ˌənsenˈsāSHənl/ ▶ **adj.** not sensational or seeking to provoke interest or excitement at the expense of accuracy.
– DERIVATIVES **un·sen·sa·tion·al·ly** **adv.**

un·sen·ti·men·tal /ˌənˌsentəˈmen(t)l/ ▶ **adj.** not displaying or influenced by sentimental feelings.
– DERIVATIVES **un·sen·ti·men·tal·ly** **adv.**

un·sep·a·rat·ed /ˌənˈsepəˌrātid/ ▶ **adj.** not separated or divided: *unseparated mixtures of gases.*

Un·ser /ˈənsər/ the name of a family of US race car drivers, including: ■ **Bobby** (1934–), the first to exceed an average of 190 mph at the Indy 500; full name *Robert William Unser.* Indy 500 champion 1968, 1975, 1981. ■ **Al** (1939–), Bobby's brother; full name *Alfred Unser.* Indy 500 champion 1970, 1971, 1978, 1987. ■ **Al, Jr.** (1962–), Al's son; full name *Alfred Unser, Jr.* Indy 500 champion 1992, 1994.

un·se·ri·ous /ˌənˈsi(ə)rēəs/ ▶ **adj.** not serious; lighthearted.

un·served /ənˈsərvd/ ▶ **adj.** **1** (of a person or section of society) not attended to: *the needs of unserved and underserved audiences.*
2 Law (of a writ or summons) not officially delivered to a person: *there is no point in leaving a writ unserved.*

un·ser·vice·a·ble /ˌənˈsərvəsəbəl/ ▶ **adj.** not in working order or fulfilling its function adequately; unfit for use.
– DERIVATIVES **un·ser·vice·a·bil·i·ty** /-ˌsərvəsəˈbilətē/ **n.**

un·set /ˌənˈset/ ▶ **adj.** **1** (of a jewel) not yet placed in a setting; unmounted: *ten unset sapphires.*
2 (of cement) not yet hardened.

un·set·tle /ˌənˈsetl/ ▶ **v.** [with obj.] cause to feel anxious or uneasy; disturb: *the crisis has unsettled financial markets* | (as adj. **unsettling**) *an unsettling conversation.*
– DERIVATIVES **un·set·tle·ment** **n.**, **un·set·tling·ly** **adv.**

un·set·tled /ˌənˈsetld/ ▶ **adj.** **1** lacking stability: *an unsettled childhood.* ■ worried and uneasy: *she felt edgy and unsettled.* ■ liable to change; unpredictable: *a spell of unsettled weather.* ■ not yet resolved: *one important question remains unsettled.* ■ (of a bill) not yet paid.
2 (of an area) having no settlers or inhabitants.
– DERIVATIVES **un·set·tled·ness** **n.**

un·sex /ˌənˈseks/ ▶ **v.** [with obj.] deprive of gender, sexuality, or the characteristic attributes or qualities of one or other sex.

un·sexed /ˌənˈsekst/ ▶ **adj.** having no sexual characteristics.

un·sex·y /ˌənˈseksē/ ▶ **adj.** (**unsexier**, **unsexiest**) not sexually attractive or exciting.

un·shack·le /ˌənˈSHakəl/ ▶ **v.** [with obj.] (usu. **be unshackled**) release from shackles, chains, or other physical restraints: *his feet were unshackled.* ■ liberate; set free.

un·shad·ed /ˌənˈSHādid/ ▶ **adj.** **1** (of a light bulb or lamp) not having a shade or cover. ■ not screened from direct light.
2 (of an area of a diagram) not shaded with pencil lines or a block of color.

un·shad·owed /ˌənˈSHadōd/ ▶ **adj.** not covered or darkened by a shadow or shadows.

un·shak·a·ble /ˌənˈSHākəbəl/ (also **unshakeable**) ▶ **adj.** (of a belief, feeling, or opinion) strongly felt and unable to be changed: *an unshakeable faith in the righteousness of their cause.* ■ unable to be disputed or questioned: *an unshakable alibi.*
– DERIVATIVES **un·shak·a·bil·i·ty** /-ˌSHākəˈbilətē/ **n.**, **un·shak·a·bly** /-blē/ **adv.**

un·shak·en /ˌənˈSHākən/ ▶ **adj.** not disturbed from a firm position or state; steadfast and unwavering: *their trust in him remained unshaken.*
– DERIVATIVES **un·sha·ken·ly** **adv.**

un·shaped /ˌənˈSHāpt/ ▶ **adj.** having a vague, ill-formed, or unfinished shape.

un·shared /ˌənˈSHe(ə)rd/ ▶ **adj.** not shared with or by another or others.

un·sharp /ˌənˈSHärp/ ▶ **adj.** Photography (of a picture or image) not well defined.
– DERIVATIVES **un·sharp·ness** **n.**

un·shaved /ˌənˈSHāvd/ ▶ **adj.** unshaven.

un·shav·en /ˌənˈSHāvən/ ▶ **adj.** not having recently shaved or been shaved.

un·sheathe /ˌənˈSHēT͟H/ ▶ **v.** [with obj.] draw or pull out (a knife, sword, or similar weapon) from its sheath or covering.

un·shed /ˌənˈSHed/ ▶ **adj.** (of tears) welling in a person's eyes but not falling on their cheeks.

un·shelled /ˌənˈSHeld/ ▶ **adj.** not extracted from its shell: *unshelled peanuts.*

un·shel·tered /ˌənˈSHeltərd/ ▶ **adj.** not sheltered or protected: *I'm standing in the freezing rain at an unsheltered bus stop.*

un·shield·ed /ˌənˈSHēldid/ ▶ **adj.** not protected or shielded. ■ (of cables or wires) having no layer to contain radiation.

un·ship /ˌənˈSHip/ ▶ **v.** (**unships**, **unshipping**, **unshipped**) [with obj.] chiefly Nautical remove (an oar, mast, or other object) from its fixed or regular position: *they unshipped the oars.* ■ unload (a cargo) from a ship or boat.

un·shod /ˌənˈSHäd/ ▶ **adj.** not wearing shoes.

un·shorn /ˌənˈSHôrn/ ▶ **adj.** (of a person's hair) not cut.

un·show·y /ənˈSHōi/ ▶ **adj.** not showy in appearance or style; restrained or understated.

un·shrink·a·ble /ˌənˈSHriNGkəbəl/ ▶ **adj.** (of fabric, etc.) not liable to shrink.
– DERIVATIVES **un·shrink·a·bil·i·ty** /-ˌSHriNGkəˈbilətē/ **n.**

un·shrink·ing /ˌənˈSHriNGkiNG/ ▶ **adj.** unhesitating; fearless.
– DERIVATIVES **un·shrink·ing·ly** **adv.**

un·sight·ed /ˌənˈsītid/ ▶ **adj.** lacking the power of sight: *blind or unsighted people.* ■ not seen: *a distant unsighted object.* ■ (esp. in sports) prevented from having a clear view of something.

un·sight·ly /ˌənˈsītlē/ ▶ **adj.** unpleasant to look at; ugly: *unsightly warts.*
– DERIVATIVES **un·sight·li·ness** **n.**

un·signed /ˌənˈsīnd/ ▶ **adj.** **1** not identified or authorized by a person's signature: *an unsigned check.* ■ (of a musician or sports player) not having signed a contract of employment.
2 Mathematics & Computing not having a plus or minus sign, or a bit representing this.

un·sink·a·ble /ˌənˈsiNGkəbəl/ ▶ **adj.** (of a ship or boat) unable to be sunk: *the supposedly unsinkable ship hit an iceberg.*
- DERIVATIVES **un·sink·a·bil·i·ty** /-ˌsiNGkəˈbilətē/ **n.**

un·sis·ter·ly /ˌənˈsistərlē/ ▶ **adj.** not showing the support and affection that is thought to be characteristic of a sister.

un·sized /ˌənˈsīzd/ ▶ **adj.** (of fabric, paper, or a wall) not treated with size (see SIZE²).

un·skilled /ˌənˈskild/ ▶ **adj.** not having or requiring special skill or training: *unskilled manual workers.*

un·skill·ful /ˌənˈskilfəl/ ▶ **adj.** not having or showing skill.
- DERIVATIVES **un·skill·ful·ly** **adv.**, **un·skill·ful·ness** **n.**

un·skimmed /ˌənˈskimd/ ▶ **adj.** (of milk) not skimmed.

un·slak·a·ble /ˌənˈslākəbəl/ (also **unslakeable**) ▶ **adj.** not able to be quenched or satisfied: *her unslakable desire.*

un·sleep·ing /ˌənˈslēpiNG/ ▶ **adj.** not or never sleeping: *much of that night she lay unsleeping.*
- DERIVATIVES **un·sleep·ing·ly** **adv.**

un·sliced /ˌənˈslīst/ ▶ **adj.** (esp. of a commercially produced loaf of bread) not having been cut into slices.

un·sling /ˌənˈsliNG/ ▶ **v.** (**unslings, unslinging;** past and past participle **unslung**) [with obj.] remove (something) from the place where it has been slung or suspended.

un·smil·ing /ˌənˈsmīliNG/ ▶ **adj.** (of a person or their manner or expression) serious or unfriendly; not smiling.
- DERIVATIVES **un·smil·ing·ly** **adv.**, **un·smil·ing·ness** **n.**

un·smoked /ˌənˈsmōkt/ ▶ **adj.** **1** (of meat or fish) not cured by exposure to smoke: *smoked and unsmoked bacon.*
2 (of tobacco or a cigarette) not having been smoked.

un·snap /ˌənˈsnap/ ▶ **v.** (**unsnaps, unsnapping, unsnapped**) [with obj.] unfasten or open with a brisk movement and a sharp sound: *he put the case on the table and unsnapped the clasps.*

un·snarl /ˌənˈsnärl/ ▶ **v.** [with obj.] disentangle; sort out.

un·so·cia·ble /ˌənˈsōSHəbəl/ ▶ **adj.** not enjoying or making an effort to behave sociably in the company of others: *Terry was grumpy and unsociable.* ■ not conducive to friendly social relations: *watching TV is a fairly unsociable activity.*
- DERIVATIVES **un·so·cia·bil·i·ty** /-ˌsōSHəˈbilətē/ **n.**, **un·so·cia·ble·ness** **n.**, **un·so·cia·bly** /-blē/ **adv.**

> **USAGE** There is some overlap in the use of the adjectives **unsociable, unsocial,** and **antisocial,** but they also have distinct core meanings. Generally speaking, **unsociable** means 'not enjoying, or avoiding, the company of others': *Terry was grumpy and* **unsociable.** **Antisocial** can be used as a synonym for **unsociable,** but can further be used to mean 'contrary to the laws and customs of a society': *aggressive and* **antisocial** *behavior.* **Unsocial** can be used as a synonym for **unsociable** as well, but it may also denote a preference for solitude and not hostility toward company: *Ben's feeling a little tired and* **unsocial** *tonight.*

un·so·cial /ˌənˈsōSHəl/ ▶ **adj.** not seeking the company of others: *woodchucks lead a relatively unsocial life.* ■ causing annoyance and disapproval in others; antisocial: *the unsocial behavior of young teenagers.*
- DERIVATIVES **un·so·cial·ly** **adv.**

> **USAGE** See usage at UNSOCIABLE.

un·soiled /ˌənˈsoild/ ▶ **adj.** not stained or dirty.

un·sold /ˌənˈsōld/ ▶ **adj.** (of an item) not sold: *numerous copies of the book remained unsold | please return any unsold tickets by November 9.*

un·sol·der /ˌənˈsädər, -ˈsôdər/ ▶ **v.** [with obj.] undo the soldering of.

un·sol·dier·ly /ˌənˈsōljərlē/ ▶ **adj.** inappropriate to or not befitting a soldier: *prisoners of war in their unsoldierly uniforms.*

un·so·lic·it·ed /ˌənsəˈlisitid/ ▶ **adj.** not asked for; given or done voluntarily: *unsolicited junk mail.*
- DERIVATIVES **un·so·lic·it·ed·ly** **adv.**

un·solv·a·ble /ˌənˈsälvəbəl/ ▶ **adj.** not able to be solved.
- DERIVATIVES **un·solv·a·bil·i·ty** **n.**

un·solved /ˌənˈsälvd/ ▶ **adj.** not solved: *an unsolved mystery.*

un·so·phis·ti·cat·ed /ˌənsəˈfistəˌkātid/ ▶ **adj.** lacking refined worldly knowledge or tastes. ■ not complicated or highly developed; basic: *unsophisticated computer software.* ■ not artificial: *the village has remained unspoiled and unsophisticated.*
- DERIVATIVES **un·so·phis·ti·cat·ed·ly** **adv.**, **un·so·phis·ti·cat·ed·ness** **n.**, **un·so·phis·ti·ca·tion** /-ˌfistiˈkāSHən/ **n.**

un·sort·ed /ˌənˈsôrtid/ ▶ **adj.** not sorted or arranged: *a mass of unsorted papers.*

un·sought /ˌənˈsôt/ ▶ **adj.** not searched for, requested, or desired.

un·sound /ˌənˈsound/ ▶ **adj.** not safe or robust; in poor condition: *the tower is structurally unsound.* ■ not based on sound evidence or reasoning and therefore unreliable or unacceptable: *unsafe and unsound banking practices.* ■ (of a person) not competent, reliable, or holding acceptable views. ■ injured, ill, or diseased, esp. (of a horse) lame.
- DERIVATIVES **un·sound·ly** **adv.**, **un·sound·ness** **n.**

un·sound·ed¹ /ˌənˈsoundid/ ▶ **adj.** not uttered, pronounced, or made to sound.

un·sound·ed² ▶ **adj.** unfathomed.

un·sourced /ənˈsôrst/ ▶ **adj.** (of information) not having or attributed to a known source or origin: *an unsourced story in an Italian newspaper.*

un·sown /ˌənˈsōn/ ▶ **adj.** not having been sown: *a strip of unsown soil.*

un·spar·ing /ˌənˈspe(ə)riNG/ ▶ **adj.** **1** merciless; severe: *he is unsparing in his criticism of the arms trade.*
2 given freely and generously: *she had won her mother's unsparing approval.*
- DERIVATIVES **un·spar·ing·ly** **adv.**, **un·spar·ing·ness** **n.**

un·speak·a·ble /ˌənˈspēkəbəl/ ▶ **adj.** not able to be expressed in words: *I felt an unspeakable tenderness toward her.* ■ too bad or horrific to express in words.
- DERIVATIVES **un·speak·a·ble·ness** **n.**, **un·speak·a·bly** /-blē/ **adv.**

un·speak·ing /ˌənˈspēkiNG/ ▶ **adj.** not speaking; silent.

un·spe·cial·ized /ˌənˈspesHəˌlīzd/ ▶ **adj.** not specialized.

un·spe·cif·ic /ˌənspəˈsifik/ ▶ **adj.** not specific; vague: *he was unspecific about his relationship with Marian.*

un·spec·i·fied /ˌənˈspesəˌfīd/ ▶ **adj.** not stated clearly or exactly: *an unspecified number of people.*

un·spec·tac·u·lar /ˌənspekˈtakyələr, -spək-/ ▶ **adj.** not spectacular; unremarkable: *she had been an unspectacular student.*
- DERIVATIVES **un·spec·tac·u·lar·ly** **adv.**

un·spent /ˌənˈspent/ ▶ **adj.** not spent. ■ not exhausted or used up: *he shook with unspent rage.*

un·spilled /ˌənˈspild/ (also **unspilt** /-ˈspilt/) ▶ **adj.** not spilled.

un·spir·i·tu·al /ˌənˈspiriCHo͞oəl/ ▶ **adj.** not spiritual; worldly: *the clergymen were deplorably unspiritual.*
- DERIVATIVES **un·spir·i·tu·al·i·ty** /-ˌspiriCHo͞oˈalitē/ **n.**, **un·spir·i·tu·al·ly** **adv.**

un·spoiled /ˌənˈspoild/ (Brit. also **unspoilt** /ˌənˈspoilt/) ▶ **adj.** not spoiled, in particular (of a place) not marred by development: *unspoiled countryside.*

un·spo·ken /ˌənˈspōkən/ ▶ **adj.** not expressed in speech; tacit: *an unspoken assumption.*

un·spon·sored /ˌənˈspänsərd/ ▶ **adj.** not supported or promoted by a sponsor.

un·spool /ˌənˈspo͞ol/ ▶ **v.** [no obj.] unwind from or as if from a spool. ■ (of a film) be screened. ■ [with obj.] show (a film).

un·sport·ing /ˌənˈspôrtiNG/ ▶ **adj.** unsportsmanlike.
- DERIVATIVES **un·sport·ing·ly** **adv.**

un·sports·man·like /ˌənˈspôrtsmənˌlīk/ ▶ **adj.** not fair, generous, or sportsmanlike: *a penalty against us for unsportsmanlike conduct.*

un·spot·ted /ˌənˈspätid/ ▶ **adj.** **1** not marked with spots.
2 unnoticed: *the network of avian enthusiasts ensures that no rarity goes unspotted.*

un·sprayed /ˌənˈsprād/ ▶ **adj.** not having been sprayed, esp. with pesticides or other chemicals.

un·sprung /ˌənˈsprəNG/ ▶ **adj.** not provided with springs.

un·sta·ble /ˌənˈstābəl/ ▶ **adj.** (**unstabler, unstablest**) prone to change, fail, or give way; not stable: *the unstable cliff tops | an unstable government.* ■ prone to psychiatric problems or sudden changes of mood: *he was mentally unstable.*
- DERIVATIVES **un·sta·ble·ness** **n.**, **un·sta·bly** /-blē/ **adv.**

un·staffed /ˌənˈstaft/ ▶ **adj.** not provided with a staff or official personnel: *the kitchen on the seventh floor is an unstaffed facility.*

un·stage·a·ble /ˌənˈstājəbəl/ ▶ **adj.** (of a play) impossible or very difficult to present to an audience.

un·stained /ˌənˈstānd/ ▶ **adj.** not stained.

un·stamped /ˌənˈstam(p)t/ ▶ **adj.** **1** not marked by stamping.
2 not having a postage stamp affixed.

un·sta·pled /ənˈstāpəld/ ▶ **adj.** (of sheets of paper) not stapled together.

un·starched /ˌənˈstärCHt/ ▶ **adj.** (esp. of fabric or clothing) not starched.

un·stat·ed /ˌənˈstātid/ ▶ **adj.** not stated or declared: *a series of unstated assumptions.*

un·states·man·like /ˌənˈstātsmənˌlīk/ ▶ **adj.** not suitable for or befitting a statesman.

un·stayed /ˌənˈstād/ ▶ **adj.** (esp. of masts and rigging) not provided with stays; unsupported.

un·stead·y /ˌənˈstedē/ ▶ **adj.** (**unsteadier, unsteadiest**) **1** liable to fall or shake; not firm: *he was very unsteady on his feet.*
2 not uniform or regular: *a soft unsteady voice.*
- DERIVATIVES **un·stead·i·ly** /-ˈstedl-ē/ **adv.**, **un·stead·i·ness** **n.**

un·step /ˌənˈstep/ ▶ **v.** (**unsteps, unstepping, unstepped**) [with obj.] remove (a vessel's mast) from its step.

un·ster·ile /ˌənˈsterəl/ ▶ **adj.** chiefly Medicine not sterile; not sterilized: *unsterile needles.*

un·stick /ˌənˈstik/ ▶ **v.** (**unsticks, unsticking;** past and past participle **unstuck**) [with obj.] cause to become no longer stuck together.
- PHRASES **come** (or **get**) **unstuck** become separated or unfastened. ■ informal fail completely: *all their clever ideas came unstuck.*

un·stint·ed /ˌənˈstintid/ ▶ **adj.** given without restraint; liberal: *we received unstinted support.*
- DERIVATIVES **un·stint·ed·ly** **adv.**

un·stint·ing /ˌənˈstintiNG/ ▶ **adj.** given or giving without restraint; unsparing: *he was unstinting in his praise.*
- DERIVATIVES **un·stint·ing·ly** **adv.**

un·stirred /ənˈstərd/ ▶ **adj.** not moved, agitated, or stirred.

un·stitch /ˌənˈstiCH/ ▶ **v.** [with obj.] undo the stitches of.

un·stop /ˌənˈstäp/ ▶ **v.** (**unstops, unstopping, unstopped**) [with obj.] free (something) from obstruction: *he must unstop the sink.* ■ remove the stopper from (a bottle or other container).

un·stop·pa·ble /ˌənˈstäpəbəl/ ▶ **adj.** impossible to stop or prevent: *an unstoppable army.*
- DERIVATIVES **un·stop·pa·bil·i·ty** /-ˌstäpəˈbilətē/ **n.**, **un·stop·pa·bly** /-blē/ **adv.**

un·stop·per /ˌənˈstäpər/ ▶ **v.** [with obj.] remove the stopper from (a bottle or other container): *he unstoppered the jar.*

un·strained /ˌənˈstrānd/ ▶ **adj.** **1** not forced or produced by effort: *a lovely warm unstrained smile.*
2 not subjected or reacting to straining or stretching.

un·strap /ˌənˈstrap/ ▶ **v.** (**unstraps, unstrapping, unstrapped**) [with obj.] undo the strap or straps of. ■ release (someone or something) by undoing straps: *they unstrapped themselves.*

un·stressed /ˌənˈstrest/ ▶ **adj.** **1** Phonetics (of a syllable) not pronounced with stress: *an unstressed syllable.*
2 not subjected to stress: *a well-balanced, unstressed person.*

un·string /ˌənˈstriNG/ ▶ **v.** (**unstrings, unstringing;** past and past participle **unstrung**) [with obj.] **1** (usu. as adj. **unstrung**) unnerve: *a mind unstrung by loneliness.*
2 remove or relax the string or strings of (a bow or musical instrument).
3 remove from a string: *unstringing the beads from the rosary.*

un·struc·tured /ˌənˈstrəkCHərd/ ▶ **adj.** without formal organization or structure: *an unstructured interview.*

un·stuck /ˌənˈstək/ past and past participle of UNSTICK.

PRONUNCIATION KEY ə *ago, up;* ər *over, fur;* a *hat;* ā *ate;* ä *car;* e *let;* ē *see;* i *fit;* ī *by;* NG *sing;* ō *go;* ô *law, for;* oi *toy;* o͝o *good;* o͞o *goo;* ou *out;* TH *thin;* T͟H *then;* ZH *vision*

U

un·stud·ied /ˌənˈstədēd/ ▶ **adj.** not labored or artificial; natural: *she had an unstudied grace in every step.*
– DERIVATIVES **un·stud·ied·ly adv.**

un·stuffed /ənˈstəft/ ▶ **adj.** not containing stuffing.

un·stuff·y /ˌənˈstəfē/ ▶ **adj. 1** friendly, informal, and approachable: *colorful and unstuffy periodicals.* **2** having fresh air or ventilation.

un·styl·ish /ˌənˈstīlisH/ ▶ **adj.** not elegant, fashionable, or stylish.

un·sub·scribe /ˌənsəbˈskrīb/ ▶ **v.** [no obj.] cancel a subscription to an electronic mailing list or online service.

un·sub·stan·tial /ˌənsəbˈstancHəl/ ▶ **adj.** having little or no solidity, reality, or factual basis.
– DERIVATIVES **un·sub·stan·ti·al·i·ty** /-ˌstancHēˈalitē/ **n.**, **un·sub·stan·tial·ly adv.**

un·sub·stan·ti·at·ed /ˌənsəbˈstancHēˌātid/ ▶ **adj.** not supported or proven by evidence: *unsubstantiated claims.*

un·sub·tle /ˌənˈsətl/ ▶ **adj.** not subtle; obvious; clumsy: *a grindingly unsubtle joke.*
– DERIVATIVES **un·sub·tly** /-ˈsətl-ē/ **adv.**

un·suc·cess·ful /ˌənsəkˈsesfəl/ ▶ **adj.** not successful: *an unsuccessful transition period.*
– DERIVATIVES **un·suc·cess·ful·ly adv.**, **un·suc·cess·ful·ness n.**

un·sug·ared /ˌənˈsHo͝ogərd/ ▶ **adj.** not sweetened or sprinkled with sugar.

un·suit·a·ble /ˌənˈso͞otəbəl/ ▶ **adj.** not fitting or appropriate: *the display is unsuitable for young children.*
– DERIVATIVES **un·suit·a·bil·i·ty** /-ˌso͞otəˈbilətē/ **n.**, **un·suit·a·ble·ness n.**, **un·suit·a·bly** /-blē/ **adv.**

un·suit·ed /ˌənˈso͞otid/ ▶ **adj.** [predic.] not right or appropriate: *he was totally* **unsuited for** *the job.*

un·sul·lied /ˌənˈsəlēd/ ▶ **adj.** not spoiled or made impure: *an unsullied reputation.*

un·sung /ˌənˈsəNG/ ▶ **adj.** not celebrated or praised: *Harvey is one of the unsung heroes of the industrial revolution.*

un·su·per·vised /ˌənˈso͞opərˌvīzd/ ▶ **adj.** not done or acting under supervision: *unsupervised visits | a safe garden where children may play unsupervised.* ■ (of a person) not watched over in the interest of their or others' security: *roaming, unsupervised youths pose a threat.*

un·sup·port·a·ble /ˌənsəˈpôrtəbəl/ ▶ **adj.** another term for **INSUPPORTABLE**.
– DERIVATIVES **un·sup·port·a·bly** /-blē/ **adv.**

un·sup·port·ed /ˌənsəˈpôrtid/ ▶ **adj.** (of a structure, object, or person) not supported physically: *a toddler who can stand unsupported.* ■ not borne out by evidence or facts: *the assumption was unsupported by evidence.* ■ (of a person or activity) not given financial or other assistance. ■ Computing (of a program, language, or device) not having assistance for the user available from a manufacturer or systems manager.

un·sup·port·ive /ˌənsəˈpôrdiv/ ▶ **adj.** not providing encouragement or emotional help: *the family environment is unsupportive.*

un·sure /ˌənˈsHo͝or/ ▶ **adj.** not feeling, showing, or done with confidence and certainty: *she was feeling nervous,* **unsure of herself** | [with clause] *she was unsure how to reply.* ■ (of a fact) not fixed or certain: *the date is unsure.*
– DERIVATIVES **un·sure·ly adv.**, **un·sure·ness n.**

un·sur·faced /ˌənˈsərfist/ ▶ **adj.** (of a road or path) not provided with a durable finished upper layer.

un·sur·mount·a·ble /ˌənsərˈmoun(t)əbəl/ ▶ **adj.** not able to be overcome; insurmountable: *unsurmountable problems.*

un·sur·pass·a·ble /ˌənsərˈpasəbəl/ ▶ **adj.** not able to be exceeded in quality or degree.
– DERIVATIVES **un·sur·pass·a·bly adv.**

un·sur·passed /ˌənsərˈpast/ ▶ **adj.** as good as or better than any other: *the quality of workmanship is unsurpassed.*

un·sur·prised /ˌənsə(r)ˈprīzd/ ▶ **adj.** not feeling or showing surprise at something unexpected: *he replied in a flat and unsurprised voice.*

un·sur·pris·ing /ˌənsə(r)ˈprīziNG/ ▶ **adj.** not unexpected and so not causing surprise: *the outcome of this somber film is unsurprising.*
– DERIVATIVES **un·sur·pris·ing·ly adv.** [sentence adverb] *unsurprisingly, recession is the theme of most reports.*

un·sus·cep·ti·ble /ˌənsəˈseptəbəl/ ▶ **adj. 1** not likely or liable to be influenced or harmed by a particular thing: *infants are relatively* **unsusceptible** *to infections.* **2** [predic.] (**unsusceptible of**) not capable or admitting of: *their meaning is unsusceptible of analysis.*
– DERIVATIVES **un·sus·cep·ti·bil·i·ty** /-ˌseptəˈbilitē/ **n.**

un·sus·pect·ed /ˌənsəˈspektid/ ▶ **adj.** not known or thought to exist or be present; not imagined possible: *the actor displays an unsuspected talent for comedy.* ■ (of a person) not regarded with suspicion.
– DERIVATIVES **un·sus·pect·ed·ly adv.**

un·sus·pect·ing /ˌənsəˈspektiNG/ ▶ **adj.** (of a person or animal) not aware of the presence of danger; feeling no suspicion: *antipersonnel mines lie in wait for their unsuspecting victims.*
– DERIVATIVES **un·sus·pect·ing·ly adv.**, **un·sus·pect·ing·ness n.**

un·sus·pi·cious /ˌənsəˈspisHəs/ ▶ **adj.** not having or showing suspicion.
– DERIVATIVES **un·sus·pi·cious·ly** /ˌənsəˈspisHəslē/ **adv.**, **un·sus·pi·cious·ness** /ˌənsəˈspisHəsnəs/ **n.**

un·sus·tain·a·ble /ˌənsəˈstānəbəl/ ▶ **adj.** not able to be maintained at the current rate or level: *macroeconomic instability led to an unsustainable boom.* ■ Ecology upsetting the ecological balance by depleting natural resources: *unsustainable fishing practices.* ■ not able to be upheld or defended: *the old idea was unsustainable.*
– DERIVATIVES **un·sus·tain·a·bly** /-blē/ **adv.**

un·sus·tained /ˌənsəˈstānd/ ▶ **adj.** not prolonged for an extended period or without interruption.

un·swayed /ˌənˈswād/ ▶ **adj.** [predic.] (of a person) not influenced or affected: *investors are unswayed by suggestions that the numbers are overblown.*

un·sweet·ened /ˌənˈswētnd/ ▶ **adj.** (of food or drink) without sugar or a similar substance having been added: *unsweetened grapefruit juice.*

un·swept /ˌənˈswept/ ▶ **adj.** (of an area) not cleaned by having the dirt or litter on it swept up: *the walls were damp, the floor unswept.*

un·swerv·ing /ˌənˈswərviNG/ ▶ **adj.** not changing or becoming weaker; steady or constant: *unswerving loyalty.*
– DERIVATIVES **un·swerv·ing·ly adv.**

un·sworn /ˌənˈswôrn/ ▶ **adj.** Law (of testimony or evidence) not given under oath.

un·sym·met·ri·cal /ˌənsəˈmetrikəl/ ▶ **adj.** another term for **ASYMMETRICAL**.
– DERIVATIVES **un·sym·met·ri·cal·ly** /-trik(ə)lē/ **adv.**

un·sym·pa·thet·ic /ˌənˌsimpəˈTHetik/ ▶ **adj.** not feeling, showing, or expressing sympathy: *I'm not being unsympathetic, but I can't see why you put up with him.* ■ [predic.] not showing approval or favor toward an idea or action: *they were initially* **unsympathetic toward** *the cause of Irish freedom.* ■ (of a person) not friendly or cooperative; unlikable: *a totally unsympathetic character.*
– DERIVATIVES **un·sym·pa·thet·i·cal·ly** /-ik(ə)lē/ **adv.**

un·sys·tem·at·ic /ˌənˌsistəˈmatik/ ▶ **adj.** not done or acting according to a fixed plan or system; unmethodical: *the burial mound was excavated in an unsystematic way | they were relatively unsystematic in their use of the data.*
– DERIVATIVES **un·sys·tem·at·i·cal·ly** /-ik(ə)lē/ **adv.**

un·tack[1] /ˌənˈtak/ ▶ **v.** [with obj.] detach (something) by the removal of tacks.

un·tack[2] ▶ **v.** [with obj.] remove the saddle and bridle from (a horse).

un·taint·ed /ˌənˈtān(t)id/ ▶ **adj.** not contaminated, polluted, or tainted: *the paper was untainted by age.*

un·tak·en /ˌənˈtākən/ ▶ **adj. 1** (of a region or person) not taken by force; uncaptured. **2** (of an action) not put into effect: *hard decisions have been left untaken.*

un·tal·ent·ed /ˌənˈtaləntid/ ▶ **adj.** (of a person) not having a natural aptitude or skill.

un·tam·a·ble /ˌənˈtāməbəl/ (also **untameable**) ▶ **adj.** (of an animal) not capable of being domesticated. ■ not capable of being controlled: *her untamable mop of thick black hair.*

un·tamed /ˌənˈtāmd/ ▶ **adj.** not domesticated or otherwise controlled.

un·tan·gle /ˌənˈtaNGgəl/ ▶ **v.** [with obj.] free from a tangled or twisted state: *fishermen untangle their nets.* ■ make (something complicated or confusing) easier to understand or deal with.

un·tanned /ˌənˈtand/ ▶ **adj. 1** (of a person or their skin) not tanned by exposure to the sun. **2** (of animal skin) not converted into leather by tanning: *untanned hides.*

un·tapped /ˌənˈtapt/ ▶ **adj. 1** (of a resource) not yet exploited or used: *a huge, untapped market for bagels.* **2** (of a telephone, etc.) free from listening devices.

un·tar·nished /ˌənˈtärnisHt/ ▶ **adj.** (of metal or metalware) not having lost its luster, esp. as a result of exposure to air or moisture. ■ not made less valuable or respected: *his ministers enjoyed an untarnished reputation.*

un·tast·ed /ˌənˈtāstid/ ▶ **adj.** (of food or drink) not sampled or tested for flavor: *Louis's untasted food was scraped into the dog's bowl.*

un·taught /ˌənˈtôt/ ▶ **adj.** (of a person) not trained by teaching: *she is totally untaught and will not listen.* ■ not acquired by teaching; natural or spontaneous: *by untaught instinct they know that scent means food.*

un·taxed /ˌənˈtakst/ ▶ **adj. 1** not subject to taxation. **2** (of an item, income, etc.) not having had the required tax paid on it.

un·teach /ˌənˈtēcH/ ▶ **v.** (past and past participle **untaught**) **1** cause (someone) to forget or discard previous knowledge. **2** remove from the mind (something known or taught) by different teaching.

un·teach·a·ble /ˌənˈtēcHəbəl/ ▶ **adj.** (of a student or skill) unable to be taught.

un·tech·ni·cal /ˌənˈteknikəl/ ▶ **adj.** not having or requiring technical knowledge.

un·tem·pered /ˌənˈtempərd/ ▶ **adj.** not moderated or lessened by anything: *the products of a technological mastery untempered by political imagination.* ■ (of a material) not brought to the proper hardness or consistency.

un·ten·a·ble /ˌənˈtenəbəl/ ▶ **adj.** (esp. of a position or view) not able to be maintained or defended against attack or objection: *this argument is clearly untenable.*
– DERIVATIVES **un·ten·a·bil·i·ty** /-ˌtenəˈbilitē/ **n.**, **un·ten·a·bly** /-blē/ **adv.**

un·tend·ed /ˌənˈtendid/ ▶ **adj.** not cared for or looked after; neglected: *untended gravestones.*

un·ten·ured /ˌənˈtenyərd/ ▶ **adj.** (of a teacher, lecturer, or other professional) not having a permanent post. ■ (of an academic or other post) not permanent.

Un·ter·mensch /ˈo͝ontərˌmencH/ ▶ **n.** (pl. **Untermenschen** /-ˌmencHən/) a person considered racially or socially inferior.
– ORIGIN German, literally 'underperson.'

Un·ter·mey·er /ˈəntərˌmīər/, Louis (1885–1977) US writer and poet. He published critical anthologies, including *Modern American Poetry* (1919) and *The World's Great Stories* (1964), as well as his own poetry such as "Long Feud" (1962).

un·test·ed /ˌənˈtestid/ ▶ **adj.** (of an idea, product, or person) not subjected to examination, experiment, or experience; unproven: *analyses based on dubious and untested assumptions.*
– DERIVATIVES **un·test·a·ble** /-ˈtestəbəl/ **adj.**

un·teth·er /ˌənˈteT͟Hər/ ▶ **v.** [with obj.] release or free from a tether: *I reached the horses and untethered them.*

un·thanked /ˌənˈTHaNGkt/ ▶ **adj.** without receiving thanks: *the women's kind gesture did not go unthanked.*

un·thank·ful /ˌənˈTHaNGkfəl/ ▶ **adj.** not feeling or showing pleasure, relief, or gratitude.
– DERIVATIVES **un·thank·ful·ly** /ˌənˈTHaNGkfəlē/ **adv.**, **un·thank·ful·ness** /ˌənˈTHaNGkfəlnəs/ **n.**

un·thaw /ˌənˈTHô/ ▶ **v. 1** melt or thaw: [with obj.] *the warm weather helped unthaw the rail lines.* **2** (as adj. **unthawed**) still frozen; unmelted: *it could not explain how future science might revive the unthawed dead.*

un·think·a·ble /ˌənˈTHiNGkəbəl/ ▶ **adj.** (of a situation or event) too unlikely or undesirable to be considered a possibility: *it was unthinkable that John could be dead* | (as noun **the unthinkable**) *the unthinkable happened—I spoke up.*
– DERIVATIVES **un·think·a·bil·i·ty** /-ˌTHiNGkəˈbilitē/ **n.**, **un·think·a·bly** /-blē/ **adv.** [as submodifier] *a land of unthinkably vast spaces.*

un·think·ing /ˌənˈTHiNGkiNG/ ▶ **adj.** expressed, done, or acting without proper consideration of the consequences: *she was at pains to correct unthinking prejudices.*
– DERIVATIVES **un·think·ing·ly adv.**, **un·think·ing·ness n.**

un·thought /ˌənˈTHôt/ ▶ **adj. 1** (**unthought of**) not imagined or dreamed of: *the old develop interests unthought of in earlier years.* **2** not formed by the process of thinking.

un·thread /ˌənˈTHred/ ▶ **v.** [with obj.] take (a thread) out of a needle. ■ remove (an object) from a thread.

un·threat·en·ing /ˌənˈTHretniNG/ ▶ **adj.** not having a hostile or frightening quality or manner; not causing someone to feel vulnerable or at risk: *a quiet and unthreatening place.*
– DERIVATIVES **un·threat·ened** /ˌənˈTHretnd/ **adj.**

un·thrift·y /ˌənˈTHriftē/ ▶ **adj. 1** not using money and other resources carefully; wasteful. **2** chiefly archaic or dialect (of livestock or plants) not strong and healthy.

– DERIVATIVES **un·thrift·i·ly** /-təlē/ **adv.**, **un·thrift·i·ness n.**

un·throne /ˌən'THrōn/ ▶ **v.** archaic term for DETHRONE.

un·ti·dy /ˌən'tīdē/ ▶ **adj.** (**untidier, untidiest**) not arranged neatly and in order: *the place was dreadfully untidy.* ■ (of a person) not inclined to keep one's possessions or appearance neat and in order.
– DERIVATIVES **un·ti·di·ly** /-'tīdilē/ **adv.**, **un·ti·di·ness n.**

un·tie /ˌən'tī/ ▶ **v.** (**unties, untying, untied**) [with obj.] undo or unfasten (a cord or knot): *she knelt to untie her laces.* ■ undo a cord or similar fastening that binds (someone or something): *Morton untied the parcel.*
– ORIGIN Old English *untīgan* (see UN-², TIE).

un·tied /ˌən'tīd/ ▶ **adj.** not fastened or knotted.

un·til /ˌən'til, ən-/ ▶ **prep. & conj.** up to (the point in time or the event mentioned): [as prep.] *the kidnappers have given us until October 11th to deliver the documents | he held the office until his death* | [as conjunction] *you don't know what you can achieve until you try.*
– ORIGIN Middle English: from Old Norse *und* 'as far as' + TILL¹ (the sense thus duplicated).

> **USAGE** On the differences between **until** and **till**, see usage at TILL¹.

un·tilled /ˌən'tild/ ▶ **adj.** (of land) not prepared and cultivated for crops.

un·time·ly /ˌən'tīmlē/ ▶ **adj.** (of an event or act) happening or done at an unsuitable time: *Dave's untimely return.* ■ (of a death or end) happening too soon or sooner than normal: *his untimely death in military action.*
▶ **adv.** archaic at a time that is unsuitable or premature: *the moment was very untimely chosen.*
– DERIVATIVES **un·time·li·ness n.**

un·tinged /ˌən'tinjd/ ▶ **adj.** [predic.] (**untinged by/with**) not in the slightest affected by: *a cold-blooded killing untinged by any remorse on your part.*

un·tir·ing /ˌən'tīriNG/ ▶ **adj.** (of a person or their actions) continuing at the same rate without loss of vigor; indefatigable: *his untiring efforts on their behalf.*
– DERIVATIVES **un·tir·ing·ly adv.**

un·ti·tled /ˌən'tītld/ ▶ **adj. 1** (of a book, composition, or other artistic work) having no name.
2 (of a person) not having a title indicating high social or official rank: *lesser untitled officials.*

un·to /'əntōō/ ▶ **prep. 1** archaic term for TO: *do unto others as you would have them do unto you | I say unto you, be gone.*
2 archaic term for UNTIL: *marriage was forever—unto death.*
– ORIGIN Middle English: from UNTIL, with TO replacing TILL¹ (in its northern dialect meaning 'to').

un·told /ˌən'tōld/ ▶ **adj. 1** [attrib.] too much or too many to be counted or measured: *thieves caused untold damage.*
2 (of a story or event) not narrated or recounted: *no event, however boring, is left untold.*
– ORIGIN Old English *unteald* 'not counted' (see UN-¹, TOLD).

un·toned /ˌən'tōnd/ ▶ **adj. 1** (of a person's body) lacking in tone or muscular definition.
2 (esp. of music) lacking in variation of tone or subtlety.

un·touch·a·ble /ˌən'təCHəbəl/ ▶ **adj. 1** not able or allowing to be touched or affected: *a receptionist looking gorgeous and untouchable.* ■ unable to be matched or rivaled: *we took the silver medal behind the untouchable US team.* ■ above approach; incorruptible.
2 of or belonging to the lowest-caste Hindu group or the people outside the caste system.
▶ **n.** a member of the lowest-caste Hindu group or a person outside the caste system. Contact with untouchables is traditionally held to defile members of higher castes.
– DERIVATIVES **un·touch·a·bil·i·ty** /-ˌtəCHə'bilitē/ **n.**

> **USAGE** In senses relating to the traditional Hindu caste system, the term **untouchable** and the social restrictions accompanying it were declared illegal in the constitution of India in 1949 and of Pakistan in 1953. The official term today is **scheduled caste.**

un·touched /ˌən'təCHt/ ▶ **adj. 1** not handled, used, or tasted: *Annabel pushed aside her untouched plate.* ■ (of a subject) not treated in writing or speech; not discussed: *no detail is left untouched.*
2 not affected, changed, or damaged in any way: *Prague was relatively untouched by the war.*

un·tour·ist·ed /ən'tŏŏristid/ ▶ **adj.** (of a place) rarely visited by tourists: *a charming, untouristed village.*

un·to·ward /ˌən'tôrd, -t(ə)'wôrd/ ▶ **adj.** unexpected and inappropriate or inconvenient: *both tried to behave as if nothing untoward had happened | untoward jokes and racial remarks.*
– DERIVATIVES **un·to·ward·ly adv.**, **un·to·ward·ness n.**

un·trace·a·ble /ˌən'trāsəbəl/ ▶ **adj.** unable to be found, discovered, or traced: *many use false addresses and are untraceable.*
– DERIVATIVES **un·trace·a·bly** /-blē/ **adv.**

un·traced /ˌən'trāst/ ▶ **adj.** not found or discovered by investigation: *patients with untraced records.*

un·tracked /ˌən'trakt/ ▶ **adj.** (of land) not previously explored or traversed; without a path or tracks: *the Saxons usually hid in the untracked marshlands.* ■ (of snow) not marked by skis, vehicles, or footprints: *experts can go heli-skiing in untracked powder.*
– PHRASES **get untracked** get into one's stride or find good form, esp. in sporting contexts.

un·tra·di·tion·al /ˌəntrə'disHənl/ ▶ **adj.** not existing in or as part of a tradition; not customary or long-established.

un·trained /ˌən'trānd/ ▶ **adj.** not having been trained in a particular skill: *self-styled doctors untrained in diagnosis | to the untrained eye, the two products look remarkably similar.*
– DERIVATIVES **un·train·a·ble** /-'trānəbəl/ **adj.**

un·tram·meled /ˌən'traməld/ (Brit. also **untrammelled**) ▶ **adj.** not deprived of freedom of action or expression; not restricted or hampered: *a mind untrammeled by convention.*

un·trans·fer·a·ble /ˌənˌtrans'fərəbəl, -'transfərə-/ ▶ **adj.** not able to be transferred to another place, occupation, or person.

un·trans·formed /ˌəntrans'fôrmd/ ▶ **adj.** not having been transformed in form, appearance, or character.

un·trans·lat·a·ble /ˌənˌtrans'lātəbəl, -ˌtranz-/ ▶ **adj.** (of a word, phrase, or text) not able to have its sense satisfactorily expressed in another language: *an untranslatable German pun.*
– DERIVATIVES **un·trans·lat·a·bil·i·ty** /-transˌlātə'bilitē, -tranz-/ **n.**

un·trans·lat·ed /ˌən'tranzˌlātid, -'trans-/ ▶ **adj.** (of words or text) not having their sense expressed in another language: *a nine-volume work, as yet untranslated from the Icelandic.* ■ (of a sequence of nucleotides in messenger RNA) not converted to the amino acid sequence of a protein or polypeptide during synthesis.

un·trav·eled /ˌən'travəld/ (Brit. also **untravelled**) ▶ **adj.** (of a person) not having traveled much. ■ (of a road or region) not journeyed along or through: *an unknown and untraveled wilderness.*

un·treat·a·ble /ˌən'trētəbəl/ ▶ **adj.** (of a patient, a disease or other condition) for whom or which no medical care is available or possible.

un·treat·ed /ˌən'trētid/ ▶ **adj. 1** (of a patient, disease, or other condition) not given medical care: *untreated cholera can kill up to half of those infected.*
2 not preserved, improved, or altered by the use of a chemical, physical, or biological agent: *untreated sewage is pumped directly into the sea.*

un·trend·y /ˌən'trendē/ ▶ **adj.** informal not very fashionable or up to date: *his untrendy long hair.*

un·tried /ˌən'trīd/ ▶ **adj. 1** not yet tested to discover quality or reliability; inexperienced: *he chose two untried actors for leading roles.*
2 Law (of an accused person) not yet subjected to a trial in court.

un·trimmed /ˌən'trimd/ ▶ **adj.** not having been trimmed.

un·trod·den /ˌən'trädn/ ▶ **adj.** (of a surface) not having been walked on: *untrodden snow.*

un·trou·bled /ən'trəbəld/ ▶ **adj.** not feeling, showing, or affected by anxiety or problems: *a man untroubled by a guilty conscience | an untroubled gaze.*

un·true /ˌən'trōō/ ▶ **adj. 1** not in accordance with fact or reality; false or incorrect: *these suggestions are totally untrue | a malicious and untrue story.*
2 [predic.] not faithful or loyal.
3 incorrectly positioned or balanced; not upright or level.
– DERIVATIVES **un·tru·ly** /-'trōōlē/ **adv.**
– ORIGIN Old English *untrēowe* 'unfaithful' (see UN-¹, TRUE).

un·truss /ən'trəs/ ▶ **v.** [with obj.] unfasten (esp. a trussed fowl).

un·trussed /ən'trəst/ ▶ **adj.** (of a chicken or other bird prepared for eating) having had its wings and legs unfastened before cooking: *an untrussed chicken.*

un·trust·ing /ˌən'trəstiNG/ ▶ **adj.** not tending to believe in other people's honesty or sincerity; suspicious.

un·trust·wor·thy /ˌən'trəstˌwərT͟Hē/ ▶ **adj.** not able to be relied on as honest or truthful: *Thomas considered her to be devious and untrustworthy | these untrustworthy impressions were instinctive.*
– DERIVATIVES **un·trust·wor·thi·ness n.**

un·truth /ˌən'trōōTH/ ▶ **n.** (pl. **untruths** /-'trōōT͟HZ, -'trōōTHS/) a lie or false statement (often used euphemistically): *they go off and tell untruths about organizations for which they worked.* ■ the quality of being false.
– ORIGIN Old English *untrēowth* 'unfaithfulness' (see UN-¹, TRUTH).

un·truth·ful /ˌən'trōōTHfəl/ ▶ **adj.** saying or consisting of something that is false or incorrect: *companies issuing untruthful recruitment brochures.*
– DERIVATIVES **un·truth·ful·ly adv.**, **un·truth·ful·ness n.**

un·tuck /ən'tək/ ▶ **v.** [with obj.] free the edges or ends of (something) from being hidden or held in place.

un·tucked /ən'təkt/ ▶ **adj.** with the edges or ends hanging loose; not tucked in: *an untucked shirt.*

un·tun·a·ble /ˌən't(y)ōōnəbəl/ ▶ **adj.** (of a piano, etc.) that cannot be tuned.

un·tuned /ˌən't(y)ōōnd/ ▶ **adj.** not tuned or properly adjusted.

un·tune·ful /ˌən't(y)ōōnfəl/ ▶ **adj.** not having a pleasing melody; unmusical: *an untuneful hymn.*
– DERIVATIVES **un·tune·ful·ly adv.**

un·turned /ˌən'tərnd/ ▶ **adj. 1** not turned: *unturned soil.*
2 (of a wooden object) not shaped on a lathe.

un·tu·tored /ˌən't(y)ōōtərd/ ▶ **adj.** not formally taught or trained: *the species are all much the same to the untutored eye.*

un·twine /ˌən'twīn/ ▶ **v.** make or become unwound or untwisted: [with obj.] *Robyn untwined her fingers.*

un·twist /ˌən'twist/ ▶ **v.** open or cause to open from a twisted position: [with obj.] *he untwisted the wire and straightened it out.*

un·ty·ing /ˌən'tī-iNG/ present participle of UNTIE.

un·typ·i·cal /ˌən'tipikəl/ ▶ **adj.** not having the distinctive qualities of a particular type of person or thing; unusual or uncharacteristic: *the harsh dissonances give a sound that is quite* **untypical of** *that period.*
– DERIVATIVES **un·typ·i·cal·ly** /-ik(ə)lē/ **adv.** [as submodifier] *I'll keep this review untypically short* | [sentence adverb] **not untypically,** *one large painting took her five months.*

un·us·a·ble /ˌən'yōōzəbəl/ ▶ **adj.** not fit to be used: *the steps were overgrown and unusable.*

un·used /ˌən'yōōzd/ ▶ **adj. 1** not being, or never having been, used: *any unused equipment will be welcomed back.*
2 /-'yōōst/ [predic.] (**unused to**) not familiar with or accustomed to something: *unused to spicy food, she took a long mouthful of water.*

un·u·su·al /ˌən'yōōZHōōəl/ ▶ **adj.** not habitually or commonly occurring or done: *the government has taken the unusual step of calling home its ambassador | it was unusual for Dennis to be late.* ■ remarkable or interesting because different from or better than others: *a man of unusual talent.*
– DERIVATIVES **un·u·su·al·ly adv.** [sentence adverb] **unusually for** *a city hotel, it is set around a lovely garden* | [as submodifier] *he made an unusually large number of mistakes.* **un·u·su·al·ness n.**

un·ut·ter·a·ble /ˌən'ətərəbəl/ ▶ **adj.** too great, intense, or awful to describe: *those private moments of unutterable grief.*
– DERIVATIVES **un·ut·ter·a·bly** /-blē/ **adv.** [as submodifier] *Juliet climbed the stairs, feeling unutterably weary.*

un·ut·tered /ˌən'ətərd/ ▶ **adj.** (of words or thoughts) not spoken or expressed: *her lips mouthed unuttered thanks.*

un·vac·ci·nat·ed /ˌən'vaksəˌnātid/ ▶ **adj.** (of a person) not inoculated with a vaccine to provide immunity against a disease: *pockets of unvaccinated children.*

un·val·ued /ˌən'valyōōd/ ▶ **adj. 1** not considered to be important or beneficial: *he felt unvalued.*
2 archaic not valued or appraised with regard to monetary worth.

U

un·van·quished /ˌənˈvaNGkwisHt/ ▶ **adj.** (of an opponent or obstacle) not conquered or overcome: *the idea of humbling the hitherto unvanquished islanders.*

un·var·ied /ˌənˈve(ə)rēd/ ▶ **adj.** not involving change; monotonous: *a plain, unvaried diet.*

un·var·nished /ˌənˈvärnisHt/ ▶ **adj.** not covered with varnish. ■ (of a statement or manner) plain and straightforward: *please tell me the unvarnished truth.*

un·var·y·ing /ˌənˈve(ə)rē-iNG/ ▶ **adj.** not changing; constant or uniform: *the unvarying routine of parsonage life.*
– DERIVATIVES **un·var·y·ing·ly adv.** [as submodifier] *they found her to be unvaryingly polite,* **un·var·y·ing·ness n.**

un·veil /ˌənˈvāl/ ▶ **v.** [with obj.] remove a veil or covering from, esp. uncover (a new monument or work of art) as part of a public ceremony: *the mayor unveiled a plaque* | (as noun **unveiling**) *the unveiling of the memorial.* ■ show or announce publicly for the first time: *the manufacturer unveiled plans for expanding into aviation.*

un·vent·ed /ˌənˈventid/ ▶ **adj. 1** not provided with ventilation.
2 (of strong, usually negative feelings) not expressed: *unvented rage.*

un·ven·ti·lat·ed /ˌənˈventlˌātid/ ▶ **adj.** (of a room or space) not provided with fresh air.

un·ver·i·fi·a·ble /ˌənverəˈfīəbəl/ ▶ **adj.** not able to be verified: *an unverifiable hypothesis.*

un·ver·i·fied /ˌənˈverəˌfīd/ ▶ **adj.** not having been verified.

un·versed /ənˈvərst/ ▶ **adj.** [predic.] (**unversed in**) not experienced or skilled in; not knowledgeable about: *he was unversed in Washington ways.*

un·vi·a·ble /ˌənˈvīəbəl/ ▶ **adj.** not capable of working successfully; not feasible: *the commission found the plan to be financially unviable.*
– DERIVATIVES **un·vi·a·bil·i·ty** /-ˌvīəˈbilitē/ **n.**

un·vi·o·lat·ed /ˌənˈvīəˌlātid/ ▶ **adj.** not violated or desecrated: *the ground above the stone was undisturbed, the stone unviolated.* ■ (of a woman) virginal.

un·vis·it·ed /ˌənˈvizitid/ ▶ **adj.** (of a place) having had no people visit it: *Antarctica remained unvisited until the late 18th century.*

un·vi·ti·at·ed /ˌənˈvisHēˌātid/ ▶ **adj.** archaic pure and uncorrupted.

un·voiced /ˌənˈvoist/ ▶ **adj. 1** not expressed in words; unuttered: *a person's unvoiced thoughts.*
2 Phonetics (of a speech sound) uttered without vibration of the vocal cords.

un·waist·ed /ənˈwāstid/ ▶ **adj.** (of a dress) not having a structured waistline; loose-fitting.

un·walled /ˌənˈwôld/ ▶ **adj.** (of a place) without enclosing or defensive walls.

un·want·ed /ˌənˈwäntid, -ˈwônt-/ ▶ **adj.** not or no longer desired: *affairs can lead to unwanted pregnancies* | *she felt unwanted.*

un·warned /ˌənˈwôrnd/ ▶ **adj.** (of a person) not warned in advance about something.

un·war·rant·a·ble /ˌənˈwôrəntəbəl, -ˈwär-/ ▶ **adj.** not able to be authorized or sanctioned; unjustifiable: *an unwarrantable intrusion into personal matters.*
– DERIVATIVES **un·war·rant·a·bly** /-blē/ **adv.**

un·war·rant·ed /ˌənˈwôrəntid, -ˈwär-/ ▶ **adj.** not justified or authorized: *I am sure your fears are unwarranted.*
– DERIVATIVES **un·war·rant·ed·ly adv.**

un·war·y /ˌənˈwe(ə)rē/ ▶ **adj.** not cautious; not aware of possible dangers or problems: *accidents can happen to the unwary traveler* | (as plural noun **the unwary**) *hidden traps for the unwary.*
– DERIVATIVES **un·war·i·ly** /-ˈwe(ə)rəlē/ **adv.**, **un·war·i·ness n.**

un·washed /ˌənˈwôsHt, -ˈwäsHt/ ▶ **adj.** not having been washed.
– PHRASES **the (great) unwashed** derogatory the mass or multitude of ordinary people.

un·watch·a·ble /ˌənˈwäCHəbəl/ ▶ **adj.** (of a film or television program) too poor, tedious, or disturbing to be viewed.

un·watched /ˌənˈwäCHt/ ▶ **adj.** not looked at or observed.

un·wa·tered /ˌənˈwôtərd, -ˈwät-/ ▶ **adj.** not supplied or sprinkled with water.

un·wa·ver·ing /ˌənˈwāvəriNG/ ▶ **adj.** steady or resolute; not wavering: *she fixed him with an unwavering stare.*
– DERIVATIVES **un·wa·ver·ing·ly adv.**

un·weaned /ˌənˈwēnd/ ▶ **adj.** (of an infant or other young mammal) not accustomed to food other than its mother's milk.

un·wear·a·ble /ˌənˈwe(ə)rəbəl/ ▶ **adj.** (of a garment) not fit to be worn.

un·wea·ried /ˌənˈwi(ə)rēd/ ▶ **adj.** not tired or becoming tired.
– DERIVATIVES **un·wea·ried·ly adv.**

un·wea·ry·ing /ˌənˈwi(ə)rē-iNG/ ▶ **adj.** never tiring or slackening.
– DERIVATIVES **un·wea·ry·ing·ly adv.**

un·wed /ˌənˈwed/ (also **unwedded**) ▶ **adj.** not married: *an unwed teenage mother.*
– DERIVATIVES **un·wed·ded·ness n.**

un·weed·ed /ˌənˈwēdid/ ▶ **adj.** not cleared of weeds.

un·weighed /ˌənˈwād/ ▶ **adj. 1** not considered; hasty.
2 (of goods) not weighed.

un·weight /ˌənˈwāt/ ▶ **v.** [with obj.] momentarily stop pressing heavily on (a ski or skateboard) in order to make a turn more easily.
– ORIGIN 1930s: back-formation from **UNWEIGHTED**.

un·weight·ed /ˌənˈwātid/ ▶ **adj. 1** without a weight attached.
2 Statistics (of a figure or sample) not adjusted or biased to reflect importance or value.

un·wel·come /ˌənˈwelkəm/ ▶ **adj.** (of a guest or new arrival) not gladly received: *guards kept out unwelcome visitors.* ■ not much needed or desired: *unwelcome attentions from men.*
– DERIVATIVES **un·wel·come·ly adv.**, **un·wel·come·ness n.**

un·wel·com·ing /ˌənˈwelkəmiNG/ ▶ **adj.** having an inhospitable or uninviting atmosphere or appearance: *Jean crept into her cold and unwelcoming bed.* ■ (of a person or their manner) not friendly toward someone arriving or approaching.

un·well /ˌənˈwel/ ▶ **adj.** [predic.] sick: *consult a doctor if you feel unwell.*

un·wept /ˌənˈwept/ ▶ **adj.** chiefly literary (of a person) not mourned or lamented.

un·whole·some /ˌənˈhōlsəm/ ▶ **adj.** not characterized by or conducive to health or moral well-being: *the use of the living room as sleeping quarters led to unwholesome crowding.*
– DERIVATIVES **un·whole·some·ly adv.**, **un·whole·some·ness n.**

un·wield·y /ˌənˈwēldē/ ▶ **adj.** (**unwieldier, unwieldiest**) difficult to carry or move because of its size, shape, or weight: *the first mechanical clocks were large and unwieldy.* ■ (of a system or bureaucracy) too big or badly organized to function efficiently.
– DERIVATIVES **un·wield·i·ly adv.**, **un·wield·i·ness n.**
– ORIGIN late Middle English (in the sense 'lacking strength, infirm'): from **UN-**[1] 'not' + **WIELDY** (in the obsolete sense 'active').

un·will·ing /ˌənˈwiliNG/ ▶ **adj.** [often with infinitive] not ready, eager, or prepared to do something: *he was unwilling to take on that responsibility* | *unwilling conscripts.*
– DERIVATIVES **un·will·ing·ly adv.**
– ORIGIN Old English *unwillende* (see **UN-**[1], **WILLING**).

un·will·ing·ness /ˌənˈwiliNGnis/ ▶ **n.** the quality or state of being unwilling to do something; reluctance: *he deplored the government's unwillingness to provide adequate funds.*

un·wind /ˌənˈwīnd/ ▶ **v.** (past and past participle **unwound** /-ˈwound/) undo or be undone after winding or being wound: [with obj.] *Ella unwound the long woolen scarf from her neck* | [no obj.] *the net unwinds from the reel.* ■ [no obj.] relax after a period of work or tension: *the Grand Hotel is a superb place to unwind.*

un·wink·ing /ˌənˈwiNGkiNG/ ▶ **adj.** (of a stare or a shining light) steady; unwavering: *the lights shone unwinking in the still air* | *unwinking blue eyes.*
– DERIVATIVES **un·wink·ing·ly adv.**

un·win·na·ble /ˌənˈwinəbəl/ ▶ **adj.** not able to be won: *an immoral and unwinnable war.*

un·wired /ˌənˈwī(ə)rd/ ▶ **adj. 1** wireless: *photosharing between Macs on wired and unwired networks.*
2 disengaged or disconnected from electronic media: *the geographic terrain and the remoteness force you to be unwired.*

un·wis·dom /ˌənˈwizdəm/ ▶ **n.** folly; lack of wisdom: *it stresses the unwisdom of fathers leaving their children.*
– ORIGIN Old English *unwīsdōm* (see **UN-**[1], **WISDOM**).

un·wise /ˌənˈwīz/ ▶ **adj.** (of a person or action) not wise or sensible; foolish: *it is unwise to rely on hearsay evidence* | *unwise policy decisions.*
– DERIVATIVES **un·wise·ly adv.** [sentence adverb] *unwisely, she repeated the remark to her mother.*
– ORIGIN Old English *unwīs* (see **UN-**[1], **WISE**[1]).

un·wished /ˌənˈwisHt/ ▶ **adj.** (usu. **unwished-for**) not wanted or desired: *an unwished-for child.*

un·wit·nessed /ˌənˈwitnist/ ▶ **adj.** (esp. of an event) not witnessed.

un·wit·ting /ˌənˈwitiNG/ ▶ **adj.** (of a person) not aware of the full facts: *an unwitting accomplice.* ■ not done on purpose; unintentional: *we are anxious to rectify the unwitting mistakes made in the past.*
– DERIVATIVES **un·wit·ting·ly adv.** [sentence adverb] *quite unwittingly, you played right into my hands that night,* **un·wit·ting·ness n.**
– ORIGIN Old English *unwitende* 'not knowing or realizing' (see **UN-**[1], **WIT**[2]).

un·wom·an·ly /ˌənˈwŏŏmənlē/ ▶ **adj.** not having or showing qualities traditionally associated with women: *initiative of any overt sort was considered unwomanly.*
– DERIVATIVES **un·wom·an·li·ness n.**

un·wont·ed /ˌənˈwôntid/ ▶ **adj.** [attrib.] unaccustomed or unusual: *there was an unwonted gaiety in her manner.*
– DERIVATIVES **un·wont·ed·ly adv.** [as submodifier] *she was unwontedly shy and subdued,* **un·wont·ed·ness n.**

un·wood·ed /ˌənˈwŏŏdid/ ▶ **adj. 1** having few trees.
2 (of a wine) not having been stored in a wooden cask.

un·work·a·ble /ˌənˈwərkəbəl/ ▶ **adj.** not able to function or be carried out successfully; impractical: *complex, unworkable theories.* ■ (of a material) not able to be worked: *the alloy becomes brittle and almost unworkable.*
– DERIVATIVES **un·work·a·bil·i·ty** /-ˌwərkəˈbilitē/ **n.**, **un·work·a·bly** /-blē/ **adv.**

un·worked /ənˈwərkt/ ▶ **adj.** not cultivated, mined, or carved: *unworked fields* | *an unworked vein of rich ore.*

un·work·man·like /ˌənˈwərkmənˌlīk/ ▶ **adj.** badly done or made.

un·world·ly /ˌənˈwərldlē/ ▶ **adj.** (of a person) not having much awareness of the realities of life, in particular, not motivated by material or practical considerations: *she was so shrewd in some ways, but hopelessly unworldly in others.* ■ not seeming to belong to this planet; strange: *the unworldly monolith loomed four stories high.*
– DERIVATIVES **un·world·li·ness n.**

un·worn /ˌənˈwôrn/ ▶ **adj.** not damaged or shabby-looking as a result of much use: *the tires appear unworn, even after many fast miles* | *unworn carpeting.* ■ (of a garment) never worn.

un·wor·ried /ˌənˈwərēd/ ▶ **adj.** [predic.] not anxious or uneasy: *foreign investors are largely unworried by the government's fall.*

un·wor·thy /ˌənˈwər<u>TH</u>ē/ ▶ **adj.** (**unworthier, unworthiest**) not deserving effort, attention, or respect: *he was unworthy of trust and unfit to hold office.* ■ (of a person's action or behavior) not acceptable, esp. from someone with a good reputation or social position: *the expression of anger was frowned upon as being unworthy.* ■ having little value or merit: *many pieces are unworthy and ungrammatical.*
– DERIVATIVES **un·wor·thi·ly** /-<u>TH</u>əlē/ **adv.**, **un·wor·thi·ness n.**

un·wound /ˌənˈwound/ past and past participle of **UNWIND**.
▶ **adj.** (of a clock or watch) not wound or wound up.

un·wound·ed /ˌənˈwŏŏndid/ ▶ **adj.** not hurt or injured.

un·wo·ven /ˌənˈwōvən/ ▶ **adj.** (of fabric) not woven.

un·wrap /ˌənˈrap/ ▶ **v.** (**unwraps, unwrapping, unwrapped**) [with obj.] remove the wrapping from a package: *children excitedly unwrapping and playing with their new presents.*

un·wrin·kled /ˌənˈriNGkəld/ ▶ **adj.** (esp. of fabric or a person's skin) free from wrinkles.

un·writ·ten /ˌənˈritn/ ▶ **adj.** not recorded in writing: *documenting unwritten languages.* ■ (esp. of a law) resting originally on custom or judicial decision rather than on statute: *an unwritten constitution.* ■ (of a convention) understood and accepted by everyone, although not formally established: *the unwritten rules of social life.*

un·wrought /ˌənˈrôt/ ▶ **adj.** (of metals or other materials) not worked into a finished condition. ■ (of a mine or ore deposit) not worked or mined.

un·yield·ing /ˌənˈyēldiNG/ ▶ **adj.** (of a mass or structure) not giving way to pressure; hard or solid: *the Atlantic hurled its waves at the unyielding rocks.* ■ (of a person or their behavior) unlikely to be swayed; resolute: *his unyielding faith.*

– DERIVATIVES **un·yield·ing·ly** adv., **un·yield·ing·ness** n.

un·yoke /ˌənˈyōk/ ▶ v. [with obj.] release (a pair of animals) from a yoke. ■ [no obj.] archaic cease work.

un·zip /ˌənˈzip/ ▶ v. (**unzips, unzipping, unzipped**) [with obj.] unfasten the zipper of (an item of clothing): *he unzipped his black jacket.* ■ Computing decompress (a file) that has previously been compressed.

up /əp/ ▶ adv. **1** toward the sky or a higher position: *he jumped up | two of the men hoisted her up | the curtain went up.* ■ upstairs: *she made her way up to bed.* ■ out of bed: *Miranda hardly ever got up for breakfast | he had been up for hours.* ■ (of the sun) visible in the sky after daybreak: *the sun was already up when they set off.* ■ expressing movement toward or position in the north: *I drove up to Detroit.* ■ to or at a place perceived as higher: *going for a walk up to the stores.* ■ Brit. toward or in the capital or a major city: *give me a ring when you're up in London.* ■ Brit. at or to a university, esp. Oxford or Cambridge: *they were up at Cambridge about the same time.* ■ (of food that has been eaten) regurgitated from the stomach: *I was sick and vomited up everything.* ■ [as exclamation] used as a command to a soldier or an animal to stand up and be ready to move or attack: *up, boys, and at 'em.*
2 to the place where someone is: *Dot didn't hear Mrs. Parvis come creeping up behind her.*
3 at or to a higher level of intensity, volume, or activity: *she turned the volume up | liven up the graphics | U.S. environmental groups had been stepping up their attack on GATT.* ■ at or to a higher price, value, or rank: *sales are up 22.8 percent at $50.2 million | unemployment is up and rising.* ■ winning or at an advantage by a specified margin: *there they were in the fourth quarter, up by 11 points | we came away 300 bucks up on the evening.*
4 into the desired or a proper condition: *the mayor agreed to set up a committee.* ■ so as to be finished or closed: *I've got a bit of paperwork to finish up | I zipped up my sweater.*
5 into a happy mood: *I don't think anything's going to cheer me up.*
6 displayed on a bulletin board or other publicly visible site: *he put up posters around the city.*
7 (of sailing) against the current or the wind. ■ (of a ship's helm) moved so that the rudder is to leeward.
8 Baseball at bat: *every time up, he had a different stance.*
▶ prep. from a lower to a higher point on (something); upward along: *she climbed up a flight of steps.* ■ from one end to another of (a street or other area), not necessarily on an upward slope: *bicycling up Pleasant Avenue toward Maywood Avenue | walking up the street.* ■ to a higher part of (a river or stream), away from the sea: *a cruise up the Rhine.*
▶ adj. **1** [attrib.] directed or moving toward a higher place or position: *the up escalator.* ■ Physics denoting a flavor of quark having a charge of $+^2/_3$. Protons and neutrons are thought to be composed of combinations of up and down quarks.
2 [predic.] in a cheerful mood; ebullient: *the mood here is resolutely up.*
3 [predic.] (of a computer system or industrial process) functioning properly: *the system is now up.*
4 [predic.] at an end: *his contract was up in three weeks | time's up.*
5 (of a jockey) in the saddle.
▶ n. informal a period of good fortune: *you can't have ups all the time in football.*
▶ v. (**ups, upping, upped**) **1** [no obj.] (**up and do something**) informal do something abruptly or boldly: *she upped and left him.*
2 [with obj.] cause (a level or amount) to be increased: *capacity will be upped by 70 percent next year.*
3 [with obj.] lift (something) up: *everybody was cheering and upping their glasses.* ■ [no obj.] (**up with**) informal raise or pick up (something): *this woman ups with a stone.*
– PHRASES **get it up** vulgar slang have a penile erection. **it is all up with** informal it is the end of or there is no hope for (someone or something). **on the up and up** informal **1** honest or sincere. **2** Brit. steadily improving or becoming more successful. **something is up** informal something unusual or undesirable is happening or afoot. **up against** close to or in contact with: *crowds pressed up against the police barricades.* ■ informal confronted with or opposed by: *I began to think of what teachers are up against today.* ■ (**up against it**) informal facing some serious but unspecified difficulty: *they play better when they're up against it.* **up and about** no longer in bed (after sleep or an illness). **up and down 1** moving upward and downward: *bouncing up and down.* **2** to and fro: *pacing up and down in front of her desk.* ■ [as prep.] to and fro along: *strolling up and down the corridor.* **3** in various places throughout: *in clubs up and down the country.* **4** informal in varying states or moods; changeable: *my relationship with her was up and down.* **up and running** (esp. of a computer system) in operation; functioning: *the new computer is up and running.* **up the ante** see ANTE. **up before** appearing for a hearing in the presence of: *we'll have to come up before a magistrate.* **up for 1** available for: *the house next door is up for sale.* **2** being considered for: *he had been up for promotion.* **3** due for: *his contract is up for renewal in June.* **up for it** informal ready to take part in a particular activity: *Nick wasn't really up for it.* **up hill and down dale** all over the place: *he led me up hill and down dale till my feet were dropping off.* **up on** well informed about: *he was up on the latest methods.* **up to 1** as far as: *I could reach just up to his waist.* ■ (also **up until**) until: *up to now I hadn't had a relationship.* **2** indicating a maximum amount: *the process is expected to take up to two years.* **3** [with negative or in questions] as good as; good enough for: *I was not up to her standards.* ■ capable of or fit for: *he is simply not up to the job.* **4** the duty, responsibility, or choice of (someone): *it was up to them to gauge the problem.* **5** informal occupied or busy with: *what's he been up to?* **up top** Brit. informal in the brain (with reference to intelligence): *a man with nothing much up top.* **up with ——** an exclamation expressing support for a stated person or thing. **up yours** (also **up your ass**) vulgar slang an exclamation expressing contemptuous defiance or rejection of someone. **what's up?** informal **1** what is going on? **2** what is the matter?: *what's up with you?*
– ORIGIN Old English *up(p)*, *uppe*, of Germanic origin; related to Dutch *op* and German *auf*.

up- ▶ prefix **1** (added to verbs and their derivatives) upward: *upturned | upthrow.* ■ to a more recent time; to a newer or better state: *upbeat | update | upgrade | upscale.*
2 (added to nouns) denoting (direction of) motion up: *upriver | uphill | upwind.*
3 (added to nouns) higher: *upland | upstroke.* ■ increased: *up-tempo.*

up·an·chor ▶ v. [no obj.] (of a ship) weigh anchor.

up-and-com·ing ▶ adj. (of a person beginning a particular activity or occupation) making good progress and likely to become successful: *up-and-coming young players.*
– DERIVATIVES **up-and-com·er** n.

U·pan·i·shad /(y)o͞oˈpanəˌsʜad, o͞oˈpəniˌsʜəd/ ▶ n. each of a series of Hindu sacred treatises written in Sanskrit *c.*800–200 BC, expounding the Vedas in predominantly mystical and monistic terms.
– ORIGIN from Sanskrit, literally 'sitting near (i.e., at the feet of a master),' from *upa* 'near' + *ni-ṣad* 'sit down.'

u·pas /ˈyo͞opəs/ (also **upas tree**) ▶ n. a tropical Asian tree, the milky sap of which has been used as arrow poison and for ritual purposes. ● *Antiaris toxicaria*, family Moraceae. ■ (in folklore) a Javanese tree alleged to poison its surroundings and said to be fatal to approach.
– ORIGIN late 18th cent.: from Malay (*pohun*) *upas* 'poison (tree).'

up·beat /ˈəpˌbēt/ ▶ n. (in music) an unaccented beat preceding an accented beat.
▶ adj. informal cheerful; optimistic.

up·bow /bō/ ▶ n. (on a stringed instrument) a stroke begun with the tip of the bow and proceeding toward the base. Compare with DOWN-BOW.

up·braid /ˌəpˈbrād/ ▶ v. [with obj.] find fault with (someone); scold: *he was upbraided for his slovenly appearance.*
– ORIGIN late Old English *upbrēdan* 'allege (something) as a basis for censure,' based on BRAID in the obsolete sense 'brandish.' The current sense dates from Middle English.

up·bring·ing /ˈəpˌbriNGiNG/ ▶ n. the treatment and instruction received by a child from its parents throughout its childhood: *his Quaker upbringing influenced his character.*
– ORIGIN late 15th cent.: from obsolete *upbring* 'to rear' (see UP-, BRING).

up·build /ˌəpˈbild/ ▶ v. (past and past participle **upbuilt**) [with obj.] chiefly literary construct or develop (something).

UPC ▶ abbr. Universal Product Code.

up card ▶ n. a playing card turned face up on the table, esp. the top card of the waste heap in rummy or a card turned face up in stud poker.

up·cast /ˈəpˌkast/ ▶ n. (also **upcast shaft**) a shaft through which air leaves a mine.
▶ v. (past and past participle **upcast**) [with obj.] cast (something) upward: (as adj. **upcast**) *upcast light.*

up·chuck /ˈəpˌCHək/ informal ▶ v. vomit: [no obj.] *don't let her upchuck on him* | [with obj.] *I almost upchucked my toasted marshmallows.*
▶ n. matter vomited from the stomach.

up·close /klōs/ ▶ adv. at very close range: *he was able to experience glaciers calving up-close.*
▶ adj. showing or allowing considerable detail: *an up-close look at a panorama of products and services.*

up·coast /ˌəpˈkōst/ ▶ adv. & adj. further up the coast.

up·code /ˌəpˈkōd/ ▶ v. [with obj.] assign an inaccurate billing code to (a medical procedure or treatment) to increase reimbursement: *if you are asked to upcode drug charges to increase reimbursement, will you refuse to do so or go along with the flow?* | [no obj.] *auditors discovered that they had been upcoding for years.*

up·com·ing /ˈəpˌkəmiNG/ ▶ adj. forthcoming; about to happen: *the upcoming election.*

up·coun·try /ˌəpˈkəntrē, ˈəpˌkəntrē/ ▶ adv. & adj. in or toward the interior of a country; inland: [as adv.] *she comes from somewhere upcountry* | [as adj.] *a little upcountry town.*

up·date ▶ v. /ˌəpˈdāt, ˈəpˌdāt/ [with obj.] make (something) more modern or up to date: *security measures are continually updated and improved* | (as adj. **updated**) *an updated list of subscribers.* ■ give (someone) the latest information about something: *the reporter promised to keep the viewers updated.*
▶ n. /ˈəpˌdāt/ an act of bringing something or someone up to date, or an updated version of something: *an update on recently published crime figures.*
– DERIVATIVES **up·dat·a·ble** adj. (Computing).

Up·dike /ˈəpˌdīk/, John (Hoyer) (1932–2009), US novelist, poet, and short-story writer. He is noted for his quartet of novels *Rabbit, Run* (1960), *Rabbit Redux* (1971), *Rabbit is Rich* (1981), and *Rabbit at Rest* (1990), the last two earning him Pulitzer Prizes. Other novels include *The Witches of Eastwick* (1984) and *S* (1998).

up·do /ˈəpdo͞o/ ▶ n. (pl. **updos**) informal a women's hairstyle in which the hair is swept up and fastened away from the face and neck.

up·dom·ing /ˈəpˌdōmiNG/ ▶ n. Geology the upward deformation of a rock mass into a dome shape.

up·draft /ˈəpˌdraft/ (Brit. **updraught**) ▶ n. an upward current or draft of air.

up·end /ˌəpˈend/ ▶ v. [with obj.] set or turn (something) on its end or upside down: *Kitty upended her purse, dumping out all her money* | (as adj. **upended**) *an upended box.* ■ [no obj.] (of a swimming duck or other waterbird) submerge the head and foreparts in order to feed, so that the tail is raised in the air.

up·field /ˌəpˈfēld/ ▶ adv.adj. Football another term for DOWNFIELD.

up·flung /ˈəpˌfləNG/ ▶ adj. chiefly literary (esp. of limbs) flung upward, esp. in a gesture of helplessness or alarm.

up·front /ˌəpˈfrənt/ informal ▶ adv. (usu. **up front**) **1** at the front; in front: *I was sitting up front.*
2 (of a payment) in advance: *the salesmen are paid commission up front.*
▶ adj. **1** bold, honest, and frank: *he'd been upfront about his intentions.*
2 [attrib.] (of a payment) made in advance.
3 at the front or the most prominent position: *a literary weekly with an upfront section modeled on The New Yorker.*

up·grade ▶ v. /ˈəpˌgrād, ˌəpˈgrād/ [with obj.] raise (something) to a higher standard, in particular improve (equipment or machinery) by adding or replacing components: *the cost of upgrading each workstation is around $300* | (as adj. **upgraded**) *upgraded computers.* ■ raise (an employee) to a higher grade or rank.
▶ n. /ˈəpˌgrād/ an act of upgrading something. ■ an improved or more modern version of something, esp. a piece of computing equipment.
– PHRASES **on the upgrade** improving; progressing.
– DERIVATIVES **up·grad·a·bil·i·ty** /ˌəpˌgrādəˈbilitē/ (also **upgradeability**) n., **up·grad·a·ble** /ˌəpˈgrādəbəl/ (also **upgradeable**) adj.

up·growth /ˈəpˌgrōTH/ ▶ n. the process or result of growing upward. ■ an upward growth.

up·heav·al /ˌəpˈhēvəl/ ▶ n. a violent or sudden change or disruption to something: *major upheavals in the financial markets | times of political upheaval.* ■ an upward displacement of part of the earth's crust.

up·heave /ˌəpˈhēv/ ▶ v. [with obj.] literary heave or lift up (something, esp. part of the earth's surface): *the area was first upheaved from the primeval ocean.*

up·hill ▶ adv. /ˌəpˈhil/ in an ascending direction up a hill or slope: *follow the track uphill.*
▶ adj. /ˈəpˌhil/ sloping upward; ascending: *the journey is slightly uphill.* ■ requiring great effort; difficult: *an uphill struggle to gain worldwide recognition.*

▶ n. /ˈəpˌhil/ an upward slope.

up·hold /ˌəpˈhōld/ ▶ v. (past and past participle **upheld**) [with obj.] confirm or support (something that has been questioned): *the court upheld his claim for damages.* ■ maintain (a custom or practice): *many furniture makers uphold the tradition of fine design.*
– DERIVATIVES **up·hold·er** n.

up·hol·ster /əpˈhōlstər, əˈpōl-/ ▶ v. [with obj.] provide (furniture) with a soft, padded covering: *the chairs were upholstered in red velvet* | (as adj. **upholstered**) *an upholstered stool.* ■ cover the walls or furniture in (a room) with textiles.
– ORIGIN mid 19th cent.: back-formation from UPHOLSTERER.

up·hol·ster·er /əpˈhōlstərər, əˈpōl-/ ▶ n. a person who upholsters furniture, esp. professionally.
– ORIGIN early 17th cent.: from the obsolete noun *upholster* (from UPHOLD in the obsolete sense 'keep in repair') + -STER.

up·hol·ster·y /əpˈhōlst(ə)rē, əˈpōl-/ ▶ n. soft, padded textile covering that is fixed to furniture such as armchairs and sofas. ■ the art or practice of fitting such a covering.

UPI ▶ abbr. United Press International.

Up·john /ˈəpˌjän/, Richard (1802–78), US architect; born in England. He is best known for his buildings, such as Trinity Church 1839–46 in New York City, designed in Gothic Revival style.

up·keep /ˈəpˌkēp/ ▶ n. the process of keeping something in good condition: *we will be responsible for the upkeep of the access road.* ■ financial or material support of a person or animal: *payments for the children's upkeep.*

Up·land /ˈəplənd/ a city in southwestern California, east of Los Angeles and north of Ontario; pop. 72,091 (est. 2008).

up·land /ˈəplənd, -ˌland/ ▶ n. (also **uplands**) an area of high or hilly land: *conservation of areas of upland.*

up·land cot·ton ▶ n. cotton of a type grown in the US that typically yields medium- and short-staple forms of cotton. ● *Gossypium hirsutum* var. *latifolium*, family Malvaceae.

up·land sand·pip·er ▶ n. a North American sandpiper that breeds on upland fields. Also called **upland plover**. ● *Bartramia longicauda.*

up·lift ▶ v. /ˌəpˈlift/ [with obj.] **1** (usu. as adj. **uplifted**) lift (something) up; raise: *her uplifted face.* ■ (**be uplifted**) (of an island, mountain, etc.) be created by an upward movement of the earth's surface.
2 (often as adj. **uplifted**) elevate or stimulate (someone) morally or spiritually: *people leave my shows feeling uplifted.*
▶ n. /ˈəpˌlift/ **1** an act of raising something. ■ Geology the upward movement of part of the earth's surface. ■ [often as modifier] support, esp. for a woman's bust, from a garment: *an uplift bra.*
2 a morally or spiritually elevating influence: *their love will prove an enormous uplift.*
– DERIVATIVES **up·lift·er** /ˌəpˈliftər/ n.

up·lift·ing /əpˈliftiNG/ ▶ adj. morally or spiritually elevating; inspiring happiness or hope: *an uplifting tune.*

up·light /ˈəpˌlīt/ (also **uplighter** /-ˌlītər/) ▶ n. a light placed or designed to throw illumination upward.
– DERIVATIVES **up·light·ing** n.

up·link /ˈəpˌliNGk/ ▶ n. a communications link to a satellite.
▶ v. [with obj.] provide (someone) with or send (something) by such a link: *I can uplink fax transmissions to a satellite.*

up·load Computing ▶ v. /ˈəpˌlōd, ˌəpˈlōd/ [with obj.] transfer (data) to another computer system; transmit (data). Compare with DOWNLOAD.
▶ n. /ˈəpˌlōd/ the action or process of transferring data in such a way.

up·mar·ket /ˌəpˈmärkit, ˈəpˌmär-/ ▶ adj. & adv. upscale.

up·most /ˈəpˌmōst/ ▶ adj. another term for UPPERMOST.

up·on /əˈpän, əˈpôn/ ▶ prep. more formal term for ON, esp. in abstract senses: *it was based upon two principles* | *a school's dependence upon parental support.*
– ORIGIN Middle English: from UP + ON, suggested by Old Norse *upp á.*

> **USAGE** The preposition **upon** has the same core meaning as the preposition **on**. **Upon** is sometimes more formal than **on**, however, and is preferred in the phrases *once upon a time* and *upon my word*, and in uses such as *row upon row of seats* and *Christmas is almost upon us.*

up·per¹ /ˈəpər/ ▶ adj. **1** situated above another part: *his upper arm* | *the upper atmosphere.* ■ higher in position or status: *the upper end of the social scale.*
2 situated on higher ground. ■ situated to the north: [in place names] *Upper California.*
3 Geology & Archaeology denoting a younger (and hence usually shallower) part of a stratigraphic division or archaeological deposit or the period in which it was formed or deposited: *the Upper Paleolithic age.*
▶ n. **1** the part of a boot or shoe above the sole.
2 (**uppers**) upper dentures or teeth.
– PHRASES **have** (or **gain**) **the upper hand** have or gain advantage or control over someone or something. **on one's uppers** informal, chiefly Brit. extremely short of money.
– ORIGIN Middle English: from the adjective UP + -ER².

up·per² ▶ n. (usu. **uppers**) informal a stimulating drug, esp. amphetamine.
– ORIGIN 1960s: from the verb UP + -ER¹.

Up·per Can·a·da the mainly English-speaking region of Canada north of the Great Lakes and west of the Ottawa River, in what is now southern Ontario.

up·per·case /ˈəpərˈ kās/ (also **upper case**) ▶ n. capital letters as opposed to small letters (lowercase): *the keywords must be in uppercase* | [as modifier] *uppercase letters.*
– ORIGIN referring originally to two type cases positioned on an angled stand, the case containing the capital letters being higher and further away from the compositor.

up·per cham·ber ▶ n. another term for UPPER HOUSE.

up·per class ▶ n. [treated as sing. or pl.] the social group that has the highest status in society, esp. the aristocracy.
▶ adj. (**upper-class**) of, relating to, or characteristic of such a group: *upper-class accents.*

up·per·class·man /ˌəpərˈklasmən/ ▶ n. (pl. **upperclassmen**) a junior or senior in high school or college.

up·per crust ▶ n. (**the upper crust**) informal the upper classes.

up·per·cut /ˈəpərˌkət/ ▶ n. a punch delivered with an upward motion and the arm bent. ■ Baseball an upward batting stroke, typically resulting in a fly ball.
▶ v. (**uppercuts, uppercutting**; past and past participle **uppercut**) [with obj.] hit with an uppercut.

Up·per Dar·by /ˈdärbē/ a township in southern Pennsylvania, southwest of Philadelphia; pop. 78,443 (est. 2008).

up·per house ▶ n. the smaller house in a bicameral legislature or parliament. ■ (**the Upper House**) (in the UK) the House of Lords.

up·per·most /ˈəpərˌmōst/ ▶ adj. (also **upmost**) highest in place, rank, or importance: *the uppermost windows* | *her father was uppermost in her mind.*
▶ adv. at or to the highest or most important position: *investors put environmental concerns uppermost on their list.*

Up·per Pe·nin·su·la (abbr.: **UP**) the northern section of Michigan that is separated from the southern part of the state by Lake Michigan, the Straits of Mackinac, and Lake Huron. Lake Superior is to the north.

up·per re·gions ▶ plural n. archaic or literary the sky or heavens.

up·per school ▶ n. a secondary school for children aged from about fourteen upward, generally following on from a middle school. ■ the section of a school that comprises or caters to the older students.

Up·per Vol·ta former name (until 1984) for BURKINA FASO.

up·pish /ˈəpisH/ ▶ adj. informal arrogantly self-assertive.
– DERIVATIVES **up·pish·ly** adv., **up·pish·ness** n.

up·pi·ty /ˈəpətē/ ▶ adj. informal self-important; arrogant: *an uppity sister-in-law.*
– ORIGIN late 19th cent.: a fanciful formation from UP.

Upp·sa·la /ˈo͝opˌsälə/ a city in eastern Sweden; pop. 190,668 (2008).

up·raise /ˌəpˈrāz/ ▶ v. [with obj.] raise (something) to a higher level: *concentration upraises things* | (as adj. **upraised**) *an upraised arm.*

up·right /ˈəpˌrīt/ ▶ adj. **1** vertical; erect: *the posts must be in an upright position.* ■ (of a piano) having vertical strings. ■ greater in height than breadth: *an upright freezer.* ■ denoting a device designed to be used in a vertical position: *an upright vacuum cleaner.*
2 (of a person or their behavior) strictly honorable or honest: *an upright member of the community.*
▶ adv. in or into a vertical position: *she was sitting upright in bed.*
▶ n. **1** a post or rod fixed vertically, esp. as a structural support: *the stone uprights of the parapet.* ■ (**uprights**) Football the vertical posts extending up from the crossbar of the goalpost, between which a field goal must pass to score.
2 an upright piano.
– DERIVATIVES **up·right·ly** adv.
– ORIGIN Old English *upriht*, of Germanic origin; related to Dutch *oprecht* and German *aufrecht* (see UP, RIGHT).

up·right·ness /ˈəpˌrītnis/ ▶ n. **1** the state of being in a vertical position.
2 the condition or quality of being honorable or honest; rectitude: *there is a general lack of uprightness in these postmodern times.*

up·rise /ˌəpˈrīz/ ▶ v. (past **uprose**; past participle **uprisen**) [no obj.] archaic or literary rise to a standing or elevated position: *bright and red uprose the morning sun.*

up·ris·ing /ˈəpˌrīziNG/ ▶ n. an act of resistance or rebellion; a revolt: *an armed uprising.*

up·riv·er /ˈəpˈrivər/ ▶ adv. & adj. toward or situated at a point nearer the source of a river: [as adv.] *the salmon head upriver to spawn* | [as adj.] *they headed for the upriver side.*

up·roar /ˈəpˌrôr/ ▶ n. a loud and impassioned noise or disturbance: *the room was in an uproar* | *the assembly dissolved in uproar.* ■ a public expression of protest or outrage: *it caused an uproar in the press.*
– ORIGIN early 16th cent.: from Middle Dutch *uproer*, from *op* 'up' + *roer* 'confusion,' assimilated to ROAR.

up·roar·i·ous /ˌəpˈrôrēəs/ ▶ adj. characterized by or provoking loud noise or uproar: *an uproarious party* ■ provoking loud laughter; very funny.
– DERIVATIVES **up·roar·i·ous·ly** adv., **up·roar·i·ous·ness** n.

up·root /ˌəpˈro͞ot, -ˈro͝ot/ ▶ v. [with obj.] **1** pull (something, esp. a tree or plant) out of the ground: *the elephant's trunk is powerful enough to uproot trees.* ■ eradicate; destroy: *a revolution is necessary to uproot the social order.*
2 ■ move (someone) from their home or a familiar location: *my father traveled constantly and uprooted his family several times.*
– DERIVATIVES **up·root·er** n.

up·rose /ˌəpˈrōz/ past of UPRISE.

up·rush /ˈəpˌrəsH/ ▶ n. a sudden upward surge or flow, esp. of a feeling: *an uprush of joy.*

UPS ▶ abbr. uninterruptible power supply.

ups-a-dai·sy /ˈəps ə ˌdāzē/ (also **upsa-daisy**) ▶ exclam. variant spelling of UPSY-DAISY.

ups and downs ▶ plural n. a succession of both good and bad experiences: *I have my ups and downs.* ■ rises and falls, esp. in the value or success of something: *the ups and downs of the market.*

up·scale /ˌəpˈskāl, ˈəpˌskāl/ ▶ adj. & adv. toward or relating to the more expensive or affluent sector of the market: [as adj.] *Hawaii's upscale boutique hotels* | [as adv.] *once known as the low-cost cousin of beef, fish has moved upscale.*

up·set /ˌəpˈset/ ▶ v. (**upsets, upsetting**; past and past participle **upset**) [with obj.] **1** make (someone) unhappy, disappointed, or worried: *the accusation upset her* | (as adj. **upsetting**) *a painful and upsetting divorce.*
2 knock (something) over: *he upset a tureen of soup.* ■ cause disorder in (something); disrupt: *the dam will upset the ecological balance.* ■ disturb the digestion of (a person's stomach); cause (someone) to feel nauseous or unwell.
3 (often as noun **upsetting**) shorten and thicken the end or edge of (a metal bar, wheel rim, or other object), esp. by hammering or pressure when heated.
▶ n. /ˈəpset/ **1** a state of being unhappy, disappointed, or worried: *domestic upsets* | *a legal dispute will cause worry and upset.*
2 an unexpected result or situation, esp. in a sports competition: *they caused one of last season's biggest upsets by winning 27–15.*
3 a disturbance of a person's digestive system: *a stomach upset.*
▶ adj. /ˌəpˈset/ **1** [predic.] unhappy, disappointed, or worried: *she looked pale and upset.*
2 (of a person's stomach) having disturbed digestion, esp. because of something eaten.
– DERIVATIVES **up·set·ter** /ˌəpˈsetər/ n., **up·set·ting·ly** adv.

up·set price /ˈəpˌset/ ▶ n. the lowest acceptable selling price for a property in an auction; a reserve price.

up·shift /ˈəpˌsHift/ ▶ v. [no obj.] change to a higher gear in a motor vehicle. ■ [with obj.] increase: *stricter driving laws that upshifted the penalties for drunken driving.*
▶ n. a change to a higher gear.

up·shot /ˈəpˌsHät/ ▶ n. [in sing.] the final or eventual outcome or conclusion of a discussion, action, or series of events: *the upshot of the meeting was that he was on the next plane to New York.*

U

up·side /ˈəpˌsīd/ ▶ **n.** [in sing.] **1** the positive or favorable aspect of something.
2 an upward movement of stock prices.
– PHRASES **upside the head** on the side of head: *she slapped him upside the head.*

up·side down ▶ **adv. & adj.** with the upper part where the lower part should be; in an inverted position: [as adv.] *the bar staff put the chairs upside down on the tables* | [as adj.] *an upside-down canoe.* ■ in or into total disorder or confusion: [as adv.] *burglars have **turned** our house **upside down**.*
– ORIGIN Middle English: originally *up so down*, perhaps in the sense 'up as if down.'

up·side-down cake ▶ **n.** a cake that is baked over a layer of fruit in syrup and inverted for serving.

up·si·lon /ˈəpsəˌlän, ˈ(y)o͞op-/ ▶ **n.** the twentieth letter of the Greek alphabet (Υ, υ), transliterated in the traditional Latin style as 'y' (as in *cycle*) or in the modern style as 'u' (as in the etymologies of this dictionary). ■ (**Upsilon**) [followed by Latin genitive] Astronomy the twentieth star in a constellation: *Upsilon Scorpii.* ■ (also **upsilon particle**) Physics a meson thought to contain a *b* quark bound to its antiparticle, produced in particle accelerators.
– ORIGIN mid 17th cent.: Greek, literally 'plain or simple U,' from *psilos* 'plain,' referring to the need to distinguish upsilon from the diphthong *oi*: in late Greek the two had (and in modern Greek still have) the same pronunciation.

up·size /ˈəpˌsīz/ ▶ **v.** increase or cause to increase in size or complexity.

up·skill /ˈəpˌskil/ ▶ **v.** [with obj.] teach (an employee) additional skills: *this is an opportunity to upskill staff and expand their capabilities.* ■ [no obj.] (of an employee) learn additional skills: *they will provide grants of up to 75% for staff who decide to upskill.*

up·slope ▶ **n.** /ˈəpˌslōp/ an upward slope.
▶ **adv. & adj.** /ˌəpˈslōp/ at or toward a higher point on a slope.

up·stage /ˌəpˈstāj/ ▶ **adv. & adj.** at or toward the back of a theater stage: [as adv.] *Hamlet turns to face upstage* | [as adj.] *an upstage exit.* ■ [as adj.] informal, dated superior; aloof.
▶ **v.** [with obj.] divert attention from (someone) toward oneself; outshine: *they were totally upstaged by their costar in the film.* ■ (of an actor) move toward the back of a stage to make (another actor) face away from the audience.

up·stairs ▶ **adv.** /ˌəpˈste(ə)rz/ on or to an upper floor of a building: *I tiptoed upstairs.* ■ used to refer to someone's mental health: *is he, uh, all right upstairs?*
▶ **adj.** /ˈəpˈsterz/ [attrib.] situated on an upper floor: *an upstairs bedroom.*
▶ **n.** /ˌəpˈsterz, ˈəpˌsterz/ an upper floor: *she was cleaning the upstairs.*
– PHRASES **the man upstairs** a humorous name for God.

up·stand·ing /ˌəpˈstandiNG, ˈəpˌstan-/ ▶ **adj.**
1 honest; respectable: *an upstanding member of the community.*
2 standing up; erect: *upstanding feathered plumes.*

up·start /ˈəpˌstärt/ ▶ **n.** derogatory a person who has risen suddenly to wealth or high position, esp. one who behaves arrogantly: *the upstarts who dare to challenge the legitimacy of his rule* | [as modifier] *an upstart leader.*

up·state /ˈəpˈstāt/ ▶ **adj. & adv.** of, in, or to a part of a state remote from its large cities, esp. the northern part: [as adj.] *the Watermans bought 27 acres in upstate Vermont.*
▶ **n.** such an area: *visiting farmers from upstate.* ■ (also **Upstate**) in New York, parts of the state north of New York City, thought of as distinct culturally and politically: *Concord table grapes from upstate* | [as modifier] *the small community college in upstate New York.*
– DERIVATIVES **up·stat·er** n.

up·stream /ˌəpˈstrēm/ ▶ **adv. & adj.** moving or situated in the opposite direction from that in which a stream or river flows; nearer to the source: [as adv.] *a salmon swimming upstream* | [as adj.] *the upstream stretch of the Platte.* ■ Biology situated in or toward the part of a sequence of genetic material where transcription takes place earlier than at a given point. ■ at a stage in the process of gas or oil extraction and production before the raw material is ready for refining.

up·stroke /ˈəpˌstrōk/ ▶ **n.** a stroke made upward: *the upstroke of the whale's tail.*

up·surge /ˈəpˌsərj/ ▶ **n.** an upward surge in the strength or quantity of something; an increase: *an upsurge in violent crime.*

up·sweep ▶ **v.** /ˌəpˈswēp/ [no obj.] be arranged in an upswept fashion. ■ [with obj.] sweep upward.
▶ **n.** /ˈəpˌswēp/ **1** an upward rise or sweep: *the gentle upsweep of the city wall.* ■ a marked rise in activity: *catching the market at the start of its upsweep.*
2 an upswept hairdo.

up·swell /ˈəpˌswel/ ▶ **n.** an increase or upsurge.

up·swept /ˈəpˌswept/ ▶ **adj.** curved, sloping, or directed upward: *an upswept mustache.* ■ (of the hair) brushed or held upward and off the face: *an elegant upswept style.*

up·swing /ˈəpˌswiNG/ ▶ **n.** an increase in strength or quantity; an upward trend: *cigar smoking has been **on the upswing**.*

up·sy-dai·sy /ˈəpsēˌdāzē/ (also **ups-a-daisy, upsa-daisy** /ˈəpsə ˈdāzē/) ▶ **exclam.** used to express encouragement to a child who has fallen or is being lifted.
– ORIGIN mid 19th cent.: alteration of earlier *up-a-daisy*; compare with LACKADAISICAL.

up·take /ˈəpˌtāk/ ▶ **n. 1** the action of taking up or making use of something that is available: *a recent uptake in cigar smoking* | *the uptake and usage of computers.* ■ the taking in or absorption of a substance by a living organism or bodily organ: *the uptake of glucose into the muscles.*
2 a pipe or flue leading air, smoke, or gases up to a chimney.
– PHRASES **be quick** (or **slow**) **on the uptake** informal be quick (or slow) to understand something.

up·talk /ˈəpˌtôk/ ▶ **n.** a manner of speaking in which declarative sentences are uttered with rising intonation at the end, as if they were questions.

up·tem·po /ˈəpˌtempō/ ▶ **adj. & adv.** Music played with a fast or increased tempo: [as adj.] *uptempo guitar work.*

up·throw /ˈəpˌTHrō/ Geology ▶ **v.** [with obj.] (usu. as adj. **upthrown**) displace (a body of rock) upward on one side of a fault relative to the other.
▶ **n.** an upward displacement of a body of rock on one side of a fault.

up·thrust /ˈəpˌTHrəst/ ▶ **n.** Physics the upward force that a liquid or gas exerts on a body floating in it. ■ Geology another term for UPLIFT. ■ an upward thrust: *the upthrust of Manhattan skyscrapers.*
▶ **v.** [with obj.] (usu. as adj. **upthrust**) thrust (something) upward: *Turco's upthrust beard.*

up·tick /ˈəpˌtik/ ▶ **n.** a small increase.

up·tight /ˌəpˈtīt/ ▶ **adj.** informal anxious or angry in a tense and overly controlled way: *don't get so uptight about everything.*

up·time /ˈəpˌtīm/ ▶ **n.** time during which a machine, esp. a computer, is in operation.

up to date ▶ **adj.** incorporating the latest developments and trends: *a modern, up-to-date hospital.* ■ incorporating or aware of the latest information: *the book will keep you up to date.*

up-to-the-min·ute ▶ **adj.** incorporating the very latest information or developments: *an up-to-the-minute news broadcast.*

up·town ▶ **adj.** /ˌəpˈtoun/ of, in, or characteristic of the residential area of a city or town. ■ of or characteristic of an affluent area or people: *I don't pay uptown prices.*
▶ **adv.** /ˌəpˈtoun/ in or into such an area.
▶ **n.** /ˈəpˌtoun/ a residential area in a town or city.
– DERIVATIVES **up·town·er** /ˌəpˈtounər/ **n.**

up·trend /ˈəpˌtrend/ ▶ **n.** an upward tendency.

up·turn ▶ **n.** /ˈəpˌtərn/ an improvement or upward trend, esp. in economic conditions or someone's fortunes: *an upturn in the economy.*
▶ **v.** /ˈəpˌtərn, ˌəpˈtərn/ [with obj.] (usu. as adj. **upturned**) turn (something) upward or upside down: *a sea of upturned faces.*

uPVC ▶ **abbr.** unplasticized polyvinyl chloride, a rigid, chemically resistant form of PVC used for piping, window frames, and other structures.

up·ward /ˈəpwərd/ ▶ **adv.** (also **upwards**) toward a higher place, point, or level: *she peered upward at the sky.*
▶ **adj.** moving, pointing, or leading to a higher place, point, or level: *an upward trend in sales.*
– PHRASES **upwards** (or **upward**) **of** more than: *upwards of 3,500 copies* | *Gooden can throw the ball at upward of 95 miles per hour.*
– DERIVATIVES **up·ward·ly** adv.
– ORIGIN Old English *upweard(es)* (see UP, -WARD).

up·ward·ly mo·bile /ˈəpwərdlē/ ▶ **adj.** moving to a higher social class; acquiring wealth and status.
– DERIVATIVES **up·ward mo·bil·i·ty** n.

up·weight /ˈəpˌwāt/ ▶ **v.** [with obj.] **1** give increased importance, rank or weighting to: *some advertisers upweighted TV, while others upweighted press.*
2 Finance increase the proportion of (an asset or asset class) in a portfolio or fund: *an opportunity to upweight equities where feasible within your risk profile.*

up·well·ing /ˌəpˈweliNG/ ▶ **n.** a rising of seawater, magma, or other liquid.
▶ **adj.** (esp. of emotion) building up or gathering strength: *upwelling grief.*

up·wind /ˌəpˈwind/ ▶ **adv. & adj.** against the direction of the wind: [as adv.] *you learn how to sail upwind* | [as adj.] *the upwind wing tip.*

Ur /ər, o͝or/ an ancient Sumerian city, formerly on the Euphrates River, in southern Iraq. One of the oldest cities in Mesopotamia, dating from the 4th millennium BC, it reached its zenith in the late 3rd millennium BC.

ur- ▶ **comb. form** primitive; original; earliest: *urtext.*
– ORIGIN from German.

u·ra·cil /ˈyo͝orəˌsil/ ▶ **n.** Biochemistry a compound found in living tissue as a constituent base of RNA. In DNA its place is taken by thymine. ● A pyrimidine derivative; chem. formula: $C_4H_4N_2O_2$.
– ORIGIN late 19th cent.: from *ur(ea)* + *ac(etic)* + -IL.

u·rae·mi·a ▶ **n.** British spelling of UREMIA.

u·rae·us /yo͝oˈrēəs/ ▶ **n.** (pl. **uraei** /yo͝oˈrēˌī, -ˈrēˌē/) a representation of a sacred serpent as an emblem of supreme power, worn on the headdresses of ancient Egyptian deities and sovereigns.
– ORIGIN mid 19th cent.: modern Latin, from Greek *ouraios*, representing the Egyptian word for 'cobra.'

U·ral-Al·ta·ic /ˌyo͝orəl alˈtāik/ ▶ **adj.** of, relating to, or denoting a hypothetical language group formerly proposed to include both the Uralic and the Altaic languages.

U·ral·ic /yo͝oˈralik/ ▶ **adj. 1** of, relating to, or denoting a family of languages spoken from northern Scandinavia to western Siberia, comprising the Finno-Ugric and Samoyedic groups.
2 of or relating to the Ural Mountains or the surrounding areas.
▶ **n.** the Uralic languages collectively.

U·ral Moun·tains /ˈyo͝orəl/ (also **the Urals**) a mountain range in Russia that extends 1,000 miles (1,600 km) from the Arctic Ocean to the Aral Sea. It forms part of the conventional boundary between Europe and Asia.

U·ral Riv·er /ˈyo͝orəl/ a river, 1,575 miles (2,534 km) long, that rises at the southern end of the Ural Mountains in western Russia and flows through western Kazakhstan to the Caspian Sea at Atyraū.

U·ra·ni·a /yo͝oˈrānēə/ Greek & Roman Mythology the Muse of astronomy.
– ORIGIN Greek, literally 'heavenly (female).'

U·ra·ni·an /yo͝oˈrānēən/ ▶ **adj. 1** of or relating to the planet Uranus.
2 literary homosexual. [late 19th cent.: with allusion to a reference to Aphrodite in Plato's *Symposium*.]
▶ **n.** a homosexual.

u·ran·i·nite /yo͝oˈrānəˌnīt, -ˈranə-/ ▶ **n.** a black, gray, or brown mineral that consists mainly of uranium dioxide and is the chief ore of uranium. PITCHBLENDE is a variety of uraninite.
– ORIGIN late 19th cent.: from URANO-² + -ITE¹.

u·ra·ni·um /yo͝oˈrānēəm/ ▶ **n.** the chemical element of atomic number 92, a gray, dense radioactive metal used as a fuel in nuclear reactors. (Symbol: **U**)

> Uranium is a chemically reactive metal belonging to the actinide series. Becquerel discovered radioactivity in uranium in 1896, and its capacity to undergo fission led to its use as a source of energy, though the fissile isotope, uranium-235, has to be separated from the more common uranium-238 before it can be used in nuclear weapons. The atom bomb exploded over Hiroshima in 1945 contained uranium-235.

– ORIGIN late 18th cent.: modern Latin, from URANUS + -IUM.

urano-¹ ▶ **comb. form** relating to the heavens: *uranography.*
– ORIGIN from Greek *ouranos* 'heavens, sky.'

urano-² ▶ **comb. form** representing URANIUM.

u·ra·nog·ra·phy /ˌyo͝orəˈnägrəfē/ ▶ **n.** archaic the branch of astronomy concerned with describing and mapping the heavens.
– DERIVATIVES **u·ra·nog·ra·pher** n., **u·ra·no·graph·ic** /-nəˈgrafik/ **adj.**

U·ran·us /ˈyo͝orənəs, yo͝oˈrā-/ **1** Greek Mythology a personification of heaven or the sky, the most ancient of the Greek gods and first ruler of the universe. He was overthrown and castrated by his son Cronus.
2 Astronomy a distant planet of the solar system, seventh in order from the sun, discovered by William Herschel in 1781.

> Uranus orbits between Jupiter and Neptune at an average distance of 1,785 million miles (2,872 km) from the sun. It has an equatorial diameter of 31,763 miles (51,118 km) and is one of the gas giants. The planet is bluish-green in color, having an upper atmosphere consisting almost entirely of hydrogen and helium. There are at least seventeen satellites, the largest of which are Oberon and Titania, and a faint ring system.

u·ra·nyl /ˈyo͝orəˌnil/ ▶ **n.** [as modifier] Chemistry the cation UO_2^{2+}, present in some compounds of uranium: *uranyl acetate.*
– ORIGIN mid 19th cent.: from **URANIUM** + **-YL**.

U·rar·ti·an /o͝oˈrärtēən/ ▶ **adj.** of or relating to the ancient kingdom of Urartu in eastern Anatolia (c.1500–585 BC).
▶ **n. 1** a native or inhabitant of ancient Urartu. **2** the language of Urartu, related to Hurrian.

u·rate /ˈyo͝orˌāt/ ▶ **n.** a salt or ester of uric acid.

ur·ban /ˈərbən/ ▶ **adj. 1** in, relating to, or characteristic of a city or town: *the urban population.*
2 (also **urban contemporary**) denoting or relating to popular dance music of black origin: *a party that features the best in urban music.* ■ denoting popular black culture in general.
– ORIGIN early 17th cent.: from Latin *urbanus*, from *urbs*, *urb-* 'city.'

Ur·ban·dale /ˈərbənˌdāl/ a city in south central Iowa, a northwestern suburb of Des Moines; pop. 38,369 (est. 2008).

ur·bane /ˌərˈbān/ ▶ **adj.** (of a person, esp. a man) suave, courteous, and refined in manner.
– DERIVATIVES **ur·bane·ly adv.**
– ORIGIN mid 16th cent. (in the sense 'urban'): from French *urbain* or Latin *urbanus* (see **URBAN**).

ur·ban for·est ▶ **n.** a densely wooded area located in a city.

ur·ban·ism /ˈərbəˌnizəm/ ▶ **n. 1** the lifestyle of city dwellers.
2 urbanization.

ur·ban·ist /ˈərbənist/ ▶ **n.** an advocate of or expert in city planning.

ur·ban·ite /ˈərbəˌnīt/ ▶ **n.** informal a person who lives in a city or town.

ur·ban·i·ty /ˌərˈbanitē/ ▶ **n. 1** suavity, courteousness, and refinement of manner.
2 urban life.
– ORIGIN mid 16th cent.: from French *urbanité* or Latin *urbanitas*, from *urbanus* 'belonging to the city' (see **URBAN**).

ur·ban·ize /ˈərbəˌnīz/ ▶ **v.** make or become urban in character: [with obj.] *once an agrarian society, the island has recently been urbanized* | (as adj. **urbanized**) *urbanized areas.*
– DERIVATIVES **ur·ban·i·za·tion** /ˌərbənəˈzāsʜən/ **n.**

ur·ban leg·end (also chiefly Brit. **urban myth**) ▶ **n.** a humorous or horrific story or piece of information circulated as though true, esp. one purporting to involve someone vaguely related or known to the teller.

ur·ban re·new·al ▶ **n.** the redevelopment of areas within a large city, typically involving the clearance of slums.

ur·ban sprawl ▶ **n.** the uncontrolled expansion of urban areas.

urbs /ərbz/ ▶ **n.** chiefly literary the city, esp. as a symbol of harsh or busy modern life.
– ORIGIN Latin.

URC ▶ **abbr.** United Reformed Church.

ur·chin /ˈərcʜin/ ▶ **n. 1** a mischievous young child, esp. one who is poorly or raggedly dressed. ■ archaic a goblin.
2 short for **SEA URCHIN**. ■ Brit. chiefly dialect a hedgehog.
– ORIGIN Middle English *hirchon*, *urchon* 'hedgehog,' from Old Northern French *herichon*, based on Latin *hericius* 'hedgehog.'

U

Ur·du /ˈo͝ordo͞o, ˈər-/ ▶ **n.** a form of Hindustani written in Persian script, with many loanwords from Persian and Arabic. It is an official language of Pakistan and is widely used in India and elsewhere.
– ORIGIN from Persian (*zabān-i-*)*urdū* '(language of the) camp' (because it developed after the Muslim invasions as a lingua franca between the occupying armies and the local people of the region around Delhi), *urdū* being from Turkic *ordu* (see **HORDE**).

-ure ▶ **suffix** forming nouns: **1** denoting an action, process, or result: *censure* | *closure* | *scripture.*
2 denoting an office or function: *judicature.*
3 denoting a collective: *legislature.*
– ORIGIN from Old French *-ure*, from Latin *-ura*.

u·re·a /yo͞oˈrēə/ ▶ **n.** Biochemistry a colorless crystalline compound that is the main nitrogenous breakdown product of protein metabolism in mammals and is excreted in urine. ● Chem. formula: $CO(NH_2)_2$.
– ORIGIN early 19th cent.: modern Latin, from French *urée*, from Greek *ouron* 'urine.'

u·re·a·plas·ma /yo͞oˌrēəˈplazmə/ ▶ **n.** a small bacterium related to the mycoplasmas, characterized by the ability to metabolize urea.
● Genus *Ureaplasma*, order Mycoplasmatales.

u·re·ase /ˈyo͞orēˌās, -ˌāz/ ▶ **n.** a naturally occurring enzyme that hydrolyzes urea into ammonium carbonate.

u·re·ide /ˈyo͞orēˌīd, -id/ ▶ **n.** Chemistry any of a group of compounds that are acyl derivatives of urea.

u·re·mi·a /yo͞oˈrēmēə/ (Brit. **uraemia**) ▶ **n.** Medicine a raised level in the blood of urea and other nitrogenous waste compounds that are normally eliminated by the kidneys.
– DERIVATIVES **u·re·mic** /yo͞oˈrēmik/ **adj.**
– ORIGIN mid 19th cent.: modern Latin, from Greek *ouron* 'urine' + *haima* 'blood.'

u·re·ter /ˈyo͞oritər, yo͞oˈrētər/ ▶ **n.** Anatomy & Zoology the duct by which urine passes from the kidney to the bladder or cloaca.
– DERIVATIVES **u·re·ter·al** /yo͞oˈrētərəl/ **adj.**, **u·re·ter·ic** /ˌyo͞oriˈterik/ **adj.**
– ORIGIN late 16th cent.: from French *uretère* or modern Latin *ureter*, from Greek *ourētēr*, from *ourein* 'urinate.'

u·re·thane /ˈyo͞orəˌᴛʜān/ ▶ **n.** Chemistry a synthetic crystalline compound used in making pesticides and fungicides, and formerly as an anesthetic.
● Alternative name: **ethyl carbamate**; chem. formula: $CO(NH_2)OC_2H_5$. ■ short for **POLYURETHANE**.
– ORIGIN mid 19th cent.: from French *uréthane* (see **UREA**, **ETHANE**).

u·re·thra /yo͞oˈrēᴛʜrə/ ▶ **n.** Anatomy & Zoology the duct by which urine is conveyed out of the body from the bladder, and which in male vertebrates also conveys semen.
– DERIVATIVES **u·re·thral adj.**
– ORIGIN mid 17th cent.: from late Latin, from Greek *ourēthra*, from *ourein* 'urinate.'

u·re·thri·tis /ˌyo͞orəˈᴛʜrītis/ ▶ **n.** Medicine inflammation of the urethra.

U·rey /ˈyo͞orē/, Harold Clayton (1893–1981), US chemist. He discovered deuterium in 1932, pioneered the use of isotope labeling, and served as director of the Manhattan Project at Columbia University. Nobel Prize for Chemistry (1934).

Ur·ga /ˈo͞orgə/ former name (until 1924) of **ULAANBAATAR**.

urge /ərj/ ▶ **v.** [with obj. and usu. infinitive] try earnestly or persistently to persuade (someone) to do something: *he urged her to come and stay with us* | [with direct speech] *"Try to relax," she urged.* ■ recommend or advocate (something) strongly: *I urge caution in interpreting these results* | [with clause] *they are urging that more treatment facilities be provided.* ■ [with obj.] encourage (a person or animal) to move more quickly or in a particular direction: *drawing up outside the house, he urged her inside.* ■ (**urge someone on**) encourage someone to continue or succeed in something: *he could hear her voice urging him on.*
▶ **n.** a strong desire or impulse: *the urge for revenge.*
– ORIGIN mid 16th cent.: from Latin *urgere* 'press, drive.'

ur·gen·cy /ˈərjənsē/ ▶ **n. 1** importance requiring swift action: *the discovery of the ozone hole gave urgency to the issue of CFCs.*
2 an earnest and persistent quality; insistence: *Emilia heard the urgency in his voice.*

ur·gent /ˈərjənt/ ▶ **adj.** (of a state or situation) requiring immediate action or attention: *the situation is far more urgent than politicians are admitting.* ■ (of action or an event) done or arranged in response to such a situation: *she needs urgent treatment.* ■ (of a person or their manner) earnest and persistent in response to such a situation: *an urgent whisper.*
– DERIVATIVES **ur·gent·ly adv.**
– ORIGIN late 15th cent.: from Old French, from Latin *urgent-* 'pressing, driving,' from the verb *urgere* (see **URGE**).

-uria ▶ **comb. form** in nouns denoting that a substance is present in the urine, esp. in excess: *glycosuria.*
– ORIGIN modern Latin, from Greek *-ouria*, from *ouron* 'urine.'

U·ri·ah /yo͞oˈrīə/ (in the Bible) a Hittite officer in David's army, whom David, desiring his wife Bathsheba, caused to be killed in battle.

ur·i·al /ˈo͝orēəl/ ▶ **n.** (pl. **same**) a wild sheep with long legs and relatively small horns, native to central Asia. ● *Ovis vignei*, family Bovidae.
– ORIGIN mid 19th cent.: from Punjabi *ūrīal*.

u·ric ac·id /ˈyo͞orik/ ▶ **n.** Biochemistry an almost insoluble compound that is a breakdown product of nitrogenous metabolism. It is the main excretory product in birds, reptiles, and insects. ● A bicyclic acid derived from purine; chem. formula: $C_5H_4N_4O_3$.
– ORIGIN early 19th cent.: *uric* from French *urique*, from *urine* (see **URINE**).

u·ri·dine /ˈyo͝orəˌdēn, -dn/ ▶ **n.** Biochemistry a compound formed by partial hydrolysis of RNA. It is a nucleoside containing uracil linked to ribose.
– ORIGIN early 20th cent.: from *ur(acil)* + **-IDE** + **-INE**[4].

U·rim and Thum·mim /ˈ(y)o͝orim, o͞oˈrēm and ˈᴛʜəmim, to͞oˈmēm/ ▶ **plural n.** historical two objects of a now unknown nature, possibly used for divination, worn on the breastplate of a Jewish high priest.
– ORIGIN from Hebrew.

u·ri·nal /ˈyo͝orənl/ ▶ **n.** a bowl or other receptacle, typically attached to a wall in a public toilet, into which men may urinate.
– ORIGIN Middle English (denoting a glass container for the medical inspection of urine): via Old French from Latin *urinal*, from *urina* (see **URINE**).

u·ri·nal·y·sis /ˌyo͝orəˈnaləsis/ ▶ **n.** (pl. **urinalyses** /-ˌsēz/) Medicine analysis of urine by physical, chemical, and microscopical means to test for the presence of disease, drugs, etc.

u·ri·nar·y /ˈyo͝orəˌnerē/ ▶ **adj.** of or relating to urine. ■ of, relating to, or denoting the system of organs, structures, and ducts by which urine is produced and discharged, in mammals comprising the kidneys, ureters, bladder, and urethra.

u·ri·nate /ˈyo͝orəˌnāt/ ▶ **v.** [no obj.] discharge urine; pass water.
– DERIVATIVES **u·ri·na·tion** /ˌyo͝orəˈnāsʜən/ **n.**
– ORIGIN late 16th cent.: from medieval Latin *urinat-* 'urinated,' from the verb *urinare*.

u·rine /ˈyo͝orən/ ▶ **n.** a watery, typically yellowish fluid stored in the bladder and discharged through the urethra. It is one of the body's chief means of eliminating excess water and salt and also contains nitrogen compounds such as urea and other waste substances removed from the blood by the kidneys.
– ORIGIN Middle English: via Old French from Latin *urina*.

u·ri·nif·er·ous tu·bule /ˌyo͝orəˈnif(ə)rəs ˈt(y)o͞oˌbyo͞ol/ ▶ **n.** another term for **KIDNEY TUBULE**.

Ur·is /ˈyo͝orəs/, Leon (Marcus) (1924–2003) US writer. His works include *Battle Cry* (1953), *Exodus* (1958), *QB VII* (1970), *Trinity* (1976), *The Haj* (1984), and *Redemption* (1995).

URL ▶ **abbr.** Computing uniform (or universal) resource locator, the address of a web page.

urn /ərn/ ▶ **n. 1** a tall, rounded vase with a base, and often a stem, esp. one used for storing the ashes of a cremated person.
2 a large metal container with a tap, in which tea or coffee is made and kept hot, or water for making such drinks is boiled: *a tea urn.*
▶ **v.** [with obj.] archaic place (something) in an urn.
– ORIGIN late Middle English: from Latin *urna*; related to *urceus* 'pitcher.'

urn 1

uro-[1] ▶ **comb. form** of or relating to urine or the urinary organs: *urogenital.*
– ORIGIN from Greek *ouron* 'urine.'

uro-[2] ▶ **comb. form** Zoology relating to a tail or the caudal region: *urodele.*
– ORIGIN from Greek *oura* 'tail.'

u·ro·bo·ros /ˌ(y)o͝orəˈbôrəs/ (also **ouroboros**) ▶ **n.** a circular symbol depicting a snake, or less commonly a dragon, swallowing its tail, as an emblem of wholeness or infinity.
– DERIVATIVES **u·ro·bo·ric** /-ˈbôrik/ **adj.**
– ORIGIN 1940s: from Greek (*drakōn*) *ouroboros* '(snake) devouring its tail.'

Ur·o·chor·da·ta /ˌyo͝orəkôrˈdätə, -ˈdātə/ Zoology a group of chordate animals that comprises the tunicates. ● Subphylum Urochordata, phylum Chordata.
– ORIGIN modern Latin (plural), from **URO-**[2] 'tail' + **CHORDATA**.

u·ro·chor·date /ˌyo͝orəˈkôrdət, -ˌdāt/ Zoology ▶ **n.** a marine invertebrate of the group Urochordata, which comprises the tunicates.
▶ **adj.** relating to or denoting urochordates.

Ur·o·de·la /ˌyo͝orəˈdēlə/ Zoology an order of amphibians that comprises the newts and salamanders, which retain the tail as adults. Also called **CAUDATA**.
– ORIGIN modern Latin (plural), from **URO-**[2] 'tail' + Greek *dēlos* 'evident.'

u·ro·dele /'yo͞orə,dēl/ ▸ **n.** Zoology an amphibian of the order Urodela; a newt or salamander.

u·ro·dy·nam·ics /,yo͞orədī'namiks/ ▸ **plural n.** [treated as sing.] Medicine the diagnostic study of pressure in the bladder, in treating incontinence.
- DERIVATIVES **u·ro·dy·nam·ic adj.**

u·ro·gen·i·tal /,yo͞orō'jenətl, ,yo͞orə-/ ▸ **adj.** of, relating to, or denoting both the urinary and genital organs.

u·rog·ra·phy /yo͞o'rägrəfē/ ▸ **n.** another term for **PYELOGRAPHY**.
- DERIVATIVES **u·ro·gram** /'yo͞orə,gram/ **n.**

u·ro·ki·nase /,yo͞orō'kī,nās, -,nāz/ ▸ **n.** Biochemistry an enzyme produced in the kidneys that promotes the conversion of plasminogen to plasmin and can be used to dissolve blood clots.

u·ro·lag·nia /,yo͞orō'lagnēə/ ▸ **n.** a tendency to derive sexual pleasure from the sight or thought of urination. Also called **UROPHILIA**.
- ORIGIN early 20th cent.: from **URO-**[1] 'of urine' + Greek *lagneia* 'lust.'

u·ro·li·thi·a·sis /,yo͞orələ'THīəsis/ ▸ **n.** Medicine the formation of stony concretions in the bladder or urinary tract.

u·rol·o·gy /yo͞o'räləjē/ ▸ **n.** the branch of medicine and physiology concerned with the function and disorders of the urinary system.
- DERIVATIVES **u·ro·log·ic** /,yo͞orə'läjik/ **adj.**, **u·ro·log·i·cal adj.**, **u·rol·o·gist** /-jist/ **n.**

u·ron·ic ac·id /yo͞o'ränik/ ▸ **n.** Biochemistry any of a class of compounds that are derived from sugars by oxidizing a $-CH_2OH$ group to an acid group ($-COOH$).
- ORIGIN 1920s: *uronic* from **URO-**[1] 'urine' + **-IC**, with the insertion of *-n-*.

u·ro·phil·i·a /,yo͞orō'filēə/ ▸ **n.** another term for **UROLAGNIA**.

u·ro·pod /'yo͞orə,päd/ ▸ **n.** Zoology the sixth and last pair of abdominal appendages of lobsters and related crustaceans, forming part of the tail fan.
- ORIGIN late 19th cent.: from **URO-**[2] 'tail' + Greek *pous, pod-* 'pod.'

u·ro·pyg·i·al gland /,yo͞orə'pijēəl/ ▸ **n.** another term for **PREEN GLAND**.

u·ro·pyg·i·um /,yo͞orə'pijēəm/ ▸ **n.** Zoology the rump of a bird, supporting the tail feathers.
- DERIVATIVES **u·ro·pyg·i·al adj.**
- ORIGIN late 18th cent.: via medieval Latin from Greek *ouropugion*.

u·ros·co·py /yo͞o'räskəpē/ ▸ **n.** Medicine, historical the diagnostic examination of urine by simple inspection.

u·ro·style /'yo͞orə,stīl/ ▸ **n.** Zoology a long bone formed from fused vertebrae at the base of the vertebral column in some lower vertebrates, esp. frogs and toads.

Ur·sa Ma·jor /'ərsə 'mājər/ Astronomy one of the largest and most prominent northern constellations (the Great Bear). The seven brightest stars form a familiar asterism known by various names (esp. the Big Dipper and the Plow) and include the Pointers. ■ (as genitive **Ursae Majoris** /'ərsē mə'jôris/) used with a preceding letter or numeral to designate a star in this constellation: *the star Delta Ursae Majoris*.
- ORIGIN Latin, 'Big Bear,' from the story in Greek mythology that the nymph Callisto was turned into a bear and placed as a constellation in the heavens by Zeus.

Ur·sa Mi·nor /'ərsə 'mīnər/ Astronomy a northern constellation (the Little Bear) that contains the north celestial pole and the polar star Polaris. The brightest stars form a shape that is also known as the Little Dipper. ■ (as genitive **Ursae Minoris** /'ərsē mi'nôris/) used with a preceding letter or numeral to designate a star in this constellation: *the star Alpha Ursae Minoris*.
- ORIGIN Latin 'Little Bear.'

ur·sine /'ər,sīn, -,sēn/ ▸ **adj.** of, relating to, or resembling bears.
- ORIGIN mid 16th cent.: from Latin *ursinus*, from *ursus* 'bear.'

Ur·su·la, St. /'ərs(y)ələ/ a legendary British saint and martyr, said to have been put to death with 11,000 virgins after being captured by Huns near Cologne while on a pilgrimage.

Ur·su·line /'ərs(y)əlin, -,līn, -,lēn/ ▸ **n.** a nun of an order founded by **St. Angela Merici** (1470–1540) at Brescia in 1535 for nursing the sick and teaching girls.
▸ **adj.** of or relating to this order.
- ORIGIN from St. *Ursula*, the founder's patron saint (see **URSULA, ST.**), + **-INE**[1].

ur·text /'o͞or,tekst/ ▸ **n.** (pl. **urtexte** /-,tekstə/ or **urtexts**) an original or the earliest version of a text, to which later versions can be compared.
- ORIGIN from German.

ur·ti·car·i·a /,ərti'ke(ə)rēə/ ▸ **n.** Medicine a rash of round, red welts on the skin that itch intensely, sometimes with dangerous swelling, caused by an allergic reaction, typically to specific foods. Also called **NETTLERASH** or **HIVES**.
- ORIGIN late 18th cent.: modern Latin, from Latin *urtica* 'nettle,' from *urere* 'to burn.'

ur·ti·cate /'ərti,kāt/ ▸ **v.** [no obj.] cause a stinging or prickling sensation like that given by a nettle: (as adj. **urticating**) *the urticating hairs*.
- DERIVATIVES **ur·ti·ca·tion** /,ərti'kāSHən/ **n.**
- ORIGIN mid 19th cent.: from medieval Latin *urticat-* 'stung,' from the verb *urticare*, from Latin *urtica* (see **URTICARIA**).

U·ru·guay /'(y)o͞orə,gwī, -,gwā/ a country on the Atlantic coast of South America south of Brazil; pop. 3,494,400 (est. 2009); official language, Spanish; capital, Montevideo.

> Uruguay was liberated from Spanish colonial rule in 1825, and in the early 20th century was molded into South America's first welfare state. Civil unrest beginning in the 1960s, and particularly fighting against the Marxist Tupamaro guerrillas, led to a period of military rule, but civilian government was restored in 1985.

- DERIVATIVES **U·ru·guay·an** /,(y)o͞orə'gwīən, -'gwā-/ **adj. & n.**

U·ruk /'o͞oro͝ok/ an ancient city in southern Mesopotamia, northwest of Ur, one of the greatest cities of Sumer. Built in the 5th millennium BC, it is associated with the hero Gilgamesh. Arabic name **WARKA**; biblical name **ERECH**.

U·rum·qi /'o͞o'ro͝om'CHē/ (also **Urumchi**) the capital of Xinjiang autonomous region in northwestern China; pop. 1,504,300 (est. 2006). Former name (until 1954) **TIHWA**.

u·rus /'yo͞orəs/ ▸ **n.** another term for **AUROCHS**.
- ORIGIN early 17th cent.: from Latin, from Greek *ouros*.

u·ru·shi·ol /(y)o͞o'ro͞oshē,ôl, -,ōl, -,äl/ ▸ **n.** Biochemistry an oily liquid that is the main constituent of Japanese lacquer and is responsible for the irritant properties of poison ivy and other plants. It consists of a mixture of catechol derivatives.
- ORIGIN early 20th cent.: from Japanese *urushi* 'Japanese lacquer' + **-OL**.

US ▸ **abbr.** ■ (also **U.S.**) United States. ■ Brit. undersecretary. ■ Brit. informal unserviceable; useless.

us /əs/ ▸ **pron.** [first person plural] **1** used by a speaker to refer to himself or herself and one or more other people as the object of a verb or preposition: *let us know* | *we asked him to come with us* | *both of us*. Compare with **WE**. ■ used after the verb "to be" and after "than" or "as": *it's us or them* | *they are richer than us*. ■ informal to or for ourselves: *we got us some good hunting*.
2 informal me: *give us a kiss*.
- PHRASES **one of us** a person recognized as an accepted member of a particular group, typically one that is exclusive in some way. **us and them** (or **them and us**) expressing a sense of division within a group of people: *negotiations were hampered by an "us and them" attitude between management and unions*.
- ORIGIN Old English *ūs*, accusative and dative of **WE**, of Germanic origin; related to Dutch *ons* and German *uns*.

> **USAGE** Is it correct to say *they are richer than us*, or is it better to say *they are richer than we (are)*? See usage at **PERSONAL PRONOUN** and **THAN**.

USA (also **U.S.A.**) ▸ **abbr.** ■ United States of America. ■ United States Army.

us·a·ble /'yo͞ozəbəl/ (also **useable**) ▸ **adj.** able or fit to be used: *usable information*.
- DERIVATIVES **us·a·bil·i·ty** /,yo͞ozə'bilətē/ **n.**

USAF (also **U.S.A.F.**) ▸ **abbr.** United States Air Force.

us·age /'yo͞osij, -zij/ ▸ **n.** the action of using something or the fact of being used: *a survey of water usage* | *the usage of equipment*. ■ the way in which a word or phrase is normally and correctly used. ■ habitual or customary practice, esp. as creating a right, obligation, or standard.
- ORIGIN Middle English (in the sense 'customary practice'): from Old French, from *us* 'a use' (see **USE**).

us·ance /'yo͞ozəns/ ▸ **n.** archaic **1** another term for **USAGE**.
2 the time allowed for the payment of foreign bills of exchange, according to law or commercial practice.
- ORIGIN late Middle English: from Old French, from the base of the verb *user* 'to use.'

USB ▸ **abbr.** Computing universal serial bus, a standardized technology for attaching peripheral devices to a computer.

USB flash drive (also **USB stick**) ▸ **n.** Computing an external flash drive, small enough to carry on a key ring, that can be used with any computer that has a USB port.

USC ▸ **abbr.** Law United States Code.

USCG (also **U.S.C.G.**) ▸ **abbr.** United States Coast Guard.

USD ▸ **abbr.** United States dollar.

USDA (also **U.S.D.A.**) ▸ **abbr.** United States Department of Agriculture.

use ▸ **v. 1** /yo͞oz/ [with obj.] take, hold, or deploy (something) as a means of accomplishing a purpose or achieving a result; employ: *she used her key to open the front door* | *the poem uses simple language*. ■ take or consume (an amount) from a limited supply of something: *we have used all the available funds*. ■ exploit (a person or situation) for one's own advantage: *I couldn't help feeling that she was using me*. ■ treat (someone) in a particular way: *use your troops well and they will not let you down*. ■ apply (a name or title) to oneself: *she still used her maiden name professionally*. ■ (**one could use**) informal one would like or benefit from: *I could use another cup of coffee*. ■ informal take (an illegal drug): *they were using heroin daily* | [no obj.] *had she been using again?*
2 /yo͞ost/ [in past] (**used to**) describing an action or state of affairs that was done repeatedly or existed for a period in the past: *this road used to be a dirt track* | *I used to give him lifts home*.
3 /yo͞ost/ (**be/get used to**) be or become familiar with someone or something through experience: *she was used to getting what she wanted* | *he's weird, but you just have to get used to him*.
▸ **n.** /yo͞os/ the action of using something or the state of being used for some purpose: *a member of staff is present when the pool is **in use*** | *theater owners were charging too much for **the use of** their venues*. ■ the ability or power to exercise or manipulate something, esp. one's mind or body: *the horse lost **the use of** his hind legs*. ■ a purpose for or way in which something can be used: *the herb has various culinary uses*. ■ the value or advantage of something: *it was no use trying to persuade her* | *what's the use of crying?* ■ Law, historical the benefit or profit of lands, esp. lands that are in the possession of another who holds them solely for the beneficiary. ■ the characteristic ritual and liturgy of a church or diocese. ■ the action of taking or habitual consumption of a drug.
- PHRASES **have its** (or **one's**) **uses** informal be useful on certain occasions or in certain respects. **have no use for** be unable to find a purpose for; have no need for: *he had no use for a single glove*. ■ informal dislike or be impatient with. **make use of** use for a purpose. ■ benefit from: *they were educated enough to make use of further training*. **use and wont** formal established custom. **use someone's name** quote someone as an authority or reference.
- PHRASAL VERBS **use something up** consume or expend the whole of something: *the money was soon used up*. ■ find a purpose for something that is left over: *I might use up all my odd scraps of wool to make a scarf*. ■ (**be used up**) informal (of a person) be worn out, esp. with overwork: *she was tired and used up*.
- ORIGIN Middle English: the noun from Old French *us*, from Latin *usus*, from *uti* 'to use'; the verb from Old French *user*, based on Latin *uti*.

> **USAGE 1** The construction **used to** is standard, but difficulties arise with the formation of negatives and questions. Traditionally, **used to** behaves as a modal verb, so that questions and negatives are formed without the auxiliary verb **do**, as in *it **used not to** be like that* and ***used** she **to** come here?* In modern English, this question form is now regarded as very formal or awkwardly old-fashioned, and the use with **do** is broadly accepted as standard, as in ***did** she **use to** come here?* Negative constructions with **do**, on the other hand (as in *it **didn't use to** be like that*), although common, are informal and are not generally accepted. **2** There is sometimes confusion over whether to use the form **used to** or **use to**, which has arisen largely because the pronunciation is the same in both cases. Except in negatives and questions, the correct form is **used to**: *we **used to** go to the movies all the time* (not *we **use to** go to the movies*). However, in negatives and questions using the auxiliary verb **do**, the correct form is **use to**, because the form of the verb required is the infinitive: ***I didn't use to** like mushrooms* (not ***I didn't used to** like mushrooms*). See also usage at **UTILIZE**.

PRONUNCIATION KEY ə **ago, up**; ər **over, fur**; a **hat**; ā **ate**; ä **car**; e **let**; ē **see**; i **fit**; ī **by**; NG **sing**; ō **go**; ô **law, for**; oi **toy**; o͝o **good**; o͞o **goo**; ou **out**; TH **thin**; T͟H **then**; ZH **vision**

U

use·a·ble ▶ adj. variant spelling of USABLE.

used /yo͞ozd/ ▶ adj. **1** having already been used: *scrawling on the back of a used envelope.* **2** secondhand: *a used car.*

use·ful /ˈyo͞osfəl/ ▶ adj. able to be used for a practical purpose or in several ways: *aspirin is useful for headaches.*
– PHRASES **make oneself useful** do something that is of some value or benefit to someone: *make yourself useful—get Jenny a drink.*
– DERIVATIVES **use·ful·ly** adv.

use·ful load ▶ n. the load able to be carried by an aircraft in addition to its own weight.

use·ful·ness /ˈyo͞osfəlnis/ ▶ n. the quality or fact of being useful: *faults that affect the book's usefulness.*

use·less /ˈyo͞osləs/ ▶ adj. not fulfilling or not expected to achieve the intended purpose or desired outcome: *a piece of useless knowledge | we tried to pacify him, but it was useless.* ■ informal having no ability or skill in a specified activity or area: *he was useless at football.*
– DERIVATIVES **use·less·ly** adv., **use·less·ness** n.

Use·net /ˈyo͞oz,net/ ▶ n. an early non-centralized computer network for the discussion of particular topics and the sharing of files via newsgroups.

us·er /ˈyo͞ozər/ ▶ n. **1** a person who uses or operates something, esp. a computer or other machine. ■ a person who takes illegal drugs; a drug user: *the drug causes long-term brain damage in users | a heroin user.* ■ a person who manipulates others for personal gain: *he was a gifted user of other people.* **2** Law the continued use or enjoyment of a right.

us·er-de·fin·a·ble ▶ adj. Computing having a function or meaning that can be specified and varied by a user.
– DERIVATIVES **us·er-de·fined** adj.

us·er-friend·ly ▶ adj. (of a machine or system) easy to use or understand: *the search software is user-friendly.*
– DERIVATIVES **us·er-friend·li·ness** n.

us·er-hos·tile ▶ adj. (of a machine or system) difficult to use or understand.

us·er in·ter·face ▶ n. Computing the means by which the user and a computer system interact, in particular the use of input devices and software.

us·er·name /ˈyo͞ozər,nām/ ▶ n. an identification used by a person with access to a computer, network, or online service.

us·er-o·ri·ent·ed ▶ adj. (of a machine or system) designed primarily for the user's convenience.

ush·er /ˈəsHər/ ▶ n. **1** a person who shows people to their seats, esp. in a theater or at a wedding. ■ an official in a court whose duties include swearing in jurors and witnesses and keeping order. ■ Brit. a person employed to walk before a person of high rank on special occasions. **2** Brit. archaic an assistant teacher.
▶ v. [with obj.] **1** show or guide (someone) somewhere: *a waiter ushered me to a table.* **2** (**usher something in**) cause or mark the start of something new: *the railroads ushered in an era of cheap mass travel.*
– ORIGIN late Middle English (denoting a doorkeeper): from Anglo-Norman French *usser*, from medieval Latin *ustiarius*, from Latin *ostiarius*, from *ostium* 'door.'

ush·er·ette /,əsHəˈret/ ▶ n. a woman who shows people to their seats in a theater.

Us·hua·ia /o͞oˈswīə/ a port in Argentina, in Tierra del Fuego; pop. 74,400 (est. 2009). It is the southernmost town in the world.

USIA (also **U.S.I.A.**) ▶ abbr. United States Information Agency.

Üs·kü·dar /,o͞oskəˈdär/ a city in northwestern Turkey, across from Istanbul on the Bosporus where it joins the Sea of Marmara; pop. 643,800 (est. 2009). Former name SCUTARI.

USMC (also **U.S.M.C.**) ▶ abbr. United States Marine Corps.

USN (also **U.S.N.**) ▶ abbr. United States Navy.

us·nic ac·id /ˈəsnik/ ▶ n. Biochemistry a yellow crystalline compound that is present in many lichens and is used as an antibiotic. ● A tricyclic phenol; chem. formula: $C_{18}H_{16}O_7$.
– ORIGIN mid 19th cent.: *usnic* from medieval Latin *usnea* (from Arabic *ushnah* 'moss') + -IC.

USO ▶ abbr. ■ ultra stable oscillator. ■ United Service Organizations.

U·so·ni·an /yo͞oˈsōnēən/ ▶ adj. of or relating to the United States: *the Usonian city.* ■ relating to or denoting the style of buildings designed in the 1930s by Frank Lloyd Wright, characterized by inexpensive construction and flat roofs.
▶ n. a native or inhabitant of the United States. ■ a house built in the 1930s by Frank Lloyd Wright.
– ORIGIN early 20th cent.: an acronym from *United States* + *-onian* after *Amazonian, Devonian*, etc.

USP ▶ n. (pl. **USPs**) unique selling point.

Us·pa·lla·ta Pass /,o͞ospäˈyätə/ a pass over the Andes near Santiago in Chile, in southern South America. It links Argentina with Chile.

USPS (also **U.S.P.S.**) ▶ abbr. United States Postal Service.

us·que·baugh /ˈəskwə,bô, -,bä/ ▶ n. chiefly Irish Scottish whiskey.
– ORIGIN late 16th cent.: from Irish and Scottish Gaelic *uisge beatha* 'water of life'; compare with WHISKEY.

USS (also **U.S.S.**) ▶ abbr. United States Ship, used in the names of ships in the US Navy: *the U.S.S. Maine was launched in 1895.*

USSR ▶ abbr. historical Union of Soviet Socialist Republics.

Ust-A·ba·kan·sko·e /,o͞ost ,äbəˈkänskəyə/ former name (until 1931) of ABAKAN.

U·sta·she /o͞oˈstäsHē/ (also **Ustashas** or **Ustashi**) ▶ plural n. [treated as sing. or pl.] the members of a Croatian extreme nationalist movement that engaged in terrorist activity before World War II and ruled Croatia with Nazi support after Yugoslavia was invaded and divided by the Germans in 1941.
– ORIGIN Croatian *Ustaše* 'rebels.'

U·sti·nov /ˈyo͞ostə,nôf, -,nôv, o͞oˈstēnəf/ former name (1984–87) of IZHEVSK.

usu. ▶ abbr. usual; usually.

u·su·al /ˈyo͞ozHo͞oəl/ ▶ adj. habitually or typically occurring or done; customary: *he carried out his usual evening routine | their room was a shambles as usual.*
▶ n. (**the/one's usual**) informal the drink someone habitually orders or prefers. ■ the thing that is typically done or present: *it's a nice change from the usual.*
– DERIVATIVES **u·su·al·ness** n.
– ORIGIN late Middle English: from Old French, or from late Latin *usualis*, from Latin *usus* 'a use' (see USE).

u·su·al·ly /ˈyo͞ozHo͞oəlē/ ▶ adv. under normal conditions; generally: *he usually arrives home about one o'clock.*

u·su·fruct /ˈyo͞ozə,frəkt, -sə-/ ▶ n. Roman Law the right to enjoy the use and advantages of another's property short of the destruction or waste of its substance.
– DERIVATIVES **u·su·fruc·tu·ar·y** /,yo͞ozəˈfrəkCHo͞o,erē, -sə-/ adj. & n.
– ORIGIN early 17th cent.: from medieval Latin *usufructus*, from Latin *usus (et) fructus* 'use (and) enjoyment,' from *usus* 'a use' + *fructus* 'fruit.'

U·sum·bu·ra /,o͞osəmˈbo͝orə/ former name (until 1962) of BUJUMBURA.

u·su·rer /ˈyo͞ozHərər/ ▶ n. a person who lends money at unreasonably high rates of interest.
– ORIGIN Middle English: from Anglo-Norman French, from Old French *usure*, from Latin *usura* (see USURY).

u·su·ri·ous /yo͞oˈzHo͝orēəs/ ▶ adj. of or relating to the practice of usury: *they lend money at usurious rates.*
– DERIVATIVES **u·su·ri·ous·ly** adv.

u·surp /yo͞oˈsərp/ ▶ v. [with obj.] take (a position of power or importance) illegally or by force: *Richard usurped the throne.* ■ take the place of (someone in a position of power) illegally; supplant: *the Hanoverian dynasty had usurped the Stuarts.* ■ [no obj.] (**usurp on/upon**) archaic encroach or infringe upon (someone's rights): *the Church had usurped upon the domain of the state.*
– DERIVATIVES **u·sur·pa·tion** /,yo͞osərˈpāsHən/ n., **u·surp·er** n.
– ORIGIN Middle English (in the sense 'appropriate (a right) wrongfully'): from Old French *usurper*, from Latin *usurpare* 'seize for use.'

u·su·ry /ˈyo͞ozH(ə)rē/ ▶ n. the illegal action or practice of lending money at unreasonably high rates of interest. ■ archaic interest at such rates.
– ORIGIN Middle English: from Anglo-Norman French *usurie*, or from medieval Latin *usuria*, from Latin *usura*, from *usus* 'a use' (see USE).

UT ▶ abbr. ■ Universal Time. ■ Utah (in official postal use).

U·tah /ˈyo͞o,tô, -,tä/ a state in the western US; pop. 2,736,424 (est. 2008); capital, Salt Lake City; statehood, Jan. 4, 1896 (45). The region, a part of Mexico from 1821, was ceded to the US in 1848. The first permanent settlers, who arrived in 1847, were Mormons fleeing persecution. Statehood was refused until the Mormons renounced polygamy—a dispute that led to the Utah War 1857–58.
– DERIVATIVES **U·tah·an** /-tô(ə)n, -ˈtä(ə)n/ adj. & n.

U·tah Beach a name given to the westernmost of the beaches, north of Carentan in Normandy, where US troops landed on D-day in June 1944.

u·tah·rap·tor /ˈyo͞o,tô,raptər, -,tä-/ ▶ n. a large dromaeosaurid dinosaur, the remains of which were discovered in Utah in 1992. It was twice the size of deinonychus. ● Genus *Utahraptor*, family Dromaeosauridae, suborder Theropoda.
– ORIGIN modern Latin, from UTAH + RAPTOR.

U·ta·ma·ro /,o͞otəˈmärō/, Kitagawa (1753–1806), Japanese painter and printmaker; born *Kitagawa Netsuyoshi*. A leading exponent of the ukiyo-e school, he was noted for his sensual depictions of women.

UTC ▶ abbr. Universal Time Coordinated. Also expanded as COORDINATED UNIVERSAL TIME.

Ute /yo͞ot/ ▶ n. (pl. **same** or **Utes**) **1** a member of an American Indian people living chiefly in Colorado and Utah. **2** the Uto-Aztecan language of this people.
▶ adj. of or relating to this people or their language.
– ORIGIN from earlier *Utah*, from Spanish *Yuta*; compare with PAIUTE.

ute /yo͞ot/ ▶ n. informal a utility vehicle: *ordinary families buy pickups and sport utes.*
– ORIGIN 1940s: abbreviation.

u·ten·sil /yo͞oˈtensəl/ ▶ n. an implement, container, or other article, esp. for household use.
– ORIGIN late Middle English (denoting domestic implements or vessels collectively): from Old French *utensile*, from medieval Latin, neuter of Latin *utensilis* 'usable,' from *uti* 'to use' (see USE).

u·ter·i /ˈyo͞otə,rī, -,rē/ plural form of UTERUS.

u·ter·ine /ˈyo͞otərin, -,rīn/ ▶ adj. of or relating to the uterus or womb: *uterine contractions.* ■ [attrib.] born of the same mother but not having the same father: *a uterine sister.*
– ORIGIN late Middle English: from UTERUS + -INE[1], or, in the sense 'born of the same mother,' from late Latin *uterinus*.

u·ter·us /ˈyo͞otərəs/ ▶ n. (pl. **uteri** /ˈyo͞otə,rī, -,rē/) the organ in the lower body of a woman or female mammal where offspring are conceived and in which they gestate before birth; the womb.
– ORIGIN Latin; related to Greek *hustera*. Compare with HYSTERIC.

U·ther Pen·drag·on /ˈ(y)o͞oTHər penˈdragən/ (in Arthurian legend) king of the Britons and father of Arthur.

U·ti·ca /ˈyo͞otikə/ an industrial city in central New York, on the Mohawk River; pop. 58,082 (est. 2008).

u·tile[1] /ˈyo͞otl, ˈyo͞o,tīl/ ▶ adj. rare advantageous.
– ORIGIN late 15th cent.: via Old French from Latin *utilis*, from *uti* 'to use.'

u·ti·le[2] /ˈyo͞otl-ē/ ▶ n. a large tropical African hardwood tree with timber that is widely used as a substitute for mahogany. ● *Entandrophragma utile*, family Meliaceae.
– ORIGIN 1950s: modern Latin, specific epithet; see UTILE[1].

u·til·i·tar·i·an /yo͞o,tiliˈte(ə)rēən/ ▶ adj. **1** designed to be useful or practical rather than attractive. **2** Philosophy of, relating to, or adhering to the doctrine of utilitarianism: *a utilitarian theorist.*
▶ n. Philosophy an adherent of utilitarianism.

u·til·i·tar·i·an·ism /yo͞o,tiləˈte(ə)rēə,nizəm/ ▶ n. the doctrine that actions are right if they are useful or for the benefit of a majority. ■ the doctrine that an action is right insofar as it promotes happiness, and that the greatest happiness of the greatest number should be the guiding principle of conduct.

u·til·i·ty /yo͞oˈtilətē/ ▶ n. (pl. **utilities**) **1** the state of being useful, profitable, or beneficial: *he had a poor opinion of the utility of book learning.* ■ (in game theory or economics) a measure of that which is sought to be maximized in any situation involving a choice. **2** a public utility. ■ (**utilities**) stocks and bonds in public utilities. **3** Computing a utility program.
▶ adj. [attrib.] **1** useful, esp. through being able to perform several functions: *a utility truck.* ■ denoting a player capable of playing in several different positions in a sport. **2** functional rather than attractive: *utility clothing.* **3** of or relating to the lowest US government grade of beef.
– ORIGIN late Middle English: from Old French *utilite*, from Latin *utilitas*, from *utilis* 'useful.'

u·til·i·ty func·tion ▶ n. Economics a mathematical function that ranks alternatives according to their utility to an individual.

u·til·i·ty knife ▶ n. a knife with a small sharp blade, often retractable, designed to cut wood, cardboard, and other materials.

u·til·i·ty pole ▶ n. another term for TELEPHONE POLE.

U

u·til·i·ty pro·gram ▶ **n.** Computing a program for carrying out a routine function.

u·til·i·ty room ▶ **n.** a room equipped with appliances for washing and other domestic work.

u·til·i·ty ve·hi·cle (also **utility truck**) ▶ **n.** a truck with low sides designed for carrying small loads.

u·ti·lize /ˈyo͞otl,īz/ ▶ **v.** [with obj.] make practical and effective use of: *vitamin C helps your body utilize the iron present in your diet.*
– DERIVATIVES **u·ti·liz·a·ble** /,yo͞otlˈīzəbəl, ˈyo͞otl,ī-/ **adj.**, **u·ti·li·za·tion** /,yo͞otl-əˈzāsʜən/ **n.**, **u·ti·liz·er n.**
– ORIGIN early 19th cent.: from French *utiliser*, from Italian *utilizzare*, from *utile* (see UTILE[1]).

> **USAGE Utilize,** borrowed in the 19th century from the French *utiliser*, means 'make practical or effective use of.' Because it is a more formal word than **use** and is often used in contexts (as in business writing) where the ordinary verb **use** would be simpler and more direct, **utilize** may strike readers as pretentious jargon and should therefore be used sparingly.

-ution ▶ **suffix** (forming nouns) equivalent to -ATION (as in *solution*).
– ORIGIN via French from Latin *-utio(n-)*.

ut·most /ˈət,mōst/ ▶ **adj.** [attrib.] most extreme; greatest: *a matter of the utmost importance.*
▶ **n.** (**the utmost**) the greatest or most extreme extent or amount: *a plot that stretches credulity to the utmost.*
– PHRASES **do one's utmost** do the most that one is able: *Dan was doing his utmost to be helpful.*
– ORIGIN Old English *ūt(e)mest* 'outermost' (see OUT, -MOST).

U·to-Az·tec·an /ˈyo͞otō'az,tekən/ ▶ **n.** a language family of Central America and western North America including Comanche, Hopi, Nahuatl (the language of the Aztecs), Paiute, Pima, and Shoshone.
▶ **adj.** of, relating to, or denoting this language family.

U·to·pi·a /yo͞oˈtōpēə/ (also **utopia**) ▶ **n.** an imagined place or state of things in which everything is perfect. The word was first used in the book *Utopia* (1516) by Sir Thomas More. The opposite of DYSTOPIA.
– ORIGIN based on Greek *ou* 'not' + *topos* 'place.'

U·to·pi·an /yo͞oˈtōpēən/ ▶ **adj.** modeled on or aiming for a state in which everything is perfect; idealistic.
▶ **n.** an idealistic reformer.
– DERIVATIVES **u·to·pi·an·ism** /-,nizəm/ **n.**

U·to·pi·an so·cial·ism ▶ **n.** socialism achieved by the moral persuasion of capitalists to surrender the means of production peacefully to the people.

U·trecht /ˈyo͞o,trekt, ˈY,trekʜt/ a city in the central Netherlands, capital of a province of the same name; pop. 294,737 (2008).

U·trecht vel·vet ▶ **n.** a strong, thick plush velvet, used in upholstery.

u·tri·cle /ˈyo͞otrəkəl/ ▶ **n.** a small cell, sac, or bladderlike protuberance in an animal or plant. ■ (also **utriculus** /yo͞oˈtrikyələs/) the larger of the two fluid-filled cavities forming part of the labyrinth of the inner ear (the other being the sacculus). It contains hair cells and otoliths that send signals to the brain concerning the orientation of the head.
– DERIVATIVES **u·tric·u·lar** /yo͞oˈtrikyələr/ **adj.**
– ORIGIN mid 18th cent.: from French *utricule* or Latin *utriculus*, diminutive of *uter* 'leather bag.'

U·tril·lo /o͞oˈtrē(y)ō, yo͞oˈtrilō/, Maurice (1883–1955), French painter, chiefly known for his depictions of Paris street scenes, esp. of the Montmartre district.

Ut·tar·ak·hand /,o͞otərˈəkhənd/ a state in northern India, formed in 2000 from the northern part of Uttar Pradesh; capital, Dehra Dun. Former name (until 2007) **Uttaranchal** /,o͞otərˈəncʜəl/.

Ut·tar Pra·desh /ˈo͞otər prəˈdāsʜ, -ˈdesʜ/ a state in northern India that borders on Tibet and Nepal; capital, Lucknow. It was formed in 1950 from the United Provinces of Agra and Oudh.

ut·ter[1] /ˈətər/ ▶ **adj.** [attrib.] complete; absolute: *Charles stared at her in utter amazement.*
– ORIGIN Old English *ūtera, ūttra* 'outer,' comparative of *ūt* 'out'; compare with OUTER.

ut·ter[2] ▶ **v.** [with obj.] **1** make (a sound) with one's voice: *he uttered an exasperated snort.* ■ say (something) aloud: *they are busily scribbling down every word she utters.*
2 Law put (forged money) into circulation.
– DERIVATIVES **ut·ter·a·ble adj.**, **ut·ter·er n.**
– ORIGIN late Middle English: from Middle Dutch *ūteren* 'speak, make known, give currency to (coins).'

ut·ter·ance /ˈətərəns/ ▶ **n.** a spoken word, statement, or vocal sound. ■ the action of saying or expressing something aloud: *the simple utterance of a few platitudes.* ■ Linguistics an uninterrupted chain of spoken or written language.

ut·ter·ly /ˈətərlē/ ▶ **adv.** [usu. as submodifier] completely and without qualification; absolutely: *he looked utterly ridiculous.*

ut·ter·most /ˈətər,mōst/ ▶ **adj.** & **n.** another term for UTMOST.

U-turn ▶ **n.** the turning of a vehicle in a U-shaped course so as to face in the opposite direction. ■ a change of plan, esp. a reversal of political policy: *another U-turn by the government.*

UV ▶ **abbr.** ultraviolet.

UVA ▶ **abbr.** ultraviolet radiation of relatively long wavelengths.

u·va·rov·ite /(y)o͞oˈvärə,vīt/ ▶ **n.** an emerald green variety of garnet, containing chromium.
– ORIGIN mid 19th cent.: from the name of Count Sergei S. *Uvarov* (1785–1855), Russian statesman, + -ITE[1].

UVB ▶ **abbr.** ultraviolet radiation of relatively short wavelengths.

u·ve·a /ˈyo͞ovēə/ ▶ **n.** the pigmented layer of the eye, lying beneath the sclera and cornea, and comprising the iris, choroid, and ciliary body.
– DERIVATIVES **u·ve·al adj.**
– ORIGIN late Middle English (denoting the choroid layer of the eye): from medieval Latin, from Latin *uva* 'grape.'

u·ve·i·tis /,yo͞ovēˈītis/ ▶ **n.** Medicine inflammation of the uvea.

u·vu·la /ˈyo͞ovyələ/ ▶ **n.** (pl. **uvulae** /-,lē, -,lī/ or **uvulas**) Anatomy (also **palatine uvula**) a fleshy extension at the back of the soft palate that hangs above the throat. ■ a similar fleshy hanging structure in any organ of the body, particularly one at the opening of the bladder.
– ORIGIN late Middle English: from late Latin, diminutive of Latin *uva* 'grape.'

u·vu·lar /ˈyo͞ovyələr/ ▶ **adj.** **1** Phonetics (of a sound) articulated with the back of the tongue and the uvula, as *r* in French and *q* in Arabic.
2 Anatomy of or relating to the uvula.
▶ **n.** Phonetics a uvular consonant.

UWB ▶ **abbr.** ultra wideband.

UXO ▶ **abbr.** unexploded ordnance.

ux·o·ri·al /,əkˈsôrēəl, əgˈzôr-/ ▶ **adj.** of or relating to a wife.
– ORIGIN early 19th cent.: from Latin *uxor* 'wife' + -IAL.

ux·o·ri·cide /,əkˈsôrə,sīd, ,əgˈzôr-/ ▶ **n.** the killing of one's wife. ■ a man who kills his wife.
– DERIVATIVES **ux·o·ri·cid·al** /ək,sôrəˈsīdl, əg,zôr-/ **adj.**
– ORIGIN mid 19th cent.: from Latin *uxor* 'wife' + -CIDE.

ux·o·ri·ous /,əkˈsôrēəs, ,əgˈzôr-/ ▶ **adj.** having or showing an excessive or submissive fondness for one's wife.
– DERIVATIVES **ux·o·ri·ous·ly adv.**, **ux·o·ri·ous·ness n.**
– ORIGIN late 16th cent.: from Latin *uxoriosus*, from *uxor* 'wife.'

Uy·gur ▶ **n.** & **adj.** variant spelling of UIGHUR.

Uz·bek /ˈo͞oz,bek, ˈəz-, o͞ozˈbek/ ▶ **n.** **1** a member of a Turkic people living mainly in the republic of Uzbekistan and elsewhere in southwestern Asia. ■ a native or inhabitant of Uzbekistan.
2 the Turkic language of Uzbekistan.
▶ **adj.** of or relating to Uzbekistan, the Uzbeks, or their language.
– ORIGIN the name in Uzbek.

Uz·bek·i·stan /o͞ozˈbekə,stan, əz-, -,stän/ an independent republic in central Asia that lies south and southeast of the Aral Sea; pop. 27,606,000 (est. 2009); capital, Tashkent; languages, Uzbek and Russian.

> A constituent republic of the Soviet Union since 1924, Uzbekistan became independent within the Commonwealth of Independent States when the Soviet Union broke up in 1991.

U·zi /ˈo͞ozē/ ▶ **n.** a type of submachine gun of Israeli design.
– ORIGIN 1950s: from *Uziel* Gal, the Israeli army officer who designed it.

U

PRONUNCIATION KEY ə *ago, up*; ər *over, fur*; a *hat*; ā *ate*; ä *car*; e *let*; ē *see*; i *fit*; ī *by*; NG *sing*; ō *go*; ô *law, for*; oi *toy*; o͝o *good*; o͞o *goo*; ou *out*; TH *thin*; T͟H *then*; ZH *vision*

Vv

V[1] /vē/ (also **v**) ▶ **n.** (pl. **Vs** or **V's**) **1** the twenty-second letter of the alphabet. ■ denoting the next after U in a set of items, categories, etc.
2 (also **vee**) a shape like that of a letter V: [in combination] *deep, V-shaped valleys.* ■ [as modifier] denoting an internal combustion engine with a number of cylinders arranged in two rows at an angle to each other in a V-shape: *a V-engine | a 32-valve V8 power plant.*
3 the Roman numeral for five.

V[2] ▶ **abbr.** volt(s). ▶ **symbol** ■ the chemical element vanadium. ■ voltage or potential difference: $V = IR$. ■ (in mathematical formulae) volume: $pV = nRT$.

v. ▶ **abbr.** ■ Grammar verb. ■ (in textual references) verse. ■ verso. ■ versus. ■ very. ■ (in textual references) vide. ▶ **symbol** velocity.

V-1 ▶ **n.** a small flying bomb powered by a simple jet engine, used by the Germans in World War II. Also called **DOODLEBUG**.
– ORIGIN abbreviation of German *Vergeltungswaffe* 'reprisal weapon.'

V-2 ▶ **n.** a rocket-powered flying bomb, which was the first ballistic missile, used by the Germans in World War II.
– ORIGIN see **V-1**.

VA ▶ **abbr.** ■ (in the UK) Order of Victoria and Albert. ■ Veterans Affairs (formerly Veterans Administration). ■ Vicar Apostolic. ■ Vice Admiral. ■ Virginia (in official postal use).

Va. ▶ **abbr.** Virginia.

Vaal /väl/ a river in South Africa, the chief tributary of the Orange River, which rises in the Drakensberg Mountains and flows 750 miles (1,200 km) southwest to the Orange River near Douglas.

Vaa·sa /'väsə, -sä/ a port in western Finland, on the Gulf of Bothnia; pop. 58,607 (2009). Swedish name **VASA**.

vac /vak/ ▶ **n. 1** informal term for **VACUUM CLEANER**.
2 Brit. informal term for **VACATION**.

va·can·cy /'vākənsē/ ▶ **n.** (pl. **vacancies**) **1** an unoccupied position or job: *a vacancy for a shorthand typist.* ■ an available room in a hotel or other establishment providing accommodations.
2 empty space: *Cathy stared into vacancy, seeing nothing.* ■ emptiness of mind; lack of intelligence or understanding: *vacancy, vanity, and inane deception.* ■ Crystallography a defect in a crystal lattice, consisting of the absence of an atom or an ion from a position where there should be one.

va·cant /'vākənt/ ▶ **adj.** (of premises) having no fixtures, furniture, or inhabitants; empty. Compare with **UNOCCUPIED** (sense 1). ■ (of a position or office) not filled: *the president resigned and the post was left vacant.* ■ (of a person or their expression) having or showing no intelligence or interest: *a vacant stare.*
– DERIVATIVES **va·cant·ly adv.**
– ORIGIN Middle English: from Old French, or from Latin *vacant-* 'remaining empty,' from the verb *vacare*.

va·cate /'vā,kāt/ ▶ **v.** [with obj.] **1** leave (a place that one previously occupied): *rooms must be vacated by noon on the last day of your vacation.* ■ give up (a position or office): *he will vacate a job in government sales.*
2 Law cancel or annul (a judgment, contract, or charge).
– ORIGIN mid 17th cent. (as a legal term, also in the sense 'make ineffective'): from Latin *vacat-* 'left empty,' from the verb *vacare*.

va·ca·tion /vā'kāsHən, və-/ ▶ **n. 1** an extended period of recreation, esp. one spent away from home or in traveling: *he took a vacation in the south of France | people come here **on vacation** |* [as modifier] *a vacation home.* ■ a fixed holiday period between terms in schools and law courts.
2 the action of leaving something one previously occupied: *his marriage was the reason for the vacation of his fellowship.*
▶ **v.** [no obj.] take a vacation: *I was vacationing in Europe with my family.*
– DERIVATIVES **va·ca·tion·er n.**, **va·ca·tion·ist** /-ist/ **n.**
– ORIGIN late Middle English: from Old French, or from Latin *vacatio(n-)*, from *vacare* 'be unoccupied' (see **VACATE**).

va·ca·tion·land /vā'kāsHən,land, və-/ ▶ **n.** an area providing attractions for people on vacation.

Vac·a·ville /'vakə,vil/ a city in west central California, southwest of Sacramento; pop. 92,219 (est. 2008).

vac·ci·nate /'vaksə,nāt/ ▶ **v.** [with obj.] treat with a vaccine to produce immunity against a disease; inoculate: *all the children **were vaccinated against** diphtheria.*
– DERIVATIVES **vac·ci·na·tion** /,vaksə'nāsHən/ **n.**, **vac·ci·na·tor** /-,nātər/ **n.**

vac·cine /vak'sēn/ ▶ **n.** Medicine a substance used to stimulate the production of antibodies and provide immunity against one or several diseases, prepared from the causative agent of a disease, its products, or a synthetic substitute, treated to act as an antigen without inducing the disease: *there is no **vaccine against** HIV infection.* ■ Computing a program designed to detect computer viruses and inactivate them.
– ORIGIN late 18th cent.: from Latin *vaccinus*, from *vacca* 'cow' (because of the early use of the cowpox virus against smallpox).

vac·cin·i·a /vak'sinēə/ ▶ **n.** Medicine cowpox, or the virus that causes it.
– ORIGIN early 19th cent.: modern Latin, from Latin *vaccinus* (see **VACCINE**).

vac·ci·nol·o·gy /,vaksɪ'näləji/ ▶ **n.** the branch of medicine concerned with the development of vaccines.
– DERIVATIVES **vac·ci·nol·o·gist n.**

Va·cher·in /,vasH(ə)'ran, ,väsH-/ ▶ **n.** a type of soft French or Swiss cheese made from cow's milk.
– ORIGIN French, from earlier *vachelin*, from *vache* 'cow.'

vac·il·late /'vasə,lāt/ ▶ **v.** [no obj.] alternate or waver between different opinions or actions; be indecisive: *I had for a time vacillated between teaching and journalism.*
– DERIVATIVES **vac·il·la·tion** /,vasə'lāsHən/ **n.**, **vac·il·la·tor** /-,lātər/ **n.**
– ORIGIN late 16th cent. (in the sense 'sway unsteadily'): from Latin *vacillat-* 'swayed,' from the verb *vacillare*.

vac·u·a /'vakyəwə/ plural form of **VACUUM**.

va·cu·i·ty /va'kyo͞oətē, və-/ ▶ **n. 1** lack of thought or intelligence; empty-headedness: *full of excitement, I listened to my first student sermon – only to be taken aback by its vacuity.*
2 empty space; emptiness.

vac·u·ole /'vakyo͞o,ōl/ ▶ **n.** Biology a space or vesicle within the cytoplasm of a cell, enclosed by a membrane and typically containing fluid. ■ a small cavity or space in tissue, esp. in nervous tissue as the result of disease.
– DERIVATIVES **vac·u·o·lar** /,vakyo͞o'ōlər, 'vakyo͞oələr/ **adj.**, **vac·u·o·la·tion** /,vakyo͞oə'lāsHən/ **n.**
– ORIGIN mid 19th cent.: from French, diminutive of Latin *vacuus* 'empty.'

vac·u·ous /'vakyəwəs/ ▶ **adj.** having or showing a lack of thought or intelligence; mindless: *a vacuous smile | vacuous slogans.* ■ archaic empty.
– DERIVATIVES **vac·u·ous·ly adv.**, **vac·u·ous·ness n.**
– ORIGIN mid 17th cent. (in the sense 'empty of matter'): from Latin *vacuus* 'empty' + **-ous**.

vac·u·um /'vak,yo͞o(ə)m, -yəm/ ▶ **n.** (pl. **vacuums** or **vacua** /-yo͞oə/) **1** a space entirely devoid of matter. ■ a space or container from which the air has been completely or partly removed. ■ [usu. in sing.] a gap left by the loss, death, or departure of someone or something formerly playing a significant part in a situation or activity: *the political vacuum left by the death of the Emperor.*
2 (pl. **vacuums**) a vacuum cleaner.
▶ **v.** [with obj.] clean with a vacuum cleaner: *the room needs to be vacuumed.*
– PHRASES **in a vacuum** (of an activity or a problem to be considered) isolated from the context normal to it and in which it can best be understood or assessed.
– ORIGIN mid 16th cent.: modern Latin, neuter of Latin *vacuus* 'empty.'

vac·u·um bot·tle ▶ **n.** another term for **THERMOS**.

vac·u·um brake ▶ **n.** a railroad-vehicle brake operated by changes in pressure in a continuous pipe that is generally kept exhausted of air by a pump and controls similar brakes throughout the train.

vac·u·um clean·er ▶ **n.** an electrical apparatus that by means of suction collects dust and small particles from floors and other surfaces.
– DERIVATIVES **vac·uum-clean v.**

vac·u·um dis·til·la·tion ▶ **n.** Chemistry distillation of a liquid under reduced pressure, enabling it to boil at a lower temperature than normal.

vac·u·um ex·trac·tion ▶ **n.** the application of reduced pressure to extract something, particularly to assist childbirth or as a method of abortion, or as a technique for removing components of a chemical mixture.

vac·u·um ex·trac·tor ▶ **n.** a cup-shaped appliance for performing vacuum extraction in childbirth. Also called **VENTOUSE**.

vac·u·um flask ▶ **n.** another term for **THERMOS**.

vac·u·um gauge ▶ **n.** a gauge for testing pressure after the production of a vacuum.

vac·u·um-pack ▶ **v.** [with obj.] seal (a product) in packaging after any air has been removed so that the packaging is tight and firm: *it is quickly vacuum-packed in foil pouches to ensure freshness |* (as adj. **vacuum-packed**) *vacuum-packed cheese.*

vac·u·um pump ▶ **n.** a pump used for creating a vacuum.

vac·u·um tube ▶ **n.** an electron tube containing a near-vacuum that allows the free passage of electric current.

va·de me·cum /,vädē 'mākəm, ,vādē 'mē-/ ▶ **n.** a handbook or guide that is kept constantly at hand for consultation.
– ORIGIN early 17th cent.: modern Latin, literally 'go with me,' from Latin *vadere* 'go,' from an Indo-European root shared by **WADE**.

Va·do·da·ra /və'dōdərə, -,rä/ a city in the state of Gujarat, western India; pop. 1,513,800 (est. 2009).

va·dose /'vā,dōs/ ▶ **adj.** relating to or denoting underground water above the water table. Compare with **PHREATIC**.
– ORIGIN late 19th cent.: from Latin *vadosus*, from *vadum* 'shallow expanse of water.'

Va·duz /vä'do͞ots, fä-/ the capital of Liechtenstein; pop. 5,000 (est. 2007).

vag·a·bond /ˈvagəˌbänd/ ▶ **n.** a person who wanders from place to place without a home or job. ■ informal, dated a rascal; a rogue.
▶ **adj.** [attrib.] having no settled home.
▶ **v.** [no obj.] archaic wander about as or like a vagabond.
– DERIVATIVES **vag·a·bond·age** /-dij/ **n.**
– ORIGIN Middle English (originally denoting a criminal): from Old French, or from Latin *vagabundus*, from *vagari* 'wander.'

va·gal /ˈvāgəl/ ▶ **adj.** of or relating to the vagus nerve.

va·gar·i·ous /vəˈge(ə)rēəs, vā-/ ▶ **adj.** rare erratic and unpredictable in behavior or direction.
– ORIGIN late 18th cent. (in the sense 'changing, inconstant'): from VAGARY + -OUS.

va·gar·y /ˈvāgərē/ ▶ **n.** (pl. **vagaries**) (usu. **vagaries**) an unexpected and inexplicable change in a situation or in someone's behavior: *the vagaries of the weather.*
– ORIGIN late 16th cent. (also as a verb in the sense 'roam'): from Latin *vagari* 'wander.'

va·gi /ˈvāˌgī, -ˌjī, -ˌgē, -ˌjē/ plural form of VAGUS.

va·gi·na /vəˈjīnə/ ▶ **n.** (pl. **vaginas** or **vaginae** /-nē, -nī/) the muscular tube leading from the external genitals to the cervix of the uterus in women and most female mammals. ■ Botany & Zoology any sheathlike structure, esp. a sheath formed around a stem by the base of a leaf.
– DERIVATIVES **vag·i·nal** /ˈvajənl/ **adj.**
– ORIGIN late 17th cent.: from Latin, literally 'sheath, scabbard,' which is also the source of the word VANILLA.

va·gi·na den·ta·ta /denˈtätə/ ▶ **n.** the motif of a vagina with teeth, occurring in folklore and fantasy and said to symbolize male fears of the dangers of sexual intercourse, esp. of castration.
– ORIGIN early 20th cent.: *dentata*, feminine of Latin *dentatus* 'having teeth.'

vag·i·nal plug ▶ **n.** Zoology a secretion that blocks the vagina of some rodents and insectivores after mating.

vag·i·nis·mus /ˌvajəˈnizməs/ ▶ **n.** painful spasmodic contraction of the vagina in response to physical contact or pressure (esp. in sexual intercourse).
– ORIGIN mid 19th cent.: modern Latin, from Latin *vagina* (see VAGINA).

vag·i·ni·tis /ˌvajəˈnītis/ ▶ **n.** inflammation of the vagina.

vag·i·no·plas·ty /ˈvajənōˌplastē/ ▶ **n.** Medicine plastic surgery performed to create or repair a vagina.
– ORIGIN late 19th cent.: from *vagina* + *-plasty*.

vag·i·no·sis /ˌvajəˈnōsəs/ ▶ **n.** a bacterial infection of the vagina causing a malodorous white discharge.

va·got·o·my /vāˈgätəmē/ ▶ **n.** (pl. **vagotomies**) a surgical operation in which one or more branches of the vagus nerve are cut, typically to reduce the rate of gastric secretion (e.g., in treating peptic ulcers).
– DERIVATIVES **va·got·o·mized** /-ˌmīzd/ **adj.**

va·go·to·ni·a /ˌvagəˈtōnēə/ ▶ **n.** the condition in which there is increased influence of the parasympathetic nervous system and increased excitability of the vagus nerve, producing bradycardia and faintness.

va·gran·cy /ˈvāgrənsē/ ▶ **n.** the state of living as a vagrant; homelessness: *a descent into vagrancy and drug abuse.*

va·grant /ˈvāgrənt/ ▶ **n.** a person without a settled home or regular work who wanders from place to place and lives by begging. ■ archaic a wanderer. ■ Ornithology a bird that has strayed or been blown from its usual range or migratory route. Also called ACCIDENTAL.
▶ **adj.** [attrib.] characteristic of, relating to, or living the life of a vagrant: *vagrant beggars.* ■ moving from place to place; wandering: *vagrant whales.* ■ literary moving or occurring unpredictably; inconstant: *the vagrant heart of my mother.*
– DERIVATIVES **va·grant·ly** **adv.**
– ORIGIN late Middle English: from Anglo-Norman French *vagarant* 'wandering around,' from the verb *vagrer*.

vague /vāg/ ▶ **adj.** of uncertain, indefinite, or unclear character or meaning: *many patients suffer vague symptoms.* ■ thinking or communicating in an unfocused or imprecise way: *he had been very vague about his activities.*
– DERIVATIVES **vague·ness** **n.**, **vagu·ish** **adj.**
– ORIGIN mid 16th cent.: from French, or from Latin *vagus* 'wandering, uncertain.'

vague·ly /ˈvāglē/ ▶ **adv.** **1** in a way that is uncertain, indefinite, or unclear; roughly: *he vaguely remembered talking to her once.* ■ in a way that is unfocused or lacks attention; absentmindedly: *he nodded vaguely.*
2 [as submodifier] slightly: *he looked vaguely familiar.*

va·gus /ˈvāgəs/ ▶ **n.** (pl. **vagi** /-gī, -jī, -gē, -jē/) (also **vagus nerve**) Anatomy each of the tenth pair of cranial nerves, supplying the heart, lungs, upper digestive tract, and other organs of the chest and abdomen.
– ORIGIN mid 19th cent.: from Latin (see VAGUE).

Vail /vāl/ a town in northern Colorado, a noted ski resort; pop. 4,768 (est. 2008).

vail /vāl/ ▶ **v.** [with obj.] archaic take off or lower (one's hat or crown) as a token of respect or submission. ■ [no obj.] take off one's hat or otherwise show respect or submission to someone.
– ORIGIN Middle English (originally in the sense 'lower (one's eyes, weapon, banner, etc.) as a sign of submission'): shortening of obsolete *avale*, from Old French *avaler* 'to lower,' from *a val* 'down' (literally 'in the valley').

vain /vān/ ▶ **adj.** **1** having or showing an excessively high opinion of one's appearance, abilities, or worth: *their flattery made him vain.*
2 [attrib.] producing no result; useless: *a vain attempt to tidy up the room | the vain hope of finding work.* ■ having no meaning or likelihood of fulfillment: *a vain boast.*
– PHRASES **in vain** without success or a result: *they waited in vain for a response.* **take someone's name in vain** use someone's name in a way that shows a lack of respect.
– DERIVATIVES **vain·ly** **adv.**
– ORIGIN Middle English (in the sense 'devoid of real worth'): via Old French from Latin *vanus* 'empty, without substance.'

vain·glo·ry /ˈvānˌglôrē, ˌvānˈglôrē/ ▶ **n.** literary inordinate pride in oneself or one's achievements; excessive vanity.
– DERIVATIVES **vain·glo·ri·ous** /ˌvānˈglôrēəs/ **adj.**, **vain·glo·ri·ous·ly** /ˌvānˈglôrēəslē/ **adv.**, **vain·glo·ri·ous·ness** /ˌvānˈglôrēəsnəs/ **n.**
– ORIGIN Middle English: suggested by Old French *vaine gloire*, Latin *vana gloria*.

vair /ve(ə)r/ ▶ **n.** **1** fur, typically bluish-gray, obtained from a variety of squirrel, used in the 13th and 14th centuries as a trimming or lining for garments.
2 Heraldry fur, represented by interlocking rows of shield-shaped or bell-shaped figures that are typically alternately blue and white, as a tincture.
– ORIGIN Middle English: via Old French from Latin *varius* (see VARIOUS).

Vaish·na·va /ˈvīsHnəvə/ ▶ **n.** a member of one of the main branches of modern Hinduism, devoted to the worship of the god Vishnu as the supreme being, esp. in his incarnation as Krishna. Compare with SHAIVA.
– ORIGIN from Sanskrit *vaiṣṇava*.

Vaish·ya /ˈvīsHyə, ˈvīs-/ (also **Vaisya**) ▶ **n.** a member of the third of the four Hindu castes, comprising the merchants and farmers.
– ORIGIN from Sanskrit *vaiśya* 'peasant, laborer.'

vaj·ra /ˈvəjrə/ ▶ **n.** (in Buddhism and Hinduism) a thunderbolt or mystical weapon, esp. one wielded by the god Indra.
– ORIGIN Sanskrit.

Vaj·ra·ya·na /ˌvəjrəˈyänə/ ▶ **n.** the Tantric tradition of Buddhism, esp. when regarded as distinct from the Mahayana tradition from which it developed.
– ORIGIN Sanskrit *vajrayāna*, from *vajra* 'thunderbolt' (the god Indra's symbolic vehicle) and *yāna* 'path, journey.'

val·ance /ˈvaləns, ˈvāləns/ ▶ **n.** a length of decorative drapery attached to the canopy or frame of a bed in order to screen the structure or the space beneath it. ■ a length of decorative drapery hung above a window to screen the curtain fittings. ■ a dust ruffle.
– DERIVATIVES **val·anced** **adj.**
– ORIGIN late Middle English: perhaps Anglo-Norman French, from a shortened form of Old French *avaler* 'descend' (see VAIL).

valance

Val·dos·ta /valˈdästə/ a city in southern Georgia, southeast of Albany; pop. 48,547 (est. 2008).

vale¹ /vāl/ ▶ **n.** a valley (used in place names or as a poetic term): *the Vale of Glamorgan.*
– PHRASES **vale of tears** literary the world regarded as a scene of trouble or sorrow.
– ORIGIN Middle English: from Old French *val*, from Latin *vallis, valles*.

va·le² /ˈvälā/ archaic ▶ **exclam.** farewell.
▶ **n.** a written or spoken farewell.
– ORIGIN Latin, literally 'be well!, be strong!,' imperative of *valere*.

val·e·dic·tion /ˌvaləˈdiksHən/ ▶ **n.** the action of saying farewell: *he spread his palm in valediction.* ■ a statement or address made at or as a farewell: *his official memorial valediction.*
– ORIGIN mid 17th cent.: based on Latin *vale* 'goodbye' + *dicere* 'to say,' on the pattern of *benediction*.

val·e·dic·to·ri·an /ˌvaləˌdikˈtôrēən/ ▶ **n.** a student, typically having the highest academic achievements of the class, who delivers the valedictory at a graduation ceremony. Compare with SALUTATORIAN.

val·e·dic·to·ry /ˌvaləˈdikt(ə)rē/ ▶ **adj.** serving as a farewell: *a valedictory wave.*
▶ **n.** (pl. **valedictories**) a farewell address.

va·lence /ˈvāləns/ ▶ **n.** Chemistry the combining power of an element, esp. as measured by the number of hydrogen atoms it can displace or combine with: *carbon always has a valence of 4.* ■ [as modifier] relating to or denoting electrons involved in or available for chemical bond formation: *molecules with unpaired valence electrons.* ■ Linguistics the number of grammatical elements with which a particular word, esp. a verb, combines in a sentence.
– ORIGIN late Middle English: from late Latin *valentia* 'power, competence,' from *valere* 'be well or strong.'

Va·len·ci·a /vəˈlensēə, -ˈlenTHēə/ **1** an autonomous region of eastern Spain, on the Mediterranean coast. It was formerly a Moorish kingdom (1021–1238). ■ its capital, a port on the Mediterranean coast; pop. 807,200 (2008).
2 a city in northern Venezuela; pop. 1,408,400 (est. 2009).

Va·len·ci·ennes /vəˌlensēˈen, ˌvalən-/ ▶ **n.** a type of bobbin lace.
– ORIGIN named after a town in northeastern France, where it was made in the 17th and 18th centuries.

va·len·cy /ˈvālənsē/ ▶ **n.** (pl. **valencies**) Chemistry & Linguistics, chiefly Brit. another term for VALENCE.
– ORIGIN early 17th cent.: from late Latin *valentia* 'power' (see VALENCE).

-valent ▶ **comb. form** **1** having a valency of the specified number: *trivalent.*
2 Genetics (denoting a meiotic structure) composed of the specified number of chromosomes: *univalent.*

val·en·tine /ˈvalənˌtīn/ ▶ **n.** a card sent, often anonymously, on St. Valentine's Day (February 14) to a person one loves or is attracted to. ■ a person to whom one sends such a card or whom one asks to be one's sweetheart.
– ORIGIN late Middle English (denoting a person chosen (sometimes by lot) as a sweetheart or special friend): from Old French *Valentin*, from Latin *Valentinus*.

Val·en·tine, St. /ˈvalənˌtīn/ either of two early Italian saints (who may have been the same person) traditionally commemorated on February 14—a Roman priest martyred *c.*269 and a bishop of Terni martyred at Rome. St. Valentine was regarded as the patron of lovers.

Val·en·ti·no /ˌvalənˈtēnō/, Rudolph (1895–1926), US actor, born in Italy; born *Rodolfo Guglielmi di Valentina d'Antonguolla*. He played the romantic hero in silent movies such as *The Sheikh* (1921) and *Blood and Sand* (1922).

Rudolph Valentino

V

Va·le·ra, Eamon de, see DE VALERA.

Va·le·ri·an /vəˈli(ə)rēən/ (died 260), Roman emperor 253–260; Latin name *Publius Licinius Valerianus*. He renewed the persecution of the Christians that was initiated by Decius.

va·le·ri·an /vəˈli(ə)rēən/ ▶ **n.** a plant that typically bears clusters of small pink or white flowers. Native to Eurasia, several species have been introduced

PRONUNCIATION KEY ə *ago, up*; ər *over, fur*; a *hat*; ā *ate*; ä *car*; e *let*; ē *see*; i *fit*; ī *by*; NG *sing*; ō *go*; ô *law, for*; oi *toy*; o͝o *good*; o͞o *goo*; ou *out*; TH *thin*; T͟H *then*; ZH *vision*

to North America. • Family Valerianaceae: several species, in particular **common valerian** (*Valeriana officinalis*), a valued medicinal herb, and the Mediterranean **red valerian** (*Centranthus ruber*), grown for its spurred flowers, which attract butterflies. ■ a drug obtained from the root of common valerian, used as a sedative and antispasmodic.
– ORIGIN late Middle English: from Old French *valeriane*, from medieval Latin *valeriana (herba)*, apparently the feminine of *Valerianus* 'of Valerius' (a personal name).

va·ler·ic ac·id /və'le(ə)rik, -'li(ə)r-/ ▶ **n.** Chemistry another term for **PENTANOIC ACID**.
– DERIVATIVES **val·er·ate** /'valə,rāt/ **n.**
– ORIGIN mid 19th cent.: *valeric* from **VALERIAN** + **-IC**.

Va·lé·ry /,välā'rē/, (Ambroise) Paul (Toussaint Jules) (1871–1945), French poet, essayist, and critic. His poetry includes *La Jeune parque* (1917) and "Le Cimetière marin" (1922).

val·et /va'lā, 'valā, 'valit/ ▶ **n. 1** a man's personal male attendant, responsible for his clothes and appearance. ■ a hotel employee performing such duties for guests. ■ a rack or stand on which to hang clothing.
2 a person employed to park cars.
▶ **v.** (**valets, valeting, valeted**) [with obj.] act as a valet to (a particular man). ■ [no obj.] work as a valet.
– ORIGIN late 15th cent. (denoting a footman acting as an attendant to a horseman): from French; related to **VASSAL**.

val·et park·ing ▶ **n.** a service provided at a restaurant, club, or airport whereby an attendant parks and retrieves patrons' vehicles.

val·e·tu·di·nar·i·an /,valə,t(y)ōōdn'e(ə)rēən/ ▶ **n.** a person who is unduly anxious about their health. ■ a person suffering from poor health.
▶ **adj.** showing undue concern about one's health. ■ suffering from poor health.
– DERIVATIVES **val·e·tu·di·nar·i·an·ism** /-,nizəm/ **n.**
– ORIGIN early 18th cent.: from Latin *valetudinarius* 'in ill health' (from *valetudo* 'health,' from *valere* 'be well') + **-AN**.

val·e·tu·di·nar·y /,valə't(y)ōōdn,erē/ ▶ **adj. & n.** (pl. **valetudinaries**) another term for **VALETUDINARIAN**.

val·gus /'valgəs/ ▶ **n.** Medicine a deformity involving oblique displacement of part of a limb away from the midline. The opposite of **VARUS**.
– ORIGIN early 19th cent.: from Latin, literally 'knock-kneed.'

Val·hal·la /val'halə, väl'hälə/ Scandinavian Mythology a hall in which heroes killed in battle were believed to feast with Odin for eternity.
– ORIGIN modern Latin, from Old Norse *Valhǫll*, from *valr* 'the slain' + *hǫll* 'hall.'

val·iant /'valyənt/ ▶ **adj.** possessing or showing courage or determination: *she made a valiant effort to hold her anger in check | a valiant warrior*.
– DERIVATIVES **val·iant·ly adv.**
– ORIGIN Middle English (also in the sense 'robust, well-built'): from Old French *vailant*, based on Latin *valere* 'be strong.'

val·id /'valid/ ▶ **adj.** (of an argument or point) having a sound basis in logic or fact; reasonable or cogent: *a valid criticism*. ■ legally binding due to having been executed in compliance with the law: *a valid contract*. ■ legally or officially acceptable: *the visas are valid for thirty days | a valid password*.
– DERIVATIVES **val·id·ly adv.**
– ORIGIN late 16th cent.: from French *valide* or Latin *validus* 'strong,' from *valere* 'be strong.'

val·i·date /'valə,dāt/ ▶ **v.** [with obj.] check or prove the validity or accuracy of (something): *these estimates have been validated by periodic surveys*. ■ demonstrate or support the truth or value of: *in a healthy family a child's feelings are validated*. ■ make or declare legally valid.
– DERIVATIVES **val·i·da·tion** /,valə'dāsHən/ **n.**
– ORIGIN mid 17th cent. (in the sense 'make legally valid'): from medieval Latin *validat-* 'made legally valid,' from the verb *validare*, from Latin *validus* (see **VALID**).

V

va·lid·i·ty /və'lidətē/ ▶ **n.** the quality of being logically or factually sound; soundness or cogency: *one might question the validity of our data*. ■ the state of being legally or officially binding or acceptable: *return travel must be within the validity of the ticket*.

val·ine /'val,ēn, 'vā,lēn/ ▶ **n.** Biochemistry an amino acid that is a constituent of most proteins. It is an essential nutrient in the diet of vertebrates. • Chem. formula: $(CH_3)_2CHCH(NH_2)COOH$.
– ORIGIN early 20th cent.: from *val(eric acid)* + **-INE**[4].

va·lise /və'lēs/ ▶ **n.** a small traveling bag or suitcase.
– ORIGIN early 17th cent.: from French, from Italian *valigia*; compare with medieval Latin *valesia*, of unknown origin.

Val·i·um /'valēəm/ ▶ **n.** trademark for **DIAZEPAM**.
– ORIGIN 1960s: of unknown origin.

Val·kyr·ie /val'ki(ə)rē, 'valkərē/ ▶ **n.** Scandinavian Mythology each of Odin's twelve handmaidens who conducted the slain warriors of their choice from the battlefield to Valhalla.
– ORIGIN from Old Norse *Valkyrja*, literally 'chooser of the slain,' from *valr* 'the slain' + *kyrja* 'chooser.'

Val·la·do·lid /,valədə'lid, ,bäyədə'lēd/ **1** a city in northern Spain, capital of Castilla-León region; pop. 318,461 (2008). It was the principal residence of the kings of Castile in the 15th century.
2 former name (until 1828) of **MORELIA**.

val·lec·u·la /və'lekyələ/ ▶ **n.** (pl. **valleculae** /-,lē, -,lī/) Anatomy & Botany a groove or furrow.
– DERIVATIVES **val·lec·u·lar** /-lər/ **adj.**
– ORIGIN mid 19th cent.: from a late Latin variant of Latin *vallicula*, diminutive of Latin *vallis* 'valley.'

Val·le·jo /və'lāō, -,hō/ an industrial port city in north central California, on San Pablo Bay, northeast of San Francisco; pop. 114,729 (est. 2008).

Val·let·ta /və'letə/ the capital and chief port of Malta; pop. 6,300 (est. 2006).
– ORIGIN named after Jean de *La Valette*, grand master of the Knights of Malta, who built the town after 1565.

val·ley /'valē/ ▶ **n.** (pl. **valleys**) **1** a low area of land between hills or mountains, typically with a river or stream flowing through it.
2 Architecture an internal angle formed by the intersecting planes of a roof, or by the slope of a roof and a wall.
– ORIGIN Middle English: from Old French *valee*, based on Latin *vallis, valles*; compare with **VALE**[1].

val·ley fe·ver (also **San Joaquin Valley fever**) ▶ **n.** informal term for **COCCIDIOIDOMYCOSIS**.

Val·ley Forge the site on the Schuylkill River in Pennsylvania, about 20 miles (32 km) northwest of Philadelphia, where George Washington's Continental Army spent the winter of 1777–78 in conditions of extreme hardship during the American Revolution.

Val·ley Girl ▶ **n.** informal a fashionable and affluent teenage girl from the San Fernando Valley in southern California.

Val·ley of the Kings a valley near ancient Thebes in Egypt where the pharaohs of the New Kingdom (c.1550–1070 BC) were buried.

Va·lois /val'wä, 'val,wä/ the French royal house from the accession of Philip VI, successor to the last Capetian king, in 1328 to the death of **Henry III** in **1589**, when the throne passed to the Bourbons.

Va·lo·na /və'lōnə/ Italian name for **VLORË**.

va·lo·ni·a /və'lōnēə/ ▶ **n.** (also **valonia oak**) an evergreen oak tree native to southern Europe and western Asia. See also **ALEPPO GALL**. • *Quercus macrolepis*, family Fagaceae. ■ the acorn cups of this tree, which yield a black dye and are used in tanning.
– ORIGIN early 18th cent.: from Italian *vallonia*, based on Greek *balanos* 'acorn.'

val·or /'valər/ (Brit. **valour**) ▶ **n.** great courage in the face of danger, esp. in battle: *the medals are awarded for acts of valor*.
– DERIVATIVES **val·or·ous** /-ərəs/ **adj.**
– ORIGIN Middle English (denoting worth derived from personal qualities or rank): via Old French from late Latin *valor*, from *valere* 'be strong.'

val·or·ize /'valə,rīz/ ▶ **v.** [with obj.] give or ascribe value or validity to (something): *the culture valorizes the individual*. ■ raise or fix the price or value of (a commodity or currency) by artificial means, esp. by government action.
– DERIVATIVES **val·or·i·za·tion** /,valərə'zāsHən/ **n.**
– ORIGIN 1920s: back-formation from *valorization* (from French *valorisation*, from *valeur* 'value').

Val·pa·raí·so /,valpə'rīzō, ,bälpärə'ēsō/ the principal port of Chile, in the center of the country, near Santiago; pop. 275,000 (est. 2006).

Val·po·li·cel·la /,val,pōlə'cHelə, ,väl-/ ▶ **n.** red Italian wine made in the Val Policella district.

val·pro·ic ac·id /val'prō-ik/ ▶ **n.** Chemistry a synthetic crystalline compound with anticonvulsant properties, used (generally as salts) in the treatment of epilepsy. • Alternative name: **2-propylpentanoic acid**; chem. formula: $C_7H_{15}COOH$.
– ORIGIN 1970s: *valproic* from *valeric* (see **VALERIC ACID**) + *pro(pyl)* + **-IC**.

Val·sal·va ma·neu·ver /val'salvə/ ▶ **n.** Medicine the action of attempting to exhale with the nostrils and mouth, or the glottis, closed. This increases pressure in the middle ear and the chest, as when bracing to lift heavy objects, and is used as a means of equalizing pressure in the ears.
– ORIGIN late 19th cent.: named after Antonio M. *Valsalva* (1666–1723), Italian anatomist.

valse /väls/ ▶ **n.** (pl. **same**) French term for **WALTZ** (esp. as used in the titles of pieces of music).
– ORIGIN late 18th cent.: via French from German *Walzer*.

val·u·a·ble /'valy(ōō)əbəl/ ▶ **adj.** worth a great deal of money: *a valuable antique*. ■ extremely useful or important: *my time is valuable*.
▶ **n.** (usu. **valuables**) a thing that is of great worth, esp. a small item of personal property: *put all your valuables in the hotel safe*.
– DERIVATIVES **val·u·a·bly** /-blē/ **adv.**

val·u·a·ble con·sid·er·a·tion ▶ **n.** Law legal consideration having some economic value, which is necessary for a contract to be enforceable.

val·u·a·tion /,valyōō'āsHən/ ▶ **n.** an estimation of something's worth, esp. one carried out by a professional appraiser: *it is wise to obtain an independent valuation*. ■ the monetary worth of something, esp. as estimated by an appraiser.
– DERIVATIVES **val·u·ate** /'valyōō,āt/ **v.**

val·u·a·tor /'valyə,wātər/ ▶ **n.** archaic a person who makes valuations.

val·ue /'valyōō/ ▶ **n. 1** the regard that something is held to deserve; the importance, worth, or usefulness of something: *your support is of great value*. ■ the material or monetary worth of something: *prints seldom rise in value | equipment is included up to a total value of $500*. ■ the worth of something compared to the price paid or asked for it: *at $12.50 the book is a good value*.
2 (**values**) a person's principles or standards of behavior; one's judgment of what is important in life: *they internalize their parents' rules and values*.
3 the numerical amount denoted by an algebraic term; a magnitude, quantity, or number: *the mean value of x | an accurate value for the mass of Venus*.
4 Music the relative duration of the sound signified by a note.
5 Linguistics the meaning of a word or other linguistic unit. ■ the quality or tone of a spoken sound; the sound represented by a letter.
6 Art the relative degree of lightness or darkness of a particular color: *the artist has used adjacent color values as the landscape recedes*.
▶ **v.** (**values, valuing, valued**) [with obj.] **1** estimate the monetary worth of (something): *his estate was valued at $45,000*.
2 consider (someone or something) to be important or beneficial; have a high opinion of: *she had come to value her privacy and independence*.
– ORIGIN Middle English: from Old French, feminine past participle of *valoir* 'be worth,' from Latin *valere*.

val·ue add·ed ▶ **n.** Economics the amount by which the value of an article is increased at each stage of its production, exclusive of initial costs.
▶ **adj.** [attrib.] (**value-added**) (of goods) having features added to a basic line or model for which the buyer is prepared to pay extra. ■ (of a company) offering specialized or extended services in a commercial area.

val·ue-add·ed tax (abbr.: **VAT**) ▶ **n.** a tax on the amount by which the value of an article has been increased at each stage of its production or distribution.

val·ue a·nal·y·sis ▶ **n.** the systematic and critical assessment by an organization of every feature of a product to ensure that its cost is no greater than is necessary to carry out its functions.

val·ue chain ▶ **n.** the process or activities by which a company adds value to an article, including production, marketing, and the provision of after-sales service.

val·ued /'valyōōd/ ▶ **adj.** considered to be important or beneficial; cherished: *a valued friend*.

val·ue-free ▶ **adj.** free from criteria imposed by subjective values or standards; purely objective: *real science could and should be value-free*.

val·ue judg·ment /'valyōō ,jəjmənt/ ▶ **n.** an assessment of something as good or bad in terms of one's standards or priorities.

val·ue-lad·en ▶ **adj.** presupposing the acceptance of a particular set of values: *governments' judgments are value-laden*.

val·ue·less /'valyōōləs/ ▶ **adj.** having no value; worthless: *cherished but valueless heirlooms*.
– DERIVATIVES **val·ue·less·ness n.**

val·ue-neu·tral ▶ **adj.** not presupposing the acceptance of any particular values.

val·ue prop·o·si·tion ▶ **n.** (in marketing) an innovation, service, or feature intended to make a company or product attractive to customers.

val·ue stock ▶ **n.** Finance shares of a company with solid fundamentals that are priced below those of its peers, based on analysis of price/earnings ratio, yield, and other factors. Compare with **GROWTH STOCK**.

va·lu·ta /vəˈlo͞otə/ ▶ **n.** the value of one currency with respect to its exchange rate with another. ■ foreign currency: *these internal flights supply valuta to the cash-starved confederation.*
– ORIGIN late 19th cent.: from Italian, literally 'value.'

val·vate /ˈvalˌvāt/ ▶ **adj.** Botany (of sepals or other parts) having adjacent edges abutting rather than overlapping. Compare with **IMBRICATE**.
– ORIGIN early 19th cent.: from Latin *valvatus* 'having folding doors,' from *valva* 'valve.'

valve /valv/ ▶ **n.** a device for controlling the passage of fluid through a pipe or duct, esp. an automatic device allowing movement in one direction only. ■ (in full **thermionic valve**) Electronics British term for **THERMIONIC TUBE**. ■ Music a cylindrical mechanism in a brass instrument that, when depressed or turned, admits air into different sections of tubing and so extends the range of available notes. ■ Anatomy & Zoology a membranous fold in a hollow organ or tubular structure, such as a blood vessel or the digestive tract, that maintains the flow of the contents in one direction by closing in response to any pressure from reverse flow. ■ Zoology each of the halves of the hinged shell of a bivalve mollusk or brachiopod, or of the parts of the compound shell of a barnacle. ■ Botany each of the halves or sections into which a dry fruit (esp. a pod or capsule) dehisces.

valve

– DERIVATIVES **valved** adj. [in combination] *a branchiopod has a two-valved outer covering*, **valve·less** adj.
– ORIGIN late Middle English (denoting a leaf of a folding or double door): from Latin *valva*.

valve head ▶ **n.** the part of a vertically opening valve that is lifted off the valve aperture to open the valve.

val·vu·lar /ˈvalvyələr/ ▶ **adj.** relating to, having, or acting as a valve or valves: *valvular heart disease | three pairs of valvular apertures.*
– ORIGIN late 18th cent.: from modern Latin *valvula* (diminutive of Latin *valva* 'leaf of a door') + **-AR**[1].

val·vu·li·tis /ˌvalvyəˈlītis/ ▶ **n.** Medicine inflammation of the valves of the heart.

vam·brace /ˈvamˌbrās/ ▶ **n.** historical a piece of armor for the arm, esp. the forearm.
– ORIGIN Middle English: from an Anglo-Norman French shortening of Old French *avantbras*, from *avant* 'before' + *bras* 'arm.' Compare with **VAMPLATE**.

va·moose /vaˈmo͞os, və-/ ▶ **v.** [no obj.] informal depart hurriedly: *we'd better vamoose before we're caught.*
– ORIGIN mid 19th cent.: from Spanish *vamos* 'let us go.'

vamp[1] /vamp/ ▶ **n. 1** the upper front part of a boot or shoe.
2 (in jazz and popular music) a short, simple introductory passage, usually repeated several times until otherwise instructed.
▶ **v. 1** [with obj.] attach a new upper to (a boot or shoe). ■ (**vamp something up**) informal repair or improve something: *the production values have been vamped up.*
2 [no obj.] repeat a short, simple passage of music: *the band was vamping gently behind his busy lead guitar.*
– ORIGIN Middle English (denoting the foot of a stocking): shortening of Old French *avantpie*, from *avant* 'before' + *pie* 'foot.' The musical sense of the verb developed from the general sense 'improvise.'

vamp[2] informal ▶ **n.** a woman who uses sexual attraction to exploit men.
▶ **v.** [with obj.] blatantly set out to attract: *she had not vamped him like some wicked Jezebel.*
– DERIVATIVES **vamp·ish** adj., **vamp·ish·ly** adv., **vamp·y** adj.
– ORIGIN early 20th cent.: abbreviation of **VAMPIRE**.

vam·pire /ˈvamˌpī(ə)r/ ▶ **n. 1** a corpse supposed, in European folklore, to leave its grave at night to drink the blood of the living by biting their necks with long pointed canine teeth. ■ a person who preys ruthlessly on others: *the protectionist vampires in the Congress.*
2 (also **vampire bat**) a small bat that feeds on the blood of mammals or birds using its two sharp incisor teeth and anticoagulant saliva, found mainly in tropical America. See also **FALSE VAMPIRE**. ● Family Desmodontidae (or Phyllostomidae): three species, in particular the **common vampire** (*Desmodus rotundus*).
– DERIVATIVES **vam·pir·ic** /vamˈpirik/ adj.
– ORIGIN mid 18th cent.: from French, from Hungarian *vampir*, perhaps from Turkish *uber* 'witch.'

vam·pir·ism /ˈvampīˌrizəm/ ▶ **n.** the action or practices of a vampire.

vam·plate /ˈvamˌplāt/ ▶ **n.** historical a circular plate on a spear or lance designed to protect the hand.
– ORIGIN Middle English: from Anglo-Norman French *vauntplate*, from *avant* 'before' + *plate* 'thin plate.' Compare with **VAMBRACE**.

van[1] /van/ ▶ **n.** a covered boxlike motor vehicle, typically having a rear door and sliding doors on the side panels, used for transporting goods or people. ■ Brit. an enclosed railroad freight car. ■ Brit. a caravan.
– ORIGIN early 19th cent.: shortening of **CARAVAN**.

van[2] ▶ **n.** (**the van**) the foremost part of a company of people moving or preparing to move forward, esp. the foremost division of an advancing military force: *in the van were the foremost chiefs and some of the warriors astride horses.* ■ the forefront: *he was in the van of the movement to encourage the cultivation of wildflowers.*
– ORIGIN early 17th cent.: abbreviation of **VANGUARD**.

van[3] ▶ **n. 1** archaic a winnowing fan.
2 archaic or literary a bird's wing.
– ORIGIN late Middle English: dialect variant of **FAN**[1], probably reinforced by Old French *van* or Latin *vannus*.

Van, Lake /van, vän/ a large saltwater lake in the mountains of eastern Turkey.

van·a·date /ˈvanəˌdāt/ ▶ **n.** Chemistry a salt in which the anion contains vanadium and oxygen, esp. one of the anion VO_4^{3-}.
– ORIGIN mid 19th cent.: from **VANADIUM** + **-ATE**[1].

va·nad·i·nite /vəˈnādnˌīt, -ˈnadn-/ ▶ **n.** a rare reddish-brown mineral consisting of a vanadate and chloride of lead, typically occurring as an oxidation product of lead ores.
– ORIGIN mid 19th cent.: from **VANADIUM** + **-ITE**[1].

va·na·di·um /vəˈnādēəm/ ▶ **n.** the chemical element of atomic number 23, a hard gray metal of the transition series, used to make alloy steels. (Symbol: **V**)
– ORIGIN mid 19th cent.: modern Latin, from Old Norse *Vanadis* (a name of the Scandinavian goddess Freyja).

va·na·di·um steel ▶ **n.** a strong alloy of steel containing vanadium.

Van Al·len /van ˈalən/, James Alfred (1914–2006), US physicist. He used balloons and rockets to study cosmic radiation in the upper atmosphere and showed that specific zones of high radiation were the result of charged particles from the solar wind being trapped in two belts around the earth.

Van Al·len belt ▶ **n.** each of two regions of intense radiation partly surrounding the earth at heights of several thousand miles.

Van·brugh /ˈvanbrə/, Sir John (1664–1726), British architect and playwright. His comedies include *The Relapse* (1696) and *The Provok'd Wife* (1697). His architectural works include Castle Howard (1702) and Blenheim Palace (1705), both produced in collaboration with Nicholas Hawksmoor (1661-1736).

Van Bu·ren, Martin (1782–1862), 8th president of the US 1837–41. Before succeeding President Jackson, he served as vice president 1833–37. A Democrat, he is noted for his development of the two-party system. His measure of placing government funds, previously held in private banks, in an independent government treasury displeased many Democrats.

Martin Van Buren

van·co·my·cin /ˌvaNGkəˈmīsin/ ▶ **n.** Medicine a bacterial antibiotic used against resistant strains of streptococcus and staphylococcus. ● This antibiotic is obtained from the bacterium *Streptomyces orientalis*.
– ORIGIN 1950s: from *vanco-* (of unknown origin) + **-MYCIN**.

Van·cou·ver[1] /vanˈko͞ovər/ **1** a city and port in British Columbia, in southwestern Canada, on the mainland opposite Vancouver Island; pop. 578,041 (2006). It is the largest city and chief port in western Canada.
2 an industrial port city in southwestern Washington, on the Columbia River, north of Portland in Oregon; pop. 163,186 (est. 2008).

Van·cou·ver[2], George (1757–98), English navigator. He led an exploration of the coasts of Australia, New Zealand, and Hawaii (1791–92) and later charted much of the west coast of North America between southern Alaska and California. Vancouver Island and the city of Vancouver, Canada, are named after him.

Van·cou·ver Is·land a large island off the Pacific coast of Canada, in southwestern British Columbia. Its capital, Victoria, is the capital of British Columbia.

Van·da /ˈvändə/ Swedish name for **VANTAA**.

van·dal /ˈvandl/ ▶ **n. 1** a person who deliberately destroys or damages public or private property: *the rear window of the car was smashed by vandals.*
2 (**Vandal**) a member of a Germanic people that ravaged Gaul, Spain, and North Africa in the 4th–5th centuries and sacked Rome in AD 455.
– ORIGIN from Latin *Vandalus*, of Germanic origin. Sense 1 dates from the mid 17th cent.

van·dal·ism /ˈvandlˌizəm/ ▶ **n.** action involving deliberate destruction of or damage to public or private property.
– DERIVATIVES **van·dal·is·tic** /ˌvandlˈistik/ adj., **van·dal·is·ti·cal·ly** /ˌvandlˈistik(ə)lē/ adv.

van·dal·ize /ˈvandlˌīz/ ▶ **v.** [with obj.] deliberately destroy or damage (public or private property): *stations have been wrecked and vandalized beyond recognition.*

van de Graaff gen·er·a·tor /ˈvan də ˌgraf/ ▶ **n.** Physics a machine devised to generate electrostatic charge by means of a vertical endless belt collecting charge from a voltage source and transferring it to a large insulated metal dome, where a high voltage is produced.
– ORIGIN 1930s: named after Robert Jemison *van de Graaff* (1901–67), US physicist.

Van·der·bijl·park /ˈvandərˌbīlˌpärk/ a steel-manufacturing city in South Africa, south of Johannesburg; pop. 220,100 (est. 2009).

Van·der·bilt /ˈvandərˌbilt/, Cornelius (1794–1877), US businessman and philanthropist. He amassed a fortune from shipping and railroads and made an endowment to found Vanderbilt University in Nashville, Tennessee (1873).

Van der Post /ˌvan dər ˈpōst/, Sir Laurens (Jan) (1906–96), South African explorer and writer. His books, including *Venture to the Interior* (1952) and *The Lost World of the Kalahari* (1958), combine travel writing and descriptions of fauna with philosophical speculation.

van der Waals forc·es /ˈvan dər ˌwôlz, -ˌvälz/ ▶ **plural n.** Chemistry weak, short-range electrostatic attractive forces between uncharged molecules, arising from the interaction of permanent or transient electric dipole moments.
– ORIGIN late 19th cent.: named after Johannes *van der Waals* (1837–1923), Dutch physicist.

Van De·van·ter /van dəˈvantər/, Willis (1859–1941), US Supreme Court associate justice 1910–37. Appointed to the Court by President Taft, he was a conservative and stayed on the Court longer than he intended in hopes of blocking many of President Franklin D. Roosevelt's New Deal programs.

van de Vel·de[1] /ˌvän də ˈveldə/ the name of a family of Dutch painters. ■ **Willem** (1611–93); known as **Willem van de Velde the Elder**. He painted marine subjects, was official artist to the Dutch fleet, and worked for Britain's Charles II. ■ **Willem** (1633–1707), son of Willem the Elder; known as **Willem van de Velde the Younger**. He was also a notable marine artist who painted for Charles II. ■ **Adriaen** (1636–72); son of Willem the Elder. He painted landscapes, portraits, and biblical and genre scenes.

van de Vel·de[2], Henri (Clemens) (1863–1957), Belgian architect, designer, and teacher. He pioneered the development of art nouveau design and architecture in Europe.

Van Die·men's Land /van ˈdēmənz/ former name (until 1855) of **TASMANIA**.

Van Dor·en /van 'dôrən/ the name of a family of US writers. ■ **Carl (Clinton) Van Doren** (1885–1950), historian and literary critic, noted as the author of *Benjamin Franklin* (1938). ■ **Mark (Albert) Van Doren** (1894–1972), poet and educator; son of Carl. His work is compiled in *Collected Poems* (1939). ■ **Charles (Lincoln) Van Doren** (1926–), writer and educator; son of Mark. He was involved in a quiz show scandal for having been given the answers prior to his appearances on television's *Twenty One* in 1956.

Van Dyck /van 'dīk/ (also **Vandyke**), Sir Anthony (1599–1641), Flemish painter. He is noted for his portraits of members of the English court.

Van·dyke (also **vandyke**) ▶ **n. 1** a broad lace or linen collar with an edge deeply cut into large points (in imitation of a style frequently depicted in portraits by Sir Anthony Van Dyck), fashionable in the 18th century. ■ each of a number of large deep-cut points on the border or fringe of a garment or piece of material.
2 (also **Vandyke beard**) a neat, pointed beard.
▶ **adj.** [attrib.] denoting a style of garment or decorative design associated with the portraits of Van Dyck: *a Vandyke handkerchief.*

Vandyke beard

Van·dyke brown ▶ **n.** a deep rich brown.

vane /vān/ ▶ **n.** a broad blade attached to a rotating axis or wheel that pushes or is pushed by wind or water and forms part of a machine or device such as a windmill, propeller, or turbine. ■ short for **WEATHERVANE**. ■ the flat part on either side of the shaft of a feather. ■ a broad, flat projecting surface designed to guide the motion of a projectile, such as a feather on an arrow or a fin on a torpedo.
– DERIVATIVES **vaned adj.** [usu. in combination] *a three-vaned windmill.*
– ORIGIN late Middle English: dialect variant of obsolete *fane* 'banner,' of Germanic origin.

Vä·nern /'venə(r)n/ a lake in southwestern Sweden, the largest lake in the country and the third largest in Europe.

Van Eyck /van 'īk/, Jan (*c.*1370–1441), Flemish painter. Notable works: *The Adoration of the Lamb* (known as the Ghent Altarpiece, 1432) in the church of St. Bavon in Ghent and *The Arnolfini Marriage* (1434).

vang /vaNG/ ▶ **n.** Sailing each of two guy ropes running from the end of a gaff to opposite sides of the deck.
– ORIGIN mid 18th cent.: variant of obsolete *fang*, denoting a gripping device, from Old Norse *fang* 'grasp,' of Germanic origin.

Van Gogh /van 'gō, 'gäKH/, Vincent (Willem) (1853–90), Dutch painter. He is best known for his post-Impressionist work. His most famous pictures include several studies of sunflowers and *A Starry Night* (1889). Suffering from severe depression, he cut off part of his own ear and eventually committed suicide.

van·guard /'van,gärd/ ▶ **n.** a group of people leading the way in new developments or ideas: *the experimental spirit of the modernist vanguard.* ■ a position at the forefront of new developments or ideas: *the prototype was **in the vanguard of** technical development.* ■ the foremost part of an advancing army or naval force.
– DERIVATIVES **van·guard·ism** /-,izəm/ **n.**, **van·guard·ist n.**
– ORIGIN late Middle English (denoting the foremost part of an army): shortening of Old French *avan(t) garde*, from *avant* 'before' + *garde* 'guard.'

va·nil·la /və'nilə/ ▶ **n. 1** a substance obtained from vanilla beans or produced artificially and used to flavor sweet foods or to impart a fragrant scent to cosmetic preparations: [as modifier] *vanilla ice cream.* ■ ice cream flavored with vanilla: *four scoops of vanilla with hot fudge sauce.* ■ [as modifier] of the yellowish-white color of vanilla ice cream: *a vanilla dress.*
2 a tropical climbing orchid that has fragrant flowers and long podlike fruit. ● Genus *Vanilla*, family Orchidaceae: many species, in particular *V. planifolia*, the chief commercial source of vanilla beans. ■ (also **vanilla bean** or **vanilla pod**) the fruit of this plant, which is cured and then either used in cooking or processed to extract an essence that is used for flavor and fragrance.
▶ **adj.** having no special or extra features; ordinary: *it will be able to do tricks that **plain vanilla** CD-ROMs can't.*
– ORIGIN mid 17th cent.: from Spanish *vainilla* 'pod,' diminutive of *vaina* 'sheath, pod,' from Latin *vagina* 'sheath.' (See **VAGINA**.) The spelling change was due to association with French *vanille*.

V

va·nil·lin /və'nilin, 'vanl-/ ▶ **n.** Chemistry a fragrant compound that is the essential constituent of vanilla. ● Alternative name: **3-methoxy-4-hydroxybenzaldehyde**; chem. formula: $CH_3OC_6H_3(OH)CHO$.
– ORIGIN mid 19th cent.: from **VANILLA** + **-IN**[1].

Va·nir /'väni(ə)r/ ▶ **n.** Scandinavian Mythology a race of Norse gods, allies of the Aesir, that function as fertility divinities.

van·ish /'vaniSH/ ▶ **v.** [no obj.] **1** disappear suddenly and completely: *Mary vanished without a trace.* ■ gradually cease to exist: *the days of the extended family are vanishing.*
2 Mathematics become zero.
– ORIGIN Middle English: shortening of Old French *e(s)vaniss-*, lengthened stem of *e(s)vanir*, from Latin *evanescere* 'die away.'

van·ish·ing cream ▶ **n.** dated a cream or ointment that leaves no visible trace when rubbed into the skin.

van·ish·ing·ly /'vaniSHiNGlē/ ▶ **adv.** [as submodifier] in such a manner or to such a degree as almost to become invisible, nonexistent, or negligible: *an event of vanishingly small probability.*

van·ish·ing point ▶ **n. 1** the point at which receding parallel lines viewed in perspective appear to converge.
2 [in sing.] the point at which something that has been growing smaller or increasingly faint disappears altogether: *custody fees have dropped close to the vanishing point.*

van·i·tas /'vanə,täs/ ▶ **n.** a still-life painting of a 17th-century Dutch genre containing symbols of death or change as a reminder of their inevitability.
– ORIGIN Latin, literally 'vanity.'

van·i·ty /'vanətē/ ▶ **n.** (pl. **vanities**) **1** excessive pride in or admiration of one's own appearance or achievements: *it flattered his vanity to think I was in love with him | the personal vanities and ambitions of politicians.* ■ [as modifier] denoting a person or company that publishes works at the author's expense: *a vanity press.*
2 the quality of being worthless or futile: *the vanity of human wishes.*
3 a dressing table. ■ a bathroom unit consisting of a washbasin typically set into a counter with a cabinet beneath.
– ORIGIN Middle English: from Old French *vanite*, from Latin *vanitas*, from *vanus* 'empty' (see **VAIN**).

van·i·ty case ▶ **n.** a small case fitted with a mirror and compartments for makeup.

Van·i·ty Fair ▶ **n.** the world regarded as a place of frivolity and idle amusement (originally with reference to Bunyan's *Pilgrim's Progress*).

van·i·ty mir·ror ▶ **n.** a small mirror used for applying makeup, esp. one fitted in a visor of a motor vehicle.

van·i·ty plate ▶ **n.** a vehicle license plate bearing a distinctive or personalized combination of letters, numbers, or both.

van·i·ty siz·ing ▶ **n.** the practice of assigning smaller sizes to articles of manufactured clothing than is really the case, in order to encourage sales.

van·i·ty ta·ble ▶ **n.** a dressing table.

Van Nuys /van 'nīz/ an industrial and residential section of northwestern Los Angeles in California, a center of aerospace manufacturing.

van·pool /'van,po͞ol/ ▶ **n.** an arrangement whereby commuters travel together in a van.

van·quish /'vaNGkwiSH/ ▶ **v.** [with obj.] defeat thoroughly: *Mexican forces vanquished the French army in a battle in Puebla.*
– DERIVATIVES **van·quish·a·ble adj.**, **van·quish·er n.**
– ORIGIN Middle English: from Old French *vencus*, *venquis* (past participle and past tense of *veintre*), *vainquiss-* (lengthened stem of *vainquir*), from Latin *vincere* 'conquer.'

Van Rens·se·laer /,van ,rensə'li(ə)r, 'rensələr/, Stephen (1764–1839), US army officer and politician. He held various state positions in New York and participated in the War of 1812. A Federalist, he served in the US House of Representatives 1822–29. He also founded the technical school (1824) that became Rensselaer Polytechnic Institute in Troy, New York.

Van·taa /'vän,tä/ a city in southern Finland, a northern suburb of Helsinki; pop. 196,934 (2009). Swedish name **VANDA**.

van·tage /'vantij/ (usu. **vantage point**) ▶ **n.** a place or position affording a good view of something: *from my vantage point I could see into the front garden* | figurative *the past is continuously reinterpreted from the vantage point of the present.*
– ORIGIN Middle English: from Anglo-Norman French, shortening of Old French *avantage* 'advantage.'

Va·nu·a·tu /,vänoo͞'ätoo͞, ,vanoo͞-/ a country that consists of a group of islands in the southwestern Pacific Ocean; pop. 218,500 (est. 2009); capital, Vila; languages, Bislama, English, and French (all official).

> The islands were administered jointly by Britain and France as the New Hebrides. Vanuatu became an independent republic within the Commonwealth of Nations in 1980.

– DERIVATIVES **Va·nu·a·tu·an** /-'ätoo͞ən/ **adj. & n.**

Van·zet·ti /van'zetē/, Bartolomeo (1888–1927), US political radical; born in Italy. In 1921, along with Nicola Sacco, he was accused and convicted of murder In 1927, both men were executed in the electric chair; fifty years later, their names were cleared of any crimes.

vap·id /'vapid/ ▶ **adj.** offering nothing that is stimulating or challenging: *tuneful but vapid musical comedies.*
– DERIVATIVES **va·pid·i·ty** /va'pidətē/ **n.**, **vap·id·ly adv.**
– ORIGIN mid 17th cent. (used originally in description of drinks as 'lacking in flavor'): from Latin *vapidus*.

va·por /'vāpər/ (Brit. **vapour**) ▶ **n.** a substance diffused or suspended in the air, esp. one normally liquid or solid: *dense clouds of smoke and toxic vapor | chemical vapors.* ■ Physics a gaseous substance that is below its critical temperature, and can therefore be liquefied by pressure alone. Compare with **GAS**. ■ (**the vapors**) dated a sudden feeling of faintness or nervousness or a state of depression.
▶ **v.** [no obj.] talk in a vacuous, boasting, or pompous way: *he was vaporing on about the days of his youth.*
– DERIVATIVES **va·por·ish adj.** (archaic), **va·por·ous** /'vāpərəs/ **adj.**, **va·por·ous·ness** /'vāpərəsnəs/ **n.**, **va·por·y** /'vāpərē/ **adj.**
– ORIGIN late Middle English: from Old French *vapour*, or from Latin *vapor* 'steam, heat.' The current verb sense dates from the early 17th cent.

va·por bar·ri·er ▶ **n.** a thin layer of impermeable material, typically polyethylene sheeting, included in building construction to prevent moisture from damaging the fabric of the building.

va·por den·si·ty ▶ **n.** Chemistry the density of a particular gas or vapor relative to that of hydrogen at the same pressure and temperature.

va·po·ret·to /,väpə'retō, ,vapə-/ ▶ **n.** (pl. **vaporetti** /-'retē/ or **vaporettos**) (in Venice) a canal boat (originally a steamboat, now a motorboat) used for public transportation.
– ORIGIN Italian, diminutive of *vapore* 'steam,' from Latin *vapor*.

va·por·ize /'vāpə,rīz/ ▶ **v.** convert or be converted into vapor: [with obj.] *there is a large current that is sufficient to vaporize carbon* | [no obj.] *cold gasoline does not vaporize readily.*
– DERIVATIVES **va·por·iz·a·ble adj.**, **va·por·i·za·tion** /,vāpərə'zāSHən, -,rī'zā-/ **n.**

va·por·iz·er /'vāpə,rīzər/ ▶ **n.** a device that generates a particular substance in the form of vapor, esp. for medicinal inhalation.

va·por lock ▶ **n.** an interruption in the flow of a liquid through a fuel line or other pipe as a result of vaporization of the liquid.

va·por pres·sure ▶ **n.** Chemistry the pressure of a vapor in contact with its liquid or solid form.

va·por trail ▶ **n.** another term for **CONTRAIL**.

va·por·ware /'vāpər,wer/ (Brit. **vapourware**) ▶ **n.** Computing, informal software or hardware that has been advertised but is not yet available to buy, either because it is only a concept or because it is still being written or designed.

va·pour ▶ **n.** British spelling of **VAPOR**.

va·que·ro /vä'kerō/ ▶ **n.** (pl. **vaqueros**) (in Spanish-speaking parts of the US) a cowboy; a cattle driver.
– ORIGIN Spanish, from *vaca* 'cow.'

VAR ▶ **abbr.** ■ value-added reseller, a company that adds extra features to products it has bought before selling them on. ■ value at risk, a method of quantifying the risk of holding a financial asset.

var. ▶ **abbr.** variety.

va·ra /'värə/ ▶ **n. 1** a unit of linear measure, formerly used in Latin America and Texas, equal to about 33 inches (84 cm).
2 a long spiked lance used by a picador.

var·ac·tor /ˈve(ə)rˌaktər, vəˈraktər/ ▶ **n.** Electronics a semiconductor diode with a capacitance dependent on the applied voltage.
– ORIGIN 1950s: from elements of *variable reactor*.

Va·ra·na·si /vəˈränəsē/ a city on the Ganges River, in Uttar Pradesh, in northern India; pop. 1,200,600 (est. 2009). It is a holy city and a place of pilgrimage for Hindus, who undergo ritual purification in the Ganges. Former name **BENARES**.

Va·rang·i·an /vəˈranjēən/ ▶ **n.** any of the Scandinavian voyagers who traveled by land and up rivers into Russia in the 9th and 10th centuries AD, establishing the Rurik dynasty and gaining great influence in the Byzantine Empire.
– ORIGIN from medieval Latin *Varangus* (a name ultimately from Old Norse, probably based on *vár* 'pledge') + **-IAN**.

Var·gas /ˈvärgəs/, Getúlio Dornelles (1883–1954), Brazilian statesman; president 1930–45 and 1951–54. After seizing power, he ruled as a virtual dictator until overthrown by a coup. Returned to power in 1951, he later committed suicide after widespread calls for his resignation.

Var·gas Llo·sa /ˈvärgəs ˈyōsə/, (Jorge) Mario (Pedro) (1936–), Peruvian novelist, playwright, and essayist. His novels include *Aunt Julia and the Scriptwriter* (1977) and *The Bad Girl* (2007).

vari- ▶ **comb. form** various: *variform*.
– ORIGIN from Latin *varius*.

var·i·a·ble /ˈve(ə)rēəbəl/ ▶ **adj. 1** not consistent or having a fixed pattern; liable to change: *the quality of hospital food is highly variable* | *awards can be for variable amounts*. ■ (of a wind) tending to change direction. ■ Mathematics (of a quantity) able to assume different numerical values. ■ Botany & Zoology (of a species) liable to deviate from the typical color or form, or to occur in different colors or forms.
2 able to be changed or adapted: *the drill has variable speed*. ■ (of a gear) designed to give varying ratios or speeds.
▶ **n.** an element, feature, or factor that is liable to vary or change: *there are too many variables involved to make any meaningful predictions*. ■ Mathematics a quantity that during a calculation is assumed to vary or be capable of varying in value. ■ Computing a data item that may take on more than one value during the runtime of a program. ■ Astronomy short for **VARIABLE STAR**. ■ (**variables**) the region of light, variable winds to the north of the northeast trade winds or (in the southern hemisphere) between the southeast trade winds and the westerlies.
– DERIVATIVES **var·i·a·bil·i·ty** /ˌve(ə)rēəˈbilitē/ **n.**, **var·i·a·ble·ness n.**, **var·i·a·bly** /-blē/ **adv.**
– ORIGIN late Middle English: via Old French from Latin *variabilis*, from *variare* (see **VARY**).

var·i·a·ble cost ▶ **n.** a cost that varies with the level of output.

var·i·a·ble-ge·om·e·try ▶ **adj.** denoting a swing-wing aircraft.

var·i·a·ble-rate mort·gage ▶ **n.** another term for **ADJUSTABLE-RATE MORTGAGE**.

var·i·a·ble star ▶ **n.** Astronomy a star whose brightness changes, either irregularly or regularly.

var·i·ance /ˈve(ə)rēəns/ ▶ **n.** the fact or quality of being different, divergent, or inconsistent: *her light tone was at variance with her sudden trembling*. ■ the state or fact of disagreeing or quarreling: *they were at variance with all their previous allies*. ■ chiefly Law a discrepancy between two statements or documents. ■ Law an official dispensation from a rule or regulation, typically a building regulation. ■ Statistics a quantity equal to the square of the standard deviation.
– ORIGIN Middle English: via Old French from Latin *variantia* 'difference,' from the verb *variare* (see **VARY**).

var·i·ant /ˈve(ə)rēənt/ ▶ **n.** a form or version of something that differs in some respect from other forms of the same thing or from a standard: *clinically distinct variants of malaria* | [as modifier] *a variant spelling*.
– ORIGIN late Middle English (as an adjective in the sense 'tending to vary'): from Old French, literally 'varying,' present participle of *varier* (see **VARY**). The noun dates from the mid 19th cent.

var·i·ate /ˈve(ə)rē-it, -ˌāt/ ▶ **n.** another term for **RANDOM VARIABLE**.

var·i·a·tion /ˌve(ə)rēˈāsʜən/ ▶ **n. 1** a change or difference in condition, amount, or level, typically with certain limits: *regional variations in house prices* | *the figures showed marked variation from year to year*. ■ Astronomy a deviation of a celestial body from its mean orbit or motion. ■ Mathematics a change in the value of a function due to small changes in the values of its argument or arguments. ■ (also **magnetic variation**) the angular difference between true north and magnetic north at a particular place. ■ Biology the occurrence of an organism in more than one distinct color or form.
2 a different or distinct form or version of something: *hurling is an Irish variation of field hockey*. ■ Music a version of a theme, modified in melody, rhythm, harmony, or ornamentation, so as to present it in a new but still recognizable form: *there is an eleven-bar theme followed by seven variations and a coda* | figurative *variations on the perennial theme of marital discord*. ■ Ballet a solo dance as part of a performance.
– DERIVATIVES **var·i·a·tion·al** /-sʜənl/ **adj.**
– ORIGIN late Middle English (denoting variance or conflict): from Old French, or from Latin *variatio(n-)*, from the verb *variare* (see **VARY**).

var·i·a·tion·ist /ˌve(ə)rēˈāsʜənist/ ▶ **n.** a person who studies variations in usage among different speakers of the same language.

var·i·ce·al /ˌvarəˈsēəl/ ▶ **adj.** Zoology & Medicine of, relating to, or involving a varix.
– ORIGIN 1960s: from Latin *varix, varic-*, on the pattern of words such as *corneal* and *laryngeal*.

var·i·cel·la /ˌvarəˈselə/ ▶ **n.** Medicine technical term for **CHICKENPOX**. ■ (also **varicella-zoster**) a herpesvirus that causes chickenpox and shingles; herpes zoster.
– ORIGIN late 18th cent.: modern Latin, irregular diminutive of **VARIOLA**.

var·i·ces /ˈvarəˌsēz/ plural form of **VARIX**.

var·i·co·cele /ˈvarikōˌsēl/ ▶ **n.** Medicine a mass of varicose veins in the spermatic cord.
– ORIGIN mid 18th cent.: from Latin *varix, varic-* 'dilated vein' + **-CELE**.

var·i·col·ored /ˈve(ə)riˌkələrd/ (Brit. **varicoloured**) ▶ **adj.** consisting of several different colors.
– ORIGIN mid 17th cent.: from Latin *varius* 'diverse' + **COLORED**.

var·i·cose /ˈvarəˌkōs/ ▶ **adj.** [attrib.] affected by a condition causing the swelling and tortuous lengthening of veins, most often in the legs: *varicose veins*.
– DERIVATIVES **var·i·cosed adj.**, **var·i·cos·i·ty** /ˌvariˈkäsitē/ **n.**
– ORIGIN late Middle English: from Latin *varicosus*, from *varix* (see **VARIX**).

var·ied /ˈve(ə)rēd/ ▶ **adj.** incorporating a number of different types or elements; showing variation or variety: *a little effort to make life pleasant and varied* | *a long and varied career*.
– DERIVATIVES **var·ied·ly adv.**

var·i·e·gat·ed /ˈver(ē)əˌgātid/ ▶ **adj.** exhibiting different colors, esp. as irregular patches or streaks: *variegated yellow brricks*. ■ Botany (of a plant or foliage) having or consisting of leaves that are edged or patterned in a second color, esp. white as well as green. ■ marked by variety: *his variegated and amusing observations*.
– DERIVATIVES **var·i·e·gate** /ˈve(ə)r(ē)iˌgāt/, **var·i·e·ga·tion** /ˌver(ē)iˈgāsʜən/ **n.**
– ORIGIN mid 17th cent.: from Latin *variegat-* 'made varied' (from the verb *variegare*, from *varius* 'diverse') + **-ED**[2].

va·ri·e·tal /vəˈrīətl/ ▶ **adj. 1** (of a wine or grape) made from or belonging to a single specified variety of grape.
2 chiefly Botany & Zoology of, relating to, characteristic of, or forming a variety: *varietal names*.
▶ **n.** a varietal wine or grape.
– DERIVATIVES **va·ri·e·tal·ly adv.**

va·ri·e·ty /vəˈrīətē/ ▶ **n.** (pl. **varieties**) **1** the quality or state of being different or diverse; the absence of uniformity, sameness, or monotony: *it's the variety that makes my job so enjoyable*. ■ (**a variety of**) a number or range of things of the same general class that are different or distinct in character or quality: *the center offers a variety of leisure activities*. ■ a thing that differs in some way from others of the same general class or sort; a type: *fifty varieties of fresh and frozen pasta*. ■ a form of television or theater entertainment consisting of a series of different types of acts, such as singing, dancing, and comedy: *in 1937 she did another season of variety* | [as modifier] *a variety show*.
2 Biology a taxonomic category that ranks below subspecies (where present) or species, its members differing from others of the same subspecies or species in minor but permanent or heritable characteristics. Varieties are more often recognized in botany, in which they are designated in the style *Apium graveolens* var. dulce. Compare with **FORM** (sense 3 of the noun) and **SUBSPECIES**. ■ a cultivated form of a plant. See **CULTIVAR**. ■ a plant or animal that varies in some trivial respect from its immediate parent or type.
– PHRASES **variety is the spice of life** proverb new and exciting experiences make life more interesting.
– ORIGIN late 15th cent.: from French *variété* or Latin *varietas*, from *varius* (see **VARIOUS**).

va·ri·e·ty meats ▶ **plural n.** meat consisting of the entrails and internal organs of an animal.

va·ri·e·ty store ▶ **n.** a small store selling a wide range of inexpensive items.

var·i·form /ˈve(ə)rəˌfôrm/ ▶ **adj.** (of a group of things) differing from one another in form: *variform languages*. ■ (of a single thing or a mass) consisting of a variety of forms or things: *a variform education*.
– ORIGIN mid 17th cent.: from Latin *varius* 'diverse' + **-FORM**.

va·ri·o·la /vəˈrīələ, ˌve(ə)rēˈōlə/ ▶ **n.** Medicine technical term for **SMALLPOX**.
– DERIVATIVES **va·ri·o·lar** /-lər/ **adj.**, **va·ri·o·lous** /-ləs/ **adj.** (archaic).
– ORIGIN late 18th cent.: from medieval Latin, literally 'pustule, pock,' from Latin *varius* 'diverse.'

var·i·o·loid /ˈve(ə)rēəˌloid/ Medicine ▶ **adj.** resembling smallpox.
▶ **n.** a mild form of smallpox affecting people who have already had the disease or have been vaccinated against it.

var·i·om·e·ter /ˌve(ə)rēˈämitər/ ▶ **n. 1** a device for indicating an aircraft's rate of climb or descent.
2 an inductor whose total inductance can be varied by altering the relative position of two coaxial coils connected in series, or by permeability tuning, and so can be used to tune an electric circuit.
3 an instrument for measuring variations in the intensity of the earth's magnetic field.

var·i·o·rum /ˌve(ə)rēˈôrəm/ ▶ **adj.** (of an edition of an author's works) having notes by various editors or commentators. ■ including variant readings from manuscripts or earlier editions.
▶ **n.** a variorum edition.
– ORIGIN early 18th cent.: genitive plural of *varius* 'diverse,' from Latin *editio cum notis variorum* 'edition with notes by various (commentators).'

var·i·ous /ˈve(ə)rēəs/ ▶ **adj.** different from one another; of different kinds or sorts: *dresses of various colors* | *his grievances were many and various*. ■ having or showing different properties or qualities: *their environments are locally various*.
▶ **determiner & pron.** more than one; individual and separate: [as determiner] *various people arrived late* | [as pronoun] *various of her friends had called*.
– DERIVATIVES **var·i·ous·ness n.**
– ORIGIN late Middle English: from Latin *varius* 'changing, diverse' + **-OUS**.

> **USAGE** In standard English, the word **various** is normally used as an adjective. It is best reserved for contexts indicating variety, and should not be used as a synonym for **several**. In colloquial American speech, **various** is sometimes also used (as though it were a pronoun) followed by *of*, as in ***various of** her friends had called* —another way of saying *some of* or *several of*. This use is discouraged by some traditionalists, however, because **various** is properly an adjective, not a pronoun.

var·i·ous·ly /ˈve(ə)rēəslē/ ▶ **adv.** in several or different ways: *his early successes can be variously accounted for*.

Va·ris·can /vəˈriskən/ ▶ **adj.** Geology another term for **HERCYNIAN**.
– ORIGIN early 20th cent.: from Latin *Varisci* (the name of a Germanic tribe) + **-AN**.

var·is·tor /vəˈristər/ ▶ **n.** a semiconductor diode with resistance dependent on the applied voltage.
– ORIGIN 1930s: contraction of *varying resistor*.

var·ix /ˈve(ə)riks/ ▶ **n.** (pl. **varices** /ˈve(ə)riəˌsēz/)
1 Medicine a varicose vein.
2 Zoology each of the ridges on the shell of a gastropod mollusk, marking a former position of the aperture.
– ORIGIN late Middle English: from Latin.

var·let /ˈvärlət/ ▶ **n. 1** historical a man or boy acting as an attendant or servant. ■ a knight's page.
2 archaic a dishonest or unprincipled man.
– DERIVATIVES **var·let·ry** /-lətrē/ **n.**
– ORIGIN late Middle English: from Old French, variant of *valet* 'attendant' (see **VALET**). The sense 'rogue' dates from the mid 16th cent.

var·mint /ˈvärmənt/ ▶ **n.** dialect, informal a troublesome wild animal. ■ a troublesome and mischievous person, esp. a child.
– ORIGIN mid 16th cent.: alteration of **VERMIN**.

V

Var·na /ˈvärnə/ a port and resort in eastern Bulgaria, on the western shores of the Black Sea; pop. 318,313 (2008).

var·na /ˈvərnə, ˈvär-/ ▶ **n.** each of the four Hindu castes, Brahman, Kshatriya, Vaishya, and Shudra.
– ORIGIN Sanskrit, literally 'color, class.'

var·nish /ˈvärnisH/ ▶ **n.** resin dissolved in a liquid for applying on wood, metal, or other materials to form a hard, clear, shiny surface when dry. ■ [in sing.] archaic an external or superficially attractive appearance of a specific quality: *an outward varnish of civilization.*
▶ **v.** [with obj.] apply varnish to: *we stripped the floor and varnished it.* ■ disguise or gloss over (a fact): *the White House is* ***varnishing over*** *the defeat of the president's proposal.*
– DERIVATIVES **var·nish·er n.**
– ORIGIN Middle English: from Old French *vernis*, from medieval Latin *veronix* 'fragrant resin, sandarac' or medieval Greek *berenikē*, probably from *Berenice*, a town in Cyrenaica.

var·nish tree ▶ **n.** another term for **LACQUER TREE**.

Var·ro /ˈvarō/, Marcus Terentius (116–27 BC), Roman scholar and satirist. His works covered many subjects, including philosophy, agriculture, education, and the Latin language.

var·ro·a /ˈvarəwə/ (also **varroa mite**) ▶ **n.** a microscopic mite that is a debilitating parasite of the honeybee, causing loss of honey production. ● *Varroa jacobsoni*, order (or subclass) Acari.
– ORIGIN 1970s: modern Latin, from **VARRO** (with reference to his work on beekeeping) + **-A**[1].

var·si·ty /ˈvärsətē/ ▶ **n.** (pl. **varsities**) a sports team representing a school or college: *Miller promoted him to the varsity for his sophomore season* | [as modifier] *girls' varsity basketball.* ■ Brit. dated, S. African, or NZ university: *he had his hair cut as soon as he got back from varsity.* ■ [as modifier] Brit. (esp. of a sporting event or team) of or relating to a university, esp. Oxford or Cambridge: *a varsity match.*
– ORIGIN mid 17th cent.: shortening of **UNIVERSITY**, reflecting an archaic pronunciation.

Var·u·na /ˈvərōōnə, ˈvär-/ Hinduism one of the gods in the Rig Veda. Originally the sovereign lord of the universe and guardian of cosmic law, he is known in later Hinduism as god of the waters.

var·us /ˈve(ə)rəs/ ▶ **n.** Medicine a deformity involving oblique displacement of part of a limb toward the midline. The opposite of **VALGUS**.
– ORIGIN early 19th cent.: from Latin, literally 'bent, crooked.'

varve /ˈvärv/ ▶ **n.** Geology a pair of thin layers of clay and silt of contrasting color and texture that represent the deposit of a single year (summer and winter) in a lake. Such layers can be used to determine the chronology of glacial sediments.
– DERIVATIVES **varved adj.**
– ORIGIN early 20th cent.: from Swedish *varv* 'layer.'

var·y /ˈve(ə)rē/ ▶ **v.** (**varies, varying, varied**) [no obj.] differ in size, amount, degree, or nature from something else of the same general class: *the properties vary in price* | (as adj. **varying**) *varying degrees of success.* ■ change from one condition, form, or state to another: *your skin's moisture content varies according to climatic conditions.* ■ [with obj.] introduce modifications or changes into (something) so as to make it different or less uniform: *he tried to vary his diet.*
– DERIVATIVES **var·y·ing·ly adv.**
– ORIGIN Middle English: from Old French *varier* or Latin *variare*, from *varius* 'diverse.'

vas /vas/ ▶ **n.** (pl. **vasa** /ˈväsə, -zə/) Anatomy a vessel or duct.
– DERIVATIVES **va·sal** /ˈvāsəl, -zəl/ **adj.**
– ORIGIN late 16th cent.: from Latin, literally 'vessel.'

Va·sa /ˈväsə/ Swedish name for **VAASA**.

Va·sa·rely /ˌväsəˈrelē, ˌvas-/, Viktor (1908–97), French painter, born in Hungary. A pioneer of op art, he was best known for a style of geometric abstraction that used repeated geometric forms and interacting colors to create visual disorientation.

Va·sa·ri /vəˈsärē/, Giorgio (1511–74), Italian painter, architect, and biographer. His *Lives of the Most Excellent Painters, Sculptors, and Architects* (1550, enlarged 1568) formed the basis for the later study of art history in the West.

Vas·co da Ga·ma /ˌväskō də ˈgämə/ see **DA GAMA**.

vas·cu·lar /ˈvaskyələr/ ▶ **adj.** Anatomy, Zoology, & Medicine of, relating to, affecting, or consisting of a vessel or vessels, esp. those that carry blood: *vascular disease* | *the vascular system.* ■ Botany relating to or denoting the plant tissues (xylem and phloem) that conduct water, sap, and nutrients in flowering plants, ferns, and their relatives.
– DERIVATIVES **vas·cu·lar·i·ty** /ˌvaskyəˈlaritē/ **n.**
– ORIGIN late 17th cent.: from modern Latin *vascularis*, from Latin *vasculum* (see **VASCULUM**).

vas·cu·lar bun·dle ▶ **n.** Botany a strand of conducting vessels in the stem or leaves of a plant, typically with phloem on the outside and xylem on the inside.

vas·cu·lar cyl·in·der ▶ **n.** another term for **STELE** (sense 1).

vas·cu·lar·ize /ˈvaskyələˌrīz/ ▶ **v.** [with obj.] Biology & Anatomy provide (a tissue or structure) with vessels, esp. blood vessels; make vascular: (as adj. **vascularized**) *the endocrine glands are highly vascularized tissues.*
– DERIVATIVES **vas·cu·lar·i·za·tion** /ˌvaskyələrəˈzāsHən/ **n.**

vas·cu·lar plant ▶ **n.** Botany a plant that is characterized by the presence of conducting tissue. ● Subkingdom Tracheophyta: divisions Pteridophyta (ferns, horsetails, and club mosses) and Spermatophyta (cycads, conifers, and flowering plants).

vas·cu·lar tis·sue ▶ **n.** the tissue in higher plants that constitutes the vascular system, consisting of phloem and xylem, by which water and nutrients are conducted throughout the plant.

vas·cu·la·ture /ˈvaskyələˌCHŏŏr, -CHər/ ▶ **n.** Anatomy the vascular system of a part of the body and its arrangement: *diseases affecting the pulmonary vasculature.*

vas·cu·li·tis /ˌvaskyəˈlītis/ ▶ **n.** (pl. **vasculitides** /-ˈlitiˌdēz/) Medicine inflammation of a blood vessel or blood vessels.
– DERIVATIVES **vas·cu·lit·ic** /-ˈlitik/ **adj.**

vas·cu·lum /ˈvaskyələm/ ▶ **n.** (pl. **vascula** /-lə/) Botany a collecting box for plants, typically in the form of a flattened cylindrical metal case with a lengthwise opening, carried by a shoulder strap.
– ORIGIN late 18th cent.: from Latin, diminutive of *vas* 'vessel.'

vas de·fe·rens /ˌvas ˈdefərənz, -ˌrenz/ ▶ **n.** (pl. **vasa deferentia** /ˌväsə ˌdefəˈrensH(ē)ə, ˌväzə/) Anatomy the duct that conveys sperm from the testicle to the urethra.
– ORIGIN late 16th cent.: from **VAS** + Latin *deferens* 'carrying away,' present participle of *deferre*.

vase /vās, vāz, väz/ ▶ **n.** a decorative container, typically made of glass or china and used as an ornament or for displaying cut flowers.
– DERIVATIVES **vase·ful** /-ˌfŏŏl/ **n.** (pl. **vasefuls**).
– ORIGIN late Middle English: from French, from Latin *vas* 'vessel.'

vas·ec·to·my /vəˈsektəmē, va-/ ▶ **n.** (pl. **vasectomies**) the surgical cutting and sealing of part of each vas deferens, typically as a means of sterilization.
– DERIVATIVES **va·sec·to·mize** /-ˌmīz/ **v.**

Vas·e·line /ˌvasəˈlēn, ˈvasəˌlēn/ ▶ **n.** trademark a type of petroleum jelly used as an ointment and lubricant.
▶ **v.** [with obj.] cover or smear with this.
– ORIGIN late 19th cent.: formed irregularly from German *Wasser* 'water' + Greek *elaion* 'olive oil' + **-INE**[4].

vase shell ▶ **n.** a predatory mollusk of warm seas, with a heavy ribbed shell that has blunt spines and is typically pale with chestnut markings. ● Genus *Vasum*, family Vasidae, class Gastropoda.

vaso- ▶ **comb. form** of or relating to a vessel or vessels, esp. blood vessels: *vasoconstriction.*
– ORIGIN from Latin *vas* 'vessel.'

vas·o·ac·tive /ˌvāzōˈaktiv, ˌvasō-/ ▶ **adj.** Physiology affecting the diameter of blood vessels (and hence blood pressure).

vas·o·con·stric·tion /ˌvāzōkənˈstriksHən, ˌvasō-/ ▶ **n.** the constriction of blood vessels, which increases blood pressure.
– DERIVATIVES **vas·o·con·stric·tive** /-ˈstriktiv/ **adj.**, **vas·o·con·stric·tor** /-ˈstriktər/ **n.**

vas·o·di·la·tion /ˌvāzōdīˈlāsHən, ˌvasō-/ (also **vasodilatation** /-ˌdiləˈtāsHən/) ▶ **n.** the dilatation of blood vessels, which decreases blood pressure.
– DERIVATIVES **vas·o·di·la·tor** /-ˈdīˌlātər/ **n.**, **vas·o·dil·a·to·ry** /-ˈdiləˌtôrē/ **adj.**

vas·o·mo·tor /ˌvāzōˈmōtər, ˌvasō-/ ▶ **adj.** [attrib.] causing or relating to the constriction or dilatation of blood vessels. ■ denoting a region in the medulla of the brain (the **vasomotor center**) that regulates blood pressure by controlling reflex alterations in the heart rate and the diameter of the blood vessels, in response to stimuli from receptors in the circulatory system or from other parts of the brain.

vas·o·pres·sin /ˌvāzōˈpresən, ˌvasō-/ ▶ **n.** Biochemistry a pituitary hormone that acts to promote the retention of water by the kidneys and increase blood pressure.
– ORIGIN 1920s: from *vasopressor* 'causing constriction in blood vessels' + **-IN**[1].

va·so·pres·sor /ˈvasōˌpresər, ˈvāzō-/ ▶ **adj.** causing the constriction of blood vessels.
▶ **n.** a drug with this effect.

va·so·spasm /ˈvasōˌspazəm, ˈvāzō-/ ▶ **n.** sudden constriction of a blood vessel, reducing its diameter and flow rate.
– DERIVATIVES **va·so·spas·tic** /ˌvasōˈspastik, ˌvāzō-/ **adj.**

va·so·va·gal /ˌvāzōˈvāgəl, ˌvasō-/ ▶ **adj.** [attrib.] Medicine relating to or denoting a temporary fall in blood pressure, with pallor, fainting, sweating, and nausea, caused by overactivity of the vagus nerve, esp. as a result of stress.

vas·sal /ˈvasəl/ ▶ **n.** historical a holder of land by feudal tenure on conditions of homage and allegiance. ■ a person or country in a subordinate position to another: [as modifier] *a much stronger nation can also turn a weaker one into a vassal state.*
– DERIVATIVES **vas·sal·age** /-əlij/ **n.**
– ORIGIN late Middle English: via Old French from medieval Latin *vassallus* 'retainer,' of Celtic origin; compare with **VAVASOUR**.

vast /vast/ ▶ **adj.** of very great extent or quantity; immense: *a vast plain of buffalo grass.*
▶ **n.** archaic an immense space.
– DERIVATIVES **vast·ly adv.**, **vast·ness n.**, **vast·y adj.**
– ORIGIN late Middle English: from Latin *vastus* 'void, immense;' compare with **WASTE**.

vas·ta·tion /vaˈstāsHən/ ▶ **n.** literary the action or process of emptying or purifying someone or something, typically violently or drastically.
– ORIGIN mid 16th cent.: from Latin *vastatio(n-)*, from *vastare* 'lay waste.'

Väs·ter·ås /ˌvestəˈrōs/ a port on Lake Mälaren in eastern Sweden; pop. 134,684 (2008).

vas·ti·tude /ˈvastiˌt(y)ōōd/ ▶ **n. 1** the quality of being vast; immensity.
2 a vast extent or space.

VAT /vat/ ▶ **abbr.** value added tax.

vat /vat/ ▶ **n. 1** a large tank or tub used to hold liquid, esp. in industry: ***a vat of hot tar.***
2 (also **vat dye**) a water-insoluble dye, such as indigo, that is applied to a fabric in a reducing bath, which converts it to a soluble form, the color being obtained on subsequent oxidation in the fabric fibers.
▶ **v.** (**vats, vatting, vatted**) [with obj.] place or treat in a vat.
– ORIGIN Middle English: southern and western English dialect variant of obsolete *fat* 'container,' of Germanic origin; related to Dutch *vat* and German *Fass*.

vat dye ▶ **n.** a water-insoluble dye that is applied as an alkaline solution of a soluble leuco form, the color being obtained through oxidation.
– DERIVATIVES **vat-dyed adj.**

vat·ic /ˈvatik/ ▶ **adj.** literary describing or predicting what will happen in the future: *vatic utterances.*
– ORIGIN early 17th cent.: from Latin *vates* 'prophet' + **-IC**.

Vat·i·can /ˈvatikən/ **n.** (usu. **the Vatican**) the palace and official residence of the pope in Rome. ■ [treated as sing. or pl.] the administrative center of the Roman Catholic Church.
– ORIGIN mid 16th cent.: from French, or from Latin *Vaticanus*, the name of a hill in Rome.

Vat·i·can Cit·y an independent papal state in the city of Rome, the seat of government of the Roman Catholic Church; pop. 800 (est. 2009).

> It covers an area of 109 acres (44 hectares) around St. Peter's Basilica and the palace of the Vatican. Having been suspended after the incorporation of the former Papal States into Italy in 1870, the temporal power of the pope was restored by the Lateran Treaty of 1929.

Vat·i·can Coun·cil n. each of two general councils of the Roman Catholic Church, held in 1869–70 and 1962–65. The first (**Vatican I**) proclaimed the infallibility of the pope when speaking *ex cathedra*; the second (**Vatican II**) made numerous reforms, abandoning the universal Latin liturgy and acknowledging ecumenism.

va·tic·i·nate /vəˈtisəˌnāt/ ▶ **v.** [no obj.] rare foretell the future.
– DERIVATIVES **va·tic·i·nal** /-ənl/ **adj.**, **va·tic·i·na·tion** /-ˌtisəˈnāsHən/ **n.**, **va·tic·i·na·tor** /-ˌnātər/ **n.**, **va·tic·i·na·to·ry** /-ənəˌtôrē/ **adj.**
– ORIGIN early 17th cent.: from Latin *vaticinat-* 'prophesied,' from the verb *vaticinari*, from *vates* 'prophet.'

Vät·tern /ˈvetə(r)n/ a lake in southern Sweden.

va·tu /ˈvä,to͞o/ ▶ **n.** (pl. **same**) the basic monetary unit of Vanuatu.
– ORIGIN Bislama.

Vaud /vō/ a canton on the shores of Lake Geneva in western Switzerland; capital, Lausanne. German name **WAADT**.

vaude·ville /ˈvôd(ə),vil, -vəl/ ▶ **n.** a type of entertainment popular chiefly in the US in the early 20th century, featuring a mixture of specialty acts such as burlesque comedy and song and dance. ■ a stage play on a trivial theme with interspersed songs. ■ archaic a satirical or topical song with a refrain.
– DERIVATIVES **vaude·vil·lian** /,vôd(ə)ˈvilyən, -ˈvilēən/ **adj.** & **n.**
– ORIGIN mid 18th cent.: from French, earlier *vau de ville* (or *vire*), said to be a name given originally to songs composed by Olivier Basselin, a 15th-cent. fuller born in *Vau de Vire* in Normandy.

Vau·dois /vōˈdwä/ ▶ **n.** (pl. **same**) historical a member of the Waldenses religious sect.
▶ **adj.** of or relating to the Waldenses.
– ORIGIN mid 16th cent.: French, representing medieval Latin *Valdensis* (see **WALDENSES**).

Vaughan[1] /vôn/, Henry (1621–95), Welsh religious writer and metaphysical poet.

Vaughan[2], Sarah (Lois) (1924–90), US jazz singer and pianist. She was notable for her vocal range, her use of vibrato, and her improvisational skills.

Vaughan Wil·liams, Ralph (1872–1958), English composer. His strongly melodic music frequently reflects his interest in Tudor composers and English folk songs. Notable works: *Fantasia on a Theme by Thomas Tallis* (1910), *A London Symphony* (1914), and the *Mass in G minor* (1922).

vault[1] /vôlt/ ▶ **n. 1** a roof in the form of an arch or a series of arches, typical of churches and other large, formal buildings. ■ literary a thing resembling an arched roof, esp. the sky: *the vault of heaven*. ■ Anatomy the arched roof of a cavity, esp. that of the skull: *the cranial vault*.
2 a large room or chamber used for storage, esp. an underground one. ■ a secure room in a bank in which valuables are stored. ■ a chamber beneath a church or in a graveyard used for burials.
▶ **v.** [with obj.] (usu. as adj. **vaulted**) provide (a building or room) with an arched roof or roofs: *a vaulted arcade*. ■ make (a roof) in the form of a vault: *there was a high ceiling, vaulted with cut slate*.
– ORIGIN Middle English: from Old French *voute*, based on Latin *volvere* 'to roll.'

vault[2] ▶ **v.** [no obj.] leap or spring while supporting or propelling oneself with one or both hands or with the help of a pole: *he vaulted over the gate*. ■ [with obj.] jump over (an obstacle) in such a way: *Ryker vaulted the barrier*.
▶ **n.** an act of vaulting.
– DERIVATIVES **vault·er n.**
– ORIGIN mid 16th cent.: from Old French *volter* 'to turn (a horse), gambol,' based on Latin *volvere* 'to roll.'

vault·ing /ˈvôltiNG/ ▶ **n.** ornamental work in a vaulted roof or ceiling.

vault·ing horse ▶ **n.** a padded wooden block used for vaulting over by gymnasts and athletes.

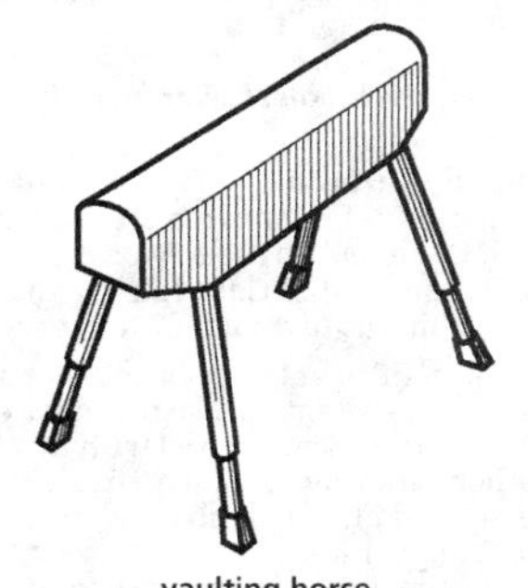
vaulting horse

vaunt /vônt, vänt/ ▶ **v.** [with obj.] (usu. as adj. **vaunted**) boast about or praise (something), esp. excessively: *the much vaunted information superhighway*.
▶ **n.** archaic a boast.
– DERIVATIVES **vaunt·er n.**, **vaunt·ing·ly adv.**
– ORIGIN late Middle English: the noun a shortening of obsolete *avaunt* 'boasting, a boast'; the verb (originally in the sense 'use boastful language') from Old French *vanter*, from late Latin *vantare*, based on Latin *vanus* 'vain, empty.'

vav /väv, vôv/ ▶ **n.** the sixth letter of the Hebrew alphabet.

vav·a·so·ry /ˈvavə,sôrē/ ▶ **n.** (pl. **vavasories**) historical the estate of a vavasour.
– ORIGIN early 17th cent.: from Old French *vavasorie* or medieval Latin *vavasoria* (see **VAVASOUR**).

vav·a·sour /ˈvavə,sôr/ ▶ **n.** historical a vassal owing allegiance to a powerful lord and having other vassals under him.
– ORIGIN Middle English: from Old French *vavas(s)our*, from medieval Latin *vavassor*, perhaps from *vassus vassorum* 'vassal of vassals.'

va-va-voom /,vä vä ˈvo͞om/ informal ▶ **n.** the quality of being exciting, vigorous, or sexually attractive: *she's lost none of her va-va-voom since giving birth to her daughter*.
▶ **adj.** sexually attractive: *her va-va-voom figure*.
– ORIGIN 1950s: representing the sound of a car engine being revved.

VC ▶ **abbr.** ■ Vice-Chairman. ■ Vice-Chancellor. ■ Vice-Consul. ■ Victoria Cross. ■ Vietcong.

vCard ▶ **n.** trademark virtual business card, an electronic representation of a business card, usually a file attached to an e-mail in place of a signature.

V-chip ▶ **n.** a computer chip installed in a television receiver that can be programmed by the user to block or scramble material containing a special code in its signal indicating that it is deemed violent or sexually explicit.

vCJD ▶ **abbr.** variant Creutzfeldt–Jakob disease, the human form of mad cow disease. Sometimes referred to as **nvCJD** (new variant Creutzfeldt–Jakob disease).

VCR ▶ **n.** (pl. **VCRs**) a videocassette recorder.

VD ▶ **abbr.** venereal disease.

V-day ▶ **n.** Victory Day, esp. with reference to the Allied victories in World War II.

VDT ▶ **abbr.** video display terminal.

've ▶ **abbr.** informal have (usually after the pronouns *I*, *you*, *we*, and *they*): *we've tried our best*.

veal /vēl/ ▶ **n.** the flesh of a calf, used as food.
– ORIGIN Middle English: from Anglo-Norman French *ve(e)l*, from Latin *vitellus*, diminutive of *vitulus* 'calf.'

veal·er /ˈvēlər/ ▶ **n.** a calf raised to become veal.

Veb·len /ˈveblən/, Thorstein (Bunde) (1857–1929), US economist and social scientist. He coined the phrase "conspicuous consumption." His works include *The Theory of the Leisure Class* (1899), a critique of capitalism, and *The Theory of Business Enterprise* (1904).

vec·tor /ˈvektər/ ▶ **n.**
1 Mathematics & Physics a quantity having direction as well as magnitude, esp. as determining the position of one point in space relative to another. Compare with **SCALAR**. ■ Mathematics a matrix with one row or one column. ■ a course to be taken by an aircraft. ■ [as modifier] Computing denoting a type of graphical representation using straight lines to construct the outlines of objects.
2 an organism, typically a biting insect or tick, that transmits a disease or parasite from one animal or plant to another. ■ Genetics a bacteriophage or plasmid that transfers genetic material into a cell, or from one bacterium to another.
▶ **v.** [with obj.] direct (an aircraft in flight) to a desired point.
– DERIVATIVES **vec·to·ri·al** /vekˈtôrēəl/ **adj.**, **vec·to·ri·al·ly** /vekˈtôrēəlē/ **adv.**, **vec·tor·i·za·tion** /,vektərəˈzāSHən/ **n.**, **vec·tor·ize** /-,rīz/ **v.**
– ORIGIN mid 19th cent.: from Latin, literally 'carrier,' from *vehere* 'convey.'

vector 1

vec·tor field ▶ **n.** Mathematics a function of a space whose value at each point is a vector quantity.

vec·tor proc·es·sor ▶ **n.** Computing a processor that is able to process sequences of data with a single instruction.

vec·tor prod·uct ▶ **n.** Mathematics the product of two real in three dimensions that is itself a vector at right angles to both the original vectors. Its magnitude is the product of the magnitudes of the original vectors and the sine of the angle between their directions. Also called **CROSS PRODUCT**. Compare with **INNER PRODUCT**. ● Written as $a \times b$.

vec·tor space ▶ **n.** Mathematics a space consisting of vectors, together with the associative and commutative operation of addition of vectors, and the associative and distributive operation of multiplication of vectors by scalars.

Ve·da /ˈvādə, ˈvēdə/ ▶ **n.** [treated as sing. or pl.] the most ancient Hindu scriptures, written in early Sanskrit and containing hymns, philosophy, and guidance on ritual for the priests of Vedic religion. Believed to have been directly revealed to seers among the early Aryans in India, and preserved by oral tradition, the four chief collections are the Rig Veda, Sama Veda, Yajur Veda, and Atharva Veda.
– ORIGIN Sanskrit, literally '(sacred) knowledge.'

Ve·dan·ta /vāˈdäntə, və-/ ▶ **n.** a Hindu philosophy based on the doctrine of the Upanishads, esp. in its monistic form.
– DERIVATIVES **Ve·dan·tic** /-tik/ **adj.**, **Ve·dan·tist** /-tist/ **n.**
– ORIGIN from Sanskrit *vedānta*, from *veda* (see **VEDA**) + *anta* 'end.'

V-E Day ▶ **n.** the day (May 8) marking the Allied victory in Europe in 1945.
– ORIGIN *V-E*, abbreviation of *Victory in Europe*.

Ved·da /ˈvedə/ ▶ **n.** a member of an aboriginal people inhabiting the forests of Sri Lanka.
– ORIGIN from Sinhalese *vaddā* 'hunter.'

ve·dette /viˈdet/ (also **vidette**) ▶ **n. 1** historical a mounted sentry positioned beyond an army's outposts to observe the movements of the enemy.
2 a leading star of stage, screen, or television.
– ORIGIN late 17th cent.: from French, literally 'scout,' from an alteration of southern Italian *veletta*, perhaps based on Spanish *velar* 'keep watch.'

Ve·dic /ˈvādik, ˈvēdik/ ▶ **adj.** of or relating to the Veda or Vedas.
▶ **n.** the language of the Vedas, an early form of Sanskrit.
– ORIGIN from French *védique* or German *vedisch* (see **VEDA**).

Ve·dic re·li·gion ▶ **n.** the ancient religion of the Aryan peoples who entered northwestern India from Persia *c.*2000–1200 BC. It was the precursor of Hinduism, and its beliefs and practices are contained in the Vedas.

> Its characteristics included ritual sacrifice to many gods, esp. Indra, Varuna, and Agni; social classes (varnas) that formed the basis of the caste system; and the emergence of the priesthood, which dominated orthodox Brahmanism from *c.*900 BC. Transition to classical Hinduism began in about the 5th century BC.

vee /vē/ ▶ **n.** the letter V. ■ a thing shaped like a V: *a broken vee of birds points for the marshes*.

vee·jay /ˈvē,jā/ ▶ **n.** informal a person who introduces and plays popular music videos.
– ORIGIN 1980s: representing a pronunciation of *VJ*, short for *video jockey*, on the pattern of *deejay*.

vee·na /ˈvēnə/ (also **vina**) ▶ **n.** an Indian stringed instrument, with four main and three auxiliary strings. The southern type has a lutelike body; the older northern type has a tubular body and a gourd fitted to each end as a resonator.
– ORIGIN from Sanskrit *vīṇā*.

veep /vēp/ ▶ **n.** informal a vice president.
– ORIGIN 1940s: from the initials *VP*.

veer[1] /vi(ə)r/ ▶ **v.** [no obj.] change direction suddenly: *an oil tanker that had veered off course*. ■ suddenly change an opinion, subject, type of behavior, etc.: *the conversation eventually veered away from theatrical things*. ■ (of the wind) change direction clockwise around the points of the compass: *the wind veered southwest*. The opposite of **BACK**.
▶ **n.** a sudden change of direction.
– ORIGIN late 16th cent.: from French *virer*, perhaps from an alteration of Latin *gyrare* (see **GYRATE**).

veer[2] ▶ **v.** [with obj.] Nautical; dated slacken or let out (a rope or cable) in a controlled way.
– ORIGIN late Middle English: from Middle Dutch *vieren*.

veer·y /ˈvi(ə)rē/ ▶ **n.** a North American woodland thrush with a brown back and speckled breast.
● *Catharus fuscescens*, subfamily Turdinae, family Muscicapidae.
– ORIGIN mid 19th cent.: perhaps imitative.

veg[1] /vej/ ▶ **v.** (**vegges, vegging, veging, vegged**) [no obj.] informal relax to the point of complete inertia: *they were vegging out in front of the TV*.
– ORIGIN 1920s: abbreviation of **VEGETATE**.

veg[2] ▶ **n.** (pl. **same**) Brit. informal a vegetable or vegetables: *meat and two veg*.
– ORIGIN late 19th cent.: abbreviation.

Ve·ga[1] /ˈvāgə/, Lope de (1562–1635), Spanish playwright and poet; full name *Lope Felix de Vega*

Carpio. He is regarded as the founder of Spanish drama.

Ve·ga² Astronomy the fifth brightest star in the sky, and the brightest in the constellation Lyra, overhead in summer to observers in the northern hemisphere.
– ORIGIN via Spanish or medieval Latin from Arabic, literally 'the falling eagle or vulture.'

ve·ga /ˈvāgə/ ▶ **n.** (in Spain and Spanish America) a large plain or valley, typically a fertile and grassy one.
– ORIGIN Spanish and Catalan.

veg·an /ˈvēgən, ˈvejən/ ▶ **n.** a person who does not eat or use animal products: *I'm a strict vegan* | [as modifier] *a vegan diet.*
– ORIGIN 1940s: from VEGETARIAN + -AN.

Ve·gas /ˈˌvāgəs/ informal name for Las Vegas.

veg·e·ta·ble /ˈvejtəbəl, ˈvəjətə-/ ▶ **n. 1** a plant or part of a plant used as food, typically as accompaniment to meat or fish, such as a cabbage, potato, carrot, or bean.
2 informal, offensive a person who is incapable of normal mental or physical activity, esp. through brain damage. ■ informal a person with a dull or inactive life: *I thought I'd sort of flop back and be a vegetable for a bit.*
▶ **adj.** [attrib.] of or relating to vegetables as food: *a vegetable garden* | *vegetable soup.* ■ of or relating to plants or plant life, esp. as distinct from animal life or mineral substances: *vegetable matter.*
– ORIGIN late Middle English (in the sense 'growing as a plant'): from Old French, or from late Latin *vegetabilis* 'animating,' from Latin *vegetare* (see VEGETATE). The noun dates from the late 16th cent.

veg·e·ta·ble but·ter ▶ **n.** vegetable fat with the consistency of butter.

veg·e·ta·ble i·vo·ry ▶ **n.** a hard white material obtained from the endosperm of the ivory nut.

veg·e·ta·ble mar·row ▶ **n.** see MARROW (sense 2).

veg·e·ta·ble oil ▶ **n.** an oil derived from plants, e.g., canola oil, olive oil, sunflower oil.

veg·e·ta·ble sheep ▶ **n.** a New Zealand plant of the daisy family that has grayish hairy leaves and forms hummocks that from a distance look like sheep.
● *Raoulia eximia*, family Compositae.

veg·e·ta·ble spa·ghet·ti ▶ **n.** another term for SPAGHETTI SQUASH.

veg·e·ta·ble sponge ▶ **n.** another term for LOOFAH.

veg·e·ta·ble tal·low ▶ **n.** vegetable fat used as tallow.

veg·e·tal /ˈvejətl/ ▶ **adj. 1** formal of or relating to plants: *a vegetal aroma.*
2 [attrib.] Embryology of or relating to that pole of the ovum or embryo that contains the less active cytoplasm, and frequently most of the yolk, in the early stages of development: *vegetal cells* | *the vegetal region.*
– ORIGIN late Middle English: from medieval Latin *vegetalis*, from Latin *vegetare* 'animate.' Sense 2 dates from the early 20th cent.

veg·e·tal pole /ˈvejitl/ ▶ **n.** Embryology the portion of an ovum opposite the animal pole, containing most of the yolk and little cytoplasm.

veg·e·tar·i·an /ˌvejiˈte(ə)rēən/ ▶ **n.** a person who does not eat meat, and sometimes other animal products, esp. for moral, religious, or health reasons.
▶ **adj.** of or relating to the exclusion of meat or other animal products from the diet: *a vegetarian restaurant.*
– DERIVATIVES **veg·e·tar·i·an·ism** /-ˌnizəm/ **n.**
– ORIGIN mid 19th cent.: formed irregularly from VEGETABLE + -ARIAN.

veg·e·tate /ˈvejəˌtāt/ ▶ **v.** [no obj.] **1** live or spend a period of time in a dull, inactive, unchallenging way: *if she left him there alone, he'd sit in front of the television set and vegetate.*
2 dated (of a plant or seed) grow; sprout. ■ [with obj.] cause plants to grow in or cover (a place).
3 Medicine (of an abnormal growth) increase in size.
– ORIGIN early 17th cent.: from Latin *vegetat-* 'enlivened,' from the verb *vegetare*, from *vegetus* 'active,' from *vegere* 'be active.'

veg·e·tat·ed /ˈvejəˌtātid/ ▶ **adj.** covered with vegetation or plant life: *densely vegetated wetlands.*

veg·e·ta·tion /ˌvejəˈtāshən/ ▶ **n. 1** plants considered collectively, esp. those found in a particular area or habitat: *the chalk cliffs are mainly sheer with little vegetation.*
2 the action or process of vegetating.
3 Medicine an abnormal growth on or in the body.
– DERIVATIVES **veg·e·ta·tion·al** /-shənl/ **adj.**
– ORIGIN mid 16th cent. (sense 2): from medieval Latin *vegetatio(n-)* 'power of growth,' from the verb *vegetare* (see VEGETATE).

veg·e·ta·tive /ˈvejəˌtātiv/ ▶ **adj. 1** Biology of, relating to, or denoting reproduction or propagation achieved by asexual means, either naturally (budding, rhizomes, runners, bulbs, etc.) or artificially (grafting, layering, or taking cuttings): *vegetative spores* | *a vegetative replicating phase.* ■ of, relating to, or concerned with growth rather than sexual reproduction: *environmental factors trigger the switch from vegetative to floral development.*
2 of or relating to vegetation or plant life: *diverse vegetative types.*
3 Medicine (of a person) alive but comatose and without apparent brain activity or responsiveness. See PERSISTENT VEGETATIVE STATE.
– DERIVATIVES **veg·e·ta·tive·ly** **adv.**, **veg·e·ta·tive·ness** **n.**
– ORIGIN late Middle English (sense 2): from Old French *vegetatif, -ive* or medieval Latin *vegetativus* (see VEGETATE).

veg·e·ta·tive cell ▶ **n.** Botany & Microbiology a cell of a bacterium or unicellular alga that is actively growing rather than forming spores.

veg·gie /ˈvejē/ (also **vegie**) ▶ **n. & adj.** informal
1 another term for VEGETABLE.
2 another term for VEGETARIAN.
– ORIGIN 1970s: abbreviation.

veg·gie burg·er ▶ **n.** a patty resembling a hamburger but made with vegetable protein, soybeans, etc., instead of meat.

ve·he·mence /ˈvēəməns/ ▶ **n.** the display of strong feeling; passion: *they speak with starry vehemence about their project.*

ve·he·ment /ˈvēəmənt/ ▶ **adj.** showing strong feeling; forceful, passionate, or intense: *her voice was low but vehement* | *vehement criticism.*
– DERIVATIVES **ve·he·ment·ly** **adv.**
– ORIGIN late Middle English (describing pain or temperature, in the sense 'intense, high in degree'): from French *véhément* or Latin *vehement-* 'impetuous, violent,' perhaps from an unrecorded adjective meaning 'deprived of mind,' influenced by *vehere* 'carry.'

ve·hi·cle /ˈvēəkəl, ˈvēˌhikəl/ ▶ **n. 1** a thing used for transporting people or goods, esp. on land, such as a car, truck, or cart.
2 a thing used to express, embody, or fulfill something: *I use paint as a* **vehicle for** *my ideas.* ■ a substance that facilitates the use of a drug, pigment, or other material mixed with it. ■ the figurative language used in a metaphor, as distinct from the metaphor's subject. Often contrasted with TENOR² (sense 1). ■ a movie, television program, song, etc., that is intended to display the leading performer to the best advantage.
– DERIVATIVES **ve·hic·u·lar** /vēˈhikyələr/ **adj.** (sense 1).
– ORIGIN early 17th cent.: from French *véhicule* or Latin *vehiculum*, from *vehere* 'carry.'

veil /vāl/ ▶ **n.** a piece of fine material worn by women to protect or conceal the face: *a white bridal veil.* ■ a piece of linen or other fabric forming part of a nun's headdress, resting on the head and shoulders. ■ a thing that conceals, disguises, or obscures something: *shrouded in an eerie veil of mist.* ■ Botany a membrane that is attached to the immature fruiting body of some toadstools and ruptures in the course of development, either (**universal veil**) enclosing the whole fruiting body or (**partial veil**) joining the edges of the cap to the stalk. ■ (in Jewish antiquity) the piece of precious cloth separating the sanctuary from the body of the Temple or the Tabernacle.
▶ **v.** [with obj.] cover with or as though with a veil: *she veiled her face.* ■ (usu. as adj. **veiled**) partially conceal, disguise, or obscure: *a thinly veiled threat.*
– PHRASES **beyond the veil** in a mysterious or hidden place or state, esp. the unknown state of life after death. **draw a veil over** avoid discussing or calling attention to (something), esp. because it is embarrassing or unpleasant. **take the veil** become a nun.
– DERIVATIVES **veil·less** **adj.**
– ORIGIN Middle English: from Anglo-Norman French *veil(e)*, from Latin *vela*, plural of *velum* (see VELUM).

veil·ing /ˈvāliNG/ ▶ **n.** a light gauzy fabric or fine lace used for veils.

vein /vān/ ▶ **n. 1** any of the tubes forming part of the blood circulation system of the body, carrying in most cases oxygen-depleted blood toward the heart. Compare with ARTERY. ■ (in general and figurative use) a blood vessel: *he felt the adrenaline course through his veins.* ■ (in plants) a slender rib running through a leaf or bract, typically dividing or branching, and containing a vascular bundle. ■ (in insects) a hardened branching rib that forms part of the supporting framework of a wing, consisting of an extension of the tracheal system; a nervure.
2 a fracture in rock containing a deposit of minerals or ore and typically having an extensive course underground. ■ a streak or stripe of a different color in wood, marble, cheese, etc. ■ a body of subsurface water, esp. as considered a source or potential source of water for a well or wells and thought of as flowing in a channel. ■ a source of a specified quality or other abstract resource: *he managed to tap into the thick vein of discontent to his own advantage.*
3 [in sing.] a distinctive quality, style, or tendency: *he closes his article in a somewhat humorous vein.*
– DERIVATIVES **vein·less** **adj.**, **vein·let** /-lit/ **n.**, **vein·like** /-ˌlīk/ **adj.**, **vein·y** **adj.** (**veinier, veiniest**).
– ORIGIN Middle English: from Old French *veine*, from Latin *vena*. The earliest senses were 'blood vessel' and 'small natural underground channel of water.'

veined /vānd/ ▶ **adj.** marked with or as if with veins: [in combination] *a blue-veined cheese.*

vein·ing /ˈvāniNG/ ▶ **n.** a pattern of lines, streaks, or veins: *the marble's characteristic surface veining.*

vein·ous /ˈvānəs/ ▶ **adj.** having prominent or noticeable veins. Compare with VENOUS.

vein·stone /ˈvānˌstōn/ ▶ **n.** another term for GANGUE.

Ve·la /ˈvēlə, ˈvā-/ Astronomy a southern constellation (the Sails), lying partly in the Milky Way between Carina and Pyxis and originally considered part of Argo. ■ (as genitive **Velorum** /viˈlôrəm/) used with a preceding letter or numeral to designate a star in this constellation: *the star Gamma Velorum.*
– ORIGIN Latin, plural of *velum* 'sail.'

ve·la /ˈvēlə/ plural form of VELUM.

ve·la·men /vəˈlāmən/ ▶ **n.** (pl. **velamina** /-ˈlamənə/) Botany an outer layer of empty cells in the aerial roots of epiphytic orchids and aroids.
– ORIGIN late 19th cent.: from Latin, from *velare* 'to cover.'

ve·lar /ˈvēlər/ ▶ **adj. 1** of or relating to a veil or velum.
2 Phonetics (of a speech sound) pronounced with the back of the tongue near the soft palate, as in *k* and *g* in English.
▶ **n.** a velar sound.
– ORIGIN early 18th cent.: from Latin *velaris*, from *velum* (see VELUM).

ve·lar·i·um /viˈle(ə)rēəm/ ▶ **n.** (pl. **velaria** /-ˈle(ə)rēə/) a large awning of a type used in ancient Rome to cover a theater or amphitheater as a protection against the weather, now more commonly used as an inner ceiling to improve acoustics.
– ORIGIN Latin.

ve·lar·i·za·tion /ˌvēlərəˈzāshən/ ▶ **n.** Phonetics a secondary articulation involving movement of the back of the tongue toward the velum.
– DERIVATIVES **ve·lar·ize** /ˈvēləˌrīz/ **v.**

Ve·láz·quez /vəˈläsˌk(w)ez, -kəs/, Diego Rodríguez de Silva y (1599–1660), Spanish painter; court painter to Philip IV. His portraits humanized the formal Spanish tradition of idealized figures. Notable works: *Pope Innocent X* (1650), *The Toilet of Venus* (known as *The Rokeby Venus*, *c.*1651), and *Las Meninas* (*c.*1656).

Ve·láz·quez de Cué·llar /vəˈläsˌk(w)ez dā ˈkwāyär/, Diego (*c.*1465–1524), Spanish conquistador. After sailing with Columbus to the New World in 1493, he began the conquest of Cuba in 1511 and later initiated expeditions to conquer Mexico.

Vel·cro /ˈvelkrō/ (also **velcro**) ▶ **n.** trademark a fastener for clothes or other items, consisting of two strips of thin plastic sheet, one covered with tiny loops and the other with tiny flexible hooks, which adhere when pressed together and can be separated when pulled apart deliberately.
▶ **v.** [with obj.] fasten, join, or fix with such a fastener.
– DERIVATIVES **Vel·croed** **adj.**
– ORIGIN 1960s: from French *velours croché* 'hooked velvet.'

veld /velt/ (also **veldt**) ▶ **n.** open, uncultivated country or grassland in southern Africa. It is conventionally classified by altitude into highveld, middleveld, and lowveld.
– ORIGIN Afrikaans, from Dutch, literally 'field.'

Vel·de, van de¹, Henri, see VAN DE VELDE².

Vel·de, van de², Willem and sons, see VAN DE VELDE¹.

ve·li·ger /ˈveləjər, ˈvēlə-/ ▶ **n.** Zoology the final larval stage of certain mollusks, having two ciliated flaps for swimming and feeding.

– ORIGIN late 19th cent.: from **velum** + Latin *-ger* 'bearing.'

vel·le·i·ty /və'lēətē, ve-/ ▶ **n.** (pl. **velleities**) formal a wish or inclination not strong enough to lead to action: *the notion intrigued me, but remained a velleity.*
– ORIGIN early 17th cent.: from medieval Latin *velleitas*, from Latin *velle* 'to wish.'

vel·lum /'veləm/ ▶ **n.** **1** fine parchment made originally from the skin of a calf.
2 smooth writing paper imitating vellum.
– ORIGIN late Middle English: from Old French *velin*, from *veel* (see **veal**).

ve·lo·cim·e·ter /ˌvelə'simitər, ˌvēlə-/ ▶ **n.** an instrument for measuring velocity.
– DERIVATIVES **ve·lo·cim·e·try** /-itrē/ **n.**
– ORIGIN mid 19th cent.: from Latin *velox, veloc-* 'swift' + **-meter**.

ve·loc·i·pede /və'läsəˌpēd/ ▶ **n.** historical an early form of bicycle propelled by working pedals on cranks fitted to the front axle. ■ a child's tricycle.
– DERIVATIVES **ve·loc·i·ped·ist** /-dist/ **n.**
– ORIGIN early 19th cent.: from French *vélocipède*, from Latin *velox, veloc-* 'swift' + *pes, ped-* 'foot.'

ve·loc·i·rap·tor /və'läsəˌraptər/ ▶ **n.** a small dromaeosaurid dinosaur of the late Cretaceous period. ● Genus *Velociraptor*, family Dromaeosauridae, suborder Theropoda.
– ORIGIN modern Latin, from Latin *velox, veloc-* 'swift' + **raptor**.

ve·loc·i·ty /və'läsətē/ ▶ **n.** (pl. **velocities**) the speed of something in a given direction: *the velocities of the emitted particles.* ■ (in general use) speed: *the tank shot backward at an incredible velocity.* ■ (also **velocity of circulation**) Economics the rate at which money changes hands within an economy.
– ORIGIN late Middle English: from French *vélocité* or Latin *velocitas*, from *velox, veloc-* 'swift.'

ve·lo·drome /'veləˌdrōm, 'vēlə-/ ▶ **n.** a cycle-racing track, typically with steeply banked curves. ■ a stadium containing such a track.
– ORIGIN late 19th cent.: from French *vélodrome*, from *vélo* 'bicycle' + *-drome* (see **-drome**).

ve·lour /və'lo͝or/ (also **velours**) ▶ **n.** a plush woven fabric resembling velvet, chiefly used for soft furnishings, casual clothing, and hats. ■ dated a hat made of such fabric.
– ORIGIN early 18th cent.: from French *velours* 'velvet,' from Old French *velour*, from Latin *villosus* 'hairy,' from *villus* (see **velvet**).

ve·lou·té /vəlo͞o'tā/ ▶ **n.** a rich white sauce made with chicken, veal, pork, or fish stock, thickened with cream and egg yolks.
– ORIGIN French, literally 'velvety.'

ve·lum /'vēləm/ ▶ **n.** (pl. **vela** /-lə/) a membrane or membranous structure, typically covering another structure or partly obscuring an opening, in particular: ■ Anatomy the soft palate. ■ Zoology a membrane, typically bordering a cavity, esp. in certain mollusks, medusae, and other invertebrates. ■ Botany the veil of a toadstool.
– ORIGIN mid 18th cent.: from Latin, literally 'sail, curtain, covering, veil.'

ve·lure /və'lo͝or/ archaic ▶ **n.** velvet.
▶ **v.** [with obj.] dress (a hat) by means of a velvet pad: *the hatter then velures the hats in a revolving device.*

vel·vet /'velvət/ ▶ **n.** a closely woven fabric of silk, cotton, or nylon, that has a thick short pile on one side. ■ soft downy skin that covers a deer's antler while it is growing.
– PHRASES **on velvet** informal, dated in an advantageous or prosperous position.
– DERIVATIVES **vel·vet·ed adj.**, **vel·vet·y adj.**
– ORIGIN Middle English: from Old French *veluotte*, from *velu* 'velvety,' from medieval Latin *villutus*, from Latin *villus* 'tuft, down.'

vel·vet ant ▶ **n.** an antlike velvety-bodied insect related to the wasps. The female is wingless, and the larvae parasitize the young of bees and wasps in the nest. ● Family Mutillidae, superfamily Scolioidea: numerous species.

vel·vet·een /'velvəˌtēn, ˌvelvə'tēn/ ▶ **n.** a cotton fabric with a pile resembling velvet. ■ (**velveteens**) dated trousers made of this fabric.

vel·vet grass ▶ **n.** a common pasture grass with soft downy leaves, native to Eurasia and naturalized in North America. ● *Holcus lanatus*, family Gramineae.

vel·vet·leaf /'velvətˌlēf/ ▶ **n.** (pl. **same** or **velvetleafs**) a Eurasian plant of the mallow family, with large heart-shaped velvety leaves and yellow flowers. It is naturalized in North America, where it has become a serious weed of farmland. ● *Abutilon theophrasti*, family Malvaceae.

vel·vet rev·o·lu·tion ▶ **n.** a nonviolent political revolution, esp. the relatively smooth change from communism to a Western-style democracy in Czechoslovakia at the end of 1989.
– ORIGIN translating Czech *sametová revoluce*.

vel·vet worm ▶ **n.** see **Onychophora**.

Ven. ▶ **abbr.** Venerable (as the title of an archdeacon): *the Ven. William Davies.*

ve·na /'vēnə/ ▶ **n.** Anatomy & Zoology a vein.

ve·na ca·va /ˌvēnə 'kävə, 'kāvə/ ▶ **n.** (pl. **venae cavae** /'vēnē 'kävē, 'kāvē, 'vēnī 'kävī, 'kāvī/) a large vein carrying deoxygenated blood into the heart. There are two in humans, the **inferior vena cava** (carrying blood from the lower body) and the **superior vena cava** (carrying blood from the head, arms, and upper body).
– ORIGIN late 16th cent.: from Latin, literally 'hollow vein.'

ve·nal /'vēnl/ ▶ **adj.** showing or motivated by susceptibility to bribery: *why should these venal politicians care how they are rated? | their generosity had been at least partly venal.*
– DERIVATIVES **ve·nal·i·ty** /vē'nalətē, və-/ **n.**, **ve·nal·ly adv.**
– ORIGIN mid 17th cent. (in the sense 'available for purchase,' referring to merchandise or a favor): from Latin *venalis*, from *venum* 'thing for sale.'

> **USAGE** Venal and venial are sometimes confused. **Venal** means 'corrupt, able to be bribed, or involving bribery': *local customs officials are notoriously venal, and smuggling thrives.* **Venial** is used to describe a sin or offense that is 'pardonable, excusable, not mortal': *in our high school, smoking cigarettes was a venial sin.*

ve·na·tion /vē'nāSHən/ ▶ **n.** Biology the arrangement of veins in a leaf or in an insect's wing. ■ the system of venous blood vessels in an animal.
– DERIVATIVES **ve·na·tion·al** /-SHənl/ **adj.**
– ORIGIN mid 17th cent.: from Latin *vena* 'vein' + **-ation**.

vend /vend/ ▶ **v.** [with obj.] offer (small items, esp. food) for sale, esp. either from a stall or from a slot machine: *there was a man vending sticky cakes and ices.* ■ Law or formal sell (something).
– DERIVATIVES **vend·i·ble** (also **vendable**) **adj.**
– ORIGIN early 17th cent. (in the sense 'be sold'): from French *vendre* or Latin *vendere* 'sell,' from *venum* 'something for sale' + a variant of *dare* 'give.'

Ven·da[1] /'vendə/ a former homeland established in South Africa for the Venda people, now part of Northern Province.

Ven·da[2] ▶ **n.** (pl. **same** or **Vendas**) **1** a member of a people living in Northern Transvaal and southern Zimbabwe.
2 the Bantu language of this people.
▶ **adj.** of or relating to this people or their language.
– ORIGIN the stem of Venda *Muvenda* (in sense 1), *Tshivenda* (in sense 2).

ven·dange /vän'dänZH, vän-/ ▶ **n.** (pl. **same**) (in France) the grape harvest.
– ORIGIN French.

Ven·dé·mi·aire /ˌvändə'myer, ˌvändā-/ (also **Vendémiaire**) ▶ **n.** the first month of the French Republican calendar (1793–1805), originally running from September 22 to October 21.
– ORIGIN French, from Latin *vindemia* 'vintage.'

vend·er /'vendər/ ▶ **n.** variant spelling of **vendor**.

ven·det·ta /ven'detə/ ▶ **n.** a blood feud in which the family of a murdered person seeks vengeance on the murderer or the murderer's family. ■ a prolonged bitter quarrel with or campaign against someone: *he has accused the British media of pursuing a vendetta against him.*
– ORIGIN mid 19th cent.: from Italian, from Latin *vindicta* 'vengeance.'

vend·ing ma·chine ▶ **n.** a machine that dispenses small articles such as food, drinks, or cigarettes when a coin, bill, or token is inserted.

ven·dor /'vendər, -ˌdôr/ (also **vender**) ▶ **n.** a person or company offering something for sale, esp. a trader in the street: *an Italian ice cream vendor.* ■ a person or company whose principal product lines are office supplies and equipment. ■ Law the seller, esp. of property.
– ORIGIN late 16th cent.: from Anglo-Norman French *vendour* (see **vend**).

ven·dor plac·ing ▶ **n.** Finance a type of placing used as a method of financing a takeover in which the purchasing company issues its own shares as payment to the company being bought, with the prearranged agreement that these shares are then placed with investors in exchange for cash.

ven·due /ven'd(y)o͞o, vän-/ ▶ **n.** a public auction.
– ORIGIN late 17th cent.: via Dutch from French dialect *vendue* 'sale,' from *vendre* 'sell.'

ve·neer /və'ni(ə)r/ ▶ **n.** a thin decorative covering of fine wood applied to a coarser wood or other material. ■ a layer of wood used to make plywood. ■ [in sing.] an attractive appearance that covers or disguises someone or something's true nature or feelings: *her veneer of composure cracked a little.*
▶ **v.** [with obj.] (usu. as adj. **veneered**) cover (something) with a decorative layer of fine wood. ■ cover or disguise (someone or something's true nature) with an attractive appearance.
– ORIGIN early 18th cent. (earlier as *fineer*): from German *furni(e)ren*, from Old French *fournir* 'furnish.'

ve·neer·ing /və'ni(ə)riNG/ ▶ **n.** material used as veneer.

ven·e·punc·ture ▶ **n.** chiefly Brit. variant spelling of **venipuncture**.

ven·er·a·ble /'venərəbəl, 'venrə-/ ▶ **adj.** accorded a great deal of respect, esp. because of age, wisdom, or character: *a venerable statesman.* ■ (in the Roman Catholic Church) a title given to a deceased person who has attained a certain degree of sanctity but has not been fully beatified or canonized. ■ (in the Anglican Church) a title given to an archdeacon.
– DERIVATIVES **ven·er·a·bil·i·ty** /ˌvenərə'bilətē/ **n.**, **ven·er·a·ble·ness n.**, **ven·er·a·bly** /-blē/ **adv.**
– ORIGIN late Middle English: from Old French, or from Latin *venerabilis*, from the verb *venerari* (see **venerate**).

ven·er·ate /'venəˌrāt/ ▶ **v.** [with obj.] regard with great respect; revere: *Mother Teresa is venerated as a saint.*
– DERIVATIVES **ven·er·a·tor** /-ˌrātər/ **n.**
– ORIGIN early 17th cent.: from Latin *venerat-* 'adored, revered,' from the verb *venerari*.

ven·er·a·tion /ˌvenə'rāSHən/ ▶ **n.** great respect; reverence: *the traditional veneration of saints.*

ve·ne·re·al /və'ni(ə)rēəl/ ▶ **adj.** of or relating to sexual desire or sexual intercourse. ■ of or relating to venereal disease.
– DERIVATIVES **ve·ne·re·al·ly adv.**
– ORIGIN late Middle English: from Latin *venereus* (from *venus, vener-* 'sexual love') + **-al**.

ve·ne·re·al dis·ease ▶ **n.** a disease typically contracted by sexual contact with a person already infected; a sexually transmitted disease.

ve·ne·re·ol·o·gy /vəˌni(ə)rē'äləjē/ ▶ **n.** the branch of medicine concerned with venereal diseases.
– DERIVATIVES **ve·ne·re·o·log·i·cal** /-ə'läjikəl/ **adj.**, **ve·ne·re·ol·o·gist** /-jist/ **n.**

ven·er·y[1] /'venərē/ ▶ **n.** archaic sexual indulgence.
– ORIGIN late Middle English: from medieval Latin *veneria*, from *venus, vener-* 'sexual love.'

ven·er·y[2] ▶ **n.** archaic hunting.
– ORIGIN Middle English: from Old French *venerie*, from *vener* 'to hunt,' from Latin *venari*.

ven·e·sec·tion /'vēnəˌsekSHən, 'venə-/ ▶ **n.** another term for **phlebotomy**.
– ORIGIN mid 17th cent.: from medieval Latin *venae sectio(n-)* 'cutting of a vein.'

Ve·ne·ti·a /və'nēSHə/ a region in northeastern Italy; capital, Venice. Italian name **Veneto**.
– ORIGIN named after the *Veneti*, the pre-Roman inhabitants of the region.

Ve·ne·tian /və'nēSHən/ ▶ **adj.** of or relating to Venice or its people.
▶ **n.** a native or citizen of Venice. ■ the dialect of Italian spoken in Venice.
– ORIGIN late Middle English: from Old French *Venicien*, assimilated to medieval Latin *Venetianus*, from Latin *Venetia* 'Venice.'

ve·ne·tian blind ▶ **n.** a window blind consisting of horizontal slats that can be pivoted to control the amount of light that passes through it.

Ve·ne·tian glass ▶ **n.** decorative glassware of a type associated with Venice, esp. the nearby island of Murano.

Ve·ne·tian red ▶ **n.** a reddish-brown pigment consisting of ferric oxide. ■ a strong reddish-brown color.

Ve·ne·tian win·dow ▶ **n.** a large window consisting of a central arched section flanked by two narrow rectangular sections.

Ve·ne·zia /və'netsēə/ Italian name for **Venice**.

Ven·e·zue·la /ˌvenəz(ə)'wālə/ a republic on the northern coast of South America, on the Caribbean Sea; pop. 26,814,800 (est. 2009); capital, Caracas; language, Spanish (official). Official name **Bolivarian Republic of Venezuela**.

PRONUNCIATION KEY ə *ago, up*; ər *over, fur*; a *hat*; ā *ate*; ä *car*; e *let*; ē *see*; i *fit*; ī *by*; NG *sing*; ō *go*; ô *law, for*; oi *toy*; o͝o *good*; o͞o *goo*; ou *out*; TH *thin*; T͟H *then*; ZH *vision*

V

Colonized by the Spanish in the 16th century, Venezuela won its independence in 1821 after a ten-year struggle. It did not, however, emerge as a separate nation until its secession from federation with Colombia in 1830. It is a major oil-exporting country, with the industry based on the area around Lake Maracaibo in the northwest.

– DERIVATIVES **Ven·e·zue·lan** adj. & n.
– ORIGIN Spanish, literally 'little Venice,' named by early explorers when they saw native houses built on stilts over water.

venge·ance /'venjəns/ ▶ n. punishment inflicted or retribution exacted for an injury or wrong.
– PHRASES **with a vengeance** used to emphasize the degree to which something occurs or is true: *her headache was back with a vengeance.*
– ORIGIN Middle English: from Old French, from *venger* 'avenge.'

venge·ful /'venjfəl/ ▶ adj. seeking to harm someone in return for a perceived injury: *a vengeful ex-con.*
– DERIVATIVES **venge·ful·ly** adv., **venge·ful·ness** n.
– ORIGIN late 16th cent.: from obsolete *venge* 'avenge' (see VENGEANCE), on the pattern of *revengeful.*

ve·ni·al /'vēnēəl, 'vēnyəl/ ▶ adj. Christian Theology denoting a sin that is not regarded as depriving the soul of divine grace. Often contrasted with MORTAL. ■ (of a fault or offense) slight and pardonable.
– DERIVATIVES **ve·ni·al·i·ty** /ˌvēnē'alətē/ n., **ve·ni·al·ly** adv.
– ORIGIN Middle English: via Old French from late Latin *venialis*, from *venia* 'forgiveness.'

USAGE See usage at VENAL.

ve·ni·al sin ▶ n. (in Roman Catholicism) a relatively slight sin that that does not entail damnation of the soul: *she lost her patience, a venial sin she must report later to Father Damien.*

Ven·ice /'venəs/ **1** a city in northeastern Italy, on a lagoon of the Adriatic Sea, capital of Venetia region; pop. 270,098 (2008). It is built on numerous islands that are separated by canals and linked by bridges. Italian name **Venezia**.
2 /'venis/ a beachfront section of Los Angeles in California, west of downtown.

ven·i·punc·ture /'vēnəˌpəNGkCHər, 'venə-/ (chiefly Brit. also **venepuncture**) ▶ n. the puncture of a vein as part of a medical procedure, typically to withdraw a blood sample or for an intravenous injection.
– ORIGIN 1920s: from Latin *vena* 'vein' + PUNCTURE.

ven·i·son /'venəsən, -zən/ ▶ n. meat from a deer.
– ORIGIN Middle English: from Old French *veneso(u)n*, from Latin *venatio(n-)* 'hunting,' from *venari* 'to hunt.'

Ve·ni·te /və'nītē, -'nētē, -'nēˌtā/ ▶ n. Psalm 95 used as a canticle in Christian liturgy, chiefly at matins.
– ORIGIN Latin, literally 'come ye,' the first word of the psalm.

Venn di·a·gram /ven/ ▶ n. a diagram representing mathematical or logical sets pictorially as circles or closed curves within an enclosing rectangle (the universal set), common elements of the sets being represented by the areas of overlap among the circles.
– ORIGIN early 20th cent.: named after John *Venn* (1834–1923), English logician.

ve·no·gram /'vēnəˌgram/ ▶ n. Medicine an image produced by venography.

ve·nog·ra·phy /vi'nägrəfē/ ▶ n. Medicine radiography of a vein after injection of a radiopaque fluid.
– DERIVATIVES **ve·no·graph·ic** /ˌvēnə'grafik/ adj., **ve·no·graph·i·cal·ly** /ˌvēnə'grafik(ə)lē/ adv.
– ORIGIN 1930s: from Latin *vena* 'vein' + -GRAPHY.

ven·om /'venəm/ ▶ n. poisonous fluid secreted by animals such as snakes and scorpions and typically injected into prey or aggressors by biting or stinging. ■ extreme malice and bitterness shown in someone's attitudes, speech, or actions: *his voice was full of venom.*
– ORIGIN Middle English: from Old French *venim*, variant of *venin*, from an alteration of Latin *venenum* 'poison.'

V

ven·om·ous /'venəməs/ ▶ adj. (of animals, esp. snakes, or their parts) secreting venom; capable of injecting venom by means of a bite or sting. ■ (of a person or their behavior) full of malice or spite: *she replied with a venomous glance.*
– DERIVATIVES **ven·om·ous·ly** adv., **ven·om·ous·ness** n.
– ORIGIN Middle English: from Old French *venimeux*, from *venim* (see VENOM).

ve·nous /'vēnəs/ ▶ adj. of or relating to a vein or the veins. ■ of or relating to the dark red, oxygen-poor blood in the veins and pulmonary artery.
– DERIVATIVES **ve·nos·i·ty** /vi'näsətē/ n., **ve·nous·ly** adv.
– ORIGIN early 17th cent.: from Latin *venosus* 'venous,' from *vena* 'vein.'

ve·nous in·suf·fi·cien·cy ▶ n. Pathology failure of the veins to adequately circulate the blood, esp. from the lower extremities.

vent[1] /vent/ ▶ n. **1** an opening that allows air, gas, or liquid to pass out of or into a confined space. ■ the opening of a volcano, through which lava and other materials are emitted. ■ historical the touch hole of a gun. ■ the anus, esp. one in a lower animal such as a fish that serves for both excretion and reproduction.
2 the expression or release of a strong emotion, energy, etc.: *children give vent to their anger in various ways.*
▶ v. [with obj.] **1** give free expression to (a strong emotion): *he had come to vent his rage and despair.*
2 provide with an outlet for air, gas, or liquid: *clothes dryers must be vented to the outside.*
■ discharge or expel (air, gas, or liquid) through an outlet: *the plant was isolated and the gas vented.*
■ permit air to enter (a beer cask).
– DERIVATIVES **vent·less** adj.
– ORIGIN late Middle English: partly from French *vent* 'wind,' from Latin *ventus*, reinforced by French *évent*, from *éventer* 'expose to air,' based on Latin *ventus* 'wind.'

vent[2] ▶ n. a slit in a garment, esp. in the lower edge of the back of a coat through the seam.
– ORIGIN late Middle English: alteration of dialect *fent*, from Old French *fente* 'slit,' based on Latin *findere* 'cleave.'

ven·tail /'venˌtāl/ ▶ n. historical the lower movable front of a medieval helmet. ■ the whole movable front of such a helmet, including the visor.

ven·ter /'ventər/ ▶ n. Zoology the underside or abdomen of an animal.
– ORIGIN early 18th cent.: from Latin, literally 'belly.'

ven·ti /'ventē/ ▶ n. [usu. as modifier] trademark a serving of a drink of coffee measuring 20 fluid ounces.
– ORIGIN Italian, literally 'twenty.'

ven·ti·fact /'ventəˌfakt/ ▶ n. Geology a stone shaped by the erosive action of windblown sand.
– ORIGIN early 20th cent.: from Latin *ventus* 'wind' + *factum*, neuter past participle of *facere* 'make.'

ven·ti·late /'ventəˌlāt/ ▶ v. [with obj.] **1** cause air to enter and circulate freely in (a room, building, etc.): *ventilate the greenhouse well* | [as adj., in combination] (**-ventilated**) *gas heaters should only ever be used in well-ventilated rooms.* ■ (of air) purify or freshen (something) by blowing on or through it: *a colossus ventilated by the dawn breeze.* ■ Medicine subject to artificial respiration. ■ archaic oxygenate (the blood).
2 discuss or examine (an opinion, issue, complaint, etc.) in public: *he used the club to ventilate an ongoing complaint.*
– ORIGIN late Middle English (in the sense 'winnow, scatter'): from Latin *ventilat-* 'blown, winnowed,' from the verb *ventilare*, from *ventus* 'wind.' The sense 'cause air to circulate in' dates from the mid 18th cent.

ven·ti·la·tion /ˌventə'lāSHən/ ▶ n. **1** the provision of fresh air to a room, building, etc. ■ Medicine the supply of air to the lungs, esp. by artificial means.
2 public discussion or examination of an opinion, issue, complaint, etc.
– ORIGIN late Middle English (in the sense 'current of air'): from Old French, or from Latin *ventilatio(n-)*, from the verb *ventilare* (see VENTILATE). Sense 1 dates from the mid 17th cent.

ven·ti·la·tor /'ventəˌlātər/ ▶ n. **1** an appliance or aperture for ventilating a room or other space.
2 Medicine an appliance for artificial respiration; a respirator.

ven·ti·la·to·ry /'ventələˌtôrē/ ▶ adj. Physiology of, relating to, or serving for the provision of air to the lungs or respiratory system.

Ven·tose /vän'tōz/ (also **Ventôse**) ▶ n. the sixth month of the French Republican calendar (1793–1805), originally running from February 19 to March 20.
– ORIGIN French *Ventôse*, from Latin *ventosus* 'windy,' from *ventus* 'wind.'

ven·touse /'venˌto͞os/ ▶ n. Medicine a vacuum extractor for use in assisting childbirth.
– ORIGIN 1960s: from French, literally 'cupping glass,' based on Latin *ventus* 'wind.'

ven·tral /'ventrəl/ ▶ adj. Anatomy, Zoology, & Botany of, on, or relating to the underside of an animal or plant; abdominal: *a ventral nerve cord* | *the ventral part of the head.* Compare with DORSAL.
– DERIVATIVES **ven·tral·ly** adv.
– ORIGIN late Middle English: from Latin *venter*, *ventr-* 'belly' + -AL.

ven·tral fin ▶ n. Zoology another term for PELVIC FIN.
■ an unpaired fin on the underside of certain fishes.
■ a single vertical fin under the fuselage or tail of an aircraft.

ven·tri·cle /'ventrəkəl/ ▶ n. Anatomy a hollow part or cavity in an organ, in particular: ■ each of the two main chambers of the heart, left and right. ■ each of the four connected fluid-filled cavities in the center of the brain.
– DERIVATIVES **ven·tric·u·lar** /ven'trikyələr/ adj.
– ORIGIN late Middle English: from Latin *ventriculus*, diminutive of *venter* 'belly.'

ven·tri·cose /'ventrəˌkōs/ ▶ adj. **1** having a protruding belly.
2 Botany distended, inflated.
– ORIGIN mid 18th cent.: formed irregularly from VENTRICLE + -OSE[1].

ven·tric·u·log·ra·phy /venˌtrikyə'lägrəfē/ ▶ n. Medicine radiography of the ventricles of the brain with the cerebral fluid replaced by air (pneumoencephalography) or radiopaque material or labeled with a radionuclide.

ven·tric·u·lus /ven'trikyələs/ ▶ n. technical term for GIZZARD.

ven·tril·o·quist /ven'triləkwist/ ▶ n. a person who can speak or utter sounds so that they seem to come from somewhere else, esp. an entertainer who makes their voice appear to come from a dummy of a person or animal.
– DERIVATIVES **ven·tri·lo·qui·al** /ˌventrə'lōkwēəl/ adj., **ven·tril·o·quism** /-ˌkwizəm/ n., **ven·tril·o·quize** /-ˌkwīz/ v., **ven·tril·o·quy** /-kwē/ n.
– ORIGIN mid 17th cent.: from modern Latin *ventriloquium* (from Latin *venter* 'belly' + *loqui* 'speak') + -IST.

ven·tro·lat·er·al /ˌventrō'latərəl, -'latrəl/ ▶ adj. Biology situated toward the junction of the ventral and lateral sides.
– DERIVATIVES **ven·tro·lat·er·al·ly** adv.

ven·tro·me·di·al /ˌventrō'mēdēəl/ ▶ adj. Biology situated toward the middle of the ventral side.
– DERIVATIVES **ven·tro·me·di·al·ly** adv.

Ven·tu·ra /ven'CHo͝orə/ (official name ***San Buenaventura***) a city in southern California, on the Pacific Ocean; pop. 103,706 (est. 2008).

ven·ture /'venCHər/ ▶ n. a risky or daring journey or undertaking: *pioneering ventures into little-known waters.* ■ a business enterprise involving considerable risk.
▶ v. [no obj.] dare to do something or go somewhere that may be dangerous or unpleasant: *she **ventured out** into the blizzard.* ■ dare to do or say something that may be considered audacious (often used as a polite expression of hesitation or apology): *may I venture to add a few comments?* | *I ventured to write to her* | [with obj.] *he ventured the opinion that Putt was now dangerously insane.* ■ [with obj.] expose (something) to the risk of loss: *his fortune is ventured in an expedition over which he has no control.*
– PHRASES **at a venture** archaic trusting to chance rather than to previous consideration or preparation: *a man drew a bow at a venture.* **nothing ventured, nothing gained** proverb you can't expect to achieve anything if you never take any risks.
– ORIGIN late Middle English (in the sense 'adventure,' also 'risk the loss of'): shortening of ADVENTURE.

ven·ture cap·i·tal ▶ n. capital invested in a project in which there is a substantial element of risk, typically a new or expanding business.
– DERIVATIVES **ven·ture cap·i·tal·ist** n.

ven·tur·er /'venCHərər/ ▶ n. archaic a person who undertakes or shares in a trading venture.

ven·ture·some /'venCHərsəm/ ▶ adj. willing to take risks or embark on difficult or unusual courses of action.
– DERIVATIVES **ven·ture·some·ly** adv., **ven·ture·some·ness** n.

Ven·tu·ri /ven'to͝orē, -'CHo͝orē/, Robert (Charles) (1925–), US architect and writer; pioneer of postmodernist architecture. Among his buildings are the Humanities Classroom Building of the State University of New York at Purchase (1973) and the Dumbarton Oaks Research Library in Washington, DC (2005).

ven·tu·ri /ven'to͝orē/ ▶ n. (pl. **venturis**) a short piece of narrow tube between wider sections for measuring flow rate or exerting suction.
– ORIGIN late 19th cent.: named after Giovanni B. *Venturi* (1746–1822), Italian physicist.

ven·ue /'venˌyo͞o/ ▶ n. the place where something happens, esp. an organized event such as a concert, conference, or sports event: *the river could soon be the venue for a powerboat world championship event.*
■ Law the county or district within which a criminal or civil case must be heard.

– ORIGIN late 16th cent. (denoting a thrust or bout in fencing; also in the Law sense): from Old French, literally 'a coming,' feminine past participle of *venir* 'come,' from Latin *venire*.

ven·ule /ˈvenˌyo͞ol/ ▶ **n.** Anatomy a very small vein, esp. one collecting blood from the capillaries.
– ORIGIN mid 19th cent.: from Latin *venula*, diminutive of *vena* 'vein.'

Ve·nus /ˈvēnəs/ **1** Roman Mythology a goddess, worshiped as the goddess of love in classical Rome though apparently a spirit of kitchen gardens in earlier times. Greek equivalent **Aphrodite**. [Latin.] ■ (as noun **a Venus**) chiefly literary a beautiful woman.
2 Astronomy the second planet from the sun in the solar system, the brightest celestial object after the sun and moon and frequently appearing in the twilight sky as the evening or morning star.

> Venus orbits between Mercury and the earth at an average distance of 67.2 million miles (108 million km) from the sun. It is almost equal in size to the earth, with a diameter of 7,521 miles (12,104 km) and shows phases similar to the moon. The planet is completely covered by clouds consisting chiefly of sulfuric acid droplets, and no surface detail can be seen by telescope. There is a dense atmosphere of carbon dioxide, which traps the heat of the sun by the greenhouse effect to produce a surface temperature of 460°C. The planet has no natural satellite.

3 (also **venus, Venus shell**, or **Venus clam**) a burrowing marine bivalve mollusk with clearly defined growth lines on the shell. ● *Venus, Venerupis*, and other genera, family Veneridae.
– DERIVATIVES **Ve·nu·si·an** /vəˈn(y)o͞oSH(ē)ən, -ZHən, -sēən/ **adj. & n.**

Ve·nus·berg /ˈvēnəsˌbərg/ ▶ **n.** (in German legend) the court of Venus.

Ve·nus de Mi·lo /də ˈmēlō, ˈmī-/ a classical sculpture of Aphrodite dated to *c.*100 BC. It was discovered on the Greek island of Melos in 1820 and is now in the Louvre in Paris.
– ORIGIN French, 'Venus of Melos.'

Ve·nus fly·trap (also **Venus's flytrap**) ▶ **n.** a small carnivorous bog plant with hinged leaves that spring shut on and digest insects that land on them. Native to the southeastern US, it is also kept as an indoor plant. ● *Dionaea muscipula*, family Droseraceae.

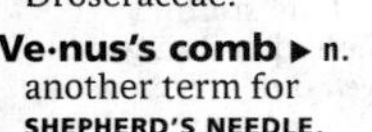

Venus flytrap

Ve·nus's comb ▶ **n.** another term for **shepherd's needle**.

Ve·nus's flow·er bas·ket ▶ **n.** a slender upright sponge with a filmy, latticelike skeleton. ● Genus *Euplectella*, class Hexactinellida.

Ve·nus's gir·dle ▶ **n.** a large, almost transparent comb jelly with a flattened ribbonlike body, living chiefly in warmer seas. ● Genus *Cestum*, phylum Ctenophora.

Ve·nus's hair ▶ **n.** the maidenhair fern *Adiantum capillus-veneris*.

Ve·nus's look·ing glass ▶ **n.** a blue-flowered plant of the bellflower family, whose shiny brown seeds inside their open capsule supposedly resemble mirrors. ● Two species in the family Campanulaceae: *Legousia hybrida* of Europe, and *Triodanis perfoliata* of North America.

ve·ra·cious /vəˈrāSHəs/ ▶ **adj.** formal speaking or representing the truth.
– DERIVATIVES **ve·ra·cious·ly adv., ve·ra·cious·ness n.**
– ORIGIN late 17th cent.: from Latin *verax, verac-* (from *verus* 'true') + **-ious**.

ve·rac·i·ty /vəˈrasətē/ ▶ **n.** conformity to facts; accuracy: *officials expressed doubts concerning the veracity of the story*. ■ habitual truthfulness: *voters should be concerned about his veracity and character*.
– ORIGIN early 17th cent.: from French *véracité* or medieval Latin *veracitas*, from *verax* 'speaking truly' (see **veracious**).

Ve·ra·cruz /ˌverəˈkro͞oz, -ˈkro͞os/ **1** a state in east central Mexico that has a long coastline on the Gulf of Mexico; capital, Jalapa Enríquez.
2 a city and port in Mexico, in Veracruz state, on the Gulf of Mexico; pop. 444,438 (2005).

ve·ran·da /vəˈrandə/ (also **verandah**) ▶ **n.** a roofed platform along the outside of a house, level with the ground floor.
– DERIVATIVES **ve·ran·daed adj.**
– ORIGIN early 18th cent.: from Hindi *varandā*, from Portuguese *varanda* 'railing, balustrade.'

ve·ra·pam·il /vəˈrapəməl/ ▶ **n.** Medicine a synthetic compound that acts as a calcium antagonist and is used to treat angina pectoris and cardiac arrhythmias.
– ORIGIN 1960s: from *v(al)er(onitr)il(e)* (from **valeric acid** + **nitrile**), with the insertion of *-apam-* (of unknown origin).

ver·a·trine /ˈverəˌtrēn, -trin/ ▶ **n.** Chemistry a poisonous substance consisting of a mixture of alkaloids that occurs in the seeds of sabadilla and related plants, used, esp. formerly, to relieve neuralgia and rheumatism.
– ORIGIN early 19th cent.: from French *vératrine*, from Latin *veratrum* 'hellebore.'

ve·ra·trum /vəˈrātrəm/ ▶ **n.** (pl. **veratrums**) a plant of a genus that includes the false hellebores. ● Genus *Veratrum*, family Liliaceae.
– ORIGIN modern Latin, from Latin, literally 'hellebore.'

verb /vərb/ ▶ **n.** Grammar a word used to describe an action, state, or occurrence, and forming the main part of the predicate of a sentence, such as *hear, become, happen*.
– DERIVATIVES **verb·less adj.**
– ORIGIN late Middle English: from Old French *verbe* or Latin *verbum* 'word, verb.'

ver·bal /ˈvərbəl/ ▶ **adj. 1** relating to or in the form of words: *the root of the problem is visual rather than verbal* | *verbal abuse*. ■ spoken rather than written; oral: *a verbal agreement*. ■ tending to talk a lot: *he's very verbal*.
2 Grammar of, relating to, or derived from a verb: *a verbal adjective*.
▶ **n.** Grammar a word or words functioning as a verb. ■ a verbal noun.
– DERIVATIVES **ver·bal·ly adv.**
– ORIGIN late 15th cent. (describing a person who deals with words rather than things): from French, or from late Latin *verbalis*, from *verbum* 'word' (see **verb**).

> **USAGE** It is sometimes said that the true sense of the adjective **verbal** is 'of or concerned with words,' whether spoken or written (as in *verbal abuse*), and that it should not be used to mean 'spoken rather than written' (as in *a verbal agreement*). For this strictly 'spoken' sense, it is said that the adjective **oral** should be used instead. In practice, however, **verbal** is well established in this sense and, even in legal contexts, *a verbal agreement* is understood to mean a contract whose accepted terms have been spoken rather than written.

ver·bal di·ar·rhe·a ▶ **n.** informal the fact or habit of talking too much: *was it necessary to have the narrator exhibit verbal diarrhea throughout the entire picture?*

ver·bal·ism /ˈvərbəˌlizəm/ ▶ **n.** concentration on forms of expression rather than content. ■ a verbal expression. ■ excessive or empty use of language.
– DERIVATIVES **ver·bal·ist n., ver·bal·is·tic** /ˌvərbəˈlistik/ **adj.**

ver·bal·ize /ˈvərbəˌlīz/ ▶ **v. 1** [with obj.] express (ideas or feelings) in words, esp. by speaking out loud: *they are unable to verbalize their real feelings*.
2 [no obj.] speak, esp. at excessive length and with little real content: *the dangers of verbalizing about art*.
3 [with obj.] make (a word, esp. a noun) into a verb.
– DERIVATIVES **ver·bal·iz·a·ble adj., ver·bal·i·za·tion** /ˌvərbələˈzāSHən, -ˌlīˈzā-/ **n., ver·bal·iz·er n.**

ver·bal noun ▶ **n.** Grammar a noun formed by inflection of a verb and partly sharing its constructions, such as *smoking* in *smoking is forbidden*. See **-ing**[1].

ver·bal o·ver·shad·ow·ing ▶ **n.** Psychology the tendency of verbalization to impair the recall of visual memories, resulting in unreliable eyewitness accounts.

ver·bas·cum /vərˈbaskəm/ ▶ **n.** a plant of a genus that comprises the mulleins. ● Genus *Verbascum*, family Scrophulariaceae.
– ORIGIN modern Latin, from Latin, literally 'mullein.'

ver·ba·tim /vərˈbātəm/ ▶ **adv. & adj.** in exactly the same words as were used originally: [as adv.] *subjects were instructed to recall the passage verbatim* | [as adj.] *your quotations must be verbatim*.
– ORIGIN late 15th cent.: from medieval Latin, from Latin *verbum* 'word.' Compare with **literatim**.

ver·be·na /vərˈbēnə/ ▶ **n.** a chiefly American herbaceous plant that bears heads of bright showy flowers, widely cultivated as a garden ornamental. ● Genus *Verbena*, family Verbenaceae: many species, in particular a group of complex cultivars (*V.* × hybrida).
– ORIGIN modern Latin, from Latin, literally 'sacred bough,' in medieval Latin 'vervain.'

ver·bi·age /ˈvərbē-ij/ ▶ **n.** speech or writing that uses too many words or excessively technical expressions.
– ORIGIN early 18th cent.: from French, from obsolete *verbeier* 'to chatter,' from *verbe* 'word' (see **verb**).

ver·bose /vərˈbōs/ ▶ **adj.** using or expressed in more words than are needed: *much academic language is obscure and verbose*.
– DERIVATIVES **ver·bose·ly adv.**
– ORIGIN late 17th cent.: from Latin *verbosus*, from *verbum* 'word.'

ver·bos·i·ty /vərˈbäsətē/ ▶ **n.** the quality of using more words than needed; wordiness: *a critic with a reputation for verbosity*.

ver·bo·ten /fərˈbōtn, vər-/ ▶ **adj.** forbidden, esp. by an authority.
– ORIGIN German.

verb phrase ▶ **n.** Grammar the part of a sentence containing the verb and any direct or indirect object, but not the subject.

ver·dant /ˈvərdnt/ ▶ **adj.** (of countryside) green with grass or other rich vegetation. ■ of the bright green color of lush grass: *a deep, verdant green*.
– DERIVATIVES **ver·dan·cy** /ˈvərdn-sē/ **n., ver·dant·ly adv.**
– ORIGIN late 16th cent.: perhaps from Old French *verdeant*, present participle of *verdoier* 'be green,' based on Latin *viridis* 'green.'

verd an·tique /ˈvərd anˈtēk/ ▶ **n.** a green ornamental marble consisting of serpentine with calcite and dolomite veins. ■ verdigris on ancient bronze or copper. ■ a green form of porphyry.
– ORIGIN mid 18th cent.: from obsolete French, literally 'antique green.'

Ver·de·lho /vərˈdelyo͞o/ ▶ **n.** (pl. **Verdelhos**) a white grape originally grown in Madeira, now also in Portugal, Sicily, Australia, and South Africa. ■ a medium Madeira made from this grape.
– ORIGIN Portuguese, literally 'little green thing;' compare with **Verdicchio**.

ver·der·er /ˈvərdərər/ ▶ **n.** Brit. a judicial officer of a royal forest.
– ORIGIN mid 16th cent.: from Anglo-Norman French, based on Latin *viridis* 'green.'

Ver·di /ˈve(ə)rdē/, Giuseppe (Fortunino Francesco) (1813–1901), Italian composer. His many operas, such as *La Traviata* (1853), *Aida* (1871), and *Otello* (1887), emphasize the dramatic element and the treatment of personal stories on a heroic scale, often against backgrounds that reflect his political interests. He is also noted for *Requiem* (1874).

Ver·dic·chi·o /vərˈdēkēˌō/ ▶ **n.** a variety of white wine grape grown in the Marche region of Italy. ■ a dry white wine made from this grape.
– ORIGIN Italian, literally 'little green thing'; compare with **Verdelho**.

ver·dict /ˈvərdikt/ ▶ **n.** a decision on a disputed issue in a civil or criminal case or an inquest: *the jury returned a verdict of 'not guilty.'* ■ an opinion or judgment: *I'm anxious to know your verdict on me*.
– ORIGIN Middle English: from Anglo-Norman French *verdit*, from Old French *veir* 'true' (from Latin *verus*) + *dit* (from Latin *dictum* 'saying').

ver·di·gris /ˈvərdəˌgrēs, -ˌgris, -ˌgrē/ ▶ **n.** a bright bluish-green encrustation or patina formed on copper or brass by atmospheric oxidation, consisting of basic copper carbonate.
– ORIGIN Middle English: from Old French *verte-gres*, earlier *vert de Grece* 'green of Greece.'

ver·din /ˈvərdn/ ▶ **n.** a small songbird with a gray body and yellowish head, found in the semideserts of southwestern North America. ● *Auriparus flaviceps*, family Remizidae.
– ORIGIN late 19th cent.: from French, literally 'yellowhammer.'

ver·di·ter /ˈvərdətər/ ▶ **n.** a light blue or bluish-green pigment, typically prepared by adding chalk or whiting to a solution of copper nitrate, used in making crayons and as a watercolor.
▶ **adj.** of this color.
– ORIGIN early 16th cent.: from Old French *verd de terre*, literally 'earth green.'

Ver·dun, Bat·tle of /vərˈdən/ a long and severe battle in 1916, during World War I, at the fortified town of Verdun in northeastern France.

V

PRONUNCIATION KEY ə *ago, up*; ər *over, fur*; a *hat*; ā *ate*; ä *car*; e *let*; ē *see*; i *fit*; ī *by*; NG *sing*; ō *go*; ô *law, for*; oi *toy*; o͝o *good*; o͞o *goo*; ou *out*; TH *thin*; T͟H *then*; ZH *vision*

ver·dure /ˈvərjər/ ▶ **n.** lush green vegetation. ■ the fresh green color of such vegetation. ■ literary a condition of freshness.
– DERIVATIVES **ver·dured adj.**, **ver·dur·ous** /-jərəs/ **adj.**
– ORIGIN late Middle English: via French from Old French *verd* 'green,' from Latin *viridis.*

Ve·ree·ni·ging /vəˈrēnəgiNG, fə-/ a city in South Africa; pop. 474,000 (est. 2009).

verge[1] /vərj/ ▶ **n.** an edge or border: *they came down to the verge of the lake.* ■ an extreme limit beyond which something specified will happen: *I was* **on the verge of** *tears.* ■ Brit. a grass edging such as that by the side of a road or path. ■ Architecture an edge of tiles projecting over a gable.
▶ **v.** [no obj.] (**verge on**) approach (something) closely; be close or similar to (something): *despair verging on the suicidal.*
– ORIGIN late Middle English: via Old French from Latin *virga* 'rod.' The current verb sense dates from the late 18th cent.

verge[2] ▶ **n.** a wand or rod carried before a bishop or dean as an emblem of office.
– ORIGIN late Middle English: from Latin *virga* 'rod.'

verge[3] ▶ **v.** [no obj.] incline in a certain direction or toward a particular state: *his style verged into the art nouveau school.*
– ORIGIN early 17th cent. (in the sense 'descend (to the horizon)'): from Latin *vergere* 'to bend, incline.'

ver·gence /ˈvərjəns/ ▶ **n. 1** Physiology the simultaneous movement of the pupils of the eyes toward or away from one another during focusing. **2** Geology the direction in which a fold is inclined or overturned: *a zone of opposing fold vergence.*
– ORIGIN 1980s: common element of **CONVERGENCE** and **DIVERGENCE**.

verg·er /ˈvərjər/ ▶ **n. 1** an official in a church who acts as a caretaker and attendant.
2 an officer who carries a rod before a bishop or dean as a symbol of office.
– DERIVATIVES **verg·er·ship** /-ˌSHip/ **n.**
– ORIGIN Middle English (sense 2): from Anglo-Norman French (see **VERGE**[2]).

Ver·gil variant spelling of **VIRGIL**.

ver·glas /verˈglä/ ▶ **n.** a thin coating of ice or frozen rain on an exposed surface.
– ORIGIN early 19th cent.: French, from *verre* 'glass' + *glas* (now *glace*) 'ice.'

ve·rid·i·cal /vəˈridikəl/ ▶ **adj.** formal truthful. ■ coinciding with reality: *such memories are not necessarily veridical.*
– DERIVATIVES **ve·rid·i·cal·i·ty** /-ˌridəˈkalətē/ **n.**, **ve·rid·i·cal·ly** /-ik(ə)lē/ **adv.**
– ORIGIN mid 17th cent.: from Latin *veridicus* (from *verus* 'true' + *dicere* 'say') + **-AL**.

ver·i·est /ˈverēist/ ▶ **adj.** [attrib.] (**the veriest**) chiefly archaic used to emphasize the degree to which a description applies to someone or something: *everyone but the veriest greenhorn knows by now.*
– ORIGIN early 16th cent.: superlative of **VERY**.

ver·i·fi·ca·tion /ˌverəfiˈkāSHən/ ▶ **n.** the process of establishing the truth, accuracy, or validity of something: *the verification of official documents.* ■ [often as modifier] Philosophy the establishment by empirical means of the validity of a proposition. ■ the process of ensuring that procedures laid down in weapons limitation agreements are followed.
– ORIGIN early 16th cent.: from Old French or from medieval Latin *verificatio(n-)*, from the verb *verificare* (see **VERIFY**).

ver·i·fy /ˈverəˌfī/ ▶ **v.** (**verifies, verifying, verified**) [with obj.] make sure or demonstrate that (something) is true, accurate, or justified: *his conclusions have been verified by later experiments* | [with clause] *"Can you verify that the guns are licensed?"* ■ Law swear to or support (a statement) by affidavit.
– DERIVATIVES **ver·i·fi·a·ble** /ˈverəˌfīəbəl, ˌverəˈfī-/ **adj.**, **ver·i·fi·a·bly** /ˈverəˌfīəblē, ˌverəˈfī-/ **adv.**, **ver·i·fi·er n.**
– ORIGIN Middle English (as a legal term): from Old French *verifier*, from medieval Latin *verificare*, from *verus* 'true.'

ver·i·ly /ˈverəlē/ ▶ **adv.** archaic truly; certainly: *I verily believed myself to be a free woman.*
– ORIGIN Middle English: from **VERY** + **-LY**[2], suggested by Old French *verrai(e)ment.*

ver·i·si·mil·i·tude /ˌverəsəˈmiliˌt(y)o͞od/ ▶ **n.** the appearance of being true or real: *the detail gives the novel some verisimilitude.*
– DERIVATIVES **ver·i·sim·i·lar** /-ˈsimələr/ **adj.**
– ORIGIN early 17th cent.: from Latin *verisimilitudo*, from *verisimilis* 'probable,' from *veri* (genitive of *verus* 'true') + *similis* 'like.'

ve·ris·mo /vəˈrizmō, ve-/ ▶ **n.** realism in the arts, esp. late 19th-century Italian opera. ■ this genre of opera, as composed principally by Puccini, Mascagni, and Leoncavallo.
– ORIGIN Italian.

ve·ris·tic /vəˈristik/ ▶ **adj.** (of art or literature) extremely or strictly naturalistic.
– DERIVATIVES **ver·ism** /ˈverˌizəm/ **n.**, **ver·ist** /ˈverist/ **n. & adj.**
– ORIGIN late 19th cent.: from Latin *verum* (neuter) 'true' or Italian *vero* 'true' + **-IST** + **-IC**.

ver·i·ta·ble /ˈveritəbəl/ ▶ **adj.** [attrib.] used as an intensifier, often to qualify a metaphor: *the early 1970s witnessed a veritable price explosion.*
– DERIVATIVES **ver·i·ta·bly** /-blē/ **adv.**
– ORIGIN late Middle English: from Old French, from *verite* 'truth' (see **VERITY**). Early senses included 'true' and 'speaking the truth,' later 'genuine, actual.'

vé·ri·té /ˌveriˈtā/ ▶ **n.** a genre of film, television, and radio programs emphasizing realism and naturalism.
– ORIGIN French, literally 'truth.'

ver·i·ty /ˈveritē/ ▶ **n.** (pl. **verities**) a true principle or belief, esp. one of fundamental importance: *the eternal verities.* ■ truth: *irrefutable, objective verity.*
– ORIGIN late Middle English: from Old French *verite*, from Latin *veritas*, from *verus* 'true.'

ver·juice /ˈvərˌjo͞os/ ▶ **n.** a sour juice obtained from crab apples, unripe grapes, or other fruit, used in cooking and formerly in medicine.
– ORIGIN Middle English: from Old French *vertjus*, from *vert* 'green' + *jus* 'juice.'

Ver·khne·u·dinsk /ˌverknəˈo͝odinsk/ former name (until 1934) of **ULAN-UDE**.

Ver·laine /vərˈlān, verˈlen/, Paul (1844–96), French symbolist poet. Notable collections of his poetry include *Poèmes saturniens* (1867), *Fêtes galantes* (1869), and *Romances sans paroles* (1874).

Ver·meer /vərˈmi(ə)r/, Jan (1632–75), Dutch painter. He generally painted domestic genre scenes, for example *The Kitchen Maid* (*c.*1658), *The Music Lesson* (*c.*1662–65), and *The Girl with a Pearl Earring* (*c.*1665–66). His work is distinguished by its clear design and simple form.

ver·meil /ˈvərməl, -ˌmāl, vərˈmā(l)/ ▶ **n.** [often as modifier] **1** gilded silver or bronze.
2 literary vermilion.
– ORIGIN late Middle English (sense 2): from Old French (see **VERMILION**).

vermi- ▶ **comb. form** of or relating to a worm or worms, esp. parasitic ones: *vermiform.*
– ORIGIN from Latin *vermis* 'worm.'

ver·mi·an /ˈvərmēən/ ▶ **adj. 1** literary relating to or resembling a worm; wormlike.
2 Anatomy of or relating to the vermis of the brain.
– ORIGIN late 19th cent.: from Latin *vermis* 'worm' + **-IAN**.

ver·mi·cel·li /ˌvərməˈCHelē, -ˈselē/ ▶ **n.** pasta made in long slender threads.
– ORIGIN Italian, plural of *vermicello*, diminutive of *verme* 'worm,' from Latin *vermis.*

ver·mi·cide /ˈvərməˌsīd/ ▶ **n.** a substance that is poisonous to worms.

ver·mi·com·post·ing /ˌvərməˈkämpōstiNG/ ▶ **n.** the use of earthworms to convert organic waste into fertilizer.
– DERIVATIVES **ver·mi·com·post·er n.**

ver·mic·u·lar /vərˈmikyələr/ ▶ **adj. 1** like a worm in form or movement; vermiform.
2 of, denoting, or caused by intestinal worms.
3 marked with close wavy lines.
– ORIGIN late 17th cent.: from medieval Latin *vermicularis*, from Latin *vermiculus*, diminutive of *vermis* 'worm.'

ver·mic·u·late /vərˈmikyəˌlāt, -lət/ ▶ **adj. 1** another term for **VERMICULAR**.
2 another term for **VERMICULATED**.
– ORIGIN early 17th cent.: from Latin *vermiculatus*, past participle of *vermiculari* 'be full of worms' (see **VERMICULAR**).

ver·mic·u·lat·ed /vərˈmikyəˌlātid/ ▶ **adj. 1** (esp. of the plumage of a bird) marked with sinuous or wavy lines.
2 archaic worm-eaten.
3 Architecture carved or molded with shallow wavy grooves resembling the tracks of worms.
– DERIVATIVES **ver·mic·u·la·tion** /vərˌmikyəˈlāSHən/ **n.**

ver·mic·u·lite /vərˈmikyəˌlīt/ ▶ **n.** a yellow or brown mineral found as an alteration product of mica and other minerals, and used for insulation or as a moisture-retentive medium for growing plants.
– ORIGIN early 19th cent.: from Latin *vermiculari* 'be full of worms' (because on expansion due to heat, it shoots out forms resembling small worms) + **-ITE**[1].

ver·mi·form /ˈvərməˌfôrm/ ▶ **adj.** chiefly Zoology or Anatomy resembling or having the form of a worm.

ver·mi·form ap·pen·dix ▶ **n.** technical term for **APPENDIX** (sense 1).

ver·mi·fuge /ˈvərməˌfyo͞oj/ ▶ **n.** Medicine an anthelmintic medicine.

ver·mil·ion /vərˈmilyən/ (also **vermillion**) ▶ **n.** a brilliant red pigment made from mercury sulfide (cinnabar). ■ a brilliant red color: *a lateral stripe of vermilion* | [as modifier] *vermilion streaks of sunset.*
– ORIGIN Middle English: from Old French *vermeillon*, from *vermeil*, from Latin *vermiculus*, diminutive of *vermis* 'worm.'

ver·min /ˈvərmən/ ▶ **n.** [treated as pl.] wild mammals and birds that are believed to be harmful to crops, farm animals, or game, or that carry disease, e.g., foxes, rodents, and insect pests. ■ parasitic worms or insects. ■ people perceived as despicable and as causing problems for the rest of society: *the vermin who ransacked her house.*
– DERIVATIVES **ver·min·ous** /-mənəs/ **adj.**
– ORIGIN Middle English (originally denoting animals such as reptiles and snakes): from Old French, based on Latin *vermis* 'worm.'

ver·mis /ˈvərməs/ ▶ **n.** Anatomy the rounded and elongated central part of the cerebellum, between the two hemispheres.
– ORIGIN late 19th cent.: from Latin, literally 'worm.'

Ver·mont /vərˈmänt/ a state in the northeastern US, on the border with Canada, one of the six New England States; pop. 621,270 (est. 2008); capital, Montpelier; statehood, Mar. 4, 1791 (14). Explored and settled by the French during the 1600s and 1700s, it became an independent republic in 1777 until it was admitted as a US state.
– DERIVATIVES **Ver·mont·er n.**

ver·mouth /vərˈmo͞oTH/ ▶ **n.** a red or white wine flavored with aromatic herbs, made chiefly in France and Italy and used in cocktails.
– ORIGIN from French *vermout*, from German *Wermut* 'wormwood.'

ver·nac·cia /vərˈnäCHə/ ▶ **n.** a variety of wine grape grown in the San Gimignano area of Italy and in Sardinia. ■ a strong dry white wine made from this grape.
– ORIGIN Italian.

ver·nac·u·lar /vərˈnakyələr/ ▶ **n. 1** (usu. **the vernacular**) the language or dialect spoken by the ordinary people in a particular country or region: *he wrote in the vernacular to reach a larger audience.* ■ [with modifier] the terminology used by people belonging to a specified group or engaging in a specialized activity: *gardening vernacular.*
2 architecture concerned with domestic and functional rather than monumental buildings: *buildings in which Gothic merged into farmhouse vernacular.*
▶ **adj. 1** (of language) spoken as one's mother tongue; not learned or imposed as a second language. ■ (of speech or written works) using such a language: *vernacular literature.*
2 (of architecture) concerned with domestic and functional rather than monumental buildings.
– DERIVATIVES **ver·nac·u·lar·ism** /-ˌrizəm/ **n.**, **ver·nac·u·lar·i·ty** /-ˌnakyəˈlaritē/ **n.**, **ver·nac·u·lar·ize** /-ˌrīz/ **v.**, **ver·nac·u·lar·ly adv.**
– ORIGIN early 17th cent.: from Latin *vernaculus* 'domestic, native' (from *verna* 'home-born slave') + **-AR**[1].

ver·nal /ˈvərnl/ ▶ **adj.** of, in, or appropriate to spring: *the vernal freshness of the land.*
– DERIVATIVES **ver·nal·ly adv.**
– ORIGIN mid 16th cent.: from Latin *vernalis*, from *vernus* 'of the spring,' from *ver* 'spring.'

ver·nal e·qui·nox ▶ **n.** the equinox in spring, on about March 20 in the northern hemisphere and September 22 in the southern hemisphere. ■ Astronomy the equinox in March. Also called **SPRING EQUINOX**. ■ Astronomy another term for **FIRST POINT OF ARIES** (see **ARIES**).

ver·nal grass ▶ **n.** a sweet-scented Eurasian grass that is sometimes grown as a meadow or hay grass. Also called **SWEET VERNAL GRASS**. ● *Anthoxanthum odoratum*, family Gramineae.

ver·nal·i·za·tion /ˌvərnl-əˈzāSHən/ ▶ **n.** the cooling of seed during germination in order to accelerate flowering when it is planted.
– DERIVATIVES **ver·nal·ize** /ˈvərnlˌīz/ **v.**
– ORIGIN 1930s: translation of Russian *yarovizatsiya.*

ver·na·tion /vərˈnāSHən/ ▶ **n.** Botany the arrangement of young leaves in a leaf bud before it opens. Compare with **ESTIVATION**.
– ORIGIN late 18th cent.: from modern Latin *vernatio(n-)*, from Latin *vernare* 'to grow (as in the spring),' from *vernus* (see **VERNAL**).

V

Verne /vərn/, Jules (1828–1905), French novelist. One of the first writers of science fiction, he often anticipated later scientific and technological developments, as in *Twenty Thousand Leagues under the Sea* (1870). Other novels include *Journey to the Center of the Earth* (1864) and *Around the World in Eighty Days* (1873).

Ver·ner's Law /'vernərz, 'vər-/ Linguistics the observation that voiceless fricatives in Germanic predicted by Grimm's Law became voiced if the preceding syllable in the corresponding Indo-European word was unstressed, as in the English words *death* and *dead*.
– ORIGIN late 19th cent.: named after Karl A. *Verner* (1846–96), Danish philologist.

ver·ni·cle /'vərnəkəl/ ▶ **n.** another term for **VERONICA** (sense 2).
– ORIGIN Middle English: from Old French, alteration of *vernique*, from medieval Latin *veronica*.

ver·nier /'vərnēər/ ▶ **n.** a small movable graduated scale for obtaining fractional parts of subdivisions on a fixed main scale of a barometer, sextant, or other measuring instrument.
– ORIGIN mid 18th cent.: named after Pierre *Vernier* (1580–1637), French mathematician.

ver·ni·er cal·i·per ▶ **n.** a linear measuring instrument consisting of a scaled rule with a projecting arm at one end, to which is attached a sliding vernier with a projecting arm that forms a jaw with the other projecting arm.

ver·nier en·gine ▶ **n.** another term for **THRUSTER**.
– ORIGIN mid 20th cent.: named after P. *Vernier* (see **VERNIER**).

ver·ni·er scale ▶ **n.** see **VERNIER**.

ver·nis·sage /ˌvernə'säzн/ ▶ **n.** (pl. **same**) a private viewing of paintings before public exhibition.
– ORIGIN French, literally 'varnishing,' originally referring to the day prior to an exhibition when artists were allowed to retouch and varnish hung work.

ver·nix /'vərniks/ ▶ **n.** (in full **vernix caseosa** /ˌkāsē'ōsə/) a greasy deposit covering the skin of a baby at birth.
– ORIGIN late 16th cent.: from medieval Latin, variant of *veronix* 'fragrant resin' (see **VARNISH**).

Ver·ny /'vernē/ former name (until 1921) of **ALMATY**.

Ve·ro·na /və'rōnə/ a city on the Adige River, in northeastern Italy; pop. 265,368 (2008).

ve·ro·nal /'verəˌnôl, -ənl/ ▶ **n.** trademark another term for **BARBITAL**.
– ORIGIN early 20th cent.: from German, from **VERONA** + **-AL**.

Ve·ro·ne·se /ˌvārə'nāzā/, Paolo (*c.*1528–88), Italian painter; born *Paolo Caliari*. He is particularly known for his richly colored feast scenes such as in *The Marriage at Cana* (1562).

ve·ron·i·ca /və'ränəkə/ ▶ **n. 1** a herbaceous plant of north temperate regions, typically with upright stems bearing narrow pointed leaves and spikes of blue or purple flowers. ● Genus *Veronica*, family Scrophulariaceae: many species, including the speedwells.
2 a cloth supposedly impressed with an image of Jesus' face. [see **VERONICA, ST.**] ■ a picture of Jesus' face similar to this.
3 (in bullfighting) a slow movement of the cape away from a charging bull by the matador, who stands in place. [said to be by association of the attitude of the matador with the depiction of St. *Veronica* holding out a cloth to Jesus (see **VERONICA, ST.**).]
– ORIGIN early 16th cent.: from medieval Latin, from the given name *Veronica*.

Ve·ron·i·ca, St. /və'ränəkə/ a woman of Jerusalem who reportedly offered her head cloth to Jesus on the way to Calvary, to wipe the blood and sweat from his face. The cloth is said to have retained the image of his features.

ve·ron·ique /ˌverə'nēk, ˌvārô-/ ▶ **adj.** [postpositive] denoting a dish, typically of fish or chicken, prepared or garnished with grapes.
– ORIGIN from the French given name *Véronique*.

Ver·ra·za·no /ˌverät'sänō/, Giovanni da (*c.*1480–1527), Italian navigator in the service of France. He was the first European to enter New York Bay 1524.

Ver·ra·za·no-Nar·rows Bridge /ˌverə'zänō/ a suspension bridge across New York Bay between Brooklyn and Staten Island, the longest in the world when it was completed in 1964.
– ORIGIN named after Giovanni da *Verrazano*.

ver·ru·ca /və'rōōkə/ ▶ **n.** (pl. **verrucae** /-kē, -kī/ or **verrucas**) a contagious and usually painful wart on the sole of the foot; a plantar wart. ■ (in medical use) a wart of any kind.
– DERIVATIVES **ver·ru·cose** /'verəˌkōs, və'rōō-/ **adj.**, **ver·ru·cous** /və'rōōkəs/ **adj.**
– ORIGIN late Middle English: from Latin.

Ver·sa·ce /vər'sächē/, Gianni (1946–97), Italian fashion designer and founder of an international house of fashion and furnishings.

Ver·sailles /vər'sī, ver-/ a palace built for Louis XIV near the town of Versailles, southwest of Paris. It was built around a chateau belonging to Louis XIII, which was transformed by additions in the grand French classical style.

Ver·sailles, Trea·ty of 1 a treaty that terminated the American Revolution in 1783.
2 a treaty signed in 1919 that brought a formal end to World War I.

> The treaty redivided the territory of the defeated Central Powers, restricted Germany's armed forces, and established the League of Nations. It left Germany smarting under what it considered a vindictive settlement while not sufficiently restricting its ability eventually to rearm and seek forcible redress.

ver·sal /'vərsəl/ ▶ **adj.** of or relating to a style of ornate capital letter used to start a verse, paragraph, etc., in a manuscript, typically built up by inking between pen strokes and with long, rather flat serifs.
▶ **n.** a versal letter.
– ORIGIN late 19th cent.: from Latin *vers-* 'turned' + **-AL**, influenced by **VERSE**.

ver·sant /'vərsənt/ ▶ **n.** a region of land sloping in one general direction.
– ORIGIN mid 19th cent.: from French, present participle (used as a noun) of *verser* 'tilt over,' from Latin *versare*.

ver·sa·tile /'vərsətl/ ▶ **adj. 1** able to adapt or be adapted to many different functions or activities: *a versatile sewing machine* | *he was versatile enough to play either position*.
2 archaic changeable; inconstant.
– DERIVATIVES **ver·sa·tile·ly adv.**, **ver·sa·til·i·ty** /ˌvərsə'tilətē/ **n.**
– ORIGIN early 17th cent. (in the sense 'inconstant, fluctuating'): from French, or from Latin *versatilis*, from *versat-* 'turned around, revolved,' from the verb *versare*, frequentative of *vertere* 'to turn.'

verse /vərs/ ▶ **n.** writing arranged with a metrical rhythm, typically having a rhyme: *a lament in verse* | [as modifier] *verse drama*. ■ a group of lines that form a unit in a poem or song; a stanza: *the second verse*. ■ each of the short numbered divisions of a chapter in the Bible or other scripture. ■ a versicle. ■ archaic a line of poetry. ■ a passage in an anthem for a soloist or a small group of voices.
▶ **v.** [no obj.] archaic speak in or compose verse; versify.
– DERIVATIVES **verse·let** /-lət/ **n.**
– ORIGIN Old English *fers*, from Latin *versus* 'a turn of the plow, a furrow, a line of writing,' from *vertere* 'to turn'; reinforced in Middle English by Old French *vers*, from Latin *versus*.

versed /vərst/ ▶ **adj.** (**versed in**) experienced or skilled in; knowledgeable about: *a native Icelander well versed in her country's medieval literature*.
– ORIGIN early 17th cent.: from French *versé* or Latin *versatus*, past participle of *versari* 'be engaged in.'

versed sine ▶ **n.** Mathematics one minus cosine. ■ Architecture the rise of an arch of a bridge.

ver·si·cle /'vərsikəl/ ▶ **n.** (usu. **versicles**) a short sentence said or sung by the minister in a church service, to which the congregation gives a response.
– ORIGIN Middle English: from Old French *versicule* or Latin *versiculus*, diminutive of *versus* (see **VERSE**).

ver·si·col·ored /ˌvərsiˌkələrd/ (Brit. **versicoloured**) ▶ **adj.** archaic **1** changing from one color to another in different lights.
2 variegated.
– ORIGIN early 18th cent.: from Latin *versicolor* (from *versus* 'turned' + *color* 'color') + **-ED**[2].

ver·si·fy /'vərsəˌfī/ ▶ **v.** (**versifies**, **versifying**, **versified**) [with obj.] turn into or express in verse: *he versifies others' ideas* | (as noun **versifying**) *a talent for versifying*.
– DERIVATIVES **ver·si·fi·ca·tion** /ˌvərsəfi'kāsнən/ **n.**, **ver·si·fi·er n.**
– ORIGIN late Middle English: from Old French *versifier*, from Latin *versificare*, from *versus* (see **VERSE**).

ver·sine /'vərˌsīn/ (also **versin**) ▶ **n.** Mathematics another term for **VERSED SINE**.
– ORIGIN early 19th cent.: abbreviation.

ver·sion /'vərzнən/ ▶ **n. 1** a particular form of something differing in certain respects from an earlier form or other forms of the same type of thing: *a revised version of the paper was produced for a later meeting* | *they produce yachts in both standard and master versions*. ■ a particular edition or translation of a book or other work: *the English version will be published next year*. ■ [usu. with modifier] an adaptation of a novel, piece of music, etc., into another medium or style: *a film version of a wonderfully funny cult novel*. ■ a particular release of a piece of computer software. ■ an account of a matter from a particular person's point of view: *he told her his version of events*.
2 Medicine the manual turning of a fetus in the uterus to make delivery easier. ■ an abnormal displacement of the uterus.
▶ **v.** [with obj.] (often as noun **versioning**) create a new version of: *it's the software for you if you need versioning and group editing*.
– DERIVATIVES **ver·sion·al** /-zнənl/ **adj.**
– ORIGIN late Middle English (in the sense 'translation'): from French, or from medieval Latin *versio(n-)*, from Latin *vertere* 'to turn.'

ver·sion con·trol ▶ **n.** Computing the task of keeping a software system consisting of many versions and configurations well organized.

vers li·bre /ˌver 'lēbrə/ ▶ **n.** another term for **FREE VERSE**.
– ORIGIN French, literally 'free verse.'

ver·so /'vərsō/ ▶ **n.** (pl. **versos**) **1** a left-hand page of an open book, or the back of a loose document. Contrasted with **RECTO**.
2 the reverse of something such as a coin or painting.
– ORIGIN mid 19th cent.: from Latin *verso (folio)* 'on the turned (leaf).'

verst /vərst/ ▶ **n.** a Russian measure of length, about 0.66 mile (1.1 km).
– ORIGIN from Russian *versta*.

Ver·ste·hen /fər'sнtāən/ ▶ **n.** Sociology empathic understanding of human behavior.
– ORIGIN German, literally 'understanding.'

ver·sus /'vərsəs, -səz/ (abbr.: **v.** or **vs.**) ▶ **prep.** against (esp. in sports and legal use): *Penn versus Princeton*. ■ as opposed to; in contrast to: *weighing the pros and cons of organic versus inorganic produce*.
– ORIGIN late Middle English: from a medieval Latin use of Latin *versus* 'toward.'

vert /vərt/ ▶ **n.** green, as a heraldic tincture: [postpositive] *three piles vert*.
– ORIGIN late Middle English (as an adjective): via Old French from Latin *viridis* 'green.'

ver·te·bra /'vərtəbrə/ ▶ **n.** (pl. **vertebrae** /-ˌbrē, -ˌbrā/) each of the series of small bones forming the backbone, having several projections for articulation and muscle attachment, and a hole through which the spinal cord passes.

> In the human spine (or vertebral column) there are seven cervical vertebrae (in the neck), twelve thoracic vertebrae (to which the ribs are attached), and five lumbar vertebrae (in the lower back). In addition, five fused vertebrae form the sacrum, and four the coccyx.

– DERIVATIVES **ver·te·bral** /-brəl, vər'tē-/ **adj.**
– ORIGIN early 17th cent.: from Latin, from *vertere* 'to turn.'

ver·te·bral col·umn ▶ **n.** another term for **SPINAL COLUMN**.

ver·te·brate /'vərtəbrət, -ˌbrāt/ ▶ **n.** an animal of a large group distinguished by the possession of a backbone or spinal column, including mammals, birds, reptiles, amphibians, and fishes. Compare with **INVERTEBRATE**. ● Subphylum Vertebrata, phylum Chordata: seven classes.
▶ **adj.** of or relating to the vertebrates.
– ORIGIN early 19th cent.: from Latin *vertebratus* 'jointed,' from *vertebra* (see **VERTEBRA**).

ver·tex /'vərˌteks/ ▶ **n.** (pl. **vertices** /-təˌsēz/ or **vertexes**) **1** the highest point; the top or apex. ■ Anatomy the crown of the head.
2 Geometry each angular point of a polygon, polyhedron, or other figure. ■ a meeting point of two lines that form an angle. ■ the point at which an axis meets a curve or surface.
– ORIGIN late Middle English: from Latin, 'whirlpool, crown of a head, vertex,' from *vertere* 'to turn.'

ver·ti·cal /'vərtikəl/ ▶ **adj. 1** at right angles to a horizontal plane; in a direction, or having an alignment, such that the top is directly above the bottom: *the vertical axis* | *keep your back vertical*.
2 archaic denoting a point at the zenith or the highest point of something.
3 Anatomy of or relating to the crown of the head.
4 involving different levels of a hierarchy or progression, in particular: ■ involving all the stages from the production to the sale of a class of goods.

V

■ (esp. of the transmission of disease or genetic traits) passed from one generation to the next.
▶ **n. 1** (usu. **the vertical**) a vertical line or plane: *the columns incline several degrees away from the vertical.*
2 an upright structure: *we remodeled the opening with a simple lintel and unadorned verticals.*
3 short for **VERTICAL TASTING.**
4 the distance between the highest and lowest points of a ski area: *the resort claims a vertical of 2100 meters.*
– DERIVATIVES **ver·ti·cal·i·ty** /ˌvərtiˈkalətē/ **n.**, **ver·ti·cal·ize** /-ˌlīz/ **v.**, **ver·ti·cal·ly** /-ik(ə)lē/ **adv.**
– ORIGIN mid 16th cent. (in the sense 'directly overhead'): from French, or from late Latin *verticalis*, from *vertex* (see **VERTEX**).

ver·ti·cal an·gles ▶ **plural n.** Mathematics each of the pairs of opposite angles made by two intersecting lines.

ver·ti·cal cir·cle ▶ **n.** a great circle of the celestial sphere whose diameter runs from zenith to nadir.

ver·ti·cal file ▶ **n.** an alphabetized file for pamphlets and other small publications that do not merit a call number in a library system.

ver·ti·cal fin ▶ **n.** Zoology any of the unpaired fins in the midline of a fish's body, i.e., a dorsal, anal, or caudal fin.

ver·ti·cal in·te·gra·tion ▶ **n.** the combination in one company of two or more stages of production normally operated by separate companies.

ver·tic·al·ly chal·lenged /ˈvərtik(ə)lē/ ▶ **adj.** humorous not tall in height; short.

ver·ti·cal sta·bi·liz·er ▶ **n.** Aeronautics a small, flattened projecting surface or attachment on an aircraft or rocket for providing aerodynamic stability.

ver·ti·cal tast·ing ▶ **n.** a tasting in order of year of several different vintages of a particular wine.

ver·ti·cal un·ion ▶ **n.** a union whose members all work in various capacities in a single industry.

ver·ti·cil·li·um /ˌvərtəˈsilēəm/ ▶ **n.** a fungus of a genus that includes a number of species that cause wilt in plants. ● Genus *Verticillium*, subdivision Deuteromycotina, in particular *V. albo-atrum* and *V. dahliae*. ■ wilt caused by such fungi.
– ORIGIN modern Latin, from Latin *verticillus* 'spindle whorl.'

ver·tig·i·nous /vərˈtijənəs/ ▶ **adj.** causing vertigo, esp. by being extremely high or steep: *vertiginous drops to the valleys below.* ■ relating to or affected by vertigo.
– DERIVATIVES **ver·tig·i·nous·ly adv.**
– ORIGIN early 17th cent.: from Latin *vertiginosus*, from *vertigo* 'whirling around' (see **VERTIGO**).

ver·ti·go /ˈvərtəgō/ ▶ **n.** a sensation of whirling and loss of balance, associated particularly with looking down from a great height, or caused by disease affecting the inner ear or the vestibular nerve; giddiness.
– ORIGIN late Middle English: from Latin, 'whirling,' from *vertere* 'to turn.'

ver·ti·sol /ˈvərtəˌsäl, -ˌsôl/ ▶ **n.** Soil Science a clayey soil with little organic matter that occurs in regions having distinct wet and dry seasons.
– ORIGIN 1960s: from **VERTICAL** + Latin *solum* 'soil.'

ver·tu ▶ **n.** variant spelling of **VIRTU.**

ver·vain /ˈvərˌvān/ ▶ **n.** a widely distributed herbaceous plant with small blue, white, or purple flowers and a long history of use as a magical and medicinal herb. ● *Verbena officinalis*, family Verbenaceae.
– ORIGIN late Middle English: from Old French *verveine*, from Latin *verbena* (see **VERBENA**).

verve /vərv/ ▶ **n.** vigor and spirit or enthusiasm: *Kollo sings with supreme verve and flexibility.*
– ORIGIN late 17th cent. (denoting special talent in writing): from French, 'vigor,' earlier 'form of expression,' from Latin *verba* 'words.'

V

ver·vet /ˈvərvət/ (also **vervet monkey**) ▶ **n.** a common African guenon with greenish-brown upper parts and a black face. Compare with **GREEN MONKEY, GRIVET.** ● *Cercopithecus aethiops*, family Cercopithecidae, in particular the race *C. a. pygerythrus* of southern and eastern Africa.
– ORIGIN late 19th cent.: from French, of unknown origin.

Ver·viers /verˈvyā/ a manufacturing town in eastern Belgium; pop 54,519 (2008).

Ver·woerd /fərˈvo͝ort/, Hendrik (Frensch) (1901–66), South African statesman; prime minister 1958–66. As minister of Bantu affairs (1950–58), he developed the segregation policy of apartheid. As premier, he banned the ANC and the Pan-Africanist Congress in 1960 and declared South Africa a republic in 1961.

ver·y /ˈverē/ ▶ **adv.** used for emphasis. ■ in a high degree: *very large | very quickly | very much so.* ■ (with superlative or **own**) used to emphasize that the following description applies without qualification: *the very best quality | his very own car.*
▶ **adj.** actual; precise (used to emphasize the exact identity of a particular person or thing): *those were his very words | he might be phoning her at this very moment | transformed **before our very eyes**.* ■ emphasizing an extreme point in time or space: *from the very beginning of the book | at the very back of the skull.* ■ with no addition of or contribution from anything else; mere: *the very thought of drink made him feel sick.* ■ archaic real; genuine: *the very God of Heaven.*
– PHRASES **not very 1** in a low degree: *"Bad news?" "Not very."* **2** far from being: *I'm not very impressed.* **the very idea!** see **IDEA. the very same** see **SAME. very good** (or **well**) an expression of consent.
– ORIGIN Middle English (as an adjective in the sense 'real, genuine'): from Old French *verai*, based on Latin *verus* 'true.'

ver·y high fre·quen·cy ▶ **n.** (abbr.: **VHF**) the band of frequencies between 30 and 300 megahertz, typically used for broadcasting television signals.

Ver·y Large Ar·ray (abbr.: **VLA**) ▶ **n.** the world's largest radio telescope, consisting of 27 dish antennas near Socorro, New Mexico.

Ver·y light /ˈverē, ˈvi(ə)rē/ ▶ **n.** a flare fired into the air from a pistol for signaling or for temporary illumination.
– ORIGIN early 20th cent.: named after Edward W. *Very* (1847–1910), American naval officer.

ver·y low fre·quen·cy ▶ **n.** (abbr.: **VLF**) the band of frequencies between 3 and 30 kilohertz.

Ver·y pis·tol ▶ **n.** a handheld gun used for firing a Very light.

VESA ▶ **abbr.** Video Electronics Standards Association, an organization that defines formats for displays and buses used in computers.

Ve·sak /ˈvāˌsäk/ (also **Wesak** or **Visākha** /viˈsäkə/) ▶ **n.** the most important Buddhist festival, commemorating the birth, enlightenment, and death of the Buddha, and celebrated at the full moon in the Indian month of Vaishaka (April–May).
– ORIGIN Sinhalese *vesak*, via Pali from Sanskrit *vaiśākha*, denoting the month April–May.

Ve·sa·li·us /vəˈsālēəs/, Andreas (1514–64), Flemish anatomist; the founder of modern anatomy.

ve·si·cal /ˈvesəkəl/ ▶ **adj.** Anatomy & Medicine of, relating to, or affecting the urinary bladder: *vesical function | the vesical artery.*
– ORIGIN late 18th cent.: from Latin *vesica* 'bladder' + **-AL.**

ves·i·cant /ˈvesəkənt/ ▶ **adj.** tending to cause blistering.
▶ **n.** an agent that causes blistering.
– ORIGIN late Middle English: from late Latin *vesicant-* 'forming pustules,' from the verb *vesicare*, from *vesica* 'bladder.'

ve·si·ca pis·cis /ˈvesikə ˈpis(k)is, ˈpīsis, vəˈsēkə, vəˈsīkə/ ▶ **n.** (pl. **vesicae piscis** /-ˌkī, -ˌkē/) another term for **MANDORLA.**
– ORIGIN Latin, literally 'fish's bladder.'

ves·i·cate /ˈvesiˌkāt/ ▶ **v.** [with obj.] chiefly Medicine raise blisters on. ■ [no obj.] form blisters.
– DERIVATIVES **ves·i·ca·tion** /ˌvesiˈkāsʜən/ **n.**, **ves·i·ca·to·ry** /ˈvesəkəˌtôrē, vəˈsikə-/ **adj. & n.**
– ORIGIN mid 17th cent.: from late Latin *vesicat-* 'having pustules,' from *vesica* 'bladder.'

ve·si·cle /ˈvesikəl/ ▶ **n.** a fluid- or air-filled cavity or sac, in particular: ■ Anatomy & Zoology a small fluid-filled bladder, sac, cyst, or vacuole within the body. ■ Botany an air-filled swelling in a plant, esp. a seaweed. ■ Geology a small cavity in volcanic rock, produced by gas bubbles in the molten lava. ■ Medicine a small blister full of clear fluid.
– DERIVATIVES **ve·sic·u·lar** /vəˈsikyələr/ **adj.**, **ve·sic·u·lat·ed** /vəˈsikyəˌlātid/ **adj.**, **ve·sic·u·la·tion** /vəˌsikyəˈlāsʜən/ **n.**
– ORIGIN late 16th cent.: from French *vésicule* or Latin *vesicula*, diminutive of *vesica* 'bladder.'

ves·i·co·u·re·ter·ic re·flux /ˌvesəkōˌyo͞oriˈterik/ ▶ **n.** Medicine flow of urine from the bladder back into the ureters, arising from defective valves and causing a high risk of kidney infection.
– ORIGIN mid 20th cent.: *vesicoureteric* from Latin *vesica* 'bladder' + *ureteric* (see **URETER**).

ve·sic·u·late ▶ **v.** /vəˈsikyəˌlāt/ make or become vesicular.
▶ **adj.** /vəˈsikyəlit, -ˌlāt/ containing or covered with vesicles or small cavities.

Ves·pa·sian /vesˈpāzʜən/ (AD 9–79), Roman emperor 69–79 and founder of the Flavian dynasty; Latin name *Titus Flavius Vespasianus*. His reign saw the restoration of financial and military order and the initiation of a public building program.

ves·per /ˈvespər/ ▶ **n.** evening prayer: [as modifier] *vesper service.* See also **VESPERS.** ■ archaic evening. ■ (**Vesper**) literary Venus as the evening star.
– ORIGIN late Middle English: from Latin *vesper* 'evening (star),' which is related to Greek *hesperos* 'western; the evening star' (see **HESPERUS.**).

ves·per·al /ˈvespərəl/ ▶ **adj. 1** of or pertaining to evening.
2 of or pertaining to vespers.
▶ **n.** a book containing the psalms, canticles, anthems and the like with their musical settings that are used at vespers.

ves·pers /ˈvespərz/ ▶ **n.** a service of evening prayer in the Divine Office of the Western Christian Church (sometimes said earlier in the day). ■ a service of evening prayer in other churches.
– ORIGIN late 15th cent.: from Old French *vespres* 'evensong,' from Latin *vesperas* (accusative plural), on the pattern of *matutinas* 'matins.'

ves·per spar·row ▶ **n.** a small North American songbird related to the buntings, having streaked brown plumage and known for its evening song. ● *Pooecetes gramineus*, family Emberizidae (subfamily Emberizidae).

ves·per·til·i·o·nid /ˌvespərˈtilēəˌnid/ ▶ **n.** Zoology a bat of a large family (Vespertilionidae) that includes most of the typical insectivorous bats of north temperate regions.
– ORIGIN late 19th cent.: from modern Latin *Vespertilionidae* (plural), from Latin *vespertilio* 'bat.'

ves·per·tine /ˈvespərˌtīn, -ˌtēn/ ▶ **adj.** technical orliterary relating to, occurring, or active in the evening.
– ORIGIN late Middle English: from Latin *vespertinus*, from *vesper* 'evening.'

ves·pi·ar·y /ˈvespēˌerē/ ▶ **n.** (pl. **vespiaries**) a nest of wasps.
– ORIGIN early 19th cent.: formed irregularly from Latin *vespa* 'wasp,' on the pattern of *apiary*.

ves·pid /ˈvespid/ ▶ **n.** any wasp of the family Vespidae, including yellow jackets and hornets.

ves·pine /ˈvesˌpīn, -pin/ ▶ **adj.** of or relating to wasps.
– ORIGIN mid 19th cent.: from Latin *vespa* 'wasp' + **-INE**[1].

Ves·puc·ci /vesˈp(y)o͞ocʜē/, Amerigo (1451–1512), Italian merchant and explorer. He reached the coast of Venezuela on his first voyage 1499–1500 and explored the Brazilian coastline 1501–02. The Latin form of his first name is believed to have given rise to the name of America.

ves·sel /ˈvesəl/ ▶ **n. 1** a ship or large boat.
2 a hollow container, esp. one used to hold liquid, such as a bowl or cask. ■ (chiefly in or alluding to biblical use) a person, esp. regarded as holding or embodying a particular quality: *giving honor unto the wife, as unto the weaker vessel.*
3 Anatomy & Zoology a duct or canal holding or conveying blood or other fluid. See also **BLOOD VESSEL.** ■ Botany any of the tubular structures in the vascular system of a plant, serving to conduct water and mineral nutrients from the root.
– ORIGIN Middle English: from Anglo-Norman French *vessel(e)*, from late Latin *vascellum*, diminutive of *vas* 'vessel.'

vest /vest/ ▶ **n.** a close-fitting waist-length garment, typically having no sleeves or collar and buttoning down the front. ■ a similar garment worn on the upper part of the body for a particular purpose or activity: *a running vest | a bulletproof vest.* ■ a piece of material showing at the neck of a woman's dress. ■ Brit. an undershirt.
▶ **v. 1** [with obj.] (usu. **be vested in**) confer or bestow (power, authority, property, etc.) on someone: *executive power is vested in the president.* ■ (usu. **be vested with**) give (someone) the legal right to power, property, etc.: *he alone is vested with the authority to steer the country's economy.* ■ [no obj.] (**vest in**) (of power, property, etc.) come into the possession of: *the bankrupt's property vests in his trustee.*
2 [no obj.] (of a chorister or member of the clergy) put on vestments. ■ [with obj.] literary dress (someone): *the Speaker vested him with a rich purple robe.*
– PHRASES **play** (or **keep**) **one's cards close to one's vest** see **CHEST.**
– ORIGIN late Middle English (as a verb): from Old French *vestu* 'clothed,' past participle of *vestir*, from Latin *vestire*; the noun (early 17th cent., denoting a loose outer garment) from French *veste*, via Italian from Latin *vestis* 'garment.'

Ves·ta /ˈvestə/ Roman Mythology the goddess of the hearth and household. Her temple in Rome contained no image but a fire that was kept constantly burning and was tended by the Vestal Virgins.

ves·ta /ˈvestə/ ▶ **n.** chiefly historical a short wooden or wax match.
– ORIGIN mid 19th cent.: from the name of the goddess VESTA.

ves·tal /ˈvestl/ ▶ **adj.** of or relating to the Roman goddess Vesta: *a vestal temple.* ■ literary chaste; pure.
▶ **n.** a vestal virgin. ■ literary a chaste woman, esp. a nun.

Ves·tal Vir·gin (also **vestal virgin**) ▶ **n.** (in ancient Rome) a virgin consecrated to Vesta and vowed to chastity, sharing the charge of maintaining the sacred fire burning on the goddess's altar.

vest·ed /ˈvestid/ ▶ **adj. 1** secured in the possession of or assigned to a person: *a state law vested the ownership of all wild birds to the individual counties.* ■ protected or established by law or contract: *parental rights are then vested by section 14 of the 1975 Act.* ■ (of a person) legally entitled to a future benefit, as from a pension: *he was completely vested after five years with the company.*
2 supplied or worn with a vest.
3 wearing vestments.

vest·ed in·ter·est ▶ **n.** [usu. in sing.] a personal stake or involvement in an undertaking or state of affairs, esp. one with an expectation of financial gain: *banks have **a vested interest** in the growth of their customers.* ■ a person or group having such a personal stake or involvement: *the problem is that the authorities are a vested interest.* ■ Law an interest (usually in land or money held in trust) recognized as belonging to a particular person.

vest·ee /ˌvesˈtē/ ▶ **n.** a vestlike piece of material showing at the neck of a woman's dress.

Ves·ter·å·len /ˈvestəˌrōlən/ a group of islands in Norway, in the Norwegian Sea, north of the Arctic Circle.

ves·ti·ar·y /ˈvestēˌerē/ ▶ **adj.** literary of or relating to clothes or dress.
▶ **n.** (pl. **vestiaries**) a room or building in a monastery or other large establishment in which clothes are kept.
– ORIGIN Middle English (denoting a vestry): from Old French *vestiarie*, from Latin *vestiarium* (see VESTRY).

ves·tib·u·lar /veˈstibyələr, və-/ ▶ **adj.** chiefly Anatomy of or relating to a vestibule, particularly that of the inner ear, or more generally to the sense of balance.

ves·ti·bule /ˈvestəˌbyo͞ol/ ▶ **n. 1** an antechamber, hall, or lobby next to the outer door of a building. ■ an enclosed entrance compartment in a railroad car.
2 Anatomy a chamber or channel communicating with or opening into another, in particular: ■ the central cavity of the labyrinth of the inner ear. ■ the part of the mouth outside the teeth. ■ the space in the vulva into which both the urethra and vagina open.
– DERIVATIVES **ves·ti·buled** adj.
– ORIGIN early 17th cent. (denoting the space in front of the main entrance of a Roman or Greek building): from French, or from Latin *vestibulum* 'entrance court.'

ves·ti·bu·lo·coch·le·ar nerve /veˌstibyəlōˈkäklēər/ ▶ **n.** Anatomy each of the eighth pair of cranial nerves, conveying sensory impulses from the organs of hearing and balance in the inner ear to the brain. The vestibulocochlear nerve on each side branches into the **vestibular nerve** and the **cochlear nerve**.

ves·tige /ˈvestij/ ▶ **n.** a trace of something that is disappearing or no longer exists: *the last vestiges of colonialism.* ■ [usu. with negative] the smallest amount (used to emphasize the absence of something): *he waited patiently, but without **a vestige of** sympathy.* ■ Biology a part or organ of an organism that has become reduced or functionless in the course of evolution.
– ORIGIN late Middle English: from French, from Latin *vestigium* 'footprint.'

ves·tig·i·al /veˈstij(ē)əl/ ▶ **adj.** forming a very small remnant of something that was once much larger or more noticeable: *he felt a vestigial flicker of anger from last night.* ■ Biology (of an organ or part of the body) degenerate, rudimentary, or atrophied, having become functionless in the course of evolution: *the vestigial wings of kiwis are entirely hidden.*
– DERIVATIVES **ves·tig·i·al·ly** adv.

ves·ti·men·ta·ry /ˌvestəˈmentərē/ ▶ **adj.** formal of or relating to clothing or dress: *lack of vestimentary rigor.*
– ORIGIN early 19th cent.: from Latin *vestimentum* 'clothing' + -ARY[1].

ves·ti·men·tif·er·an /ˌvestəˌmenˈtifərən/ ▶ **n.** Zoology a very large marine worm that lives in upright tubes near hydrothermal vents, subsisting on the products of chemoautotrophic bacteria. ● Order Vestimentifera, phylum Pogonophora; sometimes regarded as a separate phylum.
– ORIGIN late 20th cent.: from modern Latin *Vestimentifera* (from Latin *vestimentum* 'clothing' + *-fer* 'bearing') + -AN.

vest·ing /ˈvestiNG/ ▶ **n. 1** the conveying to an employee of unconditional entitlement to a share in a pension fund.
2 medium- to heavy-weight cloth with a decorated or raised pattern, used for vests and other garments.

ves·ti·ture /ˈvestiCHər, -ˌCHo͝or/ ▶ **n.** archaic clothing.
– ORIGIN mid 19th cent.: based on Latin *vestire* 'clothe.'

Vest·man·na·ey·jar /ˈvestˌmänəˈāˌyär/ Icelandic name for WESTMANN ISLANDS.

vest·ment /ˈves(t)mənt/ ▶ **n.** (usu. **vestments**) a chasuble or other robe worn by the clergy or choristers during services. ■ archaic a garment, esp. a ceremonial or official robe.
– ORIGIN Middle English: from Old French *vestiment*, from Latin *vestimentum*, from *vestire* 'clothe' (see VEST).

vest-pock·et ▶ **adj.** [attrib.] (esp. of a reference book) small enough to fit into a pocket: *a series of popular vest-pocket dictionaries.* ■ very small in size or scale: *a vest-pocket park.*

ves·try /ˈvestrē/ ▶ **n.** (pl. **vestries**) a room or building attached to a church, used as an office and for changing into vestments. ■ a meeting of parishioners, originally in a vestry, for the conduct of parochial business. ■ a body of parishioners meeting in such a way.
– ORIGIN late Middle English: probably from an Anglo-Norman French alteration of Old French *vestiarie*, from Latin *vestiarium*.

ves·try·man /ˈvestrēmən/ ▶ **n.** (pl. **vestrymen**) a member of a parochial vestry.

ves·ture /ˈvesCHər/ ▶ **n.** literary clothing; dress: *a man garbed in ancient vesture.*
– ORIGIN Middle English: from Old French, based on Latin *vestire* 'clothe.'

ve·su·vi·an·ite /vəˈso͞ovēəˌnīt/ ▶ **n.** another term for IDOCRASE.
– ORIGIN late 19th cent.: from VESUVIUS + -AN + -ITE[1].

Ve·su·vi·us /vəˈso͞ovēəs/ an active volcano near Naples, in southern Italy, 4,190 feet (1,277 m) high. A violent eruption in AD 79 buried the towns of Pompeii and Herculaneum.

vet[1] /vet/ ▶ **n.** informal a veterinary surgeon.
▶ **v.** (**vets**, **vetting**, **vetted**) [with obj.] make a careful and critical examination of (something): *proposals for vetting large takeover bids.* ■ Brit. investigate (someone) thoroughly, esp. in order to ensure that they are suitable for a job requiring secrecy, loyalty, or trustworthiness: *each applicant will be vetted by police.*
– ORIGIN mid 19th cent: abbreviation of VETERINARY or VETERINARIAN.

vet[2] ▶ **n.** informal a veteran.
– ORIGIN mid 19th cent.: abbreviation.

vetch /veCH/ ▶ **n.** a widely distributed scrambling herbaceous plant of the pea family that is cultivated as a silage or fodder crop. See also TARE[1]. ● Genus *Vicia*, family Leguminosae: several species, in particular the **common** or (**spring**) **vetch** (*V. sativa*) and **purple vetch** (*V. americana*).
– ORIGIN Middle English: from Anglo-Norman French *veche*, from Latin *vicia*.

vetch·ling /ˈveCHliNG/ ▶ **n.** a widely distributed scrambling plant related to the vetches, typically having fewer leaflets. ● Genus *Lathyrus*, family Leguminosae: several species, including *L. palustris*.

vet·er·an /ˈvetərən, ˈvetrən/ ▶ **n.** a person who has had long experience in a particular field. ■ a person who has served in the military: *a veteran of two world wars.*
– ORIGIN early 16th cent.: from French *vétéran* or Latin *veteranus*, from *vetus* 'old.'

Vet·er·ans Day ▶ **n.** a public holiday held on the anniversary of the end of World War I (November 11) to honor US veterans and victims of all wars. It replaced Armistice Day in 1954.

vet·er·i·nar·i·an /ˌvet(ə)rəˈne(ə)rēən/ ▶ **n.** a person qualified to treat diseased or injured animals.

vet·er·i·nar·y /ˈvet(ə)rəˌnerē/ ▶ **adj.** of or relating to the diseases, injuries, and treatment of animals: *veterinary medicine* | *a veterinary nurse.*
▶ **n.** (pl. **veterinaries**) dated a veterinarian.
– ORIGIN late 18th cent.: from Latin *veterinarius*, from *veterinae* 'cattle.'

vet·er·i·nar·y sur·geon ▶ **n.** British term for VETERINARIAN.

vet·i·ver /ˈvetəvər/ (also **vetivert** /-vərt/) ▶ **n.** a fragrant extract or essential oil obtained from the root of an Indian grass, used in perfumery and aromatherapy. ● The grass is *Vetiveria zizanioides*, family Gramineae.
– ORIGIN mid 19th cent.: from French *vétiver*, from Tamil *veṭṭivēr*, from *vēr* 'root.'

ve·to /ˈvētō/ ▶ **n.** (pl. **vetoes**) a constitutional right to reject a decision or proposal made by a law-making body: *the legislature would have a veto over appointments to key posts.* ■ such a rejection. ■ a prohibition: *his veto on our drinking after the meal was annoying.*
▶ **v.** (**vetoes**, **vetoing**, **vetoed**) [with obj.] exercise a veto against (a decision or proposal made by a law-making body): *the president vetoed the bill.* ■ refuse to accept or allow: *the film star often has a right to veto the pictures used for publicity.*
– DERIVATIVES **ve·to·er** n.
– ORIGIN early 17th cent.: from Latin, literally 'I forbid,' used by Roman tribunes of the people when opposing measures of the Senate.

vex /veks/ ▶ **v.** [with obj.] make (someone) feel annoyed, frustrated, or worried, esp. with trivial matters: *the memory of the conversation still vexed him* | (as adj. **vexing**) *the most vexing questions for policymakers.* ■ archaic cause distress to: *thou shalt not vex a stranger.*
– DERIVATIVES **vex·er** n., **vex·ing·ly** adv.
– ORIGIN late Middle English: from Old French *vexer*, from Latin *vexare* 'shake, disturb.'

vex·a·tion /vekˈsāSHən/ ▶ **n.** the state of being annoyed, frustrated, or worried: *Jenny bit her lip in vexation.* ■ something that causes annoyance, frustration, or worry: *the cares and vexations of life.*
– ORIGIN late Middle English: from Old French, or from Latin *vexatio(n-)*, from *vexare* (see VEX).

vex·a·tious /vekˈsāSHəs/ ▶ **adj.** causing or tending to cause annoyance, frustration, or worry: *the vexatious questions posed by software copyrights.* ■ Law denoting an action or the bringer of an action that is brought without sufficient grounds for winning, purely to cause annoyance to the defendant.
– DERIVATIVES **vex·a·tious·ly** adv., **vex·a·tious·ness** n.

vexed /vekst/ ▶ **adj. 1** [attrib.] (of a problem or issue) difficult and much debated; problematic: *the **vexed question** of exactly how much money the government is going to spend.*
2 annoyed, frustrated, or worried: *I'm very vexed with you!*
– DERIVATIVES **vex·ed·ly** /ˈveksədlē/ adv.

vex·il·lol·o·gy /ˌveksəˈläləjē/ ▶ **n.** the study of flags.
– DERIVATIVES **vex·il·lo·log·i·cal** /-ləˈläjikəl/ adj., **vex·il·lol·o·gist** /-jist/ n.
– ORIGIN 1950s: from Latin *vexillum* 'flag' + -LOGY.

vex·il·lum /vekˈsiləm/ ▶ **n.** (pl. **vexilla** /vekˈsilə/)
1 a Roman military standard or banner, esp. one of a maniple. [Latin, from *vehere* 'carry.'] ■ a body of troops under such a standard.
2 Botany the standard of a papilionaceous flower.
3 Ornithology the vane of a feather.

VF ▶ **abbr.** ■ video frequency. ■ visual field.

VFR ▶ **abbr.** visual flight rules, used to regulate the flying and navigating of an aircraft under conditions of good visibility.

VG ▶ **abbr.** ■ very good. ■ vicar general.

VGA ▶ **abbr.** video graphics array, a standard for defining color display screens for computers.

vgc ▶ **abbr.** very good condition (used in advertisements).

VHF ▶ **abbr.** very high frequency, denoting radio waves of a frequency of about 30–300 MHz and a wavelength of about 1–10 meters.

VHS ▶ **abbr.** trademark video home system, denoting the video system and tape used by domestic video recorders and some camcorders.

VI ▶ **abbr.** Virgin Islands.

vi·a /ˈvīə, ˈvēə/ ▶ **prep.** traveling through (a place) en route to a destination: *they came to Europe via Turkey.* ■ by way of; through: *they can see the artists' works via a camera hookup.* ■ by means of: *a file sent via electronic mail.*
– ORIGIN late 18th cent.: from Latin, ablative of *via* 'way, road.'

Vi·a Ap·pi·a /ˈvēə ˈäpēə, ˈvīə/ Latin name for APPIAN WAY.

vi·a·ble /ˈvīəbəl/ ▶ **adj.** capable of working successfully; feasible: *the proposed investment was*

economically viable. ■ Botany (of a seed or spore) able to germinate. ■ Biology (of a plant, animal, or cell) capable of surviving or living successfully, esp. under particular environmental conditions. ■ Medicine (of a fetus or unborn child) able to live after birth.
– DERIVATIVES **vi·a·bil·i·ty** /ˌvīəˈbilətē/ **n.**, **vi·a·bly** /-blē/ **adv.**
– ORIGIN early 19th cent.: from French, from *vie* 'life,' from Latin *vita*.

Vi·a Cru·cis /ˈvēə ˈkro͞ocHis/ ▶ **n.** another term for THE WAY OF THE CROSS (see WAY). ■ a lengthy and distressing or painful procedure: *we embarked on a Via Crucis of tired comic formulae.*
– ORIGIN Latin.

vi·a dol·o·ro·sa /ˈvēə ˌdäləˈrōsə, ˌdōlə-/ ▶ **n.** (**the Via Dolorosa**) the route believed to have been taken by Jesus through Jerusalem to Calvary. ■ a distressing or painful journey or process: *he commenced a via dolorosa to the coast.*
– ORIGIN Latin, literally 'painful path.'

vi·a·duct /ˈvīəˌdəkt/ ▶ **n.** a long bridgelike structure, typically a series of arches, carrying a road or railroad across a valley or other low ground.
– ORIGIN early 19th cent.: from Latin *via* 'way,' on the pattern of *aqueduct*.

Vi·ag·ra ▶ **n.** trademark for SILDENAFIL CITRATE.
– ORIGIN 1990s: probably suggested by words such as *virile* and *virility*.

vi·al /ˈvī(ə)l/ ▶ **n.** a small container, typically cylindrical and made of glass, used esp. for holding liquid medicines.
– ORIGIN Middle English: alteration of PHIAL.

vi·a me·di·a /ˈvēə ˈmādēə, ˈvīə ˈmēdēə/ ▶ **n.** formal a middle way or compromise between extremes: *the settlement is a via media between Catholicism and Protestantism.*
– ORIGIN Latin.

vi·and /ˈvīənd/ ▶ **n.** (usu. **viands**) literary an item of food: *an unlimited assortment of viands.*
– ORIGIN late Middle English: from Old French *viande* 'food,' from an alteration of Latin *vivenda*, neuter plural gerundive of *vivere* 'to live.'

vi·a ne·ga·ti·va /ˈvēə ˌnegəˈtēvə, ˈvīə/ ▶ **n.** Theology a way of describing something by saying what it is not, esp. denying that any finite concept of attribute can be identified with or used of God or ultimate reality.
– ORIGIN Latin, literally 'negative path.'

vi·at·i·cal set·tle·ment /vīˈatikəl, vē-/ ▶ **n.** an arrangement whereby a person with a terminal illness sells their life insurance policy to a third party for less than its mature value, in order to benefit from the proceeds while alive.
– ORIGIN 1990s: *viatical* from Latin *viaticus* 'relating to a journey or departing' + -AL.

vi·at·i·cum /vīˈatikəm, vē-/ ▶ **n.** (pl. **viatica** /-kə/)
1 the Eucharist as given to a person near or in danger of death.
2 archaic a supply of provisions or an official allowance of money for a journey.
– ORIGIN mid 16th cent.: from Latin, neuter of *viaticus*, from *via* 'road.'

vibe /vīb/ ▶ **n.** informal **1** (usu. **vibes**) a person's emotional state or the atmosphere of a place as communicated to and felt by others: *a lot of moody people giving off bad vibes.* [abbreviation of *vibrations*.]
2 (**vibes**) another term for VIBRAPHONE.

vib·ist /ˈvībist/ ▶ **n.** a musician who plays the vibraphone.

vi·brac·u·lum /vīˈbrakyələm/ ▶ **n.** (pl. **vibracula** /-lə/) Zoology (in some bryozoans) any of a number of modified zooids that bear a long whiplike seta, serving to prevent other organisms from settling on the colony. Compare with AVICULARIUM.
– DERIVATIVES **vi·brac·u·lar** /-lər/ **adj.**
– ORIGIN mid 19th cent.: modern Latin, from Latin *vibrare* (see VIBRATE).

V

vi·bra·harp /ˈvībrəˌhärp/ ▶ **n.** another term for VIBRAPHONE.

vi·brant /ˈvībrənt/ ▶ **adj.** full of energy and enthusiasm: *a vibrant cosmopolitan city.* ■ quivering; pulsating: *Rose was vibrant with anger.* ■ (of color) bright and striking. ■ (of sound) strong or resonating: *a vibrant male voice.*
– DERIVATIVES **vi·bran·cy** /-brənsē/ **n.**, **vi·brant·ly** **adv.**
– ORIGIN early 17th cent. (in the sense 'moving rapidly, vibrating'): from Latin *vibrant-* 'shaking to and fro,' from the verb *vibrare* (see VIBRATE).

vi·bra·phone /ˈvībrəˌfōn/ ▶ **n.** a musical percussion instrument with a double row of tuned metal bars, each above a tubular resonator containing a motor-driven rotating vane, giving a vibrato effect.
– DERIVATIVES **vi·bra·phon·ist** /-ˌfōnist/ **n.**
– ORIGIN 1920s: from VIBRATO + -PHONE.

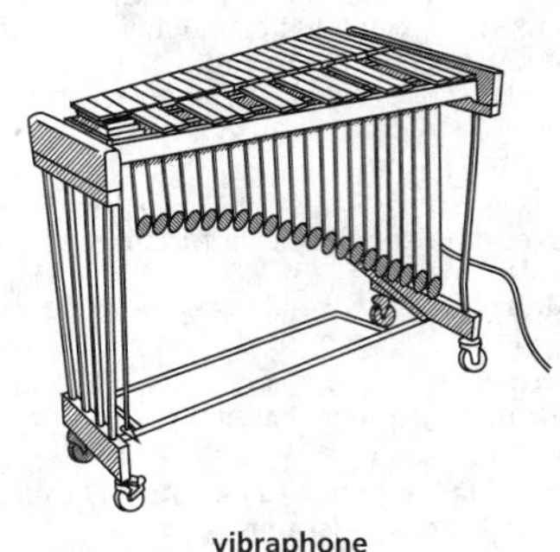

vibraphone

vi·brate /ˈvīˌbrāt/ ▶ **v.** move or cause to move continuously and rapidly to and fro: [no obj.] *the cabin started to vibrate* | [with obj.] *the bumblebee vibrated its wings for a few seconds.* ■ [no obj.] (**vibrate with**) quiver with (a quality or emotion): *his voice vibrated with terror.* ■ [no obj.] (of a sound) resonate; continue to be heard: *a low rumbling sound that began to vibrate through the car.* ■ [no obj.] (of a pendulum) swing to and fro.
– ORIGIN late Middle English (in the sense 'give out (light or sound) as if by vibration'): from Latin *vibrat-* 'moved to and fro,' from the verb *vibrare*.

vi·bra·tile /ˈvībrətl, -ˌtīl/ ▶ **adj.** Biology (of cilia, flagella, or other small appendages) capable of or characterized by oscillatory motion.
– ORIGIN early 19th cent.: alteration of VIBRATORY, on the pattern of words such as *pulsatile*.

vi·bra·tion /vīˈbrāsHən/ ▶ **n.** an instance of vibrating: *powerful vibrations from an earthquake* | *the big-capacity engine generated less vibration.* ■ Physics an oscillation of the parts of a fluid or an elastic solid whose equilibrium has been disturbed, or of an electromagnetic wave. ■ (**vibrations**) informal a person's emotional state, the atmosphere of a place, or the associations of an object, as communicated to and felt by others.
– DERIVATIVES **vi·bra·tion·al** /-sHənl/ **adj.**
– ORIGIN mid 17th -.: from Latin *vibratio(n-)*, from the verb *vibrare* (see VIBRATE).

vi·bra·tion white fin·ger ▶ **n.** Raynaud's disease, when caused by exposure to chronic vibration.

vi·bra·to /vəˈbrätō, vī-/ ▶ **n.** (pl. **vibratos**) Music a rapid, slight variation in pitch in singing or playing some musical instruments, producing a stronger or richer tone. Compare with TREMOLO.
– ORIGIN mid 19th cent.: Italian, past participle of *vibrare* 'vibrate.'

vi·bra·tor /ˈvīˌbrātər/ ▶ **n.** a device that vibrates or causes vibration, in particular: ■ a device used for massage or sexual stimulation. ■ Music a reed in a reed organ.

vi·bra·to·ry /ˈvībrəˌtôrē/ ▶ **adj.** of, relating to, or causing vibration.

vib·ri·o /ˈvibrēˌō/ ▶ **n.** (pl. **vibrios**) Medicine a waterborne bacterium of a group that includes some pathogenic kinds that cause cholera, gastroenteritis, and septicemia. ● *Vibrio* and related genera; motile Gram-negative bacteria occurring as curved flagellated rods.
– ORIGIN modern Latin, from Latin *vibrare* 'vibrate.'

vi·bris·sa /vīˈbrisə/ ▶ **n.** (pl. **vibrissae** /-brisē, -ˈbrisˌī/) Zoology any of the long stiff hairs growing around the mouth or elsewhere on the face of many mammals, used as organs of touch; whiskers. ■ Ornithology each of the coarse bristlelike feathers growing around the gape of certain insectivorous birds that catch insects in flight.
– ORIGIN late 17th cent.: from Latin, literally 'nostril hair.'

vi·bro·tac·tile /ˌvībrəˈtaktl, -ˌtīl/ ▶ **adj.** relating to or involving the perception of vibration through touch.

vi·bur·num /vīˈbərnəm/ ▶ **n.** a shrub or small tree of temperate and warm regions, typically bearing flat or rounded clusters of small white flowers. ● Genus *Viburnum*, family Caprifoliaceae: many species and ornamental hybrids, including the guelder rose and wayfaring tree.
– ORIGIN modern Latin, from Latin, 'wayfaring tree.'

Vic. ▶ **abbr.** Victoria.

vic·ar /ˈvikər/ ▶ **n.** (in the Roman Catholic Church) a representative or deputy of a bishop. ■ (in the Episcopal Church) a member of the clergy in charge of a chapel. ■ (in the Church of England) an incumbent of a parish where tithes formerly passed to a chapter or religious house or layman. ■ (in other Anglican Churches) a member of the clergy deputizing for another. ■ a cleric or choir member appointed to sing certain parts of a cathedral service.
– DERIVATIVES **vic·ar·ship** /-ˌSHip/ **n.**
– ORIGIN Middle English: via Anglo-Norman French from Old French *vicaire*, from Latin *vicarius* 'substitute,' from *vic-* 'change, turn, place' (compare with VICE[3]).

vic·ar·age /ˈvikərij/ ▶ **n.** the residence of a vicar. ■ historical the benefice or living of a vicar.

vic·ar ap·os·tol·ic ▶ **n.** a Roman Catholic missionary. ■ a titular bishop.

vic·ar gen·er·al ▶ **n.** (pl. **vicars general**) an Anglican official serving as a deputy or assistant to a bishop or archbishop. ■ (in the Roman Catholic Church) a bishop's representative in matters of jurisdiction or administration.

vi·car·i·al /vīˈke(ə)rēəl, vi-/ ▶ **adj.** archaic of, relating to, or serving as a vicar.

vi·car·i·ance /vīˈke(ə)rēəns, vi-/ ▶ **n.** Biology the geographical separation of a population, typically by a physical barrier such as a mountain range or river, resulting in a pair of closely related species.
– ORIGIN 1950s: from Latin *vicarius* 'substitute' + -ANCE.

vi·car·i·ate /viˈke(ə)rēit, vī-, -ˌāt/ ▶ **n.** the office or authority of a vicar. ■ a church or parish ministered to by a vicar.

vi·car·i·ous /vīˈkerēəs, vi-/ ▶ **adj.** experienced in the imagination through the feelings or actions of another person: *I could glean vicarious pleasure from the struggles of my imaginary film friends.* ■ acting or done for another: *a vicarious atonement.* ■ Physiology of or pertaining to the performance by one organ of the functions normally discharged by another.
– DERIVATIVES **vi·car·i·ous·ly** **adv.**, **vi·car·i·ous·ness** **n.**
– ORIGIN mid 17th cent.: from Latin *vicarius* 'substitute' (see VICAR) + -OUS.

Vic·ar of Christ ▶ **n.** (in the Roman Catholic Church) a title of the pope.

vice[1] /vīs/ ▶ **n.** immoral or wicked behavior. ■ criminal activities involving prostitution, pornography, or drugs. ■ an immoral or wicked personal characteristic. ■ a weakness of character or behavior; a bad habit: *cigars happen to be my father's vice.*
– DERIVATIVES **vice·less** **adj.**
– ORIGIN Middle English: via Old French from Latin *vitium*.

vice[2] ▶ **n.** British spelling of VISE.

vice[3] /vīs, ˈvīsē, ˈvīsə/ ▶ **prep.** as a substitute for: *the letter was drafted by David Hunt, vice Bevin who was ill.*
– ORIGIN Latin, ablative of *vic-* 'change.'

vice[4] ▶ **comb. form** acting as deputy or substitute for; next in rank: *vice regent* | *vice-consul.*
– ORIGIN from Latin *vice* 'in place of' (compare with VICE[3]).

vice ad·mi·ral /vīs/ ▶ **n.** a naval officer of very high rank, in particular an officer in the US Navy or Coast Guard ranking above rear admiral and below admiral.

vice chan·cel·lor /vīs/ ▶ **n.** **1** a deputy chancellor, esp. one of a British university who discharges most of its administrative duties.
2 Law a judge appointed to assist a chancellor, esp. in chancery court or court of equity.

vice·ge·rent /ˌvīsˈji(ə)rənt/ ▶ **n.** formal a person exercising delegated power on behalf of a sovereign or ruler. ■ a person regarded as an earthly representative of God or a god, esp. the pope.
– DERIVATIVES **vice·ge·ren·cy** **n.** (pl. **vicegerencies**).
– ORIGIN mid 16th cent.: from medieval Latin *vicegerent-* '(person) holding office,' from Latin *vic-* 'office, place, turn' + *gerere* 'carry on, hold.'

Vi·cen·te /vēˈsentā/, Gil (*c.*1465–*c.*1536), Portuguese playwright and poet.

Vi·cen·za /vēˈCHentsə/ a city in northeastern Italy; pop. 115,012 (2008).

vice pres·i·dent /vīs/ ▶ **n.** an official or executive ranking below and deputizing for a president.
– DERIVATIVES **vice pres·i·den·cy** **n.** (pl. **vice presidencies**), **vice pres·i·den·tial** /ˌpreziˈdenCHəl/ **adj.**

vice·re·gal /ˌvīsˈrēgəl/ ▶ **adj.** of or relating to a viceroy.

vice·reine /ˈvīsˌrān/ ▶ **n.** the wife of a viceroy. ■ a female viceroy.
– ORIGIN early 19th cent.: from French, from *vice-* 'in place of' + *reine* 'queen.'

vice·roy /ˈvīsˌroi/ ▶ **n.** **1** a ruler exercising authority in a colony on behalf of a sovereign.

2 a migratory orange and black butterfly that closely resembles the monarch but is typically somewhat smaller. The caterpillar feeds on willow leaves, and the adult mimics the unpalatable monarch. ● *Limenitis archippus*, subfamily Limenitidinae, family Nymphalidae.
– DERIVATIVES **vice·roy·al** /ˌvīsˈroi-əl/ **adj.**, **vice·roy·ship** /-ˌSHip/ **n.**
– ORIGIN early 16th cent.: from archaic French, from *vice-* 'in place of' + *roi* 'king.'

vice·roy·al·ty /ˌvīsˈroi-əltē, ˈvīsˌroi-/ (also **Viceroyalty**) ▶ **n.** (pl. **viceroyalties**) the office, position, or authority of a viceroy. ■ a territory governed by a viceroy.

vice squad /vīs/ ▶ **n.** a department or division of a police force that enforces laws against prostitution, drug abuse, illegal gambling, etc.

vice ver·sa /ˈvīs ˈvərsə, ˈvīsə/ ▶ **adv.** with the main items in the preceding statement the other way around: *science must be at the service of man, and not vice versa.*
– ORIGIN early 17th cent.: from Latin, literally 'in-turned position.'

Vi·chy /ˈvēSHē, ˈviSHē/ a town in south central France; pop. 26,555 (2006). A noted spa town, it is the source of an effervescent mineral water. During World War II, it was the headquarters of the regime set up after the German occupation of northern France to administer unoccupied France and the colonies. Never recognized by the Allies, the regime functioned as a puppet government for the Nazis.

vi·chys·soise /ˌvēSHēˈswäz, ˌviSHē-, ˈvēSHēˌswäz, ˈviSHē-/ ▶ **n.** a soup made with potatoes, leeks, and cream and typically served chilled.
– ORIGIN French (feminine), 'of *Vichy*' (see **VICHY**).

vic·i·nage /ˈvisənij/ ▶ **n.** another term for **VICINITY**.
– ORIGIN Middle English: from Old French *vis(e)nage*, from an alteration of Latin *vicinus* 'neighbor.'

vic·i·nal /ˈvisənl/ ▶ **adj.** rare neighboring; adjacent. ■ Chemistry relating to or denoting substituents attached to adjacent atoms in a ring or chain.
– ORIGIN early 17th cent.: from French, or from Latin *vicinalis*, from *vicinus* 'neighbor.'

vi·cin·i·ty /vəˈsinətē/ ▶ **n.** (pl. **vicinities**) the area near or surrounding a particular place: *the number of people living in the immediate vicinity was small.* ■ archaic proximity in space or relationship: *the abundance and vicinity of country seats.*
– ORIGIN mid 16th cent. (in the sense 'proximity'): from Latin *vicinitas*, from *vicinus* 'neighbor.'

vi·cious /ˈviSHəs/ ▶ **adj. 1** deliberately cruel or violent: *a vicious assault.* ■ (of an animal) wild and dangerous to people. ■ serious or dangerous: *a vicious flu bug.*
2 literary immoral: *every soul on earth, virtuous or vicious, shall perish.*
3 archaic (of language or a line of reasoning) imperfect; defective.
– DERIVATIVES **vi·cious·ly adv.**, **vi·cious·ness n.**
– ORIGIN Middle English (in the sense 'characterized by immorality'): from Old French *vicious* or Latin *vitiosus*, from *vitium* 'vice.'

vi·cious cir·cle (also **vicious cycle**) ▶ **n. 1** a sequence of reciprocal cause and effect in which two or more elements intensify and aggravate each other, leading inexorably to a worsening of the situation.
2 Logic a definition or statement that begs the question.

vi·cis·si·tude /vəˈsisəˌt(y)o͞od/ ▶ **n.** (usu. **vicissitudes**) a change of circumstances or fortune, typically one that is unwelcome or unpleasant: *her husband's sharp vicissitudes of fortune.* ■ literary alternation between opposite or contrasting things: *the vicissitude of the seasons.*
– DERIVATIVES **vi·cis·si·tu·di·nous** /-ˌsisəˈt(y)o͞odn-əs, -ˈt(y)o͞odnəs/ **adj.**
– ORIGIN early 17th cent. (in the sense 'alternation'): from French, or from Latin *vicissitudo*, from *vicissim* 'by turns,' from *vic-* 'turn, change.'

Vicks·burg /ˈviksˌbərg/ a city on the Mississippi River, in western Mississippi; pop. 24,974 (est. 2008). In 1863, during the Civil War, it was successfully besieged by Union forces. The last Confederate outpost on the river, its loss effectively split the secessionist states in half.

Vi·co·din /ˈvīkəˌdin/ ▶ **n.** trademark an analgesic drug containing acetaminophen and hydrocodone (an opioid resembling codeine), also used as a recreational drug.
– ORIGIN 1970s: from *Vi-* (of unknown origin) + *cod-* (in **CODEINE**) + **-IN**[1].

vi·comte /vēˈkôNt/ ▶ **n.** (pl. **same**) a French nobleman corresponding in rank to a viscount.
– ORIGIN French.

vi·com·tesse /ˌvēkôNˈtes/ ▶ **n.** (pl. **same**) a French noblewoman corresponding in rank to a viscountess.
– ORIGIN French.

vic·tim /ˈviktəm/ ▶ **n.** a person harmed, injured, or killed as a result of a crime, accident, or other event or action. ■ a person who is tricked or duped: *the victim of a hoax.* ■ a living creature killed as a religious sacrifice.
– PHRASES **fall victim to** be hurt, killed, damaged, or destroyed by: *many streams have fallen victim to the recent drought.*
– ORIGIN late 15th cent. (denoting a creature killed as a religious sacrifice): from Latin *victima.*

vic·tim·ize /ˈviktəˌmīz/ ▶ **v.** [with obj.] single (someone) out for cruel or unjust treatment: *scam artists who victimize senior citizens.*
– DERIVATIVES **vic·tim·i·za·tion** /ˌviktəməˈzāSHən/ **n.**, **vic·tim·iz·er n.**

vic·tim·less /ˈviktəmləs/ ▶ **adj.** denoting a crime in which there is no injured party.

vic·tim·less crime ▶ **n.** a legal offense to which all parties consent and no party is injured: *software piracy is far from a victimless crime.*

vic·tim·ol·o·gy /ˌviktəˈmäləjē/ ▶ **n.** (pl. **victimologies**) the study of the victims of crime and the psychological effects on them of their experience. ■ the possession of an outlook, arising from real or imagined victimization, that seems to glorify and indulge the state of being a victim.

vic·tor /ˈviktər/ ▶ **n. 1** a person who defeats an enemy or opponent in a battle, game, or other competition.
2 a code word representing the letter V, used in radio communication.
– ORIGIN Middle English: from Anglo-Norman French *victo(u)r* or Latin *victor*, from *vincere* 'conquer.'

Victor Em·man·u·el II /ˈviktər iˈmanyəwəl/ (1820–78), ruler of the kingdom of Sardinia 1849–61 and first king of united Italy 1861–78. He hastened the drive toward Italian unification by appointing Cavour as premier of Piedmont in 1852. He added Venetia to the kingdom in 1866 and Rome in 1870.

Victor Em·man·u·el III (1869–1947), last king of Italy 1900–46. He invited Mussolini to form a government in 1922 and lost all political power. After the loss of Sicily to the Allies in 1943, he acted to dismiss Mussolini and conclude an armistice.

Vic·to·ri·a[1] /vikˈtôrēə/ **1** a state in southeastern Australia; pop. 5,313,823 (2008); capital, Melbourne.
2 a port at the southern tip of Vancouver Island, capital of British Columbia; pop. 78,057 (2006).
3 the capital of the Seychelles, a port on the island of Mahé; pop. 26,000 (est. 2007).
4 the administrative center of Hong Kong; pop. 981,700 (2006).
5 a city in southern Texas; pop. 62,558 (est. 2008).

Vic·to·ri·a[2] (1819–1901), queen of Great Britain and Ireland 1837–1901 and empress of India 1876–1901. She took an active interest in the policies of her ministers, but largely retired from public life after Prince Albert's death in 1861. Her reign was the longest in British history.

vic·to·ri·a[3] ▶ **n.** historical a light four-wheeled horse-drawn carriage with a collapsible hood, seats for two passengers, and an elevated driver's seat in front.
– ORIGIN late 19th cent.: named after Queen *Victoria* (see **VICTORIA**[2]).

Vic·to·ri·a, Lake the largest lake in Africa, in Uganda and Tanzania and bordering on Kenya, drained by the Nile River. Also called **VICTORIA NYANZA**.

Vic·to·ri·a Cross (abbr.: **VC**) ▶ **n.** a decoration awarded for conspicuous bravery in the British Commonwealth armed services, instituted by Queen Victoria in 1856.

Vic·to·ri·a Day ▶ **n.** (in Canada) the Monday preceding May 24, observed as a national holiday to commemorate the birthday of Queen Victoria.

Vic·to·ri·a de Du·ran·go /vikˈtôrēə dā do͞oˈräNGgō, d(y)o͞oˈraNG-/ full name for **DURANGO**.

Vic·to·ri·a Falls a waterfall 355 feet (109 m) high, on the Zambezi River, on the Zimbabwe–Zambia border. Its native (Kalolo-Lozi) name is *Mosi-oa-tunya* ("the smoke that thunders").

Vic·to·ri·a Is·land an island in Canada, in the Arctic archipelago, in the Northwest Territories.

Vic·to·ri·a lil·y ▶ **n.** a tropical South American water lily that has gigantic floating leaves with raised sides. ● Genus *Victoria*, family Nymphaeaceae: two species.

Vic·to·ri·an /vikˈtôrēən/ ▶ **adj.** of or relating to the reign of Queen Victoria: *a Victorian house.* ■ of or relating to the attitudes and values of this period, regarded as characterized esp. by a stifling and prudish moral earnestness.
▶ **n.** a person who lived during the Victorian period.
– DERIVATIVES **Vic·to·ri·an·ism** /-ˌnizəm/ **n.**

Vic·to·ri·an·a /vikˌtôrēˈanə, -ˈänə/ ▶ **plural n.** articles, esp. collectors' items, from the Victorian period. ■ matters or attitudes relating to or characteristic of this period.

Vic·to·ri·a Nile the upper part of the White Nile River, between lakes Victoria and Albert.

Vic·to·ri·a Ny·an·za /nēˈanzə, nī-, ˈnyänzə/ another name for Lake Victoria (see **VICTORIA, LAKE**).

Vic·to·ri·a Peak a mountain on Hong Kong Island that rises to 1,818 ft. (554 m.).

vic·to·ri·ous /vikˈtôrēəs/ ▶ **adj.** having won a victory; triumphant: *a victorious army | the team defied the odds and emerged victorious.* ■ of or characterized by victory: *he'd participated in the victorious campaigns of the Franco-Prussian War.*
– DERIVATIVES **vic·to·ri·ous·ly adv.**, **vic·to·ri·ous·ness n.**
– ORIGIN late Middle English: from Anglo-Norman French *victorious*, from Latin *victoriosus*, from *victoria* (see **VICTORY**).

Vic·tor·ville /ˈviktərˌvil/ an industrial and residential city in southern California, northeast of Los Angeles; pop. 110,318 (est. 2008).

vic·to·ry /ˈvikt(ə)rē/ ▶ **n.** (pl. **victories**) an act of defeating an enemy or opponent in a battle, game, or other competition: *an election victory | they won their heat and went on to victory in the final |* [as modifier] *a victory celebration.*
– ORIGIN Middle English: from Anglo-Norman French *victorie*, from Latin *victoria.*

vic·to·ry bond ▶ **n.** a bond issued by a government during or immediately after a major war.

vic·to·ry gar·den ▶ **n.** a vegetable garden, esp. a home garden, planted to increase food production during a war.

vic·to·ry lap ▶ **n.** a celebratory circuit of a sports field, track, or court by the person or team that has won a contest.

vic·to·ry roll ▶ **n.** a roll performed by an aircraft as a sign of triumph, typically after a successful mission.

vic·to·ry sign ▶ **n.** a signal of triumph or celebration made by holding up the hand with the palm outward and the first two fingers spread apart to represent the letter V.

vict·ual /ˈvitl/ dated ▶ **n.** (**victuals**) food or provisions, typically as prepared for consumption.
▶ **v.** (**victuals, victualing, victualed**; Brit. **victuals, victualling, victualled**) [with obj.] provide with food or other stores: *the ship wasn't even properly victualed.* ■ [no obj.] archaic obtain or lay in food or other stores: *a voyage of such length, that no ship could victual for.* ■ [no obj.] archaic eat: *victual with me next Saturday.*
– ORIGIN Middle English: from Old French *vitaille*, from late Latin *victualia*, neuter plural of Latin *victualis*, from *victus* 'food'; related to *vivere* 'to live.' The pronunciation still represents the early spelling *vittel*; later spelling has been influenced by the Latin form.

vict·ual·er /ˈvitl-ər/ (Brit. **victualler**) ▶ **n. 1** dated a person providing or selling food or other provisions. ■ a ship providing supplies for troops or other ships.
2 (also **licensed victualer**) Brit. a person who is licensed to sell alcoholic liquor.
– ORIGIN late Middle English: from Old French *vitaill(i)er*, from *vitaille* (see **VICTUAL**).

vi·cu·ña /viˈk(y)o͞onə və-, ˈko͞onyə/ ▶ **n.** a wild relative of the llama, inhabiting mountainous regions of South America and valued for its fine silky wool. ● *Vicugna vicugna*, family Camelidae. ■ cloth made from this wool or an imitation of it.
– ORIGIN early 17th cent.: from Spanish, from Quechua.

vid /vid/ ▶ **n.** informal short for **VIDEO**.

Vi·dal /viˈdäl/, Gore (1925–), US novelist, playwright, and essayist; born *Eugene Luther Vidal.* His novels include satirical comedies such as *Myra Breckenridge* (1968) and histocial fiction such as *Lincoln* (1984).

vi·de /ˈvēdē, ˈvēˌdā, ˈvīdē/ ▶ **v.** [with obj.] see; consult (used as an instruction in a text to refer the reader to a specified passage, book, author, etc., for fuller or further information): *vide the comments cited in Schlosser.*

– ORIGIN Latin, 'see!,' imperative of *videre*.

vi·de·li·cet /və'delə,set, -sət, -'dālə,ket/ ▶ **adv.** more formal term for **VIZ**.
– ORIGIN Latin, from *videre* 'to see' + *licet* 'it is permissible.'

vid·e·o /'vidē,ō/ ▶ **n.** (pl. **videos**) the system of recording, reproducing, or broadcasting moving visual images on or from videotape. ■ a movie or other piece of material recorded on videotape. ■ a videocassette: *a blank video* | *the film will soon be released on video*. ■ a short movie made by a pop or rock group to accompany a song when broadcast on television. ■ Brit. a videocassette recorder.
▶ **v.** (**videos**, **videoing**, **videoed**) record on videotape: *he declined an invitation to be videoed*.
– ORIGIN 1930s: from Latin *videre* 'to see,' on the pattern of *audio*.

vid·e·o ar·cade ▶ **n.** an indoor area containing coin-operated video games.

vid·e·o cam·er·a ▶ **n.** a camera for recording images on videotape or for transmitting them to a monitor screen.

vid·e·o card ▶ **n.** Computing a printed circuit board controlling output to a display screen.

vid·e·o·cas·sette /,vidēōkə'set/ ▶ **n.** a cassette of videotape.

vid·e·o·con·fer·ence /'vidēō,känf(ə)rəns, -,känf(ə)rns/ ▶ **n.** a conference in which participants in different locations are able to communicate with each other in sound and vision.
– DERIVATIVES **vid·e·o·con·fer·enc·ing n.**

vid·e·o di·a·ry ▶ **n.** a record on videotape of a notable period of someone's life, or of a particular event, made using a camcorder.

vid·e·o·disc /'vidēō,disk/ (also **videodisk**) ▶ **n.** a CD-ROM or other disk used to store visual images and sound.

vid·e·o dis·play ter·min·al (abbr.: **VDT**) ▶ **n.** Computing a device for displaying input signals as characters on a screen, typically a monitor.

vid·e·o dra·ma ▶ **n.** another term for **TELEPLAY**.

vid·e·o game ▶ **n.** a game played by electronically manipulating images produced by a computer program on a television screen or other display screen.

vid·e·o·graph·ics /,vidēō'grafiks/ ▶ **plural n.** visual images produced using computer technology. ■ [treated as sing.] the manipulation of video images using a computer.

vid·e·og·ra·phy /,vidē'ägrəfē/ ▶ **n.** the process or art of making video films.
– DERIVATIVES **vid·e·og·ra·pher** /-fər/ **n.**

vid·e·o jock·ey ▶ **n.** a person who introduces and plays music videos for a broadcast, party, or other entertainment.

vid·e·o link ▶ **n.** an electronic facility that enables audiovisual communication between people in different locations.

vid·e·o-on-de·mand ▶ **n.** a system in which viewers choose their own filmed entertainment, by means of a PC or interactive TV system, from a wide selection.

vid·e·o·phone /'vidēō,fōn/ ▶ **n.** a telephone device transmitting and receiving a visual image as well as sound.

vid·e·o·play /'vidēō,plā/ ▶ **n.** another term for **TELEPLAY**.

vid·e·o re·cord·er ▶ **n.** a device that, when linked to a television set, can be used for recording on and playing videotapes.
– DERIVATIVES **vid·e·o re·cord·ing n.**

vid·e·o·scope /'vidēə,skōp/ ▶ **n.** a fiber-optic rod attached to a camera that transmits images from within the body to a television monitor, used in diagnosis and surgery.

V

vid·e·o·tape /'vidēō,tāp/ ▶ **n.** magnetic tape for recording and reproducing visual images and sound. ■ a videocassette. ■ a film or other piece of material recorded on videotape.
▶ **v.** [with obj.] make a video recording of (an event or broadcast): *his arrest was videotaped*.

vid·e·o·tex /'vidēō,teks/ (also **videotext** /-,tekst/) ▶ **n.** an electronic information system such as teletext or viewdata.
– ORIGIN 1970s: from **VIDEO** + **TEXT**.

vi·dette ▶ **n.** variant spelling of **VEDETTE**.

vid·i·con /'vidi,kän/ ▶ **n.** Electronics a small television camera tube in which the image is formed on a transparent electrode coated with photoconductive material, the current from which varies as it is scanned by a beam of low-speed electrons.

– ORIGIN 1950s: from the initial elements of **VIDEO** and *iconoscope* (an early television camera tube).

vid·i·ot /'vidēət/ ▶ **n.** informal a habitual, undiscriminating watcher of television or videotapes.
– ORIGIN 1960s: blend of **VIDEO** and **IDIOT**.

vie /vī/ ▶ **v.** (**vies**, **vying**, **vied**) [no obj.] compete eagerly with someone in order to do or achieve something: *rival mobs vying for control of the liquor business*.
– ORIGIN mid 16th cent.: probably a shortening of obsolete *envy*, via Old French from Latin *invitare* 'challenge.'

vie de Boh·ème /'vē də bō'em/ ▶ **n.** (usu. **la vie de Bohème**) an unconventional or informal way of life, esp. as practiced by an artist or writer.
– ORIGIN French, literally 'bohemian's life.'

Vi·en·na /vē'enə/ the capital of Austria, in the northeastern part of the country on the Danube River; pop. 1,661,206 (2006). From 1278 to 1918 it was the seat of the Habsburgs and has long been a center of the arts, esp. music. Mozart, Beethoven, and the Strauss family were among the composers who lived and worked there. German name **WIEN**.
– DERIVATIVES **Vi·en·nese** /,vēə'nēz, -'nēs/ **adj. & n.**

Vi·en·na, Con·gress of an international conference held 1814–15 to agree upon the settlement of Europe after the Napoleonic Wars. The guiding principle of the settlement was the restoration and strengthening of hereditary and sometimes despotic rulers; the result was a political stability that lasted for three or four decades.

Vi·en·na Cir·cle a group of empiricist philosophers, scientists, and mathematicians active in Vienna from the 1920s until 1938, including Rudolf Carnap and Kurt Gödel. Their work laid the foundations of logical positivism.

Vi·en·na sau·sage ▶ **n.** a small frankfurter made of pork, beef, or veal.

Vi·en·na Se·ces·sion ▶ **n.** see **SEZESSION**.

Vi·en·nese waltz ▶ **n.** a waltz characterized by a slight anticipation of the second beat of the bar and having a romantic quality. ■ a piece of music written in this style.

Vien·tiane /,vyen'tyän, vē,entē'än/ the capital and chief port of Laos, on the Mekong River; pop. 231,700 (est. 2009).

Vier·wald·stät·ter·see /fir'vält,SHtetər,zā/ German name for Lake Lucerne (see **LUCERNE, LAKE**).

Vi·et·cong /vē,et'kôNG, ,vyet-, ,vēət-, -'käNG/ (also **Viet Cong**) ▶ **n.** (pl. **same**) a member of the communist guerrilla movement in Vietnam that fought the South Vietnamese government forces 1954–75 with the support of the North Vietnamese army and opposed the South Vietnamese and US forces in the Vietnam War.
– ORIGIN Vietnamese, literally 'Vietnamese Communist.'

Vi·et·minh /vē,et'min, ,vyet-, ,vēət-/ ▶ **n.** (pl. **same**) a member of a communist-dominated nationalist movement, formed in 1941, that fought for Vietnamese independence from French rule. Members of the Vietminh later joined with the Vietcong.
– ORIGIN from Vietnamese *Viet*-Nam Dôc-Lâp Dông-*Minh* 'Vietnamese Independence League.'

Vi·et·nam /vē,et'näm, ,vyet-, ,vēət-, -'nam/ a country in Southeast Asia, on the South China Sea; pop. 88,576,800 (est. 2009); capital, Hanoi; language, Vietnamese (official).

> Traditionally dominated by China, Vietnam came under French influence between 1862 and 1954. After World War II, the Vietminh defeated the French, who then withdrew. Vietnam was partitioned along the 17th parallel between communist North Vietnam (capital, Hanoi) and noncommunist South Vietnam (capital, Saigon). The Vietnam War between the North and the US-backed South ended in victory for the North in 1975 and the reunification of the country under a communist regime the following year.

– ORIGIN from Vietnamese *Viet*, the name of the inhabitants, + *nam* 'south.'

Vi·et·nam·ese /vē,etnə'mēz, ,vyet-, ,vēət-, -'mēs/ ▶ **adj.** of or relating to Vietnam, its people, or their language.
▶ **n.** (pl. **same**) **1** a native or inhabitant of Vietnam, or a person of Vietnamese descent.
2 the language of Vietnam, which is probably a Mon-Khmer language although much of its vocabulary is derived from Chinese.

Viet·nam·ese pot·bel·lied pig ▶ **n.** see **POTBELLIED PIG**.

Vi·et·nam·i·za·tion /vē,etnəmə'zāSHən, ,vyet-, ,vēət-/ ▶ **n.** (in the Vietnam War) the US policy of withdrawing its troops and transferring the responsibility and direction of the war effort to the government of South Vietnam.

Vi·et·nam War a war between communist North Vietnam and US-backed South Vietnam.

> After the partition of Vietnam in 1954, the communist North attempted to unite the country as a communist state, fueling US concern over the possible spread of communism in Southeast Asia. US Army forces were sent to Vietnam in 1964, supported by contingents from South Korea, Australia, New Zealand, and Thailand, while US aircraft bombed North Vietnamese forces and areas of Cambodia. The Tet Offensive of 1968 damaged US confidence, and US forces began to be withdrawn, finally leaving in 1973. The North Vietnamese captured the southern capital Saigon to end the war in 1975.

view /vyo͞o/ ▶ **n.** **1** the ability to see something or to be seen from a particular place: *the end of the tunnel came into view* | *they stood on the bar to get a better view*. ■ a sight or prospect, typically of attractive natural scenery, that can be taken in by the eye from a particular place: *a fine view of the castle*. ■ a work of art depicting such a sight. ■ the visual appearance or an image of something when looked at in a particular way: *an aerial view of the military earthworks*. ■ an inspection of things for sale by prospective purchasers, esp. of works of art at an exhibition. ■ Law (in court proceedings) a formal inspection by the judge and jury of the scene of a crime or property mentioned in evidence.
2 a particular way of considering or regarding something; an attitude or opinion: *strong political views*.
▶ **v.** **1** [with obj.] look at or inspect (something): *the public can view the famous hall with its unique staircase*. ■ watch (something) on television. ■ Hunting see (a fox) break cover.
2 [with obj.] regard in a particular light or with a particular attitude: *farmers are viewing the rise in rabbit numbers with concern*.
– PHRASES **in full view** clearly visible. **in view** visible to someone: *the youth was keeping him in view*. ■ as one's aim or objective: *his arrest is the principal object I have in view*. ■ in one's mind when forming a judgment: *it is important to have in view the position reached at the beginning of the 1970s*. **in view of** because or as a result of. **on view** (esp. of a work of art) being shown or exhibited to the public. **with a view to** with the hope, aim, or intention of.
– DERIVATIVES **view·a·ble adj.**
– ORIGIN Middle English: from Anglo-Norman French *vieue*, feminine past participle of *veoir* 'see,' from Latin *videre*. The verb dates from the early 16th cent.

view·da·ta /'vyo͞o,datə, -,dātə/ ▶ **n.** a news and information service in which computer data is sent by a telephone link and displayed on a monitor.

view·er /'vyo͞oər/ ▶ **n.** **1** a person who looks at or inspects something. ■ a person watching television or a movie.
2 a device for looking at slides or similar photographic images.

view·er·ship /'vyo͞oər,SHip/ ▶ **n.** [treated as sing. or pl.] the audience for a particular television program or channel.

view·find·er /'vyo͞o,fīndər/ ▶ **n.** a device on a camera showing the field of view of the lens, used in framing and focusing the picture.

view·graph /'vyo͞o,graf/ ▶ **n.** a graph or other data produced as a transparency for projection onto a screen or for transmission during a teleconference.

view hal·loo ▶ **n.** a shout given by a hunter on seeing a fox break cover.

view·ing /'vyo͞oiNG/ ▶ **n.** the action of inspecting or looking at something: *the owner may allow viewing by appointment*. ■ the action of watching something on television: *it is quite unsuitable for family viewing*. ■ an opportunity to see something, esp. a work of art. ■ the act or ceremony of paying one's respect to a corpse.

view·less /'vyo͞oləs/ ▶ **adj.** **1** not having or affording a pleasant sight or prospect.
2 literary unable to be seen; invisible: *the enormous viewless mantle of the night*.

view·point /'vyo͞o,point/ ▶ **n.** another term for **POINT OF VIEW**.

view·port /'vyo͞o,pôrt/ ▶ **n.** a window in a spacecraft or in the conning tower of an oil rig. ■ Computing a framed area on a display screen for viewing information.

VIFF /vif/ (also **viff**) Aeronautics, informal ▶ **n.** a technique used by a vertical takeoff aircraft to change

direction abruptly by altering the direction of thrust of the aircraft's jet engines.
▶ **v.** [no obj.] (of a vertical takeoff aircraft) change direction in such a way.
– ORIGIN 1970s: acronym from *vectoring in forward flight*.

vig /vig/ ▶ **n.** short for VIGORISH.

vi·ga /'vēgə/ ▶ **n.** a rough-hewn roof timber or rafter, esp. in an adobe building.
– ORIGIN Spanish.

Vi·gée-Le·brun /vē,ZHā lə'brœN/, (Marie Louise) Élisabeth (1755–1842), French painter. She is known for her portraits of women and children, esp. of Marie Antoinette and of Lady Hamilton.

vi·ges·i·mal /vī'jesəməl/ ▶ **adj.** rare relating to or based on the number twenty.
– ORIGIN mid 17th cent.: from Latin *vigesimus* (from *viginti* 'twenty') + -AL.

vig·il /'vijəl/ ▶ **n. 1** a period of keeping awake during the time usually spent asleep, esp. to keep watch or pray: *my birdwatching vigils lasted for hours | as he lay in a coma the family kept vigil.* ■ a stationary, peaceful demonstration in support of a particular cause, typically without speeches.
2 (in the Christian Church) the eve of a festival or holy day as an occasion of religious observance. ■ (**vigils**) nocturnal devotions.
– ORIGIN Middle English (sense 2): via Old French from Latin *vigilia*, from *vigil* 'awake.'

vig·i·lance /'vijələns/ ▶ **n.** the action or state of keeping careful watch for possible danger or difficulties.
– ORIGIN late 16th cent.: from French, or from Latin *vigilantia*, from *vigilare* 'keep awake,' from *vigil* (see VIGIL).

vig·i·lance com·mit·tee ▶ **n.** a body of vigilantes.

vig·i·lant /'vijələnt/ ▶ **adj.** keeping careful watch for possible danger or difficulties: *the burglar was spotted by vigilant neighbors.*
– DERIVATIVES **vig·i·lant·ly** adv.
– ORIGIN late 15th cent.: from Latin *vigilant-* 'keeping awake,' from the verb *vigilare*, from *vigil* (see VIGIL).

vig·i·lan·te /,vijə'lantē/ ▶ **n.** a member of a self-appointed group of citizens who undertake law enforcement in their community without legal authority, typically because the legal agencies are thought to be inadequate.
– DERIVATIVES **vig·i·lan·tism** /-,tizəm/ n.
– ORIGIN mid 19th cent.: from Spanish, literally 'vigilant.'

vig·il light ▶ **n.** a candle lighted and placed on a shrine as an act of devotion.

vig·ne·ron /,vēnyə'rôn, -'rōn/ ▶ **n.** a person who cultivates grapes for winemaking.
– ORIGIN French, from *vigne* 'vine.'

vi·gnette /vin'yet/ ▶ **n. 1** a brief evocative description, account, or episode.
2 a small illustration or portrait photograph that fades into its background without a definite border. ■ a small ornamental design filling a space in a book or carving, typically based on foliage.
▶ **v.** [with obj.] portray (someone) in the style of a vignette. ■ produce (a photograph) in the style of a vignette by softening or shading away the edges of the subject.
– DERIVATIVES **vi·gnet·tist** /-'yetist/ n.
– ORIGIN late Middle English (sense 2 of the noun; also as an architectural term denoting a carved representation of a vine): from French, diminutive of *vigne* 'vine.'

Vi·gny /vēn'yē/, Alfred Victor, Comte de (1797–1863), French poet, novelist, and playwright. His poetry reveals his faith in "man's unconquerable mind."

Vi·go /'vēgō/ a port on the Atlantic Ocean in Galicia, in northwestern Spain; pop. 295,703 (2008).

vig·or /'vigər/ (Brit. **vigour**) ▶ **n. 1** physical strength and good health. ■ effort, energy, and enthusiasm: *they set about the new task with vigor.*
2 Law legal or binding force; validity.
– ORIGIN Middle English: from Old French *vigour*, from Latin *vigor*, from *vigere* 'be lively.'

vig·or·ish /'vigəriSH/ ▶ **n.** informal **1** [in sing.] an excessive rate of interest on a loan, typically one from an illegal moneylender.
2 the percentage deducted from a gambler's winnings by the organizers of a game.
– ORIGIN early 20th cent.: probably from Yiddish, from Russian *vyigrysh* 'gain, winnings.'

vig·or·ous /'vig(ə)rəs/ ▶ **adj.** strong, healthy, and full of energy. ■ characterized by or involving physical strength, effort, or energy: *vigorous aerobic exercise.* ■ (of language) forceful: *a vigorous denial.*
– DERIVATIVES **vig·or·ous·ness** n.
– ORIGIN Middle English: via Old French from medieval Latin *vigorosus*, from Latin *vigor* (see VIGOR).

vig·or·ous·ly /'vig(ə)rəslē/ ▶ **adv.** in a way that involves physical strength, effort, or energy; strenuously: *she shook her head vigorously.* ■ forcefully: *he vigorously denied the allegation.*

vi·ha·ra /vi'härə/ ▶ **n.** a Buddhist monastery.
– ORIGIN Sanskrit.

vi·hue·la /vē'(h)wālə/ ▶ **n.** a type of early Spanish stringed musical instrument, in particular: ■ (**vihuela de mano** /de 'mänō/) a type of guitar. ■ (**vihuela de arco** /'ärkō/) a type of viol.
– ORIGIN mid 19th cent.: Spanish.

Vi·ja·ya·wa·da /,vijəyə'wädə/ a city on the Krishna River in Andhra Pradesh, in southeastern India; pop. 971,700 (est. 2009).

Vi·king[1] /'vīkiNG/ ▶ **n.** any of the Scandinavian seafaring pirates and traders who raided and settled in many parts of northwestern Europe in the 8th–11th centuries.
▶ **adj.** of or relating to the Vikings or the period in which they lived.
– ORIGIN from Old Norse *víkingr*, from *vík* 'creek' or Old English *wīc* 'camp, dwelling place.'

Vi·king[2] either of two American space probes sent to Mars in 1975, each of which consisted of a lander that conducted experiments on the surface and an orbiter.

Vi·la /'vēlə/ (also **Port Vila**) the capital of Vanuatu, on the southwestern coast of the island of Efate; pop. 40,000 (est. 2007).

vi·la·yet /,vēlə'yet/ ▶ **n.** (in Turkey, and formerly in the Ottoman Empire) a major administrative district or province with its own governor.
– ORIGIN Turkish, from Arabic *wilāya(t)* 'government, administrative district.'

vile /vīl/ ▶ **adj.** extremely unpleasant: *he has a vile temper | vile smells.* ■ morally bad; wicked: *as vile a rogue as ever lived.* ■ archaic of little worth or value.
– DERIVATIVES **vile·ly** adv., **vile·ness** n.
– ORIGIN Middle English: via Old French from Latin *vilis* 'cheap, base.'

vil·i·fi·ca·tion /,viləfə'kāSHən/ ▶ **n.** abusively disparaging speech or writing: *the vilification of minority groupings.*

vil·i·fy /'vilə,fī/ ▶ **v.** (**vilifies**, **vilifying**, **vilified**) [with obj.] speak or write about in an abusively disparaging manner: *he has been vilified in the press.*
– DERIVATIVES **vil·i·fi·er** n.
– ORIGIN late Middle English (in the sense 'lower in value'): from late Latin *vilificare*, from Latin *vilis* 'of low value' (see VILE).

vil·i·pend /'vilə,pend/ ▶ **v.** [with obj.] archaic **1** regard as worthless or of little value; despise.
2 speak slightingly or abusively of; vilify.
– DERIVATIVES **vil·i·pend·er** n., **vil·i·pens·ive** adj.

Vil·la /'vēyə/, Pancho (1878–1923), Mexican revolutionary; born *Doroteo Arango*. He helped Venustiano Carranza to overthrow the dictatorial regime of General Victoriano Huerta in 1914, but then helped Emiliano Zapata to rebel against Carranza's regime.

vil·la /'vilə/ ▶ **n.** (esp. in continental Europe) a large and luxurious country residence. ■ a large country house of Roman times, having an estate and consisting of farm and residential buildings arranged around a courtyard. ■ Brit. a detached or semidetached house in a residential district, typically one that is Victorian or Edwardian in style.
– ORIGIN early 17th cent.: from Italian, from Latin.

Vil·la·fran·chi·an /,vilə'fraNGkēən/ ▶ **adj.** of, relating to, or denoting an age (or stage) in Europe crossing the boundary of the Upper Pliocene and Lower Pleistocene, lasting from about 3 to 1 million years ago. ■ (as noun **the Villafranchian**) the Villafranchian age or stage, or the system of deposits laid down during it.
– ORIGIN late 19th cent.: from French *villafranchien*, from *Villafranca* d'Asti, the village in northern Italy near which exposures of this period occur.

vil·lage /'vilij/ ▶ **n.** a group of houses and associated buildings, larger than a hamlet and smaller than a town, situated in a rural area. ■ a self-contained district or community within a town or city, regarded as having features characteristic of village life: *the Olympic village.* ■ (in the US) a small municipality with limited corporate powers.
– DERIVATIVES **vil·lag·er** n.
– ORIGIN late Middle English: from Old French, from Latin *villa* 'country house.'

vil·lage id·i·ot ▶ **n.** chiefly archaic a person of very low intelligence resident and well known in a village.

vil·lag·i·za·tion /,vilijə'zāSHən/ ▶ **n.** (in Africa and Asia) the concentration of the population in villages as opposed to scattered settlements, typically to ensure more efficient control and distribution of services such as health care and education. ■ the transfer of land to the communal control of villagers.

vil·lain /'vilən/ ▶ **n. 1** (in a film, novel, or play) a character whose evil actions or motives are important to the plot: *the terrorists are cartoon villains | I have played more good guys than villains.* ■ the person or thing responsible for specified trouble, harm, or damage: *the industrialized nations are the real environmental villains.*
2 archaic variant spelling of VILLEIN.
– DERIVATIVES **vil·lain·ess** /'vilənəs/ n.
– ORIGIN Middle English (in the sense 'a rustic, boor'): from Old French *vilein*, based on Latin *villa* (see VILLA).

vil·lain·ous /'vilənəs/ ▶ **adj.** relating to, constituting, or guilty of wicked or criminal behavior: *his group of villainous accomplices are wreaking havoc on the city.* ■ informal extremely bad or unpleasant: *a villainous smell.*
– DERIVATIVES **vil·lain·ous·ly** adv., **vil·lain·ous·ness** n.

vil·lain·y /'vilənē/ ▶ **n.** (pl. **villainies**) wicked or criminal behavior: *the villainy of professional racketeers | minor villainies.*
– ORIGIN Middle English: from Old French *vilenie*, from *vilein* (see VILLAIN).

vil·la·nel·la /,vilə'nelə/ ▶ **n.** (pl. **villanelle** /-'nelē/ or **villanellas**) a form of Italian part-song originating in Naples in the 16th century, in rustic style with a vigorous rhythm.
– ORIGIN Italian, feminine of *villanello* 'rural,' diminutive of *villano* 'peasant.'

vil·la·nelle /,vilə'nel/ ▶ **n.** a nineteen-line poem with two rhymes throughout, consisting of five tercets and a quatrain, with the first and third lines of the opening tercet recurring alternately at the end of the other tercets and with both repeated at the close of the concluding quatrain.
– ORIGIN late 19th cent.: from French, from Italian *villanella* (see VILLANELLA).

-ville ▶ **comb. form** informal used in fictitious place names with reference to a particular quality: *dullsville.*
– ORIGIN from French *ville* 'town,' used in many US town names.

vil·lein /'vilən, -,ān/ ▶ **n.** (in medieval England) a feudal tenant entirely subject to a lord or manor to whom he paid dues and services in return for land.
– ORIGIN Middle English: variant of VILLAIN.

vil·lein·age /'vilənij, -,ānij/ ▶ **n.** historical the tenure or status of a villein.

vil·lous /'viləs/ ▶ **adj.** Anatomy (of a structure, esp. the epithelium) covered with villi. ■ Medicine (of a condition) affecting the villi: *villous atrophy.* ■ Botany shaggy.

vil·lus /'viləs/ ▶ **n.** (pl. **villi** /'vilī, 'vilē/) **1** Anatomy any of numerous minute elongated projections set closely together on a surface, typically increasing its surface area for the absorption of substances, in particular: ■ a fingerlike projection of the lining of the small intestine. ■ a fold of the chorion.
2 [(usu. in pl.)] Botany a long slender hair.
– ORIGIN early 18th cent.: from Latin, literally 'shaggy hair.'

Vil·ni·us /'vilnēəs/ the capital of Lithuania, in the southeastern part of the country; pop. 558,165 (2009).

vim /vim/ ▶ **n.** informal energy; enthusiasm: *in his youth he was full of vim and vigor.*
– ORIGIN mid 19th cent. (originally US): perhaps from Latin, accusative of *vis* 'energy.'

Vi·my Ridge, Bat·tle of /'vēmē, 'vimē, vē'mē/ an Allied attack on the German position of Vimy Ridge, near the town of Arras, France, during World War I. One of the key points on the Western Front, it had long resisted assaults, but on April 9, 1917, it was taken by Canadian troops in fifteen minutes, at the cost of heavy casualties.

VIN /vin/ ▶ **abbr.** vehicle identification number.

vin /vaN, van/ ▶ **n.** [usu. with adj.] French wine: *vin blanc.*
– ORIGIN French, literally 'wine.'

vi·na ▶ **n.** variant spelling of VEENA.

vi·na·ceous /vī'nāSHəs, və-/ ▶ **adj.** of the color of red wine.
– ORIGIN late 17th cent.: from Latin *vinaceus* (from *vinum* 'wine') + -OUS.

vin·ai·grette /ˌvinəˈgret/ ▶ **n. 1** (also **vinaigrette dressing**) salad dressing of oil, wine vinegar, and seasoning.
2 historical a small ornamental bottle for holding smelling salts.
– ORIGIN French, diminutive of *vinaigre* 'vinegar.'

vin·blas·tine /vinˈblasˌtēn/ ▶ **n.** Medicine a cytotoxic compound of the alkaloid class obtained from the Madagascar periwinkle and used to treat Hodgkin's disease and other cancers of the lymphatic system.
– ORIGIN 1960s: from modern Latin *Vinca* (see **VINCA**) + (*leuko*)*blast* (a cell from which a leukocyte develops) + **-INE**[4].

vin·ca /ˈviNGkə/ ▶ **n.** another term for **PERIWINKLE**[1].
– ORIGIN 1930s: from modern Latin *Vinca* (genus name), from late Latin *pervinca* (see **PERIWINKLE**[1]).

Vin·cennes /vinˈsenz/ a historic commercial and industrial city in southwestern Indiana, on the Wabash River; pop. 17,976 (est. 2008).

Vin·cent de Paul, St. /ˈvinsənt də ˈpôl/ (1581–1660), French priest. He devoted his life to work among the poor and the sick and established institutions for his work, including the Daughters of Charity (Sisters of Charity of St. Vincent de Paul) 1633. Feast day, July 19.

Vin·cen·tian /vinˈsenSHən/ ▶ **n.** a member of the Congregation of the Mission, a Catholic organization founded at the priory of St. Lazare in Paris by St. Vincent de Paul to preach to the rural poor and train candidates for the priesthood. Also called **LAZARIST**.

Vin·cent's an·gi·na ▶ **n.** a painful ulcerative condition of the inside of the mouth or of the gums, associated with trench mouth.

vin·ci·ble /ˈvinsəbəl/ ▶ **adj.** literary (of an opponent or obstacle) able to be overcome or conquered.
– DERIVATIVES **vin·ci·bil·i·ty** /ˌvinsəˈbilətē/ **n.**
– ORIGIN mid 16th cent.: from Latin *vincibilis*, from *vincere* 'to overcome.'

Vin·ci, Leonardo da, see **LEONARDO DA VINCI**.

vin·cris·tine /vinˈkrisˌtēn/ ▶ **n.** Medicine a cytotoxic compound of the alkaloid class obtained from the Madagascar periwinkle and used to treat acute leukemia and other cancers.
– ORIGIN 1960s: from modern Latin *Vinca* (see **VINCA**) + a second element perhaps based on **CRISTA** + **-INE**[4].

vin·cu·lum /ˈviNGkyələm/ ▶ **n.** (pl. **vincula** /-lə/)
1 Anatomy a connecting band of tissue, such as that attaching a flexor tendon to the bone of a finger or toe.
2 Mathematics a horizontal line drawn over a group of terms in a mathematical expression to indicate that they are to be operated on as a single entity by the preceding or following operator.
– DERIVATIVES **vin·cu·lar** /-lər/ **adj.**
– ORIGIN mid 17th cent. (in the sense 'bond, tie'): from Latin, literally 'bond,' from *vincire* 'bind.' The term has been used in anatomy since the mid 19th cent.

vin·da·loo /ˈvindəˌlo͞o, ˌvindəˈlo͞o/ ▶ **n.** a highly spiced hot Indian curry.
– ORIGIN probably from Portuguese *vin d'alho* 'wine and garlic (sauce),' from *vinho* 'wine' + *alho* 'garlic.'

vin de pays /ˌvaN dɪ pāˈē, ˌvan do͞o/ (also **vin du pays**) ▶ **n.** (pl. **vins de pays** pronunc. **same**) the third-highest French classification of wine, indicating that the wine meets certain standards including area of production, strength, and quality.
– ORIGIN French, literally 'wine of the region.'

vin de ta·ble /ˌvaN də ˈtäbl(ə), ˌvan/ ▶ **n.** (pl. **vins de table** pronunc. **same**) French table wine of reasonable quality, suitable for accompanying a meal.
– ORIGIN French, literally 'table wine.'

vin·di·cate /ˈvindəˌkāt/ ▶ **v.** [with obj.] clear (someone) of blame or suspicion: *hospital staff were vindicated by the inquest verdict.* ■ show or prove to be right, reasonable, or justified: *more sober views were vindicated by events.*
– DERIVATIVES **vin·di·ca·ble** /-kəbəl/ **adj.**, **vin·di·ca·tion** /ˌvindəˈkāSHən/ **n.**, **vin·di·ca·tor** /-ˌkātər/ **n.**, **vin·di·ca·to·ry** /-kəˌtôrē/ **adj.**
– ORIGIN mid 16th cent. (in the sense 'deliver, rescue'): from Latin *vindicat-* 'claimed, avenged,' from the verb *vindicare*, from *vindex, vindic-* 'claimant, avenger.'

vin·dic·tive /vinˈdiktiv/ ▶ **adj.** having or showing a strong or unreasoning desire for revenge: *the criticism was both vindictive and personalized.*
– DERIVATIVES **vin·dic·tive·ly** **adv.**, **vin·dic·tive·ness** **n.**
– ORIGIN early 17th cent.: from Latin *vindicta* 'vengeance' + **-IVE**.

Vine /vīn/, Frederick John (1939–), English geologist. He and his colleague **Drummond H. Matthews** (1931–97) showed that magnetic data from the earth's crust under the Atlantic Ocean provided evidence for seafloor spreading.

vine /vīn/ ▶ **n. 1** a climbing or trailing woody-stemmed plant of the grape family. ● *Vitis* and other genera, family Vitaceae. ■ used in names of climbing or trailing plants of other families, e.g., **potato vine**. ■ the slender stem of a trailing or climbing plant.
2 (**vines**) informal clothes: *the hip got their vines at Wolmuth's on Market Street.*
– DERIVATIVES **vin·y** **adj.**
– ORIGIN Middle English: from Old French, from Latin *vinea* 'vineyard, vine,' from *vinum* 'wine.'

vine dress·er ▶ **n.** a person who prunes, trains, and cultivates vines.

vin·e·gar /ˈvinəgər/ ▶ **n.** a sour-tasting liquid containing acetic acid, obtained by fermenting dilute alcoholic liquids, typically wine, cider, or beer, and used as a condiment or for pickling.
■ sourness or peevishness of behavior, character, or speech: *her aggrieved tone held a touch of vinegar.*
– DERIVATIVES **vin·e·gar·ish** **adj.**, **vin·e·gar·y** **adj.**
– ORIGIN Middle English: from Old French *vyn egre*, based on Latin *vinum* 'wine' + *acer* 'sour.'

Vin·e·gar Joe see **STILWELL**.

Vine·land /ˈvīnlənd/ a commercial and industrial city in southern New Jersey; pop. 58,780 (est. 2008).

vin·er·y /ˈvīn(ə)rē/ ▶ **n.** (pl. **vineries**) a greenhouse for grapevines. ■ a vineyard.

vine·yard /ˈvinyərd/ ▶ **n.** a plantation of grapevines, typically producing grapes used in winemaking. ■ a sphere of action or labor (in allusion to Matt. 20:1): *women professors laboring in feminist vineyards.*

vingt-et-un /ˌvant ā ˈən, ˌvaNt ā ˈœN/ ▶ **n.** the card game blackjack.
– ORIGIN French, literally 'twenty-one.'

vi·nho ver·de /ˈvinyō ˈvərdē, ˈvēnyo͞o ˈverdə/ ▶ **n.** a young Portuguese wine, not allowed to mature.
– ORIGIN Portuguese, literally 'green wine.'

vini- ▶ **comb. form** of or relating to wine: *viniculture.*
– ORIGIN from Latin *vinum* 'wine.'

vin·i·cul·ture /ˈvinəˌkəlCHər/ ▶ **n.** the cultivation of grapevines for winemaking.
– DERIVATIVES **vin·i·cul·tur·al** /ˌvinəˈkəlCHərəl/ **adj.**, **vin·i·cul·tur·ist** /ˌvinəˈkəlCHərist/ **n.**
– ORIGIN late 19th cent.: from Latin *vinum* 'wine' + **CULTURE**, on the pattern of words such as *agriculture.*

vin·i·fi·ca·tion /ˌvinəfiˈkāSHən/ ▶ **n.** the conversion of grape juice or other vegetable extract into wine by fermentation.
– DERIVATIVES **vin·i·fy** /ˈvinəˌfī/ **v.** (**vinifies, vinifying, vinified**).

vin·ing /ˈvīniNG/ ▶ **adj.** [attrib.] (of a plant) growing as a vine with climbing or trailing woody stems.

Vin·land /ˈvinlənd/ the region of the northeastern coast of North America that was visited in the 11th century by Norsemen led by Leif Ericsson. It was so named from the report that grapevines were found growing there. The exact location is uncertain.

Vin·ny·tsya /ˈvēnitsyə/ a city in central Ukraine; pop. 367,800 (est. 2009). Russian name **Vinnitsa**.

vi·no /ˈvēnō/ ▶ **n.** (pl. **vinos**) informal wine, esp. that which is cheap or of inferior quality.
– ORIGIN Spanish and Italian, 'wine.'

vi·no da ta·vo·la /ˈvēno dä ˈtävōlə/ ▶ **n.** Italian wine of reasonable quality, suitable for drinking with a meal.
– ORIGIN Italian, literally 'table wine.'

vin or·di·naire /ˌvaNn ˌôrdēˈne(ə)r, ˈvan/ ▶ **n.** (pl. **vins ordinaires** /ˌvaNz ˌôrdēˈne(ə)r, ˈvanz/) cheap table wine for everyday use.
– ORIGIN French, literally 'ordinary wine.'

vi·nous /ˈvīnəs/ ▶ **adj.** resembling, associated with, or fond of wine: *a vinous smell.* ■ of the reddish color of wine.
– DERIVATIVES **vi·nos·i·ty** /vīˈnäsətē/ **n.**, **vi·nous·ly** **adv.**
– ORIGIN late Middle English: from Latin *vinum* 'wine' + **-OUS**.

Vin·son /ˈvinsən/, Frederick Moore (1890–1953), US chief justice 1946–53. Before being appointed to the chief justiceship by President Truman, he had been a member of the US House of Representatives 1924–29 and 1931–38, had held several federal positions during World War II, and had served in the president's cabinet as secretary of the Treasury 1945–46.

Vin·son Mas·sif /ˈvinsən maˈsēf/ the highest mountain in Antarctica, in Ellsworth Land. It rises to 16,863 feet (5,140 m).

vin·tage /ˈvintij/ ▶ **n.** the year or place in which wine, esp. wine of high quality, was produced. ■ a wine of high quality made from the crop of a single identified district in a good year. ■ literary wine. ■ the harvesting of grapes for winemaking. ■ the grapes or wine produced in a particular season. ■ the time that something of quality was produced: *rifles of various sizes and vintages.*
▶ **adj.** of, relating to, or denoting wine of high quality: *vintage claret.* ■ denoting something of high quality, esp. something from the past or characteristic of the best period of a person's work: *a vintage Sherlock Holmes adventure.*
– ORIGIN late Middle English: alteration (influenced by **VINTNER**) of earlier *vendage*, from Old French *vendange*, from Latin *vindemia* (from *vinum* 'wine' + *demere* 'remove').

vin·tage port ▶ **n.** port wine of special quality, all of one year, bottled early and aged in the bottle.

vin·tag·er /ˈvintijər/ ▶ **n.** a person who harvests grapes.

vin·tage year ▶ **n.** the year that a particular wine was produced. ■ a particularly successful year for some pursuit or product: *it was a vintage year for home-run hitters.*

vint·ner /ˈvintnər/ ▶ **n. 1** a wine merchant.
2 a wine maker.
– ORIGIN late Middle English: via Anglo-Latin from Old French *vinetier*, from medieval Latin *vinetarius*, from Latin *vinetum* 'vineyard,' from *vinum* 'wine.'

vin·ya·sa /vinˈyäsə/ ▶ **n.** movement between poses in yoga, typically accompanied by regulated breathing. ■ a method of yoga in which these movements form a flowing sequence in coordination with the breath.
– ORIGIN Sanskrit *vinyāsa* 'movement, position (of limbs).'

vi·nyl /ˈvīnl/ ▶ **n. 1** synthetic resin or plastic consisting of polyvinyl chloride or a related polymer, used esp. for wallpapers and other covering materials and for phonograph records: *light-reflecting vinyls can be hung in the usual way.* ■ vinyl used as the standard material for phonograph records: *fans had to wait almost a year before the song eventually appeared on vinyl.*
2 [as modifier] Chemistry of or denoting the unsaturated hydrocarbon radical $-CH=CH_2$, derived from ethylene by removal of a hydrogen atom: *a vinyl group.*
– ORIGIN mid 19th cent.: from Latin *vinum* 'wine' + **-YL**.

vi·nyl ac·e·tate ▶ **n.** Chemistry a colorless liquid ester used in the production of polyvinyl acetate and other commercially important polymers. ● Chem. formula: $CH_2CHOCOCH_3$.

vi·nyl chlo·ride ▶ **n.** Chemistry a colorless toxic gas used in the production of polyvinyl chloride and other commercially important polymers. ● Chem. formula: CH_2CHCl.

vi·ol /ˈvīəl/ ▶ **n.** a musical instrument of the Renaissance and baroque periods, typically six-stringed, held vertically and played with a bow.
– ORIGIN late 15th cent. (originally denoting a violinlike instrument): from Old French *viele*, from Provençal *viola*; probably related to **FIDDLE**.

vi·o·la[1] /vīˈōlə, vē-, ˈvīələ/ ▶ **n.** an instrument of the violin family, larger than the violin and tuned a fifth lower.
– ORIGIN early 18th cent.: from Italian and Spanish; compare with **VIOL**.

vi·o·la[2] /vēˈōlə/ ▶ **n.** a plant of a genus that includes the pansies and violets. ● Genus *Viola*, family Violaceae: many species.
– ORIGIN modern Latin, from Latin, literally 'violet.'

vi·o·la·ceous /ˌvīəˈlāSHəs/ ▶ **adj. 1** of a violet color.
2 Botany of, relating to, or denoting plants of the violet family (Violaceae).
– ORIGIN mid 17th cent.: from Latin *violaceus* (from *viola* 'violet') + **-OUS**.

vi·o·la da brac·cio /vēˈōlə də ˈbräCHō/ ▶ **n.** an early musical instrument of the violin family (as distinct from a viol), specifically one corresponding to the modern viola.
– ORIGIN Italian, literally 'viol for the arm.'

vi·o·la da gam·ba /vēˈōlə də ˈgämbə, ˈgam-/ (also **viol da gamba**) ▶ **n.** a viol, specifically a bass viol (corresponding to the modern cello).
– ORIGIN Italian, literally 'viol for the leg.'

vi·o·la d'a·mo·re /vēˈōlə däˈmôrā, də-, -ˈmôrē/ ▶ **n.** a sweet-toned 18th-century musical instrument similar to a viola, but with six or seven strings, and additional sympathetic strings below the fingerboard.
– ORIGIN Italian, literally 'viol of love.'

vi·o·late /ˈvīəˌlāt/ ▶ **v.** [with obj.] break or fail to comply with (a rule or formal agreement): *they violated the terms of a ceasefire.* ■ fail to respect

V

(someone's peace, privacy, or rights): *they denied that human rights were being violated.* ■ treat (something sacred) with irreverence or disrespect: *he was accused of violating a tomb.* ■ rape or sexually assault (someone).
– DERIVATIVES **vi·o·la·tor** /-ˌlātər/ **n.**, **vi·o·la·ble** /-ləbəl/ **adj.** (rare), **vi·o·la·tive adj.**
– ORIGIN late Middle English: from Latin *violat-* 'treated violently,' from the verb *violare*.

vi·o·la·tion /ˌvīəˈlāsнən/ ▶ **n.** the action of violating someone or something: *the aircraft were in violation of UN resolutions.*

vi·o·lence /ˈvī(ə)ləns/ ▶ **n.** behavior involving physical force intended to hurt, damage, or kill someone or something. ■ strength of emotion or an unpleasant or destructive natural force: *the violence of her own feelings.* ■ Law the unlawful exercise of physical force or intimidation by the exhibition of such force.
– PHRASES **do violence to** damage or adversely affect.
– ORIGIN Middle English: via Old French from Latin *violentia*, from *violent-* 'vehement, violent' (see VIOLENT).

vi·o·lent /ˈvī(ə)lənt/ ▶ **adj.** using or involving physical force intended to hurt, damage, or kill someone or something: *a violent confrontation with riot police.* ■ (esp. of an emotion or unpleasant or destructive natural force) very strong or powerful: *violent dislike | the violent eruption killed 1,700 people.* ■ (of a color) vivid. ■ Law involving an unlawful exercise or exhibition of force.
– DERIVATIVES **vi·o·lent·ly adv.**
– ORIGIN Middle English (in the sense 'having a marked or powerful effect'): via Old French from Latin *violent-* 'vehement, violent.'

vi·o·lent storm ▶ **n.** a wind of force 11 on the Beaufort scale (56–63 knots or 64–72 mph).

vi·o·let /ˈvī(ə)lət/ ▶ **n. 1** a herbaceous plant of temperate regions, typically having purple, blue, or white five-petaled flowers, one of which forms a landing pad for pollinating insects. ● Genus *Viola*, family Violaceae (the **violet family**): many species, including the **dog violet** and **sweet violet**. See also VIOLA². ■ used in names of similar-flowered plants of other families, e.g., **African violet**.
2 a bluish-purple color seen at the end of the spectrum opposite red.
▶ adj. of a purplish-blue color.
– ORIGIN Middle English: from Old French *violette*, diminutive of *viole*, from Latin *viola* 'violet.'

vi·o·lin /ˌvīəˈlin/ ▶ **n.** a stringed musical instrument of treble pitch, played with a horsehair bow. The classical European violin was developed in the 16th century. It has four strings and a body of characteristic rounded shape, narrowed at the middle and with two f-shaped sound holes.
– DERIVATIVES **vi·o·lin·ist** /-ist/ **n.**, **vi·o·lin·is·tic** /-linˈistik/ **adj.**
– ORIGIN late 16th cent.: from Italian *violino*, diminutive of *viola* (see VIOLA¹).

violin

vi·o·lin spi·der ▶ **n.** another term for BROWN RECLUSE.

vi·o·list ▶ **n. 1** /vēˈōlist/ a viola player.
2 /ˈvīəlist/ a viol player.

vi·o·lon·cel·lo /ˌvīələnˈcнelō, ˌvē-/ ▶ **n.** (pl. **violoncellos**) formal term for CELLO.
– DERIVATIVES **vi·o·lon·cel·list** /-ˈcнelist/ **n.**
– ORIGIN early 18th cent.: Italian, diminutive of *violone* (see VIOLONE).

vi·o·lo·ne /ˌvēəˈlōnā/ ▶ **n.** an early form of double bass, esp. a large bass viol.
– ORIGIN Italian, augmentative of *viola* (see VIOLA¹).

VIP¹ /vē ī pē/ ▶ **n.** (pl. **VIPs**) a very important person: *a party for 400 VIPs from the world of sports and showbiz.*

VIP² ▶ **abbr.** Biochemistry vasoactive intestinal polypeptide (or peptide), a substance that acts as a neurotransmitter, esp. in the brain and gastrointestinal tract.

vi·pas·sa·na /viˈpäsənə/ (also **Vipassana**) ▶ **n.** (in Theravada Buddhism) meditation involving concentration on the body or its sensations, or the insight that this provides.
– ORIGIN Pali, literally 'inward vision.'

vi·per /ˈvīpər/ ▶ **n.** a venomous snake with large hinged fangs, typically having a broad head and stout body, with dark patterns on a lighter background. ● Family Viperidae: numerous genera and species. See also PIT VIPER, ADDER. ■ a spiteful or treacherous person.
– PHRASES **viper in one's bosom** a person who betrays those who have helped them.
– DERIVATIVES **vi·per·ine** /ˈvīpəˌrīn, -rin/ **adj.**, **vi·per·ish adj.**, **vi·per·ous** /ˈvīp(ə)rəs/ **adj.**
– ORIGIN early 16th cent.: from French *vipère* or Latin *vipera*, from *vivus* 'alive' + *parere* 'bring forth.'

vi·per·fish /ˈvīpərˌfisн/ ▶ **n.** (pl. **same** or **viperfishes**) a small, elongated deep-sea fish that has large jaws with long protruding fangs. ● Family Chauliodontidae: several genera and species.

vi·per's bu·gloss ▶ **n.** a bristly plant of the borage family, with pink buds that open to blue flowers. It was formerly used in the treatment of snake bites. Native to Eurasia, it is now widespread throughout North America. ● *Echium vulgare*, family Boraginaceae.

vi·rae·mia ▶ **n.** British spelling of VIREMIA.

vi·ra·go /vəˈrägō, -ˈrā-/ ▶ **n.** (pl. **viragos** or **viragoes**) a domineering, violent, or bad-tempered woman. ■ archaic a woman of masculine strength or spirit; a female warrior.
– ORIGIN Old English (used only as the name given by Adam to Eve, following the Vulgate), from Latin, 'heroic woman, female warrior,' from *vir* 'man.' The current sense dates from late Middle English.

vi·ral /ˈvīrəl/ ▶ **adj. 1** of the nature of, caused by, or relating to a virus or viruses.
2 of or involving the rapid spread of information about a product or service by viral marketing techniques: *a viral video ad.*
▶ **n.** an image, video, advertisement, etc., that is circulated rapidly on the Internet: *the rise of virals in online marketing.*
– DERIVATIVES **vi·ral·ly adv.**

WORD TRENDS Most people are now happy to spread **viral** infections to their friends, family, and work colleagues. They do so not by sneezing on them but by forwarding e-mails, images, or videos that have amused or intrigued them. The influence of this word-of-mouth publicity on brand awareness and sales is enormous, and one of the most common compounds of **viral** is *viral marketing*. There are now entire companies, known as *viral agencies*, devoted to creating potential *viral hits* for businesses. See also MEME.

vi·ral load ▶ **n.** a measurement of the amount of a virus in an organism, typically in the bloodstream, usu. stated in virus particles per milliliter.

vi·ral mar·ket·ing ▶ **n.** a method of product promotion that relies on getting customers to market an idea, product, or service on their own by telling their friends about it, usually by e-mail: [as modifier] *a carefully designed viral marketing strategy.*

Vir·chow /ˈfirкнō/, Rudolf Karl (1821–1902), German physician and pathologist. He founded cellular pathology.

vir·e·lay /ˈvirəˌlā/ (also **virelai**) ▶ **n.** a medieval French lyric poem of indefinite length composed of stanzas of long lines rhyming with each other and short lines rhyming with each other, the short lines of each stanza furnishing the rhyme for the long lines of the next, with the short lines of the last stanza taking their rhyme from the short lines of the first.
– ORIGIN late Middle English: from Old French *virelai*.

vi·re·mi·a /vīˈrēmēə/ (Brit. also **viraemia**) ▶ **n.** Medicine the presence of viruses in the blood.
– DERIVATIVES **vi·re·mic** /-mik/ **adj.**
– ORIGIN 1940s: from VIRUS + -EMIA.

vir·e·o /ˈvirēˌō/ ▶ **n.** (pl. **vireos**) a small American songbird, typically having a green or gray back and yellow or white underparts. ● Family Vireonidae (the **vireo family**): two genera, esp. *Vireo*, and several species. The vireo family also includes the greenlets and peppershrikes.
– ORIGIN mid 19th cent.: from Latin, perhaps denoting a greenfinch.

vi·res·cent /vəˈresənt, vī-/ ▶ **adj.** literary greenish.
– DERIVATIVES **vi·res·cence n.**, **vi·res·cent·ly adv.**
– ORIGIN early 19th cent.: from Latin *virescent-* 'turning green,' inceptive of *virere* 'be green.'

vir·ga /ˈvərgə/ ▶ **n.** (pl. **virgae** /-gē, -gī/) Meteorology a mass of streaks of rain appearing to hang under a cloud and evaporating before reaching the ground.
– ORIGIN 1940s: from Latin, literally 'rod, stripe.'

vir·gate /ˈvərgət, -ˌgāt/ ▶ **n.** Brit. historical a varying measure of land, typically 30 acres.
– ORIGIN mid 17th cent.: from Latin *virgatus*, from *virga* 'rod.'

Vir·gil /ˈvərjəl/ (also **Vergil**) (70–19 BC), Roman poet; Latin name *Publius Vergilius Maro*. He wrote three major works: the *Eclogues*, ten pastoral poems that blend traditional themes of Greek bucolic poetry with contemporary political and literary themes; the *Georgics*, a didactic poem on farming; and the *Aeneid*, an epic poem about Aeneas, a Trojan (see AENEID).
– DERIVATIVES **Vir·gil·i·an** /vərˈjilēən/ **adj.**

vir·gin /ˈvərjən/ ▶ **n.** a person, typically a woman, who has never had sexual intercourse. ■ a naive, innocent, or inexperienced person, esp. in a particular context: *a political virgin.* ■ **(the Virgin)** the mother of Jesus; the Virgin Mary. ■ **(the Virgin)** the zodiacal sign or constellation Virgo. ■ Entomology a female insect that produces eggs without being fertilized.
▶ **adj. 1** [attrib.] being, relating to, or appropriate for a virgin: *his virgin bride.*
2 not yet touched, used, or exploited: *acres of virgin forests | virgin snow.* ■ (of clay) not yet fired. ■ (of wool) not yet, or only once, spun or woven. ■ (of olive oil) obtained from the first pressing of olives. ■ (of metal) made from ore by smelting.
– ORIGIN Middle English: from Old French *virgine*, from Latin *virgo*, *virgin-*.

vir·gin·al /ˈvərjənl/ ▶ **adj.** being, relating to, or appropriate for a virgin: *virginal shyness.*
▶ **n.** (usu. **virginals**) an early spinet with the strings parallel to the keyboard, typically rectangular, and popular in 16th and 17th century houses. [perhaps because usually played by young women (see origin below).]
– DERIVATIVES **vir·gin·al·ist** /-jənl-ist/ **n.**, **vir·gin·al·ly adv.**
– ORIGIN late Middle English: from Old French, or from Latin *virginalis*, from *virgo* 'young woman.'

vir·gin birth ▶ **n. 1** **(the Virgin Birth)** the doctrine of Christ's birth from a mother, Mary, who was a virgin.
2 Zoology parthenogenesis.

Vir·gin·ia¹ /vərˈjinyə/ a state in the eastern US, on the Atlantic coast; pop. 7,769,089 (est. 2008); capital, Richmond; statehood, June 25, 1788 (10). It was the site of the first permanent English settlement in North America at Jamestown in 1607. One of the original thirteen states, it saw the British surrender at Yorktown in 1781 to end the American Revolution, as well as many Civil War battles.
– DERIVATIVES **Vir·gin·ian n. & adj.**

Vir·gin·ia² ▶ **n.** a type of tobacco grown and manufactured in Virginia. ■ a cigarette made of such tobacco.
– DERIVATIVES **Vir·gin·ian n. & adj.**

Vir·gin·ia Beach a city and resort on the Atlantic coast of southeastern Virginia; pop. 433,746 (est. 2008).

Vir·gin·ia blue·bell ▶ **n.** a North American woodland plant of the borage family, bearing nodding, trumpet-shaped blue flowers. Also called VIRGINIA COWSLIP. ● *Mertensia virginica*, family Boraginaceae.

Vir·gin·ia Cit·y a historic settlement in western Nevada, south of Reno, site of the Comstock Lode gold and silver boom in the 1850s–60s.

Vir·gin·ia cow·slip ▶ **n.** another term for VIRGINIA BLUEBELL.

Vir·gin·ia creep·er ▶ **n.** a North American vine of the grape family, chiefly cultivated for its red autumn foliage. ● Genus *Parthenocissus*, family Vitaceae: several species, in particular *P. quinquefolia*.

Vir·gin·ia ham ▶ **n.** a smoke-cured ham from a hog fed on peanuts and corn.

Vir·gin·ia o·pos·sum ▶ **n.** see OPOSSUM.

Vir·gin·ia reel ▶ **n.** a lively American country dance performed by a number of couples facing each other in parallel lines.

Vir·gin·ia snake·root ▶ **n.** see SNAKEROOT.

Vir·gin·ia stock ▶ **n.** a low-growing, sweetly scented plant with white, pink, or lilac flowers, native to the Mediterranean and cultivated elsewhere. ● *Malcolmia maritima*, family Brassicaceae.

Vir·gin Is·lands /ˈvərjən/ a group of Caribbean islands at the eastern end of the Greater Antilles, divided between US and British administration. The islands were settled, mainly in the 17th century, by British and Danish sugar planters. The US islands include about 50 islands; pop. 109,800 (est. 2009); capital, Charlotte Amalie (on St. Thomas). They were purchased from Denmark in 1917 because of their strategic position. The British islands consist of about 40 islands in the northeastern part of the group; pop. 24,500 (est. 2009); capital, Road Town (on Tortola).

vir·gin·i·ty /vər'jinətē/ ▶ n. the state of never having had sexual intercourse: *he lost his virginity in college.* ■ the state of being naive, innocent, or inexperienced in a particular context: *his political virginity.*
– ORIGIN Middle English: from Old French *virginite*, from Latin *virginitas*, from *virgo* (see **VIRGIN**).

Vir·gin Mar·y the mother of Jesus (see **MARY**[1]).

vir·gin queen ▶ n. **1** an unfertilized queen bee. **2** (**the Virgin Queen**) Queen Elizabeth I of England, who died unmarried.

vir·gin's bow·er ▶ n. a North American clematis with white flowers. Also called **OLD MAN'S BEARD**, because of the fluffy gray plumes that stick to the seeds in autumn. ● *Clematis virginiana*, family Ranunculaceae.

Vir·go /'vərgō/ **1** Astronomy a large constellation (the Virgin), said to represent a maiden or goddess associated with the harvest. It contains several bright stars, the brightest of which is Spica, and a dense cluster of galaxies. ■ (as genitive **Virginis** /'vərjənis/) used with a preceding letter or numeral to designate a star in this constellation: *the star Gamma Virginis.*
2 Astrology the sixth sign of the zodiac, which the sun enters about August 23. ■ (**a Virgo**) (pl. **Virgos**) a person born when the sun is in this sign.
– DERIVATIVES **Vir·go·an** /-gōən/ n. & adj. (sense 2).
– ORIGIN Latin.

vir·go in·tac·ta /'vərgō in'taktə/ ▶ n. chiefly Law a girl or woman who has never had sexual intercourse, originally a virgin whose hymen is intact.
– ORIGIN Latin, literally 'untouched virgin.'

vir·gule /'vər,gyo͞ol/ ▶ n. another term for **SLASH**[1] (sense 2 of the noun).
– ORIGIN mid 19th cent.: from French, literally 'comma,' from Latin *virgula*, diminutive of *virga* 'rod.'

vir·i·des·cent /,virə'desənt/ ▶ adj. greenish or becoming green.
– DERIVATIVES **vir·i·des·cence** n.
– ORIGIN mid 19th cent.: from late Latin *viridescent-* 'becoming green,' from the verb *viridescere*, from Latin *viridis* 'green.'

vi·rid·i·an /və'ridēən/ ▶ n. a bluish-green pigment consisting of hydrated chromium hydroxide. ■ the bluish-green color of this.
– ORIGIN late 19th cent.: from Latin *viridis* 'green' (from *virere* 'be green') + **-IAN**.

vir·ile /'virəl/ ▶ adj. (of a man) having strength, energy, and a strong sex drive. ■ having or characterized by strength and energy: *a strong, virile performance of the Mass.*
– ORIGIN late 15th cent. (in the sense 'characteristic of a man'): from French *viril* or Latin *virilis*, from *vir* 'man.'

vir·il·ism /'virə,lizəm/ ▶ n. Medicine the condition that results from virilization.

vi·ril·i·ty /və'rilitē/ ▶ n. (in a man) the quality of having strength, energy, and a strong sex drive; manliness: *aggression and virility were highly prized in soldiers.*

vir·il·i·za·tion /,virələ'zāsHən/ ▶ n. Medicine the development of male physical characteristics (such as muscle bulk, body hair, and deep voice) in a female or precociously in a boy, typically as a result of excess androgen production.

vi·ri·no /vī'rēnō, və-/ ▶ n. (pl. **virinos**) Microbiology a hypothetical infectious particle postulated as the cause of scrapie, BSE, and Creutzfeldt–Jakob disease, consisting of noncoding nucleic acid in a protective coat made from host cell proteins. Compare with **PRION**[2].
– ORIGIN 1970s: from **VIRUS** + the diminutive suffix *-ino*.

V

vi·ri·on /'virē,än, 'vī-/ ▶ n. Microbiology the complete, infective form of a virus outside a host cell, with a core of RNA or DNA and a capsid.
– ORIGIN 1950s: from **VIRUS** + **-ON**.

vi·roid /'vī,roid/ ▶ n. Microbiology an infectious entity affecting plants, smaller than a virus and consisting only of nucleic acid without a protein coat.

vi·rol·o·gy /vī'räləjē/ ▶ n. the branch of science that deals with the study of viruses.
– DERIVATIVES **vi·ro·log·i·cal** /,vīrə'läjikəl/ adj., **vi·ro·log·i·cal·ly** adv., **vi·rol·o·gist** /-jist/ n.

vir·tu /,vər'to͞o/ (also **vertu**) ▶ n. **1** knowledge of or expertise in the fine arts. ■ curios or objets d'art collectively.
2 literary the good qualities inherent in a person or thing.
– PHRASES **article** (or **object**) **of virtu** an article that is interesting because of its antiquity, beauty, quality of workmanship, etc.
– ORIGIN early 18th cent.: from Italian *virtù* 'virtue'; the variant *vertu* is an alteration, as if from French.

vir·tu·al /'vərCHo͞oəl/ ▶ adj. almost or nearly as described, but not completely or according to strict definition: *the virtual absence of border controls.* ■ Computing not physically existing as such but made by software to appear to do so: *a virtual computer.* See also **VIRTUAL REALITY**. ■ carried out, accessed, or stored by means of a computer, esp. over a network: *a virtual library* | *virtual learning.* ■ Optics relating to the points at which rays would meet if produced backward. ■ Physics denoting particles or interactions with extremely short lifetimes and (owing to the uncertainty principle) indefinitely great energies, postulated as intermediates in some processes.
– DERIVATIVES **vir·tu·al·i·ty** /,vərCHo͞o'alitē/ n.
– ORIGIN late Middle English (also in the sense 'possessing certain virtues'): from medieval Latin *virtualis*, from Latin *virtus* 'virtue,' suggested by late Latin *virtuosus*.

vir·tu·al com·mun·i·ty ▶ n. a community of people sharing common interests, ideas, and feelings over the Internet.

vir·tu·al im·age ▶ n. Optics an optical image formed from the apparent divergence of light rays from a point, as opposed to an image formed from their actual divergence.

vir·tu·al·ize /'vərCHo͞oə,līz/ ▶ v. [with obj.] convert (something) to a computer-generated simulation of reality: *traditional universities have begun to virtualize parts of their curricula.* ■ create a virtual version of (a computing resource or facility).
– DERIVATIVES **vir·tu·al·i·za·tion** n., **vir·tu·a·li·zer** n.

vir·tu·al·ly /'vərCHə(wə)lē/ ▶ adv. **1** [as submodifier] nearly; almost: *virtually all those arrested were accused* | *the college became virtually bankrupt.*
2 by means of virtual reality techniques. ■ by means of a computer; computationally.

vir·tu·al mem·o·ry (also **virtual storage**) ▶ n. Computing memory that appears to exist as main storage although most of it is supported by data held in secondary storage, transfer between the two being made automatically as required.

vir·tu·al of·fice ▶ n. the operational domain of any business or organization whose workforce includes a significant proportion of workers using technology to perform their work at home.

vir·tu·al pet ▶ n. another term for **CYBERPET**.

vir·tu·al pri·vate net·work (abbr.: **VPN**) ▶ n. Computing a method employing encryption to provide secure access to a remote computer over the Internet.

vir·tu·al re·al·i·ty ▶ n. Computing the computer-generated simulation of a three-dimensional image or environment that can be interacted with in a seemingly real or physical way by a person using special electronic equipment, such as a helmet with a screen inside or gloves fitted with sensors.

vir·tue /'vərCHo͞o/ ▶ n. **1** behavior showing high moral standards: *paragons of virtue.* ■ a quality considered morally good or desirable in a person: *patience is a virtue.* ■ a good or useful quality of a thing: *Mike was extolling the virtues of the car* | *there's no virtue in suffering in silence.* ■ archaic virginity or chastity, esp. of a woman.
2 (**virtues**) (in traditional Christian angelology) the seventh highest order of the ninefold celestial hierarchy.
– PHRASES **by** (or **in**) **virtue of** because or as a result of. **make a virtue of** derive benefit or advantage from submitting to (an unwelcome obligation or unavoidable circumstance).
– DERIVATIVES **vir·tue·less** adj.
– ORIGIN Middle English: from Old French *vertu*, from Latin *virtus* 'valor, merit, moral perfection,' from *vir* 'man.'

vir·tu·os·i·ty /,vərCHo͞o'äsitē/ ▶ n. great skill in music or another artistic pursuit: *a performance of considerable virtuosity.*

vir·tu·o·so /,vərCHo͞o'ōsō/ ▶ n. (pl. **virtuosi** /-sē/ or **virtuosos**) a person highly skilled in music or another artistic pursuit: *a celebrated clarinet virtuoso* | [as modifier] *virtuoso guitar playing.* ■ a person with a special knowledge of or interest in works of art or curios.
– DERIVATIVES **vir·tu·os·ic** /-'äsik, -'ōsik/ adj.
– ORIGIN early 17th cent.: from Italian, literally 'learned, skillful,' from late Latin *virtuosus* (see **VIRTUOUS**).

vir·tu·ous /'vərCHəwəs/ ▶ adj. having or showing high moral standards: *she considered herself very virtuous because she neither drank nor smoked.* ■ archaic (esp. of a woman) chaste.
– DERIVATIVES **vir·tu·ous·ly** adv., **vir·tu·ous·ness** n.
– ORIGIN Middle English: from Old French *vertuous*, from late Latin *virtuosus*, from *virtus* 'virtue.'

vir·u·lence gene /'vir(y)ələns/ ▶ n. a gene whose presence or activity in an organism's genome is responsible for the pathogenicity of an infective agent.

vir·u·lent /'vir(y)ələnt/ ▶ adj. **1** (of a disease or poison) extremely severe or harmful in its effects. ■ (of a pathogen, esp. a virus) highly infective.
2 bitterly hostile: *a virulent attack on liberalism.*
– DERIVATIVES **vir·u·lence** n., **vir·u·lent·ly** adv.
– ORIGIN late Middle English (originally describing a poisoned wound): from Latin *virulentus*, from *virus* 'poison' (see **VIRUS**).

vi·rus /'vīrəs/ ▶ n. **1** an infective agent that typically consists of a nucleic acid molecule in a protein coat, is too small to be seen by light microscopy, and is able to multiply only within the living cells of a host: [as modifier] *a virus infection.* ■ an infection or disease caused by such an agent. ■ a harmful or corrupting influence: *the virus of cruelty that is latent in all human beings.*
2 (also **computer virus**) a piece of code that is capable of copying itself and typically has a detrimental effect, such as corrupting the system or destroying data.
– ORIGIN late Middle English (denoting the venom of a snake): from Latin, literally 'slimy liquid, poison.' The earlier medical sense, superseded by the current use as a result of improved scientific understanding, was 'a substance produced in the body as the result of disease, esp. one that is capable of infecting others with the same disease.'

Vis. ▶ abbr. Viscount.

vi·sa /'vēzə/ ▶ n. an endorsement on a passport indicating that the holder is allowed to enter, leave, or stay for a specified period of time in a country.
– ORIGIN mid 19th cent.: via French from Latin *visa*, past participle (neuter plural) of *videre* 'to see.'

vis·age /'vizij/ ▶ n. [usu. in sing.] literary a person's face, with reference to the form or proportions of the features: *an elegant, angular visage.* ■ a person's facial expression: *there was something hidden behind his visage of cheerfulness.* ■ the surface of an object presented to view: *the moonlit visage of the port's whitewashed buildings.*
– DERIVATIVES **vis·aged** adj. [in combination] *a stern-visaged old man.*
– ORIGIN Middle English: via Old French from Latin *visus* 'sight,' from *videre* 'to see.'

Vi·sā·kha /vi'säkə/ ▶ n. variant spelling of **VESAK**.

Vi·sa·kha·pat·nam /vi,sHäkə'pətnəm/ a port on the coast of Andhra Pradesh, in southeastern India; pop 1,058,200 (est. 2009).

Vi·sa·lia /vi'sālyə, vī-/ a city in south central California, in the San Joaquin Valley; pop. 121,040 (est. 2008).

vis-à-vis /,vēz ə 'vē/ ▶ prep. in relation to; with regard to: *many agencies now have a unit to deal with women's needs vis-à-vis employment.* ■ as compared with; as opposed to: *the advantage for U.S. exports is the value of the dollar vis-à-vis other currencies.*
▶ adv. archaic in a position facing a specified or implied subject: *he was there vis-à-vis with Miss Arundel.*
▶ n. (pl. **same**) **1** a person or group occupying a corresponding position to that of another person or group in a different area or domain; a counterpart: *his admiration for the US armed services extends to their vis-à-vis, the Russian military.*
2 a face-to-face meeting: *the dreaded vis-à-vis with his boss.*
– ORIGIN mid 18th cent.: French, literally 'face to face,' from Old French *vis* 'face.'

USAGE The expression **vis-à-vis** literally means 'face to face.' Avoid using it to mean 'about, concerning,' as in *he wanted to talk to me vis-à-vis next weekend.* In the sense 'in contrast, comparison, or relation to,' however, **vis-à-vis** is generally acceptable: *let us consider government regulations vis-à-vis employment rates.*

Visc. ▶ abbr. Viscount.

vis·ca·cha /vi'skäcHə/ ▶ n. a large South American burrowing rodent of the chinchilla family, sometimes hunted for its fur and flesh. ● Genera *Lagidium* and *Lagostomus*, family Chinchillidae: four species.
– ORIGIN early 17th cent.: via Spanish from Quechua *(h)uiscacha*.

vis·cer·a /'visərə/ ▶ plural n. (sing. **viscus** /'viskəs/) the internal organs in the main cavities of the body, esp. those in the abdomen, e.g., the intestines.
– ORIGIN mid 17th cent.: from Latin, plural of *viscus* (see **VISCUS**).

vis·cer·al /'vis(ə)rəl/ ▶ adj. of or relating to the viscera: *the visceral nervous system.* ■ relating to deep inward feelings rather than to the intellect: *the voters' visceral fear of change.*

– DERIVATIVES **vis·cer·al·ly** adv.

vis·cer·o·trop·ic /ˌvisərəˈtrōpik, -ˈträpik/ ▶ adj. (of a microorganism) tending to attack or affect the viscera.

vis·cid /ˈvisid/ ▶ adj. glutinous; sticky: *the viscid mucus lining of the intestine.*
– DERIVATIVES **vis·cid·i·ty** /vəˈsidətē/ n.
– ORIGIN mid 17th cent.: from late Latin *viscidus*, from Latin *viscum* 'birdlime.'

vis·co·e·las·tic·i·ty /ˌviskō-iˌlasˈtisitē, -ˌēla-/ ▶ n. Physics the property of a substance of exhibiting both elastic and viscous behavior, the application of stress causing temporary deformation if the stress is quickly removed but permanent deformation if it is maintained.
– DERIVATIVES **vis·co·e·las·tic** /ˌ-iˈlastik/ adj.

vis·com·e·ter /viˈskämətər/ ▶ n. an instrument for measuring the viscosity of liquids.
– DERIVATIVES **vis·co·met·ric** /ˌviskəˈmetrik/ adj., **vis·co·met·ri·cal·ly** /ˌviskəˈmetrik(ə)lē/ adv., **vis·com·e·try** /-ətrē/ n.
– ORIGIN late 19th cent.: from late Latin *viscosus* 'viscous' + -METER.

Vis·con·ti /vəˈskäntē/, Luchino (1906–76), Italian movie and theater director; full name *Don Luchino Visconti, Conte di Modrone*. His movies include *Obsession* (1942), *The Leopard* (1963), and *Death in Venice* (1971).

vis·cose /ˈvisˌkōs, -ˌkōz/ ▶ n. a viscous orange-brown solution obtained by treating cellulose with sodium hydroxide and carbon disulfide, used as the basis of manufacturing rayon fiber and transparent cellulose film. ■ rayon fabric or fiber made from this.
– ORIGIN late 19th cent.: from late Latin *viscosus*, from Latin *viscus* 'birdlime.'

vis·co·sim·e·ter /ˌviskəˈsimitər/ ▶ n. another term for VISCOMETER.

vis·cos·i·ty /ˌviˈskäsitē/ ▶ n. (pl. **viscosities**) the state of being thick, sticky, and semifluid in consistency, due to internal friction. ■ a quantity expressing the magnitude of such friction, as measured by the force per unit area resisting a flow in which parallel layers unit distance apart have unit speed relative to one another.
– ORIGIN late Middle English: from Old French *viscosite* or medieval Latin *viscositas*, from late Latin *viscosus* (see VISCOUS).

vis·count /ˈvīˌkount/ ▶ n. a British nobleman ranking above a baron and below an earl.
– DERIVATIVES **vis·count·cy** /-ˌkountsē/ n.
– ORIGIN late Middle English: from Old French *visconte*, from medieval Latin *vicecomes, vicecomit-* (see VICE[4], COUNT[2]).

vis·count·ess /ˈvīˌkountəs/ ▶ n. the wife or widow of a viscount. ■ a woman holding the rank of viscount in her own right.

vis·count·y /ˈvīˌkountē/ ▶ n. the land under the authority of a viscount.

vis·cous /ˈviskəs/ ▶ adj. having a thick, sticky consistency between solid and liquid; having a high viscosity: *viscous lava.*
– DERIVATIVES **vis·cous·ly** adv., **vis·cous·ness** n.
– ORIGIN late Middle English: from Anglo-Norman French *viscous* or late Latin *viscosus*, from Latin *viscum* 'birdlime.'

vis·cus /ˈviskəs/ singular form of VISCERA.
– ORIGIN Latin.

vise /vīs/ (Brit. **vice**) ▶ n. a metal tool with movable jaws that are used to hold an object firmly in place while work is done on it, typically attached to a workbench.
– DERIVATIVES **vise·like** adj.
– ORIGIN Middle English (denoting a screw or winch): from Old French *vis*, from Latin *vitis* 'vine.'

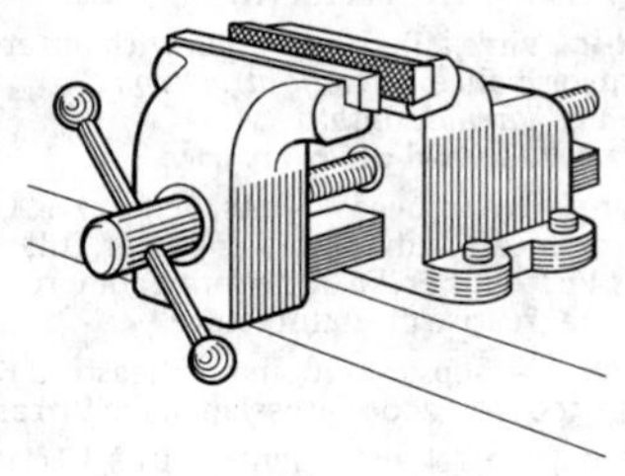
vise

Vish·nu /ˈvisHno͞o/ Hinduism a god, originally a minor Vedic god, now regarded by his worshipers as the supreme deity and savior, by others as the preserver of the cosmos in a triad with Brahma and Shiva. Vishnu is considered by Hindus to have had nine earthly incarnations or avatars, including Rama, Krishna, and the historical Buddha; the tenth avatar will herald the end of the world.
– DERIVATIVES **Vish·nu·ism** /-ˌizəm/ n., **Vish·nu·ite** /-ˌīt/ n. & adj.
– ORIGIN from Sanskrit *Viṣṇu*.

vis·i·bil·i·ty /ˌvizəˈbilitē/ ▶ n. the state of being able to see or be seen: *a reduction in police presence and visibility on the streets.* ■ the distance one can see as determined by light and weather conditions: *visibility was down to 15 yards.* ■ the degree to which something has attracted general attention; prominence: *the issue began to lose its visibility.*
– ORIGIN late Middle English: from French *visibilite* or late Latin *visibilitas*, from Latin *visibilis* (see VISIBLE).

vis·i·ble /ˈvizəbəl/ ▶ adj. **1** able to be seen: *the church spire is visible from miles away.* ■ Physics (of light) within the range of wavelengths to which the eye is sensitive. ■ able to be perceived or noticed easily: *a visible improvement.* ■ in a position of public prominence: *a highly visible member of the royal entourage.*
2 of or relating to imports or exports of tangible commodities: *the visible trade gap.*
– DERIVATIVES **vis·i·ble·ness** n., **vis·i·bly** /-blē/ adv. *he was visibly uncomfortable.*
– ORIGIN Middle English: from Old French, or from Latin *visibilis*, from *videre* 'to see.'

Vis·i·goth /ˈvizəˌgäTH/ ▶ n. a member of the branch of the Goths who invaded the Roman Empire between the 3rd and 5th centuries AD and ruled much of Spain until overthrown by the Moors in 711.
– DERIVATIVES **Vis·i·goth·ic** /ˌvizəˈgäTHik/ adj.
– ORIGIN from late Latin *Visigothus*, the first element possibly meaning 'west' (compare with OSTROGOTH).

vi·sion /ˈviZHən/ ▶ n. **1** the faculty or state of being able to see: *she had defective vision.* ■ the ability to think about or plan the future with imagination or wisdom: *the organization had lost its vision and direction.* ■ a mental image of what the future will or could be like: *a vision of retirement.* ■ the images seen on a television screen.
2 an experience of seeing someone or something in a dream or trance, or as a supernatural apparition: *the idea came to him in a vision.* ■ (often **visions**) a vivid mental image, esp. a fanciful one of the future: *he **had visions of** becoming the Elton John of his time.* ■ a person or sight of unusual beauty.
▶ v. [with obj.] rare imagine.
– DERIVATIVES **vi·sion·al** /-ZHənl/ adj., **vi·sion·less** adj.
– ORIGIN Middle English (denoting a supernatural apparition): via Old French from Latin *visio(n-)*, from *videre* 'to see.'

vi·sion·ar·y /ˈviZHəˌnerē/ ▶ adj. **1** (esp. of a person) thinking about or planning the future with imagination or wisdom: *a visionary leader.* ■ archaic (of a scheme or idea) not practical.
2 of, relating to, or able to see visions in a dream or trance, or as a supernatural apparition: *a visionary experience.* ■ archaic existing only in a vision or in the imagination.
▶ n. (pl. **visionaries**) a person with original ideas about what the future will or could be like.
– DERIVATIVES **vi·sion·ar·i·ness** n.

vi·sion·ing /ˈviZHəniNG/ ▶ n. **1** the development of a plan, goal, or vision for the future: *months of visioning and dedicated effort have culminated in the building of a cultural center.*
2 the action or fact of seeing visions.

vi·sion quest ▶ n. an attempt to achieve a vision of a future guardian spirit, traditionally undertaken at puberty by boys of the Plains Indian peoples, typically through fasting or self-torture.

vis·it /ˈvizit/ ▶ v. (**visits, visiting, visited**) [with obj.] **1** go to see and spend time with (someone) socially: *I came to visit my grandmother* | [no obj.] *he went out to visit with his pals.* ■ stay temporarily with (someone) or at (a place) as a guest or tourist: *we hope you enjoy your stay and will visit us again* | [no obj.] *I don't live here—I'm only visiting.* ■ go to see (someone or something) for a specific purpose, such as to make an inspection or to receive or give professional advice or help: *inspectors visit all the hotels.* ■ [no obj.] informal chat: *there was nothing to do but visit with one another.* ■ go to (a website or web page): *visit us at www.flycreekcidermill.com.* ■ (chiefly in biblical use) (of God) come to (a person or place) in order to bring comfort or salvation.
2 inflict (something harmful or unpleasant) on someone: *the mockery **visited upon** him by his schoolmates.* ■ (of something harmful or unpleasant) afflict (someone): *they were **visited with** epidemics of a strange disease.* ■ archaic punish (a person or a wrongful act): *offenses were visited with the loss of eyes or ears.*
▶ n. an act of going or coming to see a person or place socially, as a tourist, or for some other purpose: *a visit to the doctor.* ■ a temporary stay with a person or at a place. ■ an informal conversation.
– DERIVATIVES **vis·it·a·ble** adj.
– ORIGIN Middle English: from Old French *visiter* or Latin *visitare* 'go to see,' frequentative of *visare* 'to view,' from *videre* 'to see.'

vis·it·a·bil·i·ty /ˌvizitəˈbilitē/ ▶ n. a measure of a place's ease of access for people with disabilities: *we endeavor to create a community that is not only accessible, but is also a model of visitability.*

vis·it·ant /ˈvizətənt/ ▶ n. chiefly literary a supernatural being or agency; an apparition. ■ archaic a visitor or guest. ■ Ornithology a visitor.
▶ adj. archaic or literary paying a visit: *the housekeeper was abrupt with the poor visitant niece.*
– ORIGIN late 16th cent.: from French, or from Latin *visitant-* 'going to see,' from the verb *visitare* (see VISIT).

vis·it·a·tion /ˌvizəˈtāSHən/ ▶ n. **1** an official or formal visit, in particular: ■ (in church use) an official visit of inspection, esp. one by a bishop to a church in the bishop's diocese. ■ the appearance of a divine or supernatural being. ■ a gathering with the family of a deceased person before the funeral. ■ Law a divorced person's right to spend time with their children in the custody of a former spouse.
2 a disaster or difficulty regarded as a divine punishment: *a visitation of the plague.*
3 (**the Visitation**) the visit of the Virgin Mary to Elizabeth related in Luke 1:39–56. ■ the festival commemorating this on May 31 (formerly July 2).
– ORIGIN Middle English: from Old French, or from late Latin *visitatio(n-)*, from the verb *visitare* (see VISIT).

vis·it·a·to·ri·al /ˌvizətəˈtôrēəl/ ▶ adj. another term for VISITORIAL.

vis·it·ing /ˈvizitiNG/ ▶ adj. [attrib.] (of a person) on a visit to a person or place: *a visiting speaker.* ■ (of an academic) working for a fixed period of time at another institution: *a visiting professor.*

vis·it·ing card ▶ n. British term for CALLING CARD.

vis·it·ing fire·man ▶ n. informal an important visitor to a city or organization who is given an official welcome and especially cordial treatment. ■ a visitor or tourist who is accorded special attention because they are expected to spend extravagantly.

vis·it·ing hours ▶ plural n. a designated time when visitors may come to see a person in a hospital or other institution.

vis·it·ing nurse ▶ n. a nurse who visits and treats patients in their homes, operating as part of a social service agency.

vis·it·ing pro·fes·sor ▶ n. a professor on a short-term contract to teach at a college or university other than the one that mainly employs them.

vis·i·tor /ˈvizitər/ ▶ n. a person visiting a person or place, esp. socially or as a tourist. ■ (usu. **visitors**) a member of a sports team on tour or playing away from home. ■ chiefly Brit. a person with the right or duty of occasionally inspecting and reporting on a college or other academic institution. ■ Ornithology a migratory bird present in a locality for only part of the year.
– ORIGIN late Middle English: from Anglo-Norman French *visitour*, from Old French *visiter* (see VISIT).

vis·i·to·ri·al /ˌvizəˈtôrēəl/ ▶ adj. of or relating to an official visitor or visitation: *visitorial jurisdiction.*

Vis·king /ˈviskiNG/ (also **Visking tubing**) ▶ n. trademark a type of seamless cellulose tubing used as a membrane in dialysis and as an edible casing for sausages.
– ORIGIN 1930s: named after the *Visking* Corporation of Chicago, Illinois.

vis me·di·ca·trix na·tu·rae /ˈvis ˌmediˈkātriks nəˈto͝orē, ˈwēs ˌmediˈkätriks näˈto͝orˌī/ ▶ n. the body's natural ability to heal itself.
– ORIGIN Latin, 'the healing power of nature.'

vis·na /ˈvisnə/ ▶ n. Veterinary Medicine a fatal disease of sheep in which there is progressive demyelination of neurons in the brain and spinal cord, caused by a virus.
– ORIGIN 1950s: from Old Norse, 'to wither.'

vi·sor /ˈvīzər/ (also **vizor**) ▶ n. a stiff brim at the front of a cap. ■ a movable part of a helmet that can be pulled down to cover the face. ■ a screen for protecting the eyes from unwanted light, esp. one at the top of a vehicle windshield. ■ historical a mask.
– DERIVATIVES **vi·sored** adj.
– ORIGIN Middle English: from Anglo-Norman French *viser*, from Old French *vis* 'face,' from Latin *visus* (see VISAGE).

V

Vis·queen /ˈvisˌkwēn/ ▶ **n.** trademark a durable polyethylene sheeting, used in various building applications and in the manufacture of waterproof household articles.
– ORIGIN 1940s: from **VISKING**, with humorous alteration of *-king* to *-queen*.

VISTA /ˈvistə/ ▶ **abbr.** Volunteers in Service to America.

Vis·ta /ˈvistə/ a city in southwestern California, north of San Diego; pop. 91,144 (est. 2008).

vis·ta /ˈvistə/ ▶ **n.** a pleasing view, esp. one seen through a long, narrow opening: *a vista of church spires.* ■ a mental view of a succession of remembered or anticipated events: *vistas of freedom seemed to open ahead of him.*
– ORIGIN mid 17th cent.: from Italian, literally 'view,' from *visto* 'seen,' past participle of *vedere* 'see,' from Latin *videre*.

Vis·ta·vi·sion /ˈvistəˌvizHən/ ▶ **n.** trademark a form of widescreen cinematography employing standard 35 mm film in such a way as to give a larger projected image using ordinary methods of projection.

Vis·tu·la /ˈviscHələ/ a river in Poland that rises in the Carpathian Mountains and flows north for 592 miles (940 km) through Cracow and Warsaw, to the Baltic Sea near Gdańsk. Polish name **WISŁA**.

vis·u·al /ˈvizHo͞oəl/ ▶ **adj.** of or relating to seeing or sight: *visual perception.*
▶ **n.** (usu. **visuals**) a picture, piece of film, or display used to illustrate or accompany something.
– DERIVATIVES **vis·u·al·i·ty** /ˌvizHo͞oˈalitē/ **n.**, **vis·u·al·ly adv.**
– ORIGIN late Middle English (originally describing a beam imagined to proceed from the eye and make vision possible): from late Latin *visualis*, from Latin *visus* 'sight,' from *videre* 'to see.' The current noun sense dates from the 1950s.

vis·u·al a·cu·i·ty ▶ **n.** sharpness of vision, measured by the ability to discern letters or numbers at a given distance according to a fixed standard.

vis·u·al ag·no·sia ▶ **n.** Medicine a condition in which a person can see but cannot recognize or interpret visual information, due to a disorder in the parietal lobes.

vis·u·al aid ▶ **n.** (usu. **visual aids**) an item of illustrative matter, such as a film, slide, or model, designed to supplement written or spoken information so that it can be understood more easily.

vis·u·al an·gle ▶ **n.** Optics the angle formed at the eye by rays from the extremities of an object viewed.

vis·u·al bi·na·ry ▶ **n.** Astronomy a binary star of which the components are sufficiently far apart to be resolved by an optical telescope.

vis·u·al cor·tex ▶ **n.** Anatomy the part of the cerebral cortex that receives and processes sensory nerve impulses from the eyes.

vis·u·al field ▶ **n.** another term for **FIELD OF VISION**.

vis·u·al·ize /ˈvizH(ə)wəˌlīz/ ▶ **v.** [with obj.] **1** form a mental image of; imagine: *it is not easy to visualize the future.*
2 make (something) visible to the eye: *the cells were better visualized by staining.*
– DERIVATIVES **vis·u·al·iz·a·ble adj.**, **vis·u·al·i·za·tion** /ˌvizH(ə)wələˈzāsHən/ **n.**

vis·u·al pur·ple ▶ **n.** another term for **RHODOPSIN**.

vis·u·al ray ▶ **n.** Optics an imaginary line representing the path of light from an object to the eye.

vi·su·o·mo·tor /ˌvizHəwōˈmōtər/ ▶ **adj.** [attrib.] relating to or denoting the coordination of movement and visual perception by the brain.

vis·u·o·spa·tial /ˌvizHəwōˈspāsHəl/ ▶ **adj.** [attrib.] Psychology relating to or denoting the visual perception of the spatial relationships of objects.

vi·ta /ˈvītə, ˈvē-/ ▶ **n.** a biography or résumé.

vi·tal /ˈvītl/ ▶ **adj. 1** absolutely necessary or important; essential: *secrecy is of vital importance* | *it is vital that the system is regularly maintained.* ■ indispensable to the continuance of life: *the vital organs.*
2 full of energy; lively: *a beautiful, vital girl.*
3 archaic fatal: *the wound is vital.*
▶ **n.** (**vitals**) the body's important internal organs, esp. the gut or the genitalia. ■ short for **VITAL SIGNS**.
– DERIVATIVES **vi·tal·ly adv.**
– ORIGIN late Middle English (describing the animating principle of living beings, also sense 2 of the adjective): via Old French from Latin *vitalis*, from *vita* 'life.' The sense 'essential' dates from the early 17th cent.

vi·tal ca·pac·i·ty ▶ **n.** the greatest volume of air that can be expelled from the lungs after taking the deepest possible breath.

vi·tal force ▶ **n.** the energy or spirit that animates living creatures; the soul. ■ Philosophy (in some theories, particularly that of Bergson) a hypothetical force, independent of physical and chemical forces, regarded as being the causative factor in the evolution and development of living organisms. [translating French *élan vital*.] ■ a person or thing that gives something vitality and strength: *he was a vital force in British music.*

vi·tal·ism /ˈvītlˌizəm/ ▶ **n.** the theory that the origin and phenomena of life are dependent on a force or principle distinct from purely chemical or physical forces.
– DERIVATIVES **vi·tal·ist n. & adj.**, **vi·tal·is·tic** /ˌvītlˈistik/ **adj.**
– ORIGIN early 19th cent.: from French *vitalisme*, or from **VITAL** + **-ISM**.

vi·tal·i·ty /vīˈtalitē/ ▶ **n.** the state of being strong and active; energy: *changes that will give renewed vitality to our democracy.* ■ the power giving continuance of life, present in all living things: *the vitality of seeds.*
– ORIGIN late 16th cent.: from Latin *vitalitas*, from *vitalis* (see **VITAL**).

vi·tal·ize /ˈvītlˌīz/ ▶ **v.** [with obj.] give strength and energy to: *yoga calms and vitalizes body and mind.*
– DERIVATIVES **vi·tal·i·za·tion** /ˌvītl-əˈzāsHən/ **n.**

vi·tal signs /ˈvīdl sīnz/ ▶ **plural n.** clinical measurements, specifically pulse rate, temperature, respiration rate, and blood pressure, that indicate the state of a patient's essential body functions.

vi·tal sta·tis·tics /ˈvīdl stəˈtistiks/ ▶ **plural n.** **1** quantitative data concerning a population, such as the number of births, marriages, and deaths.
2 informal the measurements of a woman's bust, waist, and hips.

vi·ta·min /ˈvītəmən/ ▶ **n.** any of a group of organic compounds that are essential for normal growth and nutrition and are required in small quantities in the diet because they cannot be synthesized by the body.
– ORIGIN early 20th cent.: from Latin *vita* 'life' + **AMINE**, because vitamins were originally thought to contain an amino acid.

vi·ta·min A ▶ **n.** another term for **RETINOL**.

vi·ta·min B ▶ **n.** any of a group of substances (the **vitamin B complex**) that are essential for the working of certain enzymes in the body and, although not chemically related, are generally found together in the same foods. They include thiamine (**vitamin B_1**), riboflavin (**vitamin B_2**), pyridoxine (**vitamin B_6**), and cyanocobalamin (**vitamin B_{12}**).

vi·ta·min C ▶ **n.** another term for **ASCORBIC ACID**.

vi·ta·min D ▶ **n.** any of a group of vitamins found in liver and fish oils, essential for the absorption of calcium and the prevention of rickets in children and osteomalacia in adults. They include calciferol (**vitamin D_2**) and cholecalciferol (**vitamin D_3**).

vi·ta·min E ▶ **n.** another term for **TOCOPHEROL**.

vi·ta·min H ▶ **n.** another term for **BIOTIN**.

vi·ta·min K ▶ **n.** any of a group of vitamins found mainly in green leaves and essential for the blood-clotting process. They include phylloquinone (**vitamin K_1**), menaquinone (**vitamin K_2**), and menadione (**vitamin K_3**).

vi·ta·min M ▶ **n.** another term for **FOLIC ACID**.

vi·ta·min P ▶ **n.** the bioflavonoids, regarded collectively as a vitamin.

Vi·tebsk /ˈvētipsk/ Russian name for **VITSEBSK**.

vi·tel·li /vəˈtelˌī, vī-, -ˈtelē/ plural form of **VITELLUS**.

vi·tel·lin /vəˈtelən, vī-/ ▶ **n.** Biochemistry the chief protein constituent of egg yolk.
– ORIGIN mid 19th cent.: from **VITELLUS** + **-IN**[1].

vi·tel·line /vəˈtelən, vī-, -ˌēn, -ˌīn/ ▶ **adj.** Zoology or Embryology of or relating to the yolk (or yolk sac) of an egg or embryo, or to yolk-producing organs.
– ORIGIN late Middle English (in the sense 'colored like egg yolk'): from medieval Latin *vitellinus*, from *vitellus* (see **VITELLUS**).

vi·tel·line mem·brane ▶ **n.** Embryology a transparent membrane surrounding and secreted by the fertilized ovum, preventing the entry of further spermatozoa.

Vi·tel·li·us /vəˈtelēəs/, Aulus (15–69), Roman emperor. He was acclaimed emperor in January 69 by the legions in Germany during the civil wars that followed the death of Nero. He defeated Otho but was killed by the supporters of Vespasian.

vi·tel·lo·gen·in /vīˈteləˌjenən, və-/ ▶ **n.** Biochemistry a protein present in the blood, from which the substance of egg yolk is derived.
– ORIGIN 1960s: from **VITELLUS** + **-GEN** + **-IN**[1].

vi·tel·lus /vəˈteləs, vī-/ ▶ **n.** Embryology the yolk of an egg or ovum.
– ORIGIN early 18th cent.: from Latin, literally 'yolk.'

vi·tex /ˈvīteks/ ▶ **n. 1** another term for **CHASTE TREE**.
2 a medicinal preparation extracted from the berries of the chaste tree, used to treat gynecological conditions.

vi·ti·ate /ˈvisHēˌāt/ ▶ **v.** [with obj.] formal spoil or impair the quality or efficiency of: *development programs have been vitiated by the rise in population.* ■ destroy or impair the legal validity of.
– DERIVATIVES **vi·ti·a·tion** /ˌvisHēˈāsHən/ **n.**, **vi·ti·a·tor** /-ˌātər/ **n.**
– ORIGIN mid 16th cent.: from Latin *vitiat-* 'impaired,' from the verb *vitiare*, from *vitium* (see **VICE**[1]).

vit·i·cul·ture /ˈvitiˌkəlcHər/ ▶ **n.** the cultivation of grapevines. ■ the study of grape cultivation.
– DERIVATIVES **vit·i·cul·tur·al** /ˌvitiˈkəlcHərəl/ **adj.**, **vit·i·cul·tur·ist** /-rist/ **n.**
– ORIGIN late 19th cent.: from Latin *vitis* 'vine' + **CULTURE**, on the pattern of words such as *agriculture*.

Vi·ti Le·vu /ˈvētē ˈlāˌvo͞o, ˈlevˌo͞o/ the largest of the Fiji islands. Its chief settlement is Suva.

vit·i·li·go /ˌvitlˈīgō, -ˈēgō/ ▶ **n.** Medicine a condition in which the pigment is lost from areas of the skin, causing whitish patches, often with no clear cause. Also called **LEUCODERMA**.
– ORIGIN late 16th cent.: from Latin, literally 'tetter.'

Vi·to·ria /viˈtôrēə/ a city in northeastern Spain, capital of the Basque Provinces; pop. 232,477 (2008).

Vi·tó·ri·a /viˈtôrēə/ a port in eastern Brazil, capital of the state of Espírito Santo; pop. 314,042 (2007).

vit·rec·to·my /vəˈtrektəmē/ ▶ **n.** the surgical operation of removing the vitreous humor from the eyeball.

vit·re·ous /ˈvitrēəs/ ▶ **adj.** like glass in appearance or physical properties. ■ (of a substance) derived from or containing glass: *the toilet and bidet are made of vitreous china.*
– DERIVATIVES **vit·re·ous·ness n.**
– ORIGIN late Middle English: from Latin *vitreus* (from *vitrum* 'glass') + **-OUS**.

vit·re·ous hu·mor ▶ **n.** the transparent jellylike tissue filling the eyeball behind the lens. Compare with **AQUEOUS HUMOR**.

vi·tres·cent /vəˈtresənt/ ▶ **adj.** rare capable of or susceptible to being turned into glass.
– DERIVATIVES **vi·tres·cence n.**
– ORIGIN mid 18th cent.: from Latin *vitrum* 'glass' + **-ESCENT**.

vit·ri·form /ˈvitrəˌfôrm/ ▶ **adj.** having the form or appearance of glass.

vit·ri·fy /ˈvitrəˌfī/ ▶ **v.** (**vitrifies, vitrifying, vitrified**) [with obj.] convert (something) into glass or a glasslike substance, typically by exposure to heat.
– DERIVATIVES **vit·ri·fac·tion** /ˌvitrəˈfaksHən/ **n.**, **vit·ri·fi·a·ble** /ˈvitrəˌfīəbəl, ˌvitrəˈfī-/ **adj.**, **vit·ri·fi·ca·tion** /ˌvitrəfiˈkāsHən/ **n.**
– ORIGIN late Middle English: from French *vitrifier* or based on Latin *vitrum* 'glass.'

vi·trine /vəˈtrēn/ ▶ **n.** a glass display case.
– ORIGIN French, from *vitre* 'glass pane.'

vit·ri·ol /ˈvitrēəl, -ˌôl/ ▶ **n. 1** cruel and bitter criticism: *her mother's sudden gush of fury and vitriol.*
2 archaic or literary sulfuric acid.
– ORIGIN late Middle English (denoting the sulfate of various metals): from Old French, or from medieval Latin *vitriolum*, from Latin *vitrum* 'glass.'

vit·ri·ol·ic /ˌvitrēˈälik/ ▶ **adj.** filled with bitter criticism or malice: *vitriolic attacks on the politicians* | *vitriolic outbursts.*
– DERIVATIVES **vit·ri·ol·i·cal·ly adv.**

Vi·tru·vi·us /vəˈtro͞ovēəs/ (*fl.* 1st century BC), Roman architect and military engineer; full name *Marcus Vitruvius Pollio*. He wrote a comprehensive 10-volume treatise on architecture.

Vi·tsebsk /ˈvētˌsepsk/ a city in northeastern Belarus; pop. 347,500 (est. 2009). Russian name **VITEBSK**.

vit·ta /ˈvitə/ ▶ **n.** (pl. **vittae** /ˈvitē, ˈvitī/) **1** Botany an oil tube in the fruit of some plants.
2 Zoology a band or stripe of color.
– ORIGIN early 19th cent.: from Latin, literally 'band, chaplet.'

vit·tle ▶ **n.** archaic variant spelling of **VICTUAL**.

vi·tu·per·ate /vəˈt(y)o͞opəˌrāt, vī-/ ▶ **v.** [with obj.] archaic blame or insult (someone) in strong or violent language.
– DERIVATIVES **vi·tu·per·a·tor** /-ˌrātər/ **n.**

–ORIGIN mid 16th cent.: from Latin *vituperat-* 'censured, disparaged,' from the verb *vituperare*, from *vitium* 'fault' + *parare* 'prepare.'

vi·tu·per·a·tion /və,t(y)o͞opə'rāsʜən, vī-/ ▶ **n.** bitter and abusive language: *no one else attracted such vituperation from him.*

vi·tu·per·a·tive /və't(y)o͞opə,rātiv, vī-, -p(ə)rətiv/ ▶ **adj.** bitter and abusive: *the criticism soon turned into a vituperative attack.*

Vi·tus, St. /'vītəs/ (died *c.*300), Christian martyr. He is the patron of those who suffer from epilepsy and certain nervous disorders, including St. Vitus's dance (Sydenham's chorea). Feast day, June 15.

vi·va /'vēvə/ ▶ **exclam.** long live! (used to express acclaim or support for a specified person or thing): *"Viva Mexico!"*
▶ **n.** a cry of this as a salute or cheer.
–ORIGIN Italian and Spanish.

vi·va·ce /vē'vä,cʜā, -cʜē/ Music ▶ **adv. & adj.** (esp. as a direction) in a lively and brisk manner.
▶ **n.** a passage or movement marked to be performed in this manner.
–ORIGIN Italian, 'brisk, lively,' from Latin *vivax, vivac-*.

vi·va·cious /və'vāsʜəs, vī-/ ▶ **adj.** (esp. of a woman) attractively lively and animated.
–DERIVATIVES **vi·va·cious·ly adv.**, **vi·va·cious·ness n.**
–ORIGIN mid 17th cent.: from Latin *vivax, vivac-* 'lively, vigorous' (from *vivere* 'to live') + **-IOUS**.

vi·vac·i·ty /və'vasitē, vī-/ ▶ **n.** (esp. in a woman) the quality of being attractively lively and animated: *he was struck by her vivacity, humor and charm.*

Vi·val·di /vi'väldē, -'vôldē/, Antonio (Lucio) (1678–1741), Italian composer and violinist; known as **the Red Priest**. His feeling for texture and melody is evident in his numerous compositions such as *The Four Seasons* (concerto, 1725).

vi·var·i·um /vī've(ə)rēəm/ ▶ **n.** (pl. **vivaria** /-'ve(ə)rēə/) an enclosure, container, or structure adapted or prepared for keeping animals under seminatural conditions for observation or study or as pets; an aquarium or terrarium.
–ORIGIN early 17th cent.: from Latin, literally 'game enclosure, fishpond,' from *vivus* 'living,' from *vivere* 'to live.'

vi·vat /'vē,vat, -,vät, 'vī,vat/ ▶ **exclam. & n.** Latin term for **VIVA**.

vi·va vo·ce /,vēvə 'vōcʜā, ,vīvə 'vōsē/ ▶ **adj.** (esp. of an examination) oral rather than written.
▶ **adv.** orally rather than in writing.
▶ **n.** (also **viva**) Brit. an oral examination, typically for an academic qualification.
–ORIGIN mid 16th cent.: from medieval Latin, literally 'with the living voice.'

vive la dif·fé·rence /'vēv(ə) lä ,difə'räns/ ▶ **exclam.** chiefly humorous an expression of approval of difference, esp. that between the sexes.
–ORIGIN from French, literally 'long live the difference.'

vi·ver·rid /vī'verid, vi-/ ▶ **n.** Zoology a mammal of the civet family (Viverridae).
–ORIGIN early 20th cent.: from modern Latin *Viverridae*, from Latin *viverra* 'ferret.'

viv·i·an·ite /'vivēə,nīt/ ▶ **n.** a mineral consisting of a phosphate of iron that occurs as a secondary mineral in ore deposits. It is colorless when fresh but becomes blue or green with oxidization.
–ORIGIN early 19th cent.: named after John H. *Vivian* (1785–1855), British mineralogist, + **-ITE**[1].

viv·id /'vivid/ ▶ **adj. 1** producing powerful feelings or strong, clear images in the mind: *memories of that evening were still vivid | a vivid description.* ■ (of a color) intensely deep or bright.
2 archaic (of a person or animal) lively and vigorous.
–DERIVATIVES **viv·id·ly adv.**, **viv·id·ness n.**
–ORIGIN mid 17th cent.: from Latin *vividus*, from *vivere* 'to live.'

viv·i·fy /'vivə,fī/ ▶ **v.** (**vivifies, vivifying, vivified**) [with obj.] enliven or animate: *outings vivify learning for children.*
–DERIVATIVES **viv·i·fi·ca·tion** /,vivəfi'kāsʜən/ **n.**
–ORIGIN late Middle English: from French *vivifier*, from late Latin *vivificare*, from Latin *vivus* 'living,' from *vivere* 'to live.'

vi·vip·a·rous /vī'vip(ə)rəs, vi-/ ▶ **adj.** Zoology (of an animal) bringing forth live young that have developed inside the body of the parent. Compare with **OVIPAROUS** and **OVOVIVIPAROUS**. ■ Botany (of a plant) reproducing from buds that form plantlets while still attached to the parent plant, or from seeds that germinate within the fruit.
–DERIVATIVES **viv·i·par·i·ty** /,vivə'paritē, ,vīvə-/ **n.**, **vi·vip·a·rous·ly adv.**
–ORIGIN mid 17th cent.: from Latin *viviparus* (from *vivus* 'alive' + *-parus* 'bearing') + **-OUS**.

viv·i·sect /'vivə,sekt, ,vivə'sekt/ ▶ **v.** [with obj.] perform vivisection on (an animal) (used only by people who are opposed to the practice).
–DERIVATIVES **viv·i·sec·tor** /-tər/ **n.**
–ORIGIN mid 19th cent.: back-formation from **VIVISECTION**.

viv·i·sec·tion /,vivə'seksʜən/ ▶ **n.** the practice of performing operations on live animals for the purpose of experimentation or scientific research (used only by people who are opposed to such work). ■ ruthlessly sharp and detailed criticism or analysis: *the vivisection of America's seamy underbelly.*
–DERIVATIVES **viv·i·sec·tion·ist** /-ist/ **n. & adj.**
–ORIGIN early 18th cent.: from Latin *vivus* 'living,' on the pattern of *dissection*.

vix·en /'viksən/ ▶ **n.** a female fox. ■ a spiteful or quarrelsome woman.
–DERIVATIVES **vix·en·ish adj.**
–ORIGIN late Middle English *fixen*, perhaps from the Old English adjective *fyxen* 'of a fox' The *v-* is from the form of the word in southern English dialect.

Vi·yel·la /vī'elə/ ▶ **n.** trademark a fabric made from a twilled mixture of cotton and wool.
–ORIGIN late 19th cent.: from *Via Gellia*, a valley in Derbyshire, north central England, where it was first made.

viz. /viz/ or said as /'nāmlē/ ▶ **adv.** namely; in other words (used esp. to introduce a gloss or explanation): *the first music reproducing media, viz., the music box and the player piano.*
–ORIGIN abbreviation of **VIDELICET**, z being a medieval Latin symbol for *-et*.

viz·ard /'vizərd/ ▶ **n.** archaic a mask or disguise.
–ORIGIN mid 16th cent.: alteration of **VISOR**.

vi·zier /və'zi(ə)r/ ▶ **n.** historical a high official in some Muslim countries, esp. in Turkey under Ottoman rule.
–DERIVATIVES **vi·zier·ate** /-'zi(ə)rit, -'zi(ə)r,āt/ **n.**, **vi·zier·i·al** /-'zi(ə)rēəl/ **adj.**, **vi·zier·ship** /-,sʜip/ **n.**
–ORIGIN mid 16th cent.: via Turkish from Arabic *wazīr* 'caliph's chief counselor.'

vi·zor ▶ **n.** variant spelling of **VISOR**.

vizs·la /'vizʜlə, 'vēzlə/ ▶ **n.** a dog of a breed of golden-brown pointer with large drooping ears.
–ORIGIN 1940s: from the name of a town in Hungary.

VJ ▶ **abbr.** video jockey.

V-J Day ▶ **n.** the day (August 15) in 1945 on which Japan ceased fighting in World War II, or the day (September 2) when Japan formally surrendered.
–ORIGIN *V-J*, abbreviation of *Victory over Japan*.

VLA ▶ **abbr.** Very Large Array (telescope).

Vlach /vläk, vlak/ ▶ **n.** a member of the indigenous population of Romania and Moldova, claiming descent from the inhabitants of the Roman province of Dacia.
▶ **adj.** of or relating to this people.
–ORIGIN from a Slavic word meaning 'foreigner,' from a Germanic word related to Old English *Wælisc* (see **WELSH**). Compare with **WALLACHIA**.

Vla·di·kav·kaz /,vladə,käf'käz, -'käs/ a city in southwestern Russia, capital of the autonomous republic of North Ossetia; pop. 312,800 (est. 2008). Former names **ORDZHONIKIDZE** (1931–44 and 1954–93) and **DZAUDZHIKAU** (1944–54).

Vlad·i·mir /'vladə,mi(ə)r, vlə'd(y)ēmir/ a city in western Russia, east of Moscow; pop. 339,500 (est. 2008).

Vlad·i·mir I (956–1015), grand prince of Kiev 980–1015; known as **Vladimir the Great**; canonized as **St. Vladimir**. His marriage to a sister of the Byzantine emperor **Basil II** resulted in his conversion to Christianity. Feast day, July 15.

Vla·di·vos·tok /,vladə'väs,täk, -və'stäk/ a city in southeastern Russia, on the coast of the Sea of Japan, capital of Primorsky; pop. 578,800 (est. 2008).

Vla·minck /vlə'mangk, -'mank/, Maurice de (1876–1958), French painter and writer. With Derain and Matisse he became a leading exponent of Fauvism.

vlast /vläst/ ▶ **n.** (pl. **vlasti** /-tē/) (in countries of the former Soviet Union) political power or authority. ■ (**the vlasti**) members of the government; people holding political power.
–ORIGIN Russian.

VLF ▶ **abbr.** very low frequency (denoting radio waves of frequency 3–30 kHz and wavelength 10–100 km).

Vlo·rë /'vlôrə/ a port in southwestern Albania, on the Adriatic coast; pop. 95,200 (est. 2009). Also called **Vlona**. Italian name **VALONA**.

VLSI ▶ **abbr.** Electronics very large-scale integration, the process of integrating hundreds of thousands of components on a single silicon chip.

Vl·ta·va /'vəltəvə/ a river in the Czech Republic that rises in the Bohemian Forest on the German–Czech border and flows north for 270 miles (435 km), passing through Prague before joining the Elbe River north of the city. German name **MOLDAU**.

V-mail ▶ **n. 1** short for **VOICE MAIL**.
2 short for **VIDEO MAIL**.
3 a method of microfilming US soldiers' mail to and from home to cut down on shipping costs during World War II, with "V" standing for "victory."

VMD ▶ **abbr.** Doctor of Veterinary Medicine.
–ORIGIN from Latin *Veterinariae Medicinae Doctor*.

V-neck ▶ **n.** a neckline of a garment, having straight sides meeting at a point to form a V-shape. ■ a garment with a neckline of this type.
–DERIVATIVES **V-necked adj.**

voc. ▶ **abbr.** ■ vocational. ■ Grammar vocative.

vocab. ▶ **abbr.** vocabulary.

vo·ca·ble /'vōkəbəl/ ▶ **n.** a word, esp. with reference to form rather than meaning.
–ORIGIN late Middle English (denoting a name): from French, or from Latin *vocabulum*, from *vocare* 'call.'

vo·cab·u·lar·y /vō'kabyə,lerē, vi-/ ▶ **n.** (pl. **vocabularies**) the body of words used in a particular language. ■ a part of such a body of words used on a particular occasion or in a particular sphere: *the vocabulary of law | the term became part of business vocabulary.* ■ the body of words known to an individual person: *he had a wide vocabulary.* ■ a list of difficult or unfamiliar words with an explanation of their meanings, accompanying a piece of specialist or foreign-language text. ■ a range of artistic or stylistic forms, techniques, or movements: *dance companies have their own vocabularies of movement.*
–ORIGIN mid 16th cent. (denoting a list of words with definitions or translations): from medieval Latin *vocabularius*, from Latin *vocabulum* (see **VOCABLE**).

vo·cal /'vōkəl/ ▶ **adj. 1** of or relating to the human voice: *nonlinguistic vocal effects like laughs and sobs.* ■ Anatomy used in the production of speech sounds: *the vocal apparatus.* ■ Phonetics (of a sound in speech) made with the voice rather than the breath alone; voiced.
2 expressing opinions or feelings freely or loudly: *he was vocal in condemning the action.*
3 (of music) consisting of or incorporating singing.
▶ **n.** (often **vocals**) a part of a piece of music that is sung. ■ a musical performance involving singing.
–DERIVATIVES **vo·cal·i·ty** /vō'kalətē/ **n.**, **vo·cal·ly adv.**
–ORIGIN late Middle English: from Latin *vocalis*, from *vox, voc-* (see **VOICE**). Current senses of the noun date from the 1920s.

vo·cal cords (also **vocal folds**) ▶ **plural n.** folds of membranous tissue that project inward from the sides of the larynx to form a slit across the glottis in the throat, and whose edges vibrate in the airstream to produce the voice.

vo·cal·ese /,vōkə'lēz/ ▶ **n.** a style of singing in which singers put words to jazz tunes, esp. to previously improvised instrumental solos. See **SCAT**[2].

vo·cal·ic /vō'kalik, və-/ ▶ **adj.** Phonetics of, relating to, or consisting of a vowel or vowels.

vo·ca·lise /'vōkə,lēz, ,vōkə'lēz/ ▶ **n.** Music a singing exercise using individual syllables or vowel sounds to develop flexibility and control of pitch and tone. ■ a vocal passage consisting of a melody without words: *the second movement is in the spirit of a vocalise.*

vo·cal·ism /'vōkə,lizəm/ ▶ **n. 1** the use of the voice or vocal organs in speech. ■ the skill or art of exercising the voice in singing.
2 Phonetics a vowel sound or articulation. ■ a system of vowels used in a given language.

vo·cal·ist /'vōkəlist/ ▶ **n.** a singer, typically one who regularly performs with a jazz or pop group.

vo·cal·ize /'vōkə,līz/ ▶ **v.** [with obj.] **1** utter (a sound or word): *the child vocalizes a number of distinct sounds |* [no obj.] *a warbler vocalized from a reed bed.* ■ express (something) with words: *Gillie could scarcely vocalize her responses.* ■ [no obj.] Music sing with several notes to one vowel.
2 Phonetics change (a consonant) to a semivowel or vowel.
3 write (a language such as Hebrew) with vowel points.
–DERIVATIVES **vo·cal·i·za·tion** /,vōkələ'zāsʜən/ **n.**, **vo·cal·iz·er n.**

PRONUNCIATION KEY ə *ago, up;* ər *over, fur;* a *hat;* ā *ate;* ä *car;* e *let;* ē *see;* i *fit;* ī *by;* NG *sing;* ō *go;* ô *law, for;* oi *toy;* o͝o *good;* o͞o *goo;* ou *out;* TH *thin;* T͟H *then;* ZH *vision*

vo·cal sac ▶ **n.** Zoology (in many male frogs) a loose fold of skin on each side of the mouth, which can be inflated to produce sound.

vo·cal score ▶ **n.** a musical score showing the voice parts in full, but with the accompaniment reduced or omitted.

vo·ca·tion /vōˈkāsHən/ ▶ **n.** a strong feeling of suitability for a particular career or occupation: *not all of us have a vocation to be nurses or doctors.* ■ a person's employment or main occupation, esp. regarded as particularly worthy and requiring great dedication: *her vocation as a poet.* ■ a trade or profession.
– ORIGIN late Middle English: from Old French, or from Latin *vocatio(n-)*, from *vocare* 'to call.'

vo·ca·tion·al /vōˈkāsHənl/ ▶ **adj.** of or relating to an occupation or employment: *they supervised prisoners in vocational activities.* ■ (of education or training) directed at a particular occupation and its skills: *vocational school | specialized vocational courses.*
– DERIVATIVES **vo·ca·tion·al·ism** /-ˌizəm/ **n.**, **vo·ca·tion·al·ize** /-ˌīz/ **v.**, **vo·ca·tion·al·ly** **adv.**

voc·a·tive /ˈväkətiv/ Grammar ▶ **adj.** relating to or denoting a case of nouns, pronouns, and adjectives in Latin and other languages, used in addressing or invoking a person or thing.
▶ **n.** a word in the vocative case. ■ (**the vocative**) the vocative case.
– ORIGIN late Middle English: from Old French *vocatif, -ive* or Latin *vocativus*, from *vocare* 'to call.'

vo·cif·er·ate /vəˈsifəˌrāt, vō-/ ▶ **v.** [no obj.] shout, complain, or argue loudly or vehemently: *he then began to vociferate pretty loudly* | [with obj.] *he entered, vociferating curses.*
– DERIVATIVES **vo·cif·er·ant** /-rənt/ **adj.**, **vo·cif·er·a·tion** /-ˌsifəˈrāsHən/ **n.**
– ORIGIN late 16th cent.: from Latin *vociferat-* 'exclaimed,' from the verb *vociferari*, from *vox* 'voice' + *ferre* 'carry.'

vo·cif·er·ous /vəˈsifərəs, vō-/ ▶ **adj.** (esp. of a person or speech) vehement or clamorous: *he was a vociferous opponent of the takeover.*
– DERIVATIVES **vo·cif·er·ous·ly** **adv.**, **vo·cif·er·ous·ness** **n.**

vo·cod·er /ˈvōˌkōdər/ ▶ **n.** a synthesizer that produces sounds from an analysis of speech input.
– ORIGIN 1930s: from VOICE + CODE + -ER[1].

VOD ▶ **abbr.** video-on-demand.

vod·ka /ˈvädkə/ ▶ **n.** an alcoholic spirit of Russian origin made by distillation of rye, wheat, or potatoes.
– ORIGIN Russian, diminutive of *voda* 'water.'

vo·dun /vōˈdo͞on/ ▶ **n.** another term for VOODOO.
– ORIGIN Fon, 'fetish.'

vogue /vōg/ ▶ **n.** [usu. in sing.] the prevailing fashion or style at a particular time: *the vogue is to make realistic films.* ■ general acceptance or favor; popularity: *the 1920s and 30s, when art deco was much in vogue.*
▶ **adj.** [attrib.] popular; fashionable: *"citizenship" was to be the government's vogue word.*
▶ **v.** (**vogues, vogueing** or **voguing, vogued**) [no obj.] dance to music in such a way as to imitate the characteristic poses struck by a model on a catwalk. [1980s: from the name of the fashion magazine *Vogue.*]
– DERIVATIVES **vogu·ish** **adj.**
– ORIGIN late 16th cent. (in *the vogue*, denoting the foremost place in popular estimation): from French, from Italian *voga* 'rowing, fashion,' from *vogare* 'row, go well.'

voice /vois/ ▶ **n. 1** the sound produced in a person's larynx and uttered through the mouth, as speech or song: *Meg raised her voice | a worried tone of voice.* ■ an agency by which a particular point of view is expressed or represented: *once the proud voice of middle-class conservatism, the paper had fallen on hard times.* ■ [in sing.] the right to express an opinion: *the new electoral system gives minority parties a voice.* ■ a particular opinion or attitude expressed: *a dissenting voice.* ■ the ability to speak or sing: *she'd lost her voice.* ■ (usu. **voices**) the supposed utterance of a guiding spirit, typically giving instructions or advice. ■ the distinctive tone or style of a literary work or author: *she had strained and falsified her literary voice.*
2 Music the range of pitch or type of tone with which a person sings, such as soprano or tenor. ■ a vocal part in a composition. ■ a constituent part in a fugue. ■ each of the notes or sounds able to be produced simultaneously by a musical instrument (esp. an electronic one) or a computer. ■ (in an electronic musical instrument) each of a number of preset or programmable tones.
3 Phonetics sound uttered with resonance of the vocal cords (used in the pronunciation of vowels and certain consonants).
4 Grammar a form or set of forms of a verb showing the relation of the subject to the action: *the passive voice.*
▶ **v.** [with obj.] **1** express (something) in words: *get teachers to voice their opinions on important subjects.*
2 (usu. as adj. **voiced**) Phonetics utter (a speech sound) with resonance of the vocal cords (e.g., *b, d, g, v, z*).
3 Music regulate the tone quality of (organ pipes).
– PHRASES **give voice to** allow (a particular emotion, opinion, or point of view) to be expressed. ■ allow (a person or group) to express their emotions, opinion, or point of view. **in voice** in proper vocal condition for singing or speaking: *the soprano is in marvelous voice.* **with one voice** in complete agreement; unanimously.
– DERIVATIVES **voiced** **adj.** [in combination] *deep-voiced*, **voic·er** **n.**
– ORIGIN Middle English: from Old French *vois*, from Latin *vox, voc-.*

voice box ▶ **n.** the larynx.

voice chan·nel ▶ **n.** Telecommunications a channel with a bandwidth sufficiently great to accommodate speech.

voice coil ▶ **n.** Telecommunications a coil that drives the cone of a loudspeaker according to the signal current flowing in it. ■ a similar coil with the converse function in a moving-coil microphone.

voice·ful /ˈvoisfəl/ ▶ **adj.** literary possessing a voice: *the swelling of the voiceful sea.*

voice·less /ˈvoislis/ ▶ **adj.** mute; speechless: *how could he have remained voiceless in the face of her cruelty?* ■ not expressed: *the air was charged with voiceless currents of thought.* ■ (of a person or group) lacking the power or right to express an opinion or exert control over affairs. ■ Phonetics (of a speech sound) uttered without resonance of the vocal cords, e.g., *f* as opposed to *v*, *p* as opposed to *b*, and *s* as opposed to *z*.
– DERIVATIVES **voice·less·ly** **adv.**, **voice·less·ness** **n.**

voice mail (also **voicemail**) ▶ **n.** a centralized electronic system that can store messages from telephone callers.

Voice of A·mer·i·ca an official US radio station that broadcasts around the world in English and other languages. It was founded in 1942 and is operated by the Board for International Broadcasting.

voice-o·ver ▶ **n.** a piece of narration in a movie or broadcast, not accompanied by an image of the speaker.

voice·print /ˈvoisˌprint/ ▶ **n.** a visual record of speech, analyzed with respect to frequency, duration, and amplitude.
– ORIGIN 1960s: from the noun VOICE, on the pattern of *fingerprint.*

voice rec·og·ni·tion tech·nol·o·gy ▶ **n.** the technology that enables a machine or computer program to receive and interpret dictation or to understand and carry out spoken commands.

voice vote ▶ **n.** a vote taken by noting the relative strength and volume of calls of *aye* and *no.*

void /void/ ▶ **adj. 1** not valid or legally binding: *the contract was void.* ■ (of speech or action) ineffectual; useless: *all the stratagems you've worked out are rendered void.*
2 completely empty: *void spaces surround the tanks.* ■ [predic.] (**void of**) free from; lacking: *what were once the masterpieces of literature are now void of meaning.* ■ formal (of an office or position) vacant.
3 [predic.] (in bridge and whist) having been dealt no cards in a particular suit.
▶ **n. 1** a completely empty space: *the black void of space.* ■ an emptiness caused by the loss of something: *the void left by the death of his wife.* ■ an unfilled space in a wall, building, or structure.
2 (in bridge and whist) a suit in which a player is dealt no cards.
▶ **v.** [with obj.] **1** declare that (something) is not valid or legally binding: *the Supreme Court voided the statute.*
2 discharge or drain away (water, gases, etc.). ■ chiefly Medicine excrete (waste matter). ■ (usu. as adj. **voided**) empty or evacuate (a container or space).
– DERIVATIVES **void·a·ble** **adj.**, **void·ness** **n.**
– ORIGIN Middle English (in the sense 'unoccupied'): from a dialect variant of Old French *vuide*; related to Latin *vacare* 'vacate'; the verb partly a shortening of AVOID, reinforced by Old French *voider.*

void·ance /ˈvoidns/ ▶ **n.** the action of voiding something or the state of being voided: *the voidance of exhaust gases.* ■ chiefly Law an annulment of a contract. ■ Christian Church a vacancy in a benefice.
– ORIGIN late Middle English: from Old French, from the verb *voider* (see VOID).

void·ed /ˈvoidid/ ▶ **adj.** Heraldry (of a bearing) having the central area cut away so as to show the field.

voi·la /vwäˈlä/ ▶ **exclam.** there it is; there you are: *"Voilà!" she said, producing a pair of strappy white sandals.*
– ORIGIN French *voilà.*

voile /voil/ ▶ **n.** a thin, plain-weave, semitransparent fabric of cotton, wool, or silk.
– ORIGIN late 19th cent.: French, literally 'veil.'

VoIP (also **VOIP**) ▶ **abbr.** Voice over Internet Protocol, a form of technology that allows for speech communications via the Internet.

voir dire /ˈvwär ˈdi(ə)r/ ▶ **n.** Law a preliminary examination of a witness or a juror by a judge or counsel. ■ an oath taken by such a witness.
– ORIGIN Law French, from Old French *voir* 'true' + *dire* 'say.'

voix ce·leste /ˈvwä səˈlest/ ▶ **n.** French term for VOX ANGELICA.
– ORIGIN late 19th cent.: French *voix céleste*, literally 'heavenly voice.'

Voj·vo·di·na /ˈvoivəˌdēnə/ a mainly Hungarian-speaking province in northern Serbia, on the Hungarian border; capital, Novi Sad.

vol. ▶ **abbr.** volume.

Vo·lans /ˈvōlənz/ Astronomy an inconspicuous southern constellation (the Flying Fish), between Carina and the south celestial pole. ■ (as genitive **Volantis** /vəˈlantis/) used with a preceding letter or numeral to designate a star in this constellation: *the star Beta Volantis.*
– ORIGIN Latin, from the former name *Piscis Volans* 'the flying fish.'

vo·lant /ˈvōlənt/ ▶ **adj.** Zoology (of an animal) able to fly or glide: *newly volant young.* ■ of, relating to, or characterized by flight: *volant ways of life.* ■ [usu. postpositive] Heraldry represented as flying: *a falcon volant.* ■ literary moving rapidly or lightly: *her sails caught a volant wind.*
– ORIGIN mid 16th cent. (as a military term in the sense 'capable of rapid movement'): from French, literally 'flying,' present participle of *voler*, from Latin *volare* 'to fly.'

Vo·la·pük /ˈvōləˌpo͝ok, ˈvôlə-, ˈvälə-/ ▶ **n.** an artificial language devised in 1879 and proposed for international use by a German cleric, Johann M. Schleyer, and based on extremely modified forms of words from English and Romance languages.
– ORIGIN from *vol* representing English *world* + *-a-* (as a connective) + *pük* representing English *speak* or *speech.*

vo·lar /ˈvōlər/ ▶ **adj.** Anatomy relating to the palm of the hand or the sole of the foot.
– ORIGIN early 19th cent.: from Latin *vola* 'hollow of hand or foot' + -AR[1].

vol·a·tile /ˈvälətl/ ▶ **adj. 1** (of a substance) easily evaporated at normal temperatures.
2 liable to change rapidly and unpredictably, esp. for the worse: *the political situation was becoming more volatile.* ■ (of a person) liable to display rapid changes of emotion. ■ (of a computer's memory) retaining data only as long as there is a power supply connected.
▶ **n.** (usu. **volatiles**) a volatile substance.
– DERIVATIVES **vol·a·til·i·ty** /ˌväləˈtilitē/ **n.**
– ORIGIN Middle English (in the sense 'creature that flies,' also, as a collective, 'birds'): from Old French *volatil* or Latin *volatilis*, from *volare* 'to fly.'

vol·a·tile oil ▶ **n.** another term for ESSENTIAL OIL.

vol·a·til·ize /ˈvälətlˌīz/ ▶ **v.** [with obj.] cause (a substance) to evaporate or disperse in vapor. ■ [no obj.] become volatile; evaporate.
– DERIVATIVES **vol·a·til·iz·a·ble** **adj.**, **vol·a·til·i·za·tion** /ˌvälətl-əˈzāsHən/ **n.**

vol-au-vent /ˌvôl ō ˈvän/ ▶ **n.** a small round case of puff pastry filled with a savory mixture, typically of meat or fish in a richly flavored sauce.
– ORIGIN French, literally 'flight in the wind.'

vol·can·ic /välˈkanik, vôl-/ ▶ **adj.** of, relating to, or produced by a volcano or volcanoes. ■ (esp. of a feeling or emotion) bursting out or liable to burst out violently: *the kind of volcanic passion she'd felt last night.*
– DERIVATIVES **vol·can·i·cal·ly** /-ik(ə)lē/ **adv.**
– ORIGIN late 18th cent.: from French *volcanique*, from *volcan* (see VOLCANO).

vol·can·ic bomb ▶ **n.** see BOMB (sense 2 of the noun).

vol·can·ic glass ▶ **n.** another term for OBSIDIAN.

vol·can·ic·i·ty /ˌvälkəˈnisitē, ˌvôl-/ ▶ **n.** another term for VOLCANISM.

vol·can·i·clas·tic /välˌkanəˈklastik, vôl-/ ▶ **adj.** Geology relating to or denoting a clastic rock that contains volcanic material.

V

vol·can·ic neck ▶ **n.** see NECK (sense 2 of the noun).

vol·can·ism /ˈvälkəˌnizəm, ˈvôl-/ (also **vulcanism**) ▶ **n.** Geology volcanic activity or phenomena.

vol·ca·no /välˈkānō, vôl-/ ▶ **n.** (pl. **volcanoes** or **volcanos**) a mountain or hill, typically conical, having a crater or vent through which lava, rock fragments, hot vapor, and gas are being or have been erupted from the earth's crust. ■ an intense suppressed emotion or situation liable to burst out suddenly: *what volcano of emotion must have been boiling inside that youngster*.
– ORIGIN early 17th cent.: from Italian, from Latin *Volcanus* 'Vulcan.'

vol·can·ol·o·gy /ˌvälkəˈnäləjē, ˌvôl-/ (also **vulcanology**) ▶ **n.** the scientific study of volcanoes.
– DERIVATIVES **vol·can·o·log·i·cal** /ˌvälkanlˈäjikəl, ˌvôl-/ **adj.**, **vol·can·ol·o·gist** /-jist/ **n.**

vole /vōl/ ▶ **n.** a small, typically burrowing, mouselike rodent with a rounded muzzle, found in both Eurasia and North America. ● Subfamily Microtinae (or Arvicolinae), family Muridae: several genera, in particular *Microtus*, and numerous species.
– ORIGIN early 19th cent. (originally *vole-mouse*): from Norwegian *voll(mus)* 'field (mouse).'

Vol·ga /ˈvōlgə, ˈväl-, ˈvôl-/ the longest river in Europe, rising in northwestern Russia and flowing east for 2,292 miles (3,688 km) to Kazan, where it turns southeast to the Caspian Sea. It has been dammed at several points to provide hydroelectric power and is navigable for most of its length.

Vol·go·grad /ˈvōlgəˌgrad, ˈväl-, ˈvôl-/ an industrial city in southwestern Russia, at the junction of the Don and Volga rivers; pop. 983,900 (est. 2008). Former names **TSARITSYN** (until 1925) and **STALINGRAD** (1925–61).

vo·li·tion /vəˈlisHən, vō-/ ▶ **n.** the faculty or power of using one's will: *without conscious volition she backed into her office*.
– PHRASES **of** (or **by** or **on**) **one's own volition** voluntarily: *they choose to leave early of their own volition*.
– DERIVATIVES **vo·li·tion·al** /-sHənl/ **adj.**, **vo·li·tion·al·ly** /-sHənl-ē/ **adv.**, **vol·i·tive** /ˈvälətiv/ **adj.** (formal or technical).
– ORIGIN early 17th cent. (denoting a decision or choice made after deliberation): from French, or from medieval Latin *volitio(n-)*, from *volo* 'I wish.'

Völ·ker·wan·de·rung /ˈfəlkərˌvändəˌrōōNG, ˈfœl-/ ▶ **n.** a migration of peoples, esp. that of Germanic and Slavic peoples into Europe from the 2nd to the 11th centuries.
– ORIGIN German, from *Völker* 'nations' + *Wanderung* 'migration.'

völ·kisch /ˈfəlkisH, ˈfœl-/ (also **volkisch** /ˈfōkisH, ˈfōlk-/) ▶ **adj.** (of a person or ideology) populist or nationalist, and typically racist: *völkisch ideas and traditions*.
– ORIGIN German.

volks·lied /ˈfōksˌlēt, ˈfôlks-/ ▶ **n.** a German folk song, or a song in the style of one. ■ a national anthem, esp. that of the 19th-century Transvaal Republic.

vol·ley /ˈvälē/ ▶ **n.** (pl. **volleys**) **1** a number of bullets, arrows, or other projectiles discharged at one time: *the infantry let off a couple of volleys*. ■ a series of utterances directed at someone in quick succession: *he unleashed a volley of angry questions*. ■ Tennis an exchange of shots.
2 (in sports, esp. tennis or soccer) a strike or kick of the ball made before it touches the ground.
▶ **v.** (**volleys, volleying, volleyed**) [with obj.] (in sports, esp. tennis or soccer) strike or kick (the ball) before it touches the ground: *she volleyed the ball home* | [no obj.] *he took his chance well, volleying into the top corner from 25 yards*. ■ score (a goal) with such a shot. ■ [no obj.] (in tennis and similar games) play a pregame point, sometimes in order to determine who will serve first. ■ utter or discharge in quick succession: *the dog was volleying joyful barks*.
– DERIVATIVES **vol·ley·er** **n.**
– ORIGIN late 16th cent.: from French *volée*, based on Latin *volare* 'to fly.'

vol·ley·ball /ˈväléˌbôl/ ▶ **n.** a game for two teams, usually of six players, in which a large ball is hit by hand over a high net, the aim being to score points by making the ball reach the ground on the opponent's side of the court. ■ the inflated ball used in volleyball.

Vo·log·da /ˈvôləgdə/ a city in northern Russia; pop. 286,100 (est. 2008).

Vo·los /ˈvōˌläs, -ˌlôs/ a port on an inlet of the Aegean Sea, in Thessaly, in eastern Greece; pop. 82,000 (est. 2009). Greek name **Vólos**.

vol·plane /ˈvälˌplān, ˈvôl-/ Aeronautics ▶ **n.** a controlled dive or downward flight at a steep angle, esp. by an airplane with the engine shut off.
▶ **v.** [no obj.] (of an airplane) make such a dive or downward flight.
– ORIGIN early 20th cent.: from French *vol plané*, literally 'glided flight.'

vols ▶ **abbr.** volumes.

Vol·scian /ˈvälsHən, ˈvôlskēən/ ▶ **n.** **1** a member of an ancient Italic people who fought the Romans in Latium in the 5th and 4th centuries BC until absorbed into Rome after their final defeat in 304 BC.
2 the Italic language of the Volscians.
▶ **adj.** of or relating to the Volscians.

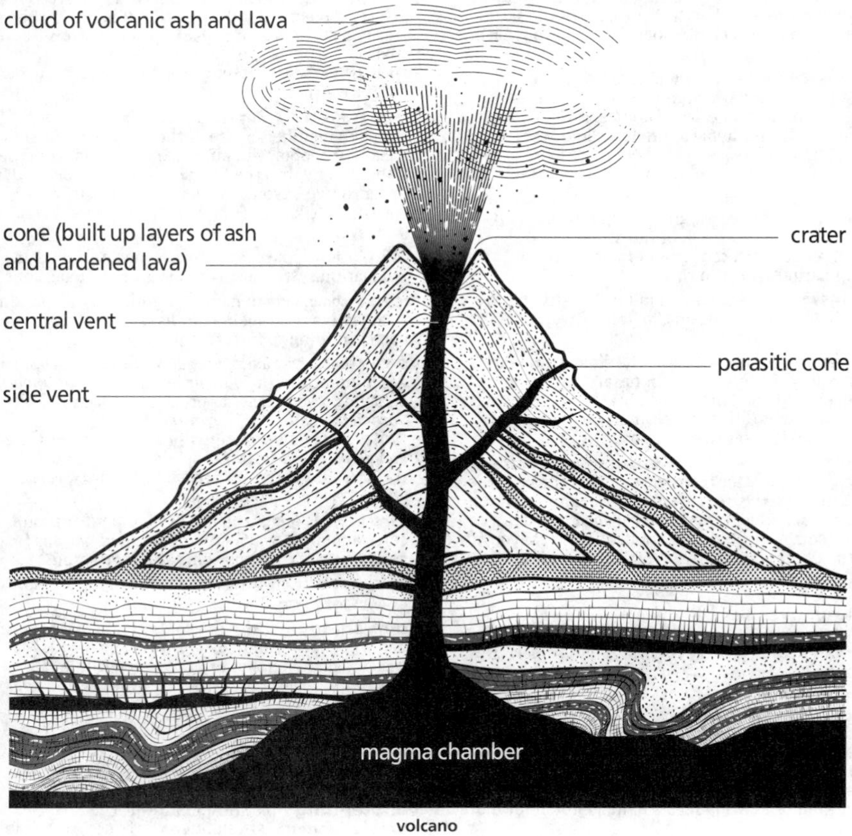

volcano

– ORIGIN from Latin *Volsci* (the name of the people) + **-AN**.

Vol·stead Act /ˈvälˌsted, ˈvôl-, ˈvōl-/ a law that enforced alcohol prohibition in the US during 1920–33.
– ORIGIN named after Andrew J. *Volstead* (1860–1947), American legislator.

volt[1] /vōlt/ (abbr.: **V**) ▶ **n.** the SI unit of electromotive force, the difference of potential that would drive one ampere of current against one ohm resistance.
– ORIGIN late 19th cent.: named after A. *Volta* (see **VOLTA**[2]).

volt[2] /vōlt, vôlt, vält/ (also **volte**) ▶ **n.** Fencing a sudden quick jump or other movement to escape a thrust.
▶ **v.** [no obj.] Fencing make a quick movement to avoid a thrust.
– ORIGIN late 17th cent.: from French *volter* (see **VOLTE**).

Vol·ta[1] /ˈvōltə, ˈväl-, ˈvôl-/ a river in West Africa that is formed in central Ghana by the junction of its headwaters and flows south to the Bight of Benin. At Akosombo in southeastern Ghana the river has been dammed to create Lake Volta, one of the world's largest man-made lakes.

Vol·ta[2] /ˈvōltə/, Alessandro Giuseppe Antonio Anastasio, Count (1745–1827), Italian physicist. He is best known for the voltaic pile or electrochemical battery in 1800, which was the first device to produce a continuous electric current.

volt·age /ˈvōltij/ ▶ **n.** Physics an electromotive force or potential difference expressed in volts.

volt·age clamp Physiology ▶ **n.** a constant electrical potential applied to a cell membrane, typically in order to measure ionic currents.
▶ **v.** (**voltage-clamp**) [with obj.] apply a voltage clamp to (a membrane, cell, etc.).

volt·age di·vid·er ▶ **n.** a series of resistors or capacitors that can be tapped at any intermediate point to produce a specific fraction of the voltage applied between its ends.

Vol·ta·ic /välˈtā-ik, vōl-, vôl-/ ▶ **adj.** & **n.** another term for **GUR**.

vol·ta·ic /välˈtā-ik, vōl-, vôl-/ ▶ **adj.** of or relating to electricity produced by chemical action in a primary battery; galvanic.
– ORIGIN early 19th cent.: from the name of A. *Volta* (see **VOLTA**[2]) + **-IC**.

Vol·taire /vōlˈte(ə)r, vôl-/ (1694–1778), French writer, playwright, and poet; pseudonym of *François-Marie Arouet*. A leading figure of the Enlightenment, he frequently came into conflict with the establishment as a result of his radical views and satirical writings. Notable works: *Lettres philosophiques* (1734) and *Candide* (1759).

volt-am·pere ▶ **n.** a unit of electrical power equal to the product of one volt and one ampere and equivalent to one watt of direct current.

volte ▶ **n.** **1** variant spelling of **VOLT**[2].
2 a movement performed in dressage and classical riding, in which a horse describes a circle of 6 yards diameter.
– ORIGIN late 17th cent. (as a fencing term): from French, from Italian *volta* 'a turn,' from *volgere* 'to turn.' Sense 2 dates from the early 18th cent.

volte-face /ˌvält(ə) ˈfäs, ˌvōlt(ə), ˌvôlt(ə)/ ▶ **n.** (pl. **same**) an act of turning around so as to face in the opposite direction. ■ an abrupt and complete reversal of attitude, opinion, or position: *a remarkable volte-face on taxes*.
– ORIGIN early 19th cent.: from French, from Italian *voltafaccia*, based on Latin *volvere* 'to roll' + *facies* 'appearance, face.'

volt·me·ter /ˈvōltˌmētər/ ▶ **n.** an instrument for measuring electric potential in volts.

vol·u·bil·i·ty /ˌvälyəˈbilətē/ ▶ **n.** the quality of talking fluently, readily, or incessantly; talkativeness: *her legendary volubility deserted her*.

vol·u·ble /ˈvälyəbəl/ ▶ **adj.** speaking or spoken incessantly and fluently: *she was as voluble as her husband was silent*.
– DERIVATIVES **vol·u·ble·ness** **n.**, **vol·u·bly** /-blē/ **adv.**
– ORIGIN late 16th cent.: from French, or from Latin *volubilis*, from *volvere* 'to roll.' Earlier use in late Middle English included the senses 'rotating around an axis' and 'having a tendency to change,' also meanings of the Latin word.

vol·ume /ˈvälyəm, -ˌyōōm/ ▶ **n.** **1** a book forming part of a work or series. ■ a single book or a bound collection of printed sheets. ■ a consecutive

sequence of issues of a periodical. ■ historical a scroll of parchment or papyrus containing written matter. **2** the amount of space that a substance or object occupies, or that is enclosed within a container, esp. when great: *the sewer could not cope with the volume of rainwater* | *a volume of air.* ■ the amount or quantity of something, esp. when great: *changes in the volume of consumer spending.* ■ (**a volume of/volumes of**) a certain, typically large amount of something: *the volumes of data handled are vast.* ■ fullness or expansive thickness of something, esp. of a person's hair.
3 quantity or power of sound; degree of loudness: *he turned the volume up on the radio.*
– ORIGIN late Middle English (originally denoting a roll of parchment containing written matter): from Old French *volum(e)*, from Latin *volumen* 'a roll,' from *volvere* 'to roll.' An obsolete meaning 'size or extent (of a book)' gave rise to sense 2.

vol·u·met·ric /ˌvälyəˈmetrik/ ▶ **adj.** of or relating to the measurement of volume. ■ (of chemical analysis) based on measuring the volumes of reagents, esp. by titration.
– DERIVATIVES **vol·u·met·ri·cal·ly** /-trik(ə)lē/ **adv.**
– ORIGIN mid 19th cent.: from VOLUME + METRIC[1].

vol·u·met·ric ef·fi·cien·cy ▶ **n.** the ratio of the volume of fluid actually displaced by a piston or plunger to its swept volume.

vol·u·met·ric sen·sor ▶ **n.** a security device that detects the movement of people or objects by sensing their shapes.

vo·lu·mi·nous /vəˈlo͞omənəs/ ▶ **adj.** occupying or containing much space; large in volume, in particular: ■ (of clothing or drapery) loose and ample. ■ (of writing) very lengthy and full. ■ (of a writer) producing many books.
– DERIVATIVES **vo·lu·mi·nous·ly adv.**, **vo·lu·mi·nous·ness n.**
– ORIGIN early 17th cent.: partly from late Latin *voluminosus* 'having many coils,' partly from Latin *volumen, volumin-* (see VOLUME).

vol·u·mize /ˈvälyəˌmīz, -yo͞o-/ ▶ **v.** [with obj.] (of a product or styling technique) give body to (hair).
– DERIVATIVES **vol·um·iz·er n.**

vol·un·tar·i·ly /ˌvälənˈte(ə)rəlē, ˈvälənˌterəlē/ ▶ **adv.** of one's own free will: *many restaurants voluntarily removed it from their menus.*

vol·un·ta·rism /ˈväləntəˌrizəm/ ▶ **n. 1** the principle of relying on voluntary action (used esp. with reference to the involvement of voluntary organizations in social welfare). ■ historical (esp. in the 19th century) the principle that churches or schools should be independent of the state and supported by voluntary contributions.
2 Philosophy the doctrine that the will is a fundamental or dominant factor in the individual or the universe.
– DERIVATIVES **vol·un·ta·rist n. & adj.**, **vol·un·ta·ris·tic** /ˌväləntəˈristik/ **adj.**
– ORIGIN mid 19th cent.: formed irregularly from VOLUNTARY.

vol·un·tar·y /ˈvälənˌterē/ ▶ **adj.** done, given, or acting of one's own free will: *we are funded by voluntary contributions.* ■ working, done, or maintained without payment: *a voluntary helper.* ■ supported by contributions rather than taxes or fees: *voluntary hospitals.* ■ Physiology under the conscious control of the brain. ■ Law (of a conveyance or disposition) made without return in money or other consideration.
▶ **n.** (pl. **voluntaries**) an organ solo played before, during, or after a church service. ■ historical a piece of music performed extempore, esp. as a prelude to other music, or composed in a free style.
– DERIVATIVES **vol·un·tar·i·ness n.**
– ORIGIN late Middle English: from Old French *volontaire* or Latin *voluntarius*, from *voluntas* 'will.'

vol·un·tar·y·ism /ˈvälənˌterēˌizəm/ ▶ **n.** less common term for VOLUNTARISM (sense 1).
– DERIVATIVES **vol·un·tar·y·ist n.**

vol·un·teer /ˌvälənˈtir/ ▶ **n.** a person who freely offers to take part in an enterprise or undertake a task. ■ a person who works for an organization without being paid. ■ a person who freely enrolls for military service rather than being conscripted, esp. a member of a force formed by voluntary enrollment and distinct from the regular army. ■ a plant that has not been deliberately planted. ■ Law a person to whom a voluntary conveyance or deposition is made.
▶ **v.** [no obj.] freely offer to do something: *he volunteered for the job* | [with infinitive] *I rashly volunteered to be a contestant.* ■ [with obj.] offer (help) in such a way: *he volunteered his services as a driver for the convoy.* ■ [reporting verb] say or suggest something without being asked: [with obj.] *it never paid to volunteer information* | [with direct speech] *"Her name's Louise," Christina volunteered.* ■ work for an organization without being paid. ■ [with obj.] commit (someone) to a particular undertaking, typically without consulting them: *he was volunteered for parachute training by friends.*
– ORIGIN late 16th cent. (as a noun, with military reference): from French *volontaire* 'voluntary.' The change in the ending was due to association with -EER.

vol·un·teer·ism /ˌvälənˈti(ə)rˌizəm/ ▶ **n.** the use or involvement of volunteer labor, esp. in community services.

Vol·un·teer State a nickname for the state of TENNESSEE.

vo·lup·tu·ar·y /vəˈləpCHo͞oˌerē/ ▶ **n.** (pl. **voluptuaries**) a person devoted to luxury and sensual pleasure.
▶ **adj.** concerned with luxury and sensual pleasure: *a voluptuary decade when high living was in style.*
– ORIGIN early 17th cent.: from Latin *volupt(u)arius*, from *voluptas* 'pleasure.'

vo·lup·tu·ous /vəˈləpCHəwəs/ ▶ **adj.** of, relating to, or characterized by luxury or sensual pleasure: *long curtains in voluptuous crimson velvet.* ■ (of a woman) curvaceous and sexually attractive.
– DERIVATIVES **vo·lup·tu·ous·ly adv.**, **vo·lup·tu·ous·ness n.**
– ORIGIN late Middle English: from Old French *voluptueux* or Latin *voluptuosus*, from *voluptas* 'pleasure.'

vo·lute /vəˈlo͞ot/ ▶ **n.**
1 Architecture a spiral scroll characteristic of Ionic capitals and also used in Corinthian and composite capitals.
2 a deep-water marine mollusk with a thick spiral shell that is colorful and prized by collectors. ● Family Volutidae, class Gastropoda: *Voluta* and other genera.
▶ **adj.** forming a spiral curve or curves: *spoked wheels with outside volute springs.*
– DERIVATIVES **vo·lut·ed adj.**
– ORIGIN mid 16th cent.: from French, or from Latin *voluta*, feminine past participle of *volvere* 'to roll.'

volute 1

vo·lu·tion /vəˈlo͞oSHən/ ▶ **n. 1** literary a rolling or revolving motion.
2 a single turn of a spiral or coil.
– ORIGIN late 15th cent.; from late Latin *volutio(n-)*, from Latin *volut-* 'rolled,' from the verb *volvere*.

vol·va /ˈvälvə, ˈvôl-/ ▶ **n.** Botany (in certain fungi) a veil that encloses the fruiting body, often persisting after rupture as a sheath at the base of the stalk.
– ORIGIN mid 18th cent.: modern Latin, from Latin *volvere* 'to roll, wrap around.'

vol·vox /ˈvälˌväks, ˈvôl-/ ▶ **n.** Biology a green, single-celled aquatic organism that forms minute, free-swimming spherical colonies. ● Genus *Volvox*, division Chlorophyta (or phylum Chlorophyta, kingdom Protista).
– ORIGIN modern Latin, from Latin *volvere* 'to roll.'

vol·vu·lus /ˈvälvyələs, ˈvôl-/ ▶ **n.** (pl. **volvuli** /-ˌlī, -ˌlē/ or **volvuluses**) Medicine an obstruction caused by twisting of the stomach or intestine.
– ORIGIN late 17th cent.: modern or medieval Latin, from Latin *volvere* 'to roll.'

Volzh·sky /ˈvôlSH(s)kē/ an industrial city in southwestern Russia, on the Volga River; pop. 306,400 (est. 2008).

vo·mer /ˈvōmər/ ▶ **n.** Anatomy the small thin bone separating the left and right nasal cavities in humans and most other vertebrates.
– ORIGIN early 18th cent.: from Latin, literally 'plowshare' (because of the shape).

vom·it /ˈvämət/ ▶ **v.** (**vomits, vomiting, vomited**) [no obj.] eject matter from the stomach through the mouth: *the sickly stench made him want to vomit* | [with obj.] *she used to vomit up her food.* ■ [with obj.] emit (something) in an uncontrolled stream or flow: *the machine vomited fold after fold of paper.*
▶ **n. 1** matter vomited from the stomach.
2 archaic an emetic.
– DERIVATIVES **vom·it·er n.**
– ORIGIN late Middle English: from Old French *vomite* (noun) or Latin *vomitus*, from *vomere* 'to vomit.'

vom·i·to·ri·um /ˌväməˈtôrēəm/ ▶ **n.** (pl. **vomitoria** /-ˈtôrēə/) **1** each of a series of entrance or exit passages in an ancient Roman amphitheater or theater.
2 a place in which, according to popular misconception, the ancient Romans are supposed to have vomited during feasts to make room for more food.
– ORIGIN Latin.

vom·i·to·ry /ˈväməˌtôrē/ ▶ **adj. 1** denoting the entrance or exit passages in a theater or amphitheater.
2 rare relating to or inducing vomiting.
▶ **n.** (pl. **vomitories**) another term for VOMITORIUM (sense 1).
– ORIGIN early 17th cent.: from Latin *vomitorius*, based on *vomere* 'to vomit,' partly as an Anglicization of Latin *vomitorium* (see VOMITORIUM).

vom·i·tous /ˈvämətəs/ ▶ **adj.** nauseating.

vom·i·tus /ˈvämətəs/ ▶ **n.** chiefly Medicine matter that has been vomited.
– ORIGIN early 20th cent.: from Latin.

von Braun /vän ˈbrôn, fôn ˈbroun/ see BRAUN[3].

Von·ne·gut /ˈvänigət/, Kurt, Jr. (1922–2007), US novelist and short-story writer. His works blend elements of realism, science fiction, fantasy, and satire and include *Cat's Cradle* (1963), *Slaughterhouse-Five* (1969), and *Hocus Pocus* (1991).

von Neu·mann /vän ˈnoiˌmän, -mən/ see NEUMANN.

von Reck·ling·hau·sen's dis·ease /ˌvän ˈrekliNGˌhouzənz/ ▶ **n. 1** a hereditary disease in which numerous benign tumors develop in various parts of the body, esp. the skin and the fibrous sheaths of the nerves. It is a form of neurofibromatosis.
2 a disease in which the bones are weakened as a result of excessive secretion of the parathyroid hormone, leading to bowing and fracture of long bones and sometimes deformities of the chest and spine. Also called OSTEITIS FIBROSA CYSTICA (see OSTEITIS).
– ORIGIN early 20th cent.: named after Friedrich *von Recklinghausen* (1833–1910), German pathologist.

von Stern·berg /vän ˈstərnˌbərg/, Josef (1894–1969), US movie director, born in Austria. His best-known movie *Der Blaue Engel* (1930; *The Blue Angel*) made Marlene Dietrich an international star. His Hollywood movies with Dietrich include *Dishonored* (1931) and *Shanghai Express* (1932).

von Wil·le·brand's dis·ease /ˌvän ˈviləˌbränts/ ▶ **n.** Medicine an inherited disorder characterized by a tendency to bleed, caused by deficiency or abnormality of a plasma coagulation factor (**von Willebrand factor**).
– ORIGIN 1940s: named after Erik A. *von Willebrand* (1870–1949), Finnish physician.

voo·doo /ˈvo͞oˌdo͞o/ ▶ **n.** a black religious cult practiced in the Caribbean and the southern US, combining elements of Roman Catholic ritual with traditional African magical and religious rites, and characterized by sorcery and spirit possession. ■ a person skilled in such practice.
▶ **v.** (**voodoos, voodooing, voodooed**) [with obj.] affect (someone) by the practice of such witchcraft.
– DERIVATIVES **voo·doo·ism** /-ˌizəm/ **n.**, **voo·doo·ist** /-ist/ **n.**
– ORIGIN early 19th cent.: from Louisiana French, from Kwa *vodũ*.

Voor·trek·ker /ˈfo͝orˌtrekər, ˈfôr-/ ▶ **n.** S. African historical a member of one of the groups of Dutch-speaking people who migrated by wagon from the Cape Colony into the interior from 1836 onward, in order to live beyond the borders of British rule.
– ORIGIN Afrikaans, from Dutch *voor* 'fore' + *trekken* 'to travel.'

VOR ▶ **abbr.** visual omnirange, denoting a type of navigation system using a series of radio beacons.

-vora ▶ **comb. form** in names of groups corresponding to adjectives ending in *-vorous* (such as *Insectivora* corresponding to *insectivorous*).

vo·ra·cious /vəˈrāSHəs/ ▶ **adj.** wanting or devouring great quantities of food: *he had a voracious appetite.* ■ having a very eager approach to an activity: *his voracious reading of literature.*
– DERIVATIVES **vo·ra·cious·ly adv.**, **vo·ra·cious·ness n.**, **vo·rac·i·ty** /-ˈrasitē/ **n.**
– ORIGIN mid 17th cent.: from Latin *vorax, vorac-* (from *vorare* 'devour') + -IOUS.

-vore ▶ **comb. form** in names of members of groups corresponding to adjectives ending in *-vorous* (such as *detritivore* corresponding to *detritivorous*).

Vo·ro·nezh /vəˈrôniSH, -ˈrō-/ a city in Russia, south of Moscow; pop. 839,900 (est. 2008).

Vo·ro·shi·lov·grad /vərəˈshēləvˌgräd, ˌvôrə-/ former name (1935–58; and 1970–91) for LUHANSK.
– ORIGIN named in honor of Marshal Kliment *Voroshilov* (1881–1969), Soviet military and political leader.

-vorous ▶ **comb. form** feeding on a specified food: *carnivorous* | *herbivorous.*
– ORIGIN from Latin *-vorus* (from *vorare* 'devour') + -OUS.

Vor·stel·lung /ˈfôrˌSHteło͝oNG/ ▶ **n.** (pl. **Vorstellungen** /-ˌSHtelo͝oNGən/) Philosophy a mental

image or idea produced by prior perception of an object, as in memory or imagination, rather than by actual perception.
– ORIGIN German.

vor·tal /ˈvôrtl/ ▶ **n.** an Internet site that provides a directory of links to information related to a particular industry.
– ORIGIN 1990s: blend of *v(ertical)* (as in *vertical industry*, an industry specializing in a narrow range of goods and services), and *(p)ortal*.

vor·tex /ˈvôrˌteks/ ▶ **n.** (pl. **vortexes** or **vortices** /-təˌsēz/) a mass of whirling fluid or air, esp. a whirlpool or whirlwind: *we were caught in a vortex of water* | figurative *a swirling vortex of emotions*. ■ something regarded as a whirling mass: *the vortex of existence*.
– DERIVATIVES **vor·ti·cal** /ˈvôrtikəl/ **adj.**, **vor·ti·cal·ly** /ˈvôrtik(ə)lē/ **adv.**, **vor·tic·i·ty** /vôrˈtisitē/ **n.**, **vor·ti·cose** /ˈvôrtəˌkōs/ **adj.**, **vor·tic·u·lar** /vôrˈtikyələr/ **adj.**
– ORIGIN mid 17th cent.: from Latin *vortex, vortic-*, literally 'eddy,' variant of **VERTEX**.

vor·ti·cel·la /ˌvôrtəˈselə/ ▶ **n.** Zoology a sedentary, single-celled aquatic animal with a contractile stalk and a bell-shaped body bearing a ring of cilia. ● Genus *Vorticella*, phylum Ciliophora, kingdom Protista.
– ORIGIN late 18th cent.: modern Latin, diminutive of Latin *vortex, vortic-* 'eddy.'

Vor·ti·cist /ˈvôrtəsist/ ▶ **n.** historical a member of a British artistic movement of 1914–15 influenced by cubism and futurism and favoring machinelike forms.
– DERIVATIVES **Vor·ti·cism** /-ˌsizəm/ **n.**
– ORIGIN from Latin *vortex, vortic-* 'eddy' + **-IST**.

Vosges /vōzh/ a mountain system in eastern France, in Alsace near the border with Germany.

Vos·tok /ˈväsˌtäk, ˌvəˈstôk/ a series of six manned Soviet orbiting spacecraft, the first of which, launched in April 1961, carried the first man in space (Yuri Gagarin).

vo·ta·ry /ˈvōtərē/ ▶ **n.** (pl. **votaries**) a person, such as a monk or nun, who has made vows of dedication to religious service. ■ a devoted follower, adherent, or advocate of someone or something: *he was a votary of John Keats*.
– DERIVATIVES **vo·ta·rist** /-rist/ **n.**
– ORIGIN mid 16th cent.: from Latin *vot-* 'vowed' (from the verb *vovere*) + **-ARY**¹.

vote /vōt/ ▶ **n.** a formal indication of a choice between two or more candidates or courses of action, expressed typically through a ballot or a show of hands or by voice. ■ an act of expressing such an indication of choice: *they are ready to put it to a vote*. ■ (**the vote**) the choice expressed collectively by a body of electors or by a specified group: *the Republican vote in Florida*. ■ (**the vote**) the right to indicate a choice in an election.
▶ **v.** [no obj.] give or register a vote: *they voted against the resolution* | [with complement] *I voted Republican*. ■ [with obj. or complement] cause (someone) to gain or lose a particular post or honor by means of a vote: *incompetent judges are voted out of office*. ■ [with clause] informal used to express a wish to follow a particular course of action: *I vote we have one more game*. ■ [with obj.] (of a legislature) grant or confer by vote. ■ [with obj.] (**vote something down**) reject (something) by means of a vote.
– PHRASES **vote of confidence** a vote showing that a majority continues to support the policy of a leader or governing body. **vote of no confidence** (or **vote of censure**) a vote showing that a majority does not support the policy of a leader or governing body. **vote with one's feet** informal indicate an opinion by being present or absent.
– DERIVATIVES **vote·less adj.**
– ORIGIN late Middle English: from Latin *votum* 'a vow, wish,' from *vovere* 'to vow.' The verb dates from the mid 16th cent.

vot·er /ˈvōtər/ ▶ **n.** a person who votes or has the right to vote at an election.

vot·ing booth ▶ **n.** a compartment with one open side in which one voter at a time stands to mark their ballot.

vot·ing ma·chine ▶ **n.** a machine for the automatic registering of votes.

vo·tive /ˈvōtiv/ ▶ **adj.** offered or consecrated in fulfillment of a vow: *votive offerings*.
▶ **n.** an object offered in this way, such as a candle used as a vigil light.
– ORIGIN late 16th cent.: from Latin *votivus*, from *votum* (see **VOTE**). The original sense was 'expressing a desire,' preserved in **VOTIVE MASS**.

vo·tive Mass ▶ **n.** (in the Roman Catholic Church) a Mass celebrated for a special purpose or occasion.

vouch /vouch/ ▶ **v.** [no obj.] (**vouch for**) assert or confirm as a result of one's own experience that something is true or accurately so described: *they say New York is the city that never sleeps, and I can certainly* ***vouch for*** *that*. ■ confirm that someone is who they say they are or that they are of good character: *he was refused entrance until someone could vouch for him*.
– ORIGIN Middle English (as a legal term in the sense 'summon (a person) to court to prove title to property'): from Old French *voucher* 'summon,' based on Latin *vocare* 'to call.'

vouch·er /ˈvouchər/ ▶ **n.** a small printed piece of paper that entitles the holder to a discount or that may be exchanged for goods or services. ■ a receipt.
– ORIGIN early 17th cent.: from **VOUCH**.

vouch·safe /vouchˈsāf, ˈvouchˌsāf/ ▶ **v.** [with two objs.] give or grant (something) to (someone) in a gracious or condescending manner: *it is a blessing vouchsafed him by heaven*. ■ [with obj.] reveal or disclose (information): *you'd never vouchsafed that interesting tidbit before*.
– ORIGIN Middle English: originally as the phrase *vouch* something *safe* on someone, i.e., 'warrant the secure conferment of (something on someone).'

vous·soir /vo͞oˈswär/ ▶ **n.** Architecture a wedge-shaped or tapered stone used to construct an arch.
– ORIGIN early 18th cent: via French from popular Latin *volsorium*, based on Latin *volvere* 'to roll.' The word, borrowed from Old French, was also used for a time in late Middle English.

Vou·vray /vo͞oˈvrā/ ▶ **n.** dry white wine, either still or sparkling, produced in the Vouvray district of the Loire valley.
– ORIGIN French.

vow /vou/ ▶ **n.** a solemn promise. ■ (**vows**) a set of such promises committing one to a prescribed role, calling, or course of action, typically to marriage or a monastic career.
▶ **v. 1** [reporting verb] solemnly promise to do a specified thing: [with clause] *he vowed that his government would not tolerate a repeat of the disorder* | [with direct speech] *one fan vowed, "I'll picket every home game."*
2 [with obj.] archaic dedicate to someone or something, esp. a deity: *I* ***vowed myself to*** *this enterprise*.
– ORIGIN Middle English: from Old French *vou*, from Latin *votum* (see **VOTE**); the verb from Old French *vouer*.

vow·el /ˈvouəl/ ▶ **n.** a speech sound that is produced by comparatively open configuration of the vocal tract, with vibration of the vocal cords but without audible friction and is a unit of the sound system of a language that forms the nucleus of a syllable. Contrasted with **CONSONANT**. ■ a letter representing such a sound, such as *a, e, i, o, u*.
– DERIVATIVES **vow·eled** /ˈvou(ə)ld/ (Brit. **vowelled**) **adj.** [usu. in combination], **vow·el·less adj.**
– ORIGIN Middle English: from Old French *vouel*, from Latin *vocalis (littera)* 'vocal (letter).'

vow·el gra·da·tion ▶ **n.** another term for **ABLAUT**.

vow·el har·mo·ny ▶ **n.** the phenomenon in some languages, e.g., Turkish, in which all the vowels in a word are members of the same subclass, for example all front vowels or all back vowels.

vow·el height ▶ **n.** Phonetics the degree to which the tongue is raised or lowered in the articulation of a particular vowel.

vow·el·ize /ˈvouəˌlīz/ ▶ **v.** [with obj.] supply (something such as a Hebrew or shorthand text) with vowel points or signs representing vowels.

vow·el point ▶ **n.** each of a set of marks indicating vowels in writing phonetically explicit text in Semitic languages such as Hebrew and Arabic.

vow·el shift ▶ **n.** Phonetics a phonetic change in a vowel or vowels. ■ (**the Great Vowel Shift**) a series of changes between medieval and modern English affecting the long vowels of the standard language.

vox /väks/ ▶ **n.** (esp. in music journalism) vocals; voice: *the barely-there falsetto vox*.
– DERIVATIVES **-voxed adj.**
– ORIGIN 1980s: shortened from *vocals*, probably after Latin *vox* 'voice.'

vox an·gel·i·ca /ˈväks anˈjelikə/ ▶ **n.** a soft stop on an organ or harmonium that is tuned slightly sharp to produce a tremolo effect.
– ORIGIN mid 19th cent.: from late Latin, literally 'angelic voice.'

vox·el /ˈväksəl/ ▶ **n.** (in computer-based modeling or graphic simulation) each of an array of elements of volume that constitute a notional three-dimensional space, esp. each of an array of discrete elements into which a representation of a three-dimensional object is divided.
– ORIGIN 1970s: from the initial letters of **VOLUME** and **ELEMENT**, with the insertion of *-x-* for ease of pronunciation.

vox hu·ma·na /ˈväks (h)yo͞oˈmänə, -ˈmanə, -ˈmānə/ ▶ **n.** an organ stop with a tone supposedly resembling the human voice.
– ORIGIN early 18th cent.: from Latin, literally 'human voice.'

vox po·pu·li /ˈväks ˈpäpyəˌlī, -ˌlē/ ▶ **n.** [in sing.] the opinions or beliefs of the majority.
– ORIGIN mid 16th cent.: from Latin, literally 'the people's voice.'

voy·age /ˈvoi-ij/ ▶ **n.** a long journey involving travel by sea or in space: *a six-year voyage to Jupiter* | figurative *writing a biography is a* ***voyage of discovery***.
▶ **v.** [no obj.] go on a long journey, typically by sea or in space: *he has voyaged through places like Venezuela and Peru*. ■ [with obj.] archaic sail over or along (a sea or river).
– DERIVATIVES **voy·age·a·ble adj.** (archaic), **voy·ag·er n.**
– ORIGIN Middle English (as a noun denoting a journey): from Old French *voiage*, from Latin *viaticum* 'provisions for a journey' (in late Latin 'journey').

Voy·ag·er /ˈvoi-ijər/ either of two American space probes launched in 1977 to investigate the outer planets. Voyager 1 encountered Jupiter and Saturn, while Voyager 2 reached Jupiter, Saturn, Uranus, and finally Neptune (1989).

vo·ya·geur /ˌvwäyəˈzhər, ˌvoi-ə-/ ▶ **n.** historical (esp. in Canada) a boatman employed by the fur companies in transporting goods and passengers to and from trading posts.
– ORIGIN French, literally 'voyager,' from *voyager* 'to travel.'

Vo·ya·geurs National Park /ˌvwäyəˈzhərz, ˌvoi-ə-/ a preserve in northern Minnesota, along the Canadian border, whose name recalls the French fur traders of the 18th century.

vo·yeur /voiˈyər, vwä-/ ▶ **n.** a person who gains sexual pleasure from watching others when they are naked or engaged in sexual activity. ■ a person who enjoys seeing the pain or distress of others.
– DERIVATIVES **vo·yeur·ism** /ˈvoiyəˌrizəm, voiˈyərˌizəm, vwäˈyər-/ **n.**, **voy·eur·is·tic** /ˌvoiyəˈristik, ˌvwäyə-/ **adj.**, **voy·eur·is·ti·cal·ly adv.**
– ORIGIN early 20th cent.: from French, from *voir* 'see.'

VP ▶ **abbr.** Vice President.

VPL ▶ **abbr.** ■ visible programming language. ■ informal visible panty line.

VPN ▶ **abbr.** Computing virtual private network.

VR ▶ **abbr.** ■ Queen Victoria. [abbreviation of Latin *Victoria Regina*.] ■ variant reading. ■ virtual reality.

VRAM /ˈvēˌram/ ▶ **n.** Electronics a type of RAM used in computer display cards.
– ORIGIN 1990s: abbreviation of *video RAM*.

VRML ▶ **abbr.** Computing virtual reality modeling language.

vroom /vro͞om, vro͝om/ informal ▶ **v.** [no obj.] (of a vehicle or its engine) make a roaring sound when traveling or running at high speed. ■ [with obj.] cause (an engine in a vehicle) to make such a sound in this way.
▶ **n.** the roaring sound of an engine or motor vehicle.
▶ **exclam.** used to express or imitate such a sound to suggest speed or acceleration: *press the ignition button and vroom!*
– ORIGIN 1960s: imitative.

VS ▶ **abbr.** Veterinary Surgeon.

vs. ▶ **abbr.** versus.

V-sign ▶ **n. 1** a sign resembling the letter V made with the palm of the hand facing outward, used as a symbol or gesture of victory.
2 Brit. a similar sign made with the first two fingers pointing up and the back of the hand facing outward, used as a gesture of abuse or contempt.

VSO ▶ **abbr.** Voluntary Service Overseas.

VSOP ▶ **abbr.** Very Special Old Pale, a kind of brandy.

VT ▶ **abbr.** Vermont (in official postal use).

Vt. ▶ **abbr.** Vermont.

VTO ▶ **abbr.** vertical takeoff.

VTOL /ˈvēˌtäl, -ˌtôl/ ▶ **abbr.** vertical takeoff and landing.

VTR ▶ **abbr.** videotape recorder.

vug /vəg/ ▶ **n.** Geology a cavity in rock, lined with mineral crystals.
– DERIVATIVES **vug·gy** /ˈvəgē/ **adj.**, **vug·u·lar** /ˈvəgyələr/ **adj.**
– ORIGIN early 19th cent.: from Cornish *vooga*.

V

Vuil·lard /vwē'yär/, (Jean) Édouard (1868–1940), French painter and graphic artist. A member of the Nabi Group, he produced decorative panels, murals, paintings, and lithographs, particularly of domestic interiors and portraits.

Vul·can /'vəlkən/ Roman Mythology the god of fire. Greek equivalent **Hephaestus**.

Vul·ca·ni·an /,vəl'kānēən/ ▶ **adj. 1** associated with the god Vulcan. ■ (also **vulcanian**) associated with metalworking or metallurgy.
2 (also **vulcanian**) Geology relating to or denoting a type of volcanic eruption marked by periodic explosive events. [early 20th cent.: from *Vulcano*, the name of a volcano in the Lipari Islands, Italy, + **-ian**.]

vul·can·ism /'vəlkə,nizəm/ ▶ **n.** variant spelling of **volcanism**.

vul·can·ite /'vəlkə,nīt/ ▶ **n.** hard black vulcanized rubber.
– ORIGIN mid 19th cent.: from **Vulcan** + **-ite**[1].

vul·can·ize /'vəlkə,nīz/ ▶ **v.** [with obj.] harden (rubber or rubberlike material) by treating it with sulfur at a high temperature.
– DERIVATIVES **vul·can·iz·a·ble adj.**, **vul·can·i·za·tion** /,vəlkənə'zāsHən/ **n.**, **vul·can·iz·er n.**
– ORIGIN early 19th cent. (in the sense 'throw into a fire'): from **Vulcan** + **-ize**.

vul·can·ol·o·gy /,vəlkə'näləjē/ ▶ **n.** variant spelling of **volcanology**.

Vulg. ▶ **abbr.** Vulgate.

vul·gar /'vəlgər/ ▶ **adj.** lacking sophistication or good taste; unrefined: *the vulgar trappings of wealth.* ■ making explicit and offensive reference to sex or bodily functions; coarse and rude: *a vulgar joke.* ■ dated characteristic of or belonging to the masses.
– DERIVATIVES **vul·gar·i·ty** /,vəl'garitē/ **n.** (pl. **vulgarities**), **vul·gar·ly adv.**
– ORIGIN late Middle English: from Latin *vulgaris*, from *vulgus* 'common people.' The original sense was 'used in ordinary calculations' (surviving in **vulgar fraction**) and 'in ordinary use, used by the people' (surviving in **vulgar Latin** and **vulgar tongue**).

vul·gar frac·tion ▶ **n.** British term for **common fraction**.

vul·gar·i·an /,vəl'ge(ə)rēən/ ▶ **n.** an unrefined person, esp. one with newly acquired power or wealth.

vul·gar·ism /'vəlgə,rizəm/ ▶ **n.** a word or expression that is considered inelegant, esp. one that makes explicit and offensive reference to sex or bodily functions. ■ archaic an instance of rude or offensive behavior.

vul·gar·ize /'vəlgə,rīz/ ▶ **v.** [with obj.] make less refined: *her voice, vulgarized by its accent, was full of caressing tones.* ■ make commonplace or less subtle or complex: (as adj. **vulgarized**) *a vulgarized version of the argument.*
– DERIVATIVES **vul·gar·i·za·tion** /,vəlgərə'zāsHən/ **n.**

vul·gar Lat·in ▶ **n.** informal Latin of classical times.

vul·gar tongue ▶ **n.** (**the vulgar tongue**) dated the national or vernacular language of a people (used typically to contrast such a language with Latin).

Vul·gate /'vəl,gāt, -gət/ ▶ **n. 1** the principal Latin version of the Bible, prepared mainly by St. Jerome in the late 4th century, and (as revised in 1592) adopted as the official text for the Roman Catholic Church. ■ (**vulgate**) a commonly recognized text or edition, as of the *Iliad*.
2 (**vulgate**) [in sing.] common or colloquial speech: *I required a new, formal language in which to address him, not the vulgate.*
– ORIGIN from Latin *vulgata* (*editio*) '(edition) prepared for the public,' feminine past participle of *vulgare*, from *vulgus* 'common people.'

vuln[1] /vəln/ ▶ **v.** [with obj.] Heraldry wound.
– ORIGIN late 16th cent.: formed irregularly from Latin *vulnerare* 'to wound.'

vuln[2] ▶ **n.** a vulnerability, esp. one associated with computer security: *the total of 10 vulns discovered are described as highly critical.*

vul·ner·a·ble /'vəln(ə)rəbəl/ ▶ **adj.** susceptible to physical or emotional attack or harm: *we were in a vulnerable position | small fish are vulnerable to predators.* ■ Bridge (of a partnership) liable to higher penalties, either by convention or through having won one game toward a rubber.
– DERIVATIVES **vul·ner·a·bil·i·ty** /,vəln(ə)rə'bilitē/ **n.** (pl. **vulnerabilities**), **vul·ner·a·ble·ness n.**, **vul·ner·a·bly** /-blē/ **adv.**
– ORIGIN early 17th cent.: from late Latin *vulnerabilis*, from Latin *vulnerare* 'to wound,' from *vulnus* 'wound.'

vul·ner·ar·y /'vəlnə,rerē/ archaic ▶ **adj.** (of a drug, plant, etc.) of use in the healing of wounds.
▶ **n.** (pl. **vulneraries**) a medicine of this kind.
– ORIGIN late 16th cent.: from Latin *vulnerarius*, from *vulnus* 'wound.'

Vul·pec·u·la /,vəl'pekyələ/ Astronomy an inconspicuous northern constellation (the Fox), lying in the Milky Way between Cygnus and Aquila. ■ (as genitive **Vulpeculae** /,vəl'pekyəlē/) used with a preceding letter or numeral to designate a star in this constellation: *the star Alpha Vulpeculae.*
– ORIGIN Latin, diminutive of *vulpes* 'fox.'

vul·pine /'vəl,pīn/ ▶ **adj.** of or relating to a fox or foxes. ■ crafty; cunning: *Karl gave a vulpine smile.*
– ORIGIN early 17th cent.: from Latin *vulpinus*, from *vulpes* 'fox.'

vul·ture /'vəlCHər/ ▶ **n. 1** a large bird of prey with the head and neck more or less bare of feathers, feeding chiefly on carrion and reputed to gather with others in anticipation of the death of a sick or injured animal or person. ● Order Accipitriformes: the **Old World vultures** (family Accipitridae, esp. *Gyps* and *Aegypius*) and the **New World vultures** (with the condors in the family Cathartidae).
2 a contemptible person who preys on or exploits others.
– DERIVATIVES **vul·tur·ine** /-,rīn/ **adj.**, **vul·tur·ish adj.**, **vul·tur·ous** /-CHərəs/ **adj.**
– ORIGIN late Middle English: from Anglo-Norman French *vultur*, from Latin *vulturius*.

vul·ture fund ▶ **n.** Finance a fund that invests in companies or properties that are performing poorly and may therefore be undervalued.

vul·va /'vəlvə/ ▶ **n.** Anatomy the female external genitals. ■ Zoology the external opening of the vagina or reproductive tract in a female mammal or nematode.
– DERIVATIVES **vul·val adj.**, **vul·var adj.**
– ORIGIN late Middle English: from Latin, literally 'womb.'

vul·vi·tis /,vəl'vītis/ ▶ **n.** Medicine inflammation of the vulva.

vul·vo·vag·in·i·tis /,vəlvō,vajə'nītis/ ▶ **n.** inflammation of the vulva and vagina.

vv. ▶ **abbr.** ■ verses. ■ volumes.

Vyat·ka /'vyätkə, vē'ät-/ an industrial town in western Russia, in the central part of European Russia, on the Vyatka River; pop. 464,500 (est. 2008). Former name (1934–92) **Kirov**.

vy·ing /'vī-iNG/ present participle of **vie**.

Ww

¹ /ˈdəbəlˌyo͞o/ (also **w**) ▶ **n.** (pl. **Ws** or **W's**) **1** the twenty-third letter of the alphabet. ■ denoting the next after V in a set of items, categories, etc. **2** a shape like that of a letter W: [in combination] *the W-shaped northern constellation of Cassiopeia.*

² ▶ **abbr.** ■ Wales. ■ Baseball WALK (sense 3 of the noun). ■ warden. ■ (in tables of sports results) games won. ■ watt(s). ■ Wednesday. ■ week. ■ **(w)** weight. ■ Welsh. ■ West or Western: *104° W | W Europe.* ■ (in personal ads) White. ■ Cricket (on scorecards) wicket(s). ■ width: *23 in. H x 20.5 in. W x 16 in. D.* ■ (in personal ads) widowed. ■ (in genealogies) wife. ■ (in shortwave transmissions) with. ■ women's (clothes size). ■ Physics work. ▶ **symbol** the chemical element tungsten. [from modern Latin *wolframium.*]

A ▶ **abbr.** ■ Washington (State) (in official postal use). ■ Western Australia.

a /wä/ ▶ **n.** (pl. **same** or **Was**) **1** a member of a hill people living on the border between China and Burma (Myanmar). **2** the Mon-Khmer language of this people. **adj.** of, relating to, or denoting this people or their language.

aac /wak/ ▶ **n.** a member of the Women's Army Auxiliary Corps (later the WAC) formed in 1942, now no longer a separate branch. ORIGIN acronym.

aadt /vät/ German name for **VAUD.**

aal /väl/ a river in the south central Netherlands. The more southern of two major distributaries of the Rhine River, it flows for 52 miles (84 km) from the point where the Rhine forks, just west of the border with Germany, to the estuary of the Meuse (Maas) River on the North Sea.

a·bash Riv·er /ˈwôˌbash/ a river that flows for 475 miles (765 km) from western Ohio across Indiana and then along the Indiana-Illinois border to the Ohio River.

a·bi /ˈwäbē/ ▶ **n.** (in Japanese art) a quality of austere and serene beauty expressing a mood of spiritual solitude recognized in Zen Buddhist philosophy. ORIGIN Japanese, literally 'solitude.'

AC /wak/ ▶ **abbr.** ■ Women's Army Corps. See **WAAC.** ■ (also **Wac**) a member of the Women's Army Corps.

ack /wak/ informal ▶ **adj.** bad; inferior: *a wack radio station.* **n. 1** a crazy or eccentric person. **2** worthless or stupid ideas, work, or talk; rubbish: *this track is a load of wack.* ORIGIN 1930s: probably a back-formation from **WACKY.**

ack·e /ˈwakə/ ▶ **n.** Geology a sandstone of which the mud matrix in which the grains are embedded amounts to between 15 and 75 percent of the mass. ORIGIN early 19th cent.: from German, from Middle High German *wacke* 'large stone,' Old High German *wacko* 'pebble.'

acked ▶ **adj.** variant spelling of **WHACKED.**

ack·o /ˈwakō/ (also **whacko**) informal ▶ **adj.** mad; insane: *his willingness to pursue every wacko idea that enters his mind.* **n.** (pl. **wackos**) a crazy person. ORIGIN 1970s: from **WACKY** + **-O.**

ack·y /ˈwakē/ (also **whacky**) ▶ **adj.** (**wackier, wackiest**) informal funny or amusing in a slightly odd or peculiar way: *a wacky chase movie.* DERIVATIVES **wack·i·ly** /ˈwakəlē/ **adv.**, **wack·i·ness n.**

– ORIGIN mid 19th cent. (originally dialect): from the noun **WHACK** + **-Y¹.**

Wa·co /ˈwākō/ a commercial and industrial city in east central Texas; pop. 124,009 (est. 2008).

wad /wäd/ ▶ **n. 1** a lump or bundle of a soft material, used for padding, stuffing, or wiping: *a wad of cotton.* ■ chiefly historical a disk of felt or another material used to keep powder or shot in place in a gun barrel. ■ a portion of chewing gum, or of tobacco or a narcotic when used for chewing. **2** a bundle of paper, banknotes, or documents: *a thick wad of index cards.* ■ informal a large amount of something, esp. money: *she was working on TV and had wads of money.*
▶ **v.** (**wads, wadding, wadded**) [with obj.] (usu. as adj. **wadded**) **1** compress (a soft material) into a lump or bundle: *a wadded handkerchief.* **2** stop up (an aperture or a gun barrel) with a bundle or lump of soft material: *he had something wadded behind his teeth.* ■ line or stuff (a garment or piece of furniture) with wadding: *a wadded sheepskin coat.*
– PHRASES **shoot one's wad** spend all one's money. [originally, to fire one's gun with only the wad for a projectile when one's ammunition is exhausted.]
– ORIGIN mid 16th cent. (denoting wadding): perhaps related to Dutch *watten,* French *ouate* 'padding, absorbent cotton.'

wad·cut·ter /ˈwädˌkətər/ ▶ **n.** a bullet designed to cut a neat hole in a paper range target.

wad·ding /ˈwädiNG/ ▶ **n.** soft, thick material used to line garments or pack fragile items, esp. absorbent cotton. ■ a material from which wads for guns are made.

wad·dle /ˈwädl/ ▶ **v.** [no obj.] walk with short steps and a clumsy swaying motion: *three geese waddled across the road.*
▶ **n.** [in sing.] a waddling gait: *I walk with a waddle.*
– DERIVATIVES **wad·dler** /ˈwädlər, ˈwädl-ər/ **n.**
– ORIGIN late 16th cent.: perhaps a frequentative of **WADE.**

wad·dy /ˈwädē/ ▶ **n.** (pl. **waddies**) an Australian Aboriginal's war club. ■ Austral./NZ a club or stick, esp. a walking stick.
– ORIGIN from Dharuk *wadi* 'tree, stick, club.'

Wade /wād/, Virginia (1945–), English tennis player; full name *Sarah Virginia Wade.* During 1968–77, she won the women's singles title at the US Open, the Australian Open, and Wimbledon.

wade /wād/ ▶ **v.** [no obj.] walk through water or another liquid or soft substance: *we waded ashore.* ■ [with obj.] walk through (something filled with water): *firefighters waded the waist-deep flood water.* ■ (**wade through**) read laboriously through (a long piece of writing). ■ (**wade into**) informal get involved in (something) vigorously or forcefully: *he waded into the yelling, fighting crowd.* ■ (**wade in**) informal make a vigorous attack or intervention: *Nicola waded in and grabbed the baby.*
▶ **n.** [in sing.] an act of wading.
– DERIVATIVES **wad·a·ble** (also **wadeable**) **adj.**
– ORIGIN Old English *wadan* 'move onward,' also 'penetrate,' from a Germanic word meaning 'go (through),' from an Indo-European root shared by Latin *vadere* 'go,' as in **VADE MECUM.**

Wade–Giles /ˈwād ˈjīlz/ ▶ **n.** a system of romanized spelling for transliterating Chinese, devised by **Sir Thomas Francis Wade** (1818–95) and **Herbert Allen Giles** (1845–1935). It has been largely superseded by Pinyin.

wad·er /ˈwādər/ ▶ **n. 1** a person or animal, esp. a bird, that wades, in particular: ■ a wading bird of the order Ciconiiformes, which comprises the herons, storks, and ibises. ■ chiefly Brit. a wading bird of the order Charadriiformes, which comprises the sandpipers, plovers, and related birds. Also called **SHOREBIRD** (esp. in North America). **2** (**waders**) high waterproof boots, or a waterproof garment for the legs and body, used esp. by anglers when fishing.

wa·di /ˈwädē/ ▶ **n.** (pl. **wadis** /-ēz/) (in certain Arabic-speaking countries) a valley, ravine, or channel that is dry except in the rainy season.
– ORIGIN early 17th cent.: from Arabic *wādī.*

wad·ing pool ▶ **n.** a shallow artificial pool for children to paddle in.

WAF /waf/ ▶ **abbr.** Women in the Air Force.
▶ **n.** a member of the WAF.

wa·fer /ˈwāfər/ ▶ **n.** a very thin, light, crisp, sweet cookie or cracker, esp. one of a kind eaten with ice cream. ■ a thin disk of unleavened bread used in the Eucharist. ■ Electronics a very thin slice of a semiconductor crystal used as the substrate for solid-state circuitry. ■ historical a small disk of dried paste formerly used for fastening letters or holding papers together. ■ a round, thin piece of something: *a wafer of ice.*
▶ **v.** [with obj.] rare fasten or seal (a letter, document, etc.) with a wafer.
– DERIVATIVES **wa·fer·y adj.**
– ORIGIN late Middle English: from an Anglo-Norman French variant of Old French *gaufre* (see **GOFFER**), from Middle Low German *wāfel* 'waffle'; compare with **WAFFLE².**

wa·fer-thin ▶ **adj. & adv.** very thin or thinly: [as adj.] *plates of wafer-thin metal* | [as adv.] *slicing meats wafer-thin.*

Waf·fen SS /ˈväfən/ ▶ **n.** (**the Waffen SS**) the combat units of the SS in Nazi Germany during World War II.
– ORIGIN German *Waffen* 'arms, weapons.'

waf·fle¹ /ˈwäfəl, ˈwô-/ informal ▶ **v.** [no obj.] **1** fail to make up one's mind: *Joseph had been waffling over where to go.* **2** chiefly Brit. speak or write, esp. at great length, without saying anything important or useful: *he waffled on about everything that didn't matter.*
▶ **n. 1** a failure to make up one's mind: *his waffle on abortion.* **2** chiefly Brit. lengthy but trivial or useless talk or writing.
– DERIVATIVES **waf·fler** /ˈwäf(ə)lər, ˈwô-/ **n.**, **waf·fly** /ˈwäf(ə)lē, ˈwô-/ **adj.**
– ORIGIN late 17th cent. (originally in the sense 'yap, yelp'): frequentative of dialect *waff* 'yelp,' of imitative origin.

waf·fle² ▶ **n.** a small crisp batter cake, baked in a waffle iron and eaten hot with butter or syrup.
▶ **adj.** denoting a style of fine honeycomb weaving or a fabric woven to give a honeycomb effect.
– ORIGIN mid 18th cent.: from Dutch *wafel*; compare with **WAFER** and **GOFFER.**

waf·fle i·ron ▶ **n.** a utensil, typically consisting of two shallow metal pans hinged together, used for baking waffles.

waft /wäft, waft/ ▶ **v.** pass or cause to pass easily or gently through or as if through the air: [no obj.] *the smell of stale fat wafted out from the cafe* | [with obj.] *each breeze would waft pollen around the house.*
▶ **n.** a gentle movement of air. ■ a scent or odor carried on such a movement of air.

PRONUNCIATION KEY ə *ago, up;* ər *over, fur;* a *hat;* ā *ate;* ä *car;* e *let;* ē *see;* i *fit;* ī *by;* NG *sing;* ō *go;* ô *law, for;* oi *toy;* o͝o *good;* o͞o *goo;* ou *out;* TH *thin;* T͟H *then;* ZH *vision*

– ORIGIN early 16th cent. (in the sense 'escort (a ship)'): back-formation from obsolete *wafter* 'armed convoy vessel,' from Low German and Dutch *wachter*, from *wachten* 'to guard.' A sense 'convey by water' gave rise to the current use of the verb.

wag[1] /wag/ ▶ **v.** (**wags, wagging, wagged**) (with reference to an animal's tail) move or cause to move rapidly to and fro: [no obj.] *his tail began to wag* | [with obj.] *the dog went out, wagging its tail.* ■ [with obj.] move (an upward-pointing finger) from side to side to signify a warning or reprimand: *she wagged a finger at Elinor.* ■ [no obj.] (used of a tongue, jaw, or chin, as representing a person) talk, esp. in order to gossip or spread rumors: *this is a small island, and tongues are beginning to wag.*
▶ **n.** a single rapid movement from side to side: *a chirpy wag of the head.*
– PHRASES **how the world wags** dated how affairs are going or being conducted. **the tail wags the dog** see TAIL[1].
– ORIGIN Middle English (as a verb): from the Germanic base of Old English *wagian* 'to sway.'

wag[2] ▶ **n.** dated a person who makes facetious jokes.
– ORIGIN mid 16th cent. (denoting a young man or mischievous boy, also used as a term of endearment to an infant): probably from obsolete *waghalter* 'person likely to be hanged' (see WAG[1], HALTER[1]).

wage /wāj/ ▶ **n.** (usu. **wages**) a fixed regular payment, typically paid on a daily or weekly basis, made by an employer to an employee, esp. to a manual or unskilled worker: *we were struggling to get better wages.* Compare with SALARY. ■ (**wages**) Economics the part of total production that is the return to labor as earned income, as distinct from the remuneration received by capital as unearned income. ■ the result or effect of doing something considered wrong or unwise: *the wages of sin is death.*
▶ **v.** [with obj.] carry on (a war or campaign): *it is necessary to destroy their capacity to wage war.*
– ORIGIN Middle English: from Anglo-Norman French and Old Northern French, of Germanic origin; related to GAGE[1] and WED.

wage drift ▶ **n.** Finance the tendency for the average level of wages actually paid to rise above wage rates through increases in overtime and other factors.

wa·ger /'wājər/ ▶ **n. & v.** more formal term for BET.
– ORIGIN Middle English (also in the sense 'solemn pledge'): from Anglo-Norman French *wageure*, from *wager* 'to wage.'

wage slave ▶ **n.** informal a person wholly dependent on income from employment, typically employment of an arduous or menial nature.
– DERIVATIVES **wage slav·er·y n.**

wag·ger·y /'wagərē/ ▶ **n.** (pl. **waggeries**) dated waggish behavior or remarks; jocularity. ■ archaic a waggish action or remark.

wag·gish /'wagiSH/ ▶ **adj.** dated humorous in a playful, mischievous, or facetious manner: *a waggish riposte.*
– DERIVATIVES **wag·gish·ly adv.**, **wag·gish·ness n.**

wag·gle /'wagəl/ ▶ **v.** informal move or cause to move with short quick movements from side to side or up and down: [no obj.] *his arm waggled* | [with obj.] *Mary waggled a glass at them.* ■ [with obj.] swing (a golf club) loosely to and fro over the ball before playing a shot.
▶ **n.** an act of waggling.
– ORIGIN late 16th cent.: frequentative of WAG[1].

wag·gle dance ▶ **n.** a waggling movement performed by a honeybee at the hive or nest, to indicate to other bees the direction and distance of a source of food.

wag·gly /'wag(ə)lē/ ▶ **adj.** moving with quick short movements from side to side or up and down: *a waggly tail.*

Wag·ner[1] /'wagnər/, Honus (1874–1955), US baseball player and coach; full name *John Peter Wagner;* known as the **Flying Dutchman**. Joining the National League in 1897 and playing shortstop for the Pittsburgh Pirates 1900–1917, he was noted for hitting, stealing bases, and speed. Baseball Hall of Fame (1936).

Wag·ner[2] /'vägnər/, Richard (1813–83), German composer; full name *Wilhelm Richard Wagner*. He developed an operatic genre that he called music drama, synthesizing music, drama, verse, legend, and spectacle. Notable works: *The Flying Dutchman* (1841), *Der Ring des Nibelungen* (1847–74), *Tristan and Isolde* (1859), and the *Siegfried Idyll* (1870).

Wag·ne·ri·an /väg'ne(ə)rēən/ ▶ **adj.** of, relating to, or characteristic of the operas of Richard Wagner. ■ having the enormous dramatic scale and intensity of a Wagner opera: *a strategic predicament of positively Wagnerian proportions.*
▶ **n.** an admirer of Wagner or his music.

Wag·ner tu·ba ▶ **n.** a brass instrument of baritone pitch with an oval shape and upward-pointing bell, combining features of the tuba and the French horn and first used in Wagner's *Der Ring des Nibelungen*.

wag·on /'wagən/ (Brit. also **waggon**) ▶ **n.** a vehicle used for transporting goods or another specified purpose: *a coal wagon* | *an ammunition wagon.* ■ a four-wheeled trailer for agricultural use, or a small version of this for use as a child's toy. ■ a horse-drawn vehicle, esp. a covered wagon used by early settlers in North America and elsewhere. ■ a wheeled cart or hut used as a food stall. ■ a small cart or wheeled table used for serving drinks or food. ■ a vehicle like a camper used by gypsies or circus performers. ■ informal short for STATION WAGON. ■ Brit. a railroad freight car.
– PHRASES **fix someone's wagon** bring about a person's downfall or spoil their chances of success. **hitch one's wagon to a star** see HITCH. **off the wagon** (of an alcoholic) drinking after a period of abstinence: *she* ***fell off the wagon*** *two days after making a resolution to quit.* **on the wagon** informal (of an alcoholic) abstaining from drinking: *Agnes was thinking of* ***going on the wagon*** *again.*
– ORIGIN late 15th cent.: from Dutch *wagen*; related to WAIN.

wag·on·er /'wagənər/ (Brit. also **waggoner**) ▶ **n.** the driver of a horse-drawn wagon.
– ORIGIN mid 16th cent.: from Dutch *wagenaar*, from *wagen* (see WAGON).

wag·on·ette /,wagə'net/ (Brit. also **waggonette**) ▶ **n.** a four-wheeled horse-drawn pleasure vehicle, typically open, with facing side seats and one or two seats arranged crosswise in front.

wag·on-lit /,vägôN 'lē/ ▶ **n.** (pl. **wagons-lits** pronunc. **same**) a sleeping car on a European railroad.
– ORIGIN from French *wagon* 'railroad car' + *lit* 'bed.'

wag·on·load /'wagən,lōd/ ▶ **n.** an amount of something that can be carried in one wagon: *a wagonload of food.*

wag·on train ▶ **n.** historical a convoy or train of covered horse-drawn wagons, as used by pioneers or settlers in North America.

wag·tail /'wag,tāl/ ▶ **n.** a slender Eurasian and African songbird with a long tail that is frequently wagged up and down, typically living by water.
● Family Motacillidae: two genera, in particular *Motacilla*, and several species.

Wag·yu /'wägyōō/ ▶ **n.** [often as modifier] a breed of Japanese cattle. ■ the tender beef obtained from such cattle, typically containing a high percentage of unsaturated fat.
– ORIGIN Japanese, from *wa* 'Japanese' + *gyu* 'cattle, beef.'

Wah·ha·bi /wə'häbē, wä-/ (also **Wahabi**) ▶ **n.** (pl. **Wahhabis** /-bēz/) a member of a strictly orthodox Sunni Muslim sect founded by **Muhammad ibn Abd al-Wahhab** (1703–92). It advocates a return to the early Islam of the Koran and Sunna, rejecting later innovations; the sect is still the predominant religious force in Saudi Arabia.
– DERIVATIVES **Wah·ha·bism** /-bizəm/ **n.**, **Wah·ha·bite n. & adj.**

wa·hi·ne /wä'hēnē/ ▶ **n. 1** a Polynesian woman or wife, esp. in Hawaii or New Zealand.
2 a young woman surfer.
– ORIGIN Hawaiian or Maori.

wa·hoo[1] /'wä,hōō, ,wä'hōō/ ▶ **n.** (also **wahoo elm**) another term for WINGED ELM.
– ORIGIN perhaps from Creek *ahá-hwa* 'walnut.'

wa·hoo[2] ▶ **n.** a North American burning bush.
● *Euonymus atropurpurea*, family Celastraceae.
– ORIGIN from Dakota.

wa·hoo[3] ▶ **n.** a large predatory tropical marine fish of the mackerel family, prized as a game fish.
● *Acanthocybium solanderi*, family Scombridae.
– ORIGIN early 20th cent.: of unknown origin.

wa·hoo[4] ▶ **exclam.** another term for YAHOO[2].
– ORIGIN 1940s: probably a natural exclamation.

wah-wah /'wä wä/ (also **wa-wa**) ▶ **n.** a musical effect achieved on brass instruments by alternately applying and removing a mute and on an electric guitar by controlling the output from the amplifier with a pedal. ■ a pedal for producing such an effect on an electric guitar.
– ORIGIN 1920s: imitative.

waif /wāf/ ▶ **n. 1** a homeless and helpless person, esp. a neglected or abandoned child: *she is foster-mother to various* ***waifs and strays.*** ■ an abandoned pet animal.
2 Law a piece of property thrown away by a fleeing thief and held by the state in trust for the owner to claim.
– DERIVATIVES **waif·ish adj.**
– ORIGIN late Middle English: from an Anglo-Norman French variant of Old Northern French *gaif*, probably of Scandinavian origin. Early use was often in *waif and stray*, as a legal term denoting a piece of property found and, if unclaimed, falling to the lord of the manor.

Wai·ka·to /wī'kätō, -'katō/ a river in New Zealand that flows northwest for 270 miles (434 km) from the center of North Island to the Tasman Sea, the country's longest river.

Wai·ki·ki /,wīkī'kē/ a beach resort, a suburb of Honolulu, on the island of Oahu in Hawaii.

wail /wāl/ ▶ **n.** a prolonged high-pitched cry of pain, grief, or anger: *Christopher let out a wail.* ■ a sound resembling this: *the wail of an air-raid siren.*
▶ **v.** [no obj.] give such a cry of pain, grief, or anger: *Tina ran off wailing* | [with direct speech] *"But why?" she wailed.* ■ make a sound resembling such a cry: *the wind wailed and buffeted the timber structure.* ■ [with obj.] literary manifest or feel deep sorrow for; lament: *she wailed her wretched life.*
– DERIVATIVES **wail·er n.**, **wail·ful** /-fəl/ **adj.** (literary), **wail·ing·ly adv.**
– ORIGIN Middle English: from Old Norse; related to WOE.

Wail·ing Wall /'wāliNG/ another name for WESTERN WALL.

Wai·mea Can·yon /wī'māə/ a deep canyon in western Kauai Island in Hawaii. Also called **Grand Canyon of the Pacific**.

Wain /wān/, John (Barrington) (1925–94), English writer and critic. One of the Angry Young Men of the early 1950s, he was later professor of poetry at Oxford 1973–78.

wain /wān/ ▶ **n.** archaic a wagon or cart. ■ (**the Wain**) short for CHARLES'S WAIN.
– ORIGIN Old English *wæg(e)n*, of Germanic origin; related to Dutch *wagen* and German *Wagen*, also to WAY and WEIGH[1].

wain·scot /'wān,skōt, -skət, -,skät/ ▶ **n.** [in sing.] an area of wooden paneling on the lower part of the walls of a room. ■ Brit. historical imported oak of fine quality, used mainly to make paneling.
▶ **v.** (**wainscots, wainscoting, wainscoted** or **wainscots, wainscotting, wainscotted**) [with obj.] line (a room or wall) with wooden paneling.
– ORIGIN Middle English: from Middle Low German *wagenschot*, apparently from *wagen* 'wagon' + *schot*, probably meaning 'partition.'

wain·scot·ing /'wān,skōtiNG, -,skä-/ (also **wainscotting**) ▶ **n.** wooden paneling that lines the lower part of the walls of a room. ■ material for such paneling.

Wain·wright /'wān,rīt/, Jonathan Mayhew (1883–1953), US army officer. The general in charge of all US troops on the Philippine Islands from March 1942, he was forced to surrender at Corregidor in May and was held as a prisoner of war by the Japanese until 1945.

wain·wright /'wān,rīt/ ▶ **n.** historical a wagon-builder.

Wai·pa·hu /wī'pähōō/ a city in Hawaii, on southern Oahu Island, west of Pearl City; pop. 33,108 (2000).

WAIS /wās/ ▶ **abbr.** Computing wide area information service, designed to provide access to information across a computer network.

waist /wāst/ ▶ **n.** the part of the human body below the ribs and above the hips. ■ the circumference of this: *her waist is 28 inches.* ■ a narrowing of the trunk of the body at this point: *the last time you had a waist was around 1978.* ■ the part of a garment encircling or covering the waist. ■ the point at which a garment is shaped so as to narrow between the rib cage and the hips: *a jacket with a high waist.* ■ a blouse or bodice. ■ a narrow part in the middle of anything, such as a violin, an hourglass, the body of wasp, etc. ■ the middle part of a ship, between the forecastle and the quarterdeck.
– DERIVATIVES **waist·ed adj.** [in combination] *high-waisted*, **waist·less adj.**
– ORIGIN late Middle English: apparently representing an Old English word from the Germanic root of WAX[2].

waist·band /'wās(t),band/ ▶ **n.** a strip of cloth forming the waist of a garment such as a skirt or a pair of trousers.

waist cloth ▶ **n.** a loincloth.

waist·coat /'wās(t),kōt, 'weskət/ ▶ **n.** Brit. a vest, esp. one worn by men over a shirt and under a jacket. ■ historical a man's quilted long-sleeved garment worn under a doublet in the 16th and 17th centuries.

waist-deep ▶ **adj. & adv.** of or at a depth to reach the waist: [as adj.] *the waist-deep water* | [as adv.] *Ellwood stood waist-deep in the water.*

waist-high ▶ **adj. & adv.** of or at a height to reach the waist: [as adj.] *a ruin surrounded by waist-high grass* | [as adv.] *weeds grew waist-high.*

waist·line /'wās(t),līn/ ▶ **n.** an imaginary line around a person's body at the waist, esp. with respect to its size: *eliminating inches from the* *waistline*. ▪ the shaping and position of the waist of a garment.

wait /wāt/ ▶ **v.** [no obj.] **1** stay where one is or delay action until a particular time or until something else happens: *he did not **wait for** a reply* | *we're waiting for Allan to get back* | *they will **wait on** a Supreme Court ruling* | [with infinitive] *Ben stood on the street corner waiting to cross* | [with obj.] *I had to wait my turn to play*. ▪ (**wait for** or **on**) stay where one is or delay action until (someone) arrives or is ready: *he sits on the corner waiting for Mary* | *she was waiting on her boyfriend*. ▪ remain in readiness for some purpose: *he found the train waiting at the platform*. ▪ be left until a later time before being dealt with: *we shall need a statement later, but that will have to wait*. ▪ [with obj.] informal defer (a meal) until a person's arrival: *he will wait supper for me*.
2 (**cannot wait**) used to indicate that one is eagerly impatient to do something or for something to happen: *I can't wait for tomorrow* | [with infinitive] *I can't wait to get started again*.
3 act as a waiter or waitress, serving food and drink: *a local man was employed to **wait on** them at table* | [with obj.] *we had to wait tables in the mess hall*.
▶ **n. 1** [in sing.] a period of waiting: *we had a long wait*.
2 (**waits**) Brit. archaic street singers of Christmas carols. ▪ historical official bands of musicians maintained by a city or town.
– PHRASES **wait and see** wait to find out what will happen before doing or deciding something. **you wait** used to convey a threat, warning, or promise: *just you wait till your father comes home!*
– PHRASAL VERBS **wait on** (or **upon**) **1** act as an attendant to (someone): *a maid was appointed to wait on her*. ▪ serve (a customer) in a store. ▪ archaic pay a respectful visit to. **2** chiefly Brit. await the convenience of: *we can't wait on the government; we have to do it ourselves*. **wait up 1** not go to bed until someone arrives or something happens. **2** go more slowly or stop until someone catches up.
– ORIGIN Middle English: from Old Northern French *waitier*, of Germanic origin; related to WAKE[1]. Early senses included 'lie in wait (for),' 'observe carefully,' and 'be watchful.'

wait-a-bit (also **wait-a-bit thorn**) ▶ **n.** chiefly S. African an African bush with hooked thorns that catch the clothing, in particular an acacia.
– ORIGIN translating Afrikaans *wag-'n-bietjie*, literally 'wait a bit.'

Waite /wāt/, Morrison Remick (1816–88), US chief justice 1874–88. Appointed to the chief justiceship by President Grant, he wrote over 100 opinions, many of which upheld the power of state governments.

wait·er /ˈwātər/ ▶ **n. 1** a man whose job is to serve customers at their tables in a restaurant.
2 a person who waits for a time, event, or opportunity.
3 a small tray; a salver.

wait·ing /ˈwātiNG/ ▶ **n. 1** the action of staying where one is or delaying action until a particular time or until something else happens.
2 official attendance at court. See also LADY-IN-WAITING.

wait·ing game ▶ **n.** a tactic in which one refrains from action for a time in order to act more effectively at a later date or stage: *policemen were playing a waiting game outside a country cottage*.

wait·ing list ▶ **n.** a list of people waiting for something, esp. housing or admission to a school.

wait·ing room ▶ **n.** a room provided for the use of people who are waiting to be seen by a doctor or dentist or who are waiting in a station for a bus or train.

wait list ▶ **n.** another term for WAITING LIST.
▶ **v.** (**wait-list**) [with obj.] put (someone) on a waiting list.

wait·per·son /ˈwātˌpərsən/ ▶ **n.** (pl. **waitpersons**) a waiter or waitress (used as a neutral alternative).

wait·ress /ˈwātris/ ▶ **n.** a woman whose job is to serve customers at their tables in a restaurant.

wait·ress·ing /ˈwātrisiNG/ ▶ **n.** the action or occupation of working as a waitress.

wait·ron /ˈwāträn, -trən/ ▶ **n.** a waiter or waitress (used as a neutral alternative).

wait·staff /ˈwātstaf/ ▶ **n.** [treated as sing. or pl.] waiters and waitresses collectively.

wait state ▶ **n.** the condition of computer software or hardware being unable to process further instructions while waiting for some event such as the completion of a data transfer.

waive /wāv/ ▶ **v.** [with obj.] refrain from insisting on or using (a right or claim): *he will waive all rights to the money*. ▪ refrain from applying or enforcing (a rule, restriction, or fee): *her tuition fees would be waived*.
– ORIGIN Middle English (originally as a legal term relating to the removal of the protection of the law): from an Anglo-Norman French variant of Old French *gaiver* 'allow to become a waif, abandon.'

> **USAGE** Waive and waiver should not be confused with wave and waver. Waive is a transitive verb that means 'surrender (a right or claim),' and waiver is its related noun, meaning 'an instance of waiving' or 'a document recording such waiving': *he **waived** potential rights in the case by signing the **waiver***. Wave, as a transitive verb, means 'move (one's hand, or something in one's hand) to and fro': *she **waved** the paper to get their attention*. Waver is an intransitive verb that means 'shake with a quivering motion' or 'be undecided about two courses of action': *the tall grass wavered silently; at the last minute, he **wavered** and said he wasn't sure whether he should go*.

waiv·er /ˈwāvər/ ▶ **n.** an act or instance of waiving a right or claim. ▪ a document recording such waiving of a right or claim.

Wa·kam·ba /wäˈkämbə/ plural form of KAMBA.

wa·ka·me /ˈwäkəˌmā, wäˈkämā/ ▶ **n.** an edible brown seaweed used, typically in dried form, in Chinese and Japanese cooking. • *Undaria pinnatifida*, class Phaeophyceae.
– ORIGIN Japanese.

Wa·kash·an /wäˈkasHən/ ▶ **adj.** of, relating to, or denoting a small family of almost extinct American Indian languages of the northern Pacific coast, including Kwakiutl and Nootka.
▶ **n.** this family of languages.
– ORIGIN formed by Captain Cook from Nootka *wakash* 'bravo!' + -AN.

wake[1] /wāk/ ▶ **v.** (past **woke** /wōk/ or **waked**; past participle **woken** /ˈwōkən/ or **waked**) **1** emerge or cause to emerge from a state of sleep; stop sleeping: [no obj.] *she **woke up** feeling better* | [with obj.] *I wake him gently*. ▪ [no obj.] (**wake up to**) become alert to or aware of: *he needs to wake up to reality*. ▪ [with obj.] cause (something) to stir or come to life: *it wakes desire in others*.
2 [with obj.] dialect hold a vigil beside (someone who has died): *we waked Jim last night*.
▶ **n. 1** a watch or vigil held beside the body of someone who has died, sometimes accompanied by ritual observances including eating and drinking.
2 (**wakes**) [treated as sing.] chiefly historical (in some parts of the UK) a festival and holiday held annually in a rural parish, originally on the feast day of the patron saint of the church. [probably from Old Norse *vaka*.]
– PHRASES **wake up and smell the coffee** [usu. in imperative] informal become aware of the realities of a situation, however unpleasant.
– DERIVATIVES **wak·er** n.
– ORIGIN Old English (recorded only in the past tense *wōc*), also partly from the weak verb *wacian* 'remain awake, hold a vigil,' of Germanic origin; related to Dutch *waken* and German *wachen*; compare with WATCH.

wake[2] ▶ **n.** a trail of disturbed water or air left by the passage of a ship or aircraft. ▪ used to refer to the aftermath or consequences of something: *the committee was set up **in the wake of** the inquiry*.
– ORIGIN late 15th cent. (denoting a track made by a person or thing): probably via Middle Low German from Old Norse *vǫk*, *vaka* 'hole or opening in ice.'

wake·board·ing /ˈwākˌbôrdiNG/ ▶ **n.** the sport of riding on a short, wide board resembling a surfboard and performing acrobatic maneuvers while being towed behind a motorboat.
– DERIVATIVES **wake·board** n., **wake·board·er** n.
– ORIGIN 1990s: from WAKE[2], on the pattern of *surfboarding*.

wake·ful /ˈwākfəl/ ▶ **adj.** (of a person) unable or not needing to sleep: *he had been wakeful all night*. ▪ alert and vigilant. ▪ (of a period of time) passed with little or no sleep: *wakeful nights*.
– DERIVATIVES **wake·ful·ly** adv., **wake·ful·ness** n.

Wake Is·land /wāk/ a coral atoll in the Pacific Ocean, north of the Marshall Islands. Controlled by the US since 1898, it was the scene of World War II fighting after the Japanese occupied it in December 1941.

wak·en /ˈwākən/ ▶ **v.** literary term for WAKE[1] (sense 1 of the verb).
– ORIGIN Old English *wæcnan* 'be aroused,' of Germanic origin; related to WAKE[1].

wake-rob·in ▶ **n. 1** another term for TRILLIUM.
2 Brit. another term for CUCKOOPINT.

wake-up ▶ **n.** [in sing.] an instance of a person waking up or being woken up.

wake-up call ▶ **n.** a telephone call made according to a prior arrangement to wake the person called. ▪ a person or thing that causes people to become fully alert to an unsatisfactory situation and to take action to remedy it: *today's statistics will be a wake-up call for the administration*.

wak·ing /ˈwākiNG/ ▶ **n.** the state of being awake: *he hangs between sleeping and waking*.

wa·ki·za·shi /ˌwäkēˈzäsHē/ ▶ **n.** (pl. **same**) a Japanese sword shorter than a katana.
– ORIGIN Japanese, from *waki* 'side' + *sasu* 'wear at one's side.'

Waks·man /ˈwäksmən, ˈwak-/, Selman Abraham (1888–1973), US microbiologist, born in Russia. He discovered the antibiotic streptomycin, for use esp. against tuberculosis. Nobel Prize for Physiology or Medicine (1952).

Wa·la·chi·a variant spelling of WALLACHIA.

Wal·cott /ˈwôlkət/, Louis Eugene, see FARRAKHAN.

Wal·den Pond /ˈwôldən/ a pond in Concord in Massachusetts, associated with the writer Henry David Thoreau, now within a state park.

Wal·den·ses /wôlˈdensēz, wä-/ ▶ **plural n.** a Christian sect that was founded in southern France *c.*1170 by **Peter Valdes** (d.1205), a merchant of Lyons, and adopted Calvinist doctrines during the Reformation, now existing chiefly in Italy and America.
– DERIVATIVES **Wal·den·si·an** /-sēən/ **adj. & n.**

Wald·heim /ˈvôldˌhīm, ˈwôld-, ˈvält-/, Kurt (1918–2007), Austrian diplomat and statesman; president 1986–92. He was secretary general of the United Nations 1972–81. His later career was blemished by revelations about his service as a German officer in World War II.

wal·do /ˈwôldō/ ▶ **n.** (pl. **waldos**) a remote manipulator, as for puppets, operated either mechanically or electronically.

Wal·dorf sal·ad /ˈwôlˌdôrf/ ▶ **n.** a salad made from apples, walnuts, celery, and mayonnaise.
– ORIGIN named after the *Waldorf*-Astoria Hotel in New York, where it was first served.

wale /wāl/ ▶ **n. 1** a ridge on a textured woven fabric such as corduroy.
2 Nautical a plank running along the side of a wooden ship, thicker than the usual planking, and strengthening and protecting the hull.
3 a horizontal band around a woven basket.
– ORIGIN late Old English *walu* 'stripe, weal.'

wale knot ▶ **n.** another term for WALL KNOT.

Wal·er /ˈwālər/ ▶ **n. 1** a horse of a typically light breed from Australia, esp. from New South Wales.
2 informal a native or inhabitant of Australia, esp. New South Wales.

Wales /wālz/ a principality of Great Britain and the United Kingdom, west of central England; pop. 2,993,000 (est. 2008); capital, Cardiff. Welsh name CYMRU.

> The Celtic inhabitants of Wales successfully maintained independence from the Anglo-Saxons who settled in England following the withdrawal of the Romans. Norman colonization from England began in the 12th century, and English control over the country was assured by Edward I's conquest 1277–84. Edward began the custom of making the English sovereign's eldest son Prince of Wales. Wales was formally brought into the English legal and parliamentary system by Henry VIII in 1536 but has retained a distinct cultural identity. In 1997, a referendum narrowly approved proposals for a Welsh assembly.

Wales, Prince of see PRINCE OF WALES; CHARLES, PRINCE.

Wa·łę·sa /vəˈlensə, vəˈwensə/, Lech (1943–), Polish labor leader and statesman; president 1990–95. The founder of the labor union called Solidarity (1980), he was imprisoned 1981–82 after the movement was banned. After Solidarity's landslide victory in the 1989 elections, he became president. Nobel Peace Prize (1983).

wa·li /ˈwälē/ ▶ **n.** the governor of a province in an Arab country.
– ORIGIN from Arabic *wālī*.

walk /wôk/ ▶ **v. 1** [no obj.] move at a regular and fairly slow pace by lifting and setting down each foot in turn, never having both feet off the ground at once: *I walked across the lawn* | *she turned and walked a few paces*. ▪ use similar movements but of a different part of one's body or a support: *he could walk on his hands, carrying a plate on one foot*. ▪ go on foot for recreation and exercise: *you can walk in 21,000 acres of mountain and moorland*. ▪ [with obj.] travel along or over (a route or area) on foot: *the police department has encouraged officers to walk the*

W

PRONUNCIATION KEY ə *ago*, *up*; ər *over*, *fur*; a *hat*; ā *ate*; ä *car*; e *let*; ē *see*; i *fit*; ī *by*; NG *sing*; ō *go*; ô *law*, *for*; oi *toy*; o͝o *good*; o͞o *goo*; ou *out*; TH *thin*; T͟H *then*; ZH *vision*

beat. ■ (of a quadruped) proceed with the slowest gait, always having at least two feet on the ground at once. ■ [with obj.] ride (a horse) at this pace: *he walked his horse toward her.* ■ informal abandon or suddenly withdraw from a job, commitment, or situation: *they can **walk away** from the deal | we were expecting the merger with Bell to go through—we didn't expect Bell to walk on the deal.* ■ informal be released from suspicion or from a charge: *had any of the others come clean during the trial, he might have walked.* ■ used to suggest that someone has achieved a state or position easily or undeservedly: *no one has the right to **walk straight into** a well-paid job for life.* ■ (of a ghost) be present and visible: *the ghosts of Bannockburn walked abroad.* ■ archaic used to describe the way in which someone lives or behaves: *walk humbly with your God.* ■ Baseball be awarded first base after not swinging at four balls pitched outside the strike zone. ■ [with obj.] Baseball allow or enable (a batter) to do this. ■ Baseball (of a pitcher) give a walk with the bases loaded so as to force in (a run). ■ Basketball another term for **TRAVEL** (sense 2 of the verb).
2 [with obj.] cause or enable (someone or something) to walk or move as though walking: *she walked her fingers over the dresses.* ■ guide, accompany, or escort (someone) on foot: *he walked her home to her door.* ■ take (a domestic animal, typically a dog) out for exercise: *a man walking his retriever.* ■ push (a bicycle or motorcycle) while walking alongside it.
▶ **n. 1** an act of traveling or an excursion on foot: *he was too restless to sleep, so he went out for a walk.* ■ [in sing.] used to indicate the time that it will take someone to reach a place on foot or the distance that they must travel: *the library is within five minutes' walk.* ■ a route recommended or marked out for recreational walking. ■ a sidewalk or path. ■ a part of a forest under one keeper. ■ chiefly Brit. the round followed by a mail carrier.
2 [in sing.] an unhurried rate of movement on foot: *they crossed the field at a leisurely walk.* ■ the slowest gait of an animal. ■ a person's manner of walking: *the spring was back in his walk.*
3 Baseball an instance of being awarded (or allowing a batter to reach) first base after not swinging at four balls pitched outside the strike zone.
– PHRASES **walk all over** informal treat in a thoughtless, disrespectful, and exploitative manner: *they thought they could come in and walk all over us.* ■ defeat easily. **walking encyclopedia** (also **walking dictionary**) informal a person who has an impressive knowledge of facts or words. **a walk in the park** informal something that is very easy to accomplish: *as any director will tell you, doing Shakespeare isn't a walk in the park.* **walk someone off their feet** walk with someone until they are exhausted. **walk of life** the position within society that someone holds or the part of society to which they belong as a result of their job or social status: *the courses attracted people from all walks of life.* **walk on air** see **AIR**. **walk on eggshells** be extremely cautious about one's words or actions. **walk the walk** (also **walk the talk**) informal suit one's actions to one's words. **walk the plank** see **PLANK**. **walk the streets 1** walk freely in a town or city. **2** work as a prostitute. **walk the wards** dated gain experience as a clinical medical student. **win in a walk** win without effort or competition.
– PHRASAL VERBS **walk away** easily, casually, or irresponsibly abandon a situation in which one is involved or for which one is responsible. **walk away with** informal another way of saying **WALK OFF WITH**. **walk in on** enter suddenly or unexpectedly. ■ intrude on: *he was clearly not expecting her to walk in on him just then.* **walk into** informal encounter or become involved in through ignorance or carelessness: *I had walked into a situation from which there was no escape.* **walk off with** informal **1** steal. **2** win: *the team walked off with a silver medal.* **walk something off** exercise on foot in order to undo the effects of a heavy meal. **walk out 1** depart suddenly or angrily. ■ leave one's job suddenly. ■ go on strike. ■ abandon someone or something toward which one has responsibilities: *he **walked out on** his wife.* **2** Brit. informal, dated go for walks in courtship: *you were **walking out with** Tom.* **walk over** informal another way of saying **WALK ALL OVER**. **walk through** rehearse (a play or other piece), reading the lines aloud from a script and performing the actions of the characters. ■ act or perform in a perfunctory or lackluster manner. **walk someone through** guide (someone) carefully through a process: *a meeting to walk parents through the complaint process.*
– DERIVATIVES **walk·a·ble** /ˈwôkəbəl/ **adj.**
– ORIGIN Old English *wealcan* 'roll, toss,' also 'wander,' of Germanic origin. The sense 'move around,' and specifically 'go around on foot,' arose in Middle English.

walk·a·bout /ˈwôkəˌbout/ ▶ **n.** Austral. a journey on foot undertaken by an Australian Aboriginal in order to live in the traditional manner. ■ chiefly Brit. an informal stroll among a crowd conducted by an important visitor. ■ a walking tour.
– PHRASES **go walkabout** (of an Australian Aboriginal) wander into the bush away from white society in order to live in the traditional manner. ■ wander around from place to place in a protracted or leisurely way.

walk·a·thon /ˈwôkəˌTHän/ ▶ **n.** informal a long-distance walk organized as a fundraising event.
– ORIGIN 1930s: from **WALK**, on the pattern of *marathon.*

Walk·er[1] /ˈwôkər/, Alice (Malsenior) (1944–), US writer and critic. She wrote the award-winning *The Color Purple* (1982), a story about a black woman rebuilding her life after being raped by her supposed father, which was made into a movie in 1985. She also wrote *Possessing the Secret of Joy* (1992) and *By the Light of My Father's Smile* (1998).

Walk·er[2], Jimmy (1881–1946), US politician; full name *James John Walker.* He was mayor of New York City 1926–32 but resigned when his involvement in fraud was exposed.

Walk·er[3], Sarah Breedlove (1867–1919), US entrepreneur and philanthropist; known as **Madame C. J. Walker**. She invented and marketed a preparation to straighten kinky hair 1905 and built her business into the largest African-American–owned firm in the US, the Madame C. J. Walker Manufacturing Co. She generously gave of her wealth, mainly to African-American educational institutions and charities.

walk·er /ˈwôkər/ ▶ **n.** a person who walks, esp. for exercise or enjoyment. ■ a device for helping a baby learn to walk, consisting of a harness set into a frame on wheels. ■ a frame used by disabled or infirm people for support while walking, typically made of metal tubing with small wheels or rubber-tipped feet.

Walk·er Cup a golf tournament held every two years and played between teams of male amateurs from the US and from Great Britain and Ireland, first held in 1922. The tournament was instituted by **George Herbert Walker**, a former president of the US Golf Association.

walk·ie-talk·ie /ˌwôkē ˈtôkē/ ▶ **n.** a portable two-way radio.

walk-in ▶ **adj. 1** (esp. of a storage area) large enough to walk into: *a walk-in closet.*
2 (of a service) available for customers or clients without the need for an appointment: *a walk-in clinic.*
▶ **n.** a walk-in customer or a walk-in storage area.

walk·ing bass /bās/ ▶ **n.** Music a bass part in 4/4 time in which a note is played on each beat of the bar and which typically moves up and down the scale in small steps.

walk·ing fern ▶ **n.** a North American fern with long slender tapering fronds that form new plantlets where the tips touch the ground, typically growing on limestone. ● *Asplenium* (or *Camptosorus*) *rhizophyllus*, family Aspleniaceae.

walk·ing frame ▶ **n.** Brit. full form of **WALKER**.

walk·ing leaf ▶ **n. 1** another term for **LEAF INSECT**.
2 another term for **WALKING FERN**.

walk·ing leg ▶ **n.** Zoology (in certain arthropods, esp. crustaceans) a limb used for walking.

walk·ing pa·pers ▶ **plural n.** informal notice of dismissal from a job: *the reporter has been given his walking papers.*

walk·ing pneu·mo·ni·a ▶ **n.** a type of pneumonia caused by mycoplasmas, with symptoms similar to but milder than those of bacterial or viral pneumonia. It spreads easily and typically affects school-age children and adults under 40.

walk·ing shoe ▶ **n.** a sturdy, practical shoe with good treads, suitable for regular or extensive walking.

walk·ing stick ▶ **n. 1** a stick, typically with a curved handle, used for support when walking.
2 (also **walkingstick**) a long, slender, slow-moving insect that resembles a twig. In many species, it appears that there are no males and that the females lay fertile eggs without mating. ● Family Phasmatidae, order Phasmida: many genera.

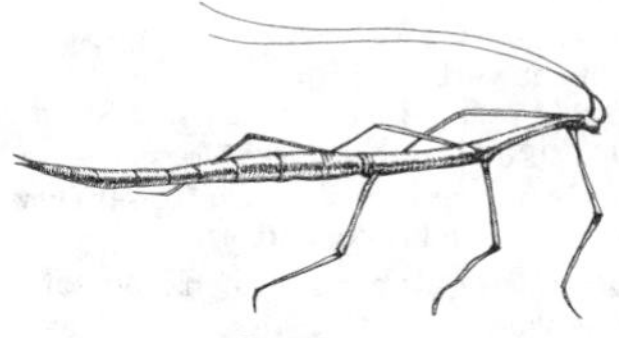

walking stick 2

walk·ing tour ▶ **n.** a sightseeing tour made on foot.

walk·ing wound·ed /ˈwo͝ondid/ ▶ **plural n.** (usu. **the walking wounded**) people who have been injured in a battle or major accident but who are still able to walk. ■ people who have suffered emotional wounds.

Walk·man /ˈwôkmən, -ˌman/ ▶ **n.** (pl. **Walkmans** or **Walkmen**) trademark a type of personal stereo.

walk-on ▶ **adj.** [attrib.] denoting a small nonspeaking part in a play or film.
▶ **n.** a person who plays such a part, or the part itself. ■ a sports player with no regular status in a team.

walk·out /ˈwôkˌout/ ▶ **n.** a sudden angry departure, esp. as a protest or strike.

walk·o·ver /ˈwôkˌōvər/ ▶ **n. 1** an easy victory: *they won in a 12–2 walkover.* ■ a win by forfeit.
2 a somersault in which a gymnast performs a handstand and then slowly moves the feet backward and down to the floor, or first arches back into a handstand and then slowly moves the feet forward and down to the floor.

walk-through ▶ **n. 1** a tour or demonstration of an area or task: *a floor-by-floor walk-through of the library.* ■ a software model of a building or other object in which the user can simulate walking around. ■ a rough rehearsal of a play, film, or other performance, without an audience or cameras. ■ Computing a product review of software carried out before release. ■ (in computer gaming) a document giving advice on how to complete a game.
2 an undemanding task or role. ■ a perfunctory or lackluster performance.
▶ **adj.** [attrib.] designed to be walked through: *a walk-through gallery | walk-through registration.*

walk-up ▶ **adj.** (of a building) allowing access to the upper floors by stairs only; having no elevator: *a walk-up hotel.* ■ (of a room or apartment) accessed in this way. ■ (of a building or service) easily accessible to pedestrians: *a walk-up food stand.* ■ (of a travel fare) at the price charged for immediate use rather than at the lower level provided when a customer makes a reservation in advance: *the one-way walk-up fare from Baltimore to San Francisco.*
▶ **n.** a building allowing access to the upper floors by stairs only.

walk·way /ˈwôkˌwā/ ▶ **n.** a passage or path for walking along, esp. a raised passageway connecting different sections of a building or a wide path in a park or garden.

wall /wôl/ ▶ **n.** a continuous vertical brick or stone structure that encloses or divides an area of land: *a garden wall | farmland traversed by drystone walls.* ■ a side of a building or room, typically forming part of the building's structure. ■ any high vertical surface or facade, esp. one that is imposing in scale: *the eastern wall of the valley |* figurative *flash floods sent a 6-foot wall of water through the village.* ■ a thing perceived as a protective or restrictive barrier: *a wall of silence.* ■ Soccer a line of defenders forming a barrier against a free kick taken near the penalty area. ■ short for **CLIMBING WALL**. ■ Mining the rock enclosing a lode or seam or forming the side of a mine-working. ■ Anatomy & Zoology the membranous outer layer or lining of an organ or cavity: *the wall of the stomach.* ■ Biology see **CELL WALL**.
▶ **v.** [with obj.] enclose (an area) within walls, esp. to protect it or lend it some privacy: *housing areas that are walled off from the indigenous population.* ■ (**wall something up**) block or seal a place by building a wall around or across it: *one doorway has been walled up.* ■ (**wall someone/something in/up**) confine or imprison someone or something in a restricted or sealed place: *the gray tenements walled in the space completely.*
– PHRASES **between you and me and the wall** see **BEDPOST**. **drive someone up the wall** informal make someone very irritated or angry. **go to the wall** informal **1** (of a business) fail; go out of business. **2** support someone or something, no matter what the cost to oneself: *the tendency for poets to go to the wall for their beliefs.* **hit the wall** (of an athlete) experience a sudden loss of energy in a long race. **off the wall** informal **1** eccentric or unconventional. **2** (of a person) angry: *the president was off the wall about the article.* **3** (of an accusation) without basis or foundation. **walls have ears** proverb be careful what you say as people may be eavesdropping. **wall-to-wall** (of a carpet or other floor covering) fitted to cover an entire floor. ■ informal denoting great extent or number: *wall-to-wall customers.*
– DERIVATIVES **wall-less adj.**
– ORIGIN Old English, from Latin *vallum* 'rampart,' from *vallus* 'stake.'

Wall·a·bout Bay /ˈwôləˌbout/ a former inlet of the East River in Brooklyn in New York City, the site of the imprisonment of thousands of American prisoners during the American Revolution, many of whom died here.

W

wal·la·by /ˈwäləbē/ ▶ **n.** (pl. **wallabies**) an Australasian marsupial that is similar to, but smaller than, a kangaroo. ● Family Macropodidae: several genera and numerous species, including the **agile wallaby** (*Macropus agilis*).
– ORIGIN early 19th cent.: from Dharuk *walabi* or *waliba*.

agile wallaby

Wal·lace[1] /ˈwôləs, ˈwäl-/, Alfred Russel (1823–1913), English naturalist; a founder of zoogeography.

Wal·lace[2], Edgar (1875–1932), English novelist, screenwriter, and playwright; full name *Richard Horatio Edgar Wallace*. He wrote the screenplay for the movie *King Kong*, which was made shortly after his death.

Wall·ace[3], George Corley (1919–98), US politician. A four-term governor of Alabama 1963–67, 1971–79, 1983–87, he gained national attention in the early 1960s when he defied the civil rights legislation that outlawed segregation in public schools. While campaigning for the 1972 Democratic presidential nomination, he was shot and paralyzed by would-be assassin Arthur Bremer (1950–).

Wall·ace[4], Henry Agard (1888–1965), US politician, agriculturist, and editor. He was editor of *Wallaces' Farmer* and its successor 1910–33. He was US secretary of agriculture 1933–40, US vice president 1941–45, and US secretary of commerce 1945–46. He was the presidential candidate for the new Progressive Party in 1948.

Wall·ace[5], Mike (1918–), US journalist; born *Myron Leon Wallace*. A news correspondent with CBS from 1963, he appeared on the television news program *60 Minutes* from 1968.

Wal·lace[6], Sir William (*c.*1270–1305), Scottish national hero. A leader of Scottish resistance to Edward I, he defeated the English army at Stirling in 1297. After Edward's second invasion of Scotland in 1298, he was defeated and subsequently executed.

Wal·lace's line Zoology a hypothetical line, proposed by Alfred Russel Wallace, marking the boundary between the Oriental and Australian zoogeographical regions. Wallace's line is now placed along the continental shelf of Southeast Asia, east of the islands of Borneo, Bali, and the Philippines. To the west of the line, Asian animals such as monkeys predominate, while to the east of it, the fauna is dominated by marsupials.

Wal·la·chi·a /wäˈlākēə, wə-/ (also **Walachia**) a former principality in southeastern Europe, between the Danube River and the Transylvanian Alps. In 1861, it was united with Moldavia to form Romania.
– DERIVATIVES **Wal·la·chi·an** adj. & n.
– ORIGIN based on a variant of **VLACH**.

wal·lah /ˈwälə/ ▶ **n.** [in combination or with modifier] Indian or informal a person concerned or involved with a specified thing or business: *ice cream wallahs.* ■ a native or inhabitant of a specified place: *Bombay wallahs.*
– ORIGIN from the Hindi suffix *-vālā* 'doer' (commonly interpreted in the sense 'fellow'), from Sanskrit *pālaka* 'keeper.'

wal·la·roo /ˌwôləˈro͞o/ ▶ **n.** a large Australian kangaroo, the female of which is paler than the male. ● Genus *Macropus*, family Macropodidae: two species, in particular the **common wallaroo** (*M. robustus*).
– ORIGIN early 19th cent.: from Dharuk *walaru*.

Wal·la Wal·la /ˌwälə ˈwälə/ a historic commercial and industrial city in southeastern Washington; pop. 30,643 (est. 2008).

wall·board /ˈwôlˌbôrd/ ▶ **n.** a type of board made from wood pulp, plaster, or other material, used for covering walls and ceilings. ■ a piece of such board.

wall chart ▶ **n.** a chart or poster designed for display on a wall as a teaching aid or source of information.

wall cov·er·ing ▶ **n.** material such as wallpaper or textured fabric used as a decorative covering for interior walls.

wall·creep·er /ˈwôlˌkrēpər/ ▶ **n.** a Eurasian songbird related to the nuthatches, having mainly gray plumage with broad bright red wings, and living among rocks in mountainous country. ● *Tichodroma muraria*, family Sittidae (or Tichodromadidae).

wall cress ▶ **n.** another term for **ARABIS**.

walled gar·den ▶ **n.** a garden or yard enclosed by high walls. ■ Computing & Telecommunications a restricted range of information to which subscribers to a particular service are limited.

Wal·len·berg /ˈwôlənˌbərg, ˈvälənˌber(yə)/, Raoul (1912–?), Swedish diplomat in Budapest. In 1944, he helped many thousands of Jews escape death by issuing them Swedish passports. Arrested by the Soviets in 1945, he was imprisoned in Moscow. Although Soviet authorities stated that he died in prison in 1947, his fate remains uncertain.

Wal·ler /ˈwälər/, Fats (1904–43), US jazz pianist, songwriter, bandleader, and singer; born *Thomas Wright Waller*. The composer of the songs "Ain't Misbehavin'" (1928) and "Honeysuckle Rose" (1929), he was the foremost exponent of the New York "stride school" of piano playing.

wal·let /ˈwälit, ˈwô-/ ▶ **n.** a pocket-sized, flat, folding holder for money and plastic cards. ■ archaic a bag for holding provisions, esp. when traveling, typically used by peddlers and pilgrims.
– ORIGIN late Middle English (denoting a bag for provisions): probably via Anglo-Norman French from a Germanic word related to **WELL**[2]. The current sense (originally US) dates from the mid 19th cent.

wall·eye /ˈwôlˌī/ ▶ **n. 1** an eye with a streaked or opaque white iris. ■ an eye directed abnormally outward.
2 a North American pikeperch with large, opaque silvery eyes. It is a commercially valuable food fish and a popular sporting fish. ● *Stizostedion vitreum*, family Percidae.
– DERIVATIVES **wall·eyed** adj.
– ORIGIN early 16th cent.: back-formation from earlier *wall-eyed*, from Old Norse *vagleygr*; related to Icelandic *vagl* 'film over the eye.'

wall·flow·er /ˈwôlˌflou(-ə)r/ ▶ **n. 1** a southern European plant of the cabbage family, with fragrant yellow, orange-red, dark red, or brown flowers, cultivated for its early spring blooming. ● *Cheiranthus cheiri*, family Brassicaceae.
2 informal a person who has no one to dance with or who feels shy, awkward, or excluded at a party.

wall hang·ing ▶ **n.** a large decorative piece of fabric or other material to be hung on the wall of a room.

wall-hung ▶ **adj.** another term for **WALL-MOUNTED**.

Wal·ling·ford /ˈwäliNGfərd/ an industrial town in south central Connecticut; pop. 44,859 (est. 2008).

Wal·lis and Fu·tu·na Is·lands /ˈwäləs and fo͞oˈto͞onə, ˈwôləs/ an overseas territory of France that consists of two groups of islands to the west of Samoa in the central Pacific Ocean; pop. 15,300 (est. 2009); capital, Mata-Utu.

wall knot (also **wale knot**) ▶ **n.** a knot made at the end of a rope by intertwining strands to prevent unraveling or act as a stopper.

wall-mount·ed ▶ **adj.** fixed to a wall.

wall of hon·or ▶ **n.** a wall on which are inscribed the names of individuals whose acts or achievements are deemed praiseworthy.

Wal·loon /wäˈlo͞on/ ▶ **n. 1** a member of a people who speak a French dialect and live in southern and eastern Belgium and neighboring parts of France. Compare with **FLEMING**[3].
2 the French dialect spoken by this people.
▶ **adj.** of or concerning the Walloons or their language.
– ORIGIN from French *Wallon*, from medieval Latin *Wallon-*, from the same Germanic origin as **WELSH**.

wal·lop /ˈwäləp/ informal ▶ **v.** (**wallops, walloping, walloped**) [with obj.] strike or hit (someone or something) very hard: *they walloped the back of his head with a stick* | figurative *they were tired of getting walloped with income taxes.* ■ heavily defeat (an opponent).
▶ **n. 1** a heavy blow or punch. ■ [in sing.] a potent effect: *the script **packs a wallop**.*
2 Brit. alcoholic drink, esp. beer.
– DERIVATIVES **wal·lop·er** n.
– ORIGIN Middle English (as a noun denoting a horse's gallop): from Old Northern French *walop* (noun), *waloper* (verb), perhaps from a Germanic phrase meaning 'run well,' from the bases of **WELL**[1] and **LEAP**. Compare with **GALLOP**. From 'gallop' the senses 'bubbling noise of a boiling liquid' and then 'sound of a clumsy movement' arose, leading to the current senses.

wal·lop·ing /ˈwäləpiNG/ informal ▶ **n.** [in sing.] a beating: *she gave him a good walloping.*
▶ **adj.** [attrib.] large and powerful: *a walloping shock.*

Wal·lops Is·land /ˈwäləps/ an island in eastern Virginia, on the Delmarva Peninsula, the site of a US rocket and high-altitude balloon facility.

wal·low /ˈwälō/ ▶ **v.** [no obj.] **1** (chiefly of large mammals) roll about or lie relaxed in mud or water, esp. to keep cool, avoid biting insects, or spread scent: *watering places where buffalo liked to wallow.* ■ (of a boat or aircraft) roll from side to side: *the small jet wallowed in the sky.*
2 (**wallow in**) (of a person) indulge in an unrestrained way in (something that creates a pleasurable sensation): *I was wallowing in the luxury of the hotel* | *he had been wallowing in self-pity.*
▶ **n. 1** an act of wallowing: *a wallow in nostalgia.*
2 an area of mud or shallow water where mammals go to wallow, typically developing into a depression in the ground over long use.
– DERIVATIVES **wal·low·er** n.
– ORIGIN Old English *walwian* 'to roll around,' of Germanic origin, from an Indo-European root shared by Latin *volvere* 'to roll.'

Wal·low·a Moun·tains /wäˈlôə/ a range in northeastern Oregon. The Wallowa River valley, on its east, is home to the Nez Perce Indians.

wall paint·ing ▶ **n.** a painting made directly on a wall, such as a fresco or mural.

wall·pa·per /ˈwôlˌpāpər/ ▶ **n.** paper that is pasted in vertical strips over the walls of a room to provide a decorative or textured surface. ■ Computing an optional background pattern or picture on a computer screen.
▶ **v.** [with obj.] apply wallpaper to (a wall or room).

wall pass ▶ **n.** Soccer a short pass to a teammate who immediately returns it.

wall·pep·per (also **wall pepper**) ▶ **n.** another term for **MOSSY STONECROP** (see **STONECROP**).

wall plate ▶ **n. 1** a piece of lumber laid horizontally in or on a wall as a support for a girder, rafter, or joist.
2 a metal plate fixed to a wall for attaching a bracket, wiring, or other device.

wall rock ▶ **n.** Geology the rock adjacent to or enclosing a vein, hydrothermal ore deposit, fault, or other geological feature.

wall rock·et ▶ **n.** a yellow-flowered European plant that resembles mustard and emits a foul smell when crushed. ● *Diplotaxis muralis*, family Brassicaceae.

wall rue ▶ **n.** a small delicate spleenwort (fern) that resembles rue, growing on walls and rocks in both Europe and North America and sensitive to atmospheric pollution. ● *Asplenium ruta-muraria*, family Aspleniaceae.

Wall Street a street at the south end of Manhattan in New York City, where the New York Stock Exchange and other leading US financial institutions are located. ■ used allusively to refer to the US money market or financial interests.
– ORIGIN named after a wooden stockade that was built in 1653 around the original Dutch settlement of New Amsterdam.

wall tent ▶ **n.** a tent with nearly perpendicular sides.

wall u·nit ▶ **n.** a piece of furniture having various sections, typically shelves and cabinets, designed to stand against a wall.

wal·nut /ˈwôlˌnət/ ▶ **n. 1** the large wrinkled edible seed of a deciduous tree, consisting of two halves contained within a hard shell that is enclosed in a green fruit.
2 (also **walnut tree**) the tall tree that produces this nut, with compound leaves and valuable ornamental timber that is used chiefly in cabinetmaking and gunstocks. ● Genus *Juglans*, family Juglandaceae: several species, including the **common** (or **English**) **walnut** (*J. regia*) and the **black walnut** (*J. nigra*).
– ORIGIN late Old English *walh-hnutu*, from a Germanic compound meaning 'foreign nut.' See also **WELSH**.

Wal·nut Creek a residential and industrial city in north central California, northeast of Oakland; pop. 63,486 (est. 2008).

Wal·pole[1] /ˈwôlˌpōl/, Horace, 4th Earl of Orford (1717–97), English writer and politician; son of Sir Robert Walpole. He wrote *The Castle of Otranto* (1764), one of the first Gothic novels.

Wal·pole[2], Sir Hugh (Seymour) (1884–1941), British novelist, born in New Zealand. He is noted for *The Herries Chronicle* (1930–33), a historical sequence.

Wal·pole[3], Sir Robert, 1st Earl of Orford (1676–1745), British statesman; first lord of the treasury and chancellor of the exchequer 1715–17 and 1721–42; father of Horace Walpole. He is generally thought of as the first British prime minister, since he presided over the cabinet for George I and George II.

Wal·pur·gis·nacht /väl'pŏŏgis,näKHt, -,näkt/ ▶ **n.** German for **WALPURGIS NIGHT**.

Wal·pur·gis night /väl'pŏŏrgis/ ▶ **n.** (in German folklore) the night of April 30 (May Day's eve), when witches meet on the Brocken mountain and hold revels with the Devil.
– ORIGIN named after St. *Walburga*, an English nun who in the 8th cent. helped to convert the Germans to Christianity; her feast day coincided with an ancient pagan festival whose rites were intended to give protection from witchcraft.

Wal·ras' law /'valrəs/ Economics a law stating that the total value of goods and money supplied equals that of goods and money demanded.
– DERIVATIVES **Wal·ra·si·an adj.**
– ORIGIN 1940s: named after M. E. Léon *Walras* (1834–1910), French economist.

wal·rus /'wôlrəs, 'wä-/ ▶ **n.** a large gregarious marine mammal related to the eared seals, having two large downward-pointing tusks and found in the Arctic Ocean. ● *Odobenus rosmarus*, the only member of the family Odobenidae.
– ORIGIN early 18th cent.: probably from Dutch *walrus*, perhaps by an inversion of elements (influenced by *walvis* 'whale-fish') of Old Norse *hrosshvalr* 'horse-whale.'

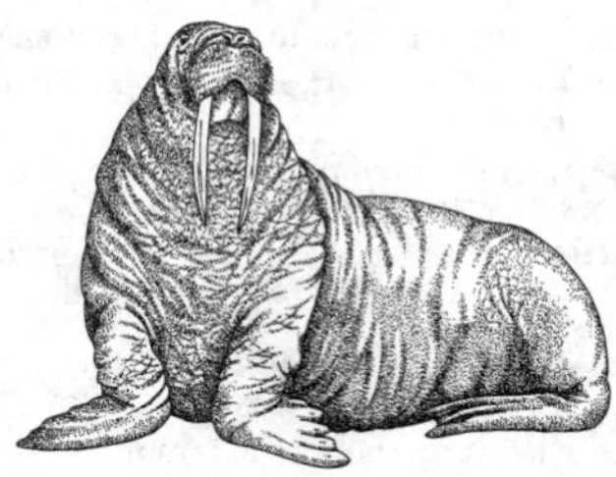

walrus

wal·rus mus·tache ▶ **n.** a long, thick, drooping mustache.

Wal·sall /'wôl,sôl, 'wäl,säl/ an industrial town in western central England; pop. 172,100 (est. 2009).

Wal·ter Mit·ty /'wôltər 'mitē/ the hero of a story (by James Thurber) who indulged in extravagant daydreams of his own triumphs. ■ [as noun often as adj.] used to refer to a person who fantasizes about a life much more exciting and glamorous than their own life.

Wal·ters /'wôltərz/, Barbara (1931–), US television journalist. Noted for her interviews of celebrities, she has appeared on the television programs *20/20* (1979–2004) and *The View* (1997–).

Wal·tham /'wôl,THam, -,THam/ a historic industrial and academic city in eastern Massachusetts, on the Charles River, west of Boston; pop. 60,236 (est. 2008).

Wal·ton¹ /'wôltn/, Ernest Thomas Sinton (1903–95), Irish physicist. In 1932 he succeeded, with Sir John Cockcroft, in splitting the atom. Nobel Prize for Physics (1951), shared with Cockcroft.

Wal·ton², Izaak (1593–1683), English writer. He is chiefly known for *The Compleat Angler* (1653; rewritten, 1655), which combines practical information on fishing with folklore and is interspersed with pastoral songs and ballads.

Wal·ton³, Sam (1918–92), US businessman. He founded Wal-Mart discount stores in 1962 and by 1966, with 20 stores, had begun to computerize inventory. By 1991, Wal-Mart was the largest retailer in the US.

waltz /wôlts/ ▶ **n.** a dance in triple time performed by a couple who as a pair turn rhythmically around and around as they progress around the dance floor. ■ a piece of music written for or in the style of this dance.
▶ **v.** [no obj.] dance a waltz: *I waltzed across the floor with the lieutenant.* ■ [with obj.] guide (someone) in or as if in a waltz: *he waltzed her around the table.* ■ [no obj.] move or act lightly, casually, or inconsiderately: *you can't just waltz in and expect to make a mark* | *it is the third time that he has waltzed off with the coveted award.*
– PHRASES **waltz Matilda** see **MATILDA²**.
– DERIVATIVES **waltz·er n.**
– ORIGIN late 18th cent.: from German *Walzer*, from *walzen* 'revolve.'

Wal·vis Bay /'wôlvəs, 'wäl-/ a port in Namibia; pop. 55,000 (est. 2009). Administratively, it was an exclave of the former Cape Province in South Africa until it was transferred to Namibia in 1994.

Wam·pa·no·ag /,wämpə'nō-ag/ ▶ **n.** (pl. **same** or **Wampanoags**) a member of a confederacy of American Indian peoples of southeastern Massachusetts who spoke the extinct Algonquian language Massachusett.
▶ **adj.** of, relating to, or denoting these people.
– ORIGIN from an Algonquian name, literally 'easterners.'

wam·pum /'wämpəm/ ▶ **n.** historical a quantity of small cylindrical beads made by North American Indians from quahog shells, strung together and worn as a decorative belt or other decoration or used as money.
– ORIGIN from Massachusett *wampumpeag*, literally 'white strings.'

WAN /wan/ ▶ **abbr.** Computing wide area network. [1980s: acronym.]

wan /wän/ ▶ **adj.** (of a person's complexion or appearance) pale and giving the impression of illness or exhaustion: *she was looking wan and bleary-eyed.* ■ (of light) pale; weak: *the wan dawn light.* ■ (of a smile) weak; strained. ■ literary (of the sea) without luster; dark and gloomy.
– DERIVATIVES **wan·ly adv.**, **wan·ness n.**
– ORIGIN Old English *wann* 'dark, black,' of unknown origin.

Wan·a·mak·er /'wänə,mākər/, John (1838–1922) US businessman. A pioneering department store merchant, he cofounded a men's clothing store in Philadelphia in 1861. After his partner's death, he made it into a department store 1877 and opened another in New York City 1896. The success of his stores was based on advertising. He also served as US postmaster general 1889–93.

wand /wänd/ ▶ **n.** a long, thin stick or rod, in particular: ■ a stick or rod thought to have magic properties, held by a magician, fairy, or conjuror and used in casting spells or performing tricks: *the fairy godmother waves her magic wand and grants the heroine's wishes.* ■ a staff or rod held as a symbol of office. ■ informal a conductor's baton. ■ a handheld electronic device that can be passed over a bar code to read the encoded data. ■ a handheld metal detector, used as a security device. ■ a device emitting a laser beam, used esp. to create a pointer on a projected image or text. ■ a small stick with a brush at one end used for the application of mascara. ■ Archery a target 6 feet (1.83 meters) high and 2 inches (5.8 cm) wide, set at 100 yards (91.44 meters) for men and 60 yards (54.86 meters) for women. ■ (**wands**) one of the suits in some tarot packs, corresponding to batons in others.
– ORIGIN Middle English: from Old Norse *vǫndr*, probably of Germanic origin and related to **WEND** and **WIND²**.

wan·der /'wändər/ ▶ **v.** [no obj.] walk or move in a leisurely, casual, or aimless way: *he wandered aimlessly through the narrow streets.* ■ move slowly away from a fixed point or place: *please don't wander off again* | figurative *his attention had wandered.* ■ (of a road or river) wind with gentle twists and turns in a particular direction; meander. ■ [with obj.] move or travel slowly through or over (a place or area): *she found her wandering the streets.* ■ be unfaithful to one's spouse or regular sexual partner.
▶ **n.** an act or instance of wandering: *she'd go on wanders like that in her nightgown.*
– ORIGIN Old English *wandrian*; related to **WEND** and **WIND²**.

wan·der·er /'wändərər/ ▶ **n.** a person who travels aimlessly; a traveler: *he is a longtime seaman, a rootless wanderer.*

wan·der·ing /'wändəriNG/ ▶ **adj.** traveling aimlessly from place to place; itinerant: *a wandering preacher.*

wan·der·ing al·ba·tross ▶ **n.** a very large albatross of southern oceans, having white plumage with black wings and a wingspan of up to 11 feet (3.3 m). ● *Diomedea exulans*, family Diomedeidae.

wan·der·ing Jew ▶ **n. 1** a legendary person said to have been condemned by Jesus Christ to wander the earth until the Second Coming. ■ a person who never settles down.
2 a tender trailing tradescantia, typically having striped leaves that are suffused with purple. ● Genus *Tradescantia*, family Commelinaceae: *T. albiflora* and *T. pendula* (formerly *Zebrina pendula*).

Wan·der·jahr /'vändər,yär/ ▶ **n.** (pl. **Wanderjahre** /-,yärə/) a year spent traveling abroad, typically immediately before or after a university or college course.
– ORIGIN late 19th cent.: German, literally 'wander year.'

wan·der·lust /'wändər,ləst/ ▶ **n.** a strong desire to travel: *a man consumed by wanderlust.*
– ORIGIN early 20th cent.: from German *Wanderlust*.

wan·der·oo /,wändə'rōō/ ▶ **n.** (in Sri Lanka) a leaf monkey or langur. ● Genus *Presbytis*, family Cercopithecidae: the purple-faced leaf monkey (*P. vetulus*), or the hanuman (*P. entellus*).
– ORIGIN late 17th cent.: from Sinhalese *wanderu* 'monkey.'

Wan·der·vo·gel /'wändər,fōgəl/ ▶ **n.** (pl. **Wandervögel** /-,fəgəl/) a member of a German youth organization founded at the end of the 19th century for the promotion of outdoor activities and folk culture. ■ a wanderer, esp. someone who travels the world on foot.
– ORIGIN German, literally 'bird of passage.'

wane¹ /wān/ ▶ **v.** [no obj.] (of the moon) have a progressively smaller part of its visible surface illuminated, so that it appears to decrease in size. ■ (esp. of a condition or feeling) decrease in vigor, power, or extent; become weaker: *confidence in the dollar waned.*
– PHRASES **on the wane** becoming weaker, less vigorous, or less extensive: *the epidemic was on the wane.*
– ORIGIN Old English *wanian* 'lessen,' of Germanic origin; related to Latin *vanus* 'vain.'

wane² ▶ **n.** the amount by which a plank or log is beveled or falls short of a squared shape.
– DERIVATIVES **wane·y adj.**
– ORIGIN mid 17th cent.: from **WANE¹**.

Wang /wäNG/, An (1920–90), US computer engineer; born in China. In 1948, he invented a magnetic core memory for computers. The founder of Wang Laboratories in 1951, he held 40 patents.

wan·gle /'waNGgəl/ informal ▶ **v.** [with obj.] obtain (something that is desired) by persuading others to comply or by manipulating events: *I wangled an invitation to her party* | *I think we should be able to wangle it so that you can start tomorrow.*
▶ **n.** an act or an instance of obtaining something in such a way: *they regarded the coalition as a wangle.*
– DERIVATIVES **wan·gler** /'waNG(ə)lər/ **n.**
– ORIGIN late 19th cent. (first recorded as printers' slang): of unknown origin; perhaps based on the verb **WAGGLE**.

wank /waNGk/ Brit. vulgar slang ▶ **v.** [no obj.] (typically of a man) masturbate.
▶ **n.** an act of masturbating.
– PHRASAL VERBS **wank oneself/someone off** (or **wank off**) masturbate.
– ORIGIN 1940s: of unknown origin.

Wan·kel en·gine /'wäNGkəl, 'waNG-/ ▶ **n.** a rotary internal combustion engine in which a curvilinear, triangular, eccentrically pivoted piston rotates in an elliptical chamber, forming three combustion spaces that vary in volume as the piston turns.
– ORIGIN 1960s: named after Felix *Wankel* (1902–88), German engineer.

wank·er /'waNGkər/ ▶ **n.** Brit. vulgar slang a person who masturbates (used as a term of abuse).

wan·ky /'wäNGkē, 'waNG-/ ▶ **adj.** (**wankier, wankiest**) Brit. vulgar slang contemptible, worthless, or stupid: *I was determined not to end up as some Nigel doing wanky beer ads.*
– ORIGIN late 20th cent.: from *wank* 'masturbate' (of unknown origin) + *-y*.

wan·na /'wônə, 'wä-/ informal ▶ **contraction** want to; want a.

wan·na·be /'wänəbē, 'wô-/ ▶ **n.** informal, derogatory a person who tries to be like someone else or to fit in with a particular group of people: *a star-struck wannabe.*
– ORIGIN 1980s: representing a pronunciation of *want to be*.

want /wänt, wônt/ ▶ **v. 1** [with obj.] have a desire to possess or do (something); wish for: *I want an apple* | [with infinitive] *we want to go to the beach* | [with obj. and infinitive] *she wanted me to go to her room* | [no obj.] *I'll give you a lift into town if you want.* ■ wish to consult or speak to (someone): *Tony wants me in the studio.* ■ (usu. **be wanted**) (of the police) desire to question or apprehend (a suspected criminal): *he is wanted by the police in connection with an arms theft.* ■ desire (someone) sexually: *I've wanted you since the first moment I saw you.* ■ [with present participle] informal, chiefly Brit. (of a thing) require to be attended to in a specified way: *the wheel wants greasing.* ■ [with infinitive] informal ought, should, or need to do something: *you don't want to believe everything you hear.* ■ [no obj.] (**want in/into/out/away**) informal desire to be in or out of a particular place or situation: *if anyone wants out, there's the door.*
2 [no obj.] chiefly archaic lack or be short of something desirable or essential: *you shall* **want** *for nothing while you are with me.* ■ [with obj.] (chiefly used in expressions of time) be short of or lack (a specified amount or thing): *it wanted twenty minutes to midnight* | *it wants a few minutes of five o'clock.*
▶ **n. 1** chiefly archaic a lack or deficiency of something: *Victorian houses which are* **in want of repair** | *it won't be through want of trying.* ■ the state of being poor and in need of essentials; poverty: *freedom from want.*

W

2 a desire for something: *the expression of our wants and desires.*
– PHRASES **for want of** because of a lack of (something): *for want of a better location we ate our picnic lunch in the cemetery.*
– ORIGIN Middle English: the noun from Old Norse *vant,* neuter of *vanr* 'lacking'; the verb from Old Norse *vanta* 'be lacking.' The original notion of "lack" was early extended to "need," and from this developed the sense 'desire.'

want ad ▶ **n.** informal a classified advertisement in a newspaper or magazine; a small ad.

want·ing /'wäntiNG, wônt-/ ▶ **adj.** [predic.] lacking in a certain required or necessary quality: *they weren't **wanting in** confidence | their products would be **found wanting** in a direct comparison.* ■ not existing or supplied; absent: *the kneecap is wanting in amphibians and reptiles.*

want list ▶ **n.** a list of stamps, books, recordings, or similar items required by a collector.

wan·ton /'wäntn/ ▶ **adj. 1** (of a cruel or violent action) deliberate and unprovoked: *sheer wanton vandalism.*
2 (esp. of a woman) sexually immodest or promiscuous. ■ literary growing profusely; luxuriant: *where wanton ivy twines.* ■ literary lively; playful: *a wanton fawn.*
▶ **n.** archaic a sexually immodest or promiscuous woman.
▶ **v.** [no obj.] archaic or literary **1** play; frolic.
2 behave in a sexually immodest or promiscuous way.
– DERIVATIVES **wan·ton·ly adv., wan·ton·ness n.**
– ORIGIN Middle English *wantowen* 'rebellious, lacking discipline,' from *wan-* 'badly' + Old English *togen* 'trained' (related to **TEAM** and **TOW**[1]).

WAP /wap/ ▶ **abbr.** Wireless Application Protocol, a set of protocols for connecting cellular phones and other radio devices to the Internet.

wap·en·take /'wäpən,tāk, 'wa-/ ▶ **n.** historical (in the UK) a subdivision of certain northern and midland English counties, corresponding to a hundred in other counties.
– ORIGIN late Old English *wǣpen(ge)tæc,* from Old Norse *vápnatak,* from *vápn* 'weapon' + *taka* 'take,' perhaps with reference to voting in an assembly by a show of weapons.

wap·i·ti /'wäpitē/ ▶ **n.** (pl. **wapitis**) another term for **ELK**.
– ORIGIN early 19th cent.: from Shawnee, literally 'white rump.'

Wap·si·pin·i·con Riv·er /,wäpsə'pinikən/ a river that flows for 225 miles (360 km) across eastern Iowa to the Mississippi River. Its valley is associated with the regional painting of Grant Wood and others.

waqf /vəkf, vəkf/ ▶ **n.** (pl. **same**) an endowment made by a Muslim to a religious, educational, or charitable cause.
– ORIGIN from Arabic, literally 'stoppage, immobilization (of ownership of property),' from *waqafa* 'come to a standstill.'

war /wôr/ ▶ **n.** a state of armed conflict between different nations or states or different groups within a nation or state: *Japan **declared war** on Germany | the two countries had been **at war** for six years.* ■ a particular armed conflict: *after the war, they emigrated to America.* ■ a state of competition, conflict, or hostility between different people or groups: *she was **at war with** her parents | a price war among discount retailers.* ■ a sustained effort to deal with or end a particular unpleasant or undesirable situation or condition: *the authorities are **waging war against** all forms of smuggling | a **war on drugs**.*
▶ **v.** (**wars, warring, warred**) [no obj.] engage in a war: *small states warred against each other |* figurative *conflicting emotions warred within her.*
– PHRASES **go to war** declare, begin, or see active service in a war. **go to the wars** archaic serve as a soldier. **war clouds** /'wôr ,kloudz/ a threatening situation of instability in international relations: *the war clouds were looming.* **war of attrition** a prolonged war or period of conflict during which each side seeks to gradually wear out the other by a series of small-scale actions. **war of nerves** see **NERVE**. **war of words** a prolonged debate conducted by means of the spoken or printed word. **war to end all wars** a war, esp. World War I, regarded as making subsequent wars unnecessary.
– ORIGIN late Old English *werre,* from an Anglo-Norman French variant of Old French *guerre,* from a Germanic base shared by **WORSE**.

war ba·by ▶ **n.** a child born in wartime, esp. one fathered by a serviceman.

war·bird /'wôr,bərd/ ▶ **n.** a vintage military aircraft.

war·ble[1] /'wôrbəl/ ▶ **v.** [no obj.] (of a bird) sing softly and with a succession of constantly changing notes: *larks were warbling in the trees.* ■ (of a person) sing in a trilling or quavering voice: *he warbled in an implausible soprano.*
▶ **n.** a warbling sound or utterance.
– ORIGIN late Middle English (as a noun in the sense 'melody'): from Old Northern French *werble* (noun), *werbler* (verb), of Germanic origin; related to **WHIRL**.

war·ble[2] ▶ **n.** a swelling or abscess beneath the skin on the back of cattle, horses, and other mammals, caused by the presence of the larva of a warble fly. ■ the larva causing this.
– ORIGIN late Middle English: of uncertain origin.

war·ble fly ▶ **n.** a large fly that lays its eggs on the legs of mammals such as cattle and horses. The larvae migrate internally to the host's back, where they form a small lump with a breathing hole, dropping to the ground later when fully grown.
● Genus *Hypoderma,* family Oestridae: several species, including the widespread *H. bovis.*

war·bler /'wôrb(ə)lər/ ▶ **n. 1** any of a number of small insectivorous songbirds that typically have a warbling song. ● (also **wood warbler**) a New World bird of the subfamily Parulinae, family Emberizidae. ● an Old World bird of the family Sylviidae, which includes the blackcap, whitethroat, and chiffchaff.
2 informal a person who sings in a trilling or quavering voice.

war·blog ▶ **n.** a weblog dealing with a war, or written by an active participant in or witness to warfare.

war bon·net ▶ **n.** see **BONNET** (sense 1).

war bride ▶ **n.** a woman who marries a man whom she met while he was on active service.

War·burg /'wôr,bərg/, Otto Heinrich (1883–1970), German biochemist. He pioneered the use of the techniques of chemistry for biochemical investigations, esp. for his work with the respiratory enzyme. Nobel Prize for Physiology or Medicine (1931); the Nazis prohibited him from accepting a second one in 1944 because of his Jewish ancestry.

war chest ▶ **n.** a reserve of funds used for fighting a war. ■ a sum of money used for conducting a campaign or business.

war col·lege ▶ **n.** a college providing advanced instruction for senior officers of the armed services.

war cor·re·spond·ent ▶ **n.** a journalist reporting from a scene of war.

war crime ▶ **n.** an action carried out during the conduct of a war that violates accepted international rules of war.
– DERIVATIVES **war crim·i·nal n.**

war cry ▶ **n.** a call made to rally soldiers for battle or to gather together participants in a campaign.

Ward[1] /wôrd/, Artemas (1727–1800), American politician and soldier. He served as a general during the American Revolution, second in command to George Washington. Later he was a member of the Continental Congress 1780–82 and of the US House of Representatives 1791–95.

Ward[2], Montgomery (1843–1913), US businessman; full name *Aaron Montgomery Ward.* In 1872, he founded a dry-goods business, which became Montgomery Ward & Co., the first mail-order firm in the US.

ward /wôrd/ ▶ **n. 1** a separate room in a hospital, typically one allocated to a particular type of patient: *a children's ward |* [as modifier] *a ward nurse.* ■ one of the divisions of a prison.
2 an administrative division of a city or borough that typically elects and is represented by a councilor or councilors. ■ a territorial division of the Mormon Church presided over by a bishop.
3 a person, usually a minor, under the care and control of a guardian appointed by their parents or a court. ■ archaic guardianship or the state of being subject to a guardian: *the ward and care of the Crown.*
4 (usu. **wards**) any of the internal ridges or bars in a lock that prevent the turning of any key that does not have grooves of corresponding form or size. ■ the corresponding grooves in the bit of a key.
5 archaic the action of keeping a lookout for danger: *I saw them keeping ward at one of those huge gates.*
6 historical an area of ground enclosed by the encircling walls of a fortress or castle.
7 Fencing a defensive position or motion.
▶ **v.** [with obj.] **1** archaic guard; protect: *it was his duty to ward the king.*
2 admit (a patient) to a hospital ward.
– PHRASES **ward of the court** a person, usually a minor or of unsound mind, for whom a guardian has been appointed by a court or who has become directly subject to the authority of that court.
– PHRASAL VERBS **ward someone/something off** prevent from harming or affecting one: *she put up a hand as if to ward him off.*
– DERIVATIVES **ward·ship** /-,SHip/ **n.**
– ORIGIN Old English *weard* (sense 5 of the noun, also 'body of guards'), *weardian* 'keep safe, guard,' of Germanic origin; reinforced in Middle English by Old Northern French *warde* (noun), *warder* (verb) 'guard,' variants of Old French *garde, garder;* compare with **GUARD**.

-ward (also **-wards**) ▶ **suffix** added to nouns of place or destination and to adverbs of direction. **1** (usu. **-wards**) (forming adverbs) toward the specified place or direction: *eastward | homewards.*
2 (usu. **-ward**) (forming adjectives) turned or tending toward: *onward | upward.*
– ORIGIN Old English *-weard,* from a Germanic base meaning 'turn.' The forms in *-s* are all remnants of the old genitive singular inflection.

war dance ▶ **n.** a ceremonial dance performed before a battle or to celebrate victory.

war·den /'wôrdn/ ▶ **n.** a person responsible for the supervision of a particular place or thing or for ensuring that regulations associated with it are obeyed: *the warden of a local nature reserve | an air-raid warden.* ■ the head official in charge of a prison. ■ a churchwarden. ■ Brit. the head of certain schools, colleges, or other institutions.
– DERIVATIVES **war·den·ship** /-,SHip/ **n.**
– ORIGIN Middle English (originally denoting a guardian or protector): from Anglo-Norman French and Old Northern French *wardein,* variant of Old French *guarden* 'guardian.'

ward·er /'wôrdər/ ▶ **n.** chiefly Brit. a guard in a prison.
– ORIGIN late Middle English (denoting a watchman or sentinel): from Anglo-Norman French *wardere,* from Old Northern French *warder* 'to guard.' The current sense dates from the mid 19th cent.

ward heel·er ▶ **n.** informal, chiefly derogatory a person who assists in a political campaign by canvassing votes for a party and performing menial tasks for its leaders.

ward·robe /'wôr,drōb/ ▶ **n.** a large, tall cabinet in which clothes may be hung or stored. ■ a person's entire collection of clothes: *her wardrobe is extensive.* ■ the costume department or costumes of a theater or movie company: [as modifier] *a wardrobe assistant.* ■ a department of a royal or noble household in charge of clothing.
– ORIGIN Middle English (in the sense 'private chamber'): from Old Northern French *warderobe,* variant of Old French *garderobe* (see **GARDEROBE**).

ward·robe mal·func·tion ▶ **n.** informal, humorous an instance of a person accidentally exposing an intimate part of their body as a result of an article of clothing slipping out of position.

ward·robe mis·tress ▶ **n.** a woman in charge of the construction and organization of the costumes in a theatrical company.

ward·robe trunk ▶ **n.** a trunk fitted with rails and shelves for use as a traveling wardrobe.

ward·room /'wôr,drōōm, -,rŏŏm/ ▶ **n.** a commissioned officers' mess on board a warship.

war drum ▶ **n.** a drum beaten as a summons or an accompaniment to battle.

-wards ▶ **suffix** variant spelling of **-WARD**.

ware[1] /we(ə)r/ ▶ **n.** [usu. with adj. or noun modifier] pottery, typically that of a specified type: *blue-and-white majolica ware |* (**wares**) *Minoan potters produced an astonishing variety of wares.* ■ manufactured articles of a specified type: *crystal ware | aluminum ware.* ■ (**wares**) articles offered for sale: *traders in the street markets displayed their wares.*
– ORIGIN Old English *waru* 'commodities,' of Germanic origin, perhaps the same word as Scots *ware* 'cautiousness,' and having the primary sense 'object of care'; related to **WARE**[2].

ware[2] ▶ **adj.** [predic.] archaic aware: *thou speak'st wiser than thou art ware of.*
– ORIGIN Old English *wær,* from the Germanic base of **WARE**[1].

ware[3] (also **'ware**) ▶ **v.** [in imperative] beware (used as a warning cry, typically in a hunting context).
– ORIGIN Old English *warian* 'be on one's guard,' from a Germanic base meaning 'observe, take care.'

-ware ▶ **comb. form 1** denoting articles made of ceramic or used in cooking and serving food: *tableware | bakeware.*
2 denoting a kind of software: *groupware.*

ware·house ▶ **n.** /'we(ə)r,hous/ a large building where raw materials or manufactured goods may be stored before their export or distribution for sale. ■ a large wholesale or retail store: *a discount warehouse.*

W

▶ **v.** /-ˌhous, -ˌhouz/ [with obj.] store (goods) in a warehouse. ■ place (imported goods) in a bonded warehouse pending the payment of import duty. ■ informal place (someone, typically a prisoner or a psychiatric patient) in a large, impersonal institution in which their problems are not satisfactorily addressed.

ware·house club ▶ **n.** an organization that operates from a large out-of-town store and sells goods in bulk at discounted prices to business and private customers who must first become club members.

ware·house·man /ˈwe(ə)rˌhousmən/ ▶ **n.** (pl. **warehousemen**) a person who is employed in, manages, or owns a warehouse.

ware·hous·ing /ˈwe(ə)rˌhouziNG/ ▶ **n.** the practice or process of storing goods in a warehouse. ■ warehouses considered collectively. ■ informal the practice of placing people, typically prisoners or psychiatric patients, in large, impersonal institutions.

warez /we(ə)rz/ ▶ **plural n.** Computing, informal software that has been illegally copied and made available.
– ORIGIN 1990s: respelling of *wares*.

war·fare /ˈwôrˌfe(ə)r/ ▶ **n.** engagement in or the activities involved in war or conflict: *guerrilla warfare*.

war·fa·rin /ˈwôrfərin/ ▶ **n.** a water-soluble compound with anticoagulant properties, used as a rat poison and in the treatment of thrombosis. ● A coumarin derivative; chem. formula: $C_{19}H_{16}O_4$.
– ORIGIN 1950s: from the initial letters of *Wisconsin Alumni Research Foundation* + *-arin* on the pattern of *coumarin*.

war·fight·er /ˈwôrˌfītər/ ▶ **n.** a soldier in combat.

war game ▶ **n.** a military exercise carried out to test or improve tactical expertise. ■ a simulated military conflict carried out as a game, leisure activity, or exercise in personal development.
▶ **v.** [with obj.] (**war-game**) engage in (a campaign or course of action) using the strategies of such a military exercise: *there seemed to be no point war-gaming an election 15 months away*.
– DERIVATIVES **war-gam·er n.**

war·gam·ing /ˈwôrˌgāmiNG/ (also **war gaming**) ▶ **n.** the action of playing a war game as a leisure activity or exercise in personal development. ■ the action of engaging in a campaign or course of action using the strategies of a military exercise.

war·head /ˈwôrˌhed/ ▶ **n.** the explosive head of a missile, torpedo, or similar weapon.

War·hol /ˈwôrˌhôl, -ˌhōl/, Andy (*c.*1928–87), US painter, graphic artist, and filmmaker; born *Andrew Warhola*. A major exponent of pop art, he achieved fame for a series of silkscreen prints and acrylic paintings of familiar objects (such as Campbell's soup cans) and famous people (such as Marilyn Monroe), that are treated with objectivity and precision.

war·horse /ˈwôrˌhôrs/ ▶ **n.** (in historical contexts) a large, powerful horse ridden in battle. ■ informal a soldier, politician, or sports player who has fought many campaigns or contests. ■ informal a musical, theatrical, or literary work that has been heard or performed repeatedly: *that old warhorse Liszt's "Hungarian Rhapsody No. 2."*

war·i·ly /ˈwe(ə)rəlē/ ▶ **adv.** cautiously; carefully: *they walk warily down the street, terrified of being caught*. ■ in a way that shows a lack of trust; suspiciously: *she looked at him warily*.

war·i·ness /ˈwe(ə)rēnis/ ▶ **n.** caution about possible dangers or problems: *her mother's wariness of computers*. ■ lack of trust; suspicion: *they had all regarded her with wariness*.

War·ka /wərˈkä/ Arabic name for **Uruk**.

war·like /ˈwôrˌlīk/ ▶ **adj.** disposed toward or threatening war; hostile: *a warlike clan*. ■ (of plans, preparations, or munitions) directed toward or prepared for war.

war·lock /ˈwôrˌläk/ ▶ **n.** a man who practices witchcraft; a sorcerer.
– ORIGIN Old English *wǣrloga* 'traitor, scoundrel, monster,' also 'the Devil,' from *wǣr* 'covenant' + an element related to *lēogan* 'belie, deny.' From its application to the Devil, the word was transferred in Middle English to a person in league with the devil, and hence a sorcerer. It was chiefly Scots until given wider currency by Sir Walter Scott.

war·lord /ˈwôrˌlôrd/ ▶ **n.** a military commander, esp. an aggressive regional commander with individual autonomy.

warm /wôrm/ ▶ **adj. 1** of or at a fairly or comfortably high temperature: *a warm September evening* | [as complement] *I walked quickly to keep warm*. ■ (of clothes or coverings) made of a material that helps the body to retain heat; suitable for cold weather: *a warm winter coat*. ■ (of a color) containing red, yellow, or orange tones: *her fair coloring suited soft, warm shades*. ■ Hunting (of a scent or trail) fresh; strong. ■ (of a soil) quick to absorb heat or retaining heat.
2 having, showing, or expressive of enthusiasm, affection, or kindness: *they exchanged warm, friendly smiles* | *a warm welcome*. ■ archaic characterized by lively or heated disagreement: *a warm debate arose*. ■ archaic sexually explicit or titillating.
3 [predic.] informal (esp. in children's games) close to discovering something or guessing the correct answer: *you're getting warmer*.
▶ **v.** make or become warm: [with obj.] *I stamped my feet to* **warm** *them* **up** | figurative *the film warmed our hearts* | [no obj.] *it's a bit chilly in here, but it'll soon* **warm up**.
– PHRASES **keep something warm for someone** hold or occupy a place or post until another person is ready to do so.
– PHRASAL VERBS **warm down** recover from strenuous physical exertion by doing gentle stretches and exercises. **warm to/toward** (or **warm up to/toward**) begin to like (someone): *she and Will had really warmed up to each other*. ■ become more interested in or enthusiastic about (something): *I never really warmed to the idea of moving*. **warm up** prepare for physical exertion or a performance by exercising or practicing gently beforehand: *the band was warming up*. ■ (of an engine or electrical appliance) reach a temperature high enough to allow it to operate efficiently. ■ become livelier or more animated: *after several more rounds, things began to warm up in the bar*. **warm something up** (or **over**) reheat previously cooked food. ■ amuse or entertain an audience or crowd so as to make them more receptive to the main act.
– DERIVATIVES **warm·er n.** [usu. in combination] *a towel-warmer*, **warm·ish adj.**, **warm·ly adv.**, **warm·ness n.**
– ORIGIN Old English *wearm* (adjective), *werman*, *wearmian* (verb), of Germanic origin; related to Dutch and German *warm*, from an Indo-European root shared by Latin *formus* 'warm' and Greek *thermos* 'hot.'

war ma·chine ▶ **n. 1** the military resources of a country organized for waging war.
2 an instrument or weapon of war.

warm·blood /ˈwôrmˌbləd/ ▶ **n.** a horse of a breed that is a cross between an Arab or similar breed and another breed of the draft or pony type.

warm-blood·ed ▶ **adj. 1** relating to or denoting animals (chiefly mammals and birds) that maintain a constant body temperature, typically above that of the surroundings, by metabolic means; homeothermic.
2 ardent; passionate.
– DERIVATIVES **warm-blood·ed·ness n.**

warm-down ▶ **n.** a series of gentle exercises designed to relax the body after strenuous physical exertion.

warmed-o·ver ▶ **adj. 1** (also **warmed-up**) (of food or drink) reheated: *warmed-over chicken and pasta*.
2 (of an idea or product) secondhand; stale: *a heap of warmed-over action film clichés*.

war me·mo·ri·al ▶ **n.** a monument commemorating those killed in a war.

warm front ▶ **n.** Meteorology the boundary of an advancing mass of warm air, in particular the leading edge of the warm sector of a low-pressure system.

warm fuz·zy ▶ **n.** see **fuzzy**.

warm·heart·ed /ˈwôrm ˈhärtəd/ ▶ **adj.** (of a person or their actions) sympathetic and kind.
– DERIVATIVES **warm·heart·ed·ly adv.**, **warm·heart·ed·ness n.**

warm·ing pan ▶ **n.** historical a wide, flat brass pan on a long handle, filled with hot coals and used for warming a bed.

war·mon·ger /ˈwôrˌməNGgər, -ˌmäNG-/ ▶ **n.** a sovereign or political leader or activist who encourages or advocates aggression or warfare toward other nations or groups.
– DERIVATIVES **war·mon·ger·ing n. & adj.**

Warm Springs a resort in northwestern Georgia, associated with Franklin D. Roosevelt and his "Little White House," where he died; pop. 477 (est. 2008).

warmth /wôrmTH/ ▶ **n.** the quality, state, or sensation of being warm; moderate and comfortable heat: *the warmth of the sun on her skin*. ■ enthusiasm, affection, or kindness: *she smiled with real warmth*. ■ vehemence or intensity of emotion: *"Of course not," he snapped, with a warmth that he regretted*.

warm-up (also **warmup**) ▶ **n.** a period or act of preparation for a game, performance, or exercise session, involving gentle exercise or practice. ■ (**warm-ups**) a garment worn during light exercise or training; a sweatsuit. ■ a period before a stage performance in which the audience is amused or entertained in order to make it more receptive to the main act.

warn /wôrn/ ▶ **v.** [reporting verb] inform someone in advance of an impending or possible danger, problem, or other unpleasant situation: [with obj.] *his father had* **warned** *him* **of** *what might happen* | [with direct speech] *"He's going to humiliate you," John warned* | [with clause] *the union warned that its members were close to going on strike*. ■ give someone forceful or cautionary advice about their actions or conduct: [with obj.] *friends* **warned** *her* **against** *the marriage* | [with obj. and infinitive] *they warned people not to keep large amounts of cash in their homes* | [no obj.] *they* **warned against** *false optimism*.
– PHRASAL VERBS **warn someone off** tell someone forcefully or threateningly to go away or stay. ■ advise someone forcefully against (a particular thing or course of action): *he has been warned off booze*.
– DERIVATIVES **warn·er n.**
– ORIGIN Old English *war(e)nian*, *wearnian*, from a West Germanic base meaning 'be cautious'; compare with **ware**[2].

War·ner Broth·ers /ˈwôrnər/ a movie production company founded in 1923 by the brothers Harry, Jack, Sam, and Albert Warner. The company produced the first full-length sound movie, *The Jazz Singer*, in 1927 and went on to release successful gangster films with Humphrey Bogart, Busby Berkeley musicals in the 1930s and 1940s, and the Looney Tunes cartoons.

War·ner Rob·ins /ˌwôrnər ˈräbinz/ an industrial city in central Georgia, site of a US Air Force base; pop. 61,336 (est. 2008).

warn·ing /ˈwôrniNG/ ▶ **n.** a statement or event that indicates a possible or impending danger, problem, or other unpleasant situation: *a warning about heavy thunderstorms* | *suddenly and without any warning, the army opened fire* | [as modifier] *a red warning light*. ■ cautionary advice: *a word of warning—don't park illegally*. ■ advance notice of something: *she had only had four days' warning before leaving Berlin*. ■ an experience or sight that serves as a cautionary example to others: *his death should be a warning to everyone*.
– DERIVATIVES **warn·ing·ly adv.**
– ORIGIN Old English *war(e)nung* (see **warn**, **-ing**[1]).

warn·ing col·or·a·tion ▶ **n.** Zoology conspicuous coloring that warns a predator that an animal is unpalatable or poisonous.

warn·ing track ▶ **n.** Baseball a grassless strip around the outside of the outfield grass that warns fielders that they are approaching the outfield wall.

War of 1812 a conflict between the US and the UK (1812–14), prompted by restrictions on US trade resulting from the British blockade of French and allied ports during the Napoleonic Wars, and by British and Canadian support for American Indians trying to resist westward expansion. It was ended by a treaty that restored all conquered territories to their owners before outbreak of war.

War of A·mer·i·can In·de·pend·ence see **American Revolution**.

War of Jen·kins's Ear see **Jenkins's Ear, War of**.

warp /wôrp/ ▶ **v. 1** become or cause to become bent or twisted out of shape, typically as a result of the effects of heat or dampness: [no obj.] *wood has a tendency to warp* | [with obj.] *moisture had warped the box*. ■ [with obj.] cause to become abnormal or strange; have a distorting effect on: *your judgment has been warped by your obvious dislike of him* | (as adj. **warped**) *a warped sense of humor*.
2 [with obj.] move (a ship) along by hauling on a rope attached to a stationary object on shore. ■ [no obj.] (of a ship) move in such a way.
3 [with obj.] (in weaving) arrange (yarn) so as to form the warp of a piece of cloth.
4 [with obj.] cover (land) with a deposit of alluvial soil by natural or artificial flooding.
▶ **n. 1** a twist or distortion in the shape or form of something: *the head of the racket had a curious warp*. ■ [as modifier] relating to or denoting (fictional or hypothetical) space travel by means of distorting space-time: *the craft possessed warp drive* | *warp speed*. ■ an abnormality or perversion in a person's character.
2 [in sing.] (in weaving) the threads on a loom over and under which other threads (the weft) are passed to make cloth: *the warp and weft are the basic constituents of all textiles* | figurative *rugby is woven into the warp and weft of South African society*.
3 a rope attached at one end to a fixed point and used for moving or mooring a ship.
4 archaic alluvial sediment; silt.
– DERIVATIVES **warp·age** /ˈwôrpij/ **n.**, **warp·er n.**

– ORIGIN Old English *weorpan* (verb), *wearp* (noun), of Germanic origin; related to Dutch *werpen* and German *werfen* 'to throw.' Early verb senses included 'throw,' 'fling open,' and 'hit (with a missile)'; the sense 'bend' dates from late Middle English. The noun was originally a term in weaving (sense 2 of the noun).

war·paint /'wôr,pānt/ ▶ n. a pigment or paint traditionally used in some societies, esp. those of North American Indians, to decorate the face and body before battle. ■ informal elaborate or excessively applied makeup.

war·path /'wôr,paTH/ ▶ n. (in phrase **on the warpath**) angry and ready or eager for confrontation: *he intends to go on the warpath with a national campaign to reverse the decision.*
– ORIGIN with reference to American Indians heading toward a battle with an enemy.

war·plane /'wôr,plān/ ▶ n. an airplane designed and equipped to engage in air combat or to drop bombs.

war po·et ▶ n. a poet writing at the time of and on the subject of war, esp. one on military service during World War I.

warp speed ▶ n. informal an extremely high speed: *these exciting developments are moving ahead at warp speed.*
– ORIGIN 1970s: popularized by the television series *Star Trek* (originally referring to a faster-than-light speed attained by a spaceship traveling in a space warp).

war·rant /'wôrənt, 'wä-/ ▶ n. **1** a document issued by a legal or government official authorizing the police or some other body to make an arrest, search premises, or carry out some other action relating to the administration of justice: *magistrates issued a warrant for his arrest* | *an extradition warrant.* ■ a document that entitles the holder to receive goods, money, or services: *we'll issue you with a travel warrant.* ■ Finance a negotiable security allowing the holder to buy shares at a specified price at or before some future date. ■ [usu. with negative] justification or authority for an action, belief, or feeling: *there is no warrant for this assumption.*
2 an official certificate of appointment issued to an officer of lower rank than a commissioned officer.
▶ v. [with obj.] justify or necessitate (a certain course of action): *that offense is serious enough to warrant a court marshal.* ■ officially affirm or guarantee: *the vendor warrants the accuracy of the report.*
– PHRASES **I** (or **I'll**) **warrant (you)** dated used to express the speaker's certainty about a fact or situation: *I'll warrant you'll thank me for it in years to come.*
– DERIVATIVES **war·rant·er** n.
– ORIGIN Middle English (in the senses 'protector' and 'safeguard,' also, as a verb, 'keep safe from danger'): from variants of Old French *guarant* (noun), *guarantir* (verb), of Germanic origin; compare with GUARANTEE.

war·rant·a·ble /'wôrəntəbəl, 'wä-/ ▶ adj. (of an action or statement) able to be authorized or sanctioned; justifiable: *a warrantable assertion.*
– DERIVATIVES **war·rant·a·ble·ness** n., **war·rant·a·bly** /-blē/ adv.

war·ran·tee /,wôrən'tē, ,wä-/ ▶ n. Law a person to whom a warranty is given.

> **USAGE** Warrantee means 'person to whom a warranty is made'; it is not a spelling variant of **warranty.**

war·rant·less /'wärəntləs/ ▶ adj. carried out without legal or official authorization: *warrantless searches and wiretaps.*

war·rant of·fi·cer ▶ n. an officer in the US armed forces ranking below the commissioned officers and above the noncommissioned officers.

war·ran·tor /'wôrəntər, 'wä-/ ▶ n. a person or company that provides a warranty.

war·ran·ty /'wôrəntē, 'wä-/ ▶ n. (pl. **warranties**) a written guarantee, issued to the purchaser of an article by its manufacturer, promising to repair or replace it if necessary within a specified period of time: *the car comes with a three-year warranty* | *as your machine is under warranty, I suggest getting it checked.* ■ (in contract law) a promise that something in furtherance of the contract is guaranteed by one of the contractors, esp. the seller's promise that the thing being sold is as promised or represented. ■ (in an insurance contract) an engagement by the insured party that certain statements are true or that certain conditions shall be fulfilled, the breach of it invalidating the policy. ■ (in property law) a covenant by which the seller binds themselves and their heirs to secure to the buyer the estate conveyed in the deed. ■ (in contract law) a term or promise in a contract, breach of which entitles the innocent party to damages but not to treat the contract as discharged by breach. ■ [usu. with negative] archaic justification or grounds for an action or belief: *you have no warranty for such an audacious doctrine.*
– ORIGIN Middle English: from Anglo-Norman French *warantie*, variant of *garantie* (see GUARANTY). Early use was as a legal term denoting a covenant annexed to a conveyance of property, in which the vendor affirmed the security of the title.

> **USAGE** See usage at WARRANTEE.

war·ran·ty deed ▶ n. Law a deed that guarantees a clear title to the buyer of real property.

War·ren[1] /'wôrən, 'wär-/ **1** an industrial city in southeastern Michigan, north of Detroit; pop. 133,939 (est. 2008).
2 an industrial city in northeastern Ohio, on the Mahoning River; pop. 43,789 (est. 2008).

War·ren[2], American family of physicians. **Joseph Warren** (1741–75), a patriot active in the events leading up to the American Revolution, was killed at the Battle of Bunker Hill. His brother, **John Warren** (1753–1815), was a leading medical practitioner in New England, a surgeon in the American Revolution, and the founder of Harvard Medical School in 1783. **John Collins Warren** (1778–1856), the son of John Warren, helped to found Massachusetts General Hospital in 1811.

War·ren[3], Earl (1891–1974), US chief justice 1953–69. He did much to extend civil liberties, including the prohibition of segregation in schools. He is also remembered for heading the Warren Commission 1964 that investigated into the assassination of President Kennedy and concluded that Lee Harvey Oswald was the sole gunman.

Earl Warren

War·ren[4], Mercy Otis (1728–1814), American writer and political satirist; the sister of James Otis. She wrote *The Adulateur* (1773) and *The Group* (1775), as well as the play *History of the Rise, Progress, and Termination of the American Revolution* (1805).

War·ren[5], Robert Penn (1905–89), US poet, novelist, and critic. The first person to win Pulitzer Prizes in both fiction and poetry categories, he was made the US's first poet laureate in 1986. Notable works: *All the King's Men* (1946), *A Place To Come To* (1977), *Promises* (1957), *Now and Then* (1978).

war·ren /'wôrən, 'wä-/ ▶ n. (also **rabbit warren**) a network of interconnecting rabbit burrows. ■ a densely populated or labyrinthine building or district: *a warren of narrow gas-lit streets.* ■ Brit. historical an enclosed piece of land set aside for breeding game, esp. rabbits.
– ORIGIN late Middle English: from an Anglo-Norman French and Old Northern French variant of Old French *garenne* 'game park,' of Gaulish origin.

war·ren·er /'wôrənər, 'wä-/ ▶ n. historical a gamekeeper. ■ a person in charge of a rabbit warren, either as owner or on behalf of its owner.
– ORIGIN late Middle English: from Anglo-Norman French *warener*, from *warenne* 'game park.'

war·ring /'wôriNG/ ▶ adj. [attrib.] (of two or more people or groups) in conflict with each other: *warring factions* | *a warring couple.*

war·ri·or /'wôrēər/ ▶ n. (esp. in former times) a brave or experienced soldier or fighter.
– ORIGIN Middle English: from Old Northern French *werreior*, variant of Old French *guerreior*, from *guerreier* 'make war,' from *guerre* 'war.'

war room ▶ n. a room from which a war is directed. ■ a room from which business or political strategy is planned.

War·saw /'wôr,sô/ the capital of Poland, in the eastern central part of the country, on the Vistula River; pop. 1,704,717 (2007). The city suffered severe damage and the loss of 700,000 lives during World War II and was almost completely rebuilt. Polish name **Warszawa**.

War·saw Pact a treaty of mutual defense and military aid signed at Warsaw on May 14, 1955, by communist states of Europe under Soviet influence, in response to the admission of West Germany to NATO. The pact was dissolved in 1991.

war·ship /'wôr,SHip/ ▶ n. a ship equipped with weapons and designed to take part in warfare at sea.

Wars of Re·li·gion another term for FRENCH WARS OF RELIGION.

Wars of the Ros·es the 15th-century English civil wars between the Houses of York and Lancaster, represented by white and red roses respectively, during the reigns of Henry VI, Edward IV, and Richard III. The struggle was largely ended in 1485 by the defeat and death of the Yorkist king Richard III at the Battle of Bosworth and the accession of the Lancastrian Henry Tudor (Henry VII), who united the two houses by marrying **Elizabeth**, daughter of Edward IV.

wart /wôrt/ ▶ n. a small, hard, benign growth on the skin, caused by a virus. ■ any rounded excrescence on the skin of an animal or the surface of a plant. ■ informal an obnoxious or objectionable person. ■ an undesirable or disfiguring feature: *few products are without their warts.*
– PHRASES **warts and all** informal including features or qualities that are not appealing or attractive: *Philip must learn to accept me, warts and all.*
– DERIVATIVES **wart·y** /'wôrtē/ adj.
– ORIGIN Old English *wearte*, of Germanic origin; related to Dutch *wrat* and German *Warze*.

wart·hog /'wôrt,häg/ ▶ n. an African wild pig with bristly gray skin, a large head, warty lumps on the face, and curved tusks. ● *Phacochoerus aethiopicus*, family Suidae.

war·time /'wôr,tīm/ ▶ n. a period during which a war is taking place.

war·torn ▶ adj. (of a place) racked or devastated by war: *a war-torn republic.*

war-wear·y ▶ adj. exhausted and dispirited by war or conflict: *an increasingly war-weary population.*

War·wick /'wôrik, 'wär-, -wik/ a city in east central Rhode Island, south of Providence; pop. 84,483 (est. 2008).

war wid·ow (or **war widower**) ▶ n. a woman (or man) whose spouse has been killed in war.

war·y /'we(ə)rē/ ▶ adj. (**warier**, **wariest**) feeling or showing caution about possible dangers or problems: *dogs that have been mistreated often remain very wary of strangers* | *a wary look.*
– ORIGIN late 15th cent.: from WARE[2] + -Y[1].

war zone ▶ n. a region in which a war is being fought: *more troops were transferred to the war zone* | figurative *for children in the ghetto, even the playground is a war zone.*

was /wəz/ first and third person singular past of BE.

wa·sa·bi /wə'säbē/ ▶ n. a Japanese plant with a thick green root that tastes like strong horseradish and is used in cooking, esp. in powder or paste form as an accompaniment to raw fish. ● *Eutrema wasabi*, family Brassicaceae.
– ORIGIN early 20th cent.: from Japanese.

Wa·satch Range /'wô,saCH/ a range of the Rocky Mountains that extends south from Idaho into central Utah, where Salt Lake City and its suburbs lie on its west.

wash /wäsH, wôsH/ ▶ v. **1** [with obj.] clean with water and, typically, soap or detergent: *I stripped and washed myself all over.* ■ [no obj.] clean oneself, esp. one's hands and face with soap and water. ■ (with reference to a stain or dirt) remove or be removed by cleaning with water and detergent: *they have to keep washing the mold off the walls* | figurative *all that hate can't wash away the guilt* | [no obj.] *the dirt on his clothes would easily wash out.* ■ [no obj.] (of fabric, a garment, or dye) withstand cleaning to a specified degree without shrinking or fading: *a linen-mix yarn that washes well.* ■ [no obj.] do one's laundry: *I need someone to cook and wash for me.* ■ literary wet or moisten (something) thoroughly: *you are beautiful with your face washed with rain.*
2 [with obj.] (of flowing water) carry (someone or something) in a particular direction: *floods washed away the bridges.* ■ [no obj.] be carried by flowing water: *an oil slick washed up on the beaches.* ■ [no obj.] (esp. of waves) sweep, move, or splash in a particular direction: *the sea began to wash along the decks.* ■ (of a river, sea, or lake) flow through or lap against (a country, coast, etc.): *offshore islands washed by warm blue seas.* ■ sift metallic particles from (earth or gravel) by running water through it.
3 [with obj.] brush with a thin coat of diluted paint or ink: *the walls were washed with shades of umber.*

W

■ (**wash something with**) coat inferior metal with (a film of gold or silver from a solution).
4 [no obj.] informal seem convincing or genuine: *charm won't wash with this crew.*
▶ **n. 1** [usu. in sing.] an act of washing something or an instance of being washed. ■ a quantity of clothes needing to be or just having been washed: *she hung out her Tuesday wash.* ■ a medicinal or cleansing solution: *mouth wash.*
2 [in sing.] the disturbed water or air behind a moving boat or aircraft or the sound made by this: *the wash of a motorboat.* ■ the surging of water or breaking of waves or the sound made by this: *the wash of waves on the pebbled beach.*
3 a layer of paint or metal spread thinly on a surface: *the walls were covered with a pale lemon wash.*
4 silt or gravel carried by a stream or river and deposited as sediment. ■ a sandbank exposed only at low tide. ■ (in the western US) a dry bed of a stream, typically in a ravine, that flows only seasonally.
5 kitchen slops and other food waste fed to pigs.
6 malt fermenting in preparation for distillation.
7 [in sing.] informal a situation or result that is of no benefit to either of two opposing sides: *the plan's impact on jobs would be a wash, creating as many as it costs.*
– PHRASES **come out in the wash** informal be resolved eventually with no lasting harm: *he's not happy, but he assures me **it'll all come out in the wash.*** **in the wash** (of clothes, bed linen, or similar) put aside for washing or in the process of being washed. **wash** (or **air**) **one's dirty linen** (or **laundry**) **in public** informal (of an individual or a member of an organization) discuss or argue about one's private affairs in public. **wash one's hands** go to the toilet (used euphemistically). **wash one's hands of** disclaim responsibility for: *the social services washed their hands of his daughter.* [originally with biblical allusion to Matt. 27:24.] **wash one's mouth out** (**with soap**) [often as imperative] stop swearing.
– PHRASAL VERBS **wash something down** accompany or follow food with a drink: *bacon and eggs washed down with a cup of tea.* **wash out** (or **wash someone out**) be excluded (or exclude someone) from a course or position after a failure to meet the required standards: *a lot of them had washed out of pilot training.* **wash something out 1** cause an event to be postponed or canceled because of rain: *the game was washed out.* **2** (of a flood or downpour) make a breach in a road. **wash over** (of a feeling) affect (someone) suddenly: *a deep feeling of sadness washed over her.* ■ occur all around without greatly affecting (someone): *she allowed the babble of conversation to wash over her.*
– ORIGIN Old English *wæscan* (verb), of Germanic origin; related to Dutch *wassen*, German *waschen*, also to WATER.

Wash. ▶ **abbr.** Washington.

wash·a·ble /ˈwäsнəbəl, ˈwôsн-/ ▶ **adj.** (esp. of fabric or clothes) able to be washed without shrinkage or other damage: *washable curtains* | [as noun] *fine washables.*
– DERIVATIVES **wash·a·bil·i·ty** /ˌwäsнəˈbilitē, ˌwôsн-/ **n.**

wash-and-wear ▶ **adj.** (of a garment or fabric) easily washed, drying quickly, and not needing to be ironed.

wash·a·ter·i·a ▶ **n.** variant form of WASHETERIA.

wash·ba·sin /ˈwäsнˌbāsən, ˈwôsн-/ ▶ **n.** a basin, typically fixed to a wall or on a pedestal, used for washing one's hands and face.

wash·board /ˈwäsнˌbôrd, ˈwôsн-/ ▶ **n. 1** a board made of ridged wood or a sheet of corrugated zinc, used when washing clothes as a surface against which to scrub them. ■ a similar board played as a percussion instrument by scraping. ■ the surface of a worn, uneven road. ■ [as modifier] denoting a man's stomach that is lean and has well-defined muscles.
2 a board fixed along the side of a boat to prevent water from spilling in over the edge.
▶ **v.** [with obj.] (usu. as adj. **washboarded**) cause ridges to develop in (a road or road surface): *a road left washboarded by winter frost.*

W

wash·bowl /ˈwäsнbōl/ ▶ **n.** another term for WASHBASIN.

wash·cloth /ˈwäsнˌklôтн, ˈwôsн-/ ▶ **n.** a cloth for washing one's face and body, typically made of terry cloth or other absorbent material.

wash·day /ˈwäsнˌdā, ˈwôsн-/ ▶ **n.** a day on which a household's clothes, bed linens, etc., are washed, esp. when the same day each week.

wash draw·ing ▶ **n.** a picture or sketch made by laying on washes of watercolor, typically in monochrome, over a pen or pencil drawing.

washed-out ▶ **adj.** faded by or as if by sunlight or repeated washing: *washed-out jeans.* ■ (of a person) pale and tired.

washed-up ▶ **adj.** deposited by the tide on a shore: *washed-up jellyfish.* ■ informal no longer effective or successful: *a washed-up actress.*

wash·er /ˈwäsнər, ˈwôsн-/ ▶ **n. 1** [usu. with modifier] a person or device that washes something: *a glass washer.* ■ a washing machine.
2 a small flat ring made of metal, rubber, or plastic fixed under a nut or the head of a bolt to spread the pressure when tightened or between two joining surfaces as a spacer or seal.

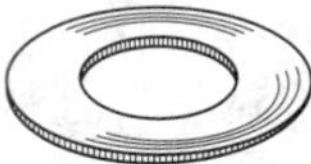
flat washer

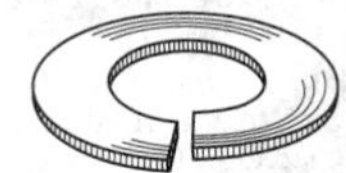
split-ring lock washer

internal tooth washer

external tooth washer

washer 2

wash·er-dry·er ▶ **n.** a washing machine with a built-in tumble-dryer.

wash·er·wom·an /ˈwäsнərˌwŏŏmən, ˈwôsн-/ ▶ **n.** (pl. **washerwomen**) a woman whose occupation is washing clothes.

wash·e·te·ri·a /ˌwäsнəˈti(ə)rēə, ˌwôsн-/ (also **washateria**) ▶ **n.** another term for LAUNDROMAT.
– ORIGIN 1950s: from WASH, on the pattern of *cafeteria.*

wash·ing /ˈwäsнiNG, ˈwôsн-/ ▶ **n.** the action of washing oneself or laundering clothes, bed linen, etc. ■ a quantity of clothes, bed linen, etc., that is to be washed or has just been washed: *she took her washing around to the laundromat.*

wash·ing ma·chine ▶ **n.** a machine for washing clothes, bed linens, etc.

wash·ing so·da ▶ **n.** sodium carbonate, used dissolved in water for washing and cleaning.

Wash·ing·ton[1] /ˈwôsнiNGtən, ˈwäsн-/ **1** a state in the northwestern US, on the Pacific coast, bordered by Canada; pop. 6,549,224 (est. 2008); capital, Olympia; statehood, Nov. 11, 1889 (42). By agreement with Britain, Washington's northern border was set at the 49th parallel in 1846.
2 the capital of the US; pop. 591,833 (est. 2008). It is coextensive with the District of Columbia, a federal district on the Potomac River bordering on the states of Virginia and Maryland. Founded in 1790, during the presidency of George Washington, the city was planned by engineer Pierre-Charles L'Enfant (1754–1825) and built as the capital. Full name **Washington, DC.**
– DERIVATIVES **Wash·ing·to·ni·an** /ˌwôsнiNGˈtōnēən, ˌwäsн-/ **n. & adj.**

Wash·ing·ton[2], Booker T. (1856–1915), US educator; full name *Booker Taliaferro Washington.* A leading commentator for black Americans, he established the Tuskegee Institute in Alabama (1881). His support for segregation and his emphasis on vocational skills for blacks were criticized by other black leaders.

Booker T. Washington

Wash·ing·ton[3], Bushrod (1762–1829), US Supreme Court associate justice 1798–1829; a nephew of George Washington. Appointed to the Court by President John Adams, he helped to establish the supremacy of the Court over states' rights.

Wash·ing·ton[4], George (1732–99), 1st president of the US 1789–97. Commander in chief of the Continental Army, he helped to win the American Revolution by keeping his army together through the winter of 1777–78 at Valley Forge and by winning a decisive battle at Yorktown in 1781. In 1787, he chaired the convention at Philadelphia that drew up the US Constitution. In his two terms as president, he followed a policy of neutrality in international affairs and of expansion on the domestic front.

George Washington

Wash·ing·ton, Mount a peak in north central New Hampshire, the highest in the Presidential Range of the White Mountains and in the northeastern US at 6,288 feet (1,918 m).

Wash·ing·ton Mon·u·ment a colossal obelisk erected in honor of George Washington as a national memorial in Washington, DC. The square base of the obelisk measures 55 feet (17 m) on a side, and the tapering hollow shaft, containing a stairway and elevator to the top, is 555 feet (169 m) high. The cornerstone to the monument was laid on July 4, 1848; the monument was finished in 1884 and opened to the public in 1886.

Washington Monument

Wash·ing·ton Square a park in lower Manhattan in New York City, a focal point of Greenwich Village.

Wash·i·ta Riv·er /ˈwôsнiˌtô, ˈwäsн-/ a river that flows for 500 miles (800 km) from the Texas Panhandle across southern Oklahoma to the Red River at Lake Texoma.

wash·out /ˈwäsнˌout, ˈwôsн-/ ▶ **n. 1** [usu. in sing.] informal an event that is spoiled by constant or heavy rain. ■ a disappointing failure: *the film was a washout.*
2 a breach in a road or railroad track caused by flooding. ■ Geology a channel cut into a sedimentary deposit by rushing water and filled with younger material.
3 Medicine the removal of material or a substance from the body or a part of it, either by washing with a fluid, or by allowing it to be eliminated over a period.

wash·rag /ˈwäsнˌrag, ˈwôsн-/ ▶ **n.** another term for WASHCLOTH.

wash·room /ˈwäsнˌro͞om, ˈwôsн-, -ˌro͝om/ ▶ **n.** a room with washing and toilet facilities.

wash·stand /ˈwäsнˌstand, ˈwôsн-/ ▶ **n.** chiefly historical a piece of furniture designed to hold a jug, bowl, or basin for the purpose of washing one's hands and face.

wash·tub /ˈwäsнˌtəb, ˈwôsн-/ ▶ **n.** a large metal tub used for washing clothes and linen.

wash-up ▶ **n.** an act of washing, esp. washing oneself or dishes.

wash·y /ˈwäsнē, ˈwôsнē/ ▶ **adj.** (**washier, washiest**) **1** archaic (of food or drink) too watery: *washy*

potatoes. ■ lacking in strength or vigor; insipid: *a weak and washy production.*
2 (of a color) having a faded look.
– DERIVATIVES **wash·i·ness** n.

was·n't /'wəzənt/ ▶ contraction was not.

Wasp /wäsp/ (also **WASP**) ▶ n. an upper- or middle-class American white Protestant, considered to be a member of the most powerful group in society.
– DERIVATIVES **Wasp·ish** adj., **Wasp·y** adj.
– ORIGIN 1950s: acronym from *white Anglo-Saxon Protestant.*

wasp /wäsp/ ▶ n. 1 a social winged insect that has a narrow waist and a sting. It constructs a paper nest from wood pulp and raises the larvae on a diet of insects. ● Family Vespidae, superfamily Vespoidea, order Hymenoptera: several genera, in particular *Vespula* and *Polistes.*
2 a solitary winged insect with a narrow waist, mostly distantly related to the social wasps and including many parasitic kinds. ● Several superfamilies in the sections Aculeata (digger, mason, and potter wasps) and Parasitica (parasitic wasps and gall wasps), order Hymenoptera.
– DERIVATIVES **wasp·like** /-ˌlīk/ adj.
– ORIGIN Old English *wæfs, wæps, wæsp,* from an Indo-European root shared by Latin *vespa*; perhaps related to WEAVE[1] (from the weblike form of its nest).

wasp·ish /'wäspisH/ ▶ adj. readily expressing anger or irritation: *he had a waspish tongue.*
– DERIVATIVES **wasp·ish·ly** adv., **wasp·ish·ness** n.

wasp waist ▶ n. a very narrow or tightly corseted waist.
– DERIVATIVES **wasp-waist·ed** adj.

was·sail /'wäsəl, -ˌsāl/ archaic ▶ n. spiced ale or mulled wine drunk during celebrations for Twelfth Night and Christmas Eve. ■ lively and noisy festivities involving the drinking of plentiful amounts of alcohol; revelry.
▶ v. 1 [no obj.] drink plentiful amounts of alcohol and enjoy oneself with others in a noisy, lively way.
2 go from house to house at Christmas singing carols: *here we go a-wassailing.*
– DERIVATIVES **was·sail·er** n.
– ORIGIN Middle English *wæs hæil* 'be in (good) health!': from Old Norse *ves heill* (compare with HAIL[2]). The drinking formula *wassail* (and the reply *drinkhail* 'drink good health') were probably introduced by Danish-speaking inhabitants of England, and then spread, so that by the 12th cent. the usage was considered by the Normans to be characteristic of Englishmen.

was·sail bowl (also **wassail cup**) ▶ n. a large bowl in which wassail was made and from which it was dispensed for the drinking of toasts.

Was·ser·mann test /'wäsərmən, 'vä-/ ▶ n. Medicine a diagnostic test for syphilis using a specific antibody reaction (the **Wassermann reaction**) of the patient's blood serum.
– ORIGIN early 20th cent.: named after August P. *Wassermann* (1866–1925), German pathologist.

Was·ser·stein /'wäsərˌstīn, -ˌstēn/, Wendy (1950–2006), US playwright. She is most noted for her award-winning play *The Heidi Chronicles* (1988). She also wrote *The Sisters Rosensweig* (1992) and *An American Daughter* (1997).

wast /wəst, wäst/ archaic or dialect second person singular past of BE.

wast·age /'wāstij/ ▶ n. 1 the action or process of losing or destroying something by using it carelessly or extravagantly: *the wastage of natural resources.* ■ the amount of something lost or destroyed in such a way: *wastage was cut by 50 percent.*
2 the weakening or deterioration of a part of the body, typically as a result of illness or lack of use: *the wastage of muscle tissue.*

waste /wāst/ ▶ v. 1 [with obj.] use or expend carelessly, extravagantly, or to no purpose: *we can't afford to waste electricity* | *I don't use the car, so why should I waste precious money on it?* ■ (usu. **be wasted on**) bestow or expend on an unappreciative recipient: *her small talk was wasted on this guest.* ■ (usu. **be wasted**) fail to make full or good use of: *we're wasted in this job.*
2 [no obj.] (of a person or a part of the body) become progressively weaker and more emaciated: *she was dying of AIDS, visibly* ***wasting away*** | (as adj. **wasting**) *a wasting disease.* ■ [with obj.] archaic cause to do this: *these symptoms wasted the patients very much.*
3 [with obj.] literary devastate or ruin (a place): *he seized their cattle and wasted their country.* ■ informal kill or severely injure (someone): *I saw them waste the guy I worked for.*
4 [no obj.] literary (of time) pass away; be spent: *the years were wasting.*
▶ adj. [attrib.] 1 (of a material, substance, or byproduct) eliminated or discarded as no longer useful or required after the completion of a process: *ensure that waste materials are disposed of responsibly* | *plants produce oxygen as a waste product.*
2 (of an area of land, typically in a city or town) not used, cultivated, or built on: *a patch of waste ground.*
▶ n. 1 an act or instance of using or expending something carelessly, extravagantly, or to no purpose: *it's a waste of time trying to argue with him* | *they had learned to avoid waste.* ■ archaic the gradual loss or diminution of something: *he was pale and weak from waste of blood.*
2 material that is not wanted; the unusable remains or byproducts of something: *bodily waste* | (**wastes**) *hazardous industrial wastes.*
3 (usu. **wastes**) a large area of barren, typically uninhabited land: *the icy wastes of the Antarctic.*
4 Law damage to an estate caused by an act or by neglect, esp. by a life-tenant.
– PHRASES **go to waste** be unused or expended to no purpose. **lay waste to** (or **lay something (to) waste**) completely destroy: *a land laid waste by war.* **waste one's breath** see BREATH. **waste not, want not** proverb if you use a commodity or resource carefully and without extravagance, you will never be in need. **waste words** see WORD.
– ORIGIN Middle English: from Old Northern French *wast(e)* (noun), *waster* (verb), based on Latin *vastus* 'unoccupied, uncultivated'; compare with VAST.

waste·bas·ket /'wāstˌbaskit/ ▶ n. a receptacle for small quantities of rubbish.

wast·ed /'wāstid/ ▶ adj. 1 used or expended carelessly, extravagantly, or to no purpose: *wasted fuel* | *a wasted opportunity.* ■ (of an action) not producing the desired result: *I'm sorry you've had a wasted journey.*
2 (of a person or a part of the body) weak and emaciated: *her wasted arm.* ■ informal under the influence of alcohol or illegal drugs: *he looked kind of wasted.*

waste·ful /'wāstfəl/ ▶ adj. (of a person, action, or process) using or expending something of value carelessly, extravagantly, or to no purpose: *wasteful energy consumption.*
– DERIVATIVES **waste·ful·ly** adv., **waste·ful·ness** n.

waste·gate /'wāstˌgāt/ ▶ n. a device in a turbocharger that regulates the pressure at which exhaust gases pass to the turbine by opening or closing a vent to the exterior.

waste·land /'wāstˌland/ ▶ n. an unused area of land that has become barren or overgrown. ■ a bleak, unattractive, and unused or neglected urban or industrial area: *the restoration of industrial wasteland* | figurative *the mid 70s are now seen as something of a cultural wasteland.*

waste·pa·per bas·ket ▶ n. a wastebasket.

waste pipe ▶ n. a pipe carrying waste water, such as that from a sink, bathtub, or shower, to a drain.

wast·er /'wāstər/ ▶ n. a wasteful person or thing: *you are a great waster of time.* ■ informal a person who does little or nothing of value. ■ a discarded piece of defective pottery.

wast·rel /'wāstrəl/ ▶ n. 1 literary a wasteful or good-for-nothing person.
2 archaic a waif; a neglected child.
– ORIGIN late 16th cent. (denoting a strip of wasteland): from the verb WASTE + -REL.

wat /wät/ ▶ n. (in Thailand, Cambodia, and Laos) a Buddhist monastery or temple.
– ORIGIN Thai, from Sanskrit, *vāṭa* 'enclosure.'

watch /wäcH/ ▶ v. 1 [with obj.] look at or observe attentively, typically over a period of time: *Lucy watched him go* | [no obj.] *as she watched, two women came into the garden* | [with clause] *everyone stopped to watch what was going on.* ■ keep under careful, protective, or secret observation: *there aren't enough staff to watch him properly* | *he told me my telephones were tapped and I was being watched.* ■ [no obj.] (**watch over**) observe and guard in a protective way: *I guess I can rest a while, with you here to watch over me .* ■ follow closely or maintain an interest in: *the girls watched the development of this relationship with incredulity.* ■ exercise care, caution, or restraint about: *most women watch their diet during pregnancy* | [with clause] *you should watch what you say!* ■ [no obj.] (**watch for**) look out or be on the alert for: *in spring and summer, watch for kingfishers* | ***watch out for*** *broken glass.* ■ [no obj., usu. in imperative] (**watch out**) be careful: *credit-card fraud is on the increase, so watch out.* ■ (**watch it/yourself**) [usu. in imperative] informal be careful (used as a warning or threat): *if anyone finds out, you're dead meat; so watch it.*
2 [no obj.] archaic remain awake for the purpose of religious observance: *she watched whole nights in the church.*
▶ n. 1 a small timepiece worn typically on a strap on one's wrist.
2 [usu. in sing.] an act or instance of carefully observing someone or something over a period of time: *the security forces have been* ***keeping a close watch on*** *our activities.* ■ a period of vigil during which a person is stationed to look out for danger or trouble, typically during the night: *Murray took the last watch before dawn.* ■ a fixed period of duty on a ship, usually lasting four hours. ■ (also **starboard** or **port watch**) the officers and crew on duty during one such period. ■ (usu. **the watch**) historical a watchman or group of watchmen who patrolled and guarded the streets of a town before the introduction of the police force. ■ a body of soldiers making up a guard.
– PHRASES **be on the watch** be carefully looking out for something, esp. a possible danger. **keep watch** stay on the lookout for danger or trouble. **watch one's mouth** see MOUTH. **watch one's** (or **someone's**) **back** protect oneself (or someone else) against danger from an unexpected source: *Because the industry is largely unregulated, you need to watch your back* |*Be careful, Ian. I'll watch your back.* **the watches of the night** literary the hours of night, portrayed as a time when one cannot sleep. **watch (one's) pennies** see PENNY. **watch one's step** used as a warning to someone to walk or act carefully. **watch this space** see SPACE. **watch the time** ensure that one is aware of the time in order to avoid being late.
– ORIGIN Old English *wæcce* 'watchfulness,' *wæccende* 'remaining awake'; related to WAKE[1]. The sense 'small timepiece' probably developed by way of a sense 'alarm device attached to a clock.'

wat·cha /'wəcHə, 'wä-/ ▶ pron. variant spelling of WHATCHA.

watch·a·ble /'wäcHəbəl/ ▶ adj. (of a film or television program) moderately enjoyable to watch.
– DERIVATIVES **watch·a·bil·i·ty** /ˌwäcHə'bilitē/ n.

watch cap ▶ n. a close-fitting knitted cap of a kind worn by members of the US Navy in cold weather.

watch·case /'wäcHˌkās/ ▶ n. a metal case enclosing the works of a watch.

watch chain ▶ n. a metal chain securing a pocket watch.

watch·dog /'wäcHˌdôg/ ▶ n. a dog kept to guard private property. ■ a person or group whose function is to monitor the practices of companies providing a particular service or utility: *a watchdog for the global banking industry.*
▶ v. (**watchdogs, watchdogging, watchdogged**) [with obj.] maintain surveillance over (a person, activity, or situation): *how can we watchdog our investments?*

watch·er /'wäcHər/ ▶ n. a person who observes something attentively or regularly: [in combination] *a whale-watcher.*

watch·fire /'wäcHˌfī(ə)r/ ▶ n. a fire maintained during the night as a signal or for the use of someone who is on watch.

watch·ful /'wäcHfəl/ ▶ adj. watching or observing someone or something closely; alert and vigilant: *they attended dances under the* ***watchful eye*** *of their father.* ■ archaic wakeful; sleepless.
– DERIVATIVES **watch·ful·ly** adv., **watch·ful·ness** n.

watch list ▶ n. a list of individuals, groups, or items that require close surveillance, typically for legal or political reasons.

watch·mak·er /'wäcHˌmākər/ ▶ n. a person who makes and repairs watches and clocks.
– DERIVATIVES **watch·mak·ing** /-kiNG/ n.

watch·man /'wäcHmən/ ▶ n. (pl. **watchmen**) a man employed to look after an empty building, esp. at night. ■ historical a member of a body of people employed to keep watch in a town at night.

watch night ▶ n. a religious service held on New Year's Eve or Christmas Eve.

watch spring ▶ n. a mainspring in a watch.

watch·tow·er /'wäcHˌtou(-ə)r/ ▶ n. a tower built to create an elevated observation point.

watch·word /'wäcHˌwərd/ ▶ n. a word or phrase expressing a person's or group's core aim or belief: *the watchword for the market is be prepared for anything.* ■ archaic a military password.

wa·ter /'wôtər, 'wä-/ ▶ n. 1 a colorless, transparent, odorless, tasteless liquid that forms the seas, lakes, rivers, and rain and is the basis of the fluids of living organisms. ■ this as supplied to houses or commercial establishments through pipes and taps: *each bedroom has a washbasin with hot and cold water* | [as modifier] *water pipes.* ■ one of the four elements in ancient and medieval philosophy and in astrology (considered essential to the nature of the signs Cancer, Scorpio, and Pisces): [as modifier] *a water sign.* ■ (usu. **the waters**) the water of a

PRONUNCIATION KEY ə ago, up; ər over, fur; a hat; ā ate; ä car; e let; ē see; i fit; ī by; NG sing; ō go; ô law, for; oi toy; o͝o good; o͞o goo; ou out; TH thin; T͟H then; ZH vision

W

mineral spring, typically as used medicinally for bathing in or drinking: *resorts where southerners came to **take the waters**.* ■ [with modifier] a solution of a specified substance in water: *ammonia water.* ■ urine: *drinking alcohol will make you need to **pass water** more often.* ■ (**waters**) the amniotic fluid surrounding a fetus in the womb, esp. as discharged in a flow shortly before birth: *I think my waters have broken.*

> Water is a compound of oxygen and hydrogen (chem. formula: H_2O) with highly distinctive physical and chemical properties: it is able to dissolve many other substances; its solid form (ice) is *less* dense than the liquid form; its boiling point, viscosity, and surface tension are unusually high for its molecular weight, and it is partially dissociated into hydrogen and hydroxyl ions.

2 (**the water**) a stretch or area of water, such as a river, sea, or lake: *the lawns ran down to the water's edge.* ■ the surface of such an area of water: *she ducked under the water.* ■ [as modifier] found in, on, or near such areas of water: *a water plant.* ■ (**waters**) the water of a particular sea, river, or lake: *the waters of Hudson Bay* | figurative *the government is taking us into unknown waters with these changes in the legislation.* ■ (**waters**) an area of sea regarded as under the jurisdiction of a particular country: *Japanese coastal waters.*
3 the quality of transparency and brilliance shown by a diamond or other gem.
4 Finance capital stock that represents a book value greater than the true assets of a company.
▶ **v. 1** [with obj.] pour or sprinkle water over (a plant or an area of ground), typically in order to encourage plant growth: *I went out to water the geraniums.* ■ give a drink of water to (an animal): *they stopped to water the horses and to refresh themselves.* ■ [no obj.] (of an animal) drink water. ■ (usu. **be watered**) (of a river) flow through (an area of land): *the valley is watered by the Pines River.* ■ take a fresh supply of water on board (a ship or steam train): *the ship was watered and fresh livestock taken aboard.* ■ Finance increase (a company's debt, or nominal capital) by the issue of new shares without a corresponding addition to assets.
2 [no obj.] (of the eyes) become full of moisture or tears: *Rory blinked, his eyes watering.* ■ (of the mouth) produce saliva, typically in response to the sight or smell of appetizing food: *the smell of frying bacon made Hilary's mouth water.*
3 [with obj.] dilute or adulterate (a drink, typically an alcoholic one) with water: *staff at the club had been **watering down** the drinks.* ■ (**water something down**) make a statement or proposal less forceful or controversial by changing or leaving out certain details: *the army's report of its investigation was considerably watered down.*
– PHRASES **by water** using a ship or boat for travel or transport: *at the end of the lake was a small gazebo, accessible only by water.* **cast one's bread upon the waters** see BREAD. **like water** in great quantities: *George was spending money like water.* **make water 1** urinate. **2** (of a ship or boat) take in water through a leak. **of the first water** (of a diamond or pearl) of the greatest brilliance and transparency. ■ (typically of someone or something perceived as undesirable or annoying) extreme or unsurpassed of their kind: *she was a bore of the first water.* **under water** submerged; flooded. **the water of life** whiskey. **water off a duck's back** see DUCK¹. **water on the brain** informal hydrocephalus. **water under the bridge** (or **water over the dam**) used to refer to events or situations that are in the past and consequently no longer to be regarded as important or as a source of concern.
– DERIVATIVES **wa·ter·er** n., **wa·ter·less** adj.
– ORIGIN Old English *wæter* (noun), *wæterian* (verb), of Germanic origin; related to Dutch *water*, German *Wasser*, from an Indo-European root shared by Russian *voda* (compare with VODKA), also by Latin *unda* 'wave' and Greek *hudōr* 'water.'

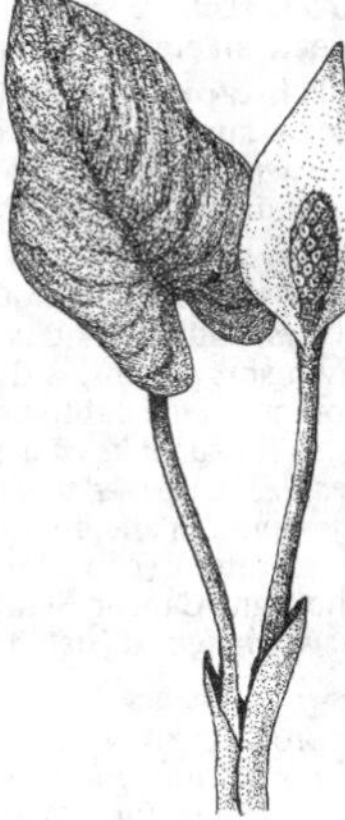
water arum

W

wa·ter ar·um ▶ n. a plant of the arum family, with heart-shaped leaves, a white spathe, and a green spadix. It grows in swamps and boggy ground in north temperate regions. Also called WILD CALLA. ● *Calla palustris*, family Araceae.

wa·ter bag /bäg, bôg/ ▶ n. a bag made of leather, canvas, or other material, used for carrying water.

wa·ter-based ▶ adj. (of a substance or solution) using or having water as a medium or main ingredient: *a water-based paint.*

wa·ter bath ▶ n. Chemistry a container of water heated to a given temperature, used for heating substances placed in smaller containers.

wa·ter bear ▶ n. a minute invertebrate with a short plump body and four pairs of stubby legs, living in water or in the film of water on plants such as mosses. ● Phylum Tardigrada.

Wa·ter Bear·er (**the Water Bearer**) the zodiacal sign or constellation Aquarius.

wa·ter·bed /ˈwôtərˌbed, ˈwä-/ ▶ n. a bed with a water-filled rubber or plastic mattress.

wa·ter bee·tle ▶ n. any of a large number of beetles that live in fresh water. ● Several families, in particular Dytiscidae (the predatory diving beetles) and Hydrophilidae (scavenging beetles).

wa·ter·bird /ˈwôtərˌbərd, ˈwä-/ ▶ n. a bird that frequents water, esp. one that habitually wades or swims in fresh water.

wa·ter birth ▶ n. a birth in which the mother spends the final stages of labor in a birthing pool, with delivery taking place either in or out of the water.

wa·ter bis·cuit ▶ n. a thin, crisp unsweetened cracker made from flour and water.

wa·ter bloom ▶ n. another term for ALGAL BLOOM (see BLOOM¹).

wa·ter·board·ing /ˈwôtərˌbôrdiNG/ ▶ n. an interrogation technique simulating the experience of drowning, in which a person is strapped, face up, to a board that slopes downward at the head, while large quantities of water are poured over the face into the breathing passages.

wa·ter boat·man ▶ n. an aquatic bug that spends much of its time on the bottom, using its front legs to sieve food from the water and its hair-fringed rear legs for swimming. ● Family Corixidae, suborder Heteroptera: *Corixa*, *Sigara*, and other genera. ■ another term for BACKSWIMMER.

wa·ter·bod·y /ˈwôtərˌbädē, ˈwä-/ ▶ n. (pl. **waterbodies**) a body of water forming a physiographical feature, for example a sea or a reservoir.

wa·ter-bomb·er ▶ n. an aircraft used for extinguishing forest fires by dropping water.

wa·ter·borne ▶ adj. conveyed by, traveling on, or involving travel or transportation on water. ■ (of a disease) communicated or propagated by contaminated water.

wa·ter·buck /ˈwôtərˌbək, ˈwä-/ ▶ n. a large African antelope occurring near rivers and lakes in the savanna. ● *Kobus ellipsiprymnus*, family Bovidae.

wa·ter buf·fa·lo ▶ n. a large black domesticated buffalo with heavy swept-back horns, used as a beast of burden throughout the tropics. ● Genus *Bubalus*, family Bovidae: the domesticated *B. bubalis*, descended from the wild *B. arnee*, which is confined to remote parts of India and Southeast Asia.

Wa·ter·bury /ˈwôtərˌberē, ˈwätər-/ an industrial city in western Connecticut, on the Naugatuck River, a historic brass-manufacturing center; pop. 107,037 (est. 2008).

wa·ter can·non ▶ n. a device that ejects a powerful jet of water, typically used to disperse a crowd.

wa·ter chest·nut ▶ n. **1** (also **Chinese water chestnut**) the tuber of a tropical sedge that is widely used in Asian cooking, its white flesh remaining crisp after cooking.
2 the sedge that yields this tuber, which is cultivated in flooded fields in Southeast Asia. ● *Eleocharis tuberosa*, family Cyperaceae.
3 (also **water caltrop**) an aquatic plant with small white flowers, producing an edible rounded seed with two large projecting horns. ● *Trapa natans*, family Trapaceae.

wa·ter clock ▶ n. historical a clock that used the flow of water to measure time.

wa·ter clos·et ▶ n. dated a flush toilet. ■ a room containing such a toilet.

wa·ter·cock /ˈwôtərˌkäk, ˈwä-/ ▶ n. a brown and gray aquatic Asian rail, the male of which develops black plumage and a red frontal shield in the breeding season. ● *Gallicrex cinerea*, family Rallidae.

wa·ter·col·or /ˈwôtərˌkələr, ˈwä-/ (Brit. **watercolour**) ▶ n. (also **watercolors**) artists' paint made with a water-soluble binder such as gum arabic, and thinned with water rather than oil, giving a transparent color. ■ a picture painted with watercolors. ■ the art of painting with watercolors, esp. using a technique of producing paler colors by diluting rather than by adding white.
– DERIVATIVES **wa·ter·col·or·ist** n.

wa·ter cool·er ▶ n. a dispenser of cooled drinking water, typically used in office workplaces. ■ informal used to refer to the type of informal conversation or socializing among office workers that takes place in the communal area in which such a dispenser is located: *the subtleties of film noir haven't exactly been a hot topic around the water cooler* | [as modifier] *a water-cooler chat about the president.*

wa·ter·course /ˈwôtərˌkôrs, ˈwä-/ ▶ n. a brook, stream, or artificially constructed water channel. ■ the bed along which this flows.

wa·ter·craft /ˈwôtərˌkraft, ˈwä-/ ▶ n. (pl. **same**) **1** a boat or other vessel that travels on water.
2 skill in sailing and other activities that take place on water.

wa·ter·cress /ˈwôtərˌkres, ˈwä-/ ▶ n. a cress that grows in running water and whose pungent leaves are used in salad. ● *Nasturtium officinale*, family Brassicaceae.

wa·ter crow·foot ▶ n. see CROWFOOT.

wa·ter cure ▶ n. chiefly historical a session of treatment by hydropathy.

wa·ter cy·cle ▶ n. the cycle of processes by which water circulates between the earth's oceans, atmosphere, and land, involving precipitation as rain and snow, drainage in streams and rivers, and return to the atmosphere by evaporation and transpiration.

wa·ter·dog /ˈwôtərˌdôg, ˈwä-/ ▶ n. an aquatic North American salamander that is a smaller relative of the mudpuppy, typically living in flowing water. ● Genus *Necturus*, family Proteidae: several species.

wa·tered silk ▶ n. silk that has been treated in such a way as to give it a wavy lustrous finish.

wa·ter·fall /ˈwôtərˌfôl, ˈwä-/ ▶ n. a cascade of water falling from a height, formed when a river or stream flows over a precipice or steep incline.

waterfall

wa·ter fern ▶ n. **1** a small aquatic or semiaquatic fern that is either free-floating or anchored by the roots, found chiefly in tropical and warm countries. ● Families Azollaceae, Marsileaceae and Salviniaceae: many species, in particular the minute floating *Azolla filiculoides* of tropical America, which has been naturalized elsewhere.
2 an Australian fern with large coarse fronds, typically growing in marshy areas and rain forests. ● Genus *Blechnum*, family Blechnaceae: several species.

wa·ter flea ▶ n. another term for DAPHNIA.

Wa·ter·ford /ˈwôtərfərd, ˈwätər-/ **1** a county in southeastern Republic of Ireland, in the province of Munster; main administrative center, Dungarvan. ■ its county town, a port on an inlet of St. George's Channel; pop. 45,748 (2006). It is noted for its clear, colorless flint glass, known as Waterford crystal.
2 a city in southeastern Michigan, northwest of Pontiac; pop. 73,150 (2000).

Wa·ter·ford glass ▶ n. fine clear, colorless flint glassware first manufactured in Waterford, Ireland in the 18th and 19th centuries.

wa·ter·fowl /ˈwôtərˌfoul, ˈwä-/ ▶ plural n. ducks, geese, or other large aquatic birds, esp. when regarded as game.

wa·ter·front /ˈwôtərˌfrənt, ˈwä-/ ▶ n. a part of a town that borders a body of water.

wa·ter gap ▶ n. a transverse gap in a mountain ridge through which a stream or river flows.

wa·ter gar·den ▶ n. a garden with pools or a stream, for growing aquatic plants.

wa·ter gas ▶ n. a fuel gas consisting mainly of carbon monoxide and hydrogen, made by passing steam over incandescent coke.

Wa·ter·gate /ˈwôtərˌgāt, ˈwä-/ a political scandal in which an attempt to bug the national headquarters of the Democratic Party (in the Watergate building in Washington, DC) led to the resignation of President Nixon (1974).

wa·ter·gate /ˈwôtərˌgāt, ˈwä-/ ▶ n. a gate of a town or castle opening on to a lake, river, or sea. ■ archaic a sluice; a floodgate.

wa·ter glass ▶ n. **1** a solution of sodium or potassium silicate. It solidifies on exposure to air and is used to make silica gel and for preserving eggs and hardening artificial stone.
2 an instrument for making observations beneath the surface of water, consisting of a bucket with a glass bottom.

wa·ter gun ▶ n. a water pistol.

wa·ter ham·mer ▶ n. a knocking noise in a water pipe that occurs when a tap is turned off briskly.

wa·ter hem·lock ▶ n. a highly poisonous plant of the parsley family that grows in ditches and marshy ground. Also called **COWBANE**. ● Genus *Cicuta*, family Umbelliferae: several species, in particular the North American *C. maculata* (also called **WATER HEMLOCK** (see **COWBANE**)).

wa·ter·hen /ˈwôtərˌhen, ˈwä-/ ▶ n. an aquatic rail, esp. a moorhen or related bird. ● Genera *Gallinula* and *Amaurornis*, family Rallidae.

wa·ter·hole /ˈwôtərˌhōl, ˈwä-/ ▶ n. a depression in which water collects, esp. one from which animals regularly drink.

wa·ter hy·a·cinth ▶ n. a free-floating tropical American water plant that has been introduced elsewhere as an ornamental and in some warmer regions has become a serious weed of waterways. ● *Eichhornia crassipes*, family Pontederiaceae.

wa·ter ice ▶ n. sorbet.

wa·ter·ing can ▶ n. a portable water container with a long spout and a detachable perforated cap, used for watering plants.

wa·ter·ing hole ▶ n. a waterhole from which animals regularly drink. ■ informal a tavern or bar.

wa·ter·ing place ▶ n. a watering hole. ■ a spa or seaside resort.

wa·ter jack·et ▶ n. a casing containing water surrounding and protecting something from extremes of temperature.
– DERIVATIVES **wa·ter-jack·et·ed** adj.

wa·ter jump ▶ n. an obstacle in a jumping competition or steeplechase, where a horse must jump over or into water.

wa·ter·leaf /ˈwôtərˌlēf, ˈwä-/ ▶ n. a North American woodland plant with bell-shaped flowers and leaves that appear to be stained with water. ● Genus *Hydrophyllum*, family Hydrophyllaceae.

wa·ter let·tuce ▶ n. a tropical aquatic plant of the arum family that forms a floating rosette of leaves. ● *Pistia stratiotes*, family Araceae.

wa·ter lev·el ▶ n. **1** the height reached by the water in a reservoir, river, storage tank, etc. ■ another term for **WATER TABLE**.
2 an instrument that uses water to indicate the horizontal.

wa·ter li·ly ▶ n. an ornamental aquatic plant with large round floating leaves and large, typically cup-shaped, floating flowers. ● Family Nymphaeaceae: several genera and many species, including the white-flowered **fragrant water lily** (*Nymphaea odorata*) of eastern North America, and the yellow-flowered **Indian pond lily** of California (*Nuphar polysepalum*).

fragrant water lily

wa·ter·line /ˈwôtərˌlīn, ˈwä-/ ▶ n. **1** the level normally reached by the water on the side of a ship. ■ the level reached by the sea or a river visible as a line on a rock face, beach, or riverbank. ■ any of a set of structural lines of a ship, parallel with the surface of the water, representing the contour of the hull at various heights above the keel and drawn on shipbuilding plans.
2 a vertical watermark made in laid paper.

wa·ter·logged /ˈwôtərˌlôgd, ˈwä-/ ▶ adj. saturated with or full of water: *the race was called off after parts of the course were found to be waterlogged.*
– ORIGIN mid 18th cent.: past participle of the verb *waterlog* 'make (a ship) unmanageable by flooding,' from **WATER** + the verb **LOG**[1].

Wa·ter·loo /ˌwôtərˈlo͞o, ˌwä-, ˈwôtərˌlo͞o, ˈwä-/ **1** an industrial and commercial city in northeastern Iowa; pop. 66,662 (est. 2008).
2 see **AUSTIN**[1].

Wa·ter·loo, Battle of /ˈwôtərˌlo͞o, ˈwä-/ a battle fought on June 18, 1815, near the village of Waterloo (in what is now Belgium), in which Napoleon's army was defeated by the British (under the Duke of Wellington) and Prussians. The allied pursuit caused Napoleon's army to disintegrate entirely, ending his bid to return to power. ■ (as noun **a Waterloo**) a decisive defeat or failure: *his team met their Waterloo.*

wa·ter main ▶ n. a main line in a water supply system.

wa·ter·man /ˈwôtərmən, ˈwä-/ ▶ n. (pl. **watermen**) a boatman. ■ an oarsman who has attained a particular level of knowledge or skill.

wa·ter·mark /ˈwôtərˌmärk, ˈwä-/ ▶ n. a faint design made in some paper during manufacture, which is visible when held against the light and typically identifies the maker.
▶ v. [with obj.] mark with such a design.

wa·ter mass ▶ n. a large body of seawater that is distinguishable esp. by its characteristic temperature and salinity range.

wa·ter meas·ur·er ▶ n. a long, thin aquatic bug that walks slowly on the surface film of water and spears small prey with its beak. ● Genus *Hydrometra*, family Hydrometridae, suborder Heteroptera: several species.

wa·ter·mel·on /ˈwôtərˌmelən, ˈwä-/ ▶ n. **1** the large melonlike fruit of a plant of the gourd family, with smooth green skin, red pulp, and watery juice.
2 the widely cultivated African plant that yields this fruit. ● *Citrullus lanatus*, family Cucurbitaceae.

wa·ter mil·foil ▶ n. see **MILFOIL** (sense 2).

wa·ter mill /ˈwôtərˌmil, ˈwä-/ ▶ n. a mill worked by a waterwheel.

wa·ter moc·ca·sin ▶ n. another term for **COTTONMOUTH**.

wa·ter mold ▶ n. any of a group of fungi-like organisms that live in water or soil, many of which are parasitic on plants. ● Phlya Chytridiomycota and Oomycota, kingdom Protista.

wa·ter nymph ▶ n. (in folklore and classical mythology) a nymph inhabiting or presiding over water, esp. a Naiad or Nereid.

wa·ter of crys·tal·li·za·tion ▶ n. Chemistry water molecules forming an essential part of the crystal structure of some compounds.

wa·ter o·pos·sum (also **water possum**) ▶ n. another term for **YAPOK**.

wa·ter ou·zel ▶ n. another term for **DIPPER** (sense 1).

wa·ter pars·nip ▶ n. a tall plant of the parsley family that lives in or near water. ● *Sium latifolium* and *Berula erecta*, family Umbelliferae.

wa·ter pep·per ▶ n. a widely distributed plant of the dock family that grows in wet ground, with peppery-tasting leaves and sap that is a skin irritant. ● Genus *Polygonum*, family Polygonaceae: several species, in particular *P. hydropiper*.

wa·ter pipe ▶ n. **1** a pipe for conveying water.
2 a pipe for smoking tobacco, cannabis, etc., that draws the smoke through water to cool it.

wa·ter pis·tol ▶ n. a toy pistol that shoots a jet of water.

wa·ter plan·tain ▶ n. an aquatic or marshland plant of north temperate regions, with leaves that resemble those of plantains and a tall stem bearing numerous white or pink flowers. ● Genus *Alisma*, family Alismataceae: several species, including *A. trivale*.

wa·ter po·lo ▶ n. a seven-a-side game played by swimmers in a pool, with a ball like a volleyball that is thrown into the opponent's net.

wa·ter pow·er ▶ n. power that is derived from the weight or motion of water, used as a force to drive machinery.
– DERIVATIVES **wa·ter-pow·ered** adj.

wa·ter·proof /ˈwôtərˌpro͞of, ˈwä-/ ▶ adj. impervious to water: *a waterproof hat.* ■ not liable to be washed away by water: *waterproof ink.*
▶ n. Brit. a garment, esp. a coat, that keeps out water.
▶ v. [with obj.] make impervious to water.
– DERIVATIVES **wa·ter·proof·er** n., **wa·ter·proof·ness** n.

wa·ter rat ▶ n. any of a number of semiaquatic rodents, in particular: ● the **Florida water rat** (*Neofiber alleni*, family Muridae) of Florida and southern Georgia, and the **MUSKRAT**.

wa·ter-re·pel·lent ▶ adj. not easily penetrated by water, esp. as a result of being treated for such a purpose with a surface coating.

wa·ter-re·sis·tant ▶ adj. able to resist the penetration of water to some degree but not entirely.
– DERIVATIVES **wa·ter-re·sis·tance** n.

wa·ter right ▶ n. **1** [usu. pl.] the right to make use of the water from a stream, lake, or irrigation canal.
2 Nautical the right to navigate on particular waters.

Wa·ters[1] /ˈwôtərz, ˈwä-/, Ethel (1896–1977), US singer and actress. A blues and jazz singer, she made songs such as "Dinah" (1925) and "Stormy Weather" (1933) popular. She acted on Broadway in *Cabin in the Sky* (1940) and *The Member of the Wedding* (1950) and in movies such as *Pinky* (1949).

Wa·ters[2], Muddy (1915–83), US blues singer and guitarist; born *McKinley Morganfield.* He recorded "Rollin' Stone" in 1950, and that year formed a blues band, with which he had such hits as "Got My Mojo Working" (1957). The Rolling Stones took their name from his 1950 song.

wa·ter·scape /ˈwôtərˌskāp, ˈwä-/ ▶ n. a landscape in which an expanse of water is a dominant feature.

wa·ter scor·pi·on ▶ n. a mainly tropical predatory water bug with grasping forelegs, breathing from the surface via a bristlelike "tail." ● Family Nepidae, suborder Heteroptera: several genera including the *Nepa* and *Ranatra.*

wa·ter·shed /ˈwôtərˌsʜed, ˈwä-/ ▶ n. **1** an area or ridge of land that separates waters flowing to different rivers, basins, or seas. ■ an area or region drained by a river, river system, or other body of water.
2 an event or period marking a turning point in a course of action or state of affairs: *these works mark a watershed in the history of music.*
– ORIGIN early 19th cent.: from **WATER** + *shed* in the sense 'ridge of high ground' (related to **SHED**[2]), suggested by German *Wasserscheide*, literally 'water-divide.'

wa·ter shrew ▶ n. a large semiaquatic shrew that preys on aquatic invertebrates. ● Four genera, family Soricidae: several species, in particular the **American water shrew** (*Sorex palustris*) and the **Eurasian water shrew** (*Neomys fodiens*).

wa·ter·side /ˈwôtərˌsīd, ˈwä-/ ▶ n. the edge of or area adjoining a sea, lake, or river.

wa·ter·ski /ˈwôtərˌskē, ˈwä-/ ▶ n. (pl. **waterskis**) each of a pair of skis enabling the wearer to skim the surface of the water when towed by a motorboat.
▶ v. [no obj.] skim the surface of water on waterskis.
– DERIVATIVES **wa·ter·ski·er** n.

wa·ter slide ▶ n. a slide into a swimming pool, typically flowing with water and incorporating a number of twists and turns.

wa·ter snake ▶ n. a harmless snake that is a powerful swimmer and spends part of its time in fresh water hunting for prey. Water snakes are found in Africa, Asia, and America. ● *Natrix* and other genera, family Colubridae: several species.

wa·ter sof·ten·er ▶ n. a device or substance that softens hard water by removing certain minerals.

wa·ter sol·dier ▶ n. an aquatic European plant with slender, spiny-toothed leaves in submerged rosettes that rise to the surface at flowering time. ● *Stratiotes aloides*, family Hydrocharitaceae.

wa·ter-sol·u·ble ▶ adj. able to be dissolved in water: *the paint is water-soluble* | *water-soluble vitamins.*

wa·ter spi·der ▶ n. a semiaquatic spider. ● Several species, including the European *Argyroneta aquatica* (family Argyronetidae), which lives in an underwater dome of silk filled with air.

wa·ter sports ▶ plural n. sports that are carried out on water, such as waterskiing and windsurfing. ■ informal sexual activity involving urination.

wa·ter·spout /ˈwôtərˌspout, ˈwä-/ ▶ n. a rotating column of water and spray formed by a whirlwind occurring over the sea or other body of water.

wa·ter stone ▶ n. a whetstone used with water rather than oil.

wa·ter strid·er ▶ n. a slender predatory bug that moves quickly across the surface film of water, using its front legs for catching prey. ● Family

Gerridae, suborder Heteroptera: *Gerris* and other genera.

wa·ter ta·ble ▶ **n.** the level below which the ground is saturated with water. Compare with **PHREATIC**, **VADOSE**.

wa·ter tax·i ▶ **n.** a small motorboat for transporting paying passengers on rivers, canals, etc.

wa·ter-thrush /ˈwôtər,THrəSH, ˈwä-/ ▶ **n.** a thrushlike North American warbler related to the ovenbird, found near woodland streams and swamps. ● Genus *Seiurus*, subfamily Parulinae, family Emberizidae: two species.

wa·ter·tight /ˈwôtər,tīt, ˈwä-/ ▶ **adj.** closely sealed, fastened, or fitted so that no water enters or passes through: *a watertight seal.* ■ (of an argument or account) unable to be disputed or questioned: *their alibis are watertight.*

wa·ter·tight com·part·ment ▶ **n.** any of the sections with intervening watertight partitions into which the interior of a large ship is now usually divided for safety.

wa·ter tor·ture ▶ **n.** a form of torture in which the victim is exposed to the incessant dripping of water on the head or to the sound of dripping.

wa·ter tow·er ▶ **n.** a tower supporting an elevated water tank, whose height creates the pressure required to distribute the water through a piped system.

wa·ter-vas·cu·lar sys·tem ▶ **n.** Zoology (in an echinoderm) a network of water vessels in the body, the tube feet being operated by hydraulic pressure within the vessels.

wa·ter·way /ˈwôtər,wā, ˈwä-/ ▶ **n. 1** a river, canal, or other route for travel by water.
2 a thick plank or angle iron at the outer edge of the deck of a vessel, which joins the vessel's side to its deck and directs water overboard via the scuppers.

wa·ter·weed /ˈwôtər,wēd, ˈwä-/ ▶ **n. 1** any aquatic plant with inconspicuous flowers, esp. a pondweed.
2 a submerged aquatic American plant that is grown in aquariums and ornamental ponds. ● Genus *Elodea*, family Hydrocharitaceae: several species, in particular *E. canadensis*.

wa·ter·wheel /ˈwôtər,(h)wēl, ˈwä-/ ▶ **n.** a large wheel driven by flowing water, used to work machinery or to raise water to a higher level.

water wheel

wa·ter wings ▶ **plural n.** inflated floats that may be fixed to the arms of someone learning to swim to give increased buoyancy.

wa·ter witch (also **water witcher**) ▶ **n.** a person who searches for underground water by using a dowsing rod.
– DERIVATIVES **wa·ter witch·ing n.**

Wa·ter Won·der·land a nickname for the state of **MICHIGAN**.

wa·ter·works /ˈwôtər,wərks, ˈwä-/ ▶ **plural n.**
1 [treated as sing.] an establishment for managing a water supply.
2 informal used to refer to the shedding of tears: *she is an expert at **turning on the waterworks** to manipulate others.*

W

wa·ter·y /ˈwôtərē, ˈwä-/ ▶ **adj.** consisting of, containing, or resembling water: *a watery fluid.* ■ thin or tasteless as a result of containing too much water: *watery coffee.* ■ weak; pale: *watery sunshine.* ■ (of a person's eyes) full of or running with tears.
– DERIVATIVES **wa·ter·i·ness n.**
– ORIGIN Old English *wæterig* (see **WATER**, **-Y**[1]).

WATS /wäts/ ▶ **abbr.** Wide Area Telecommunications Service.

Wat·son[1] /ˈwätsən/, James Dewey (1928–), US biologist. Together with Francis Crick, he proposed the double-helix model for the structure of the DNA molecule. Nobel Prize for Physiology or Medicine (1962), shared with Crick and Maurice Wilkins.

James Watson

Wat·son[2], John Broadus (1878–1958), US psychologist; founder of the school of behaviorism. He held that the role of the psychologist was to discern, through observation and experimentation, the innate behavior and acquired behavior in an individual.

Wat·son·ville /ˈwätsən,vil/ a city in west central California, south of San Jose; pop. 50,442 (est. 2008).

Wat·son-Watt /,wätsən ˈwät/, Sir Robert Alexander (1892–1973), Scottish physicist. He led a team that developed radar into a practical system for locating aircraft; this played a vital role in World War II.

Wat·su /ˈwätso͞o/ ▶ **n.** trademark a form of shiatsu massage that takes place in water.
– ORIGIN 1980s: blend of *water* and *shiatsu*.

Watt /wät/, James (1736–1819), Scottish engineer. Among his many innovations, he greatly improved the efficiency of the Newcomen steam engine, which was then adopted for a variety of purposes. He also introduced the term *horsepower*.

watt /wät/ (abbr.: **W**) ▶ **n.** the SI unit of power, equivalent to one joule per second, corresponding to the power in an electric circuit in which the potential difference is one volt and the current one ampere.
– ORIGIN late 19th cent.: named after J. **WATT**.

watt·age /ˈwätij/ ▶ **n.** a measure of electrical power expressed in watts. ■ the operating power of a lamp or other electrical appliance expressed in watts.

Wat·teau /wäˈtō/, Jean Antoine (1684–1721), French painter. An initiator of the rococo style, he is also known for his invention of the *fête galante*.

watt-hour ▶ **n.** a measure of electrical energy equivalent to a power consumption of one watt for one hour.

wat·tle[1] /ˈwätl/ ▶ **n. 1** a material for making fences, walls, etc., consisting of rods or stakes interlaced with twigs or branches.
2 chiefly Austral. an acacia. ● Genus *Acacia*, family Leguminosae: many species, including the **golden wattle**.
▶ **v.** [with obj.] make, enclose, or fill up with wattle.
– ORIGIN Old English *watul*, of unknown origin.

wat·tle[2] ▶ **n.** a colored fleshy lobe hanging from the head or neck of domestic chickens, turkeys, and some other birds.
– DERIVATIVES **wat·tled adj.**
– ORIGIN early 16th cent.: of unknown origin.

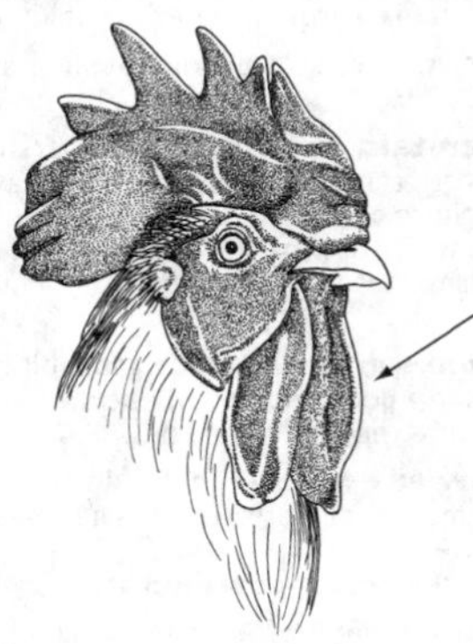
wattle[2]

wat·tle and daub ▶ **n.** a material formerly or traditionally used in building walls, consisting of a network of interwoven sticks and twigs covered with mud or clay.

wat·tle·bird /ˈwätl,bərd/ ▶ **n.** the largest of the honeyeaters found in Australia, with a wattle hanging from each cheek. ● Genus *Anthochaera* (and *Melidectes*), family Meliphagidae: four species.

watt·me·ter /ˈwät,mētər/ ▶ **n.** a meter for measuring electric power in watts.

Watts /wäts/ a district in southern Los Angeles in California, home to much of the black population of the city.

Wa·tu·si /wäˈto͞osē/ ▶ **n. 1** (also **Watutsi** /-ˈto͞otsē/) [treated as pl.] dated the Tutsi people collectively.
2 an energetic dance popular in the 1960s.
▶ **v.** [no obj.] dance the Watusi.
– ORIGIN from the Kinyarwanda language of the Bantu family, from the plural prefix *wa-* + **TUTSI**.

Waugh /wô/, Evelyn (Arthur St. John) (1903–66), English novelist. His work was profoundly influenced by his conversion to Roman Catholicism in 1930. Notable works: *Decline and Fall* (1928) and *Brideshead Revisited* (1945).

Wau·ke·gan /wôˈkēgən/ an industrial port city in northeastern Illinois, on Lake Michigan; pop. 90,788 (est. 2008).

Wau·ke·sha /ˈwôki,SHô/ an industrial city in southeastern Wisconsin, west of Milwaukee; pop. 68,008 (est. 2008).

waul /wôl/ ▶ **v.** [no obj.] give a loud plaintive cry like that of a cat.
– ORIGIN early 16th cent.: imitative.

Wau·sau /ˈwô,sô/ an industrial and commercial city in central Wisconsin; pop. 37,576 (est. 2008).

Wau·wa·to·sa /,wô-wəˈtōsə/ a city in southeastern Wisconsin, west of Milwaukee; pop. 45,004 (est. 2008).

wave /wāv/ ▶ **v. 1** [no obj.] move one's hand to and fro in greeting or as a signal: *he waved to me from the train.* ■ [with obj.] move (one's hand or arm, or something held in one's hand) to and fro: *he waved a sheaf of papers in the air.* ■ move to and fro with a swaying or undulating motion while remaining fixed to one point: *the flag waved in the wind.* ■ [with obj.] convey (a greeting or other message) by moving one's hand or something held in it to and fro: *we waved our farewells* | [with two objs.] *she waved him goodbye.* ■ [with obj.] instruct (someone) to move in a particular direction by moving one's hand: *he waved her back.*
2 [with obj.] style (hair) so that it curls slightly: *her hair had been carefully waved for the evening.* ■ [no obj.] (of hair) grow with a slight curl: (as adj. **waving**) *thick, waving gray hair sprouted back from his forehead.*
▶ **n. 1** a long body of water curling into an arched form and breaking on the shore. ■ a ridge of water between two depressions in open water: *gulls and cormorants bobbed on the waves.* ■ a shape seen as comparable to a breaking wave: *a wave of treetops stretched to the horizon.* ■ (usu. **the wave**) an effect resembling a moving wave produced by successive sections of the crowd in a stadium standing up, raising their arms, lowering them, and sitting down again. ■ (**the waves**) literary the sea. ■ a sudden occurrence of or increase in a specified phenomenon, feeling, or emotion: *a wave of strikes had effectively paralyzed the government* | *horror came over me in waves.*
2 a gesture or signal made by moving one's hand to and fro: *he gave a little wave and walked off.*
3 a slightly curling lock of hair: *his hair was drying in unruly waves.* ■ a tendency to curl in a person's hair: *her hair has a slight natural wave.*
4 Physics a periodic disturbance of the particles of a substance that may be propagated without net movement of the particles, such as in the passage of undulating motion, heat, or sound. See also **STANDING WAVE** and **TRAVELING WAVE**. ■ a single curve in the course of this motion. ■ a similar variation of an electromagnetic field in the propagation of light or other radiation through a medium or vacuum.
– PHRASES **make waves** informal create a significant impression: *he has already made waves as a sculptor.* ■ cause trouble: *I don't want to risk her welfare by making waves.*
– PHRASAL VERBS **wave something aside** dismiss something as unnecessary or irrelevant: *he waved the objection aside and carried on.* **wave someone/something down** use one's hand to give a signal to stop to a driver or vehicle.
– DERIVATIVES **wave·less adj.**, **wave·like adj. & adv.**
– ORIGIN Old English *wafian* (verb), from the Germanic base of **WAVER**; the noun by alteration (influenced by the verb) of Middle English *wawe* '(sea) wave.'

USAGE See usage at **WAIVE**.

wave·band /ˈwāv,band/ ▶ **n.** a range of wavelengths falling between two given limits, used in radio transmission.

wave e·qua·tion ▶ **n.** Mathematics a differential equation expressing the properties of motion in waves.

wave farm ▶ **n.** an area of the sea where machinery is installed to harness the energy produced by waves in order to generate electricity.

wave·form /ˈwāvˌfôrm/ ▶ **n.** Physics a curve showing the shape of a wave at a given time.

wave·front /ˈwāvˌfrənt/ ▶ **n.** Physics a surface containing points affected in the same way by a wave at a given time.

wave func·tion ▶ **n.** Physics a function that satisfies a wave equation and describes the properties of a wave.

wave·guide /ˈwāvˌgīd/ ▶ **n.** a metal tube or other device confining and conveying microwaves.

wave·length /ˈwāvˌleNG(k)TH/ ▶ **n. 1** Physics the distance between successive crests of a wave, esp. points in a sound wave or electromagnetic wave. (Symbol: λ) ■ this distance as a distinctive feature of radio waves from a transmitter.
2 a person's ideas and way of thinking, esp. as it affects their ability to communicate with others: *when we met we hit it off immediately—we're* ***on the same wavelength****.*

wave·let /ˈwāvlit/ ▶ **n.** a small wave of water; a ripple.

wave me·chan·ics ▶ **plural n.** [treated as sing.] Physics a method of analysis of the behavior of atomic phenomena with particles represented by wave equations.

wave num·ber ▶ **n.** Physics the number of waves in a unit distance.

wave pack·et ▶ **n.** Physics a group of superposed waves that together form a traveling localized disturbance, esp. one described by Schrödinger's equation and regarded as representing a particle.

wave pow·er ▶ **n.** power obtained by harnessing the energy produced by waves at sea.

wa·ver /ˈwāvər/ ▶ **v.** [no obj.] shake with a quivering motion: *the flame wavered in the draft.* ■ become unsteady or unreliable: *his love for her had never wavered.* ■ be undecided between two opinions or courses of action; be irresolute: *she never* ***wavered from*** *her intention.*
– DERIVATIVES **wa·ver·er** n., **wa·ver·ing·ly** adv., **wa·ver·y** adj.
– ORIGIN Middle English: from Old Norse *vafra* 'flicker,' of Germanic origin. Compare with WAVE.

USAGE See usage at WAIVE.

WAVES /wāvz/ ▶ **plural n.** the women's section of the US Naval Reserve, established in 1942, or, since 1948, of the US Navy.
– ORIGIN acronym from *Women Appointed* (later *Accepted*) *for Volunteer Emergency Service.*

wave·ta·ble /ˈwāvˌtābəl/ ▶ **n.** Computing a file or memory device containing data that represents a sound such as a piece of music.

wave the·o·ry ▶ **n.** Physics, historical the theory that light is propagated through the ether by a wave motion imparted to the ether by the molecular vibrations of the radiant body.

wave train ▶ **n.** a group of waves of equal or similar wavelengths traveling in the same direction.

WAV file /wāv/ (also **wave file**) ▶ **n.** Computing a format for storing uncompressed audio files.
– ORIGIN 1990s: shortened from *waveform audio format.*

wav·i·cle /ˈwāvikəl/ ▶ **n.** Physics an entity having characteristic properties of both waves and particles.
– ORIGIN 1920s: blend of WAVE and PARTICLE.

wav·y /ˈwāvē/ ▶ **adj.** (**wavier**, **waviest**) (of a line or surface) having or consisting of a series of undulating and wavelike curves: *she had long, wavy hair.* ■ [usu. postpositive] Heraldry divided or edged with a line formed of alternating shallow curves.
– DERIVATIVES **wav·i·ly** /ˈwāvəlē/ adv., **wav·i·ness** n.

wa-wa ▶ **n.** variant spelling of WAH-WAH.

wax¹ /waks/ ▶ **n.** a sticky yellowish moldable substance secreted by honeybees as the material of honeycomb; beeswax. ■ a white translucent material obtained by bleaching and purifying this substance and used for such purposes as making candles, modeling, and as a basis of polishes. ■ a similar viscous substance, typically a lipid or hydrocarbon. ■ earwax. ■ informal used in reference to phonograph records: *he didn't get* ***on wax*** *until 1959.*
▶ **v.** [with obj.] **1** cover or treat (something) with wax or a similar substance, typically to polish or protect it: *I washed and waxed the floor.* ■ remove unwanted hair from (a part of the body) by applying wax and then peeling off the wax and hairs together.
2 informal make a recording of: *he waxed a series of tracks that emphasized his lead guitar work.*
– DERIVATIVES **wax·er** n.
– ORIGIN Old English *wæx, weax*, of Germanic origin; related to Dutch *was* and German *Wachs*. The verb dates from late Middle English.

wax² ▶ **v.** [no obj.] (of the moon between new and full) have a progressively larger part of its visible surface illuminated, increasing its apparent size. ■ literary become larger or stronger: *his anger waxed.* ■ [with complement] begin to speak or write about something in the specified manner: *they* ***waxed lyrical*** *about the old days.*
– PHRASES **wax and wane** undergo alternate increases and decreases: *companies whose fortunes wax and wane with the economic cycle.*
– ORIGIN Old English *weaxan*, of Germanic origin; related to Dutch *wassen* and German *wachsen*, from an Indo-European root shared by Greek *auxanein* and Latin *augere* 'to increase.'

wax³ ▶ **n.** [usu. in sing.] Brit. informal, dated a fit of anger: *she is* ***in a wax*** *about the delay to the wedding.*
– ORIGIN mid 19th cent.: origin uncertain; perhaps from phrases such as *wax angry.*

wax bean ▶ **n.** a dwarf bean of a variety with yellow, stringless pods.

wax·ber·ry /ˈwaksˌberē/ ▶ **n.** (pl. **waxberries**) a shrub with berries that have a waxy coating, in particular a bayberry or wax myrtle.

wax·bill /ˈwaksˌbil/ ▶ **n.** a small, finchlike Old World songbird, typically brightly colored and with a red bill that resembles sealing wax in color. ● Family Estrildidae (the **waxbill family**): several genera, esp. *Estrilda*, and several species. The waxbill family also includes the avadavats, mannikins, cordon-bleu, Java sparrow, zebra finch, etc., many popular as cage birds.

waxed pa·per (also **wax paper**) ▶ **n.** paper that has been impregnated with wax to make it waterproof or greaseproof, used esp. in cooking and the wrapping of foodstuffs.

wax·en /ˈwaksən/ ▶ **adj.** having a smooth, pale, translucent surface or appearance like that of wax: *a canopy of waxen, creamy blooms.* ■ archaic or literary made of wax: *a waxen effigy.*

wax light ▶ **n.** historical a taper or candle made from wax.

wax moth ▶ **n.** a brownish moth that lays its eggs in beehives. The caterpillars cover the combs with silken tunnels and feed on beeswax. ● Genera *Galleria* and *Achroea*, family Pyralidae: several species, in particular *G. mellonella*.

wax mu·se·um ▶ **n.** an exhibition of wax dummies, typically representing famous people and fictional characters: *no wax museum is complete without its chamber of horrors.*

wax myr·tle ▶ **n.** an evergreen bayberry, esp. the common *Myrica cerifera* of the southern US. The wax covering its nutlets is used for making scented candles.

wax palm ▶ **n.** either of two South American palm trees from which wax is obtained. ● an Andean palm with a stem coated in a mixture of resin and wax (*Ceroxylon alpinum*, family Palmae). ● a carnauba.

wax re·sist ▶ **n.** a process similar to batik used in pottery and printing.

wax tree (also **Japanese wax tree**) ▶ **n.** an eastern Asian tree with white berries that produce a wax that is used as a substitute for beeswax. ● *Rhus succedanea*, family Anacardiaceae.

wax·wing /ˈwaksˌwiNG/ ▶ **n.** a crested Eurasian and American songbird with mainly pinkish-brown plumage, having small tips like red sealing wax on some wing feathers. ● Genus *Bombycilla*, family Bombycillidae: three species.

wax·work /ˈwaksˌwərk/ ▶ **n.** a lifelike dummy modeled in wax. ■ (**waxworks**) [treated as sing.] an exhibition of wax dummies.

wax·y /ˈwaksē/ ▶ **adj.** (**waxier**, **waxiest**) resembling wax in consistency or appearance: *waxy potatoes.*
– DERIVATIVES **wax·i·ly** /ˈwaksəlē/ adv., **wax·i·ness** n.

way /wā/ ▶ **n. 1** a method, style, or manner of doing something: *worry was their way of showing how much they cared* | *there are two ways of approaching this problem.* ■ a person's characteristic or habitual manner of behavior or expression: *it was not his way to wait passively for things to happen.* ■ (**ways**) the customary modes of behavior or practices of a group: *foreigners who adopt French ways.* ■ [in sing.] the typical manner in which something happens or in which someone or something behaves: *he was showing off, as is the way with adolescent boys.*
2 a road, track, path, or street for traveling along: [in place names] *No. 3, Church Way.* ■ [usu. in sing.] a course of travel or route taken in order to reach a place: *can you tell me the way to Duffy Square?* ■ a means of entry or exit from somewhere, such as a door or gate: *we're going in the back way.* ■ [in sing.] (also informal **ways**) a distance traveled or to be traveled; the distance from one place to another: *they still had a long way ahead of them* | figurative *the area's wine industry still has some way to go to full maturity.* ■ [in sing.] a period between one point in time and another: *September was a long way off.* ■ [in sing.] travel or motion along a particular route; the route along which someone or something would travel if unobstructed: *Christine tried to follow but Martin blocked her way.* ■ [in sing.] a specified direction: *we just missed another car coming the other way.* ■ (often **ways**) parts into which something divides or is divided: *the national vote split three ways* | [in combination] *a five-way bidding war.* ■ (**one's way**) used with a verb and adverbial phrase to intensify the force of an action or to denote movement or progress: *I shouldered my way to the bar.* ■ forward or backward motion of a ship or boat through water: *the dinghy lost way and drifted toward the shore.*
3 [in sing. with modifier or possessive] informal a particular area or locality: *I've got a sick cousin over Fayetteville way.*
4 a particular aspect of something; a respect: *I have changed in every way.*
5 [in sing. with adj.] a specified condition or state: *the family was in a poor way.*
6 (**ways**) a sloping structure down which a new ship is launched.
▶ **adv.** informal at or to a considerable distance or extent; far (used before an adverb or preposition for emphasis): *his understanding of what constitutes good writing is way off target* | *my grandchildren are way ahead of others their age.* ■ [as submodifier] much: *I was cycling way too fast.* ■ [usu. as submodifier] extremely; really (used for emphasis): *the guys behind the bar were way cool.* [shortening of AWAY.]
– PHRASES **across the way** nearby, esp. on the opposite side of the street. **all the way** see ALL. **be on one's way** have started one's journey. ■ [in imperative] (**(be) on your way**) informal go away: *on your way, and stop wasting my time!* **by a long way** by a great amount; by far. **by the way 1** incidentally (used to introduce a minor topic not connected with what was being spoken about previously): *by the way, pay in advance if you can.* **2** during the course of a journey: *you will have a fine view of Moray Firth by the way.* **by way of 1** so as to pass through or across; via: *we approached the Berlin Wall by way of Checkpoint Charlie.* **2** constituting; as a form of: *"I can't help it," shouted Tom by way of apology.* **3** by means of: *noncompliance with the regulations is punishable by way of a fine.* **come one's way** happen or become available to one: *he did whatever jobs came his way.* **find a way** discover a means of obtaining one's object. **get** (or **have**) **one's** (**own**) **way** get or do what one wants in spite of opposition. **give way 1** yield to someone or something: *he was not a man to* ***give way to*** *this kind of pressure.* ■ (of a support or structure) be unable to carry a load or withstand a force; collapse or break. ■ (**give way to**) allow oneself to be overcome by or to succumb to (an emotion or impulse): *she gave way to a burst of weeping.* **2** allow someone or something to be or go first: ***give way to*** *traffic coming from the right.* ■ (**give way to**) be replaced or superseded by: *Alan's discomfort gave way to anger.* **go all the** (or **go the whole**) **way** continue a course of action to its conclusion. ■ informal have sexual intercourse with someone. **go out of one's way** [usu. with infinitive] make a special effort to do something: *Mrs. Mott went out of her way to be courteous to Sara.* **go one's own way** act independently or as one wishes, esp. against contrary advice. **go one's way 1** (of events, circumstances, etc.) be favorable to one: *I was just hoping things went my way.* **2** leave: *each went his way singing hallelujahs.* **go someone's way** travel in the same direction as someone: *wait for Owen, he's going your way.* **have it your** (**own**) **way** [in imperative] informal used to indicate angrily that although one disagrees with something someone has said or proposed, one is not going to argue further: *have it your way–we'll go to Princetown.* **have it both ways** see BOTH. **have a way with** have a particular talent for dealing with or ability in: *she's got a way with animals.* **have one's way with** humorous have sexual intercourse with (someone) (typically implying that it is against their wishes or better judgment). **in more ways than one** used to indicate that a statement has more than one meaning: *Shelley let her hair down in more ways than one.* **in a way** (or **in some ways** or **in one way**) to a certain extent, but not altogether or completely (used to reduce the effect of a statement): *in some ways television is more challenging than theater.* **in**

the family way see FAMILY. **in the** (or **one's**) **way** forming an obstacle or hindrance to movement or action: *his head was in the way of my view*. **in the way of** another way of saying BY WAY OF above. **in someone/something's** (**own**) **way** if regarded from a particular standpoint appropriate to that person or thing: *it's a good enough book in its way*. **in no way** not at all: *quasars in no way resemble normal galaxies*. **keep** (or **stay**) **out of someone's way** avoid someone. **know one's way around** be familiar with (an area, procedure, or subject). **lead the way** go first along a route to show someone the way. ■ be a pioneer in a particular activity. **look the other way** deliberately avoid seeing or noticing someone or something. **no two ways about it** see NO. **one way and another** taking most aspects or considerations into account: *it's been quite a day one way and another*. **one way or another** (or **one way or the other**) used to indicate that something is the case for any of various unspecified reasons: *one way or another she brought it on herself*. ■ by some means: *he wants to get rid of me one way or another*. ■ whichever of two given alternatives is the case: *the question is not yet decided, one way or the other*. **on the** (or **one's**) **way** in the course of a journey: *I'll tell you on the way home*. **on the** (or **its**) **way** about to arrive or happen: *there's more snow on the way*. ■ informal (of a child) conceived but not yet born. **on the** (or **one's**) **way out** in the process of leaving. ■ informal going out of fashion or favor. **the other way around** in the opposite position or direction. ■ the opposite of what is expected or supposed: *it was you who sought me out, not the other way around*. **out of one's way** not on one's intended route. **put someone in the way of** dated give someone the opportunity of. **that way** dated used euphemistically to indicate that someone is homosexual: *he was a bit that way*. **to someone's** (or **one's**) **way of thinking** in someone's (or one's) opinion. **way back** (also **way back when**) informal long ago. **the way of the Cross 1** the journey of Jesus to the place of his crucifixion. **2** a set of images representing the Stations of the Cross. **3** the suffering and self-sacrifice of a Christian. **way of life** the typical pattern of behavior of a person or group: *the rural way of life*. **the way of the world** the manner in which people typically behave or things typically happen (used to express one's resignation to it): *all those millions are not going to create many jobs, but that's the way of the world*. **ways and means** the methods and resources at someone's disposal for achieving something: *the company is seeking ways and means of safeguarding jobs*. **way to go** informal used to express pleasure, approval, or excitement.
– ORIGIN Old English *weg*, of Germanic origin; related to Dutch *weg* and German *Weg*, from a base meaning 'move, carry.'

-way ▶ **suffix** equivalent to -WAYS.

wa·yang /ˈwäyäNG/ ▶ **n.** (in Indonesia and Malaysia) a theatrical performance employing puppets or human dancers. ■ (also **wayang kulit**) a Javanese and Balinese shadow puppet play.
– ORIGIN Javanese.

way·bill /ˈwāˌbil/ ▶ **n.** a list of passengers or goods being carried on a vehicle.

way·far·er /ˈwāˌfe(ə)rər/ ▶ **n.** literary a person who travels on foot.

way·far·ing /ˈwāˌfe(ə)riNG/ ▶ **adj.** (of a person) traveling on foot: *a wayfaring stranger*.
▶ **n.** the action of traveling by foot.

way·far·ing tree /ˈwāˌfe(ə)riNG/ ▶ **n.** a white-flowered Eurasian shrub that has berries at different stages of ripening (green, red, and black) occurring together, growing chiefly on calcareous soils. ● *Viburnum lantana*, family Caprifoliaceae.

way·lay /ˈwāˌlā/ ▶ **v.** (past and past participle **waylaid**) [with obj.] stop or interrupt (someone) and detain them in conversation or trouble them in some other way: *he waylaid me on the stairs*.
– DERIVATIVES **way·lay·er n.**

Wayne[1] /wān/ a residential and commercial township in northeastern New Jersey, northwest of Paterson; pop. 53,918 (est. 2008).

Wayne[2], Anthony (1745–96), American soldier; known as **Mad Anthony**. A general noted for his courage and military brilliance, he is credited with saving West Point from British occupation following Benedict Arnold's betrayal. He retired in 1783, but returned to active duty in the 1790s, defeating the Indians at the Battle of Fallen Timbers in Ohio in 1794.

Wayne[3], James Moore (c.1790–1867), US Supreme Court associate justice 1835–67. Before being appointed to the Court by President Jackson, he served in the US House of Representatives 1829–35 as a member from Georgia. On the Court, he worked to achieve a compromise between slavery and preservation of the Union.

Wayne[4], John (1907–79), US actor; born *Marion Michael Morrison*; known as **the Duke**. Associated with movie director John Ford from 1930, Wayne became a Hollywood star with *Stagecoach* (1939) and appeared in classic westerns such as *Red River* (1948), *The Searchers* (1956), and *True Grit* (1969).

John Wayne

Wayne Coun·ty a county in southeastern Michigan that includes the city of Detroit; pop. 1,949,929 (est. 2008).

way-out ▶ **adj.** informal regarded as extremely unconventional, unusual, or avant-garde.

way·point /ˈwāˌpoint/ ▶ **n.** a stopping place on a journey. ■ an endpoint of the leg of a course, esp. one whose coordinates have been generated by a computer.

-ways ▶ **suffix** forming adjectives and adverbs of direction or manner: *edgeways* | *lengthways*. Compare with -WISE.

way·side /ˈwāˌsīd/ ▶ **n.** the edge of a road.
– PHRASES **fall by the wayside** fail to persist in an endeavor or undertaking: *many readers will fall by the wayside as the terminology becomes more complicated*. [with biblical allusion to Luke 8:5.]

way sta·tion ▶ **n.** a stopping point on a journey. ■ a minor station on a railroad.

way·ward /ˈwāwərd/ ▶ **adj.** difficult to control or predict because of unusual or perverse behavior: *her wayward, difficult sister* | figurative *his wayward emotions*.
– DERIVATIVES **way·ward·ly adv.**, **way·ward·ness n.**
– ORIGIN late Middle English: shortening of obsolete *awayward* 'turned away'; compare with FROWARD.

way·worn /ˈwāˌwôrn/ ▶ **adj.** archaic weary with traveling.

wa·zir /wäˈzi(ə)r/ ▶ **n.** another term for VIZIER.

wa·zoo /wäˈzo͞o/ ▶ **n.** informal the anus.
– PHRASES **up** (or **out**) **the wazoo** very much; in great quantity; to a great degree: *he's insured out the wazoo* | *Jack and I have got work up the wazoo already*.

Wb ▶ **abbr.** weber(s).

WBA ▶ **abbr.** World Boxing Association.

WBC ▶ **abbr.** World Boxing Council.

W bo·son /ˈbōˌsän/ ▶ **n.** another term for W PARTICLE.

WC ▶ **abbr.** ■ Brit. water closet. ■ (of a region) west central.

WCC ▶ **abbr.** World Council of Churches.

we /wē/ ▶ **pron.** [first person plural] **1** used by a speaker to refer to himself or herself and one or more other people considered together: *shall we have a drink?* ■ used to refer to the speaker together with other people regarded in the same category: *nobody knows kids better than we teachers do*. ■ people in general: *we should eat as varied and well-balanced a diet as possible*.
2 used in formal contexts for or by a royal person, or by a writer or editor, to refer to himself or herself: *in this section we discuss the reasons*.
3 used condescendingly to refer to the person being addressed: *how are we today?*
– ORIGIN Old English, of Germanic origin; related to Dutch *wij* and German *wir*.

weak /wēk/ ▶ **adj. 1** lacking the power to perform physically demanding tasks; lacking physical strength and energy: *she was recovering from the flu and was very weak*. ■ lacking political or social power or influence: *the central government had grown too weak to impose order* | (as plural noun **the weak**) *the new king used his powers to protect the weak*. ■ (of a crew, team, or army) containing too few members or members of insufficient quality. ■ (of a faculty or part of the body) not able to fulfill its functions properly: *he had a weak stomach*. ■ of a low standard; performing or performed badly: *the choruses on this recording are weak*. ■ not convincing or logically forceful: *the argument is an extremely weak one* | *a weak plot*. ■ exerting only a small force: *a weak magnetic field*.
2 liable to break or give way under pressure; easily damaged: *the salamander's tail may be broken off at a weak spot near the base*. ■ lacking the force of character to hold to one's own decisions, beliefs, or principles; irresolute. ■ (of a belief, emotion, or attitude) not held or felt with such conviction or intensity as to prevent its being abandoned or dispelled: *their commitment to the project is weak*. ■ not in a secure financial position: *people have no faith in weak banks*. ■ (of prices or a market) having a downward tendency.
3 lacking intensity or brightness: *a weak light from a single street lamp*. ■ (of a liquid or solution) heavily diluted: *a cup of weak coffee*. ■ (of an acid) only slightly ionized. ■ displaying or characterized by a lack of enthusiasm or energy: *she managed a weak, nervous smile*. ■ (of features) not striking or strongly marked: *his beard covered a weak chin*. ■ (of a syllable) unstressed.
4 Grammar denoting a class of verbs in Germanic languages that form the past tense and past participle by addition of a suffix (in English, typically *-ed*); contrasted with STRONG.
5 Physics of, relating to, or denoting the weakest of the known kinds of force between particles, which acts only at distances less than about 10^{-15} cm, is very much weaker than the electromagnetic and the strong interactions, and conserves neither strangeness, parity, nor isospin.
– PHRASES **the weaker sex** [treated as sing. or pl.] dated, derogatory women regarded collectively. **weak in the knees** helpless with emotion. **the weak link** the point at which a system, sequence, or organization is most vulnerable; the least dependable element or member.
– DERIVATIVES **weak·ish adj.**
– ORIGIN Old English *wāc* 'pliant,' 'of little worth,' 'not steadfast,' reinforced in Middle English by Old Norse *veikr*, from a Germanic base meaning 'yield, give way.'

weak·en /ˈwēkən/ ▶ **v.** make or become weaker in power, resolve, or physical strength: [with obj.] *fault lines had weakened and shattered the rocks* | [no obj.] *his resistance had weakened*.
– DERIVATIVES **weak·en·er n.**

weak end·ing ▶ **n.** Prosody an unstressed syllable in a place at the end of a line of verse that normally receives a stress.

weak·fish /ˈwēkˌfisH/ ▶ **n.** (pl. **same** or **weakfishes**) a large, slender-bodied marine fish living along the east coast of North America, popular as a food fish and for sport. Also called SEA TROUT. ● *Cynoscion regalis*, family Sciaenidae.
– ORIGIN late 18th cent.: from obsolete Dutch *weekvisch*, from *week* 'soft' + *visch* 'fish.'

weak in·ter·ac·tion ▶ **n.** Physics interaction at short distances between subatomic particles mediated by the weak force.

weak-kneed ▶ **adj.** weak and shaky as a result of fear or excitement. ■ lacking in resolve or courage; cowardly.

weak·ling /ˈwēkliNG/ ▶ **n.** a person or animal that is physically weak and frail. ■ an ineffectual or cowardly person.

weak·ly /ˈwēklē/ ▶ **adv.** in a way that lacks strength or force: *she leaned weakly against the wall*.
▶ **adj.** (**weaklier**, **weakliest**) sickly; not robust.
– DERIVATIVES **weak·li·ness n.**

weak-mind·ed ▶ **adj.** lacking determination, emotional strength, or intellectual capacity.
– DERIVATIVES **weak-mind·ed·ness n.**

weak·ness /ˈwēknis/ ▶ **n.** the state or condition of lacking strength: *the country's weakness in international dealings*. ■ a quality or feature regarded as a disadvantage or fault: *you must recognize your product's strengths and weaknesses*. ■ a person or thing that one is unable to resist or likes excessively: *you're his one weakness—he should never have met you*. ■ [in sing.] (**weakness for**) a self-indulgent liking for: *he had a great weakness for Scotch whisky*.

weak side ▶ **n.** Sports (on teams with an odd number of players) the half of an offensive or defensive alignment that has one player fewer.

weak sis·ter ▶ **n.** informal a weak, ineffectual, or unreliable member of a group.

weak-willed ▶ **adj.** lacking the ability to resist influence or to restrain one's own impulses; irresolute: *he is weak-willed and indecisive*.

weal[1] /wēl/ (also chiefly Medicine **wheal**) ▶ **n.** a red, swollen mark left on flesh by a blow or pressure. ■ Medicine an area of the skin that is temporarily raised, typically reddened, and usually accompanied by itching.

– ORIGIN early 19th cent.: variant of **WALE**, influenced by obsolete *wheal* 'suppurate.'

weal[2] ▶ **n.** formal that which is best for someone or something: *I am holding this trial behind closed doors in the public weal.*
– ORIGIN Old English *wela* 'wealth, well-being'; related to **WELL**[1].

Weald /wēld/ a formerly wooded district of southeastern England that included parts of Kent, Surrey, and East Sussex.
– ORIGIN Old English, variant of *wald* (see **WOLD**).

wealth /welTH/ ▶ **n.** an abundance of valuable possessions or money: *he used his wealth to bribe officials.* ■ the state of being rich; material prosperity: *some people buy boats and cars to display their wealth.* ■ plentiful supplies of a particular resource: *the country's mineral wealth.* ■ [in sing.] a plentiful supply of a particular desirable thing: *the tables and maps contain **a wealth of** information.* ■ archaic well-being; prosperity.
– ORIGIN Middle English *welthe*, from **WELL**[1] or **WEAL**[2], on the pattern of *health.*

wealth·y /ˈwelTHē/ ▶ **adj.** (**wealthier**, **wealthiest**) having a great deal of money, resources, or assets; rich: *the wealthy nations of the world* | (as plural noun **the wealthy**) *the burden of taxation on the wealthy.*
– DERIVATIVES **wealth·i·ly** /-THəlē/ **adv.**

wean[1] /wēn/ ▶ **v.** [with obj.] accustom (an infant or other young mammal) to food other than its mother's milk. ■ accustom (someone) to managing without something on which they have become dependent or of which they have become excessively fond: *the doctor tried to wean her off the sleeping pills.* ■ (**be weaned on**) be strongly influenced by (something), esp. from an early age: *I was weaned on a regular diet of Hollywood fantasy.*
– ORIGIN Old English *wenian*, of Germanic origin; related to Dutch *wennen* and German *entwöhnen.*

wean[2] ▶ **n.** Scottish & N. English a young child.
– ORIGIN late 17th cent.: contraction of *wee ane* 'little one.'

wean·ling /ˈwēnliNG/ ▶ **n.** a newly weaned animal.

weap·on /ˈwepən/ ▶ **n.** a thing designed or used for inflicting bodily harm or physical damage: *nuclear weapons.* ■ a means of gaining an advantage or defending oneself in a conflict or contest: *resignation threats had long been a weapon in his armory.*
– DERIVATIVES **weap·oned adj.**, **weap·on·less adj.**
– ORIGIN Old English *wǣp(e)n*, of Germanic origin; related to Dutch *wapen* and German *Waffe.*

weap·on·ize ▶ **v.** [with obj.] **1** convert to use as a weapon: *a list of pathogens that terrorists might weaponize.*
2 supply or equip with weapons: *an active program to weaponize smallpox.*
– DERIVATIVES **weap·on·i·za·tion n.**

weap·on of mass de·struc·tion ▶ **n.** a chemical, biological or radioactive weapon capable of causing widespread death and destruction.

weap·on·ry /ˈwepənrē/ ▶ **n.** [treated as sing. or pl.] weapons regarded collectively.

wear[1] /we(ə)r/ ▶ **v.** (past **wore** /wôr/; past participle **worn** /wôrn/) **1** [with obj.] have on one's body or a part of one's body as clothing, decoration, protection, or for some other purpose: *he was wearing a dark suit* | *both ladies wore a bunch of violets.* ■ habitually have on one's body or be dressed in: *although she was a widow, she didn't wear black.* ■ exhibit or present (a particular facial expression or appearance): *they wear a frozen smile on their faces.* ■ [with obj. or adverbial] have (one's hair or beard) at a specified length or arranged in a specified style: *the students wore their hair long.* ■ (of a ship) fly (a flag).
2 [with obj. or complement] damage, erode, or destroy by friction or use: *the track has been worn down in part to bare rock.* ■ [no obj. or complement] undergo such damage, erosion, or destruction: *mountains are wearing down with each passing second.* ■ [with obj.] form (a hole, path, etc.) by constant friction or use: *the water was forced up through holes it had worn.* ■ [no obj.] (**wear on**) cause weariness or fatigue to: *some losses can wear on you.*
3 [no obj.] withstand continued use or life in a specified way: *a carpet-type finish seems to **wear well**.* ■ [with obj., usu. with negative] Brit. informal tolerate; accept: *the environmental health people wouldn't wear it.*
4 [no obj.] (**wear on**) (of a period of time) pass, esp. slowly or tediously: *as the afternoon wore on, he began to look unhappy.* ■ [with obj.] literary pass (a period of time) in some activity: *spinning long stories, wearing half the day.*
▶ **n. 1** the wearing of something or the state of being worn as clothing: *some new tops for wear in the evening.*
2 [with modifier] clothing suitable for a particular purpose or of a particular type: *evening wear.*
3 damage or deterioration sustained from continuous use: *you need to make a deduction for **wear and tear** on all your belongings.* ■ the capacity for withstanding continuous use without such damage: *old things were relegated to the bedrooms because there was plenty of wear left in them.*
– PHRASES **wear one's heart on one's sleeve** see **HEART**. **wear thin** be gradually used up or become less convincing or acceptable: *his patience was wearing thin* | *the joke had started to wear thin.* **wear the pants** see **PANTS**.
– PHRASAL VERBS **wear someone/something down** overcome or exhaust someone or something by persistence. **wear off** lose effectiveness or intensity. **wear something out** (or **wear out**) **1** use or be used until no longer in good condition or working order: *wearing out the stair carpet* | *the type was used again and again until it wore out.* **2** (**wear someone/something out**) exhaust or tire someone or something: *an hour of this wandering wore out Lampard's patience.*
– DERIVATIVES **wear·er n.**
– ORIGIN Old English *werian*, of Germanic origin, from an Indo-European root shared by Latin *vestis* 'clothing.'

wear[2] ▶ **v.** (past and past participle **wore**) [with obj.] Sailing bring (a ship) about by turning its head away from the wind: *Shannon gives the order to wear ship.*
– ORIGIN early 17th cent.: of unknown origin.

wear·a·ble /ˈwe(ə)rəbəl/ ▶ **adj.** capable of being worn on the body.
▶ **n.** (also **wearable computer**) a computer that is small or portable enough to be worn or carried on one's body.
– DERIVATIVES **wear·a·bil·i·ty** /ˌwe(ə)rəˈbilitē/ **n.**

wea·ri·ness /ˈwi(ə)rēnis/ ▶ **n. 1** extreme tiredness; fatigue: *he began to feel weariness.*
2 reluctance to see or experience any more of something: *hardship at home produced war-weariness.*

wear·ing /ˈwe(ə)riNG/ ▶ **adj.** mentally or physically tiring.
– DERIVATIVES **wear·ing·ly adv.**

wear·i·some /ˈwi(ə)rēsəm/ ▶ **adj.** causing one to feel tired or bored.
– DERIVATIVES **wea·ri·some·ly adv.**, **wea·ri·some·ness n.**

wear·y /ˈwi(ə)rē/ ▶ **adj.** (**wearier**, **weariest**) feeling or showing tiredness, esp. as a result of excessive exertion or lack of sleep: *he gave a long, weary sigh.* ■ reluctant to see or experience any more of; tired of: *she was **weary of** their constant arguments* | [in combination] *war-weary Americans.* ■ calling for a great amount of energy or endurance; tiring and tedious: *the weary journey began again.*
▶ **v.** (**wearies**, **wearying**, **wearied**) [with obj.] cause to become tired: *she was wearied by her persistent cough.* ■ [no obj.] (**weary of**) grow tired of or bored with: *she wearied of the sameness of her life.*
– PHRASES **no rest** (or **peace**) **for the weary** humorous one's heavy workload or lack of tranquility is due to one's own choices, or to one's sinful life. [with biblical allusion to Isa. 48:22, 57:21.]
– DERIVATIVES **wea·ri·less adj.**, **wea·ri·ly** /ˈwirəlē/ **adv.**
– ORIGIN Old English *wērig*, *wǣrig*.

wea·ry·ing /ˈwi(ə)rē-iNG/ ▶ **adj.** causing tiredness; tiring: *a long, wearying journey.*
– DERIVATIVES **wea·ry·ing·ly adv.**

wea·sel /ˈwēzəl/ ▶ **n. 1** a small, slender, carnivorous mammal related to, but generally smaller than, the stoat. ● Genus *Mustela*, family Mustelidae (the **weasel family**): several species, in particular *M. nivalis* of northern Eurasia and northern North America. The weasel family also includes the polecats, minks, martens, skunks, wolverine, otters, and badgers.
2 informal a deceitful or treacherous person.
▶ **v.** (**weasels**, **weaseling**, **weaseled**; Brit. **weasels**, **weaselling**, **weaselled**) [no obj.] achieve something by use of cunning or deceit: *she suspects me of trying **to weasel my way into** his affections.* ■ behave or talk evasively.
– DERIVATIVES **wea·sel·ly adj.**
– ORIGIN Old English *wesle*, *wesule*; related to Dutch *wezel* and German *Wiesel.*

wea·sel-faced ▶ **adj.** (of a person) having a face with unattractively thin, sharp, or pointed features.

wea·sel words ▶ **plural n.** words or statements that are intentionally ambiguous or misleading.

weath·er /ˈweT͟Hər/ ▶ **n.** the state of the atmosphere at a place and time as regards heat, dryness, sunshine, wind, rain, etc.: *if the weather's good, we can go for a walk.* ■ cold, wet, and unpleasant or unpredictable atmospheric conditions; the elements: *stone walls provide shelter from wind and weather.* ■ [as modifier] denoting the side from which the wind is blowing, esp. on board a ship; windward: *the weather side of the yacht.* Contrasted with **LEE**.
▶ **v.** [with obj.] **1** wear away or change the appearance or texture of (something) by long exposure to the air: *his skin was weathered almost black by his long outdoor life.* ■ [no obj.] (of rock or other material) be worn away or altered by such processes: *the ice sheet preserves specimens that would **weather away** more quickly in other regions.* ■ (usu. as noun **weathering**) Falconry allow (a hawk) to spend a period perched on a block in the open air.
2 come safely through (a storm). ■ withstand (a difficulty or danger): *this year has tested industry's ability to weather recession.* ■ Sailing (of a ship) get to the windward of (a cape or other obstacle).
3 make (boards or tiles) overlap downward to keep out rain. ■ (in building) slope or bevel (a surface) to throw off rain.
– PHRASES **keep a weather eye on** observe very carefully, esp. for changes or developments. **make heavy weather of** informal have unnecessary difficulty in dealing with (a task or problem). [from the nautical phrase *make good* or *bad weather of it*, referring to a ship in a storm.] **under the weather** informal slightly unwell or in low spirits.
– ORIGIN Old English *weder*, of Germanic origin; related to Dutch *weer* and German *Wetter*, probably also to the noun **WIND**[1].

weath·er bal·loon ▶ **n.** a balloon equipped with meteorological apparatus that is sent into the atmosphere to provide information about the weather.

weath·er-beat·en ▶ **adj.** damaged or worn by exposure to the weather: *a tiny weather-beaten church.* ■ (of a person or a person's face) having skin that is lined and tanned or reddened through prolonged time spent outdoors.

weath·er·board /ˈweT͟Hərˌbôrd/ ▶ **n.** each of a series of horizontal boards nailed to outside walls with edges overlapping to keep out the rain; clapboard.
▶ **v.** [with obj.] fit or supply with weatherboards.

weath·er·board·ing /ˈweT͟HərˌbôrdiNG/ ▶ **n.** weatherboards collectively.

weath·er·cock /ˈweT͟Hərˌkäk/ ▶ **n.** a weathervane in the form of a rooster.
▶ **v.** [no obj.] (of a boat or aircraft) tend to turn its head into the wind; gripe.

weath·ered /ˈweT͟Hərd/ ▶ **adj.** worn by long exposure to the air; weather-beaten: *weathered rock.*

weath·er helm ▶ **n.** Nautical a tendency in a sailing ship to head into the wind if the tiller is released.

weath·er·ize /ˈweT͟Həˌrīz/ ▶ **v.** [with obj.] make (a house or other building) resistant to cold weather by adding insulation, storm windows, etc.
– DERIVATIVES **weath·er·iz·a·tion n.**

weath·er·ly /ˈweT͟Hərlē/ ▶ **adj.** Sailing (of a boat) able to sail close to the wind without drifting much to leeward.
– DERIVATIVES **weath·er·li·ness n.**

weath·er·man /ˈweT͟Hərˌman/ ▶ **n.** (pl. **weathermen**) a man who broadcasts a description and forecast of weather conditions.

weath·er map ▶ **n.** a map showing the state of the weather over a large area.

weath·er·proof /ˈweT͟Hərˌpro͞of/ ▶ **adj.** resistant to the effects of bad weather, esp. rain: *the building is structurally sound and weatherproof.*
▶ **v.** [with obj.] make (something) resistant to the effects of bad weather, esp. rain.

weath·er sta·tion ▶ **n.** an observation post where weather conditions and meteorological data are observed and recorded.

weath·er·strip /ˈweT͟Hərˌstrip/ ▶ **n.** a strip of rubber, metal, or other material used to seal the edges of a door or window against rain and wind.
▶ **v.** (**weatherstrips**, **weatherstripping**, **weatherstripped**) [with obj.] apply such a strip to (a door or window).
– DERIVATIVES **weath·er·strip·ping n.**

weath·er·tight /ˈweT͟Hərˌtīt/ ▶ **adj.** (of a building) sealed against rain and wind.

weath·er·vane /ˈweT͟Hərˌvān/ ▶ **n.** a revolving pointer to show the direction of the wind, typically mounted on top of a building.

weathervane

W

PRONUNCIATION KEY ə *ago, up*; ər *over, fur*; a *hat*; ā *ate*; ä *car*; e *let*; ē *see*; i *fit*; ī *by*; NG *sing*; ō *go*; ô *law, for*; oi *toy*; o͝o *good*; o͞o *goo*; ou *out*; TH *thin*; T͟H *then*; ZH *vision*

weath·er·worn /ˈweTHərˌwôrn/ ▶ **adj.** eroded or altered by being exposed to the weather.

weave[1] /wēv/ ▶ **v.** (past **wove** /wōv/; past participle **woven** /ˈwōvən/ or **wove**) [with obj.] form (fabric or a fabric item) by interlacing long threads passing in one direction with others at a right angle to them: *linen was woven in the district.* ■ form (thread) into fabric in this way: *some thick mohairs can be difficult to weave.* ■ [no obj.] (usu. as noun **weaving**) make fabric in this way typically by working at a loom: *cotton spinning and weaving was done in mills.* ■ make (a complex story or pattern) from a number of interconnected elements: *he weaves colorful, cinematic plots.* ■ (**weave something into**) include an element in (such a story or pattern): *flashbacks are woven into the narrative.*
▶ **n.** [usu. with adj.] a particular style or manner in which something is woven: *scarlet cloth of a very fine weave.*
– ORIGIN Old English *wefan*, of Germanic origin, from an Indo-European root shared by Greek *huphē* 'web' and Sanskrit *ūrṇavābhi* 'spider,' literally 'wool-weaver.' The current noun sense dates from the late 19th cent.

weave[2] ▶ **v.** [no obj.] twist and turn from side to side while moving somewhere in order to avoid obstructions: *he had to weave his way through the crowds.* ■ take evasive action in an aircraft, typically by moving it from side to side. ■ (of a horse) repeatedly swing the head and forepart of the body from side to side (considered to be a vice).
– ORIGIN late 16th cent.: probably from Old Norse *veifa* 'to wave, brandish.'

weav·er /ˈwēvər/ ▶ **n.** **1** a person who weaves fabric.
2 (also **weaverbird**) a finchlike songbird of tropical Africa and Asia, related to the sparrows and building elaborately woven nests. ● Family Ploceidae: several genera, in particular *Ploceus*, and numerous species.

weav·er's knot (also **weaver's hitch**) ▶ **n.** a sheet bend used for joining threads in weaving.

web /web/ ▶ **n.** **1** a network of fine threads constructed by a spider from fluid secreted by its spinnerets, used to catch its prey. ■ a similar filmy network spun by some insect larvae, esp. communal caterpillars.
2 a complex system of interconnected elements, esp. one perceived as a trap or danger: *he found himself caught up in a web of bureaucracy.* ■ (**the Web**) short for WORLD WIDE WEB.
3 a membrane between the toes of a swimming bird or other aquatic animal. ■ a thin flat part connecting thicker or more solid parts in machinery.
4 a roll of paper used in a continuous printing process. ■ the endless wire mesh in a papermaking machine on which such paper is made.
5 a piece of woven fabric.
▶ **v.** (**webs, webbing, webbed**) [with obj.] cover with or as though with a web: *she noticed his tanned skin, webbed with fine creases.*
– DERIVATIVES **web·like** /-ˌlīk/ **adj.**
– ORIGIN Old English *web(b)* 'woven fabric,' of Germanic origin; related to Dutch *web*, also to WEAVE[1]. Early use of the verb was in the sense 'weave (fabric) on a loom.'

> **WORD TRENDS** Our lives are now so dominated by the Internet that it is difficult to think of a time when a **web** was simply the realm of lurking spiders and petrified flies. **The Web** was first seen in a computing context in 1993, as a shortening of **World Wide Web**, and the word is now widely used as a synonym for 'the Internet.' As the Oxford English Corpus shows, this sense is now the dominant one, with *site, page,* and *server* the most common collocates, and the verbs *surf, use,* and *search* pushing the spider's *weave* and *spin* down the rankings. The Corpus also shows that while **web** and **Internet** have increased in usage since 2000, the full phrase **World Wide Web** has declined.

Webb /web/, Loretta, see LYNN[2].

webbed /webd/ ▶ **adj.** **1** (of the feet of a swimming bird or other aquatic animal) having the toes connected by a membrane. ■ Medicine (of fingers or toes) abnormally united for all or part of their length by a fold of skin.
2 (of a band or strip of tough material) made from webbing or similar fabric: *a heavy webbed strap.*

web·bing /ˈwebiNG/ ▶ **n.** **1** strong, closely woven fabric used for straps, belts, etc., and for supporting the seats of upholstered chairs.
2 the part of a baseball glove between the thumb and forefinger.

web·cam /ˈwebˌkam/ ▶ **n.** trademark a video camera that inputs to a computer connected to the Internet, so that its images can be viewed by Internet users.
– ORIGIN 1990s: blend of *web* in the sense 'World Wide Web' and *cam(era)*.

web·cast /ˈwebˌkast/ (also **Webcast**) ▶ **n.** a video broadcast of an event transmitted across the Internet.
– DERIVATIVES **web·cast·ing** **n.**

web-en·able ▶ **v.** [with obj.] make accessible via or compatible with the World Wide Web: *a project to web-enable legacy accounting systems.*

We·ber[1] /ˈvābər/, Carl Maria (Friedrich Ernst) von (1786–1826), German composer. He is regarded as the founder of the German romantic school of opera. Notable works: *Der Freischütz* (1817–21) and *Euryanthe* (1822–23).

We·ber[2], Max (1864–1920), German economist and sociologist; regarded as one of the founders of modern sociology. In *The Protestant Ethic and the Spirit of Capitalism* (1904), he argued that there is a direct relationship between the Protestant work ethic and the rise of capitalism.

we·ber /ˈwebər/ (abbr.: **Wb**) ▶ **n.** the SI unit of magnetic flux, causing the electromotive force of one volt in a circuit of one turn when generated or removed in one second.
– ORIGIN late 19th cent.: named after German physicist Wilhelm Eduard *Weber* (1804–91).

We·bern /ˈvābərn/, Anton (Friedrich Ernst) von (1883–1945), Austrian composer. A leading exponent of serialism, he wrote music marked by its brevity. The atonal *Five Pieces for Orchestra* (1911–13) lasts under a minute.

web-foot·ed ▶ **adj.** (of a swimming bird or other aquatic animal) having webbed feet.

web host·ing ▶ **n.** the activity or business of providing storage space and access for websites.

web·i·nar /ˈwebinär/ ▶ **n.** a seminar conducted over the Internet.
– ORIGIN 1990s: blend of WEB and SEMINAR.

web·i·sode /ˈwebiˌsōd/ ▶ **n.** an episode, esp. from a television series, or short promotional film made for viewing online.
– ORIGIN 1990s: blend of WEB and EPISODE.

web·link /ˈwebliNGk/ ▶ **n.** Computing another term for HYPERLINK. ■ a printed address of a website in a book, newspaper, etc.

web·log /ˈwebˌlôg, -ˌläg/ ▶ **n.** another term for BLOG.
– DERIVATIVES **web·log·ger** **n.**
– ORIGIN 1990s: from *web* in the sense 'World Wide Web' and *log* in the sense 'regular record of incidents.'

web·mail /ˈwebˌmāl/ ▶ **n.** e-mail that is available for use online and stored in the Internet server mailbox, and that is not downloaded to an e-mail program or used offline.

web·mas·ter /ˈwebˌmastər/ ▶ **n.** the person who maintains a particular website.

web off·set ▶ **n.** offset printing on continuous paper fed from a reel.

web page ▶ **n.** a hypertext document connected to the World Wide Web.

web·site (also **Web site**) ▶ **n.** Computing a location connected to the Internet that maintains one or more pages on the World Wide Web.

web-spin·ner ▶ **n.** a slender mainly tropical insect with a soft brownish body, living under stones or logs in a tunnel of silk produced by glands on the front legs. ● Order Embioptera: several families.

Web·ster[1] /ˈwebstər/, Daniel (1782–1852), US statesman and lawyer. A noted orator, he represented New Hampshire 1813–17 and then Massachusetts 1823–27 in the US House of Representatives, as well as Massachusetts in the US Senate 1827–41 and 1845–50. As secretary of state 1841–43 under President W. H. Harrison, he negotiated the Webster-Ashburton Treaty, which settled boundary disputes with Canada.

Daniel Webster

Web·ster[2], John (*c.*1580–*c.*1625), English playwright. Notable works: *The White Devil* (1612) and *The Duchess of Malfi* (1623), both revenge tragedies.

Web·ster[3], Noah (1758–1843), US lexicographer. His *American Dictionary of the English Language* (1828) in two volumes and containing 70,000 words was the first dictionary to give comprehensive coverage of usage in the US.

web·work /ˈwebˌwərk/ ▶ **n.** a mesh or network of links or connecting pieces: *a webwork of beams and girders.*

web·worm /ˈwebˌwərm/ ▶ **n.** a caterpillar that spins a web in which to rest or feed. When present in large numbers, it can become a serious pest. ● *Loxostega* and other genera, family Pyralidae.

web·zine /ˈwebˌzēn/ ▶ **n.** a magazine published on the Internet.

wed /wed/ ▶ **v.** (**weds, wedding**; past and past participle **wedded** or **wed**) [with obj.] chiefly formal or archaic get married to: *he was to wed the king's daughter.* ■ [no obj.] get married: *they wed a week after meeting* | (**be wed**) *they were wed in London.* ■ give or join in marriage: *will you wed your daughter to him?* ■ (as adj. **wedded**) of or concerning marriage: *10 years of wedded bliss.* ■ combine (two factors or qualities, esp. desirable ones): *in this recording he weds an excellent program with a distinctive vocal style.* ■ (**be wedded to**) be obstinately attached or devoted to (an activity, belief, or system): *foreign policy has remained wedded to outdated assumptions.*
– ORIGIN Old English *weddian*, from the Germanic base of Scots *wed* 'a pledge'; related to Latin *vas* 'surety,' also to GAGE[1].

Wed. ▶ **abbr.** Wednesday.

we'd /wēd/ ▶ **contraction** we had: *we'd already been on board.* ■ we should or we would: *we'd like to make you an offer.*

Wed·dell Sea /ˈwedl, wəˈdel/ an arm of the Atlantic Ocean, off the coast of Antarctica.
– ORIGIN named after the British explorer James *Weddell* (1787–1834), who visited it in 1823.

Wed·dell seal ▶ **n.** a large mottled gray seal with a small head, ranging farther south than any other seal and breeding on the fast ice of Antarctica. ● *Leptonychotes weddelli*, family Phocidae.
– ORIGIN early 20th cent.: named after James *Weddell* (see WEDDELL SEA).

wed·ding /ˈwediNG/ ▶ **n.** a marriage ceremony, esp. considered as including the associated celebrations.
– ORIGIN Old English *weddung* (see WED, -ING[1]).

wed·ding band ▶ **n.** a wedding ring.

wed·ding bells ▶ **plural n.** bells rung to celebrate a wedding (used to allude to the likelihood of marriage between two people): *do we hear wedding bells for these media sweethearts?*

wed·ding cake ▶ **n.** a rich iced cake, typically in two or more tiers, served at a wedding reception. ■ [as modifier] denoting a building or architectural style that is very decorative or ornate: *a wedding-cake mansion.*

wed·ding day ▶ **n.** the day or anniversary of a wedding.

wed·ding march ▶ **n.** a piece of march music played at the entrance of the bride or the exit of the couple at a wedding.

wed·ding night ▶ **n.** the night after a wedding (esp. with reference to its consummation).

wed·ding plan·ner ▶ **n.** someone who plans and organizes weddings as a profession.

wed·ding ring ▶ **n.** a ring worn by a married person, given by the spouse at their wedding.

wedge /wej/ ▶ **n.** a piece of wood, metal, or some other material having one thick end and tapering to a thin edge, that is driven between two objects or parts of an object to secure or separate them. ■ an object or piece of something having such a shape: *a wedge of cheese.* ■ a formation of people or animals with such a shape. ■ a golf club with a low, angled face for maximum loft. ■ a shot made with such a club. ■ a shoe, typically having a fairly high heel, of which the heel and sole form a solid block, with no gap under the instep. ■ a heel of this kind. ■ Music another term for DASH.
▶ **v.** **1** [with obj.] fix in position using a wedge: [with obj. and complement] *the door was wedged open.*
2 [with obj.] force into a narrow space: *I wedged the bags into the back seat.*
– PHRASES **drive a wedge between** separate: *the general aimed to drive a wedge between the city and its northern defenses.* ■ cause disagreement or hostility between: *his parents drove a wedge between us.*
– ORIGIN Old English *wecg* (noun), of Germanic origin; related to Dutch *wig*.

wedge is·sue ▶ **n.** a divisive political issue, esp. one that is raised by a candidate for public office in hopes of attracting or alienating an opponent's supporters.

W

wedg·ie /ˈwejē/ ▶ **n.** informal **1** a shoe with a wedged heel.
2 an uncomfortable tightening of the underpants between the buttocks, typically produced when someone pulls the underpants up from the back as a practical joke.

Wedg·wood /ˈwej,wo͝od/ ▶ **n.** trademark ceramic ware made by the English potter Josiah Wedgwood (1730–95) and his successors. Wedgwood is most associated with the powder-blue stoneware pieces with white embossed cameos that first appeared in 1775. ■ a powder-blue color characteristic of this stoneware.

wed·lock /ˈwed,läk/ ▶ **n.** the state of being married.
– PHRASES **born in** (or **out of**) **wedlock** born of married (or unmarried) parents.
– ORIGIN late Old English *wedlāc* 'marriage vow,' from *wed* 'pledge' (related to WED) + the suffix *-lāc* (denoting action).

Wednes·day /ˈwenzdā, -dē/ ▶ **n.** the day of the week before Thursday and following Tuesday: *a report goes before the councilors* ***on Wednesday*** | *they finish early on Wednesdays* | [as modifier] *on a Wednesday morning.*
▶ **adv.** on Wednesday: *see you Wednesday.*
■ (**Wednesdays**) on Wednesdays; each Wednesday: *Wednesdays, the jazz DJ hosts a jam session.*
– ORIGIN Old English *Wōdnesdæg*, named after the Germanic god **ODIN**; translation of late Latin *Mercurii dies*; compare with Dutch *woensdag*.

Weds. ▶ **abbr.** Wednesday.

wee /wē/ ▶ **adj.** (**weer**, **weest**) chiefly Scottish little: *when I was just a wee bairn.*
– PHRASES **the wee hours** the early hours of the morning after midnight: *nights of dining and dancing until the wee hours.*
– ORIGIN Middle English (originally a noun use in Scots, usually as *a little wee* 'a little bit'): from Old English *wēg(e)*.

weed /wēd/ ▶ **n.** a wild plant growing where it is not wanted and in competition with cultivated plants. ■ any wild plant growing in salt or fresh water. ■ informal marijuana. ■ (**the weed**) informal tobacco. ■ informal a leggy, loosely built horse.
▶ **v.** [with obj.] remove unwanted plants from (an area of ground or the plants cultivated in it): *I was weeding a flower bed.* ■ (**weed someone/something out**) remove an inferior or unwanted component of a group or collection: *we must raise the level of research and weed out the poorest work.*
– DERIVATIVES **weed·er n.**, **weed·less adj.**
– ORIGIN Old English *wēod* (noun), *wēodian* (verb), of unknown origin; related to Dutch *wieden* (verb).

weed kill·er ▶ **n.** a substance used to destroy weeds.

weeds /wēdz/ ▶ **plural n.** short for **WIDOW'S WEEDS**.

weed whack·er ▶ **n.** an electrically powered grass trimmer with a nylon cutting cord that rotates rapidly on a spindle.

weed·y /ˈwēdē/ ▶ **adj.** (**weedier**, **weediest**)
1 containing or covered with many weeds: *a weedy path led to the gate.* ■ of the nature of or resembling a weed: *a weedy species of plant.*
2 informal (of a person) thin and physically weak in appearance.
– DERIVATIVES **weed·i·ness n.**

wee·juns /ˈwējənz/ (also **Weejuns**) trademark ▶ **plural n.** moccasin-style shoes for casual wear.
– ORIGIN 1950s: a fanciful formation.

week /wēk/ ▶ **n.** a period of seven days: *the course lasts sixteen weeks* | *he'd cut the grass a week ago.* ■ the period of seven days generally reckoned from and to midnight on Saturday night: *she has an art class twice a week.* ■ workdays as opposed to the weekend; the five days from Monday to Friday: *I work during the week, so I can only get to this shop on Saturdays.* ■ the time spent working in this period of five to seven days: *she works a 48-hour week.* ■ a period of five or seven days devoted to a specified purpose or beginning on a specified day: *Super Bowl week* | *the week of June 23.* ■ informal, chiefly Brit. used after the name of a day to indicate that something will happen seven days after that day: *the program will be broadcast on Sunday week.*
– PHRASES **week after week** during each successive week, esp. over a long period: *week after week of overcast skies.* **week by week** gradually and steadily over the weeks: *Monday evening demonstrations grew week by week.* **a week from ——** used to state that something is due to happen seven days after the specified day or date: *we'll be back a week from Friday.* **week in, week out** every week without exception.
– ORIGIN Old English *wice*, of Germanic origin; related to Dutch *week* and German *Woche*, from a base probably meaning 'sequence, series.'

week·day /ˈwēk,dā/ ▶ **n.** a day of the week other than Saturday or Sunday.

week·end /ˈwēk,end/ ▶ **n.** the period from Friday evening through Sunday evening, esp. regarded as a time for leisure: *she spent the weekend camping* | [as modifier] *a weekend break.*
▶ **v.** [no obj.] informal spend a weekend somewhere: *he was weekending in the country.*

week·end·er /ˈwēk,endər/ ▶ **n.** a person who spends time in a particular place only on weekends. ■ a bag or suitcase suitable for weekend travel. ■ a small pleasure boat.

week·end war·ri·or ▶ **n.** informal a person who participates in an activity only in their spare time.

week·long (also **weeklong**) ▶ **adj.** [attrib.] lasting for a week: *a week-long visit to New Zealand.*

week·ly /ˈwēklē/ ▶ **adj.** [attrib.] done, produced, or occurring once a week: *there was a weekly dance on Wednesdays.* ■ relating to or calculated in terms of a week: *the difference in weekly income is $290.*
▶ **adv.** once a week: *interviews were given weekly.*
▶ **n.** (pl. **weeklies**) a newspaper or periodical issued every week.

week·night /ˈwēk,nīt/ ▶ **n.** a night of the week other than Saturday or Sunday.

ween /wēn/ ▶ **v.** [no obj.] archaic be of the opinion; think or suppose: *he, I ween, is no sacred personage.*
– ORIGIN Old English *wēnan*, of Germanic origin; related to Dutch *wanen* 'imagine,' German *wähnen* 'suppose wrongly,' also to **WISH**.

wee·nie /ˈwēnē/ ▶ **n. 1** another term for **WIENER** (sense 1).
2 vulgar slang a man's penis. ■ (also **wiener**) informal a weak, socially inept, or boringly studious person: *newer programming languages are a favorite of the tech weenies.*

wee·ny /ˈwēnē/ ▶ **adj.** (**weenier**, **weeniest**) informal tiny.
– ORIGIN late 18th cent.: from **WEE**, on the pattern of *tiny*; compare with **TEENY**.

weep /wēp/ ▶ **v.** (past and past participle **wept** /wept/) [no obj.] **1** shed tears: *a grieving mother wept over the body of her daughter* | [with obj.] *he wept bitter tears at her cruelty.* ■ utter or express with tears: [with direct speech] *"No!" she wept.* ■ [with obj.] archaic mourn for; shed tears over: *a young widow weeping her lost lord.*
2 exude liquid: *she rubbed one of the sores, making it weep.*
▶ **n.** [in sing.] a fit or spell of shedding tears.
– ORIGIN Old English *wēpan* (verb), of Germanic origin, probably imitative.

weep·er /ˈwēpər/ ▶ **n. 1** a person who weeps. ■ historical a hired mourner at a funeral. ■ a small image of a mourner on a monument. ■ another term for **WEEPIE**.
2 (**weepers**) historical funeral garments, in particular: ■ a man's crepe hatband worn at funerals. ■ a widow's black crepe veil and white cuffs.

weep·ie /ˈwēpē/ ▶ **n.** (pl. **weepies**) informal a sentimental or emotional film, novel, or song.

weep·ing /ˈwēpiNG/ ▶ **adj.** [attrib.] **1** shedding tears. ■ exuding liquid.
2 used in names of tree and shrub varieties with drooping branches, e.g., **weeping cherry**.
– DERIVATIVES **weep·ing·ly adv.**

weep·ing wid·ow ▶ **n.** a mushroom that has a buff cap with purplish-black gills that appear to secrete drops of fluid when damp, found commonly in both Eurasia and North America. ● *Lacrymaria velutina*, family Coprinaceae, class Hymenomycetes.

weep·ing wil·low ▶ **n.** a Eurasian willow with trailing branches and foliage reaching down to the ground, widely grown as an ornamental in waterside settings. ● Genus *Salix*, family Salicaceae: several species and hybrids, in particular *S. babylonica*.

weep·y /ˈwēpē/ ▶ **adj.** (**weepier**, **weepiest**) informal tearful; inclined to weep: *a weepy clingy child.* ■ sentimental: *a weepy made-for-TV movie.*
– DERIVATIVES **weep·i·ly** /-əlē/ **adv.**, **weep·i·ness n.**

wee·ver /ˈwēvər/ (also **weever fish**) ▶ **n.** a small, long-bodied fish with eyes at the top of the head and venomous dorsal spines. It occurs along European Atlantic coasts, typically buried in the sand with just the eyes and spines protruding. ● Family Trachinidae: several genera and species.
– ORIGIN early 17th cent.: perhaps a transferred use of Old French *wivre* 'serpent, dragon,' from Latin *vipera* 'viper.'

wee·vil /ˈwēvəl/ ▶ **n.** a small beetle with an elongated snout, the larvae of which typically develop inside seeds, stems, or other plant parts. Many are pests of crops or stored foodstuffs. Also called **SNOUT BEETLE**. ● Curculionidae and other families in the superfamily Curculionoidea: numerous genera. ■ informal any small insect that damages stored grain.
– DERIVATIVES **wee·vil·y adj.**
– ORIGIN Old English *wifel* 'beetle,' from a Germanic base meaning 'move briskly.'

wee-wee informal ▶ **n.** a child's word for urine.
▶ **v.** [no obj.] urinate.
– ORIGIN 1930s: imitative.

w.e.f. ▶ **abbr.** Brit. with effect from: *a budget to allocate w.e.f. April 1st.*

weft /weft/ ▶ **n.** [in sing.] (in weaving) the crosswise threads on a loom over and under which other threads (the warp) are passed to make cloth.
– ORIGIN Old English *weft(a)*, of Germanic origin; related to **WEAVE**[1].

Wehr·macht /ˈver,mäkt, -,mäKHt/ the German armed forces, esp. the army, from 1921 to 1945.
– ORIGIN German, literally 'defensive force.'

Wei /wā/ the name of several dynasties that ruled in China, esp. that of AD 386–535.

Weich·sel /ˈvīksəl/ ▶ **n.** [usu. as modifier] Geology the final Pleistocene glaciation in northern Europe. ■ the system of deposits laid down at this time.
– DERIVATIVES **Weich·sel·i·an** /vīkˈsilēən/ **adj. & n.**
– ORIGIN 1930s: from the German name of the Vistula River in Poland.

Wei·fang /ˈwāˈfäNG/ a city in Shandong province, in eastern China; pop. 975,300 (est. 2006). Former name **WEIHSIEN**.

wei·ge·la /wīˈjēlə/ ▶ **n.** an Asian flowering shrub of the honeysuckle family, that has pink, red, or yellow flowers and is a popular ornamental. ● Genus *Weigela*, family Caprifoliaceae: several species, in particular *W. florida*.
– ORIGIN modern Latin, named after Christian E. *Weigel* (1748–1831), German physician.

weigh[1] /wā/ ▶ **v. 1** [with obj.] find out how heavy (someone or something) is, typically using scales: *weigh yourself on the day you begin the diet* | *the vendor weighed the vegetables.* ■ have a specified weight: *when the twins were born, they weighed ten pounds.* ■ balance in the hands to guess or as if to guess the weight of: *she picked up the brick and weighed it in her right hand.* ■ (**weigh something out**) measure and take from a larger quantity of a substance a portion of a particular weight: *she weighed out two ounces of loose tobacco.* ■ [no obj.] (**weigh on**) be depressing or burdensome to: *his unhappiness would weigh on my mind so much.*
2 assess the nature or importance of, esp. with a view to a decision or action: *the consequences of the move would need to be very carefully weighed.* ■ (**weigh something against**) compare the importance of one factor with that of (another): *they need to weigh benefit against risk.* ■ [no obj.] influence a decision or action; be considered important: *the evidence weighed heavily against him.*
– PHRASES **weigh anchor** see **ANCHOR**. **weigh one's words** carefully choose the way one expresses something.
– PHRASAL VERBS **weigh someone down** be heavy and cumbersome to someone: *my waders and fishing gear weighed me down.* ■ be oppressive or burdensome to someone: *she was weighed down by the responsibility of looking after her sisters.* **weigh in** (chiefly of a boxer or jockey) be officially weighed before or after a contest: *Mason weighed in at 203 lb.* **weigh in at** informal be of (a specified weight). ■ informal cost (a specified amount). **weigh in with** informal make a forceful contribution to a competition or argument by means of: *Baker weighed in with a three-pointer.* **weigh into** informal join in forcefully or enthusiastically: *they weighed into the election campaign.* ■ attack physically or verbally: *he weighed into the companies for their high costs.* **weigh out** (of a jockey) be weighed before a race. **weigh someone/something up** Brit. carefully assess someone or something: *investors weighed up their next move.*
– DERIVATIVES **weigh·a·ble adj.**, **weigh·er n.**
– ORIGIN Old English *wegan*, of Germanic origin; related to **WAGON** and **WAIN**, and to Dutch *wegen* 'weigh,' German *bewegen* 'move,' from an Indo-European root shared by Latin *vehere* 'convey.' Early senses included 'transport from one place to another' and 'raise up.'

weigh[2] ▶ **n.** (in phrase **under weigh**) Nautical another way of saying **UNDERWAY** (sense 2).
– ORIGIN late 18th cent.: from an erroneous association with *weigh anchor* (see **WEIGH**[1]).

weigh-in ▶ **n.** an official or regular weighing of something or someone, e.g., of boxers before a fight.

weigh sta·tion ▶ **n.** a roadside station where commercial vehicles are required to stop and be inspected, thus protecting the road from travel by overweight or unsafe vehicles.

weight /wāt/ ▶ **n. 1** a body's relative mass or the quantity of matter contained by it, giving rise

W

to a downward force; the heaviness of a person or thing: *he was at least 175 pounds in weight.* ■ Physics the force exerted on the mass of a body by a gravitational field. Compare with **MASS**. ■ the quality of being heavy: *as he came upstairs the boards creaked under his weight.* ■ a unit or system of units used for expressing how much an object or quantity of matter weighs. ■ a piece of metal known to weigh a definite amount and used on scales to determine how heavy an object or quantity of a substance is. ■ the amount that a jockey is expected or required to weigh, or the amount that a horse can easily carry. ■ the surface density of cloth, used as a measure of its quality.
2 a heavy object, esp. one being lifted or carried. ■ a heavy object used to give an impulse or act as a counterweight in a mechanism. ■ a heavy object propelled by a shot-putter. ■ (**weights**) blocks or discs of metal or other heavy material used in weightlifting or weight training.
3 the ability of someone or something to influence decisions or actions: *a recommendation by the committee will carry great weight.* ■ the importance attached to something: *individuals differ in the weight they attach to various aspects of a job.* ■ Statistics a factor associated with one of a set of numerical quantities, used to represent its importance relative to the other members of the set.
▶ **v.** [with obj.] **1** hold (something) down by placing a heavy object on top of it: *a mug half filled with coffee **weighted down** a stack of papers.* ■ make (something) heavier by attaching a heavy object to it, esp. so as to make it stay in place: *the jugs were covered with muslin veils weighted with colored beads.*
2 attach importance or value to: *speaking, reading, and writing should be weighted equally in the assessment.* ■ (**be weighted**) be planned or arranged so as to put a specified person, group, or factor in a position of advantage or disadvantage: *the balance of power is weighted in favor of the government.* ■ Statistics multiply the components of (an average) by factors to take account of their importance.
3 assign a handicap weight to (a horse).
4 treat (a fabric) with a substance to make it seem thicker and heavier.
– PHRASES **put on** (or **lose**) **weight** become fatter (or thinner). **throw one's weight around** informal be unpleasantly self-assertive. **throw one's weight behind** informal use one's influence to help support. **the weight of the world** used in reference to a very heavy burden of worry or responsibility: *he continues to carry the weight of the world on his shoulders.* **be a weight off one's mind** come as a great relief after one has been worried. **worth one's weight in gold** (of a person) exceedingly useful or helpful.
– ORIGIN Old English *(ge)wiht*, of Germanic origin; related to Dutch *wicht* and German *Gewicht*. The form of the word has been influenced by **WEIGH**[1].

weight belt ▶ **n.** a belt to which weights are attached, designed to help divers stay submerged.

weight·ed av·er·age ▶ **n.** Statistics an average resulting from the multiplication of each component by a factor reflecting its importance.

weight·ing /ˈwātiNG/ ▶ **n.** allowance or adjustment made in order to take account of special circumstances or compensate for a distorting factor. ■ an allocated proportion of something, esp. an investment: *the company continues to recommend a 35% weighting in bonds.* ■ emphasis or priority: *they will give due weighting to quality as well as price.*

weight·less /ˈwātlis/ ▶ **adj.** (of a body, esp. in an orbiting spacecraft) not apparently acted on by gravity.
– DERIVATIVES **weight·less·ly** **adv.**, **weight·less·ness** **n.**

weight·lift·ing /ˈwātˌliftiNG/ ▶ **n.** the sport or activity of lifting barbells or other heavy weights. There are two standard lifts in modern weightlifting: the single-movement lift from floor to extended position (the **snatch**), and the two-movement lift from floor to shoulder position, and from shoulders to extended position (the **clean and jerk**).
– DERIVATIVES **weight·lift·er** **n.**

weight train·ing ▶ **n.** physical training that involves lifting weights.

weight-watch·er ▶ **n.** a person who is concerned about their weight, esp. one who diets.
– DERIVATIVES **weight-watch·ing** **n. & adj.**
– ORIGIN from the proprietary name *Weight Watchers*, an organization promoting dietary control as a means of losing weight.

weight·y /ˈwātē/ ▶ **adj.** (**weightier**, **weightiest**) weighing a great deal; heavy: *a weighty candelabra.* ■ of great seriousness and importance: *he threw off all weighty considerations of state.* ■ having a great deal of influence on events or decisions.
– DERIVATIVES **weight·i·ly** /-təlē/ **adv.**, **weight·i·ness** **n.**

Wei·hsien /ˈwā-ăēˈen/ former name for **WEIFANG**.

Weil /vīl, vā/, Simone (1909–43), French essayist, philosopher, and mystic. She joined the resistance movement in England during World War II and later died of tuberculosis while weakened by voluntary starvation to call attention to the plight of her French compatriots.

Weill /vīl/, Kurt (1900–50), German composer, resident in the US from 1935. He is best known for the operas he wrote with Bertolt Brecht, political satires that include *The Threepenny Opera* (1928).

Weil's dis·ease /vīlz/ ▶ **n.** a severe, sometimes fatal, form of leptospirosis transmitted by rats via contaminated water.
– ORIGIN late 19th cent.: named after H. Adolf *Weil* (1848–1916), German physician.

Wei·mar /ˈvīˌmär/ a city in Thuringia, in central Germany; pop. 64,500 (est. 2006).

Wei·mar·an·er /ˈwīməˌränər, ˈvī-/ ▶ **n.** a dog of a thin-coated, typically gray breed of pointer used as a gun dog.
– ORIGIN 1940s: from German, from **WEIMAR** in Germany, where the breed was developed.

Wei·mar Re·pub·lic the German republic of 1919–33, so called because its constitution was drawn up at Weimar. The republic was faced with huge reparation costs deriving from the Treaty of Versailles as well as soaring inflation and high unemployment. The 1920s saw a growth in support for right-wing groups, and the Republic was eventually overthrown by the Nazi Party of Adolf Hitler.

Wein·berg /ˈwīnˌbərg/, Steven (1933–), US theoretical physicist. He devised a theory to unify electromagnetic interactions and the weak forces within the nucleus of an atom. Nobel Prize for Physics (1979), shared with Sheldon Glashow and Abdus Salam.

wei qi /wā CHē/ (also **wei ch'i**) ▶ **n.** a traditional Chinese board game of territorial possession and capture.
– ORIGIN Chinese, from *wéi* 'surround' + *qí* 'chess.'

weir /wi(ə)r/ ▶ **n.** a low dam built across a river to raise the level of water upstream or regulate its flow. ■ an enclosure of stakes set in a stream as a trap for fish.
– ORIGIN Old English *wer*, from *werian* 'dam up.'

weird /wi(ə)rd/ ▶ **adj.** suggesting something supernatural; uncanny: *the weird crying of a seal.* ■ informal very strange; bizarre: *a weird coincidence* | *all sorts of **weird and wonderful** characters.* ■ archaic connected with fate.
▶ **n.** archaic, chiefly Scottish a person's destiny.
▶ **v.** [with obj.] (**weird someone out**) informal induce a sense of disbelief or alienation in someone.
– DERIVATIVES **weird·ly** **adv.**, **weird·ness** **n.**
– ORIGIN Old English *wyrd* 'destiny,' of Germanic origin. The adjective (late Middle English) originally meant 'having the power to control destiny,' and was used esp. in *the Weird Sisters*, originally referring to the Fates, later the witches in Shakespeare's *Macbeth*; the latter use gave rise to the sense 'unearthly' (early 19th cent).

weird·o /ˈwi(ə)rdō/ ▶ **n.** (pl. **weirdos**) informal a person whose dress or behavior seems strange or eccentric.

weird sis·ters ▶ **plural n.** (usu. **the weird sisters**) the Fates. ■ witches, esp. those in Shakespeare's *Macbeth*.

Weis·mann /ˈvīsmən/, August Friedrich Leopold (1834–1914), German biologist, one of the founders of modern genetics. He expounded the theory of germ plasm and suggested that variability in individuals comes from the recombination of chromosomes during reproduction.
– DERIVATIVES **Weis·mann·ism** /-ˌnizəm/ **n.**, **Weis·mann·ist** /ˈvīsmənist/ **n. & adj.**

Weiss·mul·ler /ˈwīˌsmələr/, Johnny (1904–84), US swimmer and actor; full name *John Peter Weissmuller*. He won three Olympic gold medals in 1924 and two in 1928. He starred in the Tarzan movies in the 1930s and 1940s.

weiss·wurst /ˈvīsˌwərst, -ˌwo͝orst/ ▶ **n.** whitish German sausage made chiefly of veal.
– ORIGIN German, literally 'white sausage.'

Weiz·mann /ˈvītsmən/, Chaim (Azriel) (1874–1952), Israeli statesman, born in Russia; president 1949–52. He played an important role in persuading the US government to recognize the new state of Israel in 1948.

we·ka /ˈwekə/ ▶ **n.** a large flightless New Zealand rail with heavily built legs and feet. ● *Gallirallus australis*, family Rallidae.
– ORIGIN mid 19th cent.: from Maori, imitative of its cry.

welch /welCH/ ▶ **v.** variant spelling of **WELSH**.

wel·come /ˈwelkəm/ ▶ **n.** an instance or manner of greeting someone: *you will receive a warm welcome* | *he went to meet them with his hand stretched out in welcome.*
▶ **exclam.** used to greet someone in a glad or friendly way: ***welcome to** the Wildlife Park.*
▶ **v.** [with obj.] greet (someone arriving) in a glad, polite, or friendly way: *hotels should welcome guests in their own language* | (as adj. **welcoming**) *a welcoming smile.* ■ be glad to entertain (someone) or receive (something): *we welcome any comments.* ■ react with pleasure or approval to (an event or development): *the bank's decision to cut its rates was widely welcomed.*
▶ **adj.** (of a guest or new arrival) gladly received: *visitors with disabilities are always welcome.* ■ very pleasing because much needed or desired: *after your walk, the cafe serves a welcome pot of coffee* | *deregulation is **welcome to** consumers.* ■ [predic., with infinitive] allowed or invited to do a specified thing: *anyone is welcome to join them at their midday meal.* ■ [predic.] (**welcome to**) used to indicate that one is relieved to be relinquishing the control or possession of something to another: *the job is all yours and you're welcome to it!*
– PHRASES **make someone welcome** receive and treat someone hospitably. **wear out** (or **overstay** or **outstay**) **one's welcome** stay as a visitor longer than one is wanted. **you're welcome** used as a polite response to thanks.
– DERIVATIVES **wel·come·ly** **adv.**, **wel·come·ness** **n.**, **wel·com·er** **n.**, **wel·com·ing·ly** **adv.**
– ORIGIN Old English *wilcuma* 'a person whose coming is pleasing,' *wilcumian* (verb), from *wil-* 'desire, pleasure' + *cuman* 'come' The first element was later changed to *wel-* 'well,' influenced by Old French *bien venu* or Old Norse *velkominn*.

Wel·come Wag·on ▶ **n.** trademark a vehicle bringing gifts and samples from local merchants to newcomers in a community.

weld[1] /weld/ ▶ **v.** [with obj.] **1** join together (metal pieces or parts) by heating the surfaces to the point of melting with a blowpipe, electric arc, or other means, and uniting them by pressing, hammering, etc.: *the truck had spikes welded to the back.* ■ forge (an article) by such means. ■ unite (pieces of plastic or other material) by melting or softening of surfaces in contact.
2 cause to combine and form a harmonious or effective whole: *his efforts to **weld together** the religious parties ran into trouble.*
▶ **n.** a welded joint.
– DERIVATIVES **weld·a·bil·i·ty** /ˌweldəˈbilitē/ **n.**, **weld·a·ble** **adj.**, **weld·er** **n.**
– ORIGIN late 16th cent. (in the sense 'become united'): alteration (probably influenced by the past participle) of **WELL**[2] in the obsolete sense 'melt or weld (heated metal).'

weld[2] ▶ **n.** a widely distributed plant related to mignonette, yielding a yellow dye. ● *Reseda luteola*, family Resedaceae. ■ the yellow dye made from this plant, which has been used since Neolithic times and was a popular color for Roman wedding garments.
– ORIGIN late Middle English: related to Dutch *wouw*, perhaps also to **WOLD**.

wel·fare /ˈwelˌfe(ə)r/ ▶ **n.** the health, happiness, and fortunes of a person or group: *they don't give a damn about the welfare of their families.* ■ statutory procedure or social effort designed to promote the basic physical and material well-being of people in need: *the protection of rights to education, housing, and welfare.* ■ financial support given for this purpose.
– PHRASES **on welfare** receiving government financial assistance for basic material needs.
– ORIGIN Middle English: from the adverb **WELL**[1] + the verb **FARE**.

wel·fare re·form ▶ **n.** a movement to change the federal government's social welfare policy by shifting some of the responsibility to the states and cutting benefits.

wel·fare state ▶ **n.** a system whereby the government undertakes to protect the health and well-being of its citizens, esp. those in financial or social need, by means of grants, pensions, and other benefits. The foundations for the modern welfare state in the US were laid by the New Deal programs of President Franklin D. Roosevelt. ■ a country practicing such a system.

wel·fare-to-work ▶ **adj.** denoting government policies that encourage those receiving welfare benefits to find a job, for example by providing job training: *Wisconsin's hard-nosed welfare-to-work program.*

wel·fare work ▶ n. organized effort to promote the basic physical and material well-being of people in need.
– DERIVATIVES **wel·fare work·er** n.

wel·far·ism /ˈwelfe(ə)ˌrizəm/ ▶ n. the principles or policies associated with a welfare state.
– DERIVATIVES **wel·far·ist** n. & adj.

wel·kin /ˈwelkin/ ▶ n. literary the sky or heaven.
– PHRASES **make the welkin ring** make a very loud sound: *the crew made the welkin ring with its hurrahs.*
– ORIGIN Old English *wolcen* 'cloud, sky'; related to Dutch *wolk* and German *Wolke*.

Wel·kom /ˈvelkəm/ a town in central South Africa; pop. 584,700 (est. 2009).

well[1] /wel/ ▶ adv. (**better, best**) **1** in a good or satisfactory way: *the whole team played well.* ■ in a way that is appropriate to the facts or circumstances: *you did well to come and tell me* | [as submodifier, in combination] *a well-timed exit.* ■ so as to have a fortunate outcome: *his campaign did not go well.* ■ in a kind way: *the animals will remain loyal to humans if treated well.* ■ with praise or approval: *people spoke well of him* | *the film was quite well reviewed at the time.* ■ with equanimity: *she took it very well, all things considered.* ■ profitably; advantageously: *she would marry well or not at all.* ■ in a condition of prosperity or comfort: *they lived well and were generous with their money.* ■ archaic luckily; opportunely: *hail fellow, well met.*
2 in a thorough manner: *add the mustard and lemon juice and mix well.* ■ to a great extent or degree (often used for emphasis): *the visit had been planned well in advance* | [as submodifier, in combination] *a well-loved mother.* ■ intimately; closely: *he knew my father very well.* ■ [as submodifier] Brit. informal very; extremely: *he was well out of order.* ■ [with submodifier] used as an intensifier: *I should damn well hope so.*
3 [with modal] very probably; in all likelihood: *being short of breath may well be the first sign of asthma.* ■ without difficulty: *she could well afford to pay for the reception herself.* ■ with good reason: *"What are we doing here?" "You may well ask."*
▶ adj. (**better, best**) [predic.] **1** in good health; free or recovered from illness: *I don't feel very well* | *it would be some time before Sarah was completely well* | [attrib.] informal *he was not a well man.* ■ in a satisfactory state or position: *all is not well in her ideal-looking town.*
2 sensible; advisable: *it would be well to know just what this suggestion entails.*
▶ exclam. used to express a range of emotions including surprise, anger, resignation, or relief: *Well, really! The manners of some people!* ■ used when pausing to consider one's next words: *well, I suppose I could fit you in at 3:45.* ■ used to express agreement or acceptance, often in a qualified or slightly reluctant way: *well, all right, but be quick.* ■ used to introduce the resumption of a narrative or a change of subject. ■ used to mark the end of a conversation or activity: *well, cheers, Tom—I must run.* ■ used to indicate that one is waiting for an answer or explanation from someone: *Well? You promised to tell me all about it.*
– PHRASES **all's well that ends well** see ALL. **all very well** see ALL. **as well 1** in addition; too: *the museum provides hours of fun and a few surprises as well.* **2** (**as well** or **just as well**) with equal reason or an equally good result: *I may as well have a look.* ■ sensible, appropriate, or desirable: *it would be as well to let him go.* **as well as** and also; and in addition: *a shop that sold books as well as newspapers.* **as well he** (or **she**, etc.) **might** (or **may**) used to convey the speaker's opinion that a reaction is appropriate or unsurprising: *she sounded rather chipper, as well she might, given her bright prospects.* **be well out of** Brit. informal be fortunate to be no longer involved in (a situation). **be well in with** informal have a good relationship with (someone in a position of influence or authority): *you're well in with O'Brien, aren't you?* **leave** (or **let**) **well enough alone** refrain from interfering with or trying to improve something that is satisfactory or adequate as it is. **very well** used to express agreement or understanding, sometimes grudging: *oh very well then, come in.* (**all**) **well and good** used to express acceptance of a first statement before introducing a contradictory or confirming second statement: *well, that's all well and good, but why didn't he phone her to say so?* **well and truly** completely: *Leith was well and truly rattled.* **well enough** to a reasonable degree: *he liked Isobel well enough, but wouldn't want to make a close friend of her.* **well worth** certainly worth: *Salzburg is well worth a visit.*
– ORIGIN Old English *wel(l)*, of Germanic origin; related to Dutch *wel* and German *wohl*; probably also to the verb WILL[1].

> **USAGE 1** The adverb **well** is often used in combination with past participles to form compound adjectives: **well-adjusted, well-intentioned, well-known**, and so on. As far as hyphenation is concerned, there are three general rules: (1) if the compound adjective is placed before the noun (i.e., in the attributive position), it should be hyphenated (*a* ***well-intentioned*** *remark*); (2) if the compound adjective is preceded by an adverb (*much, very, surprisingly*, etc.), the compound adjective is open (*a thoroughly* ***well prepared*** *student*); (3) if the compound adjective is placed after the noun or verb (i.e., in the predicate position), it may, but need not, be hyphenated (*her remark was* ***well-intentioned*** or *her remark was* ***well intentioned***). Likewise, other, similar compounds with *better, best, ill, little, lesser, least*, etc., are hyphenated before the noun (*a* ***little-known*** *author*), often open after a noun or verb (*the author was* ***little known***), and open if modified by an adverb (*a* ***very little known*** *author*). **2** On uses of **well** and **good**, see usage at GOOD.

well[2] ▶ n. **1** a shaft sunk into the ground to obtain water, oil, or gas. ■ a plentiful source or supply: *she could feel a deep well of sympathy and compassion.* ■ archaic a water spring or fountain. ■ short for INKWELL. ■ a depression made to hold liquid: *put the flour on a flat surface and make a well to hold the eggs.* ■ (**Wells**) chiefly Brit. (in place names) a place where there are mineral springs: *Tunbridge Wells.*
2 an enclosed space in the middle of a building, giving room for stairs or an elevator, or to allow light or ventilation. ■ Brit. the place in a court of law where the clerks and ushers sit.
3 Physics a region of minimum potential: *a gravity well.*
▶ v. [no obj.] (of a liquid) rise to the surface and spill or be about to spill: *tears were beginning to well in her eyes.* ■ (of an emotion) arise and become more intense: *all the old bitterness began to* ***well up*** *inside her again.*
– ORIGIN Old English *wella*, of Germanic origin; related to Dutch *wel* and German *Welle* 'a wave.'

we'll /wēl/ ▶ contraction we shall; we will.

well-ad·just·ed ▶ adj. successfully altered or moved so as to achieve a desired fit, appearance, or result: *her eyes were well adjusted to the darkness.* ■ (of a person) mentally and emotionally stable: *a well-adjusted, happy child is less likely to be physically ill.*

well-ad·vised ▶ adj. [with infinitive] sensible; wise: *you would be well advised to obtain legal advice.*

Wel·land Ca·nal /ˈwelənd/ (also **Welland Ship Canal**) a canal in southern Canada, 26 mi. (42 km.) long, that links Lake Erie with Lake Ontario. It bypasses Niagara Falls and forms part of the St. Lawrence Seaway.

well-ap·point·ed ▶ adj. (of a building or room) having a high standard of equipment or furnishing.

well-at·tend·ed ▶ adj. (of an event) attended by a large number of people: *a well-attended conference.*

well a·ware ▶ adj. having full knowledge of a situation or fact: *we are well aware of the dangerous side effects that some herbs can have.*

well-bal·anced ▶ adj. (of a person) emotionally stable: *we all want well-balanced kids.*

well-be·haved ▶ adj. conducting oneself in an appropriate manner: *the crowd was very well behaved.* ■ (of a computer program) communicating with hardware via standard operating system calls rather than directly and therefore able to be used on different machines.

well-be·ing ▶ n. the state of being comfortable, healthy, or happy: *an improvement in the patient's well-being.*

well-born ▶ adj. from a noble or wealthy family.

well-bred ▶ adj. having or showing good breeding or manners.

well-built ▶ adj. (of a person) large and strong. ■ of strong, solid construction: *the well-built and massively thick walls.*

well-cho·sen ▶ adj. carefully selected, esp. for a particular effect: *he would sum up any situation with a few well-chosen words.*

well-con·duct·ed ▶ adj. properly organized or carried out: *responsible, well-conducted businesses.* ■ archaic well behaved.

well-con·nect·ed ▶ adj. acquainted with or related to people with prestige or influence.

well deck ▶ n. an open space on the main deck of a ship, lying at a lower level between the forecastle and poop.

well-dis·posed ▶ adj. having a positive, sympathetic, or friendly attitude toward someone or something: *the company is* ***well-disposed to*** *the idea of partnership.*

well-done ▶ adj. **1** (of a task or undertaking) carried out successfully or satisfactorily: *the decoration is very well done* | [postpositive] *the satisfaction of* ***a job well done.***
2 (of meat) thoroughly cooked: *well-done roast beef.*
▶ exclam. used to express congratulation or approval: *Well done—you've worked very hard!*

well-dressed ▶ adj. wearing smart or fashionable clothes.

well-earned ▶ adj. fully merited or deserved: *a well-earned rest.*

well-en·dowed ▶ adj. having plentiful supplies of a resource: *the country is* ***well endowed with*** *mineral resources.* ■ well provided with money; wealthy. ■ informal, humorous (of a man) having large genitals. ■ informal, humorous (of a woman) large-breasted.

Welles /welz/, Orson (1915–85), US writer, filmmaker, and actor; full name *George Orson Welles*. His realistic radio dramatization in 1938 of H. G. Wells's *The War of the Worlds* persuaded many listeners that a Martian invasion was really happening. Notable work as both director and actor include the movies *Citizen Kane* (1941), *The Lady from Shanghai* (1948), and *Touch of Evil* (1958).

Welles·ley /ˈwelzlē/ a town in eastern Massachusetts, west of Boston, home to Wellesley College; pop. 27,244 (est. 2008).

well-es·tab·lished ▶ adj. firmly established, esp. because of a long existence: *a well-established tradition* | *his father was now well established in his career.*

well-fa·vored ▶ adj. having special advantages, esp. good looks.

well-fed ▶ adj. having good meals regularly.

well-formed ▶ adj. correctly or attractively proportioned or shaped. ■ (esp. of a sentence or phrase) constructed according to grammatical rules. ■ conforming to the formation rules of a logical system.

well-found ▶ adj. (chiefly of a boat) well equipped and maintained.

well-found·ed ▶ adj. (esp. of a suspicion or belief) based on good evidence or reasons: *their apprehensions were well founded.*

well-groomed ▶ adj. (esp. of a person) clean, tidy, and well dressed.

well-ground·ed ▶ adj. based on good evidence or reasons. ■ having a good training in or knowledge of a subject: *boys who are* ***well grounded in*** *traditional academic subjects.*

well·head /ˈwelˌhed/ ▶ n. **1** the place where a spring comes out of the ground.
2 the structure over a well, typically an oil or gas well.

well-heeled ▶ adj. informal wealthy.

well house ▶ n. a small building or room enclosing a well and its apparatus.

well-hung ▶ adj. **1** informal, humorous (of a man) having large genitals.
2 (of meat or game) hung until sufficiently dry, tender, or high before cooking.

wel·lie ▶ n. variant spelling of WELLY.

well-in·formed ▶ adj. having or showing much knowledge about a wide range of subjects, or about one particular subject.

Wel·ling·ton[1] /ˈweliNGtən/ the capital of New Zealand, at the southern tip of North Island; pop. 179,463 (2006). It became the capital in 1865, when the seat of government was moved from Auckland.

Wel·ling·ton[2], Arthur Wellesley, 1st Duke of (1769–1852), British soldier and statesman; prime minister 1828–30 and 1834; known as **the Iron Duke**. He served as commander of the British forces against Napoleon 1808–14 and defeated him at the Battle of Waterloo 1815, which ended the Napoleonic Wars.

wel·ling·ton /ˈweliNGtən/ (also **wellington boot**) ▶ n. chiefly Brit. a knee-length waterproof rubber or plastic boot.
– ORIGIN early 19th cent.: named after the 1st Duke of *Wellington* (see WELLINGTON[2]).

wel·ling·to·nia /ˌweliNGˈtōnēə/ ▶ n. Brit. another term for *giant redwood*(see REDWOOD).
– ORIGIN mid 19th cent.: modern Latin, from the former binomial *Wellingtonia gigantea* (from WELLINGTON[2]).

W

well-in·ten·tioned ▶ adj. having or showing good intentions despite a lack of success or fortunate results: *well-intentioned advice.*

well-kept ▶ adj. (esp. of property) kept clean, tidy, and in good condition. ■ (of a secret) not told to anyone or made widely known.

well-knit ▶ adj. (of a person or animal) strongly and compactly built.

well-known ▶ adj. known widely or thoroughly: *a well-known television personality.*

well-liked ▶ adj. regarded with much affection; popular with many people: *a well-liked city landmark | he is fair-minded and well liked by his colleagues.*

well-made ▶ adj. strongly or skillfully constructed: *a well-made film.*

well-man·nered ▶ adj. having or showing good manners; polite: *they were well mannered and eager to please.*

well-matched ▶ adj. (of two or more people or items) appropriate for or very similar to each other: *a fiercely contested quarterfinal between two well-matched teams.*

well-mean·ing (also **well-meant**) ▶ adj. well intentioned: *well-meaning friends.*

well·ness /ˈwelnis/ ▶ n. the state or condition of being in good physical and mental health: *when you come right down to it, stress affects every aspect of wellness.*

well-nigh ▶ adv. chiefly literary almost: *a task that is well-nigh impossible.*

well-off ▶ adj. wealthy: *her family is quite well off.* ■ in a favorable situation or circumstances: *they were well off without her.*

well-oiled ▶ adj. **1** [predic.] informal drunk.
2 (esp. of an organization) operating smoothly: *the ruling party's well-oiled political machine.*

well-or·der·ed ▶ adj. arranged or organized in an orderly way: *the only rash decision of his well-ordered life.*

well-paid ▶ adj. earning or providing good pay: *a well-paid job.*

well-placed ▶ adj. cleverly or judiciously positioned or deployed: *I obtained the information through well-placed questions.* ■ having a fortunate or advantageous position: *the country is well placed to take advantage of the singles market.*

well-pleased ▶ adj. [predic.] highly gratified or satisfied: *Moore paused, well pleased with the effect.*

well-pre·served ▶ adj. (of something old) having remained in good condition. ■ (of an old person) showing little sign of aging.

well-read ▶ adj. (of a person) knowledgeable and informed as a result of extensive reading: *Ada was **well read in** French and German literature.*

well-round·ed ▶ adj. having a smooth, curved shape: *well-rounded quartz pebbles.* ■ (of a person) plump. ■ pleasingly varied or balanced: *a dry, robust, well-rounded wine.* ■ (of a person) having a personality that is fully developed in all aspects. ■ (of a phrase or sentence) carefully composed and balanced. ■ (of an education) covering well the necessary areas of instruction.

Wells[1] /welz/, H. G. (1866–1946), English novelist; full name *Herbert George Wells.* He wrote some of the earliest science-fiction novels, such as *The War of the Worlds* (1898), which combined political satire with warnings about the powers of science.

Wells[2], Henry, see **Wells, Fargo & Co.**

well-set ▶ adj. (of a construction) firmly established; solidly fixed or arranged. ■ (also **well-set-up**) (of a person) strongly built.

Wells, Far·go & Co. /welz ˈfärgō/ a US transportation company founded in 1852 by the businessmen **Henry Wells** (1805–78) and **William Fargo** (1818–81) and others. It carried mail to and from the newly developed West, founded a San Francisco bank, and later ran a stagecoach service.

well-spent ▶ adj. (of money or time) usefully or profitably expended: *time spent in taking stock is time well spent.*

W

well-spo·ken ▶ adj. (of a person) speaking in an educated and refined manner.

well·spring /ˈwel,spriNG/ ▶ n. literary an original and bountiful source of something: *sadness is the wellspring of creativity.*

well-tak·en ▶ adj. (of a comment, argument, etc.) shrewd and accurate: *though she often makes her case too earnestly, her points are well-taken.*

well-tem·pered ▶ adj. (of a person or animal) having a cheerful or emotionally stable disposition. ■ (of a process or activity) properly regulated, controlled, or moderated.

well-thought-of ▶ adj. having a good reputation; admired or respected by others: *he was very well-thought-of within the club.*

well-thought-out ▶ adj. carefully considered and planned: *an excellent and well-thought-out presentation.*

well-thumbed ▶ adj. (of a book, magazine, etc.) having been read often and bearing marks of frequent handling.

well-timed ▶ adj. occurring at an appropriate time; timely: *a well-timed exit.*

well-to-do ▶ adj. wealthy; prosperous: *a well-to-do family.*

well-trav·eled ▶ adj. **1** (of a person) having traveled widely.
2 (of a route) much frequented by travelers.

well-trod·den ▶ adj. much frequented by travelers: *a well-trodden path.*

well-turned ▶ adj. **1** (of a compliment, phrase, or verse) elegantly expressed.
2 (esp. of an ankle or leg) having an elegant and attractive shape.
– ORIGIN originally with reference to the turning of a piece of work on a lathe.

well-up·hol·stered ▶ adj. (of a chair or sofa) having plenty of padding. ■ humorous (of a person) fat.

well-used ▶ adj. much used: *a well-used route.* ■ worn or shabby through much use, handling, or wear: *a well-used manual typewriter.*

well-wish·er ▶ n. a person who desires happiness or success for another, or who expresses such a desire.

well-worn ▶ adj. showing the signs of extensive use or wear: *a well-worn leather armchair.* ■ (of a phrase, idea, or joke) used or repeated so often that it no longer has interest or significance.

well-wrought ▶ adj. skillfully constructed or put together: *a well-wrought argument.*

wel·ly /ˈwelē/ (also **wellie**) ▶ n. (pl. **wellies**) Brit. informal **1** short for **WELLINGTON**.
2 power or vigor: *I like big, fat voices with plenty of welly.*

Welsh /welsH/ ▶ adj. of or relating to Wales, its people, or their Celtic language.
▶ n. **1** the Celtic language of Wales, spoken by about 500,000 people (mainly bilingual in English). Descended from the Brythonic language spoken in most of Roman Britain, it has been strongly revived after a long decline.
2 (as plural noun **the Welsh**) the people of Wales collectively.
– DERIVATIVES **Welsh·ness** n.
– ORIGIN Old English *Welisc, Wælisc,* from a Germanic word meaning 'foreigner;' compare with Latin *Volcae,* the name of a Celtic people in southern Gaul.

welsh /welsH/ (also **welch**) ▶ v. [no obj.] (**welsh on**) fail to honor (a debt or obligation incurred through a promise or agreement): *banks began welshing on their agreement not to convert dollar reserves into gold.*
– DERIVATIVES **welsh·er** n.
– ORIGIN mid 19th cent.: of unknown origin.

Welsh cor·gi ▶ n. (pl. **Welsh corgis**) a dog of a short-legged breed with a foxlike head.
– ORIGIN 1920s: from Welsh, from *cor* 'dwarf' + *ci* 'dog.'

Welsh corgi

Welsh·man /ˈwelsHmən/ ▶ n. (pl. **Welshmen**) a male native or inhabitant of Wales, or a man of Welsh descent.

Welsh pop·py ▶ n. a yellow- or orange-flowered European poppy of shady rocky places. ● *Meconopsis cambrica,* family Papaveraceae.

Welsh rare·bit (also **Welsh rabbit**) ▶ n. another term for **RAREBIT**.

Welsh spring·er ▶ n. (usu. **Welsh springer spaniel**) see **SPRINGER** (sense 1).

Welsh ter·ri·er ▶ n. a stocky, rough-coated, typically black-and-tan terrier of a breed with a square muzzle and drop ears.

Welsh·wom·an /ˈwelsH,wo͝omən/ ▶ n. (pl. **Welshwomen**) a female native or inhabitant of Wales, or a woman of Welsh descent.

welt /welt/ ▶ n. **1** a leather rim sewn around the edge of a shoe upper to which the sole is attached. ■ a ribbed, reinforced, or decorative border of a garment or pocket.
2 a red, swollen mark left on flesh by a blow or pressure. ■ a heavy blow.
▶ v. [with obj.] **1** provide with a welt.
2 strike (someone or something) hard and heavily: *I could have welted her.* ■ [no obj.] develop a raised scar: *his lip was beginning to thicken and welt from the blow.*
– ORIGIN late Middle English: of unknown origin.

Welt·an·schau·ung /ˈvelt,än,sHouəNG/ ▶ n. (pl. **Weltanschauungen** /-sHouəNGən/) a particular philosophy or view of life; the worldview of an individual or group.
– ORIGIN German, from *Welt* 'world' + *Anschauung* 'perception.'

wel·ter[1] /ˈweltər/ ▶ v. [no obj.] literary move in a turbulent fashion: *the streams foam and welter.* ■ lie steeped in blood with no help or care.
▶ n. a large number of items in no order; a confused mass: *there's such a welter of conflicting rules.* ■ a state of general disorder: *the attack petered out in a welter of bloody, confused fighting.*
– ORIGIN Middle English (in the sense 'writhe, wallow'): from Middle Dutch and Middle Low German *welteren.*

wel·ter[2] ▶ n. short for **WELTERWEIGHT**.

wel·ter·weight /ˈweltər,wāt/ ▶ n. a weight in boxing and other sports intermediate between lightweight and middleweight. In the amateur boxing scale it ranges from 140 to 147 pounds (63.5–67 kg). ■ a boxer or other competitor of this weight.
– ORIGIN early 19th cent.: *welter* of unknown origin.

Welt·schmerz /ˈvelt,sHmerts/ ▶ n. a feeling of melancholy and world-weariness.
– ORIGIN German, from *Welt* 'world' + *Schmerz* 'pain.'

Wel·ty /ˈweltē/, Eudora (1909–2001), US novelist, short-story writer, and critic. Her novels chiefly focus on life in the South and contain Gothic elements; they include *Delta Wedding* (1946) and *The Optimist's Daughter* (1972), which won a Pulitzer Prize.

wel·wit·schi·a /welˈwicHēə/ ▶ n. a gymnospermous plant of desert regions in southwestern Africa that has a dwarf, massive trunk, two long strap-shaped leaves, and male and female flowers in the scales of scarlet cones. It is remarkable for its ability to extract moisture from fog. ● Genus *Welwitschia,* family Welwitschiaceae: one species, *W. mirabilis.*
– ORIGIN mid 19th cent.: modern Latin, named after Friedrich *Welwitsch* (1806–72), Austrian botanist.

wen[1] /wen/ ▶ n. a boil or other swelling or growth on the skin, esp. a sebaceous cyst. ■ archaic an outstandingly large or overcrowded city: *the great wen of London.*
– ORIGIN Old English *wen(n),* of unknown origin; compare with Low German *wehne* 'tumor, wart.'

wen[2] ▶ n. variant spelling of **WYNN**.

Wen·ces·las /ˈwensəs,läs, -,lôs/ (also **Wenceslaus**) (1361–1419), king of Bohemia (as Wenceslas IV) 1378–1419. He became king of Germany, Holy Roman Emperor, and king of Bohemia in the same year, but was deposed by the German electors in 1400.

Wen·ce·slas, St. (also **Wenceslaus**) (*c.*907–29), duke of Bohemia and patron saint of the Czech Republic; also known as **Good King Wenceslas.** He worked to Christianize the people of Bohemia but was murdered by his brother; he later became venerated as a martyr. Feast day, September 28.

wench /wencH/ ▶ n. archaic or humorous a girl or young woman. ■ archaic a prostitute.
▶ v. [no obj.] archaic (of a man) consort with prostitutes.
– DERIVATIVES **wench·er** n.
– ORIGIN Middle English: abbreviation of obsolete *wenchel* 'child, servant, prostitute'; perhaps related to Old English *wancol* 'unsteady, inconstant.'

Wen-Chou /ˈwen ˈCHō/ variant of **WENZHOU**.

Wend /wend/ ▶ n. another term for **SORB**.
– ORIGIN from German *Wende,* of unknown origin.

wend /wend/ ▶ v. [no obj.] (**wend one's way**) go in a specified direction, typically slowly or by an indirect route: *they wended their way across the city.*
– ORIGIN Old English *wendan* 'to turn, depart,' of Germanic origin; related to Dutch and German *wenden,* also to **WIND**[2].

wen·di·go ▶ n. variant spelling of **WINDIGO**.

Wend·ish /ˈwendisH/ ▶ adj. & n. another term for **SORBIAN**.

Wens·ley·dale /ˈwenzlē,dāl/ ▶ n. a light-yellow, firm-textured cow's milk cheese made in England.

went /went/ past of **GO**[1].

wen·tle·trap /ˈwentlˌtrap/ ▶ **n.** a marine mollusk that has a tall spiral shell with many whorls that are ringed with oblique ridges. ● Family Epitoniidae, class Gastropoda: numerous species.
– ORIGIN mid 18th cent.: from Dutch *wenteltrap*, literally 'winding stair.'

Wen·zhou /ˈwənˈjō, ˈwen-/ (also **Wen-Chou** /ˈwen ˈchō/) an industrial city in Zhejiang province, in eastern China; pop. 633,600 (est. 2006).

wept /wept/ past and past participle of **WEEP**.

were /wər/ second person singular past, plural past, and past subjunctive of **BE**.

we're /wi(ə)r/ ▶ **contraction** we are.

weren't /wər(ə)nt/ ▶ **contraction** were not.

were·wolf /ˈwe(ə)rˌwo͝olf/ ▶ **n.** (pl. **werewolves**) (in myth or fiction) a person who changes for periods of time into a wolf, typically when there is a full moon.
– ORIGIN late Old English *werewulf*; the first element has usually been identified with Old English *wer* 'man.' In modern use the word has been revived through folklore studies.

Wer·ner /ˈvernər/, Alfred (1866–1919), Swiss chemist, born in France. He showed that stereochemistry was general to the whole of chemistry and was a pioneer in the study of coordination compounds. Nobel Prize for Chemistry (1913).

Wer·ner's syn·drome /ˈwərnərz/ ▶ **n.** Medicine a rare hereditary syndrome causing rapid premature aging, susceptibility to cancer, and other disorders.
– ORIGIN 1930s: named after Carl O. *Werner* (1879–1936), German physician.

Wer·nick·e's ar·e·a /ˈve(ə)rnikēz, -kəz/ ▶ **n.** Anatomy a region of the brain concerned with the comprehension of language, located in the cortex of the dominant temporal lobe. Damage in this area causes **Wernicke's aphasia**, characterized by superficially fluent, grammatical speech but an inability to use or understand more than the most basic nouns and verbs.
– ORIGIN late 19th cent.: named after Karl *Wernicke* (1848–1905), German neuropsychiatrist.

Wer·nick·e's en·ceph·a·lop·a·thy (also **Wernicke's syndrome**) ▶ **n.** Medicine a neurological disorder caused by thiamine deficiency, typically from chronic alcoholism or persistent vomiting, and marked by mental confusion, abnormal eye movements, and unsteady gait.
– ORIGIN late 19th cent.: named after K. *Wernicke* (see **WERNICKE'S AREA**).

wert /wərt/ archaic second person singular past of **BE**.

We·sak ▶ **n.** variant spelling of **VESAK**.

We·ser /ˈvāzər/ a river in northwestern Germany that forms at the junction of the Werra and Fulda rivers in Lower Saxony and flows north for 182 miles (292 km) to the North Sea near Bremerhaven.

Wes·ley /ˈwezlē, ˈweslē/, John (1703–91), English preacher and cofounder of Methodism. Wesley won many working-class converts, but the opposition encountered from the establishment of the Church of England led to the Methodists forming a separate denomination in 1791. His brother **Charles** (1707–88) was also a founding Methodist.

Wes·ley·an /ˈweslēən/ ▶ **adj.** of, relating to, or denoting the teachings of John Wesley or the main branch of the Methodist Church that he founded.
▶ **n.** a follower of Wesley or adherent of the main Methodist tradition.
– DERIVATIVES **Wes·ley·an·ism** /-ˌnizəm/ **n.**

Wes·sex /ˈwesiks/ the kingdom of the West Saxons, established in Hampshire in the early 6th century and gradually extended by conquest to include much of southern England.

Wes·si /ˈwesē, ˈvesē/ informal ▶ **n.** a citizen of West Germany. Compare with **OSSI**.
– ORIGIN probably from German *Westdeutsche* 'West German.'

West[1] /west/, Benjamin (1738–1820), US painter, resident in Britain from 1763. He became historical painter to George III in 1769 and the second president of the Royal Academy in 1792.

West[2], Dorothy (1907–98), US writer. She wrote about racism and class and was a spokesman for the Harlem Renaissance during the 1920s. Her novels include *The Living Is Easy* (1948) and *The Wedding* (1995). *The Richer, the Poorer* (1995) is a collection of autobiographical pieces.

West[3], Mae (1892–1980), US actress and playwright. She established her reputation on Broadway in her own comedies, *Sex* (1926) and *Diamond Lil* (1928), which are memorable for their spirited approach to sexual matters, before she embarked on her successful Hollywood career in the 1930s.

West[4], Nathanael (1903–40), US writer; born *Nathan Wallenstein Weinstein*. He wrote mainly during the Great Depression years of the 1930s. His works include novels such as *Miss Lonelyhearts* (1933), *A Cool Million* (1934), and *The Day of the Locust* (1939).

West[5], Dame Rebecca (1892–1983), British writer and feminist, born in Ireland; born *Cicily Isabel Fairfield*. She is best remembered for *The Meaning of Treason* (1949), a study of the Nuremberg trials. Other notable works: *Black Lamb and Grey Falcon* (1942) and *The Fountain Overflows* (1957).

west /west/ ▶ **n.** (usu. **the west**) **1** the direction toward the point of the horizon where the sun sets at the equinoxes, on the left-hand side of a person facing north, or the part of the horizon lying in this direction: *the evening sun glowed from the west* | *a patrol aimed to create a diversion to the west of the city*. ■ the compass point corresponding to this.
2 the western part of the world or of a specified country, region, or town: *it will become windy in the west*. ■ (usu. **the West**) Europe and its culture seen in contrast to other civilizations. ■ (usu. **the West**) historical the noncommunist states of Europe and North America, contrasted with the former communist states of eastern Europe. ■ (usu. **the West**) the western part of the US, esp. the states west of the Mississippi.
3 [as name] (**West**) Bridge the player sitting to the right of North and partnering East.
▶ **adj.** **1** [attrib.] lying toward, near, or facing the west: *the west coast*. ■ (of a wind) blowing from the west.
2 of or denoting the western part of a specified area, city, or country or its inhabitants: *West Africa*.
▶ **adv.** to or toward the west: *he faced west and watched the sunset* | *the accident happened a mile west of Bowes*.
– ORIGIN Old English, of Germanic origin; related to Dutch and German *west*, from an Indo-European root shared by Greek *hesperos*, Latin *vesper* 'evening.'

West Af·ri·ca the western part of the African continent, esp. the countries bounded by and including Mauritania, Mali, and Niger in the north and Gabon in the south.

West Al·lis /ˈalis/ an industrial city in southeastern Wisconsin, southwest of Milwaukee; pop. 59,416 (est. 2008).

West Bank a region west of the Jordan River and northwest of the Dead Sea; pop. 2,461,300 (est. 2009). It includes Jericho, Hebron, Nablus, Bethlehem, and other settlements. It became part of Jordan in 1948 and was occupied by Israel following the Six Day War of 1967. An agreement was signed in 1993 that granted limited autonomy to the Palestinians, who comprise 97 percent of its inhabitants; withdrawal of Israeli troops began in 1994 but conflict in the area continues.

West Ben·gal a state in eastern India; capital, Kolkata (Calcutta).

West Ber·lin See **BERLIN**[1].

west·bound /ˈwestˌbound/ ▶ **adj.** leading or traveling toward the west: *I need a westbound train*.

West Brom·wich /ˈbrämich/ an industrial town in western central England; pop. 127,000 (est. 2009).

West·ches·ter Coun·ty /ˈwesˌchestər/ a suburban county in southeastern New York, northeast of New York City; pop. 953,943 (est. 2008).

West Coast ▶ **n.** the western seaboard of the US from Washington to California.

West Coun·try the southwestern counties of England.

West Co·vi·na /kōˈvēnə/ a city in southwestern California, east of Los Angeles; pop. 105,790 (est. 2008).

West Des Moines a city in south central Iowa, a western suburb of Des Moines; pop. 55,426 (est. 2008).

West End the entertainment and shopping area of London to the west of the City.

west·er·ing /ˈwestəriNG/ ▶ **adj.** literary (esp. of the sun) nearing the west.
– ORIGIN mid 17th cent.: from the literary verb *wester*, from **WEST**.

Wes·ter·ly /ˈwestərlē/ an industrial and resort town in southwestern Rhode Island, on the Connecticut border; pop. 23,377 (est. 2008).

west·er·ly /ˈwestərlē/ ▶ **adj. & adv.** in a westward position or direction: [as adj.] *the westerly end of Sunset Boulevard* | [as adv.] *our plan was to keep westerly*. ■ (of a wind) blowing from the west: [as adj.] *a stiff westerly breeze*.
▶ **n.** (often **westerlies**) a wind blowing from the west. ■ (**westerlies**) the belt of prevailing westerly winds in the mid-latitudes of the northern and southern hemispheres.
– ORIGIN late 15th cent.: from obsolete *wester* 'western' + **-LY**[1].

west·ern /ˈwestərn/ ▶ **adj.** **1** [attrib.] situated in the west, or directed toward or facing the west: *there will be showers in some western areas*. ■ (of a wind) blowing from the west.
2 (usu. **Western**) living in or originating from the west, in particular Europe or the US: *Western society*. ■ of, relating to, or characteristic of the West or its inhabitants: *the history of Western art*. ■ historical of or originating in the noncommunist states of Europe and North America in contrast to the Eastern bloc.
▶ **n.** (also **Western**) a film, television drama, or novel about cowboys in the western US, esp. in the late 19th and early 20th centuries.
– DERIVATIVES **west·ern·most** /-ˌmōst/ **adj.**
– ORIGIN Old English *westerne* (see **WEST**, **-ERN**).

West·ern Aus·tra·lia a state in western Australia; pop. 2,171,197 (2008); capital, Perth. It was colonized by the British in 1826 and was federated with the other states of Australia in 1901.

West·ern blot ▶ **n.** Biochemistry an adaptation of the Southern blot procedure, used to identify specific amino-acid sequences in proteins.
– ORIGIN suggested by **SOUTHERN BLOT**.

West·ern Cape a province in southwestern South Africa, formerly part of Cape Province; capital, Cape Town.

West·ern Church the part of the Christian Church historically originating in the Latin Church of the Western Roman Empire, including the Roman Catholic Church and the Anglican, Lutheran, and Reformed Churches, esp. as distinct from the Eastern Orthodox Church.

West·ern Des·ert Egyptian name for **LIBYAN DESERT**.

West·ern Em·pire the western part of the Roman Empire, after its division in AD 395.

west·ern·er /ˈwestərnər/ (also **Westerner**) ▶ **n.** a native or inhabitant of the west, esp. of western Europe or North America.

West·ern Front the zone of fighting in western Europe in World War I, in which the German army engaged the armies to its west, i.e., France, the UK (and its dominions), and, from 1917, the US. For most of the war the front line stretched from the Vosges mountains in eastern France through Amiens to Ostend in Belgium.

west·ern hem·i·sphere the half of the earth that contains the Americas.

west·ern hem·lock ▶ **n.** a large coniferous tree with flattened needles of two different sizes, grown for pulp and as an ornamental. It occurs chiefly along the Pacific coast from northern California to Alaska and in the northern Rocky Mountains. ● *Tsuga heterophylla*, family Pinaceae.

West·ern Isles another name for **HEBRIDES**.

west·ern·ize /ˈwestərˌnīz/ ▶ **v.** [with obj.] (usu. **be westernized**) cause (a country, person, or system) to adopt or be influenced by the cultural, economic, or political systems of Europe and North America: *the agreement provided for the legal system to be westernized* | (as adj. **westernized**) *the more westernized parts of the city*. ■ [no obj.] be in the process of adopting or being influenced by the systems of the West: (as adj. **westernizing**) *a westernizing tribe*.
– DERIVATIVES **west·ern·i·za·tion** /ˌwestərniˈzāshən/ **n.**, **west·ern·iz·er** **n.**

west·ern om·e·let ▶ **n.** an omelet containing a filling of onion, green pepper, and ham.

West·ern Ro·man Em·pire see **ROMAN EMPIRE**.

West·ern sad·dle ▶ **n.** a saddle with a deep seat, high pommel and cantle, and broad stirrups.

West·ern Sa·har·a a region in northwestern Africa, on the Atlantic coast between Morocco and Mauritania; pop. 405,200 (est. 2009); capital, Laayoune. Formerly an overseas Spanish province called Spanish Sahara, it was renamed and annexed by Morocco and Mauritania in 1976. Mauritania withdrew in 1979 and Morocco extended its control over the entire region. A liberation movement, the Polisario Front, which had launched a guerrilla war against the Spanish in 1973, continued its struggle against Morocco in an attempt to establish an independent Saharawi Arab Democratic Republic; a ceasefire came into effect in 1991.

West·ern Sa·mo·a see **SAMOA**.

west·ern sand·wich ▶ **n.** a sandwich having a western omelet as a filling.

West·ern swing ▶ **n.** a style of country music influenced by jazz, popular in the 1930s.

West·ern Wall a high wall in Jerusalem said to stand on the site of Herod's temple, where Jews traditionally pray and lament on Fridays. Also called **Wailing Wall**.

Western Wall

West·ern Zhou see **Zhou**.

Wes·ter·ville /ˈwestərˌvil/ a city in central Ohio, northeast of Columbus; pop. 36,231 (est. 2008).

West·fa·len /vestˈfälən/ German name for **Westphalia**.

West Far·go a city in southwestern North Dakota, a western suburb of Fargo; pop. 23,708 (est. 2008).

West Flan·ders a province of northwestern Belgium; capital, Bruges.

West Fri·sian Is·lands see **Frisian Islands**.

West Ger·man·ic ▶ n. the western group of Germanic languages, comprising High and Low German, Dutch, Frisian, and English.
▶ adj. of or relating to West Germanic.

West Ger·ma·ny see **Germany**.

West Hart·ford a town in central Connecticut, west of Hartford; pop. 60,495 (est. 2008).

West Ha·ven a town in southwestern Connecticut, west of New Haven; pop. 52,420 (est. 2008).

West High·land ter·ri·er (also **West Highland white terrier**) ▶ n. a dog of a small, short-legged breed of terrier with a white coat and erect ears and tail, developed in the West Highlands.

West Hol·ly·wood a city in southwestern California, northeast of Beverly Hills; pop. 36,005 (est. 2008).

West In·di·an ▶ n. a native or inhabitant of any of the islands of the West Indies. ■ a person of West Indian descent.
▶ adj. of or relating to the West Indies or its people.

West In·di·an sat·in·wood ▶ n. see **satinwood**.

West In·dies a chain of islands that extends from the Florida peninsula to the coast of Venezuela and lies between the Caribbean Sea and the Atlantic Ocean. They consist of three main island groups: the Greater and Lesser Antilles and the Bahamas, with Bermuda lying further to the north. Originally inhabited by Arawak and Carib Indians, the islands were visited by Columbus in 1492 and named by him in the belief that he had reached the coast of India. The islands now consist of a number of independent states and British, French, Dutch, and US dependencies.

west·ing /ˈwestiNG/ ▶ n. distance traveled or measured westward, esp. at sea. ■ a figure or line representing westward distance on a map.

West·ing·house /ˈwestiNGˌhous/, George (1846–1914), US engineer. He is best known for developing vacuum-operated safety brakes and electrically controlled signals for railroads. He held over 400 patents and built up a huge company to manufacture his products.

West I·ri·an another name for **Irian Jaya**.

W

West Jor·dan a city in north central Utah, south of Salt Lake City; pop. 104,447 (est. 2008).

West La·fay·ette a city in west central Indiana, across the Wabash River from Lafayette, home to Purdue University; pop. 30,847 (est. 2008).

West·land /ˈwestlənd/ a city in southeastern Michigan, a western suburb of Detroit; pop. 78,961 (est. 2008).

West·mann Is·lands /ˈwes(t)mən, ˈves(t)-/ a group of fifteen volcanic islands off the southern coast of Iceland. Icelandic name **Vestmannaeyjar**.

West·meath /ˌwes(t)ˈmēTH, -ˈmē<u>TH</u>/ a county of the Republic of Ireland, in the province of Leinster; county town, Mullingar.

West·min·ster /ˈwes(t)ˌminstər, ˌwes(t)ˈmin-/ **1** an industrial and commercial city in southwestern California, southeast of Los Angeles; pop. 88,975 (est. 2008).
2 a city in north central Colorado, northwest of Denver; pop. 107,056 (est. 2008).
3 an inner London borough that contains the Houses of Parliament and many government offices. Full name **City of Westminster**. ■ used in reference to the British Parliament: *Westminster enforced successive cuts in pay.*

West·min·ster Ab·bey the collegiate church of St. Peter in Westminster, London, originally the abbey church of a Benedictine monastery. Nearly all the kings and queens of England have been crowned in Westminster Abbey; it is also the burial place of many of England's monarchs and other leading figures.

West New York an industrial and residential town in northeastern New Jersey, on the Hudson River, across from New York City; pop. 46,472 (est. 2008).

West Nile vi·rus ▶ n. a flavivirus of African origin that can be spread to humans and other mammals via mosquitoes, causing encephalitis and flulike symptoms, with some fatalities.

west-north·west ▶ n. the direction or compass point midway between west and northwest.

West Or·ange a suburban township in northeastern New Jersey, northwest of Newark; pop. 42,617 (est. 2008).

West Palm Beach a resort city in southeastern Florida; pop. 98,779 (est. 2008).

West Pap·u·a a province of Indonesia in the western part of the island of New Guinea.

West·pha·lia /wes(t)ˈfālyə, -ˈfālēə/ a former province of northwestern Germany. German name **Westfalen**.
– DERIVATIVES **West·pha·lian** adj. & n.

West·pha·li·a, Trea·ty of the peace accord (1648) that ended the Thirty Years War, signed simultaneously in Osnabrück and Münster.

West Point the US Military Academy, founded in 1802, located on the site of a former strategic fort on the west bank of the Hudson River in New York.

West·port /ˈwestˌpôrt/ **1** a town in southwestern Connecticut, an affluent suburb southwest of Bridgeport; pop. 26,592 (est. 2008).
2 a former town, now part of Kansas City in Missouri, that was a 19th-century gateway to the westbound Santa Fe Trail.

West Quod·dy Head /ˈkwädē/ the easternmost (66° 57′ W) point in the US, in Lubec in Maine, south of Passamaquoddy Bay.

West Rox·bury a southwestern district of Boston, Massachusetts. It was a separate town until 1874 and was the site of the experimental Brook Farm.

West Sax·on ▶ n. **1** a native or inhabitant of the Anglo-Saxon kingdom of Wessex.
2 the dialect of Old English used by the West Saxons, the chief literary dialect of Old English.
▶ adj. of or relating to the West Saxons or their dialect.

West Sen·e·ca a town in western New York, southeast of Buffalo; pop. 43,795 (est. 2008).

West Side the residential and commercial districts west of Fifth Avenue in Manhattan in New York City.

west-south·west ▶ n. the direction or compass point midway between west and southwest.

West Val·ley Cit·y a city in north central Utah, south of Salt Lake City; pop. 123,447 (est. 2008).

West Vir·gin·ia a state in the eastern US; pop. 1,814,468 (est. 2008); capital, Charleston; statehood, June 20, 1863 (35). It separated from Virginia in 1861, at the beginning of the Civil War, because the two areas were at odds over the questions of secession and of slavery.
– DERIVATIVES **West Vir·gin·ian** n. & adj.

west·ward /ˈwestwərd/ ▶ adj. toward the west: *the journey covers eight time zones in a westward direction.*
▶ adv. (also **westwards**) in a westerly direction: *the vast prairie lands extending from northern Ohio westward.*
▶ n. (**the westward**) a direction or region toward the west: *he sees a light to the westward.*
– DERIVATIVES **west·ward·ly** adv.

West·wood /ˈwestˌwo͝od/ a section in western Los Angeles in California, home to the University of California at Los Angeles (UCLA).

wet /wet/ ▶ adj. (**wetter, wettest**) **1** covered or saturated with water or another liquid: *she followed, slipping on the wet rock.* ■ (of the weather) rainy: *a wet, windy evening.* ■ (of paint, ink, plaster, or a similar substance) not yet having dried or hardened. ■ (of a baby or young child) having urinated in its diaper or underwear. ■ involving the use of water or liquid: *wet methods of photography.*
2 informal (of a country or region or of its legislation) allowing the sale of alcoholic beverages. ■ (of a person) addicted to alcohol.
3 Brit. informal showing a lack of forcefulness or strength of character; feeble: *they thought the cadets were a bit wet.*
▶ v. (**wets, wetting**; past and past participle **wet** or **wetted**) [with obj.] cover or touch with liquid; moisten: *he wet a finger and flicked through the pages* | (as noun **wetting**) *the wetting caused an aggravation of his gout.* ■ (esp. of a baby or young child) urinate in or on: *the child wet the bed.* ■ (**wet oneself**) urinate involuntarily.
▶ n. **1** liquid that makes something damp: *I could feel the wet of his tears.* ■ (**the wet**) rainy weather: *the race was held in the wet.* ■ a person opposed to the prohibition of alcoholic beverages.
2 Brit. informal a person lacking forcefulness or strength of character.
– PHRASES **all wet** completely wrong. **wet behind the ears** informal lacking experience; immature. **wet through** (or **to the skin**) with one's clothes soaked; completely drenched. **wet one's whistle** informal have a drink.
– DERIVATIVES **wet·ly** adv., **wet·ness** n., **wet·ta·ble** adj., **wet·tish** adj.
– ORIGIN Old English *wǣt* (adjective and noun), *wǣtan* (verb); related to **water**.

we·ta /ˈwetə/ ▶ n. a large brown wingless insect related to the grasshoppers, with long spiny legs and wood-boring larvae, found only in New Zealand. ● Family Stenopelmatidae: several genera, including *Deinacrida* (the **giant wetas**).
– ORIGIN mid 19th cent.: from Maori.

wet·back /ˈwetˌbak/ ▶ n. informal, derogatory a Mexican living in the US, esp. one who is an illegal immigrant.
– ORIGIN 1920s: so named from the practice of swimming the Rio Grande to reach the US.

wet bar ▶ n. a bar or counter equipped with running water and a sink, for serving alcoholic drinks at home.

wet blan·ket ▶ n. informal a person who spoils other people's fun by failing to join in with or by disapproving of their activities.

wet bulb ▶ n. one of the two thermometers of a psychrometer, the bulb of which is enclosed in wetted material so that water is constantly evaporating from it and cooling the bulb.

wet cell ▶ n. a primary electric cell in which the electrolyte is a liquid. Compare with **dry cell**.

wet dock ▶ n. a dock in which water is maintained at a level that keeps a vessel afloat.

wet dream ▶ n. an erotic dream associated with involuntary ejaculation of semen.

wet fly ▶ n. an artificial fishing fly designed to sink below the surface of the water.

weth·er /ˈwe<u>TH</u>ər/ ▶ n. a castrated ram.
– ORIGIN Old English, of Germanic origin; related to Dutch *weer* and German *Widder*.

Weth·ers·field /ˈwe<u>TH</u>ərzˌfēld/ a historic town in central Connecticut, south of Hartford on the Connecticut River; pop. 25,719 (est. 2008).

wet·land /ˈwetˌland, -lənd/ ▶ n. (also **wetlands**) land consisting of marshes or swamps; saturated land.

wet look ▶ n. [in sing.] an artificially wet or shiny appearance, in particular one possessed by a clothing fabric or achieved by applying a type of gel to the hair.

wet nurse ▶ n. chiefly historical a woman employed to suckle another woman's child.
▶ v. (**wet-nurse**) [with obj.] act as a wet nurse to.
■ informal look after (someone) as though they were a helpless infant.

wet pack ▶ n. a session of hydrotherapy in which the body is wrapped in wet cloth.

wet plate ▶ n. Photography a sensitized collodion plate exposed in the camera while the collodion is moist.

wet room ▶ n. a bathroom in which the shower is open or set behind a single wall, its floor area being flush with the floor of the rest of the room and the water draining away through an outlet set into the floor.

wet·suit /ˈwetˌso͞ot/ ▶ n. a close-fitting garment of neoprene or similar material typically covering most of the body but not designed to exclude water, worn for warmth in water sports or diving. Compare with **drysuit**.

wet·ting a·gent ▶ n. a chemical that can be added to a liquid to reduce its surface tension and make it more effective in spreading over and penetrating surfaces.

wet·ware /ˈwetˌwe(ə)r/ ▶ **n.** humorous human brain cells or thought processes regarded as analogous to, or in contrast with, computer systems. ■ (chiefly in science fiction) computer technology in which the brain is linked to artificial systems, or used as a model for artificial systems based on biochemical processes.

we've /wēv/ ▶ **contraction** we have.

Wex·ford /ˈweksfərd/ a county in southeastern Republic of Ireland, in the province of Leinster. ■ its county town, a port on the Irish Sea; pop. 8,894 (2006).

Wey·mouth /ˈwāməTH/ a town in eastern Massachusetts, southeast of Boston; pop. 53,261 (est. 2008).

w.f. ▶ **abbr.** Printing wrong font (used as a proofreading mark).

whack /(h)wak/ informal ▶ **v.** [with obj.] strike forcefully with a sharp blow: *his attacker whacked him on the head* | [no obj.] *she found a stick to **whack at** the branches.* ■ murder: *he was whacked while sitting in his car.*
▶ **n. 1** a sharp or resounding blow.
2 a try or attempt: *we decided to **take a whack at** spotting the decade's trends.*
3 Brit. a specified share of or contribution to something: *motorists **pay a fair whack** for the use of the roads through taxes.*
– PHRASES **at a** (or **one**) **whack** at one time: *he built twenty houses at one whack.* **out of whack** out of order; not working: *all their calculations were out of whack.*
– PHRASAL VERBS **whack off** vulgar slang masturbate.
– DERIVATIVES **whack·er** n.
– ORIGIN early 18th cent.: imitative, or perhaps an alteration of THWACK.

whacked /(h)wakt/ (also **whacked out**) ▶ **adj.** informal completely exhausted: *I'm not staying long—I'm whacked.* ■ under the influence of drugs: *a whacked-out, drug-addicted child.*

whack·ing /ˈ(h)wakiNG/ ▶ **adj.** [attrib.] Brit. informal very large: *she poured us two whacking drinks* | [as submodifier] *he dug a whacking great hole.*

whack·o ▶ **adj. & n.** (pl. **whackos**) variant spelling of WACKO.

whack·y ▶ **adj.** variant spelling of WACKY.

whale[1] /(h)wāl/ ▶ **n.** (pl. **same** or **whales**) a very large marine mammal with a streamlined hairless body, a horizontal tail fin, and a blowhole on top of the head for breathing. ● Order Cetacea. See BALEEN WHALE and TOOTHED WHALE.
– PHRASES **a whale of a ——** informal an exceedingly good example of a particular thing: *you've been doing a whale of a job.* **have a whale of a time** enjoy oneself very much.
– ORIGIN Old English *hwæl*, of Germanic origin.

whale[2] ▶ **v.** [with obj.] informal beat; hit: *Dad came upstairs and whaled me* | [no obj.] *they **whaled at** the water with their paddles.*
– ORIGIN late 18th cent.: variant of WALE.

whale·back /ˈ(h)wālˌbak/ ▶ **n.** a thing that is shaped like a whale's back, esp. an arched structure over the bow or stern part of the deck of a steamer, or a large elongated hill: [as modifier] *a whaleback ridge.*

whale·boat /ˈ(h)wālˌbōt/ ▶ **n.** a long rowboat with a bow at either end for easy maneuverability, formerly used in whaling. ■ a similar boat used as a ship's lifeboat and utility boat.

whale·bone /ˈ(h)wālˌbōn/ ▶ **n.** an elastic horny substance that grows in a series of thin parallel plates in the upper jaw of some whales and is used by them to strain plankton from the seawater. Also called BALEEN. ■ strips of this substance, much used formerly as stays in corsets and dresses: [as modifier] *a whalebone bodice.* ■ bone or ivory from a whale or walrus.

whale·bone whale ▶ **n.** another term for BALEEN WHALE.

whale oil ▶ **n.** oil obtained from the blubber of a whale, formerly used in oil lamps and for making soap.

whal·er /ˈ(h)wālər/ ▶ **n.** a whaling ship. ■ a seaman engaged in whaling.

whale shark ▶ **n.** a very large tropical shark that typically swims close to the surface, where it feeds chiefly on plankton. It is the largest known fish. ● *Rhincodon typus*, the sole member of the family Rhincodontidae.

whal·ing /ˈ(h)wāliNG/ ▶ **n.** the practice or industry of hunting and killing whales for their oil, meat, or whalebone.

wham /(h)wam/ informal ▶ **exclam.** used to express the sound of a forcible impact: *the bombs landed—wham!—right on target.* ■ used to express the idea of a sudden, dramatic, and decisive occurrence: *he asked me out for a drink, and—wham!—that was it.*
▶ **v.** (**whams, whamming, whammed**) [no obj.] strike something forcefully: *trucks whammed into each other.* ■ make a loud sound as of a forceful impact: *my heart was whamming away like a drum.*
– ORIGIN 1920s: imitative.

wham bam informal ▶ **exclam.** used to express the idea of a sudden or dramatic occurrence or change of events: *Wham bam!—we were sitting in a wreck at the foot of the cliff.*
– PHRASES **wham-bam-thank-you-ma'am** used in reference to sexual activity conducted roughly and quickly, without tenderness.
– ORIGIN 1950s (as *wham-bang*): from WHAM + BAM or the verb BANG[1].

wham·mo /ˈ(h)wamō/ ▶ **exclam.** another term for WHAM.

wham·my /ˈ(h)wamē/ ▶ **n.** (pl. **whammies**) informal an event with a powerful and unpleasant effect; a blow: *the third whammy was the degradation of the financial system.* See also DOUBLE WHAMMY. ■ an evil or unlucky influence: *I've come to **put the whammy on** them.*
– ORIGIN 1940s: from the noun WHAM + -Y[1]; associated from the 1950s with the comic strip *Li'l Abner*, in which the hillbilly Evil-Eye Fleagle could "shoot a whammy" (put a curse on somebody) by pointing a finger with one eye open, and a 'double whammy' with both eyes open.

whang /(h)waNG/ informal ▶ **v.** [no obj.] make or produce a resonant noise: *the cheerleader whanged on a tambourine.* ■ [with obj.] strike or throw heavily and loudly: *he whanged down the receiver.*
▶ **n.** a noisy blow: *he gave a whang with his hammer.*
– ORIGIN late 17th cent. (in the sense 'strike as if with a thong'): variant of THONG; senses describing noise are imitative.

whap /(h)wap/ ▶ **v.** (**whaps, whapping, whapped**) & **n.** variant spelling of WHOP.

wharf /(h)wôrf/ ▶ **n.** (pl. **wharves** /(h)wôrvz/ or **wharfs**) a level quayside area to which a ship may be moored to load and unload.
– ORIGIN late Old English *hwearf*, of Germanic origin.

wharf·age /ˈ(h)wôrfij/ ▶ **n.** accommodations provided at a wharf for the loading, unloading, or storage of goods. ■ payment made for such accommodations.

wharf·in·ger /ˈ(h)wôrfinjər/ ▶ **n.** an owner or keeper of a wharf.
– ORIGIN Middle English: from WHARFAGE + -ER[1].

Whar·ton /ˈ(h)wôrtn/, Edith (Newbold) (1862–1937), US novelist and short-story writer, resident of France from 1907. Her novels are concerned with the conflict between social and individual fulfillment. They include *Ethan Frome* (1911) and *The Age of Innocence* (1920), which won a Pulitzer Prize.

wharves /(h)wôrvz/ plural form of WHARF.

what /(h)wət, (h)wät/ ▶ **pron. 1** [interrogative pronoun] asking for information specifying something: *what is your name?* | *I'm not sure what you mean.* ■ asking for repetition of something not heard or confirmation of something not understood: *what? I can't hear you* | *you did what?*
2 [relative pronoun] the thing or things that (used in specifying something): *what we need is a commitment.* ■ (referring to the whole of an amount) whatever: *I want to do what I can to make a difference.* ■ dialect who or that: *the one what got to my house.*
3 (in exclamations) emphasizing something surprising or remarkable: *what some people do for attention!*
▶ **determiner 1** [interrogative determiner] asking for information specifying something: *what time is it?* | *do you know what excuse he gave me?*
2 [relative determiner] (referring to the whole of an amount) whatever: *he had been robbed of what little money he had.*
3 (in exclamations) how great or remarkable: [as determiner] *what luck!* | [as predeterminer] *what a fool she was.*
▶ **adv. 1** to what extent?: *what does it matter?*
2 used to indicate an estimate or approximation: *see you, what, about four?*
3 informal, dated used for emphasis or to invite agreement: *pretty poor show, what?*
– PHRASES **and** (or **or**) **what have you** informal and/or anything else similar: *for a binder try soup, gravy, cream, or what have you.* **and what not** informal and other similar things. **give someone what for** see GIVE. **what about ——? 1** used when asking for information or an opinion on something: *what about the practical angle?* **2** used to make a suggestion: *what about a walk?* **what-d'you-call-it** (or **what's-its name**) informal another term for WHATCHAMACALLIT. **what ever** used for emphasis in questions, typically expressing surprise or confusion: *what ever did I do to deserve him?* **what for?** informal for what reason? **what if ——? 1** what would result if ——?: *what if nobody shows up?* **2** what does it matter if ——?: *what if our house is a mess? I'm clean.* **what is more** and as an additional point; moreover. **what next** see NEXT. **what of ——?** what is the news concerning ——? **what of it?** why should that be considered significant? **what's-his** (or **-its**) **-name** another term for WHATSHISNAME. **what say ——?** used to make a suggestion: *what say we take a break?* **what's what** informal what is useful or important: *I'll teach her what's what.* **what with** because of (used usually to introduce several causes of something): *what with the drought and the neglect, the garden is in a sad condition.*
– ORIGIN Old English *hwæt*, of Germanic origin; related to Dutch *wat* and German *was*, from an Indo-European root shared by Latin *quod*.

> **USAGE** On the distinction between **what ever** and **whatever**, see usage at WHATEVER.

what·cha /ˈ(h)wəCHə, ˈ(h)wä-/ (also **watcha** /ˈwəCHə, ˈwä-/) ▶ **pron.** nonstandard contraction of. ■ what are you: *hey, whatcha gonna do?* ■ what have you: *whatcha got this hammer for?* ■ what do you: *whatcha want to make a mess like that for?*

what·cha·ma·call·it /ˈ(h)wəCHəməˌkôlit, ˈ(h)wä-/ ▶ **n.** informal used to refer to a person or thing whose name one cannot recall, does not know, or does not wish to specify: *she wanted me to get the whatchamacallit from her bureau.*

what·e'er /ˌ(h)wətˈe(ə)r, ˌ(h)wät-/ literary ▶ **contraction** whatever.

what·ev·er /(h)wətˈevər, ˌ(h)wät-/ ▶ **relative pron. & determiner** used to emphasize a lack of restriction in referring to any thing or amount, no matter what: [as pronoun] *do whatever you like* | [as determiner] *take whatever action is needed.* ■ regardless of what: [as pronoun] *you have our support, whatever you decide* | [as determiner] *whatever decision he made I would support it.*
▶ **pron.** used for emphasis instead of "what" in questions, typically expressing surprise or confusion: *whatever is the matter?*
▶ **adv. 1** [with negative] at all; of any kind (used for emphasis): *they received no help whatever.*
2 informal no matter what happens: *we told him we'd back him whatever.*
▶ **exclam.** informal said as a response indicating a reluctance to discuss something, implying indifference, skepticism, or exasperation: *Joseph's commentary amounted to "Yeah, well. Whatever."*
– PHRASES **or whatever** informal or anything similar: *use chopped herbs, nuts, garlic, or whatever.* **whatever next** see NEXT.

> **USAGE** In the sentence *I will do **whatever** you ask of me* (in which **whatever** = *anything*), **whatever** is correctly spelled as one word. But in the interrogative sense (***what ever** was Mary thinking?*), the emphasis is on *ever*, and it should be spelled as the two words **what ever** because *ever* is serving as an intensifier to the pronoun *what*. See also usage at HOWEVER and WHEREVER.

> **WORD TRENDS** The exclamation **whatever** is disliked intensely by many for the attitude of indifference and contempt it conveys. Popularized by the affluent Valley Girls of 1980s California, **whatever** has grown in use as a powerfully dismissive way to end a conversation ever since: *"Whatever," he said and pulled his hood up and swaggered off.* It can also be used to imply disagreement with a preceding statement (*They are telling me it's about time I earned my own money. Whatever!*) or disbelief (*We found out later that she was casting for a major motion picture, and we were all like "Oh, yeah, whatever!"*), and is even used as shorthand for everything seen to be wrong with the modern world, embodying apathy and refusal to accept responsibility: *The board will probably brush this off, and say, "Hey, whatever!"*

what·not /ˈ(h)wətˌnät, ˈ(h)wät-/ ▶ **n. 1** informal used to refer to an item or items that are not identified but are felt to have something in common with items already named: *little flashing digital displays, electric zooms and whatnots* | *pictures and books and manuscripts and whatnot.*
2 a stand with shelves for small objects.

whats·his·name /ˈ(h)wətsizˌnām, ˈ(h)wät-/ (also **whatshisname, whatshisface** /-ˌfās/, or **whatshername** /-sərˌnām/) ▶ **n.** informal used to refer to a person whose name one cannot recall,

W

sperm whale
Physeter catodon
up to 60 feet
orca
Orcinus orca
up to 30 feet
humpback whale
Megaptera novaeangliae
30 to 60 feet
narwhal
Monodon monoceros
up to 14 feet
bottlenose dolphin
Tursiops truncatus
8 to 12 feet
harbor porpoise
Phocoena phocoena
4 to 6 feet

whales

W

does not know, or does not wish to specify: *poor Mr. Whatsisname just blew a fuse.*

whats·is /ˈ(h)wətsəs, ˈ(h)wät-/ ▶ **n.** informal used to refer to a thing whose name one cannot recall, does not know, or does not wish to specify: *I am up to my whatsis in snow and slush.*

whats·it /ˈ(h)wətsit, ˈ(h)wät-/ ▶ **n.** another term for WHATCHAMACALLIT.

what·so /ˈ(h)wətˌsō, ˈ(h)wät-/ ▶ **pron. & determiner** archaic whatever: [as pronoun] *whatso goes into their brain comes out as prose.*

– ORIGIN Middle English: reduced form of Old English *swā hwæt swā* 'so what so.'

what·so·e'er /ˌ(h)wətsōˈe(ə)r, ˌ(h)wät-/ literary ▶ **contraction** whatsoever.

what·so·ev·er /ˌ(h)wətsōˈevər, ˌ(h)wät-/ ▶ **adv.** [with negative] at all (used for emphasis): *I have no doubt whatsoever.*

▶ **determiner & pron.** archaic whatever.

what-you-see-is-what-you-get ▶ **adj.** see **WYSIWYG**.

wheal /(h)wēl/ ▶ **n.** variant spelling of WEAL[1].

wheat /(h)wēt/ ▶ **n.** a cereal plant that is the most important kind grown in temperate countries, the grain of which is ground to make flour for bread, pasta, pastry, etc. ● Genus *Triticum*, family Gramineae: several species, including **bread wheat** (*T. aestivum*) and **durum wheat**, and many distinctive cultivars. ■ the grain of this plant.

– PHRASES **separate the wheat from the chaff** see CHAFF[1].

– ORIGIN Old English *hwǣte*, of Germanic origin; related to Dutch *weit*, German *Weizen*, also to WHITE.

wheat belt ▶ **n.** (**the wheat belt**) a region where wheat is the chief agricultural product.

wheat·ear /ˈ(h)wētˌir/ ▶ **n.** a mainly Eurasian and African songbird related to the chats, with black and buff or black and white plumage and a white rump. ● Genus *Oenanthe*, subfamily Turdinae, family Muscicapidae: several species, in particular the gray-backed **northern wheatear** (*O. oenanthe*), found in the arctic barrens of Eurasia and northeastern Canada.

– ORIGIN late 16th cent.: apparently from WHITE (assimilated to WHEAT) + ARSE (assimilated to EAR[2]).

wheat·en /ˈ(h)wētn/ ▶ **adj.** (esp. of bread) made of wheat. ■ of a color resembling that of wheat; a pale yellow-beige.

wheat·en ter·ri·er ▶ **n.** a terrier of a breed with a pale golden soft wavy coat.

wheat germ ▶ **n.** a nutritious foodstuff of a dry floury consistency consisting of the extracted embryos of grains of wheat.

wheat·grass /ˈ(h)wētˌgras/ ▶ **n.** another term for COUCH GRASS.

Wheat·ley /ˈ(h)wētlē/, Phillis (c.1752–84), American poet; born in Africa. She was sold as a slave at age eight to the John Wheatley family of Boston. She was educated by them and then accompanied a member of the family to London, where her first volume of poetry, *Poems on Various Subjects, Religious and Moral* (1773), was published.

wheat·meal /ˈ(h)wētˌmēl/ ▶ **n.** flour made from wheat from which some of the bran and germ has been removed.

Whea·ton /ˈ(h)wētn/ a city in northeastern Illinois, west of Chicago; pop. 54,465 (est. 2008).

Wheat State a nickname for the state of **KANSAS**.

Wheat·stone /ˈ(h)wētˌstōn/, Sir Charles (1802–75), English physicist and inventor. He is best known for his electrical inventions.

Wheat·stone bridge ▶ **n.** a simple circuit for measuring an unknown resistance by connecting it so as to form a quadrilateral with three known resistances and applying a voltage between a pair of opposite corners.

whee /(h)wē/ ▶ **exclam.** used to express delight, excitement, or exhilaration: *as the car began to bump down the track he felt a lightening of his spirits—whee!*

– ORIGIN natural exclamation: first recorded in English in the 1920s.

whee·dle /ˈ(h)wēdl/ ▶ **v.** [no obj.] employ endearments or flattery to persuade someone to do something or give one something: *you can contrive to* **wheedle your way** *onto a court* | [with direct speech] *"Please, for my sake," he wheedled.* ■ [with obj.] (**wheedle someone into doing something**) coax or persuade someone to do something. ■ [with obj.] (**wheedle something out of**) coax or persuade (someone) to say or give something.

– DERIVATIVES **whee·dler** n., **whee·dling·ly** adv.

– ORIGIN mid 17th cent.: perhaps from German *wedeln* 'cringe, fawn,' from *Wedel* 'tail, fan.'

wheel /(h)wēl/ ▶ **n. 1** a circular object that revolves on an axle and is fixed below a vehicle or other object to enable it to move easily over the ground. ■ a circular object that revolves on an axle and forms part of a machine. ■ (**the wheel**) used in reference to the cycle of a specified condition or set of events: *the final release from the wheel of life.* ■ (**the wheel**) historical a large wheel used as an instrument of punishment or torture, esp. by binding someone to it and breaking their limbs: *a man sentenced to be* **broken on the wheel**.
2 a machine or structure having a wheel as its essential part. ■ (**the wheel**) a steering wheel (used in reference to driving or steering a vehicle or vessel): *his crew knows when he wants to* **take the wheel**. ■ a vessel's propeller or paddle-wheel. ■ a device with a revolving disk or drum used in various games of chance. ■ a system, or a part of a system, regarded as a relentlessly moving machine: *the wheels of justice.*
3 (**wheels**) informal a car: *she's got wheels now.* ■ a bicycle.
4 a thing resembling a wheel in form or function, in particular a cheese made in the form of a disk.
5 an instance of wheeling; a turn or rotation.
▶ **v. 1** [with obj.] push or pull (a vehicle with wheels): *the sled was* **wheeled out** *to the flight deck.* ■ carry (someone or something) in or on a vehicle with wheels: *a young woman is wheeled into the operating room.* ■ (**wheel something in/on/out**) informal produce something that is unimpressive because it has been frequently seen or heard before: *the old journalistic arguments have to be wheeled out.*
2 [no obj.] (of a bird or aircraft) fly in a wide circle or curve: *the birds wheeled and dived.* ■ turn around quickly so as to face another way: *Robert* **wheeled around** *to see the face of Mr. Mafouz.* ■ turn or seem to turn on an axis or pivot: *the stars wheeled through the sky.*

– PHRASES **on wheels 1** by, or traveling by, car or bicycle: *a journey on wheels.* ■ (of a service) brought to one's home or district; mobile. **2** informal used to emphasize one's distaste or dislike of the person or thing mentioned: *she was a bitch on wheels.* **wheel and deal** engage in commercial or political scheming, esp. unscrupulously: (as noun **wheeling and dealing**) *the wheeling and dealing of the Wall Street boom years.* **the wheel of Fortune** the wheel that the deity Fortune is fabled to turn as a symbol of random luck or change. **wheels within wheels** used to indicate that a situation is complicated and affected by secret or indirect influences.

– DERIVATIVES **wheeled** adj. [in combination] *a four-wheeled cart*, **wheel·less** adj.

– ORIGIN Old English *hwēol* (noun), of Germanic origin, from an Indo-European root shared by Sanskrit *cakra* 'wheel, circle' and Greek *kuklos* 'circle.'

wheel and ax·le ▶ **n.** a simple lifting machine consisting of a rope that unwinds from a wheel onto a cylindrical drum or shaft joined to the wheel to provide mechanical advantage.

wheel arch ▶ **n.** an arch-shaped cavity in the body of a vehicle, which houses a wheel.

wheel·bar·row /ˈ(h)wēlˌbarō/ ▶ **n.** a small cart with a single wheel at the front and two supporting legs and two handles at the rear, used typically for carrying loads in building-work or gardening.

▶ **v.** [with obj.] carry (a load) in a wheelbarrow.

wheelbarrow

wheel·base /ˈ(h)wēlˌbās/ ▶ **n.** the distance between the front and rear axles of a vehicle: [in combination] *a short-wheelbase model.*

wheel·chair /ˈ(h)wēlˌCHe(ə)r/ ▶ **n.** a chair built on wheels for an invalid or disabled person, pushed by another person or propelled by the occupant, or motorized.

wheel dog ▶ **n.** the dog harnessed nearest to the sleigh in a dog team.

Whee·ler /ˈ(h)wēlər/, John Archibald (1911–2008), US theoretical physicist. Wheeler worked with Niels Bohr on nuclear fission and collaborated with Richard Feynman on problems concerning the retarded effects of action at a distance. He coined the term *black hole* in 1967.

wheel·er /ˈ(h)wēlər/ ▶ **n. 1** [in combination] a vehicle having a specified number of wheels: *a huge eighteen-wheeler truck.*
2 a wheelwright.
3 a horse harnessed next to the wheels of a cart and behind a leading horse.

wheel·er-deal·er (also **wheeler and dealer**) ▶ **n.** a person who engages in commercial or political scheming.

– DERIVATIVES **wheel·er-deal·ing** n.

Whee·ler Peak /ˈ(h)wēlər/ a peak in the Sangre de Cristo Mountains, northeast of Taos, the highest peak in New Mexico at 13,161 feet (4,011 m).

wheel horse ▶ **n.** a horse harnessed nearest the wheels of a vehicle. ■ a responsible and hardworking person, esp. an experienced and conscientious member of a political party.

wheel·house /ˈ(h)wēlˌhous/ ▶ **n.** a part of a boat or ship serving as a shelter for the person at the wheel.

wheel·ie /ˈ(h)wēlē/ ▶ **n.** informal a trick or maneuver whereby a bicycle or motorcycle is ridden for a short distance with the front wheel raised off the ground.

Whee·ling /ˈ(h)wēliNG/ a historic industrial city in northern West Virginia, on the Ohio River; pop. 28,913 (est. 2008).

wheel lock ▶ **n.** historical a kind of gunlock having a steel wheel that rubbed against a flint. ■ a gun having such a gunlock.

wheel·man /ˈ(h)wēlˌmən/ ▶ **n.** (pl. **wheelmen**) a person who drives a car or takes the wheel of a boat. ■ a cyclist.

wheels·man /ˈ(h)wēlzmən/ ▶ **n.** (pl. **wheelsmen**) a person who steers a ship or boat.

wheel·spin /ˈ(h)wēlˌspin/ ▶ **n.** rotation of a vehicle's wheels without traction.

wheel well ▶ **n.** a recess in a vehicle in which a wheel is located.

wheel·wright /ˈ(h)wēlˌrīt/ ▶ **n.** chiefly historical a person who makes or repairs wooden wheels.

wheeze /(h)wēz/ ▶ **v.** [no obj.] (of a person) breathe with a whistling or rattling sound in the chest, as a result of obstruction in the air passages: *the illness often leaves her wheezing.* ■ [with obj.] utter with such a sound: *he could barely wheeze out his pleas for a handout* | [with direct speech] *"Don't worry son," he wheezed.* ■ walk or move slowly with such a sound: *she wheezed up the hill toward them.* ■ (of a device) make an irregular rattling or spluttering sound: *the engine coughed, wheezed, and shrieked into life.*

▶ **n.** [usu. in sing.] **1** a sound of or as of a person wheezing: *I talk with a wheeze.*
2 an old joke, story, aphorism, act, or routine: *the old wheeze about the diner complaining about the fly in his soup.* ■ Brit. informal a clever or amusing scheme, idea, or trick: *a new wheeze to help farmers.*

– DERIVATIVES **wheez·er** n., **wheez·ing·ly** adv.

– ORIGIN late Middle English: probably from Old Norse *hvæsa* 'to hiss.'

wheez·y /ˈ(h)wēzē/ ▶ **adj.** making the sound of a person wheezing: *a wheezy laugh.*

– DERIVATIVES **wheez·i·ly** /-əlē/ adv., **wheez·i·ness** n.

whelk[1] /(h)welk/ ▶ **n.** a predatory marine mollusk with a heavy, pointed spiral shell, some kinds of which are edible. ● Family Buccinidae, class Gastropoda: *Buccinum* and other genera.

– ORIGIN Old English *wioloc, weoloc*, of unknown origin; the spelling with *wh-* was perhaps influenced by WHELK[2].

whelk[1]

whelk[2] ▶ **n.** archaic a pimple.

– ORIGIN Old English *hwylca*, related to *hwelian* 'suppurate.'

whelm /(h)welm/ ▶ **v.** [with obj.] archaic or literary engulf, submerge, or bury (someone or something): *a swimmer whelmed in a raging storm.* ■ [no obj.] flow or heap up abundantly: *the brook whelmed up from its source.*

▶ **n.** archaic or literary an act or instance of flowing or heaping up abundantly; a surge: *the whelm of the tide.*

– ORIGIN Middle English: representing an Old English form parallel to *hwelfan* 'overturn (a vessel).'

whelp /(h)welp/ ▶ **n.** a puppy. ■ a cub. ■ a boy or young man (often as a disparaging form of address). ■ (**whelps**) a set of projections on the barrel of a capstan or windlass, designed to reduce the slippage of a rope.

▶ **v.** [with obj.] (of a female dog) give birth to (a puppy): *Copper whelped seven puppies* | [no obj.] *a bitch due to whelp.*

– PHRASES **in whelp** (of a female dog) pregnant.

– ORIGIN Old English *hwelp* (noun), of Germanic origin; related to Dutch *welp* and German *Welf.*

when /(h)wen/ ▶ **adv.** at what time: *when did you last see him?* | [with preposition] *since when have you*

been interested? ■ how soon: *when can I see you?* ■ in what circumstances: *when would such a rule be justifiable?*
▶ **relative adv.** at or on which (referring to a time or circumstance): *Saturday is the day when I get my hair done.*
▶ **conj. 1** at or during the time that: *I loved math when I was in school.* ■ after: *call me when you're finished.* ■ at any time that; whenever: *can you spare five minutes when it's convenient?*
2 after which; and just then (implying suddenness): *he had just drifted off to sleep when the phone rang.*
3 in view of the fact that; considering that: *why bother to paint it when you can photograph it with the same effect?*
4 although; whereas: *I'm saying it now when I should have told you long ago.*
– ORIGIN Old English *hwanne, hwenne*, of Germanic origin; related to German *wenn* 'if,' *wann* 'when.'

whence /(h)wens/ (also **from whence**) ▶ **adv.** formal or archaic from what place or source: *whence does Congress derive this power?*
▶ **relative adv.** formal or archaic from which; from where: *the Ural mountains, whence the ore is procured.* ■ to the place from which: *he will be sent back whence he came.* ■ as a consequence of which: *whence it followed that the strategies were obsolete.*
– ORIGIN Middle English *whennes*, from earlier *whenne* (from Old English *hwanon*, of Germanic origin) + **-s**[3] (later respelled *-ce* to denote the unvoiced sound).

> **USAGE** Strictly speaking, **whence** means 'from what place,' as in *whence did you come?* Thus, the preposition **from** in *from whence did you come?* is redundant and its use is considered incorrect by some. The use with **from** is very common, though, and has been used by reputable writers since the 14th century. It is now broadly accepted in standard English.

whence·so·ev·er /ˌ(h)wensōˈevər/ ▶ **relative adv.** formal or archaic from whatever place or source.

when·e'er /(h)wənˈe(ə)r, (h)wen-/ literary ▶ **contraction** whenever.

when·ev·er /(h)wənˈevər/ ▶ **conj.** at whatever time; on whatever occasion (emphasizing a lack of restriction): *you can ask for help whenever you need it.* ■ every time that: *the springs in the armchair creak whenever I change position.*
▶ **adv.** used for emphasis instead of "when" in questions, typically expressing surprise or confusion: *whenever shall we get there?*
– PHRASES **or whenever** informal or at any time: *if you lay eyes on him, either tonight or tomorrow or whenever, call me right away.*

> **USAGE** See usage at **WHATEVER**.

when-is·sued ▶ **adj.** Finance of or relating to trading in securities that have not yet been issued.

when·so·e'er /ˌ(h)wensōˈe(ə)r/ literary ▶ **contraction** whensoever.

when·so·ev·er /ˌ(h)wensōˈevər/ ▶ **conj. & adv.** formal term for **WHENEVER**.

where /(h)we(ə)r/ ▶ **adv.** in or to what place or position: *where do you live?* | *where is she going?* | [with preposition] *where do you come from?* ■ in what direction or respect: *where does the argument lead?* ■ in or from what source: *where did you read that?* ■ in or to what situation or condition: *just where is all this leading us?*
▶ **relative adv. 1** at, in, or to which (used after reference to a place or situation): *I first saw him in Paris, where I lived in the early sixties.*
2 the place or situation in which: *this is where I live.* ■ in or to a place or situation in which: *sit where I can see you* | *where people were concerned, his threshold of boredom was low.* ■ in or to any place in which; wherever: *he was free to go where he liked.*
▶ **conj.** informal **1** that: *do you see where the men in your life are emotionally unavailable to you?* | *I see where the hotel has changed hands again.*
2 whereas: *where some caregivers burn out, others become too involved.*
▶ **n.** [(prec. by the)] the place; the scene of something. ■ (see **WHEN**).
– ORIGIN Old English *hwǣr*, of Germanic origin; related to Dutch *waar* and German *wo*.

where·a·bouts /ˈ(h)we(ə)rəˌbouts/ ▶ **adv.** where or approximately where: *whereabouts do you come from?*
▶ **n.** [treated as sing. or pl.] the place where someone or something is: *his whereabouts remain secret.*

where·af·ter /(h)we(ə)rˈaftər/ ▶ **relative adv.** formal after which: *dinner was taken at a long wooden table, whereafter we sipped liqueurs in front of a roaring fire.*

where·as /(h)we(ə)rˈaz/ ▶ **conj.** in contrast or comparison with the fact that: *you treat the matter lightly, whereas I myself was never more serious.* ■ (esp. in legal preambles) taking into consideration the fact that.

> **USAGE** See usage at **WHILE**.

where·at /(h)we(ə)rˈat/ ▶ **relative adv. & conj.** archaic or formal at which: *they demanded an equal share in the high command, whereat negotiations broke down.*

where·by /(h)we(ə)rˈbī/ ▶ **relative adv.** by which: *a system whereby people could vote by telephone.*

wher·e'er /(h)we(ə)rˈe(ə)r/ literary ▶ **contraction** wherever.

where·fore /ˈ(h)we(ə)rˌfôr/ archaic ▶ **adv.** for what reason: *she took an ill turn, but wherefore I cannot say.*
▶ **relative adv. & conj.** as a result of which: [as conjunction] *truly he cared for me, wherefore I title him with all respect.*
– PHRASES **whys and wherefores** see **WHY**.

where·from /ˌ(h)we(ə)rˈfrəm/ ▶ **relative adv.** archaic from which or from where: *one day you may lose this pride of place wherefrom you now dominate.*

where·in /(h)we(ə)rˈin/ formal ▶ **adv. 1** [relative adverb] in which: *the situation wherein the information will eventually be used.*
2 [interrogative adverb] in what place or respect?: *so wherein lies the difference?*

where·of /(h)weˈräv, -ˈəv/ ▶ **relative adv.** formal of what or which: *I know whereof I speak.*

where·on /(h)we(ə)rˈän, -ˈôn/ ▶ **relative adv.** archaic on which: *the cliff side whereon I walked.*

where·so·e'er /ˌ(h)we(ə)rsōˈe(ə)r/ literary ▶ **contraction** wheresoever.

where·so·ev·er /ˌ(h)we(ə)rsōˈevər/ ▶ **adv. & conj.** formal word for **WHEREVER**.

where·to /(h)we(ə)rˈto͞o/ ▶ **relative adv.** archaic or formal to which: *young ambition's ladder, whereto the climber-upward turns his face.*

where·up·on /ˌ(h)we(ə)rəˈpän/ ▶ **conj.** immediately after which: *he qualified in February, whereupon he was promoted to sergeant.*

wher·ev·er /(h)we(ə)rˈevər/ ▶ **relative adv.** in or to whatever place (emphasizing a lack of restriction): *meet me wherever you like.* ■ in all places; regardless of where: *it should be available wherever you go to shop.*
▶ **adv.** used for emphasis instead of "where" in questions, typically expressing surprise or confusion: *wherever can he have gone to?*
▶ **conj.** in every case when: *use whole grain breakfast cereals wherever possible.*
– PHRASES **or wherever** informal or any similar place: *they all play in England or Italy or Spain or wherever.*

> **USAGE** In formal writing, **where ever**, in which *ever* is an intensifier of the question *where* (as distinct from **wherever** in the sense of 'anywhere') is written as two words: *where ever can he have gone?* See usage at **HOWEVER** and **WHATEVER**.

where·with /(h)we(ə)rˈwiTH, -ˈwiTH/ ▶ **relative adv.** archaic or formal with or by which: *the instrumental means wherewith the action is performed.*

where·with·al /ˈ(h)we(ə)rwiTHˌôl, -wiTH-/ ▶ **n.** [usu. with infinitive] (**the wherewithal**) the money or other means needed for a particular purpose: *they lacked the wherewithal to pay.*

wher·ry /ˈ(h)werē/ ▶ **n.** (pl. **wherries**) a light rowboat used chiefly for carrying passengers. ■ Brit. a large light barge.
– DERIVATIVES **wher·ry·man** /ˈ(h)werēmən/ **n.** (pl. **wherrymen**).
– ORIGIN late Middle English: of unknown origin.

whet /(h)wet/ ▶ **v.** (**whets, whetting, whetted**) [with obj.] sharpen the blade of (a tool or weapon): *her husband is whetting his knife.* ■ excite or stimulate (someone's desire, interest, or appetite): *here's an extract to whet your appetite.*
▶ **n.** archaic a thing that stimulates appetite or desire: *he swallowed his two dozen oysters as a whet.*
– DERIVATIVES **whet·ter n.** (rare).
– ORIGIN Old English *hwettan*, of Germanic origin; related to German *wetzen*, based on an adjective meaning 'sharp.'

wheth·er /ˈ(h)weTHər/ ▶ **conj.** expressing a doubt or choice between alternatives: *he seemed undecided whether to go or stay* | *it is still not clear whether or not he realizes.* ■ expressing an inquiry or investigation (often used in indirect questions): *I'll see whether she's at home.* ■ indicating that a statement applies whichever of the alternatives mentioned is the case: *I'm going whether you like it or not.*
– PHRASES **whether or no 1** whether or not: *the only issue arising would be whether or no the publication was defamatory.* **2** archaic in any case: *God help us, whether or no!*
– ORIGIN Old English *hwæther, hwether*, of Germanic origin; related to German *weder* 'neither.'

> **USAGE** On the difference between **whether** and **if**, see usage at **IF**.

whet·stone /ˈ(h)wetˌstōn/ ▶ **n.** a fine-grained stone used for sharpening cutting tools.

whew /hyo͞o, hwyo͞o/ ▶ **exclam.** used to express surprise, relief, or a feeling of being very hot or tired: *Whew—and I thought it was serious!*
– ORIGIN late Middle English: imitative; compare with **PHEW**.

whey /(h)wā/ ▶ **n.** the watery part of milk that remains after the formation of curds.
– ORIGIN Old English *hwæg, hweg*, of Germanic origin; related to Dutch *wei*.

whey-faced ▶ **adj.** (of a person) pale, esp. as a result of ill health, shock, or fear.

which /(h)wiCH/ ▶ **interrogative pron. & determiner** asking for information specifying one or more people or things from a definite set: [as pronoun] ***which** are the best varieties of grapes for long keeping?* | ***which** of the suspects murdered him?* | [as determiner] ***which** way is the wind blowing?*
▶ **relative pron. & determiner** used referring to something previously mentioned when introducing a clause giving further information: [as pronoun] *a conference in Vienna, **which** ended on Friday* | [after prep.] *it was a crisis for **which** he was totally unprepared* | [as determiner, after prep.] *your claim ought to succeed, **in which case** the damages will be substantial.*
– PHRASES **which is which** used when two or more people or things are difficult to distinguish from each other: *there is no confusion as to which is which.*
– ORIGIN Old English *hwilc*, from the Germanic bases of **WHO** and **ALIKE**.

> **USAGE** In US English, it is usually recommended that **which** be employed only for nonrestrictive (or nonessential) clauses: *the horse, which is in the paddock, is six years old* (the *which* clause contains a nonessential fact, noted in passing; the horse would be six years old wherever it was). A *that* clause is restrictive (or essential), as it identifies a particular thing: *the horse that is in the paddock is six years old* (not any horse, but the one in the paddock). See also usage at **RESTRICTIVE** and **THAT**.

which·a·way /ˈ(h)wiCHəˌwā/ ▶ **adv.** informal or dialect
1 in which direction?
2 how? in which way?
▶ **relative adv.** however; in whatever way.
– PHRASES **every whichaway** in a disorderly fashion: *books are skewed and lounge against one another every whichaway.*

which·ev·er /ˌ(h)wiCHˈevər/ ▶ **relative determiner & pron.** used to emphasize a lack of restriction in selecting one of a definite set of alternatives: [as determiner] *choose whichever brand you prefer* | [as pronoun] *their pension should be increased annually in line with earnings or prices, whichever is the higher.* ■ regardless of which: [as determiner] *they were in a position to intercept him whichever way he ran* | [as pronoun] *whichever they choose, we must accept it.*

which·so·ev·er /ˌ(h)wiCHsōˈevər/ ▶ **determiner & pron.** archaic whichever: [as pronoun] *on any occasion whichsoever it be.*

whick·er /ˈ(h)wikər/ ▶ **v.** [no obj.] **1** utter a half-suppressed laugh; snigger; titter: *a half-loony whicker of nerves.* ■ (of a horse) give a soft breathy whinny: *the palomino whickered when she saw him and stamped her foreleg.*
2 move with a sound as of something hurtling through or beating the air: *the soft whicker of the wind flowing through the July corn.*
▶ **n. 1** a snigger; a soft, breathy whinny.
2 the sound of something beating the air.
– ORIGIN mid 17th cent. (in the sense 'to snigger, titter'): imitative.

whid·ah ▶ **n.** archaic spelling of **WHYDAH**.

Whid·bey Is·land /ˈ(h)widbē/ an island in northwestern Washington, north of Puget Sound.

whiff /(h)wif/ ▶ **n. 1** a smell that is only smelled briefly or faintly: *I caught a whiff of peachy perfume.* ■ [in sing.] an act of sniffing or inhaling, typically so as to determine or savor a scent: *one whiff of clothing and Fido was off.* ■ [in sing.] a trace or hint of something bad, menacing, or exciting: *here was a man with a whiff of danger about him.*
2 a puff or breath of air or smoke.
3 informal (chiefly in baseball or golf) an unsuccessful attempt to hit the ball.
▶ **v. 1** [with obj.] get a brief or faint smell of: *he screwed up his nose as if he'd whiffed Limburger.*
2 [no obj.] informal (chiefly in baseball or golf) try unsuccessfully to hit the ball.

unafraid. **whistle in the wind** try unsuccessfully to influence something that cannot be changed.
– ORIGIN Old English *(h)wistlian* (verb), *(h)wistle* (noun), of Germanic origin; imitative and related to Swedish *vissla* 'to whistle.'

whis·tle-blow·er (also **whistleblower**) ▶ **n.** a person who informs on someone engaged in an illicit activity.
– DERIVATIVES **whis·tle-blow·ing n.**

Whis·tler /ˈ(h)wislər/, James (Abbott) McNeill (1834–1903), US painter and etcher. He mainly painted in one or two colors and sought to achieve harmony of color and tone. Notable works: *Arrangement in Gray and Black: The Artist's Mother* (portrait known as *Whistler's Mother*, 1872) and *Old Battersea Bridge: Nocturne—Blue and Gold* (c.1872–75).

James McNeill Whistler
portrait by Walter Greaves, 1877

whis·tler /ˈ(h)wis(ə)lər/ ▶ **n. 1** a person who whistles. ■ an atmospheric radio disturbance heard as a whistle that falls in pitch, caused by lightning.
2 a robust Australasian and Indonesian songbird with a strong and typically hooked bill and a loud melodious call. Also called THICKHEAD. ● Family Pachycephalidae: four genera, in particular *Pachycephala*, and many species.
3 another term for HOARY MARMOT.

whis·tle-stop ▶ **adj.** [attrib.] very fast and with only brief pauses: *a whistle-stop tour of Britain.*
▶ **n.** a small unimportant town on a railroad. ■ a brief pause in a tour by a politician for an electioneering speech.

whis·tling duck ▶ **n.** a long-legged duck with an upright stance and a whistling call, often perching on branches. Also called TREE DUCK. ● Genus *Dendrocygna*, family Anatidae: several species.

whis·tling swan ▶ **n.** a bird of the North American race of the tundra swan, breeding in northern Canada and overwintering on the coasts of the US. ● *Cygnus columbianus columbianus*, family Anatidae.

whit /(h)wit/ ▶ **n.** [in sing.] a very small part or amount: *the last whit of warmth was drawn off by the setting sun.*
– PHRASES **every whit** wholly: *my mother was fond of her and I shall be every whit as fond.* **not** (or **never**) **a whit** not at all: *Sara had not changed a whit.*
– ORIGIN late Middle English: apparently an alteration of obsolete *wight* 'small amount.'

White[1] /(h)wīt/, Byron Raymond (1917–2002), US Supreme Court associate justice 1962–93. Appointed to the Court by President Kennedy, he was considered a moderate, or centrist, and was often the swing vote when the Court was evenly divided. Before becoming a lawyer in 1946, he played professional football and studied at Oxford University as a Rhodes scholar.

White[2], E. B. (1899–1985), US writer; full name *Elwyn Brooks White*. He was a chief contributor to *The New Yorker* magazine from 1926 and *Harper's* magazine 1938–43 and the author of the children's classics *Stuart Little* (1945), *Charlotte's Web* (1952), and *The Trumpet of the Swan* (1970).

White[3], Edward Douglass, Jr. (1845–1921), US chief justice 1910–21. Before being appointed to the Court as an associate justice 1894–1910 by President Cleveland, he served as a US senator from Louisiana 1891–94. Appointed chief justice by President Taft, he was the first associate justice to go on to that higher post. He was noted for his work on antitrust legislation.

White[4], Edward H., see GRISSOM.

White[5], Patrick (Victor Martindale) (1912–90), Australian novelist, born in Britain. He is noted for the novels *The Tree of Man* (1955) and *Voss* (1957). Nobel Prize for Literature (1973).

White[6], T. H. (1906–64), British novelist, born in India; full name *Terence Hanbury White*. He is best known for the tetralogy *The Once and Future King*, his reworking of the Arthurian legend, which began with *The Sword in the Stone* (1938).

White[7], Theodore H. (1915–86), US journalist and historian. He is best known for *The Making of the President 1960* (Pulitzer Prize, 1962). Other works include *In Search of History* (1978) and *America in Search of Itself* (1982).

white /(h)wīt/ ▶ **adj. 1** of the color of milk or fresh snow, due to the reflection of most wavelengths of visible light; the opposite of black: *a sheet of white paper.* ■ approaching such a color; very pale: *her face was white with fear.* ■ (of a plant) having white flowers or pale-colored fruit. ■ (of a tree) having light-colored bark. ■ (of wine) made from white grapes, or dark grapes with the skins removed, and having a yellowish color. ■ Brit. (of coffee or tea) served with milk or cream. ■ (of glass) transparent; colorless. ■ (of bread) made from a light-colored, sifted, or bleached flour.
2 (also **White**) belonging to or denoting a human group having light-colored skin (chiefly used of peoples of European extraction): *a white farming community.* ■ of or relating to such people: *white Australian culture.*
3 historical counterrevolutionary or reactionary. Contrasted with RED (sense 2 of the adjective).
▶ **n. 1** white color or pigment: *garnet-red flowers flecked with white | the woodwork was an immaculate white.* ■ white clothes or material: *he was dressed from head to foot in white.* ■ (**whites**) white clothes, esp. as worn for playing tennis, or as naval uniform, or in the context of washing: *wash whites separately.* ■ white wine. ■ (**White**) the player of the white pieces in chess or checkers. ■ the white pieces in chess. ■ a white thing, in particular the white ball (the cue ball) in billiards. ■ the outer part (white when cooked) that surrounds the yolk of an egg; the albumen. ■ white bread: *tuna on white.*
2 the visible pale part of the eyeball around the iris.
3 (also **White**) a member of a light-skinned people, esp. one of European extraction.
4 [with modifier] a white or cream butterfly that has dark veins or spots on the wings. It can be a serious crop pest. ● *Pieris* and other genera, family Pieridae. See also CABBAGE WHITE.
▶ **v.** [with obj.] archaic paint or turn (something) white: *your passion hath whited your face.*
– PHRASES **bleed someone/something white** drain someone or something of wealth or resources. **whited sepulcher** literary a hypocrite. [with biblical allusion to Matt. 23:27.] **white man's burden** the task that white colonizers believed they had to impose their civilization on the black inhabitants of their colonies. [from Rudyard Kipling's *The White Man's Burden* (1899).] **whiter than white** extremely white. ■ morally beyond reproach.
– PHRASAL VERBS **white out** (of vision) become impaired by exposure to sudden bright light. ■ (of a person) lose color vision as a prelude to losing consciousness. **white something out 1** obliterate a mistake with white correction fluid. ■ cover one's face or facial blemishes completely with makeup. **2** impair someone's vision with a sudden bright light.
– DERIVATIVES **white·ly adv.**, **white·ness n.**, **whit·ish adj.**
– ORIGIN late Old English *hwīt*, of Germanic origin; related to Dutch *wit* and German *weiss*, also to WHEAT.

white ad·mi·ral ▶ **n.** a North American butterfly that has black wings bearing a broad white band and a marginal row of blue dashes. ● *Limenitis arthemis*, subfamily Limenitinae, family Nymphalidae. See RED-SPOTTED PURPLE.

white ant ▶ **n.** another term for TERMITE.

White Ar·my ▶ **n.** any of the armies that opposed the Bolsheviks during the Russian Civil War of 1918–21.

white ar·se·nic ▶ **n.** an extremely toxic soluble white solid made by burning arsenic. ● Alternative name: **arsenic trioxide**; chem. formula: As_2O_3.

white·bait /ˈ(h)wītˌbāt/ ▶ **n.** the small silvery-white young of herrings, sprats, and similar marine fish, eaten in numbers as food.

white bal·ance ▶ **n.** the color balance on a digital camera.

white bass /bās/ ▶ **n.** a North American freshwater bass with dark horizontal stripes. ● *Morone chrysops*, family Percichthyidae.

White Bear Lake a city in southeastern Minnesota, northeast of St. Paul; pop. 24,095 (est. 2008).

white belt ▶ **n.** a white belt worn by a beginner in judo or karate. ■ a person wearing such a belt.

white birch ▶ **n.** a birch tree with white bark, esp. the paper birch or the European silver birch.

white blood cell ▶ **n.** less technical term for LEUKOCYTE.

white·board /ˈ(h)wītˌbôrd/ ▶ **n.** a wipeable board with a white surface used for teaching or presentations. ■ (also **interactive whiteboard**) Computing an area on a display screen common to several users, on which they can write and draw.

white book ▶ **n.** a book of rules, standards, or records, esp. an official government report, bound in white.

white-bread ▶ **adj.** informal of, belonging to, or representative of the white middle classes; not progressive, radical, or innovative: *inoffensive white-bread comedies.*

white bry·o·ny ▶ **n.** see BRYONY (sense 1).

white·cap /ˈ(h)wītˌkap/ ▶ **n.** a small wave with a foamy crest.

white ce·dar ▶ **n.** a North American tree of the cypress family. ● *Thuja* and other genera, family Cupressaceae: several species, in particular the **northern white cedar** (*T. occidentalis*), which yields timber and medicinal oil.

white cell ▶ **n.** less technical term for LEUKOCYTE.

white choc·o·late ▶ **n.** a whitish candy made with cocoa butter.

white Christ·mas ▶ **n.** a Christmas during which there is snow on the ground.

white clo·ver ▶ **n.** see CLOVER.

white-col·lar ▶ **adj.** of or relating to the work done or those who work in an office or other professional environment. ■ denoting nonviolent crime committed by white-collar workers, esp. fraud.

white cur·rant ▶ **n.** a cultivated variety of red currant with pale edible berries. The berries are insipid and generally used for jams and jellies, in combination with other fruits.

white dwarf ▶ **n.** Astronomy a small very dense star that is typically the size of a planet. A white dwarf is formed when a low-mass star has exhausted all its central nuclear fuel and lost its outer layers as a planetary nebula.

white el·e·phant ▶ **n.** a possession that is useless or troublesome, esp. one that is expensive to maintain or difficult to dispose of.
– ORIGIN from the story that the kings of Siam gave such animals as a gift to courtiers considered obnoxious, in order to ruin the recipient by the great expense incurred in maintaining the animal.

white-eye ▶ **n.** a small Old World songbird with a ring of white feathers around the eye. ● Family Zosteropidae: several genera, in particular *Zosterops*, and numerous species.

white·face /ˈ(h)wītˌfās/ ▶ **n. 1** white stage makeup. **2** a Hereford cow or bull.

White Fa·ther ▶ **n. 1** a white man regarded by people of a nonwhite race as having authority over them.
2 a member of the Society of Missionaries of Africa, a Roman Catholic order founded in Algiers in 1868.
– ORIGIN translating French *Père Blanc*.

white feath·er ▶ **n.** a white feather given to someone as a sign that the giver considers them a coward.
– PHRASES **show the white feather** Brit. dated behave in a cowardly fashion.
– ORIGIN late 18th cent.: with reference to a white feather in the tail of a game bird, being a mark of bad breeding.

white fir ▶ **n.** a North American fir that has a whitish coloration on both sides of its flat needles. White firs are common in the mountainous coastal areas of California, the Sierra Nevada, and the southern Rockies. ● *Abies concolor*, family Pinaceae.

white·fish /ˈ(h)wītˌfisн/ ▶ **n.** (pl. **same** or **whitefishes**) a mainly freshwater fish of the salmon family, widely used as food. ● *Coregonus* and other genera, family Salmonidae: several species.

white fish ▶ **n.** fish with pale flesh, such as plaice, halibut, cod, and haddock.

white flag ▶ **n.** a white flag or cloth used as a symbol of surrender, truce, or a desire to parley.

white flight ▶ **n.** the move of white city-dwellers to the suburbs to escape the influx of minorities.

white flour ▶ **n.** fine wheat flour, typically bleached, from which most of the bran and germ have been removed.

white·fly /ˈ(h)wītˌflī/ ▶ **n.** (pl. **same** or **whiteflies**) a minute winged bug covered with powdery white wax, damaging plants by feeding on the sap and coating them with honeydew. ● Family

W

Aleyrodidae, suborder Homoptera: numerous genera and species.

white-foot·ed mouse ▶ n. a common deer mouse with white feet, found in the US and Mexico. ● *Peromyscus leucopus*, family Muridae.

White Fri·ar ▶ n. a Carmelite monk.
– ORIGIN late Middle English: so named because of the white habits worn by the monks.

white·front /ˈ(h)wīt,frənt/ (also **white-fronted goose**) ▶ n. a migratory goose with mainly gray plumage and a white forehead, breeding in northern Eurasia and North America. ● Genus *Anser*, family Anatidae: two species.

white gold ▶ n. a silver-colored alloy of gold with nickel, platinum, or another metal.

white goods ▶ plural n. **1** large electrical goods used domestically such as refrigerators and washing machines, typically white in color. Compare with BROWN GOODS.
2 archaic domestic linen.

White·hall /ˈ(h)wit,hôl/ a street in Westminster, London, on which many government offices are located. ■ used as an allusive reference to the British Civil Service. ■ used as an allusive reference to the British government, its offices, or its policy: *a pledge was given by Whitehall to protect British troops in Bosnia*.

white-hand·ed gib·bon ▶ n. the common gibbon, which has white hands and feet and is found in Thailand and Malaysia. Also called LAR GIBBON. ● *Hylobates lar*, family Hylobatidae.

White·head /ˈ(h)wit,(h)ed/, Alfred North (1861–1947), English philosopher and mathematician. He is remembered chiefly for *Principia Mathematica* (1910–13), on which he collaborated with his student Bertrand Russell.

white·head /ˈ(h)wīt,hed/ ▶ n. informal a pale or white-topped pustule on the skin.

white heat ▶ n. the temperature or state of something that is so hot that it emits white light. ■ [in sing.] a state of intense passion or activity.

white hole ▶ n. Astronomy a hypothetical celestial object that expands outward from a space-time singularity and emits energy, in the manner of a time-reversed black hole.

white hope ▶ n. a person expected to bring much success to a group or organization: *he was the great white hope for many kids trapped in bad lives*. ■ formerly, a white boxer believed by fans to be able to beat a black champion.

White·horse /ˈ(h)wīt,hôrs/ the capital of Yukon Territory in northwestern Canada; pop. 20,461 (2006). Situated on the Alaska Highway, it is the center of a copper-mining and fur-trapping region.

white hors·es ▶ plural n. white-crested sea waves.

white-hot ▶ adj. at white heat: *a shower of white-hot embers*.

White House 1 the official residence of the US president in Washington, DC. ■ the US president, presidency, or government: *the White House denounced the charge*.
2 the Russian parliament building.

White House 1

white i·bis ▶ n. a white ibis with a red face and a long decurved red bill, found chiefly from the southern US to northern South America. ● *Eudocimus albus*, family Threskiornithidae.

white knight ▶ n. a person or thing that comes to someone's aid. ■ a person or company making an acceptable counteroffer for a company facing a hostile takeover bid.

white-knuck·le ▶ adj. [attrib.] (esp. of a vehicle, boat, or airplane ride) causing excitement or tension.
– ORIGIN 1970s: with reference to the effect caused by gripping tightly to steady oneself.

white ibis

white-knuck·led ▶ adj. informal (of a person) showing signs of extreme tension due to fear or anger.

white-la·bel ▶ adj. denoting a musical recording for which the fully printed commercial label is not yet available, and which has been supplied with a plain white label before general release for promotional purposes.
▶ n. (**white label**) a recording released in such a way.

White La·dy ▶ n. a cocktail made with gin, orange liqueur, and lemon juice.

white lead /led/ ▶ n. a white pigment consisting of a mixture of lead carbonate and lead hydroxide.

white lie ▶ n. a harmless or trivial lie, esp. one told to avoid hurting someone's feelings.

white light ▶ n. apparently colorless light, for example ordinary daylight. It contains all the wavelengths of the visible spectrum at equal intensity.

white light·ning ▶ n. illicit homemade whiskey, typically colorless and distilled from corn.

white list ▶ n. informal a list of people or products viewed with approval. Compare with BLACKLIST.
▶ v. [with obj.] (**white-list**) place on such a list: *it is not possible to whitelist specific users based on their e-mail address or domain name*.

white mag·ic ▶ n. magic used only for good purposes.
– DERIVATIVES **white ma·gi·cian** n.

white mat·ter ▶ n. the paler tissue of the brain and spinal cord, consisting mainly of nerve fibers with their myelin sheaths. Compare with GRAY MATTER.

white meat ▶ n. pale meat such as poultry, veal, and rabbit. Often contrasted with RED MEAT.

white met·al ▶ n. a white or silvery alloy, esp. a tin-based alloy used for the surfaces of bearings.

White Moun·tains a range that rises to 6,288 feet (1,918 m) at Mount Washington, situated in northern New Hampshire, part of the Presidential Range in the Appalachian system.

white mouse ▶ n. an albino form of the house mouse, widely bred as a pet and laboratory animal.

whit·en /ˈ(h)wītn/ ▶ v. make or become white: [with obj.] *snow whitened the mountain tops* | [no obj.] *she gripped the handle until her knuckles whitened*.
– DERIVATIVES **whit·en·er** n.

white night ▶ n. **1** a sleepless night. [translating French *nuit blanche*.]
2 a night when it is never properly dark, as in high latitudes in summer.

White Nile the name for the main, western branch of the Nile River that flows between the Uganda–Sudan border and its confluence with the Blue Nile at Khartoum.

white noise ▶ n. Physics noise containing many frequencies with equal intensities.

white·out /ˈ(h)wīt,out/ ▶ n. **1** a blizzard, esp. in polar regions, that reduces visibilities to near zero. ■ a weather condition in which the features and horizon of snow-covered country are indistinguishable due to uniform light diffusion.
2 white correction fluid for covering typing or writing mistakes.
3 a loss of color vision due to rapid acceleration, often before a loss of consciousness.

white pa·ges ▶ n. the part of the telephone book that lists residential and business telephone numbers in alphabetical order by name, usually without any advertising copy.

white pa·per ▶ n. a government or other authoritative report giving information or proposals on an issue.

White Pass a pass from Skagway in Alaska into British Columbia that provided a route for gold seekers in the 1890s Klondike rush. A railroad here, opened in 1900, draws tourists.

white pep·per ▶ n. the husked ripe or unripe berries of the pepper (see PEPPER (sense 2 of the noun)), typically ground and used as a condiment.

white phos·pho·rus ▶ n. see PHOSPHORUS.

white pine ▶ n. any of a number of coniferous trees with whitish timber, in particular: ● a North American tree that yields high-quality timber that is valued for intricate work (*Pinus strobus*, family Pinaceae). ● the kahikatea.

White Plains a commercial city in southeastern New York, the seat of Westchester County; pop. 57,342 (est. 2008).

white point·er ▶ n. another term for GREAT WHITE SHARK.

white pop·lar ▶ n. a Eurasian poplar with lobed leaves that are white underneath and gray-green above. Also called ABELE. ● *Populus alba*, family Salicaceae.

white rhi·noc·er·os ▶ n. a very large two-horned African rhinoceros with broad lips. ● *Ceratotherium simum*, family Rhinocerotidae.

White Riv·er 1 a river that flows for 720 miles (1,160 m) from northwestern Arkansas across the Ozark Plateau to the Mississippi River.
2 a river that flows in two main branches through Indiana, past Indianapolis, to the Wabash River.
3 a river that flows for 500 miles (800 km) from northwestern Nebraska into South Dakota to the Missouri River.

White Rus·sia another name for BELARUS.

White Rus·sian ▶ n. **1** a Belorussian. ■ an opponent of the Bolsheviks during the Russian Civil War.
2 a cocktail made of vodka, coffee liqueur, and milk served on ice.
▶ adj. Belorussian. ■ of or relating to the opponents of the Bolsheviks.

white sage ▶ n. see SAGE[1] (sense 2).

white sale ▶ n. a store's sale of household linens.

white san·dal·wood ▶ n. see SANDALWOOD.

White Sands an area of white gypsum salt flats in central New Mexico, designated a national monument in 1933. It is surrounded by a large missile-testing range, which, in 1945, was the site of the detonation of the first nuclear weapon.

white sauce ▶ n. a sauce of flour, melted butter, and milk or cream.

White Sea an inlet of the Barents Sea off the coast of northwestern Russia.

white sea bass /bas/ ▶ n. see SEA BASS.

white shark ▶ n. see GREAT WHITE SHARK.

white-shoe ▶ adj. informal denoting a company, esp. a law firm, owned and run by members of the WASP elite, generally regarded as cautious and conservative.
– ORIGIN with reference to the white shoes fashionable among Ivy League college students in the 1950s.

white slave ▶ n. a woman tricked or forced into prostitution, typically one taken to a foreign country for this purpose.
– DERIVATIVES **white slav·er** n., **white slav·er·y** n.

white·smith /ˈ(h)wīt,smiTH/ ▶ n. a person who makes articles out of metal, esp. tin. ■ a polisher or finisher of metal goods.
– ORIGIN Middle English: from WHITE (denoting 'white iron,' i.e., tin) + SMITH.

white snake·root ▶ n. see SNAKEROOT.

white spruce ▶ n. a North American spruce with yellow-green or blue-green needles and cylindrical cones, found principally in Canada. ● *Picea glauca*, family Pinaceae.

White·stone /ˈ(h)wīt,stōn/ a largely residential section of northern Queens in New York City, on the East River, across from the Bronx, to which it is joined by the Bronx-Whitestone Bridge.

white sug·ar ▶ n. purified sugar.

White Sul·phur Springs a historic resort city in southeastern West Virginia, in the Allegheny Mountains; pop. 2,279 (est. 2008).

white su·prem·a·cy ▶ n. the belief that white people are superior to those of all other races, esp. the black race, and should therefore dominate society.

white·tail deer /(h)wīt ,tāl/ (also **white-tailed deer** or **whitetail**) ▶ n. a reddish to grayish American deer with white on the belly and the underside of the tail. ● *Odocoileus virginianus*, family Cervidae.

whitetail deer

white·thorn /ˈ(h)wīt,THôrn/ ▶ n. the hawthorn.

white·throat /ˈ(h)wīt,THrōt/ ▶ n. a migratory Eurasian and North African warbler with a gray head and white throat. ● Genus *Sylvia*, family

Sylviidae: three species, in particular the common *S. communis*.

white-throat·ed spar·row ▶ n. a sparrow that winters in southern and eastern North America. It has prominent yellow eyebrows and a white patch at the throat. ● *Zonotrichia albicollis*, family Emberizidae.

white tie ▶ n. a white bow tie worn by men as part of full evening dress. ■ full evening dress with a white bow tie: *he was wearing immaculate white tie and tails* | [as modifier] *a white-tie dinner*.

white trash ▶ n. informal, derogatory poor white people, esp. those living in the southern US.

white truf·fle ▶ n. an underground fungus eaten in Europe as a delicacy. Also called TARTUFO. ● *Tuber magnatum*, family Tuberaceae, subdivision Ascomycotina (also called **Piedmont truffle**).

white vit·ri·ol /'vitrēəl/ ▶ n. archaic crystalline zinc sulfate.

white·wall /'(h)wīt,wôl/ ▶ n. **1** (also **whitewall tire**) a tire with a white stripe around the outside, or a white sidewall.
2 [as modifier] denoting a haircut in which the sides of the head are shaved and the top and back are left longer.

white wal·nut ▶ n. another term for BUTTERNUT (sense 1).

white·wash /'(h)wīt,wäsh, -,wôsh/ ▶ n. **1** a solution of lime and water or of whiting, size, and water, used for painting walls white. ■ (also **whitewashing**) a deliberate concealment of someone's mistakes or faults in order to clear their name.
2 a victory in a game in which the loser scores no points.
▶ v. [with obj.] **1** (usu. as adj. **whitewashed**) paint (a wall, building, or room) with whitewash. ■ deliberately attempt to conceal unpleasant facts about (a person or organization): *his wife must have wanted to whitewash his reputation*.
2 defeat (an opponent), keeping them from scoring.
– DERIVATIVES **white·wash·er** n.

white·wa·ter /(h)wīt'wôtər, 'wä-/ (also **white water**) ▶ n. [often as modifier] (also **white-water**) fast shallow stretches of water in a river: *whitewater rafting*.

white whale ▶ n. another term for BELUGA (sense 1).

white wil·low ▶ n. a Eurasian streamside willow that has narrow leaves with silky white hairs on both sides, and the bark of which contains salicin. ● *Salix alba*, family Salicaceae.

white witch ▶ n. a person, typically a woman, who practices magic for altruistic purposes.

white·wood /'(h)wīt,wo͝od/ ▶ n. **1** light-colored wood, esp. when made up into furniture and ready for staining, varnishing, or painting.
2 any of a number of trees that yield pale timber, in particular: ● a silver fir. ● a basswood. ● the tulip tree.

white·work /'(h)wīt,wərk/ ▶ n. embroidery worked in white thread on a white ground.

whit·ey /'(h)wītē/ ▶ n. (pl. **whiteys**) informal, offensive a contemptuous term used by black people to refer to a white person or to white people collectively.

whith·er /'(h)wi*th*ər/ ▶ adv. archaic or literary to what place or state: *whither are we bound?* | *they asked people whither they would emigrate*. ■ what is the likely future of: *whither modern architecture?*
▶ relative adv. archaic or literary to which (with reference to a place): *the barbecue had been set up by the lake, whither Matthew and Sara were conducted*. ■ to whatever place; wherever: *we could drive whither we pleased*.
– ORIGIN Old English *hwider*, from the Germanic base of WHICH; compare with HITHER and THITHER.

whith·er·so·ev·er /,(h)wi*th*ərsō'evər/ ▶ relative adv. archaic wherever: *she was free to drift whithersoever she chose*.

whit·ing¹ /'(h)wīting/ ▶ n. (pl. **same**) **1** a slender-bodied marine fish of the cod family, which lives in shallow European waters and is a commercially important food fish. ● *Merlangius merlangus*, family Gadidae.
2 [usu. with modifier] any of a number of similar marine fishes, in particular the northern kingfish of eastern North America.
– ORIGIN Middle English: from Middle Dutch *wijting*, from *wijt* 'white.'

whit·ing² ▶ n. ground chalk used for purposes such as whitewashing and cleaning metal plate.

whit·leath·er /'(h)wit,le*th*ər/ ▶ n. leather that has been prepared by dressing with alum and salt so as to retain its natural color.
– ORIGIN late Middle English: from WHITE + LEATHER.

whit·low /'(h)wit,lō/ ▶ n. an abscess in the soft tissue near a fingernail or toenail.
– ORIGIN late Middle English (also as *whitflaw*, *-flow*), apparently from WHITE + FLAW¹ in the sense 'crack,' but perhaps related to Dutch *fijt* 'whitlow.'

whit·low grass ▶ n. a dwarf European plant with a rosette of leaves at the base of a low flowering stem, growing widely on rocks and walls. It was formerly believed to cure whitlows. ● Genus *Erophila*, family Brassicaceae: several species, in particular *E. verna*.

Whit·man, Walt (1819–92), US poet. In 1855, he published a free verse collection, *Leaves of Grass*, that includes "I Sing the Body Electric" and "Song of Myself"; eight further editions followed during Whitman's lifetime. Other notable works: *Drum-Taps* (1865) and *Sequel to Drum-Taps* (1865).

Whit·ney¹ /'(h)witnē/, Eli (1765–1825), US inventor. He is best known for his invention of the cotton gin (patented 1794) to automate the removal of seeds from raw cotton. He also is known to have developed the idea of mass-producing interchangeable parts in order to fulfill a contract in 1797 to supply muskets for the government.

Whit·ney², Gertrude Vanderbilt (1876–1942) US sculptor and philanthropist; the daughter of Cornelius Vanderbilt. She sculpted the *Titanic* Women's Memorial in 1931 in Washington, DC, and that same year founded the Whitney Museum of American Art in New York City, the first museum in the US devoted exclusively to native art.

Whit·ney, Mount a mountain in the Sierra Nevada in California. Rising to 14,495 feet (4,418 m), it is the highest peak in the continental US outside of Alaska.

Whit·sun /'(h)witsən/ ▶ n. Whitsuntide.
– ORIGIN Middle English: from WHITSUNDAY, reduced as if from *Whitsun Day*.

Whit·sun·day /'(h)wit'sən,dā/ ▶ n. another term for PENTECOST (sense 1).
– ORIGIN late Old English *Hwīta Sunnandæg*, literally 'white Sunday,' probably with reference to the white robes of those newly baptized at Pentecost.

Whit·sun·tide /'(h)witsən,tīd/ ▶ n. the weekend or week including Whitsunday.

Whit·ta·ker /'(h)witikər/, Charles Evans (1901–73), US Supreme Court associate justice 1957–62. Appointed to the Court by President Eisenhower, he was considered a conservative, esp. regarding civil rights.

Whit·ti·er¹ /'(h)witēər/ an industrial city in southwestern California, southeast of Los Angeles; pop. 82,267 (est. 2008).

Whit·ti·er², John Greenleaf (1807–92), US poet and abolitionist. From the early 1840s, he edited various periodicals and wrote poetry for the abolitionist cause. He is best known for his poems on rural themes, esp. "Snow-Bound" (1866).

Whit·ting·ton /'(h)witingtən/, Dick (died 1423), English merchant and lord mayor of London 1397–98, 1406–07, and 1419–20; full name *Sir Richard Whittington*. The legend of his early life as a poor orphan was first recorded in 1605.

Whit·tle /'(h)witl/, Sir Frank (1907–96), English aeronautical engineer, test pilot, and inventor of the jet aircraft engine. He took out the first patent for a turbojet engine in 1930. The first flight using Whittle's jet engine was made in 1941.

whit·tle /'(h)witl/ ▶ v. [with obj.] carve (wood) into an object by repeatedly cutting small slices from it. ■ carve (an object) from wood in this way. ■ (**whittle something away/down**) reduce something in size, amount, or extent by a gradual series of steps: *the short list of fifteen was whittled down to five* | [no obj.] *the censors had whittled away at the racy dialogue*.
– DERIVATIVES **whit·tler** n.
– ORIGIN mid 16th cent.: from dialect *whittle* 'knife.'

whiz /(h)wiz/ (also **whizz**) ▶ v. (**whizs, whizzing, whizzed**) **1** [no obj.] move quickly through the air with a whistling or whooshing sound: *missiles whizzed past* | figurative *the weeks whizzed by*. ■ (**whiz through**) do or deal with quickly: *Audrey would whiz through a few chores in the shop*. ■ [no obj.] cause to rotate in a machine, esp. a food processor: *add remaining sauce and whiz until smooth*.
2 [no obj.] informal urinate.
▶ n. **1** a whistling or whooshing sound made by something moving fast through the air.
2 (also **wiz**) informal a person who is extremely clever at something: *a computer whiz*. [early 20th cent.: influenced by WIZARD.]
3 informal an act of urinating.
– ORIGIN mid 16th cent.: imitative.

whiz-bang (also **whizz-bang**) informal ▶ n. (esp. during World War I) a high-velocity shell. ■ a resounding success: *Dan was a whiz-bang at mechanical things*.
▶ adj. lively or sensational; fast-paced: *a whiz-bang publicity campaign*.

whiz kid ▶ n. informal a young person who is outstandingly skillful or successful at something: *a computer whiz kid*.

whiz·zy /'(h)wizē/ ▶ adj. technologically innovative or advanced: *a whizzy new technology*.

WHO ▶ abbr. World Health Organization.

who /ho͞o/ ▶ pron. **1** [interrogative pronoun] what or which person or people: *who is that woman?* | *I wonder who that letter was from*.
2 [relative pronoun] used to introduce a clause giving further information about a person or people previously mentioned: *Joan Fontaine plays the mouse who married the playboy*. ■ archaic the person that; whoever: *who holds the sea, perforce doth hold the land*.
– PHRASES **as who should say** archaic as if to say: *he meekly bowed to him, as who should say "Proceed."* **who am I** (or **are you, is he**, etc.) **to do something** what right or authority do I (or you, he, etc.) have to do something: *who am I to object?* **who goes there?** see GO¹.
– ORIGIN Old English *hwā*, of Germanic origin; related to Dutch *wie* and German *wer*.

> **USAGE** 1 A continuing debate in English usage is the question of when to use **who** and when to use **whom**. According to formal grammar, **who** forms the subjective case and so should be used in subject position in a sentence, as in ***who** decided this?* The form **whom**, on the other hand, forms the objective case and so should be used in object position in a sentence, as in ***whom** do you think we should support?* or *to **whom** do you wish to speak?* Although there are some speakers who still use **who** and **whom** according to the rules of formal grammar as stated here, there are many more who rarely use **whom** at all; its use has retreated steadily and is now largely restricted to formal contexts. The normal practice in modern English is to use **who** instead of **whom** (*who do you think we should support?*) and, where applicable, to put the preposition at the end of the sentence (*who do you wish to speak to?*). Such uses are today broadly accepted in standard English, but in formal writing it is best to maintain the distinction. 2 On the use of **who** and **that** in relative clauses see usage at THAT.

whoa /wō/ ▶ exclam. used as a command to a horse to make it stop or slow down. ■ informal used as a greeting, to express surprise or interest, or to command attention: *whoa, that's huge!*
– ORIGIN late Middle English: variant of HO².

who'd /ho͞od/ ▶ contraction who had: *some Americans who'd arrived after lunch*. ■ who would: *he knew many of the people who'd be there*.

who·dun·it /ho͞o'dənit/ (Brit. **whodunnit**) ▶ n. informal a story or play about a murder in which the identity of the murderer is not revealed until the end.
– ORIGIN 1930s: from *who done it?*, nonstandard form of *who did it?*

who·e'er /ho͞o'e(ə)r/ literary ▶ contraction whoever.

who·ev·er /ho͞o'evər/ ▶ relative pron. the person or people who; any person who: *whoever did it hated him*. ■ regardless of who: *come out, whoever you are*.
▶ pron. used for emphasis instead of "who" in questions, typically expressing surprise or confusion: *whoever would want to make up something like that?*

> **USAGE** In the emphatic use, **whoever** may be spelled correctly as either one word or two: ***whoever** does he think he is?* or ***who ever** does he think he is?* See also usage at HOWEVER and WHATEVER.

whole /hōl/ ▶ adj. **1** [attrib.] all of; entire: *he spent the whole day walking* | *she wasn't telling the whole truth*. ■ used to emphasize a large extent or number: *whole shelves in libraries are devoted to the subject* | ***a whole lot of** money*.
2 in an unbroken or undamaged state; in one piece: *owls usually swallow their prey whole*. ■ [attrib.] (of milk, blood, or other substances) with no part removed. ■ [predic.] healthy: *all people should be whole in body, mind, and spirit*.
▶ n. **1** a thing that is complete in itself: *the subjects of the curriculum form a coherent whole*.
2 (**the whole**) all of something: *the effects will last for the whole of his life*.
▶ adv. [as submodifier] informal used to emphasize the novelty or distinctness of something: *the man who's given a whole new meaning to the term "cowboy."*

W

– PHRASES **as a whole** as a single unit and not as separate parts; in general: *a healthy economy is in the best interests of society as a whole.* **in whole** entirely or fully: *a number of stone churches survive in whole or in part.* **in the whole (wide) world** anywhere; of all: *he was the nicest person in the whole world.* **on the whole** taking everything into account; in general. **the whole nine yards** informal everything possible or available: *send in the troops, aircraft, nuclear submarine experts, the whole nine yards.*
– DERIVATIVES **whole·ness** n.
– ORIGIN Old English *hāl*, of Germanic origin; related to Dutch *heel* and German *heil*, also to HAIL². The spelling with *wh-* (reflecting a dialect pronunciation with *w-*) first appeared in the 15th cent.

whole blood ▶ n. blood drawn directly from the body from which none of the components, such as plasma or platelets, has been removed.

whole bod·y scan ▶ n. a CT scan of the torso, esp. one obtained for health screening purposes.
– DERIVATIVES **whole bod·y scan·ning** n.

whole cloth ▶ n. cloth of the full size as manufactured, as distinguished from a piece cut off for a garment or other item.
– PHRASES **out of (the) whole cloth** informal totally false: *the allegations had been created out of whole cloth.*

whole food ▶ n. (also **whole foods**) food that has been processed or refined as little as possible and is free from additives or other artificial substances.

whole-grain ▶ adj. made with or containing whole unprocessed grain: *whole-grain cereals.*

whole·heart·ed /ˈhōlˈhärtid/ ▶ adj. showing or characterized by complete sincerity and commitment: *you have my wholehearted support.*
– DERIVATIVES **whole·heart·ed·ly** adv., **whole·heart·ed·ness** n.

whole lan·guage ▶ n. a method of teaching children to read at an early age that allows students to select their own reading matter and that emphasizes the use and recognition of words in everyday contexts.

whole-life ▶ adj. relating to or denoting a life insurance policy that pays a specified amount only on the death of the person insured.

whole life in·sur·ance ▶ n. life insurance that pays a benefit on the death of the insured and also accumulates a cash value. Compare with TERM LIFE INSURANCE.

whole note ▶ n. Music a note having the time value of two half notes or four quarter notes, represented by a ring with no stem. It is the longest note now in common use. Also called SEMIBREVE.

whole num·ber ▶ n. a number without fractions; an integer.

whole·sale /ˈhōlˌsāl/ ▶ n. the selling of goods in large quantities to be retailed by others.
▶ adv. being sold in such a way: *bottles from this region sell wholesale at about $72 a case.* ■ on a large scale: *the safety clauses seem to have been taken wholesale from union documents.*
▶ adj. done on a large scale; extensive: *the wholesale destruction of the natural order.*
▶ v. [with obj.] sell (goods) in large quantities at low prices to be retailed by others.
– DERIVATIVES **whole·sal·er** n.
– ORIGIN late Middle English: originally as *by whole sale* 'in large quantities.'

whole·some /ˈhōlsəm/ ▶ adj. conducive to or suggestive of good health and physical well-being: *the food is plentiful and very wholesome.* ■ conducive to or promoting moral well-being: *good wholesome fun.*
– DERIVATIVES **whole·some·ly** adv., **whole·some·ness** n.
– ORIGIN Middle English: probably already in Old English (see WHOLE, -SOME¹).

whole step ▶ n. Music an interval of a (whole) tone.

whole-tone scale ▶ n. Music a scale consisting entirely of intervals of a tone, with no semitones.

wholewheat /ˈhōl,(h)wēt/ ▶ adj. denoting flour or bread made from whole grains of wheat, including the husk or outer layer.
▶ n. wholewheat bread or flour.

who·lism /ˈhōlizəm/ ▶ n. variant spelling of HOLISM.
– DERIVATIVES **who·lis·tic** adj., **who·lis·ti·cal·ly** adv.

whol·ly /ˈhōl(l)ē/ ▶ adv. entirely; fully: *she found herself given over wholly to sensation* | [as submodifier] *the distinction is not wholly clear.*
– ORIGIN Middle English: probably already in Old English (see WHOLE, -LY²).

whol·ly-owned ▶ adj. denoting a company all of whose shares are owned by another company.

whom /ho͞om/ ▶ pron. used instead of "who" as the object of a verb or preposition: [interrogative pronoun] *whom did he marry?* | [relative pronoun] *her mother, in whom she confided, said it wasn't easy for her.*

> **USAGE** On the use of who and whom, see usage at WHO.

whom·ev·er /ho͞omˈevər/ ▶ pron. chiefly formal or literary used instead of "whoever" as the object of a verb or preposition: *I'll sing whatever I like to whomever I like.*

whomp /(h)wämp, (h)wômp/ informal ▶ v. [with obj.] strike heavily; thump: *whomp the club head on the ground* | [no obj.] *giant comet chunks whomped into Jupiter.* ■ defeat decisively: *that was our last fight and I whomped him good.*
▶ n. a dull heavy sound.
– PHRASAL VERBS **whomp something up** produce something quickly: *I might whomp up a couple of gallons of spaghetti sauce.*
– ORIGIN 1920s: imitative.

whom·so /ˈho͞omsō/ ▶ pron. archaic used instead of "whoso" as the object of a verb or preposition: *whomso thou meetest, say thou this to each.*

whom·so·ev·er /ˌho͞omsōˈevər/ ▶ relative pron. formal used instead of "whosoever" as the object of a verb or preposition: *they supported his right to marry whomsoever he chose.*

whoomp /(h)wo͝omp/ (also **whoomph** /(h)wo͝omf/) ▶ n. a sudden sound, such as that made by a muffled or distant explosion: *the distant whoomp of antiaircraft shells bursting.*
– ORIGIN 1950s: imitative.

whoop /(h)wo͞op/ ▶ n. a loud cry of joy or excitement. ■ /ho͞op/ a long rasping indrawn breath, typically of someone with whooping cough.
▶ v. [no obj.] give or make a whoop: *all at once they were whooping with laughter.*
– PHRASES **not give (or care) a whoop** informal, dated be totally indifferent. **whoop it up** informal enjoy oneself or celebrate in a noisy way. ■ create or stir up excitement or enthusiasm.
– ORIGIN Middle English: probably imitative.

whoop·ee /ˈ(h)wo͝opē, ˈ(h)wo͝oˈpē/ informal ▶ exclam. expressing wild excitement or joy.
▶ n. wild revelry: *hours of parades and whoopee.* ■ dated a wild party.
– PHRASES **make whoopee 1** celebrate wildly. **2** have sexual intercourse.

whoop·ee cush·ion /ˈwo͝opē/ (also **whoopie cushion**) ▶ n. a rubber cushion that makes a sound like a fart when someone sits on it.

whoop·er /ˈ(h)wo͞opər, ˈho͞opər/ ▶ n. (also **whooper swan**) **1** a large migratory swan with a black and yellow bill and a loud trumpeting call, breeding in northern Eurasia and Greenland. ● *Cygnus cygnus*, family Anatidae. **2** short for WHOOPING CRANE.

whoop·ing cough ▶ n. a contagious bacterial disease chiefly affecting children, characterized by convulsive coughs followed by a whoop. Also called PERTUSSIS. ● The organism responsible is *Bordetella pertussis*, a Gram-negative bacterium intermediate between a coccus and a bacillus.

whoop·ing crane ▶ n. a large mainly white crane with a trumpeting call, breeding in central Canada and now endangered. ● *Grus americana*, family Gruidae.

whoops /wo͝ops, wo͞ops/ ▶ exclam. informal another term for OOPS.
– ORIGIN 1920s: probably an alteration of UPSY-DAISY; compare with OOPS.

whoosh /(h)wo͞osh, (h)wo͝osh/ (also **woosh**) ▶ v. move or cause to move quickly or suddenly with a rushing sound: [no obj.] *a train whooshed by* | (as adj. **whooshing**) *there was a loud whooshing noise.*
▶ n. a sudden movement accompanied by a rushing sound: *there was a big whoosh of air.*
▶ exclam. used to imitate such a movement and sound.
– ORIGIN mid 19th cent.: imitative.

whop /(h)wäp/ (also **whap**) informal ▶ v. (**whops, whopping, whopped**) [with obj.] hit hard: *Smith whopped him on the nose.* ■ defeat; overcome: *the Astros whopped the New York Mets in Saturday's game.*
▶ n. a heavy blow, or the sound of such a blow.
– ORIGIN late Middle English (in the sense 'take or put sharply'): variant of dialect *wap* 'strike,' of unknown origin.

whop·per /ˈ(h)wäpər/ ▶ n. informal a thing that is extremely or unusually large: *the novel is a 1,079 page whopper.* ■ a gross or blatant lie.

whop·ping /ˈ(h)wäpiNG/ ▶ adj. informal very large: *a whopping $74 million loss* | [as submodifier] *a whopping big party.*

whore /hôr/ ▶ n. derogatory a prostitute. ■ a promiscuous woman.
▶ v. [no obj.] (of a woman) work as a prostitute: *she spent her life whoring for dangerous men.* ■ (often as noun **whoring**) (of a man) use the services of prostitutes: *he lived by night, indulging in his two hobbies, whoring and eating.* ■ debase oneself by doing something for unworthy motives, typically to make money: *he had never whored after money.*
– PHRASES **the Whore of Babylon** derogatory the Roman Catholic Church. [with biblical allusion to Rev. 17:1, 5, etc.]
– ORIGIN late Old English *hōre*, of Germanic origin; related to Dutch *hoer* and German *Hure*, from an Indo-European root shared by Latin *carus* 'dear.'

whore·dom /ˈhôrdəm/ ▶ n. dated prostitution or other promiscuous sexual activity.

whore·house /ˈhôrˌhous/ ▶ n. informal a brothel.

whore·mas·ter /ˈhôrˌmastər/ ▶ n. archaic a whoremonger.

whore·mon·ger /ˈhôrˌmäNGgər, -ˌməNG-/ ▶ n. archaic a person who has dealings with prostitutes, esp. a sexually promiscuous man.

whore·son /ˈhôrsən/ ▶ n. archaic an unpleasant or greatly disliked person.
– ORIGIN Middle English: from WHORE + SON, suggested by Anglo-Norman French *fiz a putain.*

Whorf /(h)wôrf/, Benjamin Lee (1897–1941), US linguist and insurance worker, known for his contribution to the Sapir-Whorf hypothesis. A student of linguistics in his spare time, Whorf studied Hopi and other American Indian languages and attended Edward Sapir's courses at Yale.

whor·ish /ˈhôrisH/ ▶ adj. belonging to or characteristic of a prostitute.
– DERIVATIVES **whor·ish·ly** adv., **whor·ish·ness** n.

whorl /(h)wôrl/ ▶ n. a coil or ring, in particular: ■ Zoology each of the turns or convolutions in the shell of a gastropod or ammonoid mollusk. ■ Botany a set of leaves, flowers, or branches springing from the stem at the same level and encircling it. ■ Botany (in a flower) each of the sets of organs, esp. the petals and sepals, arranged concentrically around the receptacle. ■ a complete circle in a fingerprint. ■ chiefly historical a small wheel or pulley in a spinning wheel, spinning machine, or spindle.
▶ v. [no obj.] literary spiral or move in a twisted and convoluted fashion: *the dances are kinetic kaleidoscopes where steps whorl into wildness.*
– DERIVATIVES **whorled** adj.
– ORIGIN late Middle English (denoting a small flywheel): apparently a variant of WHIRL, influenced by Old English *wharve* 'whorl of a spindle.'

whor·tle·ber·ry /ˈ(h)wərtl,berē/ ▶ n. (pl. **whortleberries**) a bilberry.
– ORIGIN late 16th cent.: dialect variant of Middle English *hurtleberry*, of unknown origin.

who's /ho͞oz/ ▶ contraction who is: *who's that?* ■ who has: *who's done the reading?*

> **USAGE** A common written mistake is to confuse **who's** with **whose**. The form **who's** represents a contraction of 'who is' or 'who has': ***who's*** *going to feed the dog?* | *I wonder* ***who's*** *left the light on again?* The word **whose** is a possessive pronoun or adjective: ***whose*** *is this?* | ***whose*** *turn is it?*

whose /ho͞oz/ ▶ interrogative possessive determiner & pron. belonging to or associated with which person: [as adj.] *whose round is it?* | [as pronoun] *a minivan was parked at the curb and Juliet wondered whose it was.*
▶ relative possessive determiner of whom or which (used to indicate that the following noun belongs to or is associated with the person or thing mentioned in the previous clause): *he's a man whose opinion I respect.*
– ORIGIN Old English *hwæs*, genitive of *hwā* 'who' and *hwæt* 'what.'

> **USAGE** On the differences in use between whose and who's, see usage at WHO'S.

whose·so·ev·er /ˌho͞ozsōˈevər/ ▶ relative pron. & determiner formal whoever's: [as determiner] *the story will have been told you by your fathers, whosesoever sons you are.*

whos·ev·er /ˌho͞ozˈevər/ ▶ relative pron. & adj. rare belonging to or associated with whichever person; whoever's: [as pronoun] *the choice, whosever it was, is interesting* | [as adj.] *she dialed whosever number she could still remember.*

who·sis /ˈho͞ozis/ (also **whosit** /-zit/) ▶ n. informal (often in titles) a person whose name one cannot recall, does not know, or does not wish to specify: *lunch with Senator Whosis who was so fond of bourbon.*
– ORIGIN 1920s: contraction of *who is this?*

who·so /ˈho͞osō/ ▶ pron. archaic term for WHOEVER: *whoso took such things into account was a fool.*
– ORIGIN Middle English: shortening of Old English *swā hwā swā* 'so who so.'

who·so·ev·er /ˌho͞osōˈevər/ ▶ pron. formal term for WHOEVER: *a belief that whosoever steals will be blinded.*

who's who ▶ n. a list or directory of facts about notable people.

wh-ques·tion ▶ n. a question in English introduced by a wh-word and requiring more information in reply than simply *yes* or *no*.

whump /wəmp/ ▶ n. [usu. in sing.] a dull thudding sound: *the horse fell with a great whump.*
▶ v. [no obj.] make such a sound: *he pitched a snowball that whumped into the car.* ■ [with obj.] strike (something) heavily with such a sound: *she began whumping him on his lower back.*
– ORIGIN late 19th cent.: imitative.

whup /(h)wo͝op/ ▶ v. (**whups, whupping, whupped**) [with obj.] informal beat; thrash: *they would whup him and send him home.* ■ defeat convincingly: *if you lined up our guys against the 49ers, they'd get whupped.*
– ORIGIN late 19th cent.: variant of **WHIP**.

wh-word ▶ n. Grammar any of a class of English words used to introduce questions and relative clauses. The main wh-words are *why, who, which, what, where, when,* and *how*.

why /(h)wī/ ▶ adv. for what reason or purpose: *why did he do it?* ■ [with negative] used to make or agree to a suggestion: *why don't I give you a lift?*
▶ relative adv. (with reference to a reason) on account of which; for which: ***the reason why** flu shots need repeating every year is that the virus changes.* ■ the reason for which: *each has faced similar hardships, and perhaps that is why they are friends.*
▶ exclam. **1** expressing surprise or indignation: *Why, that's absurd!*
2 used to add emphasis to a response: *"You think so?" "Why, yes."*
▶ n. (pl. **whys**) a reason or explanation: *the **whys and wherefores** of these procedures need to be explained to students.*
– PHRASES **why so?** for what reason or purpose?
– ORIGIN Old English *hwī, hwȳ* 'by what cause,' instrumental case of *hwæt* 'what,' of Germanic origin.

whyd·ah /'(h)widə/ (also **whyda**) ▶ n. an African weaverbird, the male of which has a black back and a very long black tail used in display flight. ● Genus *Vidua*, family Ploceidae: several species.
– ORIGIN late 18th cent. (originally *widow-bird*): alteration by association with *Whidah* (now Ouidah), a town in Benin.

WI ▶ abbr. ■ West Indies. ■ Wisconsin (in official postal use). ■ Brit. Women's Institute.

WIC /wik/ ▶ abbr. Women, Infants, and Children (a federal or state program to ensure proper nutrition for poor mothers and their children).

Wic·ca /'wikə/ ▶ n. the religious cult of modern witchcraft, esp. an initiatory tradition founded in England in the mid 20th century and claiming its origins in pre-Christian pagan religions.
– DERIVATIVES **Wic·can** adj. & n.
– ORIGIN representing Old English *wicca* 'witch.'

Wich·i·ta /'wicHə,tô, -,tä/ a city in southern Kansas, on the Arkansas River, the largest city in the state; pop. 366,046 (est. 2008).

Wich·i·ta Falls an industrial and commercial city in north central Texas; pop. 101,202 (est. 2008).

wick[1] /wik/ ▶ n. a strip of porous material up which liquid fuel is drawn by capillary action to the flame in a candle, lamp, or lighter. ■ Medicine a gauze strip inserted in a wound to drain it.
▶ v. [with obj.] absorb or draw off (liquid) by capillary action: *these excellent socks will **wick away** the sweat* | [no obj.] *synthetics with hollow fibers that wick well.*
– PHRASES **dip one's wick** vulgar slang (of a man) have sexual intercourse.
– ORIGIN Old English *wēoce*; related to Dutch *wiek* and German *Wieche* 'wick yarn.'

wick[2] ▶ n. **1** (in place names) a town, hamlet, or district: *Hampton Wick* | *Warwick*.
2 Brit. dialect a dairy farm.
– ORIGIN Old English *wīc* 'dwelling place,' probably based on Latin *vicus* 'street, village.'

wick·ed /'wikid/ ▶ adj. (**wickeder, wickedest**) evil or morally wrong: *a wicked and unscrupulous politician.* ■ intended to or capable of harming someone or something: *he should be punished for his wicked driving.* ■ informal extremely unpleasant: *despite the sun, the wind outside was wicked.* ■ playfully mischievous: *Ben has a wicked sense of humor.* ■ informal excellent; wonderful: *Sophie makes wicked cakes.*
– DERIVATIVES **wick·ed·ly** adv.
– ORIGIN Middle English: probably from Old English *wicca* 'witch' + **-ED**[1].

WORD TRENDS See **SICK**[1].

wick·ed·ness /'wikidnis/ ▶ n. the quality of being evil or morally wrong: *the wickedness of the regime.*

wick·er /'wikər/ ▶ n. pliable twigs, typically of willow, plaited or woven to make items such as furniture and baskets: [as modifier] *a wicker chair.*
– ORIGIN Middle English: of Scandinavian origin; compare with Swedish *viker* 'willow'; related to *vika* 'to bend.'

wick·er·work /'wikər,wərk/ ▶ n. wicker. ■ furniture or other items made of wicker.

wick·et /'wikit/ ▶ n. **1** (also **wicket door** or **wicket gate**) a small door or gate, esp. one beside or in a larger one. ■ an opening in a door or wall, often fitted with glass or a grille and used for selling tickets or a similar purpose. ■ one of the wire hoops on a croquet course.
2 Cricket each of the sets of three stumps with two bails across the top at either end of the pitch, defended by a batsman. ■ the prepared strip of ground between these two sets of stumps. ■ the dismissal of a batsman; each of ten dismissals regarded as marking a division of a side's innings: *Darlington won by four wickets.*
– PHRASES **a sticky wicket** Cricket a pitch that has been drying after rain and is difficult to bat on. ■ [in sing.] informal a tricky or awkward situation: *the problem of who sits where can create a sticky wicket.* **take a wicket** Cricket (of a bowler or a fielding side) dismiss a batsman.
– ORIGIN Middle English (in the sense 'small door or grille'): from Anglo-Norman French and Old Northern French *wiket*; origin uncertain, usually referred to the Germanic root of Old Norse *víkja* 'to turn, move.' Cricket senses date from the late 17th cent.

wick·et·keep·er /'wikit,kēpər/ ▶ n. Cricket a fielder stationed close behind a batsman's wicket and typically equipped with gloves and pads.
– DERIVATIVES **wick·et·keep·ing** n.

wick·i·up /'wikē,əp/ ▶ n. an American Indian hut consisting of an oval frame covered with brushwood or grass.
– ORIGIN Fox 'house;' compare with **WIGWAM**.

Wick·low /'wiklō/ a county in eastern Republic of Ireland, in the province of Leinster. ■ its county town, on the Irish Sea; pop. 6,930 (2006).

wid·der·shins /'widər,SHinz/ (also **withershins**) ▶ adv. chiefly Scottish in a direction contrary to the sun's course, considered as unlucky; counterclockwise.
– ORIGIN early 16th cent.: from Middle Low German *weddersins*, from Middle High German *widersinnes*, from *wider* 'against' + *sin* 'direction'; the second element was associated with Scots *sin* 'sun.'

wide /wīd/ ▶ adj. (**wider, widest**) **1** of great or more than average width: *a wide road.* ■ (after a measurement and in questions) from side to side: *it measures 15 cm long by 12 cm wide* | *how wide do you think this house is?* ■ open to the full extent: *wide eyes.* ■ considerable: *tax revenues have undershot Treasury projections by a wide margin.*
2 including a great variety of people or things: *a wide range of opinion.* ■ spread among a large number of people or over a large area: *the business is slowly gaining wider acceptance.* ■ [in combination] extending over the whole of: *an industry-wide trend.*
3 at a considerable or specified distance from a point or mark: *Bodie's shot was inches wide.* ■ Baseball (of a pitch) outside: *the ball was **wide of** the plate.* ■ Baseball (of a throw) to either side of a base: *forced a wide throw to first.* ■ (in field sports) at or near the side of the field: *he played in a wide left position.*
4 Phonetics another term for **LAX**.
▶ adv. **1** to the full extent: *his eyes opened wide.*
2 far from a particular point or mark: *a shot that went wide to the right.* ■ at or near the side of the field; toward the sideline: *he will play wide on the right.*
▶ n. Cricket a ball that is judged to be too wide of the stumps for the batsman to play, for which an extra is awarded to the batting side.
– PHRASES **give someone/something a wide berth** see **BERTH**. **wide awake** fully awake. **wide of the mark** a long way away from an intended target. ■ inaccurate: *the accusation was a little wide of the mark.* **wide open 1** fully open: *the door was wide open.* **2** (of an issue or a contest) completely unresolved or unpredictable. **3** vulnerable, esp. to attack.
– DERIVATIVES **wide·ness** n., **wid·ish** adj.
– ORIGIN Old English *wīd* 'spacious, extensive,' *wīde* 'over a large area,' of Germanic origin.

wide-an·gle ▶ adj. (of a lens) having a short focal length and hence a field covering a wide angle.

wide ar·e·a net·work (abbr.: **WAN**) ▶ n. a computer network in which the computers connected may be far apart, generally having a radius of half a mile or more. Compare with **LOCAL AREA NETWORK**.

wide-a·wake ▶ n. a soft felt hat with a low crown and wide brim.
– ORIGIN mid 19th cent.: punningly so named, because the hat does not have a nap.

wide-band ▶ adj. (of a radio, or other device or activity involving broadcasting) having or using a wide band of frequencies or wavelengths.

wide-bod·y /'wīd,bädē/ ▶ adj. [attrib.] (also **wide-bodied**) having a wide body, in particular: ■ (of a large jet airplane) having a wide fuselage. ■ (of a tennis racket) having a wide head.
▶ n. (pl. **wide-bodies**) (also **widebody**) **1** a large jet airplane with a wide fuselage.
2 a tennis racket with a wide head.
3 informal a large, heavily built person, esp. one who plays a team sport.

wide-eyed ▶ adj. having one's eyes wide open in amazement. ■ innocent: *a wide-eyed country boy.*

wide·ly /'wīdlē/ ▶ adv. **1** over a wide area or at a wide interval: *he smiled widely and held out a hand* | *a tall man with widely spaced eyes.* ■ to a large degree in nature or character (used to describe considerable variation or difference): *lending policies vary widely between different banks* | [as submodifier] *people in widely different circumstances.*
2 over a large area or range; extensively: *Deborah has traveled widely* | [as submodifier] *she was widely read.* ■ by many people or in many places: *credit cards are widely accepted.*

wid·en /'wīdn/ ▶ v. make or become wider: [with obj.] *the incentive to dredge and widen the river* | [no obj.] *his grin widened* | *the lane **widened out** into a small clearing.*
– DERIVATIVES **wid·en·er** n.

wide·out /'wīd,out/ ▶ n. a wide receiver.

wide-rang·ing ▶ adj. covering an extensive range: *a wide-ranging discussion.*

wide re·ceiv·er ▶ n. Football an offensive player who is positioned at a distance from the end and is used primarily as a pass receiver.

wide·screen /'wīd,skrēn/ (also **widescreen**) ▶ adj. [attrib.] designed with or for a screen presenting a wide field of vision in relation to its height: *a widescreen TV.*
▶ n. a movie or television screen presenting a wide field of vision in relation to its height. ■ a film format presenting a wide field of vision in relation to height.

wide·spread /'wīd'spred/ ▶ adj. found or distributed over a large area or number of people: *there was widespread support for the war.*

widg·eon ▶ n. variant spelling of **WIGEON**.

widg·et /'wijit/ ▶ n. informal a small gadget or mechanical device, esp. one whose name is unknown or unspecified. ■ Computing an application, or a component of an interface, that enables a user to perform a function or access a service.
– ORIGIN 1930s: perhaps an alteration of **GADGET**.

wid·ow /'widō/ ▶ n. **1** a woman who has lost her husband by death and has not remarried. ■ [with modifier] humorous a woman whose husband is often away participating in a specified sport or activity: *a golf widow.*
2 Printing a last word or short last line of a paragraph falling at the top of a page or column and considered undesirable.
▶ v. [with obj.] (usu. as adj. **widowed**) make into a widow or widower: *she had to care for her widowed mother.*
– ORIGIN Old English *widewe*, from an Indo-European root meaning 'be empty'; compare with Sanskrit *vidh* 'be destitute,' Latin *viduus* 'bereft, widowed,' and Greek *ēitheos* 'unmarried man.'

wid·ow·er /'widō-ər/ ▶ n. a man who has lost his wife by death and has not remarried.

wid·ow·hood /'widō,ho͝od/ ▶ n. the state or period of being a widow or widower.

wid·ow-mak·er ▶ n. informal a thing with the potential to kill men. ■ a dead branch caught precariously high in a tree which may fall on a person below.

wid·ow's mite ▶ n. a small monetary contribution from someone who is poor.
– ORIGIN with biblical allusion to Mark 12:43.

wid·ow's peak ▶ n. a V-shaped growth of hair toward the center of the forehead, esp. one left by a receding hairline in a man.
– ORIGIN mid 19th cent.: so called because it was formerly believed to be a predictor of widowhood for a woman.

W

wid·ow's walk ▶ **n.** a railed or balustraded platform built on a roof, originally in early New England houses, typically for providing an unimpeded view of the sea.
– ORIGIN 1930s: with reference to its use as a viewpoint for the hoped-for return of a seafaring husband.

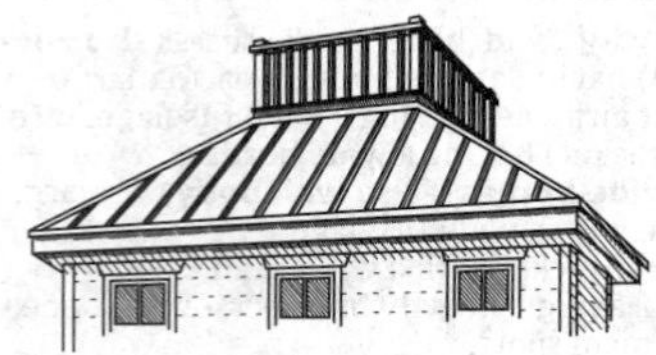
widow's walk

wid·ow's weeds ▶ **plural n.** black clothes worn by a widow in mourning.
– ORIGIN early 18th cent. (earlier as *mourning weeds*): *weeds* (obsolete in the general sense 'garments') is from Old English *wǣd(e)*, of Germanic origin.

width /widTH, witTH/ ▶ **n.** the measurement or extent of something from side to side: *the yard was about seven feet in width* | *the shoe comes in a variety of widths.* ■ a piece of something at its full extent from side to side: *a single width of hardboard.* ■ the sideways extent of a swimming pool as a measure of the distance swum. ■ the quality of covering or accepting a broad range of things; scope: *the width of experience required for these positions.*
– ORIGIN early 17th cent.: from WIDE + -TH², on the pattern of *breadth* (replacing *wideness*).

width·wise /ˈwidTH,wīz, ˈwitTH-/ (also **widthways** /-,wāz/) ▶ **adv.** in a direction parallel with a thing's width: *fold the pastry in half widthwise.*

wield /wēld/ ▶ **v.** [with obj.] hold and use (a weapon or tool): *a masked raider wielding a handgun.* ■ have and be able to use (power or influence): *faction leaders wielded enormous influence within the party.*
– DERIVATIVES **wield·er n.**
– ORIGIN Old English *wealdan*, *wieldan* 'govern, subdue, direct,' of Germanic origin; related to German *walten.*

wield·y /ˈwēldē/ ▶ **adj.** (**wieldier**, **wieldiest**) easily controlled or handled: *the beefy Bentley is far from wieldy.*
– ORIGIN late 16th cent.: back-formation from UNWIELDY.

Wien /vēn/ German name for **VIENNA**.

Wie·ner /ˈwēnər/, Norbert (1894–1964), US mathematician. He established the science of cybernetics in the late 1940s and made major contributions to the study of stochastic processes, integral equations, harmonic analysis, and related fields.

wie·ner /ˈwēnər/ (also informal **weenie**, **wienie** /-nē/) ▶ **n. 1** a frankfurter or similar sausage. **2** another term for WEENIE.
– ORIGIN early 20th cent.: abbreviation of German *Wienerwurst* 'Vienna sausage.'

Wie·ner schnit·zel /ˈvēnər ,SHnitsəl/ ▶ **n.** a dish consisting of a thin slice of veal that is breaded, fried, and garnished.
– ORIGIN from German, literally 'Vienna cutlet.'

Wies·ba·den /ˈvēs,bädn/ a city in western Germany, the capital of the state of Hesse, on the Rhine River, opposite Mainz; pop. 275,600 (est. 2006).

Wie·sel /vēˈzəl, ˈvēzəl, wiˈzel/, Elie (1928–), US human rights campaigner, novelist, and academic, born in Romania; full name *Eliezer Wiesel*. A survivor of the Auschwitz and Buchenwald concentration camps, he became an authority on the Holocaust, documenting and publicizing Nazi war crimes. Nobel Peace Prize (1986).

Wie·sen·thal /ˈvēzən,täl, -,THäl/, Simon (1908–2005), Austrian Jewish investigator of Nazi war crimes. After spending three years in concentration camps, he began a campaign to bring Nazi war criminals to justice, tracing some 1,000 unprosecuted criminals including Adolf Eichmann.

W

wife /wīf/ ▶ **n.** (pl. **wives** /wīvz/) a married woman considered in relation to her husband. ■ [with modifier] the wife of a man with a specified occupation: *a faculty wife.* ■ archaic or dialect a woman, esp. an old or uneducated one.
– PHRASES **take a woman to wife** archaic marry a woman.
– DERIVATIVES **wife·hood** /-,ho͝od/ **n.**, **wife·less adj.**, **wife·like** /-,līk/ **adj.**, **wife·li·ness** /ˈwīflēnis/ **n.**, **wife·ly adj.**
– ORIGIN Old English *wīf* 'woman,' of Germanic origin; related to Dutch *wijf* and German *Weib.*

wife-beat·er /ˈwīf ,bētər/ ▶ **n.** informal a sleeveless undershirt.
– ORIGIN apparently from the association of such a garment with men who commit domestic violence.

wife-swap·ping ▶ **n.** informal the practice within a group of married couples of exchanging sexual partners on a casual basis.

wif·ey /ˈwīfē/ ▶ **n.** (pl. **wifeys**) informal a condescending way of referring to a man's wife.

Wif·fle ball /ˈwifəl/ ▶ **n.** trademark a light perforated ball used in a type of baseball. ■ a game played with such a ball.
– ORIGIN 1950s: *Wiffle*, variant of WHIFFLE.

Wi-Fi /ˈwī fī/ ▶ **n.** trademark a facility allowing computers, smartphones, or other devices to connect to the Internet or communicate with one another wirelessly within a particular area: *add Wi-Fi, standard now on most new laptops, and your home office can be anywhere.*
▶ **v.** (**Wi-Fies**, **-Fy·ing**, **Wi-Fied**) [with obj.] convert or adapt for Wi-Fi compatibility: *what type of electronics will be immune from being Wi-Fied?*
– ORIGIN 1990s: from *wireless* + an apparently arbitrary second element, after hi-fi; sometimes incorrectly interpreted as a shortening of Wireless Fidelity.

wig¹ /wig/ ▶ **n.** a covering for the head made of real or artificial hair, typically worn by people for adornment or by people trying to conceal their baldness or in England by judges and barristers in courts of law.
– DERIVATIVES **wigged adj.**, **wig·less adj.**
– ORIGIN late 17th cent.: shortening of PERIWIG.

wig² ▶ **v.** (**wigs**, **wigging**, **wigged**) [with obj.] Brit. informal, dated rebuke (someone) severely: *I had often occasion to wig him for getting drunk.*
– PHRASAL VERBS **wig out** informal become deliriously excited; go completely wild.
– ORIGIN early 19th cent.: apparently from WIG¹, perhaps from BIGWIG and associated with a rebuke given by a person in authority.

wig·eon /ˈwijən/ (also **widgeon**) ▶ **n.** a dabbling duck with mainly reddish-brown and gray plumage, the male having a whistling call. ● Genus *Anas*, family Anatidae: several species, in particular the **American wigeon** (*A. americana*)and the **Eurasian wigeon** (*A. penelope*).
– ORIGIN early 16th cent.: perhaps of imitative origin and suggested by PIGEON¹.

wig·ger informal ▶ **n. 1** a white person who tries to emulate or acquire African-American cultural behavior and tastes: *Whites who pal around with Blacks are called "wannabes" or "wiggers"*
2 an unreliable or flaky person: *the '80s wigger is the same as the '50s greaser, the '60s hippie, or the '70s burnout.*

wig·gle /ˈwigəl/ ▶ **v.** move or cause to move up and down or from side to side with small rapid movements: [with obj.] *Stasia wiggled her toes* | [no obj.] *my tooth was wiggling around.* ■ (**wiggle out of**) avoid (something), esp. by devious means: *they're trying to wiggle out of their agreement.*
▶ **n.** a wiggling movement: *a slight wiggle of the hips.* ■ a deviation in a line: *a wiggle on a chart.*
– PHRASES **get a wiggle on** informal get moving; hurry.
– DERIVATIVES **wig·gly** /ˈwig(ə)lē/ **adj.** (**wigglier**, **wiggliest**).
– ORIGIN Middle English: from Middle Low German and Middle Dutch *wiggelen* (frequentative).

wig·gler /ˈwig(ə)lər/ ▶ **n.** a person or thing that wiggles or causes something to wiggle. ■ Physics a magnet designed to make a beam of particles in an accelerator follow a sinusoidal path, in order to increase the amount of radiation they produce. ■ dialect an earthworm. ■ informal a mosquito larva.

wig·gle room ▶ **n.** informal room to maneuver; flexibility, esp. in one's options or interpretation: *he had precious little wiggle room because of the budget deficit.*

wig·gy /ˈwigē/ ▶ **adj.** (**wiggier**, **wiggiest**) informal emotionally uncontrolled or weird: *Jerry and Susan were gloriously wiggy.*
– ORIGIN 1960s: from *wig out* (see WIG²).

wight /wīt/ ▶ **n.** [usu. with adj.] archaic or dialect a person of a specified kind, esp. one regarded as unfortunate: *he always was an unlucky wight.* ■ literary a spirit, ghost, or other supernatural being.
– ORIGIN Old English *wiht* 'thing, creature,' of Germanic origin; related to Dutch *wicht* 'little child' and German *Wicht* 'creature.'

Wight, Isle of see ISLE OF WIGHT.

wig·wag /ˈwig,wag/ ▶ **v.** (**wigwags**, **wigwagging**, **wigwagged**) [no obj.] informal move to and fro: *the dog wigwagged his way up the porch steps.* ■ signal by waving an arm, flag, light, or other object: *Ned furiously wigwagged at her.*
– ORIGIN late 16th cent.: reduplication of WAG¹.

wig·wam /ˈwig,wäm/ ▶ **n.** a dome-shaped hut or tent made by fastening mats, skins, or bark over a framework of poles, used by some North American Indian peoples.
– ORIGIN early 17th cent.: from Abnaki, 'their house,' from an Algonquian base meaning 'dwell,' shared with WICKIUP.

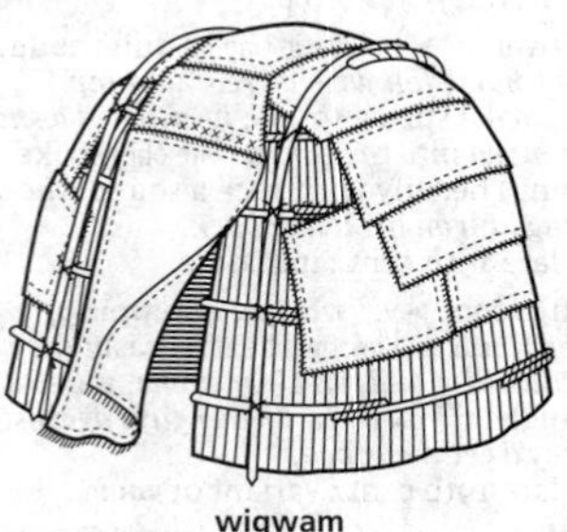
wigwam

wi·ki /ˈwikē/ ▶ **n.** a website that allows collaborative editing of its content and structure by its users.
– ORIGIN coined by programmer Ward Cunningham (1949–), from Hawaiian *wiki-wiki* 'quick-quick.'

wil·co /ˈwilkō/ ▶ **exclam.** expressing compliance or agreement, esp. acceptance of instructions received by radio: *roger, wilco.*
– ORIGIN 1940s (originally in military use): abbreviation of *will comply.*

wild /wīld/ ▶ **adj. 1** (of an animal or plant) living or growing in the natural environment; not domesticated or cultivated. ■ (of people) not civilized; barbarous: *the wild tribes from the north.* ■ (of scenery or a region) desolate-looking: *the wild coastline of Cape Wrath.*
2 uncontrolled or unrestrained, esp. in pursuit of pleasure: *she went through a wild phase of drunken parties and desperate affairs.* ■ not based on sound reasoning or probability: *a wild guess* | *who, even in their wildest dreams, could have anticipated such a victory?* ■ stormy: *the wild sea.* ■ informal very enthusiastic or excited: *I'm not wild about the music.* ■ informal very angry. ■ (of looks, appearance, etc.) indicating distraction: *her wild eyes were darting back and forth.* ■ (of a playing card) deemed to have any value, suit, color, or other property in a game at the discretion of the player holding it. See also WILD CARD.
▶ **n.** (**the wild**) a natural state or uncultivated or uninhabited region: *kiwis are virtually extinct in the wild.* ■ (**the wilds**) a remote uninhabited or sparsely inhabited area: *he spent a year in the wilds of Canada.*
– PHRASES **run wild** (of an animal, plant, or person) grow or develop without restraint or discipline: *these horses have been running wild since they were born* | figurative *her imagination had run wild.* **wild and woolly** uncouth in appearance or behavior.
– DERIVATIVES **wild·ish adj.**, **wild·ly adv.**, **wild·ness n.**
– ORIGIN Old English *wilde*, of Germanic origin; related to Dutch and German *wild.*

wild ar·um ▶ **n.** another term for CUCKOOPINT.

wild boar ▶ **n.** see BOAR (sense 1).

wild cal·la /ˈkalə/ ▶ **n.** another term for WATER ARUM.

wild cane ▶ **n.** another name for GIANT REED.

wild card ▶ **n.** a playing card that can have any value, suit, color, or other property in a game at the discretion of the player holding it. ■ a person or thing whose influence is unpredictable or whose qualities are uncertain. ■ Computing a character that will match any character or sequence of characters in a search. ■ an opportunity to enter a sports competition without having to take part in qualifying matches or be ranked at a particular level. ■ a player or team given such an opportunity.

wild car·rot ▶ **n.** another term for QUEEN ANNE'S LACE.

wild·cat /ˈwīld,kat/ ▶ **n. 1** a small native Eurasian and African cat that is typically gray with black markings and a bushy tail, noted for its ferocity. ● *Felis silvestris*, family Felidae, the African race of which is believed to be the ancestor of the domestic cat. ■ any of the smaller members of the cat family, esp. the bobcat. ■ a hot-tempered or ferocious person, typically a woman.
2 an exploratory oil well.
▶ **adj.** [attrib.] (of a strike) sudden and unofficial: *legislation to curb wildcat strikes.* ■ commercially unsound or risky.
▶ **v.** [no obj.] prospect for oil.

wild·cat·ter /ˈwīld,katər/ ▶ **n.** a prospector who sinks exploratory oil wells. ■ a risky investor.

wild-caught ▶ **adj.** (of an animal) taken from the wild rather than bred from captive stock.

wild·craft /ˈwīld,kraft/ ▶ **v.** [no obj.] gather herbs, plants, and fungi from the wild.
▶ **n.** the action or practice of wildcrafting.

wild dog ▸ n. a wild member of the dog family, esp. the hunting dog of Africa, the dhole of India, or the dingo of Australia.

Wilde /wīld/, Oscar (Fingal O'Flahertie Wills) (1854–1900), Irish playwright, novelist, poet, and wit. His advocacy of "art for art's sake" is evident in his only novel, *The Picture of Dorian Gray* (1890). As a playwright, he achieved success with the comedies *Lady Windermere's Fan* (1892) and *The Importance of Being Earnest* (1895).

Oscar Wilde

wil·de·beest /'wildə,bēst/ ▸ n. (pl. **same** or **wildebeests**) another term for GNU.
– ORIGIN early 19th cent.: from Afrikaans, literally 'wild beast.'

Wil·der[1] /'wīldər/, Billy (1906–2002), US movie director and screenwriter, born in Austria; born *Samuel Wilder*. His numerous film successes include *Double Indemnity* (1944), *The Lost Weekend* (1945), *Sunset Boulevard* (1950), *Sabrina* (1954), *Some Like It Hot* (1959), and *The Apartment* (1960).

Wil·der[2], Laura Ingalls (1867–1957), US writer. She wrote a series of children's books about her experiences growing up on the US frontier during the late 1800s. Her best known is *Little House on the Prairie* (1935), which was the basis for a television series 1974–83. Other books include *Little House in the Big Woods* (1932) and *These Happy Golden Years* (1943).

Wil·der[3], Thornton (Niven) (1897–1975), US novelist and playwright. His work is particularly concerned with the universality of human experience, irrespective of time or place. He wrote the novel *The Bridge of San Luis Rey* (1927) and the plays *Our Town* (1938) and *The Skin of Our Teeth* (1942).

wil·der /'wildər/ ▸ v. [with obj.] archaic cause to lose one's way; lead or drive astray: *unknowne Lands, where we have wildered ourselves.* ■ perplex; bewilder: *the sad Queen, wildered of thought.*
– ORIGIN early 17th cent.: origin uncertain; perhaps based on WILDERNESS.

wil·der·ness /'wildərnis/ ▸ n. [usu. in sing.] an uncultivated, uninhabited, and inhospitable region. ■ a neglected or abandoned area of a garden or town. ■ a position of disfavor, esp. in a political context: *the man who led the Green Party out of the wilderness* | [as modifier] *his wilderness years.*
– PHRASES **a voice in the wilderness** an unheeded advocate of reform (see Matt. 3:3, etc.).
– ORIGIN Old English *wildēornes* 'land inhabited only by wild animals,' from *wild dēor* 'wild deer' + -NESS.

Wil·der·ness, the a wooded region of Spotsylvania County in northeastern Virginia, site of an inconclusive Civil War battle in 1864.

Wil·der·ness Road a historic route, opened by Daniel Boone in the 1770s and used until the 1840s, that allowed western migration through the Allegheny Mountains by way of the Cumberland Gap between Tennessee and Kentucky.

wild-eyed ▸ adj. (of a person or animal) with an expression of panic or desperation in their eyes.

wild·fire /'wīld,fīr/ ▸ n. 1 a large, destructive fire that spreads quickly over woodland or brush.
2 historical a combustible liquid such as Greek fire that was readily ignited and difficult to extinguish, used esp. in warfare.
3 less common term for WILL-O'-THE-WISP.
– PHRASES **spread like wildfire** spread with great speed: *the news had spread like wildfire.*

wild·flow·er /'wīld,flou(-ə)r/ (also **wild flower**) ▸ n. a flower of an uncultivated variety or a flower growing freely without human intervention.

wild·fowl /'wīld,foul/ ▸ plural n. game birds, esp. aquatic ones; waterfowl.

wild gin·ger ▸ n. a North American plant with large heart-shaped leaves and hairy leafstalks. Its aromatic root is used as a ginger substitute. ● *Asarum canadense*, family Aristolochiaceae.

wild goose chase ▸ n. a foolish and hopeless pursuit of something unattainable.

wild horse ▸ n. a domestic horse that has returned to the wild, or that is allowed to live under natural conditions; a feral horse. ■ a horse that has not been broken in. ■ a wild animal of the horse family.
– PHRASES **wild horses wouldn't ——** used to convey that nothing could persuade or force someone to do something: *wild horses wouldn't have kept me away.*

wild·ing[1] /'wīldiNG/ ▸ n. informal the activity by a gang of youths of going on a protracted and violent rampage in a public place, attacking people at random.
– ORIGIN 1980s: from the adjective WILD + -ING[1].

wild·ing[2] (also **wildling** /-liNG/) ▸ n. a wild plant, esp. an apple tree descended from cultivated varieties, or its fruit.
– ORIGIN early 16th cent.: from the adjective WILD + -ING[3].

wild·life /'wīld,līf/ ▸ n. wild animals collectively; the native fauna (and sometimes flora) of a region.

wild·life park ▸ n. see PARK (sense 1 of the noun).

wild man ▸ n. a man with a fierce or wildly unruly nature. ■ the image of a primitive or uncivilized man as a symbol of the wild side of human nature or of seasonal fertility. ■ a supposed manlike animal such as a yeti.

wild mar·jo·ram ▸ n. see MARJORAM.

wild mus·tard ▸ n. charlock.

wild oat ▸ n. an Old World grass that is related to the cultivated oat and is commonly found as a weed of other cereal plants. ● *Avena fatua*, family Gramineae.
– PHRASES **sow one's wild oats** see OAT.

wild pitch Baseball ▸ n. an errant pitch that is not hit by the batter and cannot be stopped by the catcher, enabling a base runner to advance.
▸ v. (**wild-pitch**) [with obj.] enable (a base runner) to advance by making such a pitch: *Reed was wild-pitched to second.*

wild rice ▸ n. a tall aquatic North American grass related to rice, with edible grains. ● *Zizania aquatica*, family Gramineae. ■ the grain of this plant used as food.

wild serv·ice tree ▸ n. see SERVICE TREE.

wild silk ▸ n. coarse silk produced by wild silkworms, esp. tussore.

wild type ▸ n. Genetics a strain, gene, or characteristic that prevails among individuals in natural conditions, as distinct from an atypical mutant type.

Wild West the western US in a time of lawlessness in its early history. The Wild West was the last of a succession of frontiers formed as settlers moved gradually further west. The frontier was officially declared closed in 1890.

wild·wood /'wīld,wood/ ▸ n. chiefly literary an uncultivated wood or forest that has been allowed to grow naturally.

wile /wīl/ ▸ n. (**wiles**) devious or cunning stratagems employed in manipulating or persuading someone to do what one wants.
▸ v. [with obj.] 1 archaic lure; entice: *she could be neither driven nor wiled into the parish kirk.*
2 (**wile away the time**) another way of saying WHILE AWAY THE TIME. See WHILE.
– ORIGIN Middle English: perhaps from an Old Norse word related to *vél* 'craft.'

wil·ful ▸ adj. variant spelling of WILLFUL.

wil·ga /'wilgə/ ▸ n. a small white-flowering Australian tree that is resistant to drought and a valuable source of fodder. In North America, it is also planted as an ornamental. ● *Geijera parviflora*, family Rutaceae.
– ORIGIN late 19th cent.: from Wiradhuri *wilgar.*

Wil·helm I /'vil,helm/ (1797–1888), king of Prussia 1861–88 and emperor of Germany 1871–88. He became the first emperor of Germany after Prussia's victory against France in 1871. The latter part of his reign was marked by the rise of German socialism, to which he responded with harsh, repressive measures.

Wil·helm II (1859–1941), emperor of Germany 1888–1918; grandson of Wilhelm I and of Queen Victoria; known as **Kaiser Wilhelm**. After forcing Bismarck to resign in 1890, he proved unable to exercise a strong or consistent influence over German policies. Vilified by Allied propaganda as the instigator of World War I, he abdicated and went into exile in 1918.

Wil·hel·mi·na /,vilhel'mēnə/, (1880–1962), queen of the Netherlands 1890–1948. During World War II, she maintained a government in exile in London and through frequent radio broadcasts became a symbol of resistance for the Dutch people. She returned to the Netherlands in 1945.

Wilkes /wilks/, Charles (1798–1877), US naval officer and explorer. He determined that Antarctica is a continent during an 1838–42 expedition. Antarctica's Wilkes Land was named in his honor. In 1861, he was involved in the Trent Affair, an incident on the high seas in which Confederate commissioners to England and France were forcibly detained by the US navy.

Wilkes-Barre /'wilks ,barə, ,barē/ an industrial city in northeastern Pennsylvania, on the Susquehanna River, in the Wyoming Valley; pop. 40,932 (est. 2008).

Wilkes Land /wilks/ a region of Antarctica that has a coast on the Indian Ocean. It is claimed by Australia.
– ORIGIN named after the US naval officer Charles *Wilkes*, who sighted and surveyed it between 1838 and 1842.

Wil·kie /'wilkē/, Sir David (1785–1841), Scottish painter. He established his reputation with the painting *Village Politicians* (1806). His style contributed to the growing prestige of genre painting.

Wil·kins[1] /'wilkinz/, Maurice Hugh Frederick (1916–2004), British biochemist and molecular biologist, born in New Zealand. From X-ray diffraction analysis of DNA, he and his colleague Rosalind Franklin confirmed the double helix structure proposed by Francis Crick and James Watson in 1953. Nobel Prize for Physiology or Medicine (1962), shared with Crick and Watson.

Wil·kins[2], Roy (1901–81), US civil rights leader. He edited the NAACP's magazine, *The Crisis*, from 1934 until 1949 and then served as executive secretary of the NAACP 1955–77.

will[1] /wil/ ▸ modal v. (3rd sing. present **will**; past **would** /wood, wəd/) 1 expressing the future tense: *you will regret it when you are older.* ■ expressing a strong intention or assertion about the future: *come what may, I will succeed.*
2 expressing inevitable events: *accidents will happen.*
3 expressing a request: *will you stop here, please.* ■ expressing desire, consent, or willingness: *will you have a cognac?*
4 expressing facts about ability or capacity: *a rock so light that it will float on water* | *your tank will hold about 26 gallons.*
5 expressing habitual behavior: *she will dance for hours.* ■ (pronounced stressing "will") indicating annoyance about the habitual behavior described: *he will keep intruding.*
6 expressing probability or expectation about something in the present: *they will be miles away by now.*
– PHRASES **will do** informal expressing willingness to carry out a request or suggestion: *"Might be best to check." "OK, will do."*
– ORIGIN Old English *wyllan*, of Germanic origin; related to Dutch *willen*, German *wollen*, from an Indo-European root shared by Latin *velle* 'will, wish.'

USAGE On the differences in use between **will** and **shall**, see usage at SHALL.

will[2] ▸ n. 1 [usu. in sing.] the faculty by which a person decides on and initiates action: *she has an iron will* | *a battle of wills between children and their parents* | *an act of will.* ■ (also **willpower**) control deliberately exerted to do something or to restrain one's own impulses: *a stupendous effort of will.* ■ a deliberate or fixed desire or intention: *Jane had not wanted them to stay against their will* | [with infinitive] *the will to live.* ■ the thing that one desires or ordains: *the disaster was God's will.*
2 a legal document containing instructions as to what should be done with one's money and property after one's death.
▸ v. [with obj.] 1 chiefly formal literary intend, desire, or wish (something) to happen: *he was doing what the saint willed* | [with clause] *marijuana, dope, grass—call it what you will.* ■ [with obj. and infinitive] make or try to make (someone) do something or (something) happen by the exercise of mental powers: *reluctantly he willed himself to turn and go back* | *she stared into the fog, willing it to clear.*
2 (**will something to**) bequeath something to (someone) by the terms of one's will. ■ [with clause] leave specified instructions in one's will: *he willed that his body be given to the hospital.*
– PHRASES **at will** at whatever time or in whatever way one pleases: *it can be molded and shaped at will* | *he was shoved around at will.* **have a will of**

one's own have a willful character. **have one's will** archaic obtain what one wants. **if you will** said when politely inviting a listener or reader to do something or when using an unusual or fanciful term: *imagine, if you will, a typical silversmith's shop*. **where there's a will there's a way** proverb determination will overcome any obstacle. **with the best will in the world** however good one's intentions (used to imply that success in a particular undertaking is unlikely although desired). **with a will** energetically and resolutely.
– DERIVATIVES **willed adj.** [in combination] *I'm strong-willed*, **will·less·ness n.**, **will·er n.**
– ORIGIN Old English *willa* (noun), *willian* (verb), of Germanic origin; related to Dutch *wil*, German *Wille* (nouns), also to WILL[1] and the adverb WELL[1].

Wil·lam·ette Riv·er /wəˈlamit/ a river that flows for 300 miles (480 km) through western Oregon to the Columbia River.

Wil·lard[1] /ˈwilərd/, Emma (1787–1870), US educator. She founded a boarding school in Vermont in 1814 to teach subjects, such as mathematics and philosophy, not then available to women.

Wil·lard[2], Frances Elizabeth Caroline (1839–98), US women's rights and temperance activist. She was president of the Women's Christian Temperance Union 1879, an organizer of the Prohibition Party in 1882, and president of the National Council of Women 1890. She wrote *Woman and Temperance* (1883).

will-call ▸ **n.** relating to a place (usu. a ticket window or office) where items previously purchased can be picked up: *those picking up tickets at the will-call window must use the Trumbull entrance*.

wil·lem·ite /ˈwiləˌmīt/ ▸ **n.** a mineral, typically greenish-yellow and fluorescent, consisting of a silicate of zinc.
– ORIGIN mid 19th cent.: from the name of *Willem* I (1772–1843), king of the Netherlands, + -ITE[1].

Wil·lem·stad /ˈviləmˌstät, ˈwil-/ the capital of the Netherlands Antilles, on the southwestern coast of the island of Curaçao; pop. 120,000 (est. 2007).

wil·let /ˈwilit/ ▸ **n.** (pl. **same** or **willets**) a large North American sandpiper. ● *Catoptrophorus semipalmatus*, family Scolopacidae.
– ORIGIN mid 19th cent.: imitative of its call, *pill-will-willet*.

will·ful /ˈwilfəl/ (also **wilful**) ▸ **adj.** (of an immoral or illegal act or omission) intentional; deliberate: *willful acts of damage*. ■ having or showing a stubborn and determined intention to do as one wants, regardless of the consequences or effects: *the pettish, willful side of him*.
– DERIVATIVES **will·ful·ly** /ˈwilfəlē/ **adv.**, **will·ful·ness** /ˈwilfəlnəs/ **n.**
– ORIGIN Middle English: from the noun WILL[2] + -FUL.

Wil·liam /ˈwilyəm/ the name of two kings of England and two of Great Britain and Ireland. ■ **William I** (c.1027–87), reigned 1066–87; the first Norman king of England; known as **William the Conqueror**. He invaded England and defeated Harold II at the Battle of Hastings (1066). He introduced Norman institutions and customs (including feudalism) and instigated the Domesday Book. ■ **William II** (c.1060–1100), son of William I; reigned 1087–1100; known as **William Rufus**. He crushed rebellions in 1088 and 1095 and also campaigned against his brother **Robert**, Duke of Normandy (1089–96), ultimately acquiring the duchy. ■ **William III** (1650–1702), grandson of Charles I, husband of Mary II; reigned 1689–1702; known as **William of Orange**. In 1688, he deposed James II at the invitation of disaffected politicians and was crowned along with his wife Mary. ■ **William IV** (1765–1837), son of George III; reigned 1830–37; known as **the Sailor King**. Having served in the Royal Navy, he came to the throne after the death of his brother George IV.

Will·iam I[1] (1143–1214), grandson of David I; king of Scotland 1165–1214; known as **William the Lion**.

Will·iam I[2] (1533–84), prince of the House of Orange; first stadtholder (chief magistrate) of the United Provinces of the Netherlands 1572–84; known as **William the Silent**.

W

Will·iam of Oc·cam /ˈäkəm/ (also **Ockham**) (c.1285–1349), English philosopher and Franciscan friar. A defender of nominalism, he is known for the maxim called "Occam's razor."

Will·iam of Or·ange, William III of Great Britain and Ireland (see WILLIAM).

Will·iam Ru·fus /ˈro͞ofəs/, William II of England (see WILLIAM).

Wil·liams[1] /ˈwilyəmz/, Hank (1923–53), US country singer and songwriter; born *Hiram King Williams*. He had the first of many hits, "Lovesick Blues," in 1949 and that year joined the *Grand Ole Opry* television program. Many of his songs were successfully recorded by other artists. "Your Cheatin' Heart," recorded in 1952, was released after his sudden death.

Wil·liams[2] see LOY.

Wil·liams[3], Roger (c.1603–83), American clergyman; born in England. Banished from Massachusetts, he founded the colony of Rhode Island and, within it, the settlement of Providence in 1636 as a refuge from political and religious persecution. He served as Rhode Island's president 1654–57.

Wil·liams[4], Rowan (Douglas) (1950–), Welsh Anglican clergyman; archbishop of Canterbury from 2002. His many books include *Writing in the Dust: Reflections on 11th September and Its Aftermath* (2002) and *Anglican Identities* (2004).

Wil·liams[5], Serena (Jameka) (1981–), US tennis player; sister of Venus Williams. During 1999–2009, she won the women's singles titles at three US Open, three Wimbledon, one French Open, and four Australian Open tournaments.

Wil·liams[6], Ted (1918–2002), US baseball player; full name *Theodore Samuel Williams*; nickname the **Splendid Splinter**. His career as an outfielder for the Boston Red Sox 1939–1960 was interrupted by active duty in World War II and Korea. His 1941 batting average of .406 remains a major league record. Baseball Hall of Fame (1966).

Will·iams[7], Tennessee (1911–83), US playwright; born *Thomas Lanier Williams*. His success began with *The Glass Menagerie* (1944) and *A Streetcar Named Desire* (1947), which deal with vulnerable heroines living in fragile fantasy worlds that are shattered by brutal reality. Other notable works: *Cat on a Hot Tin Roof* (1955) and *The Night of the Iguana* (1962).

Wil·liams[8], Venus (Ebony Starr) (1980–), US tennis player; sister of Serena Williams. During 2000–08, she won the women's singles title at two US Open, one French Open, one Australian Open, and five Wimbledon tournaments.

Will·iams[9], William Carlos (1883–1963), US poet, essayist, novelist, and short-story writer. His poetry illuminates the ordinary by vivid, direct observation; it is characterized by avoidance of emotional content and the use of US vernacular. Collections include *Spring and All* (1923) and *Pictures from Brueghel* (1963).

Wil·liams·burg /ˈwilyəmzˌbərg/ **1** a city in southeastern Virginia, between the James and York rivers; pop. 12,481 (est. 2008). It was the state capital of Virginia from 1699, when it was named in honor of William III, until 1799, when Richmond became the capital. A large part of the town has been restored and reconstructed so that it appears as it was during the colonial era.
2 a residential and industrial section of northern Brooklyn in New York City, noted for its Hasidic Jewish community and arts colony.

Wil·liams·port /ˈwilyəmzˌpôrt/ an industrial city in north central Pennsylvania, on the Susquehanna River; the birthplace of Little League baseball; pop. 29,456 (est. 2008).

Will·iam the Con·quer·or, William I of England (see WILLIAM).

wil·lies /ˈwilēz/ ▸ **plural n.** (**the willies**) informal a strong feeling of nervous apprehension and discomfort: *that room gave him the willies*.
– ORIGIN late 19th cent. (originally US): of unknown origin.

will·ing /ˈwiliNG/ ▸ **adj.** [often with infinitive] ready, eager, or prepared to do something: *he was quite willing to compromise*. ■ given or done readily: *willing and prompt obedience*.

Will·ing·bo·ro /ˈwiliNGˌbərə/ a residential township in west central New Jersey, near the Delaware River; pop. 36,530 (est. 2008). It was founded as Levittown in 1959.

will·ing·ly /ˈwiliNGlē/ ▸ **adv.** readily; of one's own free will: *she went willingly*.

will·ing·ness /ˈwiliNGnis/ ▸ **n.** the quality or state of being prepared to do something; readiness: *the ability and willingness of workers to migrate*.

wil·li·waw /ˈwilēˌwô/ ▸ **n.** a sudden violent squall blowing offshore from a mountainous coast.
– ORIGIN mid 19th cent.: of unknown origin.

Will·kie, Wendell Lewis (1882–1944) US politician and lawyer. The Republican presidential candidate in 1940, he unsuccessfully ran against incumbent Franklin D. Roosevelt, who was running for his third term. He later supported Roosevelt's war effort programs and policies.

will-o'-the-wisp /ˌwil ə T͟Hə ˈwisp/ ▸ **n.** a phosphorescent light seen hovering or floating at night over marshy ground, thought to result from the combustion of natural gases; ignis fatuus. ■ a person or thing that is difficult or impossible to find, reach, or catch.
– ORIGIN early 17th cent.: originally as *Will with the wisp*, the sense of *wisp* being 'handful of (lighted) hay.'

wil·low /ˈwilō/ ▸ **n. 1** (also **willow tree**) a tree or shrub of temperate climates that typically has narrow leaves, bears catkins, and grows near water. Its pliant branches yield osiers for basketry, and its wood has various uses. ● Genus *Salix*, family Salicaceae: many species.
2 a machine with revolving spikes used for cleaning cotton, wool, or other fibers.
– ORIGIN Old English *welig*, of Germanic origin; related to Dutch *wilg*.

wil·low grouse ▸ **n.** another term for WILLOW PTARMIGAN.

wil·low herb (also **willowherb**) ▸ **n.** a plant of temperate regions that typically has willowlike leaves and pink or pale purple flowers. ● *Epilobium* and related genera, family Onagraceae: many species, including the common **hairy willow herb** (*E. hirsutum*) and the common fireweed (*E. angustifolium*).

wil·low pat·tern ▸ **n.** a conventional design representing a Chinese scene in blue on white pottery, typically showing three figures on a bridge, with a willow tree and two birds above: [as modifier] *a willow-pattern plate*.

wil·low ptar·mi·gan ▸ **n.** a common Eurasian and North American grouse with reddish-brown and white plumage, turning mainly white in winter. ● *Lagopus lagopus*, family Tetraonidae (or Phasianidae).See also RED GROUSE.

wil·low·ware /ˈwilōˌwe(ə)r/ ▸ **n.** pottery with a willow-pattern design.

wil·low·y /ˈwilōē/ ▸ **adj. 1** bordered, shaded, or covered by willows: *willowy meadow land*.
2 (of a person) tall, slim, and lithe.

will·pow·er /ˈwilˌpou(ə)r/ ▸ **n.** see WILL[2] (sense 1 of the noun).

Wills Mood·y /wilz/, Helen (1905–98), US tennis player; born *Helen Newington Wills*. During 1927–38, she won the women's singles title at eight Wimbledon, seven US Open, and four French Open tournaments.

wil·ly /ˈwilē/ (also **willie**) ▸ **n.** (pl. **willies**) informal a penis.
– ORIGIN early 20th cent.: nickname for the given name *William*.

wil·ly-nil·ly /ˌwilē ˈnilē/ ▸ **adv. 1** whether one likes it or not: *he would be forced to collaborate willy-nilly*.
2 without direction or planning; haphazardly: *politicians expanded spending programs willy-nilly*.
– ORIGIN early 17th cent.: later spelling of *will I, nill I* 'I am willing, I am unwilling.'

Wil·ming·ton /ˈwilmiNGtən/ **1** the largest city in Delaware, on the Delaware River, in the northeastern part of the state; pop. 72,592 (est. 2008).
2 an industrial port city in southeastern North Carolina, on the Cape Fear River and the Atlantic Ocean; pop. 100,192 (est. 2008).

Wilms' tu·mor /wilmz/ ▸ **n.** a malignant tumor of the kidney, of a type that occurs in young children.
– ORIGIN early 20th cent.: named after Max *Wilms* (1867–1918), German surgeon.

Wil·son[1] /ˈwilsən/ an industrial city in east central North Carolina; pop. 48,433 (est. 2008).

Wil·son[2] /ˈwilsən/, Charles Thomson Rees (1869–1959), Scottish physicist. After inventing the cloud chamber in 1895, he improved the design and by 1911 had a chamber in which the track of an ion could be made visible. This became a major tool of particle physicists. Nobel Prize for Physics (1927), shared with Arthur Compton.

Wil·son[3], Edmund (1895–1972), US critic, essayist, and short-story writer. He is remembered chiefly for works of literary and social criticism. He was a friend of F. Scott Fitzgerald and edited the latter's unfinished novel *The Last Tycoon* (1941).

Wil·son[4], Edward Osborne (1929–), US social biologist. He worked principally on social insects, notably ants and termites, extrapolating his findings to the social behavior of other animals, including humans.

Wil·son[5], Harold (1916–95), British Labour statesman; prime minister 1964–70 and 1974–76; full name *James Harold Wilson, Baron Wilson of Rievaulx*. Although faced with severe economic problems, his government introduced a number of social reforms, such as comprehensive schooling, and renegotiated Britain's terms of entry into the European Economic Community.

Wil·son[6], James (1742–98), US Supreme Court associate justice 1789–98; born in Scotland. A signer of the Declaration of Independence 1776 and a member of the Continental Congress 1775–77; 1782–83; 1785–87, he was appointed to the Court by President Washington.

Wil·son[7], John Tuzo (1908–93), Canadian geophysicist. He was a pioneer in the study of plate tectonics, introducing the term *plate* in this context in the early 1960s.

Wil·son[8], Teddy (1912–86), US jazz pianist; full name *Theodore Shaw Wilson*. He played with Benny Goodman and Gene Krupa in the 1930s and later led his own bands.

Wil·son[9], Woodrow (1856–1924), 28th president of the US 1913–21; full name *Thomas Woodrow Wilson*. A Democrat, he eventually took the US into World War I in 1917 and later played a leading role in the peace negotiations and the formation of the League of Nations. The Senate, however, failed to ratify the peace treaty. Semi-incapacitated by a stroke in 1919, he did not seek re-election. Nobel Peace Prize (1920).

Woodrow Wilson

Wil·son, Mount a peak in the San Gabriel Mountains of southwestern California, near Pasadena, site of a major astronomical observatory.

wilt[1] /wilt/ ▶ **v.** [no obj.] (of a plant, leaf, or flower) become limp through heat, loss of water, or disease; droop. ■ (of a person) lose one's energy or vigor.
▶ **n.** [usu. with modifier] any of a number of fungal or bacterial diseases of plants characterized by wilting of the foliage.
– ORIGIN late 17th cent. (originally dialect): perhaps an alteration of dialect *welk* 'lose freshness,' of Low German origin.

wilt[2] archaic second person singular of WILL[1].

Wil·ton /ˈwiltn/ ▶ **n.** a woven carpet resembling a Brussels carpet but with a velvet pile.
– ORIGIN late 18th cent.: from *Wilton*, the name of a town in southern England, noted for the manufacture of carpets.

Wilts. ▶ **abbr.** Wiltshire.

Wilt·shire /ˈwilt,sʜi(ə)r, -sʜər/ a county of southern England; county town, Trowbridge.

wil·y /ˈwīlē/ ▶ **adj.** (**wilier, wiliest**) skilled at gaining an advantage, esp. deceitfully: *his wily opponents.*
– DERIVATIVES **wil·i·ly** /ˈwīləlē/ **adv.**, **wil·i·ness n.**

Wim·ble·don /ˈwimbəldən/ an annual international tennis championship played on grass for individual players and pairs, held at the headquarters of the All England Lawn Tennis and Croquet Club in the London suburb of Wimbledon. Now one of the world's major tennis championships, it has been played since 1877.

wim·min /ˈwimin/ ▶ **plural n.** nonstandard spelling of "women" adopted by some feminists to avoid the word ending *-men*.

WIMP[1] /wimp/ ▶ **n.** [often as modifier] Computing a graphical user interface designed to simplify or demystify computing operations.
– ORIGIN 1980s: acronym from *windows, icons, menus, and pointing (device)*.

WIMP[2] ▶ **n.** Physics a hypothetical subatomic particle of large mass that interacts only weakly with ordinary matter, postulated as a constituent of the dark matter of the universe.
– ORIGIN 1980s: acronym from *weakly interacting massive particle*.

wimp /wimp/ informal ▶ **n.** a weak and cowardly or unadventurous person.
▶ **v.** [no obj.] (**wimp out**) withdraw from a course of action or a stated position in a way that is seen as feeble or cowardly.
– DERIVATIVES **wimp·ish adj.**, **wimp·ish·ly adv.**, **wimp·ish·ness n.**, **wimp·y adj.**
– ORIGIN 1920s: origin uncertain, perhaps from WHIMPER.

wim·ple /ˈwimpəl/ ▶ **n.** a cloth headdress covering the head, the neck, and the sides of the face, formerly worn by women and still worn by some nuns.
– DERIVATIVES **wim·pled adj.**
– ORIGIN late Old English *wimpel*, of Germanic origin; related to German *Wimpel* 'pennon, streamer.'

wimple

win /win/ ▶ **v.** (**wins, winning**; past and past participle **won** /wən, wän/) [with obj.] **1** be successful or victorious in (a contest or conflict): *the Mets have won four games in a row* | [no obj.] *a determination to win* | [with complement] *the Pirates won 2–1.*
2 acquire or secure as a result of a contest, conflict, bet, or other endeavor: *there are hundreds of prizes to be won* | [with two objs.] *the sort of play that won them the World Cup.* ■ gain (a person's attention, support, or love), typically gradually or by effort: *you will find it difficult to win back their attention.* ■ (**win someone over**) gain the support or favor of someone by action or persuasion: *her sense of humor had won him over at once.* ■ [no obj.] (**win out**) manage to succeed or achieve something by effort: *talent won out over bureaucracy.* ■ archaic manage to reach (a place) by effort: *many lived to win the great cave.* ■ obtain (ore) from a mine.
▶ **n.** a successful result in a contest, conflict, bet, or other endeavor; a victory: *a win against Norway.*
– PHRASES **one can't win** informal said when someone feels that no course of action open to them will bring success or please people. **win the day** be victorious in battle, sport, or argument. **win or lose** whether one succeeds or fails: *win or lose, the important thing for him is to set a good example.* **win** (or **earn**) **one's spurs** historical gain a knighthood by an act of bravery. ■ informal gain one's first distinction or honors. **you can't win them all** (or **win some, lose some**) informal said to express consolation or resignation after failure in a contest.
– DERIVATIVES **win·less n.**, **win·na·ble adj.**
– ORIGIN Old English *winnan* 'strive, contend,' also 'subdue and take possession of, acquire,' of Germanic origin.

wince[1] /wins/ ▶ **v.** [no obj.] give a slight involuntary grimace or shrinking movement of the body out of or in anticipation of pain or distress: *he winced at the disgust in her voice.*
▶ **n.** [in sing.] a slight grimace or shrinking movement caused by pain or distress.
– DERIVATIVES **winc·er n.**, **winc·ing·ly adv.**
– ORIGIN Middle English (originally in the sense 'kick restlessly from pain or impatience'): from an Anglo-Norman French variant of Old French *guenchir* 'turn aside.'

wince[2] ▶ **n.** Brit. a roller for moving textile fabric through a dyeing vat.
– ORIGIN late 17th cent. (in the sense 'winch'): variant of WINCH.

winch /wincʜ/ ▶ **n.** **1** a hauling or lifting device consisting of a rope, cable, or chain winding around a horizontal rotating drum, turned by a crank or by motor or other power source; a windlass.
2 the crank of a wheel or axle.
▶ **v.** [with obj.] hoist or haul with a winch.
– DERIVATIVES **winch·er n.**
– ORIGIN late Old English *wince* 'reel, pulley,' of Germanic origin; related to the verb WINK. The verb dates from the early 16th cent.

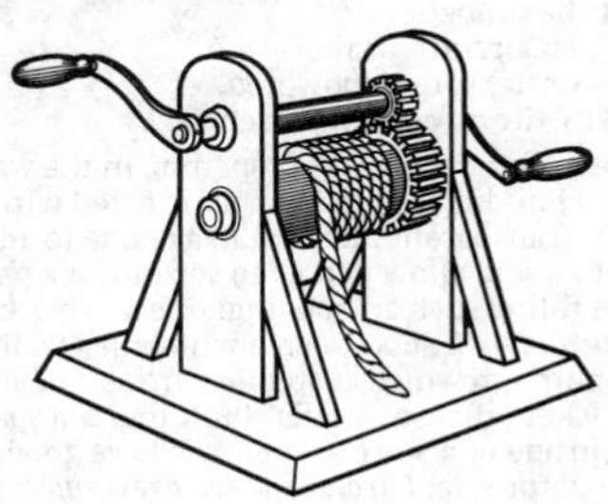

winch 1

Win·ches·ter[1] /ˈwin,cʜestər, -cʜəstər/ a historic city in northwestern Virginia, in the Shenandoah Valley; pop. 25,897 (est. 2008).

Win·ches·ter[2] ▶ **n.** **1** (also **Winchester rifle**) trademark a breech-loading side-action repeating rifle. [named after Oliver F. *Winchester* (1810–80), the US manufacturer of the rifle.]
2 (in full **Winchester disk** or **drive**) Computing a disk drive in a sealed unit containing a high-capacity hard disk and the read-write heads. [so named because its original numerical designation corresponded to the caliber of the rifle.]

wind[1] ▶ **n.** /wind/ **1** the perceptible natural movement of the air, esp. in the form of a current of air blowing from a particular direction: *the wind howled about the building* | *an easterly wind* | *gusts of wind.* ■ [as modifier] relating to or denoting energy obtained from harnessing the wind with windmills or wind turbines. ■ used to suggest something very fast, unrestrained, or changeable: *run like the wind* | *she could be as free and easy as the wind.* ■ used in reference to an influence or tendency that cannot be resisted: *a wind of change.* ■ used in reference to an impending situation: *he had seen which way the wind was blowing.* ■ the rush of air caused by a fast-moving body. ■ a scent carried by the wind, indicating the presence or proximity of an animal or person.
2 breath as needed in physical exertion or in speech. ■ the power of breathing without difficulty while running or making a similar continuous effort: *he waited while Jerry got his wind back.* See also SECOND WIND.
3 empty, pompous, or boastful talk; meaningless rhetoric. ■ air swallowed while eating or gas generated in the stomach and intestines by digestion.
4 air or breath used for sounding an organ or a wind instrument. ■ (also **winds**) [treated as sing. or pl.] wind instruments, or specifically woodwind instruments, forming a band or a section of an orchestra: *concerto for piano, violin, and thirteen winds* | [as modifier] *wind players.*
▶ **v.** /wind/ [with obj.] **1** cause (someone) to have difficulty breathing because of exertion or a blow to the stomach: *the fall nearly winded him.*
2 detect the presence of (a person or animal) by scent: *the birds could not have seen us or winded us.*
3 /wīnd/ (past and past participle **winded** /ˈwindid/ or **wound** /wound/) literary sound (a bugle or call) by blowing: *but scarce again his horn he wound.*
– PHRASES **before the wind** Sailing with the wind blowing more or less from astern. **get wind of** informal begin to suspect that (something) is happening; hear a rumor of: *Marty got wind of a plot being hatched.* [referring originally to the scent of game in hunting.] **it's an ill wind that blows no good** proverb few things are so bad that no one profits from them. **off the wind** Sailing with the wind on either quarter. **on a wind** Sailing against a wind on either bow. **put** (or **have**) **the wind up** Brit. informal alarm or frighten (or be alarmed or frightened): *he was trying to put the wind up him with stories of how hard teaching was.* **sail close to** (or **near**) **the wind** **1** Sailing sail as nearly against the wind as possible while still making headway. **2** informal verge on indecency, dishonesty, or disaster. **take the wind out of someone's sails** frustrate someone by unexpectedly anticipating an action or remark. **to the wind (s)** (or **the four winds**) in all directions: *my little flock scatters to the four winds.* ■ so as to be abandoned or neglected: *I threw my friends' advice to the winds.* [from 'And fear of death deliver to the winds' (Milton's *Paradise Lost*).]
– DERIVATIVES **wind·less adj.**
– ORIGIN Old English, of Germanic origin; related to Dutch *wind* and German *Wind*, from an Indo-European root shared by Latin *ventus*.

wind[2] /wīnd/ ▶ **v.** (past and past participle **wound** /wound/) **1** [no obj.] move in or take a twisting or spiral course: *the path wound among olive trees.*
2 [with obj.] pass (something) around a thing or person so as to encircle or enfold: *he wound a towel around his midriff.* ■ repeatedly twist or coil (a length of something) around itself or a core: *Anne wound the wool into a ball.* ■ [no obj.] be twisted or coiled in such a way: *large vines wound around every tree.* ■ wrap or surround (a core) with a coiled length of something: *devices wound with copper wire.*
3 [with obj.] make (a clock or other device, typically one operated by clockwork) operate by turning a key or handle: *he wound up the clock every Saturday night* | *she was winding the gramophone.* ■ turn (a key or handle) repeatedly around and around: *I wound the handle as fast as I could.* ■ cause (an audio or videotape or a film) to move back or forward to a desired point: *wind your tape back and listen to make sure everything is okay.* ■ hoist or draw (something) with a windlass, winch, or similar device.
▶ **n.** **1** a twist or turn in a course.
2 a single turn made when winding.
– PHRASAL VERBS **wind down** (of a mechanism, esp. one operated by clockwork) gradually lose power. ■ informal (of a person) relax after stress

or excitement. ■ (also **wind something down**) draw or bring gradually to a close: *business began to wind down as people awaited the new regime.* **wind up** informal **1** arrive or end up in a specified state, situation, or place: *Kevin winds up in New York.* **2** another way of saying **WIND SOMETHING UP**: *he wound up by attacking Nonconformists.* **3** Baseball (of a pitcher) use the windup delivery. **wind someone up 1** (usu. **be wound up**) make tense or angry: *he was clearly wound up and frantic about his daughter.* **2** Brit. informal tease or irritate someone: *she's only winding me up.* **wind something up 1** arrange the affairs of and dissolve a company: *the company has since been wound up.* **2** gradually or finally bring an activity to a conclusion: *the experiments had to be wound up because the funding stopped.* **3** informal increase the tension, intensity, or power of something: *he wound up the engine.*
– ORIGIN Old English *windan* 'go rapidly,' 'twine,' of Germanic origin; related to **WANDER** and **WEND**.

wind·age /ˈwindij/ ▶ **n.** the air resistance of a moving object, such as a vessel or a rotating machine part, or the force of the wind on a stationary object. ■ the effect of the wind in deflecting a missile such as a bullet.

Win·daus /ˈvinˌdous/, Adolf (1876–1959), German organic chemist. He did pioneering work on the chemistry and structure of steroids and their derivatives, notably cholesterol. He also investigated the D vitamins and vitamin B_1 and discovered histamine. Nobel Prize for Chemistry (1928).

wind·bag /ˈwindˌbag/ ▶ **n.** informal, derogatory a person who talks at length but says little of value.
– DERIVATIVES **wind·bag·ger·y** /-ərē/ **n.**

wind band /wind/ ▶ **n.** a group of musicians playing mainly woodwind instruments.

wind·blown /ˈwindblōn/ ▶ **adj.** carried or driven by the wind: *windblown sand | windblown pollution.* ■ exposed to or affected by the wind: *the coastline is rugged and windblown | her windblown hair.*

wind·borne ▶ **adj.** carried by the wind: *wind-borne paper bags and candy wrappers caught on a fence.*

wind·bound /ˈwindˌbound/ ▶ **adj.** (of a sailing ship) unable to sail because of extreme or contrary winds.

wind·break /ˈwindˌbrāk/ ▶ **n.** a thing, such as a row of trees or a fence, wall, or screen, that provides shelter or protection from the wind.

wind·break·er /ˈwindˌbrākər/ ▶ **n.** trademark a wind-resistant jacket with a close-fitting neck, waistband, and cuffs.

wind·burn /ˈwindˌbərn/ ▶ **n.** reddening and soreness of the skin caused by prolonged exposure to the wind.
– DERIVATIVES **wind·burned** (also chiefly Brit. **windburnt**) **adj.**

Wind Cave Na·tion·al Park /wind/ a preserve in the Black Hills of South Dakota, noted for its caves and wildlife.

wind·chill /ˈwin(d)ˌCHil/ (also **windchill factor** or **chill factor**) ▶ **n.** a quantity expressing the effective lowering of the air temperature caused by the wind, esp. as affecting the rate of heat loss from an object or human body or as perceived by an exposed person.

wind chimes /wind/ ▶ **plural n.** a decorative arrangement of small pieces of glass, metal, or shell suspended from a frame, typically hung near a door or window so as make a tinkling sound in the breeze.

wind·er /ˈwīndər/ ▶ **n.** a device or mechanism used to wind something, esp. something such as a watch or clock or the film in a camera.

Win·der·mere /ˈwində(r)ˌmi(ə)r/ a lake in northwestern England, in the southeastern part of the Lake District. About 10 miles (17 km) in length, it is the largest lake in England.

wind·fall /ˈwindˌfôl/ ▶ **n.** an apple or other fruit blown down from a tree or bush by the wind. ■ a piece of unexpected good fortune, typically one that involves receiving a large amount of money: [as modifier] *windfall profits.*

wind·fall prof·its tax (also **windfall tax**) ▶ **n.** a tax levied on an unforeseen or unexpectedly large profit, esp. one regarded to be excessive or unfairly obtained.

wind farm /wind/ ▶ **n.** an area of land with a group of energy-producing windmills or wind turbines.

wind·flow·er /ˈwindˌflou(-ə)r/ ▶ **n.** an anemone.

wind·gall /ˈwindˌgôl/ ▶ **n.** a small painless swelling just above the fetlock of a horse, caused by inflammation of the tendon sheath.

wind gap /wind/ ▶ **n.** a valley cut through a ridge by erosion by a river that no longer follows a course through the valley.

wind gauge /wind/ ▶ **n.** an anemometer. ■ an apparatus attached to the sights of a gun enabling allowance to be made for the wind in shooting.

wind harp /wind/ ▶ **n.** another term for **AEOLIAN HARP**.

Wind·hoek /ˈvintˌho͝ok, ˈwind-/ the capital of Namibia, in the center of the country; pop. 314,000 (est. 2007).

wind·hov·er /ˈwindˌhəvər/ ▶ **n.** Brit. dialect a kestrel.

win·di·go /ˈwindiˌgō/ (also **wendigo**) ▶ **n.** (pl. **windigos** or **windigoes**) (in the folklore of some northern Algonquian peoples) a cannibalistic giant; a person who has been transformed into a monster by the consumption of human flesh.
– ORIGIN from Ojibwa.

wind·ing /ˈwīndiNG/ ▶ **n.** a twisting movement or course: *the windings of the stream.* ■ an electrical conductor that is wound around a magnetic material, esp. one encircling part of the stator or rotor of an electric motor or generator or forming part of a transformer. ■ a thing that winds or is wound around something.
▶ **adj.** following a twisting or spiral course: *our bedroom was at the top of a winding staircase.*

wind·ing sheet /ˈwīndiNG/ ▶ **n.** a sheet in which a corpse is wrapped for burial; a shroud.

wind in·stru·ment /wind/ ▶ **n.** a musical instrument in which sound is produced by the vibration of air, typically by the player blowing into the instrument. ■ a woodwind instrument as distinct from a brass instrument.

wind·jam·mer /ˈwindˌjamər/ ▶ **n.** historical a merchant sailing ship.

wind·lass /ˈwindləs/ ▶ **n.** a type of winch used esp. on ships to hoist anchors and haul on mooring lines and, esp. formerly, to lower buckets into and hoist them up from wells.
▶ **v.** [with obj.] haul or lift (something) with a windlass.
– ORIGIN late Middle English: probably an alteration of obsolete *windas*, via Anglo-Norman French from Old Norse *vindáss*, literally 'winding pole.'

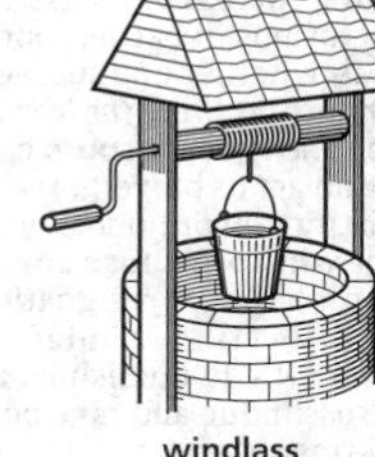

windlass

wind load /wind/ (also **wind loading**) ▶ **n.** Engineering the force on a structure arising from the impact of wind on it.

wind ma·chine /wind/ ▶ **n.** a machine used in the theater or in filmmaking for producing a blast of air or imitating the sound of wind. ■ a wind-driven turbine for producing electricity.

wind·mill /ˈwindˌmil/ ▶ **n.** a building with sails or vanes that turn in the wind and generate power to grind grain into flour. ■ a similar structure used to generate electricity or draw water. ■ Brit. a pinwheel.
▶ **v.** (with reference to a person's arms) move or be moved around in a circle in a manner suggestive of the rotating sails or vanes of a windmill. ■ [no obj.] (of the propeller or rotor of an aircraft, or the aircraft itself) spin unpowered.
– PHRASES **tilt at windmills** see **TILT**.

windmill

win·dow /ˈwindō/ ▶ **n. 1** an opening in the wall or roof of a building or vehicle that is fitted with glass or other transparent material in a frame to admit light or air and allow people to see out. ■ a pane of glass filling such an opening: *thieves smashed a window and took $600.* ■ an opening in a wall or screen through which customers are served in a bank, ticket office, or similar building. ■ a space on the inside of a store's window where goods are displayed for sale: *I prefer the red dress that's in the window* | [as modifier] *beautiful window displays.*
2 a thing resembling such an opening in form or function, in particular: ■ a transparent panel on an envelope to show an address. ■ Computing a framed area on a display screen for viewing information. ■ (**window on/into/to**) a means of observing and learning about: *television is a window on the world.* ■ Physics a range of electromagnetic wavelengths for which a medium (esp. the atmosphere) is transparent.
3 an interval or opportunity for action: *February 15 to March 15 should be the final window for new offers.* ■ an interval during which atmospheric and astronomical circumstances are suitable for the launch of a spacecraft.
4 strips of metal foil or metal filings dispersed in the air to obstruct radar detection. [military code word.]
– PHRASES **go out the window** informal (of a plan or pattern or behavior) no longer exist; disappear. **window of opportunity** a favorable opportunity for doing something that must be seized immediately if it is not to be missed. **window of vulnerability** an opportunity to attack something that is at risk (esp. as a Cold War claim that America's land-based missiles were easy targets for a Soviet first strike). **windows of the soul** organs of sense, esp. the eyes.
– DERIVATIVES **win·dow·less adj.** (sense 1).
– ORIGIN Middle English: from Old Norse *vindauga*, from *vindr* 'wind' + *auga* 'eye.'

win·dow box ▶ **n.** a long narrow box in which flowers and other plants are grown, placed on an outside windowsill.

win·dow clean·er ▶ **n.** a substance used for cleaning windows. ■ a person employed to clean windows; a window washer.

win·dow dress·ing ▶ **n.** the arrangement of an attractive display in a shop window. ■ an adroit but superficial or actually misleading presentation of something, designed to create a favorable impression: *the government's effort has amounted to little more than window dressing.*

win·dowed /ˈwindōd/ ▶ **adj. 1** having a window or windows for admitting light or air: [in combination] *a row of bay-windowed houses.*
2 Computing having or using framed areas on a display screen for viewing information.

win·dow frame ▶ **n.** a supporting frame for the glass of a window.

win·dow·ing /ˈwindō-iNG/ ▶ **n.** Computing the use of windows for the simultaneous display of more than one item on a screen.

win·dow ledge ▶ **n.** another term for **WINDOWSILL**.

win·dow·pane /ˈwindōˌpān/ ▶ **n. 1** a pane of glass in a window.
2 a broad flatfish with numerous dark spots, found in the western Atlantic. Also called **SAND DAB**. ● *Scophthalmus aquosus*, family Scophthalmidae (or Bothidae).

Win·dow Rock a community in northeastern Arizona, capital of the Navajo reservation, named for a limestone formation; pop. 3,059 (2000).

Win·dows /ˈwindōz/ ▶ **plural n.** [treated as sing.] trademark a computer operating system with a graphical user interface.

win·dow seat ▶ **n.** a seat below a window, esp. one in a bay or alcove. ■ a seat next to a window in an aircraft, train, or other vehicle.

win·dow-shop ▶ **v.** [no obj.] look at the goods displayed in shop windows, esp. without intending to buy anything: (as noun **window-shopping**) *window-shopping is the favorite pastime of all New Yorkers.*
– DERIVATIVES **win·dow-shop·per n.**

win·dow·sill /ˈwindōˌsil/ (also **window sill**) ▶ **n.** a ledge or sill forming the bottom part of a window.

win·dow treat·ment ▶ **n.** interior decoration for a window or window frame.

win·dow wash·er ▶ **n.** a person employed to clean windows.

wind·pack /ˈwindˌpak/ ▶ **n.** snow that has been compacted by the wind.

wind·pipe /ˈwindˌpīp/ ▶ **n.** the air passage from the throat to the lungs; the trachea.

wind pow·er ▶ **n.** power obtained by harnessing the energy of the wind.

Wind Riv·er Range /wind/ a range of the Rocky Mountains in western Wyoming that rises to 13,804 feet (4,207 m) at Gannett Peak, the highest in the state.

wind rose /wind/ ▶ **n.** a diagram showing the relative frequency of wind directions at a place.

wind·row /ˈwindˌrō/ ▶ **n.** a long line of raked hay or sheaves of grain laid out to dry in the wind. ■ a long line of material heaped up by the wind or by a machine.

wind·sail /ˈwindˌsāl/ ▶ **n.** historical a long wide tube or funnel of sailcloth used to convey air to the lower parts of a ship.

wind scor·pi·on /wind/ ▶ **n.** another term for **SUN SPIDER**.

wind·screen /ˈwindˌskrēn/ ▶ **n.** British term for **WINDSHIELD**.

wind shear /wind/ ▶ **n.** variation in wind velocity occurring along a direction at right angles to the wind's direction and tending to exert a turning force.

wind·shield /ˈwin(d),SHēld/ ▶ **n.** a window at the front of the passenger compartment of a motor vehicle.

wind·shield wip·er (Brit. **windscreen wiper**) ▶ **n.** a motor-driven device for keeping a windshield clear of rain, typically one with a rubber blade on an arm that moves in an arc.

wind·slab /ˈwind,slab/ ▶ **n.** a thick crust formed on the surface of soft snow by the wind, of a kind liable to slip and create an avalanche.

wind·sock /ˈwind,säk/ ▶ **n.** a light, flexible cylinder or cone mounted on a mast to show the direction and strength of the wind, esp. at an airfield.

Wind·sor[1] /ˈwinzər/ **1** a town in southern England, on the Thames River, opposite Eton; pop. 31,800 (est. 2009).
2 an industrial city and port in Ontario, southern Canada, on Lake Ontario, opposite the US city of Detroit; pop. 216,473 (2006).
3 /ˈwin(d)zər/ a commercial and residential town in north central Connecticut, north of Hartford; pop. 28,851 (est. 2008).

Wind·sor[2] the name of the British royal family since 1917. Previously Saxe-Coburg-Gotha, it was changed in response to anti-German feeling in World War I.

Wind·sor, Duke of the title conferred on Britain's Edward VIII upon his abdication in 1936.

Wind·sor Cas·tle a royal residence at Windsor, founded by William the Conqueror on the site of an earlier fortress and extended by his successors, particularly Edward III. The castle was severely damaged by fire in 1992.

Wind·sor chair ▶ **n.** a wooden dining chair with a semicircular back supported by upright rods.

Windsor chair

Wind·sor knot ▶ **n.** a large, loose triangular knot in a necktie, produced by making extra turns when tying.

Wind·sor tie ▶ **n.** dated a wide silk bias-cut necktie, tied in a loose double knot.

wind sprint /wind/ ▶ **n.** Sports a form of exercise consisting of repeated alternation between a walk or slow run and a faster run.

wind·storm /ˈwind,stôrm/ ▶ **n.** a storm with very strong wind but little or no rain or snow; a gale.

wind-suck·ing /wind/ ▶ **n.** (in a horse) habitual behavior involving repeated arching of the neck and sucking in and swallowing air, often accompanied by a grunting sound.
– DERIVATIVES **wind-suck·er** **n.**

wind·surf·er /ˈwind,sərfər/ ▶ **n.** a person who takes part in windsurfing. ■ trademark a sailboard.

wind·surf·ing /ˈwind,sərfiNG/ ▶ **n.** the sport or pastime of riding on water on a sailboard.
– DERIVATIVES **wind·surf** **v.**

wind·swept /ˈwind,swept/ ▶ **adj.** **1** (of a place) exposed to strong winds: *the windswept moors.*
2 (of a person or their appearance) affected, shaped, or mussed by exposure to the wind: *his windswept hair.*

wind tun·nel /wind/ ▶ **n.** a tunnel-like apparatus for producing an airstream of known velocity past models of aircraft, buildings, etc., in order to investigate flow or the effect of wind on the full-size object. ■ an open space through which strong winds are channeled by surrounding tall buildings.

wind tur·bine /wind/ ▶ **n.** a turbine having a large vaned wheel rotated by the wind to generate electricity.

wind·up /ˈwīnd,əp/ ▶ **n.** **1** an act of concluding or finishing something: *the windup of the convention.*
2 Baseball the motions of a pitcher immediately before delivering the ball, in which they take a step back, lift the hands over the head, and step forward.
3 Brit. informal an attempt to tease or irritate someone.
▶ **adj.** (of a toy or other device) functioning by means of winding a key or handle: *a windup clock.*

wind·ward /ˈwindwərd/ ▶ **adj. & adv.** facing the wind or on the side facing the wind: [as adj.] *the windward side of the boat.* Contrasted with LEEWARD.
▶ **n.** the side or direction from which the wind is blowing: *the ships drifted west, leaving the island quite a distance to windward.*
– PHRASES **to windward of** dated in an advantageous position in relation to: *I happen to have got to windward of the young woman.*

Wind·ward Is·lands **1** a group of islands in the eastern Caribbean Sea that constitute the southern part of the Lesser Antilles. They include Martinique, Dominica, St. Lucia, Barbados, St. Vincent and the Grenadines, and Grenada. Their name refers to their position further upwind, in terms of the prevailing southeastern winds, than the Leeward Islands.
2 an island group in the eastern Society Islands in French Polynesia that include Moorea and Tahiti. French name ILES DU VENT.

Wind·ward Pas·sage an ocean channel between Cuba on the west and Haiti on the east that connects the Caribbean Sea with the Atlantic Ocean.

wind·y[1] /ˈwindē/ ▶ **adj.** (**windier, windiest**) **1** (of weather, a period of time, or a place) marked by or exposed to strong winds: *a very windy day.*
2 Brit. suffering from, marked by, or causing an accumulation of gas in the alimentary canal.
■ informal using or expressed in many words that sound impressive but mean little: *windy speeches.*
– PHRASES **the Windy City** a nickname for Chicago.
– DERIVATIVES **wind·i·ly** /-ələ/ **adv.**, **wind·i·ness** **n.**
– ORIGIN Old English *windig* (see WIND[1], -Y[1]).

wind·y[2] /ˈwīndē/ ▶ **adj.** (of a road or river) following a curving or twisting course.

wine /wīn/ ▶ **n.** an alcoholic drink made from fermented grape juice: *he opened a bottle of red wine | the regional foods and wines of France.* ■ [with modifier] an alcoholic drink made from the fermented juice of specified other fruits or plants: *a glass of dandelion wine.* ■ short for WINE RED.
▶ **v.** [with obj.] (**wine and dine someone**) entertain someone by offering them drinks or a meal: *members of Congress have been lavishly wined and dined by lobbyists for years.* ■ [no obj.] (of a person) take part in such entertainment: *we wined and dined with Eddie's and Bernie's friends.*
– PHRASES **good wine needs no bush** proverb there's no need to advertise or boast about something of good quality as people will always discover its merits. [a *bush* was an innkeeper's sign, originally depicting a bunch of ivy used (in place of grape leaves) to show that the establishment sold wine.]
– DERIVATIVES **wine·y** (also **winy**) **adj.**
– ORIGIN Old English *wīn*, of Germanic origin; related to Dutch *wijn*, German *Wein*, based on Latin *vinum*.

wine bar ▶ **n.** a bar or small restaurant where wine is the main drink available.

wine·ber·ry /ˈwīn,berē/ ▶ **n.** (pl. **wineberries**) a bristly deciduous shrub native to China and Japan, producing scarlet berries used in cooking. ● *Rubus phoenicolasius*, family Rosaceae. ■ the fruit of this bush.

wine·bib·ber /ˈwīn,bibər/ ▶ **n.** archaic or literary a habitual drinker of alcohol.
– DERIVATIVES **wine·bib·bing** /-,bibiNG/ **n. & adj.**

wine bot·tle ▶ **n.** a glass bottle for wine, the standard size holding 750 ml or 26 ²/₃ fl. oz.

wine cel·lar ▶ **n.** a cellar in which wine is stored. ■ a stock of wine.

wine cool·er ▶ **n.** a container for chilling a bottle of wine. ■ a bottled drink made from wine, fruit juice, and carbonated water.

wine·glass /ˈwīn,glas/ ▶ **n.** a glass with a stem and foot, used for drinking wine.
– DERIVATIVES **wine·glass·ful** /ˈwīnglas,fo͝ol/ **n.** (pl. **wineglassfuls**).

wine·grow·er /ˈwīn,grōər/ ▶ **n.** a cultivator of grapes for wine.

wine list ▶ **n.** a list of the wines available in a restaurant.

wine·mak·er /ˈwīn,mākər/ ▶ **n.** a producer of wine; a winegrower.

wine·mak·ing /ˈwīn,mākiNG/ ▶ **n.** the production of wine.

wine·press /ˈwīn,pres/ ▶ **n.** a press in which grapes are squeezed in making wine.

wine red ▶ **n.** a dark red color like that of red wine.

win·er·y /ˈwīnərē/ ▶ **n.** (pl. **wineries**) an establishment where wine is made.

Wine·sap /ˈwīn,sap/ ▶ **n.** a large red apple, used for cooking and as a dessert apple.

wine·skin /ˈwīn,skin/ ▶ **n.** an animal skin sewn up and used to hold wine.

wine stew·ard ▶ **n.** a waiter responsible for serving wine.

wine tast·ing ▶ **n.** an event at which people taste and compare a number of wines. ■ the action of judging the quality of wine by tasting it.
– DERIVATIVES **wine tast·er** **n.**

wine vin·e·gar ▶ **n.** vinegar made from wine rather than malt.

Win·frey /ˈwinfrē/, Oprah (1954–), US television talk-show host, actress, and publisher. In 1984, she started as a talk-show host on *A.M. Chicago*, which evolved into the nationally televised *Oprah Winfrey Show* in 1986. She also played Sofia in the movie *The Color Purple* (1985) and began publishing *O* magazine in 2000.

Oprah Winfrey

wing /wiNG/ ▶ **n.** **1** any of a number of specialized paired appendages that enable some animals to fly, in particular: ■ (in a bird) a modified forelimb that bears large feathers. ■ (in a bat or pterosaur) a modified forelimb with skin stretched between or behind the fingers. ■ (in most insects) each of two or four flat extensions of the thoracic cuticle, either transparent or covered in scales. ■ the meat on the wing bone of a bird used as food. ■ (usu. **wings**) used with reference to ease and swiftness of movement: *time flies by on wings.*
2 a rigid horizontal structure that projects from both sides of an aircraft and supports it in the air. ■ (**wings**) a pilot's certificate of ability to fly a plane, indicated by a badge representing a pair of wings: *Michael earned his wings as a commercial pilot.*
3 a part that projects, in particular: ■ Brit. a raised part of the body of a car or other vehicle above the wheel. ■ [usu. with modifier] a part of a large building, esp. one that projects from the main part: *the maternity wing at South Cleveland Hospital.* ■ Anatomy a lateral part or projection of an organ or structure. ■ Botany a thin membranous appendage of a fruit or seed that is dispersed by the wind.
4 a group within a political party or other organization that holds particular views or has a particular function: *Sinn Fein, the political wing of the IRA.*
5 a side area, or a person or activity associated with that area, in particular: ■ (**the wings**) the sides of a theater stage out of view of the audience. ■ (in soccer, rugby, and other games) the part of the field close to the sidelines. ■ (in soccer, ice hockey, and other games) an attacking player who plays mostly forward close to one side of the field or rink. ■ a flank of a battle array.
6 an air force unit of several squadrons or groups.
▶ **v.** **1** [no obj.] travel on wings or by aircraft; fly: *a bird came winging around the corner.* ■ move, travel, or be sent quickly, as if flying: *the prize will be winging its way to you soon.* ■ [with obj.] send or convey (something) quickly, as if by air: *just jot down the title on a postcard and wing it to us.* ■ [with obj.] archaic enable (someone or something) to fly or move rapidly: *the convent was at some distance, but fear would wing her steps.*
2 [with obj.] shoot (a bird) in the wing, so as to prevent flight without causing death: *one bird was winged for every bird killed.* ■ wound (someone) superficially, esp. in the arm or shoulder.
3 (**wing it**) informal speak or act without preparation; improvise: *a little boning up puts you ahead of the job seekers who try to wing it.* [from theatrical slang, originally meaning 'to play a role without properly knowing the text' (either by relying on a prompter in the wings or by studying the part in the wings between scenes).]
– PHRASES **in the wings** ready to do something or to be used at the appropriate time: *there are no obvious successors waiting in the wings.* **on the wing** (of a bird) in flight. **on a wing and a prayer** with only the slightest chance of success. **spread** (or **stretch** or **try**) **one's wings** extend one's activities and interests or start new ones. **take wing** (of a bird, insect, or other winged creature) fly away. **under one's wing** in or into one's protective care.

–DERIVATIVES **wing·less** adj., **wing·like** /-ˌlīk/ adj.
–ORIGIN Middle English (originally in the plural): from Old Norse *vængir*, plural of *vængr*.

wing·back ▶ n. **1** Football an offensive back who lines up outside an end.
2 Soccer a player who plays in a wide position on the field, taking part both in attack and defense.

wing·beat /ˈwiNGˌbēt/ ▶ n. one complete set of motions of a wing in flying.

wing case ▶ n. each of a pair of modified toughened forewings that cover the functional wings in certain insects, esp. an elytron of a beetle.

wing chair ▶ n. a high-backed armchair with side pieces projecting from the back, originally in order to protect the sitter from drafts.

wing chair

wing col·lar ▶ n. a high stiff shirt collar with turned-down corners.

wing cov·ert ▶ n. (in a bird's wing) each of the smaller feathers covering the bases of the flight feathers.

wing dam ▶ n. a dam or barrier built into a stream to deflect the current.

wing·ding /ˈwiNGˌdiNG/ ▶ n. informal a lively event or party.
–ORIGIN 1920s (in the sense 'spasm, seizure,' esp. one associated with drug-taking): of unknown origin.

winged /wiNGd/ ▶ adj. **1** having wings for flight: *the earliest winged insects.*
2 having one or more lateral parts, appendages, or projections: *those eyeglasses with the winged frames were very popular.*

winged bean ▶ n. a tropical Asian pea plant that has four-sided pods with longitudinal flanges. The entire pod and the roots are edible and are noted for their high protein content. ● *Psophocarpus tetragonolobus*, family Leguminosae.

winged elm ▶ n. a North American elm that has extremely short leafstalks and flat corky projections on its branchlets. ● *Ulmus alata*, family Ulmaceae.

Winged Vic·to·ry ▶ n. a winged statue of Nike, the Greek goddess of victory, esp. the Nike of Samothrace (*c.*200 BC) preserved in the Louvre in Paris.

winged words ▶ plural n. literary highly apposite or significant words.

wing·er /ˈwiNGər/ ▶ n. **1** an attacking player on the wing in soccer, hockey, and other sports.
2 [in combination] a member of a specified political wing: *a left-winger.*

wing for·ward ▶ n. Soccer see WING (sense 5 of the noun).

wing·let /ˈwiNGlit/ ▶ n. a little wing. ■ a vertical projection on the tip of an aircraft wing for reducing drag.

wing·man /ˈwiNGˌmən/ ▶ n. (pl. **wingmen**) **1** a pilot whose aircraft is positioned behind and outside the leading aircraft in a formation. ■ a man who helps or supports another man; a friend or close associate: *I thought he might need a wingman—he was quite tired and emotional.*
2 another term for WINGER (sense 1).

wing nut ▶ n. **1** (also **wingnut**) a nut with a pair of projections for the fingers to screw it on.
2 an Asian tree of the walnut family, with a deeply fissured trunk, compound leaves, and characteristic broad-winged nutlets. ● Genus *Pterocarya*, family Juglandaceae.
3 (**wingnut**) informal a mad or crazy person: *some wingnut down in Finance.* ■ a person with extreme, typically right-wing, views: *McCarthyite wingnuts.*

wing·o·ver /ˈwiNGˌōvər/ ▶ n. a maneuver in which an aircraft turns at the top of a steep climb and flies back along its original path.

wing oys·ter ▶ n. an edible marine bivalve mollusk with a fragile flattened shell, the hinge of which bears winglike projections. ● Family Pteridae: *Pteria* and other genera.

W

wing sail ▶ n. a rigid or semirigid structure similar to an aircraft wing fixed vertically on a boat to provide thrust from the action of the wind.

wing shoot·ing ▶ n. the shooting of birds in flight.

wing·span /ˈwiNGˌspan/ (also **wingspread** /-ˌspred/) ▶ n. the maximum extent across the wings of an aircraft, bird, or other flying animal, measured from tip to tip.

wing·stroke /ˈwiNGˌstrōk/ ▶ n. another term for WINGBEAT.

wing tip (also **wingtip**) ▶ n. **1** the tip of the wing of an aircraft, bird, or other animal.
2 a shoe with a toe cap having a backward extending point and curving sides, resembling the shape of a wing.

wing tip 2

wing walk·ing ▶ n. acrobatic stunts performed on the wings of an airborne aircraft as a public entertainment.

wink /wiNGk/ ▶ v. [no obj.] close and open one eye quickly, typically to indicate that something is a joke or a secret or as a signal of affection or greeting: *he winked at Nicole as he passed.* ■ (**wink at**) pretend not to notice (something bad or illegal): *the authorities winked at their illegal trade.* ■ (of a bright object or a light) shine or flash intermittently.
▶ n. an act of closing and opening one eye quickly, typically as a signal: *Barney gave him a knowing wink.*
–PHRASES **as easy as winking** informal very easy or easily. **in the wink of an eye** (or **in a wink**) very quickly. **not sleep** (or **get**) **a wink** (or **not get a wink of sleep**) not sleep at all.
–ORIGIN Old English *wincian* 'close the eyes,' of Germanic origin; related to German *winken* 'to wave,' also to WINCE[1].

win·kle /ˈwiNGkəl/ ▶ n. a small herbivorous shore-dwelling mollusk with a spiral shell. Also called PERIWINKLE[2]. ● Family Littorinidae, class Gastropoda: many genera and species, including the common and edible *Littorina littorea.*
▶ v. [with obj.] (**winkle something out**) chiefly Brit. extract or obtain something with difficulty: *I swore I wasn't going to tell her, but she winkled it all out of me.*
–DERIVATIVES **win·kler** /ˈwiNGk(ə)lər/ n.
–ORIGIN late 16th cent.: shortening of PERIWINKLE[2].

win·kle-pick·er ▶ n. Brit. informal a shoe with a long pointed toe, popular in the 1950s.

Win·ne·ba·go /ˌwinəˈbāgō/ ▶ n. (pl. **same** or **Winnebagos**) **1** a member of an American Indian people formerly living in eastern Wisconsin and now mainly in southern Wisconsin and Nebraska.
2 the Siouan language of this people.
3 (pl. **Winnebagos**) trademark a motor vehicle with living accommodations used when traveling long distances or camping.
▶ adj. of or relating to the Winnebago people or their language.
–ORIGIN Algonquian, literally 'person of the dirty water,' referring to the muddy Fox River.

Win·ne·ba·go, Lake /ˌwinəˈbāgō/ the largest lake in Wisconsin, in the east central part of the state.

win·ner /ˈwinər/ ▶ n. a person or thing that wins something: *a Nobel Prize winner.* ■ a goal or shot that wins a winner or point. ■ Bridge a card that can be relied on to win a trick. ■ informal a thing that is a success or is likely to be successful: *the changes failed to make the soap opera a winner.*

win·ner's cir·cle ▶ n. a small circular area or enclosure at a racetrack where the winning horse and jockey are brought to receive their awards and have photographs taken.

win·ning /ˈwiniNG/ ▶ adj. **1** [attrib.] gaining, resulting in, or relating to victory in a contest or competition: *a winning streak.*
2 attractive; endearing: *a winning smile.*
▶ n. **1** (**winnings**) money won, esp. by gambling: *he went to collect his winnings.*
2 Mining a shaft or pit together with the apparatus for extracting coal or other minerals.
–DERIVATIVES **win·ning·ly** adv.

win·ning·est /ˈwiniNGist/ ▶ adj. informal having achieved the most success in competition: *the winningest coach in pro-football history.*

win·ning post ▶ n. a post marking the end of a race.

Win·ni·peg /ˈwinəˌpeg/ a city in southern central Canada, the capital of the province of Manitoba, at the confluence of the Assiniboine and Red rivers, south of Lake Winnipeg; pop. 633,451 (2006).

Win·ni·peg, Lake a large lake in central Canada, in southern central Manitoba, north of the city of Winnipeg. Fed by the Saskatchewan, Winnipeg, and Red rivers from the east and south, the lake is drained by the Nelson River, which flows northeast to Hudson Bay.

Win·ni·pe·sau·kee, Lake /ˌwinəpəˈsôkē, -ˈsäkē/ the largest lake in New Hampshire, a resort center in the east central part of the state.

win·now /ˈwinō/ ▶ v. **1** [with obj.] blow a current of air through (grain) in order to remove the chaff. ■ remove (chaff) from grain: *women winnow the chaff from piles of unhusked rice.* ■ remove (people or things) from a group until only the best ones are left: *the contenders had been winnowed to five | guidelines that would help winnow out those not fit to be soldiers.* ■ find or identify (a valuable or useful part of something): *amidst this welter of confusing signals, it's difficult to winnow out the truth.*
2 [no obj.] literary (of the wind) blow: *the autumn wind winnowing its way through the grass.* ■ [with obj.] (of a bird) fan (the air) with wings.
–DERIVATIVES **win·now·er** n.
–ORIGIN Old English *windwian*, from *wind* (see WIND[1]).

win·o /ˈwīnō/ ▶ n. (pl. **winos**) informal a person who drinks excessive amounts of cheap wine or other alcohol, esp. one who is homeless.

win·some /ˈwinsəm/ ▶ adj. attractive or appealing in appearance or character: *a winsome smile.*
–DERIVATIVES **win·some·ly** adv., **win·some·ness** n.
–ORIGIN Old English *wynsum*, from *wyn* 'joy' + -SOME[1].

Win·ston-Sa·lem /ˌwinstən ˈsāləm/ an industrial and commercial city in north central North Carolina, a tobacco-processing center; pop. 217,600 (est. 2008).

win·ter /ˈwintər/ ▶ n. the coldest season of the year, in the northern hemisphere from December to February and in the southern hemisphere from June to August: *the tree has a good crop of berries in winter* | [as modifier] *the winter months.* ■ Astronomy the period from the winter solstice to the vernal equinox. ■ (**winters**) literary years: *he seemed a hundred winters old.*
▶ adj. [attrib.] (of fruit and vegetables) ripening late in the growing season and suitable for storage over the winter: *a winter apple.* ■ (of wheat or other crops) sown in autumn for harvesting the following year.
▶ v. [no obj.] (esp. of a bird) spend the winter in a particular place: *birds wintering in the Caribbean.* ■ [with obj.] keep or feed (plants or cattle) during winter.
–DERIVATIVES **win·ter·er** n., **win·ter·less** adj., **win·ter·ly** adj.
–ORIGIN Old English, of Germanic origin; related to Dutch *winter* and German *Winter*, probably also to WET.

win·ter ac·o·nite ▶ n. see ACONITE.

win·ter·ber·ry /ˈwintərˌberē/ (also **winterberry holly**) ▶ n. (pl. **winterberries**) a North American holly with toothed, nonprickly leaves and berries that persist through the winter. ● Genus *Ilex*, family Aquifoliaceae: several species, in particular the **common winterberry** (*I. verticillata*) and the **smooth winterberry** (*I. laevigata*).

win·ter·bourne /ˈwintərˌbôrn/ ▶ n. Brit. a stream, typically on chalk or limestone, that flows only after wet weather.
–ORIGIN Old English *winterburna* (see WINTER, BURN[2]).

win·ter cher·ry ▶ n. a plant of the nightshade family, with cherrylike fruit that ripens in winter. ● Several species in the family Solanaceae, in particular *Physalis alkekengi*, the Chinese lantern plant.

win·ter creep·er ▶ n. an evergreen clinging vine that is native to China and cultivated elsewhere as an ornamental ground cover. It has escaped cultivation and is regarded as an ecological threat in some eastern US states. ● *Euonymus fortunei*, family Celastraceae.

win·ter cress ▶ n. a bitter-tasting cress of north temperate regions. ● Genus *Barbarea*, family Brassicaceae: several species, in particular *B. vulgaris.*

win·ter cur·rant ▶ n. another term for RED-FLOWERING CURRANT (see FLOWERING CURRANT).

win·ter floun·der ▶ n. a common flatfish of the western Atlantic, having cryptic gray-brown coloration and popular as food in winter in North America. ● *Pseudopleuronectes americanus*, family Pleuronectidae.

win·ter gar·den ▶ n. a garden of plants, such as evergreens, that flourish in winter. ■ a conservatory in which flowers and other plants are grown in winter.

win·ter·green /ˈwintərˌgrēn/ ▶ n. **1** a North American plant from which a pungent oil is obtained, in particular the checkerberry or related shrubs. ■ (also **oil of wintergreen**) a pungent oil containing methyl salicylate, now obtained chiefly from the sweet birch or made synthetically, used medicinally and as a flavoring.
2 a low-growing plant of acid soils in north temperate regions, with spikes of white bell-shaped flowers. ● *Chimaphila*, *Pyrola* and other genera,

family Pyrolaceae (the wintergreen family): several species, including the **spotted wintergreen** (*C. maculata*).
– ORIGIN mid 16th cent.: the plants so named because of remaining green in winter, suggested by Dutch *wintergroen*, German *Wintergrün*.

win·ter·ize /ˈwintəˌrīz/ ▶ **v.** [with obj.] (usu. **be winterized**) adapt or prepare (something, esp. a house or an automobile) for use in cold weather: *a waterfront cottage that Dixon had winterized.*
– DERIVATIVES **win·ter·i·za·tion** /ˌwintəriˈzāSHən/ **n.**

win·ter jas·mine ▶ **n.** a yellow-flowered Chinese jasmine that blooms during the winter. ● *Jasminum nudiflorum*, family Oleaceae.

win·ter mel·on ▶ **n.** a variety of muskmelon with a sweet, edible flesh that requires a long growing season and ripens in late autumn, making it available in many supermarkets during the winter.

win·ter moth ▶ **n.** a moth that emerges in the winter, the female of which has only vestigial wings. It was formerly a major pest of fruit trees. ● Several species in the family Geometridae.

Win·ter O·lym·pics an international contest of winter sports held every four years at a two-year interval from the Summer Games. They have been held separately from the main games since 1924.

Win·ter Pal·ace the former Russian imperial residence in St. Petersburg, stormed in the Revolution of 1917 and later used as a museum and art gallery.

win·ter quar·ters ▶ **plural n.** accommodations for the winter, esp. for soldiers.

win·ter sleep ▶ **n.** hibernation.

win·ter sol·stice ▶ **n.** the solstice that marks the onset of winter, at the time of the shortest day, about December 22 in the northern hemisphere and June 21 in the southern hemisphere. ■ Astronomy the solstice in December.

win·ter sports ▶ **plural n.** sports performed on snow or ice, such as skiing and ice skating.

win·ter squash ▶ **n.** a squash that has a hard rind and may be stored. ● Cultivars of *Cucurbita moschata* and *C. maxima*, family Cucurbitaceae.

win·ter·sweet /ˈwintərˌswēt/ ▶ **n.** a deciduous Chinese shrub that produces heavily scented yellow flowers in winter before the leaves appear, grown in North America as an ornamental. ● *Chimonanthus praecox*, family Calycanthaceae.

win·ter·tide /ˈwintərˌtīd/ ▶ **n.** literary term for **WINTERTIME**.

win·ter·time /ˈwintərˌtīm/ ▶ **n.** the season or period of winter.

Win·throp[1] /ˈwinTHrəp/, John (1588–1649), American colonial leader; born in England. He was the first governor 1630–49 of the Massachusetts Bay Colony. His son **John Winthrop, Jr.**, served as the governor of Connecticut 1657, 1659–76.

Win·throp[2], John (1714–79), American astronomer and physicist. He was the first American to practice rigorous experimental science, giving laboratory demonstrations of electricity in 1746 and predicting the return of Halley's Comet in 1759.

win·try /ˈwintrē/ (also **wintery** /ˈwint(ə)rē/) ▶ **adj.** (**wintrier**, **wintriest**) characteristic of winter, esp. in feeling or looking very cold and bleak: *a wintry landscape* | figurative *his eyes were decidedly wintry.*
– DERIVATIVES **win·tri·ly** /-trəlē/ **adv.**, **win·tri·ness** **n.**
– ORIGIN Old English *wintrig* (see **WINTER**, **-Y**[1]).

win·try mix ▶ **n.** variable precipitation consisting of rain, freezing rain, sleet, or snow: *the wintry mix slowed down drivers crossing the Blue Ridge Mountains.*

win-win ▶ **adj.** [attrib.] of or denoting a situation in which each party benefits in some way: *we are aiming for a win-win situation.*

WIP ▶ **abbr.** work in progress (chiefly in business and financial contexts).

wipe /wīp/ ▶ **v.** [with obj.] **1** clean or dry (something) by rubbing its surface with a cloth, a piece of paper, or one's hand: *Paul wiped his face with a handkerchief* | *he wiped down the kitchen wall.* ■ remove (dirt or moisture) from something by rubbing its surface with a cloth, a piece of paper, or one's hand: *she wiped away a tear.* ■ clean (something) by rubbing it against a surface: *the man wiped his hands on his hips.* ■ spread (a liquid) over a surface by rubbing: *gently wipe the lotion over the eyelids.*
2 remove or eliminate (something) completely: *things have happened to wipe the smile off Kate's face.* ■ erase (data) from a magnetic medium.
▶ **n. 1** an act of wiping.
2 a piece of disposable absorbent cloth or paper, esp. one treated with a cleansing agent, for wiping something clean.
3 a cinematographic effect in which an existing picture seems to be wiped out by a new one as the boundary between them moves across the screen.
– PHRASES **wipe the floor with** informal inflict a humiliating defeat on: *they wiped the floor with us in a 36-6 win.* **wipe the slate clean** forgive or forget past faults or offenses; make a fresh start.
– PHRASAL VERBS **wipe something off** subtract an amount from a value or debt: *the crash wiped 24 percent off stock prices.* **wipe out** informal fall over or off a vehicle. ■ be capsized by a wave while surfing. **wipe someone out 1** kill a large number of people: *the plague had wiped out whole villages.* **2** (usu. **be wiped out**) ruin someone financially. **3** informal exhaust or intoxicate someone. **wipe something out** eliminate something completely: *their life savings were wiped out.*
– DERIVATIVES **wipe·a·ble** **adj.**
– ORIGIN Old English *wīpian*, of Germanic origin; related to **WHIP**.

wipe·out /ˈwīpˌout/ ▶ **n.** informal an instance of complete destruction: *a nuclear wipeout.* ■ a complete failure. ■ the obliteration of one radio signal by another. ■ a fall from a surfboard.

wip·er /ˈwīpər/ ▶ **n. 1** a windshield wiper.
2 an electrical contact that moves across a surface.

WIPO ▶ **abbr.** World Intellectual Property Organization.

Wi·ra·dhur·i /ˌwērəˈjŏŏrē/ ▶ **n.** an Aboriginal language of southeastern Australia, now extinct.

wire /wīr/ ▶ **n. 1** metal drawn out into the form of a thin flexible thread or rod. ■ a piece of such metal. ■ a length or quantity of wire used, for example, for fencing or to carry an electric current. ■ Horse Racing a wire stretched across and above the track at the finish line of a racetrack. ■ an electronic listening device that can be concealed on a person.
2 informal a telegram or cablegram.
▶ **v.** [with obj.] **1** install electric circuits or wires in: *wiring a plug* | *they wired the place themselves.* ■ connect (someone or something) to a piece of electronic equipment: *a microphone wired to a loudspeaker.*
2 provide, fasten, or reinforce with wires: *they wired his jaw.*
3 informal send a telegram or cablegram to: *she wired her friend for advice.* ■ [with two objs.] send (money) to (someone) by means of a telegram or cablegram: *he was expecting a friend in Australia to wire him $1,500.*
4 snare (an animal) with wire.
5 Croquet obstruct (a ball, shot, or player) by a wicket.
– PHRASES **by wire** by telegraph. **down to the wire** informal used to denote a situation whose outcome is not decided until the very last minute: *it was probable that the test of nerves would go down to the wire.* **get one's wires crossed** see **CROSS**. **under the wire** informal at the last possible opportunity; just in time.
– DERIVATIVES **wir·er** **n.**
– ORIGIN Old English *wīr*, of Germanic origin, probably from the base of Latin *viere* 'plait, weave.'

wire cloth ▶ **n.** fabric woven from wire.

wire cut·ter ▶ **n.** (usu. **wire cutters**) a tool for cutting wire.

wired /wīrd/ ▶ **adj. 1** making use of computers to transfer or receive information, esp. by means of the Internet: *the economic arguments for getting your business wired.* ■ (of a device or network) using wires or cables rather than wireless technology to transmit signals.
2 [predic.] informal in a nervous, tense, or edgy state: *not much sleep lately—I'm a little wired.* ■ under the influence of drugs or alcohol.

wire-draw ▶ **v.** (past **wire-drew**; past participle **wire-drawn**) [with obj.] (often as noun **wire-drawing**)
1 draw out (metal) into wire by passing it through a series of holes of diminishing diameter in a steel plate.
2 archaic refine (an argument or idea) excessively, in such a way that it becomes strained or forced.
– DERIVATIVES **wire-draw·er** **n.**

wire·frame /ˈwīrˌfrām/ ▶ **n.** Computing a skeletal three dimensional model in which only lines and vertices are represented. ■ an image or set of images which displays the functional elements of a website or page, typically used for planning a site's structure and functionality.

wire fraud ▶ **n.** financial fraud involving the use of telecommunications or information technology.

wire gauge ▶ **n.** a gauge for measuring the diameter of wire. ■ the diameter of wire; any of a series of standard sizes in which wire is made.

wire gauze ▶ **n.** see **GAUZE**.

wire grass ▶ **n.** a grass with tough wiry stems. ● Genera *Aristida* and *Poa*, family Gramineae: several species, including the European *P. compressa*, which has become naturalized in North America.

wire-guid·ed ▶ **adj.** (of a missile) directed by means of electrical signals transmitted along fine connecting wires that uncoil during the missile's flight.

wire-haired ▶ **adj.** (esp. of a dog breed) having stiff or wiry hair: *a wire-haired terrier.*

wire·less /ˈwīrlis/ ▶ **adj.** using radio, microwaves, etc. (as opposed to wires or cables) to transmit signals: *wireless broadband.*
▶ **n. 1** broadcasting, computer networking, or other communication using radio signals, microwaves, etc.
2 (also **wireless set**) dated, chiefly Brit. a radio receiving set.
– DERIVATIVES **wire·less·ly** **adv.**

wire·less hot spot (also **wireless hotspot**) ▶ **n.** an area with a usable signal to allow wireless connection to the Internet or some other computer network.

wire·line /ˈwīrˌlīn/ ▶ **n. 1** a telegraph or telephone wire.
2 (in the oil industry) a cable for lowering and raising tools and other equipment in a well shaft. ■ an electric cable used to connect measuring devices in an oil well with indicating or recording instruments at the surface.
3 a horizontal watermark in laid paper.

wire·man /ˈwīrˌmən/ ▶ **n.** (pl. **wiremen**) **1** an electrician.
2 a journalist working for a news agency.
3 informal a professional wiretapper.

wire·pull·er /ˈwīrˌpŏŏlər/ ▶ **n.** informal a person, esp. a politician, who exerts control or influence from behind the scenes.
– DERIVATIVES **wire·pull·ing** /-ˌpŏŏliNG/ **n.**

wire rope ▶ **n.** a length of rope made from wires twisted together as strands; cable.

wire serv·ice ▶ **n.** a news agency that supplies syndicated news by wire to newspapers, radio, and television stations.

wire·tap·ping /ˈwīrˌtapiNG/ ▶ **n.** the practice of connecting a listening device to a telephone line to secretly monitor a conversation.
– DERIVATIVES **wire·tap** **n. & v.**, **wire·tap·per** /-ˌtapər/ **n.**

wire wheel ▶ **n.** a wheel on a car, esp. a sports car, having narrow metal spokes.

wire·worm /ˈwīrˌwərm/ ▶ **n.** a wormlike hard-skinned larva, esp. of a click beetle. Many wireworms feed on the underground parts of plants and can cause damage to arable and other crops. ■ a myriapod, esp. of the millipede genus *Iulus*, which damages plant roots.

wir·ing /ˈwīriNG/ ▶ **n.** a system of wires providing electric circuits for a device or building. ■ the installation of this. ■ informal the structure of the nervous system or brain perceived as determining a basic or innate pattern of behavior.

Wir·ral /ˈwi(ə)rəl/ a peninsula on the coast of northwestern England, between the estuaries of the rivers Dee and Mersey. Full name **the Wirral Peninsula**.

Wirt·schafts·wun·der /ˈvirtSHäftsˌvŏŏndər/ ▶ **n.** an economic miracle, esp. the economic recovery of the Federal Republic of West Germany after World War II.
– ORIGIN German.

wir·y /ˈwī(ə)rē/ ▶ **adj.** (**wirier**, **wiriest**) resembling wire in form and texture: *his wiry black hair.* ■ (of a person) lean, tough, and sinewy: *Bernadette was a small, wiry woman.*
– DERIVATIVES **wir·i·ly** /ˈwīrəlē/ **adv.**, **wir·i·ness** **n.**

Wis. ▶ **abbr.** Wisconsin.

Wis·con·sin[1] /wisˈkänsən/ a state in the northern US that borders on lakes Superior (in the northwest) and Michigan (in the east); pop. 5,627,967 (est. 2008); capital, Madison; statehood, May 29, 1848 (30). Ceded to Britain by the French in 1763 and acquired by the US in 1783 as part of the former Northwest Territory, it was the site of the Black Hawk War, the last armed Indian resistance to white settlement in the area, in 1832.
– DERIVATIVES **Wis·con·sin·ite** /-səˌnīt/ **n.**

Wis·con·sin[2] ▶ **n.** [usu. as modifier] Geology the last (or last two) of the Pleistocene glaciations of North America, approximating to the Weichsel of northern Europe. ■ the system of deposits laid down at this time.

Wis·con·sin Riv·er a river that flows for 430 miles (690 km) through central Wisconsin to the Mississippi River at Prairie du Chien. The ***Dells of the Wisconsin*** are a popular scenic area.

Wisd. ▶ abbr. (in biblical references) Wisdom of Solomon (Apocrypha).

wis·dom /ˈwizdəm/ ▶ n. the quality of having experience, knowledge, and good judgment; the quality of being wise. ■ the soundness of an action or decision with regard to the application of such experience, knowledge, and good judgment: *some questioned the wisdom of building the dam so close to an active volcano.* ■ the body of knowledge and principles that develops within a specified society or period: *the traditional farming wisdom of India.*
– PHRASES **in someone's wisdom** used ironically to suggest that an action is not well judged: *in their wisdom they decided to dispense with him.*
– ORIGIN Old English *wīsdōm* (see WISE¹, -DOM).

wis·dom lit·er·a·ture ▶ n. the biblical books of Job, Proverbs, Ecclesiastes, Song of Songs, Wisdom of Solomon, and Ecclesiasticus collectively. ■ similar works, esp. from the ancient Near East, containing proverbial sayings and practical maxims.

Wis·dom of Sol·o·mon a book of the Apocrypha ascribed to Solomon and containing a meditation on wisdom. The book is thought actually to date from about the 1st century BC to the 1st century AD.

wis·dom tooth ▶ n. each of the four hindmost molars in humans, which usually appear at about the age of twenty.

wise¹ /wīz/ ▶ adj. having or showing experience, knowledge, and good judgment: *she seems kind and wise* | *a wise precaution.* ■ responding sensibly or shrewdly to a particular situation: *it would be wise to discuss the matter with the chairman of the committee.* ■ [predic.] having knowledge in a specified subject: *families wise in the way of hurricane survival.* ■ [predic.] (**wise to**) informal alert to or aware of: *at seven she was already wise to the police.*
– PHRASES **get wise** become alert or aware: *the birds get wise and figure out it's just noise.* **be wise after the event** understand and assess an event or situation only after its implications have become obvious. **be none** (or **not any**) **the wiser** know no more than before.
– PHRASAL VERBS **wise off** informal make wisecracks: *Jake and I would wise off to him.* **wise up** [often in imperative] informal become alert to or aware of something: *wise up and sort yourselves out before it's too late.*
– DERIVATIVES **wise·ly** adv.
– ORIGIN Old English *wīs*, of Germanic origin; related to Dutch *wijs* and German *weise*, also to WIT².

wise² ▶ n. archaic the manner or extent of something: *he did it this wise.*
– PHRASES **in no wise** not at all.
– ORIGIN Old English *wīse*, of Germanic origin; related to WIT².

-wise ▶ suffix forming adjectives and adverbs of manner or respect such as *clockwise, otherwise.* Compare with -WAYS. ■ informal with respect to; concerning: *security-wise, there are few problems.*
– ORIGIN from WISE².

> **USAGE** In modern English, the suffix **-wise** is attached to nouns to form a sentence adverb meaning 'concerning or with respect to,' as in *tax-wise, money-wise, time-wise*, etc. The suffix is widely used, but most of the words so formed are not considered appropriate in formal writing.

wise·a·cre /ˈwīzˌākər/ ▶ n. a person with an affectation of wisdom or knowledge, regarded with scorn or irritation by others; a know-it-all.
– ORIGIN late 16th cent.: from Middle Dutch *wijsseggher* 'soothsayer,' probably from the Germanic bases of WIT² and SAY. The assimilation to ACRE remains unexplained.

wise·ass /ˈwīzˌas/ ▶ n. informal another term for SMART ALECK.

wise·crack /ˈwīzˌkrak/ informal ▶ n. a clever and pithy spoken witticism.
▶ v. [no obj.] make a wisecrack: (as noun **wisecracking**) *his warmth, boisterousness, and constant wisecracking.*
– DERIVATIVES **wise·crack·er** n.

wise guy informal ▶ n. **1** a person who speaks and behaves as if they know more than others.
2 a member of the Mafia.

wise man ▶ n. a man versed in magic, witchcraft, or astrology. See also THREE WISE MEN.

wis·en·heim·er /ˈwīzənˌhīmər/ ▶ n. informal a person who behaves in an irritatingly smug or arrogant fashion, typically by making clever remarks and displaying their knowledge.
– ORIGIN early 20th cent.: from WISE¹ + the suffix *-(n) heimer* found in surnames such as *Oppenheimer.*

wi·sent /ˈvēzent/ ▶ n. the European bison. See BISON.
– ORIGIN mid 19th cent.: from German; related to BISON.

wise saw ▶ n. a proverbial saying.

wise wom·an ▶ n. chiefly historical a woman considered to be knowledgeable in matters such as herbal healing, magic charms, or other traditional lore.

wish /wisH/ ▶ v. [no obj.] feel or express a strong desire or hope for something that is not easily attainable; want something that cannot or probably will not happen: ***we wished for peace*** | [with clause] *he wished that he had practiced the routines.* ■ silently invoke such a hope or desire, esp. in a ritualized way: *I closed my eyes and wished.* ■ [with infinitive] feel or express a desire to do something: *they wish to become involved.* ■ [with obj. and infinitive] ask (someone) to do something or that (something) be done: *I wish it to be clearly understood.* ■ [with two objs.] express a desire for (the success or good fortune) of (someone): *they wish her every success.* ■ [with obj.] (**wish something on**) hope that something unpleasant will happen to: *I would not wish it on the vilest soul.*
▶ n. a desire or hope for something to happen: *the union has reiterated its wish for an agreement* | [with infinitive] *it is their wish to continue organizing similar exhibitions.* ■ (usu. **wishes**) an expression of such a desire, typically in the form of a request or instruction: *she must carry out her late father's wishes.* ■ an invocation or recitation of a hope or desire: *he **makes a wish**.* ■ (usu. **wishes**) an expression of a desire for someone's success or good fortune: *they had received kindness and **good wishes** from total strangers.* ■ a thing or event that is or has been desired; an object of desire: *the petitioners eventually got their wish.*
– PHRASES **if wishes were horses, beggars would ride** proverb if you could achieve your aims simply by wishing for them, life would be very easy. **wish someone well** feel or express a desire for someone's well-being. **the wish is father to the thought** proverb we believe a thing because we wish it to be true.
– DERIVATIVES **wish·er** n. [in combination] *an ill-wisher.*
– ORIGIN Old English *wȳscan*, of Germanic origin; related to German *wünschen*, also to WEEN and WONT.

> **USAGE** Is it correct to say *I wish I were rich* or *I wish I was rich*? On the question of the use of the subjunctive mood, see usage at SUBJUNCTIVE.

wish·bone /ˈwisHˌbōn/ ▶ n. **1** a forked bone (the furcula) between the neck and breast of a bird. According to a popular custom, this bone from a cooked bird is broken by two people, with the holder of the longer portion being entitled to make a wish.
2 an object of similar shape, in particular: ■ Football an offensive formation in which the fullback lines up immediately behind the quarterback with the two halfbacks behind and on either side of the fullback. ■ a forked element in the suspension of a motor vehicle or aircraft, typically attached to a wheel at one end with the two arms hinged to the chassis. ■ Sailing a boom in two halves that curve outward around a sail and meet aft of it.

wish book ▶ n. informal a mail-order catalog.

wish·ful /ˈwisHfəl/ ▶ adj. having or expressing a desire or hope for something to happen. ■ expressing or containing a desire or hope for something impractical or unfeasible: *without resources the proposed measures were merely wishful thinking.*
– DERIVATIVES **wish·ful·ly** adv., **wish·ful·ness** n.

wish ful·fill·ment ▶ n. the satisfying of unconscious desires in dreams or fantasies.

wish·ing well ▶ n. a well into which one drops a coin and makes a wish.

wish list ▶ n. a list of desired things or occurrences.

wish-wash ▶ n. Brit. informal a weak or watery drink: *one pot of wish-wash called "tea."* ■ insipid or excessively sentimental talk or writing: *this isn't just emotional wish-wash.*
– ORIGIN late 18th cent.: reduplication of WASH.

wish·y-wash·y /ˈwisHēˌwäsHē, -ˌwôsHē/ ▶ adj. (of drink or liquid food such as soup) weak; watery. ■ feeble or insipid in quality or character; lacking strength or boldness: *wishy-washy liberalism.*
– ORIGIN early 18th cent.: reduplication of WASHY.

Wis·ła /ˈvēswä/ Polish name for VISTULA.

wisp /wisp/ ▶ n. a small thin or twisted bunch, piece, or amount of something: ***wisps of smoke rose into the air.*** ■ a small bunch of hay or straw used for drying or grooming a horse. ■ a small thin person, typically a child: *a fourteen-year-old wisp of a girl.*
– ORIGIN Middle English: origin uncertain; perhaps related to WHISK.

wisp·y /ˈwispē/ ▶ adj. (**wispier, wispiest**) (of hair, threads, smoke, etc.) fine; feathery: *the sky was blue with a few wispy clouds.*
– DERIVATIVES **wisp·i·ly** /ˈwispilē/ adv., **wisp·i·ness** /ˈwispēnis/ n.

Wis·sen·schaft /ˈvisənˌsHäft/ ▶ n. the systematic pursuit of knowledge, learning, and scholarship (esp. as contrasted with its application).
– ORIGIN German, literally 'knowledge, science.'

wist /wist/ past and past participle of WIT².

Wis·tar rat /ˈwistər/ ▶ n. Biology & Medicine a rat of a strain developed for laboratory purposes.
– ORIGIN 1930s: named after the *Wistar* Institute of Anatomy and Biology, Philadelphia, Pennsylvania.

wis·te·ri·a /wiˈsti(ə)rēə/ (also **wistaria** /-ˈste(ə)r-/) ▶ n. a climbing shrub of the pea family, with hanging clusters of pale bluish-lilac flowers. Native to North America and eastern Asia, ornamental varieties are widely grown on walls and pergolas. ● Genus *Wisteria*, family Leguminosae: several species.
– ORIGIN modern Latin, named after Caspar *Wistar* (or *Wister*) (1761–1818), American anatomist.

wist·ful /ˈwistfəl/ ▶ adj. having or showing a feeling of vague or regretful longing: *a wistful smile.*
– DERIVATIVES **wist·ful·ly** adv., **wist·ful·ness** n.
– ORIGIN early 17th cent.: apparently from obsolete *wistly* 'intently,' influenced by WISHFUL.

wit¹ /wit/ ▶ n. **1** mental sharpness and inventiveness; keen intelligence: *he does not lack perception or native wit.* ■ (**wits**) the intelligence required for normal activity; basic human intelligence: *he needed all his wits to figure out the way back.*
2 a natural aptitude for using words and ideas in a quick and inventive way to create humor: *a player with a sharp tongue and a quick wit.* ■ a person who has such an aptitude: *she is such a wit.*
– PHRASES **be at one's wits' end** be overwhelmed with difficulties and at a loss as to what to do next. **be frightened** (or **scared**) **out of one's wits** be extremely frightened; be immobilized by fear. **gather** (or **collect**) **one's wits** allow oneself to think calmly and clearly in a demanding situation. **have** (or **keep**) **one's wits about one** be constantly alert and vigilant. **live by one's wits** earn money by clever and sometimes dishonest means, having no regular employment. **pit one's wits against** compete with (someone or something).
– DERIVATIVES **wit·ted** adj. [in combination] *slow-witted.*
– ORIGIN Old English *wit(t), gewit(t)*, denoting the mind as the seat of consciousness, of Germanic origin; related to Dutch *weet* and German *Witz*, also to WIT².

wit² ▶ v. (**wot** /wät/, **witting**; past and past participle **wist** /wist/) [no obj.] **1** archaic have knowledge: *I addressed a few words to the lady you wot of* | [with obj.] *I wot that but too well.*
2 (**to wit**) that is to say (used to make clearer or more specific something already said or referred to): *the textbooks show an irritating parochialism, to wit an almost total exclusion of papers not in English.*
– ORIGIN Old English *witan*, of Germanic origin; related to Dutch *weten* and German *wissen*, from an Indo-European root shared by Sanskrit *veda* 'knowledge' and Latin *videre* 'see.'

wit·an /ˈwitn/ ▶ n. another term for WITENAGEMOT.
– ORIGIN representing the Old English plural of *wita* 'wise man.'

witch /wicH/ ▶ n. **1** a woman thought to have evil magic powers. Witches are popularly depicted as wearing a black cloak and pointed hat, and flying on a broomstick. ■ a follower or practitioner of modern witchcraft; a Wiccan priest or priestess. ■ informal an ugly or unpleasant old woman; a hag. ■ a girl or woman capable of enchanting or bewitching a man.
2 an edible North Atlantic flatfish that is of some commercial value. ● *Glyptocephalus cynoglossus*, family Pleuronectidae.
▶ v. [with obj.] (of a witch) cast an evil spell on: *Mrs. Mucharski had somehow witched the house.* ■ (of a girl or woman) enchant (a man): *she witched Jake.*
– PHRASES **as cold as** (or **colder than**) **a witch's tit** vulgar slang very cold.
– DERIVATIVES **witch·like** /-ˌlīk/ adj., **witch·y** adj.
– ORIGIN Old English *wicca* (masculine), *wicce* (feminine), *wiccian* (verb); current senses of the verb are probably a shortening of BEWITCH.

witch·craft /ˈwicHˌkraft/ ▶ n. the practice of magic, esp. black magic; the use of spells and the invocation of spirits. See also WICCA.

witch doc·tor ▶ n. (among tribal peoples) a magician credited with powers of healing, divination, and protection against the magic of others.

witch elm ▶ n. variant spelling of WYCH ELM.

W

witch·er·y /'wiCHərē/ ▶ **n.** the practice of magic: *warding off evil spirits and acts of witchery.* ■ compelling power exercised by beauty, eloquence, or other attractive or fascinating qualities.

witch·es' broom ▶ **n.** dense twiggy growth in a tree caused by infection with fungus (esp. rusts), mites, or viruses.

witch·es' sab·bath ▶ **n.** see SABBATH (sense 2).

witch·grass /'wiCH,gras/ (also **witch grass**) ▶ **n.** a tough creeping grass that can become an invasive weed. ● couch grass. ● a North American grass (*Panicum capillare*, family Gramineae).

witch ha·zel ▶ **n.** a shrub with fragrant yellow flowers that is widely grown as an ornamental. American species flower in autumn, and Asian species in winter. ● Genus *Hamamelis*, family Hamamelidaceae: several species, esp. *H. virginiana*, which is the source of the lotion. ■ an astringent lotion made from the bark and leaves of this plant.
– ORIGIN mid 16th cent.: *witch*, variant of *wych* (see WYCH ELM).

witch-hunt ▶ **n.** historical a search for and subsequent persecution of a supposed witch. ■ informal a campaign directed against a person or group holding unorthodox or unpopular views.
– DERIVATIVES **witch-hunt·ing n.**

witch·ing /'wiCHiNG/ ▶ **n.** the practice of witchcraft.
– PHRASES **the witching hour** midnight (with reference to the belief that witches are active and magic takes place at that time). [with allusion to *the witching time of night* from Shakespeare's *Hamlet* (III. ii. 377).]

witch·weed /'wiCH,wēd/ ▶ **n.** a small parasitic plant that attaches itself to the roots of other plants. Native to the Old World tropics and southern Africa, it has been introduced into North America and can cause serious damage to crops such as corn and sugar. ● Genus *Striga*, family Scrophulariaceae.

wit·e·na·ge·mot /'witn-əgə,mōt/ ▶ **n.** historical an Anglo-Saxon national council or parliament. Also called WITAN.
– ORIGIN Old English, from *witena*, genitive plural of *wita* 'wise man' + *gemōt* 'meeting' (compare with MOOT).

with /wiTH, wiTH/ ▶ **prep. 1** accompanied by (another person or thing): *a nice steak with a bottle of red wine.* ■ in the same direction as: *marine mammals generally swim with the current.* ■ along with (with reference to time): *wisdom comes with age.* ■ in proportion to: *the form of the light curve changes with period in a systematic way.*
2 possessing (something) as a feature or accompaniment: *a flower-sprigged blouse with a white collar.* ■ marked by or wearing: *a tall dark man with a scar on one cheek | a small man with thick glasses.*
3 indicating the instrument used to perform an action: *cut it with a knife | treatment with acid before analysis.* ■ indicating the material used for some purpose: *fill the bowl with water.*
4 in opposition to: *we started fighting with each other.*
5 indicating the manner or attitude of the person doing something: *with great reluctance.*
6 indicating responsibility: *leave it with me.*
7 in relation to: *my father will be angry with me.*
8 employed by: *she's with IBM now.* ■ as a member or employee of: *he plays with the Cincinnati Cyclones.* ■ using the services of: *I bank with the TSB.*
9 affected by (a particular fact or condition): *with no hope | in bed with lumbago.* ■ indicating the cause of an action or condition: *trembling with fear | the paper was yellow with age.*
10 indicating separation or removal from something: *to part with one's dearest possessions | their jobs could be dispensed with.*
– PHRASES **away** (or **off** or **out**, etc.) **with** used in exhortations to take or send someone or something away, in, out, etc.: *off with his head.* **be with someone 1** agree with or support someone: *we're all with you on this one.* **2** informal follow someone's meaning: *I'm not with you.* **with it 1** knowledgeable about and following modern ideas and fashions: *a young, with-it film buyer.* **2** [usu. with negative] alert and comprehending: *I'm not really with it this morning.* **with that** at that point; immediately after saying or doing something dramatic: *with that, she flounced out of the room.*
– ORIGIN Old English, probably a shortening of a Germanic preposition related to obsolete English *wither* 'adverse, opposite.'

with·al /wiTH'ôl, wiTH-/ archaic ▶ **adv.** in addition; as a further factor or consideration: *the whole is light and portable, and ornamental withal.* ■ all the same; nevertheless (used when adding something that contrasts with a previous comment): *she gave him a grateful smile, but rueful withal.*
▶ **prep.** with (used at the end of a clause): *we sat with little to nourish ourselves withal but vile water.*
– ORIGIN Middle English: originally as *with all.*

with·draw /wiTH'drô, wiTH-/ ▶ **v.** (past **withdrew**; past participle **withdrawn**) **1** [with obj.] remove or take away (something) from a particular place or position: *slowly Ruth withdrew her hand from his.* ■ take (money) out of an account: *normally you can withdraw up to $50 in cash.* ■ take back or away (something bestowed, proposed, or used): *the party threatened to withdraw its support for the government.* ■ (in parliamentary procedure) remove or recall a motion, amendment, etc., from consideration. ■ say that (a statement one has made) is untrue or unjustified: *he failed to withdraw his remarks and apologize.* ■ [no obj.] (of a man) practice coitus interruptus.
2 [no obj.] leave or come back from a place, esp. a war zone: *Allied forces* **withdrew from** *Norway in 1941.* ■ [with obj.] cause (someone) to leave or come back from a place, esp. a war zone: *both countries agreed to withdraw their troops.* ■ no longer participate in an activity or be a member of a team or organization: *his rival withdrew from the race on the second lap.* ■ depart to another room or place, esp. in search of quiet or privacy. ■ retreat from contact or communication with other people: *he went silent and* **withdrew into himself.**
3 [no obj.] cease to take an addictive drug: *for the cocaine user, it is possible to withdraw without medication.*
– ORIGIN Middle English: from the prefix *with-* 'away' + the verb DRAW.

with·draw·al /wiTH'drôl, wiTH-/ ▶ **n.** the action of withdrawing something: *the withdrawal of legal aid.* ■ an act of taking money out of an account. ■ a sum of money withdrawn from an account: *a $30,000 cash withdrawal.* ■ the action of ceasing to participate in an activity: *her withdrawal from the commercial art world.* ■ the process of ceasing to take an addictive drug. ■ coitus interruptus.
– PHRASES **withdrawal symptoms** the unpleasant physical reaction that accompanies the process of ceasing to take an addictive drug.

with·drawn /wiTH'drôn, wiTH-/ past participle of WITHDRAW.
▶ **adj.** not wanting to communicate with other people: *a disorder characterized by withdrawn and fearful behavior.*

withe /wiTH, wiTH/ ▶ **n.** variant spelling of WITHY.

with·er /'wiTHər/ ▶ **v. 1** [no obj.] (of a plant) become dry and shriveled: *the grass had withered to an unappealing brown* | (as adj. **withered**) *withered leaves.* ■ (of a person, limb, or the skin) become shrunken or wrinkled from age or disease: (as adj. **withered**) *a girl with a withered arm.* ■ cease to flourish; fall into decay or decline: *programs would* **wither away** *if they did not command local support.*
2 [with obj.] cause harm or damage to: *a business that can wither the hardiest ego.* ■ mortify (someone) with a scornful look or manner: *she withered me with a look.*
– PHRASES **wither on the vine** fail to be implemented or dealt with because of neglect or inaction.
– ORIGIN late Middle English: apparently a variant of WEATHER, ultimately differentiated for certain senses.

with·er·ing /'wiTHəriNG/ ▶ **adj. 1** intended to make someone feel mortified or humiliated: *a withering look.*
2 (of heat) intense; scorching.
▶ **n.** the action of becoming dry and shriveled. ■ the action of declining or decaying: *the withering of the PLO's revolutionary threat.*
– DERIVATIVES **with·er·ing·ly adv.**

with·er·ite /'wiTHə,rīt/ ▶ **n.** a rare white mineral consisting of barium carbonate, occurring esp. in veins with galena.
– ORIGIN late 18th cent.: from the name of William *Withering* (1741–99), the English physician and scientist who first described it, + -ITE[1].

with·ers /'wiTHərz/ ▶ **plural n.** the highest part of a horse's back, lying at the base of the neck above the shoulders. The height of a horse is measured to the withers.
– ORIGIN early 16th cent.: apparently a reduced form of *widersome*, from obsolete *wither-* 'against, contrary' (as the part that resists the strain of the collar) + a second element of obscure origin.

with·er·shins /'wiTHər,SHinz/ ▶ **adv.** variant spelling of WIDDERSHINS.

with·hold /wiTH'hōld, wiTH-/ ▶ **v.** (past and past participle **withheld**) [with obj.] refuse to give (something that is due to or is desired by another): *the name of the dead man is being withheld* | (as noun **withholding**) *the withholding of consent to treatment.* ■ suppress or hold back (an emotion or reaction). ■ (of an employer) deduct (tax) from an employee's paycheck and send it directly to the government.
– DERIVATIVES **with·hold·er n.**
– ORIGIN Middle English: from the prefix *with-* 'away' + the verb HOLD[1].

with·hold·ing tax ▶ **n.** the amount of an employee's pay withheld by the employer and sent directly to the government as partial payment of income tax.

with·in /wiTH'in, wi'TH-/ ▶ **prep.** inside (something): *the spread of fire within the building.* ■ inside the range of (an area or boundary): *a field located within the city.* ■ inside the range of (a specified action or perception): *within reach.* ■ not further off than (used with distances): *Bob lives* **within** *a few miles of Honesdale.* ■ occurring inside (a particular period of time): *sold out within two hours | 33% were rearrested* **within** *two years of their release.* ■ inside the bounds set by (a concept, argument, etc.): *full cooperation within the terms of the treaty.*
▶ **adv.** inside; indoors: *inquire within.* ■ internally or inwardly: *beauty coming from within.*
– PHRASES **within doors** indoors.
– ORIGIN late Old English *withinnan* 'on the inside.'

with·out /wiTH'out, wiTH-/ ▶ **prep. 1** in the absence of: *he went to Sweden without her.* ■ not having the use or benefit of: *the first person to make the ascent without oxygen.* ■ [often with verbal noun] in circumstances in which the action mentioned does not happen: *they sat looking at each other without speaking.*
2 archaic or literary outside: *the barbarians without the gates.*
▶ **adv.** archaic or literary outside: *the enemy without.*
▶ **conj.** archaic or dialect without it being the case that: *he won't be able to go without we know it.* ■ unless: *I'd never have known you without you spoke to me.*
– PHRASES **do without** see DO[1]. **go without** see GO[1].
– ORIGIN Old English *withūtan* 'on the outside.'

with·stand /wiTH'stand, wiTH-/ ▶ **v.** (past and past participle **withstood**) [with obj.] remain undamaged or unaffected by; resist: *the structure had been designed to withstand winds of more than 100 mph.* ■ offer strong resistance or opposition to (someone or something).
– DERIVATIVES **with·stand·er n.**
– ORIGIN Old English *withstandan*, from the prefix *with-* 'against' + the verb STAND.

with·y /'wiTHē, 'wiTHē/ (also **withe** /wiTH, wiTH, wiTH/) ▶ **n.** (pl. **withies** or **withes** /wiTHs, wiTHz/) a tough flexible branch of an osier or other willow, used for tying, binding, or basketry. ■ another term for OSIER.
– ORIGIN Old English *wīthig*, of Germanic origin; related to German *Weide.*

wit·less /'witlis/ ▶ **adj.** foolish; stupid: *a witless retort.* ■ [as complement] to such an extent that one cannot think clearly or rationally: *I was scared witless.*
– DERIVATIVES **wit·less·ly adv.**, **wit·less·ness n.**
– ORIGIN Old English *witlēas* 'crazy, dazed' (see WIT[1], -LESS).

wit·ling /'witliNG/ ▶ **n.** archaic, chiefly derogatory a person who considers themselves to be witty.

wit·loof /'wit,lōf/ ▶ **n.** chicory of a broadleaved variety grown for blanching.
– ORIGIN late 19th cent.: from Dutch, literally 'white leaf.'

wit·ness /'witnis/ ▶ **n. 1** a person who sees an event, typically a crime or accident, take place: *police are appealing for* **witnesses to** *the accident | I was witness to one of the most amazing comebacks in sprinting history.* ■ a person giving sworn testimony to a court of law or the police. ■ a person who is present at the signing of a document and signs it themselves to confirm this.
2 evidence; proof: *the memorial service was* **witness to** *the wide circle of his interest.* ■ used to refer to confirmation or evidence given by signature, under oath, or otherwise: ***in witness thereof***, *the parties sign this document.* ■ open profession of one's religious faith through words or actions: *faithful Christian witness.*
3 a member of the Jehovah's Witnesses.
▶ **v. 1** [with obj.] see (an event, typically a crime or accident) take place: *a bartender who witnessed the murder.* ■ have knowledge of (an event or change) from personal observation or experience: *what we are witnessing is the birth of a dangerously liberal orthodoxy.* ■ (of a time, place, or other context) be the setting in which (an event or development) takes place: *the 1980s witnessed an unprecedented*

W

increase in the scope of the electronic media. ■ be present as someone signs (a document) or gives (their signature) to a document and sign it oneself to confirm this: *the clerk witnessed her signature.* ■ [in imperative] look at (used to introduce a fact illustrating a preceding statement): *the nuclear family is a vulnerable institution—witness the rates of marital breakdown.*
2 [no obj.] (**witness to**) give or serve as evidence of; testify to: *his writings witness to an inner toughness.* **3** [no obj.] (of a person) openly profess one's religious faith: *our duty is to witness to God.*
– PHRASES **as God is my witness** (or **God be my witness**) an invocation of God as confirmation of the truth of a statement: *God be my witness, sir, I didn't!* **call someone or something to witness** archaic appeal or refer to someone or something for confirmation or evidence of something: *his hands extended upward as if to call the heavens to witness this injustice.*
– ORIGIN Old English *witnes* (see WIT[1], -NESS).

wit·ness stand (Brit. **witness box**) ▶ n. Law the place in a court where a witness stands to give evidence.

Witt /vit/, Katarina (1965–), German figure skater. A four-time world champion 1984, 1985, 1987, 1988, she won Olympic gold medals for East Germany in 1984 and 1988.

Wit·ten·berg /ˈwitn,bərg, ˈvitn,berk/ a town in eastern Germany, on the Elbe River northeast of Leipzig; pop. 46,100 (est. 2006). It was the scene in 1517 of Martin Luther's campaign against the Roman Catholic Church that was a major factor in the rise of the Reformation.

Witt·gen·stein /ˈvitgən,stīn, -,shtīn/, Ludwig (Josef Johann) (1889–1951), British philosopher, born in Austria. His two major works, *Tractatus Logico-Philosophicus* (1921) and *Philosophical Investigations* (1953), examine language and its relationship to the world.

wit·ti·cism /ˈwiti,sizəm/ ▶ n. a witty remark.
– ORIGIN 1677: coined by Dryden from WITTY, on the pattern of *criticism.*

wit·ting /ˈwitiNG/ ▶ adj. done in full awareness or consciousness; deliberate: *the witting and unwitting complicity of the institutions.* ■ (of a person) conscious or aware of the full facts of a situation: *he tried to implicate her as a witting accomplice.*
– DERIVATIVES **wit·ting·ly** adv.
– ORIGIN late Middle English: from WIT[2] + -ING[2].

wit·tol /ˈwitl/ ▶ n. archaic a man who is aware and tolerant of his wife's infidelity; an acquiescent cuckold.
– ORIGIN late Middle English: apparently from WIT[2] + the last syllable (with the loss of *-d*) of CUCKOLD.

wit·ty /ˈwitē/ ▶ adj. (**wittier**, **wittiest**) showing or characterized by quick and inventive verbal humor: *a witty remark | Marlowe was charming and witty.*
– DERIVATIVES **wit·ti·ly** /ˈwitəlē/ adv., **wit·ti·ness** n.
– ORIGIN Old English *wit(t)ig* 'having wisdom' (see WIT[1], -Y[1]).

Wit·wa·ters·rand /ˈwit,wôtərz,rand, -,wätərz-, -,ränd/ (**the Witwatersrand**) a region in South Africa, around the city of Johannesburg. A series of parallel rocky ridges, it forms a watershed between the Vaal and Olifant rivers. The region contains rich gold deposits that were first discovered in 1886. Also called THE RAND (see RAND[1]).
– ORIGIN Afrikaans, literally 'ridge of white waters.'

wi·vern ▶ n. archaic spelling of WYVERN.

wives /wīvz/ plural form of WIFE.

wiz /wiz/ ▶ n. variant spelling of WHIZ (sense 2 of the noun).

wiz·ard /ˈwizərd/ ▶ n. **1** a man who has magical powers, esp. in legends and fairy tales. ■ a person who is very skilled in a particular field or activity: *a financial wizard.*
2 Computing a help feature of a software package that automates complex tasks by asking the user a series of easy-to-answer questions.
▶ adj. informal, dated, chiefly Brit. wonderful; excellent.
– DERIVATIVES **wiz·ard·ly** adj.
– ORIGIN late Middle English (in the sense 'philosopher, sage'): from WISE[1] + -ARD.

W

wiz·ard·ry /ˈwizərdrē/ ▶ n. the art or practice of magic: *Merlin used his powers of wizardry for good.* ■ great skill in a particular area of activity: *his wizardry with leftovers.* ■ the product of such skill: *the car is full of hi-tech wizardry.*

wiz·en /ˈwizən, ˈwē-/ ▶ adj. archaic variant of WIZENED.

wiz·ened /ˈwizənd, ˈwē-/ ▶ adj. shriveled or wrinkled with age: *a wizened, weather-beaten old man.*
– ORIGIN early 16th cent.: past participle of archaic *wizen* 'shrivel,' of Germanic origin.

wk ▶ abbr. week: *75 mg per day for 3 wks.*

Wła·dys·ław II /vläˈdis,läf, -,wäf/ see LADISLAUS II.

WLAN ▶ abbr. Computing wireless local area network.

WLTM ▶ abbr. would like to meet (used in lonely hearts advertisements).

Wm ▶ abbr. William.

WMD ▶ abbr. weapon (or weapons) of mass destruction.

WML ▶ abbr. Computing Wireless Markup Language, a metalanguage that enables text from web pages to be displayed on cellular phones.

WMO ▶ abbr. World Meteorological Organization.

WNW ▶ abbr. west-northwest.

WO ▶ abbr. Warrant Officer.

w/o ▶ abbr. without.

woad /wōd/ ▶ n. a yellow-flowered European plant of the cabbage family. It was formerly grown as a source of blue dye, which was extracted from the leaves after they had been dried, powdered, and fermented. ● *Isatis tinctoria*, family Brassicaceae. ■ the dye obtained from this plant, now superseded by synthetic products.
– ORIGIN Old English *wād*, of Germanic origin; related to Dutch *wede* and German *Waid.*

wob·ble /ˈwäbəl/ ▶ v. [no obj.] move unsteadily from side to side: *the table wobbles where the leg is too short.* ■ [with obj.] cause to move in such a way. ■ [with adverbial of direction] move in such a way in a particular direction: *they wobble around on their bikes.* ■ (of the voice) tremble; quaver: *her voice wobbled dangerously, but she brought it under control.* ■ hesitate or waver between different courses of action; vacillate: *he is beginning to wobble on the issue.*
▶ n. an unsteady movement from side to side. ■ a tremble or quaver in the voice. ■ a moment of hesitation or vacillation.
– ORIGIN mid 17th cent. (earlier as *wabble*): of Germanic origin; compare with Old Norse *vafla* 'waver'; related to the verb WAVE.

wob·bler /ˈwäb(ə)lər/ ▶ n. a person or thing that wobbles. ■ (in angling) a lure that wobbles and does not spin.

Wob·blies /ˈwäblēz/ ▶ plural n. popular name for members of INDUSTRIAL WORKERS OF THE WORLD.
– ORIGIN early 20th cent.: of unknown origin.

wob·bly /ˈwäb(ə)lē/ ▶ adj. (**wobblier**, **wobbliest**) tending to move unsteadily from side to side: *the car had a wobbly wheel.* ■ (of a person or their legs) weak and unsteady from illness, tiredness, or anxiety. ■ (of a person, action or state) uncertain, wavering, or insecure: *the evening gets off to a wobbly start.* ■ (of a speaker, singer, or voice) having a tendency to move out of tone or slightly vary in pitch. ■ (of a line or handwriting) not straight or regular; shaky.
– DERIVATIVES **wob·bli·ness** n.

Wode·house /ˈwŏŏd,hous/, Sir P. G. (1881–1975), English writer; full name *Pelham Grenville Wodehouse*. His best-known works are humorous stories of the upper-class world of Bertie Wooster and his valet Jeeves, the first of which appeared in 1917.

Wo·den /ˈwōdn/ another name for ODIN.

woe /wō/ ▶ n. often humorous great sorrow or distress: *they had a complicated tale of woe.* ■ (**woes**) things that cause sorrow or distress; troubles: *to add to his woes, customers have been spending less.*
– PHRASES **woe betide someone** (or **woe to someone**) used humorously to warn someone that they will be in trouble if they do a specified thing: *woe betide anyone wearing the wrong color!* **woe is me!** an ironical or humorous exclamation of sorrow or distress.
– ORIGIN natural exclamation of lament: recorded as *wā* in Old English and found in several Germanic languages.

woe·be·gone /ˈwōbi,gôn, -,gän/ ▶ adj. sad or miserable in appearance: *don't look so woebegone, Joanna.*
– ORIGIN Middle English (in the sense 'afflicted with grief'): from WOE + *begone* 'surrounded' (past participle of obsolete *bego* 'go around, beset').

woe·ful /ˈwōfəl/ ▶ adj. characterized by, expressive of, or causing sorrow or misery: *her face was woeful.* ■ very bad; deplorable: *the remark was enough to establish his woeful ignorance about the theater.*
– DERIVATIVES **woe·ful·ly** adv. [as submodifier] *the police response was woefully inadequate,* **woe·ful·ness** n.

wog /wäg/ ▶ n. Brit. offensive a person who is not white.
– ORIGIN 1920s: of unknown origin.

Wöh·ler /ˈvœlər/, Friedrich (1800–82), German chemist. His synthesis of urea from ammonium cyanate in 1828 demonstrated that organic compounds could be made from inorganic compounds. He was also the first to isolate the elements aluminum and beryllium.

wok /wäk/ ▶ n. a bowl-shaped frying pan used typically in Chinese cooking.
– ORIGIN Chinese (Cantonese dialect).

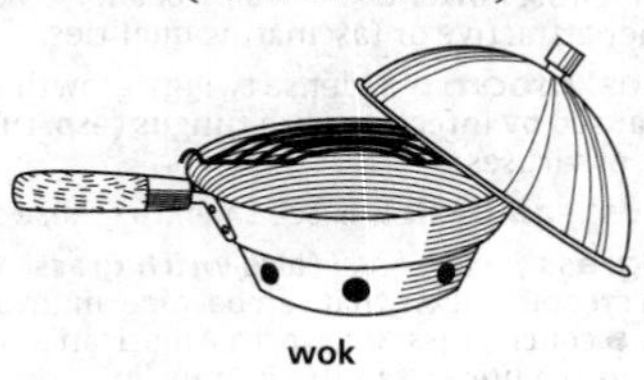
wok

woke /wōk/ past of WAKE[1].

wok·en /ˈwōkən/ past participle of WAKE[1].

wold /wōld/ ▶ n. (usu. **wolds**) (in Britain, often in place names) a piece of high, open, uncultivated land or moor: *the Lincolnshire Wolds.*
– ORIGIN Old English *wald* 'wooded upland,' of Germanic origin; perhaps related to WILD. Compare with WEALD.

wolf /wŏŏlf/ ▶ n. (pl. **wolves** /wŏŏlvz/) **1** a wild carnivorous mammal of the dog family, living and hunting in packs. It is native to both Eurasia and North America, but has been widely exterminated. ● *Canis lupus*, family Canidae; it is the chief ancestor of the domestic dog. ■ used in names of similar or related mammals, e.g., **maned wolf**, **Tasmanian wolf**.
2 used in similes and metaphors to refer to a rapacious, ferocious, or voracious person or thing. ■ informal a man who habitually seduces women.
3 a harsh or out-of-tune effect produced when playing particular notes or intervals on a musical instrument, caused either by the instrument's construction or by divergence from equal temperament.
▶ v. [with obj.] devour (food) greedily: *he* **wolfed down** *his breakfast.*
– PHRASES **cry wolf** call for help when it is not needed, with the effect that one is not believed when one really does need help. [with allusion to Aesop's fable of the shepherd boy who deluded people with false cries of "Wolf!"] **hold** (or **have**) **a wolf by the ears** be in a precarious position. **keep the wolf from the door** have enough money to avert hunger or starvation (used hyperbolically): *I work part-time to pay the mortgage and keep the wolf from the door.* **throw someone to the wolves** leave someone to be roughly treated or criticized without trying to help or defend them. **a wolf in sheep's clothing** a person or thing that appears friendly or harmless but is really hostile. [with biblical allusion to Matt. 7:15.]
– DERIVATIVES **wolf·like** /-,līk/ adj.
– ORIGIN Old English *wulf*, of Germanic origin; related to Dutch *wolf* and German *Wolf*, from an Indo-European root shared by Latin *lupus* and Greek *lukos*. The verb dates from the mid 19th cent.

wolf·ber·ry /ˈwŏŏlf,berē/ ▶ n. (pl. **wolfberries**) any of various shrubs of the genus *Lycium*, in particular the goji berry. ■ the fruit of the wolfberry.

Wolfe[1] /wŏŏlf/, James (1727–59), British general. One of the leaders of the expedition sent to seize French Canada, he commanded the attack on Quebec, the French capital, in 1759. He was fatally wounded while leading his troops to victory on the Plains of Abraham.

Wolfe[2], Thomas (Clayton) (1900–38), US novelist. His intense, romantic works, including his first autobiographical novel *Look Homeward Angel* (1929), dwell idealistically on the US Other notable works: *Of Time and the River* (1935), *The Web and the Rock* (1938), and *You Can't Go Home Again* (1940).

Wolfe[3], Tom (1931–), US writer; full name *Thomas Kennerley Wolfe, Jr.* Having been a news reporter for the *Washington Post* 1959–62 and the *Herald Tribune* 1962–66, he examined contemporary culture in the US in *The Electric Kool-Aid Acid Test* (1968), *The Bonfire of the Vanities* (1988), and *A Man in Full* (1998).

wolf·fish /ˈwŏŏlf,fisH/ ▶ n. a large long-bodied marine fish with a long-based dorsal fin and sharp doglike teeth, inhabiting the deep waters of the northern hemisphere. Also called CATFISH, SEA WOLF. ● Family Anarhichadidae: several genera and species, including the edible *Anarhichas lupus.*

wolf·hound /ˈwŏŏlf,hound/ ▶ n. a dog of a large breed originally used to hunt wolves.

wolf·ish /ˈwŏŏlfisH/ ▶ adj. resembling or likened to a wolf, esp. in being rapacious, voracious, or lascivious: *a wolfish grin.*
– DERIVATIVES **wolf·ish·ly** adv.

wolf pack ▶ n. a group of people or things that operate as a hunting and attacking pack, in particular a group of attacking submarines or aircraft.

wolf·ram /ˈwo͝olfrəm/ ▸ **n.** tungsten or its ore, esp. as a commercial commodity.
– ORIGIN mid 18th cent.: from German, assumed to be a miners' term, perhaps from *Wolf* 'wolf' + Middle High German *rām* 'soot,' probably originally a pejorative term referring to the ore's inferiority to tin, with which it occurred.

wolf·ram·ite /ˈwo͝olfrəˌmīt/ ▸ **n.** a black or brown mineral that is the chief ore of tungsten. It consists of a tungstate of iron and manganese.

Wolf Riv·er a river that flows for 210 miles (340 km) through central Wisconsin.

wolfs·bane /ˈwo͝olfsˌbān/ ▸ **n.** a northern European aconite. ● Genus *Aconitum*, family Ranunculaceae: several species, in particular the purple-flowered *A. lycoctonum*.

Wolfs·burg /ˈwo͝olfsˌbərg, ˈvôlfsˌbo͝ork/ an industrial city on the Mittelland Canal in Lower Saxony, in northwestern Germany; pop. 120,500 (est. 2006).

wolf·skin /ˈwo͝olfˌskin/ ▸ **n.** the skin or pelt of a wolf.

wolf spi·der ▸ **n.** a fast-moving ground spider that runs after and springs on its prey. ● Family Lycosidae, order Araneae.

wolf whis·tle ▸ **n.** a whistle with a rising and falling pitch, directed toward someone to express sexual attraction or admiration.
▸ **v.** (**wolf-whistle**) [with obj.] whistle in such a way at: *fans wolf-whistled her as she took off her jacket* | [no obj.] *they wolf-whistled at me*.

Wol·las·ton /ˈwo͝oləstən/, William Hyde (1766–1828), English chemist and physicist. He discovered palladium and rhodium and pioneered techniques in powder metallurgy.

wol·las·ton·ite /ˈwo͝oləstəˌnīt/ ▸ **n.** a white or grayish mineral typically occurring in tabular masses in metamorphosed limestone. It is a silicate of calcium and is used as a source of rock wool.
– ORIGIN early 19th cent.: from the name of W. H. *Wollaston* (see **WOLLASTON**) + **-ITE**[1].

Wol·lon·gong /ˈwo͝olənˌgôNG, -ˌgäNG/ a city on the coast of New South Wales, in southeastern Australia; pop. 198,324 (2008).

Woll·stone·craft /ˈwo͝olstənˌkraft/, Mary (1759–97), English writer and feminist. Her *A Vindication of the Rights of Woman* (1792) defied assumptions about male supremacy and championed educational equality for women. In 1797 she married William Godwin and died shortly after giving birth to their daughter Mary Shelley.

Wo·lof /ˈwōˌläf/ ▸ **n.** (pl. **same** or **Wolofs**) **1** a member of a people living in Senegal and Gambia. **2** the Niger–Congo language of this people.
▸ **adj.** of or relating to the Wolof or their language.
– ORIGIN the name in Wolof.

Wol·sey /ˈwo͝olzē/, Thomas (*c.*1474–1530), English prelate and statesman; known as **Cardinal Wolsey**. He incurred royal displeasure through his failure to secure the papal dispensation necessary for Henry VIII's divorce from Catherine of Aragon. He was arrested on a charge of treason and died on his way to trial.

Wol·ston·i·an /wôlˈstōnēən/ ▸ **adj.** Geology of, relating to, or denoting the penultimate Pleistocene glaciation in Britain, identified with the Saale of northern Europe (and perhaps the Riss of the Alps). ■ (as noun **the Wolstonian**) the Wolstonian glaciation or the system of deposits laid down during it.
– ORIGIN 1960s: from *Wolston*, the name of a village in central England, + **-IAN**.

Wol·ver·hamp·ton /ˈwo͝olvərˌham(p)tən, ˌwo͝olvərˈham(p)-/ an industrial city in western central England, northwest of Birmingham; pop. 246,100 (est. 2009).

wol·ver·ine /ˌwo͝olvəˈrēn/ ▸ **n. 1** a heavily built short-legged carnivorous mammal with a shaggy dark coat and a bushy tail, native to the tundra and forests of arctic and subarctic regions. ● *Gulo luscus* of North America and *G. gulo* of Europe, family Mustelidae. **2** (**Wolverine**) informal a native or inhabitant of Michigan.
– ORIGIN late 16th cent. (earlier as *wolvering*): formed obscurely from *wolv-*, plural stem of **WOLF**.

European wolverine

Wol·ver·ine State a nickname for the state of **Michigan**.

wolves /wo͝olvz/ plural form of **WOLF**.

wom·an /ˈwo͝omən/ ▸ **n.** (pl. **women** /ˈwimin/) an adult human female. ■ a female worker or employee. ■ a wife, girlfriend, or lover: *he wondered whether Billy had his woman with him*. ■ [with adj. or noun modifier] a female person associated with a particular place, activity, or occupation: *a young American woman*. ■ [in sing.] female adults in general: *woman is intuitive*. ■ a female paid to clean someone's house and carry out general domestic duties. ■ a peremptory form of address to a woman: *don't be daft, woman*.
– PHRASES **be one's own woman** see **OWN**. **the little woman** a condescending way of referring to a man's wife. **my good woman** Brit. dated a patronizing form of address to a woman: *you're mistaken, my good woman*. **woman of letters** a female scholar or author. **woman of the streets** dated used euphemistically to refer to a prostitute. **woman of the world** see **WORLD**. **woman to woman** in a direct and frank way between two women.
– DERIVATIVES **wom·an·less** adj., **wom·an·like** /-ˌlīk/ adj.
– ORIGIN Old English *wīfmon, -man* (see **WIFE**, **MAN**), a formation peculiar to English, the ancient word being **WIFE**.

-woman ▸ **comb. form** in nouns denoting. ■ a female of a specified nationality: *Frenchwoman*. ■ a woman of specified origin or place of abode: *Yorkshirewoman*. ■ a woman belonging to a distinct specified group: *laywoman*. ■ a woman having a specified occupation or professional status: *chairwoman* | *saleswoman*. ■ a woman skilled in or associated with a specified activity, esp. a craft or sport: *needlewoman* | *oarswoman*.

wom·an·hood /ˈwo͝omənˌho͝od/ ▸ **n.** the state or condition of being a woman: *she was on the very brink of womanhood*. ■ the qualities considered to be natural to or characteristic of a woman: *Mary was cultivated as an ideal of womanhood*. ■ women considered collectively: *images of African-American womanhood*.

wom·an·ish /ˈwo͝oməniSH/ ▸ **adj.** derogatory suitable to or characteristic of a woman: *he confused introspection with womanish indecision*. ■ (of a man) effeminate; unmanly: *Burden thought him a weak womanish fool*.
– DERIVATIVES **wom·an·ish·ly** adv., **wom·an·ish·ness** n.

wom·an·ism /ˈwo͝oməˌnizəm/ ▸ **n.** a form of feminism that emphasizes women's natural contribution to society (used by some in distinction to the term *feminism* and its association with white women).
– DERIVATIVES **wom·an·ist** n.

wom·an·ize /ˈwo͝oməˌnīz/ ▸ **v.** [no obj.] (of a man) engage in numerous casual sexual affairs with women: (as noun **womanizing**) *there were rumors that his womanizing had now become intolerable*.
– DERIVATIVES **wom·an·iz·er** n.

wom·an·kind /ˈwo͝omənˌkīnd/ ▸ **n.** women considered collectively: *a giant step forward for womankind*.

wom·an·ly /ˈwo͝omənlē/ ▸ **adj.** relating to or having the characteristics of a woman or women: *her smooth, womanly skin*. ■ (of a girl's or woman's body) fully developed and curvaceous: *I've got a womanly figure*.
– DERIVATIVES **wom·an·li·ness** n.

wo·man of col·or ▸ **n.** see **PERSON OF COLOR**.

womb /wo͞om/ ▸ **n.** the uterus. ■ a place of origination and development: *the womb of evil*.
– DERIVATIVES **womb·like** /-ˌlīk/ adj.
– ORIGIN Old English *wamb, womb*, of Germanic origin.

wom·bat /ˈwämˌbat/ ▸ **n.** a burrowing plant-eating Australian marsupial that resembles a small bear with short legs. ● Family Vombatidae: two genera and three species, in particular the **common wombat** (*Vombatus ursinus*).
– ORIGIN late 18th cent.: from Dharuk.

common wombat

wom·en /ˈwimin/ plural form of **WOMAN**.

wom·en·folk /ˈwiminˌfōk/ ▸ **plural n.** the women of a particular family or community considered collectively.

wom·en's lib ▸ **n.** informal short for **WOMEN'S LIBERATION**.
– DERIVATIVES **wom·en's lib·ber** n.

wom·en's lib·er·a·tion ▸ **n.** the advocacy of the liberation of women from inequalities and subservient status in relation to men, and from attitudes causing these (now generally replaced by the term *feminism*).

wom·en's move·ment ▸ **n.** a broad movement campaigning for women's liberation and rights.

wom·en's rights ▸ **plural n.** rights that promote a position of legal and social equality of women with men.

wom·en's room ▸ **n.** another term for **LADIES' ROOM**.

wom·en's stud·ies ▸ **plural n.** [usu. treated as sing.] academic courses in sociology, history, literature, and psychology that focus on the roles, experiences, and achievements of women in society.

wom·en's suf·frage ▸ **n.** the right of women to vote.

wom·ens·wear /ˈwiminzˌwe(ə)r/ (also **women's wear**) ▸ **n.** clothing for women.

wom·en's work ▸ **n.** work traditionally and historically undertaken by women, esp. tasks of a domestic nature such as cooking, needlework, and child rearing.

wom·yn /ˈwimin/ ▸ **plural n.** nonstandard spelling of "women" adopted by some feminists in order to avoid the word ending *-men*.

won[1] /wən/ past and past participle of **WIN**.

won[2] /wän/ ▸ **n.** (pl. **same**) the basic monetary unit of North and South Korea, equal to 100 jun in North Korea and 100 jeon in South Korea.
– ORIGIN from Korean *wǒn*.

Won·der /ˈwəndər/, Stevie (1950–), US singer, songwriter, and musician; born *Stevland Hardaway Judkins*. His repertoire of soul, rock, funk, and romantic ballads includes the albums *Innervisions* (1973) and *Songs in the Key of Life* (1976) and the songs "You Are the Sunshine of My Life" and "I Just Called to Say I Love You."

won·der /ˈwəndər/ ▸ **n.** a feeling of surprise mingled with admiration, caused by something beautiful, unexpected, unfamiliar, or inexplicable: *he had stood in front of it, observing the intricacy of the ironwork with the wonder of a child*. ■ the quality of a person or thing that causes such a feeling: *Athens was a place of wonder and beauty*. ■ a strange or remarkable person, thing, or event: *the electric trolley car was looked upon as the wonder of the age*. ■ [as modifier] having remarkable properties or abilities: *a wonder drug*. ■ [in sing.] a surprising event or situation: *it is a wonder that losses are not much greater*.
▸ **v.** [no obj.] **1** desire or be curious to know something: *how many times have I written that, I wonder?* | [with clause] *I can't help wondering how Stasia and Katie are feeling*. ■ [with clause] used to express a polite question or request: *I wonder whether you have thought more about it?* ■ feel doubt: *I **wonder about** such a marriage*.
2 feel admiration and amazement; marvel: *people stood by and **wondered at** such bravery* | (as adj. **wondering**) *a wondering look on her face*. ■ be surprised: *if I feel compassion for her, it is not to be wondered at*.
– PHRASES **I shouldn't wonder** informal, chiefly Brit. I think it likely. **no** (or **little** or **small**) **wonder** it is not surprising: *it is little wonder that the fax machine is so popular*. **ninety-day** (or **thirty-day** or **one-day**) **wonder** something that attracts enthusiastic interest for a short while but is then ignored or forgotten. ■ (usu. **ninety-day** (or **thirty-day**) **wonder**) a person who has had intensive military training for the specified time. **wonders will never cease** an exclamation of great surprise at something pleasing. **work** (or **do**) **wonders** have a very beneficial effect on someone or something: *a good night's sleep can work wonders for mind and body*.
– DERIVATIVES **won·der·er** n., **won·der·ing·ly** adv.
– ORIGIN Old English *wundor* (noun), *wundrian* (verb), of Germanic origin; related to Dutch *wonder* and German *Wunder*, of unknown ultimate origin.

Won·der·bra /ˈwəndərbrä/ ▸ **n.** trademark an underwire, padded bra designed to enhance the wearer's cleavage.

won·der·ful /ˈwəndərfəl/ ▸ **adj.** inspiring delight, pleasure, or admiration; extremely good; marvelous: *they all think she's wonderful* | *the climate was wonderful all the year round*.
– DERIVATIVES **won·der·ful·ly** /-f(ə)lē/ adv. [as submodifier] *the bed was wonderfully comfortable*, **won·der·ful·ness** n.
– ORIGIN late Old English *wunderfull* (see **WONDER**, **-FUL**).

W

PRONUNCIATION KEY ə *ago, up*; ər *over, fur*; a *hat*; ā *ate*; ä *car*; e *let*; ē *see*; i *fit*; ī *by*; NG *sing*; ō *go*; ô *law, for*; oi *toy*; o͝o *good*; o͞o *goo*; ou *out*; TH *thin*; T͟H *then*; ZH *vision*

won·der·land /ˈwəndərˌland/ ▶ n. a land or place full of wonderful things: *London was a wonderland of historical sites, museums, theaters, shops, and entertainment.*

won·der·ment /ˈwəndərmənt/ ▶ n. a state of awed admiration or respect: *Corbett shook his head in silent wonderment.*

won·der·struck /ˈwəndərˌstrək/ ▶ adj. (of a person) experiencing a sudden feeling of awed delight or wonder.

won·der·work·er /ˈwəndərˌwərkər/ ▶ n. a person who performs miracles or wonders.
– DERIVATIVES **won·der·work·ing** adj.

won·drous /ˈwəndrəs/ ▶ adj. literary inspiring a feeling of wonder or delight; marvelous: *this wondrous city.*
▶ adv. [as submodifier] archaic marvelously; wonderfully: *she is grown wondrous pretty.*
– DERIVATIVES **won·drous·ly** adv., **won·drous·ness** n.
– ORIGIN late 15th cent.: alteration of obsolete *wonders* (adjective and adverb), genitive of WONDER, on the pattern of *marvelous.*

wonk /wäNGk/ ▶ n. informal, derogatory a studious or hardworking person: *any kid with an interest in science was a wonk.* ■ a person who takes an excessive interest in minor details of political policy: *he is a **policy wonk** in tune with a younger generation of voters.*
– DERIVATIVES **wonk·ish** adj.
– ORIGIN 1920s: of unknown origin.

won·ky /ˈwäNGkē/ ▶ adj. (**wonkier, wonkiest**) informal crooked; off-center; askew: *you have a wonky nose and a crooked mouth.* ■ (of a thing) unsteady; shaky: *they sat drinking, perched on the wonky stools.* ■ not functioning correctly; faulty: *your sense of judgment is a bit wonky at the moment.*
– DERIVATIVES **won·ki·ly** /ˈwäNGkəlē/ adv., **won·ki·ness** n.
– ORIGIN early 20th cent.: fanciful formation.

wont /wônt, wōnt/ ▶ adj. [predic.] literary (of a person) in the habit of doing something; accustomed: *he was wont to arise at 5:30 every morning.*
▶ n. (**one's wont**) formal or humorous one's customary behavior in a particular situation: *Constance, as was her wont, had paid her little attention.*
▶ v. (3rd sing. present **wonts** or **wont**; past and past participle **wont** or **wonted**) archaic make or be or become accustomed: [with obj.] *wont thy heart to thoughts hereof* | [no obj., with infinitive] *sons wont to nurse their parents in old age.*
– ORIGIN Old English *gewunod,* past participle of *wunian,* 'dwell, be accustomed' of Germanic origin.

won't /wōnt/ ▶ contraction will not.

wont·ed /ˈwôntid, ˈwōn-/ ▶ adj. literary habitual; usual: *the place had sunk back into its wonted quiet.*
– ORIGIN late Middle English: from WONT.

won·ton /ˈwänˌtän/ (also **won ton**) ▶ n. (in Chinese cooking) a small dumpling or roll with a savory filling, often of minced pork, usually eaten boiled in soup.
– ORIGIN from Chinese (Cantonese dialect) *wān t'ān.*

woo /wo͞o/ ▶ v. (**woos, wooing, wooed**) [with obj.] try to gain the love of (someone, typically a woman), esp. with a view to marriage: *he wooed her with quotes from Shakespeare.* ■ seek the favor, support, or custom of: *pop stars are being wooed by film companies eager to sign them up.*
– DERIVATIVES **woo·a·ble** adj., **woo·er** n.
– ORIGIN late Old English *wōgian* (intransitive), *āwōgian* (transitive), of unknown origin.

Wood /wo͝od/, Grant (De Volsen) (1892–1942), US artist. He is most noted for his scenes of his native Iowa in paintings such as *Woman with Plant(s)* (1929), *American Gothic* (1930), and *Spring in Town* (1941).

wood /wo͝od/ ▶ n. **1** the hard fibrous material that forms the main substance of the trunk or branches of a tree or shrub. ■ such material when cut and used as timber or fuel: *a large table made of dark, polished wood* | *best quality woods were used for joinery* | [as modifier] *a wood cross.* ■ a golf club with a wooden or other head that is relatively broad from face to back (often with a numeral indicating the degree to which the face is angled to loft the ball). ■ a shot made with such a club.
2 (also **woods**) an area of land, smaller than a forest, that is covered with growing trees: *a thick hedge divided the wood from the field* | *a long walk in the woods.*
– PHRASES **get wood** vulgar slang have an erection. **knock on wood** said in order to prevent a confident statement from bringing bad luck: *I haven't been banned yet, knock on wood.* [with reference to the custom of touching something wooden to ward off bad luck.] **out of the wood** (or **woods**) out of danger or difficulty.
– DERIVATIVES **wood·less** adj.
– ORIGIN Old English *wudu,* from a Germanic word related to Welsh *gŵydd* 'trees.'

W

wood al·co·hol ▶ n. crude methanol made by distillation from wood.

wood a·nem·o·ne ▶ n. see ANEMONE.

wood ant ▶ n. a large reddish-brown ant found chiefly in woodlands, living in nest mounds, which it defends by spraying formic acid at the attacker. ● *Formica rufa,* family Formicidae.

wood bet·o·ny ▶ n. see LOUSEWORT.

wood·bine /ˈwo͝odˌbīn/ ▶ n. either of two climbing plants. ● Virginia creeper. ● Brit. the common honeysuckle.

wood·block /ˈwo͝odˌbläk/ ▶ n. a block of wood, esp. one from which woodcut prints are made. ■ a print made in such a way. ■ a hollow wooden block used as a percussion instrument.

Wood·bridge /ˈwo͝odˌbrij/ an industrial, commercial, and residential township in northeastern New Jersey; pop. 97,963 (est. 2008).

Wood·bur·y /ˈwo͝odˌberē, -bərē/, Levi (1789–1851), US Supreme Court associate justice 1846–51. Before being appointed to the Court by President Polk, he served as the governor of New Hampshire 1823–24 and as a US senator 1825–31, 1841–45.

wood·carv·ing /ˈwo͝odˌkärviNG/ ▶ n. the action or skill of carving wood to make functional or ornamental objects. ■ an object made in this way.
– DERIVATIVES **wood·carv·er** n.

wood·chat /ˈwo͝odˌCHat/ (also **woodchat shrike**) ▶ n. a shrike of southern Europe, North Africa, and the Middle East, having black and white plumage with a chestnut head. ● *Lanius senator,* family Laniidae.

wood·chuck /ˈwo͝odˌCHək/ ▶ n. a North American marmot with a heavy body and short legs. ● *Marmota monax,* family Sciuridae.
– ORIGIN late 17th cent.: alteration (by association with WOOD) of an American Indian name.

wood·cock /ˈwo͝odˌkäk/ ▶ n. (pl. **same**) a woodland bird of the sandpiper family, with a long bill, brown camouflaged plumage, and a distinctive display flight. ● Genus *Scolopax,* family Scolopacidae: several species, in particular the **Eurasian woodcock** (*S. rusticola*), which is sometimes regarded as a game bird.

wood·craft /ˈwo͝odˌkraft/ ▶ n. **1** skill in woodwork.
2 knowledge of the woods, esp. with reference to camping and other outdoor pursuits.

wood·cut /ˈwo͝odˌkət/ ▶ n. a print of a type made from a design cut in a block of wood, formerly widely used for illustrations in books. Compare with WOOD ENGRAVING. ■ the technique of making such prints.

wood·cut·ter /ˈwo͝odˌkətər/ ▶ n. **1** a person who cuts down trees or branches, esp. for fuel.
2 a person who makes woodcuts.
– DERIVATIVES **wood·cut·ting** n.

wood duck ▶ n. a tree-nesting North American duck, the male of which has brightly colored plumage. Also called CAROLINA DUCK. ● *Aix sponsa,* family Anatidae.

wood ear ▶ n. an edible fungus, black or brown in color, that grows on trees and is sold in dry wrinkled shapes somewhat resembling ears. ● *Auricularia auricula,* family Auriculariaceae.

wood·ed /ˈwo͝odid/ ▶ adj. (of an area of land) covered with woods or many trees: *a wooded valley.*

wood·en /ˈwo͝odn/ ▶ adj. **1** made of wood: *a wooden spoon* | *she closed the heavy wooden door.*
2 like or characteristic of wood: *a kind of dull wooden sound.* ■ stiff and awkward in movement or manner: *she is one of the most wooden actresses of all time.*
– DERIVATIVES **wood·en·ly** adv. (sense 2), **wood·en·ness** n. (sense 2).

wood en·grav·ing ▶ n. a print made from a finely detailed design cut into the end grain of a block of wood. Compare with WOODCUT. ■ the technique of making such prints.
– DERIVATIVES **wood en·grav·er** n.

wood·en·head ▶ n. informal a stupid person.
– DERIVATIVES **wood·en·head·ed** adj., **wood·en·head·ed·ness** n.

wood·fern /ˈwo͝odˌfərn/ ▶ n. an evergreen fern with leathery dark-green fronds. ● Genus *Dryopteris,* family Polypodiaceae, numerous species, including the common **evergreen** (or **marginal**) **woodfern** (*D. marginalis*).

evergreen woodfern

wood fi·ber /ˈwo͝od ˌfībər/ ▶ n. fiber obtained from wood and used esp. in the manufacture of paper.

wood·grain /ˈwo͝odˌgrān/ ▶ n. a texture seen in a cut surface of wood. ■ [as modifier] denoting a surface or finish imitating such a pattern: *the doors are available in woodgrain finish.*

wood·grouse /ˈwo͝odˌgrous/ ▶ n. a grouse that frequents woodlands, esp. a capercaillie, spruce grouse, or willow grouse.

wood·hoo·poe /ˈho͞oˌpō, -po͞o/ ▶ n. a long-tailed African bird with a long, slender, down-curved bill and blackish plumage with a blue or green gloss. ● Genus *Phoeniculus,* family Phoeniculidae: several species.

wood i·bis ▶ n. **1** a stork with a slightly down-curved bill and a bare face or head, found in America and Africa. Also called WOOD STORK. ● Genus *Mycteria,* family Ciconiidae: the black-faced *M. americana* of America, and the red-faced *M. ibis* of Africa.
2 (**crested wood ibis**) a mainly brown ibis with a greenish crest, found only in Madagascar. ● *Lophotibis cristata,* family Threskiornithidae.

wood·ie /ˈwo͝odē/ ▶ n. **1** vulgar slang (also **woody**) (of a man) a penile erection.
2 a station wagon with wood exterior paneling.

Wood·land /ˈwo͝odlənd/ a city in north central California, northwest of Sacramento; pop. 54,567 (est. 2008).

wood·land /ˈwo͝odlənd, -ˌland/ ▶ n. (also **woodlands**) land covered with trees: *large areas of ancient woodland* | [as modifier] *woodland birds are often drably colored.*

wood·land·er /ˈwo͝odləndər, -ˌlandər/ ▶ n. an inhabitant of woodland.

wood·lark /ˈwo͝odˌlärk/ ▶ n. a small European and North African lark with a short tail and melodious song, frequenting open ground with scattered trees. ● *Lullula arborea,* family Alaudidae.

Wood·lawn /ˈwo͝odˌlôn/ a residential section of the northern Bronx in New York City, site of the noted Woodlawn Cemetery.

wood louse ▶ n. (pl. **wood lice**) a small terrestrial crustacean with a grayish segmented body and seven pairs of legs, living in damp habitats. ● *Oniscus* and other genera, order Isopoda.

wood·man /ˈwo͝odmən/ ▶ n. (pl. **woodmen**) chiefly historical a person working in woodland, esp. a forester or woodcutter.

wood mouse ▶ n. a dark brown Eurasian mouse with a long tail and large eyes. Also called FIELD MOUSE. ● Genus *Apodemus,* family Muridae: several species, in particular the widespread *A. sylvaticus.*

wood mush·room ▶ n. an edible mushroom with a white cap and brown gills, smelling strongly of aniseed and found in woodland in both Eurasia and North America. ● *Agaricus silvicola,* family Agaricaceae, class Hymenomycetes.

wood·note /ˈwo͝odˌnōt/ ▶ n. literary a natural and untrained musical note resembling the song of a bird.

wood nymph ▶ n. **1** (in folklore and classical mythology) a nymph inhabiting woodland, esp. a Dryad or Hamadryad.
2 a brown American butterfly of grassy habitats and light woodlands, with large eyespots on the forewings and smaller ones on the hind wings. ● Genus *Cercyonis,* subfamily Satyrinae, family Nymphalidae: several species, in particular the widespread *C. pegala.*
3 (also **woodnymph**) a dark-colored, green-throated hummingbird, found from Mexico to Argentina. ● Genus *Thalurania,* family Trochilidae: several species, including the **common wood nymph** (*T. furcata*) and the **Mexican wood nymph** (*T. ridgwayi*).

wood nymph 2

wood·peck·er /ˈwo͝odˌpekər/ ▶ n. a bird with a strong bill and a stiff tail, that climbs tree trunks to find insects and drums on dead wood to mark territory. ● Family Picidae (the **woodpecker family**): many genera and numerous species. The woodpecker family also includes the wrynecks, piculets, flickers, and sapsuckers.

wood pi·geon ▶ n. a large Eurasian and African pigeon with mainly gray plumage, using wing claps in display flight. ● Genus *Columba*, family Columbidae: several species, in particular the widespread *C. palumbus* (also called RINGDOVE).

wood·pile /ˈwo͝odˌpīl/ ▶ n. a stack of wood stored for fuel.

wood pulp ▶ n. wood fiber reduced chemically or mechanically to pulp and used in the manufacture of paper.

wood rat ▶ n. another term for PACK RAT.

wood·ruff /ˈwo͝odˌrəf/ ▶ n. a white-flowered plant of the bedstraw family with whorled leaves, smelling of new-mown hay when dried or crushed. ● Genera *Galium* and *Asperula*, family Rubiaceae: several species, esp. **sweet woodruff** (*G. odoratum*).
– ORIGIN Old English *wudurofe*, from *wudu* 'wood' + an element of unknown meaning.

Wood·ruff key /ˈwo͝odrəf/ ▶ n. a key whose cross section is part circular, to fit into a curved keyway in a shaft, and part rectangular, used chiefly in machinery.
– ORIGIN late 19th cent.: named after the *Woodruff* Manufacturing Company, Hartford, Connecticut.

wood·rush /ˈwo͝odˌrəsн/ ▶ n. a grasslike plant that typically has long flat leaves fringed with long hairs. ● Genus *Luzula*, family Juncaceae: many species.

Woods[1] /wo͝odz/, Tiger (1975–), US golfer; full name *Eldrick Tont Woods*. Since turning professional in 1996, he has won several championships, including the Masters (1997, 2001, 2002, 2005), the PGA (1999, 2000, 2006, 2007), the US Open (2000, 2002, 2008), and the British Open (2000, 2005, 2006).

Tiger Woods

Woods[2], William Burnham (1824–87), US Supreme Court associate justice 1880–87. A judge on the circuit court, he was appointed to the Supreme Court by President Hayes.

wood sage ▶ n. another term for AMERICAN GERMANDER (see GERMANDER).

wood screw ▶ n. a tapering metal screw with a sharp point.

wood·shed /ˈwo͝odˌsнed/ ▶ n. a shed where wood for fuel is stored.
▶ v. [no obj.] informal practice a musical instrument: *he's off woodshedding again.*
– PHRASES **take someone to the woodshed** informal reprove or punish someone.

Woods Hole a village in Falmouth in southeastern Massachusetts, at the southwest corner of Cape Cod, a resort and noted ocean research center.

wood·si·a /ˈwo͝odzēə/ ▶ n. a small tufted fern that grows among rocks in mountains in temperate and cool regions. ● Genus *Woodsia*, family Woodsiaceae.
– ORIGIN modern Latin, named after Joseph *Woods* (1776–1864), English architect and botanist.

woods·man /ˈwo͝odzmən/ ▶ n. (pl. **woodsmen**) a person living or working in the woods, esp. a forester, hunter, or woodcutter.

wood·smoke /ˈwo͝odˌsmōk/ ▶ n. the smoke from a wood fire.

wood sor·rel ▶ n. a small woodland plant with cloverlike leaves and five-petaled flowers. ● Genus *Oxalis*, family Oxalidaceae: several species, including the yellow-flowered creeping **yellow wood sorrel** (*O. stricta*) and the purple-flowered **violet wood sorrel** (*O. violacea*).

wood spir·it ▶ n. another term for WOOD ALCOHOL.

Wood·stock /ˈwo͝odˌstäk/ a small town in southwestern New York, 50 miles (80 km) south of Albany. It gave its name in the summer of 1969 to a huge rock music festival held about 60 miles (96 km) to the southwest.

wood stork ▶ n. another term for WOOD IBIS.

woods·y /ˈwo͝odzē/ ▶ adj. of, relating to, or characteristic of wood or woodlands: *trails through woodsy countryside | the woodsy smells of cedar and pine.*
– ORIGIN mid 19th cent.: formed irregularly from WOOD (differentiated from *woody*).

wood thrush ▶ n. a thrush of eastern North America, with a brown back, rufous head, and dark-spotted white breast, and a loud liquid song. ● *Hylocichla mustelina*, subfamily Turdinae, family Muscicapidae.

wood tick ▶ n. a North American tick that infests wild and domestic animals, often found clinging to plants and responsible for transmitting spotted fever. ● Genus *Dermacentor*, family Ixodidae, in particular *D. andersoni*.

wood tick

wood·turn·ing /ˈwo͝odˌtərniNG/ ▶ n. the action of shaping wood with a lathe.
– DERIVATIVES **wood·turn·er** /-ˌtərnər/ n.

wood war·bler ▶ n. a migratory European leaf warbler found in woodlands, with plaintive calls and a trilling song. ● *Phylloscopus sibilatrix*, family Sylviidae. ■ any New World warbler of the subfamily Parulinae, family Emberizidae.

Wood·ward[1], Robert Burns (1917–79), US organic chemist. He was the first to synthesize quinine, cholesterol, chlorophyll, and vitamin B_{12}, and with **Roald Hoffmann** (1937–), a US chemist, born in Poland, discovered symmetry-based rules governing the course of rearrangement reactions involving cyclic intermediates. Nobel Prize for Chemistry (1965).

Wood·ward[2], Robert (Upshur) (1943–), US journalist. He was the *Washington Post* reporter who, with Carl Bernstein, broke the story of the Watergate burglary and traced the financial payoffs to President Nixon. With Bernstein, he wrote *All the President's Men* (1974) and *The Final Days* (1976). He is also the author of *The Choice* (1996), *Shadow: Five Presidents and the Legacy of Watergate* (1999), and *Plan of Attack* (2004).

wood·wasp /ˈwo͝odˌwäsp/ ▶ n. another term for HORNTAIL.

wood·wind /ˈwo͝odˌwind/ ▶ n. [treated as sing. or pl.] wind instruments other than brass instruments forming a section of an orchestra, including flutes, oboes, clarinets, and bassoons: *striking passages for woodwind and brass* | [as modifier] *a woodwind instrument.*

wood wool·ly foot ▶ n. see WOOLLY FOOT.

wood·work /ˈwo͝odˌwərk/ ▶ n. the wooden parts of a room or building, such as window frames or doors: *the woodwork was painted blue.*
– PHRASES **come out of the woodwork** (of an unpleasant person or thing) emerge from obscurity; be revealed.

wood·work·ing /ˈwo͝odˌwərkiNG/ ▶ n. the activity or skill of making things from wood.
– DERIVATIVES **wood·work·er** n.

wood·worm /ˈwo͝odˌwərm/ ▶ n. the worm or larva of a beetle that bores into wood. ■ the damaged condition of wood resulting from infestation with this larva.

wood·y /ˈwo͝odē/ ▶ adj. (**woodier**, **woodiest**) (of an area of land) covered with trees: *a woody dale.* ■ made of, resembling, or suggestive of wood: *cut out the woody central core before boiling.* ■ Botany (of a plant or its stem) of the nature of or consisting of wood; lignified.
▶ n. (pl. **woodies**) vulgar slang an erection of the penis.
– DERIVATIVES **wood·i·ness** n.

wood·yard /ˈwo͝odˌyärd/ ▶ n. a yard where wood is chopped or stored.

wood·y night·shade ▶ n. see NIGHTSHADE.

woof[1] /wo͝of/ ▶ n. the barking sound made by a dog.
▶ v. [no obj.] (of a dog) bark: *the dog started to woof.* ■ informal say something in an ostentatious or aggressive manner but with no intention to act: *King start woofing to keep folks off our case. Just woofing. Just talk.*
– ORIGIN early 19th cent.: imitative.

woof[2] ▶ n. another term for WEFT.
– ORIGIN Old English *ōwef*, a compound from the base of WEAVE[1]; Middle English *oof* later became *woof* by association with WARP in the phrase *warp and woof*.

woof·er /ˈwo͝ofər/ ▶ n. a loudspeaker designed to reproduce low frequencies.
– ORIGIN 1930s: from the verb WOOF[1] + -ER[1].

wool /wo͝ol/ ▶ n. **1** the fine soft curly or wavy hair forming the coat of a sheep, goat, or similar animal, esp. when shorn and prepared for use in making cloth or yarn. ■ yarn or textile fiber made from such hair: *carpets made of 80 percent wool and 20 percent nylon | a sampler in colored wools* | [as modifier] *her blue wool suit.*
2 a thing resembling such hair in form or texture, in particular: ■ [with modifier] the soft underfur or down of some other mammals: *beaver wool.* ■ [with modifier] a metal or mineral made into a mass of fine fibers: *lead wool.*
– PHRASES **pull the wool over someone's eyes** deceive someone by telling untruths.
– DERIVATIVES **wool·like** /-ˌlīk/ adj.
– ORIGIN Old English *wull*, of Germanic origin; related to Dutch *wol* and German *Wolle*, from an Indo-European root shared by Latin *lana* 'wool,' *vellus* 'fleece.'

wool clip ▶ n. the total quantity of wool shorn from a particular flock or in a particular area in the course of a year.

wool·en /ˈwo͝olən/ (Brit. **woollen**) ▶ adj. [attrib.] of or relating to the production of wool: *the woolen industry | a woolen mill.* ■ made wholly or partly of wool: *thick woolen blankets.*
▶ n. (usu. **woolens**) an article of clothing made of wool.
– ORIGIN late Old English *wullen* (see WOOL, -EN[2]).

Woolf /wo͝olf/, Virginia (1882–1941), English novelist, essayist, and critic; born *Adeline Virginia Stephen*. A member of the Bloomsbury Group, she gained recognition with *Jacob's Room* (1922). Subsequent novels, such as *Mrs. Dalloway* (1925) and *To the Lighthouse* (1927), established her as an exponent of modernism.

wool·gath·er·ing /ˈwo͝olˌgaTH(ə)riNG/ ▶ n. indulgence in aimless thought or dreamy imagining; absentmindedness: *he wanted to be free to indulge his woolgathering.*
– DERIVATIVES **wool·gath·er** /-ˌgaTHərər/ v.

wool·grow·er /ˈwo͝olˌgrō(ə)r/ ▶ n. a breeder of sheep for wool.

Wooll·cott /ˈwo͝olkət/, Alexander (Humpreys) (1887–1943), US critic. He was the drama critic for *The New York Times* (1914–22) and the *New York World* (1925–28) and also had a radio show called "Town Crier" (1929–42). The title character in *The Man Who Came to Dinner* (1939), a play by Moss Hart and George S. Kaufman, was based on Woollcott.

Wool·ley /ˈwo͝olē/, Leonard (1880–1960), English archaeologist; full name *Sir Charles Leonard Woolley*. He directed a British-US excavation of the Sumerian city of Ur 1922–34 that uncovered rich royal tombs and thousands of clay tablets.

wool·ly /ˈwo͝olē/ (also **wooly**) ▶ adj. (**woollier**, **woolliest**) **1** made of wool: *a red woolly hat.* ■ (of an animal, plant, or part) bearing or naturally covered with wool or hair resembling wool. ■ resembling wool in texture or appearance: *woolly wisps of cloud.*
2 vague or confused in expression or character: *woolly thinking.* ■ (of a sound) indistinct or distorted: *an opaque and woolly recording.*
▶ n. (pl. **woollies**) **1** (usu. **woollies**) informal, chiefly Brit. a garment made of wool, esp. a pullover.
2 a sheep.
– DERIVATIVES **wool·li·ness** n.

wool·ly a·del·gid /əˈdeljid/ ▶ n. any of several small aphidlike insects that feed on conifers, esp. hemlocks, spruces, and firs. By sucking the sap from young twigs, the insect retards or prevents tree growth and causes needles to discolor and drop prematurely. ● Superfamily Aphidoidea, family Adelgidae.

wool·ly bear ▶ n. a large hairy caterpillar, esp. that of a tiger moth.

wool·ly·butt /ˈwo͝olēˌbət/ ▶ n. an Australian eucalyptus with thick fibrous bark. ● Several species in the genus *Eucalyptus*, family Myrtaceae.

wool·ly foot (also **wood woolly foot**) ▶ n. a yellowish-brown toadstool with a slender stem, the base of which bears long woolly hairs, found commonly in woodlands in both Eurasia and North America. ● *Collybia peronata*, family Tricholomataceae, class Hymenomycetes.

wool·ly mam·moth ▶ n. a mammoth that was adapted to the cold periods of the Pleistocene, with a long shaggy coat, small ears, and a thick layer of fat. Individuals are sometimes found frozen in the permafrost of Siberia. ● *Mammuthus primigenius*, family Elephantidae.

woolly mammoth

wool·ly rhi·noc·er·os ▶ n. an extinct two-horned Eurasian rhinoceros that was adapted to the cold periods of the Pleistocene, with a long woolly coat. ● Genus *Coelodonta*, family Rhinocerotidae.

wool·ly spi·der mon·key ▶ n. a large spider monkey with long thin limbs and tail, dense woolly fur, and a large protruding belly, native to the rain forests of southeastern Brazil. ● *Brachyteles arachnoides*, family Cebidae.

Wool·mark /ˈwo͝olˌmärk/ ▶ n. an international quality symbol for wool instituted by the International Wool Secretariat.

Wool·sack /ˈwo͝olˌsak/ ▶ n. (in the UK) the Lord Chancellor's wool-stuffed seat in the House of Lords. It is said to have been adopted in Edward III's reign as a reminder to the Lords of the importance to England of the wool trade. ■ (**the woolsack**) the position of Lord Chancellor.

wool·sort·er's dis·ease ▶ n. see ANTHRAX.

wool·sta·pler ▶ n. archaic a person who buys wool from a producer, grades it, and sells it to a manufacturer.

wool work ▶ n. needlework executed in wool on a canvas foundation.

Wool·worth /ˈwo͝olwərTH/, Frank Winfield (1852–1919), US businessman. He pioneered the concept of low-priced retailing in 1878 and from this built a large international chain of stores.

wool·y ▶ adj. variant spelling of WOOLLY.

Woo·me·ra /ˈwo͞omərə, ˈwo͞omə-/ a town in central South Australia, the site of a vast military testing ground used in the 1950s for nuclear tests and since the 1960s for tracking space satellites.

woo·mer·a /ˈwo͞omərə/ ▶ n. Austral. an Aboriginal stick used to throw a dart or spear more forcibly.
– ORIGIN from Dharuk *wamara*.

woo·nerf /ˈvo͞onərf/ ▶ n. a road in which devices for reducing or slowing the flow of traffic have been installed.
– ORIGIN 1970s: from Dutch, from *wonen* 'reside' + *erf* 'premises, ground.'

Woon·sock·et /wo͞onˈsäkit/ an industrial city in northern Rhode Island, on the Blackstone River; pop. 43,268 (est. 2008).

woop·ie /ˈwo͞opē/ (also **woopy**) ▶ n. (pl. **woopies**) informal an affluent retired person able to pursue an active lifestyle.
– ORIGIN 1980s: elaboration of the acronym from *well-off older person*.

woosh ▶ v., n., exclam., & adv. variant spelling of WHOOSH.

Woos·ter /ˈwo͝ostər/ an industrial and academic city in north central Ohio; pop. 26,212 (est. 2008).

wooz·y /ˈwo͞ozē/ ▶ adj. (**woozier**, **wooziest**) informal unsteady, dizzy, or dazed: *I still felt woozy from all the pills*.
– DERIVATIVES **wooz·i·ly** /-zəlē/ adv., **wooz·i·ness** n.
– ORIGIN late 19th cent.: of unknown origin.

wop /wäp/ ▶ n. informal, offensive a contemptuous term for an Italian or other southern European.
– ORIGIN early 20th cent. (originally US): origin uncertain, perhaps from Italian *guappo* 'bold, showy,' from Spanish *guapo* 'dandy.'

W

Worces·ter[1] /ˈwo͝ostər/ an industrial and college city in central Massachusetts, on the Blackstone River; pop. 175,011 (est. 2008).

Worces·ter[2] /ˈwo͝ostər/ (also **Royal Worcester**) ▶ n. trademark porcelain made at Worcester, England, in a factory founded in 1751. The porcelain (largely tableware) at first showed strong influence from Chinese and Dresden designs before being produced in a wider variety of designs.

Worces·ter·shire sauce /ˈwo͝ostərˌSHi(ə)r, -SHər/ ▶ n. a pungent sauce containing soy sauce and vinegar, first made in Worcester, England.

Worcs. ▶ abbr. Worcestershire.

word /wərd/ ▶ n. a single distinct meaningful element of speech or writing, used with others (or sometimes alone) to form a sentence and typically shown with a space on either side when written or printed. ■ a single distinct conceptual unit of language, comprising inflected and variant forms. ■ (usu. **words**) something that someone says or writes; a remark or piece of information: *his grandfather's words had been meant kindly | a word of warning*. ■ speech as distinct from action: *he conforms in word and deed to the values of a society that he rejects*. ■ [with negative] (**a word**) even the smallest amount of something spoken or written: *don't believe a word of it*. ■ (**one's word**) a person's account of the truth, esp. when it differs from that of another person: *in court it would have been his word against mine*. ■ (**one's word**) a promise or assurance: *everything will be taken care of—you have my word*. ■ (**words**) the text or spoken part of a play, opera, or other performed piece; a script: *he had to learn his words*. ■ (**words**) angry talk: *her father would have **had words with** her about that*. ■ a message; news: *I was afraid to leave Washington in case there was word from the office*. ■ a command, password, or motto: *someone **gave the word** to start playing*. ■ a basic unit of data in a computer, typically 16 or 32 bits long.
▶ v. [with obj.] choose and use particular words in order to say or write (something): *he words his request in a particularly ironic way* | (as adj., with submodifier **worded**) *a strongly worded letter of protest*.
▶ exclam. informal used to express agreement: *"That Jay is one dangerous character." "Word."*
– PHRASES **at a word** as soon as requested: *ready to leave again at a word*. **be as good as one's word** do what one has promised to do. **break one's word** fail to do what one has promised. **have a word** speak briefly to someone: *I'll just **have a word with** him*. **in other words** expressed in a different way; that is to say. **in so many words** [often with negative] in the way mentioned: *I haven't told him in so many words, but he'd understand*. **in a word** briefly. **keep one's word** do what one has promised. **a man/woman of his/her word** a person who keeps their promises. **(on/upon) my word** an exclamation of surprise or emphasis: *my word, you were here quickly!* **of few words** taciturn: *he's a man of few words*. **put something into words** express something in speech or writing: *he felt a vague disappointment which he couldn't put into words*. **put words into someone's mouth** falsely or inaccurately report what someone has said. ■ prompt or encourage someone to say something that they may not otherwise have said. **take someone at their word** interpret a person's words literally or exactly, esp. by believing them or doing as they suggest. **take the words out of someone's mouth** say what someone else was about to say. **take someone's word (for it)** believe what someone says or writes without checking for oneself. **too —— for words** informal extremely ——: *going around by the road was too tedious for words*. **waste words 1** talk in vain. **2** talk at length. **the Word (of God) 1** the Bible, or a part of it. **2** Jesus Christ (see LOGOS). **word for word** in exactly the same or, when translated, exactly equivalent words. **word of honor** a solemn promise: *I'll be good to you always, I give you my word of honor*. **word of mouth** spoken language; informal or unofficial discourse. **the word on the street** informal a rumor or piece of information currently being circulated. **words fail me** used to express one's disbelief or dismay. **a word to the wise** a hint or brief explanation given, that being all that is required.
– PHRASAL VERBS **word up** [as imperative] informal listen: *word up, my brother, you got me high as a kite*.
– DERIVATIVES **word·age** /ˈwərdij/ n., **word·less** adj., **word·less·ly** adv., **word·less·ness** n.
– ORIGIN Old English, of Germanic origin; related to Dutch *woord* and German *Wort*, from an Indo-European root shared by Latin *verbum* 'word.'

-word ▶ comb. form denoting a word that may be offensive or have a negative connotation, specified by the word's first letter: *the F-word*.

word as·so·ci·a·tion ▶ n. the spontaneous and unreflective production of other words in response to a given word, as a game, a prompt to creative thought or memory, or a technique in psychiatric evaluation.

word blind·ness ▶ n. less technical term for ALEXIA, or (less accurately) for DYSLEXIA.

word·book /ˈwərdˌbo͝ok/ ▶ n. a reference book containing lists of words and meanings or other related information.

word break (also **word division**) ▶ n. Printing a point at which a word is split between two lines of text by means of a hyphen.

word class ▶ n. a category of words of similar form or function; a part of speech.

word deaf·ness ▶ n. an inability to identify spoken words, resulting from a brain defect such as Wernicke's aphasia.

word game ▶ n. a game involving the making, guessing, or selection of words.

word·ing /ˈwərdiNG/ ▶ n. the words used to express something; the way in which something is expressed: *the standard form of wording for a consent letter*.

word length ▶ n. Computing the number of bits in a word.

word or·der ▶ n. the sequence of words in a sentence, esp. as governed by grammatical rules and as affecting meaning.

word-per·fect /ˈpərfəkt/ ▶ adj. another term for LETTER-PERFECT.

word pic·ture ▶ n. a vivid description in writing.

word·play /ˈwərdˌplā/ ▶ n. the witty exploitation of the meanings and ambiguities of words, esp. in puns.

word prob·lem ▶ n. a mathematics exercise presented in the form of a hypothetical situation that requires an equation to be solved; for example, "if George earns a salary of $18,500 and 28% of it is deducted in taxes, how much take-home pay remains?"

word proc·ess·ing ▶ n. the production, storage, and manipulation of text on a computer or word processor.
– DERIVATIVES **word-proc·ess** v.

word proc·es·sor ▶ n. a program or machine for storing, manipulating, and formatting text entered from a keyboard and providing a printout.

word sal·ad ▶ n. a confused or unintelligible mixture of seemingly random words and phrases, specifically (in psychiatry) as a form of speech indicative of advanced schizophrenia.

word search ▶ n. a puzzle consisting of letters arranged in a grid, containing several hidden words written in any direction.

word·smith /ˈwərdˌsmiTH/ ▶ n. a skilled user of words.

word square ▶ n. a puzzle requiring the discovery of a set of words of equal length written one under another to read the same down as across, e.g., *too old ode*.

Words·worth[1] /ˈwərdzˌwərTH/, Dorothy (1771–1855), English diarist, sister of William Wordsworth. Her *Grasmere Journal* (1800–03) documents her intense response to nature.

Words·worth[2], William (1770–1850), English poet. Much of his work was inspired by the Lake District. "Lyrical Ballads" (1798), which was composed with Coleridge and included "Tintern Abbey," was a landmark in romanticism. He was appointed poet laureate in 1843. Other notable poems:"I Wandered Lonely as a Cloud" (1815) and "The Prelude" (1850).

word wrap ▶ n. (in word processing) a feature that automatically moves a word that is too long to fit on a line to the beginning of the next line.

word·y /ˈwərdē/ ▶ adj. (**wordier**, **wordiest**) using or expressed in too many words: *a wordy and repetitive account*. ■ archaic consisting of words: *on the publication of Worcester's dictionary, a wordy war arose*.
– DERIVATIVES **word·i·ly** /-dəlē/ adv., **word·i·ness** n.
– ORIGIN Old English *wordig* (see WORD, -Y[1]).

wore[1] /wôr/ past of WEAR[1].

wore[2] past and past participle of WEAR[2].

work /wərk/ ▶ n. **1** activity involving mental or physical effort done in order to achieve a purpose or result: *he was tired after a day's work in the fields*. ■ (**works**) [in combination] a place or premises for industrial activity, typically manufacturing: *he found a job in the ironworks*.
2 such activity as a means of earning income; employment: *I'm still looking for work*. ■ the place where one engages in such activity: *I was returning home from work on a packed subway*. ■ the period of time spent during the day engaged in such activity: *he was going to the theater after work*.
3 a task or tasks to be undertaken; something a person or thing has to do: *they made sure the work was progressing smoothly*. ■ the materials for this: *she frequently took work home with her*. ■ (**works**) Theology good or moral deeds: *the Clapham sect was concerned with works rather than with faith*.
4 something done or made: *her work hangs in all the main American collections*. ■ the result of the action of a specified person or thing: *the bombing had been the work of a German-based cell*. ■ a literary or musical composition or other piece of fine art: *a work of fiction*. ■ (**works**) all such pieces by a particular author, composer, or artist, regarded collectively: *the works of Schubert fill several feet of shelf space*. ■ a piece of embroidery,

sewing, or knitting, typically made using a specified stitch or method. ■ (usu. **works**) Military a defensive structure. ■ (**works**) an architectural or engineering structure such as a bridge or dam. ■ the record of the successive calculations made in solving a mathematical problem: *show your work on a separate sheet of paper.*
5 (**works**) the operative part of a clock or other machine: *she could almost hear the tick of its works.*
6 Physics the exertion of force overcoming resistance or producing molecular change.
7 (**the works**) informal everything needed, desired, or expected: *the heavens put on a show: sheet lightning, hailstones—the works.*
▸ **v.** (past and past participle **worked** or archaic **wrought** /rôt/) [no obj.] **1** be engaged in physical or mental activity in order to achieve a purpose or result, esp. in one's job; do work: *an engineer who had been* ***working on*** *a design for a more efficient wing | new contracts forcing employees to work longer hours.* ■ be employed, typically in a specified occupation or field: *Taylor has* ***worked in*** *education for 17 years.* ■ (**work in**) (of an artist) produce articles or pictures using (a particular material or medium): *he works in clay over a very strong frame.* ■ [with obj.] produce (an article or design) using a specified material or sewing stitch: *the castle itself is* ***worked in*** *tent stitch.* ■ [with obj.] set to or keep at work: *Jane is working you too hard.* ■ [with obj.] cultivate (land) or extract materials from (a mine or quarry): *contracts and leases to work the mines.* ■ [with obj.] solve (a puzzle or mathematical problem): *she spent her days working crosswords.* ■ [with obj.] practice one's occupation or operate in or at (a particular place): *I worked a few clubs and so forth.* ■ make efforts to achieve something; campaign: *we spend a great deal of our time* ***working for*** *the lacto-vegetarian cause.*
2 (of a machine or system) operate or function, esp. properly or effectively: *his cell phone doesn't work unless he goes to a high point.* ■ (of a machine or a part of it) run; go through regular motions: *it's designed to go into a special "rest" state when it's not working.* ■ (esp. of a person's features) move violently or convulsively: *hair wild, mouth working furiously.* ■ [with obj.] cause (a device or machine) to operate: *teaching customers how to work a VCR.* ■ (of a plan or method) have the desired result or effect: *the desperate ploy had worked.* ■ [with obj.] bring about; produce as a result: *with a dash of blusher here and there, you can work miracles.* ■ [with obj.] informal arrange or contrive: *the chairman was prepared to work it for Phillip if he was interested.* ■ (**work on/upon**) exert influence or use one's persuasive power on (someone or their feelings): *she worked upon the sympathy of her associates.* ■ [with obj.] use one's persuasive power to stir the emotions of (a person or group of people): *the born politician's art of working a crowd.*
3 [with obj. or complement] bring (a material or mixture) to a desired shape or consistency by hammering, kneading, or some other method: *work the mixture into a paste with your hands.* ■ bring into a specified state, esp. an emotional state: *Harold had worked himself into a minor rage.*
4 [with adverbial or complement] move or cause to move gradually or with difficulty into another position, typically by means of constant movement or pressure: [with obj.] *comb from tip to root, working out the knots at the end* | [no obj.] *its bases were already working loose.* ■ (of joints, such as those in a wooden ship) loosen and flex under repeated stress. ■ [with adverbial] Sailing make progress to windward, with repeated tacking: *trying to work to windward in light airs.*
– PHRASES **at work** engaged in work. ■ in action: *researchers were convinced that one infectious agent was at work.* **give someone the works** informal treat someone harshly. ■ kill someone. **have one's work cut out** be faced with a hard or lengthy task. **in the works** being planned, worked on, or produced. **out of work** unemployed. **set to work** (or **set someone to work**) begin or cause to begin work. **the work of ——** a task occupying a specified amount of time: *it was the work of a moment to discover the tiny stab wound.* **work one's ass** (**butt**, etc.) **off** vulgar slang work extremely hard. **work one's fingers to the bone** see BONE. **work one's passage** pay for one's journey on a ship with work instead of money. **work one's way through college** (or **school**, etc.) obtain the money for educational fees or one's maintenance as a student by working. **work one's will on/upon** accomplish one's purpose on: *she set a coiffeur to work his will on her hair.* **work wonders** see WONDER.
– PHRASAL VERBS **work something in** include or incorporate something, typically in something spoken or written. **work something off 1** discharge a debt by working. **2** reduce or get rid of something by work or activity: *one of those gimmicks for working off aggression.* **work out 1** (of an equation) be capable of being solved. ■ (**work out at**) be calculated at: *the losses work out at $2.94 a share.* **2** have a good or specified result: *things don't always work out that way.* **3** engage in vigorous physical exercise or training, typically at a gym. **work someone out** understand someone's character. **work something out 1** solve a sum or determine an amount by calculation. ■ solve or find the answer to something: *I couldn't work out whether it was a band playing or a record.* **2** plan or devise something in detail: *work out a seating plan.* **3** literary accomplish or attain something with difficulty: *malicious fates are bent on working out an ill intent.* **4** (usu. **be worked out**) work a mine until it is exhausted of minerals. **5** another way of saying WORK SOMETHING OFF above. **work someone over** informal treat someone with violence; beat someone severely: *the cops had worked him over a little just for the fun of it.* **work through** go through a process of understanding and accepting (a painful or difficult situation): *they should be allowed to feel the pain and work through their emotions.* **work to** follow or operate within the constraints of (a plan or system): *working to tight deadlines.* **work up to** proceed gradually toward (something more advanced or intense): *the course starts with landing technique, working up to jumps from an enclosed platform.* **work someone up** (often **get worked up**) gradually bring someone, esp. oneself, to a state of intense excitement, anger, or anxiety: *he got all worked up and started shouting and swearing.* **work something up 1** bring something gradually to a more complete or satisfactory state: *painters were accustomed to working up compositions from drawings.* **2** develop or produce by activity or effort: *despite the cold, George had already worked up a fair sweat.*
– DERIVATIVES **work·less** adj., **work·less·ness** n.
– ORIGIN Old English *weorc* (noun), *wyrcan* (verb), of Germanic origin; related to Dutch *werk* and German *Werk*, from an Indo-European root shared by Greek *ergon*.

-work ▸ comb. form denoting things or parts made of a specified material or with specified tools: *silverwork | fretwork.* ■ denoting a mechanism or structure of a specified kind: *bridgework | clockwork.* ■ denoting ornamentation of a specified kind, or articles having such ornamentation: *knotwork.*

work·a·ble /ˈwərkəbəl/ ▸ adj. **1** able to be worked, fashioned, or manipulated: *more flour and salt can be added until they make a workable dough.*
2 capable of producing the desired effect or result; practicable; feasible: *a workable peace settlement.*
– DERIVATIVES **work·a·bil·i·ty** /ˌwərkəˈbilitē/ n., **work·a·bly** /-blē/ adv.

work·a·day /ˈwərkəˌdā/ ▸ adj. of or relating to work or one's job: *the workaday world of timecards and performance reviews.* ■ not special, unusual, or interesting in any way; ordinary: *your humble workaday PC.*

work·a·hol·ic /ˌwərkəˈhôlik, -ˈhälik/ ▸ n. informal a person who compulsively works hard and long hours.
– DERIVATIVES **work·a·hol·ism** /ˈwərkəˌhôlizəm, -ˌhäl-/ n.

work·a·like /ˈwərkəˌlīk/ ▸ n. Computing a computer that is able to use the software of another specified machine without special modification. ■ a piece of software identical in function to another software package.

work·a·round /ˈwərkəˌround/ ▸ n. Computing a method for overcoming a problem or limitation in a program or system.

work·bas·ket /ˈwərkˌbaskət/ (also **workbag**) ▸ n. a basket (or bag) used for storing sewing materials.

work·bench /ˈwərkˌbenCH/ ▸ n. a bench at which carpentry or other mechanical or practical work is done.

work·boat /ˈwərkˌbōt/ ▸ n. a boat used for work such as commercial fishing or transporting freight, rather than leisure or naval service.

work·book /ˈwərkˌbo͝ok/ ▸ n. a student's book containing instruction and exercises relating to a particular subject. ■ Computing a single file containing several different types of related information as separate worksheets.

work·box /ˈwərkˌbäks/ ▸ n. a portable box used for storing or holding tools and materials for activities such as sewing.

work camp ▸ n. a camp at which community work is done, esp. by young volunteers. ■ another term for LABOR CAMP.

work·day /ˈwərkˌdā/ ▸ n. a day on which one works: *Saturdays were workdays for him.*

work·er /ˈwərkər/ ▸ n. **1** a person or animal that works, in particular: ■ [with adj. or noun modifier] a person who does a specified type of work or who works in a specified way: *a farm worker | she's a good worker.* ■ an employee, esp. one who does manual or nonexecutive work. ■ (**workers**) used in Marxist or leftist contexts to refer to the working class. ■ informal a person who works hard: *I got a reputation for being a worker.* ■ (in social insects such as bees, wasps, ants, and termites) a neuter or undeveloped female that is a member of what is usually the most numerous caste and does the basic work of the colony.
2 a person who produces or achieves a specified thing: *a worker of miracles.*

work·er priest ▸ n. a Roman Catholic priest, esp. in postwar France, or an Anglican priest who engages part-time in ordinary secular work.

work eth·ic ▸ n. [in sing.] the principle that hard work is intrinsically virtuous or worthy of reward. See also PROTESTANT ETHIC.

work·fare /ˈwərkˌfe(ə)r/ ▸ n. a welfare system that requires those receiving benefits to perform some work or to participate in job training.
– ORIGIN 1960s: from WORK + a shortened form of WELFARE.

work·flow /ˈwərkˌflō/ ▸ n. the sequence of industrial, administrative, or other processes through which a piece of work passes from initiation to completion.

work·force (also **work force**) ▸ n. [treated as sing. or pl.] the people engaged in or available for work, either in a country or area or in a particular company or industry.

work func·tion ▸ n. Physics the minimum quantity of energy that is required to remove an electron to infinity from the surface of a given solid, usually a metal. (Symbol: φ)

work·group /ˈwərkˌgro͞op/ ▸ n. a group within a workforce that normally works together. ■ Computing a group that shares data via a local network.

work-hard·en ▸ v. [with obj.] (often as noun **work-hardening**) Metallurgy toughen (a metal) by cold-working.

work·horse /ˈwərkˌhôrs/ ▸ n. a horse used for work on a farm. ■ a person or machine that dependably performs hard work over a long period of time: *he was a workhorse of an actor, often appearing in as many as forty plays in a year.*

work·house /ˈwərkˌhous/ ▸ n. **1** historical (in the UK) a public institution in which the destitute of a parish received board and lodging in return for work.
2 a prison in which petty offenders are expected to work.

work·ing /ˈwərkiNG/ ▸ adj. **1** having paid employment: *the size of the working population.* ■ engaged in manual labor: *the vote is no longer sufficient protection for the working man.* ■ relating to, suitable for, or for the purpose of work: *improvements in living and working conditions.* ■ (of an animal) used in farming, hunting, or for guard duties; not kept as a pet or for show. ■ (of something possessed) sufficient to work with: *they have a working knowledge of contract law.* ■ (of a theory, definition, or title) used as the basis for work or argument and likely to be developed, adapted, or improved later: *the working hypothesis is tested and refined through discussion.*
2 functioning or able to function: *the mill still has a working waterwheel.* ■ (of parts of a machine) moving and causing a machine to operate: *the working parts of a digital watch.*
▸ n. **1** the action of doing work. ■ (usu. **workings**) a mine or a part of a mine from which minerals are being extracted.
2 (**workings**) the way in which a machine, organization, or system operates: *we will be less secretive about the workings of government.*
– PHRASES **working lunch** (or **dinner**, etc.) a lunch (or dinner, etc.) at which those present discuss business.

work·ing cap·i·tal ▸ n. Finance the capital of a business that is used in its day-to-day trading operations, calculated as the current assets minus the current liabilities.

work·ing class ▸ n. [treated as sing. or pl.] the social group consisting of people who are employed for wages, esp. in manual or industrial work: *the housing needs of the working classes.*
▸ adj. (**working-class**) of, relating to, or characteristic of people belonging to such a group: *a working-class community.*

work·ing day ▸ n. another term for WORKDAY.

work·ing draw·ing ▸ n. a scale drawing that serves as a guide for the construction or manufacture of something such as a building or machine.

work·ing girl ▶ **n.** informal a woman who goes out to work rather than remaining at home. ■ euphemistic a prostitute.

work·ing group ▶ **n.** a committee or group appointed to study and report on a particular question and make recommendations based on its findings.

work·ing load ▶ **n.** the maximum load that a machine or other structure is designed to bear during normal operation.

work·ing·man /ˈwərkiNG,man/ ▶ **n.** (pl. **workingmen**) a man who works for wages, esp. in manual or industrial work.

work·ing mem·o·ry ▶ **n.** Psychology the part of short-term memory that is concerned with immediate conscious perceptual and linguistic processing. ■ Computing an area of high-speed memory used to store programs or data currently in use.

work·ing stor·age ▶ **n.** Computing a part of a computer's memory that is used by a program for the storage of intermediate results or other temporary items.

work·load /ˈwərk,lōd/ ▶ **n.** the amount of work to be done by someone or something: *he had been given three deputies to ease his workload.*

work·man /ˈwərkmən/ ▶ **n.** (pl. **workmen**) a man employed to do manual labor. ■ [with adj.] a person with specified skill in a job or craft: *you check it through, like all good workmen do.*

work·man·like /ˈwərkmən,lik/ ▶ **adj.** showing efficient competence: *a steady, workmanlike approach.*

work·man·ship /ˈwərkmən,sHip/ ▶ **n.** the degree of skill with which a product is made or a job done: *cracks on the bridge girders were caused by poor workmanship.*

work·mate /ˈwərk,māt/ ▶ **n.** chiefly Brit. a person with whom one works.

work of art ▶ **n.** a creative product with strong imaginative or aesthetic appeal.

work·out /ˈwərk,out/ ▶ **n.** a session of vigorous physical exercise or training.

work per·mit ▶ **n.** an official document giving a foreigner permission to take a job in a country.

work·piece /ˈwərk,pēs/ ▶ **n.** an object being worked on with a tool or machine.

work·place /ˈwərk,plās/ ▶ **n.** a place where people work, such as an office or factory.

work re·lease ▶ **n.** leave of absence from prison by day enabling a prisoner to continue in normal employment.

work·room /ˈwərk,ro͞om, -,ro͝om/ ▶ **n.** a room for working in, esp. one equipped for a particular kind of work.

works coun·cil ▶ **n.** chiefly Brit. a group of employees representing a workforce in discussions with their employers.

work·sheet /ˈwərk,sHēt/ ▶ **n. 1** a paper listing questions or tasks for students.
2 a paper for recording work done or in progress. ■ Computing a data file created and used by a spreadsheet program, which takes the form of a matrix of cells when displayed.

work·shop /ˈwərk,sHäp/ ▶ **n. 1** a room or building in which goods are manufactured or repaired.
2 a meeting at which a group of people engage in intensive discussion and activity on a particular subject or project.
▶ **v.** [with obj.] present a performance of (a dramatic work), using intensive group discussion and improvisation in order to explore aspects of the production before formal staging: *the play was workshopped briefly at the Shaw Festival.*

work-shy ▶ **adj.** (of a person) lazy and disinclined to work.

work·site /ˈwərk,sīt/ ▶ **n.** an area where an industry is located or where work takes place.

work·space /ˈwərk,spās/ ▶ **n.** space in which to work: *the kitchen is all white, with maximum workspace.* ■ an area rented or sold for commercial purposes. ■ Computing a memory storage facility for temporary use.

W

work·sta·tion /ˈwərk,stāsHən/ ▶ **n. 1** a desktop computer terminal, typically networked and more powerful than a personal computer.
2 an area where work of a particular nature is carried out, such as a specific location on a manufacturing assembly line.

work-stud·y ▶ **adj.** [attrib.] of or relating to a college program that enables students to work part-time while attending school.

work sur·face ▶ **n.** another term for COUNTERTOP.

work·ta·ble /ˈwərktābəl/ ▶ **n.** a table at which one may work, esp. one with drawers or compartments for holding tools or materials.

work·up /ˈwərk,əp/ ▶ **n. 1** a diagnostic examination of a patient: *a full neurological workup.* ■ Chemistry a series of experimental procedures carried out to separate and purify substances for analysis.
2 (in a military context) a period of training or preparation, typically for a specific operation: *an intensive predeployment workup.*

work·wear /ˈwərk,we(ə)r/ ▶ **n.** heavy-duty clothes for physical or manual work.

work·week /ˈwərk,wēk/ ▶ **n.** the total number of hours or days worked in a week: *a six-day workweek.*

world /wərld/ ▶ **n. 1** (usu. **the world**) the earth, together with all of its countries, peoples, and natural features: *he was doing his bit to save the world.* ■ (**the world**) all of the people, societies, and institutions on the earth: [as modifier] *world affairs.* ■ [as modifier] denoting one of the most important or influential people or things of its class: *they had been brought up to regard France as a world power.* ■ another planet like the earth: *the possibility of life on other worlds.* ■ the material universe or all that exists; everything.
2 a part or aspect of human life or of the natural features of the earth, in particular: ■ a region or group of countries: *the English-speaking world.* ■ a period of history: *the ancient world.* ■ a group of living things: *the animal world.* ■ the people, places, and activities to do with a particular thing: *they were a legend in the world of British theater.* ■ human and social interaction: *he has almost completely withdrawn from the world | how inexperienced she is in the ways of the world.* ■ average, respectable, or fashionable people or their customs or opinions. ■ (**one's world**) a person's life and activities: *he felt his whole world had collapsed.* ■ everything that exists outside oneself. ■ [in sing.] a stage of human life, either mortal or after death: *in this world and the next.* ■ secular interests and affairs: *parents are not viewed as the primary educators of their own children, either in the world or in the church.*
– PHRASES **be not long for this world** have only a short time to live. **the best of both** (or **all possible**) **worlds** the benefits of widely differing situations, enjoyed at the same time. **bring someone into the world** give birth to or assist at the birth of someone. **come into the world** be born. **come up** (or **go down**) **in the world** rise (or drop) in status, esp. by becoming richer (or poorer). **in the world** used for emphasis in questions, esp. to express astonishment or disbelief: *why in the world did you not reveal yourself sooner?* **look for all the world like** look precisely like (used for emphasis): *fossil imprints that look for all the world like motorcycle tracks.* **man** (or **woman**) **of the world** a person who is experienced in the ways of sophisticated society. **not do something for the world** not do something whatever the inducement: *I wouldn't miss it for the world.* **out of this world** informal extremely enjoyable or impressive: *an herb and lemon dressing that's out of this world.* **see the world** travel widely and gain wide experience. **think the world of** have a very high regard for (someone): *I thought the world of my father.* **the world, the flesh, and the devil** all forms of temptation to sin. **a** (or **the**) **world of** a very great deal of: *there's a world of difference between being alone and being lonely.* (**all**) **the world over** everywhere on the earth. **worlds apart** very different or distant.
– ORIGIN Old English *w(e)oruld*, from a Germanic compound meaning 'age of man'; related to Dutch *wereld* and German *Welt*.

World Bank an international banking organization established to control the distribution of economic aid among member nations, and to make loans to them in times of financial crisis. See also INTERNATIONAL BANK FOR RECONSTRUCTION AND DEVELOPMENT.

world beat ▶ **n.** Western music incorporating elements of traditional music from any part of the world, esp. from developing nations: *the booming sounds of world beat in the background.*

world-beat·er ▶ **n.** a person or thing that is better than all others in its field.
– DERIVATIVES **world-beat·ing** adj.

world ci·ty ▶ **n.** a cosmopolitan city, with resident and visiting foreigners.

world-class ▶ **adj.** (of a person, thing, or activity) of or among the best in the world.

World Coun·cil of Church·es (abbr.: **WCC**) an association established in 1948 to promote unity among the many different Christian Churches. Its member Churches number over 300, and include virtually all Christian traditions except Roman Catholicism and Unitarianism. Its headquarters are in Geneva.

World Cup ▶ **n.** a sports competition between teams from several countries, in particular an international soccer tournament held every four years. ■ a trophy awarded for such a competition.

world fair ▶ **n.** see WORLD'S FAIR.

world-fa·mous ▶ **adj.** known throughout the world: *the world-famous tenor José Carreras.*

World Health Or·gan·i·za·tion (abbr.: **WHO**) an agency of the United Nations, established in 1948 to promote health and control communicable diseases.

World Her·it·age Site ▶ **n.** a natural or man-made site, area, or structure recognized as being of outstanding international importance and therefore as deserving special protection. Sites are nominated to and designated by the World Heritage Convention (an organization of UNESCO).

World In·tel·lec·tu·al Pro·per·ty Or·gan·i·za·tion (abbr.: **WIPO**) an organization, established in 1967 and an agency of the United Nations from 1974, for cooperation between governments in matters concerning patents, trademarks, and copyright, and the transfer of technology between countries. Its headquarters are in Geneva.

world lan·guage ▶ **n.** a language known or spoken in many countries: *English is now the world language.* ■ an artificial language for international use: *there have been attempts to introduce a standard world language.*

world line ▶ **n.** Physics a curve in space-time joining the positions of a particle throughout its existence.

world·ling /ˈwərldliNG/ ▶ **n.** a cosmopolitan and sophisticated person.

world·ly /ˈwərldlē/ ▶ **adj.** (**worldlier**, **worldliest**) of or concerned with material values or ordinary life rather than a spiritual existence: *his ambitions for worldly success.* ■ (of a person) experienced and sophisticated.
– PHRASES **worldly goods** (or **possessions** or **wealth**) everything that someone owns.
– DERIVATIVES **world·li·ness** n.
– ORIGIN Old English *woruldlic* (see WORLD, -LY¹).

world·ly-mind·ed ▶ **adj.** intent on worldly things.

world·ly-wise ▶ **adj.** prepared by experience for life's difficulties; not easily shocked or deceived: *Lisa was sufficiently worldly-wise to understand the situation.*
– DERIVATIVES **world·ly wis·dom** n.

World Me·te·or·o·log·i·cal Or·gan·i·za·tion (abbr.: **WMO**) an agency of the United Nations, established in 1950 with the aim of facilitating worldwide cooperation in meteorological observations, research, and services. Its headquarters are in Geneva.

world mu·sic ▶ **n.** traditional music from the developing world. ■ Western popular music incorporating elements of such music.

world or·der ▶ **n.** a system controlling events in the world, esp. a set of arrangements established internationally for preserving global political stability.

world pow·er ▶ **n.** a country that has significant influence in international affairs.

World Se·ries trademark the professional championship for North American major league baseball, played at the end of the season between the champions of the American League and the National League. It was first played in 1903.

World Serv·ice a service of the British Broadcasting Corporation that transmits radio programs in English and over thirty other languages around the world twenty-four hours a day. A worldwide television station was established in 1991 on a similar basis.

world's fair (also **world fair**) ▶ **n.** an international exhibition of the industrial, scientific, technological, and artistic achievements of the participating nations.

world-shak·ing ▶ **adj.** (in hyperbolic use) of supreme importance or having a momentous effect: *a world-shaking announcement.*

world soul ▶ **n.** Philosophy the immanent cause or principle of life, order, consciousness, and self-awareness in the physical world.
– ORIGIN mid 19th cent.: translating German *Weltgeist*.

World Trade Cen·ter a complex of buildings in New York featuring twin skyscrapers 110 stories high, designed by Minoru Yamasaki and completed in 1972. The twin towers were destroyed in a terrorist attack on September 11, 2001, with the loss of about 2,700 lives.

World Trade Or·gan·i·za·tion (abbr.: **WTO**) an international body founded in 1995 to promote international trade and economic development by reducing tariffs and other restrictions.

world·view /ˈwərld,vyo͞o/ (also **world view**) ▶ **n.** a particular philosophy of life or conception of the world: *I have broadened my worldview by experiencing a whole new culture.*

world war ▶ **n.** a war involving many large nations in all different parts of the world. The name is commonly given to the wars of 1914–18 and 1939–45, although only the second of these was truly global. See **World War I**, **World War II**.

World War I a war (1914–18) in which the Central Powers (Germany and Austria–Hungary, joined later by Turkey and Bulgaria) were defeated by an alliance of Britain and its dominions, France, Russia, and others, joined later by Italy and the US.

Political tensions over the rise of the German Empire were the war's principal cause, although it was set off by the assassination of Archduke Franz Ferdinand of Austria by a Bosnian Serb nationalist in Sarajevo, an event used as a pretext by Austria for declaring war on Serbia. Most of the fighting took place on land in Europe and was generally characterized by long periods of bloody stalemate; the balance eventually shifted in the Allies' favor in 1917 when the US joined the war. Total casualties of the war are estimated at 10 million killed. One of the consequences of the war was the collapse of the German, Austro-Hungarian, Russian, and Ottoman empires.

World War II a war (1939–45) in which the Axis Powers (Germany, Italy, and Japan) were defeated by an alliance eventually including the UK and its dominions, the former Soviet Union, and the US.

Hitler's invasion of Poland in September 1939 led Great Britain and France to declare war on Germany. Germany defeated and occupied France the following year and soon overran much of Europe. Italy joined the war in 1940, and the US and Japan entered after the Japanese attack on the US fleet at Pearl Harbor. Italy surrendered in 1943, and the Allies launched a full-scale invasion in Normandy in June 1944. The war in Europe ended when Germany surrendered in May 1945; Japan surrendered after the US dropped atom bombs on Hiroshima and Nagasaki in August 1945. An estimated 55 million people were killed during the war, including a much higher proportion of civilians than in World War I.

world-wea·ry ▶ **adj.** feeling or indicating feelings of weariness, boredom, or cynicism as a result of long experience of life: *their world-weary, cynical talk.*
– DERIVATIVES **world-wea·ri·ness n.**

world·wide /ˈwərldˈwīd/ ▶ **adj.** extending or reaching throughout the world: *worldwide sales of television rights.*
▶ **adv.** throughout the world: *she travels worldwide as a consultant.*

World Wide Web Computing a widely used information system on the Internet that provides facilities for documents to be connected to other documents by hypertext links, enabling the user to search for information by moving from one document to another.

WORM /wərm/ ▶ **abbr.** write-once read-many, denoting a type of computer memory device.

worm /wərm/ ▶ **n. 1** any of a number of creeping or burrowing invertebrate animals with long, slender, soft bodies and no limbs. ● Phyla Annelida (segmented worms), Nematoda (roundworms), and Platyhelminthes (flatworms), and up to twelve minor phyla. ■ short for **earthworm**. ■ (**worms**) intestinal or other internal parasites. ■ used in names of long, slender insect larvae, esp. those in fruit or wood, e.g., **army worm**, **woodworm**. ■ used in names of other animals that resemble worms in some way, e.g., **slow-worm**, **shipworm**. ■ a maggot supposed to eat buried corpses: *food for worms.* ■ Computing a self-replicating program able to propagate itself across a network, typically having a detrimental effect.
2 informal a weak or despicable person (used as a general term of contempt).
3 a helical device or component, in particular: ■ the threaded cylinder in a worm gear. ■ the coiled pipe of a still in which the vapor is cooled and condensed.
▶ **v. 1** [no obj.] move with difficulty by crawling or wriggling: *I wormed my way along the roadside ditch.* ■ (**worm one's way into**) insinuate one's way into: *the educated dealers may later worm their way into stockbroking.* ■ [with obj.] move (something) into a confined space by wriggling it: *I wormed my right hand between my body and the earth.* ■ (**worm something out of**) obtain information from (someone) by cunning persistence: *I did manage to worm a few details out of him.*
2 [with obj.] treat (an animal) with a preparation designed to expel parasitic worms.
3 [with obj.] Nautical, archaic make (a rope) smooth by winding small cordage between the strands.
– PHRASES **(even) a worm will turn** proverb (even) a meek person will resist or retaliate if pushed too far.
– DERIVATIVES **worm·like** /-,līk/ **adj.**
– ORIGIN Old English *wyrm* (noun), of Germanic origin; related to Latin *vermis* 'worm' and Greek *rhomox* 'woodworm.'

worm cast (also **worm casting**) ▶ **n.** a convoluted mass of soil, mud, or sand thrown up by an earthworm or lugworm on the surface after passing through the worm's body.

worm-eat·en ▶ **adj.** (of organic tissue) eaten into by worms: *a worm-eaten corpse.* ■ (of wood or a wooden object) full of holes made by woodworm.

worm·er /ˈwərmər/ ▶ **n.** a substance administered to animals or birds to expel parasitic worms.

worm-fish·ing ▶ **n.** the activity or practice of angling with worms for bait.

worm gear ▶ **n.** a mechanical arrangement consisting of a toothed wheel worked by a short revolving cylinder (worm) bearing a screw thread.

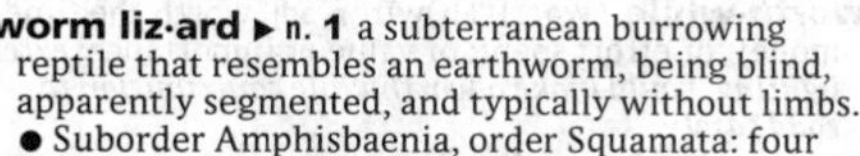
worm gear

worm·hole /ˈwərm,hōl/ ▶ **n.** a hole made by a burrowing insect larva or worm in wood, fruit, books, or other materials. ■ Physics a hypothetical connection between widely separated regions of space-time.

worm liz·ard ▶ **n. 1** a subterranean burrowing reptile that resembles an earthworm, being blind, apparently segmented, and typically without limbs. ● Suborder Amphisbaenia, order Squamata: four families and numerous species.
2 a legless lizard.

Worms /wərmz, vôrms/ an industrial town in western Germany, on the Rhine River, northwest of Mannheim; pop. 82,200 (est. 2006). The Diet of Worms 1521 condemned Martin Luther's teaching.

Worms, Di·et of see **Diet of Worms**.

worm·seed /ˈwərm,sēd/ ▶ **n.** a plant whose seeds have anthelmintic properties. ● (also **Levant wormseed**) santonica. ● (also **American wormseed**) an American plant of the goosefoot family (*Chenopodium ambrosioides*, family Chenopodiaceae).

worm's-eye view ▶ **n.** a view as seen from below or from a humble position: *being assigned to the secretariat provided a worm's-eye view of international diplomacy.*

worm snake ▶ **n. 1** a small harmless North American snake that resembles an earthworm. ● *Carphophis amoena*, family Colubridae.
2 another term for **blind snake**.

worm wheel ▶ **n.** the wheel of a worm gear.

worm·wood /ˈwərm,wo͝od/ ▶ **n. 1** a woody shrub with a bitter aromatic taste, used, esp. formerly, as an ingredient of vermouth and absinthe and in medicine. ● Genus *Artemisia*, family Compositae: several species, in particular the Eurasian *A. absinthium*.
2 a state or source of bitterness or grief.
– ORIGIN Old English *wermōd*. The change in spelling in late Middle English was due to association with **worm** and **wood**. Compare with **vermouth**.

worm·y /ˈwərmē/ ▶ **adj.** (**wormier**, **wormiest**)
1 (of organic tissue) infested with or eaten into by worms: *the prisoners received wormy vegetables.* ■ (of wood or a wooden object) full of holes made by woodworm.
2 informal (of a person) weak, abject, or revolting.
– DERIVATIVES **worm·i·ness n.**

worn /wôrn/ past participle of **wear**[1].
▶ **adj.** damaged and shabby as a result of much use: *a worn, frayed denim jacket.* ■ very tired: *his face looked worn and old.*

worn out ▶ **adj. 1** (of a person or animal) extremely tired; exhausted: *you look worn out.*
2 damaged or shabby to the point of being no longer usable: *worn-out shoes.* ■ (of an idea, method, or system) used so often or existing for so long as to be considered valueless: *he portrayed the Democrats as the party of worn-out ideas.*

wor·ri·ment /ˈwərēmənt/ ▶ **n.** archaic or humorous term for **worry**.

wor·ri·some /ˈwərē,səm/ ▶ **adj.** causing anxiety or concern: *a worrisome problem.*
– DERIVATIVES **wor·ri·some·ly adv.**

wor·ry /ˈwərē/ ▶ **v.** (**worries, worrying, worried**)
1 [no obj.] give way to anxiety or unease; allow one's mind to dwell on difficulty or troubles: *he worried about his soldier sons in the war* | [with clause] *I began to worry whether I had done the right thing.* ■ [with obj.] cause to feel anxiety or concern: *there was no need to worry her* | *I've been worrying myself sick over my mother* | [with obj. and clause] *he is worried that we are not sustaining high employment.* ■ (as adj. **worried**) expressing anxiety: *there was a worried frown on his face.* ■ [with obj.] cause annoyance to: *the noise never really stops, but it doesn't worry me.*
2 [with obj.] (of a dog or other carnivorous animal) tear at, gnaw on, or drag around with the teeth: *I found my dog contentedly worrying a bone.* ■ (of a dog) chase and attack (livestock, esp. sheep). ■ [no obj.] (**worry at**) pull at or fiddle with repeatedly: *he began to worry at the knot in the cord.*
▶ **n.** (pl. **worries**) a state of anxiety and uncertainty over actual or potential problems: *her son had been a constant source of worry to her.* ■ a source of anxiety: *the idea is to secure peace of mind for people whose greatest worry is fear of attack.*
– PHRASES **not to worry** informal used to reassure someone by telling them that a situation is not serious: *not to worry—no harm done.*
– DERIVATIVES **wor·ried·ly adv.**, **wor·ri·er n.**
– ORIGIN Old English *wyrgan* 'strangle.' In Middle English the original sense of the verb gave rise to the meaning 'seize by the throat and tear,' later figuratively 'harass,' whence 'cause anxiety to' (early 19th century, the date also of the noun).

wor·ry beads ▶ **plural n.** a string of beads that one fingers and moves in order to calm oneself.

wor·ry·ing /ˈwərē-iNG/ ▶ **adj.** causing anxiety about actual or potential problems; alarming: *a worrying health risk.*
– DERIVATIVES **wor·ry·ing·ly adv.** [as submodifier] *trade deficits are worryingly large.*

wor·ry·wart /ˈwərē,wôrt/ ▶ **n.** informal a person who tends to dwell unduly on difficulty or troubles.

worse /wərs/ ▶ **adj. 1** comparative of **bad**, **ill**.
2 of poorer quality or a lower standard; less good or desirable: *the accommodations were awful, and the food was worse.* ■ more serious or severe: *the movement made the pain worse.* ■ more reprehensible or evil: *it is worse to intend harm than to be indifferent.* ■ [predic. or as complement] in a less satisfactory or pleasant condition; more ill or unhappy: *he felt worse, and groped his way back to bed.*
▶ **adv. 1** comparative of **badly**, **ill**.
2 less well or skillfully: *the more famous I became the worse I painted.* ■ more seriously or severely: *the others had been drunk too, worse than herself.*
▶ **n.** a more serious or unpleasant event or circumstance: *the small department was already stretched to the limit, but worse was to follow.* ■ (**the worse**) a less good, favorable, or pleasant condition: *the weather changed for the worse.*
– PHRASES **none the worse for** not adversely affected by: *we were none the worse for our terrible experience.* **or worse** used to suggest a possibility that is still more serious or unpleasant than one already considered, but that the speaker does not wish or need to specify: *the child might be born blind or worse.* **so much the worse for ——** used to suggest that a problem, failure, or other unfortunate event or situation is the fault of the person specified and that the speaker does not feel any great concern about it: *if his subjects were unwilling to accept the progress her offered, so much the worse for them.* **the worse for wear** informal **1** damaged by use or weather over time; battered and shabby. **2** (of a person) feeling rather unwell, esp. as a result of drinking too much alcohol. **worse luck** see **luck**. **worse off** in a less advantageous position; less fortunate or prosperous.
– ORIGIN Old English *wyrsa*, *wiersa* (adjective), *wiers* (adverb), of Germanic origin; related to **war**.

wors·en /ˈwərsən/ ▶ **v.** make or become worse: [no obj.] *her condition worsened on the flight* | [with obj.] *arguing actually worsens the problem* | (as adj. **worsening**) *Romania's rapidly worsening economic situation.*

wor·ship /ˈwərsHəp/ ▶ **n.** the feeling or expression of reverence and adoration for a deity: *the worship of God* | *ancestor worship.* ■ the acts or rites that make up a formal expression of reverence for a deity; a religious ceremony or ceremonies: *the church was opened for public worship.* ■ adoration or devotion comparable to religious homage, shown toward a person or principle: *our society's worship of teenagers.* ■ archaic honor given to someone in recognition of their merit. ■ [as title] (**His/Your Worship**) chiefly Brit. used in addressing or referring to an important or high-ranking person, esp. a

magistrate or mayor: *we were soon joined by His Worship the Mayor.*
▶ **v.** (**worships, worshiping, worshiped**; also **worships, worshipping, worshipped**) [with obj.] show reverence and adoration for (a deity); honor with religious rites: *the Maya built jungle pyramids to worship their gods.* ■ treat (someone or something) with the reverence and adoration appropriate to a deity: *she adores her sons and they worship her.* ■ [no obj.] take part in a religious ceremony: *he went to the cathedral because he chose to worship in a spiritually inspiring building.*
– DERIVATIVES **wor·ship·er** (also **worshipper**) **n.**
– ORIGIN Old English *weorthscipe* 'worthiness, acknowledgment of worth' (see WORTH, -SHIP).

wor·ship·ful /ˈwərSHəpfəl/ ▶ **adj.** feeling or showing reverence and adoration: *her voice was full of worshipful admiration.* ■ archaic entitled to honor or respect. ■ (**Worshipful**) Brit. used in titles given to justices of the peace and to certain old corporations or their officers: *the Worshipful Company of Goldsmiths.*
– DERIVATIVES **wor·ship·ful·ly adv.**, **wor·ship·ful·ness n.**

worst /wərst/ ▶ **adj.** superlative of BAD, ILL. ■ of the poorest quality or the lowest standard; least good or desirable: *the speech was the worst he had ever made.* ■ most severe, serious, or dangerous: *at least 32 people died in Australia's worst bus accident.*
▶ **adv. 1** superlative of BADLY, ILL.
2 most severely or seriously: *manufacturing and mining are the industries worst affected by falling employment.* ■ least well, skillfully, or pleasingly: *he was voted the worst dressed celebrity.*
▶ **n.** the most serious or unpleasant thing that could happen: *when I saw the ambulance outside her front door, I began to fear the worst.* ■ the most serious, dangerous, or unpleasant part or stage of something: *there are signs that the recession is past its worst.*
▶ **v.** [with obj.] get the better of; defeat: *this was not the time for a deep discussion—she was tired and she would be worsted.*
– PHRASES **at its** (or **someone's**) **worst** in the most serious, undesirable, or unpleasant state: *nothing's working at the moment, so I suppose you've seen us at our worst.* **at worst** (or **the worst**) in the most serious case: *at worst the injury could mean months in the hospital.* ■ under the most unfavorable interpretation: *the cabinet's reaction to the crisis was at best ineffective and at worst irresponsible.* **be one's own worst enemy** see ENEMY. **do one's worst** (in the view of one's opponent) do as much damage as one can (often used to express defiance in the face of threats): *let them do their worst—he would never surrender.* **get** (or **have**) **the worst of it** be in the least advantageous or successful position; suffer the most. **if worst comes to worst** if the most serious or difficult circumstances arise. **in the worst way** informal very much: *he wants to win in the worst way.*
– ORIGIN Old English *wierresta, wyrresta* (adjective), *wierst, wyrst* (adverb), of Germanic origin; related to WORSE.

worst-case ▶ **adj.** (of a projected development) characterized by the worst of the possible foreseeable circumstances: *in the worst-case scenario, coastal resorts and communities face disaster.*

wor·sted /ˈwo͝ostid, ˈwərstid/ ▶ **n.** a fine smooth yarn spun from combed long-staple wool. ■ fabric made from such yarn, having a close-textured surface with no nap: [as modifier] *a worsted suit.*
– ORIGIN Middle English: from *Worstead*, the name of a parish in Norfolk, England.

wort /wərt, wôrt/ ▶ **n. 1** [in combination] used in names of plants and herbs, esp. those used, esp. formerly, as food or medicinally, e.g., **butterwort, woundwort.** ■ archaic such a plant or herb.
2 the sweet infusion of ground malt or other grain before fermentation, used to produce beer and distilled malt liquors.
– ORIGIN Old English *wyrt*, of Germanic origin; related to ROOT[1].

W

Worth /wərTH/, Charles Frederick (1825–95), English couturier, resident in France from 1845. Regarded as the founder of Parisian *haute couture*, he is noted for designing gowns with crinolines and for introducing the bustle.

worth /wərTH/ ▶ **adj.** [predic.] equivalent in value to the sum or item specified: *jewelry worth $450 was taken.* ■ sufficiently good, important, or interesting to justify a specified action; deserving to be treated or regarded in the way specified: *the museums in the district are well worth a visit.* ■ used to suggest that the specified course of action may be advisable: *a meat and potato dish that's worth checking out.* ■ having income or property amounting to a specified sum: *she is worth $10 million.*
▶ **n.** the value equivalent to that of someone or something under consideration; the level at which someone or something deserves to be valued or rated: *they had to listen to every piece of gossip and judge its worth.* ■ an amount of a commodity equivalent to a specified sum of money: *he admitted stealing 10,000 dollars' worth of computer systems.* ■ the amount that could be achieved or produced in a specified time: *the companies have debts greater than two years' worth of their sales.* ■ high value or merit: *he is noble and gains his position by showing his inner worth.*
– PHRASES **for all someone is worth** informal **1** as energetically or enthusiastically as someone can: *he thumps the drums for all he's worth.* **2** so as to obtain everything one can from someone: *the youths milked him for all he was worth and then disappeared.* **for what it is worth** used to present a comment, suggestion, or opinion without making a claim as to its importance or validity: *for what it's worth, she's very highly thought of abroad.* **worth it** informal sufficiently good, enjoyable, or successful to repay any effort, trouble, or expense: *it requires a bit of patience to learn, but it's well worth it.* **worth one's salt** see SALT. **worth one's while** (or **worth while**) see WHILE.
– ORIGIN Old English *w(e)orth* (adjective and noun), of Germanic origin; related to Dutch *waard* and German *wert*.

worth·less /ˈwərTHlis/ ▶ **adj.** having no real value or use: *that promise is worthless.* ■ (of a person) having no good qualities; deserving contempt: *Joan had been deserted by a worthless husband.*
– DERIVATIVES **worth·less·ly adv.**, **worth·less·ness n.**

worth·while /ˈwərTHˈ(h)wīl/ ▶ **adj.** worth the time, money, or effort spent; of value or importance: *extra lighting would make a worthwhile contribution to road safety.*
– DERIVATIVES **worth·while·ness n.**

> **USAGE** The adjective **worthwhile** is used both attributively (that is, before the noun) and predicatively (that is, when it stands alone and comes after the verb). In both positions, it is always correct as one word (*a* ***worthwhile*** *book; we didn't think it was* ***worthwhile***), but when used predicatively, it may also be written as two words: *we didn't think it was worth while.*

wor·thy /ˈwərT͟Hē/ ▶ **adj.** (**worthier, worthiest**) deserving effort, attention, or respect: *generous donations to worthy causes.* ■ having or showing the qualities or abilities that merit recognition in a specified way: *issues* ***worthy of*** *further consideration.* ■ good enough; suitable: *no composer was considered* ***worthy of*** *the name until he had written an opera.*
▶ **n.** (pl. **worthies**) often derogatory or humorous a person notable or important in a particular sphere: *schools governed by local worthies.*
– DERIVATIVES **wor·thi·ly** /-T͟Həlē/ **adv.**, **wor·thi·ness n.**
– ORIGIN Middle English: from WORTH + -Y[1].

-worthy ▶ **comb. form** deserving of a specified thing: *newsworthy.* ■ suitable or fit for a specified thing: *roadworthy.*
– ORIGIN from WORTHY.

wot[1] /wät/ ▶ **pron., determiner, & interrogative adv.** Brit. nonstandard spelling of WHAT, chiefly representing informal, dialectical, or humorous use.

wot[2] singular present of WIT[2].

Wo·tan /ˈvōˌtän/ another name for ODIN.

Wouk /wōk, wo͝ok/, Herman (1915–), US writer. His novels include *The Caine Mutiny* (1951), *Marjorie Morningstar* (1955), *The Winds of War* (1971), *War and Remembrance* (1978), and *The Glory* (1994).

would /wo͝od/ ▶ **modal v.** (3rd sing. present **would**)
1 past of WILL[1], in various senses: *he said he would be away for a couple of days | he wanted out, but she wouldn't leave | the windows would not close.*
2 (expressing the conditional mood) indicating the consequence of an imagined event or situation: *he would lose his job if he were identified.* ■ (**I would**) used to give advice: *I wouldn't drink that if I were you.*
3 expressing a desire or inclination: *I would love to work in Prague | would you like some water?*
4 expressing a polite request: *would you pour the wine, please?* ■ expressing willingness or consent: *who would live here?*
5 expressing a conjecture, opinion, or hope: *I would imagine that they'll want to keep it | I guess some people would consider it brutal | I would have to agree.*
6 used to make a comment about behavior that is typical: *every night we would hear the boy crying |* derogatory *they would say that, wouldn't they?*
7 [with clause] literary expressing a wish or regret: *would that he had lived to finish it.*
– ORIGIN Old English *wolde*, past of *wyllan* (see WILL[1]).

> **USAGE** On the differences in use between would and should, see usage at SHOULD.

would-be ▶ **adj.** [attrib.] often derogatory desiring or aspiring to be a specified type of person: *a would-be actress who dresses up as Marilyn Monroe.*

would·n't /ˈwo͝odnt/ ▶ **contraction** would not.
– PHRASES **I wouldn't know** informal used to indicate that one can't be expected to know the answer to someone's question or to comment on a matter: *"It was a lot better than last year's dance." "I wouldn't know about that."*

wouldst /wo͝odst/ (also **wouldest** /ˈwo͝odist/) archaic second person singular of WOULD.

wound[1] /wo͞ond/ ▶ **n.** an injury to living tissue caused by a cut, blow, or other impact, typically one in which the skin is cut or broken. ■ an injury to a person's feelings or reputation: *the new crisis has opened old wounds.*
▶ **v.** [with obj.] inflict an injury on (someone): *the sergeant was seriously wounded |* (as adj. **wounded**) *a wounded soldier.* ■ injure (a person's feelings): *you really wounded his pride when you turned him down |* (as adj. **wounded**) *her wounded feelings.*
– DERIVATIVES **wound·ing·ly adv.**, **wound·less adj.**
– ORIGIN Old English *wund* (noun), *wundian* (verb), of Germanic origin; related to Dutch *wond* and German *Wunde*, of unknown ultimate origin.

wound[2] /wound/ alternate past and past participle of WIND[1].

wound[3] /wound/ past and past participle of WIND[2].

Wound·ed Knee /ˈwo͞ondid/ a village in southwestern South Dakota, in the Pine Ridge Indian reservation, the site of an 1890 massacre and 1973 demonstrations.

Wound·ed Knee, Bat·tle of /ˈwo͞ondid ˈnē/ the last major confrontation (1890) between the US Army and American Indians, at the village of Wounded Knee on a reservation in South Dakota. More than 150 largely unarmed Sioux men, women, and children were massacred.

wound·wort /ˈwo͞ondˌwərt, -ˌwôrt/ ▶ **n.** a hairy Eurasian plant resembling a dead-nettle, formerly used in the treatment of wounds. ● Genus *Stachys*, family Labiatae: several species.

wove /wōv/ past of WEAVE[1].

wo·ven /ˈwōvən/ past participle of WEAVE[1].

wove pa·per ▶ **n.** paper made on a wire-gauze mesh so as to have a uniform unlined surface. Compare with LAID PAPER.
– ORIGIN early 19th cent.: *wove*, variant of WOVEN.

wow[1] /wou/ informal ▶ **exclam.** (also **wowee** /ˈwouē, ˈwou'(w)ē/) expressing astonishment or admiration: *"Wow!" he cried enthusiastically.*
▶ **n.** a sensational success: *your play's a wow.*
▶ **v.** [with obj.] impress and excite (someone) greatly: *they wowed audiences on their recent British tour.*
– ORIGIN natural exclamation: first recorded in Scots in the early 16th cent.

wow[2] ▶ **n.** slow pitch fluctuation in sound reproduction, perceptible in long notes. Compare with FLUTTER (sense 1 of the noun).
– ORIGIN mid 20th cent.: imitative.

wow fac·tor ▶ **n.** informal a quality or feature that is extremely impressive: *its funky, futuristic looks would add a definite wow factor to any kitchen.*

wow·ser /ˈwouzər/ ▶ **n.** Austral./NZ informal a person who is publicly critical of others and the pleasures they seek; a killjoy.
– ORIGIN late 19th cent.: of obscure origin.

Woz·ni·ak /ˈwäznēˌak/, Steve (1950–), US computer entrepreneur. He cofounded the Apple computer company in 1976 with Steve Jobs and helped to lead it until 1981 and again from 1983 until 1985.

WP ▶ **abbr.** word processing or word processor.

w.p. ▶ **abbr.** weather permitting: *I hope to arrive in London that evening (w.p.).*

W par·ti·cle ▶ **n.** Physics a heavy charged elementary particle considered to transmit the weak interaction between other elementary particles.
– ORIGIN *W*, the initial letter of *weak.*

wpb ▶ **abbr.** wastepaper basket.

wpm ▶ **abbr.** words per minute (used after a number to indicate typing speed).

WRAC /rak/ ▶ **abbr.** Women's Royal Army Corps (in the UK, until 1993).

wrack[1] ▶ **v.** variant spelling of RACK[1] (sense 1 of the verb).

> **USAGE** On the complicated relationship between wrack and rack, see usage at RACK[1].

wrack[2] /rak/ ▶ **n.** any of a number of coarse brown seaweeds that grow on the shoreline, frequently each kind forming a distinct band in relation to high- and low-water marks. Many have air bladders for buoyancy. ● Genera *Fucus*, *Ascophyllum*, and *Pelvetia*, class Phaeophyceae.
– ORIGIN early 16th cent.: apparently from WRACK[4].

wrack[3] ▶ **n.** variant spelling of RACK[5].
– ORIGIN late Middle English: variant of RACK[5].

wrack[4] ▶ **n.** archaic, dialect a wrecked ship; a shipwreck. ■ wreckage.
– ORIGIN late Middle English: from Middle Dutch *wrak*; related to WREAK and WRECK.

WRAF /raf/ ▶ **abbr.** Women's Royal Air Force (in the UK, until 1994).

wraith /rāTH/ ▶ **n.** a ghost or ghostlike image of someone, esp. one seen shortly before or after their death. ■ used in similes and metaphors to describe a pale, thin, or insubstantial person or thing: *heart attacks had reduced his mother to a wraith.* ■ literary a wisp or faint trace of something: *a sea breeze was sending a gray wraith of smoke up the slopes.*
– DERIVATIVES **wraith·like** /-ˌlīk/ **adj.**
– ORIGIN early 16th cent. (originally Scots): of unknown origin.

Wran·gel Is·land /ˈraNGgəl/ an island in the East Siberian Sea, off the coast of northeastern Russia. It was named after Russian admiral and explorer Baron Ferdinand Wrangel (1794–1870).

Wran·gell Moun·tains /ˈraNGgəl/ a range in southeastern Alaska, within Wrangell–St. Elias National Park, along the Pacific coast and the border of the Yukon Territory.

wran·gle /ˈraNGgəl/ ▶ **n.** a dispute or argument, typically one that is long and complicated: *an insurance wrangle is holding up compensation payments.*
▶ **v. 1** [no obj.] have such a dispute or argument: (as noun **wrangling**) *weeks of political wrangling.*
2 [with obj.] round up, herd, or take charge of (livestock): *the horses were wrangled early.*
3 another term for WANGLE.
– ORIGIN late Middle English: compare with Low German *wrangeln*, frequentative of *wrangen* 'to struggle'; related to WRING.

wran·gler /ˈraNGglər/ ▶ **n. 1** a person in charge of horses or other livestock on a ranch. ■ a person who trains and takes care of the animals used in a movie.
2 a person engaging in a lengthy and complicated quarrel or dispute.

wrap /rap/ ▶ **v.** (**wraps**, **wrapping**, **wrapped** or archaic **wrapt**) **1** [with obj.] cover or enclose (someone or something) in paper or soft material: *he wrapped the Christmas presents | Leonora wrapped herself in a large white bath towel.* ■ clasp; embrace: *she wrapped him in her arms.* ■ cover (the body) with a body wrap. ■ cover (the fingernails) with a nail wrap.
2 [with obj.] (**wrap something around**) arrange paper or soft material around (someone or something), typically as a covering or for warmth or protection: *wrap the bandage around the injured limb.* ■ place an arm, finger, or leg around (someone or something): *he wrapped an arm around her waist.* ■ informal crash a vehicle into (a stationary object): *Richard wrapped his car around a telephone pole.*
3 [with obj.] Computing cause (a word or unit of text) to be carried over to a new line automatically as the margin is reached, or to fit around embedded features such as pictures. ■ [no obj.] (of a word or unit or text) be carried over in such a way.
4 [no obj.] informal finish filming or recording: *we wrapped on schedule three days later.*
▶ **n. 1** a loose outer garment or piece of material. ■ [as modifier] denoting a garment having one part overlapping another; wraparound: *a wrap skirt.* ■ paper or soft material used for wrapping: *plastic food wrap.* ■ (usu. **wraps**) a veil of secrecy maintained about something, esp. a new project: *details of the police operation are being kept under wraps.*
2 [usu. in sing.] informal the end of a session of filming or recording: *right, it's a wrap.*
3 a sandwich in which the filling is rolled in a soft tortilla.
4 short for BODY WRAP. ■ short for NAIL WRAP.
– PHRASES **be wrapped up in** be so engrossed or absorbed in (something) that one does not notice other people or things.
– PHRASAL VERBS **wrap up** (also **wrap someone up**) put on (or dress someone in) warm clothes: *wrap up warm | Tim was well wrapped up against the weather.* **wrap something up** complete or conclude a discussion or agreement: *they hope to wrap up negotiations within sixty days.* ■ win a game or competition: *Australia wrapped up the series 4–0.*
– ORIGIN Middle English: of unknown origin.

wrap·a·round /ˈrapəˌround/ ▶ **adj.** [attrib.] curving or extending around at the edges or sides: *wraparound sunglasses.* ■ (of a garment) having one part overlapping another and fastened loosely: *a wraparound skirt.*
▶ **n. 1** a wraparound garment.
2 Computing a facility by which a linear sequence of memory locations or screen positions is treated as a continuous circular series.

wrap·a·round mort·gage ▶ **n.** a second mortgage held by a lender who collects payments on it and the first mortgage from the borrower. The lender makes the payments to the original mortgage holder.

wrap·a·round porch ▶ **n.** a shallow veranda enclosing two or more sides of a house: *three-story million-dollar houses with wraparound porches perched on pilings.*

wrap·per /ˈrapər/ ▶ **n. 1** a piece of paper, plastic, or foil covering and protecting something sold. ■ a cover enclosing a newspaper or magazine for mailing. ■ the dust jacket of a book. ■ a tobacco leaf of superior quality enclosing a cigar.
2 a loose robe or gown.

wrap·per ap·pli·ca·tion ▶ **n.** a computer program that works only with another fully developed program, which it enhances in some way: *we have created a viewer that is a simple wrapper application for the underlying multimedia system.*

wrap·ping /ˈrapiNG/ ▶ **n.** paper or soft material used to cover or enclose someone or something: *she took the cellophane wrapping off the box.*

wrap·ping pa·per ▶ **n.** strong or decorative paper for wrapping parcels or presents.

wrap-up ▶ **n.** a summary or review of an activity, sporting event, etc.: *the post-game wrap-up* | [as modifier] *200 campaign volunteers celebrated during wrap-up festivities.*

wrasse /ras/ ▶ **n.** (pl. **same** or **wrasses**) a marine fish with thick lips and strong teeth, typically brightly colored with marked differences between the male and female. ● Family Labridae: numerous genera and species.
– ORIGIN late 17th cent.: from Cornish *wrah*; related to Welsh *gwrach*, literally 'old woman.'

wrath /raTH/ ▶ **n.** extreme anger (chiefly used for humorous or rhetorical effect): *he hid his pipe for fear of incurring his father's wrath.*
– ORIGIN Old English *wrǣththu*, from *wrāth* (see WROTH).

wrathful /ˈraTHfəl/ ▶ **adj.** literary full of or characterized by intense anger: *natural calamities seemed to be the work of a wrathful deity.*
– DERIVATIVES **wrath·ful·ly adv.**, **wrath·ful·ness n.**

wrath·y /ˈraTHē/ ▶ **adj.** informal, dated another term for WRATHFUL.

wreak /rēk/ ▶ **v.** [with obj.] cause (a large amount of damage or harm): *torrential rainstorms wreaked havoc yesterday | the environmental damage wreaked by ninety years of phosphate mining.* ■ inflict (vengeance): *he was determined to wreak his revenge on the girl who had rejected him.* ■ archaic avenge (someone who has been wronged): *grant me some knight to wreak me for my son.*
– DERIVATIVES **wreak·er n.**
– ORIGIN Old English *wrecan* 'drive (out), avenge,' of Germanic origin; related to Dutch *wreken* and German *rächen*; compare with WRACK[4], WRECK, and WRETCH.

> **USAGE** The phrase **wrought havoc**, as in *they* **wrought havoc** *on the countryside*, is an acceptable variant of **wreaked havoc**. Here, **wrought** is an archaic past tense of **work**. It is not, as is sometimes assumed, a past tense of **wreak**.

wreath /rēTH/ ▶ **n.** (pl. **wreaths** /rē<u>TH</u>z, rēTHs/) **1** an arrangement of flowers, leaves, or stems fastened in a ring and used for decoration or for laying on a grave. ■ a carved representation of such a wreath. ■ a similar ring made of or resembling soft, twisted material: *a gold wreath.* ■ Heraldry a representation of such a ring below a crest (esp. where it joins a helmet). ■ a curl or ring of smoke or cloud: *wreaths of mist swirled up into the cold air.*
2 archaic, chiefly Scottish a snowdrift.
– ORIGIN Old English *writha*, related to WRITHE.

wreathe /rē<u>TH</u>/ ▶ **v.** [with obj.] **1** cover, surround, or encircle (something): *he sits wreathed in smoke.* ■ literary twist or entwine (something flexible) around or over something: *shall I once more wreathe my arms about Antonio's neck?* ■ [no obj.] (esp. of smoke) move with a curling motion: *he watched the smoke wreathe into the night air.*
2 form (flowers, leaves, or stems) into a wreath.
– PHRASES **be wreathed in smiles** be smiling broadly: *his tanned face was wreathed in smiles.*
– ORIGIN mid 16th cent.: partly a back-formation from archaic *wrethen*, past participle of WRITHE, reinforced by WREATH.

wreck /rek/ ▶ **n.** the destruction of a ship at sea; a shipwreck: *the survivors of the wreck.* ■ a ship destroyed in such a way: *the salvaging of treasure from wrecks.* ■ Law goods brought ashore by the sea from a wreck and not claimed by the owner within a specified period (usually a year): *the profits of wreck.* ■ something, esp. a vehicle or building, that has been badly damaged or destroyed: *the plane was reduced to a smoldering wreck* | figurative *the wreck of their marriage.* ■ the disorganized remains of something that has suffered damage or destruction. ■ a road or rail crash: *a train wreck.* ■ a person whose physical or mental health or strength has failed: *the scandal left the family emotional wrecks.*
▶ **v.** [with obj.] (usu. **be wrecked**) cause the destruction of (a ship) by sinking or breaking up: *he was drowned when his ship was wrecked.* ■ involve (someone) in such a wreck: *sailors who had the misfortune to be wrecked on these coasts.* ■ [no obj.] (usu. as noun **wrecking**) chiefly historical cause the destruction of a ship in order to steal the cargo: *the locals reverted to the age-old practice of wrecking.* ■ [no obj.] archaic suffer or undergo shipwreck. ■ destroy or severely damage (a structure or vehicle): *the blast wrecked more than 100 houses.* ■ spoil completely: *an eye injury wrecked his chances of a professional career.* ■ [no obj.] (usu. as noun **wrecking**) engage in breaking up badly damaged vehicles, demolishing old buildings, or similar activities to obtain usable spares or scrap.
– ORIGIN Middle English (as a legal term denoting wreckage washed ashore): from Anglo-Norman French *wrec*, from the base of Old Norse *reka* 'to drive'; related to WREAK.

wreck·age /ˈrekij/ ▶ **n.** the remains of something that has been badly damaged or destroyed: *firemen had to cut him free from the wreckage of the car.*

wrecked /rekt/ ▶ **adj. 1** having been wrecked: *an old wrecked barge lay upside down | a wrecked marriage.*
2 informal under the influence of or suffering the effects of drugs or alcohol: *they got wrecked on tequila.*

wreck·er /ˈrekər/ ▶ **n. 1** a person or thing that wrecks, damages, or destroys something: [in combination] *she was cast as a home-wrecker.* ■ a person who breaks up damaged vehicles, demolishes old buildings, salvages wrecked ships, etc., to obtain usable spares or scrap. ■ chiefly historical a person on the shore who tries to bring about a shipwreck in order to profit from the wreckage.
2 a tow truck.

wreck·ing ball (also **wrecker's ball**) ▶ **n.** a heavy metal ball swung from a crane into a building to demolish it.

Wren[1] /ren/, Sir Christopher (1632–1723), English architect. Following the Fire of London in 1666, he was responsible for the design of the new St. Paul's Cathedral 1675–1711 and many of the city's churches.

Wren[2] ▶ **n.** (in the UK) a member of the former Women's Royal Naval Service.
– ORIGIN early 20th cent.: originally in the plural, from the abbreviation **WRNS**.

wren /ren/ ▶ **n. 1** a small short-winged songbird found chiefly in the New World. ● Family Troglodytidae: many genera and numerous species, in particular the very small *Troglodytes troglodytes* (**winter wren**), which has a short cocked tail and is the only wren that occurs the Old World.
2 [usu. with modifier] any of a number of small songbirds that resemble the true wrens in size or appearance.
– ORIGIN Old English *wrenna*, of Germanic origin.

wrench /renCH/ ▶ **n. 1** [usu. in sing.] a sudden violent twist or pull: *with a wrench Tony wriggled free.*
2 a feeling of sadness or distress caused by one's own or another's departure: *it will be a real wrench to leave after eight years.*
3 a tool used for gripping and turning nuts, bolts, pipes, etc.
4 Mechanics a combination of a couple with a force along its axis.
▶ **v.** [with obj.] pull or twist (someone or something) suddenly and violently: *Casey grabbed the gun and wrenched it upward from my hand* | [with obj. and complement] *she wrenched herself free of his grip* | [no obj.] figurative *the betrayal wrenched at her heart.* ■ injure (a part of the body) as a result of a sudden twisting movement: *she slipped and wrenched her ankle.* ■ turn (something, esp. a nut or bolt) with a wrench. ■ archaic distort to fit a particular theory or interpretation: *to wrench our Bible to make it fit a misconception of facts.*

W

PRONUNCIATION KEY ə ago, up; ər over, fur; a hat; ā ate; ä car; e let; ē see; i fit; ī by; NG sing; ō go; ô law, for; oi toy; o͝o good; o͞o goo; ou out; TH thin; <u>TH</u> then; ZH vision

– PHRASES **a wrench in the works** another way of saying A MONKEY WRENCH IN THE WORKS (see MONKEY WRENCH).
– ORIGIN late Old English *wrencan* 'twist,' of unknown origin.

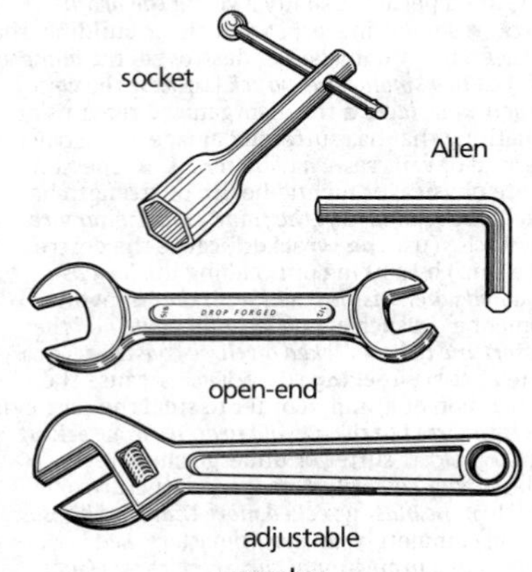

wrenches

wrench fault ▶ n. another term for STRIKE-SLIP FAULT.

wren·tit /ˈrenˌtit/ ▶ n. a long-tailed North American songbird that is the only American member of the babbler family, with dark plumage. ● *Chamaea fasciata*, family Timaliidae.

wrest /rest/ ▶ v. [with obj.] forcibly pull (something) from a person's grasp: *Leila tried to wrest her arm from his hold.* ■ take (something, esp. power or control) from someone or something else after considerable effort or difficulty: *they wanted to allow people to wrest control of their lives from impersonal bureaucracies.* ■ archaic distort the meaning or interpretation of (something) to suit one's own interests or views: *you appear convinced of my guilt, and wrest every reply I have made.*
▶ n. archaic a key for tuning a harp or piano.
– ORIGIN Old English *wrǣstan* 'twist, tighten,' of Germanic origin; related to Danish *vriste*, also to WRIST.

wres·tle /ˈresəl/ ▶ v. [no obj.] **1** take part in a fight, either as a sport or in earnest, that involves grappling with one's opponent and trying to throw or force them to the ground: *as the policeman **wrestled with** the gunman a shot rang out.* ■ [with obj.] force (someone) into a particular position or place by fighting in such a way: *the security guards wrestled them to the ground.* ■ [with obj.] move or manipulate (something) in a specified way with difficulty and some physical effort: *she wrestled the keys out of the ignition.*
2 struggle with a difficulty or problem: *for over a year David **wrestled with** a guilty conscience.*
▶ n. [in sing.] **1** a wrestling bout or contest: *a wrestle to the death.*
2 a hard struggle: *a lifelong wrestle with depression.*
– DERIVATIVES **wres·tler** /ˈres(ə)lər/ n.
– ORIGIN Old English, frequentative of *wrǣstan* 'wrest.'

wres·tling /ˈres(ə)liNG/ ▶ n. the sport or activity of grappling with an opponent and trying to throw or hold them down on the ground, typically according to a code of rules.

> Popular in ancient Egypt, China, and Greece, wrestling was introduced to the Olympic Games in 704 BC; many of the holds and throws used now are the same as those of antiquity. The two main competition styles are Greco-Roman (in which holds below the waist are prohibited) and freestyle, which has become a popular televised sport. See also SUMO.

wretch /reCH/ ▶ n. an unfortunate or unhappy person: *can the poor wretch's corpse tell us anything?* ■ informal a despicable or contemptible person: *ungrateful wretches.*
– ORIGIN Old English *wrecca* (also in the sense 'banished person'); related to German *Recke* 'warrior, hero,' also to the verb WREAK.

W

wretch·ed /ˈreCHid/ ▶ adj. (**wretcheder, wretchedest**) (of a person) in a very unhappy or unfortunate state: *I felt so wretched because I thought I might never see you again.* ■ of poor quality; very bad: *the wretched conditions of the slums.* ■ used to express anger or annoyance: *she disliked the wretched man intensely.*
– DERIVATIVES **wretch·ed·ly** adv. [as submodifier] *a wretchedly poor country*, **wretch·ed·ness** n.
– ORIGIN Middle English: formed irregularly from WRETCH + -ED[1].

wrig·gle /ˈrigəl/ ▶ v. twist and turn with quick writhing movements: [no obj.] *he kicked and wriggled but she held him firmly* | [with obj.] *she wriggled her bare, brown toes.* ■ [no obj.] move in a particular direction with wriggling movements: *Susie wriggled out of her clothes.* ■ (**wriggle out of**) avoid (something), esp. by devious means: *don't try and wriggle out of your contract.*
▶ n. [in sing.] a wriggling movement: *she gave an impatient little wriggle.*
– DERIVATIVES **wrig·gly** /ˈrig(ə)lē/ adj.
– ORIGIN late 15th cent.: from Middle Low German *wriggelen*, frequentative of *wriggen* 'twist, turn.'

wrig·gler /ˈrig(ə)lər/ ▶ n. a person or thing that wriggles. ■ a wriggling animalcule or the larva of a mosquito. Also called WIGGLER.

Wright[1] /rīt/, Frank Lloyd (1869–1959), US architect. His "prairie-style" houses, characterized by a close relationship among building, landscape, and materials used, revolutionized domestic architecture in the US. Notable buildings include the Kaufmann House (known as "Fallingwater"), which incorporated a waterfall, in Pennsylvania 1935–39 and the Guggenheim Museum of Art in New York 1956–59.

Wright[2], Orville (1871–1948) and Wilbur (1867–1912), US aviation pioneers. In 1903, the Wright brothers were the first to make brief sustained and controlled powered flights in an airplane, which was designed and built by them. They were also the first to make and fly a practical powered airplane 1905 and a passenger-carrying airplane 1908.

wright /rīt/ ▶ n. archaic a maker or builder.
– ORIGIN Old English *wryhta*, *wyrhta*; related to WORK.

wring /riNG/ ▶ v. (past **wrung** /rəNG/) [with obj.] squeeze and twist (something) to force liquid from it: *she **wrung** the cloth **out** in the sink.* ■ extract (liquid) by squeezing and twisting something: *I wrung out the excess water.* ■ break (an animal's neck) by twisting it forcibly. ■ squeeze (someone's hand) tightly, esp. with sincere emotion. ■ obtain (something) with difficulty or effort: *few concessions were wrung from the government.* ■ cause pain or distress to: *the letter must have wrung her heart.*
▶ n. [in sing.] an act of squeezing or twisting something.
– PHRASES **wring one's hands** clasp and twist one's hands together as a gesture of great distress, esp. when one is powerless to change the situation.
– ORIGIN Old English *wringan* (verb); related to Dutch *wringen*, also to WRONG.

wring·er /ˈriNGər/ ▶ n. a device for wringing water from wet clothes, mops, or other objects.
– PHRASES **put someone through the wringer** informal subject someone to a very stressful experience, esp. a severe interrogation.

wrin·kle /ˈriNGkəl/ ▶ n. **1** a slight line or fold in something, esp. fabric or the skin of the face. ■ informal a minor difficulty; a snag: *the organizers have the wrinkles pretty well ironed out.*
2 informal a clever innovation, or useful piece of information or advice: *learning the wrinkles from someone more experienced saves time.*
▶ v. [with obj.] (often as adj. **wrinkled**) make or cause lines or folds in (something, esp. fabric or the skin): *Dotty's wrinkled stockings.* ■ grimace and cause wrinkles on (a part of the face): *he sniffed and wrinkled his nose.* ■ [no obj.] form or become marked with lines or folds: *her brow wrinkled.*
– ORIGIN late Middle English: origin obscure, possibly a back-formation from the Old English past participle *gewrinclod* 'sinuous' (of which no infinitive is recorded).

wrin·kly /ˈriNGk(ə)lē/ ▶ adj. (**wrinklier, wrinkliest**) having many lines or folds: *he's old and wrinkly.*

wrist /rist/ ▶ n. **1** the joint connecting the hand with the forearm. See also CARPUS. ■ the equivalent joint (the carpal joint) in the foreleg of a quadruped or the wing of a bird. ■ the part of a garment covering the wrist; a cuff.
2 (also **wrist pin**) (in a machine) a stud projecting from a crank as an attachment for a connecting rod.
– ORIGIN Old English, of Germanic origin, probably from the base of WRITHE.

wrist·band /ˈristˌband/ ▶ n. a strip of material worn around the wrist, in particular: ■ a small strap or bracelet, esp. one used for identification or as a fashion item. ■ a strip of absorbent material worn during sports or strenuous exercise to soak up sweat. ■ the cuff of a shirt or blouse.

wrist-drop ▶ n. paralysis of the muscles that normally raise the hand at the wrist and extend the fingers, typically caused by nerve damage.

wrist·guard /ˈristˌgärd/ ▶ n. a band of leather or leatherlike material worn around the wrist for support and protection, esp. for athletic activities such as archery and fencing.

wrist·let /ˈristlit/ ▶ n. a band or bracelet worn on the wrist, typically as an ornament.

wrist pin ▶ n. another term for WRIST (sense 2).

wrist·watch /ˈristˌwäCH/ ▶ n. a watch worn on a strap around the wrist.

wrist·work /ˈristˌwərk/ ▶ n. the action of working the hand without moving the arm, esp. in fencing and ball games.

wrist·y /ˈristē/ ▶ adj. Tennis (of a stroke) performed using a pronounced movement of the wrist: *he uses a fast, wristy swing to hit his forehand.*

writ[1] /rit/ ▶ n. a form of written command in the name of a court or other legal authority to act, or abstain from acting, in some way. ■ (**one's writ**) one's power to enforce compliance or submission; one's authority: *you have business here which is out of my writ and competence.*
– ORIGIN Old English, as a general term denoting written matter, from the Germanic base of WRITE.

writ[2] ▶ v. archaic past participle of WRITE.
– PHRASES **writ large** clear and obvious: *the unspoken question writ large upon Rose's face.* ■ in a stark or exaggerated form: *bribing people by way of tax allowances is the paternalistic state writ large.*

write /rīt/ ▶ v. (past **wrote** /rōt/; past participle **written** /ˈritn/) [with obj.] **1** mark (letters, words, or other symbols) on a surface, typically paper, with a pen, pencil, or similar implement: *he wrote his name on the paper* | *Alice **wrote down** the address* | [no obj.] *he wrote very neatly in blue ink.* ■ [no obj.] have the ability to mark coherent letters or words in this way: *he couldn't read or write.* ■ fill out or complete (a sheet, check, or similar) in this way: *he had to write a check for $800.* ■ [no obj.] write in a cursive hand, as opposed to printing individual letters.
2 compose, write, and send (a letter) to someone: *I **wrote** a letter **to** Alison* | [with two objs.] *I wrote him a short letter* | [no obj.] *he wrote almost every day.* ■ write and send a letter to (someone): *Mother wrote me and told me about poor Simon's death.* ■ (**write in**) write to an organization, esp. a broadcasting station, with a question, suggestion, or opinion: *write in with your query.*
3 compose (a text or work) for written or printed reproduction or publication; put into literary form and set down in writing: *I didn't know you wrote poetry* | [no obj.] *he wrote under a pseudonym* | *he had written about the beauty of Andalucia.* ■ compose (a musical work): *he has written a song specifically for her.* ■ (**write someone into/out of**) add or remove a character to or from (a long-running story or series). ■ archaic describe in writing: *if I could write the beauty of your eyes.*
4 Computing enter (data) into a specified storage medium or location in store.
5 underwrite (an insurance policy).
– PHRASES **be nothing to write home about** informal be very mediocre or unexceptional. **be** (or **have something**) **written all over one** (or **one's face**) informal used to convey that the presence of a particular quality or feeling is clearly revealed by a person's expression: *guilt was written all over his face.* **be written in stone** see STONE. **(and) that's all she wrote** informal used to convey that there is or was nothing more to be said about a matter: *we were arguing about who should pay the bill, but he pulled out a couple of hundreds and that's all she wrote.*
– PHRASAL VERBS **write something down 1** reduce the nominal value of stock or goods. **2** write as if for those considered inferior. **write someone in** (when voting) add the name of someone not on the original list of candidates and vote for them. **write something off 1** (**write someone/something off**) dismiss someone or something as insignificant: *the boy had been written off as a nonachiever.* **2** cancel the record of a bad debt; acknowledge the loss of or failure to recover an asset: *he urged the banks to write off debt owed by poorer countries.* **write something up 1** write a full or formal account of something: *I was too tired to write up my notes.* ■ make entries to bring a diary or similar record up to date: *he wrote up a work journal which has never been published.* **2** increase the nominal value of stock or goods.
– DERIVATIVES **writ·a·ble** adj.
– ORIGIN Old English *wrītan* 'score, form (letters) by carving, write,' of Germanic origin; related to German *reissen* 'sketch, drag.'

write-back ▶ n. Finance the process of restoring to profit a provision for bad or doubtful debts previously made against profits and no longer required.

write-down ▶ n. Finance a reduction in the estimated or nominal value of an asset.

write-in ▶ n. a vote cast for an unlisted candidate by writing their name on a ballot paper: *the results showed 70 blank ballots and 770 write-ins.* ■ a candidate for whom votes are cast in such a way.

write-off ▶ n. **1** Finance a cancellation from an account of a bad debt or worthless asset.

2 a worthless or ineffectual person or thing: *she burns the toast and decides the weekend is a write-off.*

write-once ▶ **adj.** Computing denoting a memory or storage device, typically an optical one, on which data, once written, cannot be modified.

write-pro·tect ▶ **v.** [with obj.] Computing protect (a disk) from accidental writing or erasure, as by removing the cover from a notch in the plastic casing of a floppy disk.

writ·er /ˈrītər/ ▶ **n.** a person who has written a particular text: *the writer of the letter.* ■ a person who writes books, stories, or articles as a job or regular occupation: *the distinguished travel writer Freya Stark.* ■ [with adj.] a person who writes in a specified way: *Dickens was a prolific writer.* ■ a composer of musical works: *a writer of military music.* ■ Computing a device that writes data to a storage medium. ■ Stock Market a broker who makes an option available for purchase or sells options. ■ [with adj.] a person who has a specified kind of handwriting: *neat writers.* ■ Brit. historical a scribe. ■ Brit. archaic a clerk, esp. in the navy or other government offices.
– PHRASES **writer's block** the condition of being unable to think of what to write or how to proceed with writing. **writer's cramp** pain or stiffness in the hand caused by excessive writing.
– ORIGIN Old English *wrītere* (see WRITE).

writ·er-in-res·i·dence ▶ **n.** (pl. **writers-in-residence**) a writer holding a temporary residential post in an academic establishment, in order to share their professional insights.

writ·er·ly /ˈrītərlē/ ▶ **adj.** of or characteristic of a professional author: *the mixture of writerly craft and stamina that Greene had.* ■ consciously literary: *novels as tricksy and writerly as those of Robbe-Grillet.*

write-up ▶ **n. 1** a full written account. ■ a newspaper or magazine article giving the author's opinion of a recent event, performance, or product. **2** Finance an increase in the estimated or nominal value of an asset.

writhe /rīTH/ ▶ **v.** [no obj.] make continual twisting, squirming movements or contortions of the body: *he writhed in agony on the ground* | [with obj.] *a snake writhing its body.* ■ (**writhe in/with/at**) respond with great emotional or physical discomfort to (a violent or unpleasant feeling or thought): *she bit her lip, writhing in suppressed fury.*
– ORIGIN Old English *wrīthan* 'make into coils, plait, fasten with a cord,' of Germanic origin; related to WREATHE.

writh·en /ˈriTHən/ ▶ **adj. 1** literary twisted or contorted out of normal shape or form. **2** (of antique glass or silver) having spirally twisted ornamentation.
– ORIGIN Old English in the sense 'plaited, entwined,' archaic past participle of WRITHE.

writ·ing /ˈrītiNG/ ▶ **n. 1** the activity or skill of marking coherent words on paper and composing text: *parents want schools to concentrate on reading, writing, and arithmetic.* ■ the activity or occupation of composing text for publication: *she made a decent living from writing.* **2** written work, esp. with regard to its style or quality: *the writing is straightforward and accessible.* ■ (**writings**) books, stories, articles, or other written works: *he was introduced to the writings of Gertrude Stein.* ■ (**the Writings**) the Hagiographa. **3** a sequence of letters, words, or symbols marked on paper or some other surface: *a leather product with gold writing on it.* ■ handwriting: *his writing looked crabbed.*
– PHRASES **in writing** in written form, esp. as proof of an agreement or grievance: *he asked them to put their complaints in writing.* **the writing** (or **handwriting**) **is on the wall** see HANDWRITING.

writ·ing desk ▶ **n.** a piece of furniture with a surface for writing on and with drawers and other compartments for pens and paper.

writ·ing pad ▶ **n.** a pad of paper for writing on.

writ·ing pa·per ▶ **n.** paper of good quality used for writing, esp. letter-writing.

writ of ex·e·cu·tion ▶ **n.** Law a judicial order that a judgment be enforced.

writ·ten /ˈritn/ past participle of WRITE.

WRNS ▶ **abbr.** historical (in the UK) Women's Royal Naval Service.

Wro·cław /ˈvrôt,swäf, -,släf/ an industrial city on the Oder River, in western Poland; pop. 633,950 (2007). German name **BRESLAU**.

wrong /rôNG/ ▶ **adj. 1** not correct or true: *that is the wrong answer.* ■ [predic.] mistaken: *I was wrong about him being on the yacht that evening.* ■ unsuitable or undesirable: *they asked all the wrong questions.* ■ [predic.] in a bad or abnormal condition; amiss: *something was wrong with the pump.* **2** unjust, dishonest, or immoral: *they were wrong to take the law into their own hands* | *it was wrong of me to write you such an angry note.*
▶ **adv.** in an unsuitable or undesirable manner or direction: *what am I doing wrong?* ■ with an incorrect result: *she guessed wrong.*
▶ **n.** an unjust, dishonest, or immoral action: *I have done you a great wrong.* ■ Law a breach, by commission or omission, of one's legal duty. ■ Law an invasion of right to the damage or prejudice of another.
▶ **v.** [with obj.] act unjustly or dishonestly toward (someone): *please forgive me these things and the people I have wronged.* ■ mistakenly attribute bad motives to; misrepresent: *perhaps I wrong him.*
– PHRASES **get someone wrong** misunderstand someone, esp. by falsely imputing malice: *now, don't get me wrong, my fellow players are a great bunch of people.* **go down the wrong way** (of food) enter the windpipe instead of the gullet. **go wrong** make a mistake. ■ (of a device) malfunction; develop a fault. ■ develop in an undesirable way: *the government has ordered an inquiry to ascertain what went wrong.* **in the wrong** responsible for a quarrel, mistake, or offense. **two wrongs don't make a right** proverb the fact that someone has done something unjust or dishonest is no justification for acting in a similar way.
– DERIVATIVES **wrong·er** n., **wrong·ly** adv., **wrong·ness** n.
– ORIGIN late Old English *wrang*, from Old Norse *rangr* 'awry, unjust'; related to WRING.

wrong·do·er /ˈrôNG,do͞oər/ ▶ **n.** a person who behaves illegally or dishonestly; an offender: *we'd like to see wrongdoers expelled from the industry entirely.*

wrong·do·ing /ˈrôNG,do͞oiNG/ ▶ **n.** illegal or dishonest behavior: *the head of the bank has denied any wrongdoing.*

wrong-foot ▶ **v.** [with obj.] (in a game) play so as to catch (an opponent) off balance: *Cook wrong-footed the defense with a low free kick.* ■ Brit. put (someone) in a difficult or embarrassing situation by saying or doing something that they do not expect: *an announcement regarded as an attempt to wrong-foot the opposition.*

wrong·ful /ˈrôNGfəl/ ▶ **adj.** (of an act) not fair, just, or legal: *he is suing the police for wrongful arrest.*
– DERIVATIVES **wrong·ful·ly** adv., **wrong·ful·ness** n.

wrong·ful death ▶ **adj.** denoting a civil action in which damages are sought against a party for causing a death, typically when criminal action has failed or is not attempted: *a wrongful death lawsuit.*

wrong·head·ed /ˈrôNG,hedid/ ▶ **adj.** having or showing bad judgment; misguided: *this approach is both wrongheaded and naive.*
– DERIVATIVES **wrong·head·ed·ly** adv., **wrong·head·ed·ness** n.

wrong side ▶ **n.** the reverse side of a fabric.
– PHRASES **born on the wrong side of the blanket** see BLANKET. **get out of bed on the wrong side** see BED. **on the wrong side of 1** out of favor with: *she knew not to get on the wrong side of him.* **2** somewhat more than (a specified age): *he cheerfully admits he is the wrong side of fifty.* **on the wrong side of the tracks** see TRACK[1]. **wrong side out** inside out.

wrote /rōt/ past tense of WRITE.

wroth /rôTH/ ▶ **adj.** archaic angry: *Sir Leicester is majestically wroth.*
– ORIGIN Old English *wrāth*, of Germanic origin; related to Dutch *wreed* 'cruel,' also to WRITHE.

wrought /rôt/ archaic past and past participle of WORK ▶ **adj.** (of metals) beaten out or shaped by hammering.

USAGE See usage at **WREAK**.

wrought i·ron ▶ **n.** a tough, malleable form of iron suitable for forging or rolling rather than casting, obtained by puddling pig iron while molten. It is nearly pure but contains some slag in the form of filaments.

wrought up ▶ **adj.** [predic.] upset and anxious: *she didn't get too wrought up about things.*

wrung /rəNG/ past and past participle of WRING.

WRVS ▶ **abbr.** (in the UK) Women's Royal Voluntary Service.

wry /rī/ ▶ **adj.** (**wryer, wryest** or **wrier, wriest**) **1** using or expressing dry, esp. mocking, humor: *a wry smile* | *wry comments.* **2** (of a person's face or features) twisted into an expression of disgust, disappointment, or annoyance. ■ archaic (of the neck or features) distorted or turned to one side: *a remedy for wry necks.*
– DERIVATIVES **wry·ly** adv., **wry·ness** n.
– ORIGIN early 16th cent. (in the sense 'contorted'): from Old English *wrīgian* 'tend, incline,' in Middle English 'deviate, swerve, contort.'

wry·neck /ˈrī,nek/ ▶ **n. 1** an Old World bird of the woodpecker family, with brown camouflaged plumage and a habit of twisting and writhing the neck when disturbed. ● Genus *Jynx*, family Picidae: two species, in particular the **northern wryneck** (*J. torquilla*) of Eurasia. **2** another term for TORTICOLLIS.

WSW ▶ **abbr.** west-southwest.

wt ▶ **abbr.** weight.

WTF ▶ **abbr.** vulgar slang what the fuck? (used as an expression of incredulity or annoyance).

WTO ▶ **abbr.** World Trade Organization.

Wu /wo͞o/ ▶ **n.** a dialect of Chinese spoken in Jiangsu and Zhejiang provinces and the city of Shanghai.
– ORIGIN the name in Chinese.

Wu·han /ˈwo͞oˈhän/ a port in eastern China, the capital of Hubei province; pop. 8,001,500 (est. 2006). Situated at the confluence of the Han and the Yangtze rivers, it is a conurbation of three adjacent towns (Hankow, Hanyang, and Wuchang) that have been administered jointly since 1950.

wul·fen·ite /ˈwo͝olfə,nīt/ ▶ **n.** an orange-yellow mineral consisting of a molybdate of lead, typically occurring as tabular crystals.
– ORIGIN mid 19th cent.: from the name of F. X. von *Wulfen* (1728–1805), Austrian scientist, + -ITE[1].

Wun·der·kam·mer /ˈvo͝ondər,kämər/ ▶ **n.** (pl. **Wunderkammern**) a place where a collection of curiosities and rarities is exhibited.
– ORIGIN German, literally 'wonder chamber.'

wun·der·kind /ˈwo͝ondər,kind/ ▶ **n.** (pl. **wunderkinds** or **wunderkinder** /-,kindər/) a person who achieves great success when relatively young.
– ORIGIN late 19th cent.: from German, from *Wunder* 'wonder' + *Kind* 'child.'

Wundt /vo͝ont/, Wilhelm (1832–1920), German psychologist. He founded psychology as a separate discipline and established a laboratory devoted to its study.

wun·ner·ful /ˈwənərfəl/ ▶ **adj.** nonstandard spelling of WONDERFUL, representing dialect pronunciation.

Wup·per·tal /ˈvo͝opər,täl, ˈwo͝op-/ an industrial city in western Germany, in North Rhine–Westphalia northeast of Düsseldorf; pop. 358,300 (est. 2006).

Wur·litz·er /ˈwərlitsər/ ▶ **n.** trademark a large pipe organ or electric organ, esp. one used in the movie theaters of the 1930s.
– ORIGIN named after Rudolf *Wurlitzer* (1831–1914), the German-born American instrument-maker who founded the manufacturing company.

Würm /vo͝orm/ ▶ **n.** [usu. as modifier] Geology the final Pleistocene glaciation in the Alps, possibly corresponding to the Weichsel of northern Europe. ■ the system of deposits laid down at this time.
– ORIGIN early 20th cent.: the former name of the Starnberger See, a lake in Bavaria.

wurst /wərst, wo͝orst/ ▶ **n.** German or Austrian sausage.
– ORIGIN from German *Wurst*.

wurtz·ite /ˈwərt,sīt/ ▶ **n.** a mineral consisting of zinc sulfide, typically occurring as brownish-black pyramidal crystals.
– ORIGIN mid 19th cent.: from the name of Charles A. *Wurtz* (1817–84), French chemist, + -ITE[1].

Würz·burg /ˈvərtsbərg, ˈwərts-, ˈvYrts,bo͝ork/ an industrial city on the Main River in Bavaria, in southern Germany; pop. 134,900 (est. 2006).

wu·shu /ˈwo͞oˈSHo͞o/ ▶ **n.** the Chinese martial arts.
– ORIGIN from Chinese *wǔshù*, from *wǔ* 'military' + *shù* 'art.'

wuss /wo͝os/ ▶ **n.** informal a weak or ineffectual person (often used as a general term of abuse).
– DERIVATIVES **wuss·y** adj.
– ORIGIN late 20th cent.: of unknown origin.

Wu·xi /ˈwo͞oˈSHē/ (also **Wu-hsi**) a city on the Grand Canal in Jiangsu province, in eastern China; pop. 2,095,300 (est. 2006).

Wu·xia /ˈwo͞oˈSHyä/ ▶ **n.** a genre of Chinese fiction or film dealing with martial arts, sorcery, and chivalry.
– ORIGIN from Chinese *wuxia*, from *wu* 'martial art' + *xia* 'warrior.'

wuz /wəz/ ▶ **v.** nonstandard spelling of WAS, representing dialect or informal pronunciation.

WV ▶ **abbr.** West Virginia (in official postal use).

W.Va ▶ **abbr.** West Virginia.

PRONUNCIATION KEY ə *ago, up*; ər *over, fur*; a *hat*; ā *ate*; ä *car*; e *let*; ē *see*; i *fit*; ī *by*; NG *sing*; ō *go*; ô *law, for*; oi *toy*; o͝o *good*; o͞o *goo*; ou *out*; TH *thin*; T͟H *then*; ZH *vision*

WWF ▸ **abbr.** ■ World Wrestling Federation. ■ World Wildlife Fund (also **World Wide Fund for Nature**).

WWI ▸ **abbr.** World War I.

WWII ▸ **abbr.** World War II.

WWW ▸ **abbr.** World Wide Web.

WY ▸ **abbr.** Wyoming (in official postal use).

Wy·an·dot /ˈwīən,dät/ (also **Wyandotte**) ▸ **n.** **1** a member of an American Indian community formed by Huron-speaking peoples, originally in Ontario, now living mainly in Oklahoma and Quebec. **2** the Iroquoian language of this people. **3** (usu. **Wyandotte**) a domestic chicken of a medium-sized breed.
▸ **adj.** of or relating to the Wyandot people or their language.
– ORIGIN mid 18th cent.: from French *Ouendat*, from Huron *Wendat*.

wych elm /wicH/ (also **witch elm**) ▸ **n.** a European elm with large rough leaves, chiefly growing in woodland or near flowing water. ● *Ulmus glabra*, family Ulmaceae.
– ORIGIN early 17th cent.: *wych*, used in names of trees with pliant branches, from Old English *wic(e)*, apparently from a Germanic root meaning 'bend'; related to **WEAK**.

Wych·er·ley /ˈwicHərlē/, William (*c.*1640–1716), English playwright. His Restoration comedies are characterized by their acute examination of sexual morality and marriage conventions.

Wyc·lif /ˈwiklif/ (also **Wycliffe**), John (*c.*1330–84), English religious reformer. He criticized the wealth and power of the Church and upheld the Bible as the sole guide for doctrine; Wyclif instituted the first English translation of the complete Bible. His followers were known as Lollards.

Wye /wī/ a river that rises in the mountains of western Wales and flows southeast for about 132 miles (208 km) before entering the Severn estuary at Chepstow. In its lower reaches it forms part of the border between Wales and England.

wye /wī/ ▸ **n.** a support or other structure shaped like a Y, in particular: ■ a triangle of railroad track, used for turning locomotives or trains. ■ (in plumbing) a short pipe with a branch joining it at an acute angle.
– ORIGIN mid 19th cent.: the letter *Y* represented as a word.

Wy·eth /ˈwīəTH/, a US family of artists, notably **N. C.** (1882–1944), full name *Newell Convers Wyeth*, whose many illustrations appeared in publications; his son **Andrew Newell** (1917–2009), whose paintings include *Christina's World* (1948) and the Helga series (1971–85); and Andrew's son **Jamie** (1946–), full name *James Browning Wyeth*, whose notable paintings include *Portrait of J.F.K.* (1965), *Wolfbane* (1984), and his series of portraits of Orca Bates.

Wy·ler /ˈwīlər/, William (1902–81), US director; born in Germany. Notable movies: *Jezebel* (1938), *Mrs. Miniver* (1941), *The Best Years of Our Lives* (1946), *Ben-Hur* (1959), and *Funny Girl* (1968).

Wynd·ham /ˈwindəm/, John (1903–69), English writer of science fiction; pseudonym of *John Wyndham Parkes Lucas Beynon Harris*. Notable novels: *The Day of the Triffids* (1951), *The Chrysalids* (1955), and *The Midwich Cuckoos* (1957).

wynn /win/ (also **wyn, wen**) ▸ **n.** a runic letter, used in Old and Middle English, later replaced by *w*.
– ORIGIN Old English, literally 'joy'; so named because it is the first letter of this word. Compare with **THORN** (sense 3) and **ASH**[2] (sense 2).

Wyo. ▸ **abbr.** Wyoming.

Wy·o·ming /wīˈōmiNG/ **1** a state in the western central US; pop. 532,668 (est. 2008); capital, Cheyenne; statehood, July 10, 1890 (44). Acquired, in part, by the Louisiana Purchase in 1803, it gave the vote to women in 1869, the first state to do so. **2** a city in southwestern Michigan, southwest of Grand Rapids; pop. 70,462 (est. 2008).
– DERIVATIVES **Wy·o·ming·ite** /-miNG,īt/ **n.**

Wy·o·ming Val·ley a valley in northeastern Pennsylvania, along the Susquehanna River.

Wy·o·tan·a /,wīōˈtanə/ ▸ **n.** informal a region consisting largely of mountain wilderness lying partly in southern Montana and partly in northern Wyoming.
– ORIGIN blend of *Wyoming* and *Montana*.

WYSIWYG /ˈwizē,wig/ (also **wysiwyg**) ▸ **adj.** Computing denoting the representation of text on screen in a form exactly corresponding to its appearance on a printout.
– ORIGIN 1980s: acronym from *what you see is what you get*.

wythe /wiTH/ ▸ **n.** a vertical section of bricks or other masonry that is one unit thick.
– ORIGIN early 18th cent.(as *with*): probably an alteration of **WIDTH**.

wy·vern /ˈwīvərn/ ▸ **n.** Heraldry a winged two-legged dragon with a barbed tail.
– ORIGIN late Middle English (denoting a viper): from Old French *wivre*, from Latin *vipera*.

wyvern

X¹ /eks/ (also **x**) ▶ **n.** (pl. **Xs** or **X's**) **1** the twenty-fourth letter of the alphabet. ■ denoting the next after W in a set of items, categories, etc. ■ denoting an unknown or unspecified person or thing: *there is nothing in the data to tell us whether X causes Y or Y causes X.* ■ (**x**) (used in describing play in bridge) denoting an unspecified card other than an honor. ■ (usu. *x*) the first unknown quantity in an algebraic expression, usually the independent variable. [the introduction of *x*, *y*, and *z* as symbols of unknown quantities is due to Descartes (*Géométrie*, 1637), who took *z* as the first unknown and then proceeded backward in the alphabet.] ■ (usu. *x*) denoting the principal or horizontal axis in a system of coordinates.
2 a cross-shaped written symbol, in particular: ■ used to indicate a position on a map or diagram. ■ used to indicate a mistake or incorrect answer. ■ used in a letter or message to symbolize a kiss. ■ used to indicate one's vote on a ballot. ■ used in place of the signature of a person who cannot write.
3 a shape like that of a letter X: *two wires in the form of an X* | [in combination] *an X-shaped cross.*
4 the Roman numeral for ten.
▶ **v.** (**X's**, **X'ing**, **X'd**) [with obj.] mark or make a sign with an X. ■ overwrite or obliterate with an X or series of X's. ■ make void or annul; invalidate: *we're all X-ing things out of our curricula.*

X² ▶ **symbol 1** a rating assigned to movies classified as suitable for adults only. Replaced in 1990 by **NC-17**. **2** (in systematic names of organisms) hybrid. [from **CROSS** (sense 3 of the noun).]

-x ▶ **suffix** forming the plural of many nouns ending in *-u* taken from French: *tableaux.*
– ORIGIN from French.

X-act·o knife /ig'zaktō/ ▶ **n.** trademark a utility knife with a very sharp replaceable blade.
– ORIGIN 1940s: respelling of the adjective **EXACT** + **-O**.

Xan·a·du /'zanə,do͞o/ ▶ **n.** (pl. **Xanadus**) used to convey an impression of a place as almost unattainably luxurious or beautiful: *three architects and a planner combine to create a Xanadu.*
– ORIGIN alteration of *Shang-tu*, the name of an ancient city in southeastern Mongolia, as portrayed in Coleridge's poem *Kubla Khan* (1816).

Xan·ax /'zan,aks/ ▶ **n.** trademark for **ALPRAZOLAM**.

Xan·kän·di /,KHänkan'dē/ the capital of Nagorno-Karabakh in southern Azerbaijan; pop. 49,300 (est. 2005). Russian name **STEPANAKERT**.

xan·than gum /'zanTHən, -,THan/ ▶ **n.** Chemistry a substance produced by bacterial fermentation or synthetically and used in foods as a gelling agent and thickener. It is a polysaccharide composed of glucose, mannose, and glucuronic acid.
– ORIGIN 1960s: from the modern Latin name of the bacterium *Xanthomonas campestris* + **-AN**.

xan·thene /'zan,THēn/ ▶ **n.** Chemistry a yellowish crystalline compound whose molecule contains two benzene rings joined by a methylene group and an oxygen atom, and whose derivatives include brilliant, often fluorescent dyes such as fluorescein and rhodamines. ● Chem. formula: $C_{13}H_{10}O$.
– ORIGIN late 19th cent.: from Greek *xanthos* 'yellow' + **-ENE**.

xan·thic ac·id /'zanTHik/ ▶ **n.** Chemistry an organic acid containing the group $-OCS_2H$, examples of which are typically reactive solids.
– DERIVATIVES **xan·thate** /'zan,THāt/ **n.**
– ORIGIN early 19th cent.: *xanthic* from Greek *xanthos* 'yellow' + **-IC**.

xan·thine /'zan,THēn, -THin/ ▶ **n.** Biochemistry a crystalline compound that is found in blood and urine and is an intermediate in the metabolic breakdown of nucleic acids to uric acid. ● A purine derivative; chem. formula: $C_5H_4N_4O_2$. ■ any of the derivatives of this, including caffeine and related alkaloids.
– ORIGIN mid 19th cent.: from *xanthic* (from Greek *xanthos* 'yellow' + **-IC**) + **-INE⁴**.

Xan·thip·pe /zan'tipē, -'THipē/ (also **Xantippe** /-'tipē/) (5th century BC), wife of Socrates. Her allegedly bad-tempered behavior toward her husband made her proverbial as a shrew.

xan·tho·ma /zan'THōmə/ ▶ **n.** (pl. **xanthomas** or **xanthomata** /-mətə/) Medicine an irregular yellow patch or nodule on the skin, caused by deposition of lipids.
– ORIGIN mid 19th cent.: from Greek *xanthos* 'yellow' + **-OMA**.

xan·tho·phyll /'zanTHə,fil/ ▶ **n.** Biochemistry a yellow or brown carotenoid plant pigment that causes the autumn colors of leaves.
– ORIGIN mid 19th cent.: from Greek *xanthos* 'yellow' + *phullon* 'leaf.'

Xa·vi·er, St. Fran·cis /(ig)'zāvēər/ (1506–52), Spanish Catholic missionary; known as **the Apostle of the Indies**. One of the original seven Jesuits, from 1540 he traveled to southern India, Sri Lanka, Malacca, the Moluccas, and Japan, where he made thousands of converts. Feast day, December 3.

x-ax·is ▶ **n.** the principal or horizontal axis of a system of coordinates, points along which have a value of zero for all other coordinates. Compare with **Y-AXIS**.

X chro·mo·some ▶ **n.** Genetics (in humans and other mammals) a sex chromosome, two of which are normally present in female cells (designated XX) and only one in male cells (designated XY). Compare with **Y CHROMOSOME**.

xd ▶ **abbr.** ex dividend.

Xe ▶ **symbol** the chemical element xenon.

xe·bec /'zē,bek/ (also **zebec**) ▶ **n.** historical a small three-masted Mediterranean sailing ship with lateen and sometimes square sails.
– ORIGIN mid 18th cent.: alteration (influenced by Spanish *xabeque*) of French *chebec*, via Italian from Arabic *šabbāk*.

Xe·lo·da /zə'lōdə/ ▶ **n.** trademark for **CAPECITABINE**.

Xe·na·kis /ze'näkēs/, Iannis (1922–2001), French composer and architect, of Greek descent. He is noted for his use of electronic and aleatory techniques in music.

Xe·nar·thra /zə'närTHrə/ Zoology an order of mammals that comprises the edentates. Also called **EDENTATA**.
– DERIVATIVES **xe·nar·thran n. & adj.**
– ORIGIN modern Latin (plural), from **XENO-** 'strange' + Greek *arthron* 'joint' (because of the peculiar accessory articulations in the vertebrae).

xe·ni·a /'zēnēə, -nyə/ ▶ **n.** Botany the influence or effect of pollen on the endosperm or embryo, resulting in hybrid characteristics in form, color, etc., of the derived seed.

Xen·i·cal /'zenikal/ ▶ **n.** trademark a synthetic drug that blocks pancreatic enzymes used in the digestion of fats, used to treat obesity.

xeno- ▶ **comb. form** relating to a foreigner or foreigners: *xenophobia.* ■ other; different in origin: *xenograft.*
– ORIGIN from Greek *xenos* 'stranger, foreigner,' (adjective) 'strange.'

xen·o·bi·ot·ic /,zenəbī'ätik, ,zēnə-/ ▶ **adj.** relating to or denoting a substance, typically a synthetic chemical, that is foreign to the body or to an ecological system.
▶ **n.** (usu. **xenobiotics**) a substance of this kind.

xen·o·cryst /'zenə,krist, 'zēnə-/ ▶ **n.** Geology a crystal in an igneous rock that is not derived from the original magma.
– ORIGIN late 19th cent.: from **XENO-** 'foreign' + **CRYSTAL**.

xe·nog·a·my /zə'nägəmē/ ▶ **n.** Botany fertilization of a flower by pollen from a flower on a genetically different plant. Compare with **GEITONOGAMY**.
– DERIVATIVES **xe·nog·a·mous** /-məs/ **adj.**

xen·o·ge·ne·ic /,zenōjə'nē-ik, ,zēnō-/ ▶ **adj.** Immunology denoting, relating to, or involving tissues or cells belonging to individuals of different species. Compare with **ALLOGENEIC**.

xen·o·graft /'zenə,graft, 'zēnə-/ ▶ **n.** a tissue graft or organ transplant from a donor of a different species from the recipient.

xen·o·lith /'zenə,liTH, 'zēnə-/ ▶ **n.** Geology a piece of rock within an igneous rock that is not derived from the original magma but has been introduced from elsewhere, esp. the surrounding country rock.

xen·ol·o·gy /zə'näləjē/ ▶ **n.** (chiefly in science fiction) the scientific study of alien biology, cultures, etc.
– DERIVATIVES **xen·ol·o·gist n.**
– ORIGIN 1950s: from Greek *xenos* 'stranger, foreigner,' (adjective) 'strange.'

xe·non /'zē,nän, 'zen,än/ ▶ **n.** the chemical element of atomic number 54, a member of the noble gas series. It is obtained by distillation of liquid air and is used in some specialized electric lamps. (Symbol: **Xe**)
– ORIGIN late 19th cent.: from Greek, neuter of *xenos* 'strange.'

Xe·noph·a·nes /zə'näfə,nēz/ (*c.*570–*c.*480 BC), Greek philosopher. A member of the Eleatic school, he argued for a form of pantheism and criticized belief in anthropomorphic gods.

xen·o·phile /'zenə,fīl, 'zē-/ ▶ **n.** an individual who is attracted to foreign peoples, manners, or cultures.

xen·o·pho·bi·a /,zēnə'fōbēə, ,zenə-/ ▶ **n.** intense or irrational dislike or fear of people from other countries.
– DERIVATIVES **xen·o·phobe** /'zēnə,fōb, 'zenə-/ **n.**

xen·o·pho·bic /,zēnə'fōbik, ,zenə-/ ▶ **adj.** having or showing an intense or irrational dislike or fear of people from other countries: *the xenophobic undertones of this argument.*

Xen·o·phon /'zenə,fän/ (*c.*435–*c.*354 BC), Greek historian, writer, and military leader. From 401, he fought with Cyrus the Younger against Artaxerxes II. The campaign and retreat are recorded in the *Anabasis*. Other notable writings include the *Hellenica*, a history of Greece.

Xe·no·pus /'zenəpəs/ ▶ **n.** the African clawed frog, much used in embryological research and formerly in pregnancy testing, as it produces eggs in response to substances in the urine of a pregnant woman. ● *Xenopus laevis*, family Pipidae.
– ORIGIN late 19th cent.: modern Latin, from **XENO-** 'strange' + Greek *pous* 'foot.'

xen·o·time /'zenə,tīm, 'zēnə-/ ▶ **n.** a yellowish-brown mineral that occurs in some igneous rocks and consists of a phosphate of yttrium and other rare-earth elements.

– ORIGIN mid 19th cent.: from **XENO-**, apparently erroneously for Greek *kenos* 'vain, empty,' + *timē* 'honor' (because it was wrongly supposed to contain a new metal).

xen·o·trans·plan·ta·tion /ˌzenəˌtransplanˈtāsHən, ˌzēnə-/ ▶ **n.** the process of grafting or transplanting organs or tissues between members of different species.
– DERIVATIVES **xen·o·trans·plant** /-ˈtransˌplant/ **n.**

X·er /ˈeksər/ ▶ **n.** informal another term for **GEN-XER**.

xe·ric /ˈzi(ə)rik, ˈzer-/ ▶ **adj.** Ecology (of an environment or habitat) containing little moisture; very dry. Compare with **HYDRIC** and **MESIC**[1].
– ORIGIN 1920s: from **XERO-** 'dry' + **-IC**.

xe·ri·scape /ˈzi(ə)rəˌskāp, ˈzerə-/ ▶ **n.** a style of landscape design requiring little or no irrigation or other maintenance, used in arid regions. ■ a garden or landscape created in such a style.
▶ **v.** [with obj.] landscape (an area) in such a style.
– ORIGIN 1980s: from **XERIC** + **-SCAPE**.

xero- ▶ **comb. form** dry: *xeroderma* | *xerophyte*.
– ORIGIN from Greek *xēros* 'dry.'

xe·ro·der·ma /ˌzi(ə)rəˈdərmə/ ▶ **n.** any of various diseases characterized by extreme dryness of the skin, esp. a mild form of ichthyosis.
– ORIGIN mid 19th cent.: modern Latin, from **XERO-** 'dry' + Greek *derma* 'skin.'

xe·ro·der·ma pig·men·to·sum /ˌpigmənˈtōsəm, -men-/ ▶ **n.** a rare hereditary defect of the enzyme system that repairs DNA after damage from ultraviolet rays, resulting in extreme sensitivity to sunlight and a tendency to develop skin cancer.
– ORIGIN late 19th cent.: *pigmentosum*, neuter of Latin *pigmentosus* 'pigmented.'

xe·rog·ra·phy /ziˈrägrəfē/ ▶ **n.** a dry copying process in which black or colored powder adheres to parts of a surface remaining electrically charged after being exposed to light from an image of the document to be copied.
– DERIVATIVES **xe·ro·graph·ic** /ˌzi(ə)rəˈgrafik/ **adj.**, **xe·ro·graph·i·cal·ly** **adv.**

xe·roph·i·lous /ziˈräfələs/ ▶ **adj.** Botany & Zoology (of a plant or animal) adapted to a very dry climate or habitat, or to conditions where moisture is scarce.
– DERIVATIVES **xer·o·phile** /ˈzi(ə)rəˌfīl/ **n.**

xe·roph·thal·mi·a /ˌzi(ə)räfˈTHalmēə, ˌzi(ə)räp-/ ▶ **n.** Medicine abnormal dryness of the conjunctiva and cornea of the eye, with inflammation and ridge formation, typically associated with vitamin A deficiency.

xe·ro·phyte /ˈzi(ə)rəˌfīt/ ▶ **n.** Botany a plant that needs very little water.
– DERIVATIVES **xe·ro·phyt·ic** /ˌzi(ə)rəˈfitik/ **adj.**

Xerox /ˈzi(ə)rˌäks/ ▶ **n.** trademark a xerographic copying process. ■ a copy made using such a process. ■ a machine for copying by xerography.
▶ **v.** (**xerox**) [with obj.] copy (a document) by such a process.
– ORIGIN 1950s: an invented name, based on **XEROGRAPHY**.

Xerx·es I /ˈzərkˌsēz/ (c.519–465 BC), son of Darius I; king of Persia 486–465. He continued his father's attack on the Greeks but was forced to withdraw after defeats at Salamis in 480 and Plataea in 479.

X fac·tor ▶ **n.** informal **1** a variable in a given situation that could have the most significant impact on the outcome: *the young vote may turn out to be the X factor*.
2 a noteworthy special talent or quality: *there are plenty of luxury cars around, but the S-Type has that special X factor*.

x-height ▶ **n.** the height of a lower-case x, considered characteristic of a given typeface or script.

Xho·sa /ˈkōsə, ˈkô-, ˈKHō-, ˈKHô-/ ▶ **n.** (pl. **same** or **Xhosas**) **1** a member of a South African people traditionally living in the Eastern Cape Province. They form the second largest ethnic group in South Africa after the Zulus.
2 the Nguni language of this people.
▶ **adj.** of or relating to this people or their language.
– ORIGIN from the stem of Xhosa *umXhosa* (plural *amaXhosa*).

XHTML ▶ **abbr.** Computing Extensible Hypertext Markup Language, an HTML system for tagging text files to achieve font, color, graphic, and hyperlink effects on World Wide Web pages, incorporating user-defined elements.

xi /zī, ksī/ ▶ **n.** the fourteenth letter of the Greek alphabet (Ξ, ξ), transliterated as 'x.' ■ (**Xi**) [followed by Latin genitive] Astronomy the fourteenth star in a specified constellation: *Xi Cygni*.

Xia·men /ˈSH(y)äˈmən/ (also **Hsia-men**) a port in Fujian province, in southeastern China; pop. 961,800 (est. 2006). Also called **AMOY**.

Xi·an /ˈSHēˈän/ (also **Hsian**) an industrial city in central China, capital of Shaanxi province; pop. 3,094,300 (est. 2006). The city has been inhabited since the 11th century BC, having previously been the capital of the Han, Sui, and Tang dynasties. Former names **CHANGAN**, **SIKING**.

Xi·ang /SHēˈäNG/ (also **Hsiang**) ▶ **n.** a dialect of Chinese spoken by about 36 million people, mainly in Hunan province.

Xing·tai /ˈSHiNGˈtī/ a city in northeastern China, south of Shijiazhuang, in the province of Hebei; pop. 563,600 (est. 2006).

Xin·gú /SHiNGˈgo͞o/ a South American river that rises in the Mato Grosso of western Brazil and flows north for about 1,230 miles (1,979 km) to join the Amazon delta.

Xi·ning /ˈSHēˈniNG/ (also **Hsining**) a city in northern central China, capital of Qinghai province; pop. 692,500 (est. 2006).

Xin·jiang /ˈSHinjēˈäNG/ an autonomous region in northwestern China, on the border with Mongolia and Kazakhstan; pop. 20,950,000 (est. 2007); capital, Urumqi. A remote mountainous region, it includes the Tien Shan and Kunlun Shan mountains, the Taklimakan Desert, and the arid Tarim Basin.

-xion ▶ **suffix** forming nouns such as *fluxion*.
– ORIGIN from Latin participial stems (see also **-ION**).

xiph·i·ster·num /ˌzifəˈstərnəm/ ▶ **n.** Anatomy the lowest part of the sternum; the xiphoid process.
– ORIGIN mid 19th cent.: from Greek *xiphos* 'sword' + **STERNUM**.

xiph·oid proc·ess (also **xiphoid cartilage**) ▶ **n.** Anatomy the cartilaginous section at the lower end of the sternum, which is not attached to any ribs and gradually ossifies during adult life.
– ORIGIN mid 18th cent. (as *xiphoid cartilage*): *xiphoid* from Greek *xiphoeidēs*, from *xiphos* 'sword.'

X-ir·ra·di·a·tion ▶ **n.** irradiation with X-rays.

Xi·zang /ˈSHēˈzäNG/ Chinese name for **TIBET**.

XL ▶ **abbr.** extra large (as a clothes size).

Xmas /ˈkrisməs, ˈeksməs/ ▶ **n.** informal term for **CHRISTMAS**.
– ORIGIN *X* representing the initial chi of Greek *Khristos* 'Christ.'

XML ▶ **abbr.** Extensible Markup Language, a metalanguage that allows users to define their own customized markup languages, esp. in order to display documents on the Internet.

XMS ▶ **abbr.** extended memory system, a system for increasing the amount of memory available to a computer.

XO ▶ **abbr.** Military executive officer.

XOR ▶ **n.** another term for **EXCLUSIVE OR**.

x-ra·di·a·tion ▶ **n.** treatment with or exposure to X-rays. ■ radiation in the form of X-rays.

X-rat·ed /ˈeks ˌrātid/ ▶ **adj.** pornographic or indecent: *there was some X-rated humor*. ■ (of a movie) given an X classification (see **X**[2]).

X-ray /ˈeks ˌrā/ (also **x-ray** or **X ray**) ▶ **n. 1** an electromagnetic wave of high energy and very short wavelength, which is able to pass through many materials opaque to light. [X-rays were formerly defined in terms of their wavelength, radiation of shorter wavelength than theirs being classed as gamma rays. They are now usually defined in terms of the mode of production: X-rays are produced by the deceleration of charged particles, especially electrons, or by electron transitions in atoms, while gamma rays arise from the radioactive decay of atomic nuclei.] ■ [as modifier] informal denoting an apparent or supposed faculty for seeing beyond an outward form: *you didn't need X-ray eyes to know what was going on*.
2 a photographic or digital image of the internal composition of something, esp. a part of the body, produced by X-rays being passed through it and being absorbed to different degrees by different materials. ■ an act of photographing someone or something in this way: *he will have an X-ray today* | *would you send her for X-ray?*
3 a code word representing the letter X, used in radio communication.
▶ **v.** [with obj.] photograph or examine with X-rays: *luggage bound for the hold is X-rayed*.
– ORIGIN translation of German *X-Strahlen* (plural), from *X-* (because, when discovered in 1895, the nature of the rays was unknown) + *Strahl* 'ray.'

X-ray as·tron·o·my ▶ **n.** the branch of astronomy concerned with the detection and measurement of high-energy electromagnetic radiation emitted by celestial objects.

X-ray crys·tal·log·ra·phy ▶ **n.** the study of crystals and their structure by means of X-ray diffraction.

X-ray dif·frac·tion ▶ **n.** the scattering of X-rays by the regularly spaced atoms of a crystal, useful in obtaining information about the structure of the crystal.

X-ray fish ▶ **n.** a small almost transparent freshwater fish with an opaque body cavity. Native to South America, it is popular in aquariums.
● *Pristella riddlei*, family Characidae.

X-ray mi·cro·scope ▶ **n.** an instrument that uses X-rays to produce a magnified image.

X-ray tel·e·scope ▶ **n.** a telescope designed to detect sources of X-rays.

X-ray ther·a·py ▶ **n.** medical treatment of a disease using controlled doses of X-rays.

X-ray tube ▶ **n.** Physics a device for generating X-rays by accelerating electrons to high energies and causing them to strike a metal target from which the X-rays are emitted.

xu /so͞o/ ▶ **n.** (pl. **same**) a monetary unit of Vietnam, equal to one hundredth of a dong.
– ORIGIN Vietnamese, from French *sou*.

Xu·zhou /ˈSHo͞oˈjō/ (also **Hsu-chou** /ˈSHo͞oˈjō/) a city in Jiangsu province, in eastern China; pop. 1,536,500 (est. 2006). Former name (1912–45) **TONGSHAN**.

XXL ▶ **abbr.** extra extra large (as a clothes size).

xy·lan /ˈzīlan, -lən/ ▶ **n.** a polysaccharide found in plant cell walls that hydrolyzes to xylose.

xy·lem /ˈzīləm/ ▶ **n.** Botany the vascular tissue in plants that conducts water and dissolved nutrients upward from the root and also helps to form the woody element in the stem. Compare with **PHLOEM**.
– ORIGIN late 19th cent.: from Greek *xulon* 'wood' + the passive suffix *-ēma*.

xy·lene /ˈzīˌlēn/ ▶ **n.** Chemistry a volatile liquid hydrocarbon obtained by distilling wood, coal tar, or petroleum, and used in fuels and solvents, and in chemical synthesis. ● Alternative name: **dimethylbenzene**; chem. formula: $C_6H_4(CH_3)_2$; three isomers.
– ORIGIN mid 19th cent.: from **XYLO-** 'of wood' + **-ENE**.

xy·li·dine /ˈzīliˌdēn, -din, ˈzili-/ ▶ **n.** any one of six isomeric compounds that are derived from xylene and used in the manufacture of dyes. ● Chem. formula: $(CH_3)_2C_6H_3NH_2$. ■ a mixture of xylidine isomers in the form of an oily liquid.

xy·li·tol /ˈzīləˌtôl, -ˌtäl/ ▶ **n.** Chemistry a sweet-tasting crystalline alcohol derived from xylose, present in some plant tissues and used as an artificial sweetener in foods. ● Chem. formula: $CH_2OH(CHOH)_3CH_2OH$.
– ORIGIN late 19th cent.: from **XYLOSE** + **-ITE**[1] + **-OL**.

xylo- ▶ **comb. form** of or relating to wood: *xylophagous* | *xylophone*.
– ORIGIN from Greek *xulon* 'wood.'

xy·log·ra·phy /zīˈlägrəfē/ ▶ **n.** rare the art of making woodcuts or wood engravings, esp. by a relatively primitive technique.
– DERIVATIVES **xy·lo·graph·ic** /ˌzīləˈgrafik/ **adj.**

xy·loph·a·gous /zīˈläfəgəs/ ▶ **adj.** Zoology (esp. of an insect larva or mollusk) feeding on or boring into wood.

xy·lo·phone /ˈzīləˌfōn/ ▶ **n.** a musical instrument played by striking a row of wooden bars of graduated length with one or more small wooden or plastic mallets.
– DERIVATIVES **xy·lo·phon·ic** /ˌzīləˈfänik/ **adj.**, **xy·lo·phon·ist** /ˈzīləˌfōnist/ **n.**
– ORIGIN mid 19th cent.: from **XYLO-** 'of wood' + **-PHONE**.

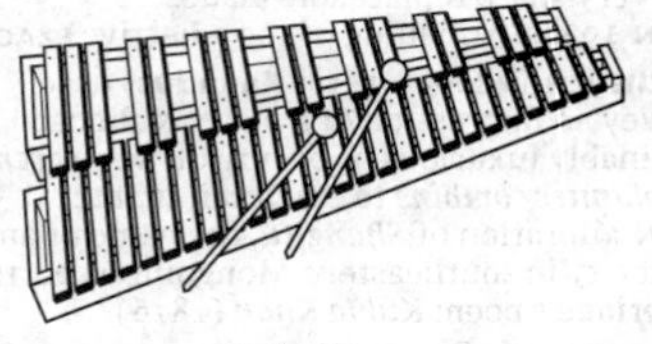

xylophone

xy·lose /ˈzīˌlōs, -ˌlōz/ ▶ **n.** Chemistry a sugar of the pentose class that occurs widely in plants, esp. as a component of hemicelluloses.

XYZ Af·fair an incident in Franco-American relations in which a bribery attempt perpetrated by French agents in 1797 led the US to the brink of formal war with France.

In 1797, President John Adams sent delegates Elbridge Gerry, John Marshall, and Charles Cotesworth Pinckney to France in order to negotiate a peaceful resolution of problems that existed between the two nations. The US delegates were informed by three French agents that negotiations could not begin until the US granted a $10 million loan to the French government and paid $250,000 to French foreign minister Talleyrand. The US delegation refused the French demands and negotiations were suspended. In 1798, the delegation's dispatches regarding the incident were made public. These documents, in which the French agents were identified only as X, Y, and Z, incited American outrage and precipitated an undeclared naval war (1798–1800) between the US and France. A treaty in 1800 finally averted a major war.

Y y

Y[1] /wī/ (also **y**) ▶ **n.** (pl. **Ys** or **Y's**) **1** the twenty-fifth letter of the alphabet. ■ denoting the next after X in a set of items, categories, etc. ■ denoting a second unknown or unspecified person or thing: *the claim that chemical X causes birth defect Y.* ■ (usu. *y*) the second unknown quantity in an algebraic expression, usually the dependent variable. [the introduction of *x, y,* and *z* as symbols of unknown quantities is due to Descartes (see **X**[1]).] ■ (usu. *y*) denoting the secondary or vertical axis in a system of coordinates: [in combination] *the y-axis.*
2 (**Y**) a shape like that of a capital Y: [in combination] *rows of tiny Y-shaped motifs.*

Y[2] ▶ **abbr.** ■ yen: *Y140.* ■ informal a YMCA, YWCA, YMHA, or YWHA facility: *Scott was living at the Y.*
▶ **symbol** the chemical element yttrium.

y ▶ **abbr.** year(s): *orbital period (Pluto): 248.5y.*

-y[1] /ē/ ▶ **suffix** [forming adjectives:] **1** (from nouns and adjectives). full of; having the quality of: *messy | milky | mousy.* ■ with depreciatory reference: *boozy | tinny.*
2 (from verbs) inclined to; apt to: *sticky.*
– ORIGIN Old English *-ig*, of Germanic origin.

-y[2] (also **-ey** or **-ie**) ▶ **suffix** forming diminutive nouns and adjectives, nicknames, hypocoristics, etc.: *aunty | Tommy | nightie.* ■ forming verbs: *shinny.*
– ORIGIN Middle English: originally Scots.

-y[3] ▶ **suffix** forming nouns: **1** denoting a state, condition, or quality: *glory | jealousy | orthodoxy.*
2 denoting an action or its result: *blasphemy | victory.*
– ORIGIN from French *-ie*, from Latin *-ia, -ium*, or Greek *-eia, -ia.*

ya /yə/ ▶ **pron. & possessive determiner** nonstandard spelling of **YOU** or **YOUR**, used to represent informal pronunciation: *see ya later.*

yab·ber /ˈyabər/ ▶ **v.** [no obj.] informal chatter.
– ORIGIN probably from Wuywurung (an Aboriginal language).

YAC ▶ **abbr.** Biology yeast artificial chromosome.

yacht /yät/ ▶ **n.** a medium-sized sailboat equipped for cruising or racing. ■ [with modifier] a powered boat or small ship equipped for cruising, typically for private or official use: *a steam yacht.*
▶ **v.** [no obj.] race or cruise in a yacht.
– ORIGIN mid 16th cent.: from early modern Dutch *jaghte*, from *jaghtschip* 'fast pirate ship,' from *jag(h)t* 'hunting' + *schip* 'ship.'

yacht·ing /ˈyätiNG/ ▶ **n.** the sport or pastime of racing or sailing in yachts.

yachts·man /ˈyätsmən/ ▶ **n.** (pl. **yachtsmen**) a man who sails yachts.

yachts·wom·an /ˈyätsˌwo͝omən/ ▶ **n.** (pl. **yachtswomen**) a woman who sails yachts.

yack /yak/ ▶ **n. & v.** variant spelling of **YAK**[2].

yack·e·ty-yak /ˌyakətē ˈyak/ (also **yackety-yack**) ▶ **n. & v.** another term for **YAK**[2].
– ORIGIN 1950s: imitative.

yad·da yad·da yad·da /ˈyädə ˈyädə ˈyädə/ ▶ **n.** informal used as a substitute for actual words where they are too lengthy or tedious to recite in full: *boy meets girl, boy loses girl, yadda yadda yadda.*
– ORIGIN 1940s: imitative of meaningless chatter.

Yad·kin Riv·er /ˈyadkin/ a river that flows for 200 miles (320 km) through western North Carolina to join the Uwharrie River to form the Pee Dee River.

Ya·fo /ˈyäfō/ Hebrew name for **JAFFA**.

YAG /yag/ ▶ **n.** a synthetic crystal of yttrium aluminum garnet, used in certain lasers and as an imitation diamond in jewelry.
– ORIGIN 1960s: acronym from *yttrium aluminum garnet.*

ya·gé /ˈyäˌZHā ˈyäˌhā/ ▶ **n.** another term for **AYAHUASCA**.
– ORIGIN 1920s: from American Spanish.

Ya·gi an·ten·na /ˈyägē, ˈyagē/ ▶ **n.** a highly directional radio antenna made of several short rods mounted across an insulating support and transmitting or receiving a narrow band of frequencies.
– ORIGIN 1940s: named after Hidetsugu *Yagi* (1886–1976), Japanese engineer.

yag·na ▶ **n.** variant spelling of **YAJNA**.

yah[1] /yä/ ▶ **n.** Brit. informal an upper-class person: *the cafe is full of yahs whose daddies own chateaux in France.*
– ORIGIN representation of a pronunciation of 'yes' in British upper-class speech.

yah[2] /yä, ya/ ▶ **exclam.** expressing derision: *yah, you missed!*
– ORIGIN natural exclamation: first recorded in English in the early 17th cent.

ya·hoo[1] /ˈyäˌhōō, yäˈhōō/ ▶ **n.** informal a rude, noisy, or violent person.
– ORIGIN mid 18th cent.: from the name of an imaginary race of brutish creatures in Swift's *Gulliver's Travels* (1726).

ya·hoo[2] /yäˈhōō/ ▶ **exclam.** expressing great joy or excitement: *yahoo—my plan worked!*
– ORIGIN natural exclamation: first recorded in English in the 1970s.

yahr·zeit /ˈyärˌtsīt, ˈyôr-/ ▶ **n.** (among Jews) the anniversary of someone's death, esp. a parent's.
– ORIGIN mid 19th cent.: Yiddish, literally 'anniversary time.'

Yah·weh /ˈyäˌwā, -ˌwe, -ˌvā/ (also **Yahveh** /-ˌvā, -ˌve/) ▶ **n.** a form of the Hebrew name of God used in the Bible. The name came to be regarded by Jews (*c.*300 BC) as too sacred to be spoken, and the vowel sounds are uncertain.
– ORIGIN from Hebrew *YHWH* with added vowels; compare with **JEHOVAH**, **YHVH**.

Yah·wist /ˈyäwist, -vist/ (also **Yahvist** /-vist/) ▶ **n.** the postulated author or authors of parts of the first six books of the Bible, in which God is regularly named *Yahweh*. Compare with **ELOHIST**.

yaj·na /ˈyəgnə, -nyə/ (also **yagna**) ▶ **n.** Hinduism a ritual sacrifice with a specific objective.
– ORIGIN from Sanskrit *yajña* 'worship, sacrifice.'

Yaj·ur Ve·da /ˈyəjo͝or ˈvādə, ˈvēdə/ Hinduism one of the four Vedas, based on a collection of sacrificial formulae in early Sanskrit used in the Vedic religion by the priest in charge of sacrificial ritual.
– ORIGIN from Sanskrit *yajus* 'sacrificial formula' and **VEDA**.

yak[1]

yak[1] /yak/ ▶ **n.** (pl. **same** or **yaks**) a large domesticated wild ox with shaggy hair, humped shoulders, and large horns, used in Tibet as a pack animal and for its milk, meat, and hide. ● Genus *Bos*, family Bovidae; the domesticated *B. grunniens*, descended from the wild *B. mutus*, which rarely is still found at high altitude.
– ORIGIN late 18th cent.: from Tibetan *gyag.*

yak[2] (also **yack** or **yackety-yak**) informal ▶ **n.** [in sing.] a trivial or unduly persistent conversation.
▶ **v.** (**yaks, yakking, yakked**) [no obj.] talk at length about trivial or boring subjects.
– ORIGIN 1950s: imitative.

Yak·i·ma[1] /ˈyakəmə, -ˌmô/ a commercial and industrial city in south central Washington; pop. 84,074 (est. 2008).

Yak·i·ma[2] ▶ **n.** (pl. **same** or **Yakimas**) **1** a member of a North American Indian people of south central Washington.
2 the Sahaptin dialect of this people.
▶ **adj.** of or relating to this people or their language.
– ORIGIN unknown, but possibly from a Salish language.

ya·ki·to·ri /ˌyäkiˈtôrē/ ▶ **n.** a Japanese dish of chicken pieces grilled on a skewer.
– ORIGIN Japanese, from *yaki* 'grilling, toasting' + *tori* 'bird.'

Ya·kut /yəˈko͞ot/ ▶ **n.** (pl. **same** or **Yakuts**) **1** a member of an indigenous people living in scattered settlements in northern Siberia.
2 the Turkic language of this people.
▶ **adj.** of or relating to this people or their language.
– ORIGIN via Russian from Yakut.

Ya·ku·tia /yəˈko͞oSH(ē)ə/ an autonomous republic in eastern Russia; pop. 948,400 (est. 2009); capital, Yakutsk. It is the coldest inhabited region in the world, with 40 percent of its territory lying north of the Arctic Circle. Official name **SAKHA, REPUBLIC OF**.

Ya·kutsk /yəˈko͞otsk/ a city in eastern Russia, on the Lena River, capital of the republic of Yakutia; pop. 255,800 (est. 2008).

ya·ku·za /yäˈko͞ozə, ˈyäko͞oˌzä/ ▶ **n.** (pl. **same**) a Japanese gangster or racketeer. ■ a Japanese organized crime syndicate similar to the Mafia.
– ORIGIN Japanese, from *ya* 'eight' + *ku* 'nine' + *za* 'three,' referring to the worst hand in a gambling game.

Yale[1] /yāl/, Elihu (1649–1721), English colonial administrator. He was a large benefactor of the Collegiate School in Saybrook, Connecticut, which was named Yale College in his honor in 1718, after its move to New Haven.

Yale[2], Linus, Jr. (1821–68), US inventor and manufacturer. He invented the pin tumbler cylinder lock and the combination lock. In 1868, he cofounded the Yale Lock Manufacturing Company.

Yale[3] (also **Yale lock**) ▶ **n.** [often as modifier] trademark a type of lock with a latch bolt and a flat key with a serrated edge.
– ORIGIN mid 19th cent.: named after Linus *Yale*, Jr., who invented the mechanism it uses.

Yale U·ni·ver·si·ty an Ivy League university in New Haven, Connecticut, founded in 1701.

Yal·ie /ˈyālē/ ▶ **n.** (pl. **Yalies**) informal a student or graduate of Yale University.

y'all /yôl/ ▶ **contraction** you-all.

Yal·ta Con·fer·ence /ˈyôltə, ˈyäl-/ a meeting between the Allied leaders Churchill, Roosevelt, and Stalin in February 1945 at Yalta, a Crimean port on the Black Sea. The leaders planned the final stages of World War II and agreed on the subsequent territorial division of Europe.

Ya·lu /ˈyä,lo͞o/ a river in eastern Asia that rises in the mountains of Jilin province in northeastern China and flows southwest for about 500 miles (800 km) to the Yellow Sea. It forms most of the border between China and North Korea. In November 1950, the advance of UN troops toward the Yalu River precipitated the Chinese invasion of North Korea.

yam /yam/ ▶ **n.** **1** the edible starchy tuber of a climbing plant, widely distributed in tropical and subtropical countries.
2 the plant that yields this tuber. ● Genus *Dioscorea*, family Dioscoreaceae: many species.
3 a sweet potato.
– ORIGIN late 16th cent.: from Portuguese *inhame* or obsolete Spanish *iñame*, probably of West African origin.

Ya·ma /ˈyəmə, ˈyämə/ (in Hindu legend) the first man to die. He became the guardian, judge, and ruler of the dead, and is represented as carrying a noose and riding a buffalo.
– ORIGIN from Sanskrit *yama* 'restraint' (from *yam* 'restrain').

Ya·ma·mo·to /,yäməˈmōtō/, Isoroku (1884–1943), Japanese admiral. As commander in chief of the combined fleet (air and naval forces) from 1939, he was responsible for planning the Japanese attack on Pearl Harbor in 1941.

Ya·ma·sa·ki /,yäməˈsäkē/, Minoru (1912–86), US architect. He designed the barrel-vaulted St. Louis Municipal Airport terminal in 1956 and the World Trade Center in New York in 1972.

Ya·ma·to-e /yäˈmätō ,ā/ ▶ **n.** a style of decorative painting in Japan during the 12th and early 13th centuries, characterized by strong color and flowing lines.
– ORIGIN Japanese, from *Yamato* 'Japan' + *e* 'picture.'

ya·men /ˈyämən/ ▶ **n.** informal the office or residence of a public official in the Chinese Empire.

yam·mer /ˈyamər/ ▶ **n.** informal or dialect loud and sustained or repetitive noise: *the yammer of their animated conversation | the yammer of enemy fire.*
▶ **v.** [no obj.] informal or dialect make a loud repetitive noise. ■ talk volubly.
– DERIVATIVES **yam·mer·er** **n.**
– ORIGIN late Middle English (as a verb meaning 'lament, cry out'): alteration of earlier *yomer* (from Old English *geōmrian* 'to lament') suggested by Middle Dutch *jammeren*.

Ya·mous·sou·kro /,yäməˈso͞okrō/ the capital of Côte d'Ivoire (Ivory Coast); pop. 110,000 (est. 2008). It replaced Abidjan as the capital in 1983.

yam·pa /ˈyampə/ ▶ **n.** a wild plant of the parsley family, native to central and western North America, that has an edible root. It has clusters of small white flowers somewhat resembling Queen Anne's lace. ● *Perideridia gairdneri*, family Umbelliferae.

Yam·pa Riv·er /ˈyampə/ a river that flows for 250 miles (400 km) across northwestern Colorado to join the Green River.

yam·pee /ˈyampē/ ▶ **n.** another term for CUSH-CUSH.

Ya·mu·na /ˈyəmo͞onə/ Hindi name for JUMNA.

Yan·cheng /ˈyanˈCHəNG/ (also **Yen-cheng** /ˈyen-/) a city in Jiangsu province, in eastern China; pop. 765,400 (est. 2006).

yang /yaNG, yäNG/ ▶ **n.** (in Chinese philosophy) the active male principle of the universe, characterized as male and creative and associated with heaven, heat, and light. Contrasted with YIN.
– ORIGIN from Chinese *yáng* 'male genitals,' 'sun,' 'positive.'

Yan·gon /,yäNGˈgōn/ Burmese name for RANGOON.

Yang·tze /ˈyaNGˈ(t)sē/ the principal river in China. It rises as the Jinsha in the Tibetan highlands and flows south and then east for 3,964 miles (6,380 km) through central China before it enters the East China Sea at Shanghai. Also called CHANG JIANG.

Yank /yaNGk/ ▶ **n.** another term for YANKEE (sense 1 and sense 2).

yank /yaNGk/ informal ▶ **v.** [with obj.] pull with a jerk: *her hair was yanked, and she screamed* | [with obj.] *he yanked her to her feet* | [no obj.] *Liz yanked at her arm.*
▶ **n.** [in sing.] a sudden hard pull: *one of the other girls gave her ponytail a yank.*
– ORIGIN late 18th cent. (as a Scots word in the sense 'sudden sharp blow'): of unknown origin.

Yan·kee /ˈyaNGkē/ ▶ **n.** informal **1** often derogatory a person who lives in, or is from, the US.
2 an inhabitant of New England or one of the northern states. ■ historical a Union soldier in the Civil War.
3 a code word representing the letter Y, used in radio communication.
4 (also **Yankee jib**) Sailing a large jib set forward of a staysail in light winds.
5 a bet on four or more horses to win (or be placed) in different races.
– ORIGIN mid 18th cent.: origin uncertain; recorded in the late 17th cent. as a nickname; perhaps from Dutch *Janke*, diminutive of *Jan* 'John.'

Yan·kee Doo·dle /ˈdo͞odl/ ▶ **n.** **1** (also **Yankee Doodle Dandy**) a song popular during the American Revolution. Informally regarded as a national song, it is the official state song of Connecticut.
2 Brit. another term for YANKEE (sense 1).

Yank·ton /ˈyaNGktən/ ▶ **n.** (pl. **same** or **Yanktons**) **1** a member of an American Indian people of the Great Plains of North and South Dakota.
2 the Siouan language of this people.
▶ **adj.** of or relating to this people or their language.
– ORIGIN from Sioux *ihą̄kthų̄wą̄*, literally 'those dwelling at the end.'

Yank·to·nai /,yaNGktəˈnī/ ▶ **n.** a Sioux people now living in the Dakotas and eastern Montana, formerly living in northern Minnesota. ■ a member of this people.

Ya·no·ma·mi /,yänəˈmämē/ (also **Yanomamö** /-ˈmämō/) ▶ **n.** (pl. **same**) **1** a member of an American Indian people living mainly in the forests of southern Venezuela and northern Brazil.
2 either of the two related languages of this people.
▶ **adj.** of or relating to this people or their language.
– ORIGIN the name in Yanomami, literally 'people.'

Yan·qui ▶ **n.** variant spelling of YANKEE, typically used in Latin American contexts.

Yan·tai /ˈyanˈtī/ (also **Yen-tai** /ˈyen-/) a port in eastern China, on the Yellow Sea, in Shandong province; pop. 1,258,100 (est. 2006). Former name CHEFOO.

yan·tra /ˈyəntrə, ˈyan-, ˈyän-/ ▶ **n.** a geometric diagram, or any object, used as an aid to meditation in tantric worship.
– ORIGIN Sanskrit, literally 'device for holding or fastening.'

Yao /you/ ▶ **n.** (pl. **same**) **1** a member of a mountain-dwelling people of southern China.
2 the language of this people.
▶ **adj.** of or relating to this people or their language.
– ORIGIN from Chinese *Yáo*, literally 'precious jade.'

Ya·oun·dé /,younˈdā/ the capital of Cameroon; pop. 1,611,000 (est. 2007).

yap /yap/ ▶ **v.** (**yaps, yapping, yapped**) [no obj.] give a sharp, shrill bark: *the dachshunds yapped at his heels.* ■ informal talk at length in an irritating manner.
▶ **n.** **1** a sharp, shrill bark.
2 informal a person's mouth: *he should keep his yap shut.* ■ loud, irritating talk: *she'll give you a lot of yap.*
– DERIVATIVES **yap·per** **n.**
– ORIGIN early 17th cent. (denoting a dog that yaps): imitative.

ya·pok /yəˈpäk/ (also **yapock**) ▶ **n.** a semiaquatic carnivorous opossum with dark-banded gray fur and webbed hind feet, native to tropical America. Also called WATER OPOSSUM. ● *Chironectes minimus*, family Didelphidae.
– ORIGIN early 19th cent.: from *Oyapock*, the name of a northern Brazilian river.

yapp /yap/ ▶ **n.** Brit. a form of bookbinding with a limp leather cover projecting to fold over the edges of the leaves, typically used for bibles.
– ORIGIN late 19th cent.: named after William *Yapp*, a London bookseller, for whom this style of binding was first made (*c.*1860).

yap·py /ˈyapē/ ▶ **adj.** (**yappier, yappiest**) informal (of a dog) inclined to bark in a sharp, shrill way. ■ inclined to talk foolishly or at length.

Ya·qui /ˈyäkē/ ▶ **n.** (pl. **same** or **Yaquis**) **1** a member of an American Indian people of northwestern Mexico and Arizona.
2 the Uto-Aztecan language of this people.
▶ **adj.** of or relating to this people or their language.
– ORIGIN Spanish, from earlier *Hiaquis*, from Yaqui *Hiaki*.

yar·ak /ˈyar,ak/ ▶ **n.** (in phrase **in yarak**) (of a trained hawk) fit and in a proper condition for hunting.
– ORIGIN mid 19th cent.: perhaps from Persian *yārakī* 'strength, ability' or from Turkish *yarağ* 'readiness.'

yar·bor·ough /ˈyär,b(ə)rə, -,bərō/ ▶ **n.** (in bridge or whist) a hand with no card above a nine.
– ORIGIN early 20th cent.: named after the Earl of *Yarborough* (died 1897), said to have bet 1000 to 1 against its occurrence.

yard[1] /yärd/ ▶ **n.** **1** (abbr.: **yd.**) a unit of linear measure equal to 3 feet (0.9144 meter). ■ (**yards of**) informal a great length: *yards and yards of fine lace.* ■ a square or cubic yard, esp. of sand or other building materials. ■ a cloth measure, of three feet in length and varying widths.
2 a cylindrical spar, tapering to each end, slung across a ship's mast for a sail to hang from.
3 informal one hundred dollars; a one hundred dollar bill.
– PHRASES **by the yard** in large numbers or quantities: *golf continues to inspire books by the yard.*
– ORIGIN Old English *gerd* (in sense 2); related to Dutch *gard* 'twig, rod' and German *Gerte*.

yard[2] ▶ **n.** a piece of ground adjoining a building or house. ■ an area of ground surrounded by walls or buildings. ■ an area of land used for a particular purpose or business: *a storage yard.* ■ an area where deer or moose gather as a herd for the winter.
▶ **v.** **1** [with obj.] store or transport (timber) in or to a log yard.
2 [no obj.] (of deer or moose) gather as a herd for the winter.
– PHRASES **the Yard** Brit. informal term for SCOTLAND YARD.
– ORIGIN Old English *geard* 'building, home, region,' from a Germanic base related to Russian *gorod* 'town.' Compare with GARDEN and ORCHARD.

yard·age /ˈyärdij/ ▶ **n.** **1** a distance or length measured in yards: *the caddie was working out yardages from tee to green.* ■ Football the distance covered in advancing the ball.
2 archaic the use of a yard for storage or the keeping of animals or payment for such use.

yar·dang /ˈyär,däNG, -,daNG/ ▶ **n.** a sharp irregular ridge of compact sand lying in the direction of the prevailing wind in exposed desert regions, formed by the wind erosion of adjacent material that is less resistant.
– ORIGIN early 20th cent.: Turkic; compare with Turkish *yar* 'steep bank.'

yard·arm /ˈyärd,ärm/ ▶ **n.** the outer extremity of a ship's yard.
– PHRASES **the sun is over the yardarm** dated used to refer to the time of day when it is permissible to begin drinking.

yard·bird /ˈyärd,bərd/ ▶ **n.** informal **1** a new military recruit, esp. one assigned to menial tasks.
2 a convict.
3 a chicken.
– ORIGIN 1940s: perhaps suggested by JAILBIRD.

yard·man /ˈyärd,man/ ▶ **n.** (pl. **yardmen**) **1** a person working in a railroad or lumberyard.
2 a person who does various outdoor jobs.

yard·mas·ter /ˈyärd,mastər/ ▶ **n.** a person who is in charge of a railroad yard.

yard of ale ▶ **n.** the amount of beer (typically two to three pints) held by a narrow glass about a yard high. ■ a glass of this kind.

yard sale ▶ **n.** a garage sale.

yard·stick /ˈyärd,stik/ ▶ **n.** a measuring rod a yard long, typically divided into inches. ■ a standard used for comparison: *the consumer price index, the government's yardstick for the cost of living.*

yare /yär, ye(ə)r/ ▶ **adj.** (of a ship) responding promptly to the helm; easily manageable.
– ORIGIN Old English *gearu* 'prepared, ready,' of Germanic origin; related to Dutch *gaar* 'done, dressed' and German *gar* 'ready.'

Yar·mouth /ˈyärməTH/ a resort town in southeastern Massachusetts, on southern Cape Cod; pop. 23,778 (est. 2008).

yar·mul·ke /ˈyämə(l)kə/ (also **yarmulka**) ▶ **n.** a skullcap worn in public by Orthodox Jewish men or during prayer by other Jewish men.
– ORIGIN early 20th cent.: from Yiddish *yarmolke*.

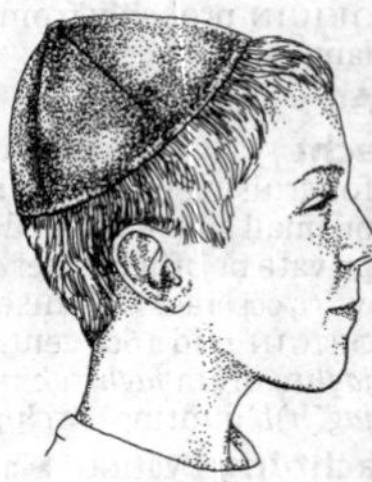
yarmulke

yarn /yärn/ ▶ **n.** **1** spun thread used for knitting, weaving, or sewing.
2 informal a long or rambling story, esp. one that is implausible.
▶ **v.** [no obj.] informal tell a long or implausible story: *they were yarning about local legends and superstitions.*
– PHRASES **spin a yarn** see SPIN.
– ORIGIN Old English *gearn*, of Germanic origin; related to Dutch *garen*.

yarn-dyed ▶ **adj.** (of fabric) dyed as yarn, before being woven.

Ya·ro·slavl /,yärəˈslävəl/ a port in western Russia, on the Volga River, northeast of Nizhni Novgorod; pop. 605,200 (est. 2008).

yar·row /ˈyarō/ ▶ **n.** a Eurasian plant of the daisy family, with feathery leaves and heads of small white, yellow, or pink aromatic

yarrow

flowers. Also called MILFOIL. ● *Achillea millefolium*, family Compositae.
– ORIGIN Old English *gearwe*; related to Dutch *gerwe*.

yash·mak /yäsн'mäk, 'yasн,mak/ ▶ n. a veil concealing all of the face except the eyes, worn by some Muslim women in public.
– ORIGIN mid 19th cent.: via Arabic from Turkish.

yat·a·ghan /'yatəgən, -,gan/ ▶ n. chiefly historical a sword without a guard and typically with a double-curved blade, used in Muslim countries.
– ORIGIN from Turkish *yatağan*.

ya·tra /'yätrə/ ▶ n. Indian a procession or pilgrimage, esp. one with a religious purpose.
– ORIGIN from Sanskrit *yātrā* 'journey,' from *yā* 'go.'

yat·ter /'yatər/ informal ▶ v. [no obj.] talk incessantly; chatter.
▶ n. incessant talk.
– ORIGIN early 19th cent.: imitative, perhaps suggested by YAMMER and CHATTER.

yau·pon /'yô,pän, 'yōō-/ (also **yaupon holly**) ▶ n. a holly of the southern US. Sometimes dried and brewed as a tea, its bitter leaves contain caffeine and have emetic properties. ● *Ilex vomitoria*, family Aquifoliaceae.
– ORIGIN early 18th cent.: from Catawba (a Siouan language spoken in South Carolina) *yopún*, diminutive of *yop* 'tree, shrub.'

yau·ti·a /you'tēə/ ▶ n. a tropical American plant of the arum family that is cultivated for its edible tubers and sometimes its leaves. ● Genus *Xanthosoma*, family Araceae: several species, in particular the fleshy-leaved **malanga** (*X. atrovirens*) of Latin America.
– ORIGIN late 19th cent.: American Spanish, from Maya *yaaj* 'wound, poison' + *té* 'mouth' with reference to its caustic properties.

yaw /yô/ ▶ v. [no obj.] (of a moving ship or aircraft) twist or oscillate about a vertical axis: [with adverbial of direction] *the jet yawed sharply to the right*.
▶ n. a twisting or oscillation of a moving ship or aircraft around a vertical axis.
– ORIGIN mid 16th cent.: of unknown origin.

yawl /yôl/ ▶ n. a two-masted fore-and-aft-rigged sailboat with the mizzenmast stepped far aft so that the mizzen boom overhangs the stern. ■ historical a ship's jolly boat with four or six oars.
– ORIGIN late 16th cent.: from Middle Low German *jolle* or Dutch *jol*, of unknown origin; compare with JOLLY².

yawn /yôn/ ▶ v. [no obj.] involuntarily open one's mouth wide and inhale deeply due to tiredness or boredom: *he began yawning and looking at his watch*. ■ (usu. as adj. **yawning**) be wide open: *a yawning chasm*.
▶ n. a reflex act of opening one's mouth wide and inhaling deeply due to tiredness or boredom. ■ informal a thing that is considered boring or tedious: *the awards show was a four-hour yawn*.
– DERIVATIVES **yawn·ing·ly** adv.
– ORIGIN Old English *geonian*, of Germanic origin, from an Indo-European root shared by Latin *hiare* and Greek *khainein*. Current noun senses date from the early 18th cent.

yawn·er /'yônər/ ▶ n. informal a thing that is considered extremely boring: *the game was a real yawner*.

yawp /yôp/ ▶ n. a harsh or hoarse cry or yelp. ■ foolish or noisy talk.
▶ v. [no obj.] shout or exclaim hoarsely. ■ talk foolishly or noisily.
– DERIVATIVES **yawp·er** n.
– ORIGIN Middle English (as a verb): imitative. The noun dates from the early 19th cent.

yaws /yôz/ ▶ plural n. [treated as sing.] a contagious disease of tropical countries, caused by a bacterium that enters skin abrasions and gives rise to small crusted lesions that may develop into deep ulcers. Also called FRAMBESIA. ● The bacterium is the spirochete *Treponema pallidum* subsp. *pertenue*.
– ORIGIN late 17th cent.: probably from Carib *yaya*.

y-ax·is ▶ n. the secondary or vertical axis of a system of coordinates, points along which have a value of zero for all other coordinates. Compare with X-AXIS.

yay[1] /yā/ ▶ exclam. informal expressing triumph, approval, or encouragement: *Yay! Great, Julie!*
– ORIGIN 1960s: perhaps an alteration of YEAH.

yay[2] (also **yea**) ▶ adv. informal (with adjectives of measure) so; to this extent: *I knew him when he was yay big*.
– ORIGIN 1960s: probably a variant of the adverb YEA¹.

ya-yas /'yäyäz/ ▶ plural n. (in phrase **get your ya-yas out**) informal enjoy yourself in an uninhibited way.
– ORIGIN 1970s: from *Get Yer Ya-Yas Out!*, the title of an album (1970) by the Rolling Stones, adapted from a reference to *yas yas*, a euphemism for ASS².

Yaz·oo Riv·er /'yazōō/ a river that flows for 190 miles (305 km) from northern Mississippi to join the Mississippi River at Vicksburg. The fertile land between the rivers is the Mississippi Delta or *Yazoo Delta*.

Yb ▶ symbol the chemical element ytterbium.

Y·bor Cit·y /'ē,bôr/ an industrial and commercial section of Tampa in Florida, noted for its Cuban culture and cigar industry.

Y chro·mo·some ▶ n. Genetics (in humans and other mammals) a sex chromosome that is normally present only in male cells, which are designated XY. Compare with X CHROMOSOME.

y·clept /i'klept/ ▶ adj. [predic.] archaic or humorous by the name of: *a lady yclept Eleanora*.
– ORIGIN Old English *gecleopod*, past participle of *cleopian* 'call,' of Germanic origin.

yd. ▶ abbr. yard (measure).

ye[1] /yē/ ▶ pron. [second person plural] archaic or dialect plural form of THOU¹: *gather ye rosebuds, while ye may*.
– PHRASES **ye gods!** an exclamation of astonishment.
– ORIGIN Old English *gē*, of Germanic origin; related to Dutch *gij* and German *ihr*.

ye[2] /yē, T͟Hē/ ▶ determiner pseudo-archaic term for THE: *Ye Olde Bookshoppe*.
– ORIGIN graphic variant; in late Middle English þ (see THORN) came to be written identically with y, so that *the* could be written *ye*. This spelling (usually yᵉ) was kept as a convenient abbreviation in handwriting until the 19th cent., and in printers' types during the 15th and 16th cent., but it was never pronounced as "ye."

yea[1] /yā/ ▶ adv. archaic or formal yes: *she has the right to say yea or nay*. ■ used for emphasis, esp. to introduce a stronger or more accurate word than one just used: *he was full, yea, crammed with anxieties*.
▶ n. archaic or formal an affirmative answer: *the assembly would give the final yea or nay*. ■ (in the US Congress) an affirmative vote.
– ORIGIN Old English *gēa*, *gē*, of Germanic origin; related to Dutch and German *ja*.

yea[2] ▶ adv. variant spelling of YAY².

Yea·ger /'yāgər/, Chuck (1923–), US pilot; full name *Charles Elwood Yeager*. He became the first person to break the sound barrier when he piloted the Bell X-1 rocket research aircraft at high altitude to a level-flight speed of 670 mph in 1947.

Chuck Yeager

yeah /ye(ə), ya(ə)/ (also **yeh**) ▶ exclam. & n. nonstandard spelling of YES, representing informal pronunciation.

yean /yēn/ ▶ v. [with obj.] archaic (of a sheep or goat) give birth to (a lamb or kid).
– ORIGIN late Middle English: perhaps representing an Old English verb related to *ēanian* 'to lamb.'

year /yi(ə)r/ ▶ n. **1** the time taken by a planet to make one revolution around the sun.

> The length of the earth's year depends on the manner of calculation. For ordinary purposes the important period is the SOLAR YEAR (also called ASTRONOMICAL YEAR, EQUINOCTIAL YEAR, or TROPICAL YEAR), which is the time between successive spring or autumnal equinoxes, or winter or summer solstices, roughly 365 days, 5 hours, 48 minutes, and 46 seconds in length. This period thus marks the regular cycle of the seasons. See also SIDEREAL YEAR, ANOMALISTIC YEAR.

2 the period of 365 days (or 366 days in leap years) starting from the first of January, used for reckoning time in ordinary affairs. Also called CALENDAR YEAR or CIVIL YEAR. ■ a period of the same length as this starting at any point: *the year starting July 1*. ■ [with adj.] such a period regarded in terms of the quality of produce, typically wine: *single-vineyard wine of a good year*. ■ a similar period used for reckoning time according to other calendars: *the Muslim year*.
3 (**one's years**) one's age or time of life: *she had a composure well beyond her years*.
4 (**years**) informal a very long time; ages: *it's going to take years to put that right*.
5 a set of students grouped together as being of roughly similar ages, mostly entering a school or college in the same academic year: *most of the girls in my year were leaving school at the end of the term*.
– PHRASES **in the year of our Lord** (or dated **in the year of grace**) —— in the year AD——: *I was born in the year of our Lord 1786*. [*year of grace*, suggested by medieval Latin *anno gratiae*, used by chroniclers.] **—— of the year** a person or thing chosen as outstanding in a specified field or of a specified kind in a particular year: *the sports personality of the year*. **put years on** (or **take years off**) **someone** make someone feel or look older (or younger). **a year and a day** the period specified in some legal matters to ensure the completion of a full year. **year in and year out** continuously or repeatedly over a period of years: *they rented the same bungalow year in and year out*.
– ORIGIN Old English *gē(a)r*, of Germanic origin; related to Dutch *jaar* and German *Jahr*, from an Indo-European root shared by Greek *hōra* 'season.'

year·book /'yi(ə)r,bo͝ok/ ▶ n. an annual publication giving current information and listing events or aspects of the previous year, esp. in a particular field: *Yearbook of Physical Anthropology*. ■ a book containing photographs of the senior class in a school or college and details of school activities in the previous year.

year end (also **year's end**) ▶ n. the end of the fiscal year: *we will discuss additional changes at year end* | [as modifier] *the year-end figures were impressive*.

year·ling /'yi(ə)rliNG/ ▶ n. an animal (esp. a sheep, calf, or foal) a year old, or in its second year. ■ a racehorse in the calendar year after its year of foaling.
▶ adj. [attrib.] having lived or existed for a year; a year old: *a yearling calf*. ■ of or relating to something that is a year old: *the yearling market*.

year·long ▶ adj. [attrib.] lasting for or throughout a year: *his yearlong battle with lung cancer*.

year·ly /'yi(ə)rlē/ ▶ adj. & adv. happening or produced once a year or every year: [as adj.] *yearly visits to Africa* | [as adv.] *rent was paid yearly*.
– ORIGIN Old English *gēarlic* (see YEAR, -LY¹).

yearn /yərn/ ▶ v. [no obj.] have an intense feeling of longing for something, typically something that one has lost or been separated from: *she yearned for a glimpse of him* | [with infinitive] *they yearned to go home*. ■ archaic be filled with compassion or warm feeling: *no fellow spirit yearned toward her*.
– DERIVATIVES **yearn·er** n.
– ORIGIN Old English *giernan*, from a Germanic base meaning 'eager.'

yearn·ing /'yərniNG/ ▶ n. a feeling of intense longing for something: *he felt a yearning for the mountains*.
▶ adj. involving or expressing yearning: *a yearning hope*.
– DERIVATIVES **yearn·ing·ly** adv.

year-round ▶ adj. & adv. happening or continuing throughout the year: [as adj.] *an indoor pool for year-round use* | [as adv.] (also **year round**) *the center is open year round*.

yea·say·er /'yā,sāər/ ▶ n. **1** a person with a positive, confident outlook.
2 a person who always agrees with or is submissive to others.

yeast /yēst/ ▶ n. a microscopic fungus consisting of single oval cells that reproduce by budding, and are capable of converting sugar into alcohol and carbon dioxide. ● Genus *Saccharomyces*, subdivision Ascomycotina. ■ a grayish-yellow preparation of this obtained chiefly from fermented beer, used as a fermenting agent, to raise bread dough, and as a food supplement. ■ Biology any unicellular fungus that reproduces vegetatively by budding or fission, including forms such as candida that can cause disease.
– DERIVATIVES **yeast·like** /-,līk/ adj.
– ORIGIN Old English, of Germanic origin; related to Dutch *gist* and German *Gischt* 'froth, yeast,' from an Indo-European root shared by Greek *zein* 'to boil.'

yeast·y /'yēstē/ ▶ adj. (**yeastier**, **yeastiest**) of, resembling, or containing yeast: *the yeasty smell of rising dough*. ■ characterized by or producing upheaval or agitation; in a state of turbulence, typically a creative or productive one: *the yeasty days of yesterday's revolution*.
– DERIVATIVES **yeast·i·ly** /'yēstəlē/ adv., **yeast·i·ness** n.

Yeats /yāts/, William Butler (1865–1939), Irish poet and playwright. His play *The Countess Cathleen* (1892) and his collection of stories *The Celtic Twilight* (1893) stimulated Ireland's theatrical, cultural, and literary revival. Notable poetry:

"Sailing to Byzantium" and "Leda and the Swan." Nobel Prize for Literature (1923).

William Butler Yeats

yech /yəKH, yək, yeKH, yek/ (also **yecch**) ▶ **exclam.** informal expressing aversion or disgust.
– DERIVATIVES **yech·y** adj.
– ORIGIN 1960s: imitative; compare with YUCK.

yee-haw /ˈyē ˌhô/ (also **yee-hah** /ˈyē ˌhä/) ▶ **exclam.** an expression of enthusiasm or exuberance, typically associated with cowboys or rural inhabitants of the southern US.
– ORIGIN natural exclamation: first recorded in American English in the 1970s.

yegg /yeg/ ▶ **n.** informal a burglar or safecracker.
– ORIGIN early 20th cent.: of unknown origin.

yeh ▶ **exclam.** /ye/ variant spelling of YEAH.
▶ **pron.** /yə/ nonstandard spelling of YOU, used to represent various accents or dialects: *are yeh all right, lads?*

Ye·ka·te·rin·burg /yiˈkatərin,bərg, yi,kətyərinˈbŏŏrk/ (also **Ekaterinburg**) an industrial city in central Russia, in the eastern foothills of the Ural Mountains; pop. 1,323,000 (est. 2008). Former name (1924–91) SVERDLOVSK.
– ORIGIN named in honor of *Ekaterina* (1684–1727), the wife of Peter the Great, who founded the city in 1721.

Ye·ka·te·ri·no·dar /yə,kätəˈrēnə,där/ (also **Ekaterinodar**) former name (until 1922) for KRASNODAR.

Ye·ka·te·ri·no·slav /yə,kätəˈrēnə,släf, -,släv/ (also **Ekaterinoslav**) former name (1787–1926) for DNIPROPETROVSK.

yell /yel/ ▶ **n.** a loud, sharp cry, esp. of pain, surprise, or delight; a shout. ■ an organized cheer, esp. one used to support a sports team.
▶ **v.** [no obj.] give a loud, sharp cry: *you heard me yelling at her* | [with direct speech] *"Happy New Year!" Ashley yelled.*
– ORIGIN Old English *g(i)ellan* (verb), of Germanic origin; related to Dutch *gillen* and German *gellen.*

yel·low /ˈyelō/ ▶ **adj. 1** of the color between green and orange in the spectrum, a primary subtractive color complementary to blue; colored like ripe lemons or egg yolks: *curly yellow hair.* ■ offensive having a naturally yellowish or olive skin (as used to describe Chinese or Japanese people). ■ denoting a warning of danger that is thought to be near but not actually imminent: *he put Camp Visoko on yellow alert.*
2 informal cowardly: *he'd better get back there quick and prove he's not yellow.* ■ archaic showing jealousy or suspicion.
3 (of a book or newspaper) unscrupulously sensational.
▶ **n. 1** yellow color or pigment: *the craft detonated in a blaze of red and yellow* | *painted in vivid blues and yellows.* ■ yellow clothes or material: *everyone dresses in yellow.*
2 the yolk of an egg.
3 (**yellows**) any of a number of plant diseases in which the leaves turn yellow, typically caused by viruses and transmitted by insects.
▶ **v.** [no obj.] become a yellow color, esp. with age: *the cream paint was beginning to yellow* | (as adj. **yellowing**) *yellowing lace curtains* | (as adj. **yellowed**) *a yellowed newspaper cutting.*
– PHRASES **the yellow peril** offensive the political or military threat regarded as being posed by the Chinese or by the peoples of Southeast Asia.
– DERIVATIVES **yel·low·ish** adj., **yel·low·ly** adv., **yel·low·ness** n., **yel·low·y** adj.
– ORIGIN Old English *geolu, geolo*; related to Dutch *geel* and German *gelb*, also to GOLD.

y

yel·low·back /ˈyelō,bak/ ▶ **n.** historical a cheap and typically sensational novel, with a yellow board or cloth binding.

yel·low-bel·lied sap·suck·er ▶ **n.** a woodpecker of eastern North America with black-and-white plumage, a pale yellow belly, and, in the male, a scarlet crown and throat. ● *Sphyrapicus varius*, family Picidae.

yel·low-bel·ly ▶ **n.** informal **1** a coward.
2 any of various animals with yellow underparts.
– DERIVATIVES **yel·low-bel·lied** adj.

yel·low bile ▶ **n.** historical another term for CHOLER.

yel·low-billed /ˈyelō ,bild/ ▶ **adj.** (of a bird) having a yellow bill. Used in the name of numerous such birds, including. ● the North American **yellow-billed cuckoo** (*Coccyzus americanus*, family Cuculidae). ● the African **yellow-billed duck** (*Anas undulata*, family Anatidae).

yel·low birch ▶ **n.** see BIRCH (sense 1 of the noun).

yel·low bunt·ing ▶ **n.** another term for YELLOWHAMMER (sense 2).

yel·low·cake /ˈyelō,kāk/ ▶ **n.** impure uranium oxide obtained during processing of uranium ore.
– ORIGIN 1950s: so named because it is obtained as a yellow precipitate.

yel·low card ▶ **n.** (in soccer and some other games) a yellow card shown by the referee to a player being cautioned. Compare with RED CARD.

yel·low dog informal ▶ **n.** a contemptible or cowardly person or thing.
▶ **adj.** (of a party-line voter, esp. a Democrat) inclined to support any candidate affiliated with one's chosen party, regardless of the candidate's personal qualities or political qualifications: *he is a self-proclaimed yellow dog Democrat.*

yel·low dog con·tract ▶ **n.** a contract between a worker and an employer in which the worker agrees not to remain in or join a union.

yel·low dog Dem·o·crat (also **Yellow Dog Democrat**) ▶ **n.** informal see YELLOW DOG. Compare with BLUE DOG DEMOCRAT.

yel·low earth ▶ **n.** a yellowish loess occurring in northern China.

yel·low fe·ver ▶ **n.** a tropical viral disease affecting the liver and kidneys, causing fever and jaundice and often fatal. It is transmitted by mosquitoes.

yel·low·fin /ˈyelō,fin/ (also **yellowfin tuna**) ▶ **n.** a widely distributed, commercially important tuna that has yellow anal and dorsal fins. ● *Thunnus albacares*, family Scombridae.

yel·low flag ▶ **n. 1** a ship's yellow flag, denoting the letter Q for 'quarantine.' When flown with another flag, it indicates disease on board; when flown alone, it indicates the absence of disease and signifies a request for customs clearance. Also called QUARANTINE FLAG. ■ Auto Racing a yellow flag used to signal to drivers that there is a hazard such as oil or a crashed car on the track.
2 a yellow-flowered iris that grows by water and in marshy places, native to Europe and naturalized in North America. ● *Iris pseudacorus*, family Iridaceae.

yel·low·ham·mer /ˈyelō,hamər/ ▶ **n. 1** another term for YELLOW-SHAFTED FLICKER (see FLICKER[2]).
2 a common Eurasian bunting, the male of which has a yellow head, neck, and breast. ● *Emberiza citrinella*, family Emberizidae (subfamily Emberizinae).
– ORIGIN mid 16th cent.: *-hammer* is perhaps from Old English *amore* (a kind of bird), possibly conflated with *hama* 'feathers.'

Yel·low·ham·mer State a nickname for the state of ALABAMA.

yel·low jack ▶ **n. 1** another term for YELLOW FLAG (sense 1).
2 archaic term for YELLOW FEVER.
3 an edible marine fish with yellowish underparts, found primarily in the Gulf of Mexico and the Caribbean Sea. ● *Caranx bartholomaei*, family Carangidae.

yel·low jack·et ▶ **n.** informal a wasp or hornet with bright yellow markings.

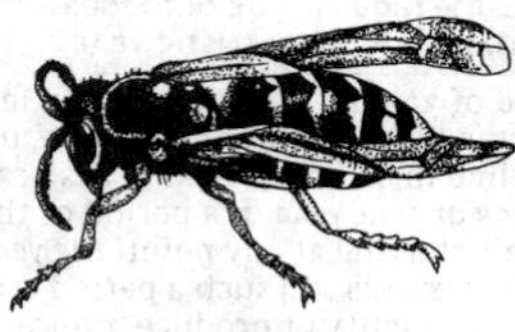
yellow jacket

yel·low jas·mine (also **yellow jessamine**) ▶ **n.** an ornamental climbing shrub with fragrant yellow flowers, native to the southeastern US. Its rhizome yields gelsemium. ● *Gelsemium sempervirens*, family Loganiaceae.

yel·low jer·sey ▶ **n.** (in a cycling race involving stages) a yellow jersey worn by the overall leader in a cycle race, at the end of any one day, and ultimately presented to the winner.

yel·low jour·nal·ism ▶ **n.** journalism that is based upon sensationalism and crude exaggeration: *equating murder and dismemberment with smoking pot is the worst yellow journalism.*
– DERIVATIVES **yel·low jour·nal·ist** n.
– ORIGIN 1895: from the appearance in an issue of the *New York World* of a cartoon in which a child in a yellow dress ('The Yellow Kid') was the central figure. The color printing was an experiment designed to attract customers.

Yel·low·knife /ˈyelō,nīf/ the capital, since 1967, of the Northwest Territories in Canada, on the northern shore of Great Slave Lake; pop. 18,700 (2006).

yel·low·legs /ˈyelō,legz/ ▶ **n.** a migratory sandpiper with bright yellow legs, breeding in Alaska and Canada. ● Genus *Tringa*, family Scolopacidae: two species, the **greater yellowlegs** (*T. melanoleuca*) and the **lesser yellowlegs** (*T. flavipes*).

yel·low mom·bin /mōmˈbēn/ ▶ **n.** see HOG PLUM.

yel·low o·cher ▶ **n.** a yellow pigment that usually contains limonite, a yellowish-brown oxide of iron. ■ a moderate orange color with yellow overtones.

Yel·low Pag·es (also **yellow pages**) ▶ **plural n.** a telephone directory, or a section of one, printed on yellow paper and listing businesses and other organizations according to the goods or services they offer. ■ a similar directory available online through the Internet.

yel·low pine ▶ **n.** any of several North American pines having a strong yellowish wood. ■ the wood of such a tree.

yel·low pop·lar ▶ **n.** another term for TULIP TREE.

yel·low rain ▶ **n.** a toxic yellow substance reported as falling in Southeast Asia, alleged to be a chemical warfare agent but now believed to consist of contaminated bee droppings.

Yel·low Riv·er the second largest river in China. It rises in the mountains of western central China and flows for more than 3,000 miles (4,830 km) in a huge semicircle before it enters Bo Hai, an inlet of the Yellow Sea. Chinese name HUANG HO.

Yel·low Sea an arm of the East China Sea that separates the Korean peninsula from the eastern coast of China. Chinese name HUANG HAI.

yel·low spot ▶ **n.** the region of greatest visual acuity around the fovea of the eye; the macula lutea (see MACULA).

Yel·low·stone Na·tion·al Park /ˈyelō,stōn/ a national park in northwestern Wyoming and Montana, known for Old Faithful geyser.

yel·low·tail /ˈyelō,tāl/ ▶ **n.** (pl. **same** or **yellowtails**) a marine fish that has yellow coloration on the fins, esp. a number of species prized as food fish. ● Several genera and species, including the large sport fish **yellowtail** (*Seriola lalandi*, family Carangidae) of southern California, the **yellowtail flounder** (*Limanda ferruginea*, family Pleuronectidae) of the Atlantic coast from Labrador to Virginia, and the **yellowtail snapper** (*Ocyurus chrysurus*, family Lutjanidae) of Bermuda and the West Indies.

yel·low·throat /ˈyelō,THrōt/ ▶ **n.** a small American warbler with a bright yellow throat. ● Genus *Geothlypis*, subfamily Parulinae, family Emberizidae: several species.

yel·low un·der·wing ▶ **n.** an underwing moth that has yellow hind wings with a black terminal band. ● *Noctua* and other genera, family Noctuidae: several species, including the **large yellow underwing** (*N. pronuba*), the larva of which is a destructive cutworm.

yel·low·wood /ˈyelō,wŏŏd/ ▶ **n.** any of a number of trees that have yellowish timber or yield a yellow dye, in particular: ● a North American tree of the pea family (*Cladrastis lutea*, family Leguminosae). ● a podocarp.

yelp /yelp/ ▶ **n.** a short sharp cry, esp. of pain or alarm: *she uttered a yelp as she bumped into a table.*
▶ **v.** [no obj.] utter such a cry: *my dogs were yelping at Linus.*
– DERIVATIVES **yelp·er** n.
– ORIGIN Old English *g(i)elpan* (verb) 'to boast,' from a Germanic imitative base. From late Middle English 'cry or sing with a loud voice' the current sense arose in the 16th cent.

Yel·tsin /ˈyeltsən/, Boris (Nikolaevich) (1931–2007), Russian statesman; president of the Russian Federation 1991–99. Impatient with the slow pace of Gorbachev's reforms, Yeltsin resigned from the Communist Party after becoming president of the Russian Soviet Federative Socialist Republic in 1990. As president of the independent Russian Federation, he faced opposition to his reforms.

Yem·en /ˈyemən/ a country in southwestern part of the Arabian peninsula; pop. 22,858,200 (est. 2009); capital, Sana'a; official language, Arabic. Official name **Yemen Republic**.

> An Islamic country since the mid 7th century, Yemen was part of the Ottoman Empire from the 16th century. During the 19th century, the port of Aden was developed as a British military base. After World War II, civil war between royalist and republican forces ended with British withdrawal and the partition of the country in 1967. South Yemen declared itself independent as the People's Democratic Republic of Yemen, and the North became the Yemen Arab Republic. In 1990, the countries reunited to form the Republic of Yemen; the South briefly seceded in 1994 but was defeated in a short civil war. Since 2004, there has been civil war in Yemen, which spread into Saudi Arabia in 2009.

– DERIVATIVES **Yem·e·ni** /ˈyemənē/ **adj. & n.**

Yem·en·ite /ˈyeməˌnīt/ ▶ **n. 1** another term for YEMENI (see YEMEN).
2 a Jew who was, or whose ancestors were, formerly resident in Yemen.
▶ **adj.** of or relating to Yemeni Arabs or Jews.
– ORIGIN from Arabic *yamanī* 'Yemeni' + -ITE[1].

yen[1] /yen/ ▶ **n.** (pl. **same**) the basic monetary unit of Japan.
– ORIGIN from Japanese *en* 'round.'

yen[2] informal ▶ **n.** [in sing.] a longing or yearning: [with infinitive] *she always had a yen to be a writer.*
▶ **v.** (**yens, yenning, yenned**) [no obj.] feel a longing or yearning: *it's no use **yenning for** the old simplicities.*
– ORIGIN late 19th cent. (in the sense 'craving (of a drug addict) for a drug'): from Chinese *yǎn*.

Yen·i·sei /ˌyenəˈsā/ (also **Yenisey**) a river in Siberia, in Russia, that rises in the mountains on the Mongolian border and flows north for 2,566 miles (4,106 km) to the Arctic coast, where it empties into the Kara Sea.

yen·ta /ˈyentə/ ▶ **n.** a woman who is a gossip or busybody.
– ORIGIN 1920s: Yiddish, originally a given name.

yeo·man /ˈyōmən/ ▶ **n.** (pl. **yeomen**) **1** historical a man holding and cultivating a small landed estate; a freeholder. ■ a person qualified for certain duties and rights, such as to serve on juries and vote for the knight of the shire, by virtue of possessing free land of an annual value of 40 shillings.
2 historical a servant in a royal or noble household, ranking between a sergeant and a groom or a squire and a page.
3 Brit. a member of the yeomanry force.
4 a petty officer in the US Navy or Coast Guard performing clerical duties on board ship. ■ (also **yeoman of signals**) (in the British Royal Navy and other Commonwealth navies) a petty officer concerned with signaling.
– PHRASES **yeoman service** efficient or useful help in need.
– DERIVATIVES **yeo·man·ly adj.**
– ORIGIN Middle English: probably from YOUNG + MAN.

Yeo·man of the Guard ▶ **n.** a member of the British sovereign's bodyguard, first established by Henry VII, now having only ceremonial duties and wearing Tudor dress as uniform. Also called BEEFEATER. ■ used erroneously to refer to a Yeoman Warder.

yeo·man·ry /ˈyōmənrē/ ▶ **n.** [treated as sing. or pl.] historical a group of men who held and cultivated small landed estates. ■ (in Britain) a volunteer cavalry force raised from such a group (1794–1908).

Yeo·man Ward·er ▶ **n.** a warder at the Tower of London. Also called BEEFEATER.

yeow /you, yēˈou/ ▶ **exclam.** another word for YOW.
– ORIGIN natural exclamation: first recorded in American English in the 1920s.

yep /yep/ (also **yup**) ▶ **exclam. & n.** nonstandard spelling of YES, representing informal pronunciation.

yer /yər/ ▶ **possessive determiner** nonstandard spelling of YOUR, used in representing dialectal speech: *eat yer dinner.*
▶ **contraction** you are, used in representing dialectal speech: *yer a dang fool.*
▶ **pron.** nonstandard spelling of YOU, used in representing dialectal speech: *well, are yer comin'?*
▶ **adv.** nonstandard spelling of HERE, used in representing dialectal speech: *I hate mighty bad to bus' up dis yer ax-helve.*

-yer ▶ **suffix** variant spelling of -IER esp. after *w* (as in *lawyer, sawyer*).

yer·ba /ˈyerbə, ˈyər-/ (also **yerba maté** /ˈmätā, mäˈtā/) ▶ **n.** another term for MATÉ.
– ORIGIN early 19th cent.: from Spanish, literally 'herb.'

Yer·ba Bue·na /ˈyərbə ˈbwānə/ an island in San Francisco Bay in California; also, the name of the 1820s mainland settlement that became the city of San Francisco.

yer·ba bue·na /ˈbwānə/ ▶ **n.** a trailing aromatic herb with whitish or lilac flowers, related to savory. Native to the western US, it has been used medicinally and as a local tea. ● *Satureja douglasii*, family Labiatae.
– ORIGIN mid 19th cent.: from Spanish, literally 'good herb.'

yer·ba ma·té /ˈye(ə)rbə mäˈtā/ ▶ **n.** see MATÉ.

Yer·by /ˈyərbē/, Frank (Garvin) (1916–91), US writer. He wrote action-packed novels such as *The Foxes of Harrow* (1946), *Judas, My Brother* (1968), and *The Dahomean* (1971). Discrimination against blacks in the US caused him to live in Spain from 1955.

Ye·re·van /ˌyeriˈvän/ (also **Erevan**) the capital of Armenia; pop. 1,107,800 (est. 2008).

yes /yes/ ▶ **exclam. 1** used to give an affirmative response: *"Do you understand?" "Yes."* ■ expressing agreement with a positive statement just made: *"That was a grand evening." "Yes, it was."* ■ expressing contradiction of a negative statement: *"You don't want to go." "Yes, I do."*
2 used as a response to someone addressing one or otherwise trying to attract one's attention: *"Oh, Mr. Lawrence." "Yes?"*
3 used to question a remark or ask for more detail about it: *"It should be easy to check." "Oh yes? How?"* ■ asked at the end of a statement to indicate the expectation of agreement: *you think I perhaps killed Westbourne, yes?*
4 encouraging someone to continue speaking: *"When you bought those photographs ..." "Yes?"*
5 expressing delight: *plenty to eat, including hot roast beef sandwiches (yes!).*
▶ **n.** (pl. **yeses** or **yesses**) an affirmative answer or decision, esp. in voting: *answering with assured and ardent yeses.*
– PHRASES **yes and no** partly and partly not: *"Did it come as a surprise to you?" "Yes and no."*
– ORIGIN Old English *gēse, gīse*, probably from an unrecorded phrase meaning 'may it be so.'

ye·shi·va /yəˈSHēvə/ ▶ **n.** an Orthodox Jewish college or seminary. ■ an Orthodox Jewish elementary or secondary school.
– ORIGIN from Hebrew *yěšīḇāh*.

yes-man ▶ **n.** (pl. **yes-men**) informal a weak person who always agrees with their political leader or their superior at work.

yes·sir /ˈyesər, ˈyesˈsər/ (also **yessiree** /-səˈrē/) informal ▶ **exclam.** used to express assent: *"Do you understand me?" "Yessir!"* ■ used to express emphatic affirmation: *yessir the food was cheap.*
– ORIGIN early 20th cent.: alteration of *yes sir*.

yes·sum /ˈyesəm/ ▶ **exclam.** dated, chiefly black English used as a polite form of assent addressed to a woman: *"You feel all right?" she asked. "Yessum."*
– ORIGIN early 20th cent.: alteration of *yes ma'am*.

yester- ▶ **comb. form** literary or archaic of yesterday: *yestereve | yesteryear.*
– ORIGIN Old English *geostran*, of Germanic origin; related to Dutch *gisteren* and German *gestern* 'yesterday,' from an Indo-European root shared by Latin *heri* and Greek *khthes*.

yes·ter·day /ˈyestərˌdā, -dē/ ▶ **adv.** on the day before today: *he returned to a hero's welcome yesterday.* ■ in the recent past: *everything seems to have been built yesterday.*
▶ **n.** the day before today: *yesterday was Tuesday.* ■ the recent past: *yesterday's bestsellers.*
– PHRASES **yesterday morning** (or **afternoon**, etc.) in the morning (or afternoon, etc.) of yesterday. **yesterday's man** a man, esp. a politician, whose career is finished or past its peak. **yesterday's news** a person or thing that is no longer of interest.
– ORIGIN Old English *giestran dæg* (see YESTER-, DAY).

yes·ter·night /ˈyestərˌnīt/ ▶ **n.** archaic last night.
▶ **adv.** during last night.

yes·ter·year /ˈyestərˌyir/ ▶ **n.** literary last year or the recent past, esp. as nostalgically recalled: *return with us now to those thrilling days of yesteryear.*

yet /yet/ ▶ **adv. 1** up until the present or a specified or implied time; by now or then: *I haven't told anyone else yet | aren't you ready to go yet? | I **have yet to** be convinced* | [with superlative] *the congress was widely acclaimed as the best yet.* ■ [with negative] as soon as the present or a specified or implied time: *wait, don't go yet.* ■ from now into the future for a specified length of time: *I hope to continue for some time yet.* ■ referring to something that will or may happen in the future: *further research may yet explain the enigma | I know she's alive and I'll find her yet.*
2 still; even (used to emphasize increase or repetition): *snow, snow, and yet more snow | yet another diet book | the rations were reduced **yet again**.*
3 nevertheless; in spite of that: *every week she gets worse, and yet it could go on for years.*
▶ **conj.** but at the same time; but nevertheless: *the path was dark, yet I slowly found my way.*
– PHRASES **as yet** see AS[1]. **nor yet** and also not.
– ORIGIN Old English *gīet(a)*, of unknown origin.

yet·i /ˈyetē, ˈyātē/ ▶ **n.** a large hairy creature resembling a human or bear, said to live in the highest part of the Himalayas.
– ORIGIN 1930s: from Tibetan *yeh-teh* 'little manlike animal.'

Yev·tu·shen·ko /ˌyevtəˈSHENGkō/, Yevgeni (Aleksandrovich) (1933–), Russian poet. *Third Snow* (1955) and *Zima Junction* (1956) were regarded as encapsulating the feelings and aspirations of the post-Stalin generation. He incurred official hostility because of the outspoken nature of some of his poetry, notably *Babi Yar* (1961).

yew /yo͞o/ ▶ **n.** (also **yew tree**) a coniferous tree that has red berrylike fruits, and most parts of which are highly poisonous. Yews are linked with folklore and superstition and can live to a great age; the timber is used in cabinetmaking and (formerly) to make longbows. ● Genus *Taxus*, family Taxaceae: several species, in particular the **American yew** (*T. canadensis*) and the **English** (or **European**) **yew** (*T. baccata*).
– ORIGIN Old English *īw, ēow*, of Germanic origin.

yez /yəz/ ▶ **pron.** nonstandard spelling of YOUSE, used in representing dialectal speech.

Ygg·dra·sil /ˈigdrəsəl, -ˌsil/ Scandinavian Mythology a huge ash tree located at the center of the earth, with three roots, one extending to Niflheim (the underworld), one to Jotunheim (land of the giants), and one to Asgard (land of the gods).
– ORIGIN from Old Norse *yg(g)drasill*, apparently from *Yggr* 'Odin' + *drasill* 'horse.'

YHVH (also **YHWH**) ▶ **abbr.** the Hebrew Tetragrammaton representing the name of God. See also TETRAGRAMMATON, YAHWEH.

yi /yi/ ▶ **pron.** nonstandard spelling of YOU, used in representing Scottish speech.

Yi·chun /ˈēˈCHo͝on/ (also **I-chun**) a city in northeastern China, in Heilongjiang province; pop. 786,400 (est. 2006).

Yid /yid/ ▶ **n.** informal, offensive a Jew.
– ORIGIN late 19th cent.: back-formation from YIDDISH.

Yid·dish /ˈyidiSH/ ▶ **n.** a language used by Jews in central and eastern Europe before the Holocaust. It was originally a German dialect with words from Hebrew and several modern languages and is today spoken mainly in the US, Israel, and Russia.
▶ **adj.** of or relating to this language.
– ORIGIN late 19th cent.: from Yiddish *yidish (daytsh)* 'Jewish German.'

Yid·dish·er /ˈyidiSHər/ ▶ **n.** a person speaking Yiddish.

Yid·dish·ism /ˈyidəˌSHizəm/ ▶ **n. 1** a Yiddish word or idiom, esp. one adopted into another language.
2 advocacy of Yiddish culture.
– DERIVATIVES **Yid·dish·ist n.** (sense 2).

Yid·dish·keit /ˈyidiSHˌkīt/ ▶ **n.** the quality of being Jewish; the Jewish way of life or its customs and practices.
– ORIGIN late 19th cent.: from Yiddish *yidishkeyt*.

yield /yēld/ ▶ **v. 1** [with obj.] produce or provide (a natural, agricultural, or industrial product): *the land yields grapes and tobacco.* ■ (of an action or process) produce or deliver (a result or gain): *this method yields the same results.* ■ (of a financial or commercial process or transaction) generate (a specified financial return): *such investments yield direct cash returns.*
2 [no obj.] give way to arguments, demands, or pressure: *the Western powers now yielded when they should have resisted | he **yielded to** the demands of his partners.* ■ [with obj.] relinquish possession of (something); give (something) up: *they might yield up their secrets | they are forced to yield ground.* ■ [with obj.] cease to argue about: *I yielded the point.* ■ (esp. in a legislature) allow another the right to speak in a debate: *I yield to the gentleman from Kentucky.* ■ give right of way to other traffic. ■ (of a mass or structure) give way under force or pressure: *he reeled into the house as the door yielded.*
▶ **n.** the full amount of an agricultural or industrial product: *the milk yield was poor.* ■ Finance the amount of money brought in, e.g., interest from an investment or revenue from a tax; return: *an annual*

dividend yield of 20 percent. ■ Chemistry the amount obtained from a process or reaction relative to the theoretical maximum amount obtainable. ■ (of a nuclear weapon) the force in tons or kilotons of TNT required to produce an equivalent explosion: *yields ranging from five kilotons to 100 tons.*
– DERIVATIVES **yield·er** n. (sense 1 of the verb).
– ORIGIN Old English *g(i)eldan* 'pay, repay,' of Germanic origin. The senses 'produce, bear' and 'surrender' arose in Middle English.

yield curve ▶ **n.** Finance a curve on a graph in which the yield of fixed-interest securities is plotted against the length of time they have to run to maturity.

yield gap ▶ **n.** Finance the difference between the return on government-issued securities and that on common stock.

yield·ing /ˈyēldiNG/ ▶ **adj.** **1** (of a substance or object) giving way under pressure; not hard or rigid: *she dropped on to the yielding cushions.* ■ (of a person) complying with the requests or desires of others: *a gentle, yielding person.*
2 [in combination] giving a product or generating a financial return of a specified amount: *higher-yielding wheat.*
– DERIVATIVES **yield·ing·ly** adv.

yield man·age·ment ▶ **n.** the process of making frequent adjustments in the price of a product in response to certain market factors, such as demand or competition.

yield point ▶ **n.** Physics the stress beyond which a material becomes plastic.

yield strength ▶ **n.** Physics (in materials that do not exhibit a well-defined yield point) the stress at which a specific amount of plastic deformation is produced, usually taken as 0.2 percent of the unstressed length.

yield stress ▶ **n.** Physics the value of stress at a yield point or at the yield strength.

yikes /yīks/ ▶ **exclam.** informal expressing shock and alarm, often for humorous effect: *I had a dip in the 40-degree pool (yikes!).*
– ORIGIN 1970s: of unknown origin; compare with **YOICKS**.

yin /yin/ ▶ **n.** (in Chinese philosophy) the passive female principle of the universe, characterized as female and sustaining and associated with earth, dark, and cold. Contrasted with **YANG**.
– ORIGIN from Chinese *yīn* 'feminine,' 'moon,' 'shade.'

symbol for yin and yang

Yin·chuan /ˈyinˈCHwän/ a city in northern central China, on the Yellow River, capital of autonomous region Ningxia; pop. 663,700 (est. 2006).

yip /yip/ ▶ **n.** a short, sharp cry or yelp, esp. of excitement or delight.
▶ **v.** (**yips, yipping, yipped**) [no obj.] give such a cry or yelp.
– ORIGIN early 20th cent. (originally US): imitative.

yipe /yīp/ ▶ **exclam.** an expression of surprise, fear, pain, etc.

yip·pee /ˈyipē, ˌyipˈē/ ▶ **exclam.** expressing wild excitement or delight.
– ORIGIN natural exclamation: first recorded in American English in the 1920s.

yip·pie /ˈyipē/ ▶ **n.** (pl. **yippies**) a member of a group of politically active hippies, originally in the US.
– ORIGIN 1960s: acronym from *Youth International Party* + the suffix *-ie*, on the pattern of *hippie*.

yips /yips/ ▶ **plural n.** (**the yips**) informal extreme nervousness causing a golfer to miss easy putts.
– ORIGIN mid 20th cent.: of unknown origin.

Yi·shuv /yiˈSHōōv/ the Jewish community or settlement in Palestine during the 19th century and until the formation of the state of Israel in 1948.
– ORIGIN from Hebrew *yiššūḇ* 'settlement.'

Yiz·kor /ˈyiskər, ˈyiz-, yēzˈkôr/ ▶ **n.** (pl. **same** or **Yizkors**) a memorial service held by Jews on certain holy days for deceased relatives or martyrs.
– ORIGIN from Hebrew *yizkōr*, literally 'may (God) remember.'

-yl ▶ **suffix** Chemistry forming names of radicals: *hydroxyl* | *phenyl.*
– ORIGIN from Greek *hulē* 'wood, material.'

y·lang-y·lang /ˌēläNG ˈēläNG/ (also **ilang-ilang**) ▶ **n.** **1** a sweet-scented essential oil obtained from the flowers of a tropical tree, used in perfumery and aromatherapy.
2 the yellow-flowered tree, native to the Malay peninsula and the Philippines, from which this oil is obtained. ● *Cananga odorata*, family Annonaceae.
– ORIGIN late 19th cent.: from Tagalog *ilang-ilang*.

y·lem /ˈīləm/ ▶ **n.** Astronomy (in the Big Bang theory) the primordial matter of the universe, originally conceived as composed of neutrons at high temperature and density.
– ORIGIN 1940s: from late Latin *hylem* (accusative) 'matter,' from Greek *hūlē*.

yl·id /ˈilid/ (also **ylide** /ˈilīd/) ▶ **n.** Chemistry a compound that has an uncharged molecule containing a negatively charged carbon atom directly bonded to a positively charged atom of sulfur, phosphorus, nitrogen, or another element.
– ORIGIN 1950s: from **-YL** + **-IDE**.

YMCA ▶ **n.** a welfare movement that began in London in 1844 and now has branches all over the world. ■ a hostel or recreational facility run by this association.
– ORIGIN abbreviation of *Young Men's Christian Association.*

YMHA ▶ **abbr.** Young Men's Hebrew Association.

Y·mir /ˈēˌmi(ə)r/ Scandinavian Mythology the primeval giant from whose body the gods created the world.

YMMV ▶ **abbr.** informal your mileage may vary (used to say that people may experience a particular thing in different ways).

-yne ▶ **suffix** Chemistry forming names of unsaturated organic compounds containing a triple bond: *ethyne.*
– ORIGIN alteration of **-INE**[4].

yng·ling /ˈiNGliNG/ ▶ **n.** a type or class of racing keelboat, designed to sail with a two- or three-person crew.
– ORIGIN Norwegian, literally 'youth.'

yo[1] /yō/ ▶ **exclam.** informal used to greet someone, attract their attention, or express excitement.
– ORIGIN natural exclamation: first recorded in late Middle English.

yo[2] ▶ **pron.** nonstandard spelling of **YOU**, used to represent black English.
▶ **possessive adj.** nonstandard spelling of **YOUR**, used to represent black English.

yob /yäb/ ▶ **n.** Brit. informal a rude, noisy, and aggressive young man.
– DERIVATIVES **yob·bish** adj., **yob·bish·ly** adv., **yob·bish·ness** n., **yob·by** adj.
– ORIGIN mid 19th cent.: backward spelling of **BOY**.

yob·bo /ˈyäbō/ ▶ **n.** (pl. **yobbos** or **yobboes**) Brit. informal another term for **YOB**.

yock /yäk/ ▶ **n.** variant form of **YUK**.

yocto- ▶ **comb. form** (used in units of measurement) denoting a factor of 10^{-24}: *yoctojoule.*
– ORIGIN adapted from **OCTO-**, on the pattern of combining forms such as *peta-* and *exa-*.

yod /yôd, yōōd, yäd/ ▶ **n.** **1** the tenth and smallest letter of the Hebrew alphabet.
2 Phonetics the semivowel or glide *y*.
3 Astrology another term for **FINGER OF GOD**.
– ORIGIN from Hebrew *yōḏ*; related to *yaḏ* 'hand.'

yo·del /ˈyōdl/ ▶ **v.** (**yodels, yodeling, yodeled**; Brit. **yodels, yodelling, yodelled**) [no obj.] practice a form of singing or calling marked by rapid alternation between the normal voice and falsetto.
▶ **n.** a song, melody, or call delivered in such a way.
– DERIVATIVES **yo·del·er** n.
– ORIGIN early 19th cent.: from German *jodeln*.

yo·ga /ˈyōgə/ ▶ **n.** a Hindu spiritual and ascetic discipline, a part of which, including breath control, simple meditation, and the adoption of specific bodily postures, is widely practiced for health and relaxation.

> The yoga widely known in the West is based on **hatha yoga**, which forms one aspect of the ancient Hindu system of religious and ascetic observance and meditation, the highest form of which is **raja yoga** and the ultimate aim of which is spiritual purification and self-understanding leading to *samadhi* or union with the divine.

– DERIVATIVES **yo·gic** /-gik/ adj.
– ORIGIN Sanskrit, literally 'union.'

yogh /yōg, yōKH/ ▶ **n.** a Middle English letter (ȝ) used mainly where modern English has *gh* or *y*.
– ORIGIN Middle English: of unknown origin.

yo·gi /ˈyōgē/ ▶ **n.** (pl. **yogis**) a person who is proficient in yoga.
– ORIGIN from Sanskrit *yogī*, from *yoga* (see **YOGA**).

yo·gic fly·ing ▶ **n.** a technique used chiefly by Transcendental Meditation practitioners that involves thrusting oneself off the ground while in the lotus position.

yo·gurt /ˈyōgərt/ (also **yoghurt** or **yoghourt**) ▶ **n.** a semisolid sourish food prepared from milk fermented by added bacteria, often sweetened and flavored.
– ORIGIN early 17th cent.: from Turkish *yoğurt*.

Yog·ya·kar·ta /ˌyägyəˈkärtə/ (also **Jogjakarta** /ˌjägyə-, jägjə-/) a city in Indonesia, on the southern coast of the island of Java; pop. 433,500 (est. 2005). It was formerly the capital of Indonesia 1945–49.

yo-heave-ho /ˌyō hēv ˈhō/ ▶ **exclam.** & **n.** another term for **HEAVE-HO**.

yo·him·be /yōˈhimbā, -bē/ ▶ **n.** a tropical West African tree of the bedstraw family, from which the drug yohimbine is obtained. ● *Pausinystalia johimbe*, family Rubiaceae.
– ORIGIN late 19th cent.: a local word.

yo·him·bine /yōˈhimˌbēn/ ▶ **n.** Chemistry a toxic crystalline compound obtained from the bark of the yohimbe tree, used as an adrenergic blocking agent and also in the treatment of impotence. ● An alkaloid; chem. formula: $C_{21}H_{26}O_3N_2$.
– ORIGIN late 19th cent.: from **YOHIMBE** + **-INE**[4].

yo-ho-ho /ˌyō hō ˈhō/ (also **yo-ho**) ▶ **exclam.** **1** dated used to attract attention.
2 Nautical, archaic a seaman's chant used while hauling ropes or performing other strenuous work.

yoicks /yoiks/ ▶ **exclam.** used by fox hunters to urge on the hounds.
– ORIGIN mid 18th cent.: of unknown origin.

yoke /yōk/ ▶ **n.** **1** a wooden crosspiece that is fastened over the necks of two animals and attached to the plow or cart that they are to pull. ■ (pl. **same** or **yokes**) a pair of animals coupled together in such a way: *a yoke of oxen.* ■ archaic the amount of land that one pair of oxen could plow in a day. ■ a frame fitting over the neck and shoulders of a person, used for carrying pails or baskets. ■ used of something that is regarded as oppressive or burdensome: *the yoke of imperialism.* ■ used of something that represents a bond between two parties: *the yoke of marriage.*
2 something resembling or likened to such a crosspiece, in particular: ■ a part of a garment that fits over the shoulders and to which the main part of the garment is attached, typically in gathers or pleats. ■ the crossbar at the head of a rudder, to whose ends ropes are fastened. ■ a bar of soft iron between the poles of an electromagnet. ■ (in ancient Rome) an arch of three spears under which a defeated army was made to march. ■ a control lever in an aircraft.
▶ **v.** [with obj.] **1** put a yoke on (a pair of animals); couple or attach with or to a yoke: *a plow drawn by a camel and donkey yoked together.* ■ cause (two people or things) to be joined in a close relationship: *Hong Kong's dollar has been **yoked to** America's.*
2 informal rob; mug: *two crackheads yoked this girl.*
– ORIGIN Old English *geoc* (noun), *geocian* (verb), of Germanic origin; related to Dutch *juk*, German *Joch*, from an Indo-European root shared by Latin *jugum* and Greek *zugon*, also by Latin *jungere* 'to join.'

yoke 1

yo·kel /ˈyōkəl/ ▶ **n.** an uneducated and unsophisticated person from the countryside.
– ORIGIN early 19th cent.: perhaps figuratively from dialect *yokel* 'green woodpecker.'

Yok·na·pa·taw·pha Coun·ty /ˌyäknəpəˈtôfə/ a fictional county in northern Mississippi, the setting for most of the work of William Faulkner.

Yo·ko·ha·ma /ˌyōkəˈhämə/ a seaport in central Japan, on the southern side of the island of Honshu; pop. 3,562,983 (2007). It is a major port and the second largest city in Japan.

yo·ko·zu·na /ˌyōkəˈzōōnə/ ▶ **n.** (pl. **same**) a grand champion sumo wrestler.
– ORIGIN Japanese, from *yoko* 'crosswise' + *tsuna* 'rope' (originally denoting a kind of belt presented to the champion).

yolk /yōk/ ▶ **n.** the yellow internal part of a bird's egg, which is surrounded by the white, is rich in protein and fat, and nourishes the developing embryo. ■ Zoology the corresponding part in the ovum or larva of all egg-laying vertebrates and many invertebrates.
– DERIVATIVES **yolked** adj. [also in combination], **yolk·less** adj., **yolk·y** adj.
– ORIGIN Old English *geol(o)ca*, from *geolu* 'yellow.'

yolk sac ▶ **n.** Zoology a membranous sac containing yolk attached to the embryos of reptiles and birds and the larvae of some fishes. ■ a sac lacking yolk in the early embryo of a mammal.

yolk stalk ▶ **n.** a tubular connection between the yolk sac and the digestive tract of a developing embryo.

Yol·la Bol·ly Moun·tains /ˈyälə ˌbälē/ a range of the Klamath Mountains, in northwestern California, noted for its wilderness and wildlife.

Yom Kip·pur /ˈyôm kiˈpo͝or, ˈyōm, ˈyäm, ˈkipər/ ▶ **n.** the most solemn religious fast of the Jewish year, the last of the ten days of penitence that begin with Rosh Hashanah (the Jewish New Year). Also called **Day of Atonement**.
– ORIGIN Hebrew.

Yom Kip·pur War the Israeli name for the Arab-Israeli conflict in 1973. Arab name **October War**.

> The war lasted for less than three weeks; it started on the festival of Yom Kippur (in that year, October 6) when Egypt and Syria simultaneously attacked Israeli forces from the south and north, respectively. The Syrians were repulsed, and the Egyptians were surrounded. A ceasefire followed, and disengagement agreements over the Suez area were signed in 1974 and 1975.

yon /yän/ ▶ **determiner & adv.** literary or dialect yonder; that: [as adj.] *you'll find some big ranches yon side of the Sierra.*
▶ **pron.** literary or dialect yonder person or thing: *what do you make of yon?*
– PHRASES **hither and yon** another term for **hither and thither**.
– ORIGIN Old English *geon*, of Germanic origin; related to German *jener* 'that one.'

yond /yänd/ ▶ **adv. & adj.** archaic yonder.

yon·der /ˈyändər/ ▶ **adv.** archaic or dialect at some distance in the direction indicated; over there: *there's a ford south of here, about nine miles yonder.*
▶ **determiner** archaic or dialect that or those (used to refer to something situated at a distance): *what light through yonder window breaks?*
▶ **n.** (**the yonder**) the far distance: *attempting to fly off into the wild blue yonder.*
– ORIGIN Middle English: of Germanic origin; related to Dutch *ginder* 'over there,' also to **yon**.

yo·ni /ˈyōnē/ ▶ **n.** (pl. **yonis**) Hinduism the vulva, esp. as a symbol of divine procreative energy conventionally represented by a circular stone. Compare with **lingam**.
– ORIGIN Sanskrit, literally 'source, womb, female genitals.'

Yon·kers /ˈyäNGkərz/ an industrial city in southeastern New York, on the Hudson River, north of the Bronx in New York City; pop. 201,588 (est. 2008).

yonks /yäNGks/ ▶ **plural n.** Brit. informal a very long time: *I haven't seen him for yonks.*
– ORIGIN 1960s: origin unknown; perhaps related to *donkey's years* (see **donkey**).

yoo-hoo /ˈyo͞o ˌho͞o/ ▶ **exclam.** a call used to attract attention to one's arrival or presence: *Yoo-hoo!—Is anyone there?*
▶ **v.** [no obj.] (of a person) make such a call.
– ORIGIN natural exclamation: first recorded in English in the 1920s.

Yor·ba Lin·da /ˌyôrbə ˈlində/ a city in southwestern California, southeast of Los Angeles; pop. 65,717 (est. 2008).

yore /yôr/ ▶ **n.** (in phrase **of yore**) literary of long ago or former times (used in nostalgic or mock-nostalgic recollection): *a great empire in days of yore.*
– ORIGIN Old English *geāra, geāre*, of unknown origin.

York /yôrk/ **1** a city in northern England, on the Ouse River; pop. 136,900 (est. 2009).
2 a commercial and industrial city in southeastern Pennsylvania; pop. 40,097 (est. 2008).
3 the southwestern tip of Hayes Peninsula, on Baffin Bay in Greenland. It served as a base for US explorer Robert E. Peary's polar expedition. A 100-ton meteorite found here was brought to the US by Peary.
– ORIGIN Danish *Jorvik*.

York, Cape a cape that extends into Torres Strait at the northeast tip of Australia, in Queensland.

York, House of the English royal house that ruled England from 1461 (Edward IV) until the defeat and death of Richard III in 1485, with a short break in 1470–01 (the restoration of Henry VI).

York·ie /ˈyôrkē/ ▶ **n.** (pl. **Yorkies**) informal **Yorkshire terrier**.

York·ist /ˈyôrkist/ historical ▶ **n.** an adherent or a supporter of the House of York, esp. in the Wars of the Roses.
▶ **adj.** of or relating to the House of York: *the town rallied itself to the Yorkist cause.*

Yorks. ▶ **abbr.** Yorkshire.

York·shire /ˈyôrk,SHi(ə)r, -SHər/ a county in northern England, traditionally divided into East, West, and North Ridings.
– DERIVATIVES **York·shire·man** /-mən/ **n.** (pl. **Yorkshiremen**), **York·shire·wom·an** /-ˌwo͝omən/ **n.** (pl. **Yorkshirewomen**).

York·shire pud·ding ▶ **n.** a popover made of baked unsweetened egg batter, typically eaten with roast beef.

York·shire ter·ri·er ▶ **n.** a dog of a small, long-haired blue-gray and tan breed of terrier.

Yorkshire terrier

York·town /ˈyôrk,toun/ a historic site in southeastern Virginia, on the York River, north of Newport News, site of both the last (October 1781) battle of the American Revolution and a Civil War battle (1862).

Yo·ru·ba /ˈyôrəbə/ ▶ **n.** (pl. **same** or **Yorubas**) **1** a member of a people of southwestern Nigeria and Benin.
2 the Kwa language of this people and an official language of Nigeria.
▶ **adj.** of or relating to the Yoruba or their language.
– ORIGIN the name in Yoruba.

Yor·vik /ˈyôrvik/ (also **Jorvik**) Viking name for **York** (sense 1).

Yo·sem·i·te Na·tion·al Park /yōˈsemətē/ a national park in the Sierra Nevada, in central California. It includes Yosemite Valley, with its sheer granite cliffs, and Yosemite Falls, the highest waterfall in the US.

Yo·shkar-O·la /yəSHˌkär əˈlä/ a city in western Russia, southeast of Nizhni Novgorod, capital of the republic of Mari El; pop. 248,700 (est. 2008).

yotta- ▶ **comb. form** (used in units of measurement) denoting a factor of 10^{24}: *yottameter*.
– ORIGIN apparently adapted from Italian *otto* 'eight' (see also **yocto-**).

you /yo͞o/ ▶ **pron.** [second person singular or pl.] **1** used to refer to the person or people that the speaker is addressing: *are you listening? | I love you.* ■ used to refer to the person being addressed together with other people regarded in the same class: *you Australians.* ■ used in exclamations to address one or more people: *you fools | hey, you!*
2 used to refer to any person in general: *after a while, you get used to it.*
– PHRASES **you and yours** you together with your family and close friends. **you-know-who** (or **you-know-what**) used to refer to someone (or something) known to the hearer without specifying their identity: *the minister was later to be sacked by you-know-who.*
– ORIGIN Old English *ēow*, accusative and dative of *gē* (see **ye**[1]); related to Dutch *u* and German *euch*. During the 14th cent. *you* began to replace **ye**[1], **thou**[1], and **thee**; by the 17th cent. it had become the ordinary second person pronoun for any number and case.

you-all /ˈyo͞o ˌôl, yôl/ (also **y'all**) ▶ **pron.** dialect (in the southern US) you (used to refer to more than one person): *how are you-all?*

you'd /yo͞od/ ▶ **contraction** you had: *you'd better remember it.* ■ you would: *I was afraid you'd ask me that.*

Yough·io·ghe·ny Riv·er /ˌyäkəˈgānē/ a river that flows for 135 miles (220 km) from West Virginia into Pennsylvania where it joins the Monongahela River at McKeesport.

you'll /yo͞ol/ ▶ **contraction** you will; you shall: *you'll find many exciting features.*

Young[1] /yəNG/, Andrew (Jackson, Jr.) (1932–), US politician, civil rights leader, and clergyman. He served in various capacities with the Southern Christian Leadership Conference 1964–70 before becoming a Democratic representative from Georgia in the US Congress 1973–79. He was the US ambassador to the United Nations 1977–79 and mayor of Atlanta 1982–90.

Young[2], Brigham (1801–77), US Mormon leader. He succeeded Joseph Smith as leader of the Mormons in 1844, led them westward, and established their headquarters at Salt Lake City, Utah. He served as governor of the territory of Utah from 1850 until 1857.

Young[3], Cy (1867–1955), US baseball player; born *Denton True Young*; also know as the **Cyclone**. The all-time pitching leader in wins (511), he pitched for the Cleveland Spiders 1890–98, the St. Louis Cardinals 1899–1900, the Boston Red Sox 1901–08, and, briefly, the Cleveland Indians and the Boston Braves before retiring in 1911. Baseball's Cy Young Award for outstanding pitchers is named for him. Baseball Hall of Fame (1937).

Cy Young

Young[4], Thomas (1773–1829), English physicist, physician, and Egyptologist. His major work in physics concerned the wave theory of light. He also played a major part in the deciphering of the Rosetta Stone.

young /yəNG/ ▶ **adj.** (**younger** /ˈyəNGgər/, **youngest** /ˈyəNGgəst/) having lived or existed for only a short time: *a young girl* | (as plural noun **the young**) *the young are amazingly resilient.* ■ not as old as the norm or as would be expected: *more people were dying young.* ■ [attrib.] relating to, characteristic of, or consisting of young people: *young love | a young authors' association.* ■ immature or inexperienced: *she's very young for her age.* ■ having the qualities popularly associated with young people, such as enthusiasm and optimism: *all those who are young at heart.* ■ (**the Younger**) used to denote the younger of two people of the same name: *Pitt the Younger.* ■ (**younger**) [postpositive] Scottish denoting the heir of a landed commoner: *Hugh Magnus Macleod, younger of Macleod.*
▶ **n.** [treated as pl.] offspring, esp. of an animal before or soon after birth: *this species carries its young.*
– PHRASES **with young** (of an animal) pregnant.
– DERIVATIVES **young·ish** /ˈyəNGiSH/ **adj.**
– ORIGIN Old English *g(e)ong*, of Germanic origin; related to Dutch *jong* and German *jung*, also to **youth**; from an Indo-European root shared by Latin *juvenis*.

young·ber·ry /ˈyəNG,berē/ ▶ **n.** (pl. **youngberries**) a bramble of a variety that bears large, edible reddish-black fruit, believed to be a hybrid of a dewberry.
– ORIGIN 1920s: named after B. M. *Young* (*fl.* 1905), the American horticulturalist who first raised it.

young fus·tic ▶ **n.** the smoke tree.

young gun ▶ **n.** informal a young man perceived as assertive and aggressively self-confident.

young la·dy ▶ **n.** a woman who is not far advanced in life; a girl. ■ a form of address used by an adult to a girl, often in anger: *I don't know what's got into you, young lady.* ■ dated a girlfriend.

young·ling /ˈyəNGliNG/ ▶ **n.** literary a young person or animal.

young man ▶ **n.** a man who is not far advanced in life; a boy. ■ a form of address used by an adult to a boy, often in anger: *don't waste my time, young man.* ■ dated a boyfriend.

Young Pre·tend·er see **Stuart**[1].

Young's mod·u·lus /yəNGz/ ▶ **n.** Physics a measure of elasticity, equal to the ratio of the stress acting on a substance to the strain produced.
– ORIGIN mid 19th cent.: named after T. *Young* (see **Young**[4]).

young·ster /ˈyəNGstər/ ▶ **n.** a child, young person, or young animal.

Youngs·town /ˈyəNGz,toun/ an industrial city in northeastern Ohio, in the Mahoning River valley; pop. 72,925 (est. 2008).

Young Turk ▶ **n.** a member of a revolutionary party in the Ottoman Empire who carried out the revolution of 1908 and deposed the sultan Abdul Hamid II. ■ a young person eager for radical change to the established order.

PRONUNCIATION KEY ə ago, up; ər over, fur; a hat; ā ate; ä car; e let; ē see; i fit; ī by; NG sing; ō go; ô law, for; oi toy; o͝o good; o͞o goo; ou out; TH thin; T͟H then; ZH vision

young 'un ▶ **n.** informal or dialect a youngster.

youn·ker /'yəNGkər/ ▶ **n.** dated a youngster.
– ORIGIN early 16th cent. (denoting a young nobleman): from Middle Dutch *jonckher*, from *jonc* 'young' + *hēre* 'lord.' Compare with **JUNKER**.

your /yôr, yo͝or/ ▶ **possessive determiner 1** belonging to or associated with the person or people that the speaker is addressing: *what is your name?*
2 belonging to or associated with any person in general: *the sight is enough to break your heart.* ■ informal used to denote someone or something that is familiar or typical of its kind: *I'm just your average Joe | she is one of your chatty types.*
3 (**Your**) used when addressing the holder of certain titles: *Your Majesty | Your Eminence.*
– ORIGIN Old English *ēower*, genitive of *gē* (see **YE**[1]), of Germanic origin; related to German *euer*.

you're /yo͝or, yôr/ ▶ **contraction** you are: *you're an angel, Deb!*

yourn /yôrn, yo͝orn/ ▶ **possessive pron.** regional or archaic form of **YOURS**.

yours /yôrz, yo͝orz/ ▶ **possessive pron. 1** used to refer to a thing or things belonging to or associated with the person or people that the speaker is addressing: *the choice is yours | it's no business of yours.* ■ dated (chiefly in commercial use) your letter: *Mr. Smythe has sent me yours of the 15th inst. regarding the vacancy.*
2 used in formulas ending a letter: *Yours sincerely, John Watson | Yours, Jim Lindsay.*
– PHRASES **up yours** see **UP**. **you and yours** see **YOU**. **yours truly** see **TRULY**.

your·self /yər'self, yôr-, yo͝or-/ ▶ **pron.** [second person singular] (pl. **yourselves** /-'selvz/) **1** [reflexive] used to refer to the person being addressed as the object of a verb or preposition when they are also the subject of the clause: *help yourselves, boys | see for yourself.*
2 [emphatic] you personally (used to emphasize the person being addressed): *you're going to have to do it yourself.*
– PHRASES (**not**) **be yourself** see **BE ONESELF, NOT BE ONESELF** at **BE**. **by yourself** see **YOURSELF** at **BY**. **how's yourself?** informal how are you? (used esp. after answering a similar inquiry).

youse /yo͞oz/ ▶ **pron.** dialect you (usually more than one person).

youth /yo͞oTH/ ▶ **n.** (pl. **youths** /yo͞oTHs, yo͞oTHz/) **1** [in sing.] the period between childhood and adult age: *he had been a keen sportsman in his youth.* ■ the state or quality of being young, esp. as associated with vigor, freshness, or immaturity: *she imagined her youth and beauty fading.* ■ an early stage in the development of something: *this publishing sector is no longer in its youth.*
2 [treated as sing. or pl.] young people considered as a group: *middle-class youth have romanticized poverty | [as modifier] youth culture.* ■ a young man: *he was attacked by a gang of youths.*
– ORIGIN Old English *geoguth*, of Germanic origin; related to Dutch *jeugd*, German *Jugend*, also to **YOUNG**.

WORD TRENDS Youth was once the ultimate state, envied and romanticized by those who had left it behind, with **youths** themselves celebrated as the possessors of beauty and potential. But that time has passed, with the Oxford English Corpus telling a sorry tale of the state of today's **youth**: *unemployed, disaffected, nuisance,* and *drunken* are some of the most common modifiers, while almost all of the verbs associated with **youths** are violent or threatening, with *attack, smash, vandalize, intimidate,* and *assault* all scoring highly. And **youths** cannot simply meet—they *congregate, gather,* and even *plague*: *intimidating gangs of baseball-capped youths congregating around the newsstands | a local parade plagued by nuisance youths.* **Teenagers** fare equally badly, commonly being the object of verbs such as *kill, stab, arrest,* and *molest* and described as *troubled, rebellious, unruly,* or *pregnant.*

youth cen·ter (also **youth club**) ▶ **n.** a place or organization providing leisure activities for young people.

youth·ful /'yo͞oTHfəl/ ▶ **adj.** young or seeming young: *people aspiring to remain youthful.* ■ typical or characteristic of young people: *youthful enthusiasm.*
– DERIVATIVES **youth·ful·ly adv.**, **youth·ful·ness n.**

youth hos·tel ▶ **n.** a place providing cheap accommodations aimed mainly at young people on hiking or cycling tours.

you've /yo͞ov/ ▶ **contraction** you have: *you've changed.*

yow /you/ (also **yeow**) ▶ **exclam.** used to express pain or shock.
– ORIGIN late Middle English: imitative. The word was not recorded again until the mid 19th cent., when it was used to express the cry of a dog or cat.

yowl /youl/ ▶ **n.** a loud wailing cry, esp. one of pain or distress.
▶ **v.** [no obj.] make such a cry: *he yowled as he touched one of the hot plates.*
– ORIGIN Middle English: imitative.

yo-yo /'yō ˌyō/ ▶ **n.** (pl. **yo-yos**) a toy consisting of a pair of joined discs with a deep groove between them in which string is attached and wound, which can be spun alternately downward and upward by its weight and momentum as the string unwinds and rewinds. ■ [often as modifier] a thing that repeatedly falls and rises again: *the yo-yo syndrome of repeatedly losing weight and gaining it again.* ■ informal a stupid, insane, or unpredictable person.
▶ **v.** (**yo-yoes, yo-yoing, yo-yoed**) [no obj.] move up and down; fluctuate: *popularity polls yo-yo up and down with the flow of events.* ■ [with obj.] manipulate or maneuver (someone or something): *I don't want the job if it means he gets to yo-yo me around.*
– ORIGIN early 20th cent.: of unknown origin.

Y·pres /'ēpr(ə)/ a town in northwestern Belgium, near the border with France, in the province of West Flanders; pop. 34,812 (2008). It was the scene of some of the most bitter fighting during World War I (see **YPRES, BATTLE OF**). Flemish name **IEPER**.

Y·pres, Bat·tle of each of three battles on the Western Front near Ypres during World War I in 1914, 1915, and 1917. See also **PASSCHENDAELE, BATTLE OF**.

Yp·si·lan·ti /ˌipsə'lantē/ an industrial city in southeastern Michigan, near Ann Arbor; pop. 21,464 (est. 2008).

Y·quem /ē'kem/ ▶ **n.** a sweet white wine from the estate of Château d'Yquem in the Sauternes region of France.

yr. ▶ **abbr.** ■ year or years. ■ younger. ■ your.

yrs. ▶ **abbr.** ■ years. ■ yours (as a formula ending a letter).

YT ▶ **abbr.** Yukon Territory (in official postal use).

YTD ▶ **abbr.** year to date.

yt·ter·bi·um /i'tərbēəm/ ▶ **n.** the chemical element of atomic number 70, a silvery-white metal of the lanthanide series. (Symbol: **Yb**)
– ORIGIN late 19th cent.: modern Latin, from *Ytterby*, the name of a Swedish town where it was first found in a quarry.

yt·tri·um /'itrēəm/ ▶ **n.** the chemical element of atomic number 39, a grayish-white metal generally included among the rare-earth elements. (Symbol: **Y**)
– ORIGIN early 19th cent.: modern Latin, from *Ytterby* (see **YTTERBIUM**).

Y2K ▶ **abbr.** the year 2000.

Yu·an /yo͞o'än/ a dynasty that ruled China AD 1259–1368, established by the Mongols under Kublai Khan. It preceded the Ming dynasty.

yu·an /yo͞o'än/ ▶ **n.** (pl. **same**) the basic monetary unit of China, equal to 10 jiao or 100 fen.
– ORIGIN Chinese, literally 'round'; compare with **YEN**[1].

Yuan Jiang /yo͞o'än jē'äNG/ Chinese name for **RED RIVER** (sense 1).

Yu·ba Cit·y /'yo͞obə/ a commercial city in north central California, northwest of Sacramento; pop. 61,226 (est. 2008).

yuc·a /'yo͞okə/ ▶ **n.** another term for **CASSAVA**.
– ORIGIN Carib.

Yu·cai·pa /yo͞o'kīpə/ a city in southern California, southeast of San Bernardino; pop. 49,750 (est. 2008).

Yu·ca·tán /ˌyo͞okə'tan, -'tän, 'yo͞okəˌtan, -ˌtän/ a state in southeastern Mexico, at the northern tip of the Yucatán Peninsula; capital, Mérida.
– ORIGIN adapted from a Mayan name for the language of the Mayan Indians in Oaxaca, Mexico.

Yu·ca·tán Pen·in·su·la a peninsula in southern Mexico that lies between the Gulf of Mexico and the Caribbean Sea.

Yu·ca·tec /'yo͞okəˌtek/ ▶ **n.** (pl. **same** or **Yucatecs**) **1** a member of an American Indian people of the Yucatán peninsula. ■ informal a native or inhabitant of the peninsula or the state of Yucatán.
2 the Mayan language of the Yucatec people.
▶ **adj.** of or relating to the Yucatec or their language.
– DERIVATIVES **Yu·ca·tec·an** /ˌyo͞okə'tekən/ **adj.**
– ORIGIN from Spanish *yucateco*.

yuc·ca /'yəkə/ ▶ **n.** a plant of the agave family with stiff swordlike leaves and spikes of white bell-shaped flowers that are dependent upon the yucca moth for fertilization, found esp. in warm regions of North America and Mexico. ● Genus *Yucca*, family Agavaceae: many species, including Spanish bayonet and Adam's needle.
– ORIGIN mid 16th cent. (denoting cassava): from Carib.

yuc·ca moth ▶ **n.** a small white American moth that lays its eggs in the ovary of a yucca plant. While doing so it deposits a ball of pollen on the stigma, thereby fertilizing the seeds on which the larvae feed. ● Genus *Tegeticula*, family Incurvariidae: several species, in particular *T. yuccasella*.

Yu·chi /'yo͞oCHē/ ▶ **n.** (pl. **same** or **Yuchis**) **1** a member of an American Indian people now incorporated into the Creek Confederacy in Oklahoma.
2 the language of this people.
– ORIGIN Creek, of uncertain origin.

yuck /yək/ informal (also **yuk**) ▶ **exclam.** used to express strong distaste or disgust: *"Raw herrings! Yuck!"*
▶ **n.** something messy or disgusting: *I can't bear the sight of blood and yuck.*
– ORIGIN 1960s (originally US): imitative.

yuck·y /'yəkē/ (also **yukky**) ▶ **adj.** (**yuckier, yuckiest**) informal messy or disgusting: *yucky green-gray slushy cabbage.*

Yu·dho·yo·no /ˌyo͞odō'yōnō/, Susilo Bambang (1949–), Indonesian statesman, president since 2004; known as **SBY**. As president, he has supported an agenda of economic and social reform.

Yue /yo͞o'ā/ ▶ **n.** another term for **CANTONESE** (the language).

yu·ga /'yo͞ogə/ ▶ **n.** Hinduism any of the four ages of the life of the world.
– ORIGIN Sanskrit.

Yu·go·slav /'yo͞ogōˌsläv, ˌyo͞ogō'släv, -gə-/ ▶ **n.** a native or inhabitant of Yugoslavia or its former constituent republics, or a person of Yugoslav descent.
▶ **adj.** of or relating to Yugoslavia, its former constituent republics, or its people.
– ORIGIN from Austrian German *Jugoslav*, from Croatian *jug* 'south' + **SLAV**.

Yu·go·sla·vi·a /ˌyo͞ogō'slävēə, ˌyo͞ogə-/ a former federation of states in southeastern Europe, in the Balkans.

The country was formed as the Kingdom of Serbs, Croats, and Slovenes in the peace settlements at the end of World War I. It included Serbia, Montenegro, and the former South Slavic provinces of the Austro-Hungarian Empire and assumed the name of Yugoslavia in 1929; its capital was Belgrade. After World War II, during which time Yugoslavia was invaded by Germany, the country emerged as a nonaligned communist federal republic under Marshal Tito. In 1990, communist rule was formally ended. Four of the six constituent republics (Slovenia, Croatia, Bosnia and Herzegovina, and Macedonia) then seceded amid serious civil and ethnic conflict. The two remaining republics, Serbia and Montenegro, declared a new Federal Republic of Yugoslavia in 1992. This was dissolved in 2003, being replaced by the Union of Serbia and Montenegro. In 2006 Serbia and Montenegro voted to become independent republics.

– DERIVATIVES **Yu·go·sla·vi·an adj. & n.**

yuh /yə/ ▶ **pron.** nonstandard spelling of **YOU**, used in representing black English speech.
▶ **possessive adj.** nonstandard spelling of **YOUR**, used in representing black English speech.

Yu·it /'yo͞oət/ ▶ **n.** (pl. **same** or **Yuits**) & **adj.** another term for **YUPIK**.
– ORIGIN Siberian Yupik, literally 'people.'

yuk ▶ **exclam.** variant spelling of **YUCK**.
▶ **n.** informal a laugh, esp. a loud hearty one. [1930s: (theatrical slang): probably imitative.]
– PHRASES **yuk it up** (**yuks, yukking, yukked**) laugh, esp. in a loud hearty way.

Yu·ka·ghir /ˌyo͞okə'gir/ ▶ **n.** (pl. **same** or **Yukaghirs**)
1 a member of a people of Arctic Siberia.
2 the language of this people, of uncertain affinity but possibly Uralic.
▶ **adj.** of or relating to this people or their language.
– ORIGIN Yakut.

yu·ka·ta /yo͞o'kätə/ ▶ **n.** (pl. **same** or **yukatas**) a light cotton kimono.
– ORIGIN Japanese, from *yu* 'hot water' (because originally worn indoors after a bath) + *kata(bira)* 'light kimono.'

yuk·ky ▶ **adj.** variant spelling of **YUCKY**.

Yu·kon /'yo͞oˌkän/ a river in northwestern North America that rises in Yukon Territory in northwestern Canada and flows west for 1,870 miles (3,020 km) through central Alaska to the Bering Sea.

Yu·kon stove ▶ **n.** a lightweight portable stove consisting of a small metal box divided into firebox and oven.

y

Yu·kon Ter·ri·to·ry a territory in northwestern Canada, on the border with Alaska; pop. 30,372 (2006); capital, Whitehorse. The population increased briefly during the Klondike gold rush 1897–99.

yu·lan /'yo͞o,lan, -lən/ ▶ **n.** a Chinese magnolia with showy white flowers. ● *Magnolia heptapeta*, family Magnoliaceae.
– ORIGIN early 19th cent.: from Chinese *yùlán*, from *yù* 'gem' + *lán* 'plant.'

Yule /yo͞ol/ ▶ **n.** archaic term for CHRISTMAS.
– ORIGIN Old English *gēol(a)* 'Christmas Day'; compare with Old Norse *jól*, originally applied to a heathen festival lasting twelve days, later to Christmas.

yule log ▶ **n.** a large log traditionally burned in the fireplace on Christmas Eve. ■ a log-shaped chocolate cake eaten at Christmas.

Yule·tide /'yo͞ol,tīd/ ▶ **n.** archaic term for CHRISTMAS.

yum /yəm/ (also **yum-yum**) informal ▶ **exclam.** used to express pleasure at eating, or at the prospect of eating, a particular food.
▶ **adj.** (of food) delicious.
– ORIGIN late 19th cent.: imitative.

Yu·ma¹ /'yo͞omə/ a city in southwestern Arizona, near the Colorado River and the Mexican border; pop. 90,041 (est. 2008).

Yu·ma² ▶ **n. 1** (pl. **same** or **Yumas**) a member of an American Indian people living mainly in southwestern Arizona.
2 the Yuman language of this people.
▶ **adj.** of or relating to this people.
– ORIGIN from Pima *yumĭ*.

Yu·man /'yo͞omən/ ▶ **n.** a family of American Indian languages including Yuma.
▶ **adj.** of or relating to the Yuman languages or their speakers.
– ORIGIN from YUMA² + -AN.

yum·my /'yəmē/ ▶ **adj.** (**yummier**, **yummiest**) informal (of food) delicious: *yummy pumpkin cakes.* ■ highly attractive and desirable: *I scooped up this yummy young man.*
– ORIGIN late 19th cent.: from YUM + -Y¹.

Yun·nan /yo͞o'nän/ a province in southwestern China, on the border with Vietnam, Laos, and Burma (Myanmar); capital, Kunming.

yup¹ /yəp/ ▶ **exclam. & n.** variant spelling of YEP.

yup² ▶ **n.** short for YUPPIE.

Yu·pik /'yo͞opik/ ▶ **n.** (pl. **same** or **Yupiks**) **1** a member of an Eskimo people of Siberia, the Aleutian Islands, and southwestern Alaska.
2 any of the Eskimo languages of this people.
▶ **adj.** of or relating to this people or their languages.
– ORIGIN from Alaskan Yupik *Yup'ik* 'real person.'

USAGE See usage at INUIT.

yup·pie /'yəpē/ (also **yuppy**) ▶ **n.** (pl. **yuppies**) informal, derogatory a well-paid young middle-class professional who works in a city job and has a luxurious lifestyle.
– DERIVATIVES **yup·pie·dom** /-dəm/ **n.**
– ORIGIN 1980s: elaboration of the acronym from *young urban professional.*

yup·pie flu (also **yuppie disease**) ▶ **n.** informal derogatory term for CHRONIC FATIGUE SYNDROME.

yup·pi·fy /'yəpə,fī/ ▶ **v.** (**yuppifies**, **yuppifying**, **yuppified**) [with obj.] informal, derogatory make more affluent and upmarket in keeping with the taste and lifestyle of yuppies: *Kreuzberg is slowly being yuppified with smart little eating places.*
– DERIVATIVES **yup·pi·fi·ca·tion** /,yəpəfi'kāSHən/ **n.**

Yu·rok /'yo͝or,äk, -ək/ ▶ **n.** (pl. **same** or **Yuroks**) **1** a member of an American Indian people of northern California.
2 the language of this people, distantly related to Algonquian.
▶ **adj.** of or relating to this people or their language.
– ORIGIN from Karok *yúruk*, literally 'downstream.'

yurt /yo͝ort, yərt/ ▶ **n.** a circular tent of felt or skins on a collapsible framework, used by nomads in Mongolia, Siberia, and Turkey.
– ORIGIN from Russian *yurta*, via French or German from Turkic *jurt*.

Yu·zov·ka /'yo͞ozəfkə/ former name (1872–1924) for DONETSK.
– ORIGIN named in honor of John Hughes (1814–89), a Welshman who established its first ironworks.

YWCA ▶ **n.** a welfare movement with branches in many countries that began in Britain in 1855. ■ a hostel or recreational facility run by this association.
– ORIGIN abbreviation of *Young Women's Christian Association.*

YWHA ▶ **abbr.** Young Women's Hebrew Association.

Zz

Z[1] /zē/ (also **z**) ▶ **n.** (pl. **Zs** or **Z's**) **1** the twenty-sixth letter of the alphabet. ■ denoting the next after Y in a set of items, categories, etc. ■ denoting a third unknown or unspecified person or thing: *X sold a car to Y (a car dealer) who in turn sold it to Z (a finance company).* ■ (usu. z) the third unknown quantity in an algebraic expression. [the introduction of *x*, *y*, and *z* as symbols of unknown quantities is due to Descartes (see **X**[1]).] ■ (usu. z) denoting the third axis in a three-dimensional system of coordinates: [in combination] *the z-axis.*
2 a shape like that of a capital Z: [in combination] *the same old Z-shaped crack in the paving stone.*
3 used in repeated form to represent the sound of buzzing or snoring: *I'm being overcome with weariness as I write ... zzzzz, zzzzz.*
– PHRASES **catch some** (or **a few**) **Zs** informal get some sleep: *I'll go back to the hotel and catch some Zs.*

Z[2] ▶ **symbol** Chemistry atomic number.

za·ba·glio·ne /ˌzäbəlˈyōnē/ ▶ **n.** an Italian dessert made of whipped and heated egg yolks, sugar, and Marsala wine, served hot or cold.
– ORIGIN Italian.

Zab·rze /ˈzäbzʜə/ an industrial and mining city in southern Poland, in Upper Silesia; pop. 189,656 (2007). From 1915 to 1945, it was a German city called Hindenburg.

Za·ca·te·cas /ˌzäkəˈtākəs, ˌsäkə-/ a state in northern central Mexico. ■ its capital, a silver-mining city located at an altitude of 8,200 feet (2,500 m); pop. 122,889 (2005).

zaf·fer /ˈzafər/ (also **zaffre**) ▶ **n.** impure cobalt oxide, formerly used to make smalt and blue enamels.
– ORIGIN mid 17th cent.: from Italian *zaffera* or French *safre.*

zaf·tig /ˈzäftig, -tik/ (also **zoftig**) ▶ **adj.** informal (of a woman) having a full, rounded figure; plump.
– ORIGIN 1930s: Yiddish, from German *saftig* 'juicy.'

zag /zag/ ▶ **n.** a sharp change of direction in a zigzag course: *we traveled in a series of zigs and zags.*
▶ **v.** (**zags, zagging, zagged**) [no obj.] make a sharp change of direction: *a long path zigged and zagged through the woods.*
– ORIGIN late 18th cent.: shortening of **ZIGZAG**.

Za·ga·zig /ˌzägäˈzēg, zäˈgäzig/ (also **Zaqaziq** /ˌzäkäˈzēk/) a city in northern Egypt, located on the Nile delta; pop. 302,800 (est. 2006).

Za·greb /ˈzäˌgreb/ a city in northern central Croatia, the country's capital; pop. 704,800 (est. 2009).

Zag·ros Moun·tains /ˈzagrəs, -ˌrōs/ a mountain range in western Iran that rises to 14,921 feet (4,548 m) at Zard Kuh. Most of Iran's oil fields lie along the western foothills.

Za·har·i·as /zəˈharēəs/, Babe (1914–56), US track and field athlete and golfer; full name *Mildred Ella Didrikson Zaharias.* After winning gold medals in the javelin throw and 80-millimeter hurdle events at the 1932 Olympic games, she turned to golf and won many major professional titles between 1936 and 1954.

zai·ba·tsu /zīˈbätˌsōō, -ˈbat-/ ▶ **n.** (pl. **same**) a large Japanese business conglomerate.
– ORIGIN Japanese, from *zai* 'wealth' + *batsu* 'clique.'

Za·ire /zäˈi(ə)r/ Former name (until 1997) of **CONGO, DEMOCRATIC REPUBLIC OF THE**.
– DERIVATIVES **Za·ir·e·an** /-ˈi(ə)rēən/ (also **Zairian**) **adj. & n.**

Za·ire Riv·er see **CONGO**.

za·kat /zəˈkät, -ˈkat/ ▶ **n.** obligatory payment made annually under Islamic law on certain kinds of property and used for charitable and religious purposes.
– ORIGIN via Persian and Urdu from Arabic *zakā(t)* 'almsgiving.'

Za·kin·thos /ˈzäkinˌTHôs, zəˈkinTHəs/ (also **Zakynthos**) a Greek island off the southwestern coast of mainland Greece, in the Ionian Sea, one of the Ionian Islands; pop. 11,000 (est. 2009). Also called **ZANTE**.

za·kus·ka /zəˈkōōskə/ (also **zakouska**) ▶ **n.** (pl. **zakuski** /-skē/ or **zakuskas**) a substantial Russian hors d'oeuvre item such as caviar sandwiches or vegetables with sour cream dip, all served with vodka.
– ORIGIN Russian.

zal·cit·a·bine /zalˈsitəˌbēn/ ▶ **n.** another term for **DIDEOXYCYTIDINE**.
– ORIGIN 1990s: from *zal-* (of unknown origin) + *-citabine* apparently formed by arbitrary alteration of **CYTIDINE**.

Zam·be·zi /zamˈbēzē/ a river in East Africa that rises in northwestern Zambia and flows for 1,600 miles (2,560 km), first south and then east, through Angola and the Democratic Republic of the Congo (formerly Zaire) to Victoria Falls where it turns to form the border between Zambia and Zimbabwe before crossing Mozambique and entering the Indian Ocean.

Zam·bi·a /ˈzambēə/ a landlocked country in central Africa, separated from Zimbabwe by the Zambezi River; pop. 11,862,700 (est. 2009); capital, Lusaka; languages, English (official) and various Bantu languages.

> Formerly a British protectorate called Northern Rhodesia, Zambia became an independent republic within the Commonwealth of Nations in 1964, under Kenneth Kaunda (president 1964–91). Zambia's economy was adversely affected by its involvement in the Zimbabwe independence struggle 1965–79.

– DERIVATIVES **Zam·bi·an adj. & n.**

Zam·bo·an·ga /ˌzambōˈäNGgə/ a port in southern Philippines, on the western coast of the island of Mindanao; pop. 774,400 (est. 2007).

Zam·bo·ni /zamˈbōnē/ ▶ **n.** trademark a machine used to resurface ice for skating.

za·mi·a /ˈzāmēə/ (Austral. also **zamia palm**) ▶ **n.** an American or Australian cycad, some kinds of which produce roots or seeds that are edible after careful preparation. ● Genera *Zamia* (of America) and *Macrozamia* (of Australia), family Zamiaceae.
– ORIGIN early 19th cent.: modern Latin, from *zamiae*, misreading (in Pliny) of *azaniae* 'pine cones.'

za·min·dar /ˈzamənˌdär, zəˌmēnˈdär/ (also **zemindar**) ▶ **n.** Indian a landowner, esp. one who leases his land to tenant farmers.
– ORIGIN via Urdu from Persian *zamīndār*, from *zamīn* 'land' + *-dār* 'holder.'

zam·in·dar·i /ˌzamənˈdärē, zəˌmēn-/ ▶ **n.** Indian historical the system under which zamindars held land. ■ the office or territory of a zamindar.
– ORIGIN Urdu.

Zan·de /ˈzandē/ (also **Azande** /əˈzandē/) ▶ **n.** (pl. **same** or **Azande**) **1** a member of a central African people of mixed ethnic origin.
2 the Niger-Congo language of this people, spoken mainly in northern Democratic Republic of the Congo (formerly Zaire) and Sudan.
▶ **adj.** of or relating to this people or their language.
– ORIGIN the name in Zande.

Zan·tac /ˈzanˌtak/ ▶ **n.** trademark for **RANITIDINE**.
– ORIGIN late 20th cent.: probably from *Z-* + **ANTACID**.

Zan·te /ˈzantē/ another name for **ZAKINTHOS**.

ZANU /ˈzanˌōō/ ▶ **abbr.** Zimbabwe African National Union.

ZANU–PF ▶ **abbr.** Zimbabwe African National Union (Patriotic Front).

Zan·uck /ˈzanək/, Darryl F. (1902–79), US movie producer; full name *Darryl Francis Zanuck.* He was the controlling executive of Twentieth Century Fox and its president from 1965 until his retirement in 1971.

za·ny /ˈzānē/ ▶ **adj.** (**zanier, zaniest**) amusingly unconventional and idiosyncratic: *zany humor.*
▶ **n.** an erratic or eccentric person. ■ historical a comic performer partnering a clown, whom he imitated in an amusing way.
– DERIVATIVES **za·ni·ly** /-nəlē/ **adv.**, **za·ni·ness n.**
– ORIGIN late 16th cent.: from French *zani* or Italian *zan(n)i*, Venetian form of *Gianni, Giovanni* 'John,' stock name of the servants acting as clowns in the *commedia dell'arte.*

Zan·zi·bar /ˈzanzəˌbär/ an island off the coast of East Africa, part of Tanzania; pop. 1,207,500 (2009, with Pemba). In 1964, it became a republic and united with Tanganyika to form Tanzania.
– DERIVATIVES **Zan·zi·ba·ri** /ˌzanzəˈbärē/ **adj. & n.**

Zao·zhuang /ˈdzouˈjwäNG, -jəˈwäNG/ (also **Tsao-chuang**) a city in eastern China, in Shandong province; pop. 762,900 (est. 2006).

zap /zap/ informal ▶ **v.** (**zaps, zapping, zapped**) **1** [with obj.] destroy or obliterate: *zap the enemy's artillery before it can damage your core units | it's vital to zap stress fast.*
2 [with obj.] cause to move suddenly and rapidly in a specified direction: *the boat zapped us up river.* ■ [no obj.] move suddenly and rapidly, esp. between television channels or sections of videotape by use of a remote control: *video recorders mean the audience will zap through the ads.*
3 [with obj.] cook or warm (food or a hot drink) in a microwave oven.
▶ **n.** a sudden effect or event that makes a dramatic impact, esp. a sudden burst of energy or sound: *the eggs get an extra zap of UV light.*
– ORIGIN 1920s (originally US): imitative.

Za·pa·ta /zəˈpätə/, Emiliano (1879–1919), Mexican revolutionary. He attempted to implement his program of agrarian reform by means of guerrilla warfare. From 1914, he and Pancho Villa fought against the regimes of General Huerta and Venustiano Carranza.

za·pa·te·a·do /ˌzäpətēˈädō, -tā-/ ▶ **n.** (pl. **zapateados**) a flamenco dance with rhythmic stamping of the feet.
– ORIGIN mid 19th cent.: Spanish, from *zapato* 'shoe.'

Za·pa·tis·ta /ˌzäpəˈtēstə/ ▶ **n.** a member or supporter of a Mexican revolutionary force working for social and agrarian reforms, which launched a popular uprising in the state of Chiapas in 1994.
– ORIGIN Spanish, named after Emiliano **ZAPATA** + **-ISTA**.

Za·po·rizhzh·ya /ˌzäpəˈrēZH(y)ə/ an industrial city in Ukraine, on the Dnieper River; pop. 781,600 (est. 2009). Russian name **Zaporozhye**. Former name (until 1921) **ALEKSANDROVSK**.

Za·po·tec /ˈzäpəˌtek/ ▶ **n.** (pl. **same** or **Zapotecs**) **1** a member of an American Indian people living in and around Oaxaca in southern Mexico.
2 the Otomanguean language of this people.
▶ **adj.** of or relating to the Zapotec or their language.
– ORIGIN from Spanish *zapoteco*, from Nahuatl *tzapoteca*, plural of *tzapotecatl*, literally 'person of the place of the sapodilla.'

zap·per /ˈzapər/ ▶ n. informal **1** a remote control for a television, video, or other piece of electronic equipment.
2 an electronic device used for killing insects: *a bug zapper*.

zap·py /ˈzapē/ ▶ adj. (**zappier, zappiest**) informal lively; energetic: *a zappy musical tapestry*.

ZAPU /ˈzapˌo͞o/ ▶ abbr. Zimbabwe African People's Union.

Za·qa·ziq /ˈzäkəˌzik/ variant spelling of **Zagazig**.

Za·ra·go·za /ˌsärəˈgōsə, ˌTHärəˈgōTHə/ Spanish name for **Saragossa**.

Zar·a·thus·tra /ˌzarəˈTHo͞ostrə/ the Avestan name for the Persian prophet Zoroaster.
– DERIVATIVES **Zar·a·thus·tri·an** /-ˈTHo͞ostrēən/ adj. & n.

za·ri /ˈzärē/ ▶ n. [usu. as modifier] a type of gold thread used decoratively on Indian clothing.
– ORIGIN from Urdu *zarī*, from Persian *zar* 'gold.'

Za·ri·a /ˈzärēə/ a city in northern Nigeria; pop. 889,000 (est. 2007).

za·ri·ba /zəˈrēbə/ (also **zareba**) ▶ n. (also **zareba, zareeba**) a protective enclosure of thorn bushes or stakes surrounding a campsite or village in northeastern Africa. ■ a cattle corral.
– ORIGIN from Arabic *zarība* 'cattle pen; stockade.'

Zar·qa /ˈzärkə/ (also **Az-Zarqa** /az/) a city in northwestern Jordan; pop. 639,469 (2004).

zar·zue·la /zärˈzwālə/ ▶ n. **1** a Spanish traditional form of musical comedy.
2 a Spanish dish of various kinds of seafood cooked in a rich sauce.
– ORIGIN Spanish, apparently from a place name.

za·yin /ˈzäyin/ ▶ n. the seventh letter of the Hebrew alphabet.

za·zen /ˌzäˈzen/ ▶ n. Zen meditation, usually performed in the lotus position.
– ORIGIN Japanese, from *za* 'sitting' + *zen* (see **Zen**).

Z bo·son ▶ n. another term for **Z particle**.

Z-DNA ▶ n. Biochemistry DNA in which the double helix has a left-handed rather than the usual right-handed twist and the sugar phosphate backbone follows a zigzag course.

zeal /zēl/ ▶ n. great energy or enthusiasm in pursuit of a cause or an objective: *his zeal for privatization | Laura brought a missionary zeal to her work*.
– ORIGIN late Middle English: via ecclesiastical Latin from Greek *zēlos*.

Zea·land /ˈzēlənd/ the principal island of Denmark, located between the Jutland peninsula and the southern tip of Sweden. Its chief city is Copenhagen. Danish name **Sjælland**.

zeal·ot /ˈzelət/ ▶ n. a person who is fanatical and uncompromising in pursuit of their religious, political, or other ideals. ■ (**Zealot**) historical a member of an ancient Jewish sect aiming at a world Jewish theocracy and resisting the Romans until AD 70.
– ORIGIN mid 16th cent. (in the sense 'member of an ancient Jewish sect'): via ecclesiastical Latin from Greek *zēlōtēs*, from *zēloun* 'be jealous,' from *zēlos* (see **zeal**).

zeal·ot·ry /zelətrē/ ▶ n. fanatical and uncompromising pursuit of religious, political, or other ideals; fanaticism.

zeal·ous /ˈzeləs/ ▶ adj. having or showing zeal: *the council was extremely zealous in the application of the regulations*.
– DERIVATIVES **zeal·ous·ly** adv., **zeal·ous·ness** n.
– ORIGIN early 16th cent.: from a medieval Latin derivative of Latin *zelus* 'zeal, jealousy.'

ze·ax·an·thin /ˌzēəˈzanTHin/ ▶ n. Biochemistry a carotenoid present in the retina of the eye and in many plants, used as a food additive and supplement.
– ORIGIN 1920s: via German from modern Latin *zea* 'maize' + *xanthin*, a yellow coloring in some plants.

ze·bec ▶ n. variant spelling of **xebec**.

ze·bra /ˈzēbrə/ ▶ n. **1** an African wild horse with black-and-white stripes and an erect mane. ● Genus *Equus*, family Equidae: three species, the **common zebra** (*E. burchellii*), **Grevy's zebra** (*E. grevyi*), and the **mountain zebra** (*E. zebra*). See also **quagga**.
2 a large butterfly with pale bold stripes on a dark background, in particular: ● a yellow and black American butterfly (*Heliconius charitonius*, subfamily Heliconiinae, family Nymphalidae).
3 (also **zebra fish**) S. African a silvery-gold sea bream with vertical black stripes. ● *Diplodus cervinus*, family Sparidae.
4 informal a person whose characteristic garb is a black-and-white striped uniform, esp. a football official or a convict.
– ORIGIN early 17th cent.: from Italian, Spanish, or Portuguese, originally in the sense 'wild ass,' perhaps ultimately from Latin *equiferus*, from *equus* 'horse' + *ferus* 'wild.'

Grevy's zebra

ze·bra cross·ing ▶ n. Brit. an area of road painted with broad white stripes, where vehicles must stop if pedestrians wish to cross; a crosswalk.

ze·bra finch ▶ n. a small Australian waxbill with black and white stripes on the face, popular as a pet bird. ● *Poephila guttata*, family Estrildidae.

ze·bra mus·sel ▶ n. a small freshwater bivalve mollusk with zigzag markings on the shell, sometimes becoming a pest because it blocks water pipes. ● *Dreissena polymorpha*, family Dreissenidae.

ze·bra·wood /ˈzēbrəˌwo͝od/ ▶ n. any of a number of tropical trees that produce ornamental striped timber that is used chiefly in cabinetmaking. ● Species in several families, such as *Connarus guianensis* (family Connaraceae) of Guyana, and *Diospyros marmorata* (family Ebenaceae) of the Andaman Islands.

ze·bu /ˈzēˌb(y)o͞o/ ▶ n. another term for **Brahman** (sense 3).
– ORIGIN late 18th cent.: from French *zébu*, of unknown origin.

Zeb·u·lun /ˈzebyələn/ (also **Zebulon**) (in the Bible) a Hebrew patriarch, son of Jacob and Leah. ■ the tribe of Israel traditionally descended from him.

Zech. ▶ abbr. Bible Zechariah.

Zech·a·ri·ah /ˌzekəˈrīə/ a Hebrew minor prophet of the 6th century BC. ■ a book of the Bible including his prophecies.

zed /zed/ ▶ n. Brit. the letter Z.
– ORIGIN late Middle English: from French *zède*, via late Latin from Greek *zēta* (see **zeta**).

Zed·e·ki·ah /ˌzedəˈkīə/ (in the Bible) the last king of Judea, who rebelled against Nebuchadnezzar and was carried off to Babylon into captivity.

zed·o·a·ry /ˈzedōˌerē/ ▶ n. an Indian plant related to turmeric, with an aromatic rhizome. ● *Curcuma zedoaria*, family Zingiberaceae. ■ a gingerlike substance made from this rhizome, used in medicine, perfumery, and dyeing.
– ORIGIN late Middle English: from medieval Latin *zedoarium*, from Persian *zadwār*.

zee /zē/ ▶ n. the letter Z.
– ORIGIN late 17th cent.: variant of **zed**.

Zee·man ef·fect /ˈzēmən, ˈzā-/ ▶ n. Physics the splitting of the spectrum line into several components by the application of a magnetic field.
– ORIGIN late 19th cent.: named after Pieter *Zeeman* (1865–1943), Dutch physicist.

Zef·fi·rel·li /ˌzefəˈrelē/, Franco (1923–), Italian movie and theater director; born *Gianfranco Corsi*. His operatic productions are noted for the opulence of their sets and costumes. Notable movies: *Romeo and Juliet* (1968), *Hamlet* (1990), and *Tea with Mussolini* (1999).

ze·in /ˈzē-in/ ▶ n. Biochemistry the principal protein of corn.
– ORIGIN early 19th cent.: from modern Latin *Zea* (genus name of corn) + **-in**¹.

zeit·ge·ber /ˈtsītˌgābər, ˈzīt-/ ▶ n. Physiology a cue given by the environment, such as a change in light or temperature, to reset the internal body clock.
– ORIGIN mid 20th cent.: from German *Zeitgeber*, from *Zeit* 'time' + *Geber* 'giver.'

zeit·geist /ˈtsītˌgīst, ˈzīt-/ ▶ n. [in sing.] the defining spirit or mood of a particular period of history as shown by the ideas and beliefs of the time: *the story captured the zeitgeist of the late 1960s*.
– ORIGIN mid 19th cent.: from German *Zeitgeist*, from *Zeit* 'time' + *Geist* 'spirit.'

Zel·ig /ˈzelig/ ▶ n. a person who is able to change their appearance, behavior, or attitudes, so as to be comfortable in any situation: *a financial Zelig, he was the only man to advise all four of the major networks on deals in one year*.
– ORIGIN 1980s: from the name of Leonard *Zelig*, the chameleonic subject of Woody Allen's film *Zelig* (1983).

zel·ko·va /zelˈkōvə/ ▶ n. an Asian tree of the elm family, often cultivated as an ornamental, for its timber, or as a bonsai tree. ● Genus *Zelkova*, family Ulmaceae: several species, in particular **Japanese zelkova** (*Z. serrata*).

ze·min·dar /zəˈmēnˌdär/ variant spelling of **zamindar**.

zem·stvo /ˈzemst-vō/ ▶ n. (pl. **zemstvos**) one of a system of elected councils established in tsarist Russia to administer local affairs after the abolition of serfdom.
– ORIGIN Russian, from *zemlya* 'land.'

Zen /zen/ (also **Zen Buddhism**) ▶ n. a Japanese school of Mahayana Buddhism emphasizing the value of meditation and intuition.

> Zen Buddhism was introduced to Japan from China in the 12th century and has had a profound cultural influence. The aim of Zen is to achieve sudden enlightenment (satori) through meditation in a seated posture (zazen), usually under the guidance of a teacher and often using paradoxical statements (koans) to transcend rational thought.

– DERIVATIVES **Zen Bud·dhist** n.
– ORIGIN Japanese, literally 'meditation,' from Chinese *chán* 'quietude,' from Sanskrit *dhyāna* 'meditation.'

ze·na·na /zəˈnänə/ ▶ n. (in India and Iran) the part of a house for the seclusion of women.
– ORIGIN from Persian and Urdu *zanānah*, from *zan* 'woman.'

Zend /zend/ ▶ n. an interpretation of the Avesta, each Zend being part of the Zend-Avesta.
– ORIGIN from Persian *zand* 'interpretation.'

Zend-A·ves·ta ▶ n. the Zoroastrian sacred writings, comprising the Avesta (the text) and Zend (the commentary).

Ze·ner /ˈzēnər/ (in full **Zener diode**) ▶ n. Electronics a form of semiconductor diode in which at a critical reverse voltage a large reverse current can flow.
– ORIGIN 1950s: named after Clarence M. *Zener* (1905–93), American physicist.

Ze·ner cards ▶ plural n. a set of 25 cards each with one of five different symbols, used in ESP research.
– ORIGIN 1930s: named after Karl E. *Zener* (1903–61), American psychologist.

ze·nith /ˈzēniTH/ ▶ n. [in sing.] the highest point reached by a celestial or other object: *the sun was well past the zenith | the missile reached its zenith and fell*. ■ the point in the sky or celestial sphere directly above an observer. The opposite of **nadir**. ■ the time at which something is most powerful or successful: *under Justinian, the Byzantine Empire reached its zenith of influence*.
– DERIVATIVES **ze·nith·al** /-nəTHəl/ adj.
– ORIGIN late Middle English: from Old French or medieval Latin *cenit*, based on Arabic *samt (ar-ra's)* 'path (over the head).'

Ze·no[1] /ˈzēnō/ (*fl.* 5th century BC), Greek philosopher. A member of the Eleatic school, he defended Parmenides' theories by formulating paradoxes that appeared to demonstrate the impossibility of motion.

Ze·no[2] (*c.*335–*c.*263 BC), Greek philosopher; founder of Stoicism; known as **Zeno of Citium**. He founded the school of Stoic philosophy *c.*300 (see **stoicism**).

Ze·no·bi·a /zəˈnōbēə/ (3rd century AD), queen of Palmyra *c.*267–272. She conquered Egypt and much of Asia Minor. When she proclaimed her son emperor, the Roman emperor Aurelian attacked, defeated, and captured her.

ze·o·lite /ˈzēəˌlīt/ ▶ n. any of a large group of minerals consisting of hydrated aluminosilicates of sodium, potassium, calcium, and barium. They can be readily dehydrated and rehydrated, and are used as cation exchangers and molecular sieves.
– DERIVATIVES **ze·o·lit·ic** /ˌzēəˈlitik/ adj.
– ORIGIN late 18th cent.: from Swedish and German *zeolit*, from Greek *zein* 'to boil' + **-lite** (from their characteristic swelling when heated in the laboratory).

Zeph. ▶ abbr. Bible Zephaniah.

Zeph·a·ni·ah /ˌzefəˈnīə/ a Hebrew minor prophet of the 7th century BC. ■ a book of the Bible containing his prophecies.

zeph·yr /ˈzefər/ ▶ n. **1** literary a soft gentle breeze.
2 historical a fine cotton gingham. ■ a very light article of clothing.
– ORIGIN late Old English *zefferus*, denoting a personification of the west wind, via Latin from Greek *zephuros* '(god of) the west wind.' Sense 1 dates from the late 17th cent.

Zep·pe·lin[1] /ˈzep(ə)lən/, Ferdinand (Adolf August Heinrich), Count von (1838–1917), German aviation pioneer. An army officer until his retirement in 1890, he devoted the rest of his life to the development of the dirigible airship named after him.

Zep·pe·lin[2] ▶ **n.** historical a large German dirigible airship of the early 20th century, long and cylindrical in shape and with a rigid framework. Zeppelins were used during World War I for reconnaissance and bombing, and after the war as passenger transports until the 1930s.

zepto- ▶ **comb. form** (used in units of measurement) denoting a factor of 10^{-21}: *zeptosecond.*
– ORIGIN adapted from **SEPTI-**, on the pattern of combining forms such as *peta-* and *exa-*.

Zer·matt /ˈzərˌmät, (t)serˈmät/ an Alpine ski resort and mountaineering center near the Matterhorn, in southern Switzerland.

ze·ro /ˈzi(ə)rō, ˈzēˌrō/ ▶ **cardinal number** (pl. **zeros**) no quantity or number; naught; the figure 0: *figures from zero to nine | you've left off a zero—it should be five hundred million.* ■ a point on a scale or instrument from which a positive or negative quantity is reckoned: *the gauge dropped to zero* | [as adj.] *a zero rate of interest.* ■ the temperature corresponding to 0° on the Celsius scale (32° Fahrenheit), marking the freezing point of water: *the temperature was below zero.* ■ the temperature corresponding to 0° on the Fahrenheit scale (approximately minus 18° Celsius), considered a very cold temperature, esp. for outdoor activities: *thirty below zero!* See also **SUBZERO**. ■ [usu. as adj.] Linguistics the absence of an actual word or morpheme to realize a syntactic or morphological phenomenon: *the zero plural in "three sheep."* ■ the lowest possible amount or level; nothing at all: *I rated my chances as zero.* ■ short for **ZERO HOUR**. ■ informal a worthless or contemptibly undistinguished person: *her husband is an absolute zero.*
▶ **v.** (**zeroes, zeroing, zeroed**) [with obj.] **1** adjust (an instrument) to zero: *zero the counter when the tape has rewound.*
2 set the sights of (a gun) for firing.
– PHRASAL VERBS **zero in** take aim with a gun or missile: *jet fighters zeroed in on the rebel positions.* ■ focus one's attention: *they zeroed in on the clues he gave away about.* **zero out** phase out or reduce to zero: *the bill would zero out capital gains taxes.*
– ORIGIN early 17th cent.: from French *zéro* or Italian *zero*, via Old Spanish from Arabic *ṣifr* 'cipher.'

ze·ro-based ▶ **adj.** Finance (of a budget or budgeting) having each item costed anew, rather than in relation to its size or status in the previous budget.

ze·ro-cou·pon ▶ **adj.** of or relating to a debt obligation that pays no interest to the holder until it reaches maturity or is sold.

ze·ro-cou·pon bond ▶ **n.** a bond that is issued at a deep discount to its face value but pays no interest.

ze·ro-e·mis·sion ▶ **adj.** denoting a road vehicle that emits no pollutants from its exhaust.

ze·ro G ▶ **abbr.** zero gravity.

ze·ro grav·i·ty ▶ **n.** Physics the state or condition in which there is no apparent force of gravity acting on a body, either because the force is locally weak, or because both the body and its surroundings are freely and equally accelerating under the force.

ze·ro hour ▶ **n.** the time at which a planned operation, typically a military one, is set to begin.

ze·ro op·tion ▶ **n.** a disarmament proposal for the total removal of certain types of weapons on both sides.

ze·ro-point ▶ **adj.** Physics relating to or denoting properties and phenomena in quantized systems at absolute zero.

ze·ro-sum ▶ **adj.** [attrib.] (of a game or situation) in which whatever is gained by one side is lost by the other: *altruism is not a zero-sum game.*

ze·roth /ˈzi(ə)rōTH, ˈzēˌrōTH/ ▶ **adj.** immediately preceding what is regarded as first in a series.
– ORIGIN late 19th cent.: from **ZERO** + **-TH**[1].

ze·ro tol·er·ance ▶ **n.** refusal to accept antisocial behavior, typically by strict and uncompromising application of the law.

zest /zest/ ▶ **n. 1** great enthusiasm and energy: *they campaigned with zest and intelligence* | [in sing.] *she had a great zest for life.* ■ a quality of excitement and piquancy: *I used to try to beat past records to add zest to my monotonous job.*
2 the outer colored part of the peel of citrus fruit, used as flavoring.
– DERIVATIVES **zest·ful** /-fəl/ **adj.**, **zest·ful·ly** /-fəlē/ **adv.**, **zest·ful·ness** /-fəlnəs/ **n.**, **zest·y** **adj.**
– ORIGIN late 15th cent.: from French *zeste* 'orange or lemon peel,' of unknown origin.

zest·er /ˈzestər/ ▶ **n.** a kitchen utensil for removing fine shreds of zest from citrus fruit.

ze·ta /ˈzātə, ˈzē-/ ▶ **n.** the sixth letter of the Greek alphabet (Ζ, ζ), transliterated as 'z.' ■ (**Zeta**) [followed by Latin genitive] Astronomy the sixth star in a constellation: *Zeta Ursae Majoris.*

ze·ta po·ten·tial ▶ **n.** Chemistry the potential difference existing between the surface of a solid particle immersed in a conducting liquid (e.g., water) and the bulk of the liquid.

ze·tet·ic /zəˈtetik/ ▶ **adj.** rare proceeding by inquiry.
– ORIGIN mid 17th cent.: from Greek *zētētikos*, from *zētein* 'seek.'

ze·tet·ics ▶ **n.** [treated as sing.] a historical branch of algebra concerned with the direct search for unknown quantities.

zetta- ▶ **comb. form** (used in units of measurement) denoting a factor of 10^{21}: *zettahertz.*
– ORIGIN apparently adapted from Italian *sette* 'seven' (see also **ZEPTO-**).

zeug·ma /ˈzo͞ogmə/ ▶ **n.** a figure of speech in which a word applies to two others in different senses (e.g., *John and his license expired last week*) or to two others of which it semantically suits only one (e.g., *with weeping eyes and hearts*). Compare with **SYLLEPSIS**.
– DERIVATIVES **zeug·mat·ic** /zo͞ogˈmatik/ **adj.**
– ORIGIN late Middle English: via Latin from Greek, from *zeugnunai* 'to yoke'; related to *zugon* 'yoke.'

Zeus /zo͞os/ Greek Mythology the supreme god, the son of Cronus (whom he dethroned) and Rhea, and brother and husband of Hera. Zeus was the protector and ruler of humankind, the dispenser of good and evil, and the god of atmospheric phenomena. Roman equivalent **JUPITER**.
– ORIGIN Greek: related to the first syllable in Latin *Jupiter* and Sanskrit *dyauḥ* 'sky.'

ZEV ▶ **abbr.** zero-emission vehicle.

Ze·ya Riv·er /ˈzāyə/ a river in eastern Russia that rises in the Stanovoy Range and flows south for 800 miles (1,290 km) into the Amur River at Blagoveshchensk.

Zhang·jia·kou /ˈjängjēˈäˈkō/ (also **Chang-chiakow**) a city in northeastern China, in Hebei province, near the Great Wall; pop. 719,800 (est. 2006). Mongolian name **KALGAN**.

Zhan·jiang /ˈjänjēˈäng/ (also **Chan-chiang**) a port in southern China, in Guangdong province; pop. 1,433,400 (est. 2006).

Zhda·nov /ˈZHdänəf/ former name (1948–89) of **MARIUPOL**.
– ORIGIN named after the Soviet Politburo official Andrei *Zhdanov* (1896–1948), the defender of Leningrad during the siege of 1941–44.

Zhe·jiang /ˈjəjēˈäng/ (also **Chekiang**) a province in eastern China; capital, Hangzhou.

Zheng·zhou /ˈjəngˈjō/ (also **Chengchow**) a city in northeastern central China, the capital of Henan province; pop. 1,883,200 (est. 2006).

Zhen·jiang /ˈjənjēˈäng/ (also **Chen-chiang**, **Chinkiang**) a port in eastern China, in Jiangsu province, on the Yangtze River; pop. 594,300 (est. 2006).

Zhi·to·mir /ZHēˈtômir/ Russian name for **ZHYTOMYR**.

Zhong·shan /jo͝ongˈSHän/ (also **Chung-shan**) a city in southeastern China, in Guangdong province; pop. 721,100 (est. 2006).

Zhou /jō/ (also **Chou**) a dynasty that ruled in China from the 11th century BC to 256 BC.

> The dynasty's rule is commonly divided into **Western Zhou** (which ruled from a capital in the west of the region near Xian until 771 BC) and **Eastern Zhou** (which ruled after 771 BC from a capital based in the east). The rule of the Eastern Zhou saw the Chinese classical age of Confucius and Lao-tzu.

Zhou En·lai /ˈjō ˈenˈlī/ (also **Chou En-lai**) (1898–1976), Chinese communist statesman; prime minister of China 1949–76. A founder of the Chinese Communist Party, he organized a communist workers' revolt in 1927 in Shanghai in support of the Kuomintang forces surrounding the city. As premier, he was a moderating influence during the Cultural Revolution and presided over the moves toward détente with the US in 1972–73.

Zhu·kov /ˈZHo͞oˌkôf, -ˌkôv, -kəf/, Georgi (Konstantinovich) (1896–1974), Soviet military leader, born in Russia. During World War II, he defeated the Germans at Stalingrad in 1943, lifted the siege of Leningrad in 1944, and led the final assault on Germany and the capture of Berlin in 1945.

Zhy·to·myr /ZHiˈtômir/ an industrial city in central Ukraine; pop. 271,900 (est. 2009). Russian name **ZHITOMIR**.

Z·ia ul-Haq /ˈzēə o͞olˈhäk/, Muhammad (1924–88), Pakistani general and statesman; president 1978–88. As chief of staff, he led the coup that deposed President Zulfikar Bhutto in 1977. He banned all political parties and introduced strict Islamic laws.

zib·e·line /ˈzibəˌlīn, -ˌlēn, -lin/ ▶ **n. 1** a thick soft fabric made of wool and other animal hair, such as mohair, with a flattened silky nap.
2 the fur of the sable.
▶ **adj.** of or relating to the sable.
– ORIGIN French 'sable,' from Italian *zibellino*, probably from a Slavic word; compare with **SABLE**[1].

Zi·bo /ˈ(d)zəˈbō/ (also **Tzu-po**) a city in eastern China, in Shandong province; pop. 1,426,600 (est. 2006).

zi·do·vu·dine /zīˈdävyəˌdēn, zə-, -ˈdō-/ ▶ **n.** Medicine an antiviral drug used in the treatment of AIDS. It slows the growth of HIV infection in the body, but is not curative. ● A thymidine derivative; chem. formula: $C_{10}H_{13}N_5O_4$.
– ORIGIN 1980s: arbitrary alteration of **AZIDOTHYMIDINE**.

Zieg·feld /ˈzēgˌfeld, -ˌfēld/, Florenz (1869–1932), US theater manager. In 1907, he produced the first of the *Ziegfeld Follies*, a series of revues in New York City that were based on those of the Folies-Bergère in Paris.

ZIF sock·et /zif/ ▶ **n.** a type of socket for mounting electronic devices that is designed not to stress or damage them during insertion.
– ORIGIN late 20th cent.: *ZIF*, acronym from *zero insertion force*.

zig /zig/ ▶ **n.** a sharp change of direction in a zigzag course: *he went round and round in zigs and zags.*
▶ **v.** (**zigs, zigging, zigged**) [no obj.] make a sharp change of direction: *we zigged to the right.*
– ORIGIN 1960s: shortening of **ZIGZAG**.

zig·gu·rat /ˈzigəˌrat/ ▶ **n.** (in ancient Mesopotamia) a rectangular stepped tower, sometimes surmounted by a temple. Ziggurats are first attested in the late 3rd millennium BC and probably inspired the biblical story of the Tower of Babel (Gen. 11:1–9).
– ORIGIN from Akkadian *ziqqurratu*.

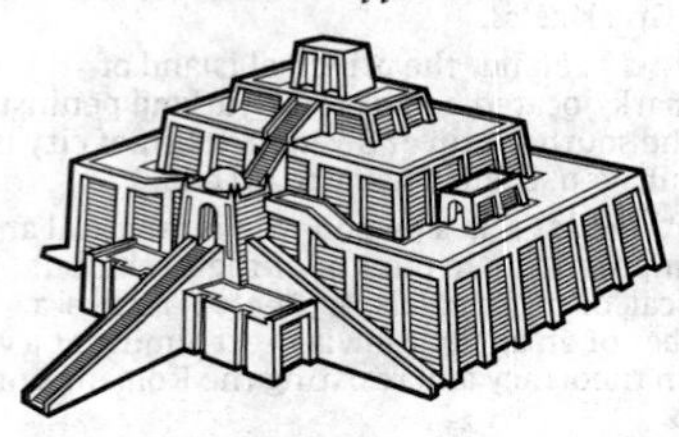

ziggurat

zig·zag /ˈzigˌzag/ ▶ **n.** a line or course having abrupt alternate right and left turns: *she traced a zigzag on the metal with her finger.* ■ a turn on such a course: *the road descends in a series of sharp zigzags.*
▶ **adj.** having the form of a zigzag; veering to right and left alternately: *when chased by a predator, some animals take a zigzag course.*
▶ **adv.** so as to move right and left alternately: *she drives zigzag across the city.*
▶ **v.** (**zigzags, zigzagging, zigzagged**) [no obj.] have or move along in a zigzag course: *the path zigzagged between dry rises in the land.*
– DERIVATIVES **zig·zag·ged·ly** /-ˌzagədlē/ **adv.**
– ORIGIN early 18th cent.: from French, from German *Zickzack*, symbolic of alternation of direction, first applied to fortifications.

zi·kr /ˈzēkər/ variant spelling of **DHIKR**.

zilch /zilCH/ informal ▶ **pron.** nothing: *I did absolutely zilch.*
▶ **determiner** not any; no: *the character has zilch class.*
– ORIGIN 1960s: of unknown origin.

zil·lion /ˈzilyən/ ▶ **cardinal number** informal an extremely large number of people or things: *we had zillions of customers.*
– DERIVATIVES **zil·lionth** /-yənTH/ **adj.**
– ORIGIN 1940s: from *Z* (perhaps as a symbol of an unknown quantity) + **MILLION**.

zil·lion·aire /ˌzilyəˈne(ə)r/ ▶ **n.** informal an extremely rich person.

Zim·bab·we /zimˈbäbwā, -wē/ a landlocked country in southeastern Africa, separated from Zambia by the Zambezi River; pop. 11,392,600 (est. 2009); capital, Harare; languages, English (official), Shona, Ndebele, and others.

Formerly known as Southern Rhodesia, Zimbabwe was a self-governing British colony from 1923. In 1965, the white minority government of the colony (then called Rhodesia) issued a unilateral declaration of independence (UDI) under its prime minister, Ian Smith. Despite UN sanctions, illegal independence lasted until 1979, when the Lancaster House Agreement led to all-party elections in 1980 and black majority rule under Robert Mugabe. The country then became an independent republic and a member of the Commonwealth of Nations. In 2002, Mugabe was returned to power in a presidential election widely regarded as undemocratic: as a result Zimbabwe was suspended from the Commonwealth for twelve months, and then chose to withdraw.

– DERIVATIVES **Zim·bab·we·an** /-wāən, -wēən/ **adj. & n.**

– ORIGIN from Shona *dzimbabwe* 'walled grave,' originally referring to *Great Zimbabwe*, a complex of stone ruins in one of the country's fertile valleys, the remains of a city at the center of a flourishing civilization in the 14th and 15th centuries.

Zim·bab·we Af·ri·can Na·tion·al Un·ion (abbr.: **ZANU** or **ZANU–PF**) a Zimbabwean political party formed in 1963 as a guerrilla organization and led from 1975 by Robert Mugabe.

The Patriotic Front, an alliance of ZANU and ZAPU formed in 1976 to coordinate opposition to white rule, ruled Zimbabwe as a coalition until a rift developed in 1982. In 1987, the parties agreed formally to merge, adopting the name ZANU–PF in 1989.

Zim·bab·we Af·ri·can Peo·ple's Un·ion (abbr.: **ZAPU**) a Zimbabwean political party formed in 1961 as a guerrilla organization. It merged with ZANU in 1987.

Zim·mer·man /'zimərmən/ see **DYLAN, MERMAN.**

zinc /ziNGk/ ▶ **n.** the chemical element of atomic number 30, a silvery-white metal that is a constituent of brass and is used for coating (galvanizing) iron and steel to protect against corrosion. (Symbol: **Zn**) ■ [usu. as modifier] galvanized iron or steel, esp. as the material of domestic utensils or corrugated roofs: *a zinc roof.*
▶ **v.** [with obj.] (usu. as adj. **zinced**) coat (iron) with zinc or a zinc compound to prevent rust.
– ORIGIN mid 17th cent.: from German *Zink*, of unknown origin.

zinc blende ▶ **n.** another term for **SPHALERITE.**

zinc fin·ger ▶ **n.** Biochemistry a fingerlike loop of peptides enclosing a bound zinc ion at one end, typically part of a larger protein molecule (in particular one regulating transcription).

zinc·ite /'ziNG,kīt/ ▶ **n.** a rare deep red or orange-yellow mineral consisting chiefly of zinc oxide, occurring typically as granular or foliated masses.
– ORIGIN mid 19th cent.: from **ZINC** + **-ITE**[1].

zin·co /'ziNGkō/ ▶ **n.** (pl. **zincos**) an etched letterpress printing plate made of zinc.

zinc oint·ment (in full **zinc oxide ointment**) ▶ **n.** ointment containing zinc oxide, used for various skin conditions.

zinc ox·ide ▶ **n.** an insoluble white solid used as a pigment and in medicinal ointments. ● Chem. formula: ZnO.

zinc white ▶ **n.** a white pigment consisting of zinc oxide.

zine /zēn/ (also **'zine**) ▶ **n.** informal a magazine, esp. a fanzine. ■ a webzine.

zin·eb /'zin,eb/ ▶ **n.** a white compound used as a fungicidal powder on vegetables and fruit. ● Alternative name: **zinc ethylene bisdithiocarbamate**; chem. formula: $C_4H_6N_2S_4Zn$.
– ORIGIN 1950s: from *zin(c)* + *e(thylene)* + *b(is-)* from the systematic name.

Zin·fan·del /'zinfən,del/ ▶ **n.** a variety of wine grape grown in California. ■ a red or blush dry wine made from this grape.
– ORIGIN of unknown origin.

zing /ziNG/ informal ▶ **n.** energy, enthusiasm, or liveliness: *he was expected to add some zing to the lackluster team.*
▶ **v.** [no obj.] move swiftly: *he could send an arrow zinging through the air.* ■ [with obj.] attack or criticize sharply: *he zinged the budget deal in interviews with journalists.*
– DERIVATIVES **zing·y** **adj.**
– ORIGIN early 20th cent.: imitative.

zing·er /'ziNGər/ ▶ **n.** informal a striking or amusing remark: *open a speech with a zinger.* ■ an outstanding person or thing: *a zinger of a shot.*

Zin·jan·thro·pus /,zin'janTHrəpəs, ,zinjan'THrō-/ ▶ **n.** a genus name sometimes applied to **AUSTRALOPITHECUS.**
– ORIGIN 1950s: modern Latin, from Arabic *Zinj*, the early medieval name for East Africa, + Greek *anthrōpos* 'man.'

Zinne·mann /'zinəmən/, Fred (1907–97), US movie director, born in Austria. Notable works include the short *That Mothers Might Live* (1938) and the feature films *From Here to Eternity* (1953) and *A Man For All Seasons* (1966).

zin·ni·a /'zinēə/ ▶ **n.** an American plant of the daisy family that is widely cultivated for its bright showy flowers. ● Numerous species and cultivars of the genus *Zinnia*, family Compositae.
– ORIGIN modern Latin, named after Johann G. *Zinn* (1727–59), German physician and botanist.

Zi·on /'zīən/ (also **Sion**) ▶ **n. 1** the hill of Jerusalem on which the city of David was built. ■ the citadel of ancient Jerusalem. ■ Jerusalem. ■ (in Christian thought) the heavenly city or kingdom of heaven. ■ the Jewish people or religion. ■ the Christian Church.
2 (among Rastafarians) Africa.
– ORIGIN Old English, from ecclesiastical Latin *Sion*, from Hebrew *ṣīyōn*.

Zi·on·ism /'zīə,nizəm/ ▶ **n.** a movement for (originally) the re-establishment and (now) the development and protection of a Jewish nation in what is now Israel. It was established as a political organization in 1897 under Theodor Herzl, and was later led by Chaim Weizmann.
– DERIVATIVES **Zi·on·ist** **n. & adj.**

zip /zip/ ▶ **v.** (**zips, zipping, zipped**) **1** [with obj.] fasten with a zipper: *I zipped up my sweater.* ■ (**zip someone up**) fasten the zipper of a garment that someone is wearing: *he zipped himself up.* ■ Computing compress (a file) so that it takes less space in storage.
2 [no obj.] informal move at high speed: *swallows zipped back and forth across the lake.* ■ [with obj.] cause to move or be delivered or dealt with rapidly: *he zipped a pass out to his receiver.*
▶ **n. 1** (also **zip fastener**) chiefly Brit. a zipper. ■ [as modifier] denoting something fastened by a zipper: *a zip pocket.*
2 informal energy; vigor: *he's full of zip.*
3 short for **ZIP CODE.**
▶ **pron.** (also **zippo**) informal nothing at all: *you got zip to do with me and my kind, buddy.*
– ORIGIN mid 19th cent.: imitative.

zip code (also **ZIP code**) ▶ **n.** a group of five or nine numbers that are added to a postal address to assist the sorting of mail.
– ORIGIN 1960s: *zip*, acronym from *zone improvement plan.*

zip·cuff /'zip,kəf/ ▶ **n.** a plastic strip with a loop on one end that is secured with notches on the other end, used as a temporary handcuff.
▶ **v.** [with obj.] restrain (someone) with zipcuffs: *one cop called someone on the phone while the other one zipcuffed me.*

zip file (also **ZIP file, zipped file**) ▶ **n.** a computer file whose contents of one or more files are compressed for storage or transmission, often carrying the extension .ZIP: *a self-extracting zip file.*

zip gun ▶ **n.** informal a cheap homemade or makeshift gun: *I made the zip gun in class out of a toy airplane launcher.*

zip·less /'ziplis/ ▶ **adj.** informal (of a sexual encounter) brief, uncomplicated, and passionate.
– ORIGIN 1970s: from the phrase *Zipless Fuck*, in Erica Jong's *Fear of Flying.*

zip line ▶ **n.** an inclined cable or rope with a suspended harness, pulley, or handle, down which a person slides for amusement.

zip·lock /'zip,läk/ (also trademark **Ziploc**) ▶ **adj.** denoting a sealable plastic bag with a two-part strip along the opening that can be pressed together and readily reopened.

zip·per /'zipər/ ▶ **n. 1** a device consisting of two flexible strips of metal or plastic with interlocking projections closed or opened by pulling a slide along them, used to fasten garments, bags, and other items.
2 a display of news or advertisements that scrolls across an illuminated screen fixed to the upper part of a building.
▶ **v.** [with obj.] fasten or provide (something) with a zipper: *he wore a running suit zippered up tight.*

zip·per·head /'zipər,hed/ ▶ **n.** offensive an Asian person.

Zip·po /'zipō/ ▶ **n.** (pl. **Zippos**) trademark a type of cigarette lighter with a hinged lid, using lighter fluid as fuel.
– ORIGIN 1930s: of unknown origin.

zip·po /'zipō/ ▶ **pron.** another term for **ZIP.**

zip·py /'zipē/ ▶ **adj.** (**zippier, zippiest**) informal bright, fresh, or lively: *a zippy, zingy, almost citrusy tang.* ■ fast or speedy: *zippy new sedans.*
– DERIVATIVES **zip·pi·ly** /'zipəlē/ **adv.**, **zip·pi·ness** **n.**

zip-up ▶ **adj.** [attrib.] chiefly Brit. (of a garment, pocket, bag, etc.) able to be fastened with a zipper: *a white zip-up jacket.*

zir·ca·loy /'zərkə,loi/ ▶ **n.** an alloy of zirconium, tin, and other metals, used chiefly as cladding for nuclear reactor fuel.
– ORIGIN 1950s: from **ZIRCONIUM** + **ALLOY.**

zir·con /'zər,kän/ ▶ **n.** a mineral occurring as prismatic crystals, typically brown but sometimes in translucent varieties of gem quality. It consists of zirconium silicate and is the chief ore of zirconium.
– ORIGIN late 18th cent.: from German *Zirkon*; compare with **JARGON**[2].

zir·co·ni·a /,zər'kōnēə/ ▶ **n.** zirconium dioxide, a white solid used in ceramic glazes and refractory coatings and as a synthetic substitute for diamonds in jewelry. See also **CUBIC ZIRCONIA.** ● Chem. formula: ZrO_2.
– ORIGIN late 18th cent.: from **ZIRCON** + **-IA**[1].

zir·co·ni·um /,zər'kōnēəm/ ▶ **n.** the chemical element of atomic number 40, a hard silver-gray metal of the transition series. (Symbol: **Zr**)
– ORIGIN early 19th cent.: modern Latin, from **ZIRCON.**

zit /zit/ ▶ **n.** informal a pimple on the skin.
– ORIGIN 1960s: of unknown origin; apparently originally American teenagers' slang.

zith·er /'ziTHər, 'ziTH-/ ▶ **n.** a musical instrument consisting of a flat wooden sound box with numerous strings stretched across it, placed horizontally and played with the fingers and a plectrum. It is used esp. in central European folk music.
– DERIVATIVES **zith·er·ist** /-ərist/ **n.**
– ORIGIN mid 19th cent.: from German, from Latin *cithara* (see **CITTERN**).

zither

zi·ti /'zētē/ ▶ **n.** pasta in the form of tubes resembling large macaroni.
– ORIGIN Italian.

zizz /ziz/ informal ▶ **n.** [in sing.] **1** a whizzing or buzzing sound: *there's a nasty zizz from the engine.*
2 chiefly Brit. a short sleep: *Philip's having a zizz.*
▶ **v.** [no obj.] **1** make a whizzing or buzzing sound: *the crane whirred and zizzed.*
2 chiefly Brit. doze; sleep: *when everyone inside the building had zizzed off he sneaked inside.*
– ORIGIN early 19th cent.: imitative.

zlo·ty /'zlôtē, 'zlä-/ ▶ **n.** (pl. **same** or **zlotys**) the basic monetary unit of Poland, equal to 100 groszy.
– ORIGIN Polish, literally 'golden.'

Zn ▶ **symbol** the chemical element zinc.

zo- ▶ **comb. form** variant spelling of zoo-, shortened before a vowel (as in *Zoantharia*).

Zo·an·thar·ia /,zōən'THe(ə)rēə/ Zoology a group of coelenterates with polyps that bear more than eight tentacles, including the sea anemones and stony corals. ● Subclass Zoantharia, class Anthozoa.
– DERIVATIVES **zo·an·thar·i·an** **n. & adj.**
– ORIGIN modern Latin (plural), from Greek *zōion* 'animal' + *anthos* 'flower.'

zo·ca·lo /'sōkə,lō, sô'kä,lō/ ▶ **n.** (in Mexico) a public square or plaza.
– ORIGIN Spanish.

zo·di·ac /'zōdē,ak/ ▶ **n.** Astrology **1** a belt of the heavens within about 8° either side of the ecliptic, including all apparent positions of the sun, moon, and most familiar planets. It is divided into twelve equal divisions or signs (Aries, Taurus, Gemini, Cancer, Leo, Virgo, Libra, Scorpio, Sagittarius, Capricorn, Aquarius, Pisces). ■ a representation of the signs of the zodiac or of a similar astrological system.

The supposed significance of the movements of the sun, moon, and planets within the zodiacal band forms the basis of astrology. However, the modern constellations do not represent equal divisions of the zodiac, and the ecliptic now passes through a thirteenth (Ophiuchus). Also, owing to precession, the signs of the zodiac now roughly correspond to the constellations that bear the names of the *preceding* signs.

2 (**Zodiac**) trademark a small inflatable boat powered by an outboard motor.
– DERIVATIVES **zo·di·a·cal** /zō'dīəkəl/ **adj.**
– ORIGIN late Middle English: from Old French *zodiaque*, via Latin from Greek *zōidiakos*, from *zōidion* 'sculptured animal figure,' diminutive of *zōion* 'animal.'

zo·di·a·cal light ▶ **n.** Astronomy a faint elongated cone of light sometimes seen in the night sky, extending from the horizon along the ecliptic. It is thought to be due to the reflection of sunlight from particles of ice and dust within the plane of the solar system.

zo·di·a·cal sign ▶ **n.** see SIGN (sense 3 of the noun).

zo·e·a /zō'ēə/ ▶ **n.** (pl. **zoeae** /zō'ē,ē/ or **zoeas**) a larval form of certain crustaceans, such as the crab, having a spiny carapace and rudimentary limbs on the abdomen and thorax.
– ORIGIN early 19th cent.: modern Latin, from Greek *zōē* 'life.'

zo·e·trope /'zō-ē,trōp/ ▶ **n.** a 19th-century optical toy consisting of a cylinder with a series of pictures on the inner surface that, when viewed through slits with the cylinder rotating, give an impression of continuous motion.
– ORIGIN mid 19th cent.: formed irregularly from Greek *zōē* 'life' + *-tropos* 'turning.'

zof·tig ▶ **adj.** variant spelling of ZAFTIG.

Zog I /zôg/ (1895–1961), Albanian statesman and ruler; prime minister 1922–24; president 1925–28; king 1928–39; full name *Ahmed Bey Zogu*. His autocratic rule resulted in relative political stability; he went into exile when the country was invaded by Italy in 1939.

Zo·har /'zō,här/ ▶ **n.** the chief text of the Jewish Kabbalah, presented as an allegorical or mystical interpretation of the Pentateuch.
– ORIGIN from Hebrew *zōhar*, literally 'light, splendor.'

-zo·ic ▶ **suffix 1** forming adjectives relating to a particular manner of animal existence (such as *cryptozoic*).
2 of or relating to a particular geologic era (such as *Paleozoic*).

zois·ite /'zoi,sīt/ ▶ **n.** a grayish-white or grayish-green crystalline mineral of the epidote group consisting of a hydroxyl silicate of calcium and aluminum.
– ORIGIN early 19th cent.: from the name of Baron S. von Edelstein *Zois* (1747–1819), Austrian scholar, + -ITE[1].

Zo·la /,zō'lä, 'zō,lä/, Émile (Édouard Charles Antoine) (1840–1902), French novelist and critic. His series of 20 novels collectively entitled *Les Rougon-Macquart* (1871–93), including *Nana* (1880), *Germinal* (1885), and *La Terre* (1887), shows how human behavior is determined by environment and heredity.

Zol·ling·er–El·li·son syn·drome /'zäliNGər 'eləsən, 'zälənjər/ ▶ **n.** Medicine a condition in which a gastrin-secreting tumor or hyperplasia of the islet cells in the pancreas causes overproduction of gastric acid, resulting in recurrent peptic ulcers.
– ORIGIN 1950s: named after Robert M. *Zollinger* (1903–92) and Edwin H. *Ellison* (1918–70), American physicians.

Zöll·ner il·lu·sion /'tsəlnər, 'zôl-/ ▶ **n.** an optical illusion in which long parallel lines appear to diverge or converge when crossed by rows of short oblique lines.
– ORIGIN late 19th cent.: named after Johann K. F. *Zöllner* (1834–82), German physicist.

Zoll·ver·ein /'tsôlfə,rīn, 'zôl-/ ▶ **n.** historical the customs union of German states in the 19th century.
– ORIGIN from German *Zoll* 'customs' + *Verein* 'union.'

zom·bie /'zämbē/ ▶ **n. 1** a corpse said to be revived by witchcraft, esp. in certain African and Caribbean religions. ■ informal a person who is or appears lifeless, apathetic, or completely unresponsive to their surroundings. ■ a computer controlled by another person without the owner's knowledge and used for sending spam or other illegal or illicit activities.
2 a tall mixed drink consisting of several kinds of rum, liqueur, and fruit juice.
– DERIVATIVES **zom·bie·like** /-,līk/ **adj.**
– ORIGIN early 19th cent.: of West African origin; compare with Kikongo *zumbi* 'fetish.'

WORD TRENDS Zombies are everywhere—on movie screens, in books, and even invading our computers and banks. The Oxford English Corpus shows steadily increasing outbreaks of the undead over the last decade. **Zombies** have been a mainstay of horror films and popular culture since *The Night of the Living Dead* in 1968, but in the last few years some new forms of **zombie** have escaped from fiction into reality. First, there were the computers taken over by hackers and used to perform malicious tasks: *a virus used to turn PCs into spam zombies.* Then came **zombie banks**, insolvent institutions kept functioning only by government support. This use exploded in the wake of the financial crisis of 2007–09, with twenty times more examples in Corpus data for 2009 than for 2008.

zom·bie bank ▶ **n.** informal a financial institution that is insolvent but that continues to operate through government support.

zom·bi·fy /'zämbə,fī/ ▶ **v.** [with obj.] (usu. as adj. **zombified**) informal deprive of energy or vitality: *exhausted, screaming kids and their zombified parents.*

zo·na pel·lu·ci·da /'zōnə pə'lōōsədə/ ▶ **n.** (pl. **zonae pellucidae** /'zō,nē pə'lōōsə,dē, 'zō,nī pə'lōōsə,dī/) Anatomy & Zoology the thick transparent membrane surrounding a mammalian ovum before implantation.
– ORIGIN mid 19th cent.: from Latin, literally 'pellucid girdle.'

zo·na·tion /zō'nāSHən/ ▶ **n.** distribution in zones or regions of definite character: *quartz grains can exhibit zonation and rounding.* ■ Ecology the distribution of plants or animals into specific zones according to such parameters as altitude or depth, each characterized by its dominant species.

zone /zōn/ ▶ **n. 1** [usu. with modifier] an area or stretch of land having a particular characteristic, purpose, or use, or subject to particular restrictions: *a pedestrian zone | the government has declared the city a disaster zone | a no-smoking zone.* ■ Geography a well-defined region extending around the earth between definite limits, esp. between two parallels of latitude: *a zone of easterly winds.* See also FRIGID ZONE, TEMPERATE ZONE, TORRID ZONE. ■ (also **time zone**) a range of longitudes where a common standard time is used. ■ Sports in basketball, football, and hockey, a specific area of the court, field, or rink, esp. one to be defended by a particular player. ■ chiefly Botany & Zoology an encircling band or stripe of distinctive color, texture, or character.
2 archaic a belt or girdle worn around a person's body.
▶ **v.** [with obj.] **1** divide into or assign to zones, in particular: ■ (often as noun **zoning**) divide (a town or stretch of land) into areas subject to particular planning restrictions: *an experimental system of zoning.* ■ designate (a specific area) for use or development in such a manner: *the land is zoned for housing.*
2 archaic encircle as or with a band or stripe.
– PHRASAL VERBS **zone out** informal fall asleep or lose concentration or consciousness: *I just zoned out for a moment.*
– DERIVATIVES **zon·al** /'zōnl/ **adj.**, **zon·al·ly** /'zōnl-ē/ **adv.**
– ORIGIN late Middle English: from French, or from Latin *zona* 'girdle,' from Greek *zōnē*.

zoned /zōnd/ ▶ **adj. 1** divided into zones, in particular (of land) designated for a particular type of use or development: *zoned industrial land.*
2 chiefly Botany & Zoology marked with circles or bands of color: *strongly zoned leaves.*
3 informal under the influence of drugs or alcohol: *she's zoned on downers | a zoned-out hippie.* [1970s: blend of ZONKED and STONED.]

zone defense ▶ **n.** (in basketball, football, and hockey) a system of defensive play in which each player guards an allotted area of the field of play and guards an opponent only when the opponent is in his area.

zone plate ▶ **n.** a plate of glass marked out into concentric zones or rings alternately transparent and opaque, used like a lens to bring light to a focus.

zone re·fin·ing ▶ **n.** a method of purifying a crystalline solid, typically a semiconductor or metal, by causing a narrow molten zone to travel slowly along an otherwise solid rod or bar to one end, at which impurities become concentrated.

zonk /zäNGk, zôNGk/ informal ▶ **v. 1** [with obj.] hit or strike: *Charley really zonked me.*
2 fall or cause to fall suddenly and heavily asleep or lose consciousness: [no obj.] *I always just zonk out and sleep straight through* | [with obj.] *I go rowing because it zonks me out.*
– ORIGIN 1940s: imitative.

zonked /zäNGkt, zôNGkt/ ▶ **adj.** informal under the influence of drugs or alcohol: *the others got zonked on acid | a zonked-out beach bum.* ■ exhausted; tired out: *we hit the sack, zonked out.*

zon·ule /'zōn,yōōl/ ▶ **n.** technical, chiefly Anatomy a small zone, band, or belt.

zoo /zōō/ ▶ **n.** an establishment that maintains a collection of wild animals, typically in a park or gardens, for study, conservation, or display to the public. ■ informal a situation characterized by confusion and disorder: *it's a zoo in the lobby.*
– ORIGIN mid 19th cent.: abbreviation of ZOOLOGICAL GARDEN, originally applied specifically to that of Regent's Park, London.

zoo- ▶ **comb. form** of animals; relating to animal life: *zoogeography.*
– ORIGIN from Greek *zōion* 'animal.'

zo·o·gen·ic /,zōə'jenik/ ▶ **adj. 1** produced by or originating in animals.
2 related or relating to animal development or evolution.

zoo·ge·o·graph·i·cal re·gion /,zōə,jēə'grafikəl/ ▶ **n.** Zoology each of a number of major areas of the earth having characteristic fauna (esp. mammals). They include the Palearctic, Ethiopian, Oriental, Australian, Nearctic, and Neotropical regions. Also called FAUNAL REGION.

zoo·ge·og·ra·phy /,zōəjē'ägrəfē/ ▶ **n.** the branch of zoology that deals with the geographical distribution of animals.
– DERIVATIVES **zo·o·ge·og·ra·pher** /-fər/ **n.**, **zo·o·ge·o·graph·ic** /-jēə'grafik/ **adj.**, **zo·o·ge·o·graph·i·cal** /-jēə'grafikəl/ **adj.**, **zo·o·ge·o·graph·i·cal·ly** /-jēə'grafik(ə)lē/ **adv.**

zo·oid /'zō,oid/ ▶ **n.** Zoology an animal arising from another by budding or division, esp. each of the individuals that make up a colonial organism and typically have different forms and functions.
– DERIVATIVES **zo·oi·dal** /,zō'oidl/ **adj.**
– ORIGIN mid 19th cent.: from ZOO- 'relating to animals' + -OID.

zoo·keep·er /'zōō,kēpər/ ▶ **n.** an animal attendant employed in a zoo.

zool. ▶ **abbr.** zoological. ■ zoologist. ■ zoology.

zo·ol·a·try /zō'älətrē, zōō-/ ▶ **n.** rare the worship of animals.

zo·o·log·i·cal /,zōə'läjikəl, ,zōōə-/ ▶ **adj.** of or relating to zoology: *zoological classification.* ■ of or relating to animals: *eighty zoological woodcuts.*
– DERIVATIVES **zo·o·log·i·cal·ly** /-ik(ə)lē/ **adv.**

zo·o·log·i·cal gar·den ▶ **n.** formal a zoo.

zo·ol·o·gy /zō'äləjē, zōō-/ ▶ **n.** the scientific study of the behavior, structure, physiology, classification, and distribution of animals. ■ the animal life of a particular area or time: *the zoology of Russia's vast interior.*
– DERIVATIVES **zo·ol·o·gist** /-jist/ **n.**
– ORIGIN mid 17th cent.: from modern Latin *zoologia* (see ZOO-, -LOGY).

zoom /zōōm/ ▶ **v.** [no obj.] **1** (esp. of a car or aircraft) move or travel very quickly: *we watched the fly zooming about | he jumped into his car and zoomed off.* ■ (of prices) rise sharply: *the share index zoomed by about 136 points.*
2 (of a camera) change smoothly from a long shot to a close-up or vice versa: *the camera zoomed in for a close-up of his face | zoom out for a wide view of the garden again.* ■ [with obj.] cause (a lens or camera) to do this.
▶ **n.** a camera shot that changes smoothly from a long shot to a close-up or vice versa: [as modifier] *the zoom button.* ■ short for ZOOM LENS.
▶ **exclam.** used to express sudden fast movement: *then suddenly, zoom!, he's off.*
– ORIGIN late 19th cent.: imitative.

zoom lens ▶ **n.** a lens allowing a camera to change smoothly from a long shot to a close-up or vice versa by varying the focal length.

zo·o·mor·phic /,zōə'môrfik/ ▶ **adj.** having or representing animal forms or gods of animal form: *pottery decorated with anthropomorphic and zoomorphic designs.*
– DERIVATIVES **zo·o·mor·phism** /-'môr,fizəm/ **n.**
– ORIGIN late 19th cent.: from ZOO- 'of animals' + Greek *morphē* 'form' + -IC.

zo·on·o·sis /zōə'nōsəs, zō'änə-/ ▶ **n.** (pl. **zoonoses** /-,sēz/) a disease that can be transmitted to humans from animals.
– DERIVATIVES **zo·o·not·ic** /,zōə'nätik/ **adj.**
– ORIGIN late 19th cent.: from ZOO- 'of animals' + Greek *nosos* 'disease.'

zo·o·phile /'zōə,fīl/ ▶ **n.** a person who is sexually attracted to animals.
– DERIVATIVES **zo·o·phil·i·a** /,zōə'filēə/ **n.**, **zo·o·phil·ic** **adj.**
– ORIGIN late 19th cent. (originally in the botanical sense 'a plant pollinated by animals'): from *zoo* +

-phile. The current senses date from the early 20th cent.

zo·o·phyte /ˈzōəˌfīt/ ▶ **n.** Zoology, dated a plantlike animal, esp. a coral, sea anemone, sponge, or sea lily.
– ORIGIN early 17th cent.: from Greek *zōiophuton* (see **ZOO-**, **-PHYTE**).

zo·o·plank·ton /ˈzōəˌplaNGktən/ ▶ **n.** Biology plankton consisting of small animals and the immature stages of larger animals.

zo·o·spore /ˈzōəˌspôr/ ▶ **n.** Biology a spore of certain algae, fungi, and protozoans, capable of swimming by means of a flagellum. Also called **SWARMER**.

zoot suit /zo͞ot/ ▶ **n.** a man's suit of an exaggerated style, characterized by a long loose jacket with padded shoulders and high-waisted tapering trousers, popular in the 1940s.
– ORIGIN 1940s: rhyming formation on **SUIT**.

zo·o·xan·thel·la /ˌzōəzanˈTHelə/ ▶ **n.** (pl. **zooxanthellae** /-ˈTHelē/) Biology a yellowish-brown symbiotic dinoflagellate present in large numbers in the cytoplasm of many marine invertebrates.
– DERIVATIVES **zo·o·xan·thel·late** /-ˈTHelˌāt/ **adj.**
– ORIGIN late 19th cent.: modern Latin, from **zoo-** 'of animals' + Greek *xanthos* 'yellow' + the diminutive suffix *-ella*.

zorb·ing /ˈzôrbiNG/ ▶ **n.** a sport in which a participant is secured inside an inner capsule in a large, transparent ball that is then rolled along the ground or down hills.
– ORIGIN 1990s: from *zorb*, the invented name for the ball, + *-ing*.

zo·ri /ˈzôrē/ ▶ **n.** (pl. **zoris**) a traditional Japanese style of sandal, much like a flip-flop, originally made with a straw sole.
– ORIGIN Japanese.

zo·ril·la /zəˈrilə/ (also **zoril** or **zorille** /ˈzôril, ˈzär-/) ▶ **n.** a black and white carnivorous mammal that resembles a skunk, inhabiting arid regions of southern Africa. Also called **STRIPED POLECAT**. ● *Ictonyx striatus*, family Mustelidae.
– ORIGIN late 18th cent.: via French from Spanish *zorrilla*, diminutive of *zorro* 'fox.'

Zo·ro·as·ter /ˈzôrōˌastər/ (*c.*628–*c.*551 BC), Persian prophet and founder of Zoroastrianism; Avestan name *Zarathustra*. Traditionally, he was born in Persia and began to preach the tenets of what was later called Zoroastrianism after receiving a vision from Ahura Mazda.

Zo·ro·as·tri·an·ism /ˌzôrōˈastrēəˌnizəm/ ▶ **n.** a monotheistic pre-Islamic religion of ancient Persia founded by Zoroaster in the 6th century BC.

> According to the teachings of Zoroaster, the supreme god, named Ahura Mazda, created twin spirits, one of which chose truth and light, the other untruth and darkness. Later writings present a more dualistic cosmology in which the struggle is between Ahura Mazda (Ormazd) and the evil spirit Ahriman. The scriptures of Zoroastrianism are the Zend-Avesta. The language survives in isolated areas of Iran and in India, where its followers are known as Parsees.

– DERIVATIVES **Zo·ro·as·tri·an adj. & n.**

zos·ter /ˈzästər/ ▶ **n. 1** short for **HERPES ZOSTER**.
2 (in ancient Greece) a belt or girdle.

Zou·ave /zo͞oˈäv, zwäv/ ▶ **n. 1** a member of a light-infantry corps in the French army, originally formed of Algerians and long retaining their oriental uniform. ■ a member of such an infantry unit patterned on the French Zouaves, esp. in the Union Army in the Civil War.
2 (**zouaves**) dated women's trousers with wide tops, tapering to a narrow ankle.
– ORIGIN mid 19th cent.: from French, from Kabyle *Zouaoua*, the name of a tribe.

Zoug /zo͞og/ French name for **ZUG**.

zouk /zo͞ok/ ▶ **n.** an exuberant style of popular music combining Caribbean and Western elements and having a fast heavy beat.
– ORIGIN 1970s: Guadeloupian Creole, literally 'to party.'

zounds /zoundz/ ▶ **exclam.** archaic or humorous expressing surprise or indignation.
– ORIGIN late 16th cent.: contraction from *(God)'s wounds* (i.e., those of Jesus Christ on the Cross).

Zo·vi·rax /zōˈvīˌraks/ ▶ **n.** trademark for **ACYCLOVIR**.

zow·ie /ˈzou-ē, zouˈē/ ▶ **exclam.** informal expressing astonishment or admiration.
– ORIGIN natural exclamation: first recorded in American English in the early 20th cent.

zoy·si·a /ˈzoisēə/ ▶ **n.** a low-growing grass of the genus *Zoysia*, native to tropical Asia and New Zealand and widely used for lawns. ● Family Gramineae: several species and cultivars, including *Z. matrella* and *Z. japonica*.
– ORIGIN 1960s: modern Latin, from the name of the Austrian botanist Carl von Zoys zu Laubach + **-IA**¹.

Z par·ti·cle ▶ **n.** Physics a heavy, uncharged elementary particle considered to transmit the weak interaction between other elementary particles.

ZPG ▶ **abbr.** zero population growth.

Z-plas·ty /ˈzē ˌplastē/ ▶ **n.** a technique in orthopedic and cosmetic surgery in which one or more Z-shaped incisions are made, the diagonals forming one straight line, and the two triangular sections so formed are drawn across the diagonal before being stitched.

Zr ▶ **symbol** the chemical element zirconium.

Zsig·mon·dy /ˈZHigˌmôndē/, Richard Adolph (1865–1929), German chemist, born in Austria. He investigated the properties of various colloidal solutions and invented the ultramicroscope for counting colloidal particles. Nobel Prize for Chemistry (1925).

zuc·chet·to /(t)so͞oˈketō, zo͞o-/ ▶ **n.** (pl. **zucchettos**) a Roman Catholic cleric's skullcap: black for a priest, purple for a bishop, red for a cardinal, and white for the pope.
– ORIGIN mid 19th cent.: from Italian *zucchetta*, diminutive of *zucca* 'gourd, head.'

zuc·chi·ni /zo͞oˈkēnē/ ▶ **n.** (pl. **same** or **zucchinis**) a green variety of smooth-skinned summer squash.
– ORIGIN Italian, plural of *zucchino*, diminutive of *zucca* 'gourd.'

Zug /tso͝ok, zo͞og/ a mainly German-speaking canton in central Switzerland. The smallest canton, it joined the confederation in 1352. ■ its capital; pop. 25,486 (2007). French name **ZOUG**.

zug·zwang /ˈzəgˌzwaNG, ˈtso͞ogˌtsvaNG/ ▶ **n.** Chess a situation in which the obligation to make a move in one's turn is a serious, often decisive, disadvantage: *black is in zugzwang*.
– ORIGIN early 20th cent.: from German *Zug* 'move' + *Zwang* 'compulsion.'

Zui·der Zee /ˌzīdər ˈzē, ˈzā/ a former shallow inlet of the North Sea, in the Netherlands. A dam across its entrance was completed in 1932, and since then large parts have been drained and reclaimed as polders. The remainder forms the IJsselmeer.
– ORIGIN Dutch, literally 'southern sea.'

Zu·kor /ˈzo͞okər/, Adolph (1873–1973), US movie producer and executive; born in Hungary. He created the Famous Players Film Company in 1912. Through mergers and name changes it evolved as Paramount Pictures with Zukor at the head.

Zu·lu /ˈzo͞oˌlo͞o/ ▶ **n. 1** a member of a South African people living mainly in KwaZulu-Natal province. ■ the Nguni language of this people.
2 a code word representing the letter Z, used in radio communication.
▶ **adj.** of or relating to the Zulu people or language.

> The Zulus formed a powerful military empire in southern Africa during the 19th century before being defeated in a series of engagements with white Afrikaner and British settlers. Some Zulus still live under the traditional clan system in the province of KwaZulu-Natal, but many now work in the cities.

– ORIGIN from the stem of Zulu *umZulu* (plural *amaZulu*).

Zu·ma /ˈzo͞omə/, Jacob (1942–), South African statesman; president since 2009.

Zu·ni /ˈzo͞onē/ (also **Zuñi** /ˈzo͞onyē/) ▶ **n.** (pl. **same** or **Zunis**) **1** a member of a Pueblo Indian people of western New Mexico.
2 the language of this people.
▶ **adj.** of or relating to this people or their language.
– ORIGIN from Spanish *Zuñi*, probably from Keresan.

zup·pa in·gle·se /ˈtso͞opə iNGˈglāzā, ˈzo͞opə, -zē/ ▶ **n.** a rich Italian dessert resembling trifle.
– ORIGIN Italian, literally 'English soup.'

Zu·rich /ˈzo͝orik/ a city in northern central Switzerland, on Lake Zurich; pop. 358,540 (2007). The largest city in Switzerland, it is a major international financial center.

Zwick·au /ˈtsvikˌou/ a mining and industrial city in southeastern Germany, in Saxony; pop. 96,800 (est. 2006).

zwie·back /ˈswēˌbak, ˈzwē-, ˈswī-, ˈzwī-/ ▶ **n.** a rusk or cracker made by baking a small loaf and then toasting slices until they are dry and crisp.
– ORIGIN German, literally 'twice-bake.'

Zwing·li /ˈzwiNG(g)lē, ˈswiNG-, ˈtsfiNG-/, Ulrich (1484–1531), Swiss religious reformer, the principal figure of the Swiss Reformation. He rejected papal authority and many orthodox doctrines and, although he had strong local support in Zurich, his ideas met with fierce resistance in some regions. Zwingli was killed in the civil war that resulted from his reforms.
– DERIVATIVES **Zwing·li·an** /-lēən/ **adj. & n.**

zwit·ter·i·on /ˈ(t)switərˌīən/ ▶ **n.** Chemistry a molecule or ion having separate positively and negatively charged groups.
– DERIVATIVES **zwit·ter·i·on·ic** /ˌ(t)switərīˈänik/ **adj.**
– ORIGIN early 20th cent.: from German, from *Zwitter* 'a hybrid' + *Ion* 'ion.'

Zwor·y·kin /ˈzwôrikən, ˈzvôr-/, Vladimir (Kuzmich) (1889–1982), US physicist and television pioneer, born in Russia. He invented a precursor to the television camera, the first to scan an image electronically. This had been developed into the first practical television camera by about 1929.

Zy·ban /ˈzīˌban/ ▶ **n.** trademark for **BUPROPION**.
– ORIGIN 1990s: an invented name, probably from *ban* or *banish*.

zy·de·co /ˈzīdəˌkō/ ▶ **n.** a kind of black American dance music originally from southern Louisiana, typically featuring accordion and guitar.
– ORIGIN 1960s: Louisiana Creole, possibly from a pronunciation of French *les haricots* in a dance-tune title.

zygo- ▶ **comb. form** relating to joining or pairing: *zygodactyl*.
– ORIGIN from Greek *zugon* 'yoke.'

zy·go·dac·tyl /ˌzīgōˈdaktl/ ▶ **adj.** (of a bird's feet) having two toes pointing forward and two backward.
▶ **n.** a bird with zygodactyl feet.
– DERIVATIVES **zy·go·dac·ty·lous** /-ˈdaktl-əs/ **adj.**

zy·go·ma /zīˈgōmə/ ▶ **n.** (pl. **zygomata** /-mətə/) Anatomy the bony arch of the cheek formed by connection of the zygomatic and temporal bones.
– DERIVATIVES **zy·go·mat·ic** /ˌzīgəˈmatik/ **adj.**
– ORIGIN late 17th cent.: from Greek *zugōma*, from *zugon* 'yoke.'

zy·go·mat·ic arch ▶ **n.** Anatomy the zygoma.

zy·go·mat·ic bone ▶ **n.** Anatomy the bone that forms the prominent part of the cheek and the outer side of the eye socket.

zy·go·mat·ic proc·ess ▶ **n.** Anatomy a projection of the temporal bone that forms part of the zygoma.

zy·go·mor·phic /ˌzīgəˈmôrfik/ ▶ **adj.** Botany (of a flower) having only one plane of symmetry, as in a pea or snapdragon; bilaterally symmetrical. Compare with **ACTINOMORPHIC**.
– DERIVATIVES **zy·go·mor·phy** /ˈzīgəˌmôrfē/ **n.**

zy·go·spore /ˈzīgəˌspôr/ ▶ **n.** Biology the thick-walled resting cell of certain fungi and algae, arising from the fusion of two similar gametes. Compare with **OOSPORE**.

zy·gote /ˈzīˌgōt/ ▶ **n.** Biology a diploid cell resulting from the fusion of two haploid gametes; a fertilized ovum.
– DERIVATIVES **zy·got·ic** /zīˈgätik/ **adj.**
– ORIGIN late 19th cent.: from Greek *zugōtos* 'yoked,' from *zugoun* 'to yoke.'

zy·go·tene /ˈzīgəˌtēn/ ▶ **n.** Biology the second stage of the prophase of meiosis, following leptotene, during which homologous chromosomes begin to pair.

Zy·klon B /ˈzīˌklän/ ▶ **n.** hydrogen cyanide adsorbed on or released from a carrier in the form of small tablets, used as an insecticidal fumigant and by the Nazis for killing concentration-camp prisoners.
– ORIGIN 1930s: from German, of unknown origin.

zy·mase /ˈzīˌmās, -ˌmāz/ ▶ **n.** Biochemistry a mixture of enzymes obtained from yeast that catalyze the breakdown of sugars in alcoholic fermentation.
– ORIGIN late 19th cent.: from French, from Greek *zumē* 'leaven.'

zymo- (also **zym-** before a vowel) ▶ **comb. form** relating to enzymes or fermentation: *zymogen* | *zymase*.
– ORIGIN from Greek *zumē* 'leaven.'

zy·mo·gen /ˈzīməjən/ ▶ **n.** Biochemistry an inactive substance that is converted into an enzyme when activated by another enzyme.

zy·mur·gy /ˈzīˌmərjē/ ▶ **n.** the study or practice of fermentation in brewing, winemaking, or distilling.
– ORIGIN mid 19th cent.: from Greek *zumē* 'leaven,' on the pattern of *metallurgy*.

007 ▶ **n.** the fictional British secret agent James Bond, or someone based on, inspired by, or reminiscent of him.

101 /ˈwənˌōˈwən/ ▶ **adj.** [postpositive] denoting an introductory course at college or university in the subject specified. ■ informal denoting the elementary or basic facts associated with the field or subject specified: *stuff that you should learn in hacking 101*.

20/20 ▶ adj. denoting vision of normal sharpness. See TWENTY-TWENTY.

24/7 (also **24-7**) ▶ adv. informal twenty-four hours a day, seven days a week; all the time: *you just can't afford to let things get you down, especially when you are on call 24/7.*

2WD ▶ abbr. two-wheel drive.

3G ▶ adj. (of telephone technology) third-generation.

404 ▶ n. Computing an error message displayed by a browser indicating that an Internet address cannot be found.

4to /ˈkwôrtō/ ▶ abbr. quarto.

4WD ▶ abbr. four-wheel drive.

8vo /äkˈtävō/ ▶ abbr. octavo.

911 (in the US and Canada) a telephone number used to contact emergency services.

9/11 the date of the terrorist attacks of September 11, 2001 (see **SEPTEMBER 11**).

999 (in the UK and elsewhere) a telephone number used to contact emergency services.

***** ▶ symbol asterisk.

" ▶ symbol ditto.

§ ▶ symbol section mark (used to indicate a section of a book).

¶ ▶ symbol paragraph sign (used to mark a new paragraph).

© ▶ symbol copyright.

® ▶ symbol registered trademark.

@ ▶ symbol 'at,' used: **1** to indicate cost or rate per unit: *30 dictionaries @$60.00 each.* **2** in Internet addresses between the user's name and the domain name: *jscott@oup.com.*

¢ ▶ symbol cent or cents.

$ ▶ symbol (preceding a numeral) dollar or dollars.
– ORIGIN from handwritten p^s, a former abbreviation for PESO used in Spanish America.

€ ▶ symbol euro or euros.

¥ ▶ symbol yen or yens.

& ▶ symbol the ampersand, used with the meaning 'and.'

▶ symbol ■ the hash sign or pound sign, used: ■ to represent a pound as a unit of weight or mass. ■ as a symbol on a phone keypad or computer keyboard. ■ before a numeral that is a number in a series: *You're breaking Rule #1.*

% ▶ symbol percent.

< ▶ symbol less than.

= ▶ symbol equals.

≠ ▶ symbol does not equal.

> ▶ symbol greater than.

° ▶ symbol degree or degrees.

£ ▶ abbr. (preceding a numeral) pound or pounds (of money).
– ORIGIN the initial letter of Latin *libra* 'pound, balance,' written in copperplate with one or two crossbars: crossbars were formerly used to indicate an abbreviation.

Illustration credits

Illustration	Source
Abdullah II	NATO Photos
Adams, Abigail	Library of Congress
Adams, John	Library of Congress
Adams, John Quincy	Library of Congress
Addams, Jane	Schlesinger Library, Radcliffe Institute, Harvard
Alamo, the	Brice Hammack
Albright, Madeleine	Courtesy of the United Nations
Alhambra, the	Brice Hammack
amphitheater	Brice Hammack
Angkor Wat	Dimitry Kushch/Shutterstock 2009
Annan, Kofi	Courtesy of the United Nations
Anthony, Susan B.	Library of Congress
aqueduct, Roman	Library of Congress
Arc de Triomphe	Library of Congress
Arlington National Cemetery	Brice Hammack
Armstrong, Neil	Roger-Viollet, Paris/The Bridgeman Art Library
Arthur, Chester Alan	Library of Congress
Aung San Suu Kyi	Reuters/Sukree Sukplang
Ball, Lucille	CBS/Landov
Barton, Clara	American Red Cross
Baryshnikov, Mikhail	20th Century Fox/Photofest
Beatles, the	Photofest
Benny, Jack	Library of Congress
Bernstein, Leonard	Library of Congress
Bradley, Omar	Library of Congress
Brandenburg Gate	Library of Congress
Brooklyn Bridge	Library of Congress
Buchanan, James	Library of Congress
Buffalo Bill	Library of Congress
Burns, George	The Museum of Modern Art
Bush, George H. W.	Library of Congress
Bush, George W.	Eric Draper, courtesy of the George W. Bush Presidential Library
Calamity Jane	Library of Congress
Capitol, US	Chris Howey/Shutterstock 2009
Capote, Truman	Library of Congress
Carter, Jimmy	Library of Congress
Carver, George Washington	Library of Congress
Castro, Fidel	Enrique de la Osa/Reuters/Landov
Chaplin, Charlie	Library of Congress
Chartres Cathedral	Library of Congress
Chiang Kai-shek	Library of Congress
Churchill, Winston	Library of Congress
Cleveland, Grover	Library of Congress
Clinton, Hillary Rodham	The White House
Clinton, William Jefferson	The White House
Cole, Nat King	Photofest
Colosseum	Library of Congress
Coolidge, Calvin	Library of Congress
Crawford, Joan	The Museum of Modern Art
Cronkite, Walter	CBS/Landov
Crosby, Bing	Library of Congress
Curie, Marie	Library of Congress
Dali, Salvador	Library of Congress
Davis, Bette	The Museum of Modern Art
Davis, Jefferson	Library of Congress
Dean, James	The Museum of Modern Art
DeNiro, Robert	The Museum of Modern Art
Dickinson, Emily	Amherst College Archives and Special Collections, by permission of the Trustees of Amherst College
Dietrich, Marlene	The Museum of Modern Art
DiMaggio, Joe	National Baseball Hall of Fame, Cooperstown, NY
Dome of the Rock	Library of Congress
Douglas, Stephen A.	Library of Congress
Douglass, Frederick	National Archives
Earhart, Amelia	Library of Congress
Easter Island	Brice Hammack
Eiffel Tower	Library of Congress
Einstein, Albert	Ferdinand Schmutzer/Wikipedia
Eisenhower, Dwight D.	Library of Congress
Elizabeth I	Library of Congress
Elizabeth II	Library of Congress
Empire State Building	Brice Hammack
Farragut, David	Library of Congress
Fillmore, Millard	Library of Congress
Fitzgerald, Ella	Library of Congress
Fonda, Henry	The Museum of Modern Art
Forbidden City	Gary718/Shutterstock 2009
Ford, Gerald	Library of Congress
Ford, Harrison	The Museum of Modern Art
Fox Quesada, Vicente	Courtesy of the United Nations
Franco, Francisco	Library of Congress
Franklin, Aretha	Photofest
Franklin, Benjamin	Library of Congress
Friedan, Betty	Library of Congress
Gable, Clark	Library of Congress
Garbo, Greta	Library of Congress
Garfield, James A.	Library of Congress
Gates, Bill	Reuters/Denis Balibouse
Gateway Arch	Marcy J. Levinson/Shutterstock
Gehrig, Lou	National Baseball Hall of Fame, Cooperstown, NY
Geronimo	Library of Congress
Gish, Lillian	Library of Congress
Golden Gate Bridge	R. Morley/PhotoLink
Gore, Al	The White House
Gordimer, Nadine	Louis Monier/Lebrecht Music & Arts
Grand Canyon	Angel's Gate Photography/Shutterstock
Grant, Ulysses S.	Library of Congress
Great Wall of China	Perkus/Shutterstock
Hamilton, Alexander	Library of Congress
Hammarskjöld, Dag	UN Photo/JO
Harding, Warren G.	US Senate Historical Office
Harlow, Jean	Museum of Modern Art
Harrison, Benjamin	Library of Congress
Harrison, William Henry	US Senate Historical Office
Hayes, Rutherford B.	Library of Congress
Hemingway, Ernest	Photofest
Hendrix, Jimi	Photofest
Henry VIII	Library of Congress
Henry, Patrick	Colonial Williamsburg Foundation
Hepburn, Katherine	The Museum of Modern Art
Hirohito	Library of Congress
Hitchcock, Alfred	Library of Congress
Ho Chi Minh	Roger-Viollet, Paris/The Bridgeman Art Library
Hoover, Herbert	Library of Congress
Houdini, Harry	Library of Congress
Houses of Parliament	Library of Congress
Houston, Samuel	Library of Congress

Illustration	Source
Humphrey, Hubert H.	Library of Congress
Jackson, Andrew	Library of Congress
Jackson, Michael	MCA/Universal Home Video/Photofest
Jackson, Thomas "Stonewall"	Library of Congress
Jagger, Mick	Photofest
Jay, John	Library of Congress
Jefferson, Thomas	Library of Congress
Jobs, Steve	Reuters/Files
Johnson, Andrew.	US Senate Historical Office
Johnson, Lyndon B.	Library of Congress
Jordan, Michael	Chicago Bulls
Joseph, Chief	Library of Congress
Kennedy, John F.	John F. Kennedy Presidential Library and Museum, Boston
King, Jr., Martin Luther	Library of Congress
Laurel and Hardy	The Museum of Modern Art
Lee, Robert E.	Library of Congress
Lenin, Vladimir	Library of Congress
Lennon, John	Photofest
Liberty Bell	Library of Congress
Lincoln, Abraham	Library of Congress
Lincoln Memorial	Dave Wetzel/Shutterstock 2009
Luther, Martin	Library of Congress
Machu Picchu	Brice Hammack
Madison, James	Library of Congress
Malcolm X	Library of Congress
Mandela, Nelson	UN photo by P. Sudhakaran
Mao Zedong	Peter Newark American Pictures/The Bridgeman Art Library
Marshall, Thurgood	Harris & Ewing, Collection of the Supreme Court of the United States
Marx, Karl	The Bridgeman Art Library
Matterhorn	Library of Congress
Mays, Willie	National Baseball Hall of Fame, Cooperstown, NY
McCartney, Paul	Photofest
McKinley, William	Library of Congress
Meir, Golda	Library of Congress
Michelangelo	Library of Congress
Monroe, James	Library of Congress
Monroe, Marilyn	20th Century-Fox/Photofest
Monticello	© 2001 PhotoDisc, Inc.
Morrison, Toni	Olga Besnard/Shutterstock 2009
Moses, Grandma	Library of Congress
Murrow, Edward R.	CBS/Photofest
Mussolini, Benito	Library of Congress
Nader, Ralph	David Alfaya
Nefertiti	Library of Congress
Nehru, Jawaharlal	Library of Congress
Newman, Paul	The Museum of Modern Art
Niagara Falls	© 2001 PhotoDisc, Inc.
Nicholson, Jack	The Museum of Modern Art
Nixon, Richard	Library of Congress
Notre Dame	Library of Congress
Oakley, Annie	Library of Congress
Obama, Barack	United States Senate
O'Keeffe, Georgia	Library of Congress
Onassis, Jacqueline Kennedy	Abbie Rowe, White House/John F. Kennedy Presidential Library and Museum, Boston
Oxford	Douglas Freer/Shutterstock 2009
Pantheon	Library of Congress
Parks, Rosa	Schomburg Center for Research in Black Culture
Parthenon	Brice Hammack
Pentagon	Library of Congress
Petronas Towers	Tourism Malaysia
Picasso, Pablo	Library of Congress
Pierce, Franklin	Library of Congress
Pisa, Leaning Tower of	Brice Hammack
Poitier, Sidney	The Museum of Modern Art
Polk, James K.	Library of Congress
pyramid of Giza	Library of Congress
Reagan, Ronald	Ronald Reagan Library
redwood	Brice Hammack
Rehnquist, William	Joe Lavenburg, National Geographic Society, Collection of the Supreme Court of the United States

Illustration	Source
Renoir, Auguste	Library of Congress
Rhodes, Cecil	Library of Congress
Ride, Sally	National Archives
Rio de Janeiro	Fanny Reno/Shutterstock 2009
Rivera, Diego (painting of Zapata)	Library of Congress
Robinson, Jackie	National Archives
Robinson, Mary	UN photo by Evan Schneider
Rodin, Auguste	Library of Congress
Roosevelt, Eleanor	FDR Library
Roosevelt, Franklin D.	FDR Library
Roosevelt, Theodore	Library of Congress
Rushmore, Mount	C. Borland/PhotoLink
Ruth, Babe	Library of Congress
Rutherford, Ernest	Library of Congress
Sacajawea	State Historical Society of North Dakota B0063
Sagrada Familia	Brice Hammack
St. Basil's Cathedral	Library of Congress
St. Paul's Cathedral	Library of Congress
Sanger, Margaret	Library of Congress
Shakespeare, William	Folger Shakespeare Library
Sherman, William Tecumseh	National Archives
Sinatra, Frank	Photofest
Sitting Bull	Library of Congress
Sphinx, the	Library of Congress
Spock, Benjamin	Photofest
Stalin, Joseph	Library of Congress
Stanton, Elizabeth Cady	Library of Congress
Statue of Liberty	Library of Congress
Steinem, Gloria	Library of Congress
Stengel, Casey	National Baseball Hall of Fame, Cooperstown, NY
Stewart, James	Library of Congress
Stonehenge	VisitBritain
Sun Yat-sen	Library of Congress
Taft, William H.	Library of Congress
Taj Mahal	Library of Congress
Taylor, Elizabeth	The Museum of Modern Art
Taylor, Zachary	Mathew Brady/Library of Congress
Tecumseh	Cincinnati Museum Center-Cincinnati Historical Society Library
Temple, Shirley	The Museum of Modern Art
Teresa, Mother	Photofest
Thant, U	Courtesy of the United Nations
Tiananmen Square	Brice Hammack
Times Square	Margaret Stephenson/Shutterstock
Tolstoy, Leo	Library of Congress
Tower of London	VisitBritain
Trevi Fountain	Amy Nichole Harris/Shutterstock
Truman, Harry S	Library of Congress
Tubman, Harriet	Library of Congress
Tutankhamen	Library of Congress
Twain, Mark	Library of Congress
Tyler, John	Library of Congress
Uncle Sam	Library of Congress
Valentino, Rudolph	Library of Congress
Van Buren, Martin	Library of Congress
Wailing Wall	Library of Congress
Warren, Earl	Abdon Daoud Ackad, Collection of the Supreme Court of the United States
Washington, Booker T.	Library of Congress
Washington, George	Library of Congress
Washington Monument	Library of Congress
waterfall	Brice Hammack
Watson, James	Photofest
Wayne, John	The Museum of Modern Art
Webster, Daniel	Library of Congress
Whistler, James McNeill	Library of Congress
White House	Library of Congress
Wilde, Oscar	William Andrews Clark Memorial Library, UCLA
Wilson, Woodrow	Library of Congress
Winfrey, Oprah	Photofest
Woods, Tiger	Reuters/Brian Snyder
Yeager, Chuck	Courtesy of the US Air Force
Yeats, William Butler	© Lebrecht Authors
Young, Cy	National Baseball Hall of Fame, Cooperstown, NY